20TH EDITION

2006

Baseball Card

PRICE GUIDE

Published by

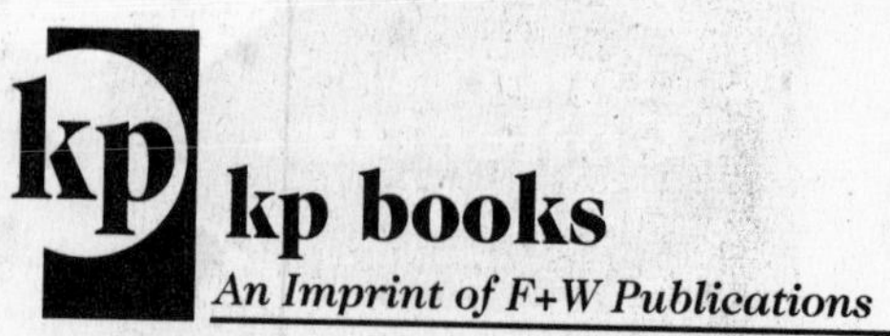

700 East State Street • Iola, WI 54990-0001
715-445-2214 • 888-457-2873

Our toll-free number to place an order or obtain
a free catalog is (800) 258-0929.

Library of Congress Catalog Number: 1549-6309

ISBN 13-digit: 978-089689-298-9

ISBN 10-digit: 0-89689-298-0

Designed by Stacy Bloch

Edited by Joe Clemens

Printed in United States of America

TABLE OF CONTENTS

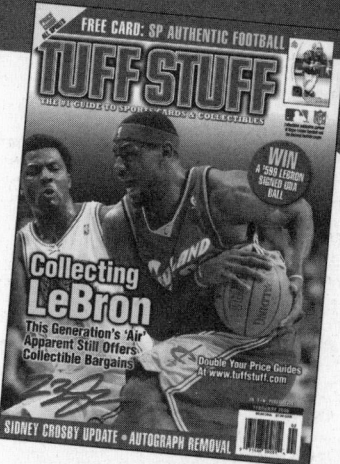

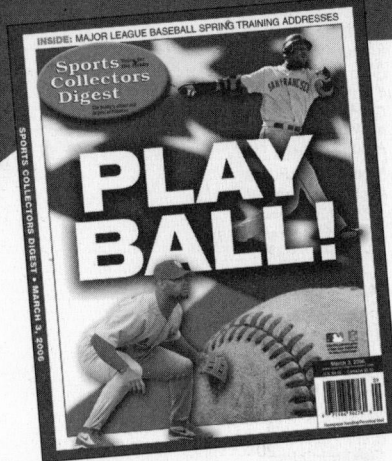

HOW TO USE THIS CATALOG

This catalog has been uniquely designed to serve the needs of collectors and dealers at all levels from beginning to advanced. It provides a comprehensive guide to more than 25 years of baseball card issues, arranged so that even the most novice hobbyist can consult it with confidence and ease.

The following explanations summarize the general practices used in preparing this catalog's listings. However, because of specialized requirements which may vary from card set to card set, these must not be considered ironclad. Where these standards have been set aside, appropriate notations are usually incorporated.

ARRANGEMENT

The most important feature in identifying and pricing a baseball card is its set of origin. Therefore, the main body of this catalog, covering cards issued from 1981-date, has been alphabetically arranged within specific eras of issue according to the name by which the set is most popularly known to collectors, or by which it can be most easily identified by a person examining a card.

Among those card issuers who produced sets for more than a single year, their sets are then listed chronologically, from earliest to most recent, again within specific eras.

Within each set, the cards are listed by their designated card number, or in the absence of card numbers, alphabetically according to the last name of the player pictured. Listing numbers found in parentheses indicate the number does not appear on the card. Certain cards which fall outside the parameters of the normal card numbering for a specific set may be found at the beginning or end of the listings for that set.

VINTAGE-MODERN ISSUES

The main body of the book details modern major league baseball card issues from 1981-2005, as produced by the major national card companies. In general, prior to about 1990, this will include issues which picture one or more baseball players, usually contemporary with their playing days, printed on paper or cardboard in a variety of shapes and sizes and given away as a premium with the purchase of another product or service. After 1990 or so the definition is broadened to remove the restriction of the card as an ancillary product and to include those printed on plastic, wood, metal, etc.

IDENTIFICATION

While most modern baseball cards are well identified on front, back or both, as to date and issue, such has not always been the case. In general, the back of the card is more useful in identifying the set of origin than the front. The issuer or sponsor's name will usually appear on the back since, after all, baseball cards were first produced as a promotional item to stimulate sales of other products. More often than not, that issuer's name is the name by which the set is known to collectors and under which it will be found listed in this catalog.

In some difficult cases, identifying a baseball card's general age, if not specific year of issue, can usually be accomplished by studying the biological or statistical information on the back of the card. The last year mentioned in either the biography or stats is usually the year which preceded the year of issue.

PHOTOGRAPHS

A photograph of the front of at least one representative card from virtually every set listed in this catalog has been incorporated into the listings to aid in identification.

Photographs have been printed in reduced size. The actual size of cards in each set is given in the introductory text preceding its listing, unless the card is the standard size (2.5" by 3.5").

DATING

The dating of baseball cards by year of issue on the front or back of the card itself is a relatively new phenomenon. In most cases, to accurately determine a date of issue for an unidentified card, it must be studied for clues. As mentioned, the biography, career summary or statistics on the back of the card are the best way to pinpoint a year of issue. In most cases, the year of issue will be the year after the last season mentioned on the card.

NUMBERING

While many baseball card issues as far back as the 1880s have contained card numbers assigned by the issuer to facilitate the collecting of a complete set, the practice has by no means been universal. Even today, not every set bears card numbers.

Logically, those baseball cards which were numbered by their manufacturer are presented in that numerical order within the listings of this catalog whenever possible. In a few cases, complete player checklists were obtained from earlier published sources which did not note card numbers, and so numbers have been arbitrarily assigned. Many other unnumbered issues have been assigned catalog numbers to facilitate their universal identification within the hobby, especially when buying and selling by mail.

In all cases, numbers which have been assigned, or which otherwise do not appear on the card through error or by design, are shown in this catalog within parentheses. In virtually all cases, unless a more natural system suggested itself by the unique matter of a particular set, the assignment of numbers by the catalog staff has been done by alphabetical arrangement of the players' last names or the card's principal title.

Significant collectible variations for any particular card are noted within the listings by the application of a suffix letter. In instances of variations, the suffix "a" is assigned to the variation which was created first, when it can be so identified.

NAMES

The identification of a player by full name on the front of his baseball card has been a common practice only since the 1920s. Prior to that, the player's last name and team were the usual information found on the card front.

As a general -- though not universally applied -- practice, the listings in this volume present the player's name exactly as it appears on the front of the card. If the player's full name only appears on the back, rather than on the front of the card, the listing may correspond to that designation.

A player's name checklisted in italic type indicates a rookie card.

Cards which contain misspelled first or last names, or even wrong initials, will have included in their listings the incorrect information, with a correction accompanying in parentheses. This extends, also, to cases where the name on the card does not correspond to the player actually pictured.

In some cases, to facilitate efficient presentations, to maintain ease of use for the reader, or to allow for proper computer sorting of data, a player's name or card title may be listed other than as it appears on the card.

GRADING

It is necessary that some sort of card grading standard be used so that buyer and seller (especially when dealing by mail) may reach an informed agreement on the value of a card.

Modern issues, which have been preserved in top condition in considerable number, are listed only in grade of Near Mint-to-Mint (NM/M), reflective of the fact that there exists in the current market little or no demand for cards of the recent past in lower grades.

Values for lower-grade cards from 1981-date may be generally figured by using a figure of 75% of the Mint price for Near Mint specimens, and 40% of the Mint price for Excellent cards.

For the benefit of the reader, we present herewith the grading guide which was originally formulated in 1981 by Baseball Cards magazine and Sports Collectors Digest, and has been continually refined since that time.

These grading definitions have been used in the pricing of cards in this book, but they are by no means a universally accepted grading standard.

The potential buyer of a baseball card should keep that in mind when encountering cards of nominally the same grade, but at a price which differs widely from that quoted in this book.

Ultimately, the collector himself must formulate his own personal grading standards in deciding whether cards available for purchase meet the needs of his own collection.

Mint (MT): A perfect card. Well-centered, with parallel borders which appear equal to the naked eye. Four sharp, square corners. No creases, edge dents, surface scratches, paper flaws, loss of luster, yellowing or fading, regardless of age. No imperfectly printed card -- out of register, badly cut or ink flawed -- or card stained by contact with gum, wax or other substances can be considered truly Mint, even if new out of the pack. Generally, to be considered in Mint condition, a card's borders must exist in a ratio of 60/40 side to side and top to bottom.

Near Mint (NR MT): A nearly perfect card. At first glance, a Near Mint card appears perfect; upon closer examination, however, a minor flaw will be discovered. On well-centered cards, three of the four corners must be perfectly sharp; only one corner shows a minor imperfection upon close inspection. A slightly off-center card with one or more borders being noticeably unequal — but no worse than in a ratio of 70/30 S/S or T/B — would also fit this grade.

Excellent (EX): Corners are still fairly sharp with only moderate wear. Card borders may be off center as much as 80/20. No creases. May have very minor gum, wax or product stains, front or back. Surfaces may show slight loss of luster from rubbing across other cards.

Very Good (VG): Shows obvious handling. Corners rounded and/or perhaps showing minor creases. Other minor creases may be visible. Surfaces may exhibit loss of luster, but all printing is intact. May show major gum, wax or other packaging stains. No major creases, tape marks or extraneous markings or writing. All four borders visible, though the ratio may be as poor as 95/5. Exhibits honest wear.

Good (G): A well-worn card, but exhibits no intentional damage or abuse. May have major or multiple creases. Corners rounded well beyond the border. A good card will generally sell for about 50% the value of a card in Very Good condition.

Fair (F or Fr.): Shows excessive wear, along with damage or abuse. Will show all the wear characteristics of a Good card, along with such damage as thumb tack holes in or near margins, evidence of having been taped or pasted, perhaps small tears around the edges, or creases so heavy as to break the cardboard. Backs may show minor added pen or pencil writing, or be missing small bits of paper. Still, basically a complete card. A Fair card will generally sell for 50% the value of a Good specimen.

Poor (P): A card that has been tortured to death. Corners or other areas may be torn off. Card may have been trimmed, show holes from a paper punch or have been used for BB gun practice. Front may have extraneous pen or pencil writing, or other defacement. Major portions of front or back design may be missing. Not a pretty sight.

In addition to these terms, collectors may encounter intermediate grades, such as NM-MT or EX-MT. These cards usually have characteristics of both the lower and higher grades, and are generally priced midway between those two values.

Grading and pricing reflected in this book are for cards which have not been authenticated, graded and encapsulated by one of the third-party certification services. Cards which have been "slabbed" by these services generally sell for a premium above the price which a "raw" card will bring.

ROOKIE CARDS

While the status (and automatic premium value) which a player's rookie card carries has fallen and risen in recent years, and though the hobby still has not reached a universal definition of a rookie card, many significant rookie cards are noted in this catalog's listings by the use of italic type. For purposes of this catalog, a player's rookie card is considered to be any card in a licensed set from a major manufacturer in the first year in which that player appears on a card.

VALUATIONS

Values quoted in this book represent the current retail market at the time of compilation (January, 2006). The quoted values are the result of a unique system of evaluation and verification created by the catalog's editors. Utilizing specialized computer analysis and drawing upon recommendations provided through their daily involvement in the publication of the hobby's leading sports collectors' periodicals, as well as the input of consultants, dealers and collectors, each listing is, in the final analysis, the interpretation of that data by one or more of the editors.

It should be stressed, however, that this book is intended to serve only as an aid in evaluating cards; actual market conditions are constantly changing. This is especially true of the cards of current players, whose on-field performance during the course of a season can greatly affect the value of their cards — upwards or downwards. Because of the extremely volatile nature of new card prices, especially high-end issues, we have chosen not to include the very latest releases such as premium-price brands from the major companies, feeling it is better to have no listings at all for those cards than to have inaccurate values in print.

Because this volume is intended to reflect the national market, users will find regional price variances caused by demand differences. Cards of Astros slugger Jeff Bagwell will, for instance, often sell at prices greater than quoted herein at shops and shows in the Houston area. Conversely, his cards may be acquired at a discount from these valuations when purchased on the East or West Coast.

Publication of this book is not intended as a solicitation to buy or sell the listed cards by the editors, publishers or contributors.

Again, the values here are retail prices — what a collector can expect to pay when buying a card from a dealer. The wholesale price, that which a collector can expect to receive from a dealer when selling cards, will be significantly lower.

Most dealers operate on a 100 percent mark-up, generally paying about 50 percent of a card's retail value for cards which they are purchasing for inventory. On some high-demand cards, dealers will pay up to 75 percent or even 100 percent or more of retail value, anticipating continued price increases. Conversely, for many low-demand cards, such as common players' cards, dealers may pay as little as 10 percent or even less of retail with many base-brand cards of recent years having no resale value at all.

SETS

Collectors may note that the complete set prices for newer issues quoted in these listings are usually significantly lower than the total of the value of the individual cards which comprise the set. This reflects two factors in the baseball card market. First, a seller is often willing to take a lower composite price for a complete set as a "volume discount" and to avoid carrying in inventory a large number of common player or other lower-demand cards.

Second, to a degree, the value of common cards can be said to be inflated as a result of having a built-in overhead charge to justify the dealer's time in sorting cards, carrying them in stock and filling orders. This accounts for the fact that even new base-brand baseball cards, which cost the dealer around one cent each when bought in bulk, carry individual price tags of five cents or higher.

Some set prices shown, especially for old cards in top condition, are merely theoretical in that it is unlikely that a complete set exists in that condition. In general among older cards the range of conditions found in even the most painstakingly assembled complete set make the set values quoted useful only as a starting point for price negotiations.

ERRORS/VARIATIONS

It is often hard for the beginning collector to understand that an error on a baseball card, in and of itself, does not usually add premium value to that card. It is usually only when the correcting of an error in the subsequent printing creates a variation that premium value attaches to an error.

Minor errors, such as wrong stats or personal data, misspellings, inconsistencies, etc. — usually affecting the back of the card — are very common, especially in recent years. Unless a corrected variation was also printed, these errors are not noted in the listings of this book because they are not generally perceived by collectors to have premium value.

Many scarce and valuable variations are included in these listings because they are widely collected and often have significant premium value.

Beginning in the early 1990s, some card companies began production of their basic sets at more than one printing facility. This frequently resulted in numerous minor variations. Combined with a general decline in quality control from the mid-1980s through the early 1990s, which allowed unprecedented numbers of uncorrected error cards to be released, this caused a softening of collector interest in errors and variations. Despite the fact most of these modern variations have no premium value, they are listed here as a matter of record.

COUNTERFEITS/REPRINTS

As the value of baseball cards has risen, certain cards and sets have become too expensive for the average collector to obtain. This, along with changes in the technology of color printing, has given rise to increasing numbers of counterfeit and reprint cards.

While both terms describe essentially the same thing — a modern day copy which attempts to duplicate as closely as possible an original baseball card — there are differences which are important to the collector.

Generally, a counterfeit is made with the intention of deceiving somebody into believing it is genuine, and thus paying large amounts of money for it. The counterfeiter takes every pain to try to make his fakes look as authentic as possible. In recent years, the 1963 Pete Rose, 1984 Donruss Don Mattingly and more than 100 superstar cards of the late 1960s-early 1990s have been counterfeited — many of which were quickly detected because of the differences in quality of cardboard on which they were printed.

A reprint, on the other hand, while it may have been made to look as close as possible to an original card, is made with the intention of allowing collectors to buy them as substitutes for cards they may never be otherwise able to afford. The big difference is that a reprint is generally marked as such, usually on the back of the card.

In other cases, like the Topps 1952 reprint set and 1953-54 Archives issues, the replicas are printed in a size markedly different from the originals. Collectors should be aware, however, that unscrupulous persons will sometimes cut off or otherwise obliterate the distinguishing word — "Reprint," "Copy," — or modern copyright date on the back of a reprint card in an attempt to pass it as genuine.

A collector's best defense against reprints and counterfeits is to acquire a knowledge of the look and feel of genuine baseball cards of various eras and issues.

MODERN MAJOR LEAGUE CARDS (1981-2005)

The vast majority of cards listed in this section were issued between 1981 and late 2005 and feature major league players only. The term "card" is used rather loosely as in this context it is construed to include virtually any series of cardboard or paper product, of whatever size and/or shape, depicting baseball players. Further, "cards" printed on wood, metal, plastic and other materials are either by their association with orhter issues or by their compatibility in size with the current 2-1/2" x 3-1/2" card standard also listed here.

Because modern cards are generally not popularly collected in lower grades, cards in this section carry only a Near Mint-to-Mint (NM/M) value quote. In general, post-1980 cards which grade Near Mint (NM) will retail at about 75% of the NM/M price, while Excellent (EX) condition cards bring 40%.

B

1988 BAZOOKA

		NM/M
Complete Set (22):		2.00
Common Player:		.05
1	George Bell	.05
2	Wade Boggs	.40
3	Jose Canseco	.20
4	Roger Clemens	.50
5	Vince Coleman	.05
6	Eric Davis	.05
7	Tony Fernandez	.05
8	Dwight Gooden	.05
9	Tony Gwynn	.40
10	Wally Joyner	.05
11	Don Mattingly	.50
12	Willie McGee	.05
13	Mark McGwire	.75
14	Kirby Puckett	.40
15	Tim Raines	.05
16	Dave Righetti	.05
17	Cal Ripken, Jr.	1.00
18	Juan Samuel	.05
19	Ryne Sandberg	.40
20	Benny Santiago	.05
21	Darryl Strawberry	.05
22	Todd Worrell	.05

1989 BAZOOKA

		NM/M
Complete Set (22):		2.00
Common Player:		.07
1	Tim Belcher	.05
2	Damon Berryhill	.05
3	Wade Boggs	.50
4	Jay Buhner	.05
5	Jose Canseco	.25
6	Vince Coleman	.05
7	Cecil Espy	.05
8	Dave Gallagher	.05
9	Ron Gant	.05
10	Kirk Gibson	.05
11	Paul Gibson	.05
12	Mark Grace	.10
13	Tony Gwynn	.50
14	Rickey Henderson	.40
15	Orel Hershiser	.05
16	Gregg Jefferies	.05
17	Ricky Jordan	.05
18	Chris Sabo	.05
19	Gary Sheffield	.15
20	Darryl Strawberry	.05
21	Frank Viola	.05
22	Walt Weiss	.05

1990 BAZOOKA

		NM/M
Complete Set (22):		3.00
Common Player:		.15
1	Kevin Mitchell	.15
2	Robin Yount	.40
3	Mark Davis	.15
4	Bret Saberhagen	.15
5	Fred McGriff	.15
6	Tony Gwynn	.50
7	Kirby Puckett	.50
8	Vince Coleman	.15
9	Rickey Henderson	.40
10	Ben McDonald	.15
11	Gregg Olson	.15
12	Todd Zeile	.15
13	Carlos Martinez	.15
14	Gregg Jefferies	.15
15	Craig Worthington	.15
16	Gary Sheffield	.25
17	Greg Briley	.15
18	Ken Griffey, Jr.	1.50
19	Jerome Walton	.15
20	Bob Geren	.15
21	Tom Gordon	.15
22	Jim Abbott	.15

1991 BAZOOKA

		NM/M
Complete Set (22):		5.00
Common Player:		.15
1	Barry Bonds	3.50
2	Rickey Henderson	.50
3	Bob Welch	.15
4	Doug Drabek	.15
5	Alex Fernandez	.15
6	Jose Offerman	.15
7	Frank Thomas	.50
8	Cecil Fielder	.15
9	Ryne Sandberg	.75
10	George Brett	1.00
11	Willie McGee	.15
12	Vince Coleman	.15
13	Hal Morris	.15
14	Delino DeShields	.15
15	Robin Ventura	.15
16	Jeff Huson	.15
17	Felix Jose	.15
18	Dave Justice	.15
19	Larry Walker	.15
20	Sandy Alomar, Jr.	.15
21	Kevin Appier	.15
22	Scott Radinsky	.15

1992 BAZOOKA

		NM/M
Complete Set (22):		8.00
Common Player:		.25
1	Joe Adcock, Bob Lemon, Willie Mays, Vic Wertz	1.50
2	Carl Furillo, Don Newcombe, Phil Rizzuto, Hank Sauer	.25
3	Ferris Fain, John Logan, Ed Mathews, Bobby Shantz	.25
4	Yogi Berra, Del Crandall, Howie Pollett, Gene Woodling	.25
5	Richie Ashburn, Leo Durocher, Allie Reynolds, Early Wynn	.25
6	Hank Aaron, Ray Boone, Luke Easter, Dick Williams	1.50
7	Ralph Branca, Bob Feller, Rogers Hornsby, Bobby Thomson	.25
8	Jim Gilliam, Billy Martin, Orestes Minoso, Hal Newhouser	.25
9	Smoky Burgess, John Mize, Preacher Roe, Warren Spahn	.25
10	Monte Irvin, Bobo Newsom, Duke Snider, Wes Westrum	.25
11	Carl Erskine, Jackie Jensen, George Kell, Al Schoendienst	.25
12	Bill Bruton, Whitey Ford, Ed Lopat, Mickey Vernon	.25
13	Joe Black, Lew Burdette, Johnny Pesky, Enos Slaughter	.25
14	Gus Bell, Mike Garcia, Mel Parnell, Jackie Robinson	1.25
15	Alvin Dark, Dick Groat, Pee Wee Reese, John Sain	.25
16	Gil Hodges, Sal Maglie, Wilmer Mizell, Billy Pierce	.45
17	Nellie Fox, Ralph Kiner, Ted Kluszewski, Eddie Stanky	.25
18	Ewell Blackwell, Vern Law, Satchell Paige, Jim Wilson	.45
19	Lou Boudreau, Roy Face, Harvey Haddix, Bill Rigney	.25
20	Roy Campanella, Walt Dropo, Harvey Kuenn, Al Rosen	.45
21	Joe Garagiola, Robin Roberts, Casey Stengel, Hoyt Wilhelm	.25
22	John Antonelli, Bob Friend, Dixie Walker, Ted Williams	1.00

1993 BAZOOKA TEAM USA

		NM/M
Complete Set (22):		100.00
Complete Tin Set (22):		150.00
Common Player:		.50
1	Terry Harvey	.50
2	Dante Powell	.50
3	Andy Barkett	.50
4	Steve Reich	2.00
5	Charlie Nelson	.50
6	Todd Walker	2.00
7	Dustin Hermanson	1.00
8	Pat Clougherty	.50
9	Danny Graves	.50
10	Paul Wilson	.75
11	Todd Helton	90.00
12	Russ Johnson	.50
13	Darren Grass	.50
14	A.J. Hinch	.50
15	Mark Merila	.50
16	John Powell	.50
17	Bob Scafa	.50
18	Matt Beaumont	.50
19	Todd Dunn	.50
20	Mike Martin	.50
21	Carlton Loewer	.50
22	Bret Wagner	.50

1995 BAZOOKA

		NM/M
Complete Set (132):		3.00
Factory Set (132+5):		5.00
Common Player:		.05
Pack (5):		.30
Wax Box (36):		7.00
1	Greg Maddux	.50
2	Cal Ripken Jr.	1.00
3	Lee Smith	.05
4	Sammy Sosa	.65
5	Jason Bere	.05
6	Dave Justice	.05
7	Kevin Mitchell	.05
8	Ozzie Guillen	.05
9	Roger Clemens	.60
10	Mike Mussina	.30
11	Sandy Alomar	.05
12	Cecil Fielder	.05
13	Dennis Martinez	.05
14	Randy Myers	.05
15	Jay Buhner	.05
16	Ivan Rodriguez	.40
17	Mo Vaughn	.05
18	Ryan Klesko	.05
19	Chuck Finley	.05
20	Barry Bonds	1.00
21	Dennis Eckersley	.40
22	Kenny Lofton	.05
23	Rafael Palmeiro	.40
24	Mike Stanley	.05
25	Gregg Jefferies	.05
26	Robin Ventura	.05
27	Mark McGwire	.75
28	Ozzie Smith	.50
29	Troy Neel	.05
30	Tony Gwynn	.50
31	Ken Griffey Jr.	.65
32	Will Clark	.10
33	Craig Biggio	.05
34	Shawon Dunston	.05
35	Wilson Alvarez	.05
36	Bobby Bonilla	.05
37	Marquis Grissom	.05
38	Ben McDonald	.05
39	Delino DeShields	.05
40	Barry Larkin	.05
41	John Olerud	.05
42	Jose Canseco	.30
43	Greg Vaughn	.05
44	Gary Sheffield	.20
45	Paul O'Neill	.05
46	Bob Hamelin	.05
47	Don Mattingly	.60
48	John Franco	.05
49	Bret Boone	.05
50	Rick Aguilera	.05
51	Tim Wallach	.05
52	Roberto Kelly	.05
53	Danny Tartabull	.05
54	Randy Johnson	.40
55	Greg McMichael	.05
56	Bip Roberts	.05
57	David Cone	.05
58	Raul Mondesi	.05
59	Travis Fryman	.05
60	Jeff Conine	.05
61	Jeff Bagwell	.40
62	Rickey Henderson	.40
63	Fred McGriff	.05
64	Matt Williams	.05
65	Rick Wilkins	.05
66	Eric Karros	.05
67	Mel Rojas	.05
68	Juan Gonzalez	.40
69	Chuck Carr	.05
70	Moises Alou	.05
71	Mark Grace	.10
72	Alex Fernandez	.05
73	Rod Beck	.05
74	Ray Lankford	.05
75	Dean Palmer	.05
76	Joe Carter	.05
77	Mike Piazza	.65
78	Eddie Murray	.40
79	Dave Nilsson	.05
80	Brett Butler	.05
81	Roberto Alomar	.10
82	Jeff Kent	.05
83	Andres Galarraga	.05
84	Brady Anderson	.05
85	Jimmy Key	.05
86	Bret Saberhagen	.05
87	Chili Davis	.05
88	Jose Rijo	.05
89	Wade Boggs	.50
90	Len Dykstra	.05
91	Steve Howe	.05
92	Hal Morris	.05
93	Larry Walker	.05
94	Jeff Montgomery	.05
95	Wil Cordero	.05
96	Jay Bell	.05
97	Tom Glavine	.15
98	Chris Hoiles	.05
99	Steve Avery	.05
100	Ruben Sierra	.05
101	Mickey Tettleton	.05
102	Paul Molitor	.40
103	Carlos Baerga	.05
104	Walt Weiss	.05
105	Darren Daulton	.05
106	Jack McDowell	.05
107	Doug Drabek	.05
108	Mark Langston	.05
109	Manny Ramirez	.40
110	Kevin Appier	.05
111	Andy Benes	.05
112	Chuck Knoblauch	.05
113	Kirby Puckett	.50
114	Dante Bichette	.05
115	Deion Sanders	.10
116	Albert Belle	.10
117	Todd Zeile	.05
118	Devon White	.05
119	Tim Salmon	.05
120	Frank Thomas	.40
121	John Wetteland	.05
122	James Mouton	.05
123	Javy Lopez	.05
124	Carlos Delgado	.25
125	Cliff Floyd	.05
126	Alex Gonzalez	.05
127	Billy Ashley	.05
128	Rondell White	.05
129	Rico Brogna	.05
130	Melvin Nieves	.05
131	Jose Oliva	.05
132	J.R. Phillips	.05

Red Hot Inserts

		NM/M
Complete Set (22):		7.00
Common Player:		.15
1	Greg Maddux	1.00
2	Cal Ripken Jr.	2.00
3	Barry Bonds	2.00
4	Kenny Lofton	.15
5	Mike Stanley	.15
6	Tony Gwynn	1.00
7	Ken Griffey Jr.	1.50
8	Barry Larkin	.15
9	Jose Canseco	.35
10	Paul O'Neill	.15
11	Randy Johnson	.50
12	David Cone	.15
13	Jeff Bagwell	.60
14	Matt Williams	.15
15	Mike Piazza	1.50
16	Roberto Alomar	.25
17	Jimmy Key	.15
18	Wade Boggs	1.00
19	Paul Molitor	.75
20	Carlos Baerga	.15
21	Albert Belle	.25
22	Frank Thomas	.60

1996 BAZOOKA

		NM/M
Unopened Factory Set (133):		9.00
Complete Set (132):		6.00
Common Player:		.05
Pack (5):		.40
Wax Box (36):		9.00
1	Ken Griffey Jr.	.75
2	J.T. Snow	.05
3	Rondell White	.05
4	Reggie Sanders	.05
5	Jeff Montgomery	.05
6	Mike Stanley	.05
7	Bernie Williams	.05
8	Mike Piazza	.75
9	Brian Hunter	.05
10	Len Dykstra	.05
11	Ray Lankford	.05
12	Kenny Lofton	.05
13	Robin Ventura	.05
14	Devon White	.05
15	Cal Ripken Jr.	1.50
16	Heathcliff Slocumb	.05
17	Ryan Klesko	.05
18	Terry Steinbach	.05
19	Travis Fryman	.05
20	Sammy Sosa	.75
21	Jim Thome	.05
22	Kenny Rogers	.05
23	Don Mattingly	.60
24	Kirby Puckett	.50
25	Matt Williams	.05
26	Larry Walker	.05
27	Tim Wakefield	.05
28	Greg Vaughn	.05
29	Denny Neagle	.05
30	Ken Caminiti	.05
31	Garret Anderson	.05
32	Brady Anderson	.05
33	Carlos Baerga	.05
34	Wade Boggs	.50
35	Roberto Alomar	.10
36	Eric Karros	.05
37	Jay Buhner	.05
38	Dante Bichette	.05
39	Darren Daulton	.05
40	Jeff Bagwell	.40
41	Jay Bell	.05
42	Dennis Eckersley	.40
43	Will Clark	.10
44	Tom Glavine	.15
45	Rick Aguilera	.05
46	Kevin Seitzer	.05
47	Bret Boone	.05
48	Mark Grace	.10
49	Ray Durham	.05
50	Rico Brogna	.05
51	Kevin Appier	.05
52	Moises Alou	.05
53	Jeff Conine	.05
54	Marty Cordova	.05
55	Jose Mesa	.05
56	Rod Beck	.05
57	Marquis Grissom	.05
58	David Cone	.05
59	Albert Belle	.10
60	Lee Smith	.05
61	Frank Thomas	.40
62	Roger Clemens	.60
63	Bobby Bonilla	.05
64	Paul Molitor	.40
65	Chuck Knoblauch	.05
66	Steve Finley	.05
67	Craig Biggio	.05
68	Ramon Martinez	.05
69	Jason Isringhausen	.05
70	Mark Wohlers	.05
71	Vinny Castilla	.05
72	Ron Gant	.05
73	Juan Gonzalez	.40
74	Mark McGwire	1.00
75	Jeff King	.05
76	Pedro Martinez	.40
77	Chad Curtis	.05
78	John Olerud	.05
79	Greg Maddux	.50
80	Derek Jeter	1.50
81	Mike Mussina	.25
82	Gregg Jefferies	.05

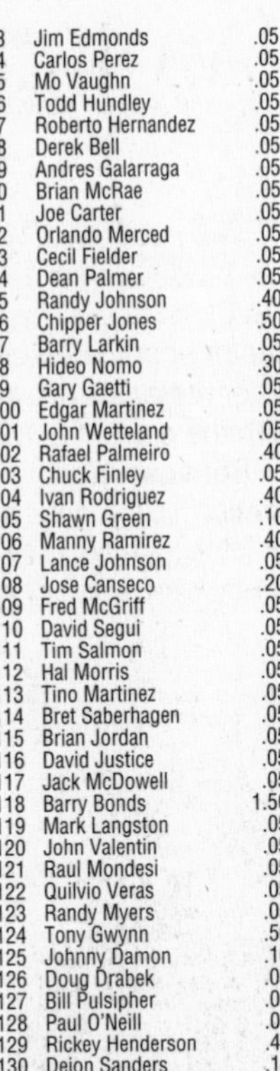

83	Jim Edmonds	.05
84	Carlos Perez	.05
85	Mo Vaughn	.05
86	Todd Hundley	.05
87	Roberto Hernandez	.05
88	Derek Bell	.05
89	Andres Galarraga	.05
90	Brian McRae	.05
91	Joe Carter	.05
92	Orlando Merced	.05
93	Cecil Fielder	.05
94	Dean Palmer	.05
95	Randy Johnson	.40
96	Chipper Jones	.50
97	Barry Larkin	.05
98	Hideo Nomo	.30
99	Gary Gaetti	.05
100	Edgar Martinez	.05
101	John Wetteland	.05
102	Rafael Palmeiro	.40
103	Chuck Finley	.05
104	Ivan Rodriguez	.40
105	Shawn Green	.10
106	Manny Ramirez	.40
107	Lance Johnson	.05
108	Jose Canseco	.20
109	Fred McGriff	.05
110	David Segui	.05
111	Tim Salmon	.05
112	Hal Morris	.05
113	Tino Martinez	.05
114	Bret Saberhagen	.05
115	Brian Jordan	.05
116	David Justice	.05
117	Jack McDowell	.05
118	Barry Bonds	1.50
119	Mark Langston	.05
120	John Valentin	.05
121	Raul Mondesi	.05
122	Quilvio Veras	.05
123	Randy Myers	.05
124	Tony Gwynn	.50
125	Johnny Damon	.10
126	Doug Drabek	.05
127	Bill Pulsipher	.05
128	Paul O'Neill	.05
129	Rickey Henderson	.40
130	Deion Sanders	.10
131	Orel Hershiser	.05
132	Gary Sheffield	.15

Mickey Mantle 1959 Reprint

	NM/M
Mickey Mantle	6.00

1989 BOWMAN

	NM/M
Unopened Factory Set (484):	20.00
Complete Set (484):	15.00
Common Player:	.05
Wax Pack (12+1):	.65
Wax Box (36):	15.00
Rack Pack (40):	1.00
Rack Box (24):	20.00

No.	Player	NM/M
1	Oswald Peraza	.05
2	Brian Holton	.05
3	Jose Bautista	.05
4	*Pete Harnisch*	.10
5	Dave Schmidt	.05
6	Gregg Olson	.05
7	Jeff Ballard	.05
8	Bob Melvin	.05
9	Cal Ripken, Jr.	.75
10	Randy Milligan	.05
11	*Juan Bell*	.05
12	Billy Ripken	.05
13	Jim Trabor	.05
14	Pete Stanicek	.05
15	*Steve Finley*	.25
16	Larry Sheets	.05
17	Phil Bradley	.05
18	Brady Anderson	.05
19	Lee Smith	.05
20	Tom Fischer	.05
21	Mike Boddicker	.05
22	Rob Murphy	.05
23	Wes Gardner	.05
24	John Dopson	.05
25	Bob Stanley	.05
26	Roger Clemens	.60
27	Rich Gedman	.05
28	Marty Barrett	.05
29	Luis Rivera	.05
30	Jody Reed	.05
31	Nick Esasky	.05
32	Wade Boggs	.50
33	Jim Rice	.15
34	Mike Greenwell	.05
35	Dwight Evans	.05
36	Ellis Burks	.05
37	Chuck Finley	.05
38	Kirk McCaskill	.05
39	Jim Abbott	.05
40	*Bryan Harvey*	.05
41	Bert Blyleven	.05
42	Mike Witt	.05
43	Bob McClure	.05
44	Bill Schroeder	.05
45	Lance Parrish	.05
46	Dick Schofield	.05
47	Wally Joyner	.05
48	Jack Howell	.05
49	Johnny Ray	.05
50	Chili Davis	.05
51	Tony Armas	.05
52	Claudell Washington	.05
53	Brian Downing	.05
54	Devon White	.05
55	Bobby Thigpen	.05
56	Bill Long	.05
57	Jerry Reuss	.05
58	Shawn Hillegas	.05
59	Melido Perez	.05
60	Jeff Bittiger.	.05
61	Jack McDowell.	.05
62	Carlton Fisk.	.40
63	Steve Lyons	.05
64	Ozzie Guillen	.05
65	Robin Ventura	.05
66	Fred Manrique	.05
67	Dan Pasqua	.05
68	Ivan Calderon	.05
69	Ron Kittle	.05
70	Daryl Boston	.05
71	Dave Gallagher	.05
72	Harold Baines	.05
73	*Charles Nagy*	.15
74	John Farrell	.05
75	Kevin Wickander	.05
76	Greg Swindell	.05
77	Mike Walker	.05
78	Doug Jones	.05
79	Rich Yett	.05
80	Tom Candiotti	.05
81	Jesse Orosco	.05
82	Bud Black	.05
83	Andy Allanson	.05
84	Pete O'Brien	.05
85	Jerry Browne	.05
86	Brook Jacoby	.05
87	*Mark Lewis*	.05
88	Luis Aguayo	.05
89	Cory Snyder	.05
90	Oddibe McDowell	.05
91	Joe Carter	.05
92	Frank Tanana	.05
93	Jack Morris	.05
94	Doyle Alexander	.05
95	Steve Searcy	.05
96	Randy Bockus	.05
97	Jeff Robinson	.05
98	Mike Henneman	.05
99	Paul Gibson	.05
100	Frank Williams	.05
101	Matt Nokes	.05
102	Rico Brogna	.05
103	Lou Whitaker	.05
104	Al Pedrique	.05
105	Alan Trammell	.05
106	Chris Brown	.05
107	Pat Sheridan	.05
108	Gary Pettis	.05
109	Keith Moreland	.05
110	Mel Stottlemyre, Jr.	.05
111	Bret Saberhagen	.05
112	Floyd Bannister	.05
113	Jeff Montgomery	.05
114	Steve Farr	.05
115	Tom Gordon	.05
116	Charlie Leibrandt	.05
117	Mark Gubicza	.05
118	Mike MacFarlane	.05
119	Bob Boone	.05
120	Kurt Stillwell	.05
121	George Brett	.60
122	Frank White	.05
123	Kevin Seitzer	.05
124	Willie Wilson	.05
125	Pat Tabler	.05
126	Bo Jackson	.10
127	Hugh Walker	.05
128	Danny Tartabull	.05
129	Teddy Higuera	.05
130	Don August	.05
131	Juan Nieves	.05
132	Mike Birkbeck	.05
133	Dan Plesac	.05
134	Chris Bosio	.05
135	Bill Wegman	.05
136	Chuck Crim	.05
137	B.J. Surhoff	.05
138	Joey Meyer	.05
139	Dale Sveum	.05
140	Paul Molitor	.40
141	Jim Gantner	.05
142	*Gary Sheffield*	.75
143	Greg Brock	.05
144	Robin Yount	.40
145	Glenn Braggs	.05
146	Rob Deer	.05
147	Fred Toliver	.05
148	Jeff Reardon	.05
149	Allan Anderson	.05
150	Frank Viola	.05
151	Shane Rawley	.05
152	Juan Berenguer	.05
153	Johnny Ard	.05
154	Tim Laudner	.05
155	Brian Harper	.05
156	Al Newman	.05
157	Kent Hrbek	.05
158	Gary Gaetti	.05
159	Wally Backman	.05
160	Gene Larkin	.05
161	Greg Gagne	.05
162	Kirby Puckett	.50
163	Danny Gladden	.05
164	Randy Bush	.05
165	Dave LaPoint	.05
166	Andy Hawkins	.05
167	Dave Righetti	.05
168	Lance McCullers	.05
169	Jimmy Jones	.05
170	Al Leiter	.05
171	John Candelaria	.05
172	Don Slaught	.05
173	Jamie Quirk	.05
174	Rafael Santana	.05
175	Mike Pagliarulo	.05
176	Don Mattingly	.60
177	Ken Phelps	.05
178	Steve Sax	.05
179	Dave Winfield	.40
180	Stan Jefferson	.05
181	Rickey Henderson	.40
182	Bob Brower	.05
183	Roberto Kelly	.05
184	Curt Young	.05
185	Gene Nelson	.05
186	Bob Welch	.05
187	Rick Honeycutt	.05
188	Dave Stewart	.05
189	Mike Moore	.05
190	Dennis Eckersley	.35
191	Eric Plunk	.05
192	Storm Davis	.05
193	Terry Steinbach	.05
194	Ron Hassey	.05
195	Stan Royer	.05
196	Walt Weiss	.05
197	Mark McGwire	.65
198	Carney Lansford	.05
199	Glenn Hubbard	.05
200	Dave Henderson	.05
201	Jose Canseco	.30
202	Dave Parker	.05
203	Scott Bankhead	.05
204	Tom Niedenfuer	.05
205	Mark Langston	.05
206	*Erik Hanson*	.05
207	Mike Jackson	.05
208	Dave Valle	.05
209	Scott Bradley	.05
210	Harold Reynolds	.05
211	Tino Martinez	.05
212	Rich Renteria	.05
213	Rey Quinones	.05
214	Jim Presley	.05
215	Alvin Davis	.05
216	Edgar Martinez	.05
217	Darnell Coles	.05
218	Jeffrey Leonard	.05
219	Jay Buhner	.05
220	*Ken Griffey, Jr.*	6.00
221	Drew Hall	.05
222	Bobby Witt	.05
223	Jamie Moyer	.05
224	Charlie Hough	.05
225	Nolan Ryan	.75
226	Jeff Russell	.05
227	Jim Sundberg	.05
228	Julio Franco	.05
229	Buddy Bell	.05
230	Scott Fletcher	.05
231	Jeff Kunkel	.05
232	Steve Buechele	.05
233	Monty Fariss	.05
234	Rick Leach	.05
235	Ruben Sierra	.05
236	Cecil Espy	.05
237	Rafael Palmeiro	.40
238	Pete Incaviglia	.05
239	Dave Steib	.05
240	Jeff Musselman	.05
241	Mike Flanagan	.05
242	Todd Stottlemyre	.05
243	Jimmy Key	.05
244	Tony Castillo	.05
245	Alex Sanchez	.05
246	Tom Henke	.05
247	John Cerutti	.05
248	Ernie Whitt	.05
249	Bob Brenly	.05
250	Rance Mulliniks	.05
251	Kelly Gruber	.05
252	Ed Sprague	.05
253	Fred McGriff	.05
254	Tony Fernandez	.05
255	Tom Lawless	.05
256	George Bell	.05
257	Jesse Barfield	.05
258	Sandy Alomar, Sr.	.05
259	Ken Griffey (with Ken Griffey, Jr.)	.30
260	Cal Ripken, Sr.	.05
261	Mel Stottlemyre, Sr.	.05
262	Zane Smith	.05
263	Charlie Puleo	.05
264	Derek Lilliquist	.05
265	Paul Assenmacher	.05
266	John Smoltz	.05
267	Tom Glavine	.25
268	*Steve Avery*	.05
269	*Pete Smith*	.05
270	Jody Davis	.05
271	Bruce Benedict	.05
272	Andres Thomas	.05
273	Gerald Perry	.05
274	Ron Gant	.05
275	Darrell Evans	.05
276	Dale Murphy	.25
277	Dion James	.05
278	Lonnie Smith	.05
279	Geronimo Berroa	.05
280	Steve Wilson	.05
281	Rick Suctcliffe	.05
282	Kevin Coffman	.05
283	Mitch Williams	.05
284	Greg Maddux	.50
285	Paul Kilgus	.05
286	Mike Harkey	.05
287	Lloyd McClendon	.05
288	Damon Berryhill	.05
289	Ty Griffin	.05
290	Ryne Sandberg	.50
291	Mark Grace	.10
292	Curt Wilkerson	.05
293	Vance Law	.05
294	Shawon Dunston	.05
295	Jerome Walton	.05
296	Mitch Webster	.05
297	Dwight Smith	.05
298	Andre Dawson	.25
299	Jeff Sellers	.05
300	Jose Rijo	.05
301	John Franco	.05
302	Rick Mahler	.05
303	Ron Robinson	.05
304	Danny Jackson	.05
305	Rob Dibble	.05
306	Tom Browning	.05
307	Bo Diaz	.05
308	Manny Trillo	.05
309	Chris Sabo	.05
310	Ron Oester	.05
311	Barry Larkin	.05
312	Todd Benzinger	.05
313	Paul O'Neill	.05
314	Kal Daniels	.05
315	Joel Youngblood	.05
316	Eric Davis	.05
317	Dave Smith	.05
318	Mark Portugal	.05
319	Brian Meyer	.05
320	Jim Deshaies	.05
321	Juan Agosto	.05
322	Mike Scott	.05
323	Rick Rhoden	.05
324	Jim Clancy	.05
325	Larry Andersen	.05
326	Alex Trevino	.05
327	Alan Ashby	.05
328	Craig Reynolds	.05
329	Bill Doran	.05
330	Rafael Ramirez	.05
331	Glenn Davis	.05
332	*Willie Ansley*	.05
333	Gerald Young	.05
334	Cameron Drew	.05
335	Jay Howell	.05
336	Tim Belcher	.05
337	Fernando Valenzuela	.05
338	Ricky Horton	.05
339	Tim Leary	.05
340	Bill Bene	.05
341	Orel Hershiser	.05
342	Mike Scioscia	.05
343	Rick Dempsey	.05
344	Willie Randolph	.05
345	Alfredo Griffin	.05
346	Eddie Murray	.40
347	Mickey Hatcher	.05
348	Mike Sharperson	.05
349	John Shelby	.05
350	Mike Marshall	.05
351	Kirk Gibson	.05
352	Mike Davis	.05
353	Bryn Smith	.05
354	Pascual Perez	.05
355	Kevin Gross	.05
356	Andy McGaffigan	.05
357	Brian Holman	.05
358	Dave Wainhouse	.05
359	Denny Martinez	.05
360	Tim Burke	.05
361	Nelson Santovenia	.05
362	Tim Wallach	.05
363	Spike Owen	.05
364	Rex Hudler	.05
365	Andres Galarraga	.05
366	Otis Nixon	.05
367	Hubie Brooks	.05
368	Mike Aldrete	.05
369	Rock Raines	.05
370	Dave Martinez	.05
371	Bob Ojeda	.05
372	Ron Darling	.05
373	Wally Whitehurst	.05
374	Randy Myers	.05
375	David Cone	.05
376	Dwight Gooden	.05
377	Sid Fernandez	.05
378	Dave Proctor	.05
379	Gary Carter	.40
380	Keith Miller	.05
381	Gregg Jefferies	.05
382	Tim Teufel	.05
383	Kevin Elster	.05
384	Dave Magadan	.05
385	Keith Hernandez	.05
386	Mookie Wilson	.05

387 Darryl Strawberry .05
388 Kevin McReynolds .05
389 Mark Carreon .05
390 Jeff Parrett .05
391 Mike Maddux .05
392 Don Carman .05
393 Bruce Ruffin .05
394 Ken Howell .05
395 Steve Bedrosian .05
396 Floyd Youmans .05
397 Larry McWilliams .05
398 Pat Combs .05
399 Steve Lake .05
400 Dickie Thon .05
401 Ricky Jordan .05
402 Mike Schmidt .60
403 Tom Herr .05
404 Chris James .05
405 Juan Samuel .05
406 Von Hayes .05
407 Ron Jones .05
408 Curt Ford .05
409 Bob Walk .05
410 Jeff Robinson .05
411 Jim Gott .05
412 Scott Medvin .05
413 John Smiley .05
414 Bob Kipper .05
415 Brian Fisher .05
416 Doug Drabek .05
417 Mike Lavalliere .05
418 Ken Oberkfell .05
419 Sid Bream .05
420 Austin Manahan .05
421 Jose Lind .05
422 Bobby Bonilla .05
423 Glenn Wilson .05
424 Andy Van Slyke .05
425 Gary Redus .05
426 Barry Bonds .75
427 Don Heinkel .05
428 Ken Dayley .05
429 Todd Worrell .05
430 Brad DuVall .05
431 Jose DeLeon .05
432 Joe Magrane .05
433 John Ericks .05
434 Frank DiPino .05
435 Tony Pena .05
436 Ozzie Smith .50
437 Terry Pendleton .05
438 Jose Oquendo .05
439 Tim Jones .05
440 Pedro Guerrero .05
441 Milt Thompson .05
442 Willie McGee .05
443 Vince Coleman .05
444 Tom Brunansky .05
445 Walt Terrell .05
446 Eric Show .05
447 Mark Davis .05
448 *Andy Benes* .10
449 Eddie Whitson .05
450 Dennis Rasmussen .05
451 Bruce Hurst .05
452 Pat Clements .05
453 Benito Santiago .05
454 Sandy Alomar, Jr. .05
455 Garry Templeton .05
456 Jack Clark .05
457 Tim Flannery .05
458 Roberto Alomar .30
459 Camelo Martinez .05
460 John Kruk .05
461 Tony Gwynn .50
462 Jerald Clark .05
463 Don Robinson .05
464 Craig Lefferts .05
465 Kelly Downs .05
466 Rick Rueschel .05
467 Scott Garrelts .05
468 Wil Tejada .05
469 Kirt Manwaring .05
470 Terry Kennedy .05
471 Jose Uribe .05
472 *Royce Clayton* .10
473 Robby Thompson .05
474 Kevin Mitchell .05
475 Ernie Riles .05
476 Will Clark .10
477 Donnell Nixon .05
478 Candy Maldonado .05
479 Tracy Jones .05
480 Brett Butler .05
481 Checklist 1-121 .05
482 Checklist 122-242 .05
483 Checklist 243-363 .05
484 Checklist 364-484 .05

Inserts

	NM/M
Complete Set (11):	3.50
Common Player:	.10
(1) Richie Ashburn	.10
(2) Yogi Berra	.10
(3) Whitey Ford	.10
(4) Gil Hodges	.10
(5) Mickey Mantle (1951)	2.00
(6) Mickey Mantle (1953)	1.50
(7) Willie Mays	.50
(8) Satchel Paige	.25
(9) Jackie Robinson	1.00
(10) Duke Snider	.10
(11) Ted Williams	1.00

Tiffany

	NM/M
Unopened Set (495):	175.00
Complete Set (495):	100.00
Common Player:	.25

(Star/rookie cards valued at 4-5X regular-issue 1989 Bowman.)

1990 BOWMAN

	NM/M
Unopened Factory Set (528):	15.00
Complete Set (528):	10.00
Common Player:	.05
Wax Pack (15):	.50
Wax Box (36):	12.50
Jumbo Pack (31):	1.00
Jumbo Box (24):	12.50
Rack Pack (39):	1.50
Rack Box (24):	20.00

1 *Tommy Greene* .05
2 Tom Glavine .25
3 Andy Nezelek .05
4 Mike Stanton .05
5 Rick Lueken .05
6 Kent Mercker .05
7 Derek Lilliquist .05
8 Charlie Liebrandt .05
9 Steve Avery .05
10 John Smoltz .05
11 Mark Lemke .05
12 Lonnie Smith .05
13 Oddibe McDowell .05
14 *Tyler Houston* .05
15 Jeff Blauser .05
16 Ernie Whitt .05
17 Alexis Infante .05
18 Jim Presley .05
19 Dale Murphy .25
20 Nick Esasky .05
21 Rick Sutcliffe .05
22 Mike Bielecki .05
23 Steve Wilson .05
24 Kevin Blankenship .05
25 Mitch Williams .05
26 Dean Wilkins .05
27 Greg Maddux .50
28 Mike Harkey .05
29 Mark Grace .10
30 Ryne Sandberg .50
31 Greg Smith .05
32 Dwight Smith .05
33 Damon Berryhill .05
34 Earl Cunningham .05
35 Jerome Walton .05
36 Lloyd McClendon .05
37 Ty Griffin .05
38 Shawon Dunston .05
39 Andre Dawson .25
40 Luis Salazar .05
41 Tim Layana .05
42 Rob Dibble .05
43 Tom Browning .05
44 Danny Jackson .05
45 Jose Rijo .05
46 Scott Scudder .05
47 Randy Myers .05
48 Brian Lane .05
49 Paul O'Neill .05
50 Barry Larkin .05
51 Reggie Jefferson .05
52 Jeff Branson .05
53 Chris Sabo .05
54 Joe Oliver .05
55 Todd Benzinger .05
56 Rolando Roomes .05
57 Hal Morris .05
58 Eric Davis .05
59 Scott Bryant .05
60 Ken Griffey .05
61 *Darryl Kile* .05
62 Dave Smith .05
63 Mark Portugal .05
64 *Jeff Juden* .05
65 Bill Gullickson .05
66 Danny Darwin .05
67 Larry Andersen .05
68 Jose Cano .05
69 Dan Schatzeder .05
70 Jim Deshaies .05
71 Mike Scott .05
72 Gerald Young .05
73 Ken Caminiti .05
74 Ken Oberkfell .05
75 Dave Rhode .05
76 Bill Doran .05
77 Andujar Cedeno .05
78 Craig Biggio .05
79 Karl Rhodes .05
80 Glenn Davis .05
81 *Eric Anthony* .05
82 John Wetteland .05
83 Jay Howell .05
84 Orel Hershiser .05
85 Tim Belcher .05
86 Kiki Jones .05
87 Mike Hartley .05
88 Ramon Martinez .05
89 Mike Scioscia .05
90 Willie Randolph .05
91 Juan Samuel .05
92 *Jose Offerman* .05
93 Dave Hansen .05
94 Jeff Hamilton .05
95 Alfredo Griffin .05
96 Tom Goodwin .05
97 Kirk Gibson .05
98 Jose Vizcaino .05
99 Kal Daniels .05
100 Hubie Brooks .05
101 Eddie Murray .40
102 Dennis Boyd .05
103 Tim Burke .05
104 Bill Sampen .05
105 Brett Gideon .05
106 Mark Gardner .05
107 Howard Farmer .05
108 Mel Rojas .05
109 Kevin Gross .05
110 Dave Schmidt .05
111 Denny Martinez .05
112 Jerry Goff .05
113 Andres Galarraga .05
114 Tim Welch .05
115 *Marquis Grissom* .25
116 Spike Owen .05
117 *Larry Walker* 1.00
118 Rock Raines .05
119 *Delino DeShields* .10
120 Tom Foley .05
121 Dave Martinez .05
122 Frank Viola .05
123 Julio Valera .05
124 Alejandro Pena .05
125 David Cone .05
126 Dwight Gooden .05
127 Kevin Brown .10
128 John Franco .05
129 Terry Bross .05
130 Blaine Beatty .05
131 Sid Fernandez .05
132 Mike Marshall .05
133 Howard Johnson .05
134 Jaime Roseboro .05
135 Alan Zinter .05
136 Keith Miller .05
137 Kevin Elster .05
138 Kevin McReynolds .05
139 Barry Lyons .05
140 Gregg Jefferies .05
141 Darryl Strawberry .05
142 *Todd Hundley* .10
143 Scott Service .05
144 Chuck Malone .05
145 Steve Ontiveros .05
146 Roger McDowell .05
147 Ken Howell .05
148 Pat Combs .05
149 Jeff Parrett .05
150 Chuck McElroy .05
151 Jason Grimsley .05
152 Len Dykstra .05
153 Mickey Morandini .05
154 John Kruk .05
155 Dickie Thon .05
156 Ricky Jordan .05
157 Jeff Jackson .05
158 Darren Daulton .05
159 Tom Herr .05
160 Von Hayes .05
161 *Dave Hollins* .05
162 Carmelo Martinez .05
163 Bob Walk .05
164 Doug Drabek .05
165 Walt Terrell .05
166 Bill Landrum .05
167 Scott Ruskin .05
168 Bob Patterson .05
169 Bobby Bonilla .05
170 Jose Lind .05
171 Andy Van Slyke .05
172 Mike LaValliere .05
173 *Willie Greene* .05
174 Jay Bell .05
175 Sid Bream .05
176 Tom Prince .05
177 Wally Backman .05
178 *Moises Alou* .25
179 Steve Carter .05
180 Gary Redus .05
181 Barry Bonds 1.00
182 Don Slaught .05
183 Joe Magrane .05
184 Bryn Smith .05
185 Todd Worrell .05
186 Jose Deleon .05
187 Frank DiPino .05
188 John Tudor .05
189 Howard Hilton .05
190 John Ericks .05
191 Ken Dayley .05
192 *Ray Lankford* .10
193 Todd Zeile .05
194 Willie McGee .05
195 Ozzie Smith .50
196 Milt Thompson .05
197 Terry Pendleton .05
198 Vince Coleman .05
199 Paul Coleman .05
200 Jose Oquendo .05
201 Pedro Guerrero .05
202 Tom Brunansky .05
203 Roger Smithberg .05
204 Eddie Whitson .05
205 Dennis Rasmussen .05
206 Craig Lefferts .05
207 Andy Benes .05
208 Bruce Hurst .05
209 Eric Show .05
210 Rafael Valdez .05
211 Joey Cora .05
212 Thomas Howard .05
213 Rob Nelson .05
214 Jack Clark .05
215 Garry Templeton .05
216 Fred Lynn .05
217 Tony Gwynn .50
218 Benny Santiago .05
219 Mike Pagliarulo .05
220 Joe Carter .05

221	Roberto Alomar	.25
222	Bip Roberts	.05
223	Rick Reuschel	.05
224	Russ Swan	.05
225	Eric Gunderson	.05
226	Steve Bedrosian	.05
227	Mike Remlinger	.05
228	Scott Garrelts	.05
229	Ernie Camacho	.05
230	Andres Santana	.05
231	Will Clark	.10
232	Kevin Mitchell	.05
233	Robby Thompson	.05
234	Bill Bathe	.05
235	Tony Perezchica	.05
236	Gary Carter	.40
237	Brett Butler	.05
238	Matt Williams	.05
239	Ernie Riles	.05
240	Kevin Bass	.05
241	Terry Kennedy	.05
242	*Steve Hosey*	.05
243	*Ben McDonald*	.15
244	Jeff Ballard	.05
245	Joe Price	.05
246	Curt Schilling	.25
247	Pete Harnisch	.05
248	Mark Williamson	.05
249	Gregg Olson	.05
250	Chris Myers	.05
251a	David Segui (no bio. data on back)	3.50
251b	David Segui (bio. data on back)	.10
252	Joe Orsulak	.05
253	Craig Worthington	.05
254	Mickey Tettleton	.05
255	Cal Ripken, Jr.	1.00
256	Billy Ripken	.05
257	Randy Milligan	.05
258	Brady Anderson	.05
259	*Chris Hoiles*	.05
260	Mike Devereaux	.05
261	Phil Bradley	.05
262	*Leo Gomez*	.05
263	Lee Smith	.05
264	Mike Rochford	.05
265	Jeff Reardon	.05
266	Wes Gardner	.05
267	Mike Boddicker	.05
268	Roger Clemens	.60
269	Rob Murphy	.05
270	Mickey Pina	.05
271	Tony Pena	.05
272	Jody Reed	.05
273	Kevin Romine	.05
274	Mike Greenwell	.05
275	*Mo Vaughn*	.60
276	Danny Heep	.05
277	Scott Cooper	.05
278	*Greg Blosser*	.05
279	Dwight Evans	.05
280	Ellis Burks	.05
281	Wade Boggs	.50
282	Marty Barrett	.05
283	Kirk McCaskill	.05
284	Mark Langston	.05
285	Bert Blyleven	.05
286	Mike Fetters	.05
287	Kyle Abbott	.05
288	Jim Abbott	.05
289	Chuck Finley	.05
290	Gary DiSarcina	.05
291	Dick Schofield	.05
292	Devon White	.05
293	Bobby Rose	.05
294	Brian Downing	.05
295	Lance Parrish	.05
296	Jack Howell	.05
297	Claudell Washington	.05
298	John Orton	.05
299	Wally Joyner	.05
300	Lee Stevens	.05
301	Chili Davis	.05
302	Johnny Ray	.05
303	Greg Hibbard	.05
304	Eric King	.05
305	Jack McDowell	.05
306	Bobby Thigpen	.05
307	Adam Peterson	.05
308	*Scott Radinsky*	.05
309	Wayne Edwards	.05
310	Melido Perez	.05
311	Robin Ventura	.05
312	*Sammy Sosa*	5.00
313	Dan Pasqua	.05
314	Carlton Fisk	.40
315	Ozzie Guillen	.05
316	Ivan Calderon	.05
317	Daryl Boston	.05
318	Craig Grebeck	.05
319	Scott Fletcher	.05
320	*Frank Thomas*	2.00
321	Steve Lyons	.05
322	Carlos Martinez	.05
323	Joe Skalski	.05
324	Tom Candiotti	.05
325	Greg Swindell	.05
326	Steve Olin	.05
327	Kevin Wickander	.05
328	Doug Jones	.05
329	Jeff Shaw	.05
330	Kevin Bearse	.05
331	Dion James	.05
332	Jerry Browne	.05
333	Albert Belle	.15
334	Felix Fermin	.05
335	Candy Maldonado	.05
336	Cory Snyder	.05
337	Sandy Alomar	.05
338	Mark Lewis	.05
339	*Carlos Baerga*	.10
340	Chris James	.05
341	Brook Jacoby	.05
342	Keith Hernandez	.05
343	Frank Tanana	.05
344	Scott Aldred	.05
345	Mike Henneman	.05
346	Steve Wapnick	.05
347	Greg Gohr	.05
348	Eric Stone	.05
349	Brian DuBois	.05
350	Kevin Ritz	.05
351	Rico Brogna	.05
352	Mike Heath	.05
353	Alan Trammell	.05
354	Chet Lemon	.05
355	Dave Bergman	.05
356	Lou Whitaker	.05
357	Cecil Fielder	.05
358	Milt Cuyler	.05
359	Tony Phillips	.05
360	*Travis Fryman*	.10
361	Ed Romero	.05
362	Lloyd Moseby	.05
363	Mark Gubicza	.05
364	Bret Saberhagen	.05
365	Tom Gordon	.05
366	Steve Farr	.05
367	Kevin Appier	.05
368	Storm Davis	.05
369	Mark Davis	.05
370	Jeff Montgomery	.05
371	Frank White	.05
372	Brent Mayne	.05
373	Bob Boone	.05
374	Jim Eisenreich	.05
375	Danny Tartabull	.05
376	Kurt Stillwell	.05
377	Bill Pecota	.05
378	Bo Jackson	.10
379	*Bob Hamelin*	.05
380	Kevin Seitzer	.05
381	Rey Palacios	.05
382	George Brett	.60
383	Gerald Perry	.05
384	Teddy Higuera	.05
385	Tom Filer	.05
386	Dan Plesac	.05
387	*Cal Eldred*	.05
388	Jaime Navarro	.05
389	Chris Bosio	.05
390	Randy Veres	.05
391	Gary Sheffield	.25
392	George Canale	.05
393	B.J. Surhoff	.05
394	Tim McIntosh	.05
395	Greg Brock	.05
396	Greg Vaughn	.05
397	Darryl Hamilton	.05
398	Dave Parker	.05
399	Paul Molitor	.40
400	Jim Gantner	.05
401	Rob Deer	.05
402	Billy Spiers	.05
403	Glenn Braggs	.05
404	Robin Yount	.40
405	Rick Aguilera	.05
406	Johnny Ard	.05
407	*Kevin Tapani*	.10
408	Park Pittman	.05
409	Allan Anderson	.05
410	Juan Berenguer	.05
411	Willie Banks	.05
412	Rich Yett	.05
413	Dave West	.05
414	Greg Gagne	.05
415	*Chuck Knoblauch*	.50
416	Randy Bush	.05
417	Gary Gaetti	.05
418	Kent Hrbek	.05
419	Al Newman	.05
420	Danny Gladden	.05
421	Paul Sorrento	.05
422	Derek Parks	.05
423	Scott Leius	.05
424	Kirby Puckett	.60
425	Willie Smith	.05
426	Dave Righetti	.05
427	Jeff Robinson	.05
428	Alan Mills	.05
429	Tim Leary	.05
430	Pascual Perez	.05
431	Alvaro Espinoza	.05
432	Dave Winfield	.40
433	Jesse Barfield	.05
434	Randy Velarde	.05
435	Rick Cerone	.05
436	Steve Balboni	.05
437	Mel Hall	.05
438	Bob Geren	.05
439	*Bernie Williams*	1.00
440	Kevin Maas	.05
441	Mike Blowers	.05
442	Steve Sax	.05
443	Don Mattingly	.60
444	Roberto Kelly	.05
445	Mike Moore	.05
446	Reggie Harris	.05
447	Scott Sanderson	.05
448	Dave Otto	.05
449	Dave Stewart	.05
450	Rick Honeycutt	.05
451	Dennis Eckersley	.40
452	Carney Lansford	.05
453	Scott Hemond	.05
454	Mark McGwire	.75
455	Felix Jose	.05
456	Terry Steinbach	.05
457	Rickey Henderson	.40
458	Dave Henderson	.05
459	Mike Gallego	.05
460	Jose Canseco	.30
461	Walt Weiss	.05
462	Ken Phelps	.05
463	*Darren Lewis*	.05
464	Ron Hassey	.05
465	*Roger Salkeld*	.05
466	Scott Bankhead	.05
467	Keith Comstock	.05
468	Randy Johnson	.40
469	Erik Hanson	.05
470	Mike Schooler	.05
471	Gary Eave	.05
472	Jeffrey Leonard	.05
473	Dave Valle	.05
474	Omar Vizquel	.05
475	Pete O'Brien	.05
476	Henry Cotto	.05
477	Jay Buhner	.05
478	Harold Reynolds	.05
479	Alvin Davis	.05
480	Darnell Coles	.05
481	Ken Griffey, Jr.	.65
482	Greg Briley	.05
483	Scott Bradley	.05
484	Tino Martinez	.05
485	Jeff Russell	.05
486	Nolan Ryan	1.00
487	Robb Nen	.05
488	Kevin Brown	.05
489	Brian Bohanon	.05
490	Ruben Sierra	.05
491	Pete Incaviglia	.05
492	*Juan Gonzalez*	1.50
493	Steve Buechele	.05
494	Scott Coolbaugh	.05
495	Geno Petralli	.05
496	Rafael Palmeiro	.40
497	Julio Franco	.05
498	Gary Pettis	.05
499	Donald Harris	.05
500	Monty Fariss	.05
501	Harold Baines	.05
502	Cecil Espy	.05
503	Jack Daugherty	.05
504	Willie Blair	.05
505	Dave Steib	.05
506	Tom Henke	.05
507	John Cerutti	.05
508	Paul Kilgus	.05
509	Jimmy Key	.05
510	*John Olerud*	.75
511	Ed Sprague	.05
512	Manny Lee	.05
513	Fred McGriff	.05
514	Glenallen Hill	.05
515	George Bell	.05
516	Mookie Wilson	.05
517	Luis Sojo	.05
518	Nelson Liriano	.05
519	Kelly Gruber	.05
520	Greg Myers	.05
521	Pat Borders	.05
522	Junior Felix	.05
523	Eddie Zosky	.05
524	Tony Fernandez	.05
525	Checklist	.05
526	Checklist	.05
527	Checklist	.05
528	Checklist	.05

Tiffany

	NM/M
Unopened Set (539):	300.00
Complete Set (539):	60.00
Common Player:	.25

(Star/rookie cards valued about 4-5X regular-issue 1990 Bowman.)

1991 BOWMAN

	NM/M
Unopened Factory Set (704):	30.00
Complete Set (704):	20.00
Common Player:	.05
Box (36):	15.00
Pack (14):	.65
Jumbo Box (24):	25.00
Jumbo Pack (40):	1.50

1	Rod Carew-I	.10
2	Rod Carew-II	.10
3	Rod Carew-III	.10
4	Rod Carew-IV	.10
5	Rod Carew-V	.10
6	Willie Fraser	.05
7	John Olerud	.05
8	William Suero	.05
9	Roberto Alomar	.30
10	Todd Stottlemyre	.05
11	Joe Carter	.05
12	*Steve Karsay*	.10
13	Mark Whiten	.05
14	Pat Borders	.05
15	Mike Timlin	.05
16	Tom Henke	.05
17	Eddie Zosky	.05
18	Kelly Gruber	.05
19	Jimmy Key	.05
20	Jerry Schunk	.05
21	Manny Lee	.05
22	Dave Steib	.05
23	Pat Hentgen	.05
24	Glenallen Hill	.05
25	Rene Gonzales	.05
26	Ed Sprague	.05
27	Ken Dayley	.05
28	Pat Tabler	.05
29	*Denis Boucher*	.05
30	Devon White	.05
31	Dante Bichette	.05
32	Paul Molitor	.40
33	Greg Vaughn	.05
34	Dan Plesac	.05
35	Chris George	.05
36	Tim McIntosh	.05
37	Franklin Stubbs	.05
38	Bo Dodson	.05
39	Ron Robinson	.05
40	Ed Nunez	.05
41	Greg Brock	.05
42	Jaime Navarro	.05
43	Chris Bosio	.05
44	B.J. Surhoff	.05
45	Chris Johnson	.05
46	Willie Randolph	.05
47	Narciso Elvira	.05

48 Jim Gantner .05
49 Kevin Brown .05
50 Julio Machado .05
51 Chuck Crim .05
52 Gary Sheffield .30
53 Angel Miranda .05
54 Teddy Higuera .05
55 Robin Yount .40
56 Cal Eldred .05
57 Sandy Alomar .05
58 Greg Swindell .05
59 Brook Jacoby .05
60 Efrain Valdez .05
61 Ever Magallanes .05
62 Tom Candiotti .05
63 Eric King .05
64 Alex Cole .05
65 Charles Nagy .05
66 Mitch Webster .05
67 Chris James .05
68 *Jim Thome* 1.50
69 Carlos Baerga .05
70 Mark Lewis .05
71 Jerry Browne .05
72 Jesse Orosco .05
73 Mike Huff .05
74 Jose Escobar .05
75 Jeff Manto .05
76 *Turner Ward* .05
77 Doug Jones .05
78 *Bruce Egloff* .05
79 Tim Costo .05
80 Beau Allred .05
81 Albert Belle .15
82 John Farrell .05
83 Glenn Davis .05
84 Joe Orsulak .05
85 Mark Williamson .05
86 Ben McDonald .05
87 Billy Ripken .05
88 Leo Gomez .05
89 Bob Melvin .05
90 Jeff Robinson .05
91 Jose Mesa .05
92 Gregg Olson .05
93 Mike Devereaux .05
94 Luis Mercedes .05
95 *Arthur Rhodes* .10
96 Juan Bell .05
97 *Mike Mussina* 1.50
98 Jeff Ballard .05
99 Chris Hoiles .05
100 Brady Anderson .05
101 Bob Milacki .05
102 David Segui .05
103 Dwight Evans .05
104 Cal Ripken, Jr. 1.00
105 Mike Linskey .05
106 *Jeff Tackett* .05
107 Jeff Reardon .05
108 Dana Kiecker .05
109 Ellis Burks .05
110 Dave Owen .05
111 Danny Darwin .05
112 Mo Vaughn .05
113 Jeff McNeely .05
114 Tom Bolton .05
115 Greg Blosser .05
116 Mike Greenwell .05
117 *Phil Plantier* .05
118 Roger Clemens .50
119 John Marzano .05
120 Jody Reed .05
121 Scott Taylor .05
122 Jack Clark .05
123 Derek Livernois .05
124 Tony Pena .05
125 Tom Brunansky .05
126 Carlos Quintana .05
127 Tim Naehring .05
128 Matt Young .05
129 Wade Boggs .45
130 Kevin Morton .05
131 Pete Incaviglia .05
132 Rob Deer .05
133 Bill Gullickson .05
134 Rico Brogna .05
135 Lloyd Moseby .05
136 Cecil Fielder .05
137 Tony Phillips .05
138 Mark Leiter .05
139 John Cerutti .05
140 Mickey Tettleton .05
141 Milt Cuyler .05
142 Greg Gohr .05
143 Tony Bernazard .05
144 Dan Gakeler .05
145 Travis Fryman .05
146 Dan Petry .05
147 Scott Aldred .05
148 John DeSilva .05
149 Rusty Meacham .05
150 Lou Whitaker .05
151 Dave Haas .05
152 Luis de los Santos .05
153 Ivan Cruz .05
154 Alan Trammell .05
155 Pat Kelly .05
156 *Carl Everett* .30
157 Greg Cadaret .05
158 Kevin Maas .05
159 Jeff Johnson .05
160 Willie Smith .05
161 Gerald Williams .05
162 Mike Humphreys .05
163 Alvaro Espinoza .05
164 Matt Nokes .05
165 Wade Taylor .05
166 Roberto Kelly .05
167 John Habyan .05
168 Steve Farr .05
169 Jesse Barfield .05
170 Steve Sax .05
171 Jim Leyritz .05
172 Robert Eenhoorn .05
173 Bernie Williams .20
174 Scott Lusader .05
175 Torey Lovullo .05
176 Chuck Cary .05
177 Scott Sanderson .05
178 Don Mattingly .50
179 Mel Hall .05
180 Juan Gonzalez .40
181 Hensley Meulens .05
182 Jose Offerman .05
183 *Jeff Bagwell* 2.00
184 *Jeff Conine* .25
185 *Henry Rodriguez* .05
186 Jimmie Reese .05
187 Kyle Abbott .05
188 Lance Parrish .05
189 Rafael Montalvo .05
190 Floyd Bannister .05
191 Dick Schofield .05
192 Scott Lewis .05
193 Jeff Robinson .05
194 Kent Anderson .05
195 Wally Joyner .05
196 Chuck Finley .05
197 Luis Sojo .05
198 Jeff Richardson .05
199 Dave Parker .05
200 Jim Abbott .05
201 Junior Felix .05
202 Mark Langston .05
203 *Tim Salmon* 1.00
204 Cliff Young .05
205 Scott Bailes .05
206 Bobby Rose .05
207 Gary Gaetti .05
208 Ruben Amaro .05
209 Luis Polonia .05
210 Dave Winfield .40
211 Bryan Harvey .05
212 Mike Moore .05
213 Rickey Henderson .40
214 Steve Chitren .05
215 Bob Welch .05
216 Terry Steinbach .05
217 Ernie Riles .05
218 *Todd Van Poppel* .10
219 Mike Gallego .05
220 Curt Young .05
221 Todd Burns .05
222 Vance Law .05
223 Eric Show .05
224 *Don Peters* .05
225 Dave Stewart .05
226 Dave Henderson .05
227 Jose Canseco .30
228 Walt Weiss .05
229 Dann Howitt .05
230 Willie Wilson .05
231 Harold Baines .05
232 Scott Hemond .05
233 Joe Slusarski .05
234 Mark McGwire .75
235 *Kirk Dressendorfer* .05
236 *Craig Paquette* .05
237 Dennis Eckersley .35
238 Dana Allison .05
239 Scott Bradley .05
240 Brian Holman .05
241 Mike Schooler .05
242 Rich Delucia .05
243 Edgar Martinez .05
244 Henry Cotto .05
245 Omar Vizquel .05
246a Ken Griffey, Jr. .60
246b Ken Griffey Sr. (should be #255) .10
247 Jay Buhner .05
248 Bill Krueger .05
249 *Dave Fleming* .05
250 *Patrick Lennon* .05
251 Dave Valle .05
252 Harold Reynolds .05
253 Randy Johnson .40
254 Scott Bankhead .05
255 (Not issued, see #246b)
256 Greg Briley .05
257 Tino Martinez .05
258 Alvin Davis .05
259 Pete O'Brien .05
260 Erik Hanson .05
261 *Bret Boone* 1.50
262 Roger Salkeld .05
263 Dave Burba .05
264 *Kerry Woodson* .05
265 Julio Franco .05
266 Dan Peltier .05
267 Jeff Russell .05
268 Steve Buechele .05
269 Donald Harris .05
270 Robb Nen .05
271 Rich Gossage .05
272 *Ivan Rodriguez* 2.00
273 Jeff Huson .05
274 Kevin Brown .10
275 *Dan Smith* .05
276 Gary Pettis .05
277 Jack Daugherty .05
278 Mike Jeffcoat .05
279 Brad Arnsberg .05
280 Nolan Ryan 1.00
281 Eric McCray .05
282 Scott Chiamparino .05
283 Ruben Sierra .05
284 Geno Petralli .05
285 Monty Fariss .05
286 Rafael Palmeiro .40
287 Bobby Witt .05
288 Dean Palmer .05
289 Tony Scruggs .05
290 Kenny Rogers .05
291 Bret Saberhagen .05
292 *Brian McRae* .05
293 Storm Davis .05
294 Danny Tartabull .05
295 David Howard .05
296 Mike Boddicker .05
297 Joel Johnston .05
298 Tim Spehr .05
299 Hector Wagner .05
300 George Brett .50
301 Mike Macfarlane .05
302 Kirk Gibson .05
303 Harvey Pulliam .05
304 Jim Eisenreich .05
305 Kevin Seitzer .05
306 Mark Davis .05
307 Kurt Stillwell .05
308 Jeff Montgomery .05
309 Kevin Appier .05
310 Bob Hamelin .05
311 Tom Gordon .05
312 *Kerwin Moore* .05
313 Hugh Walker .05
314 Terry Shumpert .05
315 Warren Cromartie .05
316 Gary Thurman .05
317 Steve Bedrosian .05
318 Danny Gladden .05
319 Jack Morris .05
320 Kirby Puckett .45
321 Kent Hrbek .05
322 Kevin Tapani .05
323 Denny Neagle .05
324 Rich Garces .05
325 Larry Casian .05
326 Shane Mack .05
327 Allan Anderson .05
328 Junior Ortiz .05
329 *Paul Abbott* .05
330 Chuck Knoblauch .05
331 Chili Davis .05
332 *Todd Ritchie* .05
333 Brian Harper .05
334 Rick Aguilera .05
335 Scott Erickson .05
336 Pedro Munoz .05
337 Scott Leuis .05
338 Greg Gagne .05
339 Mike Pagliarulo .05
340 Terry Leach .05
341 Willie Banks .05
342 Bobby Thigpen .05
343 *Roberto Hernandez* .10
344 Melido Perez .05
345 Carlton Fisk .40
346 *Norberto Martin* .05
347 *Johnny Ruffin* .05
348 *Jeff Carter* .05
349 Lance Johnson .05
350 Sammy Sosa .60
351 Alex Fernandez .05
352 Jack McDowell .05
353 Bob Wickman .05
354 Wilson Alvarez .05
355 Charlie Hough .05
356 Ozzie Guillen .05
357 Cory Snyder .05
358 Robin Ventura .05
359 Scott Fletcher .05
360 Cesar Bernhardt .05
361 Dan Pasqua .05
362 Tim Raines .05
363 Brian Drahman .05
364 Wayne Edwards .05
365 Scott Radinsky .05
366 Frank Thomas .40
367 Cecil Fielder .05
368 Julio Franco .05
369 Kelly Gruber .05
370 Alan Trammell .05
371 Rickey Henderson .20
372 Jose Canseco .15
373 Ellis Burks .05
374 Lance Parrish .05
375 Dave Parker .05
376 Eddie Murray .20
377 Ryne Sandberg .20
378 Matt Williams .05
379 Barry Larkin .05
380 Barry Bonds .50
381 Bobby Bonilla .05
382 Darryl Strawberry .05
383 Benny Santiago .05
384 Don Robinson .05
385 Paul Coleman .05
386 Milt Thompson .05
387 Lee Smith .05
388 Ray Lankford .05
389 Tom Pagnozzi .05
390 Ken Hill .05
391 Jamie Moyer .05
392 *Greg Carmona* .05
393 John Ericks .05
394 Bob Tewksbury .05
395 Jose Oquendo .05
396 Rheal Cormier .05
397 *Mike Milchin* .05
398 Ozzie Smith .45
399 *Aaron Holbert* .05
400 Jose DeLeon .05
401 Felix Jose .05
402 Juan Agosto .05
403 Pedro Guerrero .05
404 Todd Zeile .05
405 Gerald Perry .05
406 Not issued
407 Bryn Smith .05
408 Bernard Gilkey .05
409 Rex Hudler .05
410a Ralph Branca, Bobby Thomson .10
410b Donovan Osborne .05
411 Lance Dickson .05
412 Danny Jackson .05
413 Jerome Walton .05
414 Sean Cheetham .05
415 Joe Girardi .05
416 Ryne Sandberg .45
417 Mike Harkey .05
418 George Bell .05
419 *Rick Wilkins* .05
420 Earl Cunningham .05
421 Heathcliff Slocumb .05
422 Mike Bielecki .05
423 *Jessie Hollins* .05
424 Shawon Dunston .05
425 Dave Smith .05
426 Greg Maddux .45
427 Jose Vizcaino .05
428 Luis Salazar .05
429 Andre Dawson .25
430 Rick Sutcliffe .05
431 Paul Assenmacher .05
432 Erik Pappas .05
433 Mark Grace .10
434 Denny Martinez .05
435 Marquis Grissom .05
436 *Wil Cordero* .05
437 Tim Wallach .05
438 *Brian Barnes* .05
439 Barry Jones .05

No.	Player	Price
440	Ivan Calderon	.05
441	*Stan Spencer*	.05
442	Larry Walker	.05
443	*Chris Haney*	.05
444	Hector Rivera	.05
445	Delino DeShields	.05
446	Andres Galarraga	.05
447	Gilberto Reyes	.05
448	Willie Greene	.05
449	Greg Colbrunn	.05
450	*Rondell White*	.30
451	Steve Frey	.05
452	*Shane Andrews*	.10
453	Mike Fitzgerald	.05
454	Spike Owen	.05
455	Dave Martinez	.05
456	Dennis Boyd	.05
457	Eric Bullock	.05
458	*Reid Cornelius*	.05
459	Chris Nabholz	.05
460	David Cone	.05
461	Hubie Brooks	.05
462	Sid Fernandez	.05
463	*Doug Simons*	.05
464	Howard Johnson	.05
465	Chris Donnels	.05
466	Anthony Young	.05
467	Todd Hundley	.05
468	Rick Cerone	.05
469	Kevin Elster	.05
470	Wally Whitehurst	.05
471	Vince Coleman	.05
472	Dwight Gooden	.05
473	Charlie O'Brien	.05
474	*Jeromy Burnitz*	.50
475	John Franco	.05
476	Daryl Boston	.05
477	Frank Viola	.05
478	D.J. Dozier	.05
479	Kevin McReynolds	.05
480	Tom Herr	.05
481	Gregg Jefferies	.05
482	Pete Schourek	.05
483	Ron Darling	.05
484	Dave Magadan	.05
485	*Andy Ashby*	.05
486	Dale Murphy	.20
487	Von Hayes	.05
488	*Kim Batiste*	.05
489	*Tony Longmire*	.05
490	Wally Backman	.05
491	Jeff Jackson	.05
492	Mickey Morandini	.05
493	Darrel Akerfelds	.05
494	Ricky Jordan	.05
495	Randy Ready	.05
496	Darrin Fletcher	.05
497	Chuck Malone	.05
498	Pat Combs	.05
499	Dickie Thon	.05
500	Roger McDowell	.05
501	Len Dykstra	.05
502	Joe Boever	.05
503	John Kruk	.05
504	Terry Mulholland	.05
505	Wes Chamberlain	.05
506	*Mike Lieberthal*	.75
507	Darren Daulton	.05
508	Charlie Hayes	.05
509	John Smiley	.05
510	Gary Varsho	.05
511	Curt Wilkerson	.05
512	*Orlando Merced*	.05
513	Barry Bonds	1.00
514	Mike Lavalliere	.05
515	Doug Drabek	.05
516	Gary Redus	.05
517	*William Pennyfeather*	.05
518	Randy Tomlin	.05
519	*Mike Zimmerman*	.05
520	Jeff King	.05
521	*Kurt Miller*	.05
522	Jay Bell	.05
523	Bill Landrum	.05
524	Zane Smith	.05
525	Bobby Bonilla	.05
526	Bob Walk	.05
527	Austin Manahan	.05
528	*Joe Ausanio*	.05
529	Andy Van Slyke	.05
530	Jose Lind	.05
531	*Carlos Garcia*	.05
532	Don Slaught	.05
533	Colin Powell	.25
534	*Frank Bolick*	.05
535	*Gary Scott*	.05
536	Nikco Riesgo	.05
537	*Reggie Sanders*	.25
538	*Tim Howard*	.05
539	*Ryan Bowen*	.05
540	Eric Anthony	.05
541	Jim Deshaies	.05
542	Tom Nevers	.05
543	Ken Caminiti	.05
544	Karl Rhodes	.05
545	Xavier Hernandez	.05
546	Mike Scott	.05
547	Jeff Juden	.05
548	Darryl Kile	.05
549	Willie Ansley	.05
550	*Luis Gonzalez*	1.00
551	*Mike Simms*	.05
552	Mark Portugal	.05
553	Jimmy Jones	.05
554	Jim Clancy	.05
555	Pete Harnisch	.05
556	Craig Biggio	.05
557	Eric Yelding	.05
558	Dave Rohde	.05
559	Casey Candaele	.05
560	Curt Schilling	.25
561	Steve Finley	.05
562	Javier Ortiz	.05
563	Andujar Cedeno	.05
564	Rafael Ramirez	.05
565	*Kenny Lofton*	.50
566	Steve Avery	.05
567	Lonnie Smith	.05
568	Kent Mercker	.05
569	*Chipper Jones*	3.00
570	Terry Pendleton	.05
571	Otis Nixon	.05
572	Juan Berenguer	.05
573	Charlie Leibrandt	.05
574	Dave Justice	.05
575	Keith Mitchell	.05
576	Tom Glavine	.25
577	Greg Olson	.05
578	Rafael Belliard	.05
579	Ben Rivera	.05
580	John Smoltz	.05
581	Tyler Houston	.05
582	*Mark Wohlers*	.05
583	Ron Gant	.05
584	Ramon Caraballo	.05
585	Sid Bream	.05
586	Jeff Treadway	.05
587	*Javier Lopez*	.50
588	Deion Sanders	.10
589	Mike Heath	.05
590	*Ryan Klesko*	.20
591	Bob Ojeda	.05
592	Alfredo Griffin	.05
593	*Raul Mondesi*	.35
594	Greg Smith	.05
595	Orel Hershiser	.05
596	Juan Samuel	.05
597	Brett Butler	.05
598	Gary Carter	.40
599	Stan Javier	.05
600	Kal Daniels	.05
601	*Jamie McAndrew*	.05
602	Mike Sharperson	.05
603	Jay Howell	.05
604	*Eric Karros*	.35
605	Tim Belcher	.05
606	Dan Opperman	.05
607	Lenny Harris	.05
608	Tom Goodwin	.05
609	Darryl Strawberry	.05
610	Ramon Martinez	.05
611	Kevin Gross	.05
612	Zakary Shinall	.05
613	Mike Scioscia	.05
614	Eddie Murray	.40
615	Ronnie Walden	.05
616	Will Clark	.15
617	Adam Hyzdu	.05
618	Matt Williams	.05
619	Don Robinson	.05
620	Jeff Brantley	.05
621	Greg Litton	.05
622	Steve Decker	.05
623	Robby Thompson	.05
624	*Mark Leonard*	.05
625	Kevin Bass	.05
626	Scott Garrelts	.05
627	Jose Uribe	.05
628	Eric Gunderson	.05
629	Steve Hosey	.05
630	Trevor Wilson	.05
631	Terry Kennedy	.05
632	Dave Righetti	.05
633	Kelly Downs	.05
634	Johnny Ard	.05
635	*Eric Christopherson*	.05
636	Kevin Mitchell	.05
637	John Burkett	.05
638	*Kevin Rogers*	.05
639	Bud Black	.05
640	Willie McGee	.05
641	Royce Clayton	.05
642	Tony Fernandez	.05
643	Ricky Bones	.05
644	Thomas Howard	.05
645	Dave Staton	.05
646	Jim Presley	.05
647	Tony Gwynn	.45
648	Marty Barrett	.05
649	Scott Coolbaugh	.05
650	Craig Lefferts	.05
651	Eddie Whitson	.05
652	Oscar Azocar	.05
653	Wes Gardner	.05
654	Bip Roberts	.05
655	*Robbie Beckett*	.05
656	Benny Santiago	.05
657	Greg W. Harris	.05
658	Jerald Clark	.05
659	Fred McGriff	.05
660	Larry Andersen	.05
661	Bruce Hurst	.05
662	Steve Martin	.05
663	Rafael Valdez	.05
664	*Paul Faries*	.05
665	Andy Benes	.05
666	Randy Myers	.05
667	Rob Dibble	.05
668	Glenn Sutko	.05
669	Glenn Braggs	.05
670	Billy Hatcher	.05
671	Joe Oliver	.05
672	Freddie Benavides	.05
673	Barry Larkin	.05
674	Chris Sabo	.05
675	Mariano Duncan	.05
676	*Chris Jones*	.05
677	*Gino Minutelli*	.05
678	Reggie Jefferson	.05
679	Jack Armstrong	.05
680	Chris Hammond	.05
681	Jose Rijo	.05
682	Bill Doran	.05
683	Terry Lee	.05
684	Tom Browning	.05
685	Paul O'Neill	.05
686	Eric Davis	.05
687	*Dan Wilson*	.05
688	Ted Power	.05
689	Tim Layana	.05
690	Norm Charlton	.05
691	Hal Morris	.05
692	Rickey Henderson	.40
693	*Sam Militello*	.05
694	*Matt Mieske*	.05
695	*Paul Russo*	.05
696	*Domingo Mota*	.05
697	*Todd Guggiana*	.05
698	Marc Newfield	.10
699	Checklist	.05
700	Checklist	.05
701	Checklist	.05
702	Checklist	.05
703	Checklist	.05
704	Checklist	.05

1992 BOWMAN

	NM/M
Complete Set (705):	100.00
Common Player:	.10
Pack (15):	5.00
Wax Box (36):	150.00
Jumbo Pack (25):	10.00
Jumbo Box (36):	225.00

No.	Player	Price
1	Ivan Rodriguez	1.50
2	Kirk McCaskill	.10
3	Scott Livingstone	.10
4	*Salomon Torres*	.10
5	Carlos Hernandez	.10
6	Dave Hollins	.10
7	Scott Fletcher	.10
8	Jorge Fabregas	.10
9	Andujar Cedeno	.10
10	Howard Johnson	.10
11	*Trevor Hoffman*	2.00
12	Roberto Kelly	.10
13	Gregg Jefferies	.10
14	Marquis Grissom	.10
15	Mike Ignasiak	.10
16	Jack Morris	.10
17	William Pennyfeather	.10
18	Todd Stottlemyre	.10
19	Chito Martinez	.10
20	Roberto Alomar	.35
21	Sam Militello	.10
22	Hector Fajardo	.10
23	*Paul Quantrill*	.10
24	Chuck Knoblauch	.10
25	Reggie Jefferson	.10
26	Jeremy McGarity	.10
27	Jerome Walton	.10
28	Chipper Jones	4.00
29	*Brian Barber*	.10
30	Ron Darling	.10
31	*Roberto Petagine*	.10
32	Chuck Finley	.10
33	Edgar Martinez	.10
34	Napolean Robinson	.10
35	Andy Van Slyke	.10
36	Bobby Thigpen	.10
37	Travis Fryman	.10
38	Eric Christopherson	.10
39	Terry Mulholland	.10
40	Darryl Strawberry	.10
41	*Manny Alexander*	.10
42	*Tracey Sanders*	.10
43	Pete Incaviglia	.10
44	Kim Batiste	.10
45	Frank Rodriguez	.10
46	Greg Swindell	.10
47	Delino DeShields	.10
48	John Ericks	.10
49	Franklin Stubbs	.10
50	Tony Gwynn	2.00
51	*Clifton Garrett*	.10
52	Mike Gardella	.10
53	Scott Erickson	.10
54	Gary Caballo	.10
55	*Jose Oliva*	.10
56	Brook Fordyce	.10
57	Mark Whiten	.10
58	Joe Slusarski	.10
59	*J.R. Phillips*	.10
60	Barry Bonds	4.00
61	Bob Milacki	.10
62	Keith Mitchell	.10
63	Angel Miranda	.10
64	Raul Mondesi	.10
65	Brian Koelling	.10
66	Brian McRae	.10
67	John Patterson	.10
68	John Wetteland	.10
69	Wilson Alvarez	.10
70	Wade Boggs	2.00
71	Darryl Ratliff	.10
72	Jeff Jackson	.10
73	Jeremy Hernandez	.10
74	Darryl Hamilton	.10
75	Rafael Belliard	.10
76	Ricky Trlicek	.10
77	*Felipe Crespo*	.10
78	Carney Lansford	.10
79	Ryan Long	.10
80	Kirby Puckett	2.00
81	Earl Cunningham	.10
82	Pedro Martinez	8.00
83	Scott Hatteberg	.10
84	Juan Gonzalez	1.50
85	Robert Nutting	.10
86	*Calvin Reese*	.50
87	Dave Silvestri	.10
88	*Scott Ruffcorn*	.10
89	Rick Aguilera	.10
90	Cecil Fielder	.10
91	Kirk Dressendorfer	.10
92	Jerry DiPoto	.10
93	Mike Felder	.10
94	Craig Paquette	.10
95	Elvin Paulino	.10
96	Donovan Osborne	.10
97	Hubie Brooks	.10
98	*Derek Lowe*	4.00
99	David Zancanaro	.10
100	Ken Griffey, Jr.	2.50
101	Todd Hundley	.10
102	Mike Trombley	.10

No.	Player	Price
103	*Ricky Gutierrez*	.10
104	Braulio Castillo	.10
105	Craig Lefferts	.10
106	Rick Sutcliffe	.10
107	Dean Palmer	.10
108	Henry Rodriguez	.10
109	*Mark Clark*	.10
110	Kenny Lofton	.10
111	Mark Carreon	.10
112	*J.T. Bruett*	.10
113	Gerald Williams	.10
114	Frank Thomas	1.50
115	Kevin Reimer	.10
116	Sammy Sosa	3.00
117	Mickey Tettleton	.10
118	Reggie Sanders	.10
119	Trevor Wilson	.10
120	Cliff Brantley	.10
121	Spike Owen	.10
122	Jeff Montgomery	.10
123	Alex Sutherland	.10
124	*Brien Taylor*	.10
125	Brian Williams	.10
126	Kevin Seitzer	.10
127	*Carlos Delgado*	10.00
128	Gary Scott	.10
129	Scott Cooper	.10
130	*Domingo Jean*	.10
131	*Pat Mahomes*	.10
132	Mike Boddicker	.10
133	Roberto Hernandez	.10
134	Dave Valle	.10
135	Kurt Stillwell	.10
136	*Brad Pennington*	.10
137	Jermaine Swifton	.10
138	Ryan Hawblitzel	.10
139	Tito Navarro	.10
140	Sandy Alomar	.10
141	Todd Benzinger	.10
142	Danny Jackson	.10
143	*Melvin Nieves*	.25
144	Jim Campanis	.10
145	Luis Gonzalez	.50
146	Dave Doorneweerd	.10
147	Charlie Hayes	.10
148	Greg Maddux	2.00
149	Brian Harper	.10
150	Brent Miller	.10
151	*Shawn Estes*	.75
152	Mike Williams	.10
153	Charlie Hough	.10
154	Randy Myers	.10
155	*Kevin Young*	.25
156	Rick Wilkins	.10
157	Terry Schumpert	.10
158	Steve Karsay	.10
159	Gary DiSarcina	.10
160	Deion Sanders	.10
161	Tom Browning	.10
162	Dickie Thon	.10
163	Luis Mercedes	.10
164	Ricardo Ingram	.10
165	*Tavo Alavarez*	.10
166	Rickey Henderson	1.50
167	Jaime Navarro	.10
168	*Billy Ashley*	.10
169	Phil Dauphin	.10
170	Ivan Cruz	.10
171	Harold Baines	.10
172	Bryan Harvey	.10
173	Alex Cole	.10
174	Curtis Shaw	.10
175	Matt Williams	.10
176	Felix Jose	.10
177	Sam Horn	.10
178	Randy Johnson	1.50
179	Ivan Calderon	.10
180	Steve Avery	.10
181	William Suero	.10
182	Bill Swift	.10
183	*Howard Battle*	.10
184	Ruben Amaro	.10
185	Jim Abbott	.10
186	Mike Fitzgerald	.10
187	Bruce Hurst	.10
188	Jeff Juden	.10
189	Jeromy Burnitz	.10
190	Dave Burba	.10
191	Kevin Brown	.10
192	Patrick Lennon	.10
193	Jeffrey McNeely	.10
194	Wil Cordero	.10
195	Chili Davis	.10
196	Milt Cuyler	.10
197	Von Hayes	.10
198	*Todd Revening*	.10
199	Joel Johnson	.10
200	Jeff Bagwell	1.50
201	Alex Fernandez	.10
202	Todd Jones	.10
203	Charles Nagy	.10
204	Tim Raines	.10
205	Kevin Maas	.10
206	Julio Franco	.10
207	Randy Velarde	.10
208	Lance Johnson	.10
209	Scott Leius	.10
210	Derek Lee	.10
211	Joe Sondrini	.10
212	Royce Clayton	.10
213	Chris George	.10
214	Gary Sheffield	.60
215	Mark Gubicza	.10
216	Mike Moore	.10
217	Rick Huisman	.10
218	Jeff Russell	.10
219	D.J. Dozier	.10
220	Dave Martinez	.10
221	Al Newman	.10
222	Nolan Ryan	4.00
223	Teddy Higuera	.10
224	*Damon Buford*	.10
225	Ruben Sierra	.10
226	Tom Nevers	.10
227	Tommy Greene	.10
228	*Nigel Wilson*	.10
229	John DeSilva	.10
230	Bobby Witt	.10
231	Greg Cadaret	.10
232	John VanderWal	.10
233	Jack Clark	.10
234	Bill Doran	.10
235	Bobby Bonilla	.10
236	Steve Olin	.10
237	Derek Bell	.10
238	David Cone	.10
239	Victor Cole	.10
240	Rod Bolton	.10
241	Tom Pagnozzi	.10
242	Rob Dibble	.10
243	Michael Carter	.10
244	Don Peters	.10
245	Mike LaValliere	.10
246	Joe Perona	.10
247	Mitch Williams	.10
248	Jay Buhner	.10
249	Andy Benes	.10
250	*Alex Ochoa*	.10
251	Greg Blosser	.10
252	Jack Armstrong	.10
253	Juan Samuel	.10
254	Terry Pendleton	.10
255	Ramon Martinez	.10
256	Rico Brogna	.10
257	John Smiley	.10
258	Carl Everett	.10
259	Tim Salmon	.25
260	Will Clark	.15
261	*Ugueth Urbina*	.40
262	Jason Wood	.10
263	Dave Magadan	.10
264	Dante Bichette	.10
265	Jose DeLeon	.10
266	*Mike Neill*	.10
267	Paul O'Neill	.10
268	Anthony Young	.10
269	Greg Harris	.10
270	Todd Van Poppel	.10
271	Pete Castellano	.10
272	Tony Phillips	.10
273	Mike Gallego	.10
274	*Steve Cooke*	.10
275	Robin Ventura	.10
276	Kevin Mitchell	.10
277	Doug Linton	.10
278	Robert Eenhorn	.10
279	*Gabe White*	.10
280	Dave Stewart	.10
281	Mo Sanford	.10
282	Greg Perschke	.10
283	Kevin Flora	.10
284	Jeff Williams	.10
285	Keith Miller	.10
286	Andy Ashby	.10
287	Doug Dascenzo	.10
288	Eric Karros	.10
289	*Glenn Murray*	.10
290	*Troy Percival*	.75
291	Orlando Merced	.10
292	Peter Hoy	.10
293	Tony Fernandez	.10
294	Juan Guzman	.10
295	Jesse Barfield	.10
296	Sid Fernandez	.10
297	Scott Cepicky	.10
298	*Garret Anderson*	6.00
299	Cal Eldred	.10
300	Ryne Sandberg	2.00
301	Jim Gantner	.10
302	*Mariano Rivera*	6.00
303	Ron Lockett	.10
304	Jose Offerman	.10
305	Denny Martinez	.10
306	*Luis Ortiz*	.10
307	David Howard	.10
308	Russ Springer	.10
309	Chris Howard	.10
310	Kyle Abbott	.10
311	*Aaron Sele*	1.00
312	Dave Justice	.10
313	Pete O'Brien	.10
314	Greg Hansell	.10
315	Dave Winfield	1.50
316	Lance Dickson	.10
317	Eric King	.10
318	Vaughn Eshelman	.10
319	Tim Belcher	.10
320	Andres Galarraga	.10
321	Scott Bullett	.10
322	Doug Strange	.10
323	Jerald Clark	.10
324	Dave Righetti	.10
325	Greg Hibbard	.10
326	Eric Dillman	.10
327	*Shane Reynolds*	.20
328	Chris Hammond	.10
329	Albert Belle	.20
330	*Rich Becker*	.10
331	Eddie Williams	.10
332	Donald Harris	.10
333	Dave Smith	.10
334	Steve Fireovid	.10
335	Steve Buechele	.10
336	Mike Schooler	.10
337	Kevin McReynolds	.10
338	Hensley Meulens	.10
339	*Benji Gil*	.10
340	Don Mattingly	2.50
341	Alvin Davis	.10
342	Alan Mills	.10
343	Kelly Downs	.10
344	Leo Gomez	.10
345	*Tarrik Brock*	.10
346	Ryan Turner	.10
347	John Smoltz	.10
348	Bill Sampen	.10
349	Paul Byrd	.10
350	Mike Bordick	.10
351	Jose Lind	.10
352	David Wells	.10
353	Barry Larkin	.10
354	Bruce Ruffin	.10
355	Luis Rivera	.10
356	Sid Bream	.10
357	Julian Vasquez	.10
358	*Jason Bere*	.10
359	Ben McDonald	.10
360	Scott Stahoviak	.10
361	Kirt Manwaring	.10
362	Jeff Johnson	.10
363	Rob Deer	.10
364	Tony Pena	.10
365	Melido Perez	.10
366	Clay Parker	.10
367	Dale Sveum	.10
368	Mike Scioscia	.10
369	Roger Salkeld	.10
370	Mike Stanley	.10
371	Jack McDowell	.10
372	Tim Wallach	.10
373	Billy Ripken	.10
374	Mike Christopher	.10
375	Paul Molitor	1.50
376	Dave Stieb	.10
377	Pedro Guerrero	.10
378	Russ Swan	.10
379	Bob Ojeda	.10
380	Donn Pall	.10
381	Eddie Zosky	.10
382	Darnell Coles	.10
383	Tom Smith	.10
384	Mark McGwire	3.00
385	Gary Carter	1.50
386	Rich Amaral	.10
387	Alan Embree	.10
388	Jonathan Hurst	.10
389	*Bobby Jones*	.10
390	Rico Rossy	.10
391	Dan Smith	.10
392	Terry Steinbach	.10
393	Jon Farrell	.10
394	Dave Anderson	.10
395	Benito Santiago	.10
396	Mark Wohlers	.10
397	Mo Vaughn	.10
398	Randy Kramer	.10
399	*John Jaha*	.10
400	Cal Ripken, Jr.	4.00
401	Ryan Bowen	.10
402	Tim McIntosh	.10
403	Bernard Gilkey	.10
404	Junior Felix	.10
405	Cris Colon	.10
406	Marc Newfield	.10
407	Bernie Williams	.20
408	Jay Howell	.10
409	Zane Smith	.10
410	Jeff Shaw	.10
411	Kerry Woodson	.10
412	Wes Chamberlain	.10
413	Dave Mlicki	.10
414	Benny Distefano	.10
415	Kevin Rogers	.10
416	Tim Naehring	.10
417	Clemente Nunez	.10
418	Luis Sojo	.10
419	Kevin Ritz	.10
420	Omar Oliveras	.10
421	Manuel Lee	.10
422	Julio Valera	.10
423	Omar Vizquel	.10
424	Darren Burton	.10
425	Mel Hall	.10
426	Dennis Powell	.10
427	Lee Stevens	.10
428	Glenn Davis	.10
429	Willie Greene	.10
430	Kevin Wickander	.10
431	Dennis Eckersley	1.00
432	Joe Orsulak	.10
433	Eddie Murray	1.50
434	*Matt Stairs*	.10
435	Wally Joyner	.10
436	Rondell White	.10
437	Rob Mauer	.10
438	Joe Redfield	.10
439	Mark Lewis	.10
440	Darren Daulton	.10
441	Mike Henneman	.10
442	John Cangelosi	.10
443	*Vince Moore*	.10
444	John Wehner	.10
445	Kent Hrbek	.10
446	Mark McLemore	.10
447	Bill Wegman	.10
448	Robby Thompson	.10
449	Mark Anthony	.10
450	Archi Cianfrocco	.10
451	Johnny Ruffin	.10
452	Javier Lopez	.10
453	Greg Gohr	.10
454	Tim Scott	.10
455	Stan Belinda	.10
456	Darrin Jackson	.10
457	Chris Gardner	.10
458	Esteban Beltre	.10
459	Phil Plantier	.10
460	Jim Thome	5.00
461	*Mike Piazza*	25.00
462	Matt Sinatro	.10
463	Scott Servais	.10
464	*Brian Jordan*	.75
465	Doug Drabek	.10
466	Carl Willis	.10
467	Bret Barbarie	.10
468	Hal Morris	.10
469	Steve Sax	.10
470	Jerry Willard	.10
471	Dan Wilson	.10
472	Chris Hoiles	.10
473	Rheal Cormier	.10
474	John Morris	.10
475	Jeff Reardon	.10
476	Mark Leiter	.10
477	Tom Gordon	.10
478	*Kent Bottenfield*	.10
479	Gene Larkin	.10
480	Dwight Gooden	.10
481	B.J. Surhoff	.10
482	Andy Stankiewicz	.10
483	Tino Martinez	.10
484	Craig Biggio	.10
485	Denny Neagle	.10
486	Rusty Meacham	.10
487	Kal Daniels	.10
488	Dave Henderson	.10
489	Tim Costo	.10
490	Doug Davis	.10
491	Frank Viola	.10
492	Cory Snyder	.10
493	Chris Martin	.10
494	Dion James	.10
495	Randy Tomlin	.10
496	Greg Vaughn	.10
497	Dennis Cook	.10
498	Rosario Rodriguez	.10

#	Player	Price
499	Dave Staton	.10
500	George Brett	2.50
501	Brian Barnes	.10
502	Butch Henry	.10
503	Harold Reynolds	.10
504	*David Nied*	.10
505	Lee Smith	.10
506	Steve Chitren	.10
507	Ken Hill	.10
508	Robbie Beckett	.10
509	Troy Afenir	.10
510	Kelly Gruber	.10
511	Bret Boone	.10
512	Jeff Branson	.10
513	Mike Jackson	.10
514	Pete Harnisch	.10
515	Chad Kreuter	.10
516	Joe Vitko	.10
517	Orel Hershiser	.10
518	*John Doherty*	.10
519	Jay Bell	.10
520	Mark Langston	.10
521	Dann Howitt	.10
522	Bobby Reed	.10
523	Roberto Munoz	.10
524	Todd Ritchie	.10
525	Bip Roberts	.10
526	*Pat Listach*	.10
527	*Scott Brosius*	.10
528	*John Roper*	.10
529	*Phil Hiatt*	.10
530	Denny Walling	.10
531	Carlos Baerga	.10
532	*Manny Ramirez*	20.00
533	Pat Clements	.10
534	Ron Gant	.10
535	Pat Kelly	.10
536	Billy Spiers	.10
537	Darren Reed	.10
538	Ken Caminiti	.10
539	*Butch Huskey*	.10
540	Matt Nokes	.10
541	John Kruk	.10
542	John Jaha (Foil, SP)	.35
543	*Justin Thompson*	.10
544	Steve Hosey	.10
545	Joe Kmak	.10
546	John Franco	.10
547	Devon White	.10
548	Elston Hansen (Foil, SP)	.35
549	Ryan Klesko	.10
550	Danny Tartabull	.10
551	Frank Thomas (Foil, SP)	1.50
552	Kevin Tapani	.10
553a	Willie Banks	.10
553b	Pat Clements	.10
554	*B.J. Wallace* (Foil, SP)	.35
555	*Orlando Miller*	.10
556	*Mark Smith*	.10
557	Tim Wallach (Foil)	.10
558	Bill Gullickson	.10
559	Derek Bell (Foil)	.10
560	Joe Randa (Foil)	.10
561	Frank Seminara	.10
562	Mark Gardner	.10
563	Rick Greene (Foil)	.10
564	Gary Gaetti	.10
565	Ozzie Guillen	.10
566	Charles Nagy (Foil)	.10
567	Mike Milchin	.10
568	Ben Shelton (Foil)	.10
569	Chris Roberts (Foil)	.10
570	Ellis Burks	.10
571	Scott Scudder	.10
572	Jim Abbott (Foil)	.10
573	Joe Carter	.10
574	Steve Finley	.10
575	Jim Olander (Foil)	.10
576	Carlos Garcia	.10
577	Greg Olson	.10
578	Greg Swindell (Foil)	.10
579	Matt Williams (Foil)	.10
580	Mark Grace	.10
581	Howard House (Foil)	.10
582	Luis Polonia	.10
583	Erik Hanson	.10
584	Salomon Torres (Foil)	.10
585	Carlton Fisk	1.50
586	Bret Saberhagen	.10
587	*Chad McDonnell* (Foil)	.10
588	Jimmy Key	.10
589	Mike MacFarlane	.10
590	Barry Bonds (Foil)	3.50
591	Jamie McAndrew	.10
592	Shane Mack	.10
593	Kerwin Moore	.10
594	Joe Oliver	.10
595	Chris Sabo	.10
596	*Alex Gonzalez*	.50
597	Brett Butler	.10
598	Mark Hutton	.10
599	Andy Benes (Foil)	.10
600	Jose Canseco	.60
601	Darryl Kile	.10
602	Matt Stairs (Foil, SP)	.35
603	Rob Butler (Foil)	.10
604	Willie McGee	.10
605	Jack McDowell	.10
606	Tom Candiotti	.10
607	Ed Martel	.10
608	Matt Mieske (Foil)	.10
609	Darrin Fletcher	.10
610	Rafael Palmeiro	1.50
611	Bill Swift (Foil)	.10
612	Mike Mussina	.75
613	Vince Coleman	.10
614	Scott Cepicky (Foil)	.10
615	Mike Greenwell	.10
616	Kevin McGehee	.10
617	Jeffrey Hammonds (Foil)	.10
618	Scott Taylor	.10
619	Dave Otto	.10
620	Mark McGwire (Foil)	3.00
621	Kevin Tatar	.10
622	Steve Farr	.10
623	Ryan Klesko (Foil)	.10
624	Andre Dawson	.40
625	Tino Martinez (Foil, SP)	.35
627	*Chad Curtis*	.50
628	Mickey Morandini	.10
629	Gregg Olson (Foil, SP)	.35
630	Lou Whitaker	.10
631	Arthur Rhodes	.10
632	Brandon Wilson	.10
633	*Lance Jennings*	.10
634	*Allen Watson*	.10
635	Len Dykstra	.10
636	Joe Girardi	.10
637	Kiki Hernandez (Foil, SP)	.35
638	*Mike Hampton*	1.00
639	Al Osuna	.10
640	Kevin Appier	.10
641	Rick Helling (Foil, SP)	.35
642	Jody Reed	.10
643	Ray Lankford	.10
644	John Olerud	.10
645	Paul Molitor (Foil, SP)	1.50
646	Pat Borders	.10
647	Mike Morgan	.10
648	Larry Walker	.10
649	Pete Castellano (Foil, SP)	.35
650	Fred McGriff	.10
651	Walt Weiss	.10
652	*Calvin Murray* (Foil, SP)	.35
653	Dave Nilsson	.10
654	Greg Pirkl	.10
655	Robin Ventura (Foil, SP)	.35
656	Mark Portugal	.10
657	Roger McDowell	.10
658	Rick Hirtensteiner (Foil, SP)	.35
659	Glenallen Hill	.10
660	Greg Gagne	.10
661	Charles Johnson (Foil, SP)	.35
662	Brian Hunter	.10
663	Mark Lemke	.10
664	Tim Belcher (Foil, SP)	.35
665	Rich DeLucia	.10
666	Bob Walk	.10
667	Joe Carter (Foil, SP)	.35
668	Jose Guzman	.10
669	Otis Nixon	.10
670	Phil Nevin (Foil)	.25
671	Eric Davis	.10
672	*Damion Easley*	.25
673	Will Clark (Foil)	.25
674	Mark Kiefer	.10
675	Ozzie Smith	2.00
676	Manny Ramirez (Foil)	6.00
677	Gregg Olson	.10
678	*Cliff Floyd*	1.00
679	Duane Singleton	.10
680	Jose Rijo	.10
681	Willie Randolph	.10
682	*Michael Tucker* (Foil)	.25
683	Darren Lewis	.10
684	Dale Murphy	.35
685	Mike Pagliarulo	.10
686	Paul Miller	.10
687	Mike Robertson	.10
688	Mike Devereaux	.10
689	Pedro Astacio	.10
690	Alan Trammell	.10
691	Roger Clemens	2.25
692	Bud Black	.10
693	Turk Wendell	.10
694	Barry Larkin (Foil, SP)	.35
695	Todd Zeile	.10
696	Pat Hentgen	.10
697	*Eddie Taubensee*	.10
698	Guillermo Vasquez	.10
699	Tom Glavine	.25
700	Robin Yount	1.50
701	Checklist	.10
702	Checklist	.10
703	Checklist	.10
704	Checklist	.10
705	Checklist	.10

1993 BOWMAN

	NM/M
Complete Set (708):	35.00
Common Player:	.10
Pack (15):	1.50
Wax Box (24):	35.00
Jumbo Pack (22):	2.50
Jumbo Box (20):	40.00

#	Player	Price
1	Glenn Davis	.10
2	*Hector Roa*	.10
3	*Ken Ryan*	.10
4	*Derek Wallace*	.10
5	Jorge Fabregas	.10
6	Joe Oliver	.10
7	Brandon Wilson	.10
8	*Mark Thompson*	.10
9	Tracy Sanders	.10
10	Rich Renteria	.10
11	Lou Whitaker	.10
12	*Brian Hunter*	.10
13	Joe Vitiello	.10
14	Eric Karros	.10
15	Joe Kmak	.10
16	Tavo Alvarez	.10
17	*Steve Dunn*	.10
18	Tony Fernandez	.10
19	Melido Perez	.10
20	Mike Lieberthal	.10
21	Terry Steinbach	.10
22	Stan Belinda	.10
23	Jay Buhner	.10
24	Allen Watson	.10
25	*Daryl Henderson*	.10
26	*Ray McDavid*	.10
27	Shawn Green	.50
28	Bud Black	.10
29	*Sherman Obando*	.10
30	*Mike Hostetler*	.10
31	*Nate Hinchey*	.10
32	Randy Myers	.10
33	*Brian Grebeck*	.10
34	John Roper	.10
35	Larry Thomas	.10
36	Alex Cole	.10
37	*Tom Kramer*	.10
38	*Matt Whisenant*	.10
39	*Chris Gomez*	.10
40	Luis Gonzalez	.50
41	Kevin Appier	.10
42	*Omar Daal*	.10
43	Duane Singleton	.10
44	Bill Risley	.10
45	*Pat Meares*	.10
46	Butch Huskey	.10
47	Bobby Munoz	.10
48	Juan Bell	.10
49	*Scott Lydy*	.10
50	Dennis Moeller	.10
51	Marc Newfield	.10
52	*Tripp Cromer*	.10
53	Kurt Miller	.10
54	Jim Pena	.10
55	Juan Guzman	.10
56	Matt Williams	.10
57	Harold Reynolds	.10
58	*Donnie Elliott*	.10
59	*Jon Shave*	.10
60	*Kevin Roberson*	.10
61	*Hilly Hathaway*	.10
62	Jose Rijo	.10
63	*Kerry Taylor*	.10
64	Ryan Hawblitzel	.10
65	Glenallen Hill	.10
66	*Ramon D. Martinez*	.10
67	Travis Fryman	.10
68	Tom Nevers	.10
69	Phil Hiatt	.10
70	Tim Wallach	.10
71	B.J. Surhoff	.10
72	Rondell White	.10
73	*Denny Hocking*	.10
74	*Mike Oquist*	.10
75	Paul O'Neill	.10
76	Willie Banks	.10
77	Bob Welch	.10
78	*Jose Sandoval*	.10
79	Bill Haselman	.10
80	Rheal Cormier	.10
81	Dean Palmer	.10
82	*Pat Gomez*	.10
83	Steve Karsay	.10
84	*Carl Hanselman*	.10
85	*T.R. Lewis*	.10
86	Chipper Jones	2.00
87	Scott Hatteberg	.10
88	Greg Hibbard	.10
89	*Lance Painter*	.10
90	*Chad Mottola*	.10
91	Jason Bere	.10
92	Dante Bichette	.10
93	Sandy Alomar	.10
94	Carl Everett	.15
95	*Danny Bautista*	.10
96	Steve Finley	.10
97	David Cone	.10
98	Todd Hollandsworth	.10
99	Matt Mieske	.10
100	Larry Walker	.10
101	Shane Mack	.10
102	*Aaron Ledesma*	.10
103	*Andy Pettitte*	4.00
104	Kevin Stocker	.10
105	Mike Mobler	.10
106	Tony Menedez	.10
107	Derek Lowe	.10
108	Basil Shabazz	.10
109	Dan Smith	.10
110	*Scott Sanders*	.10
111	Todd Stottlemyre	.10
112	*Benji Sikonton*	.10
113	Rick Sutcliffe	.10
114	*Lee Heath*	.10
115	Jeff Russell	.10
116	*Dave Stevens*	.10
117	*Mark Holzemer*	.10
118	Tim Belcher	.10
119	Bobby Thigpen	.10
120	*Roger Bailey*	.10
121	*Tony Mitchell*	.10
122	Junior Felix	.10
123	*Rich Robertson*	.10
124	*Andy Cook*	.10
125	*Brian Bevil*	.10
126	Darryl Strawberry	.10
127	Cal Eldred	.10
128	Cliff Floyd	.10
129	Alan Newman	.10
130	Howard Johnson	.10
131	Jim Abbott	.10
132	Chad McConnell	.10
133	*Miguel Jimenez*	.10
134	*Brett Backlund*	.10
135	*John Cummings*	.10
136	Brian Barber	.10
137	Rafael Palmeiro	1.50
138	*Tim Worrell*	.10
139	*Jose Pett*	.10
140	Barry Bonds	4.00
141	Damon Buford	.10
142	Jeff Blauser	.10
143	Frankie Rodriguez	.10
144	Mike Morgan	.10
145	Gary DeSarcina	.10
146	Calvin Reese	.10
147	Johnny Ruffin	.10
148	David Nied	.10
149	Charles Nagy	.10
150	*Mike Myers*	.10
151	*Kenny Carlyle*	.10
152	Eric Anthony	.10
153	Jose Lind	.10
154	Pedro Martinez	1.50
155	Mark Kiefer	.10

No.	Player	Price
156	*Tim Laker*	.10
157	Pat Mahomes	.10
158	Bobby Bonilla	.10
159	Domingo Jean	.10
160	Darren Daulton	.10
161	Mark McGwire	3.00
162	*Jason Kendall*	1.00
163	Desi Relaford	.10
164	Ozzie Canseco	.10
165	Rick Helling	.10
166	*Steve Pegues*	.10
167	Paul Molitor	1.50
168	*Larry Carter*	.10
169	Arthur Rhodes	.10
170	*Damon Hollins*	.10
171	Frank Viola	.10
172	*Steve Trachsel*	.20
173	*J.T. Snow*	.50
174	*Keith Gordon*	.10
175	Carlton Fisk	1.50
176	*Jason Bates*	.10
177	*Mike Crosby*	.10
178	Benny Santiago	.10
179	Mike Moore	.10
180	Jeff Juden	.10
181	Darren Burton	.10
182	*Todd Williams*	.10
183	John Jaha	.10
184	*Mike Lansing*	.50
185	*Pedro Grifol*	.10
186	Vince Coleman	.10
187	Pat Kelly	.10
188	*Clemente Alvarez*	.10
189	Ron Darling	.10
190	Orlando Merced	.10
191	Chris Bosio	.10
192	*Steve Dixon*	.10
193	Doug Dascenzo	.10
194	*Ray Holbert*	.10
195	Howard Battle	.10
196	Willie McGee	.10
197	*John O'Donoghue*	.10
198	Steve Avery	.10
199	Greg Blosser	.10
200	Ryne Sandberg	2.00
201	Joe Grahe	.10
202	Dan Wilson	.10
203	*Domingo Martinez*	.10
204	Andres Galarraga	.10
205	*Jamie Taylor*	.10
206	*Darrell Whitmore*	.10
207	*Ben Blomdahl*	.10
208	Doug Drabek	.10
209	Keith Miller	.10
210	Billy Ashley	.10
211	*Mike Farrell*	.10
212	John Wetteland	.10
213	Randy Tomlin	.10
214	Sid Fernandez	.10
215	*Quilvio Veras*	.10
216	Dave Hollins	.10
217	Mike Neill	.10
218	Andy Van Slyke	.10
219	Bret Boone	.10
220	Tom Pagnozzi	.10
221	*Mike Welch*	.10
222	Frank Seminara	.10
223	Ron Villone	.10
224	*D.J. Thielen*	.10
225	Cal Ripken, Jr.	4.00
226	*Pedro Borbon*	.10
227	Carlos Quintana	.10
228	*Tommy Shields*	.10
229	Tim Salmon	.40
230	John Smiley	.10
231	Ellis Burks	.10
232	Pedro Castellano	.10
233	Paul Byrd	.10
234	Bryan Harvey	.10
235	Scott Livingstone	.10
236	*James Mouton*	.10
237	Joe Randa	.10
238	Pedro Astacio	.10
239	Darryl Hamilton	.10
240	*Joey Eischen*	.10
241	*Edgar Herrera*	.10
242	Dwight Gooden	.10
243	Sam Militello	.10
244	*Ron Blazier*	.10
245	Ruben Sierra	.10
246	Al Martin	.10
247	Mike Felder	.10
248	Bob Tewksbury	.10
249	Craig Lefferts	.10
250	Luis Lopez	.10
251	Devon White	.10
252	Will Clark	.15
253	Mark Smith	.10
254	Terry Pendleton	.10
255	Aaron Sele	.10
256	*Jose Viera*	.10
257	Damion Easley	.10
258	*Rod Lofton*	.10
259	*Chris Snopek*	.15
260	*Quinton McCracken*	.15
261	*Mike Matthews*	.10
262	*Hector Carrasco*	.10
263	Rick Greene	.10
264	*Chris Bolt*	.10
265	George Brett	2.50
266	*Rick Gorecki*	.10
267	*Francisco Gamez*	.10
268	Marquis Grissom	.10
269	Kevin Tapani	.10
270	Ryan Thompson	.10
271	Gerald Williams	.10
272	*Paul Fletcher*	.10
273	Lance Blankenship	.10
274	*Marty Heff*	.10
275	Shawn Estes	.15
276	*Rene Arocha*	.10
277	*Scott Evre*	.10
278	Phil Plantier	.10
279	*Paul Spoljaric*	.10
280	Chris Gahbs	.10
281	Harold Baines	.10
282	*Jose Oliva*	.10
283	Matt Whiteside	.10
284	*Brant Brown*	.10
285	Russ Springer	.10
286	Chris Sabo	.10
287	Ozzie Guillen	.10
288	*Marcus Moore*	.10
289	Chad Ogea	.10
290	Walt Weiss	.10
291	Brian Edmondson	.10
292	Jimmy Gonzalez	.10
293	*Danny Miceli*	.10
294	Jose Offerman	.10
295	Greg Vaughn	.10
296	Frank Bolick	.10
297	*Mike Maksudian*	.10
298	John Franco	.10
299	Danny Tartabull	.10
300	Len Dykstra	.10
301	Bobby Witt	.10
302	*Trey Beamon*	.10
303	Tino Martinez	.10
304	Aaron Holbert	.10
305	Juan Gonzalez	1.50
306	*Billy Hall*	.10
307	Duane Ward	.10
308	Rod Beck	.10
309	*Jose Mercedes*	.10
310	Otis Nixon	.10
311	*Gettys Glaze*	.10
312	Candy Maldonado	.10
313	Chad Curtis	.10
314	Tim Costo	.10
315	Mike Robertson	.10
316	Nigel Wilson	.10
317	*Greg McMichael*	.10
318	*Scott Pose*	.10
319	Ivan Cruz	.10
320	Greg Swindell	.10
321	Kevin McReynolds	.10
322	Tom Candiotti	.10
323	*Bob Wishnevski*	.10
324	Ken Hill	.10
325	Kirby Puckett	2.00
326	*Tim Bogar*	.10
327	Mariano Rivera	.50
328	Mitch Williams	.10
329	Craig Paquette	.10
330	Jay Bell	.10
331	*Jose Martinez*	.10
332	Rob Deer	.10
333	Brook Fordyce	.10
334	Matt Nokes	.10
335	Derek Lee	.10
336	*Paul Ellis*	.10
337	*Desi Wilson*	.10
338	Roberto Alomar	.35
339	Jim Tatum (Foil)	.10
340	J.T. Snow (Foil)	.15
341	Tim Salmon (Foil)	.25
342	*Russ Davis* (Foil)	.25
343	Javier Lopez (Foil)	.10
344	*Troy O'Leary* (Foil)	.15
345	*Marty Cordova* (Foil)	.60
346	*Bubba Smith* (Foil)	.10
347	Chipper Jones (Foil)	1.50
348	Jessie Hollins (Foil)	.10
349	Willie Greene (Foil)	.10
350	Mark Thompson (Foil)	.10
351	Nigel Wilson (Foil)	.10
352	Todd Jones (Foil)	.10
353	Raul Mondesi (Foil)	.10
354	Cliff Floyd (Foil)	.10
355	Bobby Jones (Foil)	.10
356	Kevin Stocker (Foil)	.10
357	Midre Cummings (Foil)	.10
358	Allen Watson (Foil)	.10
359	Ray McDavid (Foil)	.10
360	Steve Hosey (Foil)	.10
361	Brad Pennington (Foil)	.10
362	Frankie Rodriguez (Foil)	.10
363	Troy Percival (Foil)	.10
364	Jason Bere (Foil)	.10
365	Manny Ramirez (Foil)	.75
366	Justin Thompson (Foil)	.10
367	Joe Vitello (Foil)	.10
368	Tyrone Hill (Foil)	.10
369	David McCarty (Foil)	.10
370	Brien Taylor (Foil)	.10
371	Todd Van Poppel (Foil)	.10
372	Marc Newfield (Foil)	.10
373	*Terrell Lowery* (Foil)	.10
374	Alex Gonzalez (Foil)	.10
375	Ken Griffey, Jr.	2.50
376	Donovan Osborne	.10
377	*Ritchie Moody*	.10
378	Shane Andrews	.10
379	Carlos Delgado	.75
380	Bill Swift	.10
381	Leo Gomez	.10
382	Ron Gant	.10
383	Scott Fletcher	.10
384	*Matt Walbeck*	.10
385	Chuck Finley	.10
386	Kevin Mitchell	.10
387	Wilson Alvarez	.10
388	*John Burke*	.10
389	Alan Embree	.10
390	Trevor Hoffman	.10
391	Alan Trammell	.10
392	Todd Jones	.10
393	Felix Jose	.10
394	Orel Hershiser	.10
395	Pat Listach	.10
396	Gabe White	.10
397	*Dan Serafini*	.10
398	Todd Hundley	.10
399	Wade Boggs	2.00
400	Tyler Green	.10
401	Mike Bordick	.10
402	Scott Bullett	.10
403	*Lagrande Russell*	.10
404	Ray Lankford	.10
405	Nolan Ryan	4.00
406	Robbie Beckett	.10
407	*Brent Bowers*	.10
408	*Adell Davenport*	.10
409	Brady Anderson	.10
410	Tom Glavine	.25
411	*Doug Hecker*	.10
412	Jose Guzman	.10
413	Luis Polonia	.10
414	Brian Williams	.10
415	Bo Jackson	.15
416	Eric Young	.10
417	Kenny Lofton	.10
418	Orestes Destrade	.10
419	Tony Phillips	.10
420	Jeff Bagwell	1.50
421	Hark Gardner	.10
422	Brett Butler	.10
423	*Graeme Lloyd*	.10
424	Delino DeShields	.10
425	Scott Erickson	.10
426	Jeff Kent	.10
427	Jimmy Key	.10
428	Mickey Morandini	.10
429	*Marcos Arkas*	.10
430	Don Slaught	.10
431	Randy Johnson	1.50
432	Omar Olivares	.10
433	Charlie Leibrandt	.10
434	Kurt Stillwell	.10
435	*Scott Brow*	.10
436	Robby Thompson	.10
437	Ben McDonald	.10
438	Deion Sanders	.15
439	Tony Pena	.10
440	Mark Grace	.15
441	Eduardo Perez	.10
442	*Tim Pugh*	.10
443	Scott Ruffcorn	.10
444	*Jay Gainer*	.10
445	Albert Belle	.20
446	Bret Barberie	.10
447	Justin Mashore	.10
448	Pete Harnisch	.10
449	Greg Gagne	.10
450	Eric Davis	.10
451	Dave Mlicki	.10
452	Moises Alou	.10
453	Rick Aguilera	.10
454	Eddie Murray	1.50
455	Bob Wickman	.10
456	Wes Chamberlain	.10
457	Brent Gates	.10
458	Paul Weber	.10
459	Mike Hampton	.10
460	Ozzie Smith	2.00
461	Tom Henke	.10
462	Ricky Gutierrez	.10
463	Jack Morris	.10
464	*Joel Chimelis*	.10
465	Gregg Olson	.10
466	Javier Lopez	.10
467	Scott Cooper	.10
468	Willie Wilson	.10
469	Mark Langston	.10
470	Barry Larkin	.10
471	Rod Bolton	.10
472	Freddie Benavides	.10
473	*Ken Ramos*	.10
474	Chuck Carr	.10
475	Cecil Fielder	.10
476	Eddie Taubensee	.10
477	*Chris Eddy*	.10
478	Greg Hansell	.10
479	Kevin Reimer	.10
480	Denny Martinez	.10
481	Chuck Knoblauch	.10
482	Mike Draper	.10
483	Spike Owen	.10
484	Terry Mulholland	.10
485	Dennis Eckersley	1.00
486	Blas Minor	.10
487	Dave Fleming	.10
488	Dan Cholonsky	.10
489	Ivan Rodriguez	1.50
490	Gary Sheffield	.45
491	Ed Sprague	.10
492	Steve Hosey	.10
493	*Jimmy Haynes*	.10
494	John Smoltz	.10
495	Andre Dawson	.35
496	Rey Sanchez	.10
497	*Ty Van Burkleo*	.10
498	*Bobby Ayala*	.10
499	Tim Raines	.10
500	Charlie Hayes	.10
501	Paul Sorrento	.10
502	*Richie Lewis*	.10
503	*Jason Pfaff*	.10
504	Ken Caminiti	.10
505	Mike Macfarlane	.10
506	Jody Reed	.10
507	*Bobby Hughes*	.10
508	Wil Cordero	.10
509	*George Tsanis*	.10
510	Bret Saberhagen	.10
511	*Derek Jeter*	20.00
512	Gene Schall	.10
513	Curtis Shaw	.10
514	Steve Cooke	.10
515	Edgar Martinez	.10
516	Mike Milchin	.10
517	Billy Ripken	.10
518	Andy Benes	.10
519	*Juan de la Rosa*	.10
520	John Burkett	.10
521	Alex Ochoa	.10
522	*Tony Tarasco*	.10
523	Luis Ortiz	.10
524	Rick Williams	.10
525	*Chris Turner*	.10
526	Rob Dibble	.10
527	Jack McDowell	.10
528	Daryl Boston	.10
529	*Bill Wertz*	.10
530	Charlie Hough	.10
531	Sean Bergman	.10
532	Doug Jones	.10
533	Jeff Montgomery	.10
534	*Roger Cedeno*	.30
535	Robin Yount	1.50
536	Mo Vaughn	.10
537	Brian Harper	.10
538	Juan Castillo	.10
539	Steve Farr	.10
540	John Kruk	.10
541	Troy Neel	.10
542	*Danny Clyburn*	.10
543	*Jim Converse*	.10
544	Gregg Jefferies	.10
545	Jose Canseco	.40
546	*Julio Bruno*	.10
547	Rob Butler	.10
548	Royce Clayton	.10
549	Chris Hoiles	.10
550	Greg Maddux	2.00
551	*Joe Ciccarella*	.10

552	Ozzie Timmons	.10
553	Chili Davis	.10
554	Brian Koelling	.10
555	Frank Thomas	1.50
556	Vinny Castilla	.10
557	Reggie Jefferson	.10
558	Rob Natal	.10
559	Mike Henneman	.10
560	Craig Biggio	.10
561	*Billy Brewer*	.10
562	Dan Melendez	.10
563	*Kenny Felder*	.10
564	*Miguel Batista*	.10
565	Dave Winfield	1.50
566	Al Shirley	.10
567	Robert Eenhoorn	.10
568	Mike Williams	.10
569	*Tanyon Sturtze*	.10
570	Tim Wakefield	.10
571	Greg Pirkl	.10
572	*Sean Lowe*	.25
573	*Terry Burows*	.10
574	*Kevin Higgins*	.10
575	Joe Carter	.10
576	Kevin Rogers	.10
577	Manny Alexander	.10
578	Dave Justice	.10
579	*Brian Conroy*	.10
580	*Jessie Hollins*	.10
581	*Ron Watson*	.10
582	Bip Roberts	.10
583	*Tom Urbani*	.10
584	*Jason Hutchins*	.10
585	Carlos Baerga	.10
586	Jeff Mutis	.10
587	Justin Thompson	.10
588	Orlando Miller	.10
589	Brian McRae	.10
590	Ramon Martinez	.10
591	Dave Nilsson	.10
592	*Jose Vidro*	1.50
593	Rich Becker	.10
594	*Preston Wilson*	1.50
595	Don Mattingly	2.50
596	Tony Longmire	.10
597	Kevin Seitzer	.10
598	*Midre Cummings*	.10
599	Omar Vizquel	.10
600	Lee Smith	.10
601	*David Hulse*	.10
602	*Darrell Sherman*	.10
603	Alex Gonzalez	.10
604	Geronimo Pena	.10
605	Mike Devereaux	.10
606	*Sterling Hitchcock*	.25
607	Mike Greenwell	.10
608	Steve Buechele	.10
609	Troy Percival	.10
610	Bobby Kelly	.10
611	*James Baldwin*	.25
612	Jerald Clark	.10
613	*Albie Lopez*	.10
614	Dave Magadan	.10
615	Mickey Tettleton	.10
616	*Sean Runyan*	.10
617	Bob Hamelin	.10
618	Raul Mondesi	.10
619	Tyrone Hill	.10
620	Darrin Fletcher	.10
621	Mike Trombley	.10
622	Jeromy Burnitz	.10
623	Bernie Williams	.25
624	*Mike Farmer*	.10
625	Rickey Henderson	1.50
626	Carlos Garcia	.10
627	*Jeff Darwin*	.10
628	Todd Zeile	.10
629	Benji Gil	.10
630	Tony Gwynn	2.00
631	*Aaron Small*	.10
632	*Joe Rosselli*	.10
633	Mike Mussina	1.00
634	Ryan Klesko	.10
635	Roger Clemens	2.25
636	Sammy Sosa	2.50
637	*Orlando Palmeiro*	.10
638	Willie Greene	.10
639	George Bell	.10
640	*Garvin Alston*	.10
641	*Pete Janicki*	.10
642	*Chris Sheff*	.10
643	*Felipe Lira*	.10
644	Roberto Petagine	.10
645	Wally Joyner	.10
646	Mike Piazza	2.50
647	Jaime Navarro	.10
648	*Jeff Hartsock*	.10
649	David McCarty	.10
650	Bobby Jones	.10
651	Mark Hutton	.10
652	Kyle Abbott	.10
653	*Steve Cox*	.10
654	Jeff King	.10
655	Norm Charlton	.10
656	*Mike Gulan*	.10
657	Julio Franco	.10
658	*Cameron Cairncross*	.10
659	John Olerud	.10
660	Salomon Torres	.10
661	Brad Pennington	.10
662	Melvin Nieves	.10
663	Ivan Calderon	.10
664	Turk Wendell	.10
665	Chris Pritchett	.10
666	Reggie Sanders	.10
667	Robin Ventura	.10
668	Joe Girardi	.10
669	Manny Ramirez	1.50
670	Jeff Conine	.10
671	Greg Gohr	.10
672	Andujar Cedeno	.10
673	*Les Norman*	.10
674	*Mike James*	.10
675	*Marshall Boze*	.10
676	B.J. Wallace	.10
677	Kent Hrbek	.10
678	Jack Voight	.10
679	Brien Taylor	.10
680	Curt Schilling	.35
681	Todd Van Poppel	.10
682	Kevin Young	.10
683	Tommy Adams	.10
684	Bernard Gilkey	.10
685	Kevin Brown	.10
686	Fred McGriff	.10
687	Pat Borders	.10
688	Kirt Manwaring	.10
689	Sid Bream	.10
690	John Valentin	.10
691	*Steve Olsen*	.10
692	*Roberto Mejia*	.10
693	Carlos Delgado (Foil)	.60
694	*Steve Gibralter* (Foil)	.10
695	Gary Mota (Foil)	.10
696	*Jose Malave* (Foil)	.10
697	*Larry Sutton* (Foil)	.10
698	*Dan Frye* (Foil)	.10
699	*Tim Clark* (Foil)	.10
700	*Brian Rupp* (Foil)	.10
701	Felipe Alou, Moises Alou (Foil)	.10
702	Bobby Bonds, Barry Bonds (Foil)	1.00
703	Ken Griffey Sr., Ken Griffey Jr. (Foil)	1.00
704	Hal McRae, Brian McRae (Foil)	.10
705	Checklist 1	.10
706	Checklist 2	.10
707	Checklist 3	.10
708	Checklist 4	.10

1994 BOWMAN PREVIEWS

		NM/M
Complete Set (10):		7.00
Common Player:		.50
1	Frank Thomas	1.50
2	Mike Piazza	3.00
3	Albert Belle	.50
4	Javier Lopez	.50
5	Cliff Floyd	.50
6	Alex Gonzalez	.50
7	Ricky Bottalico	.50
8	Tony Clark	.50
9	Mac Suzuki	.50
10	James Mouton (Foil)	.50

1994 BOWMAN

		NM/M
Complete Set (682):		40.00
Common Player:		.10
Pack (12):		1.50
Wax Box (24):		25.00
1	Joe Carter	.10
2	Marcus Moore	.10
3	*Doug Creek*	.10
4	Pedro Martinez	1.00
5	Ken Griffey, Jr.	2.00
6	Greg Swindell	.10
7	J.J. Johnson	.10
8	*Homer Bush*	.25
9	*Arquimedez Pozo*	.10
10	Bryan Harvey	.10
11	J.T. Snow	.10
12	*Alan Benes*	.25
13	Chad Kreuter	.10
14	Eric Karros	.10
15	Frank Thomas	1.00
16	Bret Saberhagen	.10
17	Terrell Lowery	.10
18	Rod Bolton	.10
19	Harold Baines	.10
20	Matt Walbeck	.10
21	Tom Glavine	.25
22	Todd Jones	.10
23	Alberto Castillo	.10
24	Ruben Sierra	.10
25	Don Mattingly	1.75
26	Mike Morgan	.10
27	*Jim Musselwhite*	.10
28	*Matt Brunson*	.10
29	*Adam Meinershagen*	.10
30	Joe Girardi	.10
31	Shane Halter	.10
32	*Jose Paniagua*	.10
33	Paul Perkins	.10
34	*John Hudek*	.10
35	Frank Viola	.10
36	*David Lamb*	.10
37	Marshall Boze	.10
38	*Jorge Posada*	5.00
39	*Brian Anderson*	.25
40	Mark Whiten	.10
41	Sean Bergman	.10
42	*Jose Parra*	.10
43	Mike Robertson	.10
44	*Pete Walker*	.10
45	Juan Gonzalez	1.00
46	*Cleveland Ladell*	.10
47	Mark Smith	.10
48	*Kevin Jarvis*	.10
49	*Amaury Telemaco*	.10
50	Andy Van Slyke	.10
51	*Rikkert Faneyte*	.10
52	Curtis Shaw	.10
53	*Matt Drews*	.10
54	Wilson Alvarez	.10
55	Manny Ramirez	1.00
56	Bobby Munoz	.10
57	Ed Sprague	.10
58	*Jamey Wright*	.10
59	Jeff Montgomery	.10
60	Kirk Rueter	.10
61	Edgar Martinez	.10
62	Luis Gonzalez	.50
63	*Tim Vanegmond*	.10
64	Bip Roberts	.10
65	John Jaha	.10
66	Chuck Carr	.10
67	Chuck Finley	.10
68	Aaron Holbert	.10
69	Cecil Fielder	.10
70	*Tom Engle*	.10
71	Ron Karkovice	.10
72	Joe Orsulak	.10
73	*Duff Brumley*	.10
74	*Craig Clayton*	.10
75	Cal Ripken, Jr.	4.00
76	*Brad Fullmer*	.50
77	Tony Tarasco	.10
78	*Terry Farrar*	.10
79	Matt Williams	.10
80	Rickey Henderson	1.00
81	Terry Mulholland	.10
82	Sammy Sosa	2.00
83	Paul Sorrento	.10
84	Pete Incaviglia	.10
85	*Darren Hall*	.10
86	Scott Klingenbeck	.10
87	*Dario Perez*	.10
88	Ugueth Urbina	.10
89	*Dave Vanhof*	.10
90	Domingo Jean	.10
91	Otis Nixon	.10
92	Andres Berumen	.10
93	Jose Valentin	.10
94	*Edgar Renteria*	5.00
95	Chris Turner	.10
96	Ray Lankford	.10
97	Danny Bautista	.10
98	*Chan Ho Park*	1.00
99	*Glenn DiSarcina*	.10
100	Butch Huskey	.10
101	Ivan Rodriguez	1.00
102	Johnny Ruffin	.10
103	Alex Ochoa	.10
104	*Torii Hunter*	6.00
105	Ryan Klesko	.10
106	Jay Bell	.10
107	*Kurt Peltzer*	.10
108	Miguel Jimenez	.10
109	Russ Davis	.10
110	Derek Wallace	.10
111	*Keith Lockhart*	.10
112	Mike Lieberthal	.10
113	Dave Stewart	.10
114	Tom Schmidt	.10
115	Brian McRae	.10
116	Moises Alou	.10
117	Dave Fleming	.10
118	Jeff Bagwell	1.00
119	Luis Ortiz	.10
120	Tony Gwynn	1.50
121	Jaime Navarro	.10
122	Benny Santiago	.10
123	Darrel Whitmore	.10
124	*John Mabry*	.15
125	Mickey Tettleton	.10
126	Tom Candiotti	.10
127	Tim Raines	.10
128	Bobby Bonilla	.10
129	John Dettmer	.10
130	Hector Carrasco	.10
131	Chris Hoiles	.10
132	Rick Aguilera	.10
133	Dave Justice	.10
134	*Esteban Loaiza*	1.50
135	Barry Bonds	4.00
136	Bob Welch	.10
137	Mike Stanley	.10
138	Roberto Hernandez	.10
139	Sandy Alomar	.10
140	Darren Daulton	.10
141	*Angel Martinez*	.10
142	Howard Johnson	.10
143	Bob Hamelin	.10
144	*J.J. Thobe*	.10
145	Roger Salkeld	.10
146	Orlando Miller	.10
147	Dmitri Young	.10
148	*Tim Hyers*	.10
149	*Mark Loretta*	4.00
150	Chris Hammond	.10
151	*Joel Moore*	.10
152	Todd Zeile	.10
153	Wil Cordero	.10
154	Chris Smith	.10
155	James Baldwin	.10
156	*Edgardo Alfonzo*	1.00
157	*Kym Ashworth*	.10
158	*Paul Bako*	.10
159	*Rick Krivda*	.10
160	Pat Mahomes	.10
161	Damon Hollins	.10
162	*Felix Martinez*	.10
163	*Jason Myers*	.10
164	*Izzy Molina*	.10
165	Brien Taylor	.10
166	*Kevin Orie*	.10
167	*Casey Whitten*	.10
168	Tony Longmire	.10
169	John Olerud	.10
170	Mark Thompson	.10
171	Jorge Fabregas	.10

No.	Player	Price
172	John Wetteland	.10
173	Dan Wilson	.10
174	Doug Drabek	.10
175	Jeffrey McNeely	.10
176	Melvin Nieves	.10
177	*Doug Glanville*	.10
178	*Javier De La Hoya*	.10
179	Chad Curtis	.10
180	Brian Barber	.10
181	Mike Henneman	.10
182	Jose Offerman	.10
183	*Robert Ellis*	.10
184	John Franco	.10
185	Benji Gil	.10
186	Hal Morris	.10
187	Chris Sabo	.10
188	*Blaise Ilsley*	.10
189	Steve Avery	.10
190	*Rick White*	.10
191	Rod Beck	.10
(192)	Mark McGwire (no card number)	3.00
193	Jim Abbott	.10
194	Randy Myers	.10
195	Kenny Lofton	.10
196	Mariano Duncan	.10
197	*Lee Daniels*	.10
198	Armando Reynoso	.10
199	Joe Randa	.10
200	Cliff Floyd	.10
201	*Tim Harkrider*	.10
202	*Kevin Gallaher*	.10
203	Scott Cooper	.10
204	*Phil Stidham*	.10
205	*Jeff D'Amico*	.25
206	Matt Whisenant	.10
207	De Shawn Warren	.10
208	Rene Arocha	.10
209	*Tony Clark*	.50
210	*Jason Jacome*	.10
211	*Scott Christman*	.10
212	Bill Pulsipher	.10
213	Dean Palmer	.10
214	Chad Mottola	.10
215	Manny Alexander	.10
216	Rich Becker	.10
217	*Andre King*	.10
218	Carlos Garcia	.10
219	*Ron Pezzoni*	.10
220	Steve Karsay	.10
221	*Jose Musset*	.10
222	Karl Rhodes	.10
223	*Frank Cimorelli*	.10
224	*Kevin Jordan*	.10
225	Duane Ward	.10
226	John Burke	.10
227	Mike MacFarlane	.10
228	Mike Lansing	.10
229	Chuck Knoblauch	.10
230	Ken Caminiti	.10
231	*Gar Finnvold*	.10
232	*Derrek Lee*	12.00
233	Brady Anderson	.10
234	*Vic Darensbourg*	.10
235	Mark Langston	.10
236	*T.J. Mathews*	.10
237	Lou Whitaker	.10
238	Roger Cedeno	.10
239	Alex Fernandez	.10
240	Ryan Thompson	.10
241	*Kerry Lacy*	.10
242	Reggie Sanders	.10
243	Brad Pennington	.10
244	*Bryan Eversgerd*	.10
245	Greg Maddux	1.50
246	Jason Kendall	.10
247	J.R. Phillips	.10
248	Bobby Witt	.10
249	Paul O'Neill	.10
250	Ryne Sandberg	1.50
251	Charles Nagy	.10
252	Kevin Stocker	.10
253	Shawn Green	.35
254	Charlie Hayes	.10
255	Donnie Elliott	.10
256	*Rob Fitzpatrick*	.10
257	Tim Davis	.10
258	James Mouton	.10
259	Mike Greenwell	.10
260	Ray McDavid	.10
261	Mike Kelly	.10
262	*Andy Larkin*	.10
(263)	Marquis Riley (no card number)	.10
264	Bob Tewksbury	.10
265	Brian Edmondson	.10
266	*Eduardo Lantigua*	.10
267	Brandon Wilson	.10
268	Mike Welch	.10
269	Tom Henke	.10
270	Calvin Reese	.10
271	*Greg Zaun*	.10
272	Todd Ritchie	.10
273	Javier Lopez	.10
274	Kevin Young	.10
275	Kirt Manwaring	.10
276	*Bill Taylor*	.10
277	Robert Eenhoorn	.10
278	Jessie Hollins	.10
279	*Julian Tavarez*	.10
280	Gene Schall	.10
281	Paul Molitor	1.00
282	*Neifi Perez*	.10
283	Greg Gagne	.10
284	Marquis Grissom	.10
285	Randy Johnson	1.00
286	Pete Harnisch	.10
287	*Joel Bennett*	.10
288	Derek Bell	.10
289	Darryl Hamilton	.10
290	Gary Sheffield	.40
291	Eduardo Perez	.10
292	Basil Shabazz	.10
293	Eric Davis	.10
294	Pedro Astacio	.10
295	Robin Ventura	.10
296	Jeff Kent	.10
297	Rick Helling	.10
298	Joe Oliver	.10
299	Lee Smith	.10
300	Dave Winfield	1.00
301	Deion Sanders	.10
302	*Ravelo Manzanillo*	.10
303	Mark Portugal	.10
304	Brent Gates	.10
305	Wade Boggs	1.50
306	Rick Wilkins	.10
307	Carlos Baerga	.10
308	Curt Schilling	.35
309	Shannon Stewart	.25
310	Darren Holmes	.10
311	*Robert Toth*	.10
312	Gabe White	.10
313	*Mac Suzuki*	.10
314	*Alvin Morman*	.10
315	Mo Vaughn	.10
316	*Bryce Florie*	.10
317	*Gabby Martinez*	.10
318	Carl Everett	.10
319	Kerwin Moore	.10
320	Tom Pagnozzi	.10
321	Chris Gomez	.10
322	Todd Williams	.10
323	Pat Hentgen	.10
324	*Kirk Presley*	.10
325	Kevin Brown	.10
326	*Jason Isringhausen*	.25
327	*Rick Forney*	.10
328	*Carlos Pulido*	.10
329	*Terrell Wade*	.10
330	Al Martin	.10
331	*Dan Carlson*	.10
332	*Mark Acre*	.10
333	Sterling Hitchcock	.10
334	*Jon Ratliff*	.10
335	*Alex Ramirez*	.10
336	*Phil Geisler*	.10
337	*Eddie Zambrano* (Foil)	.10
338	Jim Thome (Foil)	.10
339	James Mouton (Foil)	.10
340	Cliff Floyd (Foil)	.10
341	Carlos Delgado (Foil)	.40
342	Roberto Petagine (Foil)	.10
343	Tim Clark (Foil)	.10
344	Bubba Smith (Foil)	.10
345	*Randy Curtis* (Foil)	.10
346	*Joe Biasucci* (Foil)	.10
347	*D.J. Boston* (Foil)	.10
348	*Ruben Rivera* (Foil)	.75
349	*Bryan Link* (Foil)	.10
350	*Mike Bell* (Foil)	.25
351	*Marty Watson* (Foil)	.10
352	Jason Myers (Foil)	.10
353	Chipper Jones (Foil)	1.00
354	Brooks Kieschnick (Foil)	.10
355	Calvin Reese (Foil)	.10
356	John Burke (Foil)	.10
357	Kurt Miller (Foil)	.10
358	Orlando Miller (Foil)	.10
359	Todd Hollandsworth (Foil)	.10
360	Rondell White (Foil)	.10
361	Bill Pulsipher (Foil)	.10
362	Tyler Green (Foil)	.10
363	Midre Cummings (Foil)	.10
364	Brian Barber (Foil)	.10
365	Melvin Nieves (Foil)	.10
366	Salomon Torres (Foil)	.10
367	Alex Ochoa (Foil)	.10
368	Frank Rodriguez (Foil)	.10
369	Brian Anderson (Foil)	.10
370	James Baldwin (Foil)	.10
371	Manny Ramirez (Foil)	.75
372	Justin Thompson (Foil)	.10
373	Johnny Damon (Foil)	.40
374	Jeff D'Amico (Foil)	.10
375	Rich Becker (Foil)	.10
376	Derek Jeter (Foil)	3.00
377	Steve Karsay (Foil)	.10
378	Mac Suzuki (Foil)	.10
379	Benji Gil (Foil)	.10
380	Alex Gonzalez (Foil)	.10
381	Jason Bere (Foil)	.10
382	Brett Butler (Foil)	.10
383	Jeff Conine (Foil)	.10
384	Darren Daulton (Foil)	.10
385	Jeff Kent (Foil)	.10
386	Don Mattingly (Foil)	1.25
387	Mike Piazza (Foil)	2.00
388	Ryne Sandberg (Foil)	1.00
389	Rich Amaral	.10
390	Craig Biggio	.10
391	*Jeff Suppan*	.35
392	Andy Benes	.10
393	Cal Eldred	.10
394	Jeff Conine	.10
395	Tim Salmon	.25
396	*Ray Suplee*	.10
397	Tony Phillips	.10
398	Ramon Martinez	.10
399	Julio Franco	.10
400	Dwight Gooden	.10
401	*Kevin Lomon*	.10
402	Jose Rijo	.10
403	Mike Devereaux	.10
404	*Mike Zolecki*	.10
405	Fred McGriff	.10
406	Danny Clyburn	.10
407	Robby Thompson	.10
408	Terry Steinbach	.10
409	Luis Polonia	.10
410	Mark Grace	.15
411	Albert Belle	.20
412	John Kruk	.10
413	*Scott Spiezio*	.25
414	Ellis Burks	.10
415	Joe Vitiello	.10
416	Tim Costo	.10
417	Marc Newfield	.10
418	*Oscar Henriquez*	.10
419	*Matt Perisho*	.10
420	Julio Bruno	.10
421	Kenny Felder	.10
422	Tyler Green	.10
423	Jim Edmonds	.10
424	Ozzie Smith	1.50
425	Rick Greene	.10
426	Todd Hollandsworth	.10
427	*Eddie Pearson*	.10
428	Quilvio Veras	.10
429	Kenny Rogers	.10
430	Willie Greene	.10
431	Vaughn Eshelman	.10
432	Pat Meares	.10
433	*Jermaine Dye*	1.00
434	Steve Cooke	.10
435	Bill Swift	.10
436	*Fausto Cruz*	.10
437	Mark Hutton	.10
438	*Brooks Kieschnick*	.10
439	Yorkis Perez	.10
440	Len Dykstra	.10
441	Pat Borders	.10
442	*Doug Walls*	.10
443	Wally Joyner	.10
444	Ken Hill	.10
445	Eric Anthony	.10
446	Mitch Williams	.10
447	*Cory Bailey*	.10
448	Dave Staton	.10
449	Greg Vaughn	.10
450	Dave Magadan	.10
451	Chili Davis	.10
452	*Gerald Santos*	.10
453	Joe Perona	.10
454	Delino DeShields	.10
455	Jack McDowell	.10
456	Todd Hundley	.10
457	Ritchie Moody	.10
458	Bret Boone	.10
459	Ben McDonald	.10
460	Kirby Puckett	1.50
461	Gregg Olson	.10
462	*Rich Aude*	.10
463	John Burkett	.10
464	Troy Neel	.10
465	Jimmy Key	.10
466	Ozzie Timmons	.10
467	Eddie Murray	1.00
468	*Mark Tranberg*	.10
469	Alex Gonzalez	.10
470	David Nied	.10
471	Barry Larkin	.10
472	*Brian Looney*	.10
473	Shawn Estes	.10
474	*A.J. Sager*	.10
475	Roger Clemens	1.75
476	Vince Moore	.10
477	*Scott Karl*	.10
478	Kurt Miller	.10
479	Garret Anderson	.10
480	Allen Watson	.10
481	*Jose Lima*	.10
482	Rick Gorecki	.10
483	*Jimmy Hurst*	.10
484	Preston Wilson	.10
485	Will Clark	.15
486	*Mike Ferry*	.10
487	*Curtis Goodwin*	.10
488	Mike Myers	.10
489	Chipper Jones	1.50
490	Jeff King	.10
491	*Bill Van Landingham*	.10
492	*Carlos Reyes*	.10
493	Andy Pettitte	.30
494	Brant Brown	.10
495	Daron Kirkreit	.10
496	*Ricky Bottalico*	.25
497	Devon White	.10
498	*Jason Johnson*	.10
499	Vince Coleman	.10
500	Larry Walker	.10
501	Bobby Ayala	.10
502	Steve Finley	.10
503	Scott Fletcher	.10
504	Brad Ausmus	.10
505	*Scott Talanoa*	.10
506	Orestes Destrade	.10
507	Gary DiSarcina	.10
508	*Willie Smith*	.10
509	Alan Trammell	.10
510	Mike Piazza	2.00
511	Ozzie Guillen	.10
512	Jeromy Burnitz	.10
513	Darren Oliver	.10
514	Kevin Mitchell	.10
515	Rafael Palmeiro	1.00
516	David McCarty	.10
517	Jeff Blauser	.10
518	Trey Beamon	.10
519	Royce Clayton	.10
520	Dennis Eckersley	.75
521	Bernie Williams	.25
522	Steve Buechele	.10
523	Denny Martinez	.10
524	Dave Hollins	.10
525	Joey Hamilton	.10
526	Andres Galarraga	.10
527	Jeff Granger	.10
528	Joey Eischen	.10
529	Desi Relaford	.10
530	Roberto Petagine	.10
531	Andre Dawson	.30
532	Ray Holbert	.10
533	Duane Singleton	.10
534	*Kurt Abbott*	.20
535	Bo Jackson	.15
536	Gregg Jefferies	.10
537	David Mysel	.10
538	Raul Mondesi	.10
539	Chris Snopek	.10
540	Brook Fordyce	.10
541	*Ron Frazier*	.10
542	Brian Koelling	.10
543	Jimmy Haynes	.10
544	Marty Cordova	.10
545	*Jason Green*	.10
546	Orlando Merced	.10
547	*Lou Pote*	.10
548	Todd Van Poppel	.10
549	Pat Kelly	.10
550	Turk Wendell	.10
551	*Herb Perry*	.10
552	*Ryan Karp*	.10
553	Juan Guzman	.10
554	*Bryan Rekar*	.10
555	Kevin Appier	.10
556	*Chris Schwab*	.10
557	Jay Buhner	.10
558	Andujar Cedeno	.10
559	*Ryan McGuire*	.10
560	Ricky Gutierrez	.10
561	*Keith Kimsey*	.10
562	Tim Clark	.10
563	Damion Easley	.10
564	*Clint Davis*	.10

No.	Player	Value
565	Mike Moore	.10
566	Orel Hershiser	.10
567	Jason Bere	.10
568	Kevin McReynolds	.10
569	*Leland Macon*	.10
570	*John Courtright*	.10
571	Sid Fernandez	.10
572	Chad Roper	.10
573	Terry Pendleton	.10
574	Danny Miceli	.10
575	Joe Rosselli	.10
576	Mike Bordick	.10
577	Danny Tartabull	.10
578	Jose Guzman	.10
579	Omar Vizquel	.10
580	Tommy Greene	.10
581	Paul Spoljaric	.10
582	Walt Weiss	.10
583	*Oscar Jimenez*	.10
584	Rod Henderson	.10
585	Derek Lowe	.10
586	*Richard Hidalgo*	1.00
587	*Shayne Bennett*	.10
588	*Tim Belk*	.10
589	Matt Mieske	.10
590	Nigel Wilson	.10
591	*Jeff Knox*	.10
592	Bernard Gilkey	.10
593	David Cone	.10
594	*Paul LoDuca*	5.00
595	Scott Ruffcorn	.10
596	Chris Roberts	.10
597	*Oscar Munoz*	.10
598	*Scott Sullivan*	.10
599	*Matt Jarvis*	.10
600	Jose Canseco	.35
601	*Tony Graffanino*	.10
602	Don Slaught	.10
603	*Brett King*	.10
604	*Jose Herrera*	.10
605	Melido Perez	.10
606	*Mike Hubbard*	.10
607	Chad Ogea	.10
608	*Wayne Gomes*	.10
609	Roberto Alomar	.35
610	*Angel Echevarria*	.10
611	Jose Lind	.10
612	Darrin Fletcher	.10
613	Chris Bosio	.10
614	Darryl Kile	.10
615	Frank Rodriguez	.10
616	Phil Plantier	.10
617	Pat Listach	.10
618	Charlie Hough	.10
619	*Ryan Hancock*	.10
620	*Darrel Deak*	.10
621	Travis Fryman	.10
622	Brett Butler	.10
623	Lance Johnson	.10
624	Pete Smith	.10
625	James Hurst	.10
626	Roberto Kelly	.10
627	Mike Mussina	.65
628	Kevin Tapani	.10
629	John Smoltz	.10
630	Midre Cummings	.10
631	Salomon Torres	.10
632	Willie Adams	.10
633	Derek Jeter	4.00
634	Steve Trachsel	.10
635	Albie Lopez	.10
636	Jason Moler	.10
637	Carlos Delgado	.65
638	Roberto Mejia	.10
639	Darren Burton	.10
640	B.J. Wallace	.10
641	*Brad Clontz*	.10
642	*Billy Wagner*	1.00
643	Aaron Sele	.10
644	Cameron Cairncross	.10
645	Brian Harper	.10
(646)	Marc Valdes (no card number)	.10
647	Mark Ratekin	.10
648	*Terry Bradshaw*	.10
649	Justin Thompson	.10
650	*Mike Busch*	.10
651	*Joe Hall*	.10
652	Bobby Jones	.10
653	*Kelly Stinnett*	.10
654	*Rod Steph*	.10
655	*Jay Powell*	.10
(656)	*Keith Garagozzo* (no card number)	.10
657	Todd Dunn	.10
658	*Charles Peterson*	.10
659	Darren Lewis	.10
660	*John Wasdin*	.10
661	*Tate Seefried*	.10
662	*Hector Trinidad*	.10
663	*John Carter*	.10
664	Larry Mitchell	.10
665	*David Catlett*	.10
666	Dante Bichette	.10
667	Felix Jose	.10
668	Rondell White	.10
669	Tino Martinez	.10
670	Brian Hunter	.10
671	Jose Malave	.10
672	Archi Cianfrocco	.10
673	*Mike Matheny*	.15
674	Bret Barberie	.10
675	*Andrew Lorraine*	.10
676	Brian Jordan	.10
677	Tim Belcher	.10
678	*Antonio Osuna*	.10
679	Checklist I	.10
680	Checklist II	.10
681	Checklist III	.10
682	Checklist IV	.10

1994 BOWMAN'S BEST

	NM/M
Complete Set (200):	35.00
Red Set (90):	10.00
Blue Set (90):	20.00
Common Player:	.15
Pack (8):	1.50
Wax Box (24):	25.00

RED SET

No.	Player	Value
1	Paul Molitor	1.50
2	Eddie Murray	1.50
3	Ozzie Smith	1.75
4	Rickey Henderson	1.50
5	Lee Smith	.15
6	Dave Winfield	1.50
7	Roberto Alomar	1.00
8	Matt Williams	.15
9	Mark Grace	.25
10	Lance Johnson	.15
11	Darren Daulton	.15
12	Tom Glavine	.30
13	Gary Sheffield	.40
14	Rod Beck	.15
15	Fred McGriff	.15
16	Joe Carter	.15
17	Dante Bichette	.15
18	Danny Tartabull	.15
19	Juan Gonzalez	1.50
20	Steve Avery	.15
21	John Wetteland	.15
22	Ben McDonald	.15
23	Jack McDowell	.15
24	Jose Canseco	1.00
25	Tim Salmon	.30
26	Wilson Alvarez	.15
27	Gregg Jefferies	.15
28	John Burkett	.15
29	Greg Vaughn	.15
30	Robin Ventura	.15
31	Paul O'Neill	.15
32	Cecil Fielder	.15
33	Kevin Mitchell	.15
34	Jeff Conine	.15
35	Carlos Baerga	.15
36	Greg Maddux	1.75
37	Roger Clemens	2.00
38	Deion Sanders	.30
39	Delino DeShields	.15
40	Ken Griffey Jr.	2.50
41	Albert Belle	.30
42	Wade Boggs	1.75
43	Andres Galarraga	.15
44	Aaron Sele	.15
45	Don Mattingly	2.00
46	David Cone	.15
47	Lenny Dykstra	.15
48	Brett Butler	.15
49	Bill Swift	.15
50	Bobby Bonilla	.15
51	Rafael Palmeiro	1.50
52	Moises Alou	.15
53	Jeff Bagwell	1.50
54	Mike Mussina	1.25
55	Frank Thomas	1.50
56	Jose Rijo	.15
57	Ruben Sierra	.15
58	Randy Myers	.15
59	Barry Bonds	3.00
60	Jimmy Key	.15
61	Travis Fryman	.15
62	John Olerud	.15
63	David Justice	.15
64	Ray Lankford	.15
65	Bob Tewksbury	.15
66	Chuck Carr	.15
67	Jay Buhner	.15
68	Kenny Lofton	.15
69	Marquis Grissom	.15
70	Sammy Sosa	2.50
71	Cal Ripken Jr.	4.00
72	Ellis Burks	.15
73	Jeff Montgomery	.15
74	Julio Franco	.15
75	Kirby Puckett	1.75
76	Larry Walker	.15
77	Andy Van Slyke	.15
78	Tony Gwynn	1.75
79	Will Clark	.25
80	Mo Vaughn	.15
81	Mike Piazza	2.50
82	James Mouton	.15
83	Carlos Delgado	1.00
84	Ryan Klesko	.15
85	Javy Lopez	.15
86	Raul Mondesi	.15
87	Cliff Floyd	.15
88	Manny Ramirez	1.50
89	Hector Carrasco	.15
90	Jeff Granger	.15

BLUE SET

No.	Player	Value
1	Chipper Jones	1.75
2	Derek Jeter	3.00
3	Bill Pulsipher	.15
4	James Baldwin	.15
5	*Brooks Kieschnick*	.50
6	Justin Thompson	.15
7	Midre Cummings	.15
8	Joey Hamilton	.15
9	Calvin Reese	.15
10	Brian Barber	.15
11	John Burke	.15
12	De Shawn Warren	.15
13	*Edgardo Alfonzo*	1.00
14	*Eddie Pearson*	.15
15	Jimmy Haynes	.15
16	Danny Bautista	.15
17	Roger Cedeno	.15
18	Jon Lieber	.15
19	*Billy Wagner*	.75
20	*Tate Seefried*	.15
21	Chad Mottola	.15
22	Jose Malave	.15
23	*Terrell Wade*	.15
24	Shane Andrews	.15
25	*Chan Ho Park*	.75
26	*Kirk Presley*	.15
27	Robbie Beckett	.15
28	Orlando Miller	.15
29	*Jorge Posada*	6.00
30	Frank Rodriguez	.15
31	Brian Hunter	.15
32	Billy Ashley	.15
33	Rondell White	.15
34	John Roper	.15
35	Marc Valdes	.15
36	Scott Ruffcorn	.15
37	Rod Henderson	.15
38	Curt Goodwin	.15
39	Russ Davis	.15
40	Rick Gorecki	.15
41	Johnny Damon	.60
42	Roberto Petagine	.15
43	Chris Snopek	.15
44	Mark Acre	.15
45	Todd Hollandsworth	.15
46	Shawn Green	1.00
47	John Carter	.15
48	Jim Pittsley	.15
49	*John Wasdin*	.15
50	D.J. Boston	.15
51	Tim Clark	.15
52	Alex Ochoa	.15
53	Chad Roper	.15
54	Mike Kelly	.15
55	*Brad Fullmer*	.60
56	Carl Everett	.40
57	*Tim Belk*	.15
58	*Jimmy Hurst*	.15
59	*Mac Suzuki*	.15
60	Michael Moore	.15
61	*Alan Benes*	.15
62	*Tony Clark*	1.00
63	*Edgar Renteria*	8.00
64	Trey Beamon	.15
65	*LaTroy Hawkins*	.15
66	*Wayne Gomes*	.15
67	Ray McDavid	.15
68	John Dettmer	.15
69	Willie Greene	.15
70	Dave Stevens	.15
71	*Kevin Orie*	.15
72	Chad Ogea	.15
73	Ben Van Ryn	.15
74	Kym Ashworth	.15
75	Dmitri Young	.15
76	Herb Perry	.15
77	Joey Eischen	.15
78	*Arquimedez Pozo*	.15
79	Ugueth Urbina	.15
80	Keith Williams	.15
81	*John Frascatore*	.15
82	Garey Ingram	.15
83	Aaron Small	.15
84	*Olmedo Saenz*	.15
85	Jesus Tavarez	.15
86	*Jose Silva*	.15
87	*Gerald Witasick Jr.*	.15
88	Jay Maldonado	.15
89	Keith Heberling	.15
90	*Rusty Greer*	.50

MIRROR IMAGES

No.	Players	Value
91	Frank Thomas, Kevin Young	.60
92	*Fred McGriff, Brooks Kieschnick*	.15
93	Matt Williams, Shane Andrews	.15
94	*Cal Ripken Jr., Kevin Orie*	1.50
95	Barry Larkin, Derek Jeter	1.50
96	Ken Griffey Jr., Johnny Damon	1.00
97	Barry Bonds, Rondell White	1.00
98	*Albert Belle, Jimmy Hurst*	.25
99	*Raul Mondesi, Ruben Rivera*	.15
100	Roger Clemens, Scott Ruffcorn	.75
101	*Greg Maddux, John Wasdin*	.75
102	Tim Salmon, Chad Mottola	.25
103	*Carlos Baerga, Arquimedez Pozo*	.15
104	Mike Piazza, Bobby Hughes	1.00
105	Carlos Delgado, Melvin Nieves	.50
106	*Javy Lopez, Jorge Posada*	2.00
107	Manny Ramirez, Jose Malave	.65
108	Travis Fryman, Chipper Jones	.75
109	Steve Avery, Bill Pulsipher	.15
110	John Olerud, Shawn Green	.50

Refractors

Superstars:	8X-10X
Stars:	4X-8X

(See 1994 Bowman's Best for checklist and base card values.)

1995 BOWMAN

		NM/M
Complete Set (439):		165.00
Common Player:		.10
Pack (10):		9.00
Wax Box (24):		190.00
Rack Pack (15):		5.00
Rack Box (24):		125.00
1	Billy Wagner	.10
2	Chris Widger	.10
3	Brent Bowers	.10
4	*Bob Abreu*	10.00
5	*Lou Collier*	.10
6	*Juan Acevedo*	.25
7	*Jason Kelley*	.10
8	Brian Sackinsky	.10
9	Scott Christman	.10
10	Damon Hollins	.10
11	*Willis Otanez*	.10
12	*Jason Ryan*	.10
13	Jason Giambi	1.00
14	*Andy Taulbee*	.10
15	Mark Thompson	.10
16	*Hugo Pivaral*	.10
17	Brien Taylor	.10
18	Antonio Osuna	.10
19	Edgardo Alfonzo	.10
20	Carl Everett	.10
21	Matt Drews	.10
22	*Bartolo Colon*	4.00
23	*Andruw Jones*	30.00
24	*Robert Person*	.40
25	Derrek Lee	.50
26	*John Ambrose*	.10
27	*Eric Knowles*	.10
28	Chris Roberts	.10
29	Don Wengert	.10
30	*Marcus Jensen*	.10
31	Brian Barber	.10
32	Kevin Brown	.10
33	Benji Gil	.10
34	Mike Hubbard	.10
35	*Bart Evans*	.10
36	*Enrique Wilson*	.50
37	*Brian Buchanan*	.10
38	*Ken Ray*	.10
39	*Micah Franklin*	.10
40	*Ricky Otero*	.10
41	Jason Kendall	.10
42	Jimmy Hurst	.10
43	*Jerry Wolak*	.10
44	*Jayson Peterson*	.10
45	*Allen Battle*	.10
46	Scott Stahoviak	.10
47	*Steve Schrenk*	.10
48	*Travis Miller*	.25
49	*Eddie Rios*	.10
50	Mike Hampton	.10
51	*Chad Frontera*	.10
52	*Tom Evans*	.10
53	C.J. Nitkowski	.10
54	*Clay Caruthers*	.10
55	Shannon Stewart	.25
56	Jorge Posada	.10
57	Aaron Holbert	.10
58	*Harry Berrios*	.10
59	Steve Rodriguez	.10
60	Shane Andrews	.10
61	*Will Cunnane*	.10
62	Richard Hidalgo	.10
63	*Bill Selby*	.10
64	*Jay Cranford*	.10
65	Jeff Suppan	.10
66	Curtis Goodwin	.10
67	*John Thomson*	.10
68	Justin Thompson	.10
69	Troy Percival	.10
70	*Matt Wagner*	.10
71	Terry Bradshaw	.10
72	Greg Hansell	.10
73	John Burke	.10
74	Jeff D'Amico	.10
75	Ernie Young	.10
76	Jason Bates	.10
77	Chris Stynes	.10
78	*Cade Gaspar*	.10
79	Melvin Nieves	.10
80	Rick Gorecki	.10
81	*Felix Rodriguez*	.50
82	Ryan Hancock	.10
83	*Chris Carpenter*	6.00
84	Ray McDavid	.10
85	Chris Wimmer	.10
86	Doug Glanville	.10
87	DeShawn Warren	.10
88	*Damian Moss*	.75
89	*Rafael Orellano*	.10
90	*Vladimir Guerrero*	50.00
91	*Raul Casanova*	.40
92	*Karim Garcia*	1.25
93	Bryce Florie	.10
94	Kevin Orie	.10
95	*Ryan Nye*	.10
96	*Matt Sachse*	.10
97	*Ivan Arteaga*	.10
98	Glenn Murray	.10
99	*Stacy Hollins*	.10
100	Jim Pittsley	.10
101	*Craig Mattson*	.10
102	Neifi Perez	.10
103	Keith Williams	.10
104	Roger Cedeno	.10
105	*Tony Terry*	.10
106	Jose Malave	.10
107	Joe Rosselli	.10
108	Kevin Jordan	.10
109	*Sid Roberson*	.10
110	Alan Embree	.10
111	Terrell Wade	.10
112	Bob Wolcott	.10
113	*Carlos Perez*	.10
114	*Mike Bovee*	.10
115	*Tommy Davis*	.10
116	*Jeremey Kendall*	.10
117	Rich Aude	.10
118	Rick Huisman	.10
119	Tim Belk	.10
120	Edgar Renteria	.10
121	*Calvin Maduro*	.10
122	*Jerry Martin*	.10
123	*Ramon Fermin*	.10
124	*Kimera Bartee*	.10
125	Mark Farris	.10
126	Frank Rodriguez	.10
127	*Bobby Higginson*	1.50
128	Bret Wagner	.10
129	*Edwin Diaz*	.10
130	Jimmy Haynes	.10
131	*Chris Weinke*	1.50
132	*Damian Jackson*	.10
133	Felix Martinez	.10
134	*Edwin Hurtado*	.25
135	*Matt Raleigh*	.10
136	Paul Wilson	.10
137	Ron Villone	.10
138	*Eric Stuckenschneider*	.10
139	Tate Seefried	.10
140	*Rey Ordonez*	1.00
141	Eddie Pearson	.10
142	Kevin Gallaher	.10
143	Torii Hunter	.10
144	Daron Kirkreit	.10
145	Craig Wilson	.10
146	Ugueth Urbina	.10
147	Chris Snopek	.10
148	Kym Ashworth	.10
149	Wayne Gomes	.10
150	Mark Loretta	.10
151	*Ramon Morel*	.10
152	Trot Nixon	.10
153	Desi Relaford	.10
154	Scott Sullivan	.10
155	Marc Barcelo	.10
156	Willie Adams	.10
157	*Derrick Gibson*	.10
158	*Brian Meadows*	.10
159	Julian Tavarez	.10
160	Bryan Rekar	.10
161	Steve Gibralter	.10
162	Esteban Loaiza	.10
163	John Wasdin	.10
164	Kirk Presley	.10
165	Mariano Rivera	.35
166	Andy Larkin	.10
167	*Sean Whiteside*	.10
168	*Matt Apana*	.10
169	*Shawn Senior*	.10
170	Scott Gentile	.10
171	Quilvio Veras	.10
172	*Elieser Marrero*	1.50
173	*Mendy Lopez*	.10
174	Homer Bush	.10
175	*Brian Stephenson*	.10
176	Jon Nunnally	.10
177	Jose Herrera	.10
178	*Corey Avrard*	.10
179	David Bell	.10
180	Jason Isringhausen	.10
181	Jamey Wright	.10
182	*Lonell Roberts*	.10
183	Marty Cordova	.10
185	Amaury Telemaco	.10
185	John Mabry	.10
186	*Andrew Vessel*	.10
187	*Jim Cole*	.10
188	Marquis Riley	.10
189	Todd Dunn	.10
190	John Carter	.10
191	*Donnie Sadler*	.25
192	Mike Bell	.10
193	*Chris Cumberland*	.10
194	Jason Schmidt	.10
195	Matt Brunson	.10
196	James Baldwin	.10
197	*Bill Simas*	.10
198	Gus Gandarillas	.10
199	Mac Suzuki	.10
200	*Rick Holifield*	.10
201	*Fernando Lunar*	.10
202	Kevin Jarvis	.10
203	*Everett Stull*	.10
204	Steve Wojciechowski	.10
205	Shawn Estes	.10
206	Jermaine Dye	.10
207	Marc Kroon	.10
208	*Peter Munro*	.10
209	Pat Watkins	.10
210	Matt Smith	.10
211	Joe Vitiello	.10
212	Gerald Witasick Jr.	.10
213	*Freddy Garcia*	.10
214	*Glenn Dishman*	.10
215	*Jay Canizaro*	.10
216	Angel Martinez	.10
217	*Yamil Benitez*	.25
218	*Fausto Macey*	.10
219	Eric Owens	.10
220	Checklist	.10
221	*Dwayne Hosey* (Minor League MVPs)	.10
222	*Brad Woodall* (Minor League MVPs)	.25
223	Billy Ashley (Minor League MVPs)	.10
224	*Mark Grudzielanek* (Minor League MVPs)	2.00
225	*Mark Johnson* (Minor League MVPs)	.10
226	*Tim Unroe* (Minor League MVPs)	.10
227	Todd Greene (Minor League MVPs)	.10
228	Larry Sutton (Minor League MVPs)	.10
229	Derek Jeter (Minor League MVPs)	3.00
230	*Sal Fasano* (Minor League MVPs)	.10
231	Ruben Rivera (Minor League MVPs)	.10
232	*Chris Truby* (Minor League MVPs)	.25
233	John Donati (Minor League MVPs)	.10
234	*Decomba Conner* (Minor League MVPs)	.10
235	*Sergio Nunez* (Minor League MVPs)	.10
236	*Ray Brown* (Minor League MVPs)	.10
237	*Juan Melo* (Minor League MVPs)	.10
238	*Hideo Nomo* (First Impressions)	4.00
239	*Jaime Bluma* (First Impressions)	.10
240	*Jay Payton* (First Impressions)	1.50
241	Paul Konerko (First Impressions)	.50
242	*Scott Elarton* (First Impressions)	1.00
243	*Jeff Abbott* (First Impressions)	.25
244	*Jim Brower* (First Impressions)	.10
245	*Geoff Blum* (First Impressions)	.40
246	*Aaron Boone* (First Impressions)	2.00
247	J.R. Phillips (Top Prospects)	.10
248	Alex Ochoa (Top Prospects)	.10
249	Nomar Garciaparra (Top Prospects)	5.00
250	Garret Anderson (Top Prospects)	.10
251	Ray Durham (Top Prospects)	.10
252	Paul Shuey (Top Prospects)	.10
253	Tony Clark (Top Prospects)	.10
254	Johnny Damon (Top Prospects)	.50
255	Duane Singleton (Top Prospects)	.10
256	LaTroy Hawkins (Top Prospects)	.10
257	Andy Pettitte (Top Prospects)	.50
258	Ben Grieve (Top Prospects)	.15
259	Marc Newfield (Top Prospects)	.10
260	Terrell Lowery (Top Prospects)	.10
261	Shawn Green (Top Prospects)	.60
262	Chipper Jones (Top Prospects)	2.00
263	Brooks Kieschnick (Top Prospects)	.10
264	Calvin Reese (Top Prospects)	.10
265	Doug Million (Top Prospects)	.10
266	Marc Valdes (Top Prospects)	.10
267	Brian Hunter (Top Prospects)	.10
268	Todd Hollandsworth (Top Prospects)	.10
269	Rod Henderson (Top Prospects)	.10
270	Bill Pulsipher (Top Prospects)	.10
271	*Scott Rolen* (Top Prospects)	15.00
272	Trey Beamon (Top Prospects)	.10
273	Alan Benes (Top Prospects)	.10
274	Dustin Hermanson (Top Prospects)	.15
275	Ricky Bottalico	.10
276	Albert Belle	.20
277	Deion Sanders	.10
278	Matt Williams	.10
279	Jeff Bagwell	1.50
280	Kirby Puckett	2.00
281	Dave Hollins	.10
282	Don Mattingly	2.00
283	Joey Hamilton	.10
284	Bobby Bonilla	.10
285	Moises Alou	.10
286	Tom Glavine	.25
287	Brett Butler	.10
288	Chris Hoiles	.10
289	Kenny Rogers	.10
290	Larry Walker	.10
291	Tim Raines	.10
292	Kevin Appier	.10
293	Roger Clemens	2.00
294a	Chuck Carr	.10
294b	Cliff Floyd (Should be #394)	.10
295	Randy Myers	.10
296	Dave Nilsson	.10
297	Joe Carter	.10
298	Chuck Finley	.10
299	Ray Lankford	.10
300	Roberto Kelly	.10
301	Jon Lieber	.10
302	Travis Fryman	.10
303	Mark McGwire	2.50
304	Tony Gwynn	2.00
305	Kenny Lofton	.10
306	Mark Whiten	.10
307	Doug Drabek	.10
308	Terry Steinbach	.10
309	Ryan Klesko	.10
310	Mike Piazza	2.00
311	Ben McDonald	.10
312	Reggie Sanders	.10
313	Alex Fernandez	.10
314	Aaron Sele	.10
315	Gregg Jefferies	.10
316	Rickey Henderson	1.50
317	Brian Anderson	.10
318	Jose Valentin	.10
319	Rod Beck	.10
320	Marquis Grissom	.10
321	Ken Griffey Jr.	2.25
322	Bret Saberhagen	.10
323	Juan Gonzalez	1.50
324	Paul Molitor	1.50
325	Gary Sheffield	.35
326	Darren Daulton	.10
327	Bill Swift	.10
328	Brian McRae	.10
329	Robin Ventura	.10
330	Lee Smith	.10
331	Fred McGriff	.10
332	Delino DeShields	.10
333	Edgar Martinez	.10

334 Mike Mussina .75
335 Orlando Merced .10
336 Carlos Baerga .10
337 Wil Cordero .10
338 Tom Pagnozzi .10
339 Pat Hentgen .10
340 Chad Curtis .10
341 Darren Lewis .10
342 Jeff Kent .10
343 Bip Roberts .10
344 Ivan Rodriguez 1.50
345 Jeff Montgomery .10
346 Hal Morris .10
347 Danny Tartabull .10
348 Raul Mondesi .10
349 Ken Hill .10
350 Pedro Martinez 1.50
351 Frank Thomas 1.50
352 Manny Ramirez 1.50
353 Tim Salmon .30
354 William Van Landingham .10
355 Andres Galarraga .10
356 Paul O'Neill .10
357 Brady Anderson .10
358 Ramon Martinez .10
359 John Olerud .10
360 Ruben Sierra .10
361 Cal Eldred .10
362 Jay Buhner .10
363 Jay Bell .10
364 Wally Joyner .10
365 Chuck Knoblauch .10
366 Len Dykstra .10
367 John Wetteland .10
368 Roberto Alomar .30
369 Craig Biggio .10
370 Ozzie Smith 2.00
371 Terry Pendleton .10
372 Sammy Sosa 2.25
373 Carlos Garcia .10
374 Jose Rijo .10
375 Chris Gomez .10
376 Barry Bonds 3.00
377 Steve Avery .10
378 Rick Wilkins .10
379 Pete Harnisch .10
380 Dean Palmer .10
381 Bob Hamelin .10
382 Jason Bere .10
383 Jimmy Key .10
384 Dante Bichette .10
385 Rafael Palmeiro 1.50
386 David Justice .10
387 Chili Davis .10
388 Mike Greenwell .10
389 Todd Zeile .10
390 Jeff Conine .10
391 Rick Aguilera .10
392 Eddie Murray 1.50
393 Mike Stanley .10
394 (NOT ISSUED, SEE #294)
395 Randy Johnson 1.50
396 David Nied .10
397 Devon White .10
398 Royce Clayton .10
399 Andy Benes .10
400 John Hudek .10
401 Bobby Jones .10
402 Eric Karros .10
403 Will Clark .15
404 Mark Langston .10
405 Kevin Brown .15
406 Greg Maddux 2.00
407 David Cone .10
408 Wade Boggs 2.00
409 Steve Trachsel .10
410 Greg Vaughn .10
411 Mo Vaughn .10
412 Wilson Alvarez .10
413 Cal Ripken Jr. 3.00
414 Rico Brogna .10
415 Barry Larkin .10
416 Cecil Fielder .10
417 Jose Canseco .50
418 Jack McDowell .10
419 Mike Lieberthal .10
420 Andrew Lorraine .10
421 Rich Becker .10
422 Tony Phillips .10
423 Scott Ruffcorn .10
424 Jeff Granger .10
425 Greg Pirkl .10
426 Dennis Eckersley 1.00
427 Jose Lima .10
428 Russ Davis .10
429 Armando Benitez .10
430 Alex Gonzalez .10
431 Carlos Delgado .75
432 Chan Ho Park .10
433 Mickey Tettleton .10
434 Dave Winfield 1.50
435 John Burkett .10
436 Orlando Miller .10
437 Rondell White .10
438 Jose Oliva .10
439 Checklist .10

Gold

NM/M
Complete Set (54): 100.00
Common Player: .50
Stars/RCs: 1.5X
(See 1995 Bowman #221-274 for checklist and base card values.)

1995 BOWMAN'S BEST

NM/M
Complete Set (195): 200.00
Common Player: .25
Pack (7): 18.00
Wax Box (24): 400.00
Complete Set Red (90): 45.00
1 Randy Johnson 1.50
2 Joe Carter .25
3 Chili Davis .25
4 Moises Alou .25
5 Gary Sheffield .40
6 Kevin Appier .25
7 Denny Neagle .25
8 Ruben Sierra .25
9 Darren Daulton .25
10 Cal Ripken Jr. 4.00
11 Bobby Bonilla .25
12 Manny Ramirez 1.50
13 Barry Bonds 4.00
14 Eric Karros .25
15 Greg Maddux 2.00
16 Jeff Bagwell 1.50
17 Paul Molitor 1.50
18 Ray Lankford .25
19 Mark Grace .35
20 Kenny Lofton .25
21 Tony Gwynn 2.00
22 Will Clark .35
23 Roger Clemens 2.25
24 Dante Bichette .25
25 Barry Larkin .25
26 Wade Boggs 2.00
27 Kirby Puckett 2.00
28 Cecil Fielder .25
29 Jose Canseco .50
30 Juan Gonzalez 1.50
31 David Cone .25
32 Craig Biggio .25
33 Tim Salmon .35
34 David Justice .25
35 Sammy Sosa 2.50
36 Mike Piazza 2.50
37 Carlos Baerga .25
38 Jeff Conine .25
39 Rafael Palmeiro 1.50
40 Bret Saberhagen .25
41 Len Dykstra .25
42 Mo Vaughn .25
43 Wally Joyner .25
44 Chuck Knoblauch .25
45 Robin Ventura .25
46 Don Mattingly 2.50
47 Dave Hollins .25
48 Andy Benes .25
49 Ken Griffey Jr. 2.50
50 Albert Belle .35
51 Matt Williams .25
52 Rondell White .25
53 Raul Mondesi .25
54 Brian Jordan .25
55 Greg Vaughn .25
56 Fred McGriff .25
57 Roberto Alomar .40
58 Dennis Eckersley 1.00
59 Lee Smith .25
60 Eddie Murray 1.50
61 Kenny Rogers .25
62 Ron Gant .25
63 Larry Walker .25
64 Chad Curtis .25
65 Frank Thomas 1.50
66 Paul O'Neill .25
67 Kevin Seitzer .25
68 Marquis Grissom .25
69 Mark McGwire 3.00
70 Travis Fryman .25
71 Andres Galarraga .25
72 *Carlos Perez* .25
73 Tyler Green .25
74 Marty Cordova .25
75 Shawn Green .50
76 Vaughn Eshelman .25
77 John Mabry .25
78 Jason Bates .25
79 Jon Nunnally .25
80 Ray Durham .25
81 Edgardo Alfonzo .25
82 Esteban Loaiza .25
83 *Hideo Nomo* 10.00
84 Orlando Miller .25
85 Alex Gonzalez .25
86 *Mark Grudzielanek* .65
87 Julian Tavarez .25
88 Benji Gil .25
89 Quilvio Veras .25
90 Ricky Bottalico .25
Complete Set Blue (90): 150.00
1 Derek Jeter 3.00
2 *Vladimir Guerrero* 80.00
3 *Bob Abreu* 25.00
4 Chan Ho Park .25
5 Paul Wilson .25
6 Chad Ogea .25
7 *Andruw Jones* 50.00
8 Brian Barber .25
9 Andy Larkin .25
10 *Richie Sexson* 10.00
11 *Everett Stull* .25
12 Brooks Kieschnick .25
13 Matt Murray .25
14 John Wasdin .25
15 Shannon Stewart .40
16 Luis Ortiz .25
17 Marc Kroon .25
18 Todd Greene .25
19 Juan Acevedo .25
20 Tony Clark .25
21 Jermaine Dye .25
22 Derrek Lee 1.00
23 Pat Watkins .25
24 Calvin Reese .25
25 Ben Grieve .35
26 *Julio Santana* .25
27 *Felix Rodriguez* .50
28 Paul Konerko .25
29 Nomar Garciaparra 3.00
30 Pat Ahearne .25
31 Jason Schmidt .25
32 Billy Wagner .25
33 *Rey Ordonez* 1.00
34 Curtis Goodwin .25
35 *Sergio Nunez* .25
36 Tim Belk .25
37 *Scott Elarton* 1.00
38 Jason Isringhausen .25
39 Trot Nixon .35
40 Sid Roberson .25
41 Ron Villone .25
42 Ruben Rivera .25
43 Rick Huisman .25
44 Todd Hollandsworth .25
45 Johnny Damon 1.00
46 Garret Anderson .25
47 Jeff D'Amico .25
48 Dustin Hermanson .25
49 *Juan Encarnacion* 4.00
50 Andy Pettitte .50
51 Chris Stynes .25
52 Troy Percival .25
53 LaTroy Hawkins .25
54 Roger Cedeno .25
55 Alan Benes .25
56 *Karim Garcia* 1.00
57 Andrew Lorraine .25
58 *Gary Rath* .25
59 Bret Wagner .25
60 Jeff Suppan .25
61 Bill Pulsipher .25
62 *Jay Payton* 3.00
63 Alex Ochoa .25
64 Ugueth Urbina .25
65 Armando Benitez .25
66 George Arias .25
67 *Raul Casanova* .50
68 Matt Drews .25
69 Jimmy Haynes .25
70 Jimmy Hurst .25
71 C.J. Nitkowski .25
72 *Tommy Davis* .25
73 *Bartolo Colon* 5.00
74 *Chris Carpenter* 10.00
75 Trey Beamon .25
76 Bryan Rekar .25
77 James Baldwin .25
78 Marc Valdes .25
79 *Tom Fordham* .25
80 Marc Newfield .25
81 Angel Martinez .25
82 Brian Hunter .25
83 Jose Herrera .25
84 *Glenn Dishman* .25
85 *Jacob Cruz* .25
86 Paul Shuey .25
87 *Scott Rolen* 25.00
88 Doug Million .25
89 Desi Relaford .25
90 Michael Tucker .25
Mirror Image: .50
1 Ben Davis, Ivan Rodriguez 1.50
2 Mark Redman, Manny Ramirez 1.50
3 Reggie Taylor, Deion Sanders .60
4 Ryan Jaroncyk, Shawn Green .60
5 Juan LeBron, Juan Gonzalez 1.50
6 Toby McKnight, Craig Biggio .50
7 Michael Barrett, Travis Fryman 1.50
8 Corey Jenkins, Mo Vaughn .50
9 Ruben Rivera, Frank Thomas 1.50
10 Curtis Goodwin, Kenny Lofton .50
11 Brian Hunter, Tony Gwynn 1.75
12 Todd Greene, Ken Griffey Jr. 2.00
13 Karim Garcia, Matt Williams .75
14 Billy Wagner, Randy Johnson 1.50
15 Pat Watkins, Jeff Bagwell 1.50

Refractors

NM/M
Complete Set (195): 1,900
Common Player: 1.00
Stars: 3-6X
Rookies: 2-3X
(See 1995 Bowman's Best for checklist and base card values.)

1996 BOWMAN

NM/M
Complete Set (385): 60.00
Common Player: .10
Foils: 1.5X
Pack (11): 2.50
Wax Box (24): 50.00
1 Cal Ripken Jr. 3.00
2 Ray Durham .10
3 Ivan Rodriguez 1.00
4 Fred McGriff .10
5 Hideo Nomo 1.25

No.	Player	Price
6	Troy Percival	.10
7	Moises Alou	.10
8	Mike Stanley	.10
9	Jay Buhner	.10
10	Shawn Green	.30
11	Ryan Klesko	.10
12	Andres Galarraga	.10
13	Dean Palmer	.10
14	Jeff Conine	.10
15	Brian Hunter	.10
16	J.T. Snow	.10
17	Larry Walker	.10
18	Barry Larkin	.10
19	Alex Gonzalez	.10
20	Edgar Martinez	.10
21	Mo Vaughn	.10
22	Mark McGwire	2.50
23	Jose Canseco	.50
24	Jack McDowell	.10
25	Dante Bichette	.10
26	Wade Boggs	1.50
27	Mike Piazza	2.00
28	Ray Lankford	.10
29	Craig Biggio	.10
30	Rafael Palmeiro	1.00
31	Ron Gant	.10
32	Javy Lopez	.10
33	Brian Jordan	.10
34	Paul O'Neill	.10
35	Mark Grace	.15
36	Matt Williams	.10
37	Pedro Martinez	1.25
38	Rickey Henderson	1.00
39	Bobby Bonilla	.10
40	Todd Hollandsworth	.10
41	Jim Thome	.10
42	Gary Sheffield	.40
43	Tim Salmon	.25
44	Gregg Jefferies	.10
45	Roberto Alomar	.30
45p	Roberto Alomar (unmarked promo card, fielding photo on front)	3.00
46	Carlos Baerga	.10
47	Mark Grudzielanek	.10
48	Randy Johnson	1.25
49	Tino Martinez	.10
50	Robin Ventura	.10
51	Ryne Sandberg	1.50
52	Jay Bell	.10
53	Jason Schmidt	.10
54	Frank Thomas	1.25
55	Kenny Lofton	.10
56	Ariel Prieto	.10
57	David Cone	.10
58	Reggie Sanders	.10
59	Michael Tucker	.10
60	Vinny Castilla	.10
61	Lenny Dykstra	.10
62	Todd Hundley	.10
63	Brian McRae	.10
64	Dennis Eckersley	.75
65	Rondell White	.10
66	Eric Karros	.10
67	Greg Maddux	1.50
68	Kevin Appier	.10
69	Eddie Murray	1.00
70	John Olerud	.10
71	Tony Gwynn	1.50
72	David Justice	.10
73	Ken Caminiti	.10
74	Terry Steinbach	.10
75	Alan Benes	.10
76	Chipper Jones	1.50
77	Jeff Bagwell	1.25
77p	Jeff Bagwell (unmarked promo card, name in gold)	6.00
78	Barry Bonds	3.00
79	Ken Griffey Jr.	2.00
80	Roger Cedeno	.10
81	Joe Carter	.10
82	Henry Rodriguez	.10
83	Jason Isringhausen	.10
84	Chuck Knoblauch	.10
85	Manny Ramirez	1.25
86	Tom Glavine	.25
87	Jeffrey Hammonds	.10
88	Paul Molitor	1.00
89	Roger Clemens	1.75
90	Greg Vaughn	.10
91	Marty Cordova	.10
92	Albert Belle	.20
93	Mike Mussina	.65
94	Garret Anderson	.10
95	Juan Gonzalez	1.25
96	John Valentin	.10
97	Jason Giambi	.65
98	Kirby Puckett	1.50
99	Jim Edmonds	.10
100	Cecil Fielder	.10
101	Mike Aldrete	.10
102	Marquis Grissom	.10
103	Derek Bell	.10
104	Raul Mondesi	.10
105	Sammy Sosa	2.00
106	Travis Fryman	.10
107	Rico Brogna	.10
108	Will Clark	.15
109	Bernie Williams	.30
110	Brady Anderson	.10
111	Torii Hunter	.10
112	Derek Jeter	3.00
113	*Mike Kusiewicz*	.10
114	Scott Rolen	.75
115	Ramon Castro	.10
116	*Jose Guillen*	4.00
117	*Wade Walker*	.10
118	Shawn Senior	.10
119	*Onan Masaoka*	.10
120	*Marlon Anderson*	1.00
121	*Katsuhiro Maeda*	.25
122	*Garrett Stephenson*	.25
123	Butch Huskey	.10
124	*D'Angelo Jimenez*	.50
125	*Tony Mounce*	.10
126	Jay Canizaro	.10
127	Juan Melo	.10
128	Steve Gibralter	.10
129	Freddy Garcia	.10
130	Julio Santana	.10
131	Richard Hidalgo	.10
132	Jermaine Dye	.10
133	Willie Adams	.10
134	Everett Stull	.10
135	Ramon Morel	.10
136	Chan Ho Park	.10
137	Jamey Wright	.10
138	*Luis Garcia*	.10
139	Dan Serafini	.10
140	*Ryan Dempster*	1.00
141	Tate Seefried	.10
142	Jimmy Hurst	.10
143	Travis Miller	.10
144	Curtis Goodwin	.10
145	*Rocky Coppinger*	.10
146	Enrique Wilson	.10
147	Jaime Bluma	.10
148	Andrew Vessel	.10
149	Damian Moss	.10
150	*Shawn Gallagher*	.10
151	Pat Watkins	.10
152	Jose Paniagua	.10
153	Danny Graves	.10
154	*Bryon Gainey*	.10
155	Steve Soderstrom	.10
156	*Cliff Brumbaugh*	.10
157	*Eugene Kingsale*	.10
158	Lou Collier	.10
159	Todd Walker	.10
160	*Kris Detmers*	.10
161	*Josh Booty*	.25
162	*Greg Whiteman*	.10
163	Damian Jackson	.10
164	Tony Clark	.10
165	Jeff D'Amico	.10
166	Johnny Damon	.25
167	Rafael Orellano	.10
168	Ruben Rivera	.10
169	Alex Ochoa	.10
170	Jay Powell	.10
171	Tom Evans	.10
172	Ron Villone	.10
173	Shawn Estes	.10
174	John Wasdin	.10
175	Bill Simas	.10
176	Kevin Brown	.15
177	Shannon Stewart	.20
178	Todd Greene	.10
179	Bob Wolcott	.10
180	Chris Snopek	.10
181	Nomar Garciaparra	2.00
182	*Cameron Smith*	.10
183	Matt Drews	.10
184	Jimmy Haynes	.10
185	Chris Carpenter	.10
186	Desi Relaford	.10
187	Ben Grieve	.20
188	Mike Bell	.10
189	*Luis Castillo*	1.00
190	Ugueth Urbina	.10
191	Paul Wilson	.10
191p	Paul Wilson (unmarked promo card, name in gold)	1.00
192	Andruw Jones	1.25
193	Wayne Gomes	.10
194	*Craig Counsell*	1.00
195	Jim Cole	.10
196	Brooks Kieshnick	.10
197	Trey Beamon	.10
198	*Marino Santana*	.10
199	Bob Abreu	.10
200	Calvin Reese	.10
201	Dante Powell	.10
202	George Arias	.10
202p	George Arias (unmarked promo card, name in gold)	1.00
203	*Jorge Velandia*	.10
204	*George Lombard*	.25
205	*Byron Browne*	.10
206	John Frascatore	.10
207	Terry Adams	.10
208	*Wilson Delgado*	.10
209	Billy McMillon	.10
210	Jeff Abbott	.10
211	Trot Nixon	.10
212	Amaury Telemaco	.10
213	Scott Sullivan	.10
214	Justin Thompson	.10
215	Decomba Conner	.10
216	Ryan McGuire	.10
217	*Matt Luke*	.10
218	Doug Million	.10
219	*Jason Dickson*	.25
220	*Ramon Hernandez*	.50
221	*Mark Bellhorn*	.10
222	*Eric Ludwick*	.10
223	*Luke Wilcox*	.10
224	*Marty Malloy*	.10
225	*Gary Coffee*	.10
226	*Wendell Magee*	.10
227	*Brett Tomko*	.50
228	Derek Lowe	.10
229	*Jose Rosado*	.10
230	*Steve Bourgeois*	.10
231	*Neil Weber*	.10
232	Jeff Ware	.10
233	Edwin Diaz	.10
234	Greg Norton	.10
235	Aaron Boone	.10
236	Jeff Suppan	.10
237	Bret Wagner	.10
238	Elieser Marrero	.10
239	Will Cunnane	.10
240	*Brian Barkley*	.10
241	Jay Payton	.10
242	Marcus Jensen	.10
243	Ryan Nye	.10
244	Chad Mottola	.10
245	*Scott McClain*	.10
246	*Jesse Ibarra*	.10
247	*Mike Darr*	.10
248	*Bobby Estalella*	1.00
249	Michael Barrett	.10
250	*Jamie Lopiccolo*	.10
251	*Shane Spencer*	1.00
252	*Ben Petrick*	1.00
253	*Jason Bell*	.10
254	*Arnold Gooch*	.10
255	T.J. Mathews	.10
256	Jason Ryan	.10
257	*Pat Cline*	.10
258	*Rafael Carmona*	.10
259	*Carl Pavano*	4.00
260	Ben Davis	.10
261	*Matt Lawton*	1.00
262	*Kevin Sefcik*	.15
263	*Chris Fussell*	.10
264	*Mike Cameron*	1.50
265	*Marty Janzen*	.10
266	*Livan Hernandez*	1.00
267	*Raul Ibanez*	1.50
268	Juan Encarnacion	.10
269	*David Yocum*	.10
270	*Jonathan Johnson*	.10
271	Reggie Taylor	.10
272	*Danny Buxbaum*	.10
273	Jacob Cruz	.10
274	*Bobby Morris*	.10
275	*Andy Fox*	.10
276	Greg Keagle	.10
277	Charles Peterson	.10
278	Derrek Lee	.40
279	*Bryant Nelson*	.10
280	Antone Williamson	.10
281	Scott Elarton	.10
282	*Shad Williams*	.10
283	*Rich Hunter*	.10
284	Chris Sheff	.10
285	Derrick Gibson	.10
286	Felix Rodriguez	.10
287	*Brian Banks*	.15
288	Jason McDonald	.10
289	*Glendon Rusch*	.75
290	Gary Rath	.10
291	Peter Munro	.10
292	Tom Fordham	.10
293	Jason Kendall	.10
294	Russ Johnson	.10
295	*Joe Long*	.10
296	*Robert Smith*	.10
297	*Jarrod Washburn*	1.00
298	*Dave Coggin*	.10
299	*Jeff Yoder*	.10
300	*Jed Hansen*	.10
301	*Matt Morris*	2.00
302	*Josh Bishop*	.10
303	Dustin Hermanson	.10
304	Mike Gulan	.10
305	Felipe Crespo	.10
306	Quinton McCracken	.10
307	*Jim Bonnici*	.10
308	Sal Fasano	.10
309	*Gabe Alvarez*	.10
310	*Heath Murray*	.10
311	*Jose Valentin*	.10
312	Bartolo Colon	.10
313	Olmedo Saenz	.10
314	*Norm Hutchins*	.10
315	*Chris Holt*	.10
316	*David Doster*	.10
317	Robert Person	.10
318	*Donne Wall*	.10
319	*Adam Riggs*	.10
320	Homer Bush	.10
321	*Brad Rigby*	.10
322	*Lou Merloni*	.50
323	Neifi Perez	.10
324	Chris Cumberland	.10
325	*Alvie Shepherd*	.10
326	*Jarrod Patterson*	.10
327	*Ray Ricken*	.10
328	*Danny Klassen*	.10
329	*David Miller*	.10
330	*Chad Alexander*	.10
331	Matt Beaumont	.10
332	Damon Hollins	.10
333	Todd Dunn	.10
334	*Mike Sweeney*	2.50
335	Richie Sexson	.10
336	Billy Wagner	.10
337	*Ron Wright*	.10
338	Paul Konerko	.10
339	*Tommy Phelps*	.10
340	Karim Garcia	.10
341	*Mike Grace*	.10
342	*Russell Branyan*	.75
343	*Randy Winn*	.50
344	*A.J. Pierzynski*	2.50
345	*Mike Busby*	.10
346	*Matt Beech*	.10
347	*Jose Cepeda*	.10
348	Brian Stephenson	.10
349	Rey Ordonez	.10
350	*Rich Aurilia*	1.00
351	*Edgard Velazquez*	.25
352	Raul Casanova	.10
353	*Carlos Guillen*	2.00
354	*Bruce Aven*	.10
355	*Ryan Jones*	.10
356	*Derek Aucoin*	.10
357	*Brian Rose*	.15
358	*Richard Almanzar*	.10
359	*Fletcher Bates*	.10
360	*Russ Ortiz*	1.50
361	*Wilton Guerrero*	.15
362	*Geoff Jenkins*	1.50
363	Pete Janicki	.10
364	Yamil Benitez	.10
365	Aaron Holbert	.10
366	Tim Belk	.10
367	Terrell Wade	.10
368	Terrence Long	.10
369	Brad Fullmer	.10

370	Matt Wagner	.10
371	Craig Wilson	.10
372	Mark Loretta	.10
373	Eric Owens	.10
374	Vladimir Guerrero	1.00
375	Tommy Davis	.10
376	Donnie Sadler	.10
377	Edgar Renteria	.10
378	Todd Helton	1.00
379	*Ralph Milliard*	.10
380	*Darin Blood*	.10
381	Shayne Bennett	.10
382	Mark Redman	.10
383	Felix Martinez	.10
384	*Sean Watkins*	.10
385	Oscar Henriquez	.10

Preview

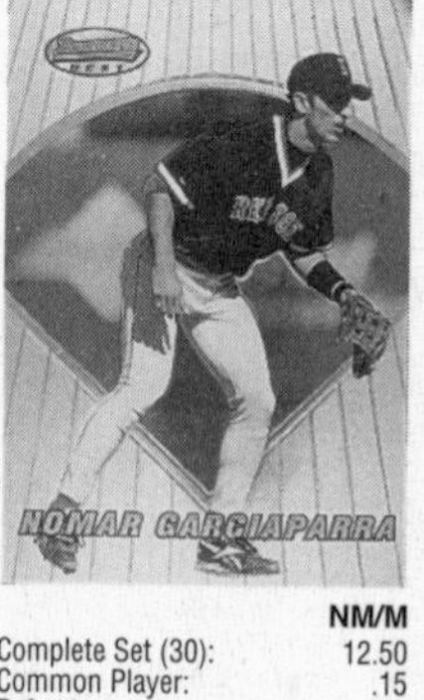

		NM/M
Complete Set (30):		12.50
Common Player:		.15
Refractors:		1.5
Atomic Refractors:		2X
1	Chipper Jones	.75
2	Alan Benes	.15
3	Brooks Kieshnick	.15
4	Barry Bonds	2.00
5	Rey Ordonez	.15
6	Tim Salmon	.25
7	Mike Piazza	1.00
8	Billy Wagner	.15
9	Andruw Jones	.60
10	Tony Gwynn	.75
11	Paul Wilson	.15
12	Calvin Reese	.15
13	Frank Thomas	.60
14	Greg Maddux	.75
15	Derek Jeter	2.00
16	Jeff Bagwell	.60
17	Barry Larkin	.15
18	Todd Greene	.15
19	Ruben Rivera	.15
20	Richard Hidalgo	.15
21	Larry Walker	.15
22	Carlos Baerga	.15
23	Derrick Gibson	.15
24	Richie Sexson	.15
25	Mo Vaughn	.15
26	Hideo Nomo	.60
27	Nomar Garciaparra	1.00
28	Cal Ripken Jr.	2.00
29	Karim Garcia	.25
30	Ken Griffey Jr.	1.00

Minor League Player of the Year

		NM/M
Complete Set (15):		12.50
Common Player:		.50
1	Andruw Jones	3.00
2	Derrick Gibson	.50
3	Bob Abreu	1.00
4	Todd Walker	.50
5	Jamey Wright	.50
6	Wes Helms	.50
7	Karim Garcia	1.50
8	Bartolo Colon	2.00
9	Alex Ochoa	.50
10	Mike Sweeney	2.00
11	Ruben Rivera	.50
12	Gabe Alvarez	.50
13	Billy Wagner	.50
14	Vladimir Guerrero	4.00
15	Edgard Velazquez	.50

1952 Mickey Mantle Reprints

		NM/M
Complete Set (4):		25.00
Common Card:		2.50
20	Mickey Mantle/Reprint	2.50
20	Mickey Mantle/Finest	5.00
20	Mickey Mantle/Refractor	7.50
20	Mickey Mantle/ Atomic Refractor	12.00

1996 BOWMAN'S BEST

		NM/M
Complete Set (180):		35.00
Common Player:		.25
Refractors:		2X
Atomics:		15X
1952 Mickey Mantle:		2.50
1952 Mantle Finest:		5.00
1952 Mantle Refractor:		7.50
1952 Mantle Atomic:		12.00
Pack (6):		2.50
Wax Box (24):		40.00
1	Hideo Nomo	1.50
2	Edgar Martinez	.25
3	Cal Ripken Jr.	4.00
4	Wade Boggs	2.00
5	Cecil Fielder	.25
6	Albert Belle	.35
7	Chipper Jones	2.00
8	Ryne Sandberg	2.00
9	Tim Salmon	.35
10	Barry Bonds	3.00
11	Ken Caminiti	.25
12	Ron Gant	.25
13	Frank Thomas	1.50
14	Dante Bichette	.25
15	Jason Kendall	.25
16	Mo Vaughn	.25
17	Rey Ordonez	.25
18	Henry Rodriguez	.25
19	Ryan Klesko	.25
20	Jeff Bagwell	1.50
21	Randy Johnson	1.50
22	Jim Edmonds	.25
23	Kenny Lofton	.25
24	Andy Pettitte	.50
25	Brady Anderson	.25
26	Mike Piazza	2.50
27	Greg Vaughn	.25
28	Joe Carter	.25
29	Jason Giambi	1.00
30	Ivan Rodriguez	1.00
31	Jeff Conine	.25
32	Rafael Palmeiro	.75
33	Roger Clemens	2.50
34	Chuck Knoblauch	.25
35	Reggie Sanders	.25
36	Andres Galarraga	.25
37	Paul O'Neill	.25
38	Tony Gwynn	2.00
39	Paul Wilson	.25
40	Garret Anderson	.25
41	David Justice	.25
42	Eddie Murray	1.50
43	*Mike Grace*	.25
44	Marty Cordova	.25
45	Kevin Appier	.25
46	Raul Mondesi	.25
47	Jim Thome	.25
48	Sammy Sosa	2.50
49	Craig Biggio	.25
50	Marquis Grissom	.25
51	Alan Benes	.25
52	Manny Ramirez	1.50
53	Gary Sheffield	.50
54	Mike Mussina	.75
55	Robin Ventura	.25
56	Johnny Damon	.40
57	Jose Canseco	.75
58	Juan Gonzalez	1.50
59	Tino Martinez	.25
60	Brian Hunter	.25
61	Fred McGriff	.25
62	Jay Buhner	.25
63	Carlos Delgado	.75
64	Moises Alou	.25
65	Roberto Alomar	.60
66	Barry Larkin	.25
67	Vinny Castilla	.25
68	Ray Durham	.25
69	Travis Fryman	.25
70	Jason Isringhausen	.25
71	Ken Griffey Jr.	2.50
72	John Smoltz	.25
73	Matt Williams	.25
74	Chan Ho Park	.25
75	Mark McGwire	3.00
76	Jeffrey Hammonds	.25
77	Will Clark	.30
78	Kirby Puckett	2.00
79	Derek Jeter	4.00
80	Derek Bell	.25
81	Eric Karros	.25
82	Lenny Dykstra	.25
83	Larry Walker	.25
84	Mark Grudzielanek	.25
85	Greg Maddux	2.00
86	Carlos Baerga	.25
87	Paul Molitor	1.50
88	John Valentin	.25
89	Mark Grace	.30
90	Ray Lankford	.25
91	Andruw Jones	1.50
92	Nomar Garciaparra	2.50
93	Alex Ochoa	.25
94	Derrick Gibson	.25
95	Jeff D'Amico	.25
96	Ruben Rivera	.25
97	Vladimir Guerrero	1.50
98	Calvin Reese	.25
99	Richard Hidalgo	.25
100	Bartolo Colon	.25
101	Karim Garcia	.25
102	Ben Davis	.25
103	Jay Powell	.25
104	Chris Snopek	.25
105	*Glendon Rusch*	1.50
106	Enrique Wilson	.25
107	*Antonio Alfonseca*	1.50
108	*Wilton Guerrero*	.50
109	*Jose Guillen*	5.00
110	*Miguel Mejia*	.25
111	Jay Payton	.25
112	Scott Elarton	.25
113	Brooks Kieschnick	.25
114	Dustin Hermanson	.25
115	Roger Cedeno	.25
116	Matt Wagner	.25
117	Lee Daniels	.25
118	Ben Grieve	.35
119	Ugueth Urbina	.25
120	Danny Graves	.25
121	*Dan Donato*	.25
122	*Matt Ruebel*	.25
123	*Mark Sievert*	.25
124	Chris Stynes	.25
125	Jeff Abbott	.25
126	*Rocky Coppinger*	.25
127	Jermaine Dye	.25
128	Todd Greene	.15
129	Chris Carpenter	.25
130	Edgar Renteria	.25
131	Matt Drews	.25
132	*Edgard Velazquez*	.50
133	Casey Whitten	.25
134	*Ryan Jones*	.25
135	Todd Walker	.20
136	*Geoff Jenkins*	3.00
137	*Matt Morris*	4.00
138	Richie Sexson	.25
139	*Todd Dunwoody*	.50
140	*Gabe Alvarez*	.50
141	J.J. Johnson	.25
142	Shannon Stewart	.25
143	Brad Fullmer	.25
144	Julio Santana	.25
145	Scott Rolen	1.00
146	Amaury Telemaco	.25
147	Trey Beamon	.25
148	Billy Wagner	.20
149	Todd Hollandsworth	.25
150	Doug Million	.25
151	*Jose Valentin*	.25
152	*Wes Helms*	.50
153	Jeff Suppan	.25
154	*Luis Castillo*	2.00
155	Bob Abreu	.30
156	Paul Konerko	.25
157	Jamey Wright	.25
158	Eddie Pearson	.25
159	Jimmy Haynes	.25
160	Derrek Lee	.40
161	Damian Moss	.15
162	*Carlos Guillen*	2.00
163	*Chris Fussell*	.25
164	*Mike Sweeney*	4.00
165	Donnie Sadler	.15
166	Desi Relaford	.15
167	Steve Gibralter	.15
168	Neifi Perez	.25
169	Antone Williamson	.15
170	*Marty Janzen*	.25
171	Todd Helton	1.50
172	*Raul Ibanez*	2.00
173	Bill Selby	.25
174	*Shane Monahan*	.35
175	*Robin Jennings*	.25
176	*Bobby Chouinard*	.25
177	Einar Diaz	.25
178	Jason Thompson	.15
179	*Rafael Medina*	.25
180	Kevin Orie	.15

Mirror Image

		NM/M
Complete Set (10):		24.00
Common Player:		1.25
Refractors:		1.5X
Atomics:		2X
1	Jeff Bagwell, Todd Helton, Frank Thomas, Richie Sexson	3.00
2	Craig Biggio, Luis Castillo, Roberto Alomar, Desi Relaford	1.50
3	Chipper Jones, Scott Rolen, Wade Boggs, George Arias	3.00
4	Barry Larkin, Neifi Perez, Cal Ripken Jr., Mark Bellhorn	4.00

5 Larry Walker, Karim Garcia, Albert Belle, Ruben Rivera 1.25
6 Barry Bonds, Andruw Jones, Kenny Lofton, Donnie Sadler 5.00
7 Tony Gwynn, Vladimir Guerrero, Ken Griffey Jr., Ben Grieve 4.00
8 Mike Piazza, Ben Davis, Ivan Rodriguez, Jose Valentin 4.00
9 Greg Maddux, Jamey Wright, Mike Mussina, Bartolo Colon 3.00
10 Tom Glavine, Billy Wagner, Randy Johnson, Jarrod Washburn 1.50

Cuts

	NM/M
Complete Set (15):	12.50
Common Player:	.20
Refractors:	1.5X
Atomic Refractors:	2X
1 Ken Griffey Jr.	2.00
2 Jason Isringhausen	.20
3 Derek Jeter	4.00
4 Andruw Jones	.75
5 Chipper Jones	1.50
6 Ryan Klesko	.20
7 Raul Mondesi	.20
8 Hideo Nomo	.75
9 Mike Piazza	2.00
10 Manny Ramirez	.75
11 Cal Ripken Jr.	4.00
12 Ruben Rivera	.20
13 Tim Salmon	.25
14 Frank Thomas	.75
15 Jim Thome	.75

1997 BOWMAN

	NM/M
Complete Set (440):	50.00
Complete Series 1 (221):	25.00
Complete Series 2 (219):	25.00
Common Player:	.10
Series 1 Pack (10):	2.00
Series 1 Wax Box (24):	35.00
Series 2 Pack (10):	2.00
Series 2 Wax Box (24):	35.00
1 Derek Jeter	2.00
2 Edgar Renteria	.10
3 Chipper Jones	1.00
4 Hideo Nomo	.50
5 Tim Salmon	.25
6 Jason Giambi	.25
7 Robin Ventura	.10
8 Tony Clark	.10
9 Barry Larkin	.10
10 Paul Molitor	.75
11 Bernard Gilkey	.10
12 Jack McDowell	.10
13 Andy Benes	.10
14 Ryan Klesko	.10
15 Mark McGwire	1.50
16 Ken Griffey Jr.	1.00
17 Robb Nen	.10
18 Cal Ripken Jr.	2.00
19 John Valentin	.10
20 Ricky Bottalico	.10
21 Mike Lansing	.10
22 Ryne Sandberg	1.00
23 Carlos Delgado	.50
24 Craig Biggio	.10
25 Eric Karros	.10
26 Kevin Appier	.10
27 Mariano Rivera	.25
28 Vinny Castilla	.10
29 Juan Gonzalez	.50
30 Al Martin	.10
31 Jeff Cirillo	.10
32 Eddie Murray	.40
33 Ray Lankford	.10
34 Manny Ramirez	.75
35 Roberto Alomar	.40
36 Will Clark	.15
37 Chuck Knoblauch	.10
38 Harold Baines	.10
39 Trevor Hoffman	.10
40 Edgar Martinez	.10
41 Geronimo Berroa	.10
42 Rey Ordonez	.10
43 Mike Stanley	.10
44 Mike Mussina	.50
45 Kevin Brown	.15
46 Dennis Eckersley	.40
47 Henry Rodriguez	.10
48 Tino Martinez	.10
49 Eric Young	.10
50 Bret Boone	.10
51 Raul Mondesi	.10
52 Sammy Sosa	1.50
53 John Smoltz	.10
54 Billy Wagner	.10
55 Jeff D'Amico	.10
56 Ken Caminiti	.10
57 Jason Kendall	.10
58 Wade Boggs	.40
59 Andres Galarraga	.10
60 Jeff Brantley	.10
61 Mel Rojas	.10
62 Brian Hunter	.10
63 Bobby Bonilla	.10
64 Roger Clemens	1.75
65 Jeff Kent	.10
66 Matt Williams	.10
67 Albert Belle	.20
68 Jeff King	.10
69 John Wetteland	.10
70 Deion Sanders	.10
71 *Bubba Trammell*	.25
72 *Felix Heredia*	.25
73 *Billy Koch*	.25
74 *Sidney Ponson*	.50
75 *Ricky Ledee*	.25
76 Brett Tomko	.10
77 *Braden Looper*	.25
78 Damian Jackson	.10
79 Jason Dickson	.10
80 *Chad Green*	.10
81 *R.A. Dickey*	.10
82 Jeff Liefer	.10
83 Matt Wagner	.10
84 Richard Hidalgo	.10
85 Adam Riggs	.10
86 Robert Smith	.10
87 *Chad Hermansen*	.10
88 Felix Martinez	.10
89 J.J. Johnson	.10
90 Todd Dunwoody	.10
91 Katsuhiro Maeda	.10
92 Darin Erstad	.25
93 Elieser Marrero	.10
94 Bartolo Colon	.10
95 Chris Fussell	.10
96 Ugueth Urbina	.10
97 *Josh Paul*	.10
98 Jaime Bluma	.10
99 *Seth Greisinger*	.10
100 *Jose Cruz*	.75
101 Todd Dunn	.10
102 *Joe Young*	.10
103 Jonathan Johnson	.10
104 *Justin Towle*	.10
105 Brian Rose	.10
106 Jose Guillen	.10
107 Andruw Jones	.50
108 *Mark Kotsay*	1.00
109 Wilton Guerrero	.10
110 Jacob Cruz	.10
111 Mike Sweeney	.10
112 Julio Mosquera	.10
113 Matt Morris	.10
114 Wendell Magee	.10
115 John Thomson	.10
116 *Javier Valentin*	.10
117 Tom Fordham	.10
118 Ruben Rivera	.10
119 *Mike Drumright*	.10
120 Chris Holt	.10
121 *Sean Maloney*	.10
122 Michael Barrett	.10
123 *Tony Saunders*	.10
124 Kevin Brown	.15
125 Richard Almanzar	.10
126 Mark Redman	.10
127 *Anthony Sanders*	.10
128 Jeff Abbott	.10
129 Eugene Kingsale	.10
130 Paul Konerko	.20
131 *Randall Simon*	.25
132 Andy Larkin	.10
133 Rafael Medina	.10
134 Mendy Lopez	.10
135 Freddy Garcia	.10
136 Karim Garcia	.15
137 *Larry Rodriguez*	.10
138 Carlos Guillen	.10
139 Aaron Boone	.10
140 Donnie Sadler	.10
141 Brooks Kieschnick	.10
142 Scott Spiezio	.10
143 Everett Stull	.10
144 Enrique Wilson	.10
145 *Milton Bradley*	3.00
146 Kevin Orie	.10
147 Derek Wallace	.10
148 Russ Johnson	.10
149 *Joe Lagarde*	.10
150 Luis Castillo	.10
151 Jay Payton	.10
152 Joe Long	.10
153 Livan Hernandez	.10
154 *Vladimir Nunez*	.15
155 Not issued	
156a George Arias	.10
156b Calvin Reese (Should be #155)	.10
157 Homer Bush	.10
158 Not issued	
159a *Eric Milton*	.50
159b Chris Carpenter (Should be #158)	.10
160 Richie Sexson	.10
161 Carl Pavano	.10
162 *Chris Gissell*	.10
163 Mac Suzuki	.10
164 Pat Cline	.10
165 Ron Wright	.10
166 Dante Powell	.10
167 Mark Bellhorn	.10
168 George Lombard	.10
169 *Pee Wee Lopez*	.10
170 *Paul Wilder*	.10
171 Brad Fullmer	.10
172 *Willie Martinez*	.10
173 *Dario Veras*	.10
174 Dave Coggin	.10
175 *Kris Benson*	1.00
176 Torii Hunter	.10
177 *D.T. Cromer*	.10
178 *Nelson Figueroa*	.10
179 *Hiram Bocachica*	.15
180 Shane Monahan	.10
181 *Jimmy Anderson*	.10
182 Juan Melo	.10
183 *Pablo Ortega*	.10
184 *Calvin Pickering*	1.00
185 Reggie Taylor	.10
186 *Jeff Farnsworth*	.10
187 Terrence Long	.10
188 Geoff Jenkins	.10
189 *Steve Rain*	.10
190 *Nerio Rodriguez*	.10
191 Derrick Gibson	.10
192 Darin Blood	.10
193 Ben Davis	.10
194 *Adrian Beltre*	6.00
195 *Damian Sapp*	.10
196 *Kerry Wood*	6.00
197 *Nate Rolison*	.10
198 *Fernando Tatis*	.25
199 *Brad Penny*	1.00
200 *Jake Westbrook*	.15
201 Edwin Diaz	.10
202 *Joe Fontenot*	.10
203 *Matt Halloran*	.10
204 *Blake Stein*	.10
205 Onan Masaoka	.10
206 Ben Petrick	.10
207 *Matt Clement*	1.00
208 Todd Greene	.10
209 Ray Ricken	.10
210 *Eric Chavez*	3.00
211 Edgard Velazquez	.10
212 *Bruce Chen*	.10
213 *Danny Patterson*	.10
214 Jeff Yoder	.10
215 *Luis Ordaz*	.10
216 Chris Widger	.10
217 Jason Brester	.10
218 Carlton Loewer	.10
219 *Chris Reitsma*	.10
220 Neifi Perez	.10
221 *Hideki Irabu*	.25
222 Ellis Burks	.10
223 Pedro Martinez	1.00
224 Kenny Lofton	.10
225 Randy Johnson	1.00
226 Terry Steinbach	.10
227 Bernie Williams	.25
228 Dean Palmer	.10
229 Alan Benes	.10
230 Marquis Grissom	.10
231 Gary Sheffield	.40
232 Curt Schilling	.50
233 Reggie Sanders	.10
234 Bobby Higginson	.10
235 Moises Alou	.10
236 Tom Glavine	.25
237 Mark Grace	.15
238 Ramon Martinez	.10
239 Rafael Palmeiro	.50
240 John Olerud	.10
241 Dante Bichette	.10
242 Greg Vaughn	.10
243 Jeff Bagwell	.50
244 Barry Bonds	2.00
245 Pat Hentgen	.10
246 Jim Thome	.10
247 Jermaine Allensworth	.10
248 Andy Pettitte	.25
249 Jay Bell	.10
250 John Jaha	.10
251 Jim Edmonds	.10
252 Ron Gant	.10
253 David Cone	.10
254 Jose Canseco	.40
255 Jay Buhner	.10
256 Greg Maddux	1.00
257 Brian McRae	.10
258 Lance Johnson	.10
259 Travis Fryman	.10
260 Paul O'Neill	.10
261 Ivan Rodriguez	.50
262 Gregg Jefferies	.10
263 Fred McGriff	.10
264 Derek Bell	.10
265 Jeff Conine	.10
266 Mike Piazza	1.00
267 Mark Grudzielanek	.10
268 Brady Anderson	.10
269 Marty Cordova	.10
270 Ray Durham	.10
271 Joe Carter	.10
272 Brian Jordan	.10
273 David Justice	.10
274 Tony Gwynn	.75
275 Larry Walker	.10
276 Cecil Fielder	.10
277 Mo Vaughn	.10
278 Alex Fernandez	.10
279 Michael Tucker	.10
280 Jose Valentin	.10
281 Sandy Alomar	.10
282 Todd Hollandsworth	.10
283 Rico Brogna	.10
284 Rusty Greer	.10
285 Roberto Hernandez	.10
286 Hal Morris	.10
287 Johnny Damon	.40
288 Todd Hundley	.10
289 Rondell White	.10
290 Frank Thomas	.50
291 *Don Denbow*	.10
292 Derrek Lee	.25
293 Todd Walker	.10
294 Scott Rolen	.75
295 Wes Helms	.10
296 Bob Abreu	.10
297 *John Patterson*	1.50
298 *Alex Gonzalez*	.25
299 *Grant Roberts*	.25
300 Jeff Suppan	.10

301 Luke Wilcox .10
302 Marlon Anderson .10
303 Ray Brown .10
304 *Mike Caruso* .25
305 *Sam Marsonek* .10
306 *Brady Raggio* .10
307 *Kevin McGlinchy* .25
308 *Roy Halladay* 2.00
309 *Jeremi Gonzalez* .25
310 *Aramis Ramirez* 4.00
311 *Dermal Brown* .10
312 Justin Thompson .10
313 *Jay Tessmer* .10
314 Mike Johnson .10
315 Danny Clyburn .10
316 Bruce Aven .10
317 *Keith Foulke* 1.50
318 *Jimmy Osting* .10
319 *Valerio De Los Santos* .10
320 Shannon Stewart .20
321 Willie Adams .10
322 Larry Barnes .10
323 Mark Johnson .10
324 *Chris Stowers* .10
325 Brandon Reed .10
326 Randy Winn .10
327 Steven Chavez .10
328 Nomar Garciaparra 1.50
329 *Jacque Jones* 1.00
330 Chris Clemons .10
331 Todd Helton .50
332 *Ryan Brannan* .10
333 *Alex Sanchez* .25
334 Arnold Gooch .10
335 Russell Branyan .10
336 Daryle Ward .10
337 *John LeRoy* .10
338 Steve Cox .10
339 Kevin Witt .10
340 Norm Hutchins .10
341 Gabby Martinez .10
342 Kris Detmers .10
343 *Mike Villano* .10
344 Preston Wilson .10
345 *Jim Manias* .10
346 *Deivi Cruz* .25
347 *Donzell McDonald* .10
348 *Rod Myers* .10
349 *Shawn Chacon* .25
350 *Elvin Hernandez* .10
351 *Orlando Cabrera* 1.00
352 Brian Banks .10
353 Robbie Bell .10
354 Brad Rigby .10
355 Scott Elarton .10
356 *Kevin Sweeney* .10
357 Steve Soderstrom .10
358 Ryan Nye .10
359 *Marlon Allen* .10
360 *Donny Leon* .10
361 *Garrett Neubart* .10
362 *Abraham Nunez* .25
363 *Adam Eaton* .75
364 *Octavio Dotel* .40
365 *Dean Crow* .10
366 *Jason Baker* .10
367 Sean Casey .10
368 *Joe Lawrence* .10
369 *Adam Johnson* .10
370 *Scott Schoeneweis* .25
371 Gerald Witasick Jr. .10
372 *Ronnie Belliard* .25
373 Russ Ortiz .10
374 *Robert Stratton* .10
375 Bobby Estalella .10
376 *Corey Lee* .10
377 Carlos Beltran .75
378 Mike Cameron .10
379 *Scott Randall* .10
380 *Corey Erickson* .10
381 Jay Canizaro .10
382 *Kerry Robinson* .20
383 *Todd Noel* .20
384 *A.J. Zapp* .20
385 Jarrod Washburn .10
386 Ben Grieve .10
387 *Javier Vazquez* 2.00
388 Tony Graffanino .10
389 *Travis Lee* .50
390 DaRond Stovall .10
391 *Dennis Reyes* .25
392 Danny Buxbaum .10
393 *Marc Lewis* .10
394 *Kelvim Escobar* .25
395 Danny Klassen .10
396 *Ken Cloude* .25
397 Gabe Alvarez .10
398 *Jaret Wright* .50
399 Raul Casanova .10
400 *Clayton Brunner* .10
401 *Jason Marquis* .50
402 Marc Kroon .10
403 Jamey Wright .10
404 *Matt Snyder* .10
405 *Josh Garrett* .10
406 Juan Encarnacion .10
407 Heath Murray .10
408 *Brett Herbison* .10
409 *Brent Butler* .25
410 *Danny Peoples* .25
411 *Miguel Tejada* 10.00
412 Damian Moss .10
413 Jim Pittsley .10
414 Dmitri Young .10
415 Glendon Rusch .10
416 Vladimir Guerrero .75
417 *Cole Liniak* .10
418 Ramon Hernandez .10
419 *Cliff Politte* .25
420 *Mel Rosario* .10
421 *Jorge Carrion* .10
422 *John Barnes* .20
423 *Chris Stowe* .25
424 *Vernon Wells* 2.00
425 *Brett Caradonna* .10
426 *Scott Hodges* .10
427 *Jon Garland* 3.00
428 *Nathan Haynes* .25
429 *Geoff Goetz* .25
430 *Adam Kennedy* .50
431 *T.J. Tucker* .10
432 *Aaron Akin* .10
433 *Jayson Werth* .75
434 *Glenn Davis* .25
435 *Mark Mangum* .10
436 *Troy Cameron* .10
437 *J.J. Davis* .10
438 *Lance Berkman* 4.00
439 *Jason Standridge* .25
440 *Jason Dellaero* .10
441 *Hideki Irabu* .25

International

NM/M

Complete Set (440): 100.00
Complete Series 1 (221): 50.00
Complete Series 2 (219): 50.00
Common Player: .25
Stars and Rookies: 1.5X

(See 1997 Bowman for checklist and base card values.)

Preview

NM/M

Complete Set (20): 30.00
Common Player: .75
Refractors: 1.5X
Atomic Refractors: 2X

1 Frank Thomas 1.50
2 Ken Griffey Jr. 3.00
3 Barry Bonds 5.00
4 Derek Jeter 5.00
5 Chipper Jones 2.00
6 Mark McGwire 4.00
7 Cal Ripken Jr. 5.00
8 Kenny Lofton .75
9 Gary Sheffield .75
10 Jeff Bagwell 1.50
11 Wilton Guerrero .75
12 Scott Rolen 1.50
13 Todd Walker .75
14 Ruben Rivera .75
15 Andruw Jones 1.50
16 Nomar Garciaparra 3.00
17 Vladimir Guerrero 1.50
18 Miguel Tejada 1.00
19 Bartolo Colon .75
20 Katsuhiro Maeda .75

Certified Autographs

NM/M

Common Blue: 2.00
Black: 1.5X
Gold: 4X
Derek Jeter Green: 1.5X

1 Jeff Abbott 2.00
2 Bob Abreu 40.00
3 Willie Adams 2.00
4 Brian Banks 2.00
5 Kris Benson 15.00
6 Darin Blood 2.00
7 Jaime Bluma 2.00
8 Kevin Brown 5.00
9 Ray Brown 2.00
10 Homer Bush 4.00
11 Mike Cameron 8.00
12 Jay Canizaro 3.00
13 Luis Castillo 5.00
14 Dave Coggin 2.00
15 Bartolo Colon 15.00
16 Rocky Coppinger 3.00
17 Jacob Cruz 5.00
18 Jose Cruz 8.00
19 Jeff D'Amico 5.00
20 Ben Davis 5.00
21 Mike Drumbright 5.00
22 Scott Elarton 5.00
23 Darin Erstad 10.00
24 Bobby Estalella 5.00
25 Joe Fontenot 4.00
26 Tom Fordham 2.00
27 Brad Fullmer 5.00
28 Chris Fussell 2.00
29 Karim Garcia 5.00
30 Kris Detmers 2.00
31 Todd Greene 4.00
32 Ben Grieve 5.00
33 Vladimir Guerrero 75.00
34 Jose Guillen 15.00
35 Roy Halladay 65.00
36 Wes Helms 5.00
37 Chad Hermansen 3.00
38 Richard Hidalgo 8.00
39 Todd Hollandsworth 3.00
40 Damian Jackson 3.00
41 Derek Jeter 120.00
42 Andruw Jones 40.00
43 Brooks Kieschnick 3.00
44 Eugene Kingsale 5.00
45 Paul Konerko 15.00
46 Marc Kroon 2.00
47 Derrek Lee 50.00
48 Travis Lee 5.00
49 Terrence Long 4.00
50 Curt Lyons 2.00
51 Elieser Marrero 3.00
52 Rafael Medina 2.00
53 Juan Melo 3.00
54 Shane Monahan 2.00
55 Julio Mosquera 2.00
56 Heath Murray 2.00
57 Ryan Nye 2.00
58 Kevin Orie 4.00
59 Russ Ortiz 5.00
60 Carl Pavano 30.00
61 Jay Payton 5.00
62 Neifi Perez 3.00
63 Sidney Ponson 10.00
64 Calvin Reese 8.00
65 Ray Ricken 3.00
66 Brad Rigby 3.00
67 Adam Riggs 3.00
68 Ruben Rivera 4.00
69 J.J. Johnson 2.00
70 Scott Rolen 40.00
71 Tony Saunders 3.00
72 Donnie Sadler 5.00
73 Richie Sexson 15.00

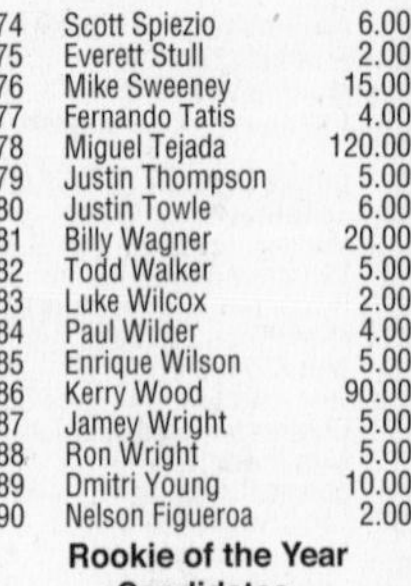

74 Scott Spiezio 6.00
75 Everett Stull 2.00
76 Mike Sweeney 15.00
77 Fernando Tatis 4.00
78 Miguel Tejada 120.00
79 Justin Thompson 5.00
80 Justin Towle 6.00
81 Billy Wagner 20.00
82 Todd Walker 5.00
83 Luke Wilcox 2.00
84 Paul Wilder 4.00
85 Enrique Wilson 5.00
86 Kerry Wood 90.00
87 Jamey Wright 5.00
88 Ron Wright 5.00
89 Dmitri Young 10.00
90 Nelson Figueroa 2.00

Rookie of the Year Candidates

NM/M

Complete Set (15): 9.00
Common Player: .50

1 Jeff Abbott .50
2 Karim Garcia 1.00
3 Todd Helton 2.50
4 Richard Hidalgo .50
5 Geoff Jenkins .50
6 Russ Johnson .50
7 Paul Konerko .75
8 Mark Kotsay .50
9 Ricky Ledee .50
10 Travis Lee .75
11 Derrek Lee .50
12 Elieser Marrero .50
13 Juan Melo .50
14 Brian Rose .50
15 Fernando Tatis .50

Scout's Honor Roll

NM/M

Complete Set (15): 12.50
Common Player: .50

1 Dmitri Young .50
2 Bob Abreu .60
3 Vladimir Guerrero 2.00
4 Paul Konerko .75
5 Kevin Orie .50
6 Todd Walker .50
7 Ben Grieve .60
8 Darin Erstad 1.50
9 Derrek Lee 1.00
10 Jose Cruz .50
11 Scott Rolen 1.50
12 Travis Lee .75
13 Andruw Jones 1.50
14 Wilton Guerrero .50
15 Nomar Garciaparra 2.50

International Best

		NM/M
Complete Set (20):		20.00
Common Player:		.60
Refractors:		1.5X
Atomic Refractors:		2X
1	Frank Thomas	1.50
2	Ken Griffey Jr.	2.50
3	Juan Gonzalez	1.50
4	Bernie Williams	.60
5	Hideo Nomo	1.50
6	Sammy Sosa	3.50
7	Larry Walker	.60
8	Vinny Castilla	.60
9	Mariano Rivera	.75
10	Rafael Palmeiro	1.00
11	Nomar Garciaparra	3.50
12	Todd Walker	.60
13	Andruw Jones	1.50
14	Vladimir Guerrero	1.50
15	Ruben Rivera	.60
16	Bob Abreu	.75
17	Karim Garcia	.75
18	Katsuhiro Maeda	.60
19	Jose Cruz Jr.	1.00
20	Damian Moss	.60

1997 BOWMAN CHROME

		NM/M
Complete Set (300):		165.00
Common Player:		.25
Pack (3):		6.00
Wax Box (24):		125.00
1	Derek Jeter	4.00
2	Chipper Jones	2.00
3	Hideo Nomo	1.50
4	Tim Salmon	.40
5	Robin Ventura	.25
6	Tony Clark	.25
7	Barry Larkin	.25
8	Paul Molitor	1.50
9	Andy Benes	.25
10	Ryan Klesko	.25
11	Mark McGwire	3.00
12	Ken Griffey Jr.	2.50
13	Robb Nen	.25
14	Cal Ripken Jr.	4.00
15	John Valentin	.25
16	Ricky Bottalico	.25
17	Mike Lansing	.25
18	Ryne Sandberg	2.00
19	Carlos Delgado	.85
20	Craig Biggio	.25
21	Eric Karros	.25
22	Kevin Appier	.25
23	Mariano Rivera	.40
24	Vinny Castilla	.25
25	Juan Gonzalez	1.50
26	Al Martin	.25
27	Jeff Cirillo	.25
28	Ray Lankford	.25
29	Manny Ramirez	1.50
30	Roberto Alomar	.50
31	Will Clark	.35
32	Chuck Knoblauch	.25
33	Harold Baines	.25
34	Edgar Martinez	.25
35	Mike Mussina	1.00
36	Kevin Brown	.35
37	Dennis Eckersley	1.00
38	Tino Martinez	.25
39	Raul Mondesi	.25
40	Sammy Sosa	2.50
41	John Smoltz	.25
42	Billy Wagner	.25
43	Ken Caminiti	.25
44	Wade Boggs	2.00
45	Andres Galarraga	.25
46	Roger Clemens	2.25
47	Matt Williams	.25
48	Albert Belle	.35
49	Jeff King	.25
50	John Wetteland	.25
51	Deion Sanders	.25
52	Ellis Burks	.25
53	Pedro Martinez	1.50
54	Kenny Lofton	.25
55	Randy Johnson	1.50
56	Bernie Williams	.40
57	Marquis Grissom	.25
58	Gary Sheffield	.50
59	Curt Schilling	.50
60	Reggie Sanders	.25
61	Bobby Higginson	.25
62	Moises Alou	.25
63	Tom Glavine	.35
64	Mark Grace	.35
65	Rafael Palmeiro	1.00
66	John Olerud	.25
67	Dante Bichette	.25
68	Jeff Bagwell	1.50
69	Barry Bonds	4.00
70	Pat Hentgen	.25
71	Jim Thome	.25
72	Andy Pettitte	.40
73	Jay Bell	.25
74	Jim Edmonds	.25
75	Ron Gant	.25
76	David Cone	.25
77	Jose Canseco	.60
78	Jay Buhner	.25
79	Greg Maddux	2.00
80	Lance Johnson	.25
81	Travis Fryman	.25
82	Paul O'Neill	.25
83	Ivan Rodriguez	1.00
84	Fred McGriff	.25
85	Mike Piazza	2.50
86	Brady Anderson	.25
87	Marty Cordova	.25
88	Joe Carter	.25
89	Brian Jordan	.25
90	David Justice	.25
91	Tony Gwynn	2.00
92	Larry Walker	.25
93	Mo Vaughn	.25
94	Sandy Alomar	.25
95	Rusty Greer	.25
96	Roberto Hernandez	.25
97	Hal Morris	.25
98	Todd Hundley	.25
99	Rondell White	.25
100	Frank Thomas	1.50
101	*Bubba Trammell*	.75
102	*Sidney Ponson*	3.00
103	*Ricky Ledee*	.50
104	Brett Tomko	.25
105	*Braden Looper*	.75
106	Jason Dickson	.25
107	*Chad Green*	.50
108	*R.A. Dickey*	.25
109	Jeff Liefer	.25
110	Richard Hidalgo	.25
111	*Chad Hermansen*	.50
112	Felix Martinez	.25
113	J.J. Johnson	.25
114	Todd Dunwoody	.25
115	Katsuhiro Maeda	.25
116	Darin Erstad	1.00
117	Elieser Marrero	.25
118	Bartolo Colon	.25
119	Ugueth Urbina	.25
120	Jaime Bluma	.25
121	*Seth Greisinger*	.50
122	*Jose Cruz Jr.*	3.00
123	Todd Dunn	.25
124	*Justin Towle*	.40
125	Brian Rose	.25
126	Jose Guillen	.25
127	Andruw Jones	1.50
128	*Mark Kotsay*	2.50
129	Wilton Guerrero	.25
130	Jacob Cruz	.25
131	Mike Sweeney	.25
132	Matt Morris	.25
133	John Thomson	.25
134	*Javier Valentin*	.25
135	*Mike Drumright*	.25
136	Michael Barrett	.25
137	*Tony Saunders*	.25
138	Kevin Brown	.25
139	*Anthony Sanders*	.25
140	Jeff Abbott	.25
141	Eugene Kingsale	.25
142	Paul Konerko	.30
143	*Randall Simon*	.50
144	Freddy Garcia	.25
145	Karim Garcia	.60
146	Carlos Guillen	.25
147	Aaron Boone	.25
148	Donnie Sadler	.25
149	Brooks Kieschnick	.25
150	Scott Spiezio	.25
151	Kevin Orie	.25
152	Russ Johnson	.25
153	Livan Hernandez	.25
154	*Vladimir Nunez*	1.00
155	Calvin Reese	.25
156	Chris Carpenter	.25
157	*Eric Milton*	1.50
158	Richie Sexson	.25
159	Carl Pavano	.25
160	Pat Cline	.25
161	Ron Wright	.25
162	Dante Powell	.25
163	Mark Bellhorn	.25
164	George Lombard	.25
165	*Paul Wilder*	.25
166	Brad Fullmer	.25
167	*Kris Benson*	2.00
168	Torii Hunter	.25
169	D.T. Cromer	.25
170	*Nelson Figueroa*	.50
171	*Hiram Bocachica*	.50
172	Shane Monahan	.25
173	Juan Melo	.25
174	*Calvin Pickering*	2.50
175	Reggie Taylor	.25
176	Geoff Jenkins	.25
177	*Steve Rain*	.25
178	Nerio Rodriguez	.25
179	Derrick Gibson	.25
180	Darin Blood	.25
181	Ben Davis	.25
182	*Adrian Beltre*	15.00
183	*Kerry Wood*	15.00
184	Nate Rolison	.25
185	*Fernando Tatis*	.50
186	*Jake Westbrook*	3.00
187	Edwin Diaz	.25
188	*Joe Fontenot*	.50
189	*Matt Halloran*	.50
190	*Matt Clement*	5.00
191	Todd Greene	.25
192	*Eric Chavez*	10.00
193	Edgard Velazquez	.25
194	*Bruce Chen*	.25
195	Jason Brester	.25
196	*Chris Reitsma*	.25
197	Neifi Perez	.25
198	*Hideki Irabu*	.75
199	*Don Denbow*	.25
200	Derrek Lee	.50
201	Todd Walker	.25
202	Scott Rolen	1.00
203	Wes Helms	.25
204	Bob Abreu	.25
205	*John Patterson*	2.00
206	*Alex Gonzalez*	1.50
207	*Grant Roberts*	.50
208	Jeff Suppan	.25
209	Luke Wilcox	.25
210	Marlon Anderson	.25
211	*Mike Caruso*	.75
212	*Roy Halladay*	8.00
213	*Jeremi Gonzalez*	.50
214	*Aramis Ramirez*	10.00
215	*Dermal Brown*	.25
216	Justin Thompson	.25
217	Danny Clyburn	.25
218	Bruce Aven	.25
219	*Keith Foulke*	2.50
220	Shannon Stewart	.35
221	Larry Barnes	.25
222	*Mark Johnson*	.25
223	Randy Winn	.25
224	Nomar Garciaparra	3.00
225	*Jacque Jones*	4.00
226	Chris Clemons	.25
227	Todd Helton	1.50
228	*Ryan Brannan*	.25
229	*Alex Sanchez*	.50
230	Russell Branyan	.25
231	Daryle Ward	.25
232	Kevin Witt	.25
233	Gabby Martinez	.25
234	Preston Wilson	.25
235	*Donzell McDonald*	.25
236	*Orlando Cabrera*	5.00
237	Brian Banks	.25
238	Robbie Bell	.25
239	Brad Rigby	.25
240	Scott Elarton	.25
241	*Donny Leon*	.25
242	*Abraham Nunez*	1.00
243	*Adam Eaton*	3.00
244	*Octavio Dotel*	1.50
245	Sean Casey	.35
246	*Joe Lawrence*	.50
247	*Adam Johnson*	.50
248	*Ronnie Belliard*	1.00
249	Bobby Estalella	.25
250	*Corey Lee*	.25
251	Mike Cameron	.25
252	*Kerry Robinson*	.25
253	*A.J. Zapp*	.25
254	Jarrod Washburn	.25
255	Ben Grieve	.30
256	*Javier Vazquez*	4.00
257	*Travis Lee*	1.50
258	*Dennis Reyes*	.50
259	Danny Buxbaum	.25
260	*Kelvim Escobar*	1.00
261	Danny Klassen	.25
262	*Ken Cloude*	.50
263	Gabe Alvarez	.25
264	*Clayton Brunner*	.25
265	*Jason Marquis*	1.50
266	Jamey Wright	.25
267	*Matt Snyder*	.50
268	*Josh Garrett*	.25
269	Juan Encarnacion	.25
270	Heath Murray	.25
271	*Brent Butler*	1.00
272	*Danny Peoples*	.50
273	*Miguel Tejada*	35.00
274	Jim Pittsley	.25
275	Dmitri Young	.25
276	Vladimir Guerrero	1.50
277	*Cole Liniak*	.50
278	Ramon Hernandez	.25
279	*Cliff Politte*	.50
280	*Mel Rosario*	.25
281	*Jorge Carrion*	.25
282	*John Barnes*	.40
283	*Chris Stowe*	.25
284	*Vernon Wells*	8.00
285	*Brett Caradonna*	.25
286	*Scott Hodges*	.25
287	*Jon Garland*	8.00
288	*Nathan Haynes*	.50
289	*Geoff Goetz*	.50
290	*Adam Kennedy*	1.00
291	*T.J. Tucker*	.25
292	*Aaron Akin*	.25
293	*Jayson Werth*	3.00
294	*Glenn Davis*	.50
295	*Mark Mangum*	.25
296	*Troy Cameron*	.25
297	*J.J. Davis*	.25
298	*Lance Berkman*	12.00
299	*Jason Standridge*	.75
300	*Jason Dellaero*	.25

International

	NM/M
Complete Set (300):	200.00
Common Player:	1.00
Stars:	3X

Inserted 1:4

(See 1997 Bowman Chrome for checklist and base card values.)

International Refractors

	NM/M
Common Player:	2.00
Stars:	6X

(See 1997 Bowman Chrome for checklist and base card values.)

Refractors

	NM/M
Complete Set (300):	625.00
Common Player:	1.00
Stars:	4X

(See 1997 Bowman Chrome for checklist and base card values.)

Scout's Honor Roll

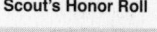

		NM/M
Complete Set (15):		12.00
Common Player:		.50
Refractors:		1.5X
1	Dmitri Young	.50
2	Bob Abreu	.60
3	Vladimir Guerrero	2.00
4	Paul Konerko	.75
5	Kevin Orie	.50
6	Todd Walker	.50
7	Ben Grieve	.60
8	Darin Erstad	1.50
9	Derrek Lee	.50
10	Jose Cruz, Jr.	.50
11	Scott Rolen	1.50
12	Travis Lee	.75
13	Andruw Jones	1.50
14	Wilton Guerrero	.50
15	Nomar Garciaparra	2.50

1997 BOWMAN'S BEST

		NM/M
Complete Set (200):		25.00
Common Player:		.25
Star Refractors:		4X
Star Atomics:		6X
Pack (6):		2.00
Wax Box (24):		45.00
1	Ken Griffey Jr.	2.00
2	Cecil Fielder	.25
3	Albert Belle	.30
4	Todd Hundley	.25
5	Mike Piazza	1.50
6	Matt Williams	.25
7	Mo Vaughn	.25
8	Ryne Sandberg	1.50
9	Chipper Jones	1.00
10	Edgar Martinez	.25
11	Kenny Lofton	.25
12	Ron Gant	.25
13	Moises Alou	.25
14	Pat Hentgen	.25
15	Steve Finley	.25
16	Mark Grace	.35
17	Jay Buhner	.25
18	Jeff Conine	.25
19	Jim Edmonds	.25
20	Todd Hollandsworth	.25
21	Andy Petitte	.50
22	Jim Thome	.25
23	Eric Young	.25
24	Ray Lankford	.25
25	Marquis Grissom	.25
26	Tony Clark	.25
27	Jermaine Allensworth	.25
28	Ellis Burks	.25
29	Tony Gwynn	1.00
30	Barry Larkin	.25
31	John Olerud	.25
32	Mariano Rivera	.40
33	Paul Molitor	.75
34	Ken Caminiti	.25
35	Gary Sheffield	.45
36	Al Martin	.25
37	John Valentin	.25
38	Frank Thomas	.75
39	John Jaha	.25
40	Greg Maddux	1.50
41	Alex Fernandez	.25
42	Dean Palmer	.25
43	Bernie Williams	.30
44	Deion Sanders	.25
45	Mark McGwire	3.00
46	Brian Jordan	.25
47	Bernard Gilkey	.25
48	Will Clark	.30
49	Kevin Appier	.25
50	Tom Glavine	.35
51	Chuck Knoblauch	.25
52	Rondell White	.25
53	Greg Vaughn	.25
54	Mike Mussina	.75
55	Brian McRae	.25
56	Chili Davis	.25
57	Wade Boggs	.75
58	Jeff Bagwell	.75
59	Roberto Alomar	.35
60	Dennis Eckersley	.50
61	Ryan Klesko	.25
62	Manny Ramirez	.75
63	John Wetteland	.25
64	Cal Ripken Jr.	3.00
65	Edgar Renteria	.25
66	Tino Martinez	.25
67	Larry Walker	.25
68	Gregg Jefferies	.25
69	Lance Johnson	.25
70	Carlos Delgado	.50
71	Craig Biggio	.25
72	Jose Canseco	.50
73	Barry Bonds	3.00
74	Juan Gonzalez	.50
75	Eric Karros	.25
76	Reggie Sanders	.25
77	Robin Ventura	.25
78	Hideo Nomo	.75
79	David Justice	.25
80	Vinny Castilla	.25
81	Travis Fryman	.25
82	Derek Jeter	3.00
83	Sammy Sosa	1.50
84	Ivan Rodriguez	.75
85	Rafael Palmeiro	.75
86	Roger Clemens	2.00
87	Jason Giambi	.50
88	Andres Galarraga	.25
89	Jermaine Dye	.25
90	Joe Carter	.25
91	Brady Anderson	.25
92	Derek Bell	.25
93	Randy Johnson	1.00
94	Fred McGriff	.25
95	John Smoltz	.25
96	Harold Baines	.25
97	Raul Mondesi	.25
98	Tim Salmon	.35
99	Carlos Baerga	.25
100	Dante Bichette	.25
101	Vladimir Guerrero	1.00
102	Richard Hidalgo	.25
103	Paul Konerko	.25
104	*Alex Gonzalez*	.50
105	Jason Dickson	.25
106	Jose Rosado	.25
107	Todd Walker	.25
108	*Seth Greisinger*	.40
109	Todd Helton	.75
110	Ben Davis	.25
111	Bartolo Colon	.25
112	Elieser Marrero	.25
113	Jeff D'Amico	.25
114	*Miguel Tejada*	8.00
115	Darin Erstad	.50
116	*Kris Benson*	1.00
117	*Adrian Beltre*	4.00
118	Neifi Perez	.25
119	Calvin Reese	.25
120	Carl Pavano	.25
121	Juan Melo	.25
122	*Kevin McGlinchy*	.50
123	Pat Cline	.25
124	*Felix Heredia*	.40
125	Aaron Boone	.25
126	Glendon Rusch	.25
127	Mike Cameron	.25
128	Justin Thompson	.25
129	*Chad Hermansen*	.25
130	*Sidney Ponson*	1.00
131	*Willie Martinez*	.25
132	*Paul Wilder*	.25
133	Geoff Jenkins	.25
134	*Roy Halladay*	2.00
135	Carlos Guillen	.25
136	Tony Batista	.25
137	Todd Greene	.25
138	Luis Castillo	.25
139	*Jimmy Anderson*	.25
140	Edgard Velazquez	.25
141	Chris Snopek	.25
142	Ruben Rivera	.25
143	*Javier Valentin*	.25
144	Brian Rose	.25
145	*Fernando Tatis*	.50
146	*Dean Crow*	.25
147	Karim Garcia	.25
148	Dante Powell	.25
149	*Hideki Irabu*	.40
150	Matt Morris	.25
151	Wes Helms	.25
152	Russ Johnson	.25
153	Jarrod Washburn	.25
154	*Kerry Wood*	6.00
155	*Joe Fontenot*	.25
156	Eugene Kingsale	.25
157	Terrence Long	.25
158	Calvin Maduro	.25
159	Jeff Suppan	.25
160	DaRond Stovall	.25
161	Mark Redman	.25
162	*Ken Cloude*	.25
163	Bobby Estalella	.25
164	*Abraham Nunez*	.75
165	Derrick Gibson	.25
166	*Mike Drumright*	.25
167	Katsuhiro Maeda	.25
168	Jeff Liefer	.25
169	Ben Grieve	.30
170	Bob Abreu	.25
171	Shannon Stewart	.25
172	*Braden Looper*	.40
173	Brant Brown	.25
174	Marlon Anderson	.25
175	Brad Fullmer	.25
176	Carlos Beltran	.25
177	Nomar Garciaparra	1.50
178	Derrek Lee	.50
179	*Valerio De Los Santos*	.25
180	Dmitri Young	.25
181	Jamey Wright	.25
182	*Hiram Bocachica*	.25
183	Wilton Guerrero	.25
184	Chris Carpenter	.25
185	Scott Spiezio	.25
186	Andruw Jones	.50
187	*Travis Lee*	.50
188	*Jose Cruz Jr.*	1.00
189	Jose Guillen	.25
190	Jeff Abbott	.25
191	*Ricky Ledee*	.40
192	Mike Sweeney	.25
193	Donnie Sadler	.25
194	Scott Rolen	.75
195	Kevin Orie	.25
196	*Jason Conti*	.25
197	*Mark Kotsay*	1.00
198	*Eric Milton*	1.00
199	Russell Branyan	.25
200	*Alex Sanchez*	.50

Autographs

		NM/M
Complete Set (10):		150.00
Common Player:		5.00
Refractors:		1.5X
Atomics:		2X
29	Tony Gwynn	30.00
33	Paul Molitor	20.00
82	Derek Jeter	90.00
91	Brady Anderson	7.50
98	Tim Salmon	10.00
107	Todd Walker	5.00
183	Wilton Guerrero	5.00
185	Scott Spiezio	5.00
188	Jose Cruz Jr.	6.00
194	Scott Rolen	30.00

Cuts

		NM/M
Complete Set (20):		20.00
Common Player:		.35
Refractors:		1.5X
Atomic Refractors:		2X
1	Derek Jeter	4.00
2	Chipper Jones	1.50
3	Frank Thomas	1.00
4	Cal Ripken Jr.	4.00
5	Mark McGwire	3.00
6	Ken Griffey Jr.	2.00
7	Jeff Bagwell	1.00
8	Mike Piazza	2.00
9	Ken Caminiti	.35
10	Albert Belle	.45
11	Jose Cruz Jr.	.35
12	Wilton Guerrero	.35
13	Darin Erstad	.75
14	Andruw Jones	1.00
15	Scott Rolen	1.00
16	Jose Guillen	.35
17	Bob Abreu	.45
18	Vladimir Guerrero	1.00
19	Todd Walker	.35
20	Nomar Garciaparra	2.00

Mirror Image

		NM/M
Complete Set (10):		35.00
Common Card:		2.00
Refractors:		1.5X
Atomic Refractors:		2X
1	Nomar Garciaparra, Derek Jeter, Hiram Bocachica, Barry Larkin	7.50
2	Travis Lee, Frank Thomas, Derrek Lee, Jeff Bagwell	3.50
3	Kerry Wood, Greg Maddux, Kris Benson, John Smoltz	3.50
4	Kevin Brown, Ivan Rodriguez, Elieser Marrero, Mike Piazza	5.00
5	Jose Cruz Jr., Ken Griffey Jr., Andruw Jones, Barry Bonds	7.50
6	Jose Guillen, Juan Gonzalez, Richard Hidalgo, Gary Sheffield	2.00
7	Paul Konerko, Mark McGwire, Todd Helton, Rafael Palmeiro	6.00
8	Wilton Guerrero, Craig Biggio, Donnie Sadler, Chuck Knoblauch	2.00
9	Russell Branyan, Matt Williams, Adrian Beltre, Chipper Jones	3.50
10	Bob Abreu, Kenny Lofton, Vladimir Guerrero, Albert Belle	3.00

1998 BOWMAN

		NM/M
Complete Set (441):		50.00
Series 1 (221):		25.00
Series 2 (220):		25.00

No.	Player	Price
	Common Player:	.10
	Series 1 Pack (10):	2.00
	Series 1 Wax Box (24):	30.00
	Series 2 Pack (10):	1.50
	Series 2 Wax Box (24):	25.00
1	Nomar Garciaparra	2.00
2	Scott Rolen	1.00
3	Andy Pettitte	.30
4	Ivan Rodriguez	.65
5	Mark McGwire	2.50
6	Jason Dickson	.10
7	Jose Cruz Jr.	.10
8	Jeff Kent	.10
9	Mike Mussina	.65
10	Jason Kendall	.10
11	Brett Tomko	.10
12	Jeff King	.10
13	Brad Radke	.10
14	Robin Ventura	.10
15	Jeff Bagwell	1.00
16	Greg Maddux	1.50
17	John Jaha	.10
18	Mike Piazza	2.00
19	Edgar Martinez	.10
20	David Justice	.10
21	Todd Hundley	.10
22	Tony Gwynn	1.50
23	Larry Walker	.10
24	Bernie Williams	.25
25	Edgar Renteria	.10
26	Rafael Palmeiro	.75
27	Tim Salmon	.25
28	Matt Morris	.10
29	Shawn Estes	.10
30	Vladimir Guerrero	1.00
31	Fernando Tatis	.10
32	Justin Thompson	.10
33	Ken Griffey Jr.	2.00
34	Edgardo Alfonzo	.10
35	Mo Vaughn	.10
36	Marty Cordova	.10
37	Craig Biggio	.10
38	Roger Clemens	1.75
39	Mark Grace	.20
40	Ken Caminiti	.10
41	Tony Womack	.10
42	Albert Belle	.20
43	Tino Martinez	.10
44	Sandy Alomar	.10
45	Jeff Cirillo	.10
46	Jason Giambi	.75
47	Darin Erstad	.65
48	Livan Hernandez	.10
49	Mark Grudzielanek	.10
50	Sammy Sosa	2.00
51	Curt Schilling	.30
52	Brian Hunter	.10
53	Neifi Perez	.10
54	Todd Walker	.10
55	Jose Guillen	.10
56	Jim Thome	.10
57	Tom Glavine	.20
58	Todd Greene	.10
59	Rondell White	.10
60	Roberto Alomar	.30
61	Tony Clark	.10
62	Vinny Castilla	.10
63	Barry Larkin	.10
64	Hideki Irabu	.10
65	Johnny Damon	.25
66	Juan Gonzalez	1.00
67	John Olerud	.10
68	Gary Sheffield	.25
69	Raul Mondesi	.10
70	Chipper Jones	1.50
71	David Ortiz	.50
72	*Warren Morris*	.50
73	Alex Gonzalez	.10
74	Nick Bierbrodt	.10
75	Roy Halladay	.10
76	Danny Buxbaum	.10
77	Adam Kennedy	.10
78	*Jared Sandberg*	.75
79	Michael Barrett	.10
80	Gil Meche	.10
81	Jayson Werth	.10
82	Abraham Nunez	.10
83	Ben Petrick	.10
84	Brett Caradonna	.10
85	*Mike Lowell*	2.00
86	*Clay Bruner*	.10
87	*John Curtice*	.10
88	Bobby Estalella	.10
89	Juan Melo	.10
90	Arnold Gooch	.10
91	*Kevin Millwood*	1.00
92	Richie Sexson	.10
93	Orlando Cabrera	.10
94	Pat Cline	.10
95	Anthony Sanders	.10
96	Russ Johnson	.10
97	Ben Grieve	.20
98	Kevin McGlinchy	.10
99	Paul Wilder	.10
100	Russ Ortiz	.10
101	*Ryan Jackson*	.10
102	Heath Murray	.10
103	Brian Rose	.10
104	*Ryan Radmanovich*	.10
105	Ricky Ledee	.10
106	*Jeff Wallace*	.10
107	*Ryan Minor*	.10
108	Dennis Reyes	.10
109	*James Manias*	.10
110	Chris Carpenter	.10
111	Daryle Ward	.10
112	Vernon Wells	.10
113	Chad Green	.10
114	*Mike Stoner*	.10
115	Brad Fullmer	.10
116	Adam Eaton	.10
117	Jeff Liefer	.10
118	*Corey Koskie*	1.00
119	Todd Helton	1.00
120	*Jaime Jones*	.10
121	Mel Rosario	.10
122	Geoff Goetz	.10
123	Adrian Beltre	.40
124	Jason Dellaero	.10
125	*Gabe Kapler*	.50
126	Scott Schoeneweis	.10
127	Ryan Brannan	.10
128	Aaron Akin	.10
129	*Ryan Anderson*	.40
130	Brad Penny	.10
131	Bruce Chen	.10
132	Eli Marrero	.10
133	Eric Chavez	.40
134	*Troy Glaus*	4.00
135	Troy Cameron	.10
136	*Brian Sikorski*	.10
137	*Mike Kinkade*	.25
138	Braden Looper	.10
139	Mark Mangum	.10
140	Danny Peoples	.10
141	J.J. Davis	.10
142	Ben Davis	.10
143	Jacque Jones	.25
144	Derrick Gibson	.10
145	Bronson Arroyo	.10
146	*Cristian Guzman*	.50
147	Jeff Abbott	.10
148	*Mike Cuddyer*	1.00
149	Jason Romano	.10
150	Shane Monahan	.10
151	*Ntema Ndungidi*	.10
152	Alex Sanchez	.10
153	*Jack Cust*	.50
154	Brent Butler	.10
155	Ramon Hernandez	.10
156	Norm Hutchins	.10
157	Jason Marquis	.10
158	Jacob Cruz	.10
159	*Rob Burger*	.10
160	Eric Milton	.10
161	Preston Wilson	.10
162	*Jason Fitzgerald*	.10
163	Dan Serafini	.10
164	Peter Munro	.10
165	Trot Nixon	.10
166	Homer Bush	.10
167	Dermal Brown	.10
168	Chad Hermansen	.10
169	*Julio Moreno*	.10
170	*John Roskos*	.10
171	Grant Roberts	.10
172	Ken Cloude	.10
173	Jason Brester	.10
174	Jason Conti	.10
175	Jon Garland	.10
176	Robbie Bell	.10
177	Nathan Haynes	.10
178	*Ramon Ortiz*	.75
179	Shannon Stewart	.20
180	Pablo Ortega	.10
181	*Jimmy Rollins*	1.00
182	Sean Casey	.40
183	*Ted Lilly*	.25
184	*Chris Enochs*	.10
185	*Magglio Ordonez*	3.00
186	Mike Drumright	.10
187	Aaron Boone	.10
188	Matt Clement	.10
189	Todd Dunwoody	.10
190	Larry Rodriguez	.10
191	Todd Noel	.10
192	Geoff Jenkins	.10
193	George Lombard	.10
194	Lance Berkman	.15
195	*Marcus McCain*	.10
196	Ryan McGuire	.10
197	*Jhensy Sandoval*	.10
198	Corey Lee	.10
199	Mario Valdez	.10
200	*Robert Fick*	.50
201	Donnie Sadler	.10
202	Marc Kroon	.10
203	David Miller	.10
204	Jarrod Washburn	.10
205	Miguel Tejada	.40
206	Raul Ibanez	.10
207	John Patterson	.10
208	Calvin Pickering	.10
209	Felix Martinez	.10
210	Mark Redman	.10
211	Scott Elarton	.10
212	*Jose Amado*	.10
213	Kerry Wood	.45
214	Dante Powell	.10
215	Aramis Ramirez	.10
216	A.J. Hinch	.10
217	*Dustin Carr*	.10
218	Mark Kotsay	.10
219	Jason Standridge	.10
220	Luis Ordaz	.10
221	*Orlando Hernandez*	.50
222	Cal Ripken Jr.	3.00
223	Paul Molitor	1.00
224	Derek Jeter	3.00
225	Barry Bonds	3.00
226	Jim Edmonds	.10
227	John Smoltz	.10
228	Eric Karros	.10
229	Ray Lankford	.10
230	Rey Ordonez	.10
231	Kenny Lofton	.10
232	Alex Rodriguez	2.50
233	Dante Bichette	.10
234	Pedro Martinez	.75
235	Carlos Delgado	.60
236	Rod Beck	.10
237	Matt Williams	.10
238	Charles Johnson	.10
239	Rico Brogna	.10
240	Frank Thomas	1.00
241	Paul O'Neill	.10
242	Jaret Wright	.10
243	Brant Brown	.10
244	Ryan Klesko	.10
245	Chuck Finley	.10
246	Derek Bell	.10
247	Delino DeShields	.10
248	Chan Ho Park	.10
249	Wade Boggs	1.50
250	Jay Buhner	.10
251	Butch Huskey	.10
252	Steve Finley	.10
253	Will Clark	.10
254	John Valentin	.10
255	Bobby Higginson	.10
256	Darryl Strawberry	.10
257	Randy Johnson	.75
258	Al Martin	.10
259	Travis Fryman	.10
260	Fred McGriff	.10
261	Jose Valentin	.10
262	Andruw Jones	1.00
263	Kenny Rogers	.10
264	Moises Alou	.10
265	Denny Neagle	.10
266	Ugueth Urbina	.10
267	Derrek Lee	.25
268	Ellis Burks	.10
269	Mariano Rivera	.30
270	Dean Palmer	.10
271	Eddie Taubensee	.10
272	Brady Anderson	.10
273	Brian Giles	.10
274	Quinton McCracken	.10
275	Henry Rodriguez	.10
276	Andres Galarraga	.10
277	Jose Canseco	.45
278	David Segui	.10
279	Bret Saberhagen	.10
280	Kevin Brown	.20
281	Chuck Knoblauch	.10
282	Jeromy Burnitz	.10
283	Jay Bell	.10
284	Manny Ramirez	1.00
285	Rick Helling	.10
286	Francisco Cordova	.10
287	Bob Abreu	.20
288	J.T. Snow Jr.	.10
289	Hideo Nomo	1.00
290	Brian Jordan	.10
291	Javy Lopez	.10
292	Travis Lee	.10
293	Russell Branyan	.10
294	Paul Konerko	.10
295	*Masato Yoshii*	.50
296	Kris Benson	.10
297	Juan Encarnacion	.10
298	Eric Milton	.10
299	Mike Caruso	.10
300	*Ricardo Aramboles*	.10
301	Bobby Smith	.10
302	Billy Koch	.10
303	Richard Hidalgo	.10
304	*Justin Baughman*	.10
305	Chris Gissell	.10
306	*Donnie Bridges*	.10
307	*Nelson Lara*	.10
308	*Randy Wolf*	1.00
309	*Jason LaRue*	.25
310	*Jason Gooding*	.10
311	*Edgar Clemente*	.10
312	Andrew Vessel	.10
313	Chris Reitsma	.10
314	*Jesus Sanchez*	.10
315	*Buddy Carlyle*	.10
316	Randy Winn	.10
317	Luis Rivera	.10
318	*Marcus Thames*	.10
319	A.J. Pierzynski	.10
320	Scott Randall	.10
321	Damian Sapp	.10
322	*Eddie Yarnell*	.10
323	*Luke Allen*	.15
324	J.D. Smart	.10
325	Willie Martinez	.10
326	Alex Ramirez	.10
327	*Eric DuBose*	.10
328	Kevin Witt	.10
329	*Dan McKinley*	.10
330	Cliff Politte	.10
331	Vladimir Nunez	.10
332	*John Halama*	.25
333	Nerio Rodriguez	.10
334	Desi Relaford	.10
335	Robinson Checo	.10
336	*John Nicholson*	.10
337	*Tom LaRosa*	.10
338	*Kevin Nicholson*	.10
339	Javier Vazquez	.40
340	A.J. Zapp	.10
341	Tom Evans	.10
342	Kerry Robinson	.10
343	*Gabe Gonzalez*	.10
344	Ralph Milliard	.10
345	Enrique Wilson	.10
346	Elvin Hernandez	.10
347	*Mike Lincoln*	.10
348	*Cesar King*	.10
349	*Cristian Guzman*	1.00
350	Donzell McDonald	.10
351	*Jim Parque*	.50
352	*Mike Saipe*	.10
353	*Carlos Febles*	.50
354	*Dernell Stenson*	.50
355	*Mark Osborne*	.10
356	*Odalis Perez*	.50
357	*Jason Dewey*	.15
358	Joe Fontenot	.10
359	*Jason Grilli*	.50
360	*Kevin Haverbusch*	.50
361	*Jay Yennaco*	.10
362	Brian Buchanan	.10
363	John Barnes	.10
364	Chris Fussell	.10
365	*Kevin Gibbs*	.10
366	Joe Lawrence	.10
367	DaRond Stovall	.10
368	*Brian Fuentes*	.10
369	Jimmy Anderson	.10
370	*Laril Gonzalez*	.10
371	*Scott Williamson*	.50
372	Milton Bradley	.10
373	*Jason Halper*	.10
374	*Brent Billingsley*	.10
375	*Joe DePastino*	.10
376	Jake Westbrook	.10
377	Octavio Dotel	.10
378	*Jason Williams*	.10
379	*Julio Ramirez*	.10
380	Seth Greisinger	.10
381	*Mike Judd*	.10
382	*Ben Ford*	.10
383	Tom Bennett	.10
384	*Adam Butler*	.10
385	*Wade Miller*	.75
386	*Kyle Peterson*	.10
387	*Tommy Peterman*	.10
388	Onan Masaoka	.10
389	*Jason Rakers*	.15
390	Rafael Medina	.10
391	Luis Lopez	.10

#	Player	Value
392	Jeff Yoder	.10
393	*Vance Wilson*	.25
394	*Fernando Seguignol*	.50
395	Ron Wright	.10
396	*Ruben Mateo*	.40
397	*Steve Lomasney*	.25
398	Damian Jackson	.10
399	*Mike Jerzembeck*	.25
400	*Luis Rivas*	.50
401	*Kevin Burford*	.20
402	Glenn Davis	.10
403	*Robert Luce*	.20
404	Cole Liniak	.10
405	*Matthew LeCroy*	.25
406	*Jeremy Giambi*	.40
407	Shawn Chacon	.10
408	*Dewayne Wise*	.20
409	*Steve Woodard*	.25
410	*Francisco Cordero*	.25
411	*Damon Minor*	.20
412	Lou Collier	.10
413	Justin Towle	.10
414	Juan LeBron	.10
415	Michael Coleman	.10
416	Felix Rodriguez	.10
417	*Paul Ah Yat*	.25
418	*Kevin Barker*	.25
419	Brian Meadows	.10
420	*Darnell McDonald*	.20
421	*Matt Kinney*	.25
422	*Mike Vavrek*	.20
423	*Courtney Duncan*	.20
424	*Kevin Millar*	.50
425	Ruben Rivera	.10
426	*Steve Shoemaker*	.25
427	*Dan Reichert*	.25
428	*Carlos Lee*	2.00
429	Rod Barajas	.10
430	*Pablo Ozuna*	.40
431	*Todd Belitz*	.20
432	Sidney Ponson	.10
433	*Steve Carver*	.20
434	Esteban Yan	.10
435	*Cedrick Bowers*	.25
436	Marlon Anderson	.10
437	Carl Pavano	.10
438	*Jae Weong Seo*	.50
439	*Jose Taveras*	.20
440	*Matt Anderson*	.25
441	*Darron Ingram*	.20

International

	NM/M
Complete Set (441):	200.00
Common Player:	.25
Stars:	1.5X
Inserted 1:1	

(See 1998 Bowman for checklist and base card values.)

Golden Anniversary

	NM/M
Common Player:	4.00
Veteran Stars:	15-30X
Young Stars:	5-10X
Rookie Cards:	5-10X

(See 1998 Bowman for checklist and base card values.)

Autographs

		NM/M
	Complete Set, Blue (70):	350.00
	Common Player:	3.00
	Inserted 1:149	
	Silvers (1:992):	1.5-2.5X
	Golds (1:2,976):	2-4X
1	Adrian Beltre	20.00
2	Brad Fullmer	6.00
3	Ricky Ledee	5.00
4	David Ortiz	35.00
5	Fernando Tatis	3.00
6	Kerry Wood	30.00
7	Mel Rosario	3.00
8	Cole Liniak	5.00
9	A.J. Hinch	5.00
10	Jhensy Sandoval	3.00
11	Jose Cruz Jr.	5.00
12	Richard Hidalgo	8.00
13	Geoff Jenkins	8.00
14	Carl Pavano	15.00
15	Richie Sexson	15.00
16	Tony Womack	5.00
17	Scott Rolen	20.00
18	Ryan Minor	5.00
19	Elieser Marrero	5.00
20	Jason Marquis	5.00
21	Mike Lowell	15.00
22	Todd Helton	20.00
23	Chad Green	3.00
24	Scott Elarton	3.00
25	Russell Branyan	5.00
26	Mike Drumright	3.00
27	Ben Grieve	5.00
28	Jacque Jones	8.00
29	Jared Sandberg	5.00
30	Grant Roberts	5.00
31	Mike Stoner	3.00
32	Brian Rose	3.00
33	Randy Winn	5.00
34	Justin Towle	3.00
35	Anthony Sanders	3.00
36	Rafael Medina	3.00
37	Corey Lee	3.00
38	Mike Kinkade	5.00
39	Norm Hutchins	3.00
40	Jason Brester	3.00
41	Ben Davis	5.00
42	Nomar Garciaparra	75.00
43	Jeff Liefer	3.00
44	Eric Milton	6.00
45	Preston Wilson	8.00
46	Miguel Tejada	50.00
47	Luis Ordaz	3.00
48	Travis Lee	5.00
49	Kris Benson	6.00
50	Jacob Cruz	5.00
51	Dermal Brown	3.00
52	Marc Kroon	3.00
53	Chad Hermansen	5.00
54	Roy Halladay	20.00
55	Eric Chavez	10.00
56	Jason Conti	3.00
57	Juan Encarnacion	5.00
58	Paul Wilder	3.00
59	Aramis Ramirez	15.00
60	Cliff Politte	3.00
61	Todd Dunwoody	5.00
62	Paul Konerko	10.00
63	Shane Monahan	3.00
64	Alex Sanchez	3.00
65	Jeff Abbott	3.00
66	John Patterson	5.00
67	Peter Munro	3.00
68	Jarrod Washburn	10.00
69	Derrek Lee	20.00
70	Ramon Hernandez	5.00

Japanese Rookies

		NM/M
	Complete Set (3):	15.00
	Common Player:	5.00
11	Hideo Nomo	10.00
17	Shigetosi Hasegawa	5.00
	Hideki Irabu	5.00

Minor League MVP

		NM/M
	Complete Set (11):	9.00
	Common Player:	.50
1	Jeff Bagwell	1.00
2	Andres Galarraga	.50
3	Juan Gonzalez	1.00
4	Tony Gwynn	1.50
5	Vladimir Guerrero	1.00
6	Derek Jeter	3.00
7	Andruw Jones	1.00
8	Tino Martinez	.50
9	Manny Ramirez	1.00
10	Gary Sheffield	.75
11	Jim Thome	.50

Rookie of the Year Favorites

		NM/M
	Complete Set (10):	4.00
	Common Player:	.25
1	Adrian Beltre	.50
2	Troy Glaus	2.50
3	Chad Hermansen	.25
4	Matt Clement	.25
5	Eric Chavez	.75
6	Kris Benson	.25
7	Richie Sexson	.25
8	Randy Wolf	.25
9	Ryan Minor	.25
10	Alex Gonzalez	.25

Scout's Choice

		NM/M
	Complete Set (21):	8.00
	Common Player:	.25
	Inserted 1:12	
1	Paul Konerko	.50
2	Richard Hidalgo	.25
3	Mark Kotsay	.25
4	Ben Grieve	.40
5	Chad Hermansen	.25
6	Matt Clement	.25
7	Brad Fullmer	.25
8	Eli Marrero	.25
9	Kerry Wood	1.50
10	Adrian Beltre	1.50
11	Ricky Ledee	.25
12	Travis Lee	.50
13	Abraham Nunez	.25
14	Ryan Anderson	.25
15	Dermal Brown	.25
16	Juan Encarnacion	.25
17	Aramis Ramirez	.50
18	Todd Helton	2.50
19	Kris Benson	.25
20	Russell Branyan	.25
21	Mike Stoner	.25

1998 BOWMAN CHROME

		NM/M
	Complete Set (441):	100.00
	Complete Series 1 (221):	60.00
	Complete Series 2 (220):	50.00
	Common Player:	.20
	Series 1 Pack (4):	2.50
	Series 2 Pack (4):	2.00
	Series 1 Box (24):	45.00
	Series 2 Box (24):	40.00
1	Nomar Garciaparra	2.00
2	Scott Rolen	1.00
3	Andy Pettitte	.40
4	Ivan Rodriguez	.75
5	Mark McGwire	2.50
6	Jason Dickson	.20
7	Jose Cruz Jr.	.20
8	Jeff Kent	.20
9	Mike Mussina	.60
10	Jason Kendall	.20
11	Brett Tomko	.20
12	Jeff King	.20
13	Brad Radke	.20
14	Robin Ventura	.20
15	Jeff Bagwell	1.00
16	Greg Maddux	1.50
17	John Jaha	.20
18	Mike Piazza	2.00
19	Edgar Martinez	.20
20	David Justice	.20
21	Todd Hundley	.20
22	Tony Gwynn	1.50
23	Larry Walker	.20
24	Bernie Williams	.50
25	Edgar Renteria	.20
26	Rafael Palmeiro	.75
27	Tim Salmon	.30
28	Matt Morris	.20
29	Shawn Estes	.20
30	Vladimir Guerrero	1.00
31	Fernando Tatis	.20
32	Justin Thompson	.20
33	Ken Griffey Jr.	2.00
34	Edgardo Alfonzo	.20
35	Mo Vaughn	.20
36	Marty Cordova	.20
37	Craig Biggio	.20
38	Roger Clemens	1.75
39	Mark Grace	.30
40	Ken Caminiti	.20
41	Tony Womack	.20
42	Albert Belle	.30
43	Tino Martinez	.20
44	Sandy Alomar	.20
45	Jeff Cirillo	.20
46	Jason Giambi	.60
47	Darin Erstad	.65
48	Livan Hernandez	.20
49	Mark Grudzielanek	.20
50	Sammy Sosa	2.00
51	Curt Schilling	.50
52	Brian Hunter	.20
53	Neifi Perez	.20
54	Todd Walker	.20
55	Jose Guillen	.20
56	Jim Thome	.20
57	Tom Glavine	.40
58	Todd Greene	.20
59	Rondell White	.20
60	Roberto Alomar	.40
61	Tony Clark	.20
62	Vinny Castilla	.20
63	Barry Larkin	.20
64	Hideki Irabu	.20
65	Johnny Damon	.50
66	Juan Gonzalez	1.00
67	John Olerud	.20
68	Gary Sheffield	.50
69	Raul Mondesi	.20
70	Chipper Jones	1.50
71	David Ortiz	1.00
72	*Warren Morris*	1.00
73	Alex Gonzalez	.20
74	Nick Bierbrodt	.20
75	Roy Halladay	.50
76	Danny Buxbaum	.20
77	Adam Kennedy	.20
78	*Jared Sandberg*	.50
79	Michael Barrett	.20
80	Gil Meche	.20
81	Jayson Werth	.20

82 Abraham Nunez .20
83 Ben Petrick .20
84 Brett Caradonna .20
85 *Mike Lowell* 4.00
86 *Clay Bruner* .20
87 *John Curtice* .20
88 Bobby Estalella .20
89 Juan Melo .20
90 Arnold Gooch .20
91 *Kevin Millwood* 4.00
92 Richie Sexson .35
93 Orlando Cabrera .20
94 Pat Cline .20
95 Anthony Sanders .20
96 Russ Johnson .20
97 Ben Grieve .20
98 Kevin McGlinchy .20
99 Paul Wilder .20
100 Russ Ortiz .20
101 *Ryan Jackson* .50
102 Heath Murray .20
103 Brian Rose .20
104 *Ryan Radmanovich* .20
105 Ricky Ledee .20
106 *Jeff Wallace* .50
107 *Ryan Minor* .50
108 Dennis Reyes .20
109 *James Manias* .20
110 Chris Carpenter .20
111 Daryle Ward .20
112 Vernon Wells .20
113 Chad Green .20
114 *Mike Stoner* .20
115 Brad Fullmer .20
116 Adam Eaton .20
117 Jeff Liefer .20
118 *Corey Koskie* 4.00
119 Todd Helton 1.00
120 *Jaime Jones* .20
121 Mel Rosario .20
122 Geoff Goetz .20
123 Adrian Beltre .50
124 Jason Dellaero .20
125 *Gabe Kapler* 1.00
126 Scott Schoeneweis .20
127 Ryan Brannan .20
128 Aaron Akin .20
129 *Ryan Anderson* 1.00
130 Brad Penny .20
131 Bruce Chen .20
132 Eli Marrero .20
133 Eric Chavez .35
134 *Troy Glaus* 12.00
135 Troy Cameron .20
136 *Brian Sikorski* .50
137 *Mike Kinkade* .75
138 Braden Looper .20
139 Mark Mangum .20
140 Danny Peoples .20
141 J.J. Davis .20
142 Ben Davis .20
143 Jacque Jones .50
144 Derrick Gibson .20
145 Bronson Arroyo .50
146 *Luis De Los Santos* .20
147 Jeff Abbott .20
148 *Mike Cuddyer* 2.00
149 Jason Romano .20
150 Shane Monahan .20
151 *Ntema Ndungidi* .20
152 Alex Sanchez .20
153 *Jack Cust* 1.00
154 Brent Butler .20
155 Ramon Hernandez .20
156 Norm Hutchins .20
157 Jason Marquis .20
158 Jacob Cruz .20
159 *Rob Burger* .20
160 Eric Milton .20
161 Preston Wilson .35
162 *Jason Fitzgerald* .20
163 Dan Serafini .20
164 Peter Munro .20
165 Trot Nixon .40
166 Homer Bush .20
167 Dermal Brown .20
168 Chad Hermansen .20
169 *Julio Moreno* .20
170 *John Roskos* .20
171 Grant Roberts .20
172 Ken Cloude .20
173 Jason Brester .20
174 Jason Conti .20
175 Jon Garland .20
176 Robbie Bell .20
177 Nathan Haynes .20
178 *Ramon Ortiz* 1.00
179 Shannon Stewart .35
180 Pablo Ortega .20
181 *Jimmy Rollins* 3.00
182 Sean Casey .60
183 *Ted Lilly* .20
184 *Chris Enochs* .20
185 *Magglio Ordonez* 6.00
186 Mike Drumright .20
187 Aaron Boone .20
188 Matt Clement .20
189 Todd Dunwoody .20
190 Larry Rodriguez .20
191 Todd Noel .20
192 Geoff Jenkins .20
193 George Lombard .20
194 Lance Berkman .20
195 *Marcus McCain* .20
196 Ryan McGuire .20
197 *Jhensy Sandoval* .20
198 Corey Lee .20
199 Mario Valdez .20
200 *Robert Fick* .50
201 Donnie Sadler .20
202 Marc Kroon .20
203 David Miller .20
204 Jarrod Washburn .20
205 Miguel Tejada .50
206 Raul Ibanez .20
207 John Patterson .20
208 Calvin Pickering .20
209 Felix Martinez .20
210 Mark Redman .20
211 Scott Elarton .20
212 *Jose Amado* .20
213 Kerry Wood .75
214 Dante Powell .20
215 Aramis Ramirez .20
216 A.J. Hinch .20
217 *Dustin Carr* .20
218 Mark Kotsay .20
219 Jason Standridge .20
220 Luis Ordaz .20
221 *Orlando Hernandez* 3.00
222 Cal Ripken Jr. 3.00
223 Paul Molitor 1.00
224 Derek Jeter 3.00
225 Barry Bonds 3.00
226 Jim Edmonds .50
227 John Smoltz .20
228 Eric Karros .20
229 Ray Lankford .20
230 Rey Ordonez .20
231 Kenny Lofton .20
232 Alex Rodriguez 2.50
233 Dante Bichette .20
234 Pedro Martinez 1.00
235 Carlos Delgado .75
236 Rod Beck .20
237 Matt Williams .20
238 Charles Johnson .20
239 Rico Brogna .20
240 Frank Thomas 1.00
241 Paul O'Neill .20
242 Jaret Wright .20
243 Brant Brown .20
244 Ryan Klesko .20
245 Chuck Finley .20
246 Derek Bell .20
247 Delino DeShields .20
248 Chan Ho Park .20
249 Wade Boggs 1.50
250 Jay Buhner .20
251 Butch Huskey .20
252 Steve Finley .20
253 Will Clark .30
254 John Valentin .20
255 Bobby Higginson .20
256 Darryl Strawberry .20
257 Randy Johnson 1.00
258 Al Martin .20
259 Travis Fryman .20
260 Fred McGriff .20
261 Jose Valentin .20
262 Andruw Jones 1.00
263 Kenny Rogers .20
264 Moises Alou .20
265 Denny Neagle .20
266 Ugueth Urbina .20
267 Derrek Lee .50
268 Ellis Burks .20
269 Mariano Rivera .40
270 Dean Palmer .20
271 Eddie Taubensee .20
272 Brady Anderson .20
273 Brian Giles .20
274 Quinton McCracken .20
275 Henry Rodriguez .20
276 Andres Galarraga .20
277 Jose Canseco .40
278 David Segui .20
279 Bret Saberhagen .20
280 Kevin Brown .40
281 Chuck Knoblauch .20
282 Jeromy Burnitz .20
283 Jay Bell .20
284 Manny Ramirez 1.00
285 Rick Helling .20
286 Francisco Cordova .20
287 Bob Abreu .30
288 J.T. Snow Jr. .20
289 Hideo Nomo 1.00
290 Brian Jordan .20
291 Javy Lopez .20
292 *Aaron Akin* .20
293 Russell Branyan .20
294 Paul Konerko .20
295 *Masato Yoshii* 1.00
296 Kris Benson .20
297 Juan Encarnacion .20
298 Eric Milton .25
299 Mike Caruso .20
300 *Ricardo Aramboles* .20
301 Bobby Smith .20
302 Billy Koch .20
303 Richard Hidalgo .20
304 *Justin Baughman* .20
305 Chris Gissell .20
306 *Donnie Bridges* .20
307 *Nelson Lara* .20
308 *Randy Wolf* 2.00
309 *Jason LaRue* .75
310 *Jason Gooding* .20
311 *Edgar Clemente* .40
312 Andrew Vessel .20
313 Chris Reitsma .20
314 *Jesus Sanchez* .20
315 *Buddy Carlyle* .20
316 Randy Winn .20
317 Luis Rivera .20
318 *Marcus Thames* .20
319 A.J. Pierzynski .20
320 Scott Randall .20
321 Damian Sapp .20
322 *Eddie Yarnell* .20
323 *Luke Allen* .20
324 J.D. Smart .20
325 Willie Martinez .20
326 Alex Ramirez .20
327 *Eric DuBose* .20
328 Kevin Witt .20
329 *Dan McKinley* .20
330 Cliff Politte .20
331 Vladimir Nunez .20
332 *John Halama* .75
333 Nerio Rodriguez .20
334 Desi Relaford .20
335 Robinson Checo .20
336 *John Nicholson* .20
337 *Tom LaRosa* .20
338 *Kevin Nicholson* .20
339 Javier Vazquez .30
340 A.J. Zapp .20
341 Tom Evans .20
342 Kerry Robinson .20
343 *Gabe Gonzalez* .20
344 Ralph Milliard .20
345 Enrique Wilson .20
346 Elvin Hernandez .20
347 *Mike Lincoln* .40
348 *Cesar King* .20
349 *Cristian Guzman* 2.00
350 Donzell McDonald .20
351 *Jim Parque* .25
352 *Mike Saipe* .20
353 *Carlos Febles* .50
354 *Dernell Stenson* .35
355 *Mark Osborne* .20
356 *Odalis Perez* 2.00
357 *Jason Dewey* .20
358 Joe Fontenot .20
359 *Jason Grilli* .50
360 *Kevin Haverbusch* .50
361 *Jay Yennaco* .20
362 Brian Buchanan .20
363 John Barnes .20
364 Chris Fussell .20
365 *Kevin Gibbs* .20
366 Joe Lawrence .20
367 DaRond Stovall .20
368 *Brian Fuentes* .20
369 Jimmy Anderson .20
370 *Laril Gonzalez* .20
371 *Scott Williamson* 1.00
372 Milton Bradley .20
373 *Jason Halper* .20
374 *Brent Billingsley* .20
375 *Joe DePastino* .20
376 Jake Westbrook .20
377 Octavio Dotel .20
378 *Jason Williams* .25
379 *Julio Ramirez* .20
380 Seth Greisinger .20
381 *Mike Judd* .20
382 *Ben Ford* .20
383 *Tom Bennett* .20
384 *Adam Butler* .20
385 *Wade Miller* 3.00
386 *Kyle Peterson* .20
387 *Tommy Peterman* .20
388 Onan Masaoka .20
389 *Jason Rakers* .20
390 Rafael Medina .20
391 Luis Lopez .20
392 Jeff Yoder .20
393 *Vance Wilson* .20
394 *Fernando Seguignol* .50
395 Ron Wright .20
396 *Ruben Mateo* 1.00
397 *Steve Lomasney* .50
398 Damian Jackson .20
399 *Mike Jerzembeck* .20
400 *Luis Rivas* 1.00
401 *Kevin Burford* .20
402 Glenn Davis .20
403 *Robert Luce* .20
404 Cole Liniak .20
405 *Matthew LeCroy* .50
406 *Jeremy Giambi* .50
407 Shawn Chacon .20
408 *Dewayne Wise* .20
409 *Steve Woodard* .50
410 *Francisco Cordero* .20
411 *Damon Minor* .20
412 Lou Collier .20
413 Justin Towle .20
414 Juan LeBron .20
415 Michael Coleman .20
416 Felix Rodriguez .20
417 *Paul Ah Yat* .20
418 *Kevin Barker* .20
419 Brian Meadows .20
420 *Darnell McDonald* .50
421 *Matt Kinney* .50
422 *Mike Vavrek* .20
423 *Courtney Duncan* .20
424 *Kevin Millar* 5.00
425 Ruben Rivera .20
426 *Steve Shoemaker* .20
427 *Dan Reichert* .20
428 *Carlos Lee* 6.00
429 *Rod Barajas* .20
430 *Pablo Ozuna* 1.00
431 *Todd Belitz* .20
432 Sidney Ponson .20
433 *Steve Carver* .20
434 *Esteban Yan* .20
435 *Cedrick Bowers* .20
436 Marlon Anderson .20
437 Carl Pavano .20
438 *Jae Weong Seo* 1.00
439 *Jose Taveras* .20
440 *Matt Anderson* .50
441 *Darron Ingram* .20

International

NM/M

Common Player: .50
Stars and rookies: 1.5X
Inserted 1:4
Refractors: 3X
Inserted 1:24
(See 1998 Bowman Chrome for checklist and base card values.)

Refractors

NM/M

Common Player: 2.00
Stars: 3X
Inserted 1:12
Int'l Refractors: 6X
Inserted 1:24
(See 1998 Bowman Chrome for checklist and base card values.)

Golden Anniversary

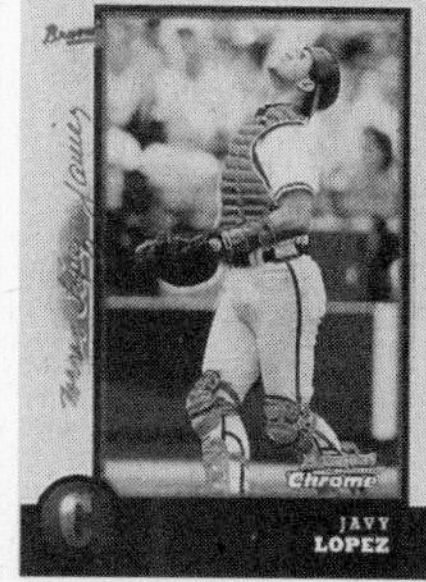

		NM/M
Common Player:		5.00
Stars:		20X
Common Refractor:		20.00

(See 1998 Bowman Chrome for checklist and base card values. Golden Anniversary Refractors cannot be accur-ately priced due to their rarity (five each).)

Reprints

		NM/M
Complete Set (50):		20.00
Common Player:		.25
Inserted 1:12		
Refractors:		1.5X
Inserted 1:36		
1	Yogi Berra	.50
2	Jackie Robinson	2.00
3	Don Newcombe	.25
4	Satchel Paige	.50
5	Willie Mays	2.00
6	Gil McDougald	.25
7	Don Larsen	.25
8	Elston Howard	.25
9	Robin Ventura	.25
10	Brady Anderson	.25
11	Gary Sheffield	.35
12	Tino Martinez	.25
13	Ken Griffey Jr.	1.00
14	John Smoltz	.25
15	Sandy Alomar Jr.	.25
16	Larry Walker	.25
17	Todd Hundley	.25
18	Mo Vaughn	.25
19	Sammy Sosa	1.00
20	Frank Thomas	.50
21	Chuck Knoblauch	.25
22	Bernie Williams	.35
23	Juan Gonzalez	.50
24	Mike Mussina	.50
25	Jeff Bagwell	.50
26	Tim Salmon	.35
27	Ivan Rodriguez	.50
28	Kenny Lofton	.25
29	Chipper Jones	1.00
30	Javier Lopez	.25
31	Ryan Klesko	.25
32	Raul Mondesi	.25
33	Jim Thome	.25
34	Carlos Delgado	.50
35	Mike Piazza	1.00
36	Manny Ramirez	.50
37	Andy Pettitte	.35
38	Derek Jeter	2.00
39	Brad Fullmer	.25
40	Richard Hidalgo	.25
41	Tony Clark	.25
42	Andruw Jones	.50
43	Vladimir Guerrero	.50
44	Nomar Garciaparra	1.00
45	Paul Konerko	.40
46	Ben Grieve	.35
47	Hideo Nomo	.50
48	Scott Rolen	.50
49	Jose Guillen	.25
50	Livan Hernandez	.25

1998 BOWMAN'S BEST

		NM/M
Complete Set (200):		30.00
Common Player:		.25
Pack (6):		2.50
Wax Box (24):		35.00
1	Mark McGwire	2.50
2	Hideo Nomo	1.00
3	Barry Bonds	3.00
4	Dante Bichette	.25
5	Chipper Jones	1.50
6	Frank Thomas	1.00
7	Kevin Brown	.25
8	Juan Gonzalez	1.00
9	Jay Buhner	.25
10	Chuck Knoblauch	.25
11	Cal Ripken Jr.	3.00
12	Matt Williams	.25
13	Jim Edmonds	.25
14	Manny Ramirez	1.00
15	Tony Clark	.25
16	Mo Vaughn	.25
17	Bernie Williams	.40
18	Scott Rolen	.75
19	Gary Sheffield	.40
20	Albert Belle	.40
21	Mike Piazza	2.00
22	John Olerud	.25
23	Tony Gwynn	1.50
24	Jay Bell	.25
25	Jose Cruz Jr.	.25
26	Justin Thompson	.25
27	Ken Griffey Jr.	2.00
28	Sandy Alomar	.25
29	Mark Grudzielanek	.25
30	Mark Grace	.35
31	Ron Gant	.25
32	Javy Lopez	.25
33	Jeff Bagwell	1.00
34	Fred McGriff	.25
35	Rafael Palmeiro	1.00
36	Vinny Castilla	.25
37	Andy Benes	.25
38	Pedro Martinez	1.00
39	Andy Pettitte	.40
40	Marty Cordova	.25
41	Rusty Greer	.25
42	Kevin Orie	.25
43	Chan Ho Park	.25
44	Ryan Klesko	.25
45	Alex Rodriguez	2.50
46	Travis Fryman	.25
47	Jeff King	.25
48	Roger Clemens	1.75
49	Darin Erstad	.75
50	Brady Anderson	.25
51	Jason Kendall	.25
52	John Valentin	.25
53	Ellis Burks	.25
54	Brian Hunter	.25
55	Paul O'Neill	.25
56	Ken Caminiti	.25
57	David Justice	.25
58	Eric Karros	.25
59	Pat Hentgen	.25
60	Greg Maddux	1.50
61	Craig Biggio	.25
62	Edgar Martinez	.25
63	Mike Mussina	.65
64	Larry Walker	.25
65	Tino Martinez	.25
66	Jim Thome	.25
67	Tom Glavine	.35
68	Raul Mondesi	.25
69	Marquis Grissom	.25
70	Randy Johnson	1.00
71	Steve Finley	.25
72	Jose Guillen	.25
73	Nomar Garciaparra	2.00
74	Wade Boggs	1.50
75	Bobby Higginson	.25
76	Robin Ventura	.25
77	Derek Jeter	3.00
78	Andruw Jones	1.00
79	Ray Lankford	.25
80	Vladimir Guerrero	1.00
81	Kenny Lofton	.25
82	Ivan Rodriguez	.75
83	Neifi Perez	.25
84	John Smoltz	.25
85	Tim Salmon	.40
86	Carlos Delgado	.50
87	Sammy Sosa	2.00
88	Jaret Wright	.25
89	Roberto Alomar	.50
90	Paul Molitor	1.00
91	Dean Palmer	.25
92	Barry Larkin	.25
93	Jason Giambi	.75
94	Curt Schilling	.35
95	Eric Young	.25
96	Denny Neagle	.25
97	Moises Alou	.25
98	Livan Hernandez	.25
99	Todd Hundley	.25
100	Andres Galarraga	.25
101	Travis Lee	.50
102	Lance Berkman	.25
103	Orlando Cabrera	.25
104	*Mike Lowell*	3.00
105	Ben Grieve	.35
106	*Jae Weong Seo*	.50
107	Richie Sexson	.25
108	Eli Marrero	.25
109	Aramis Ramirez	.25
110	Paul Konerko	.25
111	Carl Pavano	.25
112	Brad Fullmer	.25
113	Matt Clement	.25
114	Donzell McDonald	.25
115	Todd Helton	1.00
116	Mike Caruso	.25
117	Donnie Sadler	.25
118	Bruce Chen	.25
119	Jarrod Washburn	.25
120	Adrian Beltre	.50
121	*Ryan Jackson*	.50
122	*Kevin Millar*	3.00
123	*Corey Koskie*	1.00
124	Dermal Brown	.25
125	Kerry Wood	.75
126	Juan Melo	.25
127	Ramon Hernandez	.25
128	Roy Halladay	.25
129	Ron Wright	.25
130	*Darnell McDonald*	.50
131	*Odalis Perez*	.75
132	*Alex Cora*	.25
133	Justin Towle	.25
134	Juan Encarnacion	.25
135	Brian Rose	.25
136	Russell Branyan	.25
137	*Cesar King*	.25
138	Ruben Rivera	.25
139	Ricky Ledee	.25
140	Vernon Wells	.25
141	*Luis Rivas*	.50
142	Brent Butler	.25
143	Karim Garcia	.25
144	George Lombard	.25
145	*Masato Yoshii*	.75
146	Braden Looper	.25
147	Alex Sanchez	.25
148	Kris Benson	.25
149	Mark Kotsay	.25
150	Richard Hidalgo	.25
151	Scott Elarton	.25
152	*Ryan Minor*	.25
153	*Troy Glaus*	5.00
154	*Carlos Lee*	2.00
155	Michael Coleman	.25
156	*Jason Grilli*	.50
157	*Julio Ramirez*	.50
158	*Randy Wolf*	.75
159	Ryan Brannan	.25
160	*Edgar Clemente*	.50
161	Miguel Tejada	.50
162	Chad Hermansen	.25
163	*Ryan Anderson*	.75
164	Ben Petrick	.25
165	Alex Gonzalez	.25
166	Ben Davis	.25
167	John Patterson	.25
168	Cliff Politte	.25
169	Randall Simon	.25
170	Javier Vazquez	.35
171	Kevin Witt	.25
172	Geoff Jenkins	.25
173	David Ortiz	.25
174	Derrick Gibson	.25
175	Abraham Nunez	.25
176	A.J. Hinch	.25
177	*Ruben Mateo*	.75
178	*Magglio Ordonez*	2.50
179	Todd Dunwoody	.25
180	Daryle Ward	.25
181	*Mike Kinkade*	.50
182	Willie Martinez	.25
183	*Orlando Hernandez*	1.50
184	Eric Milton	.25
185	Eric Chavez	.50
186	Damian Jackson	.25
187	*Jim Parque*	.50
188	*Dan Reichert*	.25
189	Mike Drumright	.25
190	Todd Walker	.25
191	Shane Monahan	.25
192	Derrek Lee	.50
193	*Jeremy Giambi*	.75
194	*Dan McKinley*	.25
195	*Tony Armas*	.75
196	*Matt Anderson*	.50
197	*Jim Chamblee*	.25
198	*Francisco Cordero*	.25
199	Calvin Pickering	.25
200	Reggie Taylor	.25

Refractors

		NM/M
Common Player:		4.00
Stars:		10X
Production 400 sets		

(See 1998 Bowman's Best for checklist and base card values.)

Atomic Refractors

		NM/M
Common Player:		10.00
Stars:		10X
Production 100 sets		

(See 1998 Bowman's Best for checklist and base card values.)

Autographs

		NM/M
Complete Set (10):		60.00
Common Player:		5.00
Inserted 1:180		
Refractors:		1.5X
Inserted 1:2,158		
Atomics:		2X
Inserted 1:6,437		
5	Chipper Jones	30.00
10	Chuck Knoblauch	5.00
15	Tony Clark	5.00
20	Albert Belle	8.00
25	Jose Cruz Jr.	5.00
105	Ben Grieve	5.00
110	Paul Konerko	10.00
115	Todd Helton	20.00
120	Adrian Beltre	25.00
125	Kerry Wood	30.00

Performers

		NM/M
Complete Set (10):		4.00
Common Player:		.35
Refractor (1:309):		3X
Atomic Refractor (1:3237):		5X
1	Ben Grieve	.45
2	Travis Lee	.75
3	Ryan Minor	.35
4	Todd Helton	2.00
5	Brad Fullmer	.35
6	Paul Konerko	.35
7	Adrian Beltre	.75
8	Richie Sexson	.35
9	Aramis Ramirez	.35
10	Russell Branyan	.35

1999 BOWMAN

	NM/M
Complete Set (440):	85.00
Complete Series 1 (220):	40.00
Complete Series 2 (220):	45.00
Common Player:	.10
Series 1 Pack (10):	2.00
Series 1 Box (24):	25.00
Series 2 Pack (10):	3.50
Series 2 Box (24):	65.00

No.	Player	Price
1	Ben Grieve	.15
2	Kerry Wood	.50
3	Ruben Rivera	.10
4	Sandy Alomar	.10
5	Cal Ripken Jr.	2.00
6	Mark McGwire	1.75
7	Vladimir Guerrero	.75
8	Moises Alou	.10
9	Jim Edmonds	.25
10	Greg Maddux	1.00
11	Gary Sheffield	.40
12	John Valentin	.10
13	Chuck Knoblauch	.10
14	Tony Clark	.10
15	Rusty Greer	.10
16	Al Leiter	.10
17	Travis Lee	.10
18	Jose Cruz Jr.	.10
19	Pedro Martinez	.75
20	Paul O'Neill	.10
21	Todd Walker	.10
22	Vinny Castilla	.10
23	Barry Larkin	.10
24	Curt Schilling	.50
25	Jason Kendall	.10
26	Scott Erickson	.10
27	Andres Galarraga	.10
28	Jeff Shaw	.10
29	John Olerud	.10
30	Orlando Hernandez	.10
31	Larry Walker	.10
32	Andruw Jones	.75
33	Jeff Cirillo	.10
34	Barry Bonds	2.00
35	Manny Ramirez	.75
36	Mark Kotsay	.10
37	Ivan Rodriguez	.60
38	Jeff King	.10
39	Brian Hunter	.10
40	Ray Durham	.10
41	Bernie Williams	.40
42	Darin Erstad	.50
43	Chipper Jones	1.00
44	Pat Hentgen	.10
45	Eric Young	.10
46	Jaret Wright	.10
47	Juan Guzman	.10
48	Jorge Posada	.25
49	Bobby Higginson	.10
50	Jose Guillen	.10
51	Trevor Hoffman	.10
52	Ken Griffey Jr.	1.50
53	David Justice	.10
54	Matt Williams	.10
55	Eric Karros	.10
56	Derek Bell	.10
57	Ray Lankford	.10
58	Mariano Rivera	.25
59	Brett Tomko	.10
60	Mike Mussina	.50
61	Kenny Lofton	.10
62	Chuck Finley	.10
63	Alex Gonzalez	.10
64	Mark Grace	.10
65	Raul Mondesi	.10
66	David Cone	.10
67	Brad Fullmer	.10
68	Andy Benes	.10
69	John Smoltz	.10
70	Shane Reynolds	.10
71	Bruce Chen	.10
72	Adam Kennedy	.10
73	Jack Cust	.10
74	Matt Clement	.10
75	Derrick Gibson	.10
76	Darnell McDonald	.10
77	*Adam Everett*	.50
78	Ricardo Aramboles	.10
79	*Mark Quinn*	.50
80	Jason Rakers	.10
81	*Seth Etherton*	.50
82	*Jeff Urban*	.50
83	Manny Aybar	.10
84	*Mike Nannini*	.50
85	Onan Masaoka	.10
86	Rod Barajas	.10
87	Mike Frank	.10
88	Scott Randall	.10
89	*Justin Bowles*	.50
90	Chris Haas	.10
91	*Arturo McDowell*	.50
92	*Matt Belisle*	.50
93	Scott Elarton	.10
94	Vernon Wells	.20
95	Pat Cline	.10
96	Ryan Anderson	.10
97	Kevin Barker	.10
98	Ruben Mateo	.10
99	Robert Fick	.10
100	Corey Koskie	.10
101	Ricky Ledee	.10
102	*Rick Elder*	.50
103	*Jack Cressend*	.50
104	Joe Lawrence	.10
105	Mike Lincoln	.10
106	*Kit Pellow*	.50
107	*Matt Burch*	.50
108	Brent Butler	.10
109	Jason Dewey	.10
110	Cesar King	.10
111	Julio Ramirez	.10
112	Jake Westbrook	.10
113	*Eric Valent*	.50
114	*Roosevelt Brown*	.50
115	*Choo Freeman*	.50
116	Juan Melo	.10
117	Jason Grilli	.10
118	Jared Sandberg	.10
119	Glenn Davis	.10
120	*David Riske*	.50
121	Jacque Jones	.10
122	Corey Lee	.10
123	Michael Barrett	.10
124	Lariel Gonzalez	.10
125	Mitch Meluskey	.10
126	Freddy Garcia	.10
127	*Tony Torcato*	.50
128	Jeff Liefer	.10
129	Ntema Ndungidi	.10
130	*Andy Brown*	.50
131	*Ryan Mills*	.50
132	*Andy Abad*	.50
133	Carlos Febles	.10
134	*Jason Tyner*	.50
135	Mark Osborne	.10
136	*Phil Norton*	.50
137	Nathan Haynes	.10
138	Roy Halladay	.20
139	Juan Encarnacion	.10
140	Brad Penny	.10
141	Grant Roberts	.10
142	Aramis Ramirez	.25
143	Cristian Guzman	.10
144	*Mamon Tucker*	.50
145	Ryan Bradley	.10
146	Brian Simmons	.10
147	Dan Reichert	.10
148	Russ Branyon	.10
149	*Victor Valencia*	.40
150	Scott Schoeneweis	.10
151	*Sean Spencer*	.40
152	Odalis Perez	.10
153	Joe Fontenot	.10
154	Milton Bradley	.10
155	*Josh McKinley*	.25
156	Terrence Long	.10
157	Danny Klassen	.10
158	*Paul Hoover*	.25
159	Ron Belliard	.10
160	Armando Rios	.10
161	Ramon Hernandez	.10
162	Jason Conti	.10
163	Chad Hermansen	.10
164	Jason Standridge	.10
165	Jason Dellaero	.10
166	John Curtice	.10
167	*Clayton Andrews*	.25
168	Jeremy Giambi	.10
169	Alex Ramirez	.10
170	*Gabe Molina*	.25
171	*Mario Encarnacion*	.25
172	*Mike Zywica*	.25
173	*Chip Ambres*	.50
174	Trot Nixon	.10
175	*Pat Burrell*	2.00
176	Jeff Yoder	.10
177	*Chris Jones*	.50
178	Kevin Witt	.10
179	*Keith Luuloa*	.25
180	Billy Koch	.10
181	*Damaso Marte*	.25
182	*Ryan Glynn*	.25
183	Calvin Pickering	.10
184	Michael Cuddyer	.10
185	*Nick Johnson*	.75
186	*Doug Mientkiewicz*	1.00
187	*Nate Cornejo*	.40
188	Octavio Dotel	.10
189	Wes Helms	.10
190	Nelson Lara	.10
191	*Chuck Abbott*	.25
192	Tony Armas Jr.	.10
193	Gil Meche	.10
194	Ben Petrick	.10
195	*Chris George*	.25
196	*Scott Hunter*	.25
197	Ryan Brannan	.10
198	*Amaury Garcia*	.25
199	Chris Gissell	.10
200	*Austin Kearns*	1.50
201	Alex Gonzalez	.10
202	Wade Miller	.10
203	Scott Williamson	.10
204	Chris Enochs	.10
205	Fernando Seguignol	.10
206	Marlon Anderson	.10
207	*Todd Sears*	.25
208	*Nate Bump*	.25
209	*J.M. Gold*	.25
210	Matt LeCroy	.10
211	Alex Hernandez	.10
212	Luis Rivera	.10
213	Troy Cameron	.10
214	*Alex Escobar*	.75
215	Jason LaRue	.10
216	Kyle Peterson	.10
217	Brent Butler	.10
218	Dernell Stenson	.10
219	Adrian Beltre	.40
220	Daryle Ward	.10
----	Series 1 Checklist Folder	.10
221	Jim Thome	.75
222	Cliff Floyd	.10
223	Rickey Henderson	.75
224	Garret Anderson	.10
225	Ken Caminiti	.10
226	Bret Boone	.10
227	Jeromy Burnitz	.10
228	Steve Finley	.10
229	Miguel Tejada	.40
230	Greg Vaughn	.10
231	Jose Offerman	.10
232	Andy Ashby	.10
233	Albert Belle	.10
234	Fernando Tatis	.10
235	Todd Helton	.75
236	Sean Casey	.25
237	Brian Giles	.10
238	Andy Pettitte	.25
239	Fred McGriff	.10
240	Roberto Alomar	.40
241	Edgar Martinez	.10
242	Lee Stevens	.10
243	Shawn Green	.25
244	Ryan Klesko	.10
245	Sammy Sosa	1.50
246	Todd Hundley	.10
247	Shannon Stewart	.20
248	Randy Johnson	.75
249	Rondell White	.10
250	Mike Piazza	1.50
251	Craig Biggio	.10
252	David Wells	.20
253	Brian Jordan	.10
254	Edgar Renteria	.10
255	Bartolo Colon	.10
256	Frank Thomas	.75
257	Will Clark	.20
258	Dean Palmer	.10
259	Dmitri Young	.10
260	Scott Rolen	.75
261	Jeff Kent	.10
262	Dante Bichette	.10
263	Nomar Garciaparra	1.50
264	Tony Gwynn	1.00
265	Alex Rodriguez	1.50
266	Jose Canseco	.50
267	Jason Giambi	.40
268	Jeff Bagwell	.75
269	Carlos Delgado	.40
270	Tom Glavine	.40
271	Eric Davis	.10
272	Edgardo Alfonzo	.10
273	Tim Salmon	.25
274	Johnny Damon	.25
275	Rafael Palmeiro	.75
276	Denny Neagle	.10
277	Neifi Perez	.10
278	Roger Clemens	1.25
279	Brant Brown	.10
280	Kevin Brown	.25
281	Jay Bell	.10
282	Jay Buhner	.10
283	Matt Lawton	.10
284	Robin Ventura	.10
285	Juan Gonzalez	.60
286	Mo Vaughn	.10
287	Kevin Millwood	.10
288	Tino Martinez	.10
289	Justin Thompson	.10
290	Derek Jeter	2.00
291	Ben Davis	.10
292	Mike Lowell	.10
293	*Joe Crede*	.75
294	*Micah Bowie*	.25
295	Lance Berkman	.10
296	Jason Marquis	.10
297	Chad Green	.10
298	Dee Brown	.10
299	Jerry Hairston Jr.	.10
300	Gabe Kapler	.10
301	*Brent Stentz*	.50
302	*Scott Mullen*	.50
303	Brandon Reed	.10
304	*Shea Hillenbrand*	.50
305	*J.D. Closser*	.40
306	Gary Matthews Jr.	.10
307	*Toby Hall*	.50
308	*Jason Phillips*	.25
309	*Jose Macias*	.25
310	*Jung Bong*	.25
311	*Ramon Soler*	.25
312	*Kelly Dransfeldt*	.25
313	*Carlos Hernandez*	.25
314	Kevin Haverbusch	.10
315	*Aaron Myette*	.25
316	*Chad Harville*	.50
317	*Kyle Farnsworth*	.50
318	*Travis Dawkins*	.50
319	Willie Martinez	.10
320	Carlos Lee	.10
321	*Carlos Pena*	.50
322	*Peter Bergeron*	.25
323	*A.J. Burnett*	.50
324	*Bucky Jacobsen*	1.00
325	*Mo Bruce*	.25
326	Reggie Taylor	.10
327	Jackie Rexrode	.10
328	*Alvin Morrow*	.25
329	Carlos Beltran	.75
330	Eric Chavez	.25
331	John Patterson	.10
332	Jayson Werth	.10
333	Richie Sexson	.25
334	Randy Wolf	.10
335	Eli Marrero	.10
336	Paul LoDuca	.10
337	J.D. Smart	.10
338	Ryan Minor	.10
339	Kris Benson	.10
340	George Lombard	.10
341	Troy Glaus	.75
342	Eddie Yarnell	.10
343	*Kip Wells*	.50
344	*C.C. Sabathia*	1.00
345	*Sean Burroughs*	1.00
346	*Felipe Lopez*	1.50
347	*Ryan Rupe*	.25
348	*Orber Moreno*	.25
349	*Rafael Roque*	.25
350	*Alfonso Soriano*	6.00
351	Pablo Ozuna	.10
352	*Corey Patterson*	1.50
353	Braden Looper	.10
354	Robbie Bell	.10
355	*Mark Mulder*	3.00
356	Angel Pena	.10
357	Kevin McGlinchy	.10
358	*Michael Restovich*	.50
359	Eric DuBose	.10
360	Geoff Jenkins	.10
361	*Mark Harriger*	.25
362	*Junior Herndon*	.25
363	*Tim Raines Jr.*	.25
364	*Rafael Furcal*	.75
365	*Marcus Giles*	1.00
366	Ted Lilly	.10
367	*Jorge Toca*	.50
368	*David Kelton*	.50
369	*Adam Dunn*	5.00
370	*Guillermo Mota*	.50
371	*Brett Laxton*	.25
372	*Travis Harper*	.25
373	*Tom Davey*	.25
374	*Darren Blakely*	.50
375	*Tim Hudson*	3.00
376	Jason Romano	.10
377	Dan Reichert	.10
378	*Julio Lugo*	.50
379	*Jose Garcia*	.25
380	*Erubiel Durazo*	.75
381	Jose Jimenez	.10
382	Chris Fussell	.10
383	Steve Lomasney	.10
384	*Juan Pena*	.50
385	*Allen Levrault*	.25
386	*Juan Rivera*	.50
387	*Steve Colyer*	.25
388	*Joe Nathan*	.50
389	*Ron Walker*	.10
390	Nick Bierbrodt	.10
391	*Luke Prokopec*	.50
392	*Dave Roberts*	.50
393	Mike Darr	.10
394	*Abraham Nunez*	.50

395	*Giuseppe Chiaramonte*	.25
396	*Jermaine Van Buren*	.50
397	Mike Kusiewicz	.10
398	*Matt Wise*	.25
399	*Joe McEwing*	.50
400	*Matt Holliday*	.75
401	*Willi Mo Pena*	2.50
402	*Ruben Quevedo*	.25
403	*Rob Ryan*	.25
404	*Freddy Garcia*	1.00
405	*Kevin Eberwein*	.25
406	*Jesus Colome*	.50
407	*Chris Singleton*	.25
408	*Bubba Crosby*	.50
409	*Jesus Cordero*	.25
410	Donny Leon	.10
411	*Goefrey Tomlinson*	.25
412	*Jeff Winchester*	.25
413	*Adam Piatt*	.50
414	Robert Stratton	.10
415	T.J. Tucker	.10
416	*Ryan Langerhans*	.25
417	*Anthony Shumaker*	.25
418	*Matt Miller*	.25
419	*Doug Clark*	.25
420	*Kory DeHaan*	.25
421	*David Eckstein*	.50
422	*Brian Cooper*	.50
423	*Brady Clark*	1.00
424	*Chris Magruder*	.25
425	*Bobby Seay*	.25
426	*Aubrey Huff*	1.00
427	Mike Jerzembeck	.10
428	*Matt Blank*	.50
429	*Benny Agbayani*	.50
430	*Kevin Beirne*	.25
431	*Josh Hamilton*	.50
432	*Josh Girdley*	.50
433	*Kyle Snyder*	.25
434	*Mike Paradis*	.25
435	*Jason Jennings*	.50
436	*David Walling*	.40
437	*Omar Ortiz*	.25
438	*Jay Gehrke*	.25
439	*Casey Burns*	.25
440	*Carl Crawford*	1.50

International

	NM/M
Complete Set (440):	150.00
Common Player:	.25
Int'l Stars:	1.5X

(See 1999 Bowman for checklist and base card values.)

Gold

	NM/M
Common Player:	3.00
Gold Stars:	10X

(See 1999 Bowman for checklist and base card values.)

Autographs

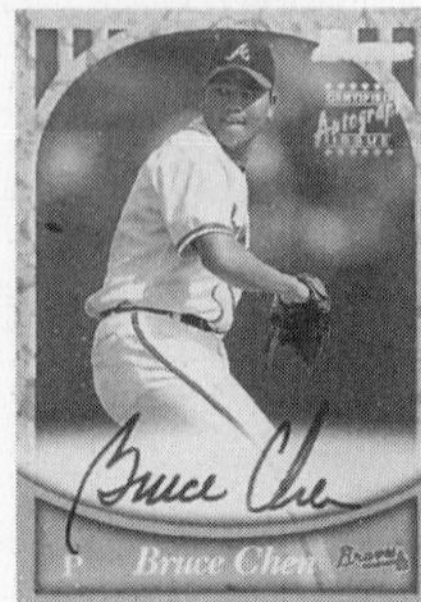

		NM/M
Common Player:		3.00
Blues inserted 1:162 or 1:85		
Silvers inserted 1:485 or 1:256		
Golds inserted 1:1954 or 1:1024		
1	Ruben Mateo B	5.00
2	Troy Glaus G	40.00
3	Ben Davis G	8.00
4	Jayson Werth B	5.00
5	Jerry Hairston Jr. S	6.00
6	Darnell McDonald B	4.00
7	Calvin Pickering S	8.00
8	Ryan Minor S	4.00
9	Alex Escobar B	6.00
10	Grant Roberts B	5.00
11	Carlos Guillen B	10.00
12	Ryan Anderson S	6.00
13	Gil Meche S	5.00
14	Russell Branyan S	5.00
15	Alex Ramirez S	5.00
16	Jason Rakers S	5.00
17	Eddie Yarnall B	5.00
18	Freddy Garcia B	20.00
19	Jason Conti B	3.00
20	Corey Koskie B	5.00
21	Roosevelt Brown B	5.00
22	Willie Martinez B	3.00
23	Mike Jerzembeck B	3.00
24	Lariel Gonzalez B	3.00
25	Fernando Seguignol B	3.00
26	Robert Fick S	5.00
27	J.D. Smart B	3.00
28	Ryan Mills B	3.00
29	Chad Hermansen G	6.00
30	Jason Grilli B	5.00
31	Michael Cuddyer B	5.00
32	Jacque Jones S	10.00
33	Reggie Taylor B	3.00
34	Richie Sexson G	15.00
35	Michael Barrett B	8.00
36	Paul LoDuca B	8.00
37	Adrian Beltre G	30.00
38	Peter Bergeron B	4.00
39	Joe Fontenot B	3.00
40	Randy Wolf B	6.00
41	Nick Johnson B	8.00
42	Ryan Bradley B	4.00
43	Mike Lowell S	10.00
44	Ricky Ledee B	5.00
45	Mike Lincoln S	4.00
46	Jeremy Giambi B	5.00
47	Dermal Brown S	3.00
48	Derrick Gibson B	3.00
49	Scott Randall B	3.00
50	Ben Petrick S	5.00
51	Jason LaRue B	3.00
52	Cole Liniak B	3.00
53	John Curtice B	3.00
54	Jackie Rexrode B	3.00
55	John Patterson B	4.00
56	Brad Penny S	6.00
57	Jared Sandberg B	6.00
58	Kerry Wood G	30.00
59	Eli Marrero B	5.00
60	Jason Marquis B	8.00
61	George Lombard S	5.00
62	Bruce Chen S	3.00
63	Kevin Witt S	4.00
64	Vernon Wells B	10.00
65	Billy Koch B	3.00
66	Roy Halladay B	20.00
67	Nathan Haynes B	3.00
68	Ben Grieve G	8.00
69	Eric Chavez G	10.00
70	Lance Berkman S	15.00

Early Risers

		NM/M
Complete Set (11):		9.00
Common Player:		.25
Inserted 1:12		
1	Mike Piazza	1.00
2	Cal Ripken Jr.	2.00
3	Jeff Bagwell	.50
4	Ben Grieve	.35
5	Kerry Wood	.50
6	Mark McGwire	1.50
7	Nomar Garciaparra	1.00
8	Derek Jeter	2.00
9	Scott Rolen	.50
10	Jose Canseco	.45
11	Raul Mondesi	.25

Late Bloomers

		NM/M
Complete Set (10):		4.00
Common Player:		.25
Inserted 1:12		
LB1	Mike Piazza	2.00
LB2	Jim Thome	.25
LB3	Larry Walker	.25
LB4	Vinny Castilla	.25
LB5	Andy Pettitte	.75
LB6	Jim Edmonds	.50
LB7	Kenny Lofton	.25
LB8	John Smoltz	.25
LB9	Mark Grace	.50
LB10	Trevor Hoffman	.25

Scout's Choice

		NM/M
Complete Set (21):		12.00
Common Player:		.40
Inserted 1:12		
SC1	Ruben Mateo	.40
SC2	Ryan Anderson	.40
SC3	Pat Burrell	3.00
SC4	Troy Glaus	4.00
SC5	Eric Chavez	1.00
SC6	Adrian Beltre	1.00
SC7	Bruce Chen	.40
SC8	Carlos Beltran	1.00
SC9	Alex Gonzalez	.40
SC10	Carlos Lee	.40
SC11	George Lombard	.40
SC12	Matt Clement	.40
SC13	Calvin Pickering	.40
SC14	Marlon Anderson	.40
SC15	Chad Hermansen	.40
SC16	Russell Branyan	.40
SC17	Jeremy Giambi	.40
SC18	Ricky Ledee	.40
SC19	John Patterson	.40
SC20	Roy Halladay	.75
SC21	Michael Barrett	.40

2000 ROOKIE OF THE YEAR

		NM/M
Complete Set (10):		7.00
Common Player:		.50
Inserted 1:12		
1	Ryan Anderson	.50
2	Pat Burrell	2.50
3	A.J. Burnett	.50
4	Ruben Mateo	.50
5	Alex Escobar	.50
6	Pablo Ozuna	.50
7	Mark Mulder	1.00
8	Corey Patterson	1.50
9	George Lombard	.50
10	Nick Johnson	1.00

1999 BOWMAN CHROME

		NM/M
Complete Set (440):		250.00
Complete Series 1 (220):		75.00
Complete Series 2 (220):		175.00
Common Player:		.25
Series 1 Pack (4):		4.00
Series 1 Wax Box (24):		80.00
Series 2 Pack (4):		6.00
Series 2 Wax Box (24):		120.00
1	Ben Grieve	.25
2	Kerry Wood	.75
3	Ruben Rivera	.25
4	Sandy Alomar	.25
5	Cal Ripken Jr.	3.00
6	Mark McGwire	2.50
7	Vladimir Guerrero	1.00
8	Moises Alou	.25
9	Jim Edmonds	.50
10	Greg Maddux	1.50
11	Gary Sheffield	.50
12	John Valentin	.25
13	Chuck Knoblauch	.25
14	Tony Clark	.25
15	Rusty Greer	.25
16	Al Leiter	.25
17	Travis Lee	.25
18	Jose Cruz Jr.	.25
19	Pedro Martinez	1.00
20	Paul O'Neill	.25
21	Todd Walker	.25
22	Vinny Castilla	.25
23	Barry Larkin	.25
24	Curt Schilling	.50
25	Jason Kendall	.25
26	Scott Erickson	.25
27	Andres Galarraga	.25
28	Jeff Shaw	.25
29	John Olerud	.25
30	Orlando Hernandez	.40
31	Larry Walker	.25
32	Andruw Jones	1.00
33	Jeff Cirillo	.25
34	Barry Bonds	3.00
35	Manny Ramirez	1.00
36	Mark Kotsay	.25
37	Ivan Rodriguez	.75
38	Jeff King	.25
39	Brian Hunter	.25
40	Ray Durham	.25
41	Bernie Williams	.50
42	Darin Erstad	.60
43	Chipper Jones	1.50
44	Pat Hentgen	.25
45	Eric Young	.25
46	Jaret Wright	.25
47	Juan Guzman	.25
48	Jorge Posada	.50
49	Bobby Higginson	.25
50	Jose Guillen	.25
51	Trevor Hoffman	.25
52	Ken Griffey Jr.	2.00
53	David Justice	.25
54	Matt Williams	.25
55	Eric Karros	.25
56	Derek Bell	.25
57	Ray Lankford	.25
58	Mariano Rivera	.40
59	Brett Tomko	.25
60	Mike Mussina	.75
61	Kenny Lofton	.25
62	Chuck Finley	.25
63	Alex Gonzalez	.25
64	Mark Grace	.40
65	Raul Mondesi	.25
66	David Cone	.25
67	Brad Fullmer	.25
68	Andy Benes	.25

69 John Smoltz .25
70 Shane Reynolds .25
71 Bruce Chen .25
72 Adam Kennedy .25
73 Jack Cust .25
74 Matt Clement .25
75 Derrick Gibson .25
76 Darnell McDonald .25
77 *Adam Everett* .75
78 Ricardo Aramboles .25
79 *Mark Quinn* .75
80 Jason Rakers .25
81 *Seth Etherton* .50
82 *Jeff Urban* .50
83 Manny Aybar .25
84 *Mike Nannini* .50
85 Onan Masaoka .25
86 Rod Barajas .25
87 Mike Frank .25
88 Scott Randall .25
89 *Justin Bowles* .50
90 Chris Haas .25
91 *Arturo McDowell* .50
92 *Matt Belisle* .50
93 Scott Elarton .25
94 Vernon Wells .40
95 Pat Cline .25
96 Ryan Anderson .25
97 Kevin Barker .25
98 Ruben Mateo .25
99 Robert Fick .25
100 Corey Koskie .25
101 Ricky Ledee .25
102 *Rick Elder* .50
103 *Jack Cressend* .50
104 Joe Lawrence .25
105 Mike Lincoln .25
106 *Kit Pellow* .50
107 *Matt Burch* .50
108 Brent Butler .25
109 Jason Dewey .25
110 Cesar King .25
111 Julio Ramirez .25
112 Jake Westbrook .25
113 *Eric Valent* 1.00
114 *Roosevelt Brown* .50
115 *Choo Freeman* 2.00
116 Juan Melo .25
117 Jason Grilli .25
118 Jared Sandberg .25
119 Glenn Davis .25
120 *David Riske* .50
121 Jacque Jones .25
122 Corey Lee .25
123 Michael Barrett .25
124 Lariel Gonzalez .25
125 Mitch Meluskey .25
126 *Freddy Garcia* .25
127 *Tony Torcato* .50
128 Jeff Liefer .25
129 Ntema Ndungidi .25
130 *Andy Brown* .50
131 *Ryan Mills* .50
132 *Andy Abad* .75
133 Carlos Febles .25
134 *Jason Tyner* .75
135 Mark Osborne .25
136 *Phil Norton* .50
137 Nathan Haynes .25
138 Roy Halladay .50
139 Juan Encarnacion .25
140 Brad Penny .25
141 Grant Roberts .25
142 Aramis Ramirez .40
143 Cristian Guzman .25
144 *Mamon Tucker* .50
145 Ryan Bradley .25
146 Brian Simmons .25
147 Dan Reichert .25
148 Russ Branyon .25
149 *Victor Valencia* .50
150 Scott Schoeneweis .25
151 *Sean Spencer* .50
152 Odalis Perez .25
153 Joe Fontenot .25
154 Milton Bradley .25
155 *Josh McKinley* .50
156 Terrence Long .25
157 Danny Klassen .25
158 *Paul Hoover* .50
159 Ron Belliard .25
160 Armando Rios .25
161 Ramon Hernandez .25
162 Jason Conti .25
163 Chad Hermansen .25
164 Jason Standridge .25
165 Jason Dellaero .25
166 John Curtice .25
167 *Clayton Andrews* .50
168 Jeremy Giambi .25
169 Alex Ramirez .25
170 *Gabe Molina* .50
171 *Mario Encarnacion* .50
172 *Mike Zywica* .25
173 *Chip Ambres* .75
174 Trot Nixon .25
175 *Pat Burrell* 10.00
176 Jeff Yoder .25
177 *Chris Jones* .50
178 Kevin Witt .25
179 *Keith Luuloa* .50
180 Billy Koch .25
181 *Damaso Marte* .50
182 *Ryan Glynn* .50
183 Calvin Pickering .25
184 Michael Cuddyer .25
185 *Nick Johnson* 6.00
186 *Doug Mientkiewicz* 4.00
187 *Nate Cornejo* 1.00
188 Octavio Dotel .25
189 Wes Helms .25
190 Nelson Lara .25
191 *Chuck Abbott* .50
192 Tony Armas Jr. .25
193 Gil Meche .25
194 Ben Petrick .25
195 *Chris George* .75
196 *Scott Hunter* .50
197 Ryan Brannan .25
198 *Amaury Garcia* .50
199 Chris Gissell .25
200 *Austin Kearns* 4.00
201 Alex Gonzalez .25
202 Wade Miller .25
203 Scott Williamson .25
204 Chris Enochs .25
205 Fernando Seguignol .25
206 Marlon Anderson .25
207 *Todd Sears* .50
208 *Nate Bump* .50
209 *J.M. Gold* .50
210 *Matt LeCroy* .25
211 Alex Hernandez .25
212 Luis Rivera .25
213 Troy Cameron .25
214 *Alex Escobar* 1.00
215 Jason LaRue .25
216 Kyle Peterson .25
217 Brent Butler .25
218 Dernell Stenson .25
219 Adrian Beltre .50
220 Daryle Ward .25
221 Jim Thome .75
222 Cliff Floyd .25
223 Rickey Henderson 1.00
224 Garret Anderson .25
225 Ken Caminiti .25
226 Bret Boone .25
227 Jeromy Burnitz .25
228 Steve Finley .25
229 Miguel Tejada .50
230 Greg Vaughn .25
231 Jose Offerman .25
232 Andy Ashby .25
233 Albert Belle .25
234 Fernando Tatis .25
235 Todd Helton 1.00
236 Sean Casey .50
237 Brian Giles .25
238 Andy Pettitte .50
239 Fred McGriff .25
240 Roberto Alomar .50
241 Edgar Martinez .25
242 Lee Stevens .25
243 Shawn Green .40
244 Ryan Klesko .25
245 Sammy Sosa 2.00
246 Todd Hundley .25
247 Shannon Stewart .35
248 Randy Johnson 1.00
249 Rondell White .25
250 Mike Piazza 2.00
251 Craig Biggio .25
252 David Wells .25
253 Brian Jordan .25
254 Edgar Renteria .25
255 Bartolo Colon .25
256 Frank Thomas 1.00
257 Will Clark .35
258 Dean Palmer .25
259 Dmitri Young .25
260 Scott Rolen 1.00
261 Jeff Kent .25
262 Dante Bichette .25
263 Nomar Garciaparra 2.00
264 Tony Gwynn 1.50
265 Alex Rodriguez 2.00
266 Jose Canseco .40
267 Jason Giambi .75
268 Jeff Bagwell 1.00
269 Carlos Delgado .75
270 Tom Glavine .50
271 Eric Davis .25
272 Edgardo Alfonzo .25
273 Tim Salmon .40
274 Johnny Damon .50
275 Rafael Palmeiro 1.00
276 Denny Neagle .25
277 Neifi Perez .25
278 Roger Clemens 1.75
279 Brant Brown .25
280 Kevin Brown .40
281 Jay Bell .25
282 Jay Buhner .25
283 Matt Lawton .25
284 Robin Ventura .25
285 Juan Gonzalez 1.00
286 Mo Vaughn .25
287 Kevin Millwood .25
288 Tino Martinez .25
289 Justin Thompson .25
290 Derek Jeter 3.00
291 Ben Davis .25
292 Mike Lowell .25
293 *Joe Crede* 2.00
294 *Micah Bowie* .50
295 Lance Berkman .25
296 Jason Marquis .25
297 Chad Green .25
298 Dee Brown .25
299 Jerry Hairston Jr. .25
300 Gabe Kapler .35
301 *Brent Stentz* .50
302 *Scott Mullen* .50
303 Brandon Reed .25
304 *Shea Hillenbrand* 2.50
305 *J.D. Closser* 1.00
306 Gary Matthews Jr. .25
307 *Toby Hall* 1.00
308 *Jason Phillips* .50
309 *Jose Macias* .50
310 *Jung Bong* .50
311 *Ramon Soler* .50
312 *Kelly Dransfeldt* .75
313 *Carlos Hernandez* .50
314 Kevin Haverbusch .25
315 *Aaron Myette* .75
316 *Chad Harville* .75
317 *Kyle Farnsworth* 1.00
318 *Travis Dawkins* .75
319 Willie Martinez .25
320 Carlos Lee .25
321 *Carlos Pena* 3.00
322 *Peter Bergeron* .75
323 *A.J. Burnett* 4.00
324 *Bucky Jacobsen* 2.00
325 *Mo Bruce* .50
326 Reggie Taylor .25
327 Jackie Rexrode .25
328 *Alvin Morrow* .50
329 Carlos Beltran 1.00
330 Eric Chavez .50
331 John Patterson .25
332 Jayson Werth .25
333 Richie Sexson .50
334 Randy Wolf .25
335 Eli Marrero .25
336 Paul LoDuca .25
337 J.D. Smart .25
338 Ryan Minor .25
339 Kris Benson .25
340 George Lombard .25
341 Troy Glaus 1.00
342 Eddie Yarnell .25
343 *Kip Wells* 1.00
344 *C.C. Sabathia* 3.00
345 *Sean Burroughs* 5.00
346 *Felipe Lopez* 5.00
347 *Ryan Rupe* .75
348 *Orber Moreno* .50
349 *Rafael Roque* .50
350 *Alfonso Soriano* 25.00
351 Pablo Ozuna .25
352 *Corey Patterson* 4.00
353 Braden Looper .25
354 Robbie Bell .25
355 *Mark Mulder* 10.00
356 Angel Pena .25
357 Kevin McGlinchy .25
358 *Michael Restovich* 3.00
359 Eric DuBose .25
360 Geoff Jenkins .25
361 *Mark Harriger* .50
362 *Junior Herndon* .50
363 *Tim Raines Jr.* .50
364 *Rafael Furcal* 4.00
365 *Marcus Giles* 4.00
366 Ted Lilly .25
367 *Jorge Toca* .75
368 *David Kelton* 2.50
369 *Adam Dunn* 25.00
370 *Guillermo Mota* .50
371 *Brett Laxton* .50
372 *Travis Harper* .50
373 *Tom Davey* .50
374 *Darren Blakely* .50
375 *Tim Hudson* 12.00
376 Jason Romano .25
377 Dan Reichert .25
378 *Julio Lugo* 1.00
379 *Jose Garcia* .50
380 *Erubiel Durazo* 3.00
381 Jose Jimenez .25
382 Chris Fussell .25
383 Steve Lomasney .25
384 *Juan Pena* .75
385 *Allen Levrault* .75
386 *Juan Rivera* 1.00
387 *Steve Colyer* .50
388 *Joe Nathan* 1.50
389 *Ron Walker* .50
390 Nick Bierbrodt .25
391 *Luke Prokopec* .50
392 *Dave Roberts* 1.00
393 Mike Darr .25
394 *Abraham Nunez* 1.00
395 *Giuseppe Chiaramonte* 1.00
396 *Jermaine Van Buren* 1.00
397 Mike Kusiewicz .25
398 *Matt Wise* .50
399 *Joe McEwing* .50
400 *Matt Holliday* 4.00
401 *Willi Mo Pena* 8.00
402 *Ruben Quevedo* .50
403 *Rob Ryan* .50
404 *Freddy Garcia* 4.00
405 *Kevin Eberwein* .50
406 *Jesus Colome* 1.00
407 *Chris Singleton* .50
408 *Bubba Crosby* 2.00
409 *Jesus Cordero* .50
410 Donny Leon .25
411 *Goefrey Tomlinson* .25
412 *Jeff Winchester* .50
413 *Adam Piatt* .75
414 Robert Stratton .25
415 T.J. Tucker .25
416 *Ryan Langerhans* 2.00
417 *Chris Wakeland* .50
418 *Matt Miller* .50
419 *Doug Clark* .50
420 *Kory DeHaan* .25
421 *David Eckstein* 2.00
422 *Brian Cooper* .50
423 *Brady Clark* 2.50
424 *Chris Magruder* .50
425 *Bobby Seay* .50
426 *Aubrey Huff* 8.00
427 Mike Jerzembeck .25
428 *Matt Blank* .50
429 *Benny Agbayani* .50
430 *Kevin Beirne* .25
431 *Josh Hamilton* .25
432 *Josh Girdley* .50
433 *Kyle Snyder* .25
434 *Mike Paradis* .50
435 *Jason Jennings* 1.00
436 *David Walling* .50
437 *Omar Ortiz* .50
438 *Jay Gehrke* .50
439 *Casey Burns* .50
440 *Carl Crawford* 6.00

Gold

	NM/M
Complete Set (440):	1,000
Complete Series 1 (220):	400.00
Complete Series 2 (220):	650.00
Common Player, Series 1:	1.50
Common Player, Series 2:	2.00
Stars:	3X
Gold Refractors:	30X

(See 1999 Bowman Chrome for checklist and base card values.)

Refractors

	NM/M
Common Player:	1.00
Refractor Stars:	5X

(See 1999 Bowman Chrome for checklist and base card values.)

International

	NM/M
Complete Set (440):	600.00

	NM/M
Complete Series 1 (220):	200.00
Complete Series 2 (220):	400.00
Common Player, Series 1:	.25
Common Player, Series 2:	.50
Stars:	1.5X
Common Refractor:	5.00
Refractors:	12X

(See 1999 Bowman Chrome for checklist and base card values.)

Diamond Aces

		NM/M
Complete Set (18):		24.00
Common Player:		.50
Inserted 1:21		
Refractors:		1.5X
Inserted 1:84		
DA1	Troy Glaus	1.50
DA2	Eric Chavez	.75
DA3	Fernando Seguignol	.50
DA4	Ryan Anderson	.50
DA5	Ruben Mateo	.50
DA6	Carlos Beltran	1.00
DA7	Adrian Beltre	.75
DA8	Bruce Chen	.50
DA9	Pat Burrell	2.00
DA10	Mike Piazza	3.00
DA11	Ken Griffey Jr.	3.00
DA12	Chipper Jones	2.00
DA13	Derek Jeter	4.00
DA14	Mark McGwire	3.50
DA15	Nomar Garciaparra	3.00
DA16	Sammy Sosa	3.00
DA17	Juan Gonzalez	1.00
DA18	Alex Rodriguez	3.50

Early Impact

		NM/M
Complete Set (20):		37.50
Common Player:		.75
Inserted 1:15		
Refractor:		1.5X
Inserted 1:75		
1	Alfonso Soriano	3.00
2	Pat Burrell	2.00
3	Ruben Mateo	.75
4	A.J. Burnett	.75
5	Corey Patterson	2.00
6	Daryle Ward	.75
7	Eric Chavez	1.00
8	Troy Glaus	2.00
9	Sean Casey	1.00
10	Joe McEwing	.75
11	Gabe Kapler	.75
12	Michael Barrett	.75
13	Sammy Sosa	3.00
14	Alex Rodriguez	4.00
15	Mark McGwire	4.00
16	Derek Jeter	5.00
17	Nomar Garciaparra	3.00
18	Mike Piazza	3.00
19	Chipper Jones	2.50
20	Ken Griffey Jr.	3.00

Scout's Choice

		NM/M
Complete Set (21):		20.00
Common Player:		.75
Inserted 1:12		
Refractors:		1.5X
Inserted 1:48		
SC1	Ruben Mateo	.75
SC2	Ryan Anderson	1.00
SC3	Pat Burrell	3.00
SC4	Troy Glaus	4.00
SC5	Eric Chavez	2.00
SC6	Adrian Beltre	1.50
SC7	Bruce Chen	.75
SC8	Carlos Beltran	2.50
SC9	Alex Gonzalez	.75
SC10	Carlos Lee	.75
SC11	George Lombard	.75
SC12	Matt Clement	.75
SC13	Calvin Pickering	.75
SC14	Marlon Anderson	.75
SC15	Chad Hermansen	.75
SC16	Russell Branyan	.75
SC17	Jeremy Giambi	.75
SC18	Ricky Ledee	.75
SC19	John Patterson	.75
SC20	Roy Halladay	1.00
SC21	Michael Barrett	.75

2000 Rookie of the Year

		NM/M
Complete Set (10):		12.00
Common Player:		1.00
Inserted 1:20		
Refractors:		1.5-3X
Inserted 1:100		
1	Ryan Anderson	1.00
2	Pat Burrell	4.00
3	A.J. Burnett	1.00
4	Ruben Mateo	1.00
5	Alex Escobar	1.00
6	Pablo Ozuna	1.00
7	Mark Mulder	1.50
8	Corey Patterson	2.50
9	George Lombard	1.00
10	Nick Johnson	2.00

1999 BOWMAN'S BEST

		NM/M
Complete Set (200):		40.00
Common Player:		.25
Pack (6):		2.50
Wax Box (24):		50.00
1	Chipper Jones	1.50
2	Brian Jordan	.25
3	David Justice	.25
4	Jason Kendall	.25
5	Mo Vaughn	.25
6	Jim Edmonds	.25
7	Wade Boggs	1.50
8	Jeromy Burnitz	.25
9	Todd Hundley	.25
10	Rondell White	.25
11	Cliff Floyd	.25
12	Sean Casey	.40
13	Bernie Williams	.50
14	Dante Bichette	.25
15	Greg Vaughn	.25
16	Andres Galarraga	.25
17	Ray Durham	.25
18	Jim Thome	.25
19	Gary Sheffield	.45
20	Frank Thomas	1.00
21	Orlando Hernandez	.35
22	Ivan Rodriguez	.75
23	Jose Cruz Jr.	.20
24	Jason Giambi	.65
25	Craig Biggio	.25
26	Kerry Wood	.60
27	Manny Ramirez	1.00
28	Curt Schilling	.40
29	Mike Mussina	.65
30	Tim Salmon	.35
31	Mike Piazza	2.00
32	Roberto Alomar	.50
33	Larry Walker	.25
34	Barry Larkin	.25
35	Nomar Garciaparra	2.00
36	Paul O'Neill	.25
37	Todd Walker	.25
38	Eric Karros	.25
39	Brad Fullmer	.25
40	John Olerud	.25
41	Todd Helton	1.00
42	Raul Mondesi	.25
43	Jose Canseco	.50
44	Matt Williams	.25
45	Ray Lankford	.25
46	Carlos Delgado	.65
47	Darin Erstad	.75
48	Vladimir Guerrero	1.00
49	Robin Ventura	.25
50	Alex Rodriguez	2.50
51	Vinny Castilla	.25
52	Tony Clark	.25
53	Pedro Martinez	.75
54	Rafael Palmeiro	.75
55	Scott Rolen	.75
56	Tino Martinez	.25
57	Tony Gwynn	1.50
58	Barry Bonds	3.00
59	Kenny Lofton	.25
60	Javy Lopez	.25
61	Mark Grace	.35
62	Travis Lee	.25
63	Kevin Brown	.35
64	Al Leiter	.25
65	Albert Belle	.35
66	Sammy Sosa	2.00
67	Greg Maddux	1.50
68	Mark Kotsay	.25
69	Dmitri Young	.25
70	Mark McGwire	2.50
71	Juan Gonzalez	1.00
72	Andruw Jones	1.00
73	Derek Jeter	3.00
74	Randy Johnson	.75
75	Cal Ripken Jr.	3.00
76	Shawn Green	.35
77	Moises Alou	.25
78	Tom Glavine	.45
79	Sandy Alomar	.25
80	Ken Griffey Jr.	2.00
81	Ryan Klesko	.25
82	Jeff Bagwell	1.00
83	Ben Grieve	.35
84	John Smoltz	.25
85	Roger Clemens	1.75
86	Ken Griffey Jr.	1.00
87	Roger Clemens	.75
88	Derek Jeter	1.50
89	Nomar Garciaparra	1.00
90	Mark McGwire	1.25
91	Sammy Sosa	1.00
92	Alex Rodriguez	1.25
93	Greg Maddux	.75
94	Vladimir Guerrero	.50
95	Chipper Jones	.75
96	Kerry Wood	.30
97	Ben Grieve	.25
98	Tony Gwynn	.75
99	Juan Gonzalez	.50
100	Mike Piazza	1.00
101	Eric Chavez	.40
102	Billy Koch	.25
103	Dernell Stenson	.25
104	Marlon Anderson	.25
105	Ron Belliard	.25
106	Bruce Chen	.25
107	Carlos Beltran	.25
108	Chad Hermansen	.25
109	Ryan Anderson	.25
110	Michael Barrett	.25
111	Matt Clement	.25
112	Ben Davis	.25
113	Calvin Pickering	.25
114	Brad Penny	.25
115	Paul Konerko	.35
116	Alex Gonzalez	.25
117	George Lombard	.25
118	John Patterson	.25
119	Rob Bell	.25
120	Ruben Mateo	.25
121	Troy Glaus	1.00
122	Ryan Bradley	.25
123	Carlos Lee	.25
124	Gabe Kapler	.25
125	Ramon Hernandez	.25
126	Carlos Febles	.25
127	Mitch Meluskey	.25
128	Michael Cuddyer	.25
129	Pablo Ozuna	.25
130	Jayson Werth	.25
131	Ricky Ledee	.25
132	Jeremy Giambi	.25
133	Danny Klassen	.25
134	Mark DeRosa	.25
135	Randy Wolf	.25
136	Roy Halladay	.35
137	Derrick Gibson	.25
138	Ben Petrick	.25
139	Warren Morris	.25
140	Lance Berkman	.25
141	Russell Branyan	.25
142	Adrian Beltre	.60
143	Juan Encarnacion	.25
144	Fernando Seguignol	.25
145	Corey Koskie	.25
146	Preston Wilson	.25
147	Homer Bush	.25
148	Daryle Ward	.25
149	*Joe McEwing*	.50
150	*Peter Bergeron*	1.00
151	*Pat Burrell*	4.00
152	*Choo Freeman*	.75
153	*Matt Belisle*	.50
154	*Carlos Pena*	1.00
155	*A.J. Burnett*	.75
156	*Doug Mientkiewicz*	1.00
157	*Sean Burroughs*	1.50
158	*Mike Zywica*	.50
159	*Corey Patterson*	2.00
160	*Austin Kearns*	2.00
161	*Chip Ambres*	.50
162	*Kelly Dransfeldt*	.50
163	*Mike Nannini*	.75
164	*Mark Mulder*	4.00
165	*Jason Tyner*	.50
166	*Bobby Seay*	.50
167	*Alex Escobar*	1.00
168	*Nick Johnson*	1.00
169	*Alfonso Soriano*	6.00
170	*Clayton Andrews*	.25
171	*C.C. Sabathia*	1.00
172	*Matt Holliday*	1.00
173	*Brad Lidge*	.75
174	*Kit Pellow*	.75
175	*J.M. Gold*	.50
176	*Roosevelt Brown*	.50
177	*Eric Valent*	.75
178	*Adam Everett*	1.00
179	*Jorge Toca*	.50
180	*Matt Roney*	.50
181	*Andy Brown*	.50
182	*Phil Norton*	.50
183	*Mickey Lopez*	.50
184	*Chris George*	.50
185	*Arturo McDowell*	.50
186	*Jose Fernandez*	.25
187	*Seth Etherton*	.50
188	*Josh McKinley*	.50
189	*Nate Cornejo*	.50
190	*Giuseppe Chiaramonte*	.50
191	*Mamon Tucker*	.50
192	*Ryan Mills*	.50
193	*Chad Moeller*	.50
194	*Tony Torcato*	.50
195	*Jeff Winchester*	.50
196	*Rick Elder*	.50
197	*Matt Burch*	.50
198	*Jeff Urban*	.50
199	*Chris Jones*	.50
200	*Masao Kida*	.50

Atomic Refractors

	NM/M
Common Player:	3.00
Stars:	15X

(See 1999 Bowman's Best for checklist and base card values.)

Refractors

	NM/M
Complete Set (200):	450.00
Common Player:	1.00
Stars:	8X

(See 1999 Bowman's Best for checklist and base card values.)

Franchise Best

	NM/M
Complete Set (10):	15.00

Common Player: .75
Production 3,000 sets
Mach II (1,000): 1.5X
Mach III (500): 2.5X
1 Mark McGwire 2.25
2 Ken Griffey Jr. 1.50
3 Sammy Sosa 1.50
4 Nomar Garciaparra 1.50
5 Alex Rodriguez 2.25
6 Derek Jeter 3.00
7 Mike Piazza 1.50
8 Frank Thomas 1.00
9 Chipper Jones 1.25
10 Juan Gonzalez .75

Franchise Favorites

NM/M
Complete Set (6): 12.00
Common Player: .50
Inserted 1:75
1A Derek Jeter 5.00
1B Don Mattingly 2.00
1C Derek Jeter, Don Mattingly 5.00
2A Scott Rolen .50
2B Mike Schmidt 1.50
2C Scott Rolen, Mike Schmidt 1.00

Franchise Favorites Autographs

NM/M
Common Player: 15.00
Version A & B 1:1548
Version C 1:6191
1A Derek Jeter 125.00
1B Don Mattingly 80.00
1C Derek Jeter, Don Mattingly 300.00
2A Scott Rolen 25.00
2B Mike Schmidt 50.00
2C Scott Rolen, Mike Schmidt 125.00

Future Foundations

NM/M
Complete Set (10): 16.00
Common Player: .75
Production 3,000 sets
Mach II (1,000): 1.5X
Mach III (500): 2.5X
1 Ruben Mateo .75
2 Troy Glaus 4.50
3 Eric Chavez 1.50
4 Pat Burrell 3.50
5 Adrian Beltre 1.50
6 Ryan Anderson .75
7 Alfonso Soriano 3.50
8 Brad Penny .75
9 Derrick Gibson .75
10 Bruce Chen .75

Rookie of the Year

NM/M
Complete Set (2): 4.00
1 Ben Grieve 2.00
2 Kerry Wood 2.00
A1 Ben Grieve (autographed) 8.00

Rookie Locker Room Autographs

NM/M
Common Player: 6.00
Inserted 1:248
1 Pat Burrell 20.00
2 Michael Barrett 6.00
3 Troy Glaus 20.00
4 Gabe Kapler 6.00
5 Eric Chavez 10.00

Rookie Locker Room Game-Worn Jerseys

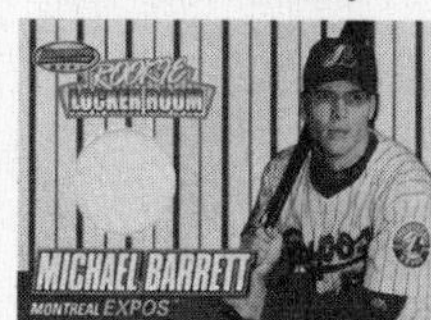

NM/M
Complete Set (4): 30.00
Common Player: 5.00
Inserted 1:270
1 Richie Sexson 8.00
2 Michael Barrett 5.00
3 Troy Glaus 20.00
4 Eric Chavez 10.00

Rookie Locker Room Game-Used Lumber

NM/M
Complete Set (6): 75.00
Common Player: 8.00
Inserted 1:258
1 Pat Burrell 15.00
2 Michael Barrett 8.00
3 Troy Glaus 30.00
4 Gabe Kapler 8.00
5 Eric Chavez 12.00
6 Richie Sexson 10.00

2000 BOWMAN

NM/M
Complete Set (440): 65.00
Common Player: .15
Common Rookie: .40
Pack (10): 2.50
Box (24): 40.00
1 Vladimir Guerrero 1.00
2 Chipper Jones 1.50
3 Todd Walker .15
4 Barry Larkin .25
5 Bernie Williams .40
6 Todd Helton 1.00
7 Jermaine Dye .15
8 Brian Giles .15
9 Freddy Garcia .15
10 Greg Vaughn .15
11 Alex Gonzalez .15
12 Luis Gonzalez .25
13 Ron Belliard .15
14 Ben Grieve .15
15 Carlos Delgado .50
16 Brian Jordan .15
17 Fernando Tatis .15
18 Ryan Rupe .15
19 Miguel Tejada .40
20 Mark Grace .30
21 Kenny Lofton .15
22 Eric Karros .15
23 Cliff Floyd .15
24 John Halama .15
25 Cristian Guzman .15
26 Scott Williamson .15
27 Mike Lieberthal .15
28 Tim Hudson .40
29 Warren Morris .15
30 Pedro Martinez 1.00
31 John Smoltz .15
32 Ray Durham .15
33 Chad Allen .15
34 Tony Clark .15
35 Tino Martinez .15
36 J.T. Snow Jr. .15
37 Kevin Brown .25
38 Bartolo Colon .15
39 Rey Ordonez .15
40 Jeff Bagwell 1.00
41 Ivan Rodriguez .60
42 Eric Chavez .25
43 Eric Milton .15
44 Jose Canseco .50
45 Shawn Green .50
46 Rich Aurilia .15
47 Roberto Alomar .40
48 Brian Daubach .15
49 Magglio Ordonez .25
50 Derek Jeter 3.00
51 Kris Benson .15
52 Albert Belle .15
53 Rondell White .15
54 Justin Thompson .15
55 Nomar Garciaparra 2.00
56 Chuck Finley .15
57 Omar Vizquel .15
58 Luis Castillo .15
59 Richard Hidalgo .15
60 Barry Bonds 3.00
61 Craig Biggio .15
62 Doug Glanville .15
63 Gabe Kapler .15
64 Johnny Damon .15
65 Pokey Reese .15
66 Andy Pettitte .25
67 B.J. Surhoff .15
68 Richie Sexson .40
69 Javy Lopez .15
70 Raul Mondesi .15
71 Darin Erstad .50
72 Kevin Millwood .15
73 Ricky Ledee .15
74 John Olerud .15
75 Sean Casey .25
76 Carlos Febles .15
77 Paul O'Neill .15
78 Bob Abreu .15
79 Neifi Perez .15
80 Tony Gwynn 1.50
81 Russ Ortiz .15
82 Matt Williams .15
83 Chris Carpenter .15
84 Roger Cedeno .15
85 Tim Salmon .30
86 Billy Koch .15
87 Jeromy Burnitz .15
88 Edgardo Alfonzo .15
89 Jay Bell .15
90 Manny Ramirez 1.00
91 Frank Thomas 1.00
92 Mike Mussina .50
93 J.D. Drew .25
94 Adrian Beltre .25
95 Alex Rodriguez 2.50
96 Larry Walker .15
97 Juan Encarnacion .15
98 Mike Sweeney .15
99 Rusty Greer .15
100 Randy Johnson 1.00
101 Jose Vidro .15
102 Preston Wilson .15
103 Greg Maddux 1.50
104 Jason Giambi .75
105 Cal Ripken Jr. 3.00
106 Carlos Beltran .50
107 Vinny Castilla .15
108 Mariano Rivera .25
109 Mo Vaughn .15
110 Rafael Palmeiro .75
111 Shannon Stewart .15
112 Mike Hampton .15
113 Joe Nathan .15
114 Ben Davis .15
115 Andruw Jones .75
116 Robin Ventura .15
117 Damion Easley .15
118 Jeff Cirillo .15
119 Kerry Wood .50
120 Scott Rolen .75
121 Sammy Sosa 2.00
122 Ken Griffey Jr. 2.00
123 Shane Reynolds .15
124 Troy Glaus 1.00
125 Tom Glavine .35
126 Michael Barrett .15
127 Al Leiter .15
128 Jason Kendall .15
129 Roger Clemens 2.00
130 Juan Gonzalez .50
131 Corey Koskie .15
132 Curt Schilling .50
133 Mike Piazza 2.00
134 Gary Sheffield .40
135 Jim Thome .40
136 Orlando Hernandez .25
137 Ray Lankford .15
138 Geoff Jenkins .15
139 Jose Lima .15
140 Mark McGwire 2.50
141 Adam Piatt .15
142 *Pat Manning* .40
143 *Marcos Castillo* .40
144 *Lesli Brea* .40
145 *Humberto Cota* .40
146 Ben Petrick .15
147 Kip Wells .15
148 Willi Mo Pena .25
149 Chris Wakeland .15
150 *Brad Baker* .50
151 *Robbie Morrison* .50
152 Reggie Taylor .15
153 *Brian Cole* .40
154 Peter Bergeron .15
155 Roosevelt Brown .15
156 *Matt Cepicky* .40
157 Ramon Castro .15
158 *Brad Baisley* .40
159 *Jeff Goldbach* .50
160 Mitch Meluskey .15
161 Chad Harville .15
162 Brian Cooper .15
163 Marcus Giles .15
164 Jim Morris .50
165 Geoff Goetz .15
166 *Bobby Bradley* .75
167 Rob Bell .15
168 Joe Crede .15
169 Michael Restovich .15
170 *Quincy Foster* .50
171 *Enrique Cruz* .50
172 Mark Quinn .15
173 Nick Johnson .15
174 Jeff Liefer .15
175 *Kevin Mench* .50
176 Steve Lomasney .15
177 Jayson Werth .15
178 Tim Drew .15
179 Chip Ambres .15
180 Ryan Anderson .15
181 Matt Blank .15
182 Giuseppe Chiaramonte .15
183 *Corey Myers* .50
184 Jeff Yoder .15
185 *Craig Dingman* .40
186 *Jon Hamilton* .40
187 Toby Hall .15
188 Russell Branyan .15
189 *Brian Falkenborg* .40
190 *Aaron Harang* .50
191 Juan Pena .15
192 *Travis Thompson* .40
193 Alfonso Soriano .50
194 *Alejandro Diaz* .40
195 Carlos Pena .15
196 Kevin Nicholson .15
197 Mo Bruce .15
198 C.C. Sabathia .15
199 Carl Crawford .15
200 Rafael Furcal .15
201 *Andrew Beinbrink* .40

No.	Player	Price
202	Jimmy Osting	.15
203	*Aaron McNeal*	.50
204	Brett Laxton	.15
205	Chris George	.15
206	Felipe Lopez	.15
207	*Ben Sheets*	3.00
208	*Mike Meyers*	.40
209	Jason Conti	.15
210	Milton Bradley	.15
211	*Chris Mears*	.40
212	*Carlos Hernandez*	.50
213	Jason Romano	.15
214	Goefrey Tomlinson	.15
215	Jimmy Rollins	.15
216	Pablo Ozuna	.15
217	Steve Cox	.15
218	Terrence Long	.15
219	*Jeff DaVanon*	.40
220	Rick Ankiel	.25
221	Jason Standridge	.15
222	Tony Armas	.15
223	Jason Tyner	.15
224	Ramon Ortiz	.15
225	Daryle Ward	.15
226	*Enger Veras*	.40
227	*Chris Jones*	.50
228	*Eric Cammack*	.40
229	Ruben Mateo	.15
230	*Ken Harvey*	1.00
231	Jake Westbrook	.15
232	*Rob Purvis*	.40
233	Choo Freeman	.15
234	Aramis Ramirez	.15
235	A.J. Burnett	.15
236	Kevin Barker	.15
237	*Chance Caple*	.50
238	Jarrod Washburn	.15
239	Lance Berkman	.15
240	*Michael Wenner*	.40
241	Alex Sanchez	.15
242	*Jake Esteves*	.40
243	Grant Roberts	.15
244	*Mark Ellis*	.50
245	Donny Leon	.15
246	David Eckstein	.15
247	*Dicky Gonzalez*	.40
248	John Patterson	.15
249	Chad Green	.15
250	*Scot Shields*	.40
251	Troy Cameron	.15
252	Jose Molina	.15
253	*Rob Pugmire*	.40
254	Rick Elder	.15
255	Sean Burroughs	.25
256	*Josh Kalinowski*	.40
257	Matt LeCroy	.15
258	*Alex Graman*	.50
259	*Tomokazu Ohka*	.50
260	Brady Clark	.15
261	*Rico Washington*	.40
262	Gary Matthews Jr.	.15
263	Matt Wise	.15
264	*Keith Reed*	.50
265	*Santiago Ramirez*	.40
266	*Ben Broussard*	.50
267	Ryan Langerhans	.15
268	Juan Rivera	.15
269	Shawn Gallagher	.15
270	Jorge Toca	.15
271	Brad Lidge	.15
272	*Leo Estrella*	.40
273	Ruben Quevedo	.15
274	Jack Cust	.15
275	T.J. Tucker	.15
276	Mike Colangelo	.15
277	Brian Schneider	.15
278	Calvin Murray	.15
279	Josh Girdley	.15
280	Mike Paradis	.15
281	Chad Hermansen	.15
282	*Ty Howington*	.50
283	Aaron Myette	.15
284	D'Angelo Jimenez	.15
285	Dernell Stenson	.15
286	Jerry Hairston Jr.	.15
287	*Gary Majewski*	.40
288	*Derrin Ebert*	.40
289	*Steve Fish*	.40
290	Carlos Hernandez	.15
291	Allen Levrault	.15
292	*Sean McNally*	.40
293	*Randey Dorame*	.40
294	*Wes Anderson*	.50
295	B.J. Ryan	.15
296	*Alan Webb*	.40
297	*Brandon Inge*	.75
298	David Walling	.15
299	*Sun-Woo Kim*	.40
300	Pat Burrell	.50
301	*Rick Guttormson*	.40
302	Gil Meche	.15
303	*Carlos Zambrano*	3.00
304	*Eric Byrnes* (photo actually Bo Porter)	1.00
305	*Robb Quinlan*	.40
306	Jackie Rexrode	.15
307	Nate Bump	.15
308	*Sean DePaula*	.40
309	Matt Riley	.15
310	Ryan Minor	.15
311	J.J. Davis	.15
312	Randy Wolf	.15
313	Jason Jennings	.15
314	*Scott Seabol*	.40
315	Doug Davis	.15
316	*Todd Moser*	.40
317	Rob Ryan	.15
318	Bubba Crosby	.15
319	*Lyle Overbay*	1.00
320	Mario Encarnacion	.15
321	*Francisco Rodriguez*	2.00
322	Michael Cuddyer	.15
323	Eddie Yarnall	.15
324	*Cesar Saba*	.40
325	Travis Dawkins	.15
326	Alex Escobar	.15
327	*Julio Zuleta*	.40
328	Josh Hamilton	.15
329	*Nick Neugebauer*	.40
330	Matt Belisle	.15
331	*Kurt Ainsworth*	.50
332	Tim Raines Jr.	.15
333	Eric Munson	.15
334	Donzell McDonald	.15
335	*Larry Bigbie*	.50
336	Matt Watson	.15
337	Aubrey Huff	.15
338	Julio Ramirez	.15
339	*Jason Grabowski*	.50
340	Jon Garland	.15
341	Austin Kearns	.50
342	Josh Pressley	.15
343	*Miguel Olivo*	.50
344	Julio Lugo	.15
345	Roberto Vaz	.15
346	Ramon Soler	.15
347	*Brandon Phillips*	.75
348	*Vince Faison*	.40
349	Mike Venafro	.15
350	*Rick Asadoorian*	.50
351	*B.J. Garbe*	.50
352	Dan Reichert	.15
353	*Jason Stumm*	.50
354	*Ruben Salazar*	.40
355	Francisco Cordero	.15
356	*Juan Guzman*	.40
357	*Mike Bacsik*	.40
358	Jared Sandberg	.15
359	Rod Barajas	.15
360	*Junior Brignac*	.40
361	J.M. Gold	.15
362	Octavio Dotel	.15
363	David Kelton	.15
364	*Scott Morgan*	.40
365	*Wascar Serrano*	.40
366	Wilton Veras	.15
367	Eugene Kingsale	.15
368	Ted Lilly	.15
369	George Lombard	.15
370	Chris Haas	.15
371	*Wilton Pena*	.50
372	Vernon Wells	.15
373	*Jason Royer*	.40
374	*Jeff Heaverlo*	.50
375	Calvin Pickering	.15
376	*Mike Lamb*	.40
377	Kyle Snyder	.15
378	*Javier Cardona*	.40
379	*Aaron Rowand*	1.00
380	Dee Brown	.15
381	*Brett Myers*	1.00
382	Abraham Nunez	.20
383	Eric Valent	.15
384	*Jody Gerut*	1.00
385	Adam Dunn	.50
386	Jay Gehrke	.15
387	Omar Ortiz	.15
388	Darnell McDonald	.15
389	Chad Alexander	.15
390	J.D. Closser	.15
391	*Ben Christensen*	.40
392	Adam Kennedy	.15
393	*Nick Green*	.40
394	Ramon Hernandez	.15
395	*Roy Oswalt*	4.00
396	*Andy Tracy*	.40
397	Eric Gagne	.15
398	*Michael Tejera*	.40
399	Adam Everett	.15
400	Corey Patterson	.25
401	*Gary Knotts*	.40
402	*Ryan Christianson*	.75
403	*Eric Ireland*	.40
404	*Andrew Good*	.40
405	Brad Penny	.15
406	Jason LaRue	.15
407	Kit Pellow	.15
408	Kevin Beirne	.15
409	Kelly Dransfeldt	.15
410	Jason Grilli	.15
411	*Scott Downs*	.40
412	Jesus Colome	.15
413	*John Sneed*	.40
414	*Tony McKnight*	.40
415	Luis Rivera	.15
416	Adam Eaton	.15
417	*Mike MacDougal*	.50
418	Mike Nannini	.15
419	*Barry Zito*	2.50
420	Dewayne Wise	.15
421	Jason Dellaero	.15
422	Chad Moeller	.15
423	Jason Marquis	.15
424	*Tim Redding*	.50
425	Mark Mulder	.15
426	Josh Paul	.15
427	Chris Enochs	.15
428	*Wilfredo Rodriguez*	.50
429	Kevin Witt	.15
430	*Scott Sobkowiak*	.40
431	McKay Christensen	.15
432	Jung Bong	.15
433	*Keith Evans*	.40
434	Garry Maddox Jr.	.15
435	*Ramon Santiago*	.50
436	Alex Cora	.15
437	Carlos Lee	.15
438	*Jason Repko*	.40
439	Matt Burch	.15
440	*Shawn Sonnier*	.40

Gold

Stars:	10-20X
Rookies:	4-8X

Production 99 sets
(See 2000 Bowman for checklist and base card values.)

Retro/Future

	NM/M
Common Player:	.25
Stars:	2-3X
Rookies:	.75-2X

Inserted 1:1
(See 2000 Bowman for checklist and base card values.)

Autographs

		NM/M
Common Autograph:		5.00
Blue Inserted 1:144		
Silver 1:312		
Gold 1:1,604		
CA	Chip Ambres B	5.00
RA	Rick Ankiel G	10.00
CB	Carlos Beltran G	40.00
LB	Lance Berkman S	20.00
DB	Dee Brown S	8.00
SB	Sean Burroughs S	15.00
JDC	J.D. Closser B	5.00
SC	Steve Cox B	5.00
MC	Michael Cuddyer S	10.00
JC	Jack Cust S	10.00
SD	Scott Downs S	10.00
JDD	J.D. Drew G	25.00
AD	Adam Dunn B	20.00
CF	Choo Freeman B	5.00
RF	Rafael Furcal S	15.00
AH	Aubrey Huff B	8.00
JJ	Jason Jennings B	8.00
NJ	Nick Johnson S	10.00
AK	Austin Kearns B	15.00
DK	David Kelton B	5.00
RM	Ruben Mateo G	15.00
MM	Mike Meyers B	5.00
CP	Corey Patterson S	20.00
BWP	Brad Penny B	5.00
BP	Ben Petrick G	10.00
AP	Adam Piatt S	8.00
MQ	Mark Quinn S	8.00
MR	Mike Restovich B	5.00
MR	Matt Riley S	8.00
JR	Jason Romano B	5.00
BS	Ben Sheets B	35.00
AS	Alfonso Soriano S	40.00
EV	Eric Valent B	5.00
JV	Jose Vidro S	10.00
VW	Vernon Wells G	20.00
SW	Scott Williamson G	10.00
KJW	Kevin Witt S	10.00
KLW	Kerry Wood S	25.00
EY	Eddie Yarnall S	10.00
JZ	Julio Zuleta B	5.00

Bowman's Best Previews

		NM/M
Complete Set (10):		20.00
Common Player:		.75
Inserted 1:18		
1	Derek Jeter	5.00
2	Ken Griffey Jr.	3.00
3	Nomar Garciaparra	3.00
4	Mike Piazza	3.00
5	Alex Rodriguez	4.00
6	Sammy Sosa	3.00
7	Mark McGwire	4.50
8	Pat Burrell	1.50
9	Josh Hamilton	.75
10	Adam Piatt	.75

Early Indications

		NM/M
Complete Set (10):		20.00
Common Player:		1.00
Inserted 1:24		
1	Nomar Garciaparra	3.00
2	Cal Ripken Jr.	5.00
3	Derek Jeter	5.00
4	Mark McGwire	4.00
5	Alex Rodriguez	4.00
6	Chipper Jones	2.50
7	Todd Helton	1.50
8	Vladimir Guerrero	1.50
9	Mike Piazza	3.00
10	Jose Canseco	1.00

Major Power

		NM/M
Complete Set (10):		20.00
Common Player:		1.00
Inserted 1:24		
1	Mark McGwire	4.00
2	Chipper Jones	2.50
3	Alex Rodriguez	4.00
4	Sammy Sosa	3.00
5	Rafael Palmeiro	1.00

6	Ken Griffey Jr.	3.00
7	Nomar Garciaparra	3.00
8	Barry Bonds	5.00
9	Derek Jeter	5.00
10	Jeff Bagwell	1.50

Tool Time

		NM/M
Complete Set (20):		8.00
Common Player:		.40
Inserted 1:8		
1	Pat Burrell	1.00
2	Aaron Rowand	.40
3	Chris Wakeland	.40
4	Ruben Mateo	.40
5	Pat Burrell	1.00
6	Adam Piatt	.50
7	Nick Johnson	.75
8	Jack Cust	.40
9	Rafael Furcal	.40
10	Julio Ramirez	.40
11	Travis Dawkins	.40
12	Corey Patterson	1.00
13	Ruben Mateo	.40
14	Jason Dellaero	.40
15	Sean Burroughs	.75
16	Ryan Langerhans	.40
17	D'Angelo Jimenez	.40
18	Corey Patterson	1.00
19	Troy Cameron	.40
20	Michael Cuddyer	.50

2000 BOWMAN CHROME

		NM/M
Complete Set (440):		120.00
Common Player:		.25
Common Rookie:		1.00
Pack (4):		3.00
Box (24):		55.00
1	Vladimir Guerrero	1.00
2	Chipper Jones	1.50
3	Todd Walker	.25
4	Barry Larkin	.25
5	Bernie Williams	.50
6	Todd Helton	1.00
7	Jermaine Dye	.25
8	Brian Giles	.25
9	Freddy Garcia	.25
10	Greg Vaughn	.25
11	Alex Gonzalez	.25
12	Luis Gonzalez	.50
13	Ron Belliard	.25
14	Ben Grieve	.25
15	Carlos Delgado	.75
16	Brian Jordan	.25
17	Fernando Tatis	.25
18	Ryan Rupe	.25
19	Miguel Tejada	.40
20	Mark Grace	.35
21	Kenny Lofton	.25
22	Eric Karros	.25
23	Cliff Floyd	.25
24	John Halama	.25
25	Cristian Guzman	.25
26	Scott Williamson	.25
27	Mike Lieberthal	.25
28	Tim Hudson	.50
29	Warren Morris	.25
30	Pedro Martinez	1.00
31	John Smoltz	.25
32	Ray Durham	.25
33	Chad Allen	.25
34	Tony Clark	.25
35	Tino Martinez	.25
36	J.T. Snow Jr.	.25
37	Kevin Brown	.40
38	Bartolo Colon	.25
39	Rey Ordonez	.25
40	Jeff Bagwell	1.00
41	Ivan Rodriguez	.75
42	Eric Chavez	.50
43	Eric Milton	.25
44	Jose Canseco	.50
45	Shawn Green	.50
46	Rich Aurilia	.25
47	Roberto Alomar	.50
48	Brian Daubach	.25
49	Magglio Ordonez	.50
50	Derek Jeter	3.00
51	Kris Benson	.25
52	Albert Belle	.25
53	Rondell White	.25
54	Justin Thompson	.25
55	Nomar Garciaparra	2.00
56	Chuck Finley	.25
57	Omar Vizquel	.25
58	Luis Castillo	.25
59	Richard Hidalgo	.25
60	Barry Bonds	3.00
61	Craig Biggio	.25
62	Doug Glanville	.25
63	Gabe Kapler	.25
64	Johnny Damon	.40
65	Pokey Reese	.25
66	Andy Pettitte	.50
67	B.J. Surhoff	.25
68	Richie Sexson	.50
69	Javy Lopez	.25
70	Raul Mondesi	.25
71	Darin Erstad	.60
72	Kevin Millwood	.40
73	Ricky Ledee	.25
74	John Olerud	.25
75	Sean Casey	.25
76	Carlos Febles	.25
77	Paul O'Neill	.25
78	Bob Abreu	.25
79	Neifi Perez	.25
80	Tony Gwynn	1.50
81	Russ Ortiz	.25
82	Matt Williams	.25
83	Chris Carpenter	.25
84	Roger Cedeno	.25
85	Tim Salmon	.35
86	Billy Koch	.25
87	Jeromy Burnitz	.25
88	Edgardo Alfonzo	.25
89	Jay Bell	.15
90	Manny Ramirez	1.00
91	Frank Thomas	1.00
92	Mike Mussina	.50
93	J.D. Drew	.40
94	Adrian Beltre	.50
95	Alex Rodriguez	2.50
96	Larry Walker	.25
97	Juan Encarnacion	.25
98	Mike Sweeney	.25
99	Rusty Greer	.25
100	Randy Johnson	1.00
101	Jose Vidro	.25
102	Preston Wilson	.25
103	Greg Maddux	1.50
104	Jason Giambi	.75
105	Cal Ripken Jr.	3.00
106	Carlos Beltran	.25
107	Vinny Castilla	.25
108	Mariano Rivera	.35
109	Mo Vaughn	.25
110	Rafael Palmeiro	.75
111	Shannon Stewart	.25
112	Mike Hampton	.25
113	Joe Nathan	.25
114	Ben Davis	.25
115	Andruw Jones	1.00
116	Robin Ventura	.25
117	Damion Easley	.25
118	Jeff Cirillo	.25
119	Kerry Wood	.75
120	Scott Rolen	.75
121	Sammy Sosa	2.00
122	Ken Griffey Jr.	2.00
123	Shane Reynolds	.25
124	Troy Glaus	1.00
125	Tom Glavine	.40
126	Michael Barrett	.25
127	Al Leiter	.25
128	Jason Kendall	.25
129	Roger Clemens	2.00
130	Juan Gonzalez	1.00
131	Corey Koskie	.25
132	Curt Schilling	.50
133	Mike Piazza	2.00
134	Gary Sheffield	.50
135	Jim Thome	.50
136	Orlando Hernandez	.40
137	Ray Lankford	.25
138	Geoff Jenkins	.25
139	Jose Lima	.25
140	Mark McGwire	2.50
141	Adam Piatt	.25
142	*Pat Manning*	1.00
143	*Marcos Castillo*	1.00
144	*Lesli Brea*	1.00
145	*Humberto Cota*	1.00
146	Ben Petrick	.25
147	Kip Wells	.25
148	Willi Mo Pena	.40
149	Chris Wakeland	.25
150	*Brad Baker*	1.00
151	*Robbie Morrison*	1.00
152	Reggie Taylor	.25
153	*Matt Ginter*	1.00
154	Peter Bergeron	.25
155	Roosevelt Brown	.25
156	*Matt Cepicky*	1.00
157	Ramon Castro	.25
158	*Brad Baisley*	1.00
159	*Jason Hart*	2.00
160	Mitch Meluskey	.25
161	Chad Harville	.25
162	Brian Cooper	.25
163	Marcus Giles	.25
164	Jim Morris	.50
165	Geoff Goetz	.25
166	*Bobby Bradley*	1.00
167	Rob Bell	.25
168	Joe Crede	.25
169	Michael Restovich	.25
170	*Quincy Foster*	1.00
171	*Enrique Cruz*	1.00
172	Mark Quinn	.25
173	Nick Johnson	.40
174	Jeff Liefer	.25
175	*Kevin Mench*	2.00
176	Steve Lomasney	.25
177	Jayson Werth	.25
178	Tim Drew	.25
179	Chip Ambres	.25
180	Ryan Anderson	.25
181	Matt Blank	.25
182	Giuseppe Chiaramonte	.25
183	*Corey Myers*	1.00
184	Jeff Yoder	.25
185	*Craig Dingman*	1.00
186	*Jon Hamilton*	1.00
187	Toby Hall	.25
188	Russell Branyan	.25
189	*Brian Falkenborg*	1.00
190	*Aaron Harang*	2.00
191	Juan Pena	.25
192	*Chin-Hui Tsao*	3.00
193	Alfonso Soriano	.75
194	*Alejandro Diaz*	1.00
195	Carlos Pena	.25
196	Kevin Nicholson	.25
197	Mo Bruce	.25
198	C.C. Sabathia	.25
199	Carl Crawford	.25
200	Rafael Furcal	.25
201	*Andrew Beinbrink*	1.00
202	Jimmy Osting	.25
203	*Aaron McNeal*	1.00
204	Brett Laxton	.25
205	Chris George	.25
206	Felipe Lopez	.25
207	*Ben Sheets*	8.00
208	*Mike Meyers*	1.00
209	Jason Conti	.25
210	Milton Bradley	.25
211	*Chris Mears*	1.00
212	*Carlos Hernandez*	1.00
213	Jason Romano	.25
214	Goefrey Tomlinson	.25
215	Jimmy Rollins	.25
216	Pablo Ozuna	.25
217	Steve Cox	.25
218	Terrence Long	.25
219	*Jeff DaVanon*	1.00
220	Rick Ankiel	.25
221	Jason Standridge	.25
222	Tony Armas	.25
223	Jason Tyner	.25
224	Ramon Ortiz	.25
225	Daryle Ward	.25
226	*Enger Veras*	1.00
227	*Chris Jones*	1.00
228	*Eric Cammack*	1.00
229	Ruben Mateo	.25
230	*Ken Harvey*	2.00
231	Jake Westbrook	.25
232	*Rob Purvis*	1.00
233	Choo Freeman	.25
234	Aramis Ramirez	.25
235	A.J. Burnett	.25
236	Kevin Barker	.25
237	*Chance Caple*	1.00
238	Jarrod Washburn	.25
239	Lance Berkman	.25
240	*Michael Wenner*	1.00
241	Alex Sanchez	.25
242	*Jake Esteves*	1.00
243	Grant Roberts	.25
244	*Mark Ellis*	1.00
245	Donny Leon	.25
246	David Eckstein	.25
247	*Dicky Gonzalez*	1.00
248	John Patterson	.25
249	Chad Green	.25
250	*Scot Shields*	1.00
251	Troy Cameron	.25
252	Jose Molina	.25
253	*Rob Pugmire*	1.00
254	Rick Elder	.25
255	Sean Burroughs	.50
256	*Josh Kalinowski*	1.00
257	Matt LeCroy	.25
258	*Alex Graman*	1.00
259	*Juan Silvestre*	1.00
260	Brady Clark	.25
261	*Rico Washington*	1.00
262	Gary Matthews Jr.	.25
263	Matt Wise	.25
264	*Keith Reed*	1.00
265	*Santiago Ramirez*	1.00
266	*Ben Broussard*	1.00
267	Ryan Langerhans	.25
268	Juan Rivera	.25
269	Shawn Gallagher	.25
270	Jorge Toca	.25
271	Brad Lidge	.25
272	*Leo Estrella*	1.00
273	Ruben Quevedo	.25
274	Jack Cust	.25
275	T.J. Tucker	.25
276	Mike Colangelo	.25
277	Brian Schneider	.25
278	Calvin Murray	.25
279	Josh Girdley	.25
280	Mike Paradis	.25
281	Chad Hermansen	.25
282	*Ty Howington*	2.00
283	Aaron Myette	.25
284	D'Angelo Jimenez	.25
285	Dernell Stenson	.25
286	Jerry Hairston Jr.	.25
287	*Gary Majewski*	1.00
288	*Derrin Ebert*	1.00
289	*Steve Fish*	1.00
290	Carlos Hernandez	.25
291	Allen Levrault	.25
292	*Sean McNally*	1.00
293	*Randey Dorame*	1.00
294	*Wes Anderson*	1.00
295	B.J. Ryan	.25
296	*Alan Webb*	1.00
297	*Brandon Inge*	2.00
298	David Walling	.25
299	*Sun-Woo Kim*	1.50
300	Pat Burrell	.75
301	*Rick Guttormson*	1.00
302	Gil Meche	.25
303	*Carlos Zambrano*	10.00
304	*Eric Byrnes* (photo actually Bo Porter)	2.00
305	*Robb Quinlan*	1.00
306	Jackie Rexrode	.25
307	Nate Bump	.25
308	*Sean DePaula*	1.00
309	Matt Riley	.25
310	Ryan Minor	.25
311	J.J. Davis	.25
312	Randy Wolf	.25
313	Jason Jennings	.25
314	*Scott Seabol*	1.00
315	Doug Davis	.25
316	*Todd Moser*	1.00

317 Rob Ryan .25
318 Bubba Crosby .25
319 *Lyle Overbay* 2.50
320 Mario Encarnacion .25
321 *Francisco Rodriguez* 6.00
322 Michael Cuddyer .25
323 Eddie Yarnall .25
324 *Cesar Saba* 1.00
325 Travis Dawkins .25
326 Alex Escobar .25
327 *Julio Zuleta* 1.00
328 Josh Hamilton .25
329 *Carlos Urquiola* 1.00
330 Matt Belisle .25
331 *Kurt Ainsworth* 1.00
332 Tim Raines Jr. .25
333 Eric Munson .25
334 Donzell McDonald .25
335 *Larry Bigbie* 1.00
336 Matt Watson .25
337 Aubrey Huff .25
338 Julio Ramirez .25
339 *Jason Grabowski* 1.00
340 Jon Garland .25
341 Austin Kearns .75
342 Josh Pressley .25
343 *Miguel Olivo* .75
344 Julio Lugo .25
345 Roberto Vaz .25
346 Ramon Soler .25
347 *Brandon Phillips* 2.00
348 *Vince Faison* .75
349 Mike Venafro .25
350 *Rick Asadoorian* 1.00
351 *B.J. Garbe* 1.00
352 Dan Reichert .25
353 *Jason Stumm* .75
354 *Ruben Salazar* .75
355 Francisco Cordero .25
356 *Juan Guzman* .75
357 *Mike Bacsik* .75
358 Jared Sandberg .25
359 Rod Barajas .25
360 *Junior Brignac* 1.00
361 J.M. Gold .25
362 Octavio Dotel .25
363 David Kelton .25
364 *Scott Morgan* 1.00
365 *Wascar Serrano* 1.00
366 Wilton Veras .25
367 Eugene Kingsale .25
368 Ted Lilly .25
369 George Lombard .25
370 Chris Haas .25
371 *Wilton Pena* 1.00
372 Vernon Wells .50
373 *Keith Ginter* 1.00
374 *Jeff Heaverlo* 1.00
375 Calvin Pickering .25
376 *Mike Lamb* 1.00
377 Kyle Snyder .25
378 *Javier Cardona* 1.00
379 *Aaron Rowand* 3.00
380 Dee Brown .25
381 *Brett Myers* 4.00
382 Abraham Nunez .25
383 Eric Valent .25
384 *Jody Gerut* 2.00
385 Adam Dunn .50
386 Jay Gehrke .25
387 Omar Ortiz .25
388 Darnell McDonald .25
389 Chad Alexander .25
390 J.D. Closser .25
391 *Ben Christensen* 1.00
392 Adam Kennedy .25
393 *Nick Green* 1.00
394 Ramon Hernandez .25
395 *Roy Oswalt* 15.00
396 *Andy Tracy* 1.00
397 Eric Gagne .25
398 *Michael Tejera* 1.00
399 Adam Everett .25
400 Corey Patterson .50
401 *Gary Knotts* 1.00
402 *Ryan Christianson* 1.00
403 *Eric Ireland* 1.00
404 *Andrew Good* 1.00
405 Brad Penny .25
406 Jason LaRue .25
407 Kit Pellow .25
408 Kevin Beirne .25
409 Kelly Dransfeldt .25
410 Jason Grilli .25
411 *Scott Downs* 1.00
412 Jesus Colome .25
413 *John Sneed* 1.00
414 *Tony McKnight* 1.00
415 Luis Rivera .25
416 Adam Eaton .25
417 *Mike MacDougal* 1.50
418 Mike Nannini .25
419 *Barry Zito* 6.00
420 Dewayne Wise .25
421 Jason Dellaero .25
422 Chad Moeller .25
423 Jason Marquis .25
424 *Tim Redding* 2.00
425 Mark Mulder .25
426 Josh Paul .25
427 Chris Enochs .25
428 *Wilfredo Rodriguez* 1.00
429 Kevin Witt .25
430 *Scott Sobkowiak* 1.00
431 McKay Christensen .25
432 Jung Bong .25
433 *Keith Evans* 1.00
434 Garry Maddox Jr. .25
435 *Ramon Santiago* 1.00
436 Alex Cora .25
437 Carlos Lee .25
438 *Jason Repko* 1.00
439 Matt Burch .25
440 *Shawn Sonnier* 1.00

Refractors

Stars: 4-8X
Rookies: 2-4X
Inserted 1:12
(See 2000 Bowman Chrome for checklist and base card values.)

Retro/Future

Stars: 1.5-3X
Rookies: .75X
Inserted 1:6
Refractors: 6-8X
Rookies: 1-3X
Inserted 1:60
(See 2000 Bowman Chrome for checklist and base values.)

Bidding for the Call

NM/M
Complete Set (15): 15.00
Common Player: 1.00
Inserted 1:16
Refractors: 2-4X
Inserted 1:160
1 Adam Piatt 1.00
2 Pat Burrell 2.00
3 Mark Mulder 1.50
4 Nick Johnson 1.50
5 Alfonso Soriano 2.00
6 Chin-Feng Chen 2.50
7 Scott Sobkowiak 1.00
8 Corey Patterson 2.00
9 Jack Cust 1.00
10 Sean Burroughs 1.50
11 Josh Hamilton 1.00
12 Corey Myers 1.00
13 Eric Munson 1.00
14 Wes Anderson 1.00
15 Lyle Overbay 1.50

Meteoric Rise

NM/M
Complete Set (10): 20.00
Common Player: 1.50
Inserted 1:24
Refractors: 2-4X
Inserted 1:240
1 Nomar Garciaparra 3.00
2 Mark McGwire 4.50
3 Ken Griffey Jr. 3.00
4 Chipper Jones 2.50
5 Manny Ramirez 2.00
6 Mike Piazza 3.00
7 Cal Ripken Jr. 5.00
8 Ivan Rodriguez 1.00
9 Greg Maddux 2.50
10 Randy Johnson 2.00

Oversize

NM/M
Complete Set (8): 8.00
Common Player: .75
Inserted 1:box
1 Pat Burrell 2.00
2 Josh Hamilton .75
3 Rafael Furcal 1.00
4 Corey Patterson 1.50
5 A.J. Burnett .75
6 Eric Munson .75
7 Nick Johnson 1.00
8 Alfonso Soriano 2.00

Rookie Class 2000

NM/M
Complete Set (10): 8.00
Common Player: 1.50
Inserted 1:24
Refractors: 2-4X
Inserted 1:240
1 Pat Burrell 2.00
2 Rick Ankiel 1.00
3 Ruben Mateo .75
4 Vernon Wells 1.50
5 Mark Mulder 1.50
6 A.J. Burnett .75
7 Chad Hermansen .75
8 Corey Patterson 1.50
9 Rafael Furcal .75
10 Mike Lamb .75

Teen Idols

NM/M
Complete Set (15): 15.00
Common Player: 1.50
Inserted 1:16
Refractors: 2-4X
Inserted 1:160
1 Alex Rodriguez 5.00
2 Andruw Jones 1.50
3 Juan Gonzalez 1.50
4 Ivan Rodriguez 1.00
5 Ken Griffey Jr. 3.00
6 Bobby Bradley .75
7 Brett Myers .75
8 C.C. Sabathia .75
9 Ty Howington .75
10 Brandon Phillips 1.00
11 Rick Asadoorian .75
12 Wily Pena 1.00
13 Sean Burroughs 1.00
14 Josh Hamilton .75
15 Rafael Furcal .75

2000 BOWMAN CHROME DRAFT PICKS AND PROSPECTS

NM/M
Complete Set (110): 50.00
Common Player: .25
1 Pat Burrell 1.00
2 Rafael Furcal .50
3 Grant Roberts .25
4 Barry Zito 2.00
5 Julio Zuleta .50
6 Mark Mulder .25
7 Rob Bell .25
8 Adam Piatt .50
9 Mike Lamb .25
10 Pablo Ozuna .25
11 Jason Tyner .25
12 Jason Marquis .25
13 Eric Munson .25
14 Seth Etherton .25
15 Milton Bradley .25
16 Nick Green .25
17 *Chin-Feng Chen* 2.50
18 *Matt Boone* .50
19 *Kevin Gregg* .50
20 *Eddy Garabito* .50
21 *Aaron Capista* .50
22 *Esteban German* .50
23 *Derek Thompson* .50
24 *Phil Merrell* .50
25 *Brian O'Connor* .50
26 Yamid Haad .25
27 *Hector Mercado* .50
28 *Jason Woolf* .50
29 *Eddie Furniss* .50
30 *Cha Sueng Baek* .50
31 *Colby Lewis* 2.00
32 *Pasqual Coco* .50
33 *Jorge Cantu* 5.00
34 *Erasmo Ramirez* .50
35 *Bobby Kielty* 2.00
36 *Joaquin Benoit* .50
37 *Brian Esposito* .50
38 Michael Wenner .25
39 *Juan Rincon* .50
40 *Yorvit Torrealba* .50
41 *Chad Durham* .50
42 *Jim Mann* .50
43 *Shane Loux* .50
44 Luis Rivas .25
45 *Ken Chenard* .50
46 *Mike Lockwood* .50
47 *Giovanni Lara* .50
48 *Bubba Carpenter* .50
49 *Ryan Dittfurth* .50
50 *John Stephens* 1.00
51 *Pedro Feliz* 2.00
52 *Kenny Kelly* .50
53 *Neil Jenkins* .50
54 *Mike Glendenning* .50
55 Bo Porter .25
56 Eric Byrnes .25
57 *Tony Alvarez* 1.50
58 *Kazuhiro Sasaki* 1.00
59 *Chad Durbin* .50
60 *Mike Bynum* .50
61 *Travis Wilson* .50
62 *Jose Leon* .50
63 *Ryan Vogelsong* .50
64 *Geraldo Guzman* .50
65 *Craig Anderson* .50
66 *Carlos Silva* 1.50
67 *Brad Thomas* .50
68 Chin-Hui Tsao 1.50
69 *Mark Buehrle* 5.00
70 *Juan Salas* .50
71 *Denny Abreu* .50
72 *Keith McDonald* .50
73 *Chris Richard* .50
74 *Tomas de la Rosa* .50
75 Vicente Padilla 1.00
76 *Justin Brunette* .50
77 *Scott Linebrink* .50
78 *Jeff Sparks* .50
79 *Tike Redman* .50
80 *John Lackey* 2.00
81 *Joe Strong* 1.00

82	*Brian Tollberg*	.50
83	*Steve Sisco*	.50
84	Chris Clapinski	.25
85	*Augie Ojeda*	.50
86	*Adrian Gonzalez* (Draft Picks)	4.00
87	*Mike Stodolka* (Draft Picks)	.50
88	*Adam Johnson* (Draft Picks)	1.00
89	*Matt Wheatland* (Draft Picks)	.75
90	*Corey Smith* (Draft Picks)	1.00
91	*Rocco Baldelli* (Draft Picks)	4.00
92	*Keith Bucktrot* (Draft Picks)	.50
93	*Adam Wainwright* (Draft Picks)	2.00
94	*Blaine Boyer* (Draft Picks)	.50
95	*Aaron Herr* (Draft Picks)	.50
96	*Scott Thorman* (Draft Picks)	1.00
97	*Brian Digby* (Draft Picks)	.50
98	*Josh Shortslef* (Draft Picks)	.50
99	*Sean Smith* (Draft Picks)	.50
100	*Alex Cruz* (Draft Picks)	.50
101	*Marc Love* (Draft Picks)	.50
102	*Kevin Lee* (Draft Picks)	.50
103	*Timoniel Perez* (Draft Picks)	.50
104	*Alex Cabrera* (Draft Picks)	1.00
105	*Shane Heams* (Draft Picks)	.50
106	*Tripper Johnson* (Draft Picks)	1.00
107	*Brent Abernathy* (Draft Picks)	.75
108	*John Cotton* (Draft Picks)	.75
109	*Brad Wilkerson* (Draft Picks)	3.00
110	*Jon Rauch* (Draft Picks)	.75

2000 BOWMAN DRAFT PICKS AND PROSPECTS

		NM/M
Complete Set (110):		30.00
Common Player:		.15
1	Pat Burrell	.50
2	Rafael Furcal	.15
3	Grant Roberts	.15
4	Barry Zito	.50
5	Julio Zuleta	.15
6	Mark Mulder	.25
7	Rob Bell	.15
8	Adam Piatt	.15
9	Mike Lamb	.15
10	Pablo Ozuna	.15
11	Jason Tyner	.15
12	Jason Marquis	.15
13	Eric Munson	.15
14	Seth Etherton	.15
15	Milton Bradley	.15
16	Nick Green	.15
17	*Chin-Feng Chen*	1.00
18	*Matt Boone*	.25
19	*Kevin Gregg*	.25
20	*Eddy Garabito*	.25
21	*Aaron Capista*	.25
22	*Esteban German*	.25
23	*Derek Thompson*	.25
24	*Phil Merrell*	.25
25	*Brian O'Connor*	.25
26	Yamid Haad	.15
27	*Hector Mercado*	.25
28	*Jason Woolf*	.25
29	*Eddie Furniss*	.25
30	*Cha Sueng Baek*	.25
31	*Colby Lewis*	.50
32	*Pasqual Coco*	.25
33	*Jorge Cantu*	3.00
34	*Erasmo Ramirez*	.40
35	*Bobby Kielty*	.75
36	*Joaquin Benoit*	.25
37	*Brian Esposito*	.25
38	Michael Wenner	.15
39	*Juan Rincon*	.25
40	*Yorvit Torrealba*	.25
41	*Chad Durham*	.25
42	*Jim Mann*	.25
43	*Shane Loux*	.25
44	Luis Rivas	.15
45	*Ken Chenard*	.25
46	*Mike Lockwood*	.25
47	*Yovanny Lara*	.25
48	*Bubba Carpenter*	.25
49	*Jeremy Griffiths*	.25
50	*John Stephens*	.50
51	*Pedro Feliz*	.50
52	*Kenny Kelly*	.25
53	*Neil Jenkins*	.25
54	*Mike Glendenning*	.25
55	Bo Porter	.15
56	Eric Byrnes	.15
57	*Tony Alvarez*	.50
58	*Kazuhiro Sasaki*	.75
59	*Chad Durbin*	.25
60	*Mike Bynum*	.25
61	*Travis Wilson*	.25
62	*Jose Leon*	.25
63	*Bill Ortega*	.25
64	*Geraldo Guzman*	.25
65	*Craig Anderson*	.25
66	*Carlos Silva*	.50
67	*Brad Thomas*	.25
68	*Chin-Hui Tsao*	.75
69	*Mark Buehrle*	2.00
70	*Juan Salas*	.25
71	*Denny Abreu*	.25
72	*Keith McDonald*	.25
73	*Chris Richard*	.25
74	*Tomas de la Rosa*	.25
75	Vicente Padilla	.50
76	*Justin Brunette*	.25
77	*Scott Linebrink*	.25
78	*Jeff Sparks*	.25
79	*Tike Redman*	.25
80	*John Lackey*	.50
81	*Joe Strong*	.25
82	*Brian Tollberg*	.25
83	*Steve Sisco*	.25
84	Chris Clapinski	.15
85	*Augie Ojeda*	.25
86	*Adrian Gonzalez* (Draft Picks)	1.50
87	*Mike Stodolka* (Draft Picks)	.25
88	*Adam Johnson* (Draft Picks)	.50
89	*Matt Wheatland* (Draft Picks)	.25
90	*Corey Smith* (Draft Picks)	.50
91	*Rocco Baldelli* (Draft Picks)	3.00
92	*Keith Bucktrot* (Draft Picks)	.25
93	*Adam Wainwright* (Draft Picks)	1.00
94	*Blaine Boyer* (Draft Picks)	.25
95	*Aaron Herr* (Draft Picks)	.25
96	*Scott Thorman* (Draft Picks)	.75
97	*Brian Digby* (Draft Picks)	.25
98	*Josh Shortslef* (Draft Picks)	.25
99	*Sean Smith* (Draft Picks)	.25
100	*Alex Cruz* (Draft Picks)	.25
101	*Marc Love* (Draft Picks)	.25
102	*Kevin Lee* (Draft Picks)	.25
103	*Victor Ramos* (Draft Picks)	.25
104	*Jason Kanoi* (Draft Picks)	.25
105	*Luis Escobar* (Draft Picks)	.25
106	*Tripper Johnson* (Draft Picks)	1.00
107	*Phil Dumatrait* (Draft Picks)	.50
108	*Bryan Edwards* (Draft Picks)	.25
109	*Grady Sizemore* (Draft Picks)	8.00
110	*Thomas Mitchell* (Draft Picks)	.25

Autograph

		NM/M
Common Autograph:		5.00
Inserted 1:set		
1	Pat Burrell	20.00
2	Rafael Furcal	8.00
3	Grant Roberts	5.00
4	Barry Zito	50.00
5	Julio Zuleta	5.00
6	Mark Mulder	20.00
7	Bob Bell	5.00
8	Adam Piatt	5.00
9	Mike Lamb	8.00
10	Pablo Ozuna	5.00
11	Jason Tyner	5.00
12	Jason Marquis	5.00
13	Eric Munson	6.00
14	Seth Etherton	5.00
15	Milton Bradley	10.00
17	Michael Wenner	5.00
18	Mike Glendenning	5.00
19	Tony Alvarez	5.00
20	Adrian Gonzalez	25.00
21	Corey Smith	10.00
22	Matt Wheatland	5.00
23	Adam Johnson	8.00
24	Mike Stodolka	5.00
25	Rocco Baldelli	40.00
26	Juan Rincon	5.00
27	Chad Durbin	5.00
28	Yorvit Torrealba	5.00
29	Nick Green	10.00
30	Derek Thompson	5.00
31	John Lackey	15.00
33	Kevin Gregg	5.00
34	NOT ISSUED	
35	Denny Abreu	5.00
36	Brian Tollberg	5.00
37	Yamid Haad	5.00
38	Grady Sizemore	120.00
39	Carlos Silva	10.00
40	Jorge Cantu	65.00
41	Bobby Kielty	8.00
42	Scott Thorman	8.00
43	Juan Salas	5.00
44	Phil Dumatrait	5.00
46	Mike Lockwood	5.00
47	Yovanny Lara	5.00
48	Tripper Johnson	10.00
49	Colby Lewis	5.00
50	Neil Jenkins	5.00
51	Keith Bucktrot	5.00
52	Eric Byrnes	10.00
53	Aaron Herr	5.00
54	Erasmo Ramirez	5.00
55	Chris Richard	5.00
57	Mike Bynum	5.00
58	Brian Esposito	5.00
59	Chris Clapinski	5.00
60	Augie Ojeda	5.00

2000 BOWMAN'S BEST

		NM/M
Complete Set (200):		275.00
Common Player:		.20
Common Rookie (151-200):		5.00
Production 2,999 sets		
Pack (4):		4.00
Box (24):		75.00
1	Nomar Garciaparra	2.00
2	Chipper Jones	1.50
3	Damion Easley	.20
4	Bernie Williams	.40
5	Barry Bonds	3.00
6	Jermaine Dye	.20
7	John Olerud	.20
8	Mike Hampton	.20
9	Cal Ripken Jr.	3.00
10	Jeff Bagwell	1.00
11	Troy Glaus	1.00
12	J.D. Drew	.40
13	Jeromy Burnitz	.20
14	Carlos Delgado	.75
15	Shawn Green	.40
16	Kevin Millwood	.40
17	Rondell White	.20
18	Scott Rolen	.75
19	Jeff Cirillo	.20
20	Barry Larkin	.20
21	Brian Giles	.20
22	Roger Clemens	1.75
23	Manny Ramirez	1.00
24	Alex Gonzalez	.20
25	Mark Grace	.35
26	Fernando Tatis	.20
27	Randy Johnson	1.00
28	Roger Cedeno	.20
29	Brian Jordan	.20
30	Kevin Brown	.40
31	Greg Vaughn	.20
32	Roberto Alomar	.50
33	Larry Walker	.20
34	Rafael Palmeiro	.75
35	Curt Schilling	.50
36	Orlando Hernandez	.20
37	Todd Walker	.20
38	Juan Gonzalez	1.00
39	Sean Casey	.35
40	Tony Gwynn	1.50
41	Albert Belle	.20
42	Gary Sheffield	.40
43	Michael Barrett	.20
44	Preston Wilson	.20
45	Jim Thome	.40
46	Shannon Stewart	.20
47	Mo Vaughn	.20
48	Ben Grieve	.20
49	Adrian Beltre	.35
50	Sammy Sosa	2.00
51	Bob Abreu	.20
52	Edgardo Alfonzo	.20
53	Carlos Febles	.20
54	Frank Thomas	1.00
55	Alex Rodriguez	2.50
56	Cliff Floyd	.20
57	Jose Canseco	.40
58	Erubiel Durazo	.20
59	Tim Hudson	.50
60	Craig Biggio	.20
61	Eric Karros	.20
62	Mike Mussina	.50
63	Robin Ventura	.20
64	Carlos Beltran	.50
65	Pedro Martinez	1.00
66	Gabe Kapler	.20
67	Jason Kendall	.20
68	Derek Jeter	3.00
69	Maglio Ordonez	.50

70 Mike Piazza 2.00
71 Mike Lieberthal .20
72 Andres Galarraga .20
73 Raul Mondesi .20
74 Eric Chavez .40
75 Greg Maddux 1.50
76 Matt Williams .30
77 Kris Benson .20
78 Ivan Rodriguez .50
79 Pokey Reese .20
80 Vladimir Guerrero 1.00
81 Mark McGwire 2.50
82 Vinny Castilla .20
83 Todd Helton 1.00
84 Andruw Jones .75
85 Ken Griffey Jr. 2.00
86 Mark McGwire (Best Performers) 1.25
87 Derek Jeter (Best Performers) 1.50
88 Chipper Jones (Best Performers) .75
89 Nomar Garciaparra (Best Performers) 1.00
90 Sammy Sosa (Best Performers) .75
91 Cal Ripken Jr. (Best Performers) 1.50
92 Juan Gonzalez (Best Performers) .50
93 Alex Rodriguez (Best Performers) 1.25
94 Barry Bonds (Best Performers) 1.50
95 Sean Casey (Best Performers) .25
96 Vladimir Guerrero (Best Performers) .50
97 Mike Piazza (Best Performers) 1.00
98 Shawn Green (Best Performers) .25
99 Jeff Bagwell (Best Performers) .50
100 Ken Griffey Jr. (Best Performers) 1.00
101 Rick Ankiel (Prospects) .35
102 John Patterson (Prospects) .20
103 David Walling (Prospects) .20
104 Michael Restovich (Prospects) .20
105 A.J. Burnett (Prospects) .20
106 Matt Riley (Prospects) .20
107 Chad Hermansen (Prospects) .20
108 Choo Freeman (Prospects) .20
109 Mark Quinn (Prospects) .20
110 Corey Patterson (Prospects) .40
111 Ramon Ortiz (Prospects) .20
112 Vernon Wells (Prospects) .40
113 Milton Bradley (Prospects) .20
114 Travis Dawkins (Prospects) .20
115 Sean Burroughs (Prospects) .35
116 Willi Mo Pena (Prospects) .40
117 Dee Brown (Prospects) .20
118 C.C. Sabathia (Prospects) .20
119 *Larry Bigbie* (Prospects) .20
120 Octavio Dotel (Prospects) .20
121 Kip Wells (Prospects) .20
122 Ben Petrick (Prospects) .20
123 Mark Mulder (Prospects) .40
124 Jason Standridge (Prospects) .20
125 Adam Piatt (Prospects) .20
126 Steve Lomasney (Prospects) .20
127 Jayson Werth (Prospects) .20
128 Alex Escobar (Prospects) .20
129 Ryan Anderson (Prospects) .20
130 Adam Dunn (Prospects) .50
131 Omar Ortiz (Prospects) .20
132 Brad Penny (Prospects) .20
133 Daryle Ward (Prospects) .20
134 Eric Munson (Prospects) .20
135 Nick Johnson (Prospects) .50
136 Jason Jennings (Prospects) .20
137 Tim Raines Jr. (Prospects) .20
138 Ruben Mateo (Prospects) .20
139 Jack Cust (Prospects) .20
140 Rafael Furcal (Prospects) .20
141 Eric Gagne (Prospects) .35
142 Tony Armas (Prospects) .20
143 Mike Paradis (Prospects) .20
144 Chris George (Prospects) .20
145 Alfonso Soriano (Prospects) .75
146 Josh Hamilton (Prospects) .35
147 Michael Cuddyer (Prospects) .35
148 Jay Gehrke (Prospects) .20
149 Josh Girdley (Prospects) .20
150 Pat Burrell (Prospects) .75
151 *Brett Myers* 15.00
152 *Scott Seabol* 5.00
153 *Keith Reed* 5.00
154 *Francisco Rodriguez* 20.00
155 *Barry Zito* 25.00
156 *Pat Manning* 5.00
157 *Ben Christensen* 5.00
158 *Corey Myers* 5.00
159 *Wascar Serrano* 5.00
160 *Wes Anderson* 5.00
161 *Andy Tracy* 5.00
162 *Cesar Saba* 5.00
163 *Mike Lamb* 5.00
164 *Bobby Bradley* 5.00
165 *Vince Faison* 5.00
166 *Ty Howington* 8.00
167 *Ken Harvey* 8.00
168 *Josh Kalinowski* 5.00
169 *Ruben Salazar* 5.00
170 *Aaron Rowand* 10.00
171 *Ramon Santiago* 5.00
172 *Scott Sobkowiak* 5.00
173 *Lyle Overbay* 10.00
174 *Rico Washington* 5.00
175 *Rick Asadoorian* 5.00
176 *Matt Ginter* 5.00
177 *Jason Stumm* 5.00
178 *B.J. Garbe* 5.00
179 *Mike MacDougal* 5.00
180 *Ryan Christianson* 5.00
181 *Kurt Ainsworth* 5.00
182 *Brad Baisley* 5.00
183 *Ben Broussard* 5.00
184 *Aaron McNeal* 5.00
185 *John Sneed* 5.00
186 *Junior Brignac* 5.00
187 *Chance Caple* 5.00
188 *Scott Downs* 5.00
189 *Matt Cepicky* 5.00
190 *Chin-Feng Chen* 30.00
191 *Johan Santana* 65.00
192 *Brad Baker* 5.00
193 *Jason Repko* 5.00
194 *Craig Dingman* 5.00
195 Chris Wakeland 5.00
196 *Rogelio Arias* 5.00
197 *Luis Matos* 8.00
198 *Robert Ramsay* 5.00
199 *Willie Bloomquist* 15.00
200 *Tony Pena Jr.* 5.00

Bets

NM/M
Complete Set (10): 10.00
Common Player: .75
Inserted 1:15
1 Pat Burrell 2.00
2 Alfonso Soriano 2.00
3 Corey Patterson 1.50
4 Eric Munson .75
5 Sean Burroughs 1.00
6 Rafael Furcal .75
7 Rick Ankiel 1.00
8 Nick Johnson 1.50
9 Ruben Mateo .75
10 Josh Hamilton .75

Franchise Favorites

NM/M
Complete Set (6): 15.00
Common Player: 1.00
Inserted 1:17
1A Sean Casey 1.00
1B Johnny Bench 3.00
1C Sean Casey, Johnny Bench 3.00
2A Cal Ripken Jr. 5.00
2B Brooks Robinson 2.00
2C Cal Ripken Jr., Brooks Robinson 5.00

Franchise Favorites Autograph

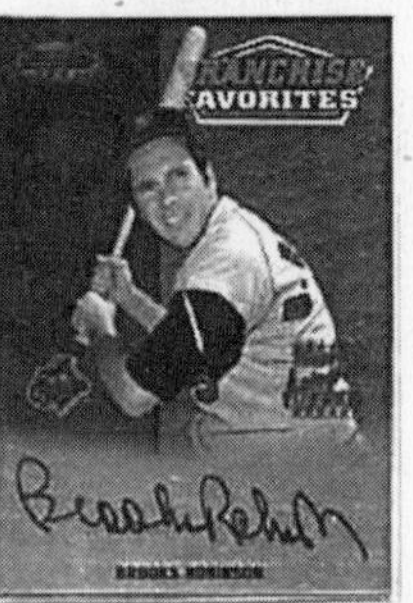

NM/M
Common Player: 20.00
Version A & B 1:1,291
Version C 1:5,153
1A Sean Casey 20.00
1B Johnny Bench 50.00
1C Sean Casey, Johnny Bench 100.00
2A Cal Ripken Jr. 125.00
2B Brooks Robinson 50.00
2C Cal Ripken Jr., Brooks Robinson 250.00

Franchise 2000

NM/M
Complete Set (25): 60.00
Common Player: 1.00
Inserted 1:18
1 Cal Ripken Jr. 8.00
2 Nomar Garciaparra 6.00
3 Frank Thomas 2.00
4 Manny Ramirez 2.00
5 Juan Gonzalez 1.50
6 Carlos Beltran 2.00
7 Derek Jeter 8.00
8 Alex Rodriguez 6.00
9 Ben Grieve 1.00
10 Jose Canseco 1.50
11 Ivan Rodriguez 1.50
12 Mo Vaughn 1.00
13 Randy Johnson 3.00
14 Chipper Jones 4.00
15 Sammy Sosa 5.00
16 Ken Griffey Jr. 5.00
17 Larry Walker 1.00
18 Preston Wilson 1.00
19 Jeff Bagwell 2.00
20 Shawn Green 1.00
21 Vladimir Guerrero 2.00
22 Mike Piazza 5.00
23 Scott Rolen 2.00
24 Tony Gwynn 3.50
25 Barry Bonds 8.00

Locker Room Collection Autographs

NM/M
Common Player: 8.00
Inserted 1:57
1 Carlos Beltran 25.00
2 Rick Ankiel 8.00

3 Vernon Wells 12.00
4 Ruben Mateo 8.00
5 Ben Petrick 8.00
6 Adam Piatt 8.00
7 Eric Munson 8.00
8 Alfonso Soriano 40.00
9 Kerry Wood 30.00
10 Jack Cust 8.00
11 Rafael Furcal 15.00
12 Josh Hamilton 8.00
13 Brad Penny 8.00
14 Dee Brown 8.00
15 Milton Bradley 12.00
16 Ryan Anderson 8.00
17 John Patterson 8.00
18 Nick Johnson 8.00
19 Peter Bergeron 8.00

Locker Room Collection Lumber

NM/M
Common Player: 5.00
Inserted 1:376
1 Carlos Beltran 15.00
2 Rick Ankiel 6.00
3 Vernon Wells 10.00
4 Adam Kennedy 5.00
5 Ben Petrick 5.00
6 Adam Piatt 5.00
7 Eric Munson 5.00
8 Rafael Furcal 5.00
9 J.D. Drew 12.00
10 Pat Burrell 15.00

Locker Room Collection Jerseys

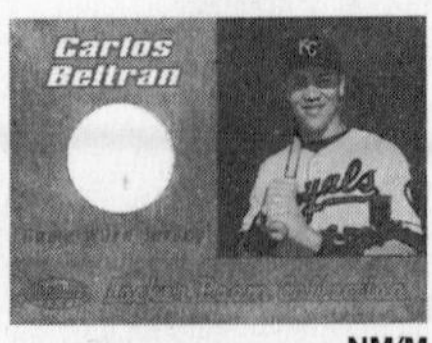

NM/M
Common Player: 4.00
Inserted 1:206
1 Carlos Beltran 12.00
2 Rick Ankiel 5.00
3 Adam Kennedy 4.00
4 Ben Petrick 4.00
5 Adam Piatt 4.00

Rookie Signed Baseballs

NM/M
Complete Set (5): 75.00
Common Player: 10.00
Inserted 1:688
1 Josh Hamilton 10.00
2 Rick Ankiel 15.00
3 Alfonso Soriano 25.00
4 Nick Johnson 15.00
5 Corey Patterson 20.00

Selections

NM/M
Complete Set (15): 50.00

Common Player:		1.00
Inserted 1:30		
1	Alex Rodriguez	7.50
2	Ken Griffey Jr.	6.00
3	Pat Burrell	2.00
4	Mark McGwire	7.50
5	Derek Jeter	10.00
6	Nomar Garciaparra	6.00
7	Mike Piazza	6.00
8	Josh Hamilton	1.00
9	Cal Ripken Jr.	10.00
10	Jeff Bagwell	2.50
11	Chipper Jones	4.50
12	Jose Canseco	1.50
13	Carlos Beltran	2.00
14	Kerry Wood	2.00
15	Ben Grieve	1.00

Year By Year

		NM/M
Complete Set (10):		25.00
Common Card:		1.50
Inserted 1:23		
1	Sammy Sosa, Ken Griffey Jr.	4.00
2	Nomar Garciaparra, Vladimir Guerrero	4.00
3	Alex Rodriguez, Jeff Cirillo	5.00
4	Mike Piazza, Pedro Martinez	4.00
5	Derek Jeter, Edgardo Alfonzo	6.00
6	Alfonso Soriano, Rick Ankiel	2.00
7	Mark McGwire, Barry Bonds	6.00
8	Juan Gonzalez, Larry Walker	1.50
9	Ivan Rodriguez, Jeff Bagwell	1.50
10	Shawn Green, Manny Ramirez	1.50

2001 BOWMAN

		NM/M
Complete Set (440):		90.00
Common Player:		.15
Common Rookie:		.50
Golds:		1-2X
Inserted 1:1		
Pack (10):		7.00
Box (24):		150.00
1	Jason Giambi	.40
2	Rafael Furcal	.15
3	Rick Ankiel	.15
4	Freddy Garcia	.15
5	Magglio Ordonez	.25
6	Bernie Williams	.40
7	Kenny Lofton	.15
8	Al Leiter	.15
9	Albert Belle	.15
10	Craig Biggio	.15
11	Mark Mulder	.15
12	Carlos Delgado	.40
13	Darin Erstad	.25
14	Richie Sexson	.15
15	Randy Johnson	.75
16	Greg Maddux	1.50
17	Cliff Floyd	.15
18	Mark Buehrle	.15
19	Chris Singleton	.15
20	Orlando Hernandez	.20
21	Javier Vazquez	.15
22	Jeff Kent	.15
23	Jim Thome	.50
24	John Olerud	.15
25	Jason Kendall	.15
26	Scott Rolen	.50
27	Tony Gwynn	.75
28	Edgardo Alfonzo	.15
29	Pokey Reese	.15
30	Todd Helton	.50
31	Mark Quinn	.15
32	*Dan Tosca*	.50
33	Dean Palmer	.15
34	Jacque Jones	.15
35	Ray Durham	.15
36	Rafael Palmeiro	.50
37	Carl Everett	.15
38	Ryan Dempster	.15
39	Randy Wolf	.15
40	Vladimir Guerrero	.75
41	Livan Hernandez	.15
42	Mo Vaughn	.15
43	Shannon Stewart	.15
44	Preston Wilson	.15
45	Jose Vidro	.15
46	Fred McGriff	.15
47	Kevin Brown	.25
48	Peter Bergeron	.15
49	Miguel Tejada	.50
50	Chipper Jones	.75
51	Edgar Martinez	.15
52	Tony Batista	.15
53	Jorge Posada	.40
54	Ricky Ledee	.15
55	Sammy Sosa	1.50
56	Steve Cox	.15
57	Tony Armas Jr.	.15
58	Gary Sheffield	.40
59	Bartolo Colon	.15
60	Pat Burrell	.50
61	Jay Payton	.15
62	Sean Casey	.25
63	Larry Walker	.15
64	Mike Mussina	.40
65	Nomar Garciaparra	1.50
66	Darren Dreifort	.15
67	Richard Hidalgo	.15
68	Troy Glaus	.50
69	Ben Grieve	.15
70	Jim Edmonds	.40
71	Raul Mondesi	.15
72	Andruw Jones	.50
73	Luis Castillo	.15
74	Mike Sweeney	.15
75	Derek Jeter	2.00
76	Ruben Mateo	.15
77	Carlos Lee	.15
78	Cristian Guzman	.15
79	Mike Hampton	.25
80	J.D. Drew	.25
81	Matt Lawton	.15
82	Moises Alou	.15
83	Terrence Long	.15
84	Geoff Jenkins	.15
85	Manny Ramirez	.75
86	Johnny Damon	.15
87	Barry Larkin	.15
88	Pedro Martinez	.75
89	Juan Gonzalez	.40
90	Roger Clemens	2.00
91	Carlos Beltran	.50
92	Brad Radke	.15
93	Orlando Cabrera	.15
94	Roberto Alomar	.50
95	Barry Bonds	3.00
96	Tim Hudson	.25
97	Tom Glavine	.25
98	Jeromy Burnitz	.15
99	Adrian Beltre	.15
100	Mike Piazza	1.50
101	Kerry Wood	.50
102	Steve Finley	.15
103	Alex Cora	.15
104	Bob Abreu	.15
105	Neifi Perez	.15
106	Mark Redman	.15
107	Paul Konerko	.15
108	Jermaine Dye	.15
109	Brian Giles	.15
110	Ivan Rodriguez	.50
111	Vinny Castilla	.15
112	Adam Kennedy	.15
113	Eric Chavez	.25
114	Billy Koch	.15
115	Shawn Green	.25
116	Matt Williams	.15
117	Greg Vaughn	.15
118	Gabe Kapler	.15
119	Jeff Cirillo	.15
120	Frank Thomas	.50
121	David Justice	.15
122	Cal Ripken Jr.	3.00
123	Rich Aurilia	.15
124	Curt Schilling	.40
125	Barry Zito	.25
126	Brian Jordan	.15
127	Chan Ho Park	.15
128	J.T. Snow Jr.	.15
129	Kazuhiro Sasaki	.15
130	Alex Rodriguez	2.00
131	Mariano Rivera	.25
132	Eric Milton	.15
133	Andy Pettitte	.25
134	Scott Elarton	.15
135	Ken Griffey Jr.	1.50
136	Bengie Molina	.15
137	Jeff Bagwell	.50
138	Kevin Millwood	.15
139	Tino Martinez	.15
140	Mark McGwire	2.00
141	Larry Barnes	.15
142	*John Buck*	.50
143	*Freddie Bynum*	.50
144	Abraham Nunez	.15
145	*Felix Diaz*	.50
146	*Horatio Estrada*	.50
147	Ben Diggins	.15
148	*Tsuyoshi Shinjo*	.50
149	Rocco Baldelli	.25
150	Rod Barajas	.15
151	Luis Terrero	.15
152	Milton Bradley	.15
153	Kurt Ainsworth	.15
154	Russell Branyan	.15
155	Ryan Anderson	.15
156	*Mitch Jones*	.50
157	Chip Ambres	.15
158	*Steve Bennett*	.50
159	Ivanon Coffie	.15
160	Sean Burroughs	.15
161	Keith Bucktrot	.15
162	Tony Alvarez	.15
163	Joaquin Benoit	.15
164	Rick Asadoorian	.15
165	Ben Broussard	.15
166	*Ryan Madson*	1.00
167	Dee Brown	.15
168	*Sergio Contreras*	.50
169	John Barnes	.15
170	*Ben Washburn*	.50
171	*Erick Almonte*	.50
172	*Shawn Fagan*	.50
173	*Gary Johnson*	.50
174	Brady Clark	.15
175	Grant Roberts	.15
176	Tony Torcato	.15
177	Ramon Castro	.15
178	Esteban German	.15
179	*Joe Hamer*	.50
180	Nick Neugebauer	.25
181	Dernell Stenson	.15
182	*Yhency Brazoban*	.50
183	Aaron Myette	.15
184	Juan Sosa	.15
185	Brandon Inge	.15
186	*Domingo Guante*	.50
187	Adrian Brown	.15
188	*Deivi Mendez*	.50
189	Luis Matos	.15
190	*Pedro Liriano*	.50
191	Donnie Bridges	.15
192	Alex Cintron	.15
193	Jace Brewer	.15
194	*Ron Davenport*	.50
195	*Jason Belcher*	.50
196	*Adrian Hernandez*	.50
197	Bobby Kielty	.15
198	*Reggie Griggs*	.50
199	*Reggie Abercrombie*	.50
200	*Troy Farnsworth*	.50
201	Matt Belisle	.15
202	*Miguel Villilo*	.50
203	Adam Everett	.15
204	John Lackey	.15
205	Pasqual Coco	.15
206	Adam Wainwright	.15
207	*Matt White*	.50
208	Chin-Feng Chen	.25
209	*Jeff Andra*	.50
210	Willie Bloomquist	.15
211	Wes Anderson	.15
212	Enrique Cruz	.15
213	Jerry Hairston Jr.	.15
214	Mike Bynum	.15
215	*Brian Hitchcox*	.50
216	Ryan Christianson	.15
217	J.J. Davis	.15
218	Jovanny Cedeno	.15
219	Elvin Nina	.15
220	Alex Graman	.15
221	Arturo McDowell	.15
222	*Deivi Santos*	.50
223	Jody Gerut	.15
224	Sun-Woo Kim	.15
225	Jimmy Rollins	.15
226	Pappy Ndungidi	.15
227	Ruben Salazar	.15
228	Josh Girdley	.15
229	Carl Crawford	.15
230	*Luis Montanez*	.50
231	*Ramon Carvajal*	.50
232	Matt Riley	.15
233	Ben Davis	.15
234	Jason Grabowski	.15
235	Chris George	.15
236	*Hank Blalock*	8.00
237	Roy Oswalt	.25
238	*Eric Reynolds*	.50
239	Brian Cole	.15
240	*Denny Bautista*	.75
241	*Hector Garcia*	.50
242	*Joe Thurston*	.75
243	Brad Cresse	.50
244	Corey Patterson	.25
245	*Brett Evert*	.50
246	*Elpidio Guzman*	.50
247	Vernon Wells	.15
248	*Roberto Miniel*	.50
249	*Brian Bass*	.50
250	*Mark Burnett*	.50
251	Juan Silvestre	.15
252	Pablo Ozuna	.15
253	Jayson Werth	.15
254	*Russ Jacobsen*	.50
255	Chad Hermansen	.15
256	*Travis Hafner*	4.00
257	Bradley Baker	.15
258	Gookie Dawkins	.15
259	Michael Cuddyer	.15
260	Mark Buehrle	.15
261	Ricardo Aramboles	.15
262	*Esix Snead*	.50
263	*Wilson Betemit*	.50
264	*Albert Pujols*	60.00
265	Joe Lawrence	.15
266	Ramon Ortiz	.15
267	Ben Sheets	.50
268	*Luke Lockwood*	.50
269	Toby Hall	.15
270	Jack Cust	.15
271	Pedro Feliz	.15
272	*Noel Devarez*	.50
273	Josh Beckett	.15
274	Alex Escobar	.15
275	*Doug Gredvig*	.75
276	Marcus Giles	.15
277	Jon Rauch	.15
278	*Brian Schmitt*	.50
279	*Seung Song*	.50
280	Kevin Mench	.15
281	Adam Eaton	.15
282	Shawn Sonnier	.15
283	*Andy Van Hekken*	.50
284	Aaron Rowand	.15
285	*Tony Blanco*	.50
286	Ryan Kohlmeier	.15
287	C.C. Sabathia	.15
288	Bubba Crosby	.15
289	Josh Hamilton	.15
290	*Dee Haynes*	.50
291	Jason Marquis	.15
292	Julio Zuleta	.15
293	Carlos Hernandez	.15
294	Matt LeCroy	.15
295	*Andy Beal*	.50
296	Carlos Pena	.15
297	Reggie Taylor	.15
298	*Bob Keppel*	.50
299	Miguel Cabrera (photo actually Manuel Esquivia)	.75
300	Ryan Franklin	.15
301	Brandon Phillips	.15
302	*Victor Hall*	.50
303	Tony Pena Jr.	.15
304	*Jim Journell*	.50
305	Cristian Guerrero	.25
306	Miguel Olivo	.15
307	Jin Ho Cho	.15
308	Choo Freeman	.15
309	*Danny Borrell*	.50

310	Doug Mientkiewicz	.15
311	Aaron Herr	.15
312	Keith Ginter	.15
313	Felipe Lopez	.15
314	*Jeff Goldbach*	.50
315	Travis Harper	.15
316	Paul LoDuca	.15
317	Joe Torres	.15
318	Eric Byrnes	.15
319	George Lombard	.15
320	David Krynzel	.15
321	Ben Christensen	.15
322	Aubrey Huff	.15
323	Lyle Overbay	.15
324	Sean McGowan	.15
325	Jeff Heaverlo	.15
326	Timo Perez	.15
327	*Octavio Martinez*	.50
328	Vince Faison	.15
329	*David Parrish*	.50
330	Bobby Bradley	.15
331	*Jason Miller*	.50
332	*Corey Spencer*	.50
333	Craig House	.15
334	*Maxim St. Pierre*	.40
335	Adam Johnson	.15
336	Joe Crede	.15
337	*Greg Nash*	.40
338	Chad Durbin	.15
339	*Pat Magness*	.50
340	Matt Wheatland	.15
341	Julio Lugo	.15
342	Grady Sizemore	.15
343	Adrian Gonzalez	.25
344	Tim Raines Jr.	.15
345	*Rainier Olmedo*	.50
346	Phil Dumatrait	.15
347	*Brandon Mims*	.50
348	Jason Jennings	.15
349	*Phil Wilson*	.50
350	Jason Hart	.25
351	Cesar Izturis	.15
352	*Matt Butler*	.50
353	David Kelton	.15
354	Luke Prokopec	.15
355	Corey Smith	.15
356	*Joel Pineiro*	.75
357	Ken Chenard	.15
358	Keith Reed	.15
359	David Walling	.15
360	*Alexis Gomez*	.75
361	*Justin Morneau*	5.00
362	*Josh Fogg*	.50
363	J.R. House	.15
364	Andy Tracy	.15
365	Kenny Kelly	.15
366	Aaron McNeal	.15
367	Nick Johnson	.15
368	Brian Esposito	.15
369	*Charles Frazier*	.50
370	Scott Heard	.15
371	Patrick Strange	.15
372	Mike Meyers	.15
373	*Ryan Ludwick*	.40
374	Brad Wilkerson	.15
375	Allen Levrault	.15
376	*Seth McClung*	.40
377	Joe Nathan	.15
378	*Rafael Soriano*	1.00
379	Chris Richard	.15
380	Xavier Nady	.15
381	Tike Redman	.15
382	Adam Dunn	.15
383	*Jared Abruzzo*	.50
384	*Jason Richardson*	.40
385	Matt Holliday	.15
386	*Darwin Cubillian*	.40
387	Mike Nannini	.15
388	*Blake Williams*	.50
389	*Valentino Pascucci*	.50
390	Jon Garland	.15
391	Josh Pressley	.15
392	Jose Ortiz	.15
393	*Ryan Hannaman*	.40
394	*Steve Smyth*	.40
395	John Patterson	.15
396	*Chad Petty*	.40
397	*Jake Peavy*	8.00
398	*Onix Mercado*	.40
399	Jason Romano	.15
400	*Luis Torres*	.40
401	*Casey Fossum*	.50
402	*Eduardo Figueroa*	.40
403	*Bryan Barnowski*	.40
404	Tim Redding	.15
405	Jason Standridge	.15
406	*Marvin Seale*	.50
407	Todd Moser	.15
408	Alex Gordon	.15
409	*Steve Smitherman*	1.00
410	Ben Petrick	.15
411	Eric Munson	.15
412	Luis Rivas	.15
413	Matt Ginter	.15
414	Alfonso Soriano	.50
415	*Rafael Boitel*	.50
416	*Dany Morban*	.40
417	*Justin Woodrowc*	.40
418	Wilfredo Rodriguez	.15
419	*Derrick Van Dusen*	.40
420	*Josh Spoerl*	.40
421	Juan Pierre	.15
422	J.C. Romero	.15
423	*Ed Rogers*	.40
424	Tomokazu Ohka	.25
425	*Ben Hendrickson*	.40
426	Carlos Zambrano	.15
427	Brett Myers	.15
428	Scott Seabol	.15
429	Thomas Mitchell	.15
430	*Jose Reyes*	5.00
431	Kip Wells	.15
432	Willi Mo Pena	.15
433	*Adam Pettyjohn*	.40
434	Austin Kearns	.15
435	Rico Washington	.15
436	*Doug Nickle*	.40
437	Steve Lomasney	.15
438	*Jason Jones*	.40
439	Bobby Seay	.15
440	*Justin Wayne*	.50

Autographs

		NM/M
Common Autograph:		5.00
Inserted 1:74		
BB	Brian Barnowski	5.00
WB	Wilson Betemit	8.00
JB	Jason Botts	30.00
SB	Sean Burroughs	8.00
FB	Freddie Bynum	5.00
ND	Noel Devarez	5.00
JD	Jose Diaz	5.00
BD	Ben Diggins	5.00
AE	Alex Escobar	8.00
RF	Rafael Furcal	10.00
AG	Adrian Gonzalez	8.00
AKG	Alex Gordon	5.00
AJG	Alex Graman	5.00
CG	Cristian Guerrero	5.00
TH	Travis Hafner	60.00
JH	Josh Hamilton	5.00
JWH	Jason Hart	5.00
JRH	J.R. House	8.00
RJ	Russ Jacobson	5.00
AJ	Adam Johnson	5.00
TJ	Tripper Johnson	8.00
DWK	David Kelton	5.00
DK	David Krynzel	5.00
PR	Pedro Liriano	5.00
SM	Sean McGowan	5.00
KM	Kevin Mench	8.00
LM	Luis Montanez	8.00
JM	Justin Morneau	70.00
LO	Lyle Overbay	10.00
ADP	Adam Piatt	8.00
JP	Josh Pressley	6.00
AP	Albert Pujols	500.00
KS	Kazuhiro Sasaki	
BS	Ben Sheets	20.00
SDS	Steve Smyth	5.00
SS	Shawn Sonnier	5.00
SU	Sixto Urena	5.00
MV	Miguel Villilo	5.00
BW	Brad Wilkerson	10.00
BZ	Barry Zito	20.00

Autographed Game-Used Bat Rookie Reprints

Inserted 1:18,259
No pricing due to scarcity

1	Willie Mays
2	Duke Snider
3	Minnie Minoso
4	Hank Bauer
5	Al Rosen

Autographed Rookie Reprints

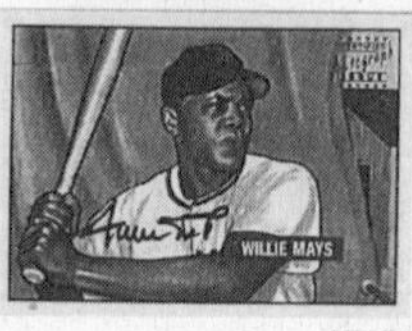

		NM/M
Common Autograph:		20.00
Inserted 1:2,467		
1	Yogi Berra	65.00
2	Willie Mays	200.00
3	Stan Musial	100.00
4	Duke Snider	35.00
5	Warren Spahn	50.00
6	Ralph Kiner	25.00
8	Don Larsen	30.00
9	Don Zimmer	20.00
10	Minnie Minoso	20.00

Autoproofs

Inserted 1:18,259H
Inserted 1:8,306HTA
Redemption Expired 4/30/03
VALUES UNDETERMINED

Hank Bauer/50 Redemp
Carlos Delgado/92 Redemp
Carl Erskine/51
Chipper Jones/91 Redemp
Ralph Kiner/48 Redemp
Don Larsen/54
Gil McDougald/52 Redemp
Ivan Rodriguez/91 Redemp
Pat Burrell/99 Redemp
Rafael Furcal/99

Futures Game-Worn Jersey

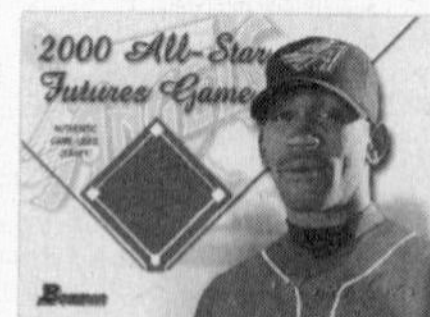

		NM/M
Common Player:		5.00
Inserted 1:82		
KA	Kurt Ainsworth	6.00
CA	Craig Anderson	5.00
RA	Ryan Anderson	5.00
BB	Bobby Bradley	5.00
MB	Mike Bynum	5.00
RC	Ramon Castro	5.00
CC	Chin-Feng Chen	25.00
JC	Jack Cust	5.00
TD	Travis Dawkins	5.00
RD	Randey Dorame	5.00
AE	Alex Escobar	5.00
CG	Chris George	5.00
MG	Marcus Giles	6.00
JH	Josh Hamilton	5.00
CH	Carlos Hernandez	5.00
SK	Sun-Woo Kim	5.00
FL	Felipe Lopez	5.00
EM	Eric Munson	5.00
AM	Aaron Myette	5.00
NN	Ntema Ndungidi	5.00
TO	Tomokazu Ohka	6.00
RO	Ramon Ortiz	5.00
DCP	Corey Patterson	8.00
CP	Carlos Pena	5.00
BP	Ben Petrick	5.00
GR	Grant Roberts	5.00
JR	Jason Romano	5.00
BS	Ben Sheets	6.00
CT	Chin-Hui Tsao	15.00
VW	Vernon Wells	8.00
BW	Brad Wilkerson	5.00
TW	Travis Wilson	5.00
BZ	Barry Zito	15.00
JZ	Julio Zuleta	5.00

Futures Game Three-Piece Game-Used

		NM/M
Common Player:		20.00
RC	Ramon Castro	20.00
CC	Chin-Feng Chen	80.00
JC	Jack Cust	20.00
TD	Travis Dawkins	20.00
AE	Alex Escobar	20.00
MG	Marcus Giles	20.00
JH	Josh Hamilton	20.00
FL	Felipe Lopez	20.00
EM	Eric Munson	25.00
NN	Ntema Ndungidi	20.00
DCP	Corey Patterson	25.00
CP	Carlos Pena	20.00
BP	Ben Petrick	20.00
JR	Jason Romano	20.00
VW	Vernon Wells	30.00
BW	Brad Wilkerson	20.00
TW	Travis Wilson	20.00
JZ	Julio Zuleta	20.00

Game-Used Bat Rookie Reprints

		NM/M
Common Player:		10.00
Inserted 1:1,954		
1	Willie Mays	60.00
2	Duke Snider	25.00
3	Minnie Minoso	10.00
4	Hank Bauer	10.00
5	Al Rosen	10.00

Rookie of the Year Dual Jersey

		NM/M
Inserted 1:2,202		
ROYR	Kazuhiro Sasaki, Rafael Furcal	30.00

Rookie Reprints

		NM/M
Complete Set (25):		50.00
Common Player:		1.50
Inserted 1:12		
1	Yogi Berra	5.00
2	Ralph Kiner	2.50
3	Stan Musial	6.00
4	Warren Spahn	4.00
5	Roy Campanella	4.00
6	Bob Lemon	1.50
7	Robin Roberts	2.00
8	Duke Snider	4.00
9	Early Wynn	1.50
10	Richie Ashburn	1.50
11	Gil Hodges	2.00
12	Hank Bauer	2.00
13	Don Newcombe	1.50

14 Al Rosen 1.50
15 Willie Mays 8.00
16 Joe Garagiola 2.00
17 Whitey Ford 4.00
18 Lew Burdette 1.50
19 Gil McDougald 1.50
20 Minnie Minoso 1.50
21 Eddie Mathews 4.00
22 Harvey Kuenn 2.00
23 Don Larsen 3.00
24 Elston Howard 2.00
25 Don Zimmer 1.50

2001 BOWMAN CHROME

NM/M

Complete Set (351):
Common (1-110, 201-310): .20
Common Ref.
(111-200, 311-330): 4.00
Inserted 1:4
Common Ref. Auto.
(331-350): 25.00
Production 500
Pack (4): 18.00
Box (24): 375.00

1 Jason Giambi .60
2 Rafael Furcal .20
3 Bernie Williams .50
4 Kenny Lofton .20
5 Al Leiter .20
6 Albert Belle .20
7 Craig Biggio .20
8 Mark Mulder .20
9 Carlos Delgado .75
10 Darin Erstad .75
11 Richie Sexson .20
12 Randy Johnson 1.00
13 Greg Maddux 1.50
14 Orlando Hernandez .20
15 Javier Vazquez .20
16 Jeff Kent .20
17 Jim Thome .40
18 John Olerud .20
19 Jason Kendall .20
20 Scott Rolen .75
21 Tony Gwynn 1.50
22 Edgardo Alfonzo .20
23 Pokey Reese .20
24 Todd Helton 1.00
25 Mark Quinn .20
26 Dean Palmer .20
27 Ray Durham .20
28 Rafael Palmeiro 1.00
29 Carl Everett .20
30 Vladimir Guerrero 1.00
31 Livan Hernandez .20
32 Preston Wilson .20
33 Jose Vidro .20
34 Fred McGriff .20
35 Kevin Brown .20
36 Miguel Tejada .40
37 Chipper Jones 1.50
38 Edgar Martinez .20
39 Tony Batista .20
40 Jorge Posada .40
41 Sammy Sosa 2.00
42 Gary Sheffield .50
43 Bartolo Colon .20
44 Pat Burrell 1.00
45 Jay Payton .20
46 Mike Mussina .60
47 Nomar Garciaparra 2.00
48 Darren Dreifort .20
49 Richard Hidalgo .20
50 Troy Glaus 1.00
51 Ben Grieve .20
52 Jim Edmonds .20
53 Raul Mondesi .20
54 Andruw Jones 1.00
55 Mike Sweeney .20
56 Derek Jeter 3.00
57 Ruben Mateo .20
58 Cristian Guzman .20
59 Mike Hampton .20
60 J.D. Drew .50
61 Matt Lawton .20
62 Moises Alou .20
63 Terrence Long .20
64 Geoff Jenkins .20
65 Manny Ramirez 1.00
66 Johnny Damon .35
67 Pedro Martinez 1.00
68 Juan Gonzalez 1.00
69 Roger Clemens 1.75
70 Carlos Beltran .75
71 Roberto Alomar .75
72 Barry Bonds 3.00
73 Tim Hudson .50
74 Tom Glavine .50
75 Jeromy Burnitz .20
76 Adrian Beltre .40
77 Mike Piazza 2.00
78 Kerry Wood .50
79 Steve Finley .20
80 Bobby Abreu .20
81 Neifi Perez .20
82 Mark Redman .20
83 Paul Konerko .20
84 Jermaine Dye .20
85 Brian Giles .20
86 Ivan Rodriguez .75
87 Adam Kennedy .20
88 Eric Chavez .40
89 Billy Koch .20
90 Shawn Green .40
91 Matt Williams .20
92 Greg Vaughn .20
93 Jeff Cirillo .20
94 Frank Thomas 1.00
95 David Justice .20
96 Cal Ripken Jr. 3.00
97 Curt Schilling .20
98 Barry Zito .40
99 Brian Jordan .20
100 Chan Ho Park .20
101 J.T. Snow Jr. .20
102 Kazuhiro Sasaki .20
103 Alex Rodriguez 2.50
104 Mariano Rivera .35
105 Eric Milton .20
106 Andy Pettitte .50
107 Ken Griffey Jr. 2.00
108 Bengie Molina .20
109 Jeff Bagwell 1.00
110 Mark McGwire 2.50
111 *Dan Tosca* 4.00
112 *Sergio Contreras* 4.00
113 *Mitch Jones* 4.00
114 *Ramon Carvajal* 4.00
115 *Ryan Madson* 8.00
116 *Hank Blalock* 60.00
117 *Ben Washburn* 4.00
118 *Erick Almonte* 4.00
119 *Shawn Fagan* 4.00
120 *Gary Johnson* 4.00
121 *Brett Evert* 4.00
122 *Joe Hamer* 4.00
123 *Yhency Brazoban* 6.00
124 *Domingo Guante* 4.00
125 *Deivi Mendez* 4.00
126 *Adrian Hernandez* 4.00
127 *Reggie Abercrombie* 6.00
128 *Steve Bennett* 4.00
129 *Matt White* 4.00
130 *Brian Hitchcox* 4.00
131 *Deivis Santos* 4.00
132 *Luis Montanez* 4.00
133 *Eric Reynolds* 4.00
134 *Denny Bautista* 25.00
135 *Hector Garcia* 4.00
136 *Joe Thurston* 8.00
137 *Tsuyoshi Shinjo* 8.00
138 *Elpidio Guzman* 4.00
139 *Brian Bass* 4.00
140 *Mark Burnett* 4.00
141 *Russ Jacobsen* 4.00
142 *Travis Hafner* 40.00
143 *Wilson Betemit* 12.00
144 *Luke Lockwood* 4.00
145 *Noel Devarez* 4.00
146 *Doug Gredvig* 4.00
147 *Seung Jun Song* 6.00
148 *Andy Van Hekken* 4.00
149 Ryan Kohlmeier 4.00
150 *Dee Haynes* 6.00
151 *Jim Journell* 6.00
152 *Chad Petty* 4.00
153 *Danny Borrell* 4.00
154 David Krynzel 4.00
155 *Octavio Martinez* 4.00
156 *David Parrish* 4.00
157 *Jason Miller* 4.00
158 *Corey Spencer* 4.00
159 *Maxim St. Pierre* 4.00
160 *Pat Magness* 4.00
161 *Rainier Olmedo* 4.00
162 *Brandon Mims* 4.00
163 *Phil Wilson* 4.00
164 *Jose Reyes* 50.00
165 *Matt Butler* 4.00
166 Joel Pineiro 4.00
167 Ken Chenard 4.00
168 *Alexis Gomez* 6.00
169 *Justin Morneau* 40.00
170 *Josh Fogg* 5.00
171 *Charles Frazier* 4.00
172 *Ryan Ludwick* 6.00
173 *Seth McClung* 6.00
174 *Justin Wayne* 6.00
175 *Rafael Soriano* 6.00
176 *Jared Abruzzo* 4.00
177 *Jason Richardson* 4.00
178 *Darwin Cubillan* 4.00
179 *Blake Williams* 4.00
180 *Valentino Pascucci* 4.00
181 *Ryan Hannaman* 4.00
182 *Steve Smyth* 4.00
183 *Jake Peavy* 60.00
184 *Onix Mercado* 4.00
185 *Luis Torres* 4.00
186 *Casey Fossum* 6.00
187 *Eduardo Figueroa* 4.00
188 *Bryan Barnowski* 4.00
189 Jason Standridge 4.00
190 *Marvin Seale* 4.00
191 *Steve Smitherman* 8.00
192 *Rafael Boitel* 4.00
193 *Dany Morban* 4.00
194 *Justin Woodrowc* 4.00
195 *Ed Rogers* 4.00
196 *Ben Hendrickson* 4.00
197 Thomas Mitchell 4.00
198 *Adam Pettyjohn* 4.00
199 *Doug Nickle* 4.00
200 *Jason Jones* 4.00
201 Larry Barnes .20
202 Ben Diggins .20
203 Dee Brown .20
204 Rocco Baldelli 1.00
205 Luis Terrero .20
206 Milton Bradley .20
207 Kurt Ainsworth .20
208 Sean Burroughs .40
209 Rick Asadoorian .20
210 Ramon Castro .20
211 Nick Neugebauer .50
212 Aaron Myette .20
213 Luis Matos .20
214 Donnie Bridges .20
215 Alex Cintron .20
216 Bobby Kielty .20
217 Matt Belisle .20
218 Adam Everett .20
219 John Lackey .20
220 Adam Wainwright .20
221 Jerry Hairston Jr. .20
222 Mike Bynum .20
223 Ryan Christianson .20
224 J.J. Davis .20
225 Alex Graman .20
226 Abraham Nunez .20
227 Sun-Woo Kim .20
228 Jimmy Rollins .20
229 Ruben Salazar .20
230 Josh Girdley .20
231 Carl Crawford .20
232 Ben Davis .20
233 Jason Grabowski .20
234 Chris George .20
235 Roy Oswalt .75
236 Brian Cole .20
237 Corey Patterson .40
238 Vernon Wells .20
239 Bradley Baker .20
240 Gookie Dawkins .20
241 Michael Cuddyer .20
242 Ricardo Aramboles .20
243 Ben Sheets .50
244 Toby Hall .20
245 Jack Cust .20
246 Pedro Feliz .20
247 Josh Beckett .50
248 Alex Escobar .20
249 Marcus Giles .20
250 Jon Rauch .40
251 Kevin Mench .20
252 Shawn Sonnier .20
253 Aaron Rowand .20
254 C.C. Sabathia .20
255 Bubba Crosby .20
256 Josh Hamilton .20
257 Carlos Hernandez .20
258 Carlos Pena .20
259 Miguel Cabrera (photo actually Manuel Esquivia) 2.50
260 Brandon Phillips .20
261 Tony Pena Jr. .20
262 Cristian Guerrero .50
263 Jin Ho Cho .20
264 Aaron Herr .20
265 Keith Ginter .20
266 Felipe Lopez .20
267 Travis Harper .20
268 Joe Torres .20
269 Eric Byrnes .20
270 Ben Christensen .20
271 Aubrey Huff .20
272 Lyle Overbay .20
273 Vince Faison .20
274 Bobby Bradley .20
275 Joe Crede .20
276 Matt Wheatland .20
277 Grady Sizemore .20
278 Adrian Gonzalez .20
279 Timothy Raines Jr. .20
280 Phil Dumatrait .20
281 Jason Hart .50
282 David Kelton .20
283 David Walling .20
284 J.R. House .50
285 Kenny Kelly .20
286 Aaron McNeal .20
287 Nick Johnson .20
288 Scott Heard .20
289 Brad Wilkerson .20
290 Allen Levrault .20
291 Chris Richard .20
292 Jared Sandberg .20
293 Tike Redman .20
294 Adam Dunn 1.00
295 Josh Pressley .20
296 Jose Ortiz .20
297 Jason Romano .20
298 Tim Redding .20
299 Alex Gordon .20
300 Ben Petrick .20
301 Eric Munson .20
302 Luis Rivas .20
303 Matt Ginter .20
304 Alfonso Soriano .50
305 Wilfredo Rodriguez .20
306 Brett Myers .20
307 Scott Seabol .20
308 Tony Alvarez .20
309 Donzell McDonald .20
310 Austin Kearns .20
311 *Will Ohman* 4.00
312 *Ryan Soules* 4.00
313 *Cody Ross* 4.00
314 *Bill Whitecotton* 4.00
315 *Mike Burns* 4.00
316 *Manuel Acosta* 4.00
317 *Lance Niekro* 20.00
318 *Travis Thompson* 4.00
319 *Zach Sorensen* 4.00
320 *Austin Evans* 4.00
321 *Brad Stiles* 4.00
322 *Joe Kennedy* 4.00
323 *Luke Martin* 4.00
324 *Juan Diaz* 4.00
325 *Pat Hallmark* 4.00
326 *Christian Parker* 4.00
327 *Ronny Corona* 4.00
328 *Jermaine Clark* 4.00
329 *Scott Dunn* 4.00
330 *Scott Chiasson* 4.00
331 *Greg Nash Auto* 25.00
332 Brad Cresse Auto 25.00
333 *John Buck Auto* 60.00
334 *Freddie Bynum Auto* 25.00
335 *Felix Diaz Auto* 25.00
336 *Jason Belcher Auto* 25.00
337 *Troy Farnsworth* 25.00
338 *Roberto Miniel* 25.00
339 *Esix Snead* 25.00
340 *Albert Pujols* 2,400
341 *Jeff Andra* 25.00
342 *Victor Hall* 25.00
343 *Pedro Liriano* 25.00
344 *Andy Beal* 25.00
345 *Bob Keppel* 40.00
346 *Brian Schmitt* 25.00
347 *Ron Davenport* 150.00
348 *Tony Blanco* 50.00
349 *Reggie Griggs* 25.00

350	*Derrick Van Dusen*	25.00
351a	*Ichiro Suzuki Eng.*	100.00
351b	*Ichiro Suzuki Japanese*	100.00

X-Fractors

Stars:	4-8X
Rookies:	.75-1.5X
Inserted 1:23	

(See 2001 Bowman Chrome for checklist and base card values.)

Gold Refractors

Stars:	8-15X
Rookies:	1.5-3X
Production 99 sets	

(See 2001 Bowman Chrome for checklist and base card values.)

Futures Game Memorabilia

		NM/M
Common Player:		6.00
Inserted 1:460		
KA	Kurt Ainsworth	8.00
CA	Craig Anderson	6.00
RA	Ryan Anderson	6.00
BB	Bobby Bradley	6.00
MB	Mike Bynum	6.00
RC	Ramon Castro	6.00
CC	Chin-Feng Chen	20.00
JC	Jack Cust	6.00
RD	Randey Dorame	6.00
AE	Alex Escobar	6.00
CG	Chris George	6.00
MG	Marcus Giles	6.00
JH	Josh Hamilton	6.00
CH	Carlos Hernandez	6.00
SK	Sun-Woo Kim	6.00
FL	Felipe Lopez	8.00
EM	Eric Munson	6.00
AM	Aaron Myette	6.00
NN	Ntema Ndungidi	6.00
TO	Tomokazu Ohka	6.00
DCP	Corey Patterson	10.00
CP	Carlos Pena	6.00
BP	Ben Petrick	6.00
JR	Jason Romano	6.00
BS	Ben Sheets	8.00
CT	Chin-Hui Tsao	10.00
BW	Brad Wilkerson	6.00
TW	Travis Wilson	6.00
BZ	Barry Zito	25.00
JZ	Julio Zuleta	6.00

Rookie Reprints

	NM/M
Complete Set (25):	50.00
Common Player:	2.00
Inserted 1:12	

Refractors:		2-3X
Production 299 sets		
1	Yogi Berra	5.00
2	Ralph Kiner	3.00
3	Stan Musial	6.00
4	Warren Spahn	4.00
5	Roy Campanella	4.00
6	Bob Lemon	2.00
7	Robin Roberts	2.00
8	Duke Snider	4.00
9	Early Wynn	2.00
10	Richie Ashburn	3.00
11	Gil Hodges	3.00
12	Hank Bauer	2.00
13	Don Newcombe	2.00
14	Al Rosen	2.00
15	Willie Mays	8.00
16	Joe Garagiola	3.00
17	Whitey Ford	4.00
18	Lew Burdette	2.00
19	Gil McDougald	2.00
20	Minnie Minoso	2.00
21	Eddie Mathews	4.00
22	Harvey Kuenn	2.00
23	Don Larsen	3.00
24	Elston Howard	2.00
25	Don Zimmer	2.00

Rookie Reprint Relics

		NM/M
Common Player:		8.00
Inserted 1:244		
1	David Justice	8.00
2	Richie Sexson	12.00
3	Sean Casey	8.00
4	Mike Piazza	50.00
5	Carlos Delgado	8.00
6	Chipper Jones	25.00

2001 BOWMAN DRAFT PICKS & PROSPECTS

		NM/M
Complete Set (110):		25.00
Complete Factory Set (112):		35.00
Common Player:		.10
1	*Alfredo Amezaga*	.50
2	Andrew Good	.10
3	*Kelly Johnson*	3.00
4	Larry Bigbie	.10
5	*Matt Thompson*	.40
6	*Wilton Chavez*	.40
7	*Joe Borchard*	1.00
8	David Espinosa	.10
9	*Zach Day*	.75
10	*Brad Hawpe*	1.50
11	Nate Cornejo	.10
12	*Jim Kavourias*	.10
13	Brad Lidge	.10
14	*Angel Berroa*	1.50
15	*Lamont Matthews*	.10
16	Jose Garcia	.10
17	*Grant Balfour*	.25
18	*Ron Chiavacci*	.20
19	Jae Seo	.10
20	Juan Rivera	.10
21	D'Angelo Jimenez	.10
22	Aaron Harang	.10
23	*Marlon Byrd*	.75
24	Sean Burnett	.10
25	*Josh Pearce*	.25
26	*Brandon Duckworth*	.25
27	*Jack Taschner*	.20
28	*Bo Robinson*	.20
29	Brent Abernathy	.10
30	*David Elder*	.20
31	*Scott Cassidy*	.20
32	*Dennis Tankersley*	.50
33	Denny Stark	.10
34	*Dave Williams*	.40
35	*Boof Bonser*	.25
36	*Kris Foster*	.20
37	*Neal Musser*	.25
38	Shawn Chacon	.10
39	*Mike Rivera*	.40
40	*Will Smith*	.40
41	*Morgan Ensberg*	3.00
42	Ken Harvey	.10
43	*Ricardo Rodriguez*	.50
44	*Jose Mieses*	.20
45	*Luis Maza*	.20
46	*Julio Perez*	.20
47	*Billy Traber*	.40
48	*David Martinez*	.20
49	*Covelli Crisp*	1.50
50	*Mario Ramos*	.10
51	*Matt Thornton*	.20
52	Xavier Nady	.10
53	Ryan Vogelsong	.10
54	*Jim Magrane*	.20
55	*Domingo Valdez*	.20
56	Brent Butler	.10
57	*Brian Tallet*	.20
58	*Brian Reith*	.20
59	*Mario Valenzuela*	.20
60	*Bobby Hill*	.50
61	*Rich Rundles*	.25
62	Rick Elder	.10
63	J.D. Closser	.10
64	Scot Shields	.10
65	Miguel Olivo	.10
66	*Stubby Clapp*	.10
67	*Jerome Williams*	2.00
68	*Jason Lane*	1.00
69	*Chase Utley*	6.00
70	*Erik Bedard*	.40
71	*Alex Herrera*	.10
72	*Juan Cruz*	.50
73	*Billy Martin*	.20
74	*Ronnie Merrill*	.20
75	*Jason Kinchen*	.20
76	*Wilken Ruan*	.20
77	*Cody Ransom*	.20
78	*Bud Smith*	.25
79	Wily Mo Pena	.10
80	*Jeff Nettles*	.20
81	*Jamal Strong*	.25
82	Bill Ortega	.10
83	Junior Zamora	.10
84	*Ichiro Suzuki*	10.00
85	*Fernando Rodney*	.20
86	*Chris Smith*	.40
87	*John VanBenschoten*	1.00
88	*Bobby Crosby*	5.00
89	*Kenny Baugh*	.25
90	*Jake Gautreau*	.50
91	*Gabe Gross*	1.50
92	*Kris Honel*	.75
93	*Daniel Denham*	.25
94	*Aaron Heilman*	.75
95	*Irvin Guzman*	5.00
96	*Mike Jones*	.50
97	*John-Ford Griffin*	.50
98	*MaCay McBride*	.25
99	*John Rheineckar*	.25
100	*Bronson Sardinha*	.50
101	*Jason Weintraub*	.25
102	*J.D. Martin*	.50
103	*Jayson Nix*	.40
104	*Noah Lowry*	3.00
105	*Richard Lewis*	.25
106	*Brad Hennessey*	.40
107	*Jeff Mathis*	1.00
108	*Jon Skaggs*	.40
109	*Justin Pope*	.25
110	*Josh Burrus*	.25

Autographs

		NM/M
Common Autograph:		5.00
Inserted 1:set		
JA	Jared Abruzzo	5.00
AA	Alfredo Amezaga	10.00
GA	Garrett Atkins	30.00
BB	Bobby Bradley	5.00
ANC	Antoine Cameron	5.00
ROC	Ramon Carvajal	5.00
RC	Ryan Church	20.00
AC	Alex Cintron	5.00
RD	Ryan Dittfurth	5.00
AE	Adam Everett	5.00
AF	Alex Fernandez	5.00
AG	Alexis Gomez	10.00
CG	Cristian Guerrero	5.00
BH	Beau Hale	5.00
SH	Scott Heard	5.00
AH	Aaron Herr	5.00
CI	Cesar Izturis	5.00
GJ	Gary Johnson	5.00
NJ	Nick Johnson	10.00
AK	Austin Kearns	15.00
JK	Joe Kennedy	5.00
JL	John Lackey	8.00
FL	Felipe Lopez	8.00
RI	Ryan Ludwick	10.00
RMM	Ryan Madson	5.00
TO	Tomo Ohka	8.00
RO	Roy Oswalt	15.00
CP	Christian Parra	5.00
BP	Brandon Phillips	8.00
JP	Joel Pineiro	15.00
NR	Nick Regilio	5.00
ER	Ed Rogers	5.00
SS	Scott Seabol	5.00
BS	Bud Smith	5.00
BJS	Brian Specht	5.00
JT	Joe Torres	5.00
JMW	Justin Wayne	8.00

Futures Game Relics

		NM/M
Common Player:		4.00
One Per Factory Set		
AA	Alfredo Amezaga	4.00
AD	Adam Dunn	10.00
AG	Adrian Gonzalez	6.00
AH	Alex Herrera	4.00
BM	Brett Myers	8.00
CD	Cody Ransom	4.00
CG	Chris George	4.00
CH	Carlos Hernandez	5.00
CU	Chase Utley	15.00
EB	Eric Bedard	4.00
GB	Grant Balfour	4.00
HB	Hank Blalock	18.00
JB	Joe Borchard	10.00
JC	Juan Cruz	5.00
JP	Josh Pearce	4.00
JR	Juan Rivera	4.00
LG	Luis Garcia	4.00
MC	Miguel Cabrera	10.00
MR	Mike Rivera	4.00
RR	Ricardo Rodriguez	4.00
SC	Scott Chiasson	4.00
SS	Seung Jun Song	6.00

TB Toby Hall 4.00
WB Wilson Betemit 4.00
WP Wily Mo Pena 5.00
JAP Juan Pena 4.00

Draft Pick Relics

NM/M

Common Player: 4.00
One Per Factory Set
CI Cesar Izturis 4.00
GJ Gary Johnson 4.00
NR Nick Regilio 4.00
RC Ryan Church 4.00
BJS Brian Specht 4.00
JRH J.R. House 4 .00

2001 BOWMAN HERITAGE

NM/M

Complete Set (440): 200.00
Common Player: .15
Common (331-440): 1.00
Inserted 1:2
Pack (10): 6.00
Box (24): 110.00
1 Chipper Jones 1.25
2 Pete Harnisch .15
3 Brian Giles .15
4 J.T. Snow .15
5 Bartolo Colon .15
6 Jorge Posada .25
7 Shawn Green .25
8 Derek Jeter 2.50
9 Benito Santiago .15
10 Ramon Hernandez .15
11 Bernie Williams .30
12 Greg Maddux 1.25
13 Barry Bonds 2.50
14 Roger Clemens 1.50
15 Miguel Tejada .40
16 Pedro Feliz .15
17 Jim Edmonds .25
18 Tom Glavine .30
19 David Justice .15
20 Rich Aurilia .15
21 Jason Giambi .65
22 Orlando Hernandez .15
23 Shawn Estes .15
24 Nelson Figueroa .15
25 Terrence Long .15
26 Mike Mussina .50
27 Eric Davis .15
28 Jimmy Rollins .15
29 Andy Pettitte .40
30 Shawon Dunston .15
31 Tim Hudson .40
32 Jeff Kent .15
33 Scott Brosius .15
34 Livan Hernandez .15
35 Alfonso Soriano 1.00
36 Mark McGwire 1.75
37 Russ Ortiz .15
38 Fernando Vina .15
39 Ken Griffey Jr. 1.50
40 Edgar Renteria .15
41 Kevin Brown .25
42 Robb Nen .15
43 Paul LoDuca .15
44 Bobby Abreu .15
45 Adam Dunn .50
46 Osvaldo Fernandez .15
47 Marvin Benard .15
48 Mark Gardner .15
49 Alex Rodriguez 2.00
50 Preston Wilson .15
51 Roberto Alomar .35
52 Ben Davis .15
53 Derek Bell .15
54 Ken Caminiti .15
55 Barry Zito .40
56 Scott Rolen .75
57 Geoff Jenkins .15
58 Mike Cameron .15
59 Ben Grieve .15
60 Chuck Knoblauch .15
61 Matt Lawton .15
62 Chan Ho Park .15
63 Lance Berkman .15
64 Carlos Beltran .50
65 Dean Palmer .15
66 Alex Gonzalez .15
67 Larry Walker .15
68 Magglio Ordonez .25
69 Ellis Burks .15
70 Mark Mulder .25
71 Randy Johnson .75
72 John Smoltz .15
73 Jerry Hairston Jr. .15
74 Pedro Martinez .75
75 Fred McGriff .15
76 Sean Casey .35
77 C.C. Sabathia .15
78 Todd Helton .75
79 Brad Penny .15
80 Mike Sweeney .15
81 Billy Wagner .15
82 Mark Buehrle .15
83 Cristian Guzman .15
84 Jose Vidro .15
85 Pat Burrell .50
86 Jermaine Dye .15
87 Brandon Inge .15
88 David Wells .15
89 Mike Piazza 1.50
90 Jose Cabrera .15
91 Cliff Floyd .15
92 Matt Morris .15
93 Raul Mondesi .15
94 *Joe Kennedy* .50
95 *Jack Wilson* 1.50
96 Andruw Jones .75
97 Mariano Rivera .25
98 Mike Hampton .15
99 Roger Cedeno .15
100 Jose Cruz .15
101 Mike Lowell .15
102 Pedro Astacio .15
103 Joe Mays .15
104 John Franco .15
105 Tim Redding .15
106 Sandy Alomar .15
107 Bret Boone .15
108 *Josh Towers* .50
109 Matt Stairs .15
110 Chris Truby .15
111 Jeff Suppan .15
112 J.C. Romero .15
113 Felipe Lopez .15
114 Ben Sheets .25
115 Frank Thomas .75
116 A.J. Burnett .15
117 Tony Clark .15
118 Mac Suzuki .15
119 Brad Radke .15
120 Jeff Shaw .15
121 Nick Neugebauer .15
122 Kenny Lofton .15
123 Jacque Jones .15
124 Brent Mayne .15
125 Carlos Hernandez .15
126 Shane Spencer .15
127 John Lackey .15
128 Sterling Hitchcock .15
129 Darren Dreifort .15
130 Rusty Greer .15
131 Michael Cuddyer .15
132 Tyler Houston .15
133 Chin-Feng Chen .15
134 Ken Harvey .15
135 Marquis Grissom .15
136 Russell Branyan .15
137 Eric Karros .15
138 Josh Beckett .15
139 Todd Zeile .15
140 Corey Koskie .15
141 Steve Sparks .15
142 Bobby Seay .15
143 Tim Raines .15
144 Julio Zuleta .15
145 Jose Lima .15
146 Dante Bichette .15
147 Randy Keisler .15
148 Brent Butler .15
149 Antonio Alfonseca .15
150 Bryan Rekar .15
151 Jeffrey Hammonds .15
152 Larry Bigbie .15
153 Blake Stein .15
154 Robin Ventura .15
155 Rondell White .15
156 Juan Silvestre .15
157 Marcus Thames .15
158 Sidney Ponson .15
159 Juan Pena .15
160 Charles Johnson .15
161 Adam Everett .15
162 Eric Munson .15
163 Jason Isringhausen .15
164 Brad Fullmer .15
165 Miguel Olivo .15
166 Fernando Tatis .15
167 Freddy Garcia .15
168 Tom Goodwin .15
169 Armando Benitez .15
170 Paul Konerko .15
171 Jeff Cirillo .15
172 Shane Reynolds .15
173 Kevin Tapani .15
174 Joe Crede .15
175 *Omar Infante* 1.00
176 *Jake Peavy* 6.00
177 Corey Patterson .15
178 *Alfredo Amezaga* .25
179 Jeromy Burnitz .15
180 David Segui .15
181 Marcus Giles .15
182 Paul O'Neill .15
183 John Olerud .15
184 Andy Benes .15
185 *Brad Cresse* .25
186 Ricky Ledee .15
187 Allen Levrault .15
188 Royce Clayton .15
189 *Kelly Johnson* 4.00
190 Quilvio Veras .15
191 Mike Williams .15
192 *Jason Lane* 1.00
193 Rick Helling .15
194 Tim Wakefield .15
195 James Baldwin .15
196 *Cody Ransom* .25
197 Bobby Kielty .15
198 Bobby Jones .15
199 Steve Cox .15
200 *Jamal Strong* .25
201 Steve Lomasney .15
202 Bill Ortega .15
203 Mike Matheny .15
204 *Jeff Randazzo* .25
205 Aubrey Huff .15
206 Chuck Finley .15
207 *Denny Bautista* 1.50
208 Terry Mulholland .15
209 Rey Ordonez .15
210 *Jason Belcher* .25
211 Orlando Cabrera .15
212 Juan Encarnacion .15
213 Dustin Hermanson .15
214 Luis Rivas .15
215 Mark Quinn .15
216 Randy Velarde .15
217 Billy Koch .15
218 Ryan Rupe .15
219 Keith Ginter .15
220 Woody Williams .15
221 *Blake Williams* .25
222 Aaron Myette .15
223 *Joe Borchard* 1.00
224 Nate Cornejo .15
225 Julian Tavarez .15
226 Kevin Millwood .15
227 *Travis Hafner* 2.50
228 Charles Nagy .15
229 Mike Lieberthal .15
230 Jeff Nelson .15
231 Ryan Dempster .15
232 Andres Galarraga .15
233 Chad Durbin .15
234 Timoniel Perez .15
235 Troy O'Leary .15
236 Kevin Young .15
237 Gabe Kapler .15
238 *Juan Cruz* .50
239 Masato Yoshii .15
240 Aramis Ramirez .15
241 *Matt Cooper* .25
242 *Randy Flores* .25
243 Rafael Furcal .15
244 David Eckstein .15
245 Matt Clement .15
246 Craig Biggio .15
247 Rick Reed .15
248 Jose Macias .15
249 Alex Escobar .15
250 Roberto Hernandez .15
251 Andy Ashby .15
252 Tony Armas .15
253 Jamie Moyer .15
254 Jason Tyner .15
255 *Ryan Ludwick* .50
256 Jeff Conine .15
257 Francisco Cordova .15
258 Ted Lilly .15
259 Joe Randa .15
260 Jeff D'Amico .15
261 Albie Lopez .15
262 Kevin Appier .15
263 Richard Hidalgo .15
264 Omar Daal .15
265 Ricky Gutierrez .15
266 John Rocker .15
267 Ray Lankford .15
268 *Beau Hale* .25
269 *Tony Blanco* .25
270 Derrick Lee .15
271 Jamey Wright .15
272 Alex Gordon .15
273 Jeff Weaver .15
274 Jaret Wright .15
275 Jose Hernandez .15
276 Bruce Chen .15
277 Todd Hollandsworth .15
278 Wade Miller .15
279 Luke Prokopec .15
280 *Rafael Soriano* 1.00
281 Damion Easley .15
282 Darren Oliver .15
283 *Brandon Duckworth* .50
284 Aaron Herr .15
285 Ray Durham .15
286 *Adrian Hernandez* .40
287 Ugueth Urbina .15
288 Scott Seabol .15
289 *Lance Niekro* 5.00
290 Trot Nixon .15
291 Adam Kennedy .15
292 *Brian Schmitt* .25
293 Grant Roberts .15
294 Benny Agbayani .15
295 Travis Lee .15
296 *Erick Almonte* .40
297 Jim Thome .35
298 Eric Young .15
299 *Daniel Denham* .25
300 *Boof Bonser* .75
301 Denny Neagle .15
302 Kenny Rogers .15
303 J.D. Closser .15
304 *Chase Utley* 6.00
305 Rey Sanchez .15
306 Sean McGowan .15
307 *Justin Pope* .25
308 Torii Hunter .15
309 B.J. Surhoff .15
310 *Aaron Heilman* .50
311 *Gabe Gross* 2.00
312 Lee Stevens .15
313 Todd Hundley .15
314 *MaCay McBride* .25
315 Edgar Martinez .15
316 Omar Vizquel .15
317 Reggie Sanders .15
318 *John-Ford Griffin* .50
319 Tim Salmon (photo actually Troy Glaus) .50
320 Pokey Reese .15
321 Jay Payton .15
322 Doug Glanville .15
323 Greg Vaughn .15
324 Ruben Sierra .15
325 Kip Wells .15
326 Carl Everett .15
327 Garret Anderson .15
328 Jay Bell .15
329 Barry Larkin .15
330 *Jeff Mathis* 1.50
331 Adrian Gonzalez 1.00
332 Juan Rivera 1.00
333 Tony Alvarez 1.00
334 Xavier Nady 1.00
335 Josh Hamilton 1.00
336 *Will Smith* 1.50
337 Israel Alcantara 1.00
338 Chris George 1.00
339 Sean Burroughs 1.25

340	Jack Cust	1.00
341	Eric Byrnes	1.00
342	Carlos Pena	1.00
343	J.R. House	1.00
344	Carlos Silva	1.00
345	*Mike Rivera*	1.00
346	Adam Johnson	1.00
347	Scott Heard	1.00
348	Alex Cintron	1.00
349	Miguel Cabrera	2.50
350	Nick Johnson	1.25
351	*Albert Pujols*	60.00
352	*Ichiro Suzuki*	35.00
353	Carlos Delgado	1.50
354	Troy Glaus	2.00
355	Sammy Sosa	4.00
356	Ivan Rodriguez	2.00
357	Vladimir Guerrero	2.00
358	Manny Ramirez	2.00
359	Luis Gonzalez	1.25
360	Roy Oswalt	1.50
361	Moises Alou	1.00
362	Juan Gonzalez	2.00
363	Tony Gwynn	2.50
364	Hideo Nomo	2.00
365	*Tsuyoshi Shinjo*	1.00
366	Kazuhiro Sasaki	1.00
367	Cal Ripken Jr.	8.00
368	Rafael Palmeiro	2.00
369	J.D. Drew	2.00
370	Doug Mientkiewicz	1.00
371	Jeff Bagwell	2.00
372	Darin Erstad	2.00
373	Tom Gordon	1.00
374	Ben Petrick	1.00
375	Eric Milton	1.00
376	Nomar Garciaparra	6.00
377	Julio Lugo	1.00
378	Tino Martinez	1.00
379	Javier Vazquez	1.00
380	Jeremy Giambi	1.00
381	Marty Cordova	1.00
382	Adrian Beltre	1.50
383	John Burkett	1.00
384	Aaron Boone	1.00
385	Eric Chavez	1.25
386	Curt Schilling	1.50
387	Cory Lidle	1.00
388	Jason Schmidt	1.00
389	Johnny Damon	1.25
390	Steve Finley	1.00
391	Edgardo Alfonzo	1.00
392	Jose Valentin	1.00
393	Jose Canseco	1.50
394	Ryan Klesko	1.00
395	David Cone	1.00
396	Jason Kendall	1.00
397	Placido Polanco	1.00
398	Glendon Rusch	1.00
399	Aaron Sele	1.00
400	D'Angelo Jimenez	1.00
401	Mark Grace	1.25
402	Al Leiter	1.00
403	Brian Jordan	1.00
404	Phil Nevin	1.00
405	Brent Abernathy	1.00
406	Kerry Wood	1.50
407	Alex Gonzalez	1.00
408	Robert Fick	1.00
409	Dmitri Young	1.00
410	Wes Helms	1.00
411	Trevor Hoffman	1.00
412	Rickey Henderson	2.00
413	Bobby Higginson	1.00
414	Gary Sheffield	1.50
415	Darryl Kile	1.00
416	Richie Sexson	1.50
417	Frank Menechino	1.00
418	Javy Lopez	1.00
419	Carlos Lee	1.00
420	Jon Lieber	1.00
421	*Hank Blalock*	10.00
422	*Marlon Byrd*	1.50
423	*Jason Kinchen*	1.00
424	*Morgan Ensberg*	6.00
425	*Greg "Toe" Nash*	1.00
426	*Dennis Tankersley*	1.00
427	Joel Pineiro	1.00
428	*Chris Smith*	1.00
429	*Jake Gautreau*	1.00
430	*John Van Benschoten*	2.00
431	Travis Thompson	1.00
432	*Orlando Hudson*	2.00
433	*Jerome Williams*	2.00
434	Kevin Reese	1.00
435	*Ed Rogers*	1.00
436	*Grant Balfour*	1.00
437	*Adam Pettyjohn*	1.00
438	*Hee Seop Choi*	3.00
439	*Justin Morneau*	8.00
440	*Mitch Jones*	1.00

Chrome

Stars: 4-8X
SPs: 2-4X
Inserted 1:12
(See 2001 Bowman Heritage for checklist and base card values.)

Autographs

		NM/M
Common Player:		35.00
BB	Barry Bonds	200.00
RC	Roger Clemens	100.00
AR	Alex Rodriguez	90.00

1948 BOWMAN REPRINTS

		NM/M
Complete Set (13):		10.00
Common Player:		.75
Inserted 1:2		
1	Ralph Kiner	.75
2	Johnny Mize	.75
3	Bobby Thomson	.75
4	Yogi Berra	1.50
5	Phil Rizzuto	1.00
6	Bob Feller	1.00
7	Enos Slaughter	.75
8	Stan Musial	2.00
9	Hank Sauer	.75
10	Ferris Fain	.75
11	Red Schoendienst	.75
12	Allie Reynolds	.75
13	Johnny Sain	.75

1948 REPRINT RELICS

		NM/M
Common Player:		8.00
Inserted 1:44		
YB1	Yogi Berra	20.00
YB2	Yogi Berra	35.00
FF	Ferris Fain	8.00
BF	Bob Feller	12.00
RK	Ralph Kiner	15.00
JM	Johnny Mize	15.00
SM1	Stan Musial	30.00
PR	Phil Rizzuto	15.00
HS	Hank Sauer	8.00
RS	Red Schoendienst	10.00
ES	Enos Slaughter	10.00
BT	Bobby Thomson	8.00

1948 Bowman Reprint Autographs

		NM/M
1	Warren Spahn	40.00
2	Bob Feller	40.00

Team Topps Legends Autographs

		NM/M
Common Autograph:		30.00
Inserted 1:332		
TT13F	Warren Spahn (1965)	40.00
TT21R	Bob Feller (1952)	30.00

2001 BOWMAN'S BEST

		NM/M
Complete Set (200):		
Common Player:		.20
Common SP (151-200):		5.00
Production 2,999		
Pack (5):		12.00
Box (24):		240.00
1	Vladimir Guerrero	1.00
2	Miguel Tejada	.40
3	Geoff Jenkins	.20
4	Jeff Bagwell	1.00
5	Todd Helton	1.00
6	Ken Griffey Jr.	2.00
7	Nomar Garciaparra	2.00
8	Chipper Jones	1.50
9	Darin Erstad	.50
10	Frank Thomas	1.00
11	Jim Thome	.35
12	Preston Wison	.20
13	Kevin Brown	.35
14	Derek Jeter	3.00
15	Scott Rolen	1.00
16	Ryan Klesko	.20
17	Jeff Kent	.20
18	Raul Mondesi	.20
19	Greg Vaughn	.20
20	Bernie Williams	.45
21	Mike Piazza	2.00
22	Richard Hidalgo	.20
23	Dean Palmer	.20
24	Roberto Alomar	.45
25	Sammy Sosa	2.00
26	Randy Johnson	1.00
27	Manny Ramirez	1.00
28	Roger Clemens	1.75
29	Terrence Long	.20
30	Jason Kendall	.20
31	Richie Sexson	.35
32	David Wells	.20
33	Andruw Jones	1.00
34	Pokey Reese	.20
35	Juan Gonzalez	1.00
36	Carlos Beltran	.75
37	Shawn Green	.40
38	Mariano Rivera	.35
39	John Olerud	.20
40	Jim Edmonds	.40
41	Andres Galarraga	.20
42	Carlos Delgado	.75
43	Kris Benson	.20
44	Andy Pettitte	.40
45	Jeff Cirillo	.20
46	Magglio Ordonez	.40
47	Tom Glavine	.45
48	Garret Anderson	.20
49	Cal Ripken Jr.	3.00
50	Pedro Martinez	1.00
51	Barry Bonds	3.00
52	Alex Rodriguez	2.50
53	Ben Grieve	.20
54	Edgar Martinez	.20
55	Jason Giambi	.75
56	Jeromy Burnitz	.20
57	Mike Mussina	.75
58	Moises Alou	.20
59	Sean Casey	.40
60	Greg Maddux	1.50
61	Tim Hudson	.50
62	Mark McGwire	2.50
63	Rafael Palmeiro	.75
64	Tony Batista	.20
65	Kazuhiro Sasaki	.20
66	Jorge Posada	.35
67	Johnny Damon	.40
68	Brian Giles	.20
69	Jose Vidro	.20
70	Jermaine Dye	.20
71	Craig Biggio	.20
72	Larry Walker	.20
73	Eric Chavez	.40
74	David Segui	.20
75	Tim Salmon	.35
76	Javy Lopez	.20
77	Paul Konerko	.20
78	Barry Larkin	.20
79	Mike Hampton	.20
80	Bobby Higginson	.20
81	Mark Mulder	.35
82	Pat Burrell	.60
83	Kerry Wood	.50
84	J.T. Snow	.20
85	Ivan Rodriguez	.65
86	Edgardo Alfonzo	.20
87	Orlando Hernandez	.20
88	Gary Sheffield	.40
89	Mike Sweeney	.20
90	Carlos Lee	.20
91	Rafael Furcal	.20
92	Troy Glaus	1.00
93	Bartolo Colon	.20
94	Cliff Floyd	.20
95	Barry Zito	.50
96	J.D. Drew	.40
97	Eric Karros	.20
98	Jose Valentin	.20
99	Ellis Burks	.20
100	David Justice	.20
101	Larry Barnes	.20
102	Rod Barajas	.20
103	Tony Pena	.20
104	Jerry Hairston Jr.	.20
105	Keith Ginter	.20
106	Corey Patterson	.50
107	Aaron Rowand	.20
108	Miguel Olivo	.20
109	Gookie Dawkins	.20
110	C.C. Sabathia	.20
111	Ben Petrick	.20
112	Eric Munson	.20
113	Ramon Castro	.20
114	Alex Escobar	.20
115	Josh Hamilton	.20
116	Jason Marquis	.20
117	Ben Davis	.20
118	Alex Cintron	.20
119	Julio Zuleta	.20
120	Ben Broussard	.20
121	Adam Everett	.20
122	*Ramon Carvajal*	.75
123	Felipe Lopez	.20
124	Alfonso Soriano	1.50
125	Jayson Werth	.20
126	Donzell McDonald	.20
127	Jason Hart	.25
128	Joe Crede	.20
129	Sean Burroughs	.20
130	Jack Cust	.20
131	Corey Smith	.20
132	Adrian Gonzalez	.35
133	J.R. House	.20
134	Steve Lomasney	.20
135	Tim Raines Jr.	.20
136	Tony Alvarez	.20
137	Doug Mientkiewicz	.20
138	Rocco Baldelli	1.50
139	Jason Romano	.20
140	Vernon Wells	.20

141	Mike Bynum	.20
142	Xavier Nady	.20
143	Brad Wilkerson	.20
144	Ben Diggins	.20
145	Aubrey Huff	.20
146	Eric Byrnes	.20
147	Alex Gordon	.20
148	Roy Oswalt	.50
149	Brian Esposito	.20
150	Scott Seabol	.20
151	*Erick Almonte*	5.00
152	*Gary Johnson*	5.00
153	*Pedro Liriano*	5.00
154	*Matt White*	5.00
155	*Luis Montanez*	5.00
156	Brad Cresse	5.00
157	*Wilson Betemit*	6.00
158	*Octavio Martinez*	5.00
159	*Adam Pettyjohn*	5.00
160	*Corey Spencer*	5.00
161	*Mark Burnett*	5.00
162	*Ichiro Suzuki*	60.00
163	*Alexis Gomez*	5.00
164	*Greg "Toe" Nash*	5.00
165	*Roberto Miniel*	5.00
166	*Justin Morneau*	25.00
167	*Ben Washburn*	5.00
168	*Bob Keppel*	5.00
169	*Deivi Mendez*	5.00
170	*Tsuyoshi Shinjo*	8.00
171	*Jared Abruzzo*	5.00
172	*Derrick Van Dusen*	6.00
173	*Hee Seop Choi*	10.00
174	*Albert Pujols*	240.00
175	*Travis Hafner*	25.00
176	*Ron Davenport*	6.00
177	*Luis Torres*	5.00
178	*Jake Peavy*	40.00
179	*Elvis Corporan*	5.00
180	David Krynzel	5.00
181	*Tony Blanco*	5.00
182	*Elpidio Guzman*	5.00
183	*Matt Butler*	5.00
184	*Joe Thurston*	5.00
185	*Andy Beal*	5.00
186	*Kevin Nulton*	5.00
187	*Sneideer Santos*	5.00
188	*Joe Dillon*	5.00
189	*Jeremy Blevins*	5.00
190	*Chris Amador*	5.00
191	*Mark Hendrickson*	5.00
192	*Willy Aybar*	8.00
193	*Antoine Cameron*	5.00
194	*Jonathan Johnson*	5.00
195	*Ryan Ketchner*	10.00
196	*Bjorn Ivy*	5.00
197	*Josh Kroeger*	10.00
198	*Ty Wigginton*	6.00
199	*Stubby Clapp*	5.00
200	*Jerrod Riggan*	5.00

Autographs

		NM/M
Common Player:		8.00
Inserted 1:95		
SB	Sean Burroughs	8.00
BC	Brad Cresse	8.00
AG	Adrian Gonzalez	8.00
JH	Josh Hamilton	8.00
JRH	J.R. House	8.00
TL	Terrence Long	8.00
JR	Jon Rauch	8.00

Exclusive Rookie Autographs

		NM/M
Common Player:		6.00
Inserted 1:50		
WA	Willy Aybar	15.00

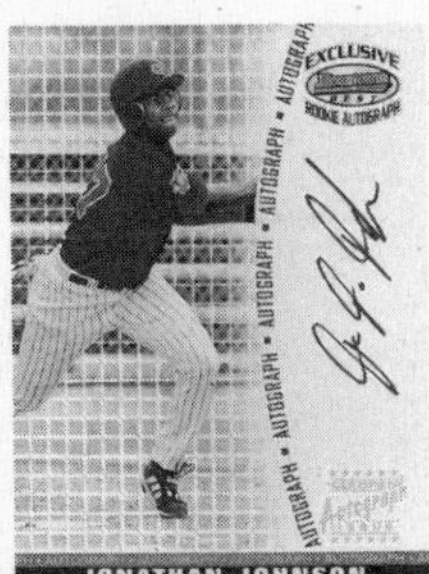

SC	Stubby Clapp	6.00
BI	Bjorn Ivy	6.00
JJ	Jonathan Johnson	6.00
TW	Ty Wigginton	10.00
JR	Jerrod Riggan	6.00
SS	Sneideer Santos	6.00
JB	Jeremy Blevins	6.00
MH	Mark Hendrickson	6.00

Franchise Favorites

		NM/M
Complete Set (8):		30.00
Common Player:		1.50
Inserted 1:16		
DM	Don Mattingly	6.00
AR	Alex Rodriguez	6.00
DE	Darin Erstad	1.50
DW	Dave Winfield	1.50
NR	Nolan Ryan	8.00
RJ	Reggie Jackson	2.00
MW	Don Mattingly, Dave Winfield	4.00
RR	Nolan Ryan, Alex Rodriguez	8.00
EJ	Darin Erstad, Reggie Jackson	2.00

Franchise Favorites Autographs

		NM/M
Common Player:		25.00
Inserted 1:556		
Combo 1:4,436		
DE	Darin Erstad	20.00
RJ	Reggie Jackson	40.00
EJ	Darin Erstad, Reggie Jackson	65.00
DM	Don Mattingly	60.00
MW	Don Mattingly, Dave Winfield	125.00
AR	Alex Rodriguez	75.00
NR	Nolan Ryan	80.00
RR	Nolan Ryan, Alex Rodriguez	300.00
DW	Dave Winfield	25.00

Franchise Favorites Relics

		NM/M
Common Player:		6.00
Jersey 1:139		
Pants 1:307		
Combo Relic 1:1,114		
JB	Jeff Bagwell	10.00
CB	Craig Biggio	6.00
BB	Craig Biggio, Jeff Bagwell	25.00
DE	Darin Erstad	6.00
RJ	Reggie Jackson	10.00
EJ	Reggie Jackson, Darin Erstad	25.00
DM	Don Mattingly	30.00
MW	Don Mattingly, Dave Winfield	65.00
AR	Alex Rodriguez	20.00
NR	Nolan Ryan	40.00
RR	Nolan Ryan, Alex Rodriguez	60.00
DW	Dave Winfield	8.00

Franchise Futures

		NM/M
Complete Set (12):		15.00
Common Player:		1.00
Inserted 1:24		
FF1	Josh Hamilton	1.00
FF2	Wes Helms	1.00
FF3	Alfonso Soriano	4.00
FF4	Nick Johnson	1.50
FF5	Jose Ortiz	1.00
FF6	Ben Sheets	1.50
FF7	Sean Burroughs	1.50
FF8	Ben Petrick	1.00
FF9	Corey Patterson	1.50
FF10	J.R. House	1.00
FF11	Alex Escobar	1.00
FF12	Travis Hafner	1.50

Game-Used Bats

		NM/M
Common Player:		6.00
Inserted 1:267		
PB	Pat Burrell	15.00
SB	Sean Burroughs	8.00
AG	Adrian Gonzalez	6.00
EM	Eric Munson	6.00
CP	Corey Patterson	8.00

Game-Worn Jerseys

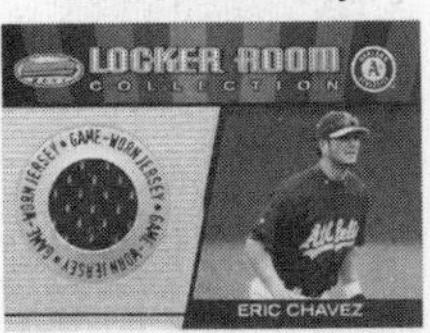

		NM/M
Common Player:		5.00
Inserted 1:133		
EC	Eric Chavez	8.00
MM	Mark Mulder	8.00
JP	Jay Payton	5.00
PR	Pokey Reese	5.00
PW	Preston Wilson	5.00

Impact Players

		NM/M
Complete Set (20):		15.00
Common Player:		.50
Inserted 1:7		
IP1	Mark McGwire	3.00
IP2	Sammy Sosa	2.00
IP3	Manny Ramirez	1.00
IP4	Troy Glaus	1.00
IP5	Ken Griffey Jr.	2.00
IP6	Gary Sheffield	.75
IP7	Vladimir Guerrero	1.00
IP8	Carlos Delgado	.75
IP9	Jason Giambi	.75
IP10	Frank Thomas	1.50
IP11	Vernon Wells	.60
IP12	Carlos Pena	.50
IP13	Joe Crede	.50
IP14	Keith Ginter	.50
IP15	Aubrey Huff	.50
IP16	Brad Cresse	.50
IP17	Austin Kearns	.75
IP18	Nick Johnson	.50
IP19	Josh Hamilton	.50
IP20	Corey Patterson	.60

Rookie Fever

		NM/M
Complete Set (10):		10.00
Common Player:		.50
Inserted 1:10		
RF1	Chipper Jones	2.00
RF2	Preston Wilson	.50
RF3	Todd Helton	1.00
RF4	Jay Payton	.50
RF5	Ivan Rodriguez	.75
RF6	Manny Ramirez	1.00
RF7	Derek Jeter	4.00
RF8	Orlando Hernandez	.50
RF9	Marcus Quinn	.50
RF10	Terrence Long	.50

Team Topps

		NM/M
Common Player:		10.00
Overall odds 1:71		
13R	Warren Spahn (1952)	40.00
37R	Tug McGraw (1965)	10.00
48R	Bobby Richardson (1957)	15.00
25R	Luis Tiant (1965 + Exchange)	10.00
31R	Clete Boyer (1957)	15.00
23R	Gil McDougald (1952)	15.00
27R	Andy Pafko (1952)	15.00
28R	Herb Score (1956)	15.00
18R	Bob Gibson (1959)	40.00
29R	Moose Skowron (1954)	15.00
37F	Tug McGraw (1985)	10.00
28F	Herb Score(1962)	15.00

2002 BOWMAN

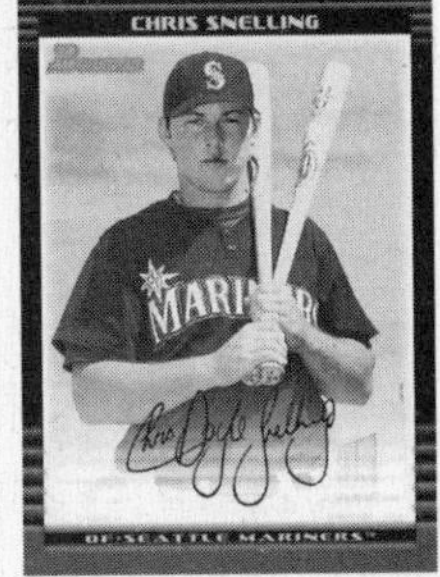

		NM/M
Complete Set (440):		70.00
Common Player:		.15
Common Rookie:		.40
Pack (10):		2.50
Box (24):		40.00
1	Adam Dunn	.50
2	Derek Jeter	2.00
3	Alex Rodriguez	1.50
4	Miguel Tejada	.30
5	Nomar Garciaparra	1.25
6	Toby Hall	.15
7	Brandon Duckworth	.15
8	Paul LoDuca	.15

9 Brian Giles .15
10 C.C. Sabathia .15
11 Curt Schilling .40
12 Tsuyoshi Shinjo .15
13 Ramon Hernandez .15
14 Jose Cruz Jr. .15
15 Albert Pujols 1.50
16 Joe Mays .15
17 Javy Lopez .15
18 J.T. Snow .15
19 David Segui .15
20 Jorge Posada .30
21 Doug Mientkiewicz .15
22 Jerry Hairston Jr. .15
23 Bernie Williams .30
24 Mike Sweeney .15
25 Jason Giambi .50
26 Ryan Dempster .15
27 Ryan Klesko .15
28 Mark Quinn .15
29 Jeff Kent .15
30 Eric Chavez .30
31 Adrian Beltre .25
32 Andruw Jones .50
33 Alfonso Soriano 1.00
34 Aramis Ramirez .15
35 Greg Maddux 1.00
36 Andy Pettitte .40
37 Bartolo Colon .15
38 Ben Sheets .40
39 Bobby Higginson .15
40 Ivan Rodriguez .50
41 Brad Penny .15
42 Carlos Lee .15
43 Damion Easley .15
44 Preston Wilson .15
45 Jeff Bagwell .50
46 Eric Milton .15
47 Rafael Palmeiro .50
48 Gary Sheffield .30
49 J.D. Drew .25
50 Jim Thome .50
51 Ichiro Suzuki 1.50
52 Bud Smith .15
53 Chan Ho Park .15
54 D'Angelo Jimenez .15
55 Ken Griffey Jr. 1.25
56 Wade Miller .15
57 Vladimir Guerrero .50
58 Troy Glaus .50
59 Shawn Green .40
60 Kerry Wood .40
61 Jack Wilson .15
62 Kevin Brown .25
63 Marcus Giles .15
64 Pat Burrell .40
65 Larry Walker .15
66 Sammy Sosa 1.25
67 Raul Mondesi .15
68 Tim Hudson .25
69 Lance Berkman .15
70 Mike Mussina .40
71 Barry Zito .40
72 Jimmy Rollins .15
73 Barry Bonds 2.00
74 Craig Biggio .15
75 Todd Helton .50
76 Roger Clemens 1.00
77 Frank Catalanotto .15
78 Josh Towers .15
79 Roy Oswalt .40
80 Chipper Jones 1.00
81 Cristian Guzman .15
82 Darin Erstad .45
83 Freddy Garcia .15
84 Jason Tyner .15
85 Carlos Delgado .40
86 Jon Lieber .15
87 Juan Pierre .15
88 Matt Morris .15
89 Phil Nevin .15
90 Jim Edmonds .30
91 Magglio Ordonez .30
92 Mike Hampton .15
93 Rafael Furcal .15
94 Richie Sexson .35
95 Luis Gonzalez .25
96 Scott Rolen .50
97 Tim Redding .15
98 Moises Alou .15
99 Jose Vidro .15
100 Mike Piazza 1.25
101 Pedro Martinez .75
102 Geoff Jenkins .15
103 Johnny Damon .25
104 Mike Cameron .15
105 Randy Johnson .75
106 David Eckstein .15
107 Javier Vazquez .15
108 Mark Mulder .25
109 Robert Fick .15
110 Roberto Alomar .35
111 Wilson Betemit .15
112 *Chris Tritle* .50
113 Ed Rogers .15
114 Juan Pena .15
115 Josh Beckett .50
116 Juan Cruz .15
117 *Noochie Varner* .50
118 *Taylor Buchholz* .50
119 Mike Rivera .15
120 Hank Blalock .40
121 *Hansel Izquierdo* .50
122 Orlando Hudson .15
123 Bill Hall .15
124 Jose Reyes .50
125 Juan Rivera .15
126 Eric Valent .15
127 *Scotty Layfield* .40
128 Austin Kearns .50
129 *Nic Jackson* .50
130 *Chris Baker* .50
131 *Chad Qualls* .40
132 Marcus Thames .15
133 Nathan Haynes .15
134 Brett Evert .15
135 Joe Borchard .15
136 Ryan Christianson .15
137 Josh Hamilton .15
138 Corey Patterson .15
139 Travis Wilson .15
140 Alex Escobar .15
141 Alexis Gomez .15
142 Nick Johnson .15
143 Kenny Kelly .15
144 Marlon Byrd .15
145 Kory DeHaan .15
146 Matt Belisle .15
147 Carlos Hernandez .15
148 Sean Burroughs .15
149 Angel Berroa .15
150 Aubrey Huff .15
151 Travis Hafner .15
152 Brandon Berger .15
153 David Kryznel .15
154 Ruben Salazar .15
155 J.R. House .15
156 Juan Silvestre .15
157 Dewon Brazelton .15
158 Jayson Werth .15
159 Larry Barnes .15
160 Elvis Pena .15
161 *Ruben Gotay* .40
162 *Tommy Marx* .50
163 *John Suomi* .40
164 Javier Colina .15
165 *Greg Sain* .40
166 *Robert Cosby* .40
167 *Angel Pagan* .40
168 *Ralph Santana* .40
169 *Joe Orloski* .40
170 *Shayne Wright* .40
171 *Jay Caligiuri* .25
172 *Greg Montalbano* .50
173 *Rich Harden* 4.00
174 *Rich Thompson* .40
175 *Fred Bastardo* .40
176 *Alejandro Giron* .40
177 *Jesus Medrano* .40
178 *Kevin Deaton* .40
179 *Mike Rosamond* .50
180 *Jon Guzman* .40
181 *Gerard Oakes* .40
182 *Francisco Liriano* 4.00
183 *Matt Allegra* .50
184 *Mike Snyder* .40
185 *James Shanks* .40
186 *Anderson Hernandez* .40
187 *Dan Trumble* .40
188 *Luis DePaula* .40
189 *Randall Shelley* .40
190 *Richard Lane* .40
191 *Antwon Rollins* .50
192 *Ryan Bukvich* .40
193 Derrick Lewis .15
194 *Eric Miller* .40
195 *Justin Schuda* .40
196 *Brian West* .40
197 *Adam Roller* .40
198 *Neal Frendling* .40
199 *Jeremy Hill* .40
200 *James Barrett* .50
201 *Brett Kay* .50
202 *Ryan Mottl* .50
203 *Brad Nelson* 1.50
204 Juan Gonzalez .15
205 *Curtis Legendre* .40
206 *Ronald Acuna* .40
207 *Chris Flinn* .40
208 *Nick Alvarez* .40
209 *Jason Ellison* .40
210 *Blake McGinley* .40
211 *Dan Phillips* .50
212 *Demetrius Heath* .40
213 *Eric Bruntlett* .40
214 *Joe Jiannetti* .40
215 *Mike Hill* .40
216 *Ricardo Cordova* .40
217 *Mark Hamilton* .50
218 *David Mattox* .40
219 *Jose Morban* .50
220 *Scott Wiggins* .50
221 Steve Green .15
222 Brian Rogers .15
223 Chin-Hui Tsao .40
224 Kenny Baugh .15
225 Nate Teut .15
226 *Josh Wilson* .40
227 Christian Parker .15
228 Tim Raines Jr. .15
229 *Anastacio Martinez* .40
230 Richard Lewis .15
231 *Tim Kalita* .40
232 *Edwin Almonte* .40
233 Hee Seop Choi .25
234 Ty Howington .15
235 *Victor Alvarez* .40
236 Morgan Ensberg .15
237 *Jeff Austin* .40
238 Luis Terrero .15
239 Adam Wainwright .15
240 *Clint Weibl* .40
241 *Eric Cyr* .40
242 *Marlyn Tisdale* .40
243 John VanBenschoten .15
244 *Ryan Raburn* .40
245 Miguel Cabrera .75
246 Jung Bong .15
247 *Raul Chavez* .50
248 Erik Bedard .15
249 *Chris Snelling* .50
250 *Joe Rogers* .40
251 *Nate Field* .40
252 Matt Herges .15
253 *Matt Childers* .50
254 Erick Almonte .15
255 Nick Neugebauer .15
256 *Ron Calloway* .40
257 Seung Jun Song .15
258 Brandon Phillips .15
259 Cole Barthel .25
260 Jason Lane .15
261 Jae Weong Seo .15
262 Randy Flores .15
263 Scott Chiasson .15
264 Chase Utley .15
265 Tony Alvarez .15
266 *Ben Howard* .40
267 *Nelson Castro* .40
268 Mark Lukasiewicz .15
269 *Eric Glaser* .40
270 *Rob Henkel* .40
271 *Jose Valverde* .40
272 Ricardo Rodriguez .15
273 Chris Smith .15
274 Mark Prior 1.50
275 Miguel Olivo .15
276 Ben Broussard .15
277 Zach Sorensen .15
278 *Brian Mallette* .40
279 Brad Wilkerson .15
280 Carl Crawford .15
281 *Chone Figgins* .40
282 *Jimmy Alvarez* .40
283 Gavin Floyd 2.00
284 *Josh Bonifay* .50
285 *Garrett Guzman* .50
286 Blake Williams .15
287 Matt Holliday .15
288 Ryan Madson .15
289 Luis Torres .15
290 *Jeff Verplancke* .40
291 *Nate Espy* .50
292 *Jeff Lincoln* .40
293 *Ryan Snare* .40
294 Jose Ortiz .15
295 Eric Munson .15
296 Denny Bautista .15
297 Willy Aybar .15
298 Kelly Johnson .15
299 Justin Morneau .15
300 Derrick Van Dusen .15
301 Chad Petty .15
302 Mike Restovich .15
303 Shawn Fagan .15
304 *Yurendell DeCaster* .40
305 Justin Wayne .15
306 *Mike Peeples* .40
307 *Joel Guzman* .40
308 Ryan Vogelsong .15
309 *Jorge Padilla* .50
310 Grady Sizemore .15
311 *Joe Jester* .40
312 Jim Journell .15
313 Bobby Seay .15
314 *Ryan Church* 1.50
315 Grant Balfour .15
316 Mitch Jones .15
317 Travis Foley .50
318 Bobby Crosby .15
319 Adrian Gonzalez .15
320 Ronnie Merrill .15
321 Joel Pineiro .15
322 John-Ford Griffin .15
323 *Brian Forystek* .40
324 Sean Douglass .15
325 *Manny Delcarmen* .40
326 Donnie Bridges .15
327 Jim Kavourias .15
328 Gabe Gross .15
329 Greg "Toe" Nash .15
330 Bill Ortega .15
331 *Joey Hammond* .40
332 *Ramon Moreta* .40
333 Ron Davenport .15
334 Brett Myers .15
335 Carlos Pena .15
336 *Ezequiel Astacio* .40
337 *Edwin Yan* .50
338 Josh Girdley .15
339 Shaun Boyd .15
340 Juan Rincon .15
341 *Chris Duffy* .50
342 Jason Kinchen .15
343 Brad Thomas .15
344 David Kelton .15
345 Rafael Soriano .15
346 *Colin Young* .50
347 Eric Byrnes .15
348 *Chris Narveson* .50
349 *John Rheinecker* .40
350 *Mike Wilson* .40
351 *Justin Sherrod* .50
352 Deivi Mendez .15
353 Wily Mo Pena .15
354 *Brett Roneberg* .50
355 *Trey Lunsford* .40
356 *Jimmy Gobble* .75
357 Brent Butler .15
358 Aaron Heilman .15
359 Wilkin Ruan .15
360 *Brian Wolfe* .40
361 Cody Ransom .15
362 Koyie Hill .40
363 Scott Cassidy .15
364 *Tony Fontana* .50
365 Mark Teixeira .40
366 *Doug Sessions* .40
367 Victor Hall .15
368 *Josh Cisneros* .40
369 Kevin Mench .15
370 Tike Redman .15
371 Jeff Heaverlo .15
372 *Carlos Brackley* .40
373 Brad Hawpe .50
374 Jesus Colome .15
375 David Espinosa .15
376 Jesse Foppert .75
377 *Ross Peeples* .40
378 *Alexander Requena* .40
379 *Joe Mauer* 6.00
380 Carlos Silva .15
381 David Wright 15.00
382 *Craig Kuzmic* .50
383 *Peter Zamora* .40
384 *Matt Parker* .40
385 Ricardo Rodriguez .15
386 *Gary Cates Jr.* .40
387 *Justin Reid* .50
388 *Jake Mauer* .50
389 John-Ford Griffin .15
390 Josh Barfield 2.00
391 Luis Maza .15
392 *Henry Pichardo* .40
393 *Michael Floyd* .40
394 *Clint Nageotte* 1.00
395 Jim Warden .15
396 *Mauricio Lara* .50
397 *Alejandro Cadena* .40
398 *Jonny Gomes* 3.00
399 *Jason Bulger* .50
400 *Bobby Jenks* 1.00
401 *David Gil* .40
402 *Joel Crump* .40
403 *Kazuhisa Ishii* 1.00

404 *So Taguchi* .75
405 *Ryan Doumit* 1.50
406 MaCay McBride .15
407 Brandon Claussen .15
408 Chin-Feng Chen .15
409 Josh Phelps .25
410 *Freddie Money* .40
411 *Clifford Bartosh* .40
412 Josh Pearce .15
413 Lyle Overbay .15
414 Ryan Anderson .15
415 *Terrance Hill* .40
416 *John Rodriguez* .40
417 *Richard Stahl* .40
418 Brian Specht .15
419 *Chris Latham* .50
420 *Carlos Cabrera* .40
421 *Jose Bautista* .50
422 *Kevin Frederick* .40
423 Jerome Williams .50
424 *Napoleon Calzado* .50
425 Benito Baez .15
426 Xavier Nady .15
427 *Jason Botts* .40
428 *Steve Bechler* .50
429 *Reed Johnson* .50
430 *Mark Outlaw* .40
431 Billy Sylvester .15
432 Luke Lockwood .15
433 Jake Peavy .15
434 Alfredo Amezega .15
435 *Aaron Cook* .50
436 *Josh Shaffer* .40
437 Dan Wright .15
438 *Ryan Gripp* .50
439 Alex Herrera .15
440 *Jason Bay* 3.00

Gold

Stars: 1-2.5X
Rookies: 1-2X
Inserted 1:1

Uncirculated

NM/M
Common Player: 4.00
Production 1,000 sets
112 Chris Tritle 6.00
113 Ed Rogers 4.00
114 Juan Pena 4.00
115 Josh Beckett 8.00
116 Juan Cruz 4.00
117 Noochie Varner 6.00
118 Taylor Buchholz 4.00
119 Mike Rivera 4.00
120 Hank Blalock 8.00
121 Hansel Izquierdo 4.00
122 Orlando Hudson 4.00
123 Bill Hall 4.00
124 Jose Reyes 8.00
125 Juan Rivera 4.00
126 Eric Valent 4.00
127 Scotty Layfield 4.00
128 Austin Kearns 8.00
129 Nic Jackson 4.00
130 Chris Baker 4.00
131 Chad Qualls 4.00

Autographs

NM/M
Common Autograph: 5.00
Inserted 1:37
AA Alfredo Amezaga 5.00
GA Garrett Atkins 8.00
JB Josh Beckett 25.00
WB Wilson Betemit 5.00
LB Larry Bigbie 5.00
HB Hank Blalock 25.00
TB Tony Blanco 5.00
JAB Jason Botts 5.00
MB Marlon Byrd 10.00
BDC Brian Cardwell 5.00
BC Ben Christensen 5.00
BAC Brandon Claussen 12.00
JD Jeff Davanon 5.00
MD Manny Delcarmen 15.00
RF Randy Flores 5.00
RF Ryan Franklin 5.00
KG Keith Ginter 5.00
TH Toby Hall 5.00
AH Aubrey Huff 8.00
GJ Gary Johnson 5.00
NJ Nick Johnson 10.00
CK Charles Kegley 5.00
JL Jason Lane 8.00
NN Nick Neugebauer 5.00
RO Roy Oswalt 15.00
JP Juan Pena 5.00
MP Mark Prior 50.00
CR Cody Ransom 5.00
JS Juan Silvestre 5.00
TS Terrmel Sledge 8.00
BS Bud Smith 5.00
CS Chris Smith 5.00
WS Will Smith 5.00
BJS Brian Specht 5.00
CT Chris Tritle 8.00
CU Chase Utley 35.00
DV Domingo Valdez 5.00
NV Noochie Varner 8.00
RV Ryan Vogelsong 8.00
JLW Jerome Williams 10.00
DW Dan Wright 5.00

Autographed Futures Game Game-Worn Jersey

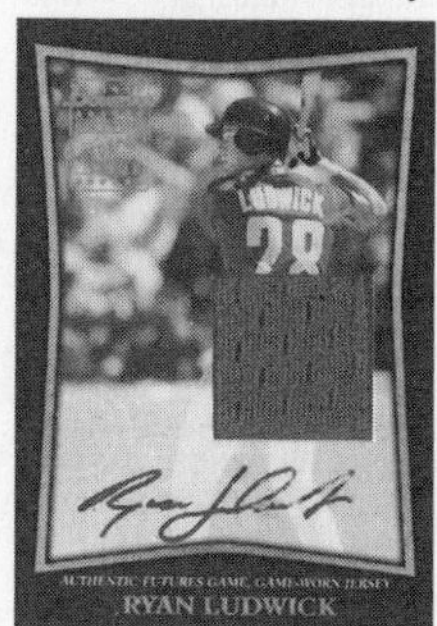

NM/M
Common Player: 15.00
Inserted 1:193
WB Wilson Betemit 15.00
CH Carlos Hernandez 15.00
JRH J.R. House 15.00
NJ Nick Johnson 20.00
RL Ryan Ludwick 15.00
CP Carlos Pena 15.00
DT Dennis Tankersley 15.00
JW Jerome Williams 20.00

Autographed Futures Game Game-Used Base

NM/M
Randomly inserted
TB Toby Hall 15.00

Game-Used Relics

NM/M
Common Player: 4.00
Inserted 1:165
JA1 Jared Abruzzo 4.00
JA2 Jared Abruzzo 4.00
GA Garrett Atkins 6.00
AB Angel Berroa 6.00
AC Antoine Cameron 4.00
RC Ryan Church 8.00
ALC Alex Cintron 4.00
NC Nate Cornejo 4.00
RD Ryan Dittfurth 4.00
AE Adam Everett 4.00
AF1 Alex Fernandez 4.00
AF2 Alex Fernandez 4.00
AG Alexis Gomez 6.00
CG Cristian Guerrero 4.00
CI Cesar Izturis 4.00
DJ D'Angelo Jimenez 4.00
FJ Forrest Johnson 4.00
AK Austin Kearns 10.00
JL Jason Lane 4.00
RM Ryan Madson 4.00
NN Nick Neugebauer 4.00
CP Corey Patterson 6.00
RS Ruben Salazar 4.00
RST Richard Stahl 4.00
JS Jamal Strong 4.00
CY Colin Young 4.00

2002 BOWMAN CHROME

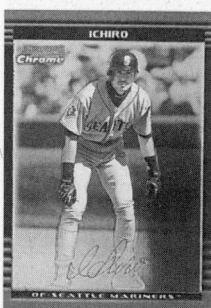

NM/M
Complete Set (405):
Common Player: .25
Common SP: 3.00
Inserted 1:3
Common Auto
(384-402,405) 10.00
Inserted 1:18
Pack (4): 8.00
Box (18): 120.00
1 Adam Dunn .50
2 Derek Jeter 3.00
3 Alex Rodriguez 2.50
4 Miguel Tejada .50
5 Nomar Garciaparra 2.00
6 Toby Hall .25
7 Brandon Duckworth .25
8 Paul LoDuca .25
9 Brian Giles .25
10 C.C. Sabathia .25
11 Curt Schilling .75
12 Tsuyoshi Shinjo .25
13 Ramon Hernandez .25
14 Jose Cruz Jr. .25
15 Albert Pujols 2.00
16 Joe Mays .25
17 Javy Lopez .25
18 J.T. Snow .25
19 David Segui .25
20 Jorge Posada .40
21 Doug Mientkiewicz .25
22 Jerry Hairston Jr. .25
23 Bernie Williams .40
24 Mike Sweeney .25
25 Jason Giambi .75
26 Ryan Dempster .25
27 Ryan Klesko .25
28 Mark Quinn .25
29 Jeff Kent .25
30 Eric Chavez .40
31 Adrian Beltre .40
32 Andruw Jones 1.00
33 Alfonso Soriano 1.00
34 Aramis Ramirez .25
35 Greg Maddux 1.50
36 Andy Pettitte .50
37 Bartolo Colon .25
38 Ben Sheets .25
39 Bobby Higginson .25
40 Ivan Rodriguez .60
41 Brad Penny .25
42 Carlos Lee .25
43 Damion Easley .25
44 Preston Wilson .25
45 Jeff Bagwell 1.00
46 Eric Milton .25
47 Rafael Palmeiro .75
48 Gary Sheffield .50
49 J.D. Drew .40
50 Jim Thome .75
51 Ichiro Suzuki 2.00
52 Bud Smith .25
53 Chan Ho Park .25
54 D'Angelo Jimenez .25
55 Ken Griffey Jr. 2.00
56 Wade Miller .25
57 Vladimir Guerrero 1.00
58 Troy Glaus 1.00
59 Shawn Green .40
60 Kerry Wood .75
61 Jack Wilson .25
62 Kevin Brown .40
63 Marcus Giles .25
64 Pat Burrell .50
65 Larry Walker .25
66 Sammy Sosa 2.00
67 Raul Mondesi .25
68 Tim Hudson .40
69 Lance Berkman .25
70 Mike Mussina .50
71 Barry Zito .50
72 Jimmy Rollins .25
73 Barry Bonds 3.00
74 Craig Biggio .25
75 Todd Helton 1.00
76 Roger Clemens 1.75
77 Frank Catalanotto .25
78 Josh Towers .25
79 Roy Oswalt .40
80 Chipper Jones 1.50
81 Cristian Guzman .25
82 Darin Erstad .60
83 Freddy Garcia .25
84 Jason Tyner .25
85 Carlos Delgado .50
86 Jon Lieber .25
87 Juan Pierre .25
88 Matt Morris .25
89 Phil Nevin .25
90 Jim Edmonds .40
91 Magglio Ordonez .50
92 Mike Hampton .25
93 Rafael Furcal .25
94 Richie Sexson .35
95 Luis Gonzalez .40
96 Scott Rolen .75
97 Tim Redding .25
98 Moises Alou .25
99 Jose Vidro .25
100 Mike Piazza 2.00
101 Pedro Martinez 1.00
102 Geoff Jenkins .25
103 Johnny Damon .40
104 Mike Cameron .25
105 Randy Johnson 1.00
106 David Eckstein .25
107 Javier Vazquez .25
108 Mark Mulder .40
109 Robert Fick .25
110 Roberto Alomar .40
111 Wilson Betemit .25
112 *Chris Tritle/SP* 4.00
113 Ed Rogers .25
114 Juan Pena .25
115 Josh Beckett .50
116 Juan Cruz .25
117 *Noochie Varner/SP* 6.00
118 Blake Williams .25
119 Mike Rivera .25
120 Hank Blalock .50
121 *Hansel Izquierdo/SP* 4.00
122 Orlando Hudson .25
123 Bill Hall .25
124 Jose Reyes 1.00
125 Juan Rivera .25
126 Eric Valent .25
127 *Scotty Layfield/SP* 3.00
128 Austin Kearns 1.00
129 *Nic Jackson/SP* 6.00
130 Scott Chiasson .25
131 *Chad Qualls/SP* 4.00
132 Marcus Thames .25
133 Nathan Haynes .25
134 Joe Borchard .25
135 Josh Hamilton .25
136 Corey Patterson .25
137 Travis Wilson .25
138 Alex Escobar .25
139 Alexis Gomez .25
140 Nick Johnson .50
141 Marlon Byrd .50
142 Kory DeHaan .25
143 Carlos Hernandez .25
144 Sean Burroughs .50
145 Angel Berroa .25
146 Aubrey Huff .25
147 Travis Hafner .25
148 Brandon Berger .25
149 J.R. House .25
150 Dewon Brazelton .25
151 Jayson Werth .25
152 Larry Barnes .25
153 *Ruben Gotay/SP* 6.00
154 *Tommy Marx/SP* 3.00
155 *John Suomi/SP* 4.00
156 Javier Colina/SP 3.00
157 *Greg Sain* 3.00
158 *Robert Cosby* 4.00
159 *Angel Pagan* 3.00
160 *Ralph Santana* 3.00
161 *Joe Orloski* 3.00

162	*Shayne Wright*	3.00
163	*Jay Caligiuri*	4.00
164	*Greg Montalbano*	5.00
165	*Rich Harden*	40.00
166	*Rich Thompson*	3.00
167	*Fred Bastardo*	3.00
168	*Alejandro Giron*	3.00
169	*Jesus Medrano*	3.00
170	*Kevin Deaton*	4.00
171	*Mike Rosamond*	2.00
172	*Jon Guzman*	3.00
173	*Gerard Oakes*	4.00
174	*Francisco Liriano*	25.00
175	*Matt Allegra*	4.00
176	*Mike Snyder*	4.00
177	*James Shanks*	3.00
178	*Anderson Hernandez*	5.00
179	*Dan Trumble*	3.00
180	*Luis DePaula*	4.00
181	*Randall Shelley*	5.00
182	*Richard Lane*	3.00
183	*Antwon Rollins*	5.00
184	*Ryan Bukvich*	5.00
185	Derrick Lewis	.25
186	*Eric Miller*	3.00
187	*Justin Schuda*	3.00
188	*Brian West*	4.00
189	Brad Wilkerson	.25
190	*Neal Frendling*	3.00
191	*Jeremy Hill*	3.00
192	*James Barrett*	5.00
193	*Brett Kay*	3.00
194	*Ryan Mottl*	4.00
195	*Brad Nelson*	15.00
196	Juan Gonzalez	.25
197	*Curtis Legendre*	3.00
198	*Ronald Acuna*	3.00
199	*Chris Flinn*	3.00
200	*Nick Alvarez*	3.00
201	*Jason Ellison*	4.00
202	*Blake McGinley*	3.00
203	*Dan Phillips*	3.00
204	*Demetrius Heath*	3.00
205	*Eric Bruntlett*	3.00
206	*Joe Jiannetti*	3.00
207	*Mike Hill*	3.00
208	*Ricardo Cordova*	3.00
209	*Mark Hamilton*	3.00
210	*David Mattox*	3.00
211	*Jose Morban*	5.00
212	*Scott Wiggins*	3.00
213	Steve Green	.25
214	Brian Rogers	.25
215	Kenny Baugh	.25
216	*Anastacio Martinez*	3.00
217	Richard Lewis	.25
218	*Tim Kalita*	3.00
219	*Edwin Almonte*	3.00
220	Hee Seop Choi	.25
221	Ty Howington	.25
222	*Victor Alvarez*	3.00
223	Morgan Ensberg	.25
224	*Jeff Austin*	3.00
225	*Clint Weibl*	4.00
226	*Eric Cyr*	4.00
227	*Marlyn Tisdale*	3.00
228	John VanBenschoten	.25
229	Ruben Salazar	.25
230	*Raul Chavez*	4.00
231	Brett Evert	.25
232	*Joe Rogers*	4.00
233	Adam Wainwright	.25
234	Matt Herges	.25
235	*Matt Childers*	4.00
236	Nick Neugebauer	.25
237	Carl Crawford	.25
238	Seung Jun Song	.25
239	Randy Flores	.25
240	Jason Lane	.25
241	Chase Utley	.25
242	*Ben Howard*	3.00
243	*Eric Glaser*	3.00
244	*Josh Wilson*	3.00
245	*Jose Valverde*	3.00
246	Chris Smith	.25
247	Mark Prior	4.00
248	*Brian Mallette*	3.00
249	*Chone Figgins*	5.00
250	*Jimmy Alvarez*	3.00
251	Luis Terrero	.25
252	*Josh Bonifay*	4.00
253	*Garrett Guzman*	3.00
254	*Jeff Verplancke*	3.00
255	*Nate Espy*	4.00
256	*Jeff Lincoln*	3.00
257	*Ryan Snare*	4.00
258	Jose Ortiz	.25
259	Denny Bautista	.25
260	Willy Aybar	.25
261	Kelly Johnson	.25
262	Shawn Fagan	.25
263	*Yurendell DeCaster*	3.00
264	*Mike Peeples*	3.00
265	*Joel Guzman*	3.00
266	Ryan Vogelsong	.25
267	*Jorge Padilla*	3.00
268	*Joe Jester*	3.00
269	*Ryan Church*	12.00
270	Mitch Jones	.25
271	Travis Foley	3.00
272	Bobby Crosby	2.00
273	Adrian Gonzalez	.25
274	Ronnie Merrill	.25
275	Joel Pineiro	.25
276	John-Ford Griffin	.25
277	*Brian Forystek*	3.00
278	Sean Douglass	.25
279	*Manny Delcarmen*	3.00
280	Jim Kavourias	3.00
281	Gabe Gross	.25
282	Bill Ortega	.25
283	*Joey Hammond*	3.00
284	Brett Myers	.25
285	Carlos Pena	.25
286	*Ezequiel Astacio*	3.00
287	*Edwin Yan*	3.00
288	*Chris Duffy*	6.00
289	Jason Kinchen	.25
290	Rafael Soriano	.25
291	*Colin Young*	.25
292	Eric Byrnes	.25
293	*Chris Narveson*	5.00
294	*John Rheinecker*	3.00
295	*Mike Wilson*	4.00
296	*Justin Sherrod*	5.00
297	Deivi Mendez	.25
298	Wily Mo Pena	.25
299	*Brett Roneberg*	4.00
300	*Trey Lunsford*	3.00
301	Christian Parker	.25
302	Brent Butler	.25
303	Aaron Heilman	.25
304	Wilkin Ruan	.25
305	Kenny Kelly	.25
306	Cody Ransom	.25
307	Koyie Hill	.25
308	*Tony Fontana*	3.00
309	Mark Teixeira	.75
310	*Doug Sessions*	3.00
311	*Josh Cisneros*	3.00
312	*Carlos Brackley*	3.00
313	Tim Raines Jr.	.25
314	*Ross Peeples*	5.00
315	*Alexander Requena*	5.00
316	Chin-Hui Tsao	.25
317	Tony Alvarez	.25
318	*Craig Kuzmic*	3.00
319	*Peter Zamora*	3.00
320	*Matt Parker*	3.00
321	Keith Ginter	.25
322	*Gary Cates Jr.*	3.00
323	Matt Belisle	.25
324	Ben Broussard	.25
325	Dennis Tankersley	.25
326	Juan Silvestre	.25
327	*Henry Pichardo*	3.00
328	*Michael Floyd*	3.00
329	*Clint Nageotte*	10.00
330	*Raymond Cabrera*	3.00
331	*Mauricio Lara*	4.00
332	*Alejandro Cadena*	3.00
333	*Jonny Gomes*	15.00
334	*Jason Bulger*	4.00
335	Nate Teut	.25
336	*David Gil*	3.00
337	*Joel Crump*	3.00
338	Brandon Phillips	.25
339	MaCay McBride	.25
340	Brandon Claussen	1.50
341	Josh Phelps	.25
342	*Freddie Money*	4.00
343	*Clifford Bartosh*	3.00
344	*Terrance Hill*	3.00
345	*John Rodriguez*	4.00
346	*Chris Latham*	3.00
347	*Carlos Cabrera*	3.00
348	*Jose Bautista*	5.00
349	*Kevin Frederick*	3.00
350	Jerome Williams	.75
351	*Napoleon Calzado*	3.00
352	Benito Baez	3.00
353	Xavier Nady	.25
354	*Jason Botts*	8.00
355	*Steve Bechler*	4.00
356	*Reed Johnson*	4.00
357	*Mark Outlaw*	3.00
358	Jake Peavy	.25
359	*Josh Shaffer*	3.00
360	Dan Wright	3.00
361	*Ryan Gripp*	3.00
362	*Nelson Castro*	3.00
363	*Jason Bay*	25.00
364	*Franklin German*	3.00
365	Corwin Malone	3.00
366	*Kelly Ramos*	3.00
367	*John Ennis*	3.00
368	George Perez	3.00
369	*Rene Reyes*	3.00
370	*Rolando Viera*	3.00
371	*Earl Snyder*	4.00
372	*Kyle Kane*	3.00
373	Mario Ramos	3.00
374	*Tyler Yates*	3.00
375	*Jason Young*	5.00
376	*Chris Bootcheck*	5.00
377	*Jesus Cota*	5.00
378	Corky Miller	3.00
379	*Matt Erickson*	3.00
380	*Justin Huber*	5.00
381	*Felix Escalona*	3.00
382	*Kevin Cash*	3.00
383	*J.J. Putz*	3.00
384	*Chris Snelling*	25.00
385	David Wright	190.00
386	*Brian Wolfe*	10.00
387	*Justin Reid*	10.00
388	*Jake Mauer*	10.00
389	*Ryan Raburn*	10.00
390	Josh Barfield	25.00
391	*Joe Mauer*	80.00
392	*Bobby Jenks*	20.00
393	*Rob Henkel*	10.00
394	*Jimmy Gobble*	10.00
395	Jesse Foppert	20.00
396	Gavin Floyd	30.00
397	*Nate Field*	10.00
398	*Ryan Doumit*	30.00
399	*Ron Calloway*	10.00
400	*Taylor Buchholz*	10.00
401	*Adam Roller*	10.00
402	Cole Barthel	10.00
403	*Kazuhisa Ishii*	6.00
404	*So Taguchi*	4.00
405	*Chris Baker*	5.00

Refractors

Star Refractors (1-220):	2-3X
SP Refractors:	.5-1.5X
Production 500	
X-Fractors (1-220):	3-5X
SP X-Fractors:	.75-2X
Production 250:	
Gold Refractors (1-220):	8-15X
SP Gold Refractors:	2-4X
Production 50	
Refractor Autos. (384-402,405)	.75-1.5X
Production 500	
X-Fractor Autos.:	.75-2X
Production 250	
Gold Autographs:	2-4X
Production 50	

Uncirculated

Cards:	1-3X
Production 350	
Autos. 10 cards of each player	
No Pricing	

Rookie Reprints

		NM/M
Complete Set (20):		25.00
Common Player:		1.00
Inserted 1:6		
Refractors:		1.5-2X
Inserted 1:18		
JB	Jeff Bagwell	1.50
BC	Bartolo Colon	1.00
CD	Carlos Delgado	1.00
JG	Juan Gonzalez	1.50
LG	Luis Gonzalez	1.00
KG	Ken Griffey Jr.	3.00
VG	Vladimir Guerrero	2.00
DJ	Derek Jeter	5.00
AJ	Andruw Jones	1.50
CJ	Chipper Jones	2.50
JK	Jason Kendall	1.00
MP	Mike Piazza	3.00
JP	Jorge Posada	1.00
IR	Ivan Rodriguez	1.00
SR	Scott Rolen	1.00
GS	Gary Sheffield	1.00
MS	Mike Sweeney	1.00
FT	Frank Thomas	1.50
LW	Larry Walker	1.00
BW	Bernie Williams	1.00

Ishii & Taguchi Autographs

		NM/M
Refractors:		.75-1.5X
Production 100		
X-Fractors:		2-4X
Production 50		
Golds: production 10		
403	Kazuhisa Ishii	50.00
404	So Taguchi	25.00

2002 BOWMAN CHROME DRAFT PICKS & PROSPECTS

		NM/M
Complete Set (175):		275.00
Common Player:		.25
Common RC:		.75
1-165 two per pack		
Common Auto (166-175):		10.00
Auto's inserted 1:45		
BDP1	*Clint Everts*	3.00
BDP2	*Fred Lewis*	1.00
BDP3	*Jonathan Broxton*	1.50
BDP4	*Jason Anderson*	.75
BDP5	*Mike Eusebio*	.75
BDP6	*Zack Greinke*	8.00
BDP7	*Joe Blanton*	6.00
BDP8	*Sergio Santos*	4.00
BDP9	*Jason Cooper*	1.50
BDP10	*Delwyn Young*	3.00
BDP11	*Jeremy Hermida*	20.00
BDP12	*Dan Ortmeyer*	1.50
BDP13	*Kevin Jepsen*	2.00
BDP14	*Russ Adams*	4.00
BDP15	*Mike Nixon*	.75
BDP16	*Nick Swisher*	8.00
BDP17	*Cole Hamels*	8.00
BDP18	*Brian Dopirak*	5.00
BDP19	*James Loney*	4.00
BDP20	*Denard Span*	2.00
BDP21	*Billy Petrick*	.75
BDP22	*Jared Doyle*	.75
BDP23	*Jeff Francoeur*	50.00
BDP24	*Nick Bourgeois*	.75
BDP25	*Matt Cain*	15.00
BDP26	*John McCurdy*	.75
BDP27	*Mark Kiger*	.75
BDP28	*Bill Murphy*	1.00
BDP29	*Matt Craig*	1.00
BDP30	*Mike Megrew*	2.50
BDP31	*Ben Crockett*	.75
BDP32	*Luke Hagerty*	1.50
BDP33	*Matt Whitney*	2.50
BDP34	*Dan Meyer*	2.00
BDP35	*Jeremy Brown*	2.00
BDP36	*Doug Johnson*	.75
BDP37	*Steve Obenchain*	.75
BDP38	*Matt Clanton*	1.00
BDP39	*Mark Teahen*	3.00
BDP40	*Thomas Carrow*	.75

BDP41	*Micah Schilling*	1.00
BDP42	*Blair Johnson*	1.00
BDP43	*Jason Pridie*	1.50
BDP44	*Joey Votto*	3.00
BDP45	*Taber Lee*	.75
BDP46	*Adam Peterson*	.75
BDP47	*Adam Donachie*	1.00
BDP48	*Josh Murray*	1.00
BDP49	*Brent Clevlen*	1.50
BDP50	*Chad Pleiness*	1.00
BDP51	*Zach Hammes*	1.50
BDP52	*Chris Snyder*	2.00
BDP53	Chris Smith	.25
BDP54	*Justin Maureau*	.75
BDP55	*David Bush*	3.00
BDP56	*Tim Gilhooly*	.75
BDP57	*Blair Barbier*	.75
BDP58	*Zach Segovia*	1.00
BDP59	*Jeremy Reed*	8.00
BDP60	*Matt Pender*	.75
BDP61	*Eric Thomas*	.75
BDP62	*Justin Jones*	2.00
BDP63	*Brian Slocum*	1.00
BDP64	*Larry Broadway*	2.00
BDP65	*Bo Flowers*	.75
BDP66	*Scott White*	1.00
BDP67	*Steve Stanley*	.75
BDP68	*Alex Merricks*	.75
BDP69	*Josh Womack*	.75
BDP70	*Dave Jensen*	.75
BDP71	*Curtis Granderson*	4.00
BDP72	*Pat Osborn*	1.50
BDP73	*Nic Carter*	.75
BDP74	*Mitch Talbot*	.75
BDP75	*Don Murphy*	.75
BDP76	*Val Majewski*	1.50
BDP77	*Javy Rodriguez*	.75
BDP78	*Fernando Pacheco*	1.00
BDP79	*Steve Russell*	.75
BDP80	*Jon Slack*	.75
BDP81	*John Baker*	.75
BDP82	*Aaron Coonrod*	.75
BDP83	*Josh Johnson*	.75
BDP84	*Jake Blalock*	3.00
BDP85	*Alex Hart*	1.50
BDP86	*Wes Bankston*	4.00
BDP87	*Josh Rupe*	1.00
BDP88	*Dan Cevette*	1.00
BDP89	*Kiel Fisher*	1.00
BDP90	*Alan Rick*	.75
BDP91	*Charlie Morton*	1.00
BDP92	*Chad Spann*	2.00
BDP93	*Kyle Boyer*	1.00
BDP94	*Bob Malek*	.75
BDP95	*Ryan Rodriguez*	.75
BDP96	*Jordan Renz*	.75
BDP97	*Randy Frye*	.75
BDP98	*Rich Hill*	4.00
BDP99	*B.J. Upton*	15.00
BDP100	*Dan Christensen*	1.00
BDP101	Casey Kotchman	8.00
BDP102	*Eric Good*	.75
BDP103	*Mike Fontenot*	1.50
BDP104	*John Webb*	.75
BDP105	*Jason Dubois*	2.00
BDP106	*Ryan Kibler*	.75
BDP107	*Jhonny Peralta*	10.00
BDP108	Kirk Saarloos	1.50
BDP109	*Rhett Parrott*	.75
BDP110	*Jason Grove*	.75
BDP111	Colt Griffin	2.00
BDP112	Dallas McPherson	8.00
BDP113	*Oliver Perez*	4.00
BDP114	*Marshall McDougall*	.75
BDP115	*Mike Wood*	1.00
BDP116	Scott Hairston	2.00
BDP117	*Jason Simontacchi*	1.00
BDP118	*Taggert Bozied*	2.00
BDP119	Shelly Duncan	.75
BDP120	*Dontrelle Willis*	20.00
BDP121	Sean Burnett	.25
BDP122	*Aaron Cook*	.75
BPD123	Brett Evert	.25
BDP124	Jimmy Journell	.25
BDP125	Brett Myers	.25
BDP126	Brad Baker	.25
BDP127	Billy Traber	1.50
BDP128	Adam Wainwright	.25
BDP129	Jason Young	1.00
BDP130	John Buck	.25
BDP131	Kevin Cash	.25
BDP132	*Jason Stokes*	5.00
BDP133	Drew Henson	.50
BDP134	*Chad Tracy*	3.00
BDP135	Orlando Hudson	.25
BDP136	Brandon Phillips	.25
BDP137	Joe Borchard	.25
BDP138	Marlon Byrd	.25
BDP139	Carl Crawford	.25
BDP140	Michael Restovich	.25
BDP141	*Corey Hart*	4.00
BDP142	Edwin Almonte	.25
BDP143	*Francis Beltran*	.75
BDP144	*Jorge De La Rosa*	.75
BDP145	*Gerardo Garcia*	.75
BDP146	*Franklyn German*	.75
BDP147	Francisco Liriano	6.00
BDP148	Francisco Rodriguez	.50
BDP149	Ricardo Rodriguez	.25
BDP150	Seung Jun Song	.25
BDP151	John Stephens	.25
BDP152	Justin Huber	2.00
BDP153	Victor Martinez	.40
BDP154	Hee Seop Choi	.25
BDP155	Justin Morneau	.25
BDP156	Miguel Cabrera	2.00
BDP157	*Victor Diaz*	2.00
BDP158	Jose Reyes	.75
BDP159	*Omar Infante*	.75
BDP160	Angel Berroa	.25
BDP161	Tony Alvarez	.25
BDP162	*Shin-Soo Choo*	2.00
BDP163	Wily Mo Pena	.25
BDP164	Andres Torres	.25
BDP165	*Jose Lopez*	4.00
BDP166	*Scott Moore/auto*	15.00
BDP167	*Chris Gruler/auto*	15.00
BDP168	*Joe Saunders/auto*	10.00
BDP169	*Jeff Francis/auto*	30.00
BDP170	*Royce Ring/auto*	15.00
BDP171	Greg Miller/auto	20.00
BDP172	*Brandon Weeden/ auto*	10.00
BDP173	*Drew Meyer/auto*	15.00
BDP174	*Khalil Greene/auto*	60.00
BDP175	*Mark Schramek/ auto*	15.00

Refractor

Cards 1-165:	2-4X
Rookies 1-175:	2-3X
1-165 production 300 sets	
166-175 inserted 1:154	

Gold Refract

Cards 1-165:	8-15X
Rookies 1-165:	5-10X
1-165 production 50 sets	
166-175 no pricing	

X-Fractor

Cards 1-165:	2-5X
Rookies 1-165:	3-4X
Rookies 166-175:	.75-1.5X
1-165 production 150 sets	
166-175 inserted 1:309	

2002 BOWMAN DRAFT PICKS & PROSPECTS

		NM/M
Complete Set (165):		35.00
Common Player:		.15
Common RC:		.25
Pack 4 Bowman + 2 Chrome:		12.00
Box (24):		250.00
BDP1	*Clint Everts*	1.00
BDP2	*Fred Lewis*	.40
BDP3	*Jonathan Broxton*	.40
BDP4	*Jason Anderson*	.25
BDP5	*Mike Eusebio*	.25
BDP6	*Zack Greinke*	3.00
BDP7	*Joe Blanton*	2.00
BDP8	*Sergio Santos*	1.50
BDP9	*Jason Cooper*	.50
BDP10	*Delwyn Young*	1.00
BDP11	*Jeremy Hermida*	3.00
BDP12	*Dan Ortmeyer*	.40
BDP13	*Kevin Jepsen*	.50
BDP14	*Russ Adams*	1.50
BDP15	*Mike Nixon*	.40
BDP16	*Nick Swisher*	2.50
BDP17	*Cole Hamels*	3.00
BDP18	*Brian Dopirak*	2.00
BDP19	*James Loney*	2.00
BDP20	*Denard Span*	.50
BDP21	*Billy Petrick*	.25
BDP22	*Jared Doyle*	.25
BDP23	*Jeff Francoeur*	20.00
BDP24	*Nick Bourgeois*	.25
BDP25	*Matt Cain*	3.00
BDP26	*John McCurdy*	.40
BDP27	*Mark Kiger*	.15
BDP28	*Bill Murphy*	.40
BDP29	*Matt Craig*	.25
BDP30	*Mike Megrew*	.50
BDP31	*Ben Crockett*	.25
BDP32	*Luke Hagerty*	.50
BDP33	*Matt Whitney*	1.00
BDP34	*Dan Meyer*	.50
BDP35	*Jeremy Brown*	.50
BDP36	*Doug Johnson*	.25
BDP37	*Steve Obenchain*	.25
BDP38	*Matt Clanton*	.40
BDP39	*Mark Teahen*	1.50
BDP40	*Thomas Carrow*	.25
BDP41	*Micah Schilling*	.50
BDP42	*Blair Johnson*	.25
BDP43	*Jason Pridie*	1.00
BDP44	*Joey Votto*	.50
BDP45	*Taber Lee*	.25
BDP46	*Adam Peterson*	.25
BDP47	*Adam Donachie*	.40
BDP48	*Josh Murray*	.40
BDP49	*Brent Clevlen*	.75
BDP50	*Chad Pleiness*	.40
BDP51	*Zach Hammes*	.50
BDP52	*Chris Snyder*	.50
BDP53	Chris Smith	.25
BDP54	*Justin Maureau*	.25
BDP55	*David Bush*	.75
BDP56	*Tim Gilhooly*	.25
BDP57	*Blair Barbier*	.25
BDP58	*Zach Segovia*	.50
BDP59	*Jeremy Reed*	3.00
BDP60	*Matt Pender*	.25
BDP61	*Eric Thomas*	.25
BDP62	*Justin Jones*	1.00
BDP63	*Brian Slocum*	.40
BDP64	*Larry Broadway*	1.00
BDP65	*Bo Flowers*	.25
BDP66	*Scott White*	.75
BDP67	*Steve Stanley*	.25
BDP68	*Alex Merricks*	.25
BDP69	*Josh Womack*	.40
BDP70	*Dave Jensen*	.25
BDP71	*Curtis Granderson*	1.00
BDP72	*Pat Osborn*	.40
BDP73	*Nic Carter*	.25
BDP74	*Mitch Talbot*	.25
BDP75	*Don Murphy*	.25
BDP76	*Val Majewski*	.50
BDP77	*Javy Rodriguez*	.25
BDP78	*Fernando Pacheco*	.40
BDP79	*Steve Russell*	.25
BDP80	*Jon Slack*	.25
BDP81	*John Baker*	.25
BDP82	*Aaron Coonrod*	.25
BDP83	*Josh Johnson*	.40
BDP84	*Jake Blalock*	1.50
BDP85	*Alex Hart*	.50
BDP86	*Wes Bankston*	1.00
BDP87	*Josh Rupe*	.40
BDP88	*Dan Cevette*	.75
BDP89	*Kiel Fisher*	.50
BDP90	*Alan Rick*	.25
BDP91	*Charlie Morton*	.50
BDP92	*Chad Spann*	.75
BDP93	*Kyle Boyer*	.25
BDP94	*Bob Malek*	.25
BDP95	*Ryan Rodriguez*	.25
BDP96	*Jordan Renz*	.25
BDP97	*Randy Frye*	.25
BDP98	*Rich Hill*	.25
BDP99	*B.J. Upton*	6.00
BDP100	*Dan Christensen*	.50
BDP101	Casey Kotchman	2.50
BDP102	*Eric Good*	.25
BDP103	*Mike Fontenot*	.50
BDP104	*John Webb*	.25
BDP105	*Jason Dubois*	1.50
BDP106	*Ryan Kibler*	.25
BDP107	*Jhonny Peralta*	3.00
BDP108	Kirk Saarloos	.75
BDP109	*Rhett Parrott*	.25
BDP110	*Jason Grove*	.25
BDP111	Colt Griffin	.50
BDP112	Dallas McPherson	3.00
BDP113	*Oliver Perez*	1.50
BDP114	*Marshall McDougall*	.25
BDP115	*Mike Wood*	.40
BDP116	Scott Hairston	1.00
BDP117	*Jason Simontacchi*	.50
BDP118	*Taggert Bozied*	1.00
BDP119	Shelly Duncan	.15
BDP120	*Dontrelle Willis*	10.00
BDP121	Sean Burnett	.15
BDP122	*Aaron Cook*	.25
BPD123	Brett Evert	.15
BDP124	Jimmy Journell	.15
BDP125	Brett Myers	.15
BDP126	Brad Baker	.15
BDP127	Billy Traber	.50
BDP128	Adam Wainwright	.15
BDP129	*Jason Young*	.40
BDP130	John Buck	.15
BDP131	*Kevin Cash*	.25
BDP132	*Jason Stokes*	2.00
BDP133	Drew Henson	.25
BDP134	*Chad Tracy*	1.50
BDP135	Orlando Hudson	.15
BDP136	Brandon Phillips	.15
BDP137	Joe Borchard	.15
BDP138	Marlon Byrd	.15
BDP139	Carl Crawford	.15
BDP140	Michael Restovich	.15
BDP141	*Corey Hart*	1.00
BDP142	Edwin Almonte	.15
BDP143	*Francis Beltran*	.25
BDP144	*Jorge De La Rosa*	.25
BDP145	*Gerardo Garcia*	.25
BDP146	*Franklyn German*	.25
BDP147	Francisco Liriano	.50
BDP148	Francisco Rodriguez	.50
BDP149	Ricardo Rodriguez	.15
BDP150	Seung Jun Song	.15
BDP151	John Stephens	.15
BDP152	*Justin Huber*	1.00
BDP153	Victor Martinez	.25
BDP154	Hee Seop Choi	.15
BDP155	Justin Morneau	.15
BDP156	Miguel Cabrera	.75
BDP157	*Victor Diaz*	1.00
BDP158	Jose Reyes	.40
BDP159	*Omar Infante*	.25
BDP160	Angel Berroa	.15
BDP161	Tony Alvarez	.15
BDP162	*Shin-Soo Choo*	1.00
BDP163	Wily Mo Pena	.15
BDP164	Andres Torres	.15
BDP165	*Jose Lopez*	2.00

Gold

Rookies:	.75-1.5X
Inserted 1:1	

Fabric of Future

		NM/M
Common Player:		4.00
Inserted 1:55		
EA	Edwin Almonte	4.00
TA	Tony Alvarez	4.00
FB	Francis Beltran	4.00
AB	Angel Berroa	5.00
SB	Sean Burnett	4.00
KC	Kevin Cash	4.00
HC	Hee Seop Choi	6.00
SC	Shin-Soo Choo	8.00
CC	Carl Crawford	6.00
JR	Jorge de la Rosa	4.00
VD	Victor Diaz	4.00
GG	Gerardo Garcia	4.00
FG	Franklyn German	4.00
CH	Corey Hart	4.00
DH	Drew Henson	6.00
JH	Justin Huber	6.00
JK	Josh Karp	4.00
FL	Francisco Liriano	4.00
JL	Jose Lopez	8.00
BM	Brett Meyers	6.00
WP	Wily Mo Pena	6.00
MR	Michael Restovich	4.00
JS	John Stephens	4.00
JS	Jason Stokes	10.00
AT	Andres Torres	4.00
BT	Billy Traber	6.00
CT	Chad Tracy	8.00
AW	Adam Wainwright	4.00

Freshman Fiber

		NM/M
Common Player:		4.00
Bat inserted 1:605		
Jersey 1:45		
BA	Brent Abernathy	4.00
DB	Dewon Brazelton	4.00
MB	Marlon Byrd/bat	8.00

TH Toby Hall 4.00
JH Josh Hamilton 4.00
AH Aubrey Huff 4.00
AK Austin Kearns/bat 8.00
JK Joe Kennedy 4.00
JS Jared Sandberg 4.00
JWS Jason Standridge 4.00
MT Mark Teixeira/bat 10.00
JV John Van Benschoten 4.00

Signs of the Future

NM/M
Common Autograph: 5.00
EB Erik Bedard 5.00
LB Larry Bigbie 5.00
TB Taylor Buchholz 5.00
DD Daniel Denham 5.00
ME Morgan Ensberg 8.00
MF Mike Fontenot 8.00
KH Kris Honel 5.00
BI Brandon Inge 5.00
NJ Nic Jackson 10.00
MJ Mitch Jones 5.00
BK Bob Keppel 5.00
TL Todd Linden 15.00
JM Jake Mauer 8.00
JEM Justin Morneau 10.00
LN Lance Niekro 5.00
CP Christian Parra 5.00
BP Brandon Phillips 5.00
JR Juan Rivera 5.00
BS Bud Smith 5.00
AT Chad Tracy 10.00
JW Jerome Williams 10.00

2002 BOWMAN HERITAGE

NM/M
Complete Set (439): 190.00
Common Player: .25
Common SP: 1.00
Inserted 1:2
Black Box variations: 2-3X
Inserted 1:2
Pack (10): 3.00
Box (24): 50.00
1 Brent Abernathy .25
2 Jermaine Dye .25
3 *James Shanks* .40
4 *Chris Flinn* .40
5 *Mike Peeples/SP* 1.50
6 Gary Sheffield .50
7 Livan Hernandez/SP 1.00
8 *Jeff Austin* .40
9 Jeremy Giambi .25
10 *Adam Roller* .50
11 Sandy Alomar Jr/SP 1.00
12 Matt Williams/SP 1.00
13 Hee Seop Choi .25
14 Jose Offerman .25
15 Robin Ventura .25
16 Craig Biggio .25
17 *Boomer Wells* .40
18 *Rob Henkel* .40
19 Edgar Martinez .25
20 Matt Morris/SP 2.00
21 Jose Valentin .25
22 Barry Bonds 3.00
23 *Justin Schuda* .50
24 Josh Phelps .25
25 *John Rodriguez* .50
26 *Angel Pagan* .50
27 Aramis Ramirez .25
28 Jack Wilson .25
29 Roger Clemens 1.50
30 *Kazuhisa Ishii* 2.00
31 Carlos Beltran .50
32 Drew Henson/SP 1.50
33 Kevin Young/SP 1.00
34 Juan Cruz .25
35 *Curtis Legendre* .40
36 *Jose Morban* .50
37 *Ricardo Cordova/SP* 1.50
38 Adam Everett .25
39 Mark Prior 1.50
40 *Jose Bautista* .75
41 Travis Foley .25
42 Kerry Wood .50
43 B.J. Surhoff .25
44 Moises Alou .25
45 *Joey Hammond* .50
46 *Eric Bruntlett* .50
47 Carlos Guillen .25
48 Joe Crede .25
49 *Dan Phillips* .50
50 Jason LaRue .25
51 Javy Lopez .25
52 Larry Bigbie/SP 1.00
53 *Chris Baker* .75
54 Marty Cordova .25
55 C.C. Sabathia .25
56 Mike Piazza 2.00
57 Brian Giles .25
58 Mike Bordick/SP 1.00
59 Tyler Houston/SP 1.00
60 Gabe Kapler .25
61 Ben Broussard .25
62 Steve Finley/SP 1.50
63 Koyie Hill .25
64 Jeff D'Amico .25
65 *Edwin Almonte* .50
66 Pedro J. Martinez 1.00
67 Travis Fryman/SP 1.50
68 Brady Clark .25
69 *Reed Johnson/SP* 2.00
70 Mark Grace/SP 4.00
71 Tony Batista/SP 1.00
72 Roy Oswalt .50
73 Pat Burrell .50
74 Dennis Tankersley .25
75 Ramon Ortiz .25
76 *Neal Frendling/SP* 1.50
77 Omar Vizquel/SP 2.00
78 Hideo Nomo .50
79 Orlando Hernandez/SP 1.50
80 Andy Pettitte .50
81 Cole Barthel .25
82 Bret Boone .25
83 Alfonso Soriano 1.00
84 Brandon Duckworth .25
85 Ben Grieve .25
86 *Mike Rosamond/SP* 1.50
87 Luke Prokopec .25
88 *Chone Figgins* .40
89 Rick Ankiel/SP 1.50
90 David Eckstein .25
91 Corey Koskie .25
92 David Justice .25
93 *Jimmy Alvarez* .40
94 Jason Schmidt .25
95 Reggie Sanders .25
96 *Victor Alvarez* .40
97 *Brett Roneberg* .40
98 D'Angelo Jimenez .25
99 Hank Blalock .50
100 Juan Rivera .25
101 Mark Buehrle/SP 1.50
102 Juan Uribe .25
103 Royce Clayton/SP 1.00
104 *Brett Kay* .50
105 John Olerud .25
106 Richie Sexson .35
107 Chipper Jones 1.50
108 Adam Dunn .75
109 Tim Salmon/SP 1.50
110 Eric Karros .25
111 Jose Vidro .25
112 Jerry Hairston Jr. .25
113 *Anastacio Martinez* .50
114 Robert Fick/SP 1.50
115 Randy Johnson 1.00
116 Trot Nixon/SP 2.00
117 Nick Bierbrodt/SP 1.00
118 Jim Edmonds .35
119 Rafael Palmeiro .75
120 Jose Macias .25
121 Josh Beckett .50
122 Sean Douglass .25
123 Jeff Kent .25
124 Tim Redding .25
125 Xavier Nady .25
126 Carl Everett .25
127 Joe Randa .25
128 Luke Hudson/SP 1.00
129 *Eric Miller* .40
130 Melvin Mora .25
131 Adrian Gonzalez .25
132 Larry Walker/SP 1.50
133 *Nic Jackson/SP* 3.00
134 Mike Lowell/SP 1.00
135 Jim Thome .50
136 Eric Milton .25
137 *Rich Thompson/SP* 1.50
138 Placido Polanco/SP 1.00
139 Juan Pierre .25
140 David Segui .25
141 Chuck Finley .25
142 Felipe Lopez .25
143 Toby Hall .25
144 *Fred Bastardo* .50
145 Troy Glaus 1.00
146 Todd Helton 1.00
147 *Ruben Gotay/SP* 1.50
148 Darin Erstad .60
149 *Ryan Gripp/SP* 1.50
150 Orlando Cabrera .25
151 *Jason Young* .50
152 Sterling Hitchcock/SP 1.00
153 Miguel Tejada .50
154 Al Leiter .25
155 *Taylor Buchholz* .40
156 Juan Gonzalez 1.00
157 Damion Easley .25
158 *Jimmy Gobble* 1.00
159 Dennis Ulacia/SP 1.00
160 Shane Reynolds/SP 1.00
161 Javier Colina .25
162 Frank Thomas 1.00
163 Chuck Knoblauch .25
164 Sean Burroughs .25
165 Greg Maddux 1.50
166 *Jason Ellison* .50
167 Tony Womack .25
168 *Randall Shelley/SP* 1.50
169 Jason Marquis .25
170 Brian Jordan .25
171 Darryl Kile .25
172 Barry Zito .50
173 *Matt Allegra/SP* 1.50
174 *Ralph Santana/SP* 1.50
175 Carlos Lee .25
176 Richard Hidalgo/SP 1.00
177 *Kevin Deaton* .50
178 Juan Encarnacion .25
179 Mark Quinn .25
180 Rafael Furcal .25
181 Garret Anderson .50
182 David Wright 8.00
183 Jose Reyes .50
184 Mario Ramos/SP 1.00
185 J.D. Drew .50
186 Juan Gonzalez .75
187 Nick Neugebauer .25
188 *Alejandro Giron* .50
189 John Burkett .25
190 Ben Sheets .50
191 Vinny Castilla/SP 1.00
192 Cory Lidle .25
193 Fernando Vina .25
194 Russell Branyan/SP 1.00
195 Ben Davis .25
196 Angel Berroa .25
197 Alex Gonzalez .25
198 Jared Sandberg .25
199 Travis Lee/SP 1.00
200 *Luis DePaula/SP* 1.50
201 Ramon Hernandez/SP 1.00
202 Brandon Inge .25
203 Aubrey Huff .25
204 Mike Rivera .25
205 *Brad Nelson* 1.50
206 Colt Griffin/SP 3.00
207 Joel Pineiro .25
208 Adam Pettyjohn .25
209 Mark Redman .25
210 Roberto Alomar/SP 3.00
211 Denny Neagle .25
212 Adam Kennedy .25
213 Jason Arnold/SP 4.00
214 Jamie Moyer .25
215 Aaron Boone .25
216 Doug Glanville .25
217 Nick Johnson/SP 1.00
218 Mike Cameron/SP 1.50
219 Tim Wakefield/SP 1.50
220 Todd Stottlemyre/SP 1.00
221 Mo Vaughn .25
222 Vladimir Guerrero 1.00
223 Bill Ortega .25
224 Kevin Brown .35
225 Peter Bergeron/SP 1.00
226 Shannon Stewart/SP 1.50
227 Eric Chavez .50
228 *Clint Weibl* .40
229 Todd Hollandsworth/SP 1.00
230 Jeff Bagwell 1.00
231 *Chad Qualls* .40
232 *Ben Howard* 1.00
233 Rondell White/SP 1.50
234 Fred McGriff .20
235 Steve Cox/SP 1.00
236 *Chris Tritle* 1.50
237 Eric Valent .25
238 *Joe Mauer* 6.00
239 Shawn Green .50
240 Jimmy Rollins .25
241 Edgar Renteria .25
242 *Edwin Yan* .40
243 *Noochie Varner* .40
244 Kris Benson/SP 1.50
245 Mike Hampton .25
246 *So Taguchi* 1.00
247 Sammy Sosa 2.00
248 Terrence Long .25
249 *Jason Bay* 1.00
250 Kevin Millar/SP 1.00
251 Albert Pujols 2.50
252 *Chris Latham* .40
253 Eric Byrnes .25
254 *Napoleon Calzado/SP* 1.50
255 Bobby Higginson .25
256 Ben Molina .25
257 Torii Hunter/SP 3.00
258 Jason Giambi .75
259 Bartolo Colon .20
260 Benito Baez .25
261 Ichiro Suzuki 2.50
262 Mike Sweeney .25
263 *Brian West* .40
264 Brad Penny .25
265 Kevin Millwood/SP 2.00
266 Orlando Hudson .25
267 Doug Mientkiewicz .25
268 Luis Gonzalez/SP 1.50
269 *Jay Caligiuri* .40
270 Nate Cornejo/SP 1.00
271 Lee Stevens .25
272 Eric Hinske .25
273 *Antwon Rollins* .50
274 *Bobby Jenks* 1.00
275 Joe Mays .25
276 *Josh Shaffer* .40
277 *Jonny Gomes* 2.00
278 Bernie Williams .40
279 Ed Rogers .25
280 Carlos Delgado .50
281 Raul Mondesi/SP 1.50
282 Jose Ortiz .25
283 Cesar Izturis .25
284 Ryan Dempster/SP 1.00
285 Brian Daubach .25
286 *Hansel Izquierdo* .40
287 Mike Lieberthal/SP 1.00
288 Marcus Thames .25
289 Nomar Garciaparra 2.00
290 Brad Fullmer .25
291 Tino Martinez .25
292 *James Barrett* .40
293 Jacque Jones .25
294 *Nick Alvarez/SP* 1.50
295 *Jason Grove/SP* 1.50
296 *Mike Wilson/SP* 1.50
297 J.T. Snow .25
298 Cliff Floyd .25
299 Todd Hundley/SP 1.00
300 Tony Clark/SP 1.00
301 *Demetrius Heath* .40
302 Morgan Ensberg .25
303 Cristian Guzman .25
304 Frank Catalanotto .25
305 Jeff Weaver .25
306 Tim Hudson .50
307 *Scott Wiggins/SP* 1.50
308 Shea Hillenbrand/SP 2.00
309 Todd Walker/SP 1.00
310 Tsuyoshi Shinjo .25
311 Adrian Beltre .40
312 *Craig Kuzmic* .40
313 Paul Konerko .40
314 Scott Hairston 1.50
315 Chan Ho Park .25
316 Jorge Posada .40
317 *Chris Snelling* .75
318 Keith Foulke .25
319 John Smoltz .25
320 *Ryan Church/SP* 3.00
321 Mike Mussina .75
322 Tony Armas Jr/SP 1.00
323 Craig Counsell .25
324 Marcus Giles .25
325 Greg Vaughn .25
326 Curt Schilling .75
327 Jeromy Burnitz .25
328 Eric Byrnes .25
329 Johnny Damon .40
330 *Michael Floyd/SP* 1.50

331	Edgardo Alfonzo	.25
332	*Jeremy Hill*	.40
333	*Josh Bonifay*	.40
334	Byung-Hyun Kim	.25
335	Keith Ginter	.25
336	*Ronald Acuna/SP*	1.50
337	*Mike Hill/SP*	1.50
338	Sean Casey	.25
339	Matt Anderson/SP	1.00
340	Dan Wright	.25
341	Ben Petrick	.25
342	Mike Sirotka/SP	1.00
343	Alex Rodriguez	2.50
344	Einar Diaz	.25
345	Derek Jeter	3.00
346	Jeff Conine	.25
347	Ray Durham/SP	1.00
348	Wilson Betemit/SP	1.00
349	Jeffrey Hammonds	.25
350	*Dan Trumble*	.40
351	Phil Nevin/SP	1.50
352	A.J. Burnett	.25
353	Bill Mueller	.25
354	Charles Nagy	.25
355	Rusty Greer/SP	1.00
356	*Jason Botts*	.25
357	Magglio Ordonez	.50
358	Kevin Appier	.25
359	Brad Radke	.25
360	Chris George	.25
361	*Chris Piersoll*	.25
362	Ivan Rodriguez	.60
363	Jim Kavourias	.25
364	Rick Helling/SP	1.00
365	Dean Palmer	.25
366	Rich Aurilia/SP	1.00
367	Ryan Vogelsong	.25
368	Matt Lawton	.25
369	Wade Miller	.25
370	Dustin Hermanson	.25
371	Craig Wilson	.25
372	Todd Zeile/SP	1.00
373	*Jon Guzman*	.40
374	Ellis Burks	.25
375	*Robert Cosby/SP*	1.50
376	Jason Kendall	.25
377	Scott Rolen/SP	4.00
378	Andruw Jones	1.00
379	*Greg Sain*	.40
380	Paul LoDuca	.25
381	*Scotty Layfield*	.40
382	Drew Henson	.50
383	*Garrett Guzman*	.40
384	Jack Cust	.25
385	*Shayne Wright*	.40
386	Derrek Lee	.25
387	*Jesus Medrano*	.40
388	Javier Vazquez	.25
389	Preston Wilson/SP	1.50
390	Gavin Floyd	1.50
391	Sidney Ponson/SP	1.00
392	Jose Hernandez	.25
393	Scott Erickson/SP	1.00
394	*Jose Valverde*	.40
395	*Mark Hamilton/SP*	1.50
396	Brad Cresse	.25
397	Danny Bautista	.25
398	Ray Lankford/SP	1.00
399	Miguel Batista/SP	1.00
400	Brent Butler	.25
401	*Manny Delcarmen/SP*	1.50
402	Kyle Farnsworth/SP	1.00
403	Freddy Garcia	.25
404	*Joe Jiannetti*	.40
405	Josh Barfield	2.00
406	Corey Patterson	.25
407	Josh Towers	.25
408	Carlos Pena	.25
409	Jeff Cirillo	.25
410	Jon Lieber	.25
411	Woody Williams/SP	1.00
412	*Richard Lane/SP*	1.50
413	Alex Gonzalez	.25
414	Wilkin Ruan	.25
415	Geoff Jenkins	.25
416	Carlos Hernandez	.25
417	Matt Clement/SP	1.50
418	Jose Cruz Jr.	.25
419	*Jake Mauer*	.75
420	*Matt Childers*	.50
421	Tom Glavine/SP	2.50
422	Ken Griffey Jr.	2.00
423	*Anderson Hernandez*	.40
424	*John Suomi*	.40
425	*Doug Sessions*	.40
426	Jaret Wright	.25
427	*Rolando Viera/SP*	1.50
428	Aaron Sele	.25
429	Dmitri Young	.25
430	Ryan Klesko	.25
431	Kevin Tapani/SP	1.00
432	Joe Kennedy	.25
433	Austin Kearns	.50
434	Roger Cedeno	.25
435	Lance Berkman	.25
436	Frank Menechino	.25
437	Brett Myers	.25
438	Bobby Abreu	.25
439	Shawn Estes	.25

Chrome Refractor

Stars:	3-6X
SP's:	1-2X
Inserted 1:16	
Gold Refractors:	4-8X
SP's	2-3X
Inserted 1:32	

Autographs

		NM/M
Common Player:		8.00
Inserted 1:45		
LB	Lance Berkman	15.00
HB	Hank Blalock	20.00
KG	Keith Ginter	8.00
TH	Toby Hall	8.00
DH	Drew Henson	15.00
KI	Kazuhisa Ishii	25.00
CI	Cesar Izturis	10.00
PL	Paul LoDuca	15.00
JM	Joe Mauer	50.00
RO	Roy Oswalt	15.00
MP	Mark Prior	50.00
AP	Albert Pujols	160.00
JR	Juan Rivera	8.00

Relics

		NM/M
Common Player:		4.00
Inserted 1:47		
EA	Edgardo Alfonzo	4.00
JB	Josh Beckett	8.00
BB	Barry Bonds	20.00
EC	Eric Chavez	8.00
CD	Carlos Delgado	6.00
JE	Jim Edmonds	8.00
DE	Darin Erstad	5.00
NG	Nomar Garciaparra	25.00
TG	Tony Gwynn	10.00
TH	Todd Helton	8.00
CJ	Chipper Jones	10.00
PK	Paul Konerko	5.00
GM	Greg Maddux	15.00
EM	Edgar Martinez	8.00
MP	Mike Piazza	15.00
AP	Albert Pujols	15.00
MR	Mariano Rivera	6.00
IR	Ivan Rodriguez	8.00
SR	Scott Rolen	10.00
TS	Tim Salmon	5.00
KS	Kazuhiro Sasaki	4.00
JS	John Smoltz	8.00
FT	Frank Thomas	8.00
JT	Jim Thome	10.00
LW	Larry Walker	4.00
PW	Preston Wilson	4.00

1954 Bowman Reprints

		NM/M
Complete Set (20):		40.00
Common Player:		2.00
Inserted 1:12		
RA	Richie Ashburn	2.00
YB	Yogi Berra	4.00
DC	Del Crandell	2.00
BF	Bob Feller	2.50
WF	Whitey Ford	4.00
NF	Nellie Fox	2.00
CL	Clem Labine	2.00
DL	Don Larsen	3.00
JL	Johnny Logan	2.00
WM	Willie Mays	6.00
GM	Gil McDougald	2.00
DM	Don Mueller	2.00
JP	Jimmy Piersall	2.00
AR	Allie Reynolds	2.00
PR	Phil Rizzuto	3.00
ES	Enos Slaughter	2.00
DS	Duke Snider	4.00
WW	Wes Westrum	2.00
HW	Hoyt Wilhelm	2.00
DW	Davey Williams	2.00

1954 Bowman Reprint Autographs

		NM/M
Common Player:		10.00
Inserted 1:118		
YB	Yogi Berra	40.00
DC	Del Crandell	15.00
CL	Clem Labine	15.00
JL	Johnny Logan	12.00
DM	Don Mueller	10.00
DW	Davey Williams	10.00

Team Topps Legends Autographs

	NM/M
Common Player:	8.00
Gil McDougald	8.00
Joe Pepitone	8.00
Bobby Richardson	8.00
Robin Roberts	12.00
Warren Spahn	30.00
Luis Tiant	8.00
Carl Yastrzemski	40.00

2002 BOWMAN'S BEST

	NM/M
Complete Set (181):	
Common Player:	.40
Common (91-181):	4.00
Inserted 1:pack	
Blue (1-90):	1-2X
Production 300	
Red (1-90):	1-2X
Production 200	
Gold (1-90):	3-6X
Production 50	
Blue (91-181):	.75-1X
Production 500	
Red (91-181):	1-1.5X
Production 150	
Gold (91-181):	1-2X
Production 50	
Pack (5):	12.00
Box (10):	100.00

1	Josh Beckett	.75
2	Derek Jeter	4.00
3	Alex Rodriguez	3.00
4	Miguel Tejada	.65
5	Nomar Garciaparra	2.50
6	Aramis Ramirez	.40
7	Jeremy Giambi	.40
8	Bernie Williams	.50
9	Juan Pierre	.40
10	Chipper Jones	2.00
11	Jimmy Rollins	.40
12	Alfonso Soriano	1.00
13	Daryle Ward	.40
14	Paul Konerko	.40
15	Tim Hudson	.75
16	Doug Mientkiewicz	.40
17	Todd Helton	1.00
18	Moises Alou	.40
19	Juan Gonzalez	1.00
20	Jorge Posada	.50
21	Jeff Kent	.40
22	Roger Clemens	2.25
23	Phil Nevin	.40
24	Brian Giles	.40
25	Carlos Delgado	1.00
26	Jason Giambi	.75
27	Vladimir Guerrero	1.50
28	Cliff Floyd	.40
29	Shea Hillenbrand	.40
30	Ken Griffey Jr.	2.50
31	Mike Piazza	2.50
32	Carlos Pena	.40
33	Larry Walker	.40
34	Magglio Ordonez	.60
35	Mike Mussina	.75
36	Andruw Jones	1.00
37	Mark Teixeira	.60
38	Curt Schilling	.75
39	Eric Chavez	.60
40	Bartolo Colon	.40
41	Eric Hinske	.40
42	Sean Burroughs	.40
43	Randy Johnson	1.00
44	Adam Dunn	.75
45	Pedro Martinez	1.50
46	Garret Anderson	.40
47	Jim Thome	.50
48	Gary Sheffield	.60
49	Tsuyoshi Shinjo	.40
50	Albert Pujols	3.00
51	Ichiro Suzuki	3.00
52	C.C. Sabathia	.40
53	Bobby Abreu	.40
54	Ivan Rodriguez	.75
55	J.D. Drew	.75
56	Jacque Jones	.40
57	Jason Kendall	.40
58	Javier Vazquez	.40
59	Jeff Bagwell	1.00
60	Greg Maddux	2.00
61	Jim Edmonds	.50
62	Austin Kearns	.75
63	Jose Vidro	.40
64	Kevin Brown	.40
65	Preston Wilson	.40
66	Sammy Sosa	2.50
67	Lance Berkman	.40
68	Mark Mulder	.60
69	Marty Cordova	.40
70	Frank Thomas	1.00
71	Mike Cameron	.40
72	Mike Sweeney	.40
73	Barry Bonds	4.00
74	Troy Glaus	1.00
75	Barry Zito	.75
76	Pat Burrell	.75
77	Paul LoDuca	.40
78	Rafael Palmeiro	1.00
79	Mark Prior	2.00
80	Darin Erstad	.75
81	Richie Sexson	.60
82	Roberto Alomar	.75
83	Roy Oswalt	.50
84	Ryan Klesko	.40
85	Luis Gonzalez	.50
86	Scott Rolen	1.00
87	Shannon Stewart	.40
88	Shawn Green	.60
89	Toby Hall	.40
90	Bret Boone	.40
91	Casey Kotchman/bat	12.00
92	*Jose Valverde/auto*	8.00
93	Cole Barthel/bat	4.00
94	*Brad Nelson/auto*	15.00
95	*Mauricio Lara/auto*	8.00
96	*Ryan Gripp/bat*	4.00
97	*Brian West/auto.*	8.00
98	*Chris Piersoll/auto.*	8.00
99	*Ryan Church/auto.*	20.00

100 Javier Colina/auto. 8.00
101 Juan Gonzalez/auto. 8.00
102 Benito Baez/auto. 8.00
103 Mike Hill/bat 4.00
104 Jason Grove/auto. 8.00
105 Koyie Hill/auto. 8.00
106 Mark Outlaw/auto. 8.00
107 Jason Bay/bat 15.00
108 Jorge Padilla/auto. 8.00
109 Peter Zamora/auto. 8.00
110 Joe Mauer/auto. 60.00
111 Franklyn German/auto. 8.00
112 Chris Flinn/auto. 8.00
113 David Wright/bat 30.00
114 Anastacio Martinez/auto. 8.00
115 Nic Jackson/bat 8.00
116 Rene Reyes/auto. 8.00
117 Colin Young/auto. 8.00
118 Joe Orloski/auto. 8.00
119 Mike Wilson/auto. 8.00
120 Rich Thompson/auto. 8.00
121 Jake Mauer/auto. 8.00
122 Mario Ramos/auto. 8.00
123 Doug Sessions/auto. 8.00
124 Doug Devore/bat 4.00
125 Travis Foley/auto. 10.00
126 Chris Baker/auto. 8.00
127 Michael Floyd/auto. 8.00
128 Josh Barfield/bat 10.00
129 Jose Bautista/bat 6.00
130 Gavin Floyd/auto. 20.00
131 Jason Botts/bat 4.00
132 Clint Nageotte/auto. 10.00
133 Jesus Cota/auto. 10.00
134 Ron Calloway/bat 4.00
135 Kevin Cash/bat 4.00
136 Jonny Gomes/auto. 35.00
137 Dennis Ulacia/auto. 8.00
138 Ryan Snare/auto 8.00
139 Kevin Deaton/auto. 8.00
140 Bobby Jenks/auto. 15.00
141 Casey Kotchman/auto. 30.00
142 Adam Walker/auto. 8.00
143 Mike Gonzalez/auto. 8.00
144 Ruben Gotay/bat 6.00
145 Jason Grove/bat 4.00
146 Freddy Sanchez/auto. 10.00
147 Jason Arnold/auto. 10.00
148 Scott Hairston/auto. 10.00
149 Jason St. Clair/auto. 8.00
150 Chris Tritle/bat 4.00
151 Edwin Yan/bat 4.00
152 Freddy Sanchez/bat 5.00
153 Greg Sain/bat 4.00
154 Yurendell DeCaster/bat 6.00
155 Noochie Varner/bat 6.00
156 Nelson Castro/auto. 8.00
157 Randall Shelley/bat 6.00
158 Reed Johnson/bat 5.00
159 Ryan Raburn/auto. 8.00
160 Jose Morban/bat 5.00
161 Justin Schuda/auto. 8.00
162 Henry Pichardo/auto. 8.00
163 Josh Bard/auto. 8.00
164 Josh Bonifay/auto. 8.00
165 Brandon League/auto. 8.00
166 Julio DePaula/auto. 10.00
167 Todd Linden/auto. 15.00
168 Francisco Liriano/auto. 50.00
169 Chris Snelling/auto. 15.00
170 Blake McGinley/auto. 8.00
171 Cody McKay/auto. 8.00
172 Jason Stanford/auto. 8.00
173 Lenny Dinardo/auto. 8.00
174 Greg Montalbano/auto. 8.00
175 Earl Snyder/auto. 8.00
176 Justin Huber/auto. 10.00
177 Chris Narveson/auto. 8.00
178 Jon Switzer/auto. 8.00
179 Ronald Acuna/auto. 8.00
180 Chris Duffy/bat 8.00
181 Kazuhisa Ishii/bat 8.00

2003 BOWMAN

NM/M
Complete Set (330): 75.00
Common Player: .15
Common Rookie: .40
Pack (10): 2.50
Box (24): 50.00
1 Garret Anderson .15
2 Derek Jeter 2.00
3 Gary Sheffield .30
4 Matt Morris .25
5 Derek Lowe .15
6 Andy Van Hekken .15
7 Sammy Sosa 1.50
8 Ken Griffey Jr. 1.50

9 Omar Vizquel .15
10 Jorge Posada .25
11 Lance Berkman .15
12 Mike Sweeney .15
13 Adrian Beltre .25
14 Richie Sexson .25
15 A.J. Pierzynski .15
16 Bartolo Colon .15
17 Mike Mussina .40
18 Paul Byrd .15
19 Bobby Abreu .15
20 Miguel Tejada .25
21 Aramis Ramirez .15
22 Edgardo Alfonzo .15
23 Edgar Martinez .15
24 Albert Pujols 1.50
25 Carl Crawford .15
26 Eric Hinske .15
27 Tim Salmon .25
28 Luis Gonzalez .25
29 Jay Gibbons .15
30 John Smoltz .15
31 Tim Wakefield .15
32 Mark Prior 1.00
33 Magglio Ordonez .35
34 Adam Dunn .50
35 Larry Walker .15
36 Luis Castillo .15
37 Wade Miller .15
38 Carlos Beltran .50
39 Odalis Perez .15
40 Alex Sanchez .15
41 Torii Hunter .25
42 Cliff Floyd .15
43 Andy Pettitte .25
44 Francisco Rodriguez .15
45 Eric Chavez .35
46 Kevin Millwood .25
47 Dennis Tankersley .15
48 Hideo Nomo .25
49 Freddy Garcia .15
50 Randy Johnson .75
51 Aubrey Huff .15
52 Carlos Delgado .40
53 Troy Glaus .75
54 Junior Spivey .15
55 Mike Hampton .15
56 Sidney Ponson .15
57 Aaron Boone .15
58 Kerry Wood .40
59 Willie Harris .15
60 Nomar Garciaparra 1.50
61 Todd Helton .75
62 Mike Lowell .15
63 Roy Oswalt .25
64 Raul Ibanez .15
65 Brian Jordan .15
66 Geoff Jenkins .15
67 Jermaine Dye .15
68 Tom Glavine .25
69 Bernie Williams .35
70 Vladimir Guerrero .60
71 Mark Mulder .15
72 Jimmy Rollins .15
73 Oliver Perez .15
74 Rich Aurilia .15
75 Joel Pineiro .15
76 J.D. Drew .40
77 Ivan Rodriguez .50
78 Josh Phelps .15
79 Darin Erstad .45
80 Curt Schilling .40
81 Paul LoDuca .15
82 Marty Cordova .15
83 Manny Ramirez .75
84 Bobby Hill .15
85 Paul Konerko .15
86 Austin Kearns .50
87 Jason Jennings .15
88 Brad Penny .15
89 Jeff Bagwell .75
90 Shawn Green .40
91 Jason Schmidt .15
92 Doug Mientkiewicz .15
93 Jose Vidro .15
94 Bret Boone .15
95 Jason Giambi .50
96 Barry Zito .40
97 Roy Halliday .15
98 Pat Burrell .40
99 Sean Burroughs .15
100 Barry Bonds 2.00
101 Kazuhiro Sasaki .15
102 Fernando Vina .15
103 Chan Ho Park .15
104 Andruw Jones .75
105 Adam Kennedy .15
106 Shea Hillenbrand .15
107 Greg Maddux 1.00
108 Jim Edmonds .25
109 Pedro J. Martinez .75
110 Moises Alou .15
111 Jeff Weaver .15
112 C.C. Sabathia .15
113 Robert Fick .15
114 A.J. Burnett .15
115 Jeff Kent .15
116 Kevin Brown .25
117 Rafael Furcal .15
118 Cristian Guzman .15
119 Brad Wilkerson .15
120 Mike Piazza 1.50
121 Alfonso Soriano .75
122 Mark Ellis .15
123 Vicente Padilla .15
124 Eric Gagne .15
125 Ryan Klesko .15
126 Ichiro Suzuki 1.50
127 Tony Batista .15
128 Roberto Alomar .35
129 Alex Rodriguez 1.50
130 Jim Thome .35
131 Jarrod Washburn .15
132 Orlando Hudson .15
133 Chipper Jones 1.00
134 Rodrigo Lopez .15
135 Johnny Damon .15
136 Matt Clement .15
137 Frank Thomas .75
138 Ellis Burks .15
139 Carlos Pena .15
140 Josh Beckett .15
141 Joe Randa .15
142 Brian Giles .15
143 Kazuhisa Ishii .15
144 Corey Koskie .15
145 Orlando Cabrera .15
146 Mark Buehrle .15
147 Roger Clemens 1.25
148 Tim Hudson .25
149 Randy Wolf .15
150 Josh Fogg .15
151 Phil Nevin .15
152 John Olerud .15
153 Scott Rolen .60
154 Joe Kennedy .15
155 Rafael Palmeiro .75
156 Chad Hutchinson .40
157 Quincy Carter .40
158 Hee Seop Choi .25
159 Joe Borchard .15
160 Brandon Phillips .15
161 Wily Mo Pena .15
162 Victor Martinez .15
163 Jason Stokes .15
164 Ken Harvey .15
165 Juan Rivera .15
166 Jose Contreras 1.00
167 Dan Haren .50
168 Michel Hernandez .50
169 Eider Torres .40
170 Chris De La Cruz .50
171 Ramon A. Martinez .75
172 Mike Adams .40
173 Justin Arneson .50
174 Jamie Athas .40
175 Dwaine Bacon .40
176 Clint Barmes 2.00
177 B.J. Barns .40
178 Tyler Johnson .40
179 Bobby Basham .50
180 T.J. Bohn .50
181 J.D. Durbin .75
182 Brandon Bowe .40
183 Craig Brazell .75
184 Dusty Brown .75
185 Brian Bruney .50
186 Greg Bruso .40
187 Jaime Bubela .50
188 Bryan Bullington 1.50
189 Brian Burgamy .40
190 Eny Cabreja .50
191 Daniel Cabrera .40
192 Ryan Cameron .40
193 Lance Caraccioli .75
194 David Cash .40
195 Bernie Castro .40
196 Ismael Castro .40
197 Daryl Clark .50
198 Jeff Clark .50
199 Chris Colton .40
200 Dexter Cooper .40
201 Callix Crabbe .40
202 Chien-Ming Wang 1.50
203 Eric Crozier .75
204 Nook Logan .40
205 David DeJesus .50
206 Matt DeMarco .40
207 Chris Duncan .40
208 Eric Eckenstahler .40
209 Willie Eyre .40
210 Evel Bastida-Martinez .40
211 Chris Fallon .75
212 Mike Flannery .40
213 Mike O'Keefe .40
214 Ben Francisco .50
215 Kason Gabbard .40
216 Mike Gallo .40
217 Jairo Garcia .40
218 Angel Garcia .40
219 Michael Garciaparra .50
220 Joey Gomes .40
221 Dusty Gomon .40
222 Bryan Grace .40
223 Tyson Graham .40
224 Henry Guerrero .40
225 Franklin Gutierrez 2.00
226 Carlos Guzman .75
227 Matthew Hagen .40
228 Josh Hall .75
229 Rob Hammock .50
230 Brendan Harris .75
231 Gary Harris .40
232 Clay Hensley .50
233 Michael Hinckley .40
234 Luis Hodge .40
235 Donnie Hood .75
236 Travis Ishikawa .75
237 Edwin Jackson 2.00
238 Ardley Jansen .75
239 Ferenc Jongejan .40
240 Matt Kata .75
241 Kazuhiro Takeoka .40
242 Beau Kemp .40
243 Il Kim .50
244 Brennan King .40
245 Cris Kroski .40
246 Jason Kubel 1.50
247 Pete LaForest .40
248 Wilfredo Ledezma .40
249 Jeremy Bonderman 1.00
250 Gonzalo Lopez .40
251 Brian Luderer .50
252 Ruddy Lugo .40
253 Wayne Lydon .40
254 Mark Malaska .40
255 Andy Marte 2.50
256 Tyler Martin .40
257 Branden Florence .40
258 Aneudis Mateo .40
259 Derell McCall .40
260 Brian McCann .50
261 Mike McNutt .40
262 Jacabo Meque .40
263 Derek Michaelis .50
264 Aaron Miles 1.00
265 Jose Morales .40
266 Dustin Moseley .40
267 Adrian Myers .40
268 Dan Neil .40
269 Jon Nelson .75
270 Mike Neu .40
271 Leigh Neuage .40
272 Weston O'Brien .40
273 Trent Oeltjen .75
274 Tim Olson .75
275 David Pahucki .40
276 Nathan Panther .75
277 Arnie Munoz .40
278 David Pember .40
279 Jason Perry .75
280 Matthew Peterson .40
281 Ryan Shealy .75
282 Jorge Piedra .40
283 Simon Pond .40
284 Aaron Rakers .40
285 Hanley Ramirez 1.50

286 *Manuel Ramirez* .40
287 *Kevin Randel* .50
288 Darrell Rasner .40
289 *Prentice Redman* .75
290 *Eric Reed* .75
291 *Wilton Reynolds* .40
292 *Eric Riggs* .40
293 *Carlos Rijo* .40
294 *Rajai Davis* .50
295 *Aron Weston* .40
296 *Arturo Rivas* .50
297 *Kyle Roat* .40
298 *Bubba Nelson* .50
299 *Levi Robinson* .40
300 *Ray Sadler* .40
301 *Gary Schneidmiller* .50
302 *Jon Schuerholz* .40
303 *Corey Shafer* .50
304 *Brian Shackelford* .40
305 *Bill Simon* .40
306 *Haj Turay* .40
307 Sean Smith .40
308 *Ryan Spataro* .40
309 *Jemel Spearman* .50
310 *Keith Stamler* .40
311 *Luke Steidlmayer* .40
312 Adam Stern .50
313 *Jay Sitzman* .40
314 *Thomari Story-Harden* .50
315 *Terry Tiffee* .40
316 *Nick Trzesniak* .50
317 *Denny Tussen* .40
318 Scott Tyler .40
319 *Shane Victorino* .40
320 *Doug Waechter* .50
321 *Brandon Watson* .75
322 *Todd Wellemeyer* .50
323 *Eli Whiteside* .50
324 *Josh Willingham* .75
325 *Travis Wong* .75
326 *Brian Wright* .40
327 *Kevin Youkilis* 2.00
328 Andy Sisco .50
329 *Dustin Yount* .75
330 *Andrew Dominique* .40

Gold

Stars (1-165): 1-2X
Rookies (166-330): 1-2X
Inserted 1:1

Uncirculated

Stars (1-165): 3-5X
Rookies (166-330): 2-4X
Production 250 sets

Dual Signs of the Future Autograph

NM/M
Inserted 1:9,220
CH Quincy Carter, Chad Hutchinson 85.00

Future Fiber Relics

NM/M
Common Player: 4.00
RB Rocco Baldelli 10.00
WB Wilson Betemit 6.00
HB Hank Blalock 10.00
JB Jason Botts 5.00
SB Sean Burroughs 8.00
KC Kevin Cash 4.00
KD Kory DeHaan 5.00
CD Chris Duffy 4.00
PF Pedro Feliz 5.00
AG Adrian Gonzalez 5.00
JG Jason Grove 5.00
JH Josh Hamilton 4.00
NH Nathan Haynes 4.00
DH Drew Henson 8.00
AH Aubrey Huff 5.00
RJ Reed Johnson 6.00
AK Austin Kearns 10.00
CK Casey Kotchman 8.00
RK Ryan Langerhans 5.00
JDM Jake Mauer 6.00
JM Joe Mauer 15.00
XN Xavier Nady 8.00
MR Michael Restovich 8.00
WR Wilkin Ruan 8.00
FS Freddy Sanchez 8.00
RS Randall Shelley 4.00
BS Bud Smith 4.00
ES Esix Snead 6.00
ST So Taguchi 8.00
JW Justin Wayne 8.00
TW Travis Wilson 6.00
DW David Wright 10.00
EY Edwin Yan 4.00

Futures Game Gear Relics

NM/M
Common Player: 4.00
Inserted 1:26
EA Edwin Almonte 4.00
TA Tony Alvarez 4.00
BB Brad Baker 4.00
FB Francis Beltran 4.00
JEB Joe Borchard 4.00
JB John Buck 4.00
SB Sean Burnett 6.00
MB Marlon Byrd 4.00
MC Miguel Cabrera 10.00
KC Kevin Cash 4.00
HC Hee Seop Choi 8.00
SC Shin-Soo Choo 6.00
AC Aaron Cook 5.00
CC Carl Crawford 5.00
JDR Jorge De La Rosa 4.00
VD Victor Diaz 4.00
RD Ryan Dittfurth 4.00
BE Brett Evert 4.00
GG Gerardo Garcia 4.00
BH Bill Hall 4.00
CH Corey Hart 4.00
DH Drew Henson 8.00
JH Justin Huber 6.00
OH Orlando Hudson 4.00
OI Omar Infante 4.00
JJ Jimmy Journell 4.00
JK Josh Karp 4.00
FL Francisco Liriano 4.00
JL Jose Lopez 4.00
VM Victor Martinez 8.00
JM Justin Morneau 10.00
BM Brett Myers 6.00
LO Lyle Overbay 6.00
WP Wily Mo Pena 6.00
BP Brandon Phillips 6.00
MR Mike Restovich 8.00
JR Jose Reyes 10.00
FR Francisco Rodriguez 5.00
RR Ricardo Rodriguez 4.00
SS Seung Jun Song 6.00
JMS John Stephens 4.00
JS Jason Stokes 8.00
BT Billy Traber 5.00
CT Chad Tracey 4.00
AW Adam Wainwright 5.00
JY Jason Young 4.00

Futures Game MVP Autograph

NM/M
Complete Set (1):
JR Jose Reyes 30.00

ROY Dual Relic

NM/M
Inserted 1:765
JH Eric Hinske, Jason Jennings 10.00

Signs of the Future

NM/M
Common Autograph: 5.00
Red Autographs: 1-2.5X
Production 50 sets
JA Jason Arnold 8.00
JB John Buck 5.00
BB Bryan Bullington 15.00
QC Quincy Carter 15.00
NC Nelson Castro 8.00
RC Ryan Church 10.00
JC Jesus Cota 5.00
JOG Jonny Gomes 25.00
DG Doug Gredvig 5.00
KG Khalil Greene 25.00
ZG Zack Greinke 10.00
JG Jason Grove 5.00
JGU Jeremy Guthrie 10.00
CH Cole Hamels 20.00
JRH Joel Hanrahan 8.00
CJH Corey Hart 20.00
KH Koyie Hill 8.00
CMH Chad Hutchinson 15.00
BJ Bobby Jenks 5.00
BK Ben Kozlowski 5.00
BL Brandon League 5.00
DL Donald Levinski 5.00
FL Fred Lewis 5.00
TL Todd Linden 5.00
JL James Loney 10.00
VM Val Majewski 8.00
DHM Dustin McGowan 5.00
CP Chris Piersoll 8.00
HR Hanley Ramirez 25.00
PR Prentice Redman 8.00
JR Jose Reyes 15.00
JSC Jason St. Clair 6.00
FS Freddy Sanchez 8.00
ZS Zach Segovia 8.00
DS Doug Sessions 5.00
BS Brian Slocum 6.00
RS Ryan Snare 8.00
MT Mitch Talbot 5.00
AT Andres Torres 5.00
AV Andy Van Hekken 5.00
OV Oscar Villarreal 8.00

2003 BOWMAN CHROME

NM/M
Complete Set (351): 400.00
Common Player: .25
Common Rookie: 1.00
Common RC Auto. (331-350): 15.00
Pack (4): 5.00
Box (18): 75.00
1 Garret Anderson .25
2 Derek Jeter 3.00
3 Gary Sheffield .50
4 Matt Morris .35
5 Derek Lowe .25
6 Andy Van Hekken .25
7 Sammy Sosa 2.00
8 Ken Griffey Jr. 2.00
9 Omar Vizquel .25
10 Jorge Posada .40
11 Lance Berkman .25
12 Mike Sweeney .25
13 Adrian Beltre .50
14 Richie Sexson .40
15 A.J. Pierzynski .25
16 Bartolo Colon .25
17 Mike Mussina .75
18 Paul Byrd .25
19 Bobby Abreu .25
20 Miguel Tejada .40
21 Aramis Ramirez .25
22 Edgardo Alfonzo .25
23 Edgar Martinez .25
24 Albert Pujols 2.50
25 Carl Crawford .25
26 Eric Hinske .25
27 Tim Salmon .40
28 Luis Gonzalez .40
29 Jay Gibbons .25
30 John Smoltz .25
31 Tim Wakefield .25
32 Mark Prior 1.50
33 Magglio Ordonez .40
34 Adam Dunn .75
35 Larry Walker .25
36 Luis Castillo .25
37 Wade Miller .25
38 Carlos Beltran .75
39 Odalis Perez .25
40 Alex Sanchez .25
41 Torii Hunter .50
42 Cliff Floyd .25
43 Andy Pettitte .50
44 Francisco Rodriguez .25
45 Eric Chavez .50
46 Kevin Millwood .50
47 Dennis Tankersley .25
48 Hideo Nomo .50
49 Freddy Garcia .25
50 Randy Johnson 1.00
51 Aubrey Huff .25
52 Carlos Delgado .50
53 Troy Glaus 1.00
54 Junior Spivey .25
55 Mike Hampton .25
56 Sidney Ponson .25
57 Aaron Boone .25
58 Kerry Wood .75
59 Willie Harris .25
60 Nomar Garciaparra 2.00
61 Todd Helton 1.00
62 Mike Lowell .25
63 Roy Oswalt .40
64 Raul Ibanez .25
65 Brian Jordan .25
66 Geoff Jenkins .25
67 Jermaine Dye .25
68 Tom Glavine .50
69 Bernie Williams .50
70 Vladimir Guerrero 1.00
71 Mark Mulder .40
72 Jimmy Rollins .25
73 Oliver Perez .25
74 Rich Aurilia .25
75 Joel Pineiro .25
76 J.D. Drew .45
77 Ivan Rodriguez .65
78 Josh Phelps .25
79 Darin Erstad .60
80 Curt Schilling .50
81 Paul LoDuca .25
82 Marty Cordova .25
83 Manny Ramirez 1.00
84 Bobby Hill .25
85 Paul Konerko .25
86 Austin Kearns .50
87 Jason Jennings .25
88 Brad Penny .25
89 Jeff Bagwell 1.00
90 Shawn Green .50
91 Jason Schmidt .25
92 Doug Mientkiewicz .25
93 Jose Vidro .25
94 Bret Boone .25
95 Jason Giambi .75
96 Barry Zito .50
97 Roy Halliday .50
98 Pat Burrell .50
99 Sean Burroughs .25
100 Barry Bonds 3.00
101 Kazuhiro Sasaki .25
102 Fernando Vina .25
103 Chan Ho Park .25
104 Andruw Jones 1.00
105 Adam Kennedy .25
106 Shea Hillenbrand .25
107 Greg Maddux 1.50
108 Jim Edmonds .40
109 Pedro J. Martinez 1.00
110 Moises Alou .25
111 Jeff Weaver .25
112 C.C. Sabathia .25
113 Robert Fick .25
114 A.J. Burnett .25
115 Jeff Kent .25
116 Kevin Brown .40
117 Rafael Furcal .25
118 Cristian Guzman .25
119 Brad Wilkerson .25
120 Mike Piazza 2.00
121 Alfonso Soriano 1.00
122 Mark Ellis .25
123 Vicente Padilla .25
124 Eric Gagne .50
125 Ryan Klesko .25
126 Ichiro Suzuki 2.00
127 Tony Batista .25

128 Roberto Alomar .50
129 Alex Rodriguez 2.50
130 Jim Thome .40
131 Jarrod Washburn .25
132 Orlando Hudson .25
133 Chipper Jones 1.50
134 Rodrigo Lopez .25
135 Johnny Damon .50
136 Matt Clement .25
137 Frank Thomas 1.00
138 Ellis Burks .25
139 Carlos Pena .25
140 Josh Beckett .50
141 Joe Randa .25
142 Brian Giles .25
143 Kazuhisa Ishii .25
144 Corey Koskie .25
145 Orlando Cabrera .25
146 Mark Buehrle .25
147 Roger Clemens 1.75
148 Tim Hudson .50
149 Randy Wolf .25
150 Josh Fogg .25
151 Phil Nevin .25
152 John Olerud .25
153 Scott Rolen 1.00
154 Joe Kennedy .25
155 Rafael Palmeiro .75
156 Chad Hutchinson .75
157 Quincy Carter 1.00
158 Hee Seop Choi .50
159 Joe Borchard .25
160 Brandon Phillips .25
161 Wily Mo Pena .25
162 Victor Martinez .25
163 Jason Stokes .25
164 Ken Harvey .25
165 Juan Rivera .25
166 *Joe Valentine* 1.50
167 Dan Haren 2.50
168 *Michel Hernandez* 1.00
169 *Eider Torres* 1.00
170 *Chris De La Cruz* 1.00
171 *Ramon A. Martinez* 2.00
172 *Mike Adams* 1.00
173 *Justin Arneson* 1.00
174 *Jamie Athas* 1.00
175 *Dwaine Bacon* 1.00
176 *Clint Barmes* 5.00
177 *B.J. Barns* 1.00
178 *Tyler Johnson* 1.00
179 *Brandon Webb* 4.00
180 *T.J. Bohn* 1.00
181 *Ozzie Chavez* 1.50
182 *Brandon Bowe* 1.00
183 *Craig Brazell* 2.00
184 *Dusty Brown* 1.50
185 *Brian Bruney* 1.00
186 *Greg Bruso* 1.00
187 *Jaime Bubela* 1.00
188 *Matt Diaz* 2.00
189 *Brian Burgamy* 1.00
190 *Eny Cabreja* 1.00
191 *Daniel Cabrera* 3.00
192 *Ryan Cameron* 1.00
193 *Lance Caraccioli* 1.50
194 *David Cash* 1.00
195 *Bernie Castro* 1.00
196 *Ismael Castro* 1.00
197 *Cory Doyne* 2.00
198 *Jeff Clark* 1.00
199 *Chris Colton* 1.00
200 *Dexter Cooper* 1.00
201 *Callix Crabbe* 1.00
202 *Chien-Ming Wang* 10.00
203 *Eric Crozier* 1.50
204 *Nook Logan* 1.50
205 *David DeJesus* 4.00
206 *Matt DeMarco* 1.00
207 *Chris Duncan* 1.00
208 Eric Eckenstahler 1.00
209 *Willie Eyre* 1.00
210 *Evel Bastida-Martinez* 1.00
211 *Chris Fallon* 1.50
212 *Mike Flannery* 1.00
213 *Mike O'Keefe* 1.00
214 *Lew Ford* 4.00
215 *Kason Gabbard* 1.00
216 *Mike Gallo* 1.00
217 *Jairo Garcia* 1.00
218 *Angel Garcia* 1.00
219 Michael Garciaparra 3.00
220 Jeremy Griffiths 1.50
221 *Dusty Gomon* 1.50
222 *Bryan Grace* 1.00
223 *Tyson Graham* 1.00
224 *Henry Guerrero* 1.00
225 *Franklin Gutierrez* 5.00
226 *Carlos Guzman* 2.00
227 *Matthew Hagen* 2.00
228 *Josh Hall* 1.50
229 *Rob Hammock* 1.50
230 *Brendan Harris* 2.00
231 *Gary Harris* 1.00
232 *Clay Hensley* 1.50
233 *Michael Hinckley* 5.00
234 *Luis Hodge* 1.00
235 *Donnie Hood* 2.00
236 *Matt Hensley* 2.00
237 *Edwin Jackson* 4.00
238 *Ardley Jansen* 2.00
239 *Ferenc Jongejan* 1.00
240 *Matt Kata* 3.00
241 *Kazuhiro Takeoka* 1.00
242 *Charlie Manning* 1.00
243 *Il Kim* 1.00
244 *Brennan King* 1.00
245 *Cris Kroski* 1.00
246 David Martinez 2.00
247 *Pete LaForest* 1.00
248 *Wilfredo Ledezma* 1.00
249 Jeremy Bonderman 6.00
250 *Gonzalo Lopez* 1.00
251 *Brian Luderer* 1.50
252 *Ruddy Lugo* 1.00
253 *Wayne Lydon* 1.00
254 *Mark Malaska* 1.00
255 *Andy Marte* 10.00
256 *Tyler Martin* 1.00
257 *Branden Florence* 1.00
258 *Aneudis Mateo* 1.00
259 *Derell McCall* 1.00
260 *Elizardo Ramirez* 2.00
261 *Mike McNutt* 1.00
262 *Jacabo Meque* 1.00
263 *Derek Michaelis* 1.50
264 *Aaron Miles* 3.00
265 Jose Morales 1.00
266 *Dustin Moseley* 1.00
267 *Adrian Myers* 1.00
268 *Dan Neil* 1.00
269 *Jon Nelson* 2.00
270 *Mike Neu* 1.00
271 *Leigh Neuage* 1.00
272 *Weston O'Brien* 1.00
273 *Trent Oeltjen* 2.00
274 *Tim Olson* 2.00
275 *David Pahucki* 1.00
276 *Nathan Panther* 2.50
277 *Arnie Munoz* 1.00
278 *David Pember* 1.00
279 *Jason Perry* 2.00
280 *Matthew Peterson* 1.00
281 *Greg Aquino* 1.50
282 *Jorge Piedra* 1.00
283 *Simon Pond* 2.00
284 *Aaron Rakers* 1.00
285 *Felix Sanchez* 1.50
286 *Manuel Ramirez* 1.00
287 *Kevin Randel* 1.00
288 *Kelly Shoppach* 3.00
289 *Prentice Redman* 2.00
290 *Eric Reed* 3.00
291 *Wilton Reynolds* 1.00
292 *Eric Riggs* 1.00
293 *Carlos Rijo* 1.00
294 *Tyler Adamczyk* 2.00
295 *Jon-Mark Sprowl* 2.00
296 *Arturo Rivas* 2.00
297 *Kyle Roat* 1.00
298 *Bubba Nelson* 2.00
299 *Levi Robinson* 1.00
300 *Ray Sadler* 1.00
301 *Rylan Reed* 1.00
302 *Jon Schuerholz* 1.00
303 *Nobuaki Yoshida* 1.50
304 *Brian Shackelford* 1.00
305 *Bill Simon* 1.00
306 *Haj Turay* 1.00
307 Sean Smith 1.00
308 *Ryan Spataro* 1.00
309 *Jemel Spearman* 1.50
310 *Keith Stamler* 1.00
311 *Luke Steidlmayer* 1.00
312 Adam Stern 1.00
313 *Jay Sitzman* 1.00
314 *Mike Wodnicki* 1.50
315 *Terry Tiffee* 1.00
316 *Nick Trzesniak* 1.00
317 *Denny Tussen* 1.00
318 Scott Tyler 1.00
319 *Shane Victorino* 1.00
320 *Doug Waechter* 1.50
321 *Brandon Watson* 1.50
322 *Todd Wellemeyer* 1.50
323 *Eli Whiteside* 1.50
324 *Josh Willingham* 2.00
325 *Travis Wong* 1.50
326 *Brian Wright* 1.00
327 *Felix Pie* 10.00
328 Andy Sisco 4.00
329 *Dustin Yount* 2.50
330 *Andrew Dominique* 1.50
331 Brian McCann 30.00
332 *Jose Contreras* 150.00
333 *Corey Shafer* 15.00
334 *Hanley Ramirez* 60.00
335 *Ryan Shealy* 20.00
336 *Kevin Youkilis* 25.00
337 *Jason Kubel* 25.00
338 *Aron Weston* 15.00
339 *J.D. Durbin* 20.00
340 *Gary Schneidmiller* 15.00
341 *Travis Ishikawa* 20.00
342 *Ben Francisco* 20.00
343 *Bobby Basham* 20.00
344 Joey Gomes 15.00
345 *Beau Kemp* 15.00
346 *Thomari Story-Harden* 15.00
347 *Daryl Clark* 15.00
348 *Bryan Bullington* 25.00
349 *Rajai Davis* 15.00
350 Darrell Rasner 15.00
351 Willie Mays 3.00

Refractors

NM/M

Stars (1-165, 351): 2-4X
Rookies (166-350): .5-1.5X
X-Fractors (1-165, 351): 3-6X
X-Fractors (166-350): 1-2X
Uncirc.Gold Refractors (1-165): 5-10X
Gold Refractors (166-350): 2-3X
Production 170 sets
Gold Refractors (331-350): 1-3X

Willie Mays Autograph

NM/M

Production 150
351AU Willie Mays 220.00

2003 BOWMAN CHROME DRAFT PICKS & PROSPECTS

NM/M

Complete Set (176): 300.00
Common Player: .25
Common Rookie: 1.00
Common Rk Autograph (166-176): 15.00
BDP1 Dontrelle Willis .75
BDP2 Freddy Sanchez .25
BDP3 Miguel Cabrera .75
BDP4 Ryan Ludwick .25
BDP5 Ty Wigginton .25
BDP6 Mark Teixeira .75
BDP7 Trey Hodges .25
BDP8 Laynce Nix .25
BDP9 Antonio Perez .25
BDP10 Jody Gerut .25
BDP11 Jae Weong Seo .25
BDP12 Erick Almonte .25
BDP13 Lyle Overbay .25
BDP14 Billy Traber .25
BDP15 Andres Torres .25
BDP16 Jose Valverde .25
BDP17 Aaron Heilman .25
BDP18 Brandon Larson .25
BDP19 Jung Bong .25
BDP20 Jesse Foppert .25
BDP21 Angel Berroa .25
BDP22 Jeff DaVanon .25
BDP23 Kurt Ainsworth .25
BDP24 Brandon Claussen .25
BDP25 Xavier Nady .25
BDP26 Travis Hafner .25
BDP27 Jerome Williams .25
BDP28 Jose Reyes .25
BDP29 *Sergio Mitre* 1.00
BDP30 *Bo Hart* 2.00
BDP31 *Adam Miller* 8.00
BDP32 *Brian Finch* 1.00
BDP33 *Taylor Mattingly* 3.00
BDP34 *Daric Barton* 10.00
BDP35 *Chris Ray* 1.00
BDP36 *Jarrod Saltalamacchia* 8.00
BDP37 *Dennis Dove* 1.00
BDP38 *James Houser* 1.50
BDP39 *Clinton King* 2.00
BDP40 *Lou Palmisano* 2.00
BDP41 *Dan Moore* 1.00
BDP42 *Craig Stansberry* 1.50
BDP43 *Jo Jo Reyes* 2.00
BDP44 *Jake Stevens* 2.00
BDP45 *Tom Gorzelanny* 2.00
BDP46 *Brian Marshall* 1.50
BDP47 *Scott Beerer* 1.00
BDP48 *Javi Herrera* 1.50
BDP49 *Steve Lerud* 2.50
BDP50 *Josh Banks* 3.00
BDP51 *Jon Papelbon* 12.00
BDP52 *Juan Valdes* 1.50
BDP53 Beau Vaghan 1.50
BDP54 *Matt Chico* 2.00
BDP55 *Todd Jennings* 1.50
BDP56 *Anthony Gwynn* 2.00
BDP57 *Matt Harrison* 3.00
BDP58 Aaron Mardsen 1.00
BDP59 *Casey Abrams* 1.00
BDP60 *Cory Stuart* 1.00
BDP61 *Mike Wagner* 1.00
BDP62 *Jordan Pratt* 1.50
BDP63 *Andre Randolph* 1.00
BDP64 *Blake Balkcom* 1.00
BDP65 *Josh Muecke* 1.00
BDP66 *Jamie D'Antona* 3.00
BDP67 *Cole Seifrig* 2.50
BDP68 *Josh Anderson* 2.00
BDP69 *Matt Lorenzo* 1.00
BDP70 *Nate Spears* 1.50
BDP71 *Chris Goodman* 1.50
BDP72 *Brian McFall* 1.50
BDP73 *Billy Hogan* 1.50
BDP74 *Jamie Romak* 1.50
BDP75 *Jeff Cook* 1.50
BDP76 *Brooks McNiven* 1.00
BDP77 *Xavier Paul* 2.00
BDP78 *Bob Zimmerman* 1.00
BDP79 *Mickey Hall* 1.00
BDP80 *Shaun Marcum* 1.00
BDP81 *Matt Nachreiner* 1.00
BDP82 *Chris Kinsey* 1.00
BDP83 *Jonathan Fulton* 1.50
BDP84 *Edgardo Baez* 2.00
BDP85 *Robert Valido* 2.00
BDP86 *Kenny Lewis* 1.50
BDP87 *Trent Peterson* 1.00
BDP88 *Johnny Woodard* 1.00
BDP89 *Wes Littleton* 1.50
BDP90 *Sean Rodriguez* 2.00
BDP91 *Kyle Pearson* 1.00
BDP92 *Josh Rainwater* 2.50
BDP93 *Travis Schlichting* 1.50
BDP94 *Tim Battle* 1.00
BDP95 *Aaron Hill* 4.00
BDP96 *Bob McCrory* 1.00
BDP97 *Rick Guarno* 1.00
BDP98 *Brandon Yarbrough* 1.00
BDP99 *Peter Stonard* 1.50
BDP100 *Darin Downs* 1.50
BDP101 *Matt Bruback* 1.00
BDP102 *Danny Garcia* 1.00
BDP103 *Cory Stewart* 1.00
BDP104 *Ferdin Tejeda* 1.50
BDP105 *Kade Johnson* 1.00
BDP106 *Andrew Brown* 2.00
BDP107 *Aquilino Lopez* 1.00
BDP108 *Stephen Randolph* 1.00
BDP109 *Dave Matranga* 1.00
BDP110 *Dustin McGowan* 2.00
BDP111 *Juan Camacho* 1.50
BDP112 Cliff Lee .15
BDP113 *Jeff Duncan* 1.00
BDP114 C.J. Wilson .50
BDP115 *Brandon Roberson* 1.00
BDP116 *David Corrente* 1.00
BDP117 *Kevin Beavers* 1.00
BDP118 *Anthony Webster* 1.50
BDP119 *Oscar Villarreal* 1.00
BDP120 *Hong-Chih Kuo* 3.00
BDP121 Josh Barfield .15
BDP122 Denny Bautista .15
BDP123 Chris Burke 4.00

BDP124	*Robinson Cano*	15.00
BDP125	Jose Castillo	.15
BDP126	Neal Cotts	.15
BDP127	Jorge De La Rosa	.15
BDP128	J.D. Durbin	.15
BDP129	Edwin Encarnacion	2.00
BDP130	Gavin Floyd	.15
BDP131	Alexis Gomez	.15
BDP132	*Edgar Gonzalez*	1.00
BDP133	Khalil Greene	.50
BDP134	Zack Greinke	.15
BDP135	Franklin Gutierrez	2.00
BDP136	Rich Harden	.15
BDP137	J.J. Hardy	4.00
BDP138	Ryan Howard	15.00
BDP139	Justin Huber	.15
BDP140	David Kelton	.15
BDP141	David Krynzel	.15
BDP142	Pete LaForest	.15
BDP143	Adam LaRoche	.15
BDP144	Preston Larrison	1.00
BDP145	*John Maine*	3.00
BDP146	Andy Marte	5.00
BDP147	Jeff Mathis	.15
BDP148	Joe Mauer	1.00
BDP149	Clint Nageotte	.15
BDP150	Chris Narveson	.15
BDP151	*Ramon Nivar*	1.00
BDP152	*Felix Pie*	8.00
BDP153	*Guillermo Quiroz*	2.50
BDP154	Rene Reyes	.15
BDP155	Royce Ring	.15
BDP156	Alexis Rios	1.00
BDP157	Grady Sizemore	.15
BDP158	Stephen Smitherman	.15
BDP159	Seung Jun Song	.15
BDP160	Scott Thorman	.15
BDP161	Chad Tracy	.15
BDP162	Chin-Hui Tsao	.15
BDP163	John Van Benschoten	.15
BDP164	Kevin Youkilis	2.00
BDP165	Chien-Ming Wang	2.00
BDP166	*Chris Lubanski/ auto*	30.00
BDP167	*Ryan Harvey/auto*	30.00
BDP168	*Matt Murton/auto*	25.00
BDP169	*Jay Sborz/auto*	15.00
BDP170	*Brandon Wood/ auto*	80.00
BDP171	*Nicholas Markakis/ auto*	30.00
BDP172	*Rickie Weeks/auto*	80.00
BDP173	*Eric Duncan/auto*	30.00
BDP174	*Chad Billingsley/ auto*	25.00
BDP175	*Ryan Wagner/auto*	20.00
BDP176	*Delmon Young/ auto*	120.00

Refractor

Rookies (29-165):	2-4X
Inserted 1:11	
Autos (166-176):	.75-1.5X
Inserted 1:196	

X-Fractor

Rookies (29-165):	2-4X
Production 130 sets	
Autos (166-176):	.75-2X
Inserted 1:393	

Gold Refract

Rookies (29-165):	3-5X
Production 50 sets	
Autos (166-176):	No Pricing
Inserted 1:1,479	

2003 BOWMAN DRAFT PICKS & PROSPECTS

		NM/M
Complete Set (165):		35.00
Common Player:		.15
Common Rookie:		.25
Pack (5 Bowman + 2 Chrome):		6.00
Box (24):		125.00
BDP1	Dontrelle Willis	.40
BDP2	Freddy Sanchez	.15
BDP3	Miguel Cabrera	.50
BDP4	Ryan Ludwick	.15
BDP5	Ty Wigginton	.15
BDP6	Mark Teixeira	.40
BDP7	Trey Hodges	.15
BDP8	Laynce Nix	.15
BDP9	Antonio Perez	.15
BDP10	Jody Gerut	.15
BDP11	Jae Weong Seo	.15
BDP12	Erick Almonte	.15
BDP13	Lyle Overbay	.15
BDP14	Billy Traber	.15
BDP15	Andres Torres	.15
BDP16	Jose Valverde	.15
BDP17	Aaron Heilman	.15
BDP18	Brandon Larson	.15
BDP19	Jung Bong	.15
BDP20	Jesse Foppert	.15
BDP21	Angel Berroa	.15
BDP22	Jeff DaVanon	.15
BDP23	Kurt Ainsworth	.15
BDP24	Brandon Claussen	.15
BDP25	Xavier Nady	.15
BDP26	Travis Hafner	.15
BDP27	Jerome Williams	.15
BDP28	Jose Reyes	.15
BDP29	*Sergio Mitre*	.25
BDP30	*Bo Hart*	1.00
BDP31	*Adam Miller*	2.00
BDP32	*Brian Finch*	.25
BDP33	*Taylor Mattingly*	2.00
BDP34	*Daric Barton*	3.00
BDP35	*Chris Ray*	.25
BDP36	*Jarrod Saltalamacchia*	1.50
BDP37	*Dennis Dove*	.25
BDP38	*James Houser*	.50
BDP39	*Clinton King*	.50
BDP40	*Lou Palmisano*	1.50
BDP41	*Dan Moore*	.25
BDP42	*Craig Stansberry*	.50
BDP43	*Jo Jo Reyes*	.50
BDP44	*Jake Stevens*	.25
BDP45	*Tom Gorzelanny*	.50
BDP46	*Brian Marshall*	.50
BDP47	*Scott Beerer*	.25
BDP48	*Javi Herrera*	.50
BDP49	*Steve Lerud*	.75
BDP50	*Josh Banks*	.75
BDP51	*Jon Papelbon*	.25
BDP52	*Juan Valdes*	.50
BDP53	Beau Vaghan	.50
BDP54	*Matt Chico*	.25
BDP55	*Todd Jennings*	.50
BDP56	*Anthony Gwynn*	1.00
BDP57	*Matt Harrison*	.25
BDP58	Aaron Mardsen	.25
BDP59	*Casey Abrams*	.25
BDP60	*Cory Stuart*	.25
BDP61	*Mike Wagner*	.25
BDP62	*Jordan Pratt*	.50
BDP63	*Andre Randolph*	.25
BDP64	*Blake Balkcom*	.25
BDP65	*Josh Muecke*	.25
BDP66	*Jamie D'Antona*	1.50
BDP67	*Cole Seifrig*	1.50
BDP68	*Josh Anderson*	.25
BDP69	*Matt Lorenzo*	.25
BDP70	*Nate Spears*	.50
BDP71	*Chris Goodman*	.50
BDP72	*Brian McFall*	.50
BDP73	*Billy Hogan*	.50
BDP74	*Jamie Romak*	.50
BDP75	*Jeff Cook*	.50
BDP76	*Brooks McNiven*	.25
BDP77	*Xavier Paul*	1.50
BDP78	*Bob Zimmerman*	.25
BDP79	*Mickey Hall*	.50
BDP80	*Shaun Marcum*	.25
BDP81	*Matt Nachreiner*	.25
BDP82	*Chris Kinsey*	.25
BDP83	*Jonathan Fulton*	.50
BDP84	*Edgardo Baez*	.50
BDP85	*Robert Valido*	1.50
BDP86	*Kenny Lewis*	.50
BDP87	*Trent Peterson*	.25
BDP88	*Johnny Woodard*	.25
BDP89	*Wes Littleton*	.50
BDP90	*Sean Rodriguez*	.50
BDP91	*Kyle Pearson*	.25
BDP92	*Josh Rainwater*	.75
BDP93	*Travis Schlichting*	.50
BDP94	*Tim Battle*	.75
BDP95	*Aaron Hill*	1.00
BDP96	*Bob McCrory*	.25
BDP97	*Rick Guarno*	.25
BDP98	*Brandon Yarbrough*	.25
BDP99	*Peter Stonard*	.50
BDP100	*Darin Downs*	.50
BDP101	*Matt Bruback*	.25
BDP102	*Danny Garcia*	.25
BDP103	*Cory Stewart*	.25
BDP104	*Ferdin Tejeda*	.50
BDP105	*Kade Johnson*	.25
BDP106	*Andrew Brown*	.25
BDP107	*Aquilino Lopez*	.25
BDP108	*Stephen Randolph*	.25
BDP109	*Dave Matranga*	.25
BDP110	*Dustin McGowan*	.75
BDP111	*Juan Camacho*	.50
BDP112	Cliff Lee	.15
BDP113	*Jeff Duncan*	.25
BDP114	C.J. Wilson	.25
BDP115	*Brandon Roberson*	.25
BDP116	*David Corrente*	.25
BDP117	*Kevin Beavers*	.25
BDP118	*Anthony Webster*	.50
BDP119	*Oscar Villarreal*	.25
BDP120	*Hong-Chih Kuo*	.75
BDP121	Josh Barfield	.15
BDP122	Denny Bautista	.15
BDP123	Chris Burke	.75
BDP124	*Robinson Cano*	3.00
BDP125	Jose Castillo	.15
BDP126	Neal Cotts	.15
BDP127	Jorge De La Rosa	.15
BDP128	J.D. Durbin	.15
BDP129	Edwin Encarnacion	.75
BDP130	Gavin Floyd	.15
BDP131	Alexis Gomez	.15
BDP132	*Edgar Gonzalez*	.25
BDP133	Khalil Greene	.15
BDP134	Zack Greinke	.15
BDP135	Franklin Gutierrez	.15
BDP136	Rich Harden	.15
BDP137	J.J. Hardy	1.50
BDP138	Ryan Howard	3.00
BDP139	Justin Huber	.15
BDP140	David Kelton	.15
BDP141	David Krynzel	.15
BDP142	Pete LaForest	.15
BDP143	Adam LaRoche	.15
BDP144	Preston Larrison	.15
BDP145	*John Maine*	1.00
BDP146	Andy Marte	1.00
BDP147	Jeff Mathis	.15
BDP148	Joe Mauer	.50
BDP149	Clint Nageotte	.15
BDP150	Chris Narveson	.15
BDP151	*Ramon Nivar*	.25
BDP152	*Felix Pie*	3.00
BDP153	*Guillermo Quiroz*	1.00
BDP154	Rene Reyes	.15
BDP155	Royce Ring	.15
BDP156	Alexis Rios	.15
BDP157	Grady Sizemore	.15
BDP158	Stephen Smitherman	.15
BDP159	Seung Jun Song	.15
BDP160	Scott Thorman	.15
BDP161	Chad Tracy	.15
BDP162	Chin-Hui Tsao	.15
BDP163	John Van Benschoten	.15
BDP164	Kevin Youkilis	.75
BDP165	Chien-Ming Wang	.50

Gold

Cards (1-165):	1-2X
Inserted 1:1	

Fabric of Future

		NM/M
Common Player:		5.00
JB	Josh Barfield	5.00
RC	Robinson Cano	8.00
JD	J.D. Durbin	8.00
GF	Gavin Floyd	8.00
EG	Edgar Gonzalez	5.00
KG	Khalil Greene	8.00
ZG	Zack Greinke	6.00
FG	Franklin Gutierrez	5.00
RH	Rich Harden	6.00
RJH	Ryan Howard	8.00
JH	Justin Huber	5.00
AL	Adam LaRoche	8.00
AM	Andy Marte	8.00
JSM	Jeff Mathis	8.00
JM	Joe Mauer	10.00
CN	Chris Narveson	5.00
FP	Felix Pie	10.00
RR	Rene Reyes	5.00
RRR	Royce Ring	5.00
GS	Grady Sizemore	8.00

Prospect Premiums

		NM/M
Common Player:		5.00
RB	Rocco Baldelli	15.00
HB	Hank Blalock	10.00
CC	Carl Crawford	5.00
TH	Travis Hafner	8.00
BH	Brendan Harris	5.00
NH	Nathan Haynes	6.00
JM	Justin Morneau	8.00
CS	Chris Snelling	6.00
JT	Joe Thurston	5.00
CU	Chase Utley	8.00

Signs of the Future

		NM/M
Common Player:		5.00
JA	Jason Arnold	5.00
ZG	Zack Greinke	30.00
CS	Cory Stewart	5.00
DT	Dennis Tankersley	5.00
AT	Andres Torres	8.00

2003 BOWMAN HERITAGE

		NM/M
Complete Set (280):		60.00
Common Player:		.25
Cards 171-180 have 3 versions		
Pack (8):		2.50
Box (24):		50.00
1	Jorge Posada	.40
2	Todd Helton	1.00
3	Marcus Giles	.25
4	Eric Chavez	.40
5	Edgar Martinez	.25
6	Luis Gonzalez	.40
7	Corey Patterson	.25
8	Preston Wilson	.25
9	Ryan Klesko	.25
10	Randy Johnson	1.00
11	Eric Byrnes	.25
12	Carlos Lee	.25
13	Steve Finley	.25
14	A.J. Pierzynski	.25
15	Troy Glaus	1.00
16	Darin Erstad	.60
17	Moises Alou	.25
18	Torii Hunter	.50
19	Marlon Byrd	.25
20	Mark Prior	1.50
21	Shannon Stewart	.25

22 Craig Biggio .25
23 Johnny Damon .40
24 Robert Fick .25
25 Jason Giambi .75
26 Fernando Vina .25
27 Aubrey Huff .25
28 Benito Santiago .25
29 Jay Gibbons .25
30 Ken Griffey Jr. 2.00
31 Rocco Baldelli .50
32 Pat Burrell .50
33 A.J. Burnett .25
34 Omar Vizquel .25
35 Greg Maddux 1.50
36 Jae Weong Seo .25
37 C.C. Sabathia .25
38 Geoff Jenkins .25
39 Ty Wigginton .25
40 Jeff Kent .25
41 Orlando Hudson .25
42 Edgardo Alfonzo .25
43 Greg Myers .25
44 Melvin Mora .25
45 Sammy Sosa 2.00
46 Russ Ortiz .25
47 Josh Beckett .50
48 Boomer Wells .25
49 Woody Williams .25
50 Alex Rodriguez 2.50
51 Randy Wolf .25
52 Carlos Beltran .60
53 Austin Kearns .40
54 Trot Nixon .25
55 Ivan Rodriguez .75
56 Shea Hillenbrand .25
57 Roberto Alomar .40
58 John Olerud .25
59 Michael Young .25
60 Garret Anderson .25
61 Mike Lieberthal .25
62 Adam Dunn .50
63 Raul Ibanez .25
64 Kenny Lofton .25
65 Ichiro Suzuki 1.50
66 Jarrod Washburn .25
67 Shawn Chacon .25
68 Alex Gonzalez .25
69 Roy Halladay .40
70 Vladimir Guerrero 1.00
71 Hee Seop Choi .25
72 Brandon Phillips .25
73 Ray Durham .25
74 Mark Teixeira .50
75 Hank Blalock .50
76 Jerry Hairston Jr. .25
77 Erubiel Durazo .25
78 Frank Catalanotto .25
79 Jacque Jones .25
80 Bobby Abreu .25
81 Mike Hampton .25
82 Zach Day .25
83 Jimmy Rollins .25
84 Joel Pineiro .25
85 Brett Myers .25
86 Frank Thomas 1.00
87 Aramis Ramirez .25
88 Paul LoDuca .25
89 Bobby Higginson .25
90 Brian Giles .25
91 Jose Cruz Jr. .25
92 Derek Lowe .25
93 Mark Buehrle .25
94 Wade Miller .25
95 Derek Jeter 3.00
96 Bret Boone .25
97 Tony Batista .25
98 Sean Casey .25
99 Eric Hinske .25
100 Albert Pujols 2.00
101 Runelvys Hernandez .25
102 Vernon Wells .25
103 Kerry Wood .75
104 Lance Berkman .25
105 Alfonso Soriano 1.00
106 Ken Harvey .25
107 Bartolo Colon .25
108 Andy Pettitte .40
109 Rafael Furcal .25
110 Dontrelle Willis .40
111 Carl Crawford .25
112 Scott Rolen .75
113 Chipper Jones 1.50
114 Magglio Ordonez .50
115 Bernie Williams .35
116 Roy Oswalt .40
117 Kevin Brown .35
118 Cristian Guzman .25
119 Kazuhisa Ishii .25
120 Larry Walker .25
121 Miguel Tejada .50
122 Manny Ramirez 1.00
123 Mike Mussina .50
124 Mike Lowell .25
125 Barry Bonds 3.00
126 Aaron Boone .25
127 Carlos Delgado .60
128 Jose Vidro .25
129 Brad Radke .25
130 Rafael Palmeiro .75
131 Mark Mulder .40
132 Jason Schmidt .25
133 Gary Sheffield .40
134 Richie Sexson .40
135 Barry Zito .50
136 Tom Glavine .40
137 Jim Edmonds .40
138 Andruw Jones 1.00
139 Pedro J. Martinez 1.00
140 Curt Schilling .50
141 Joe Kennedy .25
142 Nomar Garciaparra 2.00
143 Vicente Padilla .25
144 Kevin Millwood .40
145 Shawn Green .40
146 Jeff Bagwell 1.00
147 Hideo Nomo .50
148 Fred McGriff .25
149 Matt Morris .25
150 Roger Clemens 1.75
151 Damian Moss .25
152 Orlando Cabrera .25
153 Tim Hudson .40
154 Mike Sweeney .25
155 Jim Thome .35
156 Rich Aurilia .25
157 Mike Piazza 2.00
158 Edgar Renteria .25
159 Javy Lopez .25
160 Jamie Moyer .25
161 Miguel Cabrera .50
162 *Adam Loewen* 1.00
163 Jose Reyes .25
164 Zack Greinke .25
165 Cole Hamels .25
166 Jeremy Guthrie .25
167 Victor Martinez .25
168 Rich Harden .25
169 Joe Mauer .50
170 Khalil Greene .25
171 Willie Mays 2.00
172 Phil Rizzuto .50
173 Al Kaline 1.00
174 Warren Spahn 1.00
175 Jimmy Piersall .25
176 Luis Aparicio .25
177 Whitey Ford 1.00
178 Harmon Killebrew 1.00
179 Duke Snider 1.00
180 Bobby Richardson .25
181 David Martinez .25
182 *Felix Pie* 3.00
183 *Kevin Correia* .50
184 *Brandon Webb* 1.00
185 *Matt Diaz* .50
186 *Lew Ford* 1.50
187 Jeremy Griffiths .25
188 *Matt Hensley* .50
189 *Danny Garcia* .50
190 *Elizardo Ramirez* .50
191 *Greg Aquino* .50
192 *Felix Sanchez* .50
193 *Kelly Shoppach* .50
194 *Bubba Nelson* .50
195 *Mike O'Keefe* .50
196 *Hanley Ramirez* 3.00
197 *Todd Wellemeyer* .75
198 *Dustin Moseley* .75
199 *Eric Crozier* .50
200 *Ryan Shealy* .75
201 Jeremy Bonderman 1.00
202 *Bo Hart* 1.00
203 *Dusty Brown* .50
204 *Rob Hammock* .50
205 *Jorge Piedra* .50
206 *Jason Kubel* 2.00
207 *Stephen Randolph* .50
208 Andy Sisco 1.00
209 *Matt Kata* .75
210 *Robinson Cano* .50
211 *Ben Francisco* .50
212 *Arnie Munoz* .50
213 *Ozzie Chavez* .50
214 *Beau Kemp* .75
215 *Travis Wong* .50
216 Brian McCann .75
217 *Aquilino Lopez* .50
218 *Bobby Basham* .75
219 *Tim Olson* .75
220 *Nathan Panther* .75
221 *Wilfredo Ledezma* .50
222 *Josh Willingham* .75
223 *David Cash* .50
224 *Oscar Villarreal* .50
225 *Jeff Duncan* .75
226 Dan Haren .50
227 *Michel Hernandez* .50
228 *Matt Murton* 1.00
229 *Clay Hensley* .50
230 *Tyler Johnson* .50
231 *Tyler Martin* .50
232 *J.D. Durbin* 1.00
233 *Shane Victorino* .50
234 *Rajai Davis* .50
235 *Chien-Ming Wang* 1.50
236 *Travis Ishikawa* .50
237 Eric Eckenstahler .25
238 *Dustin McGowan* .50
239 *Prentice Redman* .50
240 *Haj Turay* .50
241 *Matt DeMarco* .50
242 *Lou Palmisano* 1.50
243 *Eric Reed* .50
244 *Willie Eyre* .50
245 *Ferdin Tejeda* .75
246 Michael Garciaparra .25
247 *Michael Hinckley* .75
248 *Branden Florence* .50
249 *Trent Oeltjen* .50
250 *Mike Neu* .75
251 *Chris Lubanski* 2.00
252 *Brandon Wood* 3.00
253 *Delmon Young* 5.00
253 *Delmon Young/auto* 70.00
254 *Matt Harrison* .50
255 *Chad Billingsley* .75
256 *Josh Anderson* .75
257 Brian McFall .75
258 *Ryan Wagner* 1.00
259 *Billy Hogan* .50
260 *Nate Spears* .50
261 *Ryan Harvey* 2.00
262 *Wes Littleton* .50
263 *Xavier Paul* 2.00
264 *Sean Rodriguez* .50
265 *Brian Finch* .50
266 *Josh Rainwater* 1.00
267 *Brian Snyder* .75
268 *Eric Duncan* 1.00
269 *Rickie Weeks* 4.00
270 *Tim Battle* .50
271 *Scott Beerer* .50
272 *Aaron Hill* 1.00
273 *Casey Abrams* .50
274 *Jonathan Fulton* .50
275 *Todd Jennings* .50
276 *Jordan Pratt* .50
277 *Tom Gorzelanny* .50
278 *Matt Lorenzo* .75
279 *Jarrod Saltalamacchia* 1.50
280 *Mike Wagner* .50

Diamond Cuts

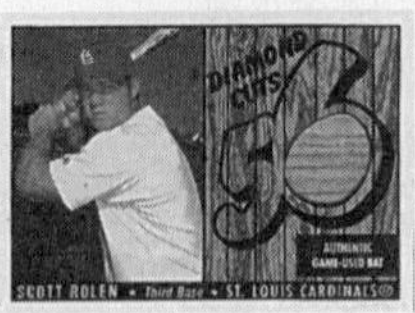

NM/M

Common Player: 4.00
Red: 1-2X
Production 56 sets
JA Jeremy Affeldt 4.00
MA Moises Alou 5.00
TA Tony Armas Jr. 4.00
JB Jeff Bagwell 8.00
CB Craig Biggio 4.00
HB Hank Blalock 6.00
BB Bret Boone 4.00
EC Eric Chavez 4.00
JE Jim Edmonds 6.00
JG Jason Giambi 8.00
TG Troy Glaus 6.00
MG Mark Grace 6.00
VG Vladimir Guerrero 8.00
CG Cristian Guzman 4.00
TH Todd Helton 6.00
RH Rickey Henderson 12.00
JJ Jason Jennings 4.00
AJ Andruw Jones 6.00
CJ1 Chipper Jones/jsy 8.00
CJ2 Chipper Jones/bat 8.00
AK Austin Kearns 6.00
PL Paul LoDuca 4.00
JL Javy Lopez 4.00
PM Pedro J. Martinez 8.00
KM Kevin Millwood 4.00
MM Mark Mulder 4.00
BM Brett Myers 4.00
HN Hideo Nomo 8.00
RP1 Rafael Palmeiro/jsy 8.00
RP2 Rafael Palmeiro/bat 8.00
JLP Josh Phelps 4.00
AP Albert Pujols 12.00
JR Jose Reyes 4.00
AR1 Alex Rodriguez/jsy 10.00
AR2 Alex Rodriguez/bat 10.00
SR1 Scott Rolen/jsy 8.00
SR2 Scott Rolen/bat 10.00
KI Kazuhiro Sasaki 4.00
GS Gary Sheffield 6.00
AS Alfonso Soriano 8.00
SS1 Sammy Sosa/jsy 10.00
SS2 Sammy Sosa/bat 10.00
MS Mike Sweeney 4.00
MT Miguel Tejada 5.00
JV Javier Vazquez 4.00
JW Jarrod Washburn 4.00
VW Vernon Wells 4.00
BW Bernie Williams 6.00
KW Kerry Wood 8.00
BZ Barry Zito 6.00

Keith Olbermann Autograph

NM/M

Inserted 1:1,421
KO Keith Olbermann 50.00

Signs of Greatness

NM/M

Common Player: 6.00
Inserted 1:30
Red Ink: No Pricing
Production one set
CB Chad Billingsley 10.00
RC Robinson Cano 100.00
JD Jeff Duncan 8.00
BF Brian Finch 8.00
TG Tom Gorzelanny 6.00
RH Rich Harden 20.00
MM Matt Murton 25.00
FP Felix Pie 30.00
BS Brian Snyder 8.00
RW Rickie Weeks 40.00
DW Dontrelle Willis 30.00
KY Kevin Youkilis 15.00

2003 BOWMAN'S BEST

NM/M

Complete Set:
Common Player: .50

Pack (5): 10.00
Box (10): 90.00
Veterans
GJA Garret Anderson .50
LB Lance Berkman .50
BLB Barry Bonds 4.00
PB Pat Burrell .75
WRC Roger Clemens 2.25
NG Nomar Garciaparra 2.50
JGG Jason Giambi 1.00
BSG Brian Giles .50
SG Shawn Green .50
KG Ken Griffey Jr. 2.50
VG Vladimir Guerrero 1.50
TH Todd Helton 1.00
TKH Torii Hunter .75
DJ Derek Jeter 4.00
RJ Randy Johnson 1.50
CJ Chipper Jones 2.00
AK Austin Kearns 1.00
JFK Jeff Kent .50
GM Greg Maddux 2.00
PM Pedro J. Martinez 1.50
MOR Magglio Ordonez .50
MJP Mike Piazza 2.50
MP Mark Prior 1.50
AP Albert Pujols 2.00
MR Manny Ramirez 1.50
AR Alex Rodriguez 3.00
CMS Curt Schilling .75
AS Alfonso Soriano 1.00
SS Sammy Sosa 2.50
IS Ichiro Suzuki 2.00
MS Mike Sweeney .50
MT Miguel Tejada .75
JT Jim Thome .50
LW Larry Walker .50
BZ Barry Zito .75
First-Year Players
JB Jeremy Bonderman 3.00
TJB T.J. Bohn 3.00
MB *Matt Bruback* 2.00
BC *Bernie Castro* 2.00
JC *Jose Contreras* 4.00
MD *Matt Diaz* 3.00
BJH *Bo Hart* 1.00
RM Ramon Martinez 3.00
MO *Mike O'Keefe* 2.00
JMS *Jon-Mark Sprowl* 2.00
TT Terry Tiffee 3.00
HT *Haj Turay* 3.00
SV *Shane Victorino* 3.00
CW *Chien-Ming Wang* 4.00
DY *Dustin Yount* 2.00
First-Year Player Autographs
Common Auto: 8.00
Inserted 1:1
TA *Tyler Adamczyk* 8.00
GA *Greg Aquino* 8.00
BWB *Bobby Basham* 10.00
GB *Gregor Blanco* 10.00
AB *Andrew Brown* 8.00
BB *Bryan Bullington* 15.00
RC *Ryan Cameron* 8.00
DC *David Cash* 8.00
OC *Ozzie Chavez* 8.00
RD *Rajai Davis* 10.00
CDC *Chris De La Cruz* 10.00
MD *Matt Diaz* 10.00
CAD *Carlos Duran* 10.00
JDD *J.D. Durbin* 10.00
WE *Willie Eyre* 8.00
BF *Branden Florence* 8.00
LF *Lew Ford* 10.00
BLF *Ben Francisco* 10.00
JG Joey Gomes 10.00
JRG Jeremy Griffiths 10.00
MNH *Matt Hagen* 10.00
RWH *Robby Hammock* 10.00
DH Dan Haren 20.00
BH *Brendan Harris* 10.00
MDH *Matt Hensley* 8.00
MH *Michel Hernandez* 10.00
MHI *Michael Hinckley* 10.00
RH Ryan Howard 90.00
TI *Travis Ishikawa* 10.00
KJ *Kade Johnson* 8.00
TJ *Tyler Johnson* 8.00
MK *Matt Kata* 10.00
BK *Beau Kemp* 8.00
JK *Jason Kubel* 15.00
PL *Pete LaForest* 10.00
WL *Wilfredo Ledezma* 10.00
NL *Nook Logan* 10.00
MDM *Mark Malaska* 8.00
CM *Charlie Manning* 8.00
DM David Martinez 10.00
AM *Aneudis Mateo* 8.00
BM Brian McCann 15.00

DMM *Dustin McGowan* 10.00
JM Jose Morales 10.00
DAM *Dustin Moseley* 10.00
TO *Tim Olson* 10.00
FP *Felix Pie* 50.00
ER *Elizardo Ramirez* 10.00
HR *Hanley Ramirez* 40.00
DR Darrell Rasner 8.00
PR *Prentice Redman* 8.00
FS *Felix Sanchez* 10.00
GS *Gary Schneidmiller* 8.00
CSS *Corey Shafer* 10.00
RS *Ryan Shealy* 10.00
KS *Kelly Shoppach* 10.00
CS *Cory Stewart* 10.00
TSH *Thomari Story-Harden* 8.00
FT *Ferdin Tejeda* 10.00
ET *Eider Torres* 10.00
ST Scott Tyler 10.00
JV *Joe Valentine* 8.00
OV *Oscar Villarreal*
DW *Doug Waechter* 10.00
AW *Aron Weston* 8.00
JW *Josh Willingham* 10.00
CJW C.J. Wilson 8.00
KY *Kevin Youkilis* 15.00
CW *Chien-Ming Wang* 65.00

Blue

Blue Autographs: 1-1.5X
Inserted 1:32
Blue base card: 3-5X
Blue Rookies: 1-2X
Production 100

Red

Red Autographs: 2-4X
Inserted 1:63
Red base card: 4-8X
Red Rookies: 2-3X
Production 50

First-Year Player Relics

NM/M
Common Player: 5.00
RLD Rajai Davis 5.00
JLF Lew Ford 5.00
JGG Joey Gomes 5.00
RJH Ryan Howard 20.00
JJK Jason Kubel 5.00
HRB Hanley Ramirez 15.00
RNS Ryan Shealy 5.00
KBS Kelly Shoppach 8.00
KEY Kevin Youkilis 8.00

Double Play

NM/M
Common Card: 20.00
Inserted 1:55
EB Elizardo Ramirez, Bryan Bullington 25.00
GK Joey Gomes, Jason Kubel 50.00
SR Felix Sanchez, Darrell Rasner 15.00
YS Kevin Youkilis, Kelly Shoppach 40.00
HV Dan Haren, Joe Valentine 25.00
GM Jeremy Griffiths, David Martinez 15.00
HM Michael Hinckley, Brian McCann 15.00
RS Prentice Redman, Gary Schneidmiller 15.00
LL Nook Logan, Wilfredo Ledezma 25.00
SB Corey Shafer, Gregor Blanco 25.00

Triple Play

NM/M
Inserted 1:219
DRS Rajai Davis, Hanley Ramirez, Ryan Shealy 85.00
BCS Andrew Brown, David Cash, Cory Stewart 30.00

2004 BOWMAN

NM/M
Complete Set (330): 65.00
Common Player: .15
Common Rookie: .50
Pack (10): 3.00
Box (24): 60.00
1 Garret Anderson .15
2 Larry Walker .15
3 Derek Jeter 2.00
4 Curt Schilling .50
5 Carlos Zambrano .25
6 Shawn Green .25

7 Manny Ramirez .75
8 Randy Johnson .75
9 Jeremy Bonderman .15
10 Alfonso Soriano .75
11 Scott Rolen .75
12 Kerry Wood .75
13 Eric Gagne .25
14 Ryan Klesko .15
15 Kevin Millar .15
16 Ty Wigginton .15
17 David Ortiz .40
18 Luis Castillo .15
19 Bernie Williams .30
20 Edgar Renteria .15
21 Matt Kata .15
22 Bartolo Colon .15
23 Derrek Lee .15
24 Gary Sheffield .25
25 Nomar Garciaparra 1.50
26 Kevin Millwood .25
27 Corey Patterson .25
28 Carlos Beltran .50
29 Mike Lieberthal .15
30 Troy Glaus .75
31 Preston Wilson .15
32 Jorge Posada .30
33 Bo Hart .15
34 Mark Prior 1.00
35 Hideo Nomo .25
36 Jason Kendall .15
37 Shea Hillenbrand .15
38 Dmitri Young .15
39 Aaron Boone .15
40 Jim Edmonds .30
41 Ryan Ludwick .15
42 Brandon Webb .15
43 Todd Helton .75
44 Jacque Jones .15
45 Xavier Nady .15
46 Tim Salmon .25
47 Kelvim Escobar .15
48 Tony Batista .15
49 Nick Johnson .15
50 Jim Thome .50
51 Casey Blake .15
52 Trot Nixon .25
53 Luis Gonzalez .25
54 Dontrelle Willis .25
55 Mike Mussina .40
56 Carl Crawford .15
57 Mark Buehrle .15
58 Scott Podsednik .50
59 Brian Giles .15
60 Rafael Furcal .15
61 Miguel Cabrera .50
62 Rich Harden .15
63 Mark Teixeira .25
64 Frank Thomas .75
65 Johan Santana .15
66 Jason Schmidt .25
67 Aramis Ramirez .25
68 Jose Reyes .15
69 Magglio Ordonez .25
70 Mike Sweeney .15
71 Eric Chavez .25
72 Rocco Baldelli .25
73 Jerry Hairston .15
74 Javy Lopez .15
75 Roy Oswalt .25
76 Raul Ibanez .15
77 Ivan Rodriguez .60
78 Jerome Williams .15
79 Carlos Lee .15
80 Geoff Jenkins .15
81 Sean Burroughs .15
82 Marcus Giles .15
83 Mike Lowell .15
84 Barry Zito .40
85 Aubrey Huff .15
86 Esteban Loaiza .15

87 Torii Hunter .25
88 Phil Nevin .15
89 Andruw Jones .75
90 Josh Beckett .50
91 Mark Mulder .25
92 Hank Blalock .25
93 Jason Phillips .15
94 Russ Ortiz .15
95 Juan Pierre .15
96 Tom Glavine .25
97 Gil Meche .15
98 Ramon Ortiz .15
99 Richie Sexson .40
100 Albert Pujols 1.50
101 Javier Vazquez .15
102 Johnny Damon .25
103 Alex Rodriguez 1.50
104 Omar Vizquel .15
105 Chipper Jones 1.00
106 Lance Berkman .15
107 Tim Hudson .25
108 Carlos Delgado .40
109 Austin Kearns .25
110 Orlando Cabrera .25
111 Edgar Martinez .15
112 Melvin Mora .15
113 Jeff Bagwell .75
114 Marlon Byrd .15
115 Vernon Wells .25
116 C.C. Sabathia .15
117 Cliff Floyd .15
118 Ichiro Suzuki 1.00
119 Miguel Olivo .15
120 Mike Piazza 1.00
121 Adam Dunn .40
122 Paul Lo Duca .15
123 Brett Myers .15
124 Michael Young .15
125 Larry Bigbie .15
126 Greg Maddux 1.00
127 Vladimir Guerrero .75
128 Miguel Tejada .40
129 Andy Pettitte .25
130 Jose Cruz .15
131 Ken Griffey Jr. 1.50
132 Shannon Stewart .15
133 Joel Pineiro .15
134 Luis Matos .15
135 Jeff Kent .15
136 Randy Wolf .15
137 Chris Woodward .15
138 Jody Gerut .15
139 Jose Vidro .15
140 Bret Boone .15
141 Bill Mueller .15
142 Angel Berroa .15
143 Bobby Abreu .15
144 Roy Halladay .25
145 Delmon Young .50
146 Jonny Gomes .15
147 Rickie Weeks .50
148 Edwin Jackson .15
149 Neal Cotts .15
150 Jason Bay .15
151 Khalil Greene .25
152 Joe Mauer .40
153 Bobby Jenks .15
154 Chin-Feng Chen .15
154 Chin-Feng Chen/jersey 10.00
155 Chien-Ming Wang .15
155 Chien-Ming Wang/jersey 10.00
156 Mickey Hall .15
156 Mickey Hall/jersey 6.00
157 James Houser .15
157 James Houser/jersey 5.00
158 Jay Sborz .15
158 Jay Sborz/jersey 6.00
159 Jonathan Fulton .15
159 Jonathan Fulton/jersey 8.00
160 Steve Lerud .15
160 Steve Lerud/jersey 5.00
161 Grady Sizemore .15
161 Grady Sizemore/auto 15.00
162 Felix Pie .15
162 Felix Pie/auto 15.00
163 Dustin McGowan .15
163 Dustin McGowan/auto 10.00
164 Chris Lubanski .15
164 Chris Lubanski/auto 10.00
164 Chris Lubanski/jersey 5.00
165 Tom Gorzelanny .15
165 Tom Gorzelanny/auto 8.00
166 *Rudy Guillen* 1.50
166 *Rudy Guillen/auto* 10.00
167 *Bobby Brownlie* 1.00
167 *Bobby Brownlie/auto* 15.00
168 Conor Jackson 1.00
168 Conor Jackson/auto 35.00
169 Matt Moses 1.00

169	Matt Moses/auto	20.00
170	Ervin Santana	1.50
170	Ervin Santana/auto	25.00
171	Merkin Valdez	1.00
171	Merkin Valdez/auto	15.00
172	Erick Aybar	.75
172	Erick Aybar/auto	15.00
173	Brad Sullivan	.50
173	Brad Sullivan/auto	15.00
174	David Aardsma	.50
174	David Aardsma/auto	10.00
175	Brad Snyder	.75
175	Brad Snyder/auto	15.00
176	Alberto Callaspo	.75
177	Brandon Medders	.50
178	Zach Miner	.50
179	Charlie Zink	1.00
180	Adam Greenberg	.75
181	Kevin Howard	.50
182	Wanell Severino	.50
183	Kevin Kouzmanoff	.50
184	Joel Zumaya	1.50
185	Skip Schumaker	.50
186	Nic Ungs	.50
187	Todd Self	.75
188	Brian Steffek	.50
189	Brock Peterson	1.00
190	Greg Thissen	.50
191	Frank Brooks	.50
192	Estee Harris	.75
192	Estee Harris/jersey	10.00
193	Chris Mabeus	.50
194	Daniel Giese	.75
195	Jared Wells	.50
196	Carlos Sosa	.75
197	Bobby Madritsch	.75
198	Calvin Hayes	.50
199	Omar Quintanilla	.75
200	Chris O'Riordan	.50
201	Tim Hutting	.50
202	Carlos Quentin	1.00
203	Brayan Pena	.50
204	Jeff Salazar	1.50
205	David Murphy	1.00
206	Alberto Garcia	.50
207	Ramon Ramirez	.75
208	Luis Bolivar	.50
209	Rodney Choy Foo	.50
210	Kyle Sleeth	1.50
211	Anthony Acevedo	.75
212	Chad Santos	.50
213	Jason Frasor	.50
214	Jesse Roman	.50
215	James Tomlin	.50
216	Josh Labandeira	.75
217	Joaquin Arias	.50
218	Don Sutton (photo actually Nick Swisher)	1.50
219	Danny Gonzalez	.50
220	Javier Guzman	.75
221	Anthony Lerew	.75
221	Anthony Lerew/jersey	8.00
222	Jon Knott	.75
223	Jesse English	.50
224	Felix Hernandez	15.00
225	Travis Hanson	.75
226	Jesse Floyd	.50
227	Nick Gorneault	.50
228	Craig Ansman	.50
229	Wardell Starling	.50
230	Carl Loadenthal	.50
231	David Crouthers	.50
232	Harvey Garcia	.50
233	Casey Kopitzke	.50
234	Ricky Nolasco	.50
235	Miguel Perez	.50
236	Ryan Mulhern	.50
237	Chris Aguila	.50
238	Brooks Conrad	.50
239	Damaso Espino	.50
240	Jereme Milons	.50
241	Luke Hughes	.50
242	Kory Casto	.50
243	Jose Valdez	.50
244	J.T. Stotts	.75
245	Lee Gwaltney	.75
246	Yoann Torrealba	.50
247	Omar Falcon	.50
248	Jon Coutlangus	.50
249	George Sherrill	.75
250	John Santor	.50
251	Tony Richie	.50
252	Kevin Richardson	.50
253	Tim Bittner	.50
254	Dustin Nippert	1.00
255	Jose Capellan	1.50
256	Donald Levinski	.50
257	Jerome Gamble	.50
258	Jeff Keppinger	.50
259	Jason Szuminski	.50
260	Akinori Otsuka	1.50
261	Ryan Budde	.50
262	Shingo Takatsu	1.50
263	Jeffrey Allison	1.00
264	Hector Gimenez	.50
265	Tim Frend	.50
266	Tom Farmer	.50
267	Shawn Hill	.50
268	Lastings Milledge	2.00
269	Scott Proctor	1.00
270	Jorge Mejia	.50
271	Terry Jones	.50
272	Zachary Duke	5.00
273	Tim Stauffer	1.00
274	Luke Anderson	.50
275	Hunter Brown	.75
276	Matt Lemanczyk	.50
277	Fernando Cortez	.50
278	Vince Perkins	.50
279	Tommy Murphy	.50
280	Mike Gosling	.50
281	Paul Bacot	.50
282	Matt Capps	1.00
283	Juan Gutierrez	.50
284	Teodoro Encarnacion	.50
285	Juan Cedeno	.50
286	Matt Creighton	.75
287	Ryan Hankins	.50
288	Leo Nunez	.50
289	Dave Wallace	.50
290	Rob Tejeda	.50
291	Lincoln Holdzkom	.50
292	Jason Hirsh	.50
293	Tydus Meadows	.50
294	Khalid Ballouli	.50
295	Benji DeQuin	.75
296	Tyler Davidson	1.00
297	Brent Colamarino	1.00
298	Marcus McBeth	.50
299	Brad Eldred	3.00
300	David Pauley	.50
301	Yadier Molina	1.00
302	Chris Shelton	2.00
303	Travis Blackley	1.00
304	Jon DeVries	.50
305	Sheldon Fulse	.50
306	Vito Chiaravalloti	1.00
307	Warner Madrigal	.75
308	Reid Gorecki	.50
309	Sung Jung	.50
310	Peter Shier	.50
311	Michael Mooney	.50
312	Kenny Perez	.50
313	Mike Mallory	.50
314	Ben Himes	.50
315	Ivan Ochoa	.50
316	Donald Kelly	.50
317	Logan Kensing	.50
318	Kevin Davidson	.75
319	Brian Pilkington	.50
320	Alex Romero	.50
321	Chad Chop	.50
322	Dioner Navarro	1.50
323	Casey Myers	.50
324	Mike Rouse	.50
325	Sergio Silva	.50
326	J.J. Furmaniak	1.00
327	Brad Vericker	.50
328	Blake Hawksworth	1.00
329	Brock Jacobsen	.50
330	Alec Zumwalt	.50

1st Edition

	NM/M
Stars:	3-5X
Rookies:	1-2X
HTA Exclusive	
Pack (10):	4.00
Box (20):	75.00

Gold

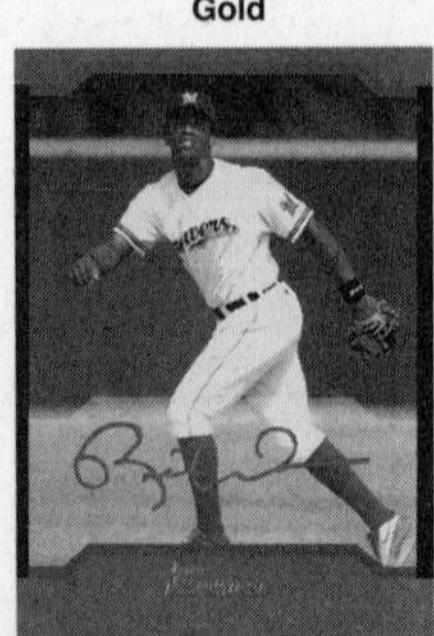

Stars:	1-2X
Rookies:	1-2X
Inserted 1:1	

Uncirculated

Stars:	4-8X
Rookies:	3-5X
Production 245 sets	

Base of the Future Autographed Relic

		NM/M
HTA Exclusive		
GS	Grady Sizemore	25.00

Futures Game Gear

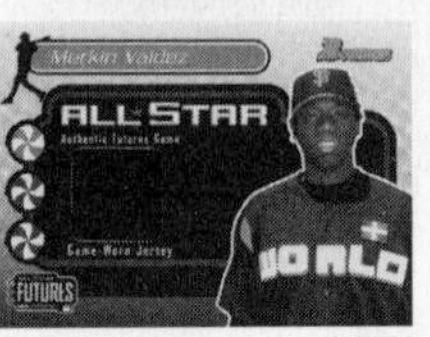

		NM/M
Common Player:		5.00
DB	Denny Bautista	8.00
CB	Chris Burke	8.00
JC	Jose Castillo	5.00
NC	Neal Cotts	5.00
JD	Jorge De La Rosa	5.00
EE	Edwin Encarnacion	8.00
SH	Shawn Hill	5.00
EJ	Edwin Jackson	8.00
DK	David Kelton	8.00
DBK	David Krynzel	5.00
PL	Pete LaForest	5.00
JM	John Maine	5.00
CN	Clint Nageotte	10.00
RN	Ramon Nivar	5.00
GQ	Guillermo Quiroz	5.00
AR	Alexis Rios	6.00
ES	Ervin Santana	8.00
SS	Stephen Smitherman	5.00
SJS	Seung Jun Song	5.00
CT	Chad Tracy	5.00
ST	Scott Thorman	5.00
MV	Merkin Valdez	5.00
JV	John VanBenschoten	5.00
CW	Chien-Ming Wang	20.00
KY	Kevin Youkilis	10.00

Rookie of the Year Dual Relic

		NM/M
Inserted 1:829		
BW	Angel Berroa, Dontrelle Willis	15.00

Signs of Future

		NM/M
Common Autograph:		8.00
Red Ink:		No Pricing
Production 25 sets		
JB	Justin Backsmeyer	12.00
IC	Ismael Castro	8.00
BC	Brent Clevelen	10.00
ED	Eric Duncan	15.00
BF	Brian Finch	8.00
RH	Ryan Harvey	15.00
AH	Aaron Hill	12.00
JH	James Houser	10.00
TJ	Tyler Johnson	8.00
TL	Todd Linden	8.00
NM	Nicholas Markakis	10.00
BM	Brandon Medders	8.00
MM	Matt Murton	8.00
CS	Corey Shafer	10.00
GS	Grady Sizemore	15.00
BS	Brian Snyder	8.00
DS	Denard Span	10.00
JV	Joey Votto	10.00
BW	Brandon Wood	15.00

2004 BOWMAN CHROME

		NM/M
Complete Set (350):		
Common Player:		.25
Common Rookie:		1.00
Common Rookie Auto. (331-350):		15.00
Inserted 1:18		
Pack (4):		5.00
Box (18):		80.00
1	Garret Anderson	.50
2	Larry Walker	.50
3	Derek Jeter	3.00

4	Curt Schilling	.75
5	Carlos Zambrano	.50
6	Shawn Green	.50
7	Manny Ramirez	.75
8	Randy Johnson	1.00
9	Jeremy Bonderman	.25
10	Alfonso Soriano	1.00
11	Scott Rolen	1.00
12	Kerry Wood	1.00
13	Eric Gagne	.50
14	Ryan Klesko	.25
15	Kevin Millar	.25
16	Ty Wigginton	.25
17	David Ortiz	.50
18	Luis Castillo	.25
19	Bernie Williams	.50
20	Edgar Renteria	.50
21	Matt Kata	.25
22	Bartolo Colon	.50
23	Derrek Lee	.50
24	Gary Sheffield	.50
25	Nomar Garciaparra	2.00
26	Kevin Millwood	.25
27	Corey Patterson	.50
28	Carlos Beltran	.50
29	Mike Lieberthal	.25
30	Troy Glaus	.50
31	Preston Wilson	.25
32	Jorge Posada	.50
33	Bo Hart	.25
34	Mark Prior	1.50
35	Hideo Nomo	.50
36	Jason Kendall	.25
37	Roger Clemens	2.50
38	Dmitri Young	.25
39	Jason Giambi	.75
40	Jim Edmonds	.75
41	Ryan Ludwick	.25
42	Brandon Webb	.25
43	Todd Helton	.75
44	Jacque Jones	.25
45	Jamie Moyer	.25
46	Tim Salmon	.50
47	Kelvim Escobar	.25
48	Tony Batista	.25
49	Nick Johnson	.25
50	Jim Thome	1.00
51	Casey Blake	.25
52	Trot Nixon	.50
53	Luis Gonzalez	.50
54	Dontrelle Willis	.50
55	Mike Mussina	.50
56	Carl Crawford	.25
57	Mark Buehrle	.25
58	Scott Podsednik	.25
59	Brian Giles	.50
60	Rafael Furcal	.25
61	Miguel Cabrera	1.00
62	Rich Harden	.25
63	Mark Teixeira	.50
64	Frank Thomas	.75
65	Johan Santana	.25
66	Jason Schmidt	.50
67	Aramis Ramirez	.50
68	Jose Reyes	.50
69	Magglio Ordonez	.50
70	Mike Sweeney	.25
71	Eric Chavez	.50
72	Rocco Baldelli	.50
73	Sammy Sosa	1.50
74	Javy Lopez	.50
75	Roy Oswalt	.50
76	Raul Ibanez	.25
77	Ivan Rodriguez	.75
78	Jerome Williams	.25
79	Carlos Lee	.50
80	Geoff Jenkins	.50
81	Sean Burroughs	.25
82	Marcus Giles	.25

83	Mike Lowell	.50
84	Barry Zito	.50
85	Aubrey Huff	.25
86	Esteban Loaiza	.25
87	Torii Hunter	.50
88	Phil Nevin	.25
89	Andruw Jones	.75
90	Josh Beckett	.75
91	Mark Mulder	.50
92	Hank Blalock	.75
93	Jason Phillips	.25
94	Russ Ortiz	.25
95	Juan Pierre	.25
96	Tom Glavine	.50
97	Gil Meche	.25
98	Ramon Ortiz	.25
99	Richie Sexson	.50
100	Albert Pujols	2.50
101	Javier Vazquez	.25
102	Johnny Damon	.50
103	Alex Rodriguez	3.00
104	Omar Vizquel	.25
105	Chipper Jones	1.00
106	Lance Berkman	.50
107	Tim Hudson	.50
108	Carlos Delgado	.50
109	Austin Kearns	.50
110	Orlando Cabrera	.25
111	Edgar Martinez	.50
112	Melvin Mora	.25
113	Jeff Bagwell	.75
114	Marlon Byrd	.25
115	Vernon Wells	.50
116	C.C. Sabathia	.25
117	Cliff Floyd	.25
118	Ichiro Suzuki	2.00
119	Miguel Olivo	.25
120	Mike Piazza	1.50
121	Adam Dunn	.50
122	Paul Lo Duca	.25
123	Brett Myers	.25
124	Michael Young	.25
125	Sidney Ponson	.25
126	Greg Maddux	1.50
127	Vladimir Guerrero	1.00
128	Miguel Tejada	.50
129	Andy Pettitte	.50
130	Rafael Palmeiro	.75
131	Ken Griffey Jr.	1.50
132	Shannon Stewart	.25
133	Joel Pineiro	.25
134	Luis Matos	.25
135	Jeff Kent	.50
136	Randy Wolf	.25
137	Chris Woodward	.25
138	Jody Gerut	.25
139	Jose Vidro	.25
140	Bret Boone	.25
141	Bill Mueller	.25
142	Angel Berroa	.25
143	Bobby Abreu	.50
144	Roy Halladay	.50
145	Delmon Young	.50
146	Jonny Gomes	.25
147	Rickie Weeks	.50
148	Edwin Jackson	.25
149	Neal Cotts	.25
150	Jason Bay	.25
151	Khalil Greene	.50
152	Joe Mauer	.50
153	Bobby Jenks	.25
154	Chin-Feng Chen	.25
155	Chien-Ming Wang	.25
156	Mickey Hall	.25
157	James Houser	.25
158	Jay Sborz	.25
159	Jonathan Fulton	.25
160	Steve Lerud	.25
161	Grady Sizemore	.50
162	Felix Pie	.50
163	Dustin McGowan	.25
164	Chris Lubanski	.25
165	Tom Gorzelanny	.25
166	*Rudy Guillen*	4.00
167	*Aarom Baldiris*	2.00
168	Conor Jackson	10.00
169	Matt Moses	4.00
170	*Ervin Santana*	5.00
171	*Merkin Valdez*	4.00
172	*Erick Aybar*	5.00
173	Brad Sullivan	1.00
174	*Joey Gathright*	5.00
175	Brad Snyder	4.00
176	*Alberto Callaspo*	2.00
177	*Brandon Medders*	1.00
178	*Zach Miner*	1.00
179	*Charlie Zink*	2.00
180	Adam Greenberg	2.00
181	*Kevin Howard*	1.00
182	*Wanell Severino*	1.00
183	*Chin-Lung Hu*	3.00
184	*Joel Zumaya*	5.00
185	*Skip Schumaker*	1.00
186	*Nic Ungs*	1.00
187	*Todd Self*	2.00
188	*Brian Steffek*	1.00
189	*Brock Peterson*	2.00
190	*Greg Thissen*	1.00
191	*Frank Brooks*	1.00
192	*Scott Olsen*	4.00
193	*Chris Mabeus*	1.00
194	*Daniel Giese*	2.00
195	*Jared Wells*	1.00
196	*Carlos Sosa*	2.00
197	Bobby Madritsch	1.50
198	*Calvin Hayes*	1.00
199	Omar Quintanilla	3.00
200	*Chris O'Riordan*	1.00
201	*Tim Hutting*	1.00
202	Carlos Quentin	8.00
203	*Brayan Pena*	1.00
204	*Jeff Salazar*	5.00
205	David Murphy	3.00
206	*Alberto Garcia*	1.00
207	*Ramon Ramirez*	2.00
208	*Luis Bolivar*	1.00
209	*Rodney Choy Foo*	1.00
210	*Fausto Carmona*	3.00
211	*Anthony Acevedo*	2.00
212	*Chad Santos*	1.00
213	*Jason Frasor*	1.00
214	*Jesse Roman*	1.00
215	*James Tomlin*	1.00
216	*Josh Labandeira*	2.00
217	*Ryan Meaux*	1.00
218	*Don Sutton*	5.00
219	*Danny Gonzalez*	1.00
220	*Javier Guzman*	2.00
221	*Anthony Lerew*	2.00
222	*Jon Connolly*	4.00
223	*Jesse English*	1.00
224	*Hector Made*	2.00
225	Travis Hanson	1.50
226	*Jesse Floyd*	1.00
227	*Nick Gorneault*	1.00
228	*Craig Ansman*	1.00
229	*Paul McAnulty*	2.50
230	*Carl Loadenthal*	1.00
231	David Crouthers	1.00
232	*Harvey Garcia*	1.00
233	*Casey Kopitzke*	1.00
234	Ricky Nolasco	1.00
235	*Miguel Perez*	1.00
236	*Ryan Mulhern*	1.00
237	*Chris Aguila*	1.00
238	*Brooks Conrad*	1.00
239	*Damaso Espino*	1.00
240	*Jereme Milons*	1.00
241	*Luke Hughes*	1.00
242	Kory Casto	1.00
243	*Jose Valdez*	1.00
244	J.T. Stotts	2.00
245	*Lee Gwaltney*	2.00
246	*Yoann Torrealba*	1.00
247	*Omar Falcon*	1.00
248	*Jon Coutlangus*	1.00
249	*George Sherrill*	2.00
250	*John Santor*	1.00
251	*Tony Richie*	1.00
252	*Kevin Richardson*	1.00
253	*Tim Bittner*	1.00
254	*Chris Saenz*	1.50
255	*Jose Capellan*	6.00
256	Donald Levinski	1.00
257	*Jerome Gamble*	1.00
258	*Jeff Keppinger*	1.00
259	*Jason Szuminski*	1.00
260	*Akinori Otsuka*	2.00
261	Ryan Budde	1.00
262	*Marland Williams*	2.00
263	Jeffrey Allison	1.00
264	*Hector Gimenez*	1.00
265	*Tim Frend*	1.00
266	*Tom Farmer*	1.00
267	*Shawn Hill*	1.00
268	*Mike Huggins*	2.00
269	*Scott Proctor*	1.50
270	*Jorge Mejia*	1.00
271	*Terry Jones*	1.00
272	*Zachary Duke*	20.00
273	Jesse Crain	3.00
274	*Luke Anderson*	1.00
275	*Hunter Brown*	1.50
276	*Matt Lemanczyk*	1.00
277	*Fernando Cortez*	1.00
278	*Vince Perkins*	1.00
279	*Tommy Murphy*	1.00
280	Mike Gosling	1.00
281	Paul Bacot	1.00
282	*Matt Capps*	2.00
283	*Juan Gutierrez*	1.00
284	*Teodoro Encarnacion*	1.00
285	*Chad Bentz*	1.00
286	*Kazuo Matsui*	3.00
287	*Ryan Hankins*	1.00
288	*Leo Nunez*	1.00
289	*Dave Wallace*	1.00
290	*Rob Tejeda*	1.00
291	*Paul Maholm*	2.00
292	*Casey Daigle*	1.00
293	*Tydus Meadows*	1.00
294	*Khalid Ballouli*	1.00
295	*Benji DeQuin*	2.00
296	Tyler Davidson	2.00
297	*Brent Colamarino*	3.00
298	*Marcus McBeth*	1.00
299	*Brad Eldred*	10.00
300	*David Pauley*	1.00
301	*Yadier Molina*	3.00
302	*Chris Shelton*	8.00
303	*Nyjer Morgan*	1.00
304	Jon DeVries	1.00
305	*Sheldon Fulse*	1.00
306	*Vito Chiaravalloti*	3.00
307	*Warner Madrigal*	3.00
308	*Reid Gorecki*	1.00
309	*Sung Jung*	1.00
310	*Peter Shier*	1.00
311	*Michael Mooney*	1.00
312	*Kenny Perez*	1.00
313	*Mike Mallory*	1.00
314	*Ben Himes*	1.00
315	*Ivan Ochoa*	1.00
316	*Donald Kelly*	1.00
317	*Tom Mastny*	1.00
318	*Kevin Davidson*	1.50
319	Brian Pilkington	1.00
320	*Alex Romero*	1.00
321	*Chad Chop*	1.00
322	*Kody Kirkland*	2.50
323	*Casey Myers*	1.00
324	Mike Rouse	1.00
325	*Sergio Silva*	1.00
326	*J.J. Furmaniak*	3.00
327	*Brad Vericker*	1.00
328	*Blake Hawksworth*	2.00
329	*Brock Jacobsen*	1.00
330	*Alec Zumwalt*	1.00
331	*Wardell Starling*	15.00
332	*Estee Harris*	20.00
333	Kyle Sleeth	20.00
334	*Dioner Navarro*	30.00
335	*Logan Kensing*	15.00
336	*Travis Blackley*	20.00
337	*Lincoln Holdzkom*	15.00
338	Jason Hirsh	15.00
339	*Juan Cedeno*	15.00
340	*Matt Creighton*	15.00
341	Tim Stauffer	25.00
342	*Shingo Takatsu*	25.00
343	Lastings Milledge	65.00
344	*Dustin Nippert*	15.00
345	*Felix Hernandez*	200.00
346	*Joaquin Arias*	15.00
347	Kevin Kouzmanoff	20.00
348	*Bobby Brownlie*	25.00
349	David Aardsma	15.00
350	*Jon Knott*	15.00

Refractor

Stars (1-165):	2-4X
Rookies (166-330):	1-2X
Inserted 1:4	
Autograph (331-350):	1-2X
Inserted 1:100	

Gold Refractor

Stars (1-165):	4-8X
Rookies (166-330):	3-5X
Production 50	
Autograph (331-350):	No Pricing
Inserted 1:1,003	

X-Fractor

	NM/M
Stars (1-165):	3-5X
Rookies (166-330):	2-4X
Production 173	
Autograph (331-350):	No Pricing
Inserted 1:200	

Stars of the Future

		NM/M
Inserted 1:600		
YSS	Delmon Young, Kyle Sleeth, Tim Stauffer	80.00
LHC	Chris Lubanski, Ryan Harvey, Chad Cordero	60.00
MHD	Nicholas Markakis, Aaron Hill, Eric Duncan	50.00

2004 BOWMAN CHROME DRAFT PICKS & PROSPECTS

		NM/M
Complete Set (175):		
Common Player:		.25
Common Rookie:		1.00
Common RC Auto. (166-175):		15.00
Inserted 1:60		
BDP1	Lyle Overbay	.50
BDP2	David Newhan	.25
BDP3	J.R. House	.25
BDP4	Chad Tracy	.25
BDP5	Humberto Quintero	.25
BDP6	David Bush	.25
BDP7	Scott Hairston	.25
BDP8	Mike Wood	.25
BDP9	Alexis Rios	.50
BDP10	Sean Burnett	.25
BDP11	Wilson Valdez	.25
BDP12	Lew Ford	.25
BDP13	*Freddie Thon*	1.00
BDP14	Zack Greinke	.25
BDP15	Bucky Jacobsen	.25
BDP16	Kevin Youkilis	.25
BDP17	Grady Sizemore	.25
BDP18	Denny Bautista	.25
BDP19	David DeJesus	.25
BDP20	Casey Kotchman	.25
BDP21	David Kelton	.25
BDP22	*Charles Thomas*	1.00
BDP23	*Kazuhito Tadano*	2.00
BDP24	*Justin Leone*	1.00
BDP25	*Eduardo Villacis*	1.00
BDP26	*Brian Dallimore*	1.00
BDP27	*Nick Green*	1.00
BDP28	*Sam McConnell*	1.00
BDP29	*Brad Halsey*	1.00
BDP30	*Roman Colon*	1.00
BDP31	*Josh Fields*	4.00
BDP32	*Cody Bunkelman*	2.00
BDP33	*Jay Rainville*	4.00
BDP34	*Richie Robnett*	4.00
BDP35	*Jon Poterson*	2.50
BDP36	*Huston Street*	5.00
BDP37	*Erick San Pedro*	1.00
BDP38	*Cory Dunlap*	3.00
BDP39	*Kurt Suzuki*	4.00
BDP40	*Anthony Swarzak*	2.00
BDP41	*Ian Desmond*	2.00
BDP42	*Chris Covington*	1.50
BDP43	*Christian Garcia*	1.50
BDP44	*Gaby Hernandez*	5.00
BDP45	*Steven Register*	1.00
BDP46	*Eduardo Morlan*	1.00
BDP47	*Collin Balester*	1.00
BDP48	*Nathan Phillips*	1.00
BDP49	*Dan Schwartzbauer*	1.00
BDP50	*Rafael Gonzalez*	1.00
BDP51	*K.C. Herren*	2.00
BDP52	*William Susdorf*	1.00
BDP53	*Rob Johnson*	1.00
BDP54	*Louis Marson*	2.00
BDP55	*Joe Koshansky*	2.00
BDP56	*Jamar Walton*	4.00
BDP57	*Mark Lowe*	1.00
BDP58	*Matt Macri*	3.00
BDP59	*Donny Lucy*	1.00
BDP60	*Mike Ferris*	2.00
BDP61	*Mike Nickeas*	2.00
BDP62	*Eric Hurley*	2.00
BDP63	*Scott Elbert*	2.00
BDP64	*Blake DeWitt*	5.00
BDP65	*Danny Putnam*	2.00
BDP66	*J.P. Howell*	3.00
BDP67	*John Wiggins*	1.00
BDP68	*Justin Orenduff*	2.00
BDP69	*Ray Liotta*	2.00
BDP70	*Billy Buckner*	1.00
BDP71	*Eric Campbell*	6.00

BDP72	*Olin Wick*	2.00
BDP73	*Sean Gamble*	1.50
BDP74	*Seth Smith*	3.00
BDP75	*Wade Davis*	1.00
BDP76	*Joe Jacobitz*	1.00
BDP77	*J.A. Happ*	2.00
BDP78	*Eric Ridener*	1.00
BDP79	*Matt Tuiasosopo*	8.00
BDP80	*Bradley Bergesen*	1.00
BDP81	*Javy Guerra*	1.50
BDP82	*Buck Shaw*	2.00
BDP83	*Paul Janish*	1.50
BDP84	*Sean Kazmar*	1.00
BDP85	*Josh Johnson*	1.50
BDP86	*Angel Salome*	2.00
BDP87	*Jordan Parraz*	1.00
BDP88	*Kelvin Vazquez*	1.00
BDP89	*Grant Hansen*	1.00
BDP90	*Matt Fox*	2.00
BDP91	*Trevor Plouffe*	4.00
BDP92	*Wes Whisler*	1.00
BDP93	*Curtis Thigpen*	2.00
BDP94	*Donnie Smith*	1.00
BDP95	*Luis Rivera*	1.50
BDP96	*Jesse Hoover*	1.00
BDP97	*Jason Vargas*	4.00
BDP98	*Clary Carlsen*	1.00
BDP99	*Mark Robinson*	1.00
BDP100	*J.C. Holt*	1.50
BDP101	*Chad Blackwell*	1.00
BDP102	*Daryl Jones*	2.00
BDP103	*Jonathan Tierce*	1.00
BDP104	*Patrick Bryant*	1.00
BDP105	*Eddie Prasch*	1.50
BDP106	*Mitch Einertson*	6.00
BDP107	*Kyle Waldrop*	4.00
BDP108	*Jeff Marquez*	2.00
BDP109	*Zach Jackson*	2.00
BDP110	*Josh Wahpepah*	1.00
BDP111	*Adam Lind*	4.00
BDP112	*Kyle Bloom*	1.00
BDP113	*Ben Harrison*	1.00
BDP114	*Taylor Tankersley*	2.00
BDP115	*Steven Jackson*	1.00
BDP116	*David Purcey*	1.50
BDP117	*Jacob McGee*	2.00
BDP118	*Lucas Harrell*	1.00
BDP119	*Brandon Allen*	2.50
BDP120	*Van Pope*	1.50
BDP121	Jeff Francis	.25
BDP122	Joe Blanton	.25
BDP123	Wilfredo Ledezma	.25
BDP124	Bryan Bullington	.25
BDP125	Jairo Garcia	.25
BDP126	Matt Cain	.25
BDP127	Arnie Munoz	.25
BDP128	Clint Everts	.25
BDP129	Jesus Cota	.25
BDP130	Gavin Floyd	.25
BDP131	Edwin Encarnacion	.25
BDP132	Koyie Hill	.25
BDP133	Ruben Gotay	.25
BDP134	Jeff Mathis	.25
BDP135	Andy Marte	.25
BDP136	Dallas McPherson	.25
BDP137	Justin Morneau	.25
BDP138	Rickie Weeks	.25
BDP139	Joel Guzman	.25
BDP140	Shin-Soo Choo	.25
BDP141	*Yusmeiro Petit*	6.00
BDP142	*Jorge Cortes*	1.00
BDP143	Val Majewski	.25
BDP144	Felix Pie	.25
BDP145	Aaron Hill	.25
BDP146	*Jose Capellan*	1.50
BDP147	*Dioner Navarro*	1.00
BDP148	*Fausto Carmona*	1.00
BDP149	*Robinzon Diaz*	1.00
BDP150	Felix Hernandez	20.00
BDP151	*Andres Blanco*	1.00
BDP152	Jason Kubel	.25
BDP153	Willy Taveras	1.50
BDP154	Merkin Valdez	1.00
BDP155	Robinson Cano	.25
BDP156	*Bill Murphy*	1.00
BDP157	Chris Burke	.25
BDP158	Kyle Sleeth	.75
BDP159	B.J. Upton	.50
BDP160	Tim Stauffer	1.00
BDP161	David Wright	.50
BDP162	Conor Jackson	2.50
BDP163	*Brad Thompson*	2.00
BDP164	Delmon Young	.25
BDP165	Jeremy Reed	.25
BDP166	*Matt Bush*	35.00
BDP167	*Mark Rogers*	20.00
BDP168	*Thomas Diamond*	30.00
BDP169	*Greg Golson*	25.00
BDP170	*Homer Bailey*	30.00
BDP171	*Chris Lambert*	20.00
BDP172	*Neil Walker*	30.00
BDP173	*Bill Bray*	15.00
BDP174	*Phillip Hughes*	35.00
BDP175	*Gio Gonzalez*	20.00

Refractor

Rookies: 2-4X
Inserted 1:11
Rookie Autos. (166-175): .75-1.5X
Inserted 1:204

X-Fractor

Rookies: 3-6X
Production 125
Rookie Autos. (166-175): 1-2X
Inserted 1:407

Gold Refract

Rookies: 10-20X
Production 50
Rookie Autos. (166-175): 3-5X
Inserted 1:2,045

2004 BOWMAN DRAFT PICKS & PROSPECTS

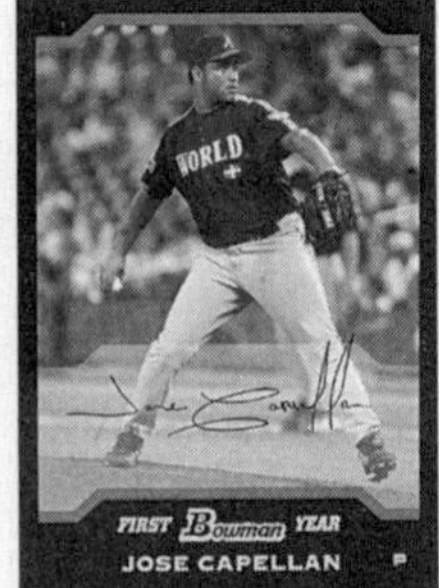

		NM/M
Complete Set (1-165):		30.00
Common Player:		.15
Common Rookie:		.25
Pack (5 Bowman + 2 Chrome):		6.00
Box (24):		100.00
BDP1	Lyle Overbay	.25
BDP2	David Newhan	.15
BDP3	J.R. House	.15
BDP4	Chad Tracy	.15
BDP5	Humberto Quintero	.15
BDP6	David Bush	.15
BDP7	Scott Hairston	.15
BDP8	Mike Wood	.15
BDP9	Alexis Rios	.25
BDP10	Sean Burnett	.15
BDP11	Wilson Valdez	.15
BDP12	Lew Ford	.15
BDP13	*Freddy Thon*	.25
BDP14	Zack Greinke	.15
BDP15	Bucky Jacobsen	.15
BDP16	Kevin Youkilis	.15
BDP17	Grady Sizemore	.15
BDP18	Denny Bautista	.15
BDP19	David DeJesus	.15
BDP20	Casey Kotchman	.15
BDP21	David Kelton	.15
BDP22	*Charles Thomas*	.25
BDP23	*Kazuhito Tadano*	.50
BDP24	*Justin Leone*	.25
BDP25	Eduardo Villacis	.25
BDP26	*Brian Dallimore*	.25
BDP27	Nick Green	.25
BDP28	Sam McConnell	.25
BDP29	*Brad Halsey*	.25
BDP30	*Roman Colon*	.25
BDP31	*Josh Fields*	1.00
BDP32	Cody Bunkelman	.50
BDP33	*Jay Rainville*	.75
BDP34	*Richie Robnett*	1.00
BDP35	*Jon Poterson*	.75
BDP36	*Huston Street*	1.00
BDP37	*Erick San Pedro*	.25
BDP38	Cory Dunlap	1.00
BDP39	*Kurt Suzuki*	.75
BDP40	Anthony Swarzak	.50
BDP41	Ian Desmond	1.00
BDP42	Chris Covington	.40
BDP43	Christian Garcia	.40
BDP44	*Gaby Hernandez*	1.00
BDP45	Steven Register	.25
BDP46	Eduardo Morlan	.25
BDP47	Collin Balester	.25
48	Nathan Phillips	.25
49	Dan Schwartzbauer	.25
50	Rafael Gonzalez	.25
51	*K.C. Herren*	.50
52	William Susdorf	.25
53	Rob Johnson	.25
54	Louis Marson	.50
55	Joe Koshansky	.40
56	Jamar Walton	1.00
57	Mark Lowe	.25
58	*Matt Macri*	.75
59	Donny Lucy	.25
60	Mike Ferris	.50
61	Mike Nickeas	.50
62	*Eric Hurley*	.50
63	*Scott Elbert*	.75
64	*Blake DeWitt*	1.50
65	*Danny Putnam*	.50
66	*J.P. Howell*	.50
67	John Wiggins	.25
68	*Justin Orenduff*	.50
69	*Ray Liotta*	.40
70	*Billy Buckner*	.25
71	*Eric Campbell*	1.00
72	Olin Wick	.25
73	Sean Gamble	.40
74	Seth Smith	1.00
75	*Wade Davis*	.25
76	Joe Jacobitz	.25
77	J.A. Happ	.50
78	Eric Ridener	.25
79	*Matt Tuiasosopo*	3.00
80	Bradley Bergesen	.25
81	Javy Guerra	.40
82	Buck Shaw	.50
83	Paul Janish	.40
84	Sean Kazmar	.25
85	*Josh Johnson*	.40
86	Angel Salome	.40
87	*Jordan Parraz*	.25
88	Kelvin Vazquez	.25
89	Grant Hansen	.25
90	*Matt Fox*	.50
91	*Trevor Plouffe*	1.50
92	Wes Whisler	.25
93	Curtis Thigpen	.50
94	*Donnie Smith*	.25
95	Luis Rivera	.40
96	Jesse Hoover	.25
97	*Jason Vargas*	.40
98	Clary Carlsen	.25
99	Mark Robinson	.25
100	*J.C. Holt*	.40
101	Chad Blackwell	.25
102	*Daryl Jones*	.50
103	Jonathan Tierce	.25
104	Patrick Bryant	.25
105	Eddie Prasch	.40
106	*Mitch Einertson*	3.00
107	*Kyle Waldrop*	.50
108	*Jeff Marquez*	.50
109	*Zach Jackson*	.25
110	Josh Wahpepah	.25
111	*Adam Lind*	1.00
112	Kyle Bloom	.25
113	Ben Harrison	.25
114	*Taylor Tankersley*	.75
115	Steven Jackson	.25
116	*David Purcey*	.40
117	Jacob McGee	.50
118	*Lucas Harrell*	.25
119	Brandon Allen	.50
120	Van Pope	.50
121	Jeff Francis	.15
122	Joe Blanton	.15
123	Wilfredo Ledezma	.15
124	Bryan Bullington	.15
125	Jairo Garcia	.15
126	Matt Cain	.15
127	Arnie Munoz	.15
128	Clint Everts	.15
129	Jesus Cota	.15
130	Gavin Floyd	.15
131	Edwin Encarnacion	.15
132	Koyie Hill	.15
133	Ruben Gotay	.15
134	Jeff Mathis	.15
135	Andy Marte	.15
136	Dallas McPherson	.15
137	Justin Morneau	.15
138	Rickie Weeks	.15
139	Joel Guzman	.15
140	Shin-Soo Choo	.15
141	*Yusmeiro Petit*	2.00
142	Jorge Cortes	.25
143	Val Majewski	.15
144	Felix Pie	.15
145	Aaron Hill	.15
146	*Jose Capellan*	.40
147	*Dioner Navarro*	.25
148	*Fausto Carmona*	.25
149	Robinzon Diaz	.25
150	Felix Hernandez	5.00
151	Andres Blanco	.25
152	Jason Kubel	.15
153	Willy Taveras	.75
154	Merkin Valdez	.25
155	Robinson Cano	.15
156	Bill Murphy	.25
157	Chris Burke	.15
158	Kyle Sleeth	.25
159	B.J. Upton	.25
160	Tim Stauffer	.25
161	David Wright	.25
162	Conor Jackson	.25
163	*Brad Thompson*	.25
164	Delmon Young	.15
165	Jeremy Reed	.15

Gold

Rookies: .75-1.5X
Inserted 1:1

Red

No Pricing
Production one set

Printing Plates

No Pricing
Production one for each color

Signs of the Future

		NM/M
Common Player:		8.00
TB	Taylor Buchholz	
CC	Chad Cordero	8.00
FH	Felix Hernandez	
JH	James Houser	8.00
JJ	Justin Jones	
AL	Adam Loewen	8.00
PM	Paul Maholm	8.00
TP	Tyler Pelland	8.00
OQ	Omar Quintanilla	
TT	Terry Tiffee	8.00

Prospect Premiums

		NM/M
Common Player:		4.00
AB	Angel Berroa	4.00
KC	Kevin Cash	4.00
RH	Ryan Harvey	6.00
CJ	Conor Jackson	10.00
EJ	Edwin Jackson	6.00
LM	Lastings Milledge	8.00
DN	Dioner Navarro	10.00
CQ	Carlos Quentin	8.00
JR	Jeremy Reed	10.00
NS	Nick Swisher	8.00
BU	B.J. Upton	6.00
DY	Delmon Young	6.00

2004 BOWMAN HERITAGE

	NM/M
Complete Set (347):	
Common Player:	.15
Common SP:	4.00
Common SP Rookie:	4.00
SP's inserted 1:3	
Pack (8):	4.00

Box (24): 80.00
1 Tom Glavine .30
2 Mike Piazza/SP 8.00
3 Sidney Ponson .15
4 Jerry Hairston Jr. .15
5 Jermaine Dye .15
6 Bobby Crosby .15
7 Carlos Zambrano .15
8 Moises Alou .15
9 Alex Rodriguez/SP 10.00
10 Derek Jeter 2.00
11 Rafael Furcal .15
12 J.D. Drew .25
13 Joe Mauer/SP 6.00
14 Brad Radke .15
15 Johnny Damon .40
16 Derek Lowe .15
17 Pat Burrell .25
18 Mike Lieberthal .15
19 Cliff Lee .15
20 Ronnie Belliard .15
21 Eric Gagne/SP 4.00
22 Brad Penny .15
23 Al Kaline .50
24 Mike Maroth .15
25 Magglio Ordonez/SP 4.00
26 Mark Buehrle .15
27 Jack Wilson .15
28 Oliver Perez .15
29 Al "Red" Schoendienst .15
30 *Yadier Molina* 1.50
31 Ryan Freel .15
32 Adam Dunn .50
33 Paul Konerko .25
34 Esteban Loaiza .15
35 Ivan Rodriguez .60
36 Carlos Guillen .15
37 Adrian Beltre .50
38 C.C. Sabathia .15
39 Hideo Nomo .40
40 Victor Martinez/SP 4.00
41 Bobby Abreu .15
42 Randy Wolf .15
43 Johnny Estrada .15
44 Russ Ortiz .15
45 Kenny Rogers .15
46 Hank Blalock/SP 4.00
47 David Ortiz .50
48 Pedro Martinez/SP 6.00
49 Austin Kearns .25
50 Ken Griffey Jr./SP 6.00
51 Mark Prior .75
52 Kerry Wood .50
53 Eric Chavez .25
54 Tim Hudson .25
55 Rafael Palmeiro/SP 5.00
56 Javy Lopez .15
57 Jason Bay .15
58 Craig Wilson .15
59 Ed "Whitey" Ford .50
60 Jason Giambi .25
61 Scott Rolen/SP 6.00
62 Matt Morris .15
63 Javier Vazquez .15
64 Jim Thome .25
65 Don Zimmer .15
66 Shawn Green .25
67 Don Larsen .15
68 Gary Sheffield .40
69 Jorge Posada .35
70 Bernie Williams .35
71 Chipper Jones 1.00
72 Andruw Jones .75
73 John Thomson .15
74 Jim Edmonds .35
75 Albert Pujols 1.50
76 Chris Carpenter .15
77 Aubrey Huff/SP 4.00
78 Carl Crawford .15
79 Victor Zambrano .15
80 Alfonso Soriano/SP 5.00
81 Lance Berkman .15
82 Mike Sweeney .15
83 Ken Harvey .15
84 Angel Berroa .15
85 A.J. Burnett .15
86 Mike Lowell .15
87 Miguel Cabrera/SP 5.00
88 Preston Wilson .15
89 Todd Helton/SP 4.00
90 Larry Walker .15
91 Vladimir Guerrero .75
92 Garret Anderson .15
93 Bartolo Colon .15
94 Scott Hairston .15
95 Richie Sexson/SP 4.00
96 Sean Casey .25
97 Johnny Podres .15
98 Andy Pettitte .25
99 Roy Oswalt .25
100 Roger Clemens/SP 8.00
101 Scott Podsednik .25
102 Ben Sheets .25
103 Lyle Overbay .15
104 Nick Johnson/SP 4.00
105 Zach Day .15
106 Jose Reyes .25
107 Khalil Greene .25
108 Sean Burroughs .15
109 David Wells/SP 4.00
110 Jason Schmidt .25
111 Neifi Perez .15
112 Edgar Renteria .15
113 Rich Aurilia .15
114 Edgar Martinez .15
115 Joel Pineiro .15
116 Mark Teixeira .25
117 Michael Young .15
118 Ricardo Rodriguez .15
119 Carlos Delgado .25
120 Roy Halladay .25
121 Jose Guillen .15
122 Troy Glaus .65
123 Shea Hillenbrand .15
124 Luis Gonzalez .25
125 Horacio Ramirez .15
126 Melvin Mora .15
127 Miguel Tejada/SP 4.00
128 Manny Ramirez .75
129 Tim Wakefield .15
130 Curt Schilling/SP 5.00
131 Aramis Ramirez .25
132 Sammy Sosa/SP 8.00
133 Matt Clement .15
134 Juan Uribe .15
135 Dontrelle Willis .25
136 Paul LoDuca .15
137 Juan Pierre .15
138 Kevin Brown .15
139 Brian Giles, Marcus Giles .15
140 Brian Giles .15
141 Nomar Garciaparra/SP 8.00
142 Cesar Izturis .15
143 Don Newcombe .15
144 Craig Biggio .15
145 Carlos Beltran .50
146 Torii Hunter .25
147 Livan Hernandez .15
148 Cliff Floyd .15
149 Barry Zito .25
150 Mark Mulder .25
151 Rocco Baldelli .25
152 Bret Boone .15
153 Jamie Moyer .15
154 Ichiro Suzuki 1.50
155 Brett Myers .15
156 Carl Pavano .15
157 Josh Beckett .25
158 Randy Johnson .75
159 Trot Nixon .15
160 Dmitri Young .15
161 Jacque Jones .15
162 Lew Ford .15
163 Jose Vidro .15
164 Mark Kotsay .15
165 A.J. Pierzynski .15
166 Dewon Brazelton .15
167 Jeromy Burnitz .15
168 Johan Santana .50
169 Greg Maddux 1.00
170 Carl Erskine .15
171 Robin Roberts .15
172 Freddy Garcia .15
173 Carlos Lee .15
174 Jeff Bagwell .75
175 Jeff Kent .15
176 Kazuhisa Ishii .15
177 Orlando Cabrera .25
178 Shannon Stewart .15
179 Mike Cameron .15
180 Mike Mussina .40
181 Frank Thomas .75
182 Jaret Wright .15
183 Alex Gonzalez/SP 4.00
184 Matt Lawton .15
185 Derrek Lee .15
186 Omar Vizquel .15
187 Jeremy Bonderman .15
188 Jake Westbrook .15
189 Zack Greinke/SP 4.00
190 Chad Tracy .15
191 Rondell White .15
192 Alex Gonzalez .15
193 Geoff Jenkins .15
194 Ralph Kiner .15
195 Al Leiter .15
196 Kevin Millwood .15
197 Jason Kendall .15
198 Kris Benson .15
199 Ryan Klesko .15
200 Mark Loretta .15
201 Richard Hidalgo .15
202 Reed Johnson .15
203 Luis Castillo .15
204 *Jon Zeringue/SP* 6.00
205 *Matt Bush* 4.00
206 *Kurt Suzuki/SP* 5.00
207 *Mark Rogers* 2.00
208 *Jason Vargas/SP* 8.00
209 *Homer Bailey* 3.00
210 *Ray Liotta/SP* 5.00
211 *Eric Campbell* 2.00
212 *Thomas Diamond* 3.00
213 *Gaby Hernandez/SP* 8.00
214 *Neil Walker* 2.00
215 *Bill Bray* 1.50
216 *Wade Davis/SP* 4.00
217 *David Purcey* 2.00
218 *Scott Elbert* 2.00
219 *Josh Fields* 2.00
220 *Josh Johnson/SP* 4.00
221 *Chris Lambert* 2.00
222 *Trevor Plouffe* 3.00
223 Bruce Froemming .15
224 *Matt Macri/SP* 5.00
225 *Greg Golson* 2.00
226 *Phillip Hughes* 3.00
227 *Kyle Waldrop* 2.00
228 *Matt Tuiasosopo/SP* 10.00
229 *Richie Robnett* 2.00
230 *Taylor Tankersley* 1.50
231 *Blake DeWitt* 2.50
232 Charlie Reliford .15
233 *Eric Hurley* 1.00
234 *Jordan Parraz/SP* 4.00
235 *J.P. Howell* 2.00
236 Dana DeMuth .15
237 *Zach Jackson* 1.00
238 *Justin Orenduff* 1.00
239 *Brad Thompson* 1.00
240 *J.C. Holt/SP* 5.00
241 *Matt Fox* 2.00
242 *Danny Putnam* 2.00
243 *Daryl Jones/SP* 5.00
244 *Jon Poterson* 1.00
245 *Gio Gonzalez* 1.00
246 *Lucas Harrell/SP* 4.00
247 Jerry Crawford .15
248 *Jay Rainville* 2.00
249 *Donnie Smith/SP* 5.00
250 *Huston Street* 2.00
251 *Jeff Marquez* 2.00
252 *Reid Brignac* 2.00
253 *Yusmeiro Petit* 2.00
254 *K.C. Herren* 1.00
255 Dale Scott .15
256 *Erick San Pedro* 1.50
257 Ed Montague .15
258 *Billy Buckner* 1.50
259 *Mitch Einertson/SP* 8.00
260 *Aarom Baldiris* 1.00
261 Conor Jackson 2.00
262 Rick Reed .15
263 *Ervin Santana* 2.00
264 Gerry Davis .15
265 *Merkin Valdez* 1.00
266 *Joey Gathright* 1.00
267 *Alberto Callaspo* .50
268 Carlos Quentin/SP 8.00
269 Gary Darling .15
270 *Jeff Salazar/SP* 8.00
271 *Akinori Otsuka/SP* 4.00
272 Joe Brinkman .15
273 Omar Quintanilla .50
274 Brian Runge .15
275 *Tom Mastny* .50
276 John Hirschbeck .15
277 *Warner Madrigal* .50
278 Joe West .15
279 *Paul Maholm* 1.00
280 Larry Young .15
281 Mike Reilly .15
282 *Kazuo Matsui/SP* 5.00
283 Randy Marsh .15
284 *Frank Francisco* .50
285 *Zachary Duke* 6.00
286 Tim McClelland .15
287 Jesse Crain 1.00
288 *Hector Gimenez* 1.00
289 *Marland Williams* .50
290 Brian Gorman .15
291 *Jose Capellan/SP* 4.00
292 Tim Welke .15
293 *Javier Guzman* .50
294 *Paul McAnulty* .50
295 *Hector Made* .50
296 *Jon Connolly* .50
297 *Don Sutton* 2.00
298 *Fausto Carmona* 1.00
299 *Ramon Ramirez* .50
300 Brad Snyder 1.00
301 *Chin-Lung Hu* 1.00
302 *Rudy Guillen* .50
303 Matt Moses 1.00
304 *Brad Halsey/SP* 4.00
305 *Erick Aybar* 1.00
306 Brad Sullivan 1.00
307 *Nick Gorneault* 1.00
308 *Craig Ansman* 1.00
309 Ricky Nolasco .50
310 *Luke Hughes* 1.00
311 *Danny Gonzalez* 1.00
312 *Josh Labandeira* .50
313 Donald Levinski 1.00
314 *Vince Perkins* .50
315 *Tommy Murphy* .50
316 *Chad Bentz* .50
317 *Chris Shelton* 3.00
318 *Nyjer Morgan/SP* 4.00
319 *Kody Kirkland* 1.00
320 *Blake Hawksworth* .50
321 *Alex Romero* .50
322 Mike Gosling .50
323 Ryan Budde .50
324 *Kevin Howard* 1.00
325 *Wanell Macia* .50
326 *Travis Blackley* 1.00
327 *Kazuhito Tadano/SP* 4.00
328 *Shingo Takatsu* 1.00
329 *Joaquin Arias* 1.00
330 *Juan Cedeno* .75
331 *Bobby Brownlie* 1.00
332 Lastings Milledge 3.00
333 *Estee Harris* 2.00
334 Tim Stauffer/SP 8.00
335 Jon Knott 1.00
336 David Aardsma .50
337 *Wardell Starling* .50
338 *Dioner Navarro* 1.50
339 *Logan Kensing* .50
340 Jason Hirsh .50
341 *Matt Creighton* .50
342 *Felix Hernandez/SP* 25.00
343 Kyle Sleeth .50
344 *Dustin Nippert* .50
345 *Anthony Lerew* .50
346 *Chris Saenz* .50
347 Steve Palermo .15

Threads of Greatness

NM/M
Common Player: 4.00
Inserted 1:12
Gold: 2-3X
Production 55 sets
MA Moises Alou 6.00
JB Jeff Bagwell 8.00
JB2 Jeff Bagwell 8.00
RB Rocco Baldelli 4.00
TB Tony Batista 4.00
JB Josh Beckett 6.00
JB2 Josh Beckett 6.00
AB Adrian Beltre 6.00
AGB Armando Benitez 4.00
LB Lance Berkman 4.00
LB2 Lance Berkman 4.00
AMB Angel Berroa 4.00
HB Hank Blalock 6.00
HB2 Hank Blalock 6.00
WB3 Wade Boggs 8.00
BB Bret Boone 4.00
BB2 Bret Boone 4.00
PB Pat Burrell 4.00
MC Miguel Cabrera 8.00
EC Eric Chavez 4.00
EC2 Eric Chavez 4.00
RC Roger Clemens 10.00
BC Bobby Cox 4.00
JD Johnny Damon 15.00
CE Carl Everett 4.00
NG Nomar Garciaparra 8.00
JG Jason Giambi 6.00
JG2 Jason Giambi 6.00
JAG Juan Gonzalez 6.00
RH Roy Halladay 4.00
TH Todd Helton 8.00

AJ	Andruw Jones	4.00
DJ	David Justice	4.00
PL	Paul LoDuca	4.00
JL	Javy Lopez	4.00
ML	Mike Lowell	4.00
JM	Joe Mauer	10.00
MCD	Mike McDougal	4.00
KM	Kevin Millwood	4.00
MM	Mark Mulder	4.00
MM2	Mark Mulder	4.00
HN	Hideo Nomo	8.00
JO	John Olerud	4.00
JO2	John Olerud	4.00
AEP	Andy Pettitte	4.00
MP	Mike Piazza	10.00
MP2	Mike Piazza	10.00
AP	Albert Pujols	15.00
AP2	Albert Pujols	15.00
MR	Manny Ramirez	8.00
MR2	Manny Ramirez	8.00
JR	Jose Reyes	4.00
AR	Alex Rodriguez	20.00
CS	C.C. Sabathia	4.00
JDS	Jason Schmidt	6.00
GS	Gary Sheffield	6.00
RS	Ruben Sierra	4.00
JS	John Smoltz	6.00
JS2	John Smoltz	6.00
AS	Alfonso Soriano	6.00
SS	Sammy Sosa	10.00
SS2	Sammy Sosa	10.00
SS3	Sammy Sosa	10.00
MS	Mike Sweeney	4.00
MCT	Mark Teixeira	6.00
MT	Miguel Tejada	6.00
MT2	Miguel Tejada	6.00
MT3	Miguel Tejada	6.00
FT	Frank Thomas	8.00
JT	Jim Thome	8.00
JT2	Jim Thome	8.00
OV	Omar Vizquel	4.00
JW	Jarrod Washburn	4.00
VW	Vernon Wells	4.00
BW	Bernie Williams	4.00
DW	Dontrelle Willis	4.00
KW	Kerry Wood	8.00
KW2	Kerry Wood	8.00
MY	Michael Young	4.00
BZ	Barry Zito	4.00

Black & White

Stars:	2X
SP Stars:	.5-1X
Rookies:	1-2X
SP Rookies:	.5-.75X
Inserted 1:1	

Mohagany

Stars:	15-25X
SP Stars:	3-4X
Rookies:	4-8X
SP Rookies:	3-5X
Production 25 sets	

Printing Plates

No Pricing
Production one set

Commissioner's Cut

Production one
FF Ford Frick

Signs of Authority

		NM/M
Common Autograph:		15.00
Inserted 1:49		
Red Ink:		2X
Production 55 sets		
JB	Joe Brinkman	15.00
JC	Jerry Crawford	15.00
GDA	Gary Darling	15.00
GD	Gerry Davis	15.00
DD	Dana DeMuth	15.00
BF	Bruce Froemming	20.00
BG	Brian Gorman	15.00
JH	John Hirschbeck	15.00
RM	Randy Marsh	15.00
TM	Tim McClelland	15.00
EM	Ed Montague	15.00
SP	Steve Palermo	15.00
ER	Rick Reed	15.00
MR	Mike Reilly	15.00
CM	Charlie Reliford	15.00
BR	Brian Runge	15.00
DS	Dale Scott	20.00
TW	Tim Welke	15.00
JW	Joe West	20.00
LY	Larry Young	15.00

Signs of Glory

		NM/M
Common Autograph:		25.00
Inserted 1:246		
Red Ink:		2X
Production 55 sets		
GK	George Kell	25.00
BK	Bob Kuzava	25.00
PR	Elwin "Preacher" Roe	30.00
BS	Bobby Shantz	25.00
MS	Bill "Moose" Skowron	30.00

Signs of Greatness

		NM/M
Common Autograph:		15.00
Inserted 1:57		
Red Ink:		2-4X
Production 55 sets		
BB	Bill Bray	
MB	Matt Bush	30.00
TD	Thomas Diamond	15.00
GG	Greg Golson	20.00
PH	Phillip Hughes	15.00
CL	Chris Lambert	15.00
JM	Jeff Marquez	15.00
TP	Trevor Plouffe	15.00
JR	Jay Rainville	20.00
MR	Mark Rogers	25.00
TT	Taylor Tankersley	
NW	Neil Walker	20.00

2004 BOWMAN STERLING

		NM/M
Common Rookie:		5.00
Pack (5):		70.00
Box (6):		375.00
ABA	*Aarom Baldiris*	5.00
BBR	*Bill Bray*	5.00
RBR	*Reid Brignac*	8.00
BBU	*Billy Buckner*	5.00
JC	*Jose Capellan*	8.00
FC	*Fausto Carmona*	8.00
JCR	*Jesse Crain*	10.00
TD	*Thomas Diamond*	12.00
ZD	*Zachary Duke*	30.00
ME	*Mitch Einertson*	15.00
BE	*Brad Eldred*	15.00
MF	*Mike Ferris*	5.00
JFI	*Josh Fields*	10.00
MFO	*Matt Fox*	8.00
JG	*Joey Gathright*	5.00
GG	*Greg Golson*	5.00
GIG	*Gio Gonzalez*	8.00
FG	*Freddy Guzman*	5.00
GH	*Gaby Hernandez*	8.00
FH	*Felix Hernandez*	40.00
KCH	*K.C. Herren*	5.00
JH	*Jesse Hoover*	5.00
JPH	*J.P. Howell*	5.00
PH	*Phillip Hughes*	8.00
EH	*Eric Hurley*	8.00
CJ	*Conor Jackson*	25.00
ZJ	*Zach Jackson*	10.00
CLA	*Chris Lambert*	5.00
CH	*Chin-Lung Hu*	5.00
MMC	*Matt Macri*	5.00
HM	*Hector Made*	5.00
PGM	*Paul Maholm*	5.00
NM	*Nyjer Morgan*	5.00
CN	*Chris Nelson*	15.00
JO	*Justin Orenduff*	8.00
YP	*Yusmeiro Petit*	15.00
DPU	*David Purcey*	5.00
OQ	*Omar Quintanilla*	5.00
MRO	*Mark Rogers*	15.00
ESP	*Erick San Pedro*	5.00
NS	*Nate Schierholtz*	25.00
SSM	*Seth Smith*	10.00
KS	*Kurt Suzuki*	12.00
KT	*Kazuhito Tadano*	5.00
CT	*Curtis Thigpen*	8.00
BT	*Brad Thompson*	8.00
NW	*Neil Walker*	10.00
AWH	*Anthony Whittington*	5.00
MW	*Marland Williams*	5.00
JZ	*Jon Zeringue*	5.00
Rookie Relic Autographs		
HB	*Homer Bailey*	25.00
BB	*Brian Bixler*	10.00
MB	*Matt Bush*	25.00
BD	*Blake DeWitt*	25.00
CG	*Christian Garcia*	15.00
SK	*Scott Kazmir*	30.00
JM	*Jeff Marquez*	10.00
SO	*Scott Olsen*	25.00
TP	*Trevor Plouffe*	25.00
DP	*Danny Putnam*	20.00
HS	*Huston Street*	50.00
TT	*Taylor Tankersley*	20.00
MT	*Matt Tuiasosopo*	40.00
KWA	*Kyle Waldrop*	20.00
Prospect Relic Autographs		
RC	Robinson Cano	60.00
CC	Chad Cordero	15.00
DD	David DeJesus	15.00
RH	Ryan Harvey	15.00
CL	Chris Lubanski	15.00
FP	Felix Pie	20.00
BU	B.J. Upton	25.00
AW	Adam Wainwright	10.00
DW	David Wright	50.00
DY	Delmon Young	30.00
Rookie Autographs:		
CA	*Chris Aguila*	10.00
AC	*Alberto Callaspo*	15.00
HG	*Hector Gimenez*	10.00
BH	*Blake Hawksworth*	10.00
LH	*Lincoln Holdzkom*	10.00
RM	*Ryan Meaux*	10.00
MM	*Matt Moses*	20.00
VP	*Vince Perkins*	10.00
CQ	*Carlos Quentin*	30.00
JR	*Jay Rainville*	20.00
AR	*Alex Romero*	10.00
MR	*Mike Rouse*	10.00
JS	*Jeremy Sowers*	25.00
AZ	*Alec Zumwalt*	10.00
Relics:		5.00
MA	Moises Alou	5.00
JB	Jeff Bagwell	8.00
RB	Rocco Baldelli	5.00
CIB	Carlos Beltran	10.00
LB	Lance Berkman	5.00
AB	Angel Berroa	5.00
CB	Craig Biggio	5.00
HJB	Hank Blalock	8.00
MC	Miguel Cabrera	8.00
LC	Luis Castillo	5.00
HC	Hee Seop Choi	5.00
BC2	Bobby Crosby	10.00
JD	Johnny Damon	10.00
AD	Adam Dunn	8.00
JE	Johnny Estrada	5.00
EG	Eric Gagne	5.00
TG	Troy Glaus	5.00
TMG	Tom Glavine	5.00
VG	Vladimir Guerrero	10.00
TLH	Todd Helton	8.00
RJH	Richard Hidalgo	5.00
NJ	Nick Johnson	5.00
AJ	Andruw Jones	5.00
AK	Austin Kearns	5.00
JK	Jason Kendall	5.00
PL	Paul LoDuca	5.00
TM	Tino Martinez	5.00
MAM	Mark Mulder	5.00
LN	Laynce Nix	5.00
RO	Russ Ortiz	5.00
RP	Rafael Palmeiro	8.00
MJP	Mike Piazza	10.00
JP	Juan Pierre	5.00
MP	Mark Prior	10.00
AP	Albert Pujols	20.00
ANR	Aramis Ramirez	5.00
MAR	Manny Ramirez	8.00
PR	Pokey Reese	5.00
AER	Alex Rodriguez	15.00
IR	Ivan Rodriguez	8.00
GS	Gary Sheffield	8.00
SS	Sammy Sosa	10.00
MCT	Mark Teixeira	5.00
MT1	Miguel Tejada/bat	8.00
MT2	Miguel Tejada/jsy	8.00
FT	Frank Thomas	10.00
BW	Bernie Williams	8.00
DWW	Dontrelle Willis	5.00
KW	Kerry Wood	10.00
MY	Michael Young	5.00

Refractors

Regular Rookies:	1.5-2X
Rookie Relic Autos.:	1-2X
Rookie Autos.:	1-2X
Prospect Relic Autos.:	1-2X
Relics:	1-2X
Production 199 sets	

Black Refractors

No Pricing
Production 25 sets

Red Refractor

No Pricing
Production one set

Uncirculated

No Pricing
Production 16 sets

2004 BOWMAN'S BEST

		NM/M
Complete Set:		
Common Player:		.25
Pack (5):		14.00
Box (10):		100.00
Veterans		
GA	Garret Anderson	.25
CB	Carlos Beltran	.75
HB	Hank Blalock	.75
MTC	Miguel Cabrera	1.00
EC	Eric Chavez	.50
RC	Roger Clemens	1.75
CD	Carlos Delgado	.50
NAG	Nomar Garciaparra	2.00
JGG	Jason Giambi	.75
BG	Brian Giles	.25
VG	Vladimir Guerrero	1.00
TLH	Todd Helton	1.00
RJ	Randy Johnson	1.00
LWJ	Chipper Jones	1.50
JLO	Javy Lopez	.25
MO	Magglio Ordonez	.25
LO	Lyle Overbay	.25
MJP	Mike Piazza	2.00
JP	Jorge Posada	.25
MWP	Mark Prior	1.00
AP	Albert Pujols	2.50
MAR	Manny Ramirez	1.00
AER	Alex Rodriguez	2.50
IR	Ivan Rodriguez	.65

SR	Scott Rolen	1.00
CMS	Curt Schilling	.50
JDS	Jason Schmidt	.25
RS	Richie Sexson	.25
AS	Alfonso Soriano	1.00
SS	Sammy Sosa	2.00
IS	Ichiro Suzuki	2.00
MT	Miguel Tejada	.50
JT	Jim Thome	.25
JAV	Jose Vidro	.25
MY	Michael Young	.25

First-Year Players

Common Rookie		2.00
JJC	*Jon Connolly*	3.00
JRG	*Joey Gathright*	2.00
DG	*Danny Gonzalez*	1.50
NG	*Nick Gorneault*	2.00
MG	Mike Gosling	1.50
CH	*Chin-Lung Hu*	2.00
TJ	Terry Jones	1.50
AL	*Anthony Lerew*	2.00
HM	*Hector Made*	2.00
WM	*Warner Madrigal*	2.00
PMM	*Paul McAnulty*	2.00
AO	*Akinori Otsuka*	2.00
TS	*Todd Self*	1.50
KS	Kyle Sleeth	2.00
DS	*Don Sutton*	3.00

First-Year Player Autographs

Common Autograph:		8.00
DA	David Aardsma	10.00
CMA	*Craig Ansman*	15.00
JA	*Joaquin Arias*	10.00
EA	*Erick Aybar*	20.00
BB	*Bobby Brownlie*	20.00
RB	Ryan Budde	10.00
KC	Kory Casto	8.00
JC	*Juan Cedeno*	10.00
VC	*Vito Chiaravalloti*	10.00
MDC	*Matt Creighton*	8.00
DC	David Crouthers	10.00
TD	Tyler Davidson	15.00
ZD	*Zachary Duke*	90.00
JE	*Jesse English*	10.00
AG	Adam Greenberg	15.00
RG	*Rudy Guillen*	10.00
TOH	Travis Hanson	10.00
EH	*Estee Harris*	10.00
FH	*Felix Hernandez*	130.00
SH	Shawn Hill	10.00
JH	Jason Hirsh	10.00
LTH	*Luke Hughes*	8.00
CJ	Conor Jackson	40.00
LK	*Logan Kensing*	10.00
JK	*Jon Knott*	10.00
KK	Kevin Kouzmanoff	15.00
JL	*Josh Labandeira*	8.00
DL	Donald Levinski	10.00
PM	*Paul Maholm*	10.00
TRM	*Tom Mastny*	10.00
BEM	*Brandon Medders*	8.00
LM	Lastings Milledge	40.00
YM	*Yadier Molina*	25.00
DM	David Murphy	15.00
DN	*Dioner Navarro*	20.00
DDN	*Dustin Nippert*	10.00
RN	Ricky Nolasco	10.00
BP	*Brayan Pena*	8.00
QQ	Omar Quintanilla	15.00
RR	*Ramon Ramirez*	10.00
JS	*Jeff Salazar*	15.00
ES	*Ervin Santana*	20.00
BMS	Brad Snyder	15.00
WS	*Wardell Starling*	10.00
TJS	Tim Stauffer	20.00
BS	Brad Sullivan	10.00
JSZ	*Jason Szuminski*	10.00
RT	*Rob Tejeda*	15.00
NU	*Nic Ungs*	10.00
MV	*Merkin Valdez*	15.00
CZ	*Charlie Zink*	10.00

First-Year Player Relics

TB	*Travis Blackley*	5.00
KRK	*Kody Kirkland*	6.00
KM	*Kazuo Matsui*	8.00
KT	*Kazuhito Tadano*	6.00
ST	*Shingo Takatsu*	8.00

Green

Green Stars:	4-8X
Green Non-Auto RC's:	1.5-3X
Production 100	
Green RC Autos.:	1-2X

Red

Red Stars:	No Pricing
Production 20	
Red Non-Auto. RC's:	No Pricing
Red RC Autos.:	No Pricing

Double Play Autographs

		NM/M
Common Duo:		20.00
Inserted 1:33		
MH	Lastings Milledge, Estee Harris	35.00
QS	Omar Quintanilla, Brad Snyder	30.00
SC	Tim Stauffer, Vito Chiaravalloti	30.00
HJ	Travis Hanson, Conor Jackson	30.00
MN	Brandon Medders, Dustin Nippert	30.00
UK	Nic Ungs, Kevin Kouzmanoff	30.00
CC	Matt Creighton, David Crouthers	30.00
EN	Jesse English, Ricky Nolasco	20.00
SV	Ervin Santana, Merkin Valdez	30.00
SK	Jeff Salazar, Jon Knott	20.00

Triple Play Autographs

		NM/M
Common Trio:		30.00
Inserted 1:109		
CBA	Juan Cedeno, Bobby Brownlie, Joaquin Arias	30.00
ALS	David Aardsma, Donald Levinski, Brad Sullivan	25.00
SSV	Tim Stauffer, Ervin Santana, Merkin Valdez	50.00

2005 BOWMAN

		NM/M
Complete Set (330):		60.00
Common Player:		.15
Common Rookie:		.50
Pack (10):		3.50
Box (24):		65.00
1	Gavin Floyd	.15
2	Eric Chavez	.25
3	Miguel Tejada	.50
4	Dmitri Young	.15
5	Hank Blalock	.50
6	Kerry Wood	.75
7	Andy Pettitte	.40
8	Pat Burrell	.25
9	Johnny Estrada	.15
10	Frank Thomas	.50
11	Juan Pierre	.15
12	Tom Glavine	.40
13	Lyle Overbay	.25
14	Jim Edmonds	.40
15	Steve Finley	.15
16	Jermaine Dye	.15
17	Omar Vizquel	.15
18	Nick Johnson	.15
19	Brian Giles	.25
20	Justin Morneau	.25
21	Preston Wilson	.15
22	Wily Mo Pena	.15
23	Rafael Palmeiro	.50
24	Scott Kazmir	.25
25	Derek Jeter	2.00
26	Barry Zito	.25
27	Mike Lowell	.15
28	Jason Bay	.25
29	Ken Harvey	.15
30	Nomar Garciaparra	1.00
31	Roy Halladay	.25
32	Todd Helton	.50
33	Mark Kotsay	.15
34	Jake Peavy	.40
35	David Wright	.75
36	Dontrelle Willis	.40
37	Marcus Giles	.15
38	Chone Figgins	.15
39	Sidney Ponson	.15
40	Randy Johnson	.75
41	John Smoltz	.25
42	Kevin Millar	.15
43	Mark Teixeira	.50
44	Alex Rios	.15
45	Mike Piazza	1.00
46	Victor Martinez	.15
47	Jeff Bagwell	.50
48	Shawn Green	.25
49	Ivan Rodriguez	.50
50	Alex Rodriguez	1.50
51	Kazuo Matsui	.15
52	Mark Mulder	.40
53	Michael Young	.15
54	Javy Lopez	.25
55	Johnny Damon	.75
56	Jeff Francis	.15
57	Rich Harden	.25
58	Bobby Abreu	.40
59	Mark Loretta	.15
60	Gary Sheffield	.40
61	Jamie Moyer	.15
62	Garret Anderson	.15
63	Vernon Wells	.15
64	Orlando Cabrera	.15
65	Magglio Ordonez	.15
66	Ronnie Belliard	.15
67	Carlos Lee	.25
68	Carl Pavano	.25
69	Jon Lieber	.15
70	Aubrey Huff	.15
71	Rocco Baldelli	.15
72	Jason Schmidt	.25
73	Bernie Williams	.40
74	Hideki Matsui	1.50
75	Ken Griffey Jr.	1.50
76	Josh Beckett	.25
77	Mark Buehrle	.25
78	David Ortiz	.75
79	Luis Gonzalez	.25
80	Scott Rolen	.75
81	Joe Mauer	.50
82	Jose Reyes	.15
83	Adam Dunn	.50
84	Greg Maddux	1.00
85	Bartolo Colon	.15
86	Bret Boone	.15
87	Mike Mussina	.50
88	Ben Sheets	.40
89	Lance Berkman	.25
90	Miguel Cabrera	.75
91	C.C. Sabathia	.15
92	Mike Maroth	.15
93	Andruw Jones	.40
94	Jack Wilson	.15
95	Ichiro Suzuki	1.50
96	Geoff Jenkins	.15
97	Zack Greinke	.15
98	Jorge Posada	.40
99	Travis Hafner	.15
100	Barry Bonds	2.50
101	Aaron Rowand	.15
102	Aramis Ramirez	.40
103	Curt Schilling	.75
104	Melvin Mora	.15
105	Albert Pujols	2.00
106	Austin Kearns	.15
107	Shannon Stewart	.15
108	Carl Crawford	.15
109	Carlos Zambrano	.40
110	Roger Clemens	2.00
111	Javier Vazquez	.15
112	Randy Wolf	.15
113	Chipper Jones	.75
114	Larry Walker	.25
115	Alfonso Soriano	.75
116	Brad Wilkerson	.15
117	Bobby Crosby	.15
118	Jim Thome	.75
119	Oliver Perez	.25
120	Vladimir Guerrero	.75
121	Roy Oswalt	.40
122	Torii Hunter	.25
123	Rafael Furcal	.25
124	Luis Castillo	.15
125	Carlos Beltran	.50
126	Mike Sweeney	.15
127	Johan Santana	.50
128	Tim Hudson	.40
129	Troy Glaus	.40
130	Manny Ramirez	.75
131	Jeff Kent	.15
132	Jose Vidro	.15
133	Edgar Renteria	.25
134	Russ Ortiz	.15
135	Sammy Sosa	1.25
136	Carlos Delgado	.40
137	Richie Sexson	.25
138	Pedro Martinez	.75
139	Adrian Beltre	.40
140	Mark Prior	.75
141	Omar Quintanilla	.15
142	Carlos Quentin	.25
143	Dan Johnson	.15
144	Jake Stevens	.15
145	Nate Schierholtz	.15
146	Neil Walker	.15
147	Bill Bray	.15
148	Taylor Tankersley	.15
149	Trevor Plouffe	.15
150	Felix Hernandez	.50
151	Phillip Hughes	.15
152	James Houser	.15
153	David Murphy	.15
154	Ervin Santana	.15
155	Anthony Whittington	.15
156	Chris Lambert	.15
157	Jeremy Sowers	.15
158	Gio Gonzalez	.15
159	Blake DeWitt	.15
160	Thomas Diamond	.15
161	Greg Golson	.15
162	David Aardsma	.15
163	Paul Maholm	.15
164	Mark Rogers	.15
165	Homer Bailey	.15
166	*Chip Cannon*	.50
167	*Tony Giarratano*	2.00
168	*Darren Fenster*	.50
169	*Elvys Quezada*	.75
170	*Glen Perkins*	1.00
171	*Ian Kinsler*	1.50
172	Michael Bourn	1.00
173	*Jeremy West*	.75
174	*Justin Verlander*	1.50
175	*Kevin West*	.50
176	*Luis Hernandez*	1.00
177	*Matt Campbell*	.75
178	*Nate McLouth*	.50
179	*Ryan Goleski*	.50
180	*Matt Lindstrom*	.50
181	*Matt DeSalvo*	.50
182	Kole Strayhorn	.50
183	*Jose Vaquedano*	.50
184	*James Jurries*	.50
185	*Ian Bladergroen*	.75
186	*Eric Nielsen*	.75
187	*Chris Vines*	1.00
188	*Chris Denorfia*	.50
189	*Kevin Melillo*	.50
190	*Melky Cabrera*	2.00
191	Ryan Sweeney	1.50
192	*Sean Marshall*	1.00
193	*Andy LaRoche*	3.00
194	*Tyler Pelland*	1.50
195	*Mike Morse*	2.00
196	*Wes Swackhamer*	.50
197	*Wade Robinson*	.50
198	*Dan Santin*	.50
199	*Steven Doetsch*	.50
200	Shane Costa	.50
201	*Scott Mathieson*	.75
202	*Ben Jones*	.75
203	*Michael Rogers*	.50
204	*Matt Rogelstad*	.50
205	*Luis Ramirez*	1.00
206	*Landon Powell*	.75
207	*Erik Cordier*	1.50
208	*Chris Seddon*	.50
209	*Chris Roberson*	.75
210	*Tom Oldham*	.50
211	*Dana Eveland*	1.00
212	*Cody Haerther*	.75
213	*Danny Core*	.50
214	*Craig Tatum*	.75
215	*Elliot Johnson*	.50
216	*Ender Chavez*	.75
217	*Errol Simonitsch*	.75
218	*Matt Van Der Bosch*	.75
219	*Eulogio de la Cruz*	.50
220	C.J. Smith	.50
221	*Adam Boeve*	.75
222	*Adam Harben*	.75
223	*Baltazar Lopez*	.75
224	*Russ Martin*	1.00
225	*Brian Bannister*	1.00
226	*Brian Miller*	.50
227	*Casey McGehee*	.50
228	*Humberto Sanchez*	.75
229	*Javon Moran*	.50
230	*Brandon McCarthy*	2.00
231	*Danny Zell*	.50
232	*Jake Postlewait*	.50

233 *Juan Tejeda* .50
234 *Keith Ramsey* .50
235 *Lorenzo Scott* .75
236 *Wladimir Balentien* 1.50
237 *Martin Prado* .50
238 *Matt Albers* .50
239 *Brian Schweiger* .50
240 *Brian Stavisky* .50
241 *Pat Misch* .50
242 *Pat Osborn* .50
243 *Ryan Feierabend* 1.00
244 Shaun Marcum .50
245 *Kevin Collins* .50
246 *Stuart Pomeranz* .50
247 *Tetsu Yofu* .75
248 *Hernan Iribarren* 1.50
249 *Mike Spiegel* .50
250 *Tony Arnerich* .50
251 *Manny Parra* .75
252 *Drew Anderson* .75
253 *T.J. Beam* .50
254 *Pedro Lopez* .75
255 *Andy Sides* .75
256 *Bear Bay* .50
257 *Bill McCarthy* 1.00
258 *Daniel Haigwood* 1.50
259 *Brian Sprout* .50
260 *Bryan Triplett* .75
261 Steve Bondurant .50
262 *Darwinson Salazar* .75
263 *David Shepard* .50
264 *Johan Silva* .75
265 *J.B. Thurmond* .50
266 *Brandon Moorhead* .50
267 *Kyle Nichols* .50
268 *Jonathan Sanchez* .50
269 *Mike Esposito* .50
270 *Erik Schindewolf* .75
271 *Peeter Ramos* .75
272 *Juan Senreiso* .50
273 *Matthew Kemp* 1.50
274 *Vinny Rottino* .50
275 *Micah Furtado* .50
276 *George Kottaras* 1.00
277 *Billy Butler* 4.00
278 *Buck Coats* .50
279 *Ken Durost* .50
280 *Nic Touchstone* .50
281 *Jerry Owens* 1.00
282 Stefan Bailie .50
283 *Jesse Gutierrez* .75
284 *Chuck Tiffany* 1.00
285 *Brendan Ryan* .50
286 *Hayden Penn* 2.00
287 *Shawn Bowman* .50
288 *Alexander Smit* .50
289 *Micah Schnurstein* .75
290 *Jared Gothreaux* .50
291 *Jair Jurrjens* 1.50
292 *Bobby Livingston* .75
293 *Ryan Speier* .50
294 *Zachary Parker* .50
295 *Christian Colonel* .75
296 *Scott Mitchinson* .50
297 *Neil Wilson* .50
298 *Chuck James* 2.50
299 *Heath Totten* .50
300 *Sean Tracey* .75
301 *Ismael Ramirez* .50
302 *Matt Brown* .50
303 *Franklin Morales* .50
304 *Brandon Sing* 1.00
305 *D.J. Houlton* .50
306 *Jayce Tingler* .50
307 *Mitchell Arnold* .50
308 *Jim Burt* .75
309 *Jason Motte* .50
310 *David Gassner* .75
311 *Andy Santana* .50
312 *Kelvin Pichardo* .50
313 *Carlos Carrasco* .75
314 *Willy Mota* .50
315 *Frank Mata* .50
316 *Carlos Gonzalez* 2.00
317 *Jeff Niemann* 1.00
318 *Chris Young* 1.50
319 Billy Sadler .50
320 Ricky Barrett .50
321 Benjamin Harrison .50
322 *Steve Nelson* .50
323 *Daryl Thompson* .75
324 *Philip Humber* 1.50
325 *Jeremy Harts* .50
326 *Nick Masset* .50
327 *Mike Rodriguez* .50
328 *Mike Garber* .50
329 *Kennard Bibbs* .50
330 *Ryan Garko* 1.50

Gold

Stars: 1-2X
Rookies: 1-2X
Inserted 1:1

White

Stars: 3-6X
Rookies: 3-6X
Production 240 Sets

Signs of the Future

NM/M

BB Brian Bixler 10.00
MC Melky Cabrera 15.00
RC Robinson Cano 40.00
CC Chad Cordero 10.00
BC Bobby Crosby 20.00
BD Blake DeWitt 20.00
CG Christian Garcia 15.00
TG Tom Gorzelanny 10.00
PH Phillip Hughes 15.00
TH Tim Hutting 15.00
SK Scott Kazmir 15.00
AL Adam Loewen 15.00
PM Paul Maholm 15.00
DM Dallas McPherson 20.00
SO Scott Olson 8.00
TP Trevor Plouffe 15.00
DP Dan Putnam 10.00
JR Jay Rainville 15.00
RR Richie Robnett 8.00
ES Ervin Santana 20.00
JS Jay Sborz 10.00
BMS Brad Snyder 15.00
HS Huston Street 40.00
BS Brad Sullivan 10.00
TT Taylor Tankersley 12.00
RW Ryan Wagner 15.00
KW Kyle Waldrop 15.00
AW Anthony Whittington 10.00
DW David Wright 70.00

Printing Plates

No Pricing
Production One Set

1st Edition

NM/M

Stars: 3-5X
Rookies: 1-2X
HTA Exclusive
Pack (10): 3.50
Box (20): 60.00

Autographed Base Card Variations

NM/M

Inserted 1:1,599
141 Omar Quintanilla 8.00
142 Carlos Quentin 20.00
143 Dan Johnson 10.00
144 Jake Stevens 10.00
145 Nate Schierholtz 15.00
146 Neil Walker 15.00
147 Bill Bray 8.00
148 Taylor Tankersley 12.00
149 Trevor Plouffe 12.00
150 Felix Hernandez 40.00
151 Phillip Hughes 15.00
152 James Houser 10.00
153 David Murphy 12.00
154 Ervin Santana 15.00
155 Anthony Whittington 8.00
156 Chris Lambert 12.00
157 Jeremy Sowers 15.00
158 Gio Gonzalez 15.00
159 Blake DeWitt 25.00
160 Thomas Diamond 20.00
161 Greg Golson 12.00
162 David Aardsma 15.00
163 Paul Maholm 12.00
164 Mark Rogers 20.00
165 Homer Bailey 20.00

A-Rod Throwbacks

NM/M

Complete Set (4): 6.00
Common A-Rod: 2.00
94-AR Alex Rodriguez 2.00
95-AR Alex Rodriguez 2.00
96-AR Alex Rodriguez 2.00
97-AR Alex Rodriguez 2.00

A-Rod Throwbacks Autographs

NM/M

Production 1-225
94A-AR Alex Rodriguez/1
95A-AR Alex Rodriguez/25
96A-AR Alex Rodriguez/99 150.00
97A-AR Alex Rodriguez/225 150.00

A-Rod Throwbacks Relic

NM/M

Quantity produced listed
94R-AR Alex Rodriguez/1
95R-AR Alex Rodriguez/25
96R-AR Alex Rodriguez/99 20.00
97R-AR Alex Rodriguez/800 15.00

Futures Game Gear

NM/M

JB Joe Blanton 5.00
BB Bryan Bullington 5.00
MC Matt Cain 5.00
SC Shin-Soo Choo 6.00
JCO Jorge Cortes 5.00
JC Jesus Cota 5.00
EE Edwin Encarnacion 5.00
CE Clint Everts 5.00
GF Gavin Floyd 5.00
JF Jeff Francis 5.00
JG Jairo Garcia 5.00
RG Ruben Gotay 5.00
JGU Joel Guzman 5.00
AH Aaron Hill 5.00
KH Koyie Hill 5.00
WL Wilfredo Ledezma 5.00
VM Val Majewski 5.00
AMA Andy Marte 8.00
JM Jeff Mathis 5.00
DM Dallas McPherson 8.00
JMO Justin Morneau 8.00
AM Arnie Munoz 5.00
YP Yusmeiro Petit 8.00
FP Felix Pie 8.00
RW Rickie Weeks 8.00

Relic Base Card Variations

NM/M

Inserted 1:50
2 Eric Chavez 5.00
5 Hank Blalock 8.00
23 Rafael Palmeiro 8.00
43 Mark Teixeira 8.00
49 Ivan Rodriguez 8.00
50 Alex Rodriguez 15.00
60 Gary Sheffield 8.00
65 Magglio Ordonez 5.00
78 David Ortiz 10.00
83 Adam Dunn 8.00
90 Miguel Cabrera 8.00
93 Andruw Jones 5.00
100 Barry Bonds 25.00
104 Melvin Mora 5.00
105 Albert Pujols 20.00
115 Alfonso Soriano 8.00
120 Vladimir Guerrero 8.00
125 Carlos Beltran 10.00
130 Manny Ramirez 8.00
135 Sammy Sosa 12.00

Two of a Kind Autograph

No Pricing
Production 13
Hank Aaron, Alex Rodriguez

2005 BOWMAN CHROME

NM/M

Complete Set (352):
Common Player: .25
Common Rookie: 1.00
Common RC Auto. (331-352): 15.00
Pack (4): 6.00
Box (18): 85.00
1 Gavin Floyd .25
2 Eric Chavez .50
3 Miguel Tejada .75
4 Dmitri Young .25
5 Hank Blalock .50
6 Kerry Wood .75
7 Andy Pettitte .50
8 Pat Burrell .50
9 Johnny Estrada .25
10 Frank Thomas .75
11 Juan Pierre .25
12 Tom Glavine .50
13 Lyle Overbay .25
14 Jim Edmonds .50
15 Steve Finley .25
16 Jermaine Dye .25
17 Omar Vizquel .25
18 Nick Johnson .25
19 Brian Giles .25
20 Justin Morneau .50
21 Preston Wilson .25
22 Wily Mo Pena .25
23 Rafael Palmeiro .75
24 Scott Kazmir .50
25 Derek Jeter 3.00
26 Barry Zito .50
27 Mike Lowell .25
28 Jason Bay .50
29 Ken Harvey .25
30 Nomar Garciaparra 1.50
31 Roy Halladay .40
32 Todd Helton .75
33 Mark Kotsay .25
34 Jake Peavy .50
35 David Wright 1.00
36 Dontrelle Willis .50
37 Marcus Giles .25
38 Chone Figgins .25
39 Sidney Ponson .25
40 Randy Johnson 1.00
41 John Smoltz .50
42 Kevin Millar .25

43 Mark Teixeira .75
44 Alex Rios .25
45 Mike Piazza 1.50
46 Victor Martinez .25
47 Jeff Bagwell .75
48 Shawn Green .50
49 Ivan Rodriguez .75
50 Alex Rodriguez 2.50
51 Kazuo Matsui .25
52 Mark Mulder .50
53 Michael Young .50
54 Javy Lopez .25
55 Johnny Damon 1.00
56 Jeff Francis .25
57 Rich Harden .50
58 Bobby Abreu .50
59 Mark Loretta .25
60 Gary Sheffield .50
61 Jamie Moyer .25
62 Garret Anderson .50
63 Vernon Wells .25
64 Orlando Cabrera .25
65 Magglio Ordonez .25
66 Ronnie Belliard .25
67 Carlos Lee .50
68 Carl Pavano .25
69 Jon Lieber .25
70 Aubrey Huff .25
71 Rocco Baldelli .25
72 Jason Schmidt .50
73 Bernie Williams .50
74 Hideki Matsui 2.00
75 Ken Griffey Jr. 2.00
76 Josh Beckett .50
77 Mark Buehrle .25
78 David Ortiz 1.00
79 Luis Gonzalez .25
80 Scott Rolen 1.00
81 Joe Mauer .50
82 Jose Reyes .50
83 Adam Dunn .75
84 Greg Maddux 2.00
85 Bartolo Colon .40
86 Bret Boone .25
87 Mike Mussina .50
88 Ben Sheets .50
89 Ben Sheets .25
90 Miguel Cabrera 1.00
91 C.C. Sabathia .25
92 Mike Maroth .25
93 Andruw Jones .50
94 Jack Wilson .25
95 Ichiro Suzuki 2.00
96 Geoff Jenkins .25
97 Zack Greinke .25
98 Jorge Posada .50
99 Travis Hafner .25
100 Barry Bonds 3.00
101 Aaron Rowand .25
102 Aramis Ramirez .75
103 Curt Schilling 1.00
104 Melvin Mora .25
105 Albert Pujols 3.00
106 Austin Kearns .25
107 Shannon Stewart .25
108 Carl Crawford .25
109 Carlos Zambrano .50
110 Roger Clemens 3.00
111 Javier Vazquez .25
112 Randy Wolf .25
113 Chipper Jones 1.00
114 Larry Walker .50
115 Alfonso Soriano 1.00
116 Brad Wilkerson .25
117 Bobby Crosby .50
118 Jim Thome .75
119 Oliver Perez .25
120 Vladimir Guerrero 1.00
121 Roy Oswalt .50
122 Torii Hunter .40
123 Rafael Furcal .25
124 Luis Castillo .25
125 Carlos Beltran .75
126 Mike Sweeney .25
127 Johan Santana .75
128 Tim Hudson .50
129 Troy Glaus .50
130 Manny Ramirez 1.00
131 Jeff Kent .40
132 Jose Vidro .25
133 Edgar Renteria .40
134 Russ Ortiz .25
135 Sammy Sosa 1.50
136 Carlos Delgado .50
137 Richie Sexson .50
138 Pedro Martinez 1.00
139 Adrian Beltre .50
140 Mark Prior 1.00
141 Omar Quintanilla .25
142 Carlos Quentin .25
143 Dan Johnson .25
144 Jake Stevens .25
145 Nate Schierholtz .25
146 Neil Walker .25
147 Bill Bray .25
148 Taylor Tankersley .25
149 Trevor Plouffe .25
150 Felix Hernandez 1.00
151 Phillip Hughes .25
152 James Houser .25
153 David Murphy .25
154 Ervin Santana .25
155 Anthony Whittington .25
156 Chris Lambert .25
157 Jeremy Sowers .25
158 Gio Gonzalez .25
159 Blake DeWitt .25
160 Thomas Diamond .25
161 Greg Golson .25
162 David Aardsma .25
163 Paul Maholm .25
164 Mark Rogers .25
165 Homer Bailey .25
166 *Elvin Puello* 1.00
167 *Tony Giarratano* 2.00
168 *Darren Fenster* 1.00
169 *Elvys Quezada* 1.00
170 *Glen Perkins* 1.50
171 *Ian Kinsler* 5.00
172 *Adam Bostick* 1.00
173 *Jeremy West* 2.00
174 *Brett Harper* 2.00
175 *Kevin West* 1.00
176 *Luis Hernandez* 1.00
177 *Matt Campbell* 1.00
178 *Nate McLouth* 1.50
179 *Ryan Goleski* 2.00
180 *Matt Lindstrom* 1.00
181 *Matt DeSalvo* 1.50
182 *Kole Strayhorn* 1.00
183 *Jose Vaquedano* 1.00
184 *James Jurries* 2.00
185 *Ian Bladergroen* 2.50
186 *Kila Kaaihue* 4.00
187 *Luke Scott* 2.00
188 *Chris Denorfia* 1.00
189 *Jai Miller* 1.50
190 *Melky Cabrera* 4.00
191 *Ryan Sweeney* 4.00
192 *Sean Marshall* 1.00
193 *Eric Abreu* 2.00
194 *Tyler Pelland* 1.00
195 *Cole Armstrong* 2.00
196 *John Hudgins* 1.00
197 *Wade Robinson* 1.00
198 *Dan Santin* 1.50
199 *Steven Doetsch* 1.50
200 *Shane Costa* 1.00
201 *Scott Mathieson* 1.00
202 *Ben Jones* 1.00
203 *Michael Rogers* 1.00
204 *Matt Rogelstad* 1.50
205 *Luis Ramirez* 1.00
206 *Landon Powell* 2.00
207 *Erik Cordier* 1.50
208 *Chris Seddon* 1.00
209 *Chris Roberson* 1.50
210 *Tom Oldham* 1.00
211 *Dana Eveland* 1.50
212 *Cody Haerther* 1.00
213 *Danny Core* 1.00
214 *Craig Tatum* 1.00
215 *Elliot Johnson* 1.00
216 *Ender Chavez* 1.00
217 *Errol Simonitsch* 1.50
218 *Matt Van Der Bosch* 1.00
219 *Eulogio de la Cruz* 1.00
220 *Drew Toussaint* 1.50
221 *Adam Boeve* 2.00
222 *Adam Harben* 1.50
223 *Baltazar Lopez* 2.00
224 *Russell Martin* 3.00
225 *Brian Bannister* 1.50
226 *Chris Walker* 1.50
227 *Casey McGehee* 1.50
228 *Humberto Sanchez* 1.00
229 *Javon Moran* 1.00
230 *Brandon McCarthy* 5.00
231 *Danny Zell* 1.00
232 *Kevin Barry* 1.00
233 *Juan Tejeda* 1.50
234 *Keith Ramsey* 1.00
235 *Lorenzo Scott* 1.00
236 *Jonathan Barratt* 1.00
237 *Martin Prado* 1.50
238 *Matt Albers* 1.00
239 *Brian Schweiger* 1.00
240 *Raul Tablado* 1.00
241 *Pat Misch* 1.00
242 *Pat Osborn* 1.00
243 *Ryan Feierabend* 1.00
244 *Shaun Marcum* 1.00
245 *Kevin Collins* 1.00
246 *Stuart Pomeranz* 1.00
247 *Tetsu Yofu* 1.00
248 *Hernan Iribarren* 5.00
249 *Michael Spidale* 1.00
250 *Tony Americh* 1.00
251 *Manny Parra* 1.00
252 *Drew Anderson* 1.00
253 *T.J. Beam* 3.00
254 *Claudio Arias* 2.00
255 *Andy Sides* 1.00
256 *Bear Bay* 2.00
257 *Bill McCarthy* 1.00
258 *Daniel Haigwood* 3.00
259 *Brian Sprout* 1.00
260 *Bryan Triplett* 1.00
261 *Steve Bondurant* 1.00
262 *Darwinson Salazar* 1.00
263 *David Shepard* 1.00
264 *Johan Silva* 1.50
265 *J.B. Thurmond* 1.00
266 *Brandon Moorhead* 1.00
267 *Kyle Nichols* 2.00
268 *Jonathan Sanchez* 1.00
269 *Mike Esposito* 1.00
270 *Erik Schindewolf* 2.00
271 *Peeter Ramos* 1.00
272 *Juan Senreiso* 1.00
273 *Travis Chick* 2.00
274 *Vinny Rottino* 1.00
275 *Micah Furtado* 1.00
276 *George Kottaras* 2.00
277 *Abel Gomez* 1.00
278 *Buck Coats* 1.00
279 *Ken Durost* 1.00
280 *Nick Touchstone* 1.00
281 *Jerry Owens* 2.00
282 *Stefan Bailie* 1.00
283 *Jesse Gutierrez* 1.00
284 *Chuck Tiffany* 3.00
285 *Brendan Ryan* 1.00
286 *Julio Pimentel* 1.00
287 *Shawn Bowman* 1.00
288 *Alexander Smit* 1.50
289 *Micah Schnurstein* 1.50
290 *Jared Gothreaux* 1.00
291 *Jair Jurrjens* 1.50
292 *Bobby Livingston* 1.00
293 *Ryan Speier* 1.00
294 *Zachary Parker* 1.00
295 *Christian Colonel* 1.00
296 *Scott Mitchinson* 1.00
297 *Neil Wilson* 1.00
298 *Chuck James* 8.00
299 *Heath Totten* 1.00
300 *Sean Tracey* 1.00
301 *Tadahito Iguchi* 2.50
302 *Matt Brown* 1.00
303 *Franklin Morales* 1.00
304 *Brandon Sing* 3.00
305 *D.J. Houlton* 1.50
306 *Jayce Tingler* 1.00
307 *Mitchell Arnold* 1.00
308 *Jim Burt* 1.00
309 *Jason Motte* 1.00
310 *David Gassner* 1.00
311 *Andy Santana* 1.00
312 *Kelvin Pichardo* 1.00
313 *Carlos Carrasco* 2.00
314 *Willy Mota* 2.00
315 *Frank Mata* 1.00
316 *Carlos Gonzalez* 8.00
317 *Jesse Floyd* 1.00
318 *Chris Young* 6.00
319 *Billy Sadler* 1.00
320 *Ricky Barrett* 1.00
321 *Benjamin Harrison* 1.00
322 *Steve Nelson* 1.00
323 *Daryl Thompson* 1.00
324 *Davis Romero* 1.00
325 *Jeremy Harts* 1.00
326 *Nick Masset* 1.00
327 *Thomas Pauly* 1.00
328 *Mike Garber* 1.00
329 *Kennard Bibbs* 1.00
330 *Colter Bean* 1.00
331 *Justin Verlander* 60.00
332 *Chip Cannon* 20.00
333 *Kevin Melillo* 25.00
334 *Jake Postlewait* 20.00
335 *Wes Swackhamer* 20.00
336 *Mike Rodriguez* 20.00
337 *Philip Humber* 40.00
338 *Jeff Niemann* 25.00
339 *Brian Miller* 20.00
340 *Chris Vines* 20.00
341 *Andy LaRoche* 65.00
342 Michael Bourn 25.00
343 *Eric Nielsen* 20.00
344 *Wladimir Balentien* 35.00
345 *Ismael Ramirez* 15.00
346 *Pedro Lopez* 20.00
347 *Shawn Bowman* 25.00
348 *Hayden Penn* 25.00
349 *Matthew Kemp* 30.00
350 *Brian Stavisky* 20.00
351 *C.J. Smith* 20.00
352 *Mike Morse* 35.00
353 *Billy Butler* 75.00

Refractor

Stars (1-165): 2-4X
Rookies (166-330): 1-2X
Inserted 1:4
Autograph (331-353): 1-2X
Production 500

X-Fractor

Stars (1-165): 3-5X
Rookies (166-330): 2-5X
Autograph (331-353): 1-2.5X
Production 225 sets

Blue Refractor

Stars (1-165): 3-5X
Rookies (166-330): 3-5X
Autograph (331-353): 1-2.5X
Production 150 sets

Gold Refractor

Stars (1-165): 8-15X
Rookies (166-330): 15-25X
Autograph (331-353): 3-6X
Production 50 sets

Red Refractor

No Pricing
Production 5 sets

Superfractor

No Pricing
Production one set

Printing Plates

No Pricing
Production one set per color

A-Rod Throwback

NM/M

Complete Set (4): 6.00
Common A-Rod 2.00
Inserted 1:9
Refractor: 2-3X
Production 499 sets
X-Fractor: 3-5X
Production 99 sets
Superfractor: No Pricing
Production one set
94AR Alex Rodriguez
95AR Alex Rodriguez
96AR Alex Rodriguez
97AR Alex Rodriguez

A-Rod Throwback Autograph

NM/M

Quantity produced listed
94AR Alex Rodriguez/1
95AR Alex Rodriguez/25
96AR Alex Rodriguez/50 160.00
97AR Alex Rodriguez/99 150.00

One of A Kind Autograph

No Pricing
Production 13
Cal Ripken Jr., Alex Rodriguez

2005 BOWMAN CHROME DRAFT PICKS & PROSPECTS

NM/M

Complete Set (180):
Common Player: .25
Common Rookie: 1.00
Common Rk Auto (166-180): 15.00
BDP1 Rickie Weeks .25
BDP2 Kyle Davies .25
BDP3 Garrett Atkins .25
BDP4 Chien-Ming Wang .25
BDP5 Dallas McPherson .25
BDP6 Dan Johnson .25
BDP7 Andy Sisco .25
BDP8 Ryan Doumit .25
BDP9 J.P. Howell .25
BDP10 Tim Stauffer .25
BDP11 Willy Taveras .25
BDP12 Aaron Hill .25
BDP13 Victor Diaz .25
BDP14 Wilson Betemit .25
BDP15 Ervin Santana .25
BDP16 Mike Morse .25
BDP17 Yadier Molina .25
BDP18 Kelly Johnson .25
BDP19 Clint Barmes .25
BDP20 Robinson Cano .25
BDP21 Brad Thompson .25
BDP22 Jorge Cantu .25
BDP23 Brad Halsey .25
BDP24 Lance Niekro .25
BDP25 D.J. Houlton .25
BDP26 Ryan Church .25
BDP27 Hayden Penn .25
BDP28 Chris Young .25
BDP29 Chad Orvella .25
BDP30 Mark Teahen .25
BDP31 *Mark McCormick* 1.00
BDP32 *Jay Bruce* 5.00
BDP33 *Beau Jones* 2.50
BDP34 *Tyler Greene* 1.50
BDP35 *Zach Ward* 1.00
BDP36 *Josh Bell* 2.50
BDP37 *Josh Wall* 2.00
BDP38 *Nick Webber* 1.00
BDP39 *Travis Buck* 2.50
BDP40 *Kyle Winters* 1.00
BDP41 *Mitch Boggs* 1.00
BDP42 *Tommy Mendoza* 1.50
BDP43 *Brad Corley* 1.50
BDP44 *Drew Butera* 1.00
BDP45 *Ryan Mount* 1.50
BDP46 *Tyler Herron* 1.00
BDP47 *Nick Weglarz* 4.00
BDP48 *Brandon Erbe* 4.00
BDP49 *Cody Allen* 1.00
BDP50 *Eric Fowler* 1.00
BDP51 *James Boone* 1.50
BDP52 *Josh Flores* 1.50
BDP53 *Brandon Monk* 2.00
BDP54 *Kieron Pope* 2.50
BDP55 *Kyle Cofield* 1.50
BDP56 *Brent Lillibridge* 1.00
BDP57 *Daryl Jones* 1.50
BDP58 *Eli Iorg* 2.00
BDP59 *Brett Hayes* 1.00
BDP60 *Mike Durant* 3.00
BDP61 *Michael Bowden* 3.00
BDP62 *Paul Kelly* 2.00
BDP63 *Andrew McCutchen* 5.00
BDP64 *Travis Wood* 2.00
BDP65 *Cesar Ramos* 1.00
BDP66 *Chaz Roe* 1.50
BDP67 *Matt Torra* 2.00
BDP68 *Kevin Slowey* 2.00
BDP69 *Trayvon Robinson* 1.50
BDP70 *Reid Engel* 1.50
BDP71 *Kris Harvey* 2.00
BDP72 *Craig Italiano* 2.50
BDP73 *Matt Maloney* 1.50
BDP74 *Sean West* 1.50
BDP75 *Henry Sanchez* 2.50
BDP76 *Scott Blue* 1.00
BDP77 *Jordan Schafer* 2.00
BDP78 *Chris Robinson* 1.00
BDP79 *Chris Hobdy* 1.00
BDP80 *Brandon Durden* 1.00
BDP81 *Clay Buchholz* 1.50
BDP82 *Josh Geer* 1.00
BDP83 *Sam LeCure* 1.00
BDP84 *Justin Thomas* 1.00
BDP85 *Brett Gardner* 1.00
BDP86 *Tommy Manzella* 1.00
BDP87 *Matt Green* 1.00
BDP88 *Yunel Escobar* 3.00
BDP89 *Mike Costanzo* 2.50
BDP90 *Nick Hundley* 1.00
BDP91 *Zach Simons* 1.00
BDP92 *Jacob Marceaux* 1.00
BDP93 *Jed Lowrie* 1.50
BDP94 *Brandon Snyder* 4.00
BDP95 *Matt Goyen* 1.00
BDP96 *Jon Egan* 1.50
BDP97 *Drew Thompson* 1.50
BDP98 *Bryan Anderson* 4.00
BDP99 *Clayton Richard* 1.00
BDP100 *Jimmy Shull* 1.00
BDP101 *Mark Pawelek* 5.00
BDP102 *P.J. Phillips* 1.50
BDP103 *John Drennen* 3.00
BDP104 *Nolan Reimold* 5.00
BDP105 *Troy Tulowitzki* 4.00
BDP106 *Kevin Whelan* 1.00
BDP107 *Wade Townsend* 2.00
BDP108 *Micah Owings* 1.00
BDP109 *Ryan Tucker* 1.50
BDP110 *Jeff Clement* 6.00
BDP111 *Josh Sullivan* 1.00
BDP112 *Jeff Lyman* 1.00
BDP113 *Brian Bogusevic* 1.50
BDP114 *Trevor Bell* 1.50
BDP115 *Brent Cox* 1.50
BDP116 *Michael Billek* 1.00
BDP117 *Garrett Olson* 1.50
BDP118 *Steven Johnson* 1.00
BDP119 *Chase Headley* 2.00
BDP120 *Daniel Carte* 1.50
BDP121 Francisco Liriano .25
BDP122 Fausto Carmona .25
BDP123 Zach Jackson .25
BDP124 Adam Loewen .25
BDP125 Chris Lambert .25
BDP126 *Scott Mathieson* 1.00
BDP127 Paul Maholm .25
BDP128 Fernando Nieve .25
BDP129 *Justin Verlander* 2.00
BDP130 Yusmeiro Petit .25
BDP131 Joel Zumaya .25
BDP132 Merkin Valdez .25
BDP133 *Ryan Garko* 2.50
BDP134 *Edison Volquez* 2.00
BDP135 *Russell Martin* 1.00
BDP136 Conor Jackson .25
BDP137 *Miguel Montero* 2.00
BDP138 Josh Barfield .25
BDP139 Delmon Young .50
BDP140 *Andy LaRoche* 3.00
BDP141 William Bergolla .25
BDP142 B.J. Upton .25
BDP143 *Hernan Iribarren* 1.00
BDP144 Brandon Wood 1.00
BDP145 Jose Bautista .25
BDP146 Edwin Encarnacion .25
BDP147 *Javier Herrera* 5.00
BDP148 Jeremy Hermida .25
BDP149 *Frank Diaz* 1.00
BDP150 *Chris Young* 1.00
BDP151 Shin-Soo Choo .25
BDP152 Kevin Thompson .25
BDP153 Hanley Ramirez .25
BDP154 Lastings Milledge .25
BDP155 Luis Montanez .25
BDP156 Justin Huber .25
BDP157 Zachary Duke .25
BDP158 Jeff Francoeur .50
BDP159 *Melky Cabrera* 1.00
BDP160 Bobby Jenks .25
BDP161 Ian Snell .25
BDP162 Fernando Cabrera .25
BDP163 Troy Patton .25
BDP164 Anthony Lerew .25
BDP165 *Nelson Cruz* 1.50
BDP166 *Stephen Drew* 100.00
BDP167 *Jered Weaver* 60.00
BDP168 *Ryan Braun* 40.00
BDP169 *John Mayberry* 25.00
BDP170 *Aaron Thompson* 20.00
BDP171 *Cesar Carrillo* 25.00
BDP172 *Jacoby Ellsbury* 30.00
BDP173 *Matt Garza* 20.00
BDP174 *Cliff Pennington* 25.00
BDP175 *Colby Rasmus* 40.00
BDP176 *Chris Volstad* 30.00
BDP177 *Ricky Romero* 20.00
BDP178 *Ryan Zimmerman* 80.00
BDP179 *C.J. Henry* 30.00
BDP180 *Eddy Martinez* 25.00

Refractor

Rookies: 2-4X
Inserted 1:11
Rk Autos (166-180): 1-1.5X
Production 500

X-Fractor

Rookies: 4-6X
Rk Autos (166-180): 1-2X
Production 250 sets

Blue Refract

Rookies: 4-6X
Rk Autos (166-180): 1.5-3X
Production 150 sets

Gold Refract

Rookies: 8-15X
Rk Autos (166-180): 4-6X
Production 50 sets

Red Refract

No Pricing
Production one set

SuperFractor

No Pricing
Production one set

2005 BOWMAN DRAFT PICKS & PROSPECTS

NM/M

Complete Set (165): 30.00
Commmon Player: .15
Common Rookie .25
Pack (5 + 2 Chrome): 5.00
Box (24): 100.00
BDP1 Rickie Weeks .15
BDP2 Kyle Davies .15
BDP3 Garrett Atkins .15
BDP4 Chien-Ming Wang .15
BDP5 Dallas McPherson .15
BDP6 Dan Johnson .15
BDP7 Andy Sisco .15
BDP8 Ryan Doumit .15
BDP9 J.P. Howell .15
BDP10 Tim Stauffer .15
BDP11 Willy Taveras .15
BDP12 Aaron Hill .15
BDP13 Victor Diaz .15
BDP14 Wilson Betemit .15
BDP15 Ervin Santana .15
BDP16 Mike Morse .15
BDP17 Yadier Molina .15
BDP18 Kelly Johnson .15
BDP19 Clint Barmes .15
BDP20 Robinson Cano .15
BDP21 Brad Thompson .15
BDP22 Jorge Cantu .15
BDP23 Brad Halsey .15
BDP24 Lance Niekro .15
BDP25 D.J. Houlton .15
BDP26 Ryan Church .15
BDP27 Hayden Penn .15
BDP28 Chris Young .15
BDP29 Chad Orvella .15
BDP30 Mark Teahen .15
BDP31 *Mark McCormick* .25
BDP32 *Jay Bruce* 1.50
BDP33 *Beau Jones* .75
BDP34 *Tyler Greene* .40
BDP35 *Zach Ward* .25
BDP36 *Josh Bell* .75
BDP37 *Josh Wall* .50
BDP38 *Nick Webber* .25
BDP39 *Travis Buck* .75
BDP40 *Kyle Winters* .25
BDP41 *Mitch Boggs* .25
BDP42 *Tommy Mendoza* .40
BDP43 *Brad Corley* .40
BDP44 *Drew Butera* .25
BDP45 *Ryan Mount* .40
BDP46 *Tyler Herron* .25
BDP47 *Nick Weglarz* 1.00
BDP48 *Brandon Erbe* 1.00
BDP49 *Cody Allen* .25
BDP50 *Eric Fowler* .25
BDP51 *James Boone* .40
BDP52 *Josh Flores* .40
BDP53 *Brandon Monk* .50
BDP54 *Kieron Pope* .75
BDP55 *Kyle Cofield* .40
BDP56 *Brent Lillibridge* .25
BDP57 *Daryl Jones* .40
BDP58 *Eli Iorg* .50
BDP59 *Brett Hayes* .25
BDP60 *Mike Durant* .75
BDP61 *Michael Bowden* .75
BDP62 *Paul Kelly* .50
BDP63 *Andrew McCutchen* 1.00
BDP64 *Travis Wood* .50
BDP65 *Cesar Ramos* .25
BDP66 *Chaz Roe* .40
BDP67 *Matt Torra* .50
BDP68 *Kevin Slowey* .50
BDP69 *Trayvon Robinson* .40
BDP70 *Reid Engel* .40
BDP71 *Kris Harvey* .50
BDP72 *Craig Italiano* .50
BDP73 *Matt Maloney* .40
BDP74 *Sean West* .40
BDP75 *Henry Sanchez* .50
BDP76 *Scott Blue* .25
BDP77 *Jordan Schafer* .50
BDP78 *Chris Robinson* .25
BDP79 *Chris Hobdy* .25
BDP80 *Brandon Durden* .25
BDP81 *Clay Buchholz* .40
BDP82 *Josh Geer* .25
BDP83 *Sam LeCure* .25
BDP84 *Justin Thomas* .25
BDP85 *Brett Gardner* .25
BDP86 *Tommy Manzella* .25
BDP87 *Matt Green* .25
BDP88 *Yunel Escobar* .75
BDP89 *Mike Costanzo* .75
BDP90 *Nick Hundley* .25
BDP91 *Zach Simons* .25
BDP92 *Jacob Marceaux* .25
BDP93 *Jed Lowrie* .40
BDP94 *Brandon Snyder* 1.00
BDP95 *Matt Goyen* .25
BDP96 *Jon Egan* .40
BDP97 *Drew Thompson* .40
BDP98 *Bryan Anderson* 1.00
BDP99 *Clayton Richard* .25
BDP100 *Jimmy Shull* .25
BDP101 *Mark Pawelek* 1.00
BDP102 *P.J. Phillips* .40
BDP103 *John Drennen* .75
BDP104 *Nolan Reimold* 1.00
BDP105 *Troy Tulowitzki* 1.00
BDP106 *Kevin Whelan* .25
BDP107 *Wade Townsend* .50
BDP108 *Micah Owings* .25
BDP109 *Ryan Tucker* .40
BDP110 *Jeff Clement* 1.50
BDP111 *Josh Sullivan* .25
BDP112 *Jeff Lyman* .25
BDP113 *Brian Bogusevic* .40
BDP114 *Trevor Bell* .40
BDP115 *Brent Cox* 1.50
BDP116 *Michael Billek* .25
BDP117 *Garrett Olson* .40
BDP118 *Steven Johnson* .25
BDP119 *Chase Headley* .50
BDP120 *Daniel Carte* .40
BDP121 Francisco Liriano .15
BDP122 Fausto Carmona .15
BDP123 Zach Jackson .15
BDP124 Adam Loewen .15
BDP125 Chris Lambert .15
BDP126 *Scott Mathieson* .25
BDP127 Paul Maholm .15
BDP128 Fernando Nieve .15
BDP129 *Justin Verlander* .50
BDP130 Yusmeiro Petit .15
BDP131 Joel Zumaya .15
BDP132 Merkin Valdez .15
BDP133 *Ryan Garko* .75
BDP134 *Edison Volquez* .50
BDP135 *Russell Martin* .25
BDP136 Conor Jackson .15
BDP137 *Miguel Montero* .50
BDP138 Josh Barfield .15
BDP139 Delmon Young .25
BDP140 *Andy LaRoche* .75
BDP141 William Bergolla .15
BDP142 B.J. Upton .15
BDP143 *Hernan Iribarren* .25
BDP144 Brandon Wood .25
BDP145 Jose Bautista .15
BDP146 Edwin Encarnacion .15
BDP147 *Javier Herrera* 1.00
BDP148 Jeremy Hermida .15
BDP149 *Frank Diaz* .25
BDP150 *Chris Young* .25
BDP151 Shin-Soo Choo .15
BDP152 Kevin Thompson .15
BDP153 Hanley Ramirez .15
BDP154 Lastings Milledge .15
BDP155 Luis Montanez .15
BDP156 Justin Huber .15
BDP157 Zachary Duke .15
BDP158 Jeff Francoeur .25
BDP159 *Melky Cabrera* .25
BDP160 Bobby Jenks .15
BDP161 Ian Snell .15
BDP162 Fernando Cabrera .15
BDP163 Troy Patton .15
BDP164 Anthony Lerew .15
BDP165 *Nelson Cruz* .40

White

Rookies: 3-5X
Production 225 sets

Red

No Pricing
Production one set

Base Relic Variat.

		NM/M
Common Player:		4.00
BDP121	Francisco Liriano	8.00
BDP122	Fausto Carmona	4.00
BDP123	Zach Jackson	4.00
BDP124	Adam Loewen	4.00
BDP125	Chris Lambert	4.00
BDP126	Scott Mathieson	4.00
BDP127	Paul Maholm	4.00
BDP128	Fernando Nieve	4.00
BDP129	Justin Verlander	6.00
BDP130	Yusmeiro Petit	6.00
BDP131	Joel Zumaya	4.00
BDP132	Merkin Valdez	4.00
BDP133	Ryan Garko	4.00
BDP134	Edison Volquez	4.00
BDP135	Russell Martin	4.00
BDP136	Conor Jackson	4.00
BDP137	Miguel Montero	6.00
BDP138	Josh Barfield	4.00
BDP139	Delmon Young	6.00
BDP140	Andy LaRoche	6.00
BDP141	William Bergolla	4.00
BDP142	B.J. Upton	4.00
BDP143	Hernan Iribarren	4.00
BDP144	Brandon Wood	10.00
BDP145	Jose Bautista	4.00
BDP146	Edwin Encarnacion	4.00
BDP147	Javier Herrera	6.00
BDP148	Jeremy Hermida	4.00
BDP149	Frank Diaz	4.00
BDP150	Chris Young	6.00

Signs of the Future

		NM/M
Common Player:		8.00
HB	Homer Bailey	10.00
BB	Bill Bray	8.00
JF	Jeff Frazier	8.00
GG	Greg Golson	8.00
AG	Angel Guzman	10.00
JH	Justin Hoyman	8.00
JJ	Justin Jones	8.00
DL	Donald Lucey	
TL	Tyler Lumsden	8.00
DM	David Murphy	10.00
JP	Jonathan Poterson	8.00
DP	David Purcey	8.00
RR	Richie Robnett	8.00
JS	Jeremy Sowers	8.00

2005 BOWMAN'S BEST

		NM/M
Common Player:		.25
Common Rookie:		1.00
Common Rookie Auto. (101-143):		10.00
Pack (5):		10.00
Box (10):		90.00
1	Jose Vidro	.25
2	Adam Dunn	.50
3	Manny Ramirez	.75
4	Miguel Tejada	.50
5	Ken Griffey Jr.	1.00
6	Pedro Martinez	1.00
7	Alex Rodriguez	1.50
8	Ichiro Suzuki	1.50
9	Alfonso Soriano	.75
10	Brian Giles	.25
11	Roger Clemens	2.00
12	Todd Helton	.50
13	Ivan Rodriguez	.50
14	David Ortiz	.75
15	Sammy Sosa	1.00
16	Chipper Jones	.75
17	Mark Buehrle	1.00
18	Miguel Cabrera	.75
19	Johan Santana	.75
20	Randy Johnson	.75
21	Jim Thome	.50
22	Vladimir Guerrero	.75
23	Dontrelle Willis	.50
24	Nomar Garciaparra	1.00
25	Barry Bonds	2.00
26	Curt Schilling	.75
27	Carlos Beltran	.50
28	Albert Pujols	2.00
29	Mark Prior	.75
30	Derek Jeter	2.00
31	*Ryan Garko*	4.00
32	*Eulogio de la Cruz*	1.00
33	*Luke Scott*	2.00
34	*Shane Costa*	2.00
35	*Casey McGehee*	1.00
36	*Jered Weaver*	8.00
37	*Kevin Melillo*	2.00
38	*D.J. Houlton*	2.00
39	*Brandon Moorhead*	1.00
40	*Jerry Owens*	1.00
41	*Elliot Johnson*	1.00
42	*Kevin West*	2.00
43	*Hernan Iribarren*	1.00
44	*Miguel Montero*	8.00
45	*Craig Tatum*	1.00
46	*Ryan Sweeney*	2.00
47	*Micah Furtado*	1.00
48	*Cody Haerther*	1.00
49	*Erik Abreu*	1.00
50	*Chuck Tiffany*	2.00
51	*Tadahito Iguchi*	4.00
52	*Frank Diaz*	3.00
53	*Errol Simonitsch*	1.00
54	*Wade Robinson*	2.00
55	*Adam Boeve*	1.00
56	*Steve Bondurant*	1.00
57	*Jason Motte*	1.00
58	*Juan Senreiso*	1.00
59	*Vinny Rottino*	1.00
60	*Jai Miller*	1.00
61	*Thomas Pauly*	1.00
62	*Tony Giarratano*	1.00
63	*Alexander Smit*	1.00
64	*Keiichi Yabu*	1.00
65	*Brian Bannister*	1.00
66	*Kennard Bibbs*	1.00
67	*Anthony Reyes*	4.00
68	*Tom Oldham*	1.00
69	*Benjamin Harrison*	1.00
70	*Daryl Thompson*	1.00
71	*Kevin Collins*	1.00
72	*Wes Swackhamer*	2.00
73	*Landon Powell*	2.00
74	*Matt Brown*	1.00
75	*Russell Martin*	1.00
76	*Nick Touchstone*	1.00
77	*Steven White*	1.00
78	*Ian Bladergroen*	1.00
79	*Sean Marshall*	1.00
80	*Nick Masset*	1.00
81	*Ryan Goleski*	2.00
82	*Matt Campbell*	1.00
83	*Manny Parra*	1.00
84	*Melky Cabrera*	3.00
85	*Ryan Feierabend*	3.00
86	*Nate McLouth*	2.00
87	*Glen Perkins*	2.00
88	*Kila Kaaihue*	1.00
89	*Dana Eveland*	1.00
90	*Tyler Pelland*	1.00
91	*Matt Van Der Bosch*	1.00
92	*Andy Santana*	1.00
93	*Eric Nielsen*	1.00
94	*Brendan Ryan*	1.00
95	*Ian Kinsler*	2.00
96	*Matthew Kemp*	3.00
97	*Stephen Drew*	12.00
98	*Peeter Ramos*	2.00
99	*Chris Seddon*	2.00
100	*Chuck James*	10.00
101	*Travis Chick*	10.00
102	*Justin Verlander*	25.00
103	*Billy Butler*	60.00
104	*Chris Young*	25.00
105	*Jake Postlewait*	15.00
106	*C.J. Smith*	10.00
107	*Mike Rodriguez*	12.00
108	*Philip Humber*	20.00
109	*Jeff Niemann*	20.00
110	*Brian Miller*	10.00
111	*Chris Vines*	12.00
112	*Andy LaRoche*	40.00
113	*Mike Bourne*	12.00
114	*Wladimir Balentien*	15.00
115	*Ismael Ramirez*	15.00
116	*Hayden Penn*	15.00
117	*Pedro Lopez*	12.00
118	*Shawn Bowman*	15.00
119	*Chad Orvella*	12.00
120	*Sean Tracey*	10.00
121	*Bobby Livingston*	15.00
122	*Michael Rogers*	10.00
123	*Willy Mota*	15.00
124	*Brandon McCarthy*	25.00
125	*Mike Morse*	20.00
126	*Matt Lindstrom*	15.00
127	*Brian Stavisky*	10.00
128	*Rich Gardner*	12.00
129	*Scott Mitchinson*	12.00
130	*Billy McCarthy*	12.00
131	*Brandon Sing*	15.00
132	*Matt Albers*	10.00
133	*George Kottaras*	15.00
134	*Luis Hernandez*	10.00
135	*Humberto Sanchez*	10.00
136	*Buck Coats*	12.00
137	*Jonathan Barratt*	12.00
138	*Raul Tablado*	12.00
139	*Jake Mullinax*	15.00
140	*Edgar Varela*	12.00
141	*Ryan Garko*	20.00
142	*Nate McLouth*	10.00
143	*Shane Costa*	10.00

Green Refractor

Stars:	2-3X
Rookies:	1-2X
Production 899	
Rookie Autos.	1-1.5X
Production 399	

Blue Refractor

Stars:	2-4X
Rookies:	1-2X
Production 499	
Rookie Autos.	1-1.5X
Production 299	

Red Refractor

Stars:	3-5X
Rookies:	2-3X
Rookie Autos.	1.5-2X
Production 199 sets	

Silver Refractor

Stars:	4-6X
Rookies:	2-3X
Rookie Autos.	1.5-3X
Production 99 sets	

Gold Refractor

No Pricing
Production 25 sets

Printing Plates

No Pricing
Production one set for each color

Printing Plates Autograph

No Pricing
Production one set for each color

A-Rod Throwback

		NM/M
Production 100		
AR	Alex Rodriguez	160.00

Bowman's Best Shortstops

Production 25		
RRB	Cal Ripken Jr., Alex Rodriguez, Matt Bush	

Mirror Image Spokesmen

Production 10		
BR	Barry Bonds, Alex Rodriguez	

Mirror Image Throwback

		NM/M
Production 50		
RR	Cal Ripken Jr., Alex Rodriguez	450.00

1996 CIRCA

		NM/M
Complete Set (200):		15.00
Common Player:		.10
Pack (8):		1.50
Wax Box (24):		30.00
1	Roberto Alomar	.40
2	Brady Anderson	.10
3	*Rocky Coppinger*	.10
4	Eddie Murray	.75
5	Mike Mussina	.50
6	Randy Myers	.10
7	Rafael Palmeiro	.75
8	Cal Ripken Jr.	2.00
9	Jose Canseco	.50
10	Roger Clemens	1.00
11	Mike Greenwell	.10
12	Tim Naehring	.10
13	John Valentin	.10
14	Mo Vaughn	.10
15	Tim Wakefield	.10
16	Jim Abbott	.10
17	Garret Anderson	.10
18	Jim Edmonds	.10
19	*Darin Erstad*	2.00
20	Chuck Finley	.10
21	Troy Percival	.10
22	Tim Salmon	.15
23	J.T. Snow	.10
24	Wilson Alvarez	.10
25	Harold Baines	.10
26	Ray Durham	.10
27	Alex Fernandez	.10
28	Tony Phillips	.10
29	Frank Thomas	.75
30	Robin Ventura	.10
31	Sandy Alomar Jr.	.10
32	Albert Belle	.15
33	Kenny Lofton	.10
34	Dennis Martinez	.10
35	Jose Mesa	.10
36	Charles Nagy	.10
37	Manny Ramirez	.75
37p	Manny Ramirez (overprinted "PROMOTIONAL SAMPLE")	2.00
38	Jim Thome	.10
39	Travis Fryman	.10
40	Bob Higginson	.10
41	Melvin Nieves	.10
42	Alan Trammell	.10
43	Kevin Appier	.10
44	Johnny Damon	.20
45	Keith Lockhart	.10
46	Jeff Montgomery	.10
47	Joe Randa	.10
48	Bip Roberts	.10
49	Ricky Bones	.10
50	Jeff Cirillo	.10
51	Marc Newfield	.10
52	Dave Nilsson	.10
53	Kevin Seitzer	.10
54	Ron Coomer	.10
55	Marty Cordova	.10
56	Roberto Kelly	.10
57	Chuck Knoblauch	.10
58	Paul Molitor	.75
59	Kirby Puckett	1.00
60	Scott Stahoviak	.10
61	Wade Boggs	1.00
62	David Cone	.10
63	Cecil Fielder	.10
64	Dwight Gooden	.10
65	Derek Jeter	2.00
66	Tino Martinez	.10
67	Paul O'Neill	.10
68	Andy Pettitte	.35
69	Ruben Rivera	.10
70	Bernie Williams	.20
71	Geronimo Berroa	.10
72	Jason Giambi	.45
73	Mark McGwire	1.50

74	Terry Steinbach	.10
75	Todd Van Poppel	.10
76	Jay Buhner	.10
77	Norm Charlton	.10
78	Ken Griffey Jr.	1.25
79	Randy Johnson	.75
80	Edgar Martinez	.10
81	Alex Rodriguez	1.50
82	Paul Sorrento	.10
83	Dan Wilson	.10
84	Will Clark	.15
85	Kevin Elster	.10
86	Juan Gonzalez	.75
87	Rusty Greer	.10
88	Ken Hill	.10
89	Mark McLemore	.10
90	Dean Palmer	.10
91	Roger Pavlik	.10
92	Ivan Rodriguez	.75
93	Joe Carter	.10
94	Carlos Delgado	.35
95	Juan Guzman	.10
96	John Olerud	.10
97	Ed Sprague	.10
98	Jermaine Dye	.10
99	Tom Glavine	.25
100	Marquis Grissom	.10
101	Andruw Jones	.75
102	Chipper Jones	1.00
103	David Justice	.10
104	Ryan Klesko	.10
105	Greg Maddux	1.00
106	Fred McGriff	.10
107	John Smoltz	.10
108	Brant Brown	.10
109	Mark Grace	.25
110	Brian McRae	.10
111	Ryne Sandberg	1.00
112	Sammy Sosa	1.25
113	Steve Trachsel	.10
114	Bret Boone	.10
115	Eric Davis	.10
116	Steve Gibralter	.10
117	Barry Larkin	.10
118	Reggie Sanders	.10
119	John Smiley	.10
120	Dante Bichette	.10
121	Ellis Burks	.10
122	Vinny Castilla	.10
123	Andres Galarraga	.10
124	Larry Walker	.10
125	Eric Young	.10
126	Kevin Brown	.10
127	Greg Colbrunn	.10
128	Jeff Conine	.10
129	Charles Johnson	.10
130	Al Leiter	.10
131	Gary Sheffield	.50
132	Devon White	.10
133	Jeff Bagwell	.75
134	Derek Bell	.10
135	Craig Biggio	.10
136	Doug Drabek	.10
137	Brian Hunter	.10
138	Darryl Kile	.10
139	Shane Reynolds	.10
140	Brett Butler	.10
141	Eric Karros	.10
142	Ramon Martinez	.10
143	Raul Mondesi	.10
144	Hideo Nomo	.75
145	Chan Ho Park	.10
146	Mike Piazza	1.25
147	Moises Alou	.10
148	Yamil Benitez	.10
149	Mark Grudzielanek	.10
150	Pedro Martinez	.75
151	Henry Rodriguez	.10
152	David Segui	.10
153	Rondell White	.10
154	Carlos Baerga	.10
155	John Franco	.10
156	Bernard Gilkey	.10
157	Todd Hundley	.10
158	Jason Isringhausen	.10
159	Lance Johnson	.10
160	Alex Ochoa	.10
161	Rey Ordonez	.10
162	Paul Wilson	.10
163	Ron Blazier	.10
164	Ricky Bottalico	.10
165	Jim Eisenreich	.10
166	Pete Incaviglia	.10
167	Mickey Morandini	.10
168	Ricky Otero	.10
169	Curt Schilling	.25
170	Jay Bell	.10
171	Charlie Hayes	.10
172	Jason Kendall	.10
173	Jeff King	.10
174	Al Martin	.10
175	Alan Benes	.10
176	Royce Clayton	.10
177	Brian Jordan	.10
178	Ray Lankford	.10
179	John Mabry	.10
180	Willie McGee	.10
181	Ozzie Smith	1.00
182	Todd Stottlemyre	.10
183	Andy Ashby	.10
184	Ken Caminiti	.10
185	Steve Finley	.10
186	Tony Gwynn	1.00
187	Rickey Henderson	.75
188	Wally Joyner	.10
189	Fernando Valenzuela	.10
190	Greg Vaughn	.10
191	Rod Beck	.10
192	Barry Bonds	2.00
193	Shawon Dunston	.10
194	Chris Singleton	.10
195	Robby Thompson	.10
196	Matt Williams	.10
197	Barry Bonds Checklist	.75
198	Ken Griffey Jr. Checklist	.65
199	Cal Ripken Jr. Checklist	.75
200	Frank Thomas Checklist	.40

Rave

	NM/M
Complete Set (200):	500.00
Common Player:	2.00
Stars:	30X

(See 1996 Circa for checklist and base card values.)

Access

		NM/M
Complete Set (30):		50.00
Common Player:		.60
1	Cal Ripken Jr.	6.00
2	Mo Vaughn	.60
3	Tim Salmon	.75
4	Frank Thomas	2.00
5	Albert Belle	.75
6	Kenny Lofton	.60
7	Manny Ramirez	2.00
8	Paul Molitor	2.00
9	Kirby Puckett	3.00
10	Paul O'Neill	.60
11	Mark McGwire	5.00
12	Ken Griffey Jr.	4.00
13	Randy Johnson	2.00
14	Greg Maddux	3.00
15	John Smoltz	.60
16	Sammy Sosa	4.00
17	Barry Larkin	.60
18	Gary Sheffield	1.00
19	Jeff Bagwell	2.00
20	Hideo Nomo	2.00
21	Mike Piazza	4.00
22	Moises Alou	.60
23	Henry Rodriguez	.60
24	Rey Ordonez	.60
25	Jay Bell	.60
26	Ozzie Smith	3.00
27	Tony Gwynn	3.00
28	Rickey Henderson	2.00
29	Barry Bonds	6.00
30	Matt Williams	.60

Boss

		NM/M
Complete Set (50):		50.00
Common Player:		.45
1	Roberto Alomar	1.00
2	Cal Ripken Jr.	5.00
2p	Cal Ripken Jr. (overprinted "PROMOTIONAL SAMPLE")	3.00
3	Jose Canseco	1.50
4	Mo Vaughn	.45
5	Tim Salmon	.60
6	Frank Thomas	2.00
7	Robin Ventura	.45
8	Albert Belle	.60
9	Kenny Lofton	.45
10	Manny Ramirez	2.00
11	Dave Nilsson	.45
12	Chuck Knoblauch	.45
13	Paul Molitor	2.00
14	Kirby Puckett	3.00
15	Wade Boggs	3.00
16	Dwight Gooden	.45
17	Paul O'Neill	.45
18	Mark McGwire	4.00
19	Jay Buhner	.45
20	Ken Griffey Jr.	3.50
21	Randy Johnson	2.00
22	Will Clark	.60
23	Juan Gonzalez	2.00
24	Joe Carter	.45
25	Tom Glavine	.45
26	Ryan Klesko	.45
27	Greg Maddux	3.00
28	John Smoltz	.45
29	Ryne Sandberg	3.00
30	Sammy Sosa	3.50
31	Barry Larkin	.45
32	Reggie Sanders	.45
33	Dante Bichette	.45
34	Andres Galarraga	.45
35	Charles Johnson	.45
36	Gary Sheffield	1.50
37	Jeff Bagwell	2.00
38	Hideo Nomo	2.00
39	Mike Piazza	3.50
40	Moises Alou	.45
41	Henry Rodriguez	.45
42	Rey Ordonez	.45
43	Ricky Otero	.45
44	Jay Bell	.45
45	Royce Clayton	.45
46	Ozzie Smith	3.00
47	Tony Gwynn	3.00
48	Rickey Henderson	2.00
49	Barry Bonds	5.00
50	Matt Williams	.45

1997 CIRCA

		NM/M
Complete Set (400):		16.00
Common Player:		.10
Pack (8):		1.00
Retail Wax Box (18):		15.00
Hobby Wax Box (36):		30.00
1	Kenny Lofton	.10
2	Ray Durham	.10
3	Mariano Rivera	.20
4	Jon Lieber	.10
5	Tim Salmon	.15
6	Mark Grudzielanek	.10
7	Neifi Perez	.10
8	Cal Ripken Jr.	3.00
9	John Olerud	.10
10	Edgar Renteria	.10
11	Jose Rosado	.10
12	Mickey Morandini	.10
13	Orlando Miller	.10
14	Ben McDonald	.10
15	Hideo Nomo	.75
16	Fred McGriff	.10
17	Sean Berry	.10
18	Roger Pavlik	.10
19	Aaron Sele	.10
20	Joey Hamilton	.10
21	Roger Clemens	1.25
22	Jose Herrera	.10
23	Ryne Sandberg	1.00
24	Ken Griffey Jr.	1.50
25	Barry Bonds	3.00
26	Dan Naulty	.10
27	Wade Boggs	1.00
28	Ray Lankford	.10
29	Rico Brogna	.10
30	Wally Joyner	.10
31	F.P. Santangelo	.10
32	Vinny Castilla	.10
33	Eddie Murray	.75
34	Kevin Elster	.10
35	Mike Macfarlane	.10
36	Jeff Kent	.10
37	Orlando Merced	.10
38	Jason Isringhausen	.10
39	Chad Ogea	.10
40	Greg Gagne	.10
41	Curt Lyons	.10
42	Mo Vaughn	.10
43	Rusty Greer	.10
44	Shane Reynolds	.10
45	Frank Thomas	.75
46	Chris Hoiles	.10
47	Scott Sanders	.10
48	Mark Lemke	.10
49	Fernando Vina	.10
50	Mark McGwire	2.00
51	Bernie Williams	.15
52	Bobby Higginson	.10
53	Kevin Tapani	.10
54	Rich Becker	.10
55	*Felix Heredia*	.30
56	Delino DeShields	.10
57	Rick Wilkins	.10
58	Edgardo Alfonzo	.10
59	Brett Butler	.10
60	Ed Sprague	.10
61	Joe Randa	.10
62	Ugueth Urbina	.10
63	Todd Greene	.10
64	Devon White	.10
65	Bruce Ruffin	.10
66	Mark Gardner	.10
67	Omar Vizquel	.10
68	Luis Gonzalez	.25
69	Tom Glavine	.25
70	Cal Eldred	.10
71	William VanLandingham	.10
72	Jay Buhner	.10
73	James Baldwin	.10
74	Robin Jennings	.10
75	Terry Steinbach	.10
76	Billy Taylor	.10
77	Armando Benitez	.10
78	Joe Girardi	.10
79	Jay Bell	.10
80	Damon Buford	.10
81	Deion Sanders	.15
82	Bill Haselman	.10
83	John Flaherty	.10
84	Todd Stottlemyre	.10
85	J.T. Snow	.10
86	Felipe Lira	.10
87	Steve Avery	.10
88	Trey Beamon	.10
89	Alex Gonzalez	.10
90	Mark Clark	.10
91	Shane Andrews	.10
92	Randy Myers	.10
93	Gary Gaetti	.10
94	Jeff Blauser	.10
95	Tony Batista	.10
96	Todd Worrell	.10
97	Jim Edmonds	.10
98	Eric Young	.10
99	Roberto Kelly	.10
100	Alex Rodriguez	2.00
100p	Alex Rodriguez (overprinted "PROMOTIONAL SAMPLE")	2.00
101	Julio Franco	.10
102	Jeff Bagwell	.75
103	Bobby Witt	.10
104	Tino Martinez	.10
105	Shannon Stewart	.15
106	Brian Banks	.10
107	Eddie Taubensee	.10
108	Terry Mulholland	.10
109	Lyle Mouton	.10
110	Jeff Conine	.10
111	Johnny Damon	.20
112	Quilvio Veras	.10
113	Wilton Guerrero	.10
114	Dmitri Young	.10
115	Garret Anderson	.10
116	Bill Pulsipher	.10
117	Jacob Brumfield	.10
118	Mike Lansing	.10
119	Jose Canseco	.50
120	Mike Bordick	.10
121	Kevin Stocker	.10
122	Frank Rodriguez	.10
123	Mike Cameron	.10
124	*Tony Womack*	.25
125	Bret Boone	.10
126	Moises Alou	.10
127	Tim Naehring	.10
128	Brant Brown	.10
129	Todd Zeile	.10
130	Dave Nilsson	.10
131	Donne Wall	.10
132	Jose Mesa	.10
133	Mark McLemore	.10
134	Mike Stanton	.10
135	Dan Wilson	.10
136	Jose Offerman	.10
137	David Justice	.10

#	Player	Value
138	Kirt Manwaring	.10
139	Raul Casanova	.10
140	Ron Coomer	.10
141	Dave Hollins	.10
142	Shawn Estes	.10
143	Darren Daulton	.10
144	Turk Wendell	.10
145	Darrin Fletcher	.10
146	Marquis Grissom	.10
147	Andy Benes	.10
148	Nomar Garciaparra	1.50
149	Andy Pettitte	.30
150	Tony Gwynn	1.00
151	Robb Nen	.10
152	Kevin Seitzer	.10
153	Ariel Prieto	.10
154	Scott Karl	.10
155	Carlos Baerga	.10
156	Wilson Alvarez	.10
157	Thomas Howard	.10
158	Kevin Appier	.10
159	Russ Davis	.10
160	Justin Thompson	.10
161	Pete Schourek	.10
162	John Burkett	.10
163	Roberto Alomar	.25
164	Darren Holmes	.10
165	Travis Miller	.10
166	Mark Langston	.10
167	Juan Guzman	.10
168	Pedro Astacio	.10
169	Mark Johnson	.10
170	Mark Leiter	.10
171	Heathcliff Slocumb	.10
172	Dante Bichette	.10
173	*Brian Giles*	1.00
174	Paul Wilson	.10
175	Eric Davis	.10
176	Charles Johnson	.10
177	Willie Greene	.10
178	Geronimo Berroa	.10
179	Mariano Duncan	.10
180	Robert Person	.10
181	David Segui	.10
182	Ozzie Guillen	.10
183	Osvaldo Fernandez	.10
184	Dean Palmer	.10
185	Bob Wickman	.10
186	Eric Karros	.10
187	Travis Fryman	.10
188	Andy Ashby	.10
189	Scott Stahoviak	.10
190	Norm Charlton	.10
191	Craig Paquette	.10
192	John Smoltz	.10
193	Orel Hershiser	.10
194	Glenallen Hill	.10
195	George Arias	.10
196	Brian Jordan	.10
197	Greg Vaughn	.10
198	Rafael Palmeiro	.75
199	Darryl Kile	.10
200	Derek Jeter	3.00
201	Jose Vizcaino	.10
202	Rick Aguilera	.10
203	Jason Schmidt	.10
204	Trot Nixon	.10
205	Tom Pagnozzi	.10
206	Mark Wohlers	.10
207	Lance Johnson	.10
208	Carlos Delgado	.40
209	Cliff Floyd	.10
210	Kent Mercker	.10
211	Matt Mieske	.10
212	Ismael Valdes	.10
213	Shawon Dunston	.10
214	Melvin Nieves	.10
215	Tony Phillips	.10
216	Scott Spiezio	.10
217	Michael Tucker	.10
218	Matt Williams	.10
219	Ricky Otero	.10
220	Kevin Ritz	.10
221	Darryl Strawberry	.10
222	Troy Percival	.10
223	Eugene Kingsale	.10
224	Julian Tavarez	.10
225	Jermaine Dye	.10
226	Jason Kendall	.10
227	Sterling Hitchcock	.10
228	Jeff Cirillo	.10
229	Roberto Hernandez	.10
230	Ricky Bottalico	.10
231	Bobby Bonilla	.10
232	Edgar Martinez	.10
233	John Valentin	.10
234	Ellis Burks	.10
235	Benito Santiago	.10
236	Terrell Wade	.10
237	Armando Reynoso	.10
238	Danny Graves	.10
239	Ken Hill	.10
240	Dennis Eckersley	.65
241	Darin Erstad	.65
242	Lee Smith	.10
243	Cecil Fielder	.10
244	Tony Clark	.10
245	Scott Erickson	.10
246	Bob Abreu	.10
247	Ruben Sierra	.10
248	Chili Davis	.10
249	Darryl Hamilton	.10
250	Albert Belle	.15
251	Todd Hollandsworth	.10
252	Terry Adams	.10
253	Rey Ordonez	.10
254	Steve Finley	.10
255	Jose Valentin	.10
256	Royce Clayton	.10
257	Sandy Alomar	.10
258	Mike Lieberthal	.10
259	Ivan Rodriguez	.65
260	Rod Beck	.10
261	Ron Karkovice	.10
262	Mark Gubicza	.10
263	Chris Holt	.10
264	Jaime Bluma	.10
265	Francisco Cordova	.10
266	Javy Lopez	.10
267	Reggie Jefferson	.10
268	Kevin Brown	.10
269	Scott Brosius	.10
270	Dwight Gooden	.10
271	Marty Cordova	.10
272	Jeff Brantley	.10
273	Joe Carter	.10
274	Todd Jones	.10
275	Sammy Sosa	1.50
276	Randy Johnson	.75
277	B.J. Surhoff	.10
278	Chan Ho Park	.10
279	Jamey Wright	.10
280	Manny Ramirez	.75
281	John Franco	.10
282	Tim Worrell	.10
283	Scott Rolen	.60
284	Reggie Sanders	.10
285	Mike Fetters	.10
286	Tim Wakefield	.10
287	Trevor Hoffman	.10
288	Donovan Osborne	.10
289	Phil Nevin	.10
290	Jermaine Allensworth	.10
291	Rocky Coppinger	.10
292	Tim Raines	.10
293	Henry Rodriguez	.10
294	Paul Sorrento	.10
295	Tom Goodwin	.10
296	Raul Mondesi	.10
297	Allen Watson	.10
298	Derek Bell	.10
299	Gary Sheffield	.45
300	Paul Molitor	.75
301	Shawn Green	.15
302	Darren Oliver	.10
303	Jack McDowell	.10
304	Denny Neagle	.10
305	Doug Drabek	.10
306	Mel Rojas	.10
307	Andres Galarraga	.10
308	Alex Ochoa	.10
309	Gary DiSarcina	.10
310	Ron Gant	.10
311	Gregg Jefferies	.10
312	Ruben Rivera	.10
313	Vladimir Guerrero	.75
314	Willie Adams	.10
315	Bip Roberts	.10
326	Mark Grace	.15
317	Bernard Gilkey	.10
318	Marc Newfield	.10
319	Al Leiter	.10
320	Otis Nixon	.10
321	Tom Candiotti	.10
322	Mike Stanley	.10
323	Jeff Fassero	.10
324	Billy Wagner	.10
325	Todd Walker	.10
326	Chad Curtis	.10
327	Quinton McCracken	.10
328	Will Clark	.15
329	Andruw Jones	.75
330	Robin Ventura	.10
331	Curtis Pride	.10
332	Barry Larkin	.10
333	Jimmy Key	.10
334	David Wells	.10
335	Mike Holtz	.10
336	Paul Wagner	.10
337	Greg Maddux	1.00
338	Curt Schilling	.35
339	Steve Trachsel	.10
340	John Wetteland	.10
341	Rickey Henderson	.75
342	Ernie Young	.10
343	Harold Baines	.10
344	Bobby Jones	.10
345	Jeff D'Amico	.10
346	John Mabry	.10
347	Pedro Martinez	.75
348	Mark Lewis	.10
349	Dan Miceli	.10
350	Chuck Knoblauch	.10
351	John Smiley	.10
352	Brady Anderson	.10
353	Jim Leyritz	.10
354	Al Martin	.10
355	Pat Hentgen	.10
356	Mike Piazza	1.50
357	Charles Nagy	.10
358	Luis Castillo	.10
359	Paul O'Neill	.10
360	Steve Reed	.10
361	Tom Gordon	.10
362	Craig Biggio	.10
363	Jeff Montgomery	.10
364	Jamie Moyer	.10
365	Ryan Klesko	.10
366	Todd Hundley	.10
367	Bobby Estalella	.10
368	Jason Giambi	.65
369	Brian Hunter	.10
370	Ramon Martinez	.10
371	Carlos Garcia	.10
372	Hal Morris	.10
373	Juan Gonzalez	.75
374	Brian McRae	.10
375	Mike Mussina	.60
376	John Ericks	.10
377	Larry Walker	.10
378	Chris Gomez	.10
379	John Jaha	.10
380	Rondell White	.10
381	Chipper Jones	1.00
382	David Cone	.10
383	Alan Benes	.10
384	Troy O'Leary	.10
385	Ken Caminiti	.10
386	Jeff King	.10
387	Mike Hampton	.10
388	Jaime Navarro	.10
389	Brad Radke	.10
390	Joey Cora	.10
391	Jim Thome	.10
392	Alex Fernandez	.10
393	Chuck Finley	.10
394	Andruw Jones Checklist	.35
395	Ken Griffey Jr. Checklist	.60
396	Frank Thomas Checklist	.35
397	Alex Rodriguez Checklist	.75
398	Cal Ripken Jr. Checklist	1.00
399	Mike Piazza Checklist	.60
400	Greg Maddux Checklist	.45

Rave

		NM/M
Complete Set (400):		500.00
Common Player:		2.00
Veteran Stars:		25-35X
Young Stars:		10-20X

(See 1997 Circa for checklist and base card values.)

Boss

		NM/M
Complete Set (20):		10.00
Common Player:		.15
Super Boss:		1.5X
1	Jeff Bagwell	.60
2	Albert Belle	.25
3	Barry Bonds	2.00
4	Ken Caminiti	.15
5	Juan Gonzalez	.60
6	Ken Griffey Jr.	1.00
7	Tony Gwynn	.75
8	Derek Jeter	2.00
9	Andruw Jones	.60
10	Chipper Jones	.75
11	Greg Maddux	.75
12	Mark McGwire	1.50
13	Mike Piazza	1.00
14	Manny Ramirez	.60
15	Cal Ripken Jr.	2.00
16	Alex Rodriguez	1.50
17	John Smoltz	.15
18	Frank Thomas	.60
19	Mo Vaughn	.15
20	Bernie Williams	.25

Emerald Autographs

		NM/M
Complete Set (6):		100.00
Common Player:		7.50
100	Alex Rodriguez	65.00
241	Darin Erstad	12.00
251	Todd Hollandsworth	6.00
283	Scott Rolen	15.00
308	Alex Ochoa	6.00
325	Todd Walker	6.00

Fast Track

		NM/M
Complete Set (10):		8.00
Common Player:		.30
1	Vladimir Guerrero	1.00
2	Todd Hollandsworth	.30
3	Derek Jeter	2.50
4	Andruw Jones	1.00
5	Chipper Jones	1.50
6	Andy Pettitte	.60
7	Mariano Rivera	.45
8	Alex Rodriguez	2.00
9	Scott Rolen	.75
10	Todd Walker	.30

Icons

		NM/M
Complete Set (12):		12.50
Common Player:		.25
1	Juan Gonzalez	.75
2	Ken Griffey Jr.	1.50
3	Tony Gwynn	1.00
4	Derek Jeter	2.50
5	Chipper Jones	1.00
6	Greg Maddux	1.00
7	Mark McGwire	2.00
8	Mike Piazza	1.50
9	Cal Ripken Jr.	2.50
10	Alex Rodriguez	2.00
11	Frank Thomas	.75
12	Matt Williams	.25

Limited Access

		NM/M
Complete Set (15):		20.00
Common Player:		.75
1	Jeff Bagwell	1.00
2	Albert Belle	.75
3	Barry Bonds	3.00
4	Juan Gonzalez	1.00
5	Ken Griffey Jr.	2.00
6	Tony Gwynn	1.50
7	Derek Jeter	3.00
8	Chipper Jones	1.50
9	Greg Maddux	1.50
10	Mark McGwire	2.50
11	Mike Piazza	2.00

12	Cal Ripken Jr.	3.00
13	Alex Rodriguez	2.50
14	Frank Thomas	1.00
15	Mo Vaughn	.75

Rave Reviews

		NM/M
Complete Set (12):		50.00
Common Player:		2.00
1	Albert Belle	2.00
2	Barry Bonds	7.50
3	Juan Gonzalez	2.50
4	Ken Griffey Jr.	5.00
5	Tony Gwynn	4.00
6	Greg Maddux	4.00
7	Mark McGwire	6.00
8	Eddie Murray	2.50
9	Mike Piazza	5.00
10	Cal Ripken Jr.	7.50
11	Alex Rodriguez	6.00
12	Frank Thomas	2.50

1998 CIRCA THUNDER

		NM/M
Complete Set (300):		10.00
Common Player:		.10
Pack (8):		1.00
Wax Box (36):		20.00
1	Ben Grieve	.15
2	Derek Jeter	2.50
3	Alex Rodriguez	2.00
4	Paul Molitor	.75
5	Nomar Garciaparra	1.50
6	Fred McGriff	.10
7	Kenny Lofton	.10
8a	Cal Ripken Jr.	2.50
8b	Marquis Grissom (should be #280)	.10
8s	Cal Ripken Jr. ("PROMOTIONAL SAMPLE" on back)	2.50
9	Matt Williams	.10
10	Chipper Jones	1.00
11	Barry Larkin	.10
12	Steve Finley	.10
13	Billy Wagner	.10
14	Rico Brogna	.10
15	Tim Salmon	.15
16	Hideo Nomo	.75
17	Tony Clark	.10
18	Jason Kendall	.10
19	Juan Gonzalez	.75
20	Jeromy Burnitz	.10
21	Roger Clemens	1.25
22	Mark Grace	.20
23	Robin Ventura	.10
24	Manny Ramirez	.75
25	Mark McGwire	2.00
26	Gary Sheffield	.50
27	Vladimir Guerrero	.75
28	Butch Huskey	.10
29	Cecil Fielder	.10
30	Roderick Myers	.10
31	Greg Maddux	1.00
32	Bill Mueller	.10
33	Larry Walker	.10
34	Henry Rodriguez	.10
35	Mike Mussina	.60
36	Ricky Ledee	.10
37	Bobby Bonilla	.10
38	Curt Schilling	.35
39	Luis Gonzalez	.25
40	Troy Percival	.10
41	Eric Milton	.10
42	Mo Vaughn	.10
43	Raul Mondesi	.10
44	Kenny Rogers	.10
45	Frank Thomas	.75
46	Jose Canseco	.50
47	Tom Glavine	.35
48	*Rich Butler*	.10
49	Jay Buhner	.10
50	Jose Cruz Jr.	.10
51	Bernie Williams	.20
52	Doug Glanville	.10
53	Travis Fryman	.10
54	Rey Ordonez	.10
55	Jeff Conine	.10
56	Trevor Hoffman	.10
57	Kirk Rueter	.10
58	Ron Gant	.10
59	Carl Everett	.10
60	Joe Carter	.10
61	Livan Hernandez	.10
62	John Jaha	.10
63	Ivan Rodriguez	.65
64	Willie Blair	.10
65	Todd Helton	.75
66	Kevin Young	.10
67	Mike Caruso	.10
68	Steve Trachsel	.10
69	Marty Cordova	.10
70	Alex Fernandez	.10
71	Eric Karros	.10
72	Reggie Sanders	.10
73	Russ Davis	.10
74	Roberto Hernandez	.10
75	Barry Bonds	2.50
76	Alex Gonzalez	.10
77	Roberto Alomar	.30
78	Troy O'Leary	.10
79	Bernard Gilkey	.10
80	Ismael Valdes	.10
81	Travis Lee	.10
82	Brant Brown	.10
83	Gary DiSarcina	.10
84	Joe Randa	.10
85	Jaret Wright	.10
86	Quilvio Veras	.10
87	Rickey Henderson	.75
88	Randall Simon	.10
89	Mariano Rivera	.25
90	Ugueth Urbina	.10
91	Fernando Vina	.10
92	Alan Benes	.10
93	Dante Bichette	.10
94	Karim Garcia	.10
95	A.J. Hinch	.10
96	Shane Reynolds	.10
97	Kevin Stocker	.10
98	John Wetteland	.10
99	Terry Steinbach	.10
100	Ken Griffey Jr.	1.50
101	Mike Cameron	.10
102	Damion Easley	.10
103	Randy Myers	.10
104	Jason Schmidt	.10
105	Jeff King	.10
106	Gregg Jefferies	.10
107	Sean Casey	.15
108	Mark Kotsay	.10
109	Brad Fullmer	.10
110	Wilson Alvarez	.10
111	Sandy Alomar Jr.	.10
112	Walt Weiss	.10
113	Doug Jones	.10
114	Andy Benes	.10
115	Paul O'Neill	.10
116	Dennis Eckersley	.65
117	Todd Greene	.10
118	Bobby Jones	.10
119	Darrin Fletcher	.10
120	Eric Young	.10
121	Jeffrey Hammonds	.10
122	Mickey Morandini	.10
123	Chuck Knoblauch	.10
124	Moises Alou	.10
125	Miguel Tejada	.15
126	Brian Anderson	.10
127	Edgar Renteria	.10
128	Mike Lansing	.10
129	Quinton McCracken	.10
130	Ray Lankford	.10
131	Andy Ashby	.10
132	Kelvim Escobar	.10
133	*Mike Lowell*	.40
134	Randy Johnson	.75
135	Andres Galarraga	.10
136	Armando Benitez	.10
137	Rusty Greer	.10
138	Jose Guillen	.10
139	Paul Konerko	.10
140	Edgardo Alfonzo	.10
141	Jim Leyritz	.10
142	Mark Clark	.10
143	Brian Johnson	.10
144	Scott Rolen	.75
145	David Cone	.10
146	Jeff Shaw	.10
147	Shannon Stewart	.15
148	Brian Hunter	.10
149	Garret Anderson	.10
150	Jeff Bagwell	.75
151	James Baldwin	.10
152	Devon White	.10
153	Jim Thome	.10
154	Wally Joyner	.10
155	Mark Wohlers	.10
156	Jeff Cirillo	.10
157	Jason Giambi	.60
158	Royce Clayton	.10
159	Dennis Reyes	.10
160	Raul Casanova	.10
161	Pedro Astacio	.10
162	Todd Dunwoody	.10
163	Sammy Sosa	1.50
164	Todd Hundley	.10
165	Wade Boggs	1.00
166	Robb Nen	.10
167	Dan Wilson	.10
168	Hideki Irabu	.10
169	B.J. Surhoff	.10
170	Carlos Delgado	.40
171	Fernando Tatis	.10
172	Bob Abreu	.10
173	David Ortiz	.10
174	Tony Womack	.10
175	*Magglio Ordonez*	2.00
176	Aaron Boone	.10
177	Brian Giles	.10
178	Kevin Appier	.10
179	Chuck Finley	.10
180	Brian Rose	.10
181	Ryan Klesko	.10
182	Mike Stanley	.10
183	Dave Nilsson	.10
184	Carlos Perez	.10
185	Jeff Blauser	.10
186	Richard Hidalgo	.10
187	Charles Johnson	.10
188	Vinny Castilla	.10
189	Joey Hamilton	.10
190	Bubba Trammell	.10
191	Eli Marrero	.10
192	Scott Erickson	.10
193	Pat Hentgen	.10
194	Jorge Fabregas	.10
195	Tino Martinez	.10
196	Bobby Higginson	.10
197	Dave Hollins	.10
198	*Rolando Arrojo*	.25
199	Joey Cora	.10
200	Mike Piazza	1.50
201	Reggie Jefferson	.10
202	John Smoltz	.10
203	Bobby Smith	.10
204	Tom Goodwin	.10
205	Omar Vizquel	.10
206	John Olerud	.10
207	Matt Stairs	.10
208	Bobby Estalella	.10
209	Miguel Cairo	.10
210	Shawn Green	.20
211	Jon Nunnally	.10
212	Al Leiter	.10
213	Matt Lawton	.10
214	Brady Anderson	.10
215	Jeff Kent	.10
216	Ray Durham	.10
217	Al Martin	.10
218	Jeff D'Amico	.10
219	Kevin Tapani	.10
220	Jim Edmonds	.10
221	Jose Vizcaino	.10
222	Jay Bell	.10
223	Ken Caminiti	.10
224	Craig Biggio	.10
225	Bartolo Colon	.10
226	Neifi Perez	.10
227	Delino DeShields	.10
228	Javier Lopez	.10
229	David Wells	.10
230	Brad Rigby	.10
231	John Franco	.10
232	Michael Coleman	.10
233	Edgar Martinez	.10
234	Francisco Cordova	.10
235	Johnny Damon	.20
236	Deivi Cruz	.10
237	J.T. Snow	.10
238	Enrique Wilson	.10
239	Rondell White	.10
240	Aaron Sele	.10
241	Tony Saunders	.10
242	Ricky Bottalico	.10
243	Cliff Floyd	.10
244	Chili Davis	.10
245	Brian McRae	.10
246	Brad Radke	.10
247	Chan Ho Park	.10
248	Lance Johnson	.10
249	Rafael Palmeiro	.75
250	Tony Gwynn	1.00
251	Denny Neagle	.10
252	Dean Palmer	.10
253	Jose Valentin	.10
254	Matt Morris	.10
255	Ellis Burks	.10
256	Jeff Suppan	.10
257	Jimmy Key	.10
258	Justin Thompson	.10
259	Brett Tomko	.10
260	Mark Grudzielanek	.10
261	Mike Hampton	.10
262	Jeff Fassero	.10
263	Charles Nagy	.10
264	Pedro Martinez	.75
265	Todd Zeile	.10
266	Will Clark	.15
267	Abraham Nunez	.10
268	Dave Martinez	.10
269	Jason Dickson	.10
270	Eric Davis	.10
271	Kevin Orie	.10
272	Derrek Lee	.10
273	Andruw Jones	.75
274	Juan Encarnacion	.10
275	Carlos Baerga	.10
276	Andy Pettitte	.40
277	Brent Brede	.10
278	Paul Sorrento	.10
279	Mike Lieberthal	.10
280	(Not issued, see #8)	.10
281	Darin Erstad	.60
282	Willie Greene	.10
283	Derek Bell	.10
284	Scott Spiezio	.10
285	David Segui	.10
286	Albert Belle	.20
287	Ramon Martinez	.10
288	Jeremi Gonzalez	.10
289	Shawn Estes	.10
290	Ron Coomer	.10
291	John Valentin	.10
292	Kevin Brown	.10
293	Michael Tucker	.10
294	Brian Jordan	.10
295	Darryl Kile	.10
296	David Justice	.10
297	Jose Cruz Jr. Checklist	.10
298	Alex Rodriguez Checklist	1.00
299	Ken Griffey Jr. Checklist	.75
300	Frank Thomas Checklist	.65

Rave

	NM/M
Common Player:	2.00
Stars:	10X

(See 1998 Circa Thunder for checklist andbase card values.)

Super Rave

	NM/M
Common Player:	6.00
Stars:	40X

(See 1998 Circa Thunder for checklist andbase card values.)

Boss

		NM/M
Complete Set (20):		10.00
Common Player:		.25
Inserted 1:6		
1B	Jeff Bagwell	.75

2B	Barry Bonds	2.00
3B	Roger Clemens	1.00
4B	Jose Cruz Jr.	.25
5B	Nomar Garciaparra	1.25
6B	Juan Gonzalez	.75
7B	Ken Griffey Jr.	1.25
8B	Tony Gwynn	1.00
9B	Derek Jeter	2.00
10B	Chipper Jones	1.00
11B	Travis Lee	.25
12B	Greg Maddux	1.00
13B	Pedro Martinez	.75
14B	Mark McGwire	1.50
15B	Mike Piazza	1.25
16B	Cal Ripken Jr.	2.00
17B	Alex Rodriguez	1.50
18B	Scott Rolen	.65
19B	Frank Thomas	.75
20B	Larry Walker	.25

Fast Track

		NM/M
Complete Set (10):		8.00
Common Player:		.25
Inserted 1:24		
1FT	Jose Cruz Jr.	.25
2FT	Juan Encarnacion	.25
3FT	Brad Fullmer	.25
4FT	Nomar Garciaparra	4.00
5FT	Todd Helton	2.50
6FT	Livan Hernandez	.25
7FT	Travis Lee	.25
8FT	Neifi Perez	.25
9FT	Scott Rolen	1.50
10FT	Jaret Wright	.25

Limited Access

		NM/M
Complete Set (15):		15.00
Common Player:		.40
Inserted 1:18		
1LA	Jeff Bagwell	1.00
2LA	Roger Clemens	1.25
3LA	Jose Cruz Jr.	.40
4LA	Nomar Garciaparra	1.50
5LA	Juan Gonzalez	1.00
6LA	Ken Griffey Jr.	1.50
7LA	Tony Gwynn	1.25
8LA	Derek Jeter	2.50
9LA	Greg Maddux	1.25
10LA	Pedro Martinez	1.00
11LA	Mark McGwire	2.00
12LA	Mike Piazza	1.50
13LA	Alex Rodriguez	2.00
14LA	Frank Thomas	1.00
15LA	Larry Walker	.40

Quick Strike

		NM/M
Complete Set (12):		20.00
Common Player:		.50
Inserted 1:36		
1QS	Jeff Bagwell	2.00
2QS	Roger Clemens	2.50
3QS	Jose Cruz Jr.	.50
4QS	Nomar Garciaparra	3.00
5QS	Ken Griffey Jr.	3.00
6QS	Greg Maddux	2.50
7QS	Pedro Martinez	2.00
8QS	Mark McGwire	4.00
9QS	Mike Piazza	3.00
10QS	Alex Rodriguez	4.00
11QS	Frank Thomas	2.00
12QS	Larry Walker	.50

Rave Reviews

		NM/M
Complete Set (15):		100.00
Common Player:		2.00
Inserted 1:288		
1RR	Jeff Bagwell	5.00
2RR	Barry Bonds	15.00
3RR	Roger Clemens	7.50
4RR	Jose Cruz Jr.	2.00
5RR	Nomar Garciaparra	10.00
6RR	Juan Gonzalez	5.00
7RR	Ken Griffey Jr.	10.00
8RR	Tony Gwynn	6.00
9RR	Derek Jeter	15.00
10RR	Greg Maddux	6.00
11RR	Mark McGwire	12.50
12RR	Mike Piazza	10.00
13RR	Alex Rodriguez	12.50
14RR	Frank Thomas	5.00
15RR	Larry Walker	2.00

Thunder Boomers

		NM/M
Complete Set (12):		35.00
Common Player:		1.00
Inserted 1:96		
1TB	Jeff Bagwell	2.50
2TB	Barry Bonds	7.50
3TB	Jay Buhner	1.00
4TB	Andres Galarraga	1.00
5TB	Juan Gonzalez	2.50
6TB	Ken Griffey Jr.	5.00
7TB	Tino Martinez	1.00
8TB	Mark McGwire	6.00
9TB	Mike Piazza	5.00
10TB	Frank Thomas	4.00
11TB	Jim Thome	1.00
12TB	Larry Walker	1.00

1994 COLLECTOR'S CHOICE

	NM/M
Unopened Factory Set (675):	12.50
Complete Set (670):	10.00
Common Player:	.05
Series 1 Pack (12):	.35
Series 2 Pack (12):	8.00
Series 1 Box (36):	.75
Series 2 Box (36):	17.50

1	*Rich Becker*	.05
2	Greg Blosser	.05
3	Midre Cummings	.05
4	Carlos Delgado	.30
5	*Steve Dreyer*	.05
6	*Carl Everett*	.50
7	Cliff Floyd	.05
8	Alex Gonzalez	.05
9	Shawn Green	.10
10	Butch Huskey	.05
11	Mark Hutton	.05
12	Miguel Jimenez	.05
13	Steve Karsay	.05
14	Marc Newfield	.05
15	Luis Ortiz	.05
16	Manny Ramirez	.60
17	Johnny Ruffin	.05
18	*Scott Stahoviak*	.05
19	Salomon Torres	.05
20	*Gabe White*	.10
21	*Brian Anderson*	.05
22	*Wayne Gomes*	.05
23	Jeff Granger	.05
24	*Steve Soderstrom*	.05
25	*Trot Nixon*	.25
26	*Kirk Presley*	.05
27	*Matt Brunson*	.05
28	*Brooks Kieschnick*	.05
29	*Billy Wagner*	.20
30	*Matt Drews*	.05
31	*Kurt Abbott*	.05
32	Luis Alicea	.05
33	Roberto Alomar	.20
34	Sandy Alomar Jr.	.05
35	Moises Alou	.05
36	Wilson Alvarez	.05
37	Rich Amaral	.05
38	Eric Anthony	.05
39	Luis Aquino	.05
40	Jack Armstrong	.05
41	Rene Arocha	.05
42	*Rich Aude*	.05
43	Brad Ausmus	.05
44	Steve Avery	.05
45	Bob Ayrault	.05
46	Willie Banks	.05
47	Bret Barberie	.05
48	Kim Batiste	.05
49	Rod Beck	.05
50	Jason Bere	.05
51	Sean Berry	.05
52	Dante Bichette	.05
53	Jeff Blauser	.05
54	Mike Blowers	.05
55	Tim Bogar	.05
56	Tom Bolton	.05
57	Ricky Bones	.05
58	Bobby Bonilla	.05
59	Bret Boone	.05
60	Pat Borders	.05
61	Mike Bordick	.05
62	Daryl Boston	.05
63	Ryan Bowen	.05
64	Jeff Branson	.05
65	George Brett	.85
66	Steve Buechele	.05
67	Dave Burba	.05
68	John Burkett	.05
69	Jeromy Burnitz	.05
70	Brett Butler	.05
71	Rob Butler	.05
72	Ken Caminiti	.05
73	Cris Carpenter	.05
74	Vinny Castilla	.05
75	Andujar Cedeno	.05
76	Wes Chamberlain	.05
77	Archi Cianfrocco	.05
78	Dave Clark	.05
79	Jerald Clark	.05
80	Royce Clayton	.05
81	David Cone	.05
82	Jeff Conine	.05
83	Steve Cooke	.05
84	Scott Cooper	.05
85	Joey Cora	.05
86	Tim Costa	.05
87	Chad Curtis	.05
88	Ron Darling	.05
89	Danny Darwin	.05
90	Rob Deer	.05
91	Jim Deshaies	.05
92	Delino DeShields	.05
93	Rob Dibble	.05
94	Gary DiSarcina	.05
95	Doug Drabek	.05
96	Scott Erickson	.05
97	*Rikkert Faneyte*	.05
98	Jeff Fassero	.05
99	Alex Fernandez	.05
100	Cecil Fielder	.05
101	Dave Fleming	.05
102	Darrin Fletcher	.05
103	Scott Fletcher	.05
104	Mike Gallego	.05
105	Carlos Garcia	.05
106	Jeff Gardner	.05
107	Brent Gates	.05
108	Benji Gil	.05
109	Bernard Gilkey	.05
110	Chris Gomez	.05
111	Luis Gonzalez	.25
112	Tom Gordon	.05
113	Jim Gott	.05
114	Mark Grace	.20
115	Tommy Greene	.05
116	Willie Greene	.05
117	Ken Griffey, Jr.	1.00
118	Bill Gullickson	.05
119	Ricky Gutierrez	.05
120	Juan Guzman	.05
121	Chris Gwynn	.05
122	Tony Gwynn	.75
123	Jeffrey Hammonds	.05
124	Erik Hanson	.05
125	Gene Harris	.05
126	Greg Harris	.05
127	Bryan Harvey	.05
128	Billy Hatcher	.05
129	Hilly Hathaway	.05
130	Charlie Hayes	.05
131	Rickey Henderson	.60
132	Mike Henneman	.05
133	Pat Hentgen	.05
134	Roberto Hernandez	.05
135	Orel Hershiser	.05
136	Phil Hiatt	.05
137	Glenallen Hill	.05
138	Ken Hill	.05
139	Eric Hillman	.05
140	Chris Hoiles	.05
141	Dave Hollins	.05
142	David Hulse	.05
143	Todd Hundley	.05
144	Pete Incaviglia	.05
145	Danny Jackson	.05
146	John Jaha	.05
147	Domingo Jean	.05
148	Gregg Jefferies	.05
149	Reggie Jefferson	.05
150	Lance Johnson	.05
151	Bobby Jones	.05
152	Chipper Jones	.75
153	Todd Jones	.05
154	Brian Jordan	.05
155	Wally Joyner	.05
156	Dave Justice	.05
157	Ron Karkovice	.05
158	Eric Karros	.05
159	Jeff Kent	.05
160	Jimmy Key	.05
161	Mark Kiefer	.05
162	Darryl Kile	.05
163	Jeff King	.05
164	Wayne Kirby	.05
165	Ryan Klesko	.05
166	Chuck Knoblauch	.05
167	Chad Kreuter	.05
168	John Kruk	.05
169	Mark Langston	.05
170	Mike Lansing	.05
171	Barry Larkin	.05
172	Manuel Lee	.05
173	*Phil Leftwich*	.05
174	Darren Lewis	.05
175	Derek Lilliquist	.05
176	Jose Lind	.05
177	Albie Lopez	.05
178	Javier Lopez	.05
179	Torey Lovullo	.05
180	Scott Lydy	.05
181	Mike Macfarlane	.05
182	Shane Mack	.05
183	Greg Maddux	.75
184	Dave Magadan	.05
185	Joe Magrane	.05
186	Kirt Manwaring	.05
187	Al Martin	.05
188	*Pedro A. Martinez*	.05
189	Pedro Martinez	.60
190	Ramon Martinez	.05
191	Tino Martinez	.05
192	Don Mattingly	.85
193	Derrick May	.05
194	David McCarty	.05
195	Ben McDonald	.05
196	Roger McDowell	.05
197	Fred McGriff	.05
198	Mark McLemore	.05

No.	Player	Price
199	Greg McMichael	.05
200	Jeff McNeely	.05
201	Brian McRae	.05
202	Pat Meares	.05
203	Roberto Mejia	.05
204	Orlando Merced	.05
205	Jose Mesa	.05
206	Blas Minor	.05
207	Angel Miranda	.05
208	Paul Molitor	.60
209	Raul Mondesi	.05
210	Jeff Montgomery	.05
211	Mickey Morandini	.05
212	Mike Morgan	.05
213	Jamie Moyer	.05
214	Bobby Munoz	.05
215	Troy Neel	.05
216	Dave Nilsson	.05
217	John O'Donoghue	.05
218	Paul O'Neill	.05
219	Jose Offerman	.05
220	Joe Oliver	.05
221	Greg Olson	.05
222	Donovan Osborne	.05
223	Jayhawk Owens	.05
224	Mike Pagliarulo	.05
225	Craig Paquette	.05
226	Roger Pavlik	.05
227	Brad Pennington	.05
228	Eduardo Perez	.05
229	Mike Perez	.05
230	Tony Phillips	.05
231	Hipolito Pichardo	.05
232	Phil Plantier	.05
233	*Curtis Pride*	.05
234	Tim Pugh	.05
235	Scott Radinsky	.05
236	Pat Rapp	.05
237	Kevin Reimer	.05
238	Armando Reynoso	.05
239	Jose Rijo	.05
240	Cal Ripken, Jr.	2.00
241	Kevin Roberson	.05
242	Kenny Rogers	.05
243	Kevin Rogers	.05
244	Mel Rojas	.05
245	John Roper	.05
246	Kirk Rueter	.05
247	Scott Ruffcorn	.05
248	Ken Ryan	.05
249	Nolan Ryan	2.00
250	Bret Saberhagen	.05
251	Tim Salmon	.10
252	Reggie Sanders	.05
253	Curt Schilling	.20
254	David Segui	.05
255	Aaron Sele	.05
256	Scott Servais	.05
257	Gary Sheffield	.30
258	Ruben Sierra	.05
259	Don Slaught	.05
260	Lee Smith	.05
261	Cory Snyder	.05
262	Paul Sorrento	.05
263	Sammy Sosa	1.00
264	Bill Spiers	.05
265	Mike Stanley	.05
266	Dave Staton	.05
267	Terry Steinbach	.05
268	Kevin Stocker	.05
269	Todd Stottlemyre	.05
270	Doug Strange	.05
271	Bill Swift	.05
272	Kevin Tapani	.05
273	Tony Tarasco	.05
274	*Julian Tavarez*	.05
275	Mickey Tettleton	.05
276	Ryan Thompson	.05
277	Chris Turner	.05
278	John Valentin	.05
279	Todd Van Poppel	.05
280	Andy Van Slyke	.05
281	Mo Vaughn	.05
282	Robin Ventura	.05
283	Frank Viola	.05
284	Jose Vizcaino	.05
285	Omar Vizquel	.05
286	Larry Walker	.05
287	Duane Ware	.05
288	Allen Watson	.05
289	Bill Wegman	.05
290	Turk Wendell	.05
291	Lou Whitaker	.05
292	Devon White	.05
293	Rondell White	.05
294	Mark Whiten	.05
295	Darrell Whitmore	.05
296	Bob Wickman	.05
297	Rick Wilkins	.05
298	Bernie Williams	.15
299	Matt Williams	.05
300	Woody Williams	.05
301	Nigel Wilson	.05
302	Dave Winfield	.60
303	Anthony Young	.05
304	Eric Young	.05
305	Todd Zeile	.05
306	Jack McDowell, John Burkett, Tom Glavine (Top Performers)	.05
307	Randy Johnson (Top Performers)	.25
308	Randy Myers (Top Performers)	.05
309	Jack McDowell (Top Performers)	.05
310	Mike Piazza (Top Performers)	.40
311	Barry Bonds (Top Performers)	.60
312	Andres Galarraga (Top Performers)	.05
313	Juan Gonzalez, Barry Bonds (Top Performers)	.45
314	Albert Belle (Top Performers)	.10
315	Kenny Lofton (Top Performers)	.05
316	Barry Bonds Checklist 1-64	.50
317	Ken Griffey, Jr. Checklist 65-128	.35
318	Mike Piazza Checklist 129-192	.35
319	Kirby Puckett Checklist 193-256	.25
320	Nolan Ryan Checklist 257-320	.50
321	Roberto Alomar Checklist 321-370	.10
322	Roger Clemens Checklist 371-420	.30
323	Juan Gonzalez Checklist 421-470	.20
324	Ken Griffey, Jr. Checklist 471-520	.35
325	David Justice Checklist 521-570	.05
326	John Kruk Checklist 571-620	.05
327	Frank Thomas Checklist 621-670	.20
328	Tim Salmon Angels Checklist	.05
329	Jeff Bagwell Astros Checklist	.20
330	Mark McGwire Athletics Checklist	.45
331	Roberto Alomar Blue Jays Checklist	.10
332	David Justice Braves Checklist	.05
333	Pat Listach Brewers Checklist	.05
334	Ozzie Smith Cardinals Checklist	.25
335	Ryne Sandberg Cubs Checklist	.25
336	Mike Piazza Dodgers Checklist	.35
337	Cliff Floyd Expos Checklist	.05
338	Barry Bonds Giants Checklist	.50
339	Albert Belle Indians Checklist	.10
340	Ken Griffey, Jr. Mariners Checklist	.35
341	Gary Sheffield Marlins Checklist	.10
342	Dwight Gooden Mets Checklist	.05
343	Cal Ripken, Jr. Orioles Checklist	.50
344	Tony Gwynn Padres Checklist	.25
345	Lenny Dykstra Phillies Checklist	.05
346	Andy Van Slyke Pirates Checklists	.05
347	Juan Gonzalez Rangers Checklist	.20
348	Roger Clemens Red Sox Checklist	.30
349	Barry Larkin Reds Checklist	.05
350	Andres Galarraga Rockies Checklist	.05
351	Kevin Appier Royals Checklist	.05
352	Cecil Fielder Tigers Checklist	.05
353	Kirby Puckett Twins Checklist	.25
354	Frank Thomas White Sox Checklist	.20
355	Don Mattingly Yankees Checklist	.30
356	Bo Jackson	.10
357	Randy Johnson	.60
358	Darren Daulton	.05
359	Charlie Hough	.05
360	Andres Galarraga	.05
361	Mike Felder	.05
362	Chris Hammond	.05
363	Shawon Dunston	.05
364	Junior Felix	.05
365	Ray Lankford	.05
366	Darryl Strawberry	.05
367	Dave Magadan	.05
368	Gregg Olson	.05
369	Len Dykstra	.05
370	Darrin Jackson	.05
371	Dave Stewart	.05
372	Terry Pendleton	.05
373	Arthur Rhodes	.05
374	Benito Santiago	.05
375	Travis Fryman	.05
376	Scott Brosius	.05
377	Stan Belinda	.05
378	Derek Parks	.05
379	Kevin Seitzer	.05
380	Wade Boggs	.75
381	Wally Whitehurst	.05
382	Scott Leius	.05
383	Danny Tartabull	.05
384	Harold Reynolds	.05
385	Tim Raines	.05
386	Darryl Hamilton	.05
387	Felix Fermin	.05
388	Jim Eisenreich	.05
389	Kurt Abbott	.05
390	Kevin Appier	.05
391	Chris Bosio	.05
392	Randy Tomlin	.05
393	Bob Hamelin	.05
394	Kevin Gross	.05
395	Wil Cordero	.05
396	Joe Girardi	.05
397	Orestes Destrade	.05
398	Chris Haney	.05
399	Xavier Hernandez	.05
400	Mike Piazza	1.00
401	Alex Arias	.05
402	Tom Candiotti	.05
403	Kirk Gibson	.05
404	Chuck Carr	.05
405	Brady Anderson	.05
406	Greg Gagne	.05
407	Bruce Ruffin	.05
408	Scott Hemond	.05
409	Keith Miller	.05
410	John Wetteland	.05
411	Eric Anthony	.05
412	Andre Dawson	.20
413	Doug Henry	.05
414	John Franco	.05
415	Julio Franco	.05
416	Dave Hansen	.05
417	Mike Harkey	.05
418	Jack Armstrong	.05
419	Joe Orsulak	.05
420	John Smoltz	.05
421	Scott Livingstone	.05
422	Darren Holmes	.05
423	Ed Sprague	.05
424	Jay Buhner	.05
425	Kirby Puckett	.75
426	Phil Clark	.05
427	Anthony Young	.05
428	Reggie Jefferson	.05
429	Mariano Duncan	.05
430	Tom Glavine	.20
431	Dave Henderson	.05
432	Melido Perez	.05
433	Paul Wagner	.05
434	Tim Worrell	.05
435	Ozzie Guillen	.05
436	Mike Butcher	.05
437	Jim Deshaies	.05
438	Kevin Young	.05
439	Tom Browning	.05
440	Mike Greenwell	.05
441	Mike Stanton	.05
442	John Doherty	.05
443	John Dopson	.05
444	Carlos Baerga	.05
445	Jack McDowell	.05
446	Kent Mercker	.05
447	Ricky Jordan	.05
448	Jerry Browne	.05
449	Fernando Vina	.05
450	Jim Abbott	.05
451	Teddy Higuera	.05
452	Tim Naehring	.05
453	Jim Leyritz	.05
454	Frank Castillo	.05
455	Joe Carter	.05
456	Craig Biggio	.05
457	Geronimo Pena	.05
458	Alejandro Pena	.05
459	Mike Moore	.05
460	Randy Myers	.05
461	Greg Myers	.05
462	Greg Hibbard	.05
463	Jose Guzman	.05
464	Tom Pagnozzi	.05
465	Marquis Grissom	.05
466	Tim Wallach	.05
467	Joe Grahe	.05
468	Bob Tewksbury	.05
469	B.J. Surhoff	.05
470	Kevin Mitchell	.05
471	Bobby Witt	.05
472	Milt Thompson	.05
473	John Smiley	.05
474	Alan Trammell	.05
475	Mike Mussina	.40
476	Rick Aguilera	.05
477	Jose Valentin	.05
478	Harold Baines	.05
479	Bip Roberts	.05
480	Edgar Martinez	.05
481	Rheal Cormier	.05
482	Hal Morris	.05
483	Pat Kelly	.05
484	Roberto Kelly	.05
485	Chris Sabo	.05
486	Kent Hrbek	.05
487	Scott Kamieniecki	.05
488	Walt Weiss	.05
489	Karl Rhodes	.05
490	Derek Bell	.05
491	Chili Davis	.05
492	Brian Harper	.05
493	Felix Jose	.05
494	Trevor Hoffman	.05
495	Dennis Eckersley	.50
496	Pedro Astacio	.05
497	Jay Bell	.05
498	Randy Velarde	.05
499	David Wells	.05
500	Frank Thomas	.60
501	Mark Lemke	.05
502	Mike Devereaux	.05
503	Chuck McElroy	.05
504	Luis Polonia	.05
505	Damion Easley	.05
506	Greg A. Harris	.05
507	Chris James	.05
508	Terry Mulholland	.05
509	Pete Smith	.05
510	Rickey Henderson	.60
511	Sid Fernandez	.05
512	Al Leiter	.05
513	Doug Jones	.05
514	Steve Farr	.05
515	Chuck Finley	.05
516	Bobby Thigpen	.05
517	Jim Edmonds	.05
518	Graeme Lloyd	.05
519	Dwight Gooden	.05
520	Pat Listach	.05
521	Kevin Bass	.05
522	Willie Banks	.05
523	Steve Finley	.05
524	Delino DeShields	.05
525	Mark McGwire	1.50
526	Greg Swindell	.05
527	Chris Nabholz	.05
528	Scott Sanders	.05
529	David Segui	.05
530	Howard Johnson	.05
531	Jaime Navarro	.05
532	Jose Vizcaino	.05
533	Mark Lewis	.05
534	Pete Harnisch	.05
535	Robby Thompson	.05
536	Marcus Moore	.05
537	Kevin Brown	.05
538	Mark Clark	.05
539	Sterling Hitchcock	.05
540	Will Clark	.10
541	Denis Boucher	.05
542	Jack Morris	.05
543	Pedro Munoz	.05

544 Bret Boone .05
545 Ozzie Smith .75
546 Dennis Martinez .05
547 Dan Wilson .05
548 Rick Sutcliffe .05
549 Kevin McReynolds .05
550 Roger Clemens .85
551 Todd Benzinger .05
552 Bill Haselman .05
553 Bobby Munoz .05
554 Ellis Burks .05
555 Ryne Sandberg .75
556 Lee Smith .05
557 Danny Bautista .05
558 Rey Sanchez .05
559 Norm Charlton .05
560 Jose Canseco .35
561 Tim Belcher .05
562 Denny Neagle .05
563 Eric Davis .05
564 Jody Reed .05
565 Kenny Lofton .05
566 Gary Gaetti .05
567 Todd Worrell .05
568 Mark Portugal .05
569 Dick Schofield .05
570 Andy Benes .05
571 Zane Smith .05
572 Bobby Ayala .05
573 Chip Hale .05
574 Bob Welch .05
575 Deion Sanders .10
576 Dave Nied .05
577 Pat Mahomes .05
578 Charles Nagy .05
579 Otis Nixon .05
580 Dean Palmer .05
581 Roberto Petagine .05
582 Dwight Smith .05
583 Jeff Russell .05
584 Mark Dewey .05
585 Greg Vaughn .05
586 Brian Hunter .05
587 Willie McGee .05
588 Pedro J. Martinez .60
589 Roger Salkeld .05
590 Jeff Bagwell .60
591 Spike Owen .05
592 Jeff Reardon .05
593 Erik Pappas .05
594 Brian Williams .05
595 Eddie Murray .60
596 Henry Rodriguez .05
597 Erik Hanson .05
598 Stan Javier .05
599 Mitch Williams .05
600 John Olerud .05
601 Vince Coleman .05
602 Damon Berryhill .05
603 Tom Brunansky .05
604 Robb Nen .05
605 Rafael Palmeiro .60
606 Cal Eldred .05
607 Jeff Brantley .05
608 Alan Mills .05
609 Jeff Nelson .05
610 Barry Bonds 2.00
611 *Carlos Pulido* .05
612 *Tim Hyers* .05
613 Steve Howe .05
614 *Brian Turang* .05
615 Leo Gomez .05
616 Jesse Orosco .05
617 Dan Pasqua .05
618 Marvin Freeman .05
619 Tony Fernandez .05
620 Albert Belle .15
621 Eddie Taubensee .05
622 Mike Jackson .05
623 Jose Bautista .05
624 Jim Thome .05
625 Ivan Rodriguez .60
626 Ben Rivera .05
627 Dave Valle .05
628 Tom Henke .05
629 Omar Vizquel .05
630 Juan Gonzalez .60
631 Roberto Alomar (Up Close) .10
632 Barry Bonds (Up Close) .60
633 Juan Gonzalez (Up Close) .25
634 Ken Griffey, Jr. (Up Close) .50
635 Michael Jordan (Up Close) 1.50
636 Dave Justice (Up Close) .05
637 Mike Piazza (Up Close) .50
638 Kirby Puckett (Up Close) .25
639 Tim Salmon (Up Close) .05
640 Frank Thomas (Up Close) .35
641 *Alan Benes* (Future Foundation) .05
642 Johnny Damon (Future Foundation) .25
643 *Brad Fullmer* (Future Foundation) .25
644 Derek Jeter (Future Foundation) 2.00
645 *Derrek Lee* (Future Foundation) .50
646 Alex Ochoa (Future Foundation) .05
647 *Alex Rodriguez* (Future Foundation) 5.00
648 *Jose Silva* (Future Foundation) .05
649 *Terrell Wade* (Future Foundation) .05
650 Preston Wilson (Future Foundation) .15
651 Shane Andrews (Rookie Class) .05
652 James Baldwin (Rookie Class) .05
653 *Ricky Bottalico* (Rookie Class) .10
654 Tavo Alvarez (Rookie Class) .05
655 Donnie Elliott (Rookie Class) .05
656 Joey Eischen (Rookie Class) .05
657 Jason Giambi (Rookie Class) .50
658 Todd Hollandsworth (Rookie Class) .05
659 Brian Hunter (Rookie Class) .05
660 Charles Johnson (Rookie Class) .05
661 *Michael Jordan* (Rookie Class) 3.00
662 Jeff Juden (Rookie Class) .05
663 Mike Kelly (Rookie Class) .05
664 James Mouton (Rookie Class) .05
665 Ray Holbert (Rookie Class) .05
666 Pokey Reese (Rookie Class) .05
667 *Ruben Santana* (Rookie Class) .05
668 Paul Spoljaric (Rookie Class) .05
669 Luis Lopez (Rookie Class) .05
670 Matt Walbeck (Rookie Class) .05

1994 COLLECTOR'S CHOICE GOLD SIGNATURE

	NM/M
Common Player:	2.00
Stars:	15X

(See 1994 Collector's Choice for checklist and base card values.)

1994 COLLECTOR'S CHOICE SILVER SIGNATURE

	NM/M
Complete Set (670):	200.00
Common Player:	.15
Stars:	2.5X

(See 1994 Collector's Choice for checklist and base card values.)

647 Alex Rodriguez (White Letters. Some A-Rod Silver Signature parallels were mistakenly printed on base cards with his name and other details on front and back printed in white, rather than gray.) 200.00

Home Run All-Stars

	NM/M
Complete Set (8):	4.00
Common Player:	.25
1HA Juan Gonzalez	.75
2HA Ken Griffey, Jr.	1.50
3HA Barry Bonds	2.50
4HAa Bobby Bonilla	.25
4HAb Cecil Fielder	.25
6HA Albert Belle	.25
7HA David Justice	.25
8HA Mike Piazza	1.50

1995 COLLECTOR'S CHOICE

	NM/M
Complete Set (530):	9.00
Unopened Factory Set (545):	15.00
Common Player:	.05
Pack (12):	1.00
Wax Box (36):	20.00

1 Charles Johnson (Rookie Class) .05
2 Scott Ruffcorn (Rookie Class) .05
3 Ray Durham (Rookie Class) .05
4 Armando Benitez (Rookie Class) .05
5 Alex Rodriguez (Rookie Class) 1.25
6 Julian Tavarez (Rookie Class) .05
7 Chad Ogea (Rookie Class) .05
8 Quilvio Veras (Rookie Class) .05
9 Phil Nevin (Rookie Class) .05
10 Michael Tucker (Rookie Class) .05
11 Mark Thompson (Rookie Class) .05
12 Rod Henderson (Rookie Class) .05
13 Andrew Lorraine (Rookie Class) .05
14 Joe Randa (Rookie Class) .05
15 Derek Jeter (Rookie Class) 1.50
16 Tony Clark (Rookie Class) .05
17 Juan Castillo (Rookie Class) .05
18 Mark Acre (Rookie Class) .05
19 Orlando Miller (Rookie Class) .05
20 Paul Wilson (Rookie Class) .05
21 John Mabry (Rookie Class) .05
22 Garey Ingram (Rookie Class) .05
23 Garret Anderson (Rookie Class) .05
24 Dave Stevens (Rookie Class) .05
25 Dustin Hermanson (Rookie Class) .05
26 Paul Shuey (Rookie Class) .05
27 J.R. Phillips (Rookie Class) .05
28 Ruben Rivera (Future Foundation) .05
29 Nomar Garciaparra (Future Foundation) 1.00
30 John Wasdin (Future Foundation) .05
31 Jim Pittsley (Future Foundation) .05
32 *Scott Elarton* (Future Foundation) .15
33 *Raul Casanova* (Future Foundation) .05
34 Todd Greene (Future Foundation) .05
35 Bill Pulsipher (Future Foundation) .05
36 Trey Beamon (Future Foundation) .05
37 Curtis Goodwin (Future Foundation) .05
38 Doug Million (Future Foundation) .05
39 *Karim Garcia* (Future Foundation) 1.00
40 Ben Grieve (Future Foundation) .10
41 Mark Farris (Future Foundation) .05
42 *Juan Acevedo* (Future Foundation) .05
43 C.J. Nitkowski (Future Foundation) .05
44 *Travis Miller* (Future Foundation) .10
45 Reid Ryan (Future Foundation) .10
46 Nolan Ryan 1.50
47 Robin Yount .50
48 Ryne Sandberg .75
49 George Brett .85
50 Mike Schmidt .85
51 Cecil Fielder (Best of the 90's) .05
52 Nolan Ryan (Best of the 90's) .75
53 Rickey Henderson (Best of the 90's) .20
54 George Brett, Robin Yount, Dave Winfield (Best of the 90's) .25
55 Sid Bream (Best of the 90's) .05
56 Carlos Baerga (Best of the 90's) .05
57 Lee Smith (Best of the 90's) .05
58 Mark Whiten (Best of the 90's) .05
59 Joe Carter (Best of the 90's) .05
60 Barry Bonds (Best of the 90's) .75
61 Tony Gwynn (Best of the 90's) .40
62 Ken Griffey Jr. (Best of the 90's) .50
63 Greg Maddux (Best of the 90's) .40
64 Frank Thomas (Best of the 90's) .35
65 Dennis Martinez, Kenny Rogers (Best of the 90's) .05
66 David Cone (Cy Young) .05
67 Greg Maddux (Cy Young) .75
68 Jimmy Key (Most Victories) .05
69 Fred McGriff (All-Star MVP) .05
70 Ken Griffey Jr. (HR Champ) 1.00
71 Matt Williams (HR Champ) .05
72 Paul O'Neill (Batting Title) .05
73 Tony Gwynn (Batting Title) .40
74 Randy Johnson (Ks Leader) .60
75 Frank Thomas (MVP) .60
76 Jeff Bagwell (MVP) .60

No.	Player	Price
77	Kirby Puckett (RBI leader)	.75
78	Bob Hamelin (ROY)	.05
79	Raul Mondesi (ROY)	.05
80	Mike Piazza (All-Star)	1.00
81	Kenny Lofton (SB Leader)	.05
82	Barry Bonds (Gold Glove)	1.50
83	Albert Belle (All-Star)	.10
84	Juan Gonzalez (HR Champ)	.60
85	Cal Ripken Jr. (2,000 Straight Games)	1.50
86	Barry Bonds (What's the Call?)	.75
87	Mike Piazza (What's the Call?)	.60
88	Ken Griffey Jr. (What's the Call?)	.50
89	Frank Thomas (What's the Call?)	.35
90	Juan Gonzalez (What's the Call?)	.20
91	Jorge Fabregas	.05
92	J.T. Snow	.05
93	Spike Owen	.05
94	Eduardo Perez	.05
95	Bo Jackson	.10
96	Damion Easley	.05
97	Gary DiSarcina	.05
98	Jim Edmonds	.05
99	Chad Curtis	.05
100	Tim Salmon	.10
101	Chili Davis	.05
102	Chuck Finley	.05
103	Mark Langston	.05
104	Brian Anderson	.05
105	Lee Smith	.05
106	Phil Leftwich	.05
107	Chris Donnels	.05
108	John Hudek	.05
109	Craig Biggio	.05
110	Luis Gonzalez	.25
111	Brian L. Hunter	.05
112	James Mouton	.05
113	Scott Servais	.05
114	Tony Eusebio	.05
115	Derek Bell	.05
116	Doug Drabek	.05
117	Shane Reynolds	.05
118	Darryl Kile	.05
119	Greg Swindell	.05
120	Phil Plantier	.05
121	Todd Jones	.05
122	Steve Ontiveros	.05
123	Bobby Witt	.05
124	Brent Gates	.05
125	Rickey Henderson	.60
126	Scott Brosius	.05
127	Mike Bordick	.05
128	Fausto Cruz	.05
129	Stan Javier	.05
130	Mark McGwire	1.25
131	Geronimo Berroa	.05
132	Terry Steinbach	.05
133	Steve Karsay	.05
134	Dennis Eckersley	.50
135	Ruben Sierra	.05
136	Ron Darling	.05
137	Todd Van Poppel	.05
138	Alex Gonzalez	.05
139	John Olerud	.05
140	Roberto Alomar	.20
141	Darren Hall	.05
142	Ed Sprague	.05
143	Devon White	.05
144	Shawn Green	.20
145	Paul Molitor	.60
146	Pat Borders	.05
147	Carlos Delgado	.35
148	Juan Guzman	.05
149	Pat Hentgen	.05
150	Joe Carter	.05
151	Dave Stewart	.05
152	Todd Stottlemyre	.05
153	Dick Schofield	.05
154	Chipper Jones	.75
155	Ryan Klesko	.05
156	Dave Justice	.05
157	Mike Kelly	.05
158	Roberto Kelly	.05
159	Tony Tarasco	.05
160	Javier Lopez	.05
161	Steve Avery	.05
162	Greg McMichael	.05
163	Kent Mercker	.05
164	Mark Lemke	.05
165	Tom Glavine	.20
166	Jose Oliva	.05
167	John Smoltz	.05
168	Jeff Blauser	.05
169	Troy O'Leary	.05
170	Greg Vaughn	.05
171	Jody Reed	.05
172	Kevin Seitzer	.05
173	Jeff Cirillo	.05
174	B.J. Surhoff	.05
175	Cal Eldred	.05
176	Jose Valentin	.05
177	Turner Ward	.05
178	Darryl Hamilton	.05
179	Pat Listach	.05
180	Matt Mieske	.05
181	Brian Harper	.05
182	Dave Nilsson	.05
183	Mike Fetters	.05
184	John Jaha	.05
185	Ricky Bones	.05
186	Geronimo Pena	.05
187	Bob Tewksbury	.05
188	Todd Zeile	.05
189	Danny Jackson	.05
190	Ray Lankford	.05
191	Bernard Gilkey	.05
192	Brian Jordan	.05
193	Tom Pagnozzi	.05
194	Rick Sutcliffe	.05
195	Mark Whiten	.05
196	Tom Henke	.05
197	Rene Arocha	.05
198	Allen Watson	.05
199	Mike Perez	.05
200	Ozzie Smith	.75
201	Anthony Young	.05
202	Rey Sanchez	.05
203	Steve Buechele	.05
204	Shawon Dunston	.05
205	Mark Grace	.15
206	Glenallen Hill	.05
207	Eddie Zambrano	.05
208	Rick Wilkins	.05
209	Derrick May	.05
210	Sammy Sosa	1.00
211	Kevin Roberson	.05
212	Steve Trachsel	.05
213	Willie Banks	.05
214	Kevin Foster	.05
215	Randy Myers	.05
216	Mike Morgan	.05
217	Rafael Bournigal	.05
218	Delino DeShields	.05
219	Tim Wallach	.05
220	Eric Karros	.05
221	Jose Offerman	.05
222	Tom Candiotti	.05
223	Ismael Valdes	.05
224	Henry Rodriguez	.05
225	Billy Ashley	.05
226	Darren Dreifort	.05
227	Ramon Martinez	.05
228	Pedro Astacio	.05
229	Orel Hershiser	.05
230	Brett Butler	.05
231	Todd Hollandsworth	.05
232	Chan Ho Park	.05
233	Mike Lansing	.05
234	Sean Berry	.05
235	Rondell White	.05
236	Ken Hill	.05
237	Marquis Grissom	.05
238	Larry Walker	.05
239	John Wetteland	.05
240	Cliff Floyd	.05
241	Joey Eischen	.05
242	Lou Frazier	.05
243	Darrin Fletcher	.05
244	Pedro J. Martinez	.60
245	Wil Cordero	.05
246	Jeff Fassero	.05
247	Butch Henry	.05
248	Mel Rojas	.05
249	Kirk Rueter	.05
250	Moises Alou	.05
251	Rod Beck	.05
252	John Patterson	.05
253	Robby Thompson	.05
254	Royce Clayton	.05
255	William Van Landingham	.05
256	Darren Lewis	.05
257	Kirt Manwaring	.05
258	Mark Portugal	.05
259	Bill Swift	.05
260	Rikkert Faneyte	.05
261	Mike Jackson	.05
262	Todd Benzinger	.05
263	Bud Black	.05
264	Salomon Torres	.05
265	Eddie Murray	.60
266	Mark Clark	.05
267	Paul Sorrento	.05
268	Jim Thome	.05
269	Omar Vizquel	.05
270	Carlos Baerga	.05
271	Jeff Russell	.05
272	Herbert Perry	.05
273	Sandy Alomar Jr.	.05
274	Dennis Martinez	.05
275	Manny Ramirez	.60
276	Wayne Kirby	.05
277	Charles Nagy	.05
278	Albie Lopez	.05
279	Jeromy Burnitz	.05
280	Dave Winfield	.60
281	Tim Davis	.05
282	Marc Newfield	.05
283	Tino Martinez	.05
284	Mike Blowers	.05
285	Goose Gossage	.05
286	Luis Sojo	.05
287	Edgar Martinez	.05
288	Rich Amaral	.05
289	Felix Fermin	.05
290	Jay Buhner	.05
291	Dan Wilson	.05
292	Bobby Ayala	.05
293	Dave Fleming	.05
294	Greg Pirkl	.05
295	Reggie Jefferson	.05
296	Greg Hibbard	.05
297	Yorkis Perez	.05
298	Kurt Miller	.05
299	Chuck Carr	.05
300	Gary Sheffield	.30
301	Jerry Browne	.05
302	Dave Magadan	.05
303	Kurt Abbott	.05
304	Pat Rapp	.05
305	Jeff Conine	.05
306	Benito Santiago	.05
307	Dave Weathers	.05
308	Robb Nen	.05
309	Chris Hammond	.05
310	Bryan Harvey	.05
311	Charlie Hough	.05
312	Greg Colbrunn	.05
313	David Segui	.05
314	Rico Brogna	.05
315	Jeff Kent	.05
316	Jose Vizcaino	.05
317	Jim Lindeman	.05
318	Carl Everett	.05
319	Ryan Thompson	.05
320	Bobby Bonilla	.05
321	Joe Orsulak	.05
322	Pete Harnisch	.05
323	Doug Linton	.05
324	Todd Hundley	.05
325	Bret Saberhagen	.05
326	Kelly Stinnett	.05
327	Jason Jacome	.05
328	Bobby Jones	.05
329	John Franco	.05
330	Rafael Palmeiro	.60
331	Chris Hoiles	.05
332	Leo Gomez	.05
333	Chris Sabo	.05
334	Brady Anderson	.05
335	Jeffrey Hammonds	.05
336	Dwight Smith	.05
337	Jack Voigt	.05
338	Harold Baines	.05
339	Ben McDonald	.05
340	Mike Mussina	.40
341	Bret Barberie	.05
342	Jamie Moyer	.05
343	Mike Oquist	.05
344	Sid Fernandez	.05
345	Eddie Williams	.05
346	Joey Hamilton	.05
347	Brian Williams	.05
348	Luis Lopez	.05
349	Steve Finley	.05
350	Andy Benes	.05
351	Andujar Cedeno	.05
352	Bip Roberts	.05
353	Ray McDavid	.05
354	Ken Caminiti	.05
355	Trevor Hoffman	.05
356	Mel Nieves	.05
357	Brad Ausmus	.05
358	Andy Ashby	.05
359	Scott Sanders	.05
360	Gregg Jefferies	.05
361	Mariano Duncan	.05
362	Dave Hollins	.05
363	Kevin Stocker	.05
364	Fernando Valenzuela	.05
365	Lenny Dykstra	.05
366	Jim Eisenreich	.05
367	Ricky Bottalico	.05
368	Doug Jones	.05
369	Ricky Jordan	.05
370	Darren Daulton	.05
371	Mike Lieberthal	.05
372	Bobby Munoz	.05
373	John Kruk	.05
374	Curt Schilling	.20
375	Orlando Merced	.05
376	Carlos Garcia	.05
377	Lance Parrish	.05
378	Steve Cooke	.05
379	Jeff King	.05
380	Jay Bell	.05
381	Al Martin	.05
382	Paul Wagner	.05
383	Rick White	.05
384	Midre Cummings	.05
385	Jon Lieber	.05
386	Dave Clark	.05
387	Don Slaught	.05
388	Denny Neagle	.05
389	Zane Smith	.05
390	Andy Van Slyke	.05
391	Ivan Rodriguez	.60
392	David Hulse	.05
393	John Burkett	.05
394	Kevin Brown	.05
395	Dean Palmer	.05
396	Otis Nixon	.05
397	Rick Helling	.05
398	Kenny Rogers	.05
399	Darren Oliver	.05
400	Will Clark	.10
401	Jeff Frye	.05
402	Kevin Gross	.05
403	John Dettmer	.05
404	Manny Lee	.05
405	Rusty Greer	.05
406	Aaron Sele	.05
407	Carlos Rodriguez	.05
408	Scott Cooper	.05
409	John Valentin	.05
410	Roger Clemens	.85
411	Mike Greenwell	.05
412	Tim Vanegmond	.05
413	Tom Brunansky	.05
414	Steve Farr	.05
415	Jose Canseco	.35
416	Joe Hesketh	.05
417	Ken Ryan	.05
418	Tim Naehring	.05
419	Frank Viola	.05
420	Andre Dawson	.20
421	Mo Vaughn	.05
422	Jeff Brantley	.05
423	Pete Schourek	.05
424	Hal Morris	.05
425	Deion Sanders	.10
426	Brian L. Hunter	.05
427	Bret Boone	.05
428	Willie Greene	.05
429	Ron Gant	.05
430	Barry Larkin	.05
431	Reggie Sanders	.05
432	Eddie Taubensee	.05
433	Jack Morris	.05
434	Jose Rijo	.05
435	Johnny Ruffin	.05
436	John Smiley	.05
437	John Roper	.05
438	David Nied	.05
439	Roberto Mejia	.05
440	Andres Galarraga	.05
441	Mike Kingery	.05
442	Curt Leskanic	.05
443	Walt Weiss	.05
444	Marvin Freeman	.05
445	Charlie Hayes	.05
446	Eric Young	.05
447	Ellis Burks	.05
448	Joe Girardi	.05
449	Lance Painter	.05
450	Dante Bichette	.05
451	Bruce Ruffin	.05
452	Jeff Granger	.05
453	Wally Joyner	.05
454	Jose Lind	.05
455	Jeff Montgomery	.05
456	Gary Gaetti	.05
457	Greg Gagne	.05
458	Vince Coleman	.05
459	Mike Macfarlane	.05
460	Brian McRae	.05
461	Tom Gordon	.05
462	Kevin Appier	.05
463	Billy Brewer	.05
464	Mark Gubicza	.05
465	Travis Fryman	.05
466	Danny Bautista	.05

467	Sean Bergman	.05
468	Mike Henneman	.05
469	Mike Moore	.05
470	Cecil Fielder	.05
471	Alan Trammell	.05
472	Kirk Gibson	.05
473	Tony Phillips	.05
474	Mickey Tettleton	.05
475	Lou Whitaker	.05
476	Chris Gomez	.05
477	John Doherty	.05
478	Greg Gohr	.05
479	Bill Gullickson	.05
480	Rick Aguilera	.05
481	Matt Walbeck	.05
482	Kevin Tapani	.05
483	Scott Erickson	.05
484	Steve Dunn	.05
485	David McCarty	.05
486	Scott Leius	.05
487	Pat Meares	.05
488	Jeff Reboulet	.05
489	Pedro Munoz	.05
490	Chuck Knoblauch	.05
491	Rich Becker	.05
492	Alex Cole	.05
493	Pat Mahomes	.05
494	Ozzie Guillen	.05
495	Tim Raines	.05
496	Kirk McCaskill	.05
497	Olmedo Saenz	.05
498	Scott Sanderson	.05
499	Lance Johnson	.05
500	Michael Jordan	1.50
501	Warren Newson	.05
502	Ron Karkovice	.05
503	Wilson Alvarez	.05
504	Jason Bere	.05
505	Robin Ventura	.05
506	Alex Fernandez	.05
507	Roberto Hernandez	.05
508	Norberto Martin	.05
509	Bob Wickman	.05
510	Don Mattingly	.85
511	Melido Perez	.05
512	Pat Kelly	.05
513	Randy Velarde	.05
514	Tony Fernandez	.05
515	Jack McDowell	.05
516	Luis Polonia	.05
517	Bernie Williams	.15
518	Danny Tartabull	.05
519	Mike Stanley	.05
520	Wade Boggs	.75
521	Jim Leyritz	.05
522	Steve Howe	.05
523	Scott Kamieniecki	.05
524	Russ Davis	.05
525	Jim Abbott	.05
526	Eddie Murray Checklist 1-106	.20
527	Alex Rodriguez Checklist 107-212	.40
528	Jeff Bagwell Checklist 213-318	.20
529	Joe Carter Checklist 319-424	.05
530	Fred McGriff Checklist 425-530	.05
---	National Packtime offer card	.05

Gold Signature

	NM/M
Common Player:	.50
Stars:	6X

(See 1995 Collector's Choice for checklist and base card values.)

Silver Signature

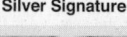

	NM/M
Common Player:	.10
Stars:	2X

(See 1995 Collector's Choice for checklist and base card values.)

Michael Jordan Jumbo

		NM/M
661	Michael Jordan	15.00

1995 COLLECTOR'S CHOICE/SE

	NM/M
Complete Set (265):	12.00
Common Player:	.05
Pack (12):	1.25
Wax Box (36):	25.00

1	Alex Rodriguez	1.50
2	Derek Jeter	2.00
3	Dustin Hermanson	.05
4	Bill Pulsipher	.05
5	Terrell Wade	.05
6	Darren Dreifort	.05
7	LaTroy Hawkins	.05
8	Alex Ochoa	.05
9	Paul Wilson	.05
10	Ernie Young	.05
11	Alan Benes	.05
12	Garret Anderson	.05
13	Armando Benitez	.05
14	Robert Perez	.05
15	Herbert Perry	.05
16	Jose Silva	.05
17	Orlando Miller	.05
18	Russ Davis	.05
19	Jason Isringhausen	.05
20	Ray McDavid	.05
21	Duane Singleton	.05
22	Paul Shuey	.05
23	Steve Dunn	.05
24	Mike Lieberthal	.05
25	Chan Ho Park	.05
26	Ken Griffey Jr. (Record Pace)	.65
27	Tony Gwynn (Record Pace)	.40
28	Chuck Knoblauch (Record Pace)	.05
29	Frank Thomas (Record Pace)	.35
30	Matt Williams (Record Pace)	.05
31	Chili Davis	.05
32	Chad Curtis	.05
33	Brian Anderson	.05
34	Chuck Finley	.05
35	Tim Salmon	.10
36	Bo Jackson	.10
37	Doug Drabek	.05
38	Craig Biggio	.05
39	Ken Caminiti	.05
40	Jeff Bagwell	.65
41	Darryl Kile	.05
42	John Hudek	.05
43	Brian L. Hunter	.05
44	Dennis Eckersley	.50
45	Mark McGwire	1.50
46	Brent Gates	.05
47	Steve Karsay	.05
48	Rickey Henderson	.65
49	Terry Steinbach	.05
50	Ruben Sierra	.05
51	Roberto Alomar	.25
52	Carlos Delgado	.25
53	Alex Gonzalez	.05
54	Joe Carter	.05
55	Paul Molitor	.65
56	Juan Guzman	.05
57	John Olerud	.05
58	Shawn Green	.25
59	Tom Glavine	.25
60	Greg Maddux	.75
61	Roberto Kelly	.05
62	Ryan Klesko	.05
63	Javier Lopez	.05
64	Jose Oliva	.05
65	Fred McGriff	.05
66	Steve Avery	.05
67	Dave Justice	.05
68	Ricky Bones	.05
69	Cal Eldred	.05
70	Greg Vaughn	.05
71	Dave Nilsson	.05
72	Jose Valentin	.05
73	Matt Mieske	.05
74	Todd Zeile	.05
75	Ozzie Smith	.75
76	Bernard Gilkey	.05
77	Ray Lankford	.05
78	Bob Tewksbury	.05
79	Mark Whiten	.05
80	Gregg Jefferies	.05
81	Randy Myers	.05
82	Shawon Dunston	.05
83	Mark Grace	.10
84	Derrick May	.05
85	Sammy Sosa	1.00
86	Steve Trachsel	.05
87	Brett Butler	.05
88	Delino DeShields	.05
89	Orel Hershiser	.05
90	Mike Piazza	1.00
91	Todd Hollandsworth	.05
92	Eric Karros	.05
93	Ramon Martinez	.05
94	Tim Wallach	.05
95	Raul Mondesi	.05
96	Larry Walker	.05
97	Wil Cordero	.05
98	Marquis Grissom	.05
99	Ken Hill	.05
100	Cliff Floyd	.05
101	Pedro J. Martinez	.65
102	John Wetteland	.05
103	Rondell White	.05
104	Moises Alou	.05
105	Barry Bonds	2.00
106	Darren Lewis	.05
107	Mark Portugal	.05
108	Matt Williams	.05
109	William VanLandingham	.05
110	Bill Swift	.05
111	Robby Thompson	.05
112	Rod Beck	.05
113	Darryl Strawberry	.05
114	Jim Thome	.05
115	Dave Winfield	.65
116	Eddie Murray	.65
117	Manny Ramirez	.65
118	Carlos Baerga	.05
119	Kenny Lofton	.05
120	Albert Belle	.10
121	Mark Clark	.05
122	Dennis Martinez	.05
123	Randy Johnson	.65
124	Jay Buhner	.05
125	Ken Griffey Jr.	1.00
125a	Ken Griffey Jr. (overprinted "For Promotional Use Only")	1.50
126	Rich Gossage	.05
127	Tino Martinez	.05
128	Reggie Jefferson	.05
129	Edgar Martinez	.05
130	Gary Sheffield	.30
131	Pat Rapp	.05
132	Bret Barberie	.05
133	Chuck Carr	.05
134	Jeff Conine	.05
135	Charles Johnson	.05
136	Benito Santiago	.05
137	Matt Williams (Stat Leaders)	.05
138	Jeff Bagwell (Stat Leaders)	.35
139	Kenny Lofton (Stat Leaders)	.05
140	Tony Gwynn (Stat Leaders)	.40
141	Jimmy Key (Stat Leaders)	.05
142	Greg Maddux (Stat Leaders)	.40
143	Randy Johnson (Stat Leaders)	.25
144	Lee Smith (Stat Leaders)	.05
145	Bobby Bonilla	.05
146	Jason Jacome	.05
147	Jeff Kent	.05
148	Ryan Thompson	.05
149	Bobby Jones	.05
150	Bret Saberhagen	.05
151	John Franco	.05
152	Lee Smith	.05
153	Rafael Palmeiro	.65
154	Brady Anderson	.05
155	Cal Ripken Jr.	2.00
156	Jeffrey Hammonds	.05
157	Mike Mussina	.50
158	Chris Hoiles	.05
159	Ben McDonald	.05
160	Tony Gwynn	.75
161	Joey Hamilton	.05
162	Andy Benes	.05
163	Trevor Hoffman	.05
164	Phil Plantier	.05
165	Derek Bell	.05
166	Bip Roberts	.05
167	Eddie Williams	.05
168	Fernando Valenzuela	.05
169	Mariano Duncan	.05
170	Lenny Dykstra	.05
171	Darren Daulton	.05
172	Danny Jackson	.05
173	Bobby Munoz	.05
174	Doug Jones	.05
175	Jay Bell	.05
176	Zane Smith	.05
177	Jon Lieber	.05
178	Carlos Garcia	.05
179	Orlando Merced	.05
180	Andy Van Slyke	.05
181	Rick Helling	.05
182	Rusty Greer	.05
183	Kenny Rogers	.05
184	Will Clark	.10
185	Jose Canseco	.40
186	Juan Gonzalez	.65
187	Dean Palmer	.05
188	Ivan Rodriguez	.60
189	John Valentin	.05
190	Roger Clemens	.85
191	Aaron Sele	.05
192	Scott Cooper	.05
193	Mike Greenwell	.05
194	Mo Vaughn	.05
195	Andre Dawson	.20
196	Ron Gant	.05
197	Jose Rijo	.05
198	Bret Boone	.05
199	Deion Sanders	.10
200	Barry Larkin	.05
201	Hal Morris	.05
202	Reggie Sanders	.05
203	Kevin Mitchell	.05
204	Marvin Freeman	.05
205	Andres Galarraga	.05
206	Walt Weiss	.05
207	Charlie Hayes	.05
208	David Nied	.05
209	Dante Bichette	.05
210	David Cone	.05
211	Jeff Montgomery	.05
212	Felix Jose	.05
213	Mike Macfarlane	.05
214	Wally Joyner	.05
215	Bob Hamelin	.05
216	Brian McRae	.05
217	Kirk Gibson	.05
218	Lou Whitaker	.05
219	Chris Gomez	.05
220	Cecil Fielder	.05
221	Mickey Tettleton	.05
222	Travis Fryman	.05
223	Tony Phillips	.05
224	Rick Aguilera	.05
225	Scott Erickson	.05
226	Chuck Knoblauch	.05
227	Kent Hrbek	.05
228	Shane Mack	.05
229	Kevin Tapani	.05
230	Kirby Puckett	.75
231	Julio Franco	.05
232	Jack McDowell	.05
233	Jason Bere	.05
234	Alex Fernandez	.05
235	Frank Thomas	.65
236	Ozzie Guillen	.05
237	Robin Ventura	.05
238	Michael Jordan	2.00
239	Wilson Alvarez	.05
240	Don Mattingly	.85
241	Jim Abbott	.05
242	Jim Leyritz	.05
243	Paul O'Neill	.05

No.	Player	Price
244	Melido Perez	.05
245	Wade Boggs	.75
246	Mike Stanley	.05
247	Danny Tartabull	.05
248	Jimmy Key	.05
249	Greg Maddux (Fantasy Team)	.40
250	Randy Johnson (Fantasy Team)	.20
251	Bret Saberhagen (Fantasy Team)	.05
252	John Wetteland (Fantasy Team)	.05
253	Mike Piazza (Fantasy Team)	.50
254	Jeff Bagwell (Fantasy Team)	.35
255	Craig Biggio (Fantasy Team)	.05
256	Matt Williams (Fantasy Team)	.05
257	Wil Cordero (Fantasy Team)	.05
258	Kenny Lofton (Fantasy Team)	.05
259	Barry Bonds (Fantasy Team)	.75
260	Dante Bichette (Fantasy Team)	.05
261	Ken Griffey Jr. Checklist 1-53	.35
262	Goose Gossage Checklist 54-106	.05
263	Cal Ripken Jr. Checklist 107-159	.45
264	Kenny Rogers Checklist 160-212	.05
265	John Valentin Checklist 213-265	.05

Gold

	NM/M
Common Player:	1.00
Stars:	6X

(For checklist and base card values, see 1995 Collector's Choice SE.)

Silver

	NM/M
Common Player:	.15
Stars:	1.5X

(For checklist and base card values, see 1995 Collector's Choice SE.)

1996 COLLECTOR'S CHOICE

	NM/M
Complete Set: (760):	7.50
Complete Factory Set (790):	10.00
Traded Set (366T-395T):	3.00
Common Player:	.05
Series 1 Pack (12):	1.00
Series 1 Wax Box (36):	28.00
Series 2 Pack (14):	1.00
Series 2 Wax Box (40):	30.00

No.	Player	Price
1	Cal Ripken Jr.	2.00
2	Edgar Martinez, Tony Gwynn (1995 Stat Leaders)	.05
3	Albert Belle, Dante Bichette (1995 Stat Leaders)	.05
4	Albert Belle, Mo Vaughn, Dante Bichette (1995 Stat Leaders)	.05
5	Kenny Lofton, Quilvio Veras (1995 Stat Leaders)	.05
6	Mike Mussina, Greg Maddux (1995 Stat Leaders)	.40
7	Randy Johnson, Hideo Nomo (1995 Stat Leaders)	.25
8	Randy Johnson, Greg Maddux (1995 Stat Leaders)	.40
9	Jose Mesa, Randy Myers (1995 Stat Leaders)	.05
10	Johnny Damon (Rookie Class)	.25
11	Rick Krivda (Rookie Class)	.05
12	Roger Cedeno (Rookie Class)	.05
13	Angel Martinez (Rookie Class)	.05
14	Ariel Prieto (Rookie Class)	.05
15	John Wasdin (Rookie Class)	.05
16	Edwin Hurtado (Rookie Class)	.05
17	Lyle Mouton (Rookie Class)	.05
18	Chris Snopek (Rookie Class)	.05
19	Mariano Rivera (Rookie Class)	.15
20	Ruben Rivera (Rookie Class)	.05
21	*Juan Castro* (Rookie Class)	.05
22	Jimmy Haynes (Rookie Class)	.05
23	Bob Wolcott (Rookie Class)	.05
24	Brian Barber (Rookie Class)	.05
25	Frank Rodriguez (Rookie Class)	.05
26	Jesus Tavarez (Rookie Class)	.05
27	Glenn Dishman (Rookie Class)	.05
28	Jose Herrera (Rookie Class)	.05
29	Chan Ho Park (Rookie Class)	.05
30	Jason Isringhausen (Rookie Class)	.05
31	Doug Johns (Rookie Class)	.05
32	Gene Schall (Rookie Class)	.05
33	Kevin Jordan (Rookie Class)	.05
34	*Matt Lawton* (Rookie Class)	.10
35	Karim Garcia (Rookie Class)	.10
36	George Williams (Rookie Class)	.05
37	Orlando Palmeiro (Rookie Class)	.05
38	Jamie Brewington (Rookie Class)	.05
39	Robert Person (Rookie Class)	.05
40	Greg Maddux	.75
41	Marquis Grissom	.05
42	Chipper Jones	.75
43	David Justice	.05
44	Mark Lemke	.05
45	Fred McGriff	.05
46	Javy Lopez	.05
47	Mark Wohlers	.05
48	Jason Schmidt	.05
49	John Smoltz	.05
50	Curtis Goodwin	.05
51	Greg Zaun	.05
52	Armando Benitez	.05
53	Manny Alexander	.05
54	Chris Hoiles	.05
55	Harold Baines	.05
56	Ben McDonald	.05
57	Scott Erickson	.05
58	Jeff Manto	.05
59	Luis Alicea	.05
60	Roger Clemens	.85
61	Rheal Cormier	.05
62	Vaughn Eshelman	.05
63	Zane Smith	.05
64	Mike Macfarlane	.05
65	Erik Hanson	.05
66	Tim Naehring	.05
67	Lee Tinsley	.05
68	Troy O'Leary	.05
69	Garret Anderson	.05
70	Chili Davis	.05
71	Jim Edmonds	.05
72	Troy Percival	.05
73	Mark Langston	.05
74	Spike Owen	.05
75	Tim Salmon	.10
76	Brian Anderson	.05
77	Lee Smith	.05
78	Jim Abbott	.05
79	Jim Bullinger	.05
80	Mark Grace	.10
81	Todd Zeile	.05
82	Kevin Foster	.05
83	Howard Johnson	.05
84	Brian McRae	.05
85	Randy Myers	.05
86	Jaime Navarro	.05
87	Luis Gonzalez	.05
88	Ozzie Timmons	.05
89	Wilson Alvarez	.05
90	Frank Thomas	.65
91	James Baldwin	.05
92	Ray Durham	.05
93	Alex Fernandez	.05
94	Ozzie Guillen	.05
95	Tim Raines	.05
96	Roberto Hernandez	.05
97	Lance Johnson	.05
98	John Kruk	.05
99	Mark Portugal	.05
100	Don Mattingly (Traditional Threads)	.60
101	Jose Canseco (Traditional Threads)	.15
102	Raul Mondesi (Traditional Threads)	.05
103	Cecil Fielder (Traditional Threads)	.05
104	Ozzie Smith (Traditional Threads)	.40
105	Frank Thomas (Traditional Threads)	.45
106	Sammy Sosa (Traditional Threads)	.60
107	Fred McGriff (Traditional Threads)	.05
108	Barry Bonds (Traditional Threads)	1.00
109	Thomas Howard	.05
110	Ron Gant	.05
111	Eddie Taubensee	.05
112	Hal Morris	.05
113	Jose Rijo	.05
114	Pete Schourek	.05
115	Reggie Sanders	.05
116	Benito Santiago	.05
117	Jeff Brantley	.05
118	Julian Tavarez	.05
119	Carlos Baerga	.05
120	Jim Thome	.05
121	Jose Mesa	.05
122	Dennis Martinez	.05
123	Dave Winfield	.60
124	Eddie Murray	.60
125	Manny Ramirez	.60
126	Paul Sorrento	.05
127	Kenny Lofton	.05
128	Eric Young	.05
129	Jason Bates	.05
130	Bret Saberhagen	.05
131	Andres Galarraga	.05
132	Joe Girardi	.05
133	John Vander Wal	.05
134	David Nied	.05
135	Dante Bichette	.05
136	Vinny Castilla	.05
137	Kevin Ritz	.05
138	Felipe Lira	.05
139	Joe Boever	.05
140	Cecil Fielder	.05
141	John Flaherty	.05
142	Kirk Gibson	.05
143	Brian Maxcy	.05
144	Lou Whitaker	.05
145	Alan Trammell	.05
146	Bobby Higginson	.05
147	Chad Curtis	.05
148	Quilvio Veras	.05
149	Jerry Browne	.05
150	Andre Dawson	.20
151	Robb Nen	.05
152	Greg Colbrunn	.05
153	Chris Hammond	.05
154	Kurt Abbott	.05
155	Charles Johnson	.05
156	Terry Pendleton	.05
157	Dave Weathers	.05
158	Mike Hampton	.05
159	Craig Biggio	.05
160	Jeff Bagwell	.60
161	Brian L. Hunter	.05
162	Mike Henneman	.05
163	Dave Magadan	.05
164	Shane Reynolds	.05
165	Derek Bell	.05
166	Orlando Miller	.05
167	James Mouton	.05
168	Melvin Bunch	.05
169	Tom Gordon	.05
170	Kevin Appier	.05
171	Tom Goodwin	.05
172	Greg Gagne	.05
173	Gary Gaetti	.05
174	Jeff Montgomery	.05
175	Jon Nunnally	.05
176	Michael Tucker	.05
177	Joe Vitiello	.05
178	Billy Ashley	.05
179	Tom Candiotti	.05
180	Hideo Nomo	.60
181	Chad Fonville	.05
182	Todd Hollandsworth	.05
183	Eric Karros	.05
184	Roberto Kelly	.05
185	Mike Piazza	1.00
186	Ramon Martinez	.05
187	Tim Wallach	.05
188	Jeff Cirillo	.05
189	Sid Roberson	.05
190	Kevin Seitzer	.05
191	Mike Fetters	.05
192	Steve Sparks	.05
193	Matt Mieske	.05
194	Joe Oliver	.05
195	B.J. Surhoff	.05
196	Alberto Reyes	.05
197	Fernando Vina	.05
198	LaTroy Hawkins	.05
199	Marty Cordova	.05
200	Kirby Puckett	.75
201	Brad Radke	.05
202	Pedro Munoz	.05
203	Scott Klingenbeck	.05
204	Pat Meares	.05
205	Chuck Knoblauch	.05
206	Scott Stahoviak	.05
207	Dave Stevens	.05
208	Shane Andrews	.05
209	Moises Alou	.05
210	David Segui	.05
211	Cliff Floyd	.05
212	Carlos Perez	.05
213	Mark Grudzielanek	.05
214	Butch Henry	.05
215	Rondell White	.05
216	Mel Rojas	.05
217	Ugueth Urbina	.05
218	Edgardo Alfonzo	.05
219	Carl Everett	.05
220	John Franco	.05
221	Todd Hundley	.05
222	Bobby Jones	.05
223	Bill Pulsipher	.05
224	Rico Brogna	.05
225	Jeff Kent	.05
226	Chris Jones	.05
227	Butch Huskey	.05
228	Robert Eenhoorn	.05
229	Sterling Hitchcock	.05
230	Wade Boggs	.75
231	Derek Jeter	2.00
232	Tony Fernandez	.05
233	Jack McDowell	.05
234	Andy Pettitte	.35
235	David Cone	.05
236	Mike Stanley	.05
237	Don Mattingly	.85
238	Geronimo Berroa	.05
239	Scott Brosius	.05
240	Rickey Henderson	.60
241	Terry Steinbach	.05

242 Mike Gallego .05
243 Jason Giambi .50
244 Steve Ontiveros .05
245 Dennis Eckersley .50
246 Dave Stewart .05
247 Don Wengert .05
248 Paul Quantrill .05
249 Ricky Bottalico .05
250 Kevin Stocker .05
251 Lenny Dykstra .05
252 Tony Longmire .05
253 Tyler Green .05
254 Mike Mimbs .05
255 Charlie Hayes .05
256 Mickey Morandini .05
257 Heathcliff Slocumb .05
258 Jeff King .05
259 Midre Cummings .05
260 Mark Johnson .05
261 Freddy Garcia .05
262 Jon Lieber .05
263 Esteban Loaiza .05
264 Danny Miceli .05
265 Orlando Merced .05
266 Denny Neagle .05
267 Steve Parris .05
268 Greg Maddux Fantasy Team '95 .35
269 Randy Johnson Fantasy Team '95 .15
270 Hideo Nomo Fantasy Team '95 .25
271 Jose Mesa Fantasy Team '95 .05
272 Mike Piazza Fantasy Team '95 .60
273 Mo Vaughn Fantasy Team '95 .10
274 Craig Biggio Fantasy Team '95 .05
275 Edgar Martinez Fantasy Team '95 .05
276 Barry Larkin Fantasy Team '95 .05
277 Sammy Sosa Fantasy Team '95 .50
278 Dante Bichette Fantasy Team '95 .05
279 Albert Belle Fantasy Team '95 .05
280 Ozzie Smith .75
281 Mark Sweeney .05
282 Terry Bradshaw .05
283 Allen Battle .05
284 Danny Jackson .05
285 Tom Henke .05
286 Scott Cooper .05
287 Tripp Cromer .05
288 Bernard Gilkey .05
289 Brian Jordan .05
290 Tony Gwynn .75
291 Brad Ausmus .05
292 Bryce Florie .05
293 Andres Berumen .05
294 Ken Caminiti .05
295 Bip Roberts .05
296 Trevor Hoffman .05
297 Roberto Petagine .05
298 Jody Reed .05
299 Fernando Valenzuela .05
300 Barry Bonds 2.00
301 Mark Leiter .05
302 Mark Carreon .05
303 Royce Clayton .05
304 Kirt Manwaring .05
305 Glenallen Hill .05
306 Deion Sanders .10
307 Joe Rosselli .05
308 Robby Thompson .05
309 William VanLandingham .05
310 Ken Griffey Jr. 1.00
311 Bobby Ayala .05
312 Joey Cora .05
313 Mike Blowers .05
314 Darren Bragg .05
315 Randy Johnson .60
316 Alex Rodriguez 1.50
317 Andy Benes .05
318 Tino Martinez .05
319 Dan Wilson .05
320 Will Clark .10
321 Jeff Frye .05
322 Benji Gil .05
323 Rick Helling .05
324 Mark McLemore .05
325 Dave Nilsson (International Flavor) .05
326 Larry Walker (International Flavor) .05
327 Jose Canseco (International Flavor) .15
328 Raul Mondesi (International Flavor) .05
329 Manny Ramirez (International Flavor) .30
330 Robert Eenhoorn (International Flavor) .05
331 Chili Davis (International Flavor) .05
332 Hideo Nomo (International Flavor) .30
333 Benji Gil (International Flavor) .05
334 Fernando Valenzuela (International Flavor) .05
335 Dennis Martinez (International Flavor) .05
336 Roberto Kelly (International Flavor) .05
337 Carlos Baerga (International Flavor) .05
338 Juan Gonzalez (International Flavor) .30
339 Roberto Alomar (International Flavor) .10
340 Chan Ho Park (International Flavor) .05
341 Andres Galarraga (International Flavor) .05
342 Midre Cummings (International Flavor) .05
343 Otis Nixon .05
344 Jeff Russell .05
345 Ivan Rodriguez .50
346 Mickey Tettleton .05
347 Bob Tewksbury .05
348 Domingo Cedeno .05
349 Lance Parrish .05
350 Joe Carter .05
351 Devon White .05
352 Carlos Delgado .35
353 Alex Gonzalez .05
354 Darren Hall .05
355 Paul Molitor .60
356 Al Leiter .05
357 Randy Knorr .05
358 Checklist 1-46 (12-player Astros-Padres trade) .05
359 Hideo Nomo Checklist 47-92 .25
360 Ramon Martinez Checklist 93-138 .05
361 Robin Ventura Checklist 139-184 .05
362 Cal Ripken Jr. Checklist 185-230 .30
363 Ken Caminiti Checklist 231-275 .05
364 Eddie Murray Checklist 276-320 .15
365 Randy Johnson Checklist 321-365 .10
366 Tony Pena A.L. Divisional Series .10
367 Jim Thome A.L. Divisional Series .10
368 Don Mattingly A.L. Divisional Series .40
369 Jim Leyritz A.L. Divisional Series .10
370 Ken Griffey Jr. A.L. Divisional Series .60
371 Edgar Martinez A.L. Divisional Series .10
372 Pete Schourek N.L. Divisional Series .10
373 Mark Lewis N.L. Divisional Series .10
374 Chipper Jones N.L. Divisonal Series .50
375 Fred McGriff N.L. Divisonal Series .10
376 Javy Lopez N.L. Championship Series .10
377 Fred McGriff N.L. Championship Series .10
378 Charlie O'Brien N.L. Championship Series .10
379 Mike Devereaux N.L. Championship Series .10
380 Mark Wohlers N.L. Championship Series .10
381 Bob Wolcott A.L. Championship Series .10
382 Manny Ramirez A.L. Championship Series .20
383 Jay Buhner A.L. Championship Series .10
384 Orel Hershiser A.L. Championship Series .10
385 Kenny Lofton A.L. Championship Series .10
386 Greg Maddux World Series .50
387 Javy Lopez World Series .10
388 Kenny Lofton World Series .10
389 Eddie Murray World Series .10
390 Luis Polonia World Series .10
391 Pedro Borbon World Series .10
392 Jim Thome World Series .10
393 Orel Hershiser World Series .10
394 David Justice World Series .10
395 Tom Glavine World Series .10
396 Greg Maddux Braves Team Checklist .20
397 Brett Butler Mets Team Checklist .05
398 Darren Daulton Phillies Team Checklist .05
399 Gary Sheffield Marlins Team Checklist .05
400 Moises Alou Expos Team Checklist .05
401 Barry Larkin Reds Team Checklist .05
402 Jeff Bagwell Astros Team Checklist .15
403 Sammy Sosa Cubs Team Checklist .35
404 Ozzie Smith Cardinals Team Checklist .20
405 Jeff King Pirates Team Checklist .05
406 Mike Piazza Dodgers Team Checklist .50
407 Dante Bichette Rockies Team Checklist .05
408 Tony Gwynn Padres Team Checklist .20
409 Barry Bonds Giants Team Checklist .45
410 Kenny Lofton Indians Team Checklist .05
411 Jon Nunnally Royals Team Checklist .05
412 Frank Thomas White Sox Team Checklist .20
413 Greg Vaughn Brewers Team Checklist .05
414 Paul Molitor Twins Team Checklist .10
415 Ken Griffey Jr. Mariners Team Checklist .35
416 Jim Edmonds Angels Team Checklist .05
417 Juan Gonzalez Rangers Team Checklist .25
418 Mark McGwire Athletics Team Checklist .75
419 Roger Clemens Red Sox Team Checklist .20
420 Wade Boggs Yankees Team Checklist .35
421 Cal Ripken Jr. Orioles Team Checklist .40
422 Cecil Fielder Tigers Team Checklist .05
423 Joe Carter Blue Jays Team Checklist .05
424 *Osvaldo Fernandez* (Rookie Class) .15
425 Billy Wagner (Rookie Class) .05
426 George Arias (Rookie Class) .05
427 Mendy Lopez (Rookie Class) .05
428 Jeff Suppan (Rookie Class) .05
429 Rey Ordonez (Rookie Class) .10
430 Brooks Kieschnick (Rookie Class) .05
431 *Raul Ibanez* (Rookie Class) .05
432 *Livan Hernandez* (Rookie Class) .20
433 Shannon Stewart (Rookie Class) .10
434 Steve Cox (Rookie Class) .05
435 Trey Beamon (Rookie Class) .05
436 Sergio Nunez (Rookie Class) .05
437 Jermaine Dye (Rookie Class) .05
438 *Mike Sweeney* (Rookie Class) .45
439 Richard Hidalgo (Rookie Class) .10
440 Todd Greene (Rookie Class) .05
441 *Robert Smith* (Rookie Class) .10
442 Rafael Orellano (Rookie Class) .05
443 *Wilton Guerrero* (Rookie Class) .05
444 *David Doster* (Rookie Class) .05
445 Jason Kendall (Rookie Class) .05
446 Edgar Renteria (Rookie Class) .05
447 Scott Spiezio (Rookie Class) .05
448 Jay Canizaro (Rookie Class) .05
449 Enrique Wilson (Rookie Class) .05
450 Bob Abreu (Rookie Class) .10
451 Dwight Smith .05
452 Jeff Blauser .05
453 Steve Avery .05
454 Brad Clontz .05
455 Tom Glavine .20
456 Mike Mordecai .05
457 Rafael Belliard .05
458 Greg McMichael .05
459 Pedro Borbon .05
460 Ryan Klesko .05
461 Terrell Wade .05
462 Brady Anderson .05
463 Roberto Alomar .20
464 Bobby Bonilla .05
465 Mike Mussina .45
466 *Cesar Devarez* .05
467 Jeffrey Hammonds .05
468 Mike Devereaux .05
469 B.J. Surhoff .05
470 Rafael Palmeiro .60
471 John Valentin .05
472 Mike Greenwell .05
473 Dwayne Hosey .05
474 Tim Wakefield .05
475 Jose Canseco .35
476 Aaron Sele .05
477 Stan Belinda .05
478 Mike Stanley .05
479 Jamie Moyer .05
480 Mo Vaughn .05
481 Randy Velarde .05
482 Gary DiSarcina .05
483 Jorge Fabregas .05
484 Rex Hudler .05
485 Chuck Finley .05
486 Tim Wallach .05
487 Eduardo Perez .05
488 Scott Sanderson .05
489 J.T. Snow .05
490 Sammy Sosa 1.00
491 Terry Adams .05
492 Matt Franco .05
493 Scott Servais .05
494 Frank Castillo .05
495 Ryne Sandberg .75
496 Rey Sanchez .05
497 Steve Trachsel .05
498 Jose Hernandez .05
499 Dave Martinez .05
500 Babe Ruth (First Class) 1.00
501 Ty Cobb (First Class) .50
502 Walter Johnson (First Class) .10
503 Christy Mathewson (First Class) .10
504 Honus Wagner (First Class) .25
505 Robin Ventura .05
506 Jason Bere .05
507 *Mike Cameron* .25
508 Ron Karkovice .05
509 Matt Karchner .05
510 Harold Baines .05
511 Kirk McCaskill .05
512 Larry Thomas .05

513 Danny Tartabull .05
514 Steve Gibralter .05
515 Bret Boone .05
516 Jeff Branson .05
517 Kevin Jarvis .05
518 Xavier Hernandez .05
519 Eric Owens .05
520 Barry Larkin .05
521 Dave Burba .05
522 John Smiley .05
523 Paul Assenmacher .05
524 Chad Ogea .05
525 Orel Hershiser .05
526 Alan Embree .05
527 Tony Pena .05
528 Omar Vizquel .05
529 Mark Clark .05
530 Albert Belle .15
531 Charles Nagy .05
532 Herbert Perry .05
533 Darren Holmes .05
534 Ellis Burks .05
535 Bill Swift .05
536 Armando Reynoso .05
537 Curtis Leskanic .05
538 Quinton McCracken .05
539 Steve Reed .05
540 Larry Walker .05
541 Walt Weiss .05
542 Bryan Rekar .05
543 Tony Clark .05
544 Steve Rodriguez .05
545 C.J. Nitkowski .05
546 Todd Steverson .05
547 Jose Lima .05
548 Phil Nevin .05
549 Chris Gomez .05
550 Travis Fryman .05
551 Mark Lewis .05
552 Alex Arias .05
553 Marc Valdes .05
554 Kevin Brown .05
555 Jeff Conine .05
556 John Burkett .05
557 Devon White .05
558 Pat Rapp .05
559 Jay Powell .05
560 Gary Sheffield .30
561 Jim Dougherty .05
562 Todd Jones .05
563 Tony Eusebio .05
564 Darryl Kile .05
565 Doug Drabek .05
566 Mike Simms .05
567 Derrick May .05
568 *Donne Wall* .05
569 Greg Swindell .05
570 Jim Pittsley .05
571 Bob Hamelin .05
572 Mark Gubicza .05
573 Chris Haney .05
574 Keith Lockhart .05
575 Mike Macfarlane .05
576 Les Norman .05
577 Joe Randa .05
578 Chris Stynes .05
579 Greg Gagne .05
580 Raul Mondesi .05
581 Delino DeShields .05
582 Pedro Astacio .05
583 Antonio Osuna .05
584 Brett Butler .05
585 Todd Worrell .05
586 Mike Blowers .05
587 Felix Rodriguez .05
588 Ismael Valdes .05
589 Ricky Bones .05
590 Greg Vaughn .05
591 Mark Loretta .05
592 Cal Eldred .05
593 Chuck Carr .05
594 Dave Nilsson .05
595 John Jaha .05
596 Scott Karl .05
597 Pat Listach .05
598 *Jose Valentin* .05
599 Mike Trombley .05
600 Paul Molitor .60
601 Dave Hollins .05
602 Ron Coomer .05
603 Matt Walbeck .05
604 Roberto Kelly .05
605 Rick Aguilera .05
606 Pat Mahomes .05
607 Jeff Reboulet .05
608 Rich Becker .05
609 Tim Scott .05
610 Pedro J. Martinez .60
611 Kirk Rueter .05
612 Tavo Alvarez .05
613 Yamil Benitez .05
614 Darrin Fletcher .05
615 Mike Lansing .05
616 Henry Rodriguez .05
617 Tony Tarasco .05
618 Alex Ochoa .05
619 Tim Bogar .05
620 Bernard Gilkey .05
621 Dave Mlicki .05
622 Brent Mayne .05
623 Ryan Thompson .05
624 Pete Harnisch .05
625 Lance Johnson .05
626 Jose Vizcaino .05
627 Doug Henry .05
628 Scott Kamieniecki .05
629 Jim Leyritz .05
630 Ruben Sierra .05
631 Pat Kelly .05
632 Joe Girardi .05
633 John Wetteland .05
634 Melido Perez .05
635 Paul O'Neill .05
636 Jorge Posada .05
637 Bernie Williams .15
638 Mark Acre .05
639 Mike Bordick .05
640 Mark McGwire 1.50
641 Fausto Cruz .05
642 Ernie Young .05
643 Todd Van Poppel .05
644 Craig Paquette .05
645 Brent Gates .05
646 Pedro Munoz .05
647 Andrew Lorraine .05
648 Sid Fernandez .05
649 Jim Eisenreich .05
650 Johnny Damon (Arizona Fall League) .20
651 Dustin Hermanson (Arizona Fall League) .05
652 Joe Randa (Arizona Fall League) .05
653 Michael Tucker (Arizona Fall League) .05
654 Alan Benes (Arizona Fall League) .05
655 Chad Fonville (Arizona Fall League) .05
656 David Bell (Arizona Fall League) .05
657 Jon Nunnally (Arizona Fall League) .05
658 Chan Ho Park (Arizona Fall League) .05
659 LaTroy Hawkins (Arizona Fall League) .05
660 Jamie Brewington (Arizona Fall League) .05
661 Quinton McCracken (Arizona Fall League) .05
662 Tim Unroe (Arizona Fall League) .05
663 Jeff Ware (Arizona Fall League) .05
664 Todd Greene (Arizona Fall League) .05
665 Andrew Lorraine (Arizona Fall League) .05
666 Ernie Young (Arizona Fall League) .05
667 Toby Borland .05
668 Lenny Webster .05
669 Benito Santiago .05
670 Gregg Jefferies .05
671 Darren Daulton .05
672 Curt Schilling .25
673 Mark Whiten .05
674 Todd Zeile .05
675 Jay Bell .05
676 Paul Wagner .05
677 Dave Clark .05
678 Nelson Liriano .05
679 Ramon Morel .05
680 Charlie Hayes .05
681 Angelo Encaracion .05
682 Al Martin .05
683 Jacob Brumfield .05
684 Mike Kingery .05
685 Carlos Garcia .05
686 Tom Pagnozzi .05
687 David Bell .05
688 Todd Stottlemyre .05
689 Jose Oliva .05
690 Ray Lankford .05
691 Mike Morgan .05
692 John Frascatore .05
693 John Mabry .05
694 Mark Petkovsek .05
695 Alan Benes .05
696 Steve Finley .05
697 Marc Newfield .05
698 Andy Ashby .05
699 Marc Kroon .05
700 Wally Joyner .05
701 Joey Hamilton .05
702 Dustin Hermanson .05
703 Scott Sanders .05
704 Marty Cordova (Award Win.-ROY) .05
705 Hideo Nomo (Award Win.-ROY) .25
706 Mo Vaughn (Award Win.-MVP) .05
707 Barry Larkin (Award Win.-MVP) .05
708 Randy Johnson (Award Win.-CY) .15
709 Greg Maddux (Award Win.-CY) .35
710 Mark McGwire (Award-Comeback) .75
711 Ron Gant (Award-Comeback) .05
712 Andujar Cedeno .05
713 Brian Johnson .05
714 J.R. Phillips .05
715 Rod Beck .05
716 Sergio Valdez .05
717 *Marvin Benard* .25
718 Steve Scarsone .05
719 *Rich Aurilia* .10
720 Matt Williams .05
721 John Patterson .05
722 Shawn Estes .05
723 Russ Davis .05
724 Rich Amaral .05
725 Edgar Martinez .05
726 Norm Charlton .05
727 Paul Sorrento .05
728 Luis Sojo .05
729 Arquimedez Pozo .05
730 Jay Buhner .05
731 Chris Bosio .05
732 Chris Widger .05
733 Kevin Gross .05
734 Darren Oliver .05
735 Dean Palmer .05
736 Matt Whiteside .05
737 Luis Ortiz .05
738 Roger Pavlik .05
739 Damon Buford .05
740 Juan Gonzalez .60
741 Rusty Greer .05
742 Lou Frazier .05
743 Pat Hentgen .05
744 Tomas Perez .05
745 Juan Guzman .05
746 Otis Nixon .05
747 Robert Perez .05
748 Ed Sprague .05
749 Tony Castillo .05
750 John Olerud .05
751 Shawn Green .10
752 Jeff Ware .05
753 Dante Bichette, Larry Walker, Andres Galarraga, Vinny Castilla Checklist 396-441/ Blake St. Bombers .05
754 Greg Maddux Checklist 442-487 .25
755 Marty Cordova Checklist 488-533 .05
756 Ozzie Smith Checklist 534-579 .35
757 John Vander Wal Checklist 580-625 .05
758 Andres Galarraga Checklist 626-670 .05
759 Frank Thomas Checklist 671-715 .20
760 Tony Gwynn Checklist 716-760 .25
761 Randy Myers .10
762 Kent Mercker .10
763 David Wells .05
764 Tom Gordon .10
765 Wil Cordero .10
766 Dave Magadan .10
767 Doug Jones .10
768 Kevin Tapani .10
769 Curtis Goodwin .10
770 Julio Franco .10
771 Jack McDowell .10
772 Al Leiter .10
773 Sean Berry .10
774 Bip Roberts .10
775 Jose Offerman .10
776 Ben McDonald .10
777 Dan Serafini .10
778 Ryan McGuire .10
779 Tim Raines .10
780 Tino Martinez .10
781 Kenny Rogers .10
782 Bob Tewksbury .10
783 Rickey Henderson .60
784 Ron Gant .10
785 Gary Gaetti .10
786 Andy Benes .10
787 Royce Clayton .10
788 Darryl Hamilton .10
789 Ken Hill .10
790 Erik Hanson .10

Gold Signature

NM/M

Common Player: 1.00
Stars: 10X
(See 1996 Collector's Choice for checklist and base card values.)

Silver Signature

NM/M

Complete Set (730): 50.00
Common Player: .10
Stars: 1.5X
(See 1996 Collector's Choice for checklist and base card values.)

A Cut Above

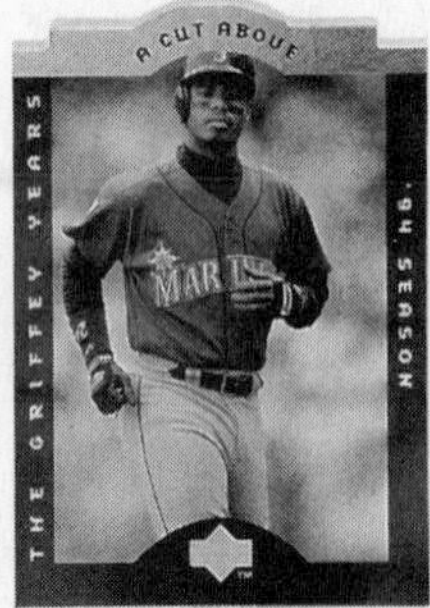

NM/M

Complete Set (10): 8.00
Common Card: 1.00

Nomo Scrapbook

NM/M

Complete Set (5): 10.00
Common Card: 2.00
Japanese: 3X
1-5 Hideo Nomo 2.00

Ripken Collection

NM/M

Complete Set (1-4, 9-12) 15.00

Common Card: 2.00
Header Card: 2.00
(See also Upper Deck Series 1 and 2, and Upper Deck/SP)

1997 COLLECTOR'S CHOICE

NM/M
Factory Set (516): 12.00
Complete Set (506): 10.00
Common Player: .05
Pack (12): 1.00
Wax Box (36): 20.00

1 Andruw Jones (Rookie Class) 1.00
2 Rocky Coppinger (Rookie Class) .05
3 Jeff D'Amico (Rookie Class) .05
4 Dmitri Young (Rookie Class) .05
5 Darin Erstad (Rookie Class) .75
6 Jermaine Allensworth (Rookie Class) .05
7 Damian Jackson (Rookie Class) .05
8 Bill Mueller (Rookie Class) .05
9 Jacob Cruz (Rookie Class) .05
10 Vladimir Guerrero (Rookie Class) 1.00
11 Marty Janzen (Rookie Class) .05
12 Kevin L. Brown (Rookie Class) .05
13 Willie Adams (Rookie Class) .05
14 Wendell Magee (Rookie Class) .05
15 Scott Rolen (Rookie Class) .65
16 Matt Beech (Rookie Class) .05
17 Neifi Perez (Rookie Class) .05
18 Jamey Wright (Rookie Class) .05
19 Jose Paniagua (Rookie Class) .05
20 Todd Walker (Rookie Class) .05
21 Justin Thompson (Rookie Class) .05
22 Robin Jennings (Rookie Class) .05
23 *Dario Veras* (Rookie Class) .05
24 Brian Lesher (Rookie Class) .05
25 Nomar Garciaparra (Rookie Class) 1.50
26 Luis Castillo (Rookie Class) .05
27 *Brian Giles* (Rookie Class) .75
28 Jermaine Dye .05
29 Terrell Wade .05
30 Fred McGriff .05
31 Marquis Grissom .05
32 Ryan Klesko .05
33 Javier Lopez .05
34 Mark Wohlers .05
35 Tom Glavine .20
36 Denny Neagle .05
37 Scott Erickson .05
38 Chris Hoiles .05
39 Roberto Alomar .35
40 Eddie Murray .75
41 Cal Ripken Jr. 2.00
42 Randy Myers .05
43 B.J. Surhoff .05
44 Rick Krivda .05
45 Jose Canseco .50
46 Heathcliff Slocumb .05
47 Jeff Suppan .05
48 Tom Gordon .05
49 Aaron Sele .05
50 Mo Vaughn .05
51 Darren Bragg .05
52 Wil Cordero .05
53 Scott Bullett .05
54 Terry Adams .05
55 Jackie Robinson .35
56 Tony Gwynn, Alex Rodriguez (Batting Leaders) .35
57 Andres Galarraga, Mark McGwire (Homer Leaders) .50
58 Andres Galarraga, Albert Belle (RBI Leaders) .05
59 Eric Young, Kenny Lofton (SB Leaders) .05
60 John Smoltz, Andy Pettitte (Victory Leaders) .05
61 John Smoltz, Roger Clemens (Strikout Leaders) .15
62 Kevin Brown, Juan Guzman (ERA Leaders) .05
63 John Wetteland, Todd Worrell, Jeff Brantley (Save Leaders) .05
64 Scott Servais .05
65 Sammy Sosa 1.25
66 Ryne Sandberg 1.00
67 Frank Castillo .05
68 Rey Sanchez .05
69 Steve Trachsel .05
70 Robin Ventura .05
71 Wilson Alvarez .05
72 Tony Phillips .05
73 Lyle Mouton .05
74 Mike Cameron .05
75 Harold Baines .05
76 Albert Belle .15
77 Chris Snopek .05
78 Reggie Sanders .05
79 Jeff Brantley .05
80 Barry Larkin .05
81 Kevin Jarvis .05
82 John Smiley .05
83 Pete Schourek .05
84 Thomas Howard .05
85 Lee Smith .05
86 Omar Vizquel .05
87 Julio Franco .05
88 Orel Hershiser .05
89 Charles Nagy .05
90 Matt Williams .05
91 Dennis Martinez .05
92 Jose Mesa .05
93 Sandy Alomar Jr. .05
94 Jim Thome .05
95 Vinny Castilla .05
96 Armando Reynoso .05
97 Kevin Ritz .05
98 Larry Walker .05
99 Eric Young .05
100 Dante Bichette .05
101 Quinton McCracken .05
102 John Vander Wal .05
103 Phil Nevin .05
104 Tony Clark .05
105 Alan Trammell .05
106 Felipe Lira .05
107 Curtis Pride .05
108 Bobby Higginson .05
109 Mark Lewis .05
110 Travis Fryman .05
111 Al Leiter .05
112 Devon White .05
113 Jeff Conine .05
114 Charles Johnson .05
115 Andre Dawson .20
116 Edgar Renteria .05
117 Robb Nen .05
118 Kevin Brown .05
119 Derek Bell .05
120 Bob Abreu .05
121 Mike Hampton .05
122 Todd Jones .05
123 Billy Wagner .05
124 Shane Reynolds .05
125 Jeff Bagwell .75
126 Brian L. Hunter .05
127 Jeff Montgomery .05
128 *Rod Myers* .05
129 Tim Belcher .05
130 Kevin Appier .05
131 Mike Sweeney .05
132 Craig Paquette .05
133 Joe Randa .05
134 Michael Tucker .05
135 Raul Mondesi .05
136 Tim Wallach .05
137 Brett Butler .05
138 Karim Garcia .10
139 Todd Hollandsworth .05
140 Eric Karros .05
141 Hideo Nomo .75
142 Ismael Valdes .05
143 Cal Eldred .05
144 Scott Karl .05
145 Matt Mieske .05
146 Mike Fetters .05
147 Mark Loretta .05
148 Fernando Vina .05
149 Jeff Cirillo .05
150 Dave Nilsson .05
151 Kirby Puckett 1.00
152 Rich Becker .05
153 Chuck Knoblauch .05
154 Marty Cordova .05
155 Paul Molitor .75
156 Rick Aguilera .05
157 Pat Meares .05
158 Frank Rodriguez .05
159 David Segui .05
160 Henry Rodriguez .05
161 Shane Andrews .05
162 Pedro J. Martinez .75
163 Mark Grudzielanek .05
164 Mike Lansing .05
165 Rondell White .05
166 Ugueth Urbina .05
167 Rey Ordonez .05
168 Robert Person .05
169 Carlos Baerga .05
170 Bernard Gilkey .05
171 John Franco .05
172 Pete Harnisch .05
173 Butch Huskey .05
174 Paul Wilson .05
175 Bernie Williams .20
176 Dwight Gooden .05
177 Wade Boggs 1.00
178 Ruben Rivera .05
179 Jim Leyritz .05
180 Derek Jeter 2.00
181 Tino Martinez .05
182 Tim Raines .05
183 Scott Brosius .05
184 Jason Giambi .60
185 Geronimo Berroa .05
186 Ariel Prieto .05
187 Scott Spiezio .05
188 John Wasdin .05
189 Ernie Young .05
190 Mark McGwire 1.50
191 Jim Eisenreich .05
192 Ricky Bottalico .05
193 Darren Daulton .05
194 David Doster .05
195 Gregg Jefferies .05
196 Lenny Dykstra .05
197 Curt Schilling .20
198 Todd Stottlemyre .05
199 Willie McGee .05
200 Ozzie Smith 1.00
201 Dennis Eckersley .65
202 Ray Lankford .05
203 John Mabry .05
204 Alan Benes .05
205 Ron Gant .05
206 Archi Cianfrocco .05
207 Fernando Valenzuela .05
208 Greg Vaughn .05
209 Steve Finley .05
210 Tony Gwynn 1.00
211 Rickey Henderson .75
212 Trevor Hoffman .05
213 Jason Thompson .05
214 Osvaldo Fernandez .05
215 Glenallen Hill .05
216 William VanLandingham .05
217 Marvin Benard .05
218 Juan Gonzalez (Postseason) .20
219 Roberto Alomar (Postseason) .05
220 Brian Jordan (Postseason) .05
221 John Smoltz (Postseason) .05
222 Javy Lopez (Postseason) .05
223 Bernie Williams (Postseason) .05
224 Jim Leyritz, John Wetteland (Postseason) .05
225 Barry Bonds 2.00
226 Rich Aurilia .05
227 Jay Canizaro .05
228 Dan Wilson .05
229 Bob Wolcott .05
230 Ken Griffey Jr. 1.25
231 Sterling Hitchcock .05
232 Edgar Martinez .05
233 Joey Cora .05
234 Norm Charlton .05
235 Alex Rodriguez 1.50
236 Bobby Witt .05
237 Darren Oliver .05
238 Kevin Elster .05
239 Rusty Greer .05
240 Juan Gonzalez .75
241 Will Clark .10
242 Dean Palmer .05
243 Ivan Rodriguez .65
244 Ken Griffey Jr. Checklist .25
245 Ken Griffey Jr. Checklist .25
246 Ken Griffey Jr. Checklist .25
247 Ken Griffey Jr. Checklist .25
248 Ken Griffey Jr. Checklist .25
249 Ken Griffey Jr. Checklist .25
250 Eddie Murray .75
251 Troy Percival .05
252 Garret Anderson .05
253 Allen Watson .05
254 Jason Dickson .05
255 Jim Edmonds .05
256 Chuck Finley .05
257 Randy Velarde .05
258 Shigetosi Hasegawa .05
259 Todd Greene .05
260 Tim Salmon .10
261 Mark Langston .05
262 Dave Hollins .05
263 Gary DiSarcina .05
264 Kenny Lofton .05
265 John Smoltz .05
266 Greg Maddux 1.00
267 Jeff Blauser .05
268 Alan Embree .05
269 Mark Lemke .05
270 Chipper Jones 1.00
271 Mike Mussina .65
272 Rafael Palmeiro .65
273 Jimmy Key .05
274 Mike Bordick .05
275 Brady Anderson .05
276 Eric Davis .05
277 Jeffrey Hammonds .05
278 Reggie Jefferson .05
279 Tim Naehring .05
280 John Valentin .05
281 Troy O'Leary .05
282 Shane Mack .05
283 Mike Stanley .05
284 Tim Wakefield .05
285 Brian McRae .05
286 Brooks Kieschnick .05
287 Shawon Dunston .05
288 Kevin Foster .05
289 Mel Rojas .05
290 Mark Grace .10
291 Brant Brown .05
292 Amaury Telemaco .05
293 Dave Martinez .05
294 Jaime Navarro .05
295 Ray Durham .05
296 Ozzie Guillen .05
297 Roberto Hernandez .05
298 Ron Karkovice .05
299 James Baldwin .05
300 Frank Thomas .75
301 Eddie Taubensee .05
302 Bret Boone .05
303 Willie Greene .05
304 Dave Burba .05
305 Deion Sanders .10
306 Reggie Sanders .05
307 Hal Morris .05
308 Pokey Reese .05
309 Tony Fernandez .05
310 Manny Ramirez .75
311 Chad Ogea .05
312 Jack McDowell .05
313 Kevin Mitchell .05
314 Chad Curtis .05
315 Steve Kline .05
316 Kevin Seitzer .05
317 Kirt Manwaring .05

318	Bill Swift	.05
319	Ellis Burks	.05
320	Andres Galarraga	.05
321	Bruce Ruffin	.05
322	Mark Thompson	.05
323	Walt Weiss	.05
324	Todd Jones	.05
325	Andruw Jones (Griffey Hot List)	.50
326	Chipper Jones (Griffey Hot List)	.65
327	Mo Vaughn (Griffey Hot List)	.05
328	Frank Thomas (Griffey Hot List)	.50
329	Albert Belle (Griffey Hot List)	.10
330	Mark McGwire (Griffey Hot List)	1.00
331	Derek Jeter (Griffey Hot List)	1.50
332	Alex Rodriguez (Griffey Hot List)	1.00
333	Jay Buhner (Griffey Hot List)	.05
334	Ken Griffey Jr. (Griffey Hot List)	.75
335	Brian L. Hunter	.05
336	Brian Johnson	.05
337	Omar Olivares	.05
338	*Deivi Cruz*	.05
339	Damion Easley	.05
340	Melvin Nieves	.05
341	Moises Alou	.05
342	Jim Eisenreich	.05
343	Mark Hutton	.05
344	Alex Fernandez	.05
345	Gary Sheffield	.35
346	Pat Rapp	.05
347	Brad Ausmus	.05
348	Sean Berry	.05
349	Darryl Kile	.05
350	Craig Biggio	.05
351	Chris Holt	.05
352	Luis Gonzalez	.25
353	Pat Listach	.05
354	Jose Rosado	.05
355	Mike Macfarlane	.05
356	Tom Goodwin	.05
357	Chris Haney	.05
358	Chili Davis	.05
359	Jose Offerman	.05
360	Johnny Damon	.20
361	Bip Roberts	.05
362	Ramon Martinez	.05
363	Pedro Astacio	.05
364	Todd Zeile	.05
365	Mike Piazza	1.25
366	Greg Gagne	.05
367	Chan Ho Park	.05
368	Wilton Guerrero	.05
369	Todd Worrell	.05
370	John Jaha	.05
371	Steve Sparks	.05
372	Mike Matheny	.05
373	Marc Newfield	.05
374	Jeromy Burnitz	.05
375	Jose Valentin	.05
376	Ben McDonald	.05
377	Roberto Kelly	.05
378	Bob Tewksbury	.05
379	Ron Coomer	.05
380	Brad Radke	.05
381	Matt Lawton	.05
382	Dan Naulty	.05
383	Scott Stahoviak	.05
384	Matt Wagner	.05
385	Jim Bullinger	.05
386	Carlos Perez	.05
387	Darrin Fletcher	.05
388	Chris Widger	.05
389	F.P. Santangelo	.05
390	Lee Smith	.05
391	Bobby Jones	.05
392	John Olerud	.05
393	Mark Clark	.05
394	Jason Isringhausen	.05
395	Todd Hundley	.05
396	Lance Johnson	.05
397	Edgardo Alfonzo	.05
398	Alex Ochoa	.05
399	Darryl Strawberry	.05
400	David Cone	.05
401	Paul O'Neill	.05
402	Joe Girardi	.05
403	Charlie Hayes	.05
404	Andy Pettitte	.25
405	Mariano Rivera	.25
406	Mariano Duncan	.05
407	Kenny Rogers	.05
408	Cecil Fielder	.05
409	George Williams	.05
410	Jose Canseco	.35
411	Tony Batista	.05
412	Steve Karsay	.05
413	Dave Telgheder	.05
414	Billy Taylor	.05
415	Mickey Morandini	.05
416	Calvin Maduro	.05
417	Mark Leiter	.05
418	Kevin Stocker	.05
419	Mike Lieberthal	.05
420	Rico Brogna	.05
421	Mark Portugal	.05
422	Rex Hudler	.05
423	Mark Johnson	.05
424	Esteban Loiaza	.05
425	Lou Collier	.05
426	Kevin Elster	.05
427	Francisco Cordova	.05
428	Marc Wilkins	.05
429	Joe Randa	.05
430	Jason Kendall	.05
431	Jon Lieber	.05
432	Steve Cooke	.05
433	*Emil Brown*	.05
434	*Tony Womack*	.25
435	Al Martin	.05
436	Jason Schmidt	.05
437	Andy Benes	.05
438	Delino DeShields	.05
439	Royce Clayton	.05
440	Brian Jordan	.05
441	Donovan Osborne	.05
442	Gary Gaetti	.05
443	Tom Pagnozzi	.05
444	Joey Hamilton	.05
445	Wally Joyner	.05
446	John Flaherty	.05
447	Chris Gomez	.05
448	Sterling Hitchcock	.05
449	Andy Ashby	.05
450	Ken Caminiti	.05
451	Tim Worrell	.05
452	Jose Vizcaino	.05
453	Rod Beck	.05
454	Wilson Delgado	.05
455	Darryl Hamilton	.05
456	Mark Lewis	.05
457	Mark Gardner	.05
458	Rick Wilkins	.05
459	Scott Sanders	.05
460	Kevin Orie	.05
461	Glendon Rusch	.05
462	Juan Melo	.05
463	Richie Sexson	.05
464	Bartolo Colon	.05
465	Jose Guillen	.05
466	Heath Murray	.05
467	Aaron Boone	.05
468	*Bubba Trammell*	.25
469	Jeff Abbott	.05
470	Derrick Gibson	.05
471	Matt Morris	.05
472	Ryan Jones	.05
473	Pat Cline	.05
474	Adam Riggs	.05
475	Jay Payton	.05
476	Derrek Lee	.05
477	Elieser Marrero	.05
478	Lee Tinsley	.05
479	Jamie Moyer	.05
480	Jay Buhner	.05
481	Bob Wells	.05
482	Jeff Fassero	.05
483	Paul Sorrento	.05
484	Russ Davis	.05
485	Randy Johnson	.75
486	Roger Pavlik	.05
487	Damon Buford	.05
488	Julio Santana	.05
489	Mark McLemore	.05
490	Mickey Tettleton	.05
491	Ken Hill	.05
492	Benji Gil	.05
493	Ed Sprague	.05
494	Mike Timlin	.05
495	Pat Hentgen	.05
496	Orlando Merced	.05
497	Carlos Garcia	.05
498	Carlos Delgado	.35
499	Juan Guzman	.05
500	Roger Clemens	1.00
501	Erik Hanson	.05
502	Otis Nixon	.05
503	Shawn Green	.10
504	Charlie O'Brien	.05
505	Joe Carter	.05
506	Alex Gonzalez	.05

All-Star Connection

		NM/M
Complete Set (45):		10.00
Common Player:		.10
1	Mark McGwire	1.00
2	Chuck Knoblauch	.10
3	Jim Thome	.10
4	Alex Rodriguez	1.00
5	Ken Griffey Jr.	.75
6	Brady Anderson	.10
7	Albert Belle	.20
8	Ivan Rodriguez	.40
9	Pat Hentgen	.10
10	Frank Thomas	.45
11	Roberto Alomar	.30
12	Robin Ventura	.10
13	Cal Ripken Jr.	1.50
14	Juan Gonzalez	.45
15	Manny Ramirez	.45
16	Bernie Williams	.15
17	Terry Steinbach	.10
18	Andy Pettitte	.25
19	Jeff Bagwell	.45
20	Craig Biggio	.10
21	Ken Caminiti	.10
22	Barry Larkin	.10
23	Tony Gwynn	.60
24	Barry Bonds	1.50
25	Kenny Lofton	.10
26	Mike Piazza	.75
27	John Smoltz	.10
28	Andres Galarraga	.10
29	Ryne Sandberg	.60
30	Chipper Jones	.60
31	Mark Grudzielanek	.10
32	Sammy Sosa	.75
33	Steve Finley	.10
34	Gary Sheffield	.25
35	Todd Hundley	.10
36	Greg Maddux	.60
37	Mo Vaughn	.10
38	Eric Young	.10
39	Vinny Castilla	.10
40	Derek Jeter	1.50
41	Lance Johnson	.10
42	Ellis Burks	.10
43	Dante Bichette	.10
44	Javy Lopez	.10
45	Hideo Nomo	.45

Big Shots

		NM/M
Complete Set (19):		15.00
Common Player:		.20
Gold Signature Edition:		2X
1	Ken Griffey Jr.	2.00
2	Nomar Garciaparra	2.00
3	Brian Jordan	.20
4	Scott Rolen	.75
5	Alex Rodriguez	2.25
6	Larry Walker	.20
7	Mariano Rivera	.35
8	Cal Ripken Jr.	2.50
9	Deion Sanders	.20
10	Frank Thomas	1.00
11	Dean Palmer	.20
12	Ken Caminiti	.20
13	Derek Jeter	2.50
14	Barry Bonds	2.50
15	Chipper Jones	1.50
16	Mo Vaughn	.20
17	Jay Buhner	.20
18	Mike Piazza	2.00
19	Tony Gwynn	1.50

Big Show

		NM/M
Complete Set (45):		7.00
Common Player:		.10
World Headquarters:		8X
1	Greg Maddux	.50
2	Chipper Jones	.50
3	Andruw Jones	.35
4	John Smoltz	.10
5	Cal Ripken Jr.	1.00
6	Roberto Alomar	.30
7	Rafael Palmeiro	.35
8	Eddie Murray	.35
9	Jose Canseco	.30
10	Roger Clemens	.55
11	Mo Vaughn	.10
12	Jim Edmonds	.10
13	Tim Salmon	.15
14	Sammy Sosa	.60
15	Albert Belle	.15
16	Frank Thomas	.35
17	Barry Larkin	.10
18	Kenny Lofton	.10
19	Manny Ramirez	.35
20	Matt Williams	.10
21	Dante Bichette	.10
22	Gary Sheffield	.30
23	Craig Biggio	.10
24	Jeff Bagwell	.35
25	Todd Hollandsworth	.10
26	Raul Mondesi	.10
27	Hideo Nomo	.35
28	Mike Piazza	.60
29	Paul Molitor	.35
30	Kirby Puckett	.50
31	Rondell White	.10
32	Rey Ordonez	.10
33	Paul Wilson	.10
34	Derek Jeter	1.00
35	Andy Pettitte	.30
36	Mark McGwire	.75
37	Jason Kendall	.10
38	Ozzie Smith	.50
39	Tony Gwynn	.50
40	Barry Bonds	1.00
41	Alex Rodriguez	.75
42	Jay Buhner	.10
43	Ken Griffey Jr.	.60
44	Randy Johnson	.35
45	Juan Gonzalez	.35

Clearly Dominant

		NM/M
Complete Set (5):		16.00
Common Card:		4.00
CD1	Ken Griffey Jr.	4.00
CD2	Ken Griffey Jr.	4.00
CD3	Ken Griffey Jr.	4.00
CD4	Ken Griffey Jr.	4.00
CD5	Ken Griffey Jr.	4.00

Clearly Dominant Jumbos

		NM/M
Complete Set (5):		10.00
Common Card:		2.00
1	Ken Griffey Jr.	2.00
2	Ken Griffey Jr.	2.00
3	Ken Griffey Jr.	2.00
4	Ken Griffey Jr.	2.00
5	Ken Griffey Jr.	2.00

Hot List Jumbos

		NM/M
Complete Set (10):		15.00
Common Player:		.50
325	Andruw Jones	1.00
326	Chipper Jones	2.00
327	Mo Vaughn	.50
328	Frank Thomas	1.50
329	Albert Belle	.60
330	Mark McGwire	3.00
331	Derek Jeter	4.00
332	Alex Rodriguez	3.00
333	Jay Buhner	.50
334	Ken Griffey Jr.	2.50

New Frontier

		NM/M
Complete Set (40):		75.00
Common Player:		1.00
1	Alex Rodriguez	5.00
2	Tony Gwynn	3.00
3	Jose Canseco	1.25
4	Hideo Nomo	2.00
5	Mark McGwire	5.00
6	Barry Bonds	6.00
7	Juan Gonzalez	2.00
8	Ken Caminiti	1.00
9	Tim Salmon	1.25
10	Mike Piazza	4.00
11	Ken Griffey Jr.	4.00
12	Andres Galarraga	1.00
13	Jay Buhner	1.00
14	Dante Bichette	1.00
15	Frank Thomas	2.00
16	Ryne Sandberg	3.00
17	Roger Clemens	3.50
18	Andruw Jones	2.00
19	Jim Thome	1.00
20	Sammy Sosa	4.00
21	David Justice	1.00
22	Deion Sanders	1.00
23	Todd Walker	1.00
24	Kevin Orie	1.00
25	Albert Belle	1.25
26	Jeff Bagwell	2.00
27	Manny Ramirez	2.00
28	Brian Jordan	1.00
29	Derek Jeter	6.00
30	Chipper Jones	3.00
31	Mo Vaughn	1.00
32	Gary Sheffield	1.50
33	Carlos Delgado	1.50
34	Vladimir Guerrero	2.00
35	Cal Ripken Jr.	6.00
36	Greg Maddux	3.00
37	Cecil Fielder	1.00
38	Todd Hundley	1.00
39	Mike Mussina	1.25
40	Scott Rolen	1.50

Premier Power

		NM/M
Complete Set (20):		17.50
Common Player:		.35
Gold:		2X
1	Mark McGwire	2.50
2	Brady Anderson	.35
3	Ken Griffey Jr.	2.00
4	Albert Belle	.45
5	Juan Gonzalez	.75
6	Andres Galarraga	.35
7	Jay Buhner	.35
8	Mo Vaughn	.35
9	Barry Bonds	3.00
10	Gary Sheffield	.65
11	Todd Hundley	.35
12	Frank Thomas	1.00
13	Sammy Sosa	2.00
14	Ken Caminiti	.35
15	Vinny Castilla	.35
16	Ellis Burks	.35
17	Rafael Palmeiro	.75
18	Alex Rodriguez	2.50
19	Mike Piazza	2.00
20	Eddie Murray	.75

Premier Power Jumbo

		NM/M
Complete Set (20):		15.00
Common Player:		.50
1	Mark McGwire	2.50
2	Brady Anderson	.50
3	Ken Griffey Jr.	2.00
4	Albert Belle	.60
5	Juan Gonzalez	1.00
6	Andres Galarraga	.50
7	Jay Buhner	.50
8	Mo Vaughn	.50
9	Barry Bonds	3.00
10	Gary Sheffield	.65
11	Todd Hundley	.50
12	Frank Thomas	1.50
13	Sammy Sosa	2.00
14	Ken Caminiti	.50
15	Vinny Castilla	.50
16	Ellis Burks	.50
17	Rafael Palmeiro	1.00
18	Alex Rodriguez	2.50
19	Mike Piazza	2.00
20	Eddie Murray	1.00

Stick'Ums

		NM/M
Complete Set (30):		5.00
Common Player:		.05
1	Ozzie Smith	.50
2	Andruw Jones	.35
3	Alex Rodriguez	.75
4	Paul Molitor	.35
5	Jeff Bagwell	.35
6	Manny Ramirez	.35
7	Kenny Lofton	.05
8	Albert Belle	.10
9	Jay Buhner	.05
10	Chipper Jones	.50
11	Barry Larkin	.05
12	Dante Bichette	.05
13	Mike Piazza	.60
14	Andres Galarraga	.05
15	Barry Bonds	1.00
16	Brady Anderson	.05
17	Gary Sheffield	.20
18	Jim Thome	.05
19	Tony Gwynn	.50
20	Cal Ripken Jr.	1.00
21	Sammy Sosa	.60
22	Juan Gonzalez	.35
23	Greg Maddux	.50
24	Ken Griffey Jr.	.60
25	Mark McGwire	.75
26	Kirby Puckett	.50
27	Mo Vaughn	.05
28	Vladimir Guerrero	.35
29	Ken Caminiti	.05
30	Frank Thomas	.35

Toast of the Town

		NM/M
Complete Set (30):		35.00
Common Player:		.25
1	Andruw Jones	1.00
2	Chipper Jones	2.00
3	Greg Maddux	2.00
4	John Smoltz	.25
5	Kenny Lofton	.25
6	Brady Anderson	.25
7	Cal Ripken Jr.	5.00
8	Mo Vaughn	.25
9	Sammy Sosa	3.00
10	Albert Belle	.30
11	Frank Thomas	1.25
12	Barry Larkin	.25
13	Manny Ramirez	1.00
14	Jeff Bagwell	1.00
15	Mike Piazza	3.00
16	Paul Molitor	1.00
17	Vladimir Guerrero	1.00
18	Todd Hundley	.25
19	Derek Jeter	5.00
20	Andy Pettitte	.40
21	Bernie Williams	.30
22	Mark McGwire	4.00
23	Scott Rolen	1.00
24	Ken Caminiti	.25
25	Tony Gwynn	2.00
26	Barry Bonds	5.00
27	Ken Griffey Jr.	3.00
28	Alex Rodriguez	4.00
29	Juan Gonzalez	1.00
30	Roger Clemens	2.25

1997 COLLECTOR'S CHOICE UPDATE

		NM/M
Complete Set (30):		2.00
Common Player:		.10
1	Jim Leyritz	.10
2	Matt Perisho	.10
3	Michael Tucker	.10
4	Mike Johnson	.10
5	Jaime Navarro	.10
6	Doug Drabek	.10
7	Terry Mulholland	.10
8	Brett Tomko	.10
9	Marquis Grissom	.10
10	David Justice	.10
11	Brian Moehler	.10
12	Bobby Bonilla	.10
13	Todd Dunwoody	.10
14	Tony Saunders	.10
15	Jay Bell	.10
16	Jeff King	.10
17	Terry Steinbach	.10
18	Steve Bieser	.10
19	*Takashi Kashiwada*	.15
20	Hideki Irabu	.10
21	Damon Mashore	.10
22	Quilvio Veras	.10
23	Will Cunnane	.10
24	Jeff Kent	.50
25	J.T. Snow	.10
26	Dante Powell	.10
17	Jose Cruz Jr.	.10
28	John Burkett	.10
29	John Wetteland	.10
30	Benito Santiago	.10

1998 COLLECTOR'S CHOICE

		NM/M
Complete Set (530):		10.00
Unopened Factory Set (540):		15.00
Common Player:		.05
Pack (14):		1.00
Wax Box (36):		15.00
1	Nomar Garciaparra (Cover Glory)	.65
2	Roger Clemens (Cover Glory)	.50
3	Larry Walker (Cover Glory)	.05
4	Mike Piazza (Cover Glory)	.60
5	Mark McGwire (Cover Glory)	.75
6	Tony Gwynn (Cover Glory)	.45
7	Jose Cruz Jr. (Cover Glory)	.05
8	Frank Thomas (Cover Glory)	.50
9	Tino Martinez (Cover Glory)	.05
10	Ken Griffey Jr. (Cover Glory)	.60
11	Barry Bonds (Cover Glory)	.85
12	Scott Rolen (Cover Glory)	.30
13	Randy Johnson (Cover Glory)	.15
14	Ryne Sandberg (Cover Glory)	.35
15	Eddie Murray (Cover Glory)	.15
16	Kevin Brown (Cover Glory)	.05
17	Greg Maddux (Cover Glory)	.35
18	Sandy Alomar Jr. (Cover Glory)	.05
19	Ken Griffey Jr., Adam Riggs Checklist	.40
20	Nomar Garciaparra, Charlie O'Brien Checklist	.10
21	Ben Grieve, Ken Griffey Jr., Larry Walker, Mark McGwire Checklist	.50
22	Mark McGwire, Cal Ripken Jr. Checklist	.50
23	Tino Martinez Checklist	.05
24	Jason Dickson	.05
25	Darin Erstad	.40
26	Todd Greene	.05
27	Chuck Finley	.05
28	Garret Anderson	.05
29	Dave Hollins	.05
30	Rickey Henderson	.60
31	John Smoltz	.05
32	Michael Tucker	.05
33	Jeff Blauser	.05
34	Javier Lopez	.05
35	Andruw Jones	.60
36	Denny Neagle	.05
37	Randall Simon	.05
38	Mark Wohlers	.05
39	Harold Baines	.05
40	Cal Ripken Jr.	1.50
41	Mike Bordick	.05
42	Jimmy Key	.05
43	Armando Benitez	.05
44	Scott Erickson	.05
45	Eric Davis	.05
46	Bret Saberhagen	.05
47	Darren Bragg	.05
48	Steve Avery	.05
49	Jeff Frye	.05
50	Aaron Sele	.05
51	Scott Hatteberg	.05
52	Tom Gordon	.05
53	Kevin Orie	.05
54	Kevin Foster	.05
55	Ryne Sandberg	.75
56	Doug Glanville	.05
57	Tyler Houston	.05
58	Steve Trachsel	.05
59	Mark Grace	.10
60	Frank Thomas	.60
61	*Scott Eyre*	.05
62	Jeff Abbott	.05
63	Chris Clemons	.05
64	Jorge Fabregas	.05
65	Robin Ventura	.05
66	Matt Karchner	.05
67	Jon Nunnally	.05
68	Aaron Boone	.05
69	Pokey Reese	.05
70	Deion Sanders	.10
71	Jeff Shaw	.05
72	Eduardo Perez	.05
73	Brett Tomko	.05
74	Bartolo Colon	.05
75	Manny Ramirez	.60
76	Jose Mesa	.05
77	Brian Giles	.05
78	Richie Sexson	.05
79	Orel Hershiser	.05
80	Matt Williams	.05
81	Walt Weiss	.05
82	Jerry DiPoto	.05
83	Quinton McCracken	.05

No.	Player	Price
84	Neifi Perez	.05
85	Vinny Castilla	.05
86	Ellis Burks	.05
87	John Thomson	.05
88	Willie Blair	.05
89	Bob Hamelin	.05
90	Tony Clark	.05
91	Todd Jones	.05
92	Deivi Cruz	.05
93	*Frank Catalanotto*	.15
94	Justin Thompson	.05
95	Gary Sheffield	.25
96	Kevin Brown	.05
97	Charles Johnson	.05
98	Bobby Bonilla	.05
99	Livan Hernandez	.05
100	Paul Konerko (Rookie Class)	.10
101	Craig Counsell (Rookie Class)	.05
102	*Magglio Ordonez* (Rookie Class)	1.00
103	Garrett Stephenson (Rookie Class)	.05
104	Ken Cloude (Rookie Class)	.05
105	Miguel Tejada (Rookie Class)	.25
106	Juan Encarnacion (Rookie Class)	.05
107	Dennis Reyes (Rookie Class)	.05
108	Orlando Cabrera (Rookie Class)	.05
109	Kelvim Escobar (Rookie Class)	.05
110	Ben Grieve (Rookie Class)	.10
111	Brian Rose (Rookie Class)	.05
112	Fernando Tatis (Rookie Class)	.05
113	Tom Evans (Rookie Class)	.05
114	Tom Fordham (Rookie Class)	.05
115	Mark Kotsay (Rookie Class)	.05
116	Mario Valdez (Rookie Class)	.05
117	Jeremi Gonzalez (Rookie Class)	.05
118	Todd Dunwoody (Rookie Class)	.05
119	Javier Valentin (Rookie Class)	.05
120	Todd Helton (Rookie Class)	.50
121	Jason Varitek (Rookie Class)	.05
122	Chris Carpenter (Rookie Class)	.05
123	*Kevin Millwood* (Rookie Class)	.75
124	Brad Fullmer (Rookie Class)	.05
125	Jaret Wright (Rookie Class)	.05
126	Brad Rigby (Rookie Class)	.05
127	Edgar Renteria	.05
128	Robb Nen	.05
129	Tony Pena	.05
130	Craig Biggio	.05
131	Brad Ausmus	.05
132	Shane Reynolds	.05
133	Mike Hampton	.05
134	Billy Wagner	.05
135	Richard Hidalgo	.05
136	Jose Rosado	.05
137	Yamil Benitez	.05
138	Felix Martinez	.05
139	Jeff King	.05
140	Jose Offerman	.05
141	Joe Vitiello	.05
142	Tim Belcher	.05
143	Brett Butler	.05
144	Greg Gagne	.05
145	Mike Piazza	1.00
146	Ramon Martinez	.05
147	Raul Mondesi	.05
148	Adam Riggs	.05
149	Eddie Murray	.50
150	Jeff Cirillo	.05
151	Scott Karl	.05
152	Mike Fetters	.05
153	Dave Nilsson	.05
154	Antone Williamson	.05
155	Jeff D'Amico	.05
156	Jose Valentin	.05
157	Brad Radke	.05
158	Torii Hunter	.05
159	Chuck Knoblauch	.05
160	Paul Molitor	.60
161	Travis Miller	.05
162	Rich Robertson	.05
163	Ron Coomer	.05
164	Mark Grudzielanek	.05
165	Lee Smith	.05
166	Vladimir Guerrero	.60
167	Dustin Hermanson	.05
168	Ugueth Urbina	.05
169	F.P. Santangelo	.05
170	Rondell White	.05
171	Bobby Jones	.05
172	Edgardo Alfonzo	.05
173	John Franco	.05
174	Carlos Baerga	.05
175	Butch Huskey	.05
176	Rey Ordonez	.05
177	Matt Franco	.05
178	Dwight Gooden	.05
179	Chad Curtis	.05
180	Tino Martinez	.05
181	Charlie O'Brien (Masked Marauders)	.05
182	Sandy Alomar Jr. (Masked Marauders)	.05
183	Raul Casanova (Masked Marauders)	.05
184	Jim Leyritz (Masked Marauders)	.05
185	Mike Piazza (Masked Marauders)	.60
186	Ivan Rodriguez (Masked Marauders)	.25
187	Charles Johnson (Masked Marauders)	.05
188	Brad Ausmus (Masked Marauders)	.05
189	Brian Johnson (Masked Marauders)	.05
190	Wade Boggs	.75
191	David Wells	.05
192	Tim Raines	.05
193	Ramiro Mendoza	.05
194	Willie Adams	.05
195	Matt Stairs	.05
196	Jason McDonald	.05
197	Dave Magadan	.05
198	Mark Bellhorn	.05
199	Ariel Prieto	.05
200	Jose Canseco	.35
201	Bobby Estalella	.05
202	*Tony Barron*	.05
203	Midre Cummings	.05
204	Ricky Bottalico	.05
205	Mike Grace	.05
206	Rico Brogna	.05
207	Mickey Morandini	.05
208	Lou Collier	.05
209	*Kevin Polcovich*	.05
210	Kevin Young	.05
211	Jose Guillen	.05
212	Esteban Loaiza	.05
213	Marc Wilkins	.05
214	Jason Schmidt	.05
215	Gary Gaetti	.05
216	Fernando Valenzuela	.05
217	Willie McGee	.05
218	Alan Benes	.05
219	Eli Marrero	.05
220	Mark McGwire	1.25
221	Matt Morris	.05
222	Trevor Hoffman	.05
223	Will Cunnane	.05
224	Joey Hamilton	.05
225	Ken Caminiti	.05
226	Derrek Lee	.05
227	Mark Sweeney	.05
228	Carlos Hernandez	.05
229	Brian Johnson	.05
230	Jeff Kent	.05
231	Kirk Rueter	.05
232	Bill Mueller	.05
233	Dante Powell	.05
234	J.T. Snow	.05
235	Shawn Estes	.05
236	Dennis Martinez	.05
237	Jamie Moyer	.05
238	Dan Wilson	.05
239	Joey Cora	.05
240	Ken Griffey Jr.	1.00
241	Paul Sorrento	.05
242	Jay Buhner	.05
243	*Hanley Frias*	.05
244	John Burkett	.05
245	Juan Gonzalez	.60
246	Rick Helling	.05
247	Darren Oliver	.05
248	Mickey Tettleton	.05
249	Ivan Rodriguez	.50
250	Joe Carter	.05
251	Pat Hentgen	.05
252	Marty Janzen	.05
253	Frank Thomas, Tony Gwynn (Top of the Charts)	.25
254	Mark McGwire, Ken Griffey Jr., Larry Walker (Top of the Charts)	.50
255	Ken Griffey Jr., Andres Galarraga (Top of the Charts)	.40
256	Brian Hunter, Tony Womack (Top of the Charts)	.05
257	Roger Clemens, Denny Neagle (Top of the Charts)	.10
258	Roger Clemens, Curt Schilling (Top of the Charts)	.30
259	Roger Clemens, Pedro J. Martinez (Top of the Charts)	.25
260	Randy Myers, Jeff Shaw (Top of the Charts)	.05
261	Nomar Garciaparra, Scott Rolen (Top of the Charts)	.25
262	Charlie O'Brien	.05
263	Shannon Stewart	.10
264	Robert Person	.05
265	Carlos Delgado	.25
266	Matt Williams, Travis Lee Checklist	.05
267	Nomar Garciaparra, Cal Ripken Jr. Checklist	.50
268	Mark McGwire, Mike Piazza Checklist	.50
269	Tony Gwynn, Ken Griffey Jr. Checklist	.40
270	Fred McGriff, Jose Cruz Jr. Checklist	.05
271	Andruw Jones (Golden Jubilee)	.25
272	Alex Rodriguez (Golden Jubilee)	.65
273	Juan Gonzalez (Golden Jubilee)	.25
274	Nomar Garciaparra (Golden Jubilee)	.60
275	Ken Griffey Jr. (Golden Jubilee)	.60
276	Tino Martinez (Golden Jubilee)	.05
277	Roger Clemens (Golden Jubilee)	.40
278	Barry Bonds (Golden Jubilee)	.85
279	Mike Piazza (Golden Jubilee)	.60
280	Tim Salmon (Golden Jubilee)	.05
281	Gary DiSarcina	.05
282	Cecil Fielder	.05
283	Ken Hill	.05
284	Troy Percival	.05
285	Jim Edmonds	.05
286	Allen Watson	.05
287	Brian Anderson	.05
288	Jay Bell	.05
289	Jorge Fabregas	.05
290	Devon White	.05
291	Yamil Benitez	.05
292	Jeff Suppan	.05
293	Tony Batista	.05
294	Brent Brede	.05
295	Andy Benes	.05
296	Felix Rodriguez	.05
297	Karim Garcia	.05
298	Omar Daal	.05
299	Andy Stankiewicz	.05
300	Matt Williams	.05
301	Willie Blair	.05
302	Ryan Klesko	.05
303	Tom Glavine	.25
304	Walt Weiss	.05
305	Greg Maddux	.75
306	Chipper Jones	.75
307	Keith Lockhart	.05
308	Andres Galarraga	.05
309	Chris Hoiles	.05
310	Roberto Alomar	.25
311	Joe Carter	.05
312	Doug Drabek	.05
313	Jeffrey Hammonds	.05
314	Rafael Palmeiro	.40
315	Mike Mussina	.40
316	Brady Anderson	.05
317	B.J. Surhoff	.05
318	Dennis Eckersley	.40
319	Jim Leyritz	.05
320	Mo Vaughn	.05
321	Nomar Garciaparra	1.00
322	Reggie Jefferson	.05
323	Tim Naehring	.05
324	Troy O'Leary	.05
325	Pedro J. Martinez	.50
326	John Valentin	.05
327	Mark Clark	.05
328	Rod Beck	.05
329	Mickey Morandini	.05
330	Sammy Sosa	1.00
331	Jeff Blauser	.05
332	Lance Johnson	.05
333	Scott Servais	.05
334	Kevin Tapani	.05
335	Henry Rodriguez	.05
336	Jaime Navarro	.05
337	Benji Gil	.05
338	James Baldwin	.05
339	Mike Cameron	.05
340	Ray Durham	.05
341	Chris Snopek	.05
342	Eddie Taubensee	.05
343	Bret Boone	.05
344	Willie Greene	.05
345	Barry Larkin	.05
346	Chris Stynes	.05
347	Pete Harnisch	.05
348	Dave Burba	.05
349	Sandy Alomar Jr.	.05
350	Kenny Lofton	.05
351	Geronimo Berroa	.05
352	Omar Vizquel	.05
353	Travis Fryman	.05
354	Dwight Gooden	.05
355	Jim Thome	.05
356	David Justice	.05
357	Charles Nagy	.05
358	Chad Ogea	.05
359	Pedro Astacio	.05
360	Larry Walker	.05
361	Mike Lansing	.05
362	Kirt Manwaring	.05
363	Dante Bichette	.05
364	Jamey Wright	.05
365	Darryl Kile	.05
366	Luis Gonzalez	.25
367	Joe Randa	.05
368	Raul Casanova	.05
369	Damion Easley	.05
370	Brian L. Hunter	.05
371	Bobby Higginson	.05
372	Brian Moehler	.05
373	Scott Sanders	.05
374	Jim Eisenreich	.05
375	Derrek Lee	.05
376	Jay Powell	.05
377	Cliff Floyd	.05
378	Alex Fernandez	.05
379	Felix Heredia	.05
380	Jeff Bagwell	.60
381	Bill Spiers	.05
382	Chris Holt	.05
383	Carl Everett	.05
384	Derek Bell	.05
385	Moises Alou	.05
386	Ramon Garcia	.05
387	Mike Sweeney	.05
388	Glendon Rusch	.05
389	Kevin Appier	.05
390	Dean Palmer	.05
391	Jeff Conine	.05
392	Johnny Damon	.15
393	Jose Vizcaino	.05
394	Todd Hollandsworth	.05
395	Eric Karros	.05
396	Todd Zeile	.05
397	Chan Ho Park	.05
398	Ismael Valdes	.05
399	Eric Young	.05
400	Hideo Nomo	.50
401	Mark Loretta	.05
402	Doug Jones	.05
403	Jeromy Burnitz	.05
404	John Jaha	.05
405	Marquis Grissom	.05
406	Mike Matheny	.05
407	Todd Walker	.05
408	Marty Cordova	.05
409	Matt Lawton	.05
410	Terry Steinbach	.05
411	Pat Meares	.05
412	Rick Aguilera	.05

413 Otis Nixon .05
414 Derrick May .05
415 Carl Pavano (Rookie Class) .05
416 A.J. Hinch (Rookie Class) .05
417 *David Dellucci* (Rookie Class) .10
418 Bruce Chen (Rookie Class) .05
419 *Darron Ingram* (Rookie Class) .05
420 Sean Casey (Rookie Class) .20
421 Mark L. Johnson (Rookie Class) .05
422 Gabe Alvarez (Rookie Class) .05
423 Alex Gonzalez (Rookie Class) .05
424 Daryle Ward (Rookie Class) .05
425 Russell Branyan (Rookie Class) .05
426 Mike Caruso (Rookie Class) .05
427 *Mike Kinkade* (Rookie Class) .20
428 Ramon Hernandez (Rookie Class) .05
429 Matt Clement (Rookie Class) .05
430 Travis Lee (Rookie Class) .10
431 Shane Monahan (Rookie Class) .05
432 *Rich Butler* (Rookie Class) .05
433 Chris Widger .05
434 Jose Vidro .05
435 Carlos Perez .05
436 Ryan McGuire .05
437 Brian McRae .05
438 Al Leiter .05
439 Rich Becker .05
440 Todd Hundley .05
441 Dave Mlicki .05
442 Bernard Gilkey .05
443 John Olerud .05
444 Paul O'Neill .05
445 Andy Pettitte .30
446 David Cone .05
447 Chili Davis .05
448 Bernie Williams .20
449 Joe Girardi .05
450 Derek Jeter 1.50
451 Mariano Rivera .20
452 George Williams .05
453 Kenny Rogers .05
454 Tom Candiotti .05
455 Rickey Henderson .60
456 Jason Giambi .40
457 Scott Spiezio .05
458 Doug Glanville .05
459 Desi Relaford .05
460 Curt Schilling .20
461 Bob Abreu .05
462 Gregg Jefferies .05
463 Scott Rolen .40
464 Mike Lieberthal .05
465 Tony Womack .05
466 Jermaine Allensworth .05
467 Francisco Cordova .05
468 Jon Lieber .05
469 Al Martin .05
470 Jason Kendall .05
471 Todd Stottlemyre .05
472 Royce Clayton .05
473 Brian Jordan .05
474 John Mabry .05
475 Ray Lankford .05
476 Delino DeShields .05
477 Ron Gant .05
478 Mark Langston .05
479 Steve Finley .05
480 Tony Gwynn .75
481 Andy Ashby .05
482 Wally Joyner .05
483 Greg Vaughn .05
484 Sterling Hitchcock .05
485 J. Kevin Brown .05
486 Orel Hershiser .05
487 Charlie Hayes .05
488 Darryl Hamilton .05
489 Mark Gardner .05
490 Barry Bonds 1.50
491 Robb Nen .05
492 Kirk Rueter .05
493 Randy Johnson .50
494 Jeff Fassero .05
495 Alex Rodriguez 1.25
496 David Segui .05
497 Rich Amaral .05
498 Russ Davis .05
499 Bubba Trammell .05
500 Wade Boggs .75
501 Roberto Hernandez .05
502 Dave Martinez .05
503 Dennis Springer .05
504 Paul Sorrento .05
505 Wilson Alvarez .05
506 Mike Kelly .05
507 Albie Lopez .05
508 Tony Saunders .05
509 John Flaherty .05
510 Fred McGriff .05
511 Quinton McCracken .05
512 Terrell Wade .05
513 Kevin Stocker .05
514 Kevin Elster .05
515 Will Clark .10
516 Bobby Witt .05
517 Tom Goodwin .05
518 Aaron Sele .05
519 Lee Stevens .05
520 Rusty Greer .05
521 John Wetteland .05
522 Darrin Fletcher .05
523 Jose Canseco .35
524 Randy Myers .05
525 Jose Cruz Jr. .10
526 Shawn Green .15
527 Tony Fernandez .05
528 Alex Gonzalez .05
529 Ed Sprague .05
530 Roger Clemens .85

1998 COLLECTOR'S CHOICE COVER GLORY 5X7

NM/M
Complete Set (10): 10.00
Common Player: 1.00
1 Nomar Garciaparra 2.50
2 Roger Clemens 2.00
3 Larry Walker 1.00
4 Mike Piazza 2.50
5 Mark McGwire 3.00
6 Tony Gwynn 1.50
7 Jose Cruz Jr. 1.00
8 Frank Thomas 1.25
9 Tino Martinez 1.00
10 Ken Griffey Jr. 2.50

Evolution Revolution

NM/M
Complete Set (28): 36.00
Common Player: .40
Inserted 1:13
1 Tim Salmon .50
2 Greg Maddux 2.00
3 Cal Ripken Jr. 6.00
4 Mo Vaughn .40
5 Sammy Sosa 4.00
6 Frank Thomas 1.50
7 Barry Larkin .40
8 Jim Thome .40
9 Larry Walker .40
10 Travis Fryman .40
11 Gary Sheffield .65
12 Jeff Bagwell 1.00
13 Johnny Damon .60
14 Mike Piazza 4.00
15 Jeff Cirillo .40
16 Paul Molitor 1.00
17 Vladimir Guerrero 1.00
18 Todd Hundley .40
19 Tino Martinez .40
20 Jose Canseco .65
21 Scott Rolen .85
22 Al Martin .40
23 Mark McGwire 5.00
24 Tony Gwynn 2.00
25 Barry Bonds 6.00
26 Ken Griffey Jr. 4.00
27 Juan Gonzalez 1.00
28 Roger Clemens 2.50

Mini Bobbing Heads

NM/M
Complete Set (30): 20.00
Common Player: .25
Inserted 1:3
1 Tim Salmon .35
2 Travis Lee .35
3 Matt Williams .25
4 Chipper Jones 1.00
5 Greg Maddux 1.00
6 Cal Ripken Jr. 2.50
7 Nomar Garciaparra 1.50
8 Mo Vaughn .25
9 Sammy Sosa 1.50
10 Frank Thomas .75
11 Kenny Lofton .25
12 Jaret Wright .25
13 Larry Walker .25
14 Tony Clark .25
15 Edgar Renteria .25
16 Jeff Bagwell .75
17 Mike Piazza 1.50
18 Vladimir Guerrero .75
19 Derek Jeter 2.50
20 Ben Grieve .25
21 Scott Rolen .60
22 Mark McGwire 2.00
23 Tony Gwynn 1.00
24 Barry Bonds 2.50
25 Ken Griffey Jr. 1.50
26 Alex Rodriguez 2.00
27 Fred McGriff .25
28 Juan Gonzalez .75
29 Roger Clemens 1.25
30 Jose Cruz Jr. .25

Rookie Class: Prime Choice

NM/M
Complete Set (18): 30.00
Common Player: 2.00
415 Carl Pavano 2.00
416 A.J. Hinch 2.00
417 David Dellucci 2.00
418 Bruce Chen 2.00
419 Darron Ingram 2.00
420 Sean Casey 5.00
421 Mark L. Johnson 2.00
422 Gabe Alvarez 2.00
423 Alex Gonzalez 2.00
424 Daryle Ward 2.00
425 Russell Branyan 2.00
426 Mike Caruso 2.00
427 Mike Kinkade 2.00
428 Ramon Hernandez 2.00
429 Matt Clement 2.50
430 Travis Lee 4.00
431 Shane Monahan 2.00
432 Rich Butler 2.00

StarQuest - Series 1

NM/M
Complete Set (90): 185.00
Common Special Delivery (1-45): .20
Inserted 1:1
Common Student of the Game (46-65): .75
Inserted 1:21
Common Super Power (66-80): 2.00
Inserted 1:71
Common Superstar Domain (81-90): 3.00
Inserted 1:145
1 Nomar Garciaparra 2.00
2 Scott Rolen 1.00
3 Jason Dickson .20
4 Jaret Wright .25
5 Kevin Orie .20
6 Jose Guillen .20
7 Matt Morris .20
8 Mike Cameron .20
9 Kevin Polcovich .20
10 Jose Cruz Jr. .20
11 Miguel Tejada .50
12 Fernando Tatis .20
13 Todd Helton .75
14 Ken Cloude .20
15 Ben Grieve .25
16 Dante Powell .20
17 Bubba Trammell .20
18 Juan Encarnacion .20
19 Derrek Lee .20
20 Paul Konerko .35
21 Richard Hidalgo .20
22 Denny Neagle .20
23 David Justice .20
24 Pedro J. Martinez 1.00
25 Greg Maddux 1.50
26 Edgar Martinez .20
27 Cal Ripken Jr. 2.50
28 Tim Salmon .30
29 Shawn Estes .20
30 Ken Griffey Jr. 2.00
31 Brad Radke .20
32 Andy Pettitte .50
33 Curt Schilling .50
34 Raul Mondesi .20
35 Alex Rodriguez 2.25
36 Jeff Kent .20
37 Jeff Bagwell 1.00
38 Juan Gonzalez 1.00
39 Barry Bonds 2.50
40 Mark McGwire 2.00
41 Frank Thomas 1.00
42 Ray Lankford .20
43 Tony Gwynn 1.50
44 Mike Piazza 1.75
45 Tino Martinez .20
46 Nomar Garciaparra 5.00
47 Paul Molitor 1.50
48 Chuck Knoblauch .75
49 Rusty Greer .75
50 Cal Ripken Jr. 6.00
51 Roberto Alomar 1.00
52 Scott Rolen 1.00
53 Derek Jeter 6.00
54 Mark Grace 1.00
55 Randy Johnson 1.50
56 Craig Biggio .75
57 Kenny Lofton .75
58 Eddie Murray 1.50
59 Ryne Sandberg 2.00
60 Rickey Henderson 1.50
61 Darin Erstad 1.50

62 Jim Edmonds 1.00
63 Ken Caminiti .75
64 Ivan Rodriguez 1.25
65 Tony Gwynn 2.00
66 Tony Clark 2.00
67 Andres Galarraga 2.00
68 Rafael Palmeiro 3.00
69 Manny Ramirez 4.00
70 Albert Belle 2.00
71 Jay Buhner 2.00
72 Mo Vaughn 2.00
73 Barry Bonds 15.00
74 Chipper Jones 7.50
75 Jeff Bagwell 6.00
76 Jim Thome 2.00
77 Sammy Sosa 10.00
78 Todd Hundley 2.00
79 Matt Williams 2.00
80 Vinny Castilla 2.00
81 Jose Cruz Jr. 3.00
82 Frank Thomas 7.50
83 Juan Gonzalez 7.50
84 Mike Piazza 15.00
85 Alex Rodriguez 20.00
86 Larry Walker 3.00
87 Tino Martinez 3.00
88 Greg Maddux 12.50
89 Mark McGwire 20.00
90 Ken Griffey Jr. 15.00

StarQuest - Series 2

NM/M
Complete Set (30): 17.50
Common Player: .25
Singles 1:1
Doubles 1:21 2X
Triples 1:71 4X
Home Runs 12X
1 Ken Griffey Jr. 1.25
2 Jose Cruz Jr. .25
3 Cal Ripken Jr. 2.00
4 Roger Clemens 1.00
5 Frank Thomas .65
6 Derek Jeter 2.00
7 Alex Rodriguez 1.50
8 Andruw Jones .65
9 Vladimir Guerrero .65
10 Mark McGwire 1.50
11 Kenny Lofton .25
12 Pedro J. Martinez .65
13 Greg Maddux 1.00
14 Larry Walker .25
15 Barry Bonds 2.00
16 Chipper Jones 1.00
17 Jeff Bagwell .65
18 Juan Gonzalez .65
19 Tony Gwynn 1.00
20 Mike Piazza 1.25
21 Tino Martinez .25
22 Mo Vaughn .20
23 Ben Grieve .35
24 Scott Rolen .60
25 Nomar Garciaparra 1.25
26 Paul Konerko .35
27 Jaret Wright .25
28 Gary Sheffield .50
29 Travis Lee .25
30 Todd Helton .65

Stickums

NM/M
Complete Set (30): 7.00
Common Player: .10
Inserted 1:3
1 Andruw Jones .35
2 Chipper Jones .45
3 Cal Ripken Jr. 1.00
4 Nomar Garciaparra .60
5 Mo Vaughn .10
6 Ryne Sandberg .45
7 Sammy Sosa .60
8 Frank Thomas .35
9 Albert Belle .15
10 Jim Thome .10
11 Manny Ramirez .35
12 Larry Walker .10
13 Gary Sheffield .20
14 Jeff Bagwell .35
15 Mike Piazza .60
16 Paul Molitor .35
17 Pedro J. Martinez .35
18 Todd Hundley .10
19 Derek Jeter 1.00
20 Tino Martinez .10
21 Curt Schilling .25
22 Mark McGwire .75
23 Tony Gwynn .45
24 Barry Bonds 1.00
25 Ken Griffey Jr. .60
26 Alex Rodriguez .75
27 Juan Gonzalez .35
28 Ivan Rodriguez .30
29 Roger Clemens .50
30 Jose Cruz Jr. .10

D

1981 DONRUSS

NM/M
Complete Set (605):
Uncut Sheet Set (5):
Common Player: .06
Wax Pack (18):
Wax Box (36):
1 Ozzie Smith 1.50
2 Rollie Fingers .70
3 Rick Wise .06
4 Gene Richards .06
5 Alan Trammell .08
6 Tom Brookens .06
7a Duffy Dyer (1980 Avg. .185) .20
7b Duffy Dyer (1980 Avg. 185) .06
8 Mark Fidrych .11
9 Dave Rozema .06
10 Ricky Peters .06
11 Mike Schmidt 2.25
12 Willie Stargell .90
13 Tim Foli .06
14 Manny Sanguillen .06
15 Grant Jackson .06
16 Eddie Solomon .06
17 Omar Moreno .06
18 Joe Morgan .90
19 Rafael Landestoy .06
20 Bruce Bochy .06
21 Joe Sambito .06
22 Manny Trillo .06
23a *Dave Smith* (incomplete box around stats) .08
23b *Dave Smith* (complete box around stats) .11
24 Terry Puhl .06
25 Bump Wills .06
26a John Ellis (Danny Walton photo - with bat) .25
26b John Ellis (John Ellis photo - with glove) .06
27 Jim Kern .06
28 Richie Zisk .06
29 John Mayberry .06
30 Bob Davis .06
31 Jackson Todd .06
32 Al Woods .06
33 Steve Carlton 1.25
34 Lee Mazzilli .06
35 John Stearns .06
36 Roy Jackson .06
37 Mike Scott .06
38 Lamar Johnson .06
39 Kevin Bell .06
40 Ed Farmer .06
41 Ross Baumgarten .06
42 Leo Sutherland .06
43 Dan Meyer .06
44 Ron Reed .06
45 Mario Mendoza .06
46 Rick Honeycutt .06
47 Glenn Abbott .06
48 Leon Roberts .06
49 Rod Carew 1.25
50 Bert Campaneris .06
51a Tom Donahue (incorrect spelling) .20
51b Tom Donohue (Donohue on front) .06
52 Dave Frost .06
53 Ed Halicki .06
54 Dan Ford .06
55 Garry Maddox .06
56a Steve Garvey (Surpassed 25 HR..) .90
56b Steve Garvey (Surpassed 21 HR..) .45
57 Bill Russell .06
58 Don Sutton .70
59 Reggie Smith .06
60 Rick Monday .06
61 Ray Knight .08
62 Johnny Bench 1.25
63 Mario Soto .06
64 Doug Bair .06
65 George Foster .08
66 Jeff Burroughs .06
67 Keith Hernandez .08
68 Tom Herr .06
69 Bob Forsch .06
70 John Fulgham .06
71a Bobby Bonds (lifetime HR 986) .25
71b Bobby Bonds (lifetime HR 326) .11
72a Rennie Stennett ("...breaking broke leg..." on back) .20
72b Rennie Stennett ("...breaking leg..." on back) .06
73 Joe Strain .06
74 Ed Whitson .06
75 Tom Griffin .06
76 Bill North .06
77 Gene Garber .06
78 Mike Hargrove .06
79 Dave Rosello .06
80 Ron Hassey .06
81 Sid Monge .06
82a *Joe Charboneau* ("For some reason, Phillies..." on back) .70
82b *Joe Charboneau* ("Phillies..." on back) .20
83 Cecil Cooper .06
84 Sal Bando .06
85 Moose Haas .06
86 Mike Caldwell .06
87a Larry Hisle ("...Twins with 28 RBI." on back) .20
87b Larry Hisle ("...Twins with 28 HR" on back) .06
88 Luis Gomez .06
89 Larry Parrish .06
90 Gary Carter .90
91 *Bill Gullickson* .11
92 Fred Norman .06
93 Tommy Hutton .06
94 Carl Yastrzemski 1.25
95 Glenn Hoffman .06
96 Dennis Eckersley .90
97a Tom Burgmeier (Throws: Right) .20
97b Tom Burgmeier (Throws: Left) .06
98 Win Remmerswaal .06
99 Bob Horner .08
100 George Brett 2.25
101 Dave Chalk .06
102 Dennis Leonard .06
103 Renie Martin .06
104 Amos Otis .06
105 Graig Nettles .11
106 Eric Soderholm .06
107 Tommy John .08
108 Tom Underwood .06
109 Lou Piniella .11
110 Mickey Klutts .06
111 Bobby Murcer .08
112 Eddie Murray 1.25
113 Rick Dempsey .06
114 Scott McGregor .06
115 Ken Singleton .06
116 Gary Roenicke .06
117 Dave Revering .06
118 Mike Norris .06
119 Rickey Henderson 1.50
120 Mike Heath .06
121 Dave Cash .06
122 Randy Jones .06
123 Eric Rasmussen .06
124 Jerry Mumphrey .06
125 Richie Hebner .06
126 Mark Wagner .06
127 Jack Morris .08
128 Dan Petry .06
129 Bruce Robbins .06
130 Champ Summers .06
131a Pete Rose ("see card 251" on back) 1.50
131b Pete Rose ("see card 371" on back) 1.50
132 Willie Stargell .90
133 Ed Ott .06
134 Jim Bibby .06
135 Bert Blyleven .08
136 Dave Parker .08
137 Bill Robinson .06
138 Enos Cabell .06
139 Dave Bergman .06
140 J.R. Richard .08
141 Ken Forsch .06
142 Larry Bowa .08
143 Frank LaCorte (photo actually Randy Niemann) .06
144 Dennis Walling .06
145 Buddy Bell .08
146 Fergie Jenkins .70
147 Danny Darwin .06
148 John Grubb .06
149 Alfredo Griffin .06
150 Jerry Garvin .06
151 *Paul Mirabella* .06
152 Rick Bosetti .06
153 Dick Ruthven .06
154 Frank Taveras .06
155 Craig Swan .06
156 *Jeff Reardon* .70
157 Steve Henderson .06
158 Jim Morrison .06
159 Glenn Borgmann .06
160 *Lamarr Hoyt (LaMarr)* .08
161 Rich Wortham .06
162 Thad Bosley .06
163 Julio Cruz .06
164a Del Unser (no 3B in stat heads) .20
164b Del Unser (3B in stat heads) .06
165 Jim Anderson .06
166 Jim Beattie .06
167 Shane Rawley .06
168 Joe Simpson .06
169 Rod Carew 1.25
170 Fred Patek .06
171 Frank Tanana .06
172 Alfredo Martinez .06
173 Chris Knapp .06
174 Joe Rudi .06
175 Greg Luzinski .06
176 Steve Garvey .60
177 Joe Ferguson .06
178 Bob Welch .06
179 Dusty Baker .08
180 Rudy Law .06
181 Dave Concepcion .06
182 Johnny Bench 1.25
183 Mike LaCoss .06
184 Ken Griffey .08
185 Dave Collins .06
186 Brian Asselstine .06
187 Garry Templeton .06
188 Mike Phillips .06
189 Pete Vukovich .06
190 John Urrea .06
191 Tony Scott .06
192 Darrell Evans .08
193 Milt May .06
194 Bob Knepper .06
195 Randy Moffitt .06
196 Larry Herndon .06
197 Rick Camp .06
198 Andre Thornton .06
199 Tom Veryzer .06

No.	Player	Price
200	Gary Alexander	.06
201	Rick Waits	.06
202	Rick Manning	.06
203	Paul Molitor	.90
204	Jim Gantner	.06
205	Paul Mitchell	.06
206	Reggie Cleveland	.06
207	Sixto Lezcano	.06
208	Bruce Benedict	.06
209	Rodney Scott	.06
210	John Tamargo	.06
211	Bill Lee	.06
212	Andre Dawson	.60
213	Rowland Office	.06
214	Carl Yastrzemski	1.25
215	Jerry Remy	.06
216	Mike Torrez	.06
217	Skip Lockwood	.06
218	Fred Lynn	.08
219	Chris Chambliss	.06
220	Willie Aikens	.06
221	John Wathan	.06
222	Dan Quisenberry	.06
223	Willie Wilson	.08
224	Clint Hurdle	.06
225	Bob Watson	.06
226	Jim Spencer	.06
227	Ron Guidry	.11
228	Reggie Jackson	1.50
229	Oscar Gamble	.06
230	Jeff Cox	.06
231	Luis Tiant	.08
232	Rich Dauer	.06
233	Dan Graham	.06
234	Mike Flanagan	.06
235	John Lowenstein	.06
236	Benny Ayala	.06
237	Wayne Gross	.06
238	Rick Langford	.06
239	Tony Armas	.06
240a	Bob Lacy (incorrect spelling)	.20
240b	Bob Lacey (correct spelling)	.06
241	Gene Tenace	.06
242	Bob Shirley	.06
243	Gary Lucas	.06
244	Jerry Turner	.06
245	John Wockenfuss	.06
246	Stan Papi	.06
247	Milt Wilcox	.06
248	Dan Schatzeder	.06
249	Steve Kemp	.06
250	Jim Lentine	.06
251	Pete Rose	1.50
252	Bill Madlock	.08
253	Dale Berra	.06
254	Kent Tekulve	.06
255	Enrique Romo	.06
256	Mike Easler	.06
257	Chuck Tanner	.06
258	Art Howe	.08
259	Alan Ashby	.06
260	Nolan Ryan	3.75
261a	Vern Ruhle (Ken Forsch photo - head shot)	.20
261b	Vern Ruhle (Vern Ruhle photo - waist to head shot)	.08
262	Bob Boone	.08
263	Cesar Cedeno	.06
264	Jeff Leonard	.06
265	Pat Putnam	.06
266	Jon Matlack	.06
267	Dave Rajsich	.06
268	Billy Sample	.06
269	*Damaso Garcia*	.08
270	Tom Buskey	.06
271	Joey McLaughlin	.06
272	Barry Bonnell	.06
273	Tug McGraw	.08
274	Mike Jorgensen	.06
275	Pat Zachry	.06
276	Neil Allen	.06
277	Joel Youngblood	.06
278	Greg Pryor	.06
279	*Britt Burns*	.08
280	*Rich Dotson*	.20
281	Chet Lemon	.06
282	Rusty Kuntz	.06
283	Ted Cox	.06
284	Sparky Lyle	.06
285	Larry Cox	.06
286	Floyd Bannister	.06
287	Byron McLaughlin	.06
288	Rodney Craig	.06
289	Bobby Grich	.06
290	Dickie Thon	.06
291	Mark Clear	.06
292	Dave Lemanczyk	.06
293	Jason Thompson	.06
294	Rick Miller	.06
295	Lonnie Smith	.06
296	Ron Cey	.06
297	Steve Yeager	.06
298	Bobby Castillo	.06
299	Manny Mota	.06
300	Jay Johnstone	.06
301	Dan Driessen	.06
302	Joe Nolan	.06
303	Paul Householder	.06
304	Harry Spilman	.06
305	Cesar Geronimo	.06
306a	Gary Mathews (Mathews on front)	.25
306b	Gary Matthews (Matthews on front)	.06
307	Ken Reitz	.06
308	Ted Simmons	.06
309	John Littlefield	.06
310	George Frazier	.06
311	Dane Iorg	.06
312	Mike Ivie	.06
313	Dennis Littlejohn	.06
314	Gary LaVelle (Lavelle)	.06
315	Jack Clark	.08
316	Jim Wohlford	.06
317	Rick Matula	.06
318	Toby Harrah	.06
319a	Dwane Kuiper (Dwane on front)	.20
319b	Duane Kuiper (Duane on front)	.06
320	Len Barker	.06
321	Victor Cruz	.06
322	Dell Alston	.06
323	Robin Yount	.90
324	Charlie Moore	.06
325	Lary Sorensen	.06
326a	Gorman Thomas ("...30-HR mark 4th..." on back)	.20
326b	Gorman Thomas ("...30-HR mark 3rd..." on back)	.06
327	Bob Rodgers	.06
328	Phil Niekro	.70
329	Chris Speier	.06
330a	Steve Rodgers (Rodgers on front)	.20
330b	Steve Rogers (Rogers on front)	.06
331	Woodie Fryman	.06
332	Warren Cromartie	.06
333	Jerry White	.06
334	Tony Perez	.90
335	Carlton Fisk	.90
336	Dick Drago	.06
337	Steve Renko	.06
338	Jim Rice	.40
339	Jerry Royster	.06
340	Frank White	.06
341	Jamie Quirk	.06
342a	Paul Spittorff (Spittorff on front)	.20
342b	Paul Splittorff (Splittorff on front)	.06
343	Marty Pattin	.06
344	Pete LaCock	.06
345	Willie Randolph	.06
346	Rick Cerone	.06
347	Rich Gossage	.08
348	Reggie Jackson	1.50
349	Ruppert Jones	.06
350	Dave McKay	.06
351	Yogi Berra	.40
352	Doug Decinces (DeCinces)	.08
353	Jim Palmer	.90
354	Tippy Martinez	.06
355	Al Bumbry	.06
356	Earl Weaver	.40
357a	Bob Picciolo (Bob on front)	.20
357b	Rob Picciolo (Rob on front)	.06
358	Matt Keough	.06
359	Dwayne Murphy	.06
360	Brian Kingman	.06
361	Bill Fahey	.06
362	Steve Mura	.06
363	Dennis Kinney	.06
364	Dave Winfield	.90
365	Lou Whitaker	.08
366	Lance Parrish	.08
367	Tim Corcoran	.06
368	Pat Underwood	.06
369	Al Cowens	.06
370	Sparky Anderson	.40
371	Pete Rose	2.25
372	Phil Garner	.06
373	Steve Nicosia	.06
374	John Candelaria	.06
375	Don Robinson	.06
376	Lee Lacy	.06
377	John Milner	.06
378	Craig Reynolds	.06
379a	Luis Pujois (Pujois on front)	.20
379b	Luis Pujols (Pujols on front)	.06
380	Joe Niekro	.06
381	Joaquin Andujar	.06
382	*Keith Moreland*	.11
383	Jose Cruz	.06
384	Bill Virdon	.06
385	Jim Sundberg	.06
386	Doc Medich	.06
387	Al Oliver	.08
388	Jim Norris	.06
389	Bob Bailor	.06
390	Ernie Whitt	.06
391	Otto Velez	.06
392	Roy Howell	.06
393	*Bob Walk*	.08
394	Doug Flynn	.06
395	Pete Falcone	.06
396	Tom Hausman	.06
397	Elliott Maddox	.06
398	Mike Squires	.06
399	Marvis Foley	.06
400	Steve Trout	.06
401	Wayne Nordhagen	.06
402	Tony Larussa (LaRussa)	.08
403	Bruce Bochte	.06
404	Bake McBride	.06
405	Jerry Narron	.06
406	Rob Dressler	.06
407	Dave Heaverlo	.06
408	Tom Paciorek	.06
409	Carney Lansford	.06
410	Brian Downing	.06
411	Don Aase	.06
412	Jim Barr	.06
413	Don Baylor	.08
414	Jim Fregosi	.06
415	Dallas Green	.06
416	Dave Lopes	.06
417	Jerry Reuss	.06
418	Rick Sutcliffe	.08
419	Derrel Thomas	.06
420	Tommy LaSorda (Lasorda)	.40
421	*Charlie Leibrandt*	.20
422	Tom Seaver	1.25
423	Ron Oester	.06
424	Junior Kennedy	.06
425	Tom Seaver	1.25
426	Bobby Cox	.08
427	*Leon Durham*	.15
428	Terry Kennedy	.06
429	Silvio Martinez	.06
430	George Hendrick	.06
431	Red Schoendienst	.40
432	John LeMaster	.06
433	Vida Blue	.08
434	John Montefusco	.06
435	Terry Whitfield	.06
436	Dave Bristol	.06
437	Dale Murphy	.60
438	Jerry Dybzinski	.06
439	Jorge Orta	.06
440	Wayne Garland	.06
441	Miguel Dilone	.06
442	Dave Garcia	.06
443	Don Money	.06
444a	Buck Martinez (photo reversed)	.25
444b	Buck Martinez (photo correct)	.08
445	Jerry Augustine	.06
446	Ben Oglivie	.06
447	Jim Slaton	.06
448	Doyle Alexander	.06
449	Tony Bernazard	.06
450	Scott Sanderson	.06
451	Dave Palmer	.06
452	Stan Bahnsen	.06
453	Dick Williams	.06
454	Rick Burleson	.06
455	Gary Allenson	.06
456	Bob Stanley	.06
457a	*John Tudor* (lifetime W/L 9.7)	.30
457b	*John Tudor* (lifetime W/L 9-7)	.15
458	Dwight Evans	.08
459	Glenn Hubbard	.06
460	U L Washington	.06
461	Larry Gura	.06
462	Rich Gale	.06
463	Hal McRae	.08
464	Jim Frey	.06
465	Bucky Dent	.08
466	Dennis Werth	.06
467	Ron Davis	.06
468	Reggie Jackson	2.00
469	Bobby Brown	.06
470	*Mike Davis*	.08
471	Gaylord Perry	.90
472	Mark Belanger	.06
473	Jim Palmer	.90
474	Sammy Stewart	.06
475	Tim Stoddard	.06
476	Steve Stone	.08
477	Jeff Newman	.06
478	Steve McCatty	.06
479	Billy Martin	.08
480	Mitchell Page	.06
481	Steve Carlton (CY)	.30
482	Bill Buckner	.08
483a	Ivan DeJesus (lifetime hits 702)	.20
483b	Ivan DeJesus (lifetime hits 642)	.06
484	Cliff Johnson	.06
485	Lenny Randle	.06
486	Larry Milbourne	.06
487	Roy Smalley	.06
488	John Castino	.06
489	Ron Jackson	.06
490a	Dave Roberts (1980 highlights begins "Showed pop...")	.20
490b	Dave Roberts (1980 highlights begins "Declared himself...")	.06
491	George Brett (MVP)	1.25
492	Mike Cubbage	.06
493	Rob Wilfong	.06
494	Danny Goodwin	.06
495	Jose Morales	.06
496	Mickey Rivers	.06
497	Mike Edwards	.06
498	Mike Sadek	.06
499	Lenn Sakata	.06
500	Gene Michael	.06
501	Dave Roberts	.06
502	Steve Dillard	.06
503	Jim Essian	.06
504	Rance Mulliniks	.06
505	Darrell Porter	.06
506	Joe Torre	.40
507	Terry Crowley	.06
508	Bill Travers	.06
509	Nelson Norman	.06
510	Bob McClure	.06
511	*Steve Howe*	.11
512	Dave Rader	.06
513	Mick Kelleher	.06
514	Kiko Garcia	.06
515	Larry Biittner	.06
516a	Willie Norwood (1980 highlights begins "Spent most...")	.20
516b	Willie Norwood (1980 highlights begins "Traded to...")	.06
517	Bo Diaz	.06
518	Juan Beniquez	.06
519	Scot Thompson	.06
520	Jim Tracy	.06
521	Carlos Lezcano	.06
522	Joe Amalfitano	.06
523	Preston Hanna	.06
524a	Ray Burris (1980 highlights begins "Went on...")	.20
524b	Ray Burris (1980 highlights begins "Drafted by...")	.06
525	Broderick Perkins	.06
526	Mickey Hatcher	.06
527	John Goryl	.06
528	Dick Davis	.06
529	Butch Wynegar	.06
530	Sal Butera	.06
531	Jerry Koosman	.06
532a	Jeff (Geoff) Zahn (1980 highlights begins "Was 2nd in...")	.20
532b	Jeff (Geoff) Zahn (1980 highlights begins "Signed a 3 year ...")	.06
533	Dennis Martinez	.06
534	Gary Thomasson	.06

535	Steve Macko	.06
536	Jim Kaat	.11
537	George Brett, Rod Carew Best Hitters	1.25
538	*Tim Raines*	2.25
539	Keith Smith	.06
540	Ken Macha	.06
541	Burt Hooton	.06
542	Butch Hobson	.06
543	Bill Stein	.06
544	Dave Stapleton	.06
545	Bob Pate	.06
546	Doug Corbett	.06
547	Darrell Jackson	.06
548	Pete Redfern	.06
549	Roger Erickson	.06
550	Al Hrabosky	.06
551	Dick Tidrow	.06
552	Dave Ford	.06
553	Dave Kingman	.08
554a	Mike Vail (1980 highlights begins "After...")	.20
554b	Mike Vail (1980 highlights begins "Traded...")	.06
555a	Jerry Martin (1980 highlights begins "Overcame...")	.20
555b	Jerry Martin (1980 highlights begins "Traded...")	.06
556a	Jesus Figueroa (1980 highlights begins "Had...")	.20
556b	Jesus Figueroa (1980 highlights begins "Traded...")	.06
557	Don Stanhouse	.06
558	Barry Foote	.06
559	Tim Blackwell	.06
560	Bruce Sutter	.70
561	Rick Reuschel	.06
562	Lynn McGlothen	.06
563a	Bob Owchinko (1980 highlights begins "Traded...")	.20
563b	Bob Owchinko (1980 highlights begins "Involved...")	.06
564	John Verhoeven	.06
565	Ken Landreaux	.06
566a	Glen Adams (Glen on front)	.20
566b	Glenn Adams (Glenn on front)	.06
567	Hosken Powell	.06
568	Dick Noles	.06
569	*Danny Ainge*	1.50
570	Bobby Mattick	.06
571	Joe LeFebvre (Lefebvre)	.06
572	Bobby Clark	.06
573	Dennis Lamp	.06
574	Randy Lerch	.06
575	*Mookie Wilson*	.25
576	Ron LeFlore	.06
577	Jim Dwyer	.06
578	Bill Castro	.06
579	Greg Minton	.06
580	Mark Littell	.06
581	Andy Hassler	.06
582	Dave Stieb	.06
583	Ken Oberkfell	.06
584	Larry Bradford	.06
585	Fred Stanley	.06
586	Bill Caudill	.06
587	Doug Capilla	.06
588	George Riley	.06
589	Willie Hernandez	.06
590	Mike Schmidt (MVP)	1.25
591	Steve Stone ((Cy Young 1980))	.08
592	Rick Sofield	.06
593	Bombo Rivera	.06
594	Gary Ward	.06
595a	Dave Edwards (1980 highlights begins "Sidelined...")	.20
595b	Dave Edwards (1980 highlights begins "Traded...")	.06
596	Mike Proly	.06
597	Tommy Boggs	.06
598	Greg Gross	.06
599	Elias Sosa	.06
600	Pat Kelly	.06

1982 DONRUSS

	NM/M
Unopened Factory Set (660):	40.00
Complete Set (660):	35.00
Complete Set, Uncut Sheets (5):	175.00
Common Player:	.10
Babe Ruth Puzzle:	1.00
Wax Pack (15):	2.00
Wax Box (36):	70.00

1	Pete Rose (Diamond King)	4.00
2	Gary Carter (DK)	1.25
3	Steve Garvey (DK)	.45
4	Vida Blue (DK)	.10
5a	Alan Trammel (DK) (last name incorrect)	1.00
5b	Alan Trammell (DK)(corrected)	.30
6	Len Barker (DK)	.10
7	Dwight Evans (DK)	.15
8	Rod Carew (DK)	1.25
9	George Hendrick (DK)	.10
10	Phil Niekro (DK)	.75
11	Richie Zisk (DK)	.10
12	Dave Parker (DK)	.10
13	Nolan Ryan (DK)	5.00
14	Ivan DeJesus (DK)	.10
15	George Brett (DK)	2.00
16	Tom Seaver (DK)	1.25
17	Dave Kingman (DK)	.15
18	Dave Winfield (DK)	1.25
19	Mike Norris (DK)	.10
20	Carlton Fisk (DK)	1.25
21	Ozzie Smith (DK)	1.50
22	Roy Smalley (DK)	.10
23	Buddy Bell (DK)	.10
24	Ken Singleton (DK)	.10
25	John Mayberry (DK)	.10
26	Gorman Thomas (DK)	.10
27	Earl Weaver	.50
28	Rollie Fingers	.75
29	Sparky Anderson	.50
30	Dennis Eckersley	1.25
31	Dave Winfield	1.25
32	Burt Hooton	.10
33	Rick Waits	.10
34	George Brett	2.00
35	Steve McCatty	.10
36	Steve Rogers	.10
37	Bill Stein	.10
38	Steve Renko	.10
39	Mike Squires	.10
40	George Hendrick	.10
41	Bob Knepper	.10
42	Steve Carlton	1.25
43	Larry Biittner	.10
44	Chris Welsh	.10
45	Steve Nicosia	.10
46	Jack Clark	.10
47	Chris Chambliss	.10
48	Ivan DeJesus	.10
49	Lee Mazzilli	.10
50	Julio Cruz	.10
51	Pete Redfern	.10
52	Dave Stieb	.10
53	Doug Corbett	.10
54	*George Bell*	.50
55	Joe Simpson	.10
56	Rusty Staub	.15
57	Hector Cruz	.10
58	Claudell Washington	.10
59	Enrique Romo	.10
60	Gary Lavelle	.10
61	Tim Flannery	.10
62	Joe Nolan	.10
63	Larry Bowa	.10
64	Sixto Lezcano	.10
65	Joe Sambito	.10
66	Bruce Kison	.10
67	Wayne Nordhagen	.10
68	Woodie Fryman	.10
69	Billy Sample	.10
70	Amos Otis	.10
71	Matt Keough	.10
72	Toby Harrah	.10
73	*Dave Righetti*	.30
74	Carl Yastrzemski	1.50
75	Bob Welch	.10
76a	Alan Trammel (last name misspelled)	1.00
76b	Alan Trammell (corrected)	.15
77	Rick Dempsey	.10
78	Paul Molitor	1.25
79	Dennis Martinez	.10
80	Jim Slaton	.10
81	Champ Summers	.10
82	Carney Lansford	.10
83	Barry Foote	.10
84	Steve Garvey	.45
85	Rick Manning	.10
86	John Wathan	.10
87	Brian Kingman	.10
88	Andre Dawson	.50
89	Jim Kern	.10
90	Bobby Grich	.10
91	Bob Forsch	.10
92	Art Howe	.10
93	Marty Bystrom	.10
94	Ozzie Smith	1.50
95	Dave Parker	.10
96	Doyle Alexander	.10
97	Al Hrabosky	.10
98	Frank Taveras	.10
99	Tim Blackwell	.10
100	Floyd Bannister	.10
101	Alfredo Griffin	.10
102	Dave Engle	.10
103	Mario Soto	.10
104	Ross Baumgarten	.10
105	Ken Singleton	.10
106	Ted Simmons	.10
107	Jack Morris	.10
108	Bob Watson	.10
109	Dwight Evans	.10
110	Tom Lasorda	.50
111	Bert Blyleven	.10
112	Dan Quisenberry	.10
113	Rickey Henderson	1.25
114	Gary Carter	1.25
115	Brian Downing	.10
116	Al Oliver	.10
117	LaMarr Hoyt	.10
118	Cesar Cedeno	.10
119	Keith Moreland	.10
120	Bob Shirley	.10
121	Terry Kennedy	.10
122	Frank Pastore	.10
123	Gene Garber	.10
124	Tony Pena	.10
125	Allen Ripley	.10
126	Randy Martz	.10
127	Richie Zisk	.10
128	Mike Scott	.10
129	Lloyd Moseby	.10
130	Rob Wilfong	.10
131	Tim Stoddard	.10
132	Gorman Thomas	.10
133	Dan Petry	.10
134	Bob Stanley	.10
135	Lou Piniella	.15
136	Pedro Guerrero	.10
137	Len Barker	.10
138	Richard Gale	.10
139	Wayne Gross	.10
140	*Tim Wallach*	.50
141	Gene Mauch	.10
142	Doc Medich	.10
143	Tony Bernazard	.10
144	Bill Virdon	.10
145	John Littlefield	.10
146	Dave Bergman	.10
147	Dick Davis	.10
148	Tom Seaver	1.50
149	Matt Sinatro	.10
150	Chuck Tanner	.10
151	Leon Durham	.10
152	Gene Tenace	.10
153	Al Bumbry	.10
154	Mark Brouhard	.10
155	Rick Peters	.10
156	Jerry Remy	.10
157	Rick Reuschel	.10
158	Steve Howe	.10
159	Alan Bannister	.10
160	U L Washington	.10
161	Rick Langford	.10
162	Bill Gullickson	.10
163	Mark Wagner	.10
164	Geoff Zahn	.10
165	Ron LeFlore	.10
166	Dane Iorg	.10
167	Joe Niekro	.10
168	Pete Rose	4.00
169	Dave Collins	.10
170	Rick Wise	.10
171	Jim Bibby	.10
172	Larry Herndon	.10
173	Bob Horner	.10
174	Steve Dillard	.10
175	Mookie Wilson	.10
176	Dan Meyer	.10
177	Fernando Arroyo	.10
178	Jackson Todd	.10
179	Darrell Jackson	.10
180	Al Woods	.10
181	Jim Anderson	.10
182	Dave Kingman	.10
183	Steve Henderson	.10
184	Brian Asselstine	.10
185	Rod Scurry	.10
186	Fred Breining	.10
187	Danny Boone	.10
188	Junior Kennedy	.10
189	Sparky Lyle	.10
190	Whitey Herzog	.10
191	Dave Smith	.10
192	Ed Ott	.10
193	Greg Luzinski	.10
194	Bill Lee	.10
195	Don Zimmer	.10
196	Hal McRae	.10
197	Mike Norris	.10
198	Duane Kuiper	.10
199	Rick Cerone	.10
200	Jim Rice	.45
201	Steve Yeager	.10
202	Tom Brookens	.10
203	Jose Morales	.10
204	Roy Howell	.10
205	Tippy Martinez	.10
206	Moose Haas	.10
207	Al Cowens	.10
208	Dave Stapleton	.10
209	Bucky Dent	.10
210	Ron Cey	.10
211	Jorge Orta	.10
212	Jamie Quirk	.10
213	Jeff Jones	.10
214	Tim Raines	.50
215	Jon Matlack	.10
216	Rod Carew	1.50
217	Jim Kaat	.15
218	Joe Pittman	.10
219	Larry Christenson	.10
220	Juan Bonilla	.10
221	Mike Easler	.10
222	Vida Blue	.10
223	Rick Camp	.10
224	Mike Jorgensen	.10
225	*Jody Davis*	.15
226	Mike Parrott	.10
227	Jim Clancy	.10
228	Hosken Powell	.10
229	Tom Hume	.10
230	Britt Burns	.10
231	Jim Palmer	1.25
232	Bob Rodgers	.10
233	Milt Wilcox	.10
234	Dave Revering	.10
235	Mike Torrez	.10
236	Robert Castillo	.10
237	*Von Hayes*	.25
238	Renie Martin	.10
239	Dwayne Murphy	.10
240	Rodney Scott	.10
241	Fred Patek	.10
242	Mickey Rivers	.10
243	Steve Trout	.10
244	Jose Cruz	.10
245	Manny Trillo	.10
246	Lary Sorensen	.10
247	Dave Edwards	.10
248	Dan Driessen	.10
249	Tommy Boggs	.10
250	Dale Berra	.10
251	Ed Whitson	.10
252	*Lee Smith*	4.00
253	Tom Paciorek	.10
254	Pat Zachry	.10
255	Luis Leal	.10
256	John Castino	.10
257	Rich Dauer	.10
258	Cecil Cooper	.10
259	Dave Rozema	.10
260	John Tudor	.10
261	Jerry Mumphrey	.10
262	Jay Johnstone	.10
263	Bo Diaz	.10

264 Dennis Leonard .10
265 Jim Spencer .10
266 John Milner .10
267 Don Aase .10
268 Jim Sundberg .10
269 Lamar Johnson .10
270 Frank LaCorte .10
271 Barry Evans .10
272 Enos Cabell .10
273 Del Unser .10
274 George Foster .10
275 *Brett Butler* .50
276 Lee Lacy .10
277 Ken Reitz .10
278 Keith Hernandez .10
279 Doug DeCinces .10
280 Charlie Moore .10
281 Lance Parrish .10
282 Ralph Houk .10
283 Rich Gossage .10
284 Jerry Reuss .10
285 Mike Stanton .10
286 Frank White .10
287 Bob Owchinko .10
288 Scott Sanderson .10
289 Bump Wills .10
290 Dave Frost .10
291 Chet Lemon .10
292 Tito Landrum .10
293 Vern Ruhle .10
294 Mike Schmidt 2.00
295 Sam Mejias .10
296 Gary Lucas .10
297 John Candelaria .10
298 Jerry Martin .10
299 Dale Murphy .50
300 Mike Lum .10
301 Tom Hausman .10
302 Glenn Abbott .10
303 Roger Erickson .10
304 Otto Velez .10
305 Danny Goodwin .10
306 John Mayberry .10
307 Lenny Randle .10
308 Bob Bailor .10
309 Jerry Morales .10
310 Rufino Linares .10
311 Kent Tekulve .10
312 Joe Morgan 1.25
313 John Urrea .10
314 Paul Householder .10
315 Garry Maddox .10
316 Mike Ramsey .10
317 Alan Ashby .10
318 Bob Clark .10
319 Tony LaRussa .15
320 Charlie Lea .10
321 Danny Darwin .10
322 Cesar Geronimo .10
323 Tom Underwood .10
324 Andre Thornton .10
325 Rudy May .10
326 Frank Tanana .10
327 Davey Lopes .10
328 Richie Hebner .10
329 Mike Flanagan .10
330 Mike Caldwell .10
331 Scott McGregor .10
332 Jerry Augustine .10
333 Stan Papi .10
334 Rick Miller .10
335 Graig Nettles .15
336 Dusty Baker .10
337 Dave Garcia .10
338 Larry Gura .10
339 Cliff Johnson .10
340 Warren Cromartie .10
341 Steve Comer .10
342 Rick Burleson .10
343 John Martin .10
344 Craig Reynolds .10
345 Mike Proly .10
346 Ruppert Jones .10
347 Omar Moreno .10
348 Greg Minton .10
349 *Rick Mahler* .10
350 Alex Trevino .10
351 Mike Krukow .10
352a Shane Rawley (Jim Anderson photo - shaking hands) .50
352b Shane Rawley (correct photo - kneeling) .15
353 Garth Iorg .10
354 Pete Mackanin .10
355 Paul Moskau .10
356 Richard Dotson .10
357 Steve Stone .10
358 Larry Hisle .10
359 Aurelio Lopez .10
360 Oscar Gamble .10
361 Tom Burgmeier .10
362 Terry Forster .10
363 Joe Charboneau .15
364 Ken Brett .10
365 Tony Armas .10
366 Chris Speier .10
367 Fred Lynn .10
368 Buddy Bell .10
369 Jim Essian .10
370 Terry Puhl .10
371 Greg Gross .10
372 Bruce Sutter 1.00
373 Joe Lefebvre .10
374 Ray Knight .10
375 Bruce Benedict .10
376 Tim Foli .10
377 Al Holland .10
378 Ken Kravec .10
379 Jeff Burroughs .10
380 Pete Falcone .10
381 Ernie Whitt .10
382 Brad Havens .10
383 Terry Crowley .10
384 Don Money .10
385 Dan Schatzeder .10
386 Gary Allenson .10
387 Yogi Berra .50
388 Ken Landreaux .10
389 Mike Hargrove .10
390 Darryl Motley .10
391 Dave McKay .10
392 Stan Bahnsen .10
393 Ken Forsch .10
394 Mario Mendoza .10
395 Jim Morrison .10
396 Mike Ivie .10
397 Broderick Perkins .10
398 Darrell Evans .10
399 Ron Reed .10
400 Johnny Bench 1.50
401 *Steve Bedrosian* .20
402 Bill Robinson .10
403 Bill Buckner .10
404 Ken Oberkfell .10
405 *Cal Ripken, Jr.* 40.00
406 Jim Gantner .10
407 Kirk Gibson .10
408 Tony Perez .75
409 Tommy John .10
410 *Dave Stewart* 2.50
411 Dan Spillner .10
412 Willie Aikens .10
413 Mike Heath .10
414 Ray Burris .10
415 Leon Roberts .10
416 *Mike Witt* .15
417 Bobby Molinaro .10
418 Steve Braun .10
419 Nolan Ryan 4.00
420 Tug McGraw .10
421 Dave Concepcion .10
422a Juan Eichelberger (Gary Lucas photo - white player) .50
422b Juan Eichelberger (correct photo - black player) .10
423 Rick Rhoden .10
424 Frank Robinson .50
425 Eddie Miller .10
426 Bill Caudill .10
427 Doug Flynn .10
428 Larry Anderson (Andersen) .10
429 Al Williams .10
430 Jerry Garvin .10
431 Glenn Adams .10
432 Barry Bonnell .10
433 Jerry Narron .10
434 John Stearns .10
435 Mike Tyson .10
436 Glenn Hubbard .10
437 Eddie Solomon .10
438 Jeff Leonard .10
439 Randy Bass .10
440 Mike LaCoss .10
441 Gary Matthews .10
442 Mark Littell .10
443 Don Sutton .75
444 John Harris .10
445 Vada Pinson .10
446 Elias Sosa .10
447 Charlie Hough .10
448 Willie Wilson .10
449 Fred Stanley .10
450 Tom Veryzer .10
451 Ron Davis .10
452 Mark Clear .10
453 Bill Russell .10
454 Lou Whitaker .10
455 Dan Graham .10
456 Reggie Cleveland .10
457 Sammy Stewart .10
458 Pete Vuckovich .10
459 John Wockenfuss .10
460 Glenn Hoffman .10
461 Willie Randolph .10
462 Fernando Valenzuela .10
463 Ron Hassey .10
464 Paul Splittorff .10
465 Rob Picciolo .10
466 Larry Parrish .10
467 Johnny Grubb .10
468 Dan Ford .10
469 Silvio Martinez .10
470 Kiko Garcia .10
471 Bob Boone .10
472 Luis Salazar .10
473 Randy Niemann .10
474 Tom Griffin .10
475 Phil Niekro .75
476 Hubie Brooks .10
477 Dick Tidrow .10
478 Jim Beattie .10
479 Damaso Garcia .10
480 Mickey Hatcher .10
481 Joe Price .10
482 Ed Farmer .10
483 Eddie Murray 1.50
484 Ben Oglivie .10
485 Kevin Saucier .10
486 Bobby Murcer .10
487 Bill Campbell .10
488 Reggie Smith .10
489 Wayne Garland .10
490 Jim Wright .10
491 Billy Martin .10
492 Jim Fanning .10
493 Don Baylor .10
494 Rick Honeycutt .10
495 Carlton Fisk 1.25
496 Denny Walling .10
497 Bake McBride .10
498 Darrell Porter .10
499 Gene Richards .10
500 Ron Oester .10
501 *Ken Dayley* .10
502 Jason Thompson .10
503 Milt May .10
504 Doug Bird .10
505 Bruce Bochte .10
506 Neil Allen .10
507 Joey McLaughlin .10
508 Butch Wynegar .10
509 Gary Roenicke .10
510 Robin Yount 1.25
511 Dave Tobik .10
512 *Rich Gedman* .15
513 *Gene Nelson* .10
514 Rick Monday .10
515 Miguel Dilone .10
516 Clint Hurdle .10
517 Jeff Newman .10
518 Grant Jackson .10
519 Andy Hassler .10
520 Pat Putnam .10
521 Greg Pryor .10
522 Tony Scott .10
523 Steve Mura .10
524 Johnnie LeMaster .10
525 Dick Ruthven .10
526 John McNamara .10
527 Larry McWilliams .10
528 *Johnny Ray* .15
529 *Pat Tabler* .15
530 Tom Herr .10
531a San Diego Chicken (w/trademark symbol) .75
531b San Diego Chicken (no trademark symbol) .50
532 Sal Butera .10
533 Mike Griffin .10
534 Kelvin Moore .10
535 Reggie Jackson 2.00
536 Ed Romero .10
537 Derrel Thomas .10
538 Mike O'Berry .10
539 Jack O'Connor .10
540 *Bob Ojeda* .25
541 Roy Lee Jackson .10
542 Lynn Jones .10
543 Gaylord Perry .75
544a Phil Garner (photo reversed) .50
544b Phil Garner (photo correct) .10
545 Garry Templeton .10
546 Rafael Ramirez .10
547 Jeff Reardon .10
548 Ron Guidry .10
549 *Tim Laudner* .15
550 John Henry Johnson .10
551 Chris Bando .10
552 Bobby Brown .10
553 Larry Bradford .10
554 *Scott Fletcher* .20
555 Jerry Royster .10
556 Shooty Babbitt .10
557 *Kent Hrbek* 2.00
558 Ron Guidry, Tommy John Yankee Winners .15
559 Mark Bomback .10
560 Julio Valdez .10
561 Buck Martinez .10
562 *Mike Marshall* .15
563 Rennie Stennett .10
564 Steve Crawford .10
565 Bob Babcock .10
566 Johnny Podres .10
567 Paul Serna .10
568 Harold Baines 1.00
569 Dave LaRoche .10
570 Lee May .10
571 Gary Ward .10
572 John Denny .10
573 Roy Smalley .10
574 *Bob Brenly* .20
575 Reggie Jackson, Dave Winfield Bronx Bombers 1.50
576 Luis Pujols .10
577 Butch Hobson .10
578 Harvey Kuenn .10
579 Cal Ripken, Sr. .10
580 Juan Berenguer .10
581 Benny Ayala .10
582 Vance Law .10
583 *Rick Leach* .15
584 George Frazier .10
585 Pete Rose, Mike Schmidt Phillies Finest 1.00
586 Joe Rudi .10
587 Juan Beniquez .10
588 *Luis DeLeon* .10
589 Craig Swan .10
590 Dave Chalk .10
591 Billy Gardner .10
592 Sal Bando .10
593 Bert Campaneris .10
594 Steve Kemp .10
595a Randy Lerch (Braves) .25
595b Randy Lerch (Brewers) .10
596 Bryan Clark .10
597 Dave Ford .10
598 Mike Scioscia .10
599 John Lowenstein .10
600 Rene Lachmann (Lachemann) .10
601 Mick Kelleher .10
602 Ron Jackson .10
603 Jerry Koosman .10
604 Dave Goltz .10
605 Ellis Valentine .10
606 Lonnie Smith .10
607 Joaquin Andujar .10
608 Garry Hancock .10
609 Jerry Turner .10
610 Bob Bonner .10
611 Jim Dwyer .10
612 Terry Bulling .10
613 Joel Youngblood .10
614 Larry Milbourne .10
615 Phil Roof (photo actually Gene Roof) .10
616 Keith Drumright .10
617 Dave Rosello .10
618 Rickey Keeton .10
619 Dennis Lamp .10
620 Sid Monge .10
621 Jerry White .10
622 *Luis Aguayo* .10
623 Jamie Easterly .10
624 *Steve Sax* .50
625 Dave Roberts .10
626 Rick Bosetti .10
627 *Terry Francona* .15
628 Johnny Bench, Tom Seaver Pride of the Reds .75
629 Paul Mirabella .10
630 Rance Mulliniks .10
631 Kevin Hickey .10
632 Reid Nichols .10
633 Dave Geisel .10
634 Ken Griffey .10
635 Bob Lemon .15

636 Orlando Sanchez .10
637 Bill Almon .10
638 Danny Ainge 1.00
639 Willie Stargell 1.25
640 Bob Sykes .10
641 Ed Lynch .10
642 John Ellis .10
643 Fergie Jenkins .75
644 Lenn Sakata .10
645 Julio Gonzales .10
646 Jesse Orosco .10
647 Jerry Dybzinski .10
648 Tommy Davis .10
649 Ron Gardenhire .10
650 Felipe Alou .15
651 Harvey Haddix .10
652 Willie Upshaw .10
653 Bill Madlock .10

1983 DONRUSS

NM/M

Unopened Factory Set (660): 50.00
Complete Set (660): 40.00
Common Player: .10
Ty Cobb Puzzle: 2.50
Wax Pack (15): 2.00
Wax Box (36): 60.00

1 Fernando Valenzuela (DK) .15
2 Rollie Fingers (DK) .60
3 Reggie Jackson (DK) 2.50
4 Jim Palmer (DK) 1.00
5 Jack Morris (DK) .15
6 George Foster (DK) .15
7 Jim Sundberg (DK) .10
8 Willie Stargell (DK) 1.00
9 Dave Stieb (DK) .15
10 Joe Niekro (DK) .15
11 Rickey Henderson (DK) 1.25
12 Dale Murphy (DK) .50
13 Toby Harrah (DK) .10
14 Bill Buckner (DK) .15
15 Willie Wilson (DK) .10
16 Steve Carlton (DK) 1.25
17 Ron Guidry (DK) .15
18 Steve Rogers (DK) .10
19 Kent Hrbek (DK) .10
20 Keith Hernandez (DK) .10
21 Floyd Bannister (DK) .10
22 Johnny Bench (DK) 2.00
23 Britt Burns (DK) .10
24 Joe Morgan (DK) 1.25
25 Carl Yastrzemski (DK) 2.00
26 Terry Kennedy (DK) .10
27 Gary Roenicke .10
28 Dwight Bernard .10
29 Pat Underwood .10
30 Gary Allenson .10
31 Ron Guidry .10
32 Burt Hooton .10
33 Chris Bando .10
34 Vida Blue .10
35 Rickey Henderson 1.25
36 Ray Burris .10
37 John Butcher .10
38 Don Aase .10
39 Jerry Koosman .10
40 Bruce Sutter 1.00
41 Jose Cruz .10
42 Pete Rose 4.00
43 Cesar Cedeno .10
44 Floyd Chiffer .10
45 Larry McWilliams .10
46 Alan Fowlkes .10
47 Dale Murphy .50
48 Doug Bird .10
49 Hubie Brooks .10
50 Floyd Bannister .10
51 Jack O'Connor .10
52 Steve Senteney .10
53 *Gary Gaetti* .60
54 Damaso Garcia .10
55 Gene Nelson .10
56 Mookie Wilson .10
57 Allen Ripley .10
58 Bob Horner .10
59 Tony Pena .10
60 Gary Lavelle .10
61 Tim Lollar .10
62 Frank Pastore .10
63 Garry Maddox .10
64 Bob Forsch .10
65 Harry Spilman .10
66 Geoff Zahn .10
67 Salome Barojas .10
68 David Palmer .10
69 Charlie Hough .10
70 Dan Quisenberry .10
71 Tony Armas .10
72 Rick Sutcliffe .10
73 Steve Balboni .10
74 Jerry Remy .10
75 Mike Scioscia .10
76 John Wockenfuss .10
77 Jim Palmer 1.00
78 Rollie Fingers .60
79 Joe Nolan .10
80 Pete Vuckovich .10
81 Rick Leach .10
82 Rick Miller .10
83 Graig Nettles .15
84 Ron Cey .10
85 Miguel Dilone .10
86 John Wathan .10
87 Kelvin Moore .10
88a Byrn Smith (first name incorrect) .35
88b Bryn Smith (first name correct) .10
89 Dave Hostetler .10
90 Rod Carew 1.50
91 Lonnie Smith .10
92 Bob Knepper .10
93 Marty Bystrom .10
94 Chris Welsh .10
95 Jason Thompson .10
96 Tom O'Malley .10
97 Phil Niekro .60
98 Neil Allen .10
99 Bill Buckner .10
100 *Ed Vande Berg* .10
101 Jim Clancy .10
102 Robert Castillo .10
103 Bruce Berenyi .10
104 Carlton Fisk 1.25
105 Mike Flanagan .10
106 Cecil Cooper .10
107 Jack Morris .10
108 Mike Morgan .10
109 Luis Aponte .10
110 Pedro Guerrero .10
111 Len Barker .10
112 Willie Wilson .10
113 Dave Beard .10
114 Mike Gates .10
115 Reggie Jackson 2.50
116 George Wright .10
117 Vance Law .10
118 Nolan Ryan 4.00
119 Mike Krukow .10
120 Ozzie Smith 2.00
121 Broderick Perkins .10
122 Tom Seaver 1.50
123 Chris Chambliss .10
124 Chuck Tanner .10
125 Johnnie LeMaster .10
126 *Mel Hall* .15
127 Bruce Bochte .10
128 *Charlie Puleo* .10
129 Luis Leal .10
130 John Pacella .10
131 Glenn Gulliver .10
132 Don Money .10
133 Dave Rozema .10
134 Bruce Hurst .10
135 Rudy May .10
136 Tom LaSorda (Lasorda) .50
137 Dan Spillner (photo actually Ed Whitson) .10
138 Jerry Martin .10
139 Mike Norris .10
140 Al Oliver .10
141 Daryl Sconiers .10
142 Lamar Johnson .10
143 Harold Baines .15
144 Alan Ashby .10
145 Garry Templeton .10
146 Al Holland .10
147 Bo Diaz .10
148 Dave Concepcion .10
149 Rick Camp .10
150 Jim Morrison .10
151 Randy Martz .10
152 Keith Hernandez .10
153 John Lowenstein .10
154 Mike Caldwell .10
155 Milt Wilcox .10
156 Rich Gedman .10
157 Rich Gossage .20
158 Jerry Reuss .10
159 Ron Hassey .10
160 Larry Gura .10
161 Dwayne Murphy .10
162 Woodie Fryman .10
163 Steve Comer .10
164 Ken Forsch .10
165 Dennis Lamp .10
166 David Green .10
167 Terry Puhl .10
168 Mike Schmidt 2.50
169 *Eddie Milner* .10
170 John Curtis .10
171 Don Robinson .10
172 Richard Gale .10
173 Steve Bedrosian .10
174 Willie Hernandez .10
175 Ron Gardenhire .10
176 Jim Beattie .10
177 Tim Laudner .10
178 Buck Martinez .10
179 Kent Hrbek .10
180 Alfredo Griffin .10
181 Larry Andersen .10
182 Pete Falcone .10
183 Jody Davis .10
184 Glenn Hubbard .10
185 Dale Berra .10
186 Greg Minton .10
187 Gary Lucas .10
188 Dave Van Gorder .10
189 Bob Dernier .10
190 *Willie McGee* 1.50
191 Dickie Thon .10
192 Bob Boone .10
193 Britt Burns .10
194 Jeff Reardon .10
195 Jon Matlack .10
196 *Don Slaught* .15
197 Fred Stanley .10
198 Rick Manning .10
199 Dave Righetti .10
200 Dave Stapleton .10
201 Steve Yeager .10
202 Enos Cabell .10
203 Sammy Stewart .10
204 Moose Haas .10
205 Lenn Sakata .10
206 Charlie Moore .10
207 Alan Trammell .15
208 Jim Rice .35
209 Roy Smalley .10
210 Bill Russell .10
211 Andre Thornton .10
212 Willie Aikens .10
213 Dave McKay .10
214 Tim Blackwell .10
215 Buddy Bell .10
216 Doug DeCinces .10
217 Tom Herr .10
218 Frank LaCorte .10
219 Steve Carlton 1.25
220 Terry Kennedy .10
221 Mike Easler .10
222 Jack Clark .10
223 Gene Garber .10
224 Scott Holman .10
225 Mike Proly .10
226 Terry Bulling .10
227 Jerry Garvin .10
228 Ron Davis .10
229 Tom Hume .10
230 Marc Hill .10
231 Dennis Martinez .10
232 Jim Gantner .10
233 Larry Pashnick .10
234 Dave Collins .10
235 Tom Burgmeier .10
236 Ken Landreaux .10
237 John Denny .10
238 Hal McRae .10
239 Matt Keough .10
240 Doug Flynn .10
241 Fred Lynn .10
242 Billy Sample .10
243 Tom Paciorek .10
244 Joe Sambito .10
245 Sid Monge .10
246 Ken Oberkfell .10
247 Joe Pittman (photo actually Juan Eichelberger) .10
248 Mario Soto .10
249 Claudell Washington .10
250 Rick Rhoden .10
251 Darrell Evans .10
252 Steve Henderson .10
253 Manny Castillo .10
254 Craig Swan .10
255 Joey McLaughlin .10
256 Pete Redfern .10
257 Ken Singleton .10
258 Robin Yount 1.25
259 Elias Sosa .10
260 Bob Ojeda .10
261 Bobby Murcer .10
262 *Candy Maldonado* .10
263 Rick Waits .10
264 Greg Pryor .10
265 Bob Owchinko .10
266 Chris Speier .10
267 Bruce Kison .10
268 Mark Wagner .10
269 Steve Kemp .10
270 Phil Garner .10
271 Gene Richards .10
272 Renie Martin .10
273 Dave Roberts .10
274 Dan Driessen .10
275 Rufino Linares .10
276 Lee Lacy .10
277 *Ryne Sandberg* 15.00
278 Darrell Porter .10
279 Cal Ripken, Jr. 4.00
280 Jamie Easterly .10
281 Bill Fahey .10
282 Glenn Hoffman .10
283 Willie Randolph .10
284 Fernando Valenzuela .10
285 Alan Bannister .10
286 Paul Splittorff .10
287 Joe Rudi .10
288 Bill Gullickson .10
289 Danny Darwin .10
290 Andy Hassler .10
291 Ernesto Escarrega .10
292 Steve Mura .10
293 Tony Scott .10
294 Manny Trillo .10
295 Greg Harris .10
296 Luis DeLeon .10
297 Kent Tekulve .10
298 Atlee Hammaker .10
299 Bruce Benedict .10
300 Fergie Jenkins .60
301 Dave Kingman .10
302 Bill Caudill .10
303 John Castino .10
304 Ernie Whitt .10
305 Randy S. Johnson .10
306 Garth Iorg .10
307 Gaylord Perry .60
308 Ed Lynch .10
309 Keith Moreland .10
310 Rafael Ramirez .10
311 Bill Madlock .10
312 Milt May .10
313 John Montefusco .10
314 Wayne Krenchicki .10
315 George Vukovich .10
316 Joaquin Andujar .10
317 Craig Reynolds .10
318 Rick Burleson .10
319 Richard Dotson .10
320 Steve Rogers .10
321 Dave Schmidt .10
322 *Bud Black* .15
323 Jeff Burroughs .10
324 Von Hayes .10
325 Butch Wynegar .10
326 Carl Yastrzemski 1.50
327 Ron Roenicke .10
328 *Howard Johnson* 1.00
329 Rick Dempsey .10
330a Jim Slaton(one yellow box on back) .25
330b Jim Slaton (two yellow boxes on back) .10
331 Benny Ayala .10
332 Ted Simmons .10
333 Lou Whitaker .10
334 Chuck Rainey .10
335 Lou Piniella .15
336 Steve Sax .10
337 Toby Harrah .10
338 George Brett 2.50
339 Davey Lopes .10
340 Gary Carter 1.25

No.	Player	Price
341	John Grubb	.10
342	Tim Foli	.10
343	Jim Kaat	.15
344	Mike LaCoss	.10
345	Larry Christenson	.10
346	Juan Bonilla	.10
347	Omar Moreno	.10
348	Chili Davis	.10
349	Tommy Boggs	.10
350	Rusty Staub	.15
351	Bump Wills	.10
352	Rick Sweet	.10
353	*Jim Gott*	.15
354	Terry Felton	.10
355	Jim Kern	.10
356	Bill Almon	.10
357	Tippy Martinez	.10
358	Roy Howell	.10
359	Dan Petry	.10
360	Jerry Mumphrey	.10
361	Mark Clear	.10
362	Mike Marshall	.10
363	Lary Sorensen	.10
364	Amos Otis	.10
365	Rick Langford	.10
366	Brad Mills	.10
367	Brian Downing	.10
368	Mike Richardt	.10
369	Aurelio Rodriguez	.10
370	Dave Smith	.10
371	Tug McGraw	.10
372	Doug Bair	.10
373	Ruppert Jones	.10
374	Alex Trevino	.10
375	Ken Dayley	.10
376	Rod Scurry	.10
377	Bob Brenly	.10
378	Scot Thompson	.10
379	Julio Cruz	.10
380	John Stearns	.10
381	Dale Murray	.10
382	*Frank Viola*	1.50
383	Al Bumbry	.10
384	Ben Oglivie	.10
385	Dave Tobik	.10
386	Bob Stanley	.10
387	Andre Robertson	.10
388	Jorge Orta	.10
389	Ed Whitson	.10
390	Don Hood	.10
391	Tom Underwood	.10
392	Tim Wallach	.10
393	Steve Renko	.10
394	Mickey Rivers	.10
395	Greg Luzinski	.10
396	Art Howe	.10
397	Alan Wiggins	.10
398	Jim Barr	.10
399	Ivan DeJesus	.10
400	*Tom Lawless*	.10
401	Bob Walk	.10
402	Jimmy Smith	.10
403	Lee Smith	.20
404	George Hendrick	.10
405	Eddie Murray	1.25
406	Marshall Edwards	.10
407	Lance Parrish	.10
408	Carney Lansford	.10
409	Dave Winfield	1.25
410	Bob Welch	.10
411	Larry Milbourne	.10
412	Dennis Leonard	.10
413	Dan Meyer	.10
414	Charlie Lea	.10
415	Rick Honeycutt	.10
416	Mike Witt	.10
417	Steve Trout	.10
418	Glenn Brummer	.10
419	Denny Walling	.10
420	Gary Matthews	.10
421	Charlie Liebrandt (Leibrandt)	.10
422	Juan Eichelberger	.10
423	*Matt Guante (Cecilio)*	.10
424	Bill Laskey	.10
425	Jerry Royster	.10
426	Dickie Noles	.10
427	George Foster	.10
428	*Mike Moore*	.25
429	Gary Ward	.10
430	Barry Bonnell	.10
431	Ron Washington	.10
432	Rance Mulliniks	.10
433	Mike Stanton	.10
434	Jesse Orosco	.10
435	Larry Bowa	.10
436	Biff Pocoroba	.10
437	Johnny Ray	.10
438	Joe Morgan	1.00
439	*Eric Show*	.15
440	Larry Biittner	.10
441	Greg Gross	.10
442	Gene Tenace	.10
443	Danny Heep	.10
444	Bobby Clark	.10
445	Kevin Hickey	.10
446	Scott Sanderson	.10
447	Frank Tanana	.10
448	Cesar Geronimo	.10
449	Jimmy Sexton	.10
450	Mike Hargrove	.10
451	Doyle Alexander	.10
452	Dwight Evans	.10
453	Terry Forster	.10
454	Tom Brookens	.10
455	Rich Dauer	.10
456	Rob Picciolo	.10
457	Terry Crowley	.10
458	Ned Yost	.10
459	Kirk Gibson	.10
460	Reid Nichols	.10
461	Oscar Gamble	.10
462	Dusty Baker	.10
463	Jack Perconte	.10
464	Frank White	.10
465	Mickey Klutts	.10
466	Warren Cromartie	.10
467	Larry Parrish	.10
468	Bobby Grich	.10
469	Dane Iorg	.10
470	Joe Niekro	.10
471	Ed Farmer	.10
472	Tim Flannery	.10
473	Dave Parker	.10
474	Jeff Leonard	.10
475	Al Hrabosky	.10
476	Ron Hodges	.10
477	Leon Durham	.10
478	Jim Essian	.10
479	Roy Lee Jackson	.10
480	Brad Havens	.10
481	Joe Price	.10
482	Tony Bernazard	.10
483	Scott McGregor	.10
484	Paul Molitor	1.25
485	Mike Ivie	.10
486	Ken Griffey	.10
487	Dennis Eckersley	1.25
488	Steve Garvey	.50
489	Mike Fischlin	.10
490	U.L. Washington	.10
491	Steve McCatty	.10
492	Roy Johnson	.10
493	Don Baylor	.10
494	Bobby Johnson	.10
495	Mike Squires	.10
496	Bert Roberge	.10
497	Dick Ruthven	.10
498	Tito Landrum	.10
499	Sixto Lezcano	.10
500	Johnny Bench	1.50
501	Larry Whisenton	.10
502	Manny Sarmiento	.10
503	Fred Breining	.10
504	Bill Campbell	.10
505	Todd Cruz	.10
506	Bob Bailor	.10
507	Dave Stieb	.10
508	Al Williams	.10
509	Dan Ford	.10
510	Gorman Thomas	.10
511	Chet Lemon	.10
512	Mike Torrez	.10
513	Shane Rawley	.10
514	Mark Belanger	.10
515	Rodney Craig	.10
516	Onix Concepcion	.10
517	Mike Heath	.10
518	Andre Dawson	.50
519	Luis Sanchez	.10
520	Terry Bogener	.10
521	Rudy Law	.10
522	Ray Knight	.10
523	Joe Lefebvre	.10
524	Jim Wohlford	.10
525	*Julio Franco*	1.50
526	Ron Oester	.10
527	Rick Mahler	.10
528	Steve Nicosia	.10
529	Junior Kennedy	.10
530a	Whitey Herzog (one yellow box on back)	.25
530b	Whitey Herzog (two yellow boxes on back)	.15
531a	Don Sutton (blue frame)	.60
531b	Don Sutton (green frame)	.60
532	Mark Brouhard	.10
533a	Sparky Anderson (one yellow box on back)	.50
533b	Sparky Anderson (two yellow boxes on back)	.50
534	Roger LaFrancois	.10
535	George Frazier	.10
536	Tom Niedenfuer	.10
537	Ed Glynn	.10
538	Lee May	.10
539	Bob Kearney	.10
540	Tim Raines	.15
541	Paul Mirabella	.10
542	Luis Tiant	.10
543	Ron LeFlore	.10
544	*Dave LaPoint*	.15
545	Randy Moffitt	.10
546	Luis Aguayo	.10
547	Brad Lesley	.10
548	Luis Salazar	.10
549	John Candelaria	.10
550	Dave Bergman	.10
551	Bob Watson	.10
552	Pat Tabler	.10
553	Brent Gaff	.10
554	Al Cowens	.10
555	Tom Brunansky	.10
556	Lloyd Moseby	.10
557a	Pascual Perez (Twins)	.25
557b	Pascual Perez (Braves)	.10
558	Willie Upshaw	.10
559	Richie Zisk	.10
560	Pat Zachry	.10
561	Jay Johnstone	.10
562	Carlos Diaz	.10
563	John Tudor	.10
564	Frank Robinson	.50
565	Dave Edwards	.10
566	Paul Householder	.10
567	Ron Reed	.10
568	Mike Ramsey	.10
569	Kiko Garcia	.10
570	Tommy John	.10
571	Tony LaRussa	.10
572	Joel Youngblood	.10
573	*Wayne Tolleson*	.10
574	Keith Creel	.10
575	Billy Martin	.10
576	Jerry Dybzinski	.10
577	Rick Cerone	.10
578	Tony Perez	.75
579	*Greg Brock*	.10
580	Glen Wilson (Glenn)	.10
581	Tim Stoddard	.10
582	Bob McClure	.10
583	Jim Dwyer	.10
584	Ed Romero	.10
585	Larry Herndon	.10
586	*Wade Boggs*	15.00
587	Jay Howell	.10
588	Dave Stewart	.10
589	Bert Blyleven	.10
590	Dick Howser	.10
591	Wayne Gross	.10
592	Terry Francona	.10
593	Don Werner	.10
594	Bill Stein	.10
595	Jesse Barfield	.10
596	Bobby Molinaro	.10
597	Mike Vail	.10
598	*Tony Gwynn*	15.00
599	Gary Rajsich	.10
600	Jerry Ujdur	.10
601	Cliff Johnson	.10
602	Jerry White	.10
603	Bryan Clark	.10
604	Joe Ferguson	.10
605	Guy Sularz	.10
606a	Ozzie Virgil (green frame around photo)	.25
606b	Ozzie Virgil (orange frame around photo)	.10
607	Terry Harper	.10
608	Harvey Kuenn	.10
609	Jim Sundberg	.10
610	Willie Stargell	1.00
611	Reggie Smith	.10
612	Rob Wilfong	.10
613	Joe Niekro, Phil Niekro Niekro Brothers	.25
614	Lee Elia	.10
615	Mickey Hatcher	.10
616	Jerry Hairston Sr.	.10
617	John Martin	.10
618	Wally Backman	.10
619	*Storm Davis*	.15
620	Alan Knicely	.10
621	John Stuper	.10
622	Matt Sinatro	.10
623	*Gene Petralli*	.10
624	Duane Walker	.10
625	Dick Williams	.10
626	Pat Corrales	.10
627	Vern Ruhle	.10
628	Joe Torre	.10
629	Anthony Johnson	.10
630	Steve Howe	.10
631	Gary Woods	.10
632	Lamarr Hoyt (LaMarr)	.10
633	Steve Swisher	.10
634	Terry Leach	.10
635	Jeff Newman	.10
636	Brett Butler	.10
637	Gary Gray	.10
638	Lee Mazzilli	.10
639a	Ron Jackson (A's)	2.00
639b	Ron Jackson (Angels - green frame around photo)	.25
639c	Ron Jackson (Angels - red frame around photo)	.15
640	Juan Beniquez	.10
641	Dave Rucker	.10
642	Luis Pujols	.10
643	Rick Monday	.10
644	Hosken Powell	.10
645	San Diego Chicken	.20
646	Dave Engle	.10
647	Dick Davis	.10
648	Vida Blue, Joe Morgan, Frank Robinson MVP's	.15
649	Al Chambers	.10
650	Jesus Vega	.10
651	Jeff Jones	.10
652	Marvis Foley	.10
653	Ty Cobb (puzzle)	.10

1984 DONRUSS

		NM/M
	Unopened Factory Set (658):	100.00
	Complete Set (660):	75.00
	Common Player:	.15
	Duke Snider Puzzle:	2.00
	Wax Pack (15):	3.00
	Wax Box (36):	115.00
	Rack Pack (45):	15.00
A	Rollie Fingers, Gaylord Perry Living Legends	1.50
B	Johnny Bench, Carl Yastrzemski Living Legends	4.00
1a	Robin Yount (DK) (Steel)	2.50
1b	Robin Yount (DK) (Steele)	3.00
2a	Dave Concepcion (DK) (Steel)	.25
2b	Dave Concepcion (DK) (Steele)	.35
3a	Dwayne Murphy (DK) (Steel)	.25
3b	Dwayne Murphy (DK) (Steele)	.35
4a	John Castino (DK) (Steel)	.25
4b	John Castino (DK) (Steele)	.35
5a	Leon Durham (DK) (Steel)	.25
5b	Leon Durham (DK) (Steele)	.35
6a	Rusty Staub (DK) (Steel)	.30
6b	Rusty Staub (DK) (Steele)	.45

7a Jack Clark (DK) (Steel) .25
7b Jack Clark (DK) (Steele) .35
8a Dave Dravecky (DK) (Steel) .25
8b Dave Dravecky (DK) (Steele) .35
9a Al Oliver (DK) (Steel) .35
9b Al Oliver (DK) (Steele) .50
10a Dave Righetti (DK) (Steel) .25
10b Dave Righetti (DK) (Steele) .35
11a Hal McRae (DK) (Steel) .25
11b Hal McRae (DK) (Steele) .35
12a Ray Knight (DK) (Steel) .25
12b Ray Knight (DK) (Steele) .35
13a Bruce Sutter (DK) (Steel) 2.00
13b Bruce Sutter (DK) (Steele) 2.25
14a Bob Horner (DK) (Steel) .25
14b Bob Horner (DK) (Steele) .35
15a Lance Parrish (DK) (Steel) .25
15b Lance Parrish (DK) (Steele) .35
16a Matt Young (DK) (Steel) .25
16b Matt Young (DK) (Steele) .35
17a Fred Lynn (DK) (Steel) .35
17b Fred Lynn (DK) (Steele) .50
18a Ron Kittle (DK) (Steel) .25
18b Ron Kittle (DK) (Steele) .35
19a Jim Clancy (DK) (Steel) .25
19b Jim Clancy (DK) (Steele) .35
20a Bill Madlock (DK) (Steel) .25
20b Bill Madlock (DK) (Steele) .35
21a Larry Parrish (DK) (Steel) .25
21b Larry Parrish (DK) (Steele) .35
22a Eddie Murray (DK) (Steel) 2.50
22b Eddie Murray (DK) (Steele) 3.00
23a Mike Schmidt (DK) (Steel) 3.00
23b Mike Schmidt (DK) (Steele) 4.00
24a Pedro Guerrero (DK) (Steel) .25
24b Pedro Guerrero (DK) (Steele) .35
25a Andre Thornton (DK) (Steel) .25
25b Andre Thornton (DK) (Steele) .35
26a Wade Boggs (DK) (Steel) 2.50
26b Wade Boggs (DK) (Steele) 3.00
27 *Joel Skinner* (RR) .15
28 Tom Dunbar (RR) .15
29a Mike Stenhouse (RR) (no number on back) .15
29b Mike Stenhouse (RR)(29 on back) 1.00
30a *Ron Darling* (RR) (no number on back) 1.50
30b *Ron Darling* (RR) (30 on back) 2.50
31 *Dion James* (RR) .15
32 *Tony Fernandez* (RR) 3.00
33 Angel Salazar (RR) .15
34 *Kevin McReynolds* (RR) 1.50
35 *Dick Schofield* (RR) .20
36 *Brad Komminsk* (RR) .15
37 *Tim Teufel* (RR) .25
38 Doug Frobel (RR) .15
39 *Greg Gagne* (RR) 1.00
40 Mike Fuentes (RR) .15
41 *Joe Carter* (RR) 8.00
42 Mike Brown (RR) .15
43 Mike Jeffcoat (RR) .15
44 *Sid Fernandez* (RR) 2.00
45 Brian Dayett (RR) .15
46 Chris Smith (RR) .15
47 Eddie Murray 3.00
48 Robin Yount 3.00
49 Lance Parrish .15
50 Jim Rice .75
51 Dave Winfield 3.00
52 Fernando Valenzuela .25
53 George Brett 5.00
54 Rickey Henderson 3.00
55 Gary Carter 3.00
56 Buddy Bell .15
57 Reggie Jackson 5.00
58 Harold Baines .25
59 Ozzie Smith 4.00
60 Nolan Ryan 8.00
61 Pete Rose 8.00
62 Ron Oester .15
63 Steve Garvey .75
64 Jason Thompson .15
65 Jack Clark .15
66 Dale Murphy 1.50
67 Leon Durham .15
68 Darryl Strawberry 2.00
69 Richie Zisk .15
70 Kent Hrbek .15
71 Dave Stieb .15
72 Ken Schrom .15
73 George Bell .15
74 John Moses .15
75 Ed Lynch .15
76 Chuck Rainey .15
77 Biff Pocoroba .15
78 Cecilio Guante .15
79 Jim Barr .15
80 Kurt Bevacqua .15
81 Tom Foley .15
82 Joe Lefebvre .15
83 *Andy Van Slyke* 2.00
84 Bob Lillis .15
85 Rick Adams .15
86 Jerry Hairston Sr. .15
87 Bob James .15
88 Joe Altobelli .15
89 Ed Romero .15
90 John Grubb .15
91 John Henry Johnson .15
92 Juan Espino .15
93 Candy Maldonado .15
94 Andre Thornton .15
95 Onix Concepcion .15
96 *Don Hill* .15
97 Andre Dawson 1.50
98 Frank Tanana .15
99 *Curt Wilkerson* .15
100 Larry Gura .15
101 Dwayne Murphy .15
102 Tom Brennan .15
103 Dave Righetti .15
104 Steve Sax .15
105 Dan Petry .15
106 Cal Ripken, Jr. 8.00
107 Paul Molitor 3.00
108 Fred Lynn .15
109 Neil Allen .15
110 Joe Niekro .15
111 Steve Carlton 3.00
112 Terry Kennedy .15
113 Bill Madlock .15
114 Chili Davis .15
115 Jim Gantner .15
116 Tom Seaver 4.00
117 Bill Buckner .15
118 Bill Caudill .15
119 Jim Clancy .15
120 John Castino .15
121 Dave Concepcion .15
122 Greg Luzinski .15
123 Mike Boddicker .15
124 Pete Ladd .15
125 Juan Berenguer .15
126 John Montefusco .15
127 Ed Jurak .15
128 Tom Niedenfuer .15
129 Bert Blyleven .20
130 Bud Black .15
131 Gorman Heimueller .15
132 Dan Schatzeder .15
133 Ron Jackson .15
134 *Tom Henke* 1.00
135 Kevin Hickey .15
136 Mike Scott .15
137 Bo Diaz .15
138 Glenn Brummer .15
139 Sid Monge .15
140 Rich Gale .15
141 Brett Butler .15
142 Brian Harper .15
143 John Rabb .15
144 Gary Woods .15
145 Pat Putnam .15
146 *Jim Acker* .15
147 Mickey Hatcher .15
148 Todd Cruz .15
149 Tom Tellmann .15
150 John Wockenfuss .15
151 Wade Boggs 5.00
152 Don Baylor .15
153 Bob Welch .15
154 Alan Bannister .15
155 Willie Aikens .15
156 Jeff Burroughs .15
157 Bryan Little .15
158 Bob Boone .15
159 Dave Hostetler .15
160 Jerry Dybzinski .15
161 Mike Madden .15
162 Luis DeLeon .15
163 Willie Hernandez .15
164 Frank Pastore .15
165 Rick Camp .15
166 Lee Mazzilli .15
167 Scot Thompson .15
168 Bob Forsch .15
169 Mike Flanagan .15
170 Rick Manning .15
171 Chet Lemon .15
172 Jerry Remy .15
173 Ron Guidry .20
174 Pedro Guerrero .15
175 Willie Wilson .15
176 Carney Lansford .15
177 Al Oliver .15
178 Jim Sundberg .15
179 Bobby Grich .15
180 Richard Dotson .15
181 Joaquin Andujar .15
182 Jose Cruz .15
183 Mike Schmidt 5.00
184 *Gary Redus* .25
185 Garry Templeton .15
186 Tony Pena .15
187 Greg Minton .15
188 Phil Niekro 1.00
189 Fergie Jenkins 1.00
190 Mookie Wilson .15
191 Jim Beattie .15
192 Gary Ward .15
193 Jesse Barfield .15
194 Pete Filson .15
195 Roy Lee Jackson .15
196 Rick Sweet .15
197 Jesse Orosco .15
198 *Steve Lake* .15
199 Ken Dayley .15
200 Manny Sarmiento .15
201 Mark Davis .15
202 Tim Flannery .15
203 Bill Scherrer .15
204 Al Holland .15
205 David Von Ohlen .15
206 Mike LaCoss .15
207 Juan Beniquez .15
208 *Juan Agosto* .15
209 Bobby Ramos .15
210 Al Bumbry .15
211 Mark Brouhard .15
212 Howard Bailey .15
213 Bruce Hurst .15
214 Bob Shirley .15
215 Pat Zachry .15
216 Julio Franco .15
217 Mike Armstrong .15
218 Dave Beard .15
219 Steve Rogers .15
220 John Butcher .15
221 *Mike Smithson* .15
222 Frank White .15
223 Mike Heath .15
224 Chris Bando .15
225 Roy Smalley .15
226 Dusty Baker .15
227 Lou Whitaker .15
228 John Lowenstein .15
229 Ben Oglivie .15
230 Doug DeCinces .15
231 Lonnie Smith .15
232 Ray Knight .15
233 Gary Matthews .15
234 Juan Bonilla .15
235 Rod Scurry .15
236 Atlee Hammaker .15
237 Mike Caldwell .15
238 Keith Hernandez .15
239 Larry Bowa .15
240 Tony Bernazard .15
241 Damaso Garcia .15
242 Tom Brunansky .15
243 Dan Driessen .15
244 Ron Kittle .15
245 Tim Stoddard .15
246 Bob L. Gibson .15
247 Marty Castillo .15
248 *Don Mattingly* 35.00
249 Jeff Newman .15
250 *Alejandro Pena* .15
251 Toby Harrah .15
252 Cesar Geronimo .15
253 Tom Underwood .15
254 Doug Flynn .15
255 Andy Hassler .15
256 Odell Jones .15
257 Rudy Law .15
258 Harry Spilman .15
259 Marty Bystrom .15
260 Dave Rucker .15
261 Ruppert Jones .15
262 Jeff Jones .15
263 *Gerald Perry* .15
264 Gene Tenace .15
265 Brad Wellman .15
266 Dickie Noles .15
267 Jamie Allen .15
268 Jim Gott .15
269 Ron Davis .15
270 Benny Ayala .15
271 Ned Yost .15
272 Dave Rozema .15
273 Dave Stapleton .15
274 Lou Piniella .25
275 Jose Morales .15
276 Brod Perkins .15
277 Butch Davis .15
278 Tony Phillips .15
279 Jeff Reardon .15
280 Ken Forsch .15
281 *Pete O'Brien* .15
282 Tom Paciorek .15
283 Frank LaCorte .15
284 Tim Lollar .15
285 Greg Gross .15
286 Alex Trevino .15
287 Gene Garber .15
288 Dave Parker .15
289 Lee Smith .25
290 Dave LaPoint .15
291 *John Shelby* .15
292 Charlie Moore .15
293 Alan Trammell .25
294 Tony Armas .15
295 Shane Rawley .15
296 Greg Brock .15
297 Hal McRae .15
298 Mike Davis .15
299 Tim Raines .50
300 Bucky Dent .15
301 Tommy John .25
302 Carlton Fisk 3.00
303 Darrell Porter .15
304 Dickie Thon .15
305 Garry Maddox .15
306 Cesar Cedeno .15
307 Gary Lucas .15
308 Johnny Ray .15
309 Andy McGaffigan .15
310 Claudell Washington .15
311 Ryne Sandberg 5.00
312 George Foster .15
313 *Spike Owen* .25
314 Gary Gaetti .15
315 Willie Upshaw .15
316 Al Williams .15
317 Jorge Orta .15
318 Orlando Mercado .15
319 *Junior Ortiz* .15
320 Mike Proly .15
321 Randy S. Johnson .15
322 Jim Morrison .15
323 Max Venable .15
324 Tony Gwynn 5.00
325 Duane Walker .15
326 Ozzie Virgil .15
327 Jeff Lahti .15
328 *Bill Dawley* .15
329 Rob Wilfong .15
330 Marc Hill .15
331 Ray Burris .15
332 Allan Ramirez .15
333 Chuck Porter .15
334 Wayne Krenchicki .15
335 Gary Allenson .15
336 *Bob Meacham* .15

337 Joe Beckwith .15
338 Rick Sutcliffe .15
339 *Mark Huismann* .15
340 *Tim Conroy* .15
341 Scott Sanderson .15
342 Larry Biittner .15
343 Dave Stewart .15
344 Darryl Motley .15
345 *Chris Codiroli* .15
346 Rick Behenna .15
347 Andre Robertson .15
348 Mike Marshall .15
349 Larry Herndon .15
350 Rich Dauer .15
351 Cecil Cooper .15
352 Rod Carew 3.00
353 Willie McGee .15
354 Phil Garner .15
355 Joe Morgan 3.00
356 Luis Salazar .15
357 John Candelaria .15
358 Bill Laskey .15
359 Bob McClure .15
360 Dave Kingman .15
361 Ron Cey .15
362 *Matt Young* .15
363 Lloyd Moseby .15
364 Frank Viola .15
365 Eddie Milner .15
366 Floyd Bannister .15
367 Dan Ford .15
368 Moose Haas .15
369 Doug Bair .15
370 *Ray Fontenot* .15
371 Luis Aponte .15
372 Jack Fimple .15
373 *Neal Heaton* .15
374 Greg Pryor .15
375 Wayne Gross .15
376 Charlie Lea .15
377 Steve Lubratich .15
378 Jon Matlack .15
379 Julio Cruz .15
380 John Mizerock .15
381 *Kevin Gross* .15
382 Mike Ramsey .15
383 Doug Gwosdz .15
384 Kelly Paris .15
385 Pete Falcone .15
386 Milt May .15
387 Fred Breining .15
388 *Craig Lefferts* .25
389 Steve Henderson .15
390 Randy Moffitt .15
391 Ron Washington .15
392 Gary Roenicke .15
393 *Tom Candiotti* .75
394 Larry Pashnick .15
395 Dwight Evans .15
396 Goose Gossage .25
397 Derrel Thomas .15
398 Juan Eichelberger .15
399 Leon Roberts .15
400 Davey Lopes .15
401 Bill Gullickson .15
402 Geoff Zahn .15
403 Billy Sample .15
404 Mike Squires .15
405 Craig Reynolds .15
406 Eric Show .15
407 John Denny .15
408 Dann Bilardello .15
409 Bruce Benedict .15
410 Kent Tekulve .15
411 Mel Hall .15
412 John Stuper .15
413 Rick Dempsey .15
414 Don Sutton 1.00
415 Jack Morris .15
416 John Tudor .15
417 Willie Randolph .15
418 Jerry Reuss .15
419 Don Slaught .15
420 Steve McCatty .15
421 Tim Wallach .15
422 Larry Parrish .15
423 Brian Downing .15
424 Britt Burns .15
425 David Green .15
426 Jerry Mumphrey .15
427 Ivan DeJesus .15
428 Mario Soto .15
429 Gene Richards .15
430 Dale Berra .15
431 Darrell Evans .15
432 Glenn Hubbard .15
433 Jody Davis .15
434 Danny Heep .15
435 *Ed Nunez* .15
436 Bobby Castillo .15
437 Ernie Whitt .15
438 Scott Ullger .15
439 Doyle Alexander .15
440 Domingo Ramos .15
441 Craig Swan .15
442 Warren Brusstar .15
443 Len Barker .15
444 Mike Easler .15
445 Renie Martin .15
446 *Dennis Rasmussen* .25
447 Ted Power .15
448 *Charlie Hudson* .15
449 *Danny Cox* .15
450 Kevin Bass .15
451 Daryl Sconiers .15
452 Scott Fletcher .15
453 Bryn Smith .15
454 Jim Dwyer .15
455 Rob Picciolo .15
456 Enos Cabell .15
457 *Dennis Boyd* .20
458 Butch Wynegar .15
459 Burt Hooton .15
460 Ron Hassey .15
461 *Danny Jackson* .15
462 Bob Kearney .15
463 Terry Francona .15
464 Wayne Tolleson .15
465 Mickey Rivers .15
466 John Wathan .15
467 Bill Almon .15
468 George Vukovich .15
469 Steve Kemp .15
470 Ken Landreaux .15
471 Milt Wilcox .15
472 Tippy Martinez .15
473 Ted Simmons .15
474 Tim Foli .15
475 George Hendrick .15
476 Terry Puhl .15
477 Von Hayes .15
478 Bobby Brown .15
479 Lee Lacy .15
480 Joel Youngblood .15
481 Jim Slaton .15
482 *Mike Fitzgerald* .15
483 Keith Moreland .15
484 Ron Roenicke .15
485 Luis Leal .15
486 Bryan Oelkers .15
487 Bruce Berenyi .15
488 LaMarr Hoyt .15
489 Joe Nolan .15
490 Marshall Edwards .15
491 *Mike Laga* .15
492 Rick Cerone .15
493 Mike Miller (Rick) .15
494 Rick Honeycutt .15
495 Mike Hargrove .15
496 Joe Simpson .15
497 *Keith Atherton* .15
498 Chris Welsh .15
499 Bruce Kison .15
500 Bob Johnson .15
501 Jerry Koosman .15
502 Frank DiPino .15
503 Tony Perez 2.00
504 Ken Oberkfell .15
505 *Mark Thurmond* .15
506 Joe Price .15
507 Pascual Perez .15
508 *Marvell Wynne* .15
509 Mike Krukow .15
510 Dick Ruthven .15
511 Al Cowens .15
512 Cliff Johnson .15
513 *Randy Bush* .15
514 Sammy Stewart .15
515 *Bill Schroeder* .15
516 Aurelio Lopez .15
517 Mike Brown .15
518 Graig Nettles .25
519 Dave Sax .15
520 Gerry Willard .15
521 Paul Splittorff .15
522 Tom Burgmeier .15
523 Chris Speier .15
524 Bobby Clark .15
525 George Wright .15
526 Dennis Lamp .15
527 Tony Scott .15
528 Ed Whitson .15
529 Ron Reed .15
530 Charlie Puleo .15
531 Jerry Royster .15
532 Don Robinson .15
533 Steve Trout .15
534 Bruce Sutter 2.00
535 Bob Horner .15
536 Pat Tabler .15
537 Chris Chambliss .15
538 Bob Ojeda .15
539 Alan Ashby .15
540 Jay Johnstone .15
541 Bob Dernier .15
542 *Brook Jacoby* .15
543 U.L. Washington .15
544 Danny Darwin .15
545 Kiko Garcia .15
546 Vance Law .15
547 Tug McGraw .15
548 Dave Smith .15
549 Len Matuszek .15
550 Tom Hume .15
551 Dave Dravecky .15
552 Rick Rhoden .15
553 Duane Kuiper .15
554 Rusty Staub .20
555 Bill Campbell .15
556 Mike Torrez .15
557 Dave Henderson .15
558 Len Whitehouse .15
559 Barry Bonnell .15
560 Rick Lysander .15
561 Garth Iorg .15
562 Bryan Clark .15
563 Brian Giles .15
564 Vern Ruhle .15
565 Steve Bedrosian .15
566 Larry McWilliams .15
567 Jeff Leonard .15
568 Alan Wiggins .15
569 *Jeff Russell* .15
570 Salome Barojas .15
571 Dane Iorg .15
572 Bob Knepper .15
573 Gary Lavelle .15
574 Gorman Thomas .15
575 Manny Trillo .15
576 Jim Palmer 3.00
577 Dale Murray .15
578 Tom Brookens .15
579 Rich Gedman .15
580 *Bill Doran* .25
581 Steve Yeager .15
582 Dan Spillner .15
583 Dan Quisenberry .15
584 Rance Mulliniks .15
585 Storm Davis .15
586 Dave Schmidt .15
587 Bill Russell .15
588 *Pat Sheridan* .15
589 Rafael Ramirez .15
590 Bud Anderson .15
591 George Frazier .15
592 *Lee Tunnell* .15
593 Kirk Gibson .15
594 Scott McGregor .15
595 Bob Bailor .15
596 Tom Herr .15
597 Luis Sanchez .15
598 Dave Engle .15
599 *Craig McMurtry* .15
600 Carlos Diaz .15
601 Tom O'Malley .15
602 *Nick Esasky* .15
603 Ron Hodges .15
604 Ed Vande Berg .15
605 Alfredo Griffin .15
606 Glenn Hoffman .15
607 Hubie Brooks .15
608 Richard Barnes (photo actually Neal Heaton) .15
609 *Greg Walker* .15
610 Ken Singleton .15
611 Mark Clear .15
612 Buck Martinez .15
613 Ken Griffey .20
614 Reid Nichols .15
615 *Doug Sisk* .15
616 Bob Brenly .15
617 Joey McLaughlin .15
618 Glenn Wilson .15
619 Bob Stoddard .15
620 Len Sakata (Lenn) .15
621 *Mike Young* .15
622 John Stefero .15
623 *Carmelo Martinez* .15
624 Dave Bergman .15
625 David Green, Willie McGee, Lonnie Smith, Ozzie Smith Runnin' Reds .75
626 Rudy May .15
627 Matt Keough .15
628 *Jose DeLeon* .15
629 Jim Essian .15
630 *Darnell Coles* .15
631 Mike Warren .15
632 Del Crandall .15
633 Dennis Martinez .15
634 Mike Moore .15
635 Lary Sorensen .15
636 Ricky Nelson .15
637 Omar Moreno .15
638 Charlie Hough .15
639 Dennis Eckersley 3.00
640 *Walt Terrell* .15
641 Denny Walling .15
642 *Dave Anderson* .15
643 *Jose Oquendo* .15
644 Bob Stanley .15
645 Dave Geisel .15
646 *Scott Garrelts* .15
647 *Gary Pettis* .15
648 Duke Snider Puzzle Card .15
649 Johnnie LeMaster .15
650 Dave Collins .15
651 San Diego Chicken .25

1985 DONRUSS

	NM/M
Unopened Fact. Set (660):	60.00
Complete Set (660):	40.00
Common Player:	.10
Lou Gehrig Puzzle:	2.50
Wax Pack (15):	2.00
Wax Box (36):	80.00
Rack Pack (45):	5.00

1 Ryne Sandberg (DK) 2.50
2 Doug DeCinces (DK) .10
3 Rich Dotson (DK) .10
4 Bert Blyleven (DK) .15
5 Lou Whitaker (DK) .15
6 Dan Quisenberry (DK) .10
7 Don Mattingly (DK) 4.00
8 Carney Lansford (DK) .10
9 Frank Tanana (DK) .10
10 Willie Upshaw (DK) .10
11 Claudell Washington (DK) .10
12 Mike Marshall (DK) .10
13 Joaquin Andujar (DK) .10
14 Cal Ripken, Jr. (DK) 6.00
15 Jim Rice (DK) .40
16 Don Sutton (DK) .50
17 Frank Viola (DK) .10
18 Alvin Davis (DK) .10
19 Mario Soto (DK) .10
20 Jose Cruz (DK) .10
21 Charlie Lea (DK) .10
22 Jesse Orosco (DK) .10
23 Juan Samuel (DK) .10
24 Tony Pena (DK) .10
25 Tony Gwynn (DK) 2.50
26 Bob Brenly (DK) .10
27 *Danny Tartabull* (RR) 1.50
28 *Mike Bielecki* (RR) .10
29 *Steve Lyons* (RR) .25
30 *Jeff Reed* (RR) .15
31 Tony Brewer (RR) .10
32 *John Morris* (RR) .10
33 *Daryl Boston* (RR) .15
34 Alfonso Pulido (RR) .10
35 *Steve Kiefer* (RR) .10
36 *Larry Sheets* (RR) .10
37 *Scott Bradley* (RR) .10
38 *Calvin Schiraldi* (RR) .10
39 *Shawon Dunston* (RR) 1.50
40 Charlie Mitchell (RR) .10
41 *Billy Hatcher* (RR) .15
42 Russ Stephans (RR) .10
43 Alejandro Sanchez (RR) .10
44 *Steve Jeltz* (RR) .10
45 *Jim Traber* (RR) .10
46 Doug Loman (RR) .10
47 Eddie Murray 2.00

No.	Player	Price
48	Robin Yount	2.00
49	Lance Parrish	.10
50	Jim Rice	.40
51	Dave Winfield	2.00
52	Fernando Valenzuela	.10
53	George Brett	3.00
54	Dave Kingman	.10
55	Gary Carter	2.00
56	Buddy Bell	.10
57	Reggie Jackson	3.00
58	Harold Baines	.15
59	Ozzie Smith	2.00
60	Nolan Ryan	6.00
61	Mike Schmidt	3.00
62	Dave Parker	.10
63	Tony Gwynn	2.50
64	Tony Pena	.10
65	Jack Clark	.10
66	Dale Murphy	.60
67	Ryne Sandberg	2.50
68	Keith Hernandez	.10
69	Alvin Davis	.10
70	Kent Hrbek	.10
71	Willie Upshaw	.10
72	Dave Engle	.10
73	Alfredo Griffin	.10
74a	Jack Perconte (last line of highlights begins "Batted .346...")	.10
74b	Jack Perconte (last line of highlights begins "Led the ...")	.15
75	Jesse Orosco	.10
76	Jody Davis	.10
77	Bob Horner	.10
78	Larry McWilliams	.10
79	Joel Youngblood	.10
80	Alan Wiggins	.10
81	Ron Oester	.10
82	Ozzie Virgil	.10
83	*Ricky Horton*	.10
84	Bill Doran	.10
85	Rod Carew	2.00
86	LaMarr Hoyt	.10
87	Tim Wallach	.10
88	Mike Flanagan	.10
89	Jim Sundberg	.10
90	Chet Lemon	.10
91	Bob Stanley	.10
92	Willie Randolph	.10
93	Bill Russell	.10
94	Julio Franco	.10
95	Dan Quisenberry	.10
96	Bill Caudill	.10
97	Bill Gullickson	.10
98	Danny Darwin	.10
99	Curtis Wilkerson	.10
100	Bud Black	.10
101	Tony Phillips	.10
102	Tony Bernazard	.10
103	Jay Howell	.10
104	Burt Hooton	.10
105	Milt Wilcox	.10
106	Rich Dauer	.10
107	Don Sutton	.75
108	Mike Witt	.10
109	Bruce Sutter	1.50
110	Enos Cabell	.10
111	John Denny	.10
112	Dave Dravecky	.10
113	Marvell Wynne	.10
114	Johnnie LeMaster	.10
115	Chuck Porter	.10
116	John Gibbons	.10
117	Keith Moreland	.10
118	Darnell Coles	.10
119	Dennis Lamp	.10
120	Ron Davis	.10
121	Nick Esasky	.10
122	Vance Law	.10
123	Gary Roenicke	.10
124	Bill Schroeder	.10
125	Dave Rozema	.10
126	Bobby Meacham	.10
127	Marty Barrett	.10
128	*R.J. Reynolds*	.15
129	Ernie Camacho	.10
130	Jorge Orta	.10
131	Lary Sorensen	.10
132	Terry Francona	.10
133	Fred Lynn	.10
134	Bobby Jones	.10
135	Jerry Hairston Sr.	.10
136	Kevin Bass	.10
137	Garry Maddox	.10
138	Dave LaPoint	.10
139	Kevin McReynolds	.10
140	Wayne Krenchicki	.10
141	Rafael Ramirez	.10
142	Rod Scurry	.10
143	Greg Minton	.10
144	Tim Stoddard	.10
145	Steve Henderson	.10
146	George Bell	.10
147	Dave Meier	.10
148	Sammy Stewart	.10
149	Mark Brouhard	.10
150	Larry Herndon	.10
151	Oil Can Boyd	.10
152	Brian Dayett	.10
153	Tom Niedenfuer	.10
154	Brook Jacoby	.10
155	Onix Concepcion	.10
156	Tim Conroy	.10
157	*Joe Hesketh*	.15
158	Brian Downing	.10
159	Tommy Dunbar	.10
160	Marc Hill	.10
161	Phil Garner	.10
162	Jerry Davis	.10
163	Bill Campbell	.10
164	*John Franco*	1.50
165	Len Barker	.10
166	*Benny Distefano*	.10
167	George Frazier	.10
168	Tito Landrum	.10
169	Cal Ripken, Jr.	6.00
170	Cecil Cooper	.10
171	Alan Trammell	.15
172	Wade Boggs	2.50
173	Don Baylor	.10
174	Pedro Guerrero	.10
175	Frank White	.10
176	Rickey Henderson	2.00
177	Charlie Lea	.10
178	Pete O'Brien	.10
179	Doug DeCinces	.10
180	Ron Kittle	.10
181	George Hendrick	.10
182	Joe Niekro	.10
183	Juan Samuel	.10
184	Mario Soto	.10
185	Goose Gossage	.15
186	Johnny Ray	.10
187	Bob Brenly	.10
188	Craig McMurtry	.10
189	Leon Durham	.10
190	Dwight Gooden	.25
191	Barry Bonnell	.10
192	Tim Teufel	.10
193	Dave Stieb	.10
194	Mickey Hatcher	.10
195	Jesse Barfield	.10
196	Al Cowens	.10
197	Hubie Brooks	.10
198	Steve Trout	.10
199	Glenn Hubbard	.10
200	Bill Madlock	.10
201	*Jeff Robinson*	.10
202	Eric Show	.10
203	Dave Concepcion	.10
204	Ivan DeJesus	.10
205	Neil Allen	.10
206	Jerry Mumphrey	.10
207	Mike Brown	.10
208	Carlton Fisk	2.00
209	Bryn Smith	.10
210	Tippy Martinez	.10
211	Dion James	.10
212	Willie Hernandez	.10
213	Mike Easler	.10
214	Ron Guidry	.10
215	Rick Honeycutt	.10
216	Brett Butler	.10
217	Larry Gura	.10
218	Ray Burris	.10
219	Steve Rogers	.10
220	Frank Tanana	.10
221	Ned Yost	.10
222	Bret Saberhagen	.25
223	Mike Davis	.10
224	Bert Blyleven	.15
225	Steve Kemp	.10
226	Jerry Reuss	.10
227	Darrell Evans	.10
228	Wayne Gross	.10
229	Jim Gantner	.10
230	Bob Boone	.10
231	Lonnie Smith	.10
232	Frank DiPino	.10
233	Jerry Koosman	.10
234	Graig Nettles	.15
235	John Tudor	.10
236	John Rabb	.10
237	Rick Manning	.10
238	Mike Fitzgerald	.10
239	Gary Matthews	.10
240	*Jim Presley*	.10
241	Dave Collins	.10
242	Gary Gaetti	.10
243	Dann Bilardello	.10
244	Rudy Law	.10
245	John Lowenstein	.10
246	Tom Tellmann	.10
247	Howard Johnson	.10
248	Ray Fontenot	.10
249	Tony Armas	.10
250	Candy Maldonado	.10
251	*Mike Jeffcoat*	.10
252	Dane Iorg	.10
253	Bruce Bochte	.10
254	Pete Rose	5.00
255	Don Aase	.10
256	George Wright	.10
257	Britt Burns	.10
258	Mike Scott	.10
259	Len Matuszek	.10
260	Dave Rucker	.10
261	Craig Lefferts	.10
262	*Jay Tibbs*	.10
263	Bruce Benedict	.10
264	Don Robinson	.10
265	Gary Lavelle	.10
266	Scott Sanderson	.10
267	Matt Young	.10
268	Ernie Whitt	.10
269	Houston Jimenez	.10
270	*Ken Dixon*	.10
271	Peter Ladd	.10
272	Juan Berenguer	.10
273	Roger Clemens	50.00
274	Rick Cerone	.10
275	Dave Anderson	.10
276	George Vukovich	.10
277	Greg Pryor	.10
278	Mike Warren	.10
279	Bob James	.10
280	Bobby Grich	.10
281	*Mike Mason*	.10
282	Ron Reed	.10
283	Alan Ashby	.10
284	Mark Thurmond	.10
285	Joe Lefebvre	.10
286	Ted Power	.10
287	Chris Chambliss	.10
288	Lee Tunnell	.10
289	Rich Bordi	.10
290	Glenn Brummer	.10
291	Mike Boddicker	.10
292	Rollie Fingers	.50
293	Lou Whitaker	.10
294	Dwight Evans	.10
295	Don Mattingly	5.00
296	Mike Marshall	.10
297	Willie Wilson	.10
298	Mike Heath	.10
299	Tim Raines	.10
300	Larry Parrish	.10
301	Geoff Zahn	.10
302	Rich Dotson	.10
303	David Green	.10
304	Jose Cruz	.10
305	Steve Carlton	2.00
306	Gary Redus	.10
307	Steve Garvey	.40
308	Jose DeLeon	.10
309	Randy Lerch	.10
310	Claudell Washington	.10
311	Lee Smith	.25
312	Darryl Strawberry	.15
313	Jim Beattie	.10
314	John Butcher	.10
315	Damaso Garcia	.10
316	Mike Smithson	.10
317	Luis Leal	.10
318	Ken Phelps	.10
319	Wally Backman	.10
320	Ron Cey	.10
321	Brad Komminsk	.10
322	Jason Thompson	.10
323	*Frank Williams*	.10
324	Tim Lollar	.10
325	*Eric Davis*	1.50
326	Von Hayes	.10
327	Andy Van Slyke	.15
328	Craig Reynolds	.10
329	Dick Schofield	.10
330	Scott Fletcher	.10
331	Jeff Reardon	.10
332	Rick Dempsey	.10
333	Ben Oglivie	.10
334	Dan Petry	.10
335	Jackie Gutierrez	.10
336	Dave Righetti	.10
337	Alejandro Pena	.10
338	Mel Hall	.10
339	Pat Sheridan	.10
340	Keith Atherton	.10
341	David Palmer	.10
342	Gary Ward	.10
343	Dave Stewart	.10
344	*Mark Gubicza*	.50
345	Carney Lansford	.10
346	Jerry Willard	.10
347	Ken Griffey	.10
348	*Franklin Stubbs*	.10
349	Aurelio Lopez	.10
350	Al Bumbry	.10
351	Charlie Moore	.10
352	Luis Sanchez	.10
353	Darrell Porter	.10
354	Bill Dawley	.10
355	Charlie Hudson	.10
356	Garry Templeton	.10
357	Cecilio Guante	.10
358	Jeff Leonard	.10
359	Paul Molitor	2.00
360	Ron Gardenhire	.10
361	Larry Bowa	.10
362	Bob Kearney	.10
363	Garth Iorg	.10
364	Tom Brunansky	.10
365	Brad Gulden	.10
366	Greg Walker	.10
367	Mike Young	.10
368	Rick Waits	.10
369	Doug Bair	.10
370	Bob Shirley	.10
371	Bob Ojeda	.10
372	Bob Welch	.10
373	Neal Heaton	.10
374	Danny Jackson (photo actually Steve Farr)	.15
375	Donnie Hill	.10
376	Mike Stenhouse	.10
377	Bruce Kison	.10
378	Wayne Tolleson	.10
379	Floyd Bannister	.10
380	Vern Ruhle	.10
381	Tim Corcoran	.10
382	Kurt Kepshire	.10
383	Bobby Brown	.10
384	Dave Van Gorder	.10
385	Rick Mahler	.10
386	Lee Mazzilli	.10
387	Bill Laskey	.10
388	Thad Bosley	.10
389	Al Chambers	.10
390	Tony Fernandez	.10
391	Ron Washington	.10
392	Bill Swaggerty	.10
393	Bob L. Gibson	.10
394	Marty Castillo	.10
395	Steve Crawford	.10
396	Clay Christiansen	.10
397	Bob Bailor	.10
398	Mike Hargrove	.10
399	Charlie Leibrandt	.10
400	Tom Burgmeier	.10
401	Razor Shines	.10
402	Rob Wilfong	.10
403	Tom Henke	.10
404	Al Jones	.10
405	Mike LaCoss	.10
406	Luis DeLeon	.10
407	Greg Gross	.10
408	Tom Hume	.10
409	Rick Camp	.10
410	Milt May	.10
411	*Henry Cotto*	.10
412	Dave Von Ohlen	.10
413	Scott McGregor	.10
414	Ted Simmons	.10
415	Jack Morris	.10
416	Bill Buckner	.10
417	Butch Wynegar	.10
418	Steve Sax	.10
419	Steve Balboni	.10
420	Dwayne Murphy	.10
421	Andre Dawson	.40
422	Charlie Hough	.10
423	Tommy John	.15
424a	Tom Seaver (Floyd Bannister photo, left-hander)	2.00
424b	Tom Seaver (correct photo)	7.50
425	Tom Herr	.10
426	Terry Puhl	.10
427	Al Holland	.10
428	Eddie Milner	.10
429	Terry Kennedy	.10
430	John Candelaria	.10
431	Manny Trillo	.10
432	Ken Oberkfell	.10
433	Rick Sutcliffe	.10

434 Ron Darling .10
435 Spike Owen .10
436 Frank Viola .10
437 Lloyd Moseby .10
438 Kirby Puckett 8.00
439 Jim Clancy .10
440 Mike Moore .10
441 Doug Sisk .10
442 Dennis Eckersley 2.00
443 Gerald Perry .10
444 Dale Berra .10
445 Dusty Baker .10
446 Ed Whitson .10
447 Cesar Cedeno .10
448 *Rick Schu* .10
449 Joaquin Andujar .10
450 *Mark Bailey* .10
451 *Ron Romanick* .10
452 Julio Cruz .10
453 Miguel Dilone .10
454 Storm Davis .10
455 Jaime Cocanower .10
456 Barbaro Garbey .10
457 Rich Gedman .10
458 Phil Niekro .50
459 Mike Scioscia .10
460 Pat Tabler .10
461 Darryl Motley .10
462 Chris Codoroli (Codiroli) .10
463 Doug Flynn .10
464 Billy Sample .10
465 Mickey Rivers .10
466 John Wathan .10
467 Bill Krueger .10
468 Andre Thornton .10
469 Rex Hudler .10
470 *Sid Bream* .25
471 Kirk Gibson .10
472 John Shelby .10
473 Moose Haas .10
474 Doug Corbett .10
475 Willie McGee .10
476 Bob Knepper .10
477 Kevin Gross .10
478 Carmelo Martinez .10
479 Kent Tekulve .10
480 Chili Davis .10
481 Bobby Clark .10
482 Mookie Wilson .10
483 Dave Owen .10
484 Ed Nunez .10
485 Rance Mulliniks .10
486 Ken Schrom .10
487 Jeff Russell .10
488 Tom Paciorek .10
489 Dan Ford .10
490 Mike Caldwell .10
491 Scottie Earl .10
492 Jose Rijo .10
493 Bruce Hurst .10
494 Ken Landreaux .10
495 Mike Fischlin .10
496 Don Slaught .10
497 Steve McCatty .10
498 Gary Lucas .10
499 Gary Pettis .10
500 Marvis Foley .10
501 Mike Squires .10
502 *Jim Pankovitz* .10
503 Luis Aguayo .10
504 Ralph Citarella .10
505 Bruce Bochy .10
506 Bob Owchinko .10
507 Pascual Perez .10
508 Lee Lacy .10
509 Atlee Hammaker .10
510 Bob Dernier .10
511 Ed Vande Berg .10
512 Cliff Johnson .10
513 Len Whitehouse .10
514 Dennis Martinez .10
515 Ed Romero .10
516 Rusty Kuntz .10
517 Rick Miller .10
518 Dennis Rasmussen .10
519 Steve Yeager .10
520 Chris Bando .10
521 U.L. Washington .10
522 *Curt Young* .10
523 Angel Salazar .10
524 Curt Kaufman .10
525 Odell Jones .10
526 Juan Agosto .10
527 Denny Walling .10
528 Andy Hawkins .10
529 Sixto Lezcano .10
530 Skeeter Barnes .10
531 Randy S. Johnson .10
532 Jim Morrison .10
533 Warren Brusstar .10
534a *Jeff Pendleton* (error) 1.00
534b *Terry Pendleton* (correct) 4.50
535 Vic Rodriguez .10
536 Bob McClure .10
537 Dave Bergman .10
538 Mark Clear .10
539 *Mike Pagliarulo* .25
540 Terry Whitfield .10
541 Joe Beckwith .10
542 Jeff Burroughs .10
543 Dan Schatzeder .10
544 Donnie Scott .10
545 Jim Slaton .10
546 Greg Luzinski .10
547 *Mark Salas* .10
548 Dave Smith .10
549 John Wockenfuss .10
550 Frank Pastore .10
551 Tim Flannery .10
552 Rick Rhoden .10
553 Mark Davis .10
554 *Jeff Dedmon* .15
555 Gary Woods .10
556 Danny Heep .10
557 Mark Langston .15
558 Darrell Brown .10
559 Jimmy Key .10
560 Rick Lysander .10
561 Doyle Alexander .10
562 Mike Stanton .10
563 Sid Fernandez .10
564 Richie Hebner .10
565 Alex Trevino .10
566 Brian Harper .10
567 *Dan Gladden* .25
568 Luis Salazar .10
569 Tom Foley .10
570 Larry Andersen .10
571 Danny Cox .10
572 Joe Sambito .10
573 Juan Beniquez .10
574 Joel Skinner .10
575 *Randy St. Claire* .10
576 Floyd Rayford .10
577 Roy Howell .10
578 John Grubb .10
579 Ed Jurak .10
580 John Montefusco .10
581 *Orel Hershiser* 3.00
582 *Tom Waddell* .10
583 Mark Huismann .10
584 Joe Morgan 2.00
585 Jim Wohlford .10
586 Dave Schmidt .10
587 *Jeff Kunkel* .10
588 Hal McRae .10
589 Bill Almon .10
590 Carmen Castillo .10
591 Omar Moreno .10
592 *Ken Howell* .10
593 Tom Brookens .10
594 Joe Nolan .10
595 Willie Lozado .10
596 *Tom Nieto* .10
597 Walt Terrell .10
598 Al Oliver .10
599 Shane Rawley .10
600 *Denny Gonzalez* .10
601 *Mark Grant* .10
602 Mike Armstrong .10
603 George Foster .10
604 Davey Lopes .10
605 Salome Barojas .10
606 Roy Lee Jackson .10
607 Pete Filson .10
608 Duane Walker .10
609 Glenn Wilson .10
610 *Rafael Santana* .10
611 Roy Smith .10
612 Ruppert Jones .10
613 Joe Cowley .10
614 *Al Nipper* (photo actually Mike Brown) .15
615 Gene Nelson .10
616 Joe Carter .10
617 Ray Knight .10
618 Chuck Rainey .10
619 Dan Driessen .10
620 Daryl Sconiers .10
621 Bill Stein .10
622 Roy Smalley .10
623 Ed Lynch .10
624 *Jeff Stone* .10
625 Bruce Berenyi .10
626 Kelvin Chapman .10
627 Joe Price .10
628 Steve Bedrosian .10
629 Vic Mata .10
630 Mike Krukow .10
631 *Phil Bradley* .15
632 Jim Gott .10
633 Randy Bush .10
634 *Tom Browning* .25
635 Lou Gehrig Puzzle Card .10
636 Reid Nichols .10
637 *Dan Pasqua* .25
638 German Rivera .10
639 *Don Schulze* .10
640a Mike Jones (last line of highlights begins "Was 11- 7...") .10
640b Mike Jones (last line of highlights begins "Spent some ...") .15
641 Pete Rose 4.00
642 *Wade Rowdon* .10
643 Jerry Narron .10
644 *Darrell Miller* .10
645 *Tim Hulett* .10
646 Andy McGaffigan .10
647 Kurt Bevacqua .10
648 *John Russell* .10
649 *Ron Robinson* .10
650 Donnie Moore .10
651a Don Mattingly, Dave Winfield Two for the Title (yellow letters) 3.00
651b Don Mattingly, Dave Winfield Two for the Title (white letters) 4.50
652 Tim Laudner .10
653 *Steve Farr* .10

1986 DONRUSS

	NM/M
Unopened Factory Set (660):	40.00
Complete Set (660):	35.00
Common Player:	.05
Hank Aaron Puzzle:	2.50
Wax Pack (15):	1.25
Wax Box (36):	37.50
Rack Pack (45):	2.50

1 Kirk Gibson (DK) .15
2 Goose Gossage (DK) .15
3 Willie McGee (DK) .10
4 George Bell (DK) .05
5 Tony Armas (DK) .05
6 Chili Davis (DK) .05
7 Cecil Cooper (DK) .05
8 Mike Boddicker (DK) .05
9 Davey Lopes (DK) .05
10 Bill Doran (DK) .05
11 Bret Saberhagen (DK) .10
12 Brett Butler (DK) .10
13 Harold Baines (DK) .15
14 Mike Davis (DK) .05
15 Tony Perez (DK) 1.00
16 Willie Randolph (DK) .05
17 Bob Boone (DK) .10
18 Orel Hershiser (DK) .10
19 Johnny Ray (DK) .05
20 Gary Ward (DK) .05
21 Rick Mahler (DK) .05
22 Phil Bradley (DK) .05
23 Jerry Koosman (DK) .10
24 Tom Brunansky (DK) .05
25 Andre Dawson (DK) .50
26 Dwight Gooden (DK) .10
27 *Kal Daniels* (RR) .15
28 *Fred McGriff* (RR) 5.00
29 *Cory Snyder* (RR) .10
30 *Jose Guzman* (RR) .05
31 *Ty Gainey* (RR) .05
32 *Johnny Abrego* (RR) .05
33a *Andres Galarraga* (RR) accent mark over e of Andres on back) 2.00
33b *Andres Galarraga* (RR) no accent mark) 2.00
34 *Dave Shipanoff* (RR) .05
35 *Mark McLemore* (RR) .50
36 *Marty Clary* (RR) .05
37 *Paul O'Neill* (RR) 3.00
38 Danny Tartabull (RR) .05
39 *Jose Canseco* (RR) 8.00
40 *Juan Nieves* (RR) .05
41 *Lance McCullers* (RR) .05
42 *Rick Surhoff* (RR) .05
43 *Todd Worrell* (RR) .25
44 Bob Kipper (RR) .05
45 *John Habyan* (RR) .05
46 *Mike Woodard* (RR) .05
47 Mike Boddicker .05
48 Robin Yount 1.50
49 Lou Whitaker .05
50 Dennis Boyd .05
51 Rickey Henderson 1.50
52 Mike Marshall .05
53 George Brett 2.50
54 Dave Kingman .05
55 Hubie Brooks .05
56 *Oddibe McDowell* .15
57 Doug DeCinces .05
58 Britt Burns .05
59 Ozzie Smith 2.00
60 Jose Cruz .05
61 Mike Schmidt 2.50
62 Pete Rose 3.00
63 Steve Garvey .40
64 Tony Pena .05
65 Chili Davis .05
66 Dale Murphy .40
67 Ryne Sandberg 2.00
68 Gary Carter 1.50
69 Alvin Davis .05
70 Kent Hrbek .05
71 George Bell .05
72 Kirby Puckett 2.00
73 Lloyd Moseby .05
74 Bob Kearney .05
75 Dwight Gooden .05
76 Gary Matthews .05
77 Rick Mahler .05
78 Benny Distefano .05
79 Jeff Leonard .05
80 Kevin McReynolds .05
81 Ron Oester .05
82 John Russell .05
83 Tommy Herr .05
84 Jerry Mumphrey .05
85 Ron Romanick .05
86 Daryl Boston .05
87 Andre Dawson .50
88 Eddie Murray 1.50
89 Dion James .05
90 Chet Lemon .05
91 Bob Stanley .05
92 Willie Randolph .05
93 Mike Scioscia .05
94 Tom Waddell .05
95 Danny Jackson .05
96 Mike Davis .05
97 Mike Fitzgerald .05
98 Gary Ward .05
99 Pete O'Brien .05
100 Bret Saberhagen .05
101 Alfredo Griffin .05
102 Brett Butler .05
103 Ron Guidry .15
104 Jerry Reuss .05
105 Jack Morris .05
106 Rick Dempsey .05
107 Ray Burris .05
108 Brian Downing .05
109 Willie McGee .05
110 Bill Doran .05
111 Kent Tekulve .05
112 Tony Gwynn 2.00
113 Marvell Wynne .05
114 David Green .05
115 Jim Gantner .05
116 George Foster .05
117 Steve Trout .05
118 Mark Langston .05
119 Tony Fernandez .05
120 John Butcher .05
121 Ron Robinson .05
122 Dan Spillner .05
123 Mike Young .05
124 Paul Molitor 1.50
125 Kirk Gibson .05
126 Ken Griffey .05
127 Tony Armas .05

No.	Player	Value
128	*Mariano Duncan*	.15
129	Pat Tabler (Mr. Clutch)	.05
130	Frank White	.05
131	Carney Lansford	.05
132	Vance Law	.05
133	Dick Schofield	.05
134	Wayne Tolleson	.05
135	Greg Walker	.05
136	Denny Walling	.05
137	Ozzie Virgil	.05
138	Ricky Horton	.05
139	LaMarr Hoyt	.05
140	Wayne Krenchicki	.05
141	Glenn Hubbard	.05
142	Cecilio Guante	.05
143	Mike Krukow	.05
144	Lee Smith	.15
145	Edwin Nunez	.05
146	Dave Stieb	.05
147	Mike Smithson	.05
148	Ken Dixon	.05
149	Danny Darwin	.05
150	Chris Pittaro	.05
151	Bill Buckner	.05
152	Mike Pagliarulo	.05
153	Bill Russell	.05
154	Brook Jacoby	.05
155	Pat Sheridan	.05
156	*Mike Gallego*	.05
157	Jim Wohlford	.05
158	Gary Pettis	.05
159	Toby Harrah	.05
160	Richard Dotson	.05
161	Bob Knepper	.05
162	Dave Dravecky	.05
163	Greg Gross	.05
164	Eric Davis	.05
165	Gerald Perry	.05
166	Rick Rhoden	.05
167	Keith Moreland	.05
168	Jack Clark	.05
169	Storm Davis	.05
170	Cecil Cooper	.05
171	Alan Trammell	.10
172	Roger Clemens	2.50
173	Don Mattingly	2.50
174	Pedro Guerrero	.05
175	Willie Wilson	.05
176	Dwayne Murphy	.05
177	Tim Raines	.05
178	Larry Parrish	.05
179	Mike Witt	.05
180	Harold Baines	.15
181	*Vince Coleman*	.35
182	*Jeff Heathcock*	.05
183	Steve Carlton	1.50
184	Mario Soto	.05
185	Goose Gossage	.10
186	Johnny Ray	.05
187	Dan Gladden	.05
188	Bob Horner	.05
189	Rick Sutcliffe	.05
190	Keith Hernandez	.05
191	Phil Bradley	.05
192	Tom Brunansky	.05
193	Jesse Barfield	.05
194	Frank Viola	.05
195	Willie Upshaw	.05
196	Jim Beattie	.05
197	Darryl Strawberry	.05
198	Ron Cey	.05
199	Steve Bedrosian	.05
200	Steve Kemp	.05
201	Manny Trillo	.05
202	Garry Templeton	.05
203	Dave Parker	.05
204	John Denny	.05
205	Terry Pendleton	.05
206	Terry Puhl	.05
207	Bobby Grich	.05
208	*Ozzie Guillen*	.75
209	Jeff Reardon	.05
210	Cal Ripken, Jr.	3.00
211	Bill Schroeder	.05
212	Dan Petry	.05
213	Jim Rice	.30
214	Dave Righetti	.05
215	Fernando Valenzuela	.05
216	Julio Franco	.05
217	Darryl Motley	.05
218	Dave Collins	.05
219	Tim Wallach	.05
220	George Wright	.05
221	Tommy Dunbar	.05
222	Steve Balboni	.05
223	Jay Howell	.05
224	Joe Carter	.05
225	Ed Whitson	.05
226	Orel Hershiser	.05
227	Willie Hernandez	.05
228	Lee Lacy	.05
229	Rollie Fingers	.50
230	Bob Boone	.05
231	Joaquin Andujar	.05
232	Craig Reynolds	.05
233	Shane Rawley	.05
234	Eric Show	.05
235	Jose DeLeon	.05
236	*Jose Uribe*	.05
237	Moose Haas	.05
238	Wally Backman	.05
239	Dennis Eckersley	1.50
240	Mike Moore	.05
241	Damaso Garcia	.05
242	Tim Teufel	.05
243	Dave Concepcion	.05
244	Floyd Bannister	.05
245	Fred Lynn	.05
246	Charlie Moore	.05
247	Walt Terrell	.05
248	Dave Winfield	1.50
249	Dwight Evans	.05
250	*Dennis Powell*	.05
251	Andre Thornton	.05
252	Onix Concepcion	.05
253	Mike Heath	.05
254a	David Palmer (2B on front)	.05
254b	David Palmer (P on front)	.15
255	Donnie Moore	.05
256	Curtis Wilkerson	.05
257	Julio Cruz	.05
258	Nolan Ryan	3.00
259	Jeff Stone	.05
260a	John Tudor (1981 Games is .18)	.05
260b	John Tudor (1981 Games is 18)	.15
261	Mark Thurmond	.05
262	Jay Tibbs	.05
263	Rafael Ramirez	.05
264	Larry McWilliams	.05
265	Mark Davis	.05
266	Bob Dernier	.05
267	Matt Young	.05
268	Jim Clancy	.05
269	Mickey Hatcher	.05
270	Sammy Stewart	.05
271	Bob L. Gibson	.05
272	Nelson Simmons	.05
273	Rich Gedman	.05
274	Butch Wynegar	.05
275	Ken Howell	.05
276	Mel Hall	.05
277	Jim Sundberg	.05
278	Chris Codiroli	.05
279	*Herman Winningham*	.05
280	Rod Carew	1.50
281	Don Slaught	.05
282	Scott Fletcher	.05
283	Bill Dawley	.05
284	Andy Hawkins	.05
285	Glenn Wilson	.05
286	Nick Esasky	.05
287	Claudell Washington	.05
288	Lee Mazzilli	.05
289	Jody Davis	.05
290	Darrell Porter	.05
291	Scott McGregor	.05
292	Ted Simmons	.05
293	Aurelio Lopez	.05
294	Marty Barrett	.05
295	Dale Berra	.05
296	Greg Brock	.05
297	Charlie Leibrandt	.05
298	Bill Krueger	.05
299	Bryn Smith	.05
300	Burt Hooton	.05
301	*Stu Cliburn*	.05
302	Luis Salazar	.05
303	Ken Dayley	.05
304	Frank DiPino	.05
305	Von Hayes	.05
306a	Gary Redus (1983 2B is .20)	.05
306b	Gary Redus (1983 2B is 20)	.15
307	Craig Lefferts	.05
308	Sam Khalifa	.05
309	Scott Garrelts	.05
310	Rick Cerone	.05
311	Shawon Dunston	.05
312	Howard Johnson	.05
313	Jim Presley	.05
314	Gary Gaetti	.05
315	Luis Leal	.05
316	Mark Salas	.05
317	Bill Caudill	.05
318	Dave Henderson	.05
319	Rafael Santana	.05
320	Leon Durham	.05
321	Bruce Sutter	1.00
322	Jason Thompson	.05
323	Bob Brenly	.05
324	Carmelo Martinez	.05
325	Eddie Milner	.05
326	Juan Samuel	.05
327	Tom Nieto	.05
328	Dave Smith	.05
329	*Urbano Lugo*	.05
330	Joel Skinner	.05
331	Bill Gullickson	.05
332	Floyd Rayford	.05
333	Ben Oglivie	.05
334	Lance Parrish	.05
335	Jackie Gutierrez	.05
336	Dennis Rasmussen	.05
337	Terry Whitfield	.05
338	Neal Heaton	.05
339	Jorge Orta	.05
340	Donnie Hill	.05
341	Joe Hesketh	.05
342	Charlie Hough	.05
343	Dave Rozema	.05
344	Greg Pryor	.05
345	Mickey Tettleton	.05
346	George Vukovich	.05
347	Don Baylor	.05
348	Carlos Diaz	.05
349	Barbaro Garbey	.05
350	Larry Sheets	.05
351	*Ted Higuera*	.10
352	Juan Beniquez	.05
353	Bob Forsch	.05
354	Mark Bailey	.05
355	Larry Andersen	.05
356	Terry Kennedy	.05
357	Don Robinson	.05
358	Jim Gott	.05
359	*Earnest Riles*	.05
360	*John Christensen*	.05
361	Ray Fontenot	.05
362	Spike Owen	.05
363	Jim Acker	.05
364a	Ron Davis (last line in highlights ends with "...inMay.")	.05
364b	Ron Davis (last line in highlights ends with "...relievers (9).")	.15
365	Tom Hume	.05
366	Carlton Fisk	1.50
367	Nate Snell	.05
368	Rick Manning	.05
369	Darrell Evans	.05
370	Ron Hassey	.05
371	Wade Boggs	2.00
372	Rick Honeycutt	.05
373	Chris Bando	.05
374	Bud Black	.05
375	Steve Henderson	.05
376	Charlie Lea	.05
377	Reggie Jackson	2.50
378	Dave Schmidt	.05
379	Bob James	.05
380	Glenn Davis	.05
381	Tim Corcoran	.05
382	Danny Cox	.05
383	Tim Flannery	.05
384	Tom Browning	.05
385	Rick Camp	.05
386	Jim Morrison	.05
387	Dave LaPoint	.05
388	Davey Lopes	.05
389	Al Cowens	.05
390	Doyle Alexander	.05
391	Tim Laudner	.05
392	Don Aase	.05
393	Jaime Cocanower	.05
394	Randy O'Neal	.05
395	Mike Easler	.05
396	Scott Bradley	.05
397	Tom Niedenfuer	.05
398	Jerry Willard	.05
399	Lonnie Smith	.05
400	Bruce Bochte	.05
401	Terry Francona	.05
402	Jim Slaton	.05
403	Bill Stein	.05
404	Tim Hulett	.05
405	Alan Ashby	.05
406	Tim Stoddard	.05
407	Garry Maddox	.05
408	Ted Power	.05
409	Len Barker	.05
410	Denny Gonzalez	.05
411	George Frazier	.05
412	Andy Van Slyke	.05
413	Jim Dwyer	.05
414	Paul Householder	.05
415	Alejandro Sanchez	.05
416	Steve Crawford	.05
417	Dan Pasqua	.05
418	Enos Cabell	.05
419	Mike Jones	.05
420	Steve Kiefer	.05
421	*Tim Burke*	.05
422	Mike Mason	.05
423	Ruppert Jones	.05
424	Jerry Hairston Sr.	.05
425	Tito Landrum	.05
426	Jeff Calhoun	.05
427	*Don Carman*	.05
428	Tony Perez	1.00
429	Jerry Davis	.05
430	Bob Walk	.05
431	Brad Wellman	.05
432	Terry Forster	.05
433	Billy Hatcher	.05
434	Clint Hurdle	.05
435	*Ivan Calderon*	.05
436	Pete Filson	.05
437	Tom Henke	.05
438	Dave Engle	.05
439	Tom Filer	.05
440	Gorman Thomas	.05
441	*Rick Aguilera*	.25
442	Scott Sanderson	.05
443	Jeff Dedmon	.05
444	*Joe Orsulak*	.10
445	Atlee Hammaker	.05
446	Jerry Royster	.05
447	Buddy Bell	.05
448	Dave Rucker	.05
449	Ivan DeJesus	.05
450	Jim Pankovits	.05
451	Jerry Narron	.05
452	Bryan Little	.05
453	Gary Lucas	.05
454	Dennis Martinez	.05
455	Ed Romero	.05
456	*Bob Melvin*	.05
457	Glenn Hoffman	.05
458	Bob Shirley	.05
459	Bob Welch	.05
460	Carmen Castillo	.05
461	Dave Leeper	.05
462	*Tim Birtsas*	.05
463	Randy St. Claire	.05
464	Chris Welsh	.05
465	Greg Harris	.05
466	Lynn Jones	.05
467	Dusty Baker	.05
468	Roy Smith	.05
469	Andre Robertson	.05
470	Ken Landreaux	.05
471	Dave Bergman	.05
472	Gary Roenicke	.05
473	Pete Vuckovich	.05
474	*Kirk McCaskill*	.10
475	Jeff Lahti	.05
476	Mike Scott	.05
477	*Darren Daulton*	1.50
478	Graig Nettles	.15
479	Bill Almon	.05
480	Greg Minton	.05
481	Randy Ready	.05
482	*Len Dykstra*	1.50
483	Thad Bosley	.05
484	*Harold Reynolds*	.50
485	Al Oliver	.05
486	Roy Smalley	.05
487	John Franco	.05
488	Juan Agosto	.05
489	Al Pardo	.05
490	*Bill Wegman*	.05
491	Frank Tanana	.05
492	*Brian Fisher*	.05
493	Mark Clear	.05
494	Len Matuszek	.05
495	Ramon Romero	.05
496	John Wathan	.05
497	Rob Picciolo	.05
498	U.L. Washington	.05
499	John Candelaria	.05
500	Duane Walker	.05
501	Gene Nelson	.05
502	John Mizerock	.05
503	Luis Aguayo	.05
504	Kurt Kepshire	.05
505	Ed Wojna	.05
506	Joe Price	.05
507	*Milt Thompson*	.05
508	Junior Ortiz	.05

509 Vida Blue .05
510 Steve Engel .05
511 Karl Best .05
512 *Cecil Fielder* 2.00
513 Frank Eufemia .05
514 Tippy Martinez .05
515 *Billy Robidoux* .05
516 Bill Scherrer .05
517 Bruce Hurst .05
518 Rich Bordi .05
519 Steve Yeager .05
520 Tony Bernazard .05
521 Hal McRae .05
522 Jose Rijo .05
523 *Mitch Webster* .05
524 *Jack Howell* .05
525 Alan Bannister .05
526 Ron Kittle .05
527 Phil Garner .05
528 Kurt Bevacqua .05
529 Kevin Gross .05
530 Bo Diaz .05
531 Ken Oberkfell .05
532 Rick Reuschel .05
533 Ron Meridith .05
534 Steve Braun .05
535 Wayne Gross .05
536 Ray Searage .05
537 Tom Brookens .05
538 Al Nipper .05
539 Billy Sample .05
540 Steve Sax .05
541 Dan Quisenberry .05
542 Tony Phillips .05
543 *Floyd Youmans* .05
544 *Steve Buechele* .05
545 Craig Gerber .05
546 Joe DeSa .05
547 Brian Harper .05
548 Kevin Bass .05
549 Tom Foley .05
550 Dave Van Gorder .05
551 Bruce Bochy .05
552 R.J. Reynolds .05
553 *Chris Brown* .05
554 Bruce Benedict .05
555 Warren Brusstar .05
556 Danny Heep .05
557 Darnell Coles .05
558 Greg Gagne .05
559 Ernie Whitt .05
560 Ron Washington .05
561 Jimmy Key .05
562 Billy Swift .05
563 Ron Darling .05
564 Dick Ruthven .05
565 Zane Smith .05
566 Sid Bream .05
567a Joel Youngblood (P on front) .05
567b Joel Youngblood (IF on front) .15
568 Mario Ramirez .05
569 Tom Runnells .05
570 Rick Schu .05
571 Bill Campbell .05
572 Dickie Thon .05
573 Al Holland .05
574 Reid Nichols .05
575 Bert Roberge .05
576 Mike Flanagan .05
577 Tim Leary .05
578 Mike Laga .05
579 Steve Lyons .05
580 Phil Niekro .50
581 Gilberto Reyes .05
582 Jamie Easterly .05
583 Mark Gubicza .05
584 *Stan Javier* .15
585 Bill Laskey .05
586 Jeff Russell .05
587 Dickie Noles .05
588 Steve Farr .05
589 *Steve Ontiveros* .05
590 Mike Hargrove .05
591 Marty Bystrom .05
592 Franklin Stubbs .05
593 Larry Herndon .05
594 Bill Swaggerty .05
595 Carlos Ponce .05
596 *Pat Perry* .05
597 Ray Knight .05
598 *Steve Lombardozzi* .05
599 Brad Havens .05
600 *Pat Clements* .05
601 Joe Niekro .05
602 Hank Aaron Puzzle Card .05
603 *Dwayne Henry* .05
604 Mookie Wilson .05
605 Buddy Biancalana .05
606 Rance Mulliniks .05
607 Alan Wiggins .05
608 Joe Cowley .05
609a Tom Seaver (green stripes around name) 1.50
609b Tom Seaver (yellow stripes around name) 2.00
610 Neil Allen .05
611 Don Sutton .50
612 *Fred Toliver* .05
613 Jay Baller .05
614 Marc Sullivan .05
615 John Grubb .05
616 Bruce Kison .05
617 Bill Madlock .05
618 Chris Chambliss .05
619 Dave Stewart .05
620 Tim Lollar .05
621 Gary Lavelle .05
622 Charles Hudson .05
623 *Joel Davis* .05
624 *Joe Johnson* .05
625 Sid Fernandez .05
626 Dennis Lamp .05
627 Terry Harper .05
628 Jack Lazorko .05
629 *Roger McDowell* .25
630 Mark Funderburk .05
631 Ed Lynch .05
632 Rudy Law .05
633 *Roger Mason* .05
634 *Mike Felder* .05
635 Ken Schrom .05
636 Bob Ojeda .05
637 Ed Vande Berg .05
638 Bobby Meacham .05
639 Cliff Johnson .05
640 Garth Iorg .05
641 Dan Driessen .05
642 Mike Brown .05
643 John Shelby .05
644 Pete Rose (RB) .50
645 Joe Niekro, Phil Niekro Knuckle Brothers .25
646 Jesse Orosco .05
647 *Billy Beane* .05
648 Cesar Cedeno .05
649 Bert Blyleven .15
650 Max Venable .05
651 Vince Coleman, Willie McGee Fleet Feet .25
652 Calvin Schiraldi .05
653 Pete Rose King of Kings 3.00

Rookies

NM/M
Unopened Set (56): 40.00
Opened Set (56): 35.00
Common Player: .05
1 *Wally Joyner* .50
2 Tracy Jones .05
3 Allan Anderson .05
4 Ed Correa .05
5 Reggie Williams .05
6 Charlie Kerfeld .05
7 Andres Galarraga .25
8 Bob Tewksbury .05
9 Al Newman .05
10 Andres Thomas .05
11 *Barry Bonds* 35.00
12 Juan Nieves .05
13 Mark Eichhorn .05
14 Dan Plesac .05
15 Cory Snyder .05
16 Kelly Gruber .05
17 *Kevin Mitchell* .25
18 Steve Lombardozzi .05
19 Mitch Williams .05
20 John Cerutti .05
21 Todd Worrell .05
22 Jose Canseco 2.00
23 *Pete Incaviglia* .15
24 Jose Guzman .05
25 Scott Bailes .05
26 Greg Mathews .05
27 Eric King .05
28 Paul Assenmacher .05
29 Jeff Sellers .05
30 *Bobby Bonilla* .25
31 *Doug Drabek* .25
32 *Will Clark* 2.00
33 Bip Roberts .05
34 Jim Deshaies .05
35 Mike LaValliere .05
36 Scott Bankhead .05
37 Dale Sveum .05
38 *Bo Jackson* 2.00
39 Rob Thompson .05
40 Eric Plunk .05
41 Bill Bathe .05
42 *John Kruk* .25
43 Andy Allanson .05
44 Mark Portugal .05
45 Danny Tartabull .05
46 Bob Kipper .05
47 Gene Walter .05
48 Rey Quinonez .05
49 Bobby Witt .05
50 Bill Mooneyham .05
51 John Cangelosi .05
52 *Ruben Sierra* .25
53 Rob Woodward .05
54 Ed Hearn .05
55 Joel McKeon .05
56 Checklist 1-56 .05

1987 DONRUSS

NM/M
Unopened Fact. Set (660): 40.00
Complete Set (660): 30.00
Common Player: .05
Roberto Clemente Puzzle: 2.00
Wax Pack (15): 1.25
Wax Box (36): 35.00
Rack Pack (45): 2.00
Jumbo Rack (75): 3.00
1 Wally Joyner (DK) .25
2 Roger Clemens (DK) 1.00
3 Dale Murphy (DK) .25
4 Darryl Strawberry (DK) .10
5 Ozzie Smith (DK) .75
6 Jose Canseco (DK) .40
7 Charlie Hough (DK) .05
8 Brook Jacoby (DK) .05
9 Fred Lynn (DK) .10
10 Rick Rhoden (DK) .05
11 Chris Brown (DK) .05
12 Von Hayes (DK) .05
13 Jack Morris (DK) .10
14a Kevin McReynolds (DK) (no yellow stripe on back) .25
14b Kevin McReynolds (DK) (yellow stripe on back) .25
15 George Brett (DK) 1.00
16 Ted Higuera (DK) .05
17 Hubie Brooks (DK) .05
18 Mike Scott (DK) .05
19 Kirby Puckett (DK) .75
20 Dave Winfield (DK) .60
21 Lloyd Moseby (DK) .05
22a Eric Davis (DK) (no yellow stripe on back) .25
22b Eric Davis (DK) (yellow stripe on back) .15
23 Jim Presley (DK) .05
24 Keith Moreland (DK) .05
25a Greg Walker (DK) (no yellow stripe on back) .25
25b Greg Walker (DK) (yellow stripe on back) .10
26 Steve Sax (DK) .10
27 Checklist 1-27 .05
28 *B.J. Surhoff* (RR) .30
29 *Randy Myers* (RR) .50
30 *Ken Gerhart* (RR) .05
31 Benito Santiago (RR) .15
32 *Greg Swindell* (RR) .15
33 *Mike Birkbeck* (RR) .05
34 *Terry Steinbach* (RR) .25
35 Bo Jackson (RR) 1.50
36 *Greg Maddux* (RR) 8.00
37 *Jim Lindeman* (RR) .05
38 *Devon White* (RR) .75
39 *Eric Bell* (RR) .05
40 *Will Fraser* (RR) .05
41 *Jerry Browne* (RR) .05
42 *Chris James* (RR) .05
43 *Rafael Palmeiro* (RR) 6.00
44 *Pat Dodson* (RR) .05
45 *Duane Ward* (RR) .10
46 Mark McGwire (RR) 6.00
47 *Bruce Fields* (RR) (Photo actually Darnell Coles) .10
48 Eddie Murray .60
49 Ted Higuera .05
50 Kirk Gibson .05
51 Oil Can Boyd .05
52 Don Mattingly .75
53 Pedro Guerrero .05
54 George Brett 1.00
55 Jose Rijo .05
56 Tim Raines .05
57 *Ed Correa* .05
58 Mike Witt .05
59 Greg Walker .05
60 Ozzie Smith .75
61 Glenn Davis .05
62 Glenn Wilson .05
63 Tom Browning .05
64 Tony Gwynn .75
65 R.J. Reynolds .05
66 Will Clark .25
67 Ozzie Virgil .05
68 Rick Sutcliffe .05
69 Gary Carter .60
70 Mike Moore .05
71 Bert Blyleven .10
72 Tony Fernandez .05
73 Kent Hrbek .05
74 Lloyd Moseby .05
75 Alvin Davis .05
76 Keith Hernandez .05
77 Ryne Sandberg .75
78 Dale Murphy .40
79 Sid Bream .05
80 Chris Brown .05
81 Steve Garvey .35
82 Mario Soto .05
83 Shane Rawley .05
84 Willie McGee .05
85 Jose Cruz .05
86 Brian Downing .05
87 Ozzie Guillen .05
88 Hubie Brooks .05
89 Cal Ripken, Jr. 2.50
90 Juan Nieves .05
91 Lance Parrish .05
92 Jim Rice .20
93 Ron Guidry .10
94 Fernando Valenzuela .05
95 *Andy Allanson* .05
96 Willie Wilson .05
97 Jose Canseco .40
98 Jeff Reardon .05
99 *Bobby Witt* .20
100 Checklist 28-133 .05
101 Jose Guzman .05
102 Steve Balboni .05
103 Tony Phillips .05
104 Brook Jacoby .05
105 Dave Winfield .60
106 Orel Hershiser .05
107 Lou Whitaker .05
108 Fred Lynn .05
109 Bill Wegman .05
110 Donnie Moore .05
111 Jack Clark .05
112 Bob Knepper .05
113 Von Hayes .05
114 *Bip Roberts* .25
115 Tony Pena .05
116 Scott Garrelts .05
117 Paul Molitor .60

No.	Player	Price
118	Darryl Strawberry	.05
119	Shawon Dunston	.05
120	Jim Presley	.05
121	Jesse Barfield	.05
122	Gary Gaetti	.05
123	*Kurt Stillwell*	.10
124	Joel Davis	.05
125	Mike Boddicker	.05
126	Robin Yount	.60
127	Alan Trammell	.10
128	Dave Righetti	.05
129	Dwight Evans	.05
130	Mike Scioscia	.05
131	Julio Franco	.05
132	Bret Saberhagen	.05
133	Mike Davis	.05
134	Joe Hesketh	.05
135	Wally Joyner	.05
136	Don Slaught	.05
137	Daryl Boston	.05
138	Nolan Ryan	2.50
139	Mike Schmidt	1.00
140	Tommy Herr	.05
141	Garry Templeton	.05
142	Kal Daniels	.05
143	Billy Sample	.05
144	Johnny Ray	.05
145	*Rob Thompson*	.10
146	Bob Dernier	.05
147	Danny Tartabull	.05
148	Ernie Whitt	.05
149	Kirby Puckett	.75
150	Mike Young	.05
151	Ernest Riles	.05
152	Frank Tanana	.05
153	Rich Gedman	.05
154	Willie Randolph	.05
155a	Bill Madlock (namein brown band)	.10
155b	Bill Madlock (name in red band)	.25
156a	Joe Carter (name in brown band)	.10
156b	Joe Carter (name in red band)	.25
157	Danny Jackson	.05
158	Carney Lansford	.05
159	Bryn Smith	.05
160	Gary Pettis	.05
161	Oddibe McDowell	.05
162	*John Cangelosi*	.10
163	Mike Scott	.05
164	Eric Show	.05
165	Juan Samuel	.05
166	Nick Esasky	.05
167	Zane Smith	.05
168	Mike Brown	.05
169	Keith Moreland	.05
170	John Tudor	.05
171	Ken Dixon	.05
172	Jim Gantner	.05
173	Jack Morris	.05
174	Bruce Hurst	.05
175	Dennis Rasmussen	.05
176	Mike Marshall	.05
177	Dan Quisenberry	.05
178	Eric Plunk	.05
179	Tim Wallach	.05
180	Steve Buechele	.05
181	Don Sutton	.50
182	Dave Schmidt	.05
183	Terry Pendleton	.05
184	*Jim Deshaies*	.05
185	Steve Bedrosian	.05
186	Pete Rose	2.00
187	Dave Dravecky	.05
188	Rick Reuschel	.05
189	Dan Gladden	.05
190	Rick Mahler	.05
191	Thad Bosley	.05
192	Ron Darling	.05
193	Matt Young	.05
194	Tom Brunansky	.05
195	Dave Stieb	.05
196	Frank Viola	.05
197	Tom Henke	.05
198	Karl Best	.05
199	Dwight Gooden	.05
200	Checklist 134-239	.05
201	Steve Trout	.05
202	Rafael Ramirez	.05
203	Bob Walk	.05
204	Roger Mason	.05
205	Terry Kennedy	.05
206	Ron Oester	.05
207	John Russell	.05
208	*Greg Mathews*	.05
209	Charlie Kerfeld	.05
210	Reggie Jackson	1.00
211	Floyd Bannister	.05
212	Vance Law	.05
213	Rich Bordi	.05
214	*Dan Plesac*	.10
215	Dave Collins	.05
216	Bob Stanley	.05
217	Joe Niekro	.05
218	Tom Niedenfuer	.05
219	Brett Butler	.05
220	Charlie Leibrandt	.05
221	Steve Ontiveros	.05
222	Tim Burke	.05
223	Curtis Wilkerson	.05
224	*Pete Incaviglia*	.10
225	Lonnie Smith	.05
226	Chris Codiroli	.05
227	*Scott Bailes*	.05
228	Rickey Henderson	.60
229	Ken Howell	.05
230	Darnell Coles	.05
231	Don Aase	.05
232	Tim Leary	.05
233	Bob Boone	.05
234	Ricky Horton	.05
235	Mark Bailey	.05
236	Kevin Gross	.05
237	Lance McCullers	.05
238	Cecilio Guante	.05
239	Bob Melvin	.05
240	Billy Jo Robidoux	.05
241	Roger McDowell	.05
242	Leon Durham	.05
243	Ed Nunez	.05
244	Jimmy Key	.05
245	Mike Smithson	.05
246	Bo Diaz	.05
247	Carlton Fisk	.60
248	Larry Sheets	.05
249	*Juan Castillo*	.05
250	*Eric King*	.05
251	Doug Drabek	.05
252	Wade Boggs	.75
253	Mariano Duncan	.05
254	Pat Tabler	.05
255	Frank White	.05
256	Alfredo Griffin	.05
257	Floyd Youmans	.05
258	Rob Wilfong	.05
259	Pete O'Brien	.05
260	Tim Hulett	.05
261	Dickie Thon	.05
262	Darren Daulton	.05
263	Vince Coleman	.05
264	Andy Hawkins	.05
265	Eric Davis	.05
266	*Andres Thomas*	.05
267	*Mike Diaz*	.05
268	Chili Davis	.05
269	Jody Davis	.05
270	Phil Bradley	.05
271	George Bell	.05
272	Keith Atherton	.05
273	Storm Davis	.05
274	Rob Deer	.05
275	Walt Terrell	.05
276	Roger Clemens	1.00
277	Mike Easler	.05
278	Steve Sax	.05
279	Andre Thornton	.05
280	Jim Sundberg	.05
281	Bill Bathe	.05
282	Jay Tibbs	.05
283	Dick Schofield	.05
284	Mike Mason	.05
285	Jerry Hairston Sr.	.05
286	Bill Doran	.05
287	Tim Flannery	.05
288	Gary Redus	.05
289	John Franco	.05
290	*Paul Assenmacher*	.10
291	Joe Orsulak	.05
292	Lee Smith	.10
293	Mike Laga	.05
294	Rick Dempsey	.05
295	Mike Felder	.05
296	Tom Brookens	.05
297	Al Nipper	.05
298	Mike Pagliarulo	.05
299	Franklin Stubbs	.05
300	Checklist 240-345	.05
301	Steve Farr	.05
302	*Bill Mooneyham*	.05
303	Andres Galarraga	.10
304	Scott Fletcher	.05
305	Jack Howell	.05
306	*Russ Morman*	.05
307	Todd Worrell	.05
308	Dave Smith	.05
309	Jeff Stone	.05
310	Ron Robinson	.05
311	Bruce Bochy	.05
312	Jim Winn	.05
313	Mark Davis	.05
314	Jeff Dedmon	.05
315	*Jamie Moyer*	.10
316	Wally Backman	.05
317	Ken Phelps	.05
318	Steve Lombardozzi	.05
319	Rance Mulliniks	.05
320	Tim Laudner	.05
321	*Mark Eichhorn*	.10
322	*Lee Guetterman*	.05
323	Sid Fernandez	.05
324	Jerry Mumphrey	.05
325	David Palmer	.05
326	Bill Almon	.05
327	Candy Maldonado	.05
328	John Kruk	.05
329	John Denny	.05
330	Milt Thompson	.05
331	*Mike LaValliere*	.10
332	Alan Ashby	.05
333	Doug Corbett	.05
334	*Ron Karkovice*	.05
335	Mitch Webster	.05
336	Lee Lacy	.05
337	*Glenn Braggs*	.05
338	Dwight Lowry	.05
339	Don Baylor	.05
340	Brian Fisher	.05
341	*Reggie Williams*	.05
342	Tom Candiotti	.05
343	Rudy Law	.05
344	Curt Young	.05
345	Mike Fitzgerald	.05
346	Ruben Sierra	.05
347	*Mitch Williams*	.25
348	Jorge Orta	.05
349	Mickey Tettleton	.05
350	Ernie Camacho	.05
351	Ron Kittle	.05
352	Ken Landreaux	.05
353	Chet Lemon	.05
354	John Shelby	.05
355	Mark Clear	.05
356	Doug DeCinces	.05
357	Ken Dayley	.05
358	Phil Garner	.05
359	Steve Jeltz	.05
360	Ed Whitson	.05
361	Barry Bonds	12.00
362	Vida Blue	.05
363	Cecil Cooper	.05
364	Bob Ojeda	.05
365	Dennis Eckersley	.60
366	Mike Morgan	.05
367	Willie Upshaw	.05
368	*Allan Anderson*	.05
369	Bill Gullickson	.05
370	*Bobby Thigpen*	.10
371	Juan Beniquez	.05
372	Charlie Moore	.05
373	Dan Petry	.05
374	Rod Scurry	.05
375	Tom Seaver	.75
376	Ed Vande Berg	.05
377	Tony Bernazard	.05
378	Greg Pryor	.05
379	Dwayne Murphy	.05
380	Andy McGaffigan	.05
381	Kirk McCaskill	.05
382	Greg Harris	.05
383	Rich Dotson	.05
384	Craig Reynolds	.05
385	Greg Gross	.05
386	Tito Landrum	.05
387	Craig Lefferts	.05
388	Dave Parker	.05
389	Bob Horner	.05
390	Pat Clements	.05
391	Jeff Leonard	.05
392	Chris Speier	.05
393	John Moses	.05
394	Garth Iorg	.05
395	Greg Gagne	.05
396	Nate Snell	.05
397	*Bryan Clutterbuck*	.05
398	Darrell Evans	.05
399	Steve Crawford	.05
400	Checklist 346-451	.05
401	*Phil Lombardi*	.05
402	Rick Honeycutt	.05
403	Ken Schrom	.05
404	Bud Black	.05
405	Donnie Hill	.05
406	Wayne Krenchicki	.05
407	*Chuck Finley*	.35
408	Toby Harrah	.05
409	Steve Lyons	.05
410	Kevin Bass	.05
411	Marvell Wynne	.05
412	Ron Roenicke	.05
413	*Tracy Jones*	.05
414	Gene Garber	.05
415	Mike Bielecki	.05
416	Frank DiPino	.05
417	Andy Van Slyke	.05
418	Jim Dwyer	.05
419	Ben Oglivie	.05
420	Dave Bergman	.05
421	Joe Sambito	.05
422	*Bob Tewksbury*	.30
423	Len Matuszek	.05
424	*Mike Kingery*	.05
425	Dave Kingman	.05
426	*Al Newman*	.05
427	Gary Ward	.05
428	Ruppert Jones	.05
429	Harold Baines	.10
430	Pat Perry	.05
431	Terry Puhl	.05
432	Don Carman	.05
433	Eddie Milner	.05
434	LaMarr Hoyt	.05
435	Rick Rhoden	.05
436	Jose Uribe	.05
437	Ken Oberkfell	.05
438	Ron Davis	.05
439	Jesse Orosco	.05
440	Scott Bradley	.05
441	Randy Bush	.05
442	*John Cerutti*	.05
443	Roy Smalley	.05
444	Kelly Gruber	.05
445	Bob Kearney	.05
446	*Ed Hearn*	.05
447	Scott Sanderson	.05
448	Bruce Benedict	.05
449	Junior Ortiz	.05
450	*Mike Aldrete*	.05
451	Kevin McReynolds	.05
452	*Rob Murphy*	.05
453	Kent Tekulve	.05
454	Curt Ford	.05
455	Davey Lopes	.05
456	Bobby Grich	.05
457	Jose DeLeon	.05
458	Andre Dawson	.35
459	Mike Flanagan	.05
460	*Joey Meyer*	.05
461	*Chuck Cary*	.05
462	Bill Buckner	.05
463	Bob Shirley	.05
464	*Jeff Hamilton*	.05
465	Phil Niekro	.50
466	Mark Gubicza	.05
467	Jerry Willard	.05
468	*Bob Sebra*	.05
469	Larry Parrish	.05
470	Charlie Hough	.05
471	Hal McRae	.05
472	*Dave Leiper*	.05
473	Mel Hall	.05
474	Dan Pasqua	.05
475	Bob Welch	.05
476	Johnny Grubb	.05
477	Jim Traber	.05
478	*Chris Bosio*	.05
479	Mark McLemore	.05
480	John Morris	.05
481	Billy Hatcher	.05
482	Dan Schatzeder	.05
483	Rich Gossage	.10
484	Jim Morrison	.05
485	Bob Brenly	.05
486	Bill Schroeder	.05
487	Mookie Wilson	.05
488	*Dave Martinez*	.10
489	Harold Reynolds	.10
490	Jeff Hearron	.05
491	Mickey Hatcher	.05
492	*Barry Larkin*	2.00
493	Bob James	.05
494	John Habyan	.05
495	*Jim Adduci*	.05
496	Mike Heath	.05
497	Tim Stoddard	.05
498	Tony Armas	.05
499	Dennis Powell	.05
500	Checklist 452-557	.05
501	Chris Bando	.05
502	*David Cone*	2.00
503	Jay Howell	.05
504	Tom Foley	.05
505	*Ray Chadwick*	.05
506	*Mike Loynd*	.05
507	Neil Allen	.05

508 Danny Darwin .05
509 Rick Schu .05
510 Jose Oquendo .05
511 Gene Walter .05
512 *Terry McGriff* .05
513 Ken Griffey .05
514 Benny Distefano .05
515 *Terry Mulholland* .40
516 Ed Lynch .05
517 Bill Swift .05
518 Manny Lee .05
519 Andre David .05
520 Scott McGregor .05
521 Rick Manning .05
522 Willie Hernandez .05
523 Marty Barrett .05
524 Wayne Tolleson .05
525 *Jose Gonzalez* .05
526 Cory Snyder .05
527 Buddy Biancalana .05
528 Moose Haas .05
529 *Wilfredo Tejada* .05
530 Stu Cliburn .05
531 *Dale Mohorcic* .05
532 Ron Hassey .05
533 Ty Gainey .05
534 Jerry Royster .05
535 *Mike Maddux* .05
536 Ted Power .05
537 Ted Simmons .05
538 *Rafael Belliard* .05
539 Chico Walker .05
540 Bob Forsch .05
541 John Stefero .05
542 *Dale Sveum* .05
543 Mark Thurmond .05
544 *Jeff Sellers* .05
545 Joel Skinner .05
546 Alex Trevino .05
547 *Randy Kutcher* .05
548 Joaquin Andujar .05
549 *Casey Candaele* .10
550 Jeff Russell .05
551 John Candelaria .05
552 Joe Cowley .05
553 Danny Cox .05
554 Denny Walling .05
555 *Bruce Ruffin* .10
556 Buddy Bell .05
557 *Jimmy Jones* .05
558 Bobby Bonilla .05
559 Jeff Robinson .05
560 Ed Olwine .05
561 *Glenallen Hill* .50
562 Lee Mazzilli .05
563 Mike Brown .05
564 George Frazier .05
565 *Mike Sharperson* .10
566 *Mark Portugal* .05
567 Rick Leach .05
568 Mark Langston .05
569 Rafael Santana .05
570 Manny Trillo .05
571 Cliff Speck .05
572 Bob Kipper .05
573 *Kelly Downs* .05
574 *Randy Asadoor* .05
575 *Dave Magadan* .25
576 *Marvin Freeman* .05
577 Jeff Lahti .05
578 Jeff Calhoun .05
579 Gus Polidor .05
580 Gene Nelson .05
581 Tim Teufel .05
582 Odell Jones .05
583 Mark Ryal .05
584 Randy O'Neal .05
585 *Mike Greenwell* .50
586 Ray Knight .05
587 *Ralph Bryant* .05
588 Carmen Castillo .05
589 Ed Wojna .05
590 Stan Javier .05
591 *Jeff Musselman* .05
592 *Mike Stanley* .05
593 Darrell Porter .05
594 *Drew Hall* .05
595 *Rob Nelson* .05
596 Bryan Oelkers .05
597 *Scott Nielsen* .05
598 *Brian Holton* .05
599 Kevin Mitchell .05
600 Checklist 558-660 .05
601 Jackie Gutierrez .05
602 *Barry Jones* .05
603 Jerry Narron .05
604 Steve Lake .05
605 Jim Pankovits .05
606 Ed Romero .05
607 Dave LaPoint .05
608 Don Robinson .05
609 Mike Krukow .05
610 *Dave Valle* .05
611 Len Dykstra .05
612 Roberto Clemente Puzzle Card .25
613 Mike Trujillo .05
614 Damaso Garcia .05
615 Neal Heaton .05
616 Juan Berenguer .05
617 Steve Carlton .75
618 Gary Lucas .05
619 Geno Petralli .05
620 Rick Aguilera .05
621 Fred McGriff .20
622 Dave Henderson .05
623 *Dave Clark* .05
624 Angel Salazar .05
625 Randy Hunt .05
626 John Gibbons .05
627 *Kevin Brown* 2.50
628 Bill Dawley .05
629 Aurelio Lopez .05
630 Charlie Hudson .05
631 Ray Soff .05
632 *Ray Hayward* .05
633 Spike Owen .05
634 Glenn Hubbard .05
635 *Kevin Elster* .10
636 Mike LaCoss .05
637 Dwayne Henry .05
638 *Rey Quinones* .05
639 Jim Clancy .05
640 Larry Andersen .05
641 Calvin Schiraldi .05
642 *Stan Jefferson* .05
643 Marc Sullivan .05
644 Mark Grant .05
645 Cliff Johnson .05
646 Howard Johnson .05
647 Dave Sax .05
648 Dave Stewart .05
649 Danny Heep .05
650 Joe Johnson .05
651 *Bob Brower* .05
652 Rob Woodward .05
653 John Mizerock .05
654 *Tim Pyznarski* .05
655 *Luis Aquino* .05
656 Mickey Brantley .05
657 Doyle Alexander .05
658 Sammy Stewart .05
659 Jim Acker .05
660 Pete Ladd .05

Rookies

	NM/M
Unopened Fact. Set (56):	20.00
Complete Set (56):	15.00
Common Player:	.05

1 Mark McGwire 6.00
2 Eric Bell .05
3 Mark Williamson .05
4 Mike Greenwell .05
5 Ellis Burks .05
6 DeWayne Buice .05
7 Mark Mclemore (McLemore) .05
8 Devon White .05
9 Willie Fraser .05
10 Lester Lancaster .05
11 Ken Williams .05
12 Matt Nokes .05
13 Jeff Robinson .05
14 Bo Jackson .25
15 Kevin Seitzer .05
16 Billy Ripken .05
17 B.J. Surhoff .05
18 Chuck Crim .05
19 Mike Birbeck .05
20 Chris Bosio .05
21 Les Straker .05
22 Mark Davidson .05
23 Gene Larkin .05
24 Ken Gerhart .05
25 Luis Polonia .05
26 Terry Steinbach .05
27 Mickey Brantley .05
28 Mike Stanley .05
29 Jerry Browne .05
30 Todd Benzinger .05
31 Fred McGriff .25
32 Mike Henneman .05
33 Casey Candaele .05
34 Dave Magadan .05
35 David Cone .10
36 Mike Jackson .05
37 John Mitchell .05
38 Mike Dunne .05
39 John Smiley .05
40 Joe Magrane .05
41 Jim Lindeman .05
42 Shane Mack .05
43 Stan Jefferson .05
44 Benito Santiago .05
45 *Matt Williams* 1.50
46 Dave Meads .05
47 Rafael Palmeiro 4.00
48 Bill Long .05
49 Bob Brower .05
50 James Steels .05
51 Paul Noce .05
52 Greg Maddux 6.00
53 Jeff Musselman .05
54 Brian Holton .05
55 Chuck Jackson .05
56 Checklist 1-56 .03

1988 DONRUSS

	NM/M
Unopened Fact. Set (660):	6.00
Complete Set (660):	5.00
Common Player:	.05
Stan Musial Puzzle:	1.00
Wax Pack (15):	.25
Wax Box (36):	6.00
Cello Pack (36):	.50
Cello Box (24):	8.00
Rack Pack (45):	.75

1 Mark McGwire (DK) .50
2 Tim Raines (DK) .05
3 Benito Santiago (DK) .05
4 Alan Trammell (DK) .05
5 Danny Tartabull (DK) .05
6 Ron Darling (DK) .05
7 Paul Molitor (DK) .30
8 Devon White (DK) .05
9 Andre Dawson (DK) .15
10 Julio Franco (DK) .05
11 Scott Fletcher (DK) .05
12 Tony Fernandez (DK) .05
13 Shane Rawley (DK) .05
14 Kal Daniels (DK) .05
15 Jack Clark (DK) .05
16 Dwight Evans (DK) .05
17 Tommy John (DK) .05
18 Andy Van Slyke (DK) .05
19 Gary Gaetti (DK) .05
20 Mark Langston (DK) .05
21 Will Clark (DK) .10
22 Glenn Hubbard (DK) .05
23 Billy Hatcher (DK) .05
24 Bob Welch (DK) .05
25 Ivan Calderon (DK) .05
26 Cal Ripken, Jr. (DK) .60
27 Checklist 1-27 .05
28 *Mackey Sasser* (RR) .05
29 *Jeff Treadway* (RR) .05
30 *Mike Campbell* (RR) .05
31 *Lance Johnson* (RR) .15
32 *Nelson Liriano* (RR) .05
33 Shawn Abner (RR) .05
34 *Roberto Alomar* (RR) .75
35 *Shawn Hillegas* (RR) .05
36 Joey Meyer (RR) .05
37 Kevin Elster (RR) .05
38 *Jose Lind* (RR) .05
39 *Kirt Manwaring* (RR) .05
40 *Mark Grace* (RR) .50
41 *Jody Reed* (RR) .10
42 *John Farrell* (RR) .05
43 *Al Leiter* (RR) .20
44 *Gary Thurman* (RR) .05
45 *Vicente Palacios* (RR) .05
46 *Eddie Williams* (RR) .05
47 *Jack McDowell* (RR) .20
48 Ken Dixon .05
49 Mike Birkbeck .05
50 Eric King .05
51 Roger Clemens .40
52 Pat Clements .05
53 Fernando Valenzuela .05
54 Mark Gubicza .05
55 Jay Howell .05
56 Floyd Youmans .05
57 Ed Correa .05
58 *DeWayne Buice* .05
59 Jose DeLeon .05
60 Danny Cox .05
61 Nolan Ryan .60
62 Steve Bedrosian .05
63 Tom Browning .05
64 Mark Davis .05
65 R.J. Reynolds .05
66 Kevin Mitchell .05
67 Ken Oberkfell .05
68 Rick Sutcliffe .05
69 Dwight Gooden .05
70 Scott Bankhead .05
71 Bert Blyleven .10
72 Jimmy Key .05
73 *Les Straker* .05
74 Jim Clancy .05
75 Mike Moore .05
76 Ron Darling .05
77 Ed Lynch .05
78 Dale Murphy .15
79 Doug Drabek .05
80 Scott Garrelts .05
81 Ed Whitson .05
82 Rob Murphy .05
83 Shane Rawley .05
84 Greg Mathews .05
85 Jim Deshaies .05
86 Mike Witt .05
87 Donnie Hill .05
88 Jeff Reed .05
89 Mike Boddicker .05
90 Ted Higuera .05
91 Walt Terrell .05
92 Bob Stanley .05
93 Dave Righetti .05
94 Orel Hershiser .05
95 Chris Bando .05
96 Bret Saberhagen .05
97 Curt Young .05
98 Tim Burke .05
99 Charlie Hough .05
100a Checklist 28-137 .05
100b Checklist 28-133 .05
101 Bobby Witt .05
102 George Brett .40
103 Mickey Tettleton .05
104 Scott Bailes .05
105 Mike Pagliarulo .05
106 Mike Scioscia .05
107 Tom Brookens .05
108 Ray Knight .05
109 Dan Plesac .05
110 Wally Joyner .05
111 Bob Forsch .05
112 Mike Scott .05
113 Kevin Gross .05
114 Benito Santiago .05
115 Bob Kipper .05
116 Mike Krukow .05
117 Chris Bosio .05
118 Sid Fernandez .05
119 Jody Davis .05
120 Mike Morgan .05
121 Mark Eichhorn .05
122 Jeff Reardon .05
123 John Franco .05
124 Richard Dotson .05
125 Eric Bell .05
126 Juan Nieves .05

127 Jack Morris .05
128 Rick Rhoden .05
129 Rich Gedman .05
130 Ken Howell .05
131 Brook Jacoby .05
132 Danny Jackson .05
133 Gene Nelson .05
134 Neal Heaton .05
135 Willie Fraser .05
136 Jose Guzman .05
137 Ozzie Guillen .05
138 Bob Knepper .05
139 *Mike Jackson* .05
140 *Joe Magrane* .05
141 Jimmy Jones .05
142 Ted Power .05
143 Ozzie Virgil .05
144 *Felix Fermin* .05
145 Kelly Downs .05
146 Shawon Dunston .05
147 Scott Bradley .05
148 Dave Stieb .05
149 Frank Viola .05
150 Terry Kennedy .05
151 Bill Wegman .05
152 *Matt Nokes* .10
153 Wade Boggs .35
154 Wayne Tolleson .05
155 Mariano Duncan .05
156 Julio Franco .05
157 Charlie Leibrandt .05
158 Terry Steinbach .05
159 Mike Fitzgerald .05
160 Jack Lazorko .05
161 Mitch Williams .05
162 Greg Walker .05
163 Alan Ashby .05
164 Tony Gwynn .35
165 Bruce Ruffin .05
166 Ron Robinson .05
167 Zane Smith .05
168 Junior Ortiz .05
169 Jamie Moyer .05
170 Tony Pena .05
171 Cal Ripken, Jr. .60
172 B.J. Surhoff .05
173 Lou Whitaker .05
174 *Ellis Burks* .20
175 Ron Guidry .10
176 Steve Sax .05
177 Danny Tartabull .05
178 Carney Lansford .05
179 Casey Candaele .05
180 Scott Fletcher .05
181 Mark McLemore .05
182 Ivan Calderon .05
183 Jack Clark .05
184 Glenn Davis .05
185 Luis Aguayo .05
186 Bo Diaz .05
187 Stan Jefferson .05
188 Sid Bream .05
189 Bob Brenly .05
190 Dion James .05
191 Leon Durham .05
192 Jesse Orosco .05
193 Alvin Davis .05
194 Gary Gaetti .05
195 Fred McGriff .05
196 Steve Lombardozzi .05
197 Rance Mulliniks .05
198 Rey Quinones .05
199 Gary Carter .30
200a Checklist 138-247 .05
200b Checklist 134-239 .05
201 Keith Moreland .05
202 Ken Griffey .05
203 *Tommy Gregg* .05
204 Will Clark .10
205 John Kruk .05
206 Buddy Bell .05
207 Von Hayes .05
208 Tommy Herr .05
209 Craig Reynolds .05
210 Gary Pettis .05
211 Harold Baines .05
212 Vance Law .05
213 Ken Gerhart .05
214 Jim Gantner .05
215 Chet Lemon .05
216 Dwight Evans .05
217 Don Mattingly .40
218 Franklin Stubbs .05
219 Pat Tabler .05
220 Bo Jackson .10
221 Tony Phillips .05
222 Tim Wallach .05
223 Ruben Sierra .05
224 Steve Buechele .05
225 Frank White .05
226 Alfredo Griffin .05
227 Greg Swindell .05
228 Willie Randolph .05
229 Mike Marshall .05
230 Alan Trammell .05
231 Eddie Murray .30
232 Dale Sveum .05
233 Dick Schofield .05
234 Jose Oquendo .05
235 Bill Doran .05
236 Milt Thompson .05
237 Marvell Wynne .05
238 Bobby Bonilla .05
239 Chris Speier .05
240 Glenn Braggs .05
241 Wally Backman .05
242 Ryne Sandberg .35
243 Phil Bradley .05
244 Kelly Gruber .05
245 Tom Brunansky .05
246 Ron Oester .05
247 Bobby Thigpen .05
248 Fred Lynn .05
249 Paul Molitor .30
250 Darrell Evans .05
251 Gary Ward .05
252 Bruce Hurst .05
253 Bob Welch .05
254 Joe Carter .05
255 Willie Wilson .05
256 Mark McGwire .50
257 Mitch Webster .05
258 Brian Downing .05
259 Mike Stanley .05
260 Carlton Fisk .30
261 Billy Hatcher .05
262 Glenn Wilson .05
263 Ozzie Smith .35
264 Randy Ready .05
265 Kurt Stillwell .05
266 David Palmer .05
267 Mike Diaz .05
268 Rob Thompson .05
269 Andre Dawson .15
270 Lee Guetterman .05
271 Willie Upshaw .05
272 Randy Bush .05
273 Larry Sheets .05
274 Rob Deer .05
275 Kirk Gibson .05
276 Marty Barrett .05
277 Rickey Henderson .30
278 Pedro Guerrero .05
279 Brett Butler .05
280 Kevin Seitzer .05
281 Mike Davis .05
282 Andres Galarraga .05
283 Devon White .05
284 Pete O'Brien .05
285 Jerry Hairston Sr. .05
286 Kevin Bass .05
287 Carmelo Martinez .05
288 Juan Samuel .05
289 Kal Daniels .05
290 Albert Hall .05
291 Andy Van Slyke .05
292 Lee Smith .10
293 Vince Coleman .05
294 Tom Niedenfuer .05
295 Robin Yount .30
296 *Jeff Robinson* .05
297 *Todd Benzinger* .10
298 Dave Winfield .30
299 Mickey Hatcher .05
300a Checklist 248-357 .05
300b Checklist 240-345 .05
301 Bud Black .05
302 Jose Canseco .20
303 Tom Foley .05
304 Pete Incaviglia .05
305 Bob Boone .05
306 *Bill Long* .05
307 Willie McGee .05
308 *Ken Caminiti* .20
309 Darren Daulton .05
310 Tracy Jones .05
311 Greg Booker .05
312 Mike LaValliere .05
313 Chili Davis .05
314 Glenn Hubbard .05
315 *Paul Noce* .05
316 Keith Hernandez .05
317 Mark Langston .05
318 Keith Atherton .05
319 Tony Fernandez .05
320 Kent Hrbek .05
321 John Cerutti .05
322 Mike Kingery .05
323 Dave Magadan .05
324 Rafael Palmeiro .30
325 Jeff Dedmon .05
326 Barry Bonds .60
327 Jeffrey Leonard .05
328 Tim Flannery .05
329 Dave Concepcion .05
330 Mike Schmidt .40
331 Bill Dawley .05
332 Larry Andersen .05
333 Jack Howell .05
334 *Ken Williams* .05
335 Bryn Smith .05
336 *Billy Ripken* .10
337 Greg Brock .05
338 Mike Heath .05
339 Mike Greenwell .05
340 Claudell Washington .05
341 Jose Gonzalez .05
342 Mel Hall .05
343 Jim Eisenreich .05
344 Tony Bernazard .05
345 Tim Raines .05
346 Bob Brower .05
347 Larry Parrish .05
348 Thad Bosley .05
349 Dennis Eckersley .30
350 Cory Snyder .05
351 Rick Cerone .05
352 John Shelby .05
353 Larry Herndon .05
354 John Habyan .05
355 *Chuck Crim* .05
356 Gus Polidor .05
357 Ken Dayley .05
358 Danny Darwin .05
359 Lance Parrish .05
360 *James Steels* .05
361 *Al Pedrique* .05
362 Mike Aldrete .05
363 Juan Castillo .05
364 Len Dykstra .05
365 Luis Quinones .05
366 Jim Presley .05
367 Lloyd Moseby .05
368 Kirby Puckett .35
369 Eric Davis .05
370 Gary Redus .05
371 Dave Schmidt .05
372 Mark Clear .05
373 Dave Bergman .05
374 Charles Hudson .05
375 Calvin Schiraldi .05
376 Alex Trevino .05
377 Tom Candiotti .05
378 Steve Farr .05
379 Mike Gallego .05
380 Andy McGaffigan .05
381 Kirk McCaskill .05
382 Oddibe McDowell .05
383 Floyd Bannister .05
384 Denny Walling .05
385 Don Carman .05
386 Todd Worrell .05
387 Eric Show .05
388 Dave Parker .05
389 Rick Mahler .05
390 *Mike Dunne* .10
391 Candy Maldonado .05
392 Bob Dernier .05
393 Dave Valle .05
394 Ernie Whitt .05
395 Juan Berenguer .05
396 Mike Young .05
397 Mike Felder .05
398 Willie Hernandez .05
399 Jim Rice .20
400a Checklist 358-467 .05
400b Checklist 346-451 .05
401 Tommy John .10
402 Brian Holton .05
403 Carmen Castillo .05
404 Jamie Quirk .05
405 Dwayne Murphy .05
406 *Jeff Parrett* .05
407 Don Sutton .30
408 Jerry Browne .05
409 Jim Winn .05
410 Dave Smith .05
411 *Shane Mack* .05
412 Greg Gross .05
413 Nick Esasky .05
414 Damaso Garcia .05
415 Brian Fisher .05
416 Brian Dayett .05
417 Curt Ford .05
418 *Mark Williamson* .05
419 Bill Schroeder .05
420 *Mike Henneman* .10
421 *John Marzano* .05
422 Ron Kittle .05
423 Matt Young .05
424 Steve Balboni .05
425 *Luis Polonia* .05
426 Randy St. Claire .05
427 Greg Harris .05
428 Johnny Ray .05
429 Ray Searage .05
430 Ricky Horton .05
431 *Gerald Young* .05
432 Rick Schu .05
433 Paul O'Neill .05
434 Rich Gossage .10
435 John Cangelosi .05
436 Mike LaCoss .05
437 Gerald Perry .05
438 Dave Martinez .05
439 Darryl Strawberry .05
440 John Moses .05
441 Greg Gagne .05
442 Jesse Barfield .05
443 George Frazier .05
444 Garth Iorg .05
445 Ed Nunez .05
446 Rick Aguilera .05
447 Jerry Mumphrey .05
448 Rafael Ramirez .05
449 *John Smiley* .10
450 Atlee Hammaker .05
451 Lance McCullers .05
452 Guy Hoffman .05
453 Chris James .05
454 Terry Pendleton .05
455 *Dave Meads* .05
456 Bill Buckner .05
457 *John Pawlowski* .05
458 Bob Sebra .05
459 Jim Dwyer .05
460 *Jay Aldrich* .05
461 Frank Tanana .05
462 Oil Can Boyd .05
463 Dan Pasqua .05
464 *Tim Crews* .10
465 Andy Allanson .05
466 *Bill Pecota* .05
467 Steve Ontiveros .05
468 Hubie Brooks .05
469 *Paul Kilgus* .05
470 Dale Mohorcic .05
471 Dan Quisenberry .05
472 Dave Stewart .05
473 Dave Clark .05
474 Joel Skinner .05
475 Dave Anderson .05
476 Dan Petry .05
477 *Carl Nichols* .05
478 Ernest Riles .05
479 George Hendrick .05
480 John Morris .05
481 *Manny Hernandez* .05
482 Jeff Stone .05
483 Chris Brown .05
484 Mike Bielecki .05
485 Dave Dravecky .05
486 Rick Manning .05
487 Bill Almon .05
488 Jim Sundberg .05
489 Ken Phelps .05
490 Tom Henke .05
491 Dan Gladden .05
492 Barry Larkin .05
493 *Fred Manrique* .05
494 Mike Griffin .05
495 *Mark Knudson* .05
496 Bill Madlock .05
497 Tim Stoddard .05
498 *Sam Horn* .05
499 *Tracy Woodson* .05
500a Checklist 468-577 .05
500b Checklist 452-557 .05
501 Ken Schrom .05
502 Angel Salazar .05
503 Eric Plunk .05
504 Joe Hesketh .05
505 Greg Minton .05
506 Geno Petralli .05
507 Bob James .05
508 *Robbie Wine* .05
509 Jeff Calhoun .05
510 Steve Lake .05
511 Mark Grant .05
512 Frank Williams .05
513 *Jeff Blauser* .10
514 Bob Walk .05
515 Craig Lefferts .05
516 Manny Trillo .05
517 Jerry Reed .05
518 Rick Leach .05

519 *Mark Davidson* .05
520 *Jeff Ballard* .05
521 *Dave Stapleton* .05
522 Pat Sheridan .05
523 Al Nipper .05
524 Steve Trout .05
525 Jeff Hamilton .05
526 *Tommy Hinzo* .05
527 Lonnie Smith .05
528 *Greg Cadaret* .05
529 Rob McClure (Bob) .05
530 Chuck Finley .05
531 Jeff Russell .05
532 Steve Lyons .05
533 Terry Puhl .05
534 *Eric Nolte* .05
535 Kent Tekulve .05
536 *Pat Pacillo* .05
537 Charlie Puleo .05
538 *Tom Prince* .05
539 Greg Maddux .35
540 Jim Lindeman .05
541 *Pete Stanicek* .05
542 Steve Kiefer .05
543 Jim Morrison .05
544 Spike Owen .05
545 *Jay Buhner* .50
546 *Mike Devereaux* .10
547 Jerry Don Gleaton .05
548 Jose Rijo .05
549 Dennis Martinez .05
550 Mike Loynd .05
551 Darrell Miller .05
552 Dave LaPoint .05
553 John Tudor .05
554 *Rocky Childress* .05
555 *Wally Ritchie* .05
556 Terry McGriff .05
557 Dave Leiper .05
558 Jeff Robinson .05
559 Jose Uribe .05
560 Ted Simmons .05
561 *Lester Lancaster* .10
562 *Keith Miller* .05
563 Harold Reynolds .05
564 *Gene Larkin* .05
565 Cecil Fielder .05
566 Roy Smalley .05
567 Duane Ward .05
568 *Bill Wilkinson* .05
569 Howard Johnson .05
570 Frank DiPino .05
571 *Pete Smith* .05
572 Darnell Coles .05
573 Don Robinson .05
574 Rob Nelson .05
575 Dennis Rasmussen .05
576 Steve Jeltz (photo actually Juan Samuel) .05
577 *Tom Pagnozzi* .05
578 Ty Gainey .05
579 Gary Lucas .05
580 Ron Hassey .05
581 Herm Winningham .05
582 *Rene Gonzales* .05
583 Brad Komminsk .05
584 Doyle Alexander .05
585 Jeff Sellers .05
586 Bill Gullickson .05
587 Tim Belcher .05
588 *Doug Jones* .05
589 *Melido Perez* .05
590 Rick Honeycutt .05
591 Pascual Perez .05
592 Curt Wilkerson .05
593 Steve Howe .05
594 *John Davis* .05
595 Storm Davis .05
596 Sammy Stewart .05
597 Neil Allen .05
598 Alejandro Pena .05
599 Mark Thurmond .05
600a Checklist 578-BC26 .05
600b Checklist 558-660 .05
601 *Jose Mesa* .10
602 *Don August* .05
603 Terry Leach (SP) .10
604 *Tom Newell* .05
605 *Randall Byers* (SP) .10
606 Jim Gott .05
607 Harry Spilman .05
608 John Candelaria .05
609 *Mike Brumley* .05
610 Mickey Brantley .05
611 *Jose Nunez* (SP) .10
612 Tom Nieto .05
613 Rick Reuschel .05
614 Lee Mazzilli (SP) .10
615 *Scott Lusader* .05
616 Bobby Meacham .05
617 Kevin McReynolds (SP) .10
618 Gene Garber .05
619 *Barry Lyons* (SP) .10
620 Randy Myers .05
621 Donnie Moore .05
622 Domingo Ramos .05
623 Ed Romero .05
624 *Greg Myers* .10
625 Billy Ripken, Cal Ripken, Jr., Cal Ripken, Sr. Ripken Baseball Family .30
626 Pat Perry .05
627 Andres Thomas (SP) .10
628 Matt Williams (SP) .15
629 *Dave Hengel* .05
630 Jeff Musselman (SP) .10
631 Tim Laudner .05
632 Bob Ojeda (SP) .10
633 Rafael Santana .05
634 *Wes Gardner* .05
635 *Roberto Kelly* (SP) .15
636 Mike Flanagan (SP) .10
637 *Jay Bell* .35
638 Bob Melvin .05
639 *Damon Berryhill* .05
640 *David Wells* (SP) .40
641 Stan Musial Puzzle Card .05
642 Doug Sisk .05
643 *Keith Hughes* .05
644 *Tom Glavine* .75
645 Al Newman .05
646 Scott Sanderson .05
647 Scott Terry .05
648 Tim Teufel (SP) .10
649 Garry Templeton (SP) .10
650 Manny Lee (SP) .10
651 Roger McDowell (SP) .10
652 Mookie Wilson (SP) .10
653 David Cone (SP) .10
654 *Ron Gant* (SP) .20
655 Joe Price (SP) .10
656 George Bell (SP) .10
657 *Gregg Jefferies* (SP) .25
658 *Todd Stottlemyre* (SP) .25
659 *Geronimo Berroa* (SP) .20
660 Jerry Royster (SP) .10

Rookies

NM/M
Complete Set (56): 3.00
Common Player: .05
1 Mark Grace .25
2 Mike Campbell .05
3 Todd Frowirth .05
4 Dave Stapleton .05
5 Shawn Abner .05
6 Jose Cecena .05
7 Dave Gallagher .05
8 Mark Parent .05
9 Cecil Espy .05
10 Pete Smith .05
11 Jay Buhner .25
12 Pat Borders .05
13 Doug Jennings .05
14 *Brady Anderson* .50
15 Pete Stanicek .05
16 Roberto Kelly .05
17 Jeff Treadway .05
18 Walt Weiss .05
19 Paul Gibson .05
20 Tim Crews .05
21 Melido Perez .05
22 Steve Peters .05
23 Craig Worthington .05
24 John Trautwein .05
25 DeWayne Vaughn .05
26 David Wells .15
27 Al Leiter .15
28 Tim Belcher .05
29 Johnny Paredes .05
30 Chris Sabo .05
31 Damon Berryhill .05
32 Randy Milligan .05
33 Gary Thurman .05
34 Kevin Elster .05
35 Roberto Alomar 1.00
36 *Edgar Martinez* (photo actually Edwin Nunez) 1.00
37 Todd Stottlemyre .15
38 Joey Meyer .05
39 Carl Nichols .05
40 Jack McDowell .05
41 Jose Bautista .05
42 Sil Campusano .05
43 John Dopson .05
44 Jody Reed .05
45 Darrin Jackson .05
46 Mike Capel .05
47 Ron Gant .05
48 John Davis .05
49 Kevin Coffman .05
50 Cris Carpenter .05
51 Mackey Sasser .05
52 Luis Alicea .05
53 Bryan Harvey .05
54 Steve Ellsworth .05
55 Mike Macfarlane .05
56 Checklist 1-56 .05

1989 DONRUSS

NM/M
Unopened Fact. Set (660): 20.00
Complete Set (660): 15.00
Common Player: .05
Warren Spahn Puzzle: .50
Wax Pack (15): .50
Wax Box (36): 9.00
Cello Pack (32): .75
Cello Box (24): 12.50
Rack Pack (45): .75
1 Mike Greenwell (DK) .05
2 Bobby Bonilla (DK) .05
3 Pete Incaviglia (DK) .05
4 Chris Sabo (DK) .05
5 Robin Yount (DK) .30
6 Tony Gwynn (DK) .45
7 Carlton Fisk (DK) .30
8 Cory Snyder (DK) .05
9 David Cone (DK) .05
10 Kevin Seitzer (DK) .05
11 Rick Reuschel (DK) .05
12 Johnny Ray (DK) .05
13 Dave Schmidt (DK) .05
14 Andres Galarraga (DK) .05
15 Kirk Gibson (DK) .05
16 Fred McGriff (DK) .05
17 Mark Grace (DK) .25
18 Jeff Robinson (DK) .05
19 Vince Coleman (DK) .05
20 Dave Henderson (DK) .05
21 Harold Reynolds (DK) .10
22 Gerald Perry (DK) .05
23 Frank Viola (DK) .05
24 Steve Bedrosian (DK) .05
25 Glenn Davis (DK) .05
26 Don Mattingly (DK) .45
27 Checklist 1-27 .05
28 *Sandy Alomar, Jr.* (RR) .35
29 *Steve Searcy* (RR) .05
30 *Cameron Drew* (RR) .05
31 *Gary Sheffield* (RR) 1.00
32 *Erik Hanson* (RR) .05
33 *Ken Griffey, Jr.* (RR) 6.00
34 *Greg Harris* (RR) .05
35 Gregg Jefferies (RR) .10
36 *Luis Medina* (RR) .05
37 *Carlos Quintana* (RR) .05
38 *Felix Jose* (RR) .05
39 *Cris Carpenter* (RR) .05
40 *Ron Jones* (RR) .05
41 *Dave West* (RR) .05
42 *Randy Johnson* (RR) 3.00
43 *Mike Harkey* (RR) .05
44 *Pete Harnisch* (RR) .10
45 *Tom Gordon* (RR) .25
46 *Gregg Olson* (RR) .10
47 *Alex Sanchez* (RR) .05
48 Ruben Sierra .05
49 Rafael Palmeiro .30
50 Ron Gant .05
51 Cal Ripken, Jr. .75
52 Wally Joyner .05
53 Gary Carter .30
54 Andy Van Slyke .05
55 Robin Yount .30
56 Pete Incaviglia .05
57 Greg Brock .05
58 Melido Perez .05
59 Craig Lefferts .05
60 Gary Pettis .05
61 Danny Tartabull .05
62 Guillermo Hernandez .05
63 Ozzie Smith .45
64 Gary Gaetti .05
65 Mark Davis .05
66 Lee Smith .10
67 Dennis Eckersley .30
68 Wade Boggs .45
69 Mike Scott .05
70 Fred McGriff .05
71 Tom Browning .05
72 Claudell Washington .05
73 Mel Hall .05
74 Don Mattingly .50
75 Steve Bedrosian .05
76 Juan Samuel .05
77 Mike Scioscia .05
78 Dave Righetti .05
79 Alfredo Griffin .05
80 Eric Davis .05
81 Juan Berenguer .05
82 Todd Worrell .05
83 Joe Carter .05
84 Steve Sax .05
85 Frank White .05
86 John Kruk .05
87 Rance Mulliniks .05
88 Alan Ashby .05
89 Charlie Leibrandt .05
90 Frank Tanana .05
91 Jose Canseco .25
92 Barry Bonds .75
93 Harold Reynolds .10
94 Mark McLemore .05
95 Mark McGwire .60
96 Eddie Murray .30
97 Tim Raines .05
98 Rob Thompson .05
99 Kevin McReynolds .05
100 Checklist 28-137 .05
101 Carlton Fisk .30
102 Dave Martinez .05
103 Glenn Braggs .05
104 Dale Murphy .15
105 Ryne Sandberg .45
106 Dennis Martinez .05
107 Pete O'Brien .05
108 Dick Schofield .05
109 Henry Cotto .05
110 Mike Marshall .05
111 Keith Moreland .05
112 Tom Brunansky .05
113 Kelly Gruber .05
114 Brook Jacoby .05
115 *Keith Brown* .05
116 Matt Nokes .05
117 Keith Hernandez .05
118 Bob Forsch .05
119 Bert Blyleven .10
120 Willie Wilson .05
121 Tommy Gregg .05
122 Jim Rice .20
123 Bob Knepper .05
124 Danny Jackson .05
125 Eric Plunk .05
126 Brian Fisher .05
127 Mike Pagliarulo .05
128 Tony Gwynn .45
129 Lance McCullers .05
130 Andres Galarraga .05
131 Jose Uribe .05
132 Kirk Gibson .05
133 David Palmer .05
134 R.J. Reynolds .05

No.	Player	Price
135	Greg Walker	.05
136	Kirk McCaskill	.05
137	Shawon Dunston	.05
138	Andy Allanson	.05
139	Rob Murphy	.05
140	Mike Aldrete	.05
141	Terry Kennedy	.05
142	Scott Fletcher	.05
143	Steve Balboni	.05
144	Bret Saberhagen	.05
145	Ozzie Virgil	.05
146	Dale Sveum	.05
147	Darryl Strawberry	.05
148	Harold Baines	.10
149	George Bell	.05
150	Dave Parker	.05
151	Bobby Bonilla	.05
152	Mookie Wilson	.05
153	Ted Power	.05
154	Nolan Ryan	.75
155	Jeff Reardon	.05
156	Tim Wallach	.05
157	Jamie Moyer	.05
158	Rich Gossage	.10
159	Dave Winfield	.30
160	Von Hayes	.05
161	Willie McGee	.05
162	Rich Gedman	.05
163	Tony Pena	.05
164	Mike Morgan	.05
165	Charlie Hough	.05
166	Mike Stanley	.05
167	Andre Dawson	.15
168	Joe Boever	.05
169	Pete Stanicek	.05
170	Bob Boone	.05
171	Ron Darling	.05
172	Bob Walk	.05
173	Rob Deer	.05
174	Steve Buechele	.05
175	Ted Higuera	.05
176	Ozzie Guillen	.05
177	Candy Maldonado	.05
178	Doyle Alexander	.05
179	Mark Gubicza	.05
180	Alan Trammell	.05
181	Vince Coleman	.05
182	Kirby Puckett	.45
183	Chris Brown	.05
184	Marty Barrett	.05
185	Stan Javier	.05
186	Mike Greenwell	.05
187	Billy Hatcher	.05
188	Jimmy Key	.05
189	Nick Esasky	.05
190	Don Slaught	.05
191	Cory Snyder	.05
192	John Candelaria	.05
193	Mike Schmidt	.50
194	Kevin Gross	.05
195	John Tudor	.05
196	Neil Allen	.05
197	Orel Hershiser	.05
198	Kal Daniels	.05
199	Kent Hrbek	.05
200	Checklist 138-247	.05
201	Joe Magrane	.05
202	Scott Bailes	.05
203	Tim Belcher	.05
204	George Brett	.50
205	Benito Santiago	.05
206	Tony Fernandez	.05
207	Gerald Young	.05
208	Bo Jackson	.10
209	Chet Lemon	.05
210	Storm Davis	.05
211	Doug Drabek	.05
212	Mickey Brantley (photo actually Nelson Simmons)	.05
213	Devon White	.05
214	Dave Stewart	.05
215	Dave Schmidt	.05
216	Bryn Smith	.05
217	Brett Butler	.05
218	Bob Ojeda	.05
219	*Steve Rosenberg*	.05
220	Hubie Brooks	.05
221	B.J. Surhoff	.05
222	Rick Mahler	.05
223	Rick Sutcliffe	.05
224	Neal Heaton	.05
225	Mitch Williams	.05
226	Chuck Finley	.05
227	Mark Langston	.05
228	Jesse Orosco	.05
229	Ed Whitson	.05
230	Terry Pendleton	.05
231	Lloyd Moseby	.05
232	Greg Swindell	.05
233	John Franco	.05
234	Jack Morris	.05
235	Howard Johnson	.05
236	Glenn Davis	.05
237	Frank Viola	.05
238	Kevin Seitzer	.05
239	Gerald Perry	.05
240	Dwight Evans	.05
241	Jim Deshaies	.05
242	Bo Diaz	.05
243	Carney Lansford	.05
244	Mike LaValliere	.05
245	Rickey Henderson	.30
246	Roberto Alomar	.20
247	Jimmy Jones	.05
248	Pascual Perez	.05
249	Will Clark	.10
250	Fernando Valenzuela	.05
251	Shane Rawley	.05
252	Sid Bream	.05
253	Steve Lyons	.05
254	Brian Downing	.05
255	Mark Grace	.15
256	Tom Candiotti	.05
257	Barry Larkin	.05
258	Mike Krukow	.05
259	Billy Ripken	.05
260	Cecilio Guante	.05
261	Scott Bradley	.05
262	Floyd Bannister	.05
263	Pete Smith	.05
264	Jim Gantner	.05
265	Roger McDowell	.05
266	Bobby Thigpen	.05
267	Jim Clancy	.05
268	Terry Steinbach	.05
269	Mike Dunne	.05
270	Dwight Gooden	.05
271	Mike Heath	.05
272	Dave Smith	.05
273	Keith Atherton	.05
274	Tim Burke	.05
275	Damon Berryhill	.05
276	Vance Law	.05
277	Rich Dotson	.05
278	Lance Parrish	.05
279	Geronimo Berroa	.05
280	Roger Clemens	.50
281	Greg Mathews	.05
282	Tom Niedenfuer	.05
283	Paul Kilgus	.05
284	Jose Guzman	.05
285	Calvin Schiraldi	.05
286	Charlie Puleo	.05
287	Joe Orsulak	.05
288	Jack Howell	.05
289	Kevin Elster	.05
290	Jose Lind	.05
291	Paul Molitor	.30
292	Cecil Espy	.05
293	Bill Wegman	.05
294	Dan Pasqua	.05
295	Scott Garrelts	.05
296	Walt Terrell	.05
297	Ed Hearn	.05
298	Lou Whitaker	.05
299	Ken Dayley	.05
300	Checklist 248-357	.05
301	Tommy Herr	.05
302	Mike Brumley	.05
303	Ellis Burks	.05
304	Curt Young	.05
305	Jody Reed	.05
306	Bill Doran	.05
307	David Wells	.05
308	Ron Robinson	.05
309	Rafael Santana	.05
310	Julio Franco	.05
311	Jack Clark	.05
312	Chris James	.05
313	Milt Thompson	.05
314	John Shelby	.05
315	Al Leiter	.05
316	Mike Davis	.05
317	*Chris Sabo*	.15
318	Greg Gagne	.05
319	Jose Oquendo	.05
320	John Farrell	.05
321	Franklin Stubbs	.05
322	Kurt Stillwell	.05
323	Shawn Abner	.05
324	Mike Flanagan	.05
325	Kevin Bass	.05
326	Pat Tabler	.05
327	Mike Henneman	.05
328	Rick Honeycutt	.05
329	John Smiley	.05
330	Rey Quinones	.05
331	Johnny Ray	.05
332	Bob Welch	.05
333	Larry Sheets	.05
334	Jeff Parrett	.05
335	Rick Reuschel	.05
336	Randy Myers	.05
337	Ken Williams	.05
338	Andy McGaffigan	.05
339	Joey Meyer	.05
340	Dion James	.05
341	Les Lancaster	.05
342	Tom Foley	.05
343	Geno Petralli	.05
344	Dan Petry	.05
345	Alvin Davis	.05
346	Mickey Hatcher	.05
347	Marvell Wynne	.05
348	Danny Cox	.05
349	Dave Stieb	.05
350	Jay Bell	.05
351	Jeff Treadway	.05
352	Luis Salazar	.05
353	Len Dykstra	.05
354	Juan Agosto	.05
355	Gene Larkin	.05
356	Steve Farr	.05
357	Paul Assenmacher	.05
358	Todd Benzinger	.05
359	Larry Andersen	.05
360	Paul O'Neill	.05
361	Ron Hassey	.05
362	Jim Gott	.05
363	Ken Phelps	.05
364	Tim Flannery	.05
365	Randy Ready	.05
366	*Nelson Santovenia*	.05
367	Kelly Downs	.05
368	Danny Heep	.05
369	Phil Bradley	.05
370	Jeff Robinson	.05
371	Ivan Calderon	.05
372	Mike Witt	.05
373	Greg Maddux	.45
374	Carmen Castillo	.05
375	Jose Rijo	.05
376	Joe Price	.05
377	R.C. Gonzalez	.05
378	Oddibe McDowell	.05
379	Jim Presley	.05
380	Brad Wellman	.05
381	Tom Glavine	.20
382	Dan Plesac	.05
383	Wally Backman	.05
384	*Dave Gallagher*	.05
385	Tom Henke	.05
386	Luis Polonia	.05
387	Junior Ortiz	.05
388	David Cone	.05
389	Dave Bergman	.05
390	Danny Darwin	.05
391	Dan Gladden	.05
392	*John Dopson*	.05
393	Frank DiPino	.05
394	Al Nipper	.05
395	Willie Randolph	.05
396	Don Carman	.05
397	Scott Terry	.05
398	Rick Cerone	.05
399	Tom Pagnozzi	.05
400	Checklist 358-467	.05
401	Mickey Tettleton	.05
402	Curtis Wilkerson	.05
403	Jeff Russell	.05
404	Pat Perry	.05
405	*Jose Alvarez*	.05
406	Rick Schu	.05
407	*Sherman Corbett*	.05
408	Dave Magadan	.05
409	Bob Kipper	.05
410	Don August	.05
411	Bob Brower	.05
412	Chris Bosio	.05
413	Jerry Reuss	.05
414	Atlee Hammaker	.05
415	Jim Walewander	.05
416	*Mike Macfarlane*	.10
417	Pat Sheridan	.05
418	Pedro Guerrero	.05
419	Allan Anderson	.05
420	*Mark Parent*	.05
421	Bob Stanley	.05
422	Mike Gallego	.05
423	Bruce Hurst	.05
424	Dave Meads	.05
425	Jesse Barfield	.05
426	*Rob Dibble*	.15
427	Joel Skinner	.05
428	Ron Kittle	.05
429	Rick Rhoden	.05
430	Bob Dernier	.05
431	Steve Jeltz	.05
432	Rick Dempsey	.05
433	Roberto Kelly	.05
434	Dave Anderson	.05
435	Herm Winningham	.05
436	Al Newman	.05
437	Jose DeLeon	.05
438	Doug Jones	.05
439	Brian Holton	.05
440	Jeff Montgomery	.05
441	Dickie Thon	.05
442	Cecil Fielder	.05
443	*John Fishel*	.05
444	Jerry Don Gleaton	.05
445	*Paul Gibson*	.05
446	Walt Weiss	.05
447	Glenn Wilson	.05
448	Mike Moore	.05
449	Chili Davis	.05
450	Dave Henderson	.05
451	*Jose Bautista*	.05
452	Rex Hudler	.05
453	Bob Brenly	.05
454	Mackey Sasser	.05
455	Daryl Boston	.05
456	Mike Fitzgerald	.05
457	Jeffery Leonard	.05
458	Bruce Sutter	.25
459	Mitch Webster	.05
460	Joe Hesketh	.05
461	Bobby Witt	.05
462	Stew Cliburn	.05
463	Scott Bankhead	.05
464	*Ramon Martinez*	.25
465	Dave Leiper	.05
466	*Luis Alicea*	.05
467	John Cerutti	.05
468	Ron Washington	.05
469	Jeff Reed	.05
470	Jeff Robinson	.05
471	Sid Fernandez	.05
472	Terry Puhl	.05
473	Charlie Lea	.05
474	*Israel Sanchez*	.05
475	Bruce Benedict	.05
476	Oil Can Boyd	.05
477	Craig Reynolds	.05
478	Frank Williams	.05
479	Greg Cadaret	.05
480	*Randy Kramer*	.05
481	*Dave Eiland*	.05
482	Eric Show	.05
483	Garry Templeton	.05
484	Wallace Johnson	.05
485	Kevin Mitchell	.05
486	Tim Crews	.05
487	Mike Maddux	.05
488	Dave LaPoint	.05
489	Fred Manrique	.05
490	Greg Minton	.05
491	*Doug Dascenzo*	.05
492	Willie Upshaw	.05
493	*Jack Armstrong*	.05
494	Kirt Manwaring	.05
495	Jeff Ballard	.05
496	Jeff Kunkel	.05
497	Mike Campbell	.05
498	Gary Thurman	.05
499	Zane Smith	.05
500	Checklist 468-577	.05
501	Mike Birkbeck	.05
502	Terry Leach	.05
503	Shawn Hillegas	.05
504	Manny Lee	.05
505	*Doug Jennings*	.05
506	Ken Oberkfell	.05
507	Tim Teufel	.05
508	Tom Brookens	.05
509	Rafael Ramirez	.05
510	Fred Toliver	.05
511	*Brian Holman*	.05
512	Mike Bielecki	.05
513	*Jeff Pico*	.05
514	Charles Hudson	.05
515	Bruce Ruffin	.05
516	Larry McWilliams	.05
517	Jeff Sellers	.05
518	*John Costello*	.05
519	Brady Anderson	.05
520	Craig McMurtry	.05
521	Ray Hayward	.05
522	Drew Hall	.05
523	*Mark Lemke*	.05
524	*Oswald Peraza*	.05
525	*Bryan Harvey*	.05
526	Rick Aguilera	.05
527	Tom Prince	.05
528	Mark Clear	.05

529	Jerry Browne	.05
530	Juan Castillo	.05
531	Jack McDowell	.05
532	Chris Speier	.05
533	Darrell Evans	.05
534	Luis Aquino	.05
535	Eric King	.05
536	*Ken Hill*	.05
537	Randy Bush	.05
538	Shane Mack	.05
539	Tom Bolton	.05
540	Gene Nelson	.05
541	Wes Gardner	.05
542	Ken Caminiti	.05
543	Duane Ward	.05
544	*Norm Charlton*	.10
545	*Hal Morris*	.25
546	Rich Yett	.05
547	*Hensley Meulens*	.10
548	Greg Harris	.05
549	Darren Daulton	.05
550	Jeff Hamilton	.05
551	Luis Aguayo	.05
552	Tim Leary	.05
553	Ron Oester	.05
554	Steve Lombardozzi	.05
555	*Tim Jones*	.05
556	Bud Black	.05
557	Alejandro Pena	.05
558	*Jose DeJesus*	.05
559	Dennis Rasmussen	.05
560	*Pat Borders*	.25
561	Craig Biggio	.05
562	*Luis de los Santos*	.05
563	Fred Lynn	.05
564	*Todd Burns*	.05
565	Felix Fermin	.05
566	Darnell Coles	.05
567	Willie Fraser	.05
568	Glenn Hubbard	.05
569	*Craig Worthington*	.05
570	*Johnny Paredes*	.05
571	Don Robinson	.05
572	Barry Lyons	.05
573	Bill Long	.05
574	Tracy Jones	.05
575	Juan Nieves	.05
576	Andres Thomas	.05
577	*Rolando Roomes*	.05
578	Luis Rivera	.05
579	*Chad Kreuter*	.10
580	Tony Armas	.05
581	Jay Buhner	.05
582	Ricky Horton	.05
583	Andy Hawkins	.05
584	*Sil Campusano*	.05
585	Dave Clark	.05
586	*Van Snider*	.05
587	Todd Frohwirth	.05
588	Warren Spahn Puzzle Card	.05
589	*William Brennan*	.05
590	*German Gonzalez*	.05
591	Ernie Whitt	.05
592	Jeff Blauser	.05
593	Spike Owen	.05
594	Matt Williams	.05
595	Lloyd McClendon	.05
596	Steve Ontiveros	.05
597	*Scott Medvin*	.05
598	*Hipolito Pena*	.05
599	*Jerald Clark*	.05
600a	Checklist 578-BC26 (#635 is Kurt Schilling)	.10
600b	Checklist 578-BC26 (#635 is Curt Schilling)	.05
601	Carmelo Martinez	.05
602	Mike LaCoss	.05
603	Mike Devereaux	.05
604	*Alex Madrid*	.05
605	Gary Redus	.05
606	Lance Johnson	.05
607	*Terry Clark*	.05
608	Manny Trillo	.05
609	*Scott Jordan*	.05
610	Jay Howell	.05
611	*Francisco Melendez*	.05
612	Mike Boddicker	.05
613	Kevin Brown	.10
614	Dave Valle	.05
615	Tim Laudner	.05
616	*Andy Nezelek*	.05
617	Chuck Crim	.05
618	Jack Savage	.05
619	Adam Peterson	.05
620	Todd Stottlemyre	.05
621	*Lance Blankenship*	.05
622	*Miguel Garcia*	.05
623	Keith Miller	.05
624	*Ricky Jordan*	.05
625	Ernest Riles	.05
626	John Moses	.05
627	Nelson Liriano	.05
628	Mike Smithson	.05
629	Scott Sanderson	.05
630	Dale Mohorcic	.05
631	Marvin Freeman	.05
632	Mike Young	.05
633	Dennis Lamp	.05
634	*Dante Bichette*	.25
635	*Curt Schilling*	3.00
636	*Scott May*	.05
637	*Mike Schooler*	.05
638	Rick Leach	.05
639	*Tom Lampkin*	.05
640	*Brian Meyer*	.05
641	Brian Harper	.05
642	John Smoltz	.05
643	Jose Canseco (40/40)	.15
644	Bill Schroeder	.05
645	Edgar Martinez	.10
646	*Dennis Cook*	.05
647	Barry Jones	.05
648	Orel Hershiser (59 and Counting)	.05
649	*Rod Nichols*	.05
650	Jody Davis	.05
651	*Bob Milacki*	.05
652	Mike Jackson	.05
653	*Derek Lilliquist*	.05
654	Paul Mirabella	.05
655	Mike Diaz	.05
656	Jeff Musselman	.05
657	Jerry Reed	.05
658	*Kevin Blankenship*	.05
659	Wayne Tolleson	.05
660	*Eric Hetzel*	.05

Rookies

		NM/M
Complete Set (56):		10.00
Common Player:		.05
1	Gary Sheffield	.75
2	Gregg Jefferies	.10
3	Ken Griffey, Jr.	5.00
4	Tom Gordon	.10
5	Billy Spiers	.05
6	*Deion Sanders*	.50
7	Donn Pall	.05
8	Steve Carter	.05
9	Francisco Oliveras	.05
10	Steve Wilson	.05
11	Bob Geren	.05
12	Tony Castillo	.05
13	Kenny Rogers	.05
14	Carlos Martinez	.05
15	Edgar Martinez	.05
16	Jim Abbott	.05
17	Torey Lovullo	.05
18	Mark Carreon	.05
19	Geronimo Berroa	.05
20	Luis Medina	.05
21	Sandy Alomar, Jr.	.10
22	Bob Milacki	.05
23	*Joe Girardi*	.10
24	German Gonzalez	.05
25	Craig Worthington	.05
26	Jerome Walton	.05
27	Gary Wayne	.05
28	Tim Jones	.05
29	Dante Bichette	.05
30	Alexis Infante	.05
31	Ken Hill	.05
32	Dwight Smith	.05
33	Luis de los Santos	.05
34	Eric Yelding	.05
35	Gregg Olson	.05
36	Phil Stephenson	.05
37	Ken Patterson	.05
38	Rick Wrona	.05
39	Mike Brumley	.05
40	Cris Carpenter	.05
41	Jeff Brantley	.05
42	Ron Jones	.05
43	Randy Johnson	2.00
44	Kevin Brown	.05
45	Ramon Martinez	.05
46	Greg Harris	.05
47	Steve Finley	.05
48	Randy Kramer	.05
49	Erik Hanson	.05
50	Matt Merullo	.05
51	Mike Devereaux	.05
52	Clay Parker	.05
53	Omar Vizquel	.15
54	Derek Lilliquist	.05
55	Junior Felix	.05
56	Checklist	.05

1989 DONRUSS TRADED

		NM/M
Complete Set (56):		2.00
Common Player:		.05
1	Jeffrey Leonard	.05
2	Jack Clark	.05
3	Kevin Gross	.05
4	Tommy Herr	.05
5	Bob Boone	.05
6	Rafael Palmeiro	.30
7	John Dopson	.05
8	Willie Randolph	.05
9	Chris Brown	.05
10	Wally Backman	.05
11	Steve Ontiveros	.05
12	Eddie Murray	.40
13	Lance McCullers	.05
14	Spike Owen	.05
15	Rob Murphy	.05
16	Pete O'Brien	.05
17	Ken Williams	.05
18	Nick Esasky	.05
19	Nolan Ryan	1.50
20	Brian Holton	.05
21	Mike Moore	.05
22	Joel Skinner	.05
23	Steve Sax	.05
24	Rick Mahler	.05
25	Mike Aldrete	.05
26	Jesse Orosco	.05
27	Dave LaPoint	.05
28	Walt Terrell	.05
29	Eddie Williams	.05
30	Mike Devereaux	.05
31	Julio Franco	.05
32	Jim Clancy	.05
33	Felix Fermin	.05
34	Curtis Wilkerson	.05
35	Bert Blyleven	.05
36	Mel Hall	.05
37	Eric King	.05
38	Mitch Williams	.05
39	Jamie Moyer	.05
40	Rick Rhoden	.05
41	Phil Bradley	.05
42	Paul Kilgus	.05
43	Milt Thompson	.05
44	Jerry Browne	.05
45	Bruce Hurst	.05
46	Claudell Washington	.05
47	Todd Benzinger	.05
48	Steve Balboni	.05
49	Oddibe McDowell	.05
50	Charles Hudson	.05
51	Ron Kittle	.05
52	Andy Hawkins	.05
53	Tom Brookens	.05
54	Tom Niedenfuer	.05
55	Jeff Parrett	.05
56	Checklist	.05

1990 DONRUSS

		NM/M
Unopened Factory Set (716):		6.00
Complete Set (716):		5.00
Common Player:		.05
Carl Yastrzemski Puzzle:		1.00
Wax Pack (16):		.30
Wax Box (36):		7.00
Rack Pack (48):		.75
Blister Rack (78):		1.00
1	Bo Jackson (Diamond King)	.15
2	Steve Sax (DK)	.05
3a	Ruben Sierra (DK) (no vertical black line at top-right on back)	.25
3b	Ruben Sierra (DK) (vertical line at top-right on back)	.10
4	Ken Griffey, Jr. (DK)	.60
5	Mickey Tettleton (DK)	.05
6	Dave Stewart (DK)	.05
7	Jim Deshaies (DK)	.05
8	John Smoltz (DK)	.05
9	Mike Bielecki (DK)	.05
10a	Brian Downing (DK) (reversed negative)	.25
10b	Brian Downing (DK) (corrected)	.05
11	Kevin Mitchell (DK)	.05
12	Kelly Gruber (DK)	.05
13	Joe Magrane (DK)	.05
14	John Franco (DK)	.05
15	Ozzie Guillen (DK)	.05
16	Lou Whitaker (DK)	.05
17	John Smiley (DK)	.05
18	Howard Johnson (DK)	.05
19	Willie Randolph (DK)	.05
20	Chris Bosio (DK)	.05
21	Tommy Herr (DK)	.05
22	Dan Gladden (DK)	.05
23	Ellis Burks (DK)	.05
24	Pete O'Brien (DK)	.05
25	Bryn Smith (DK)	.05
26	Ed Whitson (DK)	.05
27	Checklist 1-27	.05
28	Robin Ventura (Rated Rookie)	.10
29	*Todd Zeile* (RR)	.15
30	Sandy Alomar, Jr.(RR)	.05
31	*Kent Mercker* (RR)	.10
32	*Ben McDonald* (RR)	.25
33a	*Juan Gonzalez (reversed negative)* (RR)	2.00
33b	*Juan Gonzalez* (RR) (corrected)	2.00
34	*Eric Anthony* (RR)	.05
35	*Mike Fetters* (RR)	.05
36	*Marquis Grissom* (RR)	.50
37	*Greg Vaughn* (RR)	.25
38	*Brian Dubois* (RR)	.05
39	*Steve Avery* (RR)	.10
40	*Mark Gardner* (RR)	.05
41	Andy Benes (RR)	.05
42	*Delino DeShields* (RR)	.15
43	*Scott Coolbaugh* (RR)	.05
44	*Pat Combs* (RR)	.10
45	*Alex Sanchez* (RR)	.05
46	*Kelly Mann* (RR)	.05
47	*Julio Machado* (RR)	.05
48	Pete Incaviglia	.05
49	Shawon Dunston	.05
50	Jeff Treadway	.05
51	Jeff Ballard	.05
52	Claudell Washington	.05
53	Juan Samuel	.05
54	John Smiley	.05

No.	Player	Price
55	Rob Deer	.05
56	Geno Petralli	.05
57	Chris Bosio	.05
58	Carlton Fisk	.30
59	Kirt Manwaring	.05
60	Chet Lemon	.05
61	Bo Jackson	.10
62	Doyle Alexander	.05
63	Pedro Guerrero	.05
64	Allan Anderson	.05
65	Greg Harris	.05
66	Mike Greenwell	.05
67	Walt Weiss	.05
68	Wade Boggs	.40
69	Jim Clancy	.05
70	*Junior Felix*	.05
71	Barry Larkin	.05
72	Dave LaPoint	.05
73	Joel Skinner	.05
74	Jesse Barfield	.05
75	Tommy Herr	.05
76	Ricky Jordan	.05
77	Eddie Murray	.30
78	Steve Sax	.05
79	Tim Belcher	.05
80	Danny Jackson	.05
81	Kent Hrbek	.05
82	Milt Thompson	.05
83	Brook Jacoby	.05
84	Mike Marshall	.05
85	Kevin Seitzer	.05
86	Tony Gwynn	.40
87	Dave Steib	.05
88	Dave Smith	.05
89	Bret Saberhagen	.05
90	Alan Trammell	.05
91	Tony Phillips	.05
92	Doug Drabek	.05
93	Jeffrey Leonard	.05
94	Wally Joyner	.05
95	Carney Lansford	.05
96	Cal Ripken, Jr.	.75
97	Andres Galarraga	.05
98	Kevin Mitchell	.05
99	Howard Johnson	.05
100a	Checklist 28-129	.05
100b	Checklist 28-125	.05
101	Melido Perez	.05
102	Spike Owen	.05
103	Paul Molitor	.30
104	Geronimo Berroa	.05
105	Ryne Sandberg	.40
106	Bryn Smith	.05
107	Steve Buechele	.05
108	Jim Abbott	.05
109	Alvin Davis	.05
110	Lee Smith	.05
111	Roberto Alomar	.20
112	Rick Reuschel	.05
113a	Kelly Gruber (Born 2/22)	.05
113b	Kelly Gruber (Born 2/26)	.20
114	Joe Carter	.05
115	Jose Rijo	.05
116	Greg Minton	.05
117	Bob Ojeda	.05
118	Glenn Davis	.05
119	Jeff Reardon	.05
120	Kurt Stillwell	.05
121	John Smoltz	.05
122	Dwight Evans	.05
123	Eric Yelding	.05
124	John Franco	.05
125	Jose Canseco	.20
126	Barry Bonds	.75
127	Lee Guetterman	.05
128	Jack Clark	.05
129	Dave Valle	.05
130	Hubie Brooks	.05
131	Ernest Riles	.05
132	Mike Morgan	.05
133	Steve Jeltz	.05
134	Jeff Robinson	.05
135	Ozzie Guillen	.05
136	Chili Davis	.05
137	Mitch Webster	.05
138	Jerry Browne	.05
139	Bo Diaz	.05
140	Robby Thompson	.05
141	Craig Worthington	.05
142	Julio Franco	.05
143	Brian Holman	.05
144	George Brett	.50
145	Tom Glavine	.20
146	Robin Yount	.30
147	Gary Carter	.30
148	Ron Kittle	.05
149	Tony Fernandez	.05
150	Dave Stewart	.05
151	Gary Gaetti	.05
152	Kevin Elster	.05
153	Gerald Perry	.05
154	Jesse Orosco	.05
155	Wally Backman	.05
156	Dennis Martinez	.05
157	Rick Sutcliffe	.05
158	Greg Maddux	.40
159	Andy Hawkins	.05
160	John Kruk	.05
161	Jose Oquendo	.05
162	John Dopson	.05
163	Joe Magrane	.05
164	Billy Ripken	.05
165	Fred Manrique	.05
166	Nolan Ryan	.75
167	Damon Berryhill	.05
168	Dale Murphy	.20
169	Mickey Tettleton	.05
170a	Kirk McCaskill (Born 4/19)	.05
170b	Kirk McCaskill (Born 4/9)	.10
171	Dwight Gooden	.05
172	Jose Lind	.05
173	B.J. Surhoff	.05
174	Ruben Sierra	.05
175	Dan Plesac	.05
176	Dan Pasqua	.05
177	Kelly Downs	.05
178	Matt Nokes	.05
179	Luis Aquino	.05
180	Frank Tanana	.05
181	Tony Pena	.05
182	Dan Gladden	.05
183	Bruce Hurst	.05
184	Roger Clemens	.50
185	Mark McGwire	.60
186	Rob Murphy	.05
187	Jim Deshaies	.05
188	Fred McGriff	.05
189	Rob Dibble	.05
190	Don Mattingly	.45
191	Felix Fermin	.05
192	Roberto Kelly	.05
193	Dennis Cook	.05
194	Darren Daulton	.05
195	Alfredo Griffin	.05
196	Eric Plunk	.05
197	Orel Hershiser	.05
198	Paul O'Neill	.05
199	Randy Bush	.05
200a	Checklist 130-231	.05
200b	Checklist 126-223	.05
201	Ozzie Smith	.40
202	Pete O'Brien	.05
203	Jay Howell	.05
204	Mark Gubicza	.05
205	Ed Whitson	.05
206	George Bell	.05
207	Mike Scott	.05
208	Charlie Leibrandt	.05
209	Mike Heath	.05
210	Dennis Eckersley	.30
211	Mike LaValliere	.05
212	Darnell Coles	.05
213	Lance Parrish	.05
214	Mike Moore	.05
215	*Steve Finley*	.20
216	Tim Raines	.05
217a	Scott Garrelts (Born 10/20)	.05
217b	Scott Garrelts (Born 10/30)	.10
218	Kevin McReynolds	.05
219	Dave Gallagher	.05
220	Tim Wallach	.05
221	Chuck Crim	.05
222	Lonnie Smith	.05
223	Andre Dawson	.20
224	Nelson Santovenia	.05
225	Rafael Palmeiro	.30
226	Devon White	.05
227	Harold Reynolds	.05
228	Ellis Burks	.05
229	Mark Parent	.05
230	Will Clark	.10
231	Jimmy Key	.05
232	John Farrell	.05
233	Eric Davis	.05
234	Johnny Ray	.05
235	Darryl Strawberry	.05
236	Bill Doran	.05
237	Greg Gagne	.05
238	Jim Eisenreich	.05
239	Tommy Gregg	.05
240	Marty Barrett	.05
241	Rafael Ramirez	.05
242	Chris Sabo	.05
243	Dave Henderson	.05
244	Andy Van Slyke	.05
245	Alvaro Espinoza	.05
246	Garry Templeton	.05
247	Gene Harris	.05
248	Kevin Gross	.05
249	Brett Butler	.05
250	Willie Randolph	.05
251	Roger McDowell	.05
252	Rafael Belliard	.05
253	Steve Rosenberg	.05
254	Jack Howell	.05
255	Marvell Wynne	.05
256	Tom Candiotti	.05
257	Todd Benzinger	.05
258	Don Robinson	.05
259	Phil Bradley	.05
260	Cecil Espy	.05
261	Scott Bankhead	.05
262	Frank White	.05
263	Andres Thomas	.05
264	Glenn Braggs	.05
265	David Cone	.05
266	Bobby Thigpen	.05
267	Nelson Liriano	.05
268	Terry Steinbach	.05
269	Kirby Puckett	.40
270	Gregg Jefferies	.05
271	Jeff Blauser	.05
272	Cory Snyder	.05
273	Roy Smith	.05
274	Tom Foley	.05
275	Mitch Williams	.05
276	Paul Kilgus	.05
277	Don Slaught	.05
278	Von Hayes	.05
279	Vince Coleman	.05
280	Mike Boddicker	.05
281	Ken Dayley	.05
282	Mike Devereaux	.05
283	*Kenny Rogers*	.05
284	Jeff Russell	.05
285	*Jerome Walton*	.10
286	Derek Lilliquist	.05
287	Joe Orsulak	.05
288	Dick Schofield	.05
289	Ron Darling	.05
290	Bobby Bonilla	.05
291	Jim Gantner	.05
292	Bobby Witt	.05
293	Greg Brock	.05
294	Ivan Calderon	.05
295	Steve Bedrosian	.05
296	Mike Henneman	.05
297	Tom Gordon	.05
298	Lou Whitaker	.05
299	Terry Pendleton	.05
300a	Checklist 232-333	.05
300b	Checklist 224-321	.05
301	Juan Berenguer	.05
302	Mark Davis	.05
303	Nick Esasky	.05
304	Rickey Henderson	.30
305	Rick Cerone	.05
306	Craig Biggio	.05
307	Duane Ward	.05
308	Tom Browning	.05
309	Walt Terrell	.05
310	Greg Swindell	.05
311	Dave Righetti	.05
312	Mike Maddux	.05
313	Len Dykstra	.05
314	Jose Gonzalez	.05
315	Steve Balboni	.05
316	Mike Scioscia	.05
317	Ron Oester	.05
318	*Gary Wayne*	.05
319	Todd Worrell	.05
320	Doug Jones	.05
321	Jeff Hamilton	.05
322	Danny Tartabull	.05
323	Chris James	.05
324	Mike Flanagan	.05
325	Gerald Young	.05
326	Bob Boone	.05
327	Frank Williams	.05
328	Dave Parker	.05
329	Sid Bream	.05
330	Mike Schooler	.05
331	Bert Blyleven	.10
332	Bob Welch	.05
333	Bob Milacki	.05
334	Tim Burke	.05
335	Jose Uribe	.05
336	Randy Myers	.05
337	Eric King	.05
338	Mark Langston	.05
339	Ted Higuera	.05
340	Oddibe McDowell	.05
341	Lloyd McClendon	.05
342	Pascual Perez	.05
343	Kevin Brown	.05
344	Chuck Finley	.05
345	Erik Hanson	.05
346	Rich Gedman	.05
347	Bip Roberts	.05
348	Matt Williams	.05
349	Tom Henke	.05
350	Brad Komminsk	.05
351	Jeff Reed	.05
352	Brian Downing	.05
353	Frank Viola	.05
354	Terry Puhl	.05
355	Brian Harper	.05
356	Steve Farr	.05
357	Joe Boever	.05
358	Danny Heep	.05
359	Larry Andersen	.05
360	Rolando Roomes	.05
361	Mike Gallego	.05
362	Bob Kipper	.05
363	Clay Parker	.05
364	Mike Pagliarulo	.05
365	Ken Griffey, Jr.	.60
366	Rex Hudler	.05
367	Pat Sheridan	.05
368a	Kirk Gibson (May 25 birthdate)	.05
368b	Kirk Gibson (May 28 birthdate)	.05
369	Jeff Parrett	.05
370	Bob Walk	.05
371	Ken Patterson	.05
372	Bryan Harvey	.05
373	Mike Bielecki	.05
374	*Tom Magrann*	.05
375	Rick Mahler	.05
376	Craig Lefferts	.05
377	Gregg Olson	.05
378	Jamie Moyer	.05
379	Randy Johnson	.30
380	Jeff Montgomery	.05
381	Marty Clary	.05
382	*Bill Spiers*	.05
383	Dave Magadan	.05
384	*Greg Hibbard*	.05
385	Ernie Whitt	.05
386	Rick Honeycutt	.05
387	Dave West	.05
388	Keith Hernandez	.05
389	Jose Alvarez	.05
390	Albert Belle	.15
391	Rick Aguilera	.05
392	Mike Fitzgerald	.05
393	*Dwight Smith*	.05
394	*Steve Wilson*	.05
395	*Bob Geren*	.05
396	Randy Ready	.05
397	Ken Hill	.05
398	Jody Reed	.05
399	Tom Brunansky	.05
400a	Checklist 334-435	.05
400b	Checklist 322-419	.05
401	Rene Gonzales	.05
402	Harold Baines	.05
403	Cecilio Guante	.05
404	Joe Girardi	.05
405a	*Sergio Valdez* (black line crosses S in Sergio)	.10
405b	Sergio Valdez (corrected)	.05
406	Mark Williamson	.05
407	Glenn Hoffman	.05
408	*Jeff Innis*	.05
409	Randy Kramer	.05
410	Charlie O'Brien	.05
411	Charlie Hough	.05
412	Gus Polidor	.05
413	Ron Karkovice	.05
414	Trevor Wilson	.05
415	*Kevin Ritz*	.05
416	Gary Thurman	.05
417	Jeff Robinson	.05
418	Scott Terry	.05
419	Tim Laudner	.05
420	Dennis Rasmussen	.05
421	Luis Rivera	.05
422	Jim Corsi	.05
423	Dennis Lamp	.05
424	Ken Caminiti	.05
425	David Wells	.05
426	Norm Charlton	.05
427	Deion Sanders	.05
428	Dion James	.05
429	Chuck Cary	.05
430	Ken Howell	.05
431	Steve Lake	.05
432	Kal Daniels	.05

433 Lance McCullers .05
434 Lenny Harris .05
435 *Scott Scudder* .05
436 Gene Larkin .05
437 Dan Quisenberry .05
438 *Steve Olin* .05
439 Mickey Hatcher .05
440 Willie Wilson .05
441 Mark Grant .05
442 Mookie Wilson .05
443 Alex Trevino .05
444 Pat Tabler .05
445 Dave Bergman .05
446 Todd Burns .05
447 R.J. Reynolds .05
448 Jay Buhner .05
449 *Lee Stevens* .05
450 Ron Hassey .05
451 Bob Melvin .05
452 Dave Martinez .05
453 *Greg Litton* .05
454 Mark Carreon .05
455 Scott Fletcher .05
456 Otis Nixon .05
457 *Tony Fossas* .05
458 John Russell .05
459 Paul Assenmacher .05
460 Zane Smith .05
461 *Jack Daugherty* .05
462 *Rich Monteleone* .05
463 Greg Briley .05
464 Mike Smithson .05
465 Benito Santiago .05
466 *Jeff Brantley* .05
467 Jose Nunez .05
468 Scott Bailes .05
469 Ken Griffey .05
470 Bob McClure .05
471 Mackey Sasser .05
472 Glenn Wilson .05
473 *Kevin Tapani* .10
474 Bill Buckner .05
475 Ron Gant .05
476 Kevin Romine .05
477 Juan Agosto .05
478 Herm Winningham .05
479 Storm Davis .05
480 Jeff King .05
481 *Kevin Mmahat* .05
482 Carmelo Martinez .05
483 Omar Vizquel .05
484 Jim Dwyer .05
485 Bob Knepper .05
486 Dave Anderson .05
487 Ron Jones .05
488 Jay Bell .05
489 *Sammy Sosa* 3.00
490 *Kent Anderson* .05
491 Domingo Ramos .05
492 Dave Clark .05
493 Tim Birtsas .05
494 Ken Oberkfell .05
495 Larry Sheets .05
496 Jeff Kunkel .05
497 Jim Presley .05
498 Mike Macfarlane .05
499 Pete Smith .05
500a Checklist 436-537 .05
500b Checklist 420-517 .05
501 Gary Sheffield .20
502 *Terry Bross* .05
503 *Jerry Kutzler* .05
504 Lloyd Moseby .05
505 Curt Young .05
506 Al Newman .05
507 Keith Miller .05
508 *Mike Stanton* .20
509 Rich Yett .05
510 *Tim Drummond* .05
511 Joe Hesketh .05
512 *Rick Wrona* .05
513 Luis Salazar .05
514 Hal Morris .05
515 Terry Mullholland .05
516 John Morris .05
517 Carlos Quintana .05
518 Frank DiPino .05
519 Randy Milligan .05
520 Chad Kreuter .05
521 Mike Jeffcoat .05
522 Mike Harkey .05
523a Andy Nezelek (Born 1985) .05
523b Andy Nezelek (Born 1965) .05
524 Dave Schmidt .05
525 Tony Armas .05
526 Barry Lyons .05
527 *Rick Reed* .05
528 Jerry Reuss .05
529 *Dean Palmer* .15
530 *Jeff Peterek* .05
531 *Carlos Martinez* .05
532 Atlee Hammaker .05
533 Mike Brumley .05
534 Terry Leach .05
535 *Doug Strange* .05
536 Jose DeLeon .05
537 Shane Rawley .05
538 Joey Cora .05
539 Eric Hetzel .05
540 Gene Nelson .05
541 Wes Gardner .05
542 Mark Portugal .05
543 Al Leiter .05
544 Jack Armstrong .05
545 Greg Cadaret .05
546 Rod Nichols .05
547 Luis Polonia .05
548 Charlie Hayes .05
549 Dickie Thon .05
550 Tim Crews .05
551 Dave Winfield .30
552 Mike Davis .05
553 Ron Robinson .05
554 Carmen Castillo .05
555 John Costello .05
556 Bud Black .05
557 Rick Dempsey .05
558 Jim Acker .05
559 Eric Show .05
560 Pat Borders .05
561 Danny Darwin .05
562 *Rick Luecken* .05
563 Edwin Nunez .05
564 Felix Jose .05
565 John Cangelosi .05
566 Billy Swift .05
567 Bill Schroeder .05
568 Stan Javier .05
569 Jim Traber .05
570 Wallace Johnson .05
571 Donell Nixon .05
572 Sid Fernandez .05
573 Lance Johnson .05
574 Andy McGaffigan .05
575 Mark Knudson .05
576 *Tommy Greene* .05
577 Mark Grace .10
578 *Larry Walker* 1.00
579 Mike Stanley .05
580 Mike Witt .05
581 Scott Bradley .05
582 Greg Harris .05
583a Kevin Hickey (black stripe over top of "K" vertical stroke) .05
583b Kevin Hickey (black stripe under "K") .05
584 Lee Mazzilli .05
585 Jeff Pico .05
586 *Joe Oliver* .05
587 Willie Fraser .05
588 Carl Yastrzemski Puzzle card .05
589 Kevin Bass .05
590 John Moses .05
591 Tom Pagnozzi .05
592 *Tony Castillo* .05
593 Jerald Clark .05
594 Dan Schatzeder .05
595 Luis Quinones .05
596 Pete Harnisch .05
597 Gary Redus .05
598 Mel Hall .05
599 Rick Schu .05
600a Checklist 538-639 .05
600b Checklist 518-617 .05
601 Mike Kingery .05
602 Terry Kennedy .05
603 Mike Sharperson .05
604 Don Carman .05
605 Jim Gott .05
606 Donn Pall .05
607 Rance Mulliniks .05
608 Curt Wilkerson .05
609 Mike Felder .05
610 Guillermo Hernandez .05
611 Candy Maldonado .05
612 Mark Thurmond .05
613 Rick Leach .05
614 Jerry Reed .05
615 Franklin Stubbs .05
616 Billy Hatcher .05
617 Don August .05
618 Tim Teufel .05
619 Shawn Hillegas .05
620 Manny Lee .05
621 Gary Ward .05
622 *Mark Guthrie* .05
623 Jeff Musselman .05
624 Mark Lemke .05
625 Fernando Valenzuela .05
626 *Paul Sorrento* .05
627 Glenallen Hill .05
628 Les Lancaster .05
629 Vance Law .05
630 Randy Velarde .05
631 Todd Frohwirth .05
632 Willie McGee .05
633 Oil Can Boyd .05
634 Cris Carpenter .05
635 Brian Holton .05
636 Tracy Jones .05
637 Terry Steinbach (AS) .05
638 Brady Anderson .05
639a Jack Morris (black line crosses J of Jack) .10
639b Jack Morris (corrected) .10
640 *Jaime Navarro* .05
641 Darrin Jackson .05
642 *Mike Dyer* .05
643 Mike Schmidt .50
644 Henry Cotto .05
645 John Cerutti .05
646 *Francisco Cabrera* .05
647 Scott Sanderson .05
648 Brian Meyer .05
649 Ray Searage .05
650 Bo Jackson (AS) .15
651 Steve Lyons .05
652 Mike LaCoss .05
653 Ted Power .05
654 Howard Johnson (AS) .05
655 *Mauro Gozzo* .05
656 *Mike Blowers* .05
657 Paul Gibson .05
658 Neal Heaton .05
659a Nolan Ryan 5,000 K's (King of Kings (#665) back) 1.50
659b Nolan Ryan 5,000 K's (correct back) .50
660a Harold Baines (AS) (black line through star on front, Recent Major League Performance on back) .25
660b Harold Baines (AS) (black line through star on front, All-Star Game Performance on back) .25
660c Harold Baines (AS) (black line behind star on front, Recent Major League Performance on back) .25
660d Harold Baines (AS) (black line behind star on front, All-Star Game Performance on back) .10
661 Gary Pettis .05
662 *Clint Zavaras* .05
663 Rick Reuschel (AS) .05
664 Alejandro Pena .05
665a Nolan Ryan (King of Kings) 5,000 K's (#659) back) 1.50
665b Nolan Ryan (King of Kings) (correct back) .75
665c Nolan Ryan (King of Kings) (no number on back) 1.00
666 Ricky Horton .05
667 Curt Schilling .05
668 Bill Landrum .05
669 Todd Stottlemyre .05
670 Tim Leary .05
671 *John Wetteland* .25
672 Calvin Schiraldi .05
673 Ruben Sierra (AS) .05
674 Pedro Guerrero (AS) .05
675 Ken Phelps .05
676 Cal Ripken (AS) .35
677 Denny Walling .05
678 Goose Gossage .05
679 *Gary Mielke* .05
680 Bill Bathe .05
681 Tom Lawless .05
682 *Xavier Hernandez* .05
683 Kirby Puckett (AS) .25
684 Mariano Duncan .05
685 Ramon Martinez .05
686 Tim Jones .05
687 Tom Filer .05
688 Steve Lombardozzi .05
689 *Bernie Williams* 1.00
690 *Chip Hale* .05
691 *Beau Allred* .05
692 Ryne Sandberg (AS) .25
693 *Jeff Huson* .05
694 Curt Ford .05
695 Eric Davis (AS) .05
696 Scott Lusader .05
697 Mark McGwire (AS) .30
698 *Steve Cummings* .05
699 *George Canale* .05
700a Checklist 640-715/ BC1-BC26 .05
700b Checklist 640-716/ BC1-BC26 .05
700c Checklist 618-716 .05
701 Julio Franco (AS) .05
702 *Dave Johnson* .05
703 Dave Stewart (AS) .05
704 *Dave Justice* .50
705 Tony Gwynn (AS) .25
706 Greg Myers .05
707 Will Clark (AS) .05
708 Benito Santiago (AS) .05
709 Larry McWilliams .05
710 Ozzie Smith (AS) .25
711 *John Olerud* .50
712 Wade Boggs (AS) .25
713 *Gary Eave* .05
714 Bob Tewksbury .05
715 Kevin Mitchell (AS) .05
716 A. Bartlett Giamatti .25

Rookies

		NM/M
Complete Set (56):		1.00
Common Player:		.05
1	Sandy Alomar	.15
2	John Olerud	.40
3	Pat Combs	.05
4	Brian Dubois	.05
5	Felix Jose	.05
6	Delino DeShields	.05
7	Mike Stanton	.05
8	Mike Munoz	.05
9	Craig Grebeck	.05
10	Joe Kraemer	.05
11	Jeff Huson	.05
12	Bill Sampen	.05
13	Brian Bohanon	.05
14	Dave Justice	.40
15	Robin Ventura	.20
16	Greg Vaughn	.05
17	Wayne Edwards	.05
18	Shawn Boskie	.05
19	*Carlos Baerga*	.20
20	Mark Gardner	.05
21	Kevin Appier	.10
22	Mike Harkey	.05
23	Tim Layana	.05
24	Glenallen Hill	.05
25	Jerry Kutzler	.05
26	Mike Blowers	.05
27	Scott Ruskin	.05
28	Dana Kiecker	.05
29	Willie Blair	.05
30	Ben McDonald	.05
31	Todd Zeile	.05
32	Scott Coolbaugh	.05
33	Xavier Hernandez	.05
34	Mike Hartley	.05
35	Kevin Tapani	.05
36	Kevin Wickander	.05
37	Carlos Hernandez	.05
38	Brian Traxler	.05
39	Marty Brown	.05
40	Scott Radinsky	.05
41	Julio Machado	.05
42	Steve Avery	.05
43	Mark Lemke	.05
44	Alan Mills	.05

45 Marquis Grissom .15
46 Greg Olson .05
47 Dave Hollins .05
48 Jerald Clark .05
49 Eric Anthony .05
50 Tim Drummond .05
51 John Burkett .05
52 Brent Knackert .05
53 Jeff Shaw .05
54 John Orton .05
55 Terry Shumpert .05
56 Checklist .05

1991 DONRUSS PREVIEWS

NM/M
Complete Set (12): 180.00
Common Player: 3.00
1 Dave Justice 5.00
2 Doug Drabek 3.00
3 Scott Chiamparino 3.00
4 Ken Griffey, Jr. 45.00
5 Bob Welch 3.00
6 Tino Martinez 5.00
7 Nolan Ryan 60.00
8 Dwight Gooden 3.00
9 Ryne Sandberg 25.00
10 Barry Bonds 50.00
11 Jose Canseco 10.00
12 Eddie Murray 15.00

1991 DONRUSS

NM/M
Un. Fact. Set w/Previews (788): 7.50
Un. Fact. Collector's Set (792): 7.50
Complete Set (770): 5.00
Common Player: .05
Willie Stargell Puzzle: .50
Series 1 or 2 Pack (15): .35
Series 1 or 2 Wax Box (36): 7.50
1 Dave Steib (Diamond King) .05
2 Craig Biggio (DK) .05
3 Cecil Fielder (DK) .05
4 Barry Bonds (DK) .75
5 Barry Larkin (DK) .05
6 Dave Parker (DK) .05
7 Len Dykstra (DK) .05
8 Bobby Thigpen (DK) .05
9 Roger Clemens (DK) .45
10 Ron Gant (DK) .05
11 Delino DeShields (DK) .05
12 Roberto Alomar (DK) .20
13 Sandy Alomar (DK) .05
14 Ryne Sandberg (DK) .40
15 Ramon Martinez (DK) .05
16 Edgar Martinez (DK) .05
17 Dave Magadan (DK) .05
18 Matt Williams (DK) .05
19 Rafael Palmeiro (DK) .30
20 Bob Welch (DK) .05
21 Dave Righetti (DK) .05
22 Brian Harper (DK) .05
23 Gregg Olson (DK) .05
24 Kurt Stillwell (DK) .05
25 Pedro Guerrero (DK) .05
26 Chuck Finley (DK) .05
27 Diamond King Checklist .05
28 Tino Martinez (Rated Rookie) .10
29 Mark Lewis (RR) .05
30 *Bernard Gilkey* (RR) .10
31 Hensley Meulens (RR) .05
32 *Derek Bell* (RR) .30
33 Jose Offerman (RR) .05
34 Terry Bross (RR) .05
35 *Leo Gomez* (RR) .10
36 Derrick May (RR) .05
37 *Kevin Morton* (RR) .05
38 Moises Alou (RR) .10
39 *Julio Valera* (RR) .05
40 Milt Cuyler (RR) .05
41 *Phil Plantier* (RR) .10
42 *Scott Chiamparino* (RR) .05
43 *Ray Lankford* (RR) .20
44 *Mickey Morandini* (RR) .10
45 Dave Hansen (RR) .05
46 *Kevin Belcher* (RR) .05
47 Darrin Fletcher (RR) .05
48 Steve Sax (All Star) .05
49 Ken Griffey, Jr. (AS) .20
50a Jose Canseco (AS) (A's in stat line on back) .10
50b Jose Canseco (AS) (AL in stat line on back) .25
51 Sandy Alomar (AS) .05
52 Cal Ripken, Jr. (AS) .30
53 Rickey Henderson (AS) .15
54 Bob Welch (AS) .05
55 Wade Boggs (AS) .20
56 Mark McGwire (AS) .25
57a Jack McDowell (Career Games 30) .05
57b Jack McDowell (Career Games 63) .25
58 Jose Lind .05
59 Alex Fernandez .05
60 Pat Combs .05
61 *Mike Walker* .05
62 Juan Samuel .05
63 Mike Blowers .05
64 Mark Guthrie .05
65 Mark Salas .05
66 Tim Jones .05
67 Tim Leary .05
68 Andres Galarraga .05
69 Bob Milacki .05
70 Tim Belcher .05
71 Todd Zeile .05
72 Jerome Walton .05
73 Kevin Seitzer .05
74 Jerald Clark .05
75 John Smoltz .05
76 Mike Henneman .05
77 Ken Griffey, Jr. .50
78 Jim Abbott .05
79 Gregg Jefferies .05
80 Kevin Reimer .05
81 Roger Clemens .45
82 Mike Fitzgerald .05
83 Bruce Hurst .05
84 Eric Davis .05
85 Paul Molitor .30
86 Will Clark .10
87 Mike Bielecki .05
88 Bret Saberhagen .05
89 Nolan Ryan .75
90 Bobby Thigpen .05
91 Dickie Thon .05
92 Duane Ward .05
93 Luis Polonia .05
94 Terry Kennedy .05
95 Kent Hrbek .05
96 Danny Jackson .05
97 Sid Fernandez .05
98 Jimmy Key .05
99 Franklin Stubbs .05
100 Checklist 28-103 .05
101 R.J. Reynolds .05
102 Dave Stewart .05
103 Dan Pasqua .05
104 Dan Plesac .05
105 Mark McGwire .60
106 John Farrell .05
107 Don Mattingly .45
108 Carlton Fisk .30
109 Ken Oberkfell .05
110 Darrel Akerfelds .05
111 Gregg Olson .05
112 Mike Scioscia .05
113 Bryn Smith .05
114 Bob Geren .05
115 Tom Candiotti .05
116 Kevin Tapani .05
117 Jeff Treadway .05
118 Alan Trammell .05
119 Pete O'Brien .05
120 Joel Skinner .05
121 Mike LaValliere .05
122 Dwight Evans .05
123 Jody Reed .05
124 Lee Guetterman .05
125 Tim Burke .05
126 Dave Johnson .05
127 Fernando Valenzuela .05
128 Jose DeLeon .05
129 Andre Dawson .20
130 Gerald Perry .05
131 Greg Harris .05
132 Tom Glavine .25
133 Lance McCullers .05
134 Randy Johnson .30
135 Lance Parrish .05
136 Mackey Sasser .05
137 Geno Petralli .05
138 Dennis Lamp .05
139 Dennis Martinez .05
140 Mike Pagliarulo .05
141 Hal Morris .05
142 Dave Parker .05
143 Brett Butler .05
144 Paul Assenmacher .05
145 Mark Gubicza .05
146 Charlie Hough .05
147 Sammy Sosa .50
148 Randy Ready .05
149 Kelly Gruber .05
150 Devon White .05
151 Gary Carter .30
152 Gene Larkin .05
153 Chris Sabo .05
154 David Cone .05
155 Todd Stottlemyre .05
156 Glenn Wilson .05
157 Bob Walk .05
158 Mike Gallego .05
159 Greg Hibbard .05
160 Chris Bosio .05
161 Mike Moore .05
162 Jerry Browne .05
163 Steve Sax .05
164 Melido Perez .05
165 Danny Darwin .05
166 Roger McDowell .05
167 Bill Ripken .05
168 Mike Sharperson .05
169 Lee Smith .05
170 Matt Nokes .05
171 Jesse Orosco .05
172 Rick Aguilera .05
173 Jim Presley .05
174 Lou Whitaker .05
175 Harold Reynolds .05
176 Brook Jacoby .05
177 Wally Backman .05
178 Wade Boggs .40
179 Chuck Cary .05
180 Tom Foley .05
181 Pete Harnisch .05
182 Mike Morgan .05
183 Bob Tewksbury .05
184 Joe Girardi .05
185 Storm Davis .05
186 Ed Whitson .05
187 Steve Avery .05
188 Lloyd Moseby .05
189 Scott Bankhead .05
190 Mark Langston .05
191 Kevin McReynolds .05
192 Julio Franco .05
193 John Dopson .05
194 Oil Can Boyd .05
195 Bip Roberts .05
196 Billy Hatcher .05
197 Edgar Diaz .05
198 Greg Litton .05
199 Mark Grace .10
200 Checklist 104-179 .05
201 George Brett .45
202 Jeff Russell .05
203 Ivan Calderon .05
204 Ken Howell .05
205 Tom Henke .05
206 Bryan Harvey .05
207 Steve Bedrosian .05
208 Al Newman .05
209 Randy Myers .05
210 Daryl Boston .05
211 Manny Lee .05
212 Dave Smith .05
213 Don Slaught .05
214 Walt Weiss .05
215 Donn Pall .05
216 Jamie Navarro .05
217 Willie Randolph .05
218 Rudy Seanez .05
219 *Jim Leyritz* .15
220 Ron Karkovice .05
221 Ken Caminiti .05
222a Von Hayes (Traded players' first names included in How Acquired on back) .05
222b Von Hayes (No first names) .05
223 Cal Ripken, Jr. .75
224 Lenny Harris .05
225 Milt Thompson .05
226 Alvaro Espinoza .05
227 Chris James .05
228 Dan Gladden .05
229 Jeff Blauser .05
230 Mike Heath .05
231 Omar Vizquel .05
232 Doug Jones .05
233 Jeff King .05
234 Luis Rivera .05
235 Ellis Burks .05
236 Greg Cadaret .05
237 Dave Martinez .05
238 Mark Williamson .05
239 Stan Javier .05
240 Ozzie Smith .40
241 *Shawn Boskie* .05
242 Tom Gordon .05
243 Tony Gwynn .40
244 Tommy Gregg .05
245 Jeff Robinson .05
246 Keith Comstock .05
247 Jack Howell .05
248 Keith Miller .05
249 Bobby Witt .05
250 Rob Murphy .05
251 Spike Owen .05
252 Garry Templeton .05
253 Glenn Braggs .05
254 Ron Robinson .05
255 Kevin Mitchell .05
256 Les Lancaster .05
257 *Mel Stottlemyre* .10
258 Kenny Rogers .05
259 Lance Johnson .05
260 John Kruk .05
261 Fred McGriff .05
262 Dick Schofield .05
263 Trevor Wilson .05
264 David West .05
265 Scott Scudder .05
266 Dwight Gooden .05
267 *Willie Blair* .05
268 Mark Portugal .05
269 Doug Drabek .05
270 Dennis Eckersley .30
271 Eric King .05
272 Robin Yount .30
273 Carney Lansford .05
274 Carlos Baerga .05
275 Dave Righetti .05
276 Scott Fletcher .05
277 Eric Yelding .05
278 Charlie Hayes .05
279 Jeff Ballard .05
280 Orel Hershiser .05
281 Jose Oquendo .05
282 Mike Witt .05
283 Mitch Webster .05
284 Greg Gagne .05
285 *Greg Olson* .05
286 Tony Phillips .05
287 Scott Bradley .05
288 Cory Snyder .05
289 Jay Bell .05
290 Kevin Romine .05
291 Jeff Robinson .05
292 Steve Frey .05
293 Craig Worthington .05
294 Tim Crews .05
295 Joe Magrane .05
296 *Hector Villanueva* .05
297 *Terry Shumpert* .05
298 Joe Carter .05
299 Kent Mercker .05
300 Checklist 180-255 .05
301 Chet Lemon .05
302 Mike Schooler .05
303 Dante Bichette .05
304 Kevin Elster .05
305 Jeff Huson .05
306 Greg Harris .05
307 Marquis Grissom .05
308 Calvin Schiraldi .05
309 Mariano Duncan .05
310 Bill Spiers .05
311 Scott Garrelts .05
312 Mitch Williams .05
313 Mike Macfarlane .05
314 Kevin Brown .05
315 Robin Ventura .05
316 Darren Daulton .05
317 Pat Borders .05
318 Mark Eichhorn .05
319 Jeff Brantley .05
320 Shane Mack .05
321 Rob Dibble .05

322 John Franco .05
323 Junior Felix .05
324 Casey Candaele .05
325 Bobby Bonilla .05
326 Dave Henderson .05
327 Wayne Edwards .05
328 Mark Knudson .05
329 Terry Steinbach .05
330 *Colby Ward* .05
331 *Oscar Azocar* .05
332 *Scott Radinsky* .10
333 Eric Anthony .05
334 Steve Lake .05
335 Bob Melvin .05
336 Kal Daniels .05
337 Tom Pagnozzi .05
338 *Alan Mills* .05
339 Steve Olin .05
340 Juan Berenguer .05
341 Francisco Cabrera .05
342 Dave Bergman .05
343 Henry Cotto .05
344 Sergio Valdez .05
345 Bob Patterson .05
346 John Marzano .05
347 *Dana Kiecker* .05
348 Dion James .05
349 Hubie Brooks .05
350 Bill Landrum .05
351 *Bill Sampen* .05
352 Greg Briley .05
353 Paul Gibson .05
354 Dave Eiland .05
355 Steve Finley .05
356 Bob Boone .05
357 Steve Buechele .05
358 Chris Hoiles .05
359 Larry Walker .05
360 Frank DiPino .05
361 Mark Grant .05
362 Dave Magadan .05
363 Robby Thompson .05
364 Lonnie Smith .05
365 Steve Farr .05
366 Dave Valle .05
367 *Tim Naehring* .05
368 Jim Acker .05
369 Jeff Reardon .05
370 Tim Teufel .05
371 Juan Gonzalez .35
372 Luis Salazar .05
373 Rick Honeycutt .05
374 Greg Maddux .40
375 Jose Uribe .05
376 Donnie Hill .05
377 Don Carman .05
378 *Craig Grebeck* .05
379 Willie Fraser .05
380 Glenallen Hill .05
381 Joe Oliver .05
382 Randy Bush .05
383 Alex Cole .05
384 Norm Charlton .05
385 Gene Nelson .05
386a Checklist 256-331 (blue borders) .05
386b Checklist 256-331 (green borders) .05
387 Rickey Henderson (MVP) .15
388 Lance Parrish (MVP) .05
389 Fred McGriff (MVP) .05
390 Dave Parker (MVP) .05
391 Candy Maldonado (MVP) .05
392 Ken Griffey, Jr. (MVP) .30
393 Gregg Olson (MVP) .05
394 Rafael Palmeiro (MVP) .15
395 Roger Clemens (MVP) .20
396 George Brett (MVP) .20
397 Cecil Fielder (MVP) .05
398 Brian Harper (MVP) .05
399 Bobby Thigpen (MVP) .05
400 Roberto Kelly (MVP) .05
401 Danny Darwin (MVP) .05
402 Dave Justice (MVP) .05
403 Lee Smith (MVP) .05
404 Ryne Sandberg (MVP) .20
405 Eddie Murray (MVP) .15
406 Tim Wallach (MVP) .05
407 Kevin Mitchell (MVP) .05
408 Darryl Strawberry (MVP) .05
409 Joe Carter (MVP) .05
410 Len Dykstra (MVP) .05
411 Doug Drabek (MVP) .05
412 Chris Sabo (MVP) .05
413 *Paul Marak* (RR) .05
414 Tim McIntosh (RR) .05
415 *Brian Barnes* (RR) .05
416 *Eric Gunderson* (RR) .05
417 *Mike Gardiner* (RR) .05
418 Steve Carter (RR) .05
419 *Gerald Alexander* (RR) .05
420 *Rich Garces* (RR) .05
421 *Chuck Knoblauch* (RR) .45
422 *Scott Aldred* (RR) .05
423 *Wes Chamberlain* (RR) .05
424 *Lance Dickson* (RR) .05
425 *Greg Colbrunn* (RR) .10
426 *Rich Delucia* (RR) .05
427 *Jeff Conine* (RR) .40
428 *Steve Decker* (RR) .05
429 *Turner Ward* (RR) .05
430 Mo Vaughn (RR) .20
431 *Steve Chitren* (RR) .05
432 Mike Benjamin (RR) .05
433 Ryne Sandberg (AS) .20
434 Len Dykstra (AS) .05
435 Andre Dawson (AS) .15
436 Mike Scioscia (AS) .05
437 Ozzie Smith (AS) .20
438 Kevin Mitchell (AS) .05
439 Jack Armstrong (AS) .05
440 Chris Sabo (AS) .05
441 Will Clark (AS) .10
442 Mel Hall .05
443 Mark Gardner .05
444 Mike Devereaux .05
445 Kirk Gibson .05
446 Terry Pendleton .05
447 Mike Harkey .05
448 Jim Eisenreich .05
449 Benito Santiago .05
450 Oddibe McDowell .05
451 Cecil Fielder .05
452 Ken Griffey, Sr. .05
453 Bert Blyleven .10
454 Howard Johnson .05
455 Monty Farris .05
456 Tony Pena .05
457 Tim Raines .05
458 Dennis Rasmussen .05
459 Luis Quinones .05
460 B.J. Surhoff .05
461 Ernest Riles .05
462 Rick Sutcliffe .05
463 Danny Tartabull .05
464 Pete Incaviglia .05
465 Carlos Martinez .05
466 Ricky Jordan .05
467 John Cerutti .05
468 Dave Winfield .30
469 Francisco Oliveras .05
470 Roy Smith .05
471 Barry Larkin .05
472 Ron Darling .05
473 David Wells .05
474 Glenn Davis .05
475 Neal Heaton .05
476 Ron Hassey .05
477 Frank Thomas .25
478 Greg Vaughn .05
479 Todd Burns .05
480 Candy Maldonado .05
481 Dave LaPoint .05
482 Alvin Davis .05
483 Mike Scott .05
484 Dale Murphy .20
485 Ben McDonald .05
486 Jay Howell .05
487 Vince Coleman .05
488 Alfredo Griffin .05
489 Sandy Alomar .05
490 Kirby Puckett .40
491 Andres Thomas .05
492 Jack Morris .05
493 Matt Young .05
494 Greg Myers .05
495 Barry Bonds .75
496 Scott Cooper .05
497 Dan Schatzeder .05
498 Jesse Barfield .05
499 Jerry Goff .05
500 Checklist 332-408 .05
501 *Anthony Telford* .05
502 Eddie Murray .30
503 *Omar Olivares* .05
504 Ryne Sandberg .40
505 Jeff Montgomery .05
506 Mark Parent .05
507 Ron Gant .05
508 Frank Tanana .05
509 Jay Buhner .05
510 Max Venable .05
511 Wally Whitehurst .05
512 Gary Pettis .05
513 Tom Brunansky .05
514 Tim Wallach .05
515 Craig Lefferts .05
516 *Tim Layana* .05
517 Darryl Hamilton .05
518 Rick Reuschel .05
519 Steve Wilson .05
520 Kurt Stillwell .05
521 Rafael Palmeiro .30
522 Ken Patterson .05
523 Len Dykstra .05
524 Tony Fernandez .05
525 Kent Anderson .05
526 *Mark Leonard* .05
527 Allan Anderson .05
528 Tom Browning .05
529 Frank Viola .05
530 John Olerud .05
531 Juan Agosto .05
532 Zane Smith .05
533 Scott Sanderson .05
534 Barry Jones .05
535 Mike Felder .05
536 Jose Canseco .20
537 Felix Fermin .05
538 Roberto Kelly .05
539 Brian Holman .05
540 Mark Davidson .05
541 Terry Mulholland .05
542 Randy Milligan .05
543 Jose Gonzalez .05
544 *Craig Wilson* .05
545 Mike Hartley .05
546 Greg Swindell .05
547 Gary Gaetti .05
548 Dave Justice .05
549 Steve Searcy .05
550 Erik Hanson .05
551 Dave Stieb .05
552 Andy Van Slyke .05
553 Mike Greenwell .05
554 Kevin Maas .05
555 Delino Deshields .05
556 Curt Schilling .20
557 Ramon Martinez .05
558 Pedro Guerrero .05
559 Dwight Smith .05
560 Mark Davis .05
561 Shawn Abner .05
562 Charlie Leibrandt .05
563 John Shelby .05
564 Bill Swift .05
565 Mike Fetters .05
566 Alejandro Pena .05
567 Ruben Sierra .05
568 Carlos Quintana .05
569 Kevin Gross .05
570 Derek Lilliquist .05
571 Jack Armstrong .05
572 Greg Brock .05
573 Mike Kingery .05
574 Greg Smith .05
575 *Brian McRae* .10
576 Jack Daugherty .05
577 Ozzie Guillen .05
578 Joe Boever .05
579 Luis Sojo .05
580 Chili Davis .05
581 Don Robinson .05
582 Brian Harper .05
583 Paul O'Neill .05
584 Bob Ojeda .05
585 Mookie Wilson .05
586 Rafael Ramirez .05
587 Gary Redus .05
588 Jamie Quirk .05
589 Shawn Hilligas .05
590 *Tom Edens* .05
591 Joe Klink .05
592 Charles Nagy .05
593 Eric Plunk .05
594 Tracy Jones .05
595 Craig Biggio .05
596 Jose DeJesus .05
597 Mickey Tettleton .05
598 Chris Gwynn .05
599 Rex Hudler .05
600 Checklist 409-506 .05
601 Jim Gott .05
602 Jeff Manto .05
603 Nelson Liriano .05
604 Mark Lemke .05
605 Clay Parker .05
606 Edgar Martinez .05
607 *Mark Whiten* .10
608 Ted Power .05
609 Tom Bolton .05
610 Tom Herr .05
611 Andy Hawkins .05
612 Scott Ruskin .05
613 Ron Kittle .05
614 John Wetteland .05
615 *Mike Perez* .05
616 Dave Clark .05
617 Brent Mayne .05
618 Jack Clark .05
619 Marvin Freeman .05
620 Edwin Nunez .05
621 Russ Swan .05
622 Johnny Ray .05
623 Charlie O'Brien .05
624 *Joe Bitker* .05
625 Mike Marshall .05
626 Otis Nixon .05
627 Andy Benes .05
628 Ron Oester .05
629 Ted Higuera .05
630 Kevin Bass .05
631 Damon Berryhill .05
632 Bo Jackson .10
633 Brad Arnsberg .05
634 Jerry Willard .05
635 Tommy Greene .05
636 *Bob MacDonald* .05
637 Kirk McCaskill .05
638 John Burkett .05
639 *Paul Abbott* .05
640 Todd Benzinger .05
641 Todd Hundley .05
642 George Bell .05
643 *Javier Ortiz* .05
644 Sid Bream .05
645 Bob Welch .05
646 Phil Bradley .05
647 Bill Krueger .05
648 Rickey Henderson .30
649 Kevin Wickander .05
650 Steve Balboni .05
651 Gene Harris .05
652 Jim Deshaies .05
653 Jason Grimsley .05
654 Joe Orsulak .05
655 *Jimmy Poole* .05
656 Felix Jose .05
657 Dennis Cook .05
658 Tom Brookens .05
659 Junior Ortiz .05
660 Jeff Parrett .05
661 Jerry Don Gleaton .05
662 Brent Knackert .05
663 Rance Mulliniks .05
664 John Smiley .05
665 Larry Andersen .05
666 Willie McGee .05
667 *Chris Nabholz* .05
668 Brady Anderson .05
669 *Darren Holmes* .10
670 Ken Hill .05
671 Gary Varsho .05
672 Bill Pecota .05
673 Fred Lynn .05
674 Kevin D. Brown .05
675 Dan Petry .05
676 Mike Jackson .05
677 Wally Joyner .05
678 Danny Jackson .05
679 *Bill Haselman* .05
680 Mike Boddicker .05
681 *Mel Rojas* .05
682 Roberto Alomar .20
683 Dave Justice (R.O.Y.) .05
684 Chuck Crim .05
685a Matt Williams (Last line of Career Highlights ends, "most DP's in") .10
685b Matt Williams (last line ends "8/24-27/87.") .25
686 Shawon Dunston .05
687 *Jeff Schulz* .05
688 *John Barfield* .05
689 Gerald Young .05
690 *Luis Gonzalez* .75
691 Frank Wills .05
692 Chuck Finley .05
693 Sandy Alomar (R.O.Y.) .05
694 Tim Drummond .05
695 Herm Winningham .05
696 Darryl Strawberry .05
697 Al Leiter .05
698 *Karl Rhodes* .05
699 Stan Belinda .05
700 Checklist 507-604 .05
701 Lance Blankenship .05
702 Willie Stargell (Puzzle Card) .05
703 Jim Gantner .05
704 *Reggie Harris* .05
705 Rob Ducey .05
706 Tim Hulett .05
707 Atlee Hammaker .05
708 Xavier Hernandez .05
709 Chuck McElroy .05

710 John Mitchell .05
711 Carlos Hernandez .05
712 Geronimo Pena .05
713 *Jim Neidlinger* .05
714 John Orton .05
715 Terry Leach .05
716 Mike Stanton .05
717 Walt Terrell .05
718 Luis Aquino .05
719 Bud Black .05
720 Bob Kipper .05
721 *Jeff Gray* .05
722 Jose Rijo .05
723 Curt Young .05
724 Jose Vizcaino .05
725 *Randy Tomlin* .05
726 Junior Noboa .05
727 Bob Welch (Award Winner) .05
728 Gary Ward .05
729 Rob Deer .05
730 *David Segui* .05
731 Mark Carreon .05
732 Vicente Palacios .05
733 Sam Horn .05
734 *Howard Farmer* .05
735 Ken Dayley .05
736 Kelly Mann .05
737 *Joe Grahe* .05
738 Kelly Downs .05
739 *Jimmy Kremers* .05
740 Kevin Appier .05
741 Jeff Reed .05
742 Jose Rijo (World Series) .05
743 *Dave Rohde* .05
744 Len Dykstra, Dale Murphy Dr. Dirt/Mr. Clean .10
745 Paul Sorrento .05
746 Thomas Howard .05
747 *Matt Stark* .05
748 Harold Baines .05
749 Doug Dascenzo .05
750 Doug Drabek (Award Winner) .05
751 Gary Sheffield .20
752 *Terry Lee* .05
753 *Jim Vatcher* .05
754 Lee Stevens .05
755 Randy Veres .05
756 Bill Doran .05
757 Gary Wayne .05
758 *Pedro Munoz* .05
759 Chris Hammond .05
760 Checklist 605-702 .05
761 Rickey Henderson (MVP) .15
762 Barry Bonds (MVP) .40
763 Billy Hatcher (World Series) .05
764 Julio Machado .05
765 Jose Mesa .05
766 Willie Randolph (World Series) .05
767 *Scott Erickson* .10
768 Travis Fryman .05
769 *Rich Rodriguez* .05
770 Checklist 703-770; BC1-BC22 .05

Elite

	NM/M
Complete Set (10):	250.00
Common Player:	15.00
1 Barry Bonds	60.00
2 George Brett	40.00
3 Jose Canseco	25.00
4 Andre Dawson	15.00
5 Doug Drabek	7.50
6 Cecil Fielder	7.50
7 Rickey Henderson	25.00
8 Matt Williams	7.50
--- Nolan Ryan (Legend)	65.00
--- Ryne Sandberg (Signature)	100.00

Rookies

	NM/M
Complete Set (56):	3.00
Common Player:	.05
1 Pat Kelly	.05
2 Rich DeLucia	.05
3 Wes Chamberlain	.05
4 Scott Leius	.05
5 Darryl Kile	.05
6 Milt Cuyler	.05
7 Todd Van Poppel	.05
8 Ray Lankford	.05
9 Brian Hunter	.05
10 Tony Perezchica	.05
11 Ced Landrum	.05
12 Dave Burba	.05
13 Ramon Garcia	.05
14 Ed Sprague	.05
15 Warren Newson	.05
16 Paul Faries	.05
17 Luis Gonzalez	.25
18 Charles Nagy	.05
19 Chris Hammond	.05
20 Frank Castillo	.05
21 Pedro Munoz	.05
22 Orlando Merced	.05
23 Jose Melendez	.05
24 Kirk Dressendorfer	.05
25 Heathcliff Slocumb	.05
26 Doug Simons	.05
27 Mike Timlin	.05
28 Jeff Fassero	.05
29 Mark Leiter	.05
30 *Jeff Bagwell*	2.00
31 Brian McRae	.05
32 Mark Whiten	.05
33 *Ivan Rodriguez*	1.50
34 Wade Taylor	.05
35 Darren Lewis	.05
36 Mo Vaughn	.25
37 Mike Remlinger	.05
38 Rick Wilkins	.05
39 Chuck Knoblauch	.05
40 Kevin Morton	.05
41 Carlos Rodriguez	.05
42 Mark Lewis	.05
43 Brent Mayne	.05
44 Chris Haney	.05
45 Denis Boucher	.05
46 Mike Gardiner	.05
47 Jeff Johnson	.05
48 Dean Palmer	.05
49 Chuck McElroy	.05
50 Chris Jones	.05
51 Scott Kamieniecki	.05
52 Al Osuna	.05
53 Rusty Meacham	.05
54 Chito Martinez	.05
55 Reggie Jefferson	.05
56 Checklist	.05

1992 DONRUSS PREVIEWS

	NM/M
Complete Set (12):	50.00
Common Player:	1.00
1 Wade Boggs	5.00
2 Barry Bonds	15.00
3 Will Clark	1.50
4 Andre Dawson	1.50
5 Dennis Eckersley	3.00
6 Robin Ventura	1.00
7 Ken Griffey, Jr.	8.00
8 Kelly Gruber	1.00
9 Ryan Klesko (Rated Rookie)	1.00
10 Cal Ripken, Jr.	15.00
11 Nolan Ryan (Highlight)	15.00
12 Todd Van Poppel	1.00

1992 DONRUSS

	NM/M
Unopened Retail Set (788):	8.00
Unopened Hobby Set (784):	7.00
Unopened "Coca-Cola" Set (784):	24.00
Complete Set (784):	6.00
Common Player:	.05
Rod Carew Puzzle:	.50
Series 1 or 2 Pack (15):	.35
Series 1 or 2 Wax Box (36):	7.50
Blister Rack (92):	1.00
1 *Mark Wohlers* (Rated Rookie)	.05
2 Wil Cordero (Rated Rookie)	.05
3 Kyle Abbott (Rated Rookie)	.05
4 *Dave Nilsson* (Rated Rookie)	.05
5 Kenny Lofton (Rated Rookie)	.15
6 *Luis Mercedes* (Rated Rookie)	.05
7 *Roger Salkeld* (Rated Rookie)	.05
8 Eddie Zosky (Rated Rookie)	.05
9 *Todd Van Poppel* (Rated Rookie)	.10
10 *Frank Seminara* (Rated Rookie)	.05
11 *Andy Ashby* (Rated Rookie)	.10
12 Reggie Jefferson (Rated Rookie)	.05
13 Ryan Klesko (Rated Rookie)	.05
14 *Carlos Garcia* (Rated Rookie)	.10
15 *John Ramos* (Rated Rookie)	.05
16 Eric Karros (Rated Rookie)	.05
17 *Pat Lennon* (Rated Rookie)	.05
18 *Eddie Taubensee* (Rated Rookie)	.05
19 *Roberto Hernandez* (Rated Rookie)	.05
20 D.J. Dozier (Rated Rookie)	.05
21 Dave Henderson (All-Star)	.05
22 Cal Ripken, Jr. (All-Star)	.40
23 Wade Boggs (All-Star)	.20
24 Ken Griffey, Jr. (All-Star)	.25
25 Jack Morris (All-Star)	.05
26 Danny Tartabull (All-Star)	.05
27 Cecil Fielder (All-Star)	.05
28 Roberto Alomar (All-Star)	.10
29 Sandy Alomar (All-Star)	.05
30 Rickey Henderson (All-Star)	.15
31 Ken Hill	.05
32 John Habyan	.05
33 Otis Nixon (Highlight)	.05
34 Tim Wallach	.05
35 Cal Ripken, Jr.	.75
36 Gary Carter	.30
37 Juan Agosto	.05
38 Doug Dascenzo	.05
39 Kirk Gibson	.05
40 Benito Santiago	.05
41 Otis Nixon	.05
42 Andy Allanson	.05
43 Brian Holman	.05
44 Dick Schofield	.05
45 Dave Magadan	.05
46 Rafael Palmeiro	.30
47 Jody Reed	.05
48 Ivan Calderon	.05
49 Greg Harris	.05
50 Chris Sabo	.05
51 Paul Molitor	.30
52 Robby Thompson	.05
53 Dave Smith	.05
54 Mark Davis	.05
55 Kevin Brown	.05
56 Donn Pall	.05
57 Len Dykstra	.05
58 Roberto Alomar	.15
59 Jeff Robinson	.05
60 Willie McGee	.05
61 Jay Buhner	.05
62 Mike Pagliarulo	.05
63 Paul O'Neill	.05
64 Hubie Brooks	.05
65 Kelly Gruber	.05
66 Ken Caminiti	.05
67 Gary Redus	.05
68 Harold Baines	.05
69 Charlie Hough	.05
70 B.J. Surhoff	.05
71 Walt Weiss	.05
72 Shawn Hillegas	.05
73 Roberto Kelly	.05
74 Jeff Ballard	.05
75 Craig Biggio	.05
76 Pat Combs	.05
77 Jeff Robinson	.05
78 Tim Belcher	.05
79 Cris Carpenter	.05
80 Checklist 1-79	.05
81 Steve Avery	.05
82 Chris James	.05
83 Brian Harper	.05
84 Charlie Leibrandt	.05
85 Mickey Tettleton	.05
86 Pete O'Brien	.05
87 Danny Darwin	.05
88 Bob Walk	.05
89 Jeff Reardon	.05
90 Bobby Rose	.05
91 Danny Jackson	.05
92 John Morris	.05
93 Bud Black	.05
94 Tommy Greene (Highlight)	.05
95 Rick Aguilera	.05
96 Gary Gaetti	.05
97 David Cone	.05
98 John Olerud	.05
99 Joel Skinner	.05
100 Jay Bell	.05
101 Bob Milacki	.05
102 Norm Charlton	.05
103 Chuck Crim	.05
104 Terry Steinbach	.05
105 Juan Samuel	.05
106 Steve Howe	.05
107 Rafael Belliard	.05
108 Joey Cora	.05
109 Tommy Greene	.05
110 Gregg Olson	.05
111 Frank Tanana	.05
112 Lee Smith	.05
113 Greg Harris	.05
114 Dwayne Henry	.05
115 Chili Davis	.05
116 Kent Mercker	.05
117 Brian Barnes	.05
118 Rich DeLucia	.05
119 Andre Dawson	.15
120 Carlos Baerga	.05
121 Mike LaValliere	.05
122 Jeff Gray	.05
123 Bruce Hurst	.05
124 Alvin Davis	.05
125 John Candelaria	.05
126 Matt Nokes	.05
127 George Bell	.05
128 Bret Saberhagen	.05
129 Jeff Russell	.05
130 Jim Abbott	.05
131 Bill Gullickson	.05
132 Todd Zeile	.05
133 Dave Winfield	.30

No.	Player	Value
134	Wally Whitehurst	.05
135	Matt Williams	.05
136	Tom Browning	.05
137	Marquis Grissom	.05
138	Erik Hanson	.05
139	Rob Dibble	.05
140	Don August	.05
141	Tom Henke	.05
142	Dan Pasqua	.05
143	George Brett	.40
144	Jerald Clark	.05
145	Robin Ventura	.05
146	Dale Murphy	.15
147	Dennis Eckersley	.30
148	Eric Yelding	.05
149	Mario Diaz	.05
150	Casey Candaele	.05
151	Steve Olin	.05
152	Luis Salazar	.05
153	Kevin Maas	.05
154	Nolan Ryan (Highlight)	.40
155	Barry Jones	.05
156	Chris Hoiles	.05
157	Bobby Ojeda	.05
158	Pedro Guerrero	.05
159	Paul Assenmacher	.05
160	Checklist 80-157	.05
161	Mike Macfarlane	.05
162	Craig Lefferts	.05
163	*Brian Hunter*	.05
164	Alan Trammell	.05
165	Ken Griffey, Jr.	.50
166	Lance Parrish	.05
167	Brian Downing	.05
168	John Barfield	.05
169	Jack Clark	.05
170	Chris Nabholz	.05
171	Tim Teufel	.05
172	Chris Hammond	.05
173	Robin Yount	.30
174	Dave Righetti	.05
175	Joe Girardi	.05
176	Mike Boddicker	.05
177	Dean Palmer	.05
178	Greg Hibbard	.05
179	Randy Ready	.05
180	Devon White	.05
181	Mark Eichhorn	.05
182	Mike Felder	.05
183	Joe Klink	.05
184	Steve Bedrosian	.05
185	Barry Larkin	.05
186	John Franco	.05
187	*Ed Sprague*	.05
188	Mark Portugal	.05
189	Jose Lind	.05
190	Bob Welch	.05
191	Alex Fernandez	.05
192	Gary Sheffield	.15
193	Rickey Henderson	.30
194	Rod Nichols	.05
195	*Scott Kamieniecki*	.05
196	Mike Flanagan	.05
197	Steve Finley	.05
198	Darren Daulton	.05
199	Leo Gomez	.05
200	Mike Morgan	.05
201	Bob Tewksbury	.05
202	Sid Bream	.05
203	Sandy Alomar	.05
204	Greg Gagne	.05
205	Juan Berenguer	.05
206	Cecil Fielder	.05
207	Randy Johnson	.30
208	Tony Pena	.05
209	Doug Drabek	.05
210	Wade Boggs	.35
211	Bryan Harvey	.05
212	Jose Vizcaino	.05
213	*Alonzo Powell*	.05
214	Will Clark	.10
215	Rickey Henderson (Highlight)	.15
216	Jack Morris	.05
217	Junior Felix	.05
218	Vince Coleman	.05
219	Jimmy Key	.05
220	Alex Cole	.05
221	Bill Landrum	.05
222	Randy Milligan	.05
223	Jose Rijo	.05
224	Greg Vaughn	.05
225	Dave Stewart	.05
226	Lenny Harris	.05
227	Scott Sanderson	.05
228	Jeff Blauser	.05
229	Ozzie Guillen	.05
230	John Kruk	.05
231	Bob Melvin	.05
232	Milt Cuyler	.05
233	Felix Jose	.05
234	Ellis Burks	.05
235	Pete Harnisch	.05
236	Kevin Tapani	.05
237	Terry Pendleton	.05
238	Mark Gardner	.05
239	Harold Reynolds	.05
240	Checklist 158-237	.05
241	Mike Harkey	.05
242	Felix Fermin	.05
243	Barry Bonds	.75
244	Roger Clemens	.40
245	Dennis Rasmussen	.05
246	Jose DeLeon	.05
247	Orel Hershiser	.05
248	Mel Hall	.05
249	*Rick Wilkins*	.05
250	Tom Gordon	.05
251	Kevin Reimer	.05
252	Luis Polonia	.05
253	Mike Henneman	.05
254	Tom Pagnozzi	.05
255	Chuck Finley	.05
256	Mackey Sasser	.05
257	John Burkett	.05
258	Hal Morris	.05
259	Larry Walker	.05
260	Billy Swift	.05
261	Joe Oliver	.05
262	Julio Machado	.05
263	Todd Stottlemyre	.05
264	Matt Merullo	.05
265	Brent Mayne	.05
266	Thomas Howard	.05
267	Lance Johnson	.05
268	Terry Mulholland	.05
269	Rick Honeycutt	.05
270	Luis Gonzalez	.15
271	Jose Guzman	.05
272	Jimmy Jones	.05
273	Mark Lewis	.05
274	Rene Gonzales	.05
275	*Jeff Johnson*	.05
276	Dennis Martinez (Highlight)	.05
277	Delino DeShields	.05
278	Sam Horn	.05
279	Kevin Gross	.05
280	Jose Oquendo	.05
281	Mark Grace	.10
282	Mark Gubicza	.05
283	Fred McGriff	.05
284	Ron Gant	.05
285	Lou Whitaker	.05
286	Edgar Martinez	.05
287	Ron Tingley	.05
288	Kevin McReynolds	.05
289	Ivan Rodriguez	.25
290	Mike Gardiner	.05
291	*Chris Haney*	.05
292	Darrin Jackson	.05
293	Bill Doran	.05
294	Ted Higuera	.05
295	Jeff Brantley	.05
296	Les Lancaster	.05
297	Jim Eisenreich	.05
298	Ruben Sierra	.05
299	Scott Radinsky	.05
300	Jose DeJesus	.05
301	*Mike Timlin*	.05
302	Luis Sojo	.05
303	Kelly Downs	.05
304	Scott Bankhead	.05
305	Pedro Munoz	.05
306	Scott Scudder	.05
307	Kevin Elster	.05
308	Duane Ward	.05
309	*Darryl Kile*	.10
310	Orlando Merced	.05
311	Dave Henderson	.05
312	Tim Raines	.05
313	Mark Lee	.05
314	Mike Gallego	.05
315	Charles Nagy	.05
316	Jesse Barfield	.05
317	Todd Frohwirth	.05
318	Al Osuna	.05
319	Darrin Fletcher	.05
320	Checklist 238-316	.05
321	David Segui	.05
322	Stan Javier	.05
323	Bryn Smith	.05
324	Jeff Treadway	.05
325	Mark Whiten	.05
326	Kent Hrbek	.05
327	Dave Justice	.05
328	Tony Phillips	.05
329	Rob Murphy	.05
330	Kevin Morton	.05
331	John Smiley	.05
332	Luis Rivera	.05
333	Wally Joyner	.05
334	*Heathcliff Slocumb*	.05
335	Rick Cerone	.05
336	*Mike Remlinger*	.05
337	Mike Moore	.05
338	Lloyd McClendon	.05
339	Al Newman	.05
340	Kirk McCaskill	.05
341	Howard Johnson	.05
342	Greg Myers	.05
343	Kal Daniels	.05
344	Bernie Williams	.15
345	Shane Mack	.05
346	Gary Thurman	.05
347	Dante Bichette	.05
348	Mark McGwire	.60
349	Travis Fryman	.05
350	Ray Lankford	.05
351	Mike Jeffcoat	.05
352	Jack McDowell	.05
353	Mitch Williams	.05
354	Mike Devereaux	.05
355	Andres Galarraga	.05
356	Henry Cotto	.05
357	Scott Bailes	.05
358	Jeff Bagwell	.25
359	Scott Leius	.05
360	Zane Smith	.05
361	Bill Pecota	.05
362	Tony Fernandez	.05
363	Glenn Braggs	.05
364	Bill Spiers	.05
365	Vicente Palacios	.05
366	Tim Burke	.05
367	Randy Tomlin	.05
368	Kenny Rogers	.05
369	Brett Butler	.05
370	Pat Kelly	.05
371	Bip Roberts	.05
372	Gregg Jefferies	.05
373	Kevin Bass	.05
374	Ron Karkovice	.05
375	Paul Gibson	.05
376	Bernard Gilkey	.05
377	Dave Gallagher	.05
378	Bill Wegman	.05
379	Pat Borders	.05
380	Ed Whitson	.05
381	Gilberto Reyes	.05
382	Russ Swan	.05
383	Andy Van Slyke	.05
384	Wes Chamberlain	.05
385	Steve Chitren	.05
386	Greg Olson	.05
387	Brian McRae	.05
388	Rich Rodriguez	.05
389	Steve Decker	.05
390	Chuck Knoblauch	.05
391	Bobby Witt	.05
392	Eddie Murray	.30
393	Juan Gonzalez	.25
394	Scott Ruskin	.05
395	Jay Howell	.05
396	Checklist 317-396	.05
397	Royce Clayton (Rated Rookie)	.05
398	*John Jaha* (Rated Rookie)	.05
399	Dan Wilson (Rated Rookie)	.05
400	*Archie Corbin* (Rated Rookie)	.05
401	*Barry Manuel* (Rated Rookie)	.05
402	Kim Batiste (Rated Rookie)	.05
403	*Pat Mahomes* (Rated Rookie)	.05
404	Dave Fleming (Rated Rookie)	.05
405	Jeff Juden (Rated Rookie)	.05
406	Jim Thome (Rated Rookie)	.25
407	Sam Militello (Rated Rookie)	.05
408	*Jeff Nelson* (Rated Rookie)	.05
409	Anthony Young (Rated Rookie)	.05
410	Tino Martinez (Rated Rookie)	.05
411	*Jeff Mutis* (Rated Rookie)	.05
412	*Rey Sanchez* (Rated Rookie)	.05
413	*Chris Gardner* (Rated Rookie)	.05
414	*John Vander Wal* (Rated Rookie)	.10
415	Reggie Sanders (Rated Rookie)	.05
416	*Brian Williams* (Rated Rookie)	.05
417	Mo Sanford (Rated Rookie)	.05
418	*David Weathers* (Rated Rookie)	.05
419	*Hector Fajardo* (Rated Rookie)	.05
420	*Steve Foster* (Rated Rookie)	.05
421	Lance Dickson (Rated Rookie)	.05
422	Andre Dawson (All-Star)	.10
423	Ozzie Smith (All-Star)	.20
424	Chris Sabo (All-Star)	.05
425	Tony Gwynn (All-Star)	.20
426	Tom Glavine (All-Star)	.05
427	Bobby Bonilla (All-Star)	.05
428	Will Clark (All-Star)	.05
429	Ryne Sandberg (All-Star)	.15
430	Benito Santiago (All-Star)	.05
431	Ivan Calderon (All-Star)	.05
432	Ozzie Smith	.35
433	Tim Leary	.05
434	Bret Saberhagen (Highlight)	.05
435	Mel Rojas	.05
436	Ben McDonald	.05
437	Tim Crews	.05
438	Rex Hudler	.05
439	Chico Walker	.05
440	Kurt Stillwell	.05
441	Tony Gwynn	.35
442	John Smoltz	.05
443	Lloyd Moseby	.05
444	Mike Schooler	.05
445	Joe Grahe	.05
446	Dwight Gooden	.05
447	Oil Can Boyd	.05
448	John Marzano	.05
449	Bret Barberie	.05
450	Mike Maddux	.05
451	Jeff Reed	.05
452	Dale Sveum	.05
453	Jose Uribe	.05
454	Bob Scanlan	.05
455	Kevin Appier	.05
456	Jeff Huson	.05
457	Ken Patterson	.05
458	Ricky Jordan	.05
459	Tom Candiotti	.05
460	Lee Stevens	.05
461	*Rod Beck*	.10
462	Dave Valle	.05
463	Scott Erickson	.05
464	Chris Jones	.05
465	Mark Carreon	.05
466	Rob Ducey	.05
467	Jim Corsi	.05
468	Jeff King	.05
469	Curt Young	.05
470	Bo Jackson	.15
471	Chris Bosio	.05
472	Jamie Quirk	.05
473	Jesse Orosco	.05
474	Alvaro Espinoza	.05
475	Joe Orsulak	.05
476	Checklist 397-477	.05
477	Gerald Young	.05
478	Wally Backman	.05
479	Juan Bell	.05
480	Mike Scioscia	.05
481	Omar Olivares	.05
482	Francisco Cabrera	.05
483	Greg Swindell	.05
484	Terry Leach	.05
485	Tommy Gregg	.05
486	Scott Aldred	.05
487	Greg Briley	.05
488	Phil Plantier	.05
489	Curtis Wilkerson	.05
490	Tom Brunansky	.05
491	Mike Fetters	.05
492	Frank Castillo	.05
493	Joe Boever	.05
494	Kirt Manwaring	.05
495	Wilson Alvarez (Highlight)	.05
496	Gene Larkin	.05
497	Gary DiSarcina	.05

498 Frank Viola .05
499 Manuel Lee .05
500 Albert Belle .10
501 Stan Belinda .05
502 Dwight Evans .05
503 Eric Davis .05
504 Darren Holmes .05
505 Mike Bordick .05
506 Dave Hansen .05
507 Lee Guetterman .05
508 *Keith Mitchell* .05
509 Melido Perez .05
510 Dickie Thon .05
511 Mark Williamson .05
512 Mark Salas .05
513 Milt Thompson .05
514 Mo Vaughn .05
515 Jim Deshaies .05
516 Rich Garces .05
517 Lonnie Smith .05
518 Spike Owen .05
519 Tracy Jones .05
520 Greg Maddux .35
521 Carlos Martinez .05
522 Neal Heaton .05
523 Mike Greenwell .05
524 Andy Benes .05
525 Jeff Schaefer .05
526 Mike Sharperson .05
527 Wade Taylor .05
528 Jerome Walton .05
529 Storm Davis .05
530 *Jose Hernandez* .05
531 Mark Langston .05
532 Rob Deer .05
533 Geronimo Pena .05
534 *Juan Guzman* .10
535 Pete Schourek .05
536 Todd Benzinger .05
537 Billy Hatcher .05
538 Tom Foley .05
539 Dave Cochrane .05
540 Mariano Duncan .05
541 Edwin Nunez .05
542 Rance Mulliniks .05
543 Carlton Fisk .30
544 Luis Aquino .05
545 Ricky Bones .05
546 Craig Grebeck .05
547 Charlie Hayes .05
548 Jose Canseco .20
549 Andujar Cedeno .05
550 Geno Petralli .05
551 Javier Ortiz .05
552 Rudy Seanez .05
553 Rich Gedman .05
554 Eric Plunk .05
555 Nolan Ryan, Rich Gossage (Highlight) .20
556 Checklist 478-555 .05
557 Greg Colbrunn .05
558 *Chito Martinez* .05
559 Darryl Strawberry .05
560 Luis Alicea .05
561 Dwight Smith .05
562 Terry Shumpert .05
563 Jim Vatcher .05
564 Deion Sanders .10
565 Walt Terrell .05
566 Dave Burba .05
567 Dave Howard .05
568 Todd Hundley .05
569 Jack Daugherty .05
570 Scott Cooper .05
571 Bill Sampen .05
572 Jose Melendez .05
573 Freddie Benavides .05
574 Jim Gantner .05
575 Trevor Wilson .05
576 Ryne Sandberg .35
577 Kevin Seitzer .05
578 Gerald Alexander .05
579 Mike Huff .05
580 Von Hayes .05
581 Derek Bell .05
582 Mike Stanley .05
583 Kevin Mitchell .05
584 Mike Jackson .05
585 Dan Gladden .05
586 Ted Power .05
587 Jeff Innis .05
588 Bob MacDonald .05
589 *Jose Tolentino* .05
590 Bob Patterson .05
591 *Scott Brosius* .10
592 Frank Thomas .25
593 Darryl Hamilton .05
594 Kirk Dressendorfer .05
595 Jeff Shaw .05
596 Don Mattingly .40
597 Glenn Davis .05
598 Andy Mota .05
599 Jason Grimsley .05
600 Jimmy Poole .05
601 Jim Gott .05
602 Stan Royer .05
603 Marvin Freeman .05
604 Denis Boucher .05
605 Denny Neagle .05
606 Mark Lemke .05
607 Jerry Don Gleaton .05
608 Brent Knackert .05
609 Carlos Quintana .05
610 Bobby Bonilla .05
611 Joe Hesketh .05
612 Daryl Boston .05
613 Shawon Dunston .05
614 Danny Cox .05
615 Darren Lewis .05
616 Alejandro Pena, Kent Mercker, Mark Wohlers (Highlight) .05
617 Kirby Puckett .35
618 Franklin Stubbs .05
619 Chris Donnels .05
620 David Wells .05
621 Mike Aldrete .05
622 Bob Kipper .05
623 Anthony Telford .05
624 Randy Myers .05
625 Willie Randolph .05
626 Joe Slusarski .05
627 John Wetteland .05
628 Greg Cadaret .05
629 Tom Glavine .20
630 Wilson Alvarez .05
631 Wally Ritchie .05
632 Mike Mussina .25
633 Mark Leiter .05
634 Gerald Perry .05
635 Matt Young .05
636 Checklist 556-635 .05
637 Scott Hemond .05
638 David West .05
639 Jim Clancy .05
640 Doug Piatt .05
641 Omar Vizquel .05
642 Rick Sutcliffe .05
643 Glenallen Hill .05
644 Gary Varsho .05
645 Tony Fossas .05
646 Jack Howell .05
647 *Jim Campanis* .05
648 Chris Gwynn .05
649 Jim Leyritz .05
650 Chuck McElroy .05
651 Sean Berry .05
652 Donald Harris .05
653 Don Slaught .05
654 *Rusty Meacham* .05
655 Scott Terry .05
656 Ramon Martinez .05
657 Keith Miller .05
658 Ramon Garcia .05
659 *Milt Hill* .05
660 Steve Frey .05
661 Bob McClure .05
662 *Ced Landrum* .05
663 *Doug Henry* .05
664 Candy Maldonado .05
665 Carl Willis .05
666 Jeff Montgomery .05
667 *Craig Shipley* .05
668 *Warren Newson* .05
669 Mickey Morandini .05
670 Brook Jacoby .05
671 *Ryan Bowen* .05
672 Bill Krueger .05
673 Rob Mallicoat .05
674 Doug Jones .05
675 Scott Livingstone .05
676 Danny Tartabull .05
677 Joe Carter (Highlight) .05
678 Cecil Espy .05
679 Randy Velarde .05
680 Bruce Ruffin .05
681 *Ted Wood* .05
682 Dan Plesac .05
683 Eric Bullock .05
684 Junior Ortiz .05
685 Dave Hollins .05
686 Dennis Martinez .05
687 Larry Andersen .05
688 Doug Simons .05
689 *Tim Spehr* .05
690 *Calvin Jones* .05
691 Mark Guthrie .05
692 Alfredo Griffin .05
693 Joe Carter .05
694 *Terry Mathews* .05
695 Pascual Perez .05
696 Gene Nelson .05
697 Gerald Williams .05
698 *Chris Cron* .05
699 Steve Buechele .05
700 Paul McClellan .05
701 Jim Lindeman .05
702 Francisco Oliveras .05
703 *Rob Maurer* .05
704 *Pat Hentgen* .15
705 Jaime Navarro .05
706 *Mike Magnante* .05
707 Nolan Ryan .75
708 Bobby Thigpen .05
709 John Cerutti .05
710 Steve Wilson .05
711 Hensley Meulens .05
712 *Rheal Cormier* .05
713 Scott Bradley .05
714 Mitch Webster .05
715 Roger Mason .05
716 Checklist 636-716 .05
717 *Jeff Fassero* .05
718 Cal Eldred .05
719 Sid Fernandez .05
720 *Bob Zupcic* .05
721 Jose Offerman .05
722 *Cliff Brantley* .05
723 Ron Darling .05
724 Dave Stieb .05
725 Hector Villanueva .05
726 Mike Hartley .05
727 *Arthur Rhodes* .05
728 Randy Bush .05
729 Steve Sax .05
730 Dave Otto .05
731 *John Wehner* .05
732 Dave Martinez .05
733 *Ruben Amaro* .05
734 Billy Ripken .05
735 Steve Farr .05
736 Shawn Abner .05
737 *Gil Heredia* .05
738 Ron Jones .05
739 Tony Castillo .05
740 Sammy Sosa .60
741 Julio Franco .05
742 Tim Naehring .05
743 *Steve Wapnick* .05
744 Craig Wilson .05
745 *Darrin Chapin* .05
746 *Chris George* .05
747 Mike Simms .05
748 Rosario Rodriguez .05
749 Skeeter Barnes .05
750 Roger McDowell .05
751 Dann Howitt .05
752 Paul Sorrento .05
753 *Braulio Castillo* .05
754 *Yorkis Perez* .05
755 Willie Fraser .05
756 *Jeremy Hernandez* .05
757 Curt Schilling .20
758 Steve Lyons .05
759 Dave Anderson .05
760 Willie Banks .05
761 Mark Leonard .05
762 Jack Armstrong .05
763 Scott Servais .05
764 Ray Stephens .05
765 Junior Noboa .05
766 *Jim Olander* .05
767 Joe Magrane .05
768 Lance Blankenship .05
769 *Mike Humphreys* .05
770 *Jarvis Brown* .05
771 Damon Berryhill .05
772 Alejandro Pena .05
773 Jose Mesa .05
774 *Gary Cooper* .05
775 Carney Lansford .05
776 Mike Bielecki .05
777 Charlie O'Brien .05
778 Carlos Hernandez .05
779 Howard Farmer .05
780 Mike Stanton .05
781 Reggie Harris .05
782 Xavier Hernandez .05
783 *Bryan Hickerson* .05
784 Checklist 717-BC8 .05

Diamond Kings

NM/M
Complete Set (27): 4.00
Common Player: .15
1 Paul Molitor .60
2 Will Clark .25

3 Joe Carter .15
4 Julio Franco .15
5 Cal Ripken, Jr. 2.00
6 Dave Justice .15
7 George Bell .15
8 Frank Thomas .75
9 Wade Boggs 1.00
10 Scott Sanderson .15
11 Jeff Bagwell .60
12 John Kruk .15
13 Felix Jose .15
14 Harold Baines .15
15 Dwight Gooden .15
16 Brian McRae .15
17 Jay Bell .15
18 Brett Butler .15
19 Hal Morris .15
20 Mark Langston .15
21 Scott Erickson .15
22 Randy Johnson .60
23 Greg Swindell .15
24 Dennis Martinez .15
25 Tony Phillips .15
26 Fred McGriff .15
27 Checklist .04

Elite

NM/M
Complete Set (12): 200.00
Common Player: 4.50
9 Wade Boggs 10.00
10 Joe Carter 5.00
11 Will Clark 6.00
12 Dwight Gooden 5.00
13 Ken Griffey, Jr. 20.00
14 Tony Gwynn 10.00
15 Howard Johnson 5.00
16 Terry Pendleton 5.00
17 Kirby Puckett 10.00
18 Frank Thomas 15.00
--- Rickey Henderson (Legend) 15.00
--- Cal Ripken, Jr. (Signature) 200.00

Rookies

NM/M
Complete Set (132): 3.50
Common Player: .05
Pack (12): 1.00
Wax Box (36): 20.00
1 Kyle Abbott .05
2 Troy Afenir .05
3 Rich Amaral .05
4 Ruben Amaro .05
5 Billy Ashley .05
6 Pedro Astacio .05
7 Jim Austin .05

8 Robert Ayrault .05
9 Kevin Baez .05
10 Estaban Beltre .05
11 Brian Bohanon .05
12 Kent Bottenfield .05
13 Jeff Branson .05
14 Brad Brink .05
15 John Briscoe .05
16 Doug Brocail .05
17 Rico Brogna .05
18 J.T. Bruett .05
19 Jacob Brumfield .05
20 Jim Bullinger .05
21 Kevin Campbell .05
22 Pedro Castellano .05
23 Mike Christopher .05
24 Archi Cianfrocco .05
25 Mark Clark .05
26 Craig Colbert .05
27 Victor Cole .05
28 Steve Cooke .05
29 Tim Costo .05
30 Chad Curtis .10
31 Doug Davis .05
32 Gary DiSarcina .05
33 John Doherty .05
34 Mike Draper .05
35 Monty Fariss .05
36 Bien Figueroa .05
37 John Flaherty .05
38 Tim Fortugno .05
39 Eric Fox .05
40 *Jeff Frye* .05
41 Ramon Garcia .05
42 Brent Gates .05
43 Tom Goodwin .05
44 Buddy Groom .05
45 Jeff Grotewold .05
46 Juan Guerrero .05
47 Johnny Guzman .05
48 Shawn Hare .05
49 Ryan Hawblitzel .05
50 Bert Heffernan .05
51 Butch Henry .05
52 Cesar Hernandez .05
53 Vince Horsman .05
54 Steve Hosey .05
55 Pat Howell .05
56 Peter Hoy .05
57 Jon Hurst .05
58 Mark Hutton .05
59 Shawn Jeter .05
60 Joel Johnston .05
61 Jeff Kent .50
62 Kurt Knudsen .05
63 Kevin Koslofski .05
64 Danny Leon .05
65 Jesse Levis .05
66 Tom Marsh .05
67 Ed Martel .05
68 Al Martin .05
69 Pedro Martinez 1.00
70 Derrick May .05
71 Matt Maysey .05
72 Russ McGinnis .05
73 Tim McIntosh .05
74 Jim McNamara .05
75 Jeff McNeely .05
76 Rusty Meacham .05
77 Tony Melendez .05
78 Henry Mercedes .05
79 Paul Miller .05
80 Joe Millette .05
81 Blas Minor .05
82 Dennis Moeller .05
83 Raul Mondesi .25
84 Rob Natal .05
85 Troy Neel .05
86 David Nied .05
87 Jerry Nielsen .05
88 Donovan Osborne .05
89 John Patterson .05
90 Roger Pavlik .05
91 Dan Peltier .05
92 Jim Pena .05
93 William Pennyfeather .05
94 Mike Perez .05
95 Hipolito Pichardo .05
96 Greg Pirkl .05
97 Harvey Pulliam .05
98 *Manny Ramirez* 2.00
99 Pat Rapp .05
100 Jeff Reboulet .05
101 Darren Reed .05
102 Shane Reynolds .05
103 Bill Risley .05
104 Ben Rivera .05
105 Henry Rodriguez .05
106 Rico Rossy .05
107 Johnny Ruffin .05
108 Steve Scarsone .05
109 Tim Scott .05
110 Steve Shifflett .05
111 Dave Silvestri .05
112 Matt Stairs .05
113 William Suero .05
114 Jeff Tackett .05
115 Eddie Taubensee .05
116 Rick Trlicek .05
117 Scooter Tucker .05
118 Shane Turner .05
119 Julio Valera .05
120 Paul Wagner .05
121 Tim Wakefield .05
122 Mike Walker .05
123 Bruce Walton .05
124 Lenny Webster .05
125 Bob Wickman .05
126 Mike Williams .05
127 Kerry Woodson .05
128 Eric Young .05
129 Kevin Young .05
130 Pete Young .05
131 Checklist .05
132 Checklist .05

Rookie Phenoms

NM/M
Complete Set (20): 12.50
Common Player: .20
1 Moises Alou .50
2 Bret Boone 1.00
3 Jeff Conine .20
4 Dave Fleming .20
5 Tyler Green .20
6 Eric Karros .20
7 Pat Listach .20
8 Kenny Lofton .30
9 Mike Piazza 10.00
10 Tim Salmon 1.00
11 Andy Stankiewicz .20
12 Dan Walters .20
13 Ramon Caraballo .20
14 Brian Jordan .30
15 Ryan Klesko .20
16 Sam Militello .20
17 Frank Seminara .20
18 Salomon Torres .20
19 John Valentin .20
20 Wil Cordero .20

Update

NM/M
Complete Set (22): 15.00
Common Player: .50
1 Pat Listach (Rated Rookie) .50
2 Andy Stankiewicz (Rated Rookie) .50
3 Brian Jordan (Rated Rookie) .75
4 Dan Walters (Rated Rookie) .50
5 Chad Curtis (Rated Rookie) .75
6 Kenny Lofton (Rated Rookie) 2.00
7 Mark McGwire (Highlight) 8.00
8 Eddie Murray (Highlight) 1.00
9 Jeff Reardon (Highlight) .50
10 Frank Viola .50
11 Gary Sheffield .75
12 George Bell .50
13 Rick Sutcliffe .50
14 Wally Joyner .50
15 Kevin Seitzer .50
16 Bill Krueger .50
17 Danny Tartabull .50
18 Dave Winfield 2.00
19 Gary Carter 1.50
20 Bobby Bonilla .50
21 Cory Snyder .50
22 Bill Swift .50

1993 DONRUSS

NM/M
Complete Set (792): 7.00
Common Player: .05
Series 1 or 2 Pack (14): .30
Series 1 or 2 Box (36): 7.00
1 Craig Lefferts .05
2 Kent Mercker .05
3 Phil Plantier .05
4 *Alex Arias* .05
5 Julio Valera .05
6 Dan Wilson .05
7 Frank Thomas .45
8 Eric Anthony .05
9 Derek Lilliquist .05
10 *Rafael Bournigal* .05
11 *Manny Alexander* (Rated Rookie) .05
12 Bret Barberie .05
13 Mickey Tettleton .05
14 Anthony Young .05
15 Tim Spehr .05
16 *Bob Ayrault* .05
17 Bill Wegman .05
18 Jay Bell .05
19 Rick Aguilera .05
20 Todd Zeile .05
21 Steve Farr .05
22 Andy Benes .05
23 Lance Blankenship .05
24 Ted Wood .05
25 Omar Vizquel .05
26 Steve Avery .05
27 Brian Bohanon .05
28 Rick Wilkins .05
29 Devon White .05
30 *Bobby Ayala* .05
31 Leo Gomez .05
32 Mike Simms .05
33 Ellis Burks .05
34 Steve Wilson .05
35 Jim Abbott .05
36 Tim Wallach .05
37 Wilson Alvarez .05
38 Daryl Boston .05
39 Sandy Alomar, Jr. .05
40 Mitch Williams .05
41 Rico Brogna .05
42 Gary Varsho .05
43 Kevin Appier .05
44 Eric Wedge (Rated Rookie) .05
45 Dante Bichette .05
46 Jose Oquendo .05
47 *Mike Trombley* .05
48 Dan Walters .05
49 Gerald Williams .05
50 Bud Black .05
51 Bobby Witt .05
52 Mark Davis .05
53 *Shawn Barton* .05
54 Paul Assenmacher .05
55 Kevin Reimer .05
56 *Billy Ashley* (Rated Rookie) .05
57 Eddie Zosky .05
58 Chris Sabo .05
59 Billy Ripken .05
60 *Scooter Tucker* .05
61 *Tim Wakefield* (Rated Rookie) .10
62 Mitch Webster .05
63 Jack Clark .05
64 Mark Gardner .05
65 Lee Stevens .05
66 Todd Hundley .05
67 Bobby Thigpen .05
68 Dave Hollins .05
69 Jack Armstrong .05
70 Alex Cole .05
71 Mark Carreon .05
72 Todd Worrell .05
73 *Steve Shifflett* .05
74 Jerald Clark .05
75 Paul Molitor .50
76 *Larry Carter* .05
77 Rich Rowland .05
78 Damon Berryhill .05
79 Willie Banks .05
80 Hector Villanueva .05
81 Mike Gallego .05
82 Tim Belcher .05
83 Mike Bordick .05
84 Craig Biggio .05
85 Lance Parrish .05
86 Brett Butler .05
87 Mike Timlin .05
88 Brian Barnes .05
89 Brady Anderson .05
90 D.J. Dozier .05
91 Frank Viola .05
92 Darren Daulton .05
93 Chad Curtis .05
94 Zane Smith .05
95 George Bell .05
96 Rex Hudler .05
97 Mark Whiten .05
98 Tim Teufel .05
99 Kevin Ritz .05
100 Jeff Brantley .05
101 Jeff Conine .05
102 Vinny Castilla .05
103 Greg Vaughn .05
104 Steve Buechele .05
105 Darren Reed .05
106 Bip Roberts .05
107 John Habyan .05
108 Scott Servais .05
109 Walt Weiss .05
110 *J.T. Snow* (Rated Rookie) .50
111 Jay Buhner .05
112 Darryl Strawberry .05
113 *Roger Pavlik* .05
114 Chris Nabholz .05
115 Pat Borders .05
116 *Pat Howell* .05
117 Gregg Olson .05
118 Curt Schilling .25
119 Roger Clemens .65
120 *Victor Cole* .05
121 Gary DiSarcina .05
122 Checklist 1-80 .05
123 Steve Sax .05
124 Chuck Carr .05
125 Mark Lewis .05
126 Tony Gwynn .60
127 Travis Fryman .05
128 Dave Burba .05
129 Wally Joyner .05
130 John Smoltz .05
131 Cal Eldred .05
132 Checklist 81-159 .05
133 Arthur Rhodes .05
134 Jeff Blauser .05
135 Scott Cooper .05
136 Doug Strange .05
137 Luis Sojo .05
138 *Jeff Branson* .05
139 Alex Fernandez .05
140 Ken Caminiti .05
141 Charles Nagy .05
142 Tom Candiotti .05
143 Willie Green (Rated Rookie) .05
144 John Vander Wal .05
145 *Kurt Knudsen* .05
146 John Franco .05
147 *Eddie Pierce* .05
148 Kim Batiste .05
149 Darren Holmes .05
150 *Steve Cooke* .05
151 Terry Jorgensen .05
152 *Mark Clark* .05
153 Randy Velarde .05
154 Greg Harris .05
155 *Kevin Campbell* .05
156 John Burkett .05
157 Kevin Mitchell .05
158 Deion Sanders .05

159 Jose Canseco .25
160 *Jeff Hartsock* .05
161 *Tom Quinlan* .05
162 *Tim Pugh* .05
163 Glenn Davis .05
164 *Shane Reynolds* .10
165 Jody Reed .05
166 Mike Sharperson .05
167 Scott Lewis .05
168 Dennis Martinez .05
169 Scott Radinsky .05
170 Dave Gallagher .05
171 Jim Thome .05
172 Terry Mulholland .05
173 Milt Cuyler .05
174 Bob Patterson .05
175 Jeff Montgomery .05
176 Tim Salmon (Rated Rookie) .30
177 Franklin Stubbs .05
178 Donovan Osborne .05
179 *Jeff Reboulet* .05
180 Jeremy Hernandez .05
181 Charlie Hayes .05
182 Matt Williams .05
183 Mike Raczka .05
184 Francisco Cabrera .05
185 Rich DeLucia .05
186 Sammy Sosa .75
187 Ivan Rodriguez .40
188 Bret Boone (Rated Rookie) .15
189 Juan Guzman .05
190 Tom Browning .05
191 Randy Milligan .05
192 Steve Finley .05
193 John Patterson (Rated Rookie) .05
194 Kip Gross .05
195 Tony Fossas .05
196 Ivan Calderon .05
197 Junior Felix .05
198 Pete Schourek .05
199 Craig Grebeck .05
200 Juan Bell .05
201 Glenallen Hill .05
202 Danny Jackson .05
203 John Kiely .05
204 Bob Tewksbury .05
205 *Kevin Koslofski* .05
206 Craig Shipley .05
207 John Jaha .05
208 Royce Clayton .05
209 Mike Piazza (Rated Rookie) 1.50
210 Ron Gant .05
211 Scott Erickson .05
212 Doug Dascenzo .05
213 Andy Stankiewicz .05
214 Geronimo Berroa .05
215 Dennis Eckersley .50
216 Al Osuna .05
217 Tino Martinez .05
218 *Henry Rodriguez* .05
219 Ed Sprague .05
220 Ken Hill .05
221 Chito Martinez .05
222 Bret Saberhagen .05
223 Mike Greenwell .05
224 Mickey Morandini .05
225 Chuck Finley .05
226 Denny Neagle .05
227 Kirk McCaskill .05
228 Rheal Cormier .05
229 Paul Sorrento .05
230 Darrin Jackson .05
231 Rob Deer .05
232 Bill Swift .05
233 Kevin McReynolds .05
234 Terry Pendleton .05
235 Dave Nilsson .05
236 Chuck McElroy .05
237 Derek Parks .05
238 Norm Charlton .05
239 Matt Nokes .05
240 *Juan Guerrero* .05
241 Jeff Parrett .05
242 Ryan Thompson (Rated Rookie) .05
243 Dave Fleming .05
244 Dave Hansen .05
245 Monty Fariss .05
246 *Archi Cianfrocco* .05
247 Pat Hentgen .05
248 Bill Pecota .05
249 Ben McDonald .05
250 Cliff Brantley .05
251 *John Valentin* .05
252 Jeff King .05
253 *Reggie Williams* .05
254 Checklist 160-238 .05
255 Ozzie Guillen .05
256 Mike Perez .05
257 Thomas Howard .05
258 Kurt Stillwell .05
259 Mike Henneman .05
260 Steve Decker .05
261 Brent Mayne .05
262 Otis Nixon .05
263 *Mark Keifer* .05
264 Checklist 239-317 .05
265 *Richie Lewis* .05
266 *Pat Gomez* .05
267 *Scott Taylor* .05
268 Shawon Dunston .05
269 Greg Myers .05
270 Tim Costo .05
271 Greg Hibbard .05
272 Pete Harnisch .05
273 *Dave Mlicki* .05
274 Orel Hershiser .05
275 Sean Berry (Rated Rookie) .05
276 Doug Simons .05
277 *John Doherty* .05
278 Eddie Murray .50
279 Chris Haney .05
280 Stan Javier .05
281 Jaime Navarro .05
282 Orlando Merced .05
283 Kent Hrbek .05
284 Bernard Gilkey .05
285 Russ Springer .05
286 Mike Maddux .05
287 *Eric Fox* .05
288 Mark Leonard .05
289 Tim Leary .05
290 Brian Hunter .05
291 Donald Harris .05
292 Bob Scanlan .05
293 Turner Ward .05
294 Hal Morris .05
295 Jimmy Poole .05
296 Doug Jones .05
297 Tony Pena .05
298 Ramon Martinez .05
299 *Tim Fortugno* .05
300 Marquis Grissom .05
301 Lance Johnson .05
302 *Jeff Kent* 1.00
303 Reggie Jefferson .05
304 Wes Chamberlain .05
305 *Shawn Hare* .05
306 Mike LaValliere .05
307 Gregg Jefferies .05
308 *Troy Neel* (Rated Rookie) .05
309 Pat Listach .05
310 Geronimo Pena .05
311 Pedro Munoz .05
312 *Guillermo Velasquez* .05
313 Roberto Kelly .05
314 Mike Jackson .05
315 Rickey Henderson .50
316 Mark Lemke .05
317 Erik Hanson .05
318 Derrick May .05
319 Geno Petralli .05
320 Melvin Nieves (Rated Rookie) .05
321 *Doug Linton* .05
322 Rob Dibble .05
323 Chris Hoiles .05
324 Jimmy Jones .05
325 Dave Staton (Rated Rookie) .05
326 Pedro Martinez .05
327 *Paul Quantrill* .05
328 Greg Colbrunn .05
329 *Hilly Hathaway* .05
330 Jeff Innis .05
331 Ron Karkovice .05
332 *Keith Shepherd* .05
333 *Alan Embree* .05
334 *Paul Wagner* .05
335 *Dave Haas* .05
336 Ozzie Canseco .05
337 Bill Sampen .05
338 Rich Rodriguez .05
339 Dean Palmer .05
340 Greg Litton .05
341 Jim Tatum (Rated Rookie) .05
342 *Todd Haney* .05
343 Larry Casian .05
344 Ryne Sandberg .60
345 *Sterling Hitchcock* .10
346 Chris Hammond .05
347 *Vince Horsman* .05
348 *Butch Henry* .05
349 Dann Howitt .05
350 Roger McDowell .05
351 Jack Morris .05
352 Bill Krueger .05
353 *Cris Colon* .05
354 *Joe Vitko* .05
355 Willie McGee .05
356 Jay Baller .05
357 Pat Mahomes .05
358 Roger Mason .05
359 *Jerry Nielsen* .05
360 Tom Pagnozzi .05
361 *Kevin Baez* .05
362 *Tim Scott* .05
363 *Domingo Martinez* .05
364 Kirt Manwaring .05
365 Rafael Palmeiro .45
366 Ray Lankford .05
367 Tim McIntosh .05
368 *Jessie Hollins* .05
369 Scott Leius .05
370 Bill Doran .05
371 *Sam Militello* .05
372 Ryan Bowen .05
373 Dave Henderson .05
374 Dan Smith (Rated Rookie) .05
375 *Steve Reed* .05
376 Jose Offerman .05
377 Kevin Brown .05
378 Darrin Fletcher .05
379 Duane Ward .05
380 Wayne Kirby (Rated Rookie) .05
381 *Steve Scarsone* .05
382 Mariano Duncan .05
383 *Ken Ryan* .05
384 Lloyd McClendon .05
385 Brian Holman .05
386 Braulio Castillo .05
387 *Danny Leon* .05
388 Omar Olivares .05
389 Kevin Wickander .05
390 Fred McGriff .05
391 Phil Clark .05
392 Darren Lewis .05
393 *Phil Hiatt* .10
394 Mike Morgan .05
395 Shane Mack .05
396 Checklist 318-396 .05
397 David Segui .05
398 Rafael Belliard .05
399 Tim Naehring .05
400 Frank Castillo .05
401 Joe Grahe .05
402 Reggie Sanders .05
403 Roberto Hernandez .05
404 Luis Gonzalez .25
405 Carlos Baerga .05
406 Carlos Hernandez .05
407 Pedro Astacio (Rated Rookie) .05
408 Mel Rojas .05
409 Scott Livingstone .05
410 Chico Walker .05
411 Brian McRae .05
412 Ben Rivera .05
413 Ricky Bones .05
414 Andy Van Slyke .05
415 Chuck Knoblauch .05
416 Luis Alicea .05
417 Bob Wickman .05
418 Doug Brocail .05
419 Scott Brosius .05
420 Rod Beck .05
421 Edgar Martinez .05
422 Ryan Klesko .05
423 Nolan Ryan 1.50
424 Rey Sanchez .05
425 Roberto Alomar .20
426 Barry Larkin .05
427 Mike Mussina .30
428 Jeff Bagwell .45
429 Mo Vaughn .05
430 Eric Karros .05
431 John Orton .05
432 Wil Cordero .05
433 Jack McDowell .05
434 Howard Johnson .05
435 Albert Belle .15
436 John Kruk .05
437 Skeeter Barnes .05
438 Don Slaught .05
439 Rusty Meacham .05
440 Tim Laker (Rated Rookie) .05
441 Robin Yount .50
442 Brian Jordan .05
443 Kevin Tapani .05
444 Gary Sheffield .25
445 Rich Monteleone .05
446 Will Clark .10
447 Jerry Browne .05
448 Jeff Treadway .05
449 Mike Schooler .05
450 Mike Harkey .05
451 Julio Franco .05
452 Kevin Young (Rated Rookie) .05
453 Kelly Gruber .05
454 Jose Rijo .05
455 Mike Devereaux .05
456 Andujar Cedeno .05
457 Damion Easley (Rated Rookie) .05
458 Kevin Gross .05
459 Matt Young .05
460 Matt Stairs .05
461 Luis Polonia .05
462 Dwight Gooden .05
463 Warren Newson .05
464 Jose DeLeon .05
465 Jose Mesa .05
466 Danny Cox .05
467 Dan Gladden .05
468 Gerald Perry .05
469 Mike Boddicker .05
470 Jeff Gardner .05
471 Doug Henry .05
472 Mike Benajmin .05
473 Dan Peltier (Rated Rookie) .05
474 Mike Stanton .05
475 John Smiley .05
476 Dwight Smith .05
477 Jim Leyritz .05
478 Dwayne Henry .05
479 Mark McGwire 1.00
480 Pete Incaviglia .05
481 Dave Cochrane .05
482 Eric Davis .05
483 John Olerud .05
484 Ken Bottenfield .05
485 Mark McLemore .05
486 Dave Magadan .05
487 John Marzano .05
488 Ruben Amaro .05
489 Rob Ducey .05
490 Stan Belinda .05
491 Dan Pasqua .05
492 Joe Magrane .05
493 Brook Jacoby .05
494 Gene Harris .05
495 Mark Leiter .05
496 Bryan Hickerson .05
497 Tom Gordon .05
498 Pete Smith .05
499 Chris Bosio .05
500 Shawn Boskie .05
501 Dave West .05
502 Milt Hill .05
503 Pat Kelly .05
504 Joe Boever .05
505 Terry Steinbach .05
506 Butch Huskey (Rated Rookie) .05
507 David Valle .05
508 Mike Scioscia .05
509 Kenny Rogers .05
510 Moises Alou .05
511 David Wells .05
512 Mackey Sasser .05
513 Todd Frohwirth .05
514 Ricky Jordan .05
515 Mike Gardiner .05
516 Gary Redus .05
517 Gary Gaetti .05
518 Checklist 397-476 .05
519 Carlton Fisk .50
520 Ozzie Smith .60
521 Rod Nichols .05
522 Benito Santiago .05
523 Bill Gullickson .05
524 Robby Thompson .05
525 Mike Macfarlane .05
526 Sid Bream .05
527 Darryl Hamilton .05
528 Checklist 477-555 .05
529 Jeff Tackett .05
530 Greg Olson .05
531 Bob Zupcic .05
532 Mark Grace .10
533 Steve Frey .05
534 Dave Martinez .05
535 Robin Ventura .05
536 Casey Candaele .05

537 Kenny Lofton .05
538 Jay Howell .05
539 Fernando Ramsey (Rated Rookie) .05
540 Larry Walker .05
541 Cecil Fielder .05
542 Lee Guetterman .05
543 Keith Miller .05
544 Len Dykstra .05
545 B.J. Surhoff .05
546 Bob Walk .05
547 Brian Harper .05
548 Lee Smith .05
549 Danny Tartabull .05
550 Frank Seminara .05
551 Henry Mercedes .05
552 Dave Righetti .05
553 Ken Griffey, Jr. .75
554 Tom Glavine .20
555 Juan Gonzalez .45
556 Jim Bullinger .05
557 Derek Bell .05
558 Cesar Hernandez .05
559 Cal Ripken, Jr. 1.50
560 Eddie Taubensee .05
561 John Flaherty .05
562 Todd Benzinger .05
563 Hubie Brooks .05
564 Delino DeShields .05
565 Tim Raines .05
566 Sid Fernandez .05
567 Steve Olin .05
568 Tommy Greene .05
569 Buddy Groom .05
570 Randy Tomlin .05
571 Hipolito Pichardo .05
572 Rene Arocha (Rated Rookie) .05
573 Mike Fetters .05
574 Felix Jose .05
575 Gene Larkin .05
576 Bruce Hurst .05
577 Bernie Williams .15
578 Trevor Wilson .05
579 Bob Welch .05
580 Dave Justice .05
581 Randy Johnson .50
582 Jose Vizcaino .05
583 Jeff Huson .05
584 Rob Maurer (Rated Rookie) .05
585 Todd Stottlemyre .05
586 Joe Oliver .05
587 Bob Milacki .05
588 Rob Murphy .05
589 Greg Pirkl (Rated Rookie) .05
590 Lenny Harris .05
591 Luis Rivera .05
592 John Wetteland .05
593 Mark Langston .05
594 Bobby Bonilla .05
595 Esteban Beltre .05
596 Mike Hartley .05
597 Felix Fermin .05
598 Carlos Garcia .05
599 Frank Tanana .05
600 Pedro Guerrero .05
601 Terry Shumpert .05
602 Wally Whitehurst .05
603 Kevin Seitzer .05
604 Chris James .05
605 Greg Gohr (Rated Rookie) .05
606 Mark Wohlers .05
607 Kirby Puckett .60
608 Greg Maddux .60
609 Don Mattingly .65
610 Greg Cadaret .05
611 Dave Stewart .05
612 Mark Portugal .05
613 Pete O'Brien .05
614 Bobby Ojeda .05
615 Joe Carter .05
616 Pete Young .05
617 Sam Horn .05
618 Vince Coleman .05
619 Wade Boggs .60
620 *Todd Pratt* .05
621 Ron Tingley .05
622 Doug Drabek .05
623 Scott Hemond .05
624 Tim Jones .05
625 Dennis Cook .05
626 Jose Melendez .05
627 Mike Munoz .05
628 Jim Pena .05
629 Gary Thurman .05
630 Charlie Leibrandt .05
631 Scott Fletcher .05
632 Andre Dawson .25
633 Greg Gagne .05
634 Greg Swindell .05
635 Kevin Maas .05
636 Xavier Hernandez .05
637 Ruben Sierra .05
638 Dimitri Young (Rated Rookie) .05
639 Harold Reynolds .05
640 Tom Goodwin .05
641 Todd Burns .05
642 Jeff Fassero .05
643 Dave Winfield .50
644 Willie Randolph .05
645 Luis Mercedes .05
646 Dale Murphy .20
647 Danny Darwin .05
648 Dennis Moeller .05
649 Chuck Crim .05
650 Checklist 556-634 .05
651 Shawn Abner .05
652 Tracy Woodson .05
653 Scott Scudder .05
654 Tom Lampkin .05
655 Alan Trammell .05
656 Cory Snyder .05
657 Chris Gwynn .05
658 Lonnie Smith .05
659 Jim Austin .05
660 Checklist 635-713 .05
661 Tim Hulett .05
662 Marvin Freeman .05
663 Greg Harris .05
664 Heathcliff Slocumb .05
665 Mike Butcher .05
666 Steve Foster .05
667 Donn Pall .05
668 Darryl Kile .05
669 Jesse Levis .05
670 Jim Gott .05
671 *Mark Hutton* .05
672 Brian Drahman .05
673 Chad Kreuter .05
674 Tony Fernandez .05
675 Jose Lind .05
676 Kyle Abbott .05
677 Dan Plesac .05
678 Barry Bonds 1.50
679 Chili Davis .05
680 Stan Royer .05
681 Scott Kamieniecki .05
682 Carlos Martinez .05
683 Mike Moore .05
684 Candy Maldanado .05
685 Jeff Nelson .05
686 Lou Whitaker .05
687 Jose Guzman .05
688 Manuel Lee .05
689 Bob MacDonald .05
690 Scott Bankhead .05
691 Alan Mills .05
692 Brian Williams .05
693 Tom Brunansky .05
694 Lenny Webster .05
695 Greg Briley .05
696 Paul O'Neill .05
697 Joey Cora .05
698 Charlie O'Brien .05
699 Junior Ortiz .05
700 Ron Darling .05
701 Tony Phillips .05
702 William Pennyfeather .05
703 Mark Gubicza .05
704 Steve Hosey (Rated Rookie) .05
705 Henry Cotto .05
706 *David Hulse* .05
707 Mike Pagliarulo .05
708 Dave Stieb .05
709 Melido Perez .05
710 Jimmy Key .05
711 Jeff Russell .05
712 David Cone .05
713 Russ Swan .05
714 Mark Guthrie .05
715 Checklist 714-792 .05
716 Al Martin (Rated Rookie) .05
717 Randy Knorr .05
718 Mike Stanley .05
719 Rick Sutcliffe .05
720 Terry Leach .05
721 Chipper Jones (Rated Rookie) 1.00
722 Jim Eisenreich .05
723 Tom Henke .05
724 Jeff Frye .05
725 Harold Baines .05
726 Scott Sanderson .05
727 Tom Foley .05
728 Bryan Harvey (Expansion Draft) .05
729 Tom Edens .05
730 Eric Young (Expansion Draft) .05
731 Dave Weathers (Expansion Draft) .05
732 Spike Owen .05
733 Scott Aldred (Expansion Draft) .05
734 Cris Carpenter (Expansion Draft) .05
735 Dion James .05
736 Joe Girardi (Expansion Draft) .05
737 Nigel Wilson (Expansion Draft) .05
738 Scott Chiamparino (Expansion Draft) .05
739 Jeff Reardon .05
740 Willie Blair (Expansion Draft) .05
741 Jim Corsi (Expansion Draft) .05
742 Ken Patterson .05
743 Andy Ashby (Expansion Draft) .05
744 Rob Natal (Expansion Draft) .05
745 Kevin Bass .05
746 Freddie Benavides (Expansion Draft) .05
747 Chris Donnels (Expansion Draft) .05
748 *Kerry Woodson* .05
749 Calvin Jones (Expansion Draft) .05
750 Gary Scott .05
751 Joe Orsulak .05
752 Armando Reynoso (Expansion Draft) .05
753 Monty Farriss (Expansion Draft) .05
754 Billy Hatcher .05
755 Denis Boucher (Expansion Draft) .05
756 Walt Weiss .05
757 Mike Fitzgerald .05
758 Rudy Seanez .05
759 Bret Barberie (Expansion Draft) .05
760 Mo Sanford (Expansion Draft) .05
761 *Pedro Castellano* (Expansion Draft) .05
762 Chuck Carr (Expansion Draft) .05
763 Steve Howe .05
764 Andres Galarraga .05
765 Jeff Conine (Expansion Draft) .05
766 Ted Power .05
767 Butch Henry (Expansion Draft) .05
768 Steve Decker (Expansion Draft) .05
769 Storm Davis .05
770 Vinny Castilla (Expansion Draft) .05
771 Junior Felix (Expansion Draft) .05
772 Walt Terrell .05
773 Brad Ausmus (Expansion Draft) .05
774 Jamie McAndrew (Expansion Draft) .05
775 Milt Thompson .05
776 Charlie Hayes (Expansion Draft) .05
777 Jack Armstrong (Expansion Draft) .05
778 Dennis Rasmussen .05
779 Darren Holmes (Expansion Draft) .05
780 *Alex Arias* .05
781 Randy Bush .05
782 Javier Lopez (Rated Rookie) .05
783 Dante Bichette .05
784 John Johnstone (Expansion Draft) .05
785 Rene Gonzales .05
786 Alex Cole (Expansion Draft) .05
787 Jeromy Burnitz (Rated Rookie) .05
788 Michael Huff .05
789 Anthony Telford .05
790 Jerald Clark (Expansion Draft) .05
791 Joel Johnston .05
792 David Nied (Rated Rookie) .05

Diamond Kings

		NM/M
Complete Set (31):		17.50
Common Player:		.25
1	Ken Griffey, Jr.	4.00
2	Ryne Sandberg	3.00
3	Roger Clemens	3.00
4	Kirby Puckett	3.00
5	Bill Swift	.25
6	Larry Walker	.25
7	Juan Gonzalez	1.50
8	Wally Joyner	.25
9	Andy Van Slyke	.25
10	Robin Ventura	.25
11	Bip Roberts	.25
12	Roberto Kelly	.25
13	Carlos Baerga	.25
14	Orel Hershiser	.25
15	Cecil Fielder	.25
16	Robin Yount	1.50
17	Darren Daulton	.25
18	Mark McGwire	4.00
19	Tom Glavine	.75
20	Roberto Alomar	.75
21	Gary Sheffield	.75
22	Bob Tewksbury	.25
23	Brady Anderson	.25
24	Craig Biggio	.25
25	Eddie Murray	1.50
26	Luis Polonia	.25
27	Nigel Wilson	.25
28	David Nied	.25
29	Pat Listach	.25
30	Eric Karros	.25
31	Checklist	.05

Elite

		NM/M
Complete Set (20):		150.00
Common Player:		5.00
19	Fred McGriff	5.00
20	Ryne Sandberg	15.00
21	Eddie Murray	10.00
22	Paul Molitor	10.00
23	Barry Larkin	5.00
24	Don Mattingly	20.00
25	Dennis Eckersley	10.00
26	Roberto Alomar	6.50
27	Edgar Martinez	5.00
28	Gary Sheffield	6.50
29	Darren Daulton	5.00
30	Larry Walker	5.00

31	Barry Bonds	30.00
32	Andy Van Slyke	5.00
33	Mark McGwire	25.00
34	Cecil Fielder	5.00
35	Dave Winfield	10.00
36	Juan Gonzalez	7.50
---	Robin Yount (Legend)	17.50
---	Will Clark (Signature)	40.00

Long Ball Leaders

		NM/M
	Complete Set (18):	5.00
	Common Player:	.10
1	Rob Deer	.10
2	Fred McGriff	.10
3	Albert Belle	.15
4	Mark McGwire	2.00
5	Dave Justice	.10
6	Jose Canseco	.25
7	Kent Hrbek	.10
8	Roberto Alomar	.20
9	Ken Griffey, Jr.	1.50
10	Frank Thomas	.50
11	Darryl Strawberry	.10
12	Felix Jose	.10
13	Cecil Fielder	.10
14	Juan Gonzalez	.25
15	Ryne Sandberg	.75
16	Gary Sheffield	.20
17	Jeff Bagwell	.50
18	Larry Walker	.10

Masters of the Game

		NM/M
	Complete Set (16):	15.00
	Common Player:	1.00
1	Frank Thomas	1.50
2	Nolan Ryan	3.00
3	Gary Sheffield	1.25
4	Fred McGriff	1.00
5	Ryne Sandberg	1.75
6	Cal Ripken, Jr.	3.00
7	Jose Canseco	1.25
8	Ken Griffey, Jr.	2.00
9	Will Clark	1.00
10	Roberto Alomar	1.00
11	Juan Gonzalez	1.50
12	David Justice	1.00
13	Kirby Puckett	1.75
14	Barry Bonds	3.00
15	Robin Yount	1.50
16	Deion Sanders	1.00

Elite Dominators

		NM/M
	Complete Set (20):	135.00
	Common Player:	3.00
1	Ryne Sandberg	10.00
2	Fred McGriff	3.00
3	Greg Maddux	10.00
4	Ron Gant	3.00
5	Dave Justice	3.00
6	Don Mattingly	12.00
7	Tim Salmon	3.00
8	Mike Piazza	12.00
9	John Olerud	3.00
10	Nolan Ryan	20.00
11	Juan Gonzalez	7.50
12	Ken Griffey, Jr.	12.00
13	Frank Thomas	7.50
14	Tom Glavine	4.50
15	George Brett	12.00
16	Barry Bonds	20.00
17	Albert Belle	3.00
18	Paul Molitor	9.00
19	Cal Ripken, Jr.	20.00
20	Roberto Alomar	5.00
	Autographed Cards:	
6	Don Mattingly	35.00
10	Nolan Ryan	65.00
11	Juan Gonzalez	20.00
18	Paul Molitor	16.00

1993 DONRUSS PREVIEWS

		NM/M
	Complete Set (22):	60.00
	Common Player:	1.50
1	Tom Glavine	2.00
2	Ryne Sandberg	5.00
3	Barry Larkin	1.50
4	Jeff Bagwell	4.00
5	Eric Karros	1.50
6	Larry Walker	1.50
7	Eddie Murray	4.00
8	Darren Daulton	1.50
9	Andy Van Slyke	1.50
10	Gary Sheffield	2.00
11	Will Clark	1.75
12	Cal Ripken Jr.	9.00
13	Roger Clemens	6.00
14	Frank Thomas	4.00
15	Cecil Fielder	1.50
16	George Brett	6.00
17	Robin Yount	4.00
18	Don Mattingly	6.00
19	Dennis Eckersley	4.00
20	Ken Griffey Jr.	7.50
21	Jose Canseco	2.50
22	Roberto Alomar	2.00

1994 DONRUSS

		NM/M
	Complete Set (660):	15.00
	Common Player:	.05
	Series 1 or 2 Pack (13):	.50
	Series 1 or 2 Box (36):	10.00
1	Nolan Ryan (Career Salute 27 Years)	2.00
2	Mike Piazza	1.00
3	Moises Alou	.05
4	Ken Griffey, Jr.	1.00
5	Gary Sheffield	.25
6	Roberto Alomar	.25
7	John Kruk	.05
8	Gregg Olson	.05
9	Gregg Jefferies	.05
10	Tony Gwynn	.65
11	Chad Curtis	.05
12	Craig Biggio	.05
13	John Burkett	.05
14	Carlos Baerga	.05
15	Robin Yount	.60
16	Dennis Eckersley	.50
17	Dwight Gooden	.05
18	Ryne Sandberg	.65
19	Rickey Henderson	.60
20	Jack McDowell	.05
21	Jay Bell	.05
22	Kevin Brown	.10
23	Robin Ventura	.05
24	Paul Molitor	.60
25	Dave Justice	.05
26	Rafael Palmeiro	.60
27	Cecil Fielder	.05
28	Chuck Knoblauch	.05
29	Dave Hollins	.05
30	Jimmy Key	.05
31	Mark Langston	.05
32	Darryl Kile	.05
33	Ruben Sierra	.05
34	Ron Gant	.05
35	Ozzie Smith	.65
36	Wade Boggs	.65
37	Marquis Grissom	.05
38	Will Clark	.10
39	Kenny Lofton	.05
40	Cal Ripken, Jr.	2.00
41	Steve Avery	.05
42	Mo Vaughn	.05
43	Brian McRae	.05
44	Mickey Tettleton	.05
45	Barry Larkin	.05
46	Charlie Hayes	.05
47	Kevin Appier	.05
48	Robby Thompson	.05
49	Juan Gonzalez	.60
50	Paul O'Neill	.05
51	Marcos Armas	.05
52	Mike Butcher	.05
53	Ken Caminiti	.05
54	Pat Borders	.05
55	Pedro Munoz	.05
56	Tim Belcher	.05
57	Paul Assenmacher	.05
58	Damon Berryhill	.05
59	Ricky Bones	.05
60	Rene Arocha	.05
61	Shawn Boskie	.05
62	Pedro Astacio	.05
63	Frank Bolick	.05
64	Bud Black	.05
65	Sandy Alomar, Jr.	.05
66	Rich Amaral	.05
67	Luis Aquino	.05
68	Kevin Baez	.05
69	Mike Devereaux	.05
70	Andy Ashby	.05
71	Larry Andersen	.05
72	Steve Cooke	.05
73	Mario Daiz	.05
74	Rob Deer	.05
75	Bobby Ayala	.05
76	Freddie Benavides	.05
77	Stan Belinda	.05
78	John Doherty	.05
79	Willie Banks	.05
80	Spike Owen	.05
81	Mike Bordick	.05
82	Chili Davis	.05
83	Luis Gonzalez	.25
84	Ed Sprague	.05
85	Jeff Reboulet	.05
86	Jason Bere	.05
87	Mark Hutton	.05
88	Jeff Blauser	.05
89	Cal Eldred	.05
90	Bernard Gilkey	.05
91	Frank Castillo	.05
92	Jim Gott	.05
93	Greg Colbrunn	.05
94	Jeff Brantley	.05
95	Jeremy Hernandez	.05
96	Norm Charlton	.05
97	Alex Arias	.05
98	John Franco	.05
99	Chris Hoiles	.05
100	Brad Ausmus	.05
101	Wes Chamberlain	.05
102	Mark Dewey	.05
103	Benji Gil (Rated Rookie)	.05
104	John Dopson	.05
105	John Smiley	.05
106	David Nied	.05
107	George Brett (Career Salute 21 Years)	.75
108	Kirk Gibson	.05
109	Larry Casian	.05
110	Ryne Sandberg 2,000 Hits Checklist	.25
111	Brent Gates	.05
112	Damion Easley	.05
113	Pete Harnisch	.05
114	Danny Cox	.05
115	Kevin Tapani	.05
116	Roberto Hernandez	.05
117	Domingo Jean	.05
118	Sid Bream	.05
119	Doug Henry	.05
120	Omar Olivares	.05
121	Mike Harkey	.05
122	Carlos Hernandez	.05
123	Jeff Fassero	.05
124	Dave Burba	.05
125	Wayne Kirby	.05
126	John Cummings	.05
127	Bret Barberie	.05
128	Todd Hundley	.05
129	Tim Hulett	.05
130	Phil Clark	.05
131	Danny Jackson	.05
132	Tom Foley	.05
133	Donald Harris	.05
134	Scott Fletcher	.05
135	Johnny Ruffin (Rated Rookie)	.05
136	Jerald Clark	.05
137	Billy Brewer	.05
138	Dan Gladden	.05
139	Eddie Guardado	.05
140	Cal Ripken, Jr. 2,000 Hits Checklist	.25
141	Scott Hemond	.05
142	Steve Frey	.05
143	Xavier Hernandez	.05
144	Mark Eichhorn	.05
145	Ellis Burks	.05
146	Jim Leyritz	.05
147	Mark Lemke	.05
148	Pat Listach	.05
149	Donovan Osborne	.05
150	Glenallen Hill	.05
151	Orel Hershiser	.05
152	Darrin Fletcher	.05
153	Royce Clayton	.05
154	Derek Lilliquist	.05
155	Mike Felder	.05
156	Jeff Conine	.05
157	Ryan Thompson	.05
158	Ben McDonald	.05
159	Ricky Gutierrez	.05
160	Terry Mulholland	.05
161	Carlos Garcia	.05
162	Tom Henke	.05
163	Mike Greenwell	.05
164	Thomas Howard	.05
165	Joe Girardi	.05
166	Hubie Brooks	.05
167	Greg Gohr	.05
168	Chip Hale	.05
169	Rick Honeycutt	.05
170	Hilly Hathaway	.05
171	Todd Jones	.05
172	Tony Fernandez	.05
173	Bo Jackson	.10
174	Bobby Munoz	.05
175	Greg McMichael	.05
176	Graeme Lloyd	.05
177	Tom Pagnozzi	.05
178	Derrick May	.05
179	Pedro Martinez	.60
180	Ken Hill	.05
181	Bryan Hickerson	.05
182	Jose Mesa	.05
183	Dave Fleming	.05
184	Henry Cotto	.05
185	Jeff Kent	.05
186	Mark McLemore	.05
187	Trevor Hoffman	.05
188	Todd Pratt	.05
189	Blas Minor	.05
190	Charlie Leibrandt	.05
191	Tony Pena	.05
192	*Larry Luebbers*	.05
193	Greg Harris	.05
194	David Cone	.05
195	Bill Gullickson	.05
196	Brian Harper	.05
197	Steve Karsay (Rated Rookie)	.05
198	Greg Myers	.05
199	Mark Portugal	.05
200	Pat Hentgen	.05
201	Mike La Valliere	.05
202	Mike Stanley	.05
203	Kent Mercker	.05
204	Dave Nilsson	.05
205	Erik Pappas	.05
206	Mike Morgan	.05
207	Roger McDowell	.05
208	Mike Lansing	.05
209	Kirt Manwaring	.05
210	Randy Milligan	.05
211	Erik Hanson	.05
212	Orestes Destrade	.05
213	Mike Maddux	.05
214	Alan Mills	.05
215	Tim Mauser	.05
216	Ben Rivera	.05
217	Don Slaught	.05
218	Bob Patterson	.05
219	Carlos Quintana	.05
220	Tim Raines 2,000 Hits Checklist	.05
221	Hal Morris	.05
222	Darren Holmes	.05
223	Chris Gwynn	.05
224	Chad Kreuter	.05
225	Mike Hartley	.05
226	Scott Lydy	.05
227	Eduardo Perez	.05
228	Greg Swindell	.05
229	Al Leiter	.05
230	Scott Radinsky	.05
231	Bob Wickman	.05

232 Otis Nixon .05
233 Kevin Reimer .05
234 Geronimo Pena .05
235 Kevin Roberson (Rated Rookie) .05
236 Jody Reed .05
237 Kirk Rueter (Rated Rookie) .05
238 Willie McGee .05
239 Charles Nagy .05
240 Tim Leary .05
241 Carl Everett .05
242 Charlie O'Brien .05
243 Mike Pagliarulo .05
244 Kerry Taylor .05
245 Kevin Stocker .05
246 Joel Johnston .05
247 Geno Petralli .05
248 Jeff Russell .05
249 Joe Oliver .05
250 Robert Mejia .05
251 Chris Haney .05
252 Bill Krueger .05
253 Shane Mack .05
254 Terry Steinbach .05
255 Luis Polonia .05
256 Eddie Taubensee .05
257 Dave Stewart .05
258 Tim Raines .05
259 Bernie Williams .10
260 John Smoltz .05
261 Kevin Seitzer .05
262 Bob Tewksbury .05
263 Bob Scanlan .05
264 Henry Rodriguez .05
265 Tim Scott .05
266 Scott Sanderson .05
267 Eric Plunk .05
268 Edgar Martinez .05
269 Charlie Hough .05
270 Joe Orsulak .05
271 Harold Reynolds .05
272 Tim Teufel .05
273 Bobby Thigpen .05
274 Randy Tomlin .05
275 Gary Redus .05
276 Ken Ryan .05
277 Tim Pugh .05
278 Jayhawk Owens .05
279 Phil Hiatt (Rated Rookie) .05
280 Alan Trammell .05
281 Dave McCarty (Rated Rookie) .05
282 Bob Welch .05
283 J.T. Snow .05
284 Brian Williams .05
285 Devon White .05
286 Steve Sax .05
287 Tony Tarasco .05
288 Bill Spiers .05
289 Allen Watson .05
290 Rickey Henderson 2,000 Hits Checklist .05
291 Joe Vizcaino .05
292 Darryl Strawberry .05
293 John Wetteland .05
294 Bill Swift .05
295 Jeff Treadway .05
296 Tino Martinez .05
297 Richie Lewis .05
298 Bret Saberhagen .05
299 Arthur Rhodes .05
300 Guillermo Velasquez .05
301 Milt Thompson .05
302 Doug Strange .05
303 Aaron Sele .05
304 Bip Roberts .05
305 Bruce Ruffin .05
306 Jose Lind .05
307 David Wells .05
308 Bobby Witt .05
309 Mark Wohlers .05
310 B.J. Surhoff .05
311 Mark Whiten .05
312 Turk Wendell .05
313 Raul Mondesi .05
314 *Brian Turang* .05
315 Chris Hammond .05
316 Tim Bogar .05
317 Brad Pennington .05
318 Tim Worrell .05
319 Mitch Williams .05
320 Rondell White (Rated Rookie) .05
321 Frank Viola .05
322 Manny Ramirez (Rated Rookie) 1.00
323 Gary Wayne .05
324 Mike Macfarlane .05
325 Russ Springer .05
326 Tim Wallach .05
327 Salomon Torres (Rated Rookie) .05
328 Omar Vizquel .05
329 *Andy Tomberlin* .05
330 Chris Sabo .05
331 Mike Mussina .35
332 Andy Benes .05
333 Darren Daulton .05
334 Orlando Merced .05
335 Mark McGwire 1.50
336 Dave Winfield .60
337 Sammy Sosa 1.00
338 Eric Karros .05
339 Greg Vaughn .05
340 Don Mattingly .75
341 Frank Thomas .60
342 Fred McGriff .05
343 Kirby Puckett .65
344 Roberto Kelly .05
345 Wally Joyner .05
346 Andres Galarraga .05
347 Bobby Bonilla .05
348 Benito Santiago .05
349 Barry Bonds 2.00
350 Delino DeShields .05
351 Albert Belle .15
352 Randy Johnson .60
353 Tim Salmon .15
354 John Olerud .05
355 Dean Palmer .05
356 Roger Clemens .85
357 Jim Abbott .05
358 Mark Grace .10
359 Ozzie Guillen .05
360 Lou Whitaker .05
361 Jose Rijo .05
362 Jeff Montgomery .05
363 Chuck Finley .05
364 Tom Glavine .25
365 Jeff Bagwell .60
366 Joe Carter .05
367 Ray Lankford .05
368 Ramon Martinez .05
369 Jay Buhner .05
370 Matt Williams .05
371 Larry Walker .05
372 Jose Canseco .30
373 Len Dykstra .05
374 Bryan Harvey .05
375 Andy Van Slyke .05
376 Ivan Rodriguez .50
377 Kevin Mitchell .05
378 Travis Fryman .05
379 Duane Ward .05
380 Greg Maddux .65
381 Scott Servais .05
382 Greg Olson .05
383 Rey Sanchez .05
384 Tom Kramer .05
385 David Valle .05
386 Eddie Murray .60
387 Kevin Higgins .05
388 Dan Wilson .05
389 Todd Frohwirth .05
390 Gerald Williams .05
391 Hipolito Pichardo .05
392 Pat Meares .05
393 Luis Lopez .05
394 Ricky Jordan .05
395 Bob Walk .05
396 Sid Fernandez .05
397 Todd Worrell .05
398 Darryl Hamilton .05
399 Randy Myers .05
400 Rod Brewer .05
401 Lance Blankenship .05
402 Steve Finley .05
403 *Phil Leftwich* .05
404 Juan Guzman .05
405 Anthony Young .05
406 Jeff Gardner .05
407 Ryan Bowen .05
408 Fernando Valenzuela .05
409 David West .05
410 Kenny Rogers .05
411 Bob Zupcic .05
412 Eric Young .05
413 Bret Boone .05
414 Danny Tartabull .05
415 Bob MacDonald .05
416 Ron Karkovice .05
417 Scott Cooper .05
418 Dante Bichette .05
419 Tripp Cromer .05
420 Billy Ashley .05
421 Roger Smithberg .05
422 Dennis Martinez .05
423 Mike Blowers .05
424 Darren Lewis .05
425 Junior Ortiz .05
426 Butch Huskey .05
427 Jimmy Poole .05
428 Walt Weiss .05
429 Scott Bankhead .05
430 Deion Sanders .05
431 Scott Bullett .05
432 Jeff Huson .05
433 Tyler Green .05
434 Billy Hatcher .05
435 Bob Hamelin .05
436 Reggie Sanders .05
437 Scott Erickson .05
438 Steve Reed .05
439 Randy Velarde .05
440 Checklist (Tony Gwynn 2,000 Hits) .15
441 Terry Leach .05
442 Danny Bautista .05
443 Kent Hrbek .05
444 Rick Wilkins .05
445 Tony Phillips .05
446 Dion James .05
447 Joey Cora .05
448 Andre Dawson .15
449 Pedro Castellano .05
450 Tom Gordon .05
451 Rob Dibble .05
452 Ron Darling .05
453 Chipper Jones .65
454 Joe Grahe .05
455 Domingo Cedeno .05
456 Tom Edens .05
457 Mitch Webster .05
458 Jose Bautista .05
459 Troy O'Leary .05
460 Todd Zeile .05
461 Sean Berry .05
462 *Brad Holman* .05
463 Dave Martinez .05
464 Mark Lewis .05
465 Paul Carey .05
466 Jack Armstrong .05
467 David Telgheder .05
468 Gene Harris .05
469 Danny Darwin .05
470 Kim Batiste .05
471 Tim Wakefield .05
472 Craig Lefferts .05
473 Jacob Brumfield .05
474 Lance Painter .05
475 Milt Cuyler .05
476 Melido Perez .05
477 Derek Parks .05
478 Gary DiSarcina .05
479 Steve Bedrosian .05
480 Eric Anthony .05
481 Julio Franco .05
482 Tommy Greene .05
483 Pat Kelly .05
484 Nate Minchey (Rated Rookie) .05
485 William Pennyfeather .05
486 Harold Baines .05
487 Howard Johnson .05
488 Angel Miranda .05
489 Scott Sanders .05
490 Shawon Dunston .05
491 Mel Rojas .05
492 Jeff Nelson .05
493 Archi Cianfrocco .05
494 Al Martin .05
495 Mike Gallego .05
496 Mike Henneman .05
497 Armando Reynoso .05
498 Mickey Morandini .05
499 Rick Renteria .05
500 Rick Sutcliffe .05
501 Bobby Jones (Rated Rookie) .05
502 Gary Gaetti .05
503 Rick Aguilera .05
504 Todd Stottlemyre .05
505 Mike Mohler .05
506 Mike Stanton .05
507 Jose Guzman .05
508 Kevin Rogers .05
509 Chuck Carr .05
510 Chris Jones .05
511 Brent Mayne .05
512 Greg Harris .05
513 Dave Henderson .05
514 Eric Hillman .05
515 Dan Peltier .05
516 Craig Shipley .05
517 John Valentin .05
518 Wilson Alvarez .05
519 Andujar Cedeno .05
520 Troy Neel .05
521 Tom Candiotti .05
522 Matt Mieske .05
523 Jim Thome .05
524 Lou Frazier .05
525 Mike Jackson .05
526 Pedro Martinez .05
527 Roger Pavlik .05
528 Kent Bottenfield .05
529 Felix Jose .05
530 Mark Guthrie .05
531 Steve Farr .05
532 Craig Paquette .05
533 Doug Jones .05
534 Luis Alicea .05
535 Cory Snyder .05
536 Paul Sorrento .05
537 Nigel Wilson .05
538 Jeff King .05
539 Willie Green .05
540 Kirk McCaskill .05
541 Al Osuna .05
542 Greg Hibbard .05
543 Brett Butler .05
544 Jose Valentin .05
545 Wil Cordero .05
546 Chris Bosio .05
547 Jamie Moyer .05
548 Jim Eisenreich .05
549 Vinny Castilla .05
550 Checklist (Dave Winfield 3,000 Hits) .05
551 John Roper .05
552 Lance Johnson .05
553 Scott Kamieniecki .05
554 Mike Moore .05
555 Steve Buechele .05
556 Terry Pendleton .05
557 Todd Van Poppel .05
558 Rob Butler .05
559 Zane Smith .05
560 David Hulse .05
561 Tim Costo .05
562 John Habyan .05
563 Terry Jorgensen .05
564 Matt Nokes .05
565 Kevin McReynolds .05
566 Phil Plantier .05
567 Chris Turner .05
568 Carlos Delgado .45
569 John Jaha .05
570 Dwight Smith .05
571 John Vander Wal .05
572 Trevor Wilson .05
573 Felix Fermin .05
574 Marc Newfield (Rated Rookie) .05
575 Jeromy Burnitz .05
576 Leo Gomez .05
577 Curt Schilling .25
578 Kevin Young .05
579 *Jerry Spradlin* .05
580 Curt Leskanic .05
581 Carl Willis .05
582 Alex Fernandez .05
583 Mark Holzemer .05
584 Domingo Martinez .05
585 Pete Smith .05
586 Brian Jordan .05
587 Kevin Gross .05
588 J.R. Phillips (Rated Rookie) .05
589 Chris Nabholz .05
590 Bill Wertz .05
591 Derek Bell .05
592 Brady Anderson .05
593 Matt Turner .05
594 Pete Incaviglia .05
595 Greg Gagne .05
596 John Flaherty .05
597 Scott Livingstone .05
598 Rod Bolton .05
599 Mike Perez .05
600 Checklist (Roger Clemens 2,000 Strikeouts) .15
601 Tony Castillo .05
602 Henry Mercedes .05
603 Mike Fetters .05
604 Rod Beck .05
605 Damon Buford .05
606 Matt Whiteside .05
607 Shawn Green .35
608 Midre Cummings (Rated Rookie) .05
609 Jeff McNeeley .05
610 Danny Sheaffer .05
611 Paul Wagner .05

612 Torey Lovullo .05
613 Javier Lopez .05
614 Mariano Duncan .05
615 Doug Brocail .05
616 Dave Hansen .05
617 Ryan Klesko .05
618 Eric Davis .05
619 Scott Ruffcorn (Rated Rookie) .05
620 Mike Trombley .05
621 Jaime Navarro .05
622 Rheal Cormier .05
623 Jose Offerman .05
624 David Segui .05
625 Robb Nen (Rated Rookie) .05
626 Dave Gallagher .05
627 *Julian Tavarez* .05
628 Chris Gomez .05
629 Jeffrey Hammonds (Rated Rookie) .05
630 Scott Brosius .05
631 Willie Blair .05
632 Doug Drabek .05
633 Bill Wegman .05
634 Jeff McKnight .05
635 Rich Rodriguez .05
636 Steve Trachsel .05
637 Buddy Groom .05
638 Sterling Hitchcock .05
639 Chuck McElroy .05
640 Rene Gonzales .05
641 Dan Plesac .05
642 Jeff Branson .05
643 Darrell Whitmore .05
644 Paul Quantrill .05
645 Rich Rowland .05
646 *Curtis Pride* .05
647 Erik Plantenberg .05
648 Albie Lopez .05
649 *Rich Batchelor* .05
650 Lee Smith .05
651 Cliff Floyd .05
652 Pete Schourek .05
653 Reggie Jefferson .05
654 Bill Haselman .05
655 Steve Hosey .05
656 Mark Clark .05
657 Mark Davis .05
658 Dave Magadan .05
659 Candy Maldonado .05
660 Checklist (Mark Langston 2,0000 Strikeouts) .05

Anniversary-1984

NM/M
Complete Set (10): 13.50
Common Player: .60
1 Joe Carter .60
2 Robin Yount 1.00
3 George Brett 1.50
4 Rickey Henderson 1.00
5 Nolan Ryan 4.50
6 Cal Ripken, Jr. 4.50
7 Wade Boggs 1.25
8 Don Mattingly 1.50
9 Ryne Sandberg 1.25
10 Tony Gwynn 1.25

Decade Dominators

NM/M
Complete Set (20): 15.00
Common Player: .35
Series 1
1 Cecil Fielder .35
2 Barry Bonds 2.50
3 Fred McGriff .35
4 Matt Williams .35
5 Joe Carter .35
6 Juan Gonzalez .75
7 Jose Canseco .50
8 Ron Gant .35
9 Ken Griffey, Jr. 1.50
10 Mark McGwire 2.00
Series 2
1 Tony Gwynn 1.00
2 Frank Thomas .65
3 Paul Molitor .75
4 Edgar Martinez .35
5 Kirby Puckett 1.00
6 Ken Griffey, Jr. 1.50
7 Barry Bonds 2.50
8 Willie McGee .35
9 Len Dykstra .35
10 John Kruk .35

Diamond Kings

NM/M
Complete Set (30): 12.00

Common Player: .25
1 Barry Bonds 2.50
2 Mo Vaughn .25
3 Steve Avery .25
4 Tim Salmon .25
5 Rick Wilkins .25
6 Brian Harper .25
7 Andres Galarraga .25
8 Albert Belle .35
9 John Kruk .25
10 Ivan Rodriguez .75
11 Tony Gwynn 1.25
12 Brian McRae .25
13 Bobby Bonilla .25
14 Ken Griffey, Jr. 2.00
15 Mike Piazza 2.00
16 Don Mattingly 1.50
17 Barry Larkin .25
18 Ruben Sierra .25
19 Orlando Merced .25
20 Greg Vaughn .25
21 Gregg Jefferies .25
22 Cecil Fielder .25
23 Moises Alou .25
24 John Olerud .25
25 Gary Sheffield .25
26 Mike Mussina .60
27 Jeff Bagwell 1.00
28 Frank Thomas 1.00
29 Dave Winfield (King of Kings) 1.00
30 Dick Perez (Checklist) .25

Elite

NM/M
Complete Set (12): 50.00
Common Player: 3.00
37 Frank Thomas 4.50
38 Tony Gwynn 5.00
39 Tim Salmon 3.50
40 Albert Belle 3.50
41 John Kruk 3.00
42 Juan Gonzalez 4.00
43 John Olerud 3.00
44 Barry Bonds 10.00
45 Ken Griffey, Jr. 6.50
46 Mike Piazza 6.50
47 Jack McDowell 3.00
48 Andres Galarraga 3.00

Long Ball Leaders

NM/M
Complete Set (10): 3.00
Common Player: .15
1 Cecil Fielder .15
2 Dean Palmer .15
3 Andres Galarraga .15
4 Bo Jackson .20

5 Ken Griffey, Jr. .75
6 Dave Justice .15
7 Mike Piazza .75
8 Frank Thomas .50
9 Barry Bonds 1.50
10 Juan Gonzalez .40

Spirit of the Game

NM/M
Complete Set (10): 10.00
Common Player: .70
1 John Olerud .50
2 Barry Bonds 2.50
3 Ken Griffey, Jr. 2.00
4 Mike Piazza 2.00
5 Juan Gonzalez .75
6 Frank Thomas 1.00
7 Tim Salmon .50
8 Dave Justice .50
9 Don Mattingly 1.50
10 Len Dykstra .50

Special Edition - Gold

NM/M
Complete Set (100): 7.50
Common Player: .10
1 Nolan Ryan 1.50
2 Mike Piazza 1.00
3 Moises Alou .10
4 Ken Griffey, Jr. 1.00
5 Gary Sheffield .25
6 Roberto Alomar .25
7 John Kruk .10
8 Gregg Olson .10
9 Gregg Jefferies .10
10 Tony Gwynn .65
11 Chad Curtis .10
12 Craig Biggio .10
13 John Burkett .10
14 Carlos Baerga .10
15 Robin Yount .60
16 Dennis Eckersley .60
17 Dwight Gooden .10
18 Ryne Sandberg .65
19 Rickey Henderson .60
20 Jack McDowell .10
21 Jay Bell .10
22 Kevin Brown .15
23 Robin Ventura .10
24 Paul Molitor .60
25 David Justice .10
26 Rafael Palmeiro .60
27 Cecil Fielder .10
28 Chuck Knoblauch .10
29 Dave Hollins .10
30 Jimmy Key .10
31 Mark Langston .10
32 Darryl Kile .10
33 Ruben Sierra .10
34 Ron Gant .10
35 Ozzie Smith .65
36 Wade Boggs .65
37 Marquis Grissom .10
38 Will Clark .15
39 Kenny Lofton .10
40 Cal Ripken, Jr. 1.50
41 Steve Avery .10
42 Mo Vaughn .10
43 Brian McRae .10
44 Mickey Tettleton .10
45 Barry Larkin .10
46 Charlie Hayes .10
47 Kevin Appier .10
48 Robby Thompson .10
49 Juan Gonzalez .60
50 Paul O'Neill .10
51 Mike Mussina .45
52 Andy Benes .10
53 Darren Daulton .10
54 Orlando Merced .10
55 Mark McGwire 1.25
56 Dave Winfield .60
57 Sammy Sosa 1.00
58 Eric Karros .10
59 Greg Vaughn .10
60 Don Mattingly .75
61 Frank Thomas .60
62 Fred McGriff .10
63 Kirby Puckett .65
64 Roberto Kelly .10
65 Wally Joyner .10
66 Andres Galarraga .10
67 Bobby Bonilla .10
68 Benito Santiago .10
69 Barry Bonds 1.50
70 Delino DeShields .10
71 Albert Belle .15
72 Randy Johnson .60
73 Tim Salmon .10
74 John Olerud .10
75 Dean Palmer .10
76 Roger Clemens .75
77 Jim Abbott .10
78 Mark Grace .15
79 Ozzie Guillen .10
80 Lou Whitaker .10
81 Jose Rijo .10
82 Jeff Montgomery .10
83 Chuck Finley .10
84 Tom Glavine .25
85 Jeff Bagwell .60
86 Joe Carter .10
87 Ray Lankford .10
88 Ramon Martinez .10
89 Jay Buhner .10
90 Matt Williams .10
91 Larry Walker .10
92 Jose Canseco .25
93 Len Dykstra .10
94 Bryan Harvey .10
95 Andy Van Slyke .10
96 Ivan Rodriguez .50
97 Kevin Mitchell .10
98 Travis Fryman .10
99 Duane Ward .10
100 Greg Maddux .65

1995 DONRUSS

NM/M
Complete Set (550): 20.00
Common Player: .05
Series 1 or 2 Pack (12): .50
Series 1 or 2 Wax Box (36): 12.50
1 Dave Justice. .05
2 Rene Arocha. .05
3 Sandy Alomar Jr. .05
4 Luis Lopez. .05
5 Mike Piazza. 1.00
6 Bobby Jones. .05
7 Damion Easley. .05
8 Barry Bonds. 2.00
9 Mike Mussina. .45
10 Kevin Seitzer. .05
11 John Smiley. .05
12 W. VanLandingham. .05
13 Ron Darling. .05
14 Walt Weiss .05

No.	Player	Price
15	Mike Lansing	.05
16	Allen Watson	.05
17	Aaron Sele	.05
18	Randy Johnson	.60
19	Dean Palmer	.05
20	Jeff Bagwell	.60
21	Curt Schilling	.25
22	Darrell Whitmore	.05
23	Steve Trachsel	.05
24	Dan Wilson	.05
25	Steve Finley	.05
26	Bret Boone	.05
27	Charles Johnson	.05
28	Mike Stanton	.05
29	Ismael Valdes	.05
30	Salomon Torres	.05
31	Eric Anthony	.05
32	Spike Owen	.05
33	Joey Cora	.05
34	Robert Eenhoorn	.05
35	Rick White	.05
36	Omar Vizquel	.05
37	Carlos Delgado	.45
38	Eddie Williams	.05
39	Shawon Dunston	.05
40	Darrin Fletcher	.05
41	Leo Gomez	.05
42	Juan Gonzalez	.60
43	Luis Alicea	.05
44	Ken Ryan	.05
45	Lou Whitaker	.05
46	Mike Blowers	.05
47	Willie Blair	.05
48	Todd Van Poppel	.05
49	Roberto Alomar	.25
50	Ozzie Smith	.75
51	Sterling Hitchcock	.05
52	Mo Vaughn	.05
53	Rick Aguilera	.05
54	Kent Mercker	.05
55	Don Mattingly	1.00
56	Bob Scanlan	.05
57	Wilson Alvarez	.05
58	Jose Mesa	.05
59	Scott Kamieniecki	.05
60	Todd Jones	.05
61	John Kruk	.05
62	Mike Stanley	.05
63	Tino Martinez	.05
64	Eddie Zambrano	.05
65	Todd Hundley	.05
66	Jamie Moyer	.05
67	Rich Amaral	.05
68	Jose Valentin	.05
69	Alex Gonzalez	.05
70	Kurt Abbott	.05
71	Delino DeShields	.05
72	Brian Anderson	.05
73	John Vander Wal	.05
74	Turner Ward	.05
75	Tim Raines	.05
76	Mark Acre	.05
77	Jose Offerman	.05
78	Jimmy Key	.05
79	Mark Whiten	.05
80	Mark Gubicza	.05
81	Darren Hall	.05
82	Travis Fryman	.05
83	Cal Ripken, Jr.	2.00
84	Geronimo Berroa	.05
85	Bret Barberie	.05
86	Andy Ashby	.05
87	Steve Avery	.05
88	Rich Becker	.05
89	John Valentin	.05
90	Glenallen Hill	.05
91	Carlos Garcia	.05
92	Dennis Martinez	.05
93	Pat Kelly	.05
q4	Orlando Miller	.05
95	Felix Jose	.05
96	Mike Kingery	.05
97	Jeff Kent	.05
98	Pete Incaviglia	.05
99	Chad Curtis	.05
100	Thomas Howard	.05
101	Hector Carrasco	.05
102	Tom Pagnozzi	.05
103	Danny Tartabull	.05
104	Donnie Elliott	.05
105	Danny Jackson	.05
106	Steve Dunn	.05
107	Roger Salkeld	.05
108	Jeff King	.05
109	Cecil Fielder	.05
110	Checklist	.05
111	Denny Neagle	.05
112	Troy Neel	.05
113	Rod Beck	.05
114	Alex Rodriguez	1.50
115	Joey Eischen	.05
116	Tom Candiotti	.05
117	Ray McDavid	.05
118	Vince Coleman	.05
119	Pete Harnisch	.05
120	David Nied	.05
121	Pat Rapp	.05
122	Sammy Sosa	1.00
123	Steve Reed	.05
124	Jose Oliva	.05
125	Rick Bottalico	.05
126	Jose DeLeon	.05
127	Pat Hentgen	.05
128	Will Clark	.10
129	Mark Dewey	.05
130	Greg Vaughn	.05
131	Darren Dreifort	.05
132	Ed Sprague	.05
133	Lee Smith	.05
134	Charles Nagy	.05
135	Phil Plantier	.05
136	Jason Jacome	.05
137	Jose Lima	.05
138	J.R. Phillips	.05
139	J.T. Snow	.05
140	Mike Huff	.05
141	Billy Brewer	.05
142	Jeromy Burnitz	.05
143	Ricky Bones	.05
144	Carlos Rodriguez	.05
145	Luis Gonzalez	.25
146	Mark Lemke	.05
147	Al Martin	.05
148	Mike Bordick	.05
149	Robb Nen	.05
150	Wil Cordero	.05
151	Edgar Martinez	.05
152	Gerald Williams	.05
153	Esteban Beltre	.05
154	Mike Moore	.05
155	Mark Langston	.05
156	Mark Clark	.05
157	Bobby Ayala	.05
158	Rick Wilkins	.05
159	Bobby Munoz	.05
160	Checklist	.05
161	Scott Erickson	.05
162	Paul Molitor	.60
163	Jon Lieber	.05
164	Jason Grimsley	.05
165	Norberto Martin	.05
166	Javier Lopez	.05
167	Brian McRae	.05
168	Gary Sheffield	.40
169	Marcus Moore	.05
170	John Hudek	.05
171	Kelly Stinett	.05
172	Chris Gomez	.05
173	Rey Sanchez	.05
174	Juan Guzman	.05
175	Chan Ho Park	.05
176	Terry Shumpert	.05
177	Steve Ontiveros	.05
178	Brad Ausmus	.05
179	Tim Davis	.05
180	Billy Ashley	.05
181	Vinny Castilla	.05
182	Bill Spiers	.05
183	Randy Knorr	.05
184	Brian Hunter	.05
185	Pat Meares	.05
186	Steve Buechele	.05
187	Kirt Manwaring	.05
188	Tim Naehring	.05
189	Matt Mieske	.05
190	Josias Manzanillo	.05
191	Greg McMichael	.05
192	Chuck Carr	.05
193	Midre Cummings	.05
194	Darryl Strawberry	.05
195	Greg Gagne	.05
196	Steve Cooke	.05
197	Woody Williams	.05
198	Ron Karkovice	.05
199	Phil Leftwich	.05
200	Jim Thome	.05
201	Brady Anderson	.05
202	Pedro Martinez	.60
203	Steve Karsay	.05
204	Reggie Sanders	.05
205	Bill Risley	.05
206	Jay Bell	.05
207	Kevin Brown	.10
208	Tim Scott	.05
209	Len Dykstra	.05
210	Willie Greene	.05
211	Jim Eisenreich	.05
212	Cliff Floyd	.05
213	Otis Nixon	.05
214	Eduardo Perez	.05
215	Manuel Lee	.05
216	*Armando Benitez*	.10
217	Dave McCarty	.05
218	Scott Livingstone	.05
219	Chad Kreuter	.05
220	Checklist	.05
221	Brian Jordan	.05
222	Matt Whiteside	.05
223	Jim Edmonds	.05
224	Tony Gwynn	.75
225	Jose Lind	.05
226	Marvin Freeman	.05
227	Ken Hill	.05
228	David Hulse	.05
229	Joe Hesketh	.05
230	Roberto Petagine	.05
231	Jeffrey Hammonds	.05
232	John Jaha	.05
233	John Burkett	.05
234	Hal Morris	.05
235	Tony Castillo	.05
236	Ryan Bowen	.05
237	Wayne Kirby	.05
238	Brent Mayne	.05
239	Jim Bullinger	.05
240	Mike Lieberthal	.05
241	Barry Larkin	.05
242	David Segui	.05
243	Jose Bautista	.05
244	Hector Fajardo	.05
245	Orel Hershiser	.05
246	James Mouton	.05
247	Scott Leius	.05
248	Tom Glavine	.25
249	Danny Bautista	.05
250	Jose Mercedes	.05
251	Marquis Grissom	.05
252	Charlie Hayes	.05
253	Ryan Klesko	.05
254	Vicente Palacios	.05
255	Matias Carillo	.05
256	Gary DiSarcina	.05
257	Kirk Gibson	.05
258	Garey Ingram	.05
259	Alex Fernandez	.05
260	John Mabry	.05
261	Chris Howard	.05
262	Miguel Jimenez	.05
263	Heath Slocumb	.05
264	Albert Belle	.15
265	Dave Clark	.05
266	Joe Orsulak	.05
267	Joey Hamilton	.05
268	Mark Portugal	.05
269	Kevin Tapani	.05
270	Sid Fernandez	.05
271	Steve Dreyer	.05
272	Denny Hocking	.05
273	Troy O'Leary	.05
274	Milt Cuyler	.05
275	Frank Thomas	.60
276	Jorge Fabregas	.05
277	Mike Gallego	.05
278	Mickey Morandini	.05
279	Roberto Hernandez	.05
280	Henry Rodriguez	.05
281	Garret Anderson	.05
282	Bob Wickman	.05
283	Gar Finnvold	.05
284	Paul O'Neill	.05
285	Royce Clayton	.05
286	Chuck Knoblauch	.05
287	Johnny Ruffin	.05
288	Dave Nilsson	.05
289	David Cone	.05
290	Chuck McElroy	.05
291	Kevin Stocker	.05
292	Jose Rijo	.05
293	Sean Berry	.05
294	Ozzie Guillen	.05
295	Chris Hoiles	.05
296	Kevin Foster	.05
297	Jeff Frye	.05
298	Lance Johnson	.05
299	Mike Kelly	.05
300	Ellis Burks	.05
301	Roberto Kelly	.05
302	Dante Bichette	.05
303	Alvaro Espinoza	.05
304	Alex Cole	.05
305	Rickey Henderson	.60
306	Dave Weathers	.05
307	Shane Reynolds	.05
308	Bobby Bonilla	.05
309	Junior Felix	.05
310	Jeff Fassero	.05
311	Darren Lewis	.05
312	John Doherty	.05
313	Scott Servais	.05
314	Rick Helling	.05
315	Pedro Martinez	.60
316	Wes Chamberlain	.05
317	Bryan Eversgerd	.05
318	Trevor Hoffman	.05
319	John Patterson	.05
320	Matt Walbeck	.05
321	Jeff Montgomery	.05
322	Mel Rojas	.05
323	Eddie Taubensee	.05
324	Ray Lankford	.05
325	Jose Vizcaino	.05
326	Carlos Baerga	.05
327	Jack Voigt	.05
328	Julio Franco	.05
329	Brent Gates	.05
330	Checklist	.05
331	Greg Maddux	.75
332	Jason Bere	.05
333	Bill Wegman	.05
334	Tuffy Rhodes	.05
335	Kevin Young	.05
336	Andy Benes	.05
337	Pedro Astacio	.05
338	Reggie Jefferson	.05
339	Tim Belcher	.05
340	Ken Griffey Jr.	1.00
341	Mariano Duncan	.05
342	Andres Galarraga	.05
343	Rondell White	.05
344	Cory Bailey	.05
345	Bryan Harvey	.05
346	John Franco	.05
347	Greg Swindell	.05
348	David West	.05
349	Fred McGriff	.05
350	Jose Canseco	.35
351	Orlando Merced	.05
352	Rheal Cormier	.05
353	Carlos Pulido	.05
354	Terry Steinbach	.05
355	Wade Boggs	.75
356	B.J. Surhoff	.05
357	Rafael Palmeiro	.60
358	Anthony Young	.05
359	Tom Brunansky	.05
360	Todd Stottlemyre	.05
361	Chris Turner	.05
362	Joe Boever	.05
363	Jeff Blauser	.05
364	Derek Bell	.05
365	Matt Williams	.05
366	Jeremy Hernandez	.05
367	Joe Girardi	.05
368	Mike Devereaux	.05
369	Jim Abbott	.05
370	Manny Ramirez	.60
371	Kenny Lofton	.05
372	Mark Smith	.05
373	Dave Fleming	.05
374	Dave Stewart	.05
375	Roger Pavlik	.05
376	Hipolito Pichardo	.05
377	Bill Taylor	.05
378	Robin Ventura	.05
379	Bernard Gilkey	.05
380	Kirby Puckett	.75
381	Steve Howe	.05
382	Devon White	.05
383	Roberto Mejia	.05
384	Darrin Jackson	.05
385	Mike Morgan	.05
386	Rusty Meacham	.05
387	Bill Swift	.05
388	Lou Frazier	.05
389	Andy Van Slyke	.05
390	Brett Butler	.05
391	Bobby Witt	.05
392	Jeff Conine	.05
393	Tim Hyers	.05
394	Terry Pendleton	.05
395	Ricky Jordan	.05
396	Eric Plunk	.05
397	Melido Perez	.05
398	Darryl Kile	.05
399	Mark McLemore	.05
400	Greg Harris	.05
401	Jim Leyritz	.05
402	Doug Strange	.05
403	Tim Salmon	.15
404	Terry Mulholland	.05
405	Robby Thompson	.05
406	Ruben Sierra	.05
407	Tony Phillips	.05
408	Moises Alou	.05
409	Felix Fermin	.05
410	Pat Listach	.05

411 Kevin Bass .05
412 Ben McDonald .05
413 Scott Cooper .05
414 Jody Reed .05
415 Deion Sanders .05
416 Ricky Gutierrez .05
417 Gregg Jefferies .05
418 Jack McDowell .05
419 Al Leiter .05
420 Tony Longmire .05
421 Paul Wagner .05
422 Geronimo Pena .05
423 Ivan Rodriguez .60
424 Kevin Gross .05
425 Kirk McCaskill .05
426 Greg Myers .05
427 Roger Clemens .90
428 Chris Hammond .05
429 Randy Myers .05
430 Roger Mason .05
431 Bret Saberhagen .05
432 Jeff Reboulet .05
433 John Olerud .05
434 Bill Gullickson .05
435 Eddie Murray .60
436 Pedro Munoz .05
437 Charlie O'Brien .05
438 Jeff Nelson .05
439 Mike Macfarlane .05
440 Checklist .05
441 Derrick May .05
442 John Roper .05
443 Darryl Hamilton .05
444 Dan Miceli .05
445 Tony Eusebio .05
446 Jerry Browne .05
447 Wally Joyner .05
448 Brian Harper .05
449 Scott Fletcher .05
450 Bip Roberts .05
451 Pete Smith .05
452 Chili Davis .05
453 Dave Hollins .05
454 Tony Pena .05
455 Butch Henry .05
456 Craig Biggio .05
457 Zane Smith .05
458 Ryan Thompson .05
459 Mike Jackson .05
460 Mark McGwire 1.50
461 John Smoltz .05
462 Steve Scarsone .05
463 Greg Colbrunn .05
464 Shawn Green .30
465 David Wells .05
466 Jose Hernandez .05
467 Chip Hale .05
468 Tony Tarasco .05
469 Kevin Mitchell .05
470 Billy Hatcher .05
471 Jay Buhner .05
472 Ken Caminiti .05
473 Tom Henke .05
474 Todd Worrell .05
475 Mark Eichhorn .05
476 Bruce Ruffin .05
477 Chuck Finley .05
478 Marc Newfield .05
479 Paul Shuey .05
480 Bob Tewksbury .05
481 Ramon Martinez .05
482 Melvin Nieves .05
483 Todd Zeile .05
484 Benito Santiago .05
485 Stan Javier .05
486 Kirk Rueter .05
487 Andre Dawson .25
488 Eric Karros .05
489 Dave Magadan .05
490 Checklist .05
491 Randy Velarde .05
492 Larry Walker .05
493 Cris Carpenter .05
494 Tom Gordon .05
495 Dave Burba .05
496 Darren Bragg .05
497 Darren Daulton .05
498 Don Slaught .05
499 Pat Borders .05
500 Lenny Harris .05
501 Joe Ausanio .05
502 Alan Trammell .05
503 Mike Fetters .05
504 Scott Ruffcorn .05
505 Rich Rowland .05
506 Juan Samuel .05
507 Bo Jackson .10
508 Jeff Branson .05
509 Bernie Williams .15
510 Paul Sorrento .05
511 Dennis Eckersley .50
512 Pat Mahomes .05
513 Rusty Greer .05
514 Luis Polonia .05
515 Willie Banks .05
516 John Wetteland .05
517 Mike LaVaillere .05
518 Tommy Greene .05
519 Mark Grace .10
520 Bob Hamelin .05
521 Scott Sanderson .05
522 Joe Carter .05
523 Jeff Brantley .05
524 Andrew Lorraine .05
525 Rico Brogna .05
526 Shane Mack .05
527 Mark Wohlers .05
528 Scott Sanders .05
529 Chris Bosio .05
530 Andujar Cedeno .05
531 Kenny Rogers .05
532 Doug Drabek .05
533 Curt Leskanic .05
534 Craig Shipley .05
535 Craig Grebeck .05
536 Cal Eldred .05
537 Mickey Tettleton .05
538 Harold Baines .05
539 Tim Wallach .05
540 Damon Buford .05
541 Lenny Webster .05
542 Kevin Appier .05
543 Raul Mondesi .05
544 Eric Young .05
545 Russ Davis .05
546 Mike Benjamin .05
547 Mike Greenwell .05
548 Scott Brosius .05
549 Brian Dorsett .05
550 Checklist .05

Press Proofs

NM/M
Complete Set (550): 150.00
Common Player: 1.00
Stars: 15X
(See 1995 Donruss for checklist and base card values.)

All-Stars

NM/M
Complete Set (18): 26.00
Common Player: .40
AL1 Jimmy Key .40
AL2 Ivan Rodriguez 1.25
AL3 Frank Thomas 1.50
AL4 Roberto Alomar .60
AL5 Wade Boggs 2.00
AL6 Cal Ripken, Jr. 4.50
AL7 Joe Carter .40
AL8 Ken Griffey, Jr. 3.00
AL9 Kirby Puckett 2.00
NL1 Greg Maddux 2.00
NL2 Mike Piazza 3.00
NL3 Gregg Jefferies .40
NL4 Mariano Duncan .40
NL5 Matt Williams .40
NL6 Ozzie Smith 2.00
NL7 Barry Bonds 4.50
NL8 Tony Gwynn 2.00
NL9 Dave Justice .40

Bomb Squad

NM/M
Complete Set (6): 3.00
Common Player: .50
1 Ken Griffey, Jr., Matt Williams 1.00

2 Frank Thomas, Jeff Bagwell .75
3 Albert Belle, Barry Bonds 1.50
4 Jose Canseco, Fred McGriff .60
5 Cecil Fielder, Andres Galarraga .50
6 Joe Carter, Kevin Mitchell .50

Diamond Kings

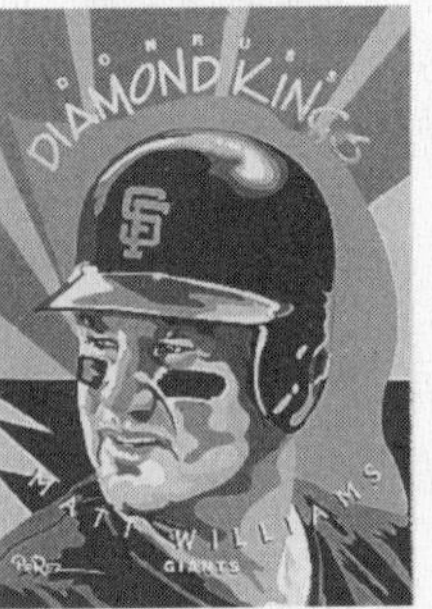

NM/M
Complete Set (29): 25.00
Common Player: .50
1 Frank Thomas 2.00
2 Jeff Bagwell 2.00
3 Chili Davis .50
4 Dante Bichette .50
5 Ruben Sierra .50
6 Jeff Conine .50
7 Paul O'Neill .50
8 Bobby Bonilla .50
9 Joe Carter .50
10 Moises Alou .50
11 Kenny Lofton .50
12 Matt Williams .50
13 Kevin Seitzer .50
14 Sammy Sosa 3.00
15 Scott Cooper .50
16 Raul Mondesi .50
17 Will Clark 1.00
18 Lenny Dykstra .50
19 Kirby Puckett 2.50
20 Hal Morris .50
21 Travis Fryman .50
22 Greg Maddux 2.50
23 Rafael Palmeiro 2.00
24 Tony Gwynn 2.50
25 David Cone .50
26 Al Martin .50
27 Ken Griffey Jr. 3.00
28 Gregg Jefferies .50
29 Checklist .10

Dominators

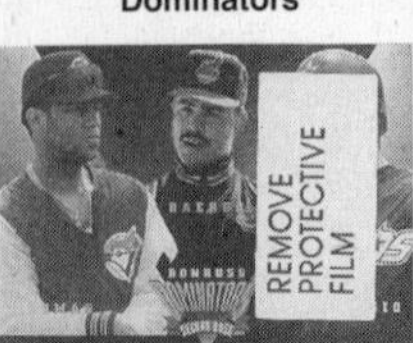

NM/M
Complete Set (9): 7.50
Common Player: .50
1 David Cone, Mike Mussina, Greg Maddux 1.00
2 Ivan Rodriguez, Mike Piazza, Darren Daulton 2.00
3 Fred McGriff, Frank Thomas, Jeff Bagwell 1.50
4 Roberto Alomar, Carlos Baerga, Craig Biggio .75
5 Robin Ventura, Travis Fryman, Matt Williams .50
6 Cal Ripken Jr., Barry Larkin, Wil Cordero 2.50
7 Albert Belle, Barry Bonds, Moises Alou 2.50
8 Ken Griffey Jr., Kenny Lofton, Marquis Grissom 2.00
9 Kirby Puckett, Paul O'Neill, Tony Gwynn 2.00

Elite

NM/M
Complete Set (12): 75.00
Common Player: 4.00
49 Jeff Bagwell 8.00
50 Paul O'Neill 4.00
51 Greg Maddux 10.00
52 Mike Piazza 12.00
53 Matt Williams 4.00
54 Ken Griffey, Jr. 12.00
55 Frank Thomas 8.00
56 Barry Bonds 15.00
57 Kirby Puckett 10.00
58 Fred McGriff 4.00
59 Jose Canseco 6.00
60 Albert Belle 4.00

Long Ball Leaders

NM/M
Complete Set (8): 7.50
Common Player: .50
1 Frank Thomas 1.50
2 Fred McGriff .50
3 Ken Griffey, Jr. 2.00
4 Matt Williams .50
5 Mike Piazza 2.00
6 Jose Canseco .75
7 Barry Bonds 2.50
8 Jeff Bagwell 1.50

Mound Marvels

NM/M
Complete Set (8): 7.50
Common Player: 1.00
1 Greg Maddux 4.00
2 David Cone 1.00
3 Mike Mussina 2.00
4 Bret Saberhagen 1.00
5 Jimmy Key 1.00
6 Doug Drabek 1.00
7 Randy Johnson 3.00
8 Jason Bere 1.00

1996 DONRUSS

NM/M
Complete Set (550): 20.00
Complete Series 1 (330): 12.00
Complete Series 2 (220): 10.00
Common Player: .05
Series 1 Pack (12): 1.00
Series 1 Wax Box (36): 20.00
Series 2 Pack (12): 1.00
Series 2 Wax Box (18): 12.50
1 Frank Thomas 1.00
2 Jason Bates .05
3 Steve Sparks .05

No.	Player	Value
4	Scott Servais	.05
5	Angelo Encarnacion	.05
6	Scott Sanders	.05
7	Billy Ashley	.05
8	Alex Rodriguez	2.00
9	Sean Bergman	.05
10	Brad Radke	.05
11	Andy Van Slyke	.05
12	Joe Girardi	.05
13	Mark Grudzielanek	.05
14	Rick Aguilera	.05
15	Randy Veres	.05
16	Tim Bogar	.05
17	Dave Veres	.05
18	Kevin Stocker	.05
19	Marquis Grissom	.05
20	Will Clark	.10
21	Jay Bell	.05
22	Allen Battle	.05
23	Frank Rodriguez	.05
24	Terry Steinbach	.05
25	Gerald Williams	.05
26	Sid Roberson	.05
27	Greg Zaun	.05
28	Ozzie Timmons	.05
29	Vaughn Eshelman	.05
30	Ed Sprague	.05
31	Gary DiSarcina	.05
32	Joe Boever	.05
33	Steve Avery	.05
34	Brad Ausmus	.05
35	Kirt Manwaring	.05
36	Gary Sheffield	.25
37	Jason Bere	.05
38	Jeff Manto	.05
39	David Cone	.05
40	Manny Ramirez	1.00
41	Sandy Alomar	.05
42	Curtis Goodwin (Rated Rookie)	.05
43	Tino Martinez	.05
44	Woody Williams	.05
45	Dean Palmer	.05
46	Hipolito Pichardo	.05
47	Jason Giambi	.60
48	Lance Johnson	.05
49	Bernard Gilkey	.05
50	Kirby Puckett	1.25
51	Tony Fernandez	.05
52	Alex Gonzalez	.05
53	Bret Saberhagen	.05
54	Lyle Mouton (Rated Rookie)	.05
55	Brian McRae	.05
56	Mark Gubicza	.05
57	Sergio Valdez	.05
58	Darrin Fletcher	.05
59	Steve Parris	.05
60	Johnny Damon (Rated Rookie)	.25
61	Rickey Henderson	1.00
62	Darrell Whitmore	.05
63	Roberto Petagine	.05
64	Trenidad Hubbard	.05
65	Heathcliff Slocumb	.05
66	Steve Finley	.05
67	Mariano Rivera	.25
68	Brian Hunter	.05
69	Jamie Moyer	.05
70	Ellis Burks	.05
71	Pat Kelly	.05
72	Mickey Tettleton	.05
73	Garret Anderson	.05
74	Andy Pettitte (Rated Rookie)	1.00
75	Glenallen Hill	.05
76	Brent Gates	.05
77	Lou Whitaker	.05
78	David Segui	.05
79	Dan Wilson	.05
80	Pat Listach	.05
81	Jeff Bagwell	1.00
82	Ben McDonald	.05
83	John Valentin	.05
84	John Jaha	.05
85	Pete Schourek	.05
86	Bryce Florie	.05
87	Brian Jordan	.05
88	Ron Karkovice	.05
89	Al Leiter	.05
90	Tony Longmire	.05
91	Nelson Liriano	.05
92	David Bell	.05
93	Kevin Gross	.05
94	Tom Candiotti	.05
95	Dave Martinez	.05
96	Greg Myers	.05
97	Rheal Cormier	.05
98	Chris Hammond	.05
99	Randy Myers	.05
100	Bill Pulsipher (Rated Rookie)	.05
101	Jason Isringhausen (Rated Rookie)	.05
102	Dave Stevens	.05
103	Roberto Alomar	.35
104	Bob Higginson (Rated Rookie)	.05
105	Eddie Murray	1.00
106	Matt Walbeck	.05
107	Mark Wohlers	.05
108	Jeff Nelson	.05
109	Tom Goodwin	.05
110	Cal Ripken Jr. Checklist 1-83 (2,131 Consecutive Games)	1.25
111	Rey Sanchez	.05
112	Hector Carrasco	.05
113	B.J. Surhoff	.05
114	Dan Miceli	.05
115	Dean Hartgraves	.05
116	John Burkett	.05
117	Gary Gaetti	.05
118	Ricky Bones	.05
119	Mike Macfarlane	.05
120	Bip Roberts	.05
121	Dave Mlicki	.05
122	Chili Davis	.05
123	Mark Whiten	.05
124	Herbert Perry	.05
125	Butch Henry	.05
126	Derek Bell	.05
127	Al Martin	.05
128	John Franco	.05
129	William VanLandingham	.05
130	Mike Bordick	.05
131	Mike Mordecai	.05
132	Robby Thompson	.05
133	Greg Colbrunn	.05
134	Domingo Cedeno	.05
135	Chad Curtis	.05
136	Jose Hernandez	.05
137	Scott Klingenbeck	.05
138	Ryan Klesko	.05
139	John Smiley	.05
140	Charlie Hayes	.05
141	Jay Buhner	.05
142	Doug Drabek	.05
143	Roger Pavlik	.05
144	Todd Worrell	.05
145	Cal Ripken Jr.	2.50
146	Steve Reed	.05
147	Chuck Finley	.05
148	Mike Blowers	.05
149	Orel Hershiser	.05
150	Allen Watson	.05
151	Ramon Martinez	.05
152	Melvin Nieves	.05
153	Tripp Cromer	.05
154	Yorkis Perez	.05
155	Stan Javier	.05
156	Mel Rojas	.05
157	Aaron Sele	.05
158	Eric Karros	.05
159	Robb Nen	.05
160	Raul Mondesi	.05
161	John Wetteland	.05
162	Tim Scott	.05
163	Kenny Rogers	.05
164	Melvin Bunch	.05
165	Rod Beck	.05
166	Andy Benes	.05
167	Lenny Dykstra	.05
168	Orlando Merced	.05
169	Tomas Perez	.05
170	Xavier Hernandez	.05
171	Ruben Sierra	.05
172	Alan Trammell	.05
173	Mike Fetters	.05
174	Wilson Alvarez	.05
175	Erik Hanson	.05
176	Travis Fryman	.05
177	Jim Abbott	.05
178	Bret Boone	.05
179	Sterling Hitchcock	.05
180	Pat Mahomes	.05
181	Mark Acre	.05
182	Charles Nagy	.05
183	Rusty Greer	.05
184	Mike Stanley	.05
185	Jim Bullinger	.05
186	Shane Andrews	.05
187	Brian Keyser	.05
188	Tyler Green	.05
189	Mark Grace	.10
190	Bob Hamelin	.05
191	Luis Ortiz	.05
192	Joe Carter	.05
193	Eddie Taubensee	.05
194	Brian Anderson	.05
195	Edgardo Alfonzo	.05
196	Pedro Munoz	.05
197	David Justice	.05
198	Trevor Hoffman	.05
199	Bobby Ayala	.05
200	Tony Eusebio	.05
201	Jeff Russell	.05
202	Mike Hampton	.05
203	Walt Weiss	.05
204	Joey Hamilton	.05
205	Roberto Hernandez	.05
206	Greg Vaughn	.05
207	Felipe Lira	.05
208	Harold Baines	.05
209	Tim Wallach	.05
210	Manny Alexander	.05
211	Tim Laker	.05
212	Chris Haney	.05
213	Brian Maxcy	.05
214	Eric Young	.05
215	Darryl Strawberry	.05
216	Barry Bonds	2.50
217	Tim Naehring	.05
218	Scott Brosius	.05
219	Reggie Sanders	.05
220	Eddie Murray Checklist 84-166 (3,000 Career Hits)	.35
221	Luis Alicea	.05
222	Albert Belle	.15
223	Benji Gil	.05
224	Dante Bichette	.05
225	Bobby Bonilla	.05
226	Todd Stottlemyre	.05
227	Jim Edmonds	.05
228	Todd Jones	.05
229	Shawn Green	.25
230	Javy Lopez	.05
231	Ariel Prieto	.05
232	Tony Phillips	.05
233	James Mouton	.05
234	Jose Oquendo	.05
235	Royce Clayton	.05
236	Chuck Carr	.05
237	Doug Jones	.05
238	Mark Mclemore (McLemore)	.05
239	Bill Swift	.05
240	Scott Leius	.05
241	Russ Davis	.05
242	Ray Durham (Rated Rookie)	.05
243	Matt Mieske	.05
244	Brent Mayne	.05
245	Thomas Howard	.05
246	Troy O'Leary	.05
247	Jacob Brumfield	.05
248	Mickey Morandini	.05
249	Todd Hundley	.05
250	Chris Bosio	.05
251	Omar Vizquel	.05
252	Mike Lansing	.05
253	John Mabry	.05
254	Mike Perez	.05
255	Delino DeShields	.05
256	Wil Cordero	.05
257	Mike James	.05
258	Todd Van Poppel	.05
259	Joey Cora	.05
260	Andre Dawson	.25
261	Jerry DiPoto	.05
262	Rick Krivda	.05
263	Glenn Dishman	.05
264	Mike Mimbs	.05
265	John Ericks	.05
266	Jose Canseco	.35
267	Jeff Branson	.05
268	Curt Leskanic	.05
269	Jon Nunnally	.05
270	Scott Stahoviak	.05
271	Jeff Montgomery	.05
272	Hal Morris	.05
273	Esteban Loaiza	.05
274	Rico Brogna	.05
275	Dave Winfield	1.00
276	J.R. Phillips	.05
277	Todd Zeile	.05
278	Tom Pagnozzi	.05
279	Mark Lemke	.05
280	Dave Magadan	.05
281	Greg McMichael	.05
282	Mike Morgan	.05
283	Moises Alou	.05
284	Dennis Martinez	.05
285	Jeff Kent	.05
286	Mark Johnson	.05
287	Darren Lewis	.05
288	Brad Clontz	.05
289	Chad Fonville (Rated Rookie)	.05
290	Paul Sorrento	.05
291	Lee Smith	.05
292	Tom Glavine	.25
293	Antonio Osuna	.05
294	Kevin Foster	.05
295	*Sandy Martinez*	.05
296	Mark Leiter	.05
297	Julian Tavarez	.05
298	Mike Kelly	.05
299	Joe Oliver	.05
300	John Flaherty	.05
301	Don Mattingly	1.50
302	Pat Meares	.05
303	John Doherty	.05
304	Joe Vitiello	.05
305	Vinny Castilla	.05
306	Jeff Brantley	.05
307	Mike Greenwell	.05
308	Midre Cummings	.05
309	Curt Schilling	.25
310	Ken Caminiti	.05
311	Scott Erickson	.05
312	Carl Everett	.05
313	Charles Johnson	.05
314	Alex Diaz	.05
315	Jose Mesa	.05
316	Mark Carreon	.05
317	Carlos Perez (Rated Rookie)	.05
318	Ismael Valdes	.05
319	Frank Castillo	.05
320	Tom Henke	.05
321	Spike Owen	.05
322	Joe Orsulak	.05
323	Paul Menhart	.05
324	Pedro Borbon	.05
325	Paul Molitor Checklist 167-249 (1,000 Career RBI)	.35
326	Jeff Cirillo	.05
327	Edwin Hurtado	.05
328	Orlando Miller	.05
329	Steve Ontiveros	.05
330	Kirby Puckett Checklist 250-330 (1,000 Career RBI)	.75
331	Scott Bullett	.05
332	Andres Galarraga	.05
333	Cal Eldred	.05
334	Sammy Sosa	1.75
335	Don Slaught	.05
336	Jody Reed	.05
337	Roger Cedeno	.05
338	Ken Griffey Jr.	1.75
339	Todd Hollandsworth	.05
340	Mike Trombley	.05
341	Gregg Jefferies	.05
342	Larry Walker	.05
343	Pedro Martinez	.05
344	Dwayne Hosey	.05
345	Terry Pendleton	.05
346	Pete Harnisch	.05
347	Tony Castillo	.05
348	Paul Quantrill	.05
349	Fred McGriff	.05
350	Ivan Rodriguez	.75
351	Butch Huskey	.05
352	Ozzie Smith	1.25
353	Marty Cordova	.05
354	John Wasdin	.05
355	Wade Boggs	1.25
356	Dave Nilsson	.05
357	Rafael Palmeiro	.75
358	Luis Gonzalez	.25
359	Reggie Jefferson	.05
360	Carlos Delgado	.60

361 Orlando Palmeiro .05
362 Chris Gomez .05
363 John Smoltz .05
364 Marc Newfield .05
365 Matt Williams .05
366 Jesus Tavarez .05
367 Bruce Ruffin .05
368 Sean Berry .05
369 Randy Velarde .05
370 Tony Pena .05
371 Jim Thome .05
372 Jeffrey Hammonds .05
373 Bob Wolcott .05
374 Juan Guzman .05
375 Juan Gonzalez 1.00
376 Michael Tucker .05
377 Doug Johns .05
378 *Mike Cameron* .75
379 Ray Lankford .05
380 Jose Parra .05
381 Jimmy Key .05
382 John Olerud .05
383 Kevin Ritz .05
384 Tim Raines .05
385 Rich Amaral .05
386 Keith Lockhart .05
387 Steve Scarsone .05
388 Cliff Floyd .05
389 Rich Aude .05
390 Hideo Nomo 1.00
391 Geronimo Berroa .05
392 Pat Rapp .05
393 Dustin Hermanson .05
394 Greg Maddux 1.25
395 Darren Daulton .05
396 Kenny Lofton .05
397 Ruben Rivera .05
398 Billy Wagner .05
399 Kevin Brown .05
400 Mike Kingery .05
401 Bernie Williams .20
402 Otis Nixon .05
403 Damion Easley .05
404 Paul O'Neill .05
405 Deion Sanders .05
406 Dennis Eckersley 1.00
407 Tony Clark .05
408 Rondell White .05
409 Luis Sojo .05
410 David Hulse .05
411 Shane Reynolds .05
412 Chris Hoiles .05
413 Lee Tinsley .05
414 Scott Karl .05
415 Ron Gant .05
416 Brian Johnson .05
417 Jose Oliva .05
418 Jack McDowell .05
419 Paul Molitor 1.00
420 Ricky Bottalico .05
421 Paul Wagner .05
422 Terry Bradshaw .05
423 Bob Tewksbury .05
424 Mike Piazza 1.75
425 *Luis Andujar* .05
426 Mark Langston .05
427 Stan Belinda .05
428 Kurt Abbott .05
429 Shawon Dunston .05
430 Bobby Jones .05
431 Jose Vizcaino .05
432 *Matt Lawton* .05
433 Pat Hentgen .05
434 Cecil Fielder .05
435 Carlos Baerga .05
436 Rich Becker .05
437 Chipper Jones 1.25
438 Bill Risley .05
439 Kevin Appier .05
440 Checklist .05
441 Jaime Navarro .05
442 Barry Larkin .05
443 *Jose Valentin* .05
444 Bryan Rekar .05
445 Rick Wilkins .05
446 Quilvio Veras .05
447 Greg Gagne .05
448 Mark Kiefer .05
449 Bobby Witt .05
450 Andy Ashby .05
451 Alex Ochoa .05
452 Jorge Fabregas .05
453 Gene Schall .05
454 Ken Hill .05
455 Tony Tarasco .05
456 Donnie Wall .05
457 Carlos Garcia .05
458 Ryan Thompson .05
459 *Marvin Benard* .05
460 Jose Herrera .05
461 Jeff Blauser .05
462 Chris Hook .05
463 Jeff Conine .05
464 Devon White .05
465 Danny Bautista .05
466 Steve Trachsel .05
467 C.J. Nitkowski .05
468 Mike Devereaux .05
469 David Wells .05
470 Jim Eisenreich .05
471 Edgar Martinez .05
472 Craig Biggio .05
473 Jeff Frye .05
474 Karim Garcia .15
475 Jimmy Haynes .05
476 Darren Holmes .05
477 Tim Salmon .20
478 Randy Johnson 1.00
479 Eric Plunk .05
480 Scott Cooper .05
481 Chan Ho Park .05
482 Ray McDavid .05
483 Mark Petkovsek .05
484 Greg Swindell .05
485 George Williams .05
486 Yamil Benitez .05
487 Tim Wakefield .05
488 Kevin Tapani .05
489 Derrick May .05
490 Ken Griffey Jr. Checklist 1.00
491 Derek Jeter 2.50
492 Jeff Fassero .05
493 Benito Santiago .05
494 Tom Gordon .05
495 Jamie Brewington .05
496 Vince Coleman .05
497 Kevin Jordan .05
498 Jeff King .05
499 Mike Simms .05
500 Jose Rijo .05
501 Denny Neagle .05
502 Jose Lima .05
503 Kevin Seitzer .05
504 Alex Fernandez .05
505 Mo Vaughn .05
506 Phil Nevin .05
507 J.T. Snow .05
508 Andujar Cedeno .05
509 Ozzie Guillen .05
510 Mark Clark .05
511 Mark McGwire 2.00
512 Jeff Reboulet .05
513 Armando Benitez .05
514 LaTroy Hawkins .05
515 Brett Butler .05
516 Tavo Alvarez .05
517 Chris Snopek .05
518 Mike Mussina .65
519 Darryl Kile .05
520 Wally Joyner .05
521 Willie McGee .05
522 Kent Mercker .05
523 Mike Jackson .05
524 Troy Percival .05
525 Tony Gwynn 1.25
526 Ron Coomer .05
527 Darryl Hamilton .05
528 Phil Plantier .05
529 Norm Charlton .05
530 Craig Paquette .05
531 Dave Burba .05
532 Mike Henneman .05
533 Terrell Wade .05
534 Eddie Williams .05
535 Robin Ventura .05
536 Chuck Knoblauch .05
537 Les Norman .05
538 Brady Anderson .05
539 Roger Clemens 1.75
540 Mark Portugal .05
541 Mike Matheny .05
542 Jeff Parrett .05
543 Roberto Kelly .05
544 Damon Buford .05
545 Chad Ogea .05
546 Jose Offerman .05
547 Brian Barber .05
548 Danny Tartabull .05
549 Duane Singleton .05
550 Tony Gwynn Checklist .75

Press Proofs

NM/M
Complete Set (550): 150.00
Common Player: .50
(Star cards valued 7X corresponding regular-issue cards.)

Diamond Kings

NM/M
Complete Set (31): 90.00
Complete Series 1 (1-14): 45.00
Complete Series 2 (15-31): 45.00
Common Player Series 1: 1.50
Common Player Series 2: 1.50
1 Frank Thomas 6.00
2 Mo Vaughn 1.50
3 Manny Ramirez 4.00
4 Mark McGwire 9.00
5 Juan Gonzalez 4.00
6 Roberto Alomar 2.00
7 Tim Salmon 1.75
8 Barry Bonds 10.00
9 Tony Gwynn 7.50
10 Reggie Sanders 1.50
11 Larry Walker 1.50
12 Pedro Martinez 4.00
13 Jeff King 1.50
14 Mark Grace 1.75
15 Greg Maddux 7.50
16 Don Mattingly 8.00
17 Gregg Jefferies 1.50
18 Chad Curtis 1.50
19 Jason Isringhausen 1.50
20 B.J. Surhoff 1.50
21 Jeff Conine 1.50
22 Kirby Puckett 7.50
23 Derek Bell 1.50
24 Wally Joyner 1.50
25 Brian Jordan 1.50
26 Edgar Martinez 1.50
27 Hideo Nomo 4.00
28 Mike Mussina 3.00
29 Eddie Murray 4.00
30 Cal Ripken Jr. 10.00
31 Checklist .25

Elite

NM/M
Complete Set (12): 45.00
Complete Series 1 (61-66): 22.50
Complete Series 2 (67-72): 24.00
Common Player Series 1: 2.00
Common Player Series 2: 1.50
61 Cal Ripken Jr. 9.00
62 Hideo Nomo 4.50
63 Reggie Sanders 2.00
64 Mo Vaughn 2.00
65 Tim Salmon 2.25
66 Chipper Jones 7.00
67 Manny Ramirez 3.50
68 Greg Maddux 6.00
69 Frank Thomas 5.00
70 Ken Griffey Jr. 7.50
71 Dante Bichette 1.50
72 Tony Gwynn 6.00

Freeze Frame

NM/M
Complete Set (8): 15.00
Common Player: 1.00
1 Frank Thomas 1.50
2 Ken Griffey Jr. 2.50
3 Cal Ripken Jr. 4.00
4 Hideo Nomo 1.50
5 Greg Maddux 2.00
6 Albert Belle 1.00
7 Chipper Jones 2.00
8 Mike Piazza 2.50

Hit List

NM/M
Complete Set (16): 40.00
Common Player: .75
1 Tony Gwynn 4.00
2 Ken Griffey Jr. 6.00
3 Will Clark 1.00
4 Mike Piazza 6.00
5 Carlos Baerga .75
6 Mo Vaughn .75
7 Mark Grace 1.00
8 Kirby Puckett 4.00
9 Frank Thomas 3.00
10 Barry Bonds 7.50
11 Jeff Bagwell 2.50
12 Edgar Martinez .75
13 Tim Salmon 1.25
14 Wade Boggs 4.00
15 Don Mattingly 5.00
16 Eddie Murray 2.50

Long Ball Leaders

NM/M
Complete Set (8): 45.00
Common Player: 1.50
1 Barry Bonds 15.00
2 Ryan Klesko 1.50
3 Mark McGwire 15.00
4 Raul Mondesi 1.50
5 Cecil Fielder 1.50
6 Ken Griffey Jr. 12.00
7 Larry Walker 1.50
8 Frank Thomas 6.00

Power Alley

NM/M
Complete Set (10): 35.00
Common Player 2.00
Die-cuts 2X
1 Frank Thomas 5.00
2 Barry Bonds 7.50
3 Reggie Sanders 2.00
4 Albert Belle 2.50
5 Tim Salmon 2.50
6 Dante Bichette 2.00
7 Mo Vaughn 2.00
8 Jim Edmonds 2.50
9 Manny Ramirez 4.00
10 Ken Griffey Jr. 6.00

Pure Power

NM/M
Complete Set (8): 20.00
Common Player: 1.50

1	Raul Mondesi	1.50
2	Barry Bonds	6.00
3	Albert Belle	2.00
4	Frank Thomas	3.00
5	Mike Piazza	5.00
6	Dante Bichette	1.50
7	Manny Ramirez	2.50
8	Mo Vaughn	1.50

Round Trippers

		NM/M
Complete Set (10):		42.50
Common Player:		3.00
1	Albert Belle	3.50
2	Barry Bonds	7.50
3	Jeff Bagwell	5.00
4	Tim Salmon	3.00
5	Mo Vaughn	3.00
6	Ken Griffey Jr.	6.00
7	Mike Piazza	6.00
8	Cal Ripken Jr.	7.50
9	Frank Thomas	5.00
9p	Frank Thomas (Promo)	3.00
10	Dante Bichette	3.00

Showdown

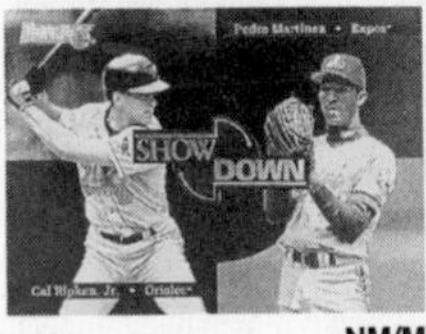

		NM/M
Complete Set (8):		22.50
Common Player:		.75
1	Frank Thomas, Hideo Nomo	3.00
2	Barry Bonds, Randy Johnson	6.00
3	Greg Maddux, Ken Griffey Jr.	5.00
4	Roger Clemens, Tony Gwynn	4.50
5	Mike Piazza, Mike Mussina	5.00
6	Cal Ripken Jr., Pedro Martinez	6.00
7	Tim Wakefield, Matt Williams	.75
8	Manny Ramirez, Carlos Perez	1.50

1997 DONRUSS

		NM/M
Complete Set (450):		20.00
Series 1 Set (270):		10.00
Update Set (180):		10.00
Common Player:		.05
Wax Pack (10):		1.50
Hobby Wax Box (18):		25.00
Retail Wax Box (36):		40.00
Magazine Pack (13):		1.50
Magazine Box (24):		20.00
Update Pack (10):		1.50
Update Wax Box (24):		30.00
1	Juan Gonzalez	.75
2	Jim Edmonds	.05
3	Tony Gwynn	1.00
4	Andres Galarraga	.05
5	Joe Carter	.05
6	Raul Mondesi	.05
7	Greg Maddux	1.00
8	Travis Fryman	.05
9	Brian Jordan	.05
10	Henry Rodriguez	.05
11	Manny Ramirez	.75
12	Mark McGwire	1.75
13	Marc Newfield	.05
14	Craig Biggio	.05
15	Sammy Sosa	1.50
16	Brady Anderson	.05
17	Wade Boggs	1.00
18	Charles Johnson	.05
19	Matt Williams	.05
20	Denny Neagle	.05
21	Ken Griffey Jr.	1.50
22	Robin Ventura	.05
23	Barry Larkin	.05
24	Todd Zeile	.05
25	Chuck Knoblauch	.05
26	Todd Hundley	.05
27	Roger Clemens	1.25
28	Michael Tucker	.05
29	Rondell White	.05
30	Osvaldo Fernandez	.05
31	Ivan Rodriguez	.65
32	Alex Fernandez	.05
33	Jason Isringhausen	.05
34	Chipper Jones	1.00
35	Paul O'Neill	.05
36	Hideo Nomo	.75
37	Roberto Alomar	.25
38	Derek Bell	.05
39	Paul Molitor	.75
40	Andy Benes	.05
41	Steve Trachsel	.05
42	J.T. Snow	.05
43	Jason Kendall	.05
44	Alex Rodriguez	1.75
45	Joey Hamilton	.05
46	Carlos Delgado	.50
47	Jason Giambi	.60
48	Larry Walker	.05
49	Derek Jeter	2.00
50	Kenny Lofton	.05
51	Devon White	.05
52	Matt Mieske	.05
53	Melvin Nieves	.05
54	Jose Canseco	.40
55	Tino Martinez	.05
56	Rafael Palmeiro	.75
57	Edgardo Alfonzo	.05
58	Jay Buhner	.05
59	Shane Reynolds	.05
60	Steve Finley	.05
61	Bobby Higginson	.05
62	Dean Palmer	.05
63	Terry Pendleton	.05
64	Marquis Grissom	.05
65	Mike Stanley	.05
66	Moises Alou	.05
67	Ray Lankford	.05
68	Marty Cordova	.05
69	John Olerud	.05
70	David Cone	.05
71	Benito Santiago	.05
72	Ryne Sandberg	1.00
73	Rickey Henderson	.75
74	Roger Cedeno	.05
75	Wilson Alvarez	.05
76	Tim Salmon	.15
77	Orlando Merced	.05
78	Vinny Castilla	.05
79	Ismael Valdes	.05
80	Dante Bichette	.05
81	Kevin Brown	.10
82	Andy Pettitte	.50
83	Scott Stahoviak	.05
84	Mickey Tettleton	.05
85	Jack McDowell	.05
86	Tom Glavine	.30
87	Gregg Jefferies	.05
88	Chili Davis	.05
89	Randy Johnson	.75
90	John Mabry	.05
91	Billy Wagner	.05
92	Jeff Cirillo	.05
93	Trevor Hoffman	.05
94	Juan Guzman	.05
95	Geronimo Berroa	.05
96	Bernard Gilkey	.05
97	Danny Tartabull	.05
98	Johnny Damon	.25
99	Charlie Hayes	.05
100	Reggie Sanders	.05
101	Robby Thompson	.05
102	Bobby Bonilla	.05
103	Reggie Jefferson	.05
104	John Smoltz	.05
105	Jim Thome	.05
106	Ruben Rivera	.05
107	Darren Oliver	.05
108	Mo Vaughn	.05
109	Roger Pavlik	.05
110	Terry Steinbach	.05
111	Jermaine Dye	.05
112	Mark Grudzielanek	.05
113	Rick Aguilera	.05
114	Jamey Wright	.05
115	Eddie Murray	.75
116	Brian Hunter	.05
117	Hal Morris	.05
118	Tom Pagnozzi	.05
119	Mike Mussina	.60
120	Mark Grace	.10
121	Cal Ripken Jr.	2.00
122	Tom Goodwin	.05
123	Paul Sorrento	.05
124	Jay Bell	.05
125	Todd Hollandsworth	.05
126	Edgar Martinez	.05
127	George Arias	.05
128	Greg Vaughn	.05
129	Roberto Hernandez	.05
130	Delino DeShields	.05
131	Bill Pulsipher	.05
132	Joey Cora	.05
133	Mariano Rivera	.15
134	Mike Piazza	1.50
135	Carlos Baerga	.05
136	Jose Mesa	.05
137	Will Clark	.10
138	Frank Thomas	.75
139	John Wetteland	.05
140	Shawn Estes	.05
141	Garret Anderson	.05
142	Andre Dawson	.25
143	Eddie Taubensee	.05
144	Ryan Klesko	.05
145	Rocky Coppinger	.05
146	Jeff Bagwell	.75
147	Donovan Osborne	.05
148	Greg Myers	.05
149	Brant Brown	.05
150	Kevin Elster	.05
151	Bob Wells	.05
152	Wally Joyner	.05
153	Rico Brogna	.05
154	Dwight Gooden	.05
155	Jermaine Allensworth	.05
156	Ray Durham	.05
157	Cecil Fielder	.05
158	Ryan Hancock	.05
159	Gary Sheffield	.25
160	Albert Belle	.15
161	Tomas Perez	.05
162	David Doster	.05
163	John Valentin	.05
164	Danny Graves	.05
165	Jose Paniagua	.05
166	*Brian Giles*	.75
167	Barry Bonds	2.00
168	Sterling Hitchcock	.05
169	Bernie Williams	.15
170	Fred McGriff	.05
171	George Williams	.05
172	Amaury Telemaco	.05
173	Ken Caminiti	.05
174	Ron Gant	.05
175	David Justice	.05
176	James Baldwin	.05
177	Pat Hentgen	.05
178	Ben McDonald	.05
179	Tim Naehring	.05
180	Jim Eisenreich	.05
181	Ken Hill	.05
182	Paul Wilson	.05
183	Marvin Benard	.05
184	Alan Benes	.05
185	Ellis Burks	.05
186	Scott Servais	.05
187	David Segui	.05
188	Scott Brosius	.05
189	Jose Offerman	.05
190	Eric Davis	.05
191	Brett Butler	.05
192	Curtis Pride	.05
193	Yamil Benitez	.05
194	Chan Ho Park	.10
195	Bret Boone	.05
196	Omar Vizquel	.05
197	Orlando Miller	.05
198	Ramon Martinez	.05
199	Harold Baines	.05
200	Eric Young	.05
201	Fernando Vina	.05
202	Alex Gonzalez	.05
203	Fernando Valenzuela	.05
204	Steve Avery	.05
205	Ernie Young	.05
206	Kevin Appier	.05
207	Randy Myers	.05
208	Jeff Suppan	.05
209	James Mouton	.05
210	Russ Davis	.05
211	Al Martin	.05
212	Troy Percival	.05
213	Al Leiter	.05
214	Dennis Eckersley	.65
215	Mark Johnson	.05
216	Eric Karros	.05
217	Royce Clayton	.05
218	Tony Phillips	.05
219	Tim Wakefield	.05
220	Alan Trammell	.05
221	Eduardo Perez	.05
222	Butch Huskey	.05
223	Tim Belcher	.05
224	Jamie Moyer	.05
225	F.P. Santangelo	.05
226	Rusty Greer	.05
227	Jeff Brantley	.05
228	Mark Langston	.05
229	Ray Montgomery	.05
230	Rich Becker	.05
231	Ozzie Smith	1.00
232	Rey Ordonez	.05
233	Ricky Otero	.05
234	Mike Cameron	.05
235	Mike Sweeney	.05
236	Mark Lewis	.05
237	Luis Gonzalez	.05
238	Marcus Jensen	.05
239	Ed Sprague	.05
240	Jose Valentin	.05
241	Jeff Frye	.05
242	Charles Nagy	.05
243	Carlos Garcia	.05
244	Mike Hampton	.05
245	B.J. Surhoff	.05
246	Wilton Guerrero	.05
247	Frank Rodriguez	.05
248	Gary Gaetti	.05
249	Lance Johnson	.05
250	Darren Bragg	.05
251	Darryl Hamilton	.05
252	John Jaha	.05
253	Craig Paquette	.05
254	Jaime Navarro	.05
255	Shawon Dunston	.05
256	Ron Wright	.05
257	Tim Belk	.05
258	Jeff Darwin	.05
259	Ruben Sierra	.05
260	Chuck Finley	.05
261	Darryl Strawberry	.05
262	Shannon Stewart	.05
263	Pedro Martinez	.05
264	Neifi Perez	.05
265	Jeff Conine	.05
266	Orel Hershiser	.05
267	Eddie Murray Checklist 1-90 (500 Career HR)	.05
268	Paul Molitor Checklist 91-180 (3,000 Career Hits)	.05
269	Barry Bonds Checklist 181-270 (300 Career HR)	.75
270	Mark McGwire Checklist - inserts (300 Career HR)	.75
271	Matt Williams	.05
272	Todd Zeile	.05
273	Roger Clemens	1.25
274	Michael Tucker	.05
275	J.T. Snow	.05
276	Kenny Lofton	.05
277	Jose Canseco	.40

278	Marquis Grissom	.05
279	Moises Alou	.05
280	Benito Santiago	.05
281	Willie McGee	.05
282	Chili Davis	.05
283	Ron Coomer	.05
284	Orlando Merced	.05
285	Delino DeShields	.05
286	John Wetteland	.05
287	Darren Daulton	.05
288	Lee Stevens	.05
289	Albert Belle	.15
290	Sterling Hitchcock	.05
291	David Justice	.05
292	Eric Davis	.05
293	Brian Hunter	.05
294	Darryl Hamilton	.05
295	Steve Avery	.05
296	Joe Vitiello	.05
297	Jaime Navarro	.05
298	Eddie Murray	.75
299	Randy Myers	.05
300	Francisco Cordova	.05
301	Javier Lopez	.05
302	Geronimo Berroa	.05
303	Jeffrey Hammonds	.05
304	Deion Sanders	.05
305	Jeff Fassero	.05
306	Curt Schilling	.25
307	Robb Nen	.05
308	Mark McLemore	.05
309	Jimmy Key	.05
310	Quilvio Veras	.05
311	Bip Roberts	.05
312	Esteban Loaiza	.05
313	Andy Ashby	.05
314	Sandy Alomar Jr.	.05
315	Shawn Green	.25
316	Luis Castillo	.05
317	Benji Gil	.05
318	Otis Nixon	.05
319	Aaron Sele	.05
320	Brad Ausmus	.05
321	Troy O'Leary	.05
322	Terrell Wade	.05
323	Jeff King	.05
324	Kevin Seitzer	.05
325	Mark Wohlers	.05
326	Edgar Renteria	.05
327	Dan Wilson	.05
328	Brian McRae	.05
329	Rod Beck	.05
330	Julio Franco	.05
331	Dave Nilsson	.05
332	Glenallen Hill	.05
333	Kevin Elster	.05
334	Joe Girardi	.05
335	David Wells	.05
336	Jeff Blauser	.05
337	Darryl Kile	.05
338	Jeff Kent	.05
339	Jim Leyritz	.05
340	Todd Stottlemyre	.05
341	Tony Clark	.05
342	Chris Hoiles	.05
343	Mike Lieberthal	.05
344	Matt Lawton	.05
345	Alex Ochoa	.05
346	Chris Snopek	.05
347	Rudy Pemberton	.05
348	Eric Owens	.05
349	Joe Randa	.05
350	John Olerud	.05
351	Steve Karsay	.05
352	Mark Whiten	.05
353	Bob Abreu	.05
354	Bartolo Colon	.05
355	Vladimir Guerrero	.75
356	Darin Erstad	.60
357	Scott Rolen	.75
358	Andruw Jones	.75
359	Scott Spiezio	.05
360	Karim Garcia	.05
361	*Hideki Irabu*	.25
362	Nomar Garciaparra	1.50
363	Dmitri Young	.05
364	*Bubba Trammell*	.25
365	Kevin Orie	.05
366	Jose Rosado	.05
367	Jose Guillen	.05
368	Brooks Kieschnick	.05
369	Pokey Reese	.05
370	Glendon Rusch	.05
371	Jason Dickson	.05
372	Todd Walker	.05
373	Justin Thompson	.05
374	Todd Greene	.05
375	Jeff Suppan	.05
376	Trey Beamon	.05
377	Damon Mashore	.05
378	Wendell Magee	.05
379	Shigetosi Hasegawa	.05
380	Bill Mueller	.05
381	Chris Widger	.05
382	Tony Grafannino	.05
383	Derrek Lee	.05
384	Brian Moehler	.05
385	Quinton McCracken	.05
386	Matt Morris	.05
387	Marvin Benard	.05
388	*Deivi Cruz*	.25
389	*Javier Valentin*	.05
390	Todd Dunwoody	.05
391	Derrick Gibson	.05
392	Raul Casanova	.05
393	George Arias	.05
394	*Tony Womack*	.25
395	Antone Williamson	.05
396	*Jose Cruz Jr.*	.75
397	Desi Relaford	.05
398	Frank Thomas (Hit List)	.40
399	Ken Griffey Jr. (Hit List)	.65
400	Cal Ripken Jr. (Hit List)	1.00
401	Chipper Jones(Hit List)	.50
402	Mike Piazza (Hit List)	.65
403	Gary Sheffield (Hit List)	.10
404	Alex Rodriguez (Hit List)	.75
405	Wade Boggs (Hit List)	.50
406	Juan Gonzalez (Hit List)	.40
407	Tony Gwynn (Hit List)	.50
408	Edgar Martinez (Hit List)	.05
409	Jeff Bagwell (Hit List)	.40
410	Larry Walker (Hit List)	.05
411	Kenny Lofton (Hit List)	.05
412	Manny Ramirez (Hit List)	.40
413	Mark McGwire (Hit List)	.75
414	Roberto Alomar (Hit List)	.15
415	Derek Jeter (Hit List)	1.00
416	Brady Anderson (Hit List)	.05
417	Paul Molitor (Hit List)	.35
418	Dante Bichette (Hit List)	.05
419	Jim Edmonds (Hit List)	.05
420	Mo Vaughn (Hit List)	.10
421	Barry Bonds (Hit List)	.75
422	Rusty Greer (Hit List)	.05
423	Greg Maddux (King of the Hill)	.50
424	Andy Pettitte (King of the Hill)	.15
425	John Smoltz (King of the Hill)	.05
426	Randy Johnson (King of the Hill)	.40
427	Hideo Nomo (King of the Hill)	.40
428	Roger Clemens (King of the Hill)	.60
429	Tom Glavine (King of the Hill)	.15
430	Pat Hentgen (King of the Hill)	.05
431	Kevin Brown (King of the Hill)	.05
432	Mike Mussina (King of the Hill)	.30
433	Alex Fernandez (King of the Hill)	.05
434	Kevin Appier (King of the Hill)	.05
435	David Cone (King of the Hill)	.05
436	Jeff Fassero (King of the Hill)	.05
437	John Wetteland (King of the Hill)	.05
438	Barry Bonds, Ivan Rodriguez (Interleague Showdown)	.75
439	Ken Griffey Jr., Andres Galarraga (Interleague Showdown)	.65
440	Fred McGriff, Rafael Palmeiro (Interleague Showdown)	.05
441	Barry Larkin, Jim Thome (Interleague Showdown)	.05
442	Sammy Sosa, Albert Belle (Interleague Showdown)	.65
443	Bernie Williams, Todd Hundley (Interleague Showdown)	.05
444	Chuck Knoblauch, Brian Jordan (Interleague Showdown)	.05
445	Mo Vaughn, Jeff Conine (Interleague Showdown)	.10
446	Ken Caminiti, Jason Giambi (Interleague Showdown)	.25
447	Raul Mondesi, Tim Salmon (Interleague Showdown)	.05
448	Cal Ripken Jr. Checklist	.75
449	Greg Maddux Checklist	.60
450	Ken Griffey Jr. Checklist	.50

Press Proofs

	NM/M
Complete Set (270):	150.00
Common Player:	.50
Stars/Rookies:	5X
Complete Gold Set (270):	350.00
Common Gold Player:	2.00
Gold Stars/Rookies:	10X

(See 1997 Donruss for checklist and base card values.)

Armed and Dangerous

		NM/M
Complete Set (15):		35.00
Common Player:		1.00
1	Ken Griffey Jr.	4.00
2	Raul Mondesi	1.00
3	Chipper Jones	3.00
4	Ivan Rodriguez	2.00
5	Randy Johnson	2.00
6	Alex Rodriguez	5.00
7	Larry Walker	1.00
8	Cal Ripken Jr.	6.00
9	Kenny Lofton	1.00
10	Barry Bonds	6.00
11	Derek Jeter	6.00
12	Charles Johnson	1.00
13	Greg Maddux	3.00
14	Roberto Alomar	1.50
15	Barry Larkin	1.00

Diamond Kings

		NM/M
Complete Set (10):		35.00
Common Player:		1.00
Canvas (1st 500):		2X
1	Ken Griffey Jr.	7.50
2	Cal Ripken Jr.	12.00
3	Mo Vaughn	1.00
4	Chuck Knoblauch	1.00
5	Jeff Bagwell	4.00
6	Henry Rodriguez	1.00
7	Mike Piazza	7.50
8	Ivan Rodriguez	3.00
9	Frank Thomas	4.00
10	Chipper Jones	6.00

Elite Inserts

	NM/M
Complete Set (12):	135.00
Common Player:	4.00

Promos:		50%
1	Frank Thomas	7.50
2	Paul Molitor	9.00
3	Sammy Sosa	17.50
4	Barry Bonds	25.00
5	Chipper Jones	12.50
6	Alex Rodriguez	20.00
7	Ken Griffey Jr.	17.50
8	Jeff Bagwell	7.50
9	Cal Ripken Jr.	25.00
10	Mo Vaughn	4.00
11	Mike Piazza	17.50
12	Juan Gonzalez	7.50

Frank Thomas The Big Heart

		NM/M
Complete Set (4):		20.00
Common Card:		5.00
1	Frank Thomas, Rod Carew	5.00
2	Frank Thomas	5.00
3	Frank Thomas	5.00
4	Frank Thomas	5.00

Longball Leaders

		NM/M
Complete Set (15):		20.00
Common Player:		.50
1	Frank Thomas	2.00
2	Albert Belle	.65
3	Mo Vaughn	.50
4	Brady Anderson	.50
5	Greg Vaughn	.50
6	Ken Griffey Jr.	3.00
7	Jay Buhner	.50
8	Juan Gonzalez	1.00
9	Mike Piazza	3.00
10	Jeff Bagwell	1.50
11	Sammy Sosa	3.00
12	Mark McGwire	4.00
13	Cecil Fielder	.50
14	Ryan Klesko	.50
15	Jose Canseco	1.00

Rocket Launchers

		NM/M
Complete Set (15):		25.00
Common Player:		.75
1	Frank Thomas	2.50
2	Albert Belle	.75
3	Chipper Jones	3.00
4	Mike Piazza	4.00
5	Mo Vaughn	.75
6	Juan Gonzalez	2.00
7	Fred McGriff	.75
8	Jeff Bagwell	2.00
9	Matt Williams	.75

10	Gary Sheffield	1.00
11	Barry Bonds	5.00
12	Manny Ramirez	2.00
13	Henry Rodriguez	.75
14	Jason Giambi	1.50
15	Cal Ripken Jr.	5.00

Rated Rookies

		NM/M
Complete Set (30):		10.00
Common Player:		.50
1	Jason Thompson	.50
2	LaTroy Hawkins	.50
3	Scott Rolen	2.00
4	Trey Beamon	.50
5	Kimera Bartee	.50
6	Nerio Rodriguez	.50
7	Jeff D'Amico	.50
8	Quinton McCracken	.50
9	John Wasdin	.50
10	Robin Jennings	.50
11	Steve Gibralter	.50
12	Tyler Houston	.50
13	Tony Clark	.50
14	Ugueth Urbina	.50
15	Billy McMillon	.50
16	Raul Casanova	.50
17	Brooks Kieschnick	.50
18	Luis Castillo	.50
19	Edgar Renteria	.50
20	Andruw Jones	2.00
21	Chad Mottola	.50
22	Makoto Suzuki	.50
23	Justin Thompson	.50
24	Darin Erstad	1.50
25	Todd Walker	.50
26	Todd Greene	.50
27	Vladimir Guerrero	2.00
28	Darren Dreifort	.50
29	John Burke	.50
30	Damon Mashore	.50

Values quoted in this guide reflect the retail price of a card, the price a collector can expect to pay when buying a card from a dealer.

Update Press Proofs

	NM/M
Complete Set (180):	200.00
Common Player:	.50
Stars:	7X
Complete Set, Gold (180):	400.00
Common Player, Gold:	2.00
Gold Stars:	15X

(See 1997 Donruss (#271-450) for checklist, base card values.)

Update Cal Ripken

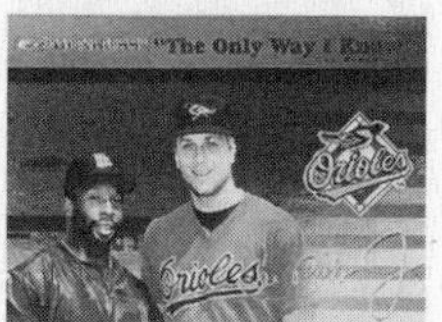

		NM/M
Complete Set (10):		75.00
Common Card:		10.00
1-9	Cal Ripken Jr.	10.00
10	Cal Ripken Jr. (book insert)	10.00

Update Dominators

		NM/M
Complete Set (20):		22.50
Common Player:		.50
1	Frank Thomas	1.25
2	Ken Griffey Jr.	2.25
3	Greg Maddux	1.50
4	Cal Ripken Jr.	3.00
5	Alex Rodriguez	2.50
6	Albert Belle	.60
7	Mark McGwire	2.50
8	Juan Gonzalez	1.00
9	Chipper Jones	1.50
10	Hideo Nomo	1.00
11	Roger Clemens	2.00
12	John Smoltz	.60
13	Mike Piazza	2.50
14	Sammy Sosa	2.00
15	Matt Williams	.50
16	Kenny Lofton	.50
17	Barry Larkin	.50
18	Rafael Palmeiro	1.00
19	Ken Caminiti	.50
20	Gary Sheffield	.75

Update Franchise Features

		NM/M
Complete Set (15):		45.00
Common Player:		2.00
1	Ken Griffey Jr., Andruw Jones	4.00
2	Frank Thomas, Darin Erstad	3.00
3	Alex Rodriguez, Nomar Garciaparra	5.00
4	Chuck Knoblauch, Wilton Guerrero	2.00
5	Juan Gonzalez, Bubba Trammell	2.50
6	Chipper Jones, Todd Walker	3.00
7	Barry Bonds, Vladimir Guerrero	6.00
8	Mark McGwire, Dmitri Young	5.00
9	Mike Piazza, Mike Sweeney	5.00
10	Mo Vaughn, Tony Clark	2.00
11	Gary Sheffield, Jose Guillen	2.00
12	Kenny Lofton, Shannon Stewart	2.00
13	Cal Ripken Jr., Scott Rolen	6.00
14	Derek Jeter, Pokey Reese	6.00
15	Tony Gwynn, Bob Abreu	3.00

Update Power Alley

		NM/M
Complete Set (24):		100.00
Common Gold:		7.50
Common Blue:		3.00
Common Green:		1.50
Die-Cuts:		1.5X
1	Frank Thomas (G)	7.50
2	Ken Griffey Jr. (G)	10.00
3	Cal Ripken Jr. (G)	15.00
4	Jeff Bagwell (B)	4.50
5	Mike Piazza (B)	7.50
6	Andruw Jones (GR)	3.50
7	Alex Rodriguez (G)	12.50
8	Albert Belle (GR)	2.00
9	Mo Vaughn (GR)	2.00
10	Chipper Jones (B)	6.00
11	Juan Gonzalez (B)	4.00
12	Ken Caminiti (GR)	1.50
13	Manny Ramirez (GR)	3.50
14	Mark McGwire (GR)	6.00
15	Kenny Lofton (B)	3.00
16	Barry Bonds (GR)	7.50
17	Gary Sheffield (GR)	1.50
18	Tony Gwynn (GR)	4.50
19	Vladimir Guerrero (B)	4.50
20	Ivan Rodriguez (B)	3.50
21	Paul Molitor (B)	5.00
22	Sammy Sosa (GR)	6.00
23	Matt Williams (GR)	1.50
24	Derek Jeter (GR)	7.50

Update Rookie Diamond Kings

		NM/M
Complete Set (10):		30.00
Common Player:		1.50
Canvas:		1.5X
1	Andruw Jones	4.00
2	Vladimir Guerrero	10.00
3	Scott Rolen	4.00
4	Todd Walker	1.50
5	Bartolo Colon	1.50
6	Jose Guillen	1.50
7	Nomar Garciaparra	7.50
8	Darin Erstad	3.00
9	Dmitri Young	1.50
10	Wilton Guerrero	1.50

1997 DONRUSS ELITE

		NM/M
Complete Set (150):		10.00
Common Player:		.10
Pack (6):		2.50
Wax Box (18):		35.00
1	Juan Gonzalez	.75
2	Alex Rodriguez	2.00
3	Frank Thomas	.75
4	Greg Maddux	1.00
5	Ken Griffey Jr.	1.50
6	Cal Ripken Jr.	2.50
7	Mike Piazza	1.50
8	Chipper Jones	1.00
9	Albert Belle	.20
10	Andruw Jones	.75
11	Vladimir Guerrero	.75
12	Mo Vaughn	.10
13	Ivan Rodriguez	.65
14	Andy Pettitte	.40
15	Tony Gwynn	1.00
16	Barry Bonds	2.50
17	Jeff Bagwell	.75
18	Manny Ramirez	.75
19	Kenny Lofton	.10
20	Roberto Alomar	.30
21	Mark McGwire	2.00
22	Ryan Klesko	.10
23	Tim Salmon	.20
24	Derek Jeter	2.50
25	Eddie Murray	.75
26	Jermaine Dye	.10
27	Ruben Rivera	.10
28	Jim Edmonds	.10
29	Mike Mussina	.50
30	Randy Johnson	.75
31	Sammy Sosa	1.50
32	Hideo Nomo	.75
33	Chuck Knoblauch	.10
34	Paul Molitor	.75
35	Rafael Palmeiro	.75
36	Brady Anderson	.10
37	Will Clark	.15
38	Craig Biggio	.10
39	Jason Giambi	.65
40	Roger Clemens	1.25
41	Jay Buhner	.10
42	Edgar Martinez	.10
43	Gary Sheffield	.35
44	Fred McGriff	.10
45	Bobby Bonilla	.10
46	Tom Glavine	.25
47	Wade Boggs	1.00
48	Jeff Conine	.10
49	John Smoltz	.10
50	Jim Thome	.10
51	Billy Wagner	.10
52	Jose Canseco	.40
53	Javy Lopez	.10
54	Cecil Fielder	.10
55	Garret Anderson	.10
56	Alex Ochoa	.10
57	Scott Rolen	.75
58	Darin Erstad	.60
59	Rey Ordonez	.10
60	Dante Bichette	.10
61	Joe Carter	.10
62	Moises Alou	.10
63	Jason Isringhausen	.10
64	Karim Garcia	.20
65	Brian Jordan	.10
66	Ruben Sierra	.10
67	Todd Hollandsworth	.10
68	Paul Wilson	.10
69	Ernie Young	.10
70	Ryne Sandberg	1.00
71	Raul Mondesi	.10
72	George Arias	.10

73	Ray Durham	.10
74	Dean Palmer	.10
75	Shawn Green	.50
76	Eric Young	.10
77	Jason Kendall	.10
78	Greg Vaughn	.10
79	Terrell Wade	.10
80	Bill Pulsipher	.10
81	Bobby Higginson	.10
82	Mark Grudzielanek	.10
83	Ken Caminiti	.10
84	Todd Greene	.10
85	Carlos Delgado	.65
86	Mark Grace	.20
87	Rondell White	.10
88	Barry Larkin	.10
89	J.T. Snow	.10
90	Alex Gonzalez	.10
91	Raul Casanova	.10
92	Marc Newfield	.10
93	Jermaine Allensworth	.10
94	John Mabry	.10
95	Kirby Puckett	1.00
96	Travis Fryman	.10
97	Kevin Brown	.15
98	Andres Galarraga	.10
99	Marty Cordova	.10
100	Henry Rodriguez	.10
101	Sterling Hitchcock	.10
102	Trey Beamon	.10
103	Brett Butler	.10
104	Rickey Henderson	.75
105	Tino Martinez	.10
106	Kevin Appier	.10
107	Brian Hunter	.10
108	Eric Karros	.10
109	Andre Dawson	.10
110	Darryl Strawberry	.10
111	James Baldwin	.10
112	Chad Mottola	.10
113	Dave Nilsson	.10
114	Carlos Baerga	.10
115	Chan Ho Park	.10
116	John Jaha	.10
117	Alan Benes	.10
118	Mariano Rivera	.20
119	Ellis Burks	.10
120	Tony Clark	.10
121	Todd Walker	.10
122	Dwight Gooden	.10
123	Ugueth Urbina	.10
124	David Cone	.10
125	Ozzie Smith	1.00
126	Kimera Bartee	.10
127	Rusty Greer	.10
128	Pat Hentgen	.10
129	Charles Johnson	.10
130	Quinton McCracken	.10
131	Troy Percival	.10
132	Shane Reynolds	.10
133	Charles Nagy	.10
134	Tom Goodwin	.10
135	Ron Gant	.10
136	Dan Wilson	.10
137	Matt Williams	.10
138	LaTroy Hawkins	.10
139	Kevin Seitzer	.10
140	Michael Tucker	.10
141	Todd Hundley	.10
142	Alex Fernandez	.10
143	Marquis Grissom	.10
144	Steve Finley	.10
145	Curtis Pride	.10
146	Derek Bell	.10
147	Butch Huskey	.10
148	Dwight Gooden	.10
149	Al Leiter	.10
150	Hideo Nomo	.75

Stars

		NM/M
Complete Set (150):		60.00
Common Player:		1.00

(Star players in the Elite Star parallel issue valued at 4X regular Elites.)

Passing the Torch

		NM/M
Complete Set (12):		110.00
Common Player:		4.50
1	Cal Ripken Jr.	20.00
2	Alex Rodriguez	15.00
3	Cal Ripken Jr., Alex Rodriguez	17.50
4	Kirby Puckett	10.00
5	Andruw Jones	7.50
6	Kirby Puckett, Andruw Jones	7.50

7	Cecil Fielder	4.50
8	Frank Thomas	7.50
9	Cecil Fielder, Frank Thomas	6.00
10	Ozzie Smith	10.00
11	Derek Jeter	20.00
12	Ozzie Smith, Derek Jeter	12.00

Passing the Torch Autographs

		NM/M
Common Card:		15.00
1	Cal Ripken Jr.	200.00
2	Alex Rodriguez	175.00
3	Cal Ripken Jr., Alex Rodriguez	500.00
4	Kirby Puckett	80.00
5	Andruw Jones	40.00
6	Kirby Puckett, Andruw Jones	125.00
7	Cecil Fielder	15.00
8	Frank Thomas	75.00
9	Cecil Fielder, Frank Thomas	125.00
10	Ozzie Smith	120.00
11	Derek Jeter	160.00
12	Ozzie Smith, Derek Jeter	250.00

Turn of the Century

		NM/M
Complete Set (20):		55.00
Common Player:		1.00
Die-Cuts:		3X
Samples:		1X
1	Alex Rodriguez	10.00
2	Andruw Jones	6.00
3	Chipper Jones	7.50
4	Todd Walker	1.00
5	Scott Rolen	4.00
6	Trey Beamon	1.00
7	Derek Jeter	12.50
8	Darin Erstad	3.00
9	Tony Clark	1.00
10	Todd Greene	1.00
11	Jason Giambi	3.00
12	Justin Thompson	1.00
13	Ernie Young	1.00
14	Jason Kendall	1.00
15	Alex Ochoa	1.00
16	Brooks Kieschnick	1.00
17	Bobby Higginson	1.00
18	Ruben Rivera	1.00
19	Chan Ho Park	1.00
20	Chad Mottola	1.00

Leather & Lumber

		NM/M
Complete Set (10):		140.00
Common Player:		4.00
1	Ken Griffey Jr.	20.00
2	Alex Rodriguez	25.00
3	Frank Thomas	9.00
4	Chipper Jones	15.00
5	Ivan Rodriguez	9.00
6	Cal Ripken Jr.	35.00
7	Barry Bonds	35.00
8	Chuck Knoblauch	4.00
9	Manny Ramirez	9.00
10	Mark McGwire	25.00

1997 DONRUSS LIMITED

		NM/M
Complete Set (200):		450.00
Common Counterpart:		.20
Common Double Team:		.75
Common Star Factor:		1.50
Common Unlimited Potential:		1.25
Pack (5):		2.00
Wax Box (24):		45.00
1	Ken Griffey Jr., Rondell White	1.00
2	Greg Maddux, David Cone	.75
3	Gary Sheffield, Moises Alou	1.25
4	Frank Thomas	10.00
5	Cal Ripken Jr., Kevin Orie	1.50
6	Vladimir Guerrero, Barry Bonds	12.00
7	Eddie Murray, Reggie Jefferson	.60
8	Manny Ramirez, Marquis Grissom	3.00
9	Mike Piazza	15.00
10	Barry Larkin, Rey Ordonez	.20
11	Jeff Bagwell, Eric Karros	.60
12	Chuck Knoblauch, Ray Durham	.20
13	Alex Rodriguez, Edgar Renteria	1.25
14	Matt Williams, Vinny Castilla	.20
15	Todd Hollandsworth, Bob Abreu	.20
16	John Smoltz, Pedro Martinez	.50
17	Jose Canseco, C hili Davis	.40
18	Jose Cruz, Jr., Ken Griffey Jr.	10.00
19	Ken Griffey Jr.	15.00
20	Paul Molitor, John Olerud	.60
21	Roberto Alomar, Luis Castillo	.35
22	Derek Jeter, Lou Collier	1.50
23	Chipper Jones, Robin Ventura	.75
24	Gary Sheffield, Ron Gant	.25
25	Ramon Martinez, Bobby Jones	.20
26	Mike Piazza, Raul Mondesi	10.00
27	Darin Erstad, Jeff Bagwell	3.50
28	Ivan Rodriguez	8.00
29	J.T. Snow, Kevin Young	.20
30	Ryne Sandberg, Julio Franco	.75
31	Travis Fryman, Chris Snopek	.20
32	Wade Boggs, Russ Davis	.75
33	Brooks Kieschnick, Marty Cordova	.20
34	Andy Pettitte, Denny Neagle	.35
35	Paul Molitor, Matt Lawton	1.50
36	Scott Rolen, Cal Ripken Jr.	20.00
37	Cal Ripken Jr.	20.00
38	Jim Thome, Dave Nilsson	.20
39	Tony Womack, Carlos Baerga	.20
40	Nomar Garciaparra, Mark Grudzielanek	1.00
41	Todd Greene, Chris Widger	.20
42	Deion Sanders, Bernard Gilkey	.20
43	Hideo Nomo, Charles Nagy	.50
44	Ivan Rodriguez, Rusty Greer	2.50
45	Todd Walker, Chipper Jones	8.00
46	Greg Maddux	12.00
47	Mo Vaughn, Cecil Fielder	.20
48	Craig Biggio, Scott Spiezio	.20
49	Pokey Reese, Jeff Blauser	.20
50	Ken Caminiti, Joe Randa	.20
51	Albert Belle, Shawn Green	.30
52	Randy Johnson, Jason Dickson	.60
53	Hideo Nomo, Chan Ho Park	6.00
54	Scott Spiezio, Chuck Knoblauch	1.25
55	Chipper Jones	12.00
56	Tino Martinez, Ryan McGuire	.20
57	Eric Young, Wilton Guerrero	.20
58	Ron Coomer, Dave Hollins	.20
59	Sammy Sosa, Angel Echevarria	1.25
60	Dennis Reyes, Jimmy Key	.20
61	Barry Larkin, Deion Sanders	.75
62	Wilton Guerrero, Roberto Alomar	2.00
63	Albert Belle	2.50
64	Mark McGwire, Andres Galarraga	1.25
65	Edgar Martinez, Todd Walker	.20
66	Steve Finley, Rich Becker	.20
67	Tom Glavine, Andy Ashby	.30
68	Sammy Sosa, Ryne Sandberg	12.00
69	Nomar Garciaparra, Alex Rodriguez	20.00
70	Jeff Bagwell	10.00
71	Darin Erstad, Mark Grace	.50
72	Scott Rolen, Edgardo Alfonzo	.60
73	Kenny Lofton, Lance Johnson	.20
74	Joey Hamilton, Brett Tomko	.20
75	Eddie Murray, Tim Salmon	2.50
76	Dmitri Young, Mo Vaughn	1.50
77	Juan Gonzalez	10.00
78	Frank Thomas, Tony Clark	.60
79	Shannon Stewart, Bip Roberts	.20
80	Shawn Estes, Alex Fernandez	.20
81	John Smoltz, Javier Lopez	.75
82	Todd Greene, Mike Piazza	16.00
83	Derek Jeter	20.00
84	Dmitri Young, Antone Williamson	.20
85	Rickey Henderson, Darryl Hamilton	.60
86	Billy Wagner, Dennis Eckersley	.50
87	Larry Walker, Eric Young	.75
88	Mark Kotsay, Juan Gonzalez	3.00
89	Barry Bonds	20.00

90 Will Clark, Jeff Conine .30
91 Tony Gwynn, Brett Butler .75
92 John Wetteland, Rod Beck .20
93 Bernie Williams, Tino Martinez 1.25
94 Andruw Jones, Kenny Lofton 3.00
95 Mo Vaughn 1.50
96 Joe Carter, Derrek Lee .20
97 John Mabry, F.P. Santangelo .20
98 Esteban Loaiza, Wilson Alvarez .20
99 Matt Williams, David Justice .75
100 Derrek Lee, Frank Thomas 3.00
101 Mark McGwire 16.00
102 Fred McGriff, Paul Sorrento .20
103 Jermaine Allensworth, Bernie Williams .20
104 Ismael Valdes, Chris Holt .20
105 Fred McGriff, Ryan Klesko .75
106 Tony Clark, Mark McGwire 16.00
107 Tony Gwynn 12.00
108 Jeffrey Hammonds, Ellis Burks .20
109 Shane Reynolds, Andy Benes .20
110 Roger Clemens, Carlos Delgado 10.00
111 Karim Garcia, Albert Belle 1.50
112 Paul Molitor 12.00
113 Trey Beamon, Eric Owens .20
114 Curt Schilling, Darryl Kile .30
115 Tom Glavine, Michael Tucker .75
116 Pokey Reese, Derek Jeter 16.00
117 Manny Ramirez 10.00
118 Juan Gonzalez, Brant Brown .60
119 Juan Guzman, Francisco Cordova .20
120 Randy Johnson, Edgar Martinez 2.00
121 Hideki Irabu, Greg Maddux 4.50
122 Alex Rodriguez 16.00
123 Barry Bonds, Quinton McCracken 1.50
124 Roger Clemens, Alan Benes .85
125 Wade Boggs, Paul O'Neill 1.75
126 Mike Cameron, Larry Walker 1.25
127 Gary Sheffield 2.00
128 Andruw Jones, Raul Mondesi .60
129 Brian Anderson, Terrell Wade .20
130 Brady Anderson, Rafael Palmeiro 2.50
131 Neifi Perez, Barry Larkin 1.25
132 Ken Caminiti 1.50
133 Larry Walker, Rusty Greer .20
134 Mariano Rivera, Mark Wohlers .30
135 Hideki Irabu, Andy Pettitte 2.00
136 Jose Guillen, Tony Gwynn 4.50
137 Hideo Nomo 6.00
138 Vladimir Guerrero, Jim Edmonds .60
139 Justin Thompson, Dwight Gooden .20
140 Andres Galarraga, Dante Bichette .75
141 Kenny Lofton 1.50
142 Tim Salmon, Manny Ramirez .60
143 Kevin Brown, Matt Morris .20
144 Craig Biggio, Bob Abreu .75
145 Roberto Alomar 4.00
146 Jose Guillen, Brian Jordan .20
147 Bartolo Colon, Kevin Appier .20
148 Ray Lankford, Brian Jordan .75
149 Chuck Knoblauch 1.50
150 Henry Rodriguez, Ray Lankford .20
151 Jaret Wright, Ben McDonald .20
152 Bobby Bonilla, Kevin Brown .75
153 Barry Larkin 1.50
154 David Justice, Reggie Sanders .20
155 Mike Mussina, Ken Hill .40
156 Mark Grace, Brooks Kieschnick 1.00
157 Jim Thome 1.50
158 Michael Tucker, Curtis Goodwin .20
159 Jeff Suppan, Jeff Fassero .20
160 Mike Mussina, Jeffrey Hammonds 1.00
161 John Smoltz 1.50
162 Moises Alou, Eric Davis .20
163 Sandy Alomar Jr., Dan Wilson .20
164 Rondell White, Henry Rodriguez .75
165 Roger Clemens 12.50
166 Brady Anderson, Al Martin .20
167 Jason Kendall, Charles Johnson .20
168 Jason Giambi, Jose Canseco 4.00
169 Larry Walker 1.50
170 Jay Buhner, Geronimo Berroa .20
171 Ivan Rodriguez, Mike Sweeney .50
172 Kevin Appier, Jose Rosado .75
173 Bernie Williams 1.75
174 *Todd Dunwoody, Brian Giles* .40
175 Javier Lopez, Scott Hatteberg .20
176 John Jaha, Jeff Cirillo .75
177 Andy Pettitte 2.00
178 Dante Bichette, Butch Huskey .20
179 Raul Casanova, Todd Hundley .20
180 Jim Edmonds, Garret Anderson .75
181 Deion Sanders 1.50
182 Ryan Klesko, Paul O'Neill .20
183 Joe Carter, Pat Hentgen .75
184 Brady Anderson 1.50
185 Carlos Delgado, Wally Joyner .50
186 Jermaine Dye, Johnny Damon .75
187 Randy Johnson 8.00
188 Todd Hundley, Carlos Baerga .75
189 Tom Glavine 3.00
190 Damon Mashore, Jason McDonald .75
191 Wade Boggs 12.00
192 Al Martin, Jason Kendall .75
193 Matt Williams 1.50
194 Will Clark, Dean Palmer 1.00
195 Sammy Sosa 15.00
196 Jose Cruz, Jr., Jay Buhner .75
197 Eddie Murray 10.00
198 Darin Erstad, Jason Dickson 1.25
199 Fred McGriff 1.50
200 Bubba Trammell, Bobby Higginson .75

Exposure

	NM/M
Complete Set (200):	1,200
Common Counterparts:	.75
Common Double Team:	3.00
Common Star Factor:	6.50
Common Unlimited:	4.50
Stars:	4X

(See 1997 Donruss Limited for checklist and base card values.)

Fabric of the Game

	NM/M
Complete Set: (69):	375.00
Common Player:	2.00
Complete Canvas Set (23):	110.00
Rickey Henderson (100)	15.00
Barry Bonds (250)	20.00

Kenny Lofton (250)	3.00
Roberto Alomar (250)	6.00
Ryne Sandberg (250)	15.00
Tony Gwynn (500)	5.00
Barry Larkin (500)	3.00
Brady Anderson (500)	3.00
Chuck Knoblauch (500)	3.00
Craig Biggio (500)	3.00
Sammy Sosa (750)	15.00
Gary Sheffield (750)	2.50
Eric Young (750)	2.00
Larry Walker (750)	2.25
Ken Griffey Jr. (750)	10.00
Deion Sanders (750)	2.25
Raul Mondesi (1,000)	2.00
Rondell White (1,000)	2.00
Derek Jeter (1,000)	12.50
Nomar Garciaparra (1,000)	10.00
Wilton Guerrero (1,000)	2.00
Pokey Reese (1,000)	2.00
Darin Erstad (1,000)	3.00
Complete Leather Set (23):	120.00
Paul Molitor (100)	20.00
Wade Boggs (250)	15.00
Cal Ripken Jr. (250)	30.00
Tony Gwynn (250)	15.00
Joe Carter (250)	4.50
Rafael Palmeiro (500)	7.50
Mark Grace (500)	4.50
Bobby Bonilla (500)	2.00
Andres Galarraga (500)	2.00
Edgar Martinez (500)	2.00
Ken Caminiti (750)	2.00
Ivan Rodriguez(750)	6.00
Frank Thomas (750)	7.50
Jeff Bagwell (750)	6.00
Albert Belle (750)	4.50
Bernie Williams(750)	4.50
Chipper Jones (1,000)	10.00
Rusty Greer (1,000)	2.00
Todd Walker (1,000)	2.00
Scott Rolen (1,000)	5.00
Bob Abreu (1,000)	2.00
Jose Guillen (1,000)	2.00
Jose Cruz, Jr. (1,000)	2.00
Complete Wood Set (23):	150.00
Eddie Murray (100)	17.50
Cal Ripken Jr. (250)	30.00
Barry Bonds (250)	30.00
Mark McGwire (250)	25.00
Fred McGriff (250)	4.50
Ken Griffey Jr. (500)	10.00
Albert Belle (500)	3.00
Frank Thomas (500)	9.00
Juan Gonzalez (500)	7.50
Matt Williams (500)	3.00
Mike Piazza (750)	10.00
Jeff Bagwell (750)	7.50
Mo Vaughn (750)	2.25
Gary Sheffield (750)	2.50
Tim Salmon (750)	2.25
David Justice (750)	2.25
Manny Ramirez (1,000)	6.00
Jim Thome (1,000)	2.25
Tino Martinez (1,000)	2.25
Andruw Jones (1,000)	4.50
Vladimir Guerrero (1,000)	5.00
Tony Clark (1,000)	2.25
Dmitri Young (1,000)	2.25

1997 DONRUSS PREFERRED

	NM/M
Complete Set (200):	225.00
Common Bronze:	.10
Common Silver:	.60
Common Gold:	1.25
Common Platinum:	6.00
Cut to the Chase:	1.5X
Tin Pack (5):	2.50
Tin Box (24):	40.00

1 Frank Thomas P 6.00
2 Ken Griffey Jr. P 10.00
3 Cecil Fielder B .10
4 Chuck Knoblauch G 1.25
5 Garret Anderson B .10

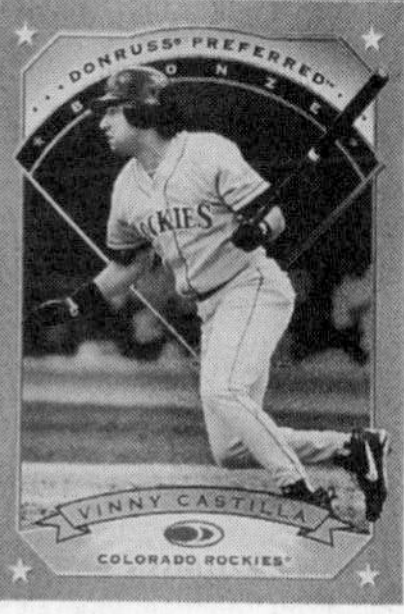

6 Greg Maddux P 8.00
7 Matt Williams S .60
8 Marquis Grissom S .60
9 Jason Isringhausen B .10
10 Larry Walker S .60
11 Charles Nagy B .10
12 Dan Wilson B .10
13 Albert Belle G 2.50
14 Javier Lopez B .10
15 David Cone B .10
16 Bernard Gilkey B .10
17 Andres Galarraga S .60
18 Bill Pulsipher B .10
19 Alex Fernandez B .10
20 Andy Pettitte S 1.25
21 Mark Grudzielanek B .10
22 Juan Gonzalez P 6.00
23 Reggie Sanders B .10
24 Kenny Lofton G 1.25
25 Andy Ashby B .10
26 John Wetteland B .10
27 Bobby Bonilla B .10
28 Hideo Nomo G 4.50
29 Joe Carter B .10
30 Jose Canseco B .40
31 Ellis Burks B .10
32 Edgar Martinez S .60
33 Chan Ho Park B .15
34 David Justice B .10
35 Carlos Delgado B .50
36 Jeff Cirillo S .60
37 Charles Johnson B .10
38 Manny Ramirez G 4.50
39 Greg Vaughn B .10
40 Henry Rodriguez B .10
41 Darryl Strawberry B .10
42 Jim Thome G 1.50
43 Ryan Klesko S .60
44 Jermaine Allensworth B .10
45 Brian Jordan G 1.25
46 Tony Gwynn P 8.00
47 Rafael Palmeiro G 4.50
48 Dante Bichette S .60
49 Ivan Rodriguez G 4.50
50 Mark McGwire G 8.00
51 Tim Salmon S .75
52 Roger Clemens B 1.50
53 Matt Lawton B .10
54 Wade Boggs S 3.00
55 Travis Fryman B .10
56 Bobby Higginson S .60
57 John Jaha S .60
58 Rondell White S .60
59 Tom Glavine S 1.25
60 Eddie Murray S 2.00
61 Vinny Castilla B .10
62 Todd Hundley B .10
63 Jay Buhner S .60
64 Paul O'Neill B .10
65 Steve Finley B .10
66 Kevin Appier B .10
67 Ray Durham B .10
68 Dave Nilsson B .10
69 Jeff Bagwell G 4.50
70 Al Martin S .60
71 Paul Molitor G 5.00
72 Kevin Brown S .90
73 Ron Gant B .10
74 Dwight Gooden B .10
75 Quinton McCracken B .10
76 Rusty Greer S .60
77 Juan Guzman B .10
78 Fred McGriff S .60
79 Tino Martinez B .10
80 Ray Lankford B .10
81 Ken Caminiti G 1.25
82 James Baldwin B .10
83 Jermaine Dye G 1.25
84 Mark Grace S .75

85	Pat Hentgen S	.60
86	Jason Giambi S	1.75
87	Brian Hunter B	.10
88	Andy Benes B	.10
89	Jose Rosado B	.10
90	Shawn Green B	.30
91	Jason Kendall B	.10
92	Alex Rodriguez P	10.00
93	Chipper Jones P	8.00
94	Barry Bonds G	10.00
95	Brady Anderson G	1.25
96	Ryne Sandberg S	2.00
97	Lance Johnson B	.10
98	Cal Ripken Jr. P	12.00
99	Craig Biggio S	.60
100	Dean Palmer B	.10
101	Gary Sheffield G	1.50
102	Johnny Damon B	.25
103	Mo Vaughn G	1.25
104	Randy Johnson S	2.50
105	Raul Mondesi S	.60
106	Roberto Alomar G	2.50
107	Mike Piazza P	9.00
108	Rey Ordonez B	.10
109	Barry Larkin G	1.25
110	Tony Clark S	.60
111	Bernie Williams S	.90
112	John Smoltz G	1.25
113	Moises Alou B	.10
114	Will Clark B	.15
115	Sammy Sosa G	8.00
116	Jim Edmonds S	.60
117	Jeff Conine B	.10
118	Joey Hamilton B	.10
119	Todd Hollandsworth B	.10
120	Troy Percival B	.10
121	Paul Wilson B	.10
122	Ken Hill B	.10
123	Mariano Rivera S	.75
124	Eric Karros B	.10
125	Derek Jeter G	10.00
126	Eric Young S	.60
127	John Mabry B	.10
128	Gregg Jefferies B	.10
129	Ismael Valdes S	.60
130	Marty Cordova B	.10
131	Omar Vizquel B	.10
132	Mike Mussina S	1.25
133	Darin Erstad B	.50
134	Edgar Renteria S	.60
135	Billy Wagner B	.10
136	Alex Ochoa B	.10
137	Luis Castillo B	.10
138	Rocky Coppinger B	.10
139	Mike Sweeney B	.10
140	Michael Tucker B	.10
141	Chris Snopek B	.10
142	Dmitri Young S	.60
143	Andruw Jones P	6.00
144	Mike Cameron S	.60
145	Brant Brown B	.10
146	Todd Walker G	1.25
147	Nomar Garciaparra G	6.00
148	Glendon Rusch B	.10
149	Karim Garcia S	.75
150	*Bubba Trammell S*	.60
151	Todd Greene B	.10
152	Wilton Guerrero G	1.25
153	Scott Spiezio B	.10
154	Brooks Kieschnick B	.10
155	Vladimir Guerrero G	4.50
156	*Brian Giles S*	1.50
157	Pokey Reese B	.10
158	Jason Dickson G	1.25
159	Kevin Orie S	.60
160	Scott Rolen G	3.50
161	Bartolo Colon S	.60
162	Shannon Stewart G	1.50
163	Wendell Magee B	.10
164	Jose Guillen S	.60
165	Bob Abreu S	.60
166	*Deivi Cruz B*	.20
167	Alex Rodriguez B	3.50
168	Frank Thomas B	.75
169	Cal Ripken Jr. B	4.00
170	Chipper Jones B	1.50
171	Mike Piazza B	3.00
172	Tony Gwynn S	2.50
173	Juan Gonzalez B	.75
174	Kenny Lofton S	.60
175	Ken Griffey Jr. B	2.50
176	Mark McGwire B	3.50
177	Jeff Bagwell B	.75
178	Paul Molitor S	2.50
179	Andruw Jones B	.75
180	Manny Ramirez S	2.00
181	Ken Caminiti S	.60
182	Barry Bonds B	4.00
183	Mo Vaughn B	.20
184	Derek Jeter B	4.00
185	Barry Larkin S	.60
186	Ivan Rodriguez B	.60
187	Albert Belle S	.75
188	John Smoltz S	.60
189	Chuck Knoblauch S	.60
190	Brian Jordan S	.60
191	Gary Sheffield S	.90
192	Jim Thome S	.75
193	Brady Anderson S	.60
194	Hideo Nomo S	1.50
195	Sammy Sosa S	4.50
196	Greg Maddux B	1.25
197	Vladimir Guerrero B Checklist	.40
198	Scott Rolen B Checklist	.15
199	Todd Walker B Checklist	.10
200	Nomar Garciaparra B Checklist	.60

Cut To The Chase

NM/M

Typical Value: 1.5X

(See 1997 Donruss Preferred for checklist and base card values.)

Tins

		NM/M
Complete Set, Blue (25):		10.00
Common Tin:		.25
Gold:		10X
1	Frank Thomas	.40
2	Ken Griffey Jr.	.60
3	Andruw Jones	.40
4	Cal Ripken Jr.	1.00
5	Mike Piazza	.60
6	Chipper Jones	.50
7	Alex Rodriguez	.75
8	Derek Jeter	1.00
9	Juan Gonzalez	.40
10	Albert Belle	.25
11	Tony Gwynn	.50
12	Greg Maddux	.50
13	Jeff Bagwell	.40
14	Roger Clemens	.55
15	Mark McGwire	.75
16	Gary Sheffield	.35
17	Manny Ramirez	.40
18	Hideo Nomo	.40
19	Kenny Lofton	.25
20	Mo Vaughn	.25
21	Ryne Sandberg	.50
22	Barry Bonds	1.00
23	Sammy Sosa	.60
24	John Smoltz	.25
25	Ivan Rodriguez	.35

Precious Metals

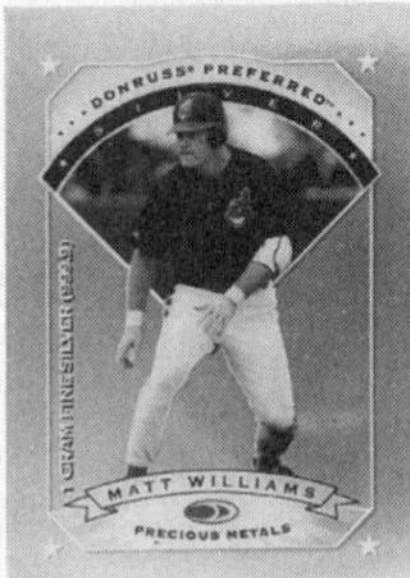

		NM/M
Complete Set (25):		800.00
Common Player:		4.00
1	Frank Thomas (P)	30.00
2	Ken Griffey Jr. (P)	60.00
3	Greg Maddux (P)	40.00
4	Albert Belle (G)	7.50
5	Juan Gonzalez (P)	30.00
6	Kenny Lofton (G)	4.00
7	Tony Gwynn (P)	40.00
8	Ivan Rodriguez (G)	25.00
9	Mark McGwire (G)	90.00
10	Matt Williams (S)	4.00
11	Wade Boggs (S)	40.00
12	Eddie Murray (S)	35.00
13	Jeff Bagwell (G)	30.00
14	Ken Caminiti (G)	4.00
15	Alex Rodriguez (P)	90.00
16	Chipper Jones (P)	40.00
17	Barry Bonds (G)	125.00
18	Cal Ripken Jr. (P)	125.00
19	Mo Vaughn (G)	4.00
20	Mike Piazza (P)	60.00
21	Derek Jeter (G)	125.00
22	Bernie Williams (S)	10.00
23	Andruw Jones (P)	30.00
24	Vladimir Guerrero (G)	30.00
25	Jose Guillen (S)	4.00

Staremasters

		NM/M
Complete Set (20):		75.00
Common Player:		1.50
Samples:		50%
1	Alex Rodriguez	7.50
2	Frank Thomas	4.00
3	Chipper Jones	5.00
4	Cal Ripken Jr.	10.00
5	Mike Piazza	6.00
6	Juan Gonzalez	4.00
7	Derek Jeter	10.00
8	Jeff Bagwell	4.00
9	Ken Griffey Jr.	6.00
10	Tony Gwynn	5.00
11	Barry Bonds	10.00
12	Albert Belle	2.00
13	Greg Maddux	5.00
14	Mark McGwire	7.50
15	Ken Caminiti	1.50
16	Hideo Nomo	3.00
17	Gary Sheffield	2.00
18	Andruw Jones	4.00
19	Mo Vaughn	1.50
20	Ivan Rodriguez	3.00

X-Ponential Power

		NM/M
Complete Set (20):		50.00
Common Player:		1.00
1A	Manny Ramirez	3.50
1B	Jim Thome	1.00
2A	Paul Molitor	3.50
2B	Chuck Knoblauch	1.00
3A	Ivan Rodriguez	2.50
3B	Juan Gonzalez	3.50
4A	Albert Belle	1.00
4B	Frank Thomas	3.50
5A	Roberto Alomar	1.25
5B	Cal Ripken Jr.	9.00
6A	Tim Salmon	1.00
6B	Jim Edmonds	1.00
7A	Ken Griffey Jr.	6.00
7B	Alex Rodriguez	7.50
8A	Chipper Jones	4.50
8B	Andruw Jones	3.50
9A	Mike Piazza	6.00
9B	Raul Mondesi	1.00
10A	Tony Gwynn	4.50
10B	Ken Caminiti	1.00

1997 DONRUSS SIGNATURE

		NM/M
Complete Set (100):		15.00
Common Player:		.10
Pack (5):		7.50
Wax Box (12):		80.00
1	Mark McGwire	1.25
2	Kenny Lofton	.10
3	Tony Gwynn	.75
4	Tony Clark	.10
5	Tim Salmon	.15
6	Ken Griffey Jr.	1.00
7	Mike Piazza	1.00
8	Greg Maddux	.75
9	Roberto Alomar	.25
10	Andres Galarraga	.10
11	Roger Clemens	.90
12	Bernie Williams	.20
13	Rondell White	.10
14	Kevin Appler	.10
15	Ray Lankford	.10
16	Frank Thomas	.60
17	Will Clark	.15
18	Chipper Jones	.75
19	Jeff Bagwell	.60
20	Manny Ramirez	.60
21	Ryne Sandberg	.75
22	Paul Molitor	.60
23	Gary Sheffield	.10
24	Jim Edmonds	.10
25	Barry Larkin	.10
26	Rafael Palmeiro	.60
27	Alan Benes	.10
28	David Justice	.10
29	Randy Johnson	.60
30	Barry Bonds	1.50
31	Mo Vaughn	.10
32	Michael Tucker	.10
33	Larry Walker	.10
34	Tino Martinez	.10
35	Jose Guillen	.10
36	Carlos Delgado	.50
37	Jason Dickson	.10
38	Tom Glavine	.25
39	Raul Mondesi	.10
40	*Jose Cruz Jr.*	.50
41	Johnny Damon	.10
42	Mark Grace	.15
43	Juan Gonzalez	.60
44	Vladimir Guerrero	.60
45	Kevin Brown	.10
46	Justin Thompson	.10
47	Eric Young	.10
48	Ron Coomer	.10
49	Mark Kotsay	.10
50	Scott Rolen	.60
51	Derek Jeter	1.50
52	Jim Thome	.10
53	Fred McGriff	.10
54	Albert Belle	.15
55	Garret Anderson	.10
56	Wilton Guerrero	.10
57	Jose Canseco	.40
58	Cal Ripken Jr.	1.50
59	Sammy Sosa	1.00
60	Dmitri Young	.10
61	Alex Rodriguez	1.25
62	Javier Lopez	.10
63	Sandy Alomar Jr.	.10
64	Joe Carter	.10
65	Dante Bichette	.10
66	Al Martin	.10
67	Darin Erstad	.50
68	Pokey Reese	.10
69	Brady Anderson	.10
70	Andruw Jones	.60
71	Ivan Rodriguez	.50

72 Nomar Garciaparra 1.00
73 Moises Alou .10
74 Andy Pettitte .35
75 Jay Buhner .10
76 Craig Biggio .10
77 Wade Boggs .75
78 Shawn Estes .10
79 Neifi Perez .10
80 Rusty Greer .10
81 Pedro Martinez .60
82 Mike Mussina .50
83 Jason Giambi .45
84 Hideo Nomo .60
85 Todd Hundley .10
86 Deion Sanders .10
87 Mike Cameron .10
88 Bobby Bonilla .10
89 Todd Greene .10
90 Kevin Orie .10
91 Ken Caminiti .10
92 Chuck Knoblauch .10
93 Matt Morris .10
94 Matt Williams .10
95 Pat Hentgen .10
96 John Smoltz .10
97 Edgar Martinez .10
98 Jason Kendall .10
99 Ken Griffey Jr. Checklist .50
100 Frank Thomas Checklist .30

Platinum Press Proofs

NM/M
Complete Set (100): 300.00
Common Player: 2.00
Stars: 12X
(See 1997 Donruss Signature for checklist and base card prices.)

Century Marks (Blue)

NM/M
Common Player: 20.00
(1) Jeff Abbott 20.00
(2) Bob Abreu 30.00
(3) Edgardo Alfonzo 20.00
(4) Roberto Alomar 75.00
(5) Sandy Alomar Jr. 25.00
(6) Moises Alou 35.00
(7) Garret Anderson 60.00
(8) Andy Ashby 20.00
(9) Jeff Bagwell 80.00
(10) Trey Beamon 20.00
(11) Albert Belle 30.00
(12) Alan Benes 20.00
(13) Geronimo Berroa 20.00
(14) Wade Boggs 100.00
(15) Barry Bonds 300.00
(16) Bobby Bonilla 20.00
(17) Kevin Brown 75.00
(18) Kevin L. Brown 20.00
(19) Jay Buhner 30.00
(20) Brett Butler 30.00
(21) Mike Cameron 25.00
(22) Giovanni Carrara 20.00
(23) Luis Castillo 20.00
(24) Tony Clark 20.00
(25) Will Clark 100.00
(26) Roger Clemens 200.00
(27) Lou Collier 20.00
(28) Bartolo Colon 30.00
(29) Ron Coomer 20.00
(30) Marty Cordova 20.00
(31) Jacob Cruz 20.00
(32) Jose Cruz Jr. 30.00
(33) Russ Davis 20.00
(34) Jason Dickson 25.00
(35) Todd Dunwoody 25.00
(36) Jermaine Dye 20.00
(37) Jim Edmonds 60.00
(38) Darin Erstad 40.00
(39) Bobby Estalella 20.00
(40) Shawn Estes 20.00
(41) Jeff Fassero 20.00
(42) Andres Galarraga 30.00
(43) Karim Garcia 20.00
(44) Nomar Garciaparra (SP/62) 225.00
(45) Derrick Gibson 20.00
(46) Brian Giles 30.00
(47) Tom Glavine 100.00
(48) Juan Gonzalez 55.00
(49) Rick Gorecki 20.00
(50) Shawn Green 90.00
(51) Todd Greene 20.00
(52) Rusty Greer 20.00
(53) Ben Grieve 20.00
(54) Mark Grudzielanek 20.00
(55) Vladimir Guerrero 100.00
(56) Wilton Guerrero 20.00
(57) Jose Guillen 30.00
(58) Tony Gwynn 95.00
(59) Jeffrey Hammonds 20.00
(60) Todd Helton 60.00
(61) Todd Hollandsworth 20.00
(62) Trenidad Hubbard 20.00
(63) Todd Hundley 25.00
(64) Derek Jeter 200.00
(65) Andruw Jones 50.00
(66) Bobby Jones 20.00
(67) Chipper Jones 100.00
(68) Brian Jordan 35.00
(69) David Justice 30.00
(70) Eric Karros 25.00
(71) Jason Kendall 30.00
(72) Jimmy Key 50.00
(73) Brooks Kieschnick 20.00
(74) Ryan Klesko 25.00
(75) Chuck Knoblauch 20.00
(76) Paul Konerko 25.00
(77) Mark Kotsay 25.00
(78) Ray Lankford 20.00
(79) Barry Larkin 60.00
(80) Derrek Lee 40.00
(81) Esteban Loaiza 20.00
(82) Javy Lopez 45.00
(83) Greg Maddux 175.00
(84) Edgar Martinez 50.00
(85) Pedro Martinez 100.00
(86) Tino Martinez 50.00
(87) Rafael Medina 20.00
(88) Raul Mondesi 35.00
(88) Raul Mondesi (Exchange card) 5.00
(89) Matt Morris 40.00
(90) Eddie Murray 75.00
(91) Mike Mussina 80.00
(92) Paul O'Neill 40.00
(93) Kevin Orie 20.00
(94) David Ortiz 100.00
(95) Rafael Palmeiro 80.00
(96) Jay Payton 20.00
(97) Neifi Perez 20.00
(98) Andy Petitte 50.00
(99) Manny Ramirez 100.00
(100) Joe Randa 20.00
(101) Calvin Reese 20.00
(102) Edgar Renteria 50.00
(102) Edgar Renteria (Exchange card) 5.00
(103) Dennis Reyes 20.00
(104) Cal Ripken Jr. 225.00
(105) Alex Rodriguez 180.00
(106) Henry Rodriguez 20.00
(107) Ivan Rodriguez 75.00
(108) Scott Rolen 75.00
(109) Kirk Rueter 20.00
(110) Ryne Sandberg 125.00
(111) Gary Sheffield 50.00
(112) Dwight Smith 20.00
(113) J.T. Snow 25.00
(114) Scott Spiezio 20.00
(115) Shannon Stewart 25.00
(116) Jeff Suppan 20.00
(117) Mike Sweeney 25.00
(118) Miguel Tejada 120.00
(119) Frank Thomas 80.00
(120) Jim Thome 75.00
(120) Jim Thome (Exchange card) 5.00
(121) Justin Thompson 20.00
(122) Brett Tomko 20.00
(123) Bubba Trammell 15.00
(124) Michael Tucker 20.00
(125) Javier Valentin 20.00
(126) Mo Vaughn 25.00
(127) Robin Ventura 30.00
(128) Terrell Wade 20.00
(129) Billy Wagner 40.00
(130) Larry Walker 80.00
(131) Todd Walker 25.00
(132) Rondell White 25.00
(133) Kevin Wickander 20.00
(134) Chris Widger 20.00
(135) Bernie Williams 75.00
(136) Matt Williams 30.00
(137) Antone Williamson 20.00
(138) Dan Wilson 20.00
(139) Tony Womack 25.00
(140) Jaret Wright 35.00
(141) Dmitri Young 30.00
(142) Eric Young 30.00
(143) Kevin Young 20.00

Autographs (Red)

NM/M
Complete Set (116): 700.00
Common Player: 2.00
(1) Jeff Abbott (3900) 2.00
(2) Bob Abreu (3900) 8.00
(3) Edgardo Alfonzo (3900) 3.00
(4) Roberto Alomar (150) 50.00
(5) Sandy Alomar Jr. (1400) 6.00
(6) Moises Alou (900) 10.00
(7) Garret Anderson (3900) 10.00
(8) Andy Ashby (3900) 3.00
(10) Trey Beamon (3900) 2.00
(12) Alan Benes (3900) 2.00
(13) Geronimo Berroa (3900) 2.00
(14) Wade Boggs (150) 60.00
(18) Kevin L. Brown (3900) 2.00
(20) Brett Butler (1400) 3.50
(21) Mike Cameron (3900) 5.00
(22) Giovanni Carrara (2900) 2.00
(23) Luis Castillo (3900) 4.00
(24) Tony Clark (3900) 3.00
(25) Will Clark (1400) 20.00
(27) Lou Collier (3900) 2.00
(28) Bartolo Colon (3900) 6.00
(29) Ron Coomer (3900) 2.00
(30) Marty Cordova (3900) 3.00
(31) Jacob Cruz (3900) 2.00
(32) Jose Cruz Jr. (900) 8.00
(33) Russ Davis (3900) 3.00
(34) Jason Dickson (3900) 2.00
(35) Todd Dunwoody (3900) 2.00
(36) Jermaine Dye (3900) 3.00
(37) Jim Edmonds (3900) 20.00
(38) Darin Erstad (900) 8.00
(39) Bobby Estalella (3900) 3.00
(40) Shawn Estes (3900) 3.00
(41) Jeff Fassero (3900) 2.00
(42) Andres Galarraga (900) 6.00
(43) Karim Garcia (3900) 3.00
(45) Derrick Gibson (3900) 2.00
(46) Brian Giles (3900) 8.00
(47) Tom Glavine (150) 50.00
(49) Rick Gorecki (900) 4.50
(50) Shawn Green (1900) 15.00
(51) Todd Greene (3900) 3.00
(52) Rusty Greer (3900) 3.00
(53) Ben Grieve (3900) 3.00
(54) Mark Grudzielanek (3900) 3.00
(55) Vladimir Guerrero (1900) 30.00
(56) Wilton Guerrero (2150) 3.00
(57) Jose Guillen (2900) 8.00
(59) Jeffrey Hammonds (2150) 3.50
(60) Todd Helton (1400) 20.00
(61) Todd Hollandsworth (2900) 3.00
(62) Trenidad Hubbard (900) 4.00
(63) Todd Hundley (1400) 3.00
(66) Bobby Jones (3900) 2.00
(68) Brian Jordan (1400) 4.00
(69) David Justice (900) 10.00
(70) Eric Karros (650) 4.50
(71) Jason Kendall (3900) 6.00
(72) Jimmy Key (3900) 5.00
(73) Brooks Kieschnick (3900) 2.00
(74) Ryan Klesko (225) 10.00
(76) Paul Konerko (3900) 10.00
(77) Mark Kotsay (2400) 3.00
(78) Ray Lankford (3900) 4.00
(79) Barry Larkin (150) 35.00
(80) Derrek Lee (3900) 15.00
(81) Esteban Loaiza (3900) 3.00
(82) Javier Lopez (1400) 10.00
(84) Edgar Martinez (150) 50.00
(85) Pedro Martinez (900) 40.00
(87) Rafael Medina (3900) 2.00
(88) Raul Mondesi (may not exist)
(88) Raul Mondesi (Exchange card) 3.00
(89) Matt Morris (3900) 10.00
(92) Paul O'Neill (900) 15.00
(93) Kevin Orie (3900) 2.00
(94) David Ortiz (3900) 35.00
(95) Rafael Palmeiro (900) 30.00
(96) Jay Payton (3900) 2.50
(97) Neifi Perez (3900) 2.00
(99) Manny Ramirez (900) 40.00
(100) Joe Randa (3900) 2.00
(101) Calvin Reese (3900) 3.00
(102) Edgar Renteria (?) 20.00
(102) Edgar Renteria (Exchange card) 3.00
(103) Dennis Reyes (3900) 2.00
(106) Henry Rodriguez (3900) 2.00
(108) Scott Rolen (1900) 25.00
(109) Kirk Rueter (2900) 3.00
(110) Ryne Sandberg (400) 60.00
(112) Dwight Smith (2900) 3.00
(113) J.T. Snow (900) 4.00
(114) Scott Spiezio (3900) 2.00
(115) Shannon Stewart (2900) 3.00
(116) Jeff Suppan (1900) 3.00
(117) Mike Sweeney (3900) 6.00
(118) Miguel Tejada (3900) 40.00
(121) Justin Thompson (2400) 3.00
(122) Brett Tomko (3900) 3.00
(123) Bubba Trammell (3900) 2.50
(124) Michael Tucker (3900) 2.00
(125) Javier Valentin (3900) 2.00
(126) Mo Vaughn (150) 10.00
(127) Robin Ventura (1400) 8.00
(128) Terrell Wade (3900) 2.00
(129) Billy Wagner (3900) 8.00
(130) Larry Walker (900) 25.00
(131) Todd Walker (2400) 3.00
(132) Rondell White (3900) 6.00
(133) Kevin Wickander (900) 4.00
(134) Chris Widger (3900) 2.00
(136) Matt Williams (150) 25.00
(137) Antone Williamson (3900) 2.00
(138) Dan Wilson (3900) 2.00
(139) Tony Womack (3900) 5.00
(140) Jaret Wright (3900) 12.00
(141) Dmitri Young (3900) 8.00
(142) Eric Young (3900) 2.50
(143) Kevin Young (3900) 2.50

Millennium Marks (Green)

	NM/M
Complete Set (143):	1,450
Common Player:	2.00
(1) Jeff Abbott	2.00
(2) Bob Abreu	8.00
(3) Edgardo Alfonzo	5.00
(4) Roberto Alomar	20.00
(5) Sandy Alomar Jr.	8.00
(6) Moises Alou	15.00
(7) Garret Anderson	15.00
(8) Andy Ashby	5.00
(9) Jeff Bagwell (400)	75.00
(10) Trey Beamon	2.00
(11) Albert Belle (400)	10.00
(12) Alan Benes	2.00
(13) Geronimo Berroa	2.00
(14) Wade Boggs	30.00
(15) Barry Bonds (400)	200.00
(16) Bobby Bonilla (900)	7.50
(17) Kevin Brown (900)	20.00
(18) Kevin L. Brown	10.00
(19) Jay Buhner (900)	10.00
(20) Brett Butler	6.00
(21) Mike Cameron	4.00
(22) Giovanni Carrara	2.00
(23) Luis Castillo	5.00
(24) Tony Clark	5.00
(25) Will Clark	20.00
(26) Roger Clemens (400)	120.00
(27) Lou Collier	2.00
(28) Bartolo Colon	8.00
(29) Ron Coomer	2.00
(30) Marty Cordova	2.00
(31) Jacob Cruz	2.00
(32) Jose Cruz Jr.	6.00
(33) Russ Davis	2.00
(34) Jason Dickson	5.00
(35) Todd Dunwoody	5.00
(36) Jermaine Dye	5.00
(37) Jim Edmonds	30.00
(38) Darin Erstad	10.00
(39) Bobby Estalella	3.00
(40) Shawn Estes	2.00
(41) Jeff Fassero	4.00
(42) Andres Galarraga	10.00
(43) Karim Garcia	3.50
(44) Nomar Garciaparra (650)	100.00
(45) Derrick Gibson	4.00
(46) Brian Giles	8.00
(47) Tom Glavine	30.00
(48) Juan Gonzalez (900)	25.00
(49) Rick Gorecki	2.00
(50) Shawn Green	20.00
(51) Todd Greene	7.50
(52) Rusty Greer	7.50
(53) Ben Grieve	5.00
(54) Mark Grudzielanek	2.00
(55) Vladimir Guerrero	30.00
(56) Wilton Guerrero	2.00
(57) Jose Guillen	6.00
(58) Tony Gwynn (900)	40.00
(59) Jeffrey Hammonds	2.00
(60) Todd Helton	30.00
(61) Todd Hollandsworth	2.00
(62) Trenidad Hubbard	2.00
(63) Todd Hundley	6.00
(64) Derek Jeter (400)	100.00
(65) Andruw Jones (900)	15.00
(66) Bobby Jones	2.00
(67) Chipper Jones	30.00
(68) Brian Jordan	7.50
(69) David Justice	10.00
(70) Eric Karros	6.00
(71) Jason Kendall	8.00
(72) Jimmy Key	2.00
(73) Brooks Kieschnick	4.00
(74) Ryan Klesko	5.00
(75) Chuck Knoblauch (900)	5.00
(76) Paul Konerko	5.00
(77) Mark Kotsay	6.00
(78) Ray Lankford	2.00
(79) Barry Larkin	30.00
(80) Derrek Lee	20.00
(81) Esteban Loaiza	2.00
(82) Javy Lopez	8.00
(83) Greg Maddux (400)	80.00
(84) Edgar Martinez	25.00
(85) Pedro Martinez	40.00
(86) Tino Martinez (900)	15.00
(87) Rafael Medina	2.00
(88) Raul Mondesi	10.00
(88) Raul Mondesi (Exchange card)	2.00
(89) Matt Morris	15.00
(90) Eddie Murray (900)	30.00
(91) Mike Mussina (900)	20.00
(92) Paul O'Neill	15.00
(93) Kevin Orie	2.00
(94) David Ortiz	40.00
(95) Rafael Palmeiro	30.00
(96) Jay Payton	5.00
(97) Neifi Perez	2.00
(98) Andy Petitte (900)	25.00
(99) Manny Ramirez	30.00
(100) Joe Randa	2.00
(101) Calvin Reese	2.00
(102) Edgar Renteria	30.00
(102) Edgar Renteria (Exchange card)	2.00
(103) Dennis Reyes	3.00
(104) Cal Ripken Jr. (400)	135.00
(105) Alex Rodriguez (400)	100.00
(106) Henry Rodriguez	3.00
(107) Ivan Rodriguez (900)	20.00
(108) Scott Rolen	25.00
(109) Kirk Rueter	2.00
(110) Ryne Sandberg	40.00
(111) Gary Sheffield (400)	25.00
(112) Dwight Smith	2.00
(113) J.T. Snow	7.50
(114) Scott Spiezio	5.00
(115) Shannon Stewart	2.00
(116) Jeff Suppan	2.00
(117) Mike Sweeney	5.00
(118) Miguel Tejada	40.00
(119) Frank Thomas (400)	50.00
(120) Jim Thome (900)	30.00
(120) Jim Thome (Exchange card)	2.00
(121) Justin Thompson	2.00
(122) Brett Tomko	2.00
(123) Bubba Trammell	4.00
(124) Michael Tucker	2.00
(125) Javier Valentin	2.00
(126) Mo Vaughn	8.00
(127) Robin Ventura	8.00
(128) Terrell Wade	2.00
(129) Billy Wagner	10.00
(130) Larry Walker	20.00
(131) Todd Walker	6.00
(132) Rondell White	6.00
(133) Kevin Wickander	2.00
(134) Chris Widger	2.00
(135) Bernie Williams (400)	60.00
(136) Matt Williams	10.00
(137) Antone Williamson	2.00
(138) Dan Wilson	2.00
(139) Tony Womack	2.00
(140) Jaret Wright	15.00
(141) Dmitri Young	5.00
(142) Eric Young	5.00
(143) Kevin Young	2.00

Notable Nicknames

	NM/M
Common Player:	20.00
(1) Ernie Banks (Mr. Cub)	150.00
(2) Tony Clark (The Tiger)	20.00
(3) Roger Clemens (The Rocket)	300.00
(4) Reggie Jackson (Mr. October)	125.00
(5) Randy Johnson (Big Unit)	250.00
(6) Stan Musial (The Man)	180.00
(7) Ivan Rodriguez (Pudge)	100.00
(8) Frank Thomas (The Big Hurt)	125.00
(9) Mo Vaughn (Hit Dog)	20.00
(10) Billy Wagner (The Kid)	40.00

Significant Signatures

	NM/M
Common Player:	15.00
(1) Ernie Banks	35.00
(2) Johnny Bench	30.00
(3) Yogi Berra	30.00
(4) George Brett	40.00
(5) Lou Brock	25.00
(6) Rod Carew	25.00
(7) Steve Carlton	20.00
(8) Larry Doby	40.00
(9) Carlton Fisk	30.00
(10) Bob Gibson	30.00
(11) Reggie Jackson	30.00
(12) Al Kaline	30.00
(13) Harmon Killebrew	30.00
(14) Don Mattingly	40.00
(15) Stan Musial	45.00
(16) Jim Palmer	15.00
(17) Brooks Robinson	30.00
(18) Frank Robinson	15.00
(19) Mike Schmidt	40.00
(20) Tom Seaver	30.00
(21) Duke Snider	25.00
(22) Carl Yastrzemski	40.00

1997 DONRUSS TEAM SETS

	NM/M
Comp. Angels Set (1-15):	1.25
Comp. Braves Set (16-30):	3.00
Comp. Orioles Set (31-45):	2.50
Comp. Red Sox Set (46-60):	1.50
Comp. White Sox Set (61-75):	2.00
Comp. Indians Set (76-90):	1.50
Comp. Rockies Set (91-105):	1.50
Comp. Dodgers Set (106-120):	2.25
Comp. Yankees Set (121-135):	4.50
Comp. Mariners Set (136-150):	4.50
Comp. Cardinals Set (151-165)	2.00
Common Player:	.05
Pennant Edition Stars:	3X
1 Jim Edmonds	.05
2 Tim Salmon	.10
3 Tony Phillips	.05
4 Garret Anderson	.05
5 Troy Percival	.05
6 Mark Langston	.05
7 Chuck Finley	.05
8 Eddie Murray	.75
9 Jim Leyritz	.05
10 Darin Erstad	.50
11 Jason Dickson	.05
12 Allen Watson	.05
13 Shigetosi Hasegawa	.05
14 Dave Hollins	.05
15 Gary DiSarcina	.05
16 Greg Maddux	1.00
17 Denny Neagle	.05
18 Chipper Jones	1.00
19 Tom Glavine	.25
20 John Smoltz	.05
21 Ryan Klesko	.05
22 Fred McGriff	.05
23 Michael Tucker	.05
24 Kenny Lofton	.05
25 Javier Lopez	.05
26 Mark Wohlers	.05
27 Jeff Blauser	.05
28 Andruw Jones	.65
29 Tony Graffanino	.05
30 Terrell Wade	.05
31 Brady Anderson	.05
32 Roberto Alomar	.15
33 Rafael Palmeiro	.65
34 Mike Mussina	.40
35 Cal Ripken Jr.	2.00
36 Rocky Coppinger	.05
37 Randy Myers	.05
38 B.J. Surhoff	.05
39 Eric Davis	.05
40 Armando Benitez	.05
41 Jeffrey Hammonds	.05
42 Jimmy Key	.05
43 Chris Hoiles	.05
44 Mike Bordick	.05
45 Pete Incaviglia	.05
46 Mike Stanley	.05
47 Reggie Jefferson	.05
48 Mo Vaughn	.20
49 John Valentin	.05
50 Tim Naehring	.05
51 Jeff Suppan	.05
52 Tim Wakefield	.05
53 Jeff Frye	.05
54 Darren Bragg	.05
55 Steve Avery	.05
56 Shane Mack	.05
57 Aaron Sele	.05
58 Troy O'Leary	.05
59 Rudy Pemberton	.05
60 Nomar Garciaparra	1.25
61 Robin Ventura	.05
62 Wilson Alvarez	.05
63 Roberto Hernandez	.05
64 Frank Thomas	.65
65 Ray Durham	.05
66 James Baldwin	.05
67 Harold Baines	.05
68 Doug Drabek	.05
69 Mike Cameron	.05
70 Albert Belle	.10
71 Jaime Navarro	.05
72 Chris Snopek	.05
73 Lyle Mouton	.05
74 Dave Martinez	.05
75 Ozzie Guillen	.05
76 Manny Ramirez	.65
77 Jack McDowell	.05
78 Jim Thome	.05
79 Jose Mesa	.05
80 Brian Giles	.05
81 Omar Vizquel	.05
82 Charles Nagy	.05
83 Orel Hershiser	.05
84 Matt Williams	.05
85 Marquis Grissom	.05
86 David Justice	.05
87 Sandy Alomar	.05
88 Kevin Seitzer	.05
89 Julio Franco	.05
90 Bartolo Colon	.05
91 Andres Galarraga	.05
92 Larry Walker	.05
93 Vinny Castilla	.05
94 Dante Bichette	.05
95 Jamey Wright	.05
96 Ellis Burks	.05
97 Eric Young	.05
98 Neifi Perez	.05
99 Quinton McCracken	.05
100 Bruce Ruffin	.05
101 Walt Weiss	.05
102 Roger Bailey	.05
103 Jeff Reed	.05
104 Bill Swift	.05
105 Kirt Manwaring	.05
106 Raul Mondesi	.05
107 Hideo Nomo	.65
108 Roger Cedeno	.05
109 Ismael Valdes	.05
110 Todd Hollandsworth	.05
111 Mike Piazza	1.50
112 Brett Butler	.05
113 Chan Ho Park	.05
114 Ramon Martinez	.05
115 Eric Karros	.05
116 Wilton Guerrero	.05
117 Todd Zeile	.05
118 Karim Garcia	.05
119 Greg Gagne	.05
120 Darren Dreifort	.05
121 Wade Boggs	.65
122 Paul O'Neill	.05

123 Derek Jeter 2.00
124 Tino Martinez .05
125 David Cone .05
126 Andy Pettitte .25
127 Charlie Hayes .05
128 Mariano Rivera .15
129 Dwight Gooden .05
130 Cecil Fielder .05
131 Not Issued
132 Darryl Strawberry .05
133 Joe Girardi .05
134 David Wells .05
135 Hideki Irabu .05
136 Ken Griffey Jr. 1.25
137 Alex Rodriguez 1.50
138 Jay Buhner .05
139 Randy Johnson .65
140 Paul Sorrento .05
141 Edgar Martinez .05
142 Joey Cora .05
143 Bob Wells .05
144 Not Issued
145 Jamie Moyer .05
146 Jeff Fassero .05
147 Dan Wilson .05
148 Jose Cruz, Jr. .40
149 Scott Sanders .05
150 Rich Amaral .05
151 Brian Jordan .05
152 Andy Benes .05
153 Ray Lankford .05
154 John Mabry .05
155 Tom Pagnozzi .05
156 Ron Gant .05
157 Alan Benes .05
158 Dennis Eckersley .75
159 Royce Clayton .05
160 Todd Stottlemyre .05
161 Gary Gaetti .05
162 Willie McGee .05
163 Delino DeShields .05
164 Dmitri Young .05
165 Matt Morris .05

MVP

NM/M
Complete Set (18): 45.00
Common Player: .50
1 Ivan Rodriguez 2.00
2 Mike Piazza 6.00
3 Frank Thomas 2.50
4 Jeff Bagwell 2.00
5 Chuck Knoblauch .50
6 Eric Young .50
7 Alex Rodriguez 6.00
8 Barry Larkin .50
9 Cal Ripken Jr. 7.50
10 Chipper Jones 4.00
11 Albert Belle .75
12 Barry Bonds 7.50
13 Ken Griffey Jr. 5.50
14 Kenny Lofton .50
15 Juan Gonzalez 2.00
16 Larry Walker .50
17 Roger Clemens 5.00
18 Greg Maddux 4.00

1998 DONRUSS

NM/M
Complete Set (420): 25.00
Complete Series 1 (170): 10.00
Complete Update 2 (250): 15.00
Common Player: .05
Pack (10): 1.00
Wax Box (24): 16.00
1 Paul Molitor .75
2 Juan Gonzalez .75
3 Darryl Kile .05
4 Randy Johnson .75

5 Tom Glavine .25
6 Pat Hentgen .05
7 David Justice .05
8 Kevin Brown .10
9 Mike Mussina .60
10 Ken Caminiti .05
11 Todd Hundley .05
12 Frank Thomas .75
13 Ray Lankford .05
14 Justin Thompson .05
15 Jason Dickson .05
16 Kenny Lofton .05
17 Ivan Rodriguez .65
18 Pedro Martinez .75
19 Brady Anderson .05
20 Barry Larkin .05
21 Chipper Jones 1.50
22 Tony Gwynn 1.50
23 Roger Clemens 1.50
24 Sandy Alomar Jr. .05
25 Tino Martinez .05
26 Jeff Bagwell .75
27 Shawn Estes .05
28 Ken Griffey Jr. 1.75
29 Javier Lopez .05
30 Denny Neagle .05
31 Mike Piazza 1.75
32 Andres Galarraga .05
33 Larry Walker .05
34 Alex Rodriguez 2.00
35 Greg Maddux 1.50
36 Albert Belle .15
37 Barry Bonds 2.50
38 Mo Vaughn .05
39 Kevin Appier .05
40 Wade Boggs 1.00
41 Garret Anderson .05
42 Jeffrey Hammonds .05
43 Marquis Grissom .05
44 Jim Edmonds .05
45 Brian Jordan .05
46 Raul Mondesi .05
47 John Valentin .05
48 Brad Radke .05
49 Ismael Valdes .05
50 Matt Stairs .05
51 Matt Williams .05
52 Reggie Jefferson .05
53 Alan Benes .05
54 Charles Johnson .05
55 Chuck Knoblauch .05
56 Edgar Martinez .05
57 Nomar Garciaparra 1.75
58 Craig Biggio .05
59 Bernie Williams .20
60 David Cone .05
61 Cal Ripken Jr. 2.50
62 Mark McGwire 2.00
63 Roberto Alomar .30
64 Fred McGriff .05
65 Eric Karros .05
66 Robin Ventura .05
67 Darin Erstad .60
68 Michael Tucker .05
69 Jim Thome .05
70 Mark Grace .10
71 Lou Collier .05
72 Karim Garcia .05
73 Alex Fernandez .05
74 J.T. Snow .05
75 Reggie Sanders .05
76 John Smoltz .05
77 Tim Salmon .15
78 Paul O'Neill .05
79 Vinny Castilla .05
80 Rafael Palmeiro .65
81 Jaret Wright .05
82 Jay Buhner .05
83 Brett Butler .05
84 Todd Greene .05
85 Scott Rolen .75
86 Sammy Sosa 1.75
87 Jason Giambi .50
88 Carlos Delgado .50
89 Deion Sanders .05
90 Wilton Guerrero .05
91 Andy Pettitte .30
92 Brian Giles .05
93 Dmitri Young .05
94 Ron Coomer .05
95 Mike Cameron .05
96 Edgardo Alfonzo .05
97 Jimmy Key .05
98 Ryan Klesko .05
99 Andy Benes .05
100 Derek Jeter 2.50
101 Jeff Fassero .05
102 Neifi Perez .05
103 Hideo Nomo .75
104 Andruw Jones .75
105 Todd Helton .45
106 Livan Hernandez .05
107 Brett Tomko .05
108 Shannon Stewart .05
109 Bartolo Colon .05
110 Matt Morris .05
111 Miguel Tejada .30
112 Pokey Reese .05
113 Fernando Tatis .05
114 Todd Dunwoody .05
115 Jose Cruz Jr. .05
116 Chan Ho Park .05
117 Kevin Young .05
118 Rickey Henderson .75
119 Hideki Irabu .05
120 Francisco Cordova .05
121 Al Martin .05
122 Tony Clark .05
123 Curt Schilling .25
124 Rusty Greer .05
125 Jose Canseco .40
126 Edgar Renteria .05
127 Todd Walker .05
128 Wally Joyner .05
129 Bill Mueller .05
130 Jose Guillen .05
131 Manny Ramirez .75
132 Bobby Higginson .05
133 Kevin Orie .05
134 Will Clark .10
135 Dave Nilsson .05
136 Jason Kendall .05
137 Ivan Cruz .05
138 Gary Sheffield .25
139 Bubba Trammell .05
140 Vladimir Guerrero .75
141 Dennis Reyes .05
142 Bobby Bonilla .05
143 Ruben Rivera .05
144 Ben Grieve .10
145 Moises Alou .05
146 Tony Womack .05
147 Eric Young .05
148 Paul Konerko .10
149 Dante Bichette .05
150 Joe Carter .05
151 Rondell White .05
152 Chris Holt .05
153 Shawn Green .30
154 Mark Grudzielanek .05
155 Jermaine Dye .05
156 Ken Griffey Jr. (Fan Club) .90
157 Frank Thomas (Fan Club) .50
158 Chipper Jones (Fan Club) .75
159 Mike Piazza (Fan Club) .75
160 Cal Ripken Jr. (Fan Club) 1.25
161 Greg Maddux (Fan Club) .75
162 Juan Gonzalez (Fan Club) .40
163 Alex Rodriguez (Fan Club) 1.00
164 Mark McGwire (Fan Club) 1.00
165 Derek Jeter (Fan Club) 1.25
166 Larry Walker Checklist .05
167 Tony Gwynn Checklist .75
168 Tino Martinez Checklist .05
169 Scott Rolen Checklist .15
170 Nomar Garciaparra Checklist .75
171 Mike Sweeney .05
172 Dustin Hermanson .05
173 Darren Dreifort .05
174 Ron Gant .05
175 Todd Hollandsworth .05
176 John Jaha .05
177 Kerry Wood .35
178 Chris Stynes .05
179 Kevin Elster .05
180 Derek Bell .05
181 Darryl Strawberry .05
182 Damion Easley .05
183 Jeff Cirillo .05
184 John Thomson .05
185 Dan Wilson .05
186 Jay Bell .05
187 Bernard Gilkey .05
188 Marc Valdes .05
189 Ramon Martinez .05
190 Charles Nagy .05
191 Derek Lowe .05
192 Andy Benes .05
193 Delino DeShields .05
194 *Ryan Jackson* .05
195 Kenny Lofton .05
196 Chuck Knoblauch .05
197 Andres Galarraga .05
198 Jose Canseco .50
199 John Olerud .05
200 Lance Johnson .05
201 Darryl Kile .05
202 Luis Castillo .05
203 Joe Carter .05
204 Dennis Eckersley .65
205 Steve Finley .05
206 Esteban Loaiza .05
207 *Ryan Christenson* .05
208 Deivi Cruz .05
209 Mariano Rivera .15
210 *Mike Judd* .05
211 Billy Wagner .05
212 Scott Spiezio .05
213 Russ Davis .05
214 Jeff Suppan .05
215 Doug Glanville .05
216 Dmitri Young .05
217 Rey Ordonez .05
218 Cecil Fielder .05
219 *Masato Yoshii* .10
220 Raul Casanova .05
221 *Rolando Arrojo* .20
222 Ellis Burks .05
223 Butch Huskey .05
224 Brian Hunter .05
225 Marquis Grissom .05
226 Kevin Brown .10
227 Joe Randa .05
228 Henry Rodriguez .05
229 Omar Vizquel .05
230 Fred McGriff .05
231 Matt Williams .05
232 Moises Alou .05
233 Travis Fryman .05
234 Wade Boggs 1.00
235 Pedro Martinez .75
236 Rickey Henderson .75
237 Bubba Trammell .05
238 Mike Caruso .05
239 Wilson Alvarez .05
240 Geronimo Berroa .05
241 Eric Milton .05
242 Scott Erickson .05
243 *Todd Erdos* .05
244 Bobby Hughes .05
245 Dave Hollins .05
246 Dean Palmer .05
247 Carlos Baerga .05
248 Jose Silva .05
249 *Jose Cabrera* .05
250 Tom Evans .05
251 Marty Cordova .05
252 *Hanley Frias* .05
253 Javier Valentin .05
254 Mario Valdez .05
255 Joey Cora .05
256 Mike Lansing .05
257 Jeff Kent .05
258 *David Dellucci* .10
259 *Curtis King* .05
260 David Segui .05
261 Royce Clayton .05
262 Jeff Blauser .05
263 *Manny Aybar* .05
264 *Mike Cather* .05
265 Todd Zeile .05
266 Richard Hidalgo .05
267 Dante Powell .05
268 *Mike DeJean* .05
269 Ken Cloude .05
270 Danny Klassen .05
271 Sean Casey .25
272 A.J. Hinch .05
273 *Rich Butler* .05
274 *Ben Ford* .05
275 Billy McMillon .05
276 Wilson Delgado .05

No.	Player	Value
277	Orlando Cabrera	.05
278	Geoff Jenkins	.05
279	Enrique Wilson	.05
280	Derrek Lee	.05
281	*Marc Pisciotta*	.05
282	Abraham Nunez	.05
283	Aaron Boone	.05
284	Brad Fullmer	.05
285	*Rob Stanifer*	.05
286	Preston Wilson	.05
287	Greg Norton	.05
288	Bobby Smith	.05
289	Josh Booty	.05
290	Russell Branyan	.05
291	Jeremi Gonzalez	.05
292	Michael Coleman	.05
293	Cliff Politte	.05
294	Eric Ludwick	.05
295	Rafael Medina	.05
296	Jason Varitek	.05
297	Ron Wright	.05
298	Mark Kotsay	.05
299	David Ortiz	.05
300	*Frank Catalanotto*	.20
301	Robinson Checo	.05
302	*Kevin Millwood*	.75
303	Jacob Cruz	.05
304	Javier Vazquez	.05
305	*Magglio Ordonez*	1.50
306	Kevin Witt	.05
307	Derrick Gibson	.05
308	Shane Monahan	.05
309	Brian Rose	.05
310	Bobby Estalella	.05
311	Felix Heredia	.05
312	Desi Relaford	.05
313	*Esteban Yan*	.05
314	Ricky Ledee	.05
315	*Steve Woodard*	.05
316	Pat Watkins	.05
317	Damian Moss	.05
318	Bob Abreu	.05
319	Jeff Abbott	.05
320	Miguel Cairo	.05
321	*Rigo Beltran*	.05
322	Tony Saunders	.05
323	Randall Simon	.05
324	Hiram Bocachica	.05
325	Richie Sexson	.05
326	Karim Garcia	.05
327	*Mike Lowell*	.75
328	Pat Cline	.05
329	Matt Clement	.05
330	Scott Elarton	.05
331	*Manuel Barrios*	.05
332	Bruce Chen	.05
333	Juan Encarnacion	.05
334	Travis Lee	.10
335	Wes Helms	.05
336	*Chad Fox*	.05
337	Donnie Sadler	.05
338	*Carlos Mendoza*	.05
339	Damian Jackson	.05
340	*Julio Ramirez*	.05
341	*John Halama*	.05
342	Edwin Diaz	.05
343	Felix Martinez	.05
344	Eli Marrero	.05
345	Carl Pavano	.05
346	Vladimir Guerrero (Hit List)	.40
347	Barry Bonds (Hit List)	1.25
348	Darin Erstad (Hit List)	.25
349	Albert Belle (Hit List)	.10
350	Kenny Lofton (Hit List)	.05
351	Mo Vaughn (Hit List)	.05
352	Jose Cruz Jr. (Hit List)	.05
353	Tony Clark (Hit List)	.05
354	Roberto Alomar (Hit List)	.15
355	Manny Ramirez (Hit List)	.40
356	Paul Molitor (Hit List)	.40
357	Jim Thome (Hit List)	.05
358	Tino Martinez (Hit List)	.05
359	Tim Salmon (Hit List)	.05
360	David Justice (Hit List)	.05
361	Raul Mondesi (Hit List)	.05
362	Mark Grace (Hit List)	.05
363	Craig Biggio (Hit List)	.05
364	Larry Walker (Hit List)	.05
365	Mark McGwire (Hit List)	1.00
366	Juan Gonzalez (Hit List)	.40
367	Derek Jeter (Hit List)	1.25
368	Chipper Jones (Hit List)	.75
369	Frank Thomas (Hit List)	.50
370	Alex Rodriguez (Hit List)	1.00
371	Mike Piazza (Hit List)	.75
372	Tony Gwynn (Hit List)	.75
373	Jeff Bagwell (Hit List)	.40
374	Nomar Garciaparra (Hit List)	.90
375	Ken Griffey Jr. (Hit List)	.90
376	Livan Hernandez (Untouchables)	.05
377	Chan Ho Park (Untouchables)	.05
378	Mike Mussina (Untouchables)	.25
379	Andy Pettitte (Untouchables)	.05
380	Greg Maddux (Untouchables)	.75
381	Hideo Nomo (Untouchables)	.40
382	Roger Clemens (Untouchables)	.75
383	Randy Johnson (Untouchables)	.40
384	Pedro Martinez (Untouchables)	.40
385	Jaret Wright (Untouchables)	.05
386	Ken Griffey Jr. (Spirit of the Game)	.90
387	Todd Helton (Spirit of the Game)	.05
388	Paul Konerko (Spirit of the Game)	.05
389	Cal Ripken Jr. (Spirit of the Game)	1.25
390	Larry Walker (Spirit of the Game)	.05
391	Ken Caminiti (Spirit of the Game)	.05
392	Jose Guillen (Spirit of the Game)	.05
393	Jim Edmonds (Spirit of the Game)	.05
394	Barry Larkin (Spirit of the Game)	.05
395	Bernie Williams (Spirit of the Game)	.05
396	Tony Clark (Spirit of the Game)	.05
397	Jose Cruz Jr. (Spirit of the Game)	.05
398	Ivan Rodriguez (Spirit of the Game)	.30
399	Darin Erstad (Spirit of the Game)	.25
400	Scott Rolen (Spirit of the Game)	.40
401	Mark McGwire (Spirit of the Game)	1.00
402	Andruw Jones (Spirit of the Game)	.40
403	Juan Gonzalez (Spirit of the Game)	.40
404	Derek Jeter (Spirit of the Game)	1.25
405	Chipper Jones (Spirit of the Game)	.75
406	Greg Maddux (Spirit of the Game)	.75
407	Frank Thomas (Spirit of the Game)	.50
408	Alex Rodriguez (Spirit of the Game)	1.00
409	Mike Piazza (Spirit of the Game)	.90
410	Tony Gwynn (Spirit of the Game)	.75
411	Jeff Bagwell (Spirit of the Game)	.40
412	Nomar Garciaparra (Spirit of the Game)	.90
413	Hideo Nomo (Spirit of the Game)	.40
414	Barry Bonds (Spirit of the Game)	1.25
415	Ben Grieve (Spirit of the Game)	.05
416	Barry Bonds Checklist	.75
417	Mark McGwire Checklist	.65
418	Roger Clemens Checklist	.50
419	Livan Hernandez Checklist	.05
420	Ken Griffey Jr. Checklist	.60

Silver Press Proofs

	NM/M
Complete Set (420):	150.00
Common Player:	.50
Stars/RCs:	3X

Production 1,500 sets

(See 1998 Donruss for checklist and base card values.)

Gold Press Proofs

	NM/M
Complete Set (420):	300.00
Common Player:	1.00
Stars/RCs:	8X

Production 500 sets

(See 1998 Donruss for checklist and base card values.)

Crusade

		NM/M
	Complete Set, Green (40):	425.00
	Common Player:	6.00
	Production:	250 sets
	Purples (100 sets):	3X
	Reds (25 sets):	12X
5	Jason Dickson	6.00
6	Todd Greene	6.00
7	Roberto Alomar	9.00
8	Cal Ripken Jr.	60.00
12	Mo Vaughn	6.00
13	Nomar Garciaparra	40.00
16	Mike Cameron	6.00
20	Sandy Alomar Jr.	6.00
21	David Justice	6.00
25	Justin Thompson	6.00
27	Kevin Appier	6.00
33	Tino Martinez	6.00
36	Hideki Irabu	6.00
37	Jose Canseco	12.50
39	Ken Griffey Jr.	40.00
42	Edgar Martinez	6.00
45	Will Clark	7.50
47	Rusty Greer	6.00
50	Shawn Green	12.50
51	Jose Cruz Jr.	6.00
52	Kenny Lofton	6.00
53	Chipper Jones	30.00
62	Kevin Orie	6.00
65	Deion Sanders	7.50
67	Larry Walker	6.00
68	Dante Bichette	6.00
71	Todd Helton	20.00
74	Bobby Bonilla	6.00
75	Kevin Brown	7.50
78	Craig Biggio	6.00
82	Wilton Guerrero	6.00
85	Pedro Martinez	20.00
86	Edgardo Alfonzo	6.00
88	Scott Rolen	15.00
89	Francisco Cordova	6.00
90	Jose Guillen	6.00
92	Ray Lankford	6.00
93	Mark McGwire	45.00
94	Matt Morris	6.00
100	Shawn Estes	6.00

Diamond Kings

		NM/M
	Complete Set (20):	45.00
	Common Player:	1.25
	Production 9,500 sets	
	Canvas (1st 500 sets):	2X
1	Cal Ripken Jr.	6.00
2	Greg Maddux	3.00
3	Ivan Rodriguez	1.50
4	Tony Gwynn	3.00
5	Paul Molitor	2.00
6	Kenny Lofton	1.25
7	Andy Pettitte	1.25
8	Darin Erstad	2.00
9	Randy Johnson	2.00
10	Derek Jeter	6.00
11	Hideo Nomo	2.00
12	David Justice	1.25
13	Bernie Williams	1.25
14	Roger Clemens	3.50
15	Barry Larkin	1.25
16	Andruw Jones	2.00
17	Mike Piazza	4.00
18	Frank Thomas	2.00
18s	Frank Thomas (sample)	2.00
19	Alex Rodriguez	5.00
20	Ken Griffey Jr.	4.00

Longball Leaders

		NM/M
	Complete Set (24):	50.00
	Common Player:	1.00
	Production 5,000 sets	
1	Ken Griffey Jr.	5.00
2	Mark McGwire	6.00
3	Tino Martinez	1.00
4	Barry Bonds	6.00
5	Frank Thomas	3.00
6	Albert Belle	1.50
7	Mike Piazza	5.00
8	Chipper Jones	4.00
9	Vladimir Guerrero	3.00
10	Matt Williams	1.00
11	Sammy Sosa	5.00
12	Tim Salmon	1.00
13	Raul Mondesi	1.00
14	Jeff Bagwell	3.00
15	Mo Vaughn	1.00
16	Manny Ramirez	3.00
17	Jim Thome	1.00
18	Jim Edmonds	1.00
19	Tony Clark	1.00
20	Nomar Garciaparra	5.00
21	Juan Gonzalez	3.00
22	Scott Rolen	2.50
23	Larry Walker	1.00
24	Andres Galarraga	1.00

Production Line-ob

		NM/M
	Complete Set (20):	85.00
	Common Player:	1.50
1	Frank Thomas (456)	6.00
2	Edgar Martinez (456)	1.50
3	Barry Bonds (446)	15.00
4	Barry Larkin (440)	1.50
5	Mike Piazza (431)	10.00
6	Jeff Bagwell (425)	6.00
7	Gary Sheffield (424)	2.00
8	Mo Vaughn (420)	1.50
9	Craig Biggio (415)	1.50
10	Kenny Lofton (409)	1.50
11	Tony Gwynn (409)	8.00
12	Bernie Williams (408)	2.00
13	Rusty Greer (405)	1.50
14	Brady Anderson (393)	1.50
15	Mark McGwire (393)	12.00
16	Chuck Knoblauch (390)	1.50
17	Roberto Alomar (390)	2.00
18	Ken Griffey Jr. (382)	10.00
19	Chipper Jones (371)	8.00
20	Derek Jeter (370)	15.00

Production Line-pi

		NM/M
	Complete Set (20):	85.00
	Common Player:	1.50
1	Larry Walker (1,172)	1.50
2	Mike Piazza (1,070)	10.00
3	Frank Thomas (1,067)	5.00
4	Mark McGwire (1,039)	12.00
5	Barry Bonds (1,031)	12.50
6	Ken Griffey Jr. (1,028)	10.00
7	Jeff Bagwell (1,017)	5.00
8	David Justice (1,013)	1.50
9	Jim Thome (1,001)	1.50
10	Mo Vaughn (980)	1.50
11	Tony Gwynn (957)	7.00
12	Manny Ramirez (953)	5.00

#	Player	NM/M
13	Bernie Williams (952)	1.50
14	Tino Martinez (948)	1.50
15	Brady Anderson (863)	1.50
16	Chipper Jones (850)	7.00
17	Scott Rolen (846)	3.00
18	Alex Rodriguez (846)	12.00
19	Vladimir Guerrero (833)	5.00
20	Albert Belle (823)	2.00

Production Line-sg

#	Player	NM/M
	Complete Set (20):	135.00
	Common Player:	3.00
1	Larry Walker (720)	3.00
2	Ken Griffey Jr. (646)	12.00
3	Mark McGwire (646)	15.00
4	Mike Piazza (638)	12.00
5	Frank Thomas (611)	7.50
6	Jeff Bagwell (592)	7.50
7	Juan Gonzalez (589)	7.50
8	Andres Galarraga (585)	3.00
9	Barry Bonds (585)	20.00
10	Jim Thome (579)	3.00
11	Tino Martinez (577)	3.00
12	Mo Vaughn (560)	3.00
13	Raul Mondesi (541)	3.00
14	Manny Ramirez (538)	7.50
15	Nomar Garciaparra (534)	12.50
16	Tim Salmon (517)	3.00
17	Tony Clark (500)	3.00
18	Jose Cruz Jr. (499)	3.00
19	Alex Rodriguez (496)	20.00
20	Cal Ripken Jr. (402)	25.00

Rated Rookies

#	Player	NM/M
	Complete Set (30):	32.50
	Common Player:	1.00
	Medalists (250 sets):	6X
1	Mark Kotsay	1.00
2	Neifi Perez	1.00
3	Paul Konerko	1.50
4	Jose Cruz Jr.	1.50
5	Hideki Irabu	1.00
6	Mike Cameron	1.00
7	Jeff Suppan	1.00
8	Kevin Orie	1.00
9	Pokey Reese	1.00
10	Todd Dunwoody	1.00
11	Miguel Tejada	2.00
12	Jose Guillen	1.00
13	Bartolo Colon	1.50
14	Derrek Lee	1.00
15	Antone Williamson	1.00
16	Wilton Guerrero	1.00
17	Jaret Wright	1.00
18	Todd Helton	4.00
19	Shannon Stewart	1.50
20	Nomar Garciaparra	6.00
21	Brett Tomko	1.00
22	Fernando Tatis	1.00
23	Raul Ibanez	1.00
24	Dennis Reyes	1.00
25	Bobby Estalella	1.00
26	Lou Collier	1.00
27	Bubba Trammell	1.00
28	Ben Grieve	1.50
29	Ivan Cruz	1.00
30	Karim Garcia	1.50

Update Crusade

#	Player	NM/M
	Complete Set, Green (30):	325.00
	Common Player:	6.00
	Production 250 sets	
	Purples (100 sets):	3X
	Reds (25 sets):	10X
1	Tim Salmon	7.50
2	Garret Anderson	6.00
9	Rafael Palmeiro	15.00
10	Brady Anderson	6.00
14	Frank Thomas	15.00
17	Robin Ventura	6.00
22	Matt Williams	6.00
23	Tony Clark	6.00
29	Chuck Knoblauch	6.00
31	Bernie Williams	7.50
32	Derek Jeter	50.00
38	Jason Giambi	10.00
43	Jay Buhner	6.00
44	Juan Gonzalez	15.00
49	Carlos Delgado	9.00
55	Greg Maddux	20.00
57	Tom Glavine	9.00
60	Mark Grace	7.50
61	Sammy Sosa	40.00
63	Barry Larkin	6.00
69	Neifi Perez	6.00
72	Gary Sheffield	7.50
77	Jeff Bagwell	15.00
80	Raul Mondesi	6.00
81	Hideo Nomo	12.50
83	Rondell White	6.00
84	Vladimir Guerrero	15.00
87	Todd Hundley	6.00
96	Brian Jordan	6.00
99	Barry Bonds	50.00

Update Dominators

#	Player	NM/M
	Complete Set (30):	25.00
	Common Player:	.25
	Approx:	1:12
1	Roger Clemens	1.50
2	Tony Clark	.25
3	Darin Erstad	.65
4	Jeff Bagwell	1.00
5	Ken Griffey Jr.	1.75
6	Andruw Jones	1.00
7	Juan Gonzalez	1.00
8	Ivan Rodriguez	.75
9	Randy Johnson	1.00
10	Tino Martinez	.25
11	Mark McGwire	2.00
12	Chuck Knoblauch	.25
13	Jim Thome	.25
14	Alex Rodriguez	2.00
15	Hideo Nomo	.75
16	Jose Cruz Jr.	.25
17	Chipper Jones	1.50
18	Tony Gwynn	1.50
19	Barry Bonds	2.50
20	Mo Vaughn	.25
21	Cal Ripken Jr.	2.50
22	Greg Maddux	1.50
23	Manny Ramirez	1.00
24	Andres Galarraga	.25
25	Vladimir Guerrero	1.00
26	Albert Belle	.35
27	Nomar Garciaparra	1.75
28	Kenny Lofton	.25
29	Mike Piazza	1.75
30	Frank Thomas	1.00

Update Elite

#	Player	NM/M
	Complete Set (20):	50.00
	Common Player:	1.50
	Production 2,500 sets	
1	Jeff Bagwell	2.00
2	Andruw Jones	2.00
3	Ken Griffey Jr.	3.00
4	Derek Jeter	6.00
5	Juan Gonzalez	2.00
6	Mark McGwire	4.00
7	Ivan Rodriguez	1.50

#	Player	NM/M
8	Paul Molitor	2.00
9	Hideo Nomo	1.50
10	Mo Vaughn	1.50
11	Chipper Jones	2.50
12	Nomar Garciaparra	3.00
13	Mike Piazza	3.00
14	Frank Thomas	2.00
15	Greg Maddux	2.50
16	Cal Ripken Jr.	6.00
17	Alex Rodriguez	4.00
18	Scott Rolen	1.75
19	Barry Bonds	6.00
20	Tony Gwynn	2.50

Update FANtasy Team

#	Player	NM/M
	Complete Set (20):	35.00
	Common Player (1-10) (1,750 sets):	1.50
	Common Player (11-20) (3,750 sets):	1.00
	Die-Cuts (250 each):	2X
1	Frank Thomas	2.00
2	Ken Griffey Jr.	3.50
3	Cal Ripken Jr.	5.00
4	Jose Cruz Jr.	1.00
5	Travis Lee	1.00
6	Greg Maddux	2.50
7	Alex Rodriguez	4.00
8	Mark McGwire	4.00
9	Chipper Jones	2.50
10	Andruw Jones	2.00
11	Mike Piazza	3.50
12	Tony Gwynn	2.50
13	Larry Walker	1.00
14	Nomar Garciaparra	3.00
15	Jaret Wright	1.00
16	Livan Hernandez	1.00
17	Roger Clemens	2.75
18	Derek Jeter	5.00
19	Scott Rolen	1.25
20	Jeff Bagwell	1.50

Update Rookie Diamond Kings

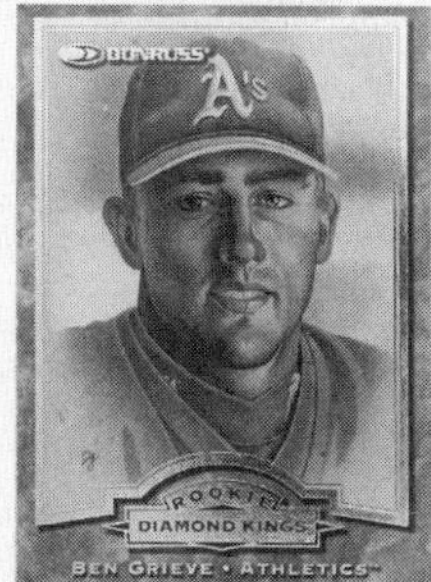

#	Player	NM/M
	Complete Set (12):	17.50
	Common Player:	1.50
	Production 9,500 sets	
	Canvas (500 sets):	2X
1	Travis Lee	2.50
2	Fernando Tatis	1.50
3	Livan Hernandez	1.50
4	Todd Helton	4.00
5	Derrek Lee	1.50
6	Jaret Wright	1.50
7	Ben Grieve	2.00
8	Paul Konerko	2.00
9	Jose Cruz Jr.	1.50
10	Mark Kotsay	1.50
11	Todd Greene	1.50
12	Brad Fullmer	1.50

1998 DONRUSS COLLECTIONS

#	Player	NM/M
	Complete Set (750):	1,000
	Complete Donruss Set (200):	135.00
	Complete Leaf Set (200):	165.00
	Complete Elite Set (150):	155.00
	Complete Preferred Set (200):	600.00
	Prized Collections Parallel:	2X
	Pack (5):	6.00
	Wax Box (20):	100.00
	Samples:	6X
	DONRUSS	
1	Paul Molitor	2.00
2	Juan Gonzalez	2.00
3	Darryl Kile	.25
4	Randy Johnson	2.00
5	Tom Glavine	.50
6	Pat Hentgen	.25
7	David Justice	.25
8	Kevin Brown	.35
9	Mike Mussina	1.00
10	Ken Caminiti	.25
11	Todd Hundley	.25
12	Frank Thomas	2.00
13	Ray Lankford	.25
14	Justin Thompson	.25
15	Jason Dickson	.25
16	Kenny Lofton	.25
17	Ivan Rodriguez	1.50
18	Pedro Martinez	2.00
19	Brady Anderson	.25
20	Barry Larkin	.25
21	Chipper Jones	3.00
22	Tony Gwynn	3.00
23	Roger Clemens	3.25
24	Sandy Alomar Jr.	.25
25	Tino Martinez	.25
26	Jeff Bagwell	2.00
27	Shawn Estes	.25
28	Ken Griffey Jr.	3.50
29	Javier Lopez	.25
30	Denny Neagle	.25
31	Mike Piazza	3.50
32	Andres Galarraga	.25
33	Larry Walker	.25
34	Alex Rodriguez	4.50
35	Greg Maddux	3.00
36	Albert Belle	.40
37	Barry Bonds	6.00
38	Mo Vaughn	.25
39	Kevin Appier	.25
40	Wade Boggs	3.00
41	Garret Anderson	.25
42	Jeffrey Hammonds	.25
43	Marquis Grissom	.25
44	Jim Edmonds	.25
45	Brian Jordan	.25
46	Raul Mondesi	.25
47	John Valentin	.25
48	Brad Radke	.25
49	Ismael Valdes	.25
50	Matt Stairs	.25
51	Matt Williams	.25
52	Reggie Jefferson	.25
53	Alan Benes	.25
54	Charles Johnson	.25
55	Chuck Knoblauch	.25
56	Edgar Martinez	.25
57	Nomar Garciaparra	3.50
58	Craig Biggio	.25
59	Bernie Williams	.50
60	David Cone	.25

61	Cal Ripken Jr.	6.00
62	Mark McGwire	4.50
63	Roberto Alomar	.60
64	Fred McGriff	.25
65	Eric Karros	.25
66	Robin Ventura	.25
67	Darin Erstad	.75
68	Michael Tucker	.25
69	Jim Thome	.25
70	Mark Grace	.35
71	Lou Collier	.25
72	Karim Garcia	.40
73	Alex Fernandez	.25
74	J.T. Snow	.25
75	Reggie Sanders	.25
76	John Smoltz	.25
77	Tim Salmon	.40
78	Paul O'Neill	.25
79	Vinny Castilla	.25
80	Rafael Palmeiro	1.50
81	Jaret Wright	.25
82	Jay Buhner	.25
83	Brett Butler	.25
84	Todd Greene	.25
85	Scott Rolen	1.50
86	Sammy Sosa	3.50
87	Jason Giambi	1.00
88	Carlos Delgado	.75
89	Deion Sanders	.25
90	Wilton Guerrero	.25
91	Andy Pettitte	.60
92	Brian Giles	.25
93	Dmitri Young	.25
94	Ron Coomer	.25
95	Mike Cameron	.25
96	Edgardo Alfonzo	.25
97	Jimmy Key	.25
98	Ryan Klesko	.25
99	Andy Benes	.25
100	Derek Jeter	6.00
101	Jeff Fassero	.25
102	Neifi Perez	.25
103	Hideo Nomo	2.00
104	Andruw Jones	2.00
105	Todd Helton	2.00
106	Livan Hernandez	.25
107	Brett Tomko	.25
108	Shannon Stewart	.35
109	Bartolo Colon	.25
110	Matt Morris	.25
111	Miguel Tejada	.50
112	Pokey Reese	.25
113	Fernando Tatis	.25
114	Todd Dunwoody	.25
115	Jose Cruz Jr.	.25
116	Chan Ho Park	.25
117	Kevin Young	.25
118	Rickey Henderson	2.00
119	Hideki Irabu	.25
120	Francisco Cordova	.25
121	Al Martin	.25
122	Tony Clark	.25
123	Curt Schilling	.40
124	Rusty Greer	.25
125	Jose Canseco	.60
126	Edgar Renteria	.25
127	Todd Walker	.25
128	Wally Joyner	.25
129	Bill Mueller	.25
130	Jose Guillen	.25
131	Manny Ramirez	2.00
132	Bobby Higginson	.25
133	Kevin Orie	.25
134	Will Clark	.35
135	Dave Nilsson	.25
136	Jason Kendall	.25
137	Ivan Cruz	.25
138	Gary Sheffield	.40
139	Bubba Trammell	.25
140	Vladimir Guerrero	2.00
141	Dennis Reyes	.25
142	Bobby Bonilla	.25
143	Ruben Rivera	.25
144	Ben Grieve	.35
145	Moises Alou	.25
146	Tony Womack	.25
147	Eric Young	.25
148	Paul Konerko	.35
149	Dante Bichette	.25
150	Joe Carter	.25
151	Rondell White	.25
152	Chris Holt	.25
153	Shawn Green	.45
154	Mark Grudzielanek	.25
155	Jermaine Dye	.25
156	Ken Griffey Jr. (Fan Club)	1.75
157	Frank Thomas (Fan Club)	1.00
158	Chipper Jones (Fan Club)	1.50
159	Mike Piazza (Fan Club)	1.75
160	Cal Ripken Jr. (Fan Club)	3.00
161	Greg Maddux (Fan Club)	1.50
162	Juan Gonzalez (Fan Club)	1.00
163	Alex Rodriguez (Fan Club)	2.25
164	Mark McGwire (Fan Club)	2.25
165	Derek Jeter (Fan Club)	3.00
166	Larry Walker (Checklist)	.25
167	Tony Gwynn (Checklist)	.75
168	Tino Martinez (Checklist)	.25
169	Scott Rolen (Checklist)	.40
170	Nomar Garciaparra (Checklist)	1.25

DONRUSS RATED ROOKIES

1	Mark Kotsay	.50
2	Neifi Perez	.50
3	Paul Konerko	1.00
4	Jose Cruz Jr.	.50
5	Hideki Irabu	.50
6	Mike Cameron	.50
7	Jeff Suppan	.50
8	Kevin Orie	.50
9	Pokey Reese	.50
10	Todd Dunwoody	.50
11	Miguel Tejada	1.00
12	Jose Guillen	.50
13	Bartolo Colon	.50
14	Derrek Lee	.50
15	Antone Williamson	.50
16	Wilton Guerrero	.50
17	Jaret Wright	.50
18	Todd Helton	2.50
19	Shannon Stewart	1.00
20	Nomar Garciaparra	6.00
21	Brett Tomko	.50
22	Fernando Tatis	.50
23	Raul Ibanez	.50
24	Dennis Reyes	.50
25	Bobby Estalella	.50
26	Lou Collier	.50
27	Bubba Trammell	.50
28	Ben Grieve	.65
29	Ivan Cruz	.50
30	Karim Garcia	1.00

LEAF

1	Rusty Greer	.25
2	Tino Martinez	.25
3	Bobby Bonilla	.25
4	Jason Giambi	.75
5	Matt Morris	.25
6	Craig Counsell	.25
7	Reggie Jefferson	.25
8	Brian Rose	.25
9	Ruben Rivera	.25
10	Shawn Estes	.25
11	Tony Gwynn	3.00
12	Jeff Abbott	.25
13	Jose Cruz Jr.	.25
14	Francisco Cordova	.25
15	Ryan Klesko	.25
16	Tim Salmon	.35
17	Brett Tomko	.25
18	Matt Williams	.25
19	Joe Carter	.25
20	Harold Baines	.25
21	Gary Sheffield	.40
22	Charles Johnson	.25
23	Aaron Boone	.35
24	Eddie Murray	2.00
25	Matt Stairs	.25
26	David Cone	.25
27	Jon Nunnally	.25
28	Chris Stynes	.25
29	Enrique Wilson	.25
30	Randy Johnson	2.00
31	Garret Anderson	.25
32	Manny Ramirez	2.00
33	Jeff Suppan	.25
34	Rickey Henderson	2.00
35	Scott Spiezio	.25
36	Rondell White	.25
37	Todd Greene	.25
38	Delino DeShields	.25
39	Kevin Brown	.35
40	Chili Davis	.25
41	Jimmy Key	.25
42	NOT ISSUED	
43	Mike Mussina	1.50
44	Joe Randa	.25
45	Chan Ho Park	.25
46	Brad Radke	.25
47	Geronimo Berroa	.25
48	Wade Boggs	3.00
49	Kevin Appier	.25
50	Moises Alou	.25
51	David Justice	.25
52	Ivan Rodriguez	2.00
53	J.T. Snow	.25
54	Brian Giles	.25
55	Will Clark	.35
56	Justin Thompson	.25
57	Javier Lopez	.25
58	Hideki Irabu	.25
59	Mark Grudzielanek	.25
60	Abraham Nunez	.25
61	Todd Hollandsworth	.25
62	Jay Bell	.25
63	Nomar Garciaparra	3.50
64	Vinny Castilla	.25
65	Lou Collier	.25
66	Kevin Orie	.25
67	John Valentin	.25
68	Robin Ventura	.25
69	Denny Neagle	.25
70	Tony Womack	.25
71	Dennis Reyes	.25
72	Wally Joyner	.25
73	Kevin Brown	.35
74	Ray Durham	.25
75	Mike Cameron	.25
76	Dante Bichette	.25
77	Jose Guillen	.25
78	Carlos Delgado	.60
79	Paul Molitor	2.00
80	Jason Kendall	.25
81	Mark Belhorn	.25
82	Damian Jackson	.25
83	Bill Mueller	.25
84	Kevin Young	.25
85	Curt Schilling	.50
86	Jeffrey Hammonds	.25
87	Sandy Alomar Jr.	.25
88	Bartolo Colon	.25
89	Wilton Guerrero	.25
90	Bernie Williams	.50
91	Deion Sanders	.25
92	Mike Piazza	3.50
93	Butch Huskey	.25
94	Edgardo Alfonzo	.25
95	Alan Benes	.25
96	Craig Biggio	.25
97	Mark Grace	.35
98	Shawn Green	.50
99	Derrek Lee	.25
100	Ken Griffey Jr.	3.50
101	Tim Raines	.25
102	Pokey Reese	.25
103	Lee Stevens	.25
104	Shannon Stewart	.35
105	John Smoltz	.25
106	Frank Thomas	2.00
107	Jeff Fassero	.25
108	Jay Buhner	.25
109	Jose Canseco	.45
110	Omar Vizquel	.25
111	Travis Fryman	.25
112	Dave Nilsson	.25
113	John Olerud	.25
114	Larry Walker	.25
115	Jim Edmonds	.25
116	Bobby Higginson	.25
117	Todd Hundley	.25
118	Paul O'Neill	.25
119	Bip Roberts	.25
120	Ismael Valdes	.25
121	Pedro Martinez	2.00
122	Jeff Cirillo	.25
123	Andy Benes	.25
124	Bobby Jones	.25
125	Brian Hunter	.25
126	Darryl Kile	.25
127	Pat Hentgen	.25
128	Marquis Grissom	.25
129	Eric Davis	.25
130	Chipper Jones	3.00
131	Edgar Martinez	.25
132	Andy Pettitte	.65
133	Cal Ripken Jr.	6.00
134	Scott Rolen	1.50
135	Ron Coomer	.25
136	Luis Castillo	.25
137	Fred McGriff	.25
138	Neifi Perez	.25
139	Eric Karros	.25
140	Alex Fernandez	.25
141	Jason Dickson	.25
142	Lance Johnson	.25
143	Ray Lankford	.25
144	Sammy Sosa	3.50
145	Eric Young	.25
146	Bubba Trammell	.25
147	Todd Walker	.25
148	Mo Vaughn	.25
149	Jeff Bagwell	2.00
150	Kenny Lofton	.25
151	Raul Mondesi	.25
152	Mike Piazza	3.50
153	Chipper Jones	3.00
154	Larry Walker	.25
155	Greg Maddux	3.00
156	Ken Griffey Jr.	3.50
157	Frank Thomas	2.00
158	Darin Erstad	3.00
159	Roberto Alomar	1.50
160	Albert Belle	1.00
161	Jim Thome	1.00
162	Tony Clark	1.00
163	Chuck Knoblauch	1.00
164	Derek Jeter	12.00
165	Alex Rodriguez	8.00
166	Tony Gwynn	6.00
167	Roger Clemens	7.00
168	Barry Larkin	1.00
169	Andres Galarraga	1.00
170	Vladimir Guerrero	4.50
171	Mark McGwire	8.00
172	Barry Bonds	12.00
173	Juan Gonzalez	4.50
174	Andruw Jones	4.50
175	Paul Molitor	4.50
176	Hideo Nomo	4.50
177	Cal Ripken Jr.	12.50
178	Brad Fullmer	1.00
179	Jaret Wright	1.00
180	Bobby Estalella	1.00
181	Ben Grieve	1.50
182	Paul Konerko	1.50
183	David Ortiz	2.00
184	Todd Helton	4.00
185	Juan Encarnacion	1.00
186	Miguel Tejada	1.50
187	Jacob Cruz	1.00
188	Mark Kotsay	1.00
189	Fernando Tatis	1.00
190	Ricky Ledee	1.00
191	Richard Hidalgo	1.00
192	Richie Sexson	1.00
193	Luis Ordaz	1.00
194	Eli Marrero	1.00
195	Livan Hernandez	1.00
196	Homer Bush	1.00
197	Raul Ibanez	1.00
198	Nomar Garciaparra Checklist	1.50
199	Scott Rolen Checklist	.75
200	Jose Cruz Jr. Checklist	.35
201	Al Martin	.25

ELITE

1	Ken Griffey Jr.	4.00
2	Frank Thomas	2.50
3	Alex Rodriguez	6.00
4	Mike Piazza	4.00
5	Greg Maddux	3.00
6	Cal Ripken Jr.	7.00
7	Chipper Jones	3.00
8	Derek Jeter	7.00
9	Tony Gwynn	3.00
10	Andruw Jones	2.50
11	Juan Gonzalez	2.50
12	Jeff Bagwell	2.50
13	Mark McGwire	6.00
14	Roger Clemens	3.00
15	Albert Belle	.65
16	Barry Bonds	7.00
17	Kenny Lofton	.50
18	Ivan Rodriguez	2.00
19	Manny Ramirez	2.50
20	Jim Thome	.50
21	Chuck Knoblauch	.50
22	Paul Molitor	2.50
23	Barry Larkin	.50
24	Andy Pettitte	1.00
25	John Smoltz	.50
26	Randy Johnson	2.50
27	Bernie Williams	.75
28	Larry Walker	.50
29	Mo Vaughn	.50
30	Bobby Higginson	.50
31	Edgardo Alfonzo	.50
32	Justin Thompson	.50
33	Jeff Suppan	.50
34	Roberto Alomar	1.00
35	Hideo Nomo	2.50
36	Rusty Greer	.50
37	Tim Salmon	.65
38	Jim Edmonds	.50
39	Gary Sheffield	.65
40	Ken Caminiti	.50
41	Sammy Sosa	4.00
42	Tony Womack	.50
43	Matt Williams	.50

44 Andres Galarraga .50
45 Garret Anderson .50
46 Rafael Palmeiro 2.50
47 Mike Mussina 1.50
48 Craig Biggio .50
49 Wade Boggs 3.00
50 Tom Glavine .75
51 Jason Giambi 1.50
52 Will Clark .65
53 David Justice .50
54 Sandy Alomar Jr. .50
55 Edgar Martinez .50
56 Brady Anderson .50
57 Eric Young .50
58 Ray Lankford .50
59 Kevin Brown .60
60 Raul Mondesi .50
61 Bobby Bonilla .50
62 Javier Lopez .50
63 Fred McGriff .50
64 Rondell White .50
65 Todd Hundley .50
66 Mark Grace .65
67 Alan Benes .50
68 Jeff Abbott .50
69 Bob Abreu .50
70 Deion Sanders .50
71 Tino Martinez .50
72 Shannon Stewart .75
73 Homer Bush .50
74 Carlos Delgado 2.00
75 Raul Ibanez .50
76 Hideki Irabu .50
77 Jose Cruz Jr. .50
78 Tony Clark .50
79 Wilton Guerrero .50
80 Vladimir Guerrero 2.50
81 Scott Rolen 2.25
82 Nomar Garciaparra 4.00
83 Darin Erstad 2.25
84 Chan Ho Park .50
85 Mike Cameron .50
86 Todd Walker .50
87 Todd Dunwoody .50
88 Neifi Perez .50
89 Brett Tomko .50
90 Jose Guillen .50
91 Matt Morris .50
92 Bartolo Colon .50
93 Jaret Wright .50
94 Shawn Estes .50
95 Livan Hernandez .50
96 Bobby Estalella .50
97 Ben Grieve .75
98 Paul Konerko .75
99 David Ortiz 1.00
100 Todd Helton 2.50
101 Juan Encarnacion .50
102 Bubba Trammell .50
103 Miguel Tejada 1.00
104 Jacob Cruz .50
105 Todd Greene .50
106 Kevin Orie .50
107 Mark Kotsay .50
108 Fernando Tatis .50
109 Jay Payton .50
110 Pokey Reese .50
111 Derrek Lee .50
112 Richard Hidalgo .50
113 Ricky Ledee .50
114 Lou Collier .50
115 Ruben Rivera .50
116 Shawn Green 1.25
117 Moises Alou .50
118 Ken Griffey Jr. 2.00
119 Frank Thomas 1.25
120 Alex Rodriguez 3.00
121 Mike Piazza 2.00
122 Greg Maddux 1.75
123 Cal Ripken Jr. 3.50
124 Chipper Jones 1.75
125 Derek Jeter 3.50
126 Tony Gwynn 1.75
127 Andruw Jones 1.25
128 Juan Gonzalez 1.25
129 Jeff Bagwell 1.25
130 Mark McGwire 3.00
131 Roger Clemens 1.75
132 Albert Belle .50
133 Barry Bonds 3.50
134 Kenny Lofton .50
135 Ivan Rodriguez 1.00
136 Manny Ramirez 1.25
137 Jim Thome .50
138 Chuck Knoblauch .50
139 Paul Molitor 1.50
140 Barry Larkin .50
141 Mo Vaughn .50
142 Hideki Irabu .50
143 Jose Cruz Jr. .50
144 Tony Clark .50
145 Vladimir Guerrero 1.25
146 Scott Rolen 1.00
147 Nomar Garciaparra 2.00
148 Nomar Garciaparra Checklist 1.25
149 Larry Walker Checklist .50
150 Tino Martinez Checklist .50

PREFERRED

1 Ken Griffey Jr. EX 12.00
2 Frank Thomas EX 7.50
3 Cal Ripken Jr. EX 17.50
4 Alex Rodriguez EX 15.00
5 Greg Maddux EX 10.00
6 Mike Piazza EX 12.00
7 Chipper Jones EX 10.00
8 Tony Gwynn FB 10.00
9 Derek Jeter FB 17.50
10 Jeff Bagwell EX 7.50
11 Juan Gonzalez EX 7.50
12 Nomar Garciaparra EX 12.00
13 Andruw Jones FB 7.50
14 Hideo Nomo FB 7.50
15 Roger Clemens FB 13.50
16 Mark McGwire FB 15.00
17 Scott Rolen FB 6.00
18 Vladimir Guerrero FB 7.50
19 Barry Bonds FB 17.50
20 Darin Erstad FB 6.00
21 Albert Belle FB 2.50
22 Kenny Lofton FB 2.00
23 Mo Vaughn FB 2.00
24 Tony Clark FB 2.00
25 Ivan Rodriguez FB 6.00
26 Larry Walker CL 2.00
27 Eddie Murray CL 7.50
28 Andy Pettitte CL 5.00
29 Roberto Alomar CL 2.00
30 Randy Johnson CL 7.50
31 Manny Ramirez CL 7.50
32 Paul Molitor FB 7.50
33 Mike Mussina CL 5.00
34 Jim Thome FB 2.00
35 Tino Martinez CL 2.00
36 Gary Sheffield CL 3.00
37 Chuck Knoblauch CL 2.00
38 Bernie Williams CL 2.50
39 Tim Salmon CL 2.50
40 Sammy Sosa CL 12.00
41 Wade Boggs MZ 10.00
42 Will Clark GS 2.50
43 Andres Galarraga CL 2.00
44 Raul Mondesi CL 2.00
45 Rickey Henderson GS 7.50
46 Jose Canseco GS 4.00
47 Pedro Martinez GS 7.50
48 Jay Buhner GS 2.00
49 Ryan Klesko GS 2.00
50 Barry Larkin CL 2.00
51 Charles Johnson GS 2.00
52 Tom Glavine GS 3.00
53 Edgar Martinez CL 2.00
54 Fred McGriff GS 2.00
55 Moises Alou MZ 2.00
56 Dante Bichette GS 2.00
57 Jim Edmonds CL 2.00
58 Mark Grace MZ 2.50
59 Chan Ho Park MZ 2.00
60 Justin Thompson MZ 2.00
61 John Smoltz MZ 2.00
62 Craig Biggio CL 2.00
63 Ken Caminiti MZ 2.00
64 Deion Sanders MZ 2.00
65 Carlos Delgado GS 4.00
66 David Justice CL 2.00
67 J.T. Snow GS 2.00
68 Jason Giambi CL 4.50
69 Garret Anderson MZ 2.00
70 Rondell White MZ 2.00
71 Matt Williams MZ 2.00
72 Brady Anderson MZ 2.00
73 Eric Karros GS 2.00
74 Javier Lopez GS 2.00
75 Pat Hentgen GS 2.00
76 Todd Hundley GS 2.00
77 Ray Lankford GS 2.00
78 Denny Neagle GS 2.00
79 Henry Rodriguez GS 2.00
80 Sandy Alomar Jr. MZ 2.00
81 Rafael Palmeiro MZ 7.50
82 Robin Ventura GS 2.00
83 John Olerud GS 2.00
84 Omar Vizquel GS 2.00
85 Joe Randa GS 2.00
86 Lance Johnson GS 2.00
87 Kevin Brown GS 2.50
88 Curt Schilling GS 4.00
89 Ismael Valdes GS 2.00
90 Francisco Cordova GS 2.00
91 David Cone GS 2.00
92 Paul O'Neill GS 2.00
93 Jimmy Key GS 2.00
94 Brad Radke GS 2.00
95 Kevin Appier GS 2.00
96 Al Martin GS 2.00
97 Rusty Greer MZ 2.00
98 Reggie Jefferson GS 2.00
99 Ron Coomer GS 2.00
100 Vinny Castilla GS 2.00
101 Bobby Bonilla MZ 2.00
102 Eric Young GS 2.00
103 Tony Womack GS 2.00
104 Jason Kendall GS 2.00
105 Jeff Suppan GS 2.00
106 Shawn Estes MZ 2.00
107 Shawn Green GS 3.00
108 Edgardo Alfonzo MZ 2.00
109 Alan Benes MZ 2.00
110 Bobby Higginson GS 2.00
111 Mark Grudzielanek GS 2.00
112 Wilton Guerrero GS 2.00
113 Todd Greene MZ 2.00
114 Pokey Reese GS 2.00
115 Jose Guillen CL 2.00
116 Neifi Perez MZ 2.00
117 Luis Castillo GS 2.00
118 Edgar Renteria GS 2.00
119 Karim Garcia GS 2.50
120 Butch Huskey GS 2.00
121 Michael Tucker GS 2.00
122 Jason Dickson GS 2.00
123 Todd Walker MZ 2.00
124 Brian Jordan GS 2.00
125 Joe Carter GS 2.00
126 Matt Morris MZ 2.00
127 Brett Tomko MZ 2.00
128 Mike Cameron CL 2.00
129 Russ Davis GS 2.00
130 Shannon Stewart MZ 2.50
131 Kevin Orie GS 2.00
132 Scott Spiezio GS 2.00
133 Brian Giles GS 2.00
134 Raul Casanova GS 2.00
135 Jose Cruz Jr. CL 2.00
136 Hideki Irabu GS 2.00
137 Bubba Trammell GS 2.00
138 Richard Hidalgo CL 2.00
139 Paul Konerko CL 2.50
140 Todd Helton FB 7.50
141 Miguel Tejada CL 3.00
142 Fernando Tatis MZ 2.00
143 Ben Grieve FB 2.50
144 Travis Lee FB 3.00
145 Mark Kotsay CL 2.00
146 Eli Marrero MZ 2.00
147 David Ortiz CL 3.50
148 Juan Encarnacion MZ 2.00
149 Jaret Wright MZ 2.00
150 Livan Hernandez CL 2.00
151 Ruben Rivera GS 2.00
152 Brad Fullmer MZ 2.00
153 Dennis Reyes GS 2.00
154 Enrique Wilson MZ 2.00
155 Todd Dunwoody MZ 2.00
156 Derrick Gibson MZ 2.00
157 Aaron Boone MZ 2.00
158 Ron Wright MZ 2.00
159 Preston Wilson MZ 2.00
160 Abraham Nunez GS 2.00
161 Shane Monahan GS 2.00
162 Carl Pavano GS 2.00
163 Derrek Lee GS 2.00
164 Jeff Abbott GS 2.00
165 Wes Helms MZ 2.00
166 Brian Rose GS 2.00
167 Bobby Estalella GS 2.00
168 Ken Griffey Jr. GS 9.00
169 Frank Thomas GS 6.00
170 Cal Ripken Jr. GS 15.00
171 Alex Rodriguez GS 12.00
172 Greg Maddux GS 7.50
173 Mike Piazza GS 9.00
174 Chipper Jones GS 7.50
175 Tony Gwynn GS 7.50
176 Derek Jeter GS 15.00
177 Jeff Bagwell GS 6.00
178 Juan Gonzalez GS 6.00
179 Nomar Garciaparra GS 9.00
180 Andruw Jones GS 6.00
181 Hideo Nomo GS 6.00
182 Roger Clemens GS 8.00
183 Mark McGwire GS 12.00
184 Scott Rolen GS 3.00
185 Barry Bonds GS 15.00
186 Darin Erstad GS 6.00
187 Mo Vaughn GS 2.00
188 Ivan Rodriguez GS 6.00
189 Larry Walker MZ 2.00
190 Andy Pettitte GS 3.50
191 Randy Johnson MZ 6.00
192 Paul Molitor GS 6.00
193 Jim Thome GS 2.00
194 Tino Martinez MZ 2.00
195 Gary Sheffield GS 3.00
196 Albert Belle GS 2.50
197 Jose Cruz Jr. GS 2.00
198 Todd Helton GS 6.00
199 Ben Grieve GS 2.50
200 Paul Konerko GS 2.50

1998 DONRUSS ELITE

	NM/M
Complete Set (150):	15.00
Common Player:	.10
Pack (5):	2.50
Wax Box (18):	40.00

1 Ken Griffey Jr. 1.25
2 Frank Thomas .75
3 Alex Rodriguez 1.50
4 Mike Piazza 1.25
5 Greg Maddux 1.00
6 Cal Ripken Jr. 2.00
7 Chipper Jones 1.00
8 Derek Jeter 2.00
9 Tony Gwynn 1.00
10 Andruw Jones .75
11 Juan Gonzalez .75
12 Jeff Bagwell .75
13 Mark McGwire 1.50
14 Roger Clemens 1.00
15 Albert Belle .15
16 Barry Bonds 2.00
17 Kenny Lofton .10
18 Ivan Rodriguez .65
19 Manny Ramirez .75
20 Jim Thome .10
21 Chuck Knoblauch .10
22 Paul Molitor .75
23 Barry Larkin .10
24 Andy Pettitte .50
25 John Smoltz .10
26 Randy Johnson .75
27 Bernie Williams .20
28 Larry Walker .10
29 Mo Vaughn .10
30 Bobby Higginson .10
31 Edgardo Alfonzo .10
32 Justin Thompson .10
33 Jeff Suppan .10
34 Roberto Alomar .40
35 Hideo Nomo .75
36 Rusty Greer .10
37 Tim Salmon .20
38 Jim Edmonds .10
39 Gary Sheffield .25
40 Ken Caminiti .10
41 Sammy Sosa 1.25
42 Tony Womack .10
43 Matt Williams .10
44 Andres Galarraga .10
45 Garret Anderson .10
46 Rafael Palmeiro .75
47 Mike Mussina .50
48 Craig Biggio .10
49 Wade Boggs 1.00
50 Tom Glavine .25
51 Jason Giambi .50
52 Will Clark .15
53 David Justice .10
54 Sandy Alomar Jr. .10
55 Edgar Martinez .10
56 Brady Anderson .10
57 Eric Young .10
58 Ray Lankford .10

59	Kevin Brown	.15
60	Raul Mondesi	.10
61	Bobby Bonilla	.10
62	Javier Lopez	.10
63	Fred McGriff	.10
64	Rondell White	.10
65	Todd Hundley	.10
66	Mark Grace	.20
67	Alan Benes	.10
68	Jeff Abbott	.10
69	Bob Abreu	.10
70	Deion Sanders	.10
71	Tino Martinez	.10
72	Shannon Stewart	.10
73	Homer Bush	.10
74	Carlos Delgado	.50
75	Raul Ibanez	.10
76	Hideki Irabu	.10
77	Jose Cruz Jr.	.10
78	Tony Clark	.10
79	Wilton Guerrero	.10
80	Vladimir Guerrero	.75
81	Scott Rolen	.65
82	Nomar Garciaparra	1.25
83	Darin Erstad	.60
84	Chan Ho Park	.10
85	Mike Cameron	.10
86	Todd Walker	.10
87	Todd Dunwoody	.10
88	Neifi Perez	.10
89	Brett Tomko	.10
90	Jose Guillen	.10
91	Matt Morris	.10
92	Bartolo Colon	.10
93	Jaret Wright	.10
94	Shawn Estes	.10
95	Livan Hernandez	.10
96	Bobby Estalella	.10
97	Ben Grieve	.15
98	Paul Konerko	.15
99	David Ortiz	.20
100	Todd Helton	.75
101	Juan Encarnacion	.10
102	Bubba Trammell	.10
103	Miguel Tejada	.30
104	Jacob Cruz	.10
105	Todd Greene	.10
106	Kevin Orie	.10
107	Mark Kotsay	.10
108	Fernando Tatis	.10
109	Jay Payton	.10
110	Pokey Reese	.10
111	Derrek Lee	.10
112	Richard Hidalgo	.10
113	Ricky Ledee	.10
114	Lou Collier	.10
115	Ruben Rivera	.10
116	Shawn Green	.20
117	Moises Alou	.10
118	Ken Griffey Jr. (Generations)	.65
119	Frank Thomas (Generations)	.40
120	Alex Rodriguez (Generations)	.75
121	Mike Piazza (Generations)	.65
122	Greg Maddux (Generations)	.50
123	Cal Ripken Jr. (Generations)	1.00
124	Chipper Jones (Generations)	.50
125	Derek Jeter (Generations)	1.00
126	Tony Gwynn (Generations)	.50
127	Andruw Jones (Generations)	.40
128	Juan Gonzalez (Generations)	.40
129	Jeff Bagwell (Generations)	.40
130	Mark McGwire (Generations)	.75
131	Roger Clemens (Generations)	.60
132	Albert Belle (Generations)	.10
133	Barry Bonds (Generations)	1.00
134	Kenny Lofton (Generations)	.10
135	Ivan Rodriguez (Generations)	.25
136	Manny Ramirez (Generations)	.40
137	Jim Thome (Generations)	.10
138	Chuck Knoblauch (Generations)	.10
139	Paul Molitor (Generations)	.40
140	Barry Larkin (Generations)	.10
141	Mo Vaughn (Generations)	.10
142	Hideki Irabu (Generations)	.10
143	Jose Cruz Jr. (Generations)	.10
144	Tony Clark (Generations)	.10
145	Vladimir Guerrero (Generations)	.40
146	Scott Rolen (Generations)	.20
147	Nomar Garciaparra (Generations)	.65
148	Nomar Garciaparra Checklist (Hit Streaks)	.45
149	Larry Walker Checklist (Long HR-Coors)	.10
150	Tino Martinez Checklist (3 HR in game)	.10

Status

	NM/M
Common Player:	1.50
Stars/Rookies:	15X

(See 1998 Donruss Elite for checklist and base card values.)

Aspirations

	NM/M
Common Player:	.50
Stars/Rookies:	2.5X

(See 1998 Donruss Elite for checklist and base card values.)

Back to the Future

		NM/M
Complete Set (8):		40.00
Common Player:		2.50
Production 1,400 sets		
1	Cal Ripken Jr., Paul Konerko	9.00
2	Jeff Bagwell, Todd Helton	4.50
3	Eddie Mathews, Chipper Jones	5.00
4	Juan Gonzalez, Ben Grieve	2.50
5	Hank Aaron, Jose Cruz Jr.	7.50
6	Frank Thomas, David Ortiz	3.00
7	Nolan Ryan, Greg Maddux	9.00
8	Alex Rodriguez, Nomar Garciaparra	9.00

Back to the Future Autographs

		NM/M
Production 100 sets		
1a	Paul Konerko	20.00
1b	Cal Ripken Jr.	200.00
2	Jeff Bagwell, Todd Helton	150.00
3	Eddie Mathews, Chipper Jones	180.00
4	Juan Gonzalez, Ben Grieve	50.00
5	Hank Aaron, Jose Cruz Jr.	160.00
6	NOT ISSUED IN AUTOGRAPHED FORM	
7	Nolan Ryan, Greg Maddux	800.00
8	Alex Rodriguez, Nomar Garciaparra	500.00
2	Frank Thomas (Specially autographed Elite)	60.00

Craftsmen

		NM/M
Complete Set (30):		20.00
Common Player:		.25
Production 3,500 sets		
Master Craftsman (100 sets):		2X
1	Ken Griffey Jr.	1.50
2	Frank Thomas	.75
3	Alex Rodriguez	2.00
4	Cal Ripken Jr.	2.50
5	Greg Maddux	1.00
6	Mike Piazza	2.00
7	Chipper Jones	1.00
8	Derek Jeter	2.50
9	Tony Gwynn	1.00
10	Nomar Garciaparra	1.50
11	Scott Rolen	.60
12	Jose Cruz Jr.	.25
13	Tony Clark	.25
14	Vladimir Guerrero	.75
15	Todd Helton	.75
16	Ben Grieve	.35
17	Andruw Jones	.75
18	Jeff Bagwell	.75
19	Mark McGwire	2.00
20	Juan Gonzalez	.75
21	Roger Clemens	1.25
22	Albert Belle	.25
23	Barry Bonds	2.50
24	Kenny Lofton	.25
25	Ivan Rodriguez	.65
26	Paul Molitor	.75
27	Barry Larkin (incorrect "CARDINALS" on front)	.25
28	Mo Vaughn	.35
29	Larry Walker	.25
30	Tino Martinez	.25

Prime Numbers

		NM/M
Common Card:		4.00
Samples:	50% player's common	
1A	Ken Griffey Jr. 2 (94)	20.00
1B	Ken Griffey Jr. 9 (204)	17.50
1C	Ken Griffey Jr. 4 (290)	13.50
2A	Frank Thomas 4 (56)	20.00
2B	Frank Thomas 5 (406)	7.00
2C	Frank Thomas 6 (450)	7.00
3A	Mark McGwire 3 (87)	25.00
3B	Mark McGwire 8 (307)	17.50
3C	Mark McGwire 7 (380)	17.50
4A	Cal Ripken Jr. 5 (17)	110.00
4B	Cal Ripken Jr. 1 (507)	11.00
4C	Cal Ripken Jr. 7 (510)	11.00
5A	Mike Piazza 5 (76)	25.00
5B	Mike Piazza 7 (506)	9.00
5C	Mike Piazza 6 (570)	9.00
6A	Chipper Jones 4 (89)	20.00
6B	Chipper Jones 8 (409)	8.00
6C	Chipper Jones 9 (480)	8.00
7A	Tony Gwynn 3 (72)	20.00
7B	Tony Gwynn 7 (302)	8.00
7C	Tony Gwynn 2 (370)	8.00
8A	Barry Bonds 3 (74)	35.00
8B	Barry Bonds 7 (304)	9.00
8C	Barry Bonds 4 (370)	9.00
9A	Jeff Bagwell 4 (25)	20.00
9B	Jeff Bagwell 2 (405)	6.00
9C	Jeff Bagwell 5 (420)	6.00
10A	Juan Gonzalez 5 (89)	15.00
10B	Juan Gonzalez 8 (509)	5.00
10C	Juan Gonzalez 9 (580)	5.00
11A	Alex Rodriguez 5 (34)	45.00
11B	Alex Rodriguez 3 (504)	9.00
11C	Alex Rodriguez 4 (530)	9.00
12A	Kenny Lofton 3 (54)	12.50
12B	Kenny Lofton 5 (304)	4.00
12C	Kenny Lofton 4 (350)	4.00

1998 DONRUSS PREFERRED

		NM/M
Complete Set (200):		75.00
Common Grand Stand (5:1):		.10
Common Mezzanine (1:6):		.20
Common Club Level (1:12):		.30
Common Field Box: (1:23)		.35
Common Executive Suite (1:65):		1.50
Tin Pack (5):		3.00
Tin Box (24):		40.00
1	Ken Griffey Jr. EX	2.50
2	Frank Thomas EX	2.00
3	Cal Ripken Jr. EX	3.50
4	Alex Rodriguez EX	3.00
5	Greg Maddux EX	2.25
6	Mike Piazza EX	2.50
7	Chipper Jones EX	2.25
8	Tony Gwynn FB	2.00
9	Derek Jeter FB	3.50
10	Jeff Bagwell EX	1.50
11	Juan Gonzalez EX	1.50
12	Nomar Garciaparra EX	2.50
13	Andruw Jones FB	1.50
14	Hideo Nomo FB	1.25
15	Roger Clemens FB	2.25
16	Mark McGwire FB	3.00
17	Scott Rolen FB	1.25
18	Vladimir Guerrero FB	1.50
19	Barry Bonds FB	3.00
20	Darin Erstad FB	1.25
21	Albert Belle FB	.40
22	Kenny Lofton FB	.35
23	Mo Vaughn FB	.35
24	Tony Clark FB	.35
25	Ivan Rodriguez FB	1.25
26	Larry Walker CL	.30
27	Eddie Murray CL	1.25
28	Andy Pettitte CL	.60
29	Roberto Alomar CL	.35
30	Randy Johnson CL	1.00
31	Manny Ramirez CL	1.00
32	Paul Molitor FB	1.50
33	Mike Mussina CL	.60
34	Jim Thome FB	.35
35	Tino Martinez CL	.30
36	Gary Sheffield CL	.35
37	Chuck Knoblauch CL	.30
38	Bernie Williams CL	.35

39	Tim Salmon CL	.35
40	Sammy Sosa CL	1.50
41	Wade Boggs MZ	.60
42	Will Clark GS	.15
43	Andres Galarraga CL	.30
44	Raul Mondesi CL	.30
45	Rickey Henderson GS	.40
46	Jose Canseco GS	.25
47	Pedro Martinez GS	.30
48	Jay Buhner GS	.10
49	Ryan Klesko GS	.10
50	Barry Larkin CL	.30
51	Charles Johnson GS	.10
52	Tom Glavine GS	.20
53	Edgar Martinez CL	.30
54	Fred McGriff GS	.10
55	Moises Alou MZ	.20
56	Dante Bichette GS	.10
57	Jim Edmonds CL	.30
58	Mark Grace MZ	.30
59	Chan Ho Park MZ	.25
60	Justin Thompson MZ	.20
61	John Smoltz MZ	.20
62	Craig Biggio CL	.30
63	Ken Caminiti MZ	.20
64	Deion Sanders MZ	.20
65	Carlos Delgado GS	.25
66	David Justice CL	.30
67	J.T. Snow GS	.10
68	Jason Giambi CL	.60
69	Garret Anderson MZ	.20
70	Rondell White MZ	.20
71	Matt Williams MZ	.20
72	Brady Anderson MZ	.20
73	Eric Karros GS	.10
74	Javier Lopez GS	.10
75	Pat Hentgen GS	.10
76	Todd Hundley GS	.10
77	Ray Lankford GS	.10
78	Denny Neagle GS	.10
79	Henry Rodriguez GS	.10
80	Sandy Alomar Jr. MZ	.20
81	Rafael Palmeiro MZ	.60
82	Robin Ventura GS	.10
83	John Olerud GS	.10
84	Omar Vizquel GS	.10
85	Joe Randa GS	.10
86	Lance Johnson GS	.10
87	Kevin Brown GS	.20
88	Curt Schilling GS	.20
89	Ismael Valdes GS	.10
90	Francisco Cordova GS	.10
91	David Cone GS	.10
92	Paul O'Neill GS	.10
93	Jimmy Key GS	.10
94	Brad Radke GS	.10
95	Kevin Appier GS	.10
96	Al Martin GS	.10
97	Rusty Greer MZ	.20
98	Reggie Jefferson GS	.10
99	Ron Coomer GS	.10
100	Vinny Castilla GS	.10
101	Bobby Bonilla MZ	.20
102	Eric Young GS	.10
103	Tony Womack GS	.10
104	Jason Kendall GS	.10
105	Jeff Suppan GS	.10
106	Shawn Estes MZ	.20
107	Shawn Green GS	.20
108	Edgardo Alfonzo MZ	.20
109	Alan Benes MZ	.20
110	Bobby Higginson GS	.10
111	Mark Grudzielanek GS	.10
112	Wilton Guerrero GS	.10
113	Todd Greene MZ	.20
114	Pokey Reese GS	.10
115	Jose Guillen CL	.30
116	Neifi Perez MZ	.20
117	Luis Castillo GS	.10
118	Edgar Renteria GS	.10
119	Karim Garcia GS	.20
120	Butch Huskey GS	.10
121	Michael Tucker GS	.10
122	Jason Dickson GS	.10
123	Todd Walker MZ	.20
124	Brian Jordan GS	.10
125	Joe Carter GS	.10
126	Matt Morris MZ	.20
127	Brett Tomko MZ	.20
128	Mike Cameron CL	.30
129	Russ Davis GS	.10
130	Shannon Stewart MZ	.25
131	Kevin Orie GS	.10
132	Scott Spiezio GS	.10
133	Brian Giles GS	.10
134	Raul Casanova GS	.10
135	Jose Cruz Jr. CL	.30
136	Hideki Irabu GS	.10
137	Bubba Trammell GS	.10
138	Richard Hidalgo CL	.30
139	Paul Konerko CL	.35
140	Todd Helton FB	1.00
141	Miguel Tejada CL	.40
142	Fernando Tatis MZ	.20
143	Ben Grieve FB	.35
144	Travis Lee FB	.75
145	Mark Kotsay CL	.30
146	Eli Marrero MZ	.20
147	David Ortiz CL	.35
148	Juan Encarnacion MZ	.20
149	Jaret Wright MZ	.20
150	Livan Hernandez CL	.30
151	Ruben Rivera GS	.10
152	Brad Fullmer MZ	.20
153	Dennis Reyes GS	.10
154	Enrique Wilson MZ	.20
155	Todd Dunwoody MZ	.20
156	Derrick Gibson MZ	.20
157	Aaron Boone MZ	.20
158	Ron Wright MZ	.20
159	Preston Wilson MZ	.25
160	Abraham Nunez GS	.10
161	Shane Monahan GS	.10
162	Carl Pavano GS	.10
163	Derrek Lee GS	.10
164	Jeff Abbott GS	.10
165	Wes Helms MZ	.10
166	Brian Rose GS	.10
167	Bobby Estalella GS	.10
168	Ken Griffey Jr. GS	.60
169	Frank Thomas GS	.35
170	Cal Ripken Jr. GS	1.00
171	Alex Rodriguez GS	.75
172	Greg Maddux GS	.50
173	Mike Piazza GS	.60
174	Chipper Jones GS	.50
175	Tony Gwynn GS	.50
176	Derek Jeter GS	1.00
177	Jeff Bagwell GS	.35
178	Juan Gonzalez GS	.35
179	Nomar Garciaparra GS	.60
180	Andruw Jones GS	.35
181	Hideo Nomo GS	.25
182	Roger Clemens GS	.55
183	Mark McGwire GS	.75
184	Scott Rolen GS	.25
185	Barry Bonds GS	1.00
186	Darin Erstad GS	.20
187	Mo Vaughn GS	.15
188	Ivan Rodriguez GS	.30
189	Larry Walker MZ	.20
190	Andy Pettitte GS	.30
191	Randy Johnson MZ	.60
192	Paul Molitor GS	.40
193	Jim Thome GS	.15
194	Tino Martinez MZ	.20
195	Gary Sheffield GS	.25
196	Albert Belle GS	.20
197	Jose Cruz Jr. GS	.15
198	Todd Helton GS	.30
199	Ben Grieve GS	.15
200	Paul Konerko GS	.20

Seating

	NM/M
Common Grand Stand:	.50
Stars and Rookies:	4X
Common Mezzanine:	.50
Stars and Rookies:	2X
Common Club Level:	.50
Stars and Rookies:	2X
Common Field Box:	1.00
Stars and Rookies:	1.5X
Common Executive Suite:	2.50
Stars and Rookies:	1X

(See 1998 Donruss Preferred for checklistand base card values.)

Double-Wide Tins

		NM/M
Complete Set (12):		12.00
Common Tin:		.75
1	Todd Helton, Ben Grieve	.75
2	Cal Ripken Jr., Alex Rodriguez	2.00
3	Greg Maddux, Mike Piazza	1.25
4	Chipper Jones, Travis Lee	1.00
5	Derek Jeter, Jeff Bagwell	1.75
6	Juan Gonzalez, Mark McGwire	1.50
7	Hideo Nomo, Roger Clemens	1.00
8	Andruw Jones, Paul Molitor	.75
9	Vladimir Guerrero, Jose Cruz Jr.	.75
10	Nomar Garciaparra, Scott Rolen	1.25
11	Ken Griffey Jr., Larry Walker	1.25
12	Tony Gwynn, Frank Thomas	1.00

Tins

		NM/M
Complete Set (24):		17.50
Common Player:		.25
Gold Tins (199):		3X
Silver Tins (999):		1.5X
1	Todd Helton	.75
2	Ben Grieve	.25
3	Cal Ripken Jr.	2.00
4	Alex Rodriguez	1.50
5	Greg Maddux	1.00
6	Mike Piazza	1.25
7	Chipper Jones	1.00
8	Travis Lee	.25
9	Derek Jeter	2.00
10	Jeff Bagwell	.75
11	Juan Gonzalez	.75
12	Mark McGwire	1.50
13	Hideo Nomo	.75
14	Roger Clemens	1.00
15	Andruw Jones	.75
16	Paul Molitor	.75
17	Vladimir Guerrero	.75
18	Jose Cruz Jr.	.25
19	Nomar Garciaparra	1.25
20	Scott Rolen	.65
21	Ken Griffey Jr.	1.25
22	Larry Walker	.25
23	Frank Thomas	.75
24	Tony Gwynn	1.00

Great X-pectations

		NM/M
Complete Set (26):		35.00
Common Player:		.75
Die-Cuts:		3X
Promos:		25%
1	Jeff Bagwell, Travis Lee	1.25
2	Jose Cruz Jr., Ken Griffey Jr.	2.00
3	Larry Walker, Ben Grieve	.75
4	Frank Thomas, Todd Helton	1.25
5	Jim Thome, Paul Konerko	.75
6	Alex Rodriguez, Miguel Tejada	2.50
7	Greg Maddux, Livan Hernandez	1.75
8	Roger Clemens, Jaret Wright	1.75
9	Albert Belle, Juan Encarnacion	.75
10	Mo Vaughn, David Ortiz	.75
11	Manny Ramirez, Mark Kotsay	1.25
12	Tim Salmon, Brad Fullmer	.75
13	Cal Ripken Jr., Fernando Tatis	3.50
14	Hideo Nomo, Hideki Irabu	1.50
15	Mike Piazza, Todd Greene	2.00
16	Gary Sheffield, Richard Hidalgo	.75
17	Paul Molitor, Darin Erstad	1.25
18	Ivan Rodriguez, Eli Marrero	1.00
19	Ken Caminiti, Todd Walker	.75
20	Tony Gwynn, Jose Guillen	1.75
21	Derek Jeter, Nomar Garciaparra	3.50
22	Chipper Jones, Scott Rolen	1.75
23	Juan Gonzalez, Andruw Jones	1.25
24	Barry Bonds, Vladimir Guerrero	3.50
25	Mark McGwire, Tony Clark	2.50
26	Bernie Williams, Mike Cameron	.75

Precious Metals

		NM/M
Complete Set (30):		850.00
Common Player:		7.50
1	Ken Griffey Jr.	50.00
2	Frank Thomas	35.00
3	Cal Ripken Jr.	75.00
4	Alex Rodriguez	60.00
5	Greg Maddux	45.00
6	Mike Piazza	50.00
7	Chipper Jones	45.00
8	Tony Gwynn	45.00
9	Derek Jeter	75.00
10	Jeff Bagwell	35.00
11	Juan Gonzalez	35.00
12	Nomar Garciaparra	50.00
13	Andruw Jones	35.00
14	Hideo Nomo	30.00
15	Roger Clemens	45.00
16	Mark McGwire	60.00
17	Scott Rolen	30.00
18	Barry Bonds	75.00
19	Darin Erstad	30.00
20	Kenny Lofton	7.50
21	Mo Vaughn	7.50
22	Ivan Rodriguez	30.00
23	Randy Johnson	35.00
24	Paul Molitor	35.00
25	Jose Cruz Jr.	7.50
26	Paul Konerko	7.50
27	Todd Helton	35.00
28	Ben Grieve	7.50
29	Travis Lee	7.50
30	Mark Kotsay	7.50

Title Waves

		NM/M
Complete Set (30):		100.00
Common Player:		1.00
1	Nomar Garciaparra	6.00

2 Scott Rolen 3.00
3 Roger Clemens 5.50
4 Gary Sheffield 1.50
5 Jeff Bagwell 3.50
6 Cal Ripken Jr. 10.00
7 Frank Thomas 3.50
8 Ken Griffey Jr. 6.00
9 Larry Walker 1.00
10 Derek Jeter 10.00
11 Juan Gonzalez 3.50
12 Bernie Williams 1.25
13 Andruw Jones 3.50
14 Andy Pettitte 2.00
15 Ivan Rodriguez 3.00
16 Alex Rodriguez 8.00
17 Mark McGwire 8.00
18 Andres Galarraga 1.00
19 Hideo Nomo 3.50
20 Mo Vaughn 1.00
21 Randy Johnson 3.50
22 Chipper Jones 5.00
23 Greg Maddux 5.00
24 Manny Ramirez 3.50
25 Tony Gwynn 5.00
26 Albert Belle 1.25
27 Kenny Lofton 1.00
28 Mike Piazza 6.00
29 Paul Molitor 3.50
30 Barry Bonds 10.00

1998 DONRUSS SIGNATURE SERIES

NM/M

Complete Set (140): 30.00
Common Player: .10
Pack (5): 12.50
Wax Box (12): 150.00
1 David Justice .10
2 Derek Jeter 2.50
3 Nomar Garciaparra 1.50
4 Ryan Klesko .10
5 Jeff Bagwell .75
6 Dante Bichette .10
7 Ivan Rodriguez .65
8 Albert Belle .15
9 Cal Ripken Jr. 2.50
10 Craig Biggio .10
11 Barry Larkin .10
12 Jose Guillen .10
13 Will Clark .15
14 J.T. Snow .10
15 Chuck Knoblauch .10
16 Todd Walker .10
17 Scott Rolen .65
18 Rickey Henderson .75
19 Juan Gonzalez .75
20 Justin Thompson .10
21 Roger Clemens 1.50
22 Ray Lankford .10
23 Jose Cruz Jr. .10
24 Ken Griffey Jr. 1.50
25 Andruw Jones .75
26 Darin Erstad .60
27 Jim Thome .10
28 Wade Boggs 1.00
29 Ken Caminiti .10
30 Todd Hundley .10
31 Mike Piazza 1.50
32 Sammy Sosa 1.50
33 Larry Walker .10
34 Matt Williams .10
35 Frank Thomas .75
36 Gary Sheffield .30
37 Alex Rodriguez 2.00
38 Hideo Nomo .75
39 Kenny Lofton .10
40 John Smoltz .10
41 Mo Vaughn .10
42 Edgar Martinez .10
43 Paul Molitor .75
44 Rafael Palmeiro .75
45 Barry Bonds 2.50
46 Vladimir Guerrero .75
47 Carlos Delgado .60
48 Bobby Higginson .10
49 Greg Maddux 1.00
50 Jim Edmonds .10
51 Randy Johnson .75
52 Mark McGwire 2.00
53 Rondell White .10
54 Raul Mondesi .10
55 Manny Ramirez .75
56 Pedro Martinez .75
57 Tim Salmon .20
58 Moises Alou .10
59 Fred McGriff .10
60 Garret Anderson .10
61 Sandy Alomar Jr. .10
62 Chan Ho Park .10
63 Mark Kotsay .10
64 Mike Mussina .50
65 Tom Glavine .25
66 Tony Clark .10
67 Mark Grace .15
68 Tony Gwynn 1.00
69 Tino Martinez .10
70 Kevin Brown .15
71 Todd Greene .10
72 Andy Pettitte .50
73 Livan Hernandez .10
74 Curt Schilling .25
75 Andres Galarraga .10
76 Rusty Greer .10
77 Jay Buhner .10
78 Bobby Bonilla .10
79 Chipper Jones 1.00
80 Eric Young .10
81 Jason Giambi .50
82 Javy Lopez .10
83 Roberto Alomar .30
84 Bernie Williams .20
85 A.J. Hinch .10
86 Kerry Wood .65
87 Juan Encarnacion .10
88 Brad Fullmer .10
89 Ben Grieve .15
90 *Magglio Ordonez* 3.00
91 Todd Helton .75
92 Richard Hidalgo .10
93 Paul Konerko .15
94 Aramis Ramirez .10
95 Ricky Ledee .10
96 Derrek Lee .10
97 Travis Lee .15
98 *Matt Anderson* .25
99 Jaret Wright .10
100 David Ortiz .25
101 Carl Pavano .10
102 *Orlando Hernandez* .50
103 Fernando Tatis .10
104 Miguel Tejada .35
105 *Rolando Arrojo* .50
106 *Kevin Millwood* 1.00
107 Ken Griffey Jr. (Checklist) .50
108 Frank Thomas (Checklist) .30
109 Cal Ripken Jr. (Checklist) .75
110 Greg Maddux (Checklist) .40
111 John Olerud .10
112 David Cone .10
113 Vinny Castilla .10
114 Jason Kendall .10
115 Brian Jordan .10
116 Hideki Irabu .10
117 Bartolo Colon .10
118 Greg Vaughn .10
119 David Segui .10
120 Bruce Chen .10
121 *Julio Ramirez* .15
122 *Troy Glaus* 6.00
123 *Jeremy Giambi* .50
124 *Ryan Minor* .15
125 Richie Sexson .10
126 Dermal Brown .10
127 Adrian Beltre .15
128 Eric Chavez .35
129 *J.D. Drew* 4.00
130 *Gabe Kapler* .50
131 *Masato Yoshii* .25
132 *Mike Lowell* 2.00
133 *Jim Parque* .25
134 Roy Halladay .25
135 *Carlos Lee* .75
136 *Jin Ho Cho* .25
137 Michael Barrett .10
138 *Fernando Seguignol* .40
139 *Odalis Perez* .50
140 Mark McGwire (Checklist) .65

Proofs

NM/M

Common Player: 1.00
Stars/Rookies: 12X

(See 1998 Donruss Signature Series for checklist and base card values.)

Autographs (Red)

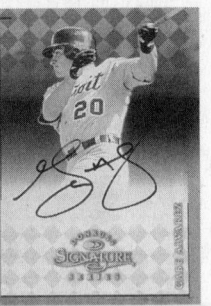

NM/M

Common Player: 2.50
(1) Roberto Alomar (150) 40.00
(2) Sandy Alomar Jr. (700) 10.00
(3) Moises Alou (900) 15.00
(4) Gabe Alvarez (2,900) 2.50
(5) Wilson Alvarez (1,600) 4.00
(6) Jay Bell (1,500) 4.00
(7) Adrian Beltre (1,900) 25.00
(8) Andy Benes (2,600) 4.00
(9) Aaron Boone (3,400) 10.00
(10) Russell Branyan (1,650) 4.00
(11) Orlando Cabrera (3,100) 8.00
(12) Mike Cameron (1,150) 6.00
(13) Joe Carter (400) 12.00
(14) Sean Casey (2,275) 8.00
(15) Bruce Chen (150) 5.00
(16) Tony Clark (2,275) 7.50
(17) Will Clark (1,400) 15.00
(18) Matt Clement (1,400) 4.00
(19) Pat Cline (400) 6.00
(20) Ken Cloude (3,400) 2.50
(21) Michael Coleman (2,800) 2.50
(22) David Cone (25) 50.00
(23) Jeff Conine (1,400) 5.00
(24) Jacob Cruz (3,200) 2.50
(25) Russ Davis (3,500) 2.50
(26) Jason Dickson (1,400) 4.00
(27) Todd Dunwoody (3,500) 2.50
(28) Juan Encarnacion (3,400) 5.00
(29) Darin Erstad (700) 15.00
(30) Bobby Estalella (3,400) 4.00
(31) Jeff Fassero (3,400) 2.50
(32) John Franco (1,800) 2.50
(33) Brad Fullmer (3,100) 5.00
(34) Jason Giambi (3,100) 15.00
(35) Derrick Gibson (1,200) 5.00
(36) Todd Greene (1,400) 5.00
(37) Ben Grieve (1,400) 6.00
(38) Mark Grudzielanek (3,200) 4.00
(39) Vladimir Guerrero (2,100) 25.00
(40) Wilton Guerrero (1,900) 4.00
(41) Jose Guillen (2,400) 5.00
(42) Todd Helton (1,300) 20.00
(43) Richard Hidalgo (3,400) 4.00
(44) A.J. Hinch (2,900) 4.00
(45) Butch Huskey (1,900) 4.00
(46) Raul Ibanez (3,300) 2.50
(47) Damian Jackson (900) 2.50
(48) Geoff Jenkins (3,100) 5.00
(49) Eric Karros (650) 10.00
(50) Ryan Klesko (400) 10.00
(51) Mark Kotsay (3,600) 5.00
(52) Ricky Ledee (2,200) 5.00
(53) Derrek Lee (3,400) 15.00
(54) Travis Lee (150) 25.00
(54s) Travis Lee (facsimile autograph, "SAMPLE" on back) 3.00
(55) Javier Lopez (650) 8.00
(56) Mike Lowell (3,500) 8.00
(57) Greg Maddux (12) 625.00
(58) Eli Marrero (3,400) 3.00
(59) Al Martin (1,300) 4.00
(60) Rafael Medina (1,400) 2.50
(61) Scott Morgan (900) 4.50
(62) Abraham Nunez (3,500) 2.50
(63) Paul O'Neill (1,000) 20.00
(64) Luis Ordaz (2,700) 2.50
(65) Magglio Ordonez (3,200) 15.00
(66) Kevin Orie (1,350) 5.00
(67) David Ortiz (3,400) 25.00
(68) Rafael Palmeiro (1,000) 25.00
(69) Carl Pavano (2,600) 8.00
(70) Neifi Perez (3,300) 2.50
(71) Dante Powell (3,050) 2.50
(72) Aramis Ramirez(2,800) 10.00
(73) Mariano Rivera (900) 35.00
(74) Felix Rodriguez (1,400) 3.00
(75) Henry Rodriguez (3,400) 3.00
(76) Scott Rolen (1,900) 30.00
(77) Brian Rose (1,400) 3.00
(78) Curt Schilling (900) 30.00
(79) Richie Sexson (3,500) 8.00
(80) Randall Simon (3,500) 3.00
(81) J.T. Snow (400) 8.00
(82) Jeff Suppan (1,400) 5.00
(83) Fernando Tatis (3,900) 3.00
(84) Miguel Tejada (3,800) 30.00
(85) Brett Tomko (3,400) 2.50
(86) Bubba Trammell (3,900) 2.50
(87) Ismael Valdez (1,900) 5.00
(88) Robin Ventura (1,400) 8.00
(89) Billy Wagner (3,900) 10.00
(90) Todd Walker (1,900) 5.00
(91) Daryle Ward (400) 4.00
(92) Rondell White (3,400) 5.00
(93) Antone Williamson (3,350) 2.50
(94) Dan Wilson (2,400) 4.00
(95) Enrique Wilson (3,400) 2.50
(96) Preston Wilson (2,100) 5.00
(97) Tony Womack (3,500) 2.50
(98) Kerry Wood (3,400) 25.00

Signature Series Preview Autographs

NM/M

Common Player: 10.00
(1) Sandy Alomar Jr. (96) 30.00
(2) Moises Alou 50.00
(3) Andy Benes (135) 15.00
(4) Russell Branyan (188) 15.00
(5) Sean Casey 85.00
(6) Tony Clark (188) 20.00

(7) Juan Encarnacion (193) 15.00
(8) Brad Fullmer (396) 10.00
(9) Juan Gonzalez (108) 115.00
(10) Ben Grieve (100) 35.00
(11) Todd Helton (101) 50.00
(12) Richard Hidalgo (380) 10.00
(13) A.J. Hinch (400) 10.00
(14) Damian Jackson (15) 65.00
(15) Geoff Jenkins 185.00
(16) Derek Jeter 1,225
(17) Chipper Jones (112) 125.00
(18) Chuck Knoblauch (98) 50.00
(19) Travis Lee (101) 20.00
(20) Mike Lowell (450) 15.00
(21) Greg Maddux (92) 165.00
(22) Kevin Millwood (395) 30.00
(23) Magglio Ordonez (420) 50.00
(24) David Ortiz (393) 75.00
(25) Rafael Palmeiro (107) 50.00
(26) Cal Ripken Jr. (22) 650.00
(27) Alex Rodriguez (23) 600.00
(28) Curt Schilling (100) 100.00
(29) Randall Simon (380) 10.00
(30) Fernando Tatis (400) 10.00
(31) Miguel Tejada (375) 40.00
(32) Robin Ventura (95) 30.00
(33) Dan Wilson 85.00
(34) Kerry Wood (373) 40.00

Century Marks (Blue)

	NM/M
Common Player:	10.00
(1) Roberto Alomar	60.00
(2) Sandy Alomar Jr.	15.00
(3) Moises Alou	40.00
(4) Gabe Alvarez	10.00
(5) Wilson Alvarez	10.00
(6) Brady Anderson	20.00
(7) Jay Bell	20.00
(8) Albert Belle	20.00
(9) Adrian Beltre	60.00
(10) Andy Benes	10.00
(11) Wade Boggs	60.00
(12) Barry Bonds	300.00
(13) Aaron Boone	40.00
(14) Russell Branyan	10.00
(15) Jay Buhner	10.00
(16) Ellis Burks	10.00
(17) Orlando Cabrera	20.00
(18) Mike Cameron	10.00
(19) Ken Caminiti	25.00
(20) Joe Carter	20.00
(21) Sean Casey	15.00
(22) Bruce Chen	10.00
(23) Tony Clark	10.00
(24) Will Clark	60.00
(25) Roger Clemens	200.00
(26) Matt Clement	20.00
(27) Pat Cline	10.00
(28) Ken Cloude	10.00
(29) Michael Coleman	10.00
(30) David Cone	25.00
(31) Jeff Conine	10.00
(32) Jacob Cruz	10.00
(33) Jose Cruz Jr.	15.00
(34) Russ Davis	10.00
(35) Jason Dickson	10.00
(36) Todd Dunwoody	10.00
(37) Scott Elarton	10.00
(38) Darin Erstad	25.00
(39) Bobby Estalella	10.00
(40) Jeff Fassero	10.00
(41) John Franco	10.00
(42) Brad Fullmer	10.00
(43) Andres Galarraga	15.00
(44) Nomar Garciaparra	100.00
(45) Jason Giambi	40.00
(46) Derrick Gibson	10.00
(47) Tom Glavine	75.00
(48) Juan Gonzalez	75.00
(49) Todd Greene	10.00
(50) Ben Grieve	10.00
(51) Mark Grudzielanek	10.00
(52) Vladimir Guerrero	75.00
(53) Wilton Guerrero	10.00
(54) Jose Guillen	10.00
(55) Tony Gwynn	100.00
(56) Todd Helton	60.00
(57) Richard Hidalgo	10.00
(58) A.J. Hinch	10.00
(59) Butch Huskey	10.00
(60) Raul Ibanez	10.00
(61) Damian Jackson	10.00
(62) Geoff Jenkins	10.00
(63) Derek Jeter	220.00
(64) Randy Johnson	150.00
(65) Chipper Jones	100.00
(66) Eric Karros (50)	15.00
(67) Jason Kendall (unsigned)	20.00
(68) Ryan Klesko	10.00
(69) Chuck Knoblauch	10.00
(70) Mark Kotsay	10.00
(71) Ricky Ledee	10.00
(72) Derrek Lee	25.00
(73) Travis Lee	15.00
(74) Javier Lopez	25.00
(75) Mike Lowell	30.00
(76) Greg Maddux	150.00
(77) Eli Marrero	10.00
(78) Al Martin	10.00
(79) Rafael Medina	10.00
(80) Paul Molitor	50.00
(81) Scott Morgan	10.00
(82) Mike Mussina	80.00
(83) Abraham Nunez	15.00
(84) Paul O'Neill	40.00
(85) Luis Ordaz	10.00
(86) Magglio Ordonez	30.00
(87) Kevin Orie	10.00
(88) David Ortiz	70.00
(89) Rafael Palmeiro	85.00
(90) Carl Pavano	25.00
(91) Neifi Perez	10.00
(92) Andy Pettitte	50.00
(93) Aramis Ramirez	25.00
(94) Cal Ripken Jr.	225.00
(95) Mariano Rivera	75.00
(96) Alex Rodriguez	200.00
(97) Felix Rodriguez	10.00
(98) Henry Rodriguez	10.00
(99) Scott Rolen	70.00
(100) Brian Rose	10.00
(101) Curt Schilling	50.00
(102) Richie Sexson	20.00
(103) Randall Simon	10.00
(104) J.T. Snow	10.00
(105) Darryl Strawberry	45.00
(106) Jeff Suppan	10.00
(107) Fernando Tatis	10.00
(108) Brett Tomko	10.00
(109) Bubba Trammell	10.00
(110) Ismael Valdez	10.00
(111) Robin Ventura	20.00
(112) Billy Wagner	40.00
(113) Todd Walker	15.00
(114) Daryle Ward	10.00
(115) Rondell White	20.00
(116) Matt Williams (80)	35.00
(117) Antone Williamson	10.00
(118) Dan Wilson	15.00
(119) Enrique Wilson	10.00
(120) Preston Wilson	25.00
(121) Tony Womack	10.00
(122) Kerry Wood	60.00

Millennium Marks (Green)

	NM/M
Common Player:	3.00
(1) Roberto Alomar	25.00
(2) Sandy Alomar Jr.	5.00
(3) Moises Alou	10.00
(4) Gabe Alvarez	3.00
(5) Wilson Alvarez	3.00
(6) Brady Anderson (800)	8.00
(7) Jay Bell	3.00
(8) Albert Belle (400)	8.00
(9) Adrian Beltre	20.00
(10) Andy Benes	3.00
(11) Wade Boggs (900)	20.00
(12) Barry Bonds (400)	150.00
(13) Aaron Boone	3.00
(14) Russell Branyan	3.00
(15) Jay Buhner (400)	15.00
(16) Ellis Burks (900)	6.00
(17) Orlando Cabrera	6.00
(18) Mike Cameron	5.00
(19) Ken Caminiti (900)	9.00
(20) Joe Carter	5.00
(21) Sean Casey	8.00
(22) Bruce Chen	3.00
(23) Tony Clark	5.00
(24) Will Clark	25.00
(25) Roger Clemens (400)	75.00
(26) Matt Clement (900)	8.00
(27) Pat Cline	3.00
(28) Ken Cloude	3.00
(29) Michael Coleman	3.00
(30) David Cone	15.00
(31) Jeff Conine	3.00
(32) Jacob Cruz	3.00
(33) Jose Cruz Jr. (850)	5.00
(34) Russ Davis (950)	3.00
(35) Jason Dickson (950)	3.00
(36) Todd Dunwoody	3.00
(37) Scott Elarton (900)	3.00
(38) Juan Encarnacion	3.00
(39) Darin Erstad	8.00
(40) Bobby Estalella	3.00
(41) Jeff Fassero	3.00
(42) John Franco (950)	7.00
(43) Brad Fullmer	3.00
(44) Andres Galarraga (900)	10.00
(45) Nomar Garciaparra (400)	75.00
(46) Jason Giambi	20.00
(47) Derrick Gibson	3.00
(48) Tom Glavine (700)	25.00
(49) Juan Gonzalez	25.00
(50) Todd Greene	3.00
(51) Ben Grieve	4.00
(52) Mark Grudzielanek	3.00
(53) Vladimir Guerrero	30.00
(54) Wilton Guerrero	3.00
(55) Jose Guillen	3.00
(56) Tony Gwynn (900)	35.00
(57) Todd Helton	20.00
(58) Richard Hidalgo	3.00
(59) A.J. Hinch	3.00
(60) Butch Huskey	3.00
(61) Raul Ibanez	3.00
(62) Damian Jackson	3.00
(63) Geoff Jenkins	3.00
(64) Derek Jeter (400)	100.00
(65) Randy Johnson (800)	60.00
(66) Chipper Jones (900)	30.00
(67) Eric Karros	7.00
(68) Ryan Klesko	6.00
(69) Chuck Knoblauch (900)	5.00
(70) Mark Kotsay	5.00
(71) Ricky Ledee	3.00
(72) Derrek Lee	20.00
(73) Travis Lee	5.00
(74) Javier Lopez (800)	10.00
(75) Mike Lowell	10.00
(76) Greg Maddux (400)	90.00
(77) Eli Marrero	3.00
(78) Al Martin (950)	3.00
(79) Rafael Medina (850)	3.00
(80) Paul Molitor (900)	20.00
(81) Scott Morgan	3.00
(82) Mike Mussina (900)	25.00
(83) Abraham Nunez	3.00
(84) Paul O'Neill (900)	20.00
(85) Luis Ordaz	3.00
(86) Magglio Ordonez	15.00
(87) Kevin Orie	3.00
(88) David Ortiz	20.00
(89) Rafael Palmeiro (900)	30.00
(90) Carl Pavano	10.00
(91) Neifi Perez	3.00
(92) Andy Pettitte (900)	20.00
(93) Dante Powell (950)	3.00
(94) Aramis Ramirez	10.00
(95) Cal Ripken Jr. (375)	100.00
(96) Mariano Rivera	30.00
(97) Alex Rodriguez (350)	75.00
(98) Felix Rodriguez	6.00
(99) Henry Rodriguez	3.00
(100) Scott Rolen	20.00
(101) Brian Rose	3.00
(102) Curt Schilling	20.00
(103) Richie Sexson	8.00
(104) Randall Simon	3.00
(105) J.T. Snow	4.00
(106) Darryl Strawberry (900)	40.00
(107) Jeff Suppan	3.00
(108) Fernando Tatis	6.00
(109) Miguel Tejada	40.00
(110) Brett Tomko	3.00
(111) Bubba Trammell	3.00
(112) Ismael Valdes	3.00
(113) Robin Ventura	6.00
(114) Billy Wagner (900)	10.00
(115) Todd Walker	4.00
(116) Daryle Ward	3.00
(117) Rondell White	6.00
(118) Matt Williams (820)	8.00
(119) Antone Williamson	3.00
(120) Dan Wilson	3.00
(121) Enrique Wilson	3.00
(122) Preston Wilson (400)	10.00
(123) Tony Womack	3.00
(124) Kerry Wood	25.00

Redemption Baseballs

	NM/M
Common Autographed Ball:	15.00
Redemption Card:	10%
(1) Roberto Alomar (60)	35.00
(2) Sandy Alomar Jr. (60)	20.00
(3) Ernie Banks (12)	85.00
(4) Ken Caminiti (60)	20.00
(5) Tony Clark (60)	20.00
(6) Jacob Cruz (12)	20.00
(7) Russ Davis (60)	15.00
(8) Juan Encarnacion (60)	20.00
(9) Bobby Estalella (60)	15.00
(10) Jeff Fassero (60)	15.00
(11) Mark Grudzielanek (60)	15.00
(12) Ben Grieve (30)	20.00
(13) Jose Guillen (120)	20.00
(14) Tony Gwynn (60)	100.00
(15) Al Kaline (12)	75.00
(16) Paul Konerko (100)	15.00
(17) Travis Lee (100)	20.00
(18) Mike Lowell (60)	15.00
(19) Eli Marrero (60)	15.00
(20) Eddie Mathews (12)	80.00
(21) Paul Molitor (60)	65.00
(22) Stan Musial (12)	125.00
(23) Abraham Nunez (12)	20.00
(24) Luis Ordaz (12)	20.00
(25) Magglio Ordonez (12)	50.00
(26) Scott Rolen (60)	45.00
(27) Bubba Trammell (24)	25.00
(28) Robin Ventura (60)	20.00
(29) Billy Wagner (60)	20.00
(30) Rondell White (60)	20.00
(31) Antone Williamson (12)	15.00
(32) Tony Womack (60)	15.00

Significant Signatures

	NM/M
Complete Set (18):	400.00
Common Player:	10.00
Ernie Banks	30.00
Yogi Berra	30.00
George Brett	45.00
Catfish Hunter	25.00
Al Kaline	30.00

Harmon Killebrew 30.00
Ralph Kiner 10.00
Sandy Koufax 150.00
Eddie Mathews 30.00
Don Mattingly 50.00
Willie McCovey 15.00
Stan Musial 40.00
Phil Rizzuto (edition of 1,000) 20.00
Nolan Ryan 75.00
Nolan Ryan (Exchange card) 5.00
Ozzie Smith 20.00
Ozzie Smith (Exchange card) 5.00
Duke Snider 25.00
Don Sutton 12.00
Billy Williams 12.00

2001 DONRUSS

NM/M

Complete Set (220): 400.00
Common Player: .15
Common Rated Rookie (151-200): 4.00
Production 2001
Hobby Pack (5): 5.00
Hobby Box (24): 100.00
The Rookies Coupon: 1.00
Inserted 1:72
Baseball's Best Coupon: 1.00
Inserted 1:720
Exchange Deadline 11/01/01

1 Alex Rodriguez 2.00
2 Barry Bonds 2.50
3 Cal Ripken Jr. 2.50
4 Chipper Jones 1.00
5 Derek Jeter 2.50
6 Troy Glaus .75
7 Frank Thomas .75
8 Greg Maddux 1.00
9 Ivan Rodriguez .50
10 Jeff Bagwell .75
11 Jose Canseco .30
12 Todd Helton .65
13 Ken Griffey Jr. 1.50
14 Manny Ramirez .75
15 Mark McGwire 2.00
16 Mike Piazza 1.50
17 Nomar Garciaparra 1.50
18 Pedro Martinez .75
19 Randy Johnson .75
20 Rick Ankiel .20
21 Ricky Henderson .75
22 Roger Clemens 1.00
23 Sammy Sosa 1.50
24 Tony Gwynn 1.00
25 Vladimir Guerrero .75
26 Eric Davis .15
27 Roberto Alomar .35
28 Mark Mulder .25
29 Pat Burrell .50
30 Harold Baines .15
31 Carlos Delgado .40
32 J.D. Drew .25
33 Jim Edmonds .25
34 Darin Erstad .45
35 Jason Giambi .50
36 Tom Glavine .30
37 Juan Gonzalez .75
38 Mark Grace .20
39 Shawn Green .25
40 Tim Hudson .40
41 Andruw Jones .75
42 David Justice .15
43 Jeff Kent .15
44 Barry Larkin .15
45 Pokey Reese .15
46 Mike Mussina .35
47 Hideo Nomo .35
48 Rafael Palmeiro .65
49 Adam Piatt .15
50 Scott Rolen .75
51 Gary Sheffield .25
52 Bernie Williams .35
53 Bob Abreu .15
54 Edgardo Alfonzo .15
55 *Jermaine Clark* .20
56 Albert Belle .25
57 Craig Biggio .15
58 Andres Galarraga .15
59 Edgar Martinez .15
60 Fred McGriff .15
61 Magglio Ordonez .25
62 Jim Thome .75
63 Matt Williams .15
64 Kerry Wood .40
65 Moises Alou .15
66 Brady Anderson .20
67 Garret Anderson .15
68 Tony Armas Jr. .15
69 Tony Batista .15
70 Jose Cruz Jr. .15
71 Carlos Beltran .50
72 Adrian Beltre .25
73 Kris Benson .15
74 Lance Berkman .15
75 Kevin Brown .20
76 Jay Buhner .15
77 Jeromy Burnitz .15
78 Ken Caminiti .15
79 Sean Casey .25
80 Luis Castillo .15
81 Eric Chavez .25
82 Jeff Cirillo .15
83 Bartolo Colon .15
84 David Cone .15
85 Freddy Garcia .15
86 Johnny Damon .25
87 Ray Durham .15
88 Jermaine Dye .15
89 Juan Encarnacion .15
90 Terrence Long .15
91 Carl Everett .15
92 Steve Finley .15
93 Cliff Floyd .15
94 Brad Fullmer .15
95 Brian Giles .15
96 Luis Gonzalez .25
97 Rusty Greer .15
98 Jeffrey Hammonds .15
99 Mike Hampton .15
100 Orlando Hernandez .15
101 Richard Hidalgo .15
102 Geoff Jenkins .15
103 Jacque Jones .15
104 Brian Jordan .15
105 Gabe Kapler .15
106 Eric Karros .15
107 Jason Kendall .15
108 Adam Kennedy .15
109 Byung-Hyun Kim .15
110 Ryan Klesko .15
111 Chuck Knoblauch .15
112 Paul Konerko .15
113 Carlos Lee .15
114 Kenny Lofton .15
115 Javy Lopez .15
116 Tino Martinez .15
117 Ruben Mateo .15
118 Kevin Millwood .15
119 Ben Molina .15
120 Raul Mondesi .15
121 Trot Nixon .15
122 John Olerud .15
123 Paul O'Neill .15
124 Chan Ho Park .15
125 Andy Pettitte .40
126 Jorge Posada .40
127 Mark Quinn .15
128 Aramis Ramirez .15
129 Mariano Rivera .25
130 Tim Salmon .25
131 Curt Schilling .40
132 Richie Sexson .25
133 John Smoltz .15
134 J.T. Snow .15
135 Jay Payton .15
136 Shannon Stewart .15
137 B.J. Surhoff .15
138 Mike Sweeney .15
139 Fernando Tatis .15
140 Miguel Tejada .40
141 Jason Varitek .15
142 Greg Vaughn .15
143 Mo Vaughn .15
144 Robin Ventura .15
145 Jose Vidro .15
146 Omar Vizquel .15
147 Larry Walker .15
148 David Wells .15
149 Rondell White .15
150 Preston Wilson .15
151 Brent Abernathy 4.00
152 *Cory Aldridge* 4.00
153 *Gene Altman* 4.00
154 Josh Beckett 4.00
155 *Wilson Betemit* 6.00
156 *Albert Pujols/500* 250.00
157 Joe Crede 4.00
158 Jack Cust 4.00
159 Ben Sheets/500 40.00
160 Alex Escobar 4.00
161 *Adrian Hernandez* 4.00
162 Pedro Feliz 4.00
163 *Nate Frese* 4.00
164 *Carlos Garcia* 4.00
165 Marcus Giles 4.00
166 *Alexis Gomez* 4.00
167 Jason Hart 4.00
168 *Eric Hinske* 8.00
169 Cesar Izturis 4.00
170 Nick Johnson 4.00
171 Mike Young 4.00
172 *Brian Lawrence* 6.00
173 Steve Lomasney 4.00
174 *Nick Maness* 4.00
175 *Jose Mieses* 4.00
176 *Greg Miller* 4.00
177 Eric Munson 4.00
178 Xavier Nady 4.00
179 *Blaine Neal* 4.00
180 Abraham Nunez 4.00
181 Jose Ortiz 4.00
182 *Jeremy Owens* 4.00
183 Pablo Ozuna 4.00
184 Corey Patterson 4.00
185 Carlos Pena 4.00
186 Wily Mo Pena 4.00
187 Timo Perez 4.00
188 *Adam Pettyjohn* 4.00
189 Luis Rivas 4.00
190 *Jackson Melian* 4.00
191 *Wilken Ruan* 4.00
192 *Duaner Sanchez* 4.00
193 Alfonso Soriano 5.00
194 *Rafael Soriano* 8.00
195 *Ichiro Suzuki* 60.00
196 *Billy Sylvester* 4.00
197 *Juan Uribe* 4.00
198 Eric Valent 4.00
199 *Carlos Valderrama* 4.00
200 *Matt White* 4.00
201 Alex Rodriguez 2.50
202 Barry Bonds 3.00
203 Cal Ripken Jr. 3.00
204 Chipper Jones 1.00
205 Derek Jeter 2.50
206 Troy Glaus .75
207 Frank Thomas .75
208 Greg Maddux 1.00
209 Ivan Rodriguez .50
210 Jeff Bagwell .75
211 Todd Helton .75
212 Ken Griffey Jr. 1.50
213 Manny Ramirez .75
214 Mark McGwire 2.00
215 Mike Piazza 1.50
216 Pedro Martinez .75
217 Sammy Sosa 2.00
218 Tony Gwynn 1.00
219 Vladimir Guerrero .75
220 Nomar Garciaparra 1.50

Stat Line Career

NM/M

Cards #1-150 print run 251-400: 3-6X
1-150 p/r 201-250: 4-8X
1-150 p/r 151-200: 4-8X
1-150 p/r 101-150: 5-10X
1-150 p/r 61-100: 10-20X
1-150 p/r 41-60: 20-30X
1-150 p/r 21-40: 25-40X
1-150 p/r 15-20: 30-60X
Common (151-200) p/r 251-400: 1.00
Common (151-200) p/r 151-250: 1.00
Common (151-200) p/r 101-150: 2.00
Common (151-200) p/r 76-100: 2.00
Common (151-200) p/r 31-75 4.00
Common (151-200) p/r 20-30 6.00
cards 201-220 p/r 201-400: 1-2X
201-220 p/r 101-200: 2-4X
201-220 p/r 75-100: 3-5X
201-220 p/r 40-74: 4-8X
156 Albert Pujols/154 150.00
190 Jackson Melian/26 50.00
195 Ichiro Suzuki/106 200.00

All-Time Diamond Kings

NM/M

Complete Set (10): 150.00
Common Player: 8.00
Production 2,500 sets
Studio Series: 2-3X
Production 250
#9 undetermined redemp.

1a Frank Robinson 8.00
1b Willie Mays (should have been ATDK-9) 25.00
2 Harmon Killebrew 8.00
3 Mike Schmidt 20.00
4 Reggie Jackson 8.00
5 Nolan Ryan 35.00
6 George Brett 25.00
7 Tom Seaver 10.00
8 Hank Aaron 25.00
9 Redemption, Willie Mays (See #1b)
10 Stan Musial 20.00

All-Time Diamond Kings Autograph

NM/M

Production 50 sets

1 Frank Robinson 100.00
1 Willie Mays 200.00
2 Harmon Killebrew 80.00
3 Mike Schmidt 200.00
4 Reggie Jackson 80.00
5 Nolan Ryan 250.00
6 George Brett 225.00
7 Tom Seaver 85.00
8 Hank Aaron 200.00
10 Stan Musial 120.00

Bat Kings

NM/M

Common Card: 20.00
Production 250 sets

1 Ivan Rodriguez 20.00
2 Tony Gwynn 35.00
3 Barry Bonds 75.00
4 Todd Helton 20.00
5 Troy Glaus 20.00
6 Mike Schmidt 50.00
7 Reggie Jackson 20.00
8 Harmon Killebrew 20.00
9 Frank Robinson 20.00
10 Hank Aaron 75.00

Bat Kings Autograph

NM/M
Production 50 sets
1 Ivan Rodriguez 75.00
2 Tony Gwynn 120.00
3 Barry Bonds/no auto 50.00
4 Todd Helton 65.00
5 Troy Glaus 65.00
6 Mike Schmidt 150.00
7 Reggie Jackson 100.00
8 Harmon Killebrew 100.00
9 Frank Robinson 85.00
10 Hank Aaron 200.00

Diamond Kings Reprints

NM/M
Complete Set (20): 160.00
Common Player: 5.00
#'d to yr. produced
1 Rod Carew 5.00
2 Nolan Ryan 25.00
3 Tom Seaver 10.00
4 Carlton Fisk 10.00
5 Reggie Jackson 12.00
6 Steve Carlton 5.00
7 Johnny Bench 10.00
8 Joe Morgan 5.00
9 Mike Schmidt 20.00
10 Wade Boggs 15.00
11 Cal Ripken Jr. 25.00
12 Tony Gwynn 15.00
13 Andre Dawson 5.00
14 Ozzie Smith 15.00
15 George Brett 20.00
16 Dave Winfield 5.00
17 Paul Molitor 10.00
18 Will Clark 5.00
19 Robin Yount 10.00
20 Ken Griffey Jr. 17.50

Diamond Kings Reprints Autograph

NM/M
Common Player:
DKR1 Rod Carew/82 40.00
DKR2 Nolan Ryan/82 150.00
DKR3 Tom SeaveR/82 75.00
DKR4 Carlton Fisk/82 65.00
DKR5 Reggie Jackson/83 60.00
DKR6 Steve Carlton/83 40.00
DKR7 Johnny Bench/83 80.00
DKR8 Joe Morgan/83 30.00
DKR9 Mike Schmidt/84 120.00
DKR10 Wade Boggs/84 60.00
DKR11 Cal Ripken Jr./85 180.00
DKR12 Tony Gwynn/86 80.00
DKR13 Andre Dawson/86 35.00
DKR14 Ozzie Smith/87 80.00
DKR15 George Brett/87 120.00
DKR16 Dave Winfield/87 40.00
DKR17 Paul Molitor/88 60.00
DKR18 Will Clark/88 75.00
DKR19 Robin Yount/89 80.00
DKR20 Ken Griffey Jr./ 89/no auto. 25.00

Elite Series

NM/M
Complete Set (20): 75.00
Common Player: 2.00
Production 2,500 sets
Dominators: 5-8X
Production 25 sets
1 Vladimir Guerrero 4.00
2 Cal Ripken Jr. 10.00
3 Greg Maddux 5.00
4 Alex Rodriguez 8.00
5 Barry Bonds 10.00
6 Chipper Jones 5.00
7 Derek Jeter 10.00

8 Ivan Rodriguez 2.50
9 Ken Griffey Jr. 7.00
10 Mark McGwire 8.00
11 Mike Piazza 7.00
12 Nomar Garciaparra 7.00
13 Pedro Martinez 4.00
14 Randy Johnson 4.00
15 Roger Clemens 6.00
16 Sammy Sosa 7.00
17 Tony Gwynn 5.00
18 Darin Erstad 3.00
19 Andruw Jones 4.00
20 Bernie Williams 2.00

Jersey Kings

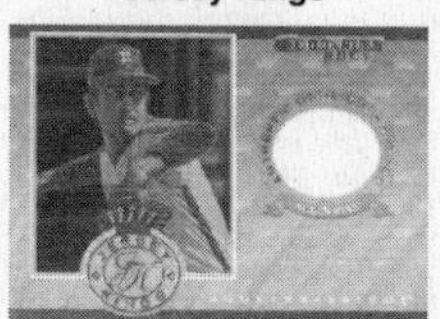

NM/M
Common Card: 25.00
Production 250 sets
1 Vladimir Guerrero 20.00
2 Cal Ripken Jr. 80.00
3 Greg Maddux 40.00
4 Chipper Jones 25.00
5 Roger Clemens 40.00
6 George Brett 50.00
7 Tom Seaver 20.00
8 Nolan Ryan 85.00
9 Stan Musial 45.00
10 Willie Mays

Jersey Kings Autographs

NM/M
Production 50 sets
1 Vladimir Guerrero 90.00
2 Cal Ripken Jr. 225.00
3 Greg Maddux 150.00
4 Chipper Jones 85.00
5 Roger Clemens 175.00
6 George Brett 200.00
7 Tom Seaver 75.00
8 Nolan Ryan 200.00
9 Stan Musial 120.00
10 Ozzie Smith 100.00

Longball Leaders

NM/M
Complete Set (20): 50.00
Common Player: 1.00
Production 1,000 sets
Die-Cut Parallel: 3-5X
#'d to '00 HR Total
1 Vladimir Guerrero 4.00
2 Alex Rodriguez 8.00
3 Barry Bonds 10.00
4 Troy Glaus 4.00
5 Frank Thomas 4.00
6 Jeff Bagwell 4.00
7 Todd Helton 4.00
8 Ken Griffey Jr. 6.00
9 Manny Ramirez 4.00
10 Mike Piazza 6.00
11 Sammy Sosa 6.00
12 Carlos Delgado 2.00
13 Jim Edmonds 1.00
14 Jason Giambi 3.00
15 David Justice 1.00
16 Rafael Palmeiro 3.00
17 Gary Sheffield 2.00
18 Jim Thome 1.00
19 Tony Batista 1.00
20 Richard Hidalgo 1.00

Production Line

NM/M
Complete Set (60): 150.00
Common Player: .50
Die-Cut OBP (1-20): 1-2X
Die-Cut SLG (21-40): 1-2.5X
Die-Cut PI (41-60): 1.5-3X
Production 100 sets
1 Jason Giambi/476 3.00
2 Carlos Delgado/470 2.00
3 Todd Helton/463 3.00
4 Manny Ramirez/457 3.00
5 Barry Bonds/440 15.00
6 Gary Sheffield/438 2.00
7 Frank Thomas/436 3.00
8 Nomar Garciaparra/ 434 10.00
9 Brian Giles/432 1.00
10 Edgardo Alfonzo/425 .50
11 Jeff Kent/424 .75
12 Jeff Bagwell/424 3.00
13 Edgar Martinez/423 .75
14 Alex Rodriguez/420 10.00
15 Luis Castillo/418 .50
16 Will Clark/418 2.50
17 Jorge Posada/417 2.00
18 Derek Jeter/416 12.00
19 Bob Abreu/416 1.00
20 Moises Alou/416 .75
21 Todd Helton/698 3.00
22 Manny Ramirez/697 3.00
23 Barry Bonds/688 15.00
24 Carlos Delgado/664 2.00
25 Vladimir Guerrero/664 3.00
26 Jason Giambi/647 3.00
27 Gary Sheffield/643 2.00
28 Richard Hidalgo/636 .50
29 Sammy Sosa/634 8.00
30 Frank Thomas/625 3.00
31 Moises Alou/623 .75
32 Jeff Bagwell/615 3.00
33 Mike Piazza/614 8.00
34 Alex Rodriguez/606 10.00
35 Troy Glaus/604 3.00
36 Nomar Garciaparra/ 599 10.00
37 Jeff Kent/596 .75
38 Brian Giles/594 .75
39 Geoff Jenkins/588 .50
40 Carl Everett/587 .50
41 Todd Helton/1161 3.00
42 Manny Ramirez/1154 3.00
43 Carlos Delgado/1134 2.00
44 Barry Bonds/1128 12.00
45 Jason Giambi/1123 3.00
46 Gary Sheffield/1081 2.00
47 Vladimir Guerrero/ 1074 3.00
48 Frank Thomas/1061 3.00
49 Sammy Sosa/1040 8.00
50 Moises Alou/1039 1.00
51 Jeff Bagwell/1039 3.00
52 Nomar Garciaparra/ 1033 10.00
53 Richard Hidalgo/1027 .50
54 Alex Rodriguez/1026 10.00
55 Brian Giles/1026 1.00
56 Jeff Kent/1020 1.00
57 Mike Piazza/1012 8.00
58 Troy Glaus/1008 3.00
59 Edgar Martinez/1002 1.00
60 Jim Edmonds/994 1.00

Rookie Reprints

NM/M
Complete Set (40): 200.00
Common Player: 3.00
#'d to Original Yr. issued
1 Cal Ripken Jr. 20.00
2 Wade Boggs 10.00
3 Tony Gwynn 10.00
4 Ryne Sandberg 10.00
5 Don Mattingly 12.00
6 Joe Carter 3.00
7 Roger Clemens 12.00
8 Kirby Puckett 10.00

9 Orel Hershiser 3.00
10 Andres Galarraga 3.00
11 Jose Canseco 5.00
12 Fred McGriff 3.00
13 Paul O'Neill 3.00
14 Mark McGwire 15.00
15 Barry Bonds 20.00
16 Kevin Brown 3.00
17 David Cone 3.00
18 Rafael Palmeiro 8.00
19 Barry Larkin 3.00
20 Bo Jackson 4.00
21 Greg Maddux 10.00
22 Roberto Alomar 4.00
23 Mark Grace 3.00
24 David Wells 3.00
25 Tom Glavine 4.00
26 Matt Williams 3.00
27 Ken Griffey Jr. 12.00
28 Randy Johnson 8.00
29 Gary Sheffield 4.00
30 Craig Biggio 3.00
31 Curt Schilling. 4.00
32 Larry Walker 3.00
33 Bernie Williams 4.00
34 Sammy Sosa 12.00
35 Juan Gonzalez 8.00
36 David Justice 3.00
37 Ivan Rodriguez 6.00
38 Jeff Bagwell 8.00
39 Jeff Kent 3.00
40 Manny Ramirez 8.00

Rookie Reprints Autographs

NM/M
Common Player:
#'d to last 2 digits of yr. issued
1 Cal Ripken/82 150.00
2 Wade Boggs/83 40.00
3 Tony Gwynn/83 75.00
4 Ryne Sandberg/83 100.00
5 Don Mattingly/84 100.00
6 Joe Carter/84 20.00
7 Roger Clemens/85 200.00
8 Kirby Puckett/85 60.00
9 Orel Hershiser/85 25.00
10 Andres Galarraga/86 30.00
15 Barry Bonds/87 200.00
16 Kevin Brown/87 30.00
17 David Cone/87 30.00
18 Rafael Palmeiro/87 50.00
20 Bo Jackson/87 85.00
21 Greg Maddux/87 150.00
22 Roberto Alomar/88 40.00
24 David Wells/88 25.00
25 Tom Glavine/88 40.00
28 Randy Johnson/89 100.00
29 Gary Sheffield/89 50.00
31 Curt Schilling/89 75.00
35 Juan Gonzalez/90 40.00
36 David Justice/90 25.00
37 Ivan Rodriguez/91 40.00
39 Manny Ramirez/92 100.00

1999 Retro

NM/M
Complete Set (100): 200.00
Common Player: .25
Inserted 1:hobby pack
Common (81-100): 3.00
Production 1,999
1 Ken Griffey Jr. 2.00
2 Nomar Garciaparra 2.00
3 Alex Rodriguez 2.50
4 Mark McGwire 2.50
5 Sammy Sosa 2.00
6 Chipper Jones 1.50
7 Mike Piazza 2.00

8 Barry Larkin .25
9 Andruw Jones 1.00
10 Albert Belle .25
11 Jeff Bagwell 1.00
12 Tony Gwynn 1.50
13 Manny Ramirez 1.00
14 Mo Vaughn .25
15 Barry Bonds 3.00
16 Frank Thomas 1.00
17 Vladimir Guerrero 1.00
18 Derek Jeter 3.00
19 Randy Johnson 1.00
20 Greg Maddux 1.50
21 Pedro Martinez 1.00
22 Cal Ripken Jr. 3.00
23 Ivan Rodriguez .75
24 Matt Williams .25
25 Javy Lopez .25
26 Tim Salmon .25
27 Raul Mondesi .25
28 Todd Helton 1.00
29 Magglio Ordonez .40
30 Sean Casey .25
31 Jeromy Burnitz .25
32 Jeff Kent .25
33 Jim Edmonds .25
34 Jim Thome .25
35 Dante Bichette .25
36 Larry Walker .25
37 Will Clark .35
38 Omar Vizquel .25
39 Mike Mussina .50
40 Eric Karros .25
41 Kenny Lofton .25
42 David Justice .25
43 Craig Biggio .25
44 J.D. Drew .25
45 Rickey Henderson 1.00
46 Bernie Williams .45
47 Brian Giles .25
48 Paul O'Neill .25
49 Orlando Hernandez .25
50 Jason Giambi .50
51 Curt Schilling .45
52 Scott Rolen 1.00
53 Mark Grace .35
54 Moises Alou .25
55 Jason Kendall .25
56 Ray Lankford .25
57 Kerry Wood .50
58 Gary Sheffield .50
59 Ruben Mateo .25
60 Darin Erstad .65
61 Troy Glaus 1.00
62 Jose Canseco .50
63 Wade Boggs 1.50
64 Tom Glavine .50
65 Gabe Kapler .25
66 Juan Gonzalez 1.00
67 Rafael Palmeiro .75
68 Richie Sexson .25
69 Carl Everett .25
70 David Wells .25
71 Carlos Delgado .75
72 Eric Davis .25
73 Shawn Green .40
74 Andres Galarraga .25
75 Edgar Martinez .25
76 Roberto Alomar .50
77 John Olerud .25
78 Luis Gonzalez .25
79 Kevin Brown .25
80 Roger Clemens 1.75
81 Josh Beckett 5.00
82 Alfonso Soriano 8.00
83 Alex Escobar 3.00
84 Pat Burrell 4.00
85 Eric Chavez 4.00
86 Erubiel Durazo 3.00
87 Abraham Nunez 3.00
88 Carlos Pena 3.00
89 Nick Johnson 4.00
90 Eric Munson 3.00
91 Corey Patterson 4.00
92 Wily Mo Pena 3.00
93 Rafael Furcal 3.00
94 Eric Valent 3.00
95 Mark Mulder 4.00
96 Chad Hutchinson 3.00
97 Freddy Garcia 3.00
98 Tim Hudson 5.00
99 Rick Ankiel 3.00
100 Kip Wells 3.00

1999 Diamond Kings

NM/M
Complete Set (5): 40.00
Common Player: 8.00
Production 2,500 sets
1 Scott Rolen 8.00
2 Sammy Sosa 10.00
3 Juan Gonzalez 8.00
4 Ken Griffey Jr. 10.00
5 Derek Jeter 20.00

2000 Retro

NM/M
Complete Set (100): 90.00
Common Player: .25
Common (81-100): 3.00
Production 2,000
1 Vladimir Guerrero .75
2 Alex Rodriguez 2.00
3 Ken Griffey Jr. 1.50
4 Nomar Garciaparra 1.50
5 Mike Piazza 1.50
6 Mark McGwire 2.00
7 Sammy Sosa 1.50
8 Chipper Jones 1.00
9 Jim Edmonds .25
10 Tony Gwynn 1.00
11 Andruw Jones .75
12 Albert Belle .25
13 Jeff Bagwell .75
14 Manny Ramirez .75
15 Mo Vaughn .25
16 Barry Bonds 2.50
17 Frank Thomas .75
18 Ivan Rodriguez .65
19 Derek Jeter 2.50
20 Randy Johnson .75
21 Greg Maddux 1.00
22 Pedro Martinez .75
23 Cal Ripken Jr. 2.50
24 Mark Grace .35
25 Javy Lopez .25
26 Ray Durham .25
27 Todd Helton .75
28 Magglio Ordonez .40
29 Sean Casey .25
30 Darin Erstad .65
31 Barry Larkin .25
32 Will Clark .35
33 Jim Thome .25
34 Dante Bichette .25
35 Larry Walker .25
36 Ken Caminiti .25
37 Omar Vizquel .25
38 Miguel Tejada .40
39 Eric Karros .25
40 Gary Sheffield .40
41 Jeff Cirillo .25
42 Rondell White .25
43 Rickey Henderson .75
44 Bernie Williams .40
45 Brian Giles .25
46 Paul O'Neill .25
47 Orlando Hernandez .25
48 Ben Grieve .25
49 Jason Giambi .50
50 Curt Schilling .40
51 Scott Rolen .75
52 Bobby Abreu .25
53 Jason Kendall .25
54 Fernando Tatis .25
55 Jeff Kent .25
56 Mike Mussina .40
57 Troy Glaus .75
58 Jose Canseco .45
59 Wade Boggs 1.00
60 Fred McGriff .25
61 Juan Gonzalez .75
62 Rafael Palmeiro .65
63 Rusty Greer .25
64 Carl Everett .25
65 David Wells .25
66 Carlos Delgado .50
67 Shawn Green .40
68 David Justice .25
69 Edgar Martinez .25
70 Andres Galarraga .25
71 Roberto Alomar .50
72 Jermaine Dye .25
73 John Olerud .25
74 Luis Gonzalez .35
75 Craig Biggio .25
76 Kevin Millwood .25
77 Kevin Brown .35
78 John Smoltz .25
79 Roger Clemens 1.25
80 Mike Hampton .25
81 Tomas De La Rosa 3.00
82 C.C. Sabathia 3.00
83 Ryan Christenson 3.00
84 Pedro Feliz 3.00
85 Jose Ortiz 3.00
86 Xavier Nady 3.00
87 Julio Zuleta 3.00
88 Jason Hart 3.00
89 Keith Ginter 3.00
90 Brent Abernathy 3.00
91 Timo Perez 3.00
92 Juan Pierre 5.00
93 Tike Redman 3.00
94 Mike Lamb 3.00
95 Ben Sheets 5.00
96 Kazuhiro Sasaki 4.00
97 Barry Zito 8.00
98 Adam Bernero 3.00
99 Chad Durbin 3.00
100 Matt Ginter 3.00

2000 Retro Stat Line Career

NM/M
Cards #1-80 print run 251-400: 2-3X
1-80 p/r 151-250: 2-4X
1-80 p/r 101-150: 3-6X
1-80 p/r 76-100: 4-8X
1-80 p/r 51-75: 5-10X
1-80 p/r 31-50: 8-15X
1-80 p/r 21-30: 15-25X
Common (81-100) p/r 251-400: 1.00
Common (81-100) p/r 151-250: 1.00
Common (81-100) p/r 101-150: 2.00
Common (81-100) p/r 76-100: 2.00
Common (81-100) p/r 31-75 3.00

2000 Diamond Kings

NM/M
Complete Set (5): 35.00
Common Player: 8.00
Production 2,500 sets
Studio: 1-2X
Production 250 sets
1 Frank Thomas 8.00
2 Greg Maddux 9.00
3 Alex Rodriguez 10.00
4 Jeff Bagwell 8.00
5 Manny Ramirez 8.00

2001 Diamond Kings

NM/M
Complete Set (20): 150.00
Common Player: 5.00
Production 2,500 sets
Studio Canvas Parallel: 1-2X
Production 250
1 Alex Rodriguez 12.50
2 Cal Ripken Jr. 15.00
3 Mark McGwire 12.50
4 Ken Griffey Jr. 10.00
5 Derek Jeter 15.00
6 Nomar Garciaparra 10.00

7 Mike Piazza 10.00
8 Roger Clemens 9.00
9 Greg Maddux 8.00
10 Chipper Jones 8.00
11 Tony Gwynn 8.00
12 Barry Bonds 15.00
13 Sammy Sosa 10.00
14 Vladimir Guerrero 6.00
15 Frank Thomas 6.00
16 Troy Glaus 6.00
17 Todd Helton 6.00
18 Ivan Rodriguez 5.00
19 Pedro Martinez 6.00
20 Carlos Delgado 5.00

2001 Diamond Kings Studio Series Autograph

NM/M
Common Autograph: 50.00
Production 50 sets
1 Alex Rodriguez 180.00
2 Cal Ripken Jr. 250.00
8 Roger Clemens 150.00
9 Greg Maddux 150.00
10 Chipper Jones 85.00
11 Tony Gwynn 80.00
12 Barry Bonds
14 Vladimir Guerrero 100.00
16 Troy Glaus 50.00
17 Todd Helton 60.00
18 Ivan Rodriguez 60.00

2001 DONRUSS CLASSICS

NM/M
Common Player: .50
Common SP (101-150): 5.00
Production 585
Common SP (151-200): 3.00
Production 1,755
Pack (6): 10.00
Box (18): 150.00
1 Alex Rodriguez 3.00
2 Barry Bonds 3.00
3 Cal Ripken Jr. 4.00
4 Chipper Jones 2.00
5 Derek Jeter 3.00
6 Troy Glaus .75
7 Frank Thomas 1.00
8 Greg Maddux 2.00
9 Ivan Rodriguez 1.00
10 Jeff Bagwell 1.00
11 Cliff Floyd .50
12 Todd Helton 1.00
13 Ken Griffey Jr. 2.00
14 Manny Ramirez 1.00
15 Mark McGwire 3.00
16 Mike Piazza 2.00
17 Nomar Garciaparra 3.00

18	Pedro Martinez	1.50
19	Randy Johnson	1.50
20	Rick Ankiel	.50
21	Rickey Henderson	.75
22	Roger Clemens	3.00
23	Sammy Sosa	2.50
24	Tony Gwynn	1.50
25	Vladimir Guerrero	1.50
26	Kazuhiro Sasaki	.50
27	Roberto Alomar	.75
28	Barry Zito	.75
29	Pat Burrell	.75
30	Harold Baines	.50
31	Carlos Delgado	.75
32	J.D. Drew	.50
33	Jim Edmonds	.75
34	Darin Erstad	.75
35	Jason Giambi	1.00
36	Tom Glavine	.75
37	Juan Gonzalez	1.00
38	Mark Grace	.75
39	Shawn Green	.75
40	Tim Hudson	.75
41	Andruw Jones	.75
42	Jeff Kent	.50
43	Barry Larkin	.75
44	Rafael Furcal	.50
45	Mike Mussina	.75
46	Hideo Nomo	.75
47	Rafael Palmeiro	1.00
48	Scott Rolen	1.00
49	Gary Sheffield	.75
50	Bernie Williams	.75
51	Bob Abreu	.50
52	Edgardo Alfonzo	.50
53	Edgar Martinez	.50
54	Magglio Ordonez	.75
55	Kerry Wood	.75
56	Adrian Beltre	.50
57	Lance Berkman	.75
58	Kevin Brown	.75
59	Sean Casey	.50
60	Eric Chavez	.75
61	Bartolo Colon	.50
62	Johnny Damon	.50
63	Jermaine Dye	.50
64	Juan Encarnacion	.50
65	Carl Everett	.50
66	Brian Giles	.75
67	Mike Hampton	.50
68	Richard Hidalgo	.50
69	Geoff Jenkins	.75
70	Jacque Jones	.50
71	Jason Kendall	.75
72	Ryan Klesko	.75
73	Chan Ho Park	.50
74	Richie Sexson	.75
75	Mike Sweeney	.50
76	Fernando Tatis	.50
77	Miguel Tejada	.75
78	Jose Vidro	.50
79	Larry Walker	.75
80	Preston Wilson	.50
81	Craig Biggio	.75
82	Fred McGriff	.75
83	Jim Thome	1.00
84	Garret Anderson	.75
85	Russell Branyan	.50
86	Tony Batista	.50
87	Terrence Long	.50
88	Brad Fullmer	.50
89	Rusty Greer	.50
90	Orlando Hernandez	.50
91	Gabe Kapler	.50
92	Paul Konerko	.50
93	Carlos Lee	.50
94	Kenny Lofton	.75
95	Raul Mondesi	.50
96	Jorge Posada	.75
97	Tim Salmon	.75
98	Greg Vaughn	.50
99	Mo Vaughn	.50
100	Omar Vizquel	.50
101	Aubrey Huff	5.00
102	Jimmy Rollins	5.00
103	*Cory Aldridge*	5.00
104	*Wilmy Caceres*	5.00
105	Josh Beckett	6.00
106	*Wilson Betemit*	5.00
107	Timo Perez	5.00
108	*Albert Pujols*	200.00
109	*Bud Smith*	5.00
110	*Jack Wilson*	10.00
111	Alex Escobar	5.00
112	*Johnny Estrada*	10.00
113	Pedro Feliz	5.00
114	*Nate Frese*	5.00
115	*Carlos Garcia*	5.00
116	*Brandon Larson*	5.00
117	*Alexis Gomez*	5.00
118	Jason Hart	5.00
119	Adam Dunn	5.00
120	Marcus Giles	5.00
121	*Christian Parker*	5.00
122	*Jackson Melian*	5.00
123	Eric Chavez	5.00
124	*Adrian Hernandez*	5.00
125	*Joe Kennedy*	5.00
126	*Jose Mieses*	5.00
127	C.C. Sabathia	5.00
128	Eric Munson	5.00
129	Xavier Nady	5.00
130	*Horacio Ramirez*	10.00
131	Abraham Nunez	5.00
132	Jose Ortiz	5.00
133	*Jeremy Owens*	5.00
134	*Claudio Vargas*	5.00
135	Corey Patterson	5.00
136	Audres Torres	5.00
137	Ben Sheets	5.00
138	Joe Crede	5.00
139	*Adam Pettyjohn*	5.00
140	*Elpidio Guzman*	5.00
141	*Jay Gibbons*	10.00
142	*Wilkin Ruan*	5.00
143	*Tsuyoshi Shinjo*	10.00
144	Alfonso Soriano	5.00
145	Nick Johnson	5.00
146	*Ichiro Suzuki*	80.00
147	*Juan Uribe*	8.00
148	Jack Cust	5.00
149	*Carlos Valderrama*	5.00
150	*Matt White*	5.00
151	Hank Aaron	10.00
152	Ernie Banks	4.00
153	Johnny Bench	6.00
154	George Brett	10.00
155	Lou Brock	3.00
156	Rod Carew	3.00
157	Steve Carlton	3.00
158	Bob Feller	3.00
159	Bob Gibson	5.00
160	Reggie Jackson	5.00
161	Al Kaline	6.00
162	Sandy Koufax	600.00
163	Don Mattingly	10.00
164	Willie Mays	10.00
165	Willie McCovey	3.00
166	Joe Morgan	3.00
167	Stan Musial	8.00
168	Jim Palmer	3.00
169	Brooks Robinson	5.00
170	Frank Robinson	3.00
171	Nolan Ryan	15.00
172	Mike Schmidt	10.00
173	Tom Seaver	5.00
174	Warren Spahn	4.00
175	Robin Yount	5.00
176	Wade Boggs	4.00
177	Ty Cobb	10.00
178	Lou Gehrig	10.00
179	Luis Aparicio	3.00
180	Babe Ruth	15.00
181	Ryne Sandberg	10.00
182	Yogi Berra	5.00
183	Roberto Clemente	10.00
184	Eddie Murray	5.00
185	Robin Roberts	3.00
186	Duke Snider	5.00
187	Orlando Cepeda	3.00
188	Billy Williams	3.00
189	Juan Marichal	3.00
190	Harmon Killebrew	5.00
191	Kirby Puckett	8.00
192	Carlton Fisk	4.00
193	Dave Winfield	3.00
194	Whitey Ford	4.00
195	Paul Molitor	4.00
196	Tony Perez	3.00
197	Ozzie Smith	6.00
198	Ralph Kiner	3.00
199	Fergie Jenkins	3.00
200	Phil Rizzuto	4.00

Benchmarks

NM/M

Common Player: 5.00
Inserted 1:18

1	Todd Helton	5.00
2	Roberto Clemente	40.00
3	Mark McGwire	30.00
4	Barry Bonds	40.00
5	Bob Gibson	10.00
6	Ken Griffey Jr.	20.00
7	Frank Robinson	8.00
8	Greg Maddux	15.00
9	Reggie Jackson	10.00
10	Sammy Sosa	20.00
11	Willie Stargell	8.00
12	Vladimir Guerrero	8.00
13	Johnny Bench	15.00
14	Tony Gwynn	10.00
15	Mike Schmidt	17.50
16	Ivan Rodriguez	6.00
17	Jeff Bagwell	10.00
18	Cal Ripken Jr.	40.00
20	Kirby Puckett	15.00
21	Frank Thomas	8.00
22	Joe Morgan	5.00
23	Mike Piazza	20.00
24	Hank Aaron	10.00
25	Andruw Jones	5.00

Benchmarks Autographs

NM/M

No pricing due to scarcity

5	Bob Gibson	60.00
7	Frank Robinson	50.00
9	Reggie Jackson	100.00
12	Vladimir Guerrero	
13	Johnny Bench	
15	Mike Schmidt	100.00
20	Kirby Puckett	
22	Joe Morgan	50.00
25	Andruw Jones	60.00

Classic Combos

NM/M

Common Card: 20.00

1	Roberto Clemente	125.00
2	Willie Stargell	25.00
3	Babe Ruth	450.00
4	Lou Gehrig	300.00
5	Hank Aaron	100.00
6	Eddie Mathews	30.00
7	Johnny Bench	40.00
8	Joe Morgan	20.00
9	Robin Yount	40.00
10	Paul Molitor	35.00
11	Steve Carlton	25.00
12	Mike Schmidt	75.00
13	Stan Musial	75.00
14	Lou Brock	20.00
15	Yogi Berra	30.00
16	Phil Rizzuto	25.00
17	Ernie Banks	40.00
18	Billy Williams	20.00
21	Jackie Robinson	60.00
22	Duke Snider	30.00
23	Frank Robinson	25.00
24	Brooks Robinson	40.00
26	Willie McCovey	30.00
27	Ryne Sandberg	60.00
29	Harmon Killebrew	40.00
30	Rod Carew	40.00
31	Roberto Clemente, Willie Stargell	200.00
32	Babe Ruth, Lou Gehrig	1,000
33	Hank Aaron, Eddie Mathews	200.00
34	Johnny Bench, Joe Morgan	80.00
35	Robin Yount, Paul Molitor	100.00
36	Steve Carlton, Mike Schmidt	200.00
37	Stan Musial, Lou Brock	150.00
38	Phil Rizzuto, Yogi Berra	100.00
39	Ernie Banks, Billy Williams	
41	Jackie Robinson, Duke Snider	150.00
42	Brooks Robinson, Frank Robinson	75.00
43	Willie McCovey, Orlando Cepeda	60.00
45	Harmon Killebrew, Rod Carew	100.00

Classic Combos Autographs

No pricing due to scarcity

Legendary Lumberjacks

NM/M

Common Player: 5.00
Inserted 1:18

1	Hack Wilson/244	150.00
2	Chipper Jones	10.00
3	Rogers Hornsby/SP/301	150.00
4	Nellie Fox	100.00
5	Ivan Rodriguez	10.00
6	Jimmie Foxx/300	150.00
7	Hank Aaron	40.00
8	Yogi Berra	15.00
9	Ernie Banks/SP/300	85.00
10	George Brett	25.00
11	Ty Cobb/SP/100	150.00
12	Roberto Clemente	85.00
13	Carlton Fisk	5.00
14	Reggie Jackson	10.00
15	Al Kaline	15.00
16	Harmon Killebrew	15.00
17	Ralph Kiner	5.00
18	Roger Maris/SP/275	150.00
19	Eddie Mathews	25.00
20	Ted Williams/SP/300	200.00
21	Willie McCovey	5.00
22	Eddie Murray	10.00
23	Joe Morgan/SP/268	20.00
24	Frank Robinson	10.00
25	Tony Perez	5.00
26	Mike Schmidt	25.00
27	Ryne Sandberg	25.00
28	Duke Snider/SP/300	25.00
29	Willie Stargell	
30	Billy Williams	5.00
31	Dave Winfield	8.00
32	Robin Yount	10.00
33	Barry Bonds	30.00
34	Stan Musial/SP/300	35.00
35	Johnny Bench/SP/300	20.00
36	Orlando Cepeda	5.00
37	Jeff Bagwell	8.00
38	Frank Thomas	8.00
39	Juan Gonzalez	8.00
40	Cal Ripken Jr.	40.00
41	Rafael Palmeiro	8.00
42	Troy Glaus/SP/100	15.00
43	Manny Ramirez	8.00
44	Paul Molitor	15.00
45	Tony Gwynn	8.00
46	Rod Carew	8.00
47	Lou Brock	8.00
48	Wade Boggs	5.00
49	Babe Ruth/SP	225.00
50	Lou Gehrig/SP	150.00

Legendary Lumberjacks Autographs

NM/M

No pricing due to scarcity

Stadium Stars

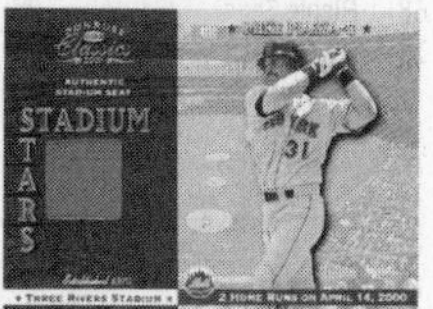

NM/M

Common Player: 4.00
Inserted 1:18

1	Babe Ruth	40.00
2	Cal Ripken Jr.	20.00
3	Brooks Robinson	8.00
4	Tony Gwynn	10.00
5	Ty Cobb	25.00

6	Vladimir Guerrero	8.00
7	Lou Gehrig	35.00
8	Nomar Garciaparra	12.00
9	Sammy Sosa	12.00
10	Reggie Jackson	8.00
11	Alex Rodriguez	12.00
12	Derek Jeter	20.00
13	Willie McCovey	4.00
14	Mark McGwire	15.00
15	Chipper Jones	10.00
16	Honus Wagner	10.00
17	Ken Griffey Jr.	12.00
18	Frank Robinson	8.00
19	Barry Bonds	20.00
20	Yogi Berra	8.00
21	Mike Piazza	12.00
22	Roger Clemens	10.00
23	Duke Snider	8.00
24	Frank Thomas	8.00
25	Andruw Jones	8.00

Stadium Stars Autographs

Common Autograph: No Pricing

Significant Signatures

		NM/M
Common Autograph:		5.00
Inserted 1:18		
101	Aubrey Huff	6.00
103	Cory Aldridge	5.00
105	Josh Beckett/SP	25.00
106	Wilson Betemit	5.00
107	Timo Perez	5.00
108	Albert Pujols	475.00
110	Jack Wilson	10.00
111	Alex Escobar	5.00
112	Johnny Estrada	20.00
113	Pedro Feliz	5.00
114	Nate Frese	5.00
115	Carlos Garcia	5.00
116	Brandon Larson	8.00
118	Jason Hart	5.00
119	Adam Dunn/SP	25.00
120	Marcus Giles	8.00
121	Christian Parker	5.00
126	Jose Mieses	5.00
127	C.C. Sabathia	10.00
129	Xavier Nady	8.00
130	Horacio Ramirez	10.00
131	Abraham Nunez	5.00
132	Jose Ortiz	5.00
133	Jeremy Owens	5.00
134	Claudio Vargas	5.00
135	Corey Patterson/SP	20.00
136	Andres Torres	5.00
137	Ben Sheets/SP	25.00
138	Joe Crede	8.00
139	Adam Pettyjohn	5.00
140	Elpidio Guzman	5.00
141	Jay Gibbons	15.00
142	Wilkin Ruan	5.00
144	Alfonso Soriano/SP	40.00
145	Nick Johnson	10.00
147	Juan Uribe	10.00
149	Carlos Valderrama	5.00
151	Hank Aaron/SP	200.00
152	Ernie Banks	35.00
153	Johnny Bench/SP	100.00
154	George Brett/SP	150.00
155	Lou Brock	15.00
156	Rod Carew	25.00
157	Steve Carlton	25.00
158	Bob Feller	15.00
159	Bob Gibson	25.00
160	Reggie Jackson/SP	65.00
161	Al Kaline	40.00
162	Nolan Ryan/SP	150.00
163	Don Mattingly	80.00
164	Willie Mays/SP	160.00
165	Willie McCovey	20.00
166	Joe Morgan	10.00
167	Stan Musial/SP	85.00
168	Jim Palmer	15.00
169	Brooks Robinson	40.00
170	Frank Robinson	20.00
171	Nolan Ryan/SP	150.00
172	Mike Schmidt	75.00
173	Tom Seaver	30.00
174	Warren Spahn	40.00
175	Robin Yount/SP	100.00
176	Wade Boggs/SP	50.00
179	Luis Aparicio	10.00
181	Ryne Sandberg	75.00
182	Yogi Berra	30.00
184	Eddie Murray	50.00
185	Ron Santo	25.00
186	Duke Snider	25.00
187	Orlando Cepeda	10.00
188	Billy Williams	10.00
189	Juan Marichal	15.00
190	Harmon Killebrew	40.00
191	Kirby Puckett/SP	60.00
192	Carlton Fisk	20.00
193	Dave Winfield/SP	50.00
194	Whitey Ford	25.00
195	Paul Molitor/SP	50.00
196	Tony Perez	15.00
197	Ozzie Smith/SP	80.00
198	Ralph Kiner	25.00
199	Fergie Jenkins	10.00
200	Phil Rizzuto	40.00

Timeless Treasures

		NM/M
Inserted 1:420		
1	Mark McGwire ball	200.00
2	Babe Ruth seat	60.00
3	Harmon Killebrew bat	30.00
4	Derek Jeter base	25.00
5	Barry Bonds ball	85.00

Timeless Tributes

	NM/M
Stars (1-100):	4-8X
SP's (101-150):	1-1.5X
SP's (151-200):	1-2.5X
Production 100 sets	

(See 2001 Donruss Classics for checklist and base cards values.)

2001 DONRUSS CLASS OF 2001

		NM/M
Complete Set (300):		
Common Player:		.20
Common (101-200):		3.00
Production 1,875		
Common (201-300):		3.00
Production 625		
Pack (3):		4.00
Box (24 + bobble head):		80.00
1	Alex Rodriguez	2.00
2	Barry Bonds	2.50
3	Vladimir Guerrero	.75
4	Jim Edmonds	.20
5	Derek Jeter	2.50
6	Jose Canseco	.40
7	Rafael Furcal	.20
8	Cal Ripken Jr.	2.50
9	Brad Radke	.20
10	Miguel Tejada	.40
11	Pat Burrell	.50
12	Ken Griffey Jr.	1.50
13	Cliff Floyd	.20
14	Luis Gonzalez	.30
15	Frank Thomas	.75
16	Mike Sweeney	.20
17	Paul LoDuca	.20
18	Lance Berkman	.20
19	Tony Gwynn	1.00
20	Chipper Jones	1.00
21	Eric Chavez	.40
22	Kerry Wood	.50
23	Jorge Posada	.40
24	J.D. Drew	.50
25	Garret Anderson	.20
26	Mike Piazza	1.50
27	Kenny Lofton	.20
28	Mike Mussina	.40
29	Paul Konerko	.20
30	Bernie Williams	.35
31	Eric Milton	.20
32	Shawn Green	.40
33	Paul O'Neill	.20
34	Juan Gonzalez	.75
35	Andres Galarraga	.20
36	Gary Sheffield	.40
37	Ben Grieve	.20
38	Scott Rolen	.75
39	Mark Grace	.30
40	Hideo Nomo	.50
41	Barry Zito	.50
42	Edgar Martinez	.20
43	Jarrod Washburn	.20
44	Greg Maddux	1.00
45	Mark Buehrle	.20
46	Larry Walker	.20
47	Trot Nixon	.20
48	Nomar Garciaparra	1.50
49	Robert Fick	.20
50	Sean Casey	.40
51	Joe Mays	.20
52	Roger Clemens	1.25
53	Chan Ho Park	.20
54	Carlos Delgado	.50
55	Phil Nevin	.20
56	Jason Giambi	.50
57	Raul Mondesi	.20
58	Roberto Alomar	.40
59	Ryan Klesko	.20
60	Andruw Jones	.75
61	Gabe Kapler	.20
62	Darin Erstad	.60
63	Cristian Guzman	.20
64	Kazuhiro Sasaki	.20
65	Doug Mientkiewicz	.20
66	Sammy Sosa	1.50
67	Mike Hampton	.20
68	Rickey Henderson	.75
69	Mark Mulder	.40
70	Mark McGwire	2.00
71	Freddy Garcia	.20
72	Ivan Rodriguez	.75
73	Terrence Long	.20
74	Jeff Bagwell	.75
75	Moises Alou	.20
76	Todd Helton	.75
77	Preston Wilson	.20
78	Pedro Martinez	.75
79	Bobby Abreu	.20
80	Manny Ramirez	.75
81	Jose Vidro	.20
82	Randy Johnson	.75
83	Richie Sexson	.20
84	Troy Glaus	.75
85	Kevin Brown	.30
86	Carlos Lee	.20
87	Adrian Beltre	.30
88	Brian Giles	.20
89	Jermaine Dye	.20
90	Craig Biggio	.20
91	Richard Hidalgo	.20
92	Magglio Ordonez	.40
93	Aramis Ramirez	.20
94	Jeff Kent	.20
95	Curt Schilling	.50
96	Tim Hudson	.40
97	Fred McGriff	.20
98	Barry Larkin	.20
99	Jim Thome	.20
100	Tom Glavine	.40
101	*Sean Douglass*	3.00
102	*Rob Mackowiak*	3.00
103	*Jeremy Fikac*	3.00
104	*Henry Mateo*	3.00
105	*Geronimo Gil*	3.00
106	*Ramon Vazquez*	5.00
107	*Pedro Santana*	3.00
108	*Ryan Jensen*	3.00
109	*Paul Phillips*	3.00
110	*Saul Rivera*	3.00
111	Larry Bigbie	3.00
112	Josh Phelps	3.00
113	*Justin Kaye*	3.00
114	*Kris Keller*	3.00
115	Adam Bernero	3.00
116	*Victor Zambrano*	3.00
117	Felipe Lopez	3.00
118	*Brian Roberts*	12.00
119	Kurt Ainsworth	3.00
120	*George Perez*	3.00
121	*Wilson Guzman*	3.00
122	*Derrick Lewis*	3.00
123	*Nate Teut*	3.00
124	*Martin Vargas*	3.00
125	Brandon Inge	3.00
126	*Travis Phelps*	3.00
127	*Les Walrond*	3.00
128	*Justin Atchley*	3.00
129	*Stubby Clapp*	3.00
130	*Bret Prinz*	3.00
131	*Bert Snow*	3.00
132	Joe Crede	3.00
133	*Nick Punto*	3.00
134	*Carlos Hernandez*	3.00
135	*Ken Vining*	3.00
136	*Luis Pineda*	3.00
137	*Winston Abreu*	3.00
138	Matt Ginter	3.00
139	*Jason Smith*	3.00
140	*Gene Altman*	3.00
141	*Brian Rogers*	3.00
142	Michael Cuddyer	3.00
143	*Mike Penney*	3.00
144	*Scott Podsednik*	10.00
145	*Esix Snead*	3.00
146	*Steve Watkins*	3.00
147	*Orlando Woodards*	3.00
148	Mike Young	3.00
149	Chris George	3.00
150	*Blaine Neal*	3.00
151	Ben Sheets	3.00
152	*Scott Stewart*	3.00
153	*Mike Koplove*	3.00
154	*Kyle Lohse*	8.00
155	Dee Brown	3.00
156	Aubrey Huff	3.00
157	Pablo Ozuna	3.00
158	Bill Ortega	3.00
159	Toby Hall	3.00
160	*Kevin Olsen*	3.00
161	*Will Ohman*	3.00
162	Nate Cornejo	3.00
163	Jack Cust	3.00
164	Juan Rivera	3.00
165	*Jerrod Riggan*	3.00
166	*Dustan Mohr*	3.00
167	*Doug Nickle*	3.00
168	*Craig Monroe*	3.00
169	Jason Jennings	3.00
170	*Bart Miadich*	3.00
171	Luis Rivas	3.00
172	*Tim Christman*	3.00
173	*Luke Hudson*	3.00
174	*Brett Jodie*	3.00
175	*Jorge Julio*	4.00
176	David Espinosa	3.00
177	*Mike Maroth*	3.00
178	Keith Ginter	3.00
179	*Juan Moreno*	3.00
180	*Brandon Knight*	3.00
181	Steve Lomasney	3.00
182	*John Grabow*	3.00
183	*Steve Green*	3.00
184	*Jason Karnuth*	3.00
185	*Bob File*	3.00
186	Brent Abernathy	3.00
187	*Morgan Ensberg*	12.00
188	Wily Mo Pena	3.00
189	Ken Harvey	3.00
190	*Josh Pearce*	3.00
191	Cesar Izturis	3.00
192	*Eric Hinske*	5.00
193	*Joe Beimel*	3.00
194	Timo Perez	3.00
195	*Troy Mattes*	3.00
196	Eric Valent	3.00
197	*Ed Rogers*	3.00
198	*Grant Balfour*	3.00
199	*Benito Baez*	3.00
200	Vernon Wells	3.00
201	*Joe Kennedy*	4.00
202	*Wilson Betemit*	5.00
203	*Christian Parker*	3.00

204	Jay Gibbons	10.00
205	Carlos Garcia	4.00
206	Jack Wilson	4.00
207	Johnny Estrada	10.00
208	Wilkin Ruan	3.00
209	Brandon Duckworth	5.00
210	Willie Harris	5.00
211	Marlon Byrd	10.00
212	C.C. Sabathia	3.00
213	Dennis Tankersley	5.00
214	Brandon Larson	5.00
215	Alexis Gomez	4.00
216	Bill Hall	5.00
217	Antonio Perez	3.00
218	Jeremy Affeldt	4.00
219	Junior Spivey	8.00
220	Casey Fossum	8.00
221	Brandon Lyon	4.00
222	Angel Santos	4.00
223	Lance Davis	3.00
224	Zach Day	4.00
225	David Williams	3.00
226	Cesar Crespo	3.00
227	Jose Acevedo	3.00
228	Travis Hafner	15.00
229	Orlando Hudson	8.00
230	Jose Mieses	3.00
231	Ricardo Rodriguez	3.00
232	Alfonso Soriano	3.00
233	Jason Hart	3.00
234	Endy Chavez	3.00
235	Delvin James	3.00
236	Ryan Drese	3.00
237	Jeremy Owens	3.00
238	Brad Voyles	3.00
239	Nate Frese	3.00
240	Josh Beckett	3.00
241	Roy Oswalt	3.00
242	Juan Uribe	5.00
243	Cory Aldridge	3.00
244	Adam Dunn	3.00
245	Bud Smith	3.00
246	Adrian Hernandez	3.00
247	Matt Guerrier	3.00
248	Jimmy Rollins	3.00
249	Wilmy Caceres	3.00
250	Jason Michaels	3.00
251	Ichiro Suzuki	60.00
252	John Buck	3.00
253	Andres Torres	3.00
254	Alfredo Amezaga	3.00
255	Corky Miller	3.00
256	Rafael Soriano	10.00
257	Donaldo Mendez	3.00
258	Victor Martinez	50.00
259	Corey Patterson	3.00
260	Horacio Ramirez	8.00
261	Elpidio Guzman	3.00
262	Juan Diaz	3.00
263	Mike Rivera	3.00
264	Brian Lawrence	3.00
265	Josue Perez	3.00
266	Jose Nunez	3.00
267	Erik Bedard	10.00
268	Albert Pujols	150.00
269	Duaner Sanchez	3.00
270	Cody Ransom	3.00
271	Greg Miller	3.00
272	Adam Pettyjohn	3.00
273	Tsuyoshi Shinjo	3.00
274	Claudio Vargas	3.00
275	Justin Duchscherer	5.00
276	Tim Spooneybarger	3.00
277	Rick Bauer	3.00
278	Josh Fogg	5.00
279	Brian Reith	3.00
280	Scott MacRae	3.00
281	Ryan Ludwick	5.00
282	Erick Almonte	3.00
283	Josh Towers	8.00
284	Juan Pena	3.00
285	David Brous	3.00
286	Erik Hiljus	3.00
287	Nick Neugebauer	3.00
288	Jackson Melian	3.00
289	Billy Sylvester	3.00
290	Carlos Valderrama	3.00
291	Jose Cueto	3.00
292	Matt White	3.00
293	Nick Maness	3.00
294	Jason Lane	10.00
295	Brandon Berger	3.00
296	Angel Berroa	6.00
297	Juan Cruz	4.00
298	Dewon Brazelton	3.00
299	Mark Prior	40.00
300	Mark Teixeira	45.00

First Class

Stars (1-100): 5-10X
Production 100
SP's (101-300): 1-3X
Production 50

Aces

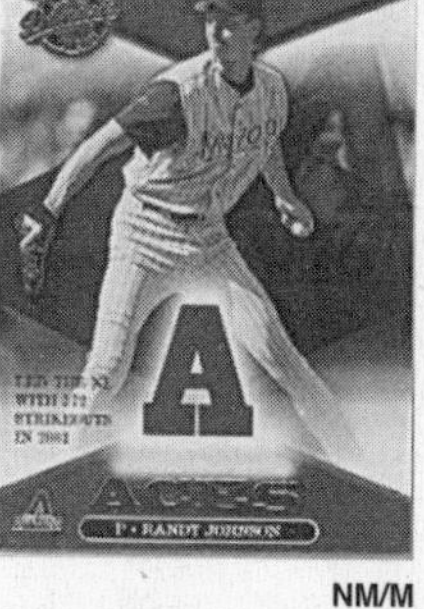

		NM/M
Complete Set (20):		70.00
Common Player:		3.00
Inserted 1:30		
1	Roger Clemens	12.00
2	Randy Johnson	7.50
3	Freddy Garcia	3.00
4	Greg Maddux	10.00
5	Tim Hudson	5.00
6	Curt Schilling	5.00
7	Mark Buehrle	3.00
8	Matt Morris	3.00
9	Joe Mays	3.00
10	Javier Vazquez	3.00
11	Mark Mulder	4.00
12	Wade Miller	3.00
13	Barry Zito	5.00
14	Pedro Martinez	7.50
15	Al Leiter	3.00
16	Chan Ho Park	3.00
17	John Burkett	3.00
18	C.C. Sabathia	3.00
19	Jamie Moyer	3.00
20	Mike Mussina	5.00

Bobblehead

		NM/M
Common Bobblehead:		10.00
One per box		
1	Ichiro Suzuki	40.00
2	Cal Ripken Jr.	40.00
3	Derek Jeter	35.00
4	Mark McGwire	35.00
5	Albert Pujols	40.00
6	Ken Griffey Jr.	20.00
7	Nomar Garciaparra	20.00
8	Mike Piazza	20.00
9	Alex Rodriguez	20.00
10	Manny Ramirez	10.00
11	Tsuyoshi Shinjo	10.00
12	Hideo Nomo	10.00
13	Chipper Jones	15.00
14	Sammy Sosa	20.00
15	Roger Clemens	17.50
16	Tony Gwynn	15.00
17	Barry Bonds	35.00
18	Kazuhiro Sasaki	10.00
19	Pedro Martinez	10.00
20	Jeff Bagwell	10.00
21	Ichiro Suzuki ROY	40.00
22	Albert Pujols ROY	40.00

Bobblehead Cards

		NM/M
Common Player:		4.00
1-20 2,000 produced		
21-22 1,000 produced		
1	Ichiro Suzuki	15.00
2	Cal Ripken Jr.	12.00
3	Derek Jeter	12.00
4	Mark McGwire	10.00
5	Albert Pujols	10.00
6	Ken Griffey Jr.	8.00
7	Nomar Garciaparra	8.00
8	Mike Piazza	8.00
9	Alex Rodriguez	8.00
10	Manny Ramirez	5.00
11	Tsuyoshi Shinjo	4.00
12	Hideo Nomo	4.00
13	Chipper Jones	6.00
14	Sammy Sosa	8.00
15	Roger Clemens	7.00
16	Tony Gwynn	6.00
17	Barry Bonds	15.00
18	Kazuhiro Sasaki	4.00
19	Pedro Martinez	5.00
20	Jeff Bagwell	5.00
21	Ichiro Suzuki	15.00
22	Albert Pujols	15.00

Crusade

		NM/M
Complete Set (25):		125.00
Common Player:		3.00
1	Roger Clemens (275)	15.00
2	Luis Gonzalez (275)	3.00
3	Troy Glaus (275)	6.00
4	Freddy Garcia (300)	3.00
5	Sean Casey (285)	5.00
6	Bobby Abreu (300)	3.00
7	Matt Morris (300)	3.00
8	Cal Ripken Jr. (275)	25.00
9	Miguel Tejada (285)	5.00
10	Vladimir Guerrero (275)	8.00
11	Mark Buehrle (100)	5.00
12	Mike Sweeney (300)	3.00
13	Ivan Rodriguez (275)	8.00
14	Jeff Bagwell (275)	8.00
15	Joe Mays (250)	3.00
16	Cliff Floyd (300)	3.00
17	Lance Berkman (300)	3.00
18	Aramis Ramirez (100)	5.00
19	Tony Gwynn (300)	10.00
20	Shannon Stewart (100)	5.00
21	Todd Helton (275)	8.00
22	Chipper Jones (275)	12.00
23	Javier Vazquez (100)	5.00
24	Shawn Green (275)	5.00
25	Barry Bonds (300)	25.00

Diamond Aces

		NM/M
Common Player:		5.00
Varying quantities produced		
1	Roger Clemens/200	30.00
2	Randy Johnson/750	10.00
3	Freddy Garcia/350	5.00
4	Greg Maddux/750	20.00
5	Tim Hudson/550	8.00
6	Curt Schilling/525	8.00
7	Mark Buehrle/750	5.00
9	Joe Mays/750	5.00
10	Javier Vazquez/500	5.00
11	Mark Mulder/300	6.00
12	Wade Miller/525	5.00
13	Barry Zito/550	8.00
14	Pedro Martinez/550	15.00
15	Al Leiter/525	5.00
16	Chan Ho Park/400	5.00
17	John Burkett/700	5.00
18	C.C. Sabathia/550	5.00
19	Jamie Moyer/700	5.00
20	Mike Mussina/75	

Crusade Autographs

		NM/M
Common Player:		
1	Roger Clemens (25)	
2	Luis Gonzalez (25)	
3	Troy Glaus (25)	
5	Sean Casey (15)	
8	Cal Ripken Jr. (25)	
9	Miguel Tejada (15)	
10	Vladimir Guerrero (25)	
11	Mark Buehrle (200)	10.00
13	Ivan Rodriguez (25)	
14	Jeff Bagwell (25)	
15	Joe Mays (50)	10.00
18	Aramis Ramirez (200)	8.00
20	Shannon Stewart (200)	8.00
21	Todd Helton (25)	
22	Chipper Jones (25)	
23	Javier Vazquez (200)	10.00
24	Shawn Green (25)	
26	Albert Pujols (50)	
27	Wilson Betemit (200)	10.00
28	C.C. Sabathia (10)	
29	Roy Oswalt (200)	12.00
30	Johnny Estrada (200)	8.00
31	Nick Johnson (200)	12.00
32	Aubrey Huff (200)	8.00
33	Corey Patterson (200)	10.00
34	Jay Gibbons (200)	20.00
35	Marcus Giles (200)	8.00
36	Juan Cruz (200)	8.00
38	Ben Sheets (15)	
39	Bud Smith (200)	8.00
40	Alex Escobar (200)	8.00
41	Joe Kennedy (200)	8.00
42	Alexis Gomez (200)	10.00
44	Josh Towers (200)	8.00
45	Joe Crede (200)	10.00
46	Brandon Duckworth (200)	12.00
48	Jose Ortiz (200)	8.00
49	Casey Fossum (200)	12.00
50	Adam Dunn (100)	30.00

Diamond Dominators

		NM/M
Common Player:		4.00
Varying quantities produced		
1	Manny Ramirez/725	8.00
2	Lance Berkman/725	4.00
3	Juan Gonzalez/500	6.00
4	Albert Pujols/125	65.00
5	Jason Giambi/250	8.00
6	Mike Sweeney/325	4.00
7	Rafael Palmeiro/550	8.00

8	Luis Gonzalez/725	4.00
9	Ichiro Suzuki/50	
10	Cliff Floyd/725	4.00
11	Roberto Alomar/200	8.00
12	Paul LoDuca/600	4.00
13	Shannon Stewart/725	6.00
14	Barry Bonds/250	30.00
15	Larry Walker/725	6.00
16	Shawn Green/500	6.00
17	Moises Alou/550	4.00
18	Cal Ripken/250	50.00
19	Brian Giles/725	5.00
20	Maggio Ordonez/725	5.00
21	Jose Vidro/725	4.00
22	Edgar Martinez/200	6.00
23	Aramis Ramirez/200	5.00
24	Tony Gwynn/500	10.00
25	Richie Sexson/725	6.00
26	Todd Helton/725	8.00
27	Garret Anderson/725	6.00
28	Chipper Jones/725	12.00
29	Troy Glaus/200	8.00
30	Jeff Bagwell/325	8.00

Dominators

		NM/M
Complete Set (30):		90.00
Common Player:		2.00
Inserted 1:20		
1	Manny Ramirez	4.00
2	Lance Berkman	2.00
3	Juan Gonzalez	4.00
4	Albert Pujols	10.00
5	Jason Giambi	3.00
6	Mike Sweeney	2.00
7	Rafael Palmeiro	4.00
8	Luis Gonzalez	2.00
9	Ichiro Suzuki	10.00
10	Cliff Floyd	2.00
11	Roberto Alomar	4.00
12	Paul LoDuca	2.00
13	Shannon Stewart	2.00
14	Barry Bonds	10.00
15	Larry Walker	2.00
16	Shawn Green	3.00
17	Moises Alou	2.00
18	Cal Ripken Jr.	10.00
19	Brian Giles	2.00
20	Magglio Ordonez	3.00
21	Jose Vidro	2.00
22	Edgar Martinez	2.00
23	Aramis Ramirez	2.00
24	Tony Gwynn	5.00
25	Richie Sexson	2.00
26	Todd Helton	4.00
27	Garret Anderson	2.00
28	Chipper Jones	5.00
29	Troy Glaus	4.00
30	Jeff Bagwell	4.00

Final Rewards

		NM/M
Common Player:		5.00
Varying quantities produced		
1	Jason Giambi/250	10.00
2	Ichiro Suzuki/50	120.00
3	Roger Clemens/200	30.00
4	Freddy Garcia/250	5.00
5	Ichiro Suzuki/50	120.00
6	Albert Pujols/125	60.00
7	Barry Bonds/250	40.00
8	Albert Pujols/125	60.00
9	Randy Johnson/250	15.00

First Class Autographs

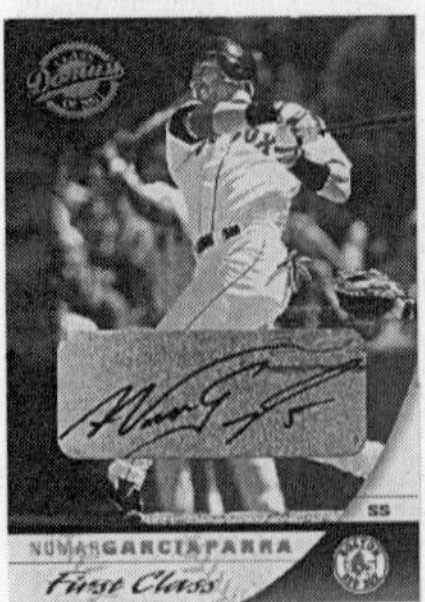

		NM/M
10	Miguel Tejada/75	50.00
21	Eric Chavez/100	20.00
41	Barry Zito/100	30.00
45	Mark Buehrle/100	15.00
50	Sean Casey/100	25.00
51	Joe Mays/100	15.00
59	Ryan Klesko/50	20.00
69	Mark Mulder/100	25.00
73	Terrence Long/100	15.00
81	Jose Vidro/100	15.00
83	Richie Sexson/100	25.00
84	Troy Glaus/100	40.00
91	Richard Hidalgo/100	15.00
96	Tim Hudson/100	25.00

Rewards

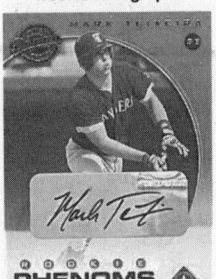

		NM/M
Common Player:		5.00
Inserted 1:212		
1	Jason Giambi	7.50
2	Ichiro Suzuki	40.00
3	Roger Clemens	20.00
4	Freddy Garcia	5.00
5	Ichiro Suzuki	40.00
6	Albert Pujols	30.00
7	Barry Bonds	30.00
8	Albert Pujols	30.00
9	Randy Johnson	10.00
10	Matt Morris	5.00

Rookie Autographs

		NM/M
Common Autograph:		8.00
109	Paul Phillips/250	8.00
114	Kris Keller/250	8.00
115	Adam Bernero/250	8.00
120	George Perez/250	8.00
123	Nate Teut/250	8.00
124	Martin Vargas/250	8.00
127	Les Walrond/250	8.00
132	Joe Crede/250	10.00
137	Winston Abreu/250	8.00
138	Matt Ginter/250	8.00
140	Gene Altman/250	8.00
142	Michael Cuddyer/250	8.00
143	Mike Penney/250	8.00
145	Esix Snead/250	8.00
147	Orlando Woodards/250	8.00
148	Jeff Deardorff/100	8.00
150	Blaine Neal/250	8.00
156	Aubrey Huff/250	10.00
157	Pablo Ozuna/250	8.00
158	Bill Ortega/250	8.00
160	Kevin Olsen/250	8.00
161	Will Ohman/250	8.00
163	Jack Cust/250	8.00
168	Craig Monroe/250	8.00
169	Jason Jennings/250	8.00
171	Luis Rivas/250	8.00
173	Luke Hudson/250	12.00
176	David Espinosa/250	8.00
177	Mike Maroth/250	8.00
178	Keith Ginter/250	8.00
181	Steve Lomasney/250	8.00
182	John Grabow/250	8.00
184	Jason Karnuth/250	8.00
186	Brent Abernathy/250	8.00
188	Wily Mo Pena/250	15.00
191	Cesar Izturis/250	8.00
192	Eric Hinske/250	10.00
194	Timo Perez/100	8.00
196	Eric Valent/250	8.00
201	Joe Kennedy/100	8.00
202	Wilson Betemit/100	15.00
203	Christian Parker/100	8.00
204	Jay Gibbons/100	20.00
205	Carlos Garcia/200	8.00
206	Jack Wilson/100	15.00
207	Johnny Estrada/100	20.00
208	Wilkin Ruan/200	8.00
209	Brandon Duckworth/100	8.00
211	Marlon Byrd/100	20.00
212	C.C. Sabathia/25	
213	Dennis Tankersley/100	10.00
214	Brandon Larson/200	8.00
215	Alexis Gomez/200	10.00
216	Bill Hall/100	8.00
217	Antonio Perez/100	8.00
218	Jeremy Affeldt/200	10.00
220	Casey Fossum/200	10.00
224	Zach Day/200	8.00
225	David Williams/200	8.00
227	Jose Acevedo/200	8.00
229	Orlando Hudson/100	15.00
230	Jose Mieses/200	8.00
231	Ric Rodriguez/200	8.00
232	Alfonso Soriano/100	40.00
233	Jason Hart/100	8.00
234	Endy Chavez/200	8.00
235	Delvin James/100	8.00
237	Jeremy Owens/200	8.00
238	Brad Voyles/200	8.00
239	Nate Frese/200	8.00
240	Josh Beckett/25	60.00
241	Roy Oswalt/100	25.00
242	Juan Uribe/150	10.00
243	Cory Aldridge/200	8.00
244	Adam Dunn/100	30.00
245	Bud Smith/100	8.00
246	Adrian Hernandez/100	8.00
249	Wilmy Caceres/200	8.00
250	Jason Michaels/200	8.00
252	John Buck/100	15.00
253	Andres Torres/100	8.00
255	Corky Miller/100	8.00
256	Rafael Soriano/200	10.00
257	Donaldo Mendez/200	8.00
259	Corey Patterson/100	15.00
260	Horacio Ramirez/200	10.00
261	Elpidio Guzman/200	8.00
262	Juan Diaz/200	8.00
264	Brian Lawrence/200	10.00
265	Josue Perez/200	8.00
266	Jose Nunez/200	8.00
268	Albert Pujols/100	500.00
269	Duaner Sanchez/200	8.00
271	Greg Miller/200	8.00
272	Adam Pettyjohn/200	8.00
274	Claudio Vargas/200	8.00
279	Brian Reith/200	8.00
283	Josh Towers/100	8.00
285	David Brous/200	8.00
287	Nick Neugebauer/100	8.00
289	Billy Sylvester/200	8.00
290	Carlos Valderrama/200	8.00
292	Matt White/200	8.00
293	Nick Maness/200	8.00
296	Angel Berroa/100	15.00
297	Juan Cruz/100	8.00
298	Dewon Brazelton/100	8.00
299	Mark Prior/100	200.00
300	Mark Teixeira/100	275.00

Rookie Crusade

		NM/M
Complete Set (25):		110.00
Common Player:		3.00
26	Albert Pujols (250)	30.00
27	Wilson Betemit (100)	3.00
28	C.C. Sabathia (290)	3.00
29	Roy Oswalt (100)	4.00
30	Johnny Estrada (100)	3.00
31	Nick Johnson (100)	4.00
32	Aubrey Huff (100)	3.00
33	Corey Patterson (200)	4.00
34	Jay Gibbons (100)	4.00
35	Marcus Giles (100)	3.00
36	Juan Cruz (100)	3.00
37	Tsuyoshi Shinjo (300)	3.00
38	Ben Sheets (285)	3.00
39	Bud Smith (100)	3.00
40	Alex Escobar (100)	3.00
41	Joe Kennedy (100)	3.00
42	Alexis Gomez (100)	3.00
43	Jimmy Rollins (300)	3.00
44	Josh Towers (100)	3.00
45	Joe Crede (100)	3.00
46	Brandon Duckworth (100)	3.00
47	Ichiro Suzuki (300)	40.00
48	Jose Ortiz (100)	3.00
49	Casey Fossum (100)	3.00
50	Adam Dunn (200)	5.00

Rookie Team

		NM/M
Complete Set (15):		65.00
Common Player:		3.00
Inserted 1:83		
1	Jay Gibbons	5.00
2	Alfonso Soriano	6.00
3	Jimmy Rollins	3.00
4	Wilson Betemit	3.00
5	Albert Pujols	20.00
6	Johnny Estrada	3.00
7	Ichiro Suzuki	15.00
8	Tsuyoshi Shinjo	4.00
9	Adam Dunn	5.00
10	C.C. Sabathia	3.00
11	Ben Sheets	3.00
12	Roy Oswalt	4.00
13	Bud Smith	3.00
14	Josh Towers	3.00
15	Juan Cruz	3.00

Rookie Team Materials

		NM/M
Common Player:		5.00
Varying quantities produced		
1	Jay Gibbons/100	8.00
2	Alfonso Soriano/100	15.00
3	Jimmy Rollins/200	5.00
4	Wilson Betemit/100	
5	Albert Pujols/100	65.00
6	Johnny Estrada/100	5.00
7	Ichiro Suzuki/50	120.00
8	Tsuyoshi Shinjo/200	10.00
9	Adam Dunn/200	8.00
10	C.C. Sabathia/200	5.00
11	Ben Sheets/200	5.00
12	Roy Oswalt/50	
13	Bud Smith/250	5.00
14	Josh Towers/200	5.00
15	Juan Cruz/200	5.00

Yearbook

		NM/M
Complete Set (25):		85.00
Common Player:		2.00
Inserted 1:24		
1	Barry Bonds	12.00
2	Mark Mulder	3.00
3	Luis Gonzalez	2.00

4 Lance Berkman 2.00
5 Matt Morris 2.00
6 Roy Oswalt 2.50
7 Todd Helton 3.00
8 Tsuyoshi Shinjo 2.00
9 C.C. Sabathia 2.00
10 Curt Schilling 3.00
11 Rickey Henderson 3.00
12 Jamie Moyer 2.00
13 Shawn Green 3.00
14 Randy Johnson 4.00
15 Jim Thome 2.00
16 Larry Walker 2.00
17 Jimmy Rollins 2.00
18 Kazuhiro Sasaki 2.00
19 Hideo Nomo 3.00
20 Roger Clemens 7.50
21 Bud Smith 2.00
22 Ichiro Suzuki 10.00
23 Albert Pujols 15.00
24 Cal Ripken Jr. 15.00
25 Tony Gwynn 5.00

Yearbook Scrapbook

NM/M
Common Player: 4.00
Varying quantities produced
1 Barry Bonds/525 30.00
2 Mark Mulder/500 6.00
3 Luis Gonzalez/500 4.00
4 Lance Berkman/525 4.00
6 Roy Oswalt/150 6.00
7 Todd Helton/525 6.00
8 Tsuyoshi Shinjo/75 15.00
9 C.C. Sabathia/500 4.00
10 Curt Schilling/525 6.00
11 Rickey Henderson/200 15.00
12 Jamie Moyer/500 4.00
13 Shawn Green/525 5.00
14 Randy Johnson/500 8.00
15 Jim Thome/400 4.00
16 Larry Walker/500 4.00
17 Jimmy Rollins/25
18 Kazuhiro Sasaki/500 4.00
19 Hideo Nomo/150 50.00
20 Roger Clemens/475 20.00
21 Bud Smith/525 4.00
22 Ichiro Suzuki/75 80.00
23 Albert Pujols/150 50.00
24 Cal Ripken/525 30.00
25 Tony Gwynn/500 10.00

2001 DONRUSS ELITE

NM/M
Complete Set (200):
Common Player: .25
Common (151-200): 5.00
Production 900
Common 201-250: 4.00
(#201-250 available by redemption)
Pack (5): 12.00
Box (18): 180.00
1 Alex Rodriguez 2.00
2 Barry Bonds 2.50
3 Cal Ripken Jr. 2.50
4 Chipper Jones 1.50
5 Derek Jeter 2.50
6 Troy Glaus 1.00
7 Frank Thomas 1.00
8 Greg Maddux 1.50
9 Ivan Rodriguez .75
10 Jeff Bagwell 1.00
11 Jose Canseco .50
12 Todd Helton 1.00
13 Ken Griffey Jr. 1.75
14 Manny Ramirez 1.00
15 Mark McGwire 2.00
16 Mike Piazza 1.75
17 Nomar Garciaparra 1.75
18 Pedro Martinez 1.00
19 Randy Johnson 1.00
20 Rick Ankiel .40
21 Ricky Henderson .75
22 Roger Clemens 1.50
23 Sammy Sosa 1.75
24 Tony Gwynn 1.50
25 Vladimir Guerrero 1.00
26 Eric Davis .25
27 Roberto Alomar .40
28 Mark Mulder .50
29 Pat Burrell .50
30 Harold Baines .25
31 Carlos Delgado .60
32 J.D. Drew .40
33 Jim Edmonds .25
34 Darin Erstad .60
35 Jason Giambi .50
36 Tom Glavine .50
37 Juan Gonzalez 1.00
38 Mark Grace .35
39 Shawn Green .40
40 Tim Hudson .40
41 Andruw Jones .75
42 David Justice .25
43 Jeff Kent .25
44 Barry Larkin .25
45 Pokey Reese .25
46 Mike Mussina .40
47 Hideo Nomo .60
48 Rafael Palmeiro .65
49 Adam Piatt .25
50 Scott Rolen 1.00
51 Gary Sheffield .40
52 Bernie Williams .40
53 Bob Abreu .25
54 Edgardo Alfonzo .25
55 *Jermaine Clark* .40
56 Albert Belle .25
57 Craig Biggio .25
58 Andres Galarraga .25
59 Edgar Martinez .25
60 Fred McGriff .25
61 Maggio Ordonez .40
62 Jim Thome .25
63 Matt Williams .25
64 Kerry Wood .50
65 Moises Alou .25
66 Brady Anderson .25
67 Garret Anderson .25
68 Tony Armas Jr. .25
69 Tony Batista .25
70 Jose Cruz Jr. .25
71 Carlos Beltran .50
72 Adrian Beltre .40
73 Kris Benson .25
74 Lance Berkman .25
75 Kevin Brown .35
76 Jay Buhner .25
77 Jeromy Burnitz .25
78 Ken Caminiti .25
79 Sean Casey .40
80 Luis Castillo .25
81 Eric Chavez .40
82 Jeff Cirillo .25
83 Bartolo Colon .25
84 David Cone .25
85 Freddy Garcia .25
86 Johnny Damon .40
87 Ray Durham .25
88 Jermaine Dye .25
89 Juan Encarnacion .25
90 Terrence Long .25
91 Carl Everett .25
92 Steve Finley .25
93 Cliff Floyd .25
94 Brad Fulmer .25
95 Brian Giles .25
96 Luis Gonzalez .35
97 Rusty Greer .25
98 Jeffrey Hammonds .25
99 Mike Hampton .25
100 Orlando Hernandez .40
101 Richard Hidalgo .25
102 Geoff Jenkins .25
103 Jacque Jones .25
104 Brian Jordan .25
105 Gabe Kapler .25
106 Eric Karros .25
107 Jason Kendall .25
108 Adam Kennedy .25
109 Byung-Hyun Kim .25
110 Ryan Klesko .25
111 Chuck Knoblauch .25
112 Paul Konerko .25
113 Carlos Lee .25
114 Kenny Lofton .25
115 Javy Lopez .25
116 Tino Martinez .25
117 Ruben Mateo .25
118 Kevin Millwood .25
119 Ben Molina .25
120 Raul Mondesi .25
121 Trot Nixon .25
122 John Olerud .25
123 Paul O'Neill .25
124 Chan Ho Park .25
125 Andy Pettitte .40
126 Jorge Posada .40
127 Mark Quinn .25
128 Aramis Ramirez .25
129 Mariano Rivera .35
130 Tim Salmon .35
131 Curt Schilling .40
132 Richie Sexson .25
133 John Smoltz .25
134 J.T. Snow .25
135 Jay Payton .25
136 Shannon Stewart .25
137 B.J. Surhoff .25
138 Mike Sweeney .25
139 Fernando Tatis .25
140 Miguel Tejada .40
141 Jason Varitek .25
142 Greg Vaughn .25
143 Mo Vaughn .25
144 Robin Ventura .25
145 Jose Vidro .25
146 Omar Vizquel .25
147 Larry Walker .25
148 David Wells .25
149 Rondell White .25
150 Preston Wilson .25
151 Brent Abernathy 5.00
152 *Cory Aldridge* 5.00
153 *Gene Altman* 5.00
154 Josh Beckett 6.00
155 *Wilson Betemit* 5.00
156 *Albert Pujols* 300.00
157 Joe Crede 5.00
158 Jack Cust 5.00
159 Ben Sheets 5.00
160 Alex Escobar 5.00
161 *Adrian Hernandez* 5.00
162 Pedro Feliz 5.00
163 *Nate Frese* 5.00
164 *Carlos Garcia* 5.00
165 Marcus Giles 5.00
166 *Alexis Gomez* 5.00
167 Jason Hart 5.00
168 Aubrey Huff 5.00
169 Cesar Izturis 5.00
170 Nick Johnson 5.00
171 *Jack Wilson* 10.00
172 *Brian Lawrence* 5.00
173 *Christian Parker* 5.00
174 *Nick Maness* 5.00
175 *Jose Mieses* 5.00
176 *Greg Miller* 5.00
177 Eric Munson 5.00
178 Xavier Nady 5.00
179 *Blaine Neal* 5.00
180 Abraham Nunez 5.00
181 Jose Ortiz 5.00
182 *Jeremy Owens* 5.00
183 *Jay Gibbons* 10.00
184 Corey Patterson 5.00
185 Carlos Pena 5.00
186 C.C. Sabathia 5.00
187 Timo Perez 5.00
188 *Adam Pettyjohn* 5.00
189 *Donaldo Mendez* 5.00
190 *Jackson Melian* 5.00
191 *Wilken Ruan* 5.00
192 *Duaner Sanchez* 5.00
193 Alfonso Soriano 5.00
194 *Rafael Soriano* 10.00
195 *Ichiro Suzuki* 150.00
196 *Billy Sylvester* 5.00
197 *Juan Uribe* 5.00
198 *Tsuyoshi Shinjo* 10.00
199 *Carlos Valderrama* 5.00
200 *Matt White* 5.00
201 Adam Dunn 6.00
202 Joe Kennedy 4.00
203 Mike Rivera 4.00
204 Erick Almonte 4.00
205 Brandon Duckworth 4.00
206 *Victor Martinez* 125.00
207 Rick Bauer 4.00
208 Jeff Deardorff 4.00
209 Antonio Perez 4.00
210 Bill Hall 4.00
211 Dennis Tankersley 6.00
212 Jeremy Affeldt 8.00
213 Junior Spivey 8.00
214 Casey Fossum 6.00
215 Brandon Lyon 4.00
216 Angel Santos 4.00
217 Cody Ransom 4.00
218 Jason Lane 35.00
219 David Williams 4.00
220 Alex Herrera 4.00
221 Ryan Drese 4.00
222 Travis Hafner 40.00
223 Bud Smith 4.00
224 Johnny Estrada 25.00
225 Ricardo Rodriguez 4.00
226 Brandon Berger 4.00
227 Claudio Vargas 4.00
228 Luis Garcia 4.00
229 Marlon Byrd 20.00
230 Hee Seop Choi 20.00
231 Corky Miller 4.00
232 Justin Duchscherer 6.00
233 Tim Spooneybarger 4.00
234 Roy Oswalt 4.00
235 Willie Harris 4.00
236 Josh Towers 4.00
237 Juan Pena 4.00
238 Alfredo Amezaga 4.00
239 Geronimo Gil 4.00
240 Juan Cruz 4.00
241 Ed Rogers 4.00
242 Joe Thurston 4.00
243 *Orlando Hudson* 10.00
244 *John Buck* 8.00
245 Martin Vargas 4.00
246 David Brous 4.00
247 Dewon Brazelton 4.00
248 Mark Prior 90.00
249 Angel Berroa 10.00
250 Mark Teixeira 100.00

Aspirations

Cards 1-150 print run 76-100: 5-10X
1-150 p/r 51-75: 8-15X
1-150 p/r 26-50: 10-25X
Cards 151-200 print run 76-100: 1X
151-200 p/r 51-75: 1.5X
151-200 p/r 26-50: 1.5-2X
Varying quantities produced

Status

Cards 1-150 print run 76-100: 5-10X
1-150 p/r 51-75: 8-15X
1-150 p/r 26-50: 10-25X
Cards 151-200 print run 76-100: 1X
151-200 p/r 51-75: 1.5X
151-200 p/r 26-50: 1.5-2X
Varying quantities produced

Back 2 Back Jacks

NM/M
Common Player: 15.00
Singles production 100
Doubles production 50
SP print runs listed
1 Ernie Banks/75 20.00
2 Ryne Sandberg/75 40.00
3 Babe Ruth 200.00
4 Lou Gehrig 150.00
5 Eddie Matthews 25.00

6	Troy Glaus	15.00
7	Don Mattingly/50	50.00
8	Todd Helton	20.00
9	Wade Boggs	15.00
10	Tony Gwynn	25.00
11	Robin Yount	25.00
12	Paul Molitor/50	25.00
13	Mike Schmidt/50	40.00
14	Scott Rolen/75	20.00
15	Reggie Jackson	20.00
16	Dave Winfield	15.00
17	Johnny Bench/50	40.00
18	Joe Morgan	15.00
19	Brooks Robinson/50	40.00
20	Cal Ripken Jr.	50.00
21	Ty Cobb	100.00
22	Al Kaline/50	40.00
23	Frank Robinson/50	25.00
24	Frank Thomas	20.00
25	Roberto Clemente	80.00
26	Vladimir Guerrero/50	25.00
27	Harmon Killebrew/50	25.00
28	Kirby Puckett	20.00
29	Yogi Berra/75	35.00
30	Phil Rizzuto/75	30.00
31	Ernie Banks, Ryne Sandberg	80.00
32	Babe Ruth, Lou Gehrig	350.00
33	Troy Glaus, Eddie Matthews	40.00
34	Don Mattingly, Todd Helton	100.00
35	Tony Gwynn, Wade Boggs	75.00
36	Paul Molitor, Robin Yount	50.00
37	Mike Schmidt, Scott Rolen	80.00
38	Dave Winfield, Reggie Jackson	40.00
39	Joe Morgan, Johnny Bench	50.00
40	Brooks Robinson, Cal Ripken Jr.	100.00
41	Al Kaline, Ty Cobb	175.00
42	Frank Robinson, Frank Thomas	40.00
43	Roberto Clemente, Vladimir Guerrero	100.00
44	Harmon Killebrew, Kirby Puckett	50.00
45	Phil Rizzuto, Yogi Berra/25	100.00

Back 2 Back Jacks Autograph

		NM/M
Common Autograph:		60.00
Print runs listed		
1	Ernie Banks/25	200.00
2	Ryne Sandberg/25	250.00
6	Troy Glaus/50	50.00
7	Don Mattingly/50	200.00
12	Paul Molitor/50	75.00
13	Mike Schmidt/50	150.00
14	Scott Rolen/25	60.00
17	Johnny Bench/50	100.00
19	Brooks Robinson/50	75.00
22	Al Kaline/50	100.00
23	Frank Robinson/50	50.00
26	Vladimir Guerrero/50	100.00
27	Harmon Killebrew/50	100.00
29	Yogi Berra/25	125.00
30	Phil Rizzuto/25	125.00
45	Phil Rizzuto, Yogi Berra/25	200.00

Passing the Torch

		NM/M
Common Player:		3.00
Singles production 1,000		
Doubles production 500		
1	Stan Musial	8.00
2	Tony Gwynn	6.00
3	Willie Mays	10.00
4	Barry Bonds	15.00
5	Mike Schmidt	10.00
6	Scott Rolen	4.00
7	Cal Ripken Jr.	15.00
8	Alex Rodriguez	10.00
9	Hank Aaron	10.00
10	Andruw Jones	4.00
11	Nolan Ryan	15.00
12	Pedro Martinez	5.00
13	Wade Boggs	6.00
14	Nomar Garciaparra	8.00
15	Don Mattingly	10.00
16	Todd Helton	5.00
17	Stan Musial, Tony Gwynn	10.00
18	Barry Bonds, Willie Mays	20.00
19	Mike Schmidt, Scott Rolen	15.00
20	Alex Rodriguez, Cal Ripken Jr.	25.00
21	Andruw Jones, Hank Aaron	15.00
22	Nolan Ryan, Pedro Martinez	25.00
23	Nomar Garciaparra, Wade Boggs	15.00
24	Don Mattingly, Todd Helton	15.00

Passing the Torch Autographs

		NM/M
Common Player:		30.00
Singles production 100		
Doubles production 50		
1	Stan Musial	100.00
2	Tony Gwynn	75.00
3	Willie Mays	200.00
4	Barry Bonds	275.00
5	Mike Schmidt	100.00
6	Scott Rolen	50.00
7	Cal Ripken Jr.	150.00
8	Alex Rodriguez	120.00
9	Hank Aaron	200.00
10	Andruw Jones	30.00
11	Nolan Ryan	125.00
12	Pedro Martinez	75.00
13	Wade Boggs	30.00
14	Nomar Garciaparra	125.00
15	Don Mattingly	100.00
16	Todd Helton	40.00
17	Stan Musial, Tony Gwynn	175.00
18	Barry Bonds, Willie Mays	900.00
19	Mike Schmidt, Scott Rolen	150.00
20	Alex Rodriguez, Cal Ripken Jr.	400.00
21	Andruw Jones, Hank Aaron	250.00
22	Nolan Ryan, Pedro Martinez	300.00
22	Nolan Ryan, Roger Clemens FB redemp.	375.00
23	Wade Boggs FB Redemp.	25.00
24	Don Mattingly, Todd Helton	200.00

Primary Colors

		NM/M
Complete Set (40):		100.00
Common Player:		1.00
Production 975 sets		
Red Die-Cut:		3-5X
Production 25		
Blues:		1-1.5X
Production 200		
Blue Die-Cut:		1.5-3X
Production 50		
Yellows:		3-5X
Production 25		
Yellow Die-Cut:		1.5-2X
Production 75		
1	Alex Rodriguez	8.00
2	Barry Bonds	10.00
3	Cal Ripken Jr.	10.00
4	Chipper Jones	5.00
5	Derek Jeter	10.00
6	Troy Glaus	4.00
7	Frank Thomas	4.00
8	Greg Maddux	5.00
9	Ivan Rodriguez	2.50
10	Jeff Bagwell	4.00
11	Todd Helton	4.00
12	Ken Griffey Jr.	6.00
13	Manny Ramirez	4.00
14	Mark McGwire	8.00
15	Mike Piazza	6.00
16	Nomar Garciaparra	6.00
17	Pedro Martinez	4.00
18	Randy Johnson	4.00
19	Rick Ankiel	1.25
20	Roger Clemens	5.50
21	Sammy Sosa	6.00
22	Tony Gwynn	5.00
23	Vladimir Guerrero	4.00
24	Carlos Delgado	2.00
25	Jason Giambi	2.50
26	Andruw Jones	4.00
27	Bernie Williams	1.50
28	Roberto Alomar	1.50
29	Shawn Green	1.50
30	Barry Larkin	1.00
31	Scott Rolen	3.00
32	Gary Sheffield	2.00
33	Rafael Palmeiro	3.00
34	Albert Belle	1.00
35	Magglio Ordonez	1.50
36	Jim Thome	1.00
37	Jim Edmonds	1.00
38	Darin Erstad	2.00
39	Kris Benson	1.00
40	Sean Casey	1.50

Prime Numbers

		NM/M
Print runs listed		
1a	Alex Rodriguez/300	8.00
1b	Alex Rodriguez/308	8.00
1c	Alex Rodriguez/350	8.00
2a	Ken Griffey Jr./400	6.00
2b	Ken Griffey Jr./408	6.00
2c	Ken Griffey Jr./430	6.00
3a	Mark McGwire/500	8.00
3b	Mark McGwire/504	8.00
3c	Mark McGwire/550	8.00
4a	Cal Ripken Jr./400	10.00
4b	Cal Ripken Jr./407	10.00
4c	Cal Ripken Jr./410	10.00
5a	Derek Jeter/300	10.00
5b	Derek Jeter/302	10.00
5c	Derek Jeter/320	10.00
6a	Mike Piazza/300	6.00
6b	Mike Piazza/302	6.00
6c	Mike Piazza/360	6.00
7a	Nomar Garciaparra/300	6.00
7b	Nomar Garciaparra/302	6.00
7c	Nomar Garciaparra/370	6.00
8a	Sammy Sosa/300	6.00
8b	Sammy Sosa/306	6.00
8c	Sammy Sosa/380	6.00
9a	Vladimir Guerrero/300	4.00
9b	Vladimir Guerrero/305	4.00
9c	Vladimir Guerrero/340	4.00
10a	Tony Gwynn/300	4.00
10b	Tony Gwynn/304	4.00
10c	Tony Gwynn/390	4.00

Throwback Threads

		NM/M
Common Player:		15.00
Singles production 100		
Doubles production 50		
SP production listed		
1	Stan Musial/75	50.00
2	Tony Gwynn/75	25.00
3	Willie McCovey	15.00
4	Barry Bonds	50.00
5	Babe Ruth	250.00
6	Lou Gehrig	200.00
7	Mike Schmidt/75	40.00
8	Scott Rolen	20.00
9	Harmon Killebrew/75	30.00
10	Kirby Puckett	20.00
11	Al Kaline/75	40.00
12	Eddie Matthews	25.00
13	Hank Aaron/75	60.00
14	Andruw Jones/50	20.00
15	Lou Brock	15.00
16	Ozzie Smith	25.00
17	Ernie Banks/75	35.00
18	Ryne Sandberg	50.00
19	Roberto Clemente	100.00
20	Vladimir Guerrero/50	30.00
21	Frank Robinson/50	25.00
22	Frank Thomas	15.00
23	Brooks Robinson/50	25.00
24	Cal Ripken Jr.	50.00
25	Roger Clemens	30.00
26	Pedro Martinez	20.00
27	Reggie Jackson	15.00
28	Dave Winfield	15.00
29	Don Mattingly/50	60.00
30	Todd Helton	15.00
31	Stan Musial, Tony Gwynn/25	120.00
32	Barry Bonds, Willie McCovey	85.00
33	Babe Ruth, Lou Gehrig	500.00
34	Mike Schmidt, Scott Rolen/25	150.00
35	Harmon Killebrew, Kirby Puckett	50.00
36	Al Kaline, Eddie Matthews	50.00
37	Andruw Jones, Hank Aaron	85.00
38	Lou Brock, Ozzie Smith	50.00
39	Ernie Banks, Ryne Sandberg/25	125.00
40	Roberto Clemente, Vladimir Guerrero	90.00
41	Frank Robinson, Frank Thomas	40.00
42	Brooks Robinson, Cal Ripken Jr.	85.00
43	Pedro Martinez, Roger Clemens	60.00
44	Dave Winfield, Reggie Jackson	30.00
45	Don Mattingly, Todd Helton	75.00

Throwback Threads Autograph

		NM/M
Production listed		
Football Exchange for 21 & 22 will be redeemed for #'s listed for 21 & 22		
1	Stan Musial/25	150.00
2	Tony Gwynn/25	100.00

7 Mike Schmidt/25 200.00
9 Harmon Killebrew/25 125.00
11 Al Kaline/25 120.00
13 Hank Aaron/25 150.00
14 Andruw Jones/50 50.00
17 Ernie Banks/25 150.00
20 Vladimir Guerrero/50 75.00
21 Frank Robinson/ 50 FB Redemp 40.00
22 Frank Thomas/ 50 FB redemp 50.00
23 Brooks Robinson/50 100.00
29 Don Mattingly/50 150.00
31 Stan Musial, Tony Gwynn/25 225.00
34 Mike Schmidt, Scott Rolen/25 225.00
39 Ernie Banks, Ryne Sandberg/ 25 250.00

Title Waves

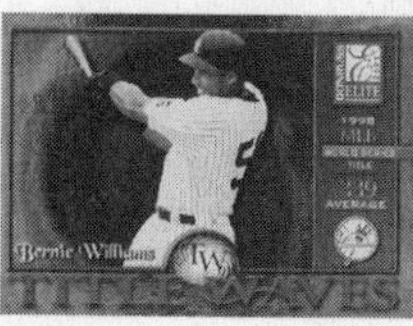

NM/M
Common Player: 1.00
numbered to title year
Holofoil: 2-3X
Production 100 sets
1 Tony Gwynn/1994 5.00
2 Todd Helton/2000 4.00
3 Nomar Garciaparra/ 2000 6.00
4 Frank Thomas/1997 4.00
5 Alex Rodriguez/1996 8.00
6 Jeff Bagwell/1994 4.00
7 Mark McGwire/1998 8.00
8 Sammy Sosa/2000 6.00
9 Ken Griffey Jr./1997 6.00
10 Albert Belle/1995 1.00
11 Barry Bonds/1993 10.00
12 Jose Canseco/1991 2.00
13 Manny Ramirez/1999 4.00
14 Sammy Sosa/1998 6.00
15 Andres Galarraga/1996 1.00
16 Todd Helton/2000 4.00
17 Ken Griffey Jr./1997 6.00
18 Jeff Bagwell/1994 4.00
19 Mike Piazza/1995 6.00
20 Alex Rodriguez/1995 8.00
21 Jason Giambi/2000 2.00
22 Ivan Rodriguez/1999 2.50
23 Greg Maddux/1997 5.00
24 Pedro Martinez/1994 4.00
25 Derek Jeter/2000 10.00
26 Bernie Williams/1998 1.50
27 Roger Clemens/1999 8.00
28 Chipper Jones/1995 4.00
29 Mark McGwire/1990 8.00
30 Cal Ripken Jr./1983 10.00

Turn of the Century Autographs

NM/M
Common Autograph: 8.00
Production 100 sets
Redemp. deadline 5/01/03
151 Brent Abernathy 8.00
152 Cory Aldridge 8.00
153 Gene Altman 8.00
154 Josh Beckett 50.00
155 Wilson Betemit 8.00
156 Albert Pujols 800.00
157 Joe Crede 10.00
158 Jack Cust 8.00
159 Ben Sheets 30.00
160 Alex Escobar 8.00
161 Adrian Hernandez 8.00
162 Pedro Feliz 8.00
163 Nate Frese 8.00
164 Carlos Garcia 8.00
165 Marcus Giles 15.00
166 Alexis Gomez 10.00
167 Jason Hart 8.00
168 Aubrey Huff 12.00
169 Cesar Izturis 10.00
170 Nick Johnson 15.00
171 Jack Wilson 10.00
172 Brian Lawrence 10.00
173 Christian Parker 8.00
174 Nick Maness 8.00
175 Jose Mieses 8.00
176 Greg Miller 8.00
177 Eric Munson 8.00
178 Xavier Nady 10.00
179 Blaine Neal 8.00
180 Abraham Nunez 8.00
181 Jose Ortiz 8.00
182 Jeremy Owens 8.00
183 Jay Gibbons 25.00
184 Corey Patterson 20.00
185 Carlos Pena 10.00
186 C.C. Sabathia 8.00
187 Timoniel Perez 8.00
188 Adam Pettyjohn 8.00
189 Donaldo Mendez 8.00
190 Jackson Melian 8.00
191 Wilken Ruan 8.00
192 Duaner Sanchez 8.00
193 Alfonso Soriano 60.00
194 Rafael Soriano 10.00
196 Billy Sylvester 8.00
197 Juan Uribe 10.00
199 Carlos Valderrama 8.00
200 Matt White 8.00

2001 DONRUSS SIGNATURE SERIES

NM/M
Complete Set (311):
Common Player: .50
Common (111-165): 8.00
Auto. print run 330
Common (166-311): 4.00
Production 800
Box: 100.00
1 Alex Rodriguez 3.00
2 Barry Bonds 4.00
3 Cal Ripken Jr. 4.00
4 Chipper Jones 2.00
5 Derek Jeter 4.00
6 Troy Glaus 1.50
7 Frank Thomas 1.50
8 Greg Maddux 2.00
9 Ivan Rodriguez 1.00
10 Jeff Bagwell 1.50
11 John Olerud .50
12 Todd Helton 1.50
13 Ken Griffey Jr. 2.50
14 Manny Ramirez 1.50
15 Mark McGwire 3.00
16 Mike Piazza 2.50
17 Nomar Garciaparra 2.50
18 Moises Alou .50
19 Aramis Ramirez .50
20 Curt Schilling .75
21 Pat Burrell .75
22 Doug Mientkiewicz .50
23 Carlos Delgado .75
24 J.D. Drew .50
25 Cliff Floyd .50
26 Freddy Garcia .50
27 Roberto Alomar .75
28 Barry Zito .75
29 Juan Encarnacion .50
30 Paul Konerko .50
31 Mark Mulder .75
32 Andy Pettitte .75
33 Jim Edmonds .50
34 Darin Erstad 1.00
35 Jason Giambi 1.00
36 Tom Glavine .75
37 Juan Gonzalez 1.50
38 Fred McGriff .50
39 Shawn Green .75
40 Tim Hudson .75
41 Andruw Jones 1.50
42 Jeff Kent .50
43 Barry Larkin .50
44 Brad Radke .50
45 Mike Mussina .75
46 Hideo Nomo .75
47 Rafael Palmeiro 1.50
48 Scott Rolen 1.50
49 Gary Sheffield .75
50 Bernie Williams .75
51 Bobby Abreu .50
52 Edgardo Alfonzo .50
53 Edgar Martinez .50
54 Magglio Ordonez .75
55 Kerry Wood .75
56 Adrian Beltre .75
57 Lance Berkman .50
58 Kevin Brown .65
59 Sean Casey .65
60 Eric Chavez .75
61 Bartolo Colon .50
62 Sammy Sosa 2.50
63 Jermaine Dye .50
64 Tony Gwynn 2.00
65 Carl Everett .50
66 Brian Giles .50
67 Mike Hampton .50
68 Richard Hidalgo .50
69 Geoff Jenkins .50
70 Tony Clark .50
71 Roger Clemens 2.25
72 Ryan Klesko .50
73 Chan Ho Park .50
74 Richie Sexson .50
75 Mike Sweeney .50
76 Kazuhiro Sasaki .50
77 Miguel Tejada .75
78 Jose Vidro .50
79 Larry Walker .50
80 Preston Wilson .50
81 Craig Biggio .50
82 Andres Galarraga .50
83 Jim Thome .50
84 Vladimir Guerrero 1.50
85 Rafael Furcal .50
86 Cristian Guzman .50
87 Terrence Long .50
88 Bret Boone .50
89 Wade Miller .50
90 Eric Milton .50
91 Gabe Kapler .50
92 Johnny Damon .75
93 Carlos Lee .50
94 Kenny Lofton .50
95 Raul Mondesi .50
96 Jorge Posada .65
97 Mark Grace .65
98 Robert Fick .50
99 Joe Mays .50
100 Aaron Sele .50
101 Ben Grieve .50
102 Luis Gonzalez .65
103 Ray Durham .50
104 Mark Quinn .50
105 Jose Canseco 1.00
106 David Justice .50
107 Pedro Martinez 1.50
108 Randy Johnson 1.50
109 Phil Nevin .50
110 Ricky Henderson 1.50
111 Alex Escobar Auto 8.00
112 *Johnny Estrada Auto* 25.00
113 Pedro Feliz Auto 8.00
114 Nate Frese Auto 8.00
115 *Ricardo Rodriguez Auto* 8.00
116 *Brandon Larson Auto* 5.00
117 *Alexis Gomez Auto* 8.00
118 Jason Hart Auto 8.00
119 C.C. Sabathia Auto 8.00
120 *Endy Chavez Auto* 8.00
121 *Christian Parker Auto* 8.00
122 *Jackson Melian* 8.00
123 *Joe Kennedy Auto* 10.00
124 *Adrian Hernandez Auto* 8.00
125 Cesar Izturis Auto 8.00
126 *Jose Mieses Auto* 8.00
127 Roy Oswalt Auto 20.00
128 Eric Munson Auto 8.00
129 Xavier Nady Auto 8.00
130 *Horacio Ramirez Auto* 15.00
131 Abraham NunezAuto 8.00
132 Jose Ortiz Auto 8.00
133 *Jeremy Owens Auto* 8.00
134 *Claudio Vargas Auto* 8.00
135 Corey Patterson Auto 20.00
136 Carlos Pena 8.00
137 *Bud Smith Auto* 8.00
138 Adam Dunn Auto 25.00
139 Adam Pettyjohn Auto 8.00
140 *Elpidio Guzman Auto* 8.00
141 *Jay Gibbons Auto* 15.00
142 *Wilken Ruan Auto* 8.00
143 *Tsuyoshi Shinjo* 8.00
144 Alfonso Soriano Auto 30.00
145 Marcus Giles Auto 10.00
146 *Ichiro Suzuki* 85.00
147 Juan Uribe Auto 10.00
148 *David Williams Auto* 8.00
149 *Carlos Valderrama Auto* 8.00
150 *Matt White Auto* 8.00
151 *Albert Pujols Auto* 600.00
152 *Donaldo Mendez Auto* 8.00
153 *Cory Aldridge Auto* 8.00
154 *Brandon Duckworth Auto* 8.00
155 Josh Beckett Auto 20.00
156 *Wilson Betemit Auto* 8.00
157 Ben Sheets Auto 25.00
158 *Andres Torres Auto* 8.00
159 Aubrey Huff Auto 10.00
160 *Jack Wilson Auto* 15.00
161 *Rafael Soriano Auto* 10.00
162 Nick Johnson Auto 8.00
163 *Carlos Garcia Auto* 8.00
164 *Josh Towers Auto* 10.00
165 *Jason Michaels Auto* 8.00
166 *Ryan Drese* 4.00
167 *Dewon Brazelton* 4.00
168 *Kevin Olsen* 4.00
169 *Benito Baez* 4.00
170 *Mark Prior* 40.00
171 *Wilmy Caceres* 4.00
172 *Mark Teixeira* 50.00
173 *Willie Harris* 4.00
174 *Mike Koplove* 4.00
175 *Brandon Knight* 4.00
176 *John Grabow* 4.00
177 *Jeremy Affeldt* 4.00
178 Brandon Inge 4.00
179 *Casey Fossum* 6.00
180 *Scott Stewart* 4.00
181 *Luke Hudson* 4.00
182 *Ken Vining* 4.00
183 Toby Hall 4.00
184 *Eric Knott* 4.00
185 *Kris Foster* 4.00
186 *David Brous* 4.00
187 *Roy Smith* 4.00
188 *Grant Balfour* 4.00
189 *Jeremy Fikac* 4.00
190 *Morgan Ensberg* 10.00
191 *Ryan Freel* 6.00
192 *Ryan Jensen* 4.00
193 *Lance Davis* 4.00
194 *Delvin James* 4.00
195 Timo Perez 4.00
196 Michael Cuddyer 4.00
197 *Bob File* 4.00
198 *Martin Vargas* 4.00
199 *Kris Keller* 4.00
200 *Tim Spooneybarger* 4.00
201 Adam Everett 4.00
202 *Josh Fogg* 6.00
203 Kip Wells 4.00
204 *Rick Bauer* 4.00
205 Brent Abernathy 4.00
206 *Erick Almonte* 4.00
207 *Pedro Santana* 4.00
208 Ken Harvey 4.00
209 *Jerrod Riggan* 4.00
210 *Nick Punto* 4.00
211 *Steve Green* 4.00
212 Nick Neugebauer 4.00
213 Chris George 4.00
214 Mike Penny 4.00
215 *Bret Prinz* 4.00
216 *Tim Christman* 4.00
217 *Sean Douglass* 4.00
218 *Brett Jodie* 4.00
219 *Juan Diaz* 4.00
220 *Carlos Hernandez* 4.00
221 Alex Cintron 4.00

222 *Juan Cruz* 4.00
223 Larry Bigbie 4.00
224 *Junior Spivey* 8.00
225 Luis Rivas 4.00
226 *Brandon Lyon* 4.00
227 *Tony Cogan* 4.00
228 *Justin Duchscherer* 6.00
229 Tike Redman 4.00
230 Jimmy Rollins 4.00
231 *Scott Podsednik* 15.00
232 *Jose Acevedo* 4.00
233 *Luis Pineda* 4.00
234 Josh Phelps 4.00
235 *Paul Phillips* 4.00
236 *Brian Roberts* 12.00
237 Orlando Woodwards 4.00
238 *Bart Miadich* 4.00
239 *Les Walrond* 4.00
240 *Brad Voyles* 4.00
241 Joe Crede 4.00
242 *Juan Moreno* 4.00
243 Matt Ginter 4.00
244 *Brian Rogers* 4.00
245 Pablo Ozuna 4.00
246 *Geronimo Gil* 4.00
247 *Mike Maroth* 4.00
248 *Josue Perez* 4.00
249 Dee Brown 4.00
250 *Victor Zambrano* 4.00
251 *Nick Maness* 4.00
252 *Kyle Lohse* 6.00
253 *Greg Miller* 4.00
254 *Henry Mateo* 4.00
255 *Duaner Sanchez* 4.00
256 *Rob Mackowiak* 4.00
257 Steve Lomasney 4.00
258 *Angel Santos* 4.00
259 *Winston Abreu* 4.00
260 *Brandon Berger* 4.00
261 Tomas De La Rosa 4.00
262 *Ramon Vazquez* 4.00
263 Mickey Callaway 4.00
264 *Corky Miller* 4.00
265 Keith Ginter 4.00
266 *Cody Ransom* 4.00
267 *Doug Nickle* 4.00
268 *Derrick Lewis* 4.00
269 *Eric Hinske* 6.00
270 *Travis Phelps* 4.00
271 Eric Valent 4.00
272 *Michael Rivera* 4.00
273 *Esix Snead* 4.00
274 *Troy Mattes* 4.00
275 Jermaine Clark 4.00
276 Nate Cornejo 4.00
277 *George Perez* 4.00
278 Juan Rivera 4.00
279 *Justin Atchley* 4.00
280 Adam Johnson 4.00
281 *Gene Altman* 4.00
282 Jason Jennings 4.00
283 *Scott MacRae* 4.00
284 *Craig Monroe* 4.00
285 *Bert Snow* 4.00
286 *Stubby Clapp* 4.00
287 Jack Cust 4.00
288 *Will Ohman* 4.00
289 Wily Mo Pena 4.00
290 *Joe Beimel* 4.00
291 *Jason Karnuth* 4.00
292 Bill Ortega 4.00
293 *Nate Teut* 4.00
294 *Erik Hiljus* 4.00
295 *Jason Smith* 4.00
296 Juan Pena 4.00
297 David Espinosa 4.00
298 Tim Redding 4.00
299 *Brian Lawrence* 4.00
300 *Brian Reith* 4.00
301 Chad Durbin 4.00
302 Kurt Ainsworth 4.00
303 *Blaine Neal* 4.00
304 *Jorge Julio* 4.00
305 Adam Bernero 4.00
306 *Travis Hafner* 15.00
307 *Dustan Mohr* 4.00
308 *Cesar Crespo* 4.00
309 *Billy Sylvester* 4.00
310 *Zach Day* 6.00
311 *Angel Berroa* 8.00

Signature Proofs

Stars (1-110): 2-3X
Production 175
Cards (111-311) production 25

Award Winning Signatures

NM/M
Common Player: 20.00

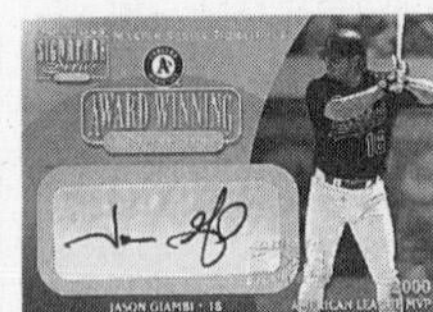

Jeff Bagwell/94 65.00
Carlos Beltran/99 40.00
Johnny Bench/68 75.00
Yogi Berra/55 50.00
Craig Biggio/97 25.00
Barry Bonds/93 200.00
Rod Carew/77 50.00
Orlando Cepeda/67 20.00
Andre Dawson/77 20.00
Dennis Eckersley/92 25.00
Dennis Eckersley/92 25.00
Whitey Ford/61 50.00
Jason Giambi/100 20.00
Bob Gibson/68 40.00
Juan Gonzalez/96 35.00
Orel Hershiser/88 25.00
Al Kaline/67 75.00
Fred Lynn/75 15.00
Fred Lynn/75 15.00
Jim Palmer/76 25.00
Cal Ripken/83 150.00
Phil Rizzuto/50 40.00
Brooks Robinson/64 40.00
Scott Rolen/97 30.00
Ryne Sandberg/84 90.00
Warren Spahn/57 50.00
Frank Thomas/94 35.00
Billy Williams/61 20.00
Kerry Wood/98 40.00
Robin Yount/89 60.00

Century Marks

NM/M
Common Autograph: 5.00
Brent Abernathy/184 5.00
Roberto Alomar/102 40.00
Rick Ankiel/119 8.00
Lance Berkman/121 15.00
Mark Buehrle/224 10.00
Wilmy Caceres/194 5.00
Eric Chavez/170 10.00
Joe Crede/154 5.00
Jack Cust/178 5.00
Brandon Duckworth/183 5.00
David Espinosa/199 5.00
Johnny Estrada/198 5.00
Pedro Feliz/180 5.00
Robert Fick/232 5.00
Cliff Floyd/146 8.00
Casey Fossum/100 10.00
Jay Gibbons/175 15.00
Keith Ginter/163 5.00
Troy Glaus/144 20.00
Luis Gonzalez/101 10.00
Vladimir Guerrero/187 30.00
Richard Hidalgo/173 5.00
Tim Hudson/145 25.00
Adam Johnson/130 5.00
Gabe Kapler/150 8.00
Joe Kennedy/219 5.00
Ryan Klesko/176 10.00
Carlos Lee/179 8.00
Terrence Long/180 5.00
Edgar Martinez/110 20.00
Joe Mays/209 5.00
Greg Miller/194 5.00
Wade Miller/180 5.00
Mark Mulder/203 20.00
Xavier Nady/180 5.00
Magglio Ordonez/104 10.00
Jose Ortiz/187 5.00
Roy Oswalt/192 20.00
Wily Mo Pena/203 10.00
Brad Penny/198 5.00
Aramis Ramirez/241 20.00
Luis Rivas/163 5.00
Alex Rodriguez/110 120.00
Scott Rolen/106 30.00
Mike Sweeney/99 10.00
Eric Valent/163 5.00
Kip Wells/223 5.00
Kerry Wood/109 25.00

Milestone Marks

NM/M
Common Player: 10.00
Ernie Banks/285 35.00
Yogi Berra/120 50.00
Wade Boggs/98 60.00
Barry Bonds/55 200.00
George Brett/27 150.00
George Brett/23 150.00
Lou Brock/83 25.00
Rod Carew/110 30.00
Steve Carlton/75 35.00
Gary Carter/213 20.00
Bobby Doerr/192 15.00
Bob Feller/202 15.00
Whitey Ford/186 25.00
Steve Garvey/175 10.00
Tony Gwynn/99 50.00
Fergie Jenkins/149 15.00
Al Kaline/149 40.00
Harmon Killebrew/127 40.00
Ralph Kiner/105 20.00
Willie McCovey/20 75.00
Paul Molitor/96 40.00
Eddie Murray/46 70.00
Eddie Murray/17
Stan Musial/109 75.00
Phil Niekro/300 10.00
Tony Perez/146 15.00
Cal Ripken/25 200.00
Frank Robinson/136 20.00
Mike Schmidt/40 125.00
Mike Schmidt/23 150.00
Enos Slaughter/117 20.00
Warren Spahn/300 40.00
Alan Trammell/154 25.00
Hoyt Wilhelm/227 10.00
Dave Winfield/31 50.00
Dave Winfield/15 80.00

Notable Nicknames

NM/M
Common Player: 30.00
Production 100
Ernie Banks 75.00
Orlando Cepeda 40.00
Will Clark 80.00
Roger Clemens/50 250.00
Andre Dawson 30.00
Bob Feller 50.00
Carlton Fisk 70.00
Andres Galarraga 40.00
Luis Gonzalez 30.00
Reggie Jackson 75.00
Harmon Killebrew 80.00
Stan Musial 120.00
Brooks Robinson 80.00
Nolan Ryan 250.00
Ryne Sandberg 150.00
Enos Slaughter 60.00
Duke Snider 75.00
Frank Thomas 100.00

Signature Stats

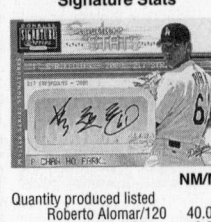

NM/M
Quantity produced listed
Roberto Alomar/120 40.00
Moises Alou/124 6.00
Luis Aparicio/313 10.00
Lance Berkman/297 15.00
Wade Boggs/51 75.00
Lou Brock/118 15.00
Gary Carter/32 50.00
Joe Carter/121 10.00
Sean Casey/103 10.00
Darin Erstad/100 15.00
Bob Feller/26 50.00
Cliff Floyd/45 15.00
Whitey Ford/72 40.00
Andres Galarraga/150 8.00
Bob Gibson/112 25.00
Brian Giles/123 10.00
Troy Glaus/102 20.00
Luis Gonzalez/114 10.00
Vladimir Guerrero/131 30.00
Tony Gwynn/17
Richard Hidalgo/314 6.00
Bo Jackson/32 85.00
Fergie Jenkins/25
Randy Johnson/20
Al Kaline/128 45.00
Gabe Kapler/302 6.00
Ralph Kiner/54 30.00
Ryan Klesko/23
Carlos Lee/261 10.00
Kenny Lofton/210 6.00
Edgar Martinez/145 20.00
Joe Mays/115 6.00
Paul Molitor/41 50.00
Mark Mulder/88 25.00
Phil Niekro/23
Magglio Ordonez/126 10.00
Jim Palmer/23
Rafael Palmeiro/47 40.00
Chan Ho Park/18
Kirby Puckett/31 100.00
Manny Ramirez/45 60.00
Alex Rodriguez/132 85.00
Ivan Rodriguez/113 30.00
Curt Schilling/15
Tom Seaver/25
Shannon Stewart/319 6.00
Mike Sweeney/144 6.00
Miguel Tejada/115 35.00
Joe Torre/230 25.00
Javier Vazquez/405 6.00
Jose Vidro/330 6.00
Hoyt Wilhelm/243 6.00

Team Trademarks

NM/M
Rick Ankiel (179) 10.00
Ernie Banks (180) 50.00
Johnny Bench (20) 75.00
Yogi Berra (124) 40.00
Wade Boggs (89) 75.00
Barry Bonds (77) 200.00
Lou Brock (29) 35.00
Steve Carlton (174) 25.00
Sean Casey (123) 15.00
Orlando Cepeda (100) 20.00
Roger Clemens (Red Sox) (30) 125.00

Roger Clemens (Yankees) (21) 150.00
Andre Dawson (176) 15.00
Bobby Doerr (193) 20.00
Whitey Ford (94) 40.00
Steve Garvey (182) 20.00
Bob Gibson (98) 30.00
Juan Gonzalez (70) 40.00
Shawn Green (109) 20.00
Orel Hershiser (210) 25.00
Reggie Jackson (73) 50.00
Fergie Jenkins (213) 15.00
Chipper Jones (74) 50.00
Pedro Martinez (27) 85.00
Don Mattingly (72) 125.00
Willie Mays (197) 125.00
Willie McCovey (26) 70.00
Joe Morgan (33) 80.00
Eddie Murray (45) 75.00
Stan Musial (65) 90.00
Mike Mussina (Orioles)(85) 40.00
Mike Mussina (Yankees)(95) 50.00
Phil Niekro (187) 10.00
Rafael Palmeiro (99) 30.00
Jim Palmer (142) 15.00
Tony Perez (73) 15.00
Manny Ramirez (57) 50.00
Cal Ripken Jr. (47) 200.00
Phil Rizzuto (98) 40.00
Brooks Robinson(146) 25.00
Frank Robinson (Orioles) (118) 25.00
Frank Robinson (Reds) (116) 25.00
Alex Rodriguez (100) 100.00
Ivan Rodriguez(62) 50.00
Scott Rolen (39) 40.00
Nolan Ryan (153) 100.00
Ryne Sandberg (52) 100.00
Curt Schilling (163) 40.00
Mike Schmidt (107) 75.00
Tom Seaver (25) 125.00
Gary Sheffield (194) 20.00
Enos Slaughter (215) 20.00
Duke Snider (47) 50.00
Warren Spahn (140) 40.00
Joe Torre (90) 40.00
Billy Williams (194) 10.00
Kerry Wood (52) 40.00

2001 DONRUSS STUDIO

NM/M
Complete Set (200):
Common Player: .25
Common SP (151-200): 4.00
Production 700
Pack (6): 8.00
Box (18) + 5x7 Auto. 140.00
1 Alex Rodriguez 2.00
2 Barry Bonds 2.50
3 Cal Ripken Jr. 2.50
4 Chipper Jones 1.00
5 Derek Jeter 2.50
6 Troy Glaus .75
7 Frank Thomas .75
8 Greg Maddux 1.00
9 Ivan Rodriguez .65
10 Jeff Bagwell .75
11 Mark Quinn .25
12 Todd Helton .75
13 Ken Griffey Jr. 1.50
14 Manny Ramirez .75
15 Mark McGwire 2.00
16 Mike Piazza 1.50
17 Nomar Garciaparra 1.50
18 Robin Ventura .25
19 Aramis Ramirez .25
20 J.T. Snow .25
21 Pat Burrell .60
22 Curt Schilling .50
23 Carlos Delgado .50
24 J.D. Drew .40
25 Cliff Floyd .25
26 Brian Jordan .25
27 Roberto Alomar .40
28 Barry Zito .50
29 Harold Baines .25
30 Brad Penny .25
31 Jose Cruz .25
32 Andy Pettitte .40
33 Jim Edmonds .25
34 Darin Erstad .60
35 Jason Giambi .60
36 Tom Glavine .50
37 Juan Gonzalez .75
38 Mark Grace .35
39 Shawn Green .50
40 Tim Hudson .50
41 Andruw Jones .75
42 Jeff Kent .25
43 Barry Larkin .25
44 Rafael Furcal .25
45 Mike Mussina .50
46 Hideo Nomo .50
47 Rafael Palmeiro .75
48 Scott Rolen .75
49 Gary Sheffield .50
50 Bernie Williams .40
51 Bobby Abreu .25
52 Edgardo Alfonzo .25
53 Edgar Martinez .25
54 Magglio Ordonez .40
55 Kerry Wood .75
56 Matt Morris .25
57 Lance Berkman .25
58 Kevin Brown .35
59 Sean Casey .40
60 Eric Chavez .40
61 Bartolo Colon .25
62 Johnny Damon .45
63 Jermaine Dye .25
64 Juan Encarnacion .25
65 Carl Everett .25
66 Brian Giles .25
67 Mike Hampton .25
68 Richard Hidalgo .25
69 Geoff Jenkins .25
70 Jacque Jones .25
71 Jason Kendall .25
72 Ryan Klesko .25
73 Chan Ho Park .25
74 Richie Sexson .25
75 Mike Sweeney .25
76 Fernando Tatis .25
77 Miguel Tejada .50
78 Jose Vidro .25
79 Larry Walker .25
80 Preston Wilson .25
81 Craig Biggio .25
82 Fred McGriff .25
83 Jim Thome .25
84 Garret Anderson .25
85 Mark Mulder .40
86 Tony Batista .25
87 Terrence Long .25
88 Brad Fullmer .25
89 Rusty Greer .25
90 Orlando Hernandez .25
91 Gabe Kapler .25
92 Paul Konerko .25
93 Carlos Lee .25
94 Kenny Lofton .25
95 Raul Mondesi .25
96 Jorge Posada .40
97 Tim Salmon .35
98 Greg Vaughn .25
99 Mo Vaughn .25
100 Omar Vizquel .25
101 Ben Grieve .25
102 Luis Gonzalez .35
103 Ray Durham .25
104 Ryan Dempster .25
105 Eric Karros .25
106 David Justice .25
107 Pedro Martinez .75
108 Randy Johnson .75
109 Rick Ankiel .25
110 Rickey Henderson .75
111 Roger Clemens 1.25
112 Sammy Sosa 1.50
113 Tony Gwynn 1.00
114 Vladimir Guerrero .75
115 Kazuhiro Sasaki .25
116 Phil Nevin .25
117 Ruben Mateo .25
118 Shannon Stewart .25
119 Matt Williams .25
120 Tino Martinez .25
121 Ken Caminiti .25
122 Edgar Renteria .25
123 Charles Johnson .25
124 Aaron Sele .25
125 Javy Lopez .25
126 Mariano Rivera .35
127 Shea Hillenbrand .25
128 Jeff D'Amico .25
129 Brady Anderson .25
130 Kevin Millwood .25
131 Trot Nixon .25
132 Mike Lieberthal .25
133 Juan Pierre .25
134 Russ Ortiz .25
135 Jose Macias .25
136 John Smoltz .25
137 Jason Varitek .25
138 Dean Palmer .25
139 Jeff Cirillo .25
140 Paul O'Neill .25
141 Andres Galarraga .25
142 David Wells .25
143 Brad Radke .25
144 Wade Miller .25
145 John Olerud .25
146 Moises Alou .25
147 Carlos Beltran .50
148 Jeromy Burnitz .25
149 Steve Finley .25
150 Joe Mays .25
151 Alex Escobar 4.00
152 *Johnny Estrada* 10.00
153 Pedro Feliz 4.00
154 *Nate Frese* 4.00
155 Dee Brown 4.00
156 *Brandon Larson* 5.00
157 *Alexis Gomez* 4.00
158 Jason Hart 4.00
159 C.C. Sabathia 4.00
160 *Josh Towers* 6.00
161 *Christian Parker* 4.00
162 *Jackson Melian* 4.00
163 *Joe Kennedy* 4.00
164 *Adrian Hernandez* 4.00
165 Jimmy Rollins 4.00
166 *Jose Mieses* 4.00
167 Roy Oswalt 5.00
168 Eric Munson 4.00
169 Xavier Nady 4.00
170 *Horacio Ramirez* 8.00
171 Abraham Nunez 4.00
172 Jose Ortiz 4.00
173 *Jeremy Owens* 4.00
174 *Claudio Vargas* 4.00
175 Corey Patterson 4.00
176 Carlos Pena 4.00
177 *Bud Smith* 4.00
178 Adam Dunn 4.00
179 *Adam Pettyjohn* 4.00
180 *Elpidio Guzman* 4.00
181 *Jay Gibbons* 10.00
182 *Wilkin Ruan* 4.00
183 *Tsuyoshi Shinjo* 4.00
184 Alfonso Soriano 6.00
185 Marcus Giles 4.00
186 *Ichiro Suzuki* 85.00
187 *Juan Uribe* 6.00
188 *David Williams* 4.00
189 *Carlos Valderrama* 4.00
190 *Matt White* 4.00
191 *Albert Pujols* 200.00
192 *Donaldo Mendez* 4.00
193 *Cory Aldridge* 4.00
194 *Endy Chavez* 4.00
195 Josh Beckett 4.00
196 *Wilson Betemit* 4.00
197 Ben Sheets 4.00
198 *Andres Torres* 4.00
199 Aubrey Huff 4.00
200 *Jack Wilson* 8.00

Proofs

VALUES UNDETERMINED
Production 25 sets
(See 2001 Studio for checklist.)

Diamond Collection

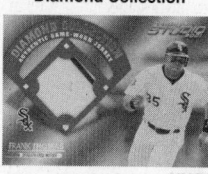

NM/M
Common Player: 5.00
1 Vladimir Guerrero 10.00
2 Barry Bonds 30.00
3 Cal Ripken Jr. 30.00
4 Nomar Garciaparra 20.00
5 Greg Maddux 15.00
6 Frank Thomas 10.00
7 Roger Clemens 20.00
8 Luis Gonzalez SP 6.00
9 Tony Gwynn 15.00
10 Carlos Lee SP 6.00
11 Troy Glaus 8.00
12 Randy Johnson 10.00
13 Manny Ramirez SP 15.00
14 Pedro Martinez 10.00
15 Todd Helton 10.00
16 Jeff Bagwell 10.00
17 Rickey Henderson 10.00
18 Kazuhiro Sasaki 5.00
19 Albert Pujols SP 50.00
20 Ivan Rodriguez 8.00
21 Darin Erstad 6.00
22 Andruw Jones 8.00
23 Roberto Alomar 6.00
25 Juan Gonzalez 10.00
26 Shawn Green 7.50
27 Lance Berkman 5.00
28 Scott Rolen 9.00
29 Rafael Palmeiro 8.00
30 J.D. Drew 5.00
31 Kerry Wood 8.00
32 Jim Edmonds 5.00
33 Tom Glavine SP 8.00
34 Hideo Nomo SP 50.00
36 Tim Hudson 5.00
37 Miguel Tejada 5.00
38 Chipper Jones 15.00
39 Edgar Martinez SP 8.00
40 Chan Ho Park 5.00
41 Magglio Ordonez 5.00
42 Sean Casey 5.00
43 Larry Walker 5.00
45 Cliff Floyd 5.00
46 Mike Sweeney 5.00
47 Kevin Brown 5.00
48 Richie Sexson 5.00
49 Jermaine Dye 5.00
50 Craig Biggio 5.00

Leather & Lumber

NM/M
Common Player: 5.00
Combos: No Pricing
Production 25 sets
1 Barry Bonds 25.00
2 Cal Ripken Jr. 25.00
3 Miguel Tejada 5.00
5 Frank Thomas 8.00
6 Greg Maddux 10.00
7 Ivan Rodriguez 8.00
8 Jeff Bagwell SP 10.00
9 Sean Casey SP 6.00
10 Todd Helton 8.00
11 Cliff Floyd 5.00
12 Hideo Nomo 40.00
13 Chipper Jones 10.00
14 Rickey Henderson 8.00
15 Richard Hidalgo 5.00
16 Mike Piazza 15.00
17 Larry Walker 5.00
18 Tony Gwynn 10.00
19 Vladimir Guerrero 8.00
20 Rafael Furcal 5.00
21 Roberto Alomar SP 8.00
23 Albert Pujols 40.00
24 Raul Mondesi 5.00
25 J.D. Drew 5.00

26	Jim Edmonds	5.00
27	Darin Erstad SP	6.00
28	Craig Biggio	5.00
29	Kenny Lofton	5.00
30	Juan Gonzalez	8.00
31	John Olerud	5.00
32	Shawn Green	5.00
33	Andruw Jones SP	8.00
34	Moises Alou	5.00
35	Jeff Kent	5.00
36	Ryan Klesko	5.00
37	Luis Gonzalez	5.00
38	Rafael Palmeiro	8.00
40	Scott Rolen	8.00
41	Carlos Lee	5.00
42	Bobby Abreu	5.00
43	Edgardo Alfonzo	5.00
44	Bernie Williams	5.00
45	Brian Giles	5.00
46	Jermaine Dye	5.00
47	Lance Berkman	5.00
48	Edgar Martinez	5.00
49	Richie Sexson	5.00
50	Magglio Ordonez	5.00

Masterstokes

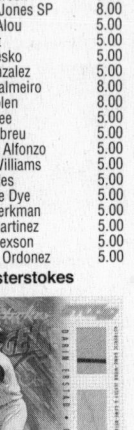

		NM/M
Common Player:		8.00
Production 200 sets		
1	Tony Gwynn	25.00
2	Ivan Rodriguez	10.00
3	J.D. Drew	8.00
4	Cal Ripken Jr.	60.00
5	Hideo Nomo	50.00
6	Darin Erstad	8.00
7	Frank Thomas	12.00
8	Andruw Jones	12.00
9	Roberto Alomar	8.00
10	Larry Walker	8.00
11	Vladimir Guerrero	12.00
12	Barry Bonds	65.00
14	Luis Gonzalez	8.00
16	Juan Gonzalez	12.00
17	Todd Helton	12.00
18	Jeff Bagwell	12.00
19	Albert Pujols	75.00
20	Shawn Green	8.00
21	Magglio Ordonez	8.00
22	Scott Rolen	12.00
23	Rafael Palmeiro	10.00
24	Sean Casey	8.00
25	Jim Edmonds	8.00
26	Chipper Jones	20.00
27	Cliff Floyd	8.00
28	Carlos Lee	8.00
29	Edgar Martinez	8.00
30	Lance Berkman	8.00

Private Signings

		NM/M
Common Player:		8.00
Inserted 1:hobby box		
1	Alex Rodriguez	75.00
2	Miguel Tejada	25.00
3	Ben Sheets	15.00
4	Tony Gwynn SP/190	60.00
5	Wilson Betemit	8.00
6	Rick Ankiel	8.00
7	Ivan Rodriguez SP/150	30.00
8	Ryan Klesko	8.00
9	Jason Giambi SP/250	15.00
10	Brad Penny	8.00
11	Gabe Kapler	8.00
12	Vladimir Guerrero	30.00
13	Alex Escobar	8.00
14	Edgar Martinez	15.00
15	Cal Ripken SP/50	200.00
16	Brian Giles	8.00
17	Todd Helton SP/125	25.00
18	Mike Sweeney	8.00
19	Cliff Floyd	8.00
20	Corey Patterson	12.00
21	Alfonso Soriano	40.00
22	Bobby Abreu	8.00
23	Shawn Green SP/190	20.00
24	C.C. Sabathia	8.00
25	Luis Gonzalez	8.00
26	Barry Bonds SP/95	200.00
27	Rafael Palmeiro SP/250	30.00
28	Mike Mussina SP/144	40.00
29	Roger Clemens SP/200	100.00
30	Greg Maddux SP/200	80.00
31	Troy Glaus	20.00
32	Kerry Wood	15.00
33	Roberto Alomar SP/200	30.00
34	Tom Glavine	30.00
35	Frank Thomas	20.00
36	Carlos Lee	8.00
37	Scott Rolen	20.00
38	Andruw Jones SP/250	20.00
39	Manny Ramirez SP/115	40.00
40	Magglio Ordonez	12.00
41	Lance Berkman	8.00
42	Josh Beckett	25.00
43	Adam Dunn	15.00
44	Albert Pujols SP/50	450.00
45	Darin Erstad	12.00
46	Curt Schilling	30.00
47	Barry Zito	12.00
48	Sean Casey	8.00

Round Trip Tickets

No Pricing
Production 25 sets

1	Mark McGwire
2	Frank Robinson
3	Joe Morgan
4	Mike Piazza
5	Barry Bonds
6	Johnny Bench
7	Vladimir Guerrero
8	Mike Schmidt
9	Andruw Jones
10	Todd Helton
11	Sammy Sosa
12	Reggie Jackson
13	Cal Ripken Jr.
15	Willie Stargell
16	Jeff Bagwell
18	Tony Gwynn
19	Ivan Rodriguez
20	Roberto Clemente

Warning Track

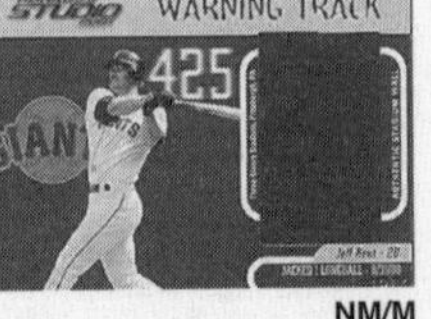

		NM/M
Common Player:		4.00
1	Andruw Jones	8.00
2	Rafael Palmeiro	7.00
3	Gary Sheffield	5.00
4	Larry Walker	4.00
5	Shawn Green	4.00
6	Mike Piazza	12.00
7	Barry Bonds	20.00
8	J.D. Drew	4.00
9	Magglio Ordonez	4.00
10	Todd Helton	8.00
11	Juan Gonzalez	8.00
12	Pat Burrell	5.00
13	Mark McGwire	15.00
14	Frank Robinson	4.00
15	Manny Ramirez	8.00
16	Lance Berkman	4.00
18	Johnny Bench	10.00
19	Chipper Jones	10.00
20	Mike Schmidt	15.00
21	Vladimir Guerrero	8.00
22	Sammy Sosa	12.00
23	Cal Ripken Jr.	20.00
24	Roberto Alomar	4.00
25	Willie Stargell	4.00
27	Scott Rolen	7.00
28	Roberto Clemente/SP	50.00
29	Tony Gwynn	10.00
30	Ivan Rodriguez	5.00
31	Sean Casey	4.00
32	Frank Thomas	8.00
33	Jeff Bagwell	8.00
34	Jeff Kent	4.00
35	Reggie Jackson	8.00

2001 DONRUSS THE ROOKIES

		NM/M
Complete Set (105):		65.00
Complete Factory Set (106):		75.00
Common Player:		.25
1	Adam Dunn	.50
2	*Ryan Drese*	.40
3	*Bud Smith*	.25
4	*Tsuyoshi Shinjo*	1.00
5	Roy Oswalt	.50
6	*Wilmy Caceres*	.25
7	*Willie Harris*	.25
8	*Andres Torres*	.25
9	*Brandon Knight*	.25
10	*Horacio Ramirez*	.75
11	*Benito Baez*	.25
12	*Jeremy Affeldt*	.25
13	*Ryan Jensen*	.25
14	*Casey Fossum*	.75
15	*Ramon Vazquez*	.50
16	*Dustan Mohr*	.25
17	*Saul Rivera*	.25
18	*Zach Day*	.50
19	*Erik Hiljus*	.25
20	*Cesar Crespo*	.25
21	*Wilson Guzman*	.25
22	*Travis Hafner*	2.00
23	*Grant Balfour*	.25
24	*Johnny Estrada*	1.50
25	*Morgan Ensberg*	1.00
26	*Jack Wilson*	1.50
27	Aubrey Huff	.25
28	*Endy Chavez*	.50
29	*Delvin James*	.25
30	Michael Cuddyer	.25
31	*Jason Michaels*	.25
32	*Martin Vargas*	.25
33	*Donaldo Mendez*	.25
34	*Jorge Julio*	.25
35	*Tim Spooneybarger*	.25
36	Kurt Ainsworth	.25
37	*Josh Fogg*	.50
38	*Brian Reith*	.25
39	*Rick Baurer*	.25
40	Tim Redding	.25
41	*Erick Almonte*	.50
42	Juan Pena	.25
43	Ken Harvey	.25
44	*David Brous*	.25
45	*Kevin Olsen*	.25
46	*Henry Mateo*	.25
47	Nick Neugebauer	.25
48	*Mike Penney*	.25
49	*Jay Gibbons*	1.00
50	*Tim Christman*	.25
51	*Brandon Duckworth*	.50
52	*Brett Jodie*	.25
53	*Christian Parker*	.25
54	*Carlos Hernandez*	.25
55	*Brandon Larson*	.50
56	*Nick Punto*	.25
57	*Elpidio Guzman*	.25
58	*Joe Beimel*	.25
59	*Junior Spivey*	1.00
60	*Will Ohman*	.25
61	*Brandon Lyon*	.25
62	*Stubby Clapp*	.25
63	*Justin Duchscherer*	.50
64	Jimmy Rollins	.25
65	*David Williams*	.40
66	*Craig Monroe*	.40
67	*Jose Acevedo*	.25
68	Jason Jennings	.25
69	Josh Phelps	.25
70	*Brian Roberts*	5.00
71	*Claudio Vargas*	.25
72	Adam Johnson	.25
73	*Bart Miadich*	.25
74	Juan Rivera	.25
75	*Brad Voyles*	.25
76	Nate Cornejo	.25
77	*Juan Moreno*	.25
78	*Brian Rogers*	.25
79	*Ricardo Rodriguez*	.40
80	*Geronimo Gil*	.25
81	*Joe Kennedy*	.40
82	*Kevin Joseph*	.25
83	*Josue Perez*	.25
84	*Victor Zambrano*	.25
85	*Josh Towers*	.40
86	*Mike Rivera*	.25
87	*Mark Prior*	15.00
88	*Juan Cruz*	.40
89	*Dewon Brazelton*	.40
90	*Angel Berroa*	1.00
91	*Mark Teixeira*	8.00
92	*Cody Ransom*	.25
93	*Angel Santos*	.25
94	*Corky Miller*	.40
95	*Brandon Berger*	.40
96	Corey Patterson	.25
97	*Albert Pujols*	35.00
98	Josh Beckett	.50
99	C.C. Sabathia	.25
100	Alfonso Soriano	.75
101	Ben Sheets	.25
102	*Rafael Soriano*	1.00
103	*Wilson Betemit*	.50
104	*Ichiro Suzuki*	12.00
105	Jose Ortiz	.25

Rookie Diamond Kings

		NM/M
Complete Set (5):		40.00
Inserted 1:Rookies Set		
106	C.C. Sabathia	5.00
107	Tsuyoshi Shinjo	8.00
108	Albert Pujols	25.00
109	Roy Oswalt	8.00
110	Ichiro Suzuki	12.00

2002 DONRUSS

	NM/M
Complete Set (220):	120.00
Common Player:	.15
Common (151-200):	1.00

Inserted 1:4		
Common (201-220):		1.00
Inserted 1:8		
Pack (5):		2.00
Box (24):		40.00
1	Alex Rodriguez	1.50
2	Barry Bonds	2.00
3	Derek Jeter	2.00
4	Robert Fick	.15
5	Juan Pierre	.20
6	Torii Hunter	.25
7	Todd Helton	.75
8	Cal Ripken Jr.	2.00
9	Manny Ramirez	.75
10	Johnny Damon	.25
11	Mike Piazza	1.25
12	Nomar Garciaparra	1.25
13	Pedro Martinez	.75
14	Brian Giles	.15
15	Albert Pujols	1.50
16	Roger Clemens	1.00
17	Sammy Sosa	1.25
18	Vladimir Guerrero	.75
19	Tony Gwynn	1.00
20	Pat Burrell	.35
21	Carlos Delgado	.50
22	Tino Martinez	.15
23	Jim Edmonds	.15
24	Jason Giambi	.50
25	Tom Glavine	.30
26	Mark Grace	.20
27	Tony Armas Jr.	.15
28	Andruw Jones	.75
29	Ben Sheets	.15
30	Jeff Kent	.15
31	Barry Larkin	.15
32	Joe Mays	.15
33	Mike Mussina	.40
34	Hideo Nomo	.60
35	Rafael Palmeiro	.65
36	Scott Brosius	.15
37	Scott Rolen	.65
38	Gary Sheffield	.35
39	Bernie Williams	.35
40	Bobby Abreu	.15
41	Edgardo Alfonzo	.15
42	C.C. Sabathia	.15
43	Jeremy Giambi	.15
44	Craig Biggio	.15
45	Andres Galarraga	.15
46	Edgar Martinez	.15
47	Fred McGriff	.25
48	Magglio Ordonez	.25
49	Jim Thome	.15
50	Matt Williams	.15
51	Kerry Wood	.50
52	Moises Alou	.15
53	Brady Anderson	.15
54	Garret Anderson	.15
55	Juan Gonzalez	.75
56	Bret Boone	.15
57	Jose Cruz Jr.	.15
58	Carlos Beltran	.50
59	Adrian Beltre	.25
60	Joe Kennedy	.15
61	Lance Berkman	.15
62	Kevin Brown	.25
63	Tim Hudson	.35
64	Jeromy Burnitz	.15
65	Jarrod Washburn	.15
66	Sean Casey	.20
67	Eric Chavez	.25
68	Bartolo Colon	.15
69	Freddy Garcia	.15
70	Jermaine Dye	.15
71	Terrence Long	.15
72	Cliff Floyd	.15
73	Luis Gonzalez	.25
74	Ichiro Suzuki	1.50
75	Mike Hampton	.15
76	Richard Hidalgo	.15
77	Geoff Jenkins	.15
78	Gabe Kapler	.15
79	Ken Griffey Jr.	1.25
80	Jason Kendall	.15
81	Josh Towers	.15
82	Ryan Klesko	.15
83	Paul Konerko	.15
84	Carlos Lee	.15
85	Kenny Lofton	.15
86	Josh Beckett	.40
87	Raul Mondesi	.15
88	Trot Nixon	.15
89	John Olerud	.15
90	Paul O'Neill	.15
91	Chan Ho Park	.15
92	Andy Pettitte	.35
93	Jorge Posada	.30
94	Mark Quinn	.15
95	Aramis Ramirez	.15
96	Curt Schilling	.40
97	Richie Sexson	.15
98	John Smoltz	.15
99	Wilson Betemit	.15
100	Shannon Stewart	.15
101	Alfonso Soriano	.75
102	Mike Sweeney	.15
103	Miguel Tejada	.40
104	Greg Vaughn	.15
105	Robin Ventura	.15
106	Jose Vidro	.15
107	Larry Walker	.15
108	Preston Wilson	.15
109	Corey Patterson	.20
110	Mark Mulder	.25
111	Tony Clark	.15
112	Roy Oswalt	.25
113	Jimmy Rollins	.15
114	Kazuhiro Sasaki	.15
115	Barry Zito	.40
116	Javier Vazquez	.15
117	Mike Cameron	.15
118	Phil Nevin	.15
119	Bud Smith	.15
120	Cristian Guzman	.15
121	Al Leiter	.15
122	Brad Radke	.15
123	Bobby Higginson	.15
124	Robert Person	.15
125	Adam Dunn	.50
126	Ben Grieve	.15
127	Rafael Furcal	.15
128	Jay Gibbons	.15
129	Paul LoDuca	.15
130	Wade Miller	.15
131	Tsuyoshi Shinjo	.15
132	Eric Milton	.15
133	Rickey Henderson	.75
134	Roberto Alomar	.40
135	Darin Erstad	.50
136	J.D. Drew	.35
137	Shawn Green	.25
138	Randy Johnson	.75
139	Mark McGwire	1.50
139		.15
140	Jose Canseco	.40
141	Jeff Bagwell	.75
142	Greg Maddux	1.00
143	Mark Buehrle	.15
144	Ivan Rodriguez	.65
145	Frank Thomas	.75
146	Rich Aurilia	.15
147	Troy Glaus	.75
148	Ryan Dempster	.15
149	Chipper Jones	1.00
150	Matt Morris	.15
151	Marlon Byrd	2.00
152	*Ben Howard*	4.00
153	*Brandon Backe*	2.00
154	*Jorge De La Rosa*	2.00
155	Corky Miller	1.00
156	Dennis Tankersley	1.00
157	*Kyle Kane*	3.00
158	Justin Duchscherer	1.00
159	*Brian Mallette*	3.00
160	*Chris Baker*	3.00
161	Jason Lane	1.00
162	Hee Seop Choi	1.50
163	Juan Cruz	1.00
164	*Rodrigo Rosario*	2.00
165	Matt Guerrier	1.00
166	*Anderson Machado*	3.00
167	Geronimo Gil	1.00
168	Dewon Brazelton	1.00
169	Mark Prior	5.00
170	Bill Hall	1.00
171	*Jorge Padilla*	4.00
172	Jose Cueto	1.00
173	*Allan Simpson*	3.00
174	*Doug Devore*	3.00
175	Josh Pearce	1.00
176	Angel Berroa	1.00
177	*Steve Bechler*	3.00
178	Antonio Perez	1.00
179	Mark Teixeira	3.00
180	Erick Almonte	1.00
181	Orlando Hudson	1.00
182	Mike Rivera	1.00
183	*Raul Chavez*	2.00
184	Juan Pena	1.00
185	*Travis Hughes*	2.00
186	Ryan Ludwick	1.00
187	Ed Rogers	1.00
188	*Andy Pratt*	2.00
189	Nick Neugebauer	1.00
190	*Tom Shearn*	3.00
191	*Eric Cyr*	3.00
192	Victor Martinez	1.00
193	Brandon Berger	1.00
194	Erik Bedard	1.00
195	Fernando Rodney	1.00
196	Joe Thurston	1.00
197	John Buck	1.00
198	*Jeff Deardorff*	2.00
199	*Ryan Jamison*	2.00
200	Alfredo Amezaga	1.00
201	Luis Gonzalez	1.00
202	Roger Clemens	4.00
203	Barry Zito	1.25
204	Bud Smith	1.00
205	Magglio Ordonez	1.25
206	Kerry Wood	1.50
207	Freddy Garcia	1.00
208	Adam Dunn	1.50
209	Curt Schilling	2.00
210	Lance Berkman	1.50
211	Rafael Palmeiro	2.00
212	Ichiro Suzuki	4.00
213	Bobby Abreu	1.00
214	Mark Mulder	1.00
215	Roy Oswalt	1.50
216	Mike Sweeney	1.00
217	Paul LoDuca	1.00
218	Aramis Ramirez	1.00
219	Randy Johnson	2.00
220	Albert Pujols	5.00

Stat Line Career

	NM/M
Cards 1-150 print run 251-400:	2-4X
1-150 p/r 151-250:	3-6X
1-150 p/r 101-150:	4-8X
1-150 p/r 61-100:	5-10X
1-150 p/r 31-60:	8-20X
1-150 p/r 15-30:	15-30X
Common 151-200 p/r 251-400:	1.00
Common 151-200 p/r 151-250:	1.00
Common 151-200 p/r 76-150:	2.00
Common 151-200 p/r 30-75:	4.00

Autographs

		NM/M
Common Autograph:		15.00
Varying quantities produced		
201	Luis Gonzalez/25	
202	Roger Clemens/25	
203	Barry Zito/200	25.00
204	Bud Smith/200	15.00
205	Magglio Ordonez/200	20.00
206	Kerry Wood/200	30.00
207	Freddy Garcia/200	15.00
208	Adam Dunn/200	25.00
209	Curt Schilling/25	
210	Lance Berkman/175	15.00
211	Rafael Palmeiro/25	20.00
213	Bobby Abreu/200	15.00
214	Mark Mulder/200	15.00
215	Roy Oswalt/200	15.00
216	Mike Sweeney/200	15.00
217	Paul LoDuca/200	15.00
218	Aramis Ramirez/200	15.00
219	Randy Johnson/10	
220	Albert Pujols/200	75.00

Bat Kings

		NM/M
Quantities produced listed		
Studio Series:		1.5-3X
Production 25 or 50		
1	Jason Giambi/250	15.00
2	Alex Rodriguez/250	25.00
3	Mike Piazza/250	20.00
4	Roberto Clemente/125	100.00
5	Babe Ruth/125	220.00

Diamond Kings

		NM/M
Complete Set (20):		80.00
Common Player:		2.00
Production 2,500 sets		
Studio Series:		2-3X
Production 250 sets		
1	Nomar Garciaparra	6.00
2	Shawn Green	2.00
3	Randy Johnson	4.00
4	Derek Jeter	7.50
5	Carlos Delgado	3.00
6	Roger Clemens	5.00
7	Jeff Bagwell	4.00
8	Vladimir Guerrero	4.00
9	Luis Gonzalez	2.00
10	Mike Piazza	6.00
11	Ichiro Suzuki	6.00
12	Pedro Martinez	4.00
13	Todd Helton	4.00
14	Sammy Sosa	6.00
15	Ivan Rodriguez	3.50
16	Barry Bonds	7.50
17	Albert Pujols	6.00
18	Jim Thome	2.00
19	Alex Rodriguez	6.00
20	Jason Giambi	3.00

Elite Series

		NM/M
Complete Set (15):		30.00
Common Player:		2.00
Production 2,500 sets		
Autographs:		No Pricing
Production 25		
1	Barry Bonds	8.00
2	Lance Berkman	2.00
3	Jason Giambi	2.50
4	Nomar Garciaparra	6.00
5	Curt Schilling	2.50
6	Vladimir Guerrero	3.00
7	Shawn Green	2.00
8	Troy Glaus	2.00
9	Jeff Bagwell	3.00
10	Manny Ramirez	3.00
11	Eric Chavez	2.00
12	Carlos Delgado	2.50
13	Mike Sweeney	2.00
14	Todd Helton	3.00
15	Luis Gonzalez	2.00

Jersey Kings

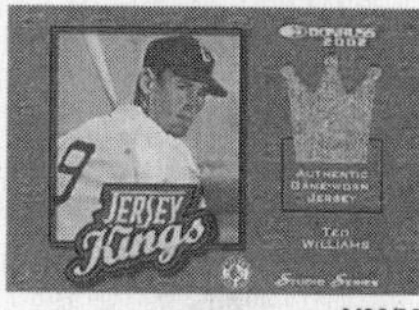

		NM/M
Quantity Produced Listed		
Studio Series:		1.5-3X
Production 25 or 50		
1	Alex Rodriguez/250	15.00
2	Jason Giambi/250	10.00
3	Carlos Delgado/250	8.00
4	Barry Bonds/250	25.00
5	Randy Johnson/250	10.00
6	Jim Thome/250	8.00
7	Shawn Green/250	8.00
8	Pedro Martinez/250	10.00
9	Jeff Bagwell/250	10.00
10	Vladimir Guerrero/250	10.00
11	Ivan Rodriguez/250	10.00
12	Nomar Garciaparra/250	15.00

13 Don Mattingly/125 80.00
14 Ted Williams/125 125.00
15 Lou Gehrig/125 200.00

Production Line

NM/M

Common Card: 2.00
Numbered to category stat
1 Barry Bonds/515 8.00
2 Jason Giambi/477 4.00
3 Larry Walker/449 2.50
4 Sammy Sosa/437 6.00
5 Todd Helton/432 3.00
6 Lance Berkman/430 2.00
7 Luis Gonzalez/429 2.00
8 Chipper Jones/427 6.00
9 Edgar Martinez/423 2.00
10 Gary Sheffield/417 2.00
11 Jim Thome/416 3.00
12 Roberto Alomar/415 3.00
13 J.D. Drew/414 2.00
14 Jim Edmonds/410 2.00
15 Carlos Delgado/408 3.00
16 Manny Ramirez/405 4.00
17 Brian Giles/404 2.00
18 Albert Pujols/403 8.00
19 John Olerud/401 2.00
20 Alex Rodriguez/399 8.00
21 Barry Bonds/863 6.00
22 Sammy Sosa/737 5.00
23 Luis Gonzalez/688 1.50
24 Todd Helton/685 2.00
25 Larry Walker/662 1.50
26 Jason Giambi/660 2.00
27 Jim Thome/624 2.00
28 Alex Rodriguez/620 5.00
29 Lance Berkman/620 1.50
30 J.D. Drew/613 1.50
31 Albert Pujols/610 5.00
32 Manny Ramirez/609 2.00
33 Chipper Jones/605 3.00
34 Shawn Green/598 1.50
35 Brian Giles/590 1.50
36 Juan Gonzalez/590 2.00
37 Phil Nevin/588 1.50
38 Gary Sheffield/583 1.50
39 Bret Boone/578 1.50
40 Cliff Floyd/578 1.50
41 Barry Bonds/1,378 5.00
42 Sammy Sosa/1,174 4.00
43 Jason Giambi/1,137 1.50
44 Todd Helton/1,117 1.50
45 Luis Gonzalez/1,117 1.00
46 Larry Walker/1,111 1.00
47 Lance Berkman/1,050 1.00
48 Jim Thome/1,040 1.50
49 Chipper Jones/1,032 2.50
50 J.D. Drew/1,027 1.00
51 Alex Rodriguez/1,021 4.00
52 Manny Ramirez/1,014 1.50
53 Albert Pujols/1,013 4.00
54 Gary Sheffield/1,000 1.50
55 Brian Giles/994 1.00
56 Phil Nevin/976 1.00
57 Jim Edmonds/974 1.50
58 Shawn Green/970 1.00
59 Cliff Floyd/968 1.00
60 Edgar Martinez/966 1.00

Longball Leaders

NM/M

Complete Set (20): 40.00
Common Player: 1.00
Production 1,000 sets
Seasonal Sum Parallel: 2-4X
Parallel #'d to 2001 HR Total
1 Barry Bonds 8.00
2 Sammy Sosa 6.00
3 Luis Gonzalez 1.00
4 Alex Rodriguez 6.00
5 Shawn Green 1.50
6 Todd Helton 3.00
7 Jim Thome 1.00
8 Rafael Palmeiro 2.50
9 Richie Sexson 1.00
10 Troy Glaus 3.00
11 Manny Ramirez 3.00
12 Phil Nevin 1.00
13 Jeff Bagwell 3.00
14 Carlos Delgado 2.00
15 Jason Giambi 2.00
16 Chipper Jones 4.00
17 Larry Walker 1.00
18 Albert Pujols 6.00
19 Brian Giles 1.00
20 Bret Boone 1.00

Rookie Year Materials - Bats

NM/M

Production 250 sets
1 Barry Bonds 40.00
2 Cal Ripken Jr. 40.00
3 Kirby Puckett 15.00
4 Johnny Bench 15.00

Rookie Year Materials - Jerseys

NM/M

Quantity produced listed
Parallel #'d to 25 or 50
1 Nomar Garciaparra/250 20.00
2 Randy Johnson/250 10.00
3 Ivan Rodriguez/250 10.00
4 Vladimir Guerrero/250 15.00
5 Stan Musial/50 80.00
6 Yogi Berra/50 50.00

Rookie Year Materials - Bats Autograph

NM/M

Numbered to debut year
1 Barry Bonds/86 125.00
2 Cal Ripken Jr/81 140.00
3 Kirby Puckett/84 120.00
4 Johnny Bench/68 75.00

2002 DONRUSS CLASSICS

NM/M

Complete Set (200):
Common Player: .50
Common (101-150): 3.00
Common (151-200): 2.00
Production 1,500
Pack (6): 5.00
Box (18): 70.00
1 Alex Rodriguez 3.00
2 Barry Bonds 4.00
3 C.C. Sabathia .50
4 Chipper Jones 2.00
5 Derek Jeter 4.00
6 Troy Glaus 1.50
7 Frank Thomas 1.50
8 Greg Maddux 2.00
9 Ivan Rodriguez 1.25
10 Jeff Bagwell 1.50
11 Mark Buehrle .50
12 Todd Helton 1.50
13 Ken Griffey Jr. 2.50
14 Manny Ramirez 1.50
15 Brad Penny .50
16 Mike Piazza 2.50
17 Nomar Garciaparra 2.50
18 Pedro J. Martinez 1.50
19 Randy Johnson 1.50
20 Bud Smith .50
21 Rickey Henderson 1.50
22 Roger Clemens 2.25
23 Sammy Sosa 2.50
24 Brandon Duckworth .50
25 Vladimir Guerrero 1.50
26 Kazuhiro Sasaki .50
27 Roberto Alomar .65
28 Barry Zito .75
29 Rich Aurilia .50
30 Ben Sheets .50
31 Carlos Delgado 1.00
32 J.D. Drew .75
33 Jermaine Dye .50
34 Darin Erstad .75
35 Jason Giambi 1.00
36 Tom Glavine .60
37 Juan Gonzalez 1.50
38 Luis Gonzalez .35
39 Shawn Green .75
40 Tim Hudson .65
41 Andruw Jones 1.50
42 Shannon Stewart .50
43 Barry Larkin .50
44 Wade Miller .50
45 Mike Mussina .65
46 Hideo Nomo 1.00
47 Rafael Palmeiro 1.25
48 Scott Rolen 1.00
49 Gary Sheffield .75
50 Bernie Williams .65
51 Bobby Abreu .50
52 Javier Vazquez .50
53 Edgar Martinez .50
54 Magglio Ordonez .75
55 Kerry Wood 1.00
56 Adrian Beltre .65
57 Lance Berkman .50
58 Kevin Brown .50
59 Sean Casey .50
60 Eric Chavez .75
61 Robert Person .50
62 Jeremy Giambi .50
63 Freddy Garcia .50
64 Alfonso Soriano 1.50
65 Doug Davis .50
66 Brian Giles .50
67 Moises Alou .50
68 Richard Hidalgo .50
69 Paul LoDuca .50
70 Aramis Ramirez .50
71 Andres Galarraga .50
72 Ryan Klesko .50
73 Chan Ho Park .50
74 Richie Sexson .50
75 Mike Sweeney .50
76 Aubrey Huff .50
77 Miguel Tejada .75
78 Jose Vidro .50
79 Larry Walker .50
80 Roy Oswalt .75
81 Craig Biggio .50
82 Juan Pierre .50
83 Jim Thome .50
84 Josh Towers .50
85 Alex Escobar .50
86 Cliff Floyd .50
87 Terrence Long .50
88 Curt Schilling .75
89 Carlos Beltran 1.00
90 Albert Pujols 2.50
91 Gabe Kapler .50
92 Mark Mulder .50
93 Carlos Lee .50
94 Robert Fick .50
95 Raul Mondesi .50
96 Ichiro Suzuki 2.50
97 Adam Dunn .75
98 Corey Patterson .75
99 Tsuyoshi Shinjo .50
100 Joe Mays .50
101 Juan Cruz 3.00
102 Marlon Byrd 5.00
103 Luis Garcia 3.00
104 *Jorge Padilla* 6.00
105 Dennis Tankersley 3.00
106 Josh Pearce 3.00
107 Ramon Vazquez 3.00
108 *Chris Baker* 5.00
109 *Eric Cyr* 3.00
110 *Reed Johnson* 5.00
111 *Ryan Jamison* 3.00
112 Antonio Perez 3.00
113 *Satoru Komiyama* 3.00
114 Austin Kearns 4.00
115 Juan Pena 3.00
116 Orlando Hudson 3.00
117 *Kazuhisa Ishii* 6.00
118 Eric Bedard 3.00
119 *Luis Ugueto* 3.00
120 *Ben Howard* 4.00
121 Morgan Ensberg 3.00
122 *Doug Devore* 4.00
123 Josh Phelps 3.00
124 Angel Berroa 4.00
125 Ed Rogers 3.00
126 *Takahito Nomura* 3.00
127 *John Ennis* 3.00
128 Bill Hall 3.00
129 Dewon Brazelton 3.00
130 Hank Blalock 5.00
131 *So Taguchi* 5.00
132 *Jorge De La Rosa* 3.00
133 Matt Thornton 3.00
134 *Brandon Backe* 3.00
135 *Jeff Deardorff* 3.00
136 Steve Smyth 3.00
137 *Anderson Machado* 5.00
138 John Buck 3.00
139 Mark Prior 15.00
140 Sean Burroughs 3.00
141 Alex Herrera 3.00
142 *Francis Beltran* 3.00
143 Jason Romano 3.00
144 Michael Cuddyer 3.00
145 *Steve Bechler* 3.00
146 Alfredo Amezaga 3.00
147 Ryan Ludwick 3.00
148 Martin Vargas 3.00
149 *Allan Simpson* 3.00
150 Mark Teixeira 4.00
151 Hank Aaron 8.00
152 Ernie Banks 6.00
153 Johnny Bench 6.00
154 George Brett 10.00
155 Lou Brock 3.00
156 Rod Carew 3.00
157 Steve Carlton 4.00
158 Joe Torre 3.00
159 Dennis Eckersley 2.50
160 Reggie Jackson 5.00
161 Al Kaline 6.00
162 Dave Parker 2.00
163 Don Mattingly 10.00
164 Tony Gwynn 6.00
165 Willie McCovey 3.00
166 Joe Morgan 3.00
167 Stan Musial 8.00
168 Jim Palmer 3.00
169 Brooks Robinson 5.00
170 Bo Jackson 6.00
171 Nolan Ryan 15.00
172 Mike Schmidt 8.00
173 Tom Seaver 6.00
174 Cal Ripken Jr. 15.00
175 Robin Yount 6.00
176 Wade Boggs 5.00
177 Gary Carter 3.00
178 Ron Santo 2.00
179 Luis Aparicio 2.00
180 Bobby Doerr 3.00
181 Ryne Sandberg 6.00
182 Yogi Berra 5.00
183 Will Clark 5.00
184 Eddie Murray 4.00
185 Andre Dawson 3.00
186 Duke Snider 5.00
187 Orlando Cepeda 3.00
188 Billy Williams 2.00
189 Juan Marichal 4.00
190 Harmon Killebrew 5.00
191 Kirby Puckett 6.00
192 Carlton Fisk 4.00
193 Dave Winfield 3.00
194 Alan Trammell 3.00
195 Paul Molitor 6.00
196 Tony Perez 3.00
197 Ozzie Smith 6.00
198 Ralph Kiner 3.00
199 Fergie Jenkins 2.00
200 Phil Rizzuto 3.00

Classic Combos

Too scarce to price

Classic Singles

NM/M

Common Player: 10.00
Some too scarce to price
1 Cal Ripken Jr/jsy/50 40.00
2 Eddie Murray/jsy/100 15.00
3 George Brett/jsy/100 35.00
4 Bo Jackson/jsy/100 20.00
5 Ted Williams/bat/50 200.00
6 Jimmie Foxx/bat/50 60.00
7 Reggie Jackson/jsy/100 15.00
8 Steve Carlton/jsy/50 30.00
9 Mel Ott/jsy/50 70.00
10 "Catfish" Hunter/jsy/100 10.00
11 Nolan Ryan/jsy/100 40.00
12 Rickey Henderson/jsy/100 25.00
13 Robin Yount/jsy/100 25.00
14 Orlando Cepeda/jsy/100 10.00
15 Ty Cobb/bat/50 150.00
16 Babe Ruth/bat/50 275.00
17 Dave Parker/jsy/100 10.00
18 Willie Stargell/jsy/100 15.00
19 Ernie Banks/bat/100 25.00
20 Mike Schmidt/jsy/100 35.00
21 Duke Snider/jsy/50 25.00
22 Jackie Robinson/jsy/50 75.00
23 Rickey Henderson/bat/100 25.00
24 TBD
25 Lou Gehrig/bat/50 175.00
26 Jimmie Foxx/bat/50 65.00

27 Reggie Jackson
28 Tony Gwynn/bat/100 20.00
29 Bobby Doerr/jsy/100 15.00
30 Joe Torre/jsy/100 10.00

Legendary Hats

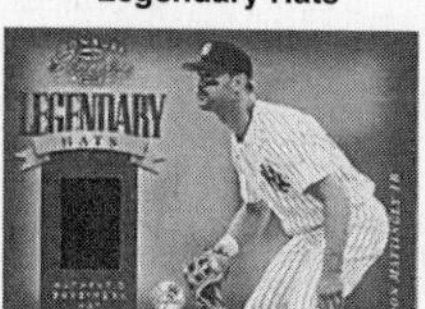

NM/M

50 sets produced
1 Don Mattingly/50 150.00
2 George Brett 150.00
3 Wade Boggs 30.00
5 Ryne Sandberg 120.00

Legendary Spikes

NM/M

50 sets produced
1 Don Mattingly 125.00
2 Eddie Murray 30.00
3 Paul Molitor 50.00
4 Harmon Killebrew 40.00
5 Mike Schmidt 100.00

Legendary Leather

NM/M

50 sets produced
1 Don Mattingly 125.00
2 Wade Boggs 30.00
4 Kirby Puckett 50.00
5 Mike Schmidt 80.00

Legendary Lumberjacks

NM/M

Varying quantities produced
1 Don Mattingly/500 20.00
2 George Brett/400 20.00
3 Stan Musial/100 35.00
4 Lou Gehrig/50 175.00
5 Mike Piazza/500 10.00
6 Mel Ott/50 75.00
7 Ted Williams/50 150.00
8 Bo Jackson/500 8.00
9 Kirby Puckett/500 15.00
10 Rafael Palmeiro/500 10.00
11 Andre Dawson/500 5.00
12 Ozzie Smith/500 15.00
13 Paul Molitor/500 15.00
14 Babe Ruth/50 220.00
15 Carlton Fisk/500 8.00
16 Rickey Henderson/500 10.00
17 Gary Carter/500 5.00
18 Cal Ripken Jr/100 40.00
19 Eddie Matthews/100 20.00
20 Luis Aparicio/500 5.00
21 Al Kaline/100 25.00
22 Eddie Murray/500 8.00
23 Yogi Berra/100 25.00
24 Alex Rodriguez/500 10.00
25 Tony Gwynn/500 10.00
26 Roberto Clemente/100 80.00
27 Mike Schmidt/400 20.00
28 Reggie Jackson/500 10.00
29 Ryne Sandberg/500 20.00
30 Joe Morgan/400 5.00
31 Joe Torre/500 5.00
32 Gary Sheffield/500 5.00
33 Nomar Garciaparra/500 10.00
34 Jeff Bagwell/500 8.00
35 Manny Ramirez/500 8.00

New Millennium Classics

NM/M

Common Player: 4.00
Varying quantities produced
All jerseys unless noted
1 Curt Schilling/500 6.00
2 Vladimir Guerrero/100 15.00
3 Jim Thome/500 8.00
4 Troy Glaus/400 6.00
5 Ivan Rodriguez/200 6.00
6 Todd Helton/400 8.00
7 Sean Casey/500 4.00
8 Scott Rolen/475 8.00
9 Ken Griffey Jr/150/base 10.00
10 Hideo Nomo/100 25.00
11 Tom Glavine/350 5.00
12 Pedro Martinez/100 15.00
13 Cliff Floyd/500 4.00
14 Shawn Green/125 8.00
15 Rafael Palmeiro/250 8.00
16 Luis Gonzalez/100 5.00
17 Lance Berkman/100 6.00
18 Frank Thomas/500 8.00
19 Randy Johnson/400 8.00
20 Moises Alou/500 4.00
21 Chipper Jones/500 8.00
22 Larry Walker/300 4.00
23 Mike Sweeney/500 4.00
24 Juan Gonzalez/300 6.00
25 Roger Clemens/100 20.00
26 Albert Pujols/300/base 15.00
27 Magglio Ordonez/500 5.00
28 Alex Rodriguez/400 10.00
29 Jeff Bagwell/125 10.00
30 Kazuhiro Sasaki/500 4.00
31 Barry Larkin/300 6.00
32 Andruw Jones/350 8.00
33 Kerry Wood/200 8.00
34 Rickey Henderson/100 10.00
35 Greg Maddux/100 15.00
36 Brian Giles/400 4.00
37 Craig Biggio/100 5.00
38 Roberto Alomar/400 6.00
39 Mike Piazza/400 10.00
40 Bernie Williams/100 10.00
41 Ichiro Suzuki/150/ball 30.00
42 Kenny Lofton/450 4.00
43 Mark Mulder/500 4.00
44 Kazuhisa Ishii/100 15.00
45 Darin Erstad/500 4.00
46 Jose Vidro/500 4.00
47 Miguel Tejada/475 6.00
48 Roy Oswalt/500 5.00
49 So Taguchi/100
50 Barry Zito/500 6.00
51 Manny Ramirez/400 8.00
52 Nomar Garciaparra/400 10.00
53 C.C. Sabathia/500 4.00
54 Carlos Delgado/500 8.00
55 Gary Sheffield/500 6.00
56 J.D. Drew/500 5.00
57 Barry Bonds/150/ball 25.00
58 Derek Jeter/150/ball 25.00
59 Edgar Martinez/400 5.00
60 Sammy Sosa/150/ball 15.00

Timeless Treasures

NM/M

Some not priced
1 Ted Williams/jsy/25
2 Ted Williams/jsy/10
3 Ted Williams/jsy/10
4 Ted Williams/jsy/10
5 Ted Williams/bat/42 140.00
6 Ted Williams/bat/47 140.00
7 Ted Williams/bat/46 140.00
8 Ted Williams/bat/49 140.00
9 Ted Williams/jsy/9
10 Cal Ripken Jr./jersey/98 50.00
11 Cal Ripken Jr./jersey/82 50.00
12 Cal Ripken Jr./jersey/83 50.00
13 Cal Ripken Jr./jersey/91 50.00
14 Cal Ripken Jr., Lou Gehrig/jsy/25
15 Cal Ripken Jr./jsy/25
16 Cal Ripken Jr./jsy/25
17 Cal Ripken Jr./jsy/8

Significant Signatures

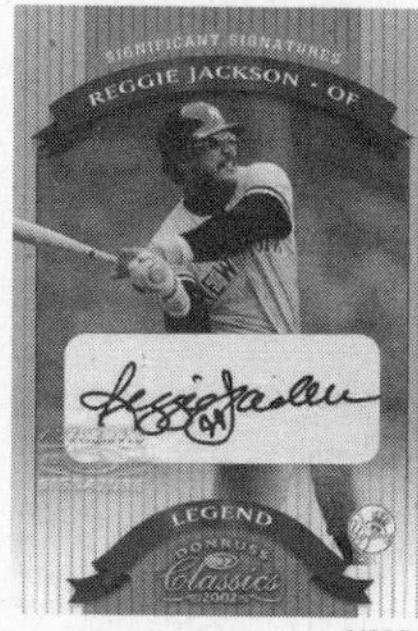

NM/M

Common Prospect Autograph: 5.00
Varying quantities produced, many not priced due to scarcity
101 Juan Cruz/400 6.00
102 Marlon Byrd/500 10.00
103 Luis Garcia/500 6.00
104 Jorge Padilla/500 10.00
105 Dennis Tankersley/250 10.00
106 Josh Pearce/500 8.00
107 Ramon Vazquez/500 5.00
108 *Chris Baker/500* 8.00
109 Eric Cyr/500 6.00
110 Reed Johnson/500 10.00
111 Ryan Jamison/500 5.00
112 Antonio Perez/500 5.00
113 Satoru Komiyama/50 50.00
114 Austin Kearns/500 15.00
115 Juan Pena/500 5.00
116 Orlando Hudson/400 10.00
117 Kazuhisa Ishii/50 40.00
118 Eric Bedard/500 5.00
119 Luis Ugueto/250 10.00
120 Ben Howard/500 8.00
121 Morgan Ensberg/500 10.00
122 Doug Devore/500 8.00
123 Josh Phelps/500 8.00
124 Angel Berroa/500 10.00
125 Ed Rogers/500 5.00
127 John Ennis/500 5.00
128 Bill Hall/400 10.00
129 Dewon Brazelton/400 8.00
130 Hank Blalock/100 25.00
131 So Taguchi/150 30.00
132 Jorge De La Rosa/500 5.00
133 Matt Thornton/500 5.00
134 Brandon Backe/500 5.00
135 Jeff Deardorff/500 5.00
136 Steve Smyth/400 5.00
137 Anderson Machado/500 10.00
138 John Buck/500 5.00
139 Mark Prior/250 60.00
140 Sean Burroughs/50 10.00
141 Alex Herrera/500 5.00
142 Francis Beltran/500 5.00
143 Jason Romano/500 5.00
144 Michael Cuddyer/400 8.00
145 Steve Bechler/500 8.00
146 Alfredo Amezaga/500 5.00
147 Ryan Ludwick/500 8.00
148 Martin Vargas/500 5.00
149 Allan Simpson/500 5.00
150 Mark Teixeira/200 30.00
152 Ernie Banks/25 100.00
153 Johnny Bench/25 125.00
154 George Brett/25 260.00
155 Lou Brock/100 30.00
157 Steve Carlton/125 35.00
159 Dennis Eckersley/500 15.00
161 Al Kaline/125 35.00
162 Dave Parker/500 10.00
163 Don Mattingly/50 75.00
168 Jim Palmer/125 25.00
169 Brooks Robinson/125 40.00
177 Gary Carter/150 25.00
178 Ron Santo/500 20.00
179 Luis Aparicio/400 10.00
180 Bobby Doerr/500 15.00
182 Yogi Berra/25 80.00
184 Eddie Murray/25 60.00
185 Andre Dawson/200 20.00
186 Duke Snider/25 70.00
187 Orlando Cepeda/125 25.00
188 Billy Williams/200 15.00
189 Juan Marichal/500 15.00
190 Harmon Killebrew/100 50.00
194 Alan Trammell/200 25.00
195 Paul Molitor/25 60.00
196 Tony Perez/150 15.00
198 Ralph Kiner/125 20.00
199 Fergie Jenkins/200 15.00
200 Phil Rizzuto/125 35.00

Timeless Tributes

Stars (1-100): 2-4X
SP's (101-150): 1-2X
SP's (151-200): 2-3X
Production 100 sets

2002 DONRUSS DIAMOND KINGS

NM/M

Complete Set (150): 150.00
Common Player: .40
Common SP (101-150): 2.00
Inserted 1:3
Pack (4): 4.50
Box (24): 80.00
1 Vladimir Guerrero 1.00
2 Adam Dunn .75
3 Tsuyoshi Shinjo .40
4 Adrian Beltre .60
5 Troy Glaus 1.00
6 Albert Pujols 2.00
7 Trot Nixon .40
8 Alex Rodriguez 2.50
9 Tom Glavine .50
10 Alfonso Soriano 1.00
11 Todd Helton 1.00
12 Joe Torre .40
13 Tim Hudson .50
14 Andruw Jones 1.00
15 Shawn Green .50
16 Aramis Ramirez .40
17 Shannon Stewart .40
18 Barry Bonds 3.00
19 Sean Casey .40
20 Barry Larkin .40
21 Scott Rolen .75
22 Barry Zito .50
23 Sammy Sosa 2.00
24 Bartolo Colon .40
25 Ryan Klesko .40
26 Ben Grieve .40
27 Roy Oswalt .50
28 Kazuhiro Sasaki .40
29 Roger Clemens 1.75
30 Bernie Williams .50
31 Roberto Alomar .50
32 Bobby Abreu .40
33 Robert Fick .40
34 Bret Boone .40
35 Rickey Henderson 1.00
36 Brian Giles .40
37 Richie Sexson .40
38 Bud Smith .40
39 Richard Hidalgo .40
40 C.C. Sabathia .40
41 Rich Aurilia .40
42 Carlos Beltran .75
43 Raul Mondesi .40
44 Carlos Delgado .50
45 Randy Johnson 1.00
46 Chan Ho Park .40
47 Rafael Palmeiro .75
48 Chipper Jones 1.50
49 Phil Nevin .40
50 Cliff Floyd .40
51 Pedro Martinez 1.00

52	Craig Biggio	.40
53	Paul LoDuca	.40
54	Cristian Guzman	.40
55	Pat Burrell	.50
56	Curt Schilling	.50
57	Orlando Cabrera	.40
58	Darin Erstad	.65
59	Omar Vizquel	.40
60	Derek Jeter	3.00
61	Nomar Garciaparra	2.00
62	Edgar Martinez	.40
63	Moises Alou	.40
64	Eric Chavez	.50
65	Mike Sweeney	.40
66	Frank Thomas	1.00
67	Mike Piazza	2.00
68	Gary Sheffield	.50
69	Mike Mussina	.50
70	Greg Maddux	1.50
71	Juan Gonzalez	1.00
72	Hideo Nomo	.65
73	Miguel Tejada	.50
74	Ichiro Suzuki	2.00
75	Matt Morris	.40
76	Ivan Rodriguez	.75
77	Mark Mulder	.40
78	J.D. Drew	.40
79	Mark Grace	.50
80	Jason Giambi	.50
81	Mark Buehrle	.40
82	Jose Vidro	.40
83	Manny Ramirez	1.00
84	Jeff Bagwell	1.00
85	Magglio Ordonez	.50
86	Ken Griffey Jr.	2.00
87	Luis Gonzalez	.40
88	Jim Edmonds	.40
89	Larry Walker	.40
90	Jim Thome	.40
91	Lance Berkman	.40
92	Jorge Posada	.50
93	Kevin Brown	.40
94	Joe Mays	.40
95	Kerry Wood	.75
96	Mark Ellis	.40
97	Austin Kearns	.75
98	*Jorge De La Rosa*	.50
99	Brandon Berger	.40
100	Ryan Ludwick	.40
101	Marlon Byrd	2.00
102	*Brandon Backe*	2.00
103	Juan Cruz	2.00
104	*Anderson Machado*	3.00
105	*So Taguchi*	4.00
106	Dewon Brazelton	2.00
107	Josh Beckett	3.00
108	John Buck	2.00
109	*Jorge Padilla*	3.00
110	Hee Seop Choi	2.00
111	Angel Berroa	2.00
112	Mark Teixeira	3.00
113	Victor Martinez	2.00
114	*Kazuhisa Ishii*	6.00
115	Dennis Tankersley	2.00
116	*Wilson Valdez*	2.00
117	Antonio Perez	2.00
118	Ed Rogers	2.00
119	Wilson Betemit	2.00
120	Mike Rivera	2.00
121	Mark Prior	6.00
122	Roberto Clemente	6.00
123	Roberto Clemente	6.00
124	Roberto Clemente	6.00
125	Roberto Clemente	6.00
126	Roberto Clemente	6.00
127	Babe Ruth	10.00
128	Ted Williams	8.00
129	Andre Dawson	2.00
130	Eddie Murray	3.00
131	Juan Marichal	3.00
132	Kirby Puckett	5.00
133	Alan Trammell	2.00
134	Bobby Doerr	2.00
135	Carlton Fisk	3.00
136	Eddie Mathews	4.00
137	Mike Schmidt	6.00
138	Jim "Catfish" Hunter	2.00
139	Nolan Ryan	10.00
140	George Brett	6.00
141	Gary Carter	2.00
142	Paul Molitor	4.00
143	Lou Gehrig	8.00
144	Ryne Sandberg	5.00
145	Tony Gwynn	5.00
146	Ron Santo	2.00
147	Cal Ripken Jr.	10.00
148	Al Kaline	4.00
149	Bo Jackson	3.00
150	Don Mattingly	8.00

Bronze Foil

Cards 1-100:	1-2X
Cards 101-150:	.5X
Inserted 1:6	
Gold Foil (1-100):	4-8X
Gold Foil (101-150):	2-3X
Production 100 sets	
Silver Foil (1-100):	3-4X
Silver Foil (101-150):	1-2X
Production 400 sets	

Diamond Cut

		NM/M
Common Signature (1-30):		5.00
1	Vladimir Guerrero/400	30.00
2	Mark Prior/400	65.00
3	Victor Martinez/500	10.00
4	Marlon Byrd/500	15.00
5	Bud Smith/400	10.00
6	Joe Mays/500	10.00
7	Troy Glaus/500	20.00
8	Ron Santo/500	15.00
9	Roy Oswalt/500	20.00
10	Angel Berroa/500	10.00
11	Mark Buehrle/500	15.00
12	John Buck/500	10.00
13	Barry Larkin/250	40.00
14	Gary Carter/300	30.00
15	Mark Teixeira/300	25.00
16	Alan Trammell/500	20.00
17	Kazuhisa Ishii/100	65.00
18	Rafael Palmeiro/125	50.00
19	Austin Kearns/500	25.00
20	Joe Torre/125	40.00
21	J.D. Drew/400	20.00
22	So Taguchi/400	20.00
23	Juan Marichal/500	15.00
24	Bobby Doerr/500	20.00
25	Carlos Beltran/500	10.00
26	Robert Fick/500	10.00
27	Albert Pujols/200	70.00
28	Shannon Stewart/500	10.00
29	Antonio Perez/500	10.00
30	Wilson Betemit/500	10.00
Jerseys (31-80):		
31	Alex Rodriguez/500	15.00
32	Curt Schilling/500	8.00
33	George Brett/300	30.00
34	Hideo Nomo/100	40.00
35	Ivan Rodriguez/500	8.00
36	Don Mattingly/200	40.00
37	Joe Mays/500	5.00
38	Lance Berkman/400	5.00
39	Tony Gwynn/500	10.00
40	Darin Erstad/400	5.00
41	Adrian Beltre/400	5.00
42	Frank Thomas/500	8.00
43	Cal Ripken Jr./300	30.00
44	Jose Vidro/500	5.00
45	Randy Johnson/300	8.00
46	Carlos Delgado/500	6.00
47	Roger Clemens/400	20.00
48	Luis Gonzalez/500	5.00
49	Marlon Byrd/500	6.00
50	Carlton Fisk/500	8.00
51	Manny Ramirez/500	8.00
52	Vladimir Guerrero/500	8.00
53	Barry Larkin/500	8.00
54	Aramis Ramirez/500	5.00
55	Todd Helton/300	8.00
56	Carlos Beltran/250	5.00
57	Jeff Bagwell/250	8.00
58	Larry Walker/500	5.00
59	Al Kaline/200	25.00
60	Chipper Jones/500	8.00
61	Bernie Williams/500	6.00
62	Bud Smith/500	5.00
63	Edgar Martinez/500	5.00
64	Pedro Martinez/500	8.00
65	Andre Dawson/200	6.00
66	Mike Piazza/100	40.00
67	Barry Zito/500	6.00
68	Bo Jackson/300	8.00
69	Nolan Ryan/400	50.00
70	Troy Glaus/500	6.00
71	Jorge Posada/500	8.00
72	Ted Williams/100	200.00
73	Nomar Garciaparra/500	15.00
74	"Catfish" Hunter/100	25.00
75	Gary Carter/500	8.00
76	Craig Biggio/500	5.00
77	Andruw Jones/500	8.00
78	Rickey Henderson/250	30.00
79	Greg Maddux/400	15.00
80	Kerry Wood/500	10.00
Bats (81-100):		
81	Alex Rodriguez/500	20.00
82	Don Mattingly/425	30.00
83	Craig Biggio/500	5.00
84	Kazuhisa Ishii/375	8.00
85	Eddie Murray/500	8.00
86	Carlton Fisk/500	8.00
87	Tsuyoshi Shinjo/500	5.00
88	Bo Jackson/500	10.00
89	Eddie Mathews/100	30.00
90	Chipper Jones/500	8.00
91	Adam Dunn/375	6.00
92	Tony Gwynn/200	10.00
93	Kirby Puckett/500	15.00
94	Andre Dawson/500	5.00
95	Bernie Williams/500	6.00
96	Roberto Clemente/300	70.00
97	Babe Ruth/100	250.00
98	Roberto Alomar/500	8.00
99	Frank Thomas/500	8.00
100	So Taguchi/500	6.00

Heritage Collection

		NM/M
Complete Set (25):		100.00
Common Player:		2.00
Inserted 1:23		
1	Lou Gehrig	8.00
2	Nolan Ryan	10.00
3	Ryne Sandberg	4.00
4	Ted Williams	8.00
5	Roberto Clemente	8.00
6	Mike Schmidt	6.00
7	Roger Clemens	5.00
8	Kirby Puckett	4.00
9	Andre Dawson	2.00
10	Carlton Fisk	2.00
11	Don Mattingly	8.00
12	Juan Marichal	2.00
13	George Brett	8.00
14	Bo Jackson	3.00
15	Eddie Mathews	3.00
16	Randy Johnson	3.00
17	Alan Trammell	2.00
18	Tony Gwynn	4.00
19	Paul Molitor	3.00
20	Barry Bonds	10.00
21	Eddie Murray	3.00
22	Jim "Catfish" Hunter	2.00
23	Rickey Henderson	3.00
24	Cal Ripken Jr.	10.00
25	Babe Ruth	10.00

DK Originals

		NM/M
Complete Set (15):		50.00
Common Player:		2.00
Production 1,000 sets		
1	Alex Rodriguez	7.00
2	Kazuhisa Ishii	2.00
3	Pedro Martinez	3.00
4	Nomar Garciaparra	6.00
5	Albert Pujols	6.00
6	Chipper Jones	5.00
7	So Taguchi	2.00
8	Jeff Bagwell	3.00
9	Vladimir Guerrero	3.00
10	Derek Jeter	8.00
11	Sammy Sosa	6.00
12	Ichiro Suzuki	6.00
13	Barry Bonds	8.00
14	Jason Giambi	3.00
15	Mike Piazza	6.00

Ramly T204

		NM/M
Complete Set (25):		120.00
Common Player:		3.00
Production 1,000 sets		
1	Vladimir Guerrero	4.00
2	Jeff Bagwell	4.00
3	Barry Bonds	15.00
4	Rickey Henderson	4.00
5	Mike Piazza	8.00
6	Derek Jeter	15.00
7	Kazuhisa Ishii	3.00
8	Ichiro Suzuki	10.00
9	Chipper Jones	5.00
10	Sammy Sosa	8.00
11	Don Mattingly	10.00
12	Shawn Green	3.00
13	Nomar Garciaparra	10.00
14	Luis Gonzalez	3.00
15	Albert Pujols	8.00
16	Cal Ripken Jr.	15.00
17	Todd Helton	4.00
18	Hideo Nomo	3.00
19	Alex Rodriguez	10.00
20	So Taguchi	3.00
21	Lance Berkman	3.00
22	Tony Gwynn	5.00
23	Roger Clemens	6.00
24	Jason Giambi	4.00
25	Ken Griffey Jr.	8.00

Timeline

		NM/M
Complete Set (10):		60.00
Common Card:		3.00
Inserted 1:60		
1	Lou Gehrig, Don Mattingly	10.00
2	Hideo Nomo, Ichiro Suzuki	6.00
3	Cal Ripken Jr., Alex Rodriguez	10.00
4	Mike Schmidt, Scott Rolen	8.00
5	Ichiro Suzuki, Albert Pujols	8.00
6	Curt Schilling, Randy Johnson	5.00
7	Chipper Jones, Eddie Mathews	5.00
8	Lou Gehrig, Cal Ripken Jr.	10.00
9	Derek Jeter, Roger Clemens	10.00
10	Kazuhiko Ishimine, So Taguchi	3.00

2002 DONRUSS ELITE

	NM/M
Complete Set (200):	
Common Player:	.25
Common (101-150):	2.00
Inserted 1:10	
Common (151-200):	3.00
Production 1,500	

Pack (5): 3.00
Box (20): 50.00
1 Vladimir Guerrero .75
2 Bernie Williams .35
3 Ichiro Suzuki 1.50
4 Roger Clemens 1.25
5 Greg Maddux 1.00
6 Fred McGriff .25
7 Jermaine Dye .25
8 Ken Griffey Jr. 1.50
9 Todd Helton .75
10 Torii Hunter .40
11 Pat Burrell .40
12 Chipper Jones 1.00
13 Ivan Rodriguez .50
14 Roy Oswalt .40
15 Shannon Stewart .25
16 Magglio Ordonez .40
17 Lance Berkman .25
18 Mark Mulder .25
19 Al Leiter .25
20 Sammy Sosa 1.50
21 Scott Rolen .75
22 Aramis Ramirez .25
23 Alfonso Soriano .75
24 Phil Nevin .25
25 Barry Bonds 2.50
26 Joe Mays .25
27 Jeff Kent .25
28 Mark Quinn .25
29 Adrian Beltre .35
30 Freddy Garcia .25
31 Pedro J. Martinez .75
32 Darryl Kile .25
33 Mike Cameron .25
34 Frank Catalanotto .25
35 Jose Vidro .25
36 Jim Thome .25
37 Javy Lopez .25
38 Paul Konerko .25
39 Jeff Bagwell .75
40 Curt Schilling .40
41 Miguel Tejada .40
42 Jim Edmonds .25
43 Ellis Burks .25
44 Mark Grace .35
45 Robb Nen .25
46 Jeff Conine .25
47 Derek Jeter 2.50
48 Mike Lowell .25
49 Javier Vazquez .25
50 Manny Ramirez .75
51 Bartolo Colon .25
52 Carlos Beltran .50
53 Tim Hudson .40
54 Rafael Palmeiro .65
55 Jimmy Rollins .25
56 Andruw Jones .75
57 Orlando Cabrera .25
58 Dean Palmer .25
59 Bret Boone .25
60 Carlos Febles .25
61 Ben Grieve .25
62 Richie Sexson .25
63 Alex Rodriguez 2.00
64 Juan Pierre .25
65 Bobby Higginson .25
66 Barry Zito .40
67 Raul Mondesi .25
68 Albert Pujols 2.00
69 Omar Vizquel .25
70 Bobby Abreu .25
71 Corey Koskie .25
72 Tom Glavine .40
73 Paul LoDuca .25
74 Terrence Long .25
75 Matt Morris .25
76 Andy Pettitte .40
77 Rich Aurilia .25
78 Todd Walker .25
79 John Olerud .25
80 Mike Sweeney .25
81 Ray Durham .25
82 Fernando Vina .25
83 Nomar Garciaparra 1.50
84 Mariano Rivera .35
85 Mike Piazza 1.50
86 Mark Buehrle .25
87 Adam Dunn .50
88 Luis Gonzalez .35
89 Richard Hidalgo .25
90 Brad Radke .25
91 Russ Ortiz .25
92 Brian Giles .25
93 Billy Wagner .25
94 Cliff Floyd .25
95 Eric Milton .25
96 Bud Smith .25
97 Wade Miller .25
98 Jon Lieber .25
99 Derrek Lee .25
100 Jose Cruz Jr. .25
101 Dmitri Young 2.00
102 Mo Vaughn 2.00
103 Tino Martinez 2.00
104 Larry Walker 2.50
105 Chuck Knoblauch 2.00
106 Troy Glaus 3.00
107 Jason Giambi 4.00
108 Travis Fryman 2.00
109 Josh Beckett 4.00
110 Edgar Martinez 2.00
111 Tim Salmon 2.00
112 C.C. Sabathia 2.00
113 Randy Johnson 5.00
114 Juan Gonzalez 4.00
115 Carlos Delgado 4.00
116 Hideo Nomo 4.00
117 Kerry Wood 4.00
118 Brian Jordan 2.00
119 Carlos Pena 2.00
120 Roger Cedeno 2.00
121 Chan Ho Park 2.00
122 Rafael Furcal 2.00
123 Frank Thomas 4.00
124 Mike Mussina 4.00
125 Rickey Henderson 5.00
126 Sean Casey 2.00
127 Barry Larkin 2.00
128 Kazuhiro Sasaki 2.00
129 Moises Alou 2.00
130 Jeff Cirillo 2.00
131 Jason Kendall 2.00
132 Gary Sheffield 3.00
133 Ryan Klesko 2.00
134 Kevin Brown 2.00
135 Darin Erstad 2.00
136 Roberto Alomar 3.00
137 Brad Fullmer 2.00
138 Eric Chavez 2.00
139 Ben Sheets 2.00
140 Trot Nixon 2.00
141 Garret Anderson 2.00
142 Shawn Green 2.50
143 Troy Percival 2.00
144 Craig Biggio 2.50
145 Jorge Posada 2.50
146 J.D. Drew 3.00
147 Johnny Damon 2.00
148 Jeromy Burnitz 2.00
149 Robin Ventura 2.00
150 Aaron Sele 2.00
151 *Cam Esslinger* 3.00
152 *Ben Howard* 4.00
153 *Brandon Backe* 3.00
154 *Jorge De La Rosa* 3.00
155 Austin Kearns 5.00
156 Carlos Zambrano 3.00
157 *Kyle Kane* 3.00
158 *So Taguchi* 5.00
159 *Brian Mallette* 3.00
160 Brett Jodie 3.00
161 *Elio Serrano* 3.00
162 Joe Thurston 3.00
163 Kevin Olsen 3.00
164 *Rodrigo Rosario* 4.00
165 Matt Guerrier 3.00
166 *Anderson Machado* 5.00
167 Bert Snow 3.00
168 *Franklyn German* 3.00
169 Brandon Claussen 3.00
170 Jason Romano 3.00
171 *Jorge Padilla* 5.00
172 Jose Cueto 3.00
173 *Allan Simpson* 3.00
174 *Doug Devore* 3.00
175 Justin Duchscherer 3.00
176 Josh Pearce 3.00
177 *Steve Bechler* 3.00
178 Josh Phelps 3.00
179 Juan Diaz 3.00
180 *Victor Alvarez* 3.00
181 Ramon Vazquez 3.00
182 Mike Rivera 3.00
183 *Kazuhisa Ishii* 6.00
184 Henry Mateo 3.00
185 *Travis Hughes* 5.00
186 Zach Day 3.00
187 Brad Voyles 3.00
188 Sean Douglass 3.00
189 Nick Neugebauer 3.00
190 *Tom Shearn* 3.00
191 *Eric Cyr* 3.00
192 Adam Johnson 3.00
193 Michael Cuddyer 3.00
194 Erik Bedard 3.00
195 Mark Ellis 3.00
196 Carlos Hernandez 3.00
197 Deivi Santos 3.00
198 Morgan Ensberg 3.00
199 *Ryan Jamison* 3.00
200 Cody Ransom 3.00

Aspirations

1-100 print run 26-50: 15-30X
1-100 p/r 51-80: 8-15X
101-150 p/r 26-50: 1.5-3X
101-150 p/r 51-99: 1-2X

Status

1-100 print run 36-70: 10-20X
1-100 p/r 71-100: 5-10X
101-150 p/r 36-70: 1-2X
101-150 p/r 71-100: 1X

Back to the Future Threads

NM/M
Common Card: 10.00
Duals 50 produced, Singles 100
1 Scott Rolen, Marlon Byrd 30.00
2 Joe Crede, Frank Thomas 40.00
3 Lance Berkman, Jeff Bagwell 40.00
4 Marcus Giles, Chipper Jones 50.00
5 Shawn Green, Paul LoDuca 30.00
7 Kerry Wood, Juan Cruz 35.00
8 Vladimir Guerrero, Orlando Cabrera 40.00
9 Scott Rolen 15.00
10 Marlon Byrd 20.00
11 Frank Thomas 25.00
12 Joe Crede 10.00
13 Jeff Bagwell 25.00
14 Lance Berkman 15.00
15 Chipper Jones 25.00
16 Marcus Giles 10.00
17 Shawn Green 15.00
18 Paul LoDuca 10.00
19 Jim Edmonds 10.00
20 So Taguchi 50.00
21 Kerry Wood 15.00
22 Juan Cruz 10.00
23 Vladimir Guerrero 25.00
24 Orlando Cabrera 10.00

All-Star Salutes

NM/M
Common Player: 1.00
Century: 1-2X
Production 100
1 Ichiro Suzuki 5.00
2 Tony Gwynn 4.00
3 Magglio Ordonez 1.50
4 Cal Ripken Jr. 8.00
5 Tony Gwynn 4.00
6 Kazuhiro Sasaki 1.00
7 Freddy Garcia 1.00
8 Luis Gonzalez 1.00
9 Lance Berkman 1.00
10 Derek Jeter 8.00
11 Chipper Jones 4.00
12 Randy Johnson 3.00
13 Andruw Jones 3.00
14 Pedro J. Martinez 3.00
15 Jim Thome 1.00
16 Rafael Palmeiro 2.50
17 Barry Larkin 1.00
18 Ivan Rodriguez 2.50
19 Omar Vizquel 1.00
20 Edgar Martinez 1.00
21 Larry Walker 1.00
22 Javy Lopez 1.00
23 Mariano Rivera 1.25
24 Frank Thomas 3.00
25 Greg Maddux 4.00

Back to the Future

NM/M
Complete Set (24): 75.00
Common Player: 2.00
Duals 500 produced, Singles 1,000
1 Scott Rolen, Marlon Byrd 5.00
2 Joe Crede, Frank Thomas 6.00
3 Lance Berkman, Jeff Bagwell 6.00
4 Marcus Giles, Chipper Jones 10.00
5 Shawn Green, Paul LoDuca 4.00
7 Kerry Wood, Juan Cruz 4.00
8 Vladimir Guerrero, Orlando Cabrera 6.00
9 Scott Rolen 3.00
10 Marlon Byrd 2.00
11 Frank Thomas 4.00
12 Joe Crede 2.00
13 Jeff Bagwell 4.00
14 Lance Berkman 2.00
15 Chipper Jones 6.00
16 Marcus Giles 2.00
17 Shawn Green 2.50
18 Paul LoDuca 2.00
19 Jim Edmonds 2.00
21 Kerry Wood 3.00
22 Juan Cruz 2.00
23 Vladimir Guerrero 4.00
24 Orlando Cabrera 2.00

Back 2 Back Jacks

NM/M
Common Card: 10.00
Dual production 75
Single production 150
1 Ivan Rodriguez, Alex Rodriguez 40.00
2 Kirby Puckett, Dave Winfield 50.00
3 Ted Williams, Nomar Garciaparra 150.00
4 Jeff Bagwell, Craig Biggio 25.00
5 Eddie Murray, Cal Ripken Jr. 125.00
6 Andruw Jones, Chipper Jones 25.00
7 Roberto Clemente, Willie Stargell 120.00
8 Lou Gehrig, Don Mattingly 180.00
9 Larry Walker, Todd Helton 20.00
10 Manny Ramirez, Trot Nixon 25.00
11 Alex Rodriguez 30.00
12 Ivan Rodriguez 15.00
13 Kirby Puckett 40.00
14 Dave Winfield 15.00

15	Ted Williams	100.00
16	Nomar Garciaparra	40.00
17	Jeff Bagwell	15.00
18	Craig Biggio	10.00
19	Eddie Murray	20.00
20	Cal Ripken Jr.	60.00
21	Andruw Jones	10.00
22	Chipper Jones	20.00
23	Roberto Clemente	80.00
25	Lou Gehrig	160.00
26	Don Mattingly	65.00
27	Larry Walker	10.00
28	Todd Helton	15.00
29	Manny Ramirez	20.00
30	Trot Nixon	10.00

Career Bests

		NM/M
	Common Player:	2.00
1	Albert Pujols/1,013	8.00
2	Alex Rodriguez/52	20.00
3	Alex Rodriguez/135	15.00
4	Andruw Jones/104	6.00
5	Barry Bonds/73	25.00
6	Barry Bonds/1379	10.00
7	Barry Bonds/177	20.00
8	C.C. Sabathia/171	4.00
9	Carlos Beltran/876	2.00
10	Chipper Jones/330	6.00
11	Derek Jeter/900	15.00
12	Eric Chavez/114	4.00
13	Frank Catalanotto/330	2.00
14	Ichiro Suzuki/838	10.00
15	Ichiro Suzuki/127	15.00
16	Ichiro Suzuki/8	
17	J.D. Drew/27	20.00
18	J.D. Drew/1027	2.00
19	Jason Giambi/660	5.00
20	Jim Thome/49	25.00
21	Jim Thome/624	4.00
22	Jorge Posada/95	8.00
23	Jose Cruz Jr/856	2.00
24	Kazuhiro Sasaki/45	15.00
25	Kerry Wood/336	5.00
26	Lance Berkman/1050	3.00
27	Magglio Ordonez/382	3.00
28	Mark Mulder/345	2.00
29	Pat Burrell/27	20.00
30	Pat Burrell/469	3.00
31	Randy Johnson/372	6.00
32	Randy Johnson/21	
33	Richie Sexson/547	3.00
34	Roberto Alomar/956	3.00
35	Sammy Sosa/160	12.00
36	Sammy Sosa/1174	6.00
37	Shawn Green/125	4.00
38	Tsuyoshi Shinjo/10	
39	Trot Nixon/150	3.00
40	Troy Glaus/108	5.00

Passing the Torch

		NM/M
	Common Card:	4.00
	Dual 500, Single 1,000 produced	
1	Fergie Jenkins, Mark Prior	10.00
2	Nolan Ryan, Roy Oswalt	25.00
3	Ozzie Smith, J.D. Drew	8.00
4	George Brett, Carlos Beltran	15.00
5	Kirby Puckett, Michael Cuddyer	10.00
6	Johnny Bench, Adam Dunn	8.00
7	Duke Snider, Paul LoDuca	6.00
8	Tony Gwynn, Xavier Nady	10.00
9	Fergie Jenkins	4.00
10	Mark Prior	8.00
11	Nolan Ryan	15.00
12	Roy Oswalt	5.00
13	Ozzie Smith	6.00
14	J.D. Drew	4.00
15	George Brett	10.00
16	Carlos Beltran	6.00
17	Kirby Puckett	6.00
18	Michael Cuddyer	4.00
19	Johnny Bench	6.00
20	Adam Dunn	6.00
21	Duke Snider	6.00
22	Paul LoDuca	4.00
23	Tony Gwynn	6.00
24	Xavier Nady	4.00

Throwback Threads

		NM/M
	Common Card:	15.00
	Dual 50, Single 100 produced	
1	Manny Ramirez, Ted Williams	125.00
2	Mike Piazza, Carlton Fisk	50.00
3	George Brett, Bo Jackson	125.00
4	Randy Johnson, Curt Schilling	40.00
5	Don Mattingly, Lou Gehrig	250.00
6	Bernie Williams, Dave Winfield	25.00
7	Rickey Henderson	75.00
8	Paul Molitor, Robin Yount	75.00
9	J.D. Drew, Stan Musial	100.00
10	Andre Dawson, Ryne Sandberg	100.00
11	Babe Ruth, Reggie Jackson	325.00
12	Brooks Robinson, Cal Ripken Jr.	120.00
13	Ted Williams, Nomar Garciaparra	125.00
14	Shawn Green, Jackie Robinson	80.00
15	Tony Gwynn, Cal Ripken Jr.	120.00
16	Ted Williams	75.00
17	Manny Ramirez	20.00
18	Carlton Fisk	25.00
19	Mike Piazza	20.00
20	Bo Jackson	20.00
21	George Brett	50.00
22	Curt Schilling	20.00
23	Randy Johnson	20.00
24	Don Mattingly	50.00
25	Lou Gehrig	200.00
26	Bernie Williams	15.00
27	Dave Winfield	15.00
29	Rickey Henderson	40.00
30	Robin Yount	30.00
31	Paul Molitor	25.00
32	Stan Musial	65.00
33	J.D. Drew	15.00
34	Andre Dawson	15.00
35	Ryne Sandberg	50.00
36	Babe Ruth	250.00
37	Reggie Jackson	25.00
38	Brooks Robinson	25.00
39	Cal Ripken Jr.	75.00
40	Nomar Garciaparra	40.00
41	Jackie Robinson	80.00
42	Shawn Green	15.00
43	Pedro J. Martinez	20.00
44	Nolan Ryan	80.00
45	Kazuhiro Sasaki	15.00
46	Tony Gwynn	25.00
47	Carlton Fisk	20.00
48	Cal Ripken Jr.	75.00
49	Rod Carew	20.00
50	Nolan Ryan	80.00
51	Alex Rodriguez	25.00
52	Greg Maddux	25.00
53	Pedro J. Martinez	20.00
54	Rickey Henderson	30.00
55	Rod Carew	20.00
56	Roberto Clemente	100.00
57	Hideo Nomo	40.00
58	Rickey Henderson	40.00
59	Dave Parker	15.00
60	Eddie Mathews	25.00
61	Eddie Murray	20.00
62	Nolan Ryan	80.00
63	Tom Seaver	25.00
64	Roger Clemens	40.00
65	Rickey Henderson	40.00

Turn of the Century

		NM/M
	Common Player:	8.00
154	Jorge De La Rosa/50	8.00
156	Carlos Zambrano/50	8.00
157	Kyle Kane/50	8.00
158	So Taguchi/25	15.00
159	Brian Mallette/50	8.00
160	Brett Jodie/50	8.00
165	Matt Guerrier/50	8.00
168	Franklyn German/50	8.00
169	Brandon Claussen/50	15.00
171	Jorge Padilla/50	10.00
172	Jose Cueto/50	8.00
176	Josh Pearce/50	8.00
177	Steve Bechler/50	8.00
178	Josh Phelps/50	8.00
180	Victor Alvarez/50	8.00
182	Michael Rivera/50	8.00
183	Kazuhisa Ishii/125	20.00
184	Henry Mateo/50	8.00
186	Zach Day/50	8.00
189	Nick Neugebauer/100	8.00
192	Adam Johnson/125	8.00
193	Michael Cuddyer/50	8.00
195	Mark Ellis/25	10.00
196	Carlos Hernandez/150	8.00
198	Morgan Ensberg/50	8.00
200	Cody Ransom/150	8.00

Turn of the Century Autographs

		NM/M
	Common Autograph:	10.00
151	Cam Esslinger/150	10.00
152	Ben Howard/150	10.00
153	Brandon Backe/150	10.00
154	Jorge De La Rosa/100	10.00
155	Austin Kearns/150	20.00
156	Carlos Zambrano/100	20.00
157	Kyle Kane/100	10.00
158	So Taguchi/125	20.00
159	Brian Mallette/100	10.00
160	Brett Jodie/100	10.00
161	Elio Serrano/150	10.00
162	Joe Thurston/150	10.00
163	Kevin Olsen/150	10.00
164	Rodrigo Rosario/150	10.00
165	Matt Guerrier/100	10.00
166	Anderson Machado/150	12.00
167	Bert Snow/150	10.00
168	Franklyn German/100	10.00
169	Brandon Claussen/100	20.00
170	Jason Romano/150	10.00
171	Jorge Padilla/100	15.00
172	Jose Cueto/100	10.00
173	Allan Simpson/150	10.00
174	Doug Devore/150	15.00
175	Justin Duchscherer/150	10.00
176	Josh Pearce/100	10.00
177	Steve Bechler/100	10.00
178	Josh Phelps/100	15.00
179	Juan Diaz/150	10.00
180	Victor Alvarez/100	10.00
181	Ramon Vazquez/150	10.00
182	Michael Rivera/100	10.00
183	Kazuhisa Ishii/25	150.00
184	Henry Mateo/100	10.00
185	Travis Hughes/150	10.00
186	Zach Day/100	10.00
187	Brad Voyles/150	10.00
188	Sean Douglass/150	10.00
189	Nick Neugebauer/50	10.00
190	Tom Shearn/150	10.00
191	Eric Cyr/150	10.00
192	Adam Johnson/25	10.00
193	Michael Cuddyer/100	10.00
194	Erik Bedard/150	10.00
195	Mark Ellis/125	10.00
197	Deivis Santos/150	10.00
198	Morgan Ensberg/100	10.00
199	Ryan Jamison/150	10.00

Passing the Torch Autographs

		NM/M
	Common Autograph:	15.00
1	Ferguson Jenkins, Mark Prior/50	125.00
2	Nolan Ryan, Roy Oswalt/50	180.00
3	Ozzie Smith, J.D. Drew/50	125.00
4	George Brett, Carlos Beltran/25	300.00
5	Kirby Puckett, Michael Cuddyer/50	100.00
6	Johnny Bench, Adam Dunn/50	100.00
7	Duke Snider, Paul LoDuca/50	80.00
8	Tony Gwynn, Xavier Nady/50	120.00
9	Fergie Jenkins/50	40.00
10	Mark Prior/100	80.00
11	Nolan Ryan/100	125.00
12	Roy Oswalt/100	25.00
13	Ozzie Smith/25	160.00
14	J.D. Drew/100	30.00
15	George Brett/25	300.00
16	Carlos Beltran/100	40.00
17	Kirby Puckett/25	120.00
18	Michael Cuddyer/100	15.00
19	Johnny Bench/100	50.00
20	Adam Dunn/50	40.00
21	Duke Snider/100	30.00
22	Paul LoDuca/100	15.00
23	Tony Gwynn/100	50.00
24	Xavier Nady/100	15.00

Throwback Threads Autographs

No Pricing

2002 DONRUSS FAN CLUB

		NM/M
	Complete Set (300):	
	Common Player:	.25
	Common (201-260):	3.00
	Production 1,350	
	Common (261-300):	2.00
	Production 2,025	
	Pack (5):	3.50
	Box (20):	60.00
1	Alex Rodriguez	2.00
2	Pedro Martinez	.75
3	Vladimir Guerrero	.75
4	Jim Edmonds	.25
5	Derek Jeter	2.50
6	Johnny Damon	.40
7	Rafael Furcal	.25
8	Cal Ripken Jr.	2.50
9	Brad Radke	.25
10	Bret Boone	.25
11	Pat Burrell	.50
12	Roy Oswalt	.50
13	Cliff Floyd	.25
14	Robin Ventura	.25
15	Frank Thomas	.75
16	Mariano Rivera	.35
17	Paul LoDuca	.25
18	Geoff Jenkins	.25
19	Tony Gwynn	1.00
20	Chipper Jones	1.00
21	Eric Chavez	.40
22	Kerry Wood	.60
23	Jorge Posada	.35
24	J.D. Drew	.40
25	Garret Anderson	.25
26	Javier Vazquez	.25

27	Kenny Lofton	.25
28	Mike Mussina	.45
29	Paul Konerko	.25
30	Bernie Williams	.45
31	Eric Milton	.25
32	Craig Wilson	.25
33	Paul O'Neill	.25
34	Dmitri Young	.25
35	Andres Galarraga	.25
36	Gary Sheffield	.40
37	Ben Grieve	.25
38	Scott Rolen	.75
39	Mark Grace	.35
40	Albert Pujols	2.00
41	Barry Zito	.40
42	Edgar Martinez	.25
43	Jarrod Washburn	.25
44	Juan Pierre	.25
45	Mark Buehrle	.25
46	Larry Walker	.25
47	Trot Nixon	.25
48	Wade Miller	.25
49	Robert Fick	.25
50	Sean Casey	.40
51	Joe Mays	.25
52	Brad Fullmer	.25
53	Chan Ho Park	.25
54	Carlos Delgado	.50
55	Phil Nevin	.25
56	Mike Cameron	.25
57	Raul Mondesi	.25
58	Roberto Alomar	.40
59	Ryan Klesko	.25
60	Andruw Jones	.75
61	Gabe Kapler	.25
62	Darin Erstad	.65
63	Cristian Guzman	.25
64	Kazuhiro Sasaki	.25
65	Doug Mientkiewicz	.25
66	Sammy Sosa	1.50
67	Mike Hampton	.25
68	Rickey Henderson	.75
69	Mark Mulder	.35
70	Jeff Conine	.25
71	Freddy Garcia	.25
72	Ivan Rodriguez	.65
73	Terrence Long	.25
74	Adam Dunn	.50
75	Moises Alou	.25
76	Todd Helton	.75
77	Preston Wilson	.25
78	Roger Cedeno	.25
79	Tony Armas Jr.	.25
80	Manny Ramirez	.75
81	Jose Vidro	.25
82	Randy Johnson	.75
83	Richie Sexson	.25
84	Troy Glaus	.75
85	Kevin Brown	.35
86	Woody Williams	.25
87	Adrian Beltre	.40
88	Brian Giles	.25
89	Jermaine Dye	.25
90	Craig Biggio	.25
91	Richard Hidalgo	.25
92	Magglio Ordonez	.40
93	Al Leiter	.25
94	Jeff Kent	.25
95	Curt Schilling	.50
96	Tim Hudson	.50
97	Fred McGriff	.25
98	Barry Larkin	.25
99	Jim Thome	.25
100	Tom Glavine	.40
101	Alfonso Soriano	.75
102	Jamie Moyer	.25
103	Vinny Castilla	.25
104	Rich Aurilia	.25
105	Matt Morris	.25
106	Rafael Palmeiro	.65
107	Joe Crede	.25
108	Barry Bonds	2.50
109	Robert Person	.25
110	Nomar Garciaparra	1.50
111	Brandon Duckworth	.25
112	Russ Ortiz	.25
113	Jeff Weaver	.25
114	Carlos Beltran	.50
115	Ellis Burks	.25
116	Jeremy Giambi	.25
117	Carlos Lee	.25
118	Ken Griffey Jr.	1.50
119	Torii Hunter	.40
120	Andy Petitte	.40
121	Jose Canseco	.40
122	Charles Johnson	.25
123	Nick Johnson	.25
124	Luis Gonzalez	.35
125	Rondell White	.25
126	Miguel Tejada	.50
127	Jose Cruz Jr.	.25
128	Brent Abernathy	.25
129	Scott Brosius	.25
130	Jon Lieber	.25
131	John Smoltz	.25
132	Mike Sweeney	.25
133	Shannon Stewart	.25
134	Derrek Lee	.25
135	Brian Jordan	.25
136	Rusty Greer	.25
137	Mike Piazza	1.50
138	Billy Wagner	.25
139	Shawn Green	.35
140	Orlando Cabrera	.25
141	Jeff Bagwell	.75
142	Aaron Sele	.25
143	Hideo Nomo	.75
144	Marlon Anderson	.25
145	Todd Walker	.25
146	Bobby Higginson	.25
147	Ichiro Suzuki	2.00
148	Juan Uribe	.25
149	Jason Kendall	.25
150	Mark Quinn	.25
151	Ben Sheets	.25
152	Paul Abbott	.25
153	Aubrey Huff	.25
154	Greg Maddux	1.00
155	Darryl Kile	.25
156	John Burkett	.25
157	Juan Gonzalez	.75
158	Javy Lopez	.25
159	Aramis Ramirez	.25
160	Lance Berkman	.25
161	David Cone	.25
162	Edgar Renteria	.25
163	Roger Clemens	1.25
164	Frank Catalanotto	.25
165	Bartolo Colon	.25
166	Mark McGwire	2.00
167	Jay Gibbons	.25
168	Tony Clark	.25
169	Tsuyoshi Shinjo	.25
170	Brad Penny	.25
171	Marcus Giles	.25
172	Matt Williams	.25
173	Bud Smith	.25
174	Tino Martinez	.25
175	Ryan Dempster	.25
176	Jimmy Rollins	.25
177	Edgardo Alfonzo	.25
178	Jason Giambi	.50
179	Aaron Boone	.25
180	Matt Dunigan	.25
181	Mike Lowell	.25
182	Jose Ortiz	.25
183	Johnny Estrada	.25
184	Shane Reynolds	.25
185	Joe Kennedy	.25
186	Corey Patterson	.25
187	Jeromy Burnitz	.25
188	C.C. Sabathia	.25
189	Doug Davis	.25
190	Omar Vizquel	.25
191	John Olerud	.25
192	Dee Brown	.25
193	Kip Wells	.25
194	A.J. Burnett	.25
195	Josh Towers	.25
196	Jason Varitek	.25
197	Jason Isringhausen	.25
198	Fernando Vina	.25
199	Ramon Ortiz	.25
200	Bobby Abreu	.25
201	Willie Harris	3.00
202	Angel Santos	3.00
203	Corky Miller	3.00
204	Mike Rivera	3.00
205	Justin Duchscherer	3.00
206	Rick Bauer	3.00
207	Angel Berroa	3.00
208	Juan Cruz	3.00
209	Dewon Brazelton	3.00
210	Mark Prior	15.00
211	Mark Teixeira	8.00
212	Geronimo Gil	3.00
213	Casey Fossum	3.00
214	Ken Harvey	3.00
215	Michael Cuddyer	3.00
216	Wilson Betemit	3.00
217	David Brous	3.00
218	Juan Pena	3.00
219	Travis Hafner	4.00
220	Erick Almonte	3.00
221	Morgan Ensberg	3.00
222	Martin Vargas	3.00
223	Brandon Berger	3.00
224	Zach Day	3.00
225	Brad Voyles	3.00
226	Jeremy Affeldt	3.00
227	Nick Neugebauer	3.00
228	Tim Redding	3.00
229	Adam Johnson	3.00
230	*Doug DeVore*	4.00
231	Cody Ransom	3.00
232	Marlon Byrd	3.00
233	Delvin James	3.00
234	Eric Munson	3.00
235	Dennis Tankersley	3.00
236	Josh Beckett	8.00
237	Bill Hall	3.00
238	Kevin Olsen	3.00
239	*Francis Beltran*	5.00
240	Antonio Perez	3.00
241	Orlando Hudson	3.00
242	*Anderson Machado*	6.00
243	*Tom Shearn*	5.00
244	*Brian Mallette*	4.00
245	*Raul Chavez*	4.00
246	*Andy Pratt*	4.00
247	*Jorge De La Rosa*	4.00
248	*Jeff Deardorff*	4.00
249	*Ben Howard*	4.00
250	*Brandon Backe*	4.00
251	Ed Rogers	3.00
252	*Travis Hughes*	5.00
253	*Rodrigo Rosario*	5.00
254	Alfredo Amezaga	3.00
255	*Jorge Padilla*	5.00
256	Victor Martinez	4.00
257	*Steve Bechler*	4.00
258	*Chris Baker*	4.00
259	Ryan Freel	3.00
260	*Allan Simpson*	3.00
261	Alex Rodriguez	6.00
262	Vladimir Guerrero	3.00
263	Bud Smith	2.00
264	Miguel Tejada	2.00
265	Craig Biggio	2.00
266	Luis Gonzalez	2.00
267	Ivan Rodriguez	3.00
268	C.C. Sabathia	2.00
269	Jeff Bagwell	3.00
270	Aramis Ramirez	2.00
271	Bobby Abreu	2.00
272	Rich Aurilia	2.00
273	Jason Giambi	3.00
274	Rickey Henderson	3.00
275	Wade Miller	2.00
276	Andruw Jones	3.00
277	Troy Glaus	3.00
278	Roy Oswalt	2.00
279	Tony Gwynn	3.00
280	Adam Dunn	3.00
281	Larry Walker	2.00
282	Jose Canseco	3.00
283	Todd Helton	3.00
284	Lance Berkman	2.00
285	Cal Ripken Jr.	10.00
286	Albert Pujols	8.00
287	Alfonso Soriano	3.00
288	Mark Mulder	2.00
289	Mike Hampton	2.00
290	Andres Galarraga	2.00
291	Barry Bonds	8.00
292	Ben Sheets	2.00
293	Ichiro Suzuki	6.00
294	J.D. Drew	2.00
295	Jose Ortiz	2.00
296	Kerry Wood	3.00
297	Mark McGwire	8.00
298	Mike Sweeney	2.00
299	Pat Burrell	3.00
300	Tim Hudson	3.00

Artist

		NM/M
Complete Set (14):		60.00
Common Player:		3.00
Production 300 sets		
1	Pedro Martinez	8.00
2	Curt Schilling	6.00
3	Kevin Brown	3.00
4	Tim Hudson	5.00
5	Kerry Wood	7.50
6	Barry Zito	4.00
7	Hideo Nomo	6.00
8	Randy Johnson	8.00
9	Greg Maddux	10.00
10	Roger Clemens	15.00
11	Kazuhiro Sasaki	3.00
12	Joe Mays	3.00
13	Mark Mulder	3.00
14	Javier Vazquez	3.00

Craftsmen

		NM/M
Complete Set (18):		80.00
Common Player:		3.00
Production 300 sets		
1	Ichiro Suzuki	10.00
2	Todd Helton	5.00
3	Manny Ramirez	5.00
4	Luis Gonzalez	3.00
5	Roberto Alomar	3.50
6	Moises Alou	3.00
7	Darin Erstad	3.00
8	Mike Piazza	10.00
9	Edgar Martinez	3.00
10	Vladimir Guerrero	6.00
11	Juan Gonzalez	5.00
12	Nomar Garciaparra	10.00
13	Tony Gwynn	6.00
14	Jeff Bagwell	5.00
15	Albert Pujols	15.00
16	Larry Walker	3.00
17	Paul LoDuca	3.00
18	Lance Berkman	3.00

Double Features

		NM/M
Complete Set (10):		80.00
Common Card:		8.00
Production 125 sets		
1	Larry Walker, Todd Helton	10.00
2	Jose Vidro, Vladimir Guerrero	10.00
3	Jason Giambi, Jeremy Giambi	8.00
4	Nomar Garciaparra, Manny Ramirez	15.00
5	Troy Glaus, Darin Erstad	8.00
6	Shawn Green, Paul LoDuca	8.00
7	Jeff Bagwell, Craig Biggio	10.00
8	Pedro Martinez, Hideo Nomo	12.00
9	Curt Schilling, Randy Johnson	10.00
10	Andruw Jones, Chipper Jones	12.50

Franchise Features

		NM/M
Complete Set (40):		180.00
Common Player:		3.00
Production 300 sets		
1	Cliff Floyd	3.00
2	Mike Piazza	12.00
3	Cal Ripken Jr.	25.00
4	Mike Sweeney	3.00
5	Curt Schilling	5.00
6	Aramis Ramirez	3.00
7	Vladimir Guerrero	8.00

8	Andruw Jones	8.00
9	Tim Hudson	3.00
10	Bernie Williams	3.00
11	Pedro Martinez	8.00
12	Roberto Alomar	3.00
13	Joe Mays	3.00
14	Jason Giambi	5.00
15	Kazuhiro Sasaki	3.00
16	Magglio Ordonez	3.00
17	Nomar Garciaparra	12.00
18	Juan Gonzalez	8.00
19	Carlos Beltran	5.00
20	Javier Vazquez	3.00
21	Miguel Tejada	3.00
22	Luis Gonzalez	3.00
23	Greg Maddux	10.00
24	Rafael Palmeiro	6.00
25	Freddy Garcia	3.00
26	Barry Zito	4.00
27	Paul LoDuca	3.00
28	Robert Fick	3.00
29	Roger Clemens	10.00
30	Eric Chavez	3.00
31	Ivan Rodriguez	6.00
32	Chipper Jones	10.00
33	Kerry Wood	6.00
34	Randy Johnson	8.00
35	Alex Rodriguez	12.00
36	Manny Ramirez	8.00
37	Mark Buehrle	3.00
38	Mark Mulder	3.00
39	Ichiro Suzuki	15.00
40	Troy Glaus	4.00

League Leaders

NM/M

Common Player: 3.00
Production 300 sets

1	Roger Clemens	12.00
2	Curt Schilling	5.00
3	Matt Morris	3.00
4	Randy Johnson	6.00
5	Mark Mulder	4.00
6	Curt Schilling	5.00
7	Mike Mussina	4.00
8	Joe Mays	3.00
9	Matt Morris	3.00
10	Tim Hudson	4.00
11	Mark Buehrle	3.00
12	Greg Maddux	10.00
13	Freddy Garcia	3.00
14	Randy Johnson	6.00
15	Curt Schilling	5.00
16	Chan Ho Park	3.00
17	Roger Clemens	12.00
18	Mike Mussina	4.00
19	Javier Vazquez	3.00
20	Kerry Wood	8.00
21	Randy Johnson	6.00
22	Barry Zito	4.00
23	Hideo Nomo	8.00
24	Ichiro Suzuki	10.00
25	Todd Helton	6.00
26	Albert Pujols	20.00
27	Alex Rodriguez	12.00
28	Shannon Stewart	3.00
29	Luis Gonzalez	3.00
30	Alex Rodriguez	12.00
31	Barry Bonds	20.00
32	Sammy Sosa	15.00
33	Luis Gonzalez	3.00
34	Todd Helton	6.00
35	Jim Thome	3.00
36	Shawn Green	4.00
37	Jeff Bagwell	7.50
38	Todd Helton	5.00
39	Luis Gonzalez	3.00
40	Lance Berkman	3.00
41	Juan Gonzalez	6.00
42	Larry Walker	3.00
43	Ichiro Suzuki	10.00
44	Lance Berkman	3.00
45	Todd Helton	5.00

Pure Power

NM/M

Complete Set (18): 65.00
Common Player: 2.00
Production 300 sets

1	Sammy Sosa	8.00
2	Lance Berkman	2.00
3	Chipper Jones	6.00
4	Troy Glaus	4.00
5	Barry Bonds	12.00
6	Todd Helton	4.00
7	Manny Ramirez	4.00
8	Jason Giambi	3.00
9	Juan Gonzalez	4.00
10	Albert Pujols	10.00
11	Jim Thome	2.00
12	Mike Piazza	8.00
13	Frank Thomas	4.00
14	Richie Sexson	2.00
15	Jeff Bagwell	4.00
16	Rafael Palmeiro	3.00
17	Luis Gonzalez	2.00
18	Shawn Green	2.50

Records

NM/M

Complete Set (5): 50.00
Common Player: 8.00
Production 300

1	Barry Bonds	15.00
2	Barry Bonds	15.00
3	Barry Bonds	15.00
4	Rickey Henderson	8.00
5	Rickey Henderson	8.00

Autographs

NM/M

Common Player: 5.00
Varying quantities produced

201	Willie Harris/500	5.00
203	Corky Miller/500	5.00
205	Justin Duchscherer/500	8.00
207	Angel Berroa/100	15.00
208	Juan Cruz/175	8.00
209	Dewon Brazelton/52	15.00
210	Mark Prior/425	50.00
211	Mark Teixeira/425	25.00
213	Casey Fossum/100	10.00
215	Michael Cuddyer/52	15.00
216	Wilson Betemit/500	8.00
217	David Brous/500	5.00
218	Juan A. Pena/188	8.00
219	Travis Hafner/375	10.00
221	Morgan Ensberg/52	15.00
222	Martin Vargas/500	5.00
223	Brandon Berger/500	5.00
224	Zach Day/500	5.00
225	Brad Voyles/500	5.00
226	Jeremy Affeldt/250	5.00
227	Nick Neugebauer/225	8.00
228	Tim Redding/500	8.00
229	Adam Johnson/425	5.00
230	Doug DeVore/300	8.00
231	Cody Ransom/500	5.00
232	Marlon Byrd/475	15.00
233	Delvin James/375	5.00
234	Eric Munson/325	8.00
235	Dennis Tankersley/500	5.00
236	Josh Beckett/25	
238	Kevin Olsen/325	5.00
240	Antonio Perez/525	5.00
241	Orlando Hudson/525	5.00
248	Jeff Deardorff/475	5.00
251	Ed Rogers/400	5.00
255	Jorge Padilla/450	15.00
260	Allan Simpson/475	8.00
278	Roy Oswalt/75	35.00

Artist Autographs

NM/M

Varying quantities produced

6	Barry Zito/100	35.00

Master Artists

NM/M

Common Player: 5.00
Production 150 sets

1	Pedro Martinez	15.00
2	Curt Schilling	10.00
3	Kevin Brown	5.00
4	Tim Hudson	5.00
5	Kerry Wood	12.00
6	Barry Zito	8.00
7	Hideo Nomo	15.00
8	Randy Johnson	15.00
9	Greg Maddux	17.50
10	Roger Clemens	20.00
11	Kazuhiro Sasaki	5.00
12	Joe Mays	5.00
13	Mark Mulder	5.00
14	Javier Vazquez	8.00

Craftsmen Autographs

NM/M

17	Paul LoDuca/100	20.00

Master Craftsmen

NM/M

Common Player: 5.00
Production 150 sets/H

1	Ichiro Suzuki/ball/51	75.00
2	Todd Helton	10.00
3	Manny Ramirez	10.00
4	Luis Gonzalez	8.00
5	Roberto Alomar	8.00

6	Moises Alou	8.00
7	Darin Erstad	8.00
8	Mike Piazza	15.00
9	Edgar Martinez	8.00
10	Vladimir Guerrero	15.00
11	Juan Gonzalez	8.00
12	Nomar Garciaparra	20.00
13	Tony Gwynn/175	20.00
14	Jeff Bagwell	10.00
15	Albert Pujols/175	25.00
16	Larry Walker/175	5.00
17	Paul LoDuca/175	5.00
18	Lance Berkman	8.00

Double Features Game-Used

NM/M

Common Card: 10.00
Production 50 sets

1	Larry Walker, Todd Helton	15.00
2	Jose Vidro, Vladimir Guerrero	20.00
3	Jason Giambi, Jeremy Giambi	15.00
4	Nomar Garciaparra, Manny Ramirez	30.00
5	Troy Glaus, Darin Erstad	15.00
6	Shawn Green, Paul LoDuca	10.00
7	Jeff Bagwell, Craig Biggio	15.00
8	Pedro Martinez, Hideo Nomo	30.00
9	Curt Schilling, Randy Johnson	20.00
10	Andruw Jones, Chipper Jones	20.00

Franchise Features Game-Used

NM/M

Common Player: 4.00
Production 150 sets
All Jerseys unless noted

1	Cliff Floyd	4.00
2	Mike Piazza	15.00
3	Cal Ripken Jr.	30.00
4	Mike Sweeney	4.00
5	Curt Schilling	8.00
6	Aramis Ramirez	6.00
7	Vladimir Guerrero	8.00
8	Andruw Jones	8.00
9	Tim Hudson	6.00
10	Bernie Williams	6.00
11	Pedro Martinez	10.00
12	Roberto Alomar	6.00
13	Joe Mays	4.00
14	Jason Giambi	8.00
15	Kazuhiro Sasaki	5.00
16	Magglio Ordonez	6.00
17	Nomar Garciaparra	20.00
18	Juan Gonzalez	8.00
19	Carlos Beltran	8.00
20	Javier Vazquez	4.00
21	Miguel Tejada	8.00
22	Luis Gonzalez	5.00
23	Greg Maddux	15.00
24	Rafael Palmeiro	10.00
25	Freddy Garcia	4.00
26	Barry Zito	8.00
27	Paul LoDuca	4.00
28	Robert Fick	4.00
29	Roger Clemens	20.00
30	Eric Chavez/bat	4.00
31	Ivan Rodriguez	8.00
32	Chipper Jones	8.00
33	Kerry Wood	10.00
34	Randy Johnson	10.00
35	Alex Rodriguez	15.00
36	Manny Ramirez	8.00
37	Mark Buehrle	4.00
38	Mark Mulder	6.00
39	Ichiro Suzuki/ball	80.00
40	Troy Glaus	6.00

Franchise Features Autographs

NM/M

Varying quantities produced

6	Aramis Ramirez/100	20.00
9	Tim Hudson/50	25.00
13	Joe Mays/75	10.00
19	Carlos Beltran/100	20.00
25	Freddy Garcia/100	20.00
26	Barry Zito/100	30.00
27	Paul LoDuca/100	15.00
28	Robert Fick/100	15.00
30	Eric Chavez/50	20.00
37	Mark Buehrle/100	15.00

League Leaders Game-Used

NM/M

Common Player: 4.00
Production 150 or 175

1	Roger Clemens	20.00
2	Curt Schilling	10.00
4	Randy Johnson	8.00
5	Mark Mulder	6.00
6	Curt Schilling	10.00
7	Mike Mussina/Shoe/50	25.00
8	Joe Mays	4.00
10	Tim Hudson	6.00
11	Mark Buehrle	4.00
12	Greg Maddux	15.00
13	Freddy Garcia	4.00
14	Randy Johnson	8.00
15	Curt Schilling	10.00
16	Chan Ho Park	4.00
17	Roger Clemens	20.00
18	Mike Mussina/Shoe/50	25.00
19	Javier Vazquez	4.00
20	Kerry Wood	10.00
21	Randy Johnson	8.00
22	Barry Zito	6.00
23	Hideo Nomo	15.00
24	Ichiro Suzuki/Ball/51	75.00
25	Todd Helton	8.00
26	Albert Pujols	20.00
27	Alex Rodriguez	15.00
28	Shannon Stewart	4.00
29	Luis Gonzalez	5.00
30	Alex Rodriguez	15.00
31	Barry Bonds	25.00
32	Sammy Sosa	15.00
33	Luis Gonzalez	4.00
34	Todd Helton	8.00
35	Jim Thome	10.00
36	Shawn Green	5.00
37	Jeff Bagwell	8.00
38	Todd Helton	8.00
39	Luis Gonzalez	4.00
40	Lance Berkman	4.00
41	Juan Gonzalez	6.00
42	Larry Walker	4.00
43	Ichiro Suzuki/Ball/51	75.00
44	Lance Berkman	4.00
45	Todd Helton	8.00

League Leaders Autographs

NM/M

Varying quantities produced

5	Mark Mulder/100	20.00
11	Mark Buehrle/100	15.00
13	Freddy Garcia/100	15.00
19	Javier Vazquez/100	15.00
26	Albert Pujols/100	80.00
28	Shannon Stewart/100	15.00

Pure Power Masters

NM/M

Complete Set (18) 125.00
Common Player: 5.00

Production 150
1 Sammy Sosa 15.00
2 Lance Berkman 5.00
3 Chipper Jones 10.00
4 Troy Glaus 8.00
5 Barry Bonds 25.00
6 Todd Helton 8.00
7 Manny Ramirez 8.00
8 Jason Giambi 6.00
9 Juan Gonzalez 8.00
10 Albert Pujols 20.00
11 Jim Thome 5.00
12 Mike Piazza 15.00
13 Frank Thomas 8.00
14 Richie Sexson 5.00
15 Jeff Bagwell 8.00
16 Rafael Palmeiro 6.00
17 Luis Gonzalez 5.00
18 Shawn Green 6.00

Pure Power Autographs

NM/M
Varying quantities produced
14 Richie Sexson/100 20.00

Records Game-Used

NM/M
Production 150
1 Barry Bonds 40.00
2 Barry Bonds 40.00
3 Barry Bonds 40.00
4 Rickey Henderson 20.00
5 Rickey Henderson 20.00

2002 DONRUSS ORIGINALS

NM/M
Complete Set (400): 75.00
Common Player: .10
Common Rated Rookie: .50
Pack (5): 2.00
Hobby Box (24): 40.00
1 *So Taguchi* (Rated Rookie) .75
2 *Allan Simpson* (Rated Rookie) .50
3 *Brian Mallette* (Rated Rookie) .50
4 *Ben Howard* (Rated Rookie) .50
5 *Kazuhisa Ishii* (Rated Rookie) 2.00
6 *Francis Beltran* (Rated Rookie) .50
7 *Jorge Padilla* (Rated Rookie) .50
8 *Brandon Puffer* (Rated Rookie) .50
9 *Oliver Perez* (Rated Rookie) 1.50
10 Kirk Saarloos (Rated Rookie) .50
11 *Travis Driskill* (Rated Rookie) .50
12 *Jeremy Lambert* (Rated Rookie) .50
13 *John Foster* (Rated Rookie) .50
14 *Steve Kent* (Rated Rookie) .50
15 *Shawn Sedlacek* (Rated Rookie) .50
16 Alex Rodriguez 1.25
17 Lance Berkman .10
18 Kevin Brown .10
19 Garret Anderson .10
20 Bobby Abreu .10
21 Richard Hidalgo .10
22 Matt Morris .10
23 Manny Ramirez .60
24 Derek Jeter 1.50
25 Kerry Wood .50
26 Mark Grace .15
27 Edgar Martinez .10
28 Nomar Garciaparra 1.00
29 Roberto Alomar .25
30 Jason Giambi .50
31 Juan Gonzalez .60
32 Albert Pujols 1.00
33 Juan Cruz .10
34 Troy Glaus .60
35 Greg Maddux .75
36 Adam Dunn .40
37 J.D. Drew .25
38 Tsuyoshi Shinjo .10
39 Vladimir Guerrero .60
40 Barry Bonds 1.50
41 Carlos Delgado .40
42 Ken Griffey Jr. 1.00
43 Carlos Pena .10
44 Jeff Kent .10
45 Roger Clemens .75
46 Frank Thomas .60
47 Larry Walker .10
48 Pedro J. Martinez .60
49 Moises Alou .10
50 Andruw Jones .60
51 Luis Gonzalez .25
52 Adrian Beltre .10
53 Bobby Hill .10
54 Roy Oswalt .20
55 Tim Hudson .20
56 Trot Nixon .10
57 Jeff Bagwell .60
58 Bernie Williams .30
59 Magglio Ordonez .25
60 Bartolo Colon .10
61 Shawn Green .20
62 Mark Buehrle .10
63 Sean Casey .10
64 Rickey Henderson .60
65 Aramis Ramirez .10
66 Ichiro Suzuki 1.00
67 Cliff Floyd .10
68 Darin Erstad .40
69 Paul LoDuca .10
70 Ivan Rodriguez .50
71 Mo Vaughn .10
72 Todd Helton .60
73 Raul Mondesi .10
74 Sammy Sosa 1.00
75 Cristian Guzman .10
76 Jimmy Rollins .10
77 Hideo Nomo .50
78 C.C. Sabathia .10
79 Wade Miller .10
80 Drew Henson .20
81 Chipper Jones .75
82 Miguel Tejada .25
83 Freddy Garcia .10
84 Richie Sexson .10
85 Robin Ventura .10
86 Jose Vidro .10
87 Rich Aurilia .10
88 Scott Rolen .60
89 Carlos Beltran .40
90 Austin Kearns .25
91 Kazuhiro Sasaki .10
92 Carlos Hernandez .10
93 Randy Johnson .60
94 Jim Thome .10
95 Curt Schilling .40
96 Alfonso Soriano .50
97 Barry Larkin .10
98 Rafael Palmeiro .50
99 Tom Glavine .25
100 Barry Zito .20
101 Craig Biggio .10
102 Mike Piazza 1.00
103 Ben Sheets .20
104 Mark Mulder .20
105 Mike Mussina .25
106 Jim Edmonds .10
107 Paul Konerko .10
108 Pat Burrell .25
109 Chan Ho Park .10
110 Mike Sweeney .10
111 Phil Nevin .10
112 Brian Giles .10
113 Eric Chavez .20
114 Corey Patterson .20
115 Gary Sheffield .25
116 Kazuhisa Ishii (Rated Rookie) 2.00
117 *Kyle Kane* (Rated Rookie) .50
118 *Eric Junge* (Rated Rookie) .50
119 *Luis Ugueto* (Rated Rookie) .50
120 *Cam Esslinger* (Rated Rookie) .50
121 *Earl Snyder* (Rated Rookie) .50
122 Oliver Perez (Rated Rookie) 1.50
123 *Victor Alvarez* (Rated Rookie) .50
124 *Tom Shearn* (Rated Rookie) .50
125 *Corey Thurman* (Rated Rookie) .50
126 *Satoru Komiyama* (Rated Rookie) .50
127 *Hansel Izquierdo* (Rated Rookie) .50
128 *Elio Serrano* (Rated Rookie) .50
129 *Michael Crudale* (Rated Rookie) .50
130 *Chris Snelling* (Rated Rookie) 1.50
131 Nomar Garciaparra 1.00
132 Roger Clemens .75
133 Hank Blalock .25
134 Eric Chavez .20
135 Corey Patterson .20
136 Richie Sexson .10
137 Freddy Garcia .10
138 Miguel Tejada .25
139 Alex Rodriguez/SP 1.50
140 Adrian Beltre .10
141 Bobby Abreu .10
142 Bret Boone .10
143 Tim Hudson .20
144 Roy Oswalt .20
145 Derek Jeter 1.50
146 Rich Aurilia .10
147 Mark Grace .15
148 Kerry Wood/SP 1.00
149 Geronimo Gil .10
150 Mark Buehrle .10
151 Jim Edmonds .10
152 Ichiro Suzuki 1.00
153 Juan Gonzalez .60
154 Darin Erstad .40
155 Barry Bonds/SP 2.50
156 Greg Maddux .75
157 Adam Dunn .40
158 Todd Helton .60
159 Roberto Alomar .25
160 Sammy Sosa 1.00
161 Sean Burroughs .10
162 Albert Pujols 1.00
163 Carlos Delgado .25
164 Frank Thomas .60
165 Ken Griffey Jr. 1.00
166 Jason Giambi/SP 1.00
167 Chipper Jones .75
168 Ivan Rodriguez .50
169 Pedro Martinez/SP 1.00
170 Gary Sheffield .25
171 Andruw Jones .60
172 Luis Gonzalez .25
173 Raul Mondesi .10
174 Jose Vidro .10
175 Garret Anderson/SP .50
176 Scott Rolen .60
177 Kazuhiro Sasaki .10
178 Jeff Bagwell .60
179 Manny Ramirez .60
180 Jim Thome .10
181 Ben Sheets .20
182 Randy Johnson .60
183 Lance Berkman .10
184 Shawn Green .20
185 Rickey Henderson .60
186 Edgar Martinez .10
187 Barry Larkin .10
188 Bernie Williams .30
189 Luis Aparicio .10
190 Troy Glaus/SP .50
191 Mike Mussina .30
192 Pee Wee Reese .20
193 Craig Biggio .10
194 Vladimir Guerrero .60
195 J.D. Drew .20
196 Jeff Kent .10
197 Dewon Brazelton .10
198 Tsuyoshi Shinjo/SP .40
199 Sean Casey .10
200 Hideo Nomo .50
201 C.C. Sabathia .10
202 Larry Walker .10
203 Mark Teixeira .20
204 Mike Sweeney .10
205 Moises Alou .10
206 Mark Prior 1.00
207 Javier Vazquez .10
208 Phil Nevin .10
209 Harmon Killebrew .50
210 Brian Giles .10
211 Carlos Beltran .40
212 Don Drysdale .40
213 Matt Morris .10
214 Trot Nixon .10
215 Magglio Ordonez .25
216 Curt Schilling/SP .75
217 Mark Mulder .20
218 Alfonso Soriano 1.00
219 Rafael Palmeiro/SP .75
220 Tom Glavine .25
221 Barry Zito .25
222 Mike Piazza 1.00
223 Bartolo Colon .10
224 Cliff Floyd .10
225 Paul LoDuca .10
226 Cristian Guzman .10
227 Mo Vaughn .10
228 Aramis Ramirez .10
229 Pat Burrell .25
230 Chan Ho Park .10
231 Satoru Komiyama (Rated Rookie) .50
232 *Brandon Backe* (Rated Rookie) .50
233 *Anderson Machado* (Rated Rookie) .50
234 *Doug Devore* (Rated Rookie) .50
235 *Steve Bechler* (Rated Rookie) .50
236 *John Ennis* (Rated Rookie) .50
237 *Rodrigo Rosario* (Rated Rookie) .50
238 *Jorge Sosa* (Rated Rookie) .50
239 *Ken Huckaby* (Rated Rookie) .50
240 *Mike Moriarty* (Rated Rookie) .50
241 Kirk Saarloos (Rated Rookie) 1.00
242 *Kevin Frederick* (Rated Rookie) .50
243 *Aaron Guiel* (Rated Rookie) .50
244 Jose Rodriguez (Rated Rookie) .50
245 So Taguchi (Rated Rookie) 1.00
246 Albert Pujols 1.00
247 Derek Jeter 1.50
248 Brian Giles .10
249 Mike Cameron .10
250 Josh Beckett .25
251 Ken Griffey Jr./SP 1.50
252 Aramis Ramirez .10
253 Miguel Tejada .25
254 Carlos Delgado .25
255 Pedro J. Martinez .60
256 Raul Mondesi .10
257 Roger Clemens .75
258 Gary Sheffield .25
259 Jose Vidro .10
260 Alex Rodriguez 1.25
261 Larry Walker .10
262 Mark Mulder .20
263 Scott Rolen .60
264 Tim Hudson .20
265 Manny Ramirez .60
266 Rich Aurilia .10
267 Roy Oswalt .20
268 Mark Grace .15
269 Lance Berkman .10
270 Nomar Garciaparra 1.00
271 Barry Bonds 1.50
272 Ryan Klesko .10
273 Ichiro Suzuki 1.00
274 Shawn Green .20
275 Darin Erstad .40
276 Bernie Williams .30
277 Greg Maddux/SP 1.00
278 Eric Hinske .10
279 Randy Johnson .60
280 Todd Helton .60
281 Sammy Sosa/SP 1.50
282 Nick Johnson .10
283 Jose Cruz Jr. .10
284 Frank Thomas .60
285 Tsuyoshi Shinjo .10
286 Troy Glaus .60
287 Jason Giambi .50
288 Chipper Jones/SP 1.00
289 Roberto Alomar .30

290 Bobby Hill .10
291 Garret Anderson .10
292 Andruw Jones .60
293 Luis Gonzalez .15
294 Mike Mussina .30
295 Ivan Rodriguez/SP .75
296 Barry Larkin .10
297 Kazuhiro Sasaki .10
298 Alfonso Soriano .50
299 Jeff Bagwell/SP .75
300 Bobby Abreu .10
301 Ben Sheets .20
302 Curt Schilling .40
303 Jim Thome .10
304 Kerry Wood .50
305 Mark Buehrle .10
306 Rickey Henderson .60
307 Rafael Palmeiro .50
308 Jim Edmonds .10
309 Mike Piazza 1.00
310 Edgar Martinez .10
311 Tom Glavine .25
312 Adrian Beltre .10
313 Adam Dunn .40
314 Craig Biggio .10
315 Vladimir Guerrero/SP 1.00
316 Bret Boone .10
317 Hideo Nomo/SP .75
318 Jeff Kent .10
319 Juan Gonzalez .60
320 Sean Casey .10
321 C.C. Sabathia .10
322 J.D. Drew .20
323 Torii Hunter/SP .40
324 Chan Ho Park .10
325 Mike Sweeney .10
326 Javier Vazquez .10
327 Jorge Posada .25
328 Barry Zito .25
329 Willie McCovey .10
330 Kevin Brown .20
331 Mo Vaughn .10
332 Carlos Beltran .40
333 Bobby Doerr .10
334 Matt Morris .10
335 Trot Nixon .10
336 Magglio Ordonez .25
337 Paul LoDuca .10
338 Phil Nevin .10
339 Eric Chavez .20
340 Corey Patterson .20
341 Richie Sexson .10
342 Pat Burrell .25
343 Freddy Garcia .10
344 Bartolo Colon .10
345 Cliff Floyd .10
346 Deivis Santos (Rated Rookie) .50
347 *Felix Escalona* (Rated Rookie) .50
348 *Miguel Asencio* (Rated Rookie) .50
349 *Takahito Nomura* (Rated Rookie) .50
350 Jorge Padilla (Rated Rookie) .50
351 Vladimir Guerrero .60
352 Ichiro Suzuki 1.00
353 Jay Gibbons .10
354 Alfonso Soriano .50
355 Mark Buehrle .10
356 Shawn Green .20
357 Barry Larkin .10
358 Josh Fogg .10
359 Shannon Stewart .10
360 Andruw Jones .60
361 Juan Gonzalez .60
362 Ken Griffey Jr. 1.00
363 Tim Hudson .20
364 Roy Oswalt/SP .50
365 Carlos Delgado .40
366 Albert Pujols/SP 2.00
367 Willie Stargell .25
368 Roger Clemens .75
369 Luis Gonzalez .25
370 Barry Zito .25
371 Alex Rodriguez 1.25
372 Troy Glaus .60
373 Vladimir Guerrero .60
374 Jeff Bagwell .60
375 Randy Johnson .60
376 Manny Ramirez .60
377 Derek Jeter/SP 2.00
378 C.C. Sabathia .10
379 Rickey Henderson .60
380 J.D. Drew .20
381 Nomar Garciaparra 1.00
382 Darin Erstad .40
383 Ben Sheets .20
384 Frank Thomas .60
385 Barry Bonds 1.50
386 Pedro J. Martinez .60
387 Mark Mulder .20
388 Greg Maddux .75
389 Todd Helton .60
390 Lance Berkman .10
391 Sammy Sosa 1.00
392 Mike Piazza 1.00
393 Chipper Jones .75
394 Adam Dunn .40
395 Jason Giambi .50
396 Eric Chavez .20
397 Bobby Abreu .10
398 Aramis Ramirez .10
399 Paul LoDuca .10
400 Miguel Tejada .25

Aqueous Glossy

Stars (1-400): 3-5X
Average of 1:box

All-Stars

NM/M

Complete Set (25): 90.00
Common Player: 2.00
Inserted 1:30
1 George Brett 8.00
2 Rickey Henderson 4.00
3 Mike Schmidt 6.00
4 Vladimir Guerrero 3.00
5 Tony Gwynn 3.00
6 Curt Schilling 2.00
7 Don Mattingly 8.00
8 Roberto Alomar 2.00
9 Cal Ripken Jr. 8.00
10 Carlton Fisk 2.00
11 Roger Clemens 5.00
12 Jeff Bagwell 3.00
13 Kirby Puckett 8.00
14 Nolan Ryan 10.00
15 Ryne Sandberg 5.00
16 Ivan Rodriguez 2.00
17 Sammy Sosa 5.00
18 Greg Maddux 5.00
19 Alex Rodriguez 8.00
20 Todd Helton 2.00
21 Randy Johnson 3.00
22 Troy Glaus 2.00
23 Ichiro Suzuki 6.00
24 Barry Bonds 8.00
25 Derek Jeter 10.00

Champions

NM/M

Complete Set (25): 75.00
Common Player: 2.00
Production 800 sets
1 Nolan Ryan 10.00
2 George Brett 6.00
3 Edgar Martinez 2.00
4 Mike Schmidt 6.00
5 Randy Johnson 3.00
6 Tony Gwynn 4.00
7 John Smoltz 2.00
8 Roger Clemens 4.00
9 Mel Ott 2.00
10 Todd Helton 3.00
11 Bernie Williams 2.00
12 Troy Glaus 3.00
13 Steve Carlton 2.00
14 Ryne Sandberg 4.00
15 Ted Williams 8.00
16 Alex Rodriguez 8.00
17 Lou Boudreau 2.00
18 Luis Gonzalez 2.00
19 Rickey Henderson 3.00
20 Jose Canseco 2.00
21 Stan Musial 5.00
22 Randy Johnson 3.00
23 Don Mattingly 6.00
24 Nomar Garciaparra 5.00
25 Wade Boggs 4.00

Champions Materials

NM/M

Common Player:
Varying quantities produced
1 Nolan Ryan/78 65.00
2 George Brett/80
3 Edgar Martinez/92 10.00
4 Mike Schmidt/80 40.00
5 Randy Johnson/94 15.00
6 Tony Gwynn/84 20.00
7 John Smoltz/96 8.00
8 Roger Clemens/88 20.00
9 Mel Ott/42
10 Todd Helton/100 10.00
11 Bernie Williams/98 10.00
12 Troy Glaus/100 10.00
13 Steve Carlton/80 15.00
14 Ryne Sandberg/90 40.00
15 Ted Williams/42 200.00
16 Alex Rodriguez/96 20.00
17 Lou Boudreau/44 15.00
18 Luis Gonzalez/99 8.00
19 Rickey Henderson/82 20.00
20 Jose Canseco/88
21 Stan Musial/50 60.00
22 Randy Johnson/88 15.00
23 Don Mattingly/84 60.00
24 Nomar Garciaparra/100 30.00
25 Wade Boggs/88 15.00

Gamers

NM/M

Common Player: 3.00
Varying quantities produced
1 Alfonso Soriano/400 8.00
2 Shawn Green/500 5.00
3 Curt Schilling/250 8.00
4 Hideo Nomo/100 20.00
5 Toby Hall/500 4.00
6 Andruw Jones/500 8.00
7 Cliff Floyd/500 3.00
8 Mark Ellis/500 4.00
9 Gabe Kapler/500 3.00
10 Andres Galarraga/500 3.00
11 Freddy Garcia/500 3.00
12 Tsuyoshi Shinjo/200 4.00
13 Robin Ventura/500 3.00
14 Paul LoDuca/500 3.00
15 Manny Ramirez/500 8.00
16 Garret Anderson/250 5.00
17 Joe Kennedy/500 3.00
18 Roger Clemens/500 15.00
19 Gary Sheffield/500 6.00
20 Vernon Wells/500 4.00
21 Matt Guerrier
22 Hideo Nomo/100 40.00
23 Tim Hudson/500 6.00
24 Larry Bigbie/500 4.00
25 Larry Walker/500 4.00
26 Ryan Ludwick
27 John Olerud/500 3.00
28 Chipper Jones/500 8.00
29 Tony Gwynn/500 10.00
30 Juan Gonzalez/500 8.00
31 Jacque Jones/500 5.00
32 Frank Thomas/500 8.00
33 Luis Gonzalez/500 4.00
34 Geoff Jenkins/500 6.00
35 J.D. Drew/500 5.00
36 Edgardo Alfonzo/500 3.00
37 Todd Helton/500 8.00
38 Brad Penny/500 4.00
39 Robert Fick/500 3.00
40 Will Clark/500 15.00
41 Tony Armas Jr./500 4.00
42 Nick Johnson/400 3.00
43 Ben Grieve/500 3.00
44 Vladimir Guerrero/500 8.00
45 Jason Jennings/500 3.00
46 Carlos Lee/500 3.00
47 Carlos Delgado/500 6.00
48 Chan Ho Park/500 3.00
49 Juan Diaz/500 3.00
50 Alex Rodriguez/400 15.00

Hit List

NM/M

Complete Set (20): 40.00
Common Player: 1.00
Production 1,500 sets
1 Ichiro Suzuki 4.00
2 Shawn Green 1.00
3 Alex Rodriguez 5.00
4 Nomar Garciaparra 4.00
5 Derek Jeter 6.00
6 Barry Bonds 6.00
7 Mike Piazza 4.00
8 Albert Pujols 4.00
9 Chipper Jones 3.00
10 Sammy Sosa 4.00
11 Rickey Henderson 2.00
12 Frank Thomas 2.00
13 Jeff Bagwell 2.00
14 Vladimir Guerrero 2.00
15 Todd Helton 2.00
16 Adam Dunn 1.00
17 Rafael Palmeiro 1.00
18 Manny Ramirez 2.00
19 Lance Berkman 1.00
20 Jason Giambi 1.50

Hit List Total Bases

NM/M

Common Player: 4.00
Numbered to career high total bases
1 Ichiro Suzuki/base/316 15.00
2 Shawn Green/bat/370 5.00
3 Alex Rodriguez/bat/393 15.00
4 Nomar Garciaparra/bat/365 10.00
5 Derek Jeter/346/base 20.00
6 Barry Bonds/base/411 20.00
7 Mike Piazza/bat/355 10.00
8 Albert Pujols/base/360 10.00
9 Chipper Jones/bat/359 8.00
10 Sammy Sosa/base/425 10.00
11 Rickey Henderson/bat/285 10.00
12 Frank Thomas/bat/364 8.00
13 Jeff Bagwell/bat/363 8.00
14 Vladimir Guerrero/bat/379 8.00
15 Todd Helton/bat/405 8.00
16 Adam Dunn/bat/141 8.00
17 Rafael Palmeiro/bat/356 8.00
18 Manny Ramirez/bat/346 8.00
19 Lance Berkman/bat/358 5.00
20 Jason Giambi/base/343 6.00

Making History

NM/M

Complete Set (10): 30.00
Common Player: 2.00
Production 800 sets
1 Rafael Palmeiro 2.00
2 Roger Clemens 5.00
3 Greg Maddux 4.00
4 Randy Johnson 3.00
5 Barry Bonds 8.00
6 Mike Piazza 6.00
7 Roberto Alomar 2.00
8 Rickey Henderson 2.00
9 Sammy Sosa 6.00
10 Tom Glavine 2.00

Making History Materials

		NM/M
Production 100 sets		
1	Rafael Palmeiro	15.00
2	Roger Clemens	20.00
3	Greg Maddux	15.00
4	Randy Johnson	10.00
5	Barry Bonds/base	20.00
6	Mike Piazza	15.00
7	Roberto Alomar	8.00
8	Rickey Henderson	25.00
9	Sammy Sosa/base	15.00
10	Tom Glavine	10.00

Mound Marvels

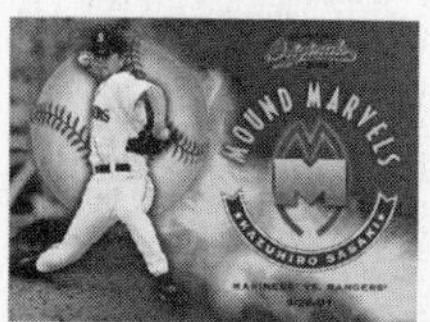

		NM/M
Complete Set (15):		30.00
Common Player:		1.00
Inserted 1:40		
1	Roger Clemens	6.00
2	Matt Morris	1.00
3	Pedro J. Martinez	5.00
4	Randy Johnson	5.00
5	Wade Miller	1.00
6	Tim Hudson	1.50
7	Mike Mussina	3.00
8	C.C. Sabathia	1.00
9	Kazuhiro Sasaki	1.00
10	Curt Schilling	4.00
11	Hideo Nomo	2.50
12	Roger Clemens	6.00
13	Mark Buehrle	1.00
14	Barry Zito	1.50
15	Roy Oswalt	1.50

Mound Marvels High Heat

		NM/M
Production 100 sets		
1	Roger Clemens	25.00
2	Matt Morris	10.00
3	Pedro J. Martinez	20.00
4	Randy Johnson	15.00
5	Wade Miller	8.00
6	Tim Hudson	10.00
7	Mike Mussina	15.00
8	C.C. Sabathia	10.00
9	Kazuhiro Sasaki	10.00
10	Curt Schilling	15.00
11	Hideo Nomo	40.00
12	Roger Clemens	25.00
13	Mark Buehrle	8.00
14	Barry Zito	15.00
15	Roy Oswalt	8.00

Nifty Fifty Bats

		NM/M
Common Player:		5.00
Production 50 sets		
1	Alex Rodriguez	20.00
2	Kerry Wood	15.00
3	Ivan Rodriguez	15.00
4	Geronimo Gil	5.00
5	Vladimir Guerrero	15.00
6	Corky Miller	5.00
7	Todd Helton	12.00
8	Rickey Henderson	15.00
9	Andruw Jones	10.00
10	Barry Bonds/ball	30.00
11	Tom Glavine	10.00
12	Mark Teixeira	10.00
13	Mike Piazza	15.00
14	Austin Kearns	8.00
15	Rickey Henderson	15.00
16	Derek Jeter/ball	20.00
17	Barry Larkin	8.00
18	Jeff Bagwell	10.00
19	Bernie Williams	10.00
20	Frank Thomas	10.00
21	Lance Berkman	8.00
22	Marlon Byrd	6.00
23	Randy Johnson	15.00
24	Ichiro Suzuki/ball	40.00
25	Darin Erstad	8.00
26	Jason Lane	5.00
27	Roberto Alomar	10.00
28	Ken Griffey Jr./ball	
29	Tsuyoshi Shinjo	8.00
30	Pedro Martinez	15.00
31	Rickey Henderson	15.00
32	Albert Pujols/ball	20.00
33	Nomar Garciaparra	15.00
34	Troy Glaus	10.00
35	Chipper Jones	15.00
36	Adam Dunn	8.00
37	Jason Giambi/ball	
38	Greg Maddux	20.00
39	Mike Piazza	15.00
40	So Taguchi	8.00
41	Manny Ramirez	10.00
42	Scott Rolen	15.00
43	Sammy Sosa/ball	15.00
44	Shawn Green	8.00
45	Rickey Henderson	15.00
46	Alex Rodriguez	20.00
47	Hideo Nomo	30.00
48	Kazuhisa Ishii	8.00
49	Luis Gonzalez	8.00
50	Jim Thome	15.00

Nifty Fifty Combos

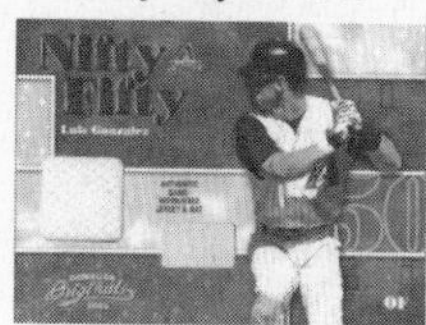

		NM/M
Production 50 sets		
All bat & jerseys unless noted		
1	Alex Rodriguez	30.00
2	Kerry Wood	20.00
3	Ivan Rodriguez	20.00
4	Geronimo Gil	10.00
5	Vladimir Guerrero	20.00
6	Corky Miller	10.00
7	Todd Helton	20.00
8	Rickey Henderson	25.00
9	Andruw Jones	15.00
10	Barry Bonds/base/ball	40.00
11	Tom Glavine	20.00
12	Mark Teixeira	20.00
13	Mike Piazza	25.00
14	Austin Kearns	15.00
15	Rickey Henderson	25.00
16	Derek Jeter/base/ball	30.00
17	Barry Larkin	15.00
18	Jeff Bagwell	20.00
19	Bernie Williams	20.00
20	Frank Thomas	20.00
21	Lance Berkman	15.00
22	Marlon Byrd	15.00
23	Randy Johnson	20.00
25	Darin Erstad	15.00
26	Jason Lane	10.00
27	Roberto Alomar	15.00
28	Ken Griffey Jr./ base/ball	25.00
29	Tsuyoshi Shinjo	10.00
30	Pedro Martinez	20.00
31	Rickey Henderson	25.00
33	Nomar Garciaparra	30.00
34	Troy Glaus	15.00
35	Chipper Jones	20.00
36	Adam Dunn	15.00
37	Jason Giambi	20.00
38	Greg Maddux	25.00
39	Mike Piazza	25.00
40	So Taguchi	15.00
41	Manny Ramirez	20.00
42	Scott Rolen	20.00
44	Shawn Green	10.00
45	Rickey Henderson	25.00
46	Alex Rodriguez	30.00
47	Hideo Nomo	
48	Kazuhisa Ishii	15.00
49	Luis Gonzalez	10.00
50	Jim Thome	20.00

Nifty Fifty Jersey

		NM/M
Common Player:		5.00
Production 50 sets		
1	Alex Rodriguez	
2	Kerry Wood	15.00
3	Ivan Rodriguez	15.00
4	Geronimo Gil	5.00
5	Vladimir Guerrero	15.00
6	Corky Miller	5.00
7	Todd Helton	12.00
8	Rickey Henderson	15.00
9	Andruw Jones	10.00
10	Barry Bonds/base	
11	Tom Glavine	10.00
12	Mark Teixeira	10.00
13	Mike Piazza	15.00
14	Austin Kearns	8.00
15	Rickey Henderson	15.00
16	Derek Jeter/base	20.00
17	Barry Larkin	8.00
18	Jeff Bagwell	10.00
19	Bernie Williams	10.00
20	Frank Thomas	10.00
21	Lance Berkman	8.00
22	Marlon Byrd	8.00
23	Randy Johnson	15.00
24	Ichiro Suzuki/base	40.00
25	Darin Erstad	8.00
26	Jason Lane	5.00
27	Roberto Alomar	10.00
28	Ken Griffey Jr./base	20.00
29	Tsuyoshi Shinjo	8.00
30	Pedro Martinez	15.00
31	Rickey Henderson	15.00
32	Albert Pujols/base	20.00
33	Nomar Garciaparra	20.00
34	Troy Glaus	10.00
35	Chipper Jones	15.00
36	Adam Dunn	8.00
39	Mike Piazza	15.00
40	So Taguchi	8.00
41	Manny Ramirez	10.00
42	Scott Rolen	15.00
43	Sammy Sosa/base	15.00
44	Shawn Green	8.00
45	Rickey Henderson	15.00
46	Alex Rodriguez	20.00
47	Hideo Nomo	30.00
48	Kazuhisa Ishii	8.00
49	Luis Gonzalez	8.00
50	Jim Thome	15.00

On The Record

		NM/M
Complete Set (15):		60.00
Common Player:		3.00
Production 800 sets		
1	Ty Cobb	6.00
2	Jimmie Foxx	4.00
3	Lou Gehrig	10.00
4	Dale Murphy	5.00
5	Steve Carlton	3.00
6	Randy Johnson	4.00
7	Greg Maddux	6.00
8	Roger Clemens	8.00
9	Yogi Berra	5.00
10	Don Mattingly	8.00
11	Rickey Henderson	4.00
12	Stan Musial	6.00
13	Jackie Robinson	6.00
14	Roberto Clemente	10.00
15	Mike Schmidt	6.00

On the Record Materials

		NM/M
Varying quantities produced		
1	Ty Cobb/9	
2	Jimmie Foxx/33	
3	Lou Gehrig/34	220.00
4	Dale Murphy/83	10.00
5	Steve Carlton/72	10.00
6	Randy Johnson/100	10.00
7	Greg Maddux/93	15.00
8	Roger Clemens/87	20.00
9	Yogi Berra/51	12.00
10	Don Mattingly/85	25.00
11	Rickey Henderson/ 90	15.00
12	Stan Musial/43	
13	Jackie Robinson/49	50.00
14	Roberto Clemente/66	75.00
15	Mike Schmidt/80	25.00

Power Alley

		NM/M
Complete Set (15):		30.00
Common Player:		1.00
Production 1,500 sets		
Die-Cut Parallel:		1.5-2X
Production 100 sets		
1	Barry Bonds	6.00
2	Sammy Sosa	3.00
3	Lance Berkman	1.00
4	Luis Gonzalez	1.00
5	Alex Rodriguez	5.00
6	Troy Glaus	2.00
7	Vladimir Guerrero	2.00
8	Jason Giambi	1.50
9	Mike Piazza	3.00
10	Todd Helton	2.00
11	Mike Schmidt	4.00
12	Don Mattingly	4.00
13	Andre Dawson	1.50
14	Reggie Jackson	2.00
15	Dale Murphy	1.50

Signature Marks

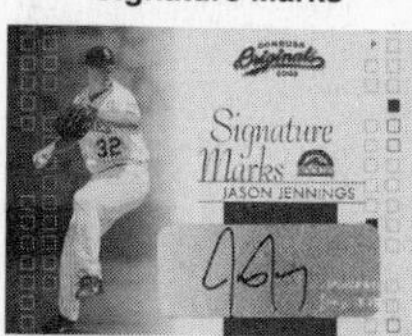

		NM/M
Common Autograph:		5.00
Varying quantities produced		
Many not priced, lack of market info		
1	Kazuhisa Ishii/50	
2	Eric Hinske/200	8.00
3	Cesar Izturis/200	5.00
4	Roy Oswalt/100	20.00
5	Jack Cust/200	5.00
6	Nick Johnson/200	8.00
7	Jason Hart/200	6.00
8	Mark Prior/100	60.00
9	Luis Garcia/200	5.00
10	Jay Gibbons/200	10.00
11	Corky Miller/200	8.00
12	Antonio Perez/100	8.00
13	Andres Torres/200	5.00
14	Brandon Claussen/200	15.00
15	Ed Rogers/200	5.00
16	Jorge Padilla/200	10.00
17	Francis Beltran/200	5.00
18	Kip Wells/200	6.00
19	Ryan Ludwick/200	8.00
20	Juan Cruz/100	8.00
21	Juan Diaz/200	5.00
22	Marcus Giles/200	10.00
23	Joe Kennedy/200	10.00
24	Wade Miller/100	15.00
25	Corey Patterson/100	15.00
26	Angel Berroa/200	10.00
27	Ricardo Rodriguez/200	5.00
28	Toby Hall/200	8.00
29	Carlos Pena/50	15.00
30	Jason Jennings/200	8.00
31	Rafael Soriano/200	10.00
32	Marlon Byrd/100	10.00
33	Rodrigo Rosario/200	5.00
34	Rick Ankiel/200	
35	Brent Abernathy/200	5.00
36	Bill Hall/200	5.00
37	Fernando Rodney/200	5.00
38	Josh Pearce/200	8.00
39	Brian Lawrence/200	8.00
40	Tim Redding/200	5.00
41	Matt Guerrier/200	
42	Jeremy Giambi/200	5.00
43	Victor Martinez/200	15.00
44	Hank Blalock/50	30.00
45	Larry Bigbie/200	
46	Geronimo Gil/200	5.00
47	So Taguchi/50	25.00
48	Austin Kearns/200	15.00
49	Alfonso Soriano/50	40.00
50	Jose Ortiz/100	

What If - '78

		NM/M
Complete Set (27):		75.00
Common Player:		1.50
Inserted 1:12		
1	Paul Molitor	4.00
2	Alan Trammell	1.50
3	Ozzie Smith	6.00
4	George Brett	10.00
5	Johnny Bench	6.00

6 Rod Carew 2.00
7 Carlton Fisk 1.50
8 Reggie Jackson 5.00
9 Dale Murphy 2.00
10 Joe Morgan 1.50
11 Eddie Murray 4.00
12 Jim Palmer 2.00
13 Tom Seaver 4.00
14 Willie Stargell 2.00
15 Dave Winfield 2.00
16 Dave Parker 1.50
17 Mike Schmidt 8.00
18 Eddie Mathews 4.00
19 Lou Brock 1.50
20 Willie McCovey 1.50
21 Andre Dawson 1.50
22 Dennis Eckersley 4.00
23 Robin Yount 4.00
24 Nolan Ryan 15.00
25 Steve Carlton 1.50
26 Paul Molitor 4.00
27 Ozzie Smith 6.00

What If - '80

NM/M
Complete Set (25): 75.00
Common Player: 1.50
Inserted 1:12
1 Rickey Henderson 3.00
2 Johnny Bench 6.00
3 George Brett 10.00
4 Steve Carlton 2.50
5 Rod Carew 2.00
6 Gary Carter 1.50
7 Carlton Fisk 1.50
8 Reggie Jackson 5.00
9 Dave Parker 1.50
10 Dale Murphy 3.00
11 Paul Molitor 4.00
12 Mike Schmidt 8.00
13 Alan Trammell 1.50
14 Dave Winfield 1.50
15 Robin Yount 4.00
16 Joe Morgan 1.50
17 Jim Palmer 1.50
18 Nolan Ryan 15.00
19 Tom Seaver 4.00
20 Ozzie Smith 6.00
21 Willie McCovey 1.50
22 Andre Dawson 1.50
23 Eddie Murray 2.00
24 Al Kaline 5.00
25 Duke Snider 4.00

What If - Rookies

NM/M
Complete Set (23): 75.00
Common Player: 1.50
Inserted 1:12
1 Wade Boggs 6.00
2 Ryne Sandberg 6.00
3 Cal Ripken Jr. 12.50
4 Tony Gwynn 6.00
5 Don Mattingly 10.00
6 Wade Boggs 6.00
7 Roger Clemens 7.50
8 Kirby Puckett 6.00
9 Eric Davis 1.50
10 Dwight Gooden 1.50
11 Eric Davis 1.50
12 Roger Clemens 7.50
13 Kirby Puckett 6.00
14 Dwight Gooden 1.50
15 Barry Bonds 12.50
16 Will Clark 1.50
17 Barry Larkin 1.50
18 Greg Maddux 6.00
19 Rafael Palmeiro 4.00
20 Craig Biggio 1.50
21 Gary Sheffield 1.50
22 Randy Johnson 5.00
23 Curt Schilling 3.00

2002 DONRUSS STUDIO

NM/M
Complete Set (250): 150.00
Common Player: .25
Common (201-250): 3.00
Production 1,500
Pack (5): 3.00
Box (18): 45.00
1 Vladimir Guerrero .75
2 Chipper Jones 1.00
3 Bobby Abreu .25
4 Barry Zito .40
5 Larry Walker .25
6 Miguel Tejada .40
7 Mike Sweeney .25
8 Shannon Stewart .25
9 Sammy Sosa 1.50
10 Bud Smith .25
11 Wilson Betemit .25
12 Kevin Brown .35
13 Ellis Burks .25
14 Pat Burrell .40
15 Cliff Floyd .25
16 Marcus Giles .25
17 Troy Glaus .75
18 Barry Larkin .25
19 Carlos Lee .25
20 Brian Lawrence .25
21 Paul LoDuca .25
22 Ben Grieve .25
23 Shawn Green .40
24 Mike Cameron .25
25 Roger Clemens 1.25
26 Joe Crede .25
27 Jose Cruz .25
28 Jeremy Affeldt .25
29 Adrian Beltre .25
30 Josh Beckett .50
31 Roberto Alomar .40
32 Toby Hall .25
33 Mike Hampton .25
34 Eric Milton .25
35 Eric Munson .25
36 Trot Nixon .25
37 Roy Oswalt .40
38 Chan Ho Park .25
39 Charles Johnson .25
40 Nick Johnson .25
41 Tim Hudson .40
42 Cristian Guzman .25
43 Drew Henson .25
44 Mark Grace .35
45 Luis Gonzalez .35
46 Pedro J. Martinez .75
47 Joe Mays .25
48 Jorge Posada .40
49 Aramis Ramirez .25
50 Kip Wells .25
51 Moises Alou .25
52 Omar Vizquel .25
53 Ichiro Suzuki 1.50
54 Jimmy Rollins .25
55 Freddy Garcia .25
56 Steve Green .25
57 Brian Jordan .25
58 Paul Konerko .35
59 Jack Cust .25
60 Sean Casey .25
61 Bret Boone .25
62 Hideo Nomo .60
63 Magglio Ordonez .40
64 Frank Thomas .75
65 Josh Towers .25
66 Javier Vazquez .25
67 Robin Ventura .25
68 Aubrey Huff .25
69 Richard Hidalgo .25
70 Brandon Claussen .25
71 Bartolo Colon .25
72 John Buck .25
73 Dee Brown .25
74 Barry Bonds 2.00
75 Jason Giambi .50
76 Erick Almonte .25
77 Ryan Dempster .25
78 Jim Edmonds .25
79 Jay Gibbons .25
80 Shigetoshi Hasegawa .25
81 Todd Helton .75
82 Erik Bedard .25
83 Carlos Beltran .50
84 Rafael Soriano .25
85 Gary Sheffield .40
86 Richie Sexson .25
87 Mike Rivera .25
88 Jose Ortiz .25
89 Abraham Nunez .25
90 Dave Williams .25
91 Preston Wilson .25
92 Jason Jennings .25
93 Juan Diaz .25
94 Steve Smyth .25
95 Phil Nevin .25
96 John Olerud .25
97 Brad Penny .25
98 Andy Pettitte .40
99 Juan Pierre .25
100 Manny Ramirez .75
101 Edgardo Alfonzo .25
102 Michael Cuddyer .25
103 Johnny Damon .40
104 Carlos Zambrano .35
105 Jose Vidro .25
106 Tsuyoshi Shinjo .25
107 Ed Rogers .25
108 Scott Rolen .75
109 Mariano Rivera .35
110 Tim Redding .25
111 Josh Phelps .25
112 Gabe Kapler .25
113 Edgar Martinez .25
114 Fred McGriff .25
115 Raul Mondesi .25
116 Wade Miller .25
117 Mike Mussina .40
118 Rafael Palmeiro .65
119 Adam Johnson .25
120 Rickey Henderson .75
121 Bill Hall .25
122 Ken Griffey Jr. 1.50
123 Geronimo Gil .25
124 Robert Fick .25
125 Darin Erstad .50
126 Brandon Duckworth .25
127 Garret Anderson .25
128 Pedro Feliz .25
129 Jeff Cirillo .25
130 Brian Giles .25
131 Craig Biggio .25
132 Willie Harris .25
133 Doug Davis .25
134 Jeff Kent .25
135 Terrence Long .25
136 Carlos Delgado .50
137 Tino Martinez .25
138 Donaldo Mendez .25
139 Sean Douglass .25
140 Eric Chavez .40
141 Rick Ankiel .25
142 Jeremy Giambi .25
143 Juan Pena .25
144 Bernie Williams .40
145 Craig Wilson .25
146 Ricardo Rodriguez .25
147 Albert Pujols 1.50
148 Antonio Perez .25
149 Russ Ortiz .25
150 Corky Miller .25
151 Rich Aurilia .25
152 Kerry Wood .50
153 Joe Thurston .25
154 *Jeff Deardorff* .25
155 Jermaine Dye .25
156 Andruw Jones .75
157 Victor Martinez .25
158 Nick Neugebauer .25
159 Matt Morris .25
160 Casey Fossum .25
161 J.D. Drew .40
162 *Matt Childers* .50
163 Mark Buehrle .25
164 Jeff Bagwell .75
165 Kazuhiro Sasaki .25
166 Ben Sheets .40
167 Alex Rodriguez 1.50
168 Adam Pettyjohn .25
169 *Chris Snelling* .50
170 Robert Person .25
171 Juan Uribe .25
172 Mo Vaughn .25
173 Alfredo Amezaga .25
174 Ryan Drese .25
175 *Corey Thurman* .25
176 Jim Thome .25
177 Orlando Cabrera .25
178 *Eric Cyr* .50
179 Greg Maddux 1.00
180 *Earl Snyder* .25
181 C.C. Sabathia .25
182 Mark Mulder .40
183 Jose Mieses .25
184 Joe Kennedy .25
185 Randy Johnson .75
186 Tom Glavine .40
187 *Eric Junge* .25
188 Mike Piazza 1.50
189 Corey Patterson .40
190 Carlos Pena .25
191 Curt Schilling .40
192 Nomar Garciaparra 1.50
193 Lance Berkman .25
194 Ryan Klesko .25
195 Ivan Rodriguez .65
196 Alfonso Soriano .75
197 Derek Jeter 2.00
198 David Justice .25
199 Juan Gonzalez .75
200 Adam Dunn .50
201 *Victor Alvarez* 3.00
202 *Miguel Asencio* 3.00
203 *Brandon Backe* 3.00
204 *Chris Baker* 4.00
205 *Steve Bechler* 4.00
206 *Francis Beltran* 4.00
207 Angel Berroa 3.00
208 Hank Blalock 4.00
209 Dewon Brazelton 3.00
210 Sean Burroughs 3.00
211 Marlon Byrd 3.00
212 *Raul Chavez* 4.00
213 Juan Cruz 3.00
214 *Jorge De La Rosa* 3.00
215 *Doug Devore* 3.00
216 *John Ennis* 3.00
217 *Felix Escalona* 3.00
218 Morgan Ensberg 3.00
219 *Cam Esslinger* 3.00
220 *Kevin Frederick* 3.00
221 *Franklyn German* 3.00
222 Eric Hinske 4.00
223 *Ben Howard* 3.00
224 Orlando Hudson 3.00
225 *Travis Hughes* 5.00
226 *Kazuhisa Ishii* 6.00
227 *Ryan Jamison* 3.00
228 *Reed Johnson* 4.00
229 *Kyle Kane* 3.00
230 Austin Kearns 3.00
231 *Satoru Komiyama* 4.00
232 Jason Lane 3.00
233 *Jeremy Lambert* 3.00
234 *Anderson Machado* 4.00
235 *Brian Mallette* 3.00
236 *Takahito Nomura* 3.00
237 *Jorge Padilla* 4.00
238 *Luis Ugueto* 3.00
239 Mark Prior 15.00
240 *Rene Reyes* 3.00
241 Deivis Santos 3.00
242 *Elio Serrano* 3.00
243 *Tom Shearn* 3.00
244 *Allan Simpson* 3.00
245 *So Taguchi* 5.00
246 Dennis Tankersley 3.00
247 Mark Teixeira 6.00
248 Matt Thornton 3.00
249 Bobby Hill 3.00
250 Ramon Vazquez 3.00

Proof

Proofs (1-200): 4-8X
Proofs (201-250): 1-2X
Production 100 sets

Classic Studio

NM/M
Complete Set (25): 90.00
Common Player: 3.00
Production 1,000 sets
First Ballot: 3-4X
Print Run based on HOF Year
1 Kirby Puckett 5.00
2 George Brett 8.00
3 Nolan Ryan 10.00

4 Mike Schmidt 8.00
5 Steve Carlton 3.00
6 Reggie Jackson 5.00
7 Tom Seaver 3.00
8 Joe Morgan 3.00
9 Jim Palmer 3.00
10 Johnny Bench 5.00
11 Willie McCovey 3.00
12 Brooks Robinson 4.00
13 Al Kaline 5.00
14 Stan Musial 6.00
15 Ozzie Smith 6.00
16 Dave Winfield 3.00
17 Robin Yount 5.00
18 Rod Carew 3.00
19 Willie Stargell 3.00
20 Lou Brock 3.00
21 Ernie Banks 5.00
22 Ted Williams 10.00
23 Jackie Robinson 8.00
24 Roberto Clemente 10.00
25 Lou Gehrig 10.00

Classic Studio Autograph

No pricing due to scarcity

Diamond Collection

NM/M
Complete Set (25): 65.00
Common Player: 1.50
Inserted 1:17
1 Todd Helton 3.00
2 Chipper Jones 4.00
3 Lance Berkman 1.50
4 Derek Jeter 8.00
5 Hideo Nomo 3.00
6 Kazuhisa Ishii 1.50
7 Barry Bonds 8.00
8 Alex Rodriguez 6.00
9 Ichiro Suzuki 5.00
10 Mike Piazza 5.00
11 Jim Thome 1.50
12 Greg Maddux 4.00
13 Jeff Bagwell 3.00
14 Vladimir Guerrero 3.00
15 Ken Griffey Jr. 5.00
16 Jason Giambi 2.50
17 Nomar Garciaparra 5.00
18 Albert Pujols 6.00
19 Manny Ramirez 3.00
20 Pedro J. Martinez 3.00
21 Roger Clemens 4.50
22 Randy Johnson 3.00
23 Mark Prior 3.00
24 So Taguchi 1.50
25 Sammy Sosa 5.00

Hats Off

NM/M
Common Player: 8.00
Production 100
MLB Logo: No Pricing
Production one set
10 Carlos Lee 10.00
14 Mark Buehrle 10.00
16 Paul LoDuca 10.00
22 Brandon Duckworth 10.00
26 J.D. Drew 12.00
28 Wade Miller 10.00
30 Brian Giles 10.00
31 Lance Berkman 10.00
32 Shannon Stewart 10.00
33 Kazuhisa Ishii/50 20.00
35 Rafael Palmeiro 20.00
36 Roy Oswalt 15.00
37 Jason Lane 10.00
38 Andruw Jones 15.00
39 Brad Penny 10.00
40 Bud Smith 8.00
41 Carlos Beltran 15.00
42 Magglio Ordonez 20.00
43 Craig Biggio 10.00
45 Jeff Bagwell 25.00
47 Juan Cruz 8.00
48 Kerry Wood 25.00
49 Brandon Berger 8.00
50 Juan Pierre 8.00

Leather & Lumber

NM/M
Common Player: 5.00
Production 200 unless noted
Artist's Proofs: 1.5-2X
Production 50
1 Nomar Garciaparra 15.00
2 Jeff Bagwell/150 8.00
3 Alex Rodriguez 15.00
4 Vladimir Guerrero/100 10.00
5 Luis Gonzalez 5.00
6 Chipper Jones 10.00
7 Shawn Green 5.00
8 Kirby Puckett/100 15.00
9 Juan Gonzalez 8.00
10 Troy Glaus 8.00
11 Don Mattingly/100 30.00
12 Todd Helton 8.00
13 Jim Thome 10.00
14 Rickey Henderson 15.00
15 Mike Schmidt/100 35.00
16 Adam Dunn/100 10.00
17 Ivan Rodriguez 10.00
18 Manny Ramirez/150 10.00
19 Tsuyoshi Shinjo 8.00
20 Andruw Jones/150 10.00
21 Roberto Alomar 8.00
22 Lance Berkman 5.00
23 Derek Jeter/50/ball 30.00
24 Ichiro Suzuki/50/ball 60.00
25 Mike Piazza 15.00

Masterstrokes

NM/M
Complete Set (25): 50.00
Common Player: 1.50
Inserted 1:17
1 Vladimir Guerrero 3.00
2 Frank Thomas 3.00
3 Alex Rodriguez 6.00
4 Manny Ramirez 3.00
5 Jeff Bagwell 3.00
6 Jim Thome 1.50
7 Ichiro Suzuki 5.00
8 Andruw Jones 3.00
9 Troy Glaus 3.00
10 Chipper Jones 4.00
11 Juan Gonzalez 3.00
12 Lance Berkman 1.50
13 Mike Piazza 5.00
14 Darin Erstad 2.00
15 Albert Pujols 6.00
16 Kazuhisa Ishii 1.50
17 Shawn Green 1.50
18 Rafael Palmeiro 2.00
19 Todd Helton 3.00
20 Carlos Delgado 1.50
21 Ivan Rodriguez 2.00
22 Luis Gonzalez 1.50
23 Derek Jeter 8.00
24 Nomar Garciaparra 5.00
15 J.D. Drew 1.50

Private Signings

NM/M
Common Autograph: 5.00
Varying quantities produced
1 Vladimir Guerrero/25 75.00
2 Chipper Jones/15 150.00
3 Bobby Abreu/50 20.00
4 Barry Zito/25 50.00
6 Miguel Tejada/50 30.00
7 Mike Sweeney/50 20.00
8 Shannon Stewart/100 10.00
10 Bud Smith/100 5.00
11 Wilson Betemit/250 8.00
12 Kevin Brown/25 45.00
15 Cliff Floyd/50 15.00
16 Marcus Giles/250 10.00
17 Troy Glaus/50 30.00
18 Barry Larkin/25
19 Carlos Lee/25 20.00
20 Brian Lawrence/250 8.00
21 Paul LoDuca/50 15.00
25 Roger Clemens/15 175.00
26 Joe Crede/250 8.00
28 Jeremy Affeldt/250 8.00
29 Adrian Beltre/25 20.00
30 Josh Beckett/25 40.00
31 Roberto Alomar/25 60.00
32 Toby Hall/250 8.00
35 Eric Munson/25
37 Roy Oswalt/50 20.00
40 Nick Johnson/250 8.00
41 Tim Hudson/25
43 Drew Henson/150 20.00
45 Luis Gonzalez/15 50.00
46 Pedro Martinez/15
47 Joe Mays/100 8.00
49 Aramis Ramirez/50 20.00
50 Kip Wells/250 8.00
51 Moises Alou/15 30.00
55 Freddy Garcia/50 15.00
56 Steve Green/250 5.00
59 Jack Cust/250 8.00
60 Sean Casey/50 15.00
63 Magglio Ordonez/15 50.00
64 Frank Thomas/15
65 Josh Towers/250 8.00
66 Javier Vazquez/100 15.00
68 Aubrey Huff/250 10.00
69 Richard Hidalgo/25 20.00
70 Brandon Claussen/250 10.00
72 John Buck/250 5.00
73 Dee Brown/250 5.00
75 Jason Giambi/25
76 Erick Almonte/250 8.00
79 Jay Gibbons/250 15.00
81 Todd Helton/15 85.00
82 Erik Bedard/250 5.00
83 Carlos Beltran/15
84 Rafael Soriano/250 10.00
85 Gary Sheffield/15 60.00
86 Richie Sexson/50 25.00
87 Mike Rivera/250 5.00
88 Jose Ortiz/250 8.00
89 Abraham Nunez/250 5.00
90 Dave Williams/250 5.00
92 Jason Jennings/250 8.00
93 Juan Diaz/250 5.00
94 Steve Smyth/250 5.00
97 Brad Penny/80 10.00
99 Juan Pierre/100 10.00
100 Manny Ramirez/15 75.00
102 Michael Cuddyer/250 10.00
104 Carlos Zambrano/250 15.00
105 Jose Vidro/100 15.00
107 Ed Rogers/250 8.00
108 Scott Rolen/15
110 Tim Redding/250 5.00
111 Josh Phelps/250 8.00
112 Gabe Kapler/100 10.00
113 Edgar Martinez/50 40.00
116 Wade Miller/250 15.00
117 Mike Mussina/15
118 Rafael Palmeiro/25 50.00
120 Rickey Henderson/15
121 Bill Hall/250 10.00
123 Geronimo Gil/250 8.00
124 Robert Fick/150 10.00
125 Darin Erstad/15
126 Brandon Duckworth/250 8.00
128 Pedro Feliz/250 8.00
130 Brian Giles/15 50.00
131 Craig Biggio/15 40.00
132 Willie Harris/250 5.00
133 Doug Davis/250 8.00
135 Terrence Long/150 10.00
138 Donaldo Mendez/250 5.00
139 Sean Douglass/250 5.00
140 Eric Chavez/15 50.00
141 Rick Ankiel/250 8.00
142 Jeremy Giambi/100 6.00
143 Juan Pena/250 8.00
144 Bernie Williams/15 75.00
145 Craig Wilson/250 20.00
146 Ricardo Rodriguez/250 10.00
147 Albert Pujols/25 120.00
148 Antonio Perez/250 5.00
150 Corky Miller/250 8.00
151 Rich Aurilia/25 20.00
152 Kerry Wood/25 70.00
153 Joe Thurston/250 5.00
154 Jeff Deardorff/250 8.00
155 Jermaine Dye/15 25.00
156 Andruw Jones/15
157 Victor Martinez/250 15.00
158 Nick Neugebauer/150 5.00
160 Casey Fossum/250 8.00
161 J.D. Drew/25 40.00
162 Matt Childers/250 5.00
163 Mark Buehrle/150 10.00
164 Jeff Bagwell/15
166 Ben Sheets/100 15.00
167 Alex Rodriguez/15 165.00
168 Adam Pettyjohn/250 5.00
169 Chris Snelling/250 10.00
170 Robert Person/250 5.00
171 Juan Uribe/250 10.00
173 Alfredo Amezaga/250 5.00
175 Corey Thurman/250 5.00
176 Jim Thome/15
178 Eric Cyr/250 5.00
179 Greg Maddux/15 200.00
180 Earl Snyder/250 5.00
181 C.C. Sabathia/50 20.00
182 Mark Mulder/50 20.00
183 Jose Mieses/250 5.00
184 Joe Kennedy/250 5.00
186 Tom Glavine/15
187 Eric Junge/250 5.00
189 Corey Patterson/205 20.00
190 Carlos Pena/250 10.00
191 Curt Schilling/15 80.00
192 Nomar Garciaparra/15
193 Lance Berkman/15
194 Ryan Klesko/15
195 Ivan Rodriguez/15 75.00
196 Alfonso Soriano/50 40.00
198 David Justice/15
199 Juan Gonzalez/15
200 Adam Dunn/25
201 Victor Alvarez/250 5.00
203 Brandon Backe/250 5.00
204 Chris Baker/250 5.00
205 Steve Bechler/250 8.00
206 Francis Beltran/250 5.00
207 Angel Berroa/250 10.00
208 Hank Blalock/100 25.00
209 Dewon Brazelton/200 5.00
210 Sean Burroughs/50 20.00
211 Marlon Byrd/200 10.00
212 Raul Chavez/250 5.00
213 Juan Cruz/50 15.00
214 Jorge De La Rosa/250 5.00
215 Doug Devore/250 5.00
216 John Ennis/250 5.00
217 Felix Escalona/250 5.00
218 Morgan Ensberg/250 10.00
219 Cam Esslinger/250 5.00
220 Kevin Frederick/250 5.00
221 Franklyn German/250 5.00
222 Eric Hinske/250 8.00
223 Ben Howard/250 8.00
224 Orlando Hudson/250 5.00
225 Travis Hughes/250 10.00
226 Kazuhisa Ishii/50 50.00
227 Ryan Jamison/250 5.00
228 Reed Johnson/250 10.00
229 Kyle Kane/250 5.00
230 Austin Kearns/250 20.00
231 Satoru Komiyama/50 10.00
232 Jason Lane/200 5.00
233 Jeremy Lambert/250 5.00
234 Anderson Machado/200 10.00
235 Brian Mallette/250 5.00
236 Takahito Nomura/100 20.00
237 Jorge Padilla/200 10.00
238 Luis Ugueto/250 5.00
239 Mark Prior/100 60.00
240 Rene Reyes/250 5.00
241 Deivis Santos/250 5.00
242 Elio Serrano/250 5.00
243 Tom Shearn/250 5.00
244 Allan Simpson/250 5.00
245 So Taguchi/100 15.00
246 Dennis Tankersley/100 10.00
247 Mark Teixeira/50 35.00
248 Matt Thornton/250 5.00
249 Bobby Hill/100 10.00
250 Ramon Vazquez/250 5.00

Spirit of the Game

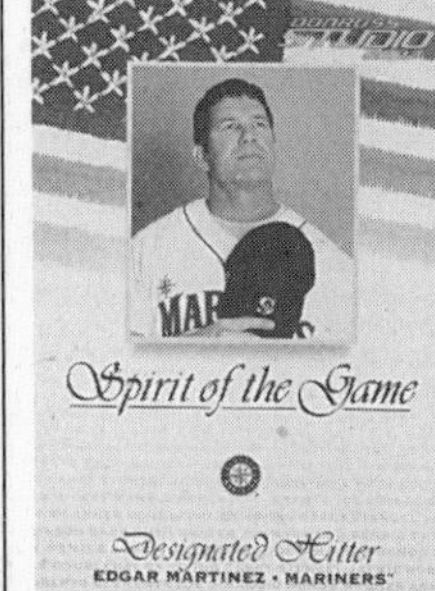

NM/M
Complete Set (50): 60.00
Common Player: 1.00

Inserted 1:9
1 Alex Rodriguez 5.00
2 Curt Schilling 1.50
3 Hideo Nomo 2.00
4 Derek Jeter 6.00
5 Mike Sweeney 1.00
6 Mike Piazza 4.00
7 Roger Clemens 3.00
8 Shawn Green 1.50
9 Vladimir Guerrero 2.00
10 Carlos Lee 1.00
11 Edgar Martinez 1.00
12 Albert Pujols 5.00
13 Mark Prior 3.00
14 Mark Buehrle 1.00
15 Chipper Jones 3.00
16 Paul LoDuca 1.00
17 Frank Thomas 2.00
18 Randy Johnson 2.00
19 Cliff Floyd 1.00
20 Todd Helton 2.00
21 Luis Gonzalez 1.00
22 Brandon Duckworth 1.00
23 Jason Giambi 1.50
24 Juan Uribe 1.00
25 Dewon Brazelton 1.00
26 J.D. Drew 1.00
27 Troy Glaus 2.00
28 Wade Miller 1.00
29 Darin Erstad 1.50
30 Brian Giles 1.00
31 Lance Berkman 1.00
32 Shannon Stewart 1.00
33 Kazuhisa Ishii 1.00
34 Corey Patterson 1.00
35 Rafael Palmeiro 1.50
36 Roy Oswalt 1.00
37 Jason Lane 1.00
38 Andruw Jones 2.00
39 Brad Penny 1.00
40 Bud Smith 1.00
41 Carlos Beltran 1.50
42 Magglio Ordonez 1.50
43 Craig Biggio 1.00
44 Hank Blalock 1.50
45 Jeff Bagwell 2.00
46 Josh Beckett 1.50
47 Juan Cruz 1.00
48 Kerry Wood 1.50
49 Brandon Berger 1.00
50 Juan Pierre 1.00

Studio Stars

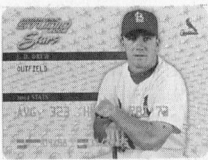

NM/M
Complete Set (50): 60.00
Common Player: 1.00
Production 700 sets
Golds: 1.5-2X
Production 250 sets
Platinums: 3-5X
Production 50 sets
1 Mike Piazza 3.00
2 Ivan Rodriguez 1.50
3 Albert Pujols 4.00
4 Scott Rolen 2.00
5 Alex Rodriguez 4.00
6 Curt Schilling 1.50
7 Vladimir Guerrero 2.00
8 Jim Thome 1.00
9 Derek Jeter 5.00
10 C.C. Sabathia 1.00
11 Sammy Sosa 3.00
12 Adam Dunn 1.50
13 Bernie Williams 1.00
14 Ichiro Suzuki 4.00
15 Barry Bonds 5.00
16 Rickey Henderson 2.00
17 Ken Griffey Jr. 3.00
18 Kazuhisa Ishii 1.00
19 Kerry Wood 1.50
20 Todd Helton 1.50
21 Hideo Nomo 2.00
22 Frank Thomas 2.00
23 Manny Ramirez 2.00
24 Luis Gonzalez 1.00
25 Rafael Palmeiro 1.50
26 Mike Mussina 1.50
27 Roy Oswalt 1.00
28 Darin Erstad 1.00
29 Barry Larkin 1.00
30 Randy Johnson 2.00
31 Tom Glavine 1.00
32 Lance Berkman 1.00
33 Juan Gonzalez 2.00
34 Shawn Green 1.00
35 Nomar Garciaparra 3.00
36 Troy Glaus 2.00
37 Tim Hudson 1.00
38 Carlos Delgado 1.50
39 Jason Giambi 1.50
40 Andruw Jones 2.00
41 Roberto Alomar 1.00
42 Greg Maddux 2.50
43 Pedro J. Martinez 2.00
44 Tony Gwynn 3.00
45 Alfonso Soriano 1.50
46 Chipper Jones 2.50
47 J.D. Drew 1.00
48 Roger Clemens 2.75
49 Barry Zito 1.00
50 Jeff Bagwell 1.50

2002 DONRUSS THE ROOKIES

NM/M
Complete Set (110): 25.00
Common Player: .15
Common Rookie: .25
Pack (5): 2.00
Box (24): 40.00
1 Kazuhisa Ishii 1.00
2 P.J. Bevis .25
3 Jason Simontacchi .75
4 John Lackey .15
5 Travis Driskill .25
6 Carl Sadler .25
7 Tim Kalita .25
8 Nelson Castro .25
9 Francis Beltran .25
10 So Taguchi .50
11 Ryan Bukvich .25
12 Brian Fitzgerald .15
13 Kevin Frederick .25
14 Chone Figgins .25
15 Marlon Byrd .15
16 Ron Calloway .25
17 Jason Lane .15
18 Satoru Komiyama .25
19 John Ennis .25
20 Juan Brito .25
21 Gustavo Chacin .25
22 Josh Bard .50
23 Brett Myers .15
24 Mike Smith .25
25 Eric Hinske .15
26 Jake Peavy .15
27 Todd Donovan .25
28 Luis Ugueto .25
29 Corey Thurman .25
30 Takahito Nomura .25
31 Andy Shibilo .25
32 Mike Crudale .25
33 Earl Snyder .25
34 Brian Tallet .50
35 Miguel Asencio .25
36 Felix Escalona .25
37 Drew Henson .40
38 Steve Kent .25
39 Rene Reyes .25
40 Edwin Almonte .25
41 Chris Snelling .75
42 Franklyn German .25
43 Jeriome Robertson .25
44 Colin Young .25
45 Jeremy Lambert .25
46 Kirk Saarloos .75
47 Matt Childers .25
48 Justin Wayne .15
49 Jose Valverde .25
50 Wily Mo Pena .15
51 Victor Alvarez .25
52 Julius Matos .25
53 Aaron Cook .40
54 Jeff Austin .25
55 Adrian Burnside .25
56 Brandon Puffer .25
57 Jeremy Hill .25
58 Jaime Cerda .25
59 Aaron Guiel .25
60 Ron Chiavacci .15
61 Kevin Cash .25
62 Elio Serrano .15
63 Julio Mateo .25
64 Cam Esslinger .25
65 Ken Huckaby .25
66 Wiki Nieves .25
67 Luis Martinez .25
68 Scotty Layfield .25
69 Jeremy Guthrie 1.00
70 Hansel Izquierdo .25
71 Shane Nance .25
72 Jeff Baker 1.00
73 Clifford Bartosh .25
74 Mitch Wylie .25
75 Oliver Perez .75
76 Matt Thornton .15
77 John Foster .25
78 Joe Borchard .15
79 Eric Junge .25
80 Jorge Sosa .25
81 Runelvys Hernandez .25
82 Kevin Mench .15
83 Ben Kozlowski .50
84 Trey Hodges .40
85 Reed Johnson .25
86 Eric Eckenstahler .25
87 Franklin Nunez .25
88 Victor Martinez .50
89 Kevin Gryboski .25
90 Jason Jennings .15
91 Jim Rushford .25
92 Jeremy Ward .25
93 Adam Walker .25
94 Freddy Sanchez .40
95 Wilson Valdez .25
96 Lee Gardner .15
97 Eric Good .25
98 Hank Blalock .50
99 Mark Corey .15
100 Jason Davis .40
101 Mike Gonzalez .25
102 David Ross .25
103 Tyler Yates .25
104 Cliff Lee .50
105 Mike Moriarty .25
106 Josh Hancock .25
107 Jason Beverlin .25
108 Clay Condrey .25
109 Shawn Sedlacek .25
110 Sean Burroughs .15
Donruss Originals
401 Runelvys Hernandez .50
402 Wilson Valdez .25
403 Brian Tallet 1.00
404 Chone Figgins .25
405 Jeriome Robertson .50
406 Shane Nance .25
407 Aaron Cook .75
408 Trey Hodges .75
409 Matt Childers .40
410 Mitch Wylie .25
411 Rene Reyes .25
412 Mike Smith .25
413 Jason Simontacchi .75
414 Luis Martinez .40
415 Kevin Cash .40
416 Todd Donovan .25
417 Scotty Layfield .25
418 Joe Borchard .25
419 Adrian Burnside .25
420 Ben Kozlowski .25
421 Clay Condrey .25
422 Cliff Lee 1.00
423 Josh Bard .25
424 Freddy Sanchez 1.00
425 Ron Calloway .25
Donruss Studio
Common Studio RC: 3.00
Production 1,500
251 Freddy Sanchez 5.00
252 Josh Bard 3.00
253 Trey Hodges 5.00
254 Jorge Sosa 3.00
255 Ben Kozlowski 3.00
256 Eric Good 3.00
257 Brian Tallet 5.00
258 P.J. Bevis 3.00
259 Rodrigo Rosario 3.00
260 Kirk Saarloos 5.00
261 Runelvys Hernandez 4.00
262 Josh Hancock 3.00
263 Tim Kalita 3.00
264 Jason Simontacchi 5.00
265 Clay Condrey 3.00
266 Cliff Lee 8.00
267 Aaron Guiel 4.00
268 Andy Pratt 4.00
269 Wilson Valdez 3.00
270 Oliver Perez 6.00
271 Joe Borchard 3.00
272 Jeriome Robertson 4.00
273 Aaron Cook 5.00
274 Kevin Cash 3.00
275 Chone Figgins 3.00
Best of Fan Club
Common Best of Fan Club RC: 3.00
Production 1,350
Best of Fan Club Spotlights: 1.5-3X
Production 100 sets
201 Kirk Saarloos 4.00
202 Oliver Perez 5.00
203 So Taguchi 6.00
204 Runelvys Hernandez 5.00
205 Freddy Sanchez 5.00
206 Cliff Lee 8.00
207 Kazuhisa Ishii 8.00
208 Kevin Cash 5.00
209 Trey Hodges 6.00
210 Wilson Valdez 3.00
211 Satoru Komiyama 3.00
212 Luis Ugueto 3.00
213 Joe Borchard 3.00
214 Brian Tallet 4.00
215 Jeriome Robertson 5.00
216 Eric Junge 4.00
217 Aaron Cook 4.00
218 Jason Simontacchi 3.00
219 Miguel Asencio 3.00
220 Josh Bard 3.00
221 Earl Snyder 3.00
222 Felix Escalona 3.00
223 Rene Reyes 3.00
224 Chone Figgins 3.00
225 Chris Snelling 5.00
Fan Club
Inserted 1:4 Retail
201 Kirk Saarloos 1.50
202 Oliver Perez 3.00
203 So Taguchi 2.00
204 Runelvys Hernandez 1.50
205 Freddy Sanchez 2.00
206 Cliff Lee 3.00
207 Kazuhisa Ishii 3.00
208 Kevin Cash 1.00
209 Trey Hodges 1.50
210 Wilson Valdez 1.00
211 Satoru Komiyama 1.00
212 Luis Ugueto 1.50
213 Joe Borchard 2.00
214 Brian Tallet 3.00
215 Jeriome Robertson 1.50
216 Eric Junge 1.50
217 Aaron Cook 1.50
218 Jason Simontacchi 1.50
219 Miguel Asencio 1.50
220 Josh Bard 1.50
221 Earl Snyder 1.50
222 Felix Escalona 1.00
223 Rene Reyes 1.00
224 Chone Figgins 1.00
225 Chris Snelling 4.00
Elite
Common Elite RC: 4.00
Production 1,000
Elite Turn of the Century: 1-2.5X
Production 100 sets
201 Chris Snelling 5.00
202 Satoru Komiyama 5.00
203 Jason Simontacchi 8.00
204 Tim Kalita 4.00
205 Runelvys Hernandez 5.00
206 Kirk Saarloos 4.00
207 Aaron Cook 6.00
208 Luis Ugueto 5.00
209 Gustavo Chacin 5.00
210 Francis Beltran 5.00
211 Takahito Nomura 5.00
212 Oliver Perez 8.00
213 Miguel Asencio 4.00
214 Rene Reyes 5.00
215 Jeff Baker 15.00
216 Jon Adkins 5.00
217 Carlos Rivera 5.00
218 Corey Thurman 5.00
219 Earl Snyder 5.00

220 *Felix Escalona* 5.00
221 *Jeremy Guthrie* 15.00
222 *Josh Hancock* 5.00
223 *Ben Kozlowski* 5.00
224 *Eric Good* 5.00
225 *Eric Junge* 5.00
226 *Andy Pratt* 5.00
227 Matt Thornton 5.00
228 *Jorge Sosa* 5.00
229 Mike Smith 5.00
230 *Mitch Wylie* 5.00
231 *John Ennis* 5.00
232 *Reed Johnson* 5.00
233 Joe Borchard 8.00
234 *Ron Calloway* 5.00
235 Brian Tallet 5.00
236 *Chris Baker* 5.00
237 *Cliff Lee* 15.00
238 *Matt Childers* 5.00
239 *Freddy Sanchez* 5.00
240 *Chone Figgins* 8.00
241 *Kevin Cash* 5.00
242 *Josh Bard* 5.00
243 *Jeriome Robertson* 5.00
244 *Jeremy Hill* 5.00
245 *Shane Nance* 5.00
246 *Wes Obermueller* 5.00
247 *Trey Hodges* 5.00
248 *Eric Eckenstahler* 5.00
249 *Jim Rushford* 5.00
250 *Jose Castillo* 10.00
251 *Garrett Atkins* 20.00
252 *Alexis Rios* 50.00
253 *Ryan Church* 10.00
254 *Jimmy Gobble* 8.00
255 Corwin Malone 6.00
257 *Nic Jackson* 6.00
258 *Tommy Whiteman* 8.00
259 Mario Ramos 5.00
260 *Rob Bowen* 8.00
261 *Josh Wilson* 5.00
262 *Tim Hummel* 5.00
264 *Gerald Laird* 15.00
265 *Vinnie Chulk* 5.00
266 *Jesus Medrano* 5.00
272 *Adam LaRoche* 20.00
273 *Adam Morrissey* 5.00
274 *Henri Stanley* 5.00
275 *Walter Young* 10.00

Donruss Classics
Common Classics RC: 3.00
Production 1,500
Classics Timeless Tributes: 1.5-3X
Production 100 sets
201 *Oliver Perez* 5.00
202 *Aaron Cook* 5.00
203 *Eric Junge* 3.00
204 *Freddy Sanchez* 5.00
205 *Cliff Lee* 5.00
206 *Runelvys Hernandez* 5.00
207 *Chone Figgins* 3.00
208 *Rodrigo Rosario* 3.00
209 *Kevin Cash* 3.00
210 *Josh Bard* 3.00
211 *Felix Escalona* 3.00
212 *Jeriome Robertson* 5.00
213 *Jason Simontacchi* 5.00
214 *Shane Nance* 3.00
215 *Ben Kozlowski* 3.00
216 Brian Tallet 5.00
217 *Earl Snyder* 3.00
218 *Andy Pratt* 3.00
219 *Trey Hodges* 5.00
220 Kirk Saarloos 5.00
221 *Rene Reyes* 3.00
222 Joe Borchard 3.00
223 *Wilson Valdez* 3.00
224 *Miguel Asencio* 3.00
225 *Chris Snelling* 5.00

Diamond Kings
Common DK RC: 3.00
Inserted 1:10
151 *Chris Snelling* 4.00
152 *Satoru Komiyama* 3.00
153 *Oliver Perez* 4.00
154 Kirk Saarloos 3.00
155 *Rene Reyes* 3.00
156 *Runelvys Hernandez* 3.00
157 *Rodrigo Rosario* 3.00
158 *Jason Simontacchi* 3.00
159 *Miguel Asencio* 3.00
160 *Aaron Cook* 3.00

Autographs

NM/M
Common Autograph: 5.00
Print runs listed
1 Kazuhisa Ishii/25
2 P.J. Bevis/50 10.00

7 Tim Kalita/25
9 Francis Beltran/100 5.00
10 So Taguchi/15
13 Kevin Frederick/100 5.00
14 Chone Figgins/100 15.00
15 Marlon Byrd/100 10.00
17 Jason Lane/100 8.00
18 Satoru Komiyama/25
19 John Ennis/100 10.00
22 Josh Bard/100 10.00
25 Eric Hinske/100 10.00
28 Luis Ugueto/100 5.00
29 Corey Thurman/100 5.00
30 Takahito Nomura/100 20.00
33 Earl Snyder/100 10.00
34 Brian Tallet/100 15.00
36 Felix Escalona/25
37 Drew Henson/50 25.00
39 Rene Reyes/50 10.00
40 Edwin Almonte/50 10.00
41 Chris Snelling/50 15.00
42 Franklyn German/100 5.00
45 Jeremy Lambert/100 5.00
46 Kirk Saarloos/50 10.00
47 Matt Childers/100 5.00
50 Wily Mo Pena/100 15.00
51 Victor Alvarez/100 10.00
61 Kevin Cash/100 8.00
62 Elio Serrano/100 5.00
64 Cam Esslinger/100 5.00
69 Jeremy Guthrie/100 25.00
71 Shane Nance/100 8.00
72 Jeff Baker/100 30.00
75 Oliver Perez/25
76 Matt Thornton/100 10.00
78 Joe Borchard/100 10.00
79 Eric Junge/25
82 Kevin Mench/100 10.00
83 Ben Kozlowski/100 8.00
84 Trey Hodges/100 10.00
85 Reed Johnson/100 15.00
88 Victor Martinez/100 20.00
90 Jason Jennings/100 8.00
95 Wilson Valdez/100 10.00
97 Eric Good/100 10.00
98 Hank Blalock/100 25.00
104 Cliff Lee/100 25.00
110 Sean Burroughs/50 20.00

Best of Fan Club Autograph

NM/M
Print Runs listed
201 Kirk Saarloos/100 10.00
208 Kevin Cash/50 10.00
209 Trey Hodges/100 10.00
210 Wilson Valdez/50 10.00
212 Luis Ugueto/75 10.00
213 Joe Borchard/50 15.00
214 Brian Tallet/50 15.00
220 Josh Bard/50 8.00
221 Earl Snyder/100 8.00
223 Rene Reyes/50 8.00
224 Chone Figgins/100 8.00
225 Chris Snelling/50 15.00

Donruss Classics Signatures

NM/M
Print Runs listed
201 Oliver Perez/50
203 Eric Junge/50 10.00
205 Cliff Lee/100 30.00
207 Chone Figgins/100 10.00
208 Rodrigo Rosario/250 10.00
209 Kevin Cash/100 10.00
210 Josh Bard/100 10.00
211 Felix Escalona/25
214 Shane Nance/200 10.00
215 Ben Kozlowski/200 10.00
216 Brian Tallet/100 15.00
217 Earl Snyder/100 10.00
218 Andy Pratt/250 10.00
219 Trey Hodges/250 15.00
220 Kirk Saarloos/100 20.00
221 Rene Reyes/50 10.00
222 Joe Borchard/100 10.00
223 Wilson Valdez/100 10.00
225 Chris Snelling/100 25.00

Donruss Studio Private Signing

NM/M
Print Runs listed
252 Josh Bard/100 10.00
253 Trey Hodges/250 10.00
255 Ben Kozlowski/200 5.00
257 Brian Tallet/100 15.00
258 P.J. Bevis/50 15.00
259 Rodrigo Rosario/250 5.00
260 Kirk Saarloos/100 10.00
263 Tim Kalita/50 8.00
266 Cliff Lee/100 25.00
268 Andy Pratt/250 8.00
269 Wilson Valdez/200 5.00
270 Oliver Perez/25
271 Joe Borchard/100 15.00
274 Kevin Cash/100 8.00
275 Chone Figgins/100 8.00

Elite Turn of the Cent. Auto.

NM/M
Print Runs listed
201 Chris Snelling/50 30.00
215 Jeff Baker/100 40.00
216 Jon Adkins/100 10.00
217 Carlos Rivera/100 20.00
221 Jeremy Guthrie/100 25.00
224 Eric Good/100 10.00
240 Chone Figgins/100 25.00
241 Kevin Cash/100 10.00
247 Trey Hodges/100 20.00
251 Garrett Atkins/100 40.00
253 Ryan Church/100 50.00
254 Jimmy Gobble/100 20.00
255 Corwin Malone/100 15.00
258 Tom Whiteman/100 15.00
259 Mario Ramos/100 10.00
260 Rob Bowen/100 15.00
261 Josh Wilson/100 15.00
262 Tim Hummel/100 10.00
264 Gerald Laird/100 25.00
266 Jesus Medrano/100 10.00
272 Adam LaRoche/100 40.00
273 Adam Morrissey/100 15.00
274 Henri Stanley/100 15.00

Fan Club Autograph

NM/M
Print Runs listed
201 Kirk Saarloos/100 10.00
208 Kevin Cash/50 8.00
209 Trey Hodges/100 10.00
210 Wilson Valdez/50 10.00
212 Luis Ugueto/75 10.00
213 Joe Borchard/50 15.00
214 Brian Tallet/50 15.00
220 Josh Bard/50 8.00
221 Earl Snyder/100 8.00
223 Rene Reyes/50 8.00
224 Chone Figgins/100 8.00
225 Chris Snelling/50

Phenoms

NM/M
Common Player: 3.00
Production 1,000 sets
1 Kazuhisa Ishii 5.00
2 Eric Hinske 3.00
3 Jason Lane 3.00
4 Victor Martinez 5.00
5 Mark Prior 8.00
6 Antonio Perez 3.00
7 John Buck 3.00
8 Joe Borchard 3.00
9 Alexis Gomez 3.00
10 Sean Burroughs 3.00
11 Carlos Pena 3.00
12 Bill Hall 3.00
13 Alfredo Amezaga 3.00
14 Ed Rogers 3.00
15 Mark Teixeira 5.00
16 Chris Snelling 4.00
17 Nick Johnson 3.00
18 Angel Berroa 3.00
19 Orlando Hudson 3.00
20 Drew Henson 3.00
21 Austin Kearns 3.00
22 Dewon Brazelton 3.00
23 Dennis Tankersley 3.00
24 Josh Beckett 4.00
25 Marlon Byrd 4.00

Phenoms Autographs

NM/M
Common Autograph: 5.00
Print runs listed
1 Kazuhisa Ishii/25
2 Eric Hinske/500 10.00
3 Jason Lane/500 5.00
4 Victor Martinez/225 10.00
5 Mark Prior/100 75.00
6 Antonio Perez/500 5.00
7 John Buck/100 8.00
8 Joe Borchard/100 10.00
9 Alexis Gomez/400 5.00
10 Sean Burroughs/150 10.00
11 Carlos Pena/150 8.00
12 Bill Hall/200 8.00
13 Alfredo Amezaga/500 5.00
14 Ed Rogers/500 5.00
15 Mark Teixeira/100 20.00
16 Chris Snelling/100 15.00
17 Nick Johnson/250 8.00
18 Angel Berroa/500 8.00
19 Orlando Hudson/400 8.00
20 Drew Henson/500 25.00
21 Austin Kearns/75 20.00
22 Dewon Brazelton/350 5.00
23 Dennis Tankersley/100 8.00
24 Josh Beckett/125 25.00
25 Marlon Byrd/500 10.00

Rookie Crusade

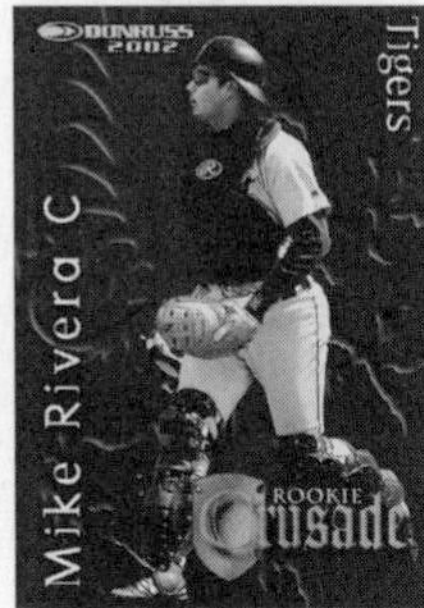

NM/M
Common Player: 3.00
Production 1,500 sets
1 Corky Miller 3.00
2 Jack Cust 3.00
3 Erik Bedard 3.00
4 Andres Torres 3.00
5 Geronimo Gil 3.00
6 Rafael Soriano 3.00
7 Johnny Estrada 3.00
8 Steve Bechler 3.00
9 Adam Johnson 3.00
10 So Taguchi 3.00
11 Dee Brown 3.00
12 Kevin Frederick 3.00
13 Allan Simpson 3.00
14 Ricardo Rodriguez 3.00
15 Jason Hart 3.00
16 Matt Childers 3.00
17 Jason Jennings 3.00
18 Anderson Machado 3.00
19 Fernando Rodney 3.00
20 Brandon Larson 3.00
21 Satoru Komiyama 3.00

#	Player	Price
22	Francis Beltran	3.00
23	Joe Thurston	3.00
24	Josh Pearce	3.00
25	Carlos Hernandez	3.00
26	Ben Howard	3.00
27	Wilson Valdez	3.00
28	Victor Alvarez	3.00
29	Cesar Izturis	3.00
30	Endy Chavez	3.00
31	Michael Cuddyer	4.00
32	Bobby Hill	3.00
33	Willie Harris	3.00
34	Joe Crede	3.00
35	Jorge Padilla	3.00
36	Brandon Backe	3.00
37	Franklyn German	3.00
38	Xavier Nady	3.00
39	Raul Chavez	3.00
40	Shane Nance	3.00
41	Brandon Claussen	4.00
42	Tom Shearn	3.00
43	Freddy Sanchez	3.00
44	Chone Figgins	3.00
45	Cliff Lee	4.00
46	Brian Mallette	3.00
47	Mike Rivera	3.00
48	Elio Serrano	3.00
49	Rodrigo Rosario	3.00
50	Earl Snyder	3.00

Rookie Crusade Autograph

		NM/M
	Common Autograph:	5.00
	Print runs listed	
1	Corky Miller/500	5.00
2	Jack Cust/500	6.00
3	Erik Bedard/100	10.00
4	Andres Torres/500	5.00
5	Geronimo Gil/500	5.00
6	Rafael Soriano/500	8.00
7	Johnny Estrada/400	5.00
8	Steve Bechler/500	6.00
9	Adam Johnson/500	5.00
11	Dee Brown/500	5.00
12	Kevin Frederick/150	5.00
13	Allan Simpson/150	5.00
14	Ricardo Rodriguez/500	5.00
15	Jason Hart/500	5.00
16	Matt Childers/150	5.00
17	Jason Jennings/500	5.00
18	Anderson Machado/500	8.00
19	Fernando Rodney/500	5.00
20	Brandon Larson/400	5.00
21	Satoru Komiyama/25	
22	Francis Beltran/500	5.00
23	Joe Thurston/500	5.00
24	Josh Pearce/500	5.00
25	Carlos Hernandez/500	5.00
26	Ben Howard/500	6.00
27	Wilson Valdez/500	5.00
28	Victor Alvarez/500	5.00
29	Cesar Izturis/500	8.00
30	Endy Chavez/500	5.00
31	Michael Cuddyer/375	10.00
32	Bobby Hill/250	5.00
33	Willie Harris/300	5.00
34	Joe Crede/100	8.00
35	Jorge Padilla/475	10.00
36	Brandon Backe/350	5.00
37	Franklyn German/500	5.00
38	Xavier Nady/500	8.00
39	Raul Chavez/500	5.00
40	Shane Nance/500	5.00
41	Brandon Claussen/150	10.00
42	Tom Shearn/500	5.00
44	Chone Figgins/500	5.00
45	Cliff Lee/500	10.00
46	Brian Mallette/150	5.00
47	Mike Rivera/400	5.00
48	Elio Serrano/500	5.00
49	Rodrigo Rosario/100	10.00
50	Earl Snyder/100	10.00

2003 DONRUSS

		NM/M
	Complete Set (400):	40.00
	Common Player:	.15
	Pack (13):	1.50
	Box (24):	30.00
1	Vladimir Guerrero	.75
2	Derek Jeter	2.00
3	Adam Dunn	.50
4	Greg Maddux	1.00
5	Lance Berkman	.40
6	Ichiro Suzuki	2.00
7	Mike Piazza	1.00
8	Alex Rodriguez	2.00
9	Tom Glavine	.25
10	Randy Johnson	.75
11	Nomar Garciaparra	1.00
12	Jason Giambi	.50
13	Sammy Sosa	1.00
14	Barry Zito	.25
15	Chipper Jones	1.00
16	Magglio Ordonez	.25
17	Larry Walker	.25
18	Alfonso Soriano	.75
19	Curt Schilling	.50
20	Barry Bonds	2.00
21	Joe Borchard	.15
22	Chris Snelling	.15
23	Brian Tallet	.15
24	Cliff Lee	.15
25	Freddy Sanchez	.15
26	Chone Figgins	.15
27	Kevin Cash	.15
28	Josh Bard	.15
29	Jeriome Robertson	.15
30	Jeremy Hill	.15
31	Shane Nance	.15
32	Jake Peavy Padres	.15
33	Trey Hodges	.15
34	Eric Eckenstahler	.15
35	Jim Rushford	.15
36	Oliver Perez	.15
37	Kirk Saarloos	.15
38	Hank Blalock	.50
39	Francisco Rodriguez	.25
40	Runelvys Hernandez	.15
41	Aaron Cook	.15
42	Josh Hancock	.15
43	P.J. Bevis	.15
44	Jon Adkins	.15
45	Tim Kalita	.15
46	Nelson Castro	.15
47	Colin Young	.15
48	Adrian Burnside	.15
49	Luis Martinez	.15
50	Peter Zamora	.15
51	Todd Donovan	.15
52	Jeremy Ward	.15
53	Wilson Valdez	.15
54	Eric Good	.15
55	Jeff Baker	.15
56	Mitch Wylie	.15
57	Ron Calloway	.15
58	Jose Valverde	.15
59	Jason Davis	.15
60	Scotty Layfield	.15
61	Matt Thornton	.15
62	Adam Walker	.15
63	Gustavo Chacin	.15
64	Ron Chiavacci	.15
65	Wiki Nieves	.15
66	Clifford Bartosh	.15
67	Mike Gonzalez	.15
68	Justin Wayne	.15
69	Eric Junge	.15
70	Ben Kozlowski	.15
71	Darin Erstad	.25
72	Garret Anderson	.40
73	Troy Glaus	.40
74	David Eckstein	.15
75	Adam Kennedy	.15
76	Kevin Appier	.15
77	Jarrod Washburn	.15
78	Scott Spiezio	.15
79	Tim Salmon	.25
80	Ramon Ortiz	.15
81	Bengie Molina	.15
82	Brad Fullmer	.15
83	Troy Percival	.15
84	David Segui	.15
85	Jay Gibbons	.15
86	Tony Batista	.15
87	Scott Erickson	.15
88	Jeff Conine	.15
89	Melvin Mora	.15
90	Buddy Groom	.15
91	Rodrigo Lopez	.15
92	Marty Cordova	.15
93	Geronimo Gil	.15
94	Kenny Lofton	.15
95	Shea Hillenbrand	.15
96	Manny Ramirez	.50
97	Pedro Martinez	.75
98	Nomar Garciaparra	1.00
99	Rickey Henderson	.40
100	Johnny Damon	.25
101	Trot Nixon	.15
102	Derek Lowe	.15
103	Hee Seop Choi	.15
104	Mark Teixeira	.40
105	Tim Wakefield	.15
106	Jason Varitek	.25
107	Frank Thomas	.50
108	Joe Crede	.15
109	Magglio Ordonez	.25
110	Ray Durham	.15
111	Mark Buehrle	.15
112	Paul Konerko	.25
113	Jose Valentin	.15
114	Carlos Lee	.15
115	Royce Clayton	.15
116	C.C. Sabathia	.15
117	Ellis Burks	.15
118	Omar Vizquel	.25
119	Jim Thome	.75
120	Matt Lawton	.15
121	Travis Fryman	.15
122	Earl Snyder	.15
123	Ricky Gutierrez	.15
124	Einar Diaz	.15
125	Danys Baez	.15
126	Robert Fick	.15
127	Bobby Higginson	.15
128	Steve Sparks	.15
129	Mike Rivera	.15
130	Wendell Magee	.15
131	Randall Simon	.15
132	Carlos Pena	.15
133	Mark Redman	.15
134	Juan Acevedo	.15
135	Mike Sweeney	.15
136	Aaron Guiel	.15
137	Carlos Beltran	.40
138	Joe Randa	.15
139	Paul Byrd	.15
140	Shawn Sedlacek	.15
141	Raul Ibanez	.15
142	Michael Tucker	.15
143	Torii Hunter	.40
144	Jacque Jones	.15
145	David Ortiz	.40
146	Corey Koskie	.15
147	Brad Radke	.15
148	Doug Mientkiewicz	.15
149	A.J. Pierzynski	.15
150	Dustan Mohr	.15
151	Michael Cuddyer	.15
152	Eddie Guardado	.15
153	Cristian Guzman	.15
154	Derek Jeter	2.00
155	Bernie Williams	.50
156	Roger Clemens	1.50
157	Mike Mussina	.50
158	Jorge Posada	.40
159	Alfonso Soriano	.75
160	Jason Giambi	.50
161	Robin Ventura	.25
162	Andy Pettitte	.25
163	David Wells	.15
164	Nick Johnson	.15
165	Jeff Weaver	.15
166	Raul Mondesi	.15
167	Rondell White	.15
168	Tim Hudson	.25
169	Barry Zito	.40
170	Mark Mulder	.25
171	Miguel Tejada	.40
172	Eric Chavez	.25
173	Billy Koch	.15
174	Jermaine Dye	.15
175	Scott Hatteberg	.15
176	Terrence Long	.15
177	David Justice	.25
178	Ramon Hernandez	.15
179	Ted Lilly	.15
180	Ichiro Suzuki	1.50
181	Edgar Martinez	.25
182	Mike Cameron	.15
183	John Olerud	.15
184	Bret Boone	.25
185	Dan Wilson	.15
186	Freddy Garcia	.15
187	Jamie Moyer	.15
188	Carlos Guillen	.15
189	Ruben Sierra	.15
190	Kazuhiro Sasaki	.15
191	Mark McLemore	.15
192	Chris Snelling	.15
193	Joel Pineiro	.15
194	Jeff Cirillo	.15
195	Rafael Soriano	.15
196	Ben Grieve	.15
197	Aubrey Huff	.15
198	Steve Cox	.15
199	Toby Hall	.15
200	Randy Winn	.15
201	Brent Abernathy	.15
202	Chris Gomez	.15
203	John Flaherty	.15
204	Paul Wilson	.15
205	Chan Ho Park	.15
206	Alex Rodriguez	2.00
207	Juan Gonzalez	.50
208	Rafael Palmeiro	.50
209	Ivan Rodriguez	.50
210	Rusty Greer	.15
211	Kenny Rogers	.15
212	Ismael Valdes	.15
213	Frank Catalanotto	.15
214	Hank Blalock	.50
215	Michael Young	.15
216	Kevin Mench	.15
217	Herbert Perry	.15
218	Gabe Kapler	.25
219	Carlos Delgado	.25
220	Shannon Stewart	.15
221	Eric Hinske	.15
222	Roy Halladay	.25
223	Felipe Lopez	.15
224	Vernon Wells	.15
225	Josh Phelps	.15
226	Jose Cruz	.15
227	Curt Schilling	.50
228	Randy Johnson	.75
229	Luis Gonzalez	.25
230	Mark Grace	.40
231	Junior Spivey	.15
232	Tony Womack	.15
233	Matt Williams	.25
234	Steve Finley	.15
235	Byung-Hyun Kim	.15
236	Craig Counsell	.15
237	Greg Maddux	1.00
238	Tom Glavine	.40
239	John Smoltz	.25
240	Chipper Jones	1.00
241	Gary Sheffield	.25
242	Andruw Jones	.40
243	Vinny Castilla	.15
244	Damian Moss	.15
245	Rafael Furcal	.15
246	Javy Lopez	.25
247	Kevin Millwood	.15
248	Kerry Wood	.75
249	Fred McGriff	.25
250	Sammy Sosa	1.00
251	Alex Gonzalez	.15
252	Corey Patterson	.25
253	Moises Alou	.25
254	Juan Cruz	.15
255	Jon Lieber	.15
256	Matt Clement	.15
257	Mark Prior	.75
258	Ken Griffey Jr.	1.00
259	Barry Larkin	.25
260	Adam Dunn	.50
261	Sean Casey	.15
262	Jose Rijo	.15
263	Elmer Dessens	.15
264	Austin Kearns	.25
265	Corky Miller	.15
266	Todd Walker	.15
267	Chris Reitsma	.15
268	Ryan Dempster	.15
269	Aaron Boone	.15
270	Danny Graves	.15
271	Brandon Larson	.15
272	Larry Walker	.25
273	Todd Helton	.50
274	Juan Uribe	.15
275	Juan Pierre	.15
276	Mike Hampton	.15
277	Todd Zeile	.15
278	Todd Hollandsworth	.15
279	Jason Jennings	.15
280	Josh Beckett	.40
281	Mike Lowell	.25
282	Derrek Lee	.25
283	A.J. Burnett	.15
284	Luis Castillo	.15
285	Tim Raines	.15

No.	Player	Price
286	Preston Wilson	.15
287	Juan Encarnacion	.15
288	Charles Johnson	.15
289	Jeff Bagwell	.50
290	Craig Biggio	.25
291	Lance Berkman	.40
292	Daryle Ward	.15
293	Roy Oswalt	.40
294	Richard Hidalgo	.15
295	Octavio Dotel	.15
296	Wade Miller	.15
297	Julio Lugo	.15
298	Billy Wagner	.15
299	Shawn Green	.40
300	Adrian Beltre	.25
301	Paul LoDuca	.15
302	Eric Karros	.15
303	Kevin Brown	.15
304	Hideo Nomo	.40
305	Odalis Perez	.15
306	Eric Gagne	.40
307	Brian Jordan	.15
308	Cesar Izturis	.15
309	Mark Grudzielanek	.15
310	Kazuhisa Ishii	.15
311	Geoff Jenkins	.15
312	Richie Sexson	.40
313	Jose Hernandez	.15
314	Ben Sheets	.25
315	Ruben Quevedo	.15
316	Jeffrey Hammonds	.15
317	Alex Sanchez	.15
318	Eric Young	.15
319	Takahito Nomura	.15
320	Vladimir Guerrero	.75
321	Jose Vidro	.15
322	Orlando Cabrera	.15
323	Michael Barrett	.15
324	Javier Vazquez	.15
325	Tony Armas Jr.	.15
326	Andres Galarraga	.15
327	Tomokazu Ohka	.15
328	Bartolo Colon	.15
329	Fernando Tatis	.15
330	Brad Wilkerson	.15
331	Masato Yoshii	.15
332	Mike Piazza	1.00
333	Jeromy Burnitz	.15
334	Roberto Alomar	.50
335	Mo Vaughn	.15
336	Al Leiter	.25
337	Pedro Astacio	.15
338	Edgardo Alfonzo	.15
339	Armando Benitez	.15
340	Timoniel Perez	.15
341	Jay Payton	.15
342	Roger Cedeno	.15
343	Rey Ordonez	.15
344	Steve Trachsel	.15
345	Satoru Komiyama	.15
346	Scott Rolen	.75
347	Pat Burrell	.40
348	Bobby Abreu	.25
349	Mike Lieberthal	.15
350	Brandon Duckworth	.15
351	Jimmy Rollins	.15
352	Marlon Anderson	.15
353	Travis Lee	.15
354	Vicente Padilla	.15
355	Randy Wolf	.15
356	Jason Kendall	.15
357	Brian Giles	.25
358	Aramis Ramirez	.40
359	Pokey Reese	.15
360	Kip Wells	.15
361	Josh Fogg	.15
362	Mike Williams	.15
363	Jack Wilson	.15
364	Craig Wilson	.15
365	Kevin Young	.15
366	Ryan Klesko	.15
367	Phil Nevin	.15
368	Brian Lawrence	.15
369	Mark Kotsay	.15
370	Brett Tomko	.15
371	Trevor Hoffman	.15
372	Deivi Cruz	.15
373	Bubba Trammell	.15
374	Sean Burroughs	.15
375	Barry Bonds	2.00
376	Jeff Kent	.25
377	Rich Aurilia	.15
378	Tsuyoshi Shinjo	.15
379	Benito Santiago	.15
380	Kirk Rueter	.15
381	Livan Hernandez	.15
382	Russ Ortiz	.15
383	David Bell	.15
384	Jason Schmidt	.40
385	Reggie Sanders	.15
386	J.T. Snow	.15
387	Robb Nen	.15
388	Ryan Jensen	.15
389	Jim Edmonds	.40
390	J.D. Drew	.25
391	Albert Pujols	1.50
392	Fernando Vina	.15
393	Tino Martinez	.15
394	Edgar Renteria	.40
395	Matt Morris	.15
396	Woody Williams	.15
397	Jason Isringhausen	.15
398	Placido Polanco	.15
399	Eli Marrero	.15
400	Jason Simontacchi	.15

Stat Line Career

Cards serial numbered 251-400: 3-6X
Print run 151-250: 4-8X
Print run 101-150: 5-10X
Print run 61-100: 8-15X
Print run 31-60: 10-20X
Numbered to career stat

All-Stars

NM/M
Complete Set (10): 25.00
Common Player: 1.50
Retail only

No.	Player	NM/M
1	Ichiro Suzuki	5.00
2	Alex Rodriguez	6.00
3	Nomar Garciaparra	3.00
4	Derek Jeter	6.00
5	Manny Ramirez	2.00
6	Barry Bonds	6.00
7	Adam Dunn	1.50
8	Mike Piazza	3.00
9	Sammy Sosa	4.00
10	Todd Helton	1.50

Anniversary 1983

NM/M
Complete Set (20): 50.00
Common Player: 1.50
Inserted 1:12

No.	Player	NM/M
1	Dale Murphy	2.00
2	Jim Palmer	2.00
3	Nolan Ryan	6.00
4	Ozzie Smith	4.00
5	Tom Seaver	4.00
6	Mike Schmidt	5.00
7	Steve Carlton	2.00
8	Robin Yount	3.00
9	Ryne Sandberg	4.00
10	Cal Ripken Jr.	8.00
11	Fernando Valenzuela	1.50
12	Andre Dawson	2.00
13	George Brett	6.00
14	Eddie Murray	3.00
15	Dave Winfield	2.00
16	Johnny Bench	4.00
17	Wade Boggs	2.00
18	Tony Gwynn	4.00
19	San Diego Chicken	1.50
20	Ty Cobb	5.00

Bat Kings

NM/M
Common Player: 10.00
Studio Series: 1.5-3X
Production 25 or 50

No.	Player	NM/M
1	Scott Rolen/250	20.00
2	Frank Thomas/250	15.00
3	Chipper Jones/250	20.00
4	Ivan Rodriguez/250	15.00
5	Stan Musial/100	40.00
6	Nomar Garciaparra/250	25.00
7	Vladimir Guerrero/250	15.00
8	Adam Dunn/250	15.00
9	Lance Berkman/250	10.00
10	Magglio Ordonez/250	10.00
11	Ernie Banks/50	40.00
12	Manny Ramirez/100	25.00
13	Mike Piazza/100	40.00
14	Alex Rodriguez/100	25.00
15	Todd Helton/100	20.00
16	Andre Dawson/100	20.00
17	Cal Ripken Jr/100	60.00
18	Tony Gwynn/100	25.00
19	Don Mattingly/100	60.00
20	Ryne Sandberg/100	45.00

Diamond Kings

NM/M
Complete Set (20): 120.00
Common Player: 2.00
Production 2,500 sets
Studio Series: 1.5-3X
Production 250 sets

No.	Player	NM/M
1	Vladimir Guerrero	5.00
2	Derek Jeter	15.00
3	Adam Dunn	5.00
4	Greg Maddux	8.00
5	Lance Berkman	3.00
6	Ichiro Suzuki	10.00
7	Mike Piazza	10.00
8	Alex Rodriguez	10.00
9	Tom Glavine	3.00
10	Randy Johnson	8.00
11	Nomar Garciaparra	10.00
12	Jason Giambi	5.00
13	Sammy Sosa	8.00
14	Barry Zito	3.00
15	Chipper Jones	8.00
16	Magglio Ordonez	2.00
17	Larry Walker	2.00
18	Alfonso Soriano	8.00
19	Curt Schilling	4.00
20	Barry Bonds	15.00

Jersey Kings

NM/M
Common Player: 10.00
Studio Series: 1.5-3X
Production 25 or 50

No.	Player	NM/M
1	Juan Gonzalez/250	15.00
2	Greg Maddux/250	20.00
3	Nomar Garciaparra/250	20.00
4	Troy Glaus/250	10.00
5	Reggie Jackson/100	20.00
6	Alex Rodriguez/250	25.00
7	Alfonso Soriano/250	15.00
8	Curt Schilling/250	12.00
9	Vladimir Guerrero/250	15.00
10	Adam Dunn/250	15.00
11	Mark Grace/100	25.00
12	Roger Clemens/100	30.00
13	Jeff Bagwell/100	25.00
14	Tom Glavine/100	20.00
15	Mike Piazza/100	25.00
16	Rod Carew/100	20.00
17	Rickey Henderson/100	25.00
18	Mike Schmidt/100	40.00
19	Cal Ripken Jr/100	60.00
20	Dale Murphy/100	15.00

Longball Leaders

NM/M
Complete Set (10): 30.00
Common Player: 1.50
Production 1,000 sets
Seasonal Sum: 4-6X
Numbered to 2002 HR total

No.	Player	NM/M
1	Alex Rodriguez	6.00
2	Alfonso Soriano	4.00
3	Rafael Palmeiro	2.00
4	Jim Thome	3.00
5	Jason Giambi	3.00
6	Sammy Sosa	5.00
7	Barry Bonds	8.00
8	Lance Berkman	2.00
9	Shawn Green	1.50
10	Vladimir Guerrero	4.00

Production Line

NM/M
Complete Set (30): 120.00
Common Player: 2.00
Numbered to selected stat
Die-Cuts: 1-3X
Production 100 sets

No.	Player	NM/M
1	Alex Rodriguez/1,015	6.00
2	Jim Thome/1,122	3.00
3	Lance Berkman/982	2.00
4	Barry Bonds/1,381	8.00
5	Sammy Sosa/993	5.00
6	Vladimir Guerrero/ 1,010	3.00
7	Barry Bonds/582	10.00
8	Jason Giambi/435	6.00
9	Vladimir Guerrero/417	4.00
10	Adam Dunn/400	3.00
11	Chipper Jones/435	6.00
12	Todd Helton/429	3.00
13	Rafael Palmeiro/571	2.00
14	Sammy Sosa/594	6.00
15	Alex Rodriguez/623	8.00
16	Larry Walker/602	2.00
17	Lance Berkman/578	2.00
18	Alfonso Soriano/547	5.00
19	Ichiro Suzuki/321	8.00
20	Mike Sweeney/340	2.00
21	Manny Ramirez/349	4.00
22	Larry Walker/338	2.00
23	Barry Bonds/370	12.00
24	Jim Edmonds/311	2.00
25	Alfonso Soriano/300	6.00
26	Jason Giambi/335	6.00
27	Miguel Tejada/336	4.00
28	Brian Giles/309	3.00
29	Vladimir Guerrero/364	5.00
30	Pat Burrell/319	8.00

Timber and Threads

NM/M
Common Player: 6.00

No.	Player	NM/M
1	Al Kaline/bat/125	25.00
2	Alex Rodriguez/ bat/350	20.00
3	Carlos Delgado/ bat/250	8.00
4	Cliff Floyd/bat/250	8.00
5	Eddie Mathews/ bat/125	25.00
6	Edgar Martinez/ bat/125	10.00
7	Ernie Banks/ bat/50	40.00
8	Ivan Rodriguez/ bat/125	15.00
9	J.D. Drew/bat/125	8.00
10	Jorge Posada/bat/300	10.00
11	Lou Brock/bat/125	20.00
12	Mike Piazza/bat/125	25.00
13	Mike Schmidt/ bat/125	50.00
14	Reggie Jackson/ bat/125	20.00
15	Rickey Henderson/ bat/125	25.00
16	Robin Yount/bat/125	35.00
17	Rod Carew/bat/125	25.00
18	Scott Rolen/bat/125	20.00
19	Shawn Green/bat/200	8.00
20	Willie Stargell/ bat/125	15.00
21	Alex Rodriguez/ jsy/175	20.00
22	Andruw Jones/jsy/275	8.00
23	Brooks Robinson/ jsy/150	25.00
24	Chipper Jones/jsy/150	20.00
25	Greg Maddux/jsy/175	20.00
26	Hideo Nomo/jsy/300	40.00
27	Ivan Rodriguez/ jsy/225	10.00
28	Jack Morris/jsy/150	8.00
29	J.D. Drew/jsy/150	8.00
30	Jeff Bagwell/jsy/500	15.00
31	Jim Thome/jsy/200	15.00
32	John Smoltz/jsy/175	8.00
33	John Olerud/jsy/450	8.00
34	Kerry Wood/jsy/200	15.00
35	Harmon Killebrew/ jsy/50	60.00
36	Larry Walker/jsy/500	6.00

37	Magglio Ordonez/ jsy/150	10.00
38	Manny Ramirez/ jsy/500	15.00
39	Mike Piazza/jsy/300	15.00
40	Mike Sweeney/jsy/200	8.00
41	Nomar Garciaparra/ jsy/200	25.00
42	Paul Konerko/jsy/500	10.00
43	Pedro Martinez/ jsy/175	15.00
44	Randy Johnson/ jsy/175	15.00
45	Roger Clemens/ jsy/350	20.00
46	Shawn Green/jsy/250	8.00
47	Todd Helton/jsy/175	8.00
48	Tom Glavine/jsy/225	12.00
49	Tony Gwynn/jsy/150	25.00
50	Vladimir Guerrero/ jsy/450	15.00

2003 DONRUSS CHAMPIONS

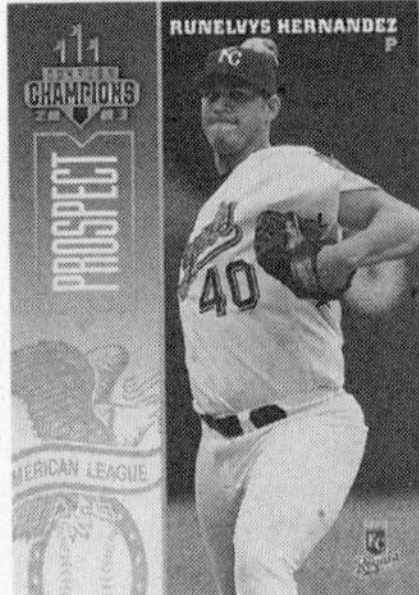

	NM/M
Complete Set (300):	40.00
Common Player:	.15
Pack (8):	2.00
Box (24):	40.00

1	Adam Kennedy	.15
2	Alfredo Amezaga	.15
3	Chone Figgins	.15
4	Darin Erstad	.25
5	David Eckstein	.15
6	Garret Anderson	.40
7	Jarrod Washburn	.15
8	Nolan Ryan	2.00
9	Tim Salmon	.25
10	Troy Glaus	.40
11	Troy Percival	.15
12	Curt Schilling	.50
13	Junior Spivey	.15
14	Luis Gonzalez	.25
15	Mark Grace	.50
16	Randy Johnson	1.00
17	Steve Finley	.15
18	Andruw Jones	.40
19	Chipper Jones	.75
20	Dale Murphy	.50
21	Gary Sheffield	.40
22	Greg Maddux	1.00
23	John Smoltz	.25
24	Andy Pratt	.15
25	Adam LaRoche	.15
26	Trey Hodges	.15
27	Warren Spahn	.75
28	Cal Ripken Jr.	3.00
29	Ed Rogers	.15
30	Brian Roberts	.15
31	Geronimo Gil	.15
32	Jay Gibbons	.15
33	Josh Towers	.15
34	Casey Fossum	.15
35	Cliff Floyd	.15
36	Derek Lowe	.15
37	Fred Lynn	.15
38	Freddy Sanchez	.15
39	Manny Ramirez	.50
40	Nomar Garciaparra	1.00
41	Pedro J. Martinez	.75
42	Rickey Henderson	.50
43	Shea Hillenbrand	.15
44	Trot Nixon	.15
45	Bobby Hill	.15
46	Corey Patterson	.25
47	Fred McGriff	.25
48	Hee Seop Choi	.15
49	Juan Cruz	.15
50	Kerry Wood	.75
51	Mark Prior	1.00
52	Moises Alou	.25
53	Nic Jackson	.15
54	Ryne Sandberg	1.00
55	Sammy Sosa	1.50
56	Carlos Lee	.15
57	Corwin Malone	.15
58	Frank Thomas	.50
59	Joe Borchard	.15
60	Joe Crede	.15
61	Magglio Ordonez	.25
62	Mark Buehrle	.15
63	Paul Konerko	.25
64	Tim Hummel	.15
65	Jon Adkins	.15
66	Adam Dunn	.50
67	Austin Kearns	.25
68	Barry Larkin	.40
69	Jose Acevedo	.15
70	Corky Miller	.15
71	Eric Davis	.15
72	Ken Griffey Jr.	1.00
73	Sean Casey	.15
74	Wily Mo Pena	.25
75	Bob Feller	.50
76	Brian Tallet	.15
77	C.C. Sabathia	.15
78	Cliff Lee	.15
79	Earl Snyder	.15
80	Ellis Burks	.15
81	Jeremy Guthrie	.15
82	Travis Hafner	.25
83	Luis Garcia	.15
84	Omar Vizquel	.25
85	Ricardo Rodriguez	.15
86	Ryan Church	.15
87	Victor Martinez	.15
88	Brandon Phillips	.15
89	Jack Cust	.15
90	Jason Jennings	.15
91	Jeff Baker	.15
92	Garrett Atkins	.15
93	Juan Uribe	.15
94	Larry Walker	.25
95	Rene Reyes	.15
96	Todd Helton	.50
97	Alan Trammell	.25
98	Fernando Rodney	.15
99	Carlos Pena	.15
100	Jack Morris	.15
101	Bobby Higginson	.15
102	Mike Maroth	.15
103	Robert Fick	.15
104	Jesus Medrano	.15
105	Josh Beckett	.40
106	Luis Castillo	.15
107	Mike Lowell	.25
108	Juan Pierre	.15
109	Josh Wilson	.15
110	Tim Redding	.15
111	Carlos Hernandez	.15
112	Craig Biggio	.25
113	Henri Stanley	.15
114	Jason Lane	.15
115	Jeff Bagwell	.50
116	John Buck	.15
117	Kirk Saarloos	.15
118	Lance Berkman	.75
119	Nolan Ryan	2.00
120	Richard Hidalgo	.15
121	Rodrigo Rosario	.15
122	Roy Oswalt	.25
123	*Tommy Whiteman*	.15
124	Wade Miller	.15
125	Alexis Gomez	.15
126	Angel Berroa	.15
127	Brandon Berger	.15
128	Carlos Beltran	.40
129	George Brett	2.00
130	Jimmy Gobble	.15
131	Dee Brown	.15
132	Mike Sweeney	.15
133	Raul Ibanez	.15
134	Runelvys Hernandez	.15
135	Adrian Beltre	.40
136	Brian Jordan	.15
137	Cesar Izturis	.15
138	Victor Alvarez	.15
139	Hideo Nomo	.50
140	Joe Thurston	.15
141	Kazuhisa Ishii	.15
142	Kevin Brown	.25
143	Odalis Perez	.15
144	Paul LoDuca	.15
145	Shawn Green	.25
146	Ben Sheets	.25
147	Bill Hall	.15
148	Nick Neugebauer	.15
149	Richie Sexson	.40
150	Robin Yount	1.00
151	Shane Nance	.15
152	Takahito Nomura	.15
153	A.J. Pierzynski	.15
154	Joe Mays	.15
155	Kirby Puckett	1.00
156	Adam Johnson	.15
157	Rob Bowen	.15
158	Torii Hunter	.40
159	Andres Galarraga	.15
160	Endy Chavez	.15
161	Javier Vazquez	.15
162	Jose Vidro	.15
163	Vladimir Guerrero	.75
164	Dwight Gooden	.15
165	Mike Piazza	1.00
166	Roberto Alomar	.40
167	Tom Glavine	.40
168	Alfonso Soriano	.75
169	Bernie Williams	.40
170	Brandon Claussen	.15
171	Derek Jeter	2.00
172	Don Mattingly	1.50
173	Drew Henson	.15
174	Jason Giambi	.50
175	Joe Torre	.25
176	Jorge Posada	.40
177	Mike Mussina	.50
178	Nick Johnson	.15
179	Roger Clemens	1.50
180	Whitey Ford	.75
181	Adam Morrissey	.15
182	Barry Zito	.40
183	David Justice	.15
184	Eric Chavez	.40
185	Jermaine Dye	.15
186	Mark Mulder	.25
187	Miguel Tejada	.40
188	Reggie Jackson	.75
189	Terrence Long	.15
190	Tim Hudson	.25
191	Anderson Machado	.15
192	Bobby Abreu	.40
193	Brandon Duckworth	.15
194	Jim Thome	.75
195	Eric Junge	.15
196	Jeremy Giambi	.15
197	Johnny Estrada	.15
198	Jorge Padilla	.15
199	Marlon Byrd	.15
200	Mike Schmidt	1.50
201	Pat Burrell	.50
202	Steve Carlton	.25
203	Aramis Ramirez	.25
204	Brian Giles	.25
205	Carlos Rivera	.15
206	Craig Wilson	.15
207	Dave Williams	.15
208	Jack Wilson	.15
209	Jose Castillo	.15
210	Kip Wells	.15
211	Roberto Clemente	1.50
212	Walter Young	.15
213	Ben Howard	.15
214	Brian Lawrence	.15
215	Clifford Bartosh	.15
216	Dennis Tankersley	.15
217	Oliver Perez	.15
218	Phil Nevin	.15
219	Ryan Klesko	.25
220	Sean Burroughs	.15
221	Tony Gwynn	.75
222	Xavier Nady	.15
223	Mike Rivera	.15
224	Barry Bonds	2.00
225	Benito Santiago	.15
226	Jason Schmidt	.40
227	Jeff Kent	.25
228	Kenny Lofton	.15
229	Rich Aurilia	.15
230	Robb Nen	.15
231	Tsuyoshi Shinjo	.15
232	Bret Boone	.15
233	Chris Snelling	.15
234	Edgar Martinez	.25
235	Freddy Garcia	.15
236	Ichiro Suzuki	1.50
237	John Olerud	.25
238	Kazuhiro Sasaki	.15
239	Mike Cameron	.15
240	Rafael Soriano	.15
241	Albert Pujols	1.50
242	J.D. Drew	.40
243	Jim Edmonds	.40
244	Ozzie Smith	1.00
245	Scott Rolen	.75
246	So Taguchi	.15
247	Stan Musial	1.00
248	Antonio Perez	.15
249	Aubrey Huff	.15
250	Dewon Brazelton	.15
251	Delvin James	.15
252	Joe Kennedy	.15
253	Toby Hall	.15
254	Alex Rodriguez	2.00
255	Ben Kozlowski	.15
256	Gerald Laird	.15
257	Hank Blalock	.50
258	Ivan Rodriguez	.50
259	Juan Gonzalez	.50
260	Kevin Mench	.15
261	Mario Ramos	.15
262	Mark Teixeira	.25
263	Nolan Ryan	2.00
264	Rafael Palmeiro	.50
265	Alexis Rios	.15
266	Carlos Delgado	.40
267	Eric Hinske	.15
268	Josh Phelps	.15
269	Kevin Cash	.15
270	Orlando Hudson	.15
271	Roy Halladay	.15
272	Shannon Stewart	.15
273	Vernon Wells	.15
274	Vinnie Chulk	.15
275	Jason Anderson	.15
276	*Craig Brazell*	.50
277	*Termel Sledge*	.50
278	*Ryan Cameron*	.50
279	*Clint Barmes*	.50
280	Jhonny Peralta	.50
281	*Todd Wellemeyer*	.50
282	*Jon Leicester*	.40
283	*Brandon Webb*	1.00
284	*Tim Olson*	.50
285	*Matt Kata*	.75
286	*Rob Hammock*	.50
287	*Pete LaForest*	.50
288	*Nook Logan*	.50
289	*Prentice Redman*	.40
290	*Joe Valentine*	.40
291	*Jose Contreras*	1.00
292	*Josh Stewart*	.40
293	*Mike Nicolas*	.40
294	Marshall McDougall	.15
295	Travis Chapman	.15
296	Jose Morban	.15
297	*Michael Hessman*	.40
298	*Buddy Hernandez*	.40
299	*Shane Victorino*	.40
300	Jason Dubois	.15
301	*Hideki Matsui*	3.00

Metalized

Stars:	4-8X
RC's:	1-3X
Production 100 sets	
Holofoils:	No Pricing
Production 25 sets	

Autographs

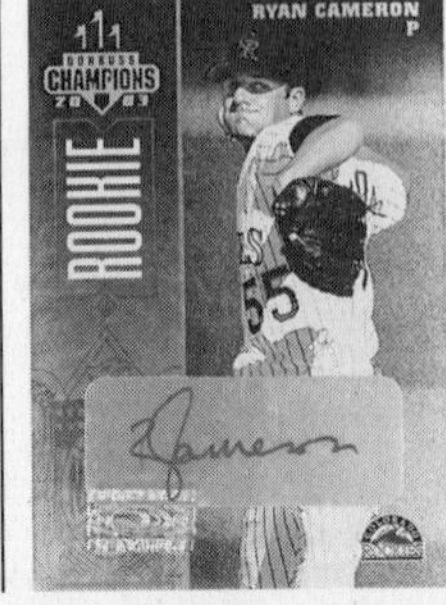

NM/M
Common Autograph: 5.00
2 Alfredo Amezaga/325 8.00
3 Chone Figgins/375 10.00
13 Junior Spivey/45 10.00
24 Andy Pratt/475 8.00
25 Adam LaRoche/400 10.00
26 Trey Hodges/305 5.00
29 Ed Rogers/305 5.00
30 Brian Roberts/500 35.00
31 Geronimo Gil/150 8.00
32 Jay Gibbons/475 8.00
33 Josh Towers/500 10.00
34 Casey Fossum/160 5.00
35 Cliff Floyd/70 20.00
37 Fred Lynn/80 25.00
38 Freddy Sanchez/400 8.00
46 Corey Patterson/100 25.00
49 Juan Cruz/250 8.00
51 Mark Prior/50 60.00
53 Nic Jackson/100 10.00
57 Corwin Malone/400 8.00
59 Joe Borchard/215 8.00
64 Tim Hummel/400 5.00
65 Jon Adkins/400 5.00
66 Adam Dunn/100 35.00
67 Austin Kearns/50 20.00
69 Jose Acevedo/315 5.00
70 Corky Miller/295 5.00
71 Eric Davis/45 25.00
74 Wily Mo Pena/450 15.00
76 Brian Tallet/250 8.00
78 Cliff Lee/330 10.00
79 Earl Snyder/225 8.00
81 Jeremy Guthrie/400 8.00
83 Luis Garcia/395 5.00
86 Ryan Church/395 10.00
87 Victor Martinez/250 25.00
88 Brandon Phillips/375 10.00
89 Jack Cust/498 8.00
90 Jason Jennings/375 8.00
91 Jeff Baker/400 8.00
92 Garrett Atkins/400 8.00
95 Rene Reyes/350 8.00
98 Fernando Rodney/500 8.00
100 Jack Morris/50 25.00
102 Mike Maroth/400 8.00
104 Jesus Medrano/500 8.00
109 Josh Wilson/400 8.00
110 Tim Redding/375 8.00
111 Carlos Hernandez/250 8.00
113 Henri Stanley/390 5.00
114 Jason Lane/250 10.00
117 Kirk Saarloos/149 8.00
120 Richard Hidalgo/120 10.00
121 Rodrigo Rosario/500 10.00
122 Roy Oswalt/100 20.00
124 Wade Miller/125 10.00
126 Angel Berroa/400 10.00
127 Brandon Berger/325 8.00
130 Jimmy Gobble/400 8.00
131 Dee Brown/500 8.00
132 Mike Sweeney/45 20.00
134 Runelvys Hernandez/400 5.00
138 Victor Alvarez/308 8.00
144 Paul LoDuca/45 20.00
146 Ben Sheets/50 20.00
147 Bill Hall/450 8.00
148 Nick Neugebauer/375 8.00
151 Shane Nance/150 8.00
152 Takahito Nomura/50 20.00
153 A.J. Pierzynski/250 10.00
156 Adam Johnson/500 8.00
157 Rob Bowen/375 8.00
158 Torii Hunter/45 20.00
160 Endy Chavez/280 10.00
161 Javier Vazquez/50 20.00
162 Jose Vidro/45 15.00
164 Dwight Gooden/45 30.00
170 Brandon Claussen/475 10.00
178 Nick Johnson/500 8.00
181 Adam Morrissey/395 8.00
185 Jermaine Dye/125 15.00
189 Terrence Long/250 10.00
191 Anderson Machado/500 8.00
193 Brandon Duckworth/100 10.00
195 Eric Junge/279 8.00
196 Jeremy Giambi/195 8.00
205 Carlos Rivera/400 8.00
206 Craig Wilson/245 15.00
207 Dave Williams/265 8.00
208 Jack Wilson/500 15.00
212 Walter Young/400 8.00
213 Ben Howard/500 8.00
214 Brian Lawrence/500 8.00
215 Clifford Bartosh/400 8.00
222 Xavier Nady/250 8.00
223 Mike Rivera/90 8.00
233 Chris Snelling/200 8.00
240 Rafael Soriano/500 8.00
248 Antonio Perez/500 8.00
249 Aubrey Huff/475 15.00
250 Dewon Brazelton/50 15.00
251 Delvin James/400 8.00
252 Joe Kennedy/250 8.00
253 Toby Hall/500 8.00
255 Ben Kozlowski/400 8.00
256 Gerald Laird/450 8.00
257 Hank Blalock/50 40.00
260 Kevin Mench/475 10.00
261 Mario Ramos/475 5.00
262 Mark Teixeira/40 40.00
265 Alexis Rios/400 15.00
267 Eric Hinske/390 10.00
269 Kevin Cash/375 8.00
274 Vinnie Chulk/100 10.00
275 Jason Anderson/493 20.00
276 Craig Brazell/500 15.00
277 Terrmel Sledge/500 10.00
278 Ryan Cameron/475 8.00
279 Clint Barmes/475 50.00
280 Jhonny Peralta/500 15.00
281 Todd Wellemeyer/477 10.00
282 Jon Leicester/480 8.00
283 Brandon Webb/500 15.00
284 Tim Olson/500 10.00
285 Matt Kata/487 10.00
286 Rob Hammock/486 10.00
287 Pete LaForest/500 10.00
288 Nook Logan/500 10.00
289 Prentice Redman/488 10.00
290 Joe Valentine/475 8.00
291 Jose Contreras/100 25.00
292 Josh Stewart/485 10.00
293 Mike Nicolas/500 10.00
295 Travis Chapman/100 15.00
296 Jose Morban/475 8.00
297 Michael Hessman/500 8.00
298 Buddy Hernandez/500 8.00
299 Shane Victorino/480 8.00
300 Jason Dubois/480 10.00
302 Ryan Wagner/100 15.00
303 Adam Loewen/100 10.00
304 Chien-Ming Wang/100 50.00
305 Hong-Chih Kuo/100 20.00
307 Dan Haren/100 20.00
309 Ramon Nivar/100 15.00

Call to the Hall

NM/M
Complete Set (10): 30.00
Common Player: 2.00
Metalized: 2-4X
Production 100 sets
Holofoils: No Pricing
Production 25 sets
1 Nolan Ryan/2,490 10.00
2 Tom Seaver/2,490 4.00
3 Phil Rizzuto/2,500 4.00
4 Orlando Cepeda/2,500 2.00
5 Al Kaline/2,500 5.00
6 Hoyt Wilhelm/2,500 2.00
7 Luis Aparicio/2,500 2.00
8 Billy Williams/2,500 2.00
9 Jim Palmer/2,500 2.00
10 Mike Schmidt/2,500 6.00

Call to the Hall Autographs

No Pricing

Grand Champions

NM/M
Complete Set (25): 80.00
Common Player: 2.00

Inserted 1:18
Metalized: 2-4X
Production 100 sets
Holo Foils: No Pricing
Production 25 sets
1 Stan Musial 6.00
2 Bob Feller 2.00
3 Reggie Jackson 3.00
4 George Brett 8.00
5 Jim Palmer 2.00
6 Harmon Killebrew 4.00
7 Ernie Banks 4.00
8 Frank Robinson 2.00
9 Greg Maddux 4.00
10 Whitey Ford 4.00
11 Bob Gibson 4.00
12 Mike Schmidt 6.00
13 Nolan Ryan 10.00
14 Warren Spahn 4.00
15 Rod Carew 3.00
16 Hoyt Wilhelm 2.00
17 Duke Snider 4.00
18 Tom Seaver 4.00
19 Steve Carlton 3.00
20 Yogi Berra 4.00
21 Cal Ripken Jr. 10.00
22 Tony Gwynn 4.00
23 Wade Boggs 2.00
24 Rickey Henderson 3.00
25 Roger Clemens 8.00

Grand Champions Autographs

No Pricing

Numbers Game

NM/M
Quantity Produced listed
1 Vladimir Guerrero/jsy/200 10.00
2 Nomar Garciaparra/jsy/200 20.00
3 Magglio Ordonez/jsy/100 8.00
4 Garret Anderson/jsy/50 15.00
5 Derek Jeter/base/200 20.00
6 Jim Thome/jsy/200 8.00
7 Torii Hunter/jsy/200 10.00
8 Todd Helton/jsy/200 10.00
9 Andruw Jones/jsy/200 6.00
10 Alfonso Soriano/jsy/25
11 Luis Gonzalez/jsy/200 5.00
12 Manny Ramirez/jsy/200 12.00
13 Paul Konerko/jsy/200 6.00
14 Alex Rodriguez/jsy/200 20.00
15 Carlos Beltran/jsy/200 4.00
16 Bernie Williams/jsy/200 8.00
17 Barry Bonds/base/200 20.00
18 Miguel Tejada/jsy/50 15.00
19 Jason Giambi/base/200 8.00
20 Ichiro Suzuki/base/200 25.00
21 Ivan Rodriguez/jsy/100 15.00
22 Rafael Palmeiro/jsy/200 10.00
23 Carlos Delgado/jsy/200 5.00
24 Vernon Wells/jsy/200 4.00
25 Sammy Sosa/jsy/200 20.00
26 Chipper Jones/jsy/200 12.00
27 Adam Dunn/jsy/44 25.00
28 Larry Walker/jsy/200 8.00
29 Shawn Green/jsy/100 10.00
30 Richie Sexson/jsy/200 6.00
31 Jose Vidro/jsy/200 4.00
32 Mike Piazza/jsy/50 40.00
33 Roberto Alomar/jsy/100 15.00
34 Bobby Abreu/jsy/200 5.00
35 Pat Burrell/jsy/200 8.00
36 Brian Giles/jsy/200 6.00
37 Albert Pujols/base/200 15.00
38 Lance Berkman/jsy/50 15.00
39 Ryan Klesko/jsy/200 6.00
40 Jeff Kent/jsy/200 4.00

Statistical Champs

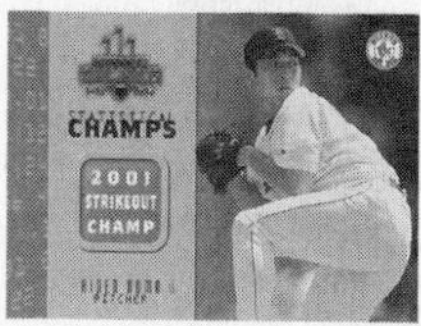

NM/M
Complete Set (30): 40.00
Common Player: 1.00
Inserted 1:10
1 Alex Rodriguez 5.00
2 Alfonso Soriano 2.00
3 Curt Schilling 1.50
4 Eddie Mathews 2.00
5 Fred Lynn 1.00
6 Harmon Killebrew 2.00
7 Hideo Nomo 1.00
8 Jim Thome 1.50
9 Kirby Puckett 3.00
10 Luis Gonzalez 1.00
11 Manny Ramirez 1.50
12 Jason Giambi 1.00
13 Mike Schmidt 4.00
14 Nomar Garciaparra 4.00
15 Lou Brock 1.50
16 Randy Johnson 2.00
17 Reggie Jackson 2.00
18 Rickey Henderson 1.50
19 Roberto Clemente 5.00
20 Barry Zito 1.50
21 Todd Helton 1.50
22 Tom Seaver 3.00
23 Tony Gwynn 2.00
24 Torii Hunter 1.00
25 Troy Glaus 1.00
26 Wade Boggs 1.50
27 Rod Carew 1.50
28 Juan Gonzalez 1.50
29 Sammy Sosa 3.00
30 Warren Spahn 2.00

Statistical Champs Materials

NM/M
Quantity Produced listed
1 Alex Rodriguez/jsy/250 20.00
2 Alfonso Soriano/jsy/25
3 Curt Schilling/jsy/225 8.00
4 Eddie Mathews/jsy/200 20.00
5 Fred Lynn/jsy/50
6 Harmon Killebrew/jsy/250 20.00
7 Hideo Nomo/jsy/110 50.00
8 Jim Thome/jsy/250 8.00
9 Kirby Puckett/jsy/250 20.00
10 Luis Gonzalez/jsy/250 5.00
11 Manny Ramirez/jsy/155 10.00
12 Jason Giambi/jsy/250 10.00
13 Mike Schmidt/jsy/250 35.00
14 Nomar Garciaparra/jsy/99 30.00
15 Lou Brock/jsy/250 15.00
16 Randy Johnson/jsy/100 15.00
17 Reggie Jackson/jsy/200 15.00
18 Rickey Henderson/jsy/184 15.00
19 Roberto Clemente/jsy/64
20 Barry Zito/jsy/100 10.00
21 Todd Helton/jsy/250 10.00
22 Tom Seaver/jsy/100 30.00
23 Tony Gwynn/jsy/200 15.00
24 Torii Hunter/jsy/250 10.00
25 Troy Glaus/jsy/125 10.00
26 Wade Boggs/jsy/250 15.00
27 Rod Carew/hat/150 15.00
28 Juan Gonzalez/jsy/250 8.00
29 Sammy Sosa/jsy/250 20.00
30 Warren Spahn/jsy/150 30.00

Team Colors

NM/M
Complete Set (30): 60.00
Common Player: 1.00
Inserted 1:10
1 Miguel Tejada 1.50
2 Mike Schmidt 5.00
3 George Brett 6.00

4	Magglio Ordonez	1.00
5	Ryne Sandberg	4.00
6	Adam Dunn	1.50
7	Mark Prior	3.00
8	Tony Gwynn	2.00
9	Troy Glaus	1.50
10	Stan Musial	4.00
11	Kirby Puckett	3.00
12	Don Mattingly	5.00
13	Bobby Abreu	1.00
14	Ichiro Suzuki	4.00
15	Cal Ripken Jr.	8.00
16	Chipper Jones	3.00
17	Carlos Beltran	1.50
18	Alfonso Soriano	2.00
19	Albert Pujols	5.00
20	Andruw Jones	1.50
21	Bernie Williams	1.50
22	Todd Helton	1.50
23	Roberto Clemente	6.00
24	Jim Thome	1.50
25	Carlos Delgado	1.00
26	Derek Jeter	6.00
27	Garret Anderson	1.00
28	Nomar Garciaparra	4.00
29	Torii Hunter	1.00
30	Vladimir Guerrero	2.00

Team Colors Materials

NM/M

Quantity Produced listed

1	Miguel Tejada/jsy/50	15.00
2	Mike Schmidt/jsy/200	35.00
3	George Brett/jsy/200	35.00
4	Magglio Ordonez/ jsy/100	8.00
5	Ryne Sandberg/ jsy/200	30.00
6	Adam Dunn/jsy/44	20.00
7	Mark Prior/jsy/200	15.00
8	Tony Gwynn/jsy/200	15.00
9	Troy Glaus/jsy/200	8.00
10	Stan Musial/jsy/200	35.00
11	Kirby Puckett/jsy/200	15.00
12	Don Mattingly/jsy/200	40.00
13	Bobby Abreu/jsy/200	5.00
14	Ichiro Suzuki/ base/200	25.00
15	Cal Ripken Jr./jsy/200	40.00
16	Chipper Jones/jsy/200	12.00
17	Carlos Beltran/jsy/200	8.00
18	Alfonso Soriano/jsy/25	
19	Albert Pujols/base/200	15.00
20	Andruw Jones/jsy/200	6.00
21	Bernie Williams/jsy/200	8.00
22	Todd Helton/jsy/200	10.00
23	Roberto Clemente/ jsy/200	80.00
24	Jim Thome/jsy/200	8.00
25	Carlos Delgado/jsy/200	5.00
26	Derek Jeter/base/200	20.00
27	Garret Anderson/ jsy/50	12.00
28	Nomar Garciaparra/ jsy/200	20.00
29	Torii Hunter/jsy/200	10.00
30	Vladimir Guerrero/ jsy/200	10.00

Total Game

NM/M

Complete Set (40):		60.00
Common Player:		1.00
Inserted 1:9		
1	Vladimir Guerrero	2.00
2	Nomar Garciaparra	4.00
3	Magglio Ordonez	1.00
4	Garret Anderson	1.00
5	Derek Jeter	6.00
6	Jim Thome	1.50
7	Torii Hunter	1.50
8	Todd Helton	1.50
9	Andruw Jones	1.50
10	Alfonso Soriano	2.00
11	Luis Gonzalez	1.00
12	Manny Ramirez	1.50
13	Paul Konerko	1.00
14	Alex Rodriguez	5.00
15	Carlos Beltran	1.00
16	Bernie Williams	1.50
17	Barry Bonds	6.00
18	Miguel Tejada	1.00
19	Jason Giambi	1.00
20	Ichiro Suzuki	4.00
21	Ivan Rodriguez	1.50
22	Rafael Palmeiro	1.50
23	Carlos Delgado	1.00
24	Vernon Wells	1.00
25	Sammy Sosa	4.00
26	Chipper Jones	2.00
27	Adam Dunn	1.50
28	Larry Walker	1.00
29	Shawn Green	1.00
30	Richie Sexson	1.00
31	Jose Vidro	1.00
32	Mike Piazza	3.00
33	Roberto Alomar	1.50
34	Bobby Abreu	1.00
35	Pat Burrell	1.00
36	Brian Giles	1.00
37	Albert Pujols	5.00
38	Lance Berkman	1.00
39	Ryan Klesko	1.00
40	Jeff Kent	1.00

World Series Champions

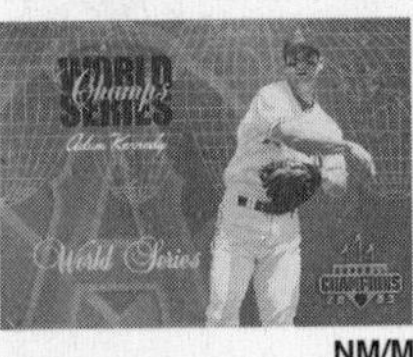

NM/M

Complete Set (15):		20.00
Common Player:		1.50
Production 2,002 sets		
Metalized:		2-3X
Production 100 sets		
Holo Foil:		No Pricing
Production 25 sets		
1	Troy Glaus	3.00
2	Jarrod Washburn	1.50
3	Darin Erstad	2.50
4	Troy Percival	1.50
5	David Eckstein	1.50
6	Francisco Rodriguez	2.00
7	Garret Anderson	2.50
8	John Lackey	1.50
9	Tim Salmon	2.00
10	Chone Figgins	1.50
11	Adam Kennedy	1.50
12	Scott Spiezio	1.50
13	Ben Molina	1.50
14	Brad Fullmer	1.50
15	Troy Glaus MVP	3.00

World Series Champions Autograph

No Pricing

1	Troy Glaus/20	
10	Chone Figgins/25	
15	Troy Glaus MVP/20	

2003 DONRUSS CLASSICS

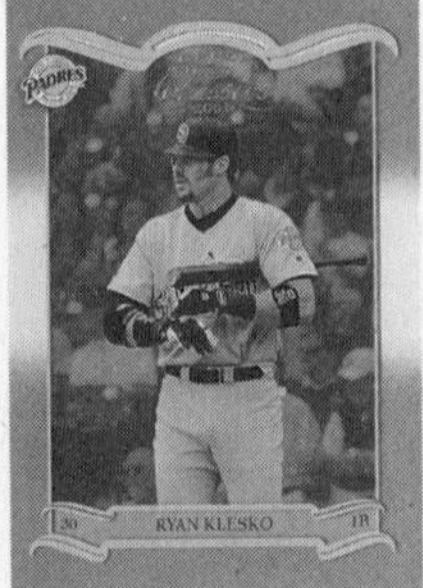

NM/M

Common Player:		.40
Common Legends (101-150):		3.00
Production 1,500		
Common Prospect (151-200):		3.00
Production 1,500		
Pack (7):		4.50
Box (18):		70.00
1	Troy Glaus	.50
2	Barry Bonds	3.00
3	Miguel Tejada	.50
4	Randy Johnson	1.00
5	Eric Hinske	.40
6	Barry Zito	.50
7	Jason Jennings	.40
8	Derek Jeter	3.00
9	Vladimir Guerrero	1.00
10	Corey Patterson	.50
11	Manny Ramirez	.75
12	Edgar Martinez	.50
13	Roy Oswalt	.50
14	Andruw Jones	.75
15	Alex Rodriguez	3.00
16	Mark Mulder	.50
17	Kazuhisa Ishii	.40
18	Gary Sheffield	.50
19	Jay Gibbons	.40
20	Roberto Alomar	.50
21	A.J. Pierzynski	.40
22	Eric Chavez	.50
23	Roger Clemens	2.00
24	C.C. Sabathia	.40
25	Jose Vidro	.40
26	Shannon Stewart	.40
27	Mark Teixeira	.50
28	Joe Thurston	.40
29	Josh Beckett	.75
30	Jeff Bagwell	.75
31	Geronimo Gil	.40
32	Curt Schilling	.75
33	Frank Thomas	.75
34	Lance Berkman	.50
35	Adam Dunn	.75
36	Christian Parker	.40
37	Jim Thome	1.00
38	Shawn Green	.50
39	Drew Henson	.40
40	Chipper Jones	1.00
41	Kevin Mench	.40
42	Hideo Nomo	.50
43	Andres Galarraga	.40
44	Doug Davis	.40
45	Mark Prior	1.00
46	Sean Casey	.40
47	Magglio Ordonez	.50
48	Tom Glavine	.50
49	Marlon Byrd	.40
50	Albert Pujols	2.00
51	Mark Buehrle	.40
52	Aramis Ramirez	.50
53	Pat Burrell	.50
54	Craig Biggio	.50
55	Alfonso Soriano	1.00
56	Kerry Wood	1.00
57	Wade Miller	.40
58	Hank Blalock	.75
59	Cliff Floyd	.40
60	Jason Giambi	.50
61	Carlos Beltran	.50
62	Brian Roberts	.40
63	Paul LoDuca	.40
64	Tim Redding	.40
65	Sammy Sosa	2.00
66	Joe Borchard	.40
67	Ryan Klesko	.40
68	Richie Sexson	.50
69	Carlos Lee	.40
70	Rickey Henderson	.75
71	Brian Tallet	.40
72	Luis Gonzalez	.50
73	Satoru Komiyama	.40
74	Tim Hudson	.50
75	Ken Griffey Jr.	1.50
76	Adam Johnson	.40
77	Bobby Abreu	.60
78	Adrian Beltre	.40
79	Rafael Palmeiro	.75
80	Ichiro Suzuki	2.00
81	Kenny Lofton	.40
82	Brian Giles	.50
83	Barry Larkin	.50
84	Robert Fick	.40
85	Ben Sheets	.50
86	Scott Rolen	1.00
87	Nomar Garciaparra	1.50
88	Brandon Phillips	.40
89	Ben Kozlowski	.40
90	Bernie Williams	.75
91	Pedro J. Martinez	1.00
92	Todd Helton	.75
93	Jermaine Dye	.40
94	Carlos Delgado	.50
95	Mike Piazza	1.50
96	Junior Spivey	.40
97	Torii Hunter	.50
98	Mike Sweeney	.40
99	Ivan Rodriguez	.75
100	Greg Maddux	1.50
101	Ernie Banks	5.00
102	Steve Garvey	3.00
103	George Brett	8.00
104	Lou Brock	3.00
105	Hoyt Wilhelm	3.00
106	Steve Carlton	4.00
107	Joe Torre	3.00
108	Dennis Eckersley	4.00
109	Reggie Jackson	5.00
110	Al Kaline	8.00
111	Harold Reynolds	3.00
112	Don Mattingly	8.00
113	Tony Gwynn	5.00
114	Willie McCovey	4.00
115	Joe Morgan	3.00
116	Stan Musial	8.00
117	Jim Palmer	3.00
118	Brooks Robinson	5.00
119	Don Sutton	3.00
120	Nolan Ryan	10.00
121	Mike Schmidt	6.00
122	Tom Seaver	5.00
123	Cal Ripken Jr.	8.00
124	Robin Yount	5.00
125	Bob Feller	3.00
126	Joe Carter	3.00
127	Jack Morris	3.00
128	Luis Aparicio	3.00
129	Bobby Doerr	3.00
130	Dave Parker	3.00
131	Yogi Berra	5.00
132	Will Clark	3.00
133	Fred Lynn	3.00
134	Andre Dawson	3.00
135	Duke Snider	4.00
136	Orlando Cepeda	3.00
137	Billy Williams	3.00
138	Dale Murphy	4.00
139	Harmon Killebrew	5.00
140	Kirby Puckett	6.00
141	Carlton Fisk	3.00
142	Eric Davis	3.00
143	Alan Trammell	3.00
144	Paul Molitor	5.00
145	Jose Canseco	3.00
146	Ozzie Smith	5.00
147	Ralph Kiner	3.00
148	Dwight Gooden	3.00
149	Phil Rizzuto	5.00
150	Lenny Dykstra	3.00
151	Adam LaRoche	4.00
152	Tim Hummel	3.00
153	*Matt Kata*	4.00
154	Jeff Baker	3.00
155	*Josh Stewart*	3.00
156	Marshall McDougall	4.00
157	Jhonny Peralta	4.00
158	*Mike Nicolas*	3.00
159	Jeremy Guthrie	3.00
160	*Craig Brazell*	4.00
161	*Joe Valentine*	4.00
162	Buddy Hernandez	3.00
163	Freddy Sanchez	4.00
164	*Shane Victorino*	4.00
165	Corwin Malone	4.00
166	Jason Dubois	3.00
167	Josh Wilson	3.00
168	*Tim Olson*	3.00
169	Clifford Bartosh	3.00
170	*Michael Hessman*	4.00
171	Ryan Church	5.00
172	Garrett Atkins	4.00
173	Jose Morban	3.00
174	*Ryan Cameron*	4.00
175	*Todd Wellemeyer*	4.00
176	Travis Chapman	3.00
177	Jason Anderson	4.00
178	Adam Morrissey	3.00
179	*Jose Contreras*	5.00
180	Nic Jackson	3.00
181	*Rob Hammock*	4.00
182	Carlos Rivera	3.00
183	Vinnie Chulk	3.00
184	*Pete LaForest*	3.00
185	*Jon Leicester*	4.00
186	*Terrmel Sledge*	3.00
187	Jose Castillo	3.00
188	Gerald Laird	3.00
189	*Nook Logan*	4.00
190	*Clint Barmes*	5.00
191	Jesus Medrano	3.00
192	Henri Stanley	4.00
193	*Hideki Matsui*	10.00
194	Walter Young	3.00
195	Jon Adkins	3.00
196	*Tommy Whiteman*	4.00

197 Rob Bowen 3.00
198 *Brandon Webb* 5.00
199 *Prentice Redman* 4.00
200 Jimmy Gobble 3.00

Combos

NM/M

Varying quantities produced
CC1 Babe Ruth, Lou Gehrig/50 475.00
CC2 Jackie Robinson, Pee Wee Reese/50 80.00
CC3 Bobby Doerr, Fred Lynn/25 65.00
CC4 Honus Wagner, Roberto Clemente/50 150.00
CC5 Kirby Puckett, Torii Hunter/25 75.00
CC6 Sammy Sosa, Ryne Sandberg/25 100.00
CC7 Hideo Nomo, Kazuhisa Ishii/25 75.00
CC8 Mike Schmidt, Steve Carlton/25 150.00
CC9 Robin Yount, Paul Molitor/25 100.00
CC10 Mike Piazza, Duke Snider/25
CC11 Al Kaline, Ty Cobb/25
CC12 Don Mattingly, Jason Giambi/25 150.00
CC13 Stan Musial, Ozzie Smith/25 100.00
CC14 Roger Clemens, Pedro Martinez/25
CC15 Thurman Munson, Yogi Berra/25

Dress Code

NM/M

Common Player: 4.00
Quantity produced listed
1 Roger Clemens/jsy/500 15.00
2 M. Tejada/jsy/hat/bat/250 20.00
3 V. Guerrero/jsy/425 8.00
4 Kazuhisa Ishii/jsy/250 10.00
5 Chipper Jones/jsy/425 10.00
6 Troy Glaus/jsy/425 8.00
7 Rafael Palmeiro/jsy/425 8.00
8 Rickey Henderson/jsy/250 10.00
9 Pedro Martinez/jsy/425 8.00
10 Andruw Jones/jsy/425 6.00
11 Nomar Garciaparra/jsy/500 12.00
12 Carlos Delgado/jsy/500 5.00
13 R.Henderson/jsy/hat/250 20.00
14 K. Wood/jsy/hat/250 20.00
15 L. Berkman/jsy/hat/50 20.00
16 Tony Gwynn/quad/100 65.00
17 Mark Mulder/jsy/425 8.00
18 Jim Thome/jsy/500 8.00
19 Mike Piazza/jsy/500 15.00
20 Mike Mussina/jsy/500 10.00
21 Luis Gonzalez/jsy/500 5.00
22 Ryan Klesko/jsy/500 5.00
23 Richie Sexson/jsy/500 6.00
24 Curt Schilling/jsy/200 10.00
25 A. Rodriguez/jsy/500 12.00
26 B. Williams/jsy/425 8.00
27 Cal Ripken Jr/jsy/500 35.00
28 C.C. Sabathia/jsy/500 4.00
29 M. Piazza/bat/jsy/200 30.00
30 Rickey Henderson/hat/jsy/250 15.00
31 Torii Hunter/jsy/425 8.00
32 Mark Teixeira/jsy/425 8.00
33 D. Murphy/jsy/bat/300 15.00
34 Todd Helton/jsy/425 8.00
35 Eric Chavez/jsy/425 8.00
36 Vernon Wells/jsy/425 5.00
37 J. Bagwell/jsy/hat/100 25.00
38 Nick Johnson/jsy/425 5.00
39 Tim Hudson/jsy/hat/250 10.00
40 Shawn Green/jsy/425 5.00
41 Mark Buehrle/jsy/500 5.00
42 Garret Anderson/jsy/100 5.00
43 Alex Rodriguez/jsy/500 12.00
44 Jason Giambi/jsy/500 8.00
45 Carlos Beltran/jsy/500 5.00
46 Adam Dunn/jsy/hat/100 30.00
47 Jorge Posada/jsy/425 8.00
48 Roy Oswalt/jsy/hat/200 15.00
49 Rich Aurilia/jsy/500 5.00
50 Jason Jennings/quad/250 15.00
51 Mark Prior/quad/250 50.00
52 Jim Edmonds/jsy/500 8.00
53 Fred McGriff/jsy/500 8.00
54 A. Soriano/jsy/shoe/100 15.00
55 Jeff Kent/jsy/425 5.00
56 Hideo Nomo/jsy/200 30.00
57 Manny Ramirez/jsy/425 8.00
58 J. Canseco/jsy/bat/350 15.00
59 M. Ordonez/jsy/500 6.00
60 A. Trammell/jsy/bat/250 10.00
61 Bobby Abreu/jsy/500 6.00
62 R.Henderson/dual jsy/200 20.00
63 Josh Beckett/jsy/500 6.00
64 Barry Larkin/jsy/500 8.00
65 Randy Johnson/jsy/200 10.00
66 Juan Gonzalez/jsy/500 8.00
67 Barry Zito/jsy/hat/125 15.00
68 Roger Clemens/jsy/500 15.00
69 Rickey Henderson/hat/jsy/100 25.00
70 Hideo Nomo/jsy/100 50.00
71 Paul Konerko/jsy/400 6.00
72 Pat Burrell/jsy/400 8.00
73 F.Thomas/jsy/pants/250 15.00
74 Sammy Sosa/jsy/500 15.00
75 G. Maddux/glove/jsy/50 60.00

Legendary Hats

NM/M

Varying quantities produced
1 Roberto Clemente/80 100.00
2 Kirby Puckett/50 50.00
3 Mike Schmidt/50 75.00
4 Tony Gwynn/50 50.00
5 Rickey Henderson/50 60.00

Legendary Spikes

NM/M

Production 50 sets
1 Kirby Puckett 60.00
2 Tony Gwynn 50.00
3 Don Mattingly 125.00
4 Frank Robinson 35.00
5 Gary Carter 30.00

Legendary Leather

NM/M

Varying quantities produced
1 Nolan Ryan/80 110.00

Legendary Lumberjacks

NM/M

Common Player: 10.00
Varying quantities produced
1 Babe Ruth/100 180.00
2 Lou Gehrig/80 125.00
3 George Brett/250 25.00
4 Duke Snider/250 20.00
5 Roberto Clemente/25 165.00
6 Ryne Sandberg/400 35.00
7 Robin Yount/300 25.00
8 Harmon Killebrew/250 25.00
9 Al Kaline/250 25.00
10 Eddie Mathews/225 20.00
11 Brooks Robinson/400 15.00
12 Stan Musial/11
13 Kirby Puckett/375 20.00
14 Jose Canseco/400 15.00
15 Nellie Fox/325 20.00
16 Don Mattingly/400 35.00
17 Joe Torre/250 10.00
18 Cal Ripken Jr/250 40.00
19 Richie Ashburn/250 20.00
20 Mike Schmidt/250 30.00
21 Dale Murphy/250 25.00
22 Thurman Munson/400 15.00
23 Tony Gwynn/400 10.00
24 Orlando Cepeda/225 10.00
25 Ty Cobb/25 225.00
26 Paul Molitor/325 10.00
27 Ralph Kiner/200 10.00
28 Frank Robinson/225 20.00
29 Yogi Berra/50 50.00
30 Reggie Jackson/375 15.00
31 Rod Carew/325 15.00
32 Carlton Fisk/325 15.00
33 Rogers Hornsby/50 60.00
34 Mel Ott/125 30.00
35 Jimmie Foxx/50 60.00

Legends of the Fall

NM/M

Complete Set (10): 40.00
Common Player: 3.00
Production 2,500 sets
1 Reggie Jackson 4.00
2 Duke Snider 4.00
3 Roberto Clemente 8.00
4 Mel Ott 5.00
5 Yogi Berra 5.00
6 Jackie Robinson 6.00
7 Enos Slaughter 3.00
8 Willie Stargell 4.00
9 Bobby Doerr 3.00
10 Thurman Munson 5.00

Legends of the Fall Fabrics

NM/M

Quantity produced listed 3.00
1 Reggie Jackson/100 20.00
2 Duke Snider/25
3 Roberto Clemente/50 120.00
4 Mel Ott/25
5 Yogi Berra/15
6 Jackie Robinson/25 80.00
7 Enos Slaughter/25
8 Willie Stargell/100 20.00
9 Bobby Doerr/100 20.00
10 Thurman Munson/25

Membership

NM/M

Complete Set (15): 65.00
Common Player: 3.00
Production 2,500 sets
1 Babe Ruth 10.00
2 Steve Carlton 3.00
3 Honus Wagner 6.00
4 Warren Spahn 5.00
5 Eddie Mathews 5.00
6 Nolan Ryan 10.00
7 Rogers Hornsby 5.00
8 Ernie Banks 5.00
9 Harmon Killebrew 5.00
10 Tom Seaver 5.00
11 Jimmie Foxx 6.00
12 Ty Cobb 6.00
13 Frank Robinson 4.00
14 Mel Ott 5.00
15 Lou Gehrig 8.00

Membership VIP Memorabilia

NM/M

Varying quantities produced
1 Babe Ruth/bat/29 325.00
2 Steve Carlton/jsy/81 25.00
3 Honus Wagner/seat/14
4 Warren Spahn/jsy/61 50.00
5 Eddie Mathews/bat/67 60.00
6 Nolan Ryan/jsy/80 75.00
7 R. Hornsby/bat/31 75.00
8 Ernie Banks/jsy/70 35.00
9 H. Killebrew/jsy/71 60.00
10 Tom Seaver/jsy/81 30.00
11 Jimmie Foxx/bat/40 60.00
12 Ty Cobb/bat/21
13 F. Robinson/jsy/71 25.00
14 Mel Ott/jsy/45 50.00
15 Lou Gehrig/bat/31

Significant Signatures

NM/M

Common Autograph: 8.00
#'s 201-211 exclusive to Donruss Rookies
5 Eric Hinske/250 15.00
6 Barry Zito/25 40.00
7 Jason Jennings/250 10.00
10 Corey Patterson/100 20.00
13 Roy Oswalt/100 15.00
16 Mark Mulder/100 35.00
19 Jay Gibbons/250 10.00
21 A.J. Pierzynski/75 20.00
22 Eric Chavez/20 50.00
25 Jose Vidro/75 15.00
27 Mark Teixeira/50 40.00
31 Geronimo Gil/50 10.00
35 Adam Dunn/100 40.00
36 Christian Parker/250 10.00
39 Drew Henson/100 30.00
41 Kevin Mench/250 10.00
45 Mark Prior/50 75.00
56 Kerry Wood/15 100.00
57 Wade Miller/200 10.00
58 Hank Blalock/50 35.00
62 Brian Roberts/250 35.00
63 Paul LoDuca/100 15.00
64 Tim Redding/250 8.00
66 Joe Borchard/100 15.00
68 Richie Sexson/20 50.00
69 Carlos Lee/25 25.00
73 Satoru Komiyama/124 20.00
76 Adam Johnson/200 8.00
84 Robert Fick/50 10.00
88 Brandon Phillips/250 10.00
89 Ben Kozlowski/150 8.00
93 Jermaine Dye/100 20.00
96 Junior Spivey/100 15.00
97 Torii Hunter/50 25.00
102 Steve Garvey/100 20.00
108 Dennis Eckersley/50 30.00
111 Harold Reynolds/50 25.00
119 Don Sutton/100 20.00
120 Nolan Ryan/50 200.00
123 Cal Ripken Jr/50 220.00
126 Joe Carter/100 25.00
127 Jack Morris/100 20.00
128 Luis Aparicio/50 20.00
132 Will Clark/20 125.00
133 Fred Lynn/50 20.00
134 Andre Dawson/50 40.00

135 Duke Snider/5
136 Orlando Cepeda/100 20.00
137 Billy Williams/100 15.00
138 Dale Murphy/20
139 Harmon Killebrew/15
140 Kirby Puckett/5
141 Carlton Fisk/5
142 Eric Davis/50 25.00
143 Alan Trammell/50 35.00
144 Paul Molitor/10
145 Jose Canseco/15
146 Ozzie Smith/5
147 Ralph Kiner/20
148 Dwight Gooden/50 40.00
149 Phil Rizzuto/20 75.00
150 Lenny Dykstra/50 25.00
151 Adam LaRoche/250 15.00
152 Tim Hummel/500 8.00
153 Matt Kata/500 15.00
154 Jeff Baker/500 10.00
155 Josh Stewart/177 10.00
156 Marshall McDougall/500 10.00
157 Jhonny Peralta/500 20.00
158 Mike Nicolas/500 8.00
159 Jeremy Guthrie/500 10.00
160 Craig Brazell/500 15.00
161 Joe Valentine/172 10.00
162 Buddy Hernandez/500 8.00
163 Freddy Sanchez/500 10.00
164 Shane Victorino/351 8.00
165 Corwin Malone/500 8.00
166 Jason Dubois/500 12.00
167 Josh Wilson/500 8.00
168 Tim Olson/500 8.00
169 Clifford Bartosh/500 8.00
170 Michael Hessman/427 8.00
171 Ryan Church/500 10.00
172 Garrett Atkins/500 8.00
173 Jose Morban/500 8.00
174 Ryan Cameron/500 10.00
175 Todd Wellemeyer/500 10.00
176 Travis Chapman/477 10.00
177 Jason Anderson/500 15.00
178 Adam Morrissey/500 8.00
179 Jose Contreras/100 20.00
180 Nic Jackson/500 8.00
181 Rob Hammock/500 10.00
182 Carlos Rivera/500 8.00
183 Vinnie Chulk/500 8.00
184 Pete LaForest/177 10.00
185 Jon Leicester/500 8.00
186 Terrmel Sledge/500 8.00
187 Jose Castillo/500 10.00
188 Gerald Laird/500 8.00
189 Nook Logan/427 8.00
190 Clint Barmes/100 40.00
191 Jesus Medrano/500 8.00
192 Henri Stanley/500 8.00
194 Walter Young/500 10.00
195 Jon Adkins/500 8.00
196 Tommy Whiteman/500 8.00
197 Rob Bowen/500 8.00
198 Brandon Webb/500 15.00
199 Prentice Redman/127 10.00
200 Jimmy Gobble/500 10.00
201 Jeremy Bonderman/100 50.00
202 Adam Loewen/100 10.00
203 Chien-Ming Wang/50 100.00
204 Hong-Chih Kuo/25
205 Ryan Wagner/100 10.00
206 Dan Haren/100 20.00
207 Dontrelle Willis/25
208 Rickie Weeks/10
209 Ramon Nivar/100 15.00
210 Chad Gaudin/25
211 Delmon Young/25

Singles

NM/M

Common Player: 10.00
Varying quantities produced
1 Babe Ruth/jsy/100 275.00
2 Lou Gehrig/jsy/80 200.00
3 Jackie Robinson/jsy/80 75.00
4 Pee Wee Reese/25
5 Bobby Doerr/jsy/100 15.00
6 Fred Lynn/jsy/100 12.00
7 Honus Wagner/seat/100 35.00
8 Roberto Clemente/jsy/80 100.00
9 Kirby Puckett/jsy/100 40.00
10 Torii Hunter/jsy/100 10.00
11 Sammy Sosa/jsy/100 25.00
12 Ryne Sandberg/jsy/100 40.00
13 Hideo Nomo/jsy/50 90.00
14 Kazuhisa Ishii/jsy/50 15.00
15 Mike Schmidt/jsy/100 45.00
16 Steve Carlton/jsy/100 15.00
17 Robin Yount/jsy/100 30.00
18 Paul Molitor/jsy/100 20.00
19 Mike Piazza/jsy/100 25.00
20 Duke Snider/jsy/50 35.00
21 Al Kaline/jsy/50 50.00
22 Ty Cobb/bat/25
23 Don Mattingly/jsy/100 60.00
24 Jason Giambi/jsy/100 10.00
25 Stan Musial/jsy/25
26 Ozzie Smith/jsy/100 40.00
27 Roger Clemens/jsy/100 25.00
28 Pedro Martinez/jsy/100 20.00
29 Thurman Munson/jsy/50 50.00
30 Yogi Berra/jsy/25 70.00

Timeless Treasures

NM/M

Varying quantities produced
1 Tony Gwynn, Stan Musial/50 100.00
2 Alex Rodriguez, Cal Ripken Jr./25
3 Vladimir Guerrero, Roberto Clemente/50 125.00
4 Sammy Sosa, Ernie Banks/25
5 Jason Giambi, Don Mattingly/50 100.00

2003 DONRUSS DIAMOND KINGS

NM/M

Complete Set (176): 90.00
Common Player: .40
Common (151-176): 1.00
Pack (5): 3.00
Box (24): 60.00
1 Darin Erstad .50
2 Garret Anderson .50
3 Troy Glaus .50
4 David Eckstein .40
5 Jarrod Washburn .40
6 Adam Kennedy .40
7 Jay Gibbons .40
8 Tony Batista .40
9 Melvin Mora .40
10 Rodrigo Lopez .40
11 Manny Ramirez .75
12 Pedro J. Martinez 1.00
13 Nomar Garciaparra 1.50
14 Rickey Henderson .60
15 Johnny Damon .50
16 Derek Lowe .40
17 Cliff Floyd .40
18 Frank Thomas .75
19 Magglio Ordonez .50
20 Paul Konerko .40
21 Mark Buehrle .40
22 C.C. Sabathia .40
23 Omar Vizquel .40
24 Jim Thome .75
25 Ellis Burks .40
26 Robert Fick .40
27 Bobby Higginson .40
28 Randall Simon .40
29 Carlos Pena .40
30 Carlos Beltran .75
31 Paul Byrd .40
32 Raul Ibanez .40
33 Mike Sweeney .50
34 Torii Hunter .50
35 Corey Koskie .40
36 A.J. Pierzynski .40
37 Cristian Guzman .40
38 Jacque Jones .40
39 Derek Jeter 3.00
40 Bernie Williams .60
41 Roger Clemens 2.00
42 Mike Mussina .60
43 Jorge Posada .50
44 Alfonso Soriano 1.00
45 Jason Giambi .50
46 Robin Ventura .40
47 David Wells .40
48 Tim Hudson .50
49 Barry Zito .50
50 Mark Mulder .50
51 Miguel Tejada .50
52 Eric Chavez .50
53 Jermaine Dye .40
54 Ichiro Suzuki 2.00
55 Edgar Martinez .50
56 John Olerud .40
57 Dan Wilson .40
58 Joel Pineiro .40
59 Kazuhiro Sasaki .40
60 Freddy Garcia .40
61 Aubrey Huff .40
62 Steve Cox .40
63 Randy Winn .40
64 Alex Rodriguez 2.50
65 Juan Gonzalez .50
66 Rafael Palmeiro .75
67 Ivan Rodriguez .75
68 Kenny Rogers .40
69 Carlos Delgado .50
70 Eric Hinske .40
71 Roy Halladay .40
72 Vernon Wells .40
73 Shannon Stewart .40
74 Curt Schilling .75
75 Randy Johnson 1.00
76 Luis Gonzalez .40
77 Mark Grace .50
78 Junior Spivey .40
79 Greg Maddux 1.50
80 Tom Glavine .50
81 John Smoltz .40
82 Chipper Jones 1.00
83 Gary Sheffield .40
84 Andruw Jones .50
85 Kerry Wood 1.00
86 Fred McGriff .40
87 Sammy Sosa 1.50
88 Mark Prior 1.00
89 Ken Griffey Jr. 1.50
90 Barry Larkin .50
91 Adam Dunn .75
92 Sean Casey .40
93 Austin Kearns .50
94 Aaron Boone .40
95 Larry Walker .40
96 Todd Helton .75
97 Jason Jennings .40
98 Jay Payton .40
99 Josh Beckett .50
100 Mike Lowell .40
101 A.J. Burnett .40
102 Jeff Bagwell .75
103 Craig da Luz .40
104 Lance Berkman .50
105 Roy Oswalt .40
106 Wade Miller .40
107 Shawn Green .50
108 Adrian Beltre .50
109 Hideo Nomo .50
110 Kazuhisa Ishii .40
111 Odalis Perez .40
112 Paul LoDuca .40
113 Ben Sheets .40
114 Richie Sexson .50
115 Jose Hernandez .40
116 Vladimir Guerrero 1.00
117 Jose Vidro .40
118 Tomokazu Ohka .40
119 Andres Galarraga .40
120 Bartolo Colon .40
121 Mike Piazza 1.50
122 Roberto Alomar .50
123 Mo Vaughn .40
124 Al Leiter .40
125 Edgardo Alfonzo .40
126 Pat Burrell .75
127 Bobby Abreu .50
128 Mike Lieberthal .40
129 Vicente Padilla .40
130 Marlon Byrd .40
131 Jason Kendall .40
132 Brian Giles .40
133 Aramis Ramirez .50
134 Kip Wells .40
135 Ryan Klesko .40
136 Phil Nevin .40
137 Brian Lawrence .40
138 Sean Burroughs .40
139 Mark Kotsay .40
140 Barry Bonds 3.00
141 Jeff Kent .40
142 Benito Santiago .40
143 Kirk Reuter .40
144 Jason Schmidt .50
145 Jim Edmonds .50
146 J.D. Drew .50
147 Albert Pujols 2.00
148 Tino Martinez .40
149 Matt Morris .40
150 Scott Rolen 1.00
151 Joe Borchard 2.00
152 Cliff Lee 1.00
153 Brian Tallet 1.00
154 Freddy Sanchez 1.00
155 Chone Figgins 1.00
156 Kevin Cash 1.00
157 Justin Wayne 1.00
158 Ben Kozlowski 1.00
159 Babe Ruth 6.00
160 Jackie Robinson 4.00
161 Ozzie Smith 4.00
162 Lou Gehrig 5.00
163 Stan Musial 4.00
164 Mike Schmidt 5.00
165 Carlton Fisk 2.00
166 George Brett 6.00
167 Dale Murphy 4.00
168 Cal Ripken Jr. 8.00
169 Tony Gwynn 3.00
170 Don Mattingly 6.00
171 Jack Morris 2.00
172 Ty Cobb 5.00
173 Nolan Ryan 6.00
174 Ryne Sandberg 5.00
175 Thurman Munson 4.00
176 *Jose Contreras* 8.00

Diamond Cut

Common Signature (1-25): 10.00
Quantity produced listed
1 Barry Zito/75 50.00
2 Edgar Martinez/125 50.00
3 Jay Gibbons/150 25.00
4 Joe Borchard/150 20.00
5 Marlon Byrd/150 20.00
6 Adam Dunn/150 40.00
7 Torii Hunter/150 40.00
8 Vladimir Guerrero/25 150.00
9 Wade Miller/150 25.00
10 Alfonso Soriano/100 60.00
11 Brian Lawrence/150 10.00
12 Cliff Floyd/100 25.00
13 Dale Murphy/75 75.00
14 Jack Morris/150 25.00
15 Eric Hinske/150 25.00
16 Jason Jennings/150 20.00
17 Mark Buehrle/150 30.00
18 Mark Prior/150 50.00
19 Mark Mulder/150 30.00
20 Mike Sweeney/150 25.00
21 Nolan Ryan/50 200.00
22 Don Mattingly/75 100.00
23 Andruw Jones/75 40.00
24 Aubrey Huff/150 20.00
25 Rickey Henderson/25
Common Jerseys (26-75): 5.00
26 Nolan Ryan/250 50.00
27 Ozzie Smith/400 15.00
28 Rickey Henderson/300 10.00
29 Jack Morris/500 5.00
30 George Brett/350 25.00
31 Cal Ripken Jr./300 40.00
32 Ryne Sandberg/450 20.00
33 Don Mattingly/400 25.00
34 Tony Gwynn/400 15.00
35 Dale Murphy/350 10.00
36 Carlton Fisk/400 10.00
37 Stan Musial/50
38 Lou Gehrig/50 240.00
39 Garret Anderson/450 8.00
40 Pedro J. Martinez/400 10.00
41 Nomar Garciaparra/350 15.00
42 Magglio Ordonez/450 8.00
43 C.C. Sabathia/500 5.00
44 Omar Vizquel/250 8.00
45 Jim Thome/500 10.00
46 Torii Hunter/500 8.00
47 Roger Clemens/500 15.00
48 Alfonso Soriano/400 10.00
49 Tim Hudson/500 8.00
50 Barry Zito/350 6.00
51 Mark Mulder/500 6.00
52 Miguel Tejada/400 8.00
53 John Olerud/350 5.00

54 Alex Rodriguez/500 15.00
55 Rafael Palmeiro/500 8.00
56 Curt Schilling/500 8.00
57 Randy Johnson/400 10.00
58 Greg Maddux/350 12.00
59 John Smoltz/400 6.00
60 Chipper Jones/450 10.00
61 Andruw Jones/500 8.00
62 Kerry Wood/500 10.00
63 Mark Prior/500 15.00
64 Adam Dunn/350 10.00
65 Larry Walker/500 5.00
66 Todd Helton/500 8.00
67 Jeff Bagwell/500 10.00
68 Roy Oswalt/500 8.00
69 Hideo Nomo/150 15.00
70 Kazuhisa Ishii/250 5.00
71 Vladimir Guerrero/500 10.00
72 Mike Piazza/500 15.00
73 Joe Borchard/500 5.00
74 Ryan Klesko/500 5.00
75 Shawn Green/500 6.00
Common Bat (76-105): 5.00
76 George Brett/350 25.00
77 Ozzie Smith/450 15.00
78 Cal Ripken Jr/150 50.00
79 Don Mattingly/400 25.00
80 Babe Ruth/50 200.00
81 Dale Murphy/350 10.00
82 Rickey Henderson/500 10.00
83 Ivan Rodriguez/500 8.00
84 Marlon Byrd/500 5.00
85 Eric Chavez/500 8.00
86 Nomar Garciaparra/500 15.00
87 Alex Rodriguez/500 15.00
88 Vladimir Guerrero/500 10.00
89 Paul LoDuca/500 5.00
90 Richie Sexson/500 6.00
91 Mike Piazza/350 15.00
92 J.D. Drew/500 8.00
93 Juan Gonzalez/500 8.00
94 Pat Burrell/500 8.00
95 Adam Dunn/250 15.00
96 Mike Schmidt/500 20.00
97 Ryne Sandberg/500 20.00
98 Edgardo Alfonzo/500 5.00
99 Andruw Jones/500 8.00
100 Carlos Beltran/500 6.00
101 Jeff Bagwell/500 10.00
102 Lance Berkman/500 8.00
103 Luis Gonzalez/500 5.00
104 Carlos Delgado/500 6.00
105 Jim Edmonds/250 8.00
Combos (106-110):
Some Combos & Autos not priced
106 Alfonso Soriano/75 40.00
107 Greg Maddux/jsy/auto/50 140.00
108 Ty Cobb/pants/bat/25
109 Adam Dunn/bat/auto/50 60.00
110 Rickey Henderson/jsy/bat/50 20.00

DK Evolution

NM/M
Complete Set (25): 85.00
Common Player: 2.00
Inserted 1:18
1 Cal Ripken Jr. 10.00
2 Ichiro Suzuki 6.00
3 Randy Johnson 4.00
4 Pedro J. Martinez 4.00
5 Nolan Ryan 10.00
6 Derek Jeter 10.00
7 Kerry Wood 4.00
8 Alex Rodriguez 8.00
9 Magglio Ordonez 2.00
10 Greg Maddux 5.00
11 Todd Helton 3.00
12 Sammy Sosa 5.00
13 Lou Gehrig 8.00
14 Lance Berkman 2.00
15 Barry Zito 2.00
16 Barry Bonds 10.00
17 Tom Glavine 2.00
18 Shawn Green 2.00
19 Roger Clemens 8.00
20 Nomar Garciaparra 6.00
21 Tony Gwynn 4.00
22 Vladimir Guerrero 3.00
23 Albert Pujols 8.00
24 Chipper Jones 4.00
25 Alfonso Soriano 4.00

Framed Portraits Bronze

Cards (1-150): 1-2.5X
Cards (151-176): .75-1.5X
Silvers (1-150): 3-5X
Silvers (151-176): 2-3X
Production 400 sets
Golds (1-150): 5-10X
Golds (151-176): 3-6X
Production 100 sets

Hall of Fame Heroes

NM/M
Complete Set (10): 40.00
Common Player: 3.00
Inserted 1:43
1 Bob Feller 3.00
2 Al Kaline 6.00
3 Lou Boudreau 3.00
4 Duke Snider 4.00
5 Jackie Robinson 6.00
6 Early Wynn 3.00
7 Yogi Berra 4.00
8 Stan Musial 6.00
9 Ty Cobb 6.00
10 Ted Williams 8.00

Heritage Collection

NM/M
Complete Set (25): 100.00
Common Player: 2.00
Inserted 1:23
1 Ozzie Smith 5.00
2 Lou Gehrig 8.00
3 Stan Musial 6.00
4 Mike Schmidt 6.00
5 Carlton Fisk 2.00
6 George Brett 10.00
7 Dale Murphy 4.00
8 Cal Ripken Jr. 10.00
9 Tony Gwynn 4.00
10 Don Mattingly 8.00
11 Jack Morris 2.00
12 Ty Cobb 8.00
13 Nolan Ryan 12.00
14 Ryne Sandberg 6.00
15 Thurman Munson 4.00
16 Ichiro Suzuki 6.00
17 Derek Jeter 10.00
18 Greg Maddux 5.00
19 Sammy Sosa 5.00
20 Pedro J. Martinez 4.00
21 Alex Rodriguez 8.00
22 Roger Clemens 5.00
23 Barry Bonds 10.00
24 Lance Berkman 2.00
25 Vladimir Guerrero 3.00

HOF Heroes Materials

NM/M
Common Player: 30.00
Production 50 sets
1 Bob Feller/jsy 70.00
2 Al Kaline/bat 45.00
3 Lou Boudreau/jsy 40.00
4 Duke Snider/bat 30.00
5 Jackie Robinson/jsy
6 Early Wynn
7 Yogi Berra/bat 40.00
8 Stan Musial/bat 100.00
9 Ty Cobb/bat 110.00
10 Ted Williams/jsy 175.00

Recollection

No Pricing

Recollection Autographs

NM/M
Common Player:
1 Adrian Beltre/40 15.00
2 Brandon Berger/99 10.00
9 Mark Buehrle/73 10.00
15 Andre Dawson/24 25.00
16 Andre Dawson/50 20.00
17 Andre Dawson/28 25.00
19 Jorge De La Rosa/148 5.00
24 Rob Fick/150 8.00
37 Tim Hudson/50 15.00
42 Ryan Ludwick/130 8.00
55 Roy Oswalt/65 15.00
56 Roy Oswalt/100 15.00
70 Bud Smith/114 5.00
72 Shannon Stewart/50 8.00

Team Timelines

NM/M
Complete Set (10): 85.00
Common Card: 4.00
Production 1,000 sets
1 Nolan Ryan, Roy Oswalt 15.00
2 Dale Murphy, Chipper Jones 8.00
3 Stan Musial, Jim Edmonds 10.00
4 George Brett, Mike Sweeney 12.00
5 Tony Gwynn, Ryan Klesko 6.00
6 Carlton Fisk, Magglio Ordonez 4.00
7 Mike Schmidt, Pat Burrell 12.00
8 Don Mattingly, Bernie Williams 12.00
9 Ryne Sandberg, Kerry Wood 10.00
10 Lou Gehrig, Alfonso Soriano 10.00

Team Timelines Materials

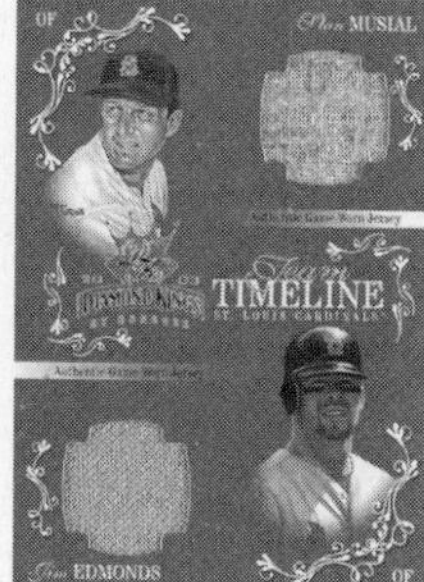

NM/M
Common Card: 30.00
Production 100 unless noted
1 Nolan Ryan, Roy Oswalt 120.00
2 Dale Murphy, Chipper Jones 40.00
3 Stan Musial, Jim Edmonds 45.00
4 George Brett, Mike Sweeney 65.00
5 Tony Gwynn, Ryan Klesko 40.00
6 Carlton Fisk, Magglio Ordonez 30.00
7 Mike Schmidt, Pat Burrell 90.00
8 Don Mattingly, Bernie Williams 70.00
9 Ryne Sandberg, Kerry Wood 60.00
10 Lou Gehrig, Alfonso Soriano/50 200.00

2003 DONRUSS ELITE

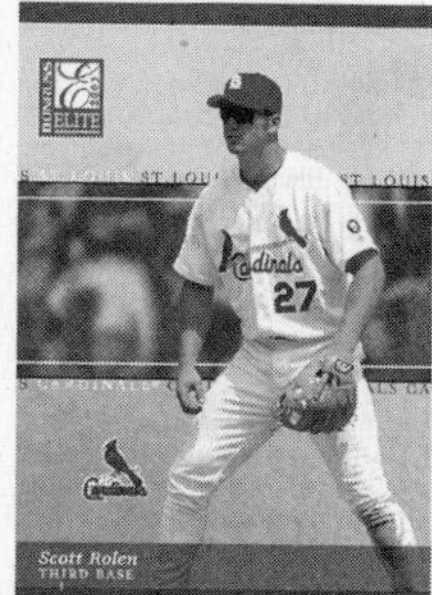

NM/M
Complete Set (200):
Common Player: .25
Common Rookie (181-200): 3.00
Production 1,750
Pack (5): 3.50
Box (20): 60.00
1 Darin Erstad .40
2 David Eckstein .25
3 Garret Anderson .40
4 Jarrod Washburn .25
5 Tim Salmon .40
6 Troy Glaus .50
7 Marty Cordova .25
8 Melvin Mora .25
9 Rodrigo Lopez .25
10 Tony Batista .25
11 Derek Lowe .25
12 Johnny Damon .40
13 Manny Ramirez .50
14 Nomar Garciaparra 1.50
15 Pedro J. Martinez .75
16 Shea Hillenbrand .25
17 Carlos Lee .25
18 Joe Crede .25
19 Frank Thomas .50
20 Magglio Ordonez .40
21 Mark Buehrle .25
22 Paul Konerko .25
23 C.C. Sabathia .25
24 Ellis Burks .25
25 Omar Vizquel .40
26 Brian Tallet .25
27 Bobby Higginson .25
28 Carlos Pena .25
29 Mark Redman .25
30 Steve Sparks .25
31 Carlos Beltran .50
32 Joe Randa .25
33 Mike Sweeney .25
34 Raul Ibanez .25
35 Runelvys Hernandez .25
36 Brad Radke .25
37 Corey Koskie .25
38 Cristian Guzman .25
39 David Ortiz .50
40 Doug Mientkiewicz .25
41 Jacque Jones .25
42 Torii Hunter .40
43 Alfonso Soriano .75
44 Andy Pettitte .40
45 Bernie Williams .50
46 David Wells .25
47 Derek Jeter 2.00
48 Jason Giambi .40
49 Jeff Weaver .25
50 Jorge Posada .40
51 Mike Mussina .50
52 Roger Clemens 1.50
53 Barry Zito .40
54 Eric Chavez .40
55 Jermaine Dye .25
56 Mark Mulder .40
57 Miguel Tejada .40
58 Tim Hudson .40
59 Bret Boone .25
60 Chris Snelling .25
61 Edgar Martinez .40
62 Freddy Garcia .25
63 Ichiro Suzuki 1.50
64 Jamie Moyer .25
65 John Olerud .25
66 Kazuhiro Sasaki .25
67 Aubrey Huff .25
68 Joe Kennedy .25
69 Paul Wilson .25
70 Alex Rodriguez 1.50

71 Chan Ho Park .25
72 Hank Blalock .50
73 Juan Gonzalez .50
74 Kevin Mench .25
75 Rafael Palmeiro .50
76 Carlos Delgado .40
77 Eric Hinske .25
78 Josh Phelps .25
79 Roy Halladay .40
80 Shannon Stewart .25
81 Vernon Wells .25
82 Curt Schilling .50
83 Junior Spivey .25
84 Luis Gonzalez .40
85 Mark Grace .50
86 Randy Johnson .75
87 Steve Finley .25
88 Andruw Jones .50
89 Chipper Jones .75
90 Gary Sheffield .50
91 Greg Maddux 1.00
92 John Smoltz .40
93 Corey Patterson .40
94 Kerry Wood .75
95 Mark Prior 1.00
96 Moises Alou .40
97 Sammy Sosa 1.50
98 Adam Dunn .50
99 Austin Kearns .40
100 Barry Larkin .40
101 Ken Griffey Jr. 1.00
102 Sean Casey .25
103 Jason Jennings .25
104 Jay Payton .25
105 Larry Walker .40
106 Todd Helton .50
107 A.J. Burnett .25
108 Josh Beckett .50
109 Juan Encarnacion .25
110 Mike Lowell .25
111 Craig Biggio .40
112 Daryle Ward .25
113 Jeff Bagwell .50
114 Lance Berkman .40
115 Roy Oswalt .40
116 Jason Lane .25
117 Adrian Beltre .50
118 Hideo Nomo .50
119 Kazuhisa Ishii .25
120 Kevin Brown .40
121 Odalis Perez .25
122 Paul LoDuca .25
123 Shawn Green .40
124 Ben Sheets .40
125 Jeffrey Hammonds .25
126 Jose Hernandez .25
127 Richie Sexson .50
128 Bartolo Colon .25
129 Brad Wilkerson .25
130 Javier Vazquez .25
131 Jose Vidro .25
132 Michael Barrett .25
133 Vladimir Guerrero .75
134 Al Leiter .25
135 Mike Piazza 1.00
136 Mo Vaughn .25
137 Pedro Astacio .25
138 Roberto Alomar .40
139 Pat Burrell .40
140 Vicente Padilla .25
141 Jimmy Rollins .25
142 Bobby Abreu .40
143 Marlon Byrd .25
144 Brian Giles .40
145 Jason Kendall .40
146 Aramis Ramirez .40
147 Josh Fogg .25
148 Ryan Klesko .40
149 Phil Nevin .25
150 Sean Burroughs .25
151 Mark Kotsay .25
152 Barry Bonds 2.00
153 Damian Moss .25
154 Jason Schmidt .50
155 Benito Santiago .25
156 Rich Aurilia .25
157 Scott Rolen .75
158 J.D. Drew .40
159 Jim Edmonds .40
160 Matt Morris .40
161 Tino Martinez .25
162 Albert Pujols 1.50
163 Russ Ortiz .25
164 Rey Ordonez .25
165 Paul Byrd .25
166 Kenny Lofton .25
167 Kenny Rogers .25
168 Rickey Henderson .50
169 Fred McGriff .40
170 Charles Johnson .25
171 Mike Hampton .25
172 Jim Thome .75
173 Travis Hafner .25
174 Ivan Rodriguez .50
175 Ray Durham .25
176 Jeremy Giambi .25
177 Jeff Kent .40
178 Cliff Floyd .25
179 Kevin Millwood .25
180 Tom Glavine .50
181 *Hideki Matsui* 10.00
182 *Jose Contreras* 5.00
183 *Terrmel Sledge* 3.00
184 *Lew Ford* 6.00
185 Jhonny Peralta 4.00
186 Alexis Rios 4.00
187 Jeff Baker 3.00
188 Jeremy Guthrie 3.00
189 Jose Castillo 3.00
190 Garrett Atkins 3.00
191 Jeremy Bonderman 3.00
192 Adam LaRoche 3.00
193 Vinnie Chulk 3.00
194 Walter Young 3.00
195 Jimmy Gobble 3.00
196 *Prentice Redman* 4.00
197 Jason Anderson 3.00
198 Nic Jackson 3.00
199 Travis Chapman 3.00
200 *Shane Victorino* 3.00

Status

NM/M

Stars print run 25-50: 10-15X
Rookies (181-200) p/r 25-50: 1-3X
Stars p/r 51-99: 5-10X
Gold Status: No Pricing
Production 24 sets
181 Hideki Matsui/55 120.00

All-Time Career Best

NM/M

Complete Set (45): 120.00
Common Player: 2.00
Inserted 1:9
Gold print run 25-50: 4-8X
Gold print run 51-100: 3-5X
Gold p/r 101-239: 1.5-3X
Numbered to career stat
1 Babe Ruth 6.00
2 Ty Cobb 4.00
3 Jackie Robinson 4.00
4 Lou Gehrig 5.00
5 Thurman Munson 2.00
6 Nolan Ryan 8.00
7 Mike Schmidt 4.00
8 Don Mattingly 5.00
9 Yogi Berra 3.00
10 Rod Carew 2.00
11 Reggie Jackson 3.00
12 Al Kaline 4.00
13 Harmon Killebrew 4.00
14 Eddie Mathews 3.00
15 Stan Musial 4.00
16 Jim Palmer 2.00
17 Phil Rizzuto 2.00
18 Brooks Robinson 3.00
19 Tom Seaver 3.00
20 Robin Yount 4.00
21 Carlton Fisk 3.00
22 Dale Murphy 4.00
23 Cal Ripken Jr. 8.00
24 Tony Gwynn 4.00
25 Andre Dawson 2.00
26 Derek Jeter 6.00
27 Ken Griffey Jr. 4.00
28 Albert Pujols 4.00
29 Sammy Sosa 4.00
30 Jason Giambi 3.00
31 Randy Johnson 3.00
32 Greg Maddux 4.00
33 Rickey Henderson 3.00
34 Pedro Martinez 3.00
35 Jeff Bagwell 3.00
36 Alex Rodriguez 5.00
37 Vladimir Guerrero 3.00
38 Chipper Jones 3.00
39 Shawn Green 2.00
40 Tom Glavine 2.00
41 Curt Schilling 2.00
42 Todd Helton 2.00
43 Roger Clemens 4.00
44 Lance Berkman 2.00
45 Nomar Garciaparra 5.00

All-Time Career Best Materials

NM/M

Common Player: 5.00
Varying quantities produced
1 Babe Ruth/bat/25 250.00
2 Ty Cobb/bat/25 150.00
3 Jackie Robinson/jsy/50 50.00
4 Lou Gehrig/bat/100 100.00
5 Thurman Munson/bat/200 15.00
6 Nolan Ryan/jsy/400 40.00
7 Mike Schmidt/jsy/400 30.00
8 Don Mattingly/jsy/250 40.00
9 Yogi Berra/bat/100 25.00
10 Rod Carew/bat/400 10.00
11 Reggie Jackson/bat/400 10.00
12 Al Kaline/bat/400 20.00
13 Harmon Killebrew/jsy/400 15.00
14 Eddie Mathews/bat/200 25.00
15 Stan Musial/bat/100 40.00
16 Jim Palmer/jsy/200 10.00
17 Phil Rizzuto/bat/400 10.00
18 Brooks Robinson/bat/400 15.00
19 Tom Seaver/jsy/400 15.00
20 Robin Yount/bat/400 15.00
21 Carlton Fisk/bat/400 10.00
22 Dale Murphy/bat/400 10.00
23 Cal Ripken Jr/bat/400 35.00
24 Tony Gwynn/jsy/400 12.00
25 Andre Dawson/bat/400 5.00
26 Derek Jeter/base/400 15.00
27 Ken Griffey Jr/base/400 10.00
28 Albert Pujols/base/400 15.00
29 Sammy Sosa/bat/400 12.00
30 Jason Giambi/bat/400 8.00
31 Randy Johnson/jsy/400 8.00
32 Greg Maddux/jsy/400 10.00
33 Rickey Henderson/bat/400 10.00
34 Pedro Martinez/jsy/400 10.00
35 Jeff Bagwell/jsy/400 8.00
36 Alex Rodriguez/bat/400 12.00
37 Vladimir Guerrero/bat/400 8.00
38 Chipper Jones/bat/400 10.00
39 Shawn Green/bat/400 5.00
40 Tom Glavine/jsy/400 5.00
41 Curt Schilling/jsy/400 8.00
42 Todd Helton/bat/400 8.00
43 Roger Clemens/jsy/400 20.00
44 Lance Berkman/bat/400 5.00
45 Nomar Garciaparra/bat/400 15.00

All-Time Career Best Materials Gold

NM/M

Numbered to career stat
Some not priced yet
1 Babe Ruth/60 125.00
2 Ty Cobb/24
3 Jackie Robinson/19
4 Lou Gehrig/49 125.00
5 Thurman Munson/105 25.00
6 Nolan Ryan/22
7 Mike Schmidt/48 50.00
8 Don Mattingly/53 60.00
9 Yogi Berra/30 50.00
10 Rod Carew/239 10.00
11 Reggie Jackson/39 25.00
12 Al Kaline/29 50.00
13 Harmon Killebrew/140 20.00
14 Eddie Mathews/31 50.00
15 Stan Musial/39 60.00
16 Jim Palmer/23
17 Phil Rizzuto/10
18 Brooks Robinson/118 20.00
19 Tom Seaver/7
20 Robin Yount/49 40.00
21 Carlton Fisk/107 15.00
22 Dale Murphy/44 40.00
23 Cal Ripken Jr./211 40.00
24 Tony Gwynn/220 10.00
25 Andre Dawson/49 15.00
26 Derek Jeter/24
27 Ken Griffey Jr./56 25.00
28 Albert Pujols/37 30.00
29 Sammy Sosa/66 35.00
30 Jason Giambi/137 10.00
31 Randy Johnson/12
32 Greg Maddux/20
33 Rickey Henderson/130 20.00
34 Pedro Martinez/23
35 Jeff Bagwell/47 15.00
36 Alex Rodriguez/393 10.00
37 Vladimir Guerrero/44 25.00
38 Chipper Jones/45 20.00
39 Shawn Green/49 15.00
40 Tom Glavine/22
41 Curt Schilling/35 20.00
42 Todd Helton/59 15.00
43 Roger Clemens/1
44 Lance Berkman/55 15.00
45 Nomar Garciaparra/35 50.00

Back to the Future

NM/M

Complete Set (15): 35.00
Common Card: 2.00
#'s 1-10 production 1,000:
#'s 11-15 production 500
1 Kerry Wood 4.00
2 Mark Prior 5.00
3 Magglio Ordonez 2.50
4 Joe Borchard 2.00
5 Lance Berkman 3.00
6 Jason Lane 2.00
7 Rafael Palmeiro 3.00
8 Mark Teixeira 3.00
9 Carlos Delgado 3.00
10 Josh Phelps 2.00
11 Kerry Wood, Mark Prior 6.00
12 Joe Borchard, Magglio Ordonez 2.50
13 Jason Lane, Lance Berkman 3.00
14 Mark Teixeira, Rafael Palmeiro 3.00
15 Carlos Delgado, Josh Phelps 3.00

Back to the Future Threads

NM/M

Common Card: 4.00
Singles production 250:
Doubles production 125:
1 Kerry Wood 10.00
2 Mark Prior 15.00
3 Magglio Ordonez 5.00
4 Joe Borchard 5.00
5 Lance Berkman 6.00
6 Jason Lane 4.00
7 Rafael Palmeiro 8.00
8 Mark Teixeira 10.00
9 Carlos Delgado 8.00
10 Josh Phelps 6.00
11 Kerry Wood, Mark Prior 25.00
12 Joe Borchard, Magglio Ordonez 8.00
13 Jason Lane, Lance Berkman 8.00
14 Mark Teixeira, Rafael Palmeiro 15.00
15 Carlos Delgado, Josh Phelps 8.00

Back 2 Back Jacks

NM/M

Common Player:
1 Adam Dunn/250 10.00
2 Alex Rodriguez/250 15.00
3 Alfonso Soriano/250 10.00
4 Andruw Jones/250 8.00
5 Chipper Jones/250 10.00
6 Jason Giambi/250 8.00
7 Jeff Bagwell/250 8.00
8 Jim Thome/250 8.00
9 Juan Gonzalez/250 8.00
10 Lance Berkman/250 6.00
11 Magglio Ordonez/250 4.00
12 Manny Ramirez/250 8.00
13 Miguel Tejada/250 6.00
14 Mike Piazza/250 15.00
15 Nomar Garciaparra/250 15.00
16 Rafael Palmeiro/250 8.00
17 Rickey Henderson/250 10.00
18 Sammy Sosa/250 15.00
19 Scott Rolen/250 8.00

20 Shawn Green/250 6.00
21 Todd Helton/250 8.00
22 Vladimir Guerrero/250 8.00
23 Ivan Rodriguez/250 8.00
24 Eric Chavez/250 6.00
25 Larry Walker/250 6.00
26 Troy Glaus/250, Garret Anderson 8.00
27 Adam Dunn, Austin Kearns/125 20.00
28 Alex Rodriguez, Rafael Palmeiro/125 20.00
29 Eric Chavez, Miguel Tejada/125 10.00
30 Frank Thomas, Magglio Ordonez/125 15.00
31 Jeff Bagwell, Lance Berkman/125 15.00
32 Manny Ramirez, Nomar Garciaparra/125 30.00
33 Jose Vidro, Vladimir Guerrero/125 15.00
34 Mike Piazza, Roberto Alomar/125 20.00
35 Larry Walker, Todd Helton/125 15.00
36 Babe Ruth/100 150.00
37 Cal Ripken Jr./100 65.00
38 Don Mattingly/100 50.00
39 Kirby Puckett/100 20.00
40 Roberto Clemente/100 75.00
41 Alfonso Soriano, Phil Rizzuto/75 25.00
42 Andre Dawson, Sammy Sosa/75 40.00
43 Ozzie Smith, Scott Rolen/75 60.00
44 Don Mattingly, Jason Giambi/75 75.00
45 Rickey Henderson, Ty Cobb/75 125.00
46 Joe Morgan, Johnny Bench/50 35.00
47 Brooks Robinson, Cal Ripken Jr./50 100.00
48 Bo Jackson, George Brett/50 100.00
49 Babe Ruth, Lou Gehrig/50 375.00
50 Thurman Munson, Yogi Berra/50 60.00

Career Best

NM/M

Common Player: 3.00
Numbered to statistic
1 Randy Johnson/24
2 Curt Schilling/23
3 Garret Anderson/56 6.00
4 Andruw Jones/83 6.00
5 Kerry Wood/4
6 Magglio Ordonez/38 6.00
7 Magglio Ordonez/135 4.00
8 Adam Dunn/26 15.00
9 Roy Oswalt/19
10 Lance Berkman/42 6.00
11 Lance Berkman/128 3.00
12 Shawn Green/385 3.00
13 Alfonso Soriano/39 12.00
14 Alfonso Soriano/300 5.00
15 Jason Giambi/120 5.00
16 Derek Jeter/32 30.00
17 Vladimir Guerrero/40 12.00
18 Vladimir Guerrero/417 5.00
19 Barry Zito/23 8.00
20 Miguel Tejada/34 8.00
21 Barry Bonds/198 15.00
22 Barry Bonds/370 15.00
23 Ichiro Suzuki/388 8.00
24 Alex Rodriguez/57 15.00
25 Alex Rodriguez/142 10.00

Career Best Materials

NM/M

Common Player: 4.00
Production 500 sets
1 Randy Johnson/jsy 8.00
2 Curt Schilling/jsy 8.00
3 Garret Anderson/bat 4.00
4 Andruw Jones/bat 6.00
5 Kerry Wood/shoe 10.00
6 Magglio Ordonez/bat 4.00
7 Magglio Ordonez/bat 4.00
8 Adam Dunn/bat 6.00
9 Roy Oswalt/jsy 5.00
10 Lance Berkman/bat 5.00
11 Lance Berkman/bat 5.00
12 Shawn Green/bat 4.00
13 Alfonso Soriano/bat 10.00
14 Alfonso Soriano/bat 10.00
15 Jason Giambi/bat 8.00
16 Derek Jeter/base 15.00
17 Vladimir Guerrero/bat 8.00
18 Vladimir Guerrero/bat 8.00
19 Barry Zito/jsy 6.00
20 Miguel Tejada/bat 6.00
21 Barry Bonds/base 15.00
22 Barry Bonds/base 15.00
23 Ichiro Suzuki/base 15.00
24 Alex Rodriguez/jsy 10.00
25 Alex Rodriguez/jsy 10.00

Career Best Materials Autograph

NM/M

Quantity produced listed
2 Curt Schilling/jsy/5
3 Garret Anderson/bat/75 35.00
4 Andruw Jones/bat/10
5 Kerry Wood/shoe/15
6 Magglio Ordonez/bat/10
7 Magglio Ordonez/bat/10
8 Adam Dunn/bat/100 50.00
9 Roy Oswalt/jsy/250 30.00
10 Lance Berkman/bat/25
11 Lance Berkman/bat/25
13 Alfonso Soriano/bat/5
14 Alfonso Soriano/bat/5
17 Vladimir Guerrero/bat/50 75.00
18 Vladimir Guerrero/bat/50 75.00
19 Barry Zito/jsy/75 40.00
20 Miguel Tejada/bat/25
24 Alex Rodriguez/jsy/5
25 Alex Rodriguez/jsy/5

Elite Dominators

No Pricing 25 sets produced

Highlights

NM/M

Production 500 sets
1 Sammy Sosa 10.00
2 Rafael Palmeiro 8.00
3 Hideki Matsui 10.00
4 Jose Contreras 4.00
5 Kevin Millwood 4.00

Highlights Autographs

NM/M

Production 50 sets
2 Rafael Palmeiro 75.00
4 Jose Contreras 25.00

Passing the Torch

NM/M

Complete Set (15): 50.00
Common Player:
1 Stan Musial 6.00
2 Jim Edmonds 2.00
3 Dale Murphy 3.00
4 Andruw Jones 3.00
5 Roger Clemens 8.00
6 Mark Prior 4.00
7 Tom Seaver 3.00
8 Tom Glavine 1.50
9 Mike Schmidt 8.00
10 Pat Burrell 2.00
11 Jim Edmonds, Stan Musial 8.00
12 Andruw Jones, Dale Murphy 5.00
13 Mark Prior, Roger Clemens 10.00
14 Tom Glavine, Tom Seaver 5.00
15 Mike Schmidt, Pat Burrell 10.00

Passing the Torch Autograph

NM/M

Common Auto (1-10): 30.00
#'s 1-10 production 50
#'s 11-15 production 25
No pricing for #'s 11-15
1 Stan Musial 80.00
2 Jim Edmonds 40.00
3 Dale Murphy 50.00
4 Andruw Jones 30.00
5 Roger Clemens 125.00
6 Mark Prior 75.00
7 Tom Seaver 60.00
8 Tom Glavine 50.00
9 Mike Schmidt 100.00
10 Pat Burrell 30.00

Recollection Autographs

NM/M

Some not priced due to scarcity
1 Jeremy Affeldt/75 15.00
2 Erick Almonte/75 8.00
4 Adrian Beltre/36 30.00
7 Brandon Berger/83 8.00
8 Angel Berroa/28 25.00
13 Jeff Deardorff/53 8.00
14 Ryan Drese/100 25.00
21 Luis Garcia/28 15.00
22 Geronimo Gil/75 8.00
28 Travis Hafner Black/52 30.00
30 Bill Hall/27 15.00
35 Gerald Laird/46 30.00
36 Jason Lane/27 15.00
44 Victor Martinez/52 100.00
46 Roy Oswalt Black/61 20.00
51 Ricardo Rodriguez/75 8.00
55 Bud Smith/50 10.00
56 Bud Smith/28 10.00
58 Junior Spivey/45 20.00
59 Tim Spooneybarger/100 8.00
60 Shannon Stewart/24
61 Shannon Stewart/35 20.00
64 Claudio Vargas/51 8.00

Throwback Threads

NM/M

Common Player: 4.00
1 Randy Johnson/jsy 8.00
2 Randy Johnson/hat 10.00
3 Roger Clemens/jsy 20.00
4 Roger Clemens/jsy 20.00
5 Manny Ramirez/jsy 8.00
6 Greg Maddux/jsy 15.00
7 Jason Giambi/jsy 6.00
8 Jason Giambi/jsy 6.00
9 Alex Rodriguez/jsy 10.00
10 Alex Rodriguez/jsy 10.00
11 Miguel Tejada/jsy 6.00
12 Alfonso Soriano/jsy 8.00
13 Nomar Garciaparra/jsy 15.00
14 Pedro J. Martinez/jsy 8.00
15 Pedro J. Martinez/jsy 8.00
16 Andruw Jones/jsy 6.00
17 Chipper Jones/jsy 8.00
18 Barry Zito/jsy 8.00
19 Mark Mulder/jsy 4.00
20 Lance Berkman/jsy 6.00
21 Magglio Ordonez/jsy 4.00
22 Mike Piazza/jsy 15.00
23 Mike Piazza/jsy 15.00
24 Rickey Henderson/jsy 8.00
25 Rickey Henderson/jsy 8.00
26 Rickey Henderson/jsy 8.00
27 Sammy Sosa/jsy 15.00
28 Shawn Green/jsy 5.00
29 Troy Glaus/jsy 6.00
30 Vladimir Guerrero/jsy 8.00
31 Adam Dunn/jsy 8.00
32 Jeff Bagwell/jsy 8.00
33 Curt Schilling/jsy 8.00
34 Hideo Nomo/jsy 20.00
35 Hideo Nomo/jsy 20.00
36 Hideo Nomo/jsy 20.00
37 Kerry Wood/jsy 10.00
38 Mark Prior/jsy 10.00
39 Roberto Alomar/jsy 6.00
40 Todd Helton/jsy 8.00
41 Jim Thome/jsy 8.00
42 Rafael Palmeiro/jsy 8.00
43 Juan Gonzalez/jsy 8.00
44 Vernon Wells/jsy 4.00
45 Torii Hunter/jsy 6.00
46 Randi Johnson/jsy 15.00
47 Roger Clemens/jsy 30.00
48 Jason Giambi/jsy 10.00
49 Alex Rodriguez/jsy 25.00
50 Pedro J. Martinez/jsy 20.00
51 Mike Piazza/jsy 25.00
52 Rickey Henderson 20.00
53 Rickey Henderson 20.00
54 Rickey Henderson/hat, Rickey Henderson/jsy 20.00
55 Hideo Nomo/jsy 40.00
56 Randy Johnson/jsy 15.00
57 Curt Schilling, Randy Johnson/jsy 15.00
58 Alfonso Soriano, Jason Giambi 20.00
59 Barry Zito, Mark Mulder 15.00
60 Andruw Jones, Chipper Jones/jsy 20.00
61 Greg Maddux, Tom Glavine 40.00
62 Jeff Bagwell, Lance Berkman/jsy 15.00
63 Mark Prior, Roger Clemens/jsy 25.00
64 Alex Rodriguez, Rafael Palmeiro/jsy 20.00
65 Jim Thome, Roberto Alomar/jsy 20.00
66 Mike Piazza, Roberto Alomar/jsy 20.00
67 Mark Grace, Sammy Sosa/jsy 25.00
68 Larry Walker, Todd Helton/jsy 20.00
69 Adam Dunn, Austin Kearns/jsy 20.00
70 Alex Rodriguez, Ivan Rodriguez/jsy 20.00
71 Bobby Abreu, Marlon Byrd/jsy 15.00
72 Eric Chavez, Miguel Tejada/jsy 15.00
73 Greg Maddux, John Smoltz/jsy 30.00
74 Kerry Wood, Mark Prior/jsy 15.00
75 Barry Zito, Tim Hudson/jsy 10.00
76 Babe Ruth 250.00
77 Ty Cobb 100.00
78 Jackie Robinson 75.00
79 Lou Gehrig 125.00
80 Thurman Munson 30.00
81 Nolan Ryan 40.00
82 Don Mattingly 50.00
83 Mike Schmidt 40.00
84 Reggie Jackson 20.00
85 George Brett 40.00
86 Cal Ripken Jr. 50.00
87 Tony Gwynn 15.00
88 Yogi Berra 25.00
89 Stan Musial 40.00
90 Jim Palmer 10.00
91 Thurman Munson 50.00
92 Chipper Jones, Dale Murphy 50.00
93 Don Mattingly, Jason Giambi 80.00
94 Andre Dawson, Sammy Sosa 40.00
95 Mark Prior, Nolan Ryan 75.00
96 Babe Ruth, Lou Gehrig 475.00
97 Joe Morgan, Tom Seaver 40.00
98 Harmon Killebrew, Rod Carew 40.00
99 Nolan Ryan 90.00
100 Reggie Jackson 35.00

Throwback Threads Autograph

NM/M

30 Vladimir Guerrero/50 75.00
31 Adam Dunn/50 75.00
37 Kerry Wood/50 75.00
38 Mark Prior/75 75.00
39 Roberto Alomar/50 75.00

Turn of the Century Autographs

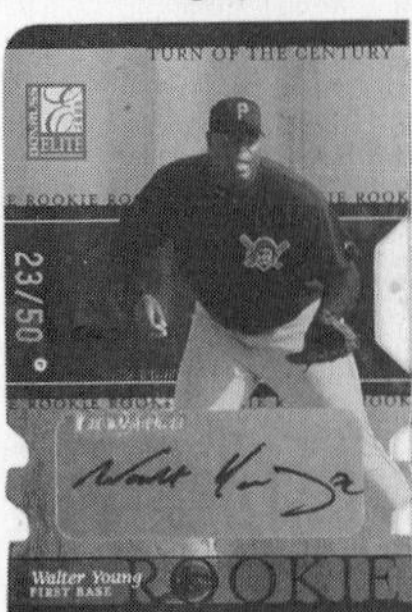

NM/M
Common Autograph: 10.00
Production 50 sets
182 Jose Contreras 40.00
183 Terrmel Sledge 20.00
184 Lew Ford 40.00
185 Jhonny Peralta 20.00
186 Alexis Rios 40.00
187 Jeff Baker 15.00
188 Jeremy Guthrie 15.00
189 Jose Castillo 15.00
190 Garrett Atkins 15.00
191 Jeremy Bonderman 25.00
192 Adam LaRoche 15.00
193 Vinnie Chulk 15.00
194 Walter Young 15.00
195 Jimmy Gobble 10.00
196 Prentice Redman 15.00
197 Jason Anderson 15.00
198 Nic Jackson 15.00
199 Travis Chapman 10.00
200 Shane Victorino 10.00

2003 DONRUSS ROOKIE & TRADED

NM/M
Complete Set (65): 8.00
Common Player: .25
Pack (8): 4.00
Box (24): 75.00
1 Jeremy Bonderman .40
2 Adam Loewen .50
3 Dan Haren .25
4 *Jose Contreras* .50
5 *Hideki Matsui* 2.00
6 Arnie Munoz .25
7 Miguel Cabrera .25
8 *Andrew Brown* .25
9 *Josh Hall* .50
10 *Josh Stewart* .25
11 *Clint Barmes* .25
12 *Luis Ayala* .25
13 *Brandon Webb* .50
14 Greg Aquino .25
15 Chien-Ming Wang .50
16 *Rickie Weeks* 1.50
17 *Edgar Gonzalez* .25
18 Dontrelle Willis .50
19 *Bo Hart* .40
20 *Rosman Garcia* .25
21 Jeremy Griffiths .25
22 *Craig Brazell* .50
23 *Daniel Cabrera* .25
24 *Fernando Cabrera* .25
25 *Terrmel Sledge* .25
26 Ramon Nivar .25
27 *Rob Hammock* .25
28 *Francisco Rosario* .25
29 Cory Stewart .25
30 Felix Sanchez .25
31 Jorge Cordova .25
32 Rocco Baldelli .50
33 *Beau Kemp* .25
34 *Micheal Nakamura* .25
35 *Rett Johnson* .25
36 *Guillermo Quiroz* .50
37 Hong-Chih Kuo .25
38 *Ian Ferguson* .25
39 Franklin Perez .25
40 *Tim Olson* .50
41 Jerome Williams .25
42 Rich Fischer .25
43 *Phil Seibel* .25
44 *Aaron Looper* .25
45 Jae Weong Seo .25
46 *Chad Gaudin* .25
47 *Matt Kata* .25
48 *Ryan Wagner* .50
49 *Michel Hernandez* .25
50 Diegomar Markwell .25
51 Doug Waechter .25
52 Mike Nicolas .25
53 *Prentice Redman* .25
54 Shane Bazzell .25
55 *Delmon Young* 2.00
56 Brian Stokes .25
57 Matt Bruback .25
58 *Nook Logan* .25
59 *Oscar Villarreal* .25
60 *Pete LaForest* .25
61 Shea Hillenbrand .25
62 Aramis Ramirez .25
63 Aaron Boone .25
64 Roberto Alomar .50
65 Rickey Henderson .50

Team Heroes
Common Player (541-548): .25
Team Heroes Glossy: 1-2X
541 *Rickie Weeks* 2.00
542 *Hideki Matsui* 1.50
543 Ramon Nivar .25
544 *Adam Loewen* .50
545 *Brandon Webb* .50
546 Dan Haren .25
547 *Delmon Young* 2.00
548 *Ryan Wagner* .25

Champions
Common Player (302-309): .25
Metalized: 4-8X
Production 100
302 *Ryan Wagner* .25
303 *Adam Loewen* .50
304 Chien-Ming Wang .25
305 Hong-Chih Kuo .25
306 *Delmon Young* 2.00
307 Dan Haren .25
308 *Rickie Weeks* 2.00
309 Ramon Nivar .25

Leaf
Common Player (321-329): .25
Leaf Red Press Proofs: 4-8X
Production 100
Leaf Blue Press Proofs: 5-10X
Production 50
321 *Hideki Matsui* 1.50
322 Ramon Nivar 1.50
323 *Adam Loewen* .50
324 *Brandon Webb* .50
325 Chien-Ming Wang 2.00
326 *Delmon Young* 2.00
327 *Ryan Wagner* .25
328 Dan Haren .25
329 *Rickie Weeks* 2.00

Playoff Prestige .25
Common Player (201-210):
Prestige X-Tra Points: 5-10X
Production 50
201 Jeremy Bonderman .50
202 *Brandon Webb* .50
203 *Adam Loewen* .50
204 Chien-Ming Wang .25
205 Hong-Chih Kuo .25
206 *Delmon Young* 2.00
207 *Ryan Wagner* .25
208 Dan Haren .25
209 *Rickie Weeks* 2.00
210 Ramon Nivar .25

Classics
Common Player (201-211): 4.00
Production 1,000
Classics Timeless Tributes: .75-1.5X
Production 100
201 Jeremy Bonderman 4.00
202 *Adam Loewen* 6.00
203 Chien-Ming Wang 4.00
204 Hong-Chih Kuo 4.00
205 *Ryan Wagner* 4.00
206 Dan Haren 4.00
207 Dontrelle Willis 4.00
208 *Rickie Weeks* 10.00
209 Ramon Nivar 4.00
210 *Chad Gaudin* 4.00
211 *Delmon Young* 10.00

Studio
Common Player (201-211): 3.00
Production 1,500
Studio Proof: 1-1.5X
Production 100
201 *Adam Loewen* 5.00
202 Jeremy Bonderman 3.00
203 *Brandon Webb* 5.00
204 Chien-Ming Wang 3.00
205 *Chad Gaudin* 3.00
206 *Ryan Wagner* 3.00
207 Hong-Chih Kuo 3.00
208 Dan Haren 3.00
209 *Rickie Weeks* 10.00
210 Ramon Nivar 3.00
211 *Delmon Young* 12.00

Diamond Kings
Common Player (177-201): 3.00
Inserted 1:30
DK Portraits Bronze: .5-1X
DK Portraits Silver: 1-1.5X
Production 100
DK Portraits Gold: 1-2X
Production 50
177 *Hideki Matsui* 6.00
178 *Jeremy Bonderman* 4.00
179 *Brandon Webb* 4.00
180 *Adam Loewen* 4.00
181 Chien-Ming Wang 4.00
182 Hong-Chih Kuo 3.00
183 *Clint Barmes* 3.00
184 *Guillermo Quiroz* 5.00
185 *Edgar Gonzalez* 3.00
186 *Todd Wellemeyer* 3.00
187 Dan Haren 3.00
188 Dustin McGowan 3.00
189 Preston Larrison 3.00
191 Kevin Youkilis 8.00
192 Bubba Nelson 3.00
193 Chris Burke 3.00
194 J.D. Durbin 4.00
195 Ryan Howard 10.00
196 Jason Kubel 8.00
197 Brendan Harris 4.00
198 Brian Bruney 3.00
199 Ramon Nivar 3.00
200 *Rickie Weeks* 10.00
201 *Delmon Young* 12.00

Leaf Certified Materials
Mirror Red Signature: .75-1.5X
Production 100 or 50
Mirror Blue Signature: 1-1.5X
Mirror Gold Signature: No Pricing
Mirror Emerald Signature: No Pricing
Mirror Reds: .2-.4X
Production 100
Mirror Blues: .4-.6X
Production 50
Mirror Golds: No Pricing
Production 25
251 *Adam Loewen/auto/250* 15.00
252 Dan Haren/auto/250 15.00
253 Dontrelle Willis/auto/150 25.00
254 Ramon Nivar/auto/250 10.00
255 Chad Gaudin/auto/250 10.00
256 *Kevin Correia/auto/250* 10.00
257 *Rickie Weeks/auto/100* 100.00
258 *Ryan Wagner/auto/250* 15.00
259 *Delmon Young/auto/100* 150.00

Playoff Absolute
Common Player (201-208): 4.00
Production 1,000
Spectrum: 1-2X
Production 100
201 *Adam Loewen* 4.00
202 Ramon Nivar 4.00
203 Dan Haren 4.00
204 Dontrelle Willis 4.00
205 Chad Gaudin 4.00
206 *Rickie Weeks* 10.00
207 *Ryan Wagner* 4.00
208 *Delmon Young* 8.00

Elite Extra Edition
Common Player (1-58): 4.00
Production 900
Elite Status: 1-3X
Numbered to Jersey Number
Elite Aspirations: 1-2X
Varying quantities produced
Turn of Century non-Auto: 1-2X
Production 100
Elite Gold Status: No Pricing
Production 24
1 *Adam Loewen* 4.00
2 *Brandon Webb* 4.00
3 Chien-Ming Wang 12.00
4 Hong-Chih Kuo 4.00
5 *Clint Barmes* 15.00
6 *Guillermo Quiroz* 3.00
7 *Edgar Gonzalez* 4.00
8 *Todd Wellemeyer* 4.00
9 *Alfredo Gonzalez* 3.00
10 *Craig Brazell* 5.00
11 *Tim Olson* 4.00
12 Rich Fischer 5.00
13 *Daniel Cabrera* 5.00
14 *Francisco Rosario* 4.00
15 *Francisco Cruceta* 4.00
16 Alejandro Machado 4.00
17 *Andrew Brown* 4.00
18 *Rob Hammock* 4.00
19 Arnie Munoz 4.00
20 Felix Sanchez 4.00
21 *Nook Logan* 4.00
22 Cory Stewart 4.00
23 *Michel Hernandez* 4.00
24 *Rett Johnson* 4.00
25 *Josh Hall* 4.00
26 Doug Waechter 4.00
27 *Matt Kata* 5.00
28 Dan Haren 4.00
29 Dontrelle Willis 4.00
30 Ramon Nivar 4.00
31 *Chad Gaudin* 4.00
32 *Rickie Weeks* 15.00
33 *Ryan Wagner* 4.00
34 *Kevin Correia* 4.00
35 *Bo Hart* 4.00
36 *Oscar Villarreal* 4.00
37 *Josh Willingham* 6.00
38 *Jeff Duncan* 6.00
39 *David DeJesus* 6.00
40 Dustin McGowan 4.00
41 Preston Larrison 4.00
43 Kevin Youkilis 8.00
44 Bubba Nelson 4.00
45 Chris Burke 6.00
46 J.D. Durbin 4.00
47 Ryan Howard 10.00
48 Jason Kubel 8.00
49 Brendan Harris 4.00
50 Brian Bruney 4.00
52 Byron Gettis 4.00
53 *Edwin Jackson* 8.00
55 Daniel Garcia 4.00
57 *Chad Cordero* 4.00
58 *Delmon Young* 12.00

Common Leaf Limited Phenom.
Silver Spotlights: 1X
Production 50
Gold Spotlights: No Pricing
Production 10 or 25
201 *Delmon Young/auto/99* 200.00
202 *Rickie Weeks/auto/99* 140.00
203 *Edwin Jackson/auto/99* 25.00
204 Dan Haren/auto/99 30.00
Signature Series:
151 *Delmon Young/auto/200* 70.00
152 *Rickie Weeks/auto/200* 65.00
153 Edwin Jackson/auto/200 25.00

Stat Line Season/Career

NM/M
Cards serial #'d from 101-150: 1-2X
Cards serial #'d from 50-100: 2-3X
Cards serial #'d from 26-49: 3-4X
Cards numbered under 25 not priced

Autographs

NM/M
Common Autograph: 5.00
1 Jeremy Bonderman/50 50.00
2 Adam Loewen/500 15.00
3 Dan Haren/100 20.00

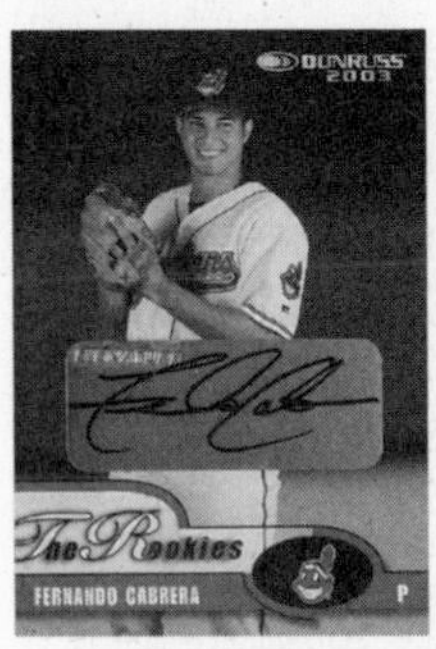

4 Jose Contreras/100 25.00
6 Arnie Munoz/584 5.00
7 Miguel Cabrera/50 50.00
8 Andrew Brown/584 5.00
9 Josh Hall/1000 10.00
10 Josh Stewart/300 5.00
11 Clint Barmes/129 35.00
12 Luis Ayala/1000 5.00
13 Brandon Webb/100 20.00
14 Greg Aquino/1000 5.00
15 Chien-Ming Wang/100 100.00
16 Rickie Weeks/10
17 Edgar Gonzalez/400 5.00
18 Dontrelle Willis/25
19 Bo Hart/150 10.00
20 Rosman Garcia/250 5.00
21 Jeremy Griffiths/812 8.00
22 Craig Brazell/205 10.00
23 Daniel Cabrera/383 35.00
24 Fernando Cabrera/1000 5.00
25 Terrmel Sledge/250 10.00
26 Ramon Nivar/100 10.00
27 Rob Hammock/201 10.00
28 Francisco Rosario/25
29 Cory Stewart/1000 5.00
30 Felix Sanchez/1000 5.00
31 Jorge Cordova/1000 5.00
32 Rocco Baldelli/25
33 Beau Kemp/1000 5.00
34 Micheal Nakamura/1000 5.00
35 Rett Johnson/1000 8.00
36 Guillermo Quiroz/90 15.00
37 Hong-Chih Kuo/50 20.00
38 Ian Ferguson/1000 5.00
39 Franklin Perez/1000 5.00
40 Tim Olson/150 8.00
41 Jerome Williams/50 20.00
42 Rich Fischer/734 5.00
43 Phil Seibel/1000 5.00
44 Aaron Looper/513 5.00
45 Jae Weong Seo/50 30.00
46 Chad Gaudin/19
47 Matt Kata/203 10.00
48 Ryan Wagner/100 15.00
49 Michel Hernandez/41
50 Diegomar Markwell/1000 5.00
51 Doug Waechter/583 10.00
52 Mike Nicolas/1000 5.00
53 Prentice Redman/425 5.00
54 Shane Bazell/1000 5.00
55 Delmon Young/75 85.00
56 Brian Stokes/1000 5.00
57 Matt Bruback/513 5.00
58 Nook Logan/150 5.00
59 Oscar Villarreal/150 8.00
60 Pete LaForest/250 8.00

Gamers

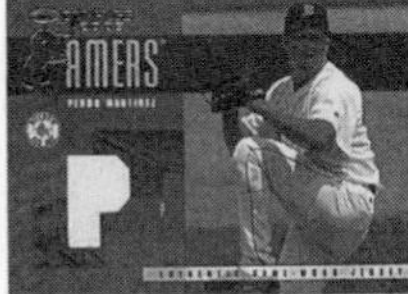

NM/M

Common Player: 4.00
Production 500
Position: 1-2X
Production 100
Number: 1-2X
Production 100
Patch: No Pricing
Production 25
Rewards: No Pricing
Production 10

1 Nomar Garciaparra 8.00
2 Alex Rodriguez 8.00
3 Mike Piazza 8.00
4 Greg Maddux 8.00
5 Roger Clemens 10.00
6 Sammy Sosa 8.00
7 Randy Johnson 6.00
8 Albert Pujols 12.00
9 Alfonso Soriano 8.00
10 Chipper Jones 8.00
11 Mark Prior 10.00
12 Hideo Nomo 6.00
13 Adam Dunn 5.00
14 Juan Gonzalez 5.00
15 Vladimir Guerrero 6.00
16 Pedro J. Martinez 6.00
17 Jim Thome 6.00
18 Brandon Webb/200 6.00
19 Mike Mussina 6.00
20 Mark Teixeira 5.00
21 Barry Larkin 5.00
22 Ivan Rodriguez 6.00
23 Hank Blalock 6.00
24 Rafael Palmeiro 6.00
25 Curt Schilling 6.00
26 Troy Glaus 5.00
27 Bernie Williams 6.00
28 Scott Rolen 6.00
29 Torii Hunter 5.00
30 Nick Johnson 4.00
31 Kazuhisa Ishii 4.00
32 Shawn Green 5.00
33 Jeff Bagwell 6.00
34 Lance Berkman 4.00
35 Roy Oswalt 4.00
36 Kerry Wood 8.00
37 Todd Helton 6.00
38 Manny Ramirez 8.00
39 Andruw Jones 5.00
40 Frank Thomas 8.00
41 Gary Sheffield 5.00
42 Magglio Ordonez 5.00
43 Mike Sweeney 4.00
44 Carlos Beltran 6.00
45 Richie Sexson 5.00
46 Jeff Kent 5.00
47 Carlos Delgado 5.00
48 Vernon Wells 4.00
49 Dontrelle Willis 8.00
50 Jae Weong Seo 4.00

Gamers Autograph

NM/M

Production 5-50 4.00
Many not priced due to scarcity
20 Mark Teixeira/50 30.00
23 Hank Blalock/50 30.00
29 Torii Hunter/50 20.00
35 Roy Oswalt/50 20.00
43 Mike Sweeney/50 15.00
48 Vernon Wells/30 20.00
49 Dontrelle Willis/50 25.00

Leaf Autographs

NM/M

Common Autograph:
304 Jose Contreras/100 25.00
322 Ramon Nivar/100 15.00
323 Adam Loewen/100 10.00
324 Brandon Webb/100 20.00
325 Chien-Ming Wang/50 65.00
326 Delmon Young/25
327 Ryan Wagner/100 10.00
328 Dan Haren/100 20.00
329 Rickie Weeks/10

Playoff Prestige Autograph

NM/M

Quantity produced listed
201 Jeremy Bonderman/100 40.00
202 Brandon Webb/100 15.00
203 Adam Loewen/100 10.00
204 Chien-Ming Wang/50 75.00
205 Hong-Chih Kuo/100 25.00
207 Ryan Wagner/100 10.00
208 Dan Haren/100 15.00
210 Ramon Nivar/100 15.00

Recollection Autographs

NM/M

7 Jack McDowell 88/75 20.00

Turn of the Century Autograph

NM/M

Common Player: 10.00
Production 100
Aspirations: .75X-1.5X
Varying quantities produced
1 Adam Loewen 15.00
2 Brandon Webb 25.00
3 Chien-Ming Wang 135.00
4 Hong-Chih Kuo 40.00
5 Clint Barmes 50.00
6 Guillermo Quiroz 20.00
7 Edgar Gonzalez 10.00
8 Todd Wellemeyer 10.00
9 Alfredo Gonzalez 10.00
10 Craig Brazell 15.00
11 Tim Olson 10.00
12 Rich Fischer 10.00
13 Daniel Cabrera 25.00
14 Francisco Rosario 10.00
15 Francisco Cruceta 10.00
16 Alejandro Machado 10.00
17 Andrew Brown 10.00
18 Rob Hammock 15.00
19 Arnie Munoz 10.00
20 Felix Sanchez 10.00
21 Nook Logan 15.00
22 Cory Stewart 10.00
23 Michel Hernandez 10.00
24 Rett Johnson 10.00
25 Josh Hall 15.00
26 Doug Waechter 15.00
27 Matt Kata 15.00
28 Dan Haren 40.00
29 Dontrelle Willis/25 60.00
30 Ramon Nivar 15.00
31 Chad Gaudin 10.00
32 Rickie Weeks/25 40.00
33 Ryan Wagner 15.00
34 Kevin Correia/25
35 Bo Hart 15.00
36 Oscar Villarreal 10.00
37 Josh Willingham 15.00
38 Jeff Duncan 15.00
40 Dustin McGowan 20.00
41 Preston Larrison 10.00
43 Kevin Youkilis 30.00
44 Bubba Nelson 15.00
45 Chris Burke 50.00
46 J.D. Durbin 15.00
47 Ryan Howard 125.00
48 Jason Kubel 25.00
49 Brendan Harris 15.00
50 Brian Bruney 10.00
52 Byron Gettis 10.00
53 Edwin Jackson 20.00
55 Daniel Garcia 10.00
58 Delmon Young 170.00

2003 DONRUSS SIGNATURE SERIES

NM/M

Complete Set (150): 150.00
Common Player: .50
Common Rk (101-150): 1.00
Inserted 1:tin
Tin: 35.00
1 Garret Anderson .75
2 Tim Salmon .75
3 Troy Glaus .75
4 Curt Schilling 1.00
5 Luis Gonzalez .75
6 Mark Grace .75
7 Matt Williams .50
8 Randy Johnson 1.50
9 Andruw Jones 1.00
10 Chipper Jones 1.50
11 Gary Sheffield .75
12 Greg Maddux 2.00
13 Johnny Damon .75
14 Manny Ramirez 1.00
15 Nomar Garciaparra 2.50
16 Pedro J. Martinez 1.50
17 Corey Patterson .75
18 Kerry Wood 1.50
19 Mark Prior 2.00
20 Sammy Sosa 2.50
21 Bartolo Colon .50
22 Frank Thomas 1.00
23 Magglio Ordonez .50
24 Paul Konerko .50
25 Adam Dunn 1.00
26 Austin Kearns .75
27 Barry Larkin .75
28 Ken Griffey Jr. 2.00
29 C.C. Sabathia .50
30 Omar Vizquel .50
31 Larry Walker .50
32 Todd Helton 1.00
33 Ivan Rodriguez 1.00
34 Josh Beckett .75
35 Craig Biggio .75
36 Jeff Bagwell 1.00
37 Jeff Kent .50
38 Lance Berkman .75
39 Richard Hidalgo .50
40 Roy Oswalt .75
41 Carlos Beltran 1.00
42 Mike Sweeney .50
43 Runelvys Hernandez .50
44 Hideo Nomo .75
45 Kazuhisa Ishii .50
46 Paul LoDuca .50
47 Shawn Green .75
48 Ben Sheets .75
49 Richie Sexson .75
50 A.J. Pierzynski .50
51 Torii Hunter .75
52 Javier Vazquez .50
53 Jose Vidro .50
54 Vladimir Guerrero 1.50
55 Cliff Floyd .50
56 David Cone .50
57 Mike Piazza 2.00
58 Roberto Alomar .75
59 Tom Glavine .75
60 Alfonso Soriano 1.50
61 Derek Jeter 4.00
62 Drew Henson .50
63 Jason Giambi .75
64 Mike Mussina 1.00
65 Nick Johnson .50
66 Roger Clemens 3.00
67 Barry Zito .75
68 Eric Chavez .75
69 Mark Mulder .75
70 Miguel Tejada .75
71 Tim Hudson .75
72 Bobby Abreu .75
73 Jim Thome 1.00
74 Kevin Millwood .50
75 Pat Burrell .50
76 Brian Giles .50
77 Jason Kendall .50
78 Kenny Lofton .50
79 Phil Nevin .50
80 Ryan Klesko .50
81 Andres Galarraga .50
82 Barry Bonds 4.00
83 Rich Aurilia .50
84 Edgar Martinez .50
85 Freddy Garcia .50
86 Ichiro Suzuki 2.50
87 Albert Pujols 3.00
88 Jim Edmonds .75
89 Scott Rolen 1.50
90 So Taguchi .50
91 Rocco Baldelli .50
92 Alex Rodriguez 3.00
93 Hank Blalock 1.00
94 Juan Gonzalez 1.00
95 Mark Teixeira .75
96 Rafael Palmeiro 1.00
97 Carlos Delgado 1.00
98 Eric Hinske .50
99 Roy Halladay .75
100 Vernon Wells .50
101 *Hideki Matsui* 10.00
102 *Jose Contreras* 3.00
103 Jeremy Bonderman 2.00
104 *Bernie Castro* 1.00
105 *Alfredo Gonzalez* 1.00
106 *Arnie Munoz* 1.00
107 *Andrew Brown* 1.50
108 *Josh Hall* 1.50
109 *Josh Stewart* 1.50
110 *Clint Barmes* 1.50
111 *Brandon Webb* 2.00
112 *Chien-Ming Wang* 5.00
113 *Edgar Gonzalez* 1.00
114 *Alejandro Machado* 1.00
115 Jeremy Griffiths 1.00
116 *Craig Brazell* 1.50
117 *Shane Bazell* 1.50
118 *Fernando Cabrera* 1.50
119 *Terrmel Sledge* 1.50
120 *Rob Hammock* 1.50
121 *Francisco Rosario* 1.50
122 *Francisco Cruceta* 1.50
123 *Rett Johnson* 1.50
124 *Guillermo Quiroz* 2.00
125 *Hong-Chih Kuo* 2.00
126 *Ian Ferguson* 1.50
127 *Tim Olson* 1.00
128 *Todd Wellemeyer* 1.50
129 *Richard Fischer* 1.00
130 *Phil Seibel* 1.00
131 *Joe Valentine* 1.00
132 *Matt Kata* 1.50
133 *Michael Hessman* 1.00
134 *Michel Hernandez* 1.00

135 *Doug Waechter* 1.50
136 *Prentice Redman* 1.50
137 *Nook Logan* 1.00
138 *Oscar Villarreal* 1.00
139 *Pete LaForest* 1.00
140 *Matt Bruback* 1.00
141 Dontrelle Willis 1.50
142 *Greg Aquino* 1.00
143 *Lew Ford* 4.00
144 *Jeff Duncan* 2.00
145 Dan Haren 1.50
146 *Miguel Ojeda* 1.00
147 *Rosman Garcia* 1.00
148 *Felix Sanchez* 1.00
149 *Jon Leicester* 1.00
150 *Roger Deago* 1.00

Century Proofs

Stars (1-100): 2-4X
Century (101-150): 1-2X
Production 100 sets

Decade Proofs

Production 10 sets
No pricing due to scarcity

Autographs

NM/M
Common Auto: 8.00
Some not priced due to scarcity
1 Garret Anderson 15.00
6 Mark Grace/141 50.00
7 Matt Williams 10.00
8 Randy Johnson/50 60.00
10 Chipper Jones/50 45.00
12 Greg Maddux/25
14 Manny Ramirez/50 40.00
16 Pedro J. Martinez/5
17 Barry Larkin/159 25.00
32 Todd Helton/5
33 Ivan Rodriguez/50 35.00
36 Jeff Bagwell/25
38 Lance Berkman/75 15.00
39 Richard Hidalgo 8.00
40 Roy Oswalt/150 15.00
42 Mike Sweeney 8.00
44 Hideo Nomo/25
45 Kazuhisa Ishii/25
50 A.J. Pierzynski 8.00
51 Torii Hunter 10.00
53 Jose Vidro 6.00
54 Vladimir Guerrero 20.00
55 Cliff Floyd 8.00
56 David Cone/35 20.00
57 Mike Piazza/5
58 Roberto Alomar/50 40.00
62 Drew Henson/28
64 Mike Mussina/5
65 Nick Johnson 10.00
67 Barry Zito/150 15.00
68 Eric Chavez 10.00
69 Mark Mulder/50 20.00
72 Bobby Abreu 10.00
78 Kenny Lofton/229 10.00
80 Ryan Klesko/150 10.00
81 Andres Galarraga 8.00
83 Rich Aurilia/122 8.00
84 Edgar Martinez 15.00
88 Jim Edmonds/25
89 Scott Rolen/200 25.00
90 So Taguchi/220 10.00
92 Alex Rodriguez/25
95 Mark Teixeira/150 20.00
96 Rafael Palmeiro/25
100 Vernon Wells 10.00
102 Jose Contreras 20.00
141 Dontrelle Willis/150 25.00

Authentic Cuts

Quantity produced listed
1 Ty Cobb/3
2 Babe Ruth/1
3 Lou Gehrig/1

Century

NM/M
Common Auto: 15.00
Production 100 sets
Decades: Not Priced
Production 10 sets
1 Garret Anderson 15.00
7 Matt Williams 15.00
27 Barry Larkin 30.00
39 Richard Hidalgo 15.00
42 Mike Sweeney 15.00
50 A.J. Pierzynski 15.00
51 Torii Hunter 20.00
53 Jose Vidro 15.00
54 Vladimir Guerrero 30.00
55 Cliff Floyd 15.00
62 Drew Henson 15.00
65 Nick Johnson 15.00
69 Mark Mulder 25.00
72 Bobby Abreu 20.00
78 Kenny Lofton 15.00
81 Andres Galarraga 15.00
84 Edgar Martinez 25.00
89 Scott Rolen 30.00
90 So Taguchi 15.00
100 Vernon Wells 15.00
102 Jose Contreras 25.00

Century Notations

NM/M
Production 100 sets
Decade Notations: No Pricing
Production 10 sets
1 Garret Anderson 20.00
7 Matt Williams 15.00
50 A.J. Pierzynski 15.00
68 Eric Chavez 15.00
78 Kenny Lofton 15.00
84 Edgar Martinez 25.00

INKredible - Three

NM/M
Production 50 sets
1 Barry Zito, Mark Mulder, Tim Hudson 300.00
2 Andruw Jones, Chipper Jones, Greg Maddux 325.00
3 Ernie Banks, Kerry Wood, Mark Prior 300.00
4 Harmon Killebrew, Kirby Puckett, Torii Hunter 175.00
5 Javier Vazquez, Jose Vidro, Vladimir Guerrero 90.00

INKredible - Six

NM/M
Production 10 sets
Limited pricing due to scarcity
3 Andre Dawson, Ernie Banks, Kerry Wood, Mark Grace, Mark Prior, Ryne Sandberg 1,500
5 Alex Rodriguez, Don Mattingly, George Brett, Hideo Nomo, Nolan Ryan, Roger Clemens 3,100

INKredible - Four

NM/M
Production 25 sets
Limited pricing due to scarcity
4 Brooks Robinson, Cal Ripken Jr., Frank Robinson, Jim Palmer 500.00
6 Bo Jackson, Carlos Beltran, George Brett, Mike Sweeney 225.00
7 Curt Schilling, Junior Spivey, Mark Grace, Randy Johnson 475.00
10 Joe Carter, Roberto Alomar, Ryan Klesko, Tony Gwynn 200.00

Legends of Summer Auto.

NM/M
Common Autograph:
1 Al Kaline 20.00
2 Alan Trammell 10.00
3 Andre Dawson 10.00
5 Billy Williams 8.00
6 Bo Jackson/100 50.00
7 Bob Feller 15.00
8 Bobby Doerr 15.00
9 Brooks Robinson 25.00
10 Dale Murphy/75 40.00
11 Dennis Eckersley 10.00
12 Don Mattingly/50 75.00
13 Duke Snider/225 20.00
14 Eric Davis 8.00
15 Frank Robinson 10.00
16 Fred Lynn 8.00
17 Gary Carter 10.00
18 Harmon Killebrew/171 20.00
19 Jack Morris 8.00
20 Jim Palmer 10.00
21 Jim Abbott 8.00
22 Joe Morgan/125 15.00
23 Joe Torre 10.00
24 Johnny Bench/75 30.00
25 Jose Canseco/75 30.00
26 Kirby Puckett/75 35.00
27 Lenny Dykstra 10.00
28 Lou Brock 15.00
29 Ralph Kiner 10.00
30 Mike Schmidt/75 60.00
31 Nolan Ryan/75 110.00
33 Orel Hershiser 20.00
34 Phil Rizzuto 15.00
35 Orlando Cepeda 15.00
36 Ryne Sandberg/75 60.00
37 Stan Musial/200 40.00
38 Steve Garvey 10.00
39 Tony Perez 10.00

Legends of Summer

NM/M
Complete Set (40): 125.00
Common Player: 3.00
Production 250 sets
Century: 1X
Production 100 sets
Decades: No Pricing
Production 10 sets
1 Al Kaline 5.00
2 Alan Trammell 3.00
3 Andre Dawson 3.00
4 Babe Ruth 10.00
5 Billy Williams 3.00
6 Bo Jackson 4.00
7 Bob Feller 3.00
8 Bobby Doerr 3.00
9 Brooks Robinson 5.00
10 Dale Murphy 5.00
11 Dennis Eckersley 3.00
12 Don Mattingly 8.00
13 Duke Snider 3.00
14 Eric Davis 3.00
15 Frank Robinson 3.00
16 Fred Lynn 3.00
17 Gary Carter 3.00
18 Harmon Killebrew 5.00
19 Jack Morris 3.00
20 Jim Palmer 3.00
21 Jim Abbott 3.00
22 Joe Morgan 3.00
23 Joe Torre 3.00
24 Johnny Bench 5.00
25 Jose Canseco 3.00
26 Kirby Puckett 5.00
27 Lenny Dykstra 3.00
28 Lou Brock 3.00
29 Ralph Kiner 3.00
30 Mike Schmidt 6.00
31 Nolan Ryan 10.00
32 Nolan Ryan 10.00
33 Orel Hershiser 3.00
34 Phil Rizzuto 3.00
35 Orlando Cepeda 3.00
36 Ryne Sandberg 8.00
37 Stan Musial 6.00
38 Steve Garvey 3.00
39 Tony Perez 3.00
40 Ty Cobb 6.00

Legends of Summer Century

NM/M
Production 100 sets
Decades: No Pricing
Production 10 sets
1 Al Kaline 25.00
2 Alan Trammell 20.00
3 Andre Dawson 15.00
5 Billy Williams 15.00
6 Bo Jackson 50.00
7 Bob Feller 25.00
8 Bobby Doerr 20.00
9 Brooks Robinson 30.00
11 Dennis Eckersley 15.00
12 Don Mattingly 65.00
14 Eric Davis 15.00
15 Frank Robinson 15.00
16 Fred Lynn 15.00
17 Gary Carter 20.00
19 Jack Morris 15.00
20 Jim Palmer 20.00
21 Jim Abbott 15.00
23 Joe Torre 15.00
27 Lenny Dykstra 15.00
28 Lou Brock 25.00
29 Ralph Kiner 15.00
33 Orel Hershiser 60.00
34 Phil Rizzuto 30.00
35 Orlando Cepeda 20.00
36 Ryne Sandberg 65.00
37 Stan Musial 60.00
38 Steve Garvey 15.00
39 Tony Perez 15.00

Legends of Summer Notations

NM/M
Common Autograph: 8.00
1 Al Kaline/200 20.00
2 Alan Trammell/250 10.00
3 Andre Dawson/165 10.00
3 Andre Dawson/250 10.00
5 Billy Williams/250 8.00
5 Billy Williams/150 8.00
7 Bob Feller/250 15.00
7 Bob Feller/200 15.00
8 Bobby Doerr/250 10.00
9 Brooks Robinson/150 20.00
9 Brooks Robinson/50 40.00
10 Dale Murphy/50 45.00
11 Dennis Eckersley/250 10.00
14 Eric Davis/250 8.00
14 Eric Davis/150 8.00
14 Eric Davis/200 8.00
16 Fred Lynn/240 10.00
16 Fred Lynn/250 10.00
18 Harmon Killebrew/75 40.00
18 Harmon Killebrew/50 40.00
18 Harmon Killebrew/125 30.00
19 Jack Morris/250 10.00
20 Jim Palmer/190 10.00
20 Jim Palmer/140 10.00
20 Jim Palmer/50 20.00
21 Jim Abbott/200 10.00
21 Jim Abbott/100 15.00
21 Jim Abbott/75 15.00
21 Jim Abbott/50 20.00
27 Lenny Dykstra/226 10.00
28 Lou Brock/50 35.00
29 Ralph Kiner/200 15.00
29 Ralph Kiner/100 15.00
29 Ralph Kiner/150 15.00
35 Orlando Cepeda/75 35.00
35 Orlando Cepeda/40 25.00
38 Steve Garvey/150 10.00
38 Steve Garvey/50 20.00
38 Steve Garvey/75 15.00
39 Tony Perez/250 10.00
39 Tony Perez/125 15.00
39 Tony Perez/75 20.00
39 Tony Perez/175 10.00

Notable Nicknames Auto.

NM/M
Quantity produced listed
Decades: No Pricing
Production 10 sets
1 Andre “The Hawk” Dawson/100 30.00
2 Torii “Spiderman” Hunter/100 30.00
3 Brooks “Hoover” Robinson 60.00
4 Carlton “Pudge” Fisk/100 50.00
5 Mike “Moose” Mussina/100 80.00
6 Don “Donnie Baseball” Mattingly/100 100.00
7 Duke “Duke of Flatbush” Snider/100 60.00
8 Eric “The Red” Davis/40 50.00
9 Frank “The Big Hurt” Thomas/100 60.00
10 Randy “Big Unit” Johnson/100 100.00
11 Lenny “Nails” Dykstra/100 20.00
12 Ivan “Pudge” Rodriguez/75 50.00
13 Nolan “The Ryan Express” Ryan/15
14 Phil “Scooter” Rizzuto/100 50.00
15 Reggie “Mr. October” Jackson/100 60.00
16 Roger “The Rocket” Clemens/100 150.00
17 Ryne “Ryno” Sandberg/100 75.00
18 Stan “The Man” Musial/100 85.00
19 Luis “Gonzo” Gonzalez/100 25.00
20 Will “The Thrill” Clark/100 60.00

Notable Nicknames

	NM/M
Complete Set (20):	75.00
Common Player:	3.00
Production 750 sets	
Century:	1-1.5X
Production 100 sets	
Decade:	No Pricing
Production 10 sets	

1	Andre Dawson	3.00
2	Torii Hunter	3.00
3	Brooks Robinson	5.00
4	Carlton Fisk	3.00
5	Mike Mussina	4.00
6	Don Mattingly	8.00
7	Duke Snider	4.00
8	Eric Davis	3.00
9	Frank Thomas	4.00
10	Randy Johnson	5.00
11	Lenny Dykstra	3.00
12	Ivan Rodriguez	3.00
13	Nolan Ryan	10.00
14	Phil Rizzuto	3.00
15	Reggie Jackson	4.00
16	Roger Clemens	8.00
17	Ryne Sandberg	8.00
18	Stan Musial	6.00
19	Luis Gonzalez	3.00
20	Will Clark	4.00

Notations

NM/M

Varying quantities produced
Many not priced due to scarcity

1	Garret Anderson/75	20.00
7	Matt Williams/250	10.00
7	Matt Williams/50	20.00
45	Kazuhisa Ishii/35	35.00
50	A.J. Pierzynski/200	10.00
53	Jose Vidro/40	15.00
62	Drew Henson/73	20.00
68	Eric Chavez/50	20.00
78	Kenny Lofton/150	10.00
80	Ryan Klesko/75	20.00
83	Rich Aurilia/61	15.00
84	Edgar Martinez/250	10.00
84	Edgar Martinez/60	20.00
100	Vernon Wells/75	15.00

Players Collection Auto.

NM/M

Quantity produced listed

Roberto Alomar/75	30.00
Adrian Beltre/104	30.00
Lance Berkman/50	20.00
Craig Biggio/26	35.00
Joe Borchard/53	10.00
J.D. Drew/52	20.00
Jim Edmonds/52	25.00
Todd Helton/50	40.00
Jason Jennings/49	10.00
Chipper Jones/51	50.00
Paul LoDuca/227	8.00
Magglio Ordonez/102	20.00
Mark Prior/27	100.00
Ivan Rodriguez/52	35.00
Richie Sexson/50	20.00
Matt Williams/482	8.00

Signature Cuts

NM/M

Some not priced due to scarcity
Decades: No Pricing
Production 10 sets

4	Curt Schilling/7	
8	Randy Johnson/40	60.00
10	Chipper Jones/9	
33	Ivan Rodriguez/122	30.00
54	Vladimir Guerrero/34	35.00
58	Roberto Alomar/100	30.00
59	Tom Glavine/9	
64	Mike Mussina/82	40.00
66	Roger Clemens/9	
73	Jim Thome/127	30.00
80	Ryan Klesko/35	20.00
81	Andres Galarraga/51	20.00
89	Scott Rolen/36	40.00
94	Juan Gonzalez/9	
96	Rafael Palmeiro/13	

Team Trademarks Autograph

NM/M

Quantity produced listed

1	Adam Dunn/50	35.00
2	Andre Dawson/250	10.00
5	Brooks Robinson/250	20.00
6	Cal Ripken Jr./50	200.00
8	Don Mattingly/75	85.00

10	Fred Lynn/250	8.00
11	Gary Carter/250	10.00
12	George Brett/50	100.00
13	Greg Maddux/50	85.00
16	Jose Contreras/250	15.00
17	Kerry Wood/50	40.00
19	Magglio Ordonez/75	15.00
20	Mark Grace/25	90.00
23	Nolan Ryan/50	110.00
24	Reggie Jackson/75	25.00
25	Rickey Henderson/50	100.00
27	Roger Clemens/50	110.00
28	Roger Clemens/50	110.00
29	Ryne Sandberg/100	60.00
31	Stan Musial/200	50.00
32	Steve Carlton/150	20.00
33	Tim Hudson/100	35.00
34	Tom Glavine/50	35.00
35	Tom Seaver/50	35.00
36	Tony Gwynn/50	60.00
37	Torii Hunter/250	10.00
39	Vladimir Guerrero/250	20.00
40	Will Clark/125	30.00

Team Trademarks Notations

NM/M

Quantity produced listed

2	Andre Dawson/250	10.00
2	Andre Dawson/150	10.00
5	Brooks Robinson/75	35.00
5	Brooks Robinson/125	30.00
10	Fred Lynn/50	20.00
11	Gary Carter/25	
12	George Brett/25	
15	Jim Palmer/32	25.00
15	Jim Palmer/128	15.00
15	Jim Palmer/150	15.00
17	Kerry Wood/25	
24	Reggie Jackson/20	
24	Reggie Jackson/5	
29	Ryne Sandberg/5	
29	Ryne Sandberg/40	80.00
29	Ryne Sandberg/55	75.00
32	Steve Carlton/50	35.00
33	Tim Hudson/5	
33	Tim Hudson/50	45.00
37	Torii Hunter/20	
40	Will Clark/52	60.00

Team Trademarks Century

NM/M

Production 100 sets
Decade: No Pricing
Production 10 sets

2	Andre Dawson	15.00
5	Brooks Robinson	30.00
9	Frank Robinson	15.00
10	Fred Lynn	15.00
11	Gary Carter	20.00
15	Jim Palmer	15.00
16	Jose Contreras	25.00
20	Mark Grace	60.00
29	Ryne Sandberg	65.00
31	Stan Musial	65.00
32	Steve Carlton	25.00
34	Tom Glavine	25.00
37	Steve Hunter	15.00
39	Vladimir Guerrero	25.00

Team Trademarks

	NM/M
Complete Set (40):	150.00
Common Player:	3.00
Production 100 sets	
Century:	1X
Production 100 sets	
Decade:	No Pricing
Production 10 sets	

1	Adam Dunn	3.00
2	Andre Dawson	3.00
3	Babe Ruth	10.00
4	Barry Bonds	10.00
5	Brooks Robinson	4.00
6	Cal Ripken Jr.	10.00
7	Derek Jeter	8.00
8	Don Mattingly	8.00
9	Frank Robinson	3.00
10	Fred Lynn	3.00
11	Gary Carter	3.00
12	George Brett	6.00
13	Greg Maddux	5.00
14	Ichiro Suzuki	6.00
15	Jim Palmer	3.00
16	Jose Contreras	3.00
17	Kerry Wood	4.00
18	Lou Gehrig	8.00
19	Magglio Ordonez	3.00
20	Mark Grace	3.00
21	Mike Schmidt	8.00
22	Nolan Ryan	10.00
23	Nolan Ryan	10.00
24	Reggie Jackson	4.00
25	Rickey Henderson	3.00
26	Roberto Clemente	6.00
27	Roger Clemens	6.00
28	Roger Clemens	6.00
29	Ryne Sandberg	6.00
30	Sammy Sosa	6.00
31	Stan Musial	6.00
32	Steve Carlton	3.00
33	Tim Hudson	3.00
34	Tom Glavine	3.00
35	Tom Seaver	4.00
36	Tony Gwynn	4.00
37	Torii Hunter	3.00
38	Ty Cobb	6.00
39	Vladimir Guerrero	4.00
40	Will Clark	4.00

2003 DONRUSS STUDIO

	NM/M
Complete Set (200):	35.00
Common Player:	.25
Pack (6):	3.00
Box (20):	50.00

1	Darin Erstad	.40
2	David Eckstein	.25
3	Garret Anderson	.50
4	Jarrod Washburn	.25
5	Tim Salmon	.50
6	Troy Glaus	.50
7	Jay Gibbons	.25
8	Melvin Mora	.25
9	Rodrigo Lopez	.25
10	Tony Batista	.25
11	Freddy Sanchez	.25
12	Derek Lowe	.25
13	Johnny Damon	.40
14	Manny Ramirez	.75
15	Nomar Garciaparra	1.50
16	Pedro J. Martinez	1.00
17	Rickey Henderson	.50
18	Shea Hillenbrand	.25
19	Carlos Lee	.25
20	Frank Thomas	.75
21	Magglio Ordonez	.40
22	Bartolo Colon	.25
23	Paul Konerko	.25
24	*Josh Stewart*	.50
25	C.C. Sabathia	.25
26	Jeremy Guthrie	.25
27	Ellis Burks	.25
28	Omar Vizquel	.40
29	Victor Martinez	.25
30	Cliff Lee	.25
31	Jhonny Peralta	.50
32	Brian Tallet	.25
33	Bobby Higginson	.25
34	Carlos Pena	.25
35	*Nook Logan*	.25
36	Steve Sparks	.25
37	Travis Chapman	.25
38	Carlos Beltran	.75
39	Joe Randa	.25
40	Mike Sweeney	.25
41	Jimmy Gobble	.25
42	Michael Tucker	.25
43	Runelvys Hernandez	.25
44	Brad Radke	.25
45	Corey Koskie	.25
46	Cristian Guzman	.25
47	J.C. Romero	.25
48	Doug Mientkiewicz	.25
49	*Lew Ford*	1.50
50	Jacque Jones	.40
51	Torii Hunter	.50
52	Alfonso Soriano	.75
53	Nick Johnson	.25
54	Bernie Williams	.50
55	*Jose Contreras*	1.50
56	Derek Jeter	3.00
57	Jason Giambi	.50
58	Brandon Claussen	.25
59	Jorge Posada	.50
60	Mike Mussina	.50
61	Roger Clemens	2.00
62	*Hideki Matsui*	5.00
63	Barry Zito	.50
64	Adam Morrissey	.25
65	Eric Chavez	.40
66	Jermaine Dye	.25
67	Mark Mulder	.40
68	Miguel Tejada	.50
69	*Joe Valentine*	.25
70	Tim Hudson	.50
71	Bret Boone	.40
72	Chris Snelling	.25
73	Edgar Martinez	.25
74	Freddy Garcia	.25
75	Ichiro Suzuki	2.00
76	Jamie Moyer	.25
77	John Olerud	.40
78	Kazuhiro Sasaki	.25
79	Aubrey Huff	.25
80	Joe Kennedy	.25
81	Dewon Brazelton	.25
82	*Pete LaForest*	.25
83	Alex Rodriguez	2.50
84	Chan Ho Park	.25
85	Hank Blalock	.75
86	Juan Gonzalez	.75
87	Kevin Mench	.25
88	Rafael Palmeiro	.75
89	Carlos Delgado	.50
90	Eric Hinske	.25
91	Josh Phelps	.25
92	Roy Halladay	.40
93	Shannon Stewart	.25
94	Vernon Wells	.40
95	Vinnie Chulk	.25
96	Curt Schilling	.75
97	Junior Spivey	.25
98	Luis Gonzalez	.50
99	Mark Grace	.50
100	Randy Johnson	1.00
101	Andruw Jones	.75
102	Chipper Jones	1.00
103	Gary Sheffield	.50
104	Greg Maddux	1.50
105	John Smoltz	.50
106	Mike Hampton	.25
107	Adam LaRoche	.25
108	*Michael Hessman*	.50
109	Corey Patterson	.40
110	Kerry Wood	1.00
111	Mark Prior	1.00
112	Moises Alou	.50
113	Sammy Sosa	1.50
114	Adam Dunn	.75
115	Austin Kearns	.40
116	Barry Larkin	.40
117	Ken Griffey Jr.	1.50
118	Sean Casey	.25
119	Jason Jennings	.25
120	Jay Payton	.25
121	Larry Walker	.40
122	Todd Helton	.75
123	Jeff Baker	.25
124	*Clint Barmes*	1.00
125	Ivan Rodriguez	.75
126	Josh Beckett	.50
127	Juan Encarnacion	.25
128	Mike Lowell	.25
129	Craig Biggio	.40
130	Jason Lane	.25
131	Jeff Bagwell	.75
132	Lance Berkman	.50
133	Roy Oswalt	.40
134	Jeff Kent	.40
135	Hideo Nomo	.50
136	Kazuhisa Ishii	.25
137	Kevin Brown	.40
138	Odalis Perez	.25
139	Paul LoDuca	.25
140	Shawn Green	.50
141	Adrian Beltre	.50

142	Ben Sheets	.40
143	Bill Hall	.25
144	Jeffrey Hammonds	.25
145	Richie Sexson	.50
146	*Terrmel Sledge*	.75
147	Brad Wilkerson	.25
148	Javier Vazquez	.25
149	Jose Vidro	.25
150	Michael Barrett	.25
151	Vladimir Guerrero	.75
152	Al Leiter	.25
153	Mike Piazza	2.00
154	Mo Vaughn	.25
155	Cliff Floyd	.25
156	Roberto Alomar	.50
157	Roger Cedeno	.25
158	Tom Glavine	.50
159	*Prentice Redman*	.50
160	Bobby Abreu	.50
161	Jimmy Rollins	.25
162	Mike Lieberthal	.25
163	Pat Burrell	.50
164	Vicente Padilla	.25
165	Jim Thome	.75
166	Kevin Millwood	.40
167	Aramis Ramirez	.50
168	Brian Giles	.40
169	Jason Kendall	.40
170	Josh Fogg	.25
171	Kip Wells	.25
172	Jose Castillo	.25
173	Mark Kotsay	.25
174	Oliver Perez	.25
175	Phil Nevin	.25
176	Ryan Klesko	.40
177	Sean Burroughs	.25
178	Brian Lawrence	.25
179	*Shane Victorino*	.25
180	Barry Bonds	3.00
181	Benito Santiago	.25
182	Ray Durham	.25
183	Rich Aurilia	.25
184	Damian Moss	.25
185	Albert Pujols	2.00
186	J.D. Drew	.25
187	Jim Edmonds	.50
188	Matt Morris	.40
189	Tino Martinez	.25
190	Scott Rolen	.75
191	Troy Glaus, Tim Salmon	.50
192	Sean Casey, Corky Miller	.25
193	Carlos Lee, Frank Thomas	.50
194	Lance Berkman, Jeff Kent	.25
195	Jose Contreras, Mariano Rivera	1.00
196	Alex Rodriguez, Juan Gonzalez	1.00
197	Andy Pettitte, David Wells	.25
198	Shawn Green, Dave Roberts	.25
199	Mike Lieberthal, Jimmy Rollins	.25
200	Mike Mussina, Hideki Matsui	2.00

Proofs

Stars (1-200): 4-8X
Rookies (1-200): 2-3X
Production 100 sets

Big League Challenge

		NM/M
Complete Set (50):		125.00
Common Player:		1.50
Production 400 sets		
Proofs		4-8X
Production 25 sets		
1	Jose Canseco	2.00
2	Magglio Ordonez	1.50
3	Alex Rodriguez	5.00
4	Lance Berkman	1.50
5	Rafael Palmeiro	3.00
6	Nomar Garciaparra	5.00
7	Nomar Garciaparra	5.00
8	Nomar Garciaparra	5.00
9	Troy Glaus	2.00
10	Mark McGwire	6.00
11	Mark McGwire	6.00
12	Mark McGwire	6.00
13	Jim Thome	3.00
14	Chipper Jones	3.00
15	Shawn Green	1.50
16	Alex Rodriguez	5.00
17	Alex Rodriguez	5.00
18	Alex Rodriguez	5.00
19	Alex Rodriguez	5.00
20	Jason Giambi	2.00
21	Pat Burrell	1.50
22	Mike Piazza	4.00
23	Mike Piazza	4.00
24	Mike Piazza	4.00
25	Frank Thomas	2.00
26	Rafael Palmeiro	2.00
27	Todd Helton	2.00
28	Jose Canseco	2.00
29	Albert Pujols	5.00
30	Troy Glaus	2.00
31	Barry Bonds	6.00
32	Barry Bonds	6.00
33	Barry Bonds	6.00
34	Todd Helton	3.00
35	Rafael Palmeiro	3.00
36	Jim Thome	3.00
37	Ozzie Smith	3.00
38	Troy Glaus	2.00
39	Shawn Green	1.50
40	Barry Bonds	6.00
41	Barry Bonds	6.00
42	Barry Bonds	6.00
43	Magglio Ordonez	1.50
44	Alex Rodriguez	5.00
45	Alex Rodriguez	5.00
46	Alex Rodriguez	5.00
47	Lance Berkman	1.50
48	Rafael Palmeiro	3.00
49	Pat Burrell	1.50
50	Albert Pujols	5.00

Big League Challenge Materials

		NM/M
Common Player:		4.00
Inserted 1:20		
2	Magglio Ordonez/jsy	4.00
3	Alex Rodriguez/jsy	10.00
4	Lance Berkman/jsy	4.00
15	Shawn Green/jsy	4.00
29	Albert Pujols/jsy	15.00
36	Jim Thome/jsy	6.00
39	Shawn Green/pants	4.00
40	Barry Bonds/base	10.00
41	Barry Bonds/base	10.00
42	Barry Bonds/base	10.00
43	Magglio Ordonez/jsy	4.00
45	Alex Rodriguez/jsy	10.00
46	Alex Rodriguez/pants	10.00
47	Lance Berkman/jsy	4.00
48	Rafael Palmeiro/jsy	6.00
50	Albert Pujols/pants	10.00

Big League Challenge Prime Material

		NM/M
Common Player:		10.00
2	Magglio Ordonez/100	10.00
3	Alex Rodriguez/100	25.00
15	Shawn Green/50	15.00
29	Albert Pujols/100	25.00
36	Jim Thome/50	20.00
45	Alex Rodriguez/100	25.00
48	Rafael Palmeiro/100	15.00

Enshrinement

		NM/M
Complete Set (50):		180.00
Common Player:		3.00
Production 750 sets		
Proofs:		5-10X
Production 20 or 21		
1	Gary Carter	4.00
2	Ozzie Smith	10.00
3	Kirby Puckett	6.00
4	Carlton Fisk	4.00
5	Tony Perez	3.00
6	Nolan Ryan	15.00
7	George Brett	12.00
8	Robin Yount	10.00
9	Orlando Cepeda	3.00
10	Phil Niekro	3.00
11	Mike Schmidt	10.00
12	Richie Ashburn	6.00
13	Steve Carlton	4.00
14	Phil Rizzuto	4.00
15	Reggie Jackson	6.00
16	Tom Seaver	5.00
17	Rollie Fingers	3.00
18	Rod Carew	5.00
19	Gaylord Perry	3.00
20	Fergie Jenkins	3.00
21	Jim Palmer	3.00
22	Joe Morgan	3.00
23	Johnny Bench	6.00
24	Willie Stargell	4.00
25	Billy Williams	3.00
26	Jim "Catfish" Hunter	3.00
27	Willie McCovey	3.00
28	Bobby Doerr	3.00
29	Lou Brock	4.00
30	Enos Slaughter	3.00
31	Hoyt Wilhelm	3.00
32	Harmon Killebrew	6.00
33	Pee Wee Reese	3.00
34	Luis Aparicio	3.00
35	Brooks Robinson	6.00
36	Juan Marichal	4.00
37	Frank Robinson	5.00
38	Bob Gibson	4.00
39	Al Kaline	6.00
40	Duke Snider	6.00
41	Eddie Mathews	5.00
42	Robin Roberts	3.00
43	Ralph Kiner	3.00
44	Whitey Ford	5.00
45	Roberto Clemente	10.00
46	Warren Spahn	4.00
47	Yogi Berra	5.00
48	Early Wynn	3.00
49	Stan Musial	6.00
50	Bob Feller	4.00

Enshrinement Autographs

		NM/M
Varying quantities produced		
1	Gary Carter/50	30.00
3	Kirby Puckett/5	
5	Tony Perez/50	50.00
6	Nolan Ryan/5	
9	Orlando Cepeda/50	25.00
10	Phil Niekro/50	20.00
13	Steve Carlton/50	40.00
14	Phil Rizzuto/15	50.00
15	Reggie Jackson/5	
20	Fergie Jenkins/50	20.00
21	Jim Palmer/25	35.00
22	Joe Morgan/10	50.00
23	Johnny Bench/10	
28	Bobby Doerr/100	20.00
29	Lou Brock/25	
31	Hoyt Wilhelm/50	25.00
34	Luis Aparicio/100	15.00
35	Brooks Robinson/25	65.00
37	Frank Robinson/25	50.00
39	Al Kaline/25	
40	Duke Snider/10	
43	Ralph Kiner/25	40.00
47	Yogi Berra/10	
49	Stan Musial	
50	Bob Feller/100	25.00

Leather & Lumber

		NM/M
Common Player:		5.00
1	Adam Dunn/400	10.00
2	Alex Rodriguez/250	12.00
3	Alfonso Soriano/250	10.00
4	Andruw Jones/400	8.00
5	Austin Kearns/400	8.00
6	Chipper Jones/400	10.00
7	Derek Jeter/100	35.00
8	Don Mattingly/100	40.00
9	Edgar Martinez	10.00
10	Frank Thomas/400	8.00
11	Fred McGriff/400	8.00
12	Garret Anderson	
13	Greg Maddux/150	15.00
14	Hideki Matsui/ball/100	40.00
15	Hideo Nomo/150	15.00
16	Ichiro Suzuki/ball/100	40.00
17	Ivan Rodriguez/250	8.00
18	Jason Giambi/400	8.00
19	Jeff Bagwell/400	8.00
20	Jim Edmonds/150	8.00
21	Jim Thome/400	10.00
22	Juan Gonzalez/400	8.00
23	Kerry Wood/250	10.00
24	Kirby Puckett/100	25.00
25	Lance Berkman/400	5.00
26	Magglio Ordonez/400	5.00
27	Manny Ramirez/250	10.00
28	Mark Prior/400	10.00
29	Miguel Tejada/200	5.00
30	Mike Piazza/400	10.00
31	Mike Schmidt/200	25.00
32	Nomar Garciaparra/400	15.00
33	Pat Burrell/400	8.00
34	Pedro Martinez/150	10.00
35	Rafael Palmeiro/400	
36	Randy Johnson/250	10.00
37	Rickey Henderson/175	10.00
38	Sammy Sosa/300	10.00
39	Shawn Green/400	5.00
40	Vladimir Guerrero/400	8.00

Leather & Lumber Dual

		NM/M
Common Player:		
Those without bat & ball are noted		
1	Adam Dunn/50	25.00
2	Alex Rodriguez/50	30.00
4	Andruw Jones/50	25.00
5	Austin Kearns/shoe/50	25.00
6	Chipper Jones/25	45.00
8	Don Mattingly/25	80.00
10	Frank Thomas/50	30.00
11	Fred McGriff/25	
13	Greg Maddux/shoe/50	35.00
14	Hideki Matsui/dual ball/25	
15	Hideo Nomo/25	
17	Ivan Rodriguez/50	25.00
18	Jason Giambi/25	
19	Jeff Bagwell/25	35.00
22	Juan Gonzalez/25	
23	Kerry Wood/50	35.00
24	Kirby Puckett/25	50.00
25	Lance Berkman/50	12.00
26	Magglio Ordonez/shoe/25	
27	Manny Ramirez/25	
28	Mark Prior/shoe/25	75.00
29	Miguel Tejada/25	15.00
30	Mike Piazza/shoe/25	
32	Nomar Garciaparra/base/25	
33	Pat Burrell/25	20.00
36	Randy Johnson/25	40.00
37	Rickey Henderson/25	
38	Sammy Sosa/shoe/25	60.00
39	Shawn Green/25	
40	Vladimir Guerrero/25	

Masterstrokes

		NM/M
Complete Set (25):		50.00
Common Player:		1.00
Production 1,000 sets		
1	Adam Dunn	2.00
2	Albert Pujols	3.00
3	Alex Rodriguez	5.00
4	Alfonso Soriano	3.00
5	Andruw Jones	1.50
6	Chipper Jones	3.00
7	Derek Jeter	6.00
8	Greg Maddux	3.00
9	Hideki Matsui	8.00
10	Hideo Nomo	1.50
11	Ivan Rodriguez	2.00
12	Jason Giambi	1.50
13	Jeff Bagwell	2.00
14	Juan Gonzalez	1.50
15	Ken Griffey Jr.	3.00
16	Lance Berkman	1.00
17	Magglio Ordonez	1.00
18	Manny Ramirez	2.00

19	Mark Prior	2.00
20	Miguel Tejada	1.00
21	Mike Piazza	4.00
22	Nomar Garciaparra	4.00
23	Pat Burrell	1.50
24	Sammy Sosa	4.00
25	Vladimir Guerrero	1.50

Masterstrokes Artist's Proof

		NM/M
Common Player:		15.00
Production 50 sets		
1	Adam Dunn	25.00
2	Albert Pujols	50.00
3	Alex Rodriguez	50.00
4	Alfonso Soriano	25.00
5	Andruw Jones	20.00
6	Chipper Jones	30.00
7	Derek Jeter	50.00
8	Greg Maddux	25.00
9	Hideki Matsui	75.00
10	Hideo Nomo	100.00
11	Ivan Rodriguez	20.00
12	Jason Giambi	15.00
13	Jeff Bagwell	25.00
14	Juan Gonzalez	25.00
15	Ken Griffey Jr.	30.00
16	Lance Berkman	15.00
17	Magglio Ordonez	15.00
18	Manny Ramirez	20.00
19	Mark Prior	30.00
20	Miguel Tejada	15.00
21	Mike Piazza	35.00
22	Nomar Garciaparra	40.00
23	Pat Burrell	15.00
24	Sammy Sosa	40.00
25	Vladimir Guerrero	25.00

Players Collection

		NM/M
Common Player:		4.00
Production 300 sets		
1	Adam Dunn	8.00
2	Adrian Beltre	6.00
3	Alex Rodriguez	10.00
4	Alfonso Soriano	8.00
5	Andruw Jones	6.00
6	Andy Pettitte	4.00
7	Barry Larkin	6.00
8	Barry Zito	4.00
9	Ben Grieve	4.00
10	Bernie Williams	8.00
11	Cal Ripken Jr.	30.00
12	Carlos Delgado	5.00
13	C.C. Sabathia	4.00
14	Chipper Jones	10.00
15	Craig Biggio	4.00
16	Curt Schilling	6.00
17	Alex Rodriguez	10.00
18	Frank Thomas	8.00
19	Freddy Garcia	4.00
20	Jay Bell	4.00
21	Roger Clemens	12.00
22	Tony Gwynn	10.00
23	Ivan Rodriguez	6.00
24	Jason Giambi	6.00
25	Jason Jennings	4.00
26	Jay Payton	4.00
27	J.D. Drew	4.00
28	Jeff Bagwell	8.00
29	Jeromy Burnitz	4.00
30	Jim Edmonds	6.00
31	Jim Thome	8.00
32	Joe Borchard	4.00
33	Joe Mays	4.00
34	John Olerud	4.00
35	David Wells	4.00
36	Juan Gonzalez	6.00
37	Kazuhiro Sasaki	4.00
38	Chan Ho Park	4.00
39	Kerry Wood	8.00
40	Kevin Brown	5.00
41	Lance Berkman	4.00
42	Larry Walker	4.00
43	Bret Boone	4.00
44	Magglio Ordonez	4.00
45	Manny Ramirez	6.00
46	Mark Mulder	4.00
47	Mark Prior	10.00
48	Matt Williams	4.00
49	Miguel Tejada	6.00
50	Mike Piazza	10.00
51	Nomar Garciaparra	10.00
52	Doug Davis	4.00
53	Paul Konerko	4.00
54	Paul LoDuca	4.00
55	Pedro J. Martinez	8.00
56	Preston Wilson	4.00
57	Rafael Palmeiro	8.00
58	Marlon Byrd	4.00
59	Reggie Sanders	4.00
60	Richie Sexson	5.00
61	Rickey Henderson	10.00
62	Rickey Henderson	10.00
63	Robert Person	4.00
64	Jeff Bagwell	8.00
65	Roger Clemens	12.00
66	Roy Oswalt	4.00
67	Ryan Klesko	4.00
68	Sammy Sosa	12.00
69	Shawn Green	5.00
70	Steve Finley	4.00
71	Terrence Long	4.00
72	Tim Hudson	5.00
73	Toby Hall	4.00
74	Todd Helton	8.00
75	Travis Lee	4.00
76	Troy Glaus	6.00
77	Tsuyoshi Shinjo	4.00
78	Vernon Wells	4.00
79	Vladimir Guerrero	8.00
80	Wes Helms	4.00
81	Alex Rodriguez	10.00
82	Alfonso Soriano	8.00
83	Barry Larkin	6.00
84	Roberto Alomar	6.00
85	Ivan Rodriguez	6.00
86	Jason Giambi	6.00
87	Jeff Bagwell	8.00
88	Juan Gonzalez	6.00
89	Larry Walker	4.00
90	Luis Gonzalez	4.00
91	Magglio Ordonez	4.00
92	Manny Ramirez	8.00
93	Marlon Byrd	4.00
94	Mike Piazza	10.00
95	Pat Burrell	8.00
96	Todd Helton	8.00
97	Rickey Henderson	10.00
98	Andruw Jones	6.00
99	Craig Biggio	4.00
100	Mark Prior	10.00

Private Signings

		NM/M
7	Jay Gibbons/100	10.00
11	Freddy Sanchez/150	8.00
24	Josh Stewart/200	8.00
26	Jeremy Guthrie/125	8.00
29	Victor Martinez/200	20.00
30	Cliff Lee/150	10.00
31	Jhonny Peralta/200	20.00
35	Nook Logan/100	8.00
37	Travis Chapman/150	8.00
41	Jimmy Gobble/200	8.00
47	J.C. Romero/200	8.00
49	Lew Ford/200	15.00
51	Torii Hunter/50	20.00
53	Nick Johnson/100	10.00
55	Jose Contreras/100	25.00
58	Brandon Claussen/200	10.00
69	Joe Valentine/200	8.00
79	Aubrey Huff/50	20.00
81	Dewon Brazelton/75	10.00
82	Pete LaForest/200	10.00
85	Hank Blalock/50	30.00
87	Kevin Mench/200	8.00
90	Eric Hinske/125	8.00
95	Vinnie Chulk/100	8.00
97	Junior Spivey/50	10.00
107	Adam LaRoche/200	8.00
108	Michael Hessman/200	8.00
111	Mark Prior/50	65.00
119	Jason Jennings/50	10.00
123	Jeff Baker/75	10.00
124	Clint Barmes/200	10.00
130	Jason Lane/100	10.00
139	Paul LoDuca/75	15.00
140	Shawn Green/5	
143	Bill Hall/50	15.00
145	Richie Sexson/15	
146	Terrmel Sledge/125	10.00
148	Javier Vazquez/25	
149	Jose Vidro/50	15.00
151	Vladimir Guerrero/15	
156	Roberto Alomar/20	
158	Tom Glavine/15	
159	Prentice Redman/200	10.00
160	Bobby Abreu/50	20.00
163	Pat Burrell/10	
165	Jim Thome/10	
167	Aramis Ramirez/15	
168	Brian Giles/25	
171	Kip Wells/100	10.00
172	Jose Castillo/175	8.00
176	Ryan Klesko/20	
178	Brian Lawrence/100	10.00
179	Shane Victorino/200	10.00
185	Albert Pujols/15	
187	Jim Edmonds/5	
201	Adam Loewen/100	20.00
202	Jeremy Bonderman/50	20.00
203	Brandon Webb/100	20.00
204	Chien-Ming Wang/50	40.00
205	Chad Gaudin/25	
206	Ryan Wagner/100	10.00
207	Hong-Chih Kuo/25	
208	Dan Haren/100	15.00
209	Rickie Weeks/10	
210	Ramon Nivar/100	15.00
211	Delmon Young/25	

Recollection Autographs 5x7

		NM/M
3	Sean Casey/125	15.00
5	Troy Glaus/82	20.00
8	Vladimir Guerrero/125	35.00
10	Todd Helton/55	35.00
12	Ryan Klesko/75	15.00
18	Ivan Rodriguez/50	40.00
19	C.C. Sabathia/50	20.00
20	Curt Schilling/75	30.00
23	Mike Sweeney/42	15.00
24	Miguel Tejada/44	30.00
26	Kerry Wood/200	25.00
27	Barry Zito/200	15.00

Spirit of the Game

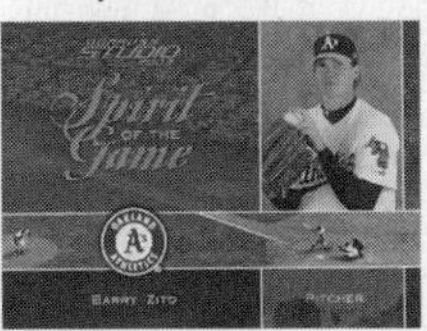

		NM/M
Complete Set (35):		60.00
Common Player:		1.00
Production 1,250 sets		
1	Garret Anderson	1.00
2	Nomar Garciaparra	3.00
3	Pedro J. Martinez	2.00
4	Rickey Henderson	1.50
5	Magglio Ordonez	1.00
6	Torii Hunter	1.50
7	Alfonso Soriano	2.00
8	Jose Contreras	1.00
9	Derek Jeter	5.00
10	Jason Giambi	1.50
11	Roger Clemens	4.00
12	Hideki Matsui	6.00
13	Barry Zito	1.50
14	Ichiro Suzuki	3.00
15	Alex Rodriguez	4.00
16	Curt Schilling	2.00
17	Randy Johnson	2.00
18	Andruw Jones	1.50
19	Chipper Jones	2.00
20	Greg Maddux	3.00
21	Sammy Sosa	3.00
22	Adam Dunn	2.00
23	Ken Griffey Jr.	3.00
24	Todd Helton	2.00
25	Ivan Rodriguez	2.00
26	Lance Berkman	1.00
27	Hideo Nomo	1.50
28	Shawn Green	1.00
29	Vladimir Guerrero	2.00
30	Mike Piazza	3.00
31	Roberto Alomar	1.50
32	Jim Thome	2.00
33	Barry Bonds	5.00
34	Albert Pujols	3.00
35	Scott Rolen	2.00

Stars

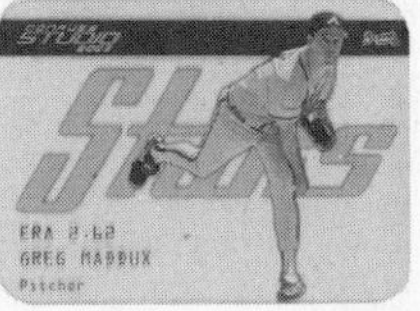

		NM/M
Complete Set (50):		65.00
Common Player:		1.00
Inserted 1:5		
Golds:		3-5X
Production 100 sets		
1	Troy Glaus	1.50
2	Manny Ramirez	2.00
3	Nomar Garciaparra	3.00
4	Pedro J. Martinez	2.00
5	Rickey Henderson	1.50
6	Torii Hunter	1.50
7	Frank Thomas	1.50
8	Magglio Ordonez	1.00
9	Alfonso Soriano	2.00
10	Jose Contreras	1.00
11	Derek Jeter	5.00
12	Jason Giambi	1.50
13	Roger Clemens	4.00
14	Mike Mussina	1.50
15	Barry Zito	1.50
16	Miguel Tejada	1.00
17	Ichiro Suzuki	4.00
18	Alex Rodriguez	1.00
19	Juan Gonzalez	1.00
20	Rafael Palmeiro	2.00
21	Hank Blalock	2.00
22	Curt Schilling	2.00
23	Randy Johnson	2.00
24	Junior Spivey	1.00
25	Andruw Jones	1.50
26	Chipper Jones	2.00
27	Greg Maddux	3.00
28	Kerry Wood	2.00
29	Mark Prior	2.00
30	Sammy Sosa	3.00
31	Adam Dunn	2.00
32	Ken Griffey Jr.	3.00
33	Austin Kearns	1.50
34	Larry Walker	1.00
35	Todd Helton	2.00
36	Ivan Rodriguez	2.00
37	Jeff Bagwell	2.00
38	Lance Berkman	1.00
39	Craig Biggio	1.00
40	Hideo Nomo	1.50
41	Shawn Green	1.00
42	Vladimir Guerrero	2.00
43	Mike Piazza	3.00
44	Tom Glavine	1.50
45	Roberto Alomar	1.50
46	Pat Burrell	1.50
47	Jim Thome	2.00
48	Barry Bonds	5.00
49	Albert Pujols	4.00
50	Scott Rolen	2.00

2003 DONRUSS TEAM HEROES

		NM/M
Complete Set (540):		55.00
Common Player:		.15
Pack (13):		1.50
Box (24):		25.00
1	Adam Kennedy	.15

No.	Player	Price
2	Steve Green	.15
3	Rod Carew	.40
4	Alfredo Amezaga	.15
5	Reggie Jackson	.50
6	Jarrod Washburn	.15
7	Nolan Ryan	3.00
8	Tim Salmon	.25
9	Garret Anderson	.25
10	Darin Erstad	.25
11	Elpidio Guzman	.15
12	David Eckstein	.15
13	Troy Percival	.15
14	Troy Glaus	.75
15	Doug Devore	.15
16	Tony Womack	.15
17	Matt Williams	.25
18	Junior Spivey	.15
19	Mark Grace	.50
20	Curt Schilling	.75
21	Erubiel Durazo	.15
22	Craig Counsell	.15
23	Byung-Hyun Kim	.15
24	Randy Johnson	1.00
25	Luis Gonzalez	.40
26	John Smoltz	.15
27	Tim Spooneybarger	.15
28	Dale Murphy	.50
29	Warren Spahn	.50
30	Jason Marquis	.15
31	Kevin Millwood	.15
32	Javy Lopez	.15
33	Vinny Castilla	.15
34	Julio Franco	.15
35	Trey Hodges	.15
36	Chipper Jones	1.50
37	Gary Sheffield	.25
38	Billy Sylvester	.15
39	Tom Glavine	.40
40	Rafael Furcal	.15
41	Cory Aldridge	.15
42	Greg Maddux	1.50
43	John Ennis	.15
44	Wes Helms	.15
45	Horacio Ramirez	.15
46	Derrick Lewis	.15
47	Marcus Giles	.15
48	Eddie Mathews	.75
49	Wilson Betemit	.15
50	Andruw Jones	.50
51	Josh Towers	.15
52	Ed Rogers	.15
53	Kris Foster	.15
54	Brooks Robinson	.75
55	Cal Ripken Jr.	3.00
56	Brian Roberts	.15
57	Luis Rivera	.15
58	Rodrigo Lopez	.15
59	Geronimo Gil	.15
60	Erik Bedard	.15
61	Jim Palmer	.40
62	Jay Gibbons	.15
63	Travis Driskill	.15
64	Larry Bigbie	.15
65	Eddie Murray	.40
66	Hoyt Wilhelm	.15
67	Bobby Doerr	.15
68	Pedro J. Martinez	1.00
69	Roger Clemens	1.50
70	Nomar Garciaparra	2.00
71	Trot Nixon	.15
72	Dennis Eckersley	.40
73	John Burkett	.15
74	Tim Wakefield	.15
75	Wade Boggs	.40
76	Cliff Floyd	.15
77	Casey Fossum	.15
78	Johnny Damon	.15
79	Fred Lynn	.15
80	Rickey Henderson	.40
81	Juan Diaz	.15
82	Manny Ramirez	.75
83	Carlton Fisk	.50
84	Jorge De La Rosa	.15
85	Shea Hillenbrand	.15
86	Derek Lowe	.15
87	Jason Varitek	.15
88	Carlos Baerga	.15
89	Freddy Sanchez	.15
90	Ugueth Urbina	.15
91	Rey Sanchez	.15
92	Josh Hancock	.15
93	Tony Clark	.15
94	Dustin Hermanson	.15
95	Ryne Sandberg	1.50
96	Fred McGriff	.25
97	Alex Gonzalez	.15
98	Mark Belhorn	.15
99	Fergie Jenkins	.25
100	Jon Lieber	.15
101	Francis Beltran	.15
102	Greg Maddux	1.50
103	Nate Frese	.15
104	Andre Dawson	.25
105	Carlos Zambrano	.15
106	Steve Smyth	.15
107	Ernie Banks	1.00
108	Will Ohman	.15
109	Kerry Wood	.50
110	Bobby Hill	.15
111	Moises Alou	.15
112	Hee Seop Choi	.15
113	Corey Patterson	.15
114	Sammy Sosa	1.50
115	Mark Prior	.50
116	Juan Cruz	.15
117	Ron Santo	.15
118	Billy Williams	.15
119	Antonio Alfonseca	.15
120	Matt Clement	.15
121	Carlton Fisk	.50
122	Joe Crede	.15
123	Magglio Ordonez	.40
124	Frank Thomas	.75
125	Joe Borchard	.15
126	Royce Clayton	.15
127	Luis Aparicio	.15
128	Willie Harris	.15
129	Kyle Kane	.15
130	Paul Konerko	.25
131	Matt Ginter	.15
132	Carlos Lee	.15
133	Mark Buehrle	.15
134	Adam Dunn	.75
135	Eric Davis	.15
136	Johnny Bench	1.00
137	Joe Morgan	.25
138	Austin Kearns	.40
139	Barry Larkin	.40
140	Ken Griffey Jr.	2.00
141	Luis Pineda	.15
142	Corky Miller	.15
143	Brandon Larson	.15
144	Wily Mo Pena	.15
145	Lance Davis	.15
146	Tom Seaver	1.00
147	Luke Hudson	.15
148	Sean Casey	.15
149	Tony Perez	.15
150	Todd Walker	.15
151	Aaron Boone	.15
152	Jose Rijo	.15
153	Ryan Dempster	.15
154	Danny Graves	.15
155	Matt Lawton	.15
156	Cliff Lee	.15
157	Ryan Drese	.15
158	Danys Baez	.15
159	Einar Diaz	.15
160	Milton Bradley	.15
161	Earl Snyder	.15
162	Ellis Burks	.15
163	Lou Boudreau	.15
164	Bob Feller	.15
165	Ricardo Rodriguez	.15
166	Victor Martinez	.15
167	Alex Herrera	.15
168	Omar Vizquel	.15
169	David Elder	.15
170	C.C. Sabathia	.15
171	Alex Escobar	.15
172	Brian Tallet	.15
173	Jim Thome	.75
174	Rene Reyes	.15
175	Juan Uribe	.15
176	Jason Romano	.15
177	Juan Pierre	.15
178	Jason Jennings	.15
179	Jose Ortiz	.15
180	Larry Walker	.25
181	Cam Esslinger	.15
182	Todd Helton	.50
183	Aaron Cook	.15
184	Jack Cust	.15
185	Jack Morris	.15
186	Mike Rivera	.15
187	Bobby Higginson	.15
188	Fernando Rodney	.15
189	Al Kaline	1.00
190	Carlos Pena	.15
191	Alan Trammell	.15
192	Mike Maroth	.15
193	Adam Pettyjohn	.15
194	David Espinosa	.15
195	Adam Bernero	.15
196	Franklyn German	.15
197	Robert Fick	.15
198	Andres Torres	.15
199	Luis Castillo	.15
200	Preston Wilson	.15
201	Pablo Ozuna	.15
202	Brad Penny	.15
203	Josh Beckett	.15
204	Charles Johnson	.15
205	Wilson Valdez	.15
206	A.J. Burnett	.15
207	Abraham Nunez	.15
208	Mike Lowell	.15
209	Jose Cueto	.15
210	Jeriome Robertson	.15
211	Jeff Bagwell	.75
212	Kirk Saarloos	.15
213	Craig Biggio	.25
214	Rodrigo Rosario	.15
215	Roy Oswalt	.25
216	John Buck	.15
217	Tim Redding	.15
218	Morgan Ensberg	.15
219	Richard Hidalgo	.15
220	Wade Miller	.15
221	Lance Berkman	.50
222	Raul Chavez	.15
223	Carlos Hernandez	.15
224	Greg Miller	.15
225	Tom Shearn	.15
226	Jason Lane	.15
227	Nolan Ryan	3.00
228	Billy Wagner	.15
229	Octavio Dotel	.15
230	Shane Reynolds	.15
231	Julio Lugo	.15
232	Daryle Ward	.15
233	Mike Sweeney	.15
234	Angel Berroa	.15
235	George Brett	1.50
236	Brad Voyles	.15
237	Brandon Berger	.15
238	Chad Durbin	.15
239	Alexis Gomez	.15
240	Jeremy Affeldt	.15
241	Bo Jackson	.75
242	Dee Brown	.15
243	Tony Cogan	.15
244	Carlos Beltran	.15
245	Joe Randa	.15
246	Pee Wee Reese	.25
247	Andy Ashby	.15
248	Cesar Izturis	.15
249	Duke Snider	.50
250	Mark Grudzielanek	.15
251	Chin-Feng Chen	.15
252	Brian Jordan	.15
253	Steve Garvey	.15
254	Odalis Perez	.15
255	Hideo Nomo	.50
256	Kevin Brown	.15
257	Eric Karros	.15
258	Joe Thurston	.15
259	Carlos Garcia	.15
260	Shawn Green	.40
261	Paul LoDuca	.15
262	Kazuhisa Ishii	.15
263	Victor Alvarez	.15
264	Eric Gagne	.15
265	Don Sutton	.15
266	Orel Hershiser	.15
267	Dave Roberts	.15
268	Adrian Beltre	.15
269	Don Drysdale	.50
270	Jackie Robinson	1.50
271	Tyler Houston	.15
272	Omar Daal	.15
273	Marquis Grissom	.15
274	Paul Quantrill	.15
275	Paul Molitor	.50
276	Jose Hernandez	.15
277	Takahito Nomura	.15
278	Nick Neugebauer	.15
279	Jose Mieses	.15
280	Richie Sexson	.40
281	Matt Childers	.15
282	Bill Hall	.15
283	Ben Sheets	.15
284	Brian Mallette	.15
285	Geoff Jenkins	.15
286	Robin Yount	.75
287	Jeff Deardorff	.15
288	Luis Rivas	.15
289	Harmon Killebrew	.50
290	Michael Cuddyer	.15
291	Torii Hunter	.15
292	Kevin Frederick	.15
293	Adam Johnson	.15
294	Jack Morris	.15
295	Rod Carew	.40
296	Kirby Puckett	1.50
297	Joe Mays	.15
298	Jacque Jones	.15
299	Cristian Guzman	.15
300	Kyle Lohse	.15
301	Eric Milton	.15
302	Brad Radke	.15
303	Doug Mientkiewicz	.15
304	Corey Koskie	.15
305	Jose Vidro	.15
306	Claudio Vargas	.15
307	Gary Carter	.15
308	Andre Dawson	.25
309	Henry Mateo	.15
310	Andres Galarraga	.15
311	Zach Day	.15
312	Bartolo Colon	.15
313	Endy Chavez	.15
314	Javier Vazquez	.15
315	Michael Barrett	.15
316	Vladimir Guerrero	1.00
317	Orlando Cabrera	.15
318	Al Leiter	.15
319	Timoniel Perez	.15
320	Rey Ordonez	.15
321	Gary Carter	.15
322	Armando Benitez	.15
323	Dwight Gooden	.15
324	Pedro Astacio	.15
325	Roberto Alomar	.50
326	Edgardo Alfonzo	.15
327	Nolan Ryan	3.00
328	Mo Vaughn	.25
329	Ryan Jamison	.15
330	Satoru Komiyama	.15
331	Mike Piazza	2.50
332	Tom Seaver	1.00
333	Jorge Posada	.40
334	Derek Jeter	2.50
335	Babe Ruth	3.00
336	Lou Gehrig	2.50
337	Andy Pettitte	.40
338	Mariano Rivera	.25
339	Robin Ventura	.15
340	Yogi Berra	1.00
341	Phil Rizzuto	.50
342	Bernie Williams	.50
343	Alfonso Soriano	1.50
344	Drew Henson	.15
345	Erick Almonte	.15
346	Rondell White	.15
347	Christian Parker	.15
348	Joe Torre	.25
349	Nick Johnson	.15
350	Raul Mondesi	.15
351	Brandon Claussen	.15
352	Reggie Jackson	.50
353	Roger Clemens	1.50
354	Don Mattingly	2.00
355	Jason Giambi	1.50
356	Adrian Hernandez	.15
357	Jeff Weaver	.15
358	Mike Mussina	.50
359	Brett Jodie	.15
360	David Wells	.15
361	Enos Slaughter	.15
362	Whitey Ford	.50
363	Eric Chavez	.25
364	Miguel Tejada	.40
365	Barry Zito	.25
366	Bert Snow	.15
367	Rickey Henderson	.50
368	Juan A. Pena	.15
369	Terrence Long	.15
370	Dennis Eckersley	.40
371	Mark Ellis	.15
372	Tim Hudson	.25
373	Jose Canseco	.50
374	Reggie Jackson	.50
375	Mark Mulder	.15
376	David Justice	.25
377	Jermaine Dye	.15
378	Brett Myers	.15
379	Lenny Dykstra	.15
380	Vicente Padilla	.15
381	Bobby Abreu	.15
382	Pat Burrell	.50
383	Jorge Padilla	.15
384	Jeremy Giambi	.15
385	Mike Lieberthal	.15
386	Anderson Machado	.15
387	Marlon Byrd	.15
388	Bud Smith	.15
389	Eric Valent	.15
390	Elio Serrano	.15
391	Jimmy Rollins	.15
392	Brandon Duckworth	.15
393	Robin Roberts	.15
394	Marlon Anderson	.15
395	Robert Person	.15
396	Johnny Estrada	.15
397	Mike Schmidt	1.00

398 Eric Junge .15
399 Jason Michaels .15
400 Steve Carlton .40
401 Placido Polanco .15
402 John Grabow .15
403 Tomas De La Rosa .15
404 Tike Redman .15
405 Willie Stargell .40
406 Dave Williams .15
407 John Candelaria .15
408 Jack Wilson .15
409 Matt Guerrier .15
410 Jason Kendall .15
411 Josh Fogg .15
412 Aramis Ramirez .15
413 Dave Parker .15
414 Roberto Clemente 2.00
415 Kip Wells .15
416 Brian Giles .25
417 Honus Wagner 1.50
418 Ramon Vazquez .15
419 Oliver Perez .15
420 Ryan Klesko .15
421 Brian Lawrence .15
422 Ben Howard .15
423 Ozzie Smith 1.00
424 Dennis Tankersley .15
425 Tony Gwynn 1.00
426 Sean Burroughs .15
427 Xavier Nady .15
428 Phil Nevin .15
429 Trevor Hoffman .15
430 Jake Peavy .15
431 Cody Ransom .15
432 Kenny Lofton .15
433 Mel Ott .50
434 Tsuyoshi Shinjo .15
435 Deivis Santos .15
436 Rich Aurilia .15
437 Will Clark .50
438 Pedro Feliz .15
439 J.T. Snow .15
440 Robb Nen .15
441 Carlos Valderrama .15
442 Willie McCovey .15
443 Jeff Kent .25
444 Orlando Cepeda .15
445 Barry Bonds 2.50
446 Alex Rodriguez 2.50
447 Allan Simpson .15
448 Antonio Perez .15
449 Edgar Martinez .15
450 Freddy Garcia .15
451 Chris Snelling .15
452 Matt Thornton .15
453 Kazuhiro Sasaki .15
454 Harold Reynolds .15
455 Randy Johnson 1.00
456 Bret Boone .15
457 Rafael Soriano .15
458 Luis Ugueto .15
459 Ken Griffey Jr. 2.00
460 Ichiro Suzuki 2.00
461 Jamie Moyer .15
462 Joel Pineiro .15
463 Jeff Cirillo .15
464 John Olerud .15
465 Mike Cameron .15
466 Ruben Sierra .15
467 Mark McLemore .15
468 Carlos Guillen .15
469 Dan Wilson .15
470 Shigetoshi Hasegawa .15
471 Ben Davis .15
472 Ozzie Smith 1.00
473 Matt Morris .15
474 Edgar Renteria .15
475 Les Walrond .15
476 Albert Pujols 1.00
477 Stan Musial 1.50
478 J.D. Drew .15
479 Josh Pearce .15
480 Enos Slaughter .15
481 Jason Simontacchi .15
482 Jeremy Lambert .15
483 Tino Martinez .15
484 Rogers Hornsby .50
485 Rick Ankiel .15
486 Jim Edmonds .25
487 Scott Rolen .50
488 Kevin Joseph .15
489 Fernando Vina .15
490 Jason Isringhausen .15
491 Lou Brock .40
492 Joe Torre .25
493 Bob Gibson .50
494 Chuck Finley .15
495 So Taguchi .15
496 Ben Grieve .15
497 Toby Hall .15
498 Brent Abernathy .15
499 Brandon Backe .15
500 Felix Escalona .15
501 Matt White .15
502 Randy Winn .15
503 Carl Crawford .15
504 Dewon Brazelton .15
505 Joe Kennedy .15
506 Wade Boggs .50
507 Aubrey Huff .15
508 Alex Rodriguez 2.50
509 Ivan Rodriguez .50
510 Will Clark .75
511 Hank Blalock .15
512 Travis Hughes .15
513 Travis Hafner .15
514 Ryan Ludwick .15
515 Doug Davis .15
516 Juan Gonzalez .50
517 Jason Hart .15
518 Mark Teixeira .40
519 Nolan Ryan 3.00
520 Rafael Palmeiro .50
521 Kevin Mench .15
522 Chan Ho Park .15
523 Kenny Rogers .15
524 Rusty Greer .15
525 Michael Young .15
526 Carlos Delgado .40
527 Vernon Wells .15
528 Orlando Hudson .15
529 Shannon Stewart .15
530 Joe Carter .15
531 Chris Baker .15
532 Eric Hinske .15
533 Corey Thurman .15
534 Josh Phelps .15
535 Reed Johnson .15
536 Brian Bowles .15
537 Roy Halladay .15
538 Jose Cruz Jr. .15
539 Kelvim Escobar .15
540 Chris Carpenter .15

Glossy

Stars: 1-2.5X
Inserted 1:1

Stat Line

Cards serial numbered 151-250: 4-8X
Print run 101-150: 5-10X
Print run 51-100: 8-15X
Print run 26-50: 10-20X

Autographs

NM/M
Common Player: 6.00
Some not priced due to scarcity
4 Alfredo Amezaga/250 6.00
11 Elpidio Guzman/100 10.00
15 Doug Devore/122 10.00
35 Trey Hodges/250 8.00
38 Billy Sylvester/250 6.00
41 Cory Aldridge/250 8.00
45 Horacio Ramirez/200 8.00
46 Derrick Lewis/250 6.00
47 Marcus Giles/200 8.00
49 Wilson Betemit/75 10.00
51 Josh Towers/110 10.00
52 Ed Rogers/250 6.00
53 Kris Foster/250 6.00
56 Brian Roberts/250 35.00
59 Geronimo Gil/60 10.00
60 Erik Bedard/250 8.00
62 Jay Gibbons/181 10.00
64 Larry Bigbie/100 10.00
77 Casey Fossum/250 6.00
79 Fred Lynn/50 20.00
81 Juan Diaz/250 6.00
84 Jorge De La Rosa/250 6.00
99 Fergie Jenkins/50 25.00
101 Francis Beltran/250 8.00
103 Nate Frese/250 6.00
105 Carlos Zambrano/150 20.00
108 Will Ohman/50 10.00
110 Bobby Hill/150 8.00
115 Mark Prior/50 65.00
116 Juan Cruz/50 10.00
122 Joe Crede/250 10.00
125 Joe Borchard/250 10.00
127 Luis Aparicio/50 20.00
128 Willie Harris/129 8.00
129 Kyle Kane/100 10.00
131 Matt Ginter/250 6.00
132 Carlos Lee/50 15.00
133 Mark Buehrle/50 20.00
135 Eric Davis/75 20.00
138 Austin Kearns/71 20.00
142 Corky Miller/250 6.00
143 Brandon Larson/143 10.00
144 Wily Mo Pena/250 15.00
147 Luke Hudson/50 12.00
149 Tony Perez/50 20.00
156 Cliff Lee/250 10.00
161 Earl Snyder/250 8.00
165 Ricardo Rodriguez/250 8.00
166 Victor Martinez/200 25.00
167 Alex Herrera/250 6.00
171 Alex Escobar/125 10.00
172 Brian Tallet/250 10.00
174 Rene Reyes/250 6.00
176 Jason Romano/50 15.00
177 Juan Pierre/66 15.00
178 Jason Jennings/250 10.00
179 Jose Ortiz/250 8.00
181 Cam Esslinger/250 6.00
182 Todd Helton/10
184 Jack Cust/250 10.00
185 Jack Morris/50 20.00
186 Mike Rivera/250 6.00
188 Fernando Rodney/250 6.00
190 Carlos Pena/96 12.00
192 Mike Maroth/250 6.00
193 Adam Pettyjohn/250 6.00
194 David Espinosa/250 6.00
195 Adam Bernero/250 6.00
196 Franklyn German/250 8.00
197 Robert Fick/50 10.00
198 Andres Torres/250 6.00
201 Pablo Ozuna/250 6.00
205 Wilson Valdez/250 6.00
207 Abraham Nunez/250 8.00
212 Kirk Saarloos/250 8.00
214 Rodrigo Rosario/250 6.00
215 Roy Oswalt/50 20.00
217 Tim Redding/250 6.00
218 Morgan Ensberg/250 6.00
219 Richard Hidalgo/100 10.00
220 Wade Miller/200 10.00
222 Raul Chavez/125 15.00
223 Carlos Hernandez/250 10.00
224 Greg Miller/90 10.00
226 Jason Lane/250 10.00
234 Angel Berroa/200 10.00
236 Brad Voyles/200 10.00
237 Brandon Berger/250 8.00
238 Chad Durbin/250 8.00
239 Alexis Gomez/165 10.00
240 Jeremy Affeldt/250 6.00
242 Dee Brown/50 12.00
243 Tony Cogan/250 6.00
248 Cesar Izturis/200 10.00
253 Steve Garvey/75 30.00
258 Joe Thurston/108 10.00
259 Carlos Garcia/100 8.00
261 Paul LoDuca/50 20.00
263 Victor Alvarez/250 6.00
265 Don Sutton/50 20.00
277 Takahito Nomura/100 20.00
279 Jose Mieses/50 15.00
281 Matt Childers/50 12.00
283 Ben Sheets/100 20.00
284 Brian Mallette/250 6.00
287 Jeff Deardorff/100 6.00
288 Luis Rivas/200 8.00
290 Michael Cuddyer/250 10.00
291 Torii Hunter/100 25.00
294 Jack Morris/50 20.00
305 Jose Vidro/50 15.00
306 Claudio Vargas/150 6.00
309 Henry Mateo/250 6.00
311 Zach Day/250 6.00
313 Endy Chavez/250 6.00
314 Javier Vazquez/50 15.00
323 Dwight Gooden/75 25.00
344 Drew Henson/50 25.00
345 Erick Almonte/250 6.00
347 Christian Parker/200 6.00
351 Brandon Claussen/250 6.00
356 Adrian Hernandez/200 6.00
359 Brett Jodie/250 8.00
366 Bert Snow/250 6.00
368 Juan Pena/250 8.00
371 Mark Ellis/150 6.00
379 Lenny Dykstra/75 25.00
383 Jorge Padilla/250 8.00
384 Jeremy Giambi/100 10.00
386 Anderson Machado/250 6.00
387 Marlon Byrd/200 10.00
388 Bud Smith/125 10.00
389 Eric Valent/100 8.00
390 Elio Serrano/250 8.00
392 Brandon Duckworth/100 10.00
395 Robert Person/100 10.00
396 Johnny Estrada/209 15.00
398 Eric Junge/250 8.00
399 Jason Michaels/221 6.00
402 John Grabow/250 6.00
406 Dave Williams/250 6.00
407 John Candelaria/100 10.00
408 Jack Wilson/250 6.00
409 Matt Guerrier/200 6.00
412 Aramis Ramirez/50 30.00
413 Dave Parker/50 20.00
415 Kip Wells/250 8.00
418 Ramon Vazquez/200 6.00
419 Oliver Perez/150 15.00
421 Brian Lawrence/250 8.00
422 Ben Howard/250 6.00
427 Xavier Nady/50 15.00
431 Cody Ransom/100 10.00
435 Deivis Santos/100 10.00
438 Pedro Feliz/50 15.00
441 Carlos Valderrama/250 6.00
447 Allan Simpson/250 6.00
448 Antonio Perez/250 6.00
451 Chris Snelling/100 10.00
452 Matt Thornton/200 6.00
454 Harold Reynolds/100 15.00
457 Rafael Soriano/250 6.00
458 Luis Ugueto/50 10.00
475 Les Walrond/50 12.00
479 Josh Pearce/200 6.00
497 Toby Hall/200 8.00
498 Brent Abernathy/250 6.00
499 Brandon Backe/250 8.00
500 Felix Escalona/50 10.00
504 Dewon Brazelton/100 10.00
505 Joe Kennedy/200 6.00
507 Aubrey Huff/100 15.00
512 Travis Hughes/200 6.00
514 Ryan Ludwick/250 6.00
515 Doug Davis/250 6.00
517 Jason Hart/123 10.00
518 Mark Teixeira/50 40.00
521 Kevin Mench/250 10.00
528 Orlando Hudson/120 10.00
531 Chris Baker/200 6.00
532 Eric Hinske/250 10.00
533 Corey Thurman/250 8.00
534 Josh Phelps/150 10.00
535 Reed Johnson/250 6.00
536 Brian Bowles/250 6.00
543 Ramon Nivar/100 15.00
544 Adam Loewen/100 10.00
545 Brandon Webb/100 20.00
546 Dan Haren/100 20.00
548 Ryan Wagner/100 15.00

Timeline Threads

NM/M
Common Player:
Quantity produced listed
1 Bobby Doerr/39 20.00
2 Phil Rizzuto/47 30.00
3 Yogi Berra/47 35.00
4 Pee Wee Reese/58 15.00
5 Stan Musial/42
6 Al Kaline/66 40.00
7 Orlando Cepeda/65 15.00
8 Eddie Mathews/66 40.00
9 Lou Brock/66 15.00
10 Juan Marichal/67 15.00
11 Ernie Banks/68 40.00

12	Willie Stargell/68	15.00
13	Jim Palmer/69	15.00
14	Luis Aparicio/69	15.00
15	Tom Seaver/69	30.00
16	Harmon Killebrew/71	50.00
17	Joe Morgan/74	15.00
18	Brooks Robinson/76	30.00
19	Mike Schmidt/81	65.00
20	Willie McCovey/77	15.00
21	Robin Yount/78	40.00
22	Reggie Jackson/79	20.00
23	Rod Carew/85	25.00
24	Nolan Ryan/91	80.00
25	Tony Gwynn/98	25.00
26	Alex Rodriguez/100	25.00
27	Carlos Delgado/101	10.00
28	Lance Berkman/102	10.00
29	Randy Johnson/100	20.00
30	Josh Beckett/101	15.00
31	Eric Davis/89	10.00
32	Todd Helton/100	15.00
33	Jose Canseco/89	25.00
34	Mike Piazza/101	25.00
35	Fred Lynn/75	10.00
36	Mike Sweeney/101	10.00
37	Miguel Tejada/101	15.00
38	Curt Schilling/101	15.00
39	Dale Murphy/87	40.00
40	Jim Thome/101	20.00
41	Adam Dunn/102	15.00
42	Nomar Garciaparra/100	25.00
43	Vladimir Guerrero/100	15.00
44	Alfonso Soriano/102	20.00
45	Wade Boggs/90	15.00
46	Randy Johnson/89	20.00
47	Hal Newhouser/55	15.00
48	Chipper Jones/93	20.00
49	Andruw Jones/96	15.00
50	Frank Thomas/94	15.00

2003 DONRUSS TIMELESS TREASURES

		NM/M
Complete Set (100):		
Common Player:		2.00
Production 900 sets		
Tin (4):		100.00
1	Adam Dunn	3.00
2	Al Kaline	5.00
3	Alan Trammell	2.00
4	Albert Pujols	8.00
5	Alex Rodriguez	8.00
6	Alfonso Soriano	4.00
7	Andre Dawson	2.00
8	Andruw Jones	3.00
9	Austin Kearns	2.00
10	Babe Ruth	10.00
11	Barry Bonds	10.00
12	Barry Larkin	2.00
13	Barry Zito	3.00
14	Bernie Williams	4.00
15	Bo Jackson	4.00
16	Brooks Robinson	4.00
17	Cal Ripken Jr.	10.00
18	Carlton Fisk	2.00
19	Chipper Jones	4.00
20	Curt Schilling	3.00
21	Dale Murphy	2.00
22	Derek Jeter	10.00
23	Don Mattingly	10.00
24	Duke Snider	3.00
25	Eddie Mathews	4.00
26	Frank Robinson	2.00
27	Frank Thomas	4.00
28	Garret Anderson	2.00
29	Gary Carter	2.00
30	George Brett	8.00
31	Greg Maddux	6.00
32	Harmon Killebrew	4.00
33	*Hideki Matsui*	10.00
34	Hideo Nomo	3.00
35	Ichiro Suzuki	6.00
36	Ivan Rodriguez	4.00
37	Jackie Robinson	6.00
38	Jason Giambi	3.00
39	Jeff Bagwell	4.00
40	Jim Edmonds	3.00
41	Jim Palmer	3.00
42	Jim Thome	4.00
43	Joe Morgan	2.00
44	Jorge Posada	3.00
45	*Jose Contreras*	5.00
46	Juan Gonzalez	3.00
47	Kazuhisa Ishii	2.00
48	Ken Griffey Jr.	5.00
49	Kerry Wood	4.00
50	Kirby Puckett	5.00
51	Lance Berkman	2.00
52	Larry Walker	2.00
53	Lou Brock	3.00
54	Lou Gehrig	8.00
55	Magglio Ordonez	2.00
56	Mark Prior	4.00
57	Miguel Tejada	3.00
58	Mike Mussina	3.00
59	Mike Piazza	6.00
60	Mike Schmidt	8.00
61	Nolan Ryan	10.00
62	Nomar Garciaparra	6.00
63	Ozzie Smith	5.00
64	Pat Burrell	2.00
65	Pedro J. Martinez	4.00
66	Pee Wee Reese	2.00
67	Phil Rizzuto	4.00
68	Rafael Palmeiro	3.00
69	Randy Johnson	5.00
70	Reggie Jackson	4.00
71	Richie Ashburn	2.00
72	Rickey Henderson	3.00
73	Roberto Alomar	3.00
74	Roberto Clemente	8.00
75	Robin Yount	4.00
76	Rod Carew	3.00
77	Roger Clemens	8.00
78	Rogers Hornsby	4.00
79	Roy Oswalt	2.00
80	Ryan Klesko	2.00
81	Ryne Sandberg	6.00
82	Sammy Sosa	6.00
83	Scott Rolen	4.00
84	Shawn Green	3.00
85	Stan Musial	6.00
86	Steve Carlton	3.00
87	Thurman Munson	5.00
88	Todd Helton	4.00
89	Tom Glavine	2.00
90	Tom Seaver	4.00
91	Tony Gwynn	4.00
92	Tony Perez	2.00
93	Torii Hunter	2.00
94	Troy Glaus	3.00
95	Ty Cobb	6.00
96	Vernon Wells	2.00
97	Vladimir Guerrero	4.00
98	Warren Spahn	4.00
99	Willie McCovey	3.00
100	Yogi Berra	5.00

Silver

Stars (1-100): 3-5X
Production 50 sets
Golds: No Pricing
Production 10 sets
Platinum 1-of-1's exist

Award Materials

		NM/M
Quantity produced listed		
1	Ivan Rodriguez/100	10.00
2	Mike Schmidt/50	60.00
3	Roberto Clemente/50	80.00
4	Roger Clemens/50	25.00
5	Randy Johnson/100	15.00
6	Pedro J. Martinez/100	15.00
7	Ivan Rodriguez/100	10.00
8	Jeff Bagwell/100	15.00
9	Frank Thomas/100	15.00
10	Cal Ripken Jr./75	50.00
11	Tom Seaver/50	25.00

Award Prime Materials

		NM/M
Quantity produced listed		
2	Mike Schmidt/25	
4	Roger Clemens/30	
5	Randy Johnson/30	
6	Pedro J. Martinez/50	30.00
9	Frank Thomas/50	25.00
11	Tom Seaver/15	

Award Winning MLB Logos

No Pricing

Classic Combos

		NM/M
Quantity produced listed		
1	Jason Giambi/100	15.00
2	Adrian Beltre/100	10.00
3	Alex Rodriguez/100	25.00
4	Alfonso Soriano/100	30.00
5	Andruw Jones/100	15.00
6	Andre Dawson/100	15.00
7	Barry Larkin/100	10.00
8	Barry Zito/100	15.00
9	Cal Ripken Jr./100	60.00
10	Chipper Jones/100	20.00
11	Don Mattingly/10	50.00
12	Eric Chavez/100	10.00
13	Frank Thomas/100	15.00
14	Greg Maddux/100	25.00
15	Ivan Rodriguez/100	15.00
16	Jeff Bagwell/100	15.00
17	Jim Thome/100	15.00
18	Juan Gonzalez/100	15.00
19	Kazuhisa Ishii/100	10.00
20	Kerry Wood/100	15.00
21	Lance Berkman/100	10.00
22	Magglio Ordonez/100	10.00
23	Manny Ramirez/100	15.00
24	Miguel Tejada/100	10.00
25	Mike Piazza/100	20.00
26	Nomar Garciaparra/100	20.00
27	Pedro J. Martinez/100	20.00
28	Randy Johnson/100	15.00
29	Rickey Henderson/100	20.00
30	Ryne Sandberg/100	30.00
31	Sammy Sosa	
32	Shawn Green/100	10.00
33	Todd Helton/100	10.00
34	Tony Gwynn/100	20.00
35	Vladimir Guerrero/100	15.00

Classic Combos Auto.

		NM/M
Quantity produced listed		
8	Barry Zito/25	100.00
22	Magglio Ordonez/25	65.00
34	Tony Gwynn/25	100.00

Classic Prime Combos

		NM/M
Quantity produced listed		
6	Andre Dawson/25	40.00
11	Don Mattingly/25	75.00
16	Jeff Bagwell/25	50.00

Game Day Materials

		NM/M
Quantity produced listed		
1	Tony Gwynn/100	15.00
2	Magglio Ordonez/100	8.00
3	George Brett/100	40.00
4	Rickey Henderson/100	15.00
5	Billy Williams/100	10.00
6	Frank Thomas/100	10.00
7	Tony Gwynn/75	20.00
8	Billy Williams/20	
9	Frank Robinson/20	
10	Ryne Sandberg/100	30.00
11	Miguel Tejada/100	10.00

Game Day Materials Auto

Quantity produced listed
No Pricing

HOF Combos

		NM/M
Quantity produced listed		
1	Al Kaline/50	50.00
2	Babe Ruth/25	
3	Eddie Mathews/50	
4	Kirby Puckett/75	40.00
5	Lou Gehrig/25	
6	Mike Schmidt/100	50.00
7	Nolan Ryan/50	100.00
8	Phil Rizzuto/50	30.00
9	Reggie Jackson/25	40.00
10	Roberto Clemente/25	
11	Rod Carew/100	25.00
12	Stan Musial/25	
13	Ty Cobb/25	
14	George Brett/50	85.00
15	Carlton Fisk/100	20.00

HOF Combos Autographs

Quantity produced listed

4	Kirby Puckett/25
6	Mike Schmidt/15
7	Nolan Ryan/25
8	Phil Rizzuto/25
11	Rod Carew/10
14	George Brett/15
15	Carlton Fisk/25

HOF Cuts

Production One set

Ty Cobb (8/03 auction)	6,500
Babe Ruth	
Lou Gehrig	
Jackie Robinson	

HOF Letters

No Pricing

HOF Materials

		NM/M
Quantity produced listed		
1	Al Kaline	25.00
2	Babe Ruth/75	140.00
3	Carlton Fisk/100	15.00
4	Eddie Mathews/100	20.00
5	Gary Carter/100	15.00
6	George Brett/100	35.00
7	Harmon Killebrew/100	25.00
8	Joe Morgan/100	10.00
9	Kirby Puckett/100	20.00
10	Lou Gehrig/100	110.00
11	Luis Aparicio/100	10.00
12	Mike Schmidt/100	25.00
13	Ozzie Smith/100	25.00
14	Phil Rizzuto/100	10.00
15	Reggie Jackson/100	15.00
16	Richie Ashburn/100	15.00
17	Roberto Clemente/100	60.00
18	Robin Yount/100	20.00
19	Rod Carew/100	15.00
20	Rogers Hornsby/100	45.00
21	Stan Musial/100	35.00
22	Ty Cobb/100	120.00
23	Willie McCovey/100	10.00
24	Yogi Berra/100	30.00
25	Al Kaline/100	25.00
26	Babe Ruth/50	300.00
27	Bobby Doerr/100	15.00
28	Brooks Robinson/100	15.00
29	Eddie Mathews/100	20.00
30	Harmon Killebrew/100	25.00
31	Ty Cobb/50	150.00
32	Joe Morgan/100	10.00
33	Lou Brock/100	10.00
34	Lou Gehrig/50	225.00
35	Mike Schmidt/100	25.00
36	Nolan Ryan/100	40.00
37	Nolan Ryan/100	40.00
38	Nolan Ryan/100	40.00
39	Phil Rizzuto/100	10.00
40	Reggie Jackson/25	25.00
41	Reggie Jackson/100	15.00
42	Roberto Clemente/50	90.00
43	Robin Yount/100	20.00
44	Rod Carew/100	15.00
45	Stan Musial/100	35.00
46	Tom Seaver/100	20.00
47	Steve Carlton/100	15.00
48	Carlton Fisk/100	15.00
49	Pee Wee Reese/100	15.00
50	Jackie Robinson/50	85.00

HOF Materials Auto.

Quantity produced listed

#	Player	NM/M
1	Al Kaline jsy/25	
1	Al Kaline bat/100	
3	Carlton Fisk/15	
5	Gary Carter/25	
6	George Brett/25	
7	Harmon Killebrew/25	80.00
8	Joe Morgan/15	
9	Kirby Puckett/25	
12	Mike Schmidt/15	180.00
13	Ozzie Smith/10	
15	Reggie Jackson/10	
18	Robin Yount/15	
23	Willie McCovey/25	
24	Yogi Berra/15	150.00
28	Brooks Robinson/25	75.00
30	Harmon Killebrew/50	75.00
33	Lou Brock/50	
35	Mike Schmidt/25	
38	Nolan Ryan/25	
39	Phil Rizzuto/25	65.00
40	Reggie Jackson/5	
41	Reggie Jackson/15	
43	Robin Yount/25	175.00
44	Rod Carew/15	
45	Stan Musial/50	
46	Tom Seaver/25	
47	Steve Carlton/25	
48	Carlton Fisk/25	

HOF Numbers

Quantity produced listed

#	Player	NM/M
35	Mike Schmidt/50	40.00
36	Nolan Ryan/35	100.00
43	Robin Yount/35	50.00
47	Steve Carlton/40	20.00
48	Carlton Fisk/35	45.00

HOF Prime Combos

Quantity produced listed

1	Al Kaline/5
2	Babe Ruth
3	Eddie Mathews/25
4	Kirby Puckett/15
6	Mike Schmidt/25
7	Nolan Ryan
8	Phil Rizzuto
10	Roberto Clemente
11	Rod Carew/5
14	George Brett/10
15	Carlton Fisk/5

HOF Logos

Quantity produced listed

#	Player	NM/M
29	Eddie Mathews/35	65.00
36	Nolan Ryan/35	100.00
37	Nolan Ryan/35	100.00
38	Nolan Ryan/35	100.00
43	Robin Yount/35	50.00

HOF Induction Year Combos

Production 25 sets

		NM/M
1	Babe Ruth, Ty Cobb/25	
2	Jimmie Foxx, Mel Ott/25	
3	Early Wynn, Yogi Berra/25	
4	Roberto Clemente, Warren Spahn/25	
5	Al Kaline, Duke Snider/25	
6	Enos Slaughter, Lou Brock/25	60.00
7	Jim Palmer, Joe Morgan/25	
8	Phil Rizzuto, Steve Carlton/25	45.00
9	Mike Schmidt, Richie Ashburn/25	
10	George Brett, Robin Yount/25	185.00

Home Run Materials

Quantity produced listed

#	Player	NM/M
1	Harmon Killebrew/100	20.00
2	Harmon Killebrew/100	20.00
3	Jose Canseco/100	15.00
4	Magglio Ordonez/100	8.00
5	Rafael Palmeiro/100	15.00
6	Rafael Palmeiro/100	15.00
7	Rafael Palmeiro/100	15.00
8	Alex Rodriguez/100	15.00
9	Alex Rodriguez/100	15.00
10	Alex Rodriguez/100	15.00
11	Alex Rodriguez/20	75.00
12	Adam Dunn/100	15.00

Home Run Materials Auto

Quantity produced listed

#	Player	NM/M
1	Harmon Killebrew/25	80.00
3	Jose Canseco/25	100.00
4	Magglio Ordonez/15	
5	Rafael Palmeiro/1	
8	Alex Rodriguez/15	
9	Alex Rodriguez/15	
10	Alex Rodriguez/15	
11	Alex Rodriguez/5	
12	Adam Dunn/25	

Past and Present

Production 100 sets

#	Player	NM/M
1	Alex Rodriguez/100	20.00
2	Hideo Nomo/100	25.00
3	Jason Giambi/100	20.00
4	Juan Gonzalez/100	15.00
5	Mike Piazza/100	20.00
6	Pedro J. Martinez/100	15.00
7	Randy Johnson/100	15.00
8	Rickey Henderson/100	20.00
9	Roberto Alomar/100	15.00
10	Roger Clemens/100	20.00
11	Sammy Sosa/100	35.00

Past & Present Letters

Quantity produced listed

#	Player	NM/M
1	Alex Rodriguez/75	30.00
2	Hideo Nomo/25	90.00
4	Juan Gonzalez/50	25.00
6	Pedro J. Martinez/75	35.00
7	Randy Johnson/75	40.00

Past & Present Numbers

Quantity produced listed

#	Player	NM/M
2	Hideo Nomo/25	75.00
3	Jason Giambi/75	40.00
6	Pedro J. Martinez/50	40.00
7	Randy Johnson/50	40.00

Past & Present Patches

No Pricing

First Season Prime Material

#	Player	NM/M
1	Ozzie Smith/75	50.00

Prime Materials

Quantity produced listed

#	Player	NM/M
1	Tony Gwynn/100	15.00
2	Magglio Ordonez/100	8.00
3	George Brett/100	
4	Rickey Henderson/100	15.00
5	Billy Williams	
6	Frank Thomas/100	10.00
7	Tony Gwynn/75	20.00
8	Billy Williams	
9	Frank Robinson/20	
10	Ryne Sandberg/100	30.00
11	Miguel Tejada/100	10.00

Prime Material Ink

Quantity produced listed

#	Player	NM/M
1	Adam Dunn/10	
2	Alan Trammell/50	50.00
4	Alex Rodriguez/5	
5	Andre Dawson/25	60.00
6	Barry Zito/10	
7	Bo Jackson/50	100.00
11	Cal Ripken Jr./50	
12	Cal Ripken Jr./50	
13	Cal Ripken Jr./50	
14	Dale Murphy/15	
15	Dave Parker/15	
16	David Cone/25	
20	Gary Carter/50	50.00
21	Harmon Killebrew/15	
23	Jim Thome/10	
24	Joe Carter/50	50.00
26	Jose Vidro/25	40.00
27	Kazuhisa Ishii/50	50.00
28	Kerry Wood/10	
29	Lance Berkman/10	
33	Nick Johnson/50	45.00
38	Paul LoDuca/25	
40	Randy Johnson/5	
41	Reggie Jackson/5	
43	Roberto Alomar/25	
44	Robin Yount/10	
45	Rod Carew/5	
48	Ryan Klesko/25	
50	Shawn Green/5	
53	Steve Carlton/50	50.00
57	Tony Gwynn/10	
58	Torii Hunter/50	50.00
59	Vladimir Guerrero/50	70.00
60	Will Clark/25	180.00

Material MLB Logo Ink

No Pricing

Material Ink

Quantity produced listed

#	Player	NM/M
1	Adam Dunn/50	45.00
2	Alan Trammell/100	30.00
3	Alex Rodriguez/25	150.00
5	Andre Dawson/100	30.00
6	Barry Zito/100	45.00
7	Bo Jackson/100	60.00
8	Bob Feller/25	70.00
9	Bobby Doerr/50	45.00
11	Cal Ripken Jr./50	200.00
12	Cal Ripken Jr./50	200.00
13	Cal Ripken Jr./25	225.00
14	Dale Murphy/50	45.00
15	Dave Parker/75	35.00
16	David Cone/100	30.00
17	Don Mattingly/100	85.00
18	Duke Snider/25	75.00
19	Edgar Martinez/50	50.00
20	Gary Carter/100	30.00
21	Harmon Killebrew/75	70.00
22	Jim Edmonds/25	55.00
23	Jim Thome/50	50.00
24	Joe Carter/100	30.00
25	Jose Canseco/50	50.00
26	Jose Vidro/100	20.00
27	Kazuhisa Ishii/100	40.00
28	Kerry Wood/50	60.00
29	Lance Berkman/50	40.00
30	Mark Mulder/25	65.00
32	Mike Schmidt/50	90.00
33	Nick Johnson/100	25.00
34	Nolan Ryan/25	225.00
35	Nolan Ryan/25	225.00
36	Nolan Ryan/25	225.00
37	Paul LoDuca/100	25.00
38	Paul Molitor/50	45.00
40	Reggie Jackson/40	85.00
41	Roberto Alomar/50	50.00
42	Roberto Alomar/100	40.00
43	Robin Yount/50	75.00
44	Rod Carew/25	
45	Roger Clemens/25	
46	Roger Clemens	
47	Ryan Klesko/75	25.00
48	Ryne Sandberg/25	140.00
49	Shawn Green/25	
50	Stan Musial/25	150.00
51	Steve Carlton/100	35.00
52	Steve Carlton/100	35.00
53	Todd Helton/50	60.00
54	Tom Seaver/50	50.00
55	Tony Gwynn/25	100.00
56	Torii Hunter/100	40.00
57	Vladimir Guerrero/100	40.00
58	Will Clark/50	85.00

Milestone Materials

Quantity produced listed

#	Player	NM/M
1	Cal Ripken Jr./24	
2	Willie McCovey/24	
3	Rickey Henderson/100	15.00

Past and Present Logos

Quantity produced listed

#	Player	NM/M
2	Hideo Nomo/25	90.00
3	Jason Giambi/75	40.00
5	Mike Piazza/50	40.00
8	Rickey Henderson/25	
10	Roger Clemens/35	
11	Sammy Sosa/25	

Rookie Year Combos

Quantity produced listed

#	Player	NM/M
1	Alfonso Soriano/25	
2	Adam Dunn/25	
4	Ivan Rodriguez/50	
5	Hank Blalock	
6	Mark Prior/50	50.00
7	Albert Pujols/50	80.00

okie Year Materials Lett

Quantity produced listed

#	Player	NM/M
4	Nomar Garciaparra/35	40.00
9	Ivan Rodriguez/35	20.00
12	Vladimir Guerrero/35	25.00
15	Andruw Jones/25	35.00
23	Ryan Klesko/15	
25	Hideo Nomo/25	
30	Albert Pujols/25	90.00

R.Y. Materials Logos

Quantity produced listed

#	Player	NM/M
9	Ivan Rodriguez/10	
12	Vladimir Guerrero/50	25.00
15	Andruw Jones/50	25.00
17	Fred Lynn/25	25.00
18	Jeff Kent/50	20.00
19	Gary Sheffield/50	25.00
22	Alfonso Soriano/20	60.00
23	Ryan Klesko/50	15.00
25	Hideo Nomo/25	
26	Mark Prior/25	
30	Albert Pujols/50	75.00

Rookie Year Materials

#	Player	NM/M
	Common Player:	8.00
1	Cal Ripken Jr./100	50.00
2	Mike Schmidt/50	40.00
3	Rafael Palmeiro/100	15.00
4	Nomar Garciaparra/100	20.00
5	Sean Casey	
6	Stan Musial/42	70.00
7	Yogi Berra/100	30.00
9	Ivan Rodriguez/100	10.00
12	Vladimir Guerrero/100	15.00
14	Ivan Rodriguez/91	10.00
15	Andruw Jones/96	15.00
16	Andruw Jones/100	15.00
17	Fred Lynn/100	10.00
18	Jeff Kent/100	8.00
19	Gary Sheffield/100	10.00
20	Ron Santo/100	15.00
21	Juan Gonzalez/100	15.00
22	Alfonso Soriano/100	25.00
23	Ryan Klesko/92	10.00
24	Adam Dunn/100	12.00
25	Hideo Nomo/100	25.00
26	Mark Prior/100	25.00
27	Pat Burrell/99	10.00
28	Magglio Ordonez/100	8.00
29	Kirby Puckett/84	25.00
30	Albert Pujols/100	30.00
31	Albert Pujols/100	30.00

R.Y. Materials Auto.

Quantity produced listed

#	Player	NM/M
1	Cal Ripken Jr./25	
2	Mike Schmidt/25	
7	Yogi Berra/15	150.00
15	Andruw Jones/10	
17	Fred Lynn/25	
19	Gary Sheffield/10	
20	Ron Santo/25	
23	Ryan Klesko/25	
26	Mark Prior/25	175.00
27	Pat Burrell/10	
28	Magglio Ordonez/25	50.00
29	Kirby Puckett/15	

R.Y. Materials Numbers

NM/M

Quantity produced listed

7	Yogi Berra/15	
9	Ivan Rodriguez/15	
12	Vladimir Guerrero/50	25.00
15	Andruw Jones/15	25.00
17	Fred Lynn/30	25.00
18	Jeff Kent/25	20.00
19	Gary Sheffield/25	30.00
21	Juan Gonzalez/30	30.00
22	Alfonso Soriano/35	50.00
23	Ryan Klesko/35	20.00
25	Hideo Nomo/25	
26	Mark Prior/35	65.00
30	Albert Pujols/25	90.00

2004 DONRUSS

		NM/M
Complete Set (400):		75.00
Common Player:		.10
Pack (10):		3.50
Box (24):		65.00
1	Derek Jeter	2.00
2	Greg Maddux	1.00
3	Albert Pujols	1.50
4	Ichiro Suzuki	1.00
5	Alex Rodriguez	1.50
6	Roger Clemens	1.50
7	Andruw Jones	.50
8	Barry Bonds	2.00
9	Jeff Bagwell	.50
10	Randy Johnson	.75
12	Scott Rolen	.50
13	Lance Berkman	.40
14	Barry Zito	.25
15	Manny Ramirez	.50
16	Carlos Delgado	.50
17	Alfonso Soriano	.75
18	Todd Helton	.50
19	Mike Mussina	.50
20	Nomar Garciaparra	1.50
21	Chipper Jones	1.00
22	Mark Prior	2.00
23	Jim Thome	.50
24	Vladimir Guerrero	.75
25	Pedro Martinez	.75
26	Sergio Mitre	.10
27	Adam Loewen	.10
28	Alfredo Gonzalez	.10
29	Miguel Ojeda	.10
30	Rosman Garcia	.10
31	Arnie Munoz	.10
32	Andrew Brown	.10
33	Josh Hall	.10
34	Josh Stewart	.10
35	Clint Barmes	.10
36	Brandon Webb	.10
37	Chien-Ming Wang	.10
38	Edgar Gonzalez	.10
39	Alejandro Machado	.10
40	Jeremy Griffiths	.10
41	Craig Brazell	.10
42	Daniel Cabrera	.10
43	Fernando Cabrera	.10
44	Termel Sledge	.10
45	Rob Hammock	.10
46	Francisco Rosario	.10
47	Francisco Cruceta	.10
48	Rett Johnson	.10
49	Guillermo Quiroz	.10
50	Hong-Chih Kuo	.10
51	Ian Ferguson	.10
52	Tim Olson	.10
53	Todd Wellemeyer	.10
54	Rich Fischer	.10
55	Phil Seibel	.10
56	Joe Valentine	.10
57	Matt Kata	.10
58	Michael Hessman	.10
59	Michel Hernandez	.10
60	Doug Waechter	.10
61	Prentice Redman	.10
62	Nook Logan	.10
63	Oscar Villarreal	.10
64	Pete LaForest	.10
65	Matt Bruback	.10
66	Dan Haren	.10
67	Greg Aquino	.10
68	Lew Ford	.10
69	Jeff Duncan	.10
70	Ryan Wagner	.10
71	Bengie Molina	.10
72	Brad Fullmer	.10
73	Darin Erstad	.25
74	David Eckstein	.10
75	Garret Anderson	.25
76	Jarrod Washburn	.10
77	Kevin Appier	.10
78	Scott Spiezio	.10
79	Tim Salmon	.25
80	Troy Glaus	.40
81	Troy Percival	.10
82	Jason Johnson	.10
83	Jay Gibbons	.25
84	Melvin Mora	.10
85	Sidney Ponson	.10
86	Tony Batista	.10
87	Bill Mueller	.10
88	Byung-Hyun Kim	.10
89	David Ortiz	.25
90	Derek Lowe	.25
91	Johnny Damon	.25
92	Casey Fossum	.10
93	Manny Ramirez	.50
94	Nomar Garciaparra	1.50
95	Pedro J. Martinez	.75
96	Todd Walker	.10
97	Trot Nixon	.10
98	Bartolo Colon	.25
99	Carlos Lee	.10
100	D'Angelo Jimenez	.10
101	Esteban Loaiza	.10
102	Frank Thomas	.50
103	Joe Crede	.10
104	Jose Valentin	.10
105	Magglio Ordonez	.25
106	Mark Buehrle	.10
107	Paul Konerko	.10
108	Brandon Phillips	.10
109	C.C. Sabathia	.10
110	Ellis Burks	.10
111	Jeremy Guthrie	.10
112	Josh Bard	.10
113	Matt Lawton	.10
114	Milton Bradley	.10
115	Omar Vizquel	.20
116	Travis Hafner	.10
117	Bobby Higginson	.10
118	Carlos Pena	.10
119	Dmitri Young	.20
120	Eric Munson	.10
121	Jeremy Bonderman	.10
122	Nate Cornejo	.10
123	Omar Infante	.10
124	Ramon Santiago	.10
125	Angel Berroa	.10
126	Carlos Beltran	.25
127	Desi Relaford	.10
128	Jeremy Affeldt	.10
129	Joe Randa	.10
130	Ken Harvey	.10
131	Mike MacDougal	.10
132	Michael Tucker	.10
133	Mike Sweeney	.20
134	Raul Ibanez	.20
135	Runelvys Hernandez	.10
136	A.J. Pierzynski	.10
137	Brad Radke	.10
138	Corey Koskie	.10
139	Cristian Guzman	.10
140	Doug Mientkiewicz	.10
141	Dustan Mohr	.10
142	Jacque Jones	.10
143	Kenny Rogers	.10
144	Bobby Kielty	.10
145	Kyle Lohse	.10
146	Luis Rivas	.10
147	Torii Hunter	.25
148	Alfonso Soriano	.75
149	Andy Pettitte	.40
150	Bernie Williams	.40
151	David Wells	.10
152	Derek Jeter	2.00
153	Hideki Matsui	2.00
154	Jason Giambi	.75
155	Jorge Posada	.50
156	Jose Contreras	.40
157	Mike Mussina	.50
158	Nick Johnson	.10
159	Robin Ventura	.20
160	Roger Clemens	1.50
161	Barry Zito	.25
162	Chris Singleton	.10
163	Eric Byrnes	.10
164	Eric Chavez	.25
165	Erubiel Durazo	.10
166	Keith Foulke	.10
167	Mark Ellis	.10
168	Miguel Tejada	.40
169	Mark Mulder	.25
170	Ramon Hernandez	.10
171	Ted Lilly	.10
172	Terrence Long	.10
173	Tim Hudson	.25
174	Bret Boone	.25
175	Carlos Guillen	.10
176	Dan Wilson	.10
177	Edgar Martinez	.25
178	Freddy Garcia	.10
179	Gil Meche	.10
180	Ichiro Suzuki	1.00
181	Jamie Moyer	.10
182	Joel Pineiro	.10
183	John Olerud	.20
184	Mike Cameron	.10
185	Randy Winn	.10
186	Ryan Franklin	.10
187	Kazuhiro Sasaki	.10
188	Aubrey Huff	.10
189	Carl Crawford	.10
190	Joe Kennedy	.10
191	Marlon Anderson	.10
192	Rey Ordonez	.10
193	Rocco Baldelli	.25
194	Toby Hall	.10
195	Travis Lee	.10
196	Alex Rodriguez	1.50
197	Carl Everett	.10
198	Chan Ho Park	.10
199	Einar Diaz	.10
200	Hank Blalock	.50
201	Ismael Valdes	.10
202	Juan Gonzalez	.50
203	Mark Teixeira	.40
204	Mike Young	.10
205	Rafael Palmeiro	.50
206	Carlos Delgado	.50
207	Kelvim Escobar	.10
208	Eric Hinske	.10
209	Frank Catalanotto	.10
210	Josh Phelps	.10
211	Orlando Hudson	.10
212	Roy Halladay	.25
213	Shannon Stewart	.10
214	Vernon Wells	.25
215	Carlos Baerga	.10
216	Curt Schilling	.40
217	Junior Spivey	.10
218	Luis Gonzalez	.25
219	Lyle Overbay	.10
220	Mark Grace	.25
221	Matt Williams	.20
222	Randy Johnson	.75
223	Shea Hillenbrand	.10
224	Steve Finley	.10
225	Andruw Jones	.50
226	Chipper Jones	1.00
227	Gary Sheffield	.40
228	Greg Maddux	1.00
229	Javy Lopez	.25
230	John Smoltz	.25
231	Marcus Giles	.20
232	Mike Hampton	.10
233	Rafael Furcal	.25
234	Robert Fick	.10
235	Russ Ortiz	.10
236	Alex Gonzalez	.10
237	Carlos Zambrano	.10
238	Corey Patterson	.10
239	Hee Seop Choi	.10
240	Kerry Wood	.50
241	Mark Belhorn	.10
242	Mark Prior	1.50
243	Moises Alou	.25
244	Sammy Sosa	1.50
245	Aaron Boone	.10
246	Adam Dunn	.40
247	Austin Kearns	.40
248	Barry Larkin	.25
249	Felipe Lopez	.10
250	Jose Guillen	.10
251	Ken Griffey Jr.	1.00
252	Jason LaRue	.10
253	Scott Williamson	.10
254	Sean Casey	.20
255	Shawn Chacon	.10
256	Chris Stynes	.10
257	Jason Jennings	.10
258	Jay Payton	.20
259	Jose Hernandez	.10
260	Larry Walker	.25
261	Preston Wilson	.20
262	Ronnie Belliard	.10
263	Todd Helton	.50
264	A.J. Burnett	.10
265	Alex Gonzalez	.10
266	Brad Penny	.10
267	Derrek Lee	.10
268	Ivan Rodriguez	.50
269	Josh Beckett	.50
270	Juan Encarnacion	.10
271	Juan Pierre	.10
272	Luis Castillo	.10
273	Mike Lowell	.10
274	Todd Hollandsworth	.10
275	Billy Wagner	.25
276	Brad Ausmus	.10
277	Craig Biggio	.25
278	Jeff Bagwell	.50
279	Jeff Kent	.25
280	Lance Berkman	.25
281	Richard Hidalgo	.10
282	Roy Oswalt	.25
283	Wade Miller	.10
284	Adrian Beltre	.10
285	Brian Jordan	.10
286	Cesar Izturis	.10
287	Dave Roberts	.10
288	Eric Gagne	.25
289	Fred McGriff	.25
290	Hideo Nomo	.40
291	Kazuhisa Ishii	.10
292	Kevin Brown	.25
293	Paul LoDuca	.10
294	Shawn Green	.40
295	Ben Sheets	.25
296	Geoff Jenkins	.25
297	Rey Sanchez	.10
298	Richie Sexson	.40
299	Wes Helms	.10
300	Brad Wilkerson	.10
301	Claudio Vargas	.10
302	Endy Chavez	.10
303	Fernando Tatis	.10
304	Javier Vazquez	.25
305	Jose Vidro	.10
306	Michael Barrett	.10
307	Orlando Cabrera	.20
308	Tony Armas Jr.	.10
309	Vladimir Guerrero	.75
310	Zach Day	.10
311	Al Leiter	.10
312	Cliff Floyd	.10
313	Jae Weong Seo	.10
314	Jeromy Burnitz	.10
315	Mike Piazza	1.00
316	Mo Vaughn	.10
317	Roberto Alomar	.40
318	Roger Cedeno	.10
319	Tom Glavine	.25
320	Jose Reyes	.10
321	Bobby Abreu	.20
322	Brett Myers	.10
323	David Bell	.10
324	Jim Thome	.50
325	Jimmy Rollins	.10
326	Kevin Millwood	.25
327	Marlon Byrd	.10
328	Mike Lieberthal	.10
329	Pat Burrell	.40
330	Randy Wolf	.10
331	Aramis Ramirez	.10
332	Brian Giles	.25
333	Jason Kendall	.20
334	Kenny Lofton	.20
335	Kip Wells	.10
336	Kris Benson	.10
337	Randall Simon	.10
338	Reggie Sanders	.10
339	Albert Pujols	2.00
340	Edgar Renteria	.10
341	Fernando Vina	.10
342	J.D. Drew	.10
343	Jim Edmonds	.25
344	Matt Morris	.10
345	Mike Matheny	.10
346	Scott Rolen	.50
347	Tino Martinez	.10
348	Woody Williams	.10
349	Brian Lawrence	.10
350	Mark Kotsay	.10
351	Mark Loretta	.10
352	Ramon Vazquez	.10
353	Rondell White	.10
354	Ryan Klesko	.25
355	Sean Burroughs	.10
356	Trevor Hoffman	.10
357	Xavier Nady	.10

358 Andres Galarraga .10
359 Barry Bonds 2.00
360 Benito Santiago .10
361 Deivi Cruz .10
362 Edgardo Alfonzo .10
363 J.T. Snow .10
364 Jason Schmidt .10
365 Kirk Rueter .10
366 Kurt Ainsworth .10
367 Marquis Grissom .10
368 Ray Durham .10
369 Rich Aurilia .10
370 Tim Worrell .10
371 Troy Glaus .20
372 Melvin Mora .10
373 Nomar Garciaparra .75
374 Magglio Ordonez .20
375 Omar Vizquel .10
376 Dmitri Young .10
377 Mike Sweeney .10
378 Torii Hunter .20
379 Derek Jeter 1.00
380 Barry Zito .20
381 Ichiro Suzuki .50
382 Rocco Baldelli .20
383 Alex Rodriguez .75
384 Carlos Delgado .25
385 Randy Johnson .40
386 Greg Maddux .50
387 Sammy Sosa .75
388 Ken Griffey Jr. .50
389 Todd Helton .25
390 Ivan Rodriguez .25
391 Jeff Bagwell .25
392 Hideo Nomo .20
393 Richie Sexson .20
394 Vladimir Guerrero .40
395 Mike Piazza .50
396 Jim Thome .25
397 Jason Kendall .10
398 Albert Pujols 1.00
399 Ryan Klesko .10
400 Barry Bonds 1.00

Career Stat Line

Cards Serial #'d from 251-500: 3-5X
Print run 101-250: 4-6X
Print run 61-100: 4-8X
Print run 26-60: 8-15X
No pricing for P/R 25 or less
Numbered to career statistic

Season Stat Line

Print run 101-261: 4-6X
Print run 61-100: 4-8X
Print run 26-60: 8-15X
No pricing for P/R 25 or less
Numbered to 2003 statistic

Black Press Proofs

No pricing due to scarcity
Production 10 sets
Hot Pack exclusive

Diamond Kings Insert

NM/M
Complete Set (25): 80.00
Common Player: 2.00
Production 2,500 sets
Studio Series: 1-2X
Production 250 sets
Black: 1.5-2X
Production 100 sets
1 Derek Jeter 8.00
2 Greg Maddux 6.00
3 Albert Pujols 8.00
4 Ichiro Suzuki 6.00
5 Alex Rodriguez 6.00
6 Roger Clemens 6.00

7 Andruw Jones 3.00
8 Barry Bonds 8.00
9 Jeff Bagwell 3.00
10 Randy Johnson 3.00
11 Scott Rolen 3.00
12 Lance Berkman 2.00
13 Barry Zito 2.00
14 Manny Ramirez 3.00
15 Carlos Delgado 2.50
16 Alfonso Soriano 4.00
17 Todd Helton 3.00
18 Mike Mussina 2.00
19 Austin Kearns 2.00
20 Nomar Garciaparra 6.00
21 Chipper Jones 4.00
22 Mark Prior 6.00
23 Jim Thome 3.00
24 Vladimir Guerrero 3.00
25 Pedro J. Martinez 3.00

Elite Series

NM/M
Complete Set (15): 60.00
Common Player: 2.00
Production 1,500 sets
Black: 1-2X
Production 150 sets
Dominators: No Pricing
Production 25 sets
1 Albert Pujols 8.00
2 Barry Zito 3.00
3 Gary Sheffield 3.00
4 Mike Mussina 3.00
5 Lance Berkman 2.00
6 Alfonso Soriano 4.00
7 Randy Johnson 4.00
8 Nomar Garciaparra 8.00
9 Austin Kearns 3.00
10 Manny Ramirez 3.00
11 Mark Prior 8.00
12 Alex Rodriguez 6.00
13 Derek Jeter 8.00
14 Barry Bonds 8.00
15 Roger Clemens 6.00

Power Alley Red

NM/M
Complete Set (20): 50.00
Common Player: 2.00
Production 2,500 sets
Red Die-Cut: 1-2X
Production 250 sets
Blues: 1X
Production 1,000 sets
Blue Die-Cuts: 1.5-2X
Production 100 sets
Purples: 1-2X
Production 250 sets
Purple Die-Cuts: No Pricing

Production 25 sets
Yellows: 1.5-2X
Production 100 sets
Yellow Die-Cuts: No Pricing
Production 10 sets
Greens: No Pricing
Production 25 sets
Green Die-Cuts: No Pricing
Production 5 sets
1 Albert Pujols 8.00
2 Mike Piazza 5.00
3 Carlos Delgado 2.00
4 Barry Bonds 8.00
5 Jim Edmonds 2.00
6 Nomar Garciaparra 6.00
7 Alfonso Soriano 4.00
8 Alex Rodriguez 6.00
9 Lance Berkman 2.00
10 Scott Rolen 3.00
11 Manny Ramirez 3.00
12 Rafael Palmeiro 3.00
13 Sammy Sosa 6.00
14 Adam Dunn 2.00
15 Andruw Jones 2.00
16 Jim Thome 3.00
17 Jason Giambi 3.00
18 Jeff Bagwell 3.00
19 Juan Gonzalez 3.00
20 Austin Kearns 2.00

Production Line OPS

NM/M
Complete Set (10): 25.00
Varying quanties produced
Black: 1-2X
Production 125 sets
Die-Cuts: 1-2X
Production 100 sets
1 Albert Pujols/1,106 5.00
2 Barry Bonds/1,278 5.00
3 Gary Sheffield/1,023 1.50
4 Todd Helton/1,088 2.00
5 Scott Rolen/910 3.00
6 Manny Ramirez/1,014 3.00
7 Alex Rodriguez/995 5.00
8 Jim Thome/958 3.00
9 Jason Giambi/939 3.00
10 Frank Thomas/952 3.00

Production Line Slugging

NM/M
Complete Set (10): 25.00
Varying quantities produced
Black: 1-2X
Production 75 sets
Die-Cuts: 1-2X
Production 100 sets
1 Alex Rodriguez/604 6.00
2 Frank Thomas/562 3.00
3 Garret Anderson/541 2.00
4 Albert Pujols/667 6.00
5 Sammy Sosa/553 5.00
6 Gary Sheffield/604 2.00
7 Manny Ramirez/587 3.00
8 Jim Edmonds/617 2.00
9 Barry Bonds/688 6.00
10 Todd Helton/630 3.00

Production Line OBP

NM/M
Complete Set (10): 25.00
Common Player: 2.00
Die-Cuts: 1-2X
Production 100 sets
Black: 2-3X
Production 40 sets
1 Todd Helton/458 3.00
2 Albert Pujols/439 6.00
3 Larry Walker/422 2.00
4 Barry Bonds/529 6.00
5 Chipper Jones/402 4.00
6 Manny Ramirez/427 3.00
7 Gary Sheffield/419 2.00
8 Lance Berkman/412 2.00
9 Alex Rodriguez/396 6.00
10 Jason Giambi/412 3.00

Production Line Average

NM/M
Complete Set (10): 35.00
Common Player:
Die-Cuts: 1-2X
Production 100 sets
Black: 2-3X
Production 35 sets
1 Gary Sheffield/330 2.00
2 Ichiro Suzuki/312 5.00
3 Todd Helton/358 3.00
4 Manny Ramirez/325 3.00
5 Garret Anderson/315 2.00
6 Barry Bonds/341 8.00
7 Albert Pujols/359 8.00
8 Derek Jeter/324 8.00
9 Nomar Garciaparra/301 6.00
10 Hank Blalock/300 3.00

All-Stars

NM/M
Complete Set (20): 40.00
Common Player: 1.50
Production 1,000 sets
Black: 1-2X
Production 250 sets
1 Alex Rodriguez 5.00
2 Roger Clemens 5.00
3 Ichiro Suzuki 3.00
4 Barry Zito 1.50
5 Garret Anderson 1.50
6 Derek Jeter 5.00
7 Manny Ramirez 2.00
8 Pedro J. Martinez 2.00
9 Alfonso Soriano 2.50
10 Carlos Delgado 1.50
11 Barry Bonds 5.00
12 Andruw Jones 2.00
13 Scott Rolen 2.00
14 Austin Kearns 1.50
15 Mark Prior 5.00
16 Vladimir Guerrero 2.00
17 Jeff Bagwell 2.00
18 Mike Piazza 3.00
19 Albert Pujols 5.00
20 Randy Johnson 2.50

Longball Leaders

NM/M
Complete Set (10): 20.00
Common Player: 1.50
Production 1,500 sets
Black: 1-2X
Production 250 sets
Die-Cuts: 1.5-3X
Production 50 sets
1 Barry Bonds 5.00
2 Alfonso Soriano 3.00
3 Adam Dunn 1.50
4 Alex Rodriguez 5.00
5 Jim Thome 2.00
6 Garret Anderson 1.50
7 Juan Gonzalez 2.00
8 Jeff Bagwell 2.00
9 Gary Sheffield 1.50
10 Sammy Sosa 4.00

Craftsmen

NM/M
Complete Set (15): 40.00
Common Player: 2.00
Production 2,000 sets

Black: 1-2X
Production 275 sets
Master Craftsmen: 1-2X
Production 150 sets
1 Alex Rodriguez 5.00
2 Mark Prior 5.00
3 Ichiro Suzuki 3.00
4 Barry Bonds 5.00
5 Ken Griffey Jr. 3.00
6 Alfonso Soriano 3.00
7 Mike Piazza 3.00
8 Chipper Jones 3.00
9 Derek Jeter 5.00
10 Randy Johnson 2.50
11 Sammy Sosa 4.00
12 Roger Clemens 4.00
13 Nomar Garciaparra 4.00
14 Greg Maddux 3.00
15 Albert Pujols 5.00

Mound Marvels

NM/M
Complete Set (15): 20.00
Common Player: 1.00
Production 750 sets
Black: 1-2X
Production 175 sets
1 Mark Prior 5.00
2 Curt Schilling 1.50
3 Mike Mussina 1.50
4 Kevin Brown 1.50
5 Pedro J. Martinez 2.50
6 Mark Mulder 1.00
7 Kerry Wood 1.50
8 Greg Maddux 3.00
9 Kevin Millwood 1.00
10 Barry Zito 1.50
11 Roger Clemens 5.00
12 Randy Johnson 2.50
13 Hideo Nomo 1.50
14 Tim Hudson 1.50
15 Tom Glavine 1.50

Inside View

NM/M
Complete Set (25): 50.00
Common Player: 1.00
Production 1,250 sets
1 Derek Jeter 5.00
2 Greg Maddux 3.00
3 Albert Pujols 5.00
4 Ichiro Suzuki 3.00
5 Alex Rodriguez 4.00
6 Roger Clemens 5.00
7 Andruw Jones 1.50
8 Barry Bonds 5.00
9 Jeff Bagwell 2.00
10 Randy Johnson 2.00
11 Scott Rolen 2.00
12 Lance Berkman 1.00
13 Barry Zito 1.50
14 Manny Ramirez 2.00
15 Carlos Delgado 1.50
16 Alfonso Soriano 2.00
17 Todd Helton 2.00
18 Mike Mussina 1.50
19 Austin Kearns 1.50
20 Nomar Garciaparra 4.00
21 Chipper Jones 3.00
22 Mark Prior 5.00
23 Jim Thome 2.00
24 Vladimir Guerrero 2.00
25 Pedro J. Martinez 2.50

Jersey Kings

NM/M
Quantity produced listed
Studio Current Player: 1.5X
Production 50
Studio Retired: No Pricing
Production 25
1 Alfonso Soriano/250 10.00
2 Sammy Sosa/250 15.00
3 Roger Clemens/250 15.00
4 Nomar Garciaparra/250 12.00
5 Mark Prior/250 15.00
6 Vladimir Guerrero/250 8.00
7 Don Mattingly/100 40.00
8 Roberto Clemente/100 80.00
9 George Brett/100 35.00
10 Nolan Ryan/100 40.00
11 Cal Ripken Jr./100 55.00
12 Mike Schmidt/100 40.00

Bat Kings

NM/M
Common Player: 5.00
Studio Current Player: 1.5X
Production 50
Studio Retired: No Pricing
Production 25
1 Alex Rodriguez/250 10.00
2 Albert Pujols/250 15.00
3 Chipper Jones/250 12.00
4 Lance Berkman/250 5.00
5 Cal Ripken Jr./100 50.00
6 George Brett/100 30.00
7 Don Mattingly/100 40.00
8 Roberto Clemente/100 75.00

Timber & Threads

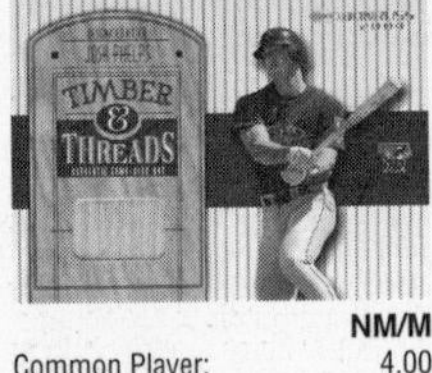

NM/M
Common Player: 4.00
Inserted 1:40
Studio Series: 1.5X
Production 50 sets
1 Adam Dunn 6.00
2 Alex Rodriguez - Blue 10.00
3 Alex Rodriguez - White 10.00
4 Andruw Jones 6.00
5 Austin Kearns 6.00
6 Carlos Beltran 4.00
7 Carlos Lee 4.00
8 Frank Thomas 8.00
9 Greg Maddux 10.00
10 Hideo Nomo 10.00
11 Jeff Bagwell 8.00
12 Lance Berkman 4.00
13 Magglio Ordonez 4.00
14 Mike Sweeney 4.00
15 Randy Johnson 8.00
16 Rocco Baldelli 10.00
17 Roger Clemens 12.00
18 Sammy Sosa 12.00
19 Shawn Green 4.00
20 Tom Glavine 6.00
21 Adam Dunn 6.00
22 Andruw Jones 6.00
23 Bobby Abreu 4.00
24 Hank Blalock 6.00
25 Ivan Rodriguez 6.00
26 Jim Edmonds 6.00
27 Josh Phelps 4.00
28 Juan Gonzalez 6.00
29 Lance Berkman 4.00
30 Larry Walker 4.00
31 Magglio Ordonez 4.00
32 Manny Ramirez 8.00
33 Mike Piazza 10.00
34 Nomar Garciaparra 10.00
35 Paul LoDuca 4.00
36 Roberto Alomar 6.00
37 Rocco Baldelli 10.00
38 Sammy Sosa 12.00
39 Vernon Wells 4.00
40 Vladimir Guerrero 8.00

2004 DONRUSS CLASSICS

NM/M
Complete Set (213):
Common Player: .40
Common (151-210): 3.00
Production 1,999
Pack (6): 6.00
Box (18): 90.00
1 Albert Pujols 2.50
2 Derek Jeter 3.00

3 Hank Blalock .50
4 Shannon Stewart .40
5 Jason Giambi 1.00
6 Carlos Lee .40
7 Trot Nixon .40
8 Bret Boone .50
9 Mark Mulder .40
10 Mariano Rivera .50
11 Scott Podsednik .75
12 Jim Edmonds .50
13 Mike Lowell .50
14 Robin Ventura .40
15 Brian Giles .50
16 Jose Vidro .40
17 Manny Ramirez .75
18 Alex Rodriquez 2.50
19 Carlos Beltran .50
20 Hideki Matsui 2.50
21 Johan Santana .40
22 Richie Sexson .50
23 Chipper Jones 1.00
24 Steve Finley .40
25 Mark Prior 2.00
26 Alexis Rios .40
27 Rafael Palmeiro .75
28 Jorge Posada .50
29 Barry Zito .50
30 Jamie Moyer .40
31 Preston Wilson .40
32 Miguel Cabrera .75
33 Pedro Martinez 1.00
34 Curt Schilling .75
35 Hee Seop Choi .40
36 Dontrelle Willis .50
37 Rafael Soriano .40
38 Richard Fischer .40
39 Brian Tallet .40
40 Jose Castillo .40
41 Wade Miller .40
42 Jose Contreras .40
43 Runelvys Hernandez .40
44 Joe Borchard .40
45 Kazuhisa Ishii .40
46 Jose Reyes .40
47 Adam Dunn .50
48 Randy Johnson 1.00
49 Brandon Phillips .40
50 Scott Rolen 1.00
51 Ken Griffey Jr. 1.50
52 Tom Glavine .50
53 Cliff Lee .40
54 Chien-Ming Wang .40
55 Roy Oswalt .50
56 Austin Kearns .50
57 Jhonny Peralta .40
58 Greg Maddux 1.50
59 Mark Grace .50
60 Jae Weong Seo .40
61 Nic Jackson .40
62 Roger Clemens 2.50
63 Jimmy Gobble .40
64 Travis Hafner .40
65 Paul Konerko .40
66 Jerome Williams .40
67 Ryan Klesko .50
68 Alexis Gomez .40
69 Omar Vizquel .40
70 Zach Day .40
71 Rickey Henderson .50
72 Morgan Ensberg .40
73 Josh Beckett .75
74 Garrett Atkins .40
75 Sean Casey .40
76 Julio Franco .40
77 Lyle Overbay .40
78 Josh Phelps .40
79 Juan Gonzalez .75
80 Rich Harden .40
81 Bernie Williams .50
82 Torii Hunter .50
83 Angel Berroa .40
84 Jody Gerut .40
85 Roberto Alomar .50
86 Byung-Hyun Kim .40
87 Jay Gibbons .40
88 Chone Figgins .40
89 Fred McGriff .50
90 Rich Aurilia .40
91 Xavier Nady .40
92 Marlon Byrd .40
93 Mike Piazza 1.50
94 Vladimir Guerrero 1.00
95 Shawn Green .50
96 Jeff Kent .50
97 Ivan Rodriguez .75
98 Jay Payton .40
99 Barry Larkin .50
100 Mike Sweeney .40
101 Adrian Beltre .40
102 Robby Hammock .40
103 Orlando Hudson .40
104 Mark Teixeira .50
105 Hong-Chih Kuo .40
106 Eric Chavez .50
107 Nick Johnson .40
108 Jacque Jones .40
109 Ken Harvey .40
110 Aramis Ramirez .40
111 Victor Martinez .40
112 Joe Crede .40
113 Jason Varitek .40
114 Troy Glaus .50
115 Billy Wagner .40
116 Kerry Wood 1.00
117 Hideo Nomo .50
118 Brandon Webb .40
119 Craig Biggio .40
120 Orlando Cabrera .40
121 Sammy Sosa 2.00
122 Bobby Abreu .50
123 Andruw Jones .75
124 Jeff Bagwell .75
125 Jim Thome 1.00
126 Javy Lopez .50
127 Luis Castillo .40
128 Todd Helton .75
129 Roy Halladay .50
130 Mike Mussina .50
131 Eric Byrnes .40
132 Eric Hinske .40
133 Nomar Garciaparra 2.00
134 Edgar Martinez .50
135 Rocco Baldelli .50
136 Miguel Tejada .50
137 Alfonso Soriano 1.00
138 Carlos Delgado .75
139 Rafael Furcal .50
140 Ichiro Suzuki 2.00
141 Aubrey Huff .40
142 Garret Anderson .50
143 Vernon Wells .40
144 Magglio Ordonez .50
145 Brett Myers .40
146 Luis Gonzalez .40
147 Lance Berkman .50
148 Frank Thomas .75
149 Gary Sheffield .50
150 Tim Hudson .50
151 Duke Snider 3.00
152 Carl Yastrzemski 4.00
153 Whitey Ford 3.00
154 Cal Ripken Jr. 8.00
155 Dwight Gooden 2.00
156 Warren Spahn 4.00
157 Bob Gibson 3.00
158 Don Mattingly 6.00
159 Jack Morris 2.00
160 Jim Bunning 2.00
161 Fergie Jenkins 2.00
162 Brooks Robinson 3.00
163 George Kell 2.00
164 Darryl Strawberry 2.00
165 Robin Roberts 2.00
166 Monte Irvin 2.00
167 Ernie Banks 4.00
168 Wade Boggs 3.00
169 Gaylord Perry 2.00
170 Keith Hernandez 2.00
171 Lou Brock 3.00
172 Frank Robinson 3.00
173 Nolan Ryan 8.00
174 Stan Musial 5.00
175 Eddie Murray 3.00
176 Byron Gettis 3.00
177 *Merkin Valdez* 5.00
178 Rickie Weeks 4.00
179 *Akinori Otsuka* 3.00
180 Brian Bruney 3.00

181 *Freddy Guzman* 3.00
182 Brendan Harris 3.00
183 *John Gall* 3.00
184 Jason Kubel 3.00
185 Delmon Young 4.00
186 Ryan Howard 3.00
187 Adam Loewen 3.00
188 J.D. Durbin 3.00
189 Dan Haren 3.00
190 Dustin McGowan 3.00
191 Chad Gaudin 3.00
192 Preston Larrison 3.00
193 Ramon Nivar 3.00
194 Ronald Belisario 3.00
195 Mike Gosling 3.00
196 Kevin Youkilis 3.00
197 Ryan Wagner 3.00
198 Bubba Nelson 3.00
199 Edwin Jackson 3.00
200 Chris Burke 3.00
201 *Carlos Hines* 3.00
202 *Greg Dobbs* 3.00
203 *Jamie Brown* 3.00
204 David Crouthers 3.00
205 *Ian Snell* 4.00
206 Gary Carter 3.00
207 Dale Murphy 3.00
208 Ryne Sandberg 5.00
209 Phil Niekro 2.00
210 Don Sutton 2.00
211 Alex Rodriguez/ Yankees/SP 5.00
212 Alfonso Soriano/ Rangers/SP 1.00
213 Greg Maddux/Cubs/SP 3.00

Timeless Tributes Green

Cards (1-150): 4-6X
Cards (151-210): 1-2X
Production 50 sets

Timeless Tributes Red

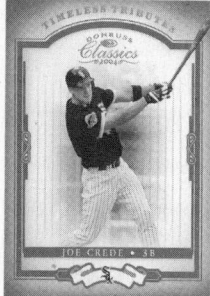

Red (1-150): 2-4X
Red (151-210): 1-1.5X
Production 100 sets

Timeless Tributes Platinum

No Pricing
Production one set

Timeless Triples Jersey

NM/M

Quantity produced listed
Prime: No Pricing
Production one set
1 Ted Williams, Carl Yastrzemski, Carlton Fisk/10
2 Lou Gehrig, Roger Maris, Thurman Munson/10
3 Brooks Robinson, Frank Robinson, Cal Ripken Jr./25 140.00

Timeless Triples Bat

NM/M

Production 25 sets
1 Ted Williams, Carl Yastrzemski, Carlton Fisk 185.00
2 Lou Gehrig, Roger Maris, Thurman Munson 200.00
3 Brooks Robinson, Frank Robinson, Cal Ripken Jr. 140.00

Timeless Triples

NM/M

Complete Set (6): 40.00
Common Player:
Production 500 sets
1 Ted Williams, Carl Yastrzemski, Carlton Fisk 10.00
2 Lou Gehrig, Roger Maris, Thurman Munson 8.00
3 Brooks Robinson, Frank Robinson, Cal Ripken Jr. 10.00
4 Roger Clemens, Andy Pettitte, Roy Oswalt 6.00
5 Greg Maddux, Mark Prior, Kerry Wood 10.00
6 Alex Rodriguez, Derek Jeter, Gary Sheffield 10.00

Team Colors Signatures

NM/M

Quantity produced listed
1 Lenny Dykstra Mets/50 15.00
2 Steve Garvey/50 25.00
3 Eric Davis/50 20.00
4 Al Oliver/50 15.00
6 Bobby Doerr/50 20.00
9 Harold Baines/50 25.00
10 Dwight Gooden/50 20.00
12 Jim Rice/50 20.00
14 Alan Trammell/50 20.00
15 Lee Smith/50 15.00
16 Dwight Evans/50 15.00
17 Tony Oliva/50 20.00
18 Dave Parker Pirates/50 15.00
19 Jack Morris/50 10.00
20 Luis Tiant/50 15.00
21 Andre Dawson Expos/25 25.00
22 Darryl Strawberry Dgr/50 20.00
23 George Foster/50 15.00
24 Marty Marion/50 15.00
25 Dennis Eckersley/50 25.00
31 Fred Lynn/50 15.00
34 Gary Carter/20 35.00
37 Keith Hernandez/25 35.00
39 Jim Palmer/20 20.00
40 Red Schoendienst/50 15.00
41 Steve Carlton/20 35.00
43 Tommy John/50 15.00
44 Luis Aparicio/50 20.00
45 Bob Feller/50 20.00
46 Andre Dawson Cubs/25 25.00
47 Bert Blyleven/50 12.00
48 Darryl Strawberry Mets/50 20.00
49 Dave Parker Reds/50 15.00
50 Lenny Dykstra Phils/50 15.00

Team Colors Jersey

NM/M

Quantity produced listed
Prime: No Pricing
Production one set
1 Lenny Dykstra Mets Fld Glv/25 15.00
2 Steve Garvey/100 6.00
3 Eric Davis/25 15.00
5 Nolan Ryan/50 30.00
6 Bobby Doerr/25 20.00
7 Paul Molitor/100 10.00
8 Dale Murphy/50 20.00
9 Harold Baines/100 8.00
10 Dwight Gooden/50 10.00
11 Jose Canseco/100 15.00
12 Jim Rice/100 8.00
13 Will Clark/50 25.00
14 Alan Trammell/100 8.00
15 Lee Smith/100 5.00
16 Dwight Evans/50 15.00
17 Tony Oliva/100 8.00
18 Dave Parker Pirates/25 10.00
19 Jack Morris/100 5.00
20 Luis Tiant/100 6.00
21 Andre Dawson Expos/100 6.00
22 Darryl Strawberry Dgr/100 8.00
23 George Foster/100 5.00
24 Marty Marion/50 6.00
25 Dennis Eckersley/100 6.00
26 Bo Jackson/50 30.00
27 Cal Ripken Jr./100 35.00
28 Deion Sanders/50 8.00
29 Don Mattingly Jacket/100 20.00
30 Mark Grace/50 15.00
31 Fred Lynn/50 8.00
32 Enos Slaughter/10
33 Ernie Banks/25 30.00
34 Gary Carter Jacket/100 8.00
35 Roger Maris/10
37 Keith Hernandez/25 15.00
38 Tony Gwynn/50 15.00
39 Jim Palmer/25 15.00
40 Red Schoendienst/25 15.00
41 Steve Carlton/25 15.00
42 Wade Boggs/25 25.00
43 Tommy John/100 5.00
44 Luis Aparicio/25 10.00
45 Bob Feller/10
46 Andre Dawson Cubs/25 15.00
47 Bert Blyleven/100 5.00
48 Darryl Strawberry Mets/100 8.00
49 Dave Parker Reds/100 5.00

Team Colors Combos Signature

NM/M

Quantity produced listed
Prime: No Pricing
Production one set
1 Lenny Dykstra Mets Fld Glv/100 15.00
2 Steve Garvey Jsy/100 15.00
3 Eric Davis Jsy/100 25.00
4 Al Oliver Bat/100 20.00
6 Bobby Doerr Jsy/100 20.00
9 Harold Baines Jsy/100 20.00
10 Dwight Gooden Jsy/100 25.00
12 Jim Rice Jsy/100 25.00
14 Alan Trammell Jsy/100 25.00
15 Lee Smith Jsy/100 20.00
16 Dwight Evans Jsy/100 25.00
17 Tony Oliva Jsy/100 20.00
18 Dave Parker Pirates Jsy/100 15.00
19 Jack Morris Jsy/100 20.00
20 Luis Tiant Jsy/100 20.00
21 Andre Dawson Expos Jsy/50 25.00
22 Darryl Strawberry Dgr Jsy/100 25.00
23 George Foster Jsy/100 20.00
24 Marty Marion Jsy/100 20.00
25 Dennis Eckersley Jsy/100 25.00
31 Fred Lynn Jsy/100 20.00
33 Ernie Banks Jsy/25 90.00
34 Gary Carter Jacket/50 40.00
36 Ron Santo Bat/25 50.00
37 Keith Hernandez Jsy/25 45.00
39 Jim PalmerJsy/50 35.00
40 Red Schoendienst Jsy/100 15.00
41 Steve Carlton Jsy/50 40.00
42 Wade Boggs Jsy/5
43 Tommy John Jsy/100 20.00
44 Luis Aparicio Jsy/100 15.00
46 Andre Dawson Cubs Jsy/50 25.00
47 Bert Blyleven Jsy/100 25.00
48 Darryl Strawberry Mets Jsy/100 25.00
49 Dave Parker Reds Jsy/100 15.00
50 Lenny Dykstra Phils Btg Glv/30 25.00

Team Colors Combos Material

NM/M

Production 25 sets
Prime: No Pricing
Production one set
2 Steve Garvey Bat-Jsy 15.00
3 Eric Davis Bat-Jsy 20.00
5 Nolan Ryan Bat-Jsy 50.00
6 Bobby Doerr Bat-Jsy 25.00
7 Paul Molitor Bat-Jsy 25.00
8 Dale Murphy Bat-Jsy 25.00
11 Jose Canseco Bat-Jsy 30.00
12 Jim Rice Bat-Jsy 25.00
13 Will Clark Bat-Jst 40.00
14 Alan Trammell Bat-Jsy 30.00
16 Dwight Evans Bat-Jsy 25.00
18 Dave Parker Pirates Bat-Jsy 20.00
21 Andre Dawson Expos Bat-Jsy 15.00
22 Darryl Strawberry Dgr Bat-Jsy 20.00
23 George Foster Bat-Jsy 10.00
26 Bo Jackson Bat-Jsy 40.00
27 Cal Ripken Jr. Bat-Jsy 65.00
28 Deion Sanders Bat-Jsy 25.00
29 Don Mattingly Bat-Jsy 45.00
30 Mark Grace Bat-Jsy 25.00
33 Ernie Banks Bat-Jsy 45.00
34 Gary Carter Bat-Jacket 25.00
35 Roger Maris Bat-Jsy/10
38 Tony Gwynn Bat-Jsy 40.00
40 Red Schoendienst Bat-Jsy 15.00
41 Steve CarltonBat-Jsy 20.00
42 Wade Boggs Bat-Jsy 25.00
44 Luis Aparicio Bat-Jsy 15.00
46 Andre Dawson Cubs Bat-Jsy 15.00
48 Darryl Strawberry Mets Bat-Jsy 20.00
49 Dave Parker Reds Bat-Jsy 20.00

Significant Signatures Red

NM/M

Quantity produced listed
3 Hank Blalock/50 30.00
4 Shannon Stewart/100 8.00
6 Carlos Lee/25 20.00
7 Trot Nixon/50 20.00
9 Mark Mulder/25 30.00
12 Jim Edmonds/25 30.00
13 Mike Lowell/50 20.00
14 Robin Ventura/50 10.00
16 Jose Vidro/25 20.00
19 Carlos Beltran/25 50.00
21 Johan Santana/100 30.00
24 Steve Finley/100 20.00
26 Alexis Rios/250 25.00
27 Rafael Palmeiro/25 65.00
28 Jorge Posada/25 45.00
32 Miguel Cabrera/100 40.00
36 Dontrelle Willis/100 25.00
37 Rafael Soriano/250 6.00
38 Richard Fischer/250 6.00
39 Brian Tallet/250 6.00
40 Jose Castillo/250 6.00
41 Wade Miller/92 15.00
42 Jose Contreras/25 25.00
43 Runelvys Hernandez/50 8.00
44 Joe Borchard/250 6.00
47 Adam Dunn/25 30.00
49 Brandon Phillips/70 6.00
50 Scott Rolen/25 35.00
53 Cliff Lee/100 8.00
54 Chien-Ming Wang/250 20.00
55 Roy Oswalt/25 30.00
56 Austin Kearns/25 20.00
57 Jhonny Peralta/250 6.00
60 Jae Weong Seo/100 10.00
61 Nic Jackson/250 8.00
63 Jimmy Gobble/200 10.00
64 Travis Hafner/100 12.00
65 Paul Konerko/25 15.00
66 Jerome Williams/250 20.00
68 Alexis Gomez/100 6.00
70 Zach Day/100 8.00
72 Morgan Ensberg/100 8.00
74 Garrett Atkins/245 6.00
76 Julio Franco/25 20.00
77 Lyle Overbay/250 15.00

78	Josh Phelps/50	8.00
79	Juan Gonzalez/25	45.00
80	Rich Harden/150	10.00
82	Torii Hunter/25	30.00
84	Jody Gerut/100	15.00
87	Jay Gibbons/100	15.00
88	Chone Figgins/100	10.00
90	Rich Aurilia/25	15.00
92	Marlon Byrd/25	15.00
98	Jay Payton/100	8.00
99	Barry Larkin/25	40.00
102	Robby Hammock/150	6.00
103	Orlando Hudson/100	6.00
105	Hong-Chih Kuo/100	20.00
106	Eric Chavez/25	35.00
107	Nick Johnson/25	15.00
108	Jacque Jones/100	10.00
109	Ken Harvey/250	8.00
110	Aramis Ramirez/100	20.00
111	Victor Martinez/99	20.00
112	Joe Crede/250	10.00
113	Jason Varitek/50	35.00
114	Troy Glaus/25	30.00
118	Brandon Webb/50	15.00
119	Craig Biggio/25	30.00
120	Orlando Cabrera50	10.00
121	Sammy Sosa/25	150.00
122	Bobby Abreu/25	15.00
123	Andruw Jones/25	30.00
124	Jeff Bagwell/25	65.00
127	Luis Castillo/50	10.00
131	Eric Byrnes/25	10.00
132	Eric Hinske/25	15.00
134	Edgar Martinez/50	30.00
135	Rocco Baldelli/25	40.00
143	Vernon Wells/25	15.00
144	Magglio Ordonez/25	30.00
145	Brett Myers/100	8.00
149	Gary Sheffield/50	20.00
150	Tim Hudson/25	40.00
151	Duke Snider/50	30.00
153	Whitey Ford/50	40.00
155	Dwight Gooden/100	20.00
156	Warren Spahn/25	45.00
158	Don Mattingly/25	100.00
159	Jack Morris/100	10.00
160	Jim Bunning/100	20.00
161	Fergie Jenkins/100	15.00
163	George Kell/100	15.00
164	Darryl Strawberry/100	20.00
165	Robin Roberts/100	15.00
166	Monte Irvin/100	15.00
167	Ernie Banks/50	50.00
168	Wade Boggs/50	30.00
169	Gaylord Perry/100	10.00
170	Keith Hernandez/ 100	20.00
171	Lou Brock/25	30.00
172	Frank Robinson/50	25.00
173	Nolan Ryan/50	85.00
174	Stan Musial/50	60.00
175	Eddie Murray/50	50.00
176	Byron Gettis/250	6.00
177	Merkin Valdez/250	15.00
178	Rickie Weeks/250	40.00
180	Brian Bruney/250	6.00
181	Freddy Guzman/250	6.00
182	Brendan Harris/250	6.00
183	John Gall/250	8.00
184	Jason Kubel/250	10.00
185	Delmon Young/100	30.00
186	Ryan Howard/250	10.00
187	Adam Loewen/250	15.00
188	J.D. Durbin/250	8.00
189	Dan Haren/250	10.00
190	Dustin McGowan/250	10.00
191	Chad Gaudin/250	6.00
192	Preston Larrison/250	6.00
193	Ramon Nivar/250	6.00
195	Mike Gosling/250	6.00
196	Kevin Youkilis/250	15.00
197	Ryan Wagner/250	10.00
198	Bubba Nelson/250	8.00
199	Edwin Jackson/250	10.00
200	Chris Burke/250	6.00
201	Carlos Hines/250	10.00
202	Greg Dobbs/150	6.00
203	Jamie Brown/250	8.00
204	David Crouthers/250	6.00
205	Ian Snell/250	20.00
206	Gary Carter/100	20.00
207	Dale Murphy/50	40.00
208	Ryne Sandberg/25	85.00
209	Phil Niekro/100	15.00
210	Don Sutton/100	15.00

Significant Signatures Green

NM/M

Quantity produced listed

3	Hank Blalock/25	40.00
4	Shannon Stewart/50	10.00
7	Trot Nixon/25	30.00
13	Mike Lowell/25	25.00
14	Robin Ventura/25	15.00
19	Carlos Beltran/25	50.00
21	Johan Santana/50	35.00
24	Steve Finley/25	25.00
26	Alexis Rios/100	25.00
32	Miguel Cabrera/50	50.00
36	Dontrelle Willis/25	25.00
37	Rafael Soriano/100	6.00
38	Richard Fischer/100	6.00
39	Brian Tallet/100	6.00
40	Jose Castillo/100	6.00
41	Wade Miller/25	20.00
43	Runelvys Hernandez/ 20	10.00
44	Joe Borchard/50	8.00
47	Adam Dunn/25	30.00
49	Brandon Phillips/50	6.00
53	Cliff Lee/50	10.00
54	Chien-Ming Wang/50	30.00
57	Jhonny Peralta/100	6.00
60	Jae Weong Seo/50	15.00
61	Nic Jackson/100	8.00
63	Jimmy Gobble/45	10.00
64	Travis Hafner/50	12.00
66	Jerome Williams/50	20.00
68	Alexis Gomez/50	6.00
70	Zach Day/50	8.00
72	Morgan Ensberg/50	8.00
74	Garrett Atkins/99	6.00
77	Lyle Overbay/100	15.00
78	Josh Phelps/25	10.00
79	Juan Gonzalez/25	45.00
80	Rich Harden/50	15.00
84	Jody Gerut/50	15.00
87	Jay Gibbons/50	15.00
88	Chone Figgins/50	10.00
98	Jay Payton/50	10.00
99	Barry Larkin/25	40.00
102	Robby Hammock/50	6.00
103	Orlando Hudson/50	6.00
105	Hong-Chih Kuo/50	20.00
106	Eric Chavez/25	35.00
108	Jacque Jones/50	10.00
109	Ken Harvey/100	8.00
110	Aramis Ramirez/50	20.00
111	Victor Martinez/50	20.00
112	Joe Crede/50	10.00
113	Jason Varitek/25	40.00
118	Brandon Webb/25	15.00
121	Sammy Sosa/21	150.00
127	Luis Castillo/25	10.00
134	Edgar Martinez/25	40.00
145	Brett Myers/50	8.00
149	Gary Sheffield/25	25.00
151	Duke Snider/25	35.00
153	Whitey Ford/25	40.00
155	Dwight Gooden/50	20.00
158	Don Mattingly/25	100.00
159	Jack Morris/50	10.00
160	Jim Bunning/25	25.00
161	Fergie Jenkins/50	15.00
163	George Kell/50	15.00
164	Darryl Strawberry/50	20.00
165	Robin Roberts/25	30.00
166	Monte Irvin/25	20.00
167	Ernie Banks/25	60.00
168	Wade Boggs/25	40.00
169	Gaylord Perry/50	10.00
170	Keith Hernandez/50	20.00
172	Frank Robinson/25	30.00
173	Nolan Ryan/25	120.00
174	Stan Musial/25	70.00
175	Eddie Murray/25	50.00
176	Byron Gettis/100	6.00
177	Merkin Valdez/100	20.00
178	Rickie Weeks/25	50.00
180	Brian Bruney/100	6.00
181	Freddy Guzman/100	6.00
182	Brendan Harris/100	6.00
183	John Gall/100	8.00
184	Jason Kubel/100	12.00
185	Delmon Young/50	30.00
186	Ryan Howard/100	20.00
187	Adam Loewen/100	15.00
188	J.D. Durbin/100	8.00
189	Dan Haren/100	10.00
190	Dustin McGowan/100	10.00
191	Chad Gaudin/100	6.00
192	Preston Larrison/100	6.00
193	Ramon Nivar/100	6.00
195	Mike Gosling/100	6.00
196	Kevin Youkilis/100	15.00
197	Ryan Wagner/100	10.00
198	Bubba Nelson/100	8.00
199	Edwin Jackson/100	10.00
200	Chris Burke/100	6.00
201	Carlos Hines/100	10.00
202	Greg Dobbs/50	6.00
203	Jamie Brown/100	8.00
204	David Crouthers/100	6.00
205	Ian Snell/100	20.00
206	Gary Carter/50	25.00
207	Dale Murphy/50	40.00
208	Ryne Sandberg/50	75.00
209	Phil Niekro/50	20.00
210	Don Sutton/50	15.00

October Heroes Signature

NM/M

Quantity produced listed

1	Reggie Jackson/5	
2	Bob Gibson/5	
3	Carlton Fisk/5	
4	Whitey Ford/50	40.00
5	George Brett/5	

October Heroes Fabric

NM/M

Quantity produced listed

2	Bob Gibson Jsy/15	30.00
3	Carlton Fisk Jsy/25	20.00
4	Whitey Ford Jsy/25	20.00
5	George Brett Jsy/25	40.00
6	Roberto Clemente Jsy/5	
7	Roy Campanella Pants/5	20.00
8	Babe Ruth Pants/5	

October Heroes Combos Signature

NM/M

Quantity produced listed

1	Reggie Jackson Bat/5	
2	Bob Gibson Jsy/5	
3	Carlton Fisk Jsy/5	
4	Whitey Ford Jsy/50	45.00
5	George Brett Jsy/5	

October Heroes Combos Material

NM/M

Quantity produced listed

1	Reggie Jackson Bat-Hat/25	40.00
3	Carlton Fisk Bat-Jsy/25	30.00
5	George Brett Bat-Jsy/25	50.00
6	Roberto Clemente Bat-Jsy/25	
7	Roy Campanella Bat-Pants/25	35.00
8	Babe Ruth Bat-Pants/3	

October Heroes Bat

NM/M

Quantity produced listed

1	Reggie Jackson/25	25.00
3	Carlton Fisk/25	25.00
5	George Brett/10	
6	Roberto Clemente/25	65.00
7	Roy Campanella/25	25.00
8	Babe Ruth/10	

October Heroes

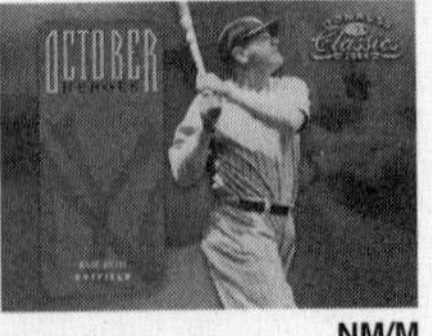

NM/M

Production 2,499 sets

1	Reggie Jackson	3.00
2	Bob Gibson	3.00
3	Carlton Fisk	2.00
4	Whitey Ford	2.00
5	George Brett	5.00
6	Roberto Clemente	5.00
7	Roy Campanella	3.00
8	Babe Ruth	6.00

Membership VIP Signatures

NM/M

Quantity produced listed

5	Al Kaline/20	50.00
9	Gaylord Perry/50	15.00
10	Fergie Jenkins/50	20.00
11	Steve Carlton/20	30.00
14	Bert Blyleven/50	10.00

Membership VIP Jersey

NM/M

Quantity produced listed

Prime: No Pricing

Production one set

1	Stan Musial/15	40.00
4	Roberto Clemente/25	75.00
5	Al Kaline Pants/25	20.00
8	Carl Yastrzemski/25	30.00
9	Gaylord Perry/25	10.00
10	Fergie Jenkins Pants/25	15.00
11	Steve Carlton/25	15.00
12	Reggie Jackson/25	25.00
13	Rod Carew/25	20.00
14	Bert Blyleven/25	10.00
15	Mike Schmidt/25	30.00
16	Nolan Ryan/25	35.00
17	Robin Yount/25	25.00
18	George Brett/25	40.00
19	Eddie Murray/25	25.00
20	Tony Gwynn/25	25.00
21	Cal Ripken Jr./25	85.00
22	Randy Johnson/25	20.00
23	Sammy Sosa/25	30.00
24	Rafael Palmeiro/25	20.00
25	Roger Clemens/25	25.00

Membership VIP Combos Signature

NM/M

Quantity produced listed

Prime: No Pricing

Production one set

5	Al Kaline Pants/25	50.00
9	Gaylord Perry Jsy/50	15.00
10	Fergie Jenkins Pants/50	20.00
11	Steve Carlton Jsy/25	40.00
14	Bert Blyleven Jsy/50	15.00

Membership VIP Combos Material

NM/M

Quantity produced listed

Prime: No Pricing

Production one set

1	Stan Musial Bat-Jsy/15	40.00
2	Ted Williams Bat-Jsy/9	
4	Roberto Clemente Bat-Jsy/25	100.00
5	Al Kaline Bat-Pants/25	30.00
7	Lou Brock Bat-Jsy/10	
8	Carl Yastrzemski Bat-Jsy/25	50.00
10	Fergie Jenkins Fld Glv-Pants/25	15.00
11	Steve Carlton Bat-Jsy/25	15.00
12	Reggie Jackson Bat-Jsy/25	30.00
13	Rod Carew Bat-Pants/25	25.00
15	Mike Schmidt Bat-Jsy/25	40.00
16	Nolan Ryan Bat-Jsy/25	50.00
17	Robin Yount Bat-Jsy/25	40.00
18	George Brett Bat-Jsy/25	50.00
19	Eddie Murray Bat-Jsy/25	30.00
20	Tony Gwynn Bat-Jsy/25	40.00

21 Cal Ripken Jr. Bat-Jsy/25 80.00
22 Randy Johnson Bat-Jsy/25 25.00
23 Sammy Sosa Bat-Jsy/25 35.00
24 Rafael Palmeiro Bat-Jsy/25 25.00
25 Roger Clemens Bat-Jsy/25 30.00

Membership VIP Bat

NM/M

Quantity produced listed
1 Stan Musial/25 40.00
2 Ted Williams/25 100.00
4 Roberto Clemente/25 65.00
5 Al Kaline/25 20.00
7 Lou Brock/25 20.00
8 Carl Yastrzemski/25 25.00
11 Steve Carlton/25 15.00
12 Reggie Jackson/25 25.00
13 Rod Carew/25 20.00
15 Mike Schmidt/25 30.00
17 Robin Yount/25 25.00
19 Eddie Murray/25 25.00
20 Tony Gwynn/25 25.00
22 Randy Johnson/25 20.00
23 Sammy Sosa/25 30.00
24 Rafael Palmeiro/25 20.00
25 Roger Clemens/25 25.00

Membership

NM/M

Complete Set (25): 70.00
Common Player: 2.00
Production 2,499 sets
1 Stan Musial 4.00
2 Ted Williams 5.00
3 Early Wynn 2.00
4 Roberto Clemente 5.00
5 Al Kaline 4.00
6 Bob Gibson 3.00
7 Lou Brock 2.00
8 Carl Yastrzemski 4.00
9 Gaylord Perry 2.00
10 Fergie Jenkins 2.00
11 Steve Carlton 2.00
12 Reggie Jackson 3.00
13 Rod Carew 3.00
14 Bert Blyleven 2.00
15 Mike Schmidt 4.00
16 Nolan Ryan 6.00
17 Robin Yount 4.00
18 George Brett 6.00
19 Eddie Murray 3.00
20 Tony Gwynn 3.00
21 Cal Ripken Jr. 8.00
22 Randy Johnson 4.00
23 Sammy Sosa 5.00
24 Rafael Palmeiro 3.00
25 Roger Clemens 5.00

Legendary Spikes Material

NM/M

Quantity produced listed
13 R Henderson Yanks/25 30.00
17 Don Mattingly/50 40.00
29 Dave Winfield/50 15.00
42 Rickey Henderson A's/25 30.00
51 Rafael Palmeiro/25 25.00
52 Sammy Sosa/50 30.00
56 Rod Carew Angels/10
60 R Henderson Angels/25 30.00

Legendary Pants Material

NM/M

Quantity produced listed
1 Tony Gwynn/25 25.00
12 Andre Dawson/25 10.00
24 Harmon Killebrew/50 20.00
26 Al Kaline/50 20.00
35 Mel Ott/10
43 Ty Cobb/5
45 Roy Campanella/25 25.00
46 Luis Aparicio/50 10.00
47 Phil Rizzuto/50 15.00
48 Roger Maris A's/25 30.00
50 Lou Gehrig/4
51 Rafael Palmeiro/25 20.00
56 Rod Carew Angels/50 15.00
57 Whitey Ford/25 25.00
58 Fergie Jenkins/25 20.00
59 Babe Ruth/3

Legendary Lumberjacks Material

NM/M

Quantity produced listed
1 Tony Gwynn/100 15.00
2 Mike Schmidt/100 15.00
3 Johnny Bench/100 12.00
4 Roger Maris Yanks/25 40.00
5 Ted Williams/25 100.00
6 George Brett/100 25.00
7 Carlton Fisk/100 10.00
8 Reggie Jackson A's/100 12.00
9 Joe Morgan/100 5.00
10 Bo Jackson/100 15.00
11 Stan Musial/25 35.00
12 Andre Dawson/100 5.00
13 R Henderson Yanks/100 10.00
14 Cal Ripken Jr./100 40.00
15 Dale Murphy/100 12.00
16 Kirby Puckett/100 15.00
17 Don Mattingly/100 20.00
18 Brooks Robinson/100 15.00
19 Orlando Cepeda/100 5.00
20 Reggie Jackson Yanks/100 12.00
21 Roberto Clemente/25 65.00
22 Ernie Banks/100 15.00
23 Frank Robinson/100 15.00
24 Harmon Killebrew/100 20.00
25 Willie Stargell/100 15.00
26 Al Kaline/100 15.00
27 Carl Yastrzemski/100 15.00
28 Duke Snider/10
29 Dave Winfield/100 5.00
30 Eddie Murray/100 15.00
31 Eddie Mathews/50 20.00
32 Gary Carter/100 8.00
33 Rod Carew Twins/100 10.00
34 Jimmie Foxx/10
35 Mel Ott/25 35.00
36 Paul Molitor/100 10.00
37 Thurman Munson/50 20.00
38 Rogers Hornsby/25 50.00
39 Robin Yount/100 15.00
40 Wade Boggs/100 10.00
42 Rickey Henderson A's/50 10.00
43 Ty Cobb/10
44 Yogi Berra/25 20.00
45 Roy Campanella/25 30.00
46 Luis Aparicio/100 8.00
48 Roger Maris A's/25 40.00
49 Reggie Jackson Angels/100 15.00
50 Lou Gehrig/25 125.00
51 Rafael Palmeiro/100 8.00
52 Sammy Sosa/100 15.00
56 Rod Carew Angels/100 8.00
59 Babe Ruth/10
60 R Henderson Angels/100 10.00

Legendary Lumberjacks

NM/M

Common Player: 2.00
Production 1,000 sets
Spikes: 1-2X
Production 100 sets
Hats: 2-3X
Production 50 sets
Jackets: 2-3X
Production 50 sets
Jerseys: 1X
Production 500 sets
Leather: 1-2X
Production 100 sets
Pants: 2-3X
Production 50 sets
1 Tony Gwynn 3.00
2 Mike Schmidt 5.00
3 Johnny Bench 4.00
4 Roger Maris Yanks 5.00
5 Ted Williams 8.00
6 George Brett 6.00
7 Carlton Fisk 2.00
8 Reggie Jackson A's 3.00
9 Joe Morgan 2.00
10 Bo Jackson 3.00
11 Stan Musial 4.00
12 Andre Dawson 2.00
13 Rickey Henderson Yanks 2.00
14 Cal Ripken Jr. 8.00
15 Dale Murphy 2.00
16 Kirby Puckett 4.00
17 Don Mattingly 5.00
18 Brooks Robinson 3.00
19 Orlando Cepeda 2.00
20 Reggie Jackson Yanks 3.00
21 Roberto Clemente 6.00
22 Ernie Banks 4.00
23 Frank Robinson 3.00
24 Harmon Killebrew 3.00
25 Willie Stargell 3.00
26 Al Kaline 4.00
27 Carl Yastrzemski 4.00
28 Duke Snider 3.00
29 Dave Winfield 2.00
30 Eddie Murray 3.00
31 Eddie Matthews 3.00
32 Gary Carter 2.00
33 Rod Carew Twins 3.00
34 Jimmie Foxx 4.00
35 Mel Ott 3.00
36 Paul Molitor 3.00
37 Thurman Munson 4.00
38 Rogers Hornsby 3.00
39 Robin Yount 4.00
40 Wade Boggs 3.00
41 Jackie Robinson 5.00
42 Rickey Henderson A's 2.00
43 Ty Cobb 5.00
44 Yogi Berra 3.00
45 Roy Campanella 3.00
46 Luis Aparicio 2.00
47 Phil Rizzuto 3.00
48 Roger Maris A's 5.00
49 Reggie Jackson Angels 3.00
50 Lou Gehrig 6.00
51 Rafael Palmeiro 3.00
52 Sammy Sosa 5.00
53 Roger Clemens 6.00
54 Nolan Ryan 8.00
55 Steve Carlton 3.00
56 Rod Carew Angels 3.00
57 Whitey Ford 3.00
58 Fergie Jenkins 2.00
59 Babe Ruth 8.00
60 R Henderson Angels 2.00

Legendary Leather Material

NM/M

Quantity produced listed
16 Kirby Puckett Fld Glv/25 40.00
32 Gary Carter Fld Glv/25 35.00
51 Rafael Palmeiro Fld Glv/25 25.00

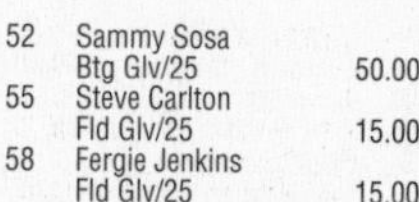

52 Sammy Sosa Btg Glv/25 50.00
55 Steve Carlton Fld Glv/25 15.00
58 Fergie Jenkins Fld Glv/25 15.00

Legendary Jerseys Material

NM/M

Quantity produced listed
Number: 1X
Production 3-50
No pricing for production 15 or less
Prime: No Pricing
Production one set
1 Tony Gwynn/50 20.00
2 Mike Schmidt/25 35.00
3 Johnny Bench/50 15.00
6 George Brett/25 50.00
7 Carlton Fisk/50 10.00
8 Reggie Jackson A's/25 30.00
9 Joe Morgan/25 15.00
10 Bo Jackson/25 50.00
12 Andre Dawson/50 10.00
13 R Henderson Yanks/25 20.00
14 Cal Ripken Jr./25 85.00
15 Dale Murphy/25 30.00
16 Kirby Puckett/50 15.00
17 Don Mattingly/50 25.00
18 Brooks Robinson/50 20.00
19 Orlando Cepeda/50 8.00
20 Reggie Jackson Yanks/25 25.00
21 Roberto Clemente/25 75.00
23 Frank Robinson/50 10.00
24 Harmon Killebrew/50 15.00
25 Willie Stargell/50 20.00
27 Carl Yastrzemski/50 25.00
29 Dave Winfield/50 10.00
30 Eddie Murray/50 20.00
31 Eddie Mathews/25 25.00
32 Gary Carter/50 8.00
33 Rod Carew Twins/25 20.00
36 Paul Molitor/50 15.00
39 Robin Yount/50 25.00
40 Wade Boggs/50 15.00
42 Rickey Henderson A's/25 25.00
44 Yogi Berra/15 35.00
46 Luis Aparicio/50 8.00
47 Phil Rizzuto/25 20.00
48 Roger Maris A's/25 40.00
49 Reggie Jackson Angels/50 15.00
51 Rafael Palmeiro/50 10.00
52 Sammy Sosa/50 20.00
53 Roger Clemens/50 25.00
p4 Nolan Ryan/50 30.00
55 Steve Carlton/50 8.00
56 Rod Carew Angels/50 15.00
57 Whitey Ford/25 35.00
59 Babe Ruth/5

Legendary Jackets Material

NM/M

Production 100 sets
2 Mike Schmidt 15.00
8 Reggie Jackson A's 15.00
17 Don Mattingly 20.00
32 Gary Carter 5.00
54 Nolan Ryan 30.00
56 Rod Carew Angels 10.00

Legendary Hats Material

NM/M

Quantity produced listed

2 Mike Schmidt/25 50.00
6 George Brett/25 60.00
14 Cal Ripken Jr./25 100.00
16 Kirby Puckett/25 30.00
20 Reggie Jackson Yanks/25 25.00
22 Ernie Banks/25 35.00
29 Dave Winfield/25 15.00
40 Wade Boggs/25 25.00
42 Rickey Henderson A'S/25 20.00
49 Reggie Jackson Angels/25 25.00
51 Rafael Palmeiro/25 20.00
52 Sammy Sosa/25 30.00
55 Steve Carlton/25 15.00
56 Rod Carew Angels/25 20.00
60 R Henderson Angels/25 20.00

Famous Foursomes Jersey

No Pricing
Production 10 sets
Prime: No Pricing
Production one set

Famous Foursomes

NM/M
Production 99 sets
1 Roy Campanella, Pee Wee Reese, Jackie Robinson, Duke Snider 15.00
2 Stan Musial, Bob Gibson, Red Schoendienst, Clete Boyer 15.00

Dress Code Jersey

NM/M
Common Player: 4.00
Production 100 sets
Number: 1X
Production 100 sets
Prime: 2X
Production 25 sets
1 Derek Jeter 25.00
2 Kerry Wood 15.00
3 Nomar Garciaparra 10.00
4 Jacque Jones 4.00
5 Mark Teixeira 5.00
6 Troy Glaus 6.00
7 Todd Helton 6.00
8 Miguel Tejada 6.00
9 Mike Piazza 10.00
11 Mike Sweeney 4.00
12 Albert Pujols 15.00
13 Rickey Henderson 8.00
14 Chipper Jones 8.00
15 Don Mattingly 25.00
16 Shawn Green 5.00
17 Mark Grace 10.00
18 Jason Giambi 8.00
19 Barry Zito 8.00
20 Sammy Sosa 12.00
21 Jay Gibbons 4.00
22 Rafael Palmeiro 8.00
23 Frank Thomas 8.00
24 Manny Ramirez 6.00
25 Mike Mussina 8.00
26 Magglio Ordonez 6.00
27 Rocco Baldelli 6.00
28 Andruw Jones 8.00
29 Torii Hunter 6.00
30 Ivan Rodriguez 8.00
31 Jeff Bagwell 8.00
32 Mark Mulder 6.00
33 Trot Nixon 5.00
34 Cal Ripken Jr./25 80.00
35 Dontrelle Willis 6.00
36 Hank Blalock 5.00
37 Brandon Webb 4.00
38 Miguel Cabrera 12.00
39 Hideo Nomo 8.00
40 Shannon Stewart 4.00
41 Tim Hudson 6.00
42 Pedro Martinez 8.00
43 Hee Seop Choi 4.00
44 Randy Johnson 8.00
45 Tony Gwynn 10.00
46 Mark Prior 20.00
47 Eric Chavez 6.00
48 Alex Rodriguez 10.00
49 Johan Santana 4.00
50 Alfonso Soriano 8.00

Dress Code Combos Signature

NM/M
Quantity produced listed
Prime: No Pricing
Production one set
4 Jacque Jones Jsy/25 15.00
21 Jay Gibbons Jsy/25 25.00
32 Mark Mulder Jsy/25 35.00
33 Trot Nixon Jsy/25 50.00
35 Dontrelle Willis Jsy/25 40.00
38 Miguel Cabrera Jsy/25 70.00
40 Shannon Stewart Jsy/25 20.00
49 Johan Santana Jsy/25 40.00

Dress Code Bat

NM/M
Common Player: 5.00
Production 50 sets
Combo Material: 1-1.5X
Production 50 sets
1 Derek Jeter 25.00
2 Kerry Wood 15.00
3 Nomar Garciaparra 15.00
4 Jacque Jones 5.00
5 Mark Teixeira 6.00
6 Troy Glaus 8.00
7 Todd Helton 10.00
8 Miguel Tejada 6.00
9 Mike Piazza 12.00
11 Mike Sweeney 5.00
12 Albert Pujols 20.00
13 Rickey Henderson 10.00
14 Chipper Jones 10.00
15 Don Mattingly 25.00
16 Shawn Green 5.00
17 Mark Grace 10.00
18 Jason Giambi 8.00
19 Barry Zito 8.00
20 Sammy Sosa 15.00
22 Rafael Palmeiro 10.00
23 Frank Thomas 10.00
24 Manny Ramirez 8.00
25 Mike Mussina 10.00
26 Magglio Ordonez 6.00
27 Rocco Baldelli 12.00
28 Andruw Jones 8.00
29 Torii Hunter 6.00
30 Ivan Rodriguez 10.00
31 Jeff Bagwell 10.00
32 Mark Mulder 6.00
33 Trot Nixon 10.00
34 Cal Ripken Jr. 60.00
35 Dontrelle Willis 8.00
36 Hank Blalock 8.00
37 Brandon Webb 8.00
38 Miguel Cabrera 10.00
39 Hideo Nomo 10.00
40 Shannon Stewart
41 Tim Hudson 8.00
42 Pedro Martinez 12.00
43 Hee Seop Choi 6.00
44 Randy Johnson 10.00
45 Tony Gwynn 15.00
46 Mark Prior 20.00
47 Eric Chavez 8.00
48 Alex Rodriguez 15.00
50 Alfonso Soriano 12.00

Classic Singles Jersey-Bat

NM/M
Quantity produced listed
Prime: No Pricing
Production one set
1 Babe Ruth Pants/5
2 Nolan Ryan/25 50.00
3 Stan Musial/15 45.00
4 Ted Williams/10
5 Lou Gehrig Pants/10
6 Eddie Murray/25 25.00
7 Roy Campanella Pants/25 35.00
8 Robin Yount/25 40.00
9 Roberto Clemente/25 125.00
10 Don Mattingly/25 40.00
12 Carl Yastrzemski/25 50.00
13 Mark Grace/25 20.00
15 Rickey Henderson/25 25.00
16 Reggie Jackson/25 25.00
17 Pee Wee Reese/25 25.00
20 Roger Maris/15 75.00
21 Cal Ripken Jr./25 75.00
23 Willie Stargell/25 20.00
24 Paul Molitor/25 25.00
26 Alan Trammell/25 20.00
27 Sammy Sosa/25 25.00
28 Bobby Doerr/25 25.00
29 Rod Carew/25 30.00
30 Yogi Berra/15 40.00
32 George Brett/25 50.00

Classic Singles Jersey

NM/M
Quantity produced listed
Prime: No Pricing
Production one set
1 Babe Ruth Pants/10
2 Nolan Ryan/50 35.00
3 Stan Musial/15 50.00
4 Ted Williams/10
5 Lou Gehrig Pants/10
6 Eddie Murray/100 10.00
7 Roy Campanella Pants/50 20.00
8 Robin Yount/100 15.00
9 Roberto Clemente/25 75.00
10 Don Mattingly/100 20.00
11 Bob Gibson/15 25.00
12 Carl Yastrzemski/50 20.00
13 Mark Grace/25 20.00
14 Jack Morris/100 6.00
15 Rickey Henderson/25 20.00
16 Reggie Jackson/50 15.00
17 Pee Wee Reese/25 25.00
18 Marty Marion/100 6.00
19 Tommy John/100 6.00
20 Roger Maris/25 50.00
21 Cal Ripken Jr./25 75.00
22 Red Schoendienst/25 10.00
23 Willie Stargell/100 15.00
24 Paul Molitor/100 10.00
25 Whitey Ford/50 25.00
26 Alan Trammell/100 10.00
27 Sammy Sosa/50 20.00
28 Bobby Doerr/50 8.00
29 Rod Carew/100 10.00
30 Yogi Berra/15 35.00
31 Phil Rizzuto/25 20.00
32 George Brett/25 40.00

Classic Singles Bat

NM/M
Quantity produced listed
1 Babe Ruth/15 250.00
2 Nolan Ryan/10
3 Stan Musial/25 30.00
4 Ted Williams/25 100.00
5 Lou Gehrig/50 125.00
6 Eddie Murray/50 15.00
7 Roy Campanella/50 20.00
8 Robin Yount/50 20.00
9 Roberto Clemente/25 70.00
10 Don Mattingly/50 25.00
12 Carl Yastrzemski/50 20.00
13 Mark Grace/50 15.00
15 Rickey Henderson/50 15.00
16 Reggie Jackson/50 15.00
17 Pee Wee Reese/50 15.00
20 Roger Maris/25 40.00
21 Cal Ripken Jr./50 60.00
23 Willie Stargell/50 15.00
24 Paul Molitor/50 20.00
26 Alan Trammell/50 12.00
27 Sammy Sosa/50 20.00
28 Bobby Doerr/50 8.00
29 Rod Carew/50 15.00
30 Yogi Berra/25 20.00
32 George Brett/50 30.00

Classic Combos Quad

NM/M
Quantity produced listed
Prime: No Pricing
Production one set
1 Babe Ruth Pants, Lou Gehrig Pants/5
2 Roy Campanella Pants, Pee Wee Reese/25 50.00
3 Ted Williams, Carl Yastrzemski/15 250.00
4 Roberto Clemente, Willie Stargell/25 200.00
5 Eddie Murray, Cal Ripken Jr./25 125.00
6 Roger Maris, Yogi Berra/15 150.00
10 Nolan Ryan, Rod Carew/25 70.00
11 Don Mattingly, Rickey Henderson/25 80.00
15 Robin Yount, Paul Molitor/25 75.00
16 Mark Grace, Sammy Sosa/25 60.00
17 Ted Williams, Bobby Doerr/15 200.00
18 Reggie Jackson, Rod Carew/25 40.00

Classic Combos Jersey

NM/M
Quantity produced listed
Prime: No Pricing
Production one set
1 Babe Ruth Pants, Lou Gehrig Pants/15 500.00
2 Roy Campanella Pants, Pee Wee Reese/25 30.00
3 Ted Williams, Carl Yastrzemski/15 200.00
4 Roberto Clemente, Willie Stargell/25 85.00
5 Eddie Murray, Cal Ripken Jr./25 75.00
6 Roger Maris, Yogi Berra/25 65.00
7 Stan Musial, Bob Gibson/10
8 Whitey Ford, Yogi Berra/25 30.00
9 Marty Marion, Stan Musial/25 40.00
10 Nolan Ryan, Rod Carew/25 40.00
11 Don Mattingly, Rickey Henderson/50 40.00
12 Jack Morris, Alan Trammell/50 15.00
13 Whitey Ford, Phil Rizzuto/25 30.00
14 Marty Marion, Red Schoendienst/25 15.00
15 Robin Yount, Paul Molitor/50 40.00
16 Mark Grace, Sammy Sosa/50 30.00
17 Ted Williams, Bobby Doerr/15 150.00
18 Reggie Jackson, Rod Carew/50 25.00

Classic Combos Bat

NM/M
Quantity produced listed
1 Babe Ruth, Lou Gehrig/25 375.00
2 Roy Campanella, Pee Wee Reese/50 25.00
3 Ted Williams, Carl Yastrzemski/25 125.00
4 Roberto Clemente, Willie Stargell/25 100.00
5 Eddie Murray, Cal Ripken Jr./50 50.00
6 Roger Maris, Yogi Berra/25 65.00
10 Nolan Ryan, Rod Carew/50 35.00
11 Don Mattingly, Rickey Henderson/50 40.00
15 Robin Yount, Paul Molitor/50 40.00
16 Mark Grace, Sammy Sosa/50 30.00
17 Ted Williams, Bobby Doerr/25 80.00
18 Reggie Jackson, Rod Carew/50 25.00

Team Colors Bat

NM/M
Quantity produced listed
2 Steve Garvey/50 10.00
3 Eric Davis/25 15.00
4 Al Oliver/50 8.00
5 Nolan Ryan/10
6 Bobby Doerr/25 20.00
7 Paul Molitor/50 15.00
8 Dale Murphy/50 20.00
11 Jose Canseco/50 20.00
12 Jim Rice/50 12.00
13 Will Clark/50 25.00
14 Alan Trammell/50 12.00

16 Dwight Evans/50 15.00
18 Dave Parker Pirates/25 10.00
21 Andre Dawson Expos/50 10.00
22 Darryl Strawberry Dgr/50 10.00
23 George Foster/50 8.00
26 Bo Jackson/50 30.00
27 Cal Ripken Jr./50 50.00
28 Deion Sanders/25 15.00
29 Don Mattingly Jacket/50 25.00
30 Mark Grace/50 15.00
31 Fred Lynn/50 8.00
33 Ernie Banks/25 30.00
34 Gary Carter/50 12.00
35 Roger Maris/25 40.00
36 Ron Santo/50 12.00
38 Tony Gwynn/50 15.00
40 Red Schoendienst/25 15.00
41 Steve Carlton/25 15.00
42 Wade Boggs/25 25.00
44 Luis Aparicio/25 10.00
46 Andre Dawson Cubs/25 12.00
48 Darryl Strawberry Mets/50 10.00
49 Dave Parker Reds/50 8.00

2004 DONRUSS DIAMOND KINGS

NM/M

Complete Set (175): 75.00
Common Player: .25
Common (151-175): 1.50
Pack (5): 7.50
Box (12): 80.00
1 Alex Rodriguez 2.50
2 Andruw Jones .75
3 Nomar Garciaparra 2.00
4 Kerry Wood .75
5 Magglio Ordonez .50
6 Victor Martinez .25
7 Jeremy Bonderman .25
8 Josh Beckett .75
9 Jeff Kent .40
10 Carlos Beltran .50
11 Hideo Nomo .50
12 Richie Sexson .50
13 Jose Vidro .25
14 Jae Weong Seo .25
15 Alfonso Soriano 1.00
16 Barry Zito .50
17 Brett Myers .25
18 Brian Giles .40
19 Edgar Martinez .40
20 Jim Edmonds .50
21 Rocco Baldelli .75
22 Mark Teixeira .50
23 Carlos Delgado .75
24 Julius Matos .25
25 Jose Reyes .50
26 Marlon Byrd .25
27 Albert Pujols 2.50
28 Vernon Wells .40
29 Garret Anderson .50
30 Jerome Williams .25
31 Chipper Jones 1.00
32 Rich Harden .25
33 Manny Ramirez .75
34 Derek Jeter 3.00
35 Brandon Webb .25
36 Mark Prior 2.00
37 Roy Halladay .50
38 Frank Thomas .75
39 Rafael Palmeiro .75
40 Adam Dunn .50
41 Aubrey Huff .25
42 Todd Helton .75
43 Matt Morris .40
44 Dontrelle Willis .40
45 Lance Berkman .50
46 Mike Sweeney .25
47 Kazuhisa Ishii .25
48 Torii Hunter .50
49 Vladimir Guerrero 1.00
50 Mike Piazza 1.50
51 Alexis Rios .25
52 Shannon Stewart .25
53 Eric Hinske .25
54 Jason Jennings .25
55 Jason Giambi 1.00
56 Brandon Claussen .25
57 Joe Thurston .25
58 Ramon Nivar .25
59 Jay Gibbons .25
60 Eric Chavez .50
61 Jimmy Gobble .25
62 Walter Young .25
63 Mark Grace .50
64 Austin Kearns .50
65 Bobby Abreu .25
66 Hee Seop Choi .25
67 Brandon Phillips .25
68 Rickie Weeks .50
69 Luis Gonzalez .50
70 Mariano Rivera .50
71 Jason Lane .25
72 Xavier Nady .25
73 Runelvys Hernandez .25
74 Aramis Ramirez .25
75 Ichiro Suzuki 2.00
76 Cliff Lee .25
77 Chris Snelling .25
78 Ryan Wagner .25
79 Miguel Tejada .50
80 Juan Gonzalez .75
81 Joe Borchard .25
82 Gary Sheffield .50
83 Wade Miller .25
84 Jeff Bagwell .75
85 Ryan Church .25
86 Adrian Beltre .25
87 Jeff Baker .25
88 Adam Loewen .25
89 Bernie Williams .50
90 Pedro J. Martinez 1.00
91 Carlos Rivera .25
92 Junior Spivey .25
93 Tim Hudson .50
94 Troy Glaus .50
95 Ken Griffey Jr. 1.50
96 Alexis Gomez .25
97 Antonio Perez .25
98 Dan Haren .25
99 Ivan Rodriguez .75
100 Randy Johnson 1.00
101 Lyle Overbay .25
102 Oliver Perez .25
103 Miguel Cabrera .75
104 Scott Rolen 1.00
105 Roger Clemens 2.00
106 Brian Tallet .25
107 Nic Jackson .25
108 Angel Berroa .25
109 Hank Blalock .50
110 Ryan Klesko .40
111 Jose Castillo .25
112 Paul Konerko .25
113 Greg Maddux 1.50
114 Mark Mulder .50
115 Pat Burrell .50
116 Garrett Atkins .25
117 Jeremy Guthrie .25
118 Orlando Cabrera .25
119 Nick Johnson .25
120 Tom Glavine .50
121 Morgan Ensberg .25
122 Sean Casey .25
123 Orlando Hudson .25
124 Hideki Matsui 2.50
125 Craig Biggio .25
126 Adam LaRoche .25
127 Hong-Chih Kuo .25
128 Paul LoDuca .25
129 Shawn Green .50
130 Luis Castillo .25
131 Joe Crede .25
132 Ken Harvey .25
133 Freddy Sanchez .25
134 Roy Oswalt .50
135 Curt Schilling .75
136 Alfredo Amezaga .25
137 Chien-Ming Wang .25
138 Barry Larkin .50
139 Trot Nixon .25
140 Jim Thome 1.00
141 Bret Boone .40
142 Jacque Jones .25
143 Travis Hafner .25
144 Sammy Sosa 2.00
145 Mike Mussina .50
146 Vinnie Chulk .25
147 Chad Gaudin .25
148 Delmon Young .50
149 Mike Lowell .40
150 Rickey Henderson .50
151 Roger Clemens 4.00
152 Mark Grace 2.00
153 Rickey Henderson 2.00
154 Alex Rodriguez 5.00
155 Rafael Palmeiro 2.00
156 Greg Maddux 3.00
157 Mike Piazza 3.00
158 Mike Mussina 1.50
159 Dale Murphy 1.50
160 Cal Ripken Jr. 6.00
161 Carl Yastrzemski 2.00
162 Marty Marion 1.50
163 Don Mattingly 4.00
164 Robin Yount 2.00
165 Andre Dawson 1.50
166 Jim Palmer 1.50
167 George Brett 5.00
168 Whitey Ford 2.00
169 Roy Campanella 2.00
170 Roger Maris 4.00
171 Duke Snider 2.00
172 Steve Carlton 2.00
173 Stan Musial 3.00
174 Nolan Ryan 6.00
175 Deion Sanders 1.50

Gallery of Stars

NM/M

Complete Set (15): 50.00
Common Player: 2.00
Inserted 1:37
1 Nolan Ryan 8.00
2 Cal Ripken Jr. 8.00
3 George Brett 6.00
4 Don Mattingly 6.00
5 Deion Sanders 2.00
6 Mike Piazza 4.00
7 Hideo Nomo 2.00
8 Rickey Henderson 2.00
9 Roger Clemens 6.00
10 Greg Maddux 4.00
11 Albert Pujols 6.00
12 Alex Rodriguez 6.00
13 Dale Murphy 3.00
14 Mark Prior 5.00
15 Dontrelle Willis 2.00

Heritage Collection

NM/M

Complete Set (25): 75.00
Common Player: 2.00
Inserted 1:22
1 Dale Murphy 3.00
2 Cal Ripken Jr. 8.00
3 Carl Yastrzemski 4.00
4 Don Mattingly 6.00
5 Jim Palmer 2.00
6 Andre Dawson 2.00
7 Roy Campanella 3.00
8 George Brett 6.00
9 Duke Snider 3.00
10 Marty Marion 2.00
11 Deion Sanders 2.00
12 Whitey Ford 3.00
13 Stan Musial 5.00
14 Nolan Ryan 8.00
15 Steve Carlton 2.00
16 Robin Yount 3.00
17 Albert Pujols 6.00
18 Alex Rodriguez 6.00
19 Mike Piazza 4.00
20 Roger Clemens 6.00
21 Hideo Nomo 2.00
22 Mark Prior 5.00
23 Roger Maris 5.00
24 Greg Maddux 4.00
25 Mark Grace 2.00

Timeline

NM/M

Common Player: 3.00
Inserted 1:92
1 Roger Clemens 6.00
2 Mark Grace 3.00
3 Mike Mussina 3.00
4 Mike Piazza 4.00
5 Nolan Ryan 8.00
6 Rickey Henderson 3.00

Team Timeline

NM/M

Complete Set (19): 65.00
Common Duo: 2.00
Inserted 1:29
1 Deion Sanders, Andruw Jones 2.00
2 Rickie Weeks, Robin Yount 3.00
3 Don Mattingly, Whitey Ford 8.00
4 Chipper Jones, Dale Murphy 4.00
5 Nomar Garciaparra, Bobby Doerr 5.00
6 Mark Prior, Sammy Sosa 6.00
7 Hideo Nomo, Kazuhisa Ishii 2.00
8 Andre Dawson, Mark Grace 3.00
9 Roger Clemens, Carl Yastrzemski 6.00
10 Mike Mussina, Cal Ripken Jr. 8.00
11 Stan Musial, Albert Pujols 6.00
12 Jim Palmer, Mike Mussina 2.00
13 Marty Marion, Stan Musial 4.00
14 George Brett, Mike Sweeney 6.00
15 Roger Clemens, Roger Maris 6.00
16 Duke Snider, Shawn Green 3.00
17 Jim Thome, Mike Schmidt 4.00
18 Nolan Ryan, Alex Rodriguez 8.00
19 Roy Campanella, Mike Piazza 4.00

HOF Heroes

NM/M

Common Player: 2.50
1 George Brett/1,000 6.00
2 George Brett/500 8.00
3 George Brett/250 12.00
4 Mike Schmidt/1,000 5.00
5 Mike Schmidt/250 8.00
6 Nolan Ryan/1,000 8.00
7 Nolan Ryan/500 10.00
8 Nolan Ryan/250 15.00
9 Roberto Clemente/1,000 6.00
10 Roberto Clemente/500 10.00
11 Roberto Clemente/250 15.00
12 Roberto Clemente/100 20.00
13 Carl Yastrzemski/1,000 4.00
14 Robin Yount/1,000 4.00
15 Whitey Ford/1,000 4.00
16 Duke Snider/1,000 4.00
17 Duke Snider/1,000 8.00
18 Carlton Fisk/1,000 3.00
19 Ozzie Smith/1,000 5.00
20 Kirby Puckett/1,000 4.00
21 Bobby Doerr/1,000 2.50
22 Frank Robinson/1,000 3.00
23 Ralph Kiner/1,000 2.50
24 Al Kaline/1,000 4.00
25 Bob Feller/1,000 3.00
26 Yogi Berra/1,000 4.00
27 Stan Musial/1,000 5.00
28 Stan Musial/500 8.00
29 Stan Musial/250 10.00
30 Jim Palmer/1,000 2.50
31 Johnny Bench/1,000 4.00
32 Steve Carlton/1,000 3.00
33 Gary Carter/1,000 3.00
34 Roy Campanella/1,000 3.00
35 Roy Campanella/250 8.00

Bronze

Bronze (1-150): 4-6X
Bronze (151-175): 2-3X
Production 100 sets
Bronze Sepia: 2-3X
Production 100

Platinum

Platinum: No Pricing
Production one set
Platinum Sepia: No Pricing
Production one set

Silver

Silver (1-150): 5-10X
Silver (151-175): 2-4X
Production 50 sets
Silver Sepia: 2-4X
Production 50

DK Combos Gold

Gold Combos: No Pricing
Production 1-5
Gold Combos Sepia: No Pricing
Production one set

DK Combos Platinum

Platinum Combos: No Pricing
Production one set
Platinum Combos Sepia: No Pricing
Production one set

DK Combos Framed Gold

Framed Gold Combos: No Pricing
Production 1-5
Framed Gold Sepia: No Pricing
Production 1-5

DK Combos Framed Platinum

Framed Platinum: No Pricing
Production one set

DK Combos Framed Silver

Framed Silver: No Pricing
Production 1-15
Framed Silver Sepia: No Pricing
Production 1-5

DK Combos Bronze

NM/M

Varying quantities produced

		NM/M
26	Marlon Byrd Bat-Jsy/30	20.00
32	Rich Harden Jsy-Jsy/15	50.00
53	Eric Hinske Bat-Jsy/30	20.00
57	Joe Thurston Bat-Jsy/25	15.00
59	Jay Gibbons Jsy-Jsy/15	35.00
65	Bob Abreu Bat-Jsy/15	25.00
74	Aramis Ramirez Bat-Bat/15	25.00
92	Junior Spivey Bat-Jsy/15	30.00
101	Lyle Overbay Bat-Jsy/30	15.00
103	Miguel Cabrera Bat-Jsy/30	35.00
108	Angel Berroa Bat-Pants/30	15.00
109	Hank Blalock Bat-Jsy/30	35.00
111	Jose Castillo Bat-Bat/15	15.00
121	Morgan Ensberg Bat-Jsy/30	15.00
123	Orlando Hudson Bat-Jsy/30	15.00
126	Adam LaRoche Bat-Bat/30	15.00
130	Luis Castillo Bat-Jsy/30	15.00
143	Travis Hafner Bat-Jsy/30	12.00
147	Chad Gaudin Jsy-Jsy/25	12.00

DK Combos Silver

Varying quantities produced

		NM/M
26	Marlon Byrd Bat-Jsy/15	15.00
101	Lyle Overbay Bat-Jsy/15	15.00
102	Miguel Cabrera Bat-Jsy/15	50.00
108	Angel Berroa Bat-Pants/15	20.00
109	Hank Blalock Bat-Jsy/15	50.00
121	Morgan Ensberg Bat-Jsy/15	20.00
123	Orlando Hudson Bat-Jsy/15	15.00
126	Adam LaRoche Bat-Bat/15	20.00

DK Combos Framed Bronze

Varying quantities produced

		NM/M
26	Marlon Byrd Bat-Jsy/25	12.00
35	Brandon Webb Bat-Jsy/25	25.00
53	Eric Hinske Bat-Jsy/25	15.00
57	Joe Thurston Bat-Jsy/25	12.00
59	Jay Gibbons Jsy-Jsy/25	15.00
62	Walter Young Bat-Bat/25	12.00
65	Bobby Abreu Bat-Jsy/25	15.00
71	Jason Lane Bat-Hat/25	15.00
74	Aramis Ramirez Bat-Bat/25	20.00
77	Chris Snelling Bat-Bat/25	12.00
81	Joe Borchard Bat-Jsy/25	10.00
92	Junior Spivey Bat-Jsy/25	12.00
97	Antonio Perez Bat-Pants/25	12.00
98	Dan Haren Bat-Jsy/25	15.00
101	Lyle Overbay Bat-Jsy/25	10.00
103	Miguel Cabrera Bat-Jsy/25	40.00
107	Nic Jackson Bat-Bat/25	10.00
108	Angel Berroa Bat-Pants/25	12.00
109	Hank Blalock Bat-Jsy/25	30.00
110	Ryan Klesko Bat-Jsy/15	20.00
111	Jose Castillo Bat-Bat/25	10.00
121	Morgan Ensberg Bat-Jsy/25	15.00
123	Orlando Hudson Bat-Jsy/25	12.00
126	Adam LaRoche Bat-Bat/25	15.00
127	Hong-Chih Kuo Bat-Bat/25	10.00
130	Luis Castillo Bat-Jsy/25	12.00
136	Alfredo Amezaga Bat-Jsy/15	15.00
143	Travis Hafner Bat-Jsy/15	15.00
147	Chad Gaudin Jsy-Jsy/25	10.00

Gallery of Stars Autograph

No Pricing

Timeline Jersey

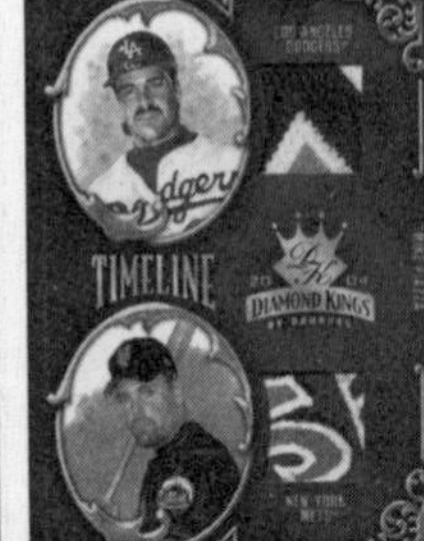

NM/M

Production 25 sets
Prime: No Pricing
Production one set

		NM/M
1	Roger Clemens	35.00
2	Mark Grace	25.00
3	Mike Mussina	20.00
4	Mike Piazza	35.00
5	Nolan Ryan	50.00
6	Rickey Henderson	20.00

Timeline Bat

Production 25 sets

		NM/M
1	Roger Clemens	35.00
2	Mark Grace	25.00
3	Mike Mussina	20.00
4	Mike Piazza	35.00
5	Nolan Ryan	50.00
6	Rickey Henderson	20.00

2004 DONRUSS ELITE

NM/M

Complete Set (205):
Common Player: .25
Common Auto. (151-180): 5.00
Production 250-1,000
Common (181-200): 2.00
Production 1,000
Pack (5): 5.00
Box (24): 100.00

		NM/M
1	Troy Glaus	.40
2	Darin Erstad	.25
3	Garret Anderson	.40
4	Tim Salmon	.40
5	Bartolo Colon	.40
6	Jose Guillen	.25
7	Miguel Tejada	.40
8	Adam Loewen	.25
9	Jay Gibbons	.25
10	Melvin Mora	.25
11	Javy Lopez	.40
12	Pedro J. Martinez	.75
13	Curt Schilling	.50
14	David Ortiz	.50
15	Keith Foulke	.25
16	Nomar Garciaparra	1.00
17	Magglio Ordonez	.40
18	Frank Thomas	.50
19	Carlos Lee	.40
20	Paul Konerko	.40
21	Mark Buehrle	.25
22	Jody Gerut	.25
23	Victor Martinez	.25
24	C.C. Sabathia	.25
25	Ellis Burks	.25
26	Bobby Higginson	.25
27	Jeremy Bonderman	.25
28	Fernando Vina	.25
29	Carlos Pena	.25
30	Dmitri Young	.25
31	Carlos Beltran	.50
32	Benito Santiago	.25
33	Mike Sweeney	.25
34	Angel Berroa	.25
35	Runelvys Hernandez	.25
36	Johan Santana	.25
37	Doug Mientkiewicz	.25
38	Shannon Stewart	.25
39	Torii Hunter	.40
40	Derek Jeter	2.00
41	Jason Giambi	.50
42	Bernie Williams	.40
43	Alfonso Soriano	.50
44	Gary Sheffield	.40
45	Mike Mussina	.50
46	Jorge Posada	.40
47	Hideki Matsui	1.00
48	Kevin Brown	.40
49	Javier Vazquez	.40
50	Mariano Rivera	.40
51	Eric Chavez	.40
52	Tim Hudson	.40
53	Mark Mulder	.40
54	Barry Zito	.40
55	Ichiro Suzuki	1.00
56	Edgar Martinez	.40
57	Bret Boone	.40
58	John Olerud	.40
59	Scott Spiezio	.25
60	Aubrey Huff	.40
61	Rocco Baldelli	.40
62	Jose Cruz Jr.	.25
63	Delmon Young	.40
64	Mark Teixeira	.40
65	Hank Blalock	.50
66	Michael Young	.40
67	Alex Rodriguez	2.00
68	Carlos Delgado	.50
69	Eric Hinske	.25
70	Roy Halladay	.40
71	Vernon Wells	.25
72	Randy Johnson	.75
73	Richie Sexson	.50
74	Brandon Webb	.25
75	Luis Gonzalez	.40
76	Steve Finley	.25
77	Chipper Jones	.75
78	Andruw Jones	.50
79	Marcus Giles	.25
80	Rafael Furcal	.25
81	J.D. Drew	.40
82	Sammy Sosa	1.50
83	Kerry Wood	.75
84	Mark Prior	1.50
85	Derrek Lee	.40
86	Moises Alou	.40
87	Corey Patterson	.40
88	Ken Griffey Jr.	1.00
89	Austin Kearns	.40
90	Adam Dunn	.50
91	Barry Larkin	.40
92	Todd Helton	.50
93	Larry Walker	.40
94	Preston Wilson	.25
95	Charles Johnson	.25
96	Luis Castillo	.25
97	Josh Beckett	.40
98	Mike Lowell	.40
99	Miguel Cabrera	.75
100	Juan Pierre	.25
101	Dontrelle Willis	.40
102	Andy Pettitte	.40
103	Wade Miller	.25
104	Jeff Bagwell	.50
105	Craig Biggio	.40
106	Lance Berkman	.40
107	Jeff Kent	.40
108	Roy Oswalt	.40
109	Hideo Nomo	.40
110	Adrian Beltre	.25
111	Paul LoDuca	.25
112	Shawn Green	.40
113	Fred McGriff	.40
114	Eric Gagne	.40
115	Geoff Jenkins	.40
116	Rickie Weeks	.40
117	Scott Podsednik	.40
118	Nick Johnson	.25
119	Orlando Cabrera	.25
120	Jose Vidro	.25
121	*Kazuo Matsui*	5.00
122	Tom Glavine	.40
123	Al Leiter	.25
124	Mike Piazza	1.00
125	Jose Reyes	.25
126	Mike Cameron	.25
127	Pat Burrell	.40
128	Jim Thome	.75
129	Mike Lieberthal	.25
130	Bobby Abreu	.40
131	Kip Wells	.25
132	Jack Wilson	.40
133	Pokey Reese	.25
134	Brian Giles	.40
135	Sean Burroughs	.25
136	Ryan Klesko	.40
137	Trevor Hoffman	.25
138	Jason Schmidt	.40
139	J.T. Snow	.25
140	A.J. Pierzynski	.25
141	Ray Durham	.25
142	Jim Edmonds	.40
143	Albert Pujols	1.50
144	Edgar Renteria	.40
145	Scott Rolen	.75
146	Matt Morris	.25
147	Ivan Rodriguez	.50

148 Vladimir Guerrero .75
149 Greg Maddux 1.00
150 Kevin Millwood .40
151 *Hector Gimenez AU/750* 5.00
152 *Willy Taveras AU/750* 5.00
153 Ruddy Yan AU/750 5.00
154 Graham Koonce AU/750 8.00
155 *Jose Capellan AU/750* 35.00
156 *Onil Joseph AU/750* 5.00
157 *John Gall AU/1000* 20.00
158 *Carlos Hines AU/750* 5.00
159 *Jerry Gil AU/750* 5.00
160 Mike Gosling AU/750 5.00
161 *Jason Frasor AU/750* 5.00
162 *Justin Knoedler AU/750* 5.00
163 *Merkin Valdez AU/500* 20.00
164 *Angel Chavez AU/1000* 5.00
165 *Ivan Ochoa AU/750* 10.00
166 *Greg Dobbs AU/750* 5.00
167 *Ronald Belisario AU/750* 5.00
168 *Aarom Baldiris AU/750* 10.00
169 *Kazuo Matsui*
170 David Crouthers AU/750 5.00
171 *Freddy Guzman AU/750* 10.00
172 *Akinori Otsuka AU/250* 50.00
173 *Ian Snell AU/750* 10.00
174 *Nick Regilio AU/1000* 5.00
175 *Jamie Brown AU/750* 5.00
176 *Jerome Gamble AU/750* 5.00
177 *Roberto Novoa AU/1000* 5.00
178 Sean Henn AU/1000 10.00
179 *Ramon Ramirez AU/1000* 15.00
180 *Jason Bartlett AU/1000* 10.00
181 Bob Gibson RET 2.00
182 Cal Ripken Jr. RET 8.00
183 Carl Yastrzemski RET 4.00
184 Dale Murphy RET 3.00
185 Don Mattingly RET 6.00
186 Eddie Murray RET 2.00
187 George Brett RET 6.00
188 Jackie Robinson RET 4.00
189 Jim Palmer RET 2.00
190 Lou Gehrig RET 5.00
191 Mike Schmidt RET 5.00
192 Ozzie Smith RET 5.00
193 Nolan Ryan RET 8.00
194 Reggie Jackson RET 3.00
195 Roberto Clemente RET 6.00
196 Robin Yount RET 4.00
197 Stan Musial RET 5.00
198 Ted Williams RET 8.00
199 Tony Gwynn RET 3.00
200 Ty Cobb RET 5.00
201 James Gandolfini FG 3.00
202 Freddy Adu FG 3.00
203 Summer Sanders FG 1.50
204 Janet Evans FG 1.50
205 Brandi Chastain FG 1.50

Aspirations

Cards (1-150) print run 61-99: 4-8X
(1-150) p/r 41-60: 6-10X
(1-150) p/r 21-40: 8-15X
Autos (151-180): .75-1.5X
(181-200): 2-3X
Production 19-99

Status

Cards (1-150) print run 61-81: 4-8X
(1-150) p/r 41-60: 6-10X
(1-150) p/r 21-40: 8-15X
Autos (151-180): .75-1X
(181-200): 3-4X
Production 1-81

Status Gold

Gold (1-150): 10-20X
Gold (151-180): No Pricing
Gold (181-200): 3-6X
Production 24 sets

Turn of the Century

Stars (1-150): 2-3X
Production 750

Stars (181-200): 1X
Production 250

Throwback Threads Autographs

NM/M

Production 25 Sets
Prime: No Pricing
Production 5-10
9 Ivan Rodriguez/25 60.00
13 Mark Prior/25 125.00
18 Sammy Sosa/25 175.00
35 Don Mattingly/25 120.00
37 Jim Palmer/25 40.00

Throwback Threads

NM/M

Quantity Produced Listed
Prime: 1.5X-3X
Prime Singles Production 10-25
Prime Duals Production 5-15
1 Albert Pujols/150 60.00
2 Alex Rodriguez Rgr/150 125.00
3 Alfonso Soriano/150 175.00
4 Chipper Jones/150 120.00
5 Derek Jeter/150 15.00
6 Greg Maddux/150 10.00
7 Hideo Nomo/150 8.00
8 Miguel Cabrera/150 8.00
9 Ivan Rodriguez/150 8.00
10 Jason Giambi/150 8.00
11 Jeff Bagwell/150 8.00
12 Lance Berkman/150 4.00
13 Mark Prior/150 10.00
14 Mike Piazza/150 10.00
15 Nomar Garciaparra/150 10.00
16 Pedro J. Martinez/150 8.00
17 Randy Johnson/150 8.00
18 Sammy Sosa/150 10.00
19 Shawn Green/150 4.00
20 Vladimir Guerrero/150 8.00
21 Adam Dunn, Austin Kearns/75 20.00
22 Barry Zito, Mark Mulder/75 10.00
23 Curt Schilling/75 10.00
24 Derek Jeter, Jason Giambi/75 25.00
25 Dontrelle Willis, Josh Beckett/75 15.00
26 Frank Thomas, Magglio Ordonez/75 15.00
27 Jim Thome/75 15.00
28 Kerry Wood, Mark Prior/75 40.00
29 Hank Blalock, Mark Teixeira/75 15.00
30 Albert Pujols, Scott Rolen/75 40.00
31 Babe Ruth/50 280.00
32 Cal Ripken Jr./100 40.00
33 Carl Yastrzemski/100 20.00
34 Deion Sanders/100 10.00
35 Don Mattingly/100 20.00
36 George Brett/100 20.00
37 Jim Palmer/100 8.00
38 Kirby Puckett/100 15.00
39 Lou Gehrig/100 125.00
40 Mark Grace/100 10.00
41 Mike Schmidt/100 20.00
42 Nolan Ryan/100 25.00
43 Ozzie Smith/100 20.00
44 Reggie Jackson/100 10.00
45 Rickey Henderson/100 10.00
46 Roberto Clemente/100 75.00
47 Roger Clemens/100 15.00
48 Roger Maris/100 40.00
49 Roy Campanella Pants/100 20.00
50 Tony Gwynn/100 15.00
51 Babe Ruth, Lou Gehrig/25 400.00
52 Cal Ripken Jr., Eddie Murray/50 50.00
53 Ted Williams, Carl Yastrzemski/50 85.00
54 Andre Dawson, Gary Carter/50 20.00
55 Reggie Jackson, Rod Carew/50 20.00
56 Derek Jeter, Phil Rizzuto/50 40.00
57 Nolan Ryan, Roy Oswalt/50 40.00
58 Roger Clemens, Mike Mussina/50 25.00
59 Albert Pujols, Stan Musial/50 40.00
60 Nomar Garciaparra, Stan Musial/50 85.00

Team Jerseys

NM/M

Production 100 Unless Noted
1 Cal Ripken Jr., Eddie Murray, Jim Palmer 50.00
2 Derek Jeter, Roger Clemens, Bernie Williams, Andy Pettitte 40.00
4 Josh Beckett, Dontrelle Willis, Ivan Rodriguez 15.00
5 Randy Johnson, Curt Schilling, Luis Gonzalez, Mark Grace 25.00
6 Derek Jeter, Wade Boggs, Darryl Strawberry 30.00
7 Chipper Jones, Tom Glavine, Greg Maddux, Ryan Klesko 25.00
9 Jackie Robinson, Roy Campanella, Duke Snider 75.00
10 Phil Rizzuto, Yogi Berra, Whitey Ford 35.00
11 Stan Musial, Curt Schilling, Marty Marion, Enos Slaughter 50.00

Team Bats

NM/M

Production 100 Sets
2 Derek Jeter, Roger Clemens, Bernie Williams, Andy Pettitte 30.00
3 Johnny Bench, Tony Perez, George Foster, Dave Concepcion 50.00
4 Josh Beckett, Dontrelle Willis, Ivan Rodriguez 15.00
5 Randy Johnson, Curt Schilling, Luis Gonzalez, Mark Grace 25.00
6 Derek Jeter, Wade Boggs, Darryl Strawberry 30.00
7 Chipper Jones, Tom Glavine, Greg Maddux, Ryan Klesko 25.00
8 Dwight Gooden, Gary Carter, Darryl Strawberry 20.00

Team

NM/M

Production 1,500 Sets
Black: 1X-2X
Production 150 Sets
Gold: 1-1.5X
Production 250 Sets
1 Cal Ripken Jr., Eddie Murray, Jim Palmer 8.00
2 Derek Jeter, Roger Clemens, Bernie Williams, Andy Pettitte 4.00
3 Johnny Bench, Tony Perez, George Foster, Dave Concepcion 4.00
4 Josh Beckett, Dontrelle Willis, Ivan Rodriguez 2.00
5 Randy Johnson, Curt Schilling, Luis Gonzalez, Mark Grace 2.00
6 Derek Jeter, Wade Boggs, Darryl Strawberry 5.00
7 Chipper Jones, Tom Glavine, Greg Maddux, Ryan Klesko 4.00
8 Dwight Gooden, Gary Carter, Darryl Strawberry 2.00
9 Jackie Robinson, Roy Campanella, Duke Snider 3.00
10 Phil Rizzuto, Yogi Berra, Whitey Ford 2.00
11 Stan Musial, Curt Schilling, Marty Marion, Enos Slaughter 4.00

Recollection Autographs

NM/M

Common Autograph: 8.00
1 Jeremy Affeldt 01/25 15.00
2 Erick Almonte 01/26 10.00
3 Rich Aurilia 02/2
4 Jeff Baker 02/25 30.00
5 Brandon Berger 01/25 8.00
6 Marlon Byrd 01/24 25.00
7 Juan Cruz 01/5
8 Ryan Drese 02/45 8.00
9 Brandon Duckworth 01/16 15.00
10 Casey Fossum 01/23 15.00
11 Geronimo Gil 01/25 8.00
12 Mark Grace 02/2
13 Jeremy Guthrie 02/25 20.00
14 Nic Jackson 02/95 8.00
15 Barry Larkin 01 PCRD/4
16 Greg Maddux 01 Ser/1
17 Antonio Perez 01/3
18 Mark Prior 02/14
19 Ivan Rodriguez 01 Ser/3
20 Ivan Rodriguez 01 SerDom/3
21 Ricardo Rodriguez 01/25 8.00
22 Ruben Sierra 97 GS/1
23 Bud Smith 01/25 8.00
24 Sammy Sosa 01/1
25 Junior Spivey 01/20 20.00
26 Tim Spooneybarger 01/25 10.00
27 Mark Teixeira 01/6
28 Martin Vargas 01/37 8.00

Passing the Torch Jerseys

NM/M

Quantity Produced Listed
1 Whitey Ford/100 15.00
2 Andy Pettitte/200 4.00
3 Willie McCovey/100 6.00
4 Will Clark/100 10.00
5 Stan Musial/100 25.00
6 Albert Pujols/200 15.00
7 Andre Dawson/200 8.00
8 Vladimir Guerrero/200 8.00
9 Dale Murphy/100 10.00
10 Chipper Jones/200 8.00
11 Joe Morgan/100 4.00
12 Barry Larkin/200 5.00
13 Jim "Catfish" Hunter/100 5.00
14 Tim Hudson/200 5.00
15 Jim Rice/200 5.00
16 Manny Ramirez/200 8.00
18 Mark Prior/200 10.00
19 Don Mattingly/100 15.00
20 Jason Giambi/200 8.00
21 Roy Campanella/50 30.00
22 Mike Piazza/200 10.00
23 Ozzie Smith/100 12.00

24 Scott Rolen/200 8.00
25 Roger Clemens/200 15.00
26 Mike Mussina/200 8.00
27 Babe Ruth/25 300.00
28 Roger Maris/50 50.00
29 Nolan Ryan/100 25.00
30 Roy Oswalt/200 4.00
31 Whitey Ford, Andy Pettitte/50 20.00
32 Willie McCovey, Will Clark/50 20.00
33 Stan Musial, Albert Pujols/50 50.00
34 Andre Dawson, Vladimir Guerrero/50 20.00
35 Dale Murphy, Chipper Jones/50 20.00
36 Joe Morgan, Barry Larkin/50 15.00
37 Jim "Catfish" Hunter, Tim Hudson/50 15.00
38 Jim Rice, Manny Ramirez/50 20.00
40 Don Mattingly, Jason Giambi/50 35.00
41 Roy Campanella, Mike Piazza 35.00
42 Ozzie Smith, Scott Rolen/50 30.00
43 Roger Clemens, Mike Mussina/50 30.00
44 Babe Ruth, Roger Maris/25
45 Nolan Ryan, Roy Oswalt/50 35.00

Passing the Torch Bats

NM/M

Quantity Produced Listed
2 Andy Pettitte/200 4.00
3 Willie McCovey/100 6.00
4 Will Clark/100 10.00
5 Stan Musial/100 25.00
6 Albert Pujols/200 15.00
7 Andre Dawson/100 8.00
8 Vladimir Guerrero/200 8.00
9 Dale Murphy/100 10.00
10 Chipper Jones/200 8.00
11 Joe Morgan/200 4.00
12 Barry Larkin/200 5.00
14 Tim Hudson/200 5.00
15 Jim Rice/200 5.00
16 Manny Ramirez/200 8.00
17 Greg Maddux/200 10.00
18 Mark Prior/200 10.00
19 Don Mattingly/100 15.00
20 Jason Giambi/200 8.00
21 Roy Campanella/50 30.00
22 Mike Piazza/200 10.00
23 Ozzie Smith/200 15.00
24 Scott Rolen/200 8.00
25 Roger Clemens/200 15.00
26 Mike Mussina/200 8.00
27 Babe Ruth/25 150.00
28 Roger Maris/50 50.00
29 Nolan Ryan/100 25.00
30 Roy Oswalt/200 4.00
32 Willie McCovey, Will Clark/50 20.00
33 Stan Musial, Albert Pujols/50 50.00
34 Andre Dawson, Vladimir Guerrero/50 20.00
35 Dale Murphy, Chipper Jones/50 20.00
36 Joe Morgan, Barry Larkin/50 15.00
38 Jim Rice, Manny Ramirez/50 20.00
39 Greg Maddux, Mark Prior/50 35.00
40 Don Mattingly, Jason Giambi/50 35.00
41 Roy Campanella, Mike Piazza/25 35.00
42 Ozzie Smith, Scott Rolen/50 30.00
43 Roger Clemens, Mike Mussina/50 30.00
44 Babe Ruth, Roger Maris/25 200.00
45 Nolan Ryan, Roy Oswalt/50 35.00

Passing the Torch Autographs

NM/M

Quantity Produced Listed
Many Not Priced Due To Scarcity

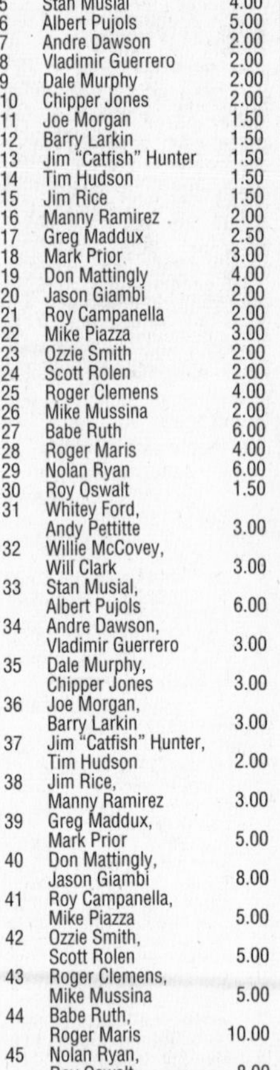

1 Whitey Ford/10
3 Willie McCovey/10
4 Will Clark/15 100.00
6 Stan Musial/10
7 Andre Dawson/50 15.00
8 Vladimir Guerrero/5
9 Dale Murphy/50 30.00
10 Chipper Jones/5
11 Joe Morgan/15 25.00
12 Barry Larkin/10
14 Tim Hudson/15 45.00
15 Jim Rice/50 15.00
16 Manny Ramirez/5
17 Greg Maddux/5
18 Mark Prior/15 125.00
19 Don Mattingly/10
20 Jason Giambi/10
21 Roy Campanella/10
22 Mike Piazza/5
23 Ozzie Smith/5
24 Scott Rolen/15 50.00
25 Roger Clemens/5
26 Mike Mussina/5
29 Nolan Ryan/10
30 Roy Oswalt/50 15.00
32 Willie McCovey, Will Clark/5
33 Stan Musial, Albert Pujols/5
34 Andre Dawson, Vladimir Guerrero/5
35 Dale Murphy, Chipper Jones/5
36 Joe Morgan, Barry Larkin/5
38 Jim Rice, Manny Ramirez/5
39 Greg Maddux, Mark Prior/5
42 Ozzie Smith, Scott Rolen/5
43 Roger Clemens, Mike Mussina/5
44 Babe Ruth, Roger Maris/1
45 Nolan Ryan, Roy Oswalt/5

Passing the Torch

NM/M

#1-30
Production 1,000
#31-45
Production 500
Black: 1X-2X
Production 50 or 100
Blue: 1X
Production 125 or 250
Gold: 1.5X-3X
Production 25 or 50
Green: .75X-1X
Production 250 or 500
1 Whitey Ford 3.00
2 Andy Pettitte 1.50
3 Willie McCovey 2.00
4 Will Clark 3.00
5 Stan Musial 4.00
6 Albert Pujols 5.00
7 Andre Dawson 2.00
8 Vladimir Guerrero 2.00
9 Dale Murphy 2.00
10 Chipper Jones 2.00
11 Joe Morgan 1.50
12 Barry Larkin 1.50
13 Jim "Catfish" Hunter 1.50
14 Tim Hudson 1.50
15 Jim Rice 1.50
16 Manny Ramirez 2.00
17 Greg Maddux 2.50
18 Mark Prior 3.00
19 Don Mattingly 4.00
20 Jason Giambi 2.00
21 Roy Campanella 2.00
22 Mike Piazza 3.00
23 Ozzie Smith 2.00
24 Scott Rolen 2.00
25 Roger Clemens 4.00
26 Mike Mussina 2.00
27 Babe Ruth 6.00
28 Roger Maris 4.00
29 Nolan Ryan 6.00
30 Roy Oswalt 1.50
31 Whitey Ford, Andy Pettitte 3.00
32 Willie McCovey, Will Clark 3.00
33 Stan Musial, Albert Pujols 6.00
34 Andre Dawson, Vladimir Guerrero 3.00
35 Dale Murphy, Chipper Jones 3.00
36 Joe Morgan, Barry Larkin 3.00
37 Jim "Catfish" Hunter, Tim Hudson 2.00
38 Jim Rice, Manny Ramirez 3.00
39 Greg Maddux, Mark Prior 5.00
40 Don Mattingly, Jason Giambi 8.00
41 Roy Campanella, Mike Piazza 5.00
42 Ozzie Smith, Scott Rolen 5.00
43 Roger Clemens, Mike Mussina 5.00
44 Babe Ruth, Roger Maris 10.00
45 Nolan Ryan, Roy Oswalt 8.00

Fans of the Game Autographs

NM/M

201 James Gandolfini 120.00
202 Freddy Adu 80.00
203 Summer Sanders 25.00
204 Janet Evans 25.00
205 Brandi Chastain 35.00

Career Best Jerseys

NM/M

Quantity Produced Listed
Prime: 1.5X-2X
Production 25-50
1 Albert Pujols/200 15.00
2 Alex Rodriguez/200 10.00
3 Alfonso Soriano/200 8.00
4 Andruw Jones/200 5.00
5 Barry Zito/200 4.00
6 Cal Ripken Jr./50 40.00
7 Chipper Jones/200 8.00
8 Curt Schilling/200 5.00
9 Derek Jeter/200 15.00
10 Don Mattingly/50 20.00
11 Dontrelle Willis/200 6.00
12 Doc Gooden/200 6.00
13 Eddie Murray/200 6.00
14 Frank Thomas/200 8.00
15 Gary Sheffield/200 5.00
16 George Brett/50 25.00
17 Greg Maddux/200 10.00
18 Hideo Nomo/200 8.00
20 Ivan Rodriguez/200 8.00
21 Jason Giambi/200 8.00
22 Jeff Bagwell/200 6.00
23 Jim Thome/200 8.00
24 Kerry Wood/200 10.00
25 Lance Berkman/200 4.00
26 Maggio Ordonez/200 4.00
27 Mark Prior/200 10.00
28 Mike Piazza/200 10.00
29 Mike Schmidt/100 10.00
30 Nomar Garciaparra/200 10.00
31 Pedro J. Martinez/200 8.00
32 Randy Johnson/200 8.00
33 Roger Clemens/200 15.00
34 Sammy Sosa/200 10.00
35 Tony Gwynn/50 15.00

Career Best Bats

NM/M

Production 100 or 200
Combo Print Run 50: 1X-2X
Combo P/R 25: 2X
Production 25 or 50
1 Albert Pujols/200 15.00
2 Alex Rodriguez/200 10.00
3 Alfonso Soriano/200 8.00
4 Andruw Jones/200 5.00
5 Barry Zito/200 4.00
6 Cal Ripken Jr./200 25.00
7 Chipper Jones/200 8.00
8 Curt Schilling/200 5.00
9 Derek Jeter/200 15.00
10 Don Mattingly/200 15.00
11 Dontrelle Willis/100 6.00
12 Doc Gooden/200 6.00
13 Eddie Murray/200 4.00
14 Frank Thomas/200 8.00
15 Gary Sheffield/200 5.00
16 George Brett/200 15.00
17 Greg Maddux/100 10.00
18 Hideo Nomo/100 8.00
20 Ivan Rodriguez/200 8.00
21 Jason Giambi/200 8.00
22 Jeff Bagwell/200 6.00
23 Jim Thome/200 8.00
24 Kerry Wood/100 10.00
25 Lance Berkman/200 4.00
26 Maggio Ordonez/200 4.00
27 Mark Prior/100 10.00
28 Mike Piazza/200 10.00
29 Mike Schmidt/200 10.00
30 Nomar Garciaparra/200 10.00
31 Pedro J. Martinez/200 8.00
32 Randy Johnson/200 8.00
33 Roger Clemens/200 15.00
34 Sammy Sosa/200 10.00
35 Tony Gwynn/200 8.00

Career Best

NM/M

Common Player: 1.00
Production 1,000 Sets
Black: 2X
Production 100 Sets
Gold Print Run 200-390: 1.5X
Gold P/R 101-200: 2X
Gold P/R 50-100: 3X
Gold P/R 26-50: 3X-5X
Gold P/R 15-25: 5X-8X
1 Albert Pujols 3.00
2 Alex Rodriguez 3.00
3 Alfonso Soriano 1.50
4 Andruw Jones 1.00
5 Barry Zito 1.00
6 Cal Ripken Jr. 5.00
7 Chipper Jones 1.50
8 Curt Schilling 1.00

9 Derek Jeter 4.00
10 Don Mattingly 4.00
11 Dontrelle Willis 1.00
12 Doc Gooden 1.00
13 Eddie Murray 1.50
14 Frank Thomas 1.50
15 Gary Sheffield 1.00
16 George Brett 4.00
17 Greg Maddux 2.00
18 Hideo Nomo 1.00
19 Ichiro Suzuki 2.00
20 Ivan Rodriguez 1.50
21 Jason Giambi 1.50
22 Jeff Bagwell 1.50
23 Jim Thome 1.50
24 Kerry Wood 1.50
25 Lance Berkman 1.00
26 Magglio Ordonez 1.00
27 Mark Prior 2.50
28 Mike Piazza 2.00
29 Mike Schmidt 3.00
30 Nomar Garciaparra 2.50
31 Pedro J. Martinez 2.00
32 Randy Johnson 2.00
33 Roger Clemens 3.00
34 Sammy Sosa 2.50
35 Tony Gwynn 1.50

Back to the Future Jerseys

NM/M

#1-6
Production 200
#7-9
Production 100
Prime: 1.5X-2X
Production 25 or 50
1 Tim Hudson 4.00
2 Rich Harden 4.00
3 Alex Rodriguez Rgr 10.00
4 Hank Blalock 6.00
5 Sammy Sosa 10.00
6 Hee Seop Choi 4.00
7 Tim Hudson, Rich Harden 8.00
8 Alex Rodriguez, Hank Blalock 12.00
9 Sammy Sosa, Hee Seop Choi 12.00

Back to the Future Bats

NM/M

#1-6
Production 200
#8-9
Production 100
1 Tim Hudson 4.00
3 Alex Rodriguez 10.00
4 Hank Blalock 6.00
5 Sammy Sosa 10.00
6 Hee Seop Choi 4.00
8 Alex Rodriguez, Hank Blalock 12.00
9 Sammy Sosa, Hee Seop Choi 12.00

Back to the Future

NM/M

#1-6
Production 500
#6-9
Production 250
Black: 1X-2X
Production 25 or 50
Gold: .75X-1.5X
Production 50 or 100
Red: 1X
Production 125 or 250
1 Tim Hudson 2.00
2 Rich Harden 1.50
3 Alex Rodriguez Rgr 5.00
4 Hank Blalock 3.00
5 Sammy Sosa 5.00
6 Hee Seop Choi 1.50
7 Tim Hudson, Rich Harden 3.00
8 Alex Rodriguez, Hank Blalock 6.00
9 Sammy Sosa, Hee Seop Choi 6.00

Back 2 Back Jacks Combos

NM/M

Singles Production 25-50
Duals Production 10-25
1 Albert Pujols Bat-Jsy/50 30.00
2 Alex Rodriguez Bat-Jsy/50 20.00
3 Alfonso Soriano Bat-Jsy/50 15.00
4 Andruw Jones Bat-Jsy/50 8.00
5 Chipper Jones Bat-Jsy/50 12.00
6 Derek Jeter Bat-Jsy/50 35.00
7 Frank Thomas Bat-Jsy/50 15.00
8 Miguel Cabrera Bat-Jsy/50 15.00
9 Jason Giambi Bat-Jsy/50 15.00
10 Jim Thome Bat-Jsy/50 15.00
11 Mike Piazza Bat-Jsy/50 20.00
12 Nomar Garciaparra Bat-Jsy/50 20.00
13 Sammy Sosa Bat-Jsy/50 20.00
14 Shawn Green Bat-Jsy/50 6.00
15 Vladimir Guerrero Bat-Jsy/50 15.00
16 Andruw Jones, Chipper Jones/25 30.00
17 Alfonso Soriano, Lance Berkman/25 50.00
18 Jeff Bagwell, Lance Berkman/25 20.00
19 Alex Rodriguez, Rafael Palmeiro/25 30.00
20 Adam Dunn, Austin Kearns/25 20.00
21 Al Kaline Bat-Jsy/50 25.00
22 Babe Ruth Bat-Jsy/25 350.00
23 Cal Ripken Jr. Bat-Jsy/50 60.00
24 Dale Murphy Bat-Jsy/50 15.00
25 Don Mattingly Bat-Jsy/50 25.00
26 George Brett Bat-Jsy/50 30.00
27 Lou Gehrig Bat-Jsy/25 150.00
28 Mike Schmidt Bat-Jsy/25 30.00
29 Roberto Clemente Bat-Jsy/50 80.00
30 Roy Campanella Bat-Jsy/50 25.00
31 Babe Ruth, Roger Maris/10 185.00
32 Harmon Killebrew, Kirby Puckett/25 50.00
33 Paul Molitor, Robin Yount/25 50.00
34 Reggie Jackson/25 25.00
35 Lou Gehrig, Ty Cobb/25 350.00
36 Don Mattingly, Jason Giambi/25 35.00
37 Ted Williams, Nomar Garciaparra 140.00
38 Andre Dawson, Sammy Sosa 40.00
39 Dale Murphy, Chipper Jones 20.00
40 Stan Musial, Jim Edmonds 35.00

Back 2 Back Jacks

NM/M

Singles Production 25-125
Duals Production 25-50
1 Albert Pujols/125 15.00
2 Alex Rodriguez/125 10.00
3 Alfonso Soriano/125 8.00
4 Andruw Jones/125 5.00
5 Chipper Jones/125 8.00
6 Derek Jeter/125 20.00
7 Frank Thomas/125 8.00
8 Miguel Cabrera/125 8.00
9 Jason Giambi/125 8.00
10 Jim Thome/125 8.00
11 Mike Piazza/125 10.00
12 Nomar Garciaparra/25 35.00
13 Sammy Sosa/125 10.00
14 Shawn Green/125 4.00
15 Vladimir Guerrero/125 8.00
16 Andruw Jones, Chipper Jones/50 20.00
17 Alfonso Soriano, Derek Jeter/50 30.00
18 Jeff Bagwell, Lance Berkman/50 15.00
19 Alex Rodriguez, Rafael Palmeiro/50 20.00
20 Adam Dunn, Austin Kearns/25 20.00
21 Al Kaline/100 15.00
22 Babe Ruth/50 140.00
23 Cal Ripken Jr./100 40.00
24 Dale Murphy/100 10.00
25 Don Mattingly/100 15.00
26 George Brett/100 20.00
27 Lou Gehrig/100 85.00
28 Mike Schmidt/100 15.00
29 Roberto Clemente/100 50.00
30 Roy Campanella/100 15.00
31 Babe Ruth, Roger Maris/25 200.00
32 Harmon Killebrew, Kirby Puckett/50 35.00
33 Paul Molitor, Robin Yount/50 40.00
34 Reggie Jackson/50 15.00
35 Lou Gehrig, Ty Cobb/50 200.00
36 Don Mattingly, Jason Giambi/50 25.00
37 Ted Williams, Nomar Garciaparra/50 75.00
38 Andre Dawson, Sammy Sosa/50 25.00
39 Dale Murphy, Chipper Jones/50 15.00
40 Stan Musial, Jim Edmonds/50 25.00

DK Signatures Platinum

No Pricing
Production one set
Framed Platinum: No Pricing
Platinum Sepia: No Pricing
Production one set

Diamond Cut Bat

NM/M

Common Player: 6.00
Production 100 unless noted
1 Alex Rodriguez 15.00
2 Nomar Garciaparra 12.00
3 Hideo Nomo 8.00
4 Alfonso Soriano 10.00
6 Edgar Martinez 8.00
7 Rocco Baldelli 10.00
8 Mark Teixeira 10.00
9 Albert Pujols 20.00
10 Vernon Wells 8.00
11 Garret Anderson 8.00
14 Brandon Webb 6.00
15 Mark Prior 20.00
16 Rafael Palmeiro 10.00
17 Adam Dunn 10.00
18 Dontrelle Willis 8.00
19 Kazuhisa Ishii 6.00
20 Torii Hunter 8.00
21 Vladimir Guerrero 10.00
22 Mike Piazza 15.00
23 Jason Giambi 10.00
26 Bobby Abreu 6.00
27 Hee Seop Choi 6.00
28 Rickie Weeks 12.00
30 Troy Glaus 8.00
31 Ivan Rodriguez 10.00
32 Hank Blalock 10.00
33 Greg Maddux 15.00
34 Nick Johnson 6.00
35 Shawn Green 8.00
36 Sammy Sosa 15.00
37 Dale Murphy/50 15.00
38 Cal Ripken Jr./50 50.00
39 Carl Yastrzemski 15.00
41 Don Mattingly 25.00
43 George Brett/50 40.00
45 Duke Snider/1
46 Steve Carlton/50 15.00
47 Stan Musial/25 40.00
48 Nolan Ryan/50 35.00
49 Deion Sanders/50 15.00
50 Roberto Clemente/25 120.00

Framed Silver

Framed Silver (1-150): 4-8X
Framed Silver (151-175): 2-3X
Production 100 sets
Framed Silver Sepia: 2-3X
Production 100

Framed Platinum

Framed Platinum: No Pricing
Production one set

DK Materials Bronze

NM/M

Common Player:
No pricing for production 15 or less
Framed Bronze: 1-1.5X
Production 5-100
Framed Bronze Sepia: 1.5-2X
Production 5-50
Silver: 1-2X
Production 5-50
Silver Sepia: 1.5-2X
Production 1-30
Framed Silver: 1-2X
Production 5-75
Framed Silver Sepia: 1.5-2X
Production 1-30
Gold: 1.5-2X
Production 1-50
Gold Sepia: No Pricing
Production 1-15
Framed Gold: 1.5-2X
Production 5-50
Framed Gold Sepia: No Pricing
Production 1-15
Platinums: No Pricing
All Platinums limited to one set
1 Alex Rodriguez Bat-Jsy/150 20.00
2 Andruw Jones Bat-Jsy/150 8.00
3 Nomar Garciaparra Bat-Jsy/150 15.00
4 Kerry Wood Bat-Jsy/150 15.00
5 Magglio Ordonez Bat-Jsy/150 8.00
6 Victor Martinez Bat-Bat/100 6.00
7 Jeremy Bonderman Jsy-Jsy/30 10.00
8 Josh Beckett Bat-Jsy/150 10.00
9 Jeff Kent Bat-Jsy/150 8.00
10 Carlos Beltran Bat-Jsy/150 8.00
11 Hideo Nomo Bat-Jsy/150 10.00
12 Richie Sexson Bat-Jsy/150 10.00
13 Jose Vidro Bat-Jsy/50 8.00
14 Jae Weong Seo Jsy-Jsy/100 8.00
15 Alfonso Soriano Bat-Jsy/150 10.00
16 Barry Zito Bat-Jsy/100 10.00
17 Brett Myers Jsy-Jsy/30 10.00
18 Brian Giles Bat-Bat/100 8.00
19 Edgar Martinez Bat-Jsy/150 8.00
20 Jim Edmonds Bat-Jsy/150 8.00
21 Rocco Baldelli Bat-Jsy/100 12.00
22 Mark Teixeira Bat-Jsy/100 8.00
23 Carlos Delgado Bat-Jsy/150 8.00
25 Jose Reyes Bat-Jsy/100 8.00
26 Marlon Byrd Bat-Jsy/100 8.00
27 Albert Pujols Bat-Jsy/150 25.00
28 Vernon Wells Bat-Jsy/150 8.00
29 Garret Anderson Bat-Jsy/15 20.00
30 Jerome Williams Jsy-Jsy/100 8.00
31 Chipper Jones Bat-Jsy/150 12.00
32 Rich Harden Jsy-Jsy/100 8.00
33 Manny Ramirez Bat-Jsy/150 10.00
34 Derek Jeter Base-Base/100 20.00
35 Brandon Webb Bat-Jsy/100 8.00
36 Mark Prior Bat-Jsy/100 20.00
37 Roy Halladay Jsy-Jsy/100 8.00
38 Frank Thomas Bat-Jsy/150 12.00

No.	Card	Price
39	Rafael Palmeiro Bat-Jsy/150	10.00
40	Adam Dunn Bat-Jsy/150	8.00
41	Aubrey Huff Bat-Jsy/30	10.00
42	Todd Helton Bat-Jsy/150	10.00
43	Matt Morris Jsy-Jsy/100	8.00
44	Dontrelle Willis Bat-Jsy/100	10.00
45	Lance Berkman Bat-Jsy/150	6.00
46	Mike Sweeney Bat-Jsy/100	8.00
47	Kazuhisa Ishii Bat-Jsy/100	8.00
48	Torii Hunter Bat-Jsy/100	8.00
49	Vladimir Guerrero Bat-Jsy/100	15.00
50	Mike Piazza Bat-Jsy/150	15.00
51	Alexis Rios Bat-Bat/150	12.00
52	Shannon Stewart Bat-Bat/100	6.00
53	Eric Hinske Bat-Jsy/100	6.00
54	Jason Jennings Bat-Jsy/150	6.00
55	Jason Giambi Bat-Jsy/150	10.00
56	Brandon Claussen Fld Glv-Shoe/5	
57	Joe Thurston Bat-Jsy/150	6.00
58	Ramon Nivar Bat-Jsy/100	6.00
59	Jay Gibbons Jsy-Jsy/100	8.00
60	Eric Chavez Bat-Jsy/150	8.00
62	Walter Young Bat-Bat/100	6.00
63	Mark Grace Bat-Jsy/150	10.00
64	Austin Kearns Bat-Jsy/150	8.00
65	Bob Abreu Bat-Jsy/150	6.00
66	Hee Seop Choi Bat-Jsy/100	6.00
67	Brandon Phillips Bat-Bat/100	6.00
68	Rickie Weeks Bat-Bat/100	15.00
69	Luis Gonzalez Bat-Jsy/150	6.00
70	Mariano Rivera Jsy-Jsy/100	10.00
71	Jason Lane	15.00
72	Xavier Nady Bat-Bat/5	
73	Runelvys Hernandez Jsy-Jsy/30	8.00
74	Aramis Ramirez Bat-Bat/1	
75	Ichiro Suzuki Ball-Base/15	50.00
77	Chris Snelling Bat-Bat/30	8.00
79	Miguel Tejada Bat-Jsy/150	8.00
80	Juan Gonzalez Bat-Jsy/150	8.00
81	Joe Borchard Bat-Jsy/15	
82	Gary Sheffield Bat-Jsy/150	8.00
83	Wade Miller Bat-Jsy/50	6.00
84	Jeff Bagwell Bat-Jsy/150	15.00
86	Adrian Beltre Bat-Jsy/100	6.00
87	Jeff Baker Bat-Bat/100	6.00
89	Bernie Williams Bat-Jsy/150	10.00
90	Pedro J. Martinez Bat-Jsy/100	15.00
92	Junior Spivey Bat-Jsy/100	8.00
93	Tim Hudson Bat-Jsy/150	8.00
94	Troy Glaus Bat-Jsy/100	8.00
95	Ken Griffey Jr. Base-Base/100	15.00
96	Alexis Gomez Bat-Bat/30	10.00
97	Antonio Perez Bat-Pants/100	6.00
98	Dan Haren Bat-Jsy/100	6.00
99	Ivan Rodriguez Bat-Jsy/150	10.00
100	Randy Johnson Bat-Jsy/100	12.00
101	Lyle Overbay Bat-Jsy/100	6.00
103	Miguel Cabrera Bat-Jsy/100	15.00
104	Scott Rolen Bat-Jsy/100	10.00
105	Roger Clemens Bat-Jsy/100	20.00
107	Nic Jackson Bat-Bat/100	6.00
108	Angel Berroa Bat-Pants/30	10.00
109	Hank Blalock Bat-Jsy/100	10.00
110	Ryan Klesko Bat-Jsy/100	8.00
111	Jose Castillo Bat-Bat/100	6.00
112	Paul Konerko Bat-Jsy/100	6.00
113	Greg Maddux Bat-Jsy/100	15.00
114	Mark Mulder Bat-Jsy/100	8.00
115	Pat Burrell Bat-Jsy/100	8.00
116	Garrett Atkins Jsy-Jsy/100	6.00
118	Orlando Cabrera Bat-Jsy/100	8.00
119	Nick Johnson Bat-Jsy/100	6.00
120	Tom Glavine Bat-Jsy/100	10.00
121	Morgan Ensberg Bat-Jsy/100	6.00
122	Sean Casey Bat-Hat/15	
123	Orlando Hudson Bat-Jsy/100	6.00
124	Hideki Matsui Ball-Base/15	70.00
125	Craig Biggio Bat-Jsy/100	8.00
126	Adam LaRoche Bat-Bat/100	8.00
127	Hong-Chih Kuo Bat-Bat/100	6.00
128	Paul LoDuca Bat-Jsy/100	6.00
129	Shawn Green Bat-Jsy/100	8.00
130	Luis Castillo Bat-Jsy/100	6.00
131	Joe Crede Bat-Btg Glv/5	
132	Ken Harvey Bat-Bat/100	6.00
133	Freddy Sanchez Bat-Bat/100	6.00
134	Roy Oswalt Bat-Jsy/100	8.00
135	Curt Schilling Bat-Jsy/100	8.00
136	Alfredo Amezaga Bat-Jsy/15	15.00
138	Barry Larkin Bat-Jsy/15	
139	Trot Nixon Bat-Bat/100	10.00
140	Jim Thome Bat-Jsy/100	15.00
141	Bret Boone Bat-Jsy/100	8.00
142	Jacque Jones Bat-Jsy/100	8.00
143	Todd Hafner Bat-Jsy/100	8.00
144	Sammy Sosa Bat-Jsy/100	20.00
145	Mike Mussina Bat-Jsy/100	12.00
147	Chad Gaudin Jsy-Jsy/100	6.00
149	Mike Lowell Bat-Jsy/100	8.00
150	Rickey Henderson Bat-Jsy/100	15.00
151	Roger Clemens FB Bat-Jsy/100	20.00
152	Mark Grace FB Bat-Jsy/15	
153	Rickey Henderson FB Bat-Jsy/30	30.00
154	Alex Rodriguez FB Bat-Jsy/100	20.00
155	Rafael Palmeiro FB Bat-Jsy/100	10.00
156	Greg Maddux FB Bat-Bat/100	15.00
157	Mike Piazza FB Bat-Jsy/100	15.00
158	Mike Mussina FB Bat-Jsy/100	12.00
159	Dale Murphy LGD Bat-Jsy/30	20.00
160	Cal Ripken Jr. LGD Bat-Jsy/100	50.00
161	Carl Yastrzemski LGD Bat-Jsy/100	25.00
162	Marty Marion LGD Jsy-Jsy/30	10.00
163	Don Mattingly LGD Bat-Jsy/100	25.00
164	Robin Yount LGD Bat-Jsy/100	25.00
165	Andre Dawson LGD Bat-Jsy/30	15.00
166	Jim Palmer LGD Jsy-Jsy/5	
167	George Brett LGD Bat-Jsy/30	50.00
168	Whitey Ford LGD Jsy-Pants/30	20.00
169	Roy Campanella LGD Bat-Pants/15	
170	Roger Maris LGD Bat-Jsy/15	
171	Duke Snider LGD Bat-Jsy/4	
172	Steve Carlton LGD Bat-Jsy/100	15.00
173	Stan Musial LGD Bat-Jsy/30	25.00
174	Nolan Ryan LGD Bat-Jsy/30	50.00
175	Deion Sanders LGD Bat-Jsy/100	12.00

Framed Bronze

Framed Bronze (1-150): 2-3X
Framed Bronze (151-175): 1-2X
Framed Bronze Sepia: 1-2X
Inserted 1:6

Diamond Cut Signature

NM/M

Many not priced due to scarcity

		NM/M
7	Rocco Baldelli/25	45.00
8	Mark Teixeira/25	30.00
13	Rich Harden/50	25.00
14	Brandon Webb/50	25.00
20	Torii Hunter/25	30.00
24	Ryan Wagner/50	20.00
25	Ramon Nivar/50	10.00
28	Rickie Weeks/50	40.00
29	Adam Loewen/50	20.00
32	Hank Blalock/25	30.00
40	Marty Marion/25	25.00
41	Don Mattingly/23	110.00
42	Jim Palmer/22	45.00
46	Steve Carlton/32	35.00
48	Nolan Ryan/34	125.00

DK Signatures Bronze

NM/M

No pricing for prod. less than 15
Framed Bronze: 1X
Production 1-50
Bronze Sepia: No Pricing
Production 1-15

		NM/M
6	Victor Martinez/200	10.00
13	Jose Vidro/200	10.00
14	Jae Weong Seo/200	15.00
17	Brett Myers/200	10.00
19	Edgar Martinez/25	40.00
26	Marlon Byrd/200	10.00
32	Rich Harden/200	15.00
35	Brandon Webb/25	30.00
41	Aubrey Huff/100	12.00
48	Torii Hunter/100	20.00
51	Alexis Rios/200	20.00
52	Shannon Stewart/200	10.00
53	Eric Hinske/25	20.00
56	Brandon Claussen/200	10.00
57	Joe Thurston/200	8.00
58	Ramon Nivar/100	10.00
59	Jay Gibbons/25	25.00
61	Jimmy Gobble/100	15.00
62	Walter Young/200	8.00
67	Brandon Phillips/100	6.00
68	Rickie Weeks/30	40.00
71	Jason Lane/200	8.00
73	Runelvys Hernandez/50	10.00
74	Aramis Ramirez/100	15.00
76	Cliff Lee/200	10.00
77	Chris Snelling/200	8.00
78	Ryan Wagner/100	15.00
81	Joe Borchard/200	8.00
85	Ryan Church/200	8.00
87	Jeff Baker/100	10.00
88	Adam Loewen/100	20.00
91	Carlos Rivera/100	8.00
92	Junior Spivey/25	20.00
96	Alexis Gomez/200	8.00
97	Antonio Perez/46	10.00
98	Dan Haren/100	12.00
101	Lyle Overbay/200	8.00
102	Oliver Perez/200	8.00
103	Miguel Cabrera/100	35.00
106	Brian Tallet/200	8.00
107	Nic Jackson/200	8.00
108	Angel Berroa/25	15.00
109	Hank Blalock/25	35.00
111	Jose Castillo/200	8.00
114	Mark Mulder/25	30.00
116	Garrett Atkins/100	8.00
117	Jeremy Guthrie/200	8.00
118	Orlando Cabrera/75	12.00
121	Morgan Ensberg/200	10.00
123	Orlando Hudson/100	8.00
126	Adam LaRoche/100	15.00
127	Hong-Chih Kuo/25	25.00
130	Luis Castillo/25	20.00
131	Joe Crede/100	8.00
132	Ken Harvey/200	8.00
133	Freddy Sanchez/50	10.00
136	Alfredo Amezaga/90	8.00
137	Chien-Ming Wang/25	35.00
142	Jacque Jones/25	20.00
143	Travis Hafner/200	10.00
146	Vinnie Chulk/200	8.00
147	Chad Gaudin/100	8.00
149	Mike Lowell/25	20.00

Diamond Cut Jersey

NM/M

Common Player: 6.00
Production 100 unless noted

		NM/M
1	Alex Rodriguez	15.00
2	Nomar Garciaparra	15.00
3	Hideo Nomo/50	15.00
4	Alfonso Soriano	10.00
5	Brett Myers/50	10.00
6	Edgar Martinez	8.00
7	Rocco Baldelli	12.00
8	Mark Teixeira	10.00
9	Albert Pujols	20.00
10	Vernon Wells	8.00
11	Garret Anderson/50	8.00
12	Jerome Williams	8.00
13	Rich Harden	8.00
14	Brandon Webb	6.00
15	Mark Prior	20.00
16	Rafael Palmeiro	10.00
17	Adam Dunn	10.00
18	Dontrelle Willis	8.00
19	Kazuhisa Ishii	6.00
20	Torii Hunter	8.00
21	Vladimir Guerrero/50	15.00
22	Mike Piazza	15.00
23	Jason Giambi	10.00
25	Ramon Nivar	6.00
26	Bobby Abreu	6.00
27	Hee Seop Choi	6.00
30	Troy Glaus	8.00
31	Ivan Rodriguez	10.00
32	Hank Blalock	10.00
33	Greg Maddux	15.00
34	Nick Johnson	6.00
35	Shawn Green	8.00
36	Sammy Sosa	15.00
37	Dale Murphy/50	20.00
38	Cal Ripken Jr./50	50.00
39	Carl Yastrzemski	20.00
40	Marty Marion/50	15.00
41	Don Mattingly	25.00
42	Jim Palmer/25	20.00
43	George Brett/50	35.00
44	Whitey Ford/25	25.00
45	Duke Snider/10	
46	Steve Carlton/50	15.00
47	Stan Musial/10	
48	Nolan Ryan/50	40.00
49	Deion Sanders/50	15.00
50	Roberto Clemente/10	

Diamond Cut Combo

NM/M

Common Player: 10.00
Production 50 unless noted

		NM/M
1	Alex Rodriguez	30.00
2	Nomar Garciaparra	25.00
3	Hideo Nomo/25	30.00

4 Alfonso Soriano 15.00
6 Edgar Martinez/25 15.00
7 Rocco Baldelli/25 25.00
8 Mark Teixeira/25 20.00
9 Albert Pujols 40.00
10 Vernon Wells/25 15.00
11 Garret Anderson/25 15.00
14 Brandon Webb/25 15.00
15 Mark Prior 30.00
16 Rafael Palmeiro/25 20.00
17 Adam Dunn/25 15.00
18 Dontrelle Willis/25 20.00
19 Kazuhisa Ishii/25 15.00
20 Torii Hunter/25 15.00
21 Vladimir Guerrero/25 25.00
22 Mike Piazza 20.00
23 Jason Giambi/25 25.00
26 Bobby Abreu 10.00
27 Hee Seop Choi 10.00
30 Troy Glaus/25 20.00
31 Ivan Rodriguez/25 20.00
32 Hank Blalock/25 20.00
33 Greg Maddux 25.00
34 Nick Johnson/25 12.00
35 Shawn Green/25 15.00
36 Sammy Sosa 25.00
41 Don Mattingly/23 50.00
42 Jim Palmer/22 20.00
46 Steve Carlton/32 20.00
48 Nolan Ryan/34 50.00
49 Deion Sanders/24 25.00
50 Roberto Clemente/21 150.00

Diamond Cut Signature Combo

NM/M

Varying quantities produced
40 Marty Marion/25 30.00
46 Steve Carlton/32 45.00

Heritage Collection Auto.

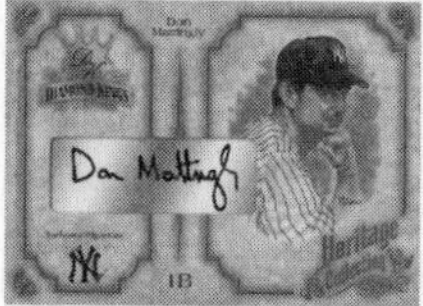

No Pricing

Heritage Collection Jersey

NM/M

Production 50 unless noted
1 Dale Murphy 15.00
2 Cal Ripken Jr. 40.00
3 Carl Yastrzemski 20.00
4 Don Mattingly 30.00
5 Jim Palmer/10
6 Andre Dawson/25 20.00
7 Roy Campanella/25 30.00
8 George Brett/25 40.00
9 Duke Snider/10
10 Marty Marion 10.00
11 Deion Sanders 10.00
12 Whitey Ford/25 25.00
13 Stan Musial/10
14 Nolan Ryan/25 40.00
15 Steve Carlton/25 20.00
16 Robin Yount 20.00
17 Albert Pujols 25.00
18 Alex Rodriguez 25.00
19 Mike Piazza 15.00
20 Roger Clemens 25.00
21 Hideo Nomo 15.00
22 Mark Prior 20.00
23 Roger Maris/25 50.00
24 Greg Maddux 15.00
25 Mark Grace 10.00

Heritage Collection Bat

NM/M

Production 50 unless noted
1 Dale Murphy 20.00
2 Cal Ripken Jr. 40.00
3 Carl Yastrzemski 20.00
4 Don Mattingly 30.00
6 Andre Dawson/25 20.00
7 Roy Campanella/25 30.00
8 George Brett/25 40.00
9 Duke Snider/1
11 Deion Sanders 10.00
13 Stan Musial/25 35.00
14 Nolan Ryan/25 40.00
15 Steve Carlton/25 20.00
16 Robin Yount 20.00
17 Albert Pujols 25.00
18 Alex Rodriguez 25.00
19 Mike Piazza 15.00
20 Roger Clemens 25.00
21 Hideo Nomo 15.00
22 Mark Prior 20.00
23 Roger Maris/25 50.00
24 Greg Maddux 15.00
25 Mark Grace 10.00

DK Signatures Silver

NM/M

No pricing for prod. less than 15
Framed Silver: 1.5-2X
Production 1-25
Silver Sepia: No Pricing
Production 1-10
6 Victor Martinez/49 15.00
13 Jose Vidro/20 20.00
14 Jae Weong Seo/80 20.00
17 Brett Myers/90 15.00
26 Marlon Byrd/100 10.00
32 Rich Harden/100 15.00
35 Brandon Webb/15 35.00
41 Aubrey Huff/40 15.00
51 Alexis Rios/100 20.00
52 Shannon Stewart/30 15.00
56 Brandon Claussen/100 10.00
57 Joe Thurston/100 8.00
58 Ramon Nivar/30 15.00
61 Jimmy Gobble/30 20.00
62 Walter Young/100 8.00
67 Brandon Phillips/30 10.00
68 Rickie Weeks/20 50.00
71 Jason Lane/100 8.00
73 Runelvys Hernandez/30 10.00
74 Aramis Ramirez/30 25.00
76 Cliff Lee/100 10.00
77 Chris Snelling/100 8.00
78 Ryan Wagner/30 20.00
81 Joe Borchard/100 8.00
85 Ryan Church/100 8.00
87 Jeff Baker/30 15.00
88 Adam Loewen/30 25.00
96 Alexis Gomez/100 8.00
98 Dan Haren/30 15.00
101 Lyle Overbay/100 8.00
102 Oliver Perez/100 8.00
103 Miguel Cabrera/30 40.00
106 Brian Tallet/100 8.00
107 Nic Jackson/100 8.00
109 Hank Blalock/30 35.00
111 Jose Castillo/100 8.00
116 Garrett Atkins/30 10.00
117 Jeremy Guthrie/30 15.00
121 Morgan Ensberg/50 15.00
123 Orlando Hudson/30 10.00
126 Adam LaRoche/30 20.00
131 Joe Crede/35 12.00
132 Ken Harvey/30 15.00
136 Alfredo Amezaga/30 10.00
143 Travis Hafner/30 15.00
146 Vinnie Chulk/100 8.00
147 Chad Gaudin/30 10.00

HOF Heroes Bat

NM/M

Production 25 unless noted
1 George Brett 35.00
2 George Brett 35.00
3 George Brett 35.00
4 Mike Schmidt 35.00
5 Mike Schmidt 35.00
6 Nolan Ryan 40.00
7 Nolan Ryan 40.00
8 Nolan Ryan 40.00
13 Carl Yastrzemski 30.00
14 Robin Yount 35.00
18 Carlton Fisk 25.00
19 Ozzie Smith 30.00
20 Kirby Puckett 30.00
21 Bobby Doerr 20.00
22 Frank Robinson 15.00
23 Ralph Kiner 15.00
24 Al Kaline 25.00
31 Johnny Bench 25.00
32 Steve Carlton 20.00
33 Gary Carter 20.00
34 Roy Campanella 30.00
35 Roy Campanella 30.00

HOF Heroes Jersey

NM/M

Production 25 unless noted
1 George Brett 35.00
2 George Brett 35.00
3 George Brett 35.00
4 Mike Schmidt 35.00
5 Mike Schmidt 35.00
6 Nolan Ryan 40.00
7 Nolan Ryan 40.00
8 Nolan Ryan 40.00
13 Carl Yastrzemski 30.00
14 Robin Yount 35.00
15 Whitey Ford 30.00
18 Carlton Fisk 25.00
19 Ozzie Smith 30.00
20 Kirby Puckett 30.00
21 Bobby Doerr 20.00
24 Al Kaline 25.00
32 Steve Carlton 20.00
33 Gary Carter 20.00
34 Roy Campanella 30.00
35 Roy Campanella 30.00

HOF Heroes Combo

NM/M

Production 25 unless noted
1 George Brett 50.00
2 George Brett 50.00
3 George Brett 50.00
4 Mike Schmidt 40.00
5 Mike Schmidt 40.00
6 Nolan Ryan 50.00
7 Nolan Ryan 50.00
8 Nolan Ryan 50.00
13 Carl Yastrzemski 40.00
14 Robin Yount 40.00
15 Whitey Ford 30.00
18 Carlton Fisk 30.00
19 Ozzie Smith 40.00
20 Kirby Puckett 40.00
21 Bobby Doerr 25.00
23 Ralph Kiner 20.00
24 Al Kaline 35.00
32 Steve Carlton 30.00
33 Gary Carter 25.00
34 Roy Campanella 40.00
35 Roy Campanella 40.00

HOF Heroes Signature

NM/M

Many not priced
14 Robin Yount/19 70.00
15 Whitey Ford/16 50.00
22 Frank Robinson/20 50.00
25 Bob Feller/19 40.00
30 Jim Palmer/22 40.00
32 Steve Carlton/32 35.00

Team Timeline Bat

NM/M

Production 25 unless noted
1 Deion Sanders, Andruw Jones 15.00
2 Rickie Weeks, Robin Yount 40.00
3 Don Mattingly, Whitey Ford 60.00
4 Chipper Jones, Dale Murphy 35.00
5 Nomar Garciaparra, Bobby Doerr 30.00
6 Mark Prior, Sammy Sosa 65.00
7 Hideo Nomo, Kazuhisa Ishii 40.00
8 Andre Dawson, Mark Grace 20.00
9 Roger Clemens, Carl Yastrzemski 50.00
10 Mike Mussina, Cal Ripken Jr. 75.00
11 Stan Musial, Albert Pujols 65.00
12 Jim Palmer, Mike Mussina 25.00
13 Marty Marion, Stan Musial
14 George Brett, Mike Sweeney 30.00
15 Roger Clemens, Roger Maris 60.00
16 Duke Snider, Shawn Green/1
17 Jim Thome, Mike Schmidt 40.00
18 Nolan Ryan, Alex Rodriguez 60.00
19 Roy Campanella, Mike Piazza 40.00

Team Timeline Jersey

NM/M

Production 25 sets
Prime: No Pricing
Production one set
1 Deion Sanders, Andruw Jones 15.00
2 Rickie Weeks, Robin Yount 40.00
3 Don Mattingly, Whitey Ford 60.00
4 Chipper Jones, Dale Murphy 35.00
5 Nomar Garciaparra, Bobby Doerr 30.00
6 Mark Prior, Sammy Sosa 65.00
7 Hideo Nomo, Kazuhisa Ishii 40.00
8 Andre Dawson, Mark Grace 20.00
9 Roger Clemens, Carl Yastrzemski 50.00
10 Mike Mussina, Cal Ripken Jr. 75.00
14 George Brett, Mike Sweeney 30.00
15 Roger Clemens, Roger Maris 60.00
17 Jim Thome, Mike Schmidt 40.00
18 Nolan Ryan, Alex Rodriguez 60.00
19 Roy Campanella, Mike Piazza 40.00

Recollection Autographs

NM/M

Varying quantities produced
6 Clint Barmes 03 DK Black/82 10.00
7 Clint Barmes 03 DK Blue/72 10.00
8 Carlos Beltran 02 DK/23 20.00
9 Carlos Beltran 03 DK/99 15.00
10 Adrian Beltre 02 DK/40 10.00
19 Chris Burke 03 DK/150 10.00
20 Marlon Byrd 02 DK/23 15.00
21 Marlon Byrd 03 DK/100 10.00
24 Kevin Cash 03 DK/103 10.00
25 Jose Cruz 85 DK/59 10.00
26 J.D. Durbin 03 DK/151 10.00
27 Jim Edmonds 03 DK/24 25.00

32 Julio Franco 87 DK/25 20.00
33 Freddy Garcia 03 DK/50 20.00
34 Jay Gibbons 03 DK/100 12.00
39 Brendan Harris 03 DK/150 8.00
42 Runelvys Hernandez 02 DK/100 8.00
43 Eric Hinske 03 DK/20 20.00
44 Tim Hudson 02 DK/25 30.00
45 Tim Hudson 03 DK/25 30.00
46 Aubrey Huff 03 DK/99 15.00
49 Jason Jennings 03 DK/50 10.00
50 Tommy John 88 DK Black/62 15.00
52 Howard Johnson 90 DK/52 10.00
54 Austin Kearns 02 DK/25 30.00
55 Austin Kearns 03 DK/25 30.00
59 Preston Larrison 03 DK Black/74 10.00
60 Preston Larrison 03 DK Blue/77 10.00
67 Dustin McGowan 03 DK/159 8.00
69 Melvin Mora 03 DK/101 8.00
71 Jack Morris 03 DK/60 10.00
72 Jack Morris 03 DK Her/19 20.00
74 Dale Murphy 03 DK Blue/47 30.00
82 Magglio Ordonez 03 DK/25 30.00
85 Dave Parker 82 DK/20 30.00
86 Dave Parker 90 DK/18 30.00
88 Jorge Posada 02 DK/25 50.00
89 Mark Prior 03 DK/25 140.00
92 Mike Rivera 02 DK/24 15.00
97 Ivan Rodriguez 03 DK/22 40.00
100 Rodrigo Rosario 02 DK/50 8.00
105 Ron Santo 02 DK/29 35.00
106 Richie Sexson 02 DK/25 25.00
107 Richie Sexson 03 DK/25 25.00
109 Chris Snelling 02 DK/46 12.00
119 Shannon Stewart 02 DK/50 15.00
120 Shannon Stewart 03 DK Black/92 12.00
126 Gorman Thomas 82 DK Black/22 20.00
127 Gorman Thomas 82 DK Blue/20 20.00
128 Alan Trammell 02 DK/29 30.00
129 Alan Trammell 02 DK Her/25 30.00
130 Robin Ventura 03 DK/25 20.00
131 Jose Vidro 03 DK/25 20.00
132 Rickie Weeks 03 DK/52 50.00
133 Kevin Youkilis 03 DK/153 15.00

DK Signatures Gold

NM/M

Many not priced due to scarcity
Framed Gold: No Pricing
Production 1-5
Gold Sepia: No Pricing
Production 1-5
32 Rich Harden/50 20.00
51 Alexis Rios/50 25.00
56 Brandon Claussen/50 15.00
57 Joe Thurston/50 10.00
62 Walter Young/50 10.00
71 Jason Lane/40 15.00
77 Chris Snelling/50 10.00
81 Joe Borchard/50 15.00
85 Ryan Church/50 10.00
96 Alexis Gomez/50 10.00
101 Lyle Overbay/50 10.00
102 Oliver Perez/50 10.00
106 Brian Tallet/50 10.00
107 Nic Jackson/50 15.00
121 Morgan Ensberg/48 15.00
146 Vinnie Chulk/50 10.00

Back to Back Picks Sign.

NM/M

Quantity Produced Listed
1 Delmon Young, Rickie Weeks/25 50.00
2 George Brett, Mike Schmidt/10
3 Adam Dunn, Austin Kearns/25 50.00
4 Bubba Crosby, Lance Berkman/10
5 Michael Young, Vernon Wells/25 35.00
6 Brian Roberts, Larry Bigbie/50 30.00
7 Ron Cey, Steve Garvey/50 35.00
8 Bill Madlock, Dave Parker/50 40.00
9 Derrek Lee, Torii Hunter, Trot Nixon/50 50.00
10 Barry Zito, Ben Sheets, Brett Myers/10
11 Chris Nelson, Matt Bush, Reid Brignac/250 65.00
12 B.J. Szymanski, Greg Golson, Jeff Frazier/250 40.00
13 Mark Trumbo, Nick Adenhart, Tyler Johnson/100 50.00
14 Chris Carter, Danny Putnam, Mark Jecmen/100 40.00
15 Billy Killian, Daryl Jones, Matt Bush/100 50.00
16 Blake DeWitt, Justin Orenduff, Scott Elbert/250 40.00
17 Jay Rainville, Kyle Waldrop, Trevor Plouffe/250 50.00
18 Jeff Marquez, Jon Poterson, Phillip Hughes/100 40.00
19 Wes Whisler, Tyler Lumsden, Wes Whisler/100 40.00
20 Curtis Thigpen, David Purcey, Zach Jackson/100 40.00

Throwback Threads

NM/M

Production 50 Sets
1 Roger Maris 60.00
2 Ted Williams 80.00
3 Cal Ripken Jr. 75.00
4 Duke Snider 20.00
5 George Brett 40.00

2004 DONRUSS ELITE EXTRA EDITION

NM/M

Complete Set (288):
Common (1-150): .25
Common (206-215): 2.00
Production 1,000
Common Auto.(216-355): 6.00
Common No Auto. (234-254): 3.00
No Auto. Production 1,000
Pack (5): 10.00
Box (12): 100.00
Note: Cards 151-205 do not exist
1 Troy Glaus .40
2 John Lackey .25
3 Garret Anderson .40
4 Francisco Rodriguez .25
5 Casey Kotchman .40
6 Jose Guillen .25
7 Miguel Tejada .50
8 Rafael Palmeiro .50
9 Jay Gibbons .25
10 Melvin Mora .25
11 Javy Lopez .25
12 Pedro Martinez .75
13 Curt Schilling .75
14 David Ortiz .75
15 Manny Ramirez .50
16 Nomar Garciaparra 1.00
17 Magglio Ordonez .25
18 Frank Thomas .50
19 Esteban Loaiza .25
20 Paul Konerko .25
21 Mark Buehrle .25
22 Jody Gerut .25
23 Victor Martinez .25
24 C.C. Sabathia .25
25 Travis Hafner .25
26 Cliff Lee .25
27 Jeremy Bonderman .25
28 Dallas McPherson .25
29 Jermaine Dye .25
30 Carlos Guillen .25
31 Carlos Beltran .50
32 Ken Harvey .25
33 Mike Sweeney .25
34 Angel Berroa .25
35 Joe Nathan .25
36 Johan Santana .50
37 Jacque Jones .25
38 Shannon Stewart .25
39 Torii Hunter .40
40 Derek Jeter 2.00
41 Jason Giambi .40
42 Danny Graves .25
43 Alfonso Soriano .75
44 Gary Sheffield .50
45 Mike Mussina .40
46 Jorge Posada .40
47 Hideki Matsui 1.00
48 Francisco Cordero .25
49 Javier Vazquez .25
50 Mariano Rivera .40
51 Eric Chavez .40
52 Tim Hudson .40
53 Mark Mulder .40
54 Barry Zito .40
55 Ichiro Suzuki 1.50
56 Edgar Martinez .25
57 Bret Boone .25
58 Lew Ford .25
59 B.J. Upton .40
60 Aubrey Huff .25
61 Rocco Baldelli .25
62 Carl Crawford .25
63 Delmon Young .40
64 Mark Teixeira .40
65 Hank Blalock .50
66 Michael Young .25
67 Alex Rodriguez 1.50
68 Carlos Delgado .40
69 Milton Bradley .25
70 Roy Halladay .25
71 Vernon Wells .25
72 Randy Johnson .75
73 Bobby Crosby .25
74 Lyle Overbay .25
75 Luis Gonzalez .25
76 Steve Finley .25
77 Chipper Jones .75
78 Andruw Jones .40
79 Marcus Giles .25
80 Rafael Furcal .25
81 J.D. Drew .40
82 Sammy Sosa 1.50
83 Kerry Wood .75
84 Mark Prior .75
85 Derrek Lee .40
86 Moises Alou .40
87 Carlos Zambrano .40
88 Ken Griffey Jr. 1.00
89 Austin Kearns .40
90 Adam Dunn .50
91 Barry Larkin .40
92 Todd Helton .50
93 Larry Walker .50
94 Preston Wilson .25
95 Sean Casey .25
96 Luis Castillo .25
97 Josh Beckett .25
98 Mike Lowell .25
99 Miguel Cabrera .50
100 Brad Penny .25
101 Dontrelle Willis .25
102 Andy Pettitte .40
103 Wade Miller .25
104 Jeff Bagwell .50
105 Craig Biggio .40
106 Lance Berkman .40
107 Jeff Kent .25
108 Roy Oswalt .40
109 Hideo Nomo .40
110 Adrian Beltre .40
111 Paul LoDuca .25
112 Shawn Green .40
113 Roger Clemens 2.00
114 Eric Gagne .40
115 Danny Kolb .25
116 Rickie Weeks .25
117 Scott Podsednik .25
118 Livan Hernandez .25
119 Orlando Cabrera .25
120 Jose Vidro .25
121 David Wright 1.50
122 Tom Glavine .40
123 Al Leiter .25
124 Mike Piazza 1.00
125 Jose Reyes .40
126 Richard Hidalgo .25
127 Eric Milton .25
128 Jim Thome .75
129 Mike Lieberthal .25
130 Bobby Abreu .40
131 Kip Wells .25
132 Jack Wilson .25
133 Jason Bay .25
134 Brian Giles .25
135 Sean Burroughs .25
136 Khalil Greene .50
137 Jake Peavy .25
138 Jason Schmidt .40
139 J.T. Snow .25
140 Craig Wilson .25
141 Chase Utley .25
142 Jim Edmonds .40
143 Albert Pujols 2.00
144 Edgar Renteria .40
145 Scott Rolen .75
146 Matt Morris .25
147 Ivan Rodriguez .50
148 Vladimir Guerrero .75
149 Greg Maddux 1.00
150 Ben Sheets .40
206 Will Clark 2.00
207 Nolan Ryan 8.00
208 Bob Feller 2.00
209 Red Schoendienst 2.00
210 Brooks Robinson 3.00
211 Al Kaline 3.00
212 Ozzie Smith 4.00
213 Maury Wills 2.00
214 Steve Carlton 2.00
215 Duke Snider 3.00
216 *Scott Lewis Auto/603* 10.00
217 *Josh Johnson Auto/597* 10.00
218 *Jeff Fiorentino Auto/597* 20.00
219 *Grant Hansen Auto/599* 6.00
220 *Yovani Gallardo Auto/803* 8.00
221 *Eddie Prasch Auto/603* 10.00
222 *Danny Hill Auto/603* 6.00
223 *Chuck Lofgren Auto/803* 8.00
224 *Blake Johnson Auto/811* 10.00
225 *Cory Dunlap Auto/599* 15.00
226 *Carlos Vasquez Auto/869* 8.00
227 *Jesse Crain Auto/1000* 10.00
228 *Yhency Brazoban Auto/1000* 6.00
229 *Abe Alvarez Auto/1000* 8.00
230 *Scott Kazmir Auto/350* 35.00
231 *J.A. Happ Auto/1195* 8.00
232 *Mark Jecmen Auto/1047* 6.00
234 *Kameron Loe/1000* 3.00
235 *Ervin Santana/1000* 5.00
239 *Josh Karp/1000* 3.00
242 *Alberto Callaspo/ 1000* 3.00
243 *Jesse Hoover Auto/1191* 8.00
246 *Justin Hoyman Auto/1124* 8.00
247 *Juan Cedeno/1000* 3.00
250 *Jake Dittler/1000* 4.00
252 *Benjamin Zobrist Auto/1178* 8.00
253 *Jeff Salazar/1000* 3.00
254 *Fausto Carmona/ 1000* 4.00
256 *Jorge Vasquez Auto/1000* 6.00

257 Rafael Gonzalez Auto/603 6.00
258 Andrew Dobies Auto/601 10.00
259 Colby Miller Auto/997 6.00
260 K.C. Herren Auto/735 10.00
261 Ryan Meaux Auto/546 6.00
262 Dustin Pedroia Auto/1114 20.00
263 Fernando Nieve Auto/1000 10.00
264 Mariano Gomez Auto/1000 6.00
265 Eric Campbell Auto/260 60.00
266 Billy Killian Auto/703 6.00
267 Mike Rouse Auto/999 6.00
268 Kyle Bono Auto/1203 8.00
269 Mitch Einertson Auto/1047 30.00
270 Scott Proctor Auto/1000 8.00
271 Tim Bittner Auto/1000 6.00
272 Christian Garcia Auto/799 10.00
273 Yadier Molina Auto/1000 25.00
275 Charles Thomas Auto/907 8.00
276 Travis Blackley Auto/1000 8.00
277 Frankie Francisco Auto/1000 6.00
278 Dioner Navarro Auto/1000 15.00
279 Joey Gathright Auto/1000 8.00
280 Kazuhito Tadano Auto/1000 15.00
281 Matt Bush Auto/1100 25.00
282 David Haehnel Auto/865 8.00
283 Tommy Hottovy Auto/825 8.00
284 Chris Carter Auto/973 20.00
285 Mark Rogers Auto/578 20.00
286 Jeremy Sowers Auto/537 25.00
287 Homer Bailey Auto/1571 15.00
288 Mike Butia Auto/825 8.00
289 Chris Nelson Auto/465 40.00
290 Thomas Diamond Auto/1055 15.00
291 Neil Walker Auto/1343 15.00
292 Sean Gamble Auto/1229 8.00
293 Bill Bray Auto/1073 6.00
294 Reid Brignac Auto/522 20.00
295 Ryan Klosterman Auto/865 6.00
296 David Purcey Auto/1485 8.00
297 Scott Elbert Auto/1617 8.00
298 Josh Fields Auto/961 15.00
299 Chris Lambert Auto/954 8.00
300 Trevor Plouffe Auto/1329 10.00
301 Greg Golson Auto/1334 10.00
302 Josh Baker Auto/525 8.00
303 Phillip Hughes Auto/1485 15.00
304 Matt Macri Auto/979 10.00
305 Kyle Waldrop Auto/823 10.00
306 Richie Robnett Auto/1575 15.00
307 Taylor Tankersley Auto/1073 8.00
308 Blake DeWitt Auto/1562 25.00
309 Daryl Jones Auto/575 15.00
310 Eric Hurley Auto/1021 8.00
311 J.P. Howell Auto/1453 10.00
312 Zach Jackson Auto/1069 8.00
313 Justin Orenduff Auto/473 10.00
314 Tyler Lumsden Auto/473 10.00
315 Matt Fox Auto/473 12.00
316 Danny Putnam Auto/473 15.00
317 Jon Poterson Auto/464 15.00
318 Gio Gonzalez Auto/473 20.00
319 Jay Rainville Auto/823 12.00
320 Huston Street Auto/709 30.00
321 Jeff Marquez Auto/493 10.00
322 Eric Beattie Auto/930 8.00
323 B.J. Szymanski Auto/1327 8.00
324 Seth Smith Auto/1065 15.00
325 Robert Johnson Auto/790 8.00
326 Wes Whisler Auto/473 8.00
327 Billy Buckner Auto/673 8.00
328 Jon Zeringue Auto/473 25.00
329 Curtis Thigpen Auto/673 10.00
330 Donny Lucy Auto/573 6.00
331 Mike Ferris Auto/558 10.00
332 Anthony Swarzak Auto/370 25.00
333 Jason Jaramillo Auto/573 8.00
334 Hunter Pence Auto/672 30.00
335 Mike Rozier Auto/628 8.00
336 Kurt Suzuki Auto/473 20.00
337 Jason Vargas Auto/621 20.00
338 Brian Bixler Auto/665 6.00
340 Dexter Fowler Auto/623 30.00
341 Mark Trumbo Auto/1321 15.00
342 Jeff Frazier Auto/423 15.00
343 Steven Register Auto/673 8.00
344 Michael Schlact Auto/477 8.00
345 Garrett Mock Auto/471 8.00
346 Eric Haberer Auto/473 8.00
347 Matt Tuiasosopo Auto/473 60.00
348 Jason Windsor Auto/473 15.00
349 Grant Johnson Auto/815 10.00
350 J.C. Holt Auto/673 10.00
351 Joseph Bauserman Auto/472 8.00
352 Jamar Walton Auto/481 15.00
353 Eric Patterson Auto/1571 15.00
354 Tyler Johnson Auto/775 15.00
355 Nick Adenhart Auto/653 15.00

Aspirations

1-150 print run 61-99: 4-8X
1-150 p/r 41-60: 6-12X
1-150 p/r 26-40: 8-15X
1-150 p/r 25 or less: No Pricing
206-355 p/r 51-99: 1-2X no auto.
216-355 p/r 61-99: .4-1X auto.
216-355 p/r 41-60: .5-1X auto.
216-355 p/r 26-40: .75-1X auto.
No pricing print run 25 or less

Aspirations Gold

Gold (1-150): 10-20X
Gold (206-215): 3-6X
Gold (216-355): No Pricing
Production 25 sets

Status

1-150 print run 61-99: 4-8X
1-150 p/r 41-60: 6-12X
1-150 p/r 26-40: 8-15X
1-150 p/r 25 or less: No Pricing
206-355 p/r 51-99: 1-2X no auto.
216-355 p/r 61-99: .4-1X auto.
216-355 p/r 41-60: .5-1X auto.
216-355 p/r 26-40: .75-1X auto.
No pricing print run 25 or less

Status Gold

No Pricing
Production 10 sets

Turn of the Century

(1-150): 3-5X
Production 250 sets
(206-215): 2-3X
(216-355 no auto): .5-1X
(216-355 auto): .2-.5X
206-355 production 100

Career Best All-Stars

NM/M

Common Player:
Production 500 Sets
1 Randy Johnson 3.00
2 David Ortiz 3.00
3 Edgar Renteria 2.00
4 Victor Martinez 2.00
5 Albert Pujols 6.00
6 Hideki Matsui 5.00
7 Mariano Rivera 2.00
8 Carlos Zambrano 2.00
9 Hank Blalock 2.00
10 Michael Young 2.00
11 Mike Piazza 4.00
12 Alfonso Soriano 3.00
13 Carl Crawford 2.00
14 Scott Rolen 3.00
15 Vladimir Guerrero 3.00
16 Lance Berkman 2.00
17 Todd Helton 3.00
18 Curt Schilling 3.00
19 Francisco Cordero 2.00
20 Mark Mulder 2.00
21 Sammy Sosa 4.00
22 Roger Clemens 6.00
23 Miguel Cabrera 3.00
24 Manny Ramirez 3.00
25 Jim Thome 3.00

Career Best A-S Jersey

NM/M

Production 50 Sets
Prime: 1X-2X
Production 5-25
No Pricing 15 or less
1 Randy Johnson 15.00
2 David Ortiz 15.00
3 Edgar Renteria 8.00
4 Victor Martinez 8.00
5 Albert Pujols 25.00
6 Hideki Matsui 40.00
7 Mariano Rivera 10.00
8 Carlos Zambrano 8.00
9 Hank Blalock 10.00
10 Michael Young 8.00
11 Mike Piazza 20.00
12 Alfonso Soriano 15.00
13 Carl Crawford 8.00
14 Scott Rolen 15.00
15 Vladimir Guerrero 15.00
16 Lance Berkman 8.00
17 Todd Helton 10.00
18 Curt Schilling 15.00
19 Francisco Cordero 8.00
20 Mark Mulder 8.00
21 Sammy Sosa 20.00
22 Roger Clemens 20.00
23 Miguel Cabrera 12.00
24 Manny Ramirez 15.00
25 Jim Thome 15.00

Career Best A-S Jersey Prime

NM/M

1 Randy Johnson/5
2 David Ortiz/25 25.00
3 Edgar Renteria/5
4 Victor Martinez/25 15.00
5 Albert Pujols/25 40.00
6 Hideki Matsui/25 75.00
7 Mariano Rivera/5
8 Carlos Zambrano/25 15.00
9 Hank Blalock/25 20.00
10 Michael Young/25 15.00
11 Mike Piazza/25 30.00
12 Alfonso Soriano/25 25.00
13 Carl Crawford/25 15.00
14 Scott Rolen/25 25.00
15 Vladimir Guerrero/25 25.00
16 Lance Berkman/25 15.00
17 Todd Helton/25 20.00
18 Curt Schilling/25 25.00
19 Francisco Cordero/5
20 Mark Mulder/25 15.00
21 Sammy Sosa/25 30.00
22 Roger Clemens/25 40.00
23 Miguel Cabrera/25 20.00
24 Manny Ramirez/25 25.00
25 Jim Thome/25 25.00

Career Best A-S Sig. Black

No Pricing
Production 1-5

Career Best A-S Sign. Gold

No Pricing
Production 1-10

Best A-S Sig. Jersey Gold

NM/M

Production 1-25
2 David Ortiz/25 75.00
3 Edgar Renteria/25 40.00
4 Victor Martinez/25 40.00
8 Carlos Zambrano/25 40.00
10 Michael Young/25 35.00
13 Carl Crawford/25 30.00
19 Francisco Cordero/25 20.00

Best A-S Sig. Jersey Prime

No Pricing
Production 1-10

Draft Class

NM/M

Common Duo:
Production 500 Sets
1 Johnny Bench, Nolan Ryan 10.00
2 Bert Blyleven, Dwight Evans 2.00
3 Jim Rice, Keith Hernandez 2.00
4 Dennis Eckersley, Gary Carter 3.00
5 Fred Lynn, Robin Yount 5.00
6 Andre Dawson, Lee Smith 2.00
7 Alan Trammell, Jack Morris 2.00
8 Harold Baines, Paul Molitor 3.00
9 Cal Ripken Jr., Kirk Gibson 10.00
10 Don Mattingly, Orel Hershiser 6.00
11 Darryl Strawberry, Eric Davis 2.00
12 Dwight Gooden, Jose Canseco 3.00
13 Rafael Palmeiro, Randy Johnson 4.00
14 Curt Schilling, Gary Sheffield 3.00
15 Mike Piazza, Robin Ventura 4.00
16 Frank Thomas, Jeff Bagwell 3.00
17 Chipper Jones, Mike Mussina 3.00
18 Garret Anderson, Jorge Posada 2.00
19 Scott Rolen, Torii Hunter 3.00
20 Kerry Wood, Todd Helton 3.00
21 Eric Chavez, Roy Oswalt 2.00
22 Johnny Estrada, Vernon Wells 2.00
23 Lance Berkman, Tim Hudson 2.00
24 Mark Buehrle, Mark Mulder 2.00
25 C.C. Sabathia, Sean Burroughs 2.00
26 Albert Pujols, Barry Zito 6.00
27 Rich Harden, Rocco Baldelli 2.00
28 Bobby Crosby, Mark Teixeira 2.00
29 Casey Kotchman, Mark Prior 3.00
30 Dewon Brazelton, Jeremy Bonderman 2.00
31 J.C. Holt, Jon Zeringue 3.00
32 Kyle Bono, Matt Fox 3.00
33 Dexter Fowler, Mike Rozier 3.00
34 Huston Street, J.P. Howell 3.00
35 Grant Johnson, Matt Macri 3.00

36 Eric Beattie, Jeff Frazier 3.00
37 Jason Windsor, Kurt Suzuki 5.00
38 Josh Fields, Matt Tuiasosopo 6.00
39 Joseph Bauserman, K.C. Herren 3.00
40 Chris Lambert, Eric Haberer, Matt Tuiasosopo 3.00

Passing the Torch

NM/M

Common Duo: 3.00
Production 500 Sets
1 Dennis Eckersley, Huston Street 4.00
2 Matt Bush, Tony Gwynn 6.00
3 Homer Bailey, Tom Seaver 4.00
4 Bob Feller, Jeremy Sowers 3.00
5 Josh Fields, Robin Ventura 3.00
6 Nolan Ryan, Thomas Diamond 8.00
7 Eric Patterson, Ryne Sandberg 6.00
8 Richie Robnett, Rickey Henderson 4.00
9 Mike Ferris, Stan Musial 5.00
10 Bobby Doerr, Dustin Pedroia 3.00

Passing the Torch Auto. Black

No Pricing
Production 5-10 Sets

Passing the Torch Auto. Gold

NM/M

Production 5-25
2 Matt Bush, Tony Gwynn/25 90.00
4 Bob Feller, Jeremy Sowers/25 60.00
10 Bobby Doerr, Dustin Pedroia/25 60.00

Round Numbers

NM/M

Common Player: 2.00
Production 500 Sets
1 Ozzie Smith 4.00
2 Derek Jeter 6.00
3 Alex Rodriguez 5.00
4 Paul Molitor 3.00
5 George Brett 6.00
6 Delmon Young 2.00
7 Dontrelle Willis 2.00
8 Gary Carter 2.00
9 Reggie Jackson 3.00
10 Andre Dawson 2.00
11 Neil Walker 2.00
12 Laynce Nix 2.00
13 Matt Bush 6.00
14 Lyle Overbay 2.00
15 Carlos Beltran 3.00
16 Todd Helton 3.00
17 Mark Grace 2.00
18 Fred Lynn 2.00
19 Robin Yount 4.00
20 Mike Schmidt 6.00
21 Roger Clemens 6.00
22 Will Clark 3.00
23 Don Mattingly 5.00
24 Blake DeWitt 2.00
25 Rafael Palmeiro 3.00
26 Wade Boggs 3.00
27 Mark Rogers 5.00
28 Billy Buckner 3.00
29 Jeff Baker 2.00
30 Nolan Ryan 8.00
31 Mike Piazza 4.00
32 Alexis Rios 2.00
33 Eddie Murray 3.00
34 Jose Canseco 3.00
35 Mike Mussina 3.00
36 Eric Beattie 3.00
37 Keith Hernandez 2.00
38 Michael Young 2.00
39 Dwight Evans 2.00
40 Scott Elbert 3.00
41 Adrian Gonzalez 2.00
42 Johnny Bench 3.00
43 Dennis Eckersley 2.00
44 Dale Murphy 3.00
45 Ryne Sandberg 4.00
46 David Wright 3.00
47 Hank Blalock 3.00
48 Orel Hershiser 2.00
49 Sean Casey 2.00
50 Albert Pujols 6.00

Round Numbers Signature

NM/M

Production 5-250
1 Ozzie Smith/25 65.00
4 Paul Molitor/25 35.00
5 George Brett/5
6 Delmon Young/50 25.00
7 Dontrelle Willis/25 20.00
8 Gary Carter/50 20.00
9 Reggie Jackson/5
10 Andre Dawson/50 20.00
11 Neil Walker/250 20.00
12 Laynce Nix/50 20.00
13 Matt Bush/100 50.00
14 Lyle Overbay/50 15.00
15 Carlos Beltran/25 50.00
16 Todd Helton/5
17 Mark Grace/25 35.00
18 Fred Lynn/50 15.00
19 Robin Yount/5
20 Mike Schmidt/25 85.00
21 Roger Clemens/5
22 Will Clark/20 60.00
23 Don Mattingly/25 80.00
24 Blake DeWitt/250 30.00
25 Rafael Palmeiro/5
26 Wade Boggs/5
27 Mark Rogers/100 40.00
28 Billy Buckner/100 15.00
29 Jeff Baker/6
30 Nolan Ryan/10
31 Mike Piazza/5
32 Alexis Rios/50 15.00
33 Eddie Murray/5
34 Jose Canseco/25 50.00
35 Mike Mussina/5
36 Eric Beattie/100 10.00
37 Keith Hernandez/50 20.00
38 Michael Young/50 20.00
39 Dwight Evans/50 25.00
40 Scott Elbert/250 15.00
41 Adrian Gonzalez/50 10.00
42 Johnny Bench/5
43 Dennis Eckersley/50 30.00
44 Dale Murphy/50 30.00
45 Ryne Sandberg/5
46 David Wright/25 75.00
47 Hank Blalock/25 20.00
48 Orel Hershiser/5
49 Sean Casey/25 15.00
50 Albert Pujols/5

Signature Aspirations

NM/M

Production 1-100
Golds: No Pricing
Production 1-25
216 Scott Lewis/50 15.00
217 Josh Johnson/50 15.00
218 Jeff Fiorentino/50 25.00
219 Grant Hansen/50 8.00
220 Yovani Gallardo/50 10.00
221 Eddie Prasch/50 10.00
222 Danny Hill/50 8.00
223 Chuck Lofgren/50 10.00
224 Blake Johnson/50 15.00
225 Cory Dunlap/50 20.00
226 Carlos Vasquez/50 10.00
227 Jesse Crain/50 15.00
228 Yhency Brazoban/50 10.00
229 Abe Alvarez/50 10.00
256 Jorge Vasquez/50 8.00
257 Rafael Gonzalez/50 8.00
258 Andrew Dobies/50 15.00
259 Colby Miller/49 10.00
260 K.C. Herren/50 15.00
261 Ryan Meaux/50 10.00
262 Dustin Pedroia/50 40.00
263 Fernando Nieve/50 8.00
264 Mariano Gomez/50 8.00
266 Billy Killian/50 8.00
267 Mike Rouse/50 10.00
268 Kyle Bono/50 10.00
269 Mitch Einertson/50 60.00
270 Scott Proctor/50 15.00
271 Tim Bittner/50 8.00
272 Christian Garcia/50 10.00
273 Yadier Molina/50 30.00
274 Justin Leone/50 15.00
275 Charles Thomas/50 15.00
276 Travis Blackley/50 10.00
277 Frankie Francisco/50 10.00
278 Dioner Navarro/50 15.00
279 Joey Gathright/50 10.00
280 Kazuhito Tadano/50 20.00
281 Matt Bush/100 50.00
282 David Haehnel/100 10.00
283 Tommy Hottovy/100 10.00
284 Chris Carter/100 35.00
285 Mark Rogers/10
286 Jeremy Sowers/100 40.00
287 Homer Bailey/100 25.00
288 Mike Butia/100 10.00
289 Chris Nelson/100 60.00
290 Thomas Diamond/100 30.00
291 Neil Walker/100 25.00
292 Sean Gamble/100 10.00
293 Bill Bray/100 8.00
294 Reid Brignac/50 25.00
295 Ryan Klosterman/100 8.00
296 David Purcey/100 10.00
297 Scott Elbert/100 10.00
298 Josh Fields/100 25.00
299 Chris Lambert/100 10.00
300 Trevor Plouffe/100 25.00
301 Greg Golson/100 15.00
302 Josh Baker/100 10.00
303 Phillip Hughes/100 25.00
304 Matt Macri/50 12.00
305 Kyle Waldrop/100 25.00
306 Richie Robnett/100 25.00
307 Taylor Tankersley/100 10.00
308 Blake DeWitt/100 50.00
309 Daryl Jones/50 25.00
310 Eric Hurley/100 15.00
311 J.P. Howell/100 10.00
312 Zach Jackson/100 20.00
313 Justin Orenduff/100 20.00
314 Tyler Lumsden/100 15.00
315 Matt Fox/100 15.00
316 Danny Putnam/100 15.00
317 Jon Poterson/100 15.00
318 Gio Gonzalez/100 25.00
319 Jay Rainville/100 25.00
320 Huston Street/100 50.00
321 Jeff Marquez/100 15.00
322 Eric Beattie/100 10.00
323 B.J. Szymanski/100 10.00
324 Seth Smith/100 25.00
325 Robert Johnson/100 10.00
326 Wes Whisler/50 10.00
327 Billy Buckner/50 10.00
328 Jon Zeringue/100 30.00
329 Curtis Thigpen/50 12.00
330 Donny Lucy/50 10.00
331 Mike Ferris/100 12.00
332 Anthony Swarzak/10
333 Jason Jaramillo/100 10.00
334 Hunter Pence/50 50.00
335 Mike Rozier/50 10.00
336 Kurt Suzuki/100 25.00
337 Jason Vargas/50 50.00
338 Brian Bixler/50 10.00
340 Dexter Fowler/50 40.00
341 Mark Trumbo/50 15.00
342 Jeff Frazier/100 20.00
343 Steven Register/50 10.00
344 Michael Schlact/50 10.00
345 Garrett Mock/50 10.00
346 Eric Haberer/50 10.00
347 Matt Tuiasosopo/100 75.00
348 Jason Windsor/50 20.00
349 Grant Johnson/50 10.00
350 J.C. Holt/50 10.00
351 Joseph Bauserman/50 10.00
352 Jamar Walton/50 10.00
353 Eric Patterson/100 25.00
354 Tyler Johnson/50 25.00
355 Nick Adenhart/100 30.00

Signature

NM/M

Production 1-50
132 Jack Wilson/25 25.00
133 Jason Bay/25 25.00
231 J.A. Happ/50 10.00
233 Mark Jecmen/50 8.00
234 Kameron Loe/50 20.00
235 Ervin Santana/50 40.00
239 Josh Karp/50 15.00
243 Jesse Hoover/50 10.00
246 Justin Hoyman/50 15.00
247 Juan Cedeno/50 15.00
252 Benjamin Zobrist/50 10.00
253 Jeff Salazar/50 30.00
254 Fausto Carmona/50 20.00

Signature Status

Production 1-50
Golds: No Pricing
Production 1-10
221 Eddie Prasch/25 15.00
224 Blake Johnson/25 20.00
229 Abe Alvarez/25 15.00
257 Rafael Gonzalez/25 10.00
268 Kyle Bono/25 15.00
272 Christian Garcia/25 15.00
276 Travis Blackley/25 15.00
281 Matt Bush/50 60.00
282 David Haehnel/50 15.00
283 Tommy Hottovy/50 15.00
284 Chris Carter/50 40.00
286 Jeremy Sowers/50 40.00
287 Homer Bailey/50 25.00
288 Mike Butia/50 15.00
289 Chris Nelson/50 60.00
290 Thomas Diamond/50 40.00
291 Neil Walker/50 25.00
292 Sean Gamble/50 15.00
293 Bill Bray/50 10.00
294 Reid Brignac/50 30.00
295 Ryan Klosterman/50 10.00
296 David Purcey/50 15.00
297 Scott Elbert/50 15.00
298 Josh Fields/50 30.00
299 Chris Lambert/50 15.00
300 Trevor Plouffe/50 25.00
301 Greg Golson/50 20.00
302 Josh Baker/50 15.00
303 Phillip Hughes/50 40.00
304 Matt Macri/50 15.00
305 Kyle Waldrop/50 25.00
306 Richie Robnett/50 25.00
307 Taylor Tankersley/50 15.00
308 Blake DeWitt/50 40.00
309 Daryl Jones/50 30.00
310 Eric Hurley/50 15.00
311 J.P. Howell/50 20.00
312 Zach Jackson/50 15.00
313 Justin Orenduff/50 20.00
314 Tyler Lumsden/50 20.00
315 Matt Fox/50 20.00
316 Danny Putnam/50 20.00
317 Jon Poterson/50 20.00
318 Gio Gonzalez/50 40.00
319 Jay Rainville/50 35.00
320 Huston Street/50 60.00
321 Jeff Marquez/50 20.00
322 Eric Beattie/50 15.00
323 B.J. Szymanski/50 15.00
324 Seth Smith/50 30.00
325 Robert Johnson/50 15.00
326 Wes Whisler/50 15.00
327 Billy Buckner/50 15.00
328 Jon Zeringue/50 35.00
329 Curtis Thigpen/50 12.00
330 Donny Lucy/50 15.00
331 Mike Ferris/50 15.00
332 Anthony Swarzak/10
333 Jason Jaramillo/50 15.00
334 Hunter Pence/50 50.00
335 Mike Rozier/50 15.00
336 Kurt Suzuki/50 25.00
337 Jason Vargas/50 50.00
338 Brian Bixler/50 15.00
340 Dexter Fowler/50 60.00
341 Mark Trumbo/50 25.00
342 Jeff Frazier/50 20.00
343 Steven Register/50 10.00
344 Michael Schlact/50 10.00
345 Garrett Mock/50 10.00
346 Eric Haberer/50 10.00
347 Matt Tuiasosopo/50 90.00
348 Jason Windsor/50 20.00
349 Grant Johnson/50 10.00
350 J.C. Holt/50 10.00
351 Joseph Bauserman/50 10.00
352 Jamar Walton/50 25.00
353 Eric Patterson/50 25.00
354 Tyler Johnson/50 15.00
355 Nick Adenhart/50 30.00

Sign. Turn of Century

NM/M

216 Scott Lewis/100 12.00
217 Josh Johnson/100 12.00
218 Jeff Fiorentino/100 10.00
219 Grant Hansen/100 8.00
220 Yovani Gallardo/100 10.00
221 Eddie Prasch/100 10.00
222 Danny Hill/100 8.00
223 Chuck Lofgren/100 10.00
224 Blake Johnson/100 15.00
225 Cory Dunlap/100 20.00
226 Carlos Vasquez/100 10.00
227 Jesse Crain/100 15.00
228 Yhency Brazoban/100 10.00
229 Abe Alvarez/100 10.00
246 Justin Hoyman/250 8.00
252 Benjamin Zobrist/150 10.00
256 Jorge Vasquez/100 8.00
257 Rafael Gonzalez/100 8.00

258 Andrew Dobies/100 15.00
259 Colby Miller/100 10.00
260 K.C. Herren/100 15.00
261 Ryan Meaux/100 10.00
262 Dustin Pedroia/100 25.00
263 Fernando Nieve/100 8.00
264 Mariano Gomez/100 8.00
266 Billy Killian/100 8.00
267 Mike Rouse/100 10.00
268 Kyle Bono/100 10.00
269 Mitch Einertson/100 60.00
270 Scott Proctor/100 10.00
271 Tim Bittner/100 8.00
272 Christian Garcia/100 10.00
273 Yadier Molina/100 25.00
274 Justin Leone/100 15.00
275 Charles Thomas/100 15.00
276 Travis Blackley/100 10.00
277 Frankie Francisco/100 10.00
278 Dioner Navarro/100 15.00
279 Joey Gathright/100 8.00
280 Kazuhito Tadano/100 15.00
281 Matt Bush/250 30.00
282 David Haehnel/250 8.00
283 Tommy Hottovy/250 8.00
284 Chris Carter/250 20.00
285 Mark Rogers/100 30.00
286 Jeremy Sowers/250 25.00
287 Homer Bailey/250 10.00
288 Mike Butia/250 8.00
289 Chris Nelson/100 50.00
290 Thomas Diamond/250 25.00
291 Neil Walker/242 10.00
292 Sean Gamble/250 8.00
293 Bill Bray/250 8.00
294 Reid Brignac/100 20.00
295 Ryan Klosterman/250 8.00
296 David Purcey/250 8.00
297 Scott Elbert/250
298 Josh Fields/250
299 Chris Lambert/250
300 Trevor Plouffe/250 15.00
301 Greg Golson/250
302 Josh Baker/100
303 Phillip Hughes/250 20.00
304 Matt Macri/250
305 Kyle Waldrop/250
306 Richie Robnett/250 15.00
307 Taylor Tankersley/250 8.00
308 Blake DeWitt/250 25.00
309 Daryl Jones/250 15.00
310 Eric Hurley/250 8.00
311 J.P. Howell/250 8.00
312 Zach Jackson/250 8.00
313 Justin Orenduff/100 15.00
314 Tyler Lumsden/250 10.00
315 Matt Fox/250 12.00
316 Danny Putnam/250 12.00
317 Jon Poterson/238 12.00
318 Gio Gonzalez/250 20.00
319 Jay Rainville/250 15.00
320 Huston Street/250 35.00
321 Jeff Marquez/250 10.00
322 Eric Beattie/250 8.00
323 B.J. Szymanski/250 8.00
324 Seth Smith/250 15.00
325 Robert Johnson/100 10.00
326 Wes Whisler/100 8.00
327 Billy Buckner/100 10.00
328 Jon Zeringue/250 20.00
329 Curtis Thigpen/100 10.00
330 Donny Lucy/100 8.00
331 Mike Ferris/250 10.00
332 Anthony Swarzak/100 25.00
333 Jason Jaramillo/250 8.00
334 Hunter Pence/200 30.00
335 Mike Rozier/250 8.00
336 Kurt Suzuki/250 20.00
337 Jason Vargas/200 20.00
338 Brian Bixler/200 8.00
340 Dexter Fowler/250 25.00
341 Mark Trumbo/250 10.00
342 Jeff Frazier/50 15.00
343 Steven Register/200 8.00
344 Michael Schlact/200 8.00
345 Garrett Mock/200 8.00
346 Eric Haberer/100 8.00
347 Matt Tuiasosopo/250 60.00
348 Jason Windsor/100 15.00
349 Grant Johnson/250 8.00
350 J.C. Holt/100 8.00
351 Joseph Bauserman/100 8.00
352 Jamar Walton/200 12.00
353 Eric Patterson/250 15.00
354 Tyler Johnson/250 10.00
355 Nick Adenhart/100 30.00

Throwback Threads Auto.

No Pricing
3 Cal Ripken Jr./8
4 Duke Snider/10
5 George Brett/5

2004 Donruss Studio

NM/M
Complete Set (220):
Common Player: .15
Common SP (201-221): 6.00
Production 400-800:
Pack (6): 4.00
Box (24): 75.00
1 Bartolo Colon .15
2 Garret Anderson .40
3 Tim Salmon .25
4 Troy Glaus .40
5 Vladimir Guerrero .75
6 Brandon Webb .15
7 Brian Bruney .15
8 Casey Fossum .15
9 Luis Gonzales .25
10 Randy Johnson 1.00
11 Richie Sexson .40
12 Robby Hammock .15
13 Roberto Alomar .40
14 Shea Hillenbrand .15
15 Steve Finley .15
16 Adam LaRoche .15
17 Andruw Jones .50
18 Bubba Nelson .15
19 Chipper Jones .75
20 Dale Murphy .50
21 J.D. Drew .25
22 Marcus Giles .15
23 Michael Hessman .15
24 Rafael Furcal .25
25 Warren Spahn .50
26 Adam Loewen .15
27 Cal Ripken Jr. 3.00
28 Javy Lopez .40
29 Jay Gibbons .15
30 Luis Matos .15
31 Miguel Tejada .40
32 Rafael Palmeiro .50
33 Curt Schilling .50
34 Jason Varitek .25
35 Kevin Youkilis .15
36 Manny Ramirez .50
37 Nomar Garciaparra 1.50
38 Pedro Martinez .75
39 Trot Nixon .25
40 Aramis Ramirez .40
41 Brendan Harris .15
42 Derrek Lee .25
43 Ernie Banks 1.00
44 Greg Maddux 1.00
45 Kerry Wood .75
46 Mark Prior 1.00
47 Ryne Sandberg 1.00
48 Sammy Sosa 1.50
49 Todd Wellemeyer .15
50 Carlos Lee .15
51 Edwin Almonte .15
52 Frank Thomas .50
53 Joe Borchard .15
54 Joe Crede .15
55 Magglio Ordonez .25
56 Adam Dunn .50
57 Austin Kearns .25
58 Barry Larkin .40
59 Brandon Larson .15
60 Ken Griffey Jr. 1.00
61 Ryan Wagner .15
62 Sean Casey .25
63 Brian Tallet .15
64 C.C. Sabathia .15
65 Jeremy Guthrie .15
66 Jody Gerut .15
67 Travis Hafner .25
68 Clint Barmes .15
69 Jeff Baker .15
70 Joe Kennedy .15
71 Larry Walker .25
72 Preston Wilson .15
73 Todd Helton .50
74 Dmitri Young .15
75 Ivan Rodriguez .50
76 Jeremy Bonderman .15
77 Preston Larrison .15
78 Dontrelle Willis .15
79 Josh Beckett .50
80 Juan Pierre .15
81 Luis Castillo .15
82 Miguel Cabrera .75
83 Mike Lowell .25
84 Andy Pettitte .25
85 Chris Burke .15
86 Craig Biggio .25
87 Jeff Bagwell .50
88 Jeff Kent .25
89 Lance Berkman .25
90 Morgan Ensberg .15
91 Richard Hidalgo .15
92 Roger Clemens 1.50
93 Roy Oswalt .25
94 Wade Miller .15
95 Angel Berroa .15
96 Byron Gettis .15
97 Carlos Beltran .25
98 Juan Gonzalez .50
99 Mike Sweeney .15
100 Duke Snider .50
101 Edwin Jackson .15
102 Eric Gagne .50
103 Hideo Nomo .40
104 Hong-Chih Kuo .15
105 Kazuhisa Ishii .15
106 Paul Lo Duca .15
107 Robin Ventura .15
108 Shawn Green .25
109 Junior Spivey .15
110 Lyle Overbay .25
111 Rickie Weeks .25
112 Scott Podsednik .25
113 J.D. Durbin .15
114 Jacque Jones .15
115 Jason Kubel .15
116 Johan Santana .15
117 Shannon Stewart .15
118 Torii Hunter .25
119 Brad Wilkerson .15
120 Jose Vidro .15
121 Nick Johnson .15
122 Orlando Cabrera .15
123 Zach Day .15
124 Gary Carter .40
125 Jae Weong Seo .15
126 *Kazuo Matsui* 5.00
127 Mike Piazza 1.00
128 Tom Glavine .40
129 Alex Rodriguez 2.00
130 Bernie Williams .40
131 Chien-Ming Wang .15
132 Derek Jeter 2.00
133 Don Mattingly 2.00
134 Gary Sheffield .40
135 Hideki Matsui 1.00
136 Jason Giambi .50
137 Javier Vazquez .25
138 Jorge Posada .40
139 Jose Contreras .15
140 Kevin Brown .25
141 Mariano Rivera .40
142 Mike Mussina .40
143 Whitey Ford .50
144 Barry Zito .25
145 Eric Chavez .25
146 Mark Mulder .25
147 Rich Harden .15
148 Tim Hudson .25
149 Bobby Abreu .25
150 Jim Thome .75
151 Kevin Millwood .25
152 Marlon Byrd .15
153 Mike Schmidt 1.00
154 Ryan Howard .15
155 Jack Wilson .15
156 Jason Kendall .15
157 *Akinori Otsuka* 1.00
158 Brian Giles .25
159 David Wells .15
160 Jay Payton .15
161 Phil Nevin .15
162 Ryan Klesko .15
163 Sean Burroughs .15
164 A.J. Pierzynski .15
165 J.T. Snow .15
166 Jason Schmidt .25
167 Jerome Williams .15
168 *Merkin Valdez* 1.00
169 Will Clark .50
170 Bret Boone .25
171 Chris Snelling .15
172 Edgar Martinez .25
173 Ichiro Suzuki 1.00
174 Jamie Moyer .15
175 Randy Winn .15
176 Rich Aurilia .15
177 Shigetoshi Hasegawa .15
178 Albert Pujols 1.50
179 Dan Haren .15
180 Edgar Renteria .25
181 Jim Edmonds .25
182 Matt Morris .25
183 Scott Rolen .75
184 Stan Musial 1.00
185 Aubrey Huff .15
186 Chad Gaudin .15
187 Delmon Young .15
188 Fred McGriff .25
189 Rocco Baldelli .25
190 Alfonso Soriano .75
191 Hank Blalock .50
192 Mark Teixeira .50
193 Nolan Ryan 2.50
194 Alexis Rios .15
195 Carlos Delgado .50
196 Dustin McGowan .15
197 Guillermo Quiroz .15
198 Josh Phelps .15
199 Roy Halladay .25
200 Vernon Wells .25
201 Mike Gosling AU/400 8.00
202 *Ronny Cedeno AU/76* 8.00
203 *Ronald Belisario AU/400* 8.00
204 *Justin Hampson AU/800* 6.00
205 *Carlos Vasquez AU/800* 6.00
206 *Lincoln Holdzkom AU/800* 6.00
207 *Casey Daigle AU/550* 6.00
208 *Jason Bartlett AU/700* 6.00
209 *Mariano Gomez AU/800* 8.00
210 *Mike House AU/800* 6.00
211 *Chris Shelton AU/800* 25.00
212 *Dennis Sarfate AU/800* 8.00
213 *Shingo Takatsu AU/400* 35.00
214 *Justin Leone AU/800* 15.00
215 *Cory Sullivan AU/800* 8.00
216 *Mike Wuertz AU/800* 8.00
217 *Tim Bausher AU/800* 8.00
218 *Jesse Harper AU/800* 8.00
219 *Ryan Meaux AU/800* 8.00
221 *Kevin Cave AU/800* 8.00

Proofs Gold

Gold (1-200): 5-10X
Gold (201-225): .5X
#220, 222-225 exist only in parallel set
Production 50 sets

Proofs Platinum

No Pricing
Production 10 sets

Proofs Silver

Silver (1-200): 3-6X
Silver (201-225): .25X
#220, 222-225 exist only in parallel set
Production 100 sets

Stars

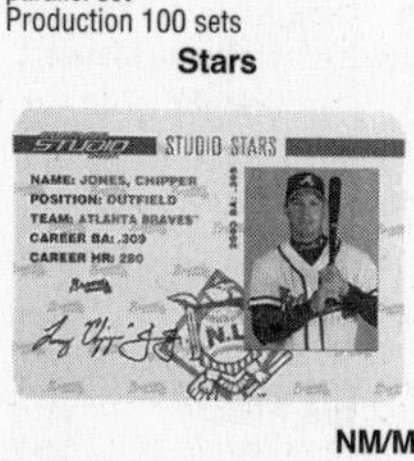

STUDIO STARS
NAME: JONES, CHIPPER
POSITION: OUTFIELD
TEAM: ATLANTA BRAVES
CAREER BA: .309
CAREER HR: 280

NM/M
Inserted 1:5
Gold: 1.5X3
Production 100 sets
Platinum: 3-5X
Production 25 sets
1 Albert Pujols 3.00
2 Alex Rodriguez 4.00
3 Alfonso Soriano 1.50
4 Andy Pettitte .50
5 Angel Berroa .50
6 Aubrey Huff .50
7 Austin Kearns .75

8	Barry Zito	.75
9	Brian Giles	.75
10	Carlos Delgado	.75
11	Chipper Jones	1.50
12	Craig Biggio	.75
13	Curt Schilling	1.00
14	Derek Jeter	4.00
15	Edgar Martinez	.50
16	Eric Gagne	1.00
17	Frank Thomas	1.00
18	Hank Blalock	1.00
19	Hideki Matsui	3.00
20	Hideo Nomo	.75
21	Ichiro Suzuki	2.00
22	Ivan Rodriguez	1.00
23	Jason Kendall	.50
24	Jason Schmidt	.75
25	Jeff Bagwell	1.00
26	Jim Edmonds	1.00
27	Jim Thome	1.50
28	Josh Beckett	.75
29	Kazuo Matsui	4.00
30	Ken Griffey Jr.	2.50
31	Larry Walker	.50
32	Magglio Ordonez	.50
33	Manny Ramirez	1.00
34	Mark Mulder	.75
35	Mark Prior	3.00
36	Mark Teixeira	1.00
37	Miguel Tejada	1.00
38	Mike Mussina	1.00
39	Mike Piazza	2.50
40	Pedro Martinez	1.50
41	Randy Johnson	1.50
42	Roger Clemens	3.00
43	Roy Halladay	.50
44	Russ Ortiz	.50
45	Sammy Sosa	3.00
46	Scott Podsednik	.50
47	Tim Hudson	.75
48	Todd Helton	1.50
49	Vernon Wells	.50
50	Vladimir Guerrero	2.00

Spirit of the Game Material Sig Jsy

NM/M

No Pricing
Production 1-5

1	Sammy Sosa/1	
2	Alex Rodriguez Rgr/1	
5	Albert Pujols/1	
7	Mark Prior/5	
11	Todd Helton/1	
12	Jeff Bagwell/1	
13	Mike Mussina/1	
14	Josh Beckett/5	
15	Hideo Nomo/1	
16	Mike Piazza/1	
17	Don Mattingly Jacket/5	
18	George Brett/1	
19	Nolan Ryan/5	
20	Cal Ripken Jr./1	

Spirit of the Game Material Jersey

NM/M

Prime: No Pricing
Production 1-5

1	Sammy Sosa/200	10.00
2	Alex Rodriguez/200	10.00
3	Nomar Garciaparra/100	10.00
4	Derek Jeter/200	20.00
5	Albert Pujols/100	20.00
7	Mark Prior/200	10.00
8	Randy Johnson/100	10.00
9	Pedro Martinez/200	10.00
11	Todd Helton/100	10.00
12	Jeff Bagwell/200	8.00
13	Mike Mussina/200	8.00
14	Josh Beckett/200	8.00
15	Hideo Nomo/200	8.00
16	Mike Piazza/200	12.00
17	Don Mattingly Jacket/200	15.00
18	George Brett/200	15.00
19	Nolan Ryan/100	40.00
20	Cal Ripken Jr./100	40.00

Spirit of the Game Material Bat

		NM/M
1	Sammy Sosa/100	15.00
2	Alex Rodriguez Rgr/100	10.00
3	Nomar Garciaparra/100	10.00
4	Derek Jeter/100	20.00
5	Albert Pujols/100	15.00
6	Roger Clemens/50	20.00
7	Mark Prior/100	10.00
8	Randy Johnson/100	10.00
9	Pedro Martinez/100	
10	Vladimir Guerrero/100	10.00
11	Todd Helton/100	10.00
12	Jeff Bagwell/100	8.00
13	Mike Mussina/50	10.00
14	Josh Beckett/100	8.00
15	Hideo Nomo/100	10.00
16	Mike Piazza/100	10.00
17	Don Mattingly/100	20.00
18	George Brett/100	20.00
19	Nolan Ryan/10	
20	Cal Ripken Jr./50	50.00

Spirit of the Game

NM/M

Production 999 sets
Die-Cut: 1X
Production 500 sets

1	Sammy Sosa	4.00
2	Alex Rodriguez Rgr	4.00
3	Nomar Garciaparra	4.00
4	Derek Jeter	6.00
5	Albert Pujols	5.00
6	Roger Clemens	5.00
7	Mark Prior	4.00
8	Randy Johnson	2.00
9	Pedro Martinez	2.00
10	Vladimir Guerrero	2.00
11	Todd Helton	2.00
12	Jeff Bagwell	2.00
13	Mike Mussina	1.50
14	Josh Beckett	1.50
15	Hideo Nomo	1.50
16	Mike Piazza	4.00
17	Don Mattingly	5.00
18	George Brett	5.00
19	Nolan Ryan	8.00
20	Cal Ripken Jr.	8.00

Rally Caps

NM/M

Production 999 sets
Die-cut: 1X
Production 500 sets

1	Adam Dunn	2.00
2	Adrian Beltre	1.50
3	Albert Pujols	5.00
4	Alex Rodriguez	5.00
5	Andruw Jones	2.00
6	Angel Berroa	1.50
7	Aubrey Huff	1.50
8	Austin Kearns	1.50
9	Ben Sheets	2.00
10	Brad Penny	1.50
11	Carlos Beltran	2.00
12	Carlos Lee	1.50
13	Casey Fossum	1.50
14	Eric Hinske	1.50
15	Geoff Jenkins	1.50
16	Jack Wilson	1.50
17	Jason Jennings	1.50
18	Joe Kennedy	1.50
19	Lance Berkman	1.50
20	Magglio Ordonez	1.50
21	Kerry Wood	3.00
22	Mark Buehrle	1.50
23	Mark Prior	4.00
24	Mark Teixeira	2.00
25	Michael Cuddyer	1.50
26	Jeff Conine	1.50
27	Mike Mussina	2.50
28	Mike Piazza	4.00
29	Jose Reyes	2.00
30	Paul Lo Duca	1.50
31	Pedro Martinez	2.00
32	Roy Oswalt	2.00
33	Ryan Klesko	1.50
34	Sammy Sosa	4.00
35	Tim Hudson	1.50
36	Todd Helton	2.00
37	Torii Hunter	2.00
38	Vernon Wells	1.50
39	Craig Wilson	1.50
40	Edgar Renteria	1.50

Private Signings Silver

		NM/M
2	Garret Anderson/25	25.00
6	Brandon Webb/25	15.00
7	Brian Bruney/200	5.00
8	Casey Fossum/63	8.00
14	Shea Hillenbrand/25	20.00
16	Adam LaRoche/26	15.00
18	Bubba Nelson/250	8.00
22	Marcus Giles/25	30.00
24	Rafael Furcal/25	25.00
26	Adam Loewen/25	20.00
29	Jay Gibbons/50	15.00
30	Luis Matos/250	10.00
35	Kevin Youkilis/250	20.00
39	Trot Nixon/25	50.00
40	Aramis Ramirez/25	25.00
41	Brendan Harris/100	8.00
43	Ernie Banks/25	75.00
48	Sammy Sosa/21	150.00
50	Carlos Lee/25	20.00
51	Edwin Almonte/227	5.00
53	Joe Borchard/100	5.00
59	Brandon Larson/100	5.00
61	Ryan Wagner/50	10.00
63	Brian Tallet/250	5.00
65	Jeremy Guthrie/89	8.00
66	Jody Gerut/100	10.00
67	Travis Hafner/100	15.00
68	Clint Barmes/100	8.00
70	Joe Kennedy/100	5.00
72	Preston Wilson/25	25.00
77	Preston Larrison/100	8.00
81	Luis Castillo/25	15.00
82	Miguel Cabrera/25	60.00
85	Chris Burke/100	5.00
90	Morgan Ensberg/50	15.00
96	Byron Gettis/250	10.00
97	Carlos Beltran/50	35.00
100	Duke Snider/50	40.00
101	Edwin Jackson/100	15.00
104	Hong-Chih Kuo/250	15.00
105	Kazuhisa Ishii/5	10.00
106	Paul Lo Duca/25	25.00
107	Robin Ventura/25	30.00
109	Junior Spivey/50	15.00
112	Scott Podsednik/100	20.00
113	J.D. Durbin/250	5.00
114	Jacque Jones/50	20.00
115	Jason Kubel/100	15.00
116	Johan Santana/25	25.00
117	Shannon Stewart/25	15.00
120	Jose Vidro/15	30.00
122	Orlando Cabrera/15	25.00
124	Gary Carter/50	25.00
131	Chien-Ming Wang/243	15.00
133	Don Mattingly/25	75.00
134	Gary Sheffield/25	25.00
147	Rich Harden/200	15.00
154	Ryan Howard/250	15.00
160	Jay Payton/50	10.00
167	Jerome Williams/57	25.00
168	Merkin Valdez/250	10.00
169	Will Clark/25	75.00
171	Chris Snelling/200	5.00
177	Shigetoshi Hasegawa/25	75.00
179	Dan Haren/250	8.00
184	Stan Musial/25	80.00
185	Aubrey Huff/250	10.00
186	Chad Gaudin/100	5.00
187	Delmon Young/25	40.00
192	Mark Teixeira/23	25.00
193	Nolan Ryan/34	100.00
194	Alexis Rios/250	15.00
196	Dustin McGowan/115	10.00
197	Guillermo Quiroz/120	8.00

Private Signings Gold

		NM/M
2	Garret Anderson/16	35.00
6	Brandon Webb/55	10.00
7	Brian Bruney/100	5.00
14	Shea Hillenbrand/28	25.00
16	Adam LaRoche/25	15.00
18	Bubba Nelson/100	10.00
22	Marcus Giles/25	30.00
23	Michael Hessman/25	15.00
29	Jay Gibbons/25	20.00
30	Luis Matos/100	10.00
35	Kevin Youkilis/100	25.00
40	Aramis Ramirez/16	35.00
41	Brendan Harris/75	10.00
49	Todd Wellemeyer/50	10.00
50	Carlos Lee/45	15.00
51	Edwin Almonte/56	10.00
53	Joe Borchard/25	10.00
54	Joe Crede/24	15.00
57	Austin Kearns/28	25.00
59	Brandon Larson/16	15.00
61	Ryan Wagner/38	10.00
63	Brian Tallet/50	10.00
65	Jeremy Guthrie/67	8.00
66	Jody Gerut/25	20.00
67	Travis Hafner/34	25.00
68	Clint Barmes/36	10.00
69	Jeff Baker/62	10.00
70	Joe Kennedy/37	15.00
73	Todd Helton/17	50.00
77	Preston Larrison/56	10.00
78	Dontrelle Willis/35	40.00
82	Miguel Cabrera/24	60.00
85	Chris Burke/46	8.00
89	Lance Berkman/17	50.00
90	Morgan Ensberg/25	15.00
96	Byron Gettis/100	8.00
97	Carlos Beltran/25	50.00
98	Juan Gonzalez/22	35.00
100	Duke Snider/25	50.00
101	Edwin Jackson/50	20.00
104	Hong-Chih Kuo/100	15.00
105	Kazuhisa Ishii/17	50.00
106	Paul Lo Duca/16	30.00
107	Robin Ventura/25	30.00
108	Shawn Green/15	30.00
109	Junior Spivey/37	15.00
112	Scott Podsednik/20	25.00
113	J.D. Durbin/31	15.00
114	Jacque Jones/25	25.00
116	Johan Santana/57	25.00
117	Shannon Stewart/23	15.00
121	Nick Johnson/21	15.00
122	Orlando Cabrera/18	25.00
124	Gary Carter/25	30.00
125	Jae Weong Seo/25	25.00
131	Chien-Ming Wang/100	20.00
147	Rich Harden/53	20.00
152	Marlon Byrd/29	15.00

154 Ryan Howard/100 20.00
160 Jay Payton/17 20.00
167 Jerome Williams/50 25.00
168 Merkin Valdez/100 15.00
171 Chris Snelling/32 10.00
177 Shigetoshi Hasegawa/17 75.00
179 Dan Haren/100 10.00
184 Stan Musial/25 80.00
185 Aubrey Huff/19 25.00
186 Chad Gaudin/100 5.00
187 Delmon Young/73 20.00
192 Mark Teixeira/25 25.00
194 Alexis Rios/50 20.00
196 Dustin McGowan/50 10.00
198 Josh Phelps/17 15.00

Masterstrokes Material Jersey

NM/M
Prime: No Pricing 4.00
Production 5 Sets
1 Todd Helton/250 8.00
2 Jose Vidro/250 4.00
3 Edgar Renteria/250 6.00
4 Mike Lowell/250 4.00
5 Gary Sheffield/250 6.00
6 Albert Pujols/250 15.00
7 Javy Lopez/250 6.00
8 Carlos Delgado/250 6.00
9 Bret Boone/250 4.00
10 Alex Rodriguez/250 10.00
11 Vernon Wells/250 4.00
12 Manny Ramirez/250 6.00
13 Jorge Posada/250 6.00
14 Edgar Martinez/250 4.00
15 Bernie Williams/250 6.00
16 Magglio Ordonez/250 4.00
17 Garret Anderson/250 4.00
18 Eric Chavez/250 4.00
19 Alfonso Soriano/150 8.00
20 Jason Giambi/250 6.00
21 Jeff Kent/250 4.00
22 Scott Rolen/250 8.00
23 Vladimir Guerrero/250 8.00
24 Sammy Sosa/250 10.00
25 Mike Piazza/250 8.00

Masterstrokes Material Bat

NM/M
Production 200 Sets 6.00
1 Todd Helton 8.00
2 Jose Vidro 4.00
3 Edgar Renteria 6.00
4 Mike Lowell 4.00
5 Gary Sheffield 6.00
6 Albert Pujols 15.00
7 Javy Lopez 6.00
8 Carlos Delgado 6.00
9 Bret Boone 4.00
10 Alex Rodriguez 10.00
11 Vernon Wells 4.00
12 Manny Ramirez 6.00
13 Jorge Posada 6.00
14 Edgar Martinez 4.00
15 Bernie Williams 6.00
16 Magglio Ordonez 4.00
17 Garret Anderson 4.00
18 Eric Chavez 4.00
19 Alfonso Soriano 8.00
20 Jason Giambi 6.00
21 Jeff Kent 4.00
22 Scott Rolen 8.00
23 Vladimir Guerrero 8.00
24 Sammy Sosa 10.00
25 Mike Piazza 8.00

Masterstrokes Combo Material Signat

No Pricing
Production 1-10

Masterstrokes Combo Material

NM/M
Production 50 Sets 10.00
1 Todd Helton Bat-Jsy/50 15.00
2 Jose Vidro Bat-Jsy/50 8.00
3 Edgar Renteria Bat-Jsy/50 10.00
4 Mike Lowell Bat-Jsy/50 10.00
5 Gary Sheffield Bat-Jsy/50 10.00
6 Albert Pujols Bat-Jsy/50 30.00
7 Javy Lopez Bat-Jsy/50 10.00
8 Carlos Delgado Bat-Jsy/50 10.00
9 Bret Boone Bat-Jsy/50 8.00
10 Alex Rodriguez Rgr Bat-Jsy/50 20.00
11 Vernon Wells Bat-Jsy/50 8.00
12 Manny Ramirez Bat-Jsy/50 10.00
13 Jorge Posada Bat-Jsy/50 10.00
14 Edgar Martinez Bat-Jsy/50 10.00
15 Bernie Williams Bat-Jsy/50 10.00
16 Magglio Ordonez Bat-Jsy/50 8.00
17 Garret Anderson Bat-Jsy/50 8.00
18 Eric Chavez Bat-Jsy/50 8.00
19 Alfonso Soriano Bat-Jsy/50 15.00
20 Jason Giambi Bat-Jsy/50 10.00
21 Jeff Kent Bat-Jsy/50 8.00
22 Scott Rolen Bat-Jsy/50 20.00
23 Vladimir Guerrero Bat-Jsy/50 20.00
24 Sammy Sosa Bat-Jsy/50 25.00
25 Mike Piazza Bat-Jsy/50 20.00

Heroes of the Hall Material Signature

No Pricing
Production 1-10

Heroes of the Hall Material Jersey

NM/M
Production 200 Unless Noted 8.00
Prime: No Pricing
Production 10 Sets
1 Fergie Jenkins Pants 8.00
2 Gary Carter 8.00
3 Gaylord Perry/100 8.00
4 George Brett 15.00
5 Jim Palmer 8.00
6 Nolan Ryan 25.00
7 Paul Molitor 10.00
8 Rod Carew 10.00
9 Steve Carlton 8.00
10 Robin Yount 15.00

Heroes of the Hall Material Bat

NM/M
Production 100 Sets 8.00
2 Gary Carter 8.00
4 George Brett 20.00
7 Paul Molitor 10.00
8 Rod Carew 8.00
9 Steve Carlton 8.00
10 Robin Yount 15.00

Heroes of the Hall

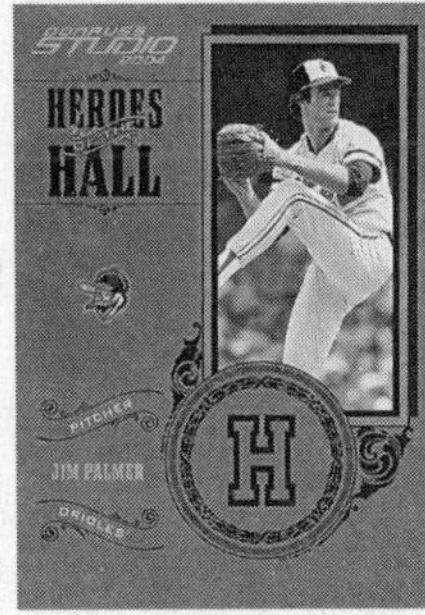

NM/M
Production 999 Sets 4.00
Die-cut: 1X
Production 500 Sets
1 Fergie Jenkins 3.00
2 Gary Carter 3.00
3 Gaylord Perry 3.00
4 George Brett 6.00
5 Jim Palmer 3.00
6 Nolan Ryan 8.00
7 Paul Molitor 4.00
8 Rod Carew 4.00
9 Steve Carlton 3.00
10 Robin Yount 5.00

Heritage Signature Material Jersey

Production 5 Sets

Heritage Material Jersey

NM/M
Quantity Produced Listed 15.00
1 George Brett/200 15.00
2 Nolan Ryan Jacket/200 20.00
3 Cal Ripken Jr./200 30.00
4 Mike Schmidt Pants/200 15.00
5 Roberto Clemente/50 60.00
6 Don Mattingly Jacket/200 15.00
7 Dale Murphy/200 8.00
8 Ryne Sandberg/200 20.00
9 Harmon Killebrew Pants/200 15.00
10 Stan Musial/100 20.00

Heritage Material Bat

NM/M
Production 50 Sets 15.00
1 George Brett 30.00
3 Cal Ripken Jr. 40.00
4 Mike Schmidt 20.00
5 Roberto Clemente 60.00
6 Don Mattingly 30.00
7 Dale Murphy 15.00
8 Ryne Sandberg 30.00
9 Harmon Killebrew 15.00
10 Stan Musial 35.00

Heritage

NM/M
Production 999 Sets 4.00
Die-Cut: 2-3X
Production 100 Sets
1 George Brett 6.00
2 Nolan Ryan 8.00
3 Cal Ripken Jr. 8.00
4 Mike Schmidt 5.00
5 Roberto Clemente 6.00
6 Don Mattingly 5.00
7 Dale Murphy 4.00
8 Ryne Sandberg 5.00
9 Harmon Killebrew 4.00
10 Stan Musial 5.00

Game Day Souvenirs Signature Number

Production 5 Sets

Game Day Souvenirs Number

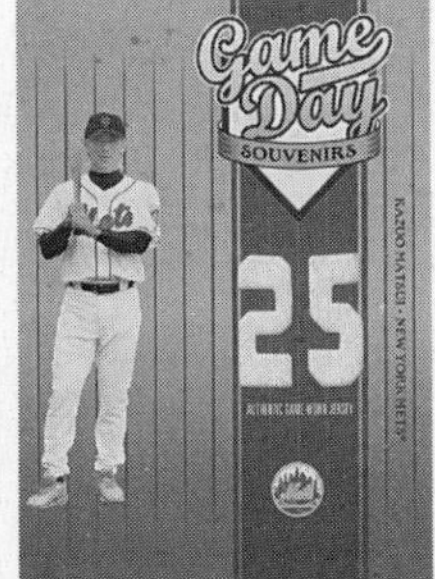

NM/M
Quantity Produced Listed 4.00
Position: .5-1X
Production 25-300
1 Garret Anderson Jsy/300 4.00
2 Troy Glaus Jsy/300 6.00
3 Vladimir Guerrero Jsy/300 8.00
4 Steve Finley Jsy/250 4.00
5 Luis Gonzalez Jsy/25 4.00
6 Richie Sexson Jsy/250 6.00
7 Andruw Jones Jsy/300 6.00
8 Chipper Jones Jsy/250 8.00
9 Rafael Furcal Jsy/250 4.00
13 Curt Schilling Jsy/300 6.00
14 Pedro Martinez Jsy/300 8.00
15 David Ortiz Jsy/300 8.00
16 Sammy Sosa Jsy/300 10.00
17 Corey Patterson Jsy/250 6.00
18 Moises Alou Jsy/300 6.00
19 Magglio Ordonez Jsy/250 4.00
20 Paul Konerko Jsy/300 4.00
21 Frank Thomas Jsy/300 8.00
22 Austin Kearns Jsy/50 8.00
23 Sean Casey Jsy/200 6.00
24 Adam Dunn Jsy/200 10.00
25 Omar Vizquel Jsy/250 4.00
26 C.C. Sabathia Jsy/300 4.00
27 Jody Gerut Jsy/250 4.00
28 Todd Helton Jsy/300 8.00
29 Vinny Castilla Jsy/300 4.00
30 Jeromy Burnitz Jsy/300 4.00
31 Fernando Vina Jsy/150 4.00
32 Ivan Rodriguez Jsy/300 8.00
33 Jeremy Bonderman Jsy/300 4.00
34 Mike Lowell Jsy/225 4.00
35 Luis Castillo Jsy/250 4.00
36 Miguel Cabrera Jsy/250 8.00
37 Roger Clemens Jsy/300 10.00
38 Andy Pettitte Jsy/300 6.00
39 Jeff Bagwell Jsy/300 6.00
40 Mike Sweeney Jsy/150 4.00
41 Carlos Beltran Jsy/200 6.00
42 Angel Berroa Jsy/100 6.00
43 Paul Lo Duca Jsy/75 6.00
44 Shawn Green Jsy/300 4.00
45 Adrian Beltre Jsy/150 4.00
46 Ben Sheets Jsy/300 6.00
47 Geoff Jenkins Jsy/250 4.00
48 Junior Spivey Jsy/300 4.00
49 Doug Mientkiewicz Jsy/100 4.00
50 Shannon Stewart Jsy/100 4.00
51 Torii Hunter Jsy/300 6.00
52 Livan Hernandez Jsy/300 4.00
53 Jose Vidro Jsy/200 4.00
54 Orlando Cabrera Jsy/300 4.00
55 Mike Piazza Jsy/250 8.00
56 Mike Cameron Jsy/250 4.00
57 Kazuo Matsui Jsy/200 30.00
58 Derek Jeter Jsy/50 30.00
59 Jason Giambi Jsy/50 10.00

61 Barry Zito Jsy/200 6.00
62 Eric Chavez Jsy/150 4.00
63 Eric Byrnes Jsy/150 4.00
65 Jim Thome Jsy/300 8.00
66 Jimmy Rollins Jsy/250 4.00
67 Jason Kendall Jsy/250 4.00
68 Craig Wilson Jsy/250 4.00
69 Jack Wilson Jsy/250 4.00
70 Ryan Klesko Jsy/300 4.00
71 Brian Giles Jsy/300 4.00
72 Sean Burroughs Jsy/300 4.00
73 A.J. Pierzynski Jsy/300 4.00
74 J.T. Snow Jsy/300 4.00
75 Michael Tucker Jsy/300 4.00
77 Edgar Martinez Jsy/50 10.00
79 Scott Rolen Jsy/300 8.00
80 Albert Pujols Jsy/300 15.00
81 Jim Edmonds Jsy/300 6.00
82 Aubrey Huff Jsy/100 4.00
83 Tino Martinez Jsy/100 4.00
84 Rocco Baldelli Jsy/100 6.00
85 Alfonso Soriano Jsy/200 8.00
86 Michael Young Jsy/250 6.00
87 Hank Blalock Jsy/200 6.00
88 Eric Hinske Jsy/200 4.00
89 Carlos Delgado Jsy/300 4.00
90 Vernon Wells Jsy/250 4.00

Fans of the Game Autographs

NM/M
20.00
216 Regis Philbin 40.00
217 Denis Leary 30.00
218 Bode Miller 20.00
219 Steve Schirripa 25.00
220 Adam Mesh 25.00

Fans of the Game

NM/M
3.00
216 Regis Philbin 3.00
217 Denis Leary 3.00
218 Bode Miller 3.00
219 Steve Schirripa 2.00
220 Adam Mesh 2.00

Diamond Cuts Material Jersey

NM/M
Production 250 Sets 8.00
1 Derek Jeter 20.00
2 Greg Maddux 10.00
3 Nomar Garciaparra 10.00
4 Miguel Cabrera 8.00
5 Mark Mulder 6.00
6 Rafael Furcal 4.00
7 Mark Prior 10.00
8 Roy Oswalt 4.00
9 Dontrelle Willis 6.00
10 Jay Gibbons 4.00
11 Josh Beckett 6.00
12 Angel Berroa 4.00
13 Adam Dunn 8.00
14 Hank Blalock 8.00
15 Carlos Beltran 6.00
16 Shannon Stewart 4.00
17 Aubrey Huff 4.00
18 Jeff Bagwell 8.00
19 Trot Nixon 6.00
20 Nolan Ryan Jacket 25.00
21 Tony Gwynn 10.00
22 Andre Dawson 6.00
23 Don Mattingly Jacket 15.00
24 Dale Murphy 10.00
25 Gary Carter 6.00

Diamond Cuts Material Bat

NM/M
Quantity Produced Listed 8.00
1 Derek Jeter/100 25.00
2 Greg Maddux/100 10.00
3 Nomar Garciaparra/200 10.00
4 Miguel Cabrera/200 8.00
5 Mark Mulder/200 6.00
6 Rafael Furcal/200 4.00
7 Mark Prior/200 10.00
8 Roy Oswalt/200 4.00
9 Dontrelle Willis/100 6.00
10 Jay Gibbons/200 4.00
11 Josh Beckett/200 6.00
12 Angel Berroa/200 4.00
13 Adam Dunn/200 8.00
14 Hank Blalock/200 8.00
15 Carlos Beltran/200 6.00
16 Shannon Stewart/200 4.00
17 Aubrey Huff/200 4.00
18 Jeff Bagwell/200 8.00
19 Trot Nixon/200 6.00
21 Tony Gwynn/200 10.00
22 Andre Dawson/200 6.00
23 Don Mattingly/200 15.00
24 Dale Murphy/200 10.00
25 Gary Carter/200 6.00

Diamond Cuts Combo Material Signature

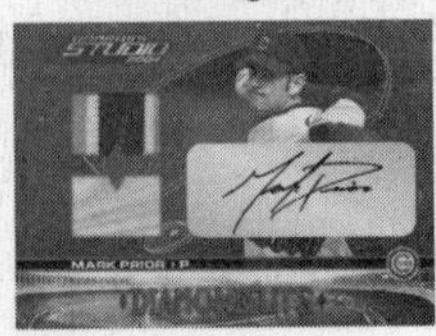

Production 1-5 Sets
4 Miguel Cabrera Bat-Jsy/5
5 Mark Mulder Bat-Jsy/5
6 Rafael Furcal Bat-Jsy/5
7 Mark Prior Bat-Jsy/5
8 Roy Oswalt Bat-Jsy/5
9 Dontrelle Willis Bat-Jsy/5
10 Jay Gibbons Bat-Jsy/5
11 Josh Beckett Bat-Jsy/5
12 Angel Berroa Bat-Jsy/5
13 Adam Dunn Bat-Jsy/5
14 Hank Blalock Bat-Jsy/5
15 Carlos Beltran Bat-Jsy/5
16 Shannon Stewart Bat-Jsy/5
17 Aubrey Huff Bat-Jsy/5
18 Jeff Bagwell Bat-Jsy/1
19 Trot Nixon Bat-Jsy/5
20 Nolan Ryan Jacket-Jsy/3
21 Tony Gwynn Bat-Jsy/3
22 Andre Dawson Bat-Jsy/5
23 Don Mattingly Bat-Jacket/5
24 Dale Murphy Bat-Jsy/5
25 Gary Carter Bat-Jsy/5

Private Signings Platinum

No Pricing
Production 1-10

Players Collection Jersey

NM/M
Common Jersey:
Production 150 Sets
Platinum: 1-2X
Production 50 Sets
1 Adam Dunn AS 6.00
2 Adam Dunn Gray 6.00
3 Adam Dunn White 6.00
4 Alex Rodriguez M's 10.00
5 Alex Rodriguez Rgr AS 10.00
6 Alex Rodriguez Rgr Blue 10.00
7 Alex Rodriguez Rgr White 10.00
8 Andruw Jones Home 6.00
9 Andruw Jones Road 6.00
10 Austin Kearns 6.00
11 Brandon Webb 4.00
12 C.C. Sabathia 4.00
13 Cal Ripken Jr. 25.00
14 Carlos Beltran 6.00
15 Carlos Delgado 6.00
16 Carlos Lee 4.00
17 Chipper Jones Home 8.00
18 Chipper Jones Road 8.00
19 Craig Biggio 6.00
20 Curt Schilling 6.00
21 David Wells 4.00
22 Don Mattingly 20.00
23 Dontrelle Willis 6.00
24 Frank Thomas Black 8.00
25 Frank Thomas White 8.00
26 Fred McGriff 4.00
27 Garret Anderson AS 6.00
28 Gary Sheffield Braves 6.00
29 Gary Sheffield Dodgers 6.00
30 Greg Maddux Gray 8.00
31 Hank Blalock Home 6.00
32 Hank Blalock Road 6.00
33 Hee Seop Choi 6.00
34 Hideo Nomo Mets 6.00
35 Hideo Nomo Dodgers Gray 6.00
36 Hideo Nomo Dodgers White 6.00
37 Ivan Rodriguez Marlins 6.00
38 Ivan Rodriguez Rgr 6.00
39 Jason Giambi Home 6.00
40 Jim Edmonds 6.00
41 Jim Thorne 8.00
42 John Olerud 4.00
43 John Smoltz 6.00
44 Josh Beckett 6.00
45 Josh Phelps 4.00
46 Juan Gonzalez Rgr 6.00
47 Juan Gonzalez Indians 6.00
48 Kazuhisa Ishii 6.00
49 Lance Berkman 6.00
50 Larry Walker Home 4.00
51 Larry Walker Road 4.00
52 Luis Gonzalez AS 4.00
53 Magglio Ordonez Home 4.00
54 Magglio Ordonez Road 4.00
55 Manny Ramirez 8.00
56 Manny Ramirez AS 8.00
57 Mark Prior Home 12.00
58 Mark Prior Road 12.00
59 Mark Teixeira 6.00
60 Mike Mussina 6.00
61 Mike Piazza AS 8.00
62 Mike Piazza Black 8.00
63 Mike Piazza White 8.00
64 Nomar Garciaparra Gray 8.00
65 Nomar Garciaparra White 8.00
66 Pat Burrell 6.00
67 Paul Konerko 4.00
68 Paul Lo Duca 4.00
69 Pedro Martinez 8.00
70 Rafael Furcal 4.00
71 Rafael Palmeiro Blue 6.00
72 Rafael Palmeiro Gray 6.00
73 Ramon Hernandez 4.00
74 Rickey Henderson 6.00
75 Rickey Henderson Black 6.00
76 Rickey Henderson White 6.00
77 Roberto Alomar Indians 6.00
78 Roberto Alomar Mets 6.00
79 Robin Ventura AS 4.00
80 Roger Clemens Away 10.00
81 Roger Clemens Home 10.00
82 Roy Halladay 6.00
83 Sammy Sosa AS 12.00
84 Sammy Sosa Gray 12.00
85 Sammy Sosa White 12.00
86 Scott Rolen 8.00
87 Shannon Stewart 4.00
88 Shawn Green Blue 4.00
89 Shawn Green Gray 4.00
90 Shawn Green White 4.00
91 Terrence Long 4.00
92 Tim Hudson 6.00
93 Todd Helton Away 8.00
94 Todd Helton Home 8.00
95 Tom Glavine Braves 6.00
96 Tom Glavine Mets 6.00
97 Torii Hunter 6.00
98 Vernon Wells 4.00
99 Vladimir Guerrero 8.00
100 Vladimir Guerrero AS 8.00

Diamond Cuts Combo Material

NM/M
Quantity Produced Listed 15.00
1 Derek Jeter Bat-Jsy/50 40.00
2 Greg Maddux Bat-Jsy/50 25.00
3 Nomar Garciaparra Bat-Jsy/25
4 Miguel Cabrera Bat-Jsy/50 20.00
5 Mark Mulder Bat-Jsy/50 15.00
6 Rafael Furcal Bat-Jsy/50 10.00
7 Mark Prior Bat-Jsy/50 25.00
8 Roy Oswalt Bat-Jsy/50 10.00
9 Dontrelle Willis Bat-Jsy/25 15.00
10 Jay Gibbons Bat-Jsy/50 10.00
11 Josh Beckett Bat-Jsy/50 15.00
12 Angel Berroa Bat-Jsy/50 10.00
13 Adam Dunn Bat-Jsy/50 15.00
14 Hank Blalock Bat-Jsy/50 15.00
15 Carlos Beltran Bat-Jsy/50 15.00
16 Shannon Stewart Bat-Jsy/50 10.00
17 Aubrey Huff Bat-Jsy/50 10.00
18 Jeff Bagwell Bat-Jsy/50 20.00
19 Trot Nixon Bat-Jsy/50 15.00
20 Nolan Ryan Jacket-Jsy/50 40.00
21 Tony Gwynn Bat-Jsy/50 30.00
22 Andre Dawson Bat-Jsy/50 15.00
23 Don Mattingly Bat-Jacket/50 40.00
24 Dale Murphy Bat-Jsy/50 20.00
25 Gary Carter Bat-Jsy/50 15.00

Big League Challenge Material

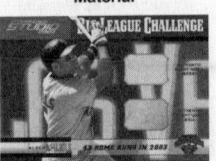

NM/M
Production 100 Sets 15.00
Combo: 1-2X
Production 50 Sets
1 Albert Pujols Jsy 15.00
2 Albert Pujols Pants 15.00
3 Alex Rodriquez Rgr Jsy 10.00
4 Alex Rodriquez Rgr Pants 10.00
5 Magglio Ordonez Jsy 5.00
6 Rafael Palmeiro Jsy 8.00
7 Troy Glaus Jsy 6.00
8 Troy Glaus Pants 6.00
9 Albert Pujols Hat 20.00
10 Alex Rodriquez Rgr Hat 15.00

Big League Challenge

NM/M
Production 999 Sets 6.00
Die-Cut: 1X
Production 500 Sets
1 Albert Pujols Left 6.00
2 Albert Pujols Right 6.00
3 Alex Rodriquez Rgr Left 5.00
4 Alex Rodriquez Rgr Right 5.00
5 Magglio Ordonez 2.00

6 Rafael Palmeiro 3.00
7 Troy Glaus Follow 2.00
8 Troy Glaus Start 2.00
9 Albert Pujols Bat Up 6.00
10 Alex Rodriquez Rgr Bat Up 5.00

2004 Donruss Leather & Lumber

NM/M

Complete Set (175):
Common Player (1-150): .25
Common Auto. (151-173): 6.00
Production 500
Pack (5): 5.00
Box (24): 100.00
1 Bartolo Colon .25
2 Garret Anderson .50
3 Tim Salmon .40
4 Troy Glaus .50
5 Vladimir Guerrero 1.00
6 Brandon Webb .25
7 Luis Gonzalez .40
8 Randy Johnson 1.00
9 Richie Sexson .50
10 Shea Hillenbrand .25
11 Adam LaRoche .25
12 Andruw Jones .50
13 Chipper Jones 1.00
14 Dale Murphy .75
15 J.D. Drew .50
16 Marcus Giles .25
17 Rafael Furcal .25
18 Cal Ripken Jr. 3.00
19 Javy Lopez .50
20 Jay Gibbons .25
21 Luis Matos .25
22 Miguel Tejada .50
23 Rafael Palmeiro .75
24 Curt Schilling .75
25 Jason Varitek .40
26 Manny Ramirez .75
27 Nomar Garciaparra 1.50
28 Pedro J. Martinez 1.00
29 Trot Nixon .25
30 Greg Maddux 1.50
31 Kerry Wood 1.00
32 Mark Prior 1.00
33 Ryne Sandberg 1.50
34 Sammy Sosa 2.00
35 Carlos Lee .25
36 Frank Thomas .75
37 Magglio Ordonez .40
38 Paul Konerko .25
39 Adam Dunn .75
40 Austin Kearns .25
41 Barry Larkin .50
42 Ken Griffey Jr. 1.50
43 Ryan Wagner .25
44 C.C. Sabathia .25
45 Jody Gerut .25
46 Omar Vizquel .25
47 Larry Walker .40
48 Preston Wilson .25
49 Todd Helton .75
50 Alan Trammell .25
51 Ivan Rodriguez. .75
52 Jeremy Bonderman. .25
53 Dontrelle Willis. .25
54 Josh Beckett. .50
55 Luis Castillo. .25
56 Miguel Cabrera. 1.00
57 Mike Lowell. .25
58 Andy Pettitte. .40
59 Craig Biggio .40
60 Jeff Bagwell .75
61 Jeff Kent .40
62 Lance Berkman .40
63 Roger Clemens 2.50
64 Roy Oswalt .40
65 Angel Berroa .25
66 Carlos Beltran .75
67 George Brett 2.00
68 Juan Gonzalez .50
69 Mike Sweeney .25
70 Eric Gagne .50
71 Hideo Nomo .50
72 Kazuhisa Ishii .25
73 Paul LoDuca .25
74 Shawn Green .50
75 Geoff Jenkins .25
76 Junior Spivey .25
77 Rickie Weeks .25
78 Robin Yount .75
79 Scott Podsednik .25
80 Jacque Jones .25
81 Johan Santana .50
82 Shannon Stewart .25
83 Torii Hunter .40
84 Andre Dawson .50
85 Chad Cordero .25
86 Jose Vidro .25
87 Nick Johnson .25
88 Orlando Cabrera .40
89 Gary Carter .50
90 Jae Weong Seo .25
91 Jose Reyes .25
92 Mike Piazza 1.50
93 Tom Glavine .50
94 Alex Rodriguez 2.50
95 Bernie Williams .50
96 Derek Jeter 2.50
97 Don Mattingly 2.00
98 Gary Sheffield .50
99 Hideki Matsui 1.50
100 Jason Giambi .50
101 Jorge Posada .50
102 Mike Mussina .50
103 Barry Zito .50
104 Bobby Crosby .25
105 Eric Chavez .40
106 Jermaine Dye .25
107 Mark Mulder .40
108 Rich Harden .25
109 Rickey Henderson .25
110 Tim Hudson .40
111 Bobby Abreu .40
112 Brett Myers .25
113 Jim Thome 1.00
114 Kevin Millwood .25
115 Marlon Byrd .25
116 Mike Schmidt 2.00
117 Pat Burrell .25
118 Dave Parker .25
119 Jason Bay .25
120 Jason Kendall .25
121 Brian Giles .25
122 Jay Payton .25
123 Ryan Klesko .25
124 Tony Gwynn 1.00
125 Edgardo Alfonzo .25
126 Jason Schmidt .50
127 Jerome Williams .25
128 Bret Boone .25
129 Edgar Martinez .25
130 Ichiro Suzuki 2.00
131 Jamie Moyer .25
132 John Olerud .25
133 Albert Pujols 2.00
134 Edgar Renteria .40
135 Jim Edmonds .50
136 Matt Morris .25
137 Scott Rolen 1.00
138 Aubrey Huff .25
139 Carl Crawford .25
140 Delmon Young .25
141 Rocco Baldelli .25
142 Alfonso Soriano 1.00
143 Hank Blalock .75
144 Mark Teixeira .50
145 Michael Young .25
146 Nolan Ryan 2.50
147 Carlos Delgado .50
148 Eric Hinske .25
149 Roy Halladay .25
150 Vernon Wells .25
151 *Andres Blanco* 8.00
152 *Kevin Cave* 6.00
153 *Ryan Meaux* 6.00
154 *Tim Bausher* 6.00
155 *Jesse Harper* 6.00
156 *Mike Wuertz* 8.00
157 *Colby Miller* 8.00
158 *Donald Kelly* 6.00
159 *Edwin Moreno* 8.00
160 *Mike Johnston* 6.00
161 *Orlando Rodriguez* 6.00
162 *Phil Stockman* 8.00
163 *Yadier Molina* 8.00
164 *Jorge Vasquez* 6.00
165 *Scott Proctor* 8.00
166 Jake Woods 6.00
167 *Aarom Baldiris* 8.00
168 *Jason Bartlett* 6.00
169 *Casey Daigle* 6.00
170 *Dennis Sarfate* 6.00
171 *Edwardo Sierra* 8.00
172 *Merkin Valdez* 8.00
173 *Eddy Rodriguez* 8.00
174 *Kazuo Matsui* 8.00
175 *David Aardsma* 4.00

Gold

Stars (1-150): 10-15X
SP's (151-175): No Pricing
Production 25 sets

Platinum

No Pricing
Production one set

Silver

Stars (1-150): 4-8X
SP's (151-175): .5X
Production 100 sets

B/W

NM/M

Common Player: 1.50
Production 1,000 sets
Gold B/W: 4-6X
Production 25 sets
Silver B/W: 2-3X
Production 100 sets
Platinum B/W: No Pricing
Production one set
13 Chipper Jones 2.00
14 Dale Murphy 1.50
18 Cal Ripken Jr. 8.00
27 Nomar Garciaparra 3.00
30 Greg Maddux 2.50
32 Mark Prior 2.00
33 Ryne Sandberg 3.00
34 Sammy Sosa 3.00
63 Roger Clemens 4.00
67 George Brett 4.00
78 Robin Yount 3.00
89 Gary Carter 1.50
92 Mike Piazza 3.00
94 Alex Rodriguez 5.00
96 Derek Jeter 5.00
97 Don Mattingly 4.00
99 Hideki Matsui 3.00
109 Rickey Henderson 1.50
116 Mike Schmidt 3.00
124 Tony Gwynn 2.00
130 Ichiro Suzuki 4.00
133 Albert Pujols 4.00
142 Alfonso Soriano 2.00
146 Nolan Ryan 5.00
174 Kazuo Matsui 6.00

Signatures Bronze B/W

No Pricing
Production 1-25

Signatures Gold B/W

No Pricing
Production 1-25

Signatures Silver B/W

No Pricing
Production 1-25

Signatures Platinum B/W

No Pricing

Signatures Platinum

No Pricing
Production one set

Materials Jersey B/W

NM/M

Common Player: 5.00
Jersey Prime B/W: No Pricing
Production 1-25
13 Chipper Jones/250 8.00
14 Dale Murphy/250 8.00
18 Cal Ripken Jr./100 35.00
30 Greg Maddux/100 10.00
32 Mark Prior/250 10.00
33 Ryne Sandberg/50 30.00
34 Sammy Sosa/250 12.00
67 George Brett/250 15.00
78 Robin Yount/150 10.00
89 Gary Carter/250 5.00
92 Mike Piazza/250 10.00
96 Derek Jeter/100 20.00
97 Don Mattingly/250 15.00
99 Hideki Matsui/250 20.00
109 Rickey Henderson/250 8.00
116 Mike Schmidt/50 25.00
124 Tony Gwynn/100 10.00
133 Albert Pujols/250 15.00
146 Nolan Ryan/100 25.00
174 Kazuo Matsui/50 25.00

Materials Bat B/W

NM/M

Production 100 unless noted
13 Chipper Jones 8.00
14 Dale Murphy 10.00
18 Cal Ripken Jr. 30.00
27 Nomar Garciaparra 10.00
30 Greg Maddux 10.00
32 Mark Prior 10.00
33 Ryne Sandberg/50 30.00
34 Sammy Sosa 12.00
63 Roger Clemens/50 20.00
67 George Brett 15.00
78 Robin Yount 12.00
89 Gary Carter 8.00
92 Mike Piazza 10.00
94 Alex Rodriguez 10.00
96 Derek Jeter 20.00
97 Don Mattingly 20.00
109 Rickey Henderson 10.00
116 Mike Schmidt 15.00
124 Tony Gwynn 10.00
133 Albert Pujols 20.00
142 Alfonso Soriano 8.00
146 Nolan Ryan/25 65.00
174 Kazuo Matsui 20.00

Signatures Silver

NM/M

Quantity produced listed
2 Garret Anderson/50 20.00
10 Shea Hillenbrand/50 15.00
11 Adam LaRoche/50 15.00
14 Dale Murphy/50 25.00
16 Marcus Giles/50 15.00
17 Rafael Furcal/50 15.00
20 Jay Gibbons/50 10.00
21 Luis Matos/50 10.00
29 Trot Nixon/25 35.00
32 Mark Prior/25 65.00
35 Carlos Lee/50 10.00
39 Adam Dunn/25 30.00
40 Austin Kearns/25 20.00
43 Ryan Wagner/50 10.00
44 C.C. Sabathia/50 15.00
45 Jody Gerut/50 15.00
48 Preston Wilson/50 15.00
50 Alan Trammell/50 20.00
52 Jeremy Bonderman/50 10.00
56 Miguel Cabrera/50 30.00
65 Angel Berroa/50 10.00
66 Carlos Beltran/50 30.00
73 Paul LoDuca/25 20.00
79 Scott Podsednik/50 15.00
80 Jacque Jones/50 15.00
81 Johan Santana/50 40.00
82 Shannon Stewart/50 15.00
83 Torii Hunter/50 15.00
84 Andre Dawson/50 15.00
85 Chad Cordero/50 8.00
86 Jose Vidro/50 10.00
88 Orlando Cabrera/50 12.00
104 Bobby Crosby/50 25.00
106 Jermaine Dye/50 15.00
107 Mark Mulder/25 20.00
108 Rich Harden/50 20.00
115 Marlon Byrd/50 10.00
119 Jason Bay/50 20.00
122 Jay Payton/50 10.00
138 Aubrey Huff/50 15.00
139 Carl Crawford/50 20.00
143 Hank Blalock/50 25.00
145 Michael Young/50 20.00
150 Vernon Wells/50 15.00
151 Andres Blanco/100 10.00
152 Kevin Cave/100 10.00
153 Ryan Meaux/100 8.00
154 Tim Bausher/100 8.00
155 Jesse Harper/100 8.00
156 Mike Wuertz/100 10.00
158 Donald Kelly/100 6.00
159 Edwin Moreno/100 6.00
160 Mike Johnston/100 6.00
161 Orlando Rodriguez/100 6.00
164 Jorge Vasquez/100 8.00
166 Jake Woods/100 8.00
167 Aarom Baldiris/100 8.00
170 Dennis Sarfate/100 6.00
173 Eddy Rodriguez/100 8.00

Signatures Gold

NM/M

Quantity produced listed
2 Garret Anderson/25 25.00
10 Shea Hillenbrand/25 20.00

11 Adam LaRoche/25 15.00
14 Dale Murphy/25 35.00
16 Marcus Giles/25 20.00
17 Rafael Furcal/25 20.00
20 Jay Gibbons/25 15.00
21 Luis Matos/25 15.00
35 Carlos Lee/25 15.00
39 Adam Dunn/25 30.00
44 C.C. Sabathia/25 20.00
45 Jody Gerut/25 20.00
48 Preston Wilson/25 20.00
50 Alan Trammell/25 25.00
52 Jeremy Bonderman/25 15.00
56 Miguel Cabrera/25 35.00
65 Angel Berroa/25 10.00
66 Carlos Beltran/25 40.00
79 Scott Podsednik/25 20.00
80 Jacque Jones/25 20.00
81 Johan Santana/25 50.00
82 Shannon Stewart/25 20.00
83 Torii Hunter/25 20.00
84 Andre Dawson/25 20.00
85 Chad Cordero/25 10.00
86 Jose Vidro/25 15.00
88 Orlando Cabrera/25 15.00
104 Bobby Crosby/25 30.00
106 Jermaine Dye/25 20.00
115 Marlon Byrd/25 15.00
119 Jason Bay/25 25.00
122 Jay Payton/25 15.00
138 Aubrey Huff/25 20.00
139 Carl Crawford/25 25.00
145 Michael Young/25 30.00
151 Andres Blanco/50 10.00
152 Kevin Cave/50 10.00
153 Ryan Meaux/50 10.00
154 Tim Bausher/50 10.00
155 Jesse Harper/50 10.00
156 Mike Wuertz/50 10.00
158 Donald Kelly/50 8.00
159 Edwin Moreno/50 8.00
160 Mike Johnston/50 8.00
161 Orlando Rodriguez/50 8.00
164 Jorge Vasquez/50 10.00
166 Jake Woods/50 10.00
167 Aarom Baldiris/50 10.00
168 Jason Bartlett/50 12.00
170 Dennis Sarfate/50 8.00
173 Eddy Rodriguez/50 10.00

Signatures Bronze

NM/M

Quantity produced listed 8.00
2 Garret Anderson/25 25.00
10 Shea Hillenbrand/100 10.00
11 Adam LaRoche/100 10.00
14 Dale Murphy/25 35.00
16 Marcus Giles/50 15.00
17 Rafael Furcal/25 20.00
20 Jay Gibbons/100 10.00
21 Luis Matos/100 10.00
35 Carlos Lee/100 10.00
39 Adam Dunn/25 30.00
44 C.C. Sabathia/100 15.00
48 Preston Wilson/50 15.00
50 Alan Trammell/50 20.00
52 Jeremy Bonderman/100 10.00
56 Miguel Cabrera/50 30.00
65 Angel Berroa/100 10.00
66 Carlos Beltran/100 25.00
79 Scott Podsednik/100 10.00
80 Jacque Jones/100 10.00
81 Johan Santana/100 40.00
82 Shannon Stewart/100 10.00
83 Torii Hunter/50 15.00
84 Andre Dawson/100 15.00
85 Chad Cordero/100 8.00
86 Jose Vidro/100 10.00
88 Orlando Cabrera/100 10.00
104 Bobby Crosby/100 20.00
106 Jermaine Dye/100 15.00
108 Rich Harden/50 20.00
115 Marlon Byrd/25 15.00
119 Jason Bay/100 15.00
122 Jay Payton/50 10.00
137 Scott Rolen/5
138 Aubrey Huff/50 15.00
139 Carl Crawford/50 20.00
145 Michael Young/100 15.00
151 Andres Blanco/50 10.00
152 Kevin Cave/50 10.00
153 Ryan Meaux/50 10.00
154 Tim Bausher/50 10.00
155 Jesse Harper/50 10.00
156 Mike Wuertz/50 10.00
158 Donald Kelly/50 8.00
159 Edwin Moreno/50 8.00
160 Mike Johnston/50 8.00
161 Orlando Rodriguez/50 8.00
164 Jorge Vasquez/50 10.00
166 Jake Woods/50 10.00
167 Aarom Baldiris/50 10.00
170 Dennis Sarfate/50 8.00
173 Eddy Rodriguez/50 10.00

Rivals Materials

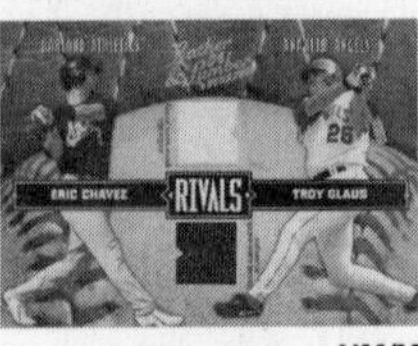

NM/M

Quantity produced listed
1 Derek Jeter Jsy, Nomar Garciaparra Bat/250 25.00
2 Mark Prior Jsy, Albert Pujols Jsy/250 25.00
3 Warren Spahn Pants, Stan Musial Jsy/100 30.00
4 Don Sutton Jsy, Reggie Jackson Jsy/10
5 Roger Clemens Jsy, Mike Piazza Jsy/250 20.00
7 Kerry Wood Jsy, Frank Thomas Jsy/250 10.00
8 Jim Palmer Jsy, Willie Stargell Jsy/250 12.00
9 Tom Seaver Jsy, Mike Schmidt Jsy/250 20.00
10 Jack Morris Jsy, George Brett Jsy/250 15.00
11 Randy Johnson Jsy, Todd Helton Jsy/250 12.00
12 Tommy John Pants, Rod Carew Jkt/250 12.00
13 Pedro J. Martinez Jsy, Jason Giambi Jsy/250 12.00
14 Dwight Gooden Jsy, Wade Boggs Jsy/250 10.00
15 Bob Gibson Jsy, Ernie Banks Pants/100 20.00
16 Hideo Nomo Jsy, Barry Larkin Jsy/250 10.00
17 Roy Halladay Jsy, Vladimir Guerrero Jsy/250 10.00
18 Greg Maddux Jsy, Jeff Bagwell Jsy/250 15.00
19 Barry Zito Jsy, Alex Rodriguez Jsy/250 15.00
20 Steve Carlton Jsy, Andre Dawson Jsy/250 10.00
21 Mariano Rivera Jsy, Chipper Jones Jsy/10
22 Tom Glavine Jsy, Manny Ramirez Jsy/250 10.00
23 Whitey Ford Pants, Harmon Killebrew Jsy/100 35.00
24 Carl Yastrzemski Jsy, Jim "Catfish" Hunter Jsy/250 20.00
25 Nolan Ryan Pants, Robin Ventura Jsy/250 25.00
26 Carlton Fisk Jsy, Joe Morgan Jsy/250 10.00
27 Phil Rizzuto Jsy, Duke Snider Jsy/5
28 Fergie Jenkins Pants, Lou Brock Jsy/100 20.00
29 Jose Canseco Bat, Will Clark Bat/250 15.00
30 Mike Mussina Jsy, Josh Beckett Jsy/250 10.00
31 Rickey Henderson Jsy, Ivan Rodriguez Jsy/250 10.00
32 Don Mattingly Pants, Eddie Murray Jsy/250 20.00
33 Troy Glaus Jsy, Eric Chavez Jsy/250 8.00
34 Ryne Sandberg Jsy, Steve Garvey Jsy/250 20.00
35 Bob Gibson Jsy, Roger Maris Jsy/100 40.00
36 Roger Clemens Jsy, Cal Ripken Jr. Pants/250 30.00
38 Curt Schilling Jsy, Paul Molitor Bat/250 12.00
39 Ichiro Suzuki Base, Hideki Matsui Base/250 40.00
40 Sammy Sosa Jsy, Jim Thome Jsy/250 12.00

Rivals

NM/M

Common Duo:
Production 1,499 Sets
Silver: 1X-2X
Production 100 Sets
1 Derek Jeter, Nomar Garciaparra 6.00
2 Mark Prior, Albert Pujols 6.00
3 Warren Spahn, Stan Musial 4.00
4 Don Sutton, Reggie Jackson 2.00
5 Roger Clemens, Mike Piazza 4.00
6 Dennis Eckersley, M. Williams 1.50
7 Kerry Wood, Frank Thomas 3.00
8 Jim Palmer, Willie Stargell 2.00
9 Tom Seaver, Mike Schmidt 5.00
10 Jack Morris, George Brett 5.00
11 Randy Johnson, Todd Helton 2.00
12 Tommy John, Rod Carew 2.00
13 Pedro J. Martinez, Jason Giambi 2.00
14 Dwight Gooden, Wade Boggs 1.50
15 Bob Gibson, Ernie Banks 3.00
16 Hideo Nomo, Barry Larkin 1.50
17 Roy Halladay, Vladimir Guerrero 2.00
18 Greg Maddux, Jeff Bagwell 3.00
19 Barry Zito, Alex Rodriguez 5.00
20 Steve Carlton, Andre Dawson 1.50
21 Mariano Rivera, Chipper Jones 2.00
22 Tom Glavine, Manny Ramirez 2.00
23 Whitey Ford, Harmon Killebrew 2.00
24 Carl Yastrzemski, Jim "Catfish" Hunter 2.00
25 Nolan Ryan, Robin Ventura 5.00
26 Carlton Fisk, Joe Morgan 1.50
27 Phil Rizzuto, Duke Snider 2.00
28 Fergie Jenkins, Lou Brock 1.50
29 Jose Canseco, Will Clark 1.50
30 Mike Mussina, Josh Beckett 1.50
31 Rickey Henderson, Ivan Rodriguez 2.00
32 Don Mattingly, Eddie Murray 5.00
33 Troy Glaus, Eric Chavez 1.50
34 Ryne Sandberg, Steve Garvey 3.00
35 Bob Gibson, Roger Maris 4.00
36 Roger Clemens, Cal Ripken Jr. 8.00
37 Orel Hershiser, Darryl Strawberry 1.50
38 Curt Schilling, Paul Molitor 2.00
39 Ichiro Suzuki, Hideki Matsui 5.00
40 Sammy Sosa, Jim Thome 4.00

Pennants/Pinstripes

NM/M

Common Player: 1.50
Production 1,499 Sets
Gold: 1X-2X
Production 100 Sets
1 Reggie Jackson 2.50
2 Mike Schmidt 5.00
3 Steve Carlton 2.00
4 Dwight Gooden 1.50
5 Darryl Strawberry 1.50
6 Roger Clemens 5.00
7 Curt Schilling 2.00
8 Mark Grace 2.00
9 Ivan Rodriguez 2.00
10 Josh Beckett 1.50

Naturals Materials Bat

NM/M

Barrel: No Pricing
Production 1-5
1 Eric Chavez/20 12.00
2 Garret Anderson/250 5.00
3 Lance Berkman/250 5.00
4 Paul Molitor/250 8.00
5 Rafael Palmeiro/250 8.00
6 Ralph Kiner/250 10.00
7 Todd Helton/250 8.00
8 Tony Gwynn/250 12.00
9 Wade Boggs/250 8.00
10 Will Clark/250 10.00

Naturals

NM/M

Common Player: 1.50
Production 1,499 Sets
Silver: 1X-2X
Production 100 Sets
1 Eric Chavez 1.50
2 Garret Anderson 1.50
3 Lance Berkman 1.50
4 Paul Molitor 3.00
5 Rafael Palmeiro 2.00
6 Ralph Kiner 3.00
7 Todd Helton 2.00
8 Tony Gwynn 4.00
9 Wade Boggs 2.00
10 Will Clark 2.00

Materials Jersey

NM/M

Common Jersey: 4.00
Quantity produced listed
MLB Logo: No Pricing
Production One Set
Prime: 1X-1.25X
Production 1-25
No pricing 15 or less
Barrel: No Pricing
Production 1-5
2 Garret Anderson/50 8.00

3	Tim Salmon/250	4.00
4	Troy Glaus/200	4.00
6	Brandon Webb/100	4.00
7	Luis Gonzalez/250	4.00
8	Randy Johnson/100	10.00
12	Andruw Jones/250	4.00
13	Chipper Jones/250	8.00
14	Dale Murphy/250	10.00
16	Marcus Giles/250	4.00
17	Rafael Furcal/250	4.00
18	Cal Ripken Jr./100	30.00
19	Javy Lopez/150	4.00
20	Jay Gibbons/250	4.00
21	Luis Matos/250	4.00
22	Miguel Tejada/250	6.00
23	Rafael Palmeiro/250	8.00
25	Jason Varitek/250	8.00
26	Manny Ramirez/250	8.00
28	Pedro J. Martinez/250	8.00
29	Trot Nixon/25	10.00
30	Greg Maddux/100	10.00
31	Kerry Wood/250	10.00
32	Mark Prior/250	10.00
33	Ryne Sandberg/50	30.00
34	Sammy Sosa/250	10.00
35	Carlos Lee/250	4.00
36	Frank Thomas/250	8.00
37	Magglio Ordonez/250	4.00
38	Paul Konerko/250	4.00
39	Adam Dunn/250	8.00
40	Austin Kearns/250	4.00
41	Barry Larkin/250	6.00
44	C.C. Sabathia/250	4.00
45	Jody Gerut/250	4.00
46	Omar Vizquel/250	4.00
47	Larry Walker/250	4.00
48	Preston Wilson/250	4.00
49	Todd Helton	8.00
50	Alan Trammell/50	10.00
51	Ivan Rodriguez/100	10.00
52	Jeremy Bonderman/150	4.00
53	Dontrelle Willis/100	4.00
54	Josh Beckett/250	4.00
55	Luis Castillo/250	4.00
56	Miguel Cabrera/50	15.00
57	Mike Lowell/25	10.00
58	Andy Pettitte/25	15.00
59	Craig Biggio/250	4.00
60	Jeff Bagwell/250	8.00
61	Jeff Kent/250	4.00
62	Lance Berkman/250	4.00
64	Roy Oswalt/250	4.00
65	Angel Berroa/50	6.00
66	Carlos Beltran/250	6.00
67	George Brett/250	15.00
69	Mike Sweeney/100	4.00
71	Hideo Nomo/250	6.00
72	Kazuhisa Ishii/250	4.00
73	Paul LoDuca/250	4.00
74	Shawn Green/250	4.00
75	Geoff Jenkins/250	4.00
78	Robin Yount/250	10.00
80	Jacque Jones/250	10.00
81	Johan Santana/250	8.00
82	Shannon Stewart/250	4.00
83	Torii Hunter/250	4.00
84	Andre Dawson/50	10.00
86	Jose Vidro/100	4.00
88	Orlando Cabrera/100	4.00
89	Gary Carter/250	8.00
90	Jae Weong Seo/100	4.00
91	Jose Reyes/250	4.00
92	Mike Piazza/250	10.00
93	Tom Glavine/250	6.00
95	Bernie Williams/250	6.00
96	Derek Jeter/150	20.00
97	Don Mattingly/250	15.00
99	Hideki Matsui/250	20.00
100	Jason Giambi/250	4.00
101	Jorge Posada/50	10.00
102	Mike Mussina/100	8.00
103	Barry Zito/250	4.00
105	Eric Chavez/100	4.00
107	Mark Mulder/250	4.00
108	Rich Harden/50	8.00
109	Rickey Henderson/100	10.00
110	Tim Hudson/250	4.00
111	Bobby Abreu/250	4.00
112	Brett Myers/250	4.00
113	Jim Thome/250	8.00
114	Kevin Millwood/250	4.00
115	Marlon Byrd/250	4.00
116	Mike Schmidt/50	25.00
117	Pat Burrell/250	4.00
118	Dave Parker/250	8.00
120	Jason Kendall/50	6.00
123	Ryan Klesko/250	4.00
124	Tony Gwynn/100	12.00
127	Jerome Williams/200	4.00
128	Bret Boone/10	
129	Edgar Martinez/250	6.00
131	Jamie Moyer/250	4.00
132	John Olerud/150	4.00
133	Albert Pujols/250	15.00
134	Edgar Renteria/100	6.00
135	Jim Edmonds/250	4.00
136	Matt Morris/250	4.00
137	Scott Rolen/250	8.00
138	Aubrey Huff/100	4.00
139	Carl Crawford/250	4.00
141	Rocco Baldelli/250	4.00
143	Hank Blalock/250	6.00
144	Mark Teixeira/1	
146	Nolan Ryan/100	30.00
147	Carlos Delgado/250	4.00
148	Eric Hinske/100	4.00
149	Roy Halladay/100	4.00
150	Vernon Wells/250	4.00

Bat-Spikes

NM/M

Bat/Glove: .75X-1.5X
Production 1-50
Bat/Ball: .75X-1.5X
Production 5-25
No pricing 15 or less
Barrel/Jersey: No Pricing
Production 1-5

1	Andruw Jones/25	15.00
2	Andy Pettitte/5	
3	Angel Berroa/25	10.00
4	Aubrey Huff/5	
5	Austin Kearns/1	
6	Barry Zito/25	15.00
7	Ben Sheets/50	10.00
8	Brad Penny/50	8.00
9	Brian Giles/50	8.00
10	Carlos Lee/50	8.00
11	Corey Patterson/50	15.00
12	Derek Jeter/10	
13	Don Mattingly/25	40.00
14	Eric Hinske/5	
15	Gary Carter/50	12.00
17	Ivan Rodriguez/50	15.00
18	Jack Cust/50	8.00
19	Jason Jennings/50	8.00
21	Jim Edmonds/50	10.00
22	Joe Borchard/50	8.00
23	Joe Crede/50	8.00
24	Josh Beckett/25	15.00
25	Josh Phelps/50	8.00
26	Juan Pierre/50	8.00
27	Kenny Lofton/50	8.00
28	Kirby Puckett/1	
29	Lance Berkman/25	15.00
30	Magglio Ordonez/25	10.00
31	Marcus Giles/50	10.00
32	Mark Buehrle/50	8.00
33	Mark Prior/25	25.00
34	Mark Teixeira/25	15.00
35	Marlon Byrd/50	8.00
36	Mike Sweeney/10	
37	Morgan Ensberg/10	
38	Nick Johnson/25	10.00
39	Orlando Hudson/50	8.00
40	Paul LoDuca/25	10.00
41	Rafael Palmeiro/25	20.00
42	Richie Sexson/5	
43	Roy Oswalt/25	15.00
44	Ryan Klesko/50	10.00
46	Sean Casey/50	10.00
47	Tony Gwynn/10	
48	Travis Hafner/50	15.00
49	Victor Martinez/50	10.00
50	Wade Miller/50	10.00

Leather Materials

NM/M

Quantity produced listed

1	Garret Anderson Ball/50	8.00
2	Albert Pujols Ball/50	25.00
3	John Smoltz Ball/50	20.00
4	Cal Ripken Jr. Ball/50	75.00
5	Ichiro Suzuki Ball/50	60.00
6	Pedro J. Martinez Ball/50	15.00
7	Shawn Green Ball/50	8.00
8	Juan Gonzalez Ball/50	10.00
9	Mariano Rivera Ball/50	10.00
10	Jason Giambi Ball/50	10.00
11	Dave Parker Btg Glv/25	20.00
12	Dwight Gooden Btg Glv/25	20.00
13	Eric Munson Btg Glv/50	8.00
14	Frank Thomas Btg Glv/50	20.00
15	Joe Carter Btg Glv/50	10.00
16	Jose Canseco Btg Glv/50	20.00
17	Paul O'Neill Btg Glv/50	20.00
18	Tony Gwynn Btg Glv/50	30.00
19	Wade Boggs Btg Glv/25	20.00
20	Xavier Nady Btg Glv/50	8.00
21	Albert Pujols Fld Glv/10	
22	Alex Rodriguez Fld Glv/25	35.00
23	Chipper Jones Fld Glv/25	30.00
24	Derek Jeter Fld Glv/25	50.00
25	Jack Wilson Fld Glv/50	8.00
26	Lenny Dykstra Fld Glv/50	10.00
27	Mark Grace Fld Glv/50	15.00
28	Steve Carlton Fld Glv/50	12.00
29	Tony Perez Fld Glv/25	15.00
30	Vladimir Guerrero Fld Glv/10	
31	Bernie Williams Spikes/50	10.00
32	Eddie Murray Spikes/50	30.00
33	Frank Robinson Spikes/50	10.00
34	Greg Maddux Spikes/25	30.00
35	Harmon Killebrew Spikes/25	35.00
36	Manny Ramirez Spikes/50	
37	Mike Piazza Spikes/25	
38	Paul Molitor Spikes/25	
39	Sammy Sosa Spikes/25	
40	Tim Hudson Spikes/50	

Leather in Leather

NM/M

Common Player:
Production 2,499 Sets
Silver: 1X-2X
Production 100 Sets

1	Garret Anderson BB	1.50
2	Albert Pujols BB	5.00
3	John Smoltz BB	1.50
4	Cal Ripken Jr. BB	8.00
5	Ichiro Suzuki BB	5.00
6	Pedro J. Martinez BB	2.00
7	Shawn Green BB	1.50
8	Juan Gonzalez BB	1.50
9	Mariano Rivera BB	1.50
10	Jason Giambi BB	1.50
11	Dave Parker BG	1.50
12	Dwight Gooden BG	1.50
13	Eric Munson BG	1.50
14	Frank Thomas BG	2.00
15	Joe Carter BG	1.50
16	Jose Canseco BG	2.00
17	Paul O'Neill BG	1.50
18	Tony Gwynn BG	3.00
19	Wade Boggs BG	2.00
20	Xavier Nady BG	1.50
21	Albert Pujols FG	5.00
22	Alex Rodriguez FG	6.00
23	Chipper Jones FG	3.00
24	Derek Jeter FG	6.00
25	Jack Wilson FG	1.50
26	Lenny Dykstra FG	1.50
27	Mark Grace FG	2.00
28	Steve Carlton FG	2.00
29	Tony Perez FG	2.00
30	Vladimir Guerrero FG	3.00
31	Bernie Williams SH	2.00
32	Eddie Murray SH	3.00
33	Frank Robinson SH	3.00
34	Greg Maddux SH	4.00
35	Harmon Killebrew SH	3.00
36	Manny Ramirez SH	2.00
37	Mike Piazza SH	4.00
38	Paul Molitor SH	3.00
39	Sammy Sosa SH	4.00
40	Tim Hudson SH	2.00

Cuts Glove

NM/M

Quantity produced listed

1	Adam Dunn/192	20.00
2	Al Kaline/192	35.00
3	Alfonso Soriano/160	40.00
4	Andre Dawson/224	15.00
5	Angel Berroa/224	10.00
6	Harmon Killebrew/192	35.00
7	Bob Gibson/96	30.00
8	Brooks Robinson/192	30.00
9	Cal Ripken Jr./32	200.00
10	Dale Murphy/224	25.00
11	Darryl Strawberry/224	15.00
12	Delmon Young/192	20.00
13	Don Mattingly/96	65.00
14	Duke Snider/96	30.00
15	Dwight Gooden/224	15.00
16	Ozzie Smith/96	60.00
18	Garret Anderson/224	15.00
19	Gary Carter/160	20.00
20	George Kell/224	15.00
21	Hank Blalock/224	20.00
22	Jim Palmer/192	20.00
23	Kirk Gibson/160	15.00
24	Lou Brock/192	25.00
25	Ryne Sandberg/160	50.00
26	Mark Prior/160	50.00
27	Miguel Cabrera/224	25.00
28	Mike Lowell/160	15.00
29	Nolan Ryan/96	100.00
30	Luis Aparicio/224	15.00
31	Paul Molitor/160	30.00
32	Red Schoendienst/224	25.00
33	Rickie Weeks/224	15.00
34	Ron Santo/224	25.00
35	Roy Oswalt/224	20.00
36	Stan Musial/96	60.00
37	Steve Carlton/192	20.00
38	Tony Gwynn/192	35.00
39	Vernon Wells/160	10.00
40	Will Clark/192	35.00
41	Bob Feller/224	25.00
42	Bobby Doerr/224	20.00
44	Ralph Kiner/224	30.00
45	Torii Hunter/224	15.00
46	Rollie Fingers/224	15.00
47	Steve Garvey/224	15.00
48	Alan Trammell/224	15.00
49	Maury Wills/224	15.00
50	Gaylord Perry/224	15.00

Hall of Fame Materials

NM/M

Quantity produced listed

1	Carl Yastrzemski Jsy/250	15.00
2	Carlton Fisk Jsy/250	10.00
3	George Brett Jsy/250	15.00
4	Johnny Bench Jsy/100	15.00
5	Mike Schmidt Jkt/250	15.00
6	Nolan Ryan Pants/100	25.00
7	Ozzie Smith Jsy/100	20.00
8	Robin Yount Jsy/250	12.00
9	Rod Carew Jkt/250	10.00
10	Tom Seaver Jsy/200	15.00

Hall of Fame

NM/M

Common Player: 2.00
Quantity produced listed
Silver: 1X-2X
Production 100 Sets

1	Carl Yastrzemski/1989	4.00
2	Carlton Fisk/2000	2.00
3	George Brett/1999	5.00
4	Johnny Bench/1989	4.00
5	Mike Schmidt/1995	5.00
6	Nolan Ryan/1999	6.00

7	Ozzie Smith/2002	4.00
8	Robin Yount/1999	4.00
9	Rod Carew/1991	3.00
10	Tom Seaver/1992	3.00

Fans of the Game Sign.

		NM/M
Common Auto.:		20.00
1	John Travolta SP EXCH	220.00
2	Dennis Haysbert	25.00
3	Chris O'Donnell	20.00
4	Abby Wambach	50.00
5	Jules Asner	50.00

Fans of the Game

		NM/M
Inserted 1:24		
1	John Travolta	4.00
2	Dennis Haysbert	2.00
3	Chris O'Donnell	2.00
4	Abby Wambach	3.00
5	Jules Asner	3.00

Cuts

		NM/M
Common Player:		
1	Adam Dunn/192	20.00
2	Al Kaline/192	35.00
3	Alfonso Soriano/160	40.00
4	Andre Dawson/224	15.00
5	Angel Berroa/224	10.00
6	Harmon Killebrew/192	35.00
7	Bob Gibson/96	30.00
8	Brooks Robinson/192	30.00
9	Cal Ripken Jr./32	200.00
10	Dale Murphy/224	25.00
11	Darryl Strawberry/224	15.00
12	Delmon Young/192	20.00
13	Don Mattingly/96	65.00
14	Duke Snider/96	30.00
15	Dwight Gooden/224	15.00
16	Ozzie Smith/96	60.00
18	Garret Anderson/224	15.00
19	Gary Carter/160	20.00
20	George Kell/224	15.00
21	Hank Blalock/224	20.00
22	Jim Palmer/192	20.00
23	Kirk Gibson/160	15.00
24	Lou Brock/192	25.00
25	Ryne Sandberg/160	50.00
26	Mark Prior/160	50.00
27	Miguel Cabrera/224	25.00
28	Mike Lowell/160	15.00
29	Nolan Ryan/96	100.00
30	Luis Aparicio/224	15.00
31	Paul Molitor/160	30.00
32	Red Schoendienst/224	25.00
33	Rickie Weeks/224	15.00
34	Ron Santo/224	25.00
35	Roy Oswalt/224	20.00
36	Stan Musial/96	60.00
37	Steve Carlton/192	20.00
38	Tony Gwynn/192	35.00
39	Vernon Wells/160	10.00
40	Will Clark/192	35.00
41	Bob Feller/224	25.00
42	Bobby Doerr/224	20.00
44	Ralph Kiner/224	30.00
45	Torii Hunter/224	15.00
46	Rollie Fingers/224	15.00
47	Steve Garvey/224	15.00
48	Alan Trammell/224	15.00
49	Maury Wills/224	15.00
50	Gaylord Perry/224	15.00

Leather Cuts Ball

No Pricing
Production 5-10

2004 DONRUSS TEAM HEROES

		NM/M
Complete Set (465):		75.00
Common Player:		.25
Common SP (441-465):		.50
Pack (8):		2.00
Box (24):		40.00
1	Troy Glaus	.40
2	Garret Anderson	.40
3	John Lackey	.25
4	Jarrod Washburn	.25
5	Bengie Molina	.25
6	Adam Kennedy	.25
7	Francisco Rodriguez	.25
8	Darin Erstad	.25
9	Ramon Ortiz	.25
10	Chone Figgins	.25
11	Rich Fischer	.25
12	David Eckstein	.25
13	Troy Percival	.25
14	Tim Salmon	.40
15	Nolan Ryan Angels	2.00
16	Luis Gonzalez	.40
17	Matt Kata	.25
18	Randy Johnson	.75
19	Oscar Villarreal	.25
20	Tim Olson	.25
21	Rob Hammock	.25
22	Alex Cintron	.25
23	Brian Bruney	.25
24	Brandon Webb	.25
25	Greg Aquino	.25
26	Shea Hillenbrand	.25
27	Steve Finley	.25
28	Rod Barajas	.25
29	Mike Hampton	.25
30	Adam LaRoche	.25
31	Russ Ortiz	.25
32	Chipper Jones	.75
33	John Smoltz	.40
34	Andruw Jones	.50
35	Bubba Nelson	.25
36	Johnny Estrada	.25
37	Marcus Giles	.25
38	Rafael Furcal	.25
39	Horacio Ramirez	.25
40	Dale Murphy	.40
41	Gaylord Perry Braves	.25
42	Mark DeRosa	.25
43	Adam Loewen	.25
44	Jerry Hairston Jr.	.25
45	Jose Morban	.25
46	Daniel Cabrera	.25
47	Jay Gibbons	.25
48	Larry Bigbie	.25
49	Luis Matos	.25
50	Rodrigo Lopez	.25
51	Melvin Mora	.25
52	Cal Ripken Jr.	2.50
53	Geronimo Gil	.25
54	Tony Batista	.25
55	Jason Johnson	.25
56	Jason Varitek	.25
57	Bill Mueller	.25
58	Todd Walker	.25
59	Trot Nixon	.40
60	Tim Wakefield	.25
61	Kevin Youkilis	.25
62	David Ortiz	.50
63	Johnny Damon	.40
64	Derek Lowe	.25
65	Pedro J. Martinez	.75
66	Carl Yastrzemski	.75
67	Bobby Doerr	.25
68	Matt Clement	.25
69	Sammy Sosa	1.50
70	Randall Simon	.25
71	Nate Frese	.25
72	Carlos Zambrano	.40
73	Moises Alou	.40
74	Mark Prior	1.50
75	Jason Dubois	.25
76	Nic Jackson	.25
77	Corey Patterson	.40
78	John Webb	.25
79	Kerry Wood	.75
80	Aramis Ramirez	.40
81	Brendan Harris	.25
82	Kenny Lofton	.40
83	Alex Gonzalez	.25
84	Gary Matthews Sr.	.25
85	Mark Grace	.40
86	Mark Grudzielanek	.25
87	Joe Borowski	.25
88	Joe Crede	.25
89	Mark Buehrle	.25
90	Paul Konerko	.40
91	Magglio Ordonez	.40
92	Corwin Malone	.25
93	Frank Thomas	.50
94	Jose Valentin	.25
95	Miguel Olivo	.25
96	Esteban Loaiza	.25
97	Carlos Lee	.40
98	Harold Baines	.25
99	Jason LaRue	.25
100	Sean Casey	.40
101	Adam Dunn	.50
102	Josh Hall	.25
103	Danny Graves	.25
104	Barry Larkin	.40
105	Ken Griffey Jr.	1.00
106	Brandon Claussen	.25
107	Austin Kearns	.40
108	D'Angelo Jimenez	.25
109	Ryan Wagner	.25
110	Tim Hummel	.25
111	Johnny Bench	1.00
112	Eric Davis	.25
113	Jose Rijo	.25
114	Travis Hafner	.40
115	Jody Gerut	.25
116	Fernando Cabrera	.25
117	Jhonny Peralta	.25
118	Ryan Church	.25
119	Francisco Cruceta	.25
120	Omar Vizquel	.40
121	Jason Davis	.25
122	Jeremy Guthrie	.25
123	C.C. Sabathia	.25
124	Milton Bradley	.25
125	Cliff Lee	.25
126	Victor Martinez	.25
127	Bob Feller	.50
128	Casey Blake	.25
129	Josh Bard	.25
130	Billy Traber	.25
131	Coco Crisp	.25
132	Larry Walker	.40
133	Jason Jennings	.25
134	Garrett Atkins	.25
135	Rene Reyes	.25
136	Chin-Hui Tsao	.25
137	Preston Wilson	.25
138	Jeff Baker	.25
139	Charles Johnson	.25
140	Shawn Chacon	.25
141	Todd Helton	.50
142	Jay Payton	.25
143	Omar Infante	.25
144	Bobby Higginson	.25
145	Dmitri Young	.25
146	Jorge Cordova	.25
147	Jeremy Bonderman	.25
148	Brandon Inge	.25
149	Franklyn German	.25
150	Nook Logan	.25
151	Alex Sanchez	.25
152	Craig Monroe	.25
153	Preston Larrison	.25
154	Carlos Pena	.25
155	Alan Trammell	.50
156	Jack Morris	.25
157	Eric Munson	.25
158	Mike Maroth	.25
159	Josh Beckett	.40
160	Josh Willingham	.25
161	Mike Lowell	.40
162	Luis Castillo	.25
163	Wilson Valdez	.25
164	Miguel Cabrera	.75
165	Alex Gonzalez	.25
166	Carl Pavano	.25
167	Dontrelle Willis	.40
168	Juan Pierre	.25
169	Juan Encarnacion	.25
170	Brad Penny	.25
171	Ivan Rodriguez Marlins	.50
172	Josh Wilson	.25
173	Jeff Conine	.25
174	Mark Redman	.25
175	A.J. Burnett	.25
176	Jeff Bagwell	.50
177	Octavio Dotel	.25
178	Craig Biggio	.40
179	John Buck	.25
180	Rodrigo Rosario	.25
181	Tommy Whiteman	.25
182	Kirk Saarloos	.25
183	Jason Lane	.25
184	Wade Miller	.25
185	Lance Berkman	.40
186	Roy Oswalt	.40
187	Tim Redding	.25
188	Jeff Kent	.40
189	Chris Burke	.25
190	Morgan Ensberg	.25
191	Nolan Ryan Astros	2.00
192	Geoff Blum	.25
193	Jeremy Affeldt	.25
194	Mike Sweeney	.25
195	Angel Berroa	.25
196	Jimmy Gobble	.25
197	Ken Harvey	.25
198	Carlos Beltran	.50
199	Alexis Gomez	.25
200	Byron Gettis	.25
201	Mike MacDougal	.25
202	David DeJesus	.25
203	Runelvys Hernandez	.25
204	George Brett	1.50
205	Amos Otis	.25
206	Joe Randa	.25
207	Aaron Guiel	.25
208	Eric Gagne	.40
209	Shawn Green	.40
210	Kevin Brown	.40
211	Cesar Izturis	.25
212	Kazuhisa Ishii	.25
213	Joe Thurston	.25
214	Odalis Perez	.25
215	Rickey Henderson	.50
216	Hideo Nomo	.40
217	Hong-Chih Kuo	.25
218	Edwin Jackson	.25
219	Paul LoDuca	.25
220	Adrian Beltre	.40
221	Duke Snider	.75
222	Steve Garvey	.50
223	Rickie Weeks	.40
224	Bill Hall	.25
225	Doug Davis	.25
226	Geoff Jenkins	.40
227	Matt Childers	.25
228	Dan Kolb	.25
229	Scott Podsednik	.40
230	Pedro Liriano	.25
231	Ben Sheets	.40
232	Robin Yount	.75
233	Gorman Thomas	.25
234	Ben Oglivie	.25
235	Matt LeCroy	.25
236	Cristian Guzman	.25
237	Lew Ford	.25
238	J.C. Romero	.25
239	Rob Bowen	.25
240	Corey Koskie	.25
241	Jacque Jones	.25
242	Brad Radke	.25
243	Shannon Stewart	.25
244	J.D. Durbin	.25
245	Doug Mientkiewicz	.25
246	Jason Kubel	.25
247	Torii Hunter	.40
248	Johan Santana	.25
249	Kirby Puckett	.75
250	Luis Rivas	.25
251	Orlando Cabrera	.25
252	Tony Armas Jr.	.25
253	Brad Wilkerson	.25
254	Endy Chavez	.25
255	Jose Vidro	.25
256	Zach Day	.25
257	Livan Hernandez	.25
258	Terrmel Sledge	.25
259	Michael Barrett	.25
260	Gary Carter	.50
261	Andre Dawson	.50
262	Craig Brazell	.25
263	Mike Piazza	1.00
264	Jeff Duncan	.25
265	Jason Anderson	.25
266	Tom Glavine	.40
267	Danny Garcia	.25
268	Ty Wigginton	.25

269 Al Leiter .25
270 Jeremy Griffiths .25
271 Jose Reyes .25
272 Prentice Redman .25
273 Cliff Floyd .25
274 Jae Weong Seo .25
275 Nolan Ryan Mets 2.00
276 Keith Hernandez .25
277 Jason Phillips .25
278 *Kazuo Matsui* 3.00
279 Jose Contreras .25
280 Aaron Boone .25
281 Mike Mussina .40
282 Jason Giambi .50
283 Hideki Matsui 1.00
284 Derek Jeter 2.00
285 Mariano Rivera .40
286 Chien-Ming Wang .25
287 Bernie Williams .40
288 Alfonso Soriano Yanks .50
289 Jorge Posada .40
290 Michel Hernandez .25
291 Erick Almonte .25
292 Don Mattingly 1.50
293 Roger Clemens Yanks 1.50
294 Gaylord Perry Rgr .25
295 Tommy John .25
296 Tim Hudson .40
297 Rich Harden .25
298 Eric Chavez .40
299 Adam Morrissey .25
300 Mark Mulder .40
301 Eric Byrnes .25
302 Jermaine Dye .25
303 Barry Zito .40
304 Erubiel Durazo .25
305 Mark Ellis .25
306 Bobby Crosby .25
307 Shane Bazzell .25
308 Mario Ramos .25
309 Jose Canseco .50
310 Placido Polanco .25
311 Jimmy Rollins .25
312 Jim Thome .75
313 Brett Myers .25
314 Jason Michaels .25
315 Vicente Padilla .25
316 Bobby Abreu .40
317 Ryan Howard .40
318 Chase Utley .25
319 Pat Burrell .40
320 Randy Wolf .25
321 Franklin Perez .25
322 Marlon Byrd .25
323 Kevin Millwood .40
324 Mike Lieberthal .25
325 Anderson Machado .25
326 Travis Chapman .25
327 Steve Carlton .50
328 Greg Luzinski .25
329 David Bell .25
330 Craig Wilson .40
331 Kris Benson .25
332 Jose Castillo .25
333 Josh Fogg .25
334 Jason Kendall .25
335 Walter Young .25
336 Oliver Perez .25
337 Jason Bay .25
338 Duaner Sanchez .25
339 Jack Wilson .40
340 Carlos Rivera .25
341 Kip Wells .25
342 Freddy Sanchez .25
343 Roberto Clemente 2.00
344 Al Oliver .25
345 Phil Nevin .25
346 Trevor Hoffman .25
347 Ryan Klesko .40
348 Khalil Greene .25
349 *Freddy Guzman* .25
350 Brian Giles .40
351 Brian Lawrence .25
352 Sean Burroughs .25
353 Ben Howard .25
354 Xavier Nady .25
355 Mark Loretta .25
356 Ramon Vazquez .25
357 Tony Gwynn .75
358 Adam Eaton .25
359 *Merkin Valdez* .75
360 Kevin Correia .25
361 Edgardo Alfonzo .25
362 Mike Cameron .25
363 Ray Durham .25
364 Jesse Foppert .25
365 Robb Nen .25
366 Marquis Grissom .25
367 Jerome Williams .25
368 Jason Schmidt .40
369 Will Clark .50
370 Bret Boone .40
371 Freddy Garcia .25
372 Dan Wilson .25
373 Rett Johnson .25
374 Kazuhiro Sasaki .25
375 Ichiro Suzuki 1.00
376 Edgar Martinez .40
377 Jamie Moyer .25
378 Joel Pineiro .25
379 Carlos Guillen .25
380 Randy Winn .25
381 J.J. Putz .25
382 John Olerud .40
383 Matt Thornton .25
384 Rafael Soriano .25
385 Gil Meche .25
386 Albert Pujols 1.50
387 Woody Williams .25
388 Dan Haren .25
389 Matt Morris .40
390 Jim Edmonds .40
391 Edgar Renteria .40
392 Scott Rolen .75
393 J.D. Drew .40
394 Bo Hart .25
395 Stan Musial 1.00
396 Red Schoendienst .25
397 Terry Pendleton .25
398 Mike Matheny .25
399 Dewon Brazelton .25
400 Chad Gaudin .25
401 Aubrey Huff .25
402 Victor Zambrano .25
403 Antonio Perez .25
404 Carl Crawford .25
405 Joe Kennedy .25
406 Pete LaForest .25
407 Delmon Young .40
408 Rocco Baldelli .40
409 Doug Waechter .25
410 Brian Stokes .25
411 Edwin Almonte .25
412 Toby Hall .25
413 Lance Carter .25
414 Greg Maddux Braves 1.00
415 Hank Blalock .50
416 Colby Lewis .25
417 Mark Teixeira .40
418 Gerald Laird .25
419 Ricardo Rodriguez .25
420 Ben Kozlowski .25
421 Kevin Mench .25
422 Michael Young .25
423 Ramon Nivar .25
424 Laynce Nix .25
425 Nolan Ryan Rgr 2.00
426 Einar Diaz .25
427 Carlos Delgado .40
428 Eric Hinske .25
429 Dustin McGowan .25
430 Frank Catalanotto .25
431 Kevin Cash .25
432 Roy Halladay .40
433 Orlando Hudson .25
434 Francisco Rosario .25
435 Guillermo Quiroz .25
436 Vernon Wells .25
437 Josh Phelps .25
438 Alexis Rios .25
439 Reed Johnson .25
440 Chris Woodward .25
441 Bartolo Colon SP .50
442 Richie Sexson SP .75
443 Greg Maddux Cubs SP 2.00
444 Javy Lopez SP .75
445 Gary Sheffield SP .75
446 Curt Schilling SP 1.00
447 Nomar Garciaparra SP 2.50
448 Manny Ramirez SP 1.50
449 Derrek Lee SP .75
450 Roberto Alomar SP .75
451 Ivan Rodriguez Tigers SP 1.50
452 Junior Spivey SP .50
453 Alfonso Soriano Rgr SP 1.00
454 Vladimir Guerrero SP 1.50
455 Nick Johnson SP .50
456 Javier Vazquez SP .50
457 Andy Pettitte SP .75
458 Miguel Tejada SP .75
459 Rich Aurilia SP .50
460 A.J. Pierzynski SP .50
461 Raul Ibanez SP .50
462 Roger Clemens Astros SP 3.00
463 Juan Gonzalez SP 1.00
464 Rafael Palmeiro SP 1.00
465 Alex Rodriguez Yanks SP 4.00

Showdown Bronze

Bronze (1-440): 3-5X
Bronze (441-465): 2-3X
Production 150 sets

Showdown Gold

No Pricing
Production 10 sets

Showdown Silver

Silver (1-440): 5-10X
Silver (441-465): 3-5X
Production 50 sets

Autographs

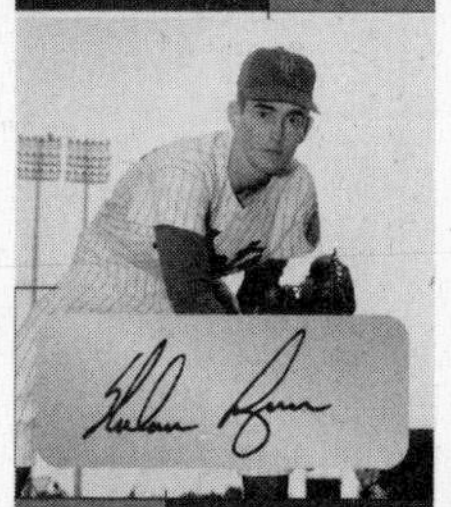

NM/M

Inserted 1:24
10 Chone Figgins 10.00
11 Rich Fischer 5.00
17 Matt Kata 5.00
19 Oscar Villarreal 5.00
20 Tim Olson 5.00
21 Rob Hammock/57 10.00
23 Brian Bruney 5.00
25 Greg Aquino 5.00
35 Bubba Nelson 5.00
45 Jose Morban 5.00
46 Daniel Cabrera 5.00
61 Kevin Youkilis/50 15.00
71 Nate Frese 5.00
75 Jason Dubois 5.00
76 Nic Jackson 5.00
78 John Webb 5.00
81 Brendan Harris 10.00
84 Gary Matthews Sr. 10.00
92 Corwin Malone 5.00
102 Josh Hall/25 15.00
106 Brandon Claussen 10.00
110 Tim Hummel 5.00
116 Francisco Cabrera 5.00
117 Jhonny Peralta 8.00
118 Ryan Church 5.00
119 Francisco Cruceta/75 8.00
146 Jorge Cordova 5.00
149 Franklyn German 5.00
150 Nook Logan 5.00
153 Preston Larrison 8.00
160 Josh Willingham 8.00
163 Wilson Valdez 5.00
172 Josh Wilson 5.00
180 Rodrigo Rosario 8.00
181 Tommy Whiteman 5.00
187 Tim Redding/22 10.00
189 Chris Burke 5.00
197 Ken Harvey 15.00
200 Byron Gettis 8.00
205 Amos Otis 10.00
211 Cesar Izturis 8.00
225 Doug Davis 8.00
227 Matt Childers 5.00
230 Pedro Liriano 5.00
233 Gorman Thomas 15.00
234 Ben Oglivie/86 15.00
237 Lew Ford 10.00
238 J.C. Romero 5.00
239 Rob Bowen 5.00
246 Jason Kubel/50 15.00
258 Terrmel Sledge 5.00
262 Craig Brazell 5.00
264 Jeff Duncan 8.00
265 Jason Anderson 5.00
267 Danny Garcia 5.00
270 Jeremy Griffiths 8.00
272 Prentice Redman 8.00
291 Erick Almonte/66 8.00
307 Shane Bazzell 5.00
308 Mario Ramos 5.00
314 Jason Michaels/42 8.00
321 Franklin Perez 5.00
325 Anderson Machado/50 10.00
326 Travis Chapman 5.00
328 Greg Luzinski 15.00
331 Kris Benson 10.00
335 Walter Young/67 10.00
338 Duaner Sanchez 5.00
353 Ben Howard 5.00
359 Merkin Valdez/50 20.00
360 Kevin Correia 5.00
373 Rett Johnson/76 8.00
381 J.J. Putz 5.00
383 Matt Thornton/50 8.00
384 Rafael Soriano 8.00
406 Pete LaForest 5.00
410 Brian Stokes 5.00
411 Edwin Almonte 5.00
419 Ricardo Rodriguez 5.00
420 Ben Kozlowski 5.00
431 Kevin Cash 5.00
434 Francisco Rosario/48 8.00

2004 DONRUSS THROWBACK THREADS

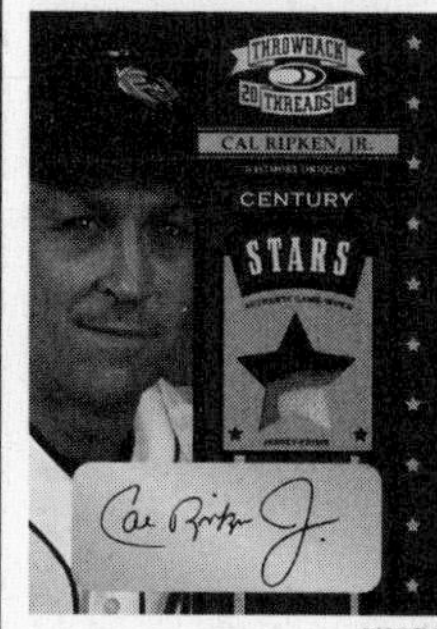

NM/M

Complete Set (250):
Common Player: .15
Common (201-225): 1.50
Common (226-250): 3.00
Production 1,000
Hobby Pack (5): 5.00
Hobby Box (24): 90.00
1 Bartolo Colon .15
2 Darin Erstad .25
3 David Eckstein .15
4 Garret Anderson .25
5 Tim Salmon .25
6 Troy Glaus .25
7 Vladimir Guerrero .75
8 Brandon Webb .15
9 Luis Gonzalez .25
10 Randy Johnson .75
11 Richie Sexson .40
12 Roberto Alomar .50
13 Shea Hillenbrand .15
14 Steve Finley .15
15 Adam LaRoche .15
16 Andruw Jones .50
17 Chipper Jones .75
18 J.D. Drew .25
19 John Smoltz .25
20 Rafael Furcal .25
21 Russ Ortiz .15
22 Javy Lopez .25
23 Jay Gibbons .15
24 Larry Bigbie .15
25 Luis Matos .15
26 Melvin Mora .15
27 Miguel Tejada .40
28 Rafael Palmeiro .50

29	Curt Schilling	.50
30	David Ortiz	.75
31	Derek Lowe	.15
32	Jason Varitek	.15
33	Johnny Damon	.25
34	Manny Ramirez	.50
35	Nomar Garciaparra	1.00
36	Pedro J. Martinez	.75
37	Trot Nixon	.15
38	Aramis Ramirez	.40
39	Corey Patterson	.25
40	Derrek Lee	.25
41	Greg Maddux	1.00
42	Kerry Wood	.75
43	Mark Prior	.75
44	Sammy Sosa	1.50
45	Carlos Lee	.15
46	Esteban Loaiza	.15
47	Frank Thomas	.50
48	Joe Borchard	.15
49	Magglio Ordonez	.25
50	Mark Buehrle	.15
51	Paul Konerko	.15
52	Adam Dunn	.50
53	Austin Kearns	.25
54	Barry Larkin	.40
55	Brandon Larson	.15
56	Ken Griffey Jr.	1.00
57	Ryan Wagner	.15
58	Sean Casey	.15
59	C.C. Sabathia	.15
60	Jody Gerut	.15
61	Omar Vizquel	.15
62	Travis Hafner	.25
63	Victor Martinez	.25
64	Charles Johnson	.15
65	Garrett Atkins	.15
66	Jason Jennings	.15
67	Joe Kennedy	.15
68	Larry Walker	.25
69	Preston Wilson	.15
70	Todd Helton	.50
71	Ivan Rodriguez	.50
72	Jeremy Bonderman	.15
73	A.J. Burnett	.15
74	Brad Penny	.15
75	Dontrelle Willis	.25
76	Josh Beckett	.50
77	Juan Pierre	.15
78	Luis Castillo	.15
79	Miguel Cabrera	.75
80	Mike Lowell	.25
81	Andy Pettitte	.25
82	Craig Biggio	.25
83	Jeff Bagwell	.50
84	Jeff Kent	.25
85	Lance Berkman	.25
86	Morgan Ensberg	.15
87	Richard Hidalgo	.15
88	Roger Clemens	1.50
89	Roy Oswalt	.25
90	Wade Miller	.15
91	Angel Berroa	.15
92	Carlos Beltran	.50
93	Juan Gonzalez	.40
94	Ken Harvey	.15
95	Mike Sweeney	.15
96	Runelvys Hernandez	.15
97	Adrian Beltre	.40
98	Edwin Jackson	.15
99	Eric Gagne	.40
100	Hideo Nomo	.25
101	Hong-Chih Kuo	.15
102	Kazuhisa Ishii	.15
103	Paul LoDuca	.15
104	Shawn Green	.25
105	Ben Sheets	.25
106	Geoff Jenkins	.15
107	Junior Spivey	.15
108	Rickie Weeks	.25
109	Scott Podsednik	.25
110	Corey Koskie	.15
111	Doug Mientkiewicz	.15
112	Jacque Jones	.15
113	Joe Mays	.15
114	Johan Santana	.25
115	Shannon Stewart	.15
116	Torii Hunter	.25
117	Brad Wilkerson	.15
118	Carl Everett	.15
119	Chad Cordero	.15
120	Jose Vidro	.15
121	Nick Johnson	.15
122	Orlando Cabrera	.25
123	Al Leiter	.15
124	Cliff Floyd	.15
125	Jae Weong Seo	.15
126	Jose Reyes	.25
127	Mike Cameron	.15
128	Mike Piazza	1.00
129	Tom Glavine	.25
130	Alex Rodriguez	2.00
131	Bernie Williams	.40
132	Chien-Ming Wang	.15
133	Derek Jeter	2.00
134	Gary Sheffield	.50
135	Hideki Matsui	1.00
136	Jason Giambi	.25
137	Javier Vazquez	.15
138	Jorge Posada	.25
139	Jose Contreras	.15
140	Kevin Brown	.15
141	Mariano Rivera	.25
142	Mike Mussina	.40
143	Barry Zito	.25
144	Bobby Crosby	.15
145	Eric Chavez	.25
146	Erubiel Durazo	.15
147	Jermaine Dye	.15
148	Mark Kotsay	.15
149	Mark Mulder	.25
150	Rich Harden	.15
151	Tim Hudson	.25
152	Billy Wagner	.15
153	Bobby Abreu	.25
154	Brett Myers	.15
155	Jim Thome	.75
156	Jimmy Rollins	.15
157	Kevin Millwood	.25
158	Marlon Byrd	.15
159	Pat Burrell	.25
160	Jason Bay	.15
161	Jason Kendall	.15
162	Brian Giles	.25
163	Jay Payton	.15
164	Ryan Klesko	.15
165	Edgardo Alfonzo	.15
166	Jason Schmidt	.40
167	Jerome Williams	.15
168	Todd Linden	.15
169	Bret Boone	.15
170	Edgar Martinez	.25
171	Freddy Garcia	.15
172	Ichiro Suzuki	1.50
173	Jamie Moyer	.15
174	John Olerud	.15
175	Shigetoshi Hasegawa	.15
176	Albert Pujols	1.50
177	Dan Haren	.15
178	Edgar Renteria	.25
179	Jim Edmonds	.25
180	Matt Morris	.25
181	Scott Rolen	.75
182	Aubrey Huff	.15
183	Carl Crawford	.15
184	Chad Gaudin	.15
185	Delmon Young	.25
186	Dewon Brazelton	.15
187	Fred McGriff	.25
188	Rocco Baldelli	.15
189	Alfonso Soriano	.75
190	Hank Blalock	.50
191	Laynce Nix	.15
192	Mark Teixeira	.25
193	Michael Young	.15
194	Carlos Delgado	.40
195	Eric Hinske	.15
196	Frank Catalanotto	.15
197	Josh Phelps	.15
198	Orlando Hudson	.15
199	Roy Halladay	.15
200	Vernon Wells	.15
201	Dale Murphy	2.00
202	Cal Ripken Jr.	10.00
203	Fred Lynn	1.50
204	Wade Boggs	2.00
205	Nolan Ryan	6.00
206	Rod Carew	2.00
207	Andre Dawson	1.50
208	Ernie Banks	3.00
209	Ryne Sandberg	5.00
210	Bo Jackson	3.00
211	Carlton Fisk	3.00
212	Dave Concepcion	1.50
213	Alan Trammell	1.50
214	George Brett	5.00
215	Robin Yount	4.00
216	Gary Carter	1.50
217	Darryl Strawberry	1.50
218	Dwight Gooden	1.50
219	Babe Ruth	6.00
220	Don Mattingly	5.00
221	Reggie Jackson	3.00
222	Mike Schmidt	5.00
223	Tony Gwynn	4.00
224	Keith Hernandez	2.00
225	*Hector Gimenez*	3.00
226	Graham Koonce	3.00
227	*John Gall*	5.00
228	*Jerry Gil*	3.00
229	*Jason Frasor*	3.00
230	*Justin Knoedler*	3.00
231	*Ivan Ochoa*	3.00
232	*Greg Dobbs*	3.00
233	*Ronald Belisario*	3.00
234	*Jerome Gamble*	3.00
235	*Roberto Novoa*	3.00
236	Sean Henn	4.00
237	*Willy Taveras*	3.00
238	*Ramon Ramirez*	3.00
239	*Kazuo Matsui*	8.00
240	*Akinori Otsuka*	4.00
241	*Jason Bartlett*	5.00
242	*Fernando Nieve*	3.00
243	*Freddy Guzman*	3.00
244	*Aarom Baldiris*	5.00
245	*Merkin Valdez*	5.00
246	*Mike Gosling*	3.00
247	*Shingo Takatsu*	8.00
248	*William Bergolla*	3.00
249	*Shawn Hill*	3.00
250	*Justin Germano*	3.00

Signature Marks

		NM/M
Common Autograph:		8.00
4	Garret Anderson/25	25.00
8	Brandon Webb/50	10.00
13	Shea Hillenbrand/50	15.00
15	Adam LaRoche/50	10.00
20	Rafael Furcal/25	25.00
23	Jay Gibbons/50	10.00
24	Larry Bigbie/50	20.00
25	Luis Matos/50	10.00
26	Melvin Mora/50	15.00
30	David Ortiz/25	40.00
37	Trot Nixon/25	30.00
40	Derrek Lee/25	30.00
43	Mark Prior/25	60.00
45	Carlos Lee/50	10.00
46	Esteban Loaiza/50	12.00
48	Joe Borchard/25	10.00
50	Mark Buehrle/25	25.00
53	Austin Kearns/25	20.00
55	Brandon Larson25	15.00
60	Jody Gerut/50	20.00
62	Travis Hafner/50	20.00
63	Victor Martinez/50	25.00
69	Preston Wilson/50	15.00
74	Brad Penny/50	10.00
79	Miguel Cabrera/25	40.00
80	Mike Lowell/25	20.00
86	Morgan Ensberg/50	12.00
89	Roy Oswalt/25	25.00
91	Angel Berroa/25	12.00
92	Carlos Beltran/25	35.00
98	Edwin Jackson/50	15.00
101	Hong-Chih Kuo/50	20.00
109	Scott Podsednik/50	15.00
112	Jacque Jones/50	15.00
114	Johan Santana/25	50.00
115	Shannon Stewart/25	20.00
116	Torii Hunter/25	25.00
119	Chad Cordero/50	8.00
120	Jose Vidro/25	15.00
122	Orlando Cabrera/50	15.00
132	Chien-Ming Wang/25	35.00
147	Jermaine Dye/50	12.00
160	Jason Bay/50	20.00
163	Jay Payton/50	15.00
168	Todd Linden/50	15.00
175	Shigetoshi Hasegawa/25	50.00
177	Dan Haren/50	15.00
181	Scott Rolen/25	50.00
182	Aubrey Huff/50	15.00
184	Chad Gaudin/50	10.00
186	Dewon Brazelton/50	10.00
187	Fred McGriff/25	40.00
189	Alfonso Soriano/25	50.00
193	Michael Young/50	20.00
203	Fred Lynn/50	15.00
207	Andre Dawson/50	20.00
216	Gary Carter/25	25.00
217	Darryl Strawberry/50	20.00
218	Dwight Gooden/50	15.00
224	Keith Hernandez/50	20.00
225	Hector Gimenez/100	8.00
226	Graham Koonce/100	8.00
228	Jerry Gil/100	8.00
229	Jason Frasor/100	8.00
230	Justin Knoedler/50	10.00
231	Ivan Ochoa/25	
232	Greg Dobbs/25	
233	Ronald Belisario/200	8.00
234	Jerome Gamble/200	8.00
235	Roberto Novoa/200	8.00
236	Sean Henn/200	10.00
237	Willy Taveras/100	8.00
238	Ramon Ramirez/200	10.00
241	Jason Bartlett/25	20.00
242	Fernando Nieve/25	12.00
243	Freddy Guzman/25	20.00
244	Aarom Baldiris/25	
245	Merkin Valdez/25	
246	Mike Gosling/25	
247	Shingo Takatsu/25	
248	William Bergolla/100	10.00
249	Shawn Hill/100	8.00
250	Justin Germano/100	8.00

Player Threads Signature

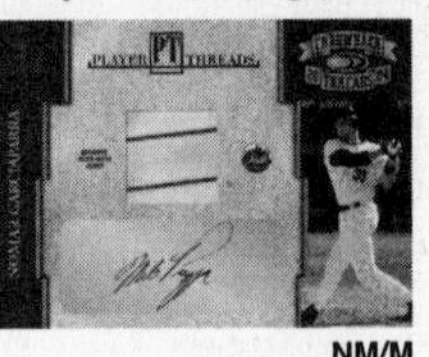

		NM/M
Quantity produced listed		
2	Alex Rodriguez M's-Rgr/5	
4	Aramis Ramirez/25	30.00
17	Darryl Strawberry Dgr-Met-Ynk/25	40.00
24	Gary Sheffield Brave-Brw-Dgr/25	40.00
28	Javier Vazquez/25	20.00
29	Jay Payton/25	15.00
33	Joe Kennedy/11	
37	Juan Gonzalez Indians-Rgr/25	40.00
39	Junior Spivey/25	15.00
50	Preston Wilson Marlins-Rockies/25	25.00
53	Reggie Jackson Jkt-Ang-Yank/5	
55	Rich Aurilia/25	15.00
62	Robin Ventura Mets-Sox-Yanks/25	40.00
67	Shawn Green Jays-Dgr/5	
68	Shea Hillenbrand/25	20.00
72	Travis Hafner Indians-Rgr/3	
74	Vladimir Guerrero/25	60.00

Player Threads

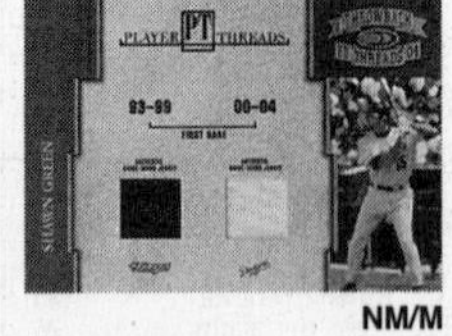

		NM/M
Common Player:		4.00
Production 250 Sets		
Prime:		2X-3X
Production 10-25		
No pricing 15 or less		
1	Aaron Boone	4.00
2	Alex Rodriguez M's-Rgr	15.00
3	Andres Galarraga Braves-Giants-Rgr	10.00
4	Aramis Ramirez	4.00
5	Bartolo Colon	4.00
6	Ben Grieve A's-D'Rays	4.00
7	Brad Fullmer	4.00

8 Bret Boone Braves-M's 4.00
9 Brian Giles 4.00
10 Brian Jordan 4.00
11 Byung-Hyun Kim 4.00
12 Casey Fossum 4.00
13 Cesar Izturis 4.00
14 Chan Ho Park 4.00
15 Charles Johnson 4.00
16 Cliff Floyd 4.00
17 Darryl Strawberry Dgr-Met-Ynk 10.00
18 David Ortiz 10.00
19 David Wells Jays-Yanks 4.00
20 Derrek Lee 6.00
21 Dmitri Young 4.00
22 Edgardo Alfonzo 4.00
23 Ellis Burks 4.00
24 Gary Sheffield Braves-Brew-Dgr 8.00
25 Hee Seop Choi 4.00
26 Ivan Rodriguez Marlins-Rgr 10.00
27 J.D. Drew 6.00
28 Javier Vazquez 4.00
29 Jay Payton 4.00
30 Jeff Kent Astros-Giants-Jays 4.00
31 Jeromy Burnitz 4.00
32 Jim Thome Indians-Phils 10.00
33 Joe Kennedy 4.00
34 Joe Torre 8.00
35 Jose Cruz Jr. 4.00
36 Juan Encarnacion 4.00
37 Juan Gonzalez Indians-Rgr 8.00
38 Juan Pierre 4.00
39 Junior Spivey 4.00
40 Kenny Lofton Brave-Tribe 8.00
41 Kevin Millwood 6.00
42 Manny Ramirez Indians-Sox 12.00
43 Mark Grace Cubs-D'backs 10.00
44 Mike Hampton 4.00
45 Mike Piazza Dgr-Marlins-Mets 20.00
46 Milton Bradley 4.00
47 Moises Alou 6.00
48 Nick Johnson 4.00
49 Nolan Ryan Ang Jkt-Ast Jkt-Rgr 50.00
50 Preston Wilson Marlins-Rockies 6.00
51 Rafael Palmeiro O's-Rgr 10.00
52 Ray Durham 4.00
53 Reggie Jackson A's-Ang-Yank 15.00
54 Reggie Sanders 4.00
55 Rich Aurilia 4.00
56 Richie Sexson 6.00
57 Rickey Henderson A's-M's-Yanks/25 50.00
58 Rickey Henderson Dgr-Mets-Padres 20.00
59 Robert Fick 4.00
60 Roberto Alomar Mets-Sox 8.00
61 Roberto Alomar Indians-O's 8.00
62 Robin Ventura Mets-Sox-Yanks 10.00
63 Rondell White Cubs-Expos 6.00
64 Ryan Klesko Braves-Padres 6.00
65 Sean Casey 6.00
66 Shannon Stewart Jays-Twins 6.00
67 Shawn Green Jays-Dgr 8.00
68 Shea Hillenbrand 4.00
69 Steve Carlton Giants-Sox 8.00
70 Terrence Long 4.00
71 Tony Batista 4.00
72 Travis Hafner Indians-Rgr 6.00
73 Travis Lee 4.00
74 Vladimir Guerrero 8.00
75 Wes Helms 4.00

Material

NM/M

Common Player: 4.00

2 Darin Erstad Jsy/100 6.00
4 Garret Anderson Jsy/100 6.00
5 Tim Salmon Jsy/100 6.00
6 Troy Glaus Jsy/100 6.00
7 Vladimir Guerrero Bat/100 10.00
8 Brandon Webb Pants/100 4.00
9 Luis Gonzalez Jsy/100 4.00
10 Randy Johnson Jsy/100 10.00
11 Richie Sexson Bat/50 8.00
12 Roberto Alomar Bat/100 8.00
14 Steve Finley Jsy/100 4.00
15 Adam LaRoche Bat/100 4.00
16 Andruw Jones Jsy/100 6.00
17 Chipper Jones Jsy/100 8.00
18 J.D. Drew Bat/100 6.00
19 John Smoltz Jsy/100 8.00
20 Rafael Furcal Jsy/100 4.00
22 Javy Lopez Bat/100 6.00
23 Jay Gibbons Jsy/100 4.00
24 Larry Bigbie Jsy/100 4.00
25 Luis Matos Jsy/100 4.00
26 Melvin Mora Jsy/100 4.00
27 Miguel Tejada Bat/100 6.00
28 Rafael Palmeiro Jsy/100 8.00
29 Curt Schilling Bat/100 6.00
30 David Ortiz Bat/100 10.00
32 Jason Varitek Jsy/100 8.00
33 Johnny Damon Bat/100 6.00
34 Manny Ramirez Jsy/100 8.00
35 Nomar Garciaparra Jsy/100 8.00
36 Pedro J. Martinez Jsy/100 8.00
37 Trot Nixon Bat/100 4.00
38 Aramis Ramirez Jsy/100 6.00
39 Corey Patterson Pants/100 6.00
41 Greg Maddux Bat/100 10.00
42 Kerry Wood Pants/100 10.00
43 Mark Prior Jsy/100 10.00
44 Sammy Sosa Jsy/100 12.00
45 Carlos Lee Jsy/100 4.00
47 Frank Thomas Pants/100 8.00
48 Joe Borchard Jsy/100 4.00
49 Magglio Ordonez Jsy/100 4.00
50 Mark Buehrle Jsy/100 4.00
51 Paul Konerko Jsy/100 4.00
52 Adam Dunn Jsy/100 8.00
53 Austin Kearns Jsy/100 6.00
54 Barry Larkin Jsy/100 6.00
55 Brandon Larson Fld Glv/100 4.00
58 Sean Casey Jsy/100 4.00
59 C.C. Sabathia Jsy/100 4.00
60 Jody Gerut Jsy/100 4.00
61 Omar Vizquel Jsy/100 4.00
62 Travis Hafner Jsy/100 4.00
63 Victor Martinez Bat/100 6.00
64 Charles Johnson Bat/100 4.00
65 Garrett Atkins Jsy/100 4.00
66 Jason Jennings Jsy/100 4.00
67 Joe Kennedy Bat/100 4.00
68 Larry Walker Jsy/100 6.00
69 Preston Wilson Jsy/100 4.00
70 Todd Helton Jsy/100 8.00
71 Ivan Rodriguez Bat/100 8.00
72 Jeremy Bonderman Jsy/100 4.00
73 A.J. Burnett Jsy/100 4.00
74 Brad Penny Jsy/100 4.00
75 Dontrelle Willis Jsy/100 4.00
76 Josh Beckett Jsy/100 6.00
77 Juan Pierre Bat/100 4.00
78 Luis Castillo Jsy/100 4.00
79 Miguel Cabrera Jsy/100 8.00
80 Mike Lowell Jsy/50 8.00
81 Andy Pettitte Bat/100 6.00
82 Craig Biggio Jsy/100 6.00
83 Jeff Bagwell Jsy/100 8.00
84 Jeff Kent Jsy/100 4.00
85 Lance Berkman Jsy/100 4.00
86 Morgan Ensberg Jsy/100 4.00
87 Richard Hidalgo Pants/100 4.00
88 Roger Clemens Bat/50 15.00
89 Roy Oswalt Jsy/100 4.00
90 Wade Miller Jsy/100 4.00
91 Angel Berroa Pants/100 4.00
92 Carlos Beltran Jsy/100 8.00
93 Juan Gonzalez Bat/100 8.00
94 Ken Harvey Bat/100 4.00
95 Mike Sweeney Jsy/100 4.00
96 Runelvys Hernandez Jsy/100 4.00
97 Adrian Beltre Jsy/100 6.00
98 Edwin Jackson Jsy/100 4.00
100 Hideo Nomo Jsy/100 8.00
101 Hong-Chih Kuo Bat/100 8.00
102 Kazuhisa Ishii Jsy/100 4.00
103 Paul LoDuca Jsy/100 4.00
104 Shawn Green Jsy/100 6.00
105 Ben Sheets Jsy/100 6.00
106 Geoff Jenkins Jsy/100 4.00
107 Junior Spivey Bat/50 4.00
108 Rickie Weeks Bat/50 8.00
111 Doug Mientkiewicz Bat/100 4.00
112 Jacque Jones Jsy/100 4.00
113 Joe Mays Jsy/100 4.00
114 Johan Santana Jsy/100 8.00
115 Shannon Stewart Jsy/100 4.00
116 Torii Hunter Jsy/100 6.00
117 Brad Wilkerson Bat/100 4.00
118 Carl Everett Bat/100 4.00
120 Jose Vidro Jsy/100 4.00
121 Nick Johnson Bat/100 4.00
122 Orlando Cabrera Jsy/100 4.00
123 Al Leiter Jsy/100 4.00
124 Cliff Floyd Bat/100 4.00
125 Jae Weong Seo Jsy/100 4.00
126 Jose Reyes Jsy/100 6.00
128 Mike Piazza Jsy/100 10.00
129 Tom Glavine Jsy/100 6.00
130 Alex Rodriguez Bat/100 10.00
131 Bernie Williams Jsy/100 6.00
133 Derek Jeter Jsy/100 20.00
134 Gary Sheffield Bat/100 6.00
135 Hideki Matsui Jsy/100 20.00
136 Jason Giambi Jsy/100 6.00
138 Jorge Posada Jsy/100 6.00
141 Mariano Rivera Jsy/50 15.00
142 Mike Mussina Jsy/100 6.00
143 Barry Zito Jsy/100 4.00
145 Eric Chavez Jsy/100 4.00
146 Erubiel Durazo Bat/100 4.00
147 Jermaine Dye Bat/100 4.00
149 Mark Mulder Jsy/100 6.00
150 Rich Harden Jsy/100 4.00
151 Tim Hudson Jsy/100 6.00
153 Bobby Abreu Jsy/100 6.00
154 Brett Myers Jsy/100 4.00
155 Jim Thome Jsy/100 8.00
157 Kevin Millwood Jsy/100 4.00
158 Marlon Byrd Jsy/100 4.00
159 Pat Burrell Jsy/100 6.00
161 Jason Kendall Jsy/100 4.00
162 Brian Giles Bat/100 4.00
164 Ryan Klesko Jsy/100 4.00
165 Edgardo Alfonzo Bat/100 4.00
167 Jerome Williams Jsy/100 4.00
169 Bret Boone Jsy/29
170 Edgar Martinez Jsy/100 8.00
171 Freddy Garcia Jsy/100 4.00
173 Jamie Moyer Jsy/100 4.00
174 John Olerud Jsy/100 4.00
176 Albert Pujols Jsy/100 20.00
177 Dan Haren Jsy/100 4.00
178 Edgar Renteria Jsy/100 6.00
179 Jim Edmonds Jsy/100 6.00
180 Matt Morris Jsy/100 4.00
181 Scott Rolen Jsy/100 8.00
182 Aubrey Huff Jsy/100 4.00
183 Carl Crawford Jsy/100 4.00
184 Chad Gaudin Jsy/100 4.00
185 Delmon Young Bat/100 6.00
186 Dewon Brazelton Jsy/100 4.00
187 Fred McGriff Jsy/100 6.00
188 Rocco Baldelli Jsy/100 4.00
189 Alfonso Soriano Bat/100 8.00
190 Hank Blalock Jsy/100 6.00
191 Laynce Nix Bat/100 4.00
192 Mark Teixeira Jsy/23 15.00
193 Michael Young Bat/100 6.00
194 Carlos Delgado Jsy/100 6.00
195 Eric Hinske Jsy/100 4.00
196 Frank Catalanotto Jsy/100 4.00
197 Josh Phelps Jsy/100 4.00
198 Orlando Hudson Jsy/100 4.00
199 Roy Halladay Jsy/100 4.00
200 Vernon Wells Jsy/100 4.00
201 Dale Murphy Jsy/100 12.00
202 Cal Ripken Jr. Jsy/100 30.00
203 Fred Lynn Bat/100 8.00
204 Wade Boggs Jsy/100 8.00
205 Nolan Ryan Jkt/100 25.00
206 Rod Carew Jkt/100 8.00
207 Andre Dawson Pants/100 6.00
208 Ernie Banks Pants/50 20.00
209 Ryne Sandberg Jsy/50 25.00
210 Bo Jackson Jsy/100 12.00
211 Carlton Fisk Jkt/100 10.00
212 Dave Concepcion Jsy/100 8.00
213 Alan Trammell Bat/100 8.00
214 George Brett Jsy/100 15.00
215 Robin Yount Jsy/100 15.00
216 Gary Carter Jsy/100 8.00
217 Darryl Strawberry Pants/100 8.00
218 Dwight Gooden Jsy/50 8.00
219 Babe Ruth Jsy/25 400.00
220 Don Mattingly Jkt/100 15.00
221 Reggie Jackson Jkt/100 10.00
222 Mike Schmidt Jkt/100 15.00
223 Tony Gwynn Jsy/100 10.00
224 Keith Hernandez Jsy/100 8.00

Generations Material

NM/M

Quantity produced listed

Prime: No Pricing

Production 5 Sets

1 George Brett, Albert Pujols/50 40.00
2 Wade Boggs, Aubrey Huff/50 10.00
3 Jim "Catfish" Hunter, Tim Hudson/25 20.00
5 Tony Gwynn, Garret Anderson/50 20.00
6 Fergie Jenkins, Mark Prior/25 25.00
7 Robin Yount, Rickie Weeks Bat/50 20.00
8 Warren Spahn, Greg Maddux/25 40.00
11 Al Kaline, Alan Trammell, Ivan Rodriguez Bat/25 40.00
14 George Foster, Dave Parker, Austin Kearns/25 20.00
16 Don Sutton, Nolan Ryan, Roger Clemens Bat/50 50.00
17 Billy Williams, Andre Dawson, Sammy Sosa/50 30.00
18 Whitey Ford, Tommy John, Andy Pettitte/25 40.00
19 Carlton Fisk, Roger Clemens, Nomar Garciaparra 40.00
20 Marty Marion, Ozzie Smith, Edgar Renteria/25 40.00
21 Reggie Jackson, Rickey Henderson, Eric Chavez/50 30.00
24 Bob Feller, Tom Seaver, Roger Clemens/25 40.00

25 Ernie Banks, Cal Ripken Jr., Alex Rodriguez 65.00
26 Pee Wee Reese, Ozzie Smith, Derek Jeter/25 50.00
27 Harmon Killebrew, Mike Schmidt, Alex Rodriguez Bat/25 50.00
28 Bob Gibson, Dwight Gooden, Josh Beckett/25 30.00

Generations

NM/M
Common Duo: 1.50
Production 1,500 Sets
Spectrum: 2X-3X
Production 100 Sets
1 George Brett, Albert Pujols 5.00
2 Wade Boggs, Aubrey Huff 2.00
3 Jim "Catfish" Hunter, Tim Hudson 2.00
4 Steve Garvey, Shawn Green 1.50
5 Tony Gwynn, Garret Anderson 4.00
6 Fergie Jenkins, Mark Prior 3.00
7 Robin Yount, Rickie Weeks 4.00
8 Warren Spahn, Greg Maddux 4.00
9 Brooks Robinson, Cal Ripken Jr., Miguel Tejada 8.00
10 Bobby Doerr, Carl Yastrzemski, Manny Ramirez 5.00
11 Al Kaline, Alan Trammell, Ivan Rodriguez 2.50
12 Tom Seaver, Dwight Gooden, Tom Glavine 3.00
13 Stan Musial, Lou Brock, Jim Edmonds 4.00
14 George Foster, Dave Parker, Austin Kearns 1.50
15 Ed Mathews, Dale Murphy, Chipper Jones 3.00
16 Don Sutton, Nolan Ryan, Roger Clemens 8.00
17 Bernie Williams, Andre Dawson, Sammy Sosa 4.00
18 Whitey Ford, Tommy John, Andy Pettitte 2.00
19 Carlton Fisk, Roger Clemens, Nomar Garciaparra 5.00
20 Shawn Marion, Ozzie Smith, Edgar Renteria 4.00
21 Reggie Jackson, Rickey Henderson, Eric Chavez 2.00
22 Babe Ruth, Don Mattingly, Derek Jeter 8.00
23 Roberto Clemente Jr., Reggie Jackson, Sammy Sosa 6.00
24 Bob Feller, Tom Seaver, Roger Clemens 5.00
25 Ernie Banks, Cal Ripken Jr., Alex Rodriguez 8.00
26 Pee Wee Reese, Ozzie Smith, Derek Jeter 6.00
27 Harmon Killebrew, Mike Schmidt, Alex Rodriguez 5.00
28 Bob Gibson, Dwight Gooden, Josh Beckett 2.00

Fans of the Game Sign.

NM/M
1 Emilio Estevez 40.00
2 Shannon Elizabeth 60.00
3 Joe Montegna UER 20.00
4 Jamie-Lynn DiScala 60.00
5 Jonathan Silverman 20.00

Fans of the Game

NM/M
Inserted 1:24
1 Emilio Estevez 3.00
2 Shannon Elizabeth 3.00
3 Joe Montegna UER 2.00
4 Jamie-Lynn DiScala 2.00
5 Jonathan Silverman 2.00

Dynasty Material

NM/M
Quantity produced listed
Prime: No Pricing
Production 5 Sets
1 Phil Rizzuto, Whitey Ford/10
2 Pee Wee Reese, Duke Snider, Tom Lasorda/5
3 Jim "Catfish" Hunter, Reggie Jackson/25 25.00
4 Roger Maris, Whitey Ford/10
5 Enos Slaughter, Shawn Marion, Stan Musial/10
6 Dwight Gooden, Gary Carter, Darryl Strawberry, Keith Hernandez/50 35.00
7 Johnny Bench, Tony Perez, Joe Morgan, George Foster/25 80.00
8 Derek Jeter, Jorge Posada, Bernie Williams, Andy Pettitte/50 50.00
9 Frank Robinson, Brooks Robinson, Jim Palmer/10
10 Willie Stargell, Dave Parker, Bill Madlock/25 30.00
11 Bob Gibson, Lou Brock, Ken Boyer/25 35.00
12 Rickey Henderson, Paul Molitor, Joe Carter, Roberto Alomar/25 60.00

Dynasty

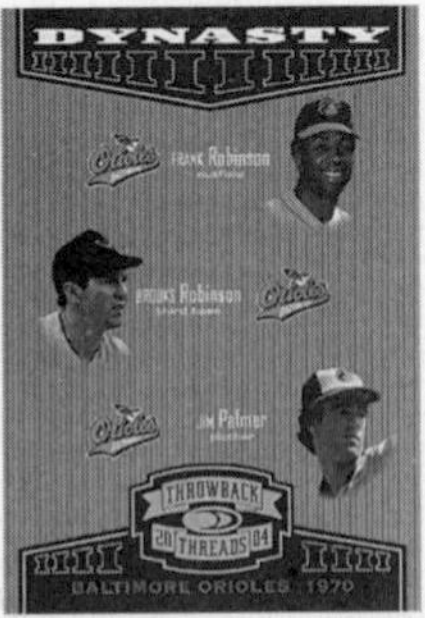

NM/M
Common Player: 3.00
Production 1,500 Sets
Spectrum: 2X-3X
Production 100 Sets
1 Phil Rizzuto, Whitey Ford 3.00
2 Pee Wee Reese, Duke Snider, Tom Lasorda 3.00
3 Jim "Catfish" Hunter, Reggie Jackson 3.00
4 Roger Maris, Whitey Ford 5.00
5 Enos Slaughter, Shawn Marion, Stan Musial 5.00
6 Dwight Gooden, Gary Carter, Darryl Strawberry, Keith Hernandez 3.00
7 Johnny Bench, Tony Perez, Joe Morgan, George Foster 3.00
8 Derek Jeter, Jorge Posada, Bernie Williams, Andy Pettitte 6.00
9 Frank Robinson, Brooks Robinson, Jim Palmer 3.00
10 Willie Stargell, Dave Parker, Bill Madlock 3.00
11 Bob Gibson, Lou Brock, Ken Boyer 3.00
12 Rickey Henderson, Paul Molitor, Joe Carter, Roberto Alomar 3.00

Century Stars Signature

NM/M
Signature Material: No Pricing
Production 5 Sets
Sig. Material Prime: No Pricing
Production 5 Sets
1 Al Kaline/25 50.00
6 Billy Williams/25 35.00
7 Bob Feller/25 30.00
8 Bob Gibson/25 35.00
12 Dale Murphy/25 40.00
13 Dave Parker/25 20.00
18 Fergie Jenkins/25 25.00
19 Gary Carter/25 25.00
24 Joe Morgan/25 30.00
28 Lou Brock/25 35.00
29 Luis Aparicio/25 20.00
35 Mike Schmidt/25 60.00
38 Ozzie Smith/25 75.00
53 Stan Musial/25 75.00

Century Stars Material

NM/M
All Jersey unless noted
Prime: No Pricing
Production 5 Sets
1 Al Kaline Pants/25 30.00
2 Albert Pujols/50 25.00
4 Barry Larkin/50 10.00
5 Barry Zito/50 6.00
6 Billy Williams/50 8.00
8 Bob Gibson/25 20.00
9 Cal Ripken Jr./50 60.00
10 Chipper Jones/50 10.00
11 Curt Schilling/50 8.00
12 Dale Murphy/50 12.00
13 Dave Parker/50 8.00
14 Derek Jeter/50 35.00
15 Don Drysdale/50 12.00
16 Don Mattingly Jkt/50 20.00
17 Eddie Murray/50 15.00
18 Fergie Jenkins Pants/25 12.00
19 Gary Carter Pants/50 8.00
20 George Brett/50 25.00
21 Greg Maddux/50 15.00
22 Ivan Rodriguez/50 12.00
23 Jeff Bagwell/50 10.00
24 Joe Morgan/25 10.00
25 Johnny Bench/50 20.00
26 Kirby Puckett/50 15.00
27 Lou Boudreau/50 8.00
28 Lou Brock/25 20.00
29 Luis Aparicio Pants/50 8.00
30 Manny Ramirez/50 10.00
31 Mark Prior/50 12.00
32 Miguel Tejada/50 8.00
33 Mike Mussina/50 10.00
34 Mike Piazza/50 20.00
35 Mike Schmidt/50 20.00
36 Nolan Ryan/50 35.00
37 Nomar Garciaparra/50 15.00
38 Ozzie Smith/50 25.00
40 Pedro J. Martinez/50 10.00
41 Rafael Palmeiro/25 15.00
42 Randy Johnson/50 12.00
43 Red Schoendienst/50 8.00
44 Reggie Jackson Pants/50 15.00
45 Rickey Henderson/50 15.00
46 Roberto Alomar/50 12.00
47 Roberto Clemente/10
48 Robin Yount/50 20.00
49 Rod Carew Jkt/50 10.00
50 Roger Clemens/50 15.00
51 Ryne Sandberg/50 20.00
52 Sammy Sosa/50 15.00
53 Stan Musial/10
54 Steve Carlton/25 15.00
55 Todd Helton/50 12.00
56 Tom Glavine/50 10.00
57 Tom Seaver/50 15.00
58 Tony Gwynn/50 15.00
59 Wade Boggs/50 10.00
60 Whitey Ford Pants/10

Century Stars

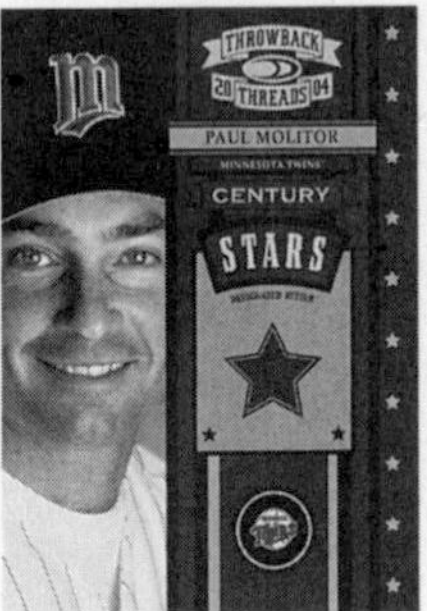

NM/M
Common Player: 1.50
Production 1,500 Sets
Spectrum: 1.5X-3X
Production 100 Sets
1 Al Kaline 2.00
2 Albert Pujols 5.00
3 Alex Rodriguez 4.00
4 Barry Larkin 2.00
5 Barry Zito 1.50
6 Billy Williams 1.50
7 Bob Feller 1.50
8 Bob Gibson 3.00
9 Cal Ripken Jr. 8.00
10 Chipper Jones 3.00
11 Curt Schilling 2.00
12 Dale Murphy 2.00
13 Dave Parker 1.50
14 Derek Jeter 6.00
15 Don Drysdale 1.50
16 Don Mattingly 5.00
17 Eddie Murray 2.00
18 Fergie Jenkins 2.00
19 Gary Carter 2.00
20 George Brett 5.00
21 Greg Maddux 3.00
22 Ivan Rodriguez 2.00
23 Jeff Bagwell 2.00
24 Joe Morgan 2.00
25 Johnny Bench 3.00
26 Kirby Puckett 3.00
27 Lou Boudreau 1.50
28 Lou Brock 1.50
29 Luis Aparicio 1.50
30 Manny Ramirez 2.00
31 Mark Prior 3.00
32 Miguel Tejada 2.00
33 Mike Mussina 2.00
34 Mike Piazza 4.00
35 Mike Schmidt 5.00
36 Nolan Ryan 6.00
37 Nomar Garciaparra 4.00
38 Ozzie Smith 4.00
39 Paul Molitor 3.00
40 Pedro J. Martinez 3.00
41 Rafael Palmeiro 2.00
42 Randy Johnson 3.00
43 Red Schoendienst 1.50
44 Reggie Jackson 3.00
45 Rickey Henderson 2.00
46 Roberto Alomar 2.00
47 Roberto Clemente 5.00
48 Robin Yount 3.00
49 Rod Carew 2.00
50 Roger Clemens 5.00
51 Ryne Sandberg 4.00
52 Sammy Sosa 4.00
53 Stan Musial 4.00
54 Steve Carlton 2.00
55 Todd Helton 2.00
56 Tom Glavine 2.00
57 Tom Seaver 3.00
58 Tony Gwynn 3.00
59 Wade Boggs 2.00
60 Whitey Ford 3.00

Cent. Coll. Sign. Mat.

NM/M
All Jersey unless noted
Prime: No Pricing
Production 5-10
Combo: .75X-1.5X

Production 5-25
No pricing 15 or less
Combo Prime: No Pricing
Production 5-10
1 Alan Trammell/50 25.00
3 Alfonso Soriano/50 40.00
4 Andre Dawson/50 25.00
6 Bert Blyleven/50 20.00
7 Bo Jackson/10
8 Bobby Doerr/50 25.00
12 Carlton Fisk Jkt/10
14 Darryl Strawberry/50 25.00
15 Dave Concepcion/50 25.00
16 Dave Parker/50 20.00
17 Dennis Eckersley/50 40.00
18 Don Sutton/50 20.00
19 Duke Snider/25 40.00
20 Dwight Gooden/50 25.00
23 Ernie Banks Pants/10
25 Frank Robinson/10
26 Frank Thomas/10
27 Garret Anderson/50 25.00
28 Gary Carter/50 25.00
29 Gary Sheffield/25 30.00
31 Harold Baines/50 20.00
33 Jack Morris/50 15.00
37 Jim Palmer/25 25.00
38 Jim Rice/50 20.00
42 Jose Canseco/25 50.00
44 Juan Marichal/50 25.00
45 Keith Hernandez/50 25.00
50 Lee Smith/50 15.00
51 Lenny Dykstra Bat/50 20.00
52 Luis Tiant/50 15.00
53 Magglio Ordonez/50 25.00
56 Mark Grace/50 40.00
57 Mark Mulder/25 25.00
58 Mark Teixeira/25 40.00
59 Marty Marion/50 25.00
63 Nolan Ryan Jkt/10
68 Phil Niekro/50 25.00
71 Ralph Kiner Bat/50 40.00
75 Roberto Alomar/25 50.00
76 Robin Ventura/50 20.00
82 Steve Garvey/50 25.00
86 Adam Dunn/10
87 Tommy John/50 15.00
90 Tony Perez Bat/25 40.00
91 Torii Hunter/25 30.00
93 Vernon Wells/25 25.00
94 Vladimir Guerrero/50 40.00
100 George Foster/50 20.00

Century Coll. Material

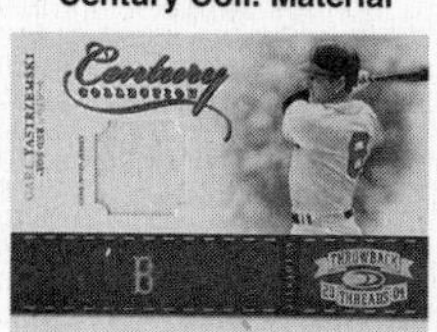

NM/M
All Jersey unless noted
Prime: 1.5X-3X
Production 10-25
Combo: .75X-2X
Production 5-50
Combo Prime: 2X-3X
Production 5-25
No pricing 15 or less
1 Alan Trammell/250 8.00
2 Alex Rodriguez/250 10.00
3 Alfonso Soriano/250 8.00
4 Andre Dawson/250 6.00
5 Andy Pettitte/250 6.00
6 Bert Blyleven/250 6.00
7 Bo Jackson/250 12.00
8 Bobby Doerr/250 8.00
9 Brooks Robinson/25 30.00
10 Carl Yastrzemski/250 15.00
11 Carlos Delgado/250 4.00
12 Carlton Fisk Jkt/250 8.00
13 Curt Schilling/250 6.00
14 Darryl Strawberry/250 6.00
15 Dave Concepcion/250 6.00
16 Dave Parker/100 8.00
17 Dennis Eckersley/250 8.00
18 Don Sutton/250 6.00
19 Duke Snider/250 10.00
20 Dwight Gooden/250 6.00
21 Eddie Mathews/25 25.00
22 Enos Slaughter/100 8.00
23 Ernie Banks Pants/250 15.00
24 Frankie Frisch Jkt/250 12.00
25 Frank Robinson/50 10.00
26 Frank Thomas/250 10.00
27 Garret Anderson/250 6.00
28 Gary Carter/250 6.00
29 Gary Sheffield/250 6.00
30 Harmon Killebrew/250 25.00
31 Harold Baines/250 6.00
32 Hideo Nomo/250 8.00
33 Jack Morris/250 6.00
34 Jason Giambi/250 6.00
35 Jeff Kent/250 4.00
36 Jim "Catfish" Hunter/250 6.00
37 Jim Palmer/50 10.00
38 Jim Rice/250 8.00
39 Jim Thome/250 10.00
40 John Smoltz/250 8.00
41 Johnny Mize Pants/250 8.00
42 Jose Canseco/250 8.00
43 Juan Gonzalez/250 6.00
44 Juan Marichal/250 8.00
45 Keith Hernandez/250 8.00
46 Kerry Wood/250 10.00
47 Kevin Brown/250 4.00
48 Lance Berkman/250 6.00
49 Larry Walker/250 6.00
50 Lee Smith/250 6.00
51 Lenny Dykstra Bat/250 6.00
52 Luis Tiant/250 6.00
53 Magglio Ordonez/250 4.00
54 Manny Ramirez/250 8.00
55 Mariano Rivera/100 8.00
56 Mark Grace/250 8.00
57 Mark Mulder/250 6.00
58 Mark Teixeira/150 6.00
59 Marty Marion/25 15.00
60 Mike Mussina Pants/250 8.00
61 Mike Piazza/250 10.00
62 Nellie Fox Bat/250 15.00
63 Nolan Ryan Jkt/250 20.00
65 Ozzie Smith/250 12.00
66 Pedro J. Martinez/250 8.00
67 Pee Wee Reese Bat/250 8.00
68 Phil Niekro/250 8.00
69 Phil Rizzuto Pants/250 10.00
70 Rafael Palmeiro/250 8.00
71 Ralph Kiner Bat/250 8.00
72 Randy Johnson/250 10.00
73 Reggie Jackson Jkt/250 8.00
74 Rickey Henderson/250 10.00
75 Roberto Alomar/250 8.00
76 Robin Ventura/250 4.00
77 Rod Carew/250 10.00
78 Roger Clemens/250 15.00
79 Ron Santo Bat/250 10.00
80 Scott Rolen/250 10.00
81 Shawn Green/250 6.00
82 Steve Garvey/250 6.00
83 Tim Hudson/250 4.00
84 Tom Glavine/250 6.00
85 Tom Seaver/25 30.00
86 Adam Dunn/250 8.00
87 Tommy John/250 6.00
88 Tommy Lasorda/250 6.00
89 Tony Oliva/250 8.00
90 Tony Perez Bat/250 8.00
91 Torii Hunter/250 4.00
92 Troy Glaus/250 4.00
93 Vernon Wells/250 4.00
94 Vladimir Guerrero/250 8.00
95 Wade Boggs/250 8.00
96 Warren Spahn/100 20.00
97 Will Clark Bat/250 10.00
98 Willie McCovey/250 8.00
99 Willie Stargell/250 8.00
100 George Foster/250 8.00

Blast From the Past Bat

NM/M
Production 250 unless noted
1 Albert Pujols 15.00
2 Alex Rodriguez 10.00
3 Babe Ruth/50 150.00
4 Cal Ripken Jr. 25.00
5 Carlton Fisk 8.00
6 Eddie Mathews 10.00
7 Eddie Murray 8.00
8 Ernie Banks 10.00
9 Frank Robinson 8.00
10 George Foster 6.00
11 Harmon Killebrew 10.00
12 Jim Rice 8.00
13 Jim Thome 8.00
14 Johnny Bench 10.00
15 Jose Canseco/100 10.00
16 Juan Gonzalez 8.00
18 Mike Piazza 10.00
19 Mike Schmidt 15.00
20 Reggie Jackson 8.00
21 Roger Maris 30.00
22 Sammy Sosa 10.00
23 Stan Musial 15.00
24 Willie McCovey 8.00
25 Willie Stargell 8.00

Blast From the Past

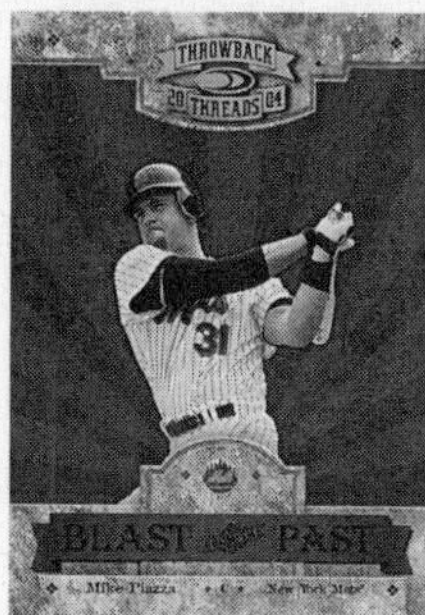

NM/M
Common Player: 1.50
Production 1,500 Sets
Spectrum: 2X-3X
Production 100 Sets
1 Albert Pujols 5.00
2 Alex Rodriguez 4.00
3 Babe Ruth 6.00
4 Cal Ripken Jr. 8.00
5 Carlton Fisk 2.00
6 Eddie Mathews 3.00
7 Eddie Murray 2.00
8 Ernie Banks 3.00
9 Frank Robinson 2.00
10 George Foster 1.50
11 Harmon Killebrew 3.00
12 Jim Rice 1.50
13 Jim Thome 2.00
14 Johnny Bench 3.00
15 Jose Canseco 2.00
16 Juan Gonzalez 2.00
17 Ken Griffey Jr. 3.00
18 Mike Piazza 4.00
19 Mike Schmidt 5.00
20 Reggie Jackson 2.00
21 Roger Maris 3.00
22 Sammy Sosa 4.00
23 Stan Musial 4.00
24 Willie McCovey 2.00
25 Willie Stargell 2.00

2004 DONRUSS TIMELESS TREASURES

NM/M
Complete Set (100): 200.00
Common Player: 1.50
Production 999 Sets
Tin (4): 125.00
1 Albert Pujols 6.00
2 Garret Anderson 2.00
3 Randy Johnson 3.00
4 Alex Rodriguez Yanks 8.00
5 Manny Ramirez 3.00
6 Mark Prior 5.00
7 Roberto Alomar 2.00
8 Barry Larkin 2.00
9 Todd Helton 2.50
10 Ivan Rodriguez 3.00
11 Jacque Jones 1.50
12 Jeff Kent 2.00
13 Mike Sweeney 1.50
14 Shawn Green 2.00
15 Richie Sexson 2.00
16 Mike Piazza 5.00
17 Vladimir Guerrero 4.00
18 Mike Mussina 2.00
19 Barry Zito 2.00
20 Don Mattingly 6.00
21 Ichiro Suzuki 5.00
22 Rocco Baldelli 2.00
23 Rafael Palmeiro 3.00
24 Carlos Delgado 2.00
25 Roger Clemens 6.00
26 Luis Gonzalez 2.00
27 Gary Sheffield 2.00
28 Jay Gibbons 1.50
29 Nomar Garciaparra 5.00
30 Aramis Ramirez 2.00
31 Frank Thomas 3.00
32 Ryan Wagner 1.50
33 Preston Wilson 1.50
34 Hideki Matsui 4.00
35 Roy Oswalt 2.00
36 Angel Berroa 1.50
37 Kazuhisa Ishii 1.50
38 Scott Podsednik 2.00
39 Torii Hunter 2.00
40 Tom Glavine 2.00
41 Jason Giambi 3.00
42 Eric Chavez 2.00
43 Jim Thome 3.00
44 Tony Gwynn 3.00
45 Edgar Martinez 2.00
46 Jim Edmonds 2.00
47 Delmon Young 2.00
48 Hank Blalock 2.00
49 Vernon Wells 1.50
50 Curt Schilling 2.50
51 Chipper Jones 3.00
52 Cal Ripken Jr. 8.00
53 Jason Varitek 1.50
54 Kerry Wood 3.00
55 Magglio Ordonez 2.00
56 Adam Dunn 2.00
57 Jay Payton 1.50
58 Josh Beckett 2.00
59 Jeff Bagwell 3.00
60 Carlos Beltran 2.00
61 Hideo Nomo 2.00
62 Rickie Weeks 2.00
63 Alfonso Soriano 2.50
64 Miguel Tejada 2.00
65 Bret Boone 2.00
66 Scott Rolen 3.00
67 Aubrey Huff 1.50
68 Juan Gonzalez 2.50
69 Roy Halladay 2.50
70 Brandon Webb 1.50
71 Andruw Jones 2.50
72 Pedro J. Martinez 3.00
73 Carlos Lee 1.50
74 Lance Berkman 2.00
75 Paul LoDuca 1.50
76 Jorge Posada 2.00
77 Tim Hudson 2.00
78 Stan Musial 4.00
79 Mark Teixeira 2.00
80 Trot Nixon 1.50
81 Fred McGriff 1.50
82 Nick Johnson 1.50
83 Nolan Ryan 8.00
84 Ken Griffey Jr. 4.00
85 Mariano Rivera 2.00
86 Mark Mulder 2.00
87 Bob Gibson 2.50
88 Dale Murphy UER 2.50
89 Bernie Williams 2.00
90 Carl Yastrzemski 3.00
91 Sammy Sosa 5.00
92 Miguel Cabrera 4.00
93 Craig Biggio 2.00
94 George Brett 6.00
95 Rickey Henderson 3.00
96 Derek Jeter 8.00
97 Greg Maddux 4.00
98 Bob Abreu 2.00
99 Troy Glaus 2.00
100 Dontrelle Willis 2.00

World Series Mat. Sig.

NM/M
Quantity Produced Listed
Prime: No Pricing
Production 9-10
1 Frank Robinson Bat/19 50.00
4 Tom Glavine Jsy/19 40.00

World Series Mat. Prime

NM/M
Quantity Produced Listed
2 Ozzie Smith Jsy/19 25.00

4 Tom Glavine Jsy/19 20.00
5 Roger Clemens Jsy/20 30.00

World Series Materials

NM/M

Quantity Produced Listed
1 Frank Robinson Bat/61 15.00
2 Ozzie Smith Jsy/87 15.00
3 Rickey Henderson Bat/93 15.00
4 Tom Glavine Jsy/96 10.00
5 Roger Clemens Jsy/100 15.00

Statistical Champ. Sig.

NM/M

Quantity Produced Listed
Number: .5X-1.5X
Production 1-47
Prime: No Pricing
Production 1-10
2 Stan Musial 43 BA Jsy/10
3 Ralph Kiner Bat/49 35.00
4 Stan Musial 57 BA Jsy/10
6 Warren Spahn Jsy/25 75.00
13 Frank Robinson Bat/66 40.00
14 Bob Gibson 68 ERA Jsy/25 50.00
15 Bob Gibson 68 K Jsy/25 50.00
16 Tom Seaver Jsy/10
17 Harmon Killebrew Jsy/71 50.00
18 Harmon Killebrew Pants/71 50.00
19 Mike Schmidt Jsy/25 75.00
20 Reggie Jackson Jsy/25 65.00
21 Phil Niekro Jsy/50 30.00
22 Rod Carew Hat/25 40.00
23 Jim Rice 78 HR Jsy/78 30.00
24 Jim Rice 78 RBI Jsy/78 30.00
25 Reggie Jackson Hat/25 65.00
26 Dale Murphy 82 RBI Jsy/25 50.00
27 Steve Carlton Jsy/25 50.00
28 Dale Murphy 85 HR Jsy/25 50.00
29 Wade Boggs 86 BA Jsy/25 40.00
30 Wade Boggs 87 BA Jsy/25 40.00
31 Will Clark Jsy/88 30.00
32 Nolan Ryan 89 K Jsy/25 120.00
33 Nolan Ryan 90 K Jsy/25 120.00
34 Nolan Ryan 90 K Pants/25 120.00
35 Ryne Sandberg Jsy/25 80.00
43 Juan Gonzalez Pants/19 40.00
50 Troy Glaus Jsy/25 35.00
52 Tom Glavine Jsy/20 40.00
53 Sammy Sosa 00 HR Jsy/25 150.00
55 Curt Schilling Jsy/25 40.00
58 Mark Mulder Jsy/25 30.00
59 Sammy Sosa 01 RBI Jsy/25 150.00
61 Lance Berkman Jsy/20 40.00
69 Sammy Sosa 02 HR Jsy/25 150.00

Statistical Champions

NM/M

Number: .75X-1.5X
Production 1-51
No Pricing 15 or Less
Prime: No Pricing
Production 5-10
2 Stan Musial 43 BA Jsy/19 40.00
3 Ralph Kiner Bat/49 10.00
4 Stan Musial 57 BA Jsy/57 30.00
5 Ted Williams Jsy/25 90.00
6 Warren Spahn Jsy/25 30.00
7 Eddie Mathews Jsy/19 40.00
8 Roger Maris 61 HR Bat/61 40.00
9 Roger Maris 61 HR Pants/61 40.00
10 Roger Maris 61 RBI Bat/61 40.00
11 Roger Maris 61 RBI Pants/61 40.00
12 Roberto Clemente Jsy/19 100.00
13 Frank Robinson Bat/66 10.00
14 Bob Gibson 68 ERA Jsy/68 15.00
15 Bob Gibson 68 K Jsy/68 15.00
16 Tom Seaver Jsy/19 25.00
17 Harmon Killebrew Jsy/3
18 Harmon Killebrew Pants/71 15.00
19 Mike Schmidt Jsy/74 15.00
20 Reggie Jackson Jsy/19 20.00
21 Phil Niekro Jsy/5
22 Rod Carew Hat/78 15.00
23 Jim Rice 78 HR Jsy/78 10.00
24 Jim Rice 78 RBI Jsy/78 10.00
25 Reggie Jackson Hat/80 15.00
26 Dale Murphy 82 RBI Jsy/82 15.00
27 Steve Carlton Jsy/83 10.00
28 Dale Murphy 85 HR Jsy/85 15.00
29 Wade Boggs 86 BA Jsy/86 15.00
30 Wade Boggs 87 BA Jsy/87 15.00
31 Will Clark Jsy/88 15.00
32 Nolan Ryan 89 K Jsy/89 20.00
33 Nolan Ryan 90 K Jsy/90 20.00
34 Nolan Ryan 90 K Pants/90 20.00
35 Ryne Sandberg Jsy/90 20.00
36 Roger Clemens 90 K Jsy/90 20.00
37 George Brett Jsy/90 20.00
38 Roger Clemens 92 ERA Jsy/100 20.00
39 Roger Clemens 96 K Jsy/100 20.00
40 Tony Gwynn Jsy/25 35.00
41 Pedro Martinez Expos Jsy/25 20.00
42 Greg Maddux Jsy/100 10.00
43 Juan Gonzalez Pants/25 20.00
44 Manny Ramirez Bat/25 15.00
45 Nomar Garciaparra 99 BA Jsy/100 10.00
46 Nomar Garciaparra 99 BA Bat/5
47 Nomar Garciaparra 00 BA Jsy/100 10.00
48 Todd Helton 00 BA Jsy/25 15.00
49 Todd Helton 00 RBI Jsy/25 15.00
50 Troy Glaus Jsy/25 10.00
51 Randy Johnson 00 K Jsy/25 15.00
52 Tom Glavine Jsy/25 10.00
53 Sammy Sosa 00 HR Jsy/100 15.00
54 Alex Rodriguez 01 HR Bat/100 15.00
55 Curt Schilling Jsy/25 10.00
56 Pedro J. Martinez 99 K Jsy/25 20.00
57 Alex Rodriguez 01 HR Jsy/100 15.00
58 Mark Mulder Jsy/25 10.00
59 Sammy Sosa 01 RBI Jsy/100 15.00
60 Manny Ramirez Jsy/25 15.00
61 Lance Berkman Jsy/25 10.00
62 Randy Johnson 02 W Jsy/25 15.00
63 Alex Rodriguez 02 HR Jsy/100 15.00
64 Alex Rodriguez 02 RBI Jsy/100 15.00
65 Alex Rodriguez 02 HR Bat/100 15.00
66 Alex Rodriguez 02 RBI Bat/100 15.00
67 Pedro J. Martinez 02 K Jsy/25 20.00
68 Pedro J. Martinez 02 ERA Jsy/25 20.00
69 Sammy Sosa 02 HR Jsy/100 15.00
70 Jim ThomeJsy/25 15.00
71 Alex Rodriguez 03 HR Bat/100 15.00
72 Albert Pujols Bat/100 20.00
73 Alex Rodriguez 03 HR Jsy/100 15.00
74 Albert Pujols Jsy/100 20.00

Silver

Silver: 2X-4X
Production 25 Sets

Rk Year Mat. Sig. Prime

No Pricing

Rookie Year Mat. Sig.

NM/M

Quantity Produced Listed
Prime: 1X
Production 1-35
Number: 1X
No Pricing 15 or Less
1 Stan Musial Jsy/9 125.00
2 Yogi Berra Stripe Jsy/9
3 Yogi Berra Grey Jsy/19 100.00
4 Whitey Ford Jsy/19 85.00
6 Johnny Bench Bat/9
7 Mike Schmidt Bat/9
8 Gary Carter Jsy/19 35.00
9 Robin Yount Jsy/9
10 Fred Lynn Jsy/75 15.00
11 Cal Ripken Jr. Bat/9
12 Kirby Puckett Bat/9
13 Roger Clemens Jsy/9
14 Lenny Dykstra Fld Glv/85 20.00
15 Gary Sheffield Jsy/11
16 Juan Gonzalez Jsy/19 40.00
17 Randy Johnson Jsy/9
18 Ivan Rodriguez Jsy/9
20 Pedro J. Martinez Jsy/1
21 Mike Piazza Jsy/1
22 Hideo Nomo Jsy/1
23 Hideo Nomo Pants/1
24 Alex Rodriguez Jsy/9
25 Garret Anderson Jsy/95 20.00
26 Scott Rolen Jsy/1
27 Andruw Jones Jsy/9
28 Vladimir Guerrero Jsy/9
30 Shannon Stewart Jsy/97 15.00
32 Albert Pujols White Jsy/5
33 Albert Pujols Grey Jsy/5
34 Albert Pujols Bat/5
35 Albert Pujols Hat/5
36 Mark Prior Blue Jsy/22 120.00
37 Mark Prior Grey Jsy/22 120.00
38 Dontrelle Willis Jsy/35 40.00
39 Rocco Baldelli Jsy/19 40.00

Rookie Year Mat. Dual

NM/M

Production 25 Sets
Prime: No Pricing
Production 10 Sets
40 Roger Clemens Jsy, Nomar Garciaparra Jsy 40.00
41 Pedro J. Martinez Jsy, Mike Piazza Jsy 35.00
42 Mike Piazza Jsy, Hideo Nomo Jsy 35.00
43 Pedro J. Martinez Jsy, Hideo Nomo Jsy 20.00
44 Yogi Berra Jsy, Whitey Ford Jsy 50.00
45 Mike Schmidt Bat, Scott Rolen Jsy 40.00
46 Stan Musial Jsy, Albert Pujols Jsy 75.00
47 Juan Gonzalez Jsy, Ivan Rodriguez Jsy 15.00

R.Y. Mat. Combo Sig. Prime

NM/M

Quantity Produced Listed
36 Mark Prior Jsy-Jsy/22 140.00
38 Dontrelle Willis Jsy-Jsy/35 40.00

R.Y. Materials Combos Sig.

NM/M

Quantity Produced Listed
36 Mark Prior Jsy-Jsy/22 140.00
38 Dontrelle Willis Jsy-Jsy/35 40.00

R.Y. Mat. Combos Prime

NM/M

Quantity Produced Listed
36 Mark Prior Jsy-Jsy/22 40.00
38 Dontrelle Willis Jsy-Jsy/35 10.00

Rookie Year Mat. Combo

NM/M

Quantity Produced Listed
2 Yogi Berra Jsy-Jsy/8 60.00
22 Hideo Nomo Jsy-Pants/16 30.00
36 Mark Prior Jsy-Jsy/22 40.00
38 Dontrelle Willis Jsy-Jsy/35 10.00

Rookie Year Materials

NM/M

Quantity Produced Listed
Prime: No Pricing
Production 5-10
Number: .75X-1.5X
Production 3-51
No Pricing 15 or Less
1 Stan Musial Jsy/19 60.00
2 Yogi Berra Stripe Jsy/19 40.00
3 Yogi Berra Grey Jsy/47 25.00
4 Whitey Ford Jsy/50 20.00
5 Jim "Catfish" Hunter Jsy/65 10.00
6 Johnny Bench Bat/68 15.00
7 Mike Schmidt Bat/72 15.00
8 Gary Carter Jsy/74 8.00
9 Robin Yount Jsy/74 20.00
11 Cal Ripken Jr. Bat/81 40.00
12 Kirby Puckett Bat/84 10.00
13 Roger Clemens Jsy/84 20.00
15 Gary Sheffield Jsy/89 8.00
16 Juan GonzalezJsy/89 10.00
17 Randy Johnson Jsy/89 10.00
18 Ivan Rodriguez Jsy/91 10.00
20 Pedro J. Martinez Jsy/92 10.00
21 Mike Piazza Jsy/93 10.00
22 Hideo Nomo Jsy/95 10.00
23 Hideo Nomo Pants/95 10.00
24 Alex Rodriguez Jsy/95 15.00
26 Scott Rolen Jsy/96 10.00
27 Andruw Jones Jsy/96 8.00
28 Nomar Garciaparra Jsy/97 10.00
29 Vladimir Guerrero Jsy/97 10.00
31 Alfonso Soriano Jsy/100 10.00
32 Albert Pujols White Jsy/100 20.00
33 Albert Pujols Grey Jsy/100 20.00
34 Albert Pujols Bat/100 20.00
35 Albert Pujols Hat/5
36 Mark Prior Blue Jsy/100 20.00
37 Mark Prior Grey Jsy/100 20.00
38 Dontrelle Willis Jsy/35 15.00
39 Rocco Baldelli Jsy/5

Platinum

Platinum: No Pricing
Production One Set

Mile. Mat. Sig. Number

NM/M

3 Rickey Henderson A's Jsy/5
4 Gaylord Perry Jsy/82 20.00
6 Rickey Henderson Padres Jsy/5

Milestone Mat. Prime

3 Rickey Henderson A's Jsy/25

4 Gaylord Perry Jsy/25
6 Rickey Henderson Padres Jsy/25

Material Ink Jersey

NM/M
Quantity Produced Listed
Number: .75X-1X
Production 1-100
No Pricing 15 or Less
Prime: .75-1.5X
Production 1-25
No Pricing 15 or Less
1 Adam Dunn/25 40.00
2 Alan Trammell/100 20.00
3 Alex Rodriguez/10
4 Andre Dawson/100 25.00
5 Bo Jackson/25 60.00
6 Cal Ripken Jr./10
7 Dale Murphy/50 35.00
8 Darryl Strawberry/100 25.00
9 Dave Parker/25 20.00
10 Deion Sanders/10
11 Doc Gooden/100 20.00
12 Don Mattingly/50 65.00
13 Dontrelle Willis/25 40.00
14 Hideo Nomo/1
15 Ivan Rodriguez/25 50.00
16 Joe Carter/25 30.00
17 Jose Canseco/25 50.00
18 Kerry Wood/15
19 Mark Grace/10
20 Mark Prior/50 90.00
21 Mark Teixeira/25 30.00
22 Marty Marion/25 25.00
23 Mike Piazza/1
24 Paul Molitor/10
26 Rocco Baldelli/25 40.00
27 Roger Clemens Yanks/5
28 Roger Clemens Sox/5
30 Ryne Sandberg/50 75.00
31 Ernie Banks/50 75.00
32 Tony Gwynn/10
33 Vladimir Guerrero/25 60.00
34 Will Clark/50 40.00

Material Ink Combos

NM/M
Quantity Produced Listed
Prime: No Pricing
Production 1-10
1 Adam Dunn Bat-Jsy/25 40.00
2 Alan Trammell Bat-Jsy/25 35.00
4 Andre Dawson Bat-Jsy/25 35.00
5 Bo Jackson Bat-Jsy/25 60.00
6 Cal Ripken Jr. Bat-Jsy/8
7 Dale Murphy Bat-Jsy/25 40.00
12 Don Mattingly Bat-Jsy/25 100.00
17 Jose Canseco Bat-Jsy/25 50.00
30 Ryne Sandberg Bat-Jsy/25 85.00
32 Tony Gwynn Bat-Jsy/25 80.00
34 Will Clark Bat-Jsy/50 40.00

Material Ink Bat

NM/M
1 Adam Dunn/25 40.00
2 Alan Trammell/25 35.00
4 Andre Dawson/25 35.00
5 Bo Jackson/25 60.00
7 Dale Murphy/25 40.00
12 Don Mattingly/50 65.00
20 Mark Prior/25 125.00
25 Paul O'Neill/25 40.00
29 Ron Santo/50 35.00
30 Ryne Sandberg/25 85.00
32 Tony Gwynn/25 80.00
34 Will Clark/25 45.00

Home Run Material Sig.

2 Ron Santo Ball/12
3 Harmon Killebrew HR 570 Bat/19
4 Harmon Killebrew HR 565 Bat/19
5 Jose Canseco Bat/9
6 Alex Rodriguez Bat/9
7 Sammy Sosa Jsy/9
8 Rafael Palmeiro Jsy/9
9 Ivan Rodriguez Jsy/9

Home Run Materials

NM/M
1 Roger Maris Bat/61 40.00
2 Ron Santo Ball/12
3 Harmon Killebrew HR 570 Bat/75 20.00
4 Harmon Killebrew HR 565 Bat/75 20.00
5 Jose Canseco Bat/96 10.00
6 Alex Rodriguez Bat/100 15.00
7 Sammy Sosa Jsy/100 15.00
8 Rafael Palmeiro Jsy/25 20.00
9 Ivan Rodriguez Jsy/25 20.00

Home Away Gamers Sig.

NM/M
5 Steve Carlton Jsy-Jsy/25 40.00
13 Mike Schmidt Jsy-Jsy/20 100.00
14 Harmon Killebrew Jsy-Jsy/25 90.00
16 Don Mattingly Jsy-Jsy/25 120.00
17 Dale Murphy Jsy-Jsy/25 70.00
19 Lou Gehrig Jsy-Jsy/1 (5/04 auction) 7,100

Home Away Gamers Combos

NM/M
Quantity Produced Listed
Prime: No Pricing
Production 3-10
1 Babe Ruth/25 800.00
2 Yogi Berra/8
3 Wade Boggs/50 25.00
4 Tony Gwynn/50 40.00
5 Steve Carlton/50 25.00
6 Stan Musial/25 85.00
7 Ryne Sandberg/50 40.00
8 Rod Carew/50 25.00
9 Rickey Henderson/50 35.00
10 Brooks Robinson/5
11 Ted Williams/100 150.00
12 Ozzie Smith/50 40.00
13 Mike Schmidt/50 50.00
14 Harmon Killebrew/25 40.00
15 George Brett/100 50.00
16 Don Mattingly/50 60.00
17 Dale Murphy/50 25.00
18 Cal Ripken Jr./100 65.00
19 Lou Gehrig/25 400.00
20 Nolan Ryan/100 65.00

Home Away Gamers

NM/M
Quantity Produced Listed
Prime: No Pricing
Production 3-5
1 Babe Ruth Jsy-Jsy/25 600.00
2 Yogi Berra Jsy-Jsy/8
3 Wade Boggs Jsy-Jsy/50 15.00
4 Tony Gwynn Jsy-Jsy/50 30.00
5 Steve Carlton Jsy-Jsy/50 15.00
6 Stan Musial Jsy-Jsy/10
7 Ryne Sandberg Jsy-Jsy/50 35.00
8 Rod Carew Jsy-Jsy/50 15.00
9 Rickey Henderson Jsy-Jsy/50 25.00
10 Brooks Robinson Jsy-Jsy/5
11 Ted Williams Jsy-Jsy/100 85.00
12 Ozzie Smith Jsy-Jsy/50 25.00
13 Mike Schmidt Jsy-Jsy/50 30.00
14 Harmon Killebrew Jsy-Jsy/50 30.00
15 George Brett Jsy-Jsy/100 30.00
16 Don Mattingly Jsy-Jsy/50 35.00
17 Dale Murphy Jsy-Jsy/50 15.00
18 Cal Ripken Jr. Jsy-Jsy/100 50.00
19 Lou Gehrig Jsy-Jsy/50 200.00
20 Nolan Ryan Jsy-Jsy/100 40.00

HOF Materials Sig.

NM/M
Quantity Produced Listed
Prime: No Pricing
Production 1-10
1 Al Kaline/25 50.00
2 Babe Ruth/1
3 Bob Feller/25 25.00
4 Bobby Doerr/1
5 Brooks Robinson/25 50.00
6 Carl Yastrzemski/8
7 Carlton Fisk/27 50.00
8 Dave Winfield/5
9 Duke Snider/25 40.00
10 Eddie Murray/5
11 Ernie Banks/25 60.00
12 Fergie Jenkins/31 30.00
13 Frank Robinson/20 40.00
14 Hal Newhouser/5
15 Hoyt Wilhelm/25 25.00
17 Jim Palmer/22 30.00
18 Joe Morgan/8
19 Johnny Bench/5
20 Juan Marichal/27 30.00
21 Kirby Puckett/34 60.00
22 Lou Brock/20 40.00
23 Lou Gehrig/1
24 Luis Aparicio/11
26 Orlando Cepeda/30 30.00
27 Pee Wee Reese/5
28 Phil Rizzuto/25 40.00
29 Red Schoendienst/25 30.00
32 Paul Molitor/25 50.00
34 Warren Spahn/21 50.00
35 Willie McCovey/25 40.00

HOF Mat. Pants Sig.

NM/M
Production 25 Sets
1 Al Kaline 50.00
12 Fergie Jenkins 30.00
24 Luis Aparicio 25.00
28 Phil Rizzuto 40.00

HOF Materials Pants

NM/M
1 Al Kaline/25 30.00
2 Babe Ruth/50 200.00
12 Fergie Jenkins/25 15.00
23 Lou Gehrig/50 125.00
24 Luis Aparicio/25 15.00
25 Mel Ott/25 40.00
31 Roy Campanella/25 30.00
33 Ty Cobb/25 125.00

HOF Materials Jsy Sig.

NM/M
Quantity Produced Listed
Prime: No Pricing
Production 1-10
Number: 1X
Production 10-25
1 Al Kaline/25 50.00
3 Bob Feller/10
4 Bobby Doerr/50 30.00
5 Brooks Robinson/25 60.00
6 Carl Yastrzemski/10
7 Carlton Fisk/10
8 Dave Winfield/10
10 Eddie Murray/10
11 Ernie Banks/10
13 Frank Robinson/50 35.00
15 Hoyt Wilhelm/25 25.00
17 Jim Palmer/50 30.00
18 Joe Morgan/25 30.00
19 Johnny Bench/5
20 Juan Marichal/50 35.00
21 Kirby Puckett/10
22 Lou Brock/50 30.00
24 Luis Aparicio/50 25.00
26 Orlando Cepeda/25 25.00
28 Phil Rizzuto/50 40.00
29 Red Schoendienst/50 20.00
32 Paul Molitor/50 30.00
34 Warren Spahn/25 65.00
35 Willie McCovey/10

HOF Materials Jersey

NM/M
Quantity Produced Listed
Prime: No Pricing
Production 1-10
Jersey Number: .75X-1.5X
Production 1-44
No Pricing 15 or Less
1 Al Kaline/6
2 Babe Ruth/25 500.00
3 Bob Feller/10 10.00
4 Bobby Doerr/25 15.00
5 Brooks Robinson/50 15.00
6 Carl Yastrzemski/50 25.00
7 Carlton Fisk/50 15.00
8 Dave Winfield/50 10.00
9 Duke Snider/10
10 Eddie Murray/25 25.00
11 Ernie Banks/10
13 Frank Robinson/25 20.00
14 Hal Newhouser/50 10.00
15 Hoyt Wilhelm/50 10.00
16 Jackie Robinson/10
17 Jim Palmer/50 10.00
18 Joe Morgan/50 10.00
20 Juan Marichal/50 10.00
21 Kirby Puckett/50 20.00
22 Lou Brock/25 15.00
23 Lou Gehrig/25 140.00
24 Luis Aparicio/25 10.00
25 Mel Ott/25 40.00
26 Orlando Cepeda/5
27 Pee Wee Reese/50 15.00
28 Phil Rizzuto/50 15.00
29 Red Schoendienst/25 15.00
30 Roberto Clemente/50 60.00
32 Paul Molitor/50 15.00
34 Warren Spahn/50 20.00
35 Willie McCovey/50 10.00
36 Willie Stargell/50 15.00

HOF Mat. Combo Jsy-Pant Sig.

NM/M
Prime: No Pricing
Production 1-5
1 Al Kaline/5
24 Luis Aparicio/25 25.00

HOF Mat. Combo Jsy-Pant Prime

1 Al Kaline/1
2 Babe Ruth/5
16 Jackie Robinson Jacket-Jsy/5
23 Lou Gehrig/5
24 Luis Aparicio/5
25 Mel Ott/5

HOF Mat. Combo Jsy-Pant

NM/M
1 Al Kaline/10
2 Babe Ruth/25 500.00
16 Jackie Robinson Jacket-Jsy/10
23 Lou Gehrig/25 220.00
24 Luis Aparicio/25 15.00
25 Mel Ott/10

HOF Mat. Combo Bat-Pant Sig

NM/M
1 Al Kaline/25 75.00
12 Fergie Jenkins Fld Glv-Pants/25 35.00
24 Luis Aparicio/25 25.00

HOF Mat. Combo Bat-Pant

NM/M
Production 25 Sets
1 Al Kaline/25 35.00
2 Babe Ruth/25 350.00
12 Fergie Jenkins Fld Glv-Pants/25 15.00
23 Lou Gehrig/25 200.00
24 Luis Aparicio/25 15.00
25 Mel Ott/25 60.00
31 Roy Campanella/25 40.00
33 Ty Cobb/25 200.00

HOF Mat. Combo Bat-Jsy Sig

NM/M
Quantity Produced Listed
Prime: No Pricing
Production 1-5
1 Al Kaline/5
4 Bobby Doerr/25 30.00
5 Brooks Robinson/25 80.00
6 Carl Yastrzemski/10
7 Carlton Fisk/10
8 Dave Winfield/10
10 Eddie Murray/10
11 Ernie Banks/25 80.00
13 Frank Robinson/25 65.00

18 Joe Morgan/25 40.00
19 Johnny Bench/1
21 Kirby Puckett/10
22 Lou Brock/25 40.00
24 Luis Aparicio/25 30.00
26 Orlando Cepeda/10
28 Phil Rizzuto/10
29 Red Schoendienst/25 40.00
32 Paul Molitor/25 60.00
35 Willie McCovey/10

HOF Mat. Combo Bat-Jsy

NM/M
Quantity Produced Listed
Prime: No Pricing
Production 1-5
1 Al Kaline/25 40.00
2 Babe Ruth/25 500.00
4 Bobby Doerr/25 15.00
5 Brooks Robinson/50 30.00
6 Carl Yastrzemski/50 40.00
7 Carlton Fisk/50 20.00
8 Dave Winfield/50 15.00
10 Eddie Murray/50 35.00
11 Ernie Banks/10
13 Frank Robinson/50 20.00
18 Joe Morgan/50 15.00
19 Johnny Bench/1
21 Kirby Puckett/50 30.00
22 Lou Brock/50 15.00
23 Lou Gehrig/25 220.00
24 Luis Aparicio/25 20.00
25 Mel Ott/25 60.00
26 Orlando Cepeda/5
27 Pee Wee Reese/50 20.00
28 Phil Rizzuto/50 20.00
29 Red Schoendienst/25 15.00
30 Roberto Clemente/50 80.00
32 Paul Molitor/50 20.00
35 Willie McCovey/50 15.00
36 Willie Stargell/50 20.00

HOF Materials Bat Sig.

NM/M
1 Al Kaline/50 40.00
4 Bobby Doerr/50 35.00
5 Brooks Robinson/50 40.00
11 Ernie Banks/25 75.00
13 Frank Robinson/50 35.00
18 Joe Morgan/25 40.00
19 Johnny Bench/25 60.00
22 Lou Brock/50 30.00
24 Luis Aparicio/50 20.00
26 Orlando Cepeda/50 25.00
28 Phil Rizzuto/50 35.00
29 Red Schoendienst/50 25.00
32 Paul Molitor/25 50.00

HOF Materials Bat

NM/M
1 Al Kaline/25 25.00
2 Babe Ruth/50 200.00
4 Bobby Doerr/25 10.00
5 Brooks Robinson/25 30.00
6 Carl Yastrzemski/25 30.00
7 Carlton Fisk/25 20.00
8 Dave Winfield/25 15.00
9 Duke Snider/5
10 Eddie Murray/25 25.00
11 Ernie Banks/25 30.00
13 Frank Robinson/25 15.00
18 Joe Morgan/25 15.00
19 Johnny Bench/25 30.00
21 Kirby Puckett/25 30.00
22 Lou Brock/25 20.00
23 Lou Gehrig/50 125.00
24 Luis Aparicio/25 10.00
25 Mel Ott/25 40.00
26 Orlando Cepeda/25 15.00
27 Pee Wee Reese/25 15.00
28 Phil Rizzuto/25 15.00
29 Red Schoendienst/25 10.00
30 Roberto Clemente/25 65.00
31 Roy Campanella/25 25.00
32 Paul Molitor/25 20.00
33 Ty Cobb/25 100.00
35 Willie McCovey/25 15.00
36 Willie Stargell/25 15.00

Gold

Gold: No Pricing
Production 10 Sets

Game Day Material Sig.

NM/M
Many Not Priced
Due To Scarcity
2 Frank Robinson Bat/25 40.00
15 Maggio Ordonez Hat/25 30.00
16 Rickey Henderson Bat/10
17 Cal Ripken Jr. Ball/8

Game Day Materials

NM/M
Quantity Produced Listed
1 Nellie Fox Bat/58 40.00
2 Frank Robinson Bat/61 10.00
3 George Brett Bat/77 20.00
4 George Brett Hat/82 30.00
5 Nolan Ryan Hat/19 80.00
6 Cal Ripken Jr. Hat/85 50.00
7 Rod Carew Hat/19 25.00
8 Ryne Sandberg Bat/91 20.00
9 Kirby Puckett Bat/92 15.00
10 Frank Thomas Bat/93 10.00
11 George Brett Ball/9
12 Tony Gwynn Pants/99 20.00
13 Vladimir Guerrero Bat/99 15.00
14 Tony Gwynn Hat/99 20.00
15 Magglio Ordonez Hat/15 15.00
16 Rickey Henderson Bat/50 10.00
17 Cal Ripken Jr. Ball/8

Bronze

Bronze: 1X-2X
Production 100 Sets

Award Materials Sig.

NM/M
Common Autograph:
Quantity Produced Listed
Number: 1X-2X
Production 1-19
No Pricing 10 or Less
Prime: No Pricing
2 Stan Musial Jsy/9
7 Bob Gibson 68 CY Jsy/19 50.00
8 Bob Gibson 68 MVP Jsy/19 50.00
9 Tom Seaver Jsy/9
10 Fred Lynn Jsy/75 15.00
11 Jim Rice Jsy/78 30.00

Award Materials Combos

NM/M
Prime: .75X-1.5X
Production 19 Sets
4 Roger Maris Bat-Pants/25 70.00
12 Mike Schmidt 80M Jsy-Pants/25 40.00
13 Mike Schmidt 80M Pant-Stir/50 30.00
14 Mike Schmidt 80M Jsy-Stir/50 30.00
15 Mike Schmidt 81M Bat-Jsy/25 40.00
16 Mike Schmidt 81M Bat-Stir/50 30.00
18 Mike Schmidt 86M Hat-Shoe/50 30.00
19 Mike Schmidt 86M Hat-Bat/50 30.00
20 Mike Schmidt 86M Hat-Stir/50 30.00
21 Mike Schmidt 86M Bat-Shoe/50 30.00
23 Frank Thomas 93M Bat-Jsy/25 25.00
25 Jeff Bagwell Bat-Jsy/25 25.00
26 Frank Thomas 94M Bat-Jsy/25 25.00
35 Miguel Tejada Bat-Jsy/25 15.00

Award Materials

NM/M
Common Player: 10.00
Quantity Produced Listed
Prime: 1X-2X
Production 1-25
No Pricing 10 or Less
Number: .75X-1.5X
Production 3-51
No Pricing 15 or Less
1 Jimmie Foxx Bat/9
2 Stan Musial Jsy/43 25.00
3 Lou Boudreau Jsy/19 15.00
4 Roger Maris Pants/61 40.00
5 Roger Maris Bat/61 40.00
6 Roberto Clemente Bat/66 60.00
7 Bob Gibson 68 CY Jsy/68 20.00
8 Bob Gibson 68 MVP Jsy/68 20.00
9 Tom Seaver Jsy/19 20.00
10 Fred Lynn Jsy/75 8.00
11 Jim Rice Jsy/78 10.00
12 Mike Schmidt 80 MVP Jsy/80 15.00
13 Mike Schmidt 80 MVP Pants/80 15.00
14 Mike Schmidt 80 MVP Stir/80 15.00
15 Mike Schmidt 81 MVP Jsy/81 15.00
16 Mike Schmidt 81 MVP Bat/81 15.00
17 Dale Murphy Jsy/82 10.00
18 Mike Schmidt 86 MVP Hat/19 35.00
19 Mike Schmidt 86 MVP Shoe/19 35.00
20 Mike Schmidt 86 MVP Bat/86 15.00
21 Mike Schmidt 86 MVP Stir/19 35.00
22 Jose Canseco Jsy/88 10.00
23 Frank Thomas 93 MVP Bat/93 10.00
24 Frank Thomas 93 MVP Jsy/93 10.00
25 Jeff Bagwell Pants/94 10.00
26 Frank Thomas 94 MVP Jsy/94 10.00
27 Frank Thomas 94 MVP Pants/94 10.00
28 Jeff Bagwell Bat/94 10.00
29 Pedro J. Martinez 97 CY Jsy/97 10.00
30 Ivan Rodriguez Bat/99 10.00
31 Randy Johnson 00 CY Jsy/25 20.00
32 Pedro J. Martinez 00 CY Jsy/25 20.00
33 Roger Clemens Jsy/50 20.00
34 Randy Johnson 02 CY Jsy/25 20.00
35 Miguel Tejada Jsy/25 15.00

Signature Bronze

NM/M
1 Albert Pujols/25 125.00
2 Garret Anderson/16 30.00
4 Alex Rodriguez/25 100.00
5 Manny Ramirez/24 40.00
6 Mark Prior/50 75.00
8 Barry Larkin/25 30.00
9 Todd Helton/17 40.00
14 Shawn Green/15 30.00
17 Vladimir Guerrero 50.00
20 Don Mattingly/50 60.00
23 Rafael Palmeiro/25 45.00
27 Gary Sheffield/50 25.00
37 Kazuhisa Ishii/17 40.00
40 Tom Glavine/25 30.00
42 Eric Chavez/25 25.00
44 Tony Gwynn/50 40.00
46 Jim Edmonds/15 35.00
47 Delmon Young/73 20.00
49 Vernon Wells/25 20.00
50 Curt Schilling/38 40.00
53 Jason Varitek/33 30.00
56 Adam Dunn/25 30.00
58 Josh Beckett/21 30.00
59 Jeff Bagwell/25 50.00
60 Carlos Beltran/15 40.00
68 Juan Gonzalez/25 40.00
71 Andruw Jones/25 30.00
76 Jorge Posada/25 40.00
78 Stan Musial/50 75.00
79 Mark Teixeira/23 35.00
83 Nolan Ryan/50 90.00
87 Bob Gibson/25 40.00
88 Dale Murphy/50 35.00
90 Carl Yastrzemski/25 60.00
91 Sammy Sosa/50 125.00
92 Miguel Cabrera/24 50.00
94 George Brett/25 100.00
95 Rickey Henderson/25 25.00
97 Greg Maddux/31 75.00
100 Dontrelle Willis/35 30.00

Signature Silver

NM/M
Quantity produced listed
2 Garret Anderson/10 10.00
6 Mark Prior/22 80.00
17 Vladimir Guerrero/27 50.00
20 Don Mattingly/23 90.00
27 Gary Sheffield/25 35.00
44 Tony Gwynn/19 75.00
47 Delmon Young/25 30.00
68 Juan Gonzalez/22 35.00
76 Jorge Posada/20 40.00
78 Stan Musial/25 75.00
83 Nolan Ryan/34 120.00
88 Dale Murphy/25 40.00
91 Sammy Sosa/21 125.00

2004 DONRUSS TIMELINES

NM/M
Complete Set (50): 40.00
Common Player: .75
Pack (5): 40.00
Box (4): 120.00
1 Adam Dunn .75
2 Albert Pujols 3.00
3 Alex Rodriguez 3.00
4 Alfonso Soriano 1.50
5 Andruw Jones 1.00
6 Austin Kearns .75
7 Miguel Cabrera 1.00
8 Barry Zito .75
9 Carlos Beltran .75
10 Carlos Delgado 1.00
11 Chipper Jones 2.00
12 Curt Schilling 1.00
13 Derek Jeter 4.00
14 Frank Thomas 1.00
15 Garret Anderson .75
16 Gary Sheffield .75
17 Greg Maddux 2.00
18 Hank Blalock .75
19 Hideki Matsui 3.00
20 Hideo Nomo .75
21 Ichiro Suzuki 2.00
22 Ivan Rodriguez 1.00
23 Jason Giambi 1.50
24 Jeff Bagwell 1.00
25 Jim Thome 1.50
26 Juan Gonzalez .75
27 Ken Griffey Jr. 2.00
28 Kevin Brown .75
29 Kerry Wood 1.00
30 Lance Berkman .75
31 Magglio Ordonez .75
32 Manny Ramirez 1.00
33 Mark Prior 3.00
34 Mike Mussina 1.00
35 Mike Piazza 2.00
36 Nomar Garciaparra 3.00
37 Pedro J. Martinez 1.50
38 Rafael Palmeiro 1.00
39 Randy Johnson 1.50
40 Richie Sexson .75
41 Roger Clemens 3.00
42 Roy Halladay .75
43 Sammy Sosa 2.50
44 Scott Rolen 1.50
45 Shawn Green .75
46 Tim Hudson .75
47 Todd Helton 1.00
48 Torii Hunter .75
49 Vernon Wells .75
50 Vladimir Guerrero 1.50

Silver

Cards (1-50): 2X
Production 100 sets

Gold

Cards (1-50): 4-6X
Production 25 sets

Platinum

No Pricing
Production one set

Boys of Summer

NM/M
Complete Set (25): 75.00
Common Player: 3.00

Production 250 sets
Silver: 1-1.5x
Production 100 sets
Gold: 3-4X
Production 25 sets
Platinum: No Pricing
Production one set

1 Alan Trammell 5.00
2 Marty Marion 3.00
3 Andre Dawson 3.00
4 Bo Jackson 5.00
5 Cal Ripken Jr. 10.00
6 Steve Garvey 3.00
7 Dale Murphy 3.00
8 Darren Daulton 3.00
9 Darryl Strawberry 3.00
10 Dave Parker 3.00
11 Doc Gooden 3.00
12 Don Mattingly 6.00
13 Eric Davis 3.00
14 Dwight Evans 3.00
15 Fred Lynn 3.00
16 Graig Nettles 3.00
17 Jay Buhner 3.00
18 Jim Rice 3.00
19 Jose Canseco 3.00
20 Keith Hernandez 3.00
21 Rickey Henderson 3.00
22 Jack Morris 3.00
23 Tony Gwynn 4.00
24 Vida Blue 3.00
25 Will Clark 3.00

Boys of Summer Autographs

NM/M
Common Autograph: 10.00
2 Marty Marion 10.00
3 Andre Dawson 15.00
6 Steve Garvey 12.00
8 Darren Daulton 10.00
9 Darryl Strawberry 15.00
10 Dave Parker 10.00
11 Doc Gooden 15.00
13 Eric Davis 10.00
15 Fred Lynn 12.00
16 Graig Nettles 15.00
17 Jay Buhner 15.00
20 Keith Hernandez 12.00
22 Jack Morris 12.00
24 Vida Blue 12.00

Boys of Summer Silver Autographs

NM/M
Common Autograph: 12.00
Production 100
2 Marty Marion 12.00
3 Andre Dawson 15.00
6 Steve Garvey 20.00
8 Darren Daulton 12.00
9 Darryl Strawberry 18.00
10 Dave Parker 12.00
11 Doc Gooden 20.00
12 Don Mattingly 65.00
13 Eric Davis 12.00
15 Fred Lynn 15.00
16 Graig Nettles 15.00
18 Jim Rice 20.00
20 Keith Hernandez 15.00
22 Jack Morris 15.00
24 Vida Blue 15.00

Boys of Summer Gold Autographs

NM/M
Common Autograph: 20.00
Production 25
1 Alan Trammell 35.00
2 Marty Marion 20.00
3 Andre Dawson 20.00
6 Steve Garvey 20.00
8 Darren Daulton 20.00
9 Darryl Strawberry 20.00
10 Dave Parker 20.00
11 Doc Gooden 20.00
12 Don Mattingly 75.00
13 Eric Davis 20.00
14 Dwight Evans 25.00
15 Fred Lynn 25.00
16 Graig Nettles 20.00
17 Jay Buhner 25.00
18 Jim Rice 25.00
20 Keith Hernandez 20.00
22 Jack Morris 20.00
24 Vida Blue 20.00
25 Will Clark 100.00

Boys of Summer Platinum Autographs

No Pricing
Production one set

Boys of Summer Materials

NM/M
Common Player: 5.00
Combos: 1-2X
Production 100 sets
Prime: 1-2X
Production 100 sets
3 Andre Dawson 5.00
4 Bo Jackson 10.00
5 Cal Ripken Jr. 20.00
7 Dale Murphy 6.00
9 Darryl Strawberry 5.00
11 Doc Gooden 5.00
12 Don Mattingly 15.00
19 Jose Canseco 6.00
21 Rickey Henderson 8.00
22 Jack Morris 5.00
23 Tony Gwynn 8.00
25 Will Clark 8.00

Boys of Summer Combo Materials

NM/M
Production 100 sets
3 Andre Dawson 10.00
4 Bo Jackson 15.00
5 Cal Ripken Jr. 30.00
7 Dale Murphy 10.00
12 Don Mattingly 25.00
19 Jose Canseco 10.00
21 Rickey Henderson 15.00
23 Tony Gwynn 10.00
25 Will Clark 10.00

Boys of Summer Material Autographs

NM/M
Varying quantities produced
3 Andre Dawson/50 25.00
9 Darryl Strawberry/150 25.00
11 Doc Gooden/100 25.00
12 Don Mattingly/25 80.00
22 Jack Morris/150 12.00

Boys of Summer Prime Materials

NM/M
Common Player: 8.00
Production 100 sets
3 Andre Dawson 8.00
4 Bo Jackson 15.00
5 Cal Ripken Jr. 30.00
9 Darryl Strawberry 8.00
11 Doc Gooden 8.00
12 Don Mattingly 25.00
21 Rickey Henderson 15.00
23 Tony Gwynn 12.00
25 Will Clark 12.00

Call to the Hall

NM/M
Complete Set (25): 80.00
Common Player: 3.00
Production 250 sets
Silver: 1X
Production 100 sets
Gold: 3-4X
Production 25 sets
Platinum: No Pricing
Production one set
1 Babe Ruth 10.00
2 Billy Williams 3.00
3 Bob Feller 3.00
4 Bobby Doerr 3.00
5 Carlton Fisk 3.00
6 Gary Carter 3.00
7 George Brett 8.00
8 Carl Yastrzemski 5.00
9 Harmon Killebrew 5.00
10 Jim Palmer 3.00
11 Joe Morgan 3.00
12 Johnny Bench 5.00
13 Kirby Puckett 5.00
14 Gaylord Perry 3.00
15 Mike Schmidt 6.00
16 Nolan Ryan 10.00
17 Ozzie Smith 5.00
18 Phil Rizzuto 3.00
19 Reggie Jackson 4.00
20 Roberto Clemente 6.00
21 Robin Yount 4.00
22 Rod Carew 3.00
23 Rollie Fingers 3.00
24 Steve Carlton 3.00
25 Tom Seaver 4.00

Call to the Hall Autographs

NM/M
Common Autograph: 15.00
Silver Autos: 1X
Production 100
3 Bob Feller 15.00
4 Bobby Doerr 15.00
14 Gaylord Perry 15.00
23 Rollie Fingers 15.00

Call to the Hall Gold Autographs

NM/M
Production 25 sets
2 Billy Williams 25.00
3 Bob Feller 40.00
4 Bobby Doerr
6 Gary Carter 40.00
10 Jim Palmer 30.00
14 Gaylord Perry
18 Phil Rizzuto 40.00
23 Rollie Fingers
24 Steve Carlton 40.00

Call to the Hall Materials

NM/M
Common Player: 6.00
1 Babe Ruth/50 575.00
4 Bobby Doerr 6.00
6 Gary Carter 8.00
7 George Brett 12.00
8 Carl Yastrzemski 12.00
13 Kirby Puckett 10.00
15 Mike Schmidt 12.00
16 Nolan Ryan 20.00
17 Ozzie Smith 8.00
19 Reggie Jackson 8.00
20 Roberto Clemente/100 50.00

Call to the Hall Combo Materials

NM/M
Production 125 sets
6 Gary Carter 12.00
7 George Brett 25.00
13 Kirby Puckett 20.00
15 Mike Schmidt 25.00
16 Nolan Ryan 35.00
19 Reggie Jackson 20.00

Call to the Hall Material Autographs

NM/M
Varying quantities produced
4 Bobby Doerr/100 25.00
6 Gary Carter/25 45.00
7 George Brett/5
8 Carl Yastrzemski/5
13 Kirby Puckett/5
16 Nolan Ryan/5
17 Ozzie Smith/5
19 Reggie Jackson/25 50.00

Gold Autographs

NM/M
Production 25 sets 30.00
1 Adam Dunn 40.00
7 Miguel Cabrera 80.00
9 Carlos Beltran 40.00
15 Garret Anderson 30.00
18 Hank Blalock 35.00
22 Ivan Rodriguez 60.00
26 Juan Gonzalez 50.00
31 Magglio Ordonez 40.00
33 Mark Prior 85.00
44 Scott Rolen 45.00
48 Torii Hunter 35.00
49 Vernon Wells 30.00
50 Vladimir Guerrero 70.00

Platinum Autographs

No Pricing
Production one set

Materials

NM/M
Common Player: 5.00
Combos: 1-2X
Production 125
Primes: 1-2X
Production 125
1 Adam Dunn 5.00
2 Albert Pujols 12.00
3 Alex Rodriguez 10.00
4 Alfonso Soriano 8.00
5 Andruw Jones 5.00
7 Miguel Cabrera/SP 10.00
10 Carlos Delgado 5.00
11 Chipper Jones 8.00
14 Frank Thomas 8.00
17 Greg Maddux 8.00
20 Hideo Nomo 6.00
22 Ivan Rodriguez 6.00
23 Jason Giambi 6.00
24 Jeff Bagwell 6.00
25 Jim Thome 8.00
26 Juan Gonzalez 6.00
30 Lance Berkman 5.00
33 Mark Prior 20.00
35 Mike Piazza 8.00
36 Nomar Garciaparra 10.00
37 Pedro J. Martinez 8.00
39 Randy Johnson 6.00
41 Roger Clemens 10.00
43 Sammy Sosa 10.00
45 Shawn Green 5.00
47 Todd Helton 6.00
49 Vernon Wells 5.00

Materials Autographs

NM/M
Varying quantities produced
7 Miguel Cabrera/25 85.00
22 Ivan Rodriguez/25 65.00
33 Mark Prior/50 125.00
49 Vernon Wells/25 25.00

Materials Combo

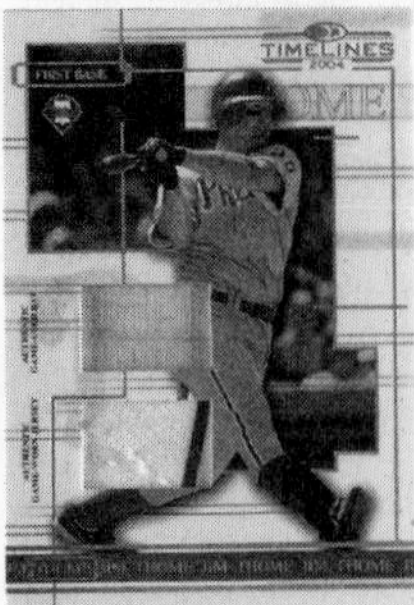

		NM/M
Common Player:		8.00
Production 125 sets		
1	Adam Dunn	8.00
2	Albert Pujols	20.00
3	Alex Rodriguez	15.00
4	Alfonso Soriano	10.00
5	Andruw Jones	8.00
7	Miguel Cabrera	20.00
11	Chipper Jones	15.00
14	Frank Thomas	12.00
17	Greg Maddux	15.00
20	Hideo Nomo	10.00
25	Jim Thome	12.00
30	Lance Berkman	8.00
33	Mark Prior	30.00
35	Mike Piazza	15.00
36	Nomar Garciaparra	15.00
37	Pedro J. Martinez	12.00
39	Randy Johnson	10.00
41	Roger Clemens	15.00
43	Sammy Sosa	15.00
45	Shawn Green	10.00
47	Todd Helton	10.00

Materials Prime

		NM/M
Common Player:		8.00
Production 125 sets		
1	Adam Dunn	8.00
2	Albert Pujols	20.00
3	Alex Rodriguez	20.00
4	Alfonso Soriano	10.00
5	Andruw Jones	8.00
7	Miguel Cabrera	20.00
10	Carlos Delgado	8.00
11	Chipper Jones	15.00
14	Frank Thomas	12.00
17	Greg Maddux	15.00
20	Hideo Nomo	10.00
25	Jim Thome	12.00
30	Lance Berkman	8.00
33	Mark Prior	30.00
35	Mike Piazza	15.00
36	Nomar Garciaparra	15.00
37	Pedro J. Martinez	12.00
39	Randy Johnson	10.00
41	Roger Clemens	15.00
43	Sammy Sosa	15.00
45	Shawn Green	10.00
47	Todd Helton	10.00
49	Vernon Wells	8.00

2004 DONRUSS WORLD SERIES

		NM/M
Complete Set (200):		
Common Player:		.15
Common SP (176-200):		8.00
Pack (6):		6.00
Box (24):		120.00
1	Bartolo Colon	.15
2	Darin Erstad	.25
3	Garret Anderson	.25
4	Tim Salmon	.25
5	Troy Glaus	.25
6	Vladimir Guerrero	.75
7	Brandon Webb	.15
8	Luis Gonzalez	.15
9	Randy Johnson	.75
10	Roberto Alomar	.40
11	Shea Hillenbrand	.15
12	Steve Finley	.15
13	Andruw Jones	.40
14	Chipper Jones	.75
15	J.D. Drew	.25
16	Marcus Giles	.15
17	Rafael Furcal	.25
18	Javy Lopez	.25
19	Jay Gibbons	.15
20	Luis Matos	.15
21	Melvin Mora	.15
22	Miguel Tejada	.40
23	Rafael Palmeiro	.50
24	Curt Schilling	.75
25	Dwight Evans	.15
26	Fred Lynn	.15
27	Jason Varitek	.25
28	Jim Rice	.25
29	Johnny Damon	.40
30	Luis Tiant	.15
31	Manny Ramirez	.50
32	Nomar Garciaparra	1.00
33	Pedro Martinez	.75
34	Trot Nixon	.15
35	Aramis Ramirez	.25
36	Corey Patterson	.25
37	Derrek Lee	.25
38	Greg Maddux	1.00
39	Kerry Wood	.75
40	Mark Prior	.75
41	Moises Alou	.25
42	Sammy Sosa	1.50
43	Carlos Lee	.15
44	Frank Thomas	.50
45	Luis Aparicio	.15
46	Magglio Ordonez	.25
47	Mark Buehrle	.15
48	Paul Konerko	.25
49	Adam Dunn	.50
50	Austin Kearns	.15
51	Barry Larkin	.25
52	Dave Concepcion	.15
53	George Foster	.15
54	Joe Morgan	.15
55	Sean Casey	.25
56	Tony Perez	.15
57	C.C. Sabathia	.15
58	Jody Gerut	.15
59	Omar Vizquel	.15
60	Victor Martinez	.15
61	Charles Johnson	.15
62	Jeromy Burnitz	.15
63	Larry Walker	.25
64	Preston Wilson	.15
65	Todd Helton	.50
66	Alan Trammell	.15
67	Dmitri Young	.15
68	Ivan Rodriguez	.50
69	Jeremy Bonderman	.15
70	A.J. Burnett	.15
71	Brad Penny	.15
72	Dontrelle Willis	.15
73	Josh Beckett	.40
74	Juan Pierre	.15
75	Luis Castillo	.15
76	Miguel Cabrera	.75
77	Mike Lowell	.25
78	Andy Pettitte	.25
79	Craig Biggio	.25
80	Jeff Bagwell	.50
81	Jeff Kent	.25
82	Lance Berkman	.25
83	Roger Clemens	2.00
84	Roy Oswalt	.25
85	Wade Miller	.15
86	Angel Berroa	.15
87	Carlos Beltran	.50
88	Juan Gonzalez	.40
89	Ken Harvey	.15
90	Mike Sweeney	.15
91	Adrian Beltre	.40
92	Hideo Nomo	.40
93	Kazuhisa Ishii	.15
94	Milton Bradley	.15
95	Orel Hershiser	.15
96	Paul LoDuca	.15
97	Shawn Green	.25
98	Ben Sheets	.25
99	Geoff Jenkins	.15
100	Junior Spivey	.15
101	Rickie Weeks	.15
102	Scott Podsednik	.15
103	Jack Morris	.15
104	Jacque Jones	.15
105	Johan Santana	.50
106	Shannon Stewart	.15
107	Torii Hunter	.25
108	Jose Vidro	.15
109	Orlando Cabrera	.25
110	Al Leiter	.25
111	Darryl Strawberry	.25
112	Dwight Gooden	.15
113	Jose Reyes	.15
114	*Kazuo Matsui*	2.00
115	Keith Hernandez	.15
116	Lenny Dykstra	.15
117	Mike Piazza	1.00
118	Tom Glavine	.40
119	Alex Rodriguez	2.00
120	Bernie Williams	.40
121	Derek Jeter	2.00
122	Gary Sheffield	.50
123	Jason Giambi	.25
124	Javier Vazquez	.25
125	Jorge Posada	.25
126	Kenny Lofton	.15
127	Kevin Brown	.25
128	Mariano Rivera	.25
129	Mike Mussina	.40
130	Barry Zito	.25
131	Eric Chavez	.25
132	Jermaine Dye	.15
133	Mark Mulder	.25
134	Rich Harden	.25
135	Tim Hudson	.25
136	Brett Myers	.15
137	Jim Thome	.75
138	Kevin Millwood	.15
139	Marlon Byrd	.15
140	Mike Lieberthal	.15
141	Pat Burrell	.15
142	Steve Carlton	.25
143	Dave Parker	.15
144	Jason Kendall	.15
145	Brian Giles	.15
146	Jay Payton	.15
147	Ryan Klesko	.15
148	J.T. Snow	.15
149	Jason Schmidt	.25
150	Bret Boone	.15
151	Edgar Martinez	.25
152	Jamie Moyer	.15
153	Rich Aurilia	.15
154	Shigetoshi Hasegawa	.15
155	Albert Pujols	2.00
156	Dan Haren	.15
157	Edgar Renteria	.25
158	Fernando Vina	.15
159	Jim Edmonds	.40
160	Matt Morris	.15
161	Scott Rolen	.75
162	Aubrey Huff	.15
163	Carl Crawford	.15
164	Dewon Brazelton	.15
165	Fred McGriff	.25
166	Rocco Baldelli	.15
167	Alfonso Soriano	.75
168	Hank Blalock	.50
169	Kenny Rogers	.15
170	Mark Teixeira	.25
171	Michael Young	.15
172	Carlos Delgado	.40
173	Eric Hinske	.15
174	Roy Halladay	.15
175	Vernon Wells	.15
176	*Ivan Ochoa Auto/487*	8.00
177	*Jason Bartlett Auto/1000*	8.00
178	*Josh Labandeira Auto/703*	8.00
179	*Phil Stockman Auto/1000*	8.00
180	*Ronny Cedeno Auto/715*	8.00
181	*Shawn Camp Auto/1000*	8.00
182	Ruddy Yan Auto/1000	8.00
183	*Roberto Novoa Auto/568*	10.00
184	*Justin Knoedler Auto/1000*	8.00
185	*Jesse Harper Auto/1000*	8.00
186	*Jason Szuminski Auto/1000*	8.00
187	*Jamie Brown Auto/800*	8.00
188	*Eddy Rodriguez Auto/1000*	8.00
189	*Dennis Sarfate Auto/1000*	8.00
190	*Ryan Meaux Auto/1000*	8.00
191	*Charles Thomas Auto/1000*	10.00
192	*Frank Francisco Auto/1000*	8.00
193	*Orlando Rodriguez Auto/500*	8.00
194	*Joey Gathright Auto/1000*	10.00
195	*Renyel Pinto Auto/1000*	10.00
196	*Justin Leone Auto/1000*	10.00
197	*Tim Bausher Auto/834*	8.00
198	*Travis Blackley Auto/1000*	10.00
199	*Yadier Molina Auto/500*	15.00
200	*Brad Halsey Auto/500*	10.00

Blue

		NM/M
Complete Set (100):		50.00
Common Player:		.50
Inserted 1:1		
HoloFoil 100:		2-4X
Production 100 sets		
HoloFoil 50:		4-6X
Production 50 sets		
HoloFoil 25:		6-10X
Production 25 sets		
HoloFoil 10:		No Pricing
Production 10 sets		
1	Josh Beckett	.50
2	Miguel Cabrera	1.00
3	Derrek Lee	.50
4	Mike Lowell	.50
5	Brad Penny	.50
6	Ivan Rodriguez	1.00
7	Dontrelle Willis	.50
8	Luis Castillo	.50
9	Garret Anderson	.75
10	Troy Glaus	.75
11	John Lackey	.50
12	Chone Figgins	.50
13	Tim Salmon	.50
14	Darin Erstad	.50
15	Troy Percival	.50
16	Steve Finley	.50
17	Mark Grace	.75
18	Randy Johnson	1.00
19	Curt Schilling	1.00
20	Luis Gonzalez	.50
21	Andy Pettitte	.75
22	Bernie Williams	.75
23	Jorge Posada	.75
24	Mariano Rivera	.75
25	Roger Clemens	3.00
26	Jose Canseco	1.00
27	David Justice	.50
28	Paul O'Neill	.75
29	Darryl Strawberry	.50
30	David Wells	.50
31	Wade Boggs	.75
32	Charles Johnson	.50
33	Cliff Floyd	.50
34	Moises Alou	.50
35	Edgar Renteria	.75
36	Chipper Jones	1.50
37	Tom Glavine	.75
38	John Smoltz	.75
39	Greg Maddux	1.50
40	Ryan Klesko	.50
41	Javy Lopez	.50
42	Fred McGriff	.50
43	Roberto Alomar	.75
44	Joe Carter	.50
45	Rickey Henderson	.50
46	Paul Molitor	1.00
47	Jack Morris	.50
48	Jack Morris	.50
49	Kirby Puckett	1.50
50	Eric Davis	.50
51	Barry Larkin	.75
52	Paul O'Neill	.75
53	Dennis Eckersley	.75
54	Jose Canseco	1.00
55	Rickey Henderson	.75
56	Dave Parker	.50
57	Orel Hershiser	.50
58	Kirk Gibson	.50
59	Bert Blyleven	.50
60	Dwight Gooden	.50

61	Gary Carter	.50
62	Lenny Dykstra	.50
63	Keith Hernandez	.50
64	Darryl Strawberry	.50
65	George Brett	3.00
66	Kirk Gibson	.50
67	Alan Trammell	.50
68	Jim Palmer	.75
69	Eddie Murray	.75
70	Cal Ripken Jr.	5.00
71	Keith Hernandez	.50
72	Ozzie Smith	1.50
73	Steve Garvey	.50
74	Steve Carlton	1.00
75	Mike Schmidt	4.00
76	John Candelaria	.50
77	Bert Blyleven	.50
78	Dave Parker	.50
79	Willie Stargell	1.00
80	Reggie Jackson	1.00
81	Johnny Bench	2.00
82	Dave Concepcion	.50
83	George Foster	.50
84	Joe Morgan	.50
85	Tony Perez	.50
86	Rollie Fingers	.50
87	Jim "Catfish" Hunter	.50
88	Reggie Jackson	1.00
89	Al Oliver	.50
90	Roberto Clemente	3.00
91	Willie Stargell	.75
92	Brooks Robinson	1.00
93	Frank Robinson	.75
94	Nolan Ryan	4.00
95	Tom Seaver	1.50
96	Al Kaline	1.00
97	Bob Gibson	1.00
98	Lou Brock	.75
99	Orlando Cepeda	.50
100	Duke Snider	1.00

Blue Material Bat

		NM/M
Common Player:		5.00
Production 50 sets		
1	Josh Beckett	8.00
2	Miguel Cabrera	12.00
3	Derrek Lee	8.00
4	Mike Lowell	5.00
5	Brad Penny	5.00
6	Ivan Rodriguez	12.00
8	Luis Castillo	5.00
9	Garret Anderson	5.00
10	Troy Glaus	8.00
13	Tim Salmon	5.00
14	Darin Erstad	5.00
17	Mark Grace	12.00
19	Curt Schilling	12.00
20	Luis Gonzalez	5.00
21	Andy Pettitte	5.00
22	Bernie Williams	8.00
23	Jorge Posada	10.00
25	Roger Clemens	20.00
27	David Justice	5.00
28	Paul O'Neill	10.00
29	Darryl Strawberry	10.00
31	Wade Boggs	15.00
32	Charles Johnson	5.00
33	Cliff Floyd	5.00
34	Moises Alou	8.00
35	Edgar Renteria	8.00
36	Chipper Jones	15.00
37	Tom Glavine	10.00
39	Greg Maddux	20.00
40	Ryan Klesko	5.00
41	Javy Lopez	5.00
42	Fred McGriff	8.00
43	Roberto Alomar	8.00
44	Joe Carter	5.00
45	Rickey Henderson	15.00
46	Paul Molitor	15.00
49	Kirby Puckett	15.00
50	Eric Davis	5.00
51	Barry Larkin	8.00
52	Paul O'Neill	8.00
55	Rickey Henderson	15.00
56	Dave Parker	8.00
58	Kirk Gibson	10.00
60	Dwight Gooden	8.00
61	Gary Carter	8.00
62	Lenny Dykstra	5.00
63	Keith Hernandez	5.00
64	Darryl Strawberry	5.00
65	George Brett	25.00
66	Kirk Gibson	8.00
67	Alan Trammell	8.00
69	Eddie Murray	20.00
70	Cal Ripken Jr.	70.00
71	Keith Hernandez	8.00
72	Ozzie Smith	20.00
73	Steve Garvey	5.00
74	Steve Carlton	10.00
75	Mike Schmidt	25.00
78	Dave Parker	8.00
79	Willie Stargell	15.00
80	Reggie Jackson	15.00
81	Johnny Bench	20.00
82	Dave Concepcion	5.00
83	George Foster	5.00
84	Joe Morgan	8.00
85	Tony Perez	8.00
88	Reggie Jackson	15.00
89	Al Oliver	5.00
90	Roberto Clemente	60.00
91	Willie Stargell	15.00
92	Brooks Robinson	15.00
93	Frank Robinson	10.00
96	Al Kaline	15.00
98	Lou Brock	15.00
99	Orlando Cepeda	10.00

Blue Material Fabric

		NM/M
Common Player:		4.00
Quantity produced listed		
1	Josh Beckett Jsy/103	4.00
2	Miguel Cabrera Jsy/103	8.00
3	Derrek Lee Jsy/103	6.00
4	Mike Lowell Jsy/103	4.00
5	Brad Penny Jsy/103	4.00
6	Ivan Rodriguez Jsy/103	8.00
7	Dontrelle Willis Jsy/103	4.00
9	Garret Anderson Jsy/102	4.00
10	Troy Glaus Jsy/102	4.00
13	Tim Salmon Jsy/102	4.00
14	Darin Erstad Jsy/102	4.00
15	Tony Percival Jsy/102	4.00
16	Steve Finley Jsy/101	4.00
18	Randy Johnson Pants/101	8.00
19	Curt Schilling Jsy/101	8.00
20	Luis Gonzalez Jsy/101	4.00
21	Andy Pettitte Jsy/100	6.00
22	Bernie Williams Jsy/100	6.00
24	Mariano Rivera Jsy/100	6.00
25	Roger Clemens Jsy/100	12.00
29	Darryl Strawberry Jsy/99	6.00
30	David Wells Jsy/99	4.00
31	Wade Boggs Jsy/96	8.00
32	Charles Johnson Jsy/97	4.00
33	Cliff Floyd Jsy/97	4.00
36	Chipper Jones Jsy/95	8.00
37	Tom Glavine Jsy/95	6.00
39	Greg Maddux Jsy/95	10.00
40	Ryan Klesko Jsy/95	4.00
41	Javy Lopez Jsy/95	4.00
51	Barry Larkin Jsy/90	8.00
54	Jose Canseco Jsy/89	10.00
55	Rickey Henderson Jsy/89	12.00
57	Orel Hershiser Jsy/88	8.00
59	Bert Blyleven Jsy/87	6.00
60	Dwight Gooden Jsy/86	6.00
61	Gary Carter Jkt/86	6.00
64	Darryl Strawberry Jsy/86	6.00
65	George Brett Jsy/85	20.00
68	Jim Palmer Pants/83	8.00
69	Eddie Murray Jsy/83	15.00
70	Cal Ripken Jr. Jsy/83	40.00
71	Keith Hernandez Jsy/82	6.00
74	Steve Carlton Jsy/80	6.00
75	Mike Schmidt Jkt/80	15.00
78	Dave Parker Jsy/79	6.00
79	Willie Stargell Jsy/79	8.00
80	Reggie Jackson Jsy/78	8.00
81	Johnny Bench Jsy/75	12.00
82	Dave Concepcion Jsy/75	4.00
83	George Foster Jsy/75	4.00
86	Rollie Fingers Jsy/74	4.00
87	Jim "Catfish" Hunter Jsy/74	8.00
88	Reggie Jackson Jkt/73	8.00
91	Willie Stargell Jsy/71	8.00
98	Lou Brock Jkt/67	8.00
100	Duke Snider Pants/55	10.00

Blue Signature

		NM/M
Quantity produced listed		
2	Miguel Cabrera/25	40.00
3	Derrek Lee/25	30.00
5	Brad Penny/25	15.00
9	Garret Anderson/25	20.00
11	John Lackey/50	10.00
12	Chone Figgins/25	15.00
16	Steve Finley/25	20.00
29	Darryl Strawberry/25	20.00
42	Fred McGriff/25	40.00
47	Jack Morris/25	20.00
48	Jack Morris/25	20.00
50	Eric Davis/25	25.00
53	Dennis Eckersley/25	40.00
56	Dave Parker/25	20.00
59	Bert Blyleven/25	25.00
60	Dwight Gooden/25	25.00
62	Lenny Dykstra/25	25.00
63	Keith Hernandez/25	25.00
64	Darryl Strawberry/25	25.00
67	Alan Trammell/25	25.00
68	Jim Palmer/25	25.00
71	Keith Hernandez/25	25.00
76	John Candelaria/25	25.00
77	Bert Blyleven/25	25.00
78	Dave Parker/25	20.00
82	Dave Concepcion/25	20.00
83	George Foster/25	20.00
85	Tony Perez/25	35.00
86	Rollie Fingers/25	25.00
89	Al Oliver/25	25.00

HoloFoil 100

HoloFoil (1-175): 4-8X
HoloFoil (176-200): .5X
Production 100 sets

HoloFoil 50

HoloFoil (1-175): 6-12X
HoloFoil (176-200): .75X
Production 50 sets

HoloFoil 25

HoloFoil (1-175): 10-20X
HoloFoil (176-200): No Pricing
Production 25 sets

HoloFoil 10

No Pricing
Production 10 sets

Face Off Material

		NM/M
Common Duo:		10.00
Quantity produced listed		
1	Roger Clemens Jsy, Mike Piazza Jsy/100	25.00
2	Mike Mussina Jsy, Ivan Rodriguez Jsy/100	20.00
3	Mark Grace Jsy, Jorge Posada Jsy/10	
4	Greg Maddux Jsy, Jim Thome Jsy/25	35.00
5	Rickey Henderson Jsy, Curt Schilling Jsy/100	15.00
6	Kirby Puckett Jsy, Tom Glavine Jsy/100	25.00
8	Bernie Williams Jsy, Randy Johnson Pants/100	20.00
9	Cal Ripken Jr. Jsy, Steve Carlton Jsy/50	75.00
11	Mike Schmidt Jkt, George Brett Jsy/50	40.00
13	Dwight Gooden Jsy, Dwight Evans Jsy/50	25.00
15	Jim Palmer Jsy, Dave Parker Jsy/50	10.00
17	Carl Yastrzemski Jsy, Lou Brock Jkt/50	40.00
18	Duke Snider Pants, Whitey Ford Jsy/50	25.00
19	Carlton Fisk Jsy, Tony Perez Fld Glv/50	20.00
20	Roberto Clemente Jsy, Frank Robinson Jsy/10	

Fans of the Game

		NM/M
Complete Set (5):		8.00
Common Player:		1.50
Inserted 1:24		
1	Val Kilmer	2.00
2	Stan Lee	2.00
3	Apolo Anton Ohno	1.50
4	Gene Shalit	1.50
5	Leeann Tweeden	1.50

Fans of the Game Signatures

		NM/M
Common Autograph:		20.00
1	Val Kilmer	50.00
2	Stan Lee	50.00
3	Apolo Anton Ohno	30.00
4	Gene Shalit	20.00
5	Leeann Tweeden	35.00

Legends of the Fall

		NM/M
Complete Set (20):		75.00
Common Player:		3.00
Production 500 sets		
HoloFoil:		2-4X
Production 25 sets		
1	Bob Gibson	4.00
2	Brooks Robinson	4.00
3	Cal Ripken Jr.	12.00
4	Carl Yastrzemski	6.00
5	Carlton Fisk	4.00
6	Derek Jeter	8.00
7	Duke Snider	4.00
8	Eddie Murray	4.00
9	Frank Robinson	3.00
10	Gary Carter	3.00
11	George Brett	8.00
12	Jim Palmer	3.00
13	Johnny Bench	4.00
14	Marco Rivera	3.00
15	Mike Schmidt	8.00
16	Phil Rizzuto	3.00
17	Red Schoendienst	3.00
18	Reggie Jackson	4.00
19	Rickey Henderson	3.00
20	Whitey Ford	4.00

Legends of the Fall Material

		NM/M
Common Player:		5.00
Quantity produced listed		
1	Bob Gibson Jsy/50	12.00
2	Brooks Robinson Bat/100	10.00
3	Cal Ripken Jr. Jkt/100	40.00
4	Carl Yastrzemski Bat/50	10.00
5	Carlton Fisk Bat/50	10.00
7	Duke Snider Pants/50	15.00
8	Eddie Murray Jsy/50	15.00
9	Frank RobinsonBat/100	5.00
10	Gary Carter Jkt/100	5.00
11	George Brett Bat/50	25.00
12	Jim Palmer Pants/25	12.00
13	Johnny Bench Bat/100	12.00
14	Marco Rivera Jsy/100	8.00
15	Mike Schmidt Jkt/50	25.00
16	Phil Rizzuto Pants/50	10.00
17	Red Schoendienst Bat/100	5.00
18	Reggie Jackson Bat/100	10.00
19	Rickey Henderson Bat/100	10.00

Legends of the Fall Signature

NM/M

Common Player:
2 Brooks Robinson/25 30.00
9 Frank Robinson/25 35.00
10 Gary Carter/25 25.00
12 Jim Palmer/25 25.00
16 Phil Rizzuto/25 30.00
17 Red Schoendienst/50 20.00

Legends of the Fall Sign. Material

NM/M

Quantity produced listed
1 Bob Gibson Jsy/25 40.00
2 Brooks Robinson Bat/50 35.00
3 Cal Ripken Jr. Jkt/5
4 Carl Yastrzemski Bat/5
5 Carlton Fisk Bat/10
7 Duke Snider Pants/50 35.00
8 Eddie Murray Jsy/5
9 Frank Robinson Bat/50 30.00
10 Gary Carter Jkt/50 25.00
11 George Brett Bat/5
12 Jim Palmer Pants/25 25.00
13 Johnny Bench Bat/25 70.00
15 Mike Schmidt Jkt/10
16 Phil Rizzuto Pants/50 35.00
17 Red Schoendienst Bat/100 20.00
18 Reggie Jackson Bat/10
19 Rickey Henderson Bat/10

Material Fabric Number

NM/M

Common Player:
5 Troy Glaus Jsy/25 10.00
6 Vladimir Guerrero Jsy/27 20.00
7 Brandon Webb Pants/55 6.00
8 Luis Gonzalez Jsy/20 8.00
9 Randy Johnson Pants/51 15.00
13 Andruw Jones Jsy/25 10.00
16 Marcus Giles Jsy/22 8.00
19 Jay Gibbons Jsy/31 8.00
23 Rafael Palmeiro Jsy/25 15.00
25 Dwight Evans Jsy/24 15.00
26 Fred Lynn Jsy/19 10.00
30 Luis Tiant Jsy/23 8.00
31 Manny Ramirez Jsy/24 20.00
33 Pedro Martinez Jsy/45 15.00
38 Greg Maddux Jsy/31 20.00
39 Kerry Wood Pants/34 20.00
40 Mark Prior Jsy/22 20.00
42 Sammy Sosa Jsy/21 25.00
43 Carlos Lee Jsy/45 6.00
44 Frank Thomas Jsy/35 15.00
46 Magglio Ordonez Jsy/30 8.00
47 Mark Buehrle Jsy/56 6.00
49 Adam Dunn Jsy/44 12.00
50 Austin Kearns Jsy/28 10.00
57 C.C. Sabathia Jsy/52 6.00
60 Victor Martinez Jsy/41 8.00
63 Larry Walker Jsy/33 10.00
64 Preston Wilson Jsy/44 6.00
65 Todd Helton Jsy/17 25.00
70 A.J. Burnett Jsy/34 6.00
71 Brad Penny Jsy/31 6.00
72 Dontrelle Willis Jsy/35 6.00
73 Josh Beckett Jsy/21 15.00
76 Miguel Cabrera Jsy/24 20.00
90 Mike Sweeney Jsy/29 10.00
91 Adrian Beltre Jsy/29 15.00
95 Orel Hershiser Jsy/55 8.00
105 Johan Santana Jsy/57 15.00
106 Shannon Stewart Jsy/23 8.00
107 Torii Hunter Jsy/48 10.00
110 Al Leiter Jsy/22 10.00
117 Mike Piazza Jsy/31 20.00
118 Tom Glavine Jsy/47 12.00
120 Bernie Williams Jsy/51 12.00
123 Jason Giambi Jsy/25 10.00
125 Jorge Posada Jsy/20 15.00
128 Mariano Rivera Jsy/42 10.00
129 Mike Mussina Jsy/35 15.00
130 Barry Zito Jsy/75 8.00
133 Mark Mulder Jsy/20 15.00
136 Brett Myers Jsy/39 6.00
137 Jim Thome Jsy/25 20.00
138 Kevin Millwood Jsy/34 8.00
139 Marlon Byrd Jsy/29 8.00
142 Steve Carlton Jsy/32 12.00
143 Dave Parker Jsy/39 8.00
147 Ryan Klesko Jsy/30 10.00
152 Jamie Moyer Jsy/50 6.00
156 Dan Haren Jsy/55 6.00
159 Jim Edmonds Jsy/15 15.00
161 Scott Rolen Jsy/27 25.00
164 Dewon Brazelton Jsy/45 6.00
165 Fred McGriff Jsy/29 15.00
174 Roy HalladayJsy/32 8.00

Material Fabric AL/NL

NM/M

Common Player: 4.00
Production 250 unless noted
2 Darin Erstad Jsy 4.00
3 Garret Anderson Jsy 4.00
4 Tim Salmon Jsy 4.00
5 Troy Glaus Jsy 4.00
6 Vladimir Guerrero Jsy 8.00
7 Brandon Webb Pants 4.00
8 Luis Gonzalez Jsy 4.00
9 Randy Johnson Pants/100 10.00
12 Steve Finley Jsy 4.00
13 Andruw Jones Jsy 6.00
14 Chipper Jones Jsy 8.00
16 Marcus Giles Jsy 4.00
17 Rafael Furcal Jsy 4.00
19 Jay Gibbons Jsy 4.00
20 Luis Matos Jsy 4.00
21 Melvin Mora Jsy 4.00
22 Miguel Tejada Jsy 6.00
23 Rafael Palmeiro Jsy/100 8.00
25 Dwight Evans Jsy 4.00
26 Fred Lynn Jsy 4.00
28 Jim Rice Jsy 6.00
31 Manny Ramirez Jsy 8.00
33 Pedro Martinez Jsy 8.00
35 Aramis Ramirez Jsy 6.00
38 Greg Maddux Jsy/100 12.00
39 Kerry Wood Pants 8.00
40 Mark Prior Jsy 8.00
42 Sammy Sosa Jsy 10.00
43 Carlos Lee Jsy 4.00
44 Frank Thomas Jsy 8.00
47 Mark Buehrle Jsy 4.00
48 Paul Konerko Jsy 4.00
49 Adam Dunn Jsy 8.00
50 Austin Kearns Jsy 4.00
52 Dave Concepcion Jsy 4.00
57 C.C. Sabathia Jsy 4.00
58 Jody Gerut Jsy 4.00
59 Omar Vizquel Jsy 4.00
60 Victor Martinez Jsy 4.00
63 Larry Walker Jsy 8.00
64 Preston Wilson Jsy 4.00
65 Todd Helton Jsy 8.00
70 A.J. Burnett Jsy 4.00
71 Brad Penny Jsy 4.00
72 Dontrelle Willis Jsy 4.00
73 Josh Beckett Jsy 6.00
76 Miguel Cabrera Jsy 8.00
77 Mike Lowell Jsy 4.00
79 Craig Biggio Jsy 6.00
80 Jeff Bagwell Pants 8.00
81 Jeff Kent Jsy 4.00
82 Lance Berkman Jsy 4.00
86 Angel Berroa Pants 4.00
90 Mike Sweeney Jsy 4.00
91 Adrian Beltre Jsy 6.00
92 Hideo Nomo Jsy 8.00
93 Kazuhisa Ishii Jsy 4.00
95 Orel Hershiser Jsy/100 6.00
96 Paul LoDuca Jsy 4.00
97 Shawn Green Jsy 6.00
98 Ben Sheets Pants 4.00
99 Geoff Jenkins Jsy 4.00
104 Jacque Jones Jsy 4.00
105 Johan Santana Jsy 8.00
106 Shannon Stewart Jsy 4.00
110 Al Leiter Jsy 4.00
111 Darryl StrawberryJsy 4.00
117 Mike Piazza Jsy 10.00
118 Tom Glavine Jsy 8.00
120 Bernie Williams Jsy 6.00
123 Jason Giambi Jsy 4.00
128 Mariano Rivera Jsy 6.00
129 Mike Mussina Jsy 8.00
130 Barry Zito Jsy 4.00
131 Eric Chavez Jsy 4.00
133 Mark Mulder Jsy 4.00
135 Tim Hudson Jsy 4.00
136 Brett Myers Jsy 4.00
137 Jim Thome Jsy 8.00
138 Kevin Millwood Jsy 4.00
139 Marlon Byrd Jsy 4.00
141 Pat Burrell Jsy 4.00
142 Steve CarltonJsy/100 6.00
143 Dave Parker Jsy/100 4.00
147 Ryan Klesko Jsy 4.00
152 Jamie Moyer Jsy 4.00
155 Albert Pujols Jsy/100 15.00
156 Dan Haren Jsy 4.00
159 Jim Edmonds Jsy 6.00
161 Scott Rolen Jsy 8.00
162 Aubrey Huff Jsy 4.00
163 Carl Crawford Jsy 4.00
164 Dewon Brazelton Jsy 4.00
165 Fred McGriff Jsy 4.00
166 Rocco Baldelli Jsy 4.00
168 Hank Blalock Jsy 8.00
174 Roy Halladay Jsy 4.00
175 Vernon Wells Jsy 4.00

Material Bat

NM/M

Common Player: 4.00
Production 100 sets
2 Darin Erstad 4.00
3 Garret Anderson 4.00
4 Tim Salmon 4.00
5 Troy Glaus 4.00
6 Vladimir Guerrero 8.00
8 Luis Gonzalez 4.00
13 Andruw Jones 6.00
14 Chipper Jones 8.00
15 J.D. Drew 4.00
16 Marcus Giles 4.00
17 Rafael Furcal 4.00
18 Javy Lopez 4.00
19 Jay Gibbons 4.00
22 Miguel Tejada 6.00
23 Rafael Palmeiro 8.00
25 Dwight Evans 4.00
26 Fred Lynn 4.00
27 Jason Varitek 8.00
28 Jim Rice 6.00
29 Johnny Damon 10.00
31 Manny Ramirez 8.00
32 Nomar Garciaparra 10.00
33 Pedro Martinez 8.00
34 Trot Nixon 4.00
35 Aramis Ramirez 6.00
37 Derrek Lee 6.00
40 Mark Prior 8.00
41 Moises Alou 4.00
42 Sammy Sosa 12.00
43 Carlos Lee 4.00
44 Frank Thomas 8.00
45 Luis Aparicio 4.00
46 Magglio Ordonez 4.00
47 Mark Buehrle 4.00
48 Paul Konerko 4.00
49 Adam Dunn Jsy 8.00
50 Austin Kearns 4.00
51 Barry Larkin 8.00
52 Dave Concepcion 4.00
53 George Foster 4.00
54 Joe Morgan 6.00
55 Sean Casey 4.00
56 Tony Perez 4.00
59 Omar Vizquel 4.00
60 Victor Martinez 4.00
61 Charles Johnson 4.00
63 Larry Walker 8.00
64 Preston Wilson 4.00
65 Todd Helton 8.00
66 Alan Trammell 4.00
68 Ivan Rodriguez 8.00
71 Brad Penny 4.00
73 Josh Beckett 6.00
74 Juan Pierre 4.00
75 Luis Castillo 4.00
76 Miguel Cabrera 8.00
77 Mike Lowell 4.00
78 Andy Pettitte 6.00
79 Craig Biggio 6.00
80 Jeff Bagwell 8.00
81 Jeff Kent 4.00
82 Lance Berkman 4.00
83 Roger Clemens 15.00
84 Roy Oswalt 4.00
86 Angel Berroa 4.00
87 Carlos Beltran 8.00
88 Juan Gonzalez 6.00
89 Ken Harvey 4.00
90 Mike Sweeney 4.00
91 Adrian Beltre 6.00
93 Kazuhisa Ishii 4.00
96 Paul LoDuca 4.00
97 Shawn Green 4.00
98 Ben Sheets 4.00
99 Geoff Jenkins 4.00
104 Jacque Jones 4.00
106 Shannon Stewart 4.00
107 Torii Hunter 6.00
108 Jose Vidro 4.00
109 Orlando Cabrera 6.00
111 Darryl Strawberry 6.00
112 Dwight Gooden 6.00
113 Jose Reyes 4.00
114 Kazuo Matsui 10.00
115 Keith Hernandez 6.00
116 Lenny Dykstra 4.00
118 Tom Glavine 8.00
122 Gary Sheffield 8.00
123 Jason Giambi 4.00
125 Jorge Posada 8.00
126 Kenny Lofton 4.00
127 Kevin Brown 4.00
129 Mike Mussina 8.00
131 Eric Chavez 4.00
132 Jermaine Dye 4.00
133 Mark Mulder 4.00
135 Tim Hudson 6.00
137 Jim Thome 8.00
139 Marlon Byrd 4.00
141 Pat Burrell 4.00
142 Steve Carlton 6.00
143 Dave Parker 4.00
145 Brian Giles 4.00
147 Ryan Klesko 4.00
151 Edgar Martinez 4.00
153 Rich Aurilia 4.00
155 Albert Pujols 15.00
156 Dan Haren 4.00
157 Edgar Renteria 6.00
159 Jim Edmonds 6.00
161 Scott Rolen 8.00
162 Aubrey Huff 4.00
165 Fred McGriff 4.00
166 Rocco Baldelli 4.00
167 Alfonso Soriano 8.00
168 Hank Blalock 8.00
170 Mark Teixeira 6.00
171 Michael Young 4.00
172 Carlos Delgado 4.00
175 Vernon Wells 4.00

MVP

NM/M

Complete Set (15): 35.00
Common Player: 2.00
Production 1,000 sets
HoloFoil: 2-4X
Production 50 sets
1 Whitey Ford 3.00
2 Bob Gibson 3.00
3 Frank Robinson 2.00
4 Brooks Robinson 3.00
5 Roberto Clemente 6.00
6 Reggie Jackson 3.00
7 Rollie Fingers 2.00
8 Johnny Bench 4.00
9 Reggie Jackson 3.00
10 Mike Schmidt 6.00
11 Alan Trammell 2.00
12 Orel Hershiser 2.00
13 Jack Morris 2.00
14 Paul Molitor 4.00
15 Tom Glavine 3.00

MVP Material

NM/M

Quantity produced listed
1 Whitey Ford Jsy/50 10.00

2 Bob Gibson Jsy/50 10.00
3 Frank Robinson Jsy/25 12.00
5 Roberto Clemente Jsy/10
6 Reggie Jackson Jkt/100 10.00
7 Rollie Fingers Jsy/100 5.00
8 Johnny Bench Jsy/10
9 Reggie Jackson Jsy/25 20.00
10 Mike Schmidt Jsy/50 25.00
12 Orel Hershiser Jsy/100 5.00
15 Tom Glavine Jsy/100 8.00

MVP Signature Material

NM/M

Quantity produced listed
1 Whitey Ford Jsy/10
2 Bob Gibson Jsy/50 35.00
3 Frank Robinson Shoe/50 40.00
7 Rollie Fingers Jsy/100 15.00
8 Johnny Bench Jsy/5
10 Mike Schmidt Jkt/5
12 Orel Hershiser Jsy/25 25.00

October Heroes

NM/M

Complete Set (20): 40.00
Common Player: 2.00
Production 500 sets
HoloFoil: 2-4X
Production 25 sets
1 Alan Trammell 2.00
2 Andy Pettitte 3.00
3 Jim "Catfish" Hunter 2.00
4 Chipper Jones 4.00
5 Dave Concepcion 2.00
6 David Wells 2.00
7 Jack Morris 2.00
8 Joe Morgan 3.00
9 Josh Beckett 2.00
10 Kirby Puckett 4.00
11 Kirk Gibson 2.00
12 Marty Marion 2.00
13 Miguel Cabrera 4.00
14 Paul Molitor 4.00
15 Paul O'Neill 2.00
16 Randy Johnson 4.00
17 Roger Clemens 6.00
18 Steve Carlton 3.00
19 Steve Garvey 2.00
20 Wade Boggs 3.00

October Heroes Material

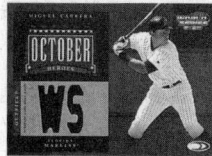

NM/M

Common Player: 4.00
1 Alan Trammell Jsy/25 10.00
2 Andy Pettitte Jsy/100 4.00
3 Jim "Catfish" Hunter Jsy/25 15.00
4 Chipper Jones Jsy/100 8.00
5 Dave Concepcion Jsy/100 4.00
6 David Wells Jsy/25 8.00
9 Josh Beckett Jsy/100 4.00
10 Kirby Puckett Jsy/25 25.00
12 Marty Marion Jsy/25 10.00
13 Miguel Cabrera Jsy/100 8.00
16 Randy Johnson Pants/50 12.00
17 Roger Clemens Jsy/100 12.00
18 Steve Carlton Jsy/100 6.00
19 Steve Garvey Jsy/100 4.00
20 Wade Boggs Jsy/100 8.00

October Heroes Signatures

NM/M

Quantity produced listed
1 Alan Trammell/25 25.00
5 Dave Concepcion/25 20.00
7 Jack Morris/25 20.00
12 Marty Marion/25 20.00
13 Miguel Cabrera/25 40.00
18 Steve Carlton/25 35.00
19 Steve Garvey/25 20.00

October Heroes Sign. Material

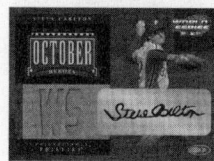

NM/M

Quantity produced listed
1 Alan Trammell Jsy/100 20.00
2 Andy Pettitte Jsy/10
5 Dave Concepcion Jsy/100 15.00
9 Josh Beckett Jsy/10
10 Kirby Puckett Jsy/10
12 Marty Marion Jsy/100 15.00
13 Miguel Cabrera Jsy/100 30.00
16 Randy Johnson Pants/5
17 Roger Clemens Jsy/5
18 Steve Carlton Jsy/50 35.00
19 Steve Garvey Jsy/100 15.00
20 Wade Boggs Jsy/5

October Legends

NM/M

Complete Set (20): 60.00
Common Player: 2.00
Production 500 sets
HoloFoil: 2-4X
Production 25 sets
1 Bob Gibson 4.00
2 Cal Ripken Jr. 10.00
3 Carl Yastrzemski 6.00
4 Carlton Fisk 3.00
5 Duke Snider 4.00
6 Eddie Murray 4.00
7 Frank Robinson 3.00
8 George Brett 8.00
9 Joe Morgan 2.00
10 Johnny Bench 4.00
11 Lou Brock 3.00
12 Mike Schmidt 8.00
13 Paul Molitor 4.00
14 Phil Rizzuto 3.00
15 Reggie Jackson 4.00
16 Robin Yount 4.00
17 Stan Musial 6.00
18 Steve Carlton 2.00
19 Whitey Ford 3.00
20 Willie McCovey 2.00

October Legends Materials

NM/M

Common Player: 5.00
Quantity produced listed
1 Bob Gibson Jsy/50 10.00
2 Cal Ripken Jr. Jsy/50 50.00
3 Carl Yastrzemski Jsy/50 20.00
4 Carlton Fisk Jsy/100 8.00
5 Duke Snider Jsy/25 20.00
6 Eddie Murray Jsy/100 10.00
7 Frank Robinson Jsy/50 8.00
8 George Brett Jsy/50 25.00
10 Johnny Bench Jsy/50 15.00
11 Lou Brock Jkt/100 8.00
12 Mike Schmidt Jkt/100 15.00
13 Paul Molitor Jsy/10
14 Phil Rizzuto Pants/25 15.00
15 Reggie Jackson Jkt/100 8.00
16 Robin Yount Jsy/100 10.00
17 Stan Musial Jsy/10
18 Steve Carlton Jsy/100 5.00
19 Whitey Ford Pants/25 15.00
20 Willie McCovey Jsy/25 15.00

October Legends Signature

NM/M

Quantity produced listed
11 Lou Brock/25 35.00
14 Phil Rizzuto/25 35.00
18 Steve Carlton/25 30.00

October Legends Sig. Material

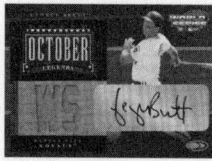

NM/M

Quantity produced listed
1 Bob Gibson Jsy/50 40.00
5 Duke Snider Jsy/50 40.00
7 Frank Robinson Jsy/50 30.00
11 Lou Brock Jkt/100 25.00
13 Paul Molitor Jsy/25 40.00
14 Phil Rizzuto Pants/50 30.00
16 Robin Yount Jsy/25 65.00
17 Stan Musial Jsy/25 90.00
18 Steve Carlton Jsy/100 25.00
19 Whitey Ford Pants/25 40.00
20 Willie McCovey Jsy/25 40.00

Playoff All-Stars

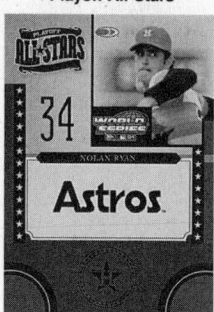

NM/M

Complete Set (20): 50.00
Common Player: 2.00
Production 500 sets
HoloFoil: 2-4X
Production 25 sets
1 Mark Prior 4.00
2 Sammy Sosa 6.00
3 Steve Finley 2.00
4 David Ortiz 4.00
5 Mike Piazza 5.00
6 Edgar Martinez 2.00
7 Roy Oswalt 2.00
8 Johan Santana 3.00
9 Jacque Jones 2.00
10 Will Clark 4.00
11 Albert Pujols 8.00
12 Andre Dawson 3.00
13 Nolan Ryan 10.00
14 Fred Lynn 2.00
15 Jim Rice 2.00
16 Dwight Evans 2.00
17 Harmon Killebrew 4.00
18 Maury Wills 2.00
19 Mark Mulder 2.00
20 Frank Thomas 4.00

Playoff All-Stars Material 1

NM/M

Quantity produced listed
1 Mark Prior Jsy/100 8.00
2 Sammy Sosa Jsy/100 10.00
3 Steve Finley Jsy/100 4.00
4 David Ortiz Jsy/100 10.00
5 Mike Piazza Jsy/100 10.00
6 Edgar Martinez Jsy/50 6.00
7 Roy Oswalt Jsy/100 4.00
8 Johan Santana Jsy/100 8.00
9 Jacque Jones Jsy/100 4.00
10 Will Clark Bat/100 10.00
11 Albert Pujols Jsy/100 20.00
12 Andre DawsonJsy/100 6.00
13 Nolan Ryan Jsy/100 25.00
14 Fred Lynn Jsy/50 6.00
15 Jim Rice Jsy/50 6.00
16 Dwight Evans Jsy/50 6.00
17 Harmon Killebrew Jsy/50 20.00
19 Mark Mulder Jsy/50 6.00
20 Frank Thomas Jsy/100 8.00

Playoff All-Stars Material 2

NM/M

Common Dual: 6.00
1 Mark Prior Jsy-Jsy/100 10.00
2 Sammy Sosa Jsy-Jsy/100 15.00
3 Steve Finley Jsy-Jsy/100 6.00
4 David Ortiz Bat-Jsy/100 20.00
5 Mike Piazza Bat-Jsy/100 15.00
6 Edgar Martinez Bat-Jsy/50 10.00
7 Roy Oswalt Bat-Jsy/100 6.00
8 Johan Santana Jsy-Jsy/100 10.00
9 Jacque Jones Bat-Jsy/100 6.00
11 Albert Pujols Jsy-Jsy/100 25.00
12 Andre Dawson Bat-Jsy/100 8.00
13 Nolan Ryan Jkt-Jsy/50 40.00
14 Fred Lynn Bat-Jsy/50 8.00
15 Jim Rice Bat-Jsy/50 10.00
16 Dwight Evans Bat-Jsy/50 6.00
17 Harmon Killebrew Bat-Jsy/50 25.00
19 Mark Mulder Bat-Jsy/10 6.00
20 Frank Thomas Bat-Jsy/100 12.00

Playoff All-Stars Material 3

NM/M

Common Triple: 10.00
1 Mark Prior Bat-Hat-Jsy/100 20.00
2 Sammy Sosa Bat-Jsy-Jsy/100 20.00
3 Steve Finley Jsy-Jsy-Jsy/100 10.00
4 David Ortiz Bat-Jsy-Jsy/100 25.00
5 Mike Piazza Bat-Jsy-Jsy/100 20.00
6 Edgar Martinez Bat-Jsy-Jsy/50 10.00
7 Roy Oswalt Bat-Fld Glv-Jsy/50 10.00
9 Jacque Jones Bat-Jsy-Jsy/50 10.00
11 Albert Pujols Bat-Jsy-Jsy/100 40.00
12 Andre Dawson Bat-Hat-Jsy/100 10.00
13 Nolan Ryan Bat-Jkt-Jsy/50 65.00
15 Jim Rice Bat-Jsy-Jsy/100 10.00
16 Dwight Evans Bat-Hat-Jsy/100 10.00
17 Harmon Killebrew Bat-Jsy-Shoe/25 50.00
20 Frank Thomas Jsy-Jsy-Pants/100 20.00

Playoff All-Stars Signature

NM/M

Quantity produced listed
1 Mark Prior/25 60.00
3 Steve Finley/25 20.00
4 David Ortiz/25 60.00
7 Roy Oswalt/25 20.00
8 Johan Santana/25 40.00
9 Jacque Jones/25 20.00
10 Will Clark/25 50.00
12 Andre Dawson/25 20.00
13 Nolan Ryan/25 125.00
14 Fred Lynn/25 20.00
15 Jim Rice/25 25.00
16 Dwight Evans/25 30.00
18 Maury Wills/25 20.00

All-Stars Sig. Material 1

NM/M

Quantity produced listed
Material 2: .75-1.5X
Production 5-100
Material 3: .75-1.5X

Production 5-100
3 Steve Finley Jsy/100 15.00
4 David Ortiz Jsy/100 50.00
6 Edgar Martinez Jsy/50 30.00
7 Roy Oswalt Jsy/100 15.00
8 Johan Santana Jsy/100 35.00
9 Jacque Jones Jsy/100 15.00
10 Will Clark Bat/25 65.00
12 Andre Dawson Jsy/100 20.00
14 Fred Lynn Jsy/25 20.00
15 Jim Rice Jsy/25 25.00
16 Dwight Evans Jsy/50 30.00
19 Mark Mulder Jsy/25 30.00
20 Frank Thomas Jsy/25 50.00

Records

NM/M
Complete Set (5): 10.00
Common Player: 3.00
Production 1,000 sets
HoloFoil: 2-4X
Production 50 sets
1 Lou Brock 3.00
2 Yogi Berra 4.00
3 Reggie Jackson 3.00
4 Bob Gibson 3.00
5 Whitey Ford 3.00

Records Signature Material

NM/M
Quantity produced listed
1 Lou Brock Bat/100 25.00
3 Reggie Jackson Bat/20 40.00

Records Signature

NM/M
1 Lou Brock/25 30.00

Records Material

NM/M
Quantity produced listed
1 Lou Brock Bat/100 10.00
2 Yogi Berra Bat/50 20.00
3 Reggie Jackson Bat/100 10.00
4 Bob Gibson Hat/10
5 Whitey Ford Pants/25 20.00

Signature

NM/M
Common Autograph: 10.00
201-222 Exclusive to Red Sox Champs Sets
3 Garret Anderson/25 25.00
7 Brandon Webb/25 10.00
11 Shea Hillenbrand/25 20.00
12 Steve Finley/25 15.00
16 Marcus Giles/25 15.00
17 Rafael Furcal/25 20.00
19 Jay Gibbons/25 10.00
20 Luis Matos/25 10.00
21 Melvin Mora/25 20.00
25 Dwight Evans/25 30.00
26 Fred Lynn/25 20.00
28 Jim Rice/25 25.00
30 Luis Tiant/25 20.00
34 Trot Nixon/25 25.00
35 Aramis Ramirez/25 35.00
37 Derrek Lee/25 30.00
40 Mark Prior/25 60.00
43 Carlos Lee/25 10.00
45 Luis Aparicio/25 20.00
46 Magglio Ordonez/25 20.00
47 Mark Buehrle/25 20.00
49 Adam Dunn/25 40.00
50 Austin Kearns/25 20.00
52 Dave Concepcion/25 15.00
53 George Foster/25 15.00
56 Tony Perez/25 35.00
57 C.C. Sabathia/25 20.00
58 Jody Gerut/25 10.00
60 Victor Martinez/25 25.00
64 Preston Wilson/25 15.00
66 Alan Trammell/25 25.00
69 Jeremy Bonderman/25 10.00
71 Brad Penny/25 10.00
76 Miguel Cabrera/25 40.00
84 Roy Oswalt/25 20.00
85 Wade Miller/25 10.00
86 Angel Berroa/25 10.00
87 Carlos Beltran/25 50.00
89 Ken Harvey/25 10.00
94 Milton Bradley/25 20.00
96 Paul LoDuca/25 25.00
101 Rickie Weeks/25 25.00
102 Scott Podsednik/25 20.00
103 Jack Morris/25 20.00
104 Jacque Jones/25 15.00
105 Johan Santana/25 50.00
106 Shannon Stewart/25 15.00
107 Torii Hunter/25 25.00
108 Jose Vidro/25 15.00
109 Orlando Cabrera/25 40.00
111 Darryl Strawberry/25 25.00
112 Dwight Gooden/25 25.00
115 Keith Hernandez/25 25.00
116 Lenny Dykstra/25 20.00
132 Jermaine Dye/25 20.00
133 Mark Mulder/25 25.00
134 Rich Harden/25 25.00
139 Marlon Byrd/25 10.00
142 Steve Carlton/25 35.00
143 Dave Parker/25 25.00
146 Jay Payton/25 10.00
148 J.T. Snow/25 15.00
154 Shigetoshi Hasegawa/25 40.00
156 Dan Haren/25 15.00
162 Aubrey Huff/25 20.00
163 Carl Crawford/25 20.00
164 Dewon Brazelton/25 10.00
168 Hank Blalock/25 25.00
170 Mark Teixeira/25 35.00
171 Michael Young/25 20.00
201 Curt Schilling SP
202 Pedro Martinez SP
210 Keith Foulke
211 Jason Varitek SP
216 Orlando Cabrera
218 Kevin Youkilis
219 Manny Ramirez SP
222 Trot Nixon

Signature Trio

NM/M
Quantity produced listed
2 Derek Lee, Brad Penny, Mike Lowell/25 40.00
3 Garret Anderson, John Lackey, Chone Figgins/25 75.00
8 Roberto Alomar, Paul Molitor, Jack Morris/25 125.00
9 Eric Davis, Barry Larkin, Paul O'Neill/25 100.00
10 Dennis Eckersley, Jose Canseco, Dave Parker/25 125.00
11 Keith Hernandez, Dwight Gooden, Gary Carter/25 75.00
12 Lenny Dykstra, George Foster, Darryl Strawberry/25 65.00
13 Alan Trammell, Kirk Gibson, Jack Morris/25 100.00
15 Bert Blyleven, John Candelaria, Dave Parker/25 75.00

Souvenirs Playoff

NM/M
Common Player: 5.00
Production 100 sets
1 Chipper Jones Ball 10.00
2 Randy Johnson Ball 10.00
3 Albert Pujols Ball 20.00
4 Jason Schmidt Ball 8.00
5 Gary Sheffield Ball 8.00
6 Miguel Tejada Ball 8.00
7 J.D. Drew Ball 5.00
8 John Smoltz Ball 10.00
9 Eric Milton Ball 5.00
10 Mark Grace Ball 10.00
11 Tim Hudson Ball 5.00
12 Jeff Bagwell Ball 10.00
13 Jim Edmonds Ball 8.00
14 Sammy Sosa Ball 15.00
15 Albert Pujols ball 20.00

Souvenirs World Series

NM/M
Common Player: 5.00
Production 100 sets
1 Jason Schmidt Ball 8.00
2 Troy Glaus Base 5.00
3 Reggie Sanders Base 5.00
4 Tim Salmon Base 5.00
5 Garret Anderson Base 5.00
6 Francisco Rodriguez Base 5.00
7 Rich Aurilia Ball 5.00
8 Jeff Kent Ball 5.00
9 Darin Erstad Base 5.00
10 Troy Glaus Base 5.00
11 Jeff Kent Ball 5.00
12 Scott Spiezio Base 5.00
13 Tony Percival Base 5.00
14 Garret Anderson Base 5.00
15 Darin Erstad Base 5.00

Triple Threads

NM/M
Common Player: 10.00
1 Josh Beckett, Miguel Cabrera, Mike Lowell/100 15.00
2 Luis Castillo, Ivan Rodriguez, Dontrelle Willis/100 20.00
3 Garret Anderson, Troy Glaus, Tim Salmon/100 20.00
4 Curt Schilling, Mark Grace, Randy Johnson/50 25.00
5 Jorge Posada, Bernie Williams, Roger Clemens/50 25.00
6 Andy Pettitte, Wade Boggs, Mariano Rivera/50 20.00
7 Charles Johnson, Cliff Floyd, Moises Alou/100 10.00
8 Chipper Jones, Tom Glavine, Greg Maddux/100 30.00
9 Joe Carter, Rickey Henderson, David Wells/100 25.00
10 Eric Davis, Barry Larkin, Paul O'Neill/100 20.00
11 Dwight Gooden, Gary Carter, Darryl Strawberry/100 20.00
12 Frank White, Willie Wilson, George Brett/100 30.00
13 Jim Palmer, Eddie Murray, Cal Ripken Jr./50 125.00
14 Willie Stargell, Dave Parker, Bill Madlock/100 20.00
15 Johnny Bench, Joe Morgan, Tony Perez/100 35.00
16 Dave Concepcion, George Foster, Johnny Bench/50 40.00
17 Al Oliver, Roberto Clemente, Willie Stargell/50 80.00
18 Jim Palmer, Frank Robinson, Brooks Robinson/50 25.00
19 Bob Gibson, Lou Brock, Orlando Cepeda/50 25.00
20 Stan Musial, Red Schoendienst, Marty Marion/50 40.00

2004 DONRUSS WORLD SERIES CHAMPIONS

NM/M
Complete Boxed Set (25): 25.00
Common Player: .50
201 Curt Schilling 3.00
202 Pedro Martinez 3.00
203 Derek Lowe .50
204 Tim Wakefield .50
205 Bronson Arroyo .50
206 Mike Timlin .50
207 Curt Leskanic .50
208 Mike Myers .50
209 Alan Embree .50
210 Keith Foulke .50
211 Jason Varitek 2.00
212 Doug Mirabelli .50
213 Doug Mientkiewicz .50
214 Mark Bellhorn .50
215 Pokey Reese .50
216 Orlando Cabrera 1.00
217 Bill Mueller .50
218 Kevin Youkilis .50
219 Manny Ramirez 3.00
220 Johnny Damon 3.00
221 Dave Roberts .50
222 Trot Nixon .50
223 Gabe Kapler .50
224 David Ortiz 3.00

Box Topper

NM/M
Inserted 1:set
WS1 World Series Champions 2.00

2005 DONRUSS

NM/M
Complete Set (400): 120.00
Common Player: .15
Common SP (1-70, 371-400): 1.00
Inserted 1:6
Pack (10): 2.50
Box (24): 50.00
1 Garret Anderson 1.00
2 Vladimir Guerrero 2.00
3 Manny Ramirez 2.00
4 Kerry Wood 2.00
5 Sammy Sosa 3.00
6 Magglio Ordonez 1.00
7 Adam Dunn 1.50
8 Todd Helton 1.50
9 Josh Beckett 1.00
10 Miguel Cabrera 2.00
11 Lance Berkman 1.00
12 Carlos Beltran 1.50
13 Shawn Green 1.00
14 Roger Clemens 4.00
15 Mike Piazza 2.50
16 Alex Rodriguez 3.00
17 Derek Jeter 4.00
18 Mark Mulder 1.00
19 Jim Thome 2.00
20 Albert Pujols 3.00
21 Scott Rolen 2.00
22 Aubrey Huff 1.00
23 Alfonso Soriano 2.00
24 Hank Blalock 1.50
25 Vernon Wells 1.00
26 Kazuo Matsui 1.50
27 B.J. Upton 1.50
28 Charles Thomas 1.00
29 Akinori Otsuka 1.00
30 David Aardsma 1.00
31 Travis Blackley 1.00
32 Brad Halsey 1.00
33 David Wright 5.00
34 Kazuhito Tadano 1.00
35 Casey Kotchman 1.50
36 Khalil Greene 2.00
37 Adrian Gonzalez 1.00
38 Zack Greinke 1.00
39 Chad Cordero 1.00
40 Scott Kazmir 4.00
41 Jeremy Guthrie 1.00
42 Noah Lowry 1.00
43 Chase Utley 1.00
44 Billy Traber 1.00
45 Aarom Baldiris 1.00
46 Abe Alvarez 1.00
47 Angel Chavez 1.00
48 Joe Mauer 1.00

49 Joey Gathright 1.00
50 John Gall 1.00
51 Ronald Belisario 1.00
52 Ryan Wing 1.00
53 Scott Proctor 1.00
54 Yadier Molina 1.00
55 Carlos Hines 1.00
56 Frankie Francisco 1.00
57 Graham Koonce 1.00
58 Jake Woods 1.00
59 Jason Bartlett 1.00
60 Mike Rouse 1.00
61 Phil Stockman 1.00
62 Renyel Pinto 1.00
63 Roberto Novoa 1.00
64 Ryan Meaux 1.00
65 David Crouthers 1.00
66 Justin Knoedler 1.00
67 Justin Leone 1.00
68 Nick Regilio 1.00
69 Mike Gosling 1.00
70 Onil Joseph 1.00
71 Bartolo Colon .15
72 Brad Fullmer .15
73 Chone Figgins .15
74 Darin Erstad .25
75 Francisco Rodriguez .15
76 Garret Anderson .25
77 Jarrod Washburn .15
78 John Lackey .15
79 Jose Guillen .15
80 Robb Quinlan .15
81 Tim Salmon .25
82 Troy Glaus .25
83 Troy Percival .15
84 Vladimir Guerrero .50
85 Brandon Webb .15
86 Casey Fossum .15
87 Luis Gonzalez .15
88 Randy Johnson .50
89 Richie Sexson .25
90 Robby Hammock .15
91 Roberto Alomar .25
92 Adam LaRoche .15
93 Andruw Jones .25
94 Bubba Nelson .15
95 Chipper Jones .50
96 J.D. Drew .25
97 John Smoltz .25
98 Johnny Estrada .15
99 Marcus Giles .15
100 Mike Hampton .15
101 Nick Green .15
102 Rafael Furcal .15
103 Russ Ortiz .15
104 Adam Loewen .15
105 Brian Roberts .15
106 Javy Lopez .25
107 Jay Gibbons .15
108 Larry Bigbie .15
109 Luis Matos .15
110 Melvin Mora .15
111 Miguel Tejada .40
112 Rafael Palmeiro .40
113 Rodrigo Lopez .15
114 Sidney Ponson .15
115 Bill Mueller .15
116 Byung-Hyun Kim .15
117 Curt Schilling .40
118 David Ortiz .40
119 Derek Lowe .15
120 Doug Mientkiewicz .15
121 Jason Varitek .25
122 Johnny Damon .25
123 Keith Foulke .15
124 Kevin Youkilis .15
125 Manny Ramirez .50
126 Orlando Cabrera .25
127 Pedro J. Martinez .50
128 Trot Nixon .15
129 Aramis Ramirez .25
130 Carlos Zambrano .25
131 Corey Patterson .25
132 Derrek Lee .25
133 Greg Maddux .75
134 Kerry Wood .50
135 Mark Prior .50
136 Matt Clement .15
137 Moises Alou .25
138 Nomar Garciaparra 1.00
139 Sammy Sosa 1.00
140 Todd Walker .15
141 Angel Guzman .15
142 Billy Koch .15
143 Carlos Lee .15
144 Frank Thomas .40
145 Magglio Ordonez .25
146 Mark Buehrle .15
147 Paul Konerko .25
148 Wilson Valdez .15
149 Adam Dunn .40
150 Austin Kearns .15
151 Barry Larkin .25
152 Benito Santiago .15
153 Jason LaRue .15
154 Ken Griffey Jr. .75
155 Ryan Wagner .15
156 Sean Casey .15
157 Brandon Phillips .15
158 Brian Tallet .15
159 C.C. Sabathia .15
160 Cliff Lee .15
161 Jeremy Guthrie .15
162 Jody Gerut .15
163 Matt Lawton .15
164 Omar Vizquel .15
165 Travis Hafner .15
166 Victor Martinez .25
167 Charles Johnson .15
168 Garrett Atkins .15
169 Jason Jennings .15
170 Jay Payton .15
171 Jeromy Burnitz .15
172 Joe Kennedy .15
173 Larry Walker .25
174 Preston Wilson .15
175 Todd Helton .40
176 Vinny Castilla .15
177 Bobby Higginson .15
178 Brandon Inge .15
179 Carlos Guillen .15
180 Carlos Pena .15
181 Craig Monroe .15
182 Dmitri Young .15
183 Eric Munson .15
184 Fernando Vina .15
185 Ivan Rodriguez .40
186 Jeremy Bonderman .15
187 Rondell White .15
188 A.J. Burnett .15
189 Dontrelle Willis .25
190 Guillermo Mota .15
191 Hee Seop Choi .15
192 Jeff Conine .15
193 Josh Beckett .25
194 Juan Encarnacion .15
195 Juan Pierre .15
196 Luis Castillo .15
197 Miguel Cabrera .50
198 Mike Lowell .15
199 Paul LoDuca .15
200 Andy Pettitte .25
201 Brad Ausmus .15
202 Carlos Beltran .40
203 Chris Burke .15
204 Craig Biggio .25
205 Jeff Bagwell .40
206 Jeff Kent .25
207 Lance Berkman .25
208 Morgan Ensberg .15
209 Octavio Dotel .15
210 Roger Clemens 1.50
211 Roy Oswalt .25
212 Tim Redding .15
213 Angel Berroa .15
214 Juan Gonzalez .25
215 Ken Harvey .15
216 Mike Sweeney .15
217 Adrian Beltre .25
218 Brad Penny .15
219 Eric Gagne .25
220 Hideo Nomo .25
221 Hong-Chih Kuo .15
222 Jeff Weaver .15
223 Kazuhisa Ishii .15
224 Milton Bradley .15
225 Shawn Green .25
226 Steve Finley .15
227 Danny Kolb .15
228 Geoff Jenkins .15
229 Junior Spivey .15
230 Lyle Overbay .15
231 Rickie Weeks .15
232 Scott Podsednik .15
233 Brad Radke .15
234 Corey Koskie .15
235 Cristian Guzman .15
236 Dustan Mohr .15
237 Eddie Guardado .15
238 J.D. Durbin .15
239 Jacque Jones .15
240 Joe Nathan .15
241 Johan Santana .40
242 Lew Ford .15
243 Michael Cuddyer .15
244 Shannon Stewart .15
245 Torii Hunter .15
246 Brad Wilkerson .15
247 Carl Everett .15
248 Jeff Fassero .15
249 Jose Vidro .15
250 Livan Hernandez .15
251 Michael Barrett .15
252 Tony Batista .15
253 Zach Day .15
254 Al Leiter .15
255 Cliff Floyd .15
256 Jae Weong Seo .15
257 John Olerud .15
258 Jose Reyes .25
259 Mike Cameron .15
260 Mike Piazza 1.00
261 Richard Hidalgo .15
262 Tom Glavine .25
263 Vance Wilson .15
264 Alex Rodriguez 1.50
265 Armando Benitez .15
266 Bernie Williams .25
267 Bubba Crosby .15
268 Chien-Ming Wang .15
269 Derek Jeter 1.50
270 Esteban Loaiza .15
271 Gary Sheffield .25
272 Hideki Matsui 1.00
273 Jason Giambi .25
274 Javier Vazquez .15
275 Jorge Posada .25
276 Jose Contreras .25
277 Kenny Lofton .15
278 Kevin Brown .15
279 Mariano Rivera .25
280 Mike Mussina .25
281 Barry Zito .25
282 Bobby Crosby .15
283 Eric Byrnes .15
284 Eric Chavez .25
285 Erubiel Durazo .15
286 Jermaine Dye .15
287 Mark Kotsay .15
288 Mark Mulder .25
289 Rich Harden .15
290 Tim Hudson .15
291 Billy Wagner .15
292 Bobby Abreu .25
293 Brett Myers .15
294 Eric Milton .15
295 Jim Thome .50
296 Jimmy Rollins .15
297 Kevin Millwood .15
298 Marlon Byrd .15
299 Mike Lieberthal .15
300 Pat Burrell .15
301 Randy Wolf .15
302 Craig Wilson .15
303 Jack Wilson .15
304 Jacob Cruz .15
305 Jason Bay .15
306 Jason Kendall .15
307 Jose Castillo .15
308 Kip Wells .15
309 Brian Giles .15
310 Brian Lawrence .15
311 Chris Oxspring .15
312 David Wells .15
313 Freddy Guzman .15
314 Jake Peavy .15
315 Mark Loretta .15
316 Ryan Klesko .15
317 Sean Burroughs .15
318 Trevor Hoffman .15
319 Xavier Nady .15
320 A.J. Pierzynski .15
321 Edgardo Alfonzo .15
322 J.T. Snow .15
323 Jason Schmidt .25
324 Jerome Williams .15
325 Kirk Rueter .15
326 Bret Boone .15
327 Bucky Jacobsen .15
328 Edgar Martinez .15
329 Freddy Garcia .15
330 Ichiro Suzuki 1.00
331 Jamie Moyer .15
332 Joel Pineiro .15
333 Scott Spiezio .15
334 Shigetoshi Hasegawa .15
335 Albert Pujols 1.50
336 Edgar Renteria .25
337 Jason Isringhausen .15
338 Jim Edmonds .25
339 Matt Morris .15
340 Mike Matheny .15
341 Reggie Sanders .15
342 Scott Rolen .50
343 Woody Williams .15
344 Jeff Suppan .15
345 Aubrey Huff .15
346 Carl Crawford .15
347 Chad Gaudin .15
348 Delmon Young .15
349 Dewon Brazelton .15
350 Jose Cruz Jr. .15
351 Rocco Baldelli .25
352 Tino Martinez .15
353 Toby Hall .15
354 Alfonso Soriano .40
355 Brian Jordan .15
356 Francisco Cordero .15
357 Hank Blalock .40
358 Kenny Rogers .15
359 Kevin Mench .15
360 Laynce Nix .15
361 Mark Teixeira .25
362 Michael Young .15
363 Alex Gonzalez .15
364 Alexis Rios .15
365 Carlos Delgado .25
366 Eric Hinske .15
367 Frank Catalanotto .15
368 Josh Phelps .15
369 Roy Halladay .15
370 Vernon Wells .15
371 Vladimir Guerrero 2.00
372 Randy Johnson 2.00
373 Chipper Jones 2.00
374 Miguel Tejada 1.50
375 Pedro Martinez 2.00
376 Sammy Sosa 3.00
377 Frank Thomas 1.50
378 Ken Griffey Jr. 3.00
379 Victor Martinez 1.00
380 Todd Helton 1.50
381 Ivan Rodriguez 1.50
382 Miguel Cabrera 2.00
383 Roger Clemens 4.00
384 Ken Harvey 1.00
385 Eric Gagne 1.50
386 Lyle Overbay 1.00
387 Shannon Stewart 1.00
388 Brad Wilkerson 1.00
389 Mike Piazza 2.50
390 Alex Rodriguez 3.00
391 Mark Mulder 1.00
392 Jim Thome 2.00
393 Jack Wilson 1.00
394 Khalil Greene 1.50
395 Jason Schmidt 1.00
396 Ichiro Suzuki 3.00
397 Albert Pujols 4.00
398 Rocco Baldelli 1.00
399 Alfonso Soriano 1.50
400 Vernon Wells 1.00

Press Proofs Black

No Pricing
Production 10 sets

Press Proofs Blue

Blue (71-370): 4-8X
Blue SP's: 2-3X
Production 100 sets

Press Proofs Gold

Gold (71-370): 10-20X
Gold SP's: 3-6X
Production 25 sets

Press Proofs Red

Red (71-370): 2-4X
Red SP's: .75-1.5X
Production 200 sets

Stat Line Career

NM/M

#71-370 print run 201-400: 2-4X
71-370 p/r 101-200: 3-6X
71-370 p/r 51-100: 4-8X
71-370 p/r 26-50: 6-12X
71-370 p/r 25 or less: No Pricing
SP's print run 200 or more: 1-2X
SP's p/r 101-200: 1.5-2X
SP's p/r 51-100: 2-4X
SP's p/r 26-50: 3-5X
SP's p/r 25 or less: No Pricing
Cards are numbered to career statistic

Stat Line Season

NM/M

#71-370 print run 101-200: 3-6X
71-370 p/r 51-100: 4-8X
71-370 p/r 26-50: 6-12X
71-370 p/r 25 or less: No Pricing
SP's p/r 101 or more 1.5-2X
SP's p/r 51-100: 2-4X
SP's p/r 26-50: 3-5X
SP's p/r 25 or less: No Pricing
Cards are numbered to season statistic

'85 Reprints

NM/M
Complete Set (12): 40.00
Common Player: 2.00
Production 1,985 Sets
1 Eddie Murray 3.00
2 George Brett 6.00
3 Nolan Ryan 8.00
4 Mike Schmidt 6.00
5 Tony Gwynn 3.00
7 Cal Ripken Jr. 10.00
8 Dwight Gooden 2.00
9 Roger Clemens 8.00
10 Don Mattingly 6.00
11 Kirby Puckett 4.00
12 Orel Hershiser 2.00

'85 Reprints Material

NM/M
Production 85 Sets
1 Eddie Murray Jsy 20.00
2 George Brett Jsy 35.00
3 Nolan Ryan Jkt 40.00
4 Mike Schmidt Jkt 35.00
5 Tony Gwynn Jsy 20.00
7 Cal Ripken Jr. Jsy 50.00
8 Dwight Gooden Jsy
9 Roger Clemens Jsy 40.00
10 Don Mattingly Jsy 35.00
11 Kirby Puckett Jsy 20.00
12 Orel Hershiser Jsy 10.00

All-Stars AL

NM/M
Common Player: 2.00
Production 1,000 Sets
Gold: 1X-2X
Production 100 Sets
1 Alex Rodriguez 6.00
2 Alfonso Soriano 3.00
3 Curt Schilling 2.00
4 Derek Jeter 8.00
5 Hank Blalock 2.00
6 Hideki Matsui 6.00
7 Ichiro Suzuki 6.00
8 Ivan Rodriguez 3.00
9 Jason Giambi 2.00
10 Manny Ramirez 3.00
11 Mark Mulder 2.00
12 Michael Young 2.00
13 Tim Hudson 2.00
14 Victor Martinez 2.00
15 Vladimir Guerrero 3.00

All-Stars NL

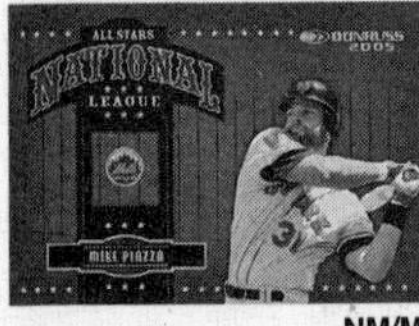

NM/M
Common Player: 2.00
Production 1,000 Sets
Gold: 1X-2X
Production 100 Sets
1 Albert Pujols 8.00
2 Ben Sheets 2.00
3 Edgar Renteria 2.00
4 Eric Gagne 2.00
5 Jack Wilson 2.00
6 Jason Schmidt 2.00
7 Jeff Kent 2.00
8 Jim Thome 3.00
9 Ken Griffey Jr. 4.00
10 Mike Piazza 4.00
11 Roger Clemens 8.00
12 Sammy Sosa 5.00
13 Scott Rolen 3.00
14 Sean Casey 2.00
15 Todd Helton 2.00

Bat Kings

NM/M
Common Player: 5.00
Quantity Produced Listed
1 Garret Anderson/250 5.00
2 Vladimir Guerrero/250 8.00
3 Cal Ripken Jr./100 50.00
4 Manny Ramirez/250 8.00
5 Kerry Wood/250 8.00
6 Sammy Sosa/250 12.00
7 Magglio Ordonez/250 5.00
8 Adam Dunn/250 8.00
9 Todd Helton/250 8.00
10 Josh Beckett/250 5.00
11 Miguel Cabrera/250 8.00
12 Lance Berkman/250 5.00
13 Carlos Beltran/250 8.00
14 Shawn Green/250 5.00
15 Roger Clemens/100 15.00
16 Mike Piazza/250 12.00
17 Nolan Ryan/100 50.00
18 Mark Mulder/250 5.00
19 Jim Thome/250 10.00
20 Albert Pujols/250 20.00
21 Scott Rolen/250 10.00
22 Aubrey Huff/250 5.00
23 Alfonso Soriano/250 8.00

Bat Kings Signatures

No Pricing
Production 5 or 10

2005 DONRUSS CAL RIPKEN 10TH ANNIVERSARY

NM/M
Cal Ripken Jr. 4.00

Craftsmen

NM/M
Complete Set (30): 40.00
Common Player: 1.00
Production 1,000 Sets
Black: 1.5X-2X
Production 100 Sets
Master: 1X-2X
Production 250 Sets
Master Black: No Pricing
Production 10 Sets
1 Albert Pujols 5.00
2 Alex Rodriguez 4.00
3 Alfonso Soriano 2.00
4 Andruw Jones 1.00
5 Carlos Beltran 1.50
6 Derek Jeter 5.00
7 Greg Maddux 2.50
8 Hank Blalock 1.50
9 Ichiro Suzuki 4.00
10 Jeff Bagwell 1.50
11 Jim Thome 2.00
12 Josh Beckett 1.00
13 Ken Griffey Jr. 2.50
14 Manny Ramirez 2.00
15 Mark Mulder 1.00
16 Mark Prior 2.00
17 Mark Teixeira 1.00
18 Miguel Tejada 1.50
19 Mike Mussina 1.50
20 Mike Piazza 2.50
21 Nomar Garciaparra 3.00
22 Pedro Martinez 2.00
23 Rafael Palmeiro 1.50
24 Randy Johnson 2.00
25 Roger Clemens 5.00
26 Sammy Sosa 3.00
27 Scott Rolen 2.00
28 Tim Hudson 1.00
29 Vernon Wells 1.00
30 Vladimir Guerrero 2.00

Diamond Kings Inserts

NM/M
Complete Set (25): 40.00
Common Player: 1.50
Production 2,005 Sets
Studio: 1.5X-2X
Production 250 Sets
Studio Black: 1.5X-3X
Production 100 Sets
1 Garret Anderson 1.50
2 Vladimir Guerrero 2.00
3 Manny Ramirez 2.00
4 Kerry Wood 1.50
5 Sammy Sosa 4.00
6 Magglio Ordonez 1.50
7 Adam Dunn 1.50
8 Todd Helton 1.50
9 Josh Beckett 1.50
10 Miguel Cabrera 2.00
11 Lance Berkman 1.50
12 Carlos Beltran 2.00
13 Shawn Green 1.50
14 Roger Clemens 6.00
15 Mike Piazza 3.00
16 Alex Rodriguez 5.00
17 Derek Jeter 6.00
18 Mark Mulder 1.50
19 Jim Thome 2.00
20 Albert Pujols 6.00
21 Scott Rolen 2.00
22 Aubrey Huff 1.50
23 Alfonso Soriano 2.00
24 Hank Blalock 1.50
25 Vernon Wells 1.50

Elite Series

NM/M
Complete Set (25): 50.00
Common Player: 2.00
Production 1,500 Sets
Black: 1X-2X
Production 100 Sets
Dominator: 1X-1.5X
Production 250 Sets
Dominator Black: 3X-5X
Production 25 Sets
1 Albert Pujols 6.00
2 Alex Rodriguez 5.00
3 Alfonso Soriano 2.00
4 Derek Jeter 6.00
5 Hank Blalock 1.50
6 Ichiro Suzuki 5.00
7 Ivan Rodriguez 2.00
8 Jim Thome 2.00
9 Ken Griffey Jr. 3.00
10 Manny Ramirez 2.00
11 Mark Mulder 1.50
12 Mark Prior 2.00
13 Michael Young 1.50
14 Miguel Cabrera 2.00
15 Miguel Tejada 2.00
16 Mike Piazza 3.00
17 Nomar Garciaparra 4.00
18 Rafael Palmeiro 2.00
19 Randy Johnson 2.00
20 Roger Clemens 6.00
21 Sammy Sosa 4.00
22 Scott Rolen 2.00
23 Tim Hudson 1.50
24 Todd Helton 1.50
25 Vladimir Guerrero 2.00

Fans of the Game

NM/M
Complete Set (5): 10.00
1 Jesse Ventura 3.00
2 John C. McGinley 2.00
3 Susie Essman 2.00
4 Dean Cain 2.00
5 Meat Loaf 3.00

Fans of the Game Signatures

NM/M
1 Jesse Ventura 50.00
2 John C. McGinley SP/300 50.00
3 Susie Essman
4 Dean Cain SP/250
5 Meat Loaf 60.00

Jersey Kings

NM/M
Common Player: 5.00
1 Garret Anderson/250 5.00
2 Vladimir Guerrero/250 8.00
3 Cal Ripken Jr./100 50.00
4 Manny Ramirez/250 8.00
5 Kerry Wood/250 10.00
6 Sammy Sosa/250 12.00
7 Magglio Ordonez/250 5.00
8 Adam Dunn/250 8.00
9 Todd Helton/250 8.00
10 Josh Beckett/250 5.00
11 Miguel Cabrera/250 8.00
12 Lance Berkman/250 5.00
13 Carlos Beltran/250 8.00
14 Shawn Green/250 5.00
15 Roger Clemens/250 15.00
16 Mike Piazza/250 10.00
17 Nolan Ryan/100 50.00
18 Mark Mulder/250 5.00
19 Jim Thome/250 8.00
20 Albert Pujols/250 20.00
21 Scott Rolen/250 10.00
22 Aubrey Huff/250 5.00
23 Alfonso Soriano/250 8.00
24 Hank Blalock/250 8.00
25 Vernon Wells/250 5.00

Jersey Kings Signatures

No Pricing
Production 5 or 10

Longball Leaders

NM/M
Complete Set (15): 30.00
Common Player: 2.00
Black: 1X-2X
Production 250 Sets
Die-Cut: 2X-3X
Production 50 Sets
Black Die-Cut: No Pricing
Production 10 Sets
1 Adam Dunn 3.00
2 Adrian Beltre 3.00
3 Albert Pujols 6.00
4 Alex Rodriguez 5.00
5 David Ortiz 3.00
6 Hank Blalock 3.00
7 J.D. Drew 2.00
8 Jeromy Burnitz 2.00
9 Jim Edmonds 2.50
10 Jim Thome 3.00
11 Manny Ramirez 3.00
12 Mark Teixeira 2.00
13 Moises Alou 2.00
14 Paul Konerko 2.00
15 Steve Finley 2.00

Mound Marvels

NM/M
Complete Set (15): 40.00
Common Player: 2.00
Production 1,000 Sets
Black: No Pricing
Production 10 Sets
1 Curt Schilling 4.00
2 Dontrelle Willis 2.00
3 Eric Gagne 4.00
4 Greg Maddux 6.00
5 John Smoltz 3.00
6 Kenny Rogers 2.00
7 Kerry Wood 4.00
8 Mariano Rivera 3.00
9 Mark Mulder 2.00
10 Mark Prior 4.00
11 Mike Mussina 3.00
12 Pedro Martinez 4.00
13 Randy Johnson 4.00

14 Roger Clemens 8.00
15 Tim Hudson 2.00

Power Alley Red

NM/M
Common Player: 1.50
Production 2,500 Sets
Black: No Pricing
Production 10 Sets
Black Die-Cut: No Pricing
Production 5 Sets
Blue: 1X
Production 1,000 Sets
Blue Die-Cut: 2X-3X
Production 100 Sets
Green: 3X-5X
Production 25 Sets
Green Die-Cut: No Pricing
Production 10 Sets
Purple: 1X-2X
Production 250 Sets
Purple Die-Cut: 2X-3X
Production 50 Sets
Red Die-Cut: 1X-2X
Production 250 Sets
Yellow: 2X-3X
Production 100 Sets
Yellow Die-Cut: 3X-5X
Production 25 Sets
1 Adam Dunn 2.00
2 Adrian Beltre 2.00
3 Albert Pujols 6.00
4 Alex Rodriguez 5.00
5 Alfonso Soriano 3.00
6 Gary Sheffield 2.00
7 Hank Blalock 2.00
8 Hideki Matsui 4.00
9 J.D. Drew 1.50
10 Jeromy Burnitz 1.50
11 Jim Edmonds 2.00
12 Jim Thome 3.00
13 Ken Griffey Jr. 3.00
14 Manny Ramirez 2.00
15 Mark Teixeira 1.50
16 Miguel Cabrera 2.00
17 Miguel Tejada 2.00
18 Mike Lowell 1.50
19 Mike Piazza 3.00
20 Moises Alou 1.50
21 Paul Konerko 1.50
22 Sammy Sosa 4.00
23 Scott Rolen 3.00
24 Todd Helton 2.00
25 Vladimir Guerrero 3.00

Production Line BA

NM/M
Common Player: 3.00
Black: 2X-3X
Production 25 Sets
Die-Cut: 1X
Production 100 Sets
Black Die-Cut: No Pricing
Production 10 Sets
1 Ichiro Suzuki/372 8.00
2 Ivan Rodriguez/334 5.00
3 Juan Pierre/326 3.00
4 Adrian Beltre/334 5.00
5 Albert Pujols/331 10.00
6 Mark Loretta/335 3.00
7 Melvin Mora/340 3.00
8 Sean Casey/324 3.00
9 Todd Helton/347 5.00
10 Vladimir Guerrero/337 5.00

Production Line OBP

NM/M
Common Player: 3.00
Black: 2X-3X
Production 25 Sets
Die-Cut: 1X
Production 100 Sets
Black Die-Cut: No Pricing
Production 10 Sets
1 Albert Pujols/415 8.00
2 Bobby Abreu/428 3.00
3 Lance Berkman/450 3.00
4 J.D. Drew/436 3.00
5 Jorge Posada/400 4.00
6 Ichiro Suzuki/414 8.00
7 Manny Ramirez/397 4.00
8 Melvin Mora/419 3.00
9 Todd Helton/469 4.00
10 Travis Hafner/410 3.00

Production Line OPS

NM/M
Common Player: 3.00
Black: 1.5X-2X
Production 50 Sets
Die-Cut: 1X
Production 100 Sets
Black Die-Cut: 2X-3X
Production 25 Sets
1 Albert Pujols/1072 8.00
2 Bobby Abreu/983 4.00
3 Lance Berkman/1017 4.00
4 J.D. Drew/1006 3.00
5 Jorge Posada/977 4.00
6 Ichiro Suzuki/1016 3.00
7 Manny Ramirez/1009 4.00
8 Melvin Mora/1007 4.00
9 Todd Helton/1088 4.00
10 Travis Hafner/993 3.00

Production Line Slugging

NM/M
Common Player: 3.00
Black: 1.5X-2X
Production 50 Sets
Die-Cut: 1X
Production 100 Sets
Black Die-Cut: 2X-3X
Production 25 Sets
1 Adrian Beltre/629 4.00
2 Albert Pujols/657 8.00
3 Todd Helton/620 4.00
4 J.D. Drew/569 3.00
5 Jim Edmonds/643 3.00
6 Jim Thome/581 4.00
7 Vladimir Guerrero/598 4.00
8 Manny Ramirez/613 4.00
9 Scott Rolen/598 4.00
10 Travis Hafner/583 3.00

Timber and Threads Bat

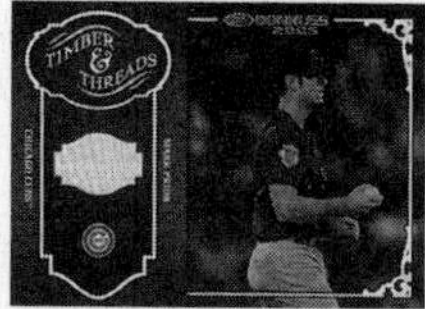

NM/M
Common Player: 5.00
1 Albert Pujols 15.00
2 Alfonso Soriano 8.00
3 Andre Dawson 8.00
4 Austin Kearns 5.00
5 Brad Penny 5.00
6 Carlos Beltran 8.00
7 Carlos Lee 5.00
8 Chipper Jones 8.00
9 Dale Murphy 8.00
10 Don Mattingly 20.00
11 Frank Thomas 8.00
12 Garret Anderson 5.00
13 Gary Carter 8.00
14 Hank Blalock 8.00
15 Jacque Jones 5.00
17 Jay Gibbons 5.00
18 Jeff Bagwell 8.00
20 Jermaine Dye 5.00
21 Jim Thome 8.00
22 Jose Vidro 5.00
23 Lance Berkman 5.00
24 Laynce Nix 5.00
25 Magglio Ordonez 5.00
26 Marcus Giles 5.00
27 Mark Prior 10.00
28 Mark Teixeira 5.00
29 Melvin Mora 5.00
30 Michael Young 5.00
31 Miguel Cabrera 8.00
32 Mike Lowell 5.00
33 Roy Oswalt 5.00
34 Sammy Sosa 10.00
35 Scott Rolen 10.00
36 Sean Burroughs 5.00
37 Sean Casey 5.00
38 Shannon Stewart 5.00
39 Torii Hunter 5.00
40 Travis Hafner 5.00

Timber and Threads Combo

NM/M
1 Albert Pujols Bat-Jsy 25.00
2 Alfonso Soriano Bat-Jsy 10.00
3 Andre Dawson Bat-Jsy 8.00
4 Austin Kearns Bat-Jsy 8.00
5 Brad Penny Bat-Jsy 6.00
6 Carlos Beltran Bat-Jsy 12.00
7 Carlos Lee Bat-Jsy 6.00
8 Chipper Jones Bat-Jsy 12.00
9 Dale Murphy Bat-Jsy 10.00
10 Don Mattingly Bat-Jsy 25.00
11 Frank Thomas Bat-Jsy 12.00
12 Garret Anderson Bat-Jsy 8.00
13 Gary Carter Bat-Jsy 10.00
14 Hank Blalock Bat-Jsy 10.00
15 Jacque Jones Bat-Jsy 6.00
17 Jay Gibbons Bat-Jsy 6.00
18 Jeff Bagwell Bat-Jsy 12.00
20 Jermaine Dye Bat-Jsy 6.00
21 Jim Thome Bat-Jsy 12.00
22 Jose Vidro Bat-Jsy 6.00
23 Lance Berkman Bat-Jsy 6.00
24 Laynce Nix Bat-Jsy 6.00
25 Magglio Ordonez Bat-Jsy 8.00
26 Marcus Giles Bat-Jsy 6.00
27 Mark Prior Bat-Jsy 15.00
28 Mark Teixeira Bat-Jsy 8.00
29 Melvin Mora Bat-Jsy 6.00
30 Michael Young Bat-Jsy 8.00
31 Miguel Cabrera Bat-Jsy 12.00
32 Mike Lowell Bat-Jsy 8.00
33 Roy Oswalt Bat-Jsy 8.00
34 Sammy Sosa Bat-Jsy 15.00
35 Scott Rolen Bat-Jsy 15.00
36 Sean Burroughs Bat-Jsy 6.00
37 Sean Casey Bat-Jsy 6.00
38 Shannon Stewart Bat-Jsy 6.00
39 Torii Hunter Bat-Jsy 8.00
40 Travis Hafner Bat-Jsy 8.00

Timber and Threads Jersey

NM/M
Common Player: 5.00
1 Albert Pujols 15.00
2 Alfonso Soriano 8.00
3 Andre Dawson
4 Austin Kearns 5.00
5 Brad Penny 5.00
6 Carlos Beltran 8.00
7 Carlos Lee 5.00
8 Chipper Jones
9 Dale Murphy 8.00
10 Don Mattingly 25.00
11 Frank Thomas 8.00
12 Garret Anderson 5.00
13 Gary Carter 8.00
14 Hank Blalock 8.00
15 Jacque Jones 5.00
17 Jay Gibbons 5.00
18 Jeff Bagwell 8.00
19 Jeremy Bonderman 5.00
20 Jermaine Dye 5.00
21 Jim Thome 8.00
22 Jose Vidro 5.00
23 Lance Berkman 5.00
24 Laynce Nix 5.00
25 Magglio Ordonez 5.00
26 Marcus Giles 5.00
27 Mark Prior 10.00
28 Mark Teixeira 5.00
29 Melvin Mora 5.00
30 Michael Young 5.00
31 Miguel Cabrera 8.00
32 Mike Lowell 5.00
33 Roy Oswalt 5.00
34 Sammy Sosa 10.00
35 Scott Rolen 10.00
36 Sean Burroughs 5.00
37 Sean Casey 5.00
38 Shannon Stewart 5.00
39 Torii Hunter 5.00
40 Travis Hafner 5.00

2005 DONRUSS CLASSICS

NM/M
Complete Set (250):
Common Player (1-200): .25
Common Auto. (201-225): 6.00
Common SP (226-250): 3.00
Production 1,000
Pack (5): 8.00
Box (18): 120.00
1 Scott Rolen 1.00
2 Derek Jeter 3.00
3 Jose Vidro .25
4 Johnny Damon 1.00
5 Nomar Garciaparra 2.00
6 Jose Guillen .25
7 Trot Nixon .25
8 Mark Loretta .25
9 Jody Gerut .25
10 Miguel Tejada .75
11 Barry Larkin .50
12 Jeff Kent .40
13 Carl Crawford .25
14 Paul Konerko .40
15 Jim Edmonds .50
16 Garret Anderson .40
17 Jay Gibbons .25
18 Moises Alou .40
19 Mike Lowell .25
20 Mark Mulder .40
21 Josh Beckett .50
22 Tim Salmon .25
23 Shannon Stewart .25
24 Miguel Cabrera 1.00
25 Jim Thome 1.00
26 Kevin Youkilis .25
27 Justin Morneau .75
28 Austin Kearns .25
29 Cliff Lee .25
30 Ken Griffey Jr. 1.50
31 Mike Piazza 1.50
32 Roy Halladay .40
33 Larry Walker .50
34 David Ortiz 1.00
35 Dontrelle Willis .50
36 Craig Wilson .25
37 Jeff Suppan .25
38 Curt Schilling 1.00
39 Larry Bigbie .25
40 Rich Harden .40
41 Victor Martinez .40
42 Jorge Posada .50
43 Joey Gathright .25
44 Adam Dunn .75
45 Pedro Martinez 1.00
46 Dallas McPherson .50
47 Tom Glavine .40
48 Torii Hunter .40
49 Angel Berroa .25
50 Mark Prior 1.00
51 Ichiro Suzuki 2.00
52 C.C. Sabathia .25
53 Bobby Abreu .50

54 Shigetoshi Hasegawa .25
55 Brandon Webb .50
56 Mark Buehrle .50
57 Johan Santana .75
58 Francisco Rodriguez .25
59 Roy Oswalt .50
60 Mike Sweeney .25
61 Jake Peavy .50
62 Akinori Otsuka .25
63 Dioner Navarro .25
64 Kazuhito Tadano .25
65 Ryan Wagner .25
66 Abe Alvarez .25
67 Mark Teixeira .75
68 Jermaine Dye .25
69 Todd Walker .25
70 Octavio Dotel .25
71 Frank Thomas .75
72 Javy Lopez .50
73 Scott Podsednik .25
74 B.J. Upton .25
75 Barry Zito .40
76 Raul Ibanez .25
77 Orlando Cabrera .25
78 Sean Burroughs .25
79 Esteban Loaiza .25
80 Jason Schmidt .50
81 Vinny Castilla .25
82 Shingo Takatsu .25
83 Juan Pierre .25
84 David Dellucci .25
85 Travis Blackley .25
86 Brad Penny .25
87 Nick Johnson .25
88 Brian Roberts .50
89 Kazuo Matsui .25
90 Mike Lieberthal .25
91 Craig Biggio .40
92 Sean Casey .25
93 Andy Pettitte .50
94 Milton Bradley .40
95 Rocco Baldelli .25
96 Adrian Gonzalez .25
97 Chad Tracy .25
98 Chad Cordero .25
99 Albert Pujols 3.00
100 Jason Kubel .25
101 Rafael Furcal .25
102 Jack Wilson .25
103 Eric Chavez .40
104 Casey Kotchman .25
105 Jeff Bagwell .75
106 Melvin Mora .25
107 Bobby Crosby .25
108 Preston Wilson .25
109 Hank Blalock .75
110 Vernon Wells .40
111 Francisco Cordero .25
112 Steve Finley .25
113 Omar Vizquel .25
114 Eric Byrnes .25
115 Tim Hudson .50
116 Aramis Ramirez .50
117 Lance Berkman .40
118 Shea Hillenbrand .25
119 Aubrey Huff .25
120 Lew Ford .25
121 Sammy Sosa 2.00
122 Marcus Giles .25
123 Rickie Weeks .25
124 Manny Ramirez 1.00
125 Jason Giambi .40
126 Adam LaRoche .25
127 Vladimir Guerrero 1.00
128 Ken Harvey .25
129 Adrian Beltre .50
130 Magglio Ordonez .25
131 Greg Maddux 1.50
132 Russ Ortiz .25
133 Jason Varitek .75
134 Kerry Wood 1.00
135 Mike Mussina .75
136 Joe Nathan .25
137 Troy Glaus .50
138 Carlos Zambrano .50
139 Ben Sheets .50
140 Jae Weong Seo .25
141 Derrek Lee .50
142 Carlos Beltran .50
143 John Lackey .25
144 Aaron Rowand .25
145 Dewon Brazelton .25
146 Jason Bay .25
147 Alfonso Soriano 1.00
148 Travis Hafner .25
149 Ryan Church .25
150 Bret Boone .25
151 Bernie Williams .50
152 Wade Miller .25
153 Zack Greinke .25
154 Scott Kazmir .25
155 Hideki Matsui 2.00
156 Livan Hernandez .25
157 Jose Capellan .25
158 David Wright 1.00
159 Chone Figgins .25
160 Jeremy Reed .25
161 J.D. Drew .40
162 Hideo Nomo .50
163 Merkin Valdez .25
164 Shawn Green .40
165 Alexis Rios .25
166 Johnny Estrada .25
167 Danny Graves .25
168 Carlos Lee .25
169 John Van Benschoten .25
170 Randy Johnson 1.00
171 Randy Wolf .25
172 Luis Gonzalez .40
173 Chipper Jones 1.00
174 Delmon Young .50
175 Edwin Jackson .25
176 Carlos Delgado .50
177 Matt Clement .25
178 Jacque Jones .25
179 Gary Sheffield .50
180 Laynce Nix .25
181 Tom Gordon .25
182 Jose Castillo .25
183 Andruw Jones .50
184 Brian Giles .40
185 Paul LoDuca .25
186 Roger Clemens 3.00
187 Todd Helton .75
188 Keith Foulke .25
189 Jeremy Bonderman .25
190 Troy Percival .25
191 Michael Young .25
192 Carlos Guillen .25
193 Rafael Palmeiro .75
194 Brett Myers .25
195 Carl Pavano .40
196 Alex Rodriguez 2.50
197 Lyle Overbay .25
198 Ivan Rodriguez .75
199 Khalil Greene .40
200 Edgar Renteria .40
201 *Justin Verlander AU/400* 20.00
202 *Miguel Negron AU/1300* 6.00
204 *Paul Reynoso AU/1200* 8.00
205 *Colter Bean AU/1200* 8.00
206 *Raul Tablado AU/1200* 8.00
207 *Mark McLemore AU/1500* 8.00
208 *Russel Rohlicek AU/1200* 8.00
210 *Chris Seddon AU/785* 8.00
213 *Mike Morse AU/1200* 6.00
215 *Randy Messenger AU/1200* 8.00
217 *Carlos Ruiz AU/1200* 8.00
218 *Chris Roberson AU/1200* 8.00
219 *Ryan Speier AU/1200* 8.00
221 *Ambiorix Burgos AU/750* 8.00
223 *David Gassner AU/1200* 6.00
224 *Sean Tracey AU/1200* 8.00
225 *Casey Rogowski AU/1500* 8.00
226 Billy Williams 3.00
227 Ralph Kiner 3.00
228 Ozzie Smith 5.00
229 Rod Carew 3.00
230 Nolan Ryan 8.00
231 Fergie Jenkins 3.00
232 Paul Molitor 4.00
233 Carlton Fisk 4.00
234 Rollie Fingers 3.00
235 Lou Brock 3.00
236 Gaylord Perry 3.00
237 Don Mattingly 6.00
238 Maury Wills 3.00
239 Luis Aparicio 3.00
240 George Brett 8.00
241 Mike Schmidt 6.00
242 Joe Morgan 3.00
243 Dennis Eckersley 3.00
244 Reggie Jackson 4.00
245 Bobby Doerr 3.00
246 Bob Feller 3.00
247 Cal Ripken Jr. 10.00
248 Harmon Killebrew 4.00
249 Frank Robinson 4.00
250 Stan Musial 5.00

Timeless Tributes Gold

Gold (1-200): 4-8X
Gold (201-225): .4-.75X
Gold (226-250): 2-4X
Production 50 sets

Timeless Tributes Silver

Gold (1-200): 2-4X
Gold (201-225): .25X
Gold (226-250): 1-2X
Production 100 sets

Timeless Tributes Platinum

No Pricing
Production one set

Classic Combos

NM/M
Common Combo: 4.00
Production 400 Sets
Gold: 2X-4X
Production 25 Sets
Platinum: No Pricing
Production One Set
33 Babe Ruth, Ted Williams 10.00
34 Roberto Clemente, Vladimir Guerrero 8.00
35 Willie Mays, Willie McCovey 8.00
36 Yogi Berra, Mike Piazza 6.00
37 Sandy Koufax, Nolan Ryan 30.00
38 Harmon Killebrew, Mike Schmidt 8.00
39 Whitey Ford, Randy Johnson 4.00
40 Cal Ripken Jr., George Brett 15.00
41 Hank Aaron, Stan Musial 8.00
42 Carl Yastrzemski, Frank Robinson 6.00
43 Bob Feller, Roger Clemens 6.00
44 Bob Gibson, Tom Seaver 4.00
45 Roger Maris, Jim Thome 4.00
46 Albert Pujols, Don Mattingly 8.00
47 Duke Snider, Sammy Sosa 4.00
48 Rickey Henderson, Bo Jackson 4.00
49 Ernie Banks, Reggie Jackson 4.00
50 Burleigh Grimes, Greg Maddux 6.00

Classic Combos Bat

No Pricing
Production 5 Sets

Classic Combos Jersey

NM/M
Production 5-50
Prime: No Pricing
Production 1-5
33 Babe Ruth, Ted Williams/5
34 Roberto Clemente, Vladimir Guerrero/5
35 Willie Mays, Willie McCovey/10
36 Yogi Berra, Mike Piazza/10
37 Sandy Koufax, Nolan Ryan/10
38 Harmon Killebrew, Mike Schmidt/50 30.00
39 Whitey Ford, Randy Johnson/25 25.00
40 Cal Ripken Jr., George Brett/50 50.00
41 Hank Aaron, Stan Musial/10
43 Bob Feller Pants, Roger Clemens/10
45 Roger Maris, Jim Thome/25 50.00
46 Albert Pujols, Don Mattingly/50 40.00
47 Duke Snider, Sammy Sosa/25 30.00
48 Rickey Henderson, Bo Jackson/50 25.00
49 Ernie Banks, Reggie Jackson/10
50 Burleigh Grimes Pants, Greg Maddux/10

Classic Combos Materials

NM/M
Production 1-25
Prime: No Pricing
Production 5 Sets
46 Albert Pujols, Don Mattingly/25 50.00
47 Duke Snider Pants, Sammy Sosa/5
48 Rickey Henderson, Bo Jackson/25 30.00

Classic Combos Materials HR

NM/M
Production 1-25
46 Albert Pujols, Don Mattingly/25 50.00
47 Duke Snider Jsy-Pants, Sammy Sosa/25
48 Rickey Henderson, Bo Jackson/25 30.00

Classic Combos Signature Jersey

No Pricing
Production 1-5

Classic Singles

NM/M
Complete Set (32): 120.00
Common Player: 3.00
Production 400 Sets
Gold: 2X-4X
Production 25 Sets
Platinum: No Pricing
Production One Set
1 Hank Aaron 8.00
2 Tom Seaver 4.00
3 Harmon Killebrew 4.00
4 Paul Molitor 4.00
5 Brooks Robinson 4.00
6 Stan Musial 5.00
7 Bobby Doerr 3.00
8 Cal Ripken Jr. 12.00
9 Phil Niekro 3.00
10 Eddie Murray 4.00
11 Randy Johnson 4.00
12 Steve Carlton 3.00
13 Rickey Henderson 3.00
14 Ernie Banks 4.00
15 Curt Schilling 4.00
16 Whitey Ford 4.00
17 Al Kaline 4.00
18 Gary Carter 3.00
19 Robin Yount 4.00
20 Johnny Bench 4.00
21 Bob Feller 3.00
22 Jim Palmer 3.00
23 Don Mattingly 6.00
24 Willie Mays 6.00
25 Dave Righetti 3.00
26 Roger Clemens 6.00
27 Juan Marichal 3.00
28 Tony Gwynn 4.00
29 Nolan Ryan 8.00
30 Carlton Fisk 3.00
31 Greg Maddux 5.00
32 Sandy Koufax 25.00

Classic Singles Bat

NM/M
Production 25-50
1 Hank Aaron/25 50.00
2 Tom Seaver/50 15.00
4 Paul Molitor/50 15.00
5 Brooks Robinson/50 15.00
6 Stan Musial/25 30.00
7 Bobby Doerr/25 10.00
8 Cal Ripken Jr./25 70.00
9 Phil Niekro/50 8.00
10 Eddie Murray/50 15.00
11 Randy Johnson/25 20.00
12 Steve Carlton/25 10.00
13 Rickey Henderson/50 15.00
14 Ernie Banks/50 20.00
17 Al Kaline/25 25.00

18 Gary Carter/50 8.00
19 Robin Yount/50 15.00
20 Johnny Bench/25 20.00
23 Don Mattingly/25 30.00
24 Willie Mays/25 50.00
28 Tony Gwynn/50 15.00
29 Nolan Ryan/25 40.00
30 Carlton Fisk/50 15.00

Classic Singles Jersey

NM/M

Production 10-100
Prime: No Pricing
Production 1-5
1 Hank Aaron/10
2 Tom Seaver/25 20.00
3 Harmon Killebrew/25 20.00
4 Paul Molitor/50 15.00
5 Brooks Robinson/50 15.00
6 Stan Musial/10
7 Bobby Doerr Pants/100 10.00
8 Cal Ripken Jr./25 70.00
9 Phil Niekro/50 8.00
10 Eddie Murray/50 15.00
11 Randy Johnson/100 12.00
12 Steve Carlton/25 12.00
13 Rickey Henderson/100 12.00
14 Ernie Banks/25 25.00
15 Curt Schilling/100 15.00
16 Whitey Ford/25 20.00
18 Gary Carter/100 8.00
19 Robin Yount/50 15.00
20 Johnny Bench/50 15.00
21 Bob Feller Pants/25 20.00
22 Jim Palmer/100 8.00
23 Don Mattingly/100 25.00
24 Willie Mays/25 50.00
25 Dave Righetti/50 8.00
26 Roger Clemens/25 25.00
27 Juan Marichal/50 10.00
28 Tony Gwynn/100 15.00
29 Nolan Ryan/50 30.00
30 Carlton Fisk/25 15.00
31 Greg Maddux/100 15.00
32 Sandy Koufax/25 375.00

Classic Singles Materials

NM/M

Production 10-25
Prime: No Pricing
Production 10-25
1 Hank Aaron Bat-Jsy/10
2 Tom Seaver Bat-Jsy/25 20.00
3 Harmon Killebrew Bat-Jys/25 25.00
4 Paul Molitor Bat-Jsy/25 20.00
5 Brooks Robinson Bat-Jsy/25 20.00
6 Stan Musial Bat-Jsy/10
7 Bobby Doerr Bat-Pants/25 10.00
11 Randy Johnson Bat-Jsy/25 20.00
12 Steve Carlton Bat-Jsy/25 15.00
13 Rickey Henderson Bat-Jsy/25 30.00
14 Ernie Banks Bat-Jsy/10
15 Curt Schilling Bat-Jsy/10
18 Gary Carter Bat-Jsy/25 15.00
19 Robin Yount Bat-Jsy/25 25.00
20 Johnny Bench Bat-Jsy/25 25.00
23 Don Mattingly Bat-Jsy/25 35.00
28 Tony Gwynn Bat-Jsy/25 25.00
29 Nolan Ryan Bat-Jsy/25 40.00
30 Carlton FiskBat-Jsy/25 15.00

Classic Singles Materials HR

NM/M

Production 10-25
1 Hank Aaron Bat-Jsy/10
2 Tom Seaver Bat-Jsy/25 20.00
3 Harmon Killebrew Bat-Jsy/25 25.00
4 Paul Molitor Bat-Jsy/25 20.00
5 Brooks Robinson Bat-Jsy/25 20.00
6 Stan Musial Bat-Jsy/10
7 Bobby Doerr Bat-Pants/25 10.00
8 Cal Ripken Jr. Bat-Jsy/10
9 Phil Niekro Bat-Jsy/10
10 Eddie Murray Bat-Jsy/10
11 Randy Johnson Bat-Jsy/25 20.00
12 Steve Carlton Bat-Pants/25 15.00
13 Rickey Henderson Bat-Jsy/25 30.00
14 Ernie Banks Bat-Jsy/10
15 Curt Schilling Bat-Jsy/10
18 Gary Carter Bat-Jsy/25 15.00
19 Robin Yount Bat-Jsy/25 25.00
20 Johnny Bench Bat-Jsy/25 25.00
23 Don Mattingly Bat-Jsy/25 35.00
24 Willie Mays Bat-Jsy/10
28 Tony Gwynn Bat-Jsy/25 25.00

Classic Singles Signature Bat

No Pricing
Production 1-10

Dress Code Bat

NM/M

Production 50-100
1 Albert Pujols/100 25.00
2 Bernie Williams/50 10.00
4 Carlos Beltran/100 10.00
5 Chipper Jones/100 10.00
7 David Ortiz/100 12.00
8 Hank Blalock/100 6.00
9 Hideki Matsui/100 30.00
10 Jim Edmonds/100 8.00
11 Jim Thome/100 10.00
14 Mark Prior/50 12.00
15 Mark Teixeira/100 6.00
16 Miguel Cabrera/100 8.00
17 Miguel Tejada/100 6.00
18 Mike Piazza/100 12.00
22 Sammy Sosa/100 12.00
23 Scott Rolen/100 10.00
26 Torii Hunter/100 6.00
30 Vladimir Guerrero/100 10.00

Dress Code Jersey Number

NM/M

Production 5-57
2 Bernie Williams/51 10.00
4 Carlos Beltran/15 20.00
6 Curt Schilling/38 15.00
7 David Ortiz/34 20.00
9 Hideki Matsui/55 30.00
11 Jim Thome/25 15.00
12 Johan Santana/57 12.00
13 Mark Mulder/20 10.00
14 Mark Prior/22 20.00
15 Mark Teixeira/23 10.00
16 Miguel Cabrera/24 15.00
18 Mike Piazza/31 20.00
19 Pedro J. Martinez/45 10.00
20 Randy Johnson Pants/51 12.00
21 Roger Clemens/23 25.00
22 Sammy Sosa/21 20.00
23 Scott Rolen/27 15.00
26 Torii Hunter/48 6.00
27 Travis Hafner/48 6.00
29 Victor Martinez/51 8.00
30 Vladimir Guerrero/27 20.00

Dress Code Jersey Prime

NM/M

Production 25 Sets
1 Albert Pujols 75.00
2 Bernie Williams 20.00
3 Carl Crawford 12.00
4 Carlos Beltran 25.00
5 Chipper Jones 30.00
6 Curt Schilling 30.00
7 David Ortiz 30.00
8 Hank Blalock 20.00
10 Jim Edmonds 20.00
11 Jim Thome 25.00
12 Johan Santana 30.00
13 Mark Mulder 20.00
14 Mark Prior 30.00
15 Mark Teixeira 15.00
16 Miguel Cabrera 25.00
17 Miguel Tejada 25.00
18 Mike Piazza 30.00
19 Pedro J. Martinez 25.00
20 Randy Johnson 30.00
21 Roger Clemens 50.00
22 Sammy Sosa 30.00
23 Scott Rolen 30.00
24 Tim Hudson 20.00
25 Todd Helton 20.00
26 Torii Hunter 15.00
27 Travis Hafner 10.00
28 Vernon Wells 10.00
29 Victor Martinez 15.00
30 Vladimir Guerrero 30.00

Dress Code Materials

NM/M

Production 5-100
Prime: No Pricing
Production 5 Sets
1 Albert Pujols Bat-Jsy/100 25.00
2 Bernie Williams Bat-Jsy/50 10.00
4 Carlos Beltran Bat-Bat/Jsy/100 10.00
5 Chipper Jones Bat-Jsy/100 12.00
6 Curt Schilling Bat-Jsy/50 15.00
7 David Ortiz Bat-Hat/100 15.00
8 Hank Blalock Bat-Jsy/100 8.00
9 Hideki Matsui Bat-Jsy/100 30.00
10 Jim Edmonds 10.00
11 Jim Thome Jsy-Jsy/100 12.00
15 Mark Teixeira Bat-Jsy/100 8.00
16 Miguel Cabrera Jsy-Jsy/100 10.00
17 Miguel Tejada Bat-Jsy/100 8.00
18 Mike Piazza Bat-Jsy/100 12.00
19 Pedro J. Martinez Bat-Jsy/100 12.00
21 Roger Clemens Bat-Jsy/5
22 Sammy Sosa Bat-Jsy/100 12.00
23 Scott Rolen Bat-Jsy/100 12.00
25 Todd Helton Jsy-Jsy/50 12.00
26 Torii Hunter Bat-Jsy/100 8.00
27 Travis Hafner Jsy-Shoes/50 8.00
28 Vernon Wells Jsy-Jsy/50 8.00
29 Victor Martinez Jsy-Jsy/50 8.00
30 Vladimir Guerrero Bat-Jsy/100 12.00

Dress Code Signature Bat

NM/M

Production 1-25
7 David Ortiz/25 50.00
8 Hank Blalock/25 30.00
16 Miguel Cabrera/25 50.00
26 Torii Hunter/25 30.00
27 Travis Hafner/25 25.00
28 Vernon Wells/25 25.00

Dress Code Signature Jersey

NM/M

Production 5-25
1 Albert Pujols/5
5 Chipper Jones/5
6 Curt Schilling/5
7 David Ortiz/25 50.00
8 Hank Blalock/25 30.00
10 Jim Edmonds/5
12 Johan Santana/25 50.00
14 Mark Prior/10
16 Miguel Cabrera/25 50.00
19 Pedro J. Martinez/5
20 Randy Johnson/5
21 Roger Clemens/5
22 Sammy Sosa/5
23 Scott Rolen/10
24 Tim Hudson/10
25 Todd Helton/5
26 Torii Hunter/25 30.00
27 Travis Hafner/25 25.00
28 Vernon Wells/25 25.00
29 Victor Martinez/25 25.00

Dress Code Sign. Jersey Number

NM/M

Production 1-25
Prime: No Pricing
Production 1-5
7 David Ortiz/25 50.00
8 Hank Blalock/25 30.00
12 Johan Santana/25 50.00
26 Torii Hunter/25 30.00
27 Travis Hafner/25 25.00
29 Victor Martinez/25 25.00

Home Run Heroes

NM/M

Complete Set (50): 90.00
Common Player: 1.50
Production 1,000 Sets
Gold: 2X-4X
Production 50 Sets
Platinum: No Pricing
Production One Set
1 Mike Schmidt 4.00
2 Ken Griffey Jr. 4.00
3 Babe Ruth 6.00
4 Duke Snider 2.00
5 Johnny Bench 3.00
6 Stan Musial 3.00
7 Willie McCovey 2.00
8 Willie Stargell 2.00
9 Ted Williams 5.00
10 Frank Thomas 2.00
11 Gary Sheffield 2.00
12 Jim Thome 2.00
13 Harmon Killebrew 2.00
14 Ernie Banks 3.00
15 George Foster 1.50
16 Albert Pujols 5.00
17 Tony Perez 1.50
18 Richie Sexson 1.50
19 Juan Gonzalez 1.50
20 Frank Robinson 2.00
21 Sammy Sosa 3.00
22 Jeff Bagwell 1.50
23 Mark Teixeira 1.50
24 Willie Mays 5.00
25 Rafael Palmeiro 2.00
26 Billy Williams 1.50
27 Vladimir Guerrero 2.00
28 Gary Carter 2.00
29 Fred McGriff 1.50
30 Orlando Cepeda 1.50
31 Dave Winfield 2.00
32 Shawn Green 1.50
33 Jose Canseco 1.50
34 Hideki Matsui 4.00
35 Roger Maris 4.00
36 Andre Dawson 2.00
37 Paul Konerko 1.50
38 Darryl Strawberry 1.50
39 Dave Parker 1.50
40 Adam Dunn 2.00
41 Ralph Kiner 2.00
42 Miguel Tejada 2.00
43 Dale Murphy 2.00
44 Hank Aaron 6.00
45 Mike Piazza 3.00
46 Reggie Jackson 2.00
47 Adrian Beltre 2.00
48 Cal Ripken Jr. 8.00
49 Manny Ramirez 3.00
50 Alex Rodriguez 5.00

Home Run Heroes Jersey HR

NM/M

Production 1-66
Prime: No Pricing
Production One Set
1 Mike Schmidt/48 25.00
3 Babe Ruth/25 165.00
4 Duke Snider Pants/14
5 Johnny Bench/45 15.00
6 Stan Musial/6
7 Willie McCovey/23 15.00
8 Willie Stargell/48 15.00
9 Ted Williams/43 60.00
10 Frank Thomas/43 12.00
11 Gary Sheffield/36 8.00
12 Jim Thome/47 15.00
13 Harmon Killebrew/49 20.00
14 Ernie Banks Pants/47 20.00
15 Gene Foster/25 10.00

16 Albert Pujols/46 35.00
18 Richie Sexson/45 8.00
19 Juan Gonzalez/47 8.00
20 Frank Robinson/1
21 Sammy Sosa/66 12.00
22 Jeff Bagwell/47 10.00
23 Mark Teixeira/38 8.00
24 Willie Mays/51 50.00
25 Rafael Palmeiro/47 10.00
26 Billy Williams/26 10.00
27 Vladimir Guerrero/44 12.00
28 Gary Carter/31 10.00
29 Fred McGriff/32 12.00
30 Orlando Cepeda Pants/46 8.00
31 Dave Winfield/34 10.00
32 Shawn Green/49 8.00
33 Jose Canseco/44 10.00
34 Hideki MatsuiPants/31 40.00
35 Roger Maris Pants/19 50.00
36 Andre Dawson/49 8.00
37 Paul Konerko/14
38 Darryl Strawberry/24 10.00
39 Dave Parker/34 8.00
40 Adam Dunn/46 10.00
42 Miguel Tejada/34 10.00
43 Dale Murphy/44 12.00
44 Hank Aaron/47 50.00
45 Mike Piazza/40 15.00
46 Reggie Jackson/39 12.00
47 Adrian Beltre/48 8.00
48 Cal Ripken Jr./34 50.00
49 Manny Ramirez/43 12.00

Home Run Heroes Materials

NM/M

Production 1-66
Prime: No Pricing
Production One Set
1 Mike Schmidt Bat-Jsy/48 30.00
3 Babe Ruth Bat-Jsy/25 300.00
5 Johnny Bench Bat-Jsy/45 20.00
6 Stan Musial Bat-Jsy/6
7 Willie McCovey Bat-Jsy/23 20.00
8 Willie Stargell Bat-Jsy/48 20.00
9 Ted Williams Bat-Jsy/43 85.00
10 Frank Thomas Jsy-Jsy/43 15.00
11 Gary Sheffield Bat-Jsy/36 10.00
12 Jim Thome Bat-Jsy/47 15.00
13 Harmon Killebrew Bat-Jsy/49 25.00
14 Ernie Banks Bat-Pants/47 25.00
15 George Foster Bat-Jsy/52 10.00
16 Albert Pujols Jsy-Jsy/46 40.00
17 Tony Perez Bat-Fld Glv/24 15.00
18 Richie Sexson Bat-Jsy/45 10.00
19 Juan Gonzalez Bat-Jsy/47 10.00
20 Frank Robinson Bat-Jsy/1
21 Sammy Sosa Bat-Jsy/66 15.00
22 Jeff Bagwell Bat-Jsy/47 12.00
23 Mark Teixeira Bat-Jsy/38 10.00
24 Willie Mays Bat-Jsy/51 50.00
25 Rafael Palmeiro Bat-Jsy/47 12.00
26 Billy Williams Bat-Jsy/26 10.00
27 Vladimir Guerrero Bat-Jsy/44 15.00
28 Gary Carter Bat-Jsy/31 12.00
29 Fred McGriff Bat-Jsy/32 15.00
30 Orlando Cepeda Bat-Pants/34 12.00
31 Dave Winfield Bat-Jsy/34 15.00
32 Shawn Green Bat-Jsy/49 10.00
33 Jose Canseco Hat-Jsy/44 12.00
34 Hideki Matsui Bat-Pants/31 60.00
35 Roger Maris Bat-Pants/19 50.00
36 Andre Dawson Bat-Jsy/49 10.00
37 Paul Konerko Bat-Jsy/14
38 Darryl Strawberry Jsy-Pants/24 12.00
39 Dave Parker Bat-Jsy/34 12.00
40 Adam Dunn Bat-Jsy/46 15.00
42 Miguel Tejada Bat-Jsy/34 15.00
43 Dale Murphy Jsy-Jsy/44 15.00
44 Hank Aaron Bat-Jsy/47 50.00
45 Mike Piazza Jsy-Jsy/40 15.00
46 Reggie Jackson Bat-Jsy/39 15.00
47 Adrian Beltre Bat-Jsy/48 12.00
48 Cal Ripken Jr. Bat-Jsy/34 60.00
49 Manny Ramirez Jsy-Jsy/43 15.00

Legendary Lumberjacks

NM/M

Common Player: 2.00
Production 400 Sets
Gold: 2X-4X
Production 50 Sets
Platinum: No Pricing
Production One Set
1 Al Kaline 4.00
2 Babe Ruth 8.00
3 Billy Williams 2.00
4 Bob Feller 3.00
5 Bob Gibson 3.00
6 Brooks Robinson 4.00
7 Cal Ripken Jr. 10.00
8 Carlton Fisk 3.00
9 Dennis Eckersley 2.00
10 Don Mattingly 6.00
11 Duke Snider 3.00
12 Eddie Murray 3.00
13 Ernie Banks 4.00
14 Fergie Jenkins 2.00
15 Frank Robinson 4.00
16 Gaylord Perry 2.00
17 George Brett 6.00
18 George Kell 2.00
19 Harmon Killebrew 4.00
20 Jim Palmer 2.00
21 Joe Morgan 2.00
22 Johnny Bench 5.00
23 Juan Marichal 2.00
24 Lou Brock 3.00
25 Maury Wills 2.00
26 Mike Schmidt 6.00
27 Nolan Ryan 8.00
28 Ozzie Smith 4.00
29 Paul Molitor 3.00
30 Pee Wee Reese 2.00
31 Phil Niekro 2.00
32 Phil Rizzuto 3.00
33 Ralph Kiner 2.00
34 Reggie Jackson 3.00
35 Rickey Henderson 3.00
36 Roberto Clemente 8.00
37 Robin Yount 4.00
38 Rod Carew 2.00
39 Roger Maris 5.00
40 Stan Musial 5.00
41 Steve Carlton 2.00
42 Ted Williams 8.00
43 Tom Seaver 3.00
44 Tony Gwynn 3.00
45 Tony Perez 2.00
46 Wade Boggs 3.00
47 Warren Spahn 4.00
48 Whitey Ford 4.00
49 Willie McCovey 3.00
50 Yogi Berra 4.00

Legendary Lumberjacks Bat

NM/M

Production 1-50
1 Al Kaline/6
2 Babe Ruth/25 200.00
6 Brooks Robinson/50 15.00
7 Cal Ripken Jr./50 50.00
8 Carlton Fisk/50 10.00
10 Don Mattingly/50 25.00
12 Eddie Murray/50 15.00
13 Ernie Banks/50 15.00
15 Frank Robinson/50 15.00
17 George Brett/50 20.00
19 Harmon Killebrew/50 15.00
21 Joe Morgan/50 10.00
22 Johnny Bench/50 15.00
24 Lou Brock/50 10.00
26 Mike Schmidt/50 20.00
28 Ozzie Smith/50 15.00
29 Paul Molitor/50 12.00
30 Pee Wee Reese/50 10.00
34 Reggie Jackson/50 12.00
35 Rickey Henderson/50 12.00
36 Roberto Clemente/50 50.00
37 Robin Yount/50 15.00
38 Rod Carew/50 10.00
39 Roger Maris/25 40.00
40 Stan Musial/25 25.00
42 Ted Williams/25 60.00
44 Tony Gwynn/50 15.00
45 Tony Perez/1
46 Wade Boggs/50 12.00
49 Willie McCovey/50 12.00
50 Yogi Berra/25 25.00

Legendary Lumberjacks Jersey

NM/M

Production 1-50
3 Billy Williams/25 12.00
6 Brooks Robinson/25 20.00
7 Cal Ripken Jr./50 50.00
8 Carlton Fisk/25 15.00
10 Don Mattingly/50 25.00
11 Duke Snider/10
12 Eddie Murray/50 15.00
13 Ernie Banks/25 20.00
17 George Brett/5
19 Harmon Killebrew/25 20.00
22 Johnny Bench/25 20.00
24 Lou Brock/25 12.00
25 Maury Wills/25 12.00
26 Mike Schmidt/25 25.00
28 Ozzie Smith/25 20.00
29 Paul Molitor/50 12.00
34 Reggie Jackson/25 15.00
35 Rickey Henderson/50 12.00
37 Robin Yount/50 15.00
38 Rod Carew/50 10.00

Legendary Lumberjacks Jersey HR

NM/M

Production 1-25
6 Brooks Robinson/25 20.00
7 Cal Ripken Jr./25 60.00
10 Don Mattingly/25 30.00
12 Eddie Murray/25 20.00
29 Paul Molitor/25 20.00
35 Rickey Henderson/25 20.00
37 Robin Yount/25 20.00
38 Rod Carew/25 15.00
44 Tony Gwynn/25 20.00
45 Tony Perez/25 15.00
46 Wade Boggs/25 15.00
49 Willie McCovey/25 15.00

Legendary Lumberjacks Materials

NM/M

Production 1-50
2 Babe Ruth Bat-Jsy/25 300.00
6 Brooks Robinson Bat-Jsy/50 20.00
7 Cal Ripken Jr. Bat-Jsy/50 60.00
8 Carlton Fisk Bat-Jsy/25 15.00
10 Don Mattingly Bat-Jsy/50 30.00
12 Eddie Murray Bat-Jsy/50 20.00
13 Ernie Banks Bat-Jsy/25 25.00
17 George Brett Bat-Jsy/5
19 Harmon Killebrew Bat-Jsy/25 20.00
21 Joe Morgan Bat-Jsy/1
22 Johnny Bench Bat-Jsy/25 20.00
24 Lou Brock Bat-Jsy/50 12.00
26 Mike Schmidt Bat-Jsy/50 25.00
28 Ozzie Smith Bat-Jsy/10
29 Paul Molitor Bat-Jsy/50 15.00
30 Pee Wee Reese Bat-Jsy/10
32 Phil Rizzuto Jsy-Pants/10
34 Reggie Jackson Bat-Jsy/25 20.00
35 Rickey Henderson Bat-Jsy/50 15.00
37 Robin Yount Bat-Jsy/50 20.00
38 Rod Carew Bat-Jsy/50 15.00
44 Tony Gwynn Bat-Jsy/50 20.00
46 Wade Boggs Bat-Jsy/50 15.00
49 Willie McCovey Bat-Jsy/44 15.00
50 Yogi Berra Bat-Jsy/8

Legendary Players

NM/M

Common Player: 1.50
Production 800 Sets
Gold: 2X-3X
Production 75 Sets
Platinum: No Pricing
Production One Set
1 Al Kaline 3.00
2 Babe Ruth 6.00
3 Billy Williams 1.50
4 Bob Feller 2.00
5 Bob Gibson 2.00
6 Brooks Robinson 3.00
7 Cal Ripken Jr. 8.00
8 Carlton Fisk 2.00
9 Dennis Eckersley 2.00
10 Don Mattingly 5.00
11 Duke Snider 2.00
12 Eddie Murray 2.00
13 Ernie Banks 3.00
14 Fergie Jenkins 1.50
15 Frank Robinson 3.00
16 Gaylord Perry 1.50
17 George Brett 5.00
18 George Kell 1.50
19 Harmon Killebrew 3.00
20 Jim Palmer 1.50
21 Joe Morgan 1.50
22 Johnny Bench 4.00
23 Juan Marichal 1.50
24 Lou Brock 2.00
25 Maury Wills 1.50
26 Mike Schmidt 5.00
27 Nolan Ryan 6.00
28 Ozzie Smith 3.00
29 Paul Molitor 2.00
30 Pee Wee Reese 1.50
31 Phil Niekro 1.50
32 Phil Rizzuto 2.00
33 Ralph Kiner 1.50
34 Reggie Jackson 2.00
35 Rickey Henderson 2.00
36 Roberto Clemente 6.00
37 Robin Yount 3.00
38 Rod Carew 2.00
39 Roger Maris 4.00
40 Stan Musial 4.00
41 Steve Carlton 1.50
42 Ted Williams 6.00
43 Tom Seaver 2.00
44 Tony Gwynn 2.00
45 Tony Perez 1.50
46 Wade Boggs 2.00
47 Warren Spahn 3.00
48 Whitey Ford 3.00
49 Willie McCovey 2.00
50 Yogi Berra 3.00

Legendary Players Hat

NM/M

Production 1-25
10 Don Mattingly/25 30.00
13 Ernie Banks/25 20.00
17 George Brett/25 30.00
20 Jim Palmer/25 10.00
26 Mike Schmidt/25 30.00
28 Ozzie Smith/25 25.00
37 Robin Yount/25 25.00
44 Tony Gwynn/25 20.00

Legendary Players Jacket

NM/M

Production 25 Sets
7 Cal Ripken Jr. 60.00
8 Carlton Fisk 12.00
10 Don Mattingly 40.00
24 Lou Brock 15.00
26 Mike Schmidt 35.00
27 Nolan Ryan 50.00
34 Reggie Jackson 15.00

35 Rickey Henderson 20.00
38 Rod Carew 20.00
42 Ted Williams 85.00

Legendary Players Jersey Number

NM/M
Production 1-44
Prime: No Pricing
Production One Set
3 Billy Williams/26 10.00
8 Carlton Fisk/72 10.00
9 Dennis Eckersley/43 10.00
10 Don Mattingly/23 30.00
12 Eddie Murray/33 15.00
16 Gaylord Perry/36 8.00
20 Jim Palmer/22 10.00
23 Juan Marichal/27 10.00
24 Lou Brock/20 15.00
25 Maury Wills/30 8.00
26 Mike Schmidt/20 30.00
27 Nolan Ryan/34 40.00
31 Phil Niekro/35 8.00
35 Rickey Henderson/24 15.00
37 Robin Yount/19 25.00
38 Rod Carew/29 15.00
41 Steve Carlton/32 10.00
43 Tom Seaver/41 15.00
44 Tony Gwynn/19 20.00
45 Tony Perez/24 10.00
46 Wade Boggs/26 15.00
47 Warren Spahn/24 20.00
49 Willie McCovey/44 12.00

Legendary Players Leather

NM/M
Production 10-25
10 Don Mattingly Btg Glv/25 40.00
14 Fergie Jenkins Fld Glv/25 15.00
26 Mike Schmidt Fld Glv/25 40.00
35 Rickey Henderson Btg Glv/25 25.00
41 Steve Carlton Fld Glv/25 15.00
44 Tony Gwynn Btg Glv/25 30.00
45 Tony Perez Fld Glv/25 15.00
46 Wade Boggs Btg Glv/10

Legendary Players Pants

NM/M
Production 1-25
4 Bob Feller/19 20.00
7 Cal Ripken Jr./25 60.00
11 Duke Snider/25 20.00
12 Eddie Murray/25 20.00
14 Fergie Jenkins/25 10.00
20 Jim Palmer/25 10.00
23 Juan Marichal/25 10.00
28 Ozzie Smith/25 25.00
29 Paul Molitor/25 15.00
35 Rickey Henderson/25 20.00
38 Rod Carew/25 15.00
39 Roger Maris/25 50.00
43 Tom Seaver/25 15.00
44 Tony Gwynn/25 20.00
47 Warren Spahn/24 20.00
49 Willie McCovey/25 15.00

Legendary Players Spikes

NM/M
Production 1-25
15 Frank Robinson/25 20.00
44 Tony Gwynn/25 30.00

Membership

NM/M
Common Player: 1.50
Production 1,000 Sets
Gold: 2X-4X
Production 50 Sets
Platinum: No Pricing
Production One Set
1 Bobby Doerr 1.50
2 Tom Seaver 2.00
3 Cal Ripken Jr. 8.00
4 Paul Molitor 2.00
5 Brooks Robinson 2.00
6 Al Kaline 4.00
7 Steve Carlton 2.00
8 Carl Yastrzemski 4.00
9 Bob Feller 2.00
10 Fred Lynn 1.50
11 Luis Aparicio 1.50
12 Hank Aaron 6.00
13 Willie Mays 6.00
14 Bob Gibson 3.00
15 Joe Morgan 2.00
16 Whitey Ford 3.00
17 Don Sutton 1.50
18 Harmon Killebrew 3.00
19 Tony Gwynn 3.00
20 Lou Brock 1.50
21 Dennis Eckersley 1.50
22 Jim Palmer 1.50
23 Don Mattingly 5.00
24 Carlton Fisk 2.00
25 Gaylord Perry 1.50
26 Mike Schmidt 5.00
27 Nolan Ryan 6.00
28 Sandy Koufax 10.00
29 Rod Carew 2.00
30 Maury Wills 1.50

Membership VIP Bat

NM/M
Production 25 Sets
1 Bobby Doerr 10.00
2 Tom Seaver 20.00
3 Cal Ripken Jr. 60.00
4 Paul Molitor 15.00
5 Brooks Robinson 15.00
6 Al Kaline 20.00
7 Steve Carlton 10.00
8 Carl Yastrzemski 20.00
10 Fred Lynn 8.00
11 Luis Aparicio 8.00
12 Hank Aaron 40.00
13 Willie Mays 50.00
15 Joe Morgan 10.00
18 Harmon Killebrew 20.00
19 Tony Gwynn 20.00
20 Lou Brock 15.00
23 Don Mattingly 30.00
24 Carlton Fisk 15.00
29 Rod Carew 12.00

Membership VIP Jersey

NM/M
Production 5-50
Prime: No Pricing
Production One Set
7 Steve Carlton/25 10.00
10 Fred Lynn/25 10.00
11 Luis Aparicio/25 10.00
15 Joe Morgan/25 10.00
17 Don Sutton/50 8.00
19 Tony Gwynn/50 15.00
20 Lou Brock/25 15.00
21 Dennis Eckersley/50 8.00
22 Jim Palmer/25 10.00
23 Don Mattingly/25 30.00
24 Carlton Fisk/25 15.00
25 Gaylord Perry/50 8.00
26 Mike Schmidt/50 20.00
27 Nolan Ryan/25 40.00
29 Rod Carew/50 10.00

Membership VIP Materials

NM/M
Production 5-25
Prime: No Pricing
Production One Set
1 Bobby Doerr Bat-Pants/25 10.00
2 Tom Seaver Bat-Jsy/25 20.00
3 Cal Ripken Jr. Bat-Jsy/25 75.00
4 Paul Molitor Bat-Jsy/25 20.00
5 Brooks Robinson Bat-Jsy/25 25.00
7 Steve Carlton Bat-Jsy/25 15.00
8 Carl Yastrzemski Bat-Jsy/10
10 Fred Lynn Bat-Jsy/25 10.00
11 Luis Aparicio Bat-Jsy/25 10.00
12 Hank Aaron Bat-Jsy/5
13 Willie Mays Bat-Jsy/5
15 Joe Morgan Bat-Jsy/25 12.00
18 Harmon Killebrew Bat-Jsy/25 25.00
19 Tony Gwynn Bat-Jsy/25 25.00
20 Lou Brock Bat-Jsy/25 25.00
23 Don Mattingly Bat-Jsy/25 35.00
27 Nolan Ryan Bat-Jsy/25 50.00
29 Rod Carew Bat-Jsy/25 20.00

Membership VIP Materials HR

NM/M
Production 6-49
1 Bobby Doerr Jsy-Pants/27 15.00
3 Cal Ripken Jr. Jsy-Pants/34 60.00
4 Paul Molitor Bat-Jsy/22 15.00
8 Carl Yastrzemski Bat-Jsy/44 25.00
10 Fred Lynn Bat-Jsy/39 8.00
11 Luis Aparicio Bat-Jsy/10
12 Hank Aaron Bat-Jsy/47 50.00
15 Joe Morgan Bat-Jsy/27 12.00
18 Harmon Killebrew Bat-Jsy/49 20.00
19 Tony Gwynn Bat-Jsy/17
20 Lou Brock Bat-Jsy/21 15.00
23 Don Mattingly Bat-Jsy/35 40.00
24 Carlton Fisk Bat-Jsy/37 15.00
26 Mike Schmidt Bat-Jsy/48 25.00
29 Rod Carew Bat-Jsy/14
30 Maury Wills Jsy-Jsy/6

Membership VIP Signature Material

NM/M
Production 1-25
Prime: No Pricing
Production One Set
1 Bobby Doerr Bat-Pants/25 35.00
10 Fred Lynn Bat-Jsy/25 30.00
11 Luis Aparicio Bat-Jsy/25 30.00
20 Lou Brock Bat-Jsy/25 50.00

Membership VIP Sign. Materials HR

No Pricing
Production 1-10

Significant Signatures Silver

NM/M
Production 1-200
Gold: .75X-1.5X
Production 1-100
No pricing 20 or less
Platinum: No Pricing
Production One Set
17 Jay Gibbons/25 15.00
22 Tim Salmon/100 15.00
26 Kevin Youkilis/25 12.00
29 Cliff Lee/200 8.00
37 Jeff Suppan/200 10.00
39 Larry Bigbie/100 15.00
40 Rich Harden/100 15.00
41 Victor Martinez/25 20.00
43 Joey Gathright/100 8.00
61 Jake Peavy/25 40.00
63 Dioner Navarro/100 15.00
64 Kazuhito Tadano/100 15.00
65 Ryan Wagner/50 10.00
66 Abe Alvarez/100 15.00
68 Jermaine Dye/25 15.00
69 Todd Walker/25 15.00
70 Octavio Dotel/25 15.00
73 Scott Podsednik/25 20.00
76 Raul Ibanez/50 10.00
77 Orlando Cabrera/25 20.00
79 Esteban Loaiza/50 15.00
84 David Dellucci/50 20.00
85 Travis Blackley/200 8.00
86 Brad Penny/25 15.00
88 Brian Roberts/100 35.00
90 Mike Lieberthal/25 15.00
94 Milton Bradley/100 15.00
96 Adrian Gonzalez/200 12.00
97 Chad Tracy/100 10.00
98 Chad Cordero/100 8.00
100 Jason Kubel/200 12.00
102 Jack Wilson/100 10.00
104 Casey Kotchman/100 12.00
106 Melvin Mora/100 15.00
107 Bobby Crosby/100 15.00
111 Francisco Cordero/50 15.00
114 Eric Byrnes/50 10.00
118 Shea Hillenbrand/25 15.00
119 Aubrey Huff/25 20.00
120 Lew Ford/25 20.00
126 Adam LaRoche/25 15.00
128 Ken Harvey/50 10.00
132 Russ Ortiz/25 15.00
133 Jason Varitek 10.00
136 Joe Nathan/100 20.00
138 Carlos Zambrano/25 35.00
143 John Lackey/200 10.00
145 Dewon Brazelton/200 10.00
146 Jason Bay/25 25.00
148 Travis Hafner/100 12.00
152 Wade Miller/50 12.00
154 Scott Kazmir/25 35.00
156 Livan Hernandez/25 15.00
158 David Wright/25 80.00
159 Chone Figgins/50 12.00
163 Merkin Valdez/200 10.00
165 Alexis Rios/50 15.00
166 Johnny Estrada/200 10.00
167 Danny Graves/50 15.00
168 Carlos Lee/25 25.00
171 Randy Wolf/25 15.00
175 Edwin Jackson/25 12.00
178 Jacque Jones/25 15.00
180 Laynce Nix/200 10.00
181 Tom Gordon/25 15.00
182 Jose Castillo/100 12.00
188 Keith Foulke/25 60.00
189 Jeremy Bonderman/50 20.00
190 Troy Percival/25 15.00
194 Brett Myers/50 15.00
197 Lyle Overbay/25 20.00
202 Miguel Negron/100 8.00
204 Paulino Reynoso/100 8.00
205 Colter Bean/100 10.00
206 Raul Tablado/100 8.00
207 Mark McLemore/100 8.00
208 Russel Rohlicek/100 8.00
210 Chris Seddon/100 8.00
213 Mike Morse/100 20.00
217 Carlos Ruiz/100 8.00
218 Chris Roberson/100 8.00
219 Ryan Speier/100 8.00
221 Ambiorix Burgos/100 8.00
223 David Gassner/100 10.00
224 Sean Tracey/100 8.00
225 Casey Rogowski/100 8.00
236 Gaylord Perry LGD/25 25.00
245 Bobby Doerr LGD/25 25.00
246 Bob Feller LGD/25 30.00

Stars of Summer

NM/M
Common Player: 1.50
Production 1,000 Sets
Gold: 2X-4X
Production 50 Sets
Platinum: No Pricing
Production One Set
1 Andre Dawson 2.00
2 Bert Blyleven 2.00
3 Bill Madlock 1.50
4 Dale Murphy 3.00
5 Darryl Strawberry 2.00
6 Dave Parker 2.00
7 Dave Righetti 2.00
8 Dwight Evans 2.00
9 Dwight Gooden 2.00
10 Fred Lynn 1.50
11 George Foster 2.00
12 Harold Baines 2.00
13 Jack Morris 1.50

14 Jim Rice 3.00
15 Keith Hernandez 2.00
16 Kirk Gibson 2.00
17 Luis Aparicio 2.00
18 Mark Grace 2.00
19 Marty Marion 1.50
20 Orel Hershiser 2.00
21 Ron Guidry 3.00
22 Ron Santo 2.00
23 Steve Garvey 2.00
24 Tony Oliva 2.00
25 Will Clark 3.00

Stars of Summer Material

NM/M

Production 100-250
1 Andre Dawson Jsy/250 8.00
2 Bert Blyleven Jsy/150 8.00
3 Bill Madlock Bat/250 5.00
4 Dale Murphy Jsy/100 12.00
5 Darryl Strawberry Jsy/250 8.00
6 Dave Parker Jsy/100 10.00
7 Dave Righetti Jsy/150 8.00
8 Dwight Evans Bat/250 8.00
9 Dwight Gooden Bat/150 8.00
10 Fred Lynn Jsy/100 5.00
11 George Foster Bat/250 5.00
12 Harold Baines Jsy/250 5.00
13 Jack Morris Jsy/100 5.00
14 Jim Rice Pants/250 8.00
15 Keith Hernandez Bat/100 5.00
16 Kirk Gibson Jsy/250 8.00
17 Luis Aparicio Bat/250 8.00
18 Mark Grace Bat/250 10.00
22 Ron Santo Bat/150 10.00
23 Steve GarveyJsy/250 8.00
24 Tony Oliva Jsy/250 8.00
25 Will Clark Bat/250 10.00

Stars of Summer Sign. Material

NM/M

Production 25-100
1 Andre Dawson Jsy/100 20.00
2 Bert Blyleven Jsy/50 20.00
3 Bill Madlock Bat/100 20.00
4 Dale Murphy Jsy/25 40.00
6 Dave Parker Jsy/50 20.00
7 Dave Righetti Jsy/50 20.00
8 Dwight Evans Bat/50 30.00
9 Dwight Gooden Bat/25 25.00
10 Fred Lynn Jsy/100 15.00
11 George Foster Bat/50 20.00
12 Harold Baines Jsy/100 25.00
13 Jack Morris Jsy/100 15.00
14 Jim Rice Pants/50 25.00
15 Keith Hernandez Jsy/50 20.00
16 Kirk Gibson Jsy/25 40.00
17 Luis Aparicio Bat/50 20.00
18 Mark Grace Bat/25 40.00
22 Ron Santo Bat/50 35.00
23 Steve Garvey Jsy/50 20.00
24 Tony Oliva Jsy/50 20.00
25 Will Clark Bat/25 40.00

Team Colors

NM/M

Common Player: 1.50
Production 800 Sets
Gold: 2X-4X
Production 50 Sets
Platinum: No Pricing
Production One Set
1 Adam Dunn 2.00
2 Albert Pujols 6.00
3 Andruw Jones 2.00
4 Aramis Ramirez 2.00
5 Aubrey Huff 1.50
6 Bobby Abreu 2.00
7 Cal Ripken Jr. 8.00
8 Carlos Lee 1.50
9 Craig Biggio 2.00
10 Derrek Lee 2.00
11 Garret Anderson 2.00
12 Gary Carter 2.00
13 Geoff Jenkins 1.50
14 Greg Maddux 4.00
15 Hank Blalock 2.00
16 Hideki Matsui 5.00
17 Jake Peavy 2.00
18 Jim Edmonds 2.00
19 Jim Palmer 2.00
20 Jose Guillen 1.50
21 Jose Vidro 1.50
22 Juan Pierre 1.50
23 Lew Ford 1.50
24 Lyle Overbay 1.50
25 Manny Ramirez 3.00
26 Mark Loretta 1.50
27 Mark Teixeira 3.00
28 Melvin Mora 1.50
29 Michael Young 2.00
30 Miguel Cabrera 4.00
31 Mike Lowell 1.50
32 Mike Mussina 2.00
33 Milton Bradley 2.00
34 Randy Johnson 4.00
35 Roger Clemens 6.00
36 Sean Casey 2.00
37 Shawn Green 2.00
38 Steve Carlton 2.00
39 Todd Helton 2.00
40 Travis Hafner 1.50

Team Colors Bat

NM/M

Production 100 Sets
1 Adam Dunn 8.00
2 Albert Pujols 20.00
3 Andruw Jones 5.00
4 Aramis Ramirez 8.00
7 Cal Ripken Jr. 30.00
9 Craig Biggio 8.00
10 Derrek Lee 8.00
11 Garret Anderson 5.00
12 Gary Carter 5.00
15 Hank Blalock 8.00
16 Hideki Matsui 30.00
18 Jim Edmonds 10.00
21 Jose Vidro 5.00
22 Juan Pierre 5.00
23 Lew Ford 5.00
27 Mark Teixeira 8.00
28 Melvin Mora 5.00
29 Michael Young 5.00
30 Miguel Cabrera 10.00
31 Mike Lowell 5.00
36 Sean Casey 5.00
37 Shawn Green 5.00

Team Colors Materials

NM/M

Production 25-100
Prime: No Pricing
Production 5 Sets
1 Adam Dunn Bat-Jsy/100 10.00
2 Albert Pujols Bat-Jsy/100 25.00
3 Andruw Jones Bat-Jsy/100 8.00
4 Aramis Ramirez Bat-Jsy/100 10.00
6 Bobby Abreu Jsy-Jsy/100 10.00
7 Cal Ripken Jr. Bat-Jsy/100 40.00
8 Carlos Lee Jsy-Jsy/100 8.00
9 Craig Biggio Bat-Jsy/100 10.00
11 Garret Anderson Bat-Jsy/50 8.00
12 Gary Carter Bat-Jsy/50 8.00
13 Geoff Jenkins Jsy-Pants/100 8.00
15 Hank Blalock Bat-Jsy/100 10.00
16 Hideki Matsui Bat-Jsy/50 45.00
18 Jim Edmonds Bat-Jkt/100 12.00
19 Jim Palmer Jsy-Pants/25 12.00
21 Jose Vidro Bat-Jsy/50 8.00
23 Lew Ford Bat-Jsy/100 8.00
25 Manny Ramirez Jsy-Jsy/100 15.00
27 Mark Teixeira Bat-Jsy/100 10.00
28 Melvin Mora Bat-Jsy/50 8.00
29 Michael Young Bat-Jsy/100 8.00
30 Miguel Cabrera Bat-Jsy/100 15.00
31 Mike Lowell Bat-Jsy/100 8.00
36 Sean Casey Bat-Jsy/100 8.00
37 Shawn Green Bat-Jsy/100 8.00
39 Todd Helton Jsy-Jsy/50 10.00

Team Colors Signature

NM/M

Production 1-25
4 Aramis Ramirez/25 40.00
5 Aubrey Huff/25 20.00
8 Carlos Lee/25 25.00
17 Jake Peavy/25 40.00
20 Jose Guillen/25 25.00
21 Jose Vidro/25 20.00
23 Lew Ford/25 20.00
24 Lyle Overbay/25 25.00
26 Mark Loretta/25 25.00
28 Melvin Mora/25 25.00
33 Milton Bradley/25 25.00
40 Travis Hafner/25 20.00

Team Colors Signature Bat

NM/M

Production 5-25
1 Adam Dunn/25 40.00
4 Aramis Ramirez/25 40.00
5 Aubrey Huff/25 20.00
10 Derrek Lee/25 35.00
11 Garret Anderson/25 25.00
15 Hank Blalock/25 30.00
21 Jose Vidro/25 20.00
23 Lew Ford/25 20.00
29 Michael Young/25 20.00

Team Colors Signature Jersey

NM/M

Production 1-25
Prime: No Pricing
Production One Set
1 Adam Dunn/25 40.00
4 Aramis Ramirez/25 40.00
5 Aubrey Huff/25 20.00
8 Carlos Lee/25 25.00
11 Garret Anderson/25 25.00
12 Gary Carter/25 25.00
15 Hank Blalock/25 30.00
21 Jose Vidro/25 20.00
23 Lew Ford/25 20.00
24 Lyle Overbay/25 25.00
28 Melvin Mora/25 25.00
29 Michael Young/25 20.00
40 Travis Hafner/25 20.00

Team Colors Signature Materials

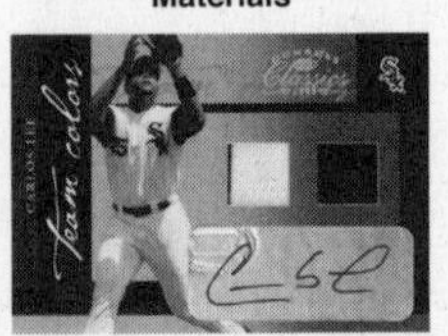

NM/M

Production 5-25
Prime: No Pricing
Production One Set
1 Adam Dunn Bat-Jsy/10
2 Albert Pujols Bat-Jsy/5
4 Aramis Ramirez Bat-Jsy/25 50.00
5 Aubrey Huff Jsy-Jsy/25 25.00
7 Cal Ripken Jr. Bat-Jsy/5
8 Carlos Lee Jsy-Jsy/25 30.00
9 Craig Biggio Bat-Jsy/10
11 Garret Anderson Bat-Jsy/25 30.00
12 Gary Carter Bat-Jsy/10
15 Hank Blalock Bat-Jsy/25 40.00
18 Jim Edmonds Bat-Jsy/5
21 Jose Vidro Bat-Jsy/25 25.00
23 Lew Ford Bat-Jsy/25 25.00
25 Manny Ramirez Bat-Jsy/5
28 Melvin Mora Bat-Jsy/25 30.00
29 Michael Young Bat-Jsy/25 30.00
30 Miguel Cabrera Bat-Jsy/10
36 Sean Casey Bat-Jsy/10
37 Shawn Green Bat-Jsy/5
39 Todd Helton Jsy-Jsy/5
40 Travis Hafner Jsy-Jsy/25 25.00

2005 DONRUSS DIAMOND KINGS

NM/M

Complete Set (300): 85.00
Complete Update Set (150): 40.00
Common Player: .25
Pack (5): 8.00
Box (12): 75.00
Update Pack (5): 5.00
Update Box (16): 75.00
1 Garret Anderson .40
2 Vladimir Guerrero .75
3 Jose Guillen .40
4 Troy Glaus .40
5 Tim Salmon .25
6 Casey Kotchman .25
7 Chone Figgins .25
8 Robb Quinlan .25
9 Francisco Rodriguez .25
10 Troy Percival .25
11 Randy Johnson .75
12 Brandon Webb .25
13 Richie Sexson .40
14 Shea Hillenbrand .25
15 Chad Tracy .25
16 Alex Cintron .25
17 Luis Gonzalez .25
18 Rafael Furcal .25
19 Andruw Jones .50
20 Marcus Giles .25
21 John Smoltz .50
22 Adam LaRoche .25
23 Russ Ortiz .25
24 J.D. Drew .25
25 Chipper Jones .75
26 Nick Green .25
27 Rafael Palmeiro .50
28 Miguel Tejada .50
29 Javy Lopez .25
30 Luis Matos .25
31 Larry Bigbie .25
32 Rodrigo Lopez .25
33 Brian Roberts .25
34 Melvin Mora .25
35 Adam Loewen .25
36 Manny Ramirez .75
37 Jason Varitek .50
38 Trot Nixon .25
39 Curt Schilling .75
40 Keith Foulke .25
41 Pedro Martinez .75

No.	Player	Price
42	Johnny Damon	.75
43	Kevin Youkilis	.25
44	Orlando Cabrera	.25
45	Abe Alvarez	.25
46	David Ortiz	.75
47	Kerry Wood	.75
48	Mark Prior	.75
49	Aramis Ramirez	.50
50	Greg Maddux	1.00
51	Carlos Zambrano	.40
52	Derrek Lee	.50
53	Corey Patterson	.40
54	Moises Alou	.40
55	Matt Clement	.25
56	Sammy Sosa	1.50
57	Nomar Garciaparra	1.00
58	Todd Walker	.25
59	Angel Guzman	.25
60	Magglio Ordonez	.25
61	Carlos Lee	.25
62	Joe Crede	.25
63	Paul Konerko	.25
64	Shingo Takatsu	.25
65	Frank Thomas	.50
66	Freddy Garcia	.25
67	Aaron Rowand	.25
68	Jose Contreras	.25
69	Adam Dunn	.50
70	Austin Kearns	.25
71	Barry Larkin	.40
72	Ken Griffey Jr.	1.00
73	Ryan Wagner	.25
74	Sean Casey	.25
75	Danny Graves	.25
76	C.C. Sabathia	.25
77	Jody Gerut	.25
78	Omar Vizquel	.25
79	Victor Martinez	.40
80	Matt Lawton	.25
81	Jake Westbrook	.25
82	Kazuhito Tadano	.25
83	Travis Hafner	.25
84	Todd Helton	.50
85	Preston Wilson	.25
86	Matt Holiday	.25
87	Jeromy Burnitz	.25
88	Vinny Castilla	.25
89	Jeremy Bonderman	.25
90	Ivan Rodriguez	.50
91	Carlos Guillen	.25
92	Brandon Inge	.25
93	Rondell White	.25
94	Dontrelle Willis	.25
95	Miguel Cabrera	.75
96	Josh Beckett	.40
97	Mike Lowell	.25
98	Luis Castillo	.25
99	Juan Pierre	.25
100	Paul LoDuca	.25
101	Guillermo Mota	.25
102	Craig Biggio	.25
103	Lance Berkman	.25
104	Roy Oswalt	.25
105	Roger Clemens	2.00
106	Jeff Kent	.25
107	Morgan Ensberg	.25
108	Jeff Bagwell	.50
109	Carlos Beltran	.50
110	Angel Berroa	.25
111	Mike Sweeney	.25
112	Jeremy Affeldt	.25
113	Zack Greinke	.25
114	Juan Gonzalez	.25
115	Andres Blanco	.25
116	Shawn Green	.25
117	Milton Bradley	.25
118	Adrian Beltre	.50
119	Hideo Nomo	.50
120	Steve Finley	.25
121	Eric Gagne	.25
122	Brad Penny	.25
123	Scott Podsednik	.25
124	Ben Sheets	.40
125	Lyle Overbay	.25
126	Junior Spivey	.25
127	Bill Hall	.25
128	Rickie Weeks	.25
129	Jacque Jones	.25
130	Torii Hunter	.40
131	Johan Santana	.50
132	Lew Ford	.25
133	Joe Mauer	.50
134	Justin Morneau	.50
135	Jason Kubel	.25
136	Jose Vidro	.25
137	Chad Cordero	.25
138	Brad Wilkerson	.25
139	Nick Johnson	.25
140	Livan Hernandez	.25
141	Tom Glavine	.40
142	Jae Weong Seo	.25
143	Jose Reyes	.25
144	Al Leiter	.25
145	Mike Piazza	1.00
146	Kazuo Matsui	.25
147	Richard Hidalgo	.25
148	David Wright	.75
149	Mariano Rivera	.50
150	Mike Mussina	.50
151	Alex Rodriguez	1.50
152	Derek Jeter	2.00
153	Jorge Posada	.50
154	Jason Giambi	.25
155	Gary Sheffield	.50
156	Bubba Crosby	.25
157	Javier Vazquez	.25
158	Kevin Brown	.25
159	Tom Gordon	.25
160	Esteban Loaiza	.25
161	Hideki Matsui	1.50
162	Eric Chavez	.40
163	Mark Mulder	.40
164	Barry Zito	.40
165	Tim Hudson	.40
166	Jermaine Dye	.25
167	Octavio Dotel	.25
168	Bobby Crosby	.25
169	Mark Kotsay	.25
170	Scott Hatteberg	.25
171	Jim Thome	.75
172	Bobby Abreu	.40
173	Kevin Millwood	.25
174	Mike Lieberthal	.25
175	Jimmy Rollins	.25
176	Chase Utley	.25
177	Randy Wolf	.25
178	Craig Wilson	.25
179	Jason Kendall	.25
180	Jack Wilson	.25
181	Jose Castillo	.25
182	Robert Mackowiak	.25
183	Oliver Perez	.25
184	Oliver Perez	.25
185	Sean Burroughs	.25
186	Jay Payton	.25
187	Brian Giles	.25
188	Akinori Otsuka	.25
189	Jake Peavy	.25
190	Phil Nevin	.25
191	Mark Loretta	.25
192	Khalil Greene	.40
193	Trevor Hoffman	.25
194	Freddy Guzman	.25
195	Jerome Williams	.25
196	Jason Schmidt	.40
197	Todd Linden	.25
198	Merkin Valdez	.25
199	J.T. Snow	.25
200	A.J. Pierzynski	.25
201	Edgar Martinez	.40
202	Ichiro Suzuki	1.50
203	Raul Ibanez	.25
204	Bret Boone	.25
205	Shigetoshi Hasegawa	.25
206	Miguel Olivo	.25
207	Bucky Jacobsen	.25
208	Jamie Moyer	.25
209	Jim Edmonds	.50
210	Scott Rolen	.75
211	Edgar Renteria	.50
212	Dan Haren	.25
213	Matt Morris	.25
214	Albert Pujols	2.00
215	Larry Walker	.40
216	Jason Isringhausen	.25
217	Chris Carpenter	.25
218	Jason Marquis	.25
219	Jeff Suppan	.25
220	Aubrey Huff	.25
221	Carl Crawford	.25
222	Rocco Baldelli	.25
223	Fred McGriff	.25
224	Dewon Brazelton	.25
225	B.J. Upton	.40
226	Joey Gathright	.25
227	Scott Kazmir	.40
228	Hank Blalock	.50
229	Mark Teixeira	.50
230	Michael Young	.25
231	Adrian Gonzalez	.25
232	Laynce Nix	.25
233	Alfonso Soriano	.75
234	Rafael Palmeiro	.50
235	Kevin Mench	.25
236	David Dellucci	.25
237	Francisco Cordero	.25
238	Kenny Rogers	.25
239	Roy Halladay	.25
240	Carlos Delgado	.40
241	Alexis Rios	.25
242	Vernon Wells	.25
243	Yadier Molina	.25
244	Rene Rivera	.25
245	Logan Kensing	.25
246	Gavin Floyd	.25
247	Russ Adams	.25
248	Dioner Navarro	.25
249	Ryan Howard	.50
250	Ryan Church	.25
251	Jeff Francis	.25
252	John Van Benschoten	.25
253	Yhency Brazoban	.25
254	David Krynzel	.25
255	Victor Diaz	.25
256	Jairo Garcia	.25
257	Scott Proctor	.25
258	Shawn Hill	.25
259	Jeff Baker	.25
260	Matt Peterson	.25
261	Josh Kroeger	.25
262	Grady Sizemore	.25
263	Clint Nageotte	.25
264	Andy Green	.25
265	*Justin Verlander*	2.00
266	Jim Thome	.75
267	Larry Walker	.40
268	Ivan Rodriguez	.50
269	Brad Penny	.25
270	Carlos Beltran	.50
271	Paul LoDuca	.25
272	Orlando Cabrera	.25
273	Nomar Garciaparra	1.00
274	Esteban Loaiza	.25
275	Richard Hidalgo	.25
276	John Olerud	.25
277	Greg Maddux	1.00
278	Roger Clemens	2.00
279	Alfonso Soriano	.75
280	Dale Murphy	.50
281	Cal Ripken Jr.	4.00
282	Dwight Evans	.25
283	Ron Santo	.25
284	Andre Dawson	.50
285	Harold Baines	.25
286	Jack Morris	.25
287	Kirk Gibson	.25
288	Bo Jackson	.75
289	Orel Hershiser	.25
290	Maury Wills	.25
291	Tony Oliva	.25
292	Darryl Strawberry	.25
293	Roger Maris	1.00
294	Don Mattingly	2.00
295	Rickey Henderson	.50
296	Dave Stewart	.25
297	Dave Parker	.25
298	Steve Garvey	.25
299	Matt Williams	.25
300	Keith Hernandez	.25
301	John Lackey	.25
302	Vladimir Guerrero	.75
303	Garret Anderson	.25
304	Dallas McPherson	.25
305	Orlando Cabrera	.25
306	Steve Finley	.25
307	Luis Gonzalez	.25
308	Randy Johnson	.75
309	Scott Hairston	.25
310	Shawn Green	.25
311	Troy Glaus	.40
312	Javier Vazquez	.25
313	Russ Ortiz	.25
314	Chipper Jones	.75
315	Johnny Estrada	.25
316	Andruw Jones	.50
317	Tim Hudson	.50
318	Danny Kolb	.25
319	Jay Gibbons	.25
320	Melvin Mora	.25
321	Rafael Palmeiro	.50
322	Val Majewski	.25
323	David Ortiz	.75
324	Manny Ramirez	.75
325	Edgar Renteria	.25
326	Matt Clement	.25
327	Curt Schilling	.75
328	Sammy Sosa	1.00
329	Mark Prior	.75
330	Greg Maddux	1.00
331	Nomar Garciaparra	1.00
332	Frank Thomas	.50
333	Mark Buehrle	.25
334	Jermaine Dye	.25
335	Scott Podsednik	.25
336	Sean Casey	.25
337	Adam Dunn	.50
338	Ken Griffey Jr.	1.00
339	Travis Hafner	.25
340	Victor Martinez	.25
341	Cliff Lee	.25
342	Todd Helton	.50
343	Preston Wilson	.25
344	Ivan Rodriguez	.50
345	Dmitri Young	.25
346	Nate Robertson	.25
347	Miguel Cabrera	.75
348	Jeff Bagwell	.40
349	Andy Pettitte	.40
350	Roger Clemens	2.00
351	Ken Harvey	.25
352	Danny Bautista	.25
353	Hideo Nomo	.50
354	Kazuhisa Ishii	.25
355	Edwin Jackson	.25
356	J.D. Drew	.25
357	Jeff Kent	.25
358	Geoff Jenkins	.25
359	Carlos Lee	.25
360	Shannon Stewart	.25
361	Joe Nathan	.25
362	Johan Santana	.50
363	Mike Piazza	1.00
364	Hideki Matsui	.25
365	Carlos Beltran	.50
366	Pedro Martinez	.75
367	*Ambiorix Concepcion*	.40
368	Hideki Matsui	1.50
369	Bernie Williams	.40
370	Gary Sheffield	.50
371	Randy Johnson	.75
372	Jaret Wright	.25
373	Carl Pavano	.25
374	Derek Jeter	2.00
375	Alex Rodriguez	1.50
376	Eric Byrnes	.25
377	Rich Harden	.25
378	Mark Mulder	.40
379	Nick Swisher	.25
380	Eric Chavez	.25
381	Jason Kendall	.25
382	Marlon Byrd	.25
383	Pat Burrell	.25
384	Brett Myers	.25
385	Jim Thome	.50
386	Jason Bay	.25
387	Jake Peavy	.25
388	Moises Alou	.25
389	Omar Vizquel	.25
390	Travis Blackley	.25
391	Jose Lopez	.25
392	Jeremy Reed	.25
393	Adrian Beltre	.25
394	Richie Sexson	.25
395	*Wladimir Balentien*	1.50
396	Ichiro Suzuki	1.50
397	Albert Pujols	2.00
398	Scott Rolen	.75
399	Mark Mulder	.40
400	David Eckstein	.25
401	Delmon Young	.25
402	Aubrey Huff	.25
403	Alfonso Soriano	.50
404	Hank Blalock	.25
405	Richard Hidalgo	.25
406	Vernon Wells	.25
407	Orlando Hudson	.25
408	Alexis Rios	.25
409	Shea Hillenbrand	.25
410	Jose Guillen	.25
411	Vinny Castilla	.25
412	Jose Vidro	.25
413	Nick Johnson	.25
414	Livan Hernandez	.25
415	Miguel Tejada	.50
416	Gary Sheffield	.50
417	Curt Schilling	.75
418	Rafael Palmeiro	.50
419	Scott Rolen	.75
420	Aramis Ramirez	.40
421	Vladimir Guerrero	.75
422	Steve Finley	.25
423	Roger Clemens	2.00
424	Mike Piazza	1.00
425	Ivan Rodriguez	.50
426	David Justice	.25
427	Mark Grace	.40
428	Alan Trammell	.25
429	Bert Blyleven	.25
430	Dwight Gooden	.25
431	Deion Sanders	.25
432	Joe Torre	.25
433	Jose Canseco	.40
434	Tony Gwynn	.75
435	Will Clark	.40
436	Marty Marion	.25
437	Nolan Ryan	3.00

438 Billy Martin .25
439 Carlos Delgado .25
440 Magglio Ordonez .25
441 Sammy Sosa 1.00
442 *Keiichi Yabu* .50
443 *Yuniesky Betancourt* 1.00
444 *Jeff Niemann* 1.50
445 *Brandon McCarthy* 1.50
446 *Philip Humber* 1.50
447 *Tadahito Iguchi* 2.00
448 Cal Ripken Jr. 4.00
449 Ryne Sandberg 2.00
450 Willie Mays 2.00

Non-Canvas

No Pricing
Production 20 sets

Bronze

Stars: 3-5X
Production 100 sets
Update Bronze (301-450): 3-5X
Production 50

Gold

Golds: 5-10X
Production 25 sets
Gold Update (301-450): No Pricing
Production 10 sets

Platinum

No pricing
Production one set
Framed Platinums: No Pricing
Production one set

Silver

Silvers: 4-8X
Production 50 sets
Update (301-450): No Pricing
Production 25 sets

Framed Black

Stars: 5-10X
Production 25 sets

Framed Blue

Stars: 5-10X
Production 25 sets

Framed Green

Stars: 4-8X
Production 50 sets

Framed Red

Stars: 1-3X
Inserted 1:3

Silver B/W

Silvers: 4-8X
Production 50 sets

Update B/W

B/W: 1X
Inserted 1:2

Diamond Cuts Bat

NM/M
Common Player: 4.00
1 Adam Dunn/200 8.00
2 Adrian Beltre/200 6.00
3 Alfonso Soriano/50 8.00
4 Andruw Jones/200 4.00
5 Andy Pettitte/50 6.00
6 Aramis Ramirez/100 6.00
7 Brian Giles/200 4.00
10 Carlos Beltran/200 8.00
12 Craig Wilson/200 4.00
13 Curt Schilling/50 10.00
14 Darin Erstad/200 4.00
16 Derrek Lee/200 6.00
17 Fred McGriff/100 4.00
19 Ivan Rodriguez/200 8.00
20 Jason Bay/200 4.00
21 Jason Giambi/100 4.00
22 Jay Gibbons/200 4.00
23 Jeff Kent/200 4.00
24 John Olerud/200 4.00
25 Juan Gonzalez/200 4.00
27 Kazuhisa Ishii/50 6.00
28 Kevin Brown/100 4.00
29 Larry Walker/200 6.00
31 Mark Teixeira/200 6.00
32 Melvin Mora/50 6.00
33 Michael Young/200 4.00
34 Miguel Tejada/100 8.00
35 Mike Mussina/50 8.00
36 Paul LoDuca/200 4.00
37 Preston Wilson/200 4.00
38 Randy Johnson/50 10.00
39 Richie Sexson/200 6.00
40 Roger Clemens/50 15.00
41 Scott Rolen/100 8.00
42 Sean Burroughs/200 4.00
43 Sean Casey/200 4.00
44 Shannon Stewart/200 4.00
45 Shawn Green/200 4.00
47 Tim Salmon/200 4.00
48 Tom Glavine/200 6.00
49 Torii Hunter/200 6.00

Diamond Cuts Combos

NM/M
Common Player: 6.00
Prime: No Pricing
Production One Set
1 Adam Dunn Bat-Jsy/100 10.00
2 Adrian Beltre Bat-Jsy/100 8.00
3 Alfonso Soriano Bat-Jsy/100 10.00
4 Andruw Jones Bat-Jsy/100 8.00
5 Andy Pettitte Jsy-Jsy/100 10.00
6 Aramis Ramirez Bat-Jsy/100 8.00
7 Brian Giles Bat-Jsy/100 6.00
10 Carlos Beltran Bat-Jsy/50 15.00
11 Carlos Lee Jsy-Jsy/100 6.00
12 Craig Wilson Bat-Jsy/100 6.00
13 Curt Schilling Bat-Jsy/100 12.00
14 Darin Erstad Bat-Jsy/100 6.00
17 Fred McGriff Bat-Jsy/100 6.00
19 Ivan Rodriguez Bat-Jsy/100 10.00
21 Jason Giambi Bat-Jsy/50 8.00
22 Jay Gibbons Bat-Jsy/50 8.00
23 Jeff Kent Bat-Jsy/100 6.00
24 John Olerud Bat-Jsy/200 6.00
25 Juan Gonzalez Bat-Pants/100 8.00
27 Kazuhisa Ishii Bat-Jsy/100 8.00
28 Kevin Brown Bat-Jsy/100 6.00
29 Larry Walker Bat-Jsy/100 8.00
31 Mark Teixeira Bat-Jsy/100 10.00
34 Miguel Tejada Jsy-Jsy/100 10.00
35 Mike Mussina Bat-Pants/50 12.00
36 Paul LoDuca Bat-Jsy/50 8.00
37 Preston Wilson Bat-Jsy/100 6.00
38 Randy Johnson Bat-Jsy/50 15.00
40 Roger Clemens Bat-Jsy/50 20.00
44 Shannon Stewart Bat-Jsy/100 6.00
45 Shawn Green Bat-Jsy/100 6.00
48 Tom Glavine Bat-Jsy/100 8.00
49 Torii Hunter Bat-Jsy/25 8.00

Diamond Cuts Jersey

NM/M
Common Player: 4.00
Prime: No Pricing
Production One Set
1 Adam Dunn/50 10.00
2 Adrian Beltre/200 6.00
3 Alfonso Soriano/50 8.00
4 Andruw Jones/200 4.00
5 Andy Pettitte/100 6.00
6 Aramis Ramirez/200 6.00
7 Brian Giles/200 4.00
8 C.C. Sabathia/200 4.00
9 Carl Crawford/200 4.00
10 Carlos Beltran/200 8.00
11 Carlos Lee/200 4.00
12 Craig Wilson/200 4.00
13 Curt Schilling/50 10.00
14 Darin Erstad/200 4.00
17 Fred McGriff/200 4.00
18 Greg Maddux/50 12.00
19 Ivan Rodriguez/200 8.00
20 Jason Bay/200 4.00
21 Jason Giambi/200 4.00
22 Jay Gibbons/100 4.00
23 Jeff Kent/200 4.00
24 John Olerud/200 4.00
25 Juan Gonzalez Pants/200 4.00
26 Junior Spivey/200 4.00
27 Kazuhisa Ishii/200 6.00
28 Kevin Brown/200 4.00
29 Larry Walker Rockies/200 6.00
30 Lyle Overbay/200 4.00
31 Mark Teixeira/100 6.00
32 Melvin Mora/200 4.00
33 Michael Young/200 4.00
34 Miguel Tejada/200 8.00
35 Mike Mussina/100 8.00
36 Paul LoDuca/50 6.00
37 Preston Wilson/200 4.00
38 Randy Johnson/200 8.00
39 Richie Sexson/200 6.00
40 Roger Clemens/50 15.00
41 Scott Rolen/50 10.00
42 Sean Burroughs/200 4.00
43 Sean Casey/200 4.00
44 Shannon Stewart/100 4.00
45 Shawn Green/200 4.00
46 Steve Finley/200 4.00
48 Tom Glavine/200 6.00
50 Travis Hafner/100 4.00

Diamond Cuts Signature

NM/M
Production 1-100
8 C.C. Sabathia/25 20.00
9 Carl Crawford/50 20.00
10 Carlos Beltran/1
11 Carlos Lee/100 15.00
20 Jason Bay/100 15.00
22 Jay Gibbons/100 10.00
30 Lyle Overbay/100 15.00
32 Melvin Mora/50 15.00
44 Shannon Stewart/25 20.00
47 Tim Salmon/100 20.00
50 Travis Hafner/100 15.00

Diamond Cuts Signature Bat

NM/M
Production 5-100
1 Adam Dunn/25 40.00
2 Adrian Beltre/50 35.00
3 Alfonso Soriano/10
4 Andruw Jones/10
6 Aramis Ramirez/100 30.00
10 Carlos Beltran/50 40.00
12 Craig Wilson/100 15.00
13 Curt Schilling/5
16 Derrek Lee/100 20.00
17 Fred McGriff/25 50.00
22 Jay Gibbons/100 10.00
25 Juan Gonzalez/10
27 Kazuhisa Ishii/10
31 Mark Teixeira/25 40.00
33 Michael Young/100 20.00
35 Mike Mussina/5
36 Paul LoDuca/25 25.00
38 Randy Johnson/5
40 Roger Clemens/5
43 Sean Casey/25 25.00
44 Shannon Stewart/25 20.00
45 Shawn Green/5
49 Torii Hunter/25 25.00
53 Carlos Beltran/25
54 Craig Biggio/5
55 Jim Edmonds/5
58 Roger Clemens/1
59 Tim Hudson/10
60 Victor Martinez/25

Diamond Cuts Sign. Combos

NM/M
Production 1-100
Prime: No Pricing
Production One Set
1 Adam Dunn Bat-Jsy/25 40.00
2 Adrian Beltre Bat-Bat/25 40.00
3 Alfonso Soriano Bat-Jsy/10
4 Andruw Jones Bat-Jsy/10
6 Aramis Ramirez Bat-Jsy/100 30.00
8 C.C. Sabathia Jsy-Jsy/50 25.00
10 Carlos Beltran Bat-Jsy/10
11 Carlos Lee Jsy-Jsy/50 20.00
12 Craig Wilson Bat-Bat/100 15.00
13 Curt Schilling Bat-Jsy/5
17 Fred McGriff Bat-Jsy/25 50.00
18 Greg Maddux Jsy-Jsy/1
22 Jay Gibbons Bat-Bat/50 10.00
25 Juan Gonzalez Bat-Jsy/100 25.00
27 Kazuhisa Ishii Bat-Jsy/25 50.00
31 Mark Teixeira Bat-Bat/25 40.00
33 Michael Young Bat-Jsy/50 25.00
35 Mike Mussina Bat-Jsy/10
36 Paul LoDuca Bat-Bat/25 25.00
38 Randy Johnson Bat-Jsy/5
40 Roger Clemens Bat-Jsy/5
41 Scott Rolen Bat-Jsy/5
43 Sean Casey Bat-Jsy/25 25.00
44 Shannon Stewart Bat-Jsy/25 20.00
45 Shawn Green Bat-Jsy/5
49 Torii Hunter Bat-Jsy/25 25.00
50 Travis Hafner Bat-Jsy/25 25.00
51 Aramis Ramirez/jsy/24 25.00
54 Craig Biggio/25
55 Jim Edmonds/5
57 Mark Mulder/10
58 Roger Clemens/1
59 Tim Hudson/10
60 Victor Martinez/25 20.00

Diamond Cuts Sign. Jersey

NM/M
Production 5-100
Prime: No Pricing
Production One Set
2 Adrian Beltre/100 25.00
6 Aramis Ramirez/100 30.00
8 C.C. Sabathia/100 15.00
9 Carl Crawford/50 20.00
11 Carlos Lee/100 15.00
12 Craig Wilson/100 15.00
30 Lyle Overbay/100 15.00
31 Mark Teixeira/25 40.00
32 Melvin Mora/50 15.00
33 Michael Young/100 20.00
36 Paul LoDuca/25 25.00
42 Sean Burroughs/50 10.00
43 Sean Casey/25 25.00
44 Shannon Stewart/25 20.00
46 Steve Finley/25 25.00
50 Travis Hafner/50 20.00
57 Mark Mulder/25 25.00
60 Victor Martinez/25 20.00

Heritage Collection

NM/M
Common Player: 1.50
Inserted 1:21
#26-35 inserted 1:76
#26-35 are DK Update exclusive
1 Andre Dawson 1.50
2 Bob Gibson 2.50
3 Cal Ripken Jr. 8.00
4 Dale Murphy 2.00
5 Darryl Strawberry 1.50
6 Dennis Eckersley 1.50
7 Don Mattingly 6.00
8 Duke Snider 3.00

9 Dwight Gooden 1.50
10 Eddie Murray 3.00
11 Frank Robinson 3.00
12 Gary Carter 2.00
13 George Brett 6.00
14 Harmon Killebrew 3.00
15 Jack Morris 1.50
16 Jim Palmer 1.50
17 Lou Brock 2.00
18 Mike Schmidt 6.00
19 Nolan Ryan 8.00
20 Ozzie Smith 4.00
21 Phil Niekro 1.50
22 Rod Carew 2.00
23 Rollie Fingers 1.50
24 Steve Carlton 1.50
25 Tony Gwynn 3.00
26 Curt Schilling 3.00
27 Bobby Doerr 1.50
28 Edgar Martinez 1.50
29 Jim Thorpe 4.00
30 Mark Grace 1.50
31 Matt Williams 1.50
32 Paul Molitor 2.50
33 Robin Yount 4.00
34 Ryne Sandberg 5.00
35 Will Clark 2.00

Heritage Collection Bat

NM/M

Production 50-100
1 Andre Dawson/50 8.00
3 Cal Ripken Jr./100 40.00
4 Dale Murphy/100 10.00
5 Darryl Strawberry/50 8.00
7 Don Mattingly/100 20.00
9 Dwight Gooden/100 5.00
10 Eddie Murray/100 15.00
11 Frank Robinson/50 8.00
12 Gary Carter/100 5.00
13 George Brett/100 15.00
14 Harmon Killebrew/100 10.00
17 Lou Brock/100 8.00
18 Mike Schmidt/100 20.00
19 Nolan Ryan/50 30.00
20 Ozzie Smith/100 15.00
21 Phil Niekro/50 8.00
22 Rod Carew/100 8.00
24 Steve Carlton/100 5.00
25 Tony Gwynn/100 10.00

Heritage Collection Combos

NM/M

Production 25-100
Prime: No Pricing
Production One Set
1 Andre Dawson Bat-Jsy/50 8.00
3 Cal Ripken Jr. Bat-Jsy/50 60.00
4 Dale Murphy Bat-Jsy/25 20.00
7 Don Mattingly Bat-Jkt/100 25.00
8 Duke Snider Jsy-Pants/25 20.00
9 Dwight Gooden Bat-Jsy/50 10.00
10 Eddie Murray Bat-Jsy/100 20.00
14 Harmon Killebrew Bat-Jsy/100 15.00
16 Jim Palmer Jsy-Pants/100 10.00
17 Lou Brock Bat-Jkt/50 10.00
18 Mike Schmidt Bat-Jsy/100 25.00
19 Nolan Ryan Jsy-Pants/50 40.00
20 Ozzie Smith Bat-Pants/100 20.00
21 Phil Niekro Bat-Jsy/50 10.00
22 Rod Carew Bat-Jsy/100 10.00
24 Steve Carlton Bat-Jsy/100 8.00
25 Tony Gwynn Bat-Jsy/50 15.00

Heritage Collection Jersey

NM/M

Production 25-100
Prime: No Pricing
Production One Set
1 Andre Dawson/100 8.00
2 Bob Gibson/50 10.00
3 Cal Ripken Jr./100 40.00
4 Dale Murphy/100 10.00
5 Darryl Strawberry/25 10.00
6 Dennis Eckersley/100 5.00
7 Don Mattingly/100 20.00
8 Duke Snider/50 15.00
9 Dwight Gooden/100 5.00
10 Eddie Murray/100 15.00
12 Gary Carter/100 5.00
13 George Brett/50 20.00
14 Harmon Killebrew/100 10.00
15 Jack Morris/100 5.00
16 Jim Palmer/100 5.00
17 Lou Brock/100 8.00
18 Mike Schmidt Jkt/100 20.00
19 Nolan Ryan/100 25.00
20 Ozzie Smith Pants/100 15.00
21 Phil Niekro/50 8.00
22 Rod Carew/100 8.00
23 Rollie Fingers/50 8.00
24 Steve Carlton/50 8.00
25 Tony Gwynn/100 10.00

Heritage Coll. Signature

NM/M

Production 1-50
1 Andre Dawson/50 25.00
5 Darryl Strawberry/50 25.00
9 Dwight Gooden/25 25.00
15 Jack Morris/50 20.00
23 Rollie Fingers/25 40.00

Heritage Coll. Sign. Bat

NM/M

Production 5-100
#26-35 are DK Update exclusive
1 Andre Dawson/50 25.00
3 Cal Ripken Jr./5
4 Dale Murphy/25 40.00
5 Darryl Strawberry/10
7 Don Mattingly/25 75.00
9 Dwight Gooden/100 25.00
11 Frank Robinson/25 40.00
13 George Brett/5
14 Harmon Killebrew/50 50.00
17 Lou Brock/50 35.00
18 Mike Schmidt/5
19 Nolan Ryan/10
20 Ozzie Smith/25 65.00
21 Phil Niekro/20 30.00
22 Rod Carew/25 40.00
24 Steve Carlton/25 40.00
25 Tony Gwynn/25 50.00
26 Curt Schilling/10
28 Edgar Martinez/25 40.00
30 Mark Grace/5
31 Matt Williams/25 35.00
32 Paul Molitor/10
33 Robin Yount/10
34 Ryne Sandberg/5
35 Will Clark/25 40.00

Heritage Coll. Sign. Combos

NM/M

Production 5-100
#26-35 are DK Update exclusive
Prime: No Pricing
Production One Set
1 Andre Dawson Bat-Jsy/50 25.00
3 Cal Ripken Jr. Bat-Jsy/5
4 Dale Murphy Bat-Jsy/25 40.00
6 Dennis Eckersley Jsy-Jsy/50 25.00
7 Don Mattingly Bat-Jkt/25 80.00
8 Duke Snider Jsy-Pants/10
9 Dwight Gooden Bat-Jsy/100 25.00
11 Frank Robinson Bat-Jsy/10
12 Gary Carter Jkt-Jsy/50 25.00
13 George Brett Bat-Jsy/5
14 Harmon Killebrew Bat-Bat/25 50.00
15 Jack Morris Jsy-Jsy/25 30.00
16 Jim Palmer Jsy-Pants/25 30.00
17 Lou Brock Bat-Jsy/50 40.00
18 Mike Schmidt Bat-Jsy/10
19 Nolan Ryan Jsy-Pants/10
20 Ozzie Smith Bat-Pants/10
21 Phil Niekro Bat-Jsy/50 25.00
22 Rod Carew Bat-Jkt/25 40.00
24 Steve Carlton Bat-Jsy/25 40.00
25 Tony Gwynn Bat-Jsy/25 50.00
26 Curt Schilling/bat/jsy/10
27 Bobby Doerr/jsy/pants/25 25.00
28 Edgar Martinez/bat/jsy/25 40.00
31 Matt Williams/bat/jsy/25 35.00
32 Paul Molitor/bat/jsy/10
33 Robin Yount/bat/jsy/10
34 Ryne Sandberg/bat/jsy/5
35 Will Clark/bat/jsy/25 40.00

Heritage Coll. Sign. Jersey

NM/M

Production 5-100
#26-35 are DK Update exclusive
Prime: No Pricing
Production one set
1 Andre Dawson/100 25.00
2 Bob Gibson/25 40.00
3 Cal Ripken Jr./5
4 Dale Murphy/50 40.00
5 Darryl Strawberry Pants/100 20.00
6 Dennis Eckersley/50 25.00
7 Don Mattingly/25 85.00
8 Duke Snider/50 35.00
9 Dwight Gooden/100 20.00
10 Eddie Murray/5
11 Frank Robinson/25 40.00
12 Gary Carter/50 25.00
13 George Brett/5
14 Harmon Killebrew/50 50.00
15 Jack Morris/100 15.00
16 Jim Palmer/25 35.00
17 Lou Brock/50 35.00
18 Mike Schmidt Jkt/5
19 Nolan Ryan/10
20 Ozzie Smith/25 60.00
21 Phil Niekro/25 30.00
22 Rod Carew/25 40.00
23 Rollie Fingers/25 30.00
24 Steve Carlton/25 40.00
25 Tony Gwynn/10
26 Curt Schilling/10
27 Bobby Doerr/25 25.00
28 Edgar Martinez/25 35.00
30 Mark Grace/10
31 Matt Williams/25 35.00
32 Paul Molitor/10
33 Robin Yount/10
34 Ryne Sandberg/5
35 Will Clark/25 40.00

HOF Heroes

NM/M

#51-100 are DK Update exclusive 100.00
Common Player: 1.50
Inserted 1:5
Non Canvas: No Pricing
Production 20 Sets
Bronze: 1X-2X
Production 100 Sets
Gold: 3X-5X
Production 25 Sets
Platinum: No Pricing
Production One Set
Silver: 2X-4X
Production 50 Sets
Frame Black: 3X-5X
Production 25 Sets
Frame Blue: 1X-2X
Production 100 Sets
Frame Green: 2X-4X
Production 50 Sets
Frame Red: 1X
Inserted 1:18
1 Phil Niekro 1.50
2 Brooks Robinson 2.00
3 Jim Palmer 2.00
4 Carl Yastrzemski 3.00
5 Ted Williams 5.00
6 Duke Snider 3.00
7 Burleigh Grimes 1.50
8 Don Sutton 1.50
9 Nolan Ryan 6.00
10 Fergie Jenkins 1.50
11 Carlton Fisk 2.00
12 Tom Seaver 2.00
13 Bob Feller 2.00
14 Nolan Ryan 6.00
15 George Brett 5.00
16 Warren Spahn 3.00
17 Paul Molitor 3.00
18 Rod Carew 3.00
19 Harmon Killebrew 3.00
20 Monte Irvin 2.00
21 Gary Carter 1.50
22 Phil Rizzuto 2.00
23 Babe Ruth 6.00
24 Reggie Jackson 2.00
25 Mike Schmidt 5.00
26 Roberto Clemente 5.00
27 Juan Marichal 1.50
28 Willie McCovey 2.00
29 Stan Musial 4.00
30 Ozzie Smith 3.00
31 Dennis Eckersley 1.50
32 Phil Niekro 1.50
33 Jim Palmer 2.00
34 Carl Yastrzemski 3.00
35 Duke Snider 3.00
36 Don Sutton 1.50
37 Nolan Ryan 6.00
38 Carlton Fisk 2.00
39 Tom Seaver 2.00
40 Bob Feller 2.00
41 Nolan Ryan 6.00
42 George Brett 5.00
43 Harmon Killebrew 3.00
44 Gary Carter 1.50
45 Mike Schmidt 5.00
46 Stan Musial 4.00
47 Ozzie Smith 3.00
48 Dennis Eckersley 1.50
49 Fergie Jenkins 1.50
50 Brooks Robinson 2.00
51 Eddie Murray 2.00
52 Frank Robinson 2.00
53 Carlton Fisk 1.50
54 Ted Williams 5.00
55 Rod Carew 2.00
56 Ernie Banks 3.00
57 Luis Aparicio 1.50
58 Johnny Bench 3.00
59 Al Kaline 2.00
60 George Kell 1.50
61 Robin Yount 3.00
62 Nolan Ryan 6.00
63 Whitey Ford 1.50
64 Reggie Jackson 2.00
65 Babe Ruth 6.00
66 Rollie Fingers 1.50
67 Steve Carlton 1.50
68 Robin Roberts 1.50
69 Ralph Kiner 1.50
70 Willie Stargell 2.00
71 Roberto Clemente 5.00
72 Gaylord Perry 1.50
73 Bob Gibson 2.00
74 Lou Brock 1.50
75 Frankie Frisch 1.50
76 Eddie Murray 2.00
77 Frank Robinson 2.00
78 Carlton Fisk 1.50
79 Ted Williams 5.00
80 Rod Carew 2.00
81 Ernie Banks 3.00
82 Luis Aparicio 1.50
83 Johnny Bench 3.00
84 Al Kaline 2.00
85 Willie Mays 5.00
86 Robin Yount 3.00
87 Nolan Ryan 5.00
88 Whitey Ford 2.00
89 Reggie Jackson 2.00
90 Babe Ruth 6.00
91 Rollie Fingers 1.50
92 Steve Carlton 1.50
93 Wade Boggs 2.00
94 Wade Boggs 2.00
95 Willie Stargell 2.00
96 Roberto Clemente 5.00
97 Gaylord Perry 1.50
98 Bob Gibson 2.00
99 Lou Brock 1.50
100 Frankie Frisch 1.50

HOF Heroes Materials Bronze

NM/M

Production 1-100
No pricing 20 or less

Gold: .75X-1.5X
Production 1-25
Silver: .75X-1.5X
Production 10-50
Framed Black: No Pricing
Production 1-10
Framed Blue: .75X-1.5X
Production 1-25
Framed Red: .75X-1.5X
Production 10-50
1 Phil Niekro Bat-Jsy/100 8.00
2 Brooks Robinson Bat-Jsy/100 12.00
3 Jim Palmer Jsy-Pants/100 8.00
4 Carl Yastrzemski Bat-Pants/50 20.00
5 Ted Williams Bat-Jsy/1
6 Duke Snider Jsy-Pants/50 15.00
7 Burleigh Grimes Pants-Pants/25 75.00
8 Don Sutton Jsy-Jsy/100 8.00
9 Nolan Ryan Bat-Jkt/50 40.00
10 Fergie Jenkins Pants-Pants/100 8.00
11 Carlton Fisk Bat-Jkt/100 12.00
12 Tom Seaver Jsy-Pants/50 15.00
13 Bob Feller Pants-Pants/25 20.00
14 Nolan Ryan Bat-Jsy/50 40.00
15 George Brett Bat-Bat/25 40.00
16 Warren Spahn Jsy-Pants/25 30.00
17 Paul Molitor Bat-Jsy/100 15.00
18 Rod Carew Bat-Jsy/50 15.00
19 Harmon Killebrew Bat-Jsy/50 20.00
21 Gary CarterBat-Jsy/100 8.00
23 Babe Ruth Bat-Pants/25 300.00
24 Reggie Jackson Bat-Jkt/100 15.00
25 Mike Schmidt Bat-Jkt/50 30.00
26 Roberto Clemente Bat-Bat/50 60.00
27 Juan Marichal Pants-Pants/25 12.00
28 Willie McCovey Jsy-Pants/100 10.00
29 Stan Musial Bat-Bat/25 30.00
30 Ozzie Smith Bat-Pants/100 20.00
31 Dennis Eckersley Jsy-Jsy/100 8.00
32 Phil Niekro Bat-Jsy/100 8.00
33 Jim Palmer Jsy-Pants/25 12.00
34 Carl Yastrzemski Bat-Pants/25 30.00
35 Duke Snider Jsy-Pants 20.00
36 Don Sutton Jsy-Jsy/100 8.00
37 Nolan Ryan Bat-Jkt/25 50.00
38 Carlton Fisk Bat-Jkt/100 12.00
39 Tom Seaver Bat-Jsy/25 20.00
40 Bob Feller Pants-Pants/25 20.00
41 Nolan Ryan Bat-Jkt/25 50.00
42 George Brett Bat-Bat/25 40.00
43 Harmon Killebrew Bat-Jsy/25 25.00
44 Gary Carter Bat-Jsy/100 8.00
45 Mike Schmidt Bat-Jsy/25 40.00
46 Stan Musial Bat-Bat/25 30.00
47 Ozzie Smith Bat-Pants/100 20.00
48 Dennis Eckersley Jsy-Jsy/100 8.00
49 Fergie Jenkins Pants-Pants/25 12.00
50 Brooks Robinson bat-Jsy/25 20.00
51 Eddie Murray/ bat/pants/50 12.00
52 Frank Robinson/ bat/bat/50 12.00
53 Carlton Fisk/ bat/bat/50 10.00
54 Ted Williams/bat/bat/50
55 Rod Carew/bat/jsy/50 12.00
56 Ernie Banks/ bat/pants/50 15.00
57 Luis Aparicio/bat/bat/50 8.00
58 Johnny Bench/ bat/jsy/50 15.00
59 Al Kaline/bat/bat/25 20.00
61 Robin Yount/bat/jsy/50 15.00
62 Nolan Ryan/bat/jsy/25 50.00
63 Whitey Ford/jsy/jsy/25 25.00
64 Reggie Jackson/ jsy/jsy/50 15.00
65 Babe Ruth/bat/pants/25
66 Rollie Fingers/ jsy/jsy/50 8.00
67 Steve Carlton/ bat/jsy/50 10.00
70 Willie Stargell/ bat/jsy/50 15.00
71 Roberto Clemente/bat/bat/25
72 Gaylord Perry/ jsy/jsy/50 8.00
73 Bob Gibson/jsy/jsy/25 15.00
74 Lou Brock/bat/jsy/50 12.00
75 Frankie Frisch/50
76 Eddie Murray/ bat/bat/50 12.00
77 Frank Robinson/ bat/bat/50 12.00
78 Carlton Fisk/bat/bat/50 12.00
79 Ted Williams/bat/bat/25
80 Rod Carew/bat/jkt/50 12.00
81 Ernie Banks/bat/jsy/25 15.00
82 Luis Aparicio/bat/bat/50 8.00
83 Johnny Bench/ bat/jsy/50 15.00
84 Al Kaline/bat/bat/10
86 Robin Yount/ bat/jsy/50 15.00
87 Nolan Ryan/ bat/jsy/25 40.00
88 Whitey Ford/ jsy/jsy/25 25.00
89 Reggie Jackson/ jsy/jsy/50 15.00
90 Babe Ruth/bat/pants/10
91 Rollie Fingers/ jsy/jsy/50 8.00
92 Steve Carlton/ bat/jsy/50 10.00
95 Willie Stargell/ jsy/jsy/50 15.00
96 Roberto Clemente/ bat/bat/10
97 Gaylord Perry/ jsy/jsy/50 8.00
98 Bob Gibson/jsy/jsy/10
99 Lou Brock/ bat/jsy/50 10.00
100 Frankie Frisch/50

HOF Heroes Signatures Bronze

NM/M

Production 1-25
No pricing 20 or less
Gold: No Pricing
Production 1-10
Platinum: No Pricing
Production One Set
Silver: 1X
Production 1-25
Framed Blue: No Pricing
Production One Set
Framed Black: No Pricing
Production One Set
Framed Green: No Pricing
Production 1-10
Framed Red: No Pricing
Production 1-25
Cards #52-99 are seeded in DK Update
13 Bob Feller/25 35.00
40 Bob Feller/25 35.00
52 Frank Robinson/25 35.00
57 Luis Aparicio/25 15.00
59 Al Kaline/25 40.00
60 George Kell/25 20.00
66 Rollie Fingers/25 15.00
67 Steve Carlton/25 20.00
68 Robin Roberts/25 20.00
69 Ralph Kiner/25 35.00
72 Gaylord Perry/15 15.00
74 Lou Brock/25 35.00
82 Luis Aparicio/25 15.00
84 Al Kaline/25 40.00
91 Rollie Fingers/25 15.00
92 Steve Carlton/25 20.00
93 Wade Boggs Yanks/25 30.00
94 Wade Boggs Sox/25 30.00
97 Gaylord Perry/25 15.00
99 Lou Brock/25 35.00

Signature Materials Bronze

NM/M

Production 5-50
No pricing 20 or less
Gold: .75X-1.5X
Production 5-25
Platinum: No Pricing
Production One Set
Silver: .75X-1X
Production 5-50
Framed Black: No Pricing
Production 5-10
Framed Blue: .75X-1.5X
Production 5-25
Framed Green: No Pricing
Production 1-10
Framed Red: .75X-1.5X
Production 1-25
#53-99 are found in DK Update
2 Brooks Robinson Bat-Jsy/25 50.00
3 Jim Palmer Jsy-Pants/25 40.00
4 Carl YastrzemskiBat-Pants/5
6 Duke Snider Jsy-Pants/25 40.00
8 Don Sutton Jsy-Jsy/25 30.00
9 Nolan Ryan Jkt-Jsy/10
10 Fergie Jenkins Pants-Pants/25 30.00
11 Carlton Fisk Bat-Jkt/10
12 Tom Seaver Bat-Jsy/10
13 Bob Feller Pants-Pants/50 35.00
14 Nolan Ryan Jkt-Jsy/10
15 George Brett Bat-Bat/5
17 Paul Molitor Bat-Jsy/50
18 Rod Carew Bat-Jsy/50 40.00
19 Harmon Killebrew Bat-Jsy/25 50.00
21 Gary Carter Bat-Jsy/50 25.00
24 Reggie Jackson Bat-Jkt/10
25 Mike Schmidt Bat-Jsy/10
27 Juan Marichal Pants-Pants/25 40.00
28 Willie McCovey Jsy-Pants/25 50.00
29 Stan Musial Bat-Bat/25 85.00
30 Ozzie Smith Bat-Pants/25 75.00
31 Dennis Eckersley Jsy-Jsy/25 35.00
32 Phil Niekro Bat-Jsy/25 30.00
33 Jim Palmer Jsy-Pants/25 40.00
34 Carl Yastrzemski Bat-Pants/5
35 Duke Snider Jsy-Pants/25 40.00
36 Don Sutton Jsy-Jsy/25 30.00
37 Nolan Ryan Bat-Jkt/10
38 Carlton Fisk Bat-Jkt/10
39 Tom Seaver Jsy-Pants/10
40 Bob Feller Pants-Pants/50 35.00
41 Nolan Ryan Jsy-Jsy/10
42 George Brett Bat-Bat/5
43 Harmon Killebrew Bat-Jsy/50 40.00
44 Gary Carter Bat-Jsy/50 25.00
45 Mike Schmidt Bat-Jkt/5
46 Stan Musial Bat-Bat/10
47 Ozzie Smith Bat-Pants/25 75.00
48 Dennis Eckersley Jsy-Jsy/50 25.00
49 Fergie Jenkins Pants-Pants/50 30.00
50 Brooks Robinson Bat-Jsy/25 50.00
53 Carlton Fisk Bat-Jsy/5
55 Rod Carew Bat-Jkt/10
58 Johnny Bench Bat-Jsy/10
61 Robin Yount Bat-Jsy/25 50.00
62 Nolan Ryan Bat-Jsy/5
63 Whitey Ford Jsy-Jsy/5
64 Reggie Jackson Bat-Pants/5
66 Rollie Fingers Jsy-Jsy/50 15.00
67 Steve Carlton Bat-Jsy/10
72 Gaylord Perry Jsy-Jsy/50 15.00
74 Lou Brock Jsy-Jsy/50 30.00
77 Frank Robinson Bat-Bat/10
78 Carlton Fisk Bat-Jsy/5
80 Rod Carew Bat-Jsy/50 25.00
83 Johnny Bench Bat-Jsy/5
86 Robin Yount Bat-Jsy/10
87 Nolan Ryan Bat-Jsy/5
88 Whitey Ford Jsy-Jsy/5
89 Reggie Jackson Bat-Pants/5
91 Rollie Fingers Jsy-Jsy/10
92 Steve Carlton Bat-Jsy/10
99 Lou Brock Bat-Jsy/25 40.00

Materials Bronze

NM/M

Production 10-200
No pricing 20 or less
Gold: .75X-1.5X
Production 25-50
Silver: .75X-1.5X
Production 25-100
Platinum: No Pricing
Production One Set
Framed Black: No Pricing
Production 10 Sets
Framed Blue: .75X-1.5X
Production 50 Sets
Framed Green:
Production 25 Sets
Framed Red: .75X-1.5X
Production 25-100
#302-450 are found in DK Update
1 Garret Anderson Bat-Jsy/200 5.00
2 Vladimir Guerrero Bat-Jsy/200 10.00
4 Troy Glaus Bat-Jsy/200 5.00
5 Tim Salmon Bat-Jsy/200 5.00
7 Chone Figgins Bat-Jsy/200 5.00
10 Tony Percival Jsy-Jsy/200 5.00
11 Randy Johnson Bat-Bat/10
12 Brandon Webb Bat-Pants/200 5.00
13 Richie Sexson Bat-Bat/200 8.00
17 Luis Gonzalez Jsy-Jsy/200 5.00
18 Rafael Furcal Bat-Jsy/200 5.00
19 Andruw Jones Bat-Jsy/200 8.00
21 John Smoltz Jsy-Jsy/200 8.00
24 J.D. Drew Bat-Bat/200 5.00
25 Chipper Jones Bat-Jsy/200 10.00
27 Rafael Palmeiro Bat-Jsy/200 8.00
28 Miguel Tejada Bat-Jsy/200 10.00
29 Javy Lopez Bat-Jsy/25 10.00
30 Luis Matos Jsy-Jsy/100 5.00
31 Larry Bigbie Jsy-Jsy/200 5.00
32 Rodrigo Lopez Jsy-Jsy/200 5.00
34 Melvin Mora Bat-Jsy/200 5.00
36 Manny Ramirez Bat-Jsy/200 10.00
38 Trot Nixon Bat-Bat/200 10.00
39 Curt Schilling Bat-Jsy/200 10.00
41 Pedro Martinez Bat-Jsy/200 10.00
42 Johnny Damon Bat-Bat/200 15.00
43 Kevin Youkilis Bat-Bat/200 5.00
46 David Ortiz Bat-Jsy/200 10.00
47 Kerry Wood Jsy-Pants/200 10.00
48 Mark Prior Bat-Jsy/200 12.00

49 Aramis Ramirez Bat-Jsy/200 8.00
50 Greg Maddux Bat-Jsy/100 15.00
51 Carlos Zambrano Jsy-Jsy/200 8.00
52 Derrek Lee Bat-Bat/200 8.00
54 Moises Alou Bat-Bat/200 8.00
56 Sammy Sosa Bat-Jsy/200 10.00
57 Nomar Garciaparra Bat-Bat/200 10.00
60 Magglio Ordonez Bat-Jsy/200 5.00
61 Carlos Lee Bat-Jsy/200 5.00
62 Joe Crede Bat-Bat/200 5.00
65 Frank Thomas Bat-Jsy/200 8.00
69 Adam Dunn Bat-Jsy/200 8.00
70 Austin Kearns Bat-Bat/200 5.00
74 Sean Casey Jsy-Pants/200 5.00
76 C.C. Sabathia Jsy-Jsy/200 5.00
77 Jody Gerut Bat-Jsy/200 5.00
78 Omar Vizquel Bat-Jsy/200 5.00
79 Victor Martinez Bat-Jsy/200 5.00
80 Matt Lawton Bat-Bat/200 5.00
84 Todd Helton Bat-Jsy/200 8.00
85 Preston Wilson Bat-Jsy/200 5.00
90 Ivan Rodriguez Bat-Jsy/200 8.00
92 Brandon Inge Bat-Jsy/200 5.00
94 Dontrelle Willis Jsy-Jsy/200 5.00
95 Miguel Cabrera Bat-Jsy/200 10.00
96 Josh Beckett Bat-Bat/100 5.00
97 Mike Lowell Bat-Jsy/100 5.00
98 Luis Castillo Bat-Bat/200 5.00
99 Juan Pierre Bat-Bat/200 5.00
100 Paul LoDuca Bat-Bat/200 5.00
102 Craig Biggio Bat-Pants/200 5.00
103 Lance Berkman Bat-Jsy/200 5.00
104 Roy Oswalt Jsy-Jsy/200 5.00
105 Roger Clemens Bat-Jsy/200 15.00
106 Jeff Kent Bat-Jsy/100 5.00
108 Jeff Bagwell Bat-Jsy/200 8.00
109 Carlos Beltran Bat-Jsy/200 8.00
110 Angel Berroa Bat-Bat/200 5.00
111 Mike Sweeney Bat-Jsy/200 5.00
112 Jeremy Affeldt Pants-Pants/200 5.00
114 Juan Gonzalez Bat-Jsy/200 8.00
116 Shawn Green Bat-Jsy/200 5.00
118 Adrian Beltre Bat-Jsy/200 8.00
119 Hideo Nomo Bat-Jsy/200 8.00
123 Scott Podsednik Jsy-Jsy/200 5.00
124 Ben Sheets Bat-Pants/200 8.00
125 Lyle Overbay Jsy-Jsy/200 5.00
126 Junior Spivey Jsy-Jsy/200 5.00
127 Bill Hall Bat-Jsy/200 5.00
129 Jacque Jones Bat-Jsy/200 5.00
130 Torii Hunter Bat-Jsy/200 5.00
131 Johan Santana Jsy-Jsy/200 10.00
132 Lew Ford Bat-Jsy/200 5.00
136 Jose Vidro Bat-Jsy/200 5.00
138 Brad Wilkerson Bat-Bat/100 5.00
139 Nick Johnson Bat-Bat/100 5.00
140 Livan Hernandez Jsy-Jsy/25 5.00
141 Tom Glavine Bat-Bat/200 8.00
143 Jose Reyes Bat-Jsy/200 5.00
144 Al Leiter Jsy-Jsy/200 5.00
145 Mike Piazza Jsy-Jsy/100 15.00
146 Kazuo Matsui Bat-Jsy/200 8.00
147 Richard Hidalgo Bat-Bat/200 5.00
149 Mariano Rivera Jsy-Jsy/100 8.00
150 Mike Mussina Bat-Jsy/200 8.00
153 Jorge Posada Bat-Jsy/200 8.00
154 Jason Giambi Bat-Jsy/200 5.00
155 Gary Sheffield Bat-Jsy/200 8.00
158 Kevin Brown Bat-Bat/100 5.00
160 Esteban Loaiza Bat-Bat/100 5.00
161 Hideki Matsui Jsy-Pants/200 20.00
162 Eric Chavez Bat-Jsy/200 5.00
163 Mark Mulder Bat-Bat/25 10.00
164 Barry Zito Bat-Jsy/200 5.00
165 Tim Hudson Bat-Jsy/200 8.00
166 Jermaine Dye Bat-Jsy/200 5.00
168 Bobby Crosby Jsy-Jsy/200 8.00
171 Jim Thome Bat-Jsy/200 8.00
172 Bobby Abreu Jsy-Jsy/200 8.00
173 Kevin Millwood Jsy-Jsy/200 5.00
178 Craig Wilson Bat-Jsy/200 5.00
180 Jack Wilson Bat-Bat/200 5.00
181 Jose Castillo Bat-Bat/200 5.00
184 Jason Bay Bat-Jsy/200 5.00
185 Sean Burroughs Bat-Jsy/200 8.00
187 Brian Giles Bat-Bat/100 5.00
193 Trevor Hoffman Jsy-Jsy/200 5.00
199 J.T. Snow Jsy-Jsy/25 5.00
200 A.J. Pierzynski Jsy-Jsy/100 5.00
201 Edgar Martinez Bat-Bat/200 5.00
204 Bret Boone Jsy-Jsy/200 5.00
208 Jamie Moyer Jsy-Jsy/50 5.00
209 Jim Edmonds Bat-Jsy/200 8.00
210 Scott Rolen Bat-Jsy/200 10.00
211 Edgar Renteria Bat-Jsy/200 8.00
212 Dan Haren Bat-Jsy/100 5.00
213 Matt Morris Jsy-Jsy/100 5.00
214 Albert Pujols Jsy-Jsy/200 20.00
215 Larry Walker Bat-Bat/200 8.00
220 Aubrey Huff Bat-Bat/100 5.00
221 Carl Crawford Jsy-Jsy/200 5.00
222 Rocco Baldelli Bat-Jsy/200 5.00
223 Fred McGriff Bat-Jsy/200 5.00
224 Dewon Brazelton Jsy-Jsy/200 5.00
225 B.J. Upton Bat-Bat/200 8.00
226 Joey Gathright Bat-Jsy/200 5.00
228 Hank Blalock Bat-Jsy/100 8.00
229 Mark Teixeira Bat-Jsy/200 8.00
230 Michael Young Bat-Jsy/200 5.00
232 Laynce Nix Bat-Jsy/200 5.00
233 Alfonso Soriano Bat-Jsy/200 8.00
234 Rafael Palmeiro Bat-Jsy/200 8.00
235 Kevin Mench Bat-Jsy/200 5.00
236 David Dellucci Jsy-Jsy/200 8.00
237 Francisco Cordero Jsy-Jsy/200 5.00
239 Roy Halladay Jsy-Jsy/200 5.00
240 Carlos Delgado Bat-Jsy/200 5.00
242 Vernon Wells Bat-Jsy/200 5.00
267 Larry Walker Jsy-Jsy/200 8.00
268 Ivan Rodriguez Jsy-Jsy/200 8.00
269 Brad Penny Bat-Jsy/200 5.00
270 Carlos Beltran Bat-Jsy/200 8.00
271 Paul LoDuca Bat-Jsy/200 5.00
273 Nomar Garciaparra Bat-Bat/100 10.00
274 Esteban Loiaza Bat-Bat/100 5.00
275 Richard Hidalgo Jkt-Pants/200 5.00
276 John Olerud Bat-Jsy/200 5.00
277 Greg Maddux Jsy-Jsy/200 12.00
278 Roger Clemens Bat-Jsy/200 15.00
279 Alfonso Soriano Bat-Jsy/200 8.00
280 Dale Murphy Jsy-Jsy/200 8.00
281 Cal Ripken Jr. Bat-Jsy/200 30.00
282 Dwight Evans Bat-Jsy/200 8.00
283 Ron Santo Bat-Bat/200 10.00
284 Andre Dawson Bat-Jsy/100 8.00
285 Harold Baines Bat-Jsy/200 8.00
286 Jack Morris Jsy-Jsy/100 8.00
287 Kirk Gibson Bat-Jsy/200 5.00
288 Bo Jackson Bat-Jsy/200 10.00
289 Orel Hershiser Jsy-Jsy/50 8.00
290 Maury Wills Jsy-Jsy/10
291 Tony Oliva Bat-Jsy/200 10.00
292 Darryl Strawberry Bat-Jsy/100 8.00
293 Roger Maris Bat-Jsy/100 50.00
294 Don Mattingly Bat-Jsy/100 25.00
295 Rickey Henderson Bat-Jsy/100 10.00
297 Dave Parker Bat-Jsy/200 8.00
298 Steve Garvey Bat-Jsy/200 8.00
299 Matt Williams Jsy-Jsy/200 8.00
300 Keith Hernandez Bat-Jsy/200 8.00
302 Vladimir Guerrero Jsy-Jsy/200 10.00
303 Garret Anderson Bat-Jsy/200 5.00
307 Luis Gonzalez Jsy-Jsy/200 5.00
308 Randy Johnson Bat/Jsy/1
310 Shawn Green Bat-Bat/200 5.00
311 Troy Glaus Bat-Bat/200 5.00
314 Chipper Jones Jsy-Jsy/100 10.00
315 Johnny Estrada Jsy-Jsy/200 5.00
316 Andruw Jones Bat-Jsy/200 8.00
319 Jay Gibbons Bat-Bat/200 5.00
320 Melvin Mora Jsy-Jsy/200 5.00
321 Rafael Palmeiro Bat-Jsy/200 8.00
323 David Ortiz Bat-Jsy/200 10.00
324 Manny Ramirez Bat-Jsy/200 10.00
327 Curt Schilling Jsy-Jsy/200 10.00
328 Sammy Sosa Bat-Jsy/100 10.00
329 Mark Prior Bat-Jsy/200 10.00
330 Greg Maddux Jsy-Jsy/25 15.00
332 Frank Thomas Bat-Pants/200 10.00
333 Mark Buehrle Bat-Jsy/200 5.00
336 Sean Casey Bat-Jsy/200 5.00
337 Adam Dunn Bat-Jsy/200 8.00
339 Travis Hafner Jsy-Jsy/100 5.00
340 Victor Martinez Bat-Jsy/100 5.00
341 Cliff Lee Jsy-Jsy/200 5.00
342 Todd Helton Bat-Jsy/25 8.00
343 Preston Wilson Jsy-Jsy/200 5.00
344 Ivan Rodriguez Bat-Jsy/200 8.00
347 Miguel Cabrera Bat-Jsy/200 10.00
348 Jeff Bagwell Bat-Jsy/200 8.00
349 Andy Pettitte Bat-Jsy/200 8.00
350 Roger Clemens Bat-Jsy/100 15.00
351 Ken Harvey Jsy-Jsy/200 5.00
353 Hideo Nomo Bat-Jsy/200 8.00
354 Kazuhisa Ishii Jsy-Jsy/200 5.00
355 Edwin Jackson Jsy-Jsy/200 5.00
356 J.D. Drew Bat-Bat/200 5.00
357 Jeff Kent Bat-Bat/25 5.00
358 Geoff Jenkins Jsy-Pants/200 5.00
359 Carlos Lee Bat-Bat/200 5.00
360 Shannon Stewart Jsy-Jsy/200 5.00
362 Johan Santana Jsy-Jsy/100 10.00
363 Mike Piazza Jsy-Jsy/100 12.00
364 Kazuo Matsui Jsy-Jsy/100 5.00
365 Carlos Beltran Bat-Bat/10
366 Pedro Martinez Bat-Bat/100 10.00
368 Hideki Matsui Bat-Jsy/100 20.00
369 Bernie Williams Bat-Jsy/200 8.00
370 Gary Sheffield Bat-Jsy/100 8.00
371 Randy Johnson Bat-Bat/25 10.00
378 Mark Mulder Bat-Bat/50 8.00
380 Eric Chavez Jsy-Jsy/100 5.00

382 Marlon Byrd Bat-Jsy/200 5.00
383 Pat Burrell Jsy-Jsy/200 5.00
385 Jim Thome Bat-Bat/200 8.00
386 Jason Bay Bat-Jsy/1
388 Moises Alou Bat-Bat/200 5.00
393 Adrian Beltre Bat-Bat/50 5.00
394 Richie Sexson Bat-Bat/200 5.00
397 Albert Pujols Bat-Jsy/200 20.00
398 Scott Rolen Bat-Jsy/200 10.00
401 Delmon Young Bat-Bat/200 5.00
402 Aubrey Huff Bat-Bat/50 5.00
403 Alfonso Soriano Bat-Jsy/200 8.00
404 Hank Blalock Bat-Jsy/200 5.00
405 Richard Hidalgo Bat-Bat/200 5.00
406 Vernon Wells Jsy-Jsy/200 5.00
407 Orlando Hudson Bat-Bat/200 5.00
412 Jose Vidro Bat-Jsy/5 5.00
415 Miguel Tejada Jsy-Jsy/200 8.00
416 Gary Sheffield Bat-Bat/200 8.00
417 Curt Schilling Jsy-Jsy/200 10.00
418 Rafael Palmeiro Bat-Pants/50 8.00
419 Scott Rolen Bat-Jsy/200 10.00
420 Aramis Ramirez Jsy-Jsy/200 8.00
421 Vladimir Guerrero Bat-Bat/200 10.00
422 Steve Finley Jsy-Jsy/200 5.00
423 Roger Clemens Bat-Jsy/200 15.00
424 Mike Piazza Jsy-Jsy/200 12.00
425 Ivan Rodriguez Bat-Jsy/200 8.00
426 David Justice Jsy-Jsy/200 5.00
427 Mark Grace Bat-Jsy/25 8.00
428 Alan Trammell Bat-Jsy/100 5.00
429 Bert Blyleven Jsy-Jsy/1
430 Dwight Gooden Bat-Jsy/200 5.00
431 Deion Sanders Bat-Jsy/200 8.00
432 Joe Torre Bat-Bat/100 5.00
433 Jose Canseco Jsy-Jsy/100 8.00
434 Tony Gwynn Bat-Pants/200 10.00
435 Will Clark Bat-Jsy/100 8.00
436 Marty Marion Jsy-Jsy/1
437 Nolan Ryan Bat-Jsy/50 15.00
438 Billy Martin Jsy-Pants/200 10.00
439 Carlos Delgado Bat-Bat/100 5.00
440 Magglio Ordonez Bat-Bat/200 5.00
441 Sammy Sosa Bat-Bat/25 10.00
449 Ryne Sandberg Bat-Jsy/100 10.00
450 Willie Mays Bat-Pants/5

Signature Bronze

NM/M

Production 1-100
No pricing 20 or less
Black: No Pricing
Production One Set
Gold: .75X-1.5X
Production 1-50
Silver: .75X-1.5X
Production 1-100
Platinum: No Pricing
Production One Set
Framed Blue: .75X-1.5X
Production 1-50
Framed Green: .75X-1.5X
Production 1-25
Framed Red: .75X-1.5X
Production 1-100
#303-450 found in DK Update
3 Jose Guillen/100 15.00
5 Tim Salmon/100 20.00
6 Casey Kotchman/100 15.00
7 Chone Figgins/100 15.00
8 Robb Quinlan/100 8.00
9 Francisco Rodriguez/50 40.00
10 Troy Percival/50 15.00
14 Shea Hillenbrand/100 10.00
15 Chad Tracy/100 10.00
16 Alex Cintron/100 8.00
22 Adam LaRoche/50 10.00
23 Russ Ortiz/50 12.00
26 Nick Green/100 8.00
30 Luis Matos/100 10.00
31 Larry Bigbie/100 10.00
32 Rodrigo Lopez/100 15.00
33 Brian Roberts/100 25.00
34 Melvin Mora/100 15.00
40 Keith Foulke/50 40.00
43 Kevin Youkilis/100 10.00
44 Orlando Cabrera/50 20.00
45 Abe Alvarez/100 8.00
51 Carlos Zambrano/50 30.00
58 Todd Walker/50 15.00
59 Angel Guzman/100 15.00
61 Carlos Lee/100 15.00
73 Ryan Wagner/100 10.00
75 Danny Graves/100 12.00
76 C.C. Sabathia/50 20.00
77 Jody Gerut/100 8.00
79 Victor Martinez/50 20.00
82 Kazuhito Tadano/100 20.00
83 Travis Hafner/100 15.00
89 Jeremy Bonderman/100 15.00
92 Brandon Inge/100 10.00
101 Guillermo Mota/50 10.00
107 Morgan Ensberg/100 10.00
112 Jeremy Affeldt/100 10.00
117 Milton Bradley/100 15.00
122 Brad Penny/100 10.00
123 Scott Podsednik/50 15.00
125 Lyle Overbay/100 12.00
127 Bill Hall/100 8.00
132 Lew Ford/100 15.00
135 Jason Kubel/100 15.00
137 Chad Cordero/100 10.00
140 Livan Hernandez/25 15.00
156 Bubba Crosby/100 10.00
159 Tom Gordon/25 20.00
160 Esteban Loaiza/100 10.00
166 Jermaine Dye/50 15.00
167 Octavio Dotel/50 15.00
168 Bobby Crosby/100 20.00
174 Mike Lieberthal/100 12.00
177 Randy Wolf/100 10.00
178 Craig Wilson/100 10.00
180 Jack Wilson/100 12.00
181 Jose Castillo/100 10.00
184 Jason Bay/100 15.00
186 Jay Payton/50 10.00
189 Jake Peavy/50 30.00
194 Freddy Guzman/100 8.00
197 Todd Linden/50 10.00
198 Merkin Valdez/100 10.00
203 Raul Ibanez/100 10.00
206 Miguel Olivo/100 8.00
207 Bucky Jacobsen/100 12.00
208 Jamie Moyer/50 15.00
212 Dan Haren/100 12.00
219 Jeff Suppan/100 10.00
220 Aubrey Huff/50 15.00
221 Carl Crawford/25 20.00
224 Dewon Brazelton/100 8.00
226 Joey Gathright/100 10.00
227 Scott Kazmir/25 25.00
230 Michael Young/50 20.00
231 Adrian Gonzalez/100 10.00
232 Laynce Nix/100 15.00
236 David Dellucci/100 20.00
237 Francisco Cordero/100 15.00
241 Alexis Rios/100 15.00
248 Dioner Navarro/100 15.00
253 Yhency Brazoban/100 10.00
257 Scott Proctor/100 8.00
260 Matt Peterson/100 8.00
269 Brad Penny/50 10.00
272 Orlando Cabrera/50 15.00
274 Esteban Loaiza/100 10.00
284 Andre Dawson/50 20.00
285 Harold Baines/100 15.00
286 Jack Morris/100 10.00
290 Maury Wills/100 15.00
292 Darryl Strawberry/100 15.00
297 Dave Parker/100 20.00
299 Matt Williams/25 25.00
303 Garret Anderson/50 15.00
304 Dallas McPherson/100 10.00
305 Orlando Cabrera/25 10.00
306 Steve Finley/50 10.00
313 Russ Ortiz/50 10.00
315 Johnny Estrada/100 8.00
318 Danny Kolb/100 8.00
319 Jay Gibbons/50 8.00
320 Melvin Mora/50 10.00
325 Edgar Renteria/50 15.00
333 Mark Buehrle/50 20.00
336 Sean Casey/25 15.00
339 Travis Hafner/50 15.00
340 Victor Martinez/50 10.00
341 Cliff Lee/100 10.00
343 Preston Wilson/50 15.00
351 Ken Harvey/100 8.00
355 Edwin Jackson/100 8.00
359 Carlos Lee/100 10.00
360 Shannon Stewart/25 15.00
361 Joe Nathan/100 15.00
376 Eric Byrnes/100 8.00
377 Rich Harden/100 15.00
378 Mark Mulder/25 20.00
380 Eric Chavez/25 15.00
382 Marlon Byrd/100 8.00
384 Brett Myers/100 10.00
386 Jason Bay/50 15.00
387 Jake Peavy/50 25.00
402 Aubrey Huff/50 15.00
407 Orlando Hudson/25 10.00
410 Jose Guillen/25 15.00
429 Bert Blyleven/50 10.00
430 Dwight Gooden/50 15.00
436 Marty Marion/50 15.00

Signature Materials Bronze

NM/M

Production 1-200
No pricing 20 or less
Platinum: No Pricing
Production One Set
Framed Black: No Pricing
Production 1-10
Framed Blue: No Pricing
Production 1-50
Framed Green: 1X-2X
Production 1-25
Framed Red: .75X-1.5X
Production 1-100
1 Garret Anderson Bat-Jsy/50 25.00
7 Chone Figgins Bat-Jsy/200 15.00
18 Rafael Furcal Bat-Jsy/50 20.00
19 Andruw Jones Bat-Jsy/25 35.00
31 Larry Bigbie Jsy-Jsy/200 15.00
32 Rodrigo Lopez Jsy-Jsy/200 15.00
38 Trot Nixon Jsy-Jsy/100 30.00
46 David Ortiz Bat-Jsy/100 50.00
48 Mark Prior Bat-Jsy/25 75.00
49 Aramis Ramirez Bat-Jsy/100 25.00
51 Carlos Zambrano Jsy-Jsy/200 25.00
52 Derrek Lee Bat-Bat/100 20.00
61 Carlos Lee Bat-Jsy/100 10.00
76 C.C. Sabathia Jsy-Jsy/100 20.00
78 Omar Vizquel Jsy-Jsy/25 40.00
95 Miguel Cabrera Bat-Jsy/25 50.00
109 Carlos Beltran Bat-Jsy/50 40.00
112 Jeremy Affeldt Pants-Pants/100 10.00
127 Bill Hall Bat-Bat/100 10.00
129 Jacque Jones Bat-Jsy/50 20.00
131 Johan Santana Jsy-Jsy/50 40.00
132 Lew Ford Bat-Jsy/200 15.00
139 Nick Johnson Bat-Bat/50 12.00
153 Jorge Posada Bat-Jsy/25 40.00
162 Eric Chavez Bat-Jsy/25 25.00
178 Craig Wilson Bat-Jsy/200 15.00
185 Sean Burroughs Bat-Jsy/100 10.00
201 Edgar Martinez Bat-Bat/25 40.00
211 Edgar Renteria Bat-Jsy/50 30.00
221 Carl Crawford Jsy-Jsy/200 15.00
229 Mark Teixeira Bat-Jsy/25 40.00
230 Michael Young Bat-Jsy/100 20.00
232 Laynce Nix Bat-Jsy/200 12.00
233 Alfonso Soriano Bat-Jsy/25 50.00
239 Roy Halladay Jsy-Jsy/25 25.00
269 Brad Penny Bat-Jsy/100 10.00
280 Dale Murphy Jsy-Jsy/50 35.00
282 Dwight Evans Bat-Jsy/50 25.00
283 Ron Santo Bat-Bat/100 35.00
284 Andre Dawson Bat-Jsy/100 25.00
286 Jack Morris Jsy-Jsy/100 20.00
287 Kirk Gibson Bat-Jsy/25 40.00
289 Orel Hershiser Jsy-Jsy/25 35.00
291 Tony Oliva Bat-Jsy/100 25.00
294 Don Mattingly Bat-Jsy/25 90.00
297 Dave Parker Bat-Jsy/100 25.00
298 Steve Garvey Bat-Jsy/50 25.00
300 Keith Hernandez Bat-Jsy/100 20.00
303 Garret Anderson Bat-Jsy/50 20.00
315 Johnny Estrada Jsy-Jsy/50 12.00
319 Jay Gibbons Bat-Bat/50 12.00
320 Melvin Mora Jsy-Jsy/50 15.00
323 David Ortiz Jsy-Jsy/25 50.00
333 Mark Buehrle Jsy-Jsy/25 25.00
339 Travis Hafner Jsy-Jsy/25 25.00
340 Victor Martinez Jsy-Jsy/25 20.00
341 Cliff Lee Jsy-Jsy/25 15.00
343 Preston Wilson Bat-Jsy/25 20.00
351 Ken Harvey Jsy-Jsy/25 12.00
382 Marlon Byrd Bat-Jsy/50 12.00
401 Delmon Young Bat-Bat/25 25.00
407 Orlando Hudson Bat-Bat/25 12.00
419 Scott Rolen Bat-Jsy/25 30.00
428 Alan Trammell Bat-Jsy/25 25.00
430 Dwight Gooden Bat-Jsy/25 25.00
434 Tony Gwynn Bat-Jsy/25 40.00

Signature Materials Gold

NM/M

Production 1-50
7 Chone Figgins Bat-Jsy/50 20.00
18 Rafael Furcal Bat-Jsy/25 30.00
31 Larry Bigbie Jsy-Jsy/50 20.00
32 Rodrigo Lopez Jsy-Jsy/50 20.00
46 David Ortiz Bat-Jsy/50 60.00
49 Aramis Ramirez Bat-Jsy/50 35.00

51 Carlos Zambrano Jsy-Jsy/50 35.00
76 C.C. Sabathia Jsy-Jsy/50 25.00
104 Roy Oswalt Jsy-Jsy/50 30.00
112 Jeremy Affeldt Pants-Pants/50 15.00
127 Bill Hall Bat-Bat/50 15.00
129 Jacque Jones Bat-Jsy/50 20.00
132 Lew Ford Bat-Jsy/50 20.00
178 Craig Wilson Bat-Jsy/50 20.00
221 Carl Crawford Jsy-Jsy/50 20.00
230 Michael Young Bat-Jsy/50 25.00
269 Brad Penny Bat-Jsy/50 15.00
280 Dale Murphy Jsy-Jsy/25 50.00
282 Dwight Evans Bat-Jsy/25 30.00
283 Ron Santo Bat-Bat/50 45.00
284 Andre Dawson Bat-Jsy/50 30.00
285 Harold Baines Bat-Jsy/50 25.00
286 Jack Morris Jsy-Jsy/50 25.00
291 Tony Oliva Bat-Jsy/50 30.00
297 Dave Parker Bat-Jsy/50 30.00
299 Matt Williams Jsy-Jsy/25 35.00

Signature Materials Silver

NM/M

Production 1-100
7 Chone Figgins Bat-Jsy/100 15.00
18 Rafael Furcal Bat-Jsy/25 30.00
31 Larry Bigbie Jsy-Jsy/100 15.00
32 Rodrigo Lopez Jsy-Jsy/100 15.00
46 David Ortiz Bat-Jsy/50 60.00
49 Aramis Ramirez Bat-Jsy/50 35.00
51 Carlos Zambrano Jsy-Jsy/100 30.00
61 Carlos Lee Bat-Jsy/100 10.00
76 C.C. Sabathia Jsy-Jsy/100 20.00
104 Roy Oswalt Jsy-Jsy/50 30.00
112 Jeremy Affeldt Pants-Pants/100 10.00
127 Bill Hall Bat-Bat/100 10.00
129 Jacque Jones Bat-Jsy/50 20.00
132 Lew Ford Bat-Jsy/100 15.00
178 Craig Wilson Bat-Jsy/100 15.00
221 Carl Crawford Jsy-Jsy/100 15.00
230 Michael Young Bat-Jsy/50 25.00
232 Laynce Nix Bat-Jsy/100 15.00
269 Brad Penny Bat-Jsy/50 15.00
280 Dale Murphy Jsy-Jsy/25 50.00
282 Dwight Evans Bat-Jsy/25 30.00
283 Ron Santo Bat-Bat/50 45.00
284 Andre Dawson Bat-Jsy/50 30.00
285 Harold Baines Bat-Jsy/50 25.00
286 Jack Morris Jsy-Jsy/50 25.00
291 Tony Oliva Bat-Jsy/50 30.00
297 Dave Parker Bat-Jsy/50 30.00
298 Steve Garvey Bat-Jsy/25 30.00
299 Matt Williams Jsy-Jsy/25 35.00
300 Keith Hernandez Bat-Jsy/50 25.00

Team Timeline

NM/M

Complete Set (25): 65.00
Common Duo: 1.50
Inserted 1:21
#26-30 found in DK Update
1 Albert Pujols, Scott Rolen 6.00
2 Roger Clemens, Andy Pettitte 6.00
3 Tim Hudson, Mark Mulder 1.50
4 Hank Blalock, Mark Teixeira 2.00
5 Miguel Cabrera, Mike Lowell 2.00
6 Greg Maddux, Sammy Sosa 4.00
7 Miguel Tejada, Cal Ripken Jr. 8.00
8 Vladimir Guerrero, Reggie Jackson 3.00
9 Mike Schmidt, Jim Thome 4.00
10 Chipper Jones, Greg Maddux 4.00
11 George Brett, Ken Harvey 5.00
12 Don Mattingly, Hideki Matsui 5.00
13 Torii Hunter, Johan Santana 2.00
14 Carlos Delgado, Vernon Wells 1.50
15 Todd Helton, Larry Walker 2.00
16 Duke Snider, Adrian Beltre 2.00
17 Al Kaline, Ivan Rodriguez 3.00
18 Rafael Palmeiro, Eddie Murray 2.00
19 Manny Ramirez, Carl Yastrzemski 3.00
20 Ralph Kiner, Jason Bay 1.50
21 Johnny Bench, Adam Dunn 3.00
22 Robin Yount, Lyle Overbay 4.00
23 Nolan Ryan, andy Johnson 8.00
24 Gary Carter, Mike Piazza 4.00
25 Carlton Fisk, Frank Thomas 3.00
26 Nolan Ryan, Mike Piazza 8.00
27 Roger Clemens, Jeff Bagwell 8.00
28 Cal Ripken Jr., Sammy Sosa 8.00
29 Willie Mays, Jim Thorpe 8.00
30 Albert Pujols, Stan Musial 8.00

Team Timeline Materials Bat

NM/M

Production 25-100
2 Roger Clemens, Andy Pettitte/50 25.00
5 Miguel Cabrera, Mike Lowell/100 15.00
8 Vladimir Guerrero, Reggie Jackson/75 20.00
9 Mike Schmidt, Jim Thome/50 30.00
12 Don Mattingly, Hideki Matsui/50 50.00
15 Todd Helton, Larry Walker/100 10.00
17 Al Kaline, Ivan Rodriguez/25 30.00
18 Rafael Palmeiro, Eddie Murray/100 15.00
21 Johnny Bench, Adam Dunn/100 15.00
22 Robin Yount, Lyle Overbay/100 20.00
23 Nolan Ryan, Randy Johnson/25 40.00

Team Timeline Materials Jersey

NM/M

Common Duo: 8.00
Production 100 Sets
Prime: No Pricing
Production One Set
#26-30 found in DK Update
1 Albert Pujols, Scott Rolen 40.00
2 Roger Clemens, Andy Pettitte 25.00
3 Tim Hudson, Mark Mulder 8.00
4 Hank Blalock, Mark Teixeira 10.00
7 Miguel Tejada, Cal Ripken Jr. 40.00
8 Vladimir Guerrero, Reggie Jackson 15.00
9 Mike Schmidt Jkt, Jim Thome 30.00
10 Chipper Jones, Greg Maddux 20.00
12 Don Mattingly Jkt, Hideki Matsui 50.00
14 Carlos Delgado, Vernon Wells 8.00
15 Todd Helton, Larry Walker 10.00
16 Duke Snider, Adrian Beltre 10.00
18 Rafael Palmeiro, Eddie Murray 15.00
19 Manny Ramirez, Carl Yastrzemski 25.00
21 Johnny Bench, Adam Dunn 15.00
22 Robin Yount, Lyle Overbay 15.00
23 Nolan Ryan, Randy Johnson
24 Gary Carter, Mike Piazza 15.00
25 Carlton Fisk, Frank Thomas 15.00
26 Nolan Ryan, Mike Piazza 30.00
27 Roger Clemens, Jeff Bagwell 20.00
29 Willie Mays, Jim Thorpe
30 Albert Pujols, Stan Musial 40.00

Timeline

NM/M

Complete Set (25): 50.00
Common Player: 1.50
Inserted 1:21
#26-30 found in DK Update
1 Roger Clemens 6.00
2 Nolan Ryan 8.00
3 Carlos Beltran 3.00
4 Ivan Rodriguez 3.00
5 Jim Thome 3.00
6 Mike Piazza 4.00
7 Miguel Tejada 3.00
8 Rafael Palmeiro 2.00
9 Greg Maddux 4.00
10 Tom Glavine 1.50
11 Vladimir Guerrero 3.00
12 Curt Schilling 3.00
13 Mike Mussina 2.00
14 Rickey Henderson 2.00
15 Scott Rolen 3.00
16 Alfonso Soriano 3.00
17 Gary Sheffield 2.00
18 Carlton Fisk 2.00
19 Aramis Ramirez 2.00
20 Mark Grace 1.50
21 Jason Giambi 1.50
22 Juan Gonzalez 1.50
23 Brad Penny 1.50
24 Nomar Garciaparra 4.00
25 Larry Walker 2.00
26 Curt Schilling 2.00
27 Reggie Jackson 2.00
28 Gary Carter 1.50
29 Roger Clemens 6.00
30 Nolan Ryan 8.00

Timeline Materials Bat

NM/M

Production 25-100
1 Roger Clemens 30.00
2 Nolan Ryan 50.00
3 Carlos Beltran 10.00
4 Ivan Rodriguez 10.00
5 Jim Thome 20.00
8 Rafael Palmeiro 10.00
9 Greg Maddux 30.00
10 Tom Glavine 10.00
11 Vladimir Guerrero 15.00
12 Curt Schilling 20.00
13 Mike Mussina 10.00
14 Rickey Henderson 10.00
15 Scott Rolen 20.00
17 Gary Sheffield 10.00
18 Carlton Fisk 10.00
19 Aramis Ramirez 10.00
20 Mark Grace 10.00
22 Juan Gonzalez 10.00
25 Larry Walker 10.00

Timeline Materials Jersey

NM/M

Production 50-200
Prime: No Pricing
Production One Set
#26-30 found in DK Update
1 Roger Clemens 15.00
2 Nolan Ryan 25.00
3 Carlos Beltran 10.00
4 Ivan Rodriguez 8.00
6 Mike Piazza 15.00
7 Miguel Tejada 10.00
8 Rafael Palmeiro 10.00
9 Greg Maddux 15.00
11 Vladimir Guerrero 15.00
12 Curt Schilling 10.00
13 Mike Mussina 10.00
14 Rickey Henderson 10.00
15 Scott Rolen 15.00
16 Alfonso Soriano 10.00
18 Carlton Fisk 10.00
19 Aramis Ramirez 10.00
21 Jason Giambi 8.00
22 Juan Gonzalez 8.00
26 Curt Schilling 10.00
27 Reggie Jackson 10.00
28 Gary Carter 8.00
29 Roger Clemens 15.00
30 Nolan Ryan 25.00

Update Gallery of Stars

NM/M

Complete Set (25): 30.00
Common Player: 1.50
Inserted 1:8
1 Andre Dawson 1.50
2 Bob Feller 2.00
3 Bobby Doerr 1.50
4 C.C. Sabathia 1.50
5 Carl Crawford 1.50
6 Dale Murphy 2.00
7 Danny Kolb 1.50
8 Darryl Strawberry 1.50
9 Dave Parker 1.50
10 David Ortiz 3.00
11 Dwight Gooden 1.50
12 Garret Anderson 1.50
13 Jack Morris 1.50
14 Jacque Jones 1.50
15 Jim Palmer 2.00
16 Johan Santana 3.00
17 Ken Harvey 1.50
18 Lyle Overbay 1.50
19 Marty Marion 1.50
20 Melvin Mora 1.50
21 Michael Young 1.50
22 Miguel Cabrera 3.00
23 Preston Wilson 1.50
24 Sean Casey 1.50
25 Victor Martinez 1.50

Update Gallery of Stars Bat

NM/M

Production 50-200
1 Andre Dawson/50 8.00
3 Bobby Doerr/100 4.00
6 Dale Murphy/100 8.00
8 Darryl Strawberry/100 4.00
9 Dave Parker/200 4.00
10 David Ortiz/200 10.00
11 Dwight Gooden/100 4.00
12 Garret Anderson/100 4.00
18 Lyle Overbay/50 4.00
21 Michael Young/200 4.00
22 Miguel Cabrera/100 8.00
23 Preston Wilson/200 4.00
24 Sean Casey/200 4.00

Update Gallery of Star Combo

NM/M

Production 50-200 5.00

Prime: No Pricing
Production one set
1 Andre Dawson/100 10.00
3 Bobby Doerr/100 8.00
4 C.C. Sabathia/100 5.00
6 Dale Murphy/100 10.00
9 Dave Parker/200 5.00
10 David Ortiz/200 12.00
11 Dwight Gooden/100 5.00
12 Garret Anderson/100 6.00
14 Jacque Jones/50 5.00
15 Jim Palmer/50 8.00
18 Lyle Overbay/50 5.00
21 Michael Young/200 5.00
22 Miguel Cabrera/200 10.00
23 Preston Wilson/200 5.00
24 Sean Casey/200 5.00

Update Gallery of Stars Jsy

NM/M

Production 25-100
Prime: No Pricing
Production one set
1 Andre Dawson/100 6.00
2 Bob Feller/50 8.00
3 Bobby Doerr/100 6.00
4 C.C. Sabathia/100 4.00
5 Carl Crawford/100 4.00
6 Dale Murphy/100 8.00
8 Darryl Strawberry/25 6.00
9 Dave Parker/100 4.00
10 David Ortiz/100 8.00
11 Dwight Gooden/25 4.00
12 Garret Anderson/50 4.00
13 Jack Morris/100 4.00
14 Jacque Jones/100 4.00
15 Jim Palmer/50 6.00
17 Ken Harvey/100 4.00
18 Lyle Overbay/100 4.00
20 Melvin Mora/100 4.00
21 Michael Young/100 4.00
22 Miguel Cabrera/100 8.00
23 Preston Wilson/100 4.00
24 Sean Casey/100 4.00
25 Victor Martinez/25 6.00

Update Gallery of Stars Auto

NM/M

Production 5-100
1 Andre Dawson/100 15.00
2 Bob Feller/100 25.00
3 Bobby Doerr/100 15.00
4 C.C. Sabathia/25 20.00
5 Carl Crawford/100 12.00
6 Dale Murphy/100 20.00
7 Danny Kolb/100 10.00
8 Darryl Strawberry/100 15.00
9 Dave Parker/100 12.00
10 David Ortiz/10
11 Dwight Gooden/100 15.00
12 Garret Anderson/10
13 Jack Morris/100 12.00
14 Jacque Jones/50 10.00
15 Jim Palmer/5
16 Johan Santana/5
17 Ken Harvey/100 8.00
18 Lyle Overbay/50 10.00
19 Marty Marion/25 20.00
20 Melvin Mora/100 12.00
21 Michael Young/5
22 Miguel Cabrera/5
24 Sean Casey/5
25 Victor Martinez/100 12.00

Update Gallery of Stars Bat Autograph

NM/M

Production 5-200
1 Andre Dawson/25 25.00
3 Bobby Doerr/200 15.00
9 Dave Parker/200 15.00
11 Dwight Gooden/100 20.00
12 Garret Anderson/100 15.00
14 Jacque Jones/100 15.00
17 Ken Harvey/25 12.00
21 Michael Young/100 15.00
22 Miguel Cabrera/50 35.00
24 Sean Casey/50 20.00

Update Gallery of Stars Combo Auto.

NM/M

Production 25-200
Prime: No Pricing
Production one set
1 Andre Dawson/50 25.00
3 Bobby Doerr/200 20.00
6 Dale Murphy/50 30.00
9 Dave Parker/100 15.00
10 David Ortiz/50 40.00
11 Dwight Gooden/100 20.00
12 Garret Anderson/50 20.00
14 Jacque Jones/50 20.00
15 Jim Palmer/25 25.00
17 Ken Harvey/25 15.00
21 Michael Young/50 20.00
22 Miguel Cabrera/50 35.00
24 Sean Casey/25 20.00
25 Victor Martinez/100 20.00

Update Gallery of Stars Jersey Auto.

NM/M

Production 25-100
Prime: No Pricing
Production one set
1 Andre Dawson/25 25.00
2 Bob Feller/50 30.00
3 Bobby Doerr/100 15.00
4 C.C. Sabathia/100 15.00
5 Carl Crawford/50 15.00
6 Dale Murphy/50 25.00
9 Dave Parker/100 15.00
10 David Ortiz/50 40.00
11 Dwight Gooden/50 20.00
12 Garret Anderson/50 20.00
13 Jack Morris/50 15.00
14 Jacque Jones/25 20.00
15 Jim Palmer/25 25.00
17 Ken Harvey/100 8.00
18 Lyle Overbay/100 10.00
19 Marty Marion/25 20.00
20 Melvin Mora/100 15.00
24 Sean Casey/25 20.00
25 Victor Martinez/100 20.00

Update HOF Sluggers

NM/M

Common Player: 2.00
1 Duke Snider 2.00
2 Eddie Murray 2.00
3 Frank Robinson 2.00
4 George Brett 5.00
5 Harmon Killebrew 3.00
6 Mike Schmidt 5.00
7 Reggie Jackson 3.00
8 Roberto Clemente 6.00
9 Stan Musial 4.00
10 Willie Mays 5.00

Update HOF Sluggers Jersey

NM/M

Production 5-50
1 Duke Snider Pants/25 10.00
2 Eddie Murray/50 10.00
5 Harmon Killebrew/25 15.00
6 Mike Schmidt/50 15.00
7 Reggie Jackson Pants/50 8.00
8 Roberto Clemente/5
9 Stan Musial Pants/25 20.00
10 Willie Mays Pants/50 25.00

Update Masters of the Game

NM/M

Common Player: 2.00
1 Albert Pujols 4.00
2 Cal Ripken Jr. 6.00
3 Don Mattingly 4.00
4 Greg Maddux 3.00
5 Jim Thorpe 4.00
6 Nolan Ryan 5.00
7 Randy Johnson 2.00
8 Roberto Clemente 6.00
9 Roger Clemens 4.00
10 Willie Mays 4.00

Update Masters of the Game Jersey

NM/M

Production 25-50
1 Albert Pujols/50 20.00
2 Cal Ripken Jr./50 30.00
3 Don Mattingly/25 20.00
4 Greg Maddux/50 10.00
5 Jim Thorpe/25 250.00
6 Nolan Ryan/50 20.00
7 Randy Johnson/25 10.00
9 Roger Clemens/50 10.00
10 Willie Mays Pants/25 30.00

2005 DONRUSS ELITE

NM/M

Complete Set (200):
Common Player (1-150): .25
Common SP (151-170): 3.00
Production 1,250
Common Auto. (171-200): 8.00
Production 500 to 1,500
Pack (5): 5.00
Box (20): 90.00
1 Bartolo Colon .25
2 Casey Kotchman .25
3 Chone Figgins .25
4 Darin Erstad .25
5 Garret Anderson .40
6 Jose Guillen .25
7 Vladimir Guerrero .75
8 Luis Gonzalez .25
9 Randy Johnson .75
10 Troy Glaus .40
11 Andruw Jones .40
12 Chipper Jones .75
13 J.D. Drew .25
14 John Smoltz .40
15 Johnny Estrada .25
16 Marcus Giles .25
17 Rafael Furcal .25
18 Javy Lopez .40
19 Jay Gibbons .25
20 Melvin Mora .25
21 Miguel Tejada .50
22 Rafael Palmeiro .50
23 Sidney Ponson .25
24 Curt Schilling .75
25 David Ortiz .75
26 Derek Lowe .25
27 Jason Varitek .40
28 Johnny Damon .75
29 Manny Ramirez .75
30 Pedro Martinez .75
31 Aramis Ramirez .40
32 Carlos Zambrano .40
33 Corey Patterson .25
34 Derrek Lee .50
35 Greg Maddux 1.00
36 Kerry Wood .50
37 Mark Prior .75
38 Moises Alou .40
39 Nomar Garciaparra 1.00
40 Sammy Sosa 1.00
41 Carlos Lee .25
42 Frank Thomas .50
43 Jermaine Dye .25
44 Magglio Ordonez .25
45 Mark Buehrle .25
46 Paul Konerko .25
47 Adam Dunn .50
48 Austin Kearns .25
49 Barry Larkin .40
50 Ken Griffey Jr. 1.00
51 Sean Casey .25
52 C.C. Sabathia .25
53 Cliff Lee .25
54 Travis Hafner .25
55 Victor Martinez .25
56 Jeromy Burnitz .25
57 Preston Wilson .25
58 Todd Helton .25
59 Brandon Inge .25
60 Ivan Rodriguez .50
61 Jeremy Bonderman .25
62 Troy Percival .25
63 Dontrelle Willis .40
64 Josh Beckett .40
65 Juan Pierre .25
66 Miguel Cabrera .75
67 Mike Lowell .25
68 Paul LoDuca .25
69 Andy Pettitte .40
70 Brad Ausmus .25
71 Carlos Beltran .50
72 Craig Biggio .40
73 Jeff Bagwell .50
74 Lance Berkman .40
75 Roger Clemens 2.00
76 Roy Oswalt .25
77 Juan Gonzalez .25
78 Mike Sweeney .25
79 Zack Greinke .25
80 Adrian Beltre .25
81 Hideo Nomo .25
82 Jeff Kent .25
83 Milton Bradley .25
84 Shawn Green .25
85 Steve Finley .25
86 Ben Sheets .25
87 Lyle Overbay .25
88 Scott Podsednik .25
89 Lew Ford .25
90 Shannon Stewart .25
91 Torii Hunter .25
92 David Wright .75
93 Jose Reyes .25
94 Kazuo Matsui .25
95 Mike Piazza 1.00
96 Tom Glavine .40
97 Alex Rodriguez 1.50
98 Bernie Williams .40
99 Derek Jeter 2.00
100 Gary Sheffield .50
101 Hideki Matsui 1.50
102 Jason Giambi .25
103 Kevin Brown .25
104 Mike Mussina .40
105 Barry Zito .25
106 Bobby Crosby .40
107 Eric Chavez .40
108 Jason Kendall .25
109 Mark Mulder .40
110 Bobby Abreu .40
111 Jim Thome .75
112 Kevin Millwood .25
113 Pat Burrell .25
114 Craig Wilson .25
115 Jack Wilson .25
116 Jason Bay .40
117 Brian Giles .25
118 Khalil Greene .40
119 Mark Loretta .25
120 Ryan Klesko .25
121 Sean Burroughs .25
122 Edgardo Alfonzo .25
123 J.T. Snow .25
124 Jason Schmidt .25
125 Omar Vizquel .25
126 Ichiro Suzuki 1.50
127 Jamie Moyer .25
128 Bret Boone .25
129 Richie Sexson .40
130 Albert Pujols 2.00
131 Edgar Renteria .40
132 Jeff Suppan .25
133 Jim Edmonds .40
134 Larry Walker .40
135 Scott Rolen .75
136 Aubrey Huff .25
137 B.J. Upton .25
138 Carl Crawford .25
139 Rocco Baldelli .25
140 Alfonso Soriano .75
141 Hank Blalock .40
142 Kenny Rogers .25
143 Laynce Nix .25
144 Mark Teixeira .50
145 Michael Young .25
146 Carlos Delgado .40
147 Eric Hinske .25
148 Roy Halladay .25
149 Vernon Wells .25
150 Jose Vidro .25
151 Bob Gibson 3.00
152 Brooks Robinson 3.00
153 Cal Ripken Jr. 10.00

154 Carl Yastrzemski 4.00
155 Don Mattingly 5.00
156 Eddie Murray 3.00
157 Ernie Banks 4.00
158 Frank Robinson 3.00
159 George Brett 5.00
160 Harmon Killebrew 4.00
161 Johnny Bench 4.00
162 Mike Schmidt 5.00
163 Nolan Ryan 6.00
164 Paul Molitor 4.00
165 Stan Musial 5.00
166 Steve Carlton 3.00
167 Tony Gwynn 4.00
168 Warren Spahn 4.00
169 Willie Mays 6.00
170 Willie McCovey 3.00
171 *Miguel Negron AU/1500* 8.00
172 *Mike Morse AU/1000* 15.00
173 *Wladimir Balentien AU/1500* 10.00
174 *Alberto Concepcion AU/651* 10.00
175 *Ubaldo Jimenez AU/500* 10.00
176 *Justin Verlander AU/500* 25.00
177 *Ryan Speier AU/1000* 8.00
178 *Geovany Soto AU/500* 8.00
179 *Mark McLemore AU/1200* 8.00
180 *Ambiorix Burgos AU/599* 8.00
181 *Chris Roberson AU/1000* 10.00
182 *Colter Bean AU/625* 10.00
183 *Erick Threets AU/500* 8.00
184 *Carlos Ruiz AU/1000* 8.00
185 *Enrique Gonzalez AU*
186 *Jared Gothreaux AU/1500* 10.00
187 *Luis Hernandez AU/1000* 8.00
188 *Agustin Montero/1000* 2.00
189 *Paulino Reynoso/1000* 2.00
190 *Garrett Jones AU/500* 8.00
191 *Sean Thompson AU/500* 8.00
192 *Matt Lindstrom AU/1500* 8.00
193 *Nate McLouth AU/500* 10.00
194 *Luke Scott AU/671* 10.00
195 Keith Hattig AU/500 10.00
196 *Jason Hammel AU/1500* 10.00
197 *Danny Rueckel AU/671* 8.00
198 *Justin Wechsler AU/500* 8.00
199 *Chris Resop AU/500* 15.00
200 *Jeff Miller AU/500* 10.00

Aspirations

NM/M
Cards (1-150) print run 61-99: 4-8X
(1-150) p/r 41-60: 6-10X
(1-150) p/r 21-40: 8-15X
(151-170) p/r 36-80: 1.5-3X
Autos (171-200) p/r 40-99: .5-1.5X
No pricing production 20 or less
Production 15-99

Status

NM/M
Cards (1-150) print run 61-81: 4-8X
(1-150) p/r 41-60: 6-10X
(1-150) p/r 21-40: 8-15X
(151-170) p/r 36-81: 1.5-3X
Autos (171-200) p/r 40-81: .5-1.5X
No pricing production 20 or less
Production 1-81

Status Gold

Gold (1-150): 10-20X
Gold (151-170): 3-5X
Gold (171-200): No Pricing
Production 24 sets

Turn of the Century

Stars (1-150): 2-3X
Production 750
(151-170): 1X
Production 250
Rookies (171-200): .25-1X
Production 500

Back 2 Back Jacks

NM/M
Production 25-200
1 Adam Dunn/200 8.00
3 Albert Pujols/100 15.00
4 Babe Ruth/50 160.00
5 Cal Ripken Jr./100 30.00
6 David Ortiz/200 10.00
7 Eddie Murray/150 8.00
8 Ernie Banks/50 15.00
9 Frank Robinson/50 8.00
10 Gary Sheffield/200 5.00
11 George Foster/125 5.00
12 Don Mattingly/10 15.00
13 Hideki Matsui/25 30.00
14 Jason Giambi/50 5.00
16 Jim Rice/125 8.00
17 Jim Thome/200 8.00
18 Johnny Bench/125 10.00
19 Lance Berkman/200 5.00
20 Manny Ramirez/200 8.00
21 Mike Piazza/200 10.00
22 Mike Schmidt/125 15.00
23 Rafael Palmeiro/200 8.00
24 Reggie Jackson/125 10.00
25 Sammy Sosa/100 10.00
26 Scott Rolen/200 8.00
27 Stan Musial/125 15.00
28 Willie Mays/50 40.00
29 Kirk Gibson/125 5.00
30 Will Clark/125 5.00
31 Willie Mays, Sammy Sosa/50 50.00
32 Eddie Murray, Mike Piazza/50 20.00
33 Mike Schmidt, Jim Thome/50 30.00
34 Rafael Palmeiro, Kirk Gibson/50 10.00
35 Jim Rice, Manny Ramirez/50 15.00
36 Adrian Beltre, Will Clark/50 15.00
37 Reggie Jackson, David Ortiz/50 15.00
38 Johnny Bench, Adam Dunn/50 20.00

Back 2 Back Jacks Combos

NM/M
1 Adam Dunn Bat-Jsy/100 10.00
2 Adrian Beltre Bat-Jsy/100 8.00
4 Babe Ruth Bat-Pants/25
5 Cal Ripken Jr. Bat-Jsy/50 40.00
6 David Ortiz Bat-Jsy/50 12.00
7 Eddie Murray Bat-Jsy/50 10.00
8 Ernie Banks Bat-Jsy/10 20.00
10 Gary Sheffield Bat-Jsy/100 8.00
11 George Foster Bat-Jsy/50 8.00
12 Don Mattingly Bat-Jsy/50 20.00
13 Hideki Matsui Bat-Jsy/25 40.00
14 Jason Giambi Bat-Jsy/50 8.00
15 Jim Edmonds Bat-Jsy/100 10.00
17 Jim Thome Bat-Jsy/100 8.00
18 Johnny Bench Bat-Jsy/50 15.00
19 Lance Berkman Bat-Jsy/100 8.00
20 Manny Ramirez Bat-Jsy/100 12.00
21 Mike Piazza Bat-Jsy/50 15.00
22 Mike Schmidt Bat-Jsy/50 20.00
23 Rafael Palmeiro Bat-Jsy/50 10.00
24 Reggie Jackson Bat-Jsy/50 15.00
25 Sammy Sosa Bat-Jsy/100 15.00
26 Scott Rolen Bat-Jsy/100 12.00
27 Stan Musial Bat-Pants/50 25.00
28 Willie Mays Bat-Jsy/50 60.00
29 Kirk Gibson Bat-Jsy/50 10.00
30 Will Clark Bat-Jsy/50 12.00
31 Willie Mays, Sammy Sosa/10
32 Eddie Murray, Mike Piazza/25 30.00
33 Mike Schmidt, Jim Thome/25 50.00
34 Rafael Palmeiro, Kirk Gibson/25 20.00
35 Jim Rice, Manny Ramirez/50 25.00
36 Adrian Beltre, Will Clark/50 15.00
37 Reggie Jackson, David Ortiz/25 30.00
38 Johnny Bench, Adam Dunn/25 30.00
40 Cal Ripken Jr., Albert Pujols/25 100.00

Career Best

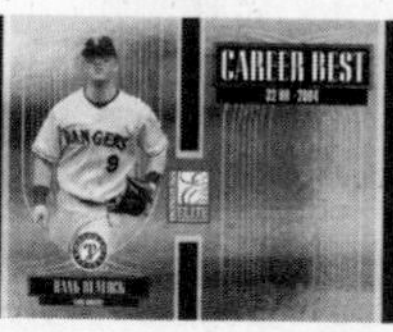

NM/M
Common Player: 1.00
Production 1,500 Sets
Black: 1X-2X
Production 150 Sets
Blue: 1X-2X
Production 250 Sets
Gold: 1X-1.5X
Production 500 Sets
1 Adam Dunn 1.50
2 Adrian Beltre 1.00
3 Albert Pujols 4.00
4 Andruw Jones 1.50
5 Ben Sheets 1.00
6 Bo Jackson 2.00
7 Brooks Robinson 2.00
8 Cal Ripken Jr. 6.00
9 Dale Murphy 1.50
10 Don Mattingly 3.00
11 Eddie Murray 1.50
12 George Brett 3.00
13 Hank Blalock 1.50
14 Ichiro Suzuki 3.00
15 Jim Thome 1.50
16 Kerry Wood 1.50
17 Lance Berkman 1.00
18 Mark Prior 2.00
19 Mark Teixeira 1.50
20 Mike Schmidt 3.00
21 Pedro Martinez 2.00
22 Randy Johnson 2.00
23 Rickey Henderson 1.50
24 Sammy Sosa 3.00
25 Tony Gwynn 2.00

Career Best Bats

NM/M
Production 50-250
1 Adam Dunn/250 8.00
2 Adrian Beltre/250 5.00
3 Albert Pujols/250 15.00
4 Andruw Jones/250 5.00
5 Ben Sheets/250 5.00
6 Bo Jackson/250 10.00
7 Brooks Robinson/250 8.00
8 Cal Ripken Jr./150 25.00
9 Dale Murphy/150 10.00
10 Don Mattingly/250 12.00
11 Eddie Murray/250 8.00
12 George Brett/250 15.00
13 Hank Blalock/250 8.00
15 Jim Thome/100 8.00
16 Kerry Wood/100 8.00
17 Lance Berkman/250 5.00
18 Mark Prior/150 10.00
19 Mark Teixeira/250 8.00
20 Mike Schmidt/250 12.00
21 Pedro Martinez/100 10.00
22 Randy Johnson/100 10.00
23 Rickey Henderson/250 8.00
24 Sammy Sosa/100 10.00
25 Tony Gwynn/100 10.00

Career Best Combos

NM/M
Production 25-150 10.00
1 Adam Dunn Bat-Jsy/150 10.00
2 Adrian Beltre Bat-Jsy/150 8.00
3 Albert Pujols Bat-Jsy/150 20.00
4 Andruw Jones Bat-Jsy/150 8.00
5 Ben Sheets Bat-Jsy/150 8.00
6 Bo Jackson Bat-Jsy/25 20.00
7 Brooks Robinson Bat-Jsy/25 20.00
8 Cal Ripken Jr. Bat-Jsy/25 40.00
9 Dale Murphy Bat-Jsy/25 10.00
10 Don Mattingly Bat-Jsy/25 20.00
11 Eddie Murray Bat-Jsy/25 12.00
12 George Brett Bat-Jsy/25 25.00
13 Hank Blalock Bat-Jsy/150 10.00
15 Jim Thome Bat-Jsy/150 10.00
16 Kerry Wood Bat-Pants/150 10.00
17 Lance Berkman Bat-Jsy/150 8.00
18 Mark Prior Bat-Jsy/150 12.00
19 Mark Teixeira Bat-Jsy/150 12.00
20 Mike Schmidt Bat-Jsy/25
21 Pedro Martinez Bat-Jsy/125 10.00
22 Randy Johnson Bat-Jsy/25
23 Rickey Henderson Bat-Jsy/25 15.00
24 Sammy Sosa Bat-Jsy/150 12.00
25 Tony Gwynn Bat-Jsy/25 15.00

Career Best Jerseys

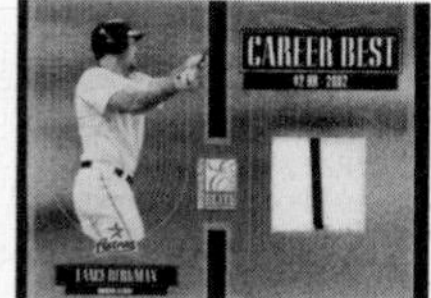

NM/M
Production 100-250
1 Adam Dunn/250 8.00
2 Adrian Beltre/250 5.00
3 Albert Pujols/250 15.00
4 Andruw Jones/250 5.00
5 Ben Sheets/250 5.00
6 Bo Jackson/250 10.00
7 Brooks Robinson/50 10.00
8 Cal Ripken Jr./150 25.00
9 Dale Murphy/100 10.00
10 Don Mattingly/150 12.00
11 Eddie Murray/100 8.00
12 George Brett/100 15.00
13 Hank Blalock/250 8.00
15 Jim Thome/250 8.00
16 Kerry Wood/250 8.00
17 Lance Berkman/250 5.00
18 Mark Prior/250 10.00
19 Mark Teixeira/250 8.00
20 Mike Schmidt/100 12.00
21 Pedro Martinez/250 8.00
22 Randy Johnson/100 10.00
23 Rickey Henderson/50 10.00
24 Sammy Sosa/250 10.00
25 Tony Gwynn/250 10.00

Face 2 Face

NM/M
Complete Set (20): 35.00
Common Duo:
Production 1,500 Sets
Black: 1X-1.5X

Production 500 Sets
Gold: 1X-2X
Production 250 Sets
Red: 1X
Production 750 Sets
1 Roger Clemens, Scott Rolen 3.00
2 Greg Maddux, Jeff Bagwell 3.00
3 Mark Prior, Mike Piazza 3.00
4 Mike Mussina, Ivan Rodriguez 2.00
5 Josh Beckett, Sammy Sosa 2.00
6 Roy Oswalt, Miguel Cabrera 2.00
7 Roger Clemens, Albert Pujols 4.00
8 Pedro Martinez, Vladimir Guerrero 2.00
9 Randy Johnson, Jim Edmonds 2.00
10 Curt Schilling, Derek Jeter 4.00
11 Kerry Wood, Lance Berkman 1.50
12 Tim Hudson, Garret Anderson 1.00
13 Pedro Martinez, Gary Sheffield 2.00
14 Barry Zito, Magglio Ordonez 1.00
15 Kerry Wood, Shawn Green 1.50
16 Mike Mussina, Miguel Tejada 2.00
17 Randy Johnson, Albert Pujols 4.00
18 Nolan Ryan, George Brett 4.00
19 Tom Seaver, Mike Schmidt 3.00
20 Jim Palmer, Harmon Killebrew 2.00

Face 2 Face Bats

NM/M

Production 25-150
3 Mark Prior, Mike Piazza/10 10.00
4 Mike Mussina, Ivan Rodriguez/100 8.00
5 Josh Beckett, Sammy Sosa/50 10.00
6 Roy Oswalt, Miguel Cabrera/100 10.00
7 Roger Clemens, Albert Pujols/25
8 Pedro Martinez, Vladimir Guerrero/50 10.00
9 Randy Johnson, Jim Edmonds/50 10.00
11 Kerry Wood, Lance Berkman/150 8.00
12 Tim Hudson, Garret Anderson/150 8.00
13 Pedro Martinez, Gary Sheffield/150 10.00
14 Barry Zito, Magglio Ordonez/50 8.00
15 Kerry Wood, Shawn Green/150 8.00
16 Mike Mussina, Miguel Tejada/25
18 Nolan Ryan, George Brett/100 25.00
19 Tom Seaver, Mike Schmidt/150 15.00

Face 2 Face Combos

NM/M

Production 25-250
1 Roger Clemens Jsy, Scott Rolen Bat/100 15.00
2 Greg Maddux Jsy, Jeff Bagwell Bat/100 10.00
3 Mark Prior Jsy, Mike Piazza Bat/250 10.00
4 Mike Mussina Jsy, Ivan Rodriguez Bat/250 8.00
5 Josh Beckett Jsy, Sammy Sosa Bat/250 10.00
6 Roy Oswalt Jsy, Miguel Cabrera Bat/250 8.00
8 Pedro Martinez Jsy, Vladimir Guerrero Bat/75 10.00
11 Kerry Wood Bat, Lance Berkman Jsy/250 8.00
12 Tim Hudson Jsy, Garret Anderson Bat/100 8.00
13 Pedro Martinez Bat, Gary Sheffield Jsy/75 12.00
14 Barry Zito Jsy, Magglio Ordonez Bat/250 8.00
15 Kerry Wood Jsy, Shawn Green Bat/250 8.00
16 Mike Mussina Jsy, Miguel Tejada Bat/250 10.00
18 Nolan Ryan Jsy, George Brett Bat/25
19 Tom Seaver Jsy, Mike Schmidt Bat/50 20.00

Face 2 Face Jerseys

NM/M

Production 25-200
1 Roger Clemens, Scott Rolen/200 15.00
2 Greg Maddux, Jeff Bagwell/75 10.00
3 Mark Prior, Mike Piazza/200 10.00
4 Mike Mussina, Ivan Rodriguez/200 8.00
5 Josh Beckett, Sammy Sosa/200 12.00
6 Roy Oswalt, Miguel Cabrera/200 8.00
7 Roger Clemens, Albert Pujols/200 20.00
8 Pedro Martinez, Vladimir Guerrero/75 10.00
11 Kerry Wood, Lance Berkman/200 8.00
12 Tim Hudson, Garret Anderson/75 8.00
13 Pedro Martinez, Gary Sheffield/75 10.00
14 Barry Zito, Magglio Ordonez/200 8.00
15 Kerry Wood, Shawn Green/200 8.00
16 Mike Mussina, Miguel Tejada/200 10.00
17 Randy Johnson, Albert Pujols/75 20.00
18 Nolan Ryan, George Brett/25
19 Tom Seaver, Mike Schmidt/50 20.00
20 Jim Palmer, Harmon Killebrew/25

Passing the Torch

NM/M

Common Player: 1.50
1-30 Production 1,000
31-45 Production 500
Black: 2X-3X
1-30 Production 50
31-45 Production 25
Gold: 1-2X
1-30 Production 100
31-45 Production 50
Green: 1X-1.5X
1-30 Production 250
31-45 Production 125
Red: 1X
1-30 Production 500
31-45 Production 250
1 Adrian Beltre 1.50
2 Albert Pujols 5.00
3 Alex Rodriguez 4.00
4 Andruw Jones 1.50
5 Babe Ruth 6.00
6 Ben Sheets 1.50
7 Brooks Robinson 2.00
8 Cal Ripken Jr. 8.00
9 Carl Yastrzemski 3.00
10 Dale Murphy 2.00
11 David Ortiz 2.00
12 Derek Jeter 5.00
13 Don Mattingly 4.00
14 George Brett 4.00
15 Greg Maddux 3.00
16 Hank Blalock 1.50
17 Jeff Bagwell 1.50
18 Johnny Bench 3.00
19 Magglio Ordonez 1.50
20 Mark Prior 2.00
21 Mark Teixeira 2.00
22 Miguel Cabrera 2.00
23 Mike Schmidt 3.00
24 Nolan Ryan 6.00
25 Pedro Martinez 2.00
26 Sammy Sosa 3.00
27 Scott Rolen 2.00
28 Tom Seaver 2.00
29 Vladimir Guerrero 2.00
30 Willie Mays 4.00
31 Carlton Fisk, Magglio Ordonez 3.00
32 Nolan Ryan, Ben Sheets 8.00
33 Babe Ruth, Alex Rodriguez 8.00
34 Cal Ripken Jr., B.J. Upton 10.00
35 Willie Mays, Andruw Jones 5.00
36 George Brett, Hank Blalock 5.00
37 Greg Maddux, Whitey Ford 4.00
38 Harmon Killebrew, Mark Prior 3.00
39 Tom Seaver, Mark Prior 3.00
40 Don Mattingly, Mark Teixeira 5.00
41 Stan Musial, Carlos Beltran 5.00
42 Dale Murphy, Lance Berkman 3.00
43 Willie McCovey, Jeff Bagwell 3.00
44 Andre Dawson, Miguel Cabrera 3.00
45 Brooks Robinson, Scott Rolen 4.00

Passing the Torch Autographs

NM/M

Production 5-100
6 Ben Sheets/75 15.00
7 Brooks Robinson/100 25.00
10 Dale Murphy/100 20.00
13 Don Mattingly/50 50.00
18 Johnny Bench/25 50.00
19 Magglio Ordonez/75 10.00
20 Mark Prior/25 40.00
21 Mark Teixeira/75 25.00
22 Miguel Cabrera/75 25.00
23 Mike Schmidt/25 50.00
27 Scott Rolen/25 50.00
44 Andre Dawson, Miguel Cabrera/25 50.00
45 Brooks Robinson, Scott Rolen/25 75.00

Passing the Torch Bats

NM/M

Production 25-250
1 Adrian Beltre/250 4.00
2 Albert Pujols/250 15.00
4 Andruw Jones/250 4.00
5 Babe Ruth/25
6 Ben Sheets/250 4.00
7 Brooks Robinson/150 10.00
8 Cal Ripken Jr./150 25.00
9 Carl Yastrzemski/150 10.00
10 Dale Murphy/150 6.00
11 David Ortiz/250 8.00
13 Don Mattingly/150 10.00
14 George Brett/150 10.00
16 Hank Blalock/250 4.00
17 Jeff Bagwell/250 6.00
18 Johnny Bench/150 10.00
19 Magglio Ordonez/250 4.00
20 Mark Prior/50 10.00
21 Mark Teixeira/250 6.00
22 Miguel Cabrera/250 8.00
23 Mike Schmidt/150 10.00
24 Nolan Ryan/50 20.00
25 Pedro Martinez/150 8.00
26 Sammy Sosa/250 8.00
27 Scott Rolen/250 8.00
28 Tom Seaver/150 8.00
29 Vladimir Guerrero/250 8.00
30 Willie Mays/50 30.00
31 Carlton Fisk, Magglio Ordonez/250 6.00
32 Nolan Ryan, Ben Sheets/50 35.00
34 Cal Ripken Jr., B.J. Upton/50 50.00
35 Willie Mays, Andruw Jones/50 35.00
36 George Brett, Hank Blalock/150 15.00
39 Tom Seaver, Mark Prior/25 20.00
40 Don Mattingly, Mark Teixeira/150 15.00
41 Stan Musial, Carlos Beltran/25
42 Dale Murphy, Lance Berkman/50 12.00
43 Willie McCovey, Jeff Bagwell/25 20.00
44 Andre Dawson, Miguel Cabrera/150 10.00
45 Brooks Robinson, Scott Rolen/150 15.00

Passing the Torch Jerseys

NM/M

Production 25-250
1 Adrian Beltre/250 4.00
2 Albert Pujols/250 15.00
4 Andruw Jones/250 4.00
5 Babe Ruth Pants/25
6 Ben Sheets/250 4.00
7 Brooks Robinson/25
8 Cal Ripken Jr./250 20.00
9 Carl Yastrzemski Pants/50 10.00
10 Dale Murphy/250 6.00
11 David Ortiz/250 8.00
13 Don Mattingly/150 10.00
14 George Brett/50 12.00
15 Greg Maddux/250 10.00
16 Hank Blalock/250 4.00
17 Jeff Bagwell/250 6.00
18 Johnny Bench Pants/150 10.00
19 Magglio Ordonez/250 4.00
20 Mark Prior/250 8.00
21 Mark Teixeira/250 6.00
22 Miguel Cabrera/250 8.00
23 Mike Schmidt/150 10.00
24 Nolan Ryan/50 20.00
25 Pedro Martinez/250 8.00
26 Sammy Sosa/250 8.00
27 Scott Rolen/250 8.00
28 Tom Seaver/50 8.00
29 Vladimir Guerrero/250 8.00
30 Willie Mays/25
31 Carlton Fisk, Magglio Ordonez/50 8.00
32 Nolan Ryan, Ben Sheets/50 35.00
34 Cal Ripken Jr., B.J. Upton/50 50.00
35 Willie Mays, Andruw Jones/50 35.00
36 George Brett, Hank Blalock/50 15.00
37 Greg Maddux, Whitey Ford/25
38 Harmon Killebrew, Adrian Beltre/50
39 Tom Seaver, Mark Prior/25 20.00
40 Don Mattingly, Mark Teixeira/100 15.00
41 Stan Musial Pants, Carlos Beltran/25
42 Dale Murphy, Lance Berkman/150 10.00
43 Willie McCovey, Jeff Bagwell/50 15.00
44 Andre Dawson, Miguel Cabrera/150 10.00
45 Brooks Robinson, Scott Rolen/25

Teams

NM/M

Common Card:
Production 1,500 Sets
Black: 1X-2X
Production 250 Sets
Blue: 1X
Production 1,000 Sets
Gold: 2X-3X
Production 100 Sets
Green: 1X-1.5X
Production 750 Sets
Red: 1X-1.5X
Production 500 Sets

1 Manny Ramirez, Pedro Martinez, David Ortiz 4.00
2 Albert Pujols, Scott Rolen, Jim Edmonds 4.00
3 Roger Clemens, Jeff Bagwell, Lance Berkman, Craig Biggio 4.00
4 Miguel Cabrera, Josh Beckett, Mike Lowell 2.00
5 Kerry Wood, Mark Prior, Sammy Sosa, Greg Maddux 4.00
6 Adrian Beltre, Shawn Green, Hideo Nomo, Kazuhisa Ishii 2.00
7 Cal Ripken Jr., Eddie Murray, Jim Palmer 8.00
8 George Brett, Bo Jackson, Frank White 4.00
9 Roger Clemens, Mike Mussina, Alfonso Soriano, Bernie Williams 4.00
10 Tom Glavine, Greg Maddux, Ryan Klesko, David Justice 4.00

Teams Bats

NM/M

Production 50-100
1 Manny Ramirez, Pedro Martinez, David Ortiz/100 20.00
2 Albert Pujols, Scott Rolen, Jim Edmonds/100 40.00
3 Roger Clemens, Jeff Bagwell, Lance Berkman, Craig Biggio/50 35.00
4 Miguel Cabrera, Josh Beckett, Mike Lowell/100 10.00
6 Adrian Beltre, Shawn Green, Hideo Nomo, Kazuhisa Ishii/50 20.00
8 George Brett, Bo Jackson, Frank White/100 25.00

Teams Jerseys

NM/M

Production 50-150
1 Manny Ramirez, Pedro Martinez, David Ortiz/150 20.00
2 Albert Pujols, Scott Rolen, Jim Edmonds/150 30.00
3 Roger Clemens, Jeff Bagwell, Lance Berkman, Craig Biggio/150 25.00
4 Miguel Cabrera, Josh Beckett, Mike Lowell/50 15.00
5 Kerry Wood, Mark Prior, Sammy Sosa, Greg Maddux/150 25.00
6 Adrian Beltre, Shawn Green, Hideo Nomo, Kazuhisa Ishii/50 20.00
7 Cal Ripken Jr., Eddie Murray, Jim Palmer/100 35.00
9 Roger Clemens, Mike Mussina, Alfonso Soriano, Bernie Williams/100 25.00
10 Tom Glavine, Greg Maddux, Ryan Klesko, David Justice/100 30.00

Throwback Threads

NM/M

Production 10-200
1 Albert Pujols/200 15.00
3 Bert Blyleven/200 4.00
4 Bobby Doerr Pants/200 6.00
6 Cal Ripken Jr./150 25.00
7 Carl Yastrzemski Pants/150 12.00
8 Dale Murphy/150 8.00
9 Dennis Eckersley/50 8.00
10 Don Mattingly/200 10.00
11 Don Sutton/100 4.00
13 Early Wynn/50 6.00
14 Eddie Murray/100 8.00
16 Greg Maddux/150 8.00
17 Harmon Killebrew/100 8.00
18 Hoyt Wilhelm/150 6.00
19 Jim Edmonds/200 8.00
21 Lou Boudreau/100 8.00
22 Lou Brock/100 8.00
23 Miguel Cabrera/200 8.00
24 Mike Mussina/150 8.00
25 Mike Piazza/150 8.00
26 Mike Schmidt/150 15.00
27 Nolan Ryan/50 20.00
28 Phil Niekro/100 6.00
29 Randy Johnson/150 8.00
30 Rickey Henderson/150 8.00
31 Sammy Sosa/150 8.00
32 Scott Rolen/200 8.00
33 Stan Musial/10
34 Steve Carlton/100 8.00
35 Ted Williams/25
36 Tommy John/150 6.00
37 Vladimir Guerrero/200 8.00
38 Whitey Ford/25 15.00
39 Willie Mays/50 40.00
40 Willie McCovey/150 8.00
46 Lou Brock, Rickey Henderson/100 15.00
49 Bo Jackson, Deion Sanders/150 15.00
50 Nolan Ryan, Curt Schilling/100 25.00
51 Don Sutton, Greg Maddux/100 15.00
52 Harmon Killebrew, Rafael Palmeiro/100 15.00
53 Dale Murphy, Dwight Evans/150 12.00
55 Carl Yastrzemski, Vladimir Guerrero/50 15.00
56 Eddie Murray, Mike Piazza/100 12.00
57 Johnny Bench, Ivan Rodriguez/50 12.00
58 Jim Palmer, Tim Hudson/50 10.00
59 Cal Ripken Jr., Hank Blalock/50 35.00
60 Jim Rice, Manny Ramirez/100 12.00

Throwback Threads Autographs

NM/M

Production 5-100
Prime: No Pricing
Production 1-10
3 Bert Blyleven/100 15.00
4 Bobby Doerr Pants/100 20.00
5 Brooks Robinson/50 30.00
8 Dale Murphy/100 25.00
9 Dennis Eckersley/75 20.00
11 Don Sutton/50 20.00
17 Harmon Killebrew/75 30.00
20 Jim Palmer/75 15.00
22 Lou Brock Jkt/75 30.00
23 Miguel Cabrera/75 30.00

2005 DONRUSS LEATHER & LUMBER

NM/M

Complete Set (177):
Common Player (1-150): .25
Common Auto. (151-175): 8.00
Production 256
Card #176 doesn't exist
Pack (5): 7.00
Box (18): 100.00
1 Adam Dunn .50
2 Adrian Beltre .40
3 Akinori Otsuka .25
4 Al Leiter .25
5 Albert Pujols 2.00
6 Alex Rodriguez 1.50
7 Alfonso Soriano .75
8 Andy Pettitte .40
9 Aramis Ramirez .40
10 Aubrey Huff .25
11 Austin Kearns .25
12 Barry Larkin .40
13 Barry Zito .40
14 Bartolo Colon .25
15 Bernie Williams .40
16 Bobby Abreu .40
17 Bobby Crosby .40
18 Brad Penny .25
19 Brian Giles .25
20 C.C. Sabathia .25
21 Carl Crawford .25
22 Carl Pavano .25
23 Carlos Beltran .50
24 Carlos Delgado .40
25 Carlos Lee .40
26 Carlos Zambrano .40
27 Casey Kotchman .25
28 Chipper Jones .75
29 Chone Figgins .25
30 Craig Biggio .40
31 Craig Monroe .25
32 Cristian Guzman .25
33 Curt Schilling .75
34 Danny Haren .25
35 Darin Erstad .25
36 David Dellucci .25
37 David Ortiz .75
38 David Wells .25
39 Derek Jeter 2.00
40 Dontrelle Willis .40
41 Edgar Renteria .40
42 Eric Gagne .40
43 Frank Thomas .50
44 Garret Anderson .40
45 Gary Sheffield .50
46 Geoff Jenkins .25
47 Greg Maddux 1.50
48 Hideo Nomo .40
49 Ichiro Suzuki 1.50
50 Ivan Rodriguez .50
51 J.D. Drew .25
52 Jake Peavy .40
53 Jamie Moyer .25
54 Jason Giambi .40
55 Jason Kendall .25
56 Jason Schmidt .40
57 Jason Varitek .40
58 Javy Lopez .40
59 Jay Gibbons .25
60 Jeff Bagwell .50
61 Jeff Bagwell .25
62 Jeremy Bonderman .25
63 Jermaine Dye .25
64 Jim Edmonds .40
65 Jim Thome .50
66 Joe Nathan .25
67 Johan Santana .50
68 John Olerud .25
69 John Smoltz .40
70 Johnny Damon .75
71 Johnny Estrada .25
72 Jose Reyes .25
73 Jose Vidro .25
74 Josh Beckett .40
75 Juan Pierre .25
76 Junior Spivey .25
77 Justin Morneau .25
78 Kazuhisa Ishii .25
79 Kazuo Matsui .25
80 Ken Griffey Jr. 1.50
81 Kerry Wood .40
82 Kevin Brown .25
83 Kevin Millwood .25
84 Khalil Greene .40
85 Lance Berkman .25
86 Larry Walker .40
87 Laynce Nix .25
88 Lyle Overbay .25
89 Magglio Ordonez .25
90 Manny Ramirez .50
91 Marcus Giles .25
92 Mark Loretta .25
93 Mark Mulder .40
94 Mark Prior .50
95 Mark Teixeira .40
96 Melvin Mora .25
97 Michael Young .25
98 Miguel Tejada .50
99 Mike Lieberthal .25
100 Mike Lowell .25
101 Mike Mussina .40
102 Mike Piazza 1.00
103 Milton Bradley .25
104 Moises Alou .40
105 Morgan Ensberg .25
106 Nomar Garciaparra 1.00
107 Omar Vizquel .25
108 Paul Konerko .40
109 Paul LoDuca .25
110 Pedro Martinez .75
111 Rafael Furcal .25
112 Rafael Palmeiro .40
113 Randy Johnson .75
114 Richie Sexson .40
115 Rocco Baldelli .25
116 Roger Clemens 2.00
117 Roy Halladay .40
118 Sammy Sosa .75
119 Scott Podsednik .25
120 Scott Rolen .75
121 Sean Burroughs .25
122 Sean Casey .25
123 Shannon Stewart .25
124 Shawn Green .40
125 Steve Finley .25
126 Tim Hudson .40
127 Tim Salmon .25
128 Todd Helton .50
129 Tom Glavine .40
130 Torii Hunter .40
131 Travis Hafner .25
132 Troy Glaus .40
133 Troy Percival .25
134 Vernon Wells .25
135 Victor Martinez .25
136 Vladimir Guerrero .75
137 Andre Dawson .40
138 Brooks Robinson .75
139 Cal Ripken Jr. 3.00
140 Dale Murphy .50
141 Darryl Strawberry .40
142 George Brett 2.00
143 Harmon Killebrew 1.00
144 Jim Palmer .50
145 Lou Brock .75
146 Mike Schmidt 2.00
147 Nolan Ryan 2.00
148 Steve Carlton .50
149 Tony Gwynn 1.00
150 Willie Mays 2.00
151 *Agustin Montero* 10.00
152 *Carlos Ruiz* 15.00
153 *Casey Rogowski* 8.00
154 *Chris Resop* 15.00
155 *Chris Roberson* 15.00
156 *Colter Bean* 15.00
157 *Danny Rueckel* 8.00
158 *David Gassner* 10.00
159 *Geovany Soto* 12.00
160 *John Hattig Jr.* 8.00
161 *Justin Wechsler* 10.00
162 *Luke Scott* 10.00
163 *Mark McLemore* 10.00
164 *Miguel Negron* 8.00
165 *Mike Morse* 20.00
166 *Nate McLouth* 8.00
167 *Philip Humber* 20.00
168 *Randy Messenger* 8.00
169 *Raul Tablado* 8.00
170 *Russel Rohlicek* 8.00
171 *Ryan Speier* 8.00
172 *Scott Munter* 10.00
173 *Sean Thompson* 10.00
174 *Sean Tracey* 10.00
175 *Wladimir Balentien* 25.00
177 *Norihiro Nakamura/128* 75.00

Gold

Gold (1-150): 4-8X
Production 50 sets

Silver

Silver (1-150): 3-5X
Production 100 sets

Platinum

Platinum: No Pricing
Production one set

Big Bang

NM/M

Common Player: 1.50

Production 2,000 Sets
Gold: 1X-2X
Production 100 Sets
Silver: 1X-2X
Production 200 Sets
Platinum: No Pricing
Production 1 Set
1 Adam Dunn 2.00
2 Adrian Beltre 1.50
3 Albert Pujols 6.00
4 Alex Rodriguez 5.00
5 Chipper Jones 2.00
6 Dale Murphy 2.00
7 Darryl Strawberry 1.50
8 Dave Parker 1.50
9 David Ortiz 2.00
10 Duke Snider 2.00
11 Frank Robinson 2.00
12 Gary Sheffield 1.50
13 George Foster 1.50
14 Harmon Killebrew 3.00
15 Jim Edmonds 2.00
16 Jim Rice 1.50
17 Jim Thome 2.00
18 Ken Griffey Jr. 4.00
19 Manny Ramirez 2.00
20 Matt Williams 1.50
21 Mike Piazza 3.00
22 Mike Schmidt 5.00
23 Rafael Palmeiro 2.00
24 Sammy Sosa 3.00
25 Ted Williams 5.00

Big Bang Bat

NM/M

Production 50-250
3 Albert Pujols/250 15.00
8 Dave Parker/250 4.00
9 David Ortiz/250 8.00
11 Frank Robinson/100 8.00
13 George Foster/250 4.00
16 Jim Rice/50 6.00
19 Manny Ramirez/250 8.00
22 Mike Schmidt/100 15.00
23 Rafael Palmeiro/250 6.00
24 Sammy Sosa/250 8.00
25 Ted Williams/100 60.00

Big Bang Combos

NM/M

Production 25-100
Prime: No Pricing
Production 5 Sets
1 Adam Dunn Bat-Jsy/25 12.00
2 Adrian Beltre Bat-Jsy/25 8.00
3 Albert Pujols Bat-Jsy/100 25.00
7 Darryl Strawberry Jsy-Pants/100 8.00
8 Dave Parker Bat-Jsy/100 8.00
9 David Ortiz Bat-Jsy/100 15.00
15 Jim Edmonds Jsy-Jsy/100 10.00
16 Jim Rice Jsy-Jsy/100 10.00
19 Manny Ramirez Bat-Jsy/100 12.00
20 Matt Williams Jsy-Jsy/100 8.00
21 Mike Piazza Bat-Jsy/50 15.00
22 Mike Schmidt Bat-Jsy/100 20.00
23 Rafael Palmeiro Bat-Jsy/100 10.00
24 Sammy Sosa Bat-Jsy/100 12.00

Big Bang Jersey

NM/M

Production 25-250
Prime: No Pricing
Production 5 Sets
1 Adam Dunn/250 6.00
3 Albert Pujols/250 15.00
5 Chipper Jones/250 8.00
6 Dale Murphy/250 8.00
7 Darryl Strawberry Pants/250 6.00
8 Dave Parker/250 4.00
9 David Ortiz/250 8.00
10 Duke Snider/25 12.00
12 Gary Sheffield/250 6.00
14 Harmon Killebrew/100 10.00
15 Jim Edmonds/250 6.00
16 Jim Rice Pants/250 6.00
17 Jim Thome/250 8.00
19 Manny Ramirez/100 8.00
20 Matt Williams/250 6.00
21 Mike Piazza/250 10.00
22 Mike Schmidt/100 15.00
23 Rafael Palmeiro Pants/250 6.00
24 Sammy Sosa/250 8.00
25 Ted Williams Jkt/250 40.00

Game Ball Signatures

NM/M

Production 1-50
1 Ben Grieve/50 10.00
3 Eli Marrero/24 12.00
4 Jeff Fassero/24 25.00
5 Jose Guillen/47 25.00
7 Mark Grudzielanek/23 30.00
9 Paul Konerko/45 25.00

Great Gloves

NM/M

Common Player: 1.50
Production 2,000 Sets
Gold: 2X-3X
Production 50 Sets
Silver: 1X-2X
Production 100 Sets
Platinum: No Pricing
Production 1 Set
1 Austin Kearns 1.50
2 Gary Carter 2.00
3 Ivan Rodriguez 2.00
4 Mark Grace 2.00
5 Mark Teixeira 2.00
6 Mike Schmidt 5.00
7 Omar Vizquel 1.50
8 Scott Rolen 3.00
9 Tony Gwynn 3.00
10 Willie Mays 5.00

Great Gloves Fielding Glv

NM/M

Production 25 Sets
1 Austin Kearns/25 10.00
2 Gary Carter/25 20.00
3 Ivan Rodriguez/25 15.00
4 Mark Grace/25 20.00
5 Mark Teixeira/25 15.00
6 Mike Schmidt/25 40.00
9 Tony Gwynn/25 20.00

Great Gloves Jersey

NM/M

Production 25-50
Prime: No Pricing
Production 5 Sets
1 Austin Kearns/50 8.00
2 Gary Carter/50 8.00
3 Ivan Rodriguez/50 8.00
4 Mark Grace/50 10.00
5 Mark Teixeira/50 8.00
6 Mike Schmidt/50 20.00
7 Omar Vizquel/50 8.00
8 Scott Rolen/50 10.00
9 Tony Gwynn/50 12.00
10 Willie Mays/25 40.00

Hitters Inc.

NM/M

Common Player: 1.50
Production 2,000 Sets
Gold: 2X-3X
Production 50 Sets
Silver: 1X-2X
Production 100 Sets
Platinum: No Pricing
Production 1 Set
1 Albert Pujols 6.00
2 Alfonso Soriano 2.00
3 Cal Ripken Jr. 8.00
4 Don Mattingly 5.00
5 Dwight Evans 1.50
6 George Brett 5.00
7 Hank Blalock 1.50
8 Ichiro Suzuki 5.00
9 Ivan Rodriguez 2.00
10 Jack Wilson 1.50
11 Keith Hernandez 1.50
12 Larry Walker 2.00
13 Lou Brock 2.00
14 Lyle Overbay 1.50
15 Michael Young 1.50
16 Paul Molitor 2.00
17 Rod Carew 2.00
18 Sean Casey 1.50
19 Steve Garvey 1.50
20 Todd Helton 2.00
21 Tony Gwynn 3.00
22 Travis Hafner 1.50
23 Ted Williams 6.00
24 Wade Boggs 2.00
25 Willie Mays 5.00

Hitters Inc. Bat

NM/M

Production 25-100
1 Albert Pujols/100 15.00
2 Alfonso Soriano/50 6.00
3 Cal Ripken Jr./100 25.00
4 Don Mattingly/100 15.00
5 Dwight Evans/100 6.00
6 George Brett/50 15.00
7 Hank Blalock/50 6.00
9 Ivan Rodriguez/100 6.00
10 Jack Wilson/100 4.00
12 Larry Walker/100 6.00
13 Lou Brock/100 8.00
15 Michael Young/100 4.00
16 Paul Molitor/100 8.00
17 Rod Carew/100 8.00
18 Sean Casey/100 4.00
19 Steve Garvey/100 6.00
21 Tony Gwynn/100 10.00
23 Ted Williams/50 60.00
24 Wade Boggs/100 8.00
25 Willie Mays/25 40.00

Hitters Inc. Jersey

NM/M

Production 25-100
1 Albert Pujols/100 15.00
2 Alfonso Soriano/100 6.00
3 Cal Ripken Jr./100 25.00
4 Don Mattingly/100 15.00
5 Dwight Evans/100 6.00
6 George Brett/20
7 Hank Blalock/100 4.00
9 Ivan Rodriguez/100 6.00
10 Jack Wilson/100 4.00
12 Larry Walker/100 6.00
13 Lou Brock/50 8.00
14 Lyle Overbay/100 4.00
16 Paul Molitor/100 8.00
17 Rod Carew/100 8.00
18 Sean Casey/100 4.00
19 Steve Garvey/100 6.00
20 Todd Helton/100 8.00
21 Tony Gwynn/100 10.00
22 Travis Hafner/100 4.00
23 Ted Williams Jkt/100 40.00
24 Wade Boggs/100 8.00
25 Willie Mays/25 40.00

Hitters Inc. Sign. Bat

NM/M

Production 5-25
5 Dwight Evans/25 20.00
7 Hank Blalock/25 25.00
10 Jack Wilson/25 15.00
13 Lou Brock/25 30.00
15 Michael Young/25 20.00
18 Sean Casey/25 15.00
19 Steve Garvey/25 30.00

Hitters Inc. Sign. Jersey

NM/M

Production 5-25
5 Dwight Evans/25 20.00
7 Hank Blalock/25 25.00
10 Jack Wilson/25 15.00
13 Lou Brock/25 30.00
14 Lyle Overbay/25 15.00
18 Sean Casey/25 15.00
19 Steve Garvey/25 30.00
22 Travis Hafner/25 20.00

Leather Cuts

NM/M

Production 1-128
2 Andre Dawson/128 15.00
3 Bert Blyleven/128 15.00
4 Lee Smith/32 15.00
5 Billy Williams/64 15.00
6 Bob Feller/128 25.00
7 Joe Pepitone/128 20.00
8 Bobby Doerr/128 15.00
9 Juan Marichal/112 20.00
12 Dale Murphy/96 25.00
13 Darryl Strawberry/128 15.00
14 Johnny Podres/128 20.00
18 Duke Snider/128 25.00
20 Dwight Gooden/128 15.00
21 Fergie Jenkins/96 15.00
23 Fred Lynn/128 15.00
24 Justin Morneau/128 15.00
25 Gaylord Perry/128 15.00
27 George Foster/128 15.00
28 Harmon Killebrew/64 30.00
29 Jack Morris/128 15.00
30 Jim Palmer/128 15.00
31 Jim Rice/128 15.00
33 John Kruk/128 20.00
34 Randy Jones/128 15.00
35 Keith Hernandez/128 15.00
36 Lenny Dykstra/128 15.00
37 Lou Brock/64 35.00
38 Luis Aparicio/128 15.00
39 Lyle Overbay/128 10.00
40 Maury Wills/128 15.00
41 Earl Weaver/128 15.00
42 Miguel Cabrera/64 40.00
44 Monte Irvin/96 20.00
47 Red Schoendienst/128 15.00
48 Rich "Goose" Gossage/128 20.00
50 Minnie Minoso/128 20.00
51 Sean Casey/64 15.00
54 Steve Stone/128 15.00
55 Tommy John/128 15.00
57 Victor Martinez/128 15.00
61 Lee Smith/128 15.00

Leather Cuts Bat

NM/M

Production 6-128
1 Al Kaline/58 40.00
10 Cal Ripken Jr./60 125.00
13 Darryl Strawberry/96 20.00
19 Dwight Evans/128 25.00
20 Dwight Gooden/128 15.00
22 Frank Robinson/40 25.00
23 Fred Lynn/96 15.00
27 George Foster/128 15.00
31 Jim Rice/32 25.00
36 Lenny Dykstra/128 15.00
37 Lou Brock/128 30.00
38 Luis Aparicio/128 15.00
39 Lyle Overbay/128 10.00
51 Sean Casey/32 15.00
55 Tommy John/128 15.00
57 Victor Martinez/128 15.00

Leather Cuts Jersey

NM/M

Production 1-128
2 Andre Dawson/128 20.00
3 Bert Blyleven/128 15.00
4 Lee Smith/96 15.00
8 Bobby Doerr Pants/128 20.00
9 Juan Marichal/112 20.00
10 Cal Ripken Jr./60 125.00
12 Dale Murphy/96 25.00
13 Darryl Strawberry/96 20.00
15 Dave Righetti/48 20.00
16 David Cone/120 15.00
19 Dwight Evans/44 30.00
20 Dwight Gooden/128 15.00
21 Fergie Jenkins Pants/96 15.00
23 Fred Lynn/96 15.00
25 Gaylord Perry/128 15.00
28 Harmon Killebrew/32 40.00
29 Jack Morris/64 15.00
31 Jim Rice Pants/128 20.00
33 John Kruk/128 20.00
35 Keith Hernandez/32 20.00
36 Lenny Dykstra/128 15.00
38 Luis Aparicio/128 15.00
39 Lyle Overbay/128 10.00
42 Miguel Cabrera/64 40.00
51 Sean Casey/32 15.00
55 Tommy John/128 15.00
57 Victor Martinez/128 15.00

Lumber Cuts

NM/M

Production 1-128
1 Al Kaline/6
2 Andre Dawson/128 15.00
3 Bert Blyleven/128 15.00
4 Lee Smith/32 20.00
5 Billy Williams/64 20.00
6 Bob Feller/128 25.00
7 Joe Pepitone/128 20.00
8 Bobby Doerr/128 20.00
9 Juan Marichal/112 20.00
12 Dale Murphy/96 25.00
13 Darryl Strawberry/128 15.00
14 Johnny Podres/128 15.00
18 Duke Snider/128 25.00
20 Dwight Gooden/128 15.00
21 Fergie Jenkins/96 15.00
23 Fred Lynn/128 15.00
24 Justin Morneau/128 15.00
25 Gaylord Perry/128 15.00
27 George Foster/128 10.00
28 Harmon Killebrew/64 30.00
29 Jack Morris/128 15.00
30 Jim Palmer/128 15.00
31 Jim Rice/128 15.00

33 John Kruk/128 20.00
34 Randy Jones/128 15.00
35 Keith Hernandez/128 15.00
36 Lenny Dykstra/128 15.00
37 Lou Brock/64 35.00
38 Luis Aparicio/128 15.00
39 Lyle Overbay/128 10.00
40 Maury Wills/128 15.00
41 Earl Weaver/128 15.00
42 Miguel Cabrera/64 40.00
44 Monte Irvin/96 20.00
46 Kent Hrbek/128 15.00
47 Red Schoendienst/128 20.00
48 Rich "Goose" Gossage/128 15.00
50 Minnie Minoso/128 20.00
51 Sean Casey/64 15.00
54 Steve Stone/128 15.00
55 Tommy John/128 15.00
57 Victor Martinez/128 15.00
61 Lee Smith/128 15.00

Lumber Cuts Bat

NM/M

Production 6-128
1 Al Kaline 40.00
10 Cal Ripken Jr./60 125.00
13 Darryl Strawberry/96 20.00
19 Dwight Evans/128 25.00
20 Dwight Gooden/128 15.00
22 Frank Robinson/40 25.00
23 Fred Lynn/96 15.00
27 George Foster/128 15.00
31 Jim Rice/32 25.00
36 Lenny Dykstra/128 15.00
37 Lou Brock/128 30.00
38 Luis Aparicio/128 15.00
39 Lyle Overbay/128 10.00
51 Sean Casey/32 15.00
55 Tommy John/128 15.00
57 Victor Martinez/128 15.00

Lumber Cuts Jersey

NM/M

Production 7-128
2 Andre Dawson/128 20.00
3 Bert Blyleven/128 15.00
4 Lee Smith/96 15.00
8 Bobby Doerr Pants/128 20.00
9 Juan Marichal/112 20.00
10 Cal Ripken Jr./60 125.00
12 Dale Murphy/96 25.00
13 Darryl Strawberry/96 20.00
15 Dave Righetti/48 20.00
16 David Cone/120 15.00
19 Dwight Evans/44 30.00
20 Dwight Gooden/128 15.00
21 Fergie Jenkins Pants/96 15.00
23 Fred Lynn/96 15.00
25 Gaylord Perry/128 15.00
28 Harmon Killebrew/32 40.00
29 Jack Morris/64 15.00
31 Jim Rice Pants/128 20.00
33 John Kruk/128 20.00
35 Keith Hernandez/32 20.00
36 Lenny Dykstra/128 15.00
38 Luis Aparicio/128 15.00
39 Lyle Overbay/128 10.00
42 Miguel Cabrera/64 40.00
51 Sean Casey/32 15.00
55 Tommy John/128 15.00
57 Victor Martinez/128 15.00

Lumber/Leather

NM/M

Common Player: 1.50
Production 2,000 Sets
Gold: 2X-3X
Production 50 Sets
Silver: 1X-2X
Production 100 Sets
Platinum: No Pricing
Production One Set
1 Albert Pujols 6.00
2 Alex Rodriguez 5.00
3 Alfonso Soriano 2.00
4 Cal Ripken Jr. 8.00
5 Carlos Lee 2.00
6 Derek Jeter 6.00
7 Don Mattingly 5.00
8 Ichiro Suzuki 4.00
9 Ivan Rodriguez 2.00
10 Jack Wilson 1.50
11 Josh Beckett 1.50
12 Ken Griffey Jr. 4.00
13 Lance Berkman 1.50
14 Magglio Ordonez 1.50
15 Mark Grace 2.00
16 Mark Prior 2.00
17 Mark Teixeira 2.00
18 Mike Schmidt 4.00
19 Nolan Ryan 6.00
20 Nomar Garciaparra 3.00
21 Paul LoDuca 1.50
22 Rafael Palmeiro 2.00
23 Randy Johnson 2.00
24 Richie Sexson 2.00
25 Rickey Henderson 2.00
26 Roger Clemens 6.00
27 Ryan Klesko 1.50
28 Stan Musial 3.00
29 Steve Carlton 2.00
30 Tim Hudson 2.00
31 Tony Gwynn 2.00
32 Travis Hafner 1.50
33 Victor Martinez 1.50
34 Wade Boggs 2.00
35 Willie Mays 5.00

L/L Bat-Btg Glove

NM/M

Production 1-25
3 Alfonso Soriano/25 15.00
4 Cal Ripken Jr./1
5 Carlos Lee/25 12.00
7 Don Mattingly/25 40.00
9 Ivan Rodriguez/25 15.00
13 Lance Berkman/25 15.00
14 Magglio Ordonez/25 10.00
18 Mike Schmidt/25 40.00
21 Paul LoDuca/25 10.00
22 Rafael Palmeiro/25 15.00
24 Richie Sexson/25 15.00
25 Rickey Henderson/25 20.00
27 Ryan Klesko/25 10.00
31 Tony Gwynn/25 20.00
34 Wade Boggs/10

L/L Bat-Fld Glove

NM/M

Production 5-25
1 Albert Pujols/5
5 Carlos Lee/25 12.00
9 Ivan Rodriguez/25 15.00
10 Jack Wilson/25 10.00
13 Lance Berkman/25 15.00
15 Mark Grace/25 20.00
16 Mark Prior/25 20.00
17 Mark Teixeira/10
18 Mike Schmidt/25 40.00
21 Paul LoDuca/25 10.00
22 Rafael Palmeiro/25 15.00
24 Richie Sexson/25 15.00
26 Roger Clemens/10
27 Ryan Klesko/25 10.00
29 Steve Carlton/25 15.00
30 Tim Hudson/25 15.00
31 Tony Gwynn/25 20.00
33 Victor Martinez/10

Lumber/Leather Bat-Spikes

NM/M

Production 1-25
1 Albert Pujols/25 40.00
3 Alfonso Soriano/1
5 Carlos Lee/25 12.00
7 Don Mattingly/10
9 Ivan Rodriguez/25 15.00
11 Josh Beckett/25 12.00
13 Lance Berkman/25 15.00
14 Magglio Ordonez/25 10.00
16 Mark Prior/25 20.00
21 Paul LoDuca/25 10.00
22 Rafael Palmeiro/25 15.00
24 Richie Sexson/25 15.00
25 Rickey Henderson/25 20.00
27 Ryan Klesko/25 10.00
30 Tim Hudson/25 15.00
31 Tony Gwynn/25 20.00

Materials Barrel

No Pricing
Production 1-4

Materials Bat

NM/M

Production 25-250
1 Adam Dunn/250 6.00
2 Adrian Beltre/100 4.00
5 Albert Pujols/250 15.00
7 Alfonso Soriano/100 6.00
8 Andy Pettitte/100 6.00
9 Aramis Ramirez/100 6.00
10 Aubrey Huff/250 4.00
11 Austin Kearns/100 4.00
12 Barry Larkin/200 6.00
13 Barry Zito/25 8.00
15 Bernie Williams/250 6.00
16 Brad Penny/75 4.00
18 Brian Giles/50 6.00
23 Carlos Beltran/100 8.00
24 Carlos Delgado/250 4.00
25 Carlos Lee/150 4.00
27 Casey Kotchman/250 4.00
29 Chone Figgins/250 4.00
30 Craig Biggio/250 6.00
31 Craig Monroe/250 4.00
33 Curt Schilling/100 8.00
35 Darin Erstad/250 4.00
37 David Ortiz/250 8.00
40 Dontrelle Willis/250 6.00
43 Frank Thomas/50 8.00
44 Garret Anderson/250 4.00
46 Geoff Jenkins/50 4.00
47 Greg Maddux/250 10.00
51 J.D. Drew/250 4.00
57 Jason Varitek/100 6.00
58 Javy Lopez/250 4.00
59 Jay Gibbons/250 4.00
60 Jeff Bagwell/250 6.00
61 Jeff Kent/250 4.00
68 John Olerud/250 4.00
72 Jose Reyes/250 4.00
73 Jose Vidro/250 4.00
75 Juan Pierre/250 4.00
81 Kerry Wood/100 6.00
82 Kevin Brown/100 4.00
85 Lance Berkman/250 4.00
87 Laynce Nix/250 4.00
89 Magglio Ordonez/250 4.00
90 Manny Ramirez/100 8.00
94 Mark Prior/100 6.00
97 Michael Young/250 4.00
104 Moises Alou/250 4.00
106 Nomar Garciaparra/100 8.00
109 Paul LoDuca/250 4.00
111 Rafael Furcal/250 4.00
112 Rafael Palmeiro/250 6.00
114 Richie Sexson/250 4.00
115 Rocco Baldelli/250 8.00
118 Sammy Sosa/100 4.00
122 Sean Casey/100 4.00
123 Shannon Stewart/50 4.00
124 Shawn Green/250 4.00
126 Tim Hudson/50 6.00
127 Tim Salmon/250 4.00
129 Tom Glavine/250 4.00
130 Torii Hunter/250 4.00
132 Troy Glaus/250 4.00
138 Brooks Robinson/100 8.00
139 Cal Ripken Jr./50 30.00
145 Lou Brock/100 8.00
146 Mike Schmidt/50 15.00
147 Nolan Ryan/50 25.00
149 Tony Gwynn/100 10.00
150 Willie Mays/25 40.00

Materials Jersey

NM/M

Production 20-250
1 Adam Dunn/150 6.00
5 Albert Pujols/250 15.00
7 Alfonso Soriano/150 6.00
8 Andy Pettitte/150 6.00
9 Aramis Ramirez/250 4.00
10 Aubrey Huff/250 4.00
12 Barry Larkin/250 6.00
13 Barry Zito/150 4.00
15 Bernie Williams/150 6.00
16 Bobby Abreu/250 4.00
17 Bobby Crosby/150 4.00
20 C.C. Sabathia/250 4.00
21 Carl Crawford/200 4.00
26 Carlos Zambrano/250 6.00
27 Casey Kotchman/140 4.00
28 Chipper Jones/250 8.00
29 Chone Figgins/200 4.00
30 Craig Biggio/200 6.00
33 Curt Schilling/250 8.00
35 Darin Erstad/150 4.00
36 David Dellucci/250 4.00
37 David Ortiz/250 8.00
40 Dontrelle Willis/250 4.00
43 Frank Thomas Pants/150 8.00
44 Garret Anderson/250 4.00
45 Gary Sheffield/250 6.00
46 Geoff Jenkins/250 4.00
47 Greg Maddux/25 15.00
48 Hideo Nomo/250 6.00
50 Ivan Rodriguez/150 6.00
53 Jamie Moyer/50 6.00
54 Jason Giambi/250 4.00
57 Jason Varitek/100 10.00
58 Javy Lopez/150 4.00
59 Jay Gibbons/75 4.00
60 Jeff Bagwell/250 6.00
62 Jeremy Bonderman/150 4.00
64 Jim Edmonds/250 6.00
65 Jim Thome/150 6.00
67 Johan Santana/250 8.00
69 John Smoltz/250 6.00
70 Johnny Damon/250 8.00
71 Johnny Estrada/250 4.00
72 Jose Reyes/150 4.00
73 Jose Vidro/150 4.00
74 Josh Beckett/50 4.00
76 Junior Spivey/250 4.00
77 Justin Morneau/250 4.00
78 Kazuhisa Ishii/250 4.00
79 Kazuo Matsui/250 4.00
81 Kerry Wood Pants/150 6.00
85 Lance Berkman/250 4.00
86 Larry Walker/250 4.00
87 Laynce Nix/250 4.00
88 Lyle Overbay/200 4.00
90 Manny Ramirez/250 8.00
91 Marcus Giles/150 4.00
94 Mark Prior/250 6.00
95 Mark Teixeira/250 6.00
96 Melvin Mora/100 4.00
97 Michael Young/25 8.00
98 Miguel Tejada/250 6.00
100 Mike Lowell/250 4.00
101 Mike Mussina/250 6.00
102 Mike Piazza/250 8.00
105 Morgan Ensberg/150 4.00
108 Paul Konerko/150 4.00
111 Rafael Furcal/150 4.00
112 Rafael Palmeiro/150 6.00
115 Rocco Baldelli/250 4.00
116 Roger Clemens/150 10.00
117 Roy Halladay/150 4.00
119 Scott Podsednik/250 4.00
120 Scott Rolen/250 6.00
121 Sean Burroughs/150 4.00
122 Sean Casey/250 4.00
123 Shannon Stewart/150 4.00
128 Todd Helton/250 6.00
130 Torii Hunter/250 4.00
131 Travis Hafner 6.00
134 Vernon Wells/250 4.00
135 Victor Martinez/150 4.00
136 Vladimir Guerrero/250 8.00
137 Andre Dawson/50 8.00
139 Cal Ripken Jr./250 20.00
140 Dale Murphy/250 6.00
141 Darryl Strawberry Pants/150 4.00
143 Harmon Killebrew/100 8.00
144 Jim Palmer Pants/20
145 Lou Brock Jkt/250 8.00
146 Mike Schmidt/50 15.00
147 Nolan Ryan/250 15.00
148 Steve Carlton/25 10.00
149 Tony Gwynn/250 8.00
150 Willie Mays Pants/25 40.00

Naturals Barrel

No Pricing
Production 1-3

Naturals Bat

NM/M

Production 25-100
1 Andruw Jones/100 6.00
2 Bernie Williams/100 6.00
3 Brooks Robinson/100 8.00
4 Cal Ripken Jr./100 25.00
5 Casey Kotchman/100 4.00
6 Craig Biggio/100 6.00
7 Craig Wilson/100 4.00
8 David Ortiz/100 10.00
9 Eddie Murray/100 8.00
10 Javy Lopez/100 4.00
11 Jeff Bagwell/100 6.00
12 Lance Berkman/100 4.00
13 Magglio Ordonez/100 4.00
14 Michael Young/100 4.00
15 Rafael Palmeiro/100 6.00
16 Reggie Jackson/100 8.00
17 Rickey Henderson/100 8.00
18 Rocco Baldelli/100 4.00
19 Sammy Sosa/100 8.00
20 Shawn Green/100 4.00
21 Ted Williams/50 50.00
22 Tony Gwynn/100 10.00

23 Wade Boggs/100 8.00
24 Will Clark/100 8.00
25 Willie Mays/25 40.00

Naturals Combos

NM/M

Production 25-100
Prime: No Pricing
Production 5 Sets
1 Andruw Jones Bat-Jsy/100 8.00
2 Bernie Williams Bat-Jsy/100 8.00
3 Brooks Robinson Bat-Jsy/25 15.00
4 Cal Ripken Jr. Bat-Jsy/100 30.00
5 Casey Kotchman Bat-Jsy/100 6.00
6 Craig Biggio Bat-Jsy/100 8.00
7 Craig Wilson Bat-Jsy/100 6.00
8 David Ortiz Bat-Jsy/100 12.00
9 Eddie Murray Bat-Jsy/100 10.00
10 Javy Lopez Bat-Jsy/100 6.00
11 Jeff Bagwell Bat-Jsy/100 8.00
12 Lance Berkman Bat-Jsy/100 6.00
13 Magglio Ordonez Bat-Jsy/25 8.00
14 Michael Young Bat-Jsy/100 6.00
15 Rafael Palmeiro Bat-Jsy/100 8.00
16 Reggie Jackson Bat-Jsy/50 12.00
17 Rickey Henderson Bat-Jkt/100 10.00
18 Rocco Baldelli Bat-Jsy/100 6.00
19 Sammy Sosa Bat-Jsy/100 10.00
20 Shawn Green Bat-Jsy/100 6.00
21 Ted Williams Bat-Jkt/50 60.00
22 Tony Gwynn Bat-Jsy/100 12.00
23 Wade Boggs Bat-Jsy/100 10.00
24 Will Clark Bat-Jsy/50 10.00
25 Willie Mays Bat-Jsy/25 50.00

Naturals

NM/M

Common Player:
Production 2,000 Sets
Gold: 2X-3X
Production 50 Sets
Silver: 1X-2X
Production 100 Sets
Platinum: No Pricing
Production One Set
1 Andruw Jones 2.00
2 Bernie Williams 1.50
3 Brooks Robinson 2.00
4 Cal Ripken Jr. 8.00
5 Casey Kotchman 1.50
6 Craig Biggio 2.00
7 Craig Wilson 1.50
8 David Ortiz 3.00
9 Eddie Murray 2.00
10 Javy Lopez 1.50
11 Jeff Bagwell 2.00
12 Lance Berkman 1.50
13 Magglio Ordonez 1.50
14 Michael Young 1.50
15 Rafael Palmeiro 2.00
16 Reggie Jackson 2.00
17 Rickey Henderson 2.00
18 Rocco Baldelli 1.50
19 Sammy Sosa 4.00
20 Shawn Green 1.50
21 Ted Williams 6.00
22 Tony Gwynn 3.00
23 Wade Boggs 2.00
24 Will Clark 2.00
25 Willie Mays 5.00

Naturals Jersey

NM/M

Production 25-100
Prime: No Pricing
Production 5 Sets
1 Andruw Jones/100 6.00
2 Bernie Williams/100 6.00
4 Cal Ripken Jr./100 25.00
5 Casey Kotchman/100 4.00
6 Craig Biggio/100 6.00
7 Craig Wilson/100 4.00
8 David Ortiz/100 10.00
9 Eddie Murray/100 8.00
10 Javy Lopez/100 4.00
11 Jeff Bagwell/100 6.00
12 Lance Berkman/100 4.00
13 Magglio Ordonez/50 4.00
14 Michael Young/50 4.00
15 Rafael Palmeiro/100 6.00
16 Reggie Jackson/100 8.00
17 Rickey Henderson Jkt/100 8.00
18 Rocco Baldelli/100 4.00
19 Sammy Sosa/100 8.00
20 Shawn Green/100 4.00
21 Ted Williams Jkt/100 40.00
22 Tony Gwynn/100 10.00
23 Wade Boggs/100 8.00
24 Will Clark/50 8.00
25 Willie Mays/25 40.00

Rivals

NM/M

Common Duo: 1.50
Production 2,000 Sets
Gold: 2X-3X
Production 50 Sets
Silver: 1X-2X
Production 100 Sets
Platinum: No Pricing
Production One Set
1 Ichiro Suzuki, Hideki Matsui 5.00
2 Mark Mulder, Vladimir Guerrero 2.00
3 Tim Hudson, Mark Teixeira 2.00
4 Roger Clemens, Albert Pujols 6.00
5 Greg Maddux, Jeff Bagwell 4.00
6 Randy Johnson, Adrian Beltre 3.00
7 Kerry Wood, Larry Walker 2.00
8 Mike Mussina, Manny Ramirez 2.00
9 C.C. Sabathia, Torii Hunter 1.50
10 Josh Beckett, Chipper Jones 2.00
11 Derek Jeter, Miguel Tejada 6.00
12 Alex Rodriguez, Hank Blalock 5.00
13 Carlos Beltran, Sammy Sosa 3.00
14 Mark Prior, Jim Thome 2.00
15 Miguel Cabrera, Andruw Jones 2.00
16 Johan Santana, Maggio Ordonez 2.00
17 Josh Beckett, Craig Biggio 2.00
18 Adam Dunn, Shawn Green 2.00
19 J. Morris, Rod Carew 2.00
20 Jim Palmer, Paul Molitor 2.00
21 Mike Schmidt, George Brett 5.00
22 Cal Ripken Jr., Don Mattingly 8.00
23 Bob Gibson, Ernie Banks 4.00
24 Eddie Murray, Bert Blyleven 3.00
25 Warren Spahn, Willie Mays 6.00

Rivals Bat

NM/M

Production 50-100
3 Tim Hudson, Mark Teixeira/50 10.00
4 Roger Clemens, Albert Pujols/100 25.00
5 Greg Maddux, Jeff Bagwell/100 15.00
7 Kerry Wood, Larry Walker/100 15.00
10 Josh Beckett, Chipper Jones/50 15.00
13 Carlos Beltran, Sammy Sosa/100 15.00
14 Mark Prior, Jim Thome/50 15.00
18 Adam Dunn, Shawn Green/100 10.00
21 Mike Schmidt, George Brett/100 20.00
22 Cal Ripken Jr., Don Mattingly/100 30.00

Rivals Jersey

NM/M

Production 50-250
Prime: No Pricing
Production 5 Sets
2 Mark Mulder, Vladimir Guerrero/100 10.00
3 Tim Hudson, Mark Teixeira/250 10.00
4 Roger Clemens, Albert Pujols/100 20.00
5 Greg Maddux, Jeff Bagwell/250 10.00
7 Kerry Wood, Larry Walker/250 8.00
9 C.C. Sabathia, Torii Hunter/150 6.00
10 Josh Beckett Pants, Chipper Jones/150 10.00
13 Carlos Beltran, Sammy Sosa/250 10.00
14 Mark Prior, Jim Thome/250 10.00
15 Miguel Cabrera, Andruw Jones/250 10.00
16 Johan Santana, Magglio Ordonez/100 10.00
18 Adam Dunn, Shawn Green/100 10.00
19 J. Morris, Rod Carew/250 10.00
21 Mike Schmidt, George Brett/100 15.00
22 Cal Ripken Jr., Don Mattingly/100 40.00
23 Bob Gibson, E rnie Banks/50 15.00
24 Eddie Murray, Bert Blyleven 10.00
25 Warren Spahn Pant, Willie Mays Pant/50 60.00

Signatures Gold

NM/M

Production 5-100
Platinum: No Pricing
Production One Set
1 Adam Dunn/25 35.00
2 Adrian Beltre/25 25.00
3 Akinori Otsuka/50 30.00
10 Aubrey Huff/50 15.00
11 Austin Kearns/25 15.00
17 Bobby Crosby/100 15.00
18 Brad Penny/100 10.00
25 Carlos Lee/100 15.00
26 Carlos Zambrano/100 25.00
27 Casey Kotchman/100 10.00
29 Chone Figgins/100 15.00
31 Craig Monroe/100 10.00
34 Danny Haren/100 10.00
36 David Dellucci/100 15.00
52 Jake Peavy/100 25.00
53 Jamie Moyer/100 15.00
59 Jay Gibbons/100 10.00
62 Jeremy Bonderman/100 10.00
63 Jermaine Dye/100 12.00
64 Jim Edmonds/5
66 Joe Nathan/100 15.00
71 Johnny Estrada/50 10.00
87 Laynce Nix/100 10.00
88 Lyle Overbay/100 10.00
92 Mark Loretta/100 15.00
99 Mike Lieberthal/100 10.00
103 Milton Bradley/100 12.00
105 Morgan Ensberg/100 12.00
108 Paul Konerko/25 20.00
111 Rafael Furcal/50 15.00
117 Roy Halladay/25 25.00
119 Scott Podsednik/50 15.00
121 Sean Burroughs/100 8.00
122 Sean Casey/25 15.00
123 Shannon Stewart/100 8.00
125 Steve Finley/50 15.00
126 Tim Hudson/25 30.00
127 Tim Salmon/100 15.00
130 Torii Hunter/25 20.00
131 Travis Hafner/100 12.00
133 Troy Percival/50 15.00
134 Vernon Wells/25 15.00
135 Victor Martinez/100 15.00
137 Andre Dawson/100 15.00
138 Brooks Robinson/25 30.00
140 Dale Murphy/50 25.00
141 Darryl Strawberry/100 15.00
143 Harmon Killebrew/50 30.00
144 Jim Palmer/25 20.00
145 Lou Brock/25 30.00
146 Mike Schmidt/25 60.00
148 Steve Carlton/50 25.00
149 Tony Gwynn/25 50.00

Signatures Lumber Cuts

NM/M

Production 256 Sets
151 Agustin Montero 8.00
152 Carlos Ruiz 8.00
153 Casey Rogowski 10.00
154 Chris Resop 15.00
155 Chris Roberson 10.00
156 Colter Bean 10.00
157 Danny Rueckel 8.00
158 David Gassner 8.00
159 Geovany Soto 8.00
160 John Hattig Jr. 8.00
161 Justin Wechsler 8.00
162 Luke Scott 8.00
163 Mark McLemore 8.00
164 Miguel Negron 8.00
165 Mike Morse 40.00
166 Nate McLouth/254 10.00
167 Philip Humber 20.00
168 Randy Messenger 8.00
169 Raul Tablado 8.00
170 Russel Rohlicek 8.00
171 Ryan Speier 8.00
172 Scott Munter 12.00
173 Sean Thompson 10.00
174 Sean Tracey 10.00
175 Wladimir Balentien 20.00
177 Norihiro Nakamura/128 75.00

2005 DONRUSS STUDIO

NM/M

Complete Set (300):
Common Player: .25
Pack (6): 4.00
Box (24): 90.00
1 Casey Kotchman .25
2 Chone Figgins .25
3 Dallas McPherson .25
4 Darin Erstad .25
5 Ervin Santana .25
6 Garret Anderson .40
7 *Norihiro Nakamura* 2.00
8 John Lackey .25
9 Orlando Cabrera .25
10 Robb Quinlan .25
11 Steve Finley .25
12 Tim Salmon .25
13 Vladimir Guerrero .75
14 Brandon Webb .25
15 Craig Counsell .25
16 Javier Vazquez .25
17 Luis Gonzalez .25
18 *Tony Pena* .40
19 Russ Ortiz .25
20 Scott Hairston .25
21 Shawn Green .25
22 Jose Cruz Jr. .25
23 Troy Glaus .40
24 Adam LaRoche .25
25 Andruw Jones .50
26 Chipper Jones .75
27 Danny Kolb .25
28 John Smoltz .40
29 Johnny Estrada .25
30 Marcus Giles .25
31 Nick Green .25
32 Rafael Furcal .25
33 Tim Hudson .40
34 Brian Roberts .25
35 Javy Lopez .25
36 Jay Gibbons .25
37 Melvin Mora .25
38 Miguel Tejada .50
39 Rafael Palmeiro .50
40 Rodrigo Lopez .25
41 Sidney Ponson .25
42 Abe Alvarez .25
43 Bill Mueller .25
44 Curt Schilling .75
45 David Ortiz .75
46 David Wells .25
47 Edgar Renteria .25
48 Jason Varitek .50

49 Jay Payton .25
50 Johnny Damon .75
51 Juan Cedeno .25
52 Manny Ramirez .75
53 Matt Clement .25
54 Trot Nixon .25
55 Wade Miller .25
56 Aramis Ramirez .40
57 Carlos Zambrano .40
58 Corey Patterson .25
59 Derrek Lee .50
60 Greg Maddux 1.50
61 Kerry Wood .40
62 Mark Prior .75
63 Nomar Garciaparra .75
64 Sammy Sosa 1.00
65 Todd Walker .25
66 A.J. Pierzynski .25
67 Aaron Rowand .25
68 Frank Thomas .50
69 Freddy Garcia .25
70 Jermaine Dye .25
71 Mark Buehrle .40
72 Paul Konerko .40
73 *Tadahito Iguchi* 3.00
74 *Pedro Lopez* .40
75 Scott Podsednik .25
76 Shingo Takatsu .25
77 Adam Dunn .50
78 Austin Kearns .25
79 Barry Larkin .50
80 Bubba Nelson .25
81 Danny Graves .25
82 Eric Milton .25
83 Ken Griffey Jr. 1.50
84 Ryan Wagner .25
85 Sean Casey .25
86 C.C. Sabathia .25
87 Cliff Lee .25
88 Fausto Carmona .25
89 Grady Sizemore .25
90 Jake Westbrook .25
91 Jody Gerut .25
92 Juan Gonzalez .40
93 Kazuhito Tadano .25
94 Travis Hafner .25
95 Victor Martinez .25
96 Charles Johnson .25
97 Clint Barmes .25
98 Cory Sullivan .25
99 Jeff Baker .25
100 Jeff Francis .25
101 Jeff Salazar .25
102 Jeromy Burnitz .25
103 Joe Kennedy .25
104 Matt Holliday .25
105 Preston Wilson .25
106 Todd Helton .50
107 *Ubaldo Jimenez* .40
108 Brandon Inge .25
109 Carlos Guillen .25
110 Carlos Pena .25
111 Craig Monroe .25
112 Ivan Rodriguez .50
113 Jeremy Bonderman .25
114 *Justin Verlander* 2.00
115 Magglio Ordonez .25
116 Troy Percival .25
117 Vance Wilson .25
118 A.J. Burnett .25
119 Al Leiter .25
120 Dontrelle Willis .40
121 Josh Beckett .40
122 Juan Pierre .25
123 Miguel Cabrera .75
124 Mike Lowell .25
125 Paul LoDuca .25
126 *Randy Messenger* .40
127 *Yorman Bazardo* .40
128 Andy Pettitte .40
129 Brad Lidge .25
130 Chris Burke .25
131 Craig Biggio .40
132 Fernando Nieve .25
133 Jason Lane .25
134 Jeff Bagwell .50
135 Lance Berkman .40
136 Morgan Ensberg .25
137 Roger Clemens 2.00
138 Roy Oswalt .25
139 *Ambiorix Burgos* .40
140 David DeJesus .25
141 Jeremy Affeldt .25
142 Jose Lima .25
143 Ken Harvey .25
144 Mike MacDougal .25
145 Mike Sweeney .25
146 Terrence Long .25
147 Zack Greinke .25
148 Brad Penny .25
149 Derek Lowe .25
150 Dioner Navarro .25
151 Edwin Jackson .25
152 Eric Gagne .25
153 Hee Seop Choi .25
154 Hideo Nomo .50
155 J.D. Drew .40
156 Jeff Kent .25
157 Jeff Weaver .25
158 Milton Bradley .25
159 Yhency Brazoban .25
160 Ben Sheets .40
161 Bill Hall .25
162 Carlos Lee .25
163 Gustavo Chacin .25
164 Geoff Jenkins .25
165 Jose Capellan .25
166 Lyle Overbay .25
167 Rickie Weeks .40
168 Jacque Jones .25
169 Joe Mauer .40
170 Joe Nathan .25
171 Johan Santana .50
172 Justin Morneau .25
173 Lew Ford .25
174 Michael Cuddyer .25
175 Shannon Stewart .25
176 Torii Hunter .25
177 Brad Radke .25
178 *Ambiorix Concepcion* .40
179 Carlos Beltran .50
180 David Wright .75
181 Jose Reyes .25
182 Kazuo Matsui .25
183 Kris Benson .25
184 Mike Piazza 1.00
185 Pedro Martinez .75
186 *Philip Humber* 1.00
187 Tom Glavine .40
188 Alex Rodriguez 1.50
189 Carl Pavano .25
190 Derek Jeter 2.00
191 *Yuniesky Betancourt* 1.00
192 Hideki Matsui 1.50
193 Jorge Posada .40
194 Kevin Brown .25
195 Mariano Rivera .40
196 Mike Mussina .40
197 Randy Johnson .75
198 Scott Proctor .25
199 Tom Gordon .25
200 Barry Zito .40
201 Bobby Crosby .40
202 Danny Haren .25
203 Eric Chavez .40
204 *Keiichi Yabu* .40
205 Jason Kendall .25
206 Joe Blanton .25
207 Mark Kotsay .25
208 Nick Swisher .25
209 Octavio Dotel .25
210 Rich Harden .40
211 Billy Wagner .25
212 Bobby Abreu .40
213 Chase Utley .40
214 Gavin Floyd .25
215 Jim Thome .50
216 Jimmy Rollins .25
217 Jon Lieber .25
218 Kenny Lofton .25
219 Mike Lieberthal .25
220 Pat Burrell .25
221 Randy Wolf .25
222 Craig Wilson .25
223 Jack Wilson .25
224 Jason Bay .25
225 John Van Benschoten .25
226 Jose Castillo .25
227 Kip Wells .25
228 Matt Lawton .25
229 Akinori Otsuka .25
230 Brian Giles .25
231 Freddy Guzman .25
232 Jake Peavy .40
233 Khalil Greene .40
234 Mark Loretta .25
235 Sean Burroughs .25
236 Trevor Hoffman .25
237 Woody Williams .25
238 Armando Benitez .25
239 Edgardo Alfonzo .25
240 *Erick Threets* .40
241 Jason Schmidt .40
242 Marquis Grissom .25
243 Merkin Valdez .25
244 Michael Tucker .25
245 Moises Alou .40
246 Omar Vizquel .25
247 Adrian Beltre .40
248 Bret Boone .25
249 Bucky Jacobsen .25
250 Clint Nageotte .25
251 Ichiro Suzuki 1.50
252 J.J. Putz .25
253 Jeremy Reed .25
254 Miguel Olivo .25
255 *Mike Morse* 2.00
256 Richie Sexson .40
257 *Wladimir Balentien* 1.00
258 Albert Pujols 2.00
259 Jason Isringhausen .25
260 Jeff Suppan .25
261 Jim Edmonds .40
262 Larry Walker .40
263 Mark Mulder .40
264 Rick Ankiel .25
265 Scott Rolen .75
266 Yadier Molina .25
267 Aubrey Huff .25
268 B.J. Upton .25
269 Carl Crawford .25
270 *Chris Seddon* .40
271 Delmon Young .25
272 Dewon Brazelton .25
273 *Jeff Niemann* 1.00
274 Rocco Baldelli .25
275 Scott Kazmir .25
276 Adrian Gonzalez .25
277 Alfonso Soriano .75
278 Francisco Cordero .25
279 Hank Blalock .40
280 Kameron Loe .25
281 Kenny Rogers .25
282 Laynce Nix .25
283 Mark Teixeira .40
284 Michael Young .25
285 Corey Koskie .25
286 David Bush .25
287 Frank Catalanotto .25
288 Gabe Gross .25
289 *Raul Tablado* .40
290 Roy Halladay .40
291 Shea Hillenbrand .25
292 Vernon Wells .25
293 Chad Cordero .25
294 Cristian Guzman .25
295 Jose Guillen .25
296 Jose Vidro .25
297 Josh Karp .25
298 Livan Hernandez .25
299 Nick Johnson .25
300 Vinny Castilla .25

Proofs Gold

Stars: 8-12X
Production 25 sets

Proofs Platinum

No Pricing
Production 10 sets

Proofs Silver

Stars: 3-5X
Production 100 sets

Diamond Cuts

NM/M
Common Player: 1.00
Production 1,250 Sets
Die-cut: 1X-1.5X
Production 250 Sets
Die-cut Gold: 1.5X-3X
Production 75 Sets
1 Roger Clemens 4.00
2 Manny Ramirez 1.50
3 Francisco Rodriguez 1.00
4 Brian Roberts 1.00
5 Javy Lopez 1.00
6 Vernon Wells 1.00
7 Johan Santana 1.50
8 Torii Hunter 1.00
9 Mike Mussina 1.50
10 Sammy Sosa 2.50
11 Ryan Wagner 1.00
12 Jack Wilson 1.00
13 Ichiro Suzuki 3.00
14 Greg Maddux 3.00
15 Albert Pujols 4.00
16 Jeremy Bonderman 1.00
17 Johnny Estrada 1.00
18 Mark Buehrle 1.00
19 Jorge Posada 1.00
20 Carl Crawford 1.00
21 Paul Konerko 1.00
22 Victor Martinez 1.00
23 Jose Vidro 1.00
24 Jim Thome 1.50
25 Andruw Jones 1.50

Diamond Cuts Bat

NM/M
Production 5-300
1 Roger Clemens/50 15.00
2 Manny Ramirez/200 8.00
5 Javy Lopez/300 4.00
6 Vernon Wells/10
8 Torii Hunter/300 4.00
10 Sammy Sosa/25 15.00
12 Jack Wilson/300 4.00
14 Greg Maddux/225 10.00
15 Albert Pujols/300 15.00
17 Johnny Estrada/25
18 Mark Buehrle/5
21 Paul Konerko/50 6.00
22 Victor Martinez/300 4.00
23 Jose Vidro/300 4.00
24 Jim Thome/10
25 Andruw Jones/300 6.00

Diamond Cuts Combo

NM/M
Production 5-50
Prime: No Pricing
Production 10 Sets
1 Roger Clemens Bat-Jsy/50 20.00
2 Manny Ramirez Bat-Jsy/50 12.00
3 Freddy Rodriguez Jsy-Jsy/50 10.00
5 Javy Lopez Bat-Jsy/50 8.00
6 Vernon Wells Jsy-Jsy/50 8.00
7 Johan Santana Jsy-Jsy/10
8 Torii Hunter Bat-Jsy/50 8.00
10 Sammy Sosa Jsy-Jsy/50 12.00
11 Ryan Wagner Jsy-Jsy/50 8.00
12 Jack Wilson Bat-Jsy/50 8.00
14 Greg Maddux Bat-Jsy/50 15.00
15 Albert Pujols Bat-Jsy/50 30.00
16 Jeremy Bonderman Jsy-Jsy/5
17 Johnny Estrada Fld Glve-Jsy/50 10.00
21 Paul Konerko Jsy-Jsy/50 10.00
22 Victor Martinez Bat-Jsy/50 10.00
23 Jose Vidro Bat-Jsy/50 8.00
24 Jim Thome Jsy-Jsy/45 12.00
25 Andruw Jones Bat-Jsy/50 10.00

Diamond Cuts Jersey

NM/M
Production 15-250
Prime: No Pricing
Production 5-10
1 Roger Clemens/125 10.00
2 Manny Ramirez/250 8.00
3 Francisco Rodriguez/250 4.00
4 Brian Roberts/250 6.00
5 Javy Lopez/250 4.00
6 Vernon Wells/250 4.00
7 Johan Santana/175 8.00
8 Torii Hunter/250 4.00
9 Mike Mussina/250 6.00
10 Sammy Sosa/250 8.00
11 Ryan Wagner/250 4.00
12 Jack Wilson/15
14 Greg Maddux/250 8.00
15 Albert Pujols/250 20.00
16 Jeremy Bonderman/250 4.00
17 Johnny Estrada/250 4.00
18 Mark Buehrle/250 4.00
19 Jorge Posada/250 4.00
20 Carl Crawford/250 4.00
21 Paul Konerko/250 4.00
22 Victor Martinez/250 4.00
23 Jose Vidro/175 4.00
24 Jim Thome/250 6.00
25 Andruw Jones/250 6.00

Diamond Cuts Signature Combo

NM/M
Production 25-50

Prime: No Pricing
Production 10 Sets
3 Freddy Rodriguez Jsy-Jsy/25 40.00
6 Vernon Wells Jsy-Jsy/25 25.00
8 Torii Hunter Bat-Jsy/50 20.00
11 Ryan Wagner Jsy-Jsy/50 15.00
12 Jack Wilson Bat-Jsy/50 20.00
16 Jeremy Bonderman Jsy-Jsy/50 20.00
17 Johnny Estrada Fld Glv-Jsy/50 15.00
21 Paul Konerko Jsy-Jsy/25 25.00

Heritage

NM/M
Common Player: 1.00
Production 1,000 Sets
Die-cut: 1X-1.5X
Production 200 Sets
Die-cut Gold: 2X-3X
Production 50 Sets
1 Rickey Henderson 1.50
2 Jeff Bagwell 1.50
3 Steve Garvey 1.00
4 Albert Pujols 5.00
5 Don Mattingly 4.00
6 Frank Thomas 1.50
7 Tony Gwynn 2.00
8 Gary Sheffield 1.50
9 Dale Murphy 1.50
10 Kerry Wood 1.50
11 Cal Ripken Jr. 6.00
12 Miguel Cabrera 2.00
13 Dwight Gooden 1.00
14 Barry Zito 1.00
15 Darryl Strawberry 1.00

Heritage Bat

NM/M
Production 150 Sets
1 Rickey Henderson 8.00
2 Jeff Bagwell 6.00
3 Steve Garvey 4.00
4 Albert Pujols 15.00
5 Don Mattingly 10.00
6 Frank Thomas 6.00
7 Tony Gwynn 8.00
8 Gary Sheffield 6.00
9 Dale Murphy 6.00
11 Cal Ripken Jr. 20.00
12 Miguel Cabrera 6.00
13 Dwight Gooden 4.00
15 Darryl Strawberry 4.00

Heritage Combo

NM/M
Production 10-50
Prime: No Pricing
Production 10 Sets
1 Rickey Henderson Bat-Jsy/50 15.00
2 Jeff Bagwell Bat-Jsy/50 10.00
3 Steve Garvey Bat-Jsy/50 10.00
4 Albert Pujols Bat-Jsy/50 25.00
5 Don Mattingly Bat-Jsy/50 20.00
6 Frank Thomas Bat-Jsy/50 10.00
7 Tony Gwynn Bat-Jsy/50 15.00
8 Gary Sheffield Bat-Jsy/50 10.00
9 Dale Murphy Bat-Jsy/50 12.00
10 Kerry Wood Jsy-Pants/25 10.00
11 Cal Ripken Jr. Bat-Jsy/50 4.00
12 Miguel Cabrera Bat-Jsy/50 12.00
13 Dwight Gooden Bat-Jsy/50 10.00
14 Barry Zito Jsy-Jsy/10
15 Darryl Strawberry Bat-Jsy/50 10.00

Heritage Jersey

NM/M
Production 50-250
Prime: No Pricing
Production 10 Sets
1 Rickey Henderson/250 8.00
2 Jeff Bagwell/250 6.00
3 Steve Garvey/250 4.00
4 Albert Pujols/250 15.00
5 Don Mattingly/250 12.00
6 Frank Thomas/250 6.00
7 Tony Gwynn/250 8.00
9 Dale Murphy/250 6.00
10 Kerry Wood/250 6.00
11 Cal Ripken Jr./250 20.00
12 Miguel Cabrera/50 8.00
13 Dwight Gooden/250 4.00
14 Barry Zito/250 4.00
15 Darryl Strawberry/250 4.00

Heritage Signature Combo

NM/M
Production 10-50
Prime: No Pricing
Production 5-10
3 Steve Garvey Bat-Jsy/50 25.00
5 Don Mattingly Bat-Jsy/25 75.00
6 Frank Thomas Bat-Jsy/10
7 Tony Gwynn Bat-Jsy/15
9 Dale Murphy Bat-Jsy/25 40.00
11 Cal Ripken Jr. Bat-Jsy/50 160.00
12 Miguel Cabrera Bat-Jsy/25 50.00
13 Dwight Gooden Bat-Jsy/25 25.00
15 Darryl Strawberry Bat-Jsy/25 25.00

Heroes of the Hall

NM/M
Common Player: 2.00
Production 350 Sets
Die-cut: 1X-1.5X
Production 75 Sets
Die-cut Gold: 2X-3X
Production 25 Sets
1 Luis Aparicio 2.00
2 Dennis Eckersley 2.00
3 Brooks Robinson 4.00
4 Carlton Fisk 4.00
5 Tom Seaver 4.00
6 Paul Molitor 4.00
7 Rod Carew 3.00
8 George Brett 6.00
9 Nolan Ryan 8.00
10 Mike Schmidt 6.00
11 Willie Mays 6.00
12 Gary Carter 2.00
13 Lou Brock 2.00
14 Steve Carlton 2.00
15 Harmon Killebrew 4.00

Heroes of the Hall Bat

NM/M
Production 100-150
1 Luis Aparicio/150 4.00
3 Brooks Robinson/150 8.00
4 Carlton Fisk/150 6.00
6 Paul Molitor/150 8.00
8 George Brett/150 12.00
10 Mike Schmidt/125 15.00
11 Willie Mays/100 35.00
12 Gary Carter/125 6.00
13 Lou Brock/150 6.00
15 Harmon Killebrew/150 8.00

Heroes of the Hall Combo

NM/M
Production 25-50
Prime: No Pricing
Production 5-10
1 Luis Aparicio Bat-Jsy/50 10.00
2 Dennis Eckersley Jsy-Pants/50 10.00
3 Brooks Robinson Bat-Jsy/25 15.00
4 Carlton Fisk Bat-Jsy/50 12.00
5 Tom Seaver Jsy-Pants/50 15.00
6 Paul Molitor Bat-Jsy/50 15.00
7 Rod Carew Bat-Jsy/50 12.00
8 George Brett Bat-Jsy/50 20.00
9 Nolan Ryan Bat-Jsy/50 25.00
10 Mike Schmidt Bat-Jsy/50 20.00
11 Willie Mays Bat-Jsy/25 60.00
12 Gary Carter Jsy-Pants/50 10.00
13 Lou Brock Bat-Jkt/50 15.00
15 Harmon Killebrew Bat-Jsy/50 15.00

Heroes of the Hall Jersey

NM/M
Production 50-150
Prime: No Pricing
Production 5-10
1 Luis Aparicio/150 4.00
2 Dennis Eckersley/150 6.00
3 Brooks Robinson/50 10.00
4 Carlton Fisk/150 6.00
5 Tom Seaver/150 8.00
6 Paul Molitor/150 8.00
7 Rod Carew/150 6.00
8 George Brett/150 12.00
9 Nolan Ryan/100 20.00
10 Mike Schmidt/100 15.00
11 Willie Mays/50 40.00
12 Gary Carter/150 6.00
14 Steve Carlton/150 4.00
15 Harmon Killebrew/150 8.00

Heroes of the Hall Signature Combo

NM/M
Production 5-50
Prime: No Pricing
Production 5-10
1 Luis Aparicio Bat-Jsy/50 20.00
2 Dennis Eckersley Jsy-Pants/25 30.00
3 Brooks Robinson Bat-Jsy/10
4 Carlton Fisk Bat-Jsy/25 40.00
5 Tom Seaver Jsy-Pants/15
6 Paul Molitor Bat-Jsy/25 35.00
11 Willie Mays Bat-Jsy/5
12 Gary Carter Jsy-Pants/15
14 Steve Carlton Bat-Jsy/25 35.00
15 Harmon Killebrew Bat-Jsy/25 40.00

Masterstrokes

NM/M
Common Player: 1.50
Production 750 Sets
Die-cut: 1X-1.5X
Production 150 Sets
Die-cut Gold: 1.5X-2X
Production 50 Sets
1 Hideki Matsui 6.00
2 David Ortiz 3.00
3 Aramis Ramirez 2.00
4 Lance Berkman 1.50
5 Ichiro Suzuki 6.00
6 Mike Piazza 4.00
7 Ivan Rodriguez 2.00
8 Hideo Nomo 2.00
9 Jeff Bagwell 2.00
10 Travis Hafner 1.50
11 Casey Kotchman 1.50
12 Jim Edmonds 2.00
13 Michael Young 1.50
14 Lyle Overbay 1.50
15 Eric Chavez 2.00
16 Jason Bay 1.50
17 Hank Blalock 2.00
18 Frank Thomas 2.00
19 Craig Biggio 2.00
20 Miguel Cabrera 3.00
21 Vladimir Guerrero 3.00
22 Sammy Sosa 4.00
23 Chipper Jones 3.00
24 Rafael Palmeiro 2.00
25 Adam Dunn 2.00

Masterstrokes Bat

NM/M
Production 25-250
1 Hideki Matsui/25 30.00
2 David Ortiz/250 8.00
3 Aramis Ramirez/35 8.00
4 Lance Berkman/250 4.00
6 Mike Piazza/100 10.00
7 Ivan Rodriguez/250 6.00
9 Jeff Bagwell/250 6.00
10 Travis Hafner/250 4.00
11 Casey Kotchman/250 4.00
13 Michael Young/250 4.00
14 Lyle Overbay/250 4.00
16 Jason Bay/250 4.00
17 Hank Blalock/50 6.00
18 Frank Thomas/250 6.00
19 Craig Biggio/250 6.00
20 Miguel Cabrera/250 6.00
21 Vladimir Guerrero/250 8.00
22 Sammy Sosa/200 8.00
23 Chipper Jones/250 6.00
25 Adam Dunn/250 6.00

Masterstrokes Combo

NM/M
Production 15-50
Prime: No Pricing
Production 10 Sets
1 Hideki Matsui Bat-Jsy/15
2 David Ortiz Bat-Jsy/50 15.00
3 Aramis Ramirez Jsy-Jsy/50 10.00
4 Lance Berkman Bat-Jsy/50 8.00
6 Mike Piazza Jsy-Jsy/50 15.00
7 Ivan Rodriguez Bat-Jsy/50 10.00
8 Hideo Nomo Jsy-Jsy/50 12.00
9 Jeff Bagwell Bat-Jsy/50 10.00
10 Travis Hafner Bat-Jsy/50 8.00
11 Casey Kotchman Bat-Jsy/50 8.00
12 Jim Edmonds Jsy-Jsy/50 10.00
13 Michael Young Bat-Jsy/50 10.00
14 Lyle Overbay Bat-Jsy/50 8.00
15 Eric Chavez Bat-Jsy/50 10.00
16 Jason Bay Bat-Jsy/50 8.00
17 Hank Blalock Jsy-Jsy/50 10.00
18 Frank Thomas Bat-Jsy/50 12.00
19 Craig Biggio Bat-Jsy/50 10.00
20 Miguel Cabrera Bat-Jsy/50 15.00
21 Vladimir Guerrero Bat-Jsy/50 15.00
22 Sammy Sosa Bat-Jsy/50 15.00
23 Chipper Jones Bat-Jsy/50 12.00
24 Rafael Palmeiro Bat-Pants/50 12.00
25 Adam Dunn Bat-Jsy/50 10.00

Masterstrokes Jersey

NM/M
Production 40-250
Prime: No Pricing
Production 10 Sets
1 Hideki Matsui/250 20.00
2 David Ortiz/250 8.00
3 Aramis Ramirez/250 6.00
4 Lance Berkman/250 4.00
6 Mike Piazza/250 8.00
7 Ivan Rodriguez/250 6.00
8 Hideo Nomo/250 6.00
9 Jeff Bagwell/250 6.00
10 Travis Hafner/200 4.00
11 Casey Kotchman/250 4.00

12 Jim Edmonds/250 6.00
13 Michael Young/150 4.00
14 Lyle Overbay/250 4.00
15 Eric Chavez/250 4.00
16 Jason Bay/150 4.00
17 Hank Blalock/250 4.00
18 Frank Thomas/250 6.00
19 Craig Biggio/250 6.00
20 Miguel Cabrera/250 6.00
21 Vladimir Guerrero/50 10.00
22 Sammy Sosa/250 8.00
23 Chipper Jones/225 6.00
24 Rafael Palmeiro/40 8.00
25 Adam Dunn/250 6.00

Masterstrokes Signature Combo

NM/M
Production 5-50
Prime: No Pricing
Production 5-10
10 Travis Hafner Bat-Jsy/50 25.00
11 Casey Kotchman Bat-Jsy/50 20.00
12 Jim Edmonds Jsy-Jsy/5
13 Michael Young Bat-Jsy/10
14 Lyle Overbay Bat-Jsy/50 12.00
15 Eric Chavez Bat-Jsy/25 25.00
16 Jason Bay Bat-Jsy/50 25.00
17 Hank Blalock Jsy-Jsy/25 30.00
18 Frank Thomas Bat-Jsy/10
20 Miguel Cabrera Bat-Jsy/25 50.00
23 Chipper Jones Bat-Jsy/5
25 Adam Dunn Bat-Jsy/10

Portraits Zenith White

NM/M
Common Player: 2.00
Production 70 Sets
Parallel #'d 40-60: .75X-1X
Parallel #'d 20-35: .75X-1.5X
No pricing 15 or less
1 Ozzie Smith 6.00
2 Derek Jeter 8.00
3 Eric Chavez 2.00
4 Duke Snider 4.00
5 Albert Pujols 8.00
6 Stan Musial 6.00
7 Ivan Rodriguez 3.00
8 Cal Ripken Jr. 15.00
9 Hank Blalock 2.00
10 Chipper Jones 3.00
11 Gary Sheffield 2.00
12 Alfonso Soriano 3.00
13 Carl Crawford 2.00
14 Lou Brock 4.00
15 Jim Edmonds 3.00
16 Bo Jackson 4.00
17 Todd Helton 3.00
18 Javy Lopez 2.00
19 Tony Gwynn 5.00
20 Mark Mulder 2.00
21 Sammy Sosa 4.00
22 Roger Clemens 6.00
23 Don Mattingly 8.00
24 Willie Mays 8.00
25 Andruw Jones 3.00
26 Steve Garvey 2.00
27 Scott Rolen 3.00
28 George Brett 8.00
29 Rod Carew 4.00
30 Ken Griffey Jr. 6.00
31 Mike Piazza 5.00
32 Steve Carlton 3.00
33 Larry Walker 3.00
34 Kerry Wood 2.00
35 Frank Thomas 3.00
36 Lance Berkman 2.00
37 Nomar Garciaparra 4.00
38 Curt Schilling 3.00
39 Carl Yastrzemski 6.00
40 Mark Grace 3.00
41 Tom Seaver 4.00
42 Mariano Rivera 3.00
43 Carlos Beltran 3.00
44 Reggie Jackson 4.00
45 Pedro Martinez 4.00
46 Richie Sexson 2.00
47 Tom Glavine 2.00
48 Torii Hunter 2.00
49 Ron Guidry 2.00
50 Michael Young 2.00
51 Ichiro Suzuki 6.00
52 C.C. Sabathia 2.00
53 Johnny Bench 4.00
54 Mark Teixeira 3.00
55 Hideki Matsui 6.00
56 Mike Mussina 3.00
57 Johan Santana 3.00
58 Fergie Jenkins 2.00
59 Hideo Nomo 3.00
60 Nolan Ryan 10.00
61 Whitey Ford 4.00
62 Jim Thome 3.00
63 Gary Carter 3.00
64 Randy Johnson 3.00
65 Vladimir Guerrero 3.00
66 Harmon Killebrew 4.00
67 Tim Hudson 3.00
68 Josh Beckett 2.00
69 Eddie Murray 4.00
70 Greg Maddux 5.00
71 J.D. Drew 2.00
72 Bob Feller 4.00
73 Adrian Beltre 2.00
74 Wade Boggs 4.00
75 Barry Zito 2.00
76 David Ortiz 3.00
77 Mike Schmidt 8.00
78 Miguel Cabrera 4.00
79 Carlos Delgado 2.00
80 Andre Dawson 2.00
81 Garret Anderson 2.00
82 Rickey Henderson 3.00
83 Shawn Green 2.00
84 Dale Murphy 3.00
85 Alex Rodriguez 6.00
86 Mark Prior 3.00
87 Paul Molitor 4.00
88 Jeff Bagwell 3.00
89 Eric Gagne 2.00
90 Troy Glaus 2.00
91 Robin Yount 4.00
92 Miguel Tejada 3.00
93 Kirk Gibson 2.00
94 Manny Ramirez 3.00
95 Rafael Palmeiro 3.00
96 Maury Wills 2.00
97 Craig Biggio 2.00
98 Jim Palmer 3.00
99 Adam Dunn 3.00
100 Carlton Fisk 3.00

Private Signings Gold

NM/M
Common Autograph: 8.00
Production 50 Sets
1 Casey Kotchman 20.00
2 Chone Figgins 10.00
5 Ervin Santana 10.00
6 Garret Anderson 15.00
9 Orlando Cabrera 15.00
10 Robb Quinlan 8.00
11 Steve Finley 15.00
12 Tim Salmon 15.00
14 Brandon Webb 10.00
18 Tony Pena 10.00
19 Russ Ortiz 10.00
24 Adam LaRoche 12.00
27 Danny Kolb 10.00
29 Johnny Estrada 10.00
31 Nick Green 8.00
32 Rafael Furcal 15.00
34 Brian Roberts 20.00
36 Jay Gibbons 10.00
40 Rodrigo Lopez 10.00
47 Edgar Renteria 25.00
49 Jay Payton 10.00
51 Juan Cedeno 8.00
53 Matt Clement 30.00
54 Trot Nixon 20.00
55 Wade Miller 10.00
57 Carlos Zambrano 25.00
59 Derrek Lee 40.00
65 Todd Walker 12.00
70 Jermaine Dye 15.00
71 Mark Buehrle 25.00
72 Paul Konerko 15.00
76 Shingo Takatsu 20.00
78 Austin Kearns 10.00
80 Bubba Nelson 8.00
81 Danny Graves 8.00
84 Ryan Wagner 8.00
87 Cliff Lee 10.00
88 Fausto Carmona 8.00
91 Jody Gerut 10.00
93 Kazuhito Tadano 15.00
94 Travis Hafner 15.00
98 Cory Sullivan 8.00
101 Jeff Salazar 8.00
103 Joe Kennedy 8.00
108 Brandon Inge 10.00
111 Craig Monroe 10.00
113 Jeremy Bonderman 15.00
114 Justin Verlander
116 Troy Percival 15.00
117 Vance Wilson 8.00
123 Miguel Cabrera 35.00
127 Yorman Bazardo 10.00
133 Jason Lane 8.00
136 Morgan Ensberg 15.00
141 Jeremy Affeldt 8.00
143 Ken Harvey 8.00
148 Brad Penny 10.00
150 Dioner Navarro 15.00
151 Edwin Jackson 10.00
158 Milton Bradley 12.00
159 Yhency Brazoban 8.00
161 Bill Hall 10.00
162 Carlos Lee 15.00
166 Lyle Overbay 8.00
168 Jacque Jones 8.00
170 Joe Nathan 12.00
173 Lew Ford 10.00
175 Shannon Stewart 10.00
191 Yuniesky Betancourt 30.00
198 Scott Proctor 10.00
199 Tom Gordon 12.00
201 Bobby Crosby 20.00
202 Danny Haren 10.00
209 Octavio Dotel 10.00
210 Rich Harden 15.00
219 Mike Lieberthal 15.00
221 Randy Wolf 8.00
222 Craig Wilson 8.00
223 Jack Wilson 10.00
224 Jason Bay 15.00
226 Jose Castillo 10.00
229 Akinori Otsuka 20.00
231 Freddy Guzman 8.00
232 Jake Peavy 30.00
234 Mark Loretta 12.00
235 Sean Burroughs 8.00
243 Merkin Valdez 10.00
246 Omar Vizquel 8.00
249 Bucky Jacobsen 10.00
250 Clint Nageotte 15.00
252 J.J. Putz 15.00
254 Miguel Olivo 8.00
260 Jeff Suppan 12.00
266 Yadier Molina 12.00
267 Aubrey Huff 12.00
268 B.J. Upton 20.00
269 Carl Crawford 20.00
271 Delmon Young 25.00
272 Dewon Brazelton 10.00
276 Adrian Gonzalez 10.00
278 Francisco Cordero 10.00
280 Kameron Loe 10.00
282 Laynce Nix 10.00
284 Michael Young 15.00
291 Shea Hillenbrand 12.00
293 Chad Cordero 12.00
295 Jose Guillen 12.00
297 Josh Karp 8.00
298 Livan Hernandez 15.00
299 Nick Johnson 15.00

Private Signings Silver

NM/M
Common Autograph: 8.00
Production 100 Sets
1 Casey Kotchman 15.00
2 Chone Figgins 8.00
5 Ervin Santana 8.00
9 Orlando Cabrera 12.00
12 Tim Salmon 12.00
18 Tony Pena 8.00
19 Russ Ortiz 8.00
24 Adam LaRoche 10.00
27 Danny Kolb 8.00
31 Nick Green 8.00
34 Brian Roberts 15.00
36 Jay Gibbons 8.00
49 Jay Payton 8.00
51 Juan Cedeno 8.00
55 Wade Miller 8.00
57 Carlos Zambrano 20.00
65 Todd Walker 10.00
70 Jermaine Dye 12.00
80 Bubba Nelson 8.00
81 Danny Graves 8.00
84 Ryan Wagner 8.00
87 Cliff Lee 8.00
88 Fausto Carmona 8.00
91 Jody Gerut 8.00
94 Travis Hafner 12.00
98 Cory Sullivan 8.00
101 Jeff Salazar 8.00
103 Joe Kennedy 8.00
108 Brandon Inge 8.00
111 Craig Monroe 8.00
113 Jeremy Bonderman 12.00
117 Vance Wilson 8.00
127 Yorman Bazardo 8.00
127 Yorman Bazardo 8.00
133 Jason Lane 8.00
136 Morgan Ensberg 12.00
141 Jeremy Affeldt 8.00
143 Ken Harvey 8.00
150 Dioner Navarro 12.00
151 Edwin Jackson 8.00
158 Milton Bradley 10.00
159 Yhency Brazoban 8.00
161 Bill Hall 8.00
162 Carlos Lee 12.00
166 Lyle Overbay 8.00
170 Joe Nathan 10.00
173 Lew Ford 8.00
191 Yuniesky Betancourt 25.00
198 Scott Proctor 8.00
201 Bobby Crosby 10.00
202 Danny Haren 8.00
209 Octavio Dotel 8.00
210 Rich Harden 12.00
219 Mike Lieberthal 12.00
221 Randy Wolf 8.00
222 Craig Wilson 8.00
223 Jack Wilson 8.00
224 Jason Bay 10.00
226 Jose Castillo 8.00
231 Freddy Guzman 8.00
232 Jake Peavy 25.00
234 Mark Loretta 10.00
250 Clint Nageotte 8.00
252 J.J. Putz 8.00
260 Jeff Suppan 10.00
276 Adrian Gonzalez 8.00
278 Francisco Cordero 8.00
280 Kameron Loe 8.00
282 Laynce Nix 8.00
291 Shea Hillenbrand 10.00
293 Chad Cordero 10.00
295 Jose Guillen 10.00
297 Josh Karp 8.00
298 Livan Hernandez 12.00

Spirit of the Game

NM/M
Common Player: 1.50
Production 600 Sets
Die-cut: 1X-1.5X
Production 125 Sets
Die-cut Gold: 2X-4X
Production 25 Sets
1 Mark Prior 3.00
2 Sean Casey 1.50
3 Ichiro Suzuki 6.00
4 Andruw Jones 2.00
5 Francisco Cordero 1.50
6 Ben Sheets 2.00
7 Rocco Baldelli 1.50
8 Rafael Furcal 1.50
9 Angel Berroa 1.50
10 Roy Oswalt 1.50
11 Jose Reyes 1.50
12 Shannon Stewart 1.50
13 Greg Maddux 5.00
14 Alfonso Soriano 3.00
15 Curt Schilling 3.00
16 Jody Gerut 1.50
17 Brandon Webb 1.50
18 Josh Beckett 2.00
19 Laynce Nix 1.50
20 Scott Rolen 3.00

Spirit of the Game Bat

NM/M
Production 75-300
1 Mark Prior/300 6.00
4 Andruw Jones/300 6.00
6 Ben Sheets/300 4.00
7 Rocco Baldelli/300 4.00
8 Rafael Furcal/300 4.00
9 Angel Berroa/300 4.00
11 Jose Reyes/300 4.00
12 Shannon Stewart/75 4.00
13 Greg Maddux/300 8.00
14 Alfonso Soriano/225 6.00
16 Jody Gerut/300 4.00
17 Brandon Webb/300 4.00
19 Laynce Nix/300 4.00

Spirit of the Game Combo

NM/M
Production 50 Sets
Prime: No Pricing
Production 10 Sets
1 Mark Prior Bat-Jsy 12.00
2 Sean Casey Jsy-Jsy 6.00
4 Andruw Jones Bat-Jsy 8.00
6 Ben Sheets Bat-Jsy 8.00
7 Rocco Baldelli Bat-Jsy 6.00
8 Rafael Furcal Bat-Jsy 6.00

10 Roy Oswalt Bat-Jsy 8.00
11 Jose Reyes Bat-Jsy 8.00
12 Shannon Stewart Jsy-Jsy 6.00
13 Greg Maddux Bat-Jsy 15.00
14 Alfonso Soriano Jsy-Jsy 12.00
15 Curt Schilling Bat-Jsy 12.00
16 Jody Gerut Bat-Jsy 6.00
19 Laynce Nix Bat-Jsy 6.00
20 Scott Rolen Jsy-Jsy 12.00

Spirit of the Game Jersey

NM/M

Production 125-250
Prime: No Pricing
Production 10 Sets
1 Mark Prior/250 6.00
2 Sean Casey/250 4.00
4 Andruw Jones/250 6.00
5 Francisco Cordero/250 4.00
6 Ben Sheets/250 4.00
7 Rocco Baldelli/250 4.00
8 Rafael Furcal/250 4.00
10 Roy Oswalt/250 4.00
11 Jose Reyes/250 4.00
12 Shannon Stewart/250 4.00
13 Greg Maddux/250 8.00
14 Alfonso Soriano/250 6.00
15 Curt Schilling/250 6.00
16 Jody Gerut/125 4.00
18 Josh Beckett/250 4.00
19 Laynce Nix/250 4.00
20 Scott Rolen/250 6.00

Spirit of the Game Signature Combo

NM/M

Production 10-25
Prime: No Pricing
Production 5-10
1 Mark Prior Bat-Jsy/15
2 Sean Casey Jsy-Jsy/25 20.00
6 Ben Sheets Bat-Jsy/10
8 Rafael Furcal Bat-Jsy/25 25.00
12 Shannon Stewart Jsy-Jsy/25 20.00
14 Alfonso Soriano Jsy-Jsy/15
16 Jody Gerut Bat-Jsy/25 15.00
19 Laynce Nix Bat-Jsy/25 15.00
20 Scott Rolen Jsy-Jsy/10

Stars

NM/M

Common Player: 1.00
Inserted 1:6
Gold: 1X-2X
Production 500 Sets
Platinum: 2X-4X
Production 50 Sets
1 Carlos Beltran 1.50
2 Sean Casey 1.00
3 Ichiro Suzuki 3.00
4 Vladimir Guerrero 1.50
5 Tim Hudson 1.50
6 Alex Rodriguez 4.00
7 Miguel Tejada 1.50
8 Curt Schilling 1.50
9 Roger Clemens 4.00
10 Ben Sheets 1.00
11 Todd Helton 1.50
12 Mark Mulder 1.00
13 Scott Podsednik 1.00
14 Victor Martinez 1.00
15 Mark Prior 1.50
16 Ivan Rodriguez 1.50
17 Dontrelle Willis 1.00
18 Andy Pettitte 1.00
19 Khalil Greene 1.50
20 Jeff Kent 1.00
21 Paul Konerko 1.00
22 Joe Mauer 1.50
23 Bobby Crosby 1.00
24 Pedro Martinez 2.00
25 John Smoltz 1.00
26 Derek Jeter 4.00
27 Moises Alou 1.00
28 Rich Harden 1.00
29 Jim Thome 1.50
30 Jason Bay 2.00
31 Aramis Ramirez 3.00
32 Carlos Lee 1.00
33 B.J. Upton 1.00
34 Nomar Garciaparra 1.00
35 Ken Griffey Jr. 1.00
36 Darin Erstad 1.00
37 Larry Walker 1.00
38 Jose Vidro 1.00
39 Zack Greinke 1.00
40 Michael Young 1.00
41 David Wright 2.00
42 Albert Pujols 4.00
43 Vernon Wells 1.00
44 Mark Teixeira 1.50
45 Jacque Jones 1.00
46 Brian Giles 1.00
47 Austin Kearns 1.00
48 Omar Vizquel 1.00
49 Randy Johnson 1.50
50 Jason Varitek 1.50

2005 DONRUSS TEAM HEROES

NM/M

Complete Set (440): 80.00
Common Player: .15
Pack (8): 1.75
Box (24): 35.00
1 Adam Kennedy .15
2 Bartolo Colon .15
3 Bengie Molina .15
4 Casey Kotchman .15
5 Chone Figgins .15
6 Dallas McPherson .25
7 Darin Erstad .15
8 David Eckstein .15
9 Francisco Rodriguez .15
10 Garret Anderson .25
11 Jarrod Washburn .15
12 John Lackey .15
13 Jose Guillen .25
14 Robb Quinlan .15
15 Tim Bittner .15
16 Tim Salmon .15
17 Vladimir Guerrero .25
18 Alex Cintron .15
19 Craig Counsell .15
20 Brandon Webb .15
21 Chad Tracy .15
22 Doug Devore .15
23 Luis Gonzalez .25
24 Mark Grace .25
25 Randy Johnson .75
26 Scott Hairston .15
27 Shea Hillenbrand .15
28 Tim Olson .15
29 Adam LaRoche .15
30 Andruw Jones .40
31 Charles Thomas .15
32 Chipper Jones .75
33 Dale Murphy .50
34 John Smoltz .25
35 Johnny Estrada .15
36 Jose Capellan .15
37 Marcus Giles .15
38 Nick Green .15
39 Phil Niekro .15
40 Rafael Furcal .25
41 Brian Roberts .50
42 Cal Ripken Jr. 4.00
43 Javy Lopez .25
44 Jay Gibbons .15
45 Larry Bigbie .15
46 Luis Matos .15
47 Melvin Mora .15
48 Miguel Tejada .50
49 Rafael Palmeiro .50
50 Rodrigo Lopez .15
51 Sidney Ponson .15
52 Abe Alvarez .15
53 Bill Mueller .15
54 Curt Schilling .75
55 David Ortiz .75
56 Doug Mientkiewicz .15
57 Dwight Evans .15
58 Fred Lynn .15
59 Jim Rice .40
60 Johnny Damon .75
61 Keith Foulke .15
62 Kevin Youkilis .15
63 Manny Ramirez .75
64 Tim Wakefield .15
65 Trot Nixon .15
66 Angel Guzman .15
67 Aramis Ramirez .40
68 Carlos Zambrano .40
69 Corey Patterson .40
70 Derrek Lee .40
71 Greg Maddux 1.00
72 Kerry Wood .75
73 Lee Smith .15
74 Mark Prior .75
75 Sammy Sosa 1.50
76 Aaron Rowand .15
77 Carlos Lee .25
78 Frank Thomas .50
79 Freddy Garcia .15
80 Harold Baines .15
81 Jose Contreras .15
82 Juan Uribe .15
83 Mark Buehrle .15
84 Paul Konerko .15
85 Shingo Takatsu .15
86 Adam Dunn .50
87 Austin Kearns .15
88 Danny Graves .15
89 Eric Davis .15
90 Jacob Cruz .15
91 Jason LaRue .15
92 Ken Griffey Jr. 1.50
93 Ryan Wagner .15
94 Sean Casey .25
95 Casey Blake .15
96 C.C. Sabathia .15
97 Cliff Lee .15
98 Grady Sizemore .15
99 Jake Westbrook .15
100 Jody Gerut .15
101 Kazuhito Tadano .15
102 Matt Lawton .15
103 Travis Hafner .15
104 Victor Martinez .15
105 Charles Johnson .15
106 Clint Barmes .25
107 Garrett Atkins .15
108 Jason Jennings .15
109 Jeff Francis .15
110 Joe Kennedy .15
111 Matt Holliday .15
112 Preston Wilson .15
113 Todd Helton .50
114 Alan Trammell .40
115 Bobby Higginson .15
116 Brandon Inge .15
117 Carlos Guillen .15
118 Carlos Pena .15
119 Craig Monroe .15
120 Dmitri Young .15
121 Eric Munson .15
122 Ivan Rodriguez .50
123 Jeremy Bonderman .15
124 Roberto Novoa .15
125 A.J. Burnett .15
126 Alex Gonzalez .15
127 Dontrelle Willis .40
128 Guillermo Mota .15
129 Josh Beckett .40
130 Juan Pierre .15
131 Luis Castillo .15
132 Miguel Cabrera .75
133 Paul LoDuca .15
134 Adam Everett .15
135 Andy Pettitte .25
136 Brad Ausmus .15
137 Chris Burke .15
138 Craig Biggio .25
139 Jeff Bagwell .50
140 Lance Berkman .15
141 Morgan Ensberg .15
142 Nolan Ryan 3.00
143 Roger Clemens 2.00
144 Roy Oswalt .25
145 Tim Redding .15
146 Wade Miller .15
147 Andres Blanco .15
148 Angel Berroa .15
149 Benito Santiago .15
150 Byron Gettis .15
151 George Brett 2.00
152 Jeremy Affeldt .15
153 Ken Harvey .15
154 Mike MacDougal .15
155 Mike Sweeney .15
156 Shawn Camp .15
157 Zack Greinke .15
158 Brad Penny .15
159 Cesar Izturis .15
160 Edwin Jackson .15
161 Eric Gagne .40
162 Jerry Hairston .15
163 Jeff Weaver .15
164 Kazuhisa Ishii .15
165 Milton Bradley .15
166 Orel Hershiser .15
167 Shawn Green .25
168 Steve Garvey .15
169 Tommy John .15
170 Yhency Brazoban .15
171 Ben Sheets .25
172 Bill Hall .15
173 Danny Kolb .15
174 Lyle Overbay .15
175 Paul Molitor .50
176 Robin Yount 1.00
177 Rollie Fingers .15
178 Rickie Weeks .15
179 Scott Podsednik .15
180 Jack Morris .15
181 Jacque Jones .15
182 Jason Kubel .15
183 Joe Mauer .25
184 Joe Nathan .15
185 Johan Santana .50
186 Justin Morneau .25
187 Lew Ford .15
188 Matthew LeCroy .15
189 Rod Carew .50
190 Shannon Stewart .15
191 Torii Hunter .25
192 Aarom Baldiris .15
193 Cliff Floyd .15
194 Darryl Strawberry .15
195 Dwight Gooden .15
196 David Wright .75
197 Victor Zambrano .15
198 Jose Reyes .15
199 Kazuo Matsui .15
200 Keith Hernandez .15
201 Mike Piazza 1.00
202 Tom Glavine .40
203 Vance Wilson .15
204 Tom Seaver .75
205 Alex Rodriguez 1.50
206 Bernie Williams .40
207 Chien-Ming Wang .15
208 Derek Jeter 2.00
209 Dioner Navarro .15
210 Don Mattingly 1.50
211 Gary Sheffield .50
212 Hideki Matsui 1.50
213 Jason Giambi .25
214 Javier Vazquez .15
215 Jim Leyritz .15
216 Jorge Posada .40
217 Kevin Brown .15
218 Mariano Rivera .40
219 Mike Mussina .40
220 Scott Proctor .15
221 Tom Gordon .15
222 Barry Zito .25
223 Bobby Crosby .25
224 Dave Stewart .15
225 Dennis Eckersley .50
226 Eric Byrnes .15
227 Eric Chavez .25
228 Erubiel Durazo .15
229 Mark Kotsay .15
230 Mark Mulder .40
231 Octavio Dotel .15
232 Rich Harden .40
233 Tim Hudson .40
234 Billy Wagner .15
235 Bobby Abreu .40
236 Brett Myers .15
237 Chase Utley .15
238 Jim Thome .75
239 Jimmy Rollins .15
240 Lenny Dykstra .15
241 Marlon Byrd .15
242 Mike Lieberthal .15
243 Mike Schmidt 1.50
244 Pat Burrell .25
245 Randy Wolf .15
246 Ryan Howard .40
247 Steve Carlton .15
248 Bert Blyleven .15
249 Bill Madlock .15
250 Dave Parker .40
251 Craig Wilson .15
252 Jack Wilson .15
253 Jason Bay .25
254 Jason Kendall .15
255 Jose Castillo .15
256 Kip Wells .15
257 Akinori Otsuka .15
258 Brian Giles .25
259 Brian Lawrence .15
260 Freddy Guzman .15
261 Gaylord Perry .15
262 Jake Peavy .40
263 Jay Payton .15
264 Khalil Greene .25
265 Mark Loretta .15
266 Phil Nevin .15
267 Ryan Klesko .15
268 Sean Burroughs .15
269 Tony Gwynn .75
270 Trevor Hoffman .15
271 A.J. Pierzynski .15
272 Dustan Mohr .15
273 Edgardo Alfonzo .15
274 Jason Schmidt .40
275 Jerome Williams .15
276 Matt Williams .40
277 Merkin Valdez .15
278 Todd Linden .15

279	Will Clark	.50
280	Bret Boone	.15
281	Bucky Jacobsen	.15
282	Clint Nageotte	.15
283	Ichiro Suzuki	1.50
284	J.J. Putz	.15
285	Jamie Moyer	.15
286	Bobby Madritsch	.15
287	*Mike Morse*	.25
288	Joel Pineiro	.15
289	Shigetoshi Hasegawa	.15
290	Travis Blackley	.15
291	Albert Pujols	2.00
292	Dan Haren	.15
293	Jason Isringhausen	.15
294	Jason Marquis	.15
295	Jeff Suppan	.15
296	Jim Edmonds	.40
297	Larry Walker	.40
298	Reggie Sanders	.15
299	Scott Rolen	.75
300	Yadier Molina	.15
301	Aubrey Huff	.15
302	B.J. Upton	.15
303	Carl Crawford	.15
304	Chad Gaudin	.15
305	Delmon Young	.40
306	Dewon Brazelton	.15
307	Joey Gathright	.15
308	Jose Cruz Jr.	.15
309	Rocco Baldelli	.15
310	Wade Boggs	.50
311	Adrian Gonzalez	.15
312	Alfonso Soriano	.75
313	Francisco Cordero	.15
314	Frankie Francisco	.15
315	Hank Blalock	.50
316	Kenny Rogers	.15
317	Laynce Nix	.15
318	Mark Teixeira	.50
319	Michael Young	.15
320	Alexis Rios	.15
321	David Bush	.15
322	Eric Hinske	.15
323	Frank Catalanotto	.15
324	Gabe Gross	.15
325	Guillermo Quiroz	.15
326	Rickey Henderson	.50
327	Orlando Hudson	.15
328	Roy Halladay	.40
329	Ted Lilly	.15
330	Vernon Wells	.15
331	Alberto Callaspo	.15
332	Jeff Mathis	.15
333	Ervin Santana	.15
334	Troy Percival	.15
335	Troy Glaus	.40
336	Greg Aquino	.15
337	*Tony Pena*	.25
338	Luis Terrero	.15
339	J.D. Drew	.15
340	Jon Lieber	.15
341	Russ Ortiz	.15
342	Daniel Cabrera	.15
343	Kenny Lofton	.15
344	Val Majewski	.15
345	Orlando Cabrera	.15
346	Hanley Ramirez	.15
347	Jason Varitek	.50
348	Pedro Martinez	.75
349	Derek Lowe	.15
350	Juan Cedeno	.15
351	Todd Walker	.15
352	Matt Clement	.25
353	Moises Alou	.25
354	Nomar Garciaparra	1.00
355	Michael Barrett	.15
356	Todd Hollandsworth	.15
357	Jose Valentin	.15
358	Magglio Ordonez	.15
359	*Pedro Lopez*	.25
360	Barry Larkin	.25
361	Jaret Wright	.15
362	Elizardo Ramirez	.15
363	Omar Vizquel	.15
364	Fausto Carmona	.15
365	Jake Dittler	.15
366	Jeff Salazar	.15
367	Jeromy Burnitz	.15
368	Jayson Nix	.15
369	*Ubaldo Jimenez*	.25
370	Vinny Castilla	.15
371	*Justin Verlander*	.75
372	Armando Benitez	.15
373	Carl Pavano	.25
374	Chris Aguila	.15
375	Logan Kensing	.15
376	Mike Lowell	.15
377	*Yorman Bazardo*	.25
378	Willy Taveras	.15
379	Jeff Kent	.25
380	Carlos Beltran	.50
381	Kevin Millwood	.15
382	Juan Gonzalez	.25
383	Steve Finley	.15
384	Hideo Nomo	.40
385	Adrian Beltre	.40
386	David Kryznel	.15
387	Richie Sexson	.40
388	Jesse Crain	.15
389	Brad Radke	.15
390	Jason Lane	.15
391	Corey Koskie	.15
392	Cristian Guzman	.15
393	Brad Wilkerson	.15
394	Brendan Harris	.15
395	Chad Cordero	.15
396	Endy Chavez	.15
397	Jose Vidro	.15
398	Josh Karp	.15
399	Livan Hernandez	.15
400	Nick Johnson	.15
401	Ryan Church	.15
402	Terrmel Sledge	.15
403	*Philip Humber*	1.50
404	*Ambiorix Concepcion*	.25
405	Al Leiter	.15
406	Richard Hidalgo	.15
407	Kris Benson	.15
408	Mike Cameron	.15
409	Victor Diaz	.15
410	Tony Womack	.15
411	Ferdin Tejeda	.15
412	Nick Swisher	.15
413	Jairo Garcia	.15
414	Jermaine Dye	.15
415	Joe Blanton	.15
416	Eric Milton	.15
417	Gavin Floyd	.15
418	John Van Benschoten	.15
419	Matt Peterson	.15
420	David Wells	.15
421	J.T. Snow	.15
422	Willie Mays	2.00
423	Jeremy Reed	.15
424	Jose Lopez	.15
425	Raul Ibanez	.15
426	*Wladimir Balentien*	1.50
427	Matt Morris	.15
428	Mike Matheny	.15
429	Edgar Renteria	.25
430	Woody Williams	.15
431	*Jeff Niemann*	4.00
432	Scott Kazmir	.15
433	Tino Martinez	.15
434	Chris Young	.15
435	David Dellucci	.15
436	Kameron Loe	.15
437	Nolan Ryan	3.00
438	John-Ford Griffin	.15
439	Carlos Delgado	.40
440	Russ Adams	.15

Showdown Blue

Blue: 3-5X

Showdown Bronze

Bronze: 4-6X
Production 100 Sets

Showdown Gold

Gold: No Pricing
Production 10 Sets

Showdown Red

Red: 1.5-3X

Showdown Silver

Silver: 6-8X
Production 50 Sets

Autographs

		NM/M
4	Casey Kotchman SP	20.00
14	Robb Quinlan	8.00
15	Tim Bittner	5.00
18	Alex Cintron SP	8.00
22	Doug Devore	5.00
28	Tim Olson	5.00
35	Johnny Estrada SP	
36	Jose Capellan SP	
37	Marcus Giles SP	
38	Nick Green	5.00
44	Jay Gibbons SP	12.00
50	Rodrigo Lopez SP	8.00
52	Abe Alvarez SP	
62	Kevin Youkilis SP	
66	Angel Guzman	12.00
80	Harold Baines SP/25	
90	Jacob Cruz	5.00
97	Cliff Lee SP	10.00
101	Kazuhito Tadano	20.00
103	Travis Hafner SP/10	
104	Victor Martinez SP	20.00
110	Joe Kennedy	5.00
116	Brandon Inge	10.00
119	Craig Monroe	8.00
121	Eric Munson SP	
124	Roberto Novoa	5.00
128	Guillermo Mota SP	
147	Andres Blanco SP	
150	Byron Gettis SP	8.00
152	Jeremy Affeldt	5.00
156	Shawn Camp	5.00
170	Yhency Brazoban	8.00
172	Bill Hall SP	8.00
182	Jason Kubel SP	12.00
192	Aarom Baldiris SP	10.00
203	Vance Wilson	5.00
220	Scott Proctor	8.00
236	Brett Myers SP	
241	Marlon Byrd SP	
246	Ryan Howard SP	
260	Freddy Guzman SP	
275	Jerome Williams SP	
277	Merkin Valdez	5.00
278	Todd Linden SP	25.00
279	Will Clark SP/5	
281	Bucky Jacobsen	5.00
282	Clint Nageotte	5.00
289	Shigetoshi Hasegawa SP/5	
290	Travis Blackley	5.00
292	Dan Haren SP	12.00
295	Jeff Suppan	10.00
300	Yadier Molina SP	15.00
302	B.J. Upton SP/25	
304	Chad Gaudin SP	
306	Dewon Brazelton	8.00
307	Joey Gathright SP	10.00
311	Adrian Gonzalez	10.00
313	Francisco Cordero SP	10.00
314	Frankie Francisco	5.00
317	Laynce Nix	8.00
320	Alexis Rios SP	
322	Eric Hinske SP	
325	Guillermo Quiroz SP	
327	Orlando Hudson SP	
333	Ervin Santana	10.00
337	Tony Pena	8.00
346	Hanley Ramirez	15.00
350	Juan Cedeno	8.00
359	Pedro Lopez	15.00
364	Fausto Carmona	5.00
365	Jake Dittler	5.00
366	Jeff Salazar	10.00
368	Jayson Nix	5.00
371	Justin Verlander SP/5	
377	Yorman Bazardo	8.00
378	Willy Taveras SP	15.00
398	Josh Karp	5.00
402	Terrmel Sledge SP	
403	Philip Humber SP/5	
411	Ferdin Tejeda	5.00
419	Matt Peterson	5.00
431	Jeff Niemann SP/5	
435	David Dellucci SP	20.00
436	Kameron Loe	5.00

2005 DONRUSS THROWBACK THREADS

		NM/M
Complete Set (300):		
Common Player:		.20
Pack (5):		3.00
Box (24):		65.00
1	Luis Castillo	.20
2	Derek Jeter	1.50
3	Eric Chavez	.20
4	Angel Berroa	.20
5	Jeff Bagwell	.40
6	J.T. Snow	.20
7	Craig Biggio	.30
8	Michael Barrett	.20
9	Hank Blalock	.40
10	Chipper Jones	.50
11	Jacque Jones	.20
12	Mark Teixeira	.50
13	Omar Vizquel	.20
14	Paul LoDuca	.20
15	Jim Edmonds	.30
16	Aramis Ramirez	.30
17	Lance Berkman	.30
18	Javy Lopez	.30
19	Adam LaRoche	.20
20	Jorge Posada	.40
21	Sean Casey	.20
22	Mark Prior	.40
23	Phil Nevin	.20
24	Manny Ramirez	.50
25	Andruw Jones	.40
26	Matt Lawton	.20
27	Vladimir Guerrero	.50
28	Austin Kearns	.20
29	John Smoltz	.40
30	Ken Griffey Jr.	1.00
31	Mike Piazza	.75
32	Jason Jennings	.20
33	Jason Varitek	.40
34	David Ortiz	.50
35	Mike Mussina	.40
36	Joe Nathan	.20
37	Kenny Rogers	.20
38	Carlos Zambrano	.30
39	Eric Byrnes	.20
40	Clint Barmes	.20
41	Danny Kolb	.20
42	Mariano Rivera	.40
43	Joey Gathright	.20
44	Adam Dunn	.40
45	Carlos Lee	.20
46	Yhency Brazoban	.20
47	Roy Oswalt	.30
48	Torii Hunter	.20
49	Scott Podsednik	.20
50	*Jason Hammel*	.40
51	Ichiro Suzuki	1.00
52	C.C. Sabathia	.20
53	Bobby Abreu	.40
54	Jon Garland	.20
55	Brandon Webb	.20
56	Mark Buehrle	.30
57	Johan Santana	.50
58	Mike Sweeney	.20
59	*Tadahito Iguchi*	1.50
60	Edgar Renteria	.20
61	Aaron Rowand	.20
62	Craig Wilson	.20
63	J.D. Drew	.30
64	Bobby Crosby	.40
65	Justin Morneau	.30
66	Scott Rolen	.50
67	Jose Vidro	.20
68	Carlos Beltran	.40
69	Jeff Weaver	.20
70	Jason Schmidt	.30
71	Brad Wilkerson	.20
72	*Yuniesky Betancourt*	1.50
73	Octavio Dotel	.20
74	Mike Cameron	.20
75	Barry Zito	.40
76	Woody Williams	.20
77	*Russel Rohlicek*	.40
78	Mark Kotsay	.20
79	Jeff Suppan	.20
80	Eric Gagne	.40
81	Tim Salmon	.40
82	Troy Glaus	.40
83	Kevin Mench	.20
84	Ivan Rodriguez	.40
85	Sean Burroughs	.20
86	Dallas McPherson	.20
87	Jamie Moyer	.20
88	Orlando Cabrera	.20
89	*Wladimir Balentien*	1.00
90	*Philip Humber*	1.00
91	Francisco Cordero	.20
92	Danny Graves	.20
93	Bucky Jacobsen	.20
94	Cliff Lee	.20
95	Oliver Perez	.20
96	Jake Peavy	.30
97	Doug Mientkiewicz	.20
98	Brad Radke	.20
99	Jeremy Reed	.20
100	Garret Anderson	.30
101	Rafael Furcal	.20
102	Jack Wilson	.20
103	Bernie Williams	.20
104	Josh Beckett	.20

105 Albert Pujols 1.50
106 *Ubaldo Jimenez* .40
107 Richard Hidalgo .20
108 *Luke Scott* .75
109 Hideo Nomo .40
110 Vernon Wells .30
111 Richie Sexson .40
112 Chad Cordero .20
113 Alex Rodriguez 1.50
114 Paul Konerko .30
115 Carlos Guillen .20
116 Francisco Rodriguez .20
117 Johnny Damon .50
118 David Wright 1.00
119 Lyle Overbay .20
120 Brian Roberts .20
121 Sammy Sosa 1.00
122 Roger Clemens 1.50
123 Rickie Weeks .50
124 Larry Bigbie .20
125 Rafael Palmeiro .40
126 Jason Giambi .30
127 Hideki Matsui 1.00
128 Brad Lidge .20
129 Jeremy Affeldt .20
130 Mike MacDougal .20
131 Troy Percival .20
132 Matt Morris .20
133 *David Gassner* .40
134 Kerry Wood .40
135 Dontrelle Willis .40
136 Michael Young .30
137 Andy Pettitte .40
138 Kris Benson .20
139 *Miguel Negron* .40
140 Rich Harden .40
141 Bret Boone .20
142 *Danny Rueckel* .40
143 *Jeff Niemann* 1.00
144 *Randy Messenger* .40
145 Pedro Martinez .50
146 Kazuhisa Ishii .20
147 Carlos Delgado .30
148 Tom Glavine .30
149 Russ Ortiz .20
150 Gavin Floyd .20
151 Randy Johnson .50
152 Prince Fielder 8.00
153 Nomar Garciaparra .75
154 Pat Burrell .30
155 Melvin Mora .20
156 Jose Reyes .30
157 Trot Nixon .20
158 B.J. Upton .20
159 Jody Gerut .20
160 Juan Pierre .20
161 Miguel Tejada .40
162 Barry Larkin .40
163 Carl Crawford .20
164 Ben Sheets .30
165 Tim Hudson .40
166 Darin Erstad .20
167 Todd Helton .40
168 Luis Gonzalez .30
169 Mark Mulder .30
170 David Dellucci .20
171 Marcus Giles .20
172 Shannon Stewart .20
173 Zack Greinke .20
174 Miguel Cabrera .50
175 Nick Johnson .20
176 Derrek Lee .50
177 Jim Thome .40
178 Ken Harvey .20
179 *Ambiorix Concepcion* .40
180 Roy Halladay .30
181 Larry Walker .40
182 Greg Maddux 1.00
183 Frank Thomas .50
184 Travis Hafner .30
185 Matt Holliday .20
186 Victor Martinez .20
187 Jason Isringhausen .20
188 Bill Mueller .20
189 Dewon Brazelton .20
190 Adrian Beltre .40
191 Tim Wakefield .20
192 Alexis Rios .20
193 Alfonso Soriano .50
194 Fernando Vina .20
195 Armando Benitez .20
196 Bartolo Colon .30
197 A.J. Burnett .20
198 Milton Bradley .20
199 Brad Penny .20
200 Rocco Baldelli .20
201 Curt Schilling .50
202 Ryan Wagner .20
203 Preston Wilson .20
204 Akinori Otsuka .20
205 *Bill McCarthy* .40
206 Edgardo Alfonzo .20
207 Mike Lieberthal .20
208 Shea Hillenbrand .20
209 Tom Gordon .20
210 Kip Wells .20
211 Frank Catalanotto .20
212 Casey Kotchman .20
213 *Justin Verlander* 1.50
214 Brandon Inge .20
215 Terrmel Sledge .20
216 Gary Sheffield .40
217 Steve Finley .20
218 Kenny Lofton .20
219 Chris Carpenter .30
220 Danny Haren .20
221 Brett Myers .20
222 Joe Mauer .40
223 David Wells .20
224 Brian Giles .20
225 Moises Alou .30
226 *Casey Rogowski* .40
227 Chase Utley .30
228 Corey Koskie .20
229 Derek Lowe .20
230 *Erick Threets* .40
231 Grady Sizemore .20
232 Jason Lane .20
233 Jeremy Bonderman .20
234 Livan Hernandez .20
235 Ryan Klesko .20
236 Sidney Ponson .20
237 Jimmy Rollins .20
238 Eric Milton .20
239 Shingo Takatsu .20
240 Scott Kazmir .20
241 Shawn Green .30
242 Nick Swisher .20
243 Shawn Chacon .20
244 Javier Vazquez .20
245 Mark Loretta .20
246 Dmitri Young .20
247 Charles Johnson .20
248 Magglio Ordonez .30
249 *Sean Thompson* .40
250 *Jared Gothreaux* .40
251 Kevin Millwood .20
252 Mike Lowell .20
253 Cristian Guzman .20
254 *Nate McLouth* .40
255 Delmon Young .40
256 Jeromy Burnitz .20
257 Garrett Atkins .20
258 Junior Spivey .20
259 Morgan Ensberg .20
260 Chone Figgins .20
261 *Hayden Penn* .50
262 Jason Bay .40
263 Jose Cruz Jr. .20
264 Khalil Greene .40
265 Ray Durham .20
266 Juan Gonzalez .40
267 Jeff Kent .20
268 Dioner Navarro .20
269 Rodrigo Lopez .20
270 Geoff Jenkins .20
271 Jermaine Dye .20
272 Orlando Hudson .20
273 Jose Lima .20
274 Jeff Francis .20
275 Luis Matos .20
276 Jason Kendall .20
277 Mike Hampton .20
278 Al Kaline .75
279 Bert Blyleven .20
280 Bill Madlock .20
281 Cal Ripken Jr. 3.00
282 Dale Murphy .50
283 Gary Carter .50
284 George Brett 2.00
285 Harmon Killebrew 1.00
286 Harold Baines .40
287 John Kruk .50
288 Keith Hernandez .40
289 Willie Mays 3.00
290 Matt Williams .20
291 Nolan Ryan 2.50
292 Paul Molitor .50
293 Reggie Jackson .75
294 Rickey Henderson .50
295 Ron Cey .20
296 Ryne Sandberg 1.00
297 Ted Williams 2.50
298 Tom Seaver .50
299 Tony Gwynn .75
300 Babe Ruth/SP 20.00

Century Proof Blue

Blue (1-299): 3-6X
Production 150 sets

Century Proof Gold

Gold (1-299): 3-6X
Production 100 sets

Century Proof Green

Green (1-299): 3-6X

Century Stars

NM/M
Common Player: 1.00
Spectrum: 1.5-3X
Production 100 sets
1 Bobby Doerr 1.00
2 Derek Jeter 4.00
3 Harmon Killebrew 1.50
4 Paul Molitor 1.50
5 Brooks Robinson 1.50
6 Steve Garvey 1.00
7 Ivan Rodriguez 1.00
8 Carl Yastrzemski 2.50
9 Nomar Garciaparra 2.00
10 Miguel Tejada 1.00
11 Edgar Martinez 1.00
12 Kevin Brown 1.00
13 Alex Rodriguez 3.00
14 Carlton Fisk 1.00
15 Craig Biggio 1.00
16 Dwight Gooden 1.00
17 Jim Palmer 1.00
18 Ken Griffey Jr. 2.00
19 Bob Feller 1.50
20 Don Sutton 1.00
21 Al Kaline 1.50
22 Roger Clemens 4.00
23 Kirk Gibson 1.00
24 Willie Mays 3.00
25 Frank Robinson 1.00
26 Randy Johnson 1.50
27 Jim "Catfish" Hunter 1.00
28 Austin Kearns 1.00
29 John Smoltz 1.00
30 Nolan Ryan 4.00
31 Duke Snider 1.50
32 Bernie Williams 1.00
33 David Wells 1.00
34 Bo Jackson 1.50
35 Mike Mussina 1.00
36 Gaylord Perry 1.00
37 Andre Dawson 1.00
38 Curt Schilling 1.50
39 Darryl Strawberry 1.00
40 Willie McCovey 1.00
41 Tom Seaver 1.50
42 Mariano Rivera 1.00
43 Dennis Eckersley 1.00
44 David Cone 1.00
45 Bret Boone 1.00
46 Will Clark 1.00
47 Jack Morris 1.00
48 Ichiro Suzuki 3.00
49 Alan Trammell 1.00
50 Cal Ripken Jr. 4.00

Century Stars Material

NM/M
Common Player: 4.00
Production 20-50
Prime: No Pricing
Production five sets
1 Bobby Doerr Pants/50 8.00
3 Harmon Killebrew Jsy/50 15.00
4 Paul Molitor Jsy/50 10.00
5 Brooks Robinson Bat/50 10.00
6 Steve Garvey Jsy/50 4.00
7 Ivan Rodriguez Jsy/50 8.00
8 Carl Yastrzemski Jsy/50 15.00
10 Miguel Tejada Jsy/50 6.00
11 Edgar Martinez Jsy/50 6.00
12 Kevin Brown Jsy/50 4.00
14 Carlton Fisk Jsy/50 8.00
15 Craig Biggio Jsy/50 8.00
16 Dwight Gooden Jsy/50 4.00
17 Jim Palmer Jsy/50 6.00
19 Bob Feller Pants/20
20 Don Sutton Jsy/50 4.00
21 Al Kaline Bat/50 15.00
22 Roger Clemens Jsy/50 15.00
23 Kirk Gibson Jsy/50 4.00
24 Willie Mays Jsy/20
25 Frank Robinson Bat/50 6.00
26 Randy Johnson Jsy/50 8.00
27 Jim "Catfish" Hunter Jsy/20
28 Austin Kearns Jsy/50 4.00
29 John Smoltz Jsy/50 8.00
30 Nolan Ryan Jkt/50 25.00
31 Duke Snider Pants/20
32 Bernie Williams Jsy/50 6.00
33 David Wells Jsy/50 4.00
34 Bo Jackson Jsy/50 10.00
35 Mike Mussina Jsy/50 8.00
36 Gaylord Perry Jsy/50 6.00
37 Andre Dawson Jsy/50 6.00
38 Curt Schilling Jsy/50 8.00
39 Darryl Strawberry Jsy/50 6.00
40 Willie McCovey Jsy/50 8.00
41 Tom Seaver Jsy/20
42 Mariano Rivera Jsy/50 10.00
43 Dennis Eckersley Jsy/50 6.00
44 David Cone Jsy/50 4.00
45 Bret Boone Jsy/50 4.00
46 Will Clark Jsy/20
47 Jack Morris Jsy/50 4.00
49 Alan Trammell Jsy/50 6.00
50 Cal Ripken Jr. Jsy/50 30.00

Dynasty

NM/M
Common Trio: 2.00
Spectrum: 1.25X
Production 100 sets
1 Reggie Jackson, Jim "Catfish" Hunter, Sparky Lyle 2.00
2 Cal Ripken Jr., Jim Palmer, Eddie Murray 8.00
3 Dwight Gooden, Gary Carter, Darryl Strawberry 2.00
4 Rickey Henderson, Dennis Eckersley, Jose Canseco 2.00
5 Chipper Jones, Greg Maddux, David Justice 3.00
6 Roger Clemens, Alfonso Soriano, Bernie Williams 6.00
7 Randy Johnson, Curt Schilling, Matt Williams 3.00
8 Troy Glaus, Garret Anderson, Francisco Rodriguez 2.00
9 Josh Beckett, Miguel Cabrera, Mike Lowell 2.00
10 Curt Schilling, Manny Ramirez, Jason Varitek 8.00

Dynasty Material

NM/M
Production 20-50
Prime: No Pricing
Production five sets
1 Reggie Jackson Pants, Jim "Catfish" Hunter Pants, Sparky Lyle Pants/50 20.00
2 Cal Ripken Jr. Jsy, Jim Palmer Jsy, Eddie Murray Jsy/50 40.00
3 Dwight Gooden Jsy, Gary Carter Jsy, Darryl Strawberry Pants/20 15.00
4 Rickey Henderson Jsy, Dennis Eckersley Pants, Jose Canseco Jsy/50 35.00
5 Chipper Jones Jsy, Greg Maddux Jsy, David Justice Jsy/50 25.00
6 Roger Clemens Jsy, Alfonso Soriano Jsy, Bernie Williams Jsy/50 30.00
7 Randy Johnson Jsy, Curt Schilling Jsy, Matt Williams Jsy/50 20.00
8 Troy Glaus Jsy, Garret Anderson Jsy, Francisco Rodriguez Jsy/50 15.00
9 Josh Beckett Jsy, Miguel Cabrera Jsy, Mike Lowell Jsy/20
10 Curt Schilling Jsy, Manny Ramirez Jsy, Jason Varitek Jsy/50 40.00

Generations

NM/M
Common Player: 2.00

Spectrum: 1-2.5X
Production 100 sets
1 Duke Snider, Reggie Jackson, Sammy Sosa 2.00
2 Rod Carew, John Kruk, Eric Chavez 2.00
3 Bo Jackson, Deion Sanders, Brian Jordan 3.00
4 Brett George, Tony Gwynn, Todd Helton 4.00
5 Babe Ruth, Ted Williams, Willie Mays 5.00
6 Rickey Henderson, Lenny Dykstra, Ichiro Suzuki 3.00
7 Keith Hernandez, Don Mattingly, Casey Kotchman 3.00
8 Wade Boggs, Mark Grace, Hank Blalock 2.00
9 Gary Carter, Ivan Rodriguez, Victor Martinez 2.00
10 Gaylord Perry, Morris, Greg Maddux 2.00
11 Joe Morgan, Ryne Sandberg, Alfonso Soriano 3.00
12 Juan Marichal, Luis Tiant, Pedro Martinez 2.00
13 Stan Musial, Carl Yastrzemski, Lance Berkman 3.00
14 Johnny Bench, Carlton Fisk, Mike Piazza 3.00
15 Harmon Killebrew, Cal Ripken Jr., Albert Pujols 5.00
16 Frank Robinson, Andre Dawson, Gary Sheffield 2.00
17 Bob Feller, Roger Clemens, Kerry Wood 4.00
18 Steve Carlton, Tom Glavine, Barry Zito 2.00
19 Murray, Rafael Palmeiro, Mark Teixeira 2.00
20 Brooks Robinson, Mike Schmidt, Scott Rolen 3.00
21 Luis Aparicio, Omar Vizquel, Rafael Furcal 2.00
22 Don Sutton, David Cone, Roy Oswalt 2.00
23 Fred Lynn, Dale Murphy, Jim Edmonds 2.00
24 Ozzie, Barry Larkin, B.J. Upton 3.00
25 Gibson, Nolan Ryan, Mark Prior 4.00

Generations Material

NM/M

Production 20-50
Prime: No Pricing
Production 10 sets
1 Duke Snider Pants, Reggie Jackson Jsy, Sammy Sosa Jsy/20
2 Rod Carew Jsy, John Kruk Jsy, Eric Chavez Jsy/50 15.00
3 Bo Jackson Jsy, Deion Sanders Jsy, Brian Jordan Jsy/50 25.00
4 Brett George Jsy, Tony Gwynn Jsy, Todd Helton Jsy/50 25.00
5 Babe Ruth Jsy, Ted Williams Jsy, Willie Mays Jsy/20
7 Keith Hernandez Jsy, Don Mattingly Pants, Casey Kotchman Jsy/20 30.00
8 Wade Boggs Jsy, Mark Grace Jsy, Hank Blalock Jsy/50 15.00
9 Gary Carter Jsy, Ivan Rodriguez Jsy, Victor Martinez Jsy/50 15.00
10 Gaylord Perry Jsy, Morris Jsy, Greg Maddux Jsy/50 25.00
11 Joe Morgan Jsy, Ryne Sandberg Jsy, Alfonso Soriano Jsy/50 35.00
12 Juan Marichal Pants, Luis Tiant Pants, Pedro Martinez Jsy/50 20.00
13 Stan Musial Pants, Carl Yastrzemski Pants, Lance Berkman Jsy/20
14 Johnny Bench Pants, Carlton Fisk Jsy, Mike Piazza Jsy/50 20.00
15 Harmon Killebrew Jsy, Cal Ripken Jr. Jsy, Albert Pujols Jsy/50 50.00
16 Frank Robinson Bat, Andre Dawson Jsy, Gary Sheffield Jsy/20 15.00
17 Bob Feller Pants, Roger Clemens Jsy, Kerry Wood Jsy/20 50.00
18 Steve Carlton Jsy, Tom Glavine Jsy, Barry Zito Jsy/50 20.00
19 Murray Jsy, Rafael Palmeiro Jsy, Mark Teixeira Jsy/50 20.00
20 Brooks Robinson Jsy, Mike Schmidt Jsy, Scott Rolen Jsy/20
21 Luis Aparicio Jsy, Omar Vizquel Jsy, Rafael Furcal Jsy/20
24 Ozzie Jsy, Barry Larkin Jsy, B.J. Upton Bat/20

Material Bat

NM/M

Common Player: 4.00
Production 5-250
1 Luis Castillo/250 4.00
4 Angel Berroa/250 4.00
5 Jeff Bagwell/250 6.00
7 Craig Biggio/250 6.00
14 Paul LoDuca/250 4.00
17 Lance Berkman/250 4.00
18 Javy Lopez/250 4.00
21 Sean Casey/50 6.00
25 Andruw Jones/250 6.00
26 Matt Lawton/250 4.00
28 Austin Kearns/250 4.00
32 Jason Jennings/250 4.00
33 Jason Varitek/50 12.00
34 David Ortiz/250 8.00
43 Joey Gathright/250 4.00
48 Torii Hunter/250 4.00
55 Brandon Webb/250 4.00
58 Mike Sweeney/250 4.00
62 Craig Wilson/250 4.00
63 J.D. Drew/250 4.00
67 Jose Vidro/250 4.00
68 Carlos Beltran/250 6.00
81 Tim Salmon/250 4.00
82 Troy Glaus/250 4.00
83 Kevin Mench/250 4.00
88 Orlando Cabrera/15
101 Rafael Furcal/150 4.00
102 Jack Wilson/25 4.00
103 Bernie Williams/250 4.00
105 Albert Pujols/10
107 Richard Hidalgo/250 4.00
111 Richie Sexson/100 6.00
117 Johnny Damon/5
121 Sammy Sosa/50 8.00
123 Rickie Weeks/25 6.00
125 Rafael Palmeiro/250 6.00
135 Dontrelle Willis/50 6.00
136 Michael Young/250 4.00
141 Bret Boone/50 4.00
147 Carlos Delgado/250 4.00
148 Tom Glavine/250 4.00
153 Nomar Garciaparra/150 8.00
154 Pat Burrell/150 4.00
156 Jose Reyes/50 4.00
157 Trot Nixon/25
158 B.J. Upton/250 6.00
159 Jody Gerut/250 4.00
160 Juan Pierre/250 4.00
162 Barry Larkin/100 6.00
164 Ben Sheets/250 4.00
165 Tim Hudson/50 6.00
166 Darin Erstad/250 4.00
168 Luis Gonzalez/25 6.00
169 Mark Mulder/35 6.00
171 Marcus Giles/20
172 Shannon Stewart/15
174 Miguel Cabrera/50 10.00
175 Nick Johnson/250 4.00
176 Derrek Lee/50 8.00
190 Adrian Beltre/10
192 Alex Rios/50 4.00
197 A.J. Burnett/250 4.00
200 Rocco Baldelli/250 4.00
203 Preston Wilson/150 4.00
206 Edgardo Alfonzo/250 4.00
212 Casey Kotchman/250 4.00
215 Terrmel Sledge/250 4.00
218 Kenny Lofton/150 4.00
224 Brian Giles/35 6.00
225 Moises Alou/250 6.00
232 Jason Lane/250 4.00
235 Ryan Klesko/25 4.00
241 Shawn Green/250 4.00
247 Charles Johnson/250 4.00
248 Magglio Ordonez/250 4.00
252 Mike Lowell/50 4.00
255 Delmon Young/250 4.00
259 Morgan Ensberg/25 6.00
260 Chone Figgins/250 4.00
262 Jason Bay/175 6.00
265 Ray Durham/200 4.00
266 Juan Gonzalez/250 6.00
267 Jeff Kent/250 4.00
272 Orlando Hudson/250 4.00
278 Al Kaline/10
280 Bill Madlock/100 4.00
281 Cal Ripken Jr./150 25.00
283 Gary Carter/25 8.00
284 George Brett/25 25.00
286 Harold Baines/50 6.00
288 Keith Hernandez/25 8.00
289 Willie Mays/25 35.00
291 Nolan Ryan/50 25.00
292 Paul Molitor/150 6.00
293 Reggie Jackson/25 10.00
294 Rickey Henderson/250 8.00
296 Ryne Sandberg/50 15.00
297 Ted Williams/25 50.00
299 Tony Gwynn/50 10.00
300 Babe Ruth/25 180.00

Material Combo

NM/M

Common Player: 6.00
Production 10-100
Prime: 1-2X
Production 5-40
No pricing 20 or less
1 Luis Castillo Bat-Jsy/90 6.00
3 Eric Chavez Bat-Jsy/25 8.00
5 Jeff Bagwell Bat-Jsy/100 8.00
7 Craig Biggio Bat-Jsy/25 10.00
12 Mark Teixeira Bat-Jsy/25 10.00
17 Lance Berkman Bat-Jsy/100 6.00
21 Sean Casey Bat-Jsy/100 6.00
22 Mark Prior Bat-Jsy/25 10.00
25 Andruw Jones Bat-Jsy/100 8.00
32 Jason Jennings Bat-Jsy/100 6.00
34 David Ortiz Bat-Jsy/25 20.00
43 Joey Gathright Bat-Jsy/50 6.00
48 Torii Hunter Bat-Jsy/10
55 Brandon Webb Bat-Pants/100 6.00
58 Mike Sweeney Bat-Jsy/65 6.00
62 Craig Wilson Bat-Jsy/100 6.00
66 Scott Rolen Bat-Jsy/10
67 Jose Vidro Bat-Jsy/100 6.00
83 Kevin Mench Bat-Jsy/100 6.00
85 Sean Burroughs Bat-Jsy/15
101 Rafael Furcal Bat-Jsy/50 6.00
103 Bernie Williams Bat-Jsy/50 8.00
104 Josh Beckett Bat-Jsy/25 8.00
110 Vernon Wells Hat-Jsy/100 6.00
124 Larry Bigbie Jsy-Jsy/100 6.00
126 Jason Giambi Jsy-Jsy/100 8.00
136 Michael Young Bat-Jsy/50 8.00
137 Andy Pettitte Bat-Jsy/15
146 Kazuhisa Ishii Hat-Jsy/25 10.00
154 Pat Burrell Bat-Jsy/50 8.00
156 Jose Reyes Bat-Jsy/25 8.00
157 Trot Nixon Bat-Jsy/25 10.00
160 Juan Pierre Bat-Fld Glv/95 6.00
162 Barry Larkin Bat-Jsy/10
164 Ben Sheets Bat-Jsy/100 8.00
167 Todd Helton Jsy-Jsy/15
168 Luis Gonzalez Jsy-Jsy/100 6.00
171 Marcus Giles Hat-Jsy/50 6.00
172 Shannon Stewart Jsy-Jsy/30 6.00
174 Miguel Cabrera Bat-Jsy/25 12.00
180 Roy Halladay Jsy-Jsy/85 8.00
183 Frank Thomas Hat-Jsy/25 15.00
186 Victor Martinez Fld Glv-Jsy/40 8.00
197 A.J. Burnett Bat-Jsy/100 6.00
200 Rocco Baldelli Bat-Jsy/100 6.00
201 Curt Schilling Bat-Jsy/25 12.00
202 Ryan Wagner Jsy-Jsy/100 6.00
203 Preston Wilson Bat-Jsy/85 6.00
212 Casey Kotchman Bat-Jsy/50 6.00
218 Kenny Lofton Bat-Fld Glv/100 6.00
232 Jason Lane Bat-Hat/50 6.00
235 Ryan Klesko Hat-Jsy/100 6.00
252 Mike Lowell Bat-Jsy/100 6.00
257 Garrett Atkins Jsy-Jsy/100 6.00
258 Junior Spivey Bat-Jsy/10
259 Morgan Ensberg Hat-Jsy/100 8.00
260 Chone Figgins Bat-Jsy/50 6.00
262 Jason Bay Bat-Jsy/40 8.00
270 Geoff Jenkins Bat-Jsy/10
272 Orlando Hudson Bat-Jsy/40 6.00
275 Luis Matos Jsy-Jsy/50 6.00
281 Cal Ripken Jr. Bat-Jsy/50 40.00
283 Gary Carter Jsy-Pants/25 15.00
284 George Brett Bat-Jsy/25 30.00
286 Harold Baines Bat-Jsy/50 10.00
288 Keith Hernandez Bat-Jsy/25 10.00
289 Willie Mays Bat-Pants/25 50.00
291 Nolan Ryan Bat-Jsy/50 25.00
292 Paul Molitor Bat-Jsy/50 15.00
293 Reggie Jackson Bat-Jsy/25 15.00
294 Rickey Henderson Bat-Jsy/50 15.00
296 Ryne Sandberg Bat-Jsy/50 25.00
297 Ted Williams Bat-Jsy/25 75.00
298 Tom Seaver Jsy-Pants/25 15.00
299 Tony Gwynn Jsy-Pants/50 15.00
300 Babe Ruth Bat-Jsy/25 375.00

Material Jersey

NM/M

Common Player: 4.00
Production 5-250
Prime: 1-2X
Production 10-100
No pricing 20 or less
1 Luis Castillo/45 4.00
3 Eric Chavez/250 4.00
5 Jeff Bagwell/250 6.00
6 J.T. Snow/250 4.00
7 Craig Biggio/50 6.00

9	Hank Blalock/25	6.00
10	Chipper Jones/250	8.00
11	Jacque Jones/250	4.00
12	Mark Teixeira/150	6.00
15	Jim Edmonds/250	6.00
16	Aramis Ramirez/250	6.00
17	Lance Berkman/250	4.00
18	Javy Lopez/250	4.00
20	Jorge Posada/250	6.00
21	Sean Casey/250	4.00
22	Mark Prior/50	8.00
23	Phil Nevin/50	4.00
24	Manny Ramirez/250	8.00
25	Andruw Jones/250	6.00
27	Vladimir Guerrero/250	8.00
28	Austin Kearns/250	4.00
29	John Smoltz/250	8.00
31	Mike Piazza/250	8.00
32	Jason Jennings/250	4.00
34	David Ortiz/250	10.00
35	Mike Mussina/250	6.00
38	Carlos Zambrano/250	6.00
42	Mariano Rivera/50	8.00
43	Joey Gathright/100	4.00
44	Adam Dunn/250	6.00
47	Roy Oswalt/250	4.00
48	Torii Hunter/100	4.00
52	C.C. Sabathia/250	4.00
53	Bobby Abreu/250	4.00
56	Mark Buehrle/250	4.00
57	Johan Santana/250	6.00
58	Mike Sweeney/75	4.00
62	Craig Wilson/250	4.00
64	Bobby Crosby/100	6.00
66	Scott Rolen/250	6.00
67	Jose Vidro/75	4.00
74	Mike Cameron/250	4.00
75	Barry Zito/250	4.00
83	Kevin Mench/250	4.00
84	Ivan Rodriguez/250	6.00
87	Jamie Moyer/50	4.00
91	Francisco Cordero/250	4.00
94	Cliff Lee/250	4.00
98	Brad Radke/250	4.00
100	Garret Anderson/50	6.00
101	Rafael Furcal/100	4.00
102	Jack Wilson/15	
103	Bernie Williams/250	6.00
104	Josh Beckett/25	6.00
105	Albert Pujols/250	15.00
109	Hideo Nomo/250	8.00
110	Vernon Wells/250	4.00
114	Paul Konerko/250	4.00
116	Francisco Rodriguez/250	4.00
117	Johnny Damon/250	8.00
118	David Wright/250	10.00
119	Lyle Overbay/250	4.00
120	Brian Roberts/100	4.00
122	Roger Clemens/100	12.00
124	Larry Bigbie/200	4.00
125	Rafael Palmeiro/250	6.00
126	Jason Giambi/250	6.00
127	Hideki Matsui/250	15.00
132	Matt Morris/20	
134	Kerry Wood/250	6.00
135	Dontrelle Willis/250	6.00
136	Michael Young/250	4.00
137	Andy Pettitte/250	6.00
140	Rich Harden/5	
141	Bret Boone/250	4.00
146	Kazuhisa Ishii/250	4.00
147	Carlos Delgado/250	4.00
148	Tom Glavine/250	4.00
154	Pat Burrell/250	4.00
155	Melvin Mora/250	4.00
156	Jose Reyes/200	6.00
157	Trot Nixon/250	4.00
158	B.J. Upton/250	4.00
159	Jody Gerut/100	4.00
161	Miguel Tejada/35	8.00
162	Barry Larkin/40	8.00
163	Carl Crawford/40	4.00
164	Ben Sheets/250	6.00
166	Darin Erstad/25	6.00
167	Todd Helton/150	6.00
168	Luis Gonzalez/250	4.00
170	David Dellucci/150	4.00
171	Marcus Giles/15	
172	Shannon Stewart/250	4.00
174	Miguel Cabrera/100	8.00
176	Derrek Lee/250	8.00
177	Jim Thome/250	6.00
178	Ken Harvey/150	4.00
180	Roy Halladay/250	4.00
182	Greg Maddux/250	8.00
184	Travis Hafner/5	
186	Victor Martinez/250	4.00
189	Dewon Brazelton/250	4.00
190	Adrian Beltre/250	4.00
193	Alfonso Soriano/250	8.00
197	A.J. Burnett/250	4.00
200	Rocco Baldelli/250	4.00
201	Curt Schilling/250	8.00
202	Ryan Wagner/250	4.00
203	Preston Wilson/250	4.00
211	Frank Catalanotto/250	4.00
212	Casey Kotchman/250	4.00
214	Brandon Inge/250	4.00
221	Brett Myers/50	4.00
224	Brian Giles/20	
232	Jason Lane/95	4.00
233	Jeremy Bonderman/250	4.00
234	Livan Hernandez/250	4.00
235	Ryan Klesko/250	4.00
237	Jimmy Rollins/35	6.00
252	Mike Lowell/250	4.00
257	Garrett Atkins/250	4.00
258	Junior Spivey/250	4.00
259	Morgan Ensberg/150	4.00
260	Chone Figgins/250	4.00
262	Jason Bay/250	6.00
269	Rodrigo Lopez/250	4.00
270	Geoff Jenkins/250	4.00
272	Orlando Hudson/20	
275	Luis Matos/250	4.00
279	Bert Blyleven/50	6.00
281	Cal Ripken Jr./50	30.00
282	Dale Murphy/25	10.00
283	Gary Carter/50	8.00
284	George Brett/50	15.00
285	Harmon Killebrew/25	15.00
286	Harold Baines/50	6.00
287	John Kruk/50	8.00
288	Keith Hernandez/10	
289	Willie Mays Pants/25	40.00
290	Matt Williams/50	8.00
291	Nolan Ryan/50	25.00
292	Paul Molitor/50	10.00
293	Reggie Jackson/25	8.00
294	Rickey Henderson/50	10.00
295	Ron Cey/50	6.00
296	Ryne Sandberg/50	15.00
297	Ted Williams/25	60.00
298	Tom Seaver/25	15.00
299	Tony Gwynn/50	12.00
300	Babe Ruth/25	200.00

Player Timelines

		NM/M
Common Player:		1.00
Spectrum:		1-2.5X
Production 100 sets		
1	Dale Murphy	2.00
2	Greg Maddux	3.00
3	Tom Glavine	2.00
4	David Ortiz	3.00
5	Bo Jackson	2.00
6	Lyle Overbay	1.00
7	Tommy John	1.00
8	Shawn Green	1.00
9	Aramis Ramirez	1.50
10	Javy Lopez	1.00
11	Vladimir Guerrero	3.00
12	Travis Hafner	1.00
13	Junior Spivey	1.00
14	Alfonso Soriano	2.00
15	Andre Dawson	1.00
16	Sammy Sosa	3.00
17	Andy Pettitte	1.50
18	Jim Edmonds	1.50
19	Willie McCovey	2.00
20	Scott Rolen	2.00
21	Jermaine Dye	1.00
22	Pedro Martinez	2.50
23	Don Sutton	1.00
24	Randy Johnson	2.00
25	Nolan Ryan	3.00
26	Dennis Eckersley	1.00
27	Reggie Jackson	2.00
28	Deion Sanders	1.00
29	Curt Schilling	2.00
30	Rickey Henderson	1.00
31	Mike Piazza	2.00
32	Gary Carter	1.00
33	Roberto Alomar	1.00
34	Hideo Nomo	1.00
35	Andres Galarraga	1.00
36	Juan Gonzalez	1.00
37	Roger Clemens	4.00
38	Jeff Kent	1.00
39	Steve Carlton	1.00
40	Wade Boggs	1.50

Player Timeline Material

		NM/M
Production 25-250		
1	Dale Murphy/50	10.00
2	Greg Maddux/100	10.00
3	Tom Glavine/50	8.00
4	David Ortiz/250	10.00
5	Bo Jackson/100	12.00
6	Lyle Overbay/250	4.00
7	Tommy John Pants/250	4.00
8	Shawn Green/100	4.00
9	Aramis Ramirez/250	6.00
10	Javy Lopez/100	4.00
11	Vladimir Guerrero/25	15.00
12	Travis Hafner/25	8.00
13	Junior Spivey/250	4.00
14	Alfonso Soriano/100	6.00
16	Sammy Sosa/250	8.00
17	Andy Pettitte/100	8.00
18	Jim Edmonds/100	8.00
19	Willie McCovey Pants/50	12.00
20	Scott Rolen/50	10.00
21	Jermaine Dye/100	4.00
22	Pedro Martinez/50	12.00
23	Don Sutton/25	10.00
24	Randy Johnson/50	15.00
25	Nolan Ryan Jkt/50	40.00
27	Reggie Jackson Pants/50	15.00
28	Deion Sanders/25	15.00
29	Curt Schilling/50	10.00
30	Rickey Henderson Pants/100	15.00
31	Mike Piazza/50	15.00
32	Gary Carter Pants/50	10.00
33	Roberto Alomar/250	8.00
34	Hideo Nomo/50	15.00
35	Andres Galarraga/250	6.00
36	Juan Gonzalez/25	8.00
37	Roger Clemens/25	30.00
38	Jeff Kent/50	6.00

Player Timelines Sign. Mat.

		NM/M
Production 5-50		
Prime:		No Pricing
Production 5-10		
1	Dale Murphy/50	30.00
5	Bo Jackson/10	
6	Lyle Overbay/50	12.00
7	Tommy John Pants/50	15.00
8	Shawn Green/10	
12	Travis Hafner/25	20.00
13	Junior Spivey/50	12.00
14	Alfonso Soriano/10	
15	Andre Dawson/25	25.00
18	Jim Edmonds/10	
19	Willie McCovey Pants/10	
20	Scott Rolen/10	
21	Jermaine Dye/50	15.00
22	Pedro Martinez/5	
23	Don Sutton/25	20.00
25	Nolan Ryan Jkt/10	
26	Dennis Eckersley/10	
27	Reggie Jackson Pants/10	
28	Deion Sanders/5	
29	Curt Schilling/5	
30	Ricky Henderson Pants/5	
32	Gary Carter Pants/50	20.00
33	Roberto Alomar/10	
36	Juan Gonzalez/25	40.00
37	Roger Clemens/5	
40	Wade Boggs/15	

Polo Grounds 85 HIT Long Fly

		NM/M
Common Player:		1.50
Production 85 sets		
Parallel #'d 40-75:		.75-1.5X
Parallel #'d 20-35:		1-2X
No pricing 15 or less		

1	Ken Griffey Jr.	4.00
2	Roger Clemens	6.00
3	Barry Zito	2.00
4	Alex Rodriguez	5.00
5	Melvin Mora	1.50
6	Kevin Brown	1.50
7	Chipper Jones	3.00
8	Scott Kazmir	2.00
9	Kip Wells	1.50
10	Khalil Greene	2.00
11	Kevin Millwood	1.50
12	Kerry Wood	2.00
13	Mark Kotsay	1.50
14	Jeff Bagwell	2.00
15	Hank Blalock	2.00
16	Scott Rolen	2.00
17	Lance Berkman	2.00
18	Mike Mussina	2.00
19	Jim Edmonds	2.00
20	Jorge Posada	2.00
21	Curt Schilling	3.00
22	Vernon Wells	1.50
23	Pedro Martinez	3.00
24	Jeremy Reed	1.50
25	Hideki Matsui	4.00
26	Steve Finley	1.50
27	Gavin Floyd	1.50
28	Darin Erstad	1.50
29	Bernie Williams	2.00
30	Mark Mulder	2.00
31	Rafael Palmeiro	2.00
32	Andruw Jones	2.00
33	Roy Halladay	2.00
34	Dontrelle Willis	2.00
35	Bret Boone	1.50
36	Andy Pettitte	2.00
37	Vladimir Guerrero	3.00
38	Randy Johnson	3.00
39	Michael Young	2.00
40	Frank Thomas	2.00
41	Todd Helton	2.00
42	Johan Santana	3.00
43	Mark Teixeira	2.00
44	Justin Morneau	1.50
45	Brad Radke	1.50
46	Dallas McPherson	1.50
47	Tim Hudson	2.00
48	Carl Crawford	1.50
49	Eric Gagne	2.00
50	Mark Prior	3.00
51	Tom Glavine	2.00
52	Craig Biggio	2.00
53	John Smoltz	2.00
54	Manny Ramirez	3.00
55	Ivan Rodriguez	2.00
56	Gary Sheffield	2.00
57	Josh Beckett	2.00
58	Miguel Tejada	2.00
59	Bobby Abreu	2.00
60	Ichiro Suzuki	4.00
61	Sammy Sosa	2.50
62	Garret Anderson	2.00
63	Sean Casey	1.50
64	Troy Glaus	2.00
65	Larry Walker	2.00
66	Alfonso Soriano	2.00
67	Luis Gonzalez	2.00
68	Eric Chavez	2.00
69	Adrian Beltre	2.00
70	Miguel Cabrera	3.00
71	Carlos Beltran	2.00
72	Jim Thome	2.00
73	David Ortiz	3.00
74	Adam Dunn	2.00
75	Jacque Jones	1.50
76	Shawn Green	1.50
77	Victor Martinez	1.50
78	Torii Hunter	1.50
79	Carlos Lee	1.50

80 C.C. Sabathia 1.50
81 Joe Mauer 2.00
82 Kris Benson 1.50
83 Zack Greinke 1.50
84 Greg Maddux 4.00
85 David Wright 4.00
86 Mike Piazza 4.00
87 Johnny Damon 3.00
88 Derek Jeter 6.00
89 B.J. Upton 1.50
90 Albert Pujols 6.00
91 Cal Ripken Jr. 6.00
92 Nolan Ryan 5.00
93 George Brett 5.00
94 Don Mattingly 4.00
95 Ryne Sandberg 4.00
96 Rickey Henderson 3.00
97 Robin Yount 3.00
98 Mike Schmidt 4.00
99 Tony Gwynn 3.00
100 Willie Mays 5.00

Signature Marks

NM/M

Production 5-1,000
4 Angel Berroa/25 12.00
19 Adam LaRoche/50 20.00
36 Joe Nathan/25 20.00
38 Carlos Zambrano/25 30.00
39 Eric Byrnes/50 10.00
41 Danny Kolb/25 10.00
45 Carlos Lee/25 20.00
49 Scott Podsednik/20 20.00
52 C.C. Sabathia/25 15.00
56 Mark Buehrle/25 30.00
62 Craig Wilson/50 10.00
64 Bobby Crosby/100 15.00
67 Jose Vidro/25 12.00
73 Octavio Dotel/25 12.00
77 Russel Rohlicek/250 5.00
81 Tim Salmon/50 20.00
85 Sean Burroughs/25 10.00
87 Jamie Moyer/25 15.00
88 Orlando Cabrera/25 20.00
90 Philip Humber/50 20.00
91 Francisco Cordero/50 10.00
92 Danny Graves/25 10.00
93 Bucky Jacobsen/64 8.00
94 Cliff Lee/50 10.00
96 Jake Peavy/25 35.00
101 Rafael Furcal/25 20.00
102 Jack Wilson/100 10.00
108 Luke Scott/250 8.00
110 Vernon Wells/25 15.00
112 Chad Cordero/25 15.00
114 Paul Konerko/25 20.00
116 Francisco Rodriguez/25 20.00
118 David Wright/25 75.00
119 Lyle Overbay/25 10.00
120 Brian Roberts/100 15.00
124 Larry Bigbie/75 8.00
129 Jeremy Affeldt/50 8.00
131 Troy Percival/25 15.00
133 David Gassner/1000 5.00
136 Michael Young/25 20.00
139 Miguel Negron/250 5.00
140 Rich Harden/50 25.00
142 Danny Rueckel/250 5.00
144 Randy Messenger/500 5.00
149 Russ Ortiz/25 15.00
157 Trot Nixon/25 25.00
158 B.J. Upton/25 20.00
159 Jody Gerut/25 10.00
170 David Dellucci/50 15.00
172 Shannon Stewart/25 15.00
174 Miguel Cabrera/15
175 Nick Johnson/25 15.00
176 Derrek Lee/25 40.00
178 Ken Harvey/50 8.00
179 Ambiorix Concepcion/500 8.00
184 Travis Hafner/50 15.00
189 Dewon Brazelton/66 8.00
192 Alexis Rios/25 15.00
198 Milton Bradley/100 12.00
199 Brad Penny/25 10.00
202 Ryan Wagner/25 10.00
204 Akinori Otsuka/25 20.00
207 Mike Lieberthal/25 10.00
208 Shea Hillenbrand/25 20.00
209 Tom Gordon/25 20.00
212 Casey Kotchman/100 10.00
213 Justin Verlander/50 25.00
220 Danny Haren/25 20.00
226 Casey Rogowski/250 5.00
230 Erick Threets/500 5.00
232 Jason Lane/25 10.00
233 Jeremy Bonderman/50 15.00
234 Livan Hernandez/25 15.00
239 Shingo Takatsu/25 20.00
245 Mark Loretta/25 20.00
250 Jared Gothreaux/1000 5.00
254 Nate McLouth/1000 8.00
258 Junior Spivey/25 10.00
259 Morgan Ensberg/25 20.00
260 Chone Figgins/50 10.00
262 Jason Bay/186 15.00
268 Dioner Navarro/75 8.00
271 Jermaine Dye/25 15.00
272 Orlando Hudson/100 8.00
275 Luis Matos/50 10.00
279 Bert Blyleven/25 15.00
280 Bill Madlock/50 15.00
281 Cal Ripken Jr./25 150.00
282 Dale Murphy/25 30.00
286 Harold Baines/25 15.00
288 Keith Hernandez/25 15.00
290 Matt Williams/25 30.00

Throwback Collection

NM/M

Common Player: 1.00
Spectrum: 1-2.5X
Production 100 sets
1 Billy Martin 2.00
2 Tony Gwynn 2.00
3 Babe Ruth 4.00
4 Angel Berroa 1.00
5 Jeff Bagwell 1.50
6 Tony Oliva 1.00
7 Ivan Rodriguez 1.50
8 Gary Carter 1.50
9 Ted Williams 4.00
10 Chipper Jones 2.00
11 Al Oliver 1.00
12 Roberto Alomar 1.00
13 Omar Vizquel 1.00
14 Ernie Banks 2.00
15 Carlos Beltran 1.50
16 Garret Anderson 1.00
17 Mark Grace 1.00
18 Jason Giambi 1.00
19 Dave Righetti 1.00
20 Mike Schmidt 3.00
21 Roger Clemens 4.00
22 Juan Gonzalez 1.50
23 Carlos Delgado 1.00
24 Manny Ramirez 2.00
25 Jim Thome 1.50
26 Wade Boggs 2.00
27 Luis Tiant 1.00
28 Kerry Wood 1.50
29 Rod Carew 1.50
30 Dwight Evans 1.00
31 Mike Piazza 2.00
32 Billy Williams 1.00
33 Larry Walker 1.00
34 Nolan Ryan 4.00
35 Edgar Renteria 1.00
36 Greg Maddux 2.50
37 Gaylord Perry 1.00
38 Curt Schilling 2.00
39 Dave Parker 1.00
40 Andruw Jones 1.50
41 Orlando Cepeda 1.50
42 Fergie Jenkins 1.00
43 Kirby Puckett 2.00
44 Reggie Jackson 2.00
45 Bob Gibson 2.00
46 Rickey Henderson 2.00
47 Lee Smith 1.00
48 Lou Brock 1.50
49 Fred Lynn 1.00
50 Lance Berkman 1.00
51 Shawn Green 1.00
52 Hoyt Wilhelm 1.00
53 Sammy Sosa 2.50
54 Tim Hudson 1.50
55 Matt Williams 1.00
56 Marty Marion 1.00
57 Eric Chavez 1.00
58 Rafael Palmeiro 1.50
59 Randy Johnson 2.00
60 David Ortiz 2.00
61 Hank Blalock 1.00
62 Jim Rice 1.00
63 Mark Mulder 1.50
64 Kazuo Matsui 1.00
65 Pedro Martinez 2.00
66 Sean Casey 1.00
67 Carlos Lee 1.00
68 Stan Musial 3.00
69 Fred McGriff 1.00
70 Darryl Strawberry 1.00
71 Tommy John 1.00
72 Hideo Nomo 1.00
73 Johnny Bench 2.00
74 Cal Ripken Jr. 5.00
75 Harold Baines 1.00

Throwback Coll. Material

NM/M

Production 5-500
Prime: 1-2X
Production 5-25
No pricing 20 or less
1 Billy Martin Pants/250 8.00
2 Tony Gwynn Jsy/250 8.00
3 Babe Ruth Pants/20
4 Angel Berroa Pants/100 4.00
5 Jeff Bagwell Jsy/250 6.00
6 Tony Oliva Jsy/250 4.00
7 Ivan Rodriguez Jsy/500 6.00
8 Gary Carter Pants/250 4.00
9 Ted Williams Jsy/20
10 Chipper Jones Jsy/250 6.00
11 Al Oliver Jsy/250 4.00
12 Roberto Alomar Jsy/500 6.00
13 Omar Vizquel Jsy/500 4.00
14 Ernie Banks Jsy/20
15 Carlos Beltran Jsy/100 6.00
16 Garret Anderson Jsy/50 4.00
17 Mark Grace Jsy/250 6.00
18 Jason Giambi Jsy/500 4.00
19 Dave Righetti Jsy/250 4.00
20 Mike Schmidt Jsy/20
21 Roger Clemens Jsy/250 10.00
22 Juan Gonzalez Jsy/150 4.00
23 Carlos Delgado Jsy/150 4.00
24 Manny Ramirez Jsy/50 10.00
25 Jim Thome Jsy/500 4.00
26 Wade Boggs Jsy/250 6.00
27 Luis Tiant Pants/500 4.00
28 Kerry Wood Jsy/50 4.00
29 Rod Carew Jkt/250 6.00
30 Dwight Evans Jsy/50 6.00
31 Mike Piazza Jsy/250 8.00
32 Billy Williams Jsy/100 4.00
33 Larry Walker Jsy/500 4.00
34 Nolan Ryan Pants/100 15.00
35 Edgar Renteria Jsy/500 4.00
36 Greg Maddux Jsy/375 8.00
37 Gaylord Perry Jsyu/250 4.00
38 Curt Schilling Jsy/500 4.00
39 Dave Parker Jsy/50 4.00
40 Andruw Jones Jsy/500 4.00
41 Orlando Cepeda Pants/250 4.00
42 Fergie Jenkins Jsy/250 4.00
43 Kirby Puckett Jsy/400 6.00
44 Reggie Jackson Jsy/250 6.00
45 Bob Gibson Jsy/100 8.00
46 Rickey Henderson Jsy/500 6.00
47 Lee Smith Jsy/250 4.00
49 Fred Lynn Jsy/250 4.00
50 Lance Berkman Jsy/500 4.00
51 Shawn Green Jsy/500 4.00
52 Hoyt Wilhelm Jsy/250 4.00
53 Sammy Sosa Jsy/500 8.00
54 Tim Hudson Jsy/500 4.00
55 Matt Williams Jsy/250 4.00
56 Marty Marion Jsy/5
57 Eric Chavez Jsy/500 4.00
58 Rafael Palmeiro Jsy/500 6.00
59 Randy Johnson Jsy/250 6.00
60 David Ortiz Jsy/500 8.00
61 Hank Blalock Jsy/50 4.00
62 Jim Rice Pants/250 4.00
63 Mark Mulder Jsy/100 4.00
64 Kazuo Matsui Jsy/500 4.00
65 Pedro Martinez Jsy/250 6.00
66 Sean Casey Jsy/500 4.00
67 Carlos Lee Jsy/500 4.00
68 Stan Musial Pants/100 20.00
69 Fred McGriff Jsy/500 4.00
70 Darryl Strawberry Jsy/250 4.00
71 Tommy John Jsy/250 4.00
72 Hideo Nomo Jsy/500 6.00
73 Johnny Bench Pants/100 8.00
74 Cal Ripken Jr. Jsy/250 20.00
75 Harold Baines Jsy/250 4.00

Throwback Col. Mat. Combo

NM/M

Production 5-100
1 Billy Martin Jsy-Pants/100 10.00
2 Tony Gwynn Jsy-Pants/100 12.00
3 Babe Ruth Bat-Pants/20
4 Angel Berroa Bat-Pants/100 4.00
5 Jeff Bagwell Jsy-Pants/100 8.00
6 Tony Oliva Bat-Jsy/100 6.00
7 Ivan Rodriguez Chest Prot-Jsy/100 8.00
8 Gary Carter Jsy-Pants/100 4.00
9 Ted Williams Bat-Jsy/20
10 Chipper Jones Bat-Jsy/100 8.00
11 Al Oliver Bat-Jsy/100 6.00
12 Roberto Alomar Bat-Jsy/100 8.00
13 Omar Vizquel Bat-Jsy/100 6.00
14 Ernie Banks Bat-Jsy/20
15 Carlos Beltran Bat-Jsy/100 8.00
17 Mark Grace Bat-Jsy/50 10.00
18 Jason Giambi Jsy-Jsy/100 6.00
19 Dave Righetti Jsy-Jsy/100 6.00
20 Mike Schmidt Bat-Jsy/5
21 Roger Clemens Jsy-Jsy/100 15.00
22 Juan Gonzalez Bat-Jsy/100 6.00
23 Carlos Delgado Bat-Jsy/100 4.00
24 Manny Ramirez Bat-Jsy/5
26 Wade Boggs Bat-Jsy/100 10.00
28 Kerry Wood Jsy-Pants/20
29 Rod Carew Jkt-Jsy/100 10.00
30 Dwight Evans Bat-Jsy/10
33 Larry Walker Jsy-Jsy/100 6.00
34 Nolan Ryan Bat-Pants/100 20.00
36 Greg Maddux Jsy-Jsy/100 12.00
38 Curt Schilling Jsy-Jsy/100 6.00
40 Andruw Jones Bat-Jsy/100 8.00
41 Orlando Cepeda Bat-Pants/100 8.00
42 Fergie Jenkins Hat-Jsy/5
43 Kirby Puckett Bat-Jsy/100 12.00
44 Reggie Jackson Bat-Jsy/100 10.00
46 Rickey Henderson Bat-Jsy/100 10.00
47 Lee Smith Jsy-Jsy/100 6.00
48 Lou Brock Bat-Jsy/5
49 Fred Lynn Bat-Jsy/100 4.00
50 Lance Berkman Bat-Jsy/100 4.00
51 Shawn Green Bat-Jsy/100 4.00
52 Hoyt Wilhelm Jsy-Jsy/100 4.00
53 Sammy Sosa Hat-Jsy/100 8.00
54 Tim Hudson Jsy-Jsy/100 4.00
57 Eric Chavez Jsy-Jsy/50 6.00
58 Rafael Palmeiro Bat-Jsy/100 8.00
59 Randy Johnson Jsy-Pants/100 10.00
60 David Ortiz Bat-Jsy/100 10.00
61 Hank Blalock Jsy-Jsy/50 6.00
62 Jim Rice Jsy-Pants/100 6.00
64 Kazuo Matsui Bat-Jsy/100 4.00
65 Pedro Martinez Jsy-Jsy/100 8.00
66 Sean Casey Jsy-Pants/100 4.00
67 Carlos Lee Hat-Jsy/100 4.00
68 Stan Musial Bat-Pants/25
69 Fred McGriff Bat-Jsy/100 8.00
70 Darryl Strawberry Jsy-Jsy/100 6.00
71 Tommy John Bat-Jsy/100 4.00
72 Hideo Nomo Jsy-Jsy/100 10.00
73 Johnny Bench Bat-Pants/100 12.00
74 Cal Ripken Jr. Bat-Jsy/100 30.00
75 Harold Baines Bat-Jsy/100 4.00

Throwback Col. Sign. Mat.

NM/M

Production 5-50
2 Tony Gwynn Jsy/50 40.00
4 Angel Berroa Pants/50 10.00
5 Jeff Bagwell Jsy/20
6 Tony Oliva Jsy/50 20.00
8 Gary Carter Pants/50 20.00
10 Chipper Jones Jsy/20
12 Roberto Alomar Jsy/50 30.00
13 Omar Vizquel Jsy/50 30.00
14 Ernie Banks Jsy/20
15 Carlos Beltran Jsy/50 30.00
16 Garret Anderson Jsy/20
17 Mark Grace Jsy/50 30.00
19 Dave Righetti Jsy/50 20.00
20 Mike Schmidt Jsy/5
21 Roger Clemens Jsy/5
24 Manny Ramirez Jsy/5
26 Wade Boggs Jsy/50 35.00
27 Luis Tiant Pants/50 20.00
28 Kerry Wood Jsy/20
29 Rod Carew Jkt/50 30.00
30 Dwight Evans Jsy/25 25.00
32 Billy Williams Jsy/50 20.00
34 Nolan Ryan Pants/20
35 Edgar Renteria Jsy/50 20.00
37 Gaylord Perry Jsy/50 15.00
38 Curt Schilling Jsy/5
39 Dave Parker Jsy/50 20.00
41 Orlando Cepeda Pants/25 25.00
42 Fergie Jenkins Jsy/50 20.00
43 Kirby Puckett Jsy/10
44 Reggie Jackson Jsy/25 50.00
45 Bob Gibson Jsy/25 40.00
46 Rickey Henderson Jsy/5
49 Fred Lynn Jsy/50 20.00
51 Shawn Green Jsy/5
54 Tim Hudson Jsy/25 25.00
55 Matt Williams Jsy/50 30.00
56 Marty Marion Jsy/20
57 Eric Chavez Jsy/50 20.00
60 David Ortiz Jsy/5
61 Hank Blalock Jsy/5
62 Jim Rice Pants/50 25.00
63 Mark Mulder Jsy/50 20.00
65 Pedro Martinez Jsy/5
66 Sean Casey Jsy/50 20.00
67 Carlos Lee Jsy/50 20.00
68 Stan Musial Pants/25 75.00
70 Darryl Strawberry Jsy/50 20.00
71 Tommy John Jsy/50 15.00
72 Hideo Nomo Jsy/5
73 Johnny Bench Pants/25
74 Cal Ripken Jr. Jsy/10
75 Harold Baines Jsy/50 15.00

Throw. Col. Sign. Mat. Combo

NM/M

Production 5-25
2 Tony Gwynn Jsy-Pants/25 50.00
4 Angel Berroa Bat-Pants/25 15.00
6 Tony Oliva Bat-Jsy/25 25.00
8 Gary Carter Jsy-Pants/25 25.00
12 Roberto Alomar Bat-Jsy/25 40.00
15 Carlos Beltran Bat-Jsy/25 35.00
17 Mark Grace Bat-Jsy/25 35.00
19 Dave Righetti Jsy-Jsy/25 25.00
26 Wade Boggs Bat-Jsy/25 40.00
29 Rod Carew Jkt-Jsy/25 40.00
44 Reggie Jackson Bat-Jsy/25 50.00
49 Fred Lynn Bat-Jsy/25 25.00
62 Jim Rice Jsy-Pants/25 30.00
67 Carlos Lee Hat-Jsy/25 25.00
68 Stan Musial Bat-Pants/25 75.00
70 Darryl Strawberry Jsy-Jsy/25 20.00
75 Harold Baines Bat-Jsy/25 20.00

2005 DONRUSS TIMELESS TREASURES

NM/M

Complete Set (100):
Common Player: 1.50
Production 799 Sets
Tin (4): 100.00
1 David Ortiz 3.00
2 Derek Jeter 8.00
3 Edgar Renteria 2.00
4 Paul Molitor 3.00
5 Jeff Bagwell 2.00
6 Melvin Mora 1.50
7 Bobby Crosby 1.50
8 Cal Ripken Jr. 10.00
9 Hank Blalock 2.00
10 Hideo Nomo 2.00
11 Gary Sheffield 2.00
12 Alfonso Soriano 3.00
13 Carl Crawford 1.50
14 Paul Konerko 1.50
15 Jim Edmonds 2.00
16 Garret Anderson 2.00
17 Lance Berkman 1.50
18 Javy Lopez 1.50
19 Tony Gwynn 3.00
20 Mark Mulder 1.50
21 Sammy Sosa 5.00
22 Roger Clemens 8.00
23 Mark Teixeira 2.00
24 Miguel Cabrera 3.00
25 Jim Thome 3.00
26 Mike Piazza 4.00
27 Vladimir Guerrero 3.00
28 Austin Kearns 1.50
29 Rod Carew 3.00
30 Ken Griffey Jr. 5.00
31 Mike Piazza 4.00
32 David Wright 3.00
33 Jason Varitek 2.00
34 Kerry Wood 3.00
35 Frank Thomas 2.00
36 Mark Prior 3.00
37 Mike Mussina 2.00
38 Curt Schilling 3.00
39 Greg Maddux 4.00
40 Miguel Tejada 3.00
41 Tom Seaver 3.00
42 Mariano Rivera 2.00
43 Jason Giambi 1.50
44 Roy Oswalt 1.50
45 Pedro Martinez 3.00
46 *Jeff Niemann* 5.00
47 Tom Glavine 1.50
48 Torii Hunter 1.50
49 Scott Rolen 3.00
50 Curt Schilling 3.00
51 Randy Johnson 3.00
52 C.C. Sabathia 1.50
53 Rafael Palmeiro 2.00
54 Jake Peavy 2.00
55 Hideki Matsui 6.00
56 Ichiro Suzuki 6.00
57 Johan Santana 3.00
58 Todd Helton 2.00
59 *Justin Verlander* 5.00
60 Kazuo Matsui 1.50
61 Rafael Palmeiro 2.00
62 Sean Casey 1.50
63 Nolan Ryan 8.00
64 Magglio Ordonez 1.50
65 Craig Biggio 2.00
66 Vernon Wells 1.50
67 Manny Ramirez 3.00
68 Aramis Ramirez 2.00
69 Omar Vizquel 1.50
70 Eric Gagne 1.50
71 Troy Glaus 2.00
72 Carlton Fisk 2.00
73 Victor Martinez 1.50
74 Adrian Beltre 2.00
75 Barry Zito 1.50
76 Josh Beckett 2.00
77 Michael Young 1.50
78 Eric Chavez 1.50
79 Hideo Nomo 2.00
80 Andruw Jones 2.00
81 Ivan Rodriguez 2.00
82 Don Mattingly 6.00
83 Larry Walker 2.00
84 *Philip Humber* 5.00
85 Juan Gonzalez 1.50
86 Tim Hudson 2.00
87 Alex Rodriguez 6.00
88 Greg Maddux 4.00
89 J.D. Drew 2.00
90 Shawn Green 1.50
91 Roger Clemens 8.00
92 Nomar Garciaparra 4.00
93 Andy Pettitte 2.00
94 Khalil Greene 1.50
95 Mike Schmidt 5.00
96 Carlos Beltran 2.00
97 Mike Mussina 2.00
98 Ben Sheets 1.50
99 Chipper Jones 3.00
100 Albert Pujols 8.00

Bronze

Bronze: 1-2X
Production 100 sets

Gold

Gold: 3-5X
Production 25 sets

Platinum

No Pricing
Production one set

Silver

Gold: 2-3X
Production 50 sets

Award Materials Number

NM/M

Production 1-29
Prime: No Pricing
Production 1-5
9 Jim Palmer Pants/22 12.00
10 Rod Carew Jsy/29 15.00
12 Mike Schmidt Jsy/20 25.00
13 Robin Yount Jsy/19 25.00
15 Roger ClemensJsy/21 25.00

Award Mat. Sign. Year

NM/M

Production 1-25
Prime: No Pricing
Production 1-5
6 Johnny Bench Jsy/25 60.00
9 Jim Palmer Pants/25 35.00
10 Rod Carew Jsy/25 50.00
12 Mike Schmidt Jsy/25 75.00
14 Dale MurphyJsy/25 50.00

Award Materials Year

NM/M

Production 1-99
1 Lou Boudreau Jsy/48 20.00
2 Roger Maris Pants/61 40.00
6 Johnny Bench Jsy/72 15.00
9 Jim Palmer Pants/76 10.00
10 Rod Carew Jsy/77 10.00
12 Mike Schmidt Jsy/81 20.00
13 Robin Yount Jsy/89 15.00
14 Dale Murphy Jsy/83 10.00
15 Roger Clemens Jsy/86 20.00
16 Cal Ripken Jr. Jsy/91 40.00
17 Tom Glavine Jsy/91 8.00
18 Frank Thomas Jsy/94 10.00
19 Jeff Bagwell Pants/94 8.00
20 Randy Johnson Jsy/95 10.00
21 Pedro Martinez Jsy/97 10.00
22 Ivan Rodriguez Jsy/99 10.00

Game Day Materials

NM/M

Production 5-100
1 Rod Carew Hat/25 20.00
2 Kirby Puckett Bat/100 15.00
5 Nellie Fox Bat/25 60.00
6 Vladimir Guerrero Fld Glv/25 15.00
7 Tony Gwynn Jsy/100 15.00
8 Rickey Henderson Bat/100 10.00
9 David Ortiz Hat/100 15.00
10 Carlos Beltran Jsy/50 10.00

Game Day Mat. Sign.

NM/M

Production 3-25
7 Tony Gwynn Jsy/25 50.00

Gamers NY

NM/M

Production 25 Sets
1 Jim Thorpe Jsy-Jsy/25 450.00
2 Willie Mays Jsy-Pants/25 75.00
3 Nolan Ryan Bat-Jsy/25 65.00

Gamers NY Signatures

NM/M

Production 25 Sets
2 Willie Mays Jsy-Pants/25 250.00
3 Nolan Ryan Bat-Jsy/25 125.00

HOF Cuts Materials

No Pricing
Production 1-10

HOF Materials Bat

NM/M

Production 5-50
1 Pee Wee Reese/25 20.00
2 Red Schoendienst/5
3 Harmon Killebrew/25 20.00
4 Hack Wilson/50 65.00
5 Brooks Robinson/50 20.00
6 Stan Musial/50 30.00
8 Carl Yastrzemski/50 20.00
9 Ted Williams/50 50.00
11 Luis Aparicio/25 15.00
12 Bobby Doerr/25 15.00
14 Ernie Banks/50 20.00
15 Ralph Kiner/25 20.00
18 Willie McCovey/5
20 Mike Schmidt/50 20.00
21 Roberto Clemente/50 75.00
24 Willie Mays/50 40.00
25 Willie Stargell/25 25.00
26 Frank Robinson/50 10.00
28 Reggie Jackson/50 15.00
30 Orlando Cepeda/50 10.00
34 Nolan Ryan/50 30.00
35 George Brett/50 25.00
39 Nellie Fox/50 40.00
43 Johnny Bench/50 20.00
44 Hank Aaron/50 40.00
48 Yogi Berra/5
50 Al Kaline/50 20.00

HOF Materials Combos

NM/M

Production 1-25
Prime: No Pricing
Production 1-5
3 Harmon Killebrew Bat-Jsy/25 25.00
5 Brooks Robinson Bat-Jsy/25 30.00
6 Stan Musial Bat-Jsy/25 40.00
8 Carl Yastrzemski Bat-Jsy/25 30.00
9 Ted Williams Bat-Jsy/25 85.00
12 Bobby Doerr Bat-Pants/25 15.00
14 Ernie Banks Bat-Jsy/25 25.00
18 Willie McCovey Jsy-Pants/25 25.00
20 Mike Schmidt Bat-Jsy/25 30.00
24 Willie Mays Bat-Jsy/25 75.00
25 Willie Stargell Bat-Jsy/25 30.00
28 Reggie Jackson Bat-Jsy/25 30.00
29 Warren Spahn Jsy-Pants/25 30.00
34 Nolan Ryan Jsy-Pants/25 50.00
35 George Brett Bat-Jsy/25 30.00
43 Johnny Bench Bat-Jsy/25 25.00
44 Hank Aaron Bat-Jsy/25 60.00

HOF Materials Jersey

NM/M

Production 1-100
Prime: No Pricing
Production 1-5
3 Harmon Killebrew/100 15.00
5 Brooks Robinson/50 15.00
6 Stan Musial/100 25.00
8 Carl Yastrzemski/100 15.00
9 Ted Williams/100 60.00

14 Ernie Banks/100 15.00
16 Whitey Ford/100 15.00
17 Duke Snider/25 20.00
18 Willie McCovey/25 20.00
20 Mike Schmidt/50 25.00
22 Jim Palmer/25 12.00
23 Enos Slaughter/50 15.00
24 Willie Mays/100 40.00
25 Willie Stargell/50 20.00
28 Reggie Jackson/25 25.00
29 Warren Spahn/25 25.00
31 Hoyt Wilhelm/50 10.00
32 Sandy Koufax/25 250.00
33 Hal Newhouser/50 10.00
34 Nolan Ryan/50 30.00
35 George Brett/50 25.00
37 Jim "Catfish" Hunter/25 15.00
38 Frankie Frisch Jkt/50 15.00
40 Lou Boudreau/25 15.00
43 Johnny Bench/50 15.00
44 Hank Aaron/100 40.00
45 Joe Cronin/50 20.00
49 Early Wynn/50 15.00

HOF Mat. Jersey Number

NM/M

Production 1-44
18 Willie McCovey/44 15.00
20 Mike Schmidt/20 30.00
22 Jim Palmer/22 12.00
24 Willie Mays/24 65.00
28 Reggie Jackson/44 15.00
29 Warren Spahn/21 25.00
31 Hoyt Wilhelm/31 10.00
32 Sandy Koufax/32 250.00
34 Nolan Ryan/34 30.00
37 Jim "Catfish" Hunter/29 15.00
44 Hank Aaron/44 50.00
49 Early Wynn/24 15.00

HOF Materials Pants

NM/M

Production 1-50
6 Stan Musial/50 30.00
8 Carl Yastrzemski/50 20.00
12 Bobby Doerr/50 10.00
17 Duke Snider/25 20.00
18 Willie McCovey/50 15.00
19 Bob Feller/25 20.00
22 Jim Palmer/25 10.00
24 Willie Mays/50 40.00
29 Warren Spahn/25 25.00
30 Orlando Cepeda/50 10.00
34 Nolan Ryan/50 25.00
42 Burleigh Grimes/50 75.00
43 Johnny Bench/50 15.00
45 Joe Cronin/50 20.00
46 Fergie Jenkins/50 10.00

HOF Mat. Sign. Bat

NM/M

Production 1-25
3 Harmon Killebrew/25 50.00
5 Brooks Robinson/25 50.00
6 Stan Musial/25 85.00
11 Luis Aparicio/25 25.00
12 Bobby Doerr/25 25.00
15 Ralph Kiner/25 50.00
20 Mike Schmidt/25 75.00
24 Willie Mays/25 240.00
26 Frank Robinson/25 40.00
30 Orlando Cepeda/25 25.00
34 Nolan Ryan/25 120.00
43 Johnny Bench/25 60.00
50 Al Kaline/25 50.00

HOF Mat. Sign. Combos

NM/M

Production 1-25
Prime: No Pricing
Production 1-5
3 Harmon Killebrew Bat-Jsy/25 65.00
5 Brooks Robinson Bat-Jsy/25 65.00
6 Stan Musial Bat-Jsy/25 100.00
12 Bobby Doerr Bat-Pants/25 30.00
18 Willie McCovey Jsy-Pants/25 60.00
20 Mike Schmidt Bat-Jsy/25 85.00
24 Willie Mays Bat-Jsy/25 250.00
30 Orlando Cepeda Bat-Pants/25 30.00
34 Nolan Ryan Jsy-Pants/25 120.00
43 Johnny Bench Bat-Jsy/25 60.00

HOF Materials Sign. Hat

Production 5-10

HOF Mat. Sign. Jersey

NM/M

Production 1-25
Prime: No Pricing
Production 1-5
3 Harmon Killebrew/25 50.00
5 Brooks Robinson/25 50.00
6 Stan Musial/25 85.00
17 Duke Snider/25 40.00
18 Willie McCovey/25 50.00
20 Mike Schmidt/25 75.00
22 Jim Palmer/25 40.00
24 Willie Mays/25 240.00
34 Nolan Ryan/25 120.00
43 Johnny Bench/25 60.00

HOF Mat. Sign. Pants

NM/M

Production 1-50
6 Stan Musial/25 85.00
12 Bobby Doerr/50 25.00
17 Duke Snider/25 40.00
18 Willie McCovey/25 50.00
22 Jim Palmer/25 40.00
24 Willie Mays/25 240.00
30 Orlando Cepeda/25 25.00
34 Nolan Ryan/25 120.00
43 Johnny Bench/25 60.00
46 Fergie Jenkins/25 30.00

HOF Silver

NM/M

Common Player: 4.00
Production 500 Sets
Gold: 2X-4X
Production 25 Sets
Platinum: No Pricing
Production One Set
1 Pee Wee Reese 4.00
2 Red Schoendienst 4.00
3 Harmon Killebrew 5.00
4 Hack Wilson 5.00
5 Brooks Robinson 5.00
6 Stan Musial 6.00
7 Al Simmons 4.00
8 Carl Yastrzemski 5.00
9 Ted Williams 8.00
10 Phil Rizzuto 4.00
11 Luis Aparicio 4.00
12 Bobby Doerr 4.00
13 Bob Lemon 4.00
14 Ernie Banks 5.00
15 Ralph Kiner 4.00
16 Whitey Ford 4.00
17 Duke Snider 4.00
18 Willie McCovey 4.00
19 Bob Feller 4.00
20 Mike Schmidt 6.00
21 Roberto Clemente 8.00
22 Jim Palmer 4.00
23 Enos Slaughter 4.00
24 Willie Mays 8.00
25 Willie Stargell 4.00
26 Frank Robinson 4.00
27 Carl Hubbell 4.00
28 Reggie Jackson 4.00
29 Warren Spahn 5.00
30 Orlando Cepeda 4.00
31 Hoyt Wilhelm 4.00
32 Sandy Koufax 15.00
33 Hal Newhouser 4.00
34 Nolan Ryan 8.00
35 George Brett 6.00
36 Bill Dickey 4.00
37 Jim "Catfish" Hunter 4.00
38 Frankie Frisch 4.00
39 Nellie Fox 4.00
40 Lou Boudreau 4.00
41 Hank Greenberg 5.00
42 Burleigh Grimes 4.00
43 Johnny Bench 5.00
44 Hank Aaron 8.00
45 Joe Cronin 4.00
46 Fergie Jenkins 4.00
47 Luke Appling 4.00
48 Yogi Berra 5.00
49 Early Wynn 4.00
50 Al Kaline 5.00

Home Road Gamers Duos

NM/M

Production 1-100
Prime: No Pricing
Production 1-10
3 Babe Ruth Jsy-Jsy/25 450.00
4 Paul Molitor Jsy-Pants/100 15.00
7 Ivan Rodriguez Jsy-Jsy/100 10.00
9 Ted Williams Jsy-Jsy/25 85.00
10 Andre Dawson Jsy-Jsy/25 15.00
11 Darryl Strawberry Jsy-Jsy/25 12.00
14 Ernie Banks Jsy-Jsy/25 30.00
15 Jim Edmonds Jsy-Jsy/25 15.00
16 Bo Jackson Jsy-Jsy/25 20.00
17 Mark Grace Jsy-Jsy/100 15.00
18 Albert Pujols Jsy-Jsy/100 25.00
19 Tony Gwynn Jsy-Jsy/100 15.00
20 Cal Ripken Jr. Jsy-Jsy/100 40.00
21 Chipper Jones Jsy-Jsy/50 15.00
23 Don Mattingly Jsy-Jsy/100 25.00
24 Willie Mays Jsy-Jsy/25 80.00
25 Tony Oliva Jsy-Jsy/50 10.00
28 Reggie Jackson Jsy-Jsy/100 15.00
29 Rod Carew Jsy-Jsy/100 15.00
30 Harmon Killebrew Jsy-Jsy/25 25.00
32 Nolan Ryan Jsy-Jsy/100 30.00
33 Eddie Murray Jsy-Pants/100 15.00
35 Rickey Henderson Jsy-Jsy/50 15.00
36 Jim Rice Jsy-Jsy/50 12.00
37 Hoyt Wilhelm Jsy-Jsy/50 10.00
38 Curt Schilling Jsy-Jsy/100 10.00
42 Greg Maddux Jsy-Jsy/100 15.00
43 Dennis Eckersley Jsy-Jsy/50 10.00
44 Willie McCovey Jsy-Pants/100 15.00
45 Willie Stargell Jsy-Jsy/50 20.00
46 Mike Mussina Jsy-Pants/50 15.00
47 Gary Carter Jsy-Jsy/50 15.00
48 Dale Murphy Jsy-Jsy/50 15.00
49 Mike Piazza Jsy-Jsy/50 20.00
50 Jim Palmer Jsy-Pants/100 10.00

Home Road Gamers Sig. Duos

NM/M

Production 1-25
4 Paul Molitor Jsy-Pants/25 60.00
11 Darryl Strawberry Jsy-Jsy/25 30.00
17 Mark Grace Jsy-Jsy/25 50.00
19 Tony Gwynn Jsy-Jsy/25 50.00
23 Don Mattingly Jsy-Jsy/25 80.00
25 Tony Oliva Jsy-Jsy/25 30.00
29 Rod Carew Jsy-Jsy/25 50.00
30 Harmon Killebrew Jsy-Jsy/25 50.00
36 Jim Rice Jsy-Jsy/25 35.00
43 Dennis Eckersley Jsy-Jsy/25 30.00
44 Willie McCovey Jsy-Pants/25 50.00
47 Gary Carter Jsy-Jsy/25 30.00
48 Dale Murphy Jsy-Jsy/25 50.00
50 Jim Palmer Jsy-Pants/25 40.00

Home Road Gamers Trios

NM/M

Production 1-100
Prime: No Pricing
Production 1-10
4 Paul Molitor Bat-Jsy-Pants/100 25.00
7 Ivan Rodriguez Jsy-Jsy-Jsy/100 15.00
9 Ted Williams Bat-Jsy-Jsy/25 120.00
11 Darryl Strawberry Fld Glv-Jsy-Jsy/25 20.00
14 Ernie Banks Bat-Jsy-Jsy/25 40.00
15 Jim Edmonds Bat-Jsy-Jsy/25 25.00
17 Mark Grace Bat-Jsy-Jsy/100 20.00
18 Albert Pujols Bat-Jsy-Jsy/100 40.00
19 Tony Gwynn Jsy-Jsy-Jsy/100 25.00
20 Cal Ripken Jr. Jsy-Jsy-Jsy/100 60.00
21 Chipper Jones Bat-Jsy-Jsy/25 20.00
23 Don Mattingly Bat-Jsy-Jsy/100 30.00
24 Willie Mays Bat-Jsy-Jsy/25 75.00
25 Tony Oliva Bat-Jsy-Jsy/25 20.00
28 Reggie Jackson Bat-Jsy-Jsy/100 20.00
29 Rod Carew Bat-Jsy-Jsy/100 20.00
30 Harmon Killebrew Bat-Jsy-Jsy/25 35.00
32 Nolan Ryan Jkt-Jsy-Jsy/100 35.00
33 Eddie Murray Jsy-Jsy-Pants/100 20.00
35 Rickey Henderson Bat-Jsy-Jsy/100 20.00
36 Jim Rice Bat-Jsy-Jsy/25 20.00
38 Curt Schilling Bat-Jsy-Jsy/50 15.00
44 Willie McCovey Bat-Jsy-Pants/100 20.00
45 Willie Stargell Bat-Jsy-Jsy/50 25.00
46 Mike Mussina Bat-Jsy-Pants/25 35.00
47 Gary Carter Bat-Jsy-Jsy/50 25.00
48 Dale Murphy Bat-Jsy-Jsy/25 30.00
49 Mike Piazza Jsy-Jsy-Jsy/25 35.00

Home Run Materials

NM/M

Production 1-100
1 Ernie Banks Bat/60 15.00
2 Roger Maris Bat/61 50.00
4 Johnny Bench Pants/71 10.00
5 Harmon Killebrew Bat/75 10.00
6 Jose Canseco Bat/25 15.00
7 Cal Ripken Jr. Ball/10
8 Sammy Sosa Jsy/100 10.00
9 Jim Thome Jsy/50 10.00
10 Rafael Palmeiro Jsy/50 8.00

Home Run Materials Sig.

NM/M

Production 3-25
1 Ernie Banks Bat/25 60.00
3 Ron Santo Ball/5
4 Johnny Bench Pants/25 60.00
5 Harmon Killebrew Bat/25 50.00
6 Jose Canseco Bat/3
7 Cal Ripken Jr. Ball/5
8 Sammy Sosa Jsy/5
10 Rafael Palmeiro Jsy/10

Material Ink Bat

No Pricing
Production 1-10

Material Ink Combos

NM/M

Production 1-25
Prime: No Pricing
Production 1-5

2 Fred Lynn Bat-Jsy/25 35.00
8 Gary Carter Bat-Jsy/25 30.00
10 Andre Dawson Bat-Jsy/25 30.00
11 Luis Aparicio Bat-Jsy/25 30.00
14 Darryl Strawberry Bat-Jsy/25 30.00
27 Carlton Fisk Bat-Jsy/25 40.00
37 Miguel Cabrera Bat-Jsy/25 50.00
39 Dave Parker Bat-Jsy/25 25.00
48 Mark Grace Bat-Jsy/25 40.00

Material Ink Jersey

NM/M

Production 1-50
2 Fred Lynn/50 15.00
3 Dale Murphy/50 30.00
4 Paul Molitor/50 30.00
5 Alan Trammell/50 15.00
8 Gary Carter/50 20.00
10 Andre Dawson/50 20.00
11 Luis Aparicio/50 15.00
14 Darryl Strawberry/50 15.00
18 Kirk Gibson/50 20.00
20 Don Sutton/25 20.00
23 Don Mattingly Jkt/25 75.00
24 Tony Perez/50 25.00
27 Carlton Fisk/25 40.00
29 Fred McGriff/25 40.00
30 John Kruk/25 50.00
32 Dwight Evans/50 25.00
33 Gary Sheffield/25 50.00
34 Bo Jackson/25 65.00
36 Gaylord Perry/50 20.00
39 Dave Parker/25 20.00
42 Harmon Killebrew/50 50.00
43 Dennis Eckersley/25 25.00
44 Willie McCovey/25 50.00
46 Luis Tiant/50 20.00
48 Mark Grace/25 40.00

Mat. Ink Jersey Number

NM/M

Production 1-44
2 Fred Lynn/19 30.00
14 Darryl Strawberry/44 20.00
20 Don Sutton/20 25.00
22 Mark Prior/22 70.00
23 Don Mattingly Jkt/23 80.00
24 Tony Perez/34 30.00
27 Carlton Fisk/27 40.00
29 Fred McGriff/29 40.00
30 John Kruk/29 50.00
32 Dwight Evans/24 35.00
36 Gaylord Perry/36 20.00
40 Mark Teixeira/23 40.00
43 Dennis Eckersley/43 20.00
44 Willie McCovey/44 40.00
46 Luis Tiant/27 25.00

Milestone Mat. Number

NM/M

Production 1-31
2 Nolan Ryan Jsy/30 35.00
10 Greg Maddux Jsy/31 20.00

Materials Signature Year

NM/M

Production 1-25
Prime: No Pricing
Production 1-10
2 Nolan Ryan Jsy/25 120.00
4 Rollie Fingers Jsy/10
5 Steve Garvey Jsy/25 25.00
6 Wade Boggs Jsy/10
7 Tony Gwynn Jsy/25 40.00
8 Sammy Sosa Jsy/1
9 Randy Johnson Jsy/5
10 Greg Maddux Jsy/1

Milestone Material Year

NM/M

Production 10-25
Prime: No Pricing
Production 1-10
1 Roger Maris Pants/25 40.00
2 Nolan Ryan Jsy/25 30.00
4 Rollie Fingers Jsy/10
5 Steve Garvey Jsy/25 10.00
6 Wade Boggs Jsy/25 20.00
7 Tony Gwynn Jsy/25 20.00
8 Sammy Sosa Jsy/25 20.00
9 Randy JohnsonJsy/25 15.00
10 Greg Maddux Jsy/25 20.00

No-Hitters

NM/M

Production 3-25
7 Dennis Eckersley, Bert Blyleven/25 35.00
8 Juan Marichal, Gaylord Perry/25 35.00
9 Jim Palmer, Bob Gibson/25 40.00

Materials Number

NM/M

Production 1-44
1 Rod Carew Jsy/29 20.00
6 Juan Marichal Jsy/27 12.00
8 Jim Palmer Hat/22 15.00
16 Kirk Gibson Hat/23 15.00
18 Roger Clemens Jsy/21 25.00
20 David Cone Jsy/44 8.00
23 Deion Sanders Jsy/21 20.00
24 Dwight Gooden Jsy/16 15.00
28 Mike Piazza Jsy/31 20.00
33 Andruw Jones Jsy/25 10.00
34 Vladimir Guerrero Jsy/27 15.00
37 Kerry Wood Jsy/34 15.00
38 Magglio Ordonez Jsy/30 8.00
40 Mark Mulder Jsy/20 10.00
41 Lance Berkman Jsy/17 10.00
42 Alfonso Soriano Jsy/33 10.00
46 Mark Prior Jsy/22 15.00
47 Mark Teixeira Jsy/23 10.00
48 Miguel Cabrera Jsy/20 15.00
50 Victor Martinez Jsy/41 8.00

Material Signature Number

NM/M

Production 1-30
1 Rod Carew Jsy/29 35.00
4 Duke Snider Jsy/25 40.00
6 Juan Marichal Jsy/25 25.00
11 Gary Carter Jsy/25 30.00
12 Robin Yount Jsy/19 65.00
13 Keith Hernandez Jsy/18 35.00
15 Ozzie Smith Jsy/25 50.00
20 David Cone Jsy/25 25.00
21 Gary Sheffield Jsy/25 40.00
24 Dwight Gooden Jsy/25 25.00
38 Magglio Ordonez Jsy/30 20.00
46 Mark Prior Jsy/22 65.00
47 Mark Teixeira Jsy/23 40.00
48 Miguel Cabrera Jsy/20 50.00
50 Victor Martinez Jsy/25 20.00

Materials Signature Year

NM/M

Production 1-25
Prime: No Pricing
Production 1-5
1 Rod Carew Jsy/25 35.00
4 Duke Snider Jsy/25 40.00
6 Juan Marichal Jsy/25 25.00
11 Gary Carter Jsy/25 30.00
12 Robin Yount Jsy/25 65.00
13 Keith Hernandez Jsy/25 30.00
15 Ozzie Smith Jsy/25 50.00
17 Dave Righetti Jsy/25 20.00
20 David Cone Jsy/25 25.00
21 Gary Sheffield Jsy/25 40.00
24 Dwight Gooden Jsy/25 25.00
32 Scott Rolen Jsy/25 50.00
35 Sean Casey Jsy/25 20.00
36 Paul LoDuca Jsy/25 20.00
38 Magglio Ordonez Jsy/25 20.00
39 Vernon Wells Jsy/25 20.00
40 Mark Mulder Jsy/25 25.00
42 Alfonso Soriano Jsy/25 35.00
44 Ben Sheets Jsy/25 25.00
46 Mark Prior Jsy/25 65.00
47 Mark Teixeira Jsy/25 40.00
48 Miguel Cabrera Jsy/25 50.00
49 Travis Hafner Jsy/25 20.00
50 Victor Martinez Jsy/25 20.00

Materials Year

NM/M

Production 1-100
Prime: No Pricing
Production 5 Sets
1 Rod Carew Jsy/100 12.00
4 Duke Snider Jsy/100 12.00
6 Juan Marichal Jsy/100 10.00
11 Gary Carter Jsy/100 8.00
12 Robin Yount Jsy/100 15.00
13 Keith Hernandez Jsy/25 10.00
15 Ozzie Smith Jsy/25 20.00
17 Dave Righetti Jsy/25 10.00
18 Roger Clemens Jsy/100 15.00
19 Greg Maddux Jsy/25 25.00
20 David Cone Jsy/100 8.00
21 Gary Sheffield Jsy/100 10.00
22 Randy Johnson Jsy/100 10.00
23 Deion Sanders Jsy/100 10.00
24 Dwight Gooden Jsy/25 10.00
25 Ivan Rodriguez Jsy/100 8.00
26 Jeff Bagwell Pants/100 8.00
27 Pedro Martinez Jsy/100 10.00
28 Mike Piazza Jsy/100 12.00
29 Chipper Jones Jsy/100 10.00
30 Hideo Nomo Jsy/100 12.00
31 Garret Anderson Jsy/5
32 Scott Rolen Jsy/100 10.00
33 Andruw Jones Jsy/100 8.00
34 Vladimir Guerrero Jsy/100 10.00
35 Sean Casey Jsy/25 10.00
36 Paul LoDuca Jsy/25 8.00
37 Kerry Wood Jsy/100 12.00
38 Magglio Ordonez Jsy/25 8.00
39 Vernon Wells Jsy/25 8.00
40 Mark Mulder Jsy/100 8.00
41 Lance Berkman Jsy/100 8.00
42 Alfonso Soriano Jsy/100 8.00
43 Albert Pujols Jsy/100 20.00
44 Ben Sheets Jsy/25 10.00
45 Roy Oswalt Jsy/25 10.00
46 Mark Prior Jsy/100 10.00
47 Mark Teixeira Jsy/100 8.00
48 Miguel Cabrera Jsy/100 10.00
49 Travis Hafner Jsy/25 10.00
50 Victor Martinez Jsy/25 10.00

Salutations Signature

NM/M

Production 1-24
1 Al Kaline/24 70.00
5 Dale Murphy/24 50.00
7 Duke Snider/24 50.00
11 Johnny Bench/24 60.00
19 Steve Carlton/24 40.00

Signature Bronze

NM/M

Production 10-100
Platinum: No Pricing
Production One Set
3 Edgar Renteria/50 30.00
4 Paul Molitor/100 25.00
7 Bobby Crosby/25 25.00
8 Cal Ripken Jr./25 200.00
9 Hank Blalock/50 20.00
11 Gary Sheffield/50 35.00
12 Alfonso Soriano/50 25.00
14 Paul Konerko/50 20.00
15 Jim Edmonds/50 30.00
16 Garret Anderson/50 20.00
19 Tony Gwynn/100 40.00
20 Mark Mulder/100 20.00
23 Mark Teixeira/50 30.00
24 Miguel Cabrera/50 30.00
28 Austin Kearns/50 15.00
29 Rod Carew/100 25.00
32 David Wright/25 65.00
34 Kerry Wood/50 35.00
36 Mark Prior/100 60.00
41 Tom Seaver/100 40.00
44 Roy Oswalt/25 20.00
46 Jeff Niemann/100 35.00
48 Torii Hunter/50 20.00
49 Scott Rolen/50 40.00
52 C.C. Sabathia/25 25.00
53 Rafael Palmeiro/25 50.00
57 Johan Santana/50 40.00
59 Justin Verlander/100 20.00
61 Rafael Palmeiro/25 50.00
62 Sean Casey/25 20.00
63 Nolan Ryan/100 85.00
64 Magglio Ordonez/50 15.00
65 Craig Biggio/50 30.00
66 Vernon Wells/25 20.00
67 Manny Ramirez/25 50.00
69 Omar Vizquel/50 40.00
72 Carlton Fisk/100 25.00
73 Victor Martinez/50 15.00
74 Adrian Beltre/50 25.00
75 Barry Zito/50 20.00
76 Josh Beckett/25 35.00
77 Michael Young/50 20.00
78 Eric Chavez/50 15.00
82 Don Mattingly/100 60.00
84 Philip Humber/100 25.00
85 Juan Gonzalez/50 25.00
86 Tim Hudson/50 30.00
90 Shawn Green/25 30.00
95 Mike Schmidt/100 50.00
98 Ben Sheets/25 25.00
99 Chipper Jones/25 60.00

Signature Gold

NM/M

Production 3-25
4 Paul Molitor/25 35.00
19 Tony Gwynn/25 50.00
20 Mark Mulder/25 30.00
29 Rod Carew/25 35.00
36 Mark Prior/25 70.00
41 Tom Seaver/25 60.00
63 Nolan Ryan/25 120.00
72 Carlton Fisk/25 35.00
82 Don Mattingly/25 80.00
95 Mike Schmidt/25 85.00

Signature Silver

NM/M

Production 5-50
3 Edgar Renteria/25 40.00
4 Paul Molitor/50 30.00
9 Hank Blalock/25 25.00
11 Gary Sheffield/25 40.00
12 Alfonso Soriano/25 35.00
14 Paul Konerko/25 25.00
15 Jim Edmonds/25 35.00
16 Garret Anderson/25 25.00
19 Tony Gwynn/50 60.00
20 Mark Mulder/50 25.00
23 Mark Teixeira/25 40.00
24 Miguel Cabrera/25 40.00
28 Austin Kearns/25 20.00
29 Rod Carew/50 30.00
34 Kerry Wood/25 40.00
36 Mark Prior/50 50.00
41 Tom Seaver/50 50.00
46 Jeff Niemann/50 40.00
48 Torii Hunter/25 25.00
49 Scott Rolen/25 50.00
57 Johan Santana/25 50.00
59 Justin Verlander/50 25.00
63 Nolan Ryan/50 100.00
64 Magglio Ordonez/25 20.00
65 Craig Biggio/25 35.00
69 Omar Vizquel/25 40.00
72 Carlton Fisk/50 25.00
73 Victor Martinez/25 20.00
74 Adrian Beltre/25 25.00
75 Barry Zito/25 20.00
77 Michael Young/25 20.00
78 Eric Chavez/25 20.00
82 Don Mattingly/50 60.00
84 Philip Humber/50 30.00
85 Juan Gonzalez/25 30.00
86 Tim Hudson/25 40.00
95 Mike Schmidt/50 65.00

Champions Material Number

NM/M

Production 1-47
1 Nolan Ryan Jsy/34 30.00
2 Lee Smith Jsy/47 8.00
4 Kerry Wood Jsy/34 12.00
6 Curt Schilling Jsy/38 10.00
20 Mark Mulder Jsy/20 10.00
21 Roger Clemens Jsy/21 25.00
22 Will Clark Jsy/22 20.00
23 Don Mattingly Jsy/23 25.00
24 Manny Ramirez Jsy/24 12.00
25 Billy Williams Jsy/26 10.00
26 Wade Boggs Jsy/26 15.00
27 Kevin Brown Jsy/27 8.00
29 Adrian Beltre Jsy/29 8.00
32 Sandy Koufax Jsy/32 250.00
33 Jose Canseco Jsy/33 12.00
34 Kirby Puckett Jsy/34 15.00
35 Rickey Henderson Jsy/35 15.00
38 Curt Schilling Jsy/38 10.00
41 Nolan Ryan Jsy/34 30.00
44 Roy Oswalt Jsy/44 8.00

Champions Materials Sign. Number

NM/M

Production 1-34
1 Nolan Ryan Jsy/34 120.00
19 Tony Gwynn Jsy/19 75.00
20 Mark Mulder Jsy/20 25.00
22 Will Clark Jsy/22 40.00
23 Don Mattingly Jsy/23 75.00

26 Wade Boggs Jsy/26 40.00
29 Adrian Beltre Jsy/29 35.00
39 Don Sutton Jsy/20 30.00
41 Nolan Ryan Jsy/34 120.00

Champions Materials Sign. Year

NM/M
Production 1-50
Prime: No Pricing
Production 1-5
1 Nolan Ryan Jsy/50 100.00
3 Harmon Killebrew Jsy/50 40.00
4 Kerry Wood Jsy/25 40.00
8 Cal Ripken Jr. Jsy/25 175.00
9 Barry Zito Jsy/25 25.00
11 Edgar Martinez Jsy/25 40.00
19 Tony Gwynn Jsy/50 60.00
20 Mark Mulder Jsy/25 25.00
22 Will Clark Jsy/25 40.00
23 Don Mattingly Jsy/50 60.00
26 Wade Boggs Jsy/25 40.00
29 Adrian Beltre Jsy/25 35.00
39 Don Sutton Jsy/25 30.00
40 Johan Santana Jsy/25 60.00
41 Nolan Ryan Jsy/50 100.00
43 Lou Brock Jsy/50 40.00
45 Dale Murphy Jsy/50 30.00

Champions Materials Year

NM/M
Production 1-100
Prime: No Pricing
Production 1-5
1 Nolan Ryan Jsy/100 25.00
2 Lee Smith Jsy/25 10.00
3 Harmon Killebrew Jsy/100 12.00
4 Kerry Wood Jsy/100 12.00
5 Albert Pujols Jsy/100 20.00
6 Curt Schilling Jsy/100 8.00
7 Joe Cronin Pants/100 12.00
8 Cal Ripken Jr. Jsy/100 30.00
9 Barry Zito Jsy/100 8.00
10 Miguel Tejada Jsy/100 10.00
11 Edgar Martinez Jsy/25 8.00
14 Andre Dawson Jsy/25 10.00
17 Todd Helton Jsy/100 8.00
19 Tony Gwynn Jsy/100 12.00
20 Mark Mulder Jsy/100 5.00
21 Roger Clemens Jsy/100 15.00
22 Will Clark Jsy/25 20.00
23 Don Mattingly Jsy/100 20.00
24 Manny Ramirez Jsy/25 10.00
25 Billy Williams Jsy/100 8.00
26 Wade Boggs Jsy/100 10.00
27 Kevin Brown Jsy/25 8.00
28 George Brett Jsy/100 20.00
29 Adrian Beltre Jsy/25 10.00
30 Lance Berkman Jsy/100 5.00
31 Sammy Sosa Jsy/100 10.00
32 Sandy Koufax Jsy/25 250.00
33 Jose Canseco Jsy/25 15.00
34 Kirby Puckett Jsy/100 10.00
35 Rickey Henderson Jsy/100 12.00
36 Juan Gonzalez Jsy/100 8.00
37 Orel Hershiser Jsy/1
38 Curt Schilling Jsy/100 8.00
39 Don Sutton Jsy/100 8.00
40 Johan Santana Jsy/100 10.00
41 Nolan Ryan Jsy/100 25.00
42 Mariano Rivera Jsy/25
43 Lou Brock Jsy/100 10.00
44 Roy Oswalt Jsy/25 8.00
45 Dale Murphy Jsy/100 10.00

World Series Materials

NM/M
Production 1-100
1 Frank Robinson Bat/100 10.00
3 Carl Yastrzemski Bat/100 25.00
4 Jack Morris Jsy/50 8.00
5 Wade Boggs Bat/100 12.00
8 Andruw Jones Jsy/100 8.00
10 Darryl Strawberry Jsy/25 10.00

Materials Signatures

NM/M
Production 1-25
Prime: No Pricing
Production 1-10
1 Frank Robinson Bat/25
2 Bob Gibson Ball/1
3 Carl Yastrzemski Bat/10
4 Jack Morris Jsy/25 25.00
5 Wade Boggs Bat/25 40.00
6 Ozzie Smith Jsy/1
7 Rickey Henderson Jsy/5
9 Tom Glavine Jsy/1
10 Darryl Strawberry Jsy/25 25.00

E

2000 E-X

NM/M
Complete Set (90): 80.00
Common Player: .25
Common Prospect (61-90): 3.00
Production 3,499 sets
Pack: 2.75
Box: 50.00
1 Alex Rodriguez 2.50
2 Jeff Bagwell 1.00
3 Mike Piazza 2.00
4 Tony Gwynn 1.50
5 Ken Griffey Jr. 2.00
6 Juan Gonzalez .40
7 Vladimir Guerrero 1.00
8 Cal Ripken Jr. 3.00
9 Mo Vaughn .25
10 Chipper Jones 1.50
11 Derek Jeter 3.00
12 Nomar Garciaparra 1.50
13 Mark McGwire 2.50
14 Sammy Sosa 1.50
15 Pedro Martinez 1.00
16 Greg Maddux 1.50
17 Frank Thomas .75
18 Shawn Green .50
19 Carlos Beltran .50
20 Roger Clemens 1.75
21 Randy Johnson 1.00
22 Bernie Williams .25
23 Carlos Delgado .50
24 Manny Ramirez .75
25 Freddy Garcia .25
26 Barry Bonds 3.00
27 Tim Hudson .40
28 Larry Walker .25
29 Raul Mondesi .25
30 Ivan Rodriguez .65
31 Magglio Ordonez .25
32 Scott Rolen .65
33 Mike Mussina .40
34 J.D. Drew .40
35 Tom Glavine .50
36 Barry Larkin .25
37 Jim Thome .65
38 Erubiel Durazo .25
39 Curt Schilling .50
40 Orlando Hernandez .25
41 Rafael Palmeiro .65
42 Gabe Kapler .25
43 Mark Grace .25
44 Jeff Cirillo .25
45 Jeromy Burnitz .25
46 Sean Casey .35
47 Kevin Millwood .25
48 Vinny Castilla .25
49 Jose Canseco .50
50 Roberto Alomar .30
51 Craig Biggio .25
52 Preston Wilson .25
53 Jeff Weaver .25
54 Robin Ventura .25
55 Ben Grieve .25
56 Troy Glaus .65
57 Jacque Jones .25
58 Brian Giles .25
59 Kevin Brown .25
60 Todd Helton .65
61 Ben Petrick (Prospects) 3.00
62 Chad Hermansen (Prospects) 3.00
63 Kevin Barker (Prospects) 3.00
64 Matt LeCroy (Prospects) 3.00
65 Brad Penny (Prospects) 4.00
66 D.T. Cromer (Prospects) 3.00
67 Steve Lomasney (Prospects) 3.00
68 Cole Liniak (Prospects) 3.00
69 B.J. Ryan (Prospects) 3.00
70 Wilton Veras (Prospects) 3.00
71 *Aaron McNeal* (Prospects) 4.00
72 Nick Johnson (Prospects) 4.00
73 Adam Piatt (Prospects) 3.00
74 Adam Kennedy (Prospects) 3.00
75 Cesar King (Prospects) 3.00
76 Peter Bergeron (Prospects) 3.00
77 Rob Bell (Prospects) 3.00
78 Wily Pena (Prospects) 4.00
79 Ruben Mateo (Prospects) 3.00
80 Kip Wells (Prospects) 3.00
81 Alex Escobar (Prospects) 3.00
82 *Danys Baez* (Prospects) 5.00
83 Travis Dawkins (Prospects) 3.00
84 Mark Quinn (Prospects) 3.00
85 Jimmy Anderson (Prospects) 3.00
86 Rick Ankiel (Prospects) 4.00
87 Alfonso Soriano (Prospects) 5.00
88 Pat Burrell (Prospects) 4.00
89 Eric Munson (Prospects) 3.00
90 Josh Beckett (Prospects) 4.00

Essential Credentials Now

NM/M
Common Player: 8.00
20 Roger Clemens (20) 50.00
21 Randy Johnson (21) 30.00
22 Bernie Williams (22) 10.00
23 Carlos Delgado (23) 25.00
24 Manny Ramirez (24) 30.00
25 Freddy Garcia (25) 10.00
26 Barry Bonds (26) 75.00
27 Tim Hudson (27) 15.00
28 Larry Walker (28) 10.00
29 Raul Mondesi (29) 10.00
30 Ivan Rodriguez (30) 15.00
31 Magglio Ordonez (31) 10.00
32 Scott Rolen (32) 20.00
33 Mike Mussina (33) 15.00
34 J.D. Drew (34) 20.00
35 Tom Glavine (35) 20.00
36 Barry Larkin (36) 15.00
37 Jim Thome (37) 25.00
38 Erubiel Durazo (38) 8.00
39 Curt Schilling (39) 20.00
40 Orlando Hernandez (40) 8.00
41 Rafael Palmeiro (41) 15.00
42 Gabe Kapler (42) 8.00
43 Mark Grace (43) 8.00
44 Jeff Cirillo (44) 8.00
45 Jeromy Burnitz (45) 8.00
46 Sean Casey (46) 8.00
47 Kevin Millwood (47) 8.00
48 Vinny Castilla (48) 8.00
49 Jose Canseco (49) 15.00
50 Roberto Alomar (50) 12.00
51 Craig Biggio (51) 15.00
52 Preston Wilson (52) 8.00
53 Jeff Weaver (53) 8.00
54 Robin Ventura (54) 8.00
55 Ben Grieve (55) 8.00
56 Troy Glaus (56) 15.00
57 Jacque Jones (57) 12.00
58 Brian Giles (58) 8.00
59 Kevin Brown (59) 8.00
60 Todd Helton (60) 20.00
74 Adam Kennedy (14) (Prospects) 15.00
75 Cesar King (15) (Prospects) 15.00
76 Peter Bergeron (16) (Prospects) 15.00
77 Rob Bell (17) (Prospects) 15.00
78 Wily Pena (18) (Prospects) 15.00
79 Ruben Mateo (19) (Prospects) 15.00
80 Kip Wells (20) (Prospects) 15.00
81 Alex Escobar (21) (Prospects) 15.00
82 Danys Baez (22) (Prospects) 15.00
83 Travis Dawkins (23) (Prospects) 15.00
84 Mark Quinn (24) (Prospects) 15.00
85 Jimmy Anderson (25) (Prospects) 15.00
86 Rick Ankiel (26) (Prospects) 15.00
87 Alfonso Soriano (27) (Prospects) 60.00
88 Pat Burrell (28) (Prospects) 30.00
89 Eric Munson (29) (Prospects) 15.00
90 Josh Beckett (30) (Prospects) 20.00

Essential Credentials Future

NM/M
Common Player: 10.00
1 Alex Rodriguez (60) 75.00
2 Jeff Bagwell (59) 30.00
3 Mike Piazza (58) 50.00
4 Tony Gwynn (57) 50.00
5 Ken Griffey Jr.(56) 50.00
6 Juan Gonzalez (55) 15.00
7 Vladimir Guerrero (54) 20.00
8 Cal Ripken Jr. (53) 85.00
9 Mo Vaughn (52) 10.00
10 Chipper Jones (51) 30.00
11 Derek Jeter (50) 85.00
12 Nomar Garciaparra (49) 45.00
13 Mark McGwire (48) 75.00
14 Sammy Sosa (47) 50.00
15 Pedro Martinez(46) 30.00
16 Greg Maddux (45) 50.00
17 Frank Thomas (44) 20.00
18 Shawn Green (43) 10.00
19 Carlos Beltran (42) 10.00
20 Roger Clemens (41) 60.00
21 Randy Johnson (40) 30.00
22 Bernie Williams (39) 10.00
23 Carlos Delgado (38) 15.00
24 Manny Ramirez (37) 20.00
25 Freddy Garcia (36) 10.00
26 Barry Bonds (35) 90.00
27 Tim Hudson (34) 20.00
28 Larry Walker (33) 10.00
29 Raul Mondesi (32) 10.00
30 Ivan Rodriguez (31) 15.00
31 Maglio Ordonez (30) 10.00
32 Scott Rolen (29) 20.00
33 Mike Mussina (28) 25.00
34 J.D. Drew (27) 20.00
35 Tom Glavine (26) 25.00
36 Barry Larkin (25) 15.00
37 Jim Thome (24) 30.00
38 Erubiel Durazo (23) 15.00
39 Curt Schilling (22) 25.00
40 Orlando Hernandez (21) 15.00
41 Rafael Palmeiro (20) 40.00
42 Gabe Kapler (19) 15.00
43 Mark Grace (18) 15.00
44 Jeff Cirillo (17) 15.00
45 Jeromy Burnitz (16) 15.00
46 Sean Casey (15) 15.00
47 Kevin Millwood (14) 20.00
48 Vinny Castilla (13) 20.00
49 Jose Canseco (12) 40.00
50 Roberto Alomar (11) 50.00
51 Craig Biggio (10) 50.00
61 Ben Petrick (30) (Prospects) 10.00
62 Chad Hermansen (29) (Prospects) 10.00
63 Kevin Barker (28) (Prospects) 10.00
64 Matt LeCroy (27) (Prospects) 10.00
65 Brad Penny (26) (Prospects) 10.00
66 D.T. Cromer (25) (Prospects) 10.00
67 Steve Lomasney (24) (Prospects) 10.00
68 Cole Liniak (23) (Prospects) 10.00

#	Player	NM/M
69	B.J. Ryan (22) (Prospects)	10.00
70	Wilton Veras (21) (Prospects)	10.00
71	Aaron McNeal(20) (Prospects)	15.00
72	Nick Johnson (19) (Prospects)	25.00
73	Adam Piatt (18) (Prospects)	15.00
74	Adam Kennedy (17) (Prospects)	15.00
75	Cesar King (16) (Prospects)	15.00
76	Peter Bergeron (15) (Prospects)	15.00
77	Rob Bell (14) (Prospects)	15.00
78	Wily Pena (13) (Prospects)	15.00
79	Ruben Mateo (12) (Prospects)	15.00
80	Kip Wells (11) (Prospects)	15.00
81	Alex Escobar (10) (Prospects)	20.00

Autographics

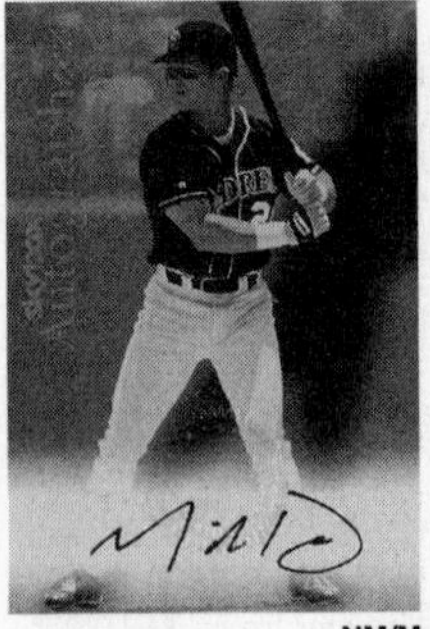

	NM/M
Common Player:	5.00
Inserted 1:24	
Bob Abreu	15.00
Moises Alou	15.00
Rick Ankiel	10.00
Michael Barrett	5.00
Josh Beckett	10.00
Rob Bell	5.00
Adrian Beltre	12.00
Carlos Beltran	15.00
Wade Boggs	25.00
Barry Bonds	150.00
Kent Bottenfield	5.00
Milton Bradley	10.00
Pat Burrell	25.00
Chris Carpenter	6.00
Sean Casey	10.00
Eric Chavez	15.00
Will Clark	25.00
Johnny Damon	20.00
Mike Darr	5.00
Ben Davis	5.00
Russ Davis	5.00
Carlos Delgado	20.00
Jason Dewey	5.00
Octavio Dotel	10.00
J.D. Drew	15.00
Ray Durham	8.00
Damion Easley	6.00
Kelvim Escobar	6.00
Carlos Febles	6.00
Freddy Garcia	10.00
Jeremy Giambi	10.00
Todd Greene	5.00
Jason Grilli	5.00
Vladimir Guerrero	30.00
Tony Gwynn	40.00
Jerry Hairston Jr.	10.00
Mike Hampton	10.00
Todd Helton	20.00
Trevor Hoffman	10.00
Tim Hudson	15.00
John Jaha	6.00
Derek Jeter	100.00
D'Angelo Jimenez	5.00
Randy Johnson	60.00
Jason Kendall	15.00
Adam Kennedy	10.00
Cesar King	5.00
Paul Konerko	8.00
Mark Kotsay	8.00
Ray Lankford	6.00
Jason LaRue	6.00
Matt Lawton	10.00
Carlos Lee	10.00
Mike Lieberthal	10.00
Cole Liniak	5.00
Steve Lomasney	5.00
Jose Macias	5.00
Greg Maddux	50.00
Edgar Martinez	20.00
Pedro Martinez	75.00
Ruben Mateo	8.00
Gary Matthews Jr.	8.00
Aaron McNeal	6.00
Raul Mondesi	10.00
Orber Moreno	5.00
Warren Morris	5.00
Eric Munson	8.00
Heath Murray	5.00
Mike Mussina	30.00
Joe Nathan	5.00
Rafael Palmeiro	30.00
Jim Parque	6.00
Angel Pena	5.00
Wily Pena	8.00
Pokey Reese	6.00
Matt Riley	5.00
Cal Ripken Jr.	100.00
Alex Rodriguez	75.00
Scott Rolen	20.00
Jimmy Rollins	10.00
B.J. Ryan	5.00
Randall Simon	8.00
Chris Singleton	5.00
Alfonso Soriano	60.00
Shannon Stewart	10.00
Mike Sweeney	15.00
Miguel Tejada	20.00
Wilton Veras	5.00
Frank Thomas	25.00
Billy Wagner	12.00
Jeff Weaver	8.00
Rondell White	10.00
Scott Williamson	8.00
Randy Wolf	10.00
Jaret Wright	5.00
Ed Yarnall	5.00
Kevin Young	10.00

E-Xplosive

#		NM/M
	Complete Set (20):	90.00
	Common Player:	2.00
	Production 2,499 sets	
1	Tony Gwynn	6.00
2	Alex Rodriguez	10.00
3	Pedro Martinez	5.00
4	Sammy Sosa	6.00
5	Cal Ripken Jr.	15.00
6	Adam Piatt	2.00
7	Pat Burrell	2.50
8	J.D. Drew	2.50
9	Mike Piazza	8.00
10	Shawn Green	2.50
11	Troy Glaus	4.00
12	Randy Johnson	5.00
13	Juan Gonzalez	2.50
14	Chipper Jones	6.00
15	Ivan Rodriguez	4.00
16	Nomar Garciaparra	6.00
17	Ken Griffey Jr.	8.00
18	Nick Johnson	2.50
19	Mark McGwire	10.00
20	Frank Thomas	5.00

E-Xceptional Red

#		NM/M
	Complete Set (15):	100.00
	Common Player:	3.00
	Inserted 1:14	
	Blue:	2-3X
	Inserted 1:288	
	Green:	1-1.5X
	Production 999 sets	
1	Ken Griffey Jr.	8.00
2	Derek Jeter	15.00
3	Nomar Garciaparra	6.00
4	Mark McGwire	10.00
5	Sammy Sosa	6.00
6	Mike Piazza	8.00
7	Alex Rodriguez	10.00
8	Cal Ripken Jr.	15.00
9	Chipper Jones	6.00
10	Pedro Martinez	4.00
11	Jeff Bagwell	4.00
12	Greg Maddux	6.00
13	Roger Clemens	7.00
14	Tony Gwynn	5.00
15	Frank Thomas	4.00

E-Xciting

#		NM/M
	Complete Set (10):	25.00
	Common Player:	1.00
	Inserted 1:24	
1	Mark McGwire	6.00
2	Ken Griffey Jr.	4.00
3	Randy Johnson	2.00
4	Sammy Sosa	3.00
5	Manny Ramirez	2.00
6	Jose Canseco	1.00
7	Derek Jeter	6.00
8	Scott Rolen	1.50
9	Juan Gonzalez	1.25
10	Barry Bonds	6.00

Generation E-X

#		NM/M
	Complete Set (15):	20.00
	Common Player:	1.00
	Inserted 1:8	
1	Rick Ankiel	1.00
2	Josh Beckett	1.50
3	Carlos Beltran	2.00
4	Pat Burrell	2.00
5	Freddy Garcia	1.00
6	Alex Rodriguez	5.00
7	Derek Jeter	6.00
8	Tim Hudson	1.50
9	Shawn Green	1.50
10	Eric Munson	1.00
11	Adam Piatt	1.00
12	Adam Kennedy	1.00
13	Nick Johnson	1.00
14	Alfonso Soriano	2.00
15	Nomar Garciaparra	4.00

Genuine Coverage

#		NM/M
	Common Player:	5.00
	Inserted 1:144	
1	Alex Rodriguez	40.00
2	Tom Glavine	10.00
3	Cal Ripken Jr.	50.00
4	Edgar Martinez	5.00
5	Raul Mondesi	5.00
6	Carlos Beltran	5.00
7	Chipper Jones	25.00
8	Barry Bonds	50.00
9	Heath Murray	5.00
10	Tim Hudson	10.00
11	Mike Mussina	10.00
12	Derek Jeter	50.00

2001 E-X

#		NM/M
	Complete Set (130):	150.00
	Common Player:	.25
	Common SP (101-130):	4.00
	Production listed	
	Pack (5):	4.00
	Box (24):	80.00
1	Jason Kendall	.25
2	Derek Jeter	3.00
3	Greg Vaughn	.25
4	Eric Chavez	.40
5	Nomar Garciaparra	2.00
6	Roberto Alomar	.50
7	Barry Larkin	.25
8	Matt Lawton	.25
9	Larry Walker	.25
10	Chipper Jones	1.50
11	Scott Rolen	.75
12	Carlos Lee	.25
13	Adrian Beltre	.40
14	Ben Grieve	.25
15	Mike Sweeney	.25
16	John Olerud	.25
17	Gabe Kapler	.25
18	Brian Giles	.25
19	Luis Gonzalez	.40
20	Sammy Sosa	2.00
21	Roger Clemens	1.75
22	Vladimir Guerrero	1.00
23	Ken Griffey Jr.	2.00
24	Mark McGwire	2.50
25	Orlando Hernandez	.25
26	Shannon Stewart	.25
27	Fred McGriff	.25
28	Lance Berkman	.25
29	Carlos Delgado	.75
30	Mike Piazza	2.00
31	Juan Encarnacion	.25
32	David Justice	.25
33	Greg Maddux	1.50
34	Frank Thomas	1.00
35	Jason Giambi	.75
36	Ruben Mateo	.25
37	Todd Helton	1.00
38	Jim Edmonds	.25
39	Steve Finley	.25
40	Tom Glavine	.40
41	Mo Vaughn	.25
42	Phil Nevin	.25
43	Richie Sexson	.25
44	Craig Biggio	.25
45	Kerry Wood	.50
46	Pat Burrell	.60
47	Edgar Martinez	.25
48	Jim Thome	.25
49	Jeff Bagwell	1.00
50	Bernie Williams	.45
51	Andruw Jones	1.00
52	Gary Sheffield	.40
53	Johnny Damon	.40
54	Rondell White	.25
55	J.D. Drew	.50
56	Tony Batista	.25
57	Paul Konerko	.25
58	Rafael Palmeiro	.75
59	Cal Ripken Jr.	3.00
60	Darin Erstad	.60
61	Ivan Rodriguez	.75
62	Barry Bonds	3.00
63	Edgardo Alfonzo	.25
64	Ellis Burks	.25

65	Mike Lieberthal	.25
66	Robin Ventura	.25
67	Richard Hidalgo	.25
68	Magglio Ordonez	.40
69	Kazuhiro Sasaki	.25
70	Miguel Tejada	.50
71	David Wells	.25
72	Troy Glaus	1.00
73	Jose Vidro	.25
74	Shawn Green	.50
75	Barry Zito	.50
76	Jermaine Dye	.25
77	Geoff Jenkins	.25
78	Jeff Kent	.25
79	Al Leiter	.25
80	Deivi Cruz	.25
81	Eric Karros	.25
82	Albert Belle	.25
83	Pedro Martinez	1.00
84	Raul Mondesi	.25
85	Preston Wilson	.25
86	Rafael Furcal	.25
87	Rick Ankiel	.25
88	Randy Johnson	1.00
89	Kevin Brown	.25
90	Sean Casey	.35
91	Mike Mussina	.50
92	Alex Rodriguez	2.50
93	Andres Galarraga	.25
94	Juan Gonzalez	1.00
95	Manny Ramirez	1.00
96	Mark Grace	.35
97	Carl Everett	.25
98	Tony Gwynn	1.50
99	Mike Hampton	.25
100	Ken Caminiti	.25
101	Jason Hart/1749	4.00
102	Corey Patterson/1199	5.00
103	Timo Perez/1999	4.00
104	Marcus Giles/1999	4.00
105	*Ichiro Suzuki/1999*	50.00
106	Aubrey Huff/1499	8.00
107	Joe Crede/1999	5.00
108	Larry Barnes/1499	4.00
109	*Esix Snead/1499*	4.00
110	Kenny Kelly/2249	4.00
111	Justin Miller/2249	4.00
112	Jack Cust/1999	4.00
113	Xavier Nady/999	4.00
114	Eric Munson/1499	4.00
115	*Elpidio Guzman/1749*	4.00
116	Juan Pierre/2189	4.00
117	*Winston Abreu/1749*	4.00
118	Keith Ginter/1999	4.00
119	Jace Brewer/2699	4.00
120	Paxton Crawford/2249	4.00
121	Jason Tyner/2249	4.00
122	Tike Redman/1999	4.00
123	John Riedling/2499	4.00
124	Jose Ortiz/1499	4.00
125	Oswaldo Mairena/2499	4.00
126	Eric Byrnes/2249	4.00
127	Brian Cole/999	4.00
128	Adam Piatt/2249	4.00
129	Nate Rolison/2499	4.00
130	Keith McDonald/2249	4.00

Essential Credentials

	NM/M
Stars (1-100):	3-6X
Production 299	
Common (101-130):	10.00
Minor Stars (101-130):	15.00
Production 29	

(See 2001 E-X for checklist and base card values.)

Prospects Autograph

	NM/M
Common Autograph:	8.00

Prod. #'s listed

101	Jason Hart/250	8.00
102	Corey Patterson/800	15.00
103	Timoniel Perez/1000	8.00
104	Marcus Giles/500	10.00
106	Aubrey Huff/500	15.00
107	Joe Crede/500	10.00
108	Larry Barnes/500	8.00
109	Esix Snead/500	8.00
110	Kenny Kelly/250	8.00
111	Justin Miller/250	8.00
112	Jack Cust/1000	8.00
113	Xavier Nady/1000	10.00
114	Eric Munson/1500	8.00
115	Elpidio Guzman/250	8.00
116	Juan Pierre/810	10.00
117	Winston Abreu/250	8.00
118	Keith Ginter/500	8.00
119	Jace Brewer/300	8.00
120	Paxton Crawford/250	8.00
121	Jason Tyner/250	8.00
122	Tike Redman/250	8.00
123	John Riedling/500	8.00
124	Jose Ortiz/500	8.00
125	Oswaldo Mairena/500	8.00
126	Eric Byrnes/250	8.00
127	Brian Cole/2000	8.00
128	Adam Piatt/250	8.00
129	Nate Rolison/500	8.00
130	Keith McDonald/250	8.00

Base Inks

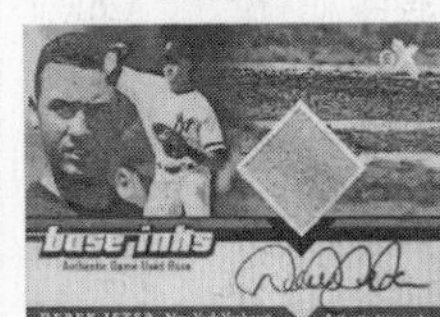

	NM/M
Random Inserts	
Derek Jeter AU/500	100.00

Behind the Numbers

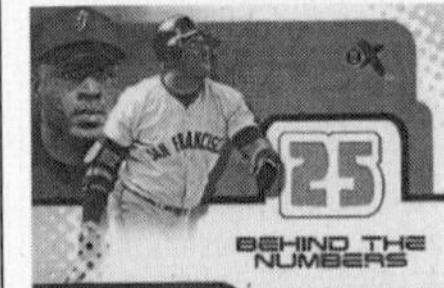

		NM/M
Common Player:		5.00
Inserted 1:33		
1BN	Johnny Bench	10.00
2BN	Wade Boggs	15.00
3BN	George Brett	20.00
4BN	Lou Brock	5.00
5BN	Rollie Fingers	5.00
6BN	Carlton Fisk	10.00
7BN	Reggie Jackson	10.00
8BN	Al Kaline	10.00
9BN	Willie Mays	
10BN	Willie McCovey	5.00
11BN	Paul Molitor	10.00
12BN	Eddie Murray	10.00
13BN	Jim Palmer	5.00
14BN	Ozzie Smith	15.00
15BN	Nolan Ryan	30.00
16BN	Mike Schmidt	20.00
17BN	Tom Seaver	10.00
18BN	Dave Winfield	5.00
19BN	Ted Williams	75.00
20BN	Robin Yount	10.00
21BN	Brady Anderson	5.00
22BN	Rick Ankiel	5.00
23BN	Albert Belle	5.00
24BN	Adrian Beltre	7.50
25BN	Barry Bonds	30.00
26BN	Eric Chavez	5.00
27BN	J.D. Drew	6.00
28BN	Darin Erstad	5.00
29BN	Troy Glaus	6.00
30BN	Mark Grace	6.00
31BN	Ben Grieve	5.00
32BN	Tony Gwynn	15.00
33BN	Todd Helton	10.00
34BN	Derek Jeter	30.00
35BN	Jeff Kent	5.00
36BN	Jason Kendall	5.00
37BN	Greg Maddux	15.00
38BN	John Olerud	5.00
39BN	Cal Ripken Jr.	30.00
40BN	Chipper Jones	15.00
41BN	John Smoltz	5.00
42BN	Frank Thomas	10.00
43BN	Robin Ventura	5.00
44BN	Bernie Williams	6.00

Behind the Numbers Autograph

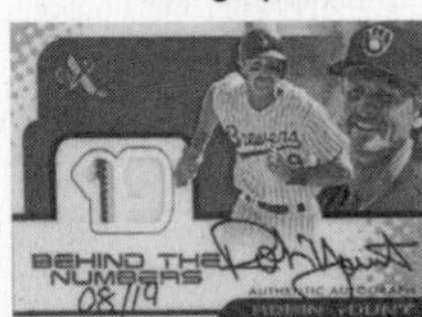

		NM/M
Quantity produced listed		
2BN	Wade Boggs/26	150.00
4BN	Lou Brock/20	100.00
5BN	Rollie Fingers/34	50.00
6BN	Carlton Fisk/27	125.00
7BN	Reggie Jackson/44	80.00
10BN	Willie McCovey/44	80.00
12BN	Eddie Murray/33	100.00
13BN	Jim Palmer/22	100.00
15BN	Nolan Ryan/34	350.00
16BN	Mike Schmidt/20	200.00
17BN	Tom Seaver/41	80.00
18BN	Dave Winfield/31	60.00
20BN	Robin Yount/19	180.00
22BN	Rick Ankiel/66	20.00
23BN	Albert Belle/88	20.00
24BN	Adrian Beltre/29	25.00
25BN	Barry Bonds/25	250.00
28BN	Darin Erstad/17	80.00
29BN	Troy Glaus/25	80.00
30BN	Mark Grace/17	100.00
32BN	Tony Gwynn/19	150.00
33BN	Todd Helton/17	125.00
35BN	Jeff Kent/21	50.00
36BN	Jason Kendall/18	40.00
37BN	Greg Maddux/31	250.00
41BN	John Smoltz/29	40.00
42BN	Frank Thomas/35	75.00
44BN	Bernie Williams/51	75.00

Derek Jeter Monumental Moments

		NM/M
2DJMM	Derek Jeter (edition of 1,996)	5.00
2DJMM	Derek Jeter (autographed edition of 96)	80.00

E-Xtra Innings

		NM/M
Complete Set (10):		30.00
Common Player:		2.00
Inserted 1:20 R		
1XI	Mark McGwire	5.00
2XI	Sammy Sosa	4.00
3XI	Chipper Jones	3.00
4XI	Mike Piazza	4.00
5XI	Cal Ripken Jr.	6.00
6XI	Ken Griffey Jr.	4.00
7XI	Alex Rodriguez	5.00
8XI	Vladimir Guerrero	2.00
9XI	Nomar Garciaparra	4.00
10XI	Derek Jeter	6.00

Wall of Fame

		NM/M
Common Player:		4.00
Inserted 1:24		
1WF	Robin Yount	8.00
2WF	Paul Molitor	8.00
3WF	Geoff Jenkins	4.00
4WF	Mark McGwire	15.00
5WF	Sammy Sosa	12.00
6WF	Greg Maddux	10.00
7WF	Mike Piazza	12.00
8WF	Cal Ripken Jr.	20.00
9WF	Todd Helton	8.00
10WF	Ken Griffey Jr.	12.00
11WF	Alex Rodriguez	15.00
12WF	Vladimir Guerrero	8.00
13WF	Jeff Bagwell	8.00
14WF	Ivan Rodriguez	6.00
15WF	Juan Gonzalez	8.00
16WF	Barry Bonds	20.00
17WF	Derek Jeter	20.00
18WF	Chipper Jones	10.00
19WF	Frank Thomas	8.00
20WF	Tony Gwynn	10.00
21WF	Nomar Garciaparra	12.00
22WF	Manny Ramirez	8.00
23WF	Andruw Jones	8.00
24WF	Scott Rolen	6.00
25WF	Jason Kendall	4.00
26WF	Roger Clemens	15.00
27WF	Troy Glaus	6.00
28WF	Pedro Martinez	8.00
29WF	Jason Giambi	5.00
30WF	Pat Burrell	5.00

1993 FINEST

		NM/M
Complete Set (199):		100.00
Common Player:		.50
Pack (6):		20.00
Wax Box (18):		300.00
1	Dave Justice	.50
2	Lou Whitaker	.50
3	Bryan Harvey	.50
4	Carlos Garcia	.50
5	Sid Fernandez	.50
6	Brett Butler	.50
7	Scott Cooper	.50
8	B.J. Surhoff	.50
9	Steve Finley	.50
10	Curt Schilling	2.00
11	Jeff Bagwell	4.50
12	Alex Cole	.50
13	John Olerud	.50
14	John Smiley	.50
15	Bip Roberts	.50
16	Albert Belle	.75
17	Duane Ward	.50
18	Alan Trammell	.50
19	Andy Benes	.50
20	Reggie Sanders	.50
21	Todd Zeile	.50
22	Rick Aguilera	.50
23	Dave Hollins	.50
24	Jose Rijo	.50
25	Matt Williams	.50
26	Sandy Alomar	.50
27	Alex Fernandez	.50
28	Ozzie Smith	6.00
29	Ramon Martinez	.50
30	Bernie Williams	1.00
31	Gary Sheffield	1.00
32	Eric Karros	.50
33	Frank Viola	.50
34	Kevin Young	.50
35	Ken Hill	.50
36	Tony Fernandez	.50
37	Tim Wakefield	.50
38	John Kruk	.50
39	Chris Sabo	.50
40	Marquis Grissom	.50
41	Glenn Davis	.50

42 Jeff Montgomery .50
43 Kenny Lofton .50
44 John Burkett .50
45 Darryl Hamilton .50
46 Jim Abbott .50
47 Ivan Rodriguez 4.50
48 Eric Young .50
49 Mitch Williams .50
50 Harold Reynolds .50
51 Brian Harper .50
52 Rafael Palmeiro 4.50
53 Bret Saberhagen .50
54 Jeff Conine .50
55 Ivan Calderon .50
56 Juan Guzman .50
57 Carlos Baerga .50
58 Charles Nagy .50
59 Wally Joyner .50
60 Charlie Hayes .50
61 Shane Mack .50
62 Pete Harnisch .50
63 George Brett 7.00
64 Lance Johnson .50
65 Ben McDonald .50
66 Bobby Bonilla .50
67 Terry Steinbach .50
68 Ron Gant .50
69 Doug Jones .50
70 Paul Molitor 4.50
71 Brady Anderson .50
72 Chuck Finley .50
73 Mark Grace .75
74 Mike Devereaux .50
75 Tony Phillips .50
76 Chuck Knoblauch .50
77 Tony Gwynn 6.00
78 Kevin Appier .50
79 Sammy Sosa 7.50
80 Mickey Tettleton .50
81 Felix Jose .50
82 Mark Langston .50
83 Gregg Jefferies .50
84 Andre Dawson (AS) 1.00
85 Greg Maddux (AS) 6.00
86 Rickey Henderson (AS) 4.50
87 Tom Glavine (AS) 2.50
88 Roberto Alomar (AS) 1.50
89 Darryl Strawberry (AS) .50
90 Wade Boggs (AS) 6.00
91 Bo Jackson (AS) 1.00
92 Mark McGwire (AS) 7.50
93 Robin Ventura (AS) .50
94 Joe Carter (AS) .50
95 Lee Smith (AS) .50
96 Cal Ripken, Jr. (AS) 8.00
97 Larry Walker (AS) .50
98 Don Mattingly (AS) 7.00
99 Jose Canseco (AS) 2.50
100 Dennis Eckersley (AS) 3.50
101 Terry Pendleton (AS) .50
102 Frank Thomas (AS) 4.50
103 Barry Bonds (AS) 8.00
104 Roger Clemens (AS) 7.00
105 Ryne Sandberg (AS) 6.00
106 Fred McGriff (AS) .50
107 Nolan Ryan (AS) 8.00
108 Will Clark (AS) .60
109 Pat Listach (AS) .50
110 Ken Griffey, Jr. (AS) 7.50
111 Cecil Fielder (AS) .50
112 Kirby Puckett (AS) 6.00
113 Dwight Gooden (AS) .50
114 Barry Larkin (AS) .50
115 David Cone (AS) .50
116 Juan Gonzalez (AS) 4.50
117 Kent Hrbek .50
118 Tim Wallach .50
119 Craig Biggio .50
120 Bobby Kelly .50
121 Greg Olson .50
122 Eddie Murray 4.50
123 Wil Cordero .50
124 Jay Buhner .50
125 Carlton Fisk 4.50
126 Eric Davis .50
127 Doug Drabek .50
128 Ozzie Guillen .50
129 John Wetteland .50
130 Andres Galarraga .50
131 Ken Caminiti .50
132 Tom Candiotti .50
133 Pat Borders .50
134 Kevin Brown .60
135 Travis Fryman .50
136 Kevin Mitchell .50
137 Greg Swindell .50
138 Benny Santiago .50
139 Reggie Jefferson .50
140 Chris Bosio .50
141 Deion Sanders .60
142 Scott Erickson .50
143 Howard Johnson .50
144 Orestes Destrade .50
145 Jose Guzman .50
146 Chad Curtis .50
147 Cal Eldred .50
148 Willie Greene .50
149 Tommy Greene .50
150 Erik Hanson .50
151 Bob Welch .50
152 John Jaha .50
153 Harold Baines .50
154 Randy Johnson 4.50
155 Al Martin .50
156 *J.T. Snow* 1.50
157 Mike Mussina 3.00
158 Ruben Sierra .50
159 Dean Palmer .50
160 Steve Avery .50
161 Julio Franco .50
162 Dave Winfield 4.50
163 Tim Salmon 1.00
164 Tom Henke .50
165 Mo Vaughn .50
166 John Smoltz .50
167 Danny Tartabull .50
168 Delino DeShields .50
169 Charlie Hough .50
170 Paul O'Neill .50
171 Darren Daulton .50
172 Jack McDowell .50
173 Junior Felix .50
174 Jimmy Key .50
175 George Bell .50
176 Mike Stanton .50
177 Len Dykstra .50
178 Norm Charlton .50
179 Eric Anthony .50
180 Bob Dibble .50
181 Otis Nixon .50
182 Randy Myers .50
183 Tim Raines .50
184 Orel Hershiser .50
185 Andy Van Slyke .50
186 *Mike Lansing* 1.00
187 Ray Lankford .50
188 Mike Morgan .50
189 Moises Alou .50
190 Edgar Martinez .50
191 John Franco .50
192 Robin Yount 4.50
193 Bob Tewksbury .50
194 Jay Bell .50
195 Luis Gonzalez .50
196 Dave Fleming .50
197 Mike Greenwell .50
198 David Nied .50
199 Mike Piazza 10.00

Refractors

NM/M
Common Player: 20.00
1 Dave Justice 20.00
2 Lou Whitaker 20.00
3 Bryan Harvey 20.00
4 Carlos Garcia 20.00
5 Sid Fernandez 20.00
6 Brett Butler 20.00
7 Scott Cooper 20.00
8 B.J. Surhoff 20.00
9 Steve Finley 20.00
10 Curt Schilling 35.00
11 Jeff Bagwell 100.00
12 Alex Cole 20.00
13 John Olerud 20.00
14 John Smiley 20.00
15 Bip Roberts 20.00
16 Albert Belle 30.00
17 Duane Ward 20.00
18 Alan Trammell 20.00
19 Andy Benes 20.00
20 Reggie Sanders 20.00
21 Todd Zeile 20.00
22 Rick Aguilera 20.00
23 Dave Hollins 20.00
24 Jose Rijo 20.00
25 Matt Williams 20.00
26 Sandy Alomar 20.00
27 Alex Fernandez 20.00
28 Ozzie Smith 150.00
29 Ramon Martinez 20.00
30 Bernie Williams 25.00
31 Gary Sheffield 45.00
32 Eric Karros 20.00
33 Frank Viola 20.00
34 Kevin Young 20.00
35 Ken Hill 20.00
36 Tony Fernandez 20.00
37 Tim Wakefield 20.00
38 John Kruk 20.00
39 Chris Sabo 20.00
40 Marquis Grissom 20.00
41 Glenn Davis 20.00
42 Jeff Montgomery 20.00
43 Kenny Lofton 20.00
44 John Burkett 20.00
45 Darryl Hamilton 20.00
46 Jim Abbott 20.00
47 Ivan Rodriguez 100.00
48 Eric Young 20.00
49 Mitch Williams 20.00
50 Harold Reynolds 20.00
51 Brian Harper 20.00
52 Rafael Palmeiro 100.00
53 Bret Saberhagen 20.00
54 Jeff Conine 20.00
55 Ivan Calderon 20.00
56 Juan Guzman 20.00
57 Carlos Baerga 20.00
58 Charles Nagy 20.00
59 Wally Joyner 20.00
60 Charlie Hayes 20.00
61 Shane Mack 20.00
62 Pete Harnisch 20.00
63 George Brett 250.00
64 Lance Johnson 20.00
65 Ben McDonald 20.00
66 Bobby Bonilla 20.00
67 Terry Steinbach 20.00
68 Ron Gant 20.00
69 Doug Jones 20.00
70 Paul Molitor 100.00
71 Brady Anderson 20.00
72 Chuck Finley 20.00
73 Mark Grace 30.00
74 Mike Devereaux 20.00
75 Tony Phillips 20.00
76 Chuck Knoblauch 20.00
77 Tony Gwynn 150.00
78 Kevin Appier 20.00
79 Sammy Sosa 250.00
80 Mickey Tettleton 20.00
81 Felix Jose 20.00
82 Mark Langston 20.00
83 Gregg Jefferies 20.00
84 Andre Dawson (AS) 35.00
85 Greg Maddux (AS) 150.00
86 Rickey Henderson (AS) 100.00
87 Tom Glavine (AS) 50.00
88 Roberto Alomar (AS) 45.00
89 Darryl Strawberry (AS) 20.00
90 Wade Boggs (AS) 150.00
91 Bo Jackson (AS) 60.00
92 Mark McGwire (AS) 450.00
93 Robin Ventura (AS) 20.00
94 Joe Carter (AS) 20.00
95 Lee Smith (AS) 20.00
96 Cal Ripken, Jr. (AS) 650.00
97 Larry Walker (AS) 20.00
98 Don Mattingly (AS) 175.00
99 Jose Canseco(AS) 60.00
100 Dennis Eckersley (AS) 75.00
101 Terry Pendleton (AS) 20.00
102 Frank Thomas(AS) 100.00
103 Barry Bonds (AS) 500.00
104 Roger Clemens 175.00
105 Ryne Sandberg (AS) 150.00
106 Fred McGriff (AS) 20.00
107 Nolan Ryan (AS) 650.00
108 Will Clark (AS) 30.00
109 Pat Listach (AS) 20.00
110 Ken Griffey, Jr. (AS) 450.00
111 Cecil Fielder (AS) 20.00
112 Kirby Puckett (AS) 150.00
113 Dwight Gooden (AS) 20.00
114 Barry Larkin (AS) 20.00
115 David Cone (AS) 20.00
116 Juan Gonzalez (AS) 100.00
117 Kent Hrbek 20.00
118 Tim Wallach 20.00
119 Craig Biggio 20.00
120 Bobby Kelly 20.00
121 Greg Olson 20.00
122 Eddie Murray 100.00
123 Wil Cordero 20.00
124 Jay Buhner 20.00
125 Carlton Fisk 100.00
126 Eric Davis 20.00
127 Doug Drabek 20.00
128 Ozzie Guillen 20.00
129 John Wetteland 20.00
130 Andres Galarraga 20.00
131 Ken Caminiti 20.00
132 Tom Candiotti 20.00
133 Pat Borders 20.00
134 Kevin Brown 20.00
135 Travis Fryman 20.00
136 Kevin Mitchell 20.00
137 Greg Swindell 20.00
138 Benny Santiago 20.00
139 Reggie Jefferson 20.00
140 Chris Bosio 20.00
141 Deion Sanders 20.00
142 Scott Erickson 20.00
143 Howard Johnson 20.00
144 Orestes Destrade 20.00
145 Jose Guzman 20.00
146 Chad Curtis 20.00
147 Cal Eldred 20.00
148 Willie Greene 20.00
149 Tommy Greene 20.00
150 Erik Hanson 20.00
151 Bob Welch 20.00
152 John Jaha 20.00
153 Harold Baines 20.00
154 Randy Johnson 100.00
155 Al Martin 20.00
156 J.T. Snow 20.00
157 Mike Mussina 45.00
158 Ruben Sierra 20.00
159 Dean Palmer 20.00
160 Steve Avery 20.00
161 Julio Franco 20.00
162 Dave Winfield 100.00
163 Tim Salmon 30.00
164 Tom Henke 20.00
165 Mo Vaughn 20.00
166 John Smoltz 20.00
167 Danny Tartabull 20.00
168 Delino DeShields 20.00
169 Charlie Hough 20.00
170 Paul O'Neill 20.00
171 Darren Daulton 20.00
172 Jack McDowell 20.00
173 Junior Felix 20.00
174 Jimmy Key 20.00
175 George Bell 20.00
176 Mike Stanton 20.00
177 Len Dykstra 20.00
178 Norm Charlton 20.00
179 Eric Anthony 20.00
180 Bob Dibble 20.00
181 Otis Nixon 20.00
182 Randy Myers 20.00
183 Tim Raines 20.00
184 Orel Hershiser 20.00
185 Andy Van Slyke 20.00
186 Mike Lansing 20.00
187 Ray Lankford 20.00
188 Mike Morgan 20.00
189 Moises Alou 20.00
190 Edgar Martinez 20.00
191 John Franco 20.00
192 Robin Yount 100.00
193 Bob Tewksbury 20.00
194 Jay Bell 20.00
195 Luis Gonzalez 20.00
196 Dave Fleming 20.00
197 Mike Greenwell 20.00
198 David Nied 20.00
199 Mike Piazza 250.00

Jumbo All-Stars

NM/M
Complete Set (33): 185.00
Common Player: 2.00
84 Andre Dawson 2.50
85 Greg Maddux 10.00
86 Rickey Henderson 7.50
87 Tom Glavine 3.00
88 Roberto Alomar 3.00
89 Darryl Strawberry 2.00
90 Wade Boggs 10.00
91 Bo Jackson 2.00
92 Mark McGwire 20.00
93 Robin Ventura 2.00

No.	Player	Price
94	Joe Carter	2.00
95	Lee Smith	2.00
96	Cal Ripken, Jr.	30.00
97	Larry Walker	2.00
98	Don Mattingly	12.00
99	Jose Canseco	3.50
100	Dennis Eckersley	6.00
101	Terry Pendleton	2.00
102	Frank Thomas	7.50
103	Barry Bonds	30.00
104	Roger Clemens	12.00
105	Ryne Sandberg	10.00
106	Fred McGriff	2.00
107	Nolan Ryan	30.00
108	Will Clark	2.50
109	Pat Listach	2.00
110	Ken Griffey, Jr.	15.00
111	Cecil Fielder	2.00
112	Kirby Puckett	10.00
113	Dwight Gooden	2.00
114	Barry Larkin	2.00
115	David Cone	2.00
116	Juan Gonzalez	7.50

1993 FINEST PROMOS

		NM/M
Complete Set (3):		15.00
Complete Set, Refractors (3):		1,500
88	Roberto Alomar	3.50
88r	Roberto Alomar (refractor)	300.00
98	Don Mattingly	7.50
98r	Don Mattingly (refractor)	500.00
107	Nolan Ryan	10.00
107r	Nolan Ryan (refractor)	750.00

1994 FINEST

		NM/M
Complete Set (440):		40.00
Common Player:		.15
Series 1 or 2 Pack (7):		1.50
Series 1 or 2 Box (24):		25.00
1	Mike Piazza	4.00
2	Kevin Stocker	.15
3	Greg McMichael	.15
4	Jeff Conine	.15
5	Rene Arocha	.15
6	Aaron Sele	.15
7	Brent Gates	.15
8	Chuck Carr	.15
9	Kirk Rueter	.15
10	Mike Lansing	.15
11	Al Martin	.15
12	Jason Bere	.15
13	Troy Neel	.15
14	Armando Reynoso	.15
15	Jeromy Burnitz	.15
16	Rich Amaral	.15
17	David McCarty	.15
18	Tim Salmon	.35
19	Steve Cooke	.15
20	Wil Cordero	.15
21	Kevin Tapani	.15
22	Deion Sanders	.15
23	Jose Offerman	.15
24	Mark Langston	.15
25	Ken Hill	.15
26	Alex Fernandez	.15
27	Jeff Blauser	.15
28	Royce Clayton	.15
29	Brad Ausmus	.15
30	Ryan Bowen	.15
31	Steve Finley	.15
32	Charlie Hayes	.15
33	Jeff Kent	.15
34	Mike Henneman	.15
35	Andres Galarraga	.15
36	Wayne Kirby	.15
37	Joe Oliver	.15
38	Terry Steinbach	.15
39	Ryan Thompson	.15
40	Luis Alicea	.15
41	Randy Velarde	.15
42	Bob Tewksbury	.15
43	Reggie Sanders	.15
44	Brian Williams	.15
45	Joe Orsulak	.15
46	Jose Lind	.15
47	Dave Hollins	.15
48	Graeme Lloyd	.15
49	Jim Gott	.15
50	Andre Dawson	.40
51	Steve Buechele	.15
52	David Cone	.15
53	Ricky Gutierrez	.15
54	Lance Johnson	.15
55	Tino Martinez	.15
56	Phil Hiatt	.15
57	Carlos Garcia	.15
58	Danny Darwin	.15
59	Dante Bichette	.15
60	Scott Kamieniecki	.15
61	Orlando Merced	.15
62	Brian McRae	.15
63	Pat Kelly	.15
64	Tom Henke	.15
65	Jeff King	.15
66	Mike Mussina	1.00
67	Tim Pugh	.15
68	Robby Thompson	.15
69	Paul O'Neill	.15
70	Hal Morris	.15
71	Ron Karkovice	.15
72	Joe Girardi	.15
73	Eduardo Perez	.15
74	Raul Mondesi	.15
75	Mike Gallego	.15
76	Mike Stanley	.15
77	Kevin Roberson	.15
78	Mark McGwire	4.00
79	Pat Listach	.15
80	Eric Davis	.15
81	Mike Bordick	.15
82	Dwight Gooden	.15
83	Mike Moore	.15
84	Phil Plantier	.15
85	Darren Lewis	.15
86	Rick Wilkins	.15
87	Darryl Strawberry	.15
88	Rob Dibble	.15
89	Greg Vaughn	.15
90	Jeff Russell	.15
91	Mark Lewis	.15
92	Gregg Jefferies	.15
93	Jose Guzman	.15
94	Kenny Rogers	.15
95	Mark Lemke	.15
96	Mike Morgan	.15
97	Andujar Cedeno	.15
98	Orel Hershiser	.15
99	Greg Swindell	.15
100	John Smoltz	.15
101	Pedro Martinez	.15
102	Jim Thome	.15
103	David Segui	.15
104	Charles Nagy	.15
105	Shane Mack	.15
106	John Jaha	.15
107	Tom Candiotti	.15
108	David Wells	.15
109	Bobby Jones	.15
110	Bob Hamelin	.15
111	Bernard Gilkey	.15
112	Chili Davis	.15
113	Todd Stottlemyre	.15
114	Derek Bell	.15
115	Mark McLemore	.15
116	Mark Whiten	.15
117	Mike Devereaux	.15
118	Terry Pendleton	.15
119	Pat Meares	.15
120	Pete Harnisch	.15
121	Moises Alou	.15
122	Jay Buhner	.15
123	Wes Chamberlain	.15
124	Mike Perez	.15
125	Devon White	.15
126	Ivan Rodriguez	1.25
127	Don Slaught	.15
128	John Valentin	.15
129	Jaime Navarro	.15
130	Dave Magadan	.15
131	Brady Anderson	.15
132	Juan Guzman	.15
133	John Wetteland	.15
134	Dave Stewart	.15
135	Scott Servais	.15
136	Ozzie Smith	2.50
137	Darrin Fletcher	.15
138	Jose Mesa	.15
139	Wilson Alvarez	.15
140	Pete Incaviglia	.15
141	Chris Hoiles	.15
142	Darryl Hamilton	.15
143	Chuck Finley	.15
144	Archi Cianfrocco	.15
145	Bill Wegman	.15
146	Joey Cora	.15
147	Darrell Whitmore	.15
148	David Hulse	.15
149	Jim Abbott	.15
150	Curt Schilling	.40
151	Bill Swift	.15
152	Tommy Greene	.15
153	Roberto Mejia	.15
154	Edgar Martinez	.15
155	Roger Pavlik	.15
156	Randy Tomlin	.15
157	J.T. Snow	.15
158	Bob Welch	.15
159	Alan Trammell	.15
160	Ed Sprague	.15
161	Ben McDonald	.15
162	Derrick May	.15
163	Roberto Kelly	.15
164	Bryan Harvey	.15
165	Ron Gant	.15
166	Scott Erickson	.15
167	Anthony Young	.15
168	Scott Cooper	.15
169	Rod Beck	.15
170	John Franco	.15
171	Gary DiSarcina	.15
172	Dave Fleming	.15
173	Wade Boggs	2.50
174	Kevin Appier	.15
175	Jose Bautista	.15
176	Wally Joyner	.15
177	Dean Palmer	.15
178	Tony Phillips	.15
179	John Smiley	.15
180	Charlie Hough	.15
181	Scott Fletcher	.15
182	Todd Van Poppel	.15
183	Mike Blowers	.15
184	Willie McGee	.15
185	Paul Sorrento	.15
186	Eric Young	.15
187	Bret Barberie	.15
188	Manuel Lee	.15
189	Jeff Branson	.15
190	Jim Deshaies	.15
191	Ken Caminiti	.15
192	Tim Raines	.15
193	Joe Grahe	.15
194	Hipolito Pichardo	.15
195	Denny Neagle	.15
196	Jeff Gardner	.15
197	Mike Benjamin	.15
198	Milt Thompson	.15
199	Bruce Ruffin	.15
200	Chris Hammond	.15
201	Tony Gwynn	2.50
202	Robin Ventura	.15
203	Frank Thomas	1.50
204	Kirby Puckett	2.50
205	Roberto Alomar	.50
206	Dennis Eckersley	1.00
207	Joe Carter	.15
208	Albert Belle	.35
209	Greg Maddux	2.50
210	Ryne Sandberg	2.50
211	Juan Gonzalez	1.50
212	Jeff Bagwell	1.50
213	Randy Johnson	1.50
214	Matt Williams	.15
215	Dave Winfield	1.50
216	Larry Walker	.15
217	Roger Clemens	3.00
218	Kenny Lofton	.15
219	Cecil Fielder	.15
220	Darren Daulton	.15
221	John Olerud	.15
222	Jose Canseco	.75
223	Rickey Henderson	1.50
224	Fred McGriff	.15
225	Gary Sheffield	.50
226	Jack McDowell	.15
227	Rafael Palmeiro	1.25
228	Travis Fryman	.15
229	Marquis Grissom	.15
230	Barry Bonds	5.00
231	Carlos Baerga	.15
232	Ken Griffey, Jr.	4.00
233	Dave Justice	.15
234	Bobby Bonilla	.15
235	Cal Ripken	5.00
236	Sammy Sosa	4.00
237	Len Dykstra	.15
238	Will Clark	.25
239	Paul Molitor	1.50
240	Barry Larkin	.15
241	Bo Jackson	.35
242	Mitch Williams	.15
243	Ron Darling	.15
244	Darryl Kile	.15
245	Geronimo Berroa	.15
246	Gregg Olson	.15
247	Brian Harper	.15
248	Rheal Cormier	.15
249	Rey Sanchez	.15
250	Jeff Fassero	.15
251	Sandy Alomar	.15
252	Chris Bosio	.15
253	Andy Stankiewicz	.15
254	Harold Baines	.15
255	Andy Ashby	.15
256	Tyler Green	.15
257	Kevin Brown	.15
258	Mo Vaughn	.15
259	Mike Harkey	.15
260	Dave Henderson	.15
261	Kent Hrbek	.15
262	Darrin Jackson	.15
263	Bob Wickman	.15
264	Spike Owen	.15
265	Todd Jones	.15
266	Pat Borders	.15
267	Tom Glavine	.45
268	Dave Nilsson	.15
269	Rich Batchelor	.15
270	Delino DeShields	.15
271	Felix Fermin	.15
272	Orestes Destrade	.15
273	Mickey Morandini	.15
274	Otis Nixon	.15
275	Ellis Burks	.15
276	Greg Gagne	.15
277	John Doherty	.15
278	Julio Franco	.15
279	Bernie Williams	.35
280	Rick Aguilera	.15
281	Mickey Tettleton	.15
282	David Nied	.15
283	Johnny Ruffin	.15
284	Dan Wilson	.15
285	Omar Vizquel	.15
286	Willie Banks	.15
287	Erik Pappas	.15
288	Cal Eldred	.15
289	Bobby Witt	.15
290	Luis Gonzalez	.35
291	Greg Pirkl	.15
292	Alex Cole	.15
293	Ricky Bones	.15
294	Denis Boucher	.15
295	John Burkett	.15
296	Steve Trachsel	.15
297	Ricky Jordan	.15
298	Mark Dewey	.15
299	Jimmy Key	.15
300	Mike MacFarlane	.15
301	Tim Belcher	.15
302	Carlos Reyes	.15
303	Greg Harris	.15
304	*Brian Anderson*	.15
305	Terry Mulholland	.15
306	Felix Jose	.15
307	Darren Holmes	.15
308	Jose Rijo	.15
309	Paul Wagner	.15
310	Bob Scanlan	.15

311	Mike Jackson	.15
312	Jose Vizcaino	.15
313	Rob Butler	.15
314	Kevin Seitzer	.15
315	Geronimo Pena	.15
316	Hector Carrasco	.15
317	Eddie Murray	1.50
318	Roger Salkeld	.15
319	Todd Hundley	.15
320	Danny Jackson	.15
321	Kevin Young	.15
322	Mike Greenwell	.15
323	Kevin Mitchell	.15
324	Chuck Knoblauch	.15
325	Danny Tartabull	.15
326	Vince Coleman	.15
327	Marvin Freeman	.15
328	Andy Benes	.15
329	Mike Kelly	.15
330	Karl Rhodes	.15
331	Allen Watson	.15
332	Damion Easley	.15
333	Reggie Jefferson	.15
334	Kevin McReynolds	.15
335	Arthur Rhodes	.15
336	Brian Hunter	.15
337	Tom Browning	.15
338	Pedro Munoz	.15
339	Billy Ripken	.15
340	Gene Harris	.15
341	Fernando Vina	.15
342	Sean Berry	.15
343	Pedro Astacio	.15
344	B.J. Surhoff	.15
345	Doug Drabek	.15
346	Jody Reed	.15
347	Ray Lankford	.15
348	Steve Farr	.15
349	Eric Anthony	.15
350	Pete Smith	.15
351	Lee Smith	.15
352	Mariano Duncan	.15
353	Doug Strange	.15
354	Tim Bogar	.15
355	Dave Weathers	.15
356	Eric Karros	.15
357	Randy Myers	.15
358	Chad Curtis	.15
359	Steve Avery	.15
360	Brian Jordan	.15
361	Tim Wallach	.15
362	Pedro Martinez	1.50
363	Bip Roberts	.15
364	Lou Whitaker	.15
365	Luis Polonia	.15
366	Benny Santiago	.15
367	Brett Butler	.15
368	Shawon Dunston	.15
369	Kelly Stinnett	.15
370	Chris Turner	.15
371	Ruben Sierra	.15
372	Greg Harris	.15
373	Xavier Hernandez	.15
374	Howard Johnson	.15
375	Duane Ward	.15
376	Roberto Hernandez	.15
377	Scott Leius	.15
378	Dave Valle	.15
379	Sid Fernandez	.15
380	Doug Jones	.15
381	Zane Smith	.15
382	Craig Biggio	.15
383	Rick White	.15
384	Tom Pagnozzi	.15
385	Chris James	.15
386	Bret Boone	.15
387	Jeff Montgomery	.15
388	Chad Kreuter	.15
389	Greg Hibbard	.15
390	Mark Grace	.35
391	Phil Leftwich	.15
392	Don Mattingly	3.00
393	Ozzie Guillen	.15
394	Gary Gaetti	.15
395	Erik Hanson	.15
396	Scott Brosius	.15
397	Tom Gordon	.15
398	Bill Gullickson	.15
399	Matt Mieske	.15
400	Pat Hentgen	.15
401	Walt Weiss	.15
402	Greg Blosser	.15
403	Stan Javier	.15
404	Doug Henry	.15
405	Ramon Martinez	.15
406	Frank Viola	.15
407	Mike Hampton	.15
408	Andy Van Slyke	.15
409	Bobby Ayala	.15
410	Todd Zeile	.15
411	Jay Bell	.15
412	Denny Martinez	.15
413	Mark Portugal	.15
414	Bobby Munoz	.15
415	Kirt Manwaring	.15
416	John Kruk	.15
417	Trevor Hoffman	.15
418	Chris Sabo	.15
419	Bret Saberhagen	.15
420	Chris Nabholz	.15
421	James Mouton	.15
422	Tony Tarasco	.15
423	Carlos Delgado	.75
424	Rondell White	.15
425	Javier Lopez	.15
426	*Chan Ho Park*	1.00
427	Cliff Floyd	.15
428	Dave Staton	.15
429	J.R. Phillips	.15
430	Manny Ramirez	1.50
431	Kurt Abbott	.15
432	Melvin Nieves	.15
433	Alex Gonzalez	.15
434	Rick Helling	.15
435	Danny Bautista	.15
436	Matt Walbeck	.15
437	Ryan Klesko	.15
438	Steve Karsay	.15
439	Salomon Torres	.15
440	Scott Ruffcorn	.15

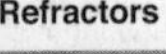

Refractors

	NM/M
Complete Set (440):	300.00
Common Player:	1.00
Stars/Rookies:	3X

(See 1994 Finest for checklist and base card prices.)

Bronze

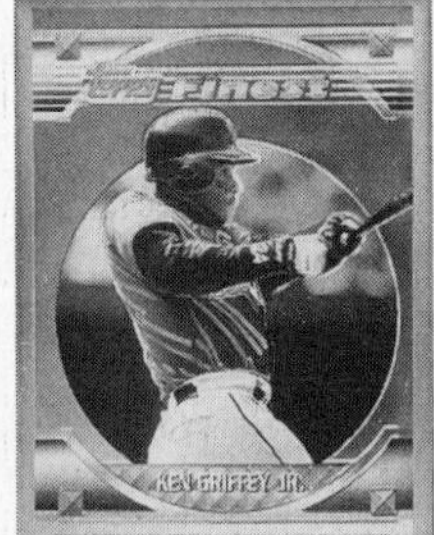

		NM/M
Complete Set (3):		75.00
Common Player:		25.00
1	Barry Bonds	35.00
2	Ken Griffey, Jr.	30.00
3	Frank Thomas	20.00

Superstar Jumbos

		NM/M
Complete Set (80):		140.00
Common Player:		1.00
1	Mike Piazza	12.50
2	Kevin Stocker	1.00
3	Greg McMichael	1.00
4	Jeff Conine	1.00
5	Rene Arocha	1.00
6	Aaron Sele	1.00
7	Brent Gates	1.00
8	Chuck Carr	1.00
9	Kirk Rueter	1.00
10	Mike Lansing	1.00
11	Al Martin	1.00
12	Jason Bere	1.00
13	Troy Neel	1.00
14	Armando Reynoso	1.00
15	Jeromy Burnitz	1.00
16	Rich Amaral	1.00
17	David McCarty	1.00
18	Tim Salmon	2.00
19	Steve Cooke	1.00
20	Wil Cordero	1.00
201	Tony Gwynn	7.50
202	Robin Ventura	1.00
203	Frank Thomas	6.00
204	Kirby Puckett	7.50
205	Roberto Alomar	2.00
206	Dennis Eckersley	5.00
207	Joe Carter	1.00
208	Albert Belle	2.00
209	Greg Maddux	7.50
210	Ryne Sandberg	7.50
211	Juan Gonzalez	6.00
212	Jeff Bagwell	6.00
213	Randy Johnson	6.00
214	Matt Williams	1.00
215	Dave Winfield	6.00
216	Larry Walker	1.00
217	Roger Clemens	9.00
218	Kenny Lofton	1.00
219	Cecil Fielder	1.00
220	Darren Daulton	1.00
221	John Olerud	1.00
222	Jose Canseco	4.00
223	Rickey Henderson	6.00
224	Fred McGriff	1.00
225	Gary Sheffield	2.00
226	Jack McDowell	1.00
227	Rafael Palmeiro	5.00
228	Travis Fryman	1.00
229	Marquis Grissom	1.00
230	Barry Bonds	20.00
231	Carlos Baerga	1.00
232	Ken Griffey Jr.	12.50
233	Dave Justice	1.00
234	Bobby Bonilla	1.00
235	Cal Ripken	20.00
236	Sammy Sosa	12.50
237	Len Dykstra	1.00
238	Will Clark	1.50
239	Paul Molitor	6.00
240	Barry Larkin	1.00
421	James Mouton	1.00
422	Tony Tarasco	1.00
423	Carlos Delgado	3.50
424	Rondell White	1.00
425	Javier Lopez	1.00
426	Chan Ho Park	1.00
427	Cliff Floyd	1.00
428	Dave Staton	1.00
429	J.R. Phillips	1.00
430	Manny Ramirez	6.00
431	Kurt Abbott	1.00
432	Melvin Nieves	1.00
433	Alex Gonzalez	1.00
434	Rick Helling	1.00
435	Danny Bautista	1.00
436	Matt Walbeck	1.00
437	Ryan Klesko	1.00
438	Steve Karsay	1.00
439	Salomon Torres	1.00
440	Scott Ruffcorn	1.00

1995 FINEST

	NM/M
Complete Set (220):	75.00
Common Player:	.25
Series 1 or 2 Pack (7):	2.00
Series 1 or 2 Wax Box (24):	30.00

1	Raul Mondesi	.25
2	Kurt Abbott	.25
3	Chris Gomez	.25
4	Manny Ramirez	1.50
5	Rondell White	.25
6	William Van Landingham	.25
7	Jon Lieber	.25
8	Ryan Klesko	.25
9	John Hudek	.25
10	Joey Hamilton	.25
11	Bob Hamelin	.25
12	Brian Anderson	.25
13	Mike Lieberthal	.25
14	Rico Brogna	.25
15	Rusty Greer	.25
16	Carlos Delgado	1.00
17	Jim Edmonds	.65
18	Steve Trachsel	.25
19	Matt Walbeck	.25
20	Armando Benitez	.25
21	Steve Karsay	.25
22	Jose Oliva	.25
23	Cliff Floyd	.25
24	Kevin Foster	.25
25	Javier Lopez	.25
26	Jose Valentin	.25
27	James Mouton	.25
28	Hector Carrasco	.25
29	Orlando Miller	.25
30	Garret Anderson	.25
31	Marvin Freeman	.25
32	Brett Butler	.25
33	Roberto Kelly	.25
34	Rod Beck	.25
35	Jose Rijo	.25
36	Edgar Martinez	.25
37	Jim Thome	.25
38	Rick Wilkins	.25
39	Wally Joyner	.25
40	Wil Cordero	.25
41	Tommy Greene	.25
42	Travis Fryman	.25
43	Don Slaught	.25
44	Brady Anderson	.25
45	Matt Williams	.25
46	Rene Arocha	.25
47	Rickey Henderson	1.50
48	Mike Mussina	1.00
49	Greg McMichael	.25
50	Jody Reed	.25
51	Tino Martinez	.25
52	Dave Clark	.25
53	John Valentin	.25
54	Bret Boone	.25
55	Walt Weiss	.25
56	Kenny Lofton	.25
57	Scott Leius	.25
58	Eric Karros	.25
59	John Olerud	.25
60	Chris Hoiles	.25
61	Sandy Alomar	.25
62	Tim Wallach	.25
63	Cal Eldred	.25
64	Tom Glavine	.50
65	Mark Grace	.35
66	Rey Sanchez	.25
67	Bobby Ayala	.25
68	Dante Bichette	.25
69	Andres Galarraga	.25
70	Chuck Carr	.25
71	Bobby Witt	.25
72	Steve Avery	.25
73	Bobby Jones	.25
74	Delino DeShields	.25
75	Kevin Tapani	.25
76	Randy Johnson	1.50
77	David Nied	.25
78	Pat Hentgen	.25
79	Tim Salmon	.50
80	Todd Zeile	.25

81	John Wetteland	.25
82	Albert Belle	.35
83	Ben McDonald	.25
84	Bobby Munoz	.25
85	Bip Roberts	.25
86	Mo Vaughn	.25
87	Chuck Finley	.25
88	Chuck Knoblauch	.25
89	Frank Thomas	1.50
90	Danny Tartabull	.25
91	Dean Palmer	.25
92	Len Dykstra	.25
93	J.R. Phillips	.25
94	Tom Candiotti	.25
95	Marquis Grissom	.25
96	Barry Larkin	.25
97	Bryan Harvey	.25
98	Dave Justice	.25
99	David Cone	.25
100	Wade Boggs	2.50
101	Jason Bere	.25
102	Hal Morris	.25
103	Fred McGriff	.25
104	Bobby Bonilla	.25
105	Jay Buhner	.25
106	Allen Watson	.25
107	Mickey Tettleton	.25
108	Kevin Appier	.25
109	Ivan Rodriguez	1.50
110	Carlos Garcia	.25
111	Andy Benes	.25
112	Eddie Murray	1.50
113	Mike Piazza	3.00
114	Greg Vaughn	.25
115	Paul Molitor	1.50
116	Terry Steinbach	.25
117	Jeff Bagwell	1.50
118	Ken Griffey Jr.	3.00
119	Gary Sheffield	.75
120	Cal Ripken Jr.	5.00
121	Jeff Kent	.25
122	Jay Bell	.25
123	Will Clark	.35
124	Cecil Fielder	.25
125	Alex Fernandez	.25
126	Don Mattingly	3.00
127	Reggie Sanders	.25
128	Moises Alou	.25
129	Craig Biggio	.25
130	Eddie Williams	.25
131	John Franco	.25
132	John Kruk	.25
133	Jeff King	.25
134	Royce Clayton	.25
135	Doug Drabek	.25
136	Ray Lankford	.25
137	Roberto Alomar	.50
138	Todd Hundley	.25
139	Alex Cole	.25
140	Shawon Dunston	.25
141	John Roper	.25
142	Mark Langston	.25
143	Tom Pagnozzi	.25
144	Wilson Alvarez	.25
145	Scott Cooper	.25
146	Kevin Mitchell	.25
147	Mark Whiten	.25
148	Jeff Conine	.25
149	Chili Davis	.25
150	Luis Gonzalez	.50
151	Juan Guzman	.25
152	Mike Greenwell	.25
153	Mike Henneman	.25
154	Rick Aguilera	.25
155	Dennis Eckersley	1.00
156	Darrin Fletcher	.25
157	Darren Lewis	.25
158	Juan Gonzalez	1.50
159	Dave Hollins	.25
160	Jimmy Key	.25
161	Roberto Hernandez	.25
162	Randy Myers	.25
163	Joe Carter	.25
164	Darren Daulton	.25
165	Mike MacFarlane	.25
166	Bret Saberhagen	.25
167	Kirby Puckett	2.50
168	Lance Johnson	.25
169	Mark McGwire	4.00
170	Jose Canseco	.75
171	Mike Stanley	.25
172	Lee Smith	.25
173	Robin Ventura	.25
174	Greg Gagne	.25
175	Brian McRae	.25
176	Mike Bordick	.25
177	Rafael Palmeiro	1.50
178	Kenny Rogers	.25
179	Chad Curtis	.25
180	Devon White	.25
181	Paul O'Neill	.25
182	Ken Caminiti	.25
183	Dave Nilsson	.25
184	Tim Naehring	.25
185	Roger Clemens	2.75
186	Otis Nixon	.25
187	Tim Raines	.25
188	Dennis Martinez	.25
189	Pedro Martinez	1.50
190	Jim Abbott	.25
191	Ryan Thompson	.25
192	Barry Bonds	5.00
193	Joe Girardi	.25
194	Steve Finley	.25
195	John Jaha	.25
196	Tony Gwynn	2.50
197	Sammy Sosa	3.00
198	John Burkett	.25
199	Carlos Baerga	.25
200	Ramon Martinez	.25
201	Aaron Sele	.25
202	Eduardo Perez	.25
203	Alan Trammell	.25
204	Orlando Merced	.25
205	Deion Sanders	.35
206	Robb Nen	.25
207	Jack McDowell	.25
208	Ruben Sierra	.25
209	Bernie Williams	.50
210	Kevin Seitzer	.25
211	Charles Nagy	.25
212	Tony Phillips	.25
213	Greg Maddux	2.50
214	Jeff Montgomery	.25
215	Larry Walker	.25
216	Andy Van Slyke	.25
217	Ozzie Smith	2.50
218	Geronimo Pena	.25
219	Gregg Jefferies	.25
220	Lou Whitaker	.25

Refractors

	NM/M
Complete Set (220):	400.00
Common Player:	1.00
Stars:	5X

(See 1995 Finest for checklist and base card values.)

Bronze League Leaders

		NM/M
Complete Set (6):		22.50
Common Player:		2.50
1	Matt Williams	2.50
2	Tony Gwynn	6.50
3	Jeff Bagwell	5.00
4	Ken Griffey Jr.	9.00
5	Paul O'Neill	2.50
6	Frank Thomas	5.00

Flame Throwers

		NM/M
Complete Set (9):		20.00
Common Player:		1.50
1	Jason Bere	1.50
2	Roger Clemens	8.00
3	Juan Guzman	1.50
4	John Hudek	1.50
5	Randy Johnson	5.00
6	Pedro Martinez	4.00
7	Jose Rijo	1.50
8	Bret Saberhagen	1.50
9	John Wetteland	1.50

Power Kings

		NM/M
Complete Set (18):		35.00
Common Player:		.75
1	Bob Hamelin	.75
2	Raul Mondesi	.75
3	Ryan Klesko	.75
4	Carlos Delgado	2.50
5	Manny Ramirez	3.50
6	Mike Piazza	5.00
7	Jeff Bagwell	3.00
8	Mo Vaughn	.75
9	Frank Thomas	3.50
10	Ken Griffey Jr.	5.00
11	Albert Belle	1.00
12	Sammy Sosa	5.00
13	Dante Bichette	.75
14	Gary Sheffield	.75
15	Matt Williams	.75
16	Fred McGriff	.75
17	Barry Bonds	7.50
18	Cecil Fielder	.75

Update

		NM/M
Complete Set (110):		20.00
Common Player:		.25
Wax Pack (7):		1.25
Wax Box (24):		20.00
221	Chipper Jones	2.50
222	Benji Gil	.25
223	Tony Phillips	.25
224	Trevor Wilson	.25
225	Tony Tarasco	.25
226	Roberto Petagine	.25
227	Mike MacFarlane	.25
228	*Hideo Nomo*	3.00
229	Mark McLemore	.25
230	Ron Gant	.25
231	Andujar Cedeno	.25
232	*Mike Mimbs*	.25
233	Jim Abbott	.25
234	Ricky Bones	.25
235	Marty Cordova	.25
236	Mark Johnson	.25
237	Marquis Grissom	.25
238	Tom Henke	.25
239	Terry Pendleton	.25
240	John Wetteland	.25
241	Lee Smith	.25
242	Jaime Navarro	.25
243	Luis Alicea	.25
244	Scott Cooper	.25
245	Gary Gaetti	.25
246	Edgardo Alfonzo	.25
247	Brad Clontz	.25
248	Dave Mlicki	.25
249	Dave Winfield	1.00
250	*Mark Grudzielanek*	1.00
251	Alex Gonzalez	.25
252	Kevin Brown	.35
253	Esteban Loaiza	.25
254	Vaughn Eshelman	.25
255	Bill Swift	.25
256	Brian McRae	.25
257	*Bobby Higginson*	1.00
258	Jack McDowell	.25
259	Scott Stahoviak	.25
260	Jon Nunnally	.25
261	Charlie Hayes	.25
262	Jacob Brumfield	.25
263	Chad Curtis	.25
264	Heathcliff Slocumb	.25
265	Mark Whiten	.25
266	Mickey Tettleton	.25
267	Jose Mesa	.25
268	Doug Jones	.25
269	Trevor Hoffman	.25
270	Paul Sorrento	.25
271	Shane Andrews	.25
272	Brett Butler	.25
273	Curtis Goodwin	.25
274	Larry Walker	.25
275	Phil Plantier	.25
276	Ken Hill	.25
277	Vinny Castilla	.25
278	Billy Ashley	.25
279	Derek Jeter	6.00
280	Bob Tewksbury	.25
281	Jose Offerman	.25
282	Glenallen Hill	.25
283	Tony Fernandez	.25
284	Mike Devereaux	.25
285	John Burkett	.25
286	Geronimo Berroa	.25
287	Quilvio Veras	.25
288	Jason Bates	.25
289	Lee Tinsley	.25
290	Derek Bell	.25
291	Jeff Fassero	.25
292	Ray Durham	.25
293	Chad Ogea	.25
294	Bill Pulsipher	.25
295	Phil Nevin	.25
296	*Carlos Perez*	.25
297	Roberto Kelly	.25
298	Tim Wakefield	.25
299	Jeff Manto	.25
300	Brian Hunter	.25
301	C.J. Nitkowski	.25
302	Dustin Hermanson	.25
303	John Mabry	.25
304	Orel Hershiser	.25
305	Ron Villone	.25
306	Sean Bergman	.25
307	Tom Goodwin	.25
308	Al Reyes	.25
309	Todd Stottlemyre	.25
310	Rich Becker	.25
311	Joey Cora	.25
312	Ed Sprague	.25
313	John Smoltz	.25
314	Frank Castillo	.25
315	Chris Hammond	.25
316	Ismael Valdes	.25
317	Pete Harnisch	.25
318	Bernard Gilkey	.25
319	John Kruk	.25
320	Marc Newfield	.25
321	Brian Johnson	.25
322	Mark Portugal	.25
323	David Hulse	.25
324	Luis Ortiz	.25
325	Mike Benjamin	.25
326	Brian Jordan	.25
327	Shawn Green	1.00
328	Joe Oliver	.25
329	Felipe Lira	.25
330	Andre Dawson	.75

Update Refractors

	NM/M
Complete Set (110):	100.00
Common Player:	1.00
Stars:	5X

(See 1995 Finest Update for checklist and base card values.)

1996 FINEST

	NM/M
Complete Set (359):	300.00
Bronze Set (220):	60.00
Common Bronze:	.15
Silver Set (91):	90.00
Typical Silver:	.50
Gold Set (47):	200.00
Typical Gold:	2.00
Series 1 Pack (6):	1.50
Series 1 Wax Box (24):	30.00
Series 2 Pack (6):	1.50
Series 2 Wax Box (24):	30.00

#	Player	NM/M
1	Greg Maddux S	3.00
2	Bernie Williams S	1.00
3	Ivan Rodriguez S	1.50
4	Marty Cordova G	2.00
5	Roberto Hernandez	.15
6	Tony Gwynn G	7.50
7	Barry Larkin S	.50
8	Terry Pendleton	.15
9	Albert Belle G	2.50
10	Ray Lankford S	.50
11	Mike Piazza S	4.00
12	Ken Caminiti	.15
13	Larry Walker S	.50
14	Matt Williams S	.50
15	Dan Miceli	.15
16	Chipper Jones	2.00
17	John Wetteland	.15
18	Kirby Puckett G	7.50
19	Tim Naehring	.15
20	Karim Garcia G	2.50
21	Eddie Murray	1.00
22	Tim Salmon S	.75
23	Kevin Appier	.15
24	Ken Griffey Jr.	3.00
25	Cal Ripken Jr. G	15.00
26	Brian McRae	.15
27	Pedro Martinez	1.00
28	Brian Jordan	.15
29	Mike Fetters	.15
30	Carlos Delgado	.65
31	Shane Reynolds	.15
32	Terry Steinbach	.15
33	Hideo Nomo G	5.00
34	Mark Leiter	.15
35	Edgar Martinez S	.50
36	David Segui	.15
37	Gregg Jefferies S	.50
38	Bill Pulsipher S	.50
39	Ryne Sandberg G	7.50
40	Fred McGriff	.15
41	Shawn Green S	1.00
42	Jeff Bagwell G	5.00
43	Jim Abbott S	.50
44	Glenallen Hill	.15
45	Brady Anderson	.15
46	Roger Clemens S	3.50
47	Jim Thome	.15
48	Frank Thomas	1.00
49	Chuck Knoblauch	.15
50	Lenny Dykstra	.15
51	Jason Isringhausen G	2.00
52	Rondell White S	.50
53	Tom Pagnozzi	.15
54	Dennis Eckersley S	1.50
55	Ricky Bones	.15
56	David Justice	.15
57	Steve Avery	.15
58	Robby Thompson	.15
59	Hideo Nomo S	2.00
60	Gary Sheffield S	.75
61	Tony Gwynn	2.00
62	Will Clark S	.60
63	Denny Neagle	.15
64	Mo Vaughn G	2.00
65	Bret Boone S	.50
66	Dante Bichette G	2.00
67	Robin Ventura	.15
68	Rafael Palmeiro S	1.50
69	Carlos Baerga S	.50
70	Kevin Seitzer	.15
71	Ramon Martinez	.15
72	Tom Glavine S	1.00
73	Garret Anderson S	.50
74	Mark McGwire G	12.00
75	Brian Hunter	.15
76	Alan Benes	.15
77	Randy Johnson S	2.00
78	Jeff King S	.50
79	Kirby Puckett S	3.00
80	Ozzie Guillen	.15
81	Kenny Lofton G	2.00
82	Benji Gil	.15
83	Jim Edmonds G	2.00
84	Cecil Fielder S	.50
85	Todd Hundley	.15
86	Reggie Sanders S	.50
87	Pat Hentgen	.15
88	Ryan Klesko S	.50
89	Chuck Finley	.15
90	Mike Mussina G	4.00
91	John Valentin S	.50
92	Derek Jeter	4.00
93	Paul O'Neill	.15
94	Darrin Fletcher	.15
95	Manny Ramirez S	2.00
96	Delino DeShields	.15
97	Tim Salmon	.25
98	John Olerud	.15
99	Vinny Castilla S	.50
100	Jeff Conine G	2.00
101	Tim Wakefield	.15
102	Johnny Damon G	3.50
103	Dave Stevens	.15
104	Orlando Merced	.15
105	Barry Bonds G	15.00
106	Jay Bell	.15
107	John Burkett	.15
108	Chris Hoiles	.15
109	Carlos Perez S	.50
110	Dave Nilsson	.15
111	Rod Beck	.15
112	Craig Biggio S	.50
113	Mike Piazza	3.00
114	Mark Langston	.15
115	Juan Gonzalez S	2.00
116	Rico Brogna	.15
117	Jose Canseco G	3.00
118	Tom Goodwin	.15
119	Bryan Rekar	.15
120	David Cone	.15
121	Ray Durham S	.50
122	Andy Pettitte	.40
123	Chili Davis	.15
124	John Smoltz	.15
125	Heathcliff Slocumb	.15
126	Dante Bichette	.15
127	C.J. Nitkowski S	.50
128	Alex Gonzalez	.15
129	Jeff Montgomery	.15
130	Raul Mondesi S	.50
131	Denny Martinez	.15
132	Mel Rojas	.15
133	Derek Bell	.15
134	Trevor Hoffman	.15
135	Ken Griffey Jr. G	9.00
136	Darren Daulton	.15
137	Pete Schourek	.15
138	Phil Nevin	.15
139	Andres Galarraga	.15
140	Chad Fonville	.15
141	Chipper Jones G	7.50
142	Lee Smith S	.50
143	Joe Carter S	.50
144	J.T. Snow	.15
145	Greg Maddux G	7.50
146	Barry Bonds	4.00
147	Orel Hershiser	.15
148	Quilvio Veras	.15
149	Will Clark	.25
150	Jose Rijo	.15
151	Mo Vaughn S	.50
152	Travis Fryman	.15
153	Frank Rodriguez S	.50
154	Alex Fernandez	.15
155	Wade Boggs	2.00
156	Troy Percival	.15
157	Moises Alou	.15
158	Javy Lopez	.15
159	Jason Giambi	.50
160	Steve Finley S	.50
161	Jeff Bagwell S	2.00
162	Mark McGwire	3.50
163	Eric Karros	.15
164	Jay Buhner G	2.00
165	Cal Ripken Jr. S	6.00
166	Mickey Tettleton	.15
167	Barry Larkin	.15
168	Lyle Mouton S	.50
169	Ruben Sierra	.15
170	Bill Swift	.15
171	Sammy Sosa S	4.00
172	Chad Curtis	.15
173	Dean Palmer	.15
174	John Franco S	.50
175	Bobby Bonilla	.15
176	Greg Colbrunn	.15
177	Jose Mesa	.15
178	Mike Greenwell	.15
179	Greg Vaughn S	.50
180	Mark Wohlers S	.50
181	Doug Drabek	.15
182	Paul O'Neill S	.50
183	Wilson Alvarez	.15
184	Marty Cordova	.15
185	Hal Morris	.15
186	Frank Thomas G	6.00
187	Carlos Garcia	.15
188	Albert Belle S	.75
189	Mark Grace S	.75
190	Marquis Grissom	.15
191	Checklist	.15
192	Chipper Jones G	7.50
193	Will Clark	.20
194	Paul Molitor	1.00
195	Kenny Rogers	.15
196	Reggie Sanders	.15
197	Roberto Alomar G	2.50
198	Dennis Eckersley G	4.00
199	Raul Mondesi	.15
200	Lance Johnson	.15
201	Alvin Mormon	.15
202	George Arias G	2.00
203	Jack McDowell	.15
204	Randy Myers	.15
205	Harold Baines	.15
206	Marty Cordova	.15
207	*Rich Hunter*	.15
208	Al Leiter	.15
209	Greg Gagne	.15
210	Ben McDonald	.15
211	Ernie Young S	.50
212	Terry Adams	.15
213	Paul Sorrento	.15
214	Albert Belle	.25
215	Mike Blowers	.15
216	Jim Edmonds	.15
217	Felipe Crespo	.15
218	Fred McGriff S	.50
219	Shawon Dunston	.15
220	Jimmy Haynes	.15
221	Jose Canseco	.50
222	Eric Davis	.15
223	Kimera Bartee S	.50
224	Tim Raines	.15
225	Tony Phillips	.15
226	Charlie Hayes	.15
227	Eric Owens	.15
228	Roberto Alomar	.50
229	Rickey Henderson S	2.00
230	Sterling Hitchcock S	.50
231	Bernard Gilkey S	.50
232	Hideo Nomo G	5.00
233	Kenny Lofton	.15
234	Ryne Sandberg S	3.00
235	Greg Maddux S	3.00
236	Mark McGwire	3.50
237	Jay Buhner	.15
238	Craig Biggio	.15
239	Todd Stottlemyre S	.50
240	Barry Bonds	4.00
241	Jason Kendall S	.50
242	Paul O'Neill S	.50
243	Chris Snopek G	2.00
244	Ron Gant	.15
245	Paul Wilson	.15
246	Todd Hollandsworth	.15
247	Todd Zeile	.15
248	David Justice	.15
249	Tim Salmon G	2.50
250	Moises Alou	.15
251	Bob Wolcott	.15
252	David Wells	.15
253	Juan Gonzalez	1.00
254	Andres Galarraga	.15
255	Dave Hollins	.15
256	Devon White S	.50
257	Sammy Sosa	3.00
258	Ivan Rodriguez	.65
259	Bip Roberts	.15
260	Tino Martinez	.15
261	Chuck Knoblauch S	.50
262	Mike Stanley	.15
263	Wally Joyner S	.50
264	Butch Huskey	.15
265	Jeff Conine	.15
266	Matt Williams G	2.00
267	Mark Grace	.25
268	Jason Schmidt	.15
269	Otis Nixon	.15
270	Randy Johnson G	5.00
271	Kirby Puckett	2.00
272	*Andy Fox S*	.50
273	Andy Benes	.15
274	Sean Berry S	.50
275	Mike Piazza	3.00
276	Rey Ordonez	.15
277	Benito Santiago S	.50
278	Gary Gaetti	.15
279	Paul Molitor G	5.00
280	Robin Ventura	.15
281	Cal Ripken Jr.	4.00
282	Carlos Baerga	.15
283	Roger Cedeno	.15
284	Chad Mottola S	.50
285	Terrell Wade	.15
286	Kevin Brown	.15
287	Rafael Palmeiro	.75
288	Mo Vaughn	.15
289	Dante Bichette S	.50
290	Cecil Fielder G	2.00
291	Doc Gooden S	.50
292	Bob Tewksbury	.15
293	Kevin Mitchell S	.50
294	*Livan Hernandez G*	2.00
295	Russ Davis S	.50
296	Chan Ho Park S	.50
297	T.J. Mathews	.15
298	Manny Ramirez	1.00
299	Jeff Bagwell	1.00
300	*Marty Janzen G*	2.00
301	Wade Boggs	2.00
302	Larry Walker S	.50
303	Steve Gibralter	.15
304	B.J. Surhoff	.15
305	Ken Griffey Jr. S	4.00
306	Royce Clayton	.15
307	Sal Fasano	.15
308	Ron Gant G	2.00
309	Gary Sheffield	.40
310	Ken Hill	.15
311	Joe Girardi	.15
312	*Matt Lawton*	.15
313	Billy Wagner S	.50
314	Julio Franco	.15
315	Joe Carter	.15
316	Brooks Kieschnick	.15
317	*Mike Grace S*	.50
318	Heathcliff Slocumb	.15
319	Barry Larkin	.15
320	Tony Gwynn	2.00
321	Ryan Klesko G	2.00
322	Frank Thomas	1.00
323	Edgar Martinez	.15
324	Jermaine Dye G	2.00
325	Henry Rodriguez	.15
326	*Marvin Benard*	.50
327	Kenny Lofton S	.50
328	Derek Bell S	.50
329	Ugueth Urbina	.15
330	Jason Giambi G	3.00
331	Roger Salkeld	.15
332	Edgar Renteria	.15
333	Ryan Klesko	.15
334	Ray Lankford	.15
335	Edgar Martinez G	2.00
336	Justin Thompson	.15
337	Gary Sheffield S	.75
338	Rey Ordonez G	2.00
339	Mark Clark	.15
340	Ruben Rivera	.15
341	Mark Grace S	.75
342	Matt Williams	.15
343	*Francisco Cordova*	.25
344	Cecil Fielder	.15
345	Andres Galarraga S	.50
346	Brady Anderson S	.50
347	Sammy Sosa G	9.00
348	Mark Grudzielanek	.15
349	Ron Coomer	.15
350	Derek Jeter S	6.00
351	Rich Aurilia	.15
352	Jose Herrera	.15
353	Jay Buhner S	.50
354	Juan Gonzalez G	5.00
355	Craig Biggio G	2.00
356	Tony Clark	.15
357	Tino Martinez S	.50
358	*Dan Naulty*	.15
359	Checklist	.15

Refractors

	NM/M
Complete Set (359):	900.00

Bronze Set (220): 300.00
Common Bronze: 1.00
Bronze Stars: 4X
Silver Set (91): 250.00
Typical Silver: 2.00
Silver Stars: 2.5X
Gold Set (48): 600.00
Typical Gold: 6.00
Gold Stars: 2X
(See 1996 Finest for checkl-ist and base card values.)

1997 FINEST

NM/M
Complete Set (350): 250.00
Bronze Set (200): 20.00
Common Bronze: .15
Silver Set (100): 75.00
Typical Silver: .50
Embossed Silvers: 2X
Gold Set (50): 150.00
Typical Gold: 2.00
Embossed Die-Cut Golds: 1.5X
Series 1 or 2 Pack (6): 1.50
Series 1 or 2 Wax Box (24): 25.00

1 Barry Bonds B 2.00
2 Ryne Sandberg B .75
3 Brian Jordan B .15
4 Rocky Coppinger B .15
5 Dante Bichette B .15
6 Al Martin B .15
7 Charles Nagy B .15
8 Otis Nixon B .15
9 Mark Johnson B .15
10 Jeff Bagwell B .60
11 Ken Hill B .15
12 Willie Adams B .15
13 Raul Mondesi B .15
14 Reggie Sanders B .15
15 Derek Jeter B 2.00
16 Jermaine Dye B .15
17 Edgar Renteria B .15
18 Travis Fryman B .15
19 Roberto Hernandez B .15
20 Sammy Sosa B 1.00
21 Garret Anderson B .15
22 Rey Ordonez B .15
23 Glenallen Hill B .15
24 Dave Nilsson B .15
25 Kevin Brown B .15
26 Brian McRae B .15
27 Joey Hamilton B .15
28 Jamey Wright B .15
29 Frank Thomas B .60
30 Mark McGwire B 1.50
31 Ramon Martinez B .15
32 Jaime Bluma B .15
33 Frank Rodriguez B .15
34 Andy Benes B .15
35 Jay Buhner B .15
36 Justin Thompson B .15
37 Darin Erstad B .50
38 Gregg Jefferies B .15
39 Jeff D'Amico B .15
40 Pedro Martinez B .60
41 Nomar Garciaparra B 1.00
42 Jose Valentin B .15
43 Pat Hentgen B .15
44 Will Clark B .20
45 Bernie Williams B .30
46 Luis Castillo B .15
47 B.J. Surhoff B .15
48 Greg Gagne B .15
49 Pete Schourek B .15
50 Mike Piazza B 1.00
51 Dwight Gooden B .15
52 Javy Lopez B .15
53 Chuck Finley B .15
54 James Baldwin B .15
55 Jack McDowell B .15
56 Royce Clayton B .15
57 Carlos Delgado B .50
58 Neifi Perez B .15
59 Eddie Taubensee B .15
60 Rafael Palmeiro B .50
61 Marty Cordova B .15
62 Wade Boggs B .75
63 Rickey Henderson B .60
64 Mike Hampton B .15
65 Troy Percival B .15
66 Barry Larkin B .15
67 Jermaine Allensworth B .15
68 Mark Clark B .15
69 Mike Lansing B .15
70 Mark Grudzielanek B .15
71 Todd Stottlemyre B .15
72 Juan Guzman B .15
73 John Burkett B .15
74 Wilson Alvarez B .15
75 Ellis Burks B .15
76 Bobby Higginson B .15
77 Ricky Bottalico B .15
78 Omar Vizquel B .15
79 Paul Sorrento B .15
80 Denny Neagle B .15
81 Roger Pavlik B .15
82 Mike Lieberthal B .15
83 Devon White B .15
84 John Olerud B .15
85 Kevin Appier B .15
86 Joe Girardi B .15
87 Paul O'Neill B .15
88 Mike Sweeney B .15
89 John Smiley B .15
90 Ivan Rodriguez B .50
91 Randy Myers B .15
92 Bip Roberts B .15
93 Jose Mesa B .15
94 Paul Wilson B .15
95 Mike Mussina B .30
96 Ben McDonald B .15
97 John Mabry B .15
98 Tom Goodwin B .15
99 Edgar Martinez B .15
100 Andruw Jones B .60
101 Jose Canseco S .75
102 Billy Wagner S .50
103 Dante Bichette S .50
104 Curt Schilling S 1.00
105 Dean Palmer S .50
106 Larry Walker S .50
107 Bernie Williams S .75
108 Chipper Jones S 2.00
109 Gary Sheffield S 1.00
110 Randy Johnson S 1.50
111 Roberto Alomar S .75
112 Todd Walker S .50
113 Sandy Alomar S .50
114 John Jaha S .50
115 Ken Caminiti S .50
116 Ryan Klesko S .50
117 Mariano Rivera S .75
118 Jason Giambi S 1.00
119 Lance Johnson S .50
120 Robin Ventura S .50
121 Todd Hollandsworth S .50
122 Johnny Damon S .75
123 William VanLandingham S .50
124 Jason Kendall S .50
125 Vinny Castilla S .50
126 Harold Baines S .50
127 Joe Carter S .50
128 Craig Biggio S .50
129 Tony Clark S .50
130 Ron Gant S .50
131 David Segui S .50
132 Steve Trachsel S .50
133 Scott Rolen S 1.50
134 Mike Stanley S .50
135 Cal Ripken Jr. S 5.00
136 John Smoltz S .50
137 Bobby Jones S .50
138 Manny Ramirez S 1.50
139 Ken Griffey Jr. S 3.00
140 Chuck Knoblauch S .50
141 Mark Grace S .65
142 Chris Snopek S .50
143 Hideo Nomo S 1.50
144 Tim Salmon S .75
145 David Cone S .50
146 Eric Young S .50
147 Jeff Brantley S .50
148 Jim Thome S .50
149 Trevor Hoffman S .50
150 Juan Gonzalez S 1.50
151 Mike Piazza G 10.00
152 Ivan Rodriguez G 4.50
153 Mo Vaughn G 2.00
154 Brady Anderson G 2.00
155 Mark McGwire G 11.00
156 Rafael Palmeiro G 4.50
157 Barry Larkin G 2.00
158 Greg Maddux G 7.50
159 Jeff Bagwell G 6.00
160 Frank Thomas G 6.00
161 Ken Caminiti G 2.00
162 Andruw Jones G 6.00
163 Dennis Eckersley G 4.50
164 Jeff Conine G 2.00
165 Jim Edmonds G 2.00
166 Derek Jeter G 12.50
167 Vladimir Guerrero G 6.00
168 Sammy Sosa G 10.00
169 Tony Gwynn G 7.50
170 Andres Galarraga G 2.00
171 Todd Hundley G 2.00
172 Jay Buhner G 2.00
173 Paul Molitor G 6.00
174 Kenny Lofton G 2.00
175 Barry Bonds G 12.50
176 Gary Sheffield B .35
177 Dmitri Young B .15
178 Jay Bell B .15
179 David Wells B .15
180 Walt Weiss B .15
181 Paul Molitor B .60
182 Jose Guillen B .15
183 Al Leiter B .15
184 Mike Fetters B .15
185 Mark Langston B .15
186 Fred McGriff B .15
187 Darrin Fletcher B .15
188 Brant Brown B .15
189 Geronimo Berroa B .15
190 Jim Thome B .15
191 Jose Vizcaino B .15
192 Andy Ashby B .15
193 Rusty Greer B .15
194 Brian Hunter B .15
195 Chris Hoiles B .15
196 Orlando Merced B .15
197 Brett Butler B .15
198 Derek Bell B .15
199 Bobby Bonilla B .15
200 Alex Ochoa B .15
201 Wally Joyner B .15
202 Mo Vaughn B .15
203 Doug Drabek B .15
204 Tino Martinez B .15
205 Roberto Alomar B .50
206 *Brian Giles B* .75
207 Todd Worrell B .15
208 Alan Benes B .15
209 Jim Leyritz B .15
210 Darryl Hamilton B .15
211 Jimmy Key B .15
212 Juan Gonzalez B .60
213 Vinny Castilla B .15
214 Chuck Knoblauch B .15
215 Tony Phillips B .15
216 Jeff Cirillo B .15
217 Carlos Garcia B .15
218 Brooks Kieschnick B .15
219 Marquis Grissom B .15
220 Dan Wilson B .15
221 Greg Vaughn B .15
222 John Wetteland B .15
223 Andres Galarraga B .15
224 Ozzie Guillen B .15
225 Kevin Elster B .15
226 Bernard Gilkey B .15
227 Mike MacFarlane B .15
228 Heathcliff Slocumb B .15
229 Wendell Magee Jr. B .15
230 Carlos Baerga B .15
231 Kevin Seitzer B .15
232 Henry Rodriguez B .15
233 Roger Clemens B .85
234 Mark Wohlers B .15
235 Eddie Murray B .60
236 Todd Zeile B .15
237 J.T. Snow B .15
238 Ken Griffey Jr. B 1.00
239 Sterling Hitchcock B .15
240 Albert Belle B .25
241 Terry Steinbach B .15
242 Robb Nen B .15
243 Mark McLemore B .15
244 Jeff King B .15
245 Tony Clark B .15
246 Tim Salmon B .25
247 Benito Santiago B .15
248 Robin Ventura B .15
249 *Bubba Trammell B* .15
250 Chili Davis B .15
251 John Valentin B .15
252 Cal Ripken Jr. B 2.00
253 Matt Williams B .15
254 Jeff Kent B .15
255 Eric Karros B .15
256 Ray Lankford B .15
257 Ed Sprague B .15
258 Shane Reynolds B .15
259 Jaime Navarro B .15
260 Eric Davis B .15
261 Orel Hershiser B .15
262 Mark Grace B .25
263 Rod Beck B .15
264 Ismael Valdes B .15
265 Manny Ramirez B .60
266 Ken Caminiti B .15
267 Tim Naehring B .15
268 Jose Rosado B .15
269 Greg Colbrunn B .15
270 Dean Palmer B .15
271 David Justice B .15
272 Scott Spiezio B .15
273 Chipper Jones B .75
274 Mel Rojas B .15
275 Bartolo Colon B .15
276 Darin Erstad S 1.00
277 Sammy Sosa S 3.00
278 Rafael Palmeiro S 1.25
279 Frank Thomas S 1.50
280 Ruben Rivera S .50
281 Hal Morris S .50
282 Jay Buhner S .50
283 Kenny Lofton S .50
284 Jose Canseco S .75
285 Alex Fernandez S .50
286 Todd Helton S 1.50
287 Andy Pettitte S 1.00
288 John Franco S .50
289 Ivan Rodriguez S 1.25
290 Ellis Burks S .50
291 Julio Franco S .50
292 Mike Piazza S 3.00
293 Brian Jordan S .50
294 Greg Maddux S 2.00
295 Bob Abreu S .50
296 Rondell White S .50
297 Moises Alou S .50
298 Tony Gwynn S 2.00
299 Deion Sanders S .50
300 Jeff Montgomery S .50
301 Ray Durham S .50
302 John Wasdin S .50
303 Ryne Sandberg S 2.00
304 Delino DeShields S .50
305 Mark McGwire S 4.00
306 Andruw Jones S 1.50
307 Kevin Orie S .50
308 Matt Williams S .50
309 Karim Garcia S .50
310 Derek Jeter S 5.00
311 Mo Vaughn S .50
312 Brady Anderson S .50
313 Barry Bonds S 5.00
314 Steve Finley S .50
315 Vladimir Guerrero S 1.50
316 Matt Morris S .50
317 Tom Glavine S 1.00
318 Jeff Bagwell S 1.50
319 Albert Belle S .65
320 *Hideki Irabu S* 1.00
321 Andres Galarraga S .50
322 Cecil Fielder S .50
323 Barry Larkin S .50
324 Todd Hundley S .50
325 Fred McGriff S .50
326 Gary Sheffield G 3.00
327 Craig Biggio G 2.00
328 Raul Mondesi G 2.00
329 Edgar Martinez G 2.00
330 Chipper Jones G 7.50
331 Bernie Williams G 2.50
332 Juan Gonzalez G 6.00
333 Ron Gant G 2.00
334 Cal Ripken Jr. G 12.50
335 Larry Walker G 2.00
336 Matt Williams G 2.00
337 Jose Cruz Jr. G 2.00
338 Joe Carter G 2.00
339 Wilton Guerrero G 2.00
340 Cecil Fielder G 2.00
341 Todd Walker G 2.00
342 Ken Griffey Jr. G 10.00
343 Ryan Klesko G 2.00
344 Roger Clemens G 9.00
345 Hideo Nomo G 6.00
346 Dante Bichette G 2.00
347 Albert Belle G 1.50
348 Randy Johnson G 6.00
349 Manny Ramirez G 6.00
350 John Smoltz G 2.00

Refractors

	NM/M
Common Bronze:	2.00
Bronze Stars:	6X
Typical Silver:	3.00
Silver Stars:	3X
Typical Gold:	8.00
Gold Stars:	2X
Typical Embossed Silver:	7.50
Embossed Silver Stars:	7X
Typical Embossed Gold:	20.00
Embossed Gold Stars:	5X

(See 1997 Finest for cheklist and base card values.)

Embossed

	NM/M
Common Embossed Silver:	1.00
Embossed Silver Stars:	2X
Common Embossed Gold:	3.00
Embossed/Die-Cut Gold Stars:	1.5X

(See 1997 Finest for checklist and base card values.)

1998 FINEST

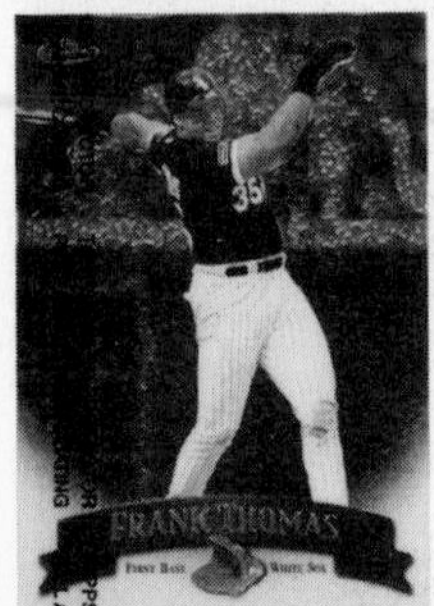

	NM/M
Complete Set (275):	30.00
Complete Series 1 Set (150):	17.50
Complete Series 2 Set (125):	12.50
Common Player:	.15
Pack (6):	1.50
Wax Box (24):	25.00
Jumbo Pack (13):	2.50
Jumbo Box (12):	25.00

1	Larry Walker	.15
2	Andruw Jones	.75
3	Ramon Martinez	.15
4	Geronimo Berroa	.15
5	David Justice	.15
6	Rusty Greer	.15
7	Chad Ogea	.15
8	Tom Goodwin	.15
9	Tino Martinez	.15
10	Jose Guillen	.15
11	Jeffrey Hammonds	.15
12	Brian McRae	.15
13	Jeremi Gonzalez	.15
14	Craig Counsell	.15
15	Mike Piazza	1.25
16	Greg Maddux	1.00
17	Todd Greene	.15
18	Rondell White	.15
19	Kirk Rueter	.15
20	Tony Clark	.15
21	Brad Radke	.15
22	Jaret Wright	.15
23	Carlos Delgado	.50
24	Dustin Hermanson	.15
25	Gary Sheffield	.40
26	Jose Canseco	.35
27	Kevin Young	.15
28	David Wells	.15
29	Mariano Rivera	.25
30	Reggie Sanders	.15
31	Mike Cameron	.15
32	Bobby Witt	.15
33	Kevin Orie	.15
34	Royce Clayton	.15
35	Edgar Martinez	.15
36	Neifi Perez	.15
37	Kevin Appier	.15
38	Darryl Hamilton	.15
39	Michael Tucker	.15
40	Roger Clemens	1.00
41	Carl Everett	.15
42	Mike Sweeney	.15
43	Pat Meares	.15
44	Brian Giles	.15
45	Matt Morris	.15
46	Jason Dickson	.15
47	Rich Loiselle	.15
48	Joe Girardi	.15
49	Steve Trachsel	.15
50	Ben Grieve	.15
51	Jose Vizcaino	.15
52	Hideki Irabu	.15
53	J.T. Snow	.15
54	Mike Hampton	.15
55	Dave Nilsson	.15
56	Alex Fernandez	.15
57	Brett Tomko	.15
58	Wally Joyner	.15
59	Kelvim Escobar	.15
60	Roberto Alomar	.30
61	Todd Jones	.15
62	Paul O'Neill	.15
63	Jamie Moyer	.15
64	Mark Wohlers	.15
65	Jose Cruz Jr.	.15
66	Troy Percival	.15
67	Rick Reed	.15
68	Will Clark	.20
69	Jamey Wright	.15
70	Mike Mussina	.35
71	David Cone	.15
72	Ryan Klesko	.15
73	Scott Hatteberg	.15
74	James Baldwin	.15
75	Tony Womack	.15
76	Carlos Perez	.15
77	Charles Nagy	.15
78	Jeromy Burnitz	.15
79	Shane Reynolds	.15
80	Cliff Floyd	.15
81	Jason Kendall	.15
82	Chad Curtis	.15
83	Matt Karchner	.15
84	Ricky Bottalico	.15
85	Sammy Sosa	1.25
86	Javy Lopez	.15
87	Jeff Kent	.15
88	Shawn Green	.25
89	Devon White	.15
90	Tony Gwynn	1.00
91	Bob Tewksbury	.15
92	Derek Jeter	2.00
93	Eric Davis	.15
94	Jeff Fassero	.15
95	Denny Neagle	.15
96	Ismael Valdes	.15
97	Tim Salmon	.20
98	Mark Grudzielanek	.15
99	Curt Schilling	.35
100	Ken Griffey Jr.	1.25
101	Edgardo Alfonzo	.15
102	Vinny Castilla	.15
103	Jose Rosado	.15
104	Scott Erickson	.15
105	Alan Benes	.15
106	Shannon Stewart	.15
107	Delino DeShields	.15
108	Mark Loretta	.15
109	Todd Hundley	.15
110	Chuck Knoblauch	.15
111	Quinton McCracken	.15
112	F.P. Santangelo	.15
113	Gerald Williams	.15
114	Omar Vizquel	.15
115	John Valentin	.15
116	Damion Easley	.15
117	Matt Lawton	.15
118	Jim Thome	.15
119	Sandy Alomar	.15
120	Albert Belle	.25
121	Chris Stynes	.15
122	Butch Huskey	.15
123	Shawn Estes	.15
124	Terry Adams	.15
125	Ivan Rodriguez	.60
126	Ron Gant	.15
127	John Mabry	.15
128	Jeff Shaw	.15
129	Jeff Montgomery	.15
130	Justin Thompson	.15
131	Livan Hernandez	.15
132	Ugueth Urbina	.15
133	Doug Glanville	.15
134	Troy O'Leary	.15
135	Cal Ripken Jr.	2.00
136	Quilvio Veras	.15
137	Pedro Astacio	.15
138	Willie Greene	.15
139	Lance Johnson	.15
140	Nomar Garciaparra	1.25
141	Jose Offerman	.15
142	Scott Rolen	.75
143	Derek Bell	.15
144	Johnny Damon	.25
145	Mark McGwire	1.50
146	Chan Ho Park	.15
147	Edgar Renteria	.15
148	Eric Young	.15
149	Craig Biggio	.15
150	Checklist 1-150	.15
151	Frank Thomas	.75
152	John Wetteland	.15
153	Mike Lansing	.15
154	Pedro Martinez	.75
155	Rico Brogna	.15
156	Kevin Brown	.15
157	Alex Rodriguez	1.50
158	Wade Boggs	1.00
159	Richard Hidalgo	.15
160	Mark Grace	.15
161	Jose Mesa	.15
162	John Olerud	.15
163	Tim Belcher	.15
164	Chuck Finley	.15
165	Brian Hunter	.15
166	Joe Carter	.15
167	Stan Javier	.15
168	Jay Bell	.15
169	Ray Lankford	.15
170	John Smoltz	.15
171	Ed Sprague	.15
172	Jason Giambi	.50
173	Todd Walker	.15
174	Paul Konerko	.15
175	Rey Ordonez	.15
176	Dante Bichette	.15
177	Bernie Williams	.25
178	Jon Nunnally	.15
179	Rafael Palmeiro	.60
180	Jay Buhner	.15
181	Devon White	.15
182	Jeff D'Amico	.15
183	Walt Weiss	.15
184	Scott Spiezio	.15
185	Moises Alou	.15
186	Carlos Baerga	.15
187	Todd Zeile	.15
188	Gregg Jefferies	.15
189	Mo Vaughn	.15
190	Terry Steinbach	.15
191	Ray Durham	.15
192	Robin Ventura	.15
193	Jeff Reed	.15
194	Ken Caminiti	.15
195	Eric Karros	.15
196	Wilson Alvarez	.15
197	Gary Gaetti	.15
198	Andres Galarraga	.15
199	Alex Gonzalez	.15
200	Garret Anderson	.15
201	Andy Benes	.15
202	Harold Baines	.15
203	Ron Coomer	.15
204	Dean Palmer	.15
205	Reggie Jefferson	.15
206	John Burkett	.15
207	Jermaine Allensworth	.15
208	Bernard Gilkey	.15
209	Jeff Bagwell	.75
210	Kenny Lofton	.15
211	Bobby Jones	.15
212	Bartolo Colon	.15
213	Jim Edmonds	.15
214	Pat Hentgen	.15
215	Matt Williams	.15
216	Bob Abreu	.15
217	Jorge Posada	.15
218	Marty Cordova	.15
219	Ken Hill	.15
220	Steve Finley	.15
221	Jeff King	.15
222	Quinton McCracken	.15
223	Matt Stairs	.15
224	Darin Erstad	.60
225	Fred McGriff	.15
226	Marquis Grissom	.15
227	Doug Glanville	.15
228	Tom Glavine	.35
229	John Franco	.15
230	Darren Bragg	.15
231	Barry Larkin	.15
232	Trevor Hoffman	.15
233	Brady Anderson	.15
234	Al Martin	.15
235	B.J. Surhoff	.15
236	Ellis Burks	.15
237	Randy Johnson	.75
238	Mark Clark	.15
239	Tony Saunders	.15
240	Hideo Nomo	.60
241	Brad Fullmer	.15
242	Chipper Jones	1.00
243	Jose Valentin	.15
244	Manny Ramirez	.75
245	Derrek Lee	.15
246	Jimmy Key	.15
247	Tim Naehring	.15
248	Bobby Higginson	.15
249	Charles Johnson	.15
250	Chili Davis	.15
251	Tom Gordon	.15
252	Mike Lieberthal	.15
253	Billy Wagner	.15
254	Juan Guzman	.15
255	Todd Stottlemyre	.15
256	Brian Jordan	.15
257	Barry Bonds	2.00
258	Dan Wilson	.15
259	Paul Molitor	.75
260	Juan Gonzalez	.75
261	Francisco Cordova	.15
262	Cecil Fielder	.15
263	Travis Lee	.15
264	Kevin Tapani	.15
265	Raul Mondesi	.15
266	Travis Fryman	.15
267	Armando Benitez	.15
268	Pokey Reese	.15
269	Rick Aguilera	.15
270	Andy Pettitte	.35
271	Jose Vizcaino	.15
272	Kerry Wood	.50
273	Vladimir Guerrero	.75
274	John Smiley	.15
275	Checklist 151-275	.15

Refractors

	NM/M
Complete Set (275):	200.00
Common Player:	1.00
Stars/Rookies:	4X

(See 1998 Finest for checklist and base card values.)

No-Protector

	NM/M
Complete Set (275):	150.00
Common Player:	.50
Stars/Rookies:	2.5X

(See 1998 Finest for checklist and base card values.)

No-Protector Refractor

	NM/M
Complete Set (275):	400.00
Common Player:	2.00
Stars/Rookies:	8X

(See 1998 Finest for checklist and base card values.)

Centurions

	NM/M
Complete Set (20):	75.00

Common Player:		1.50
Production 500 sets		
Refractors (75 sets):		4X
C1	Andruw Jones	4.50
C2	Vladimir Guerrero	4.50
C3	Nomar Garciaparra	8.00
C4	Scott Rolen	4.50
C5	Ken Griffey Jr.	8.00
C6	Jose Cruz Jr.	1.50
C7	Barry Bonds	12.00
C8	Mark McGwire	10.00
C9	Juan Gonzalez	4.50
C10	Jeff Bagwell	4.50
C11	Frank Thomas	4.50
C12	Paul Konerko	2.00
C13	Alex Rodriguez	10.00
C14	Mike Piazza	8.00
C15	Travis Lee	1.50
C16	Chipper Jones	6.00
C17	Larry Walker	1.50
C18	Mo Vaughn	1.50
C19	Livan Hernandez	1.50
C20	Jaret Wright	1.50

Jumbo

		NM/M
Complete Set (16):		30.00
Common Player:		1.00
Refractors:		1.5X
	FIRST SERIES	
1	Mark McGwire	4.00
2	Cal Ripken Jr.	5.00
3	Nomar Garciaparra	3.00
4	Mike Piazza	3.00
5	Greg Maddux	2.00
6	Jose Cruz Jr.	1.00
7	Roger Clemens	2.50
8	Ken Griffey Jr.	3.00
	SECOND SERIES	
1	Frank Thomas	1.50
2	Bernie Williams	1.00
3	Randy Johnson	1.50
4	Chipper Jones	2.00
5	Manny Ramirez	1.50
6	Barry Bonds	5.00
7	Juan Gonzalez	1.50
8	Jeff Bagwell	1.50

Power Zone

		NM/M
Complete Set (20):		25.00
Common Player:		.50
1	Ken Griffey Jr.	3.00
2	Jeff Bagwell	2.00
3	Jose Cruz Jr.	.50
4	Barry Bonds	5.00
5	Mark McGwire	4.00
6	Jim Thome	.50
7	Mo Vaughn	.50
8	Gary Sheffield	1.00
9	Andres Galarraga	.50
10	Nomar Garciaparra	3.00
11	Rafael Palmeiro	1.50
12	Sammy Sosa	3.00
13	Jay Buhner	.50
14	Tony Clark	.50
15	Mike Piazza	3.00
16	Larry Walker	.50
17	Albert Belle	.65
18	Tino Martinez	.50
19	Juan Gonzalez	2.00
20	Frank Thomas	2.00

Mystery Finest

		NM/M
Complete Set (50):		125.00
Common Player:		1.50
Refractors:		4X
M1	Frank Thomas, Ken Griffey Jr.	3.00
M2	Frank Thomas, Mike Piazza	3.00
M3	Frank Thomas, Mark McGwire	4.00
M4	Frank Thomas, Frank Thomas	2.00
M5	Ken Griffey Jr., Mike Piazza	3.00
M6	Ken Griffey Jr., Mark McGwire	4.00
M7	Ken Griffey Jr., Ken Griffey Jr.	4.00
M8	Mike Piazza, Mark McGwire	4.00
M9	Mike Piazza, Mike Piazza	4.00
M10	Mark McGwire, Mark McGwire	6.00
M11	Nomar Garciaparra, Jose Cruz Jr.	3.00
M12	Nomar Garciaparra, Derek Jeter	5.00
M13	Nomar Garciaparra, Andruw Jones	3.00
M14	Nomar Garciaparra, Nomar Garciaparra	4.00
M15	Jose Cruz Jr., Derek Jeter	5.00
M16	Jose Cruz Jr., Andruw Jones	1.50
M17	Jose Cruz Jr., Jose Cruz Jr.	1.50
M18	Derek Jeter, Andruw Jones	5.00
M19	Derek Jeter, Derek Jeter	7.50
M20	Andruw Jones, Andruw Jones	2.00
M21	Cal Ripken Jr., Tony Gwynn	5.00
M22	Cal Ripken Jr., Barry Bonds	5.00
M23	Cal Ripken Jr., Greg Maddux	5.00
M24	Cal Ripken Jr., Cal Ripken Jr.	7.50
M25	Tony Gwynn, Barry Bonds	5.00
M26	Tony Gwynn, Greg Maddux	2.50
M27	Tony Gwynn, Tony Gwynn	3.00
M28	Barry Bonds, Greg Maddux	5.00
M29	Barry Bonds, Barry Bonds	7.50
M30	Greg Maddux, Greg Maddux	3.00
M31	Juan Gonzalez, Larry Walker	1.50
M32	Juan Gonzalez, Andres Galarraga	1.50
M33	Juan Gonzalez, Chipper Jones	2.50
M34	Juan Gonzalez, Juan Gonzalez	2.00
M35	Larry Walker, Andres Galarraga	1.50
M36	Larry Walker, Chipper Jones	2.50
M37	Larry Walker, Larry Walker	1.50
M38	Andres Galarraga, Chipper Jones	2.50
M39	Andres Galarraga, Andres Galarraga	1.50
M40	Chipper Jones, Chipper Jones	3.00
M41	Gary Sheffield, Sammy Sosa	3.00
M42	Gary Sheffield, Jeff Bagwell	1.50
M43	Gary Sheffield, Tino Martinez	1.50
M44	Gary Sheffield, Gary Sheffield	2.00
M45	Sammy Sosa, Jeff Bagwell	3.00
M46	Sammy Sosa, Tino Martinez	3.00
M47	Sammy Sosa, Sammy Sosa	4.00
M48	Jeff Bagwell, Tino Martinez	1.50
M49	Jeff Bagwell, Jeff Bagwell	2.00
M50	Tino Martinez, Tino Martinez	1.50

Mystery Finest 2

		NM/M
Complete Set (40):		100.00
Common Player:		1.50
Refractors:		4X
M1	Nomar Garciaparra, Frank Thomas	3.50
M2	Nomar Garciaparra, Albert Belle	3.50
M3	Nomar Garciaparra, Scott Rolen	3.50
M4	Frank Thomas, Albert Belle	2.50
M5	Frank Thomas, Scott Rolen	2.50
M6	Albert Belle, Scott Rolen	1.50
M7	Ken Griffey Jr., Jose Cruz	4.00
M8	Ken Griffey Jr., Alex Rodriguez	6.00
M9	Ken Griffey Jr., Roger Clemens	4.50
M10	Jose Cruz, Alex Rodriguez	6.00
M11	Jose Cruz, Roger Clemens	3.00
M12	Alex Rodriguez, Roger Clemens	6.00
M13	Mike Piazza, Barry Bonds	6.00
M14	Mike Piazza, Derek Jeter	6.00
M15	Mike Piazza, Bernie Williams	5.00
M16	Barry Bonds, Derek Jeter	6.50
M17	Barry Bonds, Bernie Williams	4.00
M18	Derek Jeter, Bernie Williams	6.00
M19	Mark McGwire, Jeff Bagwell	4.50
M20	Mark McGwire, Mo Vaughn	5.00
M21	Mark McGwire, Jim Thome	5.00
M22	Jeff Bagwell, Mo Vaughn	2.00
M23	Jeff Bagwell, Jim Thome	1.50
M24	Mo Vaughn, Jim Thome	1.50
M25	Juan Gonzalez, Travis Lee	2.00
M26	Juan Gonzalez, Ben Grieve	2.00
M27	Juan Gonzalez, Fred McGriff	2.00
M28	Travis Lee, Ben Grieve	1.50
M29	Travis Lee, Fred McGriff	1.50
M30	Ben Grieve, Fred McGriff	1.50
M31	Albert Belle, Albert Belle	1.50
M32	Scott Rolen, Scott Rolen	2.00
M33	Alex Rodriguez, Alex Rodriguez	6.00
M34	Roger Clemens, Roger Clemens	4.00
M35	Bernie Williams, Bernie Williams	1.50
M36	Mo Vaughn, Mo Vaughn	1.50
M37	Jim Thome, Jim Thome	1.50
M38	Travis Lee, Travis Lee	1.50
M39	Fred McGriff, Fred McGriff	1.50
M40	Ben Grieve, Ben Grieve	1.50

Stadium Stars

		NM/M
Complete Set (24):		95.00
Common Player:		1.00
SS1	Ken Griffey Jr.	8.00
SS2	Alex Rodriguez	10.00
SS3	Mo Vaughn	1.00
SS4	Nomar Garciaparra	8.00
SS5	Frank Thomas	4.50
SS6	Albert Belle	1.00
SS7	Derek Jeter	12.00
SS8	Chipper Jones	6.00
SS9	Cal Ripken Jr.	12.00
SS10	Jim Thome	1.00
SS11	Mike Piazza	8.00
SS12	Juan Gonzalez	4.50
SS13	Jeff Bagwell	4.50
SS14	Sammy Sosa	8.00
SS15	Jose Cruz Jr.	1.00
SS16	Gary Sheffield	2.00
SS17	Larry Walker	1.00
SS18	Tony Gwynn	6.00
SS19	Mark McGwire	10.00
SS20	Barry Bonds	12.00
SS21	Tino Martinez	1.00
SS22	Manny Ramirez	4.50
SS23	Ken Caminiti	1.00
SS24	Andres Galarraga	1.00

The Man

		NM/M
Complete Set (20):		125.00

Common Player:		1.50
Refractors:		3X
TM1	Ken Griffey Jr.	10.00
TM2	Barry Bonds	15.00
TM3	Frank Thomas	6.00
TM4	Chipper Jones	7.50
TM5	Cal Ripken Jr.	15.00
TM6	Nomar Garciaparra	10.00
TM7	Mark McGwire	12.50
TM8	Mike Piazza	10.00
TM9	Derek Jeter	15.00
TM10	Alex Rodriguez	12.50
TM11	Jose Cruz Jr.	1.50
TM12	Larry Walker	1.50
TM13	Jeff Bagwell	6.00
TM14	Tony Gwynn	7.50
TM15	Travis Lee	2.00
TM16	Juan Gonzalez	6.00
TM17	Scott Rolen	4.50
TM18	Randy Johnson	6.00
TM19	Roger Clemens	9.00
TM20	Greg Maddux	7.50

1999 FINEST

		NM/M
Complete Set (300):		80.00
Complete Series 1 (150):		30.00
Complete Series 2 (150):		50.00
Common Player:		.15
Common SP (101-150, 251-300):		.50
Pack (6):		2.00
Wax Box (24):		35.00
1	Darin Erstad	.50
2	Javy Lopez	.15
3	Vinny Castilla	.15
4	Jim Thome	.15
5	Tino Martinez	.15
6	Mark Grace	.25
7	Shawn Green	.40
8	Dustin Hermanson	.15
9	Kevin Young	.15
10	Tony Clark	.15
11	Scott Brosius	.15
12	Craig Biggio	.15
13	Brian McRae	.15
14	Chan Ho Park	.15
15	Manny Ramirez	1.00
16	Chipper Jones	1.50
17	Rico Brogna	.15
18	Quinton McCracken	.15
19	J.T. Snow Jr.	.15
20	Tony Gwynn	1.50
21	Juan Guzman	.15
22	John Valentin	.15
23	Rick Helling	.15
24	Sandy Alomar	.15
25	Frank Thomas	1.00
26	Jorge Posada	.40
27	Dmitri Young	.15
28	Rick Reed	.15
29	Kevin Tapani	.15
30	Troy Glaus	1.00
31	Kenny Rogers	.15
32	Jeromy Burnitz	.15
33	Mark Grudzielanek	.15
34	Mike Mussina	.75
35	Scott Rolen	.75
36	Neifi Perez	.15
37	Brad Radke	.15
38	Darryl Strawberry	.15
39	Robb Nen	.15
40	Moises Alou	.15
41	Eric Young	.15
42	Livan Hernandez	.15
43	John Wetteland	.15
44	Matt Lawton	.15
45	Ben Grieve	.15
46	Fernando Tatis	.15
47	Travis Fryman	.15
48	David Segui	.15
49	Bob Abreu	.15
50	Nomar Garciaparra	2.00
51	Paul O'Neill	.15
52	Jeff King	.15
53	Francisco Cordova	.15
54	John Olerud	.15
55	Vladimir Guerrero	1.00
56	Fernando Vina	.15
57	Shane Reynolds	.15
58	Chuck Finley	.15
59	Rondell White	.15
60	Greg Vaughn	.15
61	Ryan Minor	.15
62	Tom Gordon	.15
63	Damion Easley	.15
64	Ray Durham	.15
65	Orlando Hernandez	.15
66	Bartolo Colon	.15
67	Jaret Wright	.15
68	Royce Clayton	.15
69	Tim Salmon	.25
70	Mark McGwire	2.50
71	Alex Gonzalez	.15
72	Tom Glavine	.40
73	David Justice	.15
74	Omar Vizquel	.15
75	Juan Gonzalez	1.00
76	Bobby Higginson	.15
77	Todd Walker	.15
78	Dante Bichette	.15
79	Kevin Millwood	.15
80	Roger Clemens	1.75
81	Kerry Wood	.75
82	Cal Ripken Jr.	3.00
83	Jay Bell	.15
84	Barry Bonds	3.00
85	Alex Rodriguez	2.50
86	Doug Glanville	.15
87	Jason Kendall	.15
88	Sean Casey	.25
89	Aaron Sele	.15
90	Derek Jeter	3.00
91	Andy Ashby	.15
92	Rusty Greer	.15
93	Rod Beck	.15
94	Matt Williams	.15
95	Mike Piazza	2.00
96	Wally Joyner	.15
97	Barry Larkin	.15
98	Eric Milton	.15
99	Gary Sheffield	.50
100	Greg Maddux	1.50
101	Ken Griffey Jr. (Gem)	4.00
102	Frank Thomas(Gem)	2.00
103	Nomar Garciaparra (Gem)	4.00
104	Mark McGwire (Gem)	5.00
105	Alex Rodriguez (Gem)	5.00
106	Tony Gwynn (Gem)	3.00
107	Juan Gonzalez (Gem)	1.50
108	Jeff Bagwell (Gem)	2.00
109	Sammy Sosa (Gem)	4.00
110	Vladimir Guerrero (Gem)	2.00
111	Roger Clemens (Gem)	3.50
112	Barry Bonds (Gem)	6.00
113	Darin Erstad (Gem)	1.00
114	Mike Piazza (Gem)	4.00
115	Derek Jeter (Gem)	6.00
116	Chipper Jones (Gem)	3.00
117	Larry Walker (Gem)	.50
118	Scott Rolen (Gem)	1.50
119	Cal Ripken Jr. (Gem)	6.00
120	Greg Maddux (Gem)	3.00
121	Troy Glaus (Sensations)	2.50
122	Ben Grieve (Sensations)	.50
123	Ryan Minor (Sensations)	.50
124	Kerry Wood (Sensations)	1.25
125	Travis Lee (Sensations)	.50
126	Adrian Beltre (Sensations)	.65
127	Brad Fullmer (Sensations)	.50
128	Aramis Ramirez (Sensations)	.50
129	Eric Chavez (Sensations)	.50
130	Todd Helton (Sensations)	2.00
131	*Pat Burrell* (Finest Rookies)	4.00
132	*Ryan Mills* (Finest Rookies)	.75
133	*Austin Kearns* (Finest Rookies)	3.00
134	*Josh McKinley* (Finest Rookies)	.75
135	*Adam Everett* (Finest Rookies)	.75
136	Marlon Anderson	.50
137	Bruce Chen	.50
138	Matt Clement	.60
139	Alex Gonzalez	.50
140	Roy Halladay	.75
141	Calvin Pickering	.50
142	Randy Wolf	.50
143	Ryan Anderson	.50
144	Ruben Mateo	.50
145	*Alex Escobar*	1.00
146	Jeremy Giambi	.50
147	Lance Berkman	.50
148	Michael Barrett	.50
149	Preston Wilson	.50
150	Gabe Kapler	.50
151	Roger Clemens	1.75
152	Jay Buhner	.15
153	Brad Fullmer	.15
154	Ray Lankford	.15
155	Jim Edmonds	.15
156	Jason Giambi	.75
157	Bret Boone	.15
158	Jeff Cirillo	.15
159	Rickey Henderson	.75
160	Edgar Martinez	.15
161	Ron Gant	.15
162	Mark Kotsay	.15
163	Trevor Hoffman	.15
164	Jason Schmidt	.15
165	Brett Tomko	.15
166	David Ortiz	.40
167	Dean Palmer	.15
168	Hideki Irabu	.15
169	Mike Cameron	.15
170	Pedro Martinez	1.00
171	Tom Goodwin	.15
172	Brian Hunter	.15
173	Al Leiter	.15
174	Charles Johnson	.15
175	Curt Schilling	.50
176	Robin Ventura	.15
177	Travis Lee	.15
178	Jeff Shaw	.15
179	Ugueth Urbina	.15
180	Roberto Alomar	.40
181	Cliff Floyd	.15
182	Adrian Beltre	.25
183	Tony Womack	.15
184	Brian Jordan	.15
185	Randy Johnson	1.00
186	Mickey Morandini	.15
187	Todd Hundley	.15
188	Jose Valentin	.15
189	Eric Davis	.15
190	Ken Caminiti	.15
191	David Wells	.15
192	Ryan Klesko	.15
193	Garret Anderson	.15
194	Eric Karros	.15
195	Ivan Rodriguez	.75
196	Aramis Ramirez	.25
197	Mike Lieberthal	.15
198	Will Clark	.25
199	Rey Ordonez	.15
200	Ken Griffey Jr.	2.00
201	Jose Guillen	.15
202	Scott Erickson	.15
203	Paul Konerko	.15
204	Johnny Damon	.40
205	Larry Walker	.15
206	Denny Neagle	.15
207	Jose Offerman	.15
208	Andy Pettitte	.40
209	Bobby Jones	.15
210	Kevin Brown	.15
211	John Smoltz	.15
212	Henry Rodriguez	.15
213	Tim Belcher	.15
214	Carlos Delgado	.50
215	Andruw Jones	1.00
216	Andy Benes	.15
217	Fred McGriff	.15
218	Edgar Renteria	.15
219	Miguel Tejada	.25
220	Bernie Williams	.40
221	Justin Thompson	.15
222	Marty Cordova	.15
223	Delino DeShields	.15
224	Ellis Burks	.15
225	Kenny Lofton	.15
226	Steve Finley	.15
227	Eric Chavez	.25
228	Jose Cruz Jr.	.15
229	Marquis Grissom	.15
230	Jeff Bagwell	1.00
231	Jose Canseco	.50
232	Edgardo Alfonzo	.15
233	Richie Sexson	.15
234	Jeff Kent	.15
235	Rafael Palmeiro	.75
236	David Cone	.15
237	Gregg Jefferies	.15
238	Mike Lansing	.15
239	Mariano Rivera	.25
240	Albert Belle	.15
241	Chuck Knoblauch	.15
242	Derek Bell	.15
243	Pat Hentgen	.15
244	Andres Galarraga	.15
245	Mo Vaughn	.15
246	Wade Boggs	1.50
247	Devon White	.15
248	Todd Helton	1.00
249	Raul Mondesi	.15
250	Sammy Sosa	2.00
251	Nomar Garciaparra (Sterling)	4.00
252	Mark McGwire (Sterling)	5.00
253	Alex Rodriguez (Sterling)	5.00
254	Juan Gonzalez (Sterling)	1.50
255	Vladimir Guerrero (Sterling)	2.00
256	Ken Griffey Jr. (Sterling)	4.00
257	Mike Piazza (Sterling)	4.00
258	Derek Jeter (Sterling)	6.00
259	Albert Belle (Sterling)	.50
260	Greg Vaughn (Sterling)	.50
261	Sammy Sosa (Sterling)	4.00
262	Greg Maddux (Sterling)	3.00
263	Frank Thomas (Sterling)	2.00
264	Mark Grace (Sterling)	.65
265	Ivan Rodriguez (Sterling)	1.25
266	Roger Clemens (Gamers)	3.50
267	Mo Vaughn (Gamers)	.50
268	Jim Thome (Gamers)	.50
269	Darin Erstad (Gamers)	.75
270	Chipper Jones (Gamers)	2.50
271	Larry Walker (Gamers)	.50
272	Cal Ripken Jr. (Gamers)	6.00
273	Scott Rolen (Gamers)	2.00
274	Randy Johnson (Gamers)	2.00
275	Tony Gwynn (Gamers)	2.50
276	Barry Bonds (Gamers)	6.00
277	*Sean Burroughs*	1.50
278	*J.M. Gold*	.50
279	Carlos Lee	.50
280	George Lombard	.50
281	Carlos Beltran	1.50
282	Fernando Seguignol	.50
283	Eric Chavez	.65
284	*Carlos Pena*	.75
285	*Corey Patterson*	2.00
286	*Alfonso Soriano*	8.00
287	*Nick Johnson*	2.00
288	*Jorge Toca*	.50
289	*A.J. Burnett*	1.00
290	*Andy Brown*	.75
291	*Doug Mientkiewicz*	1.00
292	*Bobby Seay*	.75
293	*Chip Ambres*	.75
294	*C.C. Sabathia*	1.00
295	*Choo Freeman*	1.00
296	*Eric Valent*	.75
297	*Matt Belisle*	.75
298	*Jason Tyner*	.75
299	*Masao Kida*	.50
300	Hank Aaron, Mark McGwire (Homerun Kings)	3.00

Refractors

	NM/M
Complete Set (300):	750.00
Common Player:	1.00
Stars:	6X
SPs:	3X

(See 1999 Finest for checklist and base card values.)

Gold Refractors

	NM/M
Common Player:	3.00
Stars:	15X
SPs:	10X

(See 1999 Finest for checklist and base card values.)

Complements

		NM/M
Complete Set (7):		25.00
Common Player:		2.50
Inserted 1:56		
Dual-Refractors:		2X
Inserted 1:168		
1	Mike Piazza, Ivan Rodriguez	4.00
2	Tony Gwynn, Wade Boggs	3.00
3	Kerry Wood, Roger Clemens	3.00
4	Juan Gonzalez, Sammy Sosa	4.00
5	Derek Jeter, Nomar Garciaparra	6.00
6	Mark McGwire, Frank Thomas	5.00
7	Vladimir Guerrero, Andruw Jones	2.50

Double Feature

		NM/M
Complete Set (7):		30.00
Common Player:		2.00
Dual-Refractors:		2X
1	Ken Griffey Jr., Alex Rodriguez	10.00
2	Chipper Jones, Andruw Jones	6.00
3	Darin Erstad, Mo Vaughn	2.00
4	Craig Biggio, Jeff Bagwell	4.00
5	Ben Grieve, Eric Chavez	2.00
6	Albert Belle, Cal Ripken Jr.	10.00
7	Scott Rolen, Pat Burrell	4.00

Franchise Records

		NM/M
Complete Set (10):		35.00
Common Player:		2.00
Refractors:		3X
1	Frank Thomas	2.50
2	Ken Griffey Jr.	5.00
3	Mark McGwire	6.00
4	Juan Gonzalez	2.00
5	Nomar Garciaparra	5.00
6	Mike Piazza	5.00
7	Cal Ripken Jr.	7.50
8	Sammy Sosa	5.00
9	Barry Bonds	7.50
10	Tony Gwynn	3.00

Future's Finest

		NM/M
Complete Set (10):		35.00
Common Player:		2.00
1	Pat Burrell	10.00
2	Troy Glaus	12.50
3	Eric Chavez	4.00
4	Ryan Anderson	2.00
5	Ruben Mateo	2.00
6	Gabe Kapler	2.00
7	Alex Gonzalez	2.00
8	Michael Barrett	2.00
9	Lance Berkman	2.00
10	Fernando Seguignol	2.00

Hank Aaron Award Contenders

		NM/M
Complete Set (9):		25.00
Common Player:		2.00
Refractors:		3X
1	Juan Gonzalez	2.50
2	Vladimir Guerrero	2.50
3	Nomar Garciaparra	4.00
4	Albert Belle	2.00
5	Frank Thomas	2.50
6	Sammy Sosa	4.00
7	Alex Rodriguez	5.00
8	Ken Griffey Jr.	4.00
9	Mark McGwire	5.00

Leading Indicators

		NM/M
Complete Set (10):		20.00
Common Player:		.50
Inserted 1:24		
L1	Mark McGwire	5.00
L2	Sammy Sosa	4.00
L3	Ken Griffey Jr.	4.00
L4	Greg Vaughn	.50
L5	Albert Belle	.50
L6	Juan Gonzalez	1.50
L7	Andres Galarraga	.50
L8	Alex Rodriguez	5.00
L9	Barry Bonds	6.00
L10	Jeff Bagwell	1.50

Milestones

		NM/M
Complete Set (40):		125.00
Common Hits (1-10):		.50
Common Homeruns (11-20):		2.00
Common RBI (21-30):		1.00
Common Doubles (31-40):		2.00
1	Tony Gwynn (Hits)	1.50
2	Cal Ripken Jr. (Hits)	3.00
3	Wade Boggs (Hits)	1.50
4	Ken Griffey Jr. (Hits)	2.00
5	Frank Thomas(Hits)	1.00
6	Barry Bonds (Hits)	3.00
7	Travis Lee (Hits)	.50
8	Alex Rodriguez (Hits)	2.50
9	Derek Jeter (Hits)	3.00
10	Vladimir Guerrero (Hits)	1.00
11	Mark McGwire (Home Runs)	8.00
12	Ken Griffey Jr. (Home Runs)	7.00
13	Vladimir Guerrero (Home Runs)	4.00
14	Alex Rodriguez (Home Runs)	8.00
15	Barry Bonds (Home Runs)	10.00
16	Sammy Sosa (Home Runs)	7.00
17	Albert Belle (Home Runs)	2.00
18	Frank Thomas (Home Runs)	4.00
19	Jose Canseco (Home Runs)	3.00
20	Mike Piazza (Home Runs)	7.00
21	Jeff Bagwell (RBI)	2.00
22	Barry Bonds (RBI)	6.00
23	Ken Griffey Jr. (RBI)	4.00
24	Albert Belle (RBI)	1.50
25	Juan Gonzalez (RBI)	2.00
26	Vinny Castilla (RBI)	1.00
27	Mark McGwire (RBI)	5.00
28	Alex Rodriguez (RBI)	5.00
29	Nomar Garciaparra (RBI)	4.00
30	Frank Thomas (RBI)	2.50
31	Barry Bonds (Doubles)	10.00
32	Albert Belle (Doubles)	2.00
33	Ben Grieve (Doubles)	2.00
34	Craig Biggio (Doubles)	2.00
35	Vladimir Guerrero (Doubles)	4.00
36	Nomar Garciaparra (Doubles)	7.00
37	Alex Rodriguez (Doubles)	7.00
38	Derek Jeter (Doubles)	10.00
39	Ken Griffey Jr. (Doubles)	7.00
40	Brad Fullmer (Doubles)	2.00

Peel & Reveal

		NM/M
Complete Set (20):		40.00
Common Player:		1.00
Hyperplaid:		1.5X
Stadium Stars:		2.5X
1	Kerry Wood	1.50
2	Mark McGwire	5.00
3	Sammy Sosa	4.00
4	Ken Griffey Jr.	4.00
5	Nomar Garciaparra	4.00
6	Greg Maddux	3.00
7	Derek Jeter	6.00
8	Andres Galarraga	1.00
9	Alex Rodriguez	5.00
10	Frank Thomas	2.00
11	Roger Clemens	3.50
12	Juan Gonzalez	2.00
13	Ben Grieve	1.00
14	Jeff Bagwell	2.00
15	Todd Helton	2.00
16	Chipper Jones	3.00
17	Barry Bonds	6.00
18	Travis Lee	1.00
19	Vladimir Guerrero	2.00
20	Pat Burrell	1.50

Prominent Figures

		NM/M
Complete Set (50):		250.00
Common Home Runs (1-10); #d to 70:		3.00
Common Slugging % (11-20); #d to 847:		1.00
Common Batting Ave. (21-30); #d to 424:		1.75
Common RBIs (31-40); #d to 190:		2.00
Common Total Bases (41-50); #d to 457:		1.75
1	Mark McGwire (HR)	25.00
2	Sammy Sosa (HR)	15.00
3	Ken Griffey Jr. (HR)	15.00
4	Mike Piazza (HR)	15.00
5	Juan Gonzalez (HR)	7.50
6	Greg Vaughn (HR)	3.00
7	Alex Rodriguez (HR)	25.00
8	Manny Ramirez (HR)	7.50
9	Jeff Bagwell (HR)	7.50
10	Andres Galarraga (HR)	3.00
11	Mark McGwire (S%)	6.00
12	Sammy Sosa (S%)	5.00
13	Juan Gonzalez (S%)	2.50
14	Ken Griffey Jr. (S%)	5.00
15	Barry Bonds (S%)	7.50
16	Greg Vaughn (S%)	1.00
17	Larry Walker (S%)	1.00
18	Andres Galarraga (S%)	1.00
19	Jeff Bagwell (S%)	2.50
20	Albert Belle (S%)	1.50
21	Tony Gwynn (BA)	5.00
22	Mike Piazza (BA)	6.00
23	Larry Walker (BA)	1.75
24	Alex Rodriguez (BA)	7.50
25	John Olerud (BA)	1.75
26	Frank Thomas (BA)	3.50
27	Bernie Williams (BA)	1.75
28	Chipper Jones (BA)	5.00
29	Jim Thome (BA)	1.75
30	Barry Bonds (BA)	9.00
31	Juan Gonzalez (RBI)	6.00
32	Sammy Sosa (RBI)	15.00
33	Mark McGwire (RBI)	20.00
34	Albert Belle (RBI)	2.00
35	Ken Griffey Jr. (RBI)	15.00
36	Jeff Bagwell (RBI)	6.00
37	Chipper Jones (RBI)	9.00
38	Vinny Castilla (RBI)	2.00
39	Alex Rodriguez (RBI)	20.00
40	Andres Galarraga (RBI)	2.00
41	Sammy Sosa (TB)	6.00
42	Mark McGwire (TB)	7.50
43	Albert Belle (TB)	1.75
44	Ken Griffey Jr. (TB)	6.00
45	Jeff Bagwell (TB)	3.50
46	Juan Gonzalez (TB)	3.50
47	Barry Bonds (TB)	9.00
48	Vladimir Guerrero (TB)	3.50
49	Larry Walker (TB)	1.75
50	Alex Rodriguez (TB)	7.50

Split Screen

	NM/M
Complete Set (14):	30.00
Common Card:	1.00

Dual-Refractor: 2X
1 Mark McGwire, Sammy Sosa 4.00
2 Ken Griffey Jr., Alex Rodriguez 4.00
3 Nomar Garciaparra, Derek Jeter 5.00
4 Barry Bonds, Albert Belle 4.00
5 Cal Ripken Jr., Tony Gwynn 4.00
6 Manny Ramirez, Juan Gonzalez 1.50
7 Frank Thomas, Andres Galarraga 1.50
8 Scott Rolen, Chipper Jones 1.50
9 Ivan Rodriguez, Mike Piazza 3.00
10 Kerry Wood, Roger Clemens 2.50
11 Greg Maddux, Tom Glavine 2.00
12 Troy Glaus, Eric Chavez 1.50
13 Ben Grieve, Todd Helton 1.00
14 Travis Lee, Pat Burrell 2.50

Team Finest

NM/M

Complete Set (20): 25.00
Common Blue: 1.00
Production 1,500 sets
Blue Refractors: 3X
Production 150 sets
Reds: 1.5X
Production 500 sets
Red Refractors: 7X
Production 50 sets
Golds: 2X
Production 250 sets
Gold Refractors: 10X
Production 25 sets
1 Greg Maddux 2.50
2 Mark McGwire 4.50
3 Sammy Sosa 3.50
4 Juan Gonzalez 2.00
5 Alex Rodriguez 4.50
6 Travis Lee 1.00
7 Roger Clemens 2.75
8 Darin Erstad 1.25
9 Todd Helton 2.00
10 Mike Piazza 3.50
11 Kerry Wood 1.50
12 Ken Griffey Jr. 3.50
13 Frank Thomas 2.00
14 Jeff Bagwell 2.00
15 Nomar Garciaparra 3.50
16 Derek Jeter 6.00
17 Chipper Jones 2.50
18 Barry Bonds 6.00
19 Tony Gwynn 2.50
20 Ben Grieve 1.00

2000 FINEST

NM/M

Complete Set (286): 250.00
Complete Series 1 (147) 175.00
Complete Series 2(140): 125.00
Common Player: .25
Common Rookie (101-120): 4.00
Production 2,000
Common Rookie (247-266) 4.00
Production 3,000
Common Counterpart (267-276) .75
Inserted 1:8
Common Gem (136-145): 1.50
Inserted 1:24
Pack (6): 2.00
Series 1 & 2 Box (24): 40.00
1 Nomar Garciaparra 2.00
2 Chipper Jones 1.50
3 Erubiel Durazo .25
4 Robin Ventura .25
5 Garret Anderson .25
6 Dean Palmer .25
7 Mariano Rivera .35
8 Rusty Greer .25
9 Jim Thome .25
10 Jeff Bagwell 1.00
11 Jason Giambi .75
12 Jeromy Burnitz .25
13 Mark Grace .35
14 Russ Ortiz .25
15 Kevin Brown .25
16 Kevin Millwood .25
17 Scott Williamson .25
18 Orlando Hernandez .25
19 Todd Walker .25
20 Carlos Beltran .50
21 Ruben Rivera .25
22 Curt Schilling .40
23 Brian Giles .25
24 Eric Karros .25
25 Preston Wilson .25
26 Al Leiter .25
27 Juan Encarnacion .25
28 Tim Salmon .40
29 B.J. Surhoff .25
30 Bernie Williams .45
31 Lee Stevens .25
32 Pokey Reese .25
33 Mike Sweeney .25
34 Corey Koskie .25
35 Roberto Alomar .40
36 Tim Hudson .40
37 Tom Glavine .40
38 Jeff Kent .25
39 Mike Lieberthal .25
40 Barry Larkin .25
41 Paul O'Neill .25
42 Rico Brogna .25
43 Brian Daubach .25
44 Rich Aurilia .25
45 Vladimir Guerrero 1.00
46 Luis Castillo .25
47 Bartolo Colon .25
48 Kevin Appier .25
49 Mo Vaughn .25
50 Alex Rodriguez 2.50
51 Randy Johnson 1.00
52 Kris Benson .25
53 Tony Clark .25
54 Chad Allen .25
55 Larry Walker .25
56 Freddy Garcia .25
57 Paul Konerko .35
58 Edgardo Alfonzo .25
59 Brady Anderson .25
60 Derek Jeter 3.00
61 Mike Hampton .25
62 Jeff Cirillo .25
63 Shannon Stewart .25
64 Greg Maddux 1.50
65 Mark McGwire 2.50
66 Gary Sheffield .50
67 Kevin Young .25
68 Tony Gwynn 1.50
69 Rey Ordonez .25
70 Cal Ripken Jr. 3.00
71 Todd Helton 1.00
72 Brian Jordan .25
73 Jose Canseco .50
74 Luis Gonzalez .40
75 Barry Bonds 3.00
76 Jermaine Dye .25
77 Jose Offerman .25
78 Magglio Ordonez .40
79 Fred McGriff .25
80 Ivan Rodriguez .60
81 Josh Hamilton (Prospects) .25
82 Vernon Wells (Prospects) .25
83 Mark Mulder (Prospects) .35
84 John Patterson (Prospects) .25
85 Nick Johnson (Prospects) .50
86 Pablo Ozuna (Prospects) .25
87 A.J. Burnett (Prospects) .25
88 Jack Cust (Prospects) .25
89 Adam Piatt (Prospects) .25
90 Rob Ryan (Prospects) .25
91 Sean Burroughs (Prospects) .35
92 D'Angelo Jimenez (Prospects) .25
93 Chad Hermansen (Prospects) .25
94 Rob Fick (Prospects) .25
95 Ruben Mateo (Prospects) .25
96 Alex Escobar (Prospects) .25
97 Willi Mo Pena (Prospects) .25
98 Corey Patterson (Prospects) .50
99 Eric Munson (Prospects) .25
100 Pat Burrell (Prospects) .75
101 *Michael Tejera* 4.00
102 *Bobby Bradley* 4.00
103 *Larry Bigbie* 6.00
104 *B.J. Garbe* 4.00
105 *Josh Kalinowski* 4.00
106 *Brett Myers* 15.00
107 *Chris Mears* 4.00
108 *Aaron Rowand* 10.00
109 *Corey Myers* 4.00
110 *John Sneed* 4.00
111 *Ryan Christensen* 4.00
112 *Kyle Snyder* 4.00
113 *Mike Paradis* 4.00
114 *Chance Caple* 4.00
115 *Ben Christiansen* 4.00
116 *Brad Baker* 4.00
117 *Rob Purvis* 4.00
118 *Rick Asadoorian* 4.00
119 *Ruben Salazar* 4.00
120 *Julio Zuleta* 4.00
121 Ken Griffey Jr., Alex Rodriguez (Features) 4.00
122 Nomar Garciaparra, Derek Jeter (Features) 5.00
123 Mark McGwire, Sammy Sosa (Features) 4.00
124 Randy Johnson, Pedro Martinez (Features) 2.00
125 Mike Piazza, Ivan Rodriguez (Features) 3.00
126 Manny Ramirez, Roberto Alomar (Features) 2.00
127 Chipper Jones, Andruw Jones (Features) 3.00
128 Cal Ripken Jr., Tony Gwynn (Features) 5.00
129 Jeff Bagwell, Craig Biggio (Features) 1.50
130 Vladimir Guerrero, Barry Bonds (Features) 5.00
131 Alfonso Soriano, Nick Johnson (Features) 2.00
132 Josh Hamilton, Pat Burrell (Features) 1.50
133 Corey Patterson, Ruben Mateo (Features) .75
134 Larry Walker, Todd Helton (Features) 1.50
135 Edgardo Alfonzo, Rey Ordonez (Features) .75
136 Derek Jeter (Gems) 10.00
137 Alex Rodriguez (Gems) 8.00
138 Chipper Jones (Gems) 5.00
139 Mike Piazza (Gems) 6.00
140 Mark McGwire (Gems) 8.00
141 Ivan Rodriguez (Gems) 2.00
142 Cal Ripken Jr. (Gems) 10.00
143 Vladimir Guerrero (Gems) 3.00
144 Randy Johnson (Gems) 3.00
145 Jeff Bagwell (Gems) 3.00
146 Ken Griffey Jr. field 1.50
146a Ken Griffey Jr. press 1.50
147 Andruw Jones 1.00
148 Kerry Wood .50
149 Jim Edmonds .25
150 Pedro Martinez 1.00
151 Warren Morris .25
152 Trevor Hoffman .25
153 Eric Young .25
154 Andy Pettitte .40
155 Frank Thomas 1.00
156 Damion Easley .25
157 Cliff Floyd .25
158 Ben Davis .25
159 John Valentin .25
160 Rafael Palmeiro .65
161 Andy Ashby .25
162 J.D. Drew .40
163 Jay Bell .25
164 Adam Kennedy .25
165 Manny Ramirez 1.00
166 John Halama .25
167 Octavio Dotel .25
168 Darin Erstad .40
169 Jose Lima .25
170 Andres Galarraga .25
171 Scott Rolen .75
172 Delino DeShields .25
173 J.T. Snow Jr. .25
174 Tony Womack .25
175 John Olerud .25
176 Jason Kendall .25
177 Carlos Lee .25
178 Eric Milton .25
179 Jeff Cirillo .25
180 Gabe Kapler .25
181 Greg Vaughn .25
182 Denny Neagle .25
183 Tino Martinez .25
184 Doug Mientkiewicz .25
185 Juan Gonzalez 1.00
186 Ellis Burks .25
187 Mike Hampton .25
188 Royce Clayton .25
189 Mike Mussina .50
190 Carlos Delgado .50
191 Ben Grieve .25
192 Fernando Tatis .25
193 Matt Williams .25
194 Rondell White .25
195 Shawn Green .50
196 Justin Thompson .25
197 Troy Glaus 1.00
198 Roger Cedeno .25
199 Ray Lankford .25
200 Sammy Sosa 2.00
201 Kenny Lofton .25
202 Edgar Martinez .25
203 Mark Kotsay .25
204 David Wells .25
205 Craig Biggio .25
206 Ray Durham .25
207 Troy O'Leary .25
208 Rickey Henderson .75
209 Bob Abreu .25
210 Neifi Perez .25
211 Carlos Febles .25
212 Chuck Knoblauch .25
213 Moises Alou .25
214 Omar Vizquel .25
215 Vinny Castilla .25
216 Javy Lopez .25
217 Johnny Damon .40
218 Roger Clemens 1.75
219 Miguel Tejada .40
220 Deion Sanders .35
221 Matt Lawton .25
222 Albert Belle .25
223 Adrian Beltre .50
224 Dante Bichette .25
225 Raul Mondesi .25
226 Mike Piazza 2.00
227 Brad Penny (Prospects) .25
228 Kip Wells (Prospects) .25
229 Adam Everett (Prospects) .25
230 Eddie Yarnall (Prospects) .25
231 Matt LeCroy (Prospects) .25
232 Ryan Anderson (Prospects) .25
233 Rick Ankiel (Prospects) .25
234 Daryle Ward (Prospects) .25
235 Rafael Furcal (Prospects) .25
236 Dee Brown (Prospects) .25
237 Travis Dawkins (Prospects) .25
238 Eric Valent (Prospects) .25
239 Peter Bergeron (Prospects) .25
240 Alfonso Soriano (Prospects) 1.50
241 John Patterson (Prospects) .25
242 Jorge Toca (Prospects) .25
243 Ryan Anderson (Prospects) .25
244 Jason Dallaero (Prospects) .25

245 Jason Grilli (Prospects) .25
246 Chad Hermansen (Prospects) .25
247 *Scott Downs* 4.00
248 *Keith Reed* 4.00
249 *Edgar Cruz* 4.00
250 *Wes Anderson* 4.00
251 *Lyle Overbay* 10.00
252 *Mike Lamb* 4.00
253 *Vince Faison* 4.00
254 *Chad Alexander* 4.00
255 Chris Wakeland 4.00
256 *Aaron McNeal* 4.00
257 *Tomokazu Ohka* 4.00
258 *Ty Howington* 6.00
259 *Javier Colina* 4.00
260 Jason Jennings 4.00
261 *Ramon Santiago* 4.00
262 *Johan Santana* 65.00
263 *Quincey Foster* 4.00
264 *Junior Brignac* 4.00
265 *Rico Washington* 4.00
266 *Scott Sobkowiak* 4.00
267 Pedro Martinez, Rick Ankiel (Counterparts) 2.00
268 Manny Ramirez, Vladimir Guerrero (Counterparts) 2.00
269 A.J. Burnett, Mark Mulder (Counterparts) .75
270 Mike Piazza, Eric Munson (Counterparts) 2.50
271 Josh Hamilton, Corey Patterson (Counterparts) .75
272 Ken Griffey Jr., Sammy Sosa (Counterparts) 3.00
273 Derek Jeter, Alfonso Soriano (Counterparts) 5.00
274 Mark McGwire, Pat Burrell (Counterparts) 4.00
275 Chipper Jones, Cal Ripken Jr. (Counterparts) 5.00
276 Nomar Garciaparra, Alex Rodriguez (Counterparts) 4.00
277 Pedro Martinez (Gems) 3.00
278 Tony Gwynn (Gems) 5.00
279 Barry Bonds (Gems) 10.00
280 Juan Gonzalez (Gems) 3.00
281 Larry Walker (Gems) 1.50
282 Nomar Garciaparra (Gems) 8.00
283 Ken Griffey Jr. (Gems) 6.00
284 Manny Ramirez (Gems) 3.00
285 Shawn Green (Gems) 2.00
286 Sammy Sosa (Gems) 6.00

Refractor

NM/M

Stars (1-100): 5-10X
Inserted 1:24
Rookies (101-120,247-266): .5-1X
Production 500 sets
Features (121-135): 2-3X
Inserted 1:96
Counterparts (267-276): 2-3X
Inserted 1:96
Gems (136-145,277-286): 2-3X
Inserted 1:288

Gold Refractor

NM/M

Stars (1-100): 20-40X
Inserted 1:240
Rookies (101-120, 247-266): 1-2X
Production 100 sets
Features: 4-8X
Inserted 1:960
Counterparts: 4-8X
Inserted 1:960
Gems: 5-10X
Inserted 1:2,880

Ballpark Bounties

NM/M

Complete Set (30): 85.00
Complete Series 1 (15): 45.00
Complete Series 2 (15): 45.00
Common Player: 1.50
Inserted 1:24

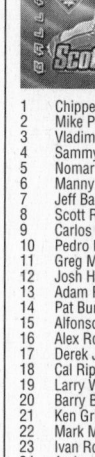

1 Chipper Jones 5.00
2 Mike Piazza 6.00
3 Vladimir Guerrero 3.00
4 Sammy Sosa 6.00
5 Nomar Garciaparra 6.00
6 Manny Ramirez 3.00
7 Jeff Bagwell 3.00
8 Scott Rolen 2.00
9 Carlos Beltran 2.50
10 Pedro Martinez 3.00
11 Greg Maddux 5.00
12 Josh Hamilton 1.50
13 Adam Piatt 1.50
14 Pat Burrell 2.00
15 Alfonso Soriano 3.00
16 Alex Rodriguez 8.00
17 Derek Jeter 10.00
18 Cal Ripken Jr. 10.00
19 Larry Walker 1.50
20 Barry Bonds 10.00
21 Ken Griffey Jr. 6.00
22 Mark McGwire 8.00
23 Ivan Rodriguez 2.00
24 Andruw Jones 2.50
25 Todd Helton 2.50
26 Randy Johnson 3.00
27 Ruben Mateo 1.50
28 Corey Patterson 1.50
29 Sean Burroughs 1.50
30 Eric Munson 1.50

Dream Cast

NM/M

Complete Set (10): 40.00
Common Player: 2.00
Inserted 1:36
1 Mark McGwire 8.00
2 Roberto Alomar 2.00
3 Chipper Jones 5.00
4 Derek Jeter 10.00
5 Barry Bonds 10.00
6 Ken Griffey Jr. 6.00
7 Sammy Sosa 6.00
8 Mike Piazza 6.00
9 Pedro Martinez 3.00
10 Randy Johnson 3.00

Values quoted in this guide reflect the retail price of a card, the price a collector can expect to pay when buying a card from a dealer.

Finest Moments

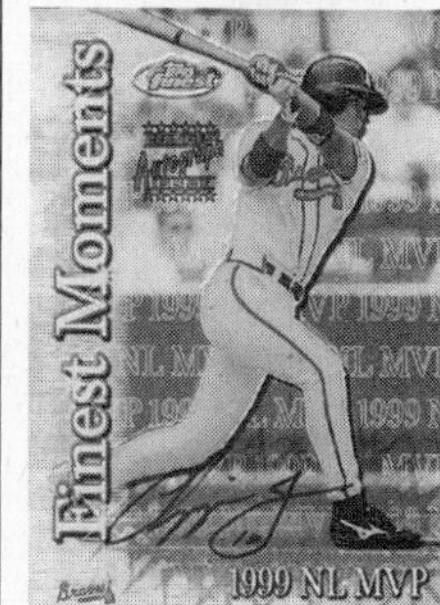

NM/M

Complete Set (4): 6.00
Common Player: 1.00
Inserted 1:9
Refractor: 1-2X
Inserted 1:20
1 Chipper Jones 3.00
2 Ivan Rodriguez 1.50
3 Tony Gwynn 3.00
4 Wade Boggs 3.00

For The Record

NM/M

Complete Set (30): 300.00
Common Player: 8.00
1A Derek Jeter (318) 20.00
1B Derek Jeter (408) 20.00
1C Derek Jeter (314) 20.00
2A Mark McGwire (330) 15.00
2B Mark McGwire (402) 15.00
2C Mark McGwire (330) 15.00
3A Ken Griffey Jr. (331) 10.00
3B Ken Griffey Jr. (405) 10.00
3C Ken Griffey Jr. (327) 10.00
4A Alex Rodriguez (331) 15.00
4B Alex Rodriguez (405) 15.00
4C Alex Rodriguez (327) 15.00
5A Nomar Garciaparra (310) 10.00
5B Nomar Garciaparra (390) 10.00
5C Nomar Garciaparra (302) 10.00
6A Cal Ripken Jr. (333) 20.00
6B Cal Ripken Jr. (410) 20.00
6C Cal Ripken Jr. (318) 20.00
7A Sammy Sosa (355) 10.00
7B Sammy Sosa (400) 10.00
7C Sammy Sosa (353) 10.00
8A Manny Ramirez (325) 8.00
8B Manny Ramirez (410) 8.00
8C Manny Ramirez (325) 8.00
9A Mike Piazza (338) 10.00
9B Mike Piazza (410) 10.00
9C Mike Piazza (338) 10.00
10A Chipper Jones (335) 9.00
10B Chipper Jones (401) 9.00
10C Chipper Jones (330) 9.00

Gems Oversized

NM/M

Complete Set (20): 50.00
Common Player: 1.00
Inserted 1:box
1 Derek Jeter 6.00
2 Alex Rodriguez 5.00
3 Chipper Jones 3.00
4 Mike Piazza 4.00
5 Mark McGwire 5.00
6 Ivan Rodriguez 1.25
7 Cal Ripken Jr. 6.00
8 Vladimir Guerrero 2.00
9 Randy Johnson 2.00
10 Jeff Bagwell 2.00
11 Nomar Garciaparra 4.00
12 Ken Griffey Jr. 4.00
13 Manny Ramirez 2.00
14 Shawn Green 1.50
15 Sammy Sosa 4.00
16 Pedro Martinez 2.00
17 Tony Gwynn 2.00
18 Barry Bonds 6.00
19 Juan Gonzalez 1.50
20 Larry Walker 1.00

Going the Distance

NM/M

Complete Set (12): 45.00
Common Player: 3.00
Inserted 1:24
1 Tony Gwynn 3.50
2 Alex Rodriguez 6.00
3 Derek Jeter 8.00
4 Chipper Jones 3.50
5 Nomar Garciaparra 4.00
6 Sammy Sosa 4.00
7 Ken Griffey Jr. 4.00
8 Vladimir Guerrero 3.00
9 Mark McGwire 6.00
10 Mike Piazza 4.00
11 Manny Ramirez 3.00
12 Cal Ripken Jr. 8.00

Moments Autographs

NM/M

Common Autograph: 25.00
Inserted 1:425
1 Chipper Jones 50.00
2 Ivan Rodriguez 25.00
3 Tony Gwynn 50.00
4 Wade Boggs 25.00

2001 FINEST

NM/M

Complete Set (140): 250.00
Common Player: .25
Common Standout Veteran (10): 5.00
Production 1999
Common Rookie (111-140): 4.00
Production 999
Pack (6): 4.00
Box (20): 65.00
1 Mike Piazza SV 10.00
2 Andruw Jones 1.00
3 Jason Giambi .75
4 Fred McGriff .25
5 Vladimir Guerrero SV 6.00
6 Adrian Gonzalez .25
7 Pedro Martinez 1.00
8 Mike Lieberthal .25
9 Warren Morris .25
10 Juan Gonzalez 1.00
11 Jose Canseco .50
12 Jose Valentin .25
13 Jeff Cirillo .25
14 Pokey Reese .25
15 Scott Rolen .75
16 Greg Maddux 1.50
17 Carlos Delgado .50
18 Rick Ankiel .25
19 Steve Finley .25
20 Shawn Green .40
21 Orlando Cabrera .25
22 Roberto Alomar .45
23 John Olerud .25

24 Albert Belle .35
25 Edgardo Alfonzo .25
26 Rafael Palmeiro .75
27 Mike Sweeney .25
28 Bernie Williams .35
29 Larry Walker .25
30 Barry Bonds SV 15.00
31 Orlando Hernandez .25
32 Randy Johnson 1.00
33 Shannon Stewart .25
34 Mark Grace .35
35 Alex Rodriguez SV 12.00
36 Tino Martinez .25
37 Carlos Febles .25
38 Al Leiter .25
39 Omar Vizquel .25
40 Chuck Knoblauch .25
41 Tim Salmon .40
42 Brian Jordan .25
43 Edgar Renteria .25
44 Preston Wilson .25
45 Mariano Rivera .40
46 Gabe Kapler .25
47 Jason Kendall .25
48 Rickey Henderson .75
49 Luis Gonzalez .40
50 Tom Glavine .40
51 Jeromy Burnitz .25
52 Garret Anderson .25
53 Craig Biggio .25
54 Vinny Castilla .25
55 Jeff Kent .25
56 Gary Sheffield .50
57 Jorge Posada .40
58 Sean Casey .40
59 Johnny Damon .40
60 Dean Palmer .25
61 Todd Helton 1.00
62 Barry Larkin .25
63 Robin Ventura .25
64 Kenny Lofton .25
65 Sammy Sosa SV 10.00
66 Rafael Furcal .25
67 Jay Bell .25
68 J.T. Snow Jr. .25
69 Jose Vidro .25
70 Ivan Rodriguez .75
71 Jermaine Dye .25
72 Chipper Jones SV 8.00
73 Fernando Vina .25
74 Ben Grieve .25
75 Mark McGwire SV 12.00
76 Matt Williams .25
77 Mark Grudzielanek .25
78 Mike Hampton .25
79 Brian Giles .25
80 Tony Gwynn 1.50
81 Carlos Beltran .50
82 Ray Durham .25
83 Brad Radke .25
84 David Justice .25
85 Frank Thomas 1.00
86 Todd Zeile .25
87 Pat Burrell .75
88 Jim Thome .25
89 Greg Vaughn .25
90 Ken Griffey Jr. SV 10.00
91 Mike Mussina .40
92 Magglio Ordonez .40
93 Bobby Abreu .25
94 Alex Gonzalez .25
95 Kevin Brown .25
96 Jay Buhner .25
97 Roger Clemens 2.00
98 Nomar Garciaparra SV 10.00
99 Derek Lee .25
100 Derek Jeter SV 15.00
101 Adrian Beltre .45
102 Geoff Jenkins .25
103 Javy Lopez .25
104 Raul Mondesi .25
105 Troy Glaus 1.00
106 Jeff Bagwell 1.00
107 Eric Karros .25
108 Mo Vaughn .25
109 Cal Ripken Jr. 3.00
110 Manny Ramirez 1.00
111 Scott Heard 4.00
112 *Luis Montanez* 5.00
113 Ben Diggins 4.00
114 *Shaun Boyd* 4.00
115 Sean Burnett 4.00
116 *Carmen Cali* 4.00
117 Derek Thompson 4.00
118 *David Parrish* 4.00
119 *Dominic Rich* 4.00
120 *Chad Petty* 4.00
121 *Steve Smyth* 4.00
122 John Lackey 4.00
123 *Matt Galante* 4.00
124 *Danny Borrell* 4.00
125 *Bob Keppel* 4.00
126 *Justin Wayne* 8.00
127 J.R. House 4.00
128 *Brian Sellier* 4.00
129 *Dan Moylan* 4.00
130 *Scott Pratt* 4.00
131 *Victor Hall* 4.00
132 Joel Pineiro 8.00
133 *Josh Axelson* 4.00
134 *Jose Reyes* 40.00
135 *Greg Runser* 4.00
136 *Bryan Hebson* 4.00
137 *Sammy Serrano* 4.00
138 *Kevin Joseph* 4.00
139 *Juan Richardson* 8.00
140 *Mark Fischer* 4.00

Refractors

Stars (1-110): 4-8X
Production 499
SP's: .5-1.5X
Production 399
Cards (111-140): 1-2X
Production 241

All-Stars

NM/M
Complete Set (10): 30.00
Common Player: 2.00
Inserted 1:10
Refractors: 1.5-2X
Inserted 1:40
1 Mark McGwire 5.00
2 Derek Jeter 6.00
3 Alex Rodriguez 5.00
4 Chipper Jones 3.00
5 Nomar Garciaparra 4.00
6 Sammy Sosa 4.00
7 Mike Piazza 4.00
8 Barry Bonds 6.00
9 Vladimir Guerrero 2.00
10 Ken Griffey Jr. 4.00

Autographed

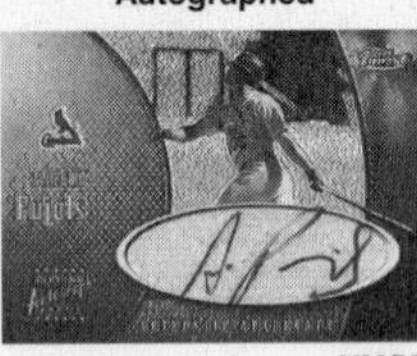

NM/M
Common Player: 5.00
Inserted 1:22
MB Milton Bradley 10.00
SB Sean Burnett 5.00
BKC Brian Cole 5.00
JC Joe Crede 6.00
BC Brad Creese 5.00
BD Ben Diggins 5.00
CD Chad Durham 5.00
TF Troy Farnsworth 5.00
RF Rafael Furcal 8.00
KG Keith Ginter 5.00
AG Adrian Gonzalez 5.00
JHH Josh Hamilton 5.00
JH Jason Hart 5.00
JRH J.R. House 5.00
AH Adam Hyzdu 5.00
DKC David Kelton 5.00
AK Adam Kennedy 5.00
DK David Krynzel 8.00
ML Mike Lamb 5.00
TL Terrence Long 5.00
KM Kevin Mench 5.00
BM Ben Molina 5.00
JM Justin Morneau 50.00
CM Chad Mottola 5.00
JO Jose Ortiz 5.00
DP David Parrish 5.00
DCP Corey Patterson 15.00
JP Jay Payton 6.00
CP Carlos Pena 5.00
AP Albert Pujols 320.00
MQ Mark Quinn 5.00
MR Mark Redman 5.00
BS Ben Sheets 15.00
JS Juan Silvestre 5.00
JNS Jamal Strong 5.00
BZ Barry Zito 20.00

Moments

NM/M
Complete Set (25): 45.00
Common Player: 1.00
Inserted 1:12
Refractors: 1.5-2X
Inserted 1:40
1 Pat Burrell 2.00
2 Adam Kennedy 1.00
3 Mike Lamb 1.00
4 Rafael Furcal 1.00
5 Terrence Long 1.00
6 Jay Payton 1.00
7 Mark Quinn 1.00
8 Ben Molina 1.00
9 Kazuhiro Sasaki 1.00
10 Mark Redman 1.00
11 Barry Bonds 8.00
12 Alex Rodriguez 6.00
13 Roger Clemens 5.00
14 Jim Edmonds 1.00
15 Jason Giambi 2.00
16 Todd Helton 2.50
17 Troy Glaus 2.50
18 Carlos Delgado 2.00
19 Darin Erstad 2.00
20 Cal Ripken Jr. 8.00
21 Paul Molitor 3.00
22 Robin Yount 2.50
23 George Brett 5.00
24 Dave Winfield 2.50
25 Wade Boggs 3.00

Moments Autographs

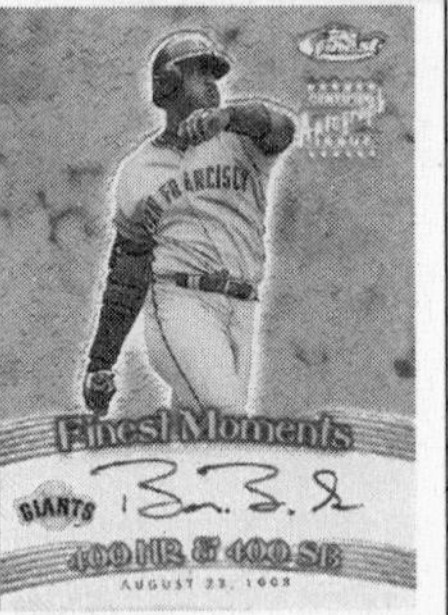

NM/M
Inserted 1:250
BB Barry Bonds 200.00
GB George Brett 75.00
JG Jason Giambi 25.00
TG Troy Glaus 20.00
TH Todd Helton 30.00
PM Paul Molitor 30.00
EM Eddie Murray 20.00
CR Cal Ripken Jr. 125.00
DW Dave Winfield 20.00
RY Robin Yount 50.00

Origins

NM/M
Complete Set (15): 18.00
Common Player: 1.00
Inserted 1:7
Refractors: 1.5-2X
Inserted 1:40
1 Derek Jeter 5.00
2 Jason Kendall 1.00
3 Jose Vidro 1.00
4 Preston Wilson 1.00
5 Jim Edmonds 1.00
6 Vladimir Guerrero 2.00
7 Andruw Jones 1.50
8 Scott Rolen 1.50

9 Edgardo Alfonzo 1.00
10 Mike Sweeney 1.00
11 Alex Rodriguez 4.00
12 Jermaine Dye 1.00
13 Charles Johnson 1.00
14 Darren Dreifort 1.00
15 Neifi Perez 1.00

2002 FINEST

NM/M
Complete Set (110): 125.00
Common Player: .25
Common SP Auto. (101-110): 8.00
Pack (5): 4.00
Box (18): 60.00
1 Mike Mussina .50
2 Steve Sparks .25
3 Randy Johnson 1.00
4 Orlando Cabrera .25
5 Jeff Kent .25
6 Carlos Delgado .75
7 Ivan Rodriguez .75
8 Jose Cruz .25
9 Jason Giambi .75
10 Brad Penny .25
11 Moises Alou .25
12 Mike Piazza 2.00
13 Ben Grieve .25
14 Derek Jeter 3.00
15 Roy Oswalt .40
16 Pat Burrell .65
17 Preston Wilson .25
18 Kevin Brown .25
19 Barry Bonds 3.00
20 Phil Nevin .25
21 Juan Gonzalez 1.00
22 Carlos Beltran .60
23 Chipper Jones 1.50
24 Curt Schilling .50
25 Jorge Posada .40
26 Alfonso Soriano 1.00
27 Cliff Floyd .25
28 Rafael Palmeiro .75
29 Terrence Long .25
30 Ken Griffey Jr. 2.00
31 Jason Kendall .25
32 Jose Vidro .25
33 Jermaine Dye .25
34 Bobby Higginson .25
35 Albert Pujols 2.50
36 Miguel Tejada .40
37 Jim Edmonds .25
38 Barry Zito .40
39 Jimmy Rollins .25
40 Rafael Furcal .25
41 Omar Vizquel .25
42 Kazuhiro Sasaki .25
43 Brian Giles .25

44 Darin Erstad .50
45 Mariano Rivera .40
46 Troy Percival .25
47 Mike Sweeney .25
48 Vladimir Guerrero 1.00
49 Troy Glaus 1.00
50 Hideo Nomo .65
51 Edgardo Alfonzo .25
52 Roger Clemens 1.75
53 Eric Chavez .40
54 Alex Rodriguez 2.50
55 Cristian Guzman .25
56 Jeff Bagwell 1.00
57 Bernie Williams .40
58 Kerry Wood .60
59 Ryan Klesko .25
60 Ichiro Suzuki 2.00
61 Larry Walker .25
62 Nomar Garciaparra 2.00
63 Craig Biggio .25
64 J.D. Drew .40
65 Juan Pierre .25
66 Roberto Alomar .50
67 Luis Gonzalez .40
68 Bud Smith .25
69 Magglio Ordonez .50
70 Scott Rolen 1.00
71 Tsuyoshi Shinjo .25
72 Reggie Sanders .25
73 Garret Anderson .25
74 Tim Hudson .40
75 Adam Dunn .75
76 Gary Sheffield .50
77 Johnny Damon .40
78 Todd Helton 1.00
79 Geoff Jenkins .25
80 Shawn Green .40
81 C.C. Sabathia .25
82 *Kazuhisa Ishii* 3.00
83 Rich Aurilia .25
84 Mike Hampton .25
85 Ben Sheets .25
86 Andruw Jones 1.00
87 Richie Sexson .25
88 Jim Thome .25
89 Sammy Sosa 2.00
90 Greg Maddux 1.50
91 Pedro Martinez 1.00
92 Jeromy Burnitz .25
93 Raul Mondesi .25
94 Bret Boone .25
95 Jerry Hairston Jr. .25
96 Carlos Pena .25
97 Juan Cruz .25
98 Morgan Ensberg .25
99 Nathan Haynes .25
100 Xavier Nady .25
101 *Nic Jackson Auto.* 10.00
102 *Mauricio Lara Auto.* 8.00
103 *Freddy Sanchez Auto.* 10.00
104 *Clint Nageotte Auto.* 15.00
105 *Beltran Perez Auto.* 8.00
106 *Garrett Gentry Auto.* 8.00
107 *Chad Qualls Auto.* 8.00
108 *Jason Bay Auto.* 40.00
109 *Michael Hill Auto.* 8.00
110 Brian Tallet Auto. 10.00

Refractors

Star Refractors: 2-5X
Numbered to 499
X-Fractors: 3-6X
Numbered to 299
X-Fractor Protector: 5-10X
X-Fract. Protector (101-110): 1-2X
Numbered to 99

Bat Relics

NM/M
Common Player: 5.00
Inserted 1:72
BB Barry Bonds 25.00
BBO Bret Boone 5.00
NG Nomar Garciaparra 15.00
LG Luis Gonzalez 5.00
TG Tony Gwynn 10.00
TH Todd Helton 8.00
AJ Andruw Jones 5.00
CJ Chipper Jones 10.00
MP Mike Piazza 10.00
AP Albert Pujols 20.00
AR Alex Rodriguez 10.00
IR Ivan Rodriguez 8.00
TS Tsuyoshi Shinjo 5.00
AS Alfonso Soriano 8.00
BW Bernie Williams 8.00

Moments Autographs

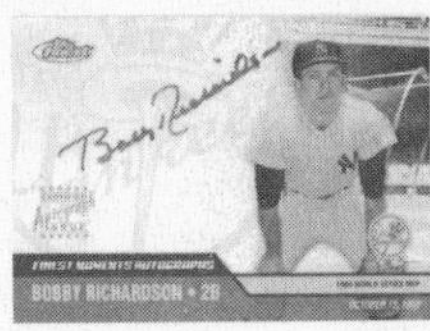

NM/M
Common Autograph: 10.00
Inserted 1:18
LA Luis Aparicio 15.00
YB Yogi Berra 30.00
JB Jim Bunning 10.00
BG Bob Gibson 25.00
GG Rich "Goose" Gossage 10.00
FJ Fergie Jenkins 15.00
DL Don Larsen 15.00
DM Don Mattingly 75.00
JM Joe Morgan
GP Gaylord Perry 10.00
BR Bobby Richardson 10.00
BRO Brooks Robinson 35.00
JS Johnny Sain 10.00
MS Mike Schmidt 50.00
RS Red Schoendienst 10.00
BT Bobby Thomson 15.00

Uniform Relics

NM/M
Common Player: 5.00
Inserted 1:24
RA Roberto Alomar 8.00
JB Jeff Bagwell 8.00
BB Barry Bonds 20.00
BBO Bret Boone 5.00
CD Carlos Delgado 8.00
LG Luis Gonzalez 5.00
MG Mark Grace 8.00
SG Shawn Green 5.00
TG Tony Gwynn 10.00
TH Todd Helton 8.00
RH Rickey Henderson 15.00
AJ Andruw Jones 8.00
CJ Chipper Jones 10.00
GM Greg Maddux 10.00
PM Pedro Martinez 10.00
HN Hideo Nomo 20.00
RP Rafael Palmeiro 10.00
MP Mike Piazza 10.00
AR Alex Rodriguez 10.00
IR Ivan Rodriguez 8.00
CS Curt Schilling 10.00
TS Tsuyoshi Shinjo 5.00
FT Frank Thomas 8.00
LW Larry Walker 5.00

2003 FINEST

NM/M
Complete Set (110):
Common Player: .25
Common Auto (101-110): 10.00
Pack (5): 5.00
Box (18): 75.00
1 Sammy Sosa 2.00
2 Paul Konerko .25
3 Todd Helton .75
4 Mike Lowell .25
5 Lance Berkman .25
6 Kazuhisa Ishii .25
7 A.J. Pierzynski .25
8 Jose Vidro .25
9 Roberto Alomar .40
10 Derek Jeter 3.00
11 Barry Zito .50
12 Jimmy Rollins .25
13 Brian Giles .25
14 Ryan Klesko .25
15 Rich Aurilia .25
16 Jim Edmonds .25
17 Aubrey Huff .25
18 Ivan Rodriguez .65
19 Eric Hinske .25
20 Barry Bonds 3.00
21 Darin Erstad .60
22 Curt Schilling .50
23 Andruw Jones .75
24 Jay Gibbons .25
25 Nomar Garciaparra 1.50
26 Kerry Wood .60
27 Magglio Ordonez .50
28 Austin Kearns .50
29 Jason Jennings .25
30 Jason Giambi .50
31 Tim Hudson .40
32 Edgar Martinez .25
33 Carl Crawford .25
34 Hee Seop Choi 35.00
35 Vladimir Guerrero .75
36 Jeff Kent .25
37 John Smoltz .25
38 Frank Thomas .75
39 Cliff Floyd .25
40 Mike Piazza 1.50
41 Mark Prior .75
42 Tim Salmon .40
43 Shawn Green .50
44 Bernie Williams .40
45 Jim Thome .25
46 John Olerud .25
47 Orlando Hudson .25
48 Mark Teixeira .75
49 Gary Sheffield .50
50 Ichiro Suzuki 2.00
51 Tom Glavine .40
52 Torii Hunter .25
53 Craig Biggio .25
54 Carlos Beltran .75
55 Bartolo Colon .25
56 Jorge Posada .35
57 Pat Burrell .65
58 Edgar Renteria .25
59 Rafael Palmeiro .65
60 Alfonso Soriano .75
61 Brandon Phillips .25
62 Luis Gonzalez .40
63 Manny Ramirez .75
64 Garret Anderson .25
65 Ken Griffey Jr. 1.50
66 A.J. Burnett .25
67 Mike Sweeney .25
68 Doug Mientkiewicz .25
69 Eric Chavez .50
70 Adam Dunn .75
71 Shea Hillenbrand .25
72 Troy Glaus .75
73 Rodrigo Lopez .25
74 Moises Alou .25
75 Chipper Jones 1.00
76 Bobby Abreu .25
77 Mark Mulder .40
78 Kevin Brown .25
79 Josh Beckett .50
80 Larry Walker .25
81 Randy Johnson .75
82 Greg Maddux 1.00
83 Johnny Damon .40
84 Omar Vizquel .25
85 Jeff Bagwell .75
86 Carlos Pena .25
87 Roy Oswalt .40
88 Richie Sexson .25
89 Roger Clemens 1.25
90 Miguel Tejada .40
91 Vicente Padilla .25
92 Phil Nevin .25
93 Edgardo Alfonzo .25
94 Bret Boone .25
95 Albert Pujols 2.00
96 Carlos Delgado .50
97 Marlon Byrd .25
98 Scott Rolen .75
99 Pedro J. Martinez .75
100 Alex Rodriguez 2.00
101 Adam LaRoche 15.00
102 *Andy Marte* 40.00
103 *Daryl Clark* 10.00
104 *J.D. Durbin* 10.00
105 *Craig Brazell* 15.00
106 *Brian Burgamy* 10.00
107 *Tyler Johnson* 10.00
108 Joey Gomes 10.00
109 *Bryan Bullington* 25.00
110 *Byron Gettis* 10.00

Refractors

Stars (1-100): 2-4X
Rookie Autos (101-110): .75-1.5X
Inserted 1:6

X-Fractors

Stars (1-100): 5-10X
Rookie Autos (101-110): 1-2.5X
Production 99 sets
X-Fractor Golds (1-100): 3-6X
Golds Rk Autos (101-110): 1-2X
Production 199 sets

Bat Relics

NM/M
Common Player: 8.00
Inserted 1:6
JB Jeff Bagwell 8.00
LB Lance Berkman 8.00
WB Wade Boggs 8.00
BB Barry Bonds 20.00
RC Rod Carew 10.00
RCL Roger Clemens 15.00
AD Adam Dunn 8.00
NG Nomar Garciaparra 20.00
TH Todd Helton 8.00
RH Rickey Henderson 10.00
CJ Chipper Jones 10.00
AK Austin Kearns 8.00
GM Greg Maddux 15.00
PM Paul Molitor 8.00
DM Dale Murphy 15.00
RP Rafael Palmeiro 8.00
MP Mike Piazza 15.00
KP Kirby Puckett 15.00
AP Albert Pujols 15.00
MR Manny Ramirez 8.00
CR Cal Ripken Jr. 35.00
AR Alex Rodriguez 12.00
IR Ivan Rodriguez 8.00
MS Mike Schmidt 20.00
AS Alfonso Soriano 10.00
MT Miguel Tejada 8.00
JT Jim Thome 10.00

Moments Autographs

NM/M
Common Player: 10.00
EB Ernie Banks 60.00
PB Paul Blair 10.00
LB Lou Brock 25.00

GC Gary Carter 15.00
OC Orlando Cepeda 15.00
GF George Foster 15.00
GG Rich "Goose" Gossage 15.00
KH Keith Hernandez 15.00
DL Don Larsen 15.00
WMA Willie Mays 150.00
JP Jim Palmer 15.00
GP Gaylord Perry 15.00
JS Johnny Sain 10.00

Team Topps Legends Autograph

NM/M

Common Autograph: 10.00
Luis Aparicio 15.00
Paul Blair 10.00
Lou Brock 25.00
Rich "Goose" Gossage 15.00
Al Kaline 35.00
Don Larsen 20.00
Vern Law 12.00
Stan Musial 75.00
Brooks Robinson

Uniform Relics

NM/M

Common Player: 5.00
BB Barry Bonds 20.00
EC Eric Chavez 5.00
AD Adam Dunn 10.00
LG Luis Gonzalez 5.00
TH Todd Helton 8.00
RJ Randy Johnson 8.00
AJ Andruw Jones 8.00
CJ Chipper Jones 10.00
GM Greg Maddux 12.00
WM Willie Mays 30.00
MM Mark Mulder 6.00
RO Roy Oswalt 5.00
RP Rafael Palmeiro 8.00
MP Mike Piazza 12.00
AP Albert Pujols 15.00
MR Manny Ramirez 8.00
AR Alex Rodriguez 15.00
CS Curt Schilling 5.00
AS Alfonso Soriano 10.00
SS Sammy Sosa 15.00
MSW Mike Sweeney 5.00
LW Larry Walker 5.00

2004 FINEST

NM/M

Complete Set (122):
Common Player: .40
Common Star Relic (101-110): 8.00
Inserted 1:42
Common FYP Autograph (111-122): 10.00
Inserted 1:18
Pack (5): 6.00
Box (18): 85.00
Mini-Box (6): 30.00

1 Juan Pierre .40
2 Derek Jeter 3.00
3 Garret Anderson .50
4 Javy Lopez .50
5 Corey Patterson .50
6 Todd Helton .75
7 Roy Oswalt .50
8 Shawn Green .50
9 Vladimir Guerrero 1.00
10 Jorge Posada .50
11 Jason Kendall .40
12 Scott Rolen 1.00
13 Randy Johnson 1.00
14 Bill Mueller .40
15 Magglio Ordonez .50
16 Larry Walker .50
17 Lance Berkman .50
18 Richie Sexson .75
19 Orlando Cabrera .40
20 Alfonso Soriano 1.00
21 Kevin Millwood .50
22 Edgar Martinez .50
23 Aubrey Huff .40
24 Carlos Delgado .75
25 Vernon Wells .40
26 Mark Teixeira .40
27 Troy Glaus .50
28 Jeff Kent .50
29 Hideo Nomo .50
30 Torii Hunter .50
31 Hank Blalock .50
32 Brandon Webb .40
33 Tony Batista .40
34 Bret Boone .50
35 Ryan Klesko .50
36 Barry Zito .50
37 Aaron Boone .40
38 Geoff Jenkins .50
39 Jeff Bagwell .75
40 Dontrelle Willis .50
41 Adam Dunn .75
42 Mark Buehrle .40
43 Esteban Loaiza .40
44 Angel Berroa .40
45 Ivan Rodriguez .75
46 Jose Vidro .40
47 Mark Mulder .50
48 Marlon Byrd .40
49 Jim Edmonds .50
50 Eric Gagne .50
51 Marcus Giles .40
52 Curt Schilling .75
53 Ken Griffey Jr. 1.50
54 Jason Schmidt .50
55 Miguel Tejada .50
56 Dmitri Young .40
57 Mike Lowell .50
58 Mike Sweeney .40
59 Scott Podsednik .75
60 Miguel Cabrera 1.00
61 Johan Santana .40
62 Bernie Williams .50
63 Eric Chavez .50
64 Bobby Abreu .50
65 Brian Giles .50
66 Michael Young .40
67 Paul LoDuca .40
68 Austin Kearns .40
69 Jody Gerut .40
70 Kerry Wood 1.00
71 Luis Matos .40
72 Greg Maddux 1.50
73 Alex Rodriguez 4.00
74 Mike Lieberthal .40
75 Jim Thome 1.00
76 Javier Vazquez .40
77 Bartolo Colon .50
78 Manny Ramirez .75
79 Jacque Jones .40
80 Johnny Damon .40
81 Carlos Beltran .75
82 C.C. Sabathia .40
83 Preston Wilson .40
84 Luis Castillo .40
85 Kevin Brown .50
86 Shannon Stewart .40
87 Cliff Floyd .40
88 Mike Mussina .50
89 Rafael Furcal .40
90 Roy Halladay .50
91 Frank Thomas .75
92 Melvin Mora .40
93 Andruw Jones .75
94 Luis Gonzalez .50
95 David Ortiz .75
96 Gary Sheffield .50
97 Tim Hudson .50
98 Phil Nevin .40
99 Ichiro Suzuki 2.00
100 Albert Pujols 2.50
101 Nomar Garciaparra 15.00
102 Sammy Sosa 15.00
103 Josh Beckett 8.00
104 Jason Giambi 8.00
105 Rocco Baldelli 8.00
106 Jose Reyes 8.00
107 Chipper Jones 10.00
108 Pedro J. Martinez 10.00
109 Mike Piazza 8.00
110 Mark Prior 10.00
111 *Craig Ansman* 10.00
112 Jeff Allison 15.00
113 David Murphy 15.00
114 Jason Hirsh 10.00
115 Matt Moses 20.00
116 *Estee Harris* 10.00
117 *Logan Kensing* 10.00
118 Lastings Milledge 35.00
119 *Merkin Valdez* 15.00
120 *Travis Blackley* 15.00
121 *Vito Chiaravalloti* 15.00
122 *Dioner Navarro* 25.00

Gold Refractor

Gold Refractor (1-100): 6-12X
Gold Refr. (101-110): 1.5-2X
Gold Refr. (111-122): 2-4X
Production 50 sets

Refractor

Refractor (1-100): 2-4X
Inserted 1:6
Refractor (101-110): 1-2X
Inserted 1:156
Refractor (111-122): 1-2X
Inserted 1:132

Uncirculated X-Fractor

Stars (1-100): 4-8X
Relics (101-110): 1-2X
Autographs (111-122): 1-2X
Inserted as a box topper
Production 139 sets

Moments Autographs

NM/M

Common Autograph: 10.00
JA Jim Abbott 15.00
VB Vida Blue 12.00
OC Orlando Cepeda 12.00
LD Lenny Dykstra 10.00
GS George Foster 10.00
EK Ed Kranepool 10.00
WM Willie Mays 100.00
JP Johnny Podres 10.00
DS Duke Snider 40.00
RY Robin Yount 75.00

Relics

NM/M

Common Player: 4.00
JB Jeff Bagwell 8.00
RB1 Rocco Baldelli/jsy 6.00
RB3 Rocco Baldelli/jsy 6.00
JPB1 Josh Beckett 8.00
LB1 Lance Berkman/bat 5.00
LB2 Lance Berkman/jsy 5.00
AB Angel Berroa 4.00
HB1 Hank Blalock/bat 8.00
HB2 Hank Blalock/jsy 8.00
PB Pat Burrell 10.00
SB Sean Burroughs 5.00
MB Marlon Byrd 4.00

MC Miguel Cabrera 10.00
EC Eric Chavez 6.00
AD Adam Dunn 8.00
DE Darin Erstad 4.00
NG Nomar Garciaparra 12.00
TG Troy Glaus 6.00
AG Adrian Gonzalez 4.00
LG Luis Gonzalez 4.00
SG Shawn Green 6.00
VG Vladimir Guerrero 8.00
CG Cristian Guzman 4.00
RH Rich Harden 5.00
TH1 Todd Helton/bat 8.00
TH2 Todd Helton/jsy 8.00
TH Tim Hudson 5.00
TKH1 Torii Hunter/bat 6.00
TKH2 Torii Hunter/jsy 6.00
KI Kazuhisa Ishii 4.00
RJ Randy Johnson 8.00
AJ Andruw Jones 6.00
JL Javy Lopez 6.00
DL Derek Lowe 6.00
ML1 Mike Lowell/jsy 5.00
ML2 Mike Lowell/jsy 5.00
GM Greg Maddux 10.00
KM Kevin Millwood 6.00
MM Mark Mulder 4.00
BM1 Brett Myers/jsy 4.00
BM2 Brett Myers/jsy 4.00
MO1 Magglio Ordonez/jsy 6.00
MO2 Magglio Ordonez/bat 6.00
RP1 Rafael Palmeiro/bat 8.00
RP2 Rafael Palmeiro/jsy 8.00
RP3 Rafael Palmeiro/jsy 8.00
AP Andy Pettitte 6.00
JP Juan Pierre 4.00
MP Mark Prior 15.00
AP1 Albert Pujols/jsy 15.00
AP2 Albert Pujols/bat 15.00
JR1 Jose Reyes/jsy 8.00
JR2 Jose Reyes/bat 8.00
JR3 Jose Reyes/jsy 8.00
MR Mariano Rivera 10.00
AR1 Alex Rodriguez/ Rangers 10.00
AR2 Alex Rodriguez/ Yankees 20.00
IR1 Ivan Rodriguez/jsy 4.00
IR2 Ivan Rodriguez/jsy 8.00
IR3 Ivan Rodriguez/bat 8.00
SR Scott Rolen 8.00
CCS C.C. Sabathia 6.00
KS Kazuhiro Sasaki 4.00
CS Curt Schilling 6.00
GS Gary Sheffield 6.00
JS John Smoltz 8.00
AS Alfonso Soriano 8.00
SS Sammy Sosa 12.00
MT1 Miguel Tejada/bat 6.00
MT2 Miguel Tejada/jsy 6.00
FT Frank Thomas 8.00
JT Jim Thome 10.00
LW Larry Walker 4.00
VW Vernon Wells 5.00
BW Bernie Williams 6.00
DW Dontrelle Willis 6.00
PW Preston Wilson 4.00
KW1 Kerry Wood/jsy 10.00
KW2 Kerry Wood/bat 10.00
DY Delmon Young 8.00
BZ Barry Zito 8.00

2005 FINEST

NM/M

Complete Set (166):
Common Player: .40
Common Auto. (141-156): 10.00
Production 970, unless noted

Pack (5):		10.00
Box (18):		150.00
1	Alexis Rios	.40
2	Hank Blalock	.75
3	Bobby Abreu	.50
4	Curt Schilling	1.00
5	Albert Pujols	3.00
6	Aaron Rowand	.40
7	B.J. Upton	.50
8	Andruw Jones	.50
9	Jeff Francis	.40
10	Sammy Sosa	2.00
11	Aramis Ramirez	.75
12	Carl Pavano	.50
13	Bartolo Colon	.40
14	Greg Maddux	2.00
15	Scott Kazmir	.50
16	Melvin Mora	.40
17	Brandon Backe	.40
18	Bobby Crosby	.40
19	Carlos Lee	.40
20	Carl Crawford	.40
21	Brian Giles	.40
22	Jeff Bagwell	.75
23	J.D. Drew	.40
24	C.C. Sabathia	.40
25	Alfonso Soriano	1.00
26	Chipper Jones	1.00
27	Austin Kearns	.40
28	Carlos Delgado	.50
29	Jack Wilson	.40
30	Dmitri Young	.40
31	Carlos Guillen	.40
32	Jim Thome	1.00
33	Eric Chavez	.50
34	Jason Schmidt	.50
35	Brad Radke	.40
36	Frank Thomas	.75
37	Darin Erstad	.40
38	Javier Vazquez	.40
39	Garret Anderson	.50
40	David Ortiz	1.00
41	Javy Lopez	.40
42	Geoff Jenkins	.40
43	Jose Vidro	.40
44	Aubrey Huff	.40
45	Bernie Williams	.50
46	Dontrelle Willis	.50
47	Jim Edmonds	.50
48	Ivan Rodriguez	.75
49	Gary Sheffield	.50
50	Alex Rodriguez	2.50
51	John Buck	.40
52	Andy Pettitte	.50
53	Ichiro Suzuki	2.50
54	Johnny Estrada	.40
55	Jake Peavy	.50
56	Carlos Zambrano	.50
57	Jose Reyes	.40
58	Bret Boone	.40
59	Jason Bay	.50
60	David Wright	1.00
61	Jeromy Burnitz	.40
62	Corey Patterson	.50
63	Juan Pierre	.40
64	Zack Greinke	.40
65	Mike Lowell	.40
66	Ken Griffey Jr.	2.00
67	Marcus Giles	.40
68	Edgar Renteria	.50
69	Ken Harvey	.40
70	Pedro Martinez	1.00
71	Johnny Damon	1.00
72	Lyle Overbay	.50
73	Mike Maroth	.40
74	Jorge Posada	.50
75	Carlos Beltran	.75
76	Mark Buehrle	.40
77	Khalil Greene	.40
78	Josh Beckett	.75
79	Mark Loretta	.40
80	Rafael Palmeiro	.75
81	Justin Morneau	.50
82	Rocco Baldelli	.40
83	Ben Sheets	.50
84	Kerry Wood	1.00
85	Miguel Tejada	.75
86	Magglio Ordonez	.40
87	Livan Hernandez	.40
88	Kazuo Matsui	.40
89	Manny Ramirez	1.00
90	Hideki Matsui	2.00
91	Jeff Kent	.40
92	Matt Lawton	.40
93	Richie Sexson	.50
94	Mike Mussina	.50
95	Adam Dunn	.75
96	Johan Santana	.75
97	Nomar Garciaparra	1.50
98	Michael Young	.40
99	Victor Martinez	.40
100	Barry Bonds	4.00
101	Oliver Perez	.40
102	Randy Johnson	1.00
103	Mark Mulder	.50
104	Pat Burrell	.40
105	Mike Sweeney	.40
106	Mark Teixeira	.75
107	Paul LoDuca	.40
108	Jon Lieber	.40
109	Mike Piazza	2.00
110	Roger Clemens	3.00
111	Rafael Furcal	.40
112	Troy Glaus	.50
113	Miguel Cabrera	1.00
114	Randy Wolf	.40
115	Lance Berkman	.40
116	Mark Prior	1.00
117	Rich Harden	.50
118	Preston Wilson	.40
119	Roy Oswalt	.40
120	Luis Gonzalez	.40
121	Ronnie Belliard	.40
122	Sean Casey	.50
123	Barry Zito	.50
124	Larry Walker	.50
125	Derek Jeter	3.00
126	Tim Hudson	.50
127	Tom Glavine	.50
128	Scott Rolen	1.00
129	Torii Hunter	.50
130	Paul Konerko	.40
131	Shawn Green	.40
132	Travis Hafner	.40
133	Vernon Wells	.40
134	Sidney Ponson	.40
135	Vladimir Guerrero	1.00
136	Mark Kotsay	.40
137	Todd Helton	.75
138	Adrian Beltre	.50
139	Wily Mo Pena	.40
140	Joe Mauer	.50
141	*Brian Stavisky*	12.00
142	*Nate McLouth*	15.00
143	*Glen Perkins*	15.00
144	*Chip Cannon*	15.00
145	*Shane Costa*	12.00
146	*Wes Swackhamer*	12.00
147	*Kevin Melillo*	15.00
148	*Billy Butler*	40.00
149	*Landon Powell*	15.00
150	*Scott Mathieson*	12.00
151	*Chris Roberson*	15.00
152	*Chad Orvella/375*	40.00
153	*Eric Nielsen*	10.00
154	*Matt Campbell*	10.00
155	*Mike Rogers*	15.00
156	*Melky Cabrera*	15.00
157	Nolan Ryan	4.00
158	Bo Jackson	1.00
159	Wade Boggs	1.00
160	Andre Dawson	.75
161	Dave Winfield	1.00
162	Reggie Jackson	1.00
163	David Justice	.50
164	Dale Murphy	1.00
165	Paul O'Neill	.75
166	Tom Seaver	1.50

Rookie cards are in *Italic.*

Printing Plates

No Pricing
Production one set for each color

Refractors

Refrac. (1-140, 157-166):	2-4X
Autograph (141-156):	.5-1X

Production 399 sets

Refractors Black

Refrac. (1-140, 157-166):	4-8X
Autograph (141-156):	1-2X

Production 99 sets

Refractors Blue

Refrac. (1-140, 157-166):	2-4X
Autograph (141-156):	.5-1X

Production 299 sets

Refractors Gold

Refrac. (1-140, 157-166):	5-10X
Autograph (141-156):	2-4X

Production 49 sets

Refractors Green

Refrac. (1-140, 157-166):	2-4X
Autograph (141-156):	.5-1.5X

Production 199 sets

Refractors White Framed

No Pricing
Production one set

X-Fractor

Refrac. (1-140, 157-166):	2-4X
Autograph (141-156):	.5-1X

Production 250 sets

X-Fractor Black

Refrac. (1-140, 157-166):	8-15X
Autograph (141-156):	No Pricing

Production 25 sets

X-Fractor Blue

Refrac. (1-140, 157-166):	3-5X
Autograph (141-156):	.5-1.5X

Production 150 sets

X-Fractor Gold

No Pricing
Production 10 sets

X-Fractor Green

Refrac. (1-140, 157-166):	5-10X
Autograph (141-156):	1.5-3X

Production 50 sets

X-Fractor White Framed

No Pricing
Production one set

Super Fractor

No Pricing
Production one set

Autographs

		NM/M
X-Fractor:		1.5X-2X
Production 25 sets		
FA-JB	Jason Bay	25.00
FA-CB	Carlos Beltran	50.00
FA-BB	Barry Bonds	350.00
FA-MB	Milton Bradley	15.00
FA-EC	Eric Chavez	20.00
FA-JE	Johnny Estrada	15.00
FA-EG	Eric Gagne	30.00
FA-KM	Kevin Millar	35.00
FA-DO	David Ortiz	50.00
FA-MR	Mariano Rivera	60.00
FA-JS	Johan Santana	40.00
FA-GS	Gary Sheffield	30.00
FA-AS	Alfonso Soriano	35.00
FA-JST	Jacob Stevens	10.00
FA-DW	David Wright	50.00

Alex Rodriguez Finest Moments Autograph

	NM/M
Production 13 Sets	
A-Rod Auto. 1-49:	150.00

Alex Rodriguez Finest Moments

	NM/M
A-Rod 1-49:	10.00

Production 190 Sets

2 of a Kind Autographs

No Pricing
Production 13
2OK-RB Alex Rodriguez, Ernie Banks

Finest Moment Autographs

No Pricing
Production 50

1993 FLAIR

		NM/M
Complete Set (300):		12.50
Common Player:		.10
Pack (10):		1.50
Wax Box (24):		20.00
1	Steve Avery	.10
2	Jeff Blauser	.10
3	Ron Gant	.10
4	Tom Glavine	.25
5	Dave Justice	.10
6	Mark Lemke	.10

No.	Player	NM/M
7	Greg Maddux	1.00
8	Fred McGriff	.10
9	Terry Pendleton	.10
10	Deion Sanders	.15
11	John Smoltz	.10
12	Mike Stanton	.10
13	Steve Buechele	.10
14	Mark Grace	.15
15	Greg Hibbard	.10
16	Derrick May	.10
17	Chuck McElroy	.10
18	Mike Morgan	.10
19	Randy Myers	.10
20	Ryne Sandberg	1.00
21	Dwight Smith	.10
22	Sammy Sosa	1.25
23	Jose Vizcaino	.10
24	Tim Belcher	.10
25	Rob Dibble	.10
26	Roberto Kelly	.10
27	Barry Larkin	.10
28	Kevin Mitchell	.10
29	Hal Morris	.10
30	Joe Oliver	.10
31	Jose Rijo	.10
32	Bip Roberts	.10
33	Chris Sabo	.10
34	Reggie Sanders	.10
35	Dante Bichette	.10
36	Willie Blair	.10
37	Jerald Clark	.10
38	Alex Cole	.10
39	Andres Galarraga	.10
40	Joe Girardi	.10
41	Charlie Hayes	.10
42	Chris Jones	.10
43	David Nied	.10
44	Eric Young	.10
45	Alex Arias	.10
46	Jack Armstrong	.10
47	Bret Barberie	.10
48	Chuck Carr	.10
49	Jeff Conine	.10
50	Orestes Destrade	.10
51	Chris Hammond	.10
52	Bryan Harvey	.10
53	Benito Santiago	.10
54	Gary Sheffield	.35
55	Walt Weiss	.10
56	Eric Anthony	.10
57	Jeff Bagwell	.75
58	Craig Biggio	.10
59	Ken Caminiti	.10
60	Andujar Cedeno	.10
61	Doug Drabek	.10
62	Steve Finley	.10
63	Luis Gonzalez	.25
64	Pete Harnisch	.10
65	Doug Jones	.10
66	Darryl Kile	.10
67	Greg Swindell	.10
68	Brett Butler	.10
69	Jim Gott	.10
70	Orel Hershiser	.10
71	Eric Karros	.10
72	Pedro Martinez	.75
73	Ramon Martinez	.10
74	Roger McDowell	.10
75	Mike Piazza	1.25
76	Jody Reed	.10
77	Tim Wallach	.10
78	Moises Alou	.10
79	Greg Colbrunn	.10
80	Wil Cordero	.10
81	Delino DeShields	.10
82	Jeff Fassero	.10
83	Marquis Grissom	.10
84	Ken Hill	.10
85	*Mike Lansing*	.30
86	Dennis Martinez	.10
87	Larry Walker	.10
88	John Wetteland	.10
89	Bobby Bonilla	.10
90	Vince Coleman	.10
91	Dwight Gooden	.10
92	Todd Hundley	.10
93	Howard Johnson	.10
94	Eddie Murray	.75
95	Joe Orsulak	.10
96	Bret Saberhagen	.10
97	Darren Daulton	.10
98	Mariano Duncan	.10
99	Len Dykstra	.10
100	Jim Eisenreich	.10
101	Tommy Greene	.10
102	Dave Hollins	.10
103	Pete Incaviglia	.10
104	Danny Jackson	.10
105	John Kruk	.10
106	Terry Mulholland	.10
107	Curt Schilling	.25
108	Mitch Williams	.10
109	Stan Belinda	.10
110	Jay Bell	.10
111	Steve Cooke	.10
112	Carlos Garcia	.10
113	Jeff King	.10
114	Al Martin	.10
115	Orlando Merced	.10
116	Don Slaught	.10
117	Andy Van Slyke	.10
118	Tim Wakefield	.10
119	*Rene Arocha*	.10
120	Bernard Gilkey	.10
121	Gregg Jefferies	.10
122	Ray Lankford	.10
123	Donovan Osborne	.10
124	Tom Pagnozzi	.10
125	Erik Pappas	.10
126	Geronimo Pena	.10
127	Lee Smith	.10
128	Ozzie Smith	1.00
129	Bob Tewksbury	.10
130	Mark Whiten	.10
131	Derek Bell	.10
132	Andy Benes	.10
133	Tony Gwynn	1.00
134	Gene Harris	.10
135	Trevor Hoffman	.10
136	Phil Plantier	.10
137	Rod Beck	.10
138	Barry Bonds	2.00
139	John Burkett	.10
140	Will Clark	.15
141	Royce Clayton	.10
142	Mike Jackson	.10
143	Darren Lewis	.10
144	Kirt Manwaring	.10
145	Willie McGee	.10
146	Bill Swift	.10
147	Robby Thompson	.10
148	Matt Williams	.10
149	Brady Anderson	.10
150	Mike Devereaux	.10
151	Chris Hoiles	.10
152	Ben McDonald	.10
153	Mark McLemore	.10
154	Mike Mussina	.40
155	Gregg Olson	.10
156	Harold Reynolds	.10
157	Cal Ripken, Jr.	2.00
158	Rick Sutcliffe	.10
159	Fernando Valenzuela	.10
160	Roger Clemens	1.00
161	Scott Cooper	.10
162	Andre Dawson	.30
163	Scott Fletcher	.10
164	Mike Greenwell	.10
165	Greg Harris	.10
166	Billy Hatcher	.10
167	Jeff Russell	.10
168	Mo Vaughn	.10
169	Frank Viola	.10
170	Chad Curtis	.10
171	Chili Davis	.10
172	Gary DiSarcina	.10
173	Damion Easley	.10
174	Chuck Finley	.10
175	Mark Langston	.10
176	Luis Polonia	.10
177	Tim Salmon	.20
178	Scott Sanderson	.10
179	*J.T. Snow*	.75
180	Wilson Alvarez	.10
181	Ellis Burks	.10
182	Joey Cora	.10
183	Alex Fernandez	.10
184	Ozzie Guillen	.10
185	Roberto Hernandez	.10
186	Bo Jackson	.20
187	Lance Johnson	.10
188	Jack McDowell	.10
189	Frank Thomas	.75
190	Robin Ventura	.10
191	Carlos Baerga	.10
192	Albert Belle	.15
193	Wayne Kirby	.10
194	Derek Lilliquist	.10
195	Kenny Lofton	.10
196	Carlos Martinez	.10
197	Jose Mesa	.10
198	Eric Plunk	.10
199	Paul Sorrento	.10
200	John Doherty	.10
201	Cecil Fielder	.10
202	Travis Fryman	.10
203	Kirk Gibson	.10
204	Mike Henneman	.10
205	Chad Kreuter	.10
206	Scott Livingstone	.10
207	Tony Phillips	.10
208	Mickey Tettleton	.10
209	Alan Trammell	.10
210	David Wells	.10
211	Lou Whitaker	.10
212	Kevin Appier	.10
213	George Brett	1.00
214	David Cone	.10
215	Tom Gordon	.10
216	Phil Hiatt	.10
217	Felix Jose	.10
218	Wally Joyner	.10
219	Jose Lind	.10
220	Mike Macfarlane	.10
221	Brian McRae	.10
222	Jeff Montgomery	.10
223	Cal Eldred	.10
224	Darryl Hamilton	.10
225	John Jaha	.10
226	Pat Listach	.10
227	*Graeme Lloyd*	.10
228	Kevin Reimer	.10
229	Bill Spiers	.10
230	B.J. Surhoff	.10
231	Greg Vaughn	.10
232	Robin Yount	.75
233	Rick Aguilera	.10
234	Jim Deshaies	.10
235	Brian Harper	.10
236	Kent Hrbek	.10
237	Chuck Knoblauch	.10
238	Shane Mack	.10
239	David McCarty	.10
240	Pedro Munoz	.10
241	Mike Pagliarulo	.10
242	Kirby Puckett	1.00
243	Dave Winfield	.75
244	Jim Abbott	.10
245	Wade Boggs	1.00
246	Pat Kelly	.10
247	Jimmy Key	.10
248	Jim Leyritz	.10
249	Don Mattingly	1.00
250	Matt Nokes	.10
251	Paul O'Neill	.10
252	Mike Stanley	.10
253	Danny Tartabull	.10
254	Bob Wickman	.10
255	Bernie Williams	.20
256	Mike Bordick	.10
257	Dennis Eckersley	.60
258	Brent Gates	.10
259	Goose Gossage	.10
260	Rickey Henderson	.75
261	Mark McGwire	1.50
262	Ruben Sierra	.10
263	Terry Steinbach	.10
264	Bob Welch	.10
265	Bobby Witt	.10
266	Rich Amaral	.10
267	Chris Bosio	.10
268	Jay Buhner	.10
269	Norm Charlton	.10
270	Ken Griffey, Jr.	1.25
271	Erik Hanson	.10
272	Randy Johnson	.75
273	Edgar Martinez	.10
274	Tino Martinez	.10
275	Dave Valle	.10
276	Omar Vizquel	.10
277	Kevin Brown	.10
278	Jose Canseco	.45
279	Julio Franco	.10
280	Juan Gonzalez	.75
281	Tom Henke	.10
282	David Hulse	.10
283	Rafael Palmeiro	.65
284	Dean Palmer	.10
285	Ivan Rodriguez	.65
286	Nolan Ryan	2.00
287	Roberto Alomar	.30
288	Pat Borders	.10
289	Joe Carter	.10
290	Juan Guzman	.10
291	Pat Hentgen	.10
292	Paul Molitor	.75
293	John Olerud	.10
294	Ed Sprague	.10
295	Dave Stewart	.10
296	Duane Ward	.10
297	Devon White	.10
298	Checklist	.05
299	Checklist	.05
300	Checklist	.05

1993 FLAIR PROMOS

	NM/M
Complete Set (8):	200.00

Common Player:		10.00
(1)	Will Clark	12.50
(2)	Darren Daulton	10.00
(3)	Andres Galarraga	10.00
(4)	Bryan Harvey	10.00
(5)	David Justice	10.00
(6)	Jody Reed	10.00
(7)	Nolan Ryan	100.00
(8)	Sammy Sosa	60.00

Wave of the Future

		NM/M
Complete Set (20):		6.00
Common Player:		.15
1	Jason Bere	.15
2	Jeremy Burnitz	.25
3	Russ Davis	.15
4	Jim Edmonds	.50
5	Cliff Floyd	.25
6	Jeffrey Hammonds	.15
7	Trevor Hoffman	.25
8	Domingo Jean	.15
9	David McCarty	.15
10	Bobby Munoz	.15
11	Brad Pennington	.15
12	Mike Piazza	3.00
13	Manny Ramirez	1.25
14	John Roper	.15
15	Tim Salmon	.60
16	Aaron Sele	.25
17	Allen Watson	.15
18	Rondell White	.25
19	Darell Whitmore	.15
20	Nigel Wilson	.15

1994 FLAIR

	NM/M
Complete Set (450):	60.00

	Common Player:	.10
	Series 1 Pack (10):	1.50
	Series 1 Box (24):	20.00
	Series 2 Pack (10):	2.50
	Series 2 Box (24):	50.00
1	Harold Baines	.10
2	Jeffrey Hammonds	.10
3	Chris Hoiles	.10
4	Ben McDonald	.10
5	Mark McLemore	.10
6	Jamie Moyer	.10
7	Jim Poole	.10
8	Cal Ripken, Jr.	3.00
9	Chris Sabo	.10
10	Scott Bankhead	.10
11	Scott Cooper	.10
12	Danny Darwin	.10
13	Andre Dawson	.30
14	Billy Hatcher	.10
15	Aaron Sele	.10
15a	Aaron Sele (overprinted "PROMOTIONAL SAMPLE")	2.00
16	John Valentin	.10
17	Dave Valle	.10
18	Mo Vaughn	.10
19	*Brian Anderson*	.50
20	Gary DiSarcina	.10
21	Jim Edmonds	.10
22	Chuck Finley	.10
23	Bo Jackson	.20
24	Mark Leiter	.10
25	Greg Myers	.10
26	Eduardo Perez	.10
27	Tim Salmon	.20
28	Wilson Alvarez	.10
29	Jason Bere	.10
30	Alex Fernandez	.10
31	Ozzie Guillen	.10
32	Joe Hall	.10
33	Darrin Jackson	.10
34	Kirk McCaskill	.10
35	Tim Raines	.10
36	Frank Thomas	1.00
37	Carlos Baerga	.10
38	Albert Belle	.15
39	Mark Clark	.10
40	Wayne Kirby	.10
41	Dennis Martinez	.10
42	Charles Nagy	.10
43	Manny Ramirez	1.00
44	Paul Sorrento	.10
45	Jim Thome	.10
46	Eric Davis	.10
47	John Doherty	.10
48	Junior Felix	.10
49	Cecil Fielder	.10
50	Kirk Gibson	.10
51	Mike Moore	.10
52	Tony Phillips	.10
53	Alan Trammell	.10
54	Kevin Appier	.10
55	Stan Belinda	.10
56	Vince Coleman	.10
57	Greg Gagne	.10
58	Bob Hamelin	.10
59	Dave Henderson	.10
60	Wally Joyner	.10
61	Mike Macfarlane	.10
62	Jeff Montgomery	.10
63	Ricky Bones	.10
64	Jeff Bronkey	.10
65	Alex Diaz	.10
66	Cal Eldred	.10
67	Darryl Hamilton	.10
68	John Jaha	.10
69	Mark Kiefer	.10
70	Kevin Seitzer	.10
71	Turner Ward	.10
72	Rich Becker	.10
73	Scott Erickson	.10
74	Keith Garagozzo	.10
75	Kent Hrbek	.10
76	Scott Leius	.10
77	Kirby Puckett	1.50
78	Matt Walkbeck	.10
79	Dave Winfield	1.00
80	Mike Gallego	.10
81	Xavier Hernandez	.10
82	Jimmy Key	.10
83	Jim Leyritz	.10
84	Don Mattingly	1.75
85	Matt Nokes	.10
86	Paul O'Neill	.10
87	Melido Perez	.10
88	Danny Tartabull	.10
89	Mike Bordick	.10
90	Ron Darling	.10
91	Dennis Eckersley	.75
92	Stan Javier	.10
93	Steve Karsay	.10
94	Mark McGwire	2.50
95	Troy Neel	.10
96	Terry Steinbach	.10
97	Bill Taylor	.10
98	Eric Anthony	.10
99	Chris Bosio	.10
100	Tim Davis	.10
101	Felix Fermin	.10
102	Dave Fleming	.10
103	Ken Griffey, Jr.	2.00
104	Greg Hibbard	.10
105	Reggie Jefferson	.10
106	Tino Martinez	.10
107	Jack Armstrong	.10
108	Will Clark	.15
109	Juan Gonzalez	1.00
110	Rick Helling	.10
111	Tom Henke	.10
112	David Hulse	.10
113	Manuel Lee	.10
114	Doug Strange	.10
115	Roberto Alomar	.25
116	Joe Carter	.10
117	Carlos Delgado	.50
118	Pat Hentgen	.10
119	Paul Molitor	1.00
120	John Olerud	.10
121	Dave Stewart	.10
122	Todd Stottlemyre	.10
123	Mike Timlin	.10
124	Jeff Blauser	.10
125	Tom Glavine	.30
126	Dave Justice	.10
127	Mike Kelly	.10
128	Ryan Klesko	.10
129	Javier Lopez	.10
130	Greg Maddux	1.50
131	Fred McGriff	.10
132	Kent Mercker	.10
133	Mark Wohlers	.10
134	Willie Banks	.10
135	Steve Buechele	.10
136	Shawon Dunston	.10
137	Jose Guzman	.10
138	Glenallen Hill	.10
139	Randy Myers	.10
140	Karl Rhodes	.10
141	Ryne Sandberg	1.50
142	Steve Trachsel	.10
143	Bret Boone	.10
144	Tom Browning	.10
145	Hector Carrasco	.10
146	Barry Larkin	.10
147	Hal Morris	.10
148	Jose Rijo	.10
149	Reggie Sanders	.10
150	John Smiley	.10
151	Dante Bichette	.10
152	Ellis Burks	.10
153	Joe Girardi	.10
154	Mike Harkey	.10
155	Roberto Mejia	.10
156	Marcus Moore	.10
157	Armando Reynoso	.10
158	Bruce Ruffin	.10
159	Eric Young	.10
160	*Kurt Abbott*	.10
161	Jeff Conine	.10
162	Orestes Destrade	.10
163	Chris Hammond	.10
164	Bryan Harvey	.10
165	Dave Magadan	.10
166	Gary Sheffield	.40
167	David Weathers	.10
168	Andujar Cedeno	.10
169	Tom Edens	.10
170	Luis Gonzalez	.25
171	Pete Harnisch	.10
172	Todd Jones	.10
173	Darryl Kile	.10
174	James Mouton	.10
175	Scott Servais	.10
176	Mitch Williams	.10
177	Pedro Astacio	.10
178	Orel Hershiser	.10
179	Raul Mondesi	.10
180	Jose Offerman	.10
181	*Chan Ho Park*	1.00
182	Mike Piazza	2.00
183	Cory Snyder	.10
184	Tim Wallach	.10
185	Todd Worrell	.10
186	Sean Berry	.10
187	Wil Cordero	.10
188	Darrin Fletcher	.10
189	Cliff Floyd	.10
190	Marquis Grissom	.10
191	Rod Henderson	.10
192	Ken Hill	.10
193	Pedro Martinez	1.00
194	Kirk Rueter	.10
195	Jeromy Burnitz	.10
196	John Franco	.10
197	Dwight Gooden	.10
198	Todd Hundley	.10
199	Bobby Jones	.10
200	Jeff Kent	.10
201	Mike Maddux	.10
202	Ryan Thompson	.10
203	Jose Vizcaino	.10
204	Darren Daulton	.10
205	Len Dykstra	.10
206	Jim Eisenreich	.10
207	Dave Hollins	.10
208	Danny Jackson	.10
209	Doug Jones	.10
210	Jeff Juden	.10
211	Ben Rivera	.10
212	Kevin Stocker	.10
213	Milt Thompson	.10
214	Jay Bell	.10
215	Steve Cooke	.10
216	Mark Dewey	.10
217	Al Martin	.10
218	Orlando Merced	.10
219	Don Slaught	.10
220	Zane Smith	.10
221	Rick White	.10
222	Kevin Young	.10
223	Rene Arocha	.10
224	Rheal Cormier	.10
225	Brian Jordan	.10
226	Ray Lankford	.10
227	Mike Perez	.10
228	Ozzie Smith	1.50
229	Mark Whiten	.10
230	Todd Zeile	.10
231	Derek Bell	.10
232	Archi Cianfrocco	.10
233	Ricky Gutierrez	.10
234	Trevor Hoffman	.10
235	Phil Plantier	.10
236	Dave Staton	.10
237	Wally Whitehurst	.10
238	Todd Benzinger	.10
239	Barry Bonds	3.00
240	John Burkett	.10
241	Royce Clayton	.10
242	Bryan Hickerson	.10
243	Mike Jackson	.10
244	Darren Lewis	.10
245	Kirt Manwaring	.10
246	Mark Portugal	.10
247	Salomon Torres	.10
248	Checklist	.10
249	Checklist	.10
250	Checklist	.10
251	Brady Anderson	.10
252	Mike Devereaux	.10
253	Sid Fernandez	.10
254	Leo Gomez	.10
255	Mike Mussina	.65
256	Mike Oquist	.10
257	Rafael Palmeiro	.75
258	Lee Smith	.10
259	Damon Berryhill	.10
260	Wes Chamberlain	.10
261	Roger Clemens	1.75
262	Gar Finnvold	.10
263	Mike Greenwell	.10
264	Tim Naehring	.10
265	Otis Nixon	.10
266	Ken Ryan	.10
267	Chad Curtis	.10
268	Chili Davis	.10
269	Damion Easley	.10
270	Jorge Fabregas	.10
271	Mark Langston	.10
272	Phil Leftwich	.10
273	Harold Reynolds	.10
274	J.T. Snow	.10
275	Joey Cora	.10
276	Julio Franco	.10
277	Roberto Hernandez	.10
278	Lance Johnson	.10
279	Ron Karkovice	.10
280	Jack McDowell	.10
281	Robin Ventura	.10
282	Sandy Alomar Jr.	.10
283	Kenny Lofton	.10
284	Jose Mesa	.10
285	Jack Morris	.10
286	Eddie Murray	1.00
287	Chad Ogea	.10
288	Eric Plunk	.10
289	Paul Shuey	.10
290	Omar Vizquel	.10
291	Danny Bautista	.10
292	Travis Fryman	.10
293	Greg Gohr	.10
294	Chris Gomez	.10
295	Mickey Tettleton	.10
296	Lou Whitaker	.10
297	David Cone	.10
298	Gary Gaetti	.10
299	Tom Gordon	.10
300	Felix Jose	.10
301	Jose Lind	.10
302	Brian McRae	.10
303	Mike Fetters	.10
304	Brian Harper	.10
305	Pat Listach	.10
306	Matt Mieske	.10
307	Dave Nilsson	.10
308	Jody Reed	.10
309	Greg Vaughn	.10
310	Bill Wegman	.10
311	Rick Aguilera	.10
312	Alex Cole	.10
313	Denny Hocking	.10
314	Chuck Knoblauch	.10
315	Shane Mack	.10
316	Pat Meares	.10
317	Kevin Tapani	.10
318	Jim Abbott	.10
319	Wade Boggs	1.50
320	Sterling Hitchcock	.10
321	Pat Kelly	.10
322	Terry Mulholland	.10
323	Luis Polonia	.10
324	Mike Stanley	.10
325	Bob Wickman	.10
326	Bernie Williams	.20
327	Mark Acre	.10
328	Geronimo Berroa	.10
329	Scott Brosius	.10
330	Brent Gates	.10
331	Rickey Henderson	1.00
332	Carlos Reyes	.10
333	Ruben Sierra	.10
334	Bobby Witt	.10
335	Bobby Ayala	.10
336	Jay Buhner	.10
337	Randy Johnson	1.00
338	Edgar Martinez	.10
339	Bill Risley	.10
340	*Alex Rodriguez*	40.00
341	Roger Salkeld	.10
342	Dan Wilson	.10
343	Kevin Brown	.10
344	Jose Canseco	.45
345	Dean Palmer	.10
346	Ivan Rodriguez	.75
347	Kenny Rogers	.10
348	Pat Borders	.10
349	Juan Guzman	.10
350	Ed Sprague	.10
351	Devon White	.10
352	Steve Avery	.10
353	Roberto Kelly	.10
354	Mark Lemke	.10
355	Greg McMichael	.10
356	Terry Pendleton	.10
357	John Smoltz	.10
358	Mike Stanton	.10
359	Tony Tarasco	.10
360	Mark Grace	.15
361	Derrick May	.10
362	Rey Sanchez	.10
363	Sammy Sosa	2.00
364	Rick Wilkins	.10
365	Jeff Brantley	.10
366	Tony Fernandez	.10
367	Chuck McElroy	.10
368	Kevin Mitchell	.10
369	John Roper	.10
370	Johnny Ruffin	.10
371	Deion Sanders	.15
372	Marvin Freeman	.10
373	Andres Galarraga	.10
374	Charlie Hayes	.10
375	Nelson Liriano	.10
376	David Nied	.10
377	Walt Weiss	.10
378	Bret Barberie	.10
379	Jerry Browne	.10
380	Chuck Carr	.10
381	Greg Colbrunn	.10
382	Charlie Hough	.10
383	Kurt Miller	.10
384	Benito Santiago	.10
385	Jeff Bagwell	1.00
386	Craig Biggio	.10
387	Ken Caminiti	.10
388	Doug Drabek	.10
389	Steve Finley	.10
390	John Hudek	.10
391	Orlando Miller	.10
392	Shane Reynolds	.10
393	Brett Butler	.10
394	Tom Candiotti	.10
395	Delino DeShields	.10
396	Kevin Gross	.10

397 Eric Karros .10
398 Ramon Martinez .10
399 Henry Rodriguez .10
400 Moises Alou .10
401 Jeff Fassero .10
402 Mike Lansing .10
403 Mel Rojas .10
404 Larry Walker .10
405 John Wetteland .10
406 Gabe White .10
407 Bobby Bonilla .10
408 Josias Manzanillo .10
409 Bret Saberhagen .10
410 David Segui .10
411 Mariano Duncan .10
412 Tommy Greene .10
413 Billy Hatcher .10
414 Ricky Jordan .10
415 John Kruk .10
416 Bobby Munoz .10
417 Curt Schilling .30
418 Fernando Valenzuela .10
419 David West .10
420 Carlos Garcia .10
421 Brian Hunter .10
422 Jeff King .10
423 Jon Lieber .10
424 Ravelo Manzanillo .10
425 Denny Neagle .10
426 Andy Van Slyke .10
427 Bryan Eversgerd .10
428 Bernard Gilkey .10
429 Gregg Jefferies .10
430 Tom Pagnozzi .10
431 Bob Tewksbury .10
432 Allen Watson .10
433 Andy Ashby .10
434 Andy Benes .10
435 Donnie Elliott .10
436 Tony Gwynn 1.50
437 Joey Hamilton .10
438 Tim Hyers .10
439 Luis Lopez .10
440 Bip Roberts .10
441 Scott Sanders .10
442 Rod Beck .10
443 Dave Burba .10
444 Darryl Strawberry .10
445 Bill Swift .10
446 Robby Thompson .10
447 *William VanLandingham* .25
448 Matt Williams .10
449 Checklist .10
450 Checklist .10

Hot Gloves

NM/M
Complete Set (10): 40.00
Common Player: 2.00
1 Barry Bonds 7.50
2 Will Clark 2.25
3 Ken Griffey, Jr. 6.00
4 Kenny Lofton 2.00
5 Greg Maddux 5.00
6 Don Mattingly 5.50
7 Kirby Puckett 5.00
8 Cal Ripken, Jr. 7.50
9 Tim Salmon 2.00
10 Matt Williams 2.00

Hot Numbers

NM/M
Complete Set (10): 17.50
Common Player: .50
1 Roberto Alomar 1.00
2 Carlos Baerga .50
3 Will Clark .75
4 Fred McGriff .50
5 Paul Molitor 3.00
6 John Olerud .50
7 Mike Piazza 4.50
8 Cal Ripken, Jr. 6.00
9 Ryne Sandberg 4.00
10 Frank Thomas 3.00

Infield Power

NM/M
Complete Set (10): 5.00
Common Player: .25
1 Jeff Bagwell .75
2 Will Clark .35
3 Darren Daulton .25
4 Don Mattingly 1.00
5 Fred McGriff .25
6 Rafael Palmeiro .65
7 Mike Piazza 1.50
8 Cal Ripken, Jr. 2.50
9 Frank Thomas .75
10 Matt Williams .25

Outfield Power

NM/M
Complete Set (10): 5.00
Common Player: .30
1 Albert Belle .45
2 Barry Bonds 2.00
3 Joe Carter .30
4 Len Dykstra .30
5 Juan Gonzalez .75
6 Ken Griffey, Jr. 1.50
7 Dave Justice .30
8 Kirby Puckett 1.00
9 Tim Salmon .45
10 Dave Winfield .75

Wave of the Future 1

NM/M
Complete Set (10): 6.00
Common Player: .25
1 Kurt Abbott .25
2 Carlos Delgado 5.00
3 Steve Karsay .25
4 Ryan Klesko .25
5 Javier Lopez .25
6 Raul Mondesi .25
7 James Mouton .25
8 Chan Ho Park .25
9 Dave Staton .25
10 Rick White .25

Wave of the Future 2

NM/M
Complete Set (10): 16.00
Common Player: .50
1 Mark Acre .50
2 Chris Gomez .50
3 Joey Hamilton .50
4 John Hudek .50
5 Jon Lieber .50
6 Matt Mieske .50
7 Orlando Miller .50
8 Alex Rodriguez 15.00
9 Tony Tarasco .50
10 Bill VanLandingham .50

1995 FLAIR

NM/M
Complete Set (432): 20.00
Common Player: .10
Series 1 or 2 Pack (9): 1.00
Series 1 or 2 Wax Box (24): 15.00
1 Brady Anderson .10
2 Harold Baines .10
3 Leo Gomez .10
4 Alan Mills .10
5 Jamie Moyer .10
6 Mike Mussina .50
7 Mike Oquist .10
8 Arthur Rhodes .10
9 Cal Ripken Jr. 3.00
10 Roger Clemens 1.75
11 Scott Cooper .10
12 Mike Greenwell .10
13 Aaron Sele .10
14 John Valentin .10
15 Mo Vaughn .10
16 Chad Curtis .10
17 Gary DiSarcina .10
18 Chuck Finley .10
19 Andrew Lorraine .10
20 Spike Owen .10
21 Tim Salmon .20
22 J.T. Snow .10
23 Wilson Alvarez .10
24 Jason Bere .10
25 Ozzie Guillen .10
26 Mike LaValliere .10
27 Frank Thomas 1.00
28 Robin Ventura .10
29 Carlos Baerga .10
30 Albert Belle .15
31 Jason Grimsley .10
32 Dennis Martinez .10
33 Eddie Murray 1.00
34 Charles Nagy .10
35 Manny Ramirez 1.00
36 Paul Sorrento .10
37 John Doherty .10
38 Cecil Fielder .10
39 Travis Fryman .10
40 Chris Gomez .10
41 Tony Phillips .10
42 Lou Whitaker .10
43 David Cone .10
44 Gary Gaetti .10
45 Mark Gubicza .10
46 Bob Hamelin .10
47 Wally Joyner .10
48 Rusty Meacham .10
49 Jeff Montgomery .10
50 Ricky Bones .10
51 Cal Eldred .10
52 Pat Listach .10
53 Matt Mieske .10
54 Dave Nilsson .10
55 Greg Vaughn .10
56 Bill Wegman .10
57 Chuck Knoblauch .10
58 Scott Leius .10
59 Pat Mahomes .10
60 Pat Meares .10
61 Pedro Munoz .10
62 Kirby Puckett 1.50
63 Wade Boggs 1.50
64 Jimmy Key .10
65 Jim Leyritz .10
66 Don Mattingly 1.75
67 Paul O'Neill .10
68 Melido Perez .10
69 Danny Tartabull .10
70 John Briscoe .10
71 Scott Brosius .10
72 Ron Darling .10
73 Brent Gates .10
74 Rickey Henderson 1.00
75 Stan Javier .10
76 Mark McGwire 2.50
77 Todd Van Poppel .10
78 Bobby Ayala .10
79 Mike Blowers .10
80 Jay Buhner .10
81 Ken Griffey Jr. 2.00
82 Randy Johnson 1.00
83 Tino Martinez .10
84 Jeff Nelson .10
85 Alex Rodriguez 2.50
86 Will Clark .15
87 Jeff Frye .10
88 Juan Gonzalez 1.00
89 Rusty Greer .10
90 Darren Oliver .10
91 Dean Palmer .10
92 Ivan Rodriguez 1.00
93 Matt Whiteside .10
94 Roberto Alomar .30
95 Joe Carter .10
96 Tony Castillo .10
97 Juan Guzman .10
98 Pat Hentgen .10
99 Mike Huff .10
100 John Olerud .10
101 Woody Williams .10
102 Roberto Kelly .10
103 Ryan Klesko .10
104 Javier Lopez .10
105 Greg Maddux 1.50
106 Fred McGriff .10
107 Jose Oliva .10
108 John Smoltz .10
109 Tony Tarasco .10
110 Mark Wohlers .10
111 Jim Bullinger .10
112 Shawon Dunston .10
113 Derrick May .10
114 Randy Myers .10
115 Karl Rhodes .10
116 Rey Sanchez .10
117 Steve Trachsel .10
118 Eddie Zambrano .10
119 Bret Boone .10
120 Brian Dorsett .10
121 Hal Morris .10
122 Jose Rijo .10
123 John Roper .10
124 Reggie Sanders .10
125 Pete Schourek .10
126 John Smiley .10
127 Ellis Burks .10
128 Vinny Castilla .10
129 Marvin Freeman .10
130 Andres Galarraga .10
131 Mike Munoz .10
132 David Nied .10
133 Bruce Ruffin .10
134 Walt Weiss .10
135 Eric Young .10
136 Greg Colbrunn .10
137 Jeff Conine .10
138 Jeremy Hernandez .10
139 Charles Johnson .10
140 Robb Nen .10
141 Gary Sheffield .40
142 Dave Weathers .10
143 Jeff Bagwell 1.00
144 Craig Biggio .10
145 Tony Eusebio .10
146 Luis Gonzalez .25
147 John Hudek .10
148 Darryl Kile .10
149 Dave Veres .10
150 Billy Ashley .10
151 Pedro Astacio .10
152 Rafael Bournigal .10
153 Delino DeShields .10
154 Raul Mondesi .10
155 Mike Piazza 2.00
156 Rudy Seanez .10
157 Ismael Valdes .10
158 Tim Wallach .10
159 Todd Worrell .10
160 Moises Alou .10
161 Cliff Floyd .10
162 Gil Heredia .10
163 Mike Lansing .10
164 Pedro Martinez 1.00
165 Kirk Rueter .10
166 Tim Scott .10
167 Jeff Shaw .10
168 Rondell White .10
169 Bobby Bonilla .10
170 Rico Brogna .10
171 Todd Hundley .10
172 Jeff Kent .10

No.	Player	NM/M
173	Jim Lindeman	.10
174	Joe Orsulak	.10
175	Bret Saberhagen	.10
176	Toby Borland	.10
177	Darren Daulton	.10
178	Lenny Dykstra	.10
179	Jim Eisenreich	.10
180	Tommy Greene	.10
181	Tony Longmire	.10
182	Bobby Munoz	.10
183	Kevin Stocker	.10
184	Jay Bell	.10
185	Steve Cooke	.10
186	Ravelo Manzanillo	.10
187	Al Martin	.10
188	Denny Neagle	.10
189	Don Slaught	.10
190	Paul Wagner	.10
191	Rene Arocha	.10
192	Bernard Gilkey	.10
193	Jose Oquendo	.10
194	Tom Pagnozzi	.10
195	Ozzie Smith	1.50
196	Allen Watson	.10
197	Mark Whiten	.10
198	Andy Ashby	.10
199	Donnie Elliott	.10
200	Bryce Florie	.10
201	Tony Gwynn	1.50
202	Trevor Hoffman	.10
203	Brian Johnson	.10
204	Tim Mauser	.10
205	Bip Roberts	.10
206	Rod Beck	.10
207	Barry Bonds	3.00
208	Royce Clayton	.10
209	Darren Lewis	.10
210	Mark Portugal	.10
211	Kevin Rogers	.10
212	William Van Landingham	.10
213	Matt Williams	.10
214	Checklist	.10
215	Checklist	.10
216	Checklist	.10
217	Bret Barberie	.10
218	Armando Benitez	.10
219	Kevin Brown	.10
220	Sid Fernandez	.10
221	Chris Hoiles	.10
222	Doug Jones	.10
223	Ben McDonald	.10
224	Rafael Palmeiro	.75
225	Andy Van Slyke	.10
226	Jose Canseco	.40
227	Vaughn Eshelman	.10
228	Mike Macfarlane	.10
229	Tim Naehring	.10
230	Frank Rodriguez	.10
231	Lee Tinsley	.10
232	Mark Whiten	.10
233	Garret Anderson	.10
234	Chili Davis	.10
235	Jim Edmonds	.10
236	Mark Langston	.10
237	Troy Percival	.10
238	Tony Phillips	.10
239	Lee Smith	.10
240	Jim Abbott	.10
241	James Baldwin	.10
242	Mike Devereaux	.10
243	Ray Durham	.10
244	Alex Fernandez	.10
245	Roberto Hernandez	.10
246	Lance Johnson	.10
247	Ron Karkovice	.10
248	Tim Raines	.10
249	Sandy Alomar Jr.	.10
250	Orel Hershiser	.10
251	Julian Tavarez	.10
252	Jim Thome	.10
253	Omar Vizquel	.10
254	Dave Winfield	1.00
255	Chad Curtis	.10
256	Kirk Gibson	.10
257	Mike Henneman	.10
258	*Bob Higginson*	.75
259	Felipe Lira	.10
260	Rudy Pemberton	.10
261	Alan Trammell	.10
262	Kevin Appier	.10
263	Pat Borders	.10
264	Tom Gordon	.10
265	Jose Lind	.10
266	Jon Nunnally	.10
267	Dilson Torres	.10
268	Michael Tucker	.10
269	Jeff Cirillo	.10
270	Darryl Hamilton	.10
271	David Hulse	.10
272	Mark Kiefer	.10
273	Graeme Lloyd	.10
274	Joe Oliver	.10
275	Al Reyes	.10
276	Kevin Seitzer	.10
277	Rick Aguilera	.10
278	Marty Cordova	.10
279	Scott Erickson	.10
280	LaTroy Hawkins	.10
281	Brad Radke	.10
282	Kevin Tapani	.10
283	Tony Fernandez	.10
284	Sterling Hitchcock	.10
285	Pat Kelly	.10
286	Jack McDowell	.10
287	Andy Pettitte	.35
288	Mike Stanley	.10
289	John Wetteland	.10
290	Bernie Williams	.25
291	Mark Acre	.10
292	Geronimo Berroa	.10
293	Dennis Eckersley	.75
294	Steve Ontiveros	.10
295	Ruben Sierra	.10
296	Terry Steinbach	.10
297	Dave Stewart	.10
298	Todd Stottlemyre	.10
299	Darren Bragg	.10
300	Joey Cora	.10
301	Edgar Martinez	.10
302	Bill Risley	.10
303	Ron Villone	.10
304	Dan Wilson	.10
305	Benji Gil	.10
306	Wilson Heredia	.10
307	Mark McLemore	.10
308	Otis Nixon	.10
309	Kenny Rogers	.10
310	Jeff Russell	.10
311	Mickey Tettleton	.10
312	Bob Tewksbury	.10
313	David Cone	.10
314	Carlos Delgado	.50
315	Alex Gonzalez	.10
316	Shawn Green	.50
317	Paul Molitor	1.00
318	Ed Sprague	.10
319	Devon White	.10
320	Steve Avery	.10
321	Jeff Blauser	.10
322	Brad Clontz	.10
323	Tom Glavine	.30
324	Marquis Grissom	.10
325	Chipper Jones	1.50
326	Dave Justice	.10
327	Mark Lemke	.10
328	Kent Mercker	.10
329	Jason Schmidt	.10
330	Steve Buechele	.10
331	Kevin Foster	.10
332	Mark Grace	.15
333	Brian McRae	.10
334	Sammy Sosa	2.00
335	Ozzie Timmons	.10
336	Rick Wilkins	.10
337	Hector Carrasco	.10
338	Ron Gant	.10
339	Barry Larkin	.10
340	Deion Sanders	.15
341	Benito Santiago	.10
342	Roger Bailey	.10
343	Jason Bates	.10
344	Dante Bichette	.10
345	Joe Girardi	.10
346	Bill Swift	.10
347	Mark Thompson	.10
348	Larry Walker	.10
349	Kurt Abbott	.10
350	John Burkett	.10
351	Chuck Carr	.10
352	Andre Dawson	.30
353	Chris Hammond	.10
354	Charles Johnson	.10
355	Terry Pendleton	.10
356	Quilvio Veras	.10
357	Derek Bell	.10
358	Jim Dougherty	.10
359	Doug Drabek	.10
360	Todd Jones	.10
361	Orlando Miller	.10
362	James Mouton	.10
363	Phil Plantier	.10
364	Shane Reynolds	.10
365	Todd Hollandsworth	.10
366	Eric Karros	.10
367	Ramon Martinez	.10
368	*Hideo Nomo*	3.00
369	Jose Offerman	.10
370	Antonio Osuna	.10
371	Todd Williams	.10
372	Shane Andrews	.10
373	Wil Cordero	.10
374	Jeff Fassero	.10
375	Darrin Fletcher	.10
376	*Mark Grudzielanek*	.50
377	*Carlos Perez*	.25
378	Mel Rojas	.10
379	Tony Tarasco	.10
380	Edgardo Alfonzo	.10
381	Brett Butler	.10
382	Carl Everett	.10
383	John Franco	.10
384	Pete Harnisch	.10
385	Bobby Jones	.10
386	Dave Mlicki	.10
387	Jose Vizcaino	.10
388	Ricky Bottalico	.10
389	Tyler Green	.10
390	Charlie Hayes	.10
391	Dave Hollins	.10
392	Gregg Jefferies	.10
393	*Michael Mimbs*	.10
394	Mickey Morandini	.10
395	Curt Schilling	.30
396	Heathcliff Slocumb	.10
397	Jason Christiansen	.10
398	Midre Cummings	.10
399	Carlos Garcia	.10
400	Mark Johnson	.10
401	Jeff King	.10
402	Jon Lieber	.10
403	Esteban Loaiza	.10
404	Orlando Merced	.10
405	*Gary Wilson*	.10
406	Scott Cooper	.10
407	Tom Henke	.10
408	Ken Hill	.10
409	Danny Jackson	.10
410	Brian Jordan	.10
411	Ray Lankford	.10
412	John Mabry	.10
413	Todd Zeile	.10
414	Andy Benes	.10
415	Andres Berumen	.10
416	Ken Caminiti	.10
417	Andujar Cedeno	.10
418	Steve Finley	.10
419	Joey Hamilton	.10
420	Dustin Hermanson	.10
421	Melvin Nieves	.10
422	Roberto Petagine	.10
423	Eddie Williams	.10
424	Glenallen Hill	.10
425	Kirt Manwaring	.10
426	Terry Mulholland	.10
427	J.R. Phillips	.10
428	Joe Rosselli	.10
429	Robby Thompson	.10
430	Checklist	.10
431	Checklist	.10
432	Checklist	.10

Cal Ripken, Jr. Enduring Flair

		NM/M
Complete Set (15):		40.00
Common Card:		3.00
1	Rookie Of The Year	3.00
2	1st MVP Season	3.00
3	World Series Highlight	3.00
4	Family Tradition	3.00
5	8,243 Consecutive Innings	3.00
6	95 Consecutive Errorless Games	3.00
7	All-Star MVP	3.00
8	1,000th RBI	3.00
9	287th Home Run	3.00
10	2,000th Consecutive Game	3.00
11	Record-tying Game	6.00
12	Record-breaking Game	6.00
13	Defensive Prowess	6.00
14	Literacy Work	6.00
15	2,153 and Counting	6.00

Hot Gloves

		NM/M
Complete Set (12):		35.00
Common Player:		1.25
1	Roberto Alomar	2.00
2	Barry Bonds	10.00
3	Ken Griffey Jr.	7.50
4	Marquis Grissom	1.25
5	Barry Larkin	1.25
6	Darren Lewis	1.25
7	Kenny Lofton	1.25
8	Don Mattingly	6.00
9	Cal Ripken Jr.	10.00
10	Ivan Rodriguez	2.50
11	Devon White	1.25
12	Matt Williams	1.25

Hot Numbers

		NM/M
Complete Set (10):		10.00
Common Player:		.50
1	Jeff Bagwell	1.00
2	Albert Belle	.60
3	Barry Bonds	2.25
4	Ken Griffey Jr.	1.50
5	Kenny Lofton	.50
6	Greg Maddux	1.25
7	Mike Piazza	2.00
8	Cal Ripken Jr.	2.25
9	Frank Thomas	1.00
10	Matt Williams	.50

Infield Power

		NM/M
Complete Set (10):		4.00
Common Player:		.25
1	Jeff Bagwell	.75
2	Darren Daulton	.25
3	Cecil Fielder	.25
4	Andres Galarraga	.25
5	Fred McGriff	.25
6	Rafael Palmeiro	.65
7	Mike Piazza	1.50
8	Frank Thomas	1.00
9	Mo Vaughn	.25
10	Matt Williams	.25

Outfield Power

		NM/M
Complete Set (10):		4.00
Common Player:		.25
1	Albert Belle	.35
2	Dante Bichette	.25
3	Barry Bonds	2.00
4	Jose Canseco	.50
5	Joe Carter	.25
6	Juan Gonzalez	.65
7	Ken Griffey Jr.	1.00
8	Kirby Puckett	.75
9	Gary Sheffield	.50
10	Ruben Sierra	.25

Today's Spotlight

		NM/M
Complete Set (12):		15.00
Common Player:		1.00
1	Jeff Bagwell	3.00
2	Jason Bere	1.00
3	Cliff Floyd	1.00
4	Chuck Knoblauch	1.00

5	Kenny Lofton	1.00
6	Javier Lopez	1.00
7	Raul Mondesi	1.00
8	Mike Mussina	2.00
9	Mike Piazza	5.00
10	Manny Ramirez	3.00
11	Tim Salmon	1.25
12	Frank Thomas	3.00

Wave of the Future

		NM/M
Complete Set (10):		7.50
Common Player:		.35
1	Jason Bates	.25
2	Armando Benitez	.25
3	Marty Cordova	.25
4	Ray Durham	.25
5	Vaughn Eshelman	.25
6	Carl Everett	.25
7	Shawn Green	1.50
8	Dustin Hermanson	.25
9	Chipper Jones	4.00
10	Hideo Nomo	2.00

1996 FLAIR

		NM/M
Complete Set (400):		50.00
Common Player:		.15
Pack (9):		3.00
Wax Box (18):		40.00
1	Roberto Alomar	.45
2	Brady Anderson	.15
3	Bobby Bonilla	.15
4	Scott Erickson	.15
5	Jeffrey Hammonds	.15
6	Jimmy Haynes	.15
7	Chris Hoiles	.15
8	Kent Mercker	.15
9	Mike Mussina	.60
10	Randy Myers	.15
11	Rafael Palmeiro	.75
12	Cal Ripken Jr.	3.00
(12p)	Cal Ripken Jr. (no card #, overprinted "PROMOTIONAL SAMPLE")	3.00
13	B.J. Surhoff	.15
14	David Wells	.15
15	Jose Canseco	.50
16	Roger Clemens	1.75
17	Wil Cordero	.15
18	Tom Gordon	.15
19	Mike Greenwell	.15
20	Dwayne Hosey	.15
21	Jose Malave	.15
22	Tim Naehring	.15
23	Troy O'Leary	.15
24	Aaron Sele	.15
25	Heathcliff Slocumb	.15
26	Mike Stanley	.15
27	Jeff Suppan	.15
28	John Valentin	.15
29	Mo Vaughn	.15
30	Tim Wakefield	.15
31	Jim Abbott	.15
32	Garret Anderson	.15
33	George Arias	.15
34	Chili Davis	.15
35	Gary DiSarcina	.15
36	Jim Edmonds	.15
37	Chuck Finley	.15
38	Todd Greene	.15
39	Mark Langston	.15
40	Troy Percival	.15
41	Tim Salmon	.25
42	Lee Smith	.15
43	J.T. Snow	.15
44	Randy Velarde	.15
45	Tim Wallach	.15
46	Wilson Alvarez	.15
47	Harold Baines	.15
48	Jason Bere	.15
49	Ray Durham	.15
50	Alex Fernandez	.15
51	Ozzie Guillen	.15
52	Roberto Hernandez	.15
53	Ron Karkovice	.15
54	Darren Lewis	.15
55	Lyle Mouton	.15
56	Tony Phillips	.15
57	Chris Snopek	.15
58	Kevin Tapani	.15
59	Danny Tartabull	.15
30	Frank Thomas	1.00
61	Robin Ventura	.15
62	Sandy Alomar	.15
63	Carlos Baerga	.15
64	Albert Belle	.25
65	Julio Franco	.15
66	Orel Hershiser	.15
67	Kenny Lofton	.15
68	Dennis Martinez	.15
69	Jack McDowell	.15
70	Jose Mesa	.15
71	Eddie Murray	1.00
72	Charles Nagy	.15
73	Tony Pena	.15
74	Manny Ramirez	1.00
75	Julian Tavarez	.15
76	Jim Thome	.15
77	Omar Vizquel	.15
78	Chad Curtis	.15
79	Cecil Fielder	.15
80	Travis Fryman	.15
81	Chris Gomez	.15
82	Bob Higginson	.15
83	Mark Lewis	.15
84	Felipe Lira	.15
85	Alan Trammell	.15
86	Kevin Appier	.15
87	Johnny Damon	.40
88	Tom Goodwin	.15
89	Mark Gubicza	.15
90	Bob Hamelin	.15
91	Keith Lockhart	.15
92	Jeff Montgomery	.15
93	Jon Nunnally	.15
94	Bip Roberts	.15
95	Michael Tucker	.15
96	Joe Vitiello	.15
97	Ricky Bones	.15
98	Chuck Carr	.15
99	Jeff Cirillo	.15
100	Mike Fetters	.15
101	John Jaha	.15
102	Mike Matheny	.15
103	Ben McDonald	.15
104	Matt Mieske	.15
105	Dave Nilsson	.15
106	Kevin Seitzer	.15
107	Steve Sparks	.15
108	Jose Valentin	.15
109	Greg Vaughn	.15
110	Rick Aguilera	.15
111	Rich Becker	.15
112	Marty Cordova	.15
113	LaTroy Hawkins	.15
114	Dave Hollins	.15
115	Roberto Kelly	.15
116	Chuck Knoblauch	.15
117	*Matt Lawton*	.50
118	Pat Meares	.15
119	Paul Molitor	1.00
120	Kirby Puckett	1.50
121	Brad Radke	.15
122	Frank Rodriguez	.15
123	Scott Stahoviak	.15
124	Matt Walbeck	.15
125	Wade Boggs	1.50
126	David Cone	.15
127	Joe Girardi	.15
128	Dwight Gooden	.15
129	Derek Jeter	3.00
130	Jimmy Key	.15
131	Jim Leyritz	.15
132	Tino Martinez	.15
133	Paul O'Neill	.15
134	Andy Pettitte	.40
135	Tim Raines	.15
136	Ruben Rivera	.15
137	Kenny Rogers	.15
138	Ruben Sierra	.15
139	John Wetteland	.15
140	Bernie Williams	.25
141	*Tony Batista*	.50
142	Allen Battle	.15
143	Geronimo Berroa	.15
144	Mike Bordick	.15
145	Scott Brosius	.15
146	Steve Cox	.15
147	Brent Gates	.15
148	Jason Giambi	.75
149	Doug Johns	.15
150	Mark McGwire	2.50
151	Pedro Munoz	.15
152	Ariel Prieto	.15
153	Terry Steinbach	.15
154	Todd Van Poppel	.15
155	Bobby Ayala	.15
156	Chris Bosio	.15
157	Jay Buhner	.15
158	Joey Cora	.15
159	Russ Davis	.15
160	Ken Griffey Jr.	2.00
161	Sterling Hitchcock	.15
162	Randy Johnson	1.00
163	Edgar Martinez	.15
164	Alex Rodriguez	2.50
165	Paul Sorrento	.15
166	Dan Wilson	.15
167	Will Clark	.20
168	Benji Gil	.15
169	Juan Gonzalez	1.00
170	Rusty Greer	.15
171	Kevin Gross	.15
172	Darryl Hamilton	.15
173	Mike Henneman	.15
174	Ken Hill	.15
175	Mark McLemore	.15
176	Dean Palmer	.15
177	Roger Pavlik	.15
178	Ivan Rodriguez	.75
179	Mickey Tettleton	.15
180	Bobby Witt	.15
181	Joe Carter	.15
182	Felipe Crespo	.15
183	Alex Gonzalez	.15
184	Shawn Green	.40
185	Juan Guzman	.15
186	Erik Hanson	.15
187	Pat Hentgen	.15
188	*Sandy Martinez*	.15
189	Otis Nixon	.15
190	John Olerud	.15
191	Paul Quantrill	.15
192	Bill Risley	.15
193	Ed Sprague	.15
194	Steve Avery	.15
195	Jeff Blauser	.15
196	Brad Clontz	.15
197	Jermaine Dye	.15
198	Tom Glavine	.40
199	Marquis Grissom	.15
200	Chipper Jones	1.50
201	David Justice	.15
202	Ryan Klesko	.15
203	Mark Lemke	.15
204	Javier Lopez	.15
205	Greg Maddux	1.50
206	Fred McGriff	.15
207	Greg McMichael	.15
208	Wonderful Monds	.15
209	Jason Schmidt	.15
210	John Smoltz	.15
211	Mark Wohlers	.15
212	Jim Bullinger	.15
213	Frank Castillo	.15
214	Kevin Foster	.15
215	Luis Gonzalez	.30
216	Mark Grace	.20
217	*Robin Jennings*	.15
218	Doug Jones	.15
219	Dave Magadan	.15
220	Brian McRae	.15
221	Jaime Navarro	.15
222	Rey Sanchez	.15
223	Ryne Sandberg	1.50
224	Scott Servais	.15
225	Sammy Sosa	2.00
226	Ozzie Timmons	.15
227	Bret Boone	.15
228	Jeff Branson	.15
229	Jeff Brantley	.15
230	Dave Burba	.15
231	Vince Coleman	.15
232	Steve Gibralter	.15
233	Mike Kelly	.15
234	Barry Larkin	.15
235	Hal Morris	.15
236	Mark Portugal	.15
237	Jose Rijo	.15
238	Reggie Sanders	.15
239	Pete Schourek	.15
240	John Smiley	.15
241	Eddie Taubensee	.15
242	Jason Bates	.15
243	Dante Bichette	.15
244	Ellis Burks	.15
245	Vinny Castilla	.15
246	Andres Galarraga	.15
247	Darren Holmes	.15
248	Curt Leskanic	.15
249	Steve Reed	.15
250	Kevin Ritz	.15
251	Bret Saberhagen	.15
252	Bill Swift	.15
253	Larry Walker	.15
254	Walt Weiss	.15
255	Eric Young	.15
256	Kurt Abbott	.15
257	Kevin Brown	.15
258	John Burkett	.15
259	Greg Colbrunn	.15
260	Jeff Conine	.15
261	Andre Dawson	.40
262	Chris Hammond	.15
263	Charles Johnson	.15
264	Al Leiter	.15
265	Robb Nen	.15
266	Terry Pendleton	.15
267	Pat Rapp	.15
268	Gary Sheffield	.50
269	Quilvio Veras	.15
270	Devon White	.15
271	Bob Abreu	.15
272	Jeff Bagwell	1.00
273	Derek Bell	.15
274	Sean Berry	.15
275	Craig Biggio	.15
276	Doug Drabek	.15
277	Tony Eusebio	.15
278	Richard Hidalgo	.15
279	Brian Hunter	.15
280	Todd Jones	.15
281	Derrick May	.15
282	Orlando Miller	.15
283	James Mouton	.15
284	Shane Reynolds	.15
285	Greg Swindell	.15
286	Mike Blowers	.15
287	Brett Butler	.15
288	Tom Candiotti	.15
289	Roger Cedeno	.15
290	Delino DeShields	.15
291	Greg Gagne	.15
292	Karim Garcia	.15
293	Todd Hollandsworth	.15
294	Eric Karros	.15
295	Ramon Martinez	.15
296	Raul Mondesi	.15
297	Hideo Nomo	1.00
298	Mike Piazza	2.00
299	Ismael Valdes	.15
300	Todd Worrell	.15
301	Moises Alou	.15
302	Shane Andrews	.15
303	Yamil Benitez	.15
304	Jeff Fassero	.15
305	Darrin Fletcher	.15
306	Cliff Floyd	.15
307	Mark Grudzielanek	.15
308	Mike Lansing	.15
309	Pedro Martinez	1.00
310	Ryan McGuire	.15
311	Carlos Perez	.15
312	Mel Rojas	.15
313	David Segui	.15
314	Rondell White	.15
315	Edgardo Alfonzo	.15
316	Rico Brogna	.15
317	Carl Everett	.15
318	John Franco	.15
319	Bernard Gilkey	.15
320	Todd Hundley	.15
321	Jason Isringhausen	.15

322 Lance Johnson .15
323 Bobby Jones .15
324 Jeff Kent .15
325 Rey Ordonez .15
326 Bill Pulsipher .15
327 Jose Vizcaino .15
328 Paul Wilson .15
329 Ricky Bottalico .15
330 Darren Daulton .15
331 *David Doster* .15
332 Lenny Dykstra .15
333 Jim Eisenreich .15
334 Sid Fernandez .15
335 Gregg Jefferies .15
336 Mickey Morandini .15
337 Benito Santiago .15
338 Curt Schilling .40
339 Kevin Stocker .15
340 David West .15
341 Mark Whiten .15
342 Todd Zeile .15
343 Jay Bell .15
344 John Ericks .15
345 Carlos Garcia .15
346 Charlie Hayes .15
347 Jason Kendall .15
348 Jeff King .15
349 Mike Kingery .15
350 Al Martin .15
351 Orlando Merced .15
352 Dan Miceli .15
353 Denny Neagle .15
354 Alan Benes .15
355 Andy Benes .15
356 Royce Clayton .15
357 Dennis Eckersley .75
358 Gary Gaetti .15
359 Ron Gant .15
360 Brian Jordan .15
361 Ray Lankford .15
362 John Mabry .15
363 T.J. Mathews .15
364 Mike Morgan .15
365 Donovan Osborne .15
366 Tom Pagnozzi .15
367 Ozzie Smith 1.50
368 Todd Stottlemyre .15
369 Andy Ashby .15
370 Brad Ausmus .15
371 Ken Caminiti .15
372 Andujar Cedeno .15
373 Steve Finley .15
374 Tony Gwynn 1.50
375 Joey Hamilton .15
376 Rickey Henderson 1.00
377 Trevor Hoffman .15
378 Wally Joyner .15
379 Marc Newfield .15
380 Jody Reed .15
381 Bob Tewksbury .15
382 Fernando Valenzuela .15
383 Rod Beck .15
384 Barry Bonds 3.00
385 Mark Carreon .15
386 Shawon Dunston .15
387 *Osvaldo Fernandez* .40
388 Glenallen Hill .15
389 Stan Javier .15
390 Mark Leiter .15
391 Kirt Manwaring .15
392 Robby Thompson .15
393 William VanLandingham .15
394 Allen Watson .15
395 Matt Williams .15
396 Checklist .15
397 Checklist .15
398 Checklist .15
399 Checklist .15
400 Checklist .15

Diamond Cuts

NM/M
Complete Set (12): 25.00
Common Player: 1.00
1 Jeff Bagwell 2.50
2 Albert Belle 1.00
3 Barry Bonds 6.00
4 Juan Gonzalez 2.50
5 Ken Griffey Jr. 3.50
6 Greg Maddux 3.00
7 Eddie Murray 2.50
8 Mike Piazza 3.50
9 Cal Ripken Jr. 6.00
10 Frank Thomas 2.50
11 Mo Vaughn 1.00
12 Matt Williams 1.00

Hot Gloves

NM/M
Complete Set (10): 60.00

Common Player: 3.00
1 Roberto Alomar 4.50
2 Barry Bonds 15.00
3 Will Clark 3.00
4 Ken Griffey Jr. 10.00
5 Kenny Lofton 3.00
6 Greg Maddux 7.50
7 Mike Piazza 10.00
8 Cal Ripken Jr. 15.00
9 Ivan Rodriguez 6.00
10 Matt Williams 3.00

Powerline

NM/M
Complete Set (10): 6.00
Common Player: .25
1 Albert Belle .25
2 Barry Bonds 1.50
3 Juan Gonzalez .50
4 Ken Griffey Jr. .75
5 Mark McGwire 1.00
6 Mike Piazza .75
7 Manny Ramirez .50
8 Sammy Sosa .75
9 Frank Thomas .50
10 Matt Williams .25

Wave of the Future

NM/M
Complete Set (20): 30.00
Common Player: 2.00
1 Bob Abreu 2.00
2 George Arias 2.00
3 Tony Batista 2.00
4 Alan Benes 2.00
5 Yamil Benitez 2.00
6 Steve Cox 2.00
7 David Doster 2.00
8 Jermaine Dye 2.00
9 Osvaldo Fernandez 2.00
10 Karim Garcia 4.00
11 Steve Gibralter 2.00
12 Todd Greene 2.00
13 Richard Hidalgo 2.00
14 Robin Jennings 2.00
15 Jason Kendall 2.00
16 Jose Malave 2.00
17 Wonderful Monds 2.00
18 Rey Ordonez 2.00
19 Ruben Rivera 2.00
20 Paul Wilson 2.00

1997 FLAIR SHOWCASE ROW 2 (STYLE)

NM/M
Complete Set (180): 15.00
Common Showtime (1-60): .15
Common Showpiece (61-120): .25
Common Showstopper (121-180): .20
A-Rod Glove Exchange: 125.00
Pack (5): 2.00
Wax Box (24): 35.00
1 Andruw Jones 1.25
2 Derek Jeter 3.00
3 Alex Rodriguez 2.25
4 Paul Molitor 1.25
5 Jeff Bagwell 1.25
6 Scott Rolen 1.00
7 Kenny Lofton .15
8 Cal Ripken Jr. 3.00
9 Brady Anderson .15
10 Chipper Jones 1.50
11 Todd Greene .15
12 Todd Walker .15
13 Billy Wagner .15
14 Craig Biggio .15
15 Kevin Orie .15
16 Hideo Nomo 1.25
17 Kevin Appier .15
18 *Bubba Trammell* .40
19 Juan Gonzalez 1.25
20 Randy Johnson 1.25
21 Roger Clemens 1.75
22 Johnny Damon .25
23 Ryne Sandberg 1.50
24 Ken Griffey Jr. 2.00
25 Barry Bonds 3.00
26 Nomar Garciaparra 2.00
27 Vladimir Guerrero 1.25
28 Ron Gant .15
29 Joe Carter .15
30 Tim Salmon .25
31 Mike Piazza 2.00
32 Barry Larkin .15
33 Manny Ramirez 1.25
34 Sammy Sosa 2.00
35 Frank Thomas 1.25
36 Melvin Nieves .15
37 Tony Gwynn 1.50
38 Gary Sheffield .35
39 Darin Erstad 1.00
40 Ken Caminiti .15
41 Jermaine Dye .15
42 Mo Vaughn .15
43 Raul Mondesi .15
44 Greg Maddux 1.50
45 Chuck Knoblauch .15
46 Andy Pettitte .60
47 Deion Sanders .25
48 Albert Belle .25
49 Jamey Wright .15
50 Rey Ordonez .15
51 Bernie Williams .25
52 Mark McGwire 2.25
53 Mike Mussina .75
54 Bob Abreu .15
55 Reggie Sanders .15
56 Brian Jordan .15
57 Ivan Rodriguez 1.00
58 Roberto Alomar .40
59 Tim Naehring .15
60 Edgar Renteria .15
61 Dean Palmer .25
62 Benito Santiago .25
63 David Cone .25
64 Carlos Delgado .75
65 *Brian Giles* .75
66 Alex Ochoa .25
67 Rondell White .25
68 Robin Ventura .25
69 Eric Karros .25
70 Jose Valentin .25
71 Rafael Palmeiro 1.00
72 Chris Snopek .25
73 David Justice .25
74 Tom Glavine .45
75 Rudy Pemberton .25
76 Larry Walker .25
77 Jim Thome .25
78 Charles Johnson .25
79 Dante Powell .25
80 Derrek Lee .25
81 Jason Kendall .25
82 Todd Hollandsworth .25
83 Bernard Gilkey .25
84 Mel Rojas .25
85 Dmitri Young .25
86 Bret Boone .25
87 Pat Hentgen .25
88 Bobby Bonilla .25
89 John Wetteland .25
90 Todd Hundley .25
91 Wilton Guerrero .25
92 Geronimo Berroa .25
93 Al Martin .25
94 Danny Tartabull .25
95 Brian McRae .25
96 Steve Finley .25
97 Todd Stottlemyre .25
98 John Smoltz .25
99 Matt Williams .25
100 Eddie Murray 1.25
101 Henry Rodriguez .25
102 Marty Cordova .25
103 Juan Guzman .25
104 Chili Davis .25
105 Eric Young .25
106 Jeff Abbott .25
107 Shannon Stewart .25
108 Rocky Coppinger .25
109 Jose Canseco .65
110 Dante Bichette .25
111 Dwight Gooden .25
112 Scott Brosius .25
113 Steve Avery .25
114 Andres Galarraga .25
115 Sandy Alomar Jr. .25
116 Ray Lankford .25
117 Jorge Posada .25
118 Ryan Klesko .25
119 Jay Buhner .25
120 Jose Guillen .25
121 Paul O'Neill .20
122 Jimmy Key .20
123 Hal Morris .20
124 Travis Fryman .20
125 Jim Edmonds .25
126 Jeff Cirillo .20
127 Fred McGriff .20
128 Alan Benes .20
129 Derek Bell .20
130 Tony Graffanino .20
131 Shawn Green .40
132 Denny Neagle .20
133 Alex Fernandez .20
134 Mickey Morandini .20
135 Royce Clayton .20
136 Jose Mesa .20
137 Edgar Martinez .20
138 Curt Schilling .40
139 Lance Johnson .20
140 Andy Benes .20
141 Charles Nagy .20
142 Mariano Rivera .40
143 Mark Wohlers .20
144 Ken Hill .20
145 Jay Bell .20
146 Bob Higginson .20
147 Mark Grudzielanek .20
148 Ray Durham .20
149 John Olerud .20
150 Joey Hamilton .20
151 Trevor Hoffman .20
152 Dan Wilson .20

153 J.T. Snow .20
154 Marquis Grissom .20
155 Yamil Benitez .20
156 Rusty Greer .20
157 Darryl Kile .20
158 Ismael Valdes .20
159 Jeff Conine .20
160 Darren Daulton .20
161 Chan Ho Park .25
162 Troy Percival .20
163 Wade Boggs 1.50
164 Dave Nilsson .20
165 Vinny Castilla .20
166 Kevin Brown .20
167 Dennis Eckersley 1.00
168 Wendell Magee Jr. .20
169 John Jaha .20
170 Garret Anderson .20
171 Jason Giambi .75
172 Mark Grace .40
173 Tony Clark .20
174 Moises Alou .20
175 Brett Butler .20
176 Cecil Fielder .20
177 Chris Widger .20
178 Doug Drabek .20
179 Ellis Burks .20
180 Shigetosi Hasegawa .20

Row 1 Grace

NM/M
Complete Set (180): 55.00
Common Showstopper (1-60): .35
Stars: 1.5X
Common Showtime (#61-120): .25
Stars: 1X
Common Showpiece (#121-180): .60
Stars: 1.5X
(See 1997 Flair Showcase Row 2 for checklist and base card values.)

Row 0 Showcase

NM/M
Complete Set (180): 250.00
Common Showpiece (1-60): 1.50
Stars: 2X
Common Showstopper (61-120): .75
Stars: 4X
Common Showtime (121-180): .35
Stars: 3X
(See 1997 Flair Showcase Row 2 for checklist and base card values.)

Legacy Masterpiece

NM/M
Common Player: 100.00
(Star values undertermined)

Legacy Collection

NM/M
Common Player: 10.00
Stars: 15X
(See 1997 Flair Showcase Row 2 for checklist and base card values.)

Diamond Cuts

NM/M
Complete Set (20): 55.00
Common Player: 1.50
1 Jeff Bagwell 2.50
2 Albert Belle 1.50
3 Ken Caminiti 1.50
4 Juan Gonzalez 2.50
5 Ken Griffey Jr. 4.00
6 Tony Gwynn 4.00
7 Todd Hundley 1.50
8 Andruw Jones 2.50
9 Chipper Jones 4.00
10 Greg Maddux 4.00
11 Mark McGwire 5.00
12 Mike Piazza 4.00
13 Derek Jeter 6.00
14 Manny Ramirez 2.50
15 Cal Ripken Jr. 6.00
16 Alex Rodriguez 5.00
17 Frank Thomas 2.50
18 Mo Vaughn 1.50
19 Bernie Williams 1.50
20 Matt Williams 1.50

Hot Gloves

Complete Set (15): 125.00
Common Player: 2.50
1 Roberto Alomar 4.00
2 Barry Bonds 20.00
3 Juan Gonzalez 10.00
4 Ken Griffey Jr. 15.00
5 Marquis Grissom 2.50
6 Derek Jeter 20.00
7 Chipper Jones 12.00
8 Barry Larkin 2.50
9 Kenny Lofton 2.50
10 Greg Maddux 12.00
11 Mike Piazza 15.00
12 Cal Ripken Jr. 20.00
13 Alex Rodriguez 17.50
14 Ivan Rodriguez 7.50
15 Frank Thomas 10.00

Wave of the Future

NM/M
Complete Set (27): 7.50
Common Player: .25
1 Todd Greene .25
2 Andruw Jones 1.50
3 Randall Simon .25
4 Wady Almonte .25

5 Pat Cline .25
6 Jeff Abbott .25
7 Justin Towle .25
8 Richie Sexson .25
9 Bubba Trammell .25
10 Bob Abreu .25
11 David Arias (last name actually Ortiz) 2.00
12 Todd Walker .25
13 Orlando Cabrera .40
14 Vladimir Guerrero 1.50
15 Ricky Ledee .25
16 Jorge Posada .40
17 Ruben Rivera .25
18 Scott Spiezio .25
19 Scott Rolen 1.50
20 Emil Brown .25
21 Jose Guillen .25
22 T.J. Staton .25
23 Elieser Marrero .25
24 Fernando Tatis .25
25 Ryan Jones .25
WF1 Hideki Irabu .25
WF2 Jose Cruz Jr. .25

1998 FLAIR SHOWCASE ROW 3

NM/M
Complete Set (120): 20.00
Common Player (1-30): .25
Common Player (31-60): .25
Common Player (61-90): .35
Common Player (91-120): .45
Pack (5): 2.50
Wax Box (24): 40.00
1 Ken Griffey Jr. 2.00
2 Travis Lee .40
3 Frank Thomas 1.25
4 Ben Grieve .25
5 Nomar Garciaparra 2.00
6 Jose Cruz Jr. .25
7 Alex Rodriguez 2.50
8 Cal Ripken Jr. 3.00
9 Mark McGwire 2.50
10 Chipper Jones 1.50
11 Paul Konerko .40
12 Todd Helton 1.00
13 Greg Maddux 1.50
14 Derek Jeter 3.00
15 Jaret Wright .25
16 Livan Hernandez .25
17 Mike Piazza 2.00
18 Juan Encarnacion .25
19 Tony Gwynn 1.50
20 Scott Rolen 1.00
21 Roger Clemens 1.75
22 Tony Clark .25
23 Albert Belle .35
24 Mo Vaughn .25
25 Andruw Jones 1.00
26 Jason Dickson .25
27 Fernando Tatis .25
28 Ivan Rodriguez .75
29 Ricky Ledee .25
30 Darin Erstad 1.00
31 Brian Rose .25
32 *Magglio Ordonez* 3.00
33 Larry Walker .25
34 Bobby Higginson .25
35 Chili Davis .25
36 Barry Bonds 3.00
37 Vladimir Guerrero 1.00
38 Jeff Bagwell 1.00
39 Kenny Lofton .25
40 Ryan Klesko .25
41 Mike Cameron .25
42 Charles Johnson .25
43 Andy Pettitte .50
44 Juan Gonzalez 1.00
45 Tim Salmon .35
46 Hideki Irabu .25
47 Paul Molitor 1.00
48 Edgar Renteria .25
49 Manny Ramirez 1.00
50 Jim Edmonds .25
51 Bernie Williams .35
52 Roberto Alomar .50
53 David Justice .25
54 Rey Ordonez .25
55 Ken Caminiti .25
56 Jose Guillen .25
57 Randy Johnson 1.00
58 Brady Anderson .25
59 Hideo Nomo 1.00
60 Tino Martinez .25
61 John Smoltz .35
62 Joe Carter .35
63 Matt Williams .35
64 Robin Ventura .35
65 Barry Larkin .35
66 Dante Bichette .35
67 Travis Fryman .35
68 Gary Sheffield .60
69 Eric Karros .35
70 Matt Stairs .35
71 Al Martin .35
72 Jay Buhner .35
73 Ray Lankford .35
74 Carlos Delgado .65
75 Edgardo Alfonzo .35
76 Rondell White .35
77 Chuck Knoblauch .35
78 Raul Mondesi .35
79 Johnny Damon .50
80 Matt Morris .35
81 Tom Glavine .60
82 Kevin Brown .35
83 Garret Anderson .35
84 Mike Mussina .50
85 Pedro Martinez 1.25
86 Craig Biggio .35
87 Darryl Kile .35
88 Rafael Palmeiro .75
89 Jim Thome .35
90 Andres Galarraga .35
91 Sammy Sosa 3.00
92 Willie Greene .45
93 Vinny Castilla .45
94 Justin Thompson .45
95 Jeff King .45
96 Jeff Cirillo .45
97 Mark Grudzielanek .45
98 Brad Radke .45
99 John Olerud .45
100 Curt Schilling .75
101 Steve Finley .45
102 J.T. Snow .45
103 Edgar Martinez .45
104 Wilson Alvarez .45
105 Rusty Greer .45
106 Pat Hentgen .45
107 David Cone .45
108 Fred McGriff .45
109 Jason Giambi 1.00
110 Tony Womack .45
111 Bernard Gilkey .45
112 Alan Benes .45
113 Mark Grace .60
114 Reggie Sanders .45
115 Moises Alou .45
116 John Jaha .45
117 Henry Rodriguez .45
118 Dean Palmer .45
119 Mike Lieberthal .45
120 Shawn Estes .45

Row 2

	NM/M
Complete Set (120):	40.00
Common Player:	.50
Stars:	1.5-2X

(See 1998 Flair Showcase Row 3 for checklist and base card values.)

Row 1

Complete Set (1-120):	100.00
Commons (1-30):	1.00
Stars:	2X
Commons (31-60):	1.25
Stars:	3X
Commons (61-90):	.35
Stars:	1X
Commons (91-120):	.75
Stars:	1.5X

(See 1998 Flair Showcase Row 3 for checklist and base cards values.)

Row 0

Complete Set (120):	350.00
Common Player (1-30):	5.00
Stars:	10X
Common Player (31-60):	3.00
Stars:	8X
Common Player (61-90):	2.00
Stars:	6X
Common Player (91-120):	1.00
Stars:	4X

(See 1998 Flair Showcase Row 3 for checklist and base card values.)

Legacy Collection

	NM/M
Common Player:	4.00
Stars:	20X

(See 1998 Flair Showcase Row 3 for checklist and base card values.)

Legacy Masterpiece

	NM/M
Common Player:	50.00

(Values undetermined)

Perfect 10

		NM/M
Complete Set (10):		1,600
Common Player:		100.00
1	Ken Griffey Jr.	200.00
2	Cal Ripken Jr.	300.00
3	Frank Thomas	125.00
4	Mike Piazza	200.00
5	Greg Maddux	150.00
6	Nomar Garciaparra	200.00
7	Mark McGwire	250.00
8	Scott Rolen	100.00

9	Alex Rodriguez	250.00
10	Roger Clemens	175.00

Wave of the Future

		NM/M
Complete Set (12):		10.00
Common Player:		.50
WF1	Travis Lee	1.00
WF2	Todd Helton	5.00
WF3	Ben Grieve	.50
WF4	Juan Encarnacion	.50
WF5	Brad Fullmer	.50
WF6	Ruben Rivera	.50
WF7	Paul Konerko	.75
WF8	Derrek Lee	.50
WF9	Mike Lowell	.50
WF10	Magglio Ordonez	3.00
WF11	Rich Butler	.50
WF12	Eli Marrero	.50

1999 FLAIR SHOWCASE ROW 3 (POWER)

		NM/M
Complete Set (144):		25.00
Common Player:		.25
Pack (5):		3.00
Wax Box (24):		45.00
1	Mark McGwire	2.50
2	Sammy Sosa	1.50
3	Ken Griffey Jr.	2.00
4	Chipper Jones	1.50
5	Ben Grieve	.25
6	J.D. Drew	.75
7	Jeff Bagwell	1.00
8	Cal Ripken Jr.	3.00
9	Tony Gwynn	1.50
10	Nomar Garciaparra	1.50
11	Travis Lee	.35
12	Troy Glaus	.75
13	Mike Piazza	2.00
14	Alex Rodriguez	2.50
15	Kevin Brown	.25
16	Darin Erstad	.50
17	Scott Rolen	.50
18	*Micah Bowie*	.25
19	Juan Gonzalez	.50
20	Kerry Wood	.50
21	Roger Clemens	1.75
22	Derek Jeter	3.00
23	*Pat Burrell*	3.00
24	Tim Salmon	.25
25	Barry Bonds	3.00
26	*Roosevelt Brown*	.25
27	Vladimir Guerrero	1.00
28	Randy Johnson	1.00
29	Mo Vaughn	.25
30	Fernando Seguignol	.25
31	Greg Maddux	1.50
32	Tony Clark	.25
33	Eric Chavez	.40
34	Kris Benson	.25
35	Frank Thomas	1.00
36	Mario Encarnacion	.25
37	Gabe Kapler	.25
38	Jeremy Giambi	.25
39	*Peter Tucci*	.25
40	Manny Ramirez	1.00
41	Albert Belle	.25
42	Warren Morris	.25
43	Michael Barrett	.25
44	Andruw Jones	1.00
45	Carlos Delgado	.60
46	Jaret Wright	.25
47	Juan Encarnacion	.25
48	Scott Hunter	.25
49	Tino Martinez	.25
50	Craig Biggio	.25
51	Jim Thome	.60
52	Vinny Castilla	.25
53	Tom Glavine	.40
54	Bob Higginson	.25
55	Moises Alou	.25
56	Robin Ventura	.25
57	Bernie Williams	.25
58	Pedro J. Martinez	1.00
59	Greg Vaughn	.25
60	Ray Lankford	.25
61	Jose Canseco	.40
62	Ivan Rodriguez	.75
63	Shawn Green	.40
64	Rafael Palmeiro	.75
65	Ellis Burks	.25
66	Jason Kendall	.25
67	David Wells	.25
68	Rondell White	.25
69	Gary Sheffield	.40
70	Ken Caminiti	.25
71	Cliff Floyd	.25
72	Larry Walker	.25
73	Bartolo Colon	.25
74	Barry Larkin	.25
75	Calvin Pickering	.25
76	Jim Edmonds	.25
77	Henry Rodriguez	.25
78	Roberto Alomar	.40
79	Andres Galarraga	.25
80	Richie Sexson	.25
81	Todd Helton	.75
82	Damion Easley	.25
83	Livan Hernandez	.25
84	Carlos Beltran	.60
85	Todd Hundley	.25
86	Todd Walker	.25
87	Scott Brosius	.25
88	Bob Abreu	.25
89	Corey Koskie	.25
90	Ruben Rivera	.25
91	Edgar Renteria	.25
92	Quinton McCracken	.25
93	Bernard Gilkey	.25
94	Shannon Stewart	.25
95	Dustin Hermanson	.25
96	Mike Caruso	.25
97	Alex Gonzalez	.25
98	Raul Mondesi	.25
99	David Cone	.25
100	Curt Schilling	.40
101	Brian Giles	.25
102	Edgar Martinez	.25
103	Rolando Arrojo	.25
104	Derek Bell	.25
105	Denny Neagle	.25
106	Marquis Grissom	.25
107	Bret Boone	.25
108	Mike Mussina	.50
109	John Smoltz	.25
110	Brett Tomko	.25
111	David Justice	.25
112	Andy Pettitte	.40
113	Eric Karros	.25
114	Dante Bichette	.25
115	Jeromy Burnitz	.25
116	Paul Konerko	.40
117	Steve Finley	.25
118	Ricky Ledee	.25
119	Edgardo Alfonzo	.25
120	Dean Palmer	.25
121	Rusty Greer	.25
122	Luis Gonzalez	.25
123	Randy Winn	.25
124	Jeff Kent	.25
125	Doug Glanville	.25
126	Justin Thompson	.25
127	Bret Saberhagen	.25
128	Wade Boggs	1.50
129	Al Leiter	.25
130	Paul O'Neill	.25
131	Chan Ho Park	.25
132	Johnny Damon	.60
133	Darryl Kile	.25
134	Reggie Sanders	.25
135	Kevin Millwood	.25
136	Charles Johnson	.25
137	Ray Durham	.25
138	Rico Brogna	.25
139	Matt Williams	.25
140	Sandy Alomar	.25
141	Jeff Cirillo	.25
142	Devon White	.25
143	Andy Benes	.25
144	Mike Stanley	.25
	Checklist card	.05

Row 2 (Passion)

	NM/M
Complete Set (144):	65.00
Common Player:	.25
Showdown (1-48):	2X
Showpiece (49-96):	1X
Showtime (97-144):	1X

(See 1999 Flair Showcase Row 3 for checklist and base card values.)

Row 1 Showcase

	NM/M
Complete Set (144):	300.00
Common Showpiece (1-48):	2.00
Showpiece Stars:	5X
Common Showtime (49-96):	1.00
Showtime Stars:	3X
Common Showdown (97-144):	.50
Showdown Stars:	2X

(See 1999 Flair Showcase Row 1 for checklist and base card values.)

Legacy Masterpiece

	NM/M
Common Legacy:	6.00
Legacy Stars:	20X
Common Masterpiece:	50.00

(See 1999 Flair Showcase for checklist.)

Measure of Greatness

		NM/M
Complete Set (15):		100.00
Common Player:		3.00
Production 500 sets		
1	Roger Clemens	7.50
2	Nomar Garciaparra	6.50
3	Juan Gonzalez	3.00
4	Ken Griffey Jr.	9.00
5	Vladimir Guerrero	5.00

6 Tony Gwynn 6.50
7 Derek Jeter 15.00
8 Chipper Jones 6.50
9 Mark McGwire 12.50
10 Mike Piazza 9.00
11 Manny Ramirez 5.00
12 Cal Ripken Jr. 15.00
13 Alex Rodriguez 12.50
14 Sammy Sosa 6.50
15 Frank Thomas 5.00

Wave of the Future

NM/M
Complete Set (15): 40.00
Common Player: 1.50
Production 1,000 sets
1 Kerry Wood 4.00
2 Ben Grieve 1.50
3 J.D. Drew 4.00
4 Juan Encarnacion 1.50
5 Travis Lee 2.00
6 Todd Helton 7.50
7 Troy Glaus 7.50
8 Ricky Ledee 1.50
9 Eric Chavez 2.00
10 Ben Davis 1.50
11 George Lombard 1.50
12 Jeremy Giambi 1.50
13 Roosevelt Brown 1.50
14 Pat Burrell 6.00
15 Preston Wilson 1.50

2003 FLAIR

NM/M
Complete Set (125):
Common Player: .25
Common SP (91-125): 4.00
Production 500
Pack (5): 3.50
Box (20): 50.00
1 Hideo Nomo .60
2 Derek Jeter 3.00
3 Junior Spivey .25
4 Rich Aurilia .25
5 Luis Gonzalez .35
6 Sean Burroughs .25
7 Pedro J. Martinez 1.00
8 Randy Winn .25
9 Carlos Delgado .50
10 Pat Burrell .50
11 Barry Larkin .25
12 Roberto Alomar .40
13 Tony Batista .25
14 Barry Bonds 3.00
15 Craig Biggio .25
16 Ivan Rodriguez .65
17 Javier Vazquez .25
18 Joe Borchard .25
19 Josh Phelps .25
20 Omar Vizquel .25
21 Tom Glavine .40
22 Darin Erstad .50
23 Hee Seop Choi .25
24 Roger Clemens 1.75
25 Michael Cuddyer .25
26 Mike Sweeney .25
27 Phil Nevin .25
28 Torii Hunter .25
29 Vladimir Guerrero 1.00
30 Ellis Burks .25
31 Jimmy Rollins .25
32 Ken Griffey Jr. 2.00
33 Maggio Ordonez .40
34 Mark Prior 1.00
35 Mike Lieberthal .25
36 Jorge Posada .30
37 Rodrigo Lopez .25
38 Todd Helton 1.00
39 Adam Kennedy .25
40 Curt Schilling .40
41 Jim Thome .25
42 Josh Beckett .25
43 Carlos Pena .25
44 Jason Kendall .25
45 Sammy Sosa 2.00
46 Scott Rolen .75
47 Alex Rodriguez 2.50
48 Aubrey Huff .25
49 Bobby Abreu .25
50 Jeff Kent .25
51 Joe Randa .25
52 Lance Berkman .25
53 Orlando Cabrera .25
54 Richie Sexson .25
55 Albert Pujols 2.00
56 Alfonso Soriano .50
57 Greg Maddux 1.50
58 Jason Giambi .75
59 Jeff Bagwell 1.00
60 Kerry Wood .50
61 Manny Ramirez 1.00
62 Eric Chavez .40
63 Preston Wilson .25
64 Shawn Green .50
65 Shea Hillenbrand .25
66 Austin Kearns .75
67 Cliff Floyd .25
68 Edgardo Alfonzo .25
69 J.D. Drew .40
70 Larry Walker .25
71 Mike Piazza 2.00
72 Andruw Jones .75
73 Ben Grieve .25
74 Eric Hinske .25
75 Geoff Jenkins .25
76 Kazuhiro Sasaki .25
77 Matt Morris .25
78 Miguel Tejada .40
79 Aramis Ramirez .25
80 Troy Glaus 1.00
81 Ichiro Suzuki 2.00
82 Mark Teixeira .50
83 Nomar Garciaparra 2.00
84 Chipper Jones 1.50
85 Frank Thomas 1.00
86 Paul LoDuca .25
87 Bernie Williams .35
88 Adam Dunn .75
89 Randy Johnson 1.00
90 Barry Zito .40
91 *Lew Ford* 8.00
92 *Joe Valentine* 3.00
93 Jhonny Peralta 4.00
94 *Hideki Matsui* 20.00
95 *Francisco Rosario* 3.00
96 Adam LaRoche 4.00
97 *Josh Hall* 6.00
98 *Chien-Ming Wang* 10.00
99 *Josh Willingham* 6.00
100 *Guillermo Quiroz* 6.00
101 *Termel Sledge* 3.00
102 *Prentice Redman* 3.00
103 *Matt Bruback* 6.00
104 *Alejandro Machado* 3.00
105 *Shane Victorino* 6.00
106 *Chris Waters* 3.00
107 *Jose Contreras* 8.00
108 *Pete LaForest* 3.00
109 *Nook Logan* 3.00
110 *Hector Luna* 8.00
111 *Daniel Cabrera* 6.00
112 *Matt Kata* 6.00
113 *Rontrez Johnson* 6.00
114 *Josh Stewart* 8.00
115 *Michael Hessman* 3.00
116 *Felix Sanchez* 6.00
117 *Michel Hernandez* 3.00
118 *Arnaldo Munoz* 3.00
119 *Ian Ferguson* 3.00
120 *Clint Barmes* 6.00
121 *Brian Stokes* 3.00
122 *Craig Brazell* 6.00
123 John Webb 3.00
124 *Tim Olson* 6.00
125 Jeremy Bonderman 6.00

Row 1

Stars (1-90): 5-10X
Rookies (91-125): .75-1.5X
Production 150 sets
Row 2: No Pricing
Production 25 sets

Diamond Cuts

NM/M
Common Player: 4.00
Inserted 1:10
Golds: 1-2X
Production 100 sets
1DC Alex Rodriguez 12.00
2DC Roberto Alomar 4.00
3DC Scott Rolen 5.00
4DC Alfonso Soriano 6.00
5DC Chipper Jones 7.50
6DC Pat Burrell 5.00
7DC Derek Jeter 15.00
8DC Mike Piazza 10.00
9DC J.D. Drew 4.00
10DC Vladimir Guerrero 6.00
11DC Greg Maddux 7.50
12DC Barry Zito 4.00
13DC Troy Glaus 5.00
14DC Roy Oswalt 4.00
15DC Roger Clemens 9.00

Hot Numbers

NM/M
Common Player: 15.00
Production 100 sets
1HN Alex Rodriguez 35.00
2HN Roberto Alomar 20.00
3HN Scott Rolen 30.00
4HN Alfonso Soriano 30.00
5HN Chipper Jones 25.00
6HN Pat Burrell 25.00
7HN Derek Jeter 40.00
8HN Mike Piazza 30.00
9HN J.D. Drew 15.00
10HN Vladimir Guerrero 20.00
11HN Greg Maddux 30.00
12HN Barry Zito 15.00
13HN Troy Glaus 15.00
14HN Roy Oswalt 15.00
15HN Roger Clemens

Hot Numbers Dual

Production 25 sets: No Pricing

Power Tools

NM/M
Common Player: 5.00
Production 500 sets
Golds: 1-1.5X
Production 100 sets
1PT Nomar Garciaparra 15.00
2PT Derek Jeter 25.00
3PT Sammy Sosa 12.00
4PT Miguel Tejada 5.00
5PT Austin Kearns 10.00
6PT Jason Giambi 8.00
7PT Adam Dunn 8.00
8PT Jim Thome 8.00
9PT Lance Berkman 6.00
10PT Alfonso Soriano 15.00
11PT Pat Burrell
12PT Alex Rodriguez 15.00
13PT Mike Piazza 10.00
14PT Bernie Williams 10.00
15PT Jeff Bagwell 8.00
16PT Andruw Jones 5.00
17PT Scott Rolen 12.00
18PT Eric Hinske
19PT Juan Gonzalez 6.00
20PT Hee Seop Choi

Power Tools - Dual

NM/M
Common Duo:

Production 200 sets
1PTD Nomar Garciaparra, Derek Jeter 40.00
2PTD Pat Burrell, Jim Thome
3PTD Adam Dunn, Austin Kearns 25.00
4PTD Jim Thome, Sammy Sosa 15.00
5PTD Alex Rodriguez, Nomar Garciaparra 20.00
6PTD Jason Giambi, Bernie Williams 15.00
7PTD Derek Jeter, Alfonso Soriano 25.00
8PTD Lance Berkman, Jeff Bagwell 10.00
9PTD Miguel Tejada, Alex Rodriguez 20.00
10PTD Jason Giambi, Mike Piazza 20.00

Sweet Swatch

NM/M
Common Player: 5.00
Production 250 sets
Derek Jeter 20.00
Sammy Sosa 15.00
Hideo Nomo 20.00
Vladimir Guerrero 6.00
Jason Giambi 8.00
Nomar Garciaparra 15.00
Randy Johnson 12.00
Miguel Tejada 5.00
Pedro J. Martinez 10.00
Adam Dunn 8.00
Roger Clemens 15.00
Mark Prior 20.00
Chipper Jones 10.00
Alex Rodriguez 15.00
Hee Seop Choi
Bernie Williams 6.00
Jorge Posada
Lance Berkman 6.00
Kazuhiro Sasaki 6.00
Alfonso Soriano 12.00

Sweet Swatch Autograph Oversized

NM/M
Common Player:
Golds: 1.5-2X
Production 25, Jeter 50
Masterpiece One-of-Ones exist
Derek Jeter/312 90.00
Randy Johnson/218 60.00
Adam Dunn/218 30.00
Jeff Bagwell/218 40.00

Sweet Swatch Dual Oversized

NM/M
Production 25 sets: No Pricing

Sweet Swatch Patch

NM/M
Common Player: 15.00
Production 50 sets
Derek Jeter
Sammy Sosa 50.00
Hideo Nomo 50.00
Vladimir Guerrero
Jason Giambi 20.00
Nomar Garciaparra 45.00
Randy Johnson 40.00
Miguel Tejada 15.00
Pedro J. Martinez 40.00
Adam Dunn 35.00
Roger Clemens 50.00
Mark Prior 45.00

Chipper Jones	
Alex Rodriguez	45.00
Hee Seop Choi	
Bernie Williams	20.00
Jorge Posada	
Lance Berkman	
Kazuhiro Sasaki	30.00
Alfonso Soriano	35.00

Sweet Swatch Patch Oversized

	NM/M
Common Player:	15.00
Derek Jeter/35	75.00
Sammy Sosa/190	40.00
Hideo Nomo/114	50.00
Vladimir Guerrero/290	35.00
Jason Giambi/26	
Nomar Garciaparra/124	40.00
Randy Johnson/46	
Miguel Tejada/183	15.00
Pedro Martinez/185	40.00
Adam Dunn/130	30.00
Roger Clemens	
Mark Prior/290	40.00
Chipper Jones/284	25.00
Alex Rodriguez/298	40.00
Hee Seop Choi	
Bernie Williams/123	25.00
Jorge Posada	
Lance Berkman/287	25.00
Kazuhiro Sasaki/90	40.00
Alfonso Soriano	

Sweet Swatch Oversized

	NM/M
Common Player:	6.00
1:hobby box	
Masterpiece One-of-One's exist	
Derek Jeter/150	20.00
Sammy Sosa/279	15.00
Hideo Nomo/970	12.00
Vladimir Guerrero	
Jason Giambi/350	15.00
Nomar Garciaparra/727	15.00
Randy Johnson/274	15.00
Miguel Tejada/518	6.00
Pedro Martinez/1,480	10.00
Adam Dunn/1,090	8.00
Roger Clemens/97	25.00
Mark Prior/1,195	15.00
Chipper Jones/80	15.00
Alex Rodriguez/150	15.00
Hee Seop Choi	
Bernie Williams/1,420	8.00
Jorge Posada	
Lance Berkman/1,465	6.00
Kazuhiro Sasaki/505	10.00
Alfonso Soriano	

Wave of the Future

		NM/M
Common Player:		3.00
Production 500 sets		
Golds:		1-2X
Production 100 sets		
1WOF	Francisco Rodriguez	3.00
2WOF	Carl Crawford	4.00
3WOF	Austin Kearns	10.00
4WOF	Hank Blalock	8.00
5WOF	Marlon Byrd	3.00
6WOF	Michael Restovich	3.00
7WOF	Joe Borchard	3.00
8WOF	Sean Burroughs	4.00
9WOF	Aubrey Huff	3.00
10WOF	Josh Phelps	5.00

2003 Flair Greats of the Game

		NM/M
Complete Set (95):		35.00
Common Player:		.40
Pack (5):		6.00
Box (20):		100.00
1	Ozzie Smith	1.00
2	Red Schoendienst	.40
3	Harmon Killebrew	1.50
4	Ralph Kiner	.40
5	Johnny Bench	2.00
6	Al Kaline	1.00
7	Bobby Doerr	.40
8	Cal Ripken Jr.	4.00
9	Enos Slaughter	.40
10	Phil Rizzuto	1.00
11	Luis Aparicio	.40
12	Pee Wee Reese	.40
13	Richie Ashburn	.40
14	Ernie Banks	2.00
15	Earl Weaver	.40
16	Whitey Ford	1.50
17	Brooks Robinson	1.00
18	Lou Boudreau	.40
19	Robin Yount	1.00
20	Mike Schmidt	2.50
21	Bob Lemon	.40
22	Stan Musial	2.50
23	Joe Morgan	.60
24	Early Wynn	.40
25	Willie Stargell	.75
26	Yogi Berra	2.00
27	Juan Marichal	.40
28	Rick Ferrell	.40
29	Rod Carew	.75
30	Jim Bunning	.40
31	Ferguson Jenkins	.40
32	Steve Carlton	.75
33	Larry Doby	.40
34	Nolan Ryan	4.00
35	Phil Niekro	.40
36	Billy Williams	.40
37	Hal Newhouser	.40
38	Bob Feller	.75
39	Lou Brock	.75
40	Monte Irvin	.75
41	Eddie Mathews	1.00
42	Rollie Fingers	.40
43	Gaylord Perry	.40
44	Reggie Jackson	1.50
45	Bob Gibson	1.00
46	Robin Roberts	.40
47	Tom Seaver	1.00
48	Willie McCovey	.40
49	Hoyt Wilhelm	.40
50	George Kell	.40
51	Warren Spahn	1.00
52	Jim "Catfish" Hunter	.40
53	Dom DiMaggio	.40
54	Joe Medwick	.40
55	Johnny Pesky	.40
56	Steve Garvey	.40
57	Harry Heilmann	.40
58	Dave Winfield	.75
59	Andre Dawson	.40
60	Jimmie Foxx	1.00
61	Buddy Bell	.40
62	Gabby Hartnett	.40
63	Babe Ruth	4.00
64	Dizzy Dean	1.50
65	Hank Greenberg	.40
66	Don Drysdale	.75
67	Gary Carter	.40
68	Wade Boggs	.75
69	Tony Perez	.40
70	Mickey Cochrane	.75
71	Bill Dickey	.40
72	George Brett	3.00
73	Honus Wagner	3.00
74	George Sisler	1.00
75	Walter Johnson	2.00
76	Ron Santo	.40
77	Roy Campanella	1.00
78	Roger Maris	2.50
79	Kirby Puckett	2.50
80	Alan Trammell	.40
81	Don Mattingly	4.00
82	Ty Cobb	3.00
83	Lou Gehrig	3.00
84	Jackie Robinson	3.00
85	Billy Martin	.75
86	Paul Molitor	.75
87	Duke Snider	1.00
88	Thurman Munson	1.50
89	Luke Appling	.40
90	Ernie Lombardi	.40
91	Rube Waddell	.40
92	Travis Jackson	.40
93	Joe Sewell	.40
94	King Kelly	.40
95	Heinie Manush	.40
Common Home Team (96-133):		2.00
96HT	Bobby Doerr	2.00
97HT	Johnny Pesky	2.00
98HT	Wade Boggs	3.00
99HT	Tony Conigliaro	2.00
100HT	Carlton Fisk	3.00
101HT	Rico Petrocelli	2.00
102HT	Jim Rice	2.00
103HT	Al Lopez	2.00
104HT	Pee Wee Reese	2.00
105HT	Tommy Lasorda	2.00
106HT	Gil Hodges	3.00
107HT	Jackie Robinson	6.00
108HT	Duke Snider	4.00
109HT	Don Drysdale	4.00
110HT	Steve Garvey	2.00
111HT	Hoyt Wilhelm	2.00
112HT	Juan Marichal	3.00
113HT	Monte Irvin	3.00
114HT	Willie McCovey	3.00
115HT	Travis Jackson	2.00
116HT	Bobby Bonds	2.00
117HT	Orlando Cepeda	2.00
118HT	Whitey Ford	4.00
119HT	Phil Rizzuto	4.00
120HT	Reggie Jackson	4.00
121HT	Yogi Berra	5.00
122HT	Roger Maris	6.00
123HT	Don Mattingly	10.00
124HT	Babe Ruth	10.00
125HT	Dave Winfield	3.00
126HT	Bob Gibson	4.00
127HT	Enos Slaughter	2.00
128HT	Joe Medwick	2.00
129HT	Lou Brock	3.00
130HT	Ozzie Smith	5.00
131HT	Stan Musial	6.00
132HT	Steve Carlton	3.00
133HT	Dizzy Dean	4.00

Cut of History

	NM/M
Common Player:	5.00
Inserted 1:10	
Paul O'Neill	5.00
Dennis Eckersley	8.00
Jim Palmer	6.00
Graig Nettles	8.00
Frank Baker	30.00
Wade Boggs	8.00
Roger Maris	60.00
Jim "Catfish" Hunter	8.00
Alan Trammell	12.00
Eddie Murray	20.00
Steve Carlton	10.00
Tom Seaver	8.00
Hank Greenberg	
Gary Carter	8.00
Phil Niekro	6.00
Luis Aparicio	8.00
Reggie Jackson	12.00
Fergie Jenkins	8.00
Kirby Puckett	15.00
Billy Martin	15.00
Joe Medwick	25.00
Buddy Bell	5.00
Early Wynn	10.00
Cal Ripken Jr.	25.00
Hoyt Wilhelm	8.00
Willie McCovey	10.00

Cut of History Auto.

	NM/M
Common Player:	
Alan Trammell/211	25.00
Steve Carlton/506	30.00
Cal Ripken Jr/155	150.00
Johnny Bench/161	50.00

Ballpark Heroes

		NM/M
Complete Set (9):		25.00
Common Player:		2.00
Inserted 1:10		
1BH	Nolan Ryan	5.00
2BH	Babe Ruth	5.00
3BH	Honus Wagner	3.00
4BH	Ty Cobb	4.00
5BH	Ernie Banks	3.00
6BH	Mike Schmidt	3.00
7BH	Duke Snider	2.00
8BH	Cal Ripken Jr.	5.00
9BH	Stan Musial	3.00

Bat Rack Triple

	NM/M
Common Card:	15.00
Production 300	
Eddie Murray, Cal Ripken Jr., Brooks Robinson	75.00
Ryne Sandberg, Ron Santo, Billy Williams	45.00
Johnny Bench, Joe Morgan, Tony Perez	35.00
Hank Greenberg, Harry Heilmann, George Kell	
Eddie Mathews, Paul Molitor, Robin Yount	40.00
Tommie Agee, Jerry Grote, Bud Harrelson	15.00
Reggie Jackson, Don Mattingly, Dave Winfield	45.00
Dave Parker, Willie Stargell	20.00

Bat Rack Quad

	NM/M
Common Card:	50.00
Numbered to 150	
Don Mattingly, Joe Morgan, Cal Ripken Jr., Brooks Robinson	90.00
Ryne Sandberg, Ron Santo, Billy Williams, Andre Dawson	60.00
Dave Winfield, Cal Ripken Jr., Paul Molitor, Robin Yount	80.00
Eddie Murray, Eddie Mathews, Reggie Jackson, Willie McCovey	50.00

Classic Numbers

		NM/M
Complete Set (13):		50.00
Common Player:		3.00
Inserted 1:20		
1CN	Jackie Robinson	6.00
2CN	Willie McCovey	3.00
3CN	Brooks Robinson	5.00
4CN	Reggie Jackson	6.00

5CN	Ozzie Smith	6.00
6CN	Johnny Bench	6.00
7CN	Yogi Berra	6.00
8CN	Cal Ripken Jr.	10.00
9CN	George Brett	8.00
10CN	Thurman Munson	5.00
11CN	Joe Morgan	3.00
12CN	Nolan Ryan	10.00
13CN	Steve Carlton	3.00

Classic Numbers Game-Used

	NM/M
Common Player:	10.00
Inserted 1:24	
Willie McCovey	12.00
George Brett	20.00
Joe Morgan	10.00
Yogi Berra	20.00
Cal Ripken Jr.	25.00
Nolan Ryan	35.00
Ozzie Smith	15.00
Johnny Bench	15.00
Ryne Sandberg	25.00
Thurman Munson	20.00
Steve Carlton	10.00

Classic Numbers Dual-side

	NM/M
Common Card:	25.00
Production 250 sets	
Yogi Berra, Thurman Munson	45.00
Nolan Ryan, Steve Carlton	65.00
Johnny Bench, Thurman Munson	35.00
Cal Ripken Jr., Ozzie Smith	60.00
Joe Morgan, Ryne Sandberg	35.00
Willie McCovey, Johnny Bench	25.00
Yogi Berra, Cal Ripken Jr.	50.00
George Brett, Nolan Ryan	75.00

Greats of the Grain

		NM/M
Production 50 sets		
1GOG	Ty Cobb	100.00
2GOG	Mike Schmidt	50.00
3GOG	Babe Ruth	140.00
4GOG	Lou Gehrig	80.00
5GOG	George Brett	160.00
6GOG	Stan Musial	75.00
7GOG	Don Mattingly	110.00
8GOG	Cal Ripken Jr.	100.00
9GOG	Eddie Mathews	75.00

Home Team Cut

	NM/M
Common Player:	8.00
Patch:	2-5X
Production 25 sets	
Wade Boggs	15.00
Carlton Fisk	20.00
Jim Rice	15.00
Pee Wee Reese	15.00
Duke Snider	20.00
Steve Garvey	10.00
Tommy Lasorda	15.00
Juan Marichal	10.00
Bobby Bonds	8.00
Willie McCovey	10.00
Billy Martin	15.00
Roger Maris	65.00
Reggie Jackson	15.00
Dave Winfield	12.00
Red Schoendienst	8.00
Ozzie Smith	35.00
Joe Medwick	25.00

HOF Postmark

	NM/M
Production 2,002	
Ozzie Smith	20.00
Ozzie Smith/auto/202	100.00

Sweet Swatch jersey

	NM/M
Common Player:	15.00
Jerry Coleman/528	20.00
Ryne Sandberg/374	25.00
Johnny Bench/410	20.00
Tony Perez	
Paul Molitor/592	15.00
Cal Ripken Jr/557	45.00
Gil Hodges/545	20.00
Carlton Fisk/1,200	15.00
Nolan Ryan/590	40.00
Tom Seaver/385	20.00
Don Mattingly/880	35.00
Jose Canseco/1,329	15.00
George Brett/384	30.00
Jim Palmer/335	15.00
Kirby Puckett/445	20.00
Juan Marichal/385	15.00
Robin Yount/340	25.00
Andre Dawson/335	15.00

Sweet Swatch bat

	NM/M
Common Player:	15.00
Cal Ripken Jr/305	40.00
George Brett/320	30.00
Johnny Bench/175	20.00
Reggie Jackson/155	20.00
Don Mattingly/340	40.00
Willie McCovey/155	15.00
Jose Canseco/175	25.00
Kirby Puckett/251	30.00
Orlando Cepeda/165	15.00
Hank Greenberg	
Eddie Mathews/185	40.00
Pee Wee Reese/165	30.00
Andre Dawson/310	15.00

Sweet Swatch Jersey Auto

	NM/M
Common Autograph:	
Cal Ripken Jr/40	240.00
Johnny Bench/40	130.00
Alan Trammell/40	75.00
Tony Kubek	

1981 FLEER

STEVE CARLTON
PITCHER OF THE YEAR

		NM/M
Complete Set (660):		30.00
Common Player:		.05
Wax Pack (17):		1.75
Wax Box (38):		45.00
Vending Box (500):		20.00
1	Pete Rose	2.25
2	Larry Bowa	.04
3	Manny Trillo	.05
4	Bob Boone	.04
5a	Mike Schmidt (portrait)	2.00
5b	Mike Schmidt (batting)	1.50
6a	Steve Carlton ("Lefty" on front)	.70
6b	Steve Carlton (Pitcher of the Year on front, date 1066 on back)	1.50
6c	Steve Carlton (Pitcher of the Year on front, date 1966 on back)	2.00
7a	Tug McGraw (Game Saver on front)	.40
7b	Tug McGraw (Pitcher on front)	.06
8	Larry Christenson	.05
9	Bake McBride	.05
10	Greg Luzinski	.06
11	Ron Reed	.05
12	Dickie Noles	.05
13	*Keith Moreland*	.11
14	*Bob Walk*	.06
15	Lonnie Smith	.05
16	Dick Ruthven	.05
17	Sparky Lyle	.06
18	Greg Gross	.05
19	Garry Maddox	.06
20	Nino Espinosa	.05
21	George Vukovich	.05
22	John Vukovich	.05
23	Ramon Aviles	.05
24a	Kevin Saucier (Ken Saucier on back)	.08
24b	Kevin Saucier (Kevin Saucier on back)	.40
25	Randy Lerch	.05
26	Del Unser	.05
27	Tim McCarver	.11
28a	George Brett (batting)	1.50
28b	George Brett (portrait)	1.50
29a	Willie Wilson (portrait)	.40
29b	Willie Wilson (batting)	.11
30	Paul Splittorff	.05
31	Dan Quisenberry	.06
32a	Amos Otis (batting)	.40
32b	Amos Otis (portrait)	.08
33	Steve Busby	.05
34	U.L. Washington	.05
35	Dave Chalk	.05
36	Darrell Porter	.05
37	Marty Pattin	.05
38	Larry Gura	.05
39	Renie Martin	.05
40	Rich Gale	.05
41a	Hal McRae (dark blue "Royals" on front)	.30
41b	Hal McRae (light blue "Royals" on front)	.08
42	Dennis Leonard	.05
43	Willie Aikens	.05
44	Frank White	.05
45	Clint Hurdle	.05
46	John Wathan	.05
47	Pete LaCock	.05
48	Rance Mulliniks	.05
49	Jeff Twitty	.05
50	Jamie Quirk	.05
51	Art Howe	.05
52	Ken Forsch	.05
53	Vern Ruhle	.05
54	Joe Niekro	.04
55	Frank LaCorte	.05
56	J.R. Richard	.04
57	Nolan Ryan	3.00
58	Enos Cabell	.05
59	Cesar Cedeno	.04
60	Jose Cruz	.04
61	Bill Virdon	.05
62	Terry Puhl	.05
63	Joaquin Andujar	.05
64	Alan Ashby	.05
65	Joe Sambito	.05
66	Denny Walling	.05
67	Jeff Leonard	.05
68	Luis Pujols	.05
69	Bruce Bochy	.05
70	Rafael Landestoy	.05
71	*Dave Smith*	.05
72	*Danny Heep*	.05
73	Julio Gonzalez	.05
74	Craig Reynolds	.05
75	Gary Woods	.05
76	Dave Bergman	.05
77	Randy Niemann	.05
78	Joe Morgan	.70
79a	Reggie Jackson (portrait)	2.00
79b	Reggie Jackson (batting)	1.50
80	Bucky Dent	.08
81	Tommy John	.08
82	Luis Tiant	.04
83	Rick Cerone	.05
84	Dick Howser	.05
85	Lou Piniella	.08
86	Ron Davis	.05
87a	Graig Nettles (Craig on back)	3.50
87b	Graig Nettles (Graig on back)	.11
88	Ron Guidry	.08
89	Rich Gossage	.08
90	Rudy May	.05
91	Gaylord Perry	.60
92	Eric Soderholm	.05
93	Bob Watson	.05
94	Bobby Murcer	.08
95	Bobby Brown	.05
96	Jim Spencer	.05
97	Tom Underwood	.05
98	Oscar Gamble	.05
99	Johnny Oates	.05
100	Fred Stanley	.05
101	Ruppert Jones	.05
102	Dennis Werth	.05
103	Joe Lefebvre	.05
104	Brian Doyle	.05
105	Aurelio Rodriguez	.05
106	Doug Bird	.05
107	Mike Griffin	.05
108	Tim Lollar	.05
109	Willie Randolph	.05
110	Steve Garvey	.25
111	Reggie Smith	.06
112	Don Sutton	.60
113	Burt Hooton	.05
114a	Davy Lopes (Davey) (no finger on back)	.05
114b	Davy Lopes (Davey) (small finger on back)	.40
115	Dusty Baker	.04
116	Tom Lasorda	.08
117	Bill Russell	.06
118	Jerry Reuss	.05
119	Terry Forster	.05
120a	Bob Welch (Bob on back)	.08
120b	Bob Welch (Robert)	.40
121	Don Stanhouse	.05
122	Rick Monday	.05
123	Derrel Thomas	.05
124	Joe Ferguson	.05
125	Rick Sutcliffe	.08
126a	Ron Cey (no finger on back)	.06
126b	Ron Cey (small finger on back)	.40
127	Dave Goltz	.05
128	Jay Johnstone	.05
129	Steve Yeager	.05
130	Gary Weiss	.05
131	*Mike Scioscia*	.40
132	Vic Davalillo	.05
133	Doug Rau	.05
134	Pepe Frias	.05
135	Mickey Hatcher	.05
136	*Steve Howe*	.08
137	Robert Castillo	.05
138	Gary Thomasson	.05
139	Rudy Law	.05
140	*Fernando Valenzuela*	1.25
141	Manny Mota	.05
142	Gary Carter	.70
143	Steve Rogers	.05
144	Warren Cromartie	.05
145	Andre Dawson	.30
146	Larry Parrish	.05
147	Rowland Office	.05
148	Ellis Valentine	.05
149	Dick Williams	.05
150	*Bill Gullickson*	.11
151	Elias Sosa	.05
152	John Tamargo	.05
153	Chris Speier	.05
154	Ron LeFlore	.05
155	Rodney Scott	.05
156	Stan Bahnsen	.05
157	Bill Lee	.06
158	Fred Norman	.05
159	Woodie Fryman	.05
160	Dave Palmer	.05
161	Jerry White	.05
162	Roberto Ramos	.05
163	John D'Acquisto	.05
164	Tommy Hutton	.05
165	*Charlie Lea*	.11
166	Scott Sanderson	.05
167	Ken Macha	.05
168	Tony Bernazard	.05
169	Jim Palmer	.70
170	Steve Stone	.08
171	Mike Flanagan	.05
172	Al Bumbry	.05
173	Doug DeCinces	.05
174	Scott McGregor	.05
175	Mark Belanger	.05
176	Tim Stoddard	.05
177a	Rick Dempsey (no finger on front)	.05
177b	Rick Dempsey (small finger on front)	.40
178	Earl Weaver	.20
179	Tippy Martinez	.05
180	Dennis Martinez	.06
181	Sammy Stewart	.05
182	Rich Dauer	.05
183	Lee May	.05
184	Eddie Murray	.70
185	Benny Ayala	.05
186	John Lowenstein	.05
187	Gary Roenicke	.05

188 Ken Singleton .06
189 Dan Graham .05
190 Terry Crowley .05
191 Kiko Garcia .05
192 Dave Ford .05
193 Mark Corey .05
194 Lenn Sakata .05
195 Doug DeCinces .05
196 Johnny Bench .70
197 Dave Concepcion .04
198 Ray Knight .04
199 Ken Griffey .08
200 Tom Seaver .70
201 Dave Collins .05
202 George Foster .04
203 Junior Kennedy .05
204 Frank Pastore .05
205 Dan Driessen .06
206 Hector Cruz .05
207 Paul Moskau .05
208 *Charlie Leibrandt* .20
209 Harry Spilman .05
210 *Joe Price* .05
211 Tom Hume .05
212 Joe Nolan .05
213 Doug Bair .05
214 Mario Soto .05
215a Bill Bonham (no finger on back) .05
215b Bill Bonham (small finger on back) .40
216a George Foster (Slugger on front) .20
216b George Foster (Outfield on front) .11
217 Paul Householder .05
218 Ron Oester .05
219 Sam Mejias .05
220 Sheldon Burnside .05
221 Carl Yastrzemski .70
222 Jim Rice .30
223 Fred Lynn .04
224 Carlton Fisk .70
225 Rick Burleson .05
226 Dennis Eckersley .60
227 Butch Hobson .05
228 Tom Burgmeier .05
229 Garry Hancock .05
230 Don Zimmer .05
231 Steve Renko .05
232 Dwight Evans .04
233 Mike Torrez .05
234 Bob Stanley .05
235 Jim Dwyer .05
236 Dave Stapleton .05
237 Glenn Hoffman .05
238 Jerry Remy .05
239 Dick Drago .05
240 Bill Campbell .05
241 Tony Perez .60
242 Phil Niekro .60
243 Dale Murphy .25
244 Bob Horner .04
245 Jeff Burroughs .05
246 Rick Camp .05
247 Bob Cox .20
248 Bruce Benedict .05
249 Gene Garber .05
250 Jerry Royster .05
251a Gary Matthews (no finger on back) .05
251b Gary Matthews (small finger on back) .40
252 Chris Chambliss .05
253 Luis Gomez .05
254 Bill Nahorodny .05
255 Doyle Alexander .05
256 Brian Asselstine .05
257 Biff Pocoroba .05
258 Mike Lum .05
259 Charlie Spikes .05
260 Glenn Hubbard .06
261 Tommy Boggs .05
262 Al Hrabosky .05
263 Rick Matula .05
264 Preston Hanna .05
265 Larry Bradford .05
266 *Rafael Ramirez* .05
267 Larry McWilliams .05
268 Rod Carew .70
269 Bobby Grich .04
270 Carney Lansford .05
271 Don Baylor .04
272 Joe Rudi .05
273 Dan Ford .05
274 Jim Fregosi .06
275 Dave Frost .05
276 Frank Tanana .05
277 Dickie Thon .05
278 Jason Thompson .05
279 Rick Miller .05
280 Bert Campaneris .05
281 Tom Donohue .05
282 Brian Downing .05
283 Fred Patek .05
284 Bruce Kison .05
285 Dave LaRoche .05
286 Don Aase .05
287 Jim Barr .05
288 Alfredo Martinez .05
289 Larry Harlow .05
290 Andy Hassler .05
291 Dave Kingman .04
292 Bill Buckner .04
293 Rick Reuschel .05
294 Bruce Sutter .60
295 Jerry Martin .05
296 Scot Thompson .05
297 Ivan DeJesus .05
298 Steve Dillard .05
299 Dick Tidrow .05
300 Randy Martz .05
301 Lenny Randle .05
302 Lynn McGlothen .05
303 Cliff Johnson .05
304 Tim Blackwell .05
305 Dennis Lamp .05
306 Bill Caudill .05
307 Carlos Lezcano .05
308 Jim Tracy .06
309 Doug Capilla .05
310 Willie Hernandez .05
311 Mike Vail .05
312 Mike Krukow .05
313 Barry Foote .05
314 Larry Biittner .05
315 Mike Tyson .05
316 Lee Mazzilli .05
317 John Stearns .05
318 Alex Trevino .05
319 Craig Swan .05
320 Frank Taveras .05
321 Steve Henderson .05
322 Neil Allen .05
323 Mark Bomback .05
324 Mike Jorgensen .05
325 Joe Torre .20
326 Elliott Maddox .05
327 Pete Falcone .05
328 Ray Burris .05
329 Claudell Washington .05
330 Doug Flynn .05
331 Joel Youngblood .05
332 Bill Almon .05
333 Tom Hausman .05
334 Pat Zachry .05
335 *Jeff Reardon* 1.50
336 *Wally Backman* .11
337 Dan Norman .05
338 Jerry Morales .05
339 Ed Farmer .05
340 Bob Molinaro .05
341 Todd Cruz .05
342a *Britt Burns* (no finger on front) .08
342b *Britt Burns* (small finger on front) .40
343 Kevin Bell .05
344 Tony LaRussa .20
345 Steve Trout .05
346 *Harold Baines* 2.25
347 Richard Wortham .05
348 Wayne Nordhagen .05
349 Mike Squires .05
350 Lamar Johnson .05
351 Rickey Henderson 2.00
352 Francisco Barrios .05
353 Thad Bosley .05
354 Chet Lemon .05
355 Bruce Kimm .05
356 *Richard Dotson* .05
357 Jim Morrison .05
358 Mike Proly .05
359 Greg Pryor .05
360 Dave Parker .04
361 Omar Moreno .05
362a Kent Tekulve (1071 Waterbury on back) .11
362b Kent Tekulve (1971 Waterbury on back) .40
363 Willie Stargell .70
364 Phil Garner .05
365 Ed Ott .05
366 Don Robinson .05
367 Chuck Tanner .05
368 Jim Rooker .05
369 Dale Berra .05
370 Jim Bibby .05
371 Steve Nicosia .05
372 Mike Easler .05
373 Bill Robinson .05
374 Lee Lacy .05
375 John Candelaria .05
376 Manny Sanguillen .05
377 Rick Rhoden .05
378 Grant Jackson .05
379 Tim Foli .05
380 *Rod Scurry* .05
381 Bill Madlock .04
382a Kurt Bevacqua (photo reversed, backwards "P" on cap) .11
382b Kurt Bevacqua (correct photo) .40
383 Bert Blyleven .08
384 Eddie Solomon .05
385 Enrique Romo .05
386 John Milner .05
387 Mike Hargrove .05
388 Jorge Orta .05
389 Toby Harrah .06
390 Tom Veryzer .05
391 Miguel Dilone .05
392 Dan Spillner .05
393 Jack Brohamer .05
394 Wayne Garland .05
395 Sid Monge .05
396 Rick Waits .05
397 *Joe Charboneau* .40
398 Gary Alexander .05
399 Jerry Dybzinski .05
400 Mike Stanton .05
401 Mike Paxton .05
402 Gary Gray .05
403 Rick Manning .05
404 Bo Diaz .05
405 Ron Hassey .05
406 Ross Grimsley .05
407 Victor Cruz .05
408 Len Barker .05
409 Bob Bailor .05
410 Otto Velez .05
411 Ernie Whitt .05
412 Jim Clancy .05
413 Barry Bonnell .05
414 Dave Stieb .04
415 *Damaso Garcia* .08
416 John Mayberry .05
417 Roy Howell .05
418 *Dan Ainge* 2.25
419a Jesse Jefferson (Pirates on back) .08
419b Jesse Jefferson (Blue Jays on back) .40
420 Joey McLaughlin .05
421 *Lloyd Moseby* .08
422 Al Woods .05
423 Garth Iorg .05
424 Doug Ault .05
425 *Ken Schrom* .05
426 Mike Willis .05
427 Steve Braun .05
428 Bob Davis .05
429 Jerry Garvin .05
430 Alfredo Griffin .05
431 Bob Mattick .05
432 Vida Blue .04
433 Jack Clark .04
434 Willie McCovey .70
435 Mike Ivie .05
436a Darrel Evans (Darrel on front) .11
436b Darrell Evans (Darrell on front) .40
437 Terry Whitfield .05
438 Rennie Stennett .05
439 John Montefusco .05
440 Jim Wohlford .05
441 Bill North .05
442 Milt May .05
443 Max Venable .05
444 Ed Whitson .05
445 *Al Holland* .05
446 Randy Moffitt .05
447 Bob Knepper .06
448 Gary Lavelle .05
449 Greg Minton .05
450 Johnnie LeMaster .05
451 Larry Herndon .05
452 Rich Murray .05
453 Joe Pettini .05
454 Allen Ripley .05
455 Dennis Littlejohn .05
456 Tom Griffin .05
457 Alan Hargesheimer .05
458 Joe Strain .05
459 Steve Kemp .05
460 Sparky Anderson .20
461 Alan Trammell .04
462 Mark Fidrych .20
463 Lou Whitaker .04
464 Dave Rozema .05
465 Milt Wilcox .05
466 Champ Summers .05
467 Lance Parrish .04
468 Dan Petry .05
469 Pat Underwood .05
470 Rick Peters .05
471 Al Cowens .05
472 John Wockenfuss .05
473 Tom Brookens .05
474 Richie Hebner .05
475 Jack Morris .04
476 Jim Lentine .05
477 Bruce Robbins .05
478 Mark Wagner .05
479 Tim Corcoran .05
480a Stan Papi (Pitcher on front) .11
480b Stan Papi (Shortstop on front) .40
481 *Kirk Gibson* 2.25
482 Dan Schatzeder .05
483 Amos Otis .04
484 Dave Winfield .70
485 Rollie Fingers .60
486 Gene Richards .05
487 Randy Jones .05
488 Ozzie Smith 1.50
489 Gene Tenace .05
490 Bill Fahey .05
491 John Curtis .05
492 Dave Cash .05
493a Tim Flannery (photo reversed, batting righty) .11
493b Tim Flannery (photo correct, batting lefty) .40
494 Jerry Mumphrey .05
495 Bob Shirley .05
496 Steve Mura .05
497 Eric Rasmussen .05
498 Broderick Perkins .05
499 Barry Evans .05
500 Chuck Baker .05
501 *Luis Salazar* .06
502 Gary Lucas .05
503 Mike Armstrong .05
504 Jerry Turner .05
505 Dennis Kinney .05
506 Willy Montanez (Willie) .05
507 Gorman Thomas .05
508 Ben Oglivie .05
509 Larry Hisle .05
510 Sal Bando .05
511 Robin Yount .70
512 Mike Caldwell .05
513 Sixto Lezcano .05
514a Jerry Augustine (Billy Travers photo) .11
514b Billy Travers (correct name with photo) .40
515 Paul Molitor .70
516 Moose Haas .05
517 Bill Castro .05
518 Jim Slaton .05
519 Lary Sorensen .05
520 Bob McClure .05
521 Charlie Moore .05
522 Jim Gantner .05
523 Reggie Cleveland .05
524 Don Money .05
525 Billy Travers .05
526 Buck Martinez .05
527 Dick Davis .05
528 Ted Simmons .05
529 Garry Templeton .05
530 Ken Reitz .05
531 Tony Scott .05
532 Ken Oberkfell .05
533 Bob Sykes .05
534 Keith Smith .05
535 John Littlefield .05
536 Jim Kaat .04
537 Bob Forsch .05
538 Mike Phillips .05
539 *Terry Landrum* .05
540 *Leon Durham* .08
541 Terry Kennedy .05
542 George Hendrick .05
543 Dane Iorg .05
544 Mark Littell (photo actually Jeff Little) .05
545 Keith Hernandez .04
546 Silvio Martinez .05
547a Pete Vuckovich (photo actually Don Hood) .11

547b Don Hood (correct name with photo) .40
548 Bobby Bonds .08
549 Mike Ramsey .05
550 Tom Herr .05
551 Roy Smalley .05
552 Jerry Koosman .05
553 Ken Landreaux .05
554 John Castino .05
555 Doug Corbett .05
556 Bombo Rivera .05
557 Ron Jackson .05
558 Butch Wynegar .05
559 Hosken Powell .05
560 Pete Redfern .05
561 Roger Erickson .05
562 Glenn Adams .05
563 Rick Sofield .05
564 Geoff Zahn .05
565 Pete Mackanin .05
566 Mike Cubbage .05
567 Darrell Jackson .05
568 Dave Edwards .05
569 Rob Wilfong .05
570 Sal Butera .05
571 Jose Morales .05
572 Rick Langford .05
573 Mike Norris .05
574 Rickey Henderson 2.00
575 Tony Armas .05
576 Dave Revering .05
577 Jeff Newman .05
578 Bob Lacey .05
579 Brian Kingman (photo actually Alan Wirth) .05
580 Mitchell Page .05
581 Billy Martin .20
582 Rob Picciolo .05
583 Mike Heath .05
584 Mickey Klutts .05
585 Orlando Gonzalez .05
586 *Mike Davis* .05
587 Wayne Gross .05
588 Matt Keough .05
589 Steve McCatty .05
590 Dwayne Murphy .05
591 Mario Guerrero .05
592 Dave McKay .05
593 Jim Essian .05
594 Dave Heaverlo .05
595 Maury Wills .08
596 Juan Beniquez .05
597 Rodney Craig .05
598 Jim Anderson .05
599 Floyd Bannister .05
600 Bruce Bochte .05
601 Julio Cruz .05
602 Ted Cox .05
603 Dan Meyer .05
604 Larry Cox .05
605 Bill Stein .05
606 Steve Garvey .25
607 Dave Roberts .05
608 Leon Roberts .05
609 Reggie Walton .05
610 Dave Edler .05
611 Larry Milbourne .05
612 Kim Allen .05
613 Mario Mendoza .05
614 Tom Paciorek .05
615 Glenn Abbott .05
616 Joe Simpson .05
617 Mickey Rivers .05
618 Jim Kern .05
619 Jim Sundberg .05
620 Richie Zisk .06
621 Jon Matlack .06
622 Fergie Jenkins .60
623 Pat Corrales .05
624 Ed Figueroa .05
625 Buddy Bell .04
626 Al Oliver .04
627 Doc Medich .05
628 Bump Wills .05
629 Rusty Staub .04
630 Pat Putnam .05
631 John Grubb .05
632 Danny Darwin .05
633 Ken Clay .05
634 Jim Norris .05
635 John Butcher .05
636 Dave Roberts .05
637 Billy Sample .05
638 Carl Yastrzemski .70
639 Cecil Cooper .05
640 Mike Schmidt 1.50
641a Checklist 1-50 (41 Hal McRae) .08
641b Checklist 1-50 (41 Hal McRae Double Threat) .08
642 Checklist 51-109 .05
643 Checklist 110-168 .05
644a Checklist 169-220 (202 George Foster) .08
644b Checklist 169-220 (202 George Foster "Slugger") .08
(645a) Larry Bowa, Pete Rose, Mike Schmidt Triple Threat (no number on back) 1.50
645b Pete Rose, Larry Bowa, Mike Schmidt Triple Threat (number on back) 1.50
646 Checklist 221-267 .05
647 Checklist 268-315 .05
648 Checklist 316-359 .05
649 Checklist 360-408 .05
650 Reggie Jackson 1.50
651 Checklist 409-458 .05
652a Checklist 459-509 (483 Aurelio Lopez) .08
652b Checklist 459-506 (no 483) .08
653 Willie Wilson .04
654a Checklist 507-550 (514 Jerry Augustine) .08
654b Checklist 507-550 (514 Billy Travers) .08
655 George Brett 2.25
656 Checklist 551-593 .05
657 Tug McGraw .04
658 Checklist 594-637 .05
659a Checklist 640-660 (last number on front is 551) .08
659b Checklist 640-660 (last number on front is 483) .11
660a Steve Carlton (date 1066 on back) .70
660b Steve Carlton (date 1966 on back) 1.50

1982 FLEER

NM/M

Complete Set (660): 40.00
Common Player: .05
Wax Pack (15): 2.00
Wax Box (36): 75.00
Cello Pack (28): 4.00
Cello Box (24): 85.00
Vending Box (500): 40.00

1 Dusty Baker .05
2 Robert Castillo .05
3 Ron Cey .05
4 Terry Forster .05
5 Steve Garvey .30
6 Dave Goltz .05
7 Pedro Guerrero .05
8 Burt Hooton .05
9 Steve Howe .05
10 Jay Johnstone .05
11 Ken Landreaux .05
12 Davey Lopes .05
13 *Mike Marshall* .15
14 Bobby Mitchell .05
15 Rick Monday .05
16 *Tom Niedenfuer* .05
17 *Ted Power* .05
18 Jerry Reuss .05
19 Ron Roenicke .05
20 Bill Russell .05
21 *Steve Sax* .45
22 Mike Scioscia .05
23 Reggie Smith .05
24 *Dave Stewart* 1.50
25 Rick Sutcliffe .05
26 Derrel Thomas .05
27 Fernando Valenzuela .10
28 Bob Welch .05
29 Steve Yeager .05
30 Bobby Brown .05
31 Rick Cerone .05
32 Ron Davis .05
33 Bucky Dent .10
34 Barry Foote .05
35 George Frazier .05
36 Oscar Gamble .05
37 Rich Gossage .10
38 Ron Guidry .10
39 Reggie Jackson 1.50
40 Tommy John .10
41 Rudy May .05
42 Larry Milbourne .05
43 Jerry Mumphrey .05
44 Bobby Murcer .10
45 *Gene Nelson* .05
46 Graig Nettles .10
47 Johnny Oates .05
48 Lou Piniella .10
49 Willie Randolph .05
50 Rick Reuschel .05
51 Dave Revering .05
52 *Dave Righetti* .45
53 Aurelio Rodriguez .05
54 Bob Watson .05
55 Dennis Werth .05
56 Dave Winfield 1.00
57 Johnny Bench 1.00
58 Bruce Berenyi .05
59 Larry Biittner .05
60 Scott Brown .05
61 Dave Collins .05
62 Geoff Combe .05
63 Dave Concepcion .05
64 Dan Driessen .05
65 Joe Edelen .05
66 George Foster .05
67 Ken Griffey .05
68 Paul Householder .05
69 Tom Hume .05
70 Junior Kennedy .05
71 Ray Knight .05
72 Mike LaCoss .05
73 Rafael Landestoy .05
74 Charlie Leibrandt .05
75 Sam Mejias .05
76 Paul Moskau .05
77 Joe Nolan .05
78 Mike O'Berry .05
79 Ron Oester .05
80 Frank Pastore .05
81 Joe Price .05
82 Tom Seaver 1.00
83 Mario Soto .05
84 Mike Vail .05
85 Tony Armas .05
86 Shooty Babitt .05
87 Dave Beard .05
88 Rick Bosetti .05
89 Keith Drumright .05
90 Wayne Gross .05
91 Mike Heath .05
92 Rickey Henderson 1.00
93 Cliff Johnson .05
94 Jeff Jones .05
95 Matt Keough .05
96 Brian Kingman .05
97 Mickey Klutts .05
98 Rick Langford .05
99 Steve McCatty .05
100 Dave McKay .05
101 Dwayne Murphy .05
102 Jeff Newman .05
103 Mike Norris .05
104 Bob Owchinko .05
105 Mitchell Page .05
106 Rob Picciolo .05
107 Jim Spencer .05
108 Fred Stanley .05
109 Tom Underwood .05
110 Joaquin Andujar .05
111 Steve Braun .05
112 Bob Forsch .05
113 George Hendrick .05
114 Keith Hernandez .05
115 Tom Herr .05
116 Dane Iorg .05
117 Jim Kaat .10
118 Tito Landrum .05
119 Sixto Lezcano .05
120 Mark Littell .05
121 John Martin .05
122 Silvio Martinez .05
123 Ken Oberkfell .05
124 Darrell Porter .05
125 Mike Ramsey .05
126 Orlando Sanchez .05
127 Bob Shirley .05
128 Lary Sorensen .05
129 Bruce Sutter .75
130 Bob Sykes .05
131 Garry Templeton .05
132 Gene Tenace .05
133 Jerry Augustine .05
134 Sal Bando .05
135 Mark Brouhard .05
136 Mike Caldwell .05
137 Reggie Cleveland .05
138 Cecil Cooper .05
139 Jamie Easterly .05
140 Marshall Edwards .05
141 Rollie Fingers .75
142 Jim Gantner .05
143 Moose Haas .05
144 Larry Hisle .05
145 Roy Howell .05
146 Rickey Keeton .05
147 Randy Lerch .05
148 Paul Molitor 1.00
149 Don Money .05
150 Charlie Moore .05
151 Ben Oglivie .05
152 Ted Simmons .05
153 Jim Slaton .05
154 Gorman Thomas .05
155 Robin Yount 1.00
156 Pete Vukovich .05
157 Benny Ayala .05
158 Mark Belanger .05
159 Al Bumbry .05
160 Terry Crowley .05
161 Rich Dauer .05
162 Doug DeCinces .05
163 Rick Dempsey .05
164 Jim Dwyer .05
165 Mike Flanagan .05
166 Dave Ford .05
167 Dan Graham .05
168 Wayne Krenchicki .05
169 John Lowenstein .05
170 Dennis Martinez .05
171 Tippy Martinez .05
172 Scott McGregor .05
173 Jose Morales .05
174 Eddie Murray 1.00
175 Jim Palmer 1.00
176 *Cal Ripken, Jr.* 30.00
177 Gary Roenicke .05
178 Lenn Sakata .05
179 Ken Singleton .05
180 Sammy Stewart .05
181 Tim Stoddard .05
182 Steve Stone .05
183 Stan Bahnsen .05
184 Ray Burris .05
185 Gary Carter 1.00
186 Warren Cromartie .05
187 Andre Dawson .50
188 *Terry Francona* .05
189 Woodie Fryman .05
190 Bill Gullickson .05
191 Grant Jackson .05
192 Wallace Johnson .05
193 Charlie Lea .05
194 Bill Lee .05
195 Jerry Manuel .05
196 Brad Mills .05
197 John Milner .05
198 Rowland Office .05
199 David Palmer .05
200 Larry Parrish .05
201 Mike Phillips .05
202 Tim Raines .25
203 Bobby Ramos .05
204 Jeff Reardon .05
205 Steve Rogers .05
206 Scott Sanderson .05
207 Rodney Scott (photo actually Tim Raines) .10
208 Elias Sosa .05
209 Chris Speier .05
210 *Tim Wallach* 1.00
211 Jerry White .05
212 Alan Ashby .05
213 Cesar Cedeno .05
214 Jose Cruz .05
215 Kiko Garcia .05
216 Phil Garner .05
217 Danny Heep .05
218 Art Howe .05
219 Bob Knepper .05
220 Frank LaCorte .05
221 Joe Niekro .05

222 Joe Pittman .05
223 Terry Puhl .05
224 Luis Pujols .05
225 Craig Reynolds .05
226 J.R. Richard .05
227 Dave Roberts .05
228 Vern Ruhle .05
229 Nolan Ryan 3.00
230 Joe Sambito .05
231 Tony Scott .05
232 Dave Smith .05
233 Harry Spilman .05
234 Don Sutton .75
235 Dickie Thon .05
236 Denny Walling .05
237 Gary Woods .05
238 *Luis Aguayo* .05
239 Ramon Aviles .05
240 Bob Boone .05
241 Larry Bowa .05
242 Warren Brusstar .05
243 Steve Carlton 1.00
244 Larry Christenson .05
245 Dick Davis .05
246 Greg Gross .05
247 Sparky Lyle .05
248 Garry Maddox .05
249 Gary Matthews .05
250 Bake McBride .05
251 Tug McGraw .05
252 Keith Moreland .05
253 Dickie Noles .05
254 Mike Proly .05
255 Ron Reed .05
256 Pete Rose 2.50
257 Dick Ruthven .05
258 Mike Schmidt 2.00
259 Lonnie Smith .05
260 Manny Trillo .05
261 Del Unser .05
262 George Vukovich .05
263 Tom Brookens .05
264 George Cappuzzello .05
265 Marty Castillo .05
266 Al Cowens .05
267 Kirk Gibson .05
268 Richie Hebner .05
269 Ron Jackson .05
270 Lynn Jones .05
271 Steve Kemp .05
272 *Rick Leach* .25
273 Aurelio Lopez .05
274 Jack Morris .05
275 Kevin Saucier .05
276 Lance Parrish .05
277 Rick Peters .05
278 Dan Petry .05
279 David Rozema .05
280 Stan Papi .05
281 Dan Schatzeder .05
282 Champ Summers .05
283 Alan Trammell .05
284 Lou Whitaker .05
285 Milt Wilcox .05
286 John Wockenfuss .05
287 Gary Allenson .05
288 Tom Burgmeier .05
289 Bill Campbell .05
290 Mark Clear .05
291 Steve Crawford .05
292 Dennis Eckersley .75
293 Dwight Evans .05
294 *Rich Gedman* .10
295 Garry Hancock .05
296 Glenn Hoffman .05
297 Bruce Hurst .05
298 Carney Lansford .05
299 Rick Miller .05
300 Reid Nichols .05
301 *Bob Ojeda* .25
302 Tony Perez .75
303 Chuck Rainey .05
304 Jerry Remy .05
305 Jim Rice .50
306 Joe Rudi .05
307 Bob Stanley .05
308 Dave Stapleton .05
309 Frank Tanana .05
310 Mike Torrez .05
311 John Tudor .05
312 Carl Yastrzemski 1.00
313 Buddy Bell .05
314 Steve Comer .05
315 Danny Darwin .05
316 John Ellis .05
317 John Grubb .05
318 Rick Honeycutt .05
319 Charlie Hough .05
320 Fergie Jenkins .75
321 John Henry Johnson .05
322 Jim Kern .05
323 Jon Matlack .05
324 Doc Medich .05
325 Mario Mendoza .05
326 Al Oliver .05
327 Pat Putnam .05
328 Mickey Rivers .05
329 Leon Roberts .05
330 Billy Sample .05
331 Bill Stein .05
332 Jim Sundberg .05
333 Mark Wagner .05
334 Bump Wills .05
335 Bill Almon .05
336 Harold Baines .05
337 Ross Baumgarten .05
338 Tony Bernazard .05
339 Britt Burns .05
340 Richard Dotson .05
341 Jim Essian .05
342 Ed Farmer .05
343 Carlton Fisk 1.00
344 Kevin Hickey .05
345 Lamarr Hoyt (LaMarr) .05
346 Lamar Johnson .05
347 Jerry Koosman .05
348 Rusty Kuntz .05
349 Dennis Lamp .05
350 Ron LeFlore .05
351 Chet Lemon .05
352 Greg Luzinski .05
353 Bob Molinaro .05
354 Jim Morrison .05
355 Wayne Nordhagen .05
356 Greg Pryor .05
357 Mike Squires .05
358 Steve Trout .05
359 Alan Bannister .05
360 Len Barker .05
361 Bert Blyleven .10
362 Joe Charboneau .10
363 John Denny .05
364 Bo Diaz .05
365 Miguel Dilone .05
366 Jerry Dybzinski .05
367 Wayne Garland .05
368 Mike Hargrove .05
369 Toby Harrah .05
370 Ron Hassey .05
371 *Von Hayes* .25
372 Pat Kelly .05
373 Duane Kuiper .05
374 Rick Manning .05
375 Sid Monge .05
376 Jorge Orta .05
377 Dave Rosello .05
378 Dan Spillner .05
379 Mike Stanton .05
380 Andre Thornton .05
381 Tom Veryzer .05
382 Rick Waits .05
383 Doyle Alexander .05
384 Vida Blue .05
385 Fred Breining .05
386 Enos Cabell .05
387 Jack Clark .05
388 Darrell Evans .05
389 Tom Griffin .05
390 Larry Herndon .05
391 Al Holland .05
392 Gary Lavelle .05
393 Johnnie LeMaster .05
394 Jerry Martin .05
395 Milt May .05
396 Greg Minton .05
397 Joe Morgan 1.00
398 Joe Pettini .05
399 Alan Ripley .05
400 Billy Smith .05
401 Rennie Stennett .05
402 Ed Whitson .05
403 Jim Wohlford .05
404 Willie Aikens .05
405 George Brett 2.00
406 Ken Brett .05
407 Dave Chalk .05
408 Rich Gale .05
409 Cesar Geronimo .05
410 Larry Gura .05
411 Clint Hurdle .05
412 Mike Jones .05
413 Dennis Leonard .05
414 Renie Martin .05
415 Lee May .05
416 Hal McRae .05
417 Darryl Motley .05
418 Rance Mulliniks .05
419 Amos Otis .05
420 *Ken Phelps* .05
421 Jamie Quirk .05
422 Dan Quisenberry .05
423 Paul Splittorff .05
424 U.L. Washington .05
425 John Wathan .05
426 Frank White .05
427 Willie Wilson .05
428 Brian Asselstine .05
429 Bruce Benedict .05
430 Tom Boggs .05
431 Larry Bradford .05
432 Rick Camp .05
433 Chris Chambliss .05
434 Gene Garber .05
435 Preston Hanna .05
436 Bob Horner .05
437 Glenn Hubbard .05
438a Al Hrabosky (All Hrabosky, 5'1" on back) 4.50
438b Al Hrabosky (Al Hrabosky, 5'1" on back) 1.00
438c Al Hrabosky (Al Hrabosky, 5'10" on back) .25
439 Rufino Linares .05
440 *Rick Mahler* .05
441 Ed Miller .05
442 John Montefusco .05
443 Dale Murphy .50
444 Phil Niekro .75
445 Gaylord Perry .75
446 Biff Pocoroba .05
447 Rafael Ramirez .05
448 Jerry Royster .05
449 Claudell Washington .05
450 Don Aase .05
451 Don Baylor .05
452 Juan Beniquez .05
453 Rick Burleson .05
454 Bert Campaneris .05
455 Rod Carew 1.00
456 Bob Clark .05
457 Brian Downing .05
458 Dan Ford .05
459 Ken Forsch .05
460 Dave Frost .05
461 Bobby Grich .05
462 Larry Harlow .05
463 John Harris .05
464 Andy Hassler .05
465 Butch Hobson .05
466 Jesse Jefferson .05
467 Bruce Kison .05
468 Fred Lynn .05
469 Angel Moreno .05
470 Ed Ott .05
471 Fred Patek .05
472 Steve Renko .05
473 *Mike Witt* .10
474 Geoff Zahn .05
475 Gary Alexander .05
476 Dale Berra .05
477 Kurt Bevacqua .05
478 Jim Bibby .05
479 John Candelaria .05
480 Victor Cruz .05
481 Mike Easler .05
482 Tim Foli .05
483 Lee Lacy .05
484 Vance Law .05
485 Bill Madlock .05
486 Willie Montanez .05
487 Omar Moreno .05
488 Steve Nicosia .05
489 Dave Parker .05
490 Tony Pena .05
491 Pascual Perez .05
492 *Johnny Ray* .05
493 Rick Rhoden .05
494 Bill Robinson .05
495 Don Robinson .05
496 Enrique Romo .05
497 Rod Scurry .05
498 Eddie Solomon .05
499 Willie Stargell 1.00
500 Kent Tekulve .05
501 Jason Thompson .05
502 Glenn Abbott .05
503 Jim Anderson .05
504 Floyd Bannister .05
505 Bruce Bochte .05
506 Jeff Burroughs .05
507 Bryan Clark .05
508 Ken Clay .05
509 Julio Cruz .05
510 Dick Drago .05
511 Gary Gray .05
512 Dan Meyer .05
513 Jerry Narron .05
514 Tom Paciorek .05
515 Casey Parsons .05
516 Lenny Randle .05
517 Shane Rawley .05
518 Joe Simpson .05
519 Richie Zisk .05
520 Neil Allen .05
521 Bob Bailor .05
522 Hubie Brooks .05
523 Mike Cubbage .05
524 Pete Falcone .05
525 Doug Flynn .05
526 Tom Hausman .05
527 Ron Hodges .05
528 Randy Jones .05
529 Mike Jorgensen .05
530 Dave Kingman .05
531 Ed Lynch .05
532 Mike Marshall .05
533 Lee Mazzilli .05
534 Dyar Miller .05
535 Mike Scott .05
536 Rusty Staub .05
537 John Stearns .05
538 Craig Swan .05
539 Frank Taveras .05
540 Alex Trevino .05
541 Ellis Valentine .05
542 Mookie Wilson .05
543 Joel Youngblood .05
544 Pat Zachry .05
545 Glenn Adams .05
546 Fernando Arroyo .05
547 John Verhoeven .05
548 Sal Butera .05
549 John Castino .05
550 Don Cooper .05
551 Doug Corbett .05
552 Dave Engle .05
553 Roger Erickson .05
554 Danny Goodwin .05
555a Darrell Jackson (black cap) .65
555b Darrell Jackson (red cap w/speck of white) 3.00
555c Darrell Jackson (red cap w/white T) .10
556 Pete Mackanin .05
557 Jack O'Connor .05
558 Hosken Powell .05
559 Pete Redfern .05
560 Roy Smalley .05
561 Chuck Baker .05
562 Gary Ward .05
563 Rob Wilfong .05
564 Al Williams .05
565 Butch Wynegar .05
566 Randy Bass .05
567 Juan Bonilla .05
568 Danny Boone .05
569 John Curtis .05
570 Juan Eichelberger .05
571 Barry Evans .05
572 Tim Flannery .05
573 Ruppert Jones .05
574 Terry Kennedy .05
575 Joe Lefebvre .05
576a John Littlefield (pitching lefty) 80.00
576b John Littlefield (pitching righty) .05
577 Gary Lucas .05
578 Steve Mura .05
579 Broderick Perkins .05
580 Gene Richards .05
581 Luis Salazar .05
582 Ozzie Smith 1.50
583 John Urrea .05
584 Chris Welsh .05
585 Rick Wise .05
586 Doug Bird .05
587 Tim Blackwell .05
588 Bobby Bonds .10
589 Bill Buckner .05
590 Bill Caudill .05
591 Hector Cruz .05
592 *Jody Davis* .10
593 Ivan DeJesus .05
594 Steve Dillard .05
595 Leon Durham .05
596 Rawly Eastwick .05
597 Steve Henderson .05
598 Mike Krukow .05
599 Mike Lum .05
600 Randy Martz .05
601 Jerry Morales .05
602 Ken Reitz .05
603a *Lee Smith* (Cubs logo reversed on back) 2.50

603b *Lee Smith* (corrected) 2.50
604 Dick Tidrow .05
605 Jim Tracy .05
606 Mike Tyson .05
607 Ty Waller .05
608 Danny Ainge .50
609 *Jorge Bell* 1.00
610 Mark Bomback .05
611 Barry Bonnell .05
612 Jim Clancy .05
613 Damaso Garcia .05
614 Jerry Garvin .05
615 Alfredo Griffin .05
616 Garth Iorg .05
617 Luis Leal .05
618 Ken Macha .05
619 John Mayberry .05
620 Joey McLaughlin .05
621 Lloyd Moseby .05
622 Dave Stieb .05
623 Jackson Todd .05
624 Willie Upshaw .05
625 Otto Velez .05
626 Ernie Whitt .05
627 Al Woods .05
628 1981 All-Star Game .05
629 Bucky Dent, Frank White All-Star Infielders .05
630 Dave Concepcion, Dan Driessen, George Foster Big Red Machine .10
631 Bruce Sutter Top N.L. Relief Pitcher .30
632 Steve Carlton, Carlton Fisk Steve & Carlton .25
633 Carl Yastrzemski 3000th Game, May 25, 1981 .35
634 Johnny Bench, Tom Seaver Dynamic Duo .30
635 Gary Carter, Fernando Valenzuela West Meets East .20
636a Fernando Valenzuela N.L. Strikeout King ("...led the National League...") .50
636b Fernando Valenzuela N.L. Strikeout King ("... led the National League) .25
637 Mike Schmidt Home Run King .50
638 Gary Carter, Dave Parker N.L. All-Stars .25
639 Len Barker, Bo Diaz Perfect Game! .05
640 Pete Rose, Pete Rose, Jr. (Re-Pete) 2.00
641 Steve Carlton, Mike Schmidt, Lonnie Smith Phillies' Finest .50
642 Dwight Evans, Fred Lynn Red Sox Reunion .10
643 Rickey Henderson Most Hits and Runs 1.00
644 Rollie Fingers Most Saves 1981 A.L. .15
645 Tom Seaver Most 1981 Wins .25
646a Reggie Jackson, Dave Winfield Yankee Powerhouse (comma after "outfielder" on back) 1.50
646b Reggie Jackson, Dave Winfield Yankee Powerhouse (no comma) 2.00
647 Checklist 1-56 .05
648 Checklist 57-109 .05
649 Checklist 110-156 .05
650 Checklist 157-211 .05
651 Checklist 212-262 .05
652 Checklist 263-312 .05
653 Checklist 313-358 .05
654 Checklist 359-403 .05
655 Checklist 404-449 .05
656 Checklist 450-501 .05
657 Checklist 502-544 .05
658 Checklist 545-585 .05
659 Checklist 586-627 .05
660 Checklist 628-646 .05

1983 FLEER

	NM/M
Complete Set (660):	40.00
Common Player:	.05
Wax Pack (15):	2.00
Wax Box (38):	65.00
Cello Pack (28):	3.50
Cello Box (24):	75.00
Vending Box (500):	25.00

1 Joaquin Andujar .05
2 Doug Bair .05
3 Steve Braun .05
4 Glenn Brummer .05
5 Bob Forsch .05
6 David Green .05
7 George Hendrick .05
8 Keith Hernandez .05
9 Tom Herr .05
10 Dane Iorg .05
11 Jim Kaat .10
12 Jeff Lahti .05
13 Tito Landrum .05
14 *Dave LaPoint* .05
15 *Willie McGee* 1.50
16 Steve Mura .05
17 Ken Oberkfell .05
18 Darrell Porter .05
19 Mike Ramsey .05
20 Gene Roof .05
21 Lonnie Smith .05
22 Ozzie Smith 1.50
23 John Stuper .05
24 Bruce Sutter .65
25 Gene Tenace .05
26 Jerry Augustine .05
27 Dwight Bernard .05
28 Mark Brouhard .05
29 Mike Caldwell .05
30 Cecil Cooper .05
31 Jamie Easterly .05
32 Marshall Edwards .05
33 Rollie Fingers .65
34 Jim Gantner .05
35 Moose Haas .05
36 Roy Howell .05
37 Peter Ladd .05
38 Bob McClure .05
39 Doc Medich .05
40 Paul Molitor .75
41 Don Money .05
42 Charlie Moore .05
43 Ben Oglivie .05
44 Ed Romero .05
45 Ted Simmons .05
46 Jim Slaton .05
47 Don Sutton .65
48 Gorman Thomas .05
49 Pete Vuckovich .05
50 Ned Yost .05
51 Robin Yount .75
52 Benny Ayala .05
53 Bob Bonner .05
54 Al Bumbry .05
55 Terry Crowley .05
56 *Storm Davis* .10
57 Rich Dauer .05
58 Rick Dempsey .05
59 Jim Dwyer .05
60 Mike Flanagan .05
61 Dan Ford .05
62 Glenn Gulliver .05
63 John Lowenstein .05
64 Dennis Martinez .05
65 Tippy Martinez .05
66 Scott McGregor .05
67 Eddie Murray .75
68 Joe Nolan .05
69 Jim Palmer .75
70 Cal Ripken, Jr. 6.00
71 Gary Roenicke .05
72 Lenn Sakata .05
73 Ken Singleton .05
74 Sammy Stewart .05
75 Tim Stoddard .05
76 Don Aase .05
77 Don Baylor .05
78 Juan Beniquez .05
79 Bob Boone .05
80 Rick Burleson .05
81 Rod Carew .75
82 Bobby Clark .05
83 Doug Corbett .05
84 John Curtis .05
85 Doug DeCinces .05
86 Brian Downing .05
87 Joe Ferguson .05
88 Tim Foli .05
89 Ken Forsch .05
90 Dave Goltz .05
91 Bobby Grich .05
92 Andy Hassler .05
93 Reggie Jackson 1.50
94 Ron Jackson .05
95 Tommy John .10
96 Bruce Kison .05
97 Fred Lynn .05
98 Ed Ott .05
99 Steve Renko .05
100 Luis Sanchez .05
101 Rob Wilfong .05
102 Mike Witt .05
103 Geoff Zahn .05
104 Willie Aikens .05
105 Mike Armstrong .05
106 Vida Blue .05
107 *Bud Black* .50
108 George Brett 2.00
109 Bill Castro .05
110 Onix Concepcion .05
111 Dave Frost .05
112 Cesar Geronimo .05
113 Larry Gura .05
114 Steve Hammond .05
115 Don Hood .05
116 Dennis Leonard .05
117 Jerry Martin .05
118 Lee May .05
119 Hal McRae .05
120 Amos Otis .05
121 Greg Pryor .05
122 Dan Quisenberry .05
123 *Don Slaught* .20
124 Paul Splittorff .05
125 U.L. Washington .05
126 John Wathan .05
127 Frank White .05
128 Willie Wilson .05
129 Steve Bedrosian .05
130 Bruce Benedict .05
131 Tommy Boggs .05
132 Brett Butler .05
133 Rick Camp .05
134 Chris Chambliss .05
135 Ken Dayley .05
136 Gene Garber .05
137 Terry Harper .05
138 Bob Horner .05
139 Glenn Hubbard .05
140 Rufino Linares .05
141 Rick Mahler .05
142 Dale Murphy .50
143 Phil Niekro .65
144 Pascual Perez .05
145 Biff Pocoroba .05
146 Rafael Ramirez .05
147 Jerry Royster .05
148 Ken Smith .05
149 Bob Walk .05
150 Claudell Washington .05
151 Bob Watson .05
152 Larry Whisenton .05
153 Porfirio Altamirano .05
154 Marty Bystrom .05
155 Steve Carlton .75
156 Larry Christenson .05
157 Ivan DeJesus .05
158 John Denny .05
159 Bob Dernier .05
160 Bo Diaz .05
161 Ed Farmer .05
162 Greg Gross .05
163 Mike Krukow .05
164 Garry Maddox .05
165 Gary Matthews .05
166 Tug McGraw .05
167 Bob Molinaro .05
168 Sid Monge .05
169 Ron Reed .05
170 Bill Robinson .05
171 Pete Rose 3.00
172 Dick Ruthven .05
173 Mike Schmidt 2.00
174 Manny Trillo .05
175 Ozzie Virgil .05
176 George Vukovich .05
177 Gary Allenson .05
178 Luis Aponte .05
179 *Wade Boggs* 10.00
180 Tom Burgmeier .05
181 Mark Clear .05
182 Dennis Eckersley .65
183 Dwight Evans .05
184 Rich Gedman .05
185 Glenn Hoffman .05
186 Bruce Hurst .05
187 Carney Lansford .05
188 Rick Miller .05
189 Reid Nichols .05
190 Bob Ojeda .05
191 Tony Perez .65
192 Chuck Rainey .05
193 Jerry Remy .05
194 Jim Rice .35
195 Bob Stanley .05
196 Dave Stapleton .05
197 Mike Torrez .05
198 John Tudor .05
199 Julio Valdez .05
200 Carl Yastrzemski .75
201 Dusty Baker .05
202 Joe Beckwith .05
203 *Greg Brock* .05
204 Ron Cey .05
205 Terry Forster .05
206 Steve Garvey .30
207 Pedro Guerrero .05
208 Burt Hooton .05
209 Steve Howe .05
210 Ken Landreaux .05
211 Mike Marshall .05
212 *Candy Maldonado* .05
213 Rick Monday .05
214 Tom Niedenfuer .05
215 Jorge Orta .05
216 Jerry Reuss .05
217 Ron Roenicke .05
218 Vicente Romo .05
219 Bill Russell .05
220 Steve Sax .05
221 Mike Scioscia .05
222 Dave Stewart .05
223 Derrel Thomas .05
224 Fernando Valenzuela .05
225 Bob Welch .05
226 Ricky Wright .05
227 Steve Yeager .05
228 Bill Almon .05
229 Harold Baines .05
230 Salome Barojas .05
231 Tony Bernazard .05
232 Britt Burns .05
233 Richard Dotson .05
234 Ernesto Escarrega .05
235 Carlton Fisk .75
236 Jerry Hairston Sr. .05
237 Kevin Hickey .05
238 LaMarr Hoyt .05
239 Steve Kemp .05
240 Jim Kern .05
241 *Ron Kittle* .25
242 Jerry Koosman .05
243 Dennis Lamp .05
244 Rudy Law .05
245 Vance Law .05
246 Ron LeFlore .05
247 Greg Luzinski .05
248 Tom Paciorek .05
249 Aurelio Rodriguez .05
250 Mike Squires .05
251 Steve Trout .05
252 Jim Barr .05
253 Dave Bergman .05
254 Fred Breining .05
255 Bob Brenly .05
256 Jack Clark .05
257 Chili Davis .05
258 Darrell Evans .05
259 Alan Fowlkes .05
260 Rich Gale .05
261 Atlee Hammaker .05
262 Al Holland .05
263 Duane Kuiper .05
264 Bill Laskey .05
265 Gary Lavelle .05
266 Johnnie LeMaster .05
267 Renie Martin .05
268 Milt May .05
269 Greg Minton .05
270 Joe Morgan .75
271 Tom O'Malley .05
272 Reggie Smith .05
273 Guy Sularz .05
274 Champ Summers .05
275 Max Venable .05
276 Jim Wohlford .05
277 Ray Burris .05

No.	Player	Value
278	Gary Carter	.75
279	Warren Cromartie	.05
280	Andre Dawson	.40
281	Terry Francona	.05
282	Doug Flynn	.05
283	Woody Fryman	.05
284	Bill Gullickson	.05
285	Wallace Johnson	.05
286	Charlie Lea	.05
287	Randy Lerch	.05
288	Brad Mills	.05
289	Dan Norman	.05
290	Al Oliver	.05
291	David Palmer	.05
292	Tim Raines	.05
293	Jeff Reardon	.05
294	Steve Rogers	.05
295	Scott Sanderson	.05
296	Dan Schatzeder	.05
297	Bryn Smith	.05
298	Chris Speier	.05
299	Tim Wallach	.05
300	Jerry White	.05
301	Joel Youngblood	.05
302	Ross Baumgarten	.05
303	Dale Berra	.05
304	John Candelaria	.05
305	Dick Davis	.05
306	Mike Easler	.05
307	Richie Hebner	.05
308	Lee Lacy	.05
309	Bill Madlock	.05
310	Larry McWilliams	.05
311	John Milner	.05
312	Omar Moreno	.05
313	Jim Morrison	.05
314	Steve Nicosia	.05
315	Dave Parker	.05
316	Tony Pena	.05
317	Johnny Ray	.05
318	Rick Rhoden	.05
319	Don Robinson	.05
320	Enrique Romo	.05
321	Manny Sarmiento	.05
322	Rod Scurry	.05
323	Jim Smith	.05
324	Willie Stargell	.75
325	Jason Thompson	.05
326	Kent Tekulve	.05
327a	Tom Brookens (narrow (1/4") brown box at bottom on back)	.45
327b	Tom Brookens (wide (1-1/4") brown box at bottom on back)	.05
328	Enos Cabell	.05
329	Kirk Gibson	.05
330	Larry Herndon	.05
331	Mike Ivie	.05
332	*Howard Johnson*	1.00
333	Lynn Jones	.05
334	Rick Leach	.05
335	Chet Lemon	.05
336	Jack Morris	.05
337	Lance Parrish	.05
338	Larry Pashnick	.05
339	Dan Petry	.05
340	Dave Rozema	.05
341	Dave Rucker	.05
342	Elias Sosa	.05
343	Dave Tobik	.05
344	Alan Trammell	.05
345	Jerry Turner	.05
346	Jerry Ujdur	.05
347	Pat Underwood	.05
348	Lou Whitaker	.05
349	Milt Wilcox	.05
350	*Glenn Wilson*	.05
351	John Wockenfuss	.05
352	Kurt Bevacqua	.05
353	Juan Bonilla	.05
354	Floyd Chiffer	.05
355	Luis DeLeon	.05
356	*Dave Dravecky*	.30
357	Dave Edwards	.05
358	Juan Eichelberger	.05
359	Tim Flannery	.05
360	*Tony Gwynn*	15.00
361	Ruppert Jones	.05
362	Terry Kennedy	.05
363	Joe Lefebvre	.05
364	Sixto Lezcano	.05
365	Tim Lollar	.05
366	Gary Lucas	.05
367	John Montefusco	.05
368	Broderick Perkins	.05
369	Joe Pittman	.05
370	Gene Richards	.05
371	Luis Salazar	.05
372	*Eric Show*	.05
373	Garry Templeton	.05
374	Chris Welsh	.05
375	Alan Wiggins	.05
376	Rick Cerone	.05
377	Dave Collins	.05
378	Roger Erickson	.05
379	George Frazier	.05
380	Oscar Gamble	.05
381	Goose Gossage	.10
382	Ken Griffey	.05
383	Ron Guidry	.10
384	Dave LaRoche	.05
385	Rudy May	.05
386	John Mayberry	.05
387	Lee Mazzilli	.05
388	Mike Morgan	.05
389	Jerry Mumphrey	.05
390	Bobby Murcer	.10
391	Graig Nettles	.10
392	Lou Piniella	.10
393	Willie Randolph	.05
394	Shane Rawley	.05
395	Dave Righetti	.05
396	Andre Robertson	.05
397	Roy Smalley	.05
398	Dave Winfield	.75
399	Butch Wynegar	.05
400	Chris Bando	.05
401	Alan Bannister	.05
402	Len Barker	.05
403	Tom Brennan	.05
404	*Carmelo Castillo*	.05
405	Miguel Dilone	.05
406	Jerry Dybzinski	.05
407	Mike Fischlin	.05
408	Ed Glynn (photo actually Bud Anderson)	.05
409	Mike Hargrove	.05
410	Toby Harrah	.05
411	Ron Hassey	.05
412	Von Hayes	.05
413	Rick Manning	.05
414	Bake McBride	.05
415	Larry Milbourne	.05
416	Bill Nahorodny	.05
417	Jack Perconte	.05
418	Larry Sorensen	.05
419	Dan Spillner	.05
420	Rick Sutcliffe	.05
421	Andre Thornton	.05
422	Rick Waits	.05
423	Eddie Whitson	.05
424	Jesse Barfield	.05
425	Barry Bonnell	.05
426	Jim Clancy	.05
427	Damaso Garcia	.05
428	Jerry Garvin	.05
429	Alfredo Griffin	.05
430	Garth Iorg	.05
431	Roy Lee Jackson	.05
432	Luis Leal	.05
433	Buck Martinez	.05
434	Joey McLaughlin	.05
435	Lloyd Moseby	.05
436	Rance Mulliniks	.05
437	Dale Murray	.05
438	Wayne Nordhagen	.05
439	*Gene Petralli*	.05
440	Hosken Powell	.05
441	Dave Stieb	.05
442	Willie Upshaw	.05
443	Ernie Whitt	.05
444	Al Woods	.05
445	Alan Ashby	.05
446	Jose Cruz	.05
447	Kiko Garcia	.05
448	Phil Garner	.05
449	Danny Heep	.05
450	Art Howe	.05
451	Bob Knepper	.05
452	Alan Knicely	.05
453	Ray Knight	.05
454	Frank LaCorte	.05
455	Mike LaCoss	.05
456	Randy Moffitt	.05
457	Joe Niekro	.05
458	Terry Puhl	.05
459	Luis Pujols	.05
460	Craig Reynolds	.05
461	Bert Roberge	.05
462	Vern Ruhle	.05
463	Nolan Ryan	4.00
464	Joe Sambito	.05
465	Tony Scott	.05
466	Dave Smith	.05
467	Harry Spilman	.05
468	Dickie Thon	.05
469	Denny Walling	.05
470	Larry Andersen	.05
471	Floyd Bannister	.05
472	Jim Beattie	.05
473	Bruce Bochte	.05
474	Manny Castillo	.05
475	Bill Caudill	.05
476	Bryan Clark	.05
477	Al Cowens	.05
478	Julio Cruz	.05
479	Todd Cruz	.05
480	Gary Gray	.05
481	Dave Henderson	.05
482	*Mike Moore*	.05
483	Gaylord Perry	.65
484	Dave Revering	.05
485	Joe Simpson	.05
486	Mike Stanton	.05
487	Rick Sweet	.05
488	*Ed Vande Berg*	.05
489	Richie Zisk	.05
490	Doug Bird	.05
491	Larry Bowa	.05
492	Bill Buckner	.05
493	Bill Campbell	.05
494	Jody Davis	.05
495	Leon Durham	.05
496	Steve Henderson	.05
497	Willie Hernandez	.05
498	Fergie Jenkins	.65
499	Jay Johnstone	.05
500	Junior Kennedy	.05
501	Randy Martz	.05
502	Jerry Morales	.05
503	Keith Moreland	.05
504	Dickie Noles	.05
505	Mike Proly	.05
506	Allen Ripley	.05
507	*Ryne Sandberg*	10.00
508	Lee Smith	1.00
509	Pat Tabler	.05
510	Dick Tidrow	.05
511	Bump Wills	.05
512	Gary Woods	.05
513	Tony Armas	.05
514	Dave Beard	.05
515	Jeff Burroughs	.05
516	John D'Acquisto	.05
517	Wayne Gross	.05
518	Mike Heath	.05
519	Rickey Henderson	.75
520	Cliff Johnson	.05
521	Matt Keough	.05
522	Brian Kingman	.05
523	Rick Langford	.05
524	Davey Lopes	.05
525	Steve McCatty	.05
526	Dave McKay	.05
527	Dan Meyer	.05
528	Dwayne Murphy	.05
529	Jeff Newman	.05
530	Mike Norris	.05
531	Bob Owchinko	.05
532	Joe Rudi	.05
533	Jimmy Sexton	.05
534	Fred Stanley	.05
535	Tom Underwood	.05
536	Neil Allen	.05
537	Wally Backman	.05
538	Bob Bailor	.05
539	Hubie Brooks	.05
540	Carlos Diaz	.05
541	Pete Falcone	.05
542	George Foster	.05
543	Ron Gardenhire	.05
544	Brian Giles	.05
545	Ron Hodges	.05
546	Randy Jones	.05
547	Mike Jorgensen	.05
548	Dave Kingman	.05
549	Ed Lynch	.05
550	Jesse Orosco	.05
551	Rick Ownbey	.05
552	*Charlie Puleo*	.05
553	Gary Rajsich	.05
554	Mike Scott	.05
555	Rusty Staub	.05
556	John Stearns	.05
557	Craig Swan	.05
558	Ellis Valentine	.05
559	Tom Veryzer	.05
560	Mookie Wilson	.05
561	Pat Zachry	.05
562	Buddy Bell	.05
563	John Butcher	.05
564	Steve Comer	.05
565	Danny Darwin	.05
566	Bucky Dent	.05
567	John Grubb	.05
568	Rick Honeycutt	.05
569	Dave Hostetler	.05
570	Charlie Hough	.05
571	Lamar Johnson	.05
572	Jon Matlack	.05
573	Paul Mirabella	.05
574	Larry Parrish	.05
575	Mike Richardt	.05
576	Mickey Rivers	.05
577	Billy Sample	.05
578	*Dave Schmidt*	.05
579	Bill Stein	.05
580	Jim Sundberg	.05
581	Frank Tanana	.05
582	Mark Wagner	.05
583	George Wright	.05
584	Johnny Bench	.75
585	Bruce Berenyi	.05
586	Larry Biittner	.05
587	Cesar Cedeno	.05
588	Dave Concepcion	.05
589	Dan Driessen	.05
590	Greg Harris	.05
591	Ben Hayes	.05
592	Paul Householder	.05
593	Tom Hume	.05
594	Wayne Krenchicki	.05
595	Rafael Landestoy	.05
596	Charlie Leibrandt	.05
597	*Eddie Milner*	.05
598	Ron Oester	.05
599	Frank Pastore	.05
600	Joe Price	.05
601	Tom Seaver	.75
602	Bob Shirley	.05
603	Mario Soto	.05
604	Alex Trevino	.05
605	Mike Vail	.05
606	Duane Walker	.05
607	Tom Brunansky	.05
608	Bobby Castillo	.05
609	John Castino	.05
610	Ron Davis	.05
611	Lenny Faedo	.05
612	Terry Felton	.05
613	*Gary Gaetti*	.35
614	Mickey Hatcher	.05
615	Brad Havens	.05
616	Kent Hrbek	.05
617	Randy S. Johnson	.05
618	Tim Laudner	.05
619	Jeff Little	.05
620	Bob Mitchell	.05
621	Jack O'Connor	.05
622	John Pacella	.05
623	Pete Redfern	.05
624	Jesus Vega	.05
625	*Frank Viola*	1.00
626	Ron Washington	.05
627	Gary Ward	.05
628	Al Williams	.05
629	Mark Clear, Dennis Eckersley, Carl Yastrzemski Red Sox All-Stars	.25
630	Terry Bulling, Gaylord Perry 300 Career Wins	.10
631	Dave Concepcion, Manny Trillo Pride of Venezuela	.10
632	Buddy Bell, Robin Yount All-Star Infielders	.20
633	Kent Hrbek, Dave Winfield Mr. Vet & Mr. Rookie	.25
634	Pete Rose, Willie Stargell Fountain of Youth	.40
635	Toby Harrah, Andre Thornton Big Chiefs	.05
636	Lonnie Smith, Ozzie Smith "Smith Bros."	.15
637	Gary Carter, Bo Diaz Base Stealers' Threat	.10
638	Gary Carter, Carlton Fisk All-Star Catchers	.15
639	Rickey Henderson (In Action)	.50
640	Reggie Jackson, Ben Oglivie Home Run Threats	.25
641	Joel Youngblood Two Teams - Same Day	.05
642	Len Barker, Ron Hassey Last Perfect Game	.05
643	Vida Blue Blue	.05
644	Bud Black Black &	.05
645	Reggie Jackson Power	.30
646	Rickey Henderson Speed &	.30
647	Checklist 1-51	.05
648	Checklist 52-103	.05
649	Checklist 104-152	.05
650	Checklist 153-200	.05

651	Checklist 201-251	.05
652	Checklist 252-301	.05
653	Checklist 302-351	.05
654	Checklist 352-399	.05
655	Checklist 400-444	.05
656	Checklist 445-489	.05
657	Checklist 490-535	.05
658	Checklist 536-583	.05
659	Checklist 584-628	.05
660	Checklist 629-646	.05

1984 FLEER

	NM/M
Complete Set (660):	50.00
Common Player:	.05
Wax Pack (15):	2.50
Wax Box (36):	70.00
Cello Pack (28):	4.50
Cello Box (24):	85.00
Vending Box (500):	40.00

1	Mike Boddicker	.05
2	Al Bumbry	.05
3	Todd Cruz	.05
4	Rich Dauer	.05
5	Storm Davis	.05
6	Rick Dempsey	.05
7	Jim Dwyer	.05
8	Mike Flanagan	.05
9	Dan Ford	.05
10	John Lowenstein	.05
11	Dennis Martinez	.05
12	Tippy Martinez	.05
13	Scott McGregor	.05
14	Eddie Murray	1.00
15	Joe Nolan	.05
16	Jim Palmer	1.00
17	Cal Ripken, Jr.	4.00
18	Gary Roenicke	.05
19	Lenn Sakata	.05
20	*John Shelby*	.05
21	Ken Singleton	.05
22	Sammy Stewart	.05
23	Tim Stoddard	.05
24	Marty Bystrom	.05
25	Steve Carlton	1.00
26	Ivan DeJesus	.05
27	John Denny	.05
28	Bob Dernier	.05
29	Bo Diaz	.05
30	Kiko Garcia	.05
31	Greg Gross	.05
32	*Kevin Gross*	.05
33	Von Hayes	.05
34	Willie Hernandez	.05
35	Al Holland	.05
36	*Charles Hudson*	.05
37	Joe Lefebvre	.05
38	Sixto Lezcano	.05
39	Garry Maddox	.05
40	Gary Matthews	.05
41	Len Matuszek	.05
42	Tug McGraw	.05
43	Joe Morgan	1.00
44	Tony Perez	.75
45	Ron Reed	.05
46	Pete Rose	3.00
47	*Juan Samuel*	.25
48	Mike Schmidt	2.50
49	Ozzie Virgil	.05
50	*Juan Agosto*	.05
51	Harold Baines	.05
52	Floyd Bannister	.05
53	Salome Barojas	.05
54	Britt Burns	.05
55	Julio Cruz	.05
56	Richard Dotson	.05
57	Jerry Dybzinski	.05
58	Carlton Fisk	1.00
59	Scott Fletcher	.05
60	Jerry Hairston Sr.	.05
61	Kevin Hickey	.05
62	Marc Hill	.05
63	LaMarr Hoyt	.05
64	Ron Kittle	.05
65	Jerry Koosman	.05
66	Dennis Lamp	.05
67	Rudy Law	.05
68	Vance Law	.05
69	Greg Luzinski	.05
70	Tom Paciorek	.05
71	Mike Squires	.05
72	Dick Tidrow	.05
73	*Greg Walker*	.05
74	Glenn Abbott	.05
75	Howard Bailey	.05
76	Doug Bair	.05
77	Juan Berenguer	.05
78	Tom Brookens	.05
79	Enos Cabell	.05
80	Kirk Gibson	.05
81	John Grubb	.05
82	Larry Herndon	.05
83	Wayne Krenchicki	.05
84	Rick Leach	.05
85	Chet Lemon	.05
86	Aurelio Lopez	.05
87	Jack Morris	.05
88	Lance Parrish	.05
89	Dan Petry	.05
90	Dave Rozema	.05
91	Alan Trammell	.05
92	Lou Whitaker	.05
93	Milt Wilcox	.05
94	Glenn Wilson	.05
95	John Wockenfuss	.05
96	Dusty Baker	.05
97	Joe Beckwith	.05
98	Greg Brock	.05
99	Jack Fimple	.05
100	Pedro Guerrero	.05
101	Rick Honeycutt	.05
102	Burt Hooton	.05
103	Steve Howe	.05
104	Ken Landreaux	.05
105	Mike Marshall	.05
106	Rick Monday	.05
107	Jose Morales	.05
108	Tom Niedenfuer	.05
109	*Alejandro Pena*	.05
110	Jerry Reuss	.05
111	Bill Russell	.05
112	Steve Sax	.05
113	Mike Scioscia	.05
114	Derrel Thomas	.05
115	Fernando Valenzuela	.05
116	Bob Welch	.05
117	Steve Yeager	.05
118	Pat Zachry	.05
119	Don Baylor	.05
120	Bert Campaneris	.05
121	Rick Cerone	.05
122	*Ray Fontenot*	.05
123	George Frazier	.05
124	Oscar Gamble	.05
125	Goose Gossage	.10
126	Ken Griffey	.05
127	Ron Guidry	.10
128	Jay Howell	.05
129	Steve Kemp	.05
130	Matt Keough	.05
131	*Don Mattingly*	20.00
132	John Montefusco	.05
133	Omar Moreno	.05
134	Dale Murray	.05
135	Graig Nettles	.05
136	Lou Piniella	.10
137	Willie Randolph	.05
138	Shane Rawley	.05
139	Dave Righetti	.05
140	Andre Robertson	.05
141	Bob Shirley	.05
142	Roy Smalley	.05
143	Dave Winfield	1.00
144	Butch Wynegar	.05
145	*Jim Acker*	.05
146	Doyle Alexander	.05
147	Jesse Barfield	.05
148	George Bell	.05
149	Barry Bonnell	.05
150	Jim Clancy	.05
151	Dave Collins	.05
152	*Tony Fernandez*	.50
153	Damaso Garcia	.05
154	Dave Geisel	.05
155	Jim Gott	.05
156	Alfredo Griffin	.05
157	Garth Iorg	.05
158	Roy Lee Jackson	.05
159	Cliff Johnson	.05
160	Luis Leal	.05
161	Buck Martinez	.05
162	Joey McLaughlin	.05
163	Randy Moffitt	.05
164	Lloyd Moseby	.05
165	Rance Mulliniks	.05
166	Jorge Orta	.05
167	Dave Stieb	.05
168	Willie Upshaw	.05
169	Ernie Whitt	.05
170	Len Barker	.05
171	Steve Bedrosian	.05
172	Bruce Benedict	.05
173	Brett Butler	.05
174	Rick Camp	.05
175	Chris Chambliss	.05
176	Ken Dayley	.05
177	Pete Falcone	.05
178	Terry Forster	.05
179	Gene Garber	.05
180	Terry Harper	.05
181	Bob Horner	.05
182	Glenn Hubbard	.05
183	Randy Johnson	.05
184	*Craig McMurtry*	.05
185	Donnie Moore	.05
186	Dale Murphy	.60
187	Phil Niekro	.75
188	Pascual Perez	.05
189	Biff Pocoroba	.05
190	Rafael Ramirez	.05
191	Jerry Royster	.05
192	Claudell Washington	.05
193	Bob Watson	.05
194	Jerry Augustine	.05
195	Mark Brouhard	.05
196	Mike Caldwell	.05
197	*Tom Candiotti*	.25
198	Cecil Cooper	.05
199	Rollie Fingers	.75
200	Jim Gantner	.05
201	Bob L. Gibson	.05
202	Moose Haas	.05
203	Roy Howell	.05
204	Pete Ladd	.05
205	Rick Manning	.05
206	Bob McClure	.05
207	Paul Molitor	1.00
208	Don Money	.05
209	Charlie Moore	.05
210	Ben Oglivie	.05
211	Chuck Porter	.05
212	Ed Romero	.05
213	Ted Simmons	.05
214	Jim Slaton	.05
215	Don Sutton	.75
216	Tom Tellmann	.05
217	Pete Vuckovich	.05
218	Ned Yost	.05
219	Robin Yount	1.00
220	Alan Ashby	.05
221	Kevin Bass	.05
222	Jose Cruz	.05
223	*Bill Dawley*	.05
224	Frank DiPino	.05
225	*Bill Doran*	.05
226	Phil Garner	.05
227	Art Howe	.05
228	Bob Knepper	.05
229	Ray Knight	.05
230	Frank LaCorte	.05
231	Mike LaCoss	.05
232	Mike Madden	.05
233	Jerry Mumphrey	.05
234	Joe Niekro	.05
235	Terry Puhl	.05
236	Luis Pujols	.05
237	Craig Reynolds	.05
238	Vern Ruhle	.05
239	Nolan Ryan	4.00
240	Mike Scott	.05
241	Tony Scott	.05
242	Dave Smith	.05
243	Dickie Thon	.05
244	Denny Walling	.05
245	Dale Berra	.05
246	Jim Bibby	.05
247	John Candelaria	.05
248	*Jose DeLeon*	.05
249	Mike Easler	.05
250	Cecilio Guante	.05
251	Richie Hebner	.05
252	Lee Lacy	.05
253	Bill Madlock	.05
254	Milt May	.05
255	Lee Mazzilli	.05
256	Larry McWilliams	.05
257	Jim Morrison	.05
258	Dave Parker	.05
259	Tony Pena	.05
260	Johnny Ray	.05
261	Rick Rhoden	.05
262	Don Robinson	.05
263	Manny Sarmiento	.05
264	Rod Scurry	.05
265	Kent Tekulve	.05
266	Gene Tenace	.05
267	Jason Thompson	.05
268	*Lee Tunnell*	.05
269	*Marvell Wynne*	.05
270	Ray Burris	.05
271	Gary Carter	1.00
272	Warren Cromartie	.05
273	Andre Dawson	.30
274	Doug Flynn	.05
275	Terry Francona	.05
276	Bill Gullickson	.05
277	Bob James	.05
278	Charlie Lea	.05
279	Bryan Little	.05
280	Al Oliver	.05
281	Tim Raines	.05
282	Bobby Ramos	.05
283	Jeff Reardon	.05
284	Steve Rogers	.05
285	Scott Sanderson	.05
286	Dan Schatzeder	.05
287	Bryn Smith	.05
288	Chris Speier	.05
289	Manny Trillo	.05
290	Mike Vail	.05
291	Tim Wallach	.05
292	Chris Welsh	.05
293	Jim Wohlford	.05
294	Kurt Bevacqua	.05
295	Juan Bonilla	.05
296	Bobby Brown	.05
297	Luis DeLeon	.05
298	Dave Dravecky	.05
299	Tim Flannery	.05
300	Steve Garvey	.25
301	Tony Gwynn	2.00
302	*Andy Hawkins*	.10
303	Ruppert Jones	.05
304	Terry Kennedy	.05
305	Tim Lollar	.05
306	Gary Lucas	.05
307	*Kevin McReynolds*	.25
308	Sid Monge	.05
309	Mario Ramirez	.05
310	Gene Richards	.05
311	Luis Salazar	.05
312	Eric Show	.05
313	Elias Sosa	.05
314	Garry Templeton	.05
315	*Mark Thurmond*	.05
316	Ed Whitson	.05
317	Alan Wiggins	.05
318	Neil Allen	.05
319	Joaquin Andujar	.05
320	Steve Braun	.05
321	Glenn Brummer	.05
322	Bob Forsch	.05
323	David Green	.05
324	George Hendrick	.05
325	Tom Herr	.05
326	Dane Iorg	.05
327	Jeff Lahti	.05
328	Dave LaPoint	.05
329	Willie McGee	.05
330	Ken Oberkfell	.05
331	Darrell Porter	.05
332	Jamie Quirk	.05
333	Mike Ramsey	.05
334	Floyd Rayford	.05
335	Lonnie Smith	.05
336	Ozzie Smith	2.00
337	John Stuper	.05
338	Bruce Sutter	.75
339	*Andy Van Slyke*	1.00
340	Dave Von Ohlen	.05
341	Willie Aikens	.05
342	Mike Armstrong	.05
343	Bud Black	.05
344	George Brett	2.50
345	Onix Concepcion	.05
346	Keith Creel	.05
347	Larry Gura	.05
348	Don Hood	.05
349	Dennis Leonard	.05
350	Hal McRae	.05
351	Amos Otis	.05
352	Gaylord Perry	.75
353	Greg Pryor	.05
354	Dan Quisenberry	.05
355	Steve Renko	.05
356	Leon Roberts	.05

357	*Pat Sheridan*	.05
358	Joe Simpson	.05
359	Don Slaught	.05
360	Paul Splittorff	.05
361	U.L. Washington	.05
362	John Wathan	.05
363	Frank White	.05
364	Willie Wilson	.05
365	Jim Barr	.05
366	Dave Bergman	.05
367	Fred Breining	.05
368	Bob Brenly	.05
369	Jack Clark	.05
370	Chili Davis	.05
371	Mark Davis	.05
372	Darrell Evans	.05
373	Atlee Hammaker	.05
374	Mike Krukow	.05
375	Duane Kuiper	.05
376	Bill Laskey	.05
377	Gary Lavelle	.05
378	Johnnie LeMaster	.05
379	Jeff Leonard	.05
380	Randy Lerch	.05
381	Renie Martin	.05
382	Andy McGaffigan	.05
383	Greg Minton	.05
384	Tom O'Malley	.05
385	Max Venable	.05
386	Brad Wellman	.05
387	Joel Youngblood	.05
388	Gary Allenson	.05
389	Luis Aponte	.05
390	Tony Armas	.05
391	Doug Bird	.05
392	Wade Boggs	2.00
393	*Dennis Boyd*	.05
394	Mike Brown	.05
395	Mark Clear	.05
396	Dennis Eckersley	.75
397	Dwight Evans	.05
398	Rich Gedman	.05
399	Glenn Hoffman	.05
400	Bruce Hurst	.05
401	John Henry Johnson	.05
402	Ed Jurak	.05
403	Rick Miller	.05
404	Jeff Newman	.05
405	Reid Nichols	.05
406	Bob Ojeda	.05
407	Jerry Remy	.05
408	Jim Rice	.05
409	Bob Stanley	.05
410	Dave Stapleton	.05
411	John Tudor	.05
412	Carl Yastrzemski	1.50
413	Buddy Bell	.05
414	Larry Biittner	.05
415	John Butcher	.05
416	Danny Darwin	.05
417	Bucky Dent	.05
418	Dave Hostetler	.05
419	Charlie Hough	.05
420	Bobby Johnson	.05
421	Odell Jones	.05
422	Jon Matlack	.05
423	*Pete O'Brien*	.05
424	Larry Parrish	.05
425	Mickey Rivers	.05
426	Billy Sample	.05
427	Dave Schmidt	.05
428	*Mike Smithson*	.05
429	Bill Stein	.05
430	Dave Stewart	.05
431	Jim Sundberg	.05
432	Frank Tanana	.05
433	Dave Tobik	.05
434	Wayne Tolleson	.05
435	George Wright	.05
436	Bill Almon	.05
437	*Keith Atherton*	.05
438	Dave Beard	.05
439	Tom Burgmeier	.05
440	Jeff Burroughs	.05
441	*Chris Codiroli*	.05
442	*Tim Conroy*	.05
443	Mike Davis	.05
444	Wayne Gross	.05
445	Garry Hancock	.05
446	Mike Heath	.05
447	Rickey Henderson	1.00
448	*Don Hill*	.05
449	Bob Kearney	.05
450	Bill Krueger	.05
451	Rick Langford	.05
452	Carney Lansford	.05
453	Davey Lopes	.05
454	Steve McCatty	.05
455	Dan Meyer	.05
456	Dwayne Murphy	.05
457	Mike Norris	.05
458	Ricky Peters	.05
459	Tony Phillips	.05
460	Tom Underwood	.05
461	Mike Warren	.05
462	Johnny Bench	1.50
463	Bruce Berenyi	.05
464	Dann Bilardello	.05
465	Cesar Cedeno	.05
466	Dave Concepcion	.05
467	Dan Driessen	.05
468	*Nick Esasky*	.05
469	Rich Gale	.05
470	Ben Hayes	.05
471	Paul Householder	.05
472	Tom Hume	.05
473	Alan Knicely	.05
474	Eddie Milner	.05
475	Ron Oester	.05
476	Kelly Paris	.05
477	Frank Pastore	.05
478	Ted Power	.05
479	Joe Price	.05
480	Charlie Puleo	.05
481	*Gary Redus*	.05
482	Bill Scherrer	.05
483	Mario Soto	.05
484	Alex Trevino	.05
485	Duane Walker	.05
486	Larry Bowa	.05
487	Warren Brusstar	.05
488	Bill Buckner	.05
489	Bill Campbell	.05
490	Ron Cey	.05
491	Jody Davis	.05
492	Leon Durham	.05
493	Mel Hall	.05
494	Fergie Jenkins	.75
495	Jay Johnstone	.05
496	*Craig Lefferts*	.10
497	*Carmelo Martinez*	.05
498	Jerry Morales	.05
499	Keith Moreland	.05
500	Dickie Noles	.05
501	Mike Proly	.05
502	Chuck Rainey	.05
503	Dick Ruthven	.05
504	Ryne Sandberg	2.00
505	Lee Smith	.05
506	Steve Trout	.05
507	Gary Woods	.05
508	Juan Beniquez	.05
509	Bob Boone	.05
510	Rick Burleson	.05
511	Rod Carew	1.00
512	Bobby Clark	.05
513	John Curtis	.05
514	Doug DeCinces	.05
515	Brian Downing	.05
516	Tim Foli	.05
517	Ken Forsch	.05
518	Bobby Grich	.05
519	Andy Hassler	.05
520	Reggie Jackson	1.50
521	Ron Jackson	.05
522	Tommy John	.10
523	Bruce Kison	.05
524	Steve Lubratich	.05
525	Fred Lynn	.05
526	*Gary Pettis*	.05
527	Luis Sanchez	.05
528	Daryl Sconiers	.05
529	Ellis Valentine	.05
530	Rob Wilfong	.05
531	Mike Witt	.05
532	Geoff Zahn	.05
533	Bud Anderson	.05
534	Chris Bando	.05
535	Alan Bannister	.05
536	Bert Blyleven	.10
537	Tom Brennan	.05
538	Jamie Easterly	.05
539	Juan Eichelberger	.05
540	Jim Essian	.05
541	Mike Fischlin	.05
542	Julio Franco	.05
543	Mike Hargrove	.05
544	Toby Harrah	.05
545	Ron Hassey	.05
546	*Neal Heaton*	.05
547	Bake McBride	.05
548	Broderick Perkins	.05
549	Lary Sorensen	.05
550	Dan Spillner	.05
551	Rick Sutcliffe	.05
552	Pat Tabler	.05
553	Gorman Thomas	.05
554	Andre Thornton	.05
555	George Vukovich	.05
556	Darrell Brown	.05
557	Tom Brunansky	.05
558	*Randy Bush*	.05
559	Bobby Castillo	.05
560	John Castino	.05
561	Ron Davis	.05
562	Dave Engle	.05
563	Lenny Faedo	.05
564	Pete Filson	.05
565	Gary Gaetti	.05
566	Mickey Hatcher	.05
567	Kent Hrbek	.05
568	Rusty Kuntz	.05
569	Tim Laudner	.05
570	Rick Lysander	.05
571	Bobby Mitchell	.05
572	Ken Schrom	.05
573	Ray Smith	.05
574	*Tim Teufel*	.05
575	Frank Viola	.05
576	Gary Ward	.05
577	Ron Washington	.05
578	Len Whitehouse	.05
579	Al Williams	.05
580	Bob Bailor	.05
581	Mark Bradley	.05
582	Hubie Brooks	.05
583	Carlos Diaz	.05
584	George Foster	.05
585	Brian Giles	.05
586	Danny Heep	.05
587	Keith Hernandez	.05
588	Ron Hodges	.05
589	Scott Holman	.05
590	Dave Kingman	.05
591	Ed Lynch	.05
592	*Jose Oquendo*	.05
593	Jesse Orosco	.05
594	*Junior Ortiz*	.05
595	Tom Seaver	1.00
596	*Doug Sisk*	.05
597	Rusty Staub	.05
598	John Stearns	.05
599	Darryl Strawberry	.25
600	Craig Swan	.05
601	*Walt Terrell*	.05
602	Mike Torrez	.05
603	Mookie Wilson	.05
604	Jamie Allen	.05
605	Jim Beattie	.05
606	Tony Bernazard	.05
607	Manny Castillo	.05
608	Bill Caudill	.05
609	Bryan Clark	.05
610	Al Cowens	.05
611	Dave Henderson	.05
612	Steve Henderson	.05
613	Orlando Mercado	.05
614	Mike Moore	.05
615	Ricky Nelson	.05
616	*Spike Owen*	.10
617	Pat Putnam	.05
618	Ron Roenicke	.05
619	Mike Stanton	.05
620	Bob Stoddard	.05
621	Rick Sweet	.05
622	Roy Thomas	.05
623	Ed Vande Berg	.05
624	*Matt Young*	.05
625	Richie Zisk	.05
626	Fred Lynn '83 All-Star Game Record Breaker	.05
627	Manny Trillo '83 All-Star Game Record Breaker	.05
628	Steve Garvey N.L. Iron Man	.10
629	Rod Carew A.L. Batting Runner-Up	.15
630	Wade Boggs A.L. Batting Champion	.50
631	Tim Raines L etting Go Of The Raines	.10
632	Al Oliver Double Trouble	.05
633	Steve Sax All-Star Second Base	.05
634	Dickie Thon All-Star Shortstop	.05
635	Tippy Martinez, Dan Quisenberry Ace Firemen	.05
636	Joe Morgan, Tony Perez, Pete Rose Reds Reunited	.75
637	Bob Boone, Lance Parrish Backstop Stars	.05
638	George Brett, Gaylord Perry The Pine Tar Incident, 7/24/83	.25
639	Bob Forsch, Dave Righetti, Mike Warren 1983 No-Hitters	.05
640	Johnny Bench, Carl Yastrzemski Retiring Superstars	.50
641	Gaylord Perry Going Out In Style	.05
642	Steve Carlton 300 Club & Strikeout Record	.10
643	Joe Altobelli, Paul Owens The Managers	.05
644	Rick Dempsey The MVP	.05
645	Mike Boddicker The Rookie Winner	.05
646	Scott McGregor The Clincher	.05
647	Joe Altobelli Checklist: Orioles/Royals	.05
648	Paul Owens Checklist: Phillies/Giants	.05
649	Tony LaRussa Checklist: White Sox/Red Sox	.05
650	Sparky Anderson Checklist: Tigers/Rangers	.10
651	Tommy Lasorda Checklist: Dodgers/A's	.10
652	Billy Martin Checklist: Yankees/Reds	.05
653	Bobby Cox Checklist: Blue Jays/Cubs	.10
654	Joe Torre Checklist: Braves/Angels	.10
655	Rene Lachemann Checklist: Brewers/Indians	.05
656	Bob Lillis Checklist: Astros/Twins	.05
657	Chuck Tanner Checklist: Pirates/Mets	.05
658	Bill Virdon Checklist: Expos/Mariners	.05
659	Dick Williams Checklist: Padres/Specials	.05
660	Whitey Herzog Checklist: Cardinals/Specials	.05

Update

		NM/M
Complete Set (132):		275.00
Common Player:		.25
1	Willie Aikens	.25
2	Luis Aponte	.25
3	Mark Bailey	.25
4	Bob Bailor	.25
5	Dusty Baker	.25
6	Steve Balboni	.25
7	Alan Bannister	.25
8	Marty Barrett	.25
9	Dave Beard	.25
10	Joe Beckwith	.25
11	Dave Bergman	.25
12	Tony Bernazard	.25
13	Bruce Bochte	.25
14	Barry Bonnell	.25
15	Phil Bradley	.25
16	Fred Breining	.25
17	Mike Brown	.25
18	Bill Buckner	.25
19	Ray Burris	.25
20	John Butcher	.25
21	Brett Butler	.25
22	Enos Cabell	.25
23	Bill Campbell	.25
24	Bill Caudill	.25
25	Bobby Clark	.25
26	Bryan Clark	.25
27	*Roger Clemens*	220.00
28	Jaime Cocanower	.25
29	*Ron Darling*	1.00

30 *Alvin Davis* .25
31 Bob Dernier .25
32 Carlos Diaz .25
33 Mike Easler .25
34 Dennis Eckersley 4.00
35 Jim Essian .25
36 Darrell Evans .25
37 Mike Fitzgerald .25
38 Tim Foli .25
39 *John Franco* 3.00
40 George Frazier .25
41 Rich Gale .25
42 Barbaro Garbey .25
43 *Dwight Gooden* 7.50
44 Goose Gossage .40
45 Wayne Gross .25
46 Mark Gubicza 1.00
47 Jackie Gutierrez .25
48 Toby Harrah .25
49 Ron Hassey .25
50 Richie Hebner .25
51 Willie Hernandez .25
52 Ed Hodge .25
53 Ricky Horton .25
54 Art Howe .25
55 Dane Iorg .25
56 Brook Jacoby .25
57 Dion James .25
58 Mike Jeffcoat .25
59 Ruppert Jones .25
60 Bob Kearney .25
61 *Jimmy Key* 1.00
62 Dave Kingman .25
63 Brad Komminsk .25
64 Jerry Koosman .25
65 Wayne Krenchicki .25
66 Rusty Kuntz .25
67 Frank LaCorte .25
68 Dennis Lamp .25
69 Tito Landrum .25
70 *Mark Langston* 4.00
71 Rick Leach .25
72 Craig Lefferts .25
73 Gary Lucas .25
74 Jerry Martin .25
75 Carmelo Martinez .25
76 Mike Mason .25
77 Gary Matthews .25
78 Andy McGaffigan .25
79 Joey McLaughlin .25
80 Joe Morgan 5.00
81 Darryl Motley .25
82 Graig Nettles .40
83 Phil Niekro 3.00
84 Ken Oberkfell .25
85 Al Oliver .25
86 Jorge Orta .25
87 Amos Otis .25
88 Bob Owchinko .25
89 Dave Parker .25
90 Jack Perconte .25
91 Tony Perez 3.00
92 Gerald Perry .25
93 *Kirby Puckett* 55.00
94 Shane Rawley .25
95 Floyd Rayford .25
96 Ron Reed .25
97 R.J. Reynolds .25
98 Gene Richards .25
99 *Jose Rijo* 1.00
100 Jeff Robinson .25
101 Ron Romanick .25
102 Pete Rose 10.00
103 *Bret Saberhagen* 5.00
104 Scott Sanderson .25
105 Dick Schofield .25
106 Tom Seaver 7.50
107 Jim Slaton .25
108 Mike Smithson .25
109 Lary Sorensen .25
110 Tim Stoddard .25
111 Jeff Stone .25
112 Champ Summers .25
113 Jim Sundberg .25
114 Rick Sutcliffe .35
115 Craig Swan .25
116 Derrel Thomas .25
117 Gorman Thomas .25
118 Alex Trevino .25
119 Manny Trillo .25
120 John Tudor .25
121 Tom Underwood .25
122 Mike Vail .25
123 Tom Waddell .25
124 Gary Ward .25
125 Terry Whitfield .25
126 Curtis Wilkerson .25
127 Frank Williams .25
128 Glenn Wilson .25
129 John Wockenfuss .25
130 Ned Yost .25
131 Mike Young .25
132 Checklist 1-132 .10

1985 FLEER

NM/M

Unopened Factory Set (660): 50.00
Complete Set (660): 40.00
Common Player: .05
Wax Pack (15): 4.00
Wax Box (36): 150.00
Cello Pack (28): 6.00
Cello Box (24): 150.00
Rack Pack (45): 12.00
Vending Box (500): 35.00

1 Doug Bair .05
2 Juan Berenguer .05
3 Dave Bergman .05
4 Tom Brookens .05
5 Marty Castillo .05
6 Darrell Evans .05
7 Barbaro Garbey .05
8 Kirk Gibson .05
9 John Grubb .05
10 Willie Hernandez .05
11 Larry Herndon .05
12 Howard Johnson .05
13 Ruppert Jones .05
14 Rusty Kuntz .05
15 Chet Lemon .05
16 Aurelio Lopez .05
17 Sid Monge .05
18 Jack Morris .05
19 Lance Parrish .05
20 Dan Petry .05
21 Dave Rozema .05
22 Bill Scherrer .05
23 Alan Trammell .05
24 Lou Whitaker .05
25 Milt Wilcox .05
26 Kurt Bevacqua .05
27 *Greg Booker* .05
28 Bobby Brown .05
29 Luis DeLeon .05
30 Dave Dravecky .05
31 Tim Flannery .05
32 Steve Garvey .40
33 Goose Gossage .10
34 Tony Gwynn 2.00
35 Greg Harris .05
36 Andy Hawkins .05
37 Terry Kennedy .05
38 Craig Lefferts .05
39 Tim Lollar .05
40 Carmelo Martinez .05
41 Kevin McReynolds .05
42 Graig Nettles .05
43 Luis Salazar .05
44 Eric Show .05
45 Garry Templeton .05
46 Mark Thurmond .05
47 Ed Whitson .05
48 Alan Wiggins .05
49 Rich Bordi .05
50 Larry Bowa .05
51 Warren Brusstar .05
52 Ron Cey .05
53 *Henry Cotto* .05
54 Jody Davis .05
55 Bob Dernier .05
56 Leon Durham .05
57 Dennis Eckersley .75
58 George Frazier .05
59 Richie Hebner .05
60 Dave Lopes .05
61 Gary Matthews .05
62 Keith Moreland .05
63 Rick Reuschel .05
64 Dick Ruthven .05
65 Ryne Sandberg 2.00
66 Scott Sanderson .05
67 Lee Smith .05
68 Tim Stoddard .05
69 Rick Sutcliffe .05
70 Steve Trout .05
71 Gary Woods .05
72 Wally Backman .05
73 Bruce Berenyi .05
74 Hubie Brooks .05
75 Kelvin Chapman .05
76 Ron Darling .05
77 Sid Fernandez .05
78 Mike Fitzgerald .05
79 George Foster .05
80 Brent Gaff .05
81 Ron Gardenhire .05
82 Dwight Gooden .25
83 Tom Gorman .05
84 Danny Heep .05
85 Keith Hernandez .05
86 Ray Knight .05
87 Ed Lynch .05
88 Jose Oquendo .05
89 Jesse Orosco .05
90 *Rafael Santana* .05
91 Doug Sisk .05
92 Rusty Staub .05
93 Darryl Strawberry .10
94 Walt Terrell .05
95 Mookie Wilson .05
96 Jim Acker .05
97 Willie Aikens .05
98 Doyle Alexander .05
99 Jesse Barfield .05
100 George Bell .05
101 Jim Clancy .05
102 Dave Collins .05
103 Tony Fernandez .05
104 Damaso Garcia .05
105 Jim Gott .05
106 Alfredo Griffin .05
107 Garth Iorg .05
108 Roy Lee Jackson .05
109 Cliff Johnson .05
110 Jimmy Key .05
111 Dennis Lamp .05
112 Rick Leach .05
113 Luis Leal .05
114 Buck Martinez .05
115 Lloyd Moseby .05
116 Rance Mulliniks .05
117 Dave Stieb .05
118 Willie Upshaw .05
119 Ernie Whitt .05
120 Mike Armstrong .05
121 Don Baylor .05
122 Marty Bystrom .05
123 Rick Cerone .05
124 Joe Cowley .05
125 Brian Dayett .05
126 Tim Foli .05
127 Ray Fontenot .05
128 Ken Griffey .05
129 Ron Guidry .10
130 Toby Harrah .05
131 Jay Howell .05
132 Steve Kemp .05
133 Don Mattingly 2.50
134 Bobby Meacham .05
135 John Montefusco .05
136 Omar Moreno .05
137 Dale Murray .05
138 Phil Niekro .75
139 *Mike Pagliarulo* .20
140 Willie Randolph .05
141 Dennis Rasmussen .05
142 Dave Righetti .05
143 Jose Rijo .05
144 Andre Robertson .05
145 Bob Shirley .05
146 Dave Winfield 1.00
147 Butch Wynegar .05
148 Gary Allenson .05
149 Tony Armas .05
150 Marty Barrett .05
151 Wade Boggs 2.00
152 Dennis Boyd .05
153 Bill Buckner .05
154 Mark Clear .05
155 Roger Clemens 40.00
156 Steve Crawford .05
157 Mike Easler .05
158 Dwight Evans .05
159 Rich Gedman .05
160 Jackie Gutierrez .05
161 Bruce Hurst .05
162 John Henry Johnson .05
163 Rick Miller .05
164 Reid Nichols .05
165 *Al Nipper* .05
166 Bob Ojeda .05
167 Jerry Remy .05
168 Jim Rice .25
169 Bob Stanley .05
170 Mike Boddicker .05
171 Al Bumbry .05
172 Todd Cruz .05
173 Rich Dauer .05
174 Storm Davis .05
175 Rick Dempsey .05
176 Jim Dwyer .05
177 Mike Flanagan .05
178 Dan Ford .05
179 Wayne Gross .05
180 John Lowenstein .05
181 Dennis Martinez .05
182 Tippy Martinez .05
183 Scott McGregor .05
184 Eddie Murray 1.00
185 Joe Nolan .05
186 Floyd Rayford .05
187 Cal Ripken, Jr. 4.00
188 Gary Roenicke .05
189 Lenn Sakata .05
190 John Shelby .05
191 Ken Singleton .05
192 Sammy Stewart .05
193 Bill Swaggerty .05
194 Tom Underwood .05
195 Mike Young .05
196 Steve Balboni .05
197 Joe Beckwith .05
198 Bud Black .05
199 George Brett 2.50
200 Onix Concepcion .05
201 *Mark Gubicza* .50
202 Larry Gura .05
203 Mark Huismann .05
204 Dane Iorg .05
205 Danny Jackson .05
206 Charlie Leibrandt .05
207 Hal McRae .05
208 Darryl Motley .05
209 Jorge Orta .05
210 Greg Pryor .05
211 Dan Quisenberry .05
212 Bret Saberhagen .25
213 Pat Sheridan .05
214 Don Slaught .05
215 U.L. Washington .05
216 John Wathan .05
217 Frank White .05
218 Willie Wilson .05
219 Neil Allen .05
220 Joaquin Andujar .05
221 Steve Braun .05
222 Danny Cox .05
223 Bob Forsch .05
224 David Green .05
225 George Hendrick .05
226 Tom Herr .05
227 *Ricky Horton* .05
228 Art Howe .05
229 Mike Jorgensen .05
230 Kurt Kepshire .05
231 Jeff Lahti .05
232 Tito Landrum .05
233 Dave LaPoint .05
234 Willie McGee .05
235 *Tom Nieto* .05
236 *Terry Pendleton* 1.00
237 Darrell Porter .05
238 Dave Rucker .05
239 Lonnie Smith .05
240 Ozzie Smith 2.00
241 Bruce Sutter .75
242 Andy Van Slyke .05
243 Dave Von Ohlen .05
244 Larry Andersen .05
245 Bill Campbell .05
246 Steve Carlton 1.00
247 Tim Corcoran .05
248 Ivan DeJesus .05
249 John Denny .05
250 Bo Diaz .05
251 Greg Gross .05
252 Kevin Gross .05
253 Von Hayes .05
254 Al Holland .05
255 Charles Hudson .05
256 Jerry Koosman .05
257 Joe Lefebvre .05
258 Sixto Lezcano .05
259 Garry Maddox .05
260 Len Matuszek .05
261 Tug McGraw .05

262 Al Oliver .05
263 Shane Rawley .05
264 Juan Samuel .05
265 Mike Schmidt 2.50
266 *Jeff Stone* .05
267 Ozzie Virgil .05
268 Glenn Wilson .05
269 John Wockenfuss .05
270 Darrell Brown .05
271 Tom Brunansky .05
272 Randy Bush .05
273 John Butcher .05
274 Bobby Castillo .05
275 Ron Davis .05
276 Dave Engle .05
277 Pete Filson .05
278 Gary Gaetti .05
279 Mickey Hatcher .05
280 Ed Hodge .05
281 Kent Hrbek .05
282 Houston Jimenez .05
283 Tim Laudner .05
284 Rick Lysander .05
285 Dave Meier .05
286 Kirby Puckett 8.00
287 Pat Putnam .05
288 Ken Schrom .05
289 Mike Smithson .05
290 Tim Teufel .05
291 Frank Viola .05
292 Ron Washington .05
293 Don Aase .05
294 Juan Beniquez .05
295 Bob Boone .05
296 Mike Brown .05
297 Rod Carew 1.00
298 Doug Corbett .05
299 Doug DeCinces .05
300 Brian Downing .05
301 Ken Forsch .05
302 Bobby Grich .05
303 Reggie Jackson 2.00
304 Tommy John .10
305 Curt Kaufman .05
306 Bruce Kison .05
307 Fred Lynn .05
308 Gary Pettis .05
309 *Ron Romanick* .05
310 Luis Sanchez .05
311 Dick Schofield .05
312 Daryl Sconiers .05
313 Jim Slaton .05
314 Derrel Thomas .05
315 Rob Wilfong .05
316 Mike Witt .05
317 Geoff Zahn .05
318 Len Barker .05
319 Steve Bedrosian .05
320 Bruce Benedict .05
321 Rick Camp .05
322 Chris Chambliss .05
323 *Jeff Dedmon* .05
324 Terry Forster .05
325 Gene Garber .05
326 *Albert Hall* .05
327 Terry Harper .05
328 Bob Horner .05
329 Glenn Hubbard .05
330 Randy Johnson .05
331 Brad Komminsk .05
332 Rick Mahler .05
333 Craig McMurtry .05
334 Donnie Moore .05
335 Dale Murphy .40
336 Ken Oberkfell .05
337 Pascual Perez .05
338 Gerald Perry .05
339 Rafael Ramirez .05
340 Jerry Royster .05
341 Alex Trevino .05
342 Claudell Washington .05
343 Alan Ashby .05
344 *Mark Bailey* .05
345 Kevin Bass .05
346 Enos Cabell .05
347 Jose Cruz .05
348 Bill Dawley .05
349 Frank DiPino .05
350 Bill Doran .05
351 Phil Garner .05
352 Bob Knepper .05
353 Mike LaCoss .05
354 Jerry Mumphrey .05
355 Joe Niekro .05
356 Terry Puhl .05
357 Craig Reynolds .05
358 Vern Ruhle .05
359 Nolan Ryan 4.00
360 Joe Sambito .05
361 Mike Scott .05
362 Dave Smith .05
363 *Julio Solano* .05
364 Dickie Thon .05
365 Denny Walling .05
366 Dave Anderson .05
367 Bob Bailor .05
368 Greg Brock .05
369 Carlos Diaz .05
370 Pedro Guerrero .05
371 *Orel Hershiser* 3.00
372 Rick Honeycutt .05
373 Burt Hooton .05
374 *Ken Howell* .05
375 Ken Landreaux .05
376 Candy Maldonado .05
377 Mike Marshall .05
378 Tom Niedenfuer .05
379 Alejandro Pena .05
380 Jerry Reuss .05
381 *R.J. Reynolds* .05
382 German Rivera .05
383 Bill Russell .05
384 Steve Sax .05
385 Mike Scioscia .05
386 *Franklin Stubbs* .05
387 Fernando Valenzuela .05
388 Bob Welch .05
389 Terry Whitfield .05
390 Steve Yeager .05
391 Pat Zachry .05
392 Fred Breining .05
393 Gary Carter 1.00
394 Andre Dawson .25
395 Miguel Dilone .05
396 Dan Driessen .05
397 Doug Flynn .05
398 Terry Francona .05
399 Bill Gullickson .05
400 Bob James .05
401 Charlie Lea .05
402 Bryan Little .05
403 Gary Lucas .05
404 David Palmer .05
405 Tim Raines .05
406 Mike Ramsey .05
407 Jeff Reardon .05
408 Steve Rogers .05
409 Dan Schatzeder .05
410 Bryn Smith .05
411 Mike Stenhouse .05
412 Tim Wallach .05
413 Jim Wohlford .05
414 Bill Almon .05
415 Keith Atherton .05
416 Bruce Bochte .05
417 Tom Burgmeier .05
418 Ray Burris .05
419 Bill Caudill .05
420 Chris Codiroli .05
421 Tim Conroy .05
422 Mike Davis .05
423 Jim Essian .05
424 Mike Heath .05
425 Rickey Henderson 1.00
426 Donnie Hill .05
427 Dave Kingman .05
428 Bill Krueger .05
429 Carney Lansford .05
430 Steve McCatty .05
431 Joe Morgan 1.00
432 Dwayne Murphy .05
433 Tony Phillips .05
434 Lary Sorensen .05
435 Mike Warren .05
436 *Curt Young* .05
437 Luis Aponte .05
438 Chris Bando .05
439 Tony Bernazard .05
440 Bert Blyleven .10
441 Brett Butler .05
442 Ernie Camacho .05
443 Joe Carter .25
444 Carmelo Castillo .05
445 Jamie Easterly .05
446 *Steve Farr* .05
447 Mike Fischlin .05
448 Julio Franco .05
449 Mel Hall .05
450 Mike Hargrove .05
451 Neal Heaton .05
452 Brook Jacoby .05
453 *Mike Jeffcoat* .05
454 *Don Schulze* .05
455 Roy Smith .05
456 Pat Tabler .05
457 Andre Thornton .05
458 George Vukovich .05
459 Tom Waddell .05
460 Jerry Willard .05
461 Dale Berra .05
462 John Candelaria .05
463 Jose DeLeon .05
464 Doug Frobel .05
465 Cecilio Guante .05
466 Brian Harper .05
467 Lee Lacy .05
468 Bill Madlock .05
469 Lee Mazzilli .05
470 Larry McWilliams .05
471 Jim Morrison .05
472 Tony Pena .05
473 Johnny Ray .05
474 Rick Rhoden .05
475 Don Robinson .05
476 Rod Scurry .05
477 Kent Tekulve .05
478 Jason Thompson .05
479 John Tudor .05
480 Lee Tunnell .05
481 Marvell Wynne .05
482 Salome Barojas .05
483 Dave Beard .05
484 Jim Beattie .05
485 Barry Bonnell .05
486 *Phil Bradley* .05
487 Al Cowens .05
488 Alvin Davis .05
489 Dave Henderson .05
490 Steve Henderson .05
491 Bob Kearney .05
492 Mark Langston .15
493 Larry Milbourne .05
494 Paul Mirabella .05
495 Mike Moore .05
496 Edwin Nunez .05
497 Spike Owen .05
498 Jack Perconte .05
499 Ken Phelps .05
500 *Jim Presley* .05
501 Mike Stanton .05
502 Bob Stoddard .05
503 Gorman Thomas .05
504 Ed Vande Berg .05
505 Matt Young .05
506 Juan Agosto .05
507 Harold Baines .05
508 Floyd Bannister .05
509 Britt Burns .05
510 Julio Cruz .05
511 Richard Dotson .05
512 Jerry Dybzinski .05
513 Carlton Fisk 1.00
514 Scott Fletcher .05
515 Jerry Hairston Sr. .05
516 Marc Hill .05
517 LaMarr Hoyt .05
518 Ron Kittle .05
519 Rudy Law .05
520 Vance Law .05
521 Greg Luzinski .05
522 Gene Nelson .05
523 Tom Paciorek .05
524 Ron Reed .05
525 Bert Roberge .05
526 Tom Seaver 1.00
527 Roy Smalley .05
528 Dan Spillner .05
529 Mike Squires .05
530 Greg Walker .05
531 Cesar Cedeno .05
532 Dave Concepcion .05
533 *Eric Davis* 2.00
534 Nick Esasky .05
535 Tom Foley .05
536 John Franco .05
537 Brad Gulden .05
538 Tom Hume .05
539 Wayne Krenchicki .05
540 Andy McGaffigan .05
541 Eddie Milner .05
542 Ron Oester .05
543 Bob Owchinko .05
544 Dave Parker .05
545 Frank Pastore .05
546 Tony Perez .75
547 Ted Power .05
548 Joe Price .05
549 Gary Redus .05
550 Pete Rose 3.00
551 Jeff Russell .05
552 Mario Soto .05
553 *Jay Tibbs* .05
554 Duane Walker .05
555 Alan Bannister .05
556 Buddy Bell .05
557 Danny Darwin .05
558 Charlie Hough .05
559 Bobby Jones .05
560 Odell Jones .05
561 *Jeff Kunkel* .05
562 *Mike Mason* .05
563 Pete O'Brien .05
564 Larry Parrish .05
565 Mickey Rivers .05
566 Billy Sample .05
567 Dave Schmidt .05
568 Donnie Scott .05
569 Dave Stewart .05
570 Frank Tanana .05
571 Wayne Tolleson .05
572 Gary Ward .05
573 Curtis Wilkerson .05
574 George Wright .05
575 Ned Yost .05
576 Mark Brouhard .05
577 Mike Caldwell .05
578 Bobby Clark .05
579 Jaime Cocanower .05
580 Cecil Cooper .05
581 Rollie Fingers .75
582 Jim Gantner .05
583 Moose Haas .05
584 Dion James .05
585 Pete Ladd .05
586 Rick Manning .05
587 Bob McClure .05
588 Paul Molitor 1.00
589 Charlie Moore .05
590 Ben Oglivie .05
591 Chuck Porter .05
592 *Randy Ready* .05
593 Ed Romero .05
594 Bill Schroeder .05
595 Ray Searage .05
596 Ted Simmons .05
597 Jim Sundberg .05
598 Don Sutton .75
599 Tom Tellmann .05
600 Rick Waits .05
601 Robin Yount 1.00
602 Dusty Baker .05
603 Bob Brenly .05
604 Jack Clark .05
605 Chili Davis .05
606 Mark Davis .05
607 *Dan Gladden* .25
608 Atlee Hammaker .05
609 Mike Krukow .05
610 Duane Kuiper .05
611 Bob Lacey .05
612 Bill Laskey .05
613 Gary Lavelle .05
614 Johnnie LeMaster .05
615 Jeff Leonard .05
616 Randy Lerch .05
617 Greg Minton .05
618 Steve Nicosia .05
619 Gene Richards .05
620 *Jeff Robinson* .05
621 Scot Thompson .05
622 Manny Trillo .05
623 Brad Wellman .05
624 *Frank Williams* .05
625 Joel Youngblood .05
626 Cal Ripken, Jr. (In Action) 1.00
627 Mike Schmidt (In Action) .50
628 Sparky Anderson Giving the Signs .05
629 Rickey Henderson, Dave Winfield A.L. Pitcher's Nightmare .50
630 Ryne Sandberg, Mike Schmidt N.L. Pitcher's Nightmare 1.00
631 Gary Carter, Steve Garvey, Ozzie Smith, Darryl Strawberry N.L. All-Stars .25
632 Gary Carter, Charlie Lea All-Star Game Winning Battery .10
633 Steve Garvey, Goose Gossage N.L. Pennant Clinchers .10
634 Dwight Gooden, Juan Samuel N.L. Rookie Phenoms .05
635 Willie Upshaw Toronto's Big Guns .05
636 Lloyd Moseby Toronto's Big Guns .05
637 Al Holland Holland .05
638 Lee Tunnell Tunnell .05
639 Reggie Jackson (In Action) .50
640 Pete Rose (In Action) .75

641	Cal Ripken, Jr., Cal Ripken, Sr. Father & Son	1.00
642	Cubs team	.10
643	Jack Morris, David Palmer, Mike Witt 1984's Two Perfect Games & One No-Hitter	.05
644	Willie Lozado, Vic Mata Major League Prospect	.05
645	*Kelly Gruber, Randy O'Neal* Major League Prospect	.15
646	*Jose Roman, Joel Skinner* Major League Prospect	.05
647	*Steve Kiefer, Danny Tartabull* Major League Prospect	.50
648	*Rob Deer, Alejandro Sanchez* Major League Prospect	.25
649	*Shawon Dunston, Bill Hatcher* Major League Prospect	1.00
650	*Mike Bielecki, Ron Robinson* Major League Prospect	.10
651	*Zane Smith, Paul Zuvella* Major League Prospect	.10
652	*Glenn Davis, Joe Hesketh* Major League Prospect	.20
653	*Steve Jeltz, John Russell* Major League Prospect	.10
654	Checklist 1-95	.05
655	Checklist 96-195	.05
656	Checklist 196-292	.05
657	Checklist 293-391	.05
658	Checklist 392-481	.05
659	Checklist 482-575	.05
660	Checklist 576-660	.05

Update

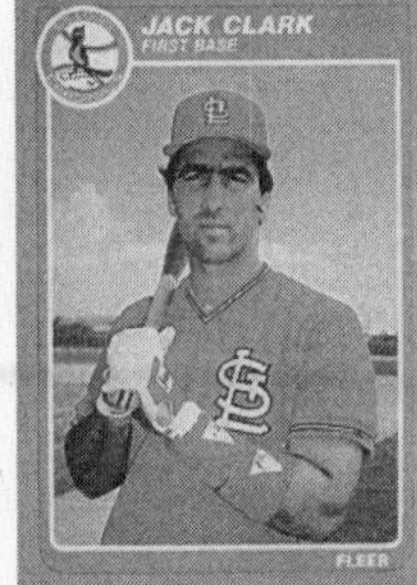

		NM/M
Complete Set (132):		5.00
Common Player:		.10
1	Don Aase	.10
2	Bill Almon	.10
3	Dusty Baker	.10
4	Dale Berra	.10
5	Karl Best	.10
6	Tim Birtsas	.10
7	Vida Blue	.10
8	Rich Bordi	.10
9	Daryl Boston	.10
10	Hubie Brooks	.10
11	Chris Brown	.10
12	Tom Browning	.10
13	Al Bumbry	.10
14	Tim Burke	.10
15	Ray Burris	.10
16	Jeff Burroughs	.10
17	Ivan Calderon	.10
18	Jeff Calhoun	.10
19	Bill Campbell	.10
20	Don Carman	.10
21	Gary Carter	.50
22	Bobby Castillo	.10
23	Bill Caudill	.10
24	Rick Cerone	.10
25	Jack Clark	.10
26	Pat Clements	.10
27	Stewart Cliburn	.10
28	Vince Coleman	.10
29	Dave Collins	.10
30	Fritz Connally	.10
31	Henry Cotto	.10
32	Danny Darwin	.10
33	*Darren Daulton*	1.00
34	Jerry Davis	.10
35	Brian Dayett	.10
36	Ken Dixon	.10
37	Tommy Dunbar	.10
38	Mariano Duncan	.10
39	Bob Fallon	.10
40	Brian Fisher	.10
41	Mike Fitzgerald	.10
42	Ray Fontenot	.10
43	Greg Gagne	.10
44	Oscar Gamble	.10
45	Jim Gott	.10
46	David Green	.10
47	Alfredo Griffin	.10
48	*Ozzie Guillen*	2.00
49	Toby Harrah	.10
50	Ron Hassey	.10
51	Rickey Henderson	3.00
52	Steve Henderson	.10
53	George Hendrick	.10
54	Teddy Higuera	.10
55	Al Holland	.10
56	Burt Hooton	.10
57	Jay Howell	.10
58	LaMarr Hoyt	.10
59	Tim Hulett	.10
60	Bob James	.10
61	Cliff Johnson	.10
62	Howard Johnson	.10
63	Ruppert Jones	.10
64	Steve Kemp	.10
65	Bruce Kison	.10
66	Mike LaCoss	.10
67	Lee Lacy	.10
68	Dave LaPoint	.10
69	Gary Lavelle	.10
70	Vance Law	.10
71	Manny Lee	.10
72	Sixto Lezcano	.10
73	Tim Lollar	.10
74	Urbano Lugo	.10
75	Fred Lynn	.10
76	Steve Lyons	.10
77	Mickey Mahler	.10
78	Ron Mathis	.10
79	Len Matuszek	.10
80	Oddibe McDowell	.10
81	Roger McDowell	.10
82	Donnie Moore	.10
83	Ron Musselman	.10
84	Al Oliver	.10
85	Joe Orsulak	.10
86	Dan Pasqua	.10
87	Chris Pittaro	.10
88	Rick Reuschel	.10
89	Earnie Riles	.10
90	Jerry Royster	.10
91	Dave Rozema	.10
92	Dave Rucker	.10
93	Vern Ruhle	.10
94	Mark Salas	.10
95	Luis Salazar	.10
96	Joe Sambito	.10
97	Billy Sample	.10
98	Alex Sanchez	.10
99	Calvin Schiraldi	.10
100	Rick Schu	.10
101	Larry Sheets	.10
102	Ron Shepherd	.10
103	Nelson Simmons	.10
104	Don Slaught	.10
105	Roy Smalley	.10
106	Lonnie Smith	.10
107	Nate Snell	.10
108	Lary Sorensen	.10
109	Chris Speier	.10
110	Mike Stenhouse	.10
111	Tim Stoddard	.10
112	John Stuper	.10
113	Jim Sundberg	.10
114	Bruce Sutter	.40
115	Don Sutton	.50
116	Bruce Tanner	.10
117	Kent Tekulve	.10
118	Walt Terrell	.10
119	*Mickey Tettleton*	1.00
120	Rich Thompson	.10
121	Louis Thornton	.10
122	Alex Trevino	.10
123	John Tudor	.10
124	Jose Uribe	.10
125	Dave Valle	.10
126	Dave Von Ohlen	.10
127	Curt Wardle	.10
128	U.L. Washington	.10
129	Ed Whitson	.10
130	Herm Winningham	.10
131	Rich Yett	.10
132	Checklist	.10

1986 FLEER

		NM/M
Unopened Fact. Set (660):		30.00
Complete Set (660):		25.00
Common Player:		.05
Wax Pack (15):		1.50
Wax Box (36):		35.00
Cello Pack (28):		2.00
Cello Box (24):		35.00
Rack Pack (45):		4.00
Rack Box (24):		60.00
1	Steve Balboni	.05
2	Joe Beckwith	.05
3	Buddy Biancalana	.05
4	Bud Black	.05
5	George Brett	2.00
6	Onix Concepcion	.05
7	Steve Farr	.05
8	Mark Gubicza	.05
9	Dane Iorg	.05
10	Danny Jackson	.05
11	Lynn Jones	.05
12	Mike Jones	.05
13	Charlie Leibrandt	.05
14	Hal McRae	.05
15	Omar Moreno	.05
16	Darryl Motley	.05
17	Jorge Orta	.05
18	Dan Quisenberry	.05
19	Bret Saberhagen	.05
20	Pat Sheridan	.05
21	Lonnie Smith	.05
22	Jim Sundberg	.05
23	John Wathan	.05
24	Frank White	.05
25	Willie Wilson	.05
26	Joaquin Andujar	.05
27	Steve Braun	.05
28	Bill Campbell	.05
29	Cesar Cedeno	.05
30	Jack Clark	.05
31	Vince Coleman	.05
32	Danny Cox	.05
33	Ken Dayley	.05
34	Ivan DeJesus	.05
35	Bob Forsch	.05
36	Brian Harper	.05
37	Tom Herr	.05
38	Ricky Horton	.05
39	Kurt Kepshire	.05
40	Jeff Lahti	.05
41	Tito Landrum	.05
42	Willie McGee	.05
43	Tom Nieto	.05
44	Terry Pendleton	.05
45	Darrell Porter	.05
46	Ozzie Smith	1.50
47	John Tudor	.05
48	Andy Van Slyke	.05
49	*Todd Worrell*	.25
50	Jim Acker	.05
51	Doyle Alexander	.05
52	Jesse Barfield	.05
53	George Bell	.05
54	Jeff Burroughs	.05
55	Bill Caudill	.05
56	Jim Clancy	.05
57	Tony Fernandez	.05
58	Tom Filer	.05
59	Damaso Garcia	.05
60	Tom Henke	.05
61	Garth Iorg	.05
62	Cliff Johnson	.05
63	Jimmy Key	.05
64	Dennis Lamp	.05
65	Gary Lavelle	.05
66	Buck Martinez	.05
67	Lloyd Moseby	.05
68	Rance Mulliniks	.05
69	Al Oliver	.05
70	Dave Stieb	.05
71	Louis Thornton	.05
72	Willie Upshaw	.05
73	Ernie Whitt	.05
74	*Rick Aguilera*	.75
75	Wally Backman	.05
76	Gary Carter	1.00
77	Ron Darling	.05
78	*Len Dykstra*	2.00
79	Sid Fernandez	.05
80	George Foster	.05
81	Dwight Gooden	.05
82	Tom Gorman	.05
83	Danny Heep	.05
84	Keith Hernandez	.05
85	Howard Johnson	.05
86	Ray Knight	.05
87	Terry Leach	.05
88	Ed Lynch	.05
89	Roger McDowell	.05
90	Jesse Orosco	.05
91	Tom Paciorek	.05
92	Ronn Reynolds	.05
93	Rafael Santana	.05
94	Doug Sisk	.05
95	Rusty Staub	.05
96	Darryl Strawberry	.05
97	Mookie Wilson	.05
98	Neil Allen	.05
99	Don Baylor	.05
100	Dale Berra	.05
101	Rich Bordi	.05
102	Marty Bystrom	.05
103	Joe Cowley	.05
104	*Brian Fisher*	.05
105	Ken Griffey	.05
106	Ron Guidry	.10
107	Ron Hassey	.05
108	Rickey Henderson	1.00
109	Don Mattingly	2.00
110	Bobby Meacham	.05
111	John Montefusco	.05
112	Phil Niekro	.75
113	Mike Pagliarulo	.05
114	Dan Pasqua	.05
115	Willie Randolph	.05
116	Dave Righetti	.05
117	Andre Robertson	.05
118	Billy Sample	.05
119	Bob Shirley	.05
120	Ed Whitson	.05
121	Dave Winfield	1.00
122	Butch Wynegar	.05
123	Dave Anderson	.05
124	Bob Bailor	.05
125	Greg Brock	.05
126	Enos Cabell	.05
127	Bobby Castillo	.05
128	Carlos Diaz	.05
129	Mariano Duncan	.05
130	Pedro Guerrero	.05
131	Orel Hershiser	.05
132	Rick Honeycutt	.05
133	Ken Howell	.05
134	Ken Landreaux	.05
135	Bill Madlock	.05
136	Candy Maldonado	.05
137	Mike Marshall	.05
138	Len Matuszek	.05
139	Tom Niedenfuer	.05
140	Alejandro Pena	.05
141	Jerry Reuss	.05
142	Bill Russell	.05
143	Steve Sax	.05
144	Mike Scioscia	.05
145	Fernando Valenzuela	.05
146	Bob Welch	.05
147	Terry Whitfield	.05
148	Juan Beniquez	.05
149	Bob Boone	.05
150	John Candelaria	.05
151	Rod Carew	1.00
152	*Stewart Cliburn*	.05
153	Doug DeCinces	.05
154	Brian Downing	.05
155	Ken Forsch	.05
156	Craig Gerber	.05
157	Bobby Grich	.05
158	George Hendrick	.05
159	Al Holland	.05
160	Reggie Jackson	1.50
161	Ruppert Jones	.05
162	*Urbano Lugo*	.05
163	*Kirk McCaskill*	.25
164	Donnie Moore	.05
165	Gary Pettis	.05
166	Ron Romanick	.05
167	Dick Schofield	.05
168	Daryl Sconiers	.05
169	Jim Slaton	.05
170	Don Sutton	.75
171	Mike Witt	.05
172	Buddy Bell	.05

No.	Player	Value
173	Tom Browning	.05
174	Dave Concepcion	.05
175	Eric Davis	.05
176	Bo Diaz	.05
177	Nick Esasky	.05
178	John Franco	.05
179	Tom Hume	.05
180	Wayne Krenchicki	.05
181	Andy McGaffigan	.05
182	Eddie Milner	.05
183	Ron Oester	.05
184	Dave Parker	.05
185	Frank Pastore	.05
186	Tony Perez	.75
187	Ted Power	.05
188	Joe Price	.05
189	Gary Redus	.05
190	Ron Robinson	.05
191	Pete Rose	2.50
192	Mario Soto	.05
193	John Stuper	.05
194	Jay Tibbs	.05
195	Dave Van Gorder	.05
196	Max Venable	.05
197	Juan Agosto	.05
198	Harold Baines	.05
199	Floyd Bannister	.05
200	Britt Burns	.05
201	Julio Cruz	.05
202	*Joel Davis*	.05
203	Richard Dotson	.05
204	Carlton Fisk	1.00
205	Scott Fletcher	.05
206	Ozzie Guillen	.05
207	Jerry Hairston Sr.	.05
208	Tim Hulett	.05
209	Bob James	.05
210	Ron Kittle	.05
211	Rudy Law	.05
212	Bryan Little	.05
213	Gene Nelson	.05
214	Reid Nichols	.05
215	Luis Salazar	.05
216	Tom Seaver	1.00
217	Dan Spillner	.05
218	Bruce Tanner	.05
219	Greg Walker	.05
220	Dave Wehrmeister	.05
221	Juan Berenguer	.05
222	Dave Bergman	.05
223	Tom Brookens	.05
224	Darrell Evans	.05
225	Barbaro Garbey	.05
226	Kirk Gibson	.05
227	John Grubb	.05
228	Willie Hernandez	.05
229	Larry Herndon	.05
230	Chet Lemon	.05
231	Aurelio Lopez	.05
232	Jack Morris	.05
233	Randy O'Neal	.05
234	Lance Parrish	.05
235	Dan Petry	.05
236	Alex Sanchez	.05
237	Bill Scherrer	.05
238	Nelson Simmons	.05
239	Frank Tanana	.05
240	Walt Terrell	.05
241	Alan Trammell	.05
242	Lou Whitaker	.05
243	Milt Wilcox	.05
244	Hubie Brooks	.05
245	*Tim Burke*	.05
246	Andre Dawson	.35
247	Mike Fitzgerald	.05
248	Terry Francona	.05
249	Bill Gullickson	.05
250	Joe Hesketh	.05
251	Bill Laskey	.05
252	Vance Law	.05
253	Charlie Lea	.05
254	Gary Lucas	.05
255	David Palmer	.05
256	Tim Raines	.05
257	Jeff Reardon	.05
258	Bert Roberge	.05
259	Dan Schatzeder	.05
260	Bryn Smith	.05
261	Randy St. Claire	.05
262	Scot Thompson	.05
263	Tim Wallach	.05
264	U.L. Washington	.05
265	*Mitch Webster*	.05
266	*Herm Winningham*	.05
267	*Floyd Youmans*	.05
268	Don Aase	.05
269	Mike Boddicker	.05
270	Rich Dauer	.05
271	Storm Davis	.05
272	Rick Dempsey	.05
273	Ken Dixon	.05
274	Jim Dwyer	.05
275	Mike Flanagan	.05
276	Wayne Gross	.05
277	Lee Lacy	.05
278	Fred Lynn	.05
279	Tippy Martinez	.05
280	Dennis Martinez	.05
281	Scott McGregor	.05
282	Eddie Murray	1.00
283	Floyd Rayford	.05
284	Cal Ripken, Jr.	3.00
285	Gary Roenicke	.05
286	Larry Sheets	.05
287	John Shelby	.05
288	Nate Snell	.05
289	Sammy Stewart	.05
290	Alan Wiggins	.05
291	Mike Young	.05
292	Alan Ashby	.05
293	Mark Bailey	.05
294	Kevin Bass	.05
295	Jeff Calhoun	.05
296	Jose Cruz	.05
297	Glenn Davis	.05
298	Bill Dawley	.05
299	Frank DiPino	.05
300	Bill Doran	.05
301	Phil Garner	.05
302	*Jeff Heathcock*	.05
303	*Charlie Kerfeld*	.05
304	Bob Knepper	.05
305	Ron Mathis	.05
306	Jerry Mumphrey	.05
307	Jim Pankovits	.05
308	Terry Puhl	.05
309	Craig Reynolds	.05
310	Nolan Ryan	3.00
311	Mike Scott	.05
312	Dave Smith	.05
313	Dickie Thon	.05
314	Denny Walling	.05
315	Kurt Bevacqua	.05
316	Al Bumbry	.05
317	Jerry Davis	.05
318	Luis DeLeon	.05
319	Dave Dravecky	.05
320	Tim Flannery	.05
321	Steve Garvey	.30
322	Goose Gossage	.05
323	Tony Gwynn	1.50
324	Andy Hawkins	.05
325	LaMarr Hoyt	.05
326	Roy Lee Jackson	.05
327	Terry Kennedy	.05
328	Craig Lefferts	.05
329	Carmelo Martinez	.05
330	*Lance McCullers*	.05
331	Kevin McReynolds	.05
332	Graig Nettles	.05
333	Jerry Royster	.05
334	Eric Show	.05
335	Tim Stoddard	.05
336	Garry Templeton	.05
337	Mark Thurmond	.05
338	Ed Wojna	.05
339	Tony Armas	.05
340	Marty Barrett	.05
341	Wade Boggs	1.50
342	Dennis Boyd	.05
343	Bill Buckner	.05
344	Mark Clear	.05
345	Roger Clemens	2.00
346	Steve Crawford	.05
347	Mike Easler	.05
348	Dwight Evans	.05
349	Rich Gedman	.05
350	Jackie Gutierrez	.05
351	Glenn Hoffman	.05
352	Bruce Hurst	.05
353	Bruce Kison	.05
354	Tim Lollar	.05
355	Steve Lyons	.05
356	Al Nipper	.05
357	Bob Ojeda	.05
358	Jim Rice	.30
359	Bob Stanley	.05
360	Mike Trujillo	.05
361	Thad Bosley	.05
362	Warren Brusstar	.05
363	Ron Cey	.05
364	Jody Davis	.05
365	Bob Dernier	.05
366	Shawon Dunston	.05
367	Leon Durham	.05
368	Dennis Eckersley	.75
369	Ray Fontenot	.05
370	George Frazier	.05
371	Bill Hatcher	.05
372	Dave Lopes	.05
373	Gary Matthews	.05
374	Ron Meredith	.05
375	Keith Moreland	.05
376	Reggie Patterson	.05
377	Dick Ruthven	.05
378	Ryne Sandberg	1.50
379	Scott Sanderson	.05
380	Lee Smith	.05
381	Lary Sorensen	.05
382	Chris Speier	.05
383	Rick Sutcliffe	.05
384	Steve Trout	.05
385	Gary Woods	.05
386	Bert Blyleven	.10
387	Tom Brunansky	.05
388	Randy Bush	.05
389	John Butcher	.05
390	Ron Davis	.05
391	Dave Engle	.05
392	Frank Eufemia	.05
393	Pete Filson	.05
394	Gary Gaetti	.05
395	Greg Gagne	.05
396	Mickey Hatcher	.05
397	Kent Hrbek	.05
398	Tim Laudner	.05
399	Rick Lysander	.05
400	Dave Meier	.05
401	Kirby Puckett	1.50
402	Mark Salas	.05
403	Ken Schrom	.05
404	Roy Smalley	.05
405	Mike Smithson	.05
406	Mike Stenhouse	.05
407	Tim Teufel	.05
408	Frank Viola	.05
409	Ron Washington	.05
410	Keith Atherton	.05
411	Dusty Baker	.05
412	*Tim Birtsas*	.05
413	Bruce Bochte	.05
414	Chris Codiroli	.05
415	Dave Collins	.05
416	Mike Davis	.05
417	Alfredo Griffin	.05
418	Mike Heath	.05
419	Steve Henderson	.05
420	Donnie Hill	.05
421	Jay Howell	.05
422	Tommy John	.10
423	Dave Kingman	.05
424	Bill Krueger	.05
425	Rick Langford	.05
426	Carney Lansford	.05
427	Steve McCatty	.05
428	Dwayne Murphy	.05
429	*Steve Ontiveros*	.05
430	Tony Phillips	.05
431	Jose Rijo	.05
432	Mickey Tettleton	.05
433	Luis Aguayo	.05
434	Larry Andersen	.05
435	Steve Carlton	1.00
436	*Don Carman*	.05
437	Tim Corcoran	.05
438	Darren Daulton	.05
439	John Denny	.05
440	Tom Foley	.05
441	Greg Gross	.05
442	Kevin Gross	.05
443	Von Hayes	.05
444	Charles Hudson	.05
445	Garry Maddox	.05
446	Shane Rawley	.05
447	Dave Rucker	.05
448	John Russell	.05
449	Juan Samuel	.05
450	Mike Schmidt	2.00
451	Rick Schu	.05
452	Dave Shipanoff	.05
453	Dave Stewart	.05
454	Jeff Stone	.05
455	Kent Tekulve	.05
456	Ozzie Virgil	.05
457	Glenn Wilson	.05
458	Jim Beattie	.05
459	Karl Best	.05
460	Barry Bonnell	.05
461	Phil Bradley	.05
462	*Ivan Calderon*	.05
463	Al Cowens	.05
464	Alvin Davis	.05
465	Dave Henderson	.05
466	Bob Kearney	.05
467	Mark Langston	.05
468	Bob Long	.05
469	Mike Moore	.05
470	Edwin Nunez	.05
471	Spike Owen	.05
472	Jack Perconte	.05
473	Jim Presley	.05
474	Donnie Scott	.05
475	Bill Swift	.05
476	Danny Tartabull	.05
477	Gorman Thomas	.05
478	Roy Thomas	.05
479	Ed Vande Berg	.05
480	Frank Wills	.05
481	Matt Young	.05
482	Ray Burris	.05
483	Jaime Cocanower	.05
484	Cecil Cooper	.05
485	Danny Darwin	.05
486	Rollie Fingers	.75
487	Jim Gantner	.05
488	Bob Gibson	.05
489	Moose Haas	.05
490	*Teddy Higuera*	.05
491	Paul Householder	.05
492	Pete Ladd	.05
493	Rick Manning	.05
494	Bob McClure	.05
495	Paul Molitor	1.00
496	Charlie Moore	.05
497	Ben Oglivie	.05
498	Randy Ready	.05
499	*Earnie Riles*	.05
500	Ed Romero	.05
501	Bill Schroeder	.05
502	Ray Searage	.05
503	Ted Simmons	.05
504	Pete Vuckovich	.05
505	Rick Waits	.05
506	Robin Yount	1.00
507	Len Barker	.05
508	Steve Bedrosian	.05
509	Bruce Benedict	.05
510	Rick Camp	.05
511	Rick Cerone	.05
512	Chris Chambliss	.05
513	Jeff Dedmon	.05
514	Terry Forster	.05
515	Gene Garber	.05
516	Terry Harper	.05
517	Bob Horner	.05
518	Glenn Hubbard	.05
519	*Joe Johnson*	.05
520	Brad Komminsk	.05
521	Rick Mahler	.05
522	Dale Murphy	.30
523	Ken Oberkfell	.05
524	Pascual Perez	.05
525	Gerald Perry	.05
526	Rafael Ramirez	.05
527	*Steve Shields*	.05
528	Zane Smith	.05
529	Bruce Sutter	.75
530	*Milt Thompson*	.05
531	Claudell Washington	.05
532	Paul Zuvella	.05
533	Vida Blue	.05
534	Bob Brenly	.05
535	*Chris Brown*	.05
536	Chili Davis	.05
537	Mark Davis	.05
538	Rob Deer	.05
539	Dan Driessen	.05
540	Scott Garrelts	.05
541	Dan Gladden	.05
542	Jim Gott	.05
543	David Green	.05
544	Atlee Hammaker	.05
545	Mike Jeffcoat	.05
546	Mike Krukow	.05
547	Dave LaPoint	.05
548	Jeff Leonard	.05
549	Greg Minton	.05
550	Alex Trevino	.05
551	Manny Trillo	.05
552	*Jose Uribe*	.05
553	Brad Wellman	.05
554	Frank Williams	.05
555	Joel Youngblood	.05
556	Alan Bannister	.05
557	Glenn Brummer	.05
558	*Steve Buechele*	.05
559	*Jose Guzman*	.05
560	Toby Harrah	.05
561	Greg Harris	.05
562	*Dwayne Henry*	.05
563	Burt Hooton	.05
564	Charlie Hough	.05
565	Mike Mason	.05
566	*Oddibe McDowell*	.05
567	Dickie Noles	.05
568	Pete O'Brien	.05

No.	Player	Price
569	Larry Parrish	.05
570	Dave Rozema	.05
571	Dave Schmidt	.05
572	Don Slaught	.05
573	Wayne Tolleson	.05
574	Duane Walker	.05
575	Gary Ward	.05
576	Chris Welsh	.05
577	Curtis Wilkerson	.05
578	George Wright	.05
579	Chris Bando	.05
580	Tony Bernazard	.05
581	Brett Butler	.05
582	Ernie Camacho	.05
583	Joe Carter	.05
584	Carmello Castillo (Carmelo)	.05
585	Jamie Easterly	.05
586	Julio Franco	.05
587	Mel Hall	.05
588	Mike Hargrove	.05
589	Neal Heaton	.05
590	Brook Jacoby	.05
591	*Otis Nixon*	.25
592	Jerry Reed	.05
593	Vern Ruhle	.05
594	Pat Tabler	.05
595	Rich Thompson	.05
596	Andre Thornton	.05
597	Dave Von Ohlen	.05
598	George Vukovich	.05
599	Tom Waddell	.05
600	Curt Wardle	.05
601	Jerry Willard	.05
602	Bill Almon	.05
603	Mike Bielecki	.05
604	Sid Bream	.05
605	Mike Brown	.05
606	*Pat Clements*	.05
607	Jose DeLeon	.05
608	Denny Gonzalez	.05
609	Cecilio Guante	.05
610	Steve Kemp	.05
611	Sam Khalifa	.05
612	Lee Mazzilli	.05
613	Larry McWilliams	.05
614	Jim Morrison	.05
615	*Joe Orsulak*	.25
616	Tony Pena	.05
617	Johnny Ray	.05
618	Rick Reuschel	.05
619	R.J. Reynolds	.05
620	Rick Rhoden	.05
621	Don Robinson	.05
622	Jason Thompson	.05
623	Lee Tunnell	.05
624	Jim Winn	.05
625	Marvell Wynne	.05
626	Dwight Gooden (In Action)	.05
627	Don Mattingly (In Action)	.50
628	Pete Rose (4,192 hits)	1.00
629	Rod Carew (3,000 Hits)	.25
630	Phil Niekro, Tom Seaver (300 Wins)	.25
631	Don Baylor Ouch!	.05
632	Tim Raines, Darryl Strawberry Instant Offense	.05
633	Cal Ripken, Jr., Alan Trammell Shortstops Supreme	1.00
634	Wade Boggs, George Brett Boggs & "Hero"	1.00
635	Bob Horner, Dale Murphy Braves Dynamic Duo	.25
636	Vince Coleman, Willie McGee Cardinal Ignitors	.25
637	Vince Coleman Terror on the Basepaths	.05
638	Dwight Gooden, Pete Rose Charlie Hustle & Dr. K	.50
639	Wade Boggs, Don Mattingly 1984 and 1985 A.L. Batting Champs	1.00
640	Steve Garvey, Dale Murphy, Dave Parker N.L. West Sluggers	.25
641	Dwight Gooden, Fernando Valenzuela Staff Aces	.10
642	Jimmy Key, Dave Stieb Blue Jay Stoppers	.05
643	Carlton Fisk, Rich Gedman A.L. All-Star Backstops	.10
644	*Benito Santiago, Gene Walter* Major League Prospect	1.00
645	*Colin Ward, Mike Woodard* Major League Prospect	.10
646	*Kal Daniels, Paul O'Neill* Major League Prospect	2.00
647	*Andres Galarraga, Fred Toliver* Major League Prospect	3.00
648	*Curt Ford, Bob Kipper* Major League Prospect	.10
649	*Jose Canseco, Eric Plunk* Major League Prospect	5.00
650	*Mark McLemore, Gus Polidor* Major League Prospect	.75
651	*Mickey Brantley, Rob Woodward* Major League Prospect	.10
652	*Mark Funderburk, Billy Joe Robidoux* Major League Prospect	.10
653	*Cecil Fielder, Cory Snyder* Major League Prospect	1.50
654	Checklist 1-97	.05
655	Checklist 98-196	.05
656	Checklist 197-291	.05
657	Checklist 292-385	.05
658	Checklist 386-482	.05
659	Checklist 483-578	.05
660	Checklist 579-660	.05

Update

		NM/M
	Unopened Fact. Set (132):	60.00
	Complete Set (132):	50.00
	Common Player:	.05
1	Mike Aldrete	.05
2	Andy Allanson	.05
3	Neil Allen	.05
4	Joaquin Andujar	.05
5	Paul Assenmacher	.05
6	Scott Bailes	.05
7	Jay Baller	.05
8	Scott Bankhead	.05
9	Bill Bathe	.05
10	Don Baylor	.05
11	Billy Beane	.05
12	Steve Bedrosian	.05
13	Juan Beniquez	.05
14	*Barry Bonds*	45.00
15	*Bobby Bonilla*	1.00
16	Rich Bordi	.05
17	Bill Campbell	.05
18	Tom Candiotti	.05
19	John Cangelosi	.05
20	Jose Canseco	4.00
21	Chuck Cary	.05
22	Juan Castillo	.05
23	Rick Cerone	.05
24	John Cerutti	.05
25	*Will Clark*	1.00
26	Mark Clear	.05
27	Darnell Coles	.05
28	Dave Collins	.05
29	Tim Conroy	.05
30	Ed Correa	.05
31	Joe Cowley	.05
32	Bill Dawley	.05
33	Rob Deer	.05
34	John Denny	.05
35	Jim DeShaies	.05
36	*Doug Drabek*	1.00
37	Mike Easler	.05
38	Mark Eichhorn	.05
39	Dave Engle	.05
40	Mike Fischlin	.05
41	Scott Fletcher	.05
42	Terry Forster	.05
43	Terry Francona	.05
44	Andres Galarraga	.50
45	Lee Guetterman	.05
46	Bill Gullickson	.05
47	Jackie Gutierrez	.05
48	Moose Haas	.05
49	Billy Hatcher	.05
50	Mike Heath	.05
51	Guy Hoffman	.05
52	Tom Hume	.05
53	*Pete Incaviglia*	.50
54	Dane Iorg	.05
55	Chris James	.05
56	Stan Javier	.05
57	Tommy John	.15
58	Tracy Jones	.05
59	*Wally Joyner*	1.00
60	Wayne Krenchicki	.05
61	*John Kruk*	1.00
62	Mike LaCoss	.05
63	Pete Ladd	.05
64	Dave LaPoint	.05
65	Mike LaValliere	.05
66	Rudy Law	.05
67	Dennis Leonard	.05
68	Steve Lombardozzi	.05
69	Aurelio Lopez	.05
70	Mickey Mahler	.05
71	Candy Maldonado	.05
72	Roger Mason	.05
73	Greg Mathews	.05
74	Andy McGaffigan	.05
75	Joel McKeon	.05
76	*Kevin Mitchell*	.50
77	Bill Mooneyham	.05
78	Omar Moreno	.05
79	Jerry Mumphrey	.05
80	Al Newman	.05
81	Phil Niekro	.50
82	Randy Niemann	.05
83	Juan Nieves	.05
84	Bob Ojeda	.05
85	Rick Ownbey	.05
86	Tom Paciorek	.05
87	David Palmer	.05
88	Jeff Parrett	.05
89	Pat Perry	.05
90	Dan Plesac	.05
91	Darrell Porter	.05
92	Luis Quinones	.05
93	Rey Quinonez	.05
94	Gary Redus	.05
95	Jeff Reed	.05
96	Bip Roberts	.05
97	Billy Joe Robidoux	.05
98	Gary Roenicke	.05
99	Ron Roenicke	.05
100	Angel Salazar	.05
101	Joe Sambito	.05
102	Billy Sample	.05
103	Dave Schmidt	.05
104	Ken Schrom	.05
105	*Ruben Sierra*	.75
106	Ted Simmons	.05
107	Sammy Stewart	.05
108	Kurt Stillwell	.05
109	Dale Sveum	.05
110	Tim Teufel	.05
111	Bob Tewksbury	.05
112	Andres Thomas	.05
113	Jason Thompson	.05
114	Milt Thompson	.05
115	Rob Thompson	.05
116	Jay Tibbs	.05
117	Fred Toliver	.05
118	Wayne Tolleson	.05
119	Alex Trevino	.05
120	Manny Trillo	.05
121	Ed Vande Berg	.05
122	Ozzie Virgil	.05
123	Tony Walker	.05
124	Gene Walter	.05
125	Duane Ward	.05
126	Jerry Willard	.05
127	Mitch Williams	.05
128	Reggie Williams	.05
129	Bobby Witt	.05
130	Marvell Wynne	.05
131	Steve Yeager	.05
132	Checklist	.05

1987 FLEER

		NM/M
	Unopened Fact. Set (672):	75.00
	Complete Set (660):	70.00
	Common Player:	.05
	Wax Pack (15/17):	3.00
	Wax Box (36):	100.00
	Cello Pack (28):	5.00
	Cello Box (24):	120.00
	Rack Pack (51):	10.00
	Rack Box (24):	200.00
1	Rick Aguilera	.05
2	Richard Anderson	.05
3	Wally Backman	.05
4	Gary Carter	.75
5	Ron Darling	.05
6	Len Dykstra	.05
7	*Kevin Elster*	.15
8	Sid Fernandez	.05
9	Dwight Gooden	.05
10	*Ed Hearn*	.05
11	Danny Heep	.05
12	Keith Hernandez	.05
13	Howard Johnson	.05
14	Ray Knight	.05
15	Lee Mazzilli	.05
16	Roger McDowell	.05
17	Kevin Mitchell	.05
18	Randy Niemann	.05
19	Bob Ojeda	.05
20	Jesse Orosco	.05
21	Rafael Santana	.05
22	Doug Sisk	.05
23	Darryl Strawberry	.05
24	Tim Teufel	.05
25	Mookie Wilson	.05
26	Tony Armas	.05
27	Marty Barrett	.05
28	Don Baylor	.05
29	Wade Boggs	1.00
30	Oil Can Boyd	.05
31	Bill Buckner	.05
32	Roger Clemens	2.00
33	Steve Crawford	.05
34	Dwight Evans	.05
35	Rich Gedman	.05
36	Dave Henderson	.05
37	Bruce Hurst	.05
38	Tim Lollar	.05
39	Al Nipper	.05
40	Spike Owen	.05
41	Jim Rice	.30
42	Ed Romero	.05
43	Joe Sambito	.05
44	Calvin Schiraldi	.05
45	Tom Seaver	.75
46	*Jeff Sellers*	.05
47	Bob Stanley	.05
48	Sammy Stewart	.05
49	Larry Andersen	.05
50	Alan Ashby	.05
51	Kevin Bass	.05
52	Jeff Calhoun	.05
53	Jose Cruz	.05
54	Danny Darwin	.05
55	Glenn Davis	.05
56	*Jim Deshaies*	.10
57	Bill Doran	.05
58	Phil Garner	.05
59	Billy Hatcher	.05
60	Charlie Kerfeld	.05
61	Bob Knepper	.05
62	Dave Lopes	.05
63	Aurelio Lopez	.05
64	Jim Pankovits	.05
65	Terry Puhl	.05
66	Craig Reynolds	.05
67	Nolan Ryan	3.00
68	Mike Scott	.05
69	Dave Smith	.05
70	Dickie Thon	.05
71	Tony Walker	.05
72	Denny Walling	.05
73	Bob Boone	.05
74	Rick Burleson	.05
75	John Candelaria	.05
76	Doug Corbett	.05
77	Doug DeCinces	.05
78	Brian Downing	.05
79	*Chuck Finley*	1.00
80	Terry Forster	.05
81	Bobby Grich	.05

No.	Player	Price
82	George Hendrick	.05
83	Jack Howell	.05
84	Reggie Jackson	1.00
85	Ruppert Jones	.05
86	Wally Joyner	.05
87	Gary Lucas	.05
88	Kirk McCaskill	.05
89	Donnie Moore	.05
90	Gary Pettis	.05
91	Vern Ruhle	.05
92	Dick Schofield	.05
93	Don Sutton	.65
94	Rob Wilfong	.05
95	Mike Witt	.05
96	Doug Drabek	.05
97	Mike Easler	.05
98	Mike Fischlin	.05
99	Brian Fisher	.05
100	Ron Guidry	.10
101	Rickey Henderson	.75
102	Tommy John	.10
103	Ron Kittle	.05
104	Don Mattingly	2.00
105	Bobby Meacham	.05
106	Joe Niekro	.05
107	Mike Pagliarulo	.05
108	Dan Pasqua	.05
109	Willie Randolph	.05
110	Dennis Rasmussen	.05
111	Dave Righetti	.05
112	Gary Roenicke	.05
113	Rod Scurry	.05
114	Bob Shirley	.05
115	Joel Skinner	.05
116	Tim Stoddard	.05
117	*Bob Tewksbury*	.35
118	Wayne Tolleson	.05
119	Claudell Washington	.05
120	Dave Winfield	.75
121	Steve Buechele	.05
122	*Ed Correa*	.05
123	Scott Fletcher	.05
124	Jose Guzman	.05
125	Toby Harrah	.05
126	Greg Harris	.05
127	Charlie Hough	.05
128	Pete Incaviglia	.05
129	Mike Mason	.05
130	Oddibe McDowell	.05
131	*Dale Mohorcic*	.05
132	Pete O'Brien	.05
133	Tom Paciorek	.05
134	Larry Parrish	.05
135	Geno Petralli	.05
136	Darrell Porter	.05
137	Jeff Russell	.05
138	Ruben Sierra	.05
139	Don Slaught	.05
140	Gary Ward	.05
141	Curtis Wilkerson	.05
142	*Mitch Williams*	.10
143	*Bobby Witt*	.10
144	Dave Bergman	.05
145	Tom Brookens	.05
146	Bill Campbell	.05
147	*Chuck Cary*	.05
148	Darnell Coles	.05
149	Dave Collins	.05
150	Darrell Evans	.05
151	Kirk Gibson	.05
152	John Grubb	.05
153	Willie Hernandez	.05
154	Larry Herndon	.05
155	*Eric King*	.05
156	Chet Lemon	.05
157	Dwight Lowry	.05
158	Jack Morris	.05
159	Randy O'Neal	.05
160	Lance Parrish	.05
161	Dan Petry	.05
162	Pat Sheridan	.05
163	Jim Slaton	.05
164	Frank Tanana	.05
165	Walt Terrell	.05
166	Mark Thurmond	.05
167	Alan Trammell	.05
168	Lou Whitaker	.05
169	Luis Aguayo	.05
170	Steve Bedrosian	.05
171	Don Carman	.05
172	Darren Daulton	.05
173	Greg Gross	.05
174	Kevin Gross	.05
175	Von Hayes	.05
176	Charles Hudson	.05
177	Tom Hume	.05
178	Steve Jeltz	.05
179	*Mike Maddux*	.05
180	Shane Rawley	.05
181	Gary Redus	.05
182	Ron Roenicke	.05
183	*Bruce Ruffin*	.10
184	John Russell	.05
185	Juan Samuel	.05
186	Dan Schatzeder	.05
187	Mike Schmidt	2.00
188	Rick Schu	.05
189	Jeff Stone	.05
190	Kent Tekulve	.05
191	Milt Thompson	.05
192	Glenn Wilson	.05
193	Buddy Bell	.05
194	Tom Browning	.05
195	Sal Butera	.05
196	Dave Concepcion	.05
197	Kal Daniels	.05
198	Eric Davis	.05
199	John Denny	.05
200	Bo Diaz	.05
201	Nick Esasky	.05
202	John Franco	.05
203	Bill Gullickson	.05
204	*Barry Larkin*	2.00
205	Eddie Milner	.05
206	*Rob Murphy*	.05
207	Ron Oester	.05
208	Dave Parker	.05
209	Tony Perez	.65
210	Ted Power	.05
211	Joe Price	.05
212	Ron Robinson	.05
213	Pete Rose	2.50
214	Mario Soto	.05
215	*Kurt Stillwell*	.05
216	Max Venable	.05
217	Chris Welsh	.05
218	*Carl Willis*	.05
219	Jesse Barfield	.05
220	George Bell	.05
221	Bill Caudill	.05
222	*John Cerutti*	.05
223	Jim Clancy	.05
224	*Mark Eichhorn*	.10
225	Tony Fernandez	.05
226	Damaso Garcia	.05
227	Kelly Gruber	.05
228	Tom Henke	.05
229	Garth Iorg	.05
230	Cliff Johnson	.05
231	Joe Johnson	.05
232	Jimmy Key	.05
233	Dennis Lamp	.05
234	Rick Leach	.05
235	Buck Martinez	.05
236	Lloyd Moseby	.05
237	Rance Mulliniks	.05
238	Dave Stieb	.05
239	Willie Upshaw	.05
240	Ernie Whitt	.05
241	*Andy Allanson*	.05
242	*Scott Bailes*	.05
243	Chris Bando	.05
244	Tony Bernazard	.05
245	John Butcher	.05
246	Brett Butler	.05
247	Ernie Camacho	.05
248	Tom Candiotti	.05
249	Joe Carter	.05
250	Carmen Castillo	.05
251	Julio Franco	.05
252	Mel Hall	.05
253	Brook Jacoby	.05
254	Phil Niekro	.65
255	Otis Nixon	.05
256	Dickie Noles	.05
257	Bryan Oelkers	.05
258	Ken Schrom	.05
259	Don Schulze	.05
260	Cory Snyder	.05
261	Pat Tabler	.05
262	Andre Thornton	.05
263	*Rich Yett*	.05
264	*Mike Aldrete*	.05
265	Juan Berenguer	.05
266	Vida Blue	.05
267	Bob Brenly	.05
268	Chris Brown	.05
269	Will Clark	.05
270	Chili Davis	.05
271	Mark Davis	.05
272	*Kelly Downs*	.05
273	Scott Garrelts	.05
274	Dan Gladden	.05
275	Mike Krukow	.05
276	*Randy Kutcher*	.05
277	Mike LaCoss	.05
278	Jeff Leonard	.05
279	Candy Maldonado	.05
280	Roger Mason	.05
281	Bob Melvin	.05
282	Greg Minton	.05
283	Jeff Robinson	.05
284	Harry Spilman	.05
285	*Rob Thompson*	.05
286	Jose Uribe	.05
287	Frank Williams	.05
288	Joel Youngblood	.05
289	Jack Clark	.05
290	Vince Coleman	.05
291	Tim Conroy	.05
292	Danny Cox	.05
293	Ken Dayley	.05
294	Curt Ford	.05
295	Bob Forsch	.05
296	Tom Herr	.05
297	Ricky Horton	.05
298	Clint Hurdle	.05
299	Jeff Lahti	.05
300	Steve Lake	.05
301	Tito Landrum	.05
302	*Mike LaValliere*	.05
303	*Greg Mathews*	.05
304	Willie McGee	.05
305	Jose Oquendo	.05
306	Terry Pendleton	.05
307	Pat Perry	.05
308	Ozzie Smith	1.50
309	Ray Soff	.05
310	John Tudor	.05
311	Andy Van Slyke	.05
312	Todd Worrell	.05
313	Dann Bilardello	.05
314	Hubie Brooks	.05
315	Tim Burke	.05
316	Andre Dawson	.35
317	Mike Fitzgerald	.05
318	Tom Foley	.05
319	Andres Galarraga	.05
320	Joe Hesketh	.05
321	Wallace Johnson	.05
322	Wayne Krenchicki	.05
323	Vance Law	.05
324	Dennis Martinez	.05
325	Bob McClure	.05
326	Andy McGaffigan	.05
327	*Al Newman*	.05
328	Tim Raines	.05
329	Jeff Reardon	.05
330	*Luis Rivera*	.05
331	*Bob Sebra*	.05
332	Bryn Smith	.05
333	Jay Tibbs	.05
334	Tim Wallach	.05
335	Mitch Webster	.05
336	Jim Wohlford	.05
337	Floyd Youmans	.05
338	*Chris Bosio*	.25
339	*Glenn Braggs*	.05
340	Rick Cerone	.05
341	Mark Clear	.05
342	*Bryan Clutterbuck*	.05
343	Cecil Cooper	.05
344	Rob Deer	.05
345	Jim Gantner	.05
346	Ted Higuera	.05
347	John Henry Johnson	.05
348	Tim Leary	.05
349	Rick Manning	.05
350	Paul Molitor	.75
351	Charlie Moore	.05
352	Juan Nieves	.05
353	Ben Oglivie	.05
354	*Dan Plesac*	.10
355	Ernest Riles	.05
356	Billy Joe Robidoux	.05
357	Bill Schroeder	.05
358	*Dale Sveum*	.05
359	Gorman Thomas	.05
360	Bill Wegman	.05
361	Robin Yount	.75
362	Steve Balboni	.05
363	*Scott Bankhead*	.05
364	Buddy Biancalana	.05
365	Bud Black	.05
366	George Brett	2.00
367	Steve Farr	.05
368	Mark Gubicza	.05
369	Bo Jackson	.75
370	Danny Jackson	.05
371	*Mike Kingery*	.05
372	Rudy Law	.05
373	Charlie Leibrandt	.05
374	Dennis Leonard	.05
375	Hal McRae	.05
376	Jorge Orta	.05
377	Jamie Quirk	.05
378	Dan Quisenberry	.05
379	Bret Saberhagen	.05
380	Angel Salazar	.05
381	Lonnie Smith	.05
382	Jim Sundberg	.05
383	Frank White	.05
384	Willie Wilson	.05
385	Joaquin Andujar	.05
386	Doug Bair	.05
387	Dusty Baker	.05
388	Bruce Bochte	.05
389	Jose Canseco	.65
390	Chris Codiroli	.05
391	Mike Davis	.05
392	Alfredo Griffin	.05
393	Moose Haas	.05
394	Donnie Hill	.05
395	Jay Howell	.05
396	Dave Kingman	.05
397	Carney Lansford	.05
398	*David Leiper*	.05
399	*Bill Mooneyham*	.05
400	Dwayne Murphy	.05
401	Steve Ontiveros	.05
402	Tony Phillips	.05
403	Eric Plunk	.05
404	Jose Rijo	.05
405	*Terry Steinbach*	.50
406	Dave Stewart	.05
407	Mickey Tettleton	.05
408	Dave Von Ohlen	.05
409	Jerry Willard	.05
410	Curt Young	.05
411	Bruce Bochy	.05
412	Dave Dravecky	.05
413	Tim Flannery	.05
414	Steve Garvey	.25
415	Goose Gossage	.10
416	Tony Gwynn	1.50
417	Andy Hawkins	.05
418	LaMarr Hoyt	.05
419	Terry Kennedy	.05
420	John Kruk	.05
421	Dave LaPoint	.05
422	Craig Lefferts	.05
423	Carmelo Martinez	.05
424	Lance McCullers	.05
425	Kevin McReynolds	.05
426	Graig Nettles	.05
427	Bip Roberts	.05
428	Jerry Royster	.05
429	Benito Santiago	.05
430	Eric Show	.05
431	Bob Stoddard	.05
432	Garry Templeton	.05
433	Gene Walter	.05
434	Ed Whitson	.05
435	Marvell Wynne	.05
436	Dave Anderson	.05
437	Greg Brock	.05
438	Enos Cabell	.05
439	Mariano Duncan	.05
440	Pedro Guerrero	.05
441	Orel Hershiser	.05
442	Rick Honeycutt	.05
443	Ken Howell	.05
444	Ken Landreaux	.05
445	Bill Madlock	.05
446	Mike Marshall	.05
447	Len Matuszek	.05
448	Tom Niedenfuer	.05
449	Alejandro Pena	.05
450	Dennis Powell	.05
451	Jerry Reuss	.05
452	Bill Russell	.05
453	Steve Sax	.05
454	Mike Scioscia	.05
455	Franklin Stubbs	.05
456	Alex Trevino	.05
457	Fernando Valenzuela	.05
458	Ed Vande Berg	.05
459	Bob Welch	.05
460	*Reggie Williams*	.05
461	Don Aase	.05
462	Juan Beniquez	.05
463	Mike Boddicker	.05
464	Juan Bonilla	.05
465	Rich Bordi	.05
466	Storm Davis	.05
467	Rick Dempsey	.05
468	Ken Dixon	.05
469	Jim Dwyer	.05
470	Mike Flanagan	.05
471	Jackie Gutierrez	.05
472	Brad Havens	.05
473	Lee Lacy	.05
474	Fred Lynn	.05
475	Scott McGregor	.05
476	Eddie Murray	.75
477	Tom O'Malley	.05

478 Cal Ripken, Jr. 3.00
479 Larry Sheets .05
480 John Shelby .05
481 Nate Snell .05
482 Jim Traber .05
483 Mike Young .05
484 Neil Allen .05
485 Harold Baines .05
486 Floyd Bannister .05
487 Daryl Boston .05
488 Ivan Calderon .05
489 *John Cangelosi* .05
490 Steve Carlton .75
491 Joe Cowley .05
492 Julio Cruz .05
493 Bill Dawley .05
494 Jose DeLeon .05
495 Richard Dotson .05
496 Carlton Fisk .75
497 Ozzie Guillen .05
498 Jerry Hairston Sr. .05
499 Ron Hassey .05
500 Tim Hulett .05
501 Bob James .05
502 Steve Lyons .05
503 *Joel McKeon* .05
504 Gene Nelson .05
505 Dave Schmidt .05
506 Ray Searage .05
507 *Bobby Thigpen* .15
508 Greg Walker .05
509 Jim Acker .05
510 Doyle Alexander .05
511 *Paul Assenmacher* .05
512 Bruce Benedict .05
513 Chris Chambliss .05
514 Jeff Dedmon .05
515 Gene Garber .05
516 Ken Griffey .05
517 Terry Harper .05
518 Bob Horner .05
519 Glenn Hubbard .05
520 Rick Mahler .05
521 Omar Moreno .05
522 Dale Murphy .35
523 Ken Oberkfell .05
524 Ed Olwine .05
525 David Palmer .05
526 Rafael Ramirez .05
527 Billy Sample .05
528 Ted Simmons .05
529 Zane Smith .05
530 Bruce Sutter .65
531 *Andres Thomas* .05
532 Ozzie Virgil .05
533 *Allan Anderson* .05
534 Keith Atherton .05
535 Billy Beane .05
536 Bert Blyleven .10
537 Tom Brunansky .05
538 Randy Bush .05
539 George Frazier .05
540 Gary Gaetti .05
541 Greg Gagne .05
542 Mickey Hatcher .05
543 Neal Heaton .05
544 Kent Hrbek .05
545 Roy Lee Jackson .05
546 Tim Laudner .05
547 Steve Lombardozzi .05
548 *Mark Portugal* .10
549 Kirby Puckett 1.50
550 Jeff Reed .05
551 Mark Salas .05
552 Roy Smalley .05
553 Mike Smithson .05
554 Frank Viola .05
555 Thad Bosley .05
556 Ron Cey .05
557 Jody Davis .05
558 Ron Davis .05
559 Bob Dernier .05
560 Frank DiPino .05
561 Shawon Dunston .05
562 Leon Durham .05
563 Dennis Eckersley .65
564 Terry Francona .05
565 Dave Gumpert .05
566 Guy Hoffman .05
567 Ed Lynch .05
568 Gary Matthews .05
569 Keith Moreland .05
570 *Jamie Moyer* .05
571 Jerry Mumphrey .05
572 Ryne Sandberg 1.00
573 Scott Sanderson .05
574 Lee Smith .05
575 Chris Speier .05
576 Rick Sutcliffe .05
577 Manny Trillo .05
578 Steve Trout .05
579 Karl Best .05
580 Scott Bradley .05
581 Phil Bradley .05
582 Mickey Brantley .05
583 Mike Brown .05
584 Alvin Davis .05
585 *Lee Guetterman* .05
586 Mark Huismann .05
587 Bob Kearney .05
588 Pete Ladd .05
589 Mark Langston .05
590 Mike Moore .05
591 Mike Morgan .05
592 John Moses .05
593 Ken Phelps .05
594 Jim Presley .05
595 *Rey Quinonez (Quinones)* .05
596 Harold Reynolds .05
597 Billy Swift .05
598 Danny Tartabull .05
599 Steve Yeager .05
600 Matt Young .05
601 Bill Almon .05
602 *Rafael Belliard* .05
603 Mike Bielecki .05
604 Barry Bonds 50.00
605 Bobby Bonilla .05
606 Sid Bream .05
607 Mike Brown .05
608 Pat Clements .05
609 *Mike Diaz* .05
610 Cecillo Guante .05
611 *Barry Jones* .05
612 Bob Kipper .05
613 Larry McWilliams .05
614 Jim Morrison .05
615 Joe Orsulak .05
616 Junior Ortiz .05
617 Tony Pena .05
618 Johnny Ray .05
619 Rick Reuschel .05
620 R.J. Reynolds .05
621 Rick Rhoden .05
622 Don Robinson .05
623 Bob Walk .05
624 Jim Winn .05
625 Jose Canseco, Pete Incaviglia Youthful Power .15
626 Phil Niekro, Don Sutton 300 Game Winners .25
627 Don Aase, Dave Righetti A.L. Firemen .05
628 Jose Canseco, Wally Joyner Rookie All-Stars .15
629 Gary Carter, Dwight Gooden, Keith Hernandez, Darryl Strawberry Magic Mets .15
630 Mike Krukow, Mike Scott N.L. Best Righties .05
631 John Franco, Fernando Valenzuela Sensational Southpaws .05
632 Bob Horner Count 'Em .05
633 Jose Canseco, Kirby Puckett, Jim Rice A.L. Pitcher's Nightmare .25
634 Gary Carter, Roger Clemens All Star Battery .50
635 Steve Carlton 4,000 Strikeouts .15
636 Glenn Davis, Eddie Murray Big Bats At First Sack .15
637 Wade Boggs, Keith Hernandez On Base .25
638 Don Mattingly, Darryl Strawberry Sluggers From Left Side .50
639 Dave Parker, Ryne Sandberg Former MVP's .25
640 Roger Clemens, Dwight Gooden Dr. K. & Super K .50
641 Charlie Hough, Mike Witt A.L. West Stoppers .05
642 Tim Raines, Juan Samuel Doubles & Triples .05
643 Harold Baines, Jesse Barfield Outfielders With Punch .05
644 *Dave Clark, Greg Swindell* Major League Prospects .35
645 *Ron Karkovice, Russ Morman* Major League Prospects .25
646 *Willie Fraser, Devon White* Major League Prospects 1.00
647 *Jerry Browne, Mike Stanley* Major League Prospects .25
648 *Phil Lombardi, Dave Magadan* Major League Prospects .20
649 *Ralph Bryant, Jose Gonzalez* Major League Prospects .10
650 *Randy Asadoor, Jimmy Jones* Major League Prospects .10
651 *Marvin Freeman, Tracy Jones* Major League Prospects .10
652 Kevin Seitzer, John Stefero Major League Prospects .25
653 *Steve Fireovid, Rob Nelson* Major League Prospects .10
654 Checklist 1-95 .05
655 Checklist 96-192 .05
656 Checklist 193-288 .05
657 Checklist 289-384 .05
658 Checklist 385-483 .05
659 Checklist 484-578 .05
660 Checklist 579-660 .05

Update

NM/M

Complete Set (132): 9.00
Common Player: .05
1 Scott Bankhead .05
2 Eric Bell .05
3 Juan Beniquez .05
4 Juan Berenguer .05
5 Mike Birkbeck .05
6 Randy Bockus .05
7 Rod Booker .05
8 Thad Bosley .05
9 Greg Brock .05
10 Bob Brower .05
11 Chris Brown .05
12 Jerry Browne .05
13 Ralph Bryant .05
14 DeWayne Buice .05
15 Ellis Burks .05
16 Casey Candaele .05
17 Steve Carlton .50
18 Juan Castillo .05
19 Chuck Crim .05
20 Mark Davidson .05
21 Mark Davis .05
22 Storm Davis .05
23 Bill Dawley .05
24 Andre Dawson .30
25 Brian Dayett .05
26 Rick Dempsey .05
27 Ken Dowell .05
28 Dave Dravecky .05
29 Mike Dunne .05
30 Dennis Eckersley .40
31 Cecil Fielder .05
32 Brian Fisher .05
33 Willie Fraser .05
34 Ken Gerhart .05
35 Jim Gott .05
36 Dan Gladden .05
37 Mike Greenwell .05
38 Cecilio Guante .05
39 Albert Hall .05
40 Atlee Hammaker .05
41 Mickey Hatcher .05
42 Mike Heath .05
43 Neal Heaton .05
44 Mike Henneman .05
45 Guy Hoffman .05
46 Charles Hudson .05
47 Chuck Jackson .05
48 Mike Jackson .05
49 Reggie Jackson .75
50 Chris James .05
51 Dion James .05
52 Stan Javier .05
53 Stan Jefferson .05
54 Jimmy Jones .05
55 Tracy Jones .05
56 Terry Kennedy .05
57 Mike Kingery .05
58 Ray Knight .05
59 Gene Larkin .05
60 Mike LaValliere .05
61 Jack Lazorko .05
62 Terry Leach .05
63 Rick Leach .05
64 Craig Lefferts .05
65 Jim Lindeman .05
66 Bill Long .05
67 Mike Loynd .05
68 *Greg Maddux* 6.00
69 Bill Madlock .05
70 Dave Magadan .05
71 Joe Magrane .05
72 Fred Manrique .05
73 Mike Mason .05
74 Lloyd McClendon .05
75 Fred McGriff .05
76 Mark McGwire 3.00
77 Mark McLemore .05
78 Kevin McReynolds .05
79 Dave Meads .05
80 Greg Minton .05
81 John Mitchell .05
82 Kevin Mitchell .05
83 John Morris .05
84 Jeff Musselman .05
85 Randy Myers .05
86 Gene Nelson .05
87 Joe Niekro .05
88 Tom Nieto .05
89 Reid Nichols .05
90 Matt Nokes .05
91 Dickie Noles .05
92 Edwin Nunez .05
93 Jose Nunez .05
94 Paul O'Neill .05
95 Jim Paciorek .05
96 Lance Parrish .05
97 Bill Pecota .05
98 Tony Pena .05
99 Luis Polonia .05
100 Randy Ready .05
101 Jeff Reardon .05
102 Gary Redus .05
103 Rick Rhoden .05
104 Wally Ritchie .05
105 Jeff Robinson .05
106 Mark Salas .05
107 Dave Schmidt .05
108 Kevin Seitzer .05
109 John Shelby .05
110 John Smiley .05
111 Lary Sorenson .05
112 Chris Speier .05
113 Randy St. Claire .05
114 Jim Sundberg .05
115 B.J. Surhoff .05
116 Greg Swindell .05
117 Danny Tartabull .05
118 Dorn Taylor .05
119 Lee Tunnell .05
120 Ed Vande Berg .05
121 Andy Van Slyke .05
122 Gary Ward .05
123 Devon White .05
124 Alan Wiggins .05
125 Bill Wilkinson .05
126 Jim Winn .05
127 Frank Williams .05
128 Ken Williams .05
129 *Matt Williams* 1.00
130 Herm Winningham .05
131 Matt Young .05
132 Checklist 1-132 .05

1987 FLEER GLOSSY TIN

NM/M

Unopened Set (672): 75.00
Complete Set (672): 50.00
Common Player: .10
(Single star cards valued at .75-1X regular-issue 1987 Fleer.)

1987 FLEER UPDATE GLOSSY TIN

	NM/M
Unopened Set (132):	12.00
Complete Set (132):	7.50
Common Player:	.10

(Star cards valued at .75-1X regular version 1987 Fleer updates.)

1988 FLEER

	NM/M
Retail Factory Set (672):	12.00
Hobby Factory Set (672):	10.00
Complete Set (660):	8.00
Common Player:	.05
Wax Pack (15):	.75
Wax Box (36):	12.00
Cello Pack (28):	1.25
Cello Box (24):	16.00

No.	Player	NM/M
1	Keith Atherton	.05
2	Don Baylor	.05
3	Juan Berenguer	.05
4	Bert Blyleven	.10
5	Tom Brunansky	.05
6	Randy Bush	.05
7	Steve Carlton	.50
8	*Mark Davidson*	.05
9	George Frazier	.05
10	Gary Gaetti	.05
11	Greg Gagne	.05
12	Dan Gladden	.05
13	Kent Hrbek	.05
14	*Gene Larkin*	.05
15	Tim Laudner	.05
16	Steve Lombardozzi	.05
17	Al Newman	.05
18	Joe Niekro	.05
19	Kirby Puckett	.65
20	Jeff Reardon	.05
21a	Dan Schatzader (incorrect spelling)	.10
21b	Dan Schatzeder (correct spelling)	.05
22	Roy Smalley	.05
23	Mike Smithson	.05
24	*Les Straker*	.05
25	Frank Viola	.05
26	Jack Clark	.05
27	Vince Coleman	.05
28	Danny Cox	.05
29	Bill Dawley	.05
30	Ken Dayley	.05
31	Doug DeCinces	.05
32	Curt Ford	.05
33	Bob Forsch	.05
34	David Green	.05
35	Tom Herr	.05
36	Ricky Horton	.05
37	*Lance Johnson*	.25
38	Steve Lake	.05
39	Jim Lindeman	.05
40	*Joe Magrane*	.10
41	Greg Mathews	.05
42	Willie McGee	.05
43	John Morris	.05
44	Jose Oquendo	.05
45	Tony Pena	.05
46	Terry Pendleton	.05
47	Ozzie Smith	.65
48	John Tudor	.05
49	Lee Tunnell	.05
50	Todd Worrell	.05
51	Doyle Alexander	.05
52	Dave Bergman	.05
53	Tom Brookens	.05
54	Darrell Evans	.05
55	Kirk Gibson	.05
56	Mike Heath	.05
57	Mike Henneman	.05
58	Willie Hernandez	.05
59	Larry Herndon	.05
60	Eric King	.05
61	Chet Lemon	.05
62	*Scott Lusader*	.05
63	Bill Madlock	.05
64	Jack Morris	.05
65	Jim Morrison	.05
66	Matt Nokes	.05
67	Dan Petry	.05
68a	*Jeff Robinson* (Born 12-13-60 on back)	.25
68b	*Jeff Robinson* (Born 12/14/61 on back)	.10
69	Pat Sheridan	.05
70	Nate Snell	.05
71	Frank Tanana	.05
72	Walt Terrell	.05
73	Mark Thurmond	.05
74	Alan Trammell	.05
75	Lou Whitaker	.05
76	Mike Aldrete	.05
77	Bob Brenly	.05
78	Will Clark	.05
79	Chili Davis	.05
80	Kelly Downs	.05
81	Dave Dravecky	.05
82	Scott Garrelts	.05
83	Atlee Hammaker	.05
84	Dave Henderson	.05
85	Mike Krukow	.05
86	Mike LaCoss	.05
87	Craig Lefferts	.05
88	Jeff Leonard	.05
89	Candy Maldonado	.05
90	Ed Milner	.05
91	Bob Melvin	.05
92	Kevin Mitchell	.05
93	*Jon Perlman*	.05
94	Rick Reuschel	.05
95	Don Robinson	.05
96	Chris Speier	.05
97	Harry Spilman	.05
98	Robbie Thompson	.05
99	Jose Uribe	.05
100	*Mark Wasinger*	.05
101	Matt Williams	.05
102	Jesse Barfield	.05
103	George Bell	.05
104	Juan Beniquez	.05
105	John Cerutti	.05
106	Jim Clancy	.05
107	*Rob Ducey*	.05
108	Mark Eichhorn	.05
109	Tony Fernandez	.05
110	Cecil Fielder	.05
111	Kelly Gruber	.05
112	Tom Henke	.05
113	Garth Iorq (Iorg)	.05
114	Jimmy Key	.05
115	Rick Leach	.05
116	Manny Lee	.05
117	*Nelson Liriano*	.05
118	Fred McGriff	.05
119	Lloyd Moseby	.05
120	Rance Mulliniks	.05
121	Jeff Musselman	.05
122	*Jose Nunez*	.05
123	Dave Stieb	.05
124	Willie Upshaw	.05
125	Duane Ward	.05
126	Ernie Whitt	.05
127	Rick Aguilera	.05
128	Wally Backman	.05
129	*Mark Carreon*	.10
130	Gary Carter	.50
131	David Cone	.05
132	Ron Darling	.05
133	Len Dykstra	.05
134	Sid Fernandez	.05
135	Dwight Gooden	.05
136	Keith Hernandez	.05
137	*Gregg Jefferies*	.50
138	Howard Johnson	.05
139	Terry Leach	.05
140	*Barry Lyons*	.05
141	Dave Magadan	.05
142	Roger McDowell	.05
143	Kevin McReynolds	.05
144	*Keith Miller*	.05
145	*John Mitchell*	.05
146	Randy Myers	.05
147	Bob Ojeda	.05
148	Jesse Orosco	.05
149	Rafael Santana	.05
150	Doug Sisk	.05
151	Darryl Strawberry	.05
152	Tim Teufel	.05
153	Gene Walter	.05
154	Mookie Wilson	.05
155	*Jay Aldrich*	.05
156	Chris Bosio	.05
157	Glenn Braggs	.05
158	Greg Brock	.05
159	Juan Castillo	.05
160	Mark Clear	.05
161	Cecil Cooper	.05
162	*Chuck Crim*	.05
163	Rob Deer	.05
164	Mike Felder	.05
165	Jim Gantner	.05
166	Ted Higuera	.05
167	Steve Kiefer	.05
168	Rick Manning	.05
169	Paul Molitor	.50
170	Juan Nieves	.05
171	Dan Plesac	.05
172	Earnest Riles	.05
173	Bill Schroeder	.05
174	*Steve Stanicek*	.05
175	B.J. Surhoff	.05
176	Dale Sveum	.05
177	Bill Wegman	.05
178	Robin Yount	.50
179	Hubie Brooks	.05
180	Tim Burke	.05
181	Casey Candaele	.05
182	Mike Fitzgerald	.05
183	Tom Foley	.05
184	Andres Galarraga	.05
185	Neal Heaton	.05
186	Wallace Johnson	.05
187	Vance Law	.05
188	Dennis Martinez	.05
189	Bob McClure	.05
190	Andy McGaffigan	.05
191	Reid Nichols	.05
192	Pascual Perez	.05
193	Tim Raines	.05
194	Jeff Reed	.05
195	Bob Sebra	.05
196	Bryn Smith	.05
197	Randy St. Claire	.05
198	Tim Wallach	.05
199	Mitch Webster	.05
200	Herm Winningham	.05
201	Floyd Youmans	.05
202	*Brad Arnsberg*	.05
203	Rick Cerone	.05
204	Pat Clements	.05
205	Henry Cotto	.05
206	Mike Easler	.05
207	Ron Guidry	.10
208	Bill Gullickson	.05
209	Rickey Henderson	.50
210	Charles Hudson	.05
211	Tommy John	.10
212	*Roberto Kelly*	.25
213	Ron Kittle	.05
214	Don Mattingly	.75
215	Bobby Meacham	.05
216	Mike Pagliarulo	.05
217	Dan Pasqua	.05
218	Willie Randolph	.05
219	Rick Rhoden	.05
220	Dave Righetti	.05
221	Jerry Royster	.05
222	Tim Stoddard	.05
223	Wayne Tolleson	.05
224	Gary Ward	.05
225	Claudell Washington	.05
226	Dave Winfield	.50
227	Buddy Bell	.05
228	Tom Browning	.05
229	Dave Concepcion	.05
230	Kal Daniels	.05
231	Eric Davis	.05
232	Bo Diaz	.05
233	Nick Esasky	.05
234	John Franco	.05
235	Guy Hoffman	.05
236	Tom Hume	.05
237	Tracy Jones	.05
238	*Bill Landrum*	.05
239	Barry Larkin	.05
240	Terry McGriff	.05
241	Rob Murphy	.05
242	Ron Oester	.05
243	Dave Parker	.05
244	Pat Perry	.05
245	Ted Power	.05
246	Dennis Rasmussen	.05
247	Ron Robinson	.05
248	Kurt Stillwell	.05
249	*Jeff Treadway*	.05
250	Frank Williams	.05
251	Steve Balboni	.05
252	Bud Black	.05
253	Thad Bosley	.05
254	George Brett	.75
255	*John Davis*	.05
256	Steve Farr	.05
257	Gene Garber	.05
258	Jerry Gleaton	.05
259	Mark Gubicza	.05
260	Bo Jackson	.10
261	Danny Jackson	.05
262	*Ross Jones*	.05
263	Charlie Leibrandt	.05
264	*Bill Pecota*	.05
265	*Melido Perez*	.05
266	Jamie Quirk	.05
267	Dan Quisenberry	.05
268	Bret Saberhagen	.05
269	Angel Salazar	.05
270	Kevin Seitzer	.05
271	Danny Tartabull	.05
272	*Gary Thurman*	.05
273	Frank White	.05
274	Willie Wilson	.05
275	Tony Bernazard	.05
276	Jose Canseco	.30
277	Mike Davis	.05
278	Storm Davis	.05
279	Dennis Eckersley	.40
280	Alfredo Griffin	.05
281	Rick Honeycutt	.05
282	Jay Howell	.05
283	Reggie Jackson	.65
284	Dennis Lamp	.05
285	Carney Lansford	.05
286	Mark McGwire	.85
287	Dwayne Murphy	.05
288	Gene Nelson	.05
289	Steve Ontiveros	.05
290	Tony Phillips	.05
291	Eric Plunk	.05
292	*Luis Polonia*	.15
293	*Rick Rodriguez*	.05
294	Terry Steinbach	.05
295	Dave Stewart	.05
296	Curt Young	.05
297	Luis Aguayo	.05
298	Steve Bedrosian	.05
299	Jeff Calhoun	.05
300	Don Carman	.05
301	*Todd Frohwirth*	.05
302	Greg Gross	.05
303	Kevin Gross	.05
304	Von Hayes	.05
305	*Keith Hughes*	.05
306	*Mike Jackson*	.05
307	Chris James	.05
308	Steve Jeltz	.05
309	Mike Maddux	.05
310	Lance Parrish	.05
311	Shane Rawley	.05
312	*Wally Ritchie*	.05
313	Bruce Ruffin	.05
314	Juan Samuel	.05
315	Mike Schmidt	.75
316	Rick Schu	.05
317	Jeff Stone	.05
318	Kent Tekulve	.05
319	Milt Thompson	.05
320	Glenn Wilson	.05
321	Rafael Belliard	.05
322	Barry Bonds	1.00
323	Bobby Bonilla	.05
324	Sid Bream	.05
325	John Cangelosi	.05
326	Mike Diaz	.05
327	Doug Drabek	.05
328	*Mike Dunne*	.05
329	Brian Fisher	.05
330	*Brett Gideon*	.05
331	Terry Harper	.05
332	Bob Kipper	.05
333	Mike LaValliere	.05
334	*Jose Lind*	.15
335	Junior Ortiz	.05
336	*Vicente Palacios*	.05
337	*Bob Patterson*	.05
338	*Al Pedrique*	.05
339	R.J. Reynolds	.05
340	John Smiley	.05
341	Andy Van Slyke	.05
342	Bob Walk	.05
343	Marty Barrett	.05
344	*Todd Benzinger*	.05
345	Wade Boggs	.65
346	*Tom Bolton*	.05
347	Oil Can Boyd	.05
348	Ellis Burks	.05
349	Roger Clemens	.75
350	Steve Crawford	.05

351 Dwight Evans .05
352 *Wes Gardner* .05
353 Rich Gedman .05
354 Mike Greenwell .05
355 *Sam Horn* .05
356 Bruce Hurst .05
357 *John Marzano* .05
358 Al Nipper .05
359 Spike Owen .05
360 *Jody Reed* .15
361 Jim Rice .20
362 Ed Romero .05
363 Kevin Romine .05
364 Joe Sambito .05
365 Calvin Schiraldi .05
366 Jeff Sellers .05
367 Bob Stanley .05
368 Scott Bankhead .05
369 Phil Bradley .05
370 Scott Bradley .05
371 Mickey Brantley .05
372 *Mike Campbell* .05
373 Alvin Davis .05
374 Lee Guetterman .05
375 *Dave Hengel* .05
376 Mike Kingery .05
377 Mark Langston .05
378 *Edgar Martinez* 1.00
379 Mike Moore .05
380 Mike Morgan .05
381 John Moses .05
382 *Donnell Nixon* .05
383 Edwin Nunez .05
384 Ken Phelps .05
385 Jim Presley .05
386 Rey Quinones .05
387 Jerry Reed .05
388 Harold Reynolds .05
389 Dave Valle .05
390 *Bill Wilkinson* .05
391 Harold Baines .05
392 Floyd Bannister .05
393 Daryl Boston .05
394 Ivan Calderon .05
395 Jose DeLeon .05
396 Richard Dotson .05
397 Carlton Fisk .50
398 Ozzie Guillen .05
399 Ron Hassey .05
400 Donnie Hill .05
401 Bob James .05
402 Dave LaPoint .05
403 *Bill Lindsey* .05
404 *Bill Long* .05
405 Steve Lyons .05
406 *Fred Manrique* .05
407 *Jack McDowell* .25
408 Gary Redus .05
409 Ray Searage .05
410 Bobby Thigpen .05
411 Greg Walker .05
412 *Kenny Williams* .05
413 Jim Winn .05
414 Jody Davis .05
415 Andre Dawson .25
416 Brian Dayett .05
417 Bob Dernier .05
418 Frank DiPino .05
419 Shawon Dunston .05
420 Leon Durham .05
421 *Les Lancaster* .10
422 Ed Lynch .05
423 Greg Maddux .75
424 Dave Martinez .05
425a Keith Moreland (bunting, photo actually Jody Davis) 2.00
425b Keith Moreland (standing upright, correct photo) .05
426 Jamie Moyer .05
427 Jerry Mumphrey .05
428 *Paul Noce* .05
429 Rafael Palmeiro .40
430 Wade Rowdon .05
431 Ryne Sandberg .65
432 Scott Sanderson .05
433 Lee Smith .05
434 Jim Sundberg .05
435 Rick Sutcliffe .05
436 Manny Trillo .05
437 Juan Agosto .05
438 Larry Andersen .05
439 Alan Ashby .05
440 Kevin Bass .05
441 *Ken Caminiti* .25
442 *Rocky Childress* .05
443 Jose Cruz .05
444 Danny Darwin .05
445 Glenn Davis .05
446 Jim Deshaies .05
447 Bill Doran .05
448 Ty Gainey .05
449 Billy Hatcher .05
450 Jeff Heathcock .05
451 Bob Knepper .05
452 *Rob Mallicoat* .05
453 *Dave Meads* .05
454 Craig Reynolds .05
455 Nolan Ryan 1.00
456 Mike Scott .05
457 Dave Smith .05
458 Denny Walling .05
459 *Robbie Wine* .05
460 *Gerald Young* .05
461 Bob Brower .05
462a Jerry Browne (white player, photo actually Bob Brower) 2.00
462b Jerry Browne (black player, correct photo) .05
463 Steve Buechele .05
464 Edwin Correa .05
465 *Cecil Espy* .05
466 Scott Fletcher .05
467 Jose Guzman .05
468 Greg Harris .05
469 Charlie Hough .05
470 Pete Incaviglia .05
471 *Paul Kilgus* .05
472 Mike Loynd .05
473 Oddibe McDowell .05
474 Dale Mohorcic .05
475 Pete O'Brien .05
476 Larry Parrish .05
477 Geno Petralli .05
478 Jeff Russell .05
479 Ruben Sierra .05
480 Mike Stanley .05
481 Curtis Wilkerson .05
482 Mitch Williams .05
483 Bobby Witt .05
484 Tony Armas .05
485 Bob Boone .05
486 Bill Buckner .05
487 *DeWayne Buice* .05
488 Brian Downing .05
489 Chuck Finley .05
490 Willie Fraser .05
491 Jack Howell .05
492 Ruppert Jones .05
493 Wally Joyner .05
494 Jack Lazorko .05
495 Gary Lucas .05
496 Kirk McCaskill .05
497 Mark McLemore .05
498 Darrell Miller .05
499 Greg Minton .05
500 Donnie Moore .05
501 Gus Polidor .05
502 Johnny Ray .05
503 Mark Ryal .05
504 Dick Schofield .05
505 Don Sutton .40
506 Devon White .05
507 Mike Witt .05
508 Dave Anderson .05
509 Tim Belcher .05
510 Ralph Bryant .05
511 *Tim Crews* .15
512 *Mike Devereaux* .10
513 Mariano Duncan .05
514 Pedro Guerrero .05
515 Jeff Hamilton .05
516 Mickey Hatcher .05
517 Brad Havens .05
518 Orel Hershiser .05
519 *Shawn Hillegas* .05
520 Ken Howell .05
521 Tim Leary .05
522 Mike Marshall .05
523 Steve Sax .05
524 Mike Scioscia .05
525 Mike Sharperson .05
526 John Shelby .05
527 Franklin Stubbs .05
528 Fernando Valenzuela .05
529 Bob Welch .05
530 Matt Young .05
531 Jim Acker .05
532 Paul Assenmacher .05
533 *Jeff Blauser* .10
534 *Joe Boever* .05
535 Martin Clary .05
536 *Kevin Coffman* .05
537 Jeff Dedmon .05
538 *Ron Gant* .50
539 *Tom Glavine* 2.00
540 Ken Griffey .05
541 Al Hall .05
542 Glenn Hubbard .05
543 Dion James .05
544 Dale Murphy .20
545 Ken Oberkfell .05
546 David Palmer .05
547 Gerald Perry .05
548 Charlie Puleo .05
549 Ted Simmons .05
550 Zane Smith .05
551 Andres Thomas .05
552 Ozzie Virgil .05
553 Don Aase .05
554 *Jeff Ballard* .05
555 Eric Bell .05
556 Mike Boddicker .05
557 Ken Dixon .05
558 Jim Dwyer .05
559 Ken Gerhart .05
560 *Rene Gonzales* .05
561 Mike Griffin .05
562 John Hayban (Habyan) .05
563 Terry Kennedy .05
564 Ray Knight .05
565 Lee Lacy .05
566 Fred Lynn .05
567 Eddie Murray .50
568 Tom Niedenfuer .05
569 *Bill Ripken* .05
570 Cal Ripken, Jr. 1.00
571 Dave Schmidt .05
572 Larry Sheets .05
573 *Pete Stanicek* .05
574 *Mark Williamson* .05
575 Mike Young .05
576 Shawn Abner .05
577 Greg Booker .05
578 Chris Brown .05
579 *Keith Comstock* .05
580 *Joey Cora* .05
581 Mark Davis .05
582 Tim Flannery .05
583 Goose Gossage .05
584 Mark Grant .05
585 Tony Gwynn .65
586 Andy Hawkins .05
587 Stan Jefferson .05
588 Jimmy Jones .05
589 John Kruk .05
590 *Shane Mack* .10
591 Carmelo Martinez .05
592 Lance McCullers .05
593 *Eric Nolte* .05
594 Randy Ready .05
595 Luis Salazar .05
596 Benito Santiago .05
597 Eric Show .05
598 Garry Templeton .05
599 Ed Whitson .05
600 Scott Bailes .05
601 Chris Bando .05
602 *Jay Bell* .50
603 Brett Butler .05
604 Tom Candiotti .05
605 Joe Carter .05
606 Carmen Castillo .05
607 *Brian Dorsett* .05
608 *John Farrell* .05
609 Julio Franco .05
610 Mel Hall .05
611 *Tommy Hinzo* .05
612 Brook Jacoby .05
613 *Doug Jones* .10
614 Ken Schrom .05
615 Cory Snyder .05
616 Sammy Stewart .05
617 Greg Swindell .05
618 Pat Tabler .05
619 Ed Vande Berg .05
620 *Eddie Williams* .05
621 Rich Yett .05
622 Wally Joyner, Cory Snyder Slugging Sophomores .10
623 George Bell, Pedro Guerrero Dominican Dynamite .05
624 Jose Canseco, Mark McGwire Oakland's Power Team .50
625 Dan Plesac, Dave Righetti Classic Relief .05
626 Jack Morris, Bret Saberhagen, Mike Witt All Star Righties .05
627 Steve Bedrosian, John Franco Game Closers .05
628 Ryne Sandberg, Ozzie Smith Masters of the Double Play .50
629 Mark McGwire Rookie Record Setter .50
630 Todd Benzinger, Ellis Burks, Mike Greenwell Changing the Guard in Boston .10
631 Tony Gwynn, Tim Raines N.L. Batting Champs .20
632 Orel Hershiser, Mike Scott Pitching Magic .05
633 Mark McGwire, Pat Tabler Big Bats At First .50
634 Tony Gwynn, Vince Coleman Hitting King and the Thief .15
635 Tony Fernandez, Cal Ripken, Jr., Alan Trammell A.L. Slugging Shortstops .40
636 Gary Carter, Mike Schmidt Tried and True Sluggers .40
637 Eric Davis Crunch Time .05
638 Matt Nokes, Kirby Puckett A.L. All Stars .25
639 Keith Hernandez, Dale Murphy N.L. All Stars .10
640 Bill Ripken, Cal Ripken, Jr. The "O's" Brothers .50
641 *Mark Grace, Darrin Jackson* Major League Prospects 1.00
642 *Damon Berryhill, Jeff Montgomery* Major League Prospects .20
643 *Felix Fermin, Jessie Reid* Major League Prospects .05
644 *Greg Myers, Greg Tabor* Major League Prospects .05
645 Jim Eppard, Joey Meyer Major League Prospects .05
646 *Adam Peterson, Randy Velarde* Major League Prospects .10
647 *Chris Gwynn, Peter Smith* Major League Prospects .15
648 *Greg Jelks, Tom Newell* Major League Prospects .05
649 *Mario Diaz, Clay Parker* Major League Prospects .05
650 *Jack Savage, Todd Simmons* Major League Prospects .05
651 *John Burkett, Kirt Manwaring* Major League Prospects .30
652 *Dave Otto, Walt Weiss* Major League Prospects .25
653 *Randell Byers (Randall), Jeff King* Major League Prospects .25
654a Checklist 1-101 (21 is Schatzader) .10
654b Checklist 1-101 (21 is Schatzeder) .05
655 Checklist 102-201 .05
656 Checklist 202-296 .05
657 Checklist 297-390 .05
658 Checklist 391-483 .05
659 Checklist 484-575 .05
660 Checklist 576-660 .05

Update

	NM/M
Complete Set (132):	5.00
Common Player:	.05
1 Jose Bautista	.05
2 Joe Orsulak	.05
3 Doug Sisk	.05
4 Craig Worthington	.05
5 Mike Boddicker	.05
6 Rick Cerone	.05
7 Larry Parrish	.05
8 Lee Smith	.10

9 Mike Smithson .05
10 John Trautwein .05
11 Sherman Corbett .05
12 Chili Davis .05
13 Jim Eppard .05
14 Bryan Harvey .05
15 John Davis .05
16 Dave Gallagher .05
17 Ricky Horton .05
18 Dan Pasqua .05
19 Melido Perez .05
20 Jose Segura .05
21 Andy Allanson .05
22 Jon Perlman .05
23 Domingo Ramos .05
24 Rick Rodriguez .05
25 Willie Upshaw .05
26 Paul Gibson .05
27 Don Heinkel .05
28 Ray Knight .05
29 Gary Pettis .05
30 Luis Salazar .05
31 Mike MacFarlane .05
32 Jeff Montgomery .05
33 Ted Power .05
34 Israel Sanchez .05
35 Kurt Stillwell .05
36 Pat Tabler .05
37 Don August .05
38 Darryl Hamilton .05
39 Jeff Leonard .05
40 Joey Meyer .05
41 Allan Anderson .05
42 Brian Harper .05
43 Tom Herr .05
44 Charlie Lea .05
45 John Moses .05
46 John Candelaria .05
47 Jack Clark .05
48 Richard Dotson .05
49 Al Leiter .05
50 Rafael Santana .05
51 Don Slaught .05
52 Todd Burns .05
53 Dave Henderson .05
54 Doug Jennings .05
55 Dave Parker .05
56 Walt Weiss .05
57 Bob Welch .05
58 Henry Cotto .05
59 Marion Diaz (Mario) .05
60 Mike Jackson .05
61 Bill Swift .05
62 Jose Cecena .05
63 Ray Hayward .05
64 Jim Steels .05
65 Pat Borders .05
66 Sil Campusano .05
67 Mike Flanagan .05
68 Todd Stottlemyre .05
69 David Wells .05
70 Jose Alvarez .05
71 Paul Runge .05
72 Cesar Jimenez (German) .05
73 Pete Smith .05
74 *John Smoltz* 1.50
75 Damon Berryhill .05
76 Goose Gossage .05
77 Mark Grace .10
78 Darrin Jackson .05
79 Vance Law .05
80 Jeff Pico .05
81 Gary Varsho .05
82 Tim Birtsas .05
83 Rob Dibble .05
84 Danny Jackson .05
85 Paul O'Neill .05
86 Jose Rijo .05
87 *Chris Sabo* .25
88 John Fishel .05
89 *Craig Biggio* 2.00
90 Terry Puhl .05
91 Rafael Ramirez .05
92 Louie Meadows .05
93 Kirk Gibson .05
94 Alfredo Griffin .05
95 Jay Howell .05
96 Jesse Orosco .05
97 Alejandro Pena .05
98 Tracy Woodson .05
99 John Dopson .05
100 Brian Holman .05
101 Rex Hudler .05
102 Jeff Parrett .05
103 Nelson Santovenia .05
104 Kevin Elster .05
105 Jeff Innis .05
106 Mackey Sasser .05
107 Phil Bradley .05
108 Danny Clay .05
109 Greg Harris .05
110 Ricky Jordan .05
111 David Palmer .05
112 Jim Gott .05
113 Tommy Gregg (photo actually Randy Milligan) .05
114 Barry Jones .05
115 Randy Milligan .05
116 Luis Alicea .05
117 Tom Brunansky .05
118 John Costello .05
119 Jose DeLeon .05
120 Bob Horner .05
121 Scott Terry .05
122 *Roberto Alomar* 1.50
123 Dave Leiper .05
124 Keith Moreland .05
125 Mark Parent .05
126 Dennis Rasmussen .05
127 Randy Bockus .05
128 Brett Butler .05
129 Donell Nixon .05
130 Earnest Riles .05
131 Roger Samuels .05
132 Checklist .05

1988 FLEER GLOSSY TIN

NM/M
Complete Set (672): 20.00
Common Player: .15
(Star cards valued 1-1.5X regular-issue 1988 Fleer.)

1988 FLEER UPDATE GLOSSY TIN

NM/M
Complete Set (132): 9.00
Common Player: .15
(Star cards valued about 2X regular-issue1988 Fleer Updates.)

1989 FLEER

NM/M
Retail Factory Set (660): 17.50
Hobby Factory Set (672): 20.00
Complete Set (660): 15.00
Common Player: .05
Wax Pack (15): .75
Wax Box (36): 15.00
Cello Pack (36): 1.25
Cello Box (24): 17.50
Rack Pack (42+1): 1.25
Rack Box (24): 20.00

1 Don Baylor .05
2 *Lance Blankenship* .05
3 *Todd Burns* .05
4 Greg Cadaret .05
5 Jose Canseco .35
6 Storm Davis .05
7 Dennis Eckersley .35
8 Mike Gallego .05
9 Ron Hassey .05
10 Dave Henderson .05
11 Rick Honeycutt .05
12 Glenn Hubbard .05
13 Stan Javier .05
14 *Doug Jennings* .05
15 *Felix Jose* .05
16 Carney Lansford .05
17 Mark McGwire .65
18 Gene Nelson .05
19 Dave Parker .05
20 Eric Plunk .05
21 Luis Polonia .05
22 Terry Steinbach .05
23 Dave Stewart .05
24 Walt Weiss .05
25 Bob Welch .05
26 Curt Young .05
27 Rick Aguilera .05
28 Wally Backman .05
29 Mark Carreon .05
30 Gary Carter .40
31 David Cone .05
32 Ron Darling .05
33 Len Dykstra .05
34 Kevin Elster .05
35 Sid Fernandez .05
36 Dwight Gooden .05
37 Keith Hernandez .05
38 Gregg Jefferies .05
39 Howard Johnson .05
40 Terry Leach .05
41 Dave Magadan .05
42 Bob McClure .05
43 Roger McDowell .05
44 Kevin McReynolds .05
45 Keith Miller .05
46 Randy Myers .05
47 Bob Ojeda .05
48 Mackey Sasser .05
49 Darryl Strawberry .05
50 Tim Teufel .05
51 *Dave West* .05
52 Mookie Wilson .05
53 Dave Anderson .05
54 Tim Belcher .05
55 Mike Davis .05
56 Mike Devereaux .05
57 Kirk Gibson .05
58 Alfredo Griffin .05
59 Chris Gwynn .05
60 Jeff Hamilton .05
61a Danny Heep (Home: San Antonio, TX) .25
61b Danny Heep (Home: Lake Hills, TX) .05
62 Orel Hershiser .05
63 Brian Holton .05
64 Jay Howell .05
65 Tim Leary .05
66 Mike Marshall .05
67 *Ramon Martinez* .25
68 Jesse Orosco .05
69 Alejandro Pena .05
70 Steve Sax .05
71 Mike Scioscia .05
72 Mike Sharperson .05
73 John Shelby .05
74 Franklin Stubbs .05
75 John Tudor .05
76 Fernando Valenzuela .05
77 Tracy Woodson .05
78 Marty Barrett .05
79 Todd Benzinger .05
80 Mike Boddicker .05
81 Wade Boggs .50
82 "Oil Can" Boyd .05
83 Ellis Burks .05
84 Rick Cerone .05
85 Roger Clemens .60
86 *Steve Curry* .05
87 Dwight Evans .05
88 Wes Gardner .05
89 Rich Gedman .05
90 Mike Greenwell .05
91 Bruce Hurst .05
92 Dennis Lamp .05
93 Spike Owen .05
94 Larry Parrish .05
95 *Carlos Quintana* .05
96 Jody Reed .05
97 Jim Rice .25
98a Kevin Romine (batting follow-thru, photo actually Randy Kutcher) .25
98b Kevin Romine (arms crossed on chest, correct photo) .25
99 Lee Smith .05
100 Mike Smithson .05
101 Bob Stanley .05
102 Allan Anderson .05
103 Keith Atherton .05
104 Juan Berenguer .05
105 Bert Blyleven .10
106 *Eric Bullock* .05
107 Randy Bush .05
108 John Christensen .05
109 Mark Davidson .05
110 Gary Gaetti .05
111 Greg Gagne .05
112 Dan Gladden .05
113 *German Gonzalez* .05
114 Brian Harper .05
115 Tom Herr .05
116 Kent Hrbek .05
117 Gene Larkin .05
118 Tim Laudner .05
119 Charlie Lea .05
120 Steve Lombardozzi .05
121a John Moses (Home: Phoenix, AZ) .25
121b John Moses (Home: Tempe, AZ) .05
122 Al Newman .05
123 Mark Portugal .05
124 Kirby Puckett .50
125 Jeff Reardon .05
126 Fred Toliver .05
127 Frank Viola .05
128 Doyle Alexander .05
129 Dave Bergman .05
130a Tom Brookens (Mike Heath stats on back) .50
130b Tom Brookens (correct stats on back) .05
131 *Paul Gibson* .05
132a Mike Heath (Tom Brookens stats on back) .50
132b Mike Heath (correct stats on back) .05
133 *Don Heinkel* .05
134 Mike Henneman .05
135 Guillermo Hernandez .05
136 Eric King .05
137 Chet Lemon .05
138 Fred Lynn .05
139 Jack Morris .05
140 Matt Nokes .05
141 Gary Pettis .05
142 Ted Power .05
143 Jeff Robinson .05
144 Luis Salazar .05
145 *Steve Searcy* .05
146 Pat Sheridan .05
147 Frank Tanana .05
148 Alan Trammell .05
149 Walt Terrell .05
150 Jim Walewander .05
151 Lou Whitaker .05
152 Tim Birtsas .05
153 Tom Browning .05
154 *Keith Brown* .05
155 *Norm Charlton* .15
156 Dave Concepcion .05
157 Kal Daniels .05
158 Eric Davis .05
159 Bo Diaz .05
160 Rob Dibble .05
161 Nick Esasky .05
162 John Franco .05
163 Danny Jackson .05
164 Barry Larkin .05
165 Rob Murphy .05
166 Paul O'Neill .05
167 Jeff Reed .05
168 Jose Rijo .05
169 Ron Robinson .05
170 Chris Sabo .05
171 *Candy Sierra* .05
172 *Van Snider* .05
173a Jeff Treadway (blue "target" above head) 75.00
173b Jeff Treadway (no "target") .05
174 Frank Williams .05
175 Herm Winningham .05
176 Jim Adduci .05
177 Don August .05
178 Mike Birkbeck .05
179 Chris Bosio .05
180 Glenn Braggs .05
181 Greg Brock .05
182 Mark Clear .05
183 Chuck Crim .05
184 Rob Deer .05
185 Tom Filer .05
186 Jim Gantner .05
187 Darryl Hamilton .05
188 Ted Higuera .05
189 Odell Jones .05
190 Jeffrey Leonard .05
191 Joey Meyer .05
192 Paul Mirabella .05
193 Paul Molitor .40
194 Charlie O'Brien .05
195 Dan Plesac .05
196 *Gary Sheffield* 1.00
197 B.J. Surhoff .05
198 Dale Sveum .05
199 Bill Wegman .05
200 Robin Yount .40
201 Rafael Belliard .05
202 Barry Bonds .75
203 Bobby Bonilla .05
204 Sid Bream .05

No.	Player	Price
205	Benny Distefano	.05
206	Doug Drabek	.05
207	Mike Dunne	.05
208	Felix Fermin	.05
209	Brian Fisher	.05
210	Jim Gott	.05
211	Bob Kipper	.05
212	Dave LaPoint	.05
213	Mike LaValliere	.05
214	Jose Lind	.05
215	Junior Ortiz	.05
216	Vicente Palacios	.05
217	Tom Prince	.05
218	Gary Redus	.05
219	R.J. Reynolds	.05
220	Jeff Robinson	.05
221	John Smiley	.05
222	Andy Van Slyke	.05
223	Bob Walk	.05
224	Glenn Wilson	.05
225	Jesse Barfield	.05
226	George Bell	.05
227	Pat Borders	.05
228	John Cerutti	.05
229	Jim Clancy	.05
230	Mark Eichhorn	.05
231	Tony Fernandez	.05
232	Cecil Fielder	.05
233	Mike Flanagan	.05
234	Kelly Gruber	.05
235	Tom Henke	.05
236	Jimmy Key	.05
237	Rick Leach	.05
238	Manny Lee	.05
239	Nelson Liriano	.05
240	Fred McGriff	.05
241	Lloyd Moseby	.05
242	Rance Mulliniks	.05
243	Jeff Musselman	.05
244	Dave Stieb	.05
245	Todd Stottlemyre	.05
246	Duane Ward	.05
247	David Wells	.05
248	Ernie Whitt	.05
249	Luis Aguayo	.05
250a	Neil Allen (Home: Sarasota, FL)	.25
250b	Neil Allen (Home: Syosset, NY)	.05
251	John Candelaria	.05
252	Jack Clark	.05
253	Richard Dotson	.05
254	Rickey Henderson	.40
255	Tommy John	.10
256	Roberto Kelly	.05
257	Al Leiter	.05
258	Don Mattingly	.60
259	Dale Mohorcic	.05
260	*Hal Morris*	.25
261	Scott Nielsen	.05
262	Mike Pagliarulo	.05
263	*Hipolito Pena*	.05
264	Ken Phelps	.05
265	Willie Randolph	.05
266	Rick Rhoden	.05
267	Dave Righetti	.05
268	Rafael Santana	.05
269	Steve Shields	.05
270	Joel Skinner	.05
271	Don Slaught	.05
272	Claudell Washington	.05
273	Gary Ward	.05
274	Dave Winfield	.40
275	Luis Aquino	.05
276	Floyd Bannister	.05
277	George Brett	.60
278	Bill Buckner	.05
279	*Nick Capra*	.05
280	*Jose DeJesus*	.05
281	Steve Farr	.05
282	Jerry Gleaton	.05
283	Mark Gubicza	.05
284	*Tom Gordon*	.25
285	Bo Jackson	.10
286	Charlie Leibrandt	.05
287	*Mike Macfarlane*	.10
288	Jeff Montgomery	.05
289	Bill Pecota	.05
290	Jamie Quirk	.05
291	Bret Saberhagen	.05
292	Kevin Seitzer	.05
293	Kurt Stillwell	.05
294	Pat Tabler	.05
295	Danny Tartabull	.05
296	Gary Thurman	.05
297	Frank White	.05
298	Willie Wilson	.05
299	Roberto Alomar	.20
300	*Sandy Alomar, Jr.*	.25
301	Chris Brown	.05
302	Mike Brumley	.05
303	Mark Davis	.05
304	Mark Grant	.05
305	Tony Gwynn	.50
306	*Greg Harris*	.05
307	Andy Hawkins	.05
308	Jimmy Jones	.05
309	John Kruk	.05
310	Dave Leiper	.05
311	Carmelo Martinez	.05
312	Lance McCullers	.05
313	Keith Moreland	.05
314	Dennis Rasmussen	.05
315	Randy Ready	.05
316	Benito Santiago	.05
317	Eric Show	.05
318	Todd Simmons	.05
319	Garry Templeton	.05
320	Dickie Thon	.05
321	Ed Whitson	.05
322	Marvell Wynne	.05
323	Mike Aldrete	.05
324	Brett Butler	.05
325	Will Clark	.05
326	Kelly Downs	.05
327	Dave Dravecky	.05
328	Scott Garrelts	.05
329	Atlee Hammaker	.05
330	*Charlie Hayes*	.10
331	Mike Krukow	.05
332	Craig Lefferts	.05
333	Candy Maldonado	.05
334	Kirt Manwaring	.05
335	Bob Melvin	.05
336	Kevin Mitchell	.05
337	Donell Nixon	.05
338	*Tony Perezchica*	.05
339	Joe Price	.05
340	Rick Reuschel	.05
341	Earnest Riles	.05
342	Don Robinson	.05
343	Chris Speier	.05
344	Robby Thompson	.05
345	Jose Uribe	.05
346	Matt Williams	.05
347	*Trevor Wilson*	.15
348	Juan Agosto	.05
349	Larry Andersen	.05
350a	Alan Ashby ("Throws Rig")	.25
350b	Alan Ashby ("Throws Right")	.05
351	Kevin Bass	.05
352	Buddy Bell	.05
353	Craig Biggio	.05
354	Danny Darwin	.05
355	Glenn Davis	.05
356	Jim Deshaies	.05
357	Bill Doran	.05
358	*John Fishel*	.05
359	Billy Hatcher	.05
360	Bob Knepper	.05
361	*Louie Meadows*	.05
362	Dave Meads	.05
363	Jim Pankovits	.05
364	Terry Puhl	.05
365	Rafael Ramirez	.05
366	Craig Reynolds	.05
367	Mike Scott	.05
368	Nolan Ryan	.75
369	Dave Smith	.05
370	Gerald Young	.05
371	Hubie Brooks	.05
372	Tim Burke	.05
373	*John Dopson*	.05
374	Mike Fitzgerald	.05
375	Tom Foley	.05
376	Andres Galarraga	.05
377	Neal Heaton	.05
378	Joe Hesketh	.05
379	*Brian Holman*	.05
380	Rex Hudler	.05
381a	*Randy Johnson* (Marlboro ad on scoreboard)	40.00
381b	Randy Johnson (ad partially obscured)	10.00
381c	*Randy Johnson* (ad completely blacked out)	3.00
382	Wallace Johnson	.05
383	Tracy Jones	.05
384	Dave Martinez	.05
385	Dennis Martinez	.05
386	Andy McGaffigan	.05
387	Otis Nixon	.05
388	*Johnny Paredes*	.05
389	Jeff Parrett	.05
390	Pascual Perez	.05
391	Tim Raines	.05
392	Luis Rivera	.05
393	*Nelson Santovenia*	.05
394	Bryn Smith	.05
395	Tim Wallach	.05
396	Andy Allanson	.05
397	*Rod Allen*	.05
398	Scott Bailes	.05
399	Tom Candiotti	.05
400	Joe Carter	.05
401	Carmen Castillo	.05
402	Dave Clark	.05
403	John Farrell	.05
404	Julio Franco	.05
405	Don Gordon	.05
406	Mel Hall	.05
407	Brad Havens	.05
408	Brook Jacoby	.05
409	Doug Jones	.05
410	*Jeff Kaiser*	.05
411	*Luis Medina*	.05
412	Cory Snyder	.05
413	Greg Swindell	.05
414	*Ron Tingley*	.05
415	Willie Upshaw	.05
416	Ron Washington	.05
417	Rich Yett	.05
418	Damon Berryhill	.05
419	Mike Bielecki	.05
420	*Doug Dascenzo*	.05
421	Jody Davis	.05
422	Andre Dawson	.25
423	Frank DiPino	.05
424	Shawon Dunston	.05
425	"Goose" Gossage	.10
426	Mark Grace	.05
427	*Mike Harkey*	.05
428	Darrin Jackson	.05
429	Les Lancaster	.05
430	Vance Law	.05
431	Greg Maddux	.50
432	Jamie Moyer	.05
433	Al Nipper	.05
434	Rafael Palmeiro	.35
435	Pat Perry	.05
436	*Jeff Pico*	.05
437	Ryne Sandberg	.50
438	Calvin Schiraldi	.05
439	Rick Sutcliffe	.05
440a	Manny Trillo ("Throws Rig")	.35
440b	Manny Trillo ("Throws Right")	.05
441	*Gary Varsho*	.05
442	Mitch Webster	.05
443	Luis Alicea	.05
444	Tom Brunansky	.05
445	Vince Coleman	.05
446	*John Costello*	.05
447	Danny Cox	.05
448	Ken Dayley	.05
449	Jose DeLeon	.05
450	Curt Ford	.05
451	Pedro Guerrero	.05
452	Bob Horner	.05
453	*Tim Jones*	.05
454	Steve Lake	.05
455	Joe Magrane	.05
456	Greg Mathews	.05
457	Willie McGee	.05
458	Larry McWilliams	.05
459	Jose Oquendo	.05
460	Tony Pena	.05
461	Terry Pendleton	.05
462	*Steve Peters*	.05
463	Ozzie Smith	.50
464	Scott Terry	.05
465	Denny Walling	.05
466	Todd Worrell	.05
467	Tony Armas	.05
468	*Dante Bichette*	.25
469	Bob Boone	.05
470	*Terry Clark*	.05
471	Stew Cliburn	.05
472	*Mike Cook*	.05
473	*Sherman Corbett*	.05
474	Chili Davis	.05
475	Brian Downing	.05
476	Jim Eppard	.05
477	Chuck Finley	.05
478	Willie Fraser	.05
479	Bryan Harvey	.05
480	Jack Howell	.05
481	Wally Joyner	.05
482	Jack Lazorko	.05
483	Kirk McCaskill	.05
484	Mark McLemore	.05
485	Greg Minton	.05
486	Dan Petry	.05
487	Johnny Ray	.05
488	Dick Schofield	.05
489	Devon White	.05
490	Mike Witt	.05
491	Harold Baines	.05
492	Daryl Boston	.05
493	Ivan Calderon	.05
494	Mike Diaz	.05
495	Carlton Fisk	.40
496	*Dave Gallagher*	.05
497	Ozzie Guillen	.05
498	Shawn Hillegas	.05
499	Lance Johnson	.05
500	Barry Jones	.05
501	Bill Long	.05
502	Steve Lyons	.05
503	Fred Manrique	.05
504	Jack McDowell	.05
505	*Donn Pall*	.05
506	Kelly Paris	.05
507	Dan Pasqua	.05
508	*Ken Patterson*	.05
509	Melido Perez	.05
510	Jerry Reuss	.05
511	Mark Salas	.05
512	Bobby Thigpen	.05
513	Mike Woodard	.05
514	Bob Brower	.05
515	Steve Buechele	.05
516	*Jose Cecena*	.05
517	Cecil Espy	.05
518	Scott Fletcher	.05
519	Cecilio Guante	.05
520	Jose Guzman	.05
521	Ray Hayward	.05
522	Charlie Hough	.05
523	Pete Incaviglia	.05
524	Mike Jeffcoat	.05
525	Paul Kilgus	.05
526	*Chad Kreuter*	.15
527	Jeff Kunkel	.05
528	Oddibe McDowell	.05
529	Pete O'Brien	.05
530	Geno Petralli	.05
531	Jeff Russell	.05
532	Ruben Sierra	.05
533	Mike Stanley	.05
534	Ed Vande Berg	.05
535	Curtis Wilkerson	.05
536	Mitch Williams	.05
537	Bobby Witt	.05
538	Steve Balboni	.05
539	Scott Bankhead	.05
540	Scott Bradley	.05
541	Mickey Brantley	.05
542	Jay Buhner	.05
543	Mike Campbell	.05
544	Darnell Coles	.05
545	Henry Cotto	.05
546	Alvin Davis	.05
547	Mario Diaz	.05
548	*Ken Griffey, Jr.*	6.00
549	*Erik Hanson*	.05
550	Mike Jackson	.05
551	Mark Langston	.05
552	Edgar Martinez	.05
553	*Bill McGuire*	.05
554	Mike Moore	.05
555	Jim Presley	.05
556	Rey Quinones	.05
557	Jerry Reed	.05
558	Harold Reynolds	.05
559	*Mike Schooler*	.05
560	Bill Swift	.05
561	Dave Valle	.05
562	Steve Bedrosian	.05
563	Phil Bradley	.05
564	Don Carman	.05
565	Bob Dernier	.05
566	Marvin Freeman	.05
567	Todd Frohwirth	.05
568	Greg Gross	.05
569	Kevin Gross	.05
570	Greg Harris	.05
571	Von Hayes	.05
572	Chris James	.05
573	Steve Jeltz	.05
574	*Ron Jones*	.05
575	*Ricky Jordan*	.05
576	Mike Maddux	.05
577	David Palmer	.05
578	Lance Parrish	.05
579	Shane Rawley	.05
580	Bruce Ruffin	.05
581	Juan Samuel	.05
582	Mike Schmidt	.60
583	Kent Tekulve	.05
584	Milt Thompson	.05
585	*Jose Alvarez*	.05
586	Paul Assenmacher	.05

#	Player	Value
587	Bruce Benedict	.05
588	Jeff Blauser	.05
589	*Terry Blocker*	.05
590	Ron Gant	.05
591	Tom Glavine	.30
592	Tommy Gregg	.05
593	Albert Hall	.05
594	Dion James	.05
595	Rick Mahler	.05
596	Dale Murphy	.25
597	Gerald Perry	.05
598	Charlie Puleo	.05
599	Ted Simmons	.05
600	Pete Smith	.05
601	Zane Smith	.05
602	John Smoltz	.50
603	Bruce Sutter	.35
604	Andres Thomas	.05
605	Ozzie Virgil	.05
606	Brady Anderson	.05
607	Jeff Ballard	.05
608	*Jose Bautista*	.05
609	Ken Gerhart	.05
610	Terry Kennedy	.05
611	Eddie Murray	.40
612	Carl Nichols	.05
613	Tom Niedenfuer	.05
614	Joe Orsulak	.05
615	*Oswaldo Peraza* (Oswald)	.05
616a	Bill Ripken (vulgarity on bat knob)	8.00
616b	Bill Ripken (scribble over vulgarity)	6.00
616c	Bill Ripken (black box over vulgarity)	.10
616d	Bill Ripken (vulgarity whited out)	75.00
616e	Billy Ripken (strip cut out of bottom of card)	.10
617	Cal Ripken, Jr.	.75
618	Dave Schmidt	.05
619	Rick Schu	.05
620	Larry Sheets	.05
621	Doug Sisk	.05
622	Pete Stanicek	.05
623	Mickey Tettleton	.05
624	Jay Tibbs	.05
625	Jim Traber	.05
626	Mark Williamson	.05
627	*Craig Worthington*	.05
628	Jose Canseco Speed and Power	.20
629	Tom Browning Pitcher Perfect	.05
630	Roberto Alomar, Sandy Alomar, Jr. Like Father Like Sons	.20
631	Will Clark, Rafael Palmeiro N.L. All-Stars	.10
632	Will Clark, Darryl Strawberry Homeruns Coast to Coast	.05
633	Wade Boggs, Carney Lansford Hot Corner's Hot Hitters	.25
634	Jose Canseco, Mark McGwire, Terry Steinbach Triple A's	.40
635	Mark Davis, Dwight Gooden Dual Heat	.05
636	David Cone, Danny Jackson N.L. Pitching Power	.05
637	Bobby Bonilla, Chris Sabo Cannon Arms	.05
638	Andres Galarraga, Gerald Perry Double Trouble	.05
639	Eric Davis Power Center	.05
640	*Cameron Drew, Steve Wilson* Major League Prospects	.05
641	*Kevin Brown, Kevin Reimer* Major League Prospects	.30
642	*Jerald Clark, Brad Pounders* Major League Prospects	.05
643	*Mike Capel, Drew Hall* Major League Prospects	.05
644	*Joe Girardi, Rolando Roomes* Major League Prospects	.20
645	*Marty Brown, Lenny Harris* Major League Prospects	.15
646	*Luis de los Santos, Jim Campbell* Major League Prospects	.05
647	*Miguel Garcia, Randy Kramer* Major League Prospects	.05
648	*Torey Lovullo, Robert Palacios* Major League Prospects	.05
649	*Jim Corsi, Bob Milacki* Major League Prospects	.05
650	*Grady Hall, Mike Rochford* Major League Prospects	.05
651	*Vance Lovelace, Terry Taylor* Major League Prospects	.05
652	*Dennis Cook, Ken Hill* Major League Prospects	.20
653	*Scott Service, Shane Turner* Major League Prospects	.05
654	Checklist 1-101	.05
655	Checklist 102-200	.05
656	Checklist 201-298	.05
657	Checklist 299-395	.05
658	Checklist 396-490	.05
659	Checklist 491-584	.05
660	Checklist 585-660	.05

Update

		NM/M
	Complete Set (132):	6.00
	Common Player:	.05
1	Phil Bradley	.05
2	Mike Devereaux	.05
3	Steve Finley	.05
4	Kevin Hickey	.05
5	Brian Holton	.05
6	Bob Milacki	.05
7	Randy Milligan	.05
8	John Dopson	.05
9	Nick Esasky	.05
10	Rob Murphy	.05
11	Jim Abbott	.05
12	Bert Blyleven	.10
13	Jeff Manto	.05
14	Bob McClure	.05
15	Lance Parrish	.05
16	Lee Stevens	.05
17	Claudell Washington	.05
18	Mark Davis	.05
19	Eric King	.05
20	Ron Kittle	.05
21	Matt Merullo	.05
22	Steve Rosenberg	.05
23	Robin Ventura	.25
24	Keith Atherton	.05
25	*Joey (Albert) Belle*	1.00
26	Jerry Browne	.05
27	Felix Fermin	.05
28	Brad Komminsk	.05
29	Pete O'Brien	.05
30	Mike Brumley	.05
31	Tracy Jones	.05
32	Mike Schwabe	.05
33	Gary Ward	.05
34	Frank Williams	.05
35	*Kevin Appier*	.25
36	Bob Boone	.05
37	Luis de los Santos	.05
38	Jim Eisenreich	.05
39	*Jaime Navarro*	.05
40	Bill Spiers	.05
41	*Greg Vaughn*	.25
42	Randy Veres	.05
43	Wally Backman	.05
44	Shane Rawley	.05
45	Steve Balboni	.05
46	Jesse Barfield	.05
47	Alvaro Espinoza	.05
48	Bob Geren	.05
49	Mel Hall	.05
50	Andy Hawkins	.05
51	Hensley Meulens	.05
52	Steve Sax	.05
53	*Deion Sanders*	.75
54	Rickey Henderson	.40
55	Mike Moore	.05
56	Tony Phillips	.05
57	Greg Briley	.05
58	Gene Harris	.05
59	Randy Johnson	2.00
60	Jeffrey Leonard	.05
61	Dennis Powell	.05
62	Omar Vizquel	.05
63	Kevin Brown	.05
64	Julio Franco	.05
65	Jamie Moyer	.05
66	Rafael Palmeiro	.35
67	Nolan Ryan	1.00
68	Francisco Cabrera	.05
69	Junior Felix	.05
70	Al Leiter	.05
71	Alex Sanchez	.05
72	Geronimo Berroa	.05
73	Derek Lilliquist	.05
74	Lonnie Smith	.05
75	Jeff Treadway	.05
76	Paul Kilgus	.05
77	Lloyd McClendon	.05
78	Scott Sanderson	.05
79	Dwight Smith	.05
80	Jerome Walton	.05
81	Mitch Williams	.05
82	Steve Wilson	.05
83	Todd Benzinger	.05
84	Ken Griffey	.05
85	Rick Mahler	.05
86	Rolando Roomes	.05
87	Scott Scudder	.05
88	Jim Clancy	.05
89	Rick Rhoden	.05
90	Dan Schatzeder	.05
91	Mike Morgan	.05
92	Eddie Murray	.40
93	Willie Randolph	.05
94	Ray Searage	.05
95	Mike Aldrete	.05
96	Kevin Gross	.05
97	Mark Langston	.05
98	Spike Owen	.05
99	Zane Smith	.05
100	Don Aase	.05
101	Barry Lyons	.05
102	Juan Samuel	.05
103	Wally Whitehurst	.05
104	Dennis Cook	.05
105	Len Dykstra	.05
106	Charlie Hayes	.05
107	Tommy Herr	.05
108	Ken Howell	.05
109	John Kruk	.05
110	Roger McDowell	.05
111	Terry Mulholland	.05
112	Jeff Parrett	.05
113	Neal Heaton	.05
114	Jeff King	.05
115	Randy Kramer	.05
116	Bill Landrum	.05
117	Cris Carpenter	.05
118	Frank DiPino	.05
119	Ken Hill	.05
120	Dan Quisenberry	.05
121	Milt Thompson	.05
122	*Todd Zeile*	.25
123	Jack Clark	.05
124	Bruce Hurst	.05
125	Mark Parent	.05
126	Bip Roberts	.05
127	Jeff Brantley	.05
128	Terry Kennedy	.05
129	Mike LaCoss	.05
130	Greg Litton	.05
131	Mike Schmidt	.65
132	Checklist	.05

1989 FLEER GLOSSY TIN

	NM/M
Unopened Set (672):	75.00
Complete Set (672):	50.00
Common Player:	.25

(Star cards valued at 3-4X regular 1989 Fleer cards.)

1990 FLEER

		NM/M
	Factory Hobby Set (672):	12.50
	Retail Hobby Set (660):	12.00
	Complete Set (660):	10.00
	Common Player:	.05
	Wax Pack (15):	.50
	Wax Box (36):	10.00
	Cello Pack (33):	1.00
	Cello Box (24):	12.00
1	Lance Blankenship	.05
2	Todd Burns	.05
3	Jose Canseco	.30
4	Jim Corsi	.05
5	Storm Davis	.05
6	Dennis Eckersley	.35
7	Mike Gallego	.05
8	Ron Hassey	.05
9	Dave Henderson	.05
10	Rickey Henderson	.40
11	Rick Honeycutt	.05
12	Stan Javier	.05
13	Felix Jose	.05
14	Carney Lansford	.05
15	Mark McGwire	.65
16	Mike Moore	.05
17	Gene Nelson	.05
18	Dave Parker	.05
19	Tony Phillips	.05
20	Terry Steinbach	.05
21	Dave Stewart	.05
22	Walt Weiss	.05
23	Bob Welch	.05
24	Curt Young	.05
25	Paul Assenmacher	.05
26	Damon Berryhill	.05
27	Mike Bielecki	.05
28	Kevin Blankenship	.05
29	Andre Dawson	.25
30	Shawon Dunston	.05
31	Joe Girardi	.05
32	Mark Grace	.05
33	Mike Harkey	.05
34	Paul Kilgus	.05
35	Les Lancaster	.05
36	Vance Law	.05
37	Greg Maddux	.50
38	Lloyd McClendon	.05
39	Jeff Pico	.05
40	Ryne Sandberg	.50
41	Scott Sanderson	.05
42	Dwight Smith	.05
43	Rick Sutcliffe	.05
44	*Jerome Walton*	.05
45	Mitch Webster	.05
46	Curt Wilkerson	.05
47	*Dean Wilkins*	.05
48	Mitch Williams	.05
49	Steve Wilson	.05
50	Steve Bedrosian	.05
51	*Mike Benjamin*	.05
52	*Jeff Brantley*	.10
53	Brett Butler	.05
54	Will Clark	.05
55	Kelly Downs	.05
56	Scott Garrelts	.05
57	Atlee Hammaker	.05
58	Terry Kennedy	.05
59	Mike LaCoss	.05
60	Craig Lefferts	.05
61	*Greg Litton*	.05
62	Candy Maldonado	.05
63	Kirt Manwaring	.05
64	*Randy McCament*	.05
65	Kevin Mitchell	.05
66	Donell Nixon	.05
67	Ken Oberkfell	.05
68	Rick Reuschel	.05
69	Ernest Riles	.05
70	Don Robinson	.05
71	Pat Sheridan	.05
72	Chris Speier	.05
73	Robby Thompson	.05
74	Jose Uribe	.05
75	Matt Williams	.05
76	George Bell	.05
77	Pat Borders	.05
78	John Cerutti	.05
79	*Junior Felix*	.05
80	Tony Fernandez	.05
81	Mike Flanagan	.05
82	*Mauro Gozzo*	.05
83	Kelly Gruber	.05
84	Tom Henke	.05
85	Jimmy Key	.05
86	Manny Lee	.05
87	Nelson Liriano	.05
88	Lee Mazzilli	.05
89	Fred McGriff	.05
90	Lloyd Moseby	.05

No.	Player	Value
91	Rance Mulliniks	.05
92	Alex Sanchez	.05
93	Dave Steib	.05
94	Todd Stottlemyre	.05
95	Duane Ward	.05
96	David Wells	.05
97	Ernie Whitt	.05
98	Frank Wills	.05
99	Mookie Wilson	.05
100	Kevin Appier	.05
101	Luis Aquino	.05
102	Bob Boone	.05
103	George Brett	.60
104	Jose DeJesus	.05
105	Luis de los Santos	.05
106	Jim Eisenreich	.05
107	Steve Farr	.05
108	Tom Gordon	.05
109	Mark Gubicza	.05
110	Bo Jackson	.10
111	Terry Leach	.05
112	Charlie Leibrandt	.05
113	*Rick Luecken*	.05
114	Mike Macfarlane	.05
115	Jeff Montgomery	.05
116	Bret Saberhagen	.05
117	Kevin Seitzer	.05
118	Kurt Stillwell	.05
119	Pat Tabler	.05
120	Danny Tartabull	.05
121	Gary Thurman	.05
122	Frank White	.05
123	Willie Wilson	.05
124	*Matt Winters*	.05
125	Jim Abbott	.05
126	Tony Armas	.05
127	Dante Bichette	.05
128	Bert Blyleven	.10
129	Chili Davis	.05
130	Brian Downing	.05
131	*Mike Fetters*	.05
132	Chuck Finley	.05
133	Willie Fraser	.05
134	Bryan Harvey	.05
135	Jack Howell	.05
136	Wally Joyner	.05
137	*Jeff Manto*	.05
138	Kirk McCaskill	.05
139	Bob McClure	.05
140	Greg Minton	.05
141	Lance Parrish	.05
142	Dan Petry	.05
143	Johnny Ray	.05
144	Dick Schofield	.05
145	*Lee Stevens*	.05
146	Claudell Washington	.05
147	Devon White	.05
148	Mike Witt	.05
149	Roberto Alomar	.20
150	Sandy Alomar, Jr.	.05
151	Andy Benes	.05
152	Jack Clark	.05
153	Pat Clements	.05
154	Joey Cora	.05
155	Mark Davis	.05
156	Mark Grant	.05
157	Tony Gwynn	.50
158	Greg Harris	.05
159	Bruce Hurst	.05
160	Darrin Jackson	.05
161	Chris James	.05
162	Carmelo Martinez	.05
163	Mike Pagliarulo	.05
164	Mark Parent	.05
165	Dennis Rasmussen	.05
166	Bip Roberts	.05
167	Benito Santiago	.05
168	Calvin Schiraldi	.05
169	Eric Show	.05
170	Garry Templeton	.05
171	Ed Whitson	.05
172	Brady Anderson	.05
173	Jeff Ballard	.05
174	Phil Bradley	.05
175	Mike Devereaux	.05
176	Steve Finley	.05
177	Pete Harnisch	.05
178	Kevin Hickey	.05
179	Brian Holton	.05
180	*Ben McDonald*	.15
181	Bob Melvin	.05
182	Bob Milacki	.05
183	Randy Milligan	.05
184	Gregg Olson	.05
185	Joe Orsulak	.05
186	Bill Ripken	.05
187	Cal Ripken, Jr.	.75
188	Dave Schmidt	.05
189	Larry Sheets	.05
190	Mickey Tettleton	.05
191	Mark Thurmond	.05
192	Jay Tibbs	.05
193	Jim Traber	.05
194	Mark Williamson	.05
195	Craig Worthington	.05
196	Don Aase	.05
197	*Blaine Beatty*	.05
198	Mark Carreon	.05
199	Gary Carter	.40
200	David Cone	.05
201	Ron Darling	.05
202	Kevin Elster	.05
203	Sid Fernandez	.05
204	Dwight Gooden	.05
205	Keith Hernandez	.05
206	*Jeff Innis*	.05
207	Gregg Jefferies	.05
208	Howard Johnson	.05
209	Barry Lyons	.05
210	Dave Magadan	.05
211	Kevin McReynolds	.05
212	Jeff Musselman	.05
213	Randy Myers	.05
214	Bob Ojeda	.05
215	Juan Samuel	.05
216	Mackey Sasser	.05
217	Darryl Strawberry	.05
218	Tim Teufel	.05
219	Frank Viola	.05
220	Juan Agosto	.05
221	Larry Anderson	.05
222	*Eric Anthony*	.10
223	Kevin Bass	.05
224	Craig Biggio	.05
225	Ken Caminiti	.05
226	Jim Clancy	.05
227	Danny Darwin	.05
228	Glenn Davis	.05
229	Jim Deshaies	.05
230	Bill Doran	.05
231	Bob Forsch	.05
232	Brian Meyer	.05
233	Terry Puhl	.05
234	Rafael Ramirez	.05
235	Rick Rhoden	.05
236	Dan Schatzeder	.05
237	Mike Scott	.05
238	Dave Smith	.05
239	Alex Trevino	.05
240	Glenn Wilson	.05
241	Gerald Young	.05
242	Tom Brunansky	.05
243	Cris Carpenter	.05
244	*Alex Cole*	.05
245	Vince Coleman	.05
246	John Costello	.05
247	Ken Dayley	.05
248	Jose DeLeon	.05
249	Frank DiPino	.05
250	Pedro Guerrero	.05
251	Ken Hill	.05
252	Joe Magrane	.05
253	Willie McGee	.05
254	John Morris	.05
255	Jose Oquendo	.05
256	Tony Pena	.05
257	Terry Pendleton	.05
258	Ted Power	.05
259	Dan Quisenberry	.05
260	Ozzie Smith	.50
261	Scott Terry	.05
262	Milt Thompson	.05
263	Denny Walling	.05
264	Todd Worrell	.05
265	Todd Zeile	.05
266	Marty Barrett	.05
267	Mike Boddicker	.05
268	Wade Boggs	.50
269	Ellis Burks	.05
270	Rick Cerone	.05
271	Roger Clemens	.60
272	John Dopson	.05
273	Nick Esasky	.05
274	Dwight Evans	.05
275	Wes Gardner	.05
276	Rich Gedman	.05
277	Mike Greenwell	.05
278	Danny Heep	.05
279	Eric Hetzel	.05
280	Dennis Lamp	.05
281	Rob Murphy	.05
282	Joe Price	.05
283	Carlos Quintana	.05
284	Jody Reed	.05
285	Luis Rivera	.05
286	Kevin Romine	.05
287	Lee Smith	.05
288	Mike Smithson	.05
289	Bob Stanley	.05
290	Harold Baines	.05
291	Kevin Brown	.05
292	Steve Buechele	.05
293	*Scott Coolbaugh*	.05
294	*Jack Daugherty*	.05
295	Cecil Espy	.05
296	Julio Franco	.05
297	*Juan Gonzalez*	2.00
298	Cecilio Guante	.05
299	Drew Hall	.05
300	Charlie Hough	.05
301	Pete Incaviglia	.05
302	Mike Jeffcoat	.05
303	Chad Kreuter	.05
304	Jeff Kunkel	.05
305	Rick Leach	.05
306	Fred Manrique	.05
307	Jamie Moyer	.05
308	Rafael Palmeiro	.35
309	Geno Petralli	.05
310	Kevin Reimer	.05
311	*Kenny Rogers*	.10
312	Jeff Russell	.05
313	Nolan Ryan	.75
314	Ruben Sierra	.05
315	Bobby Witt	.05
316	Chris Bosio	.05
317	Glenn Braggs	.05
318	Greg Brock	.05
319	Chuck Crim	.05
320	Rob Deer	.05
321	Mike Felder	.05
322	Tom Filer	.05
323	*Tony Fossas*	.05
324	Jim Gantner	.05
325	Darryl Hamilton	.05
326	Ted Higuera	.05
327	Mark Knudson	.05
328	Bill Krueger	.05
329	*Tim McIntosh*	.05
330	Paul Molitor	.40
331	Jaime Navarro	.05
332	Charlie O'Brien	.05
333	*Jeff Peterek*	.05
334	Dan Plesac	.05
335	Jerry Reuss	.05
336	Gary Sheffield	.35
337	*Bill Spiers*	.05
338	B.J. Surhoff	.05
339	Greg Vaughn	.05
340	Robin Yount	.40
341	Hubie Brooks	.05
342	Tim Burke	.05
343	Mike Fitzgerald	.05
344	Tom Foley	.05
345	Andres Galarraga	.05
346	Damaso Garcia	.05
347	*Marquis Grissom*	.50
348	Kevin Gross	.05
349	Joe Hesketh	.05
350	*Jeff Huson*	.05
351	Wallace Johnson	.05
352	Mark Langston	.05
353a	Dave Martinez (yellow 90)	6.00
353b	Dave Martinez (red 90)	.05
354	Dennis Martinez	.05
355	Andy McGaffigan	.05
356	Otis Nixon	.05
357	Spike Owen	.05
358	Pascual Perez	.05
359	Tim Raines	.05
360	Nelson Santovenia	.05
361	Bryn Smith	.05
362	Zane Smith	.05
363	*Larry Walker*	.75
364	Tim Wallach	.05
365	Rick Aguilera	.05
366	Allan Anderson	.05
367	Wally Backman	.05
368	Doug Baker	.05
369	Juan Berenguer	.05
370	Randy Bush	.05
371	Carmen Castillo	.05
372	*Mike Dyer*	.05
373	Gary Gaetti	.05
374	Greg Gagne	.05
375	Dan Gladden	.05
376	German Gonzalez	.05
377	Brian Harper	.05
378	Kent Hrbek	.05
379	Gene Larkin	.05
380	Tim Laudner	.05
381	John Moses	.05
382	Al Newman	.05
383	Kirby Puckett	.50
384	Shane Rawley	.05
385	Jeff Reardon	.05
386	Roy Smith	.05
387	*Gary Wayne*	.05
388	Dave West	.05
389	Tim Belcher	.05
390	Tim Crews	.05
391	Mike Davis	.05
392	Rick Dempsey	.05
393	Kirk Gibson	.05
394	Jose Gonzalez	.05
395	Alfredo Griffin	.05
396	Jeff Hamilton	.05
397	Lenny Harris	.05
398	Mickey Hatcher	.05
399	Orel Hershiser	.05
400	Jay Howell	.05
401	Mike Marshall	.05
402	Ramon Martinez	.05
403	Mike Morgan	.05
404	Eddie Murray	.40
405	Alejandro Pena	.05
406	Willie Randolph	.05
407	Mike Scioscia	.05
408	Ray Searage	.05
409	Fernando Valenzuela	.05
410	*Jose Vizcaino*	.10
411	*John Wetteland*	.20
412	Jack Armstrong	.05
413	Todd Benzinger	.05
414	Tim Birtsas	.05
415	Tom Browning	.05
416	Norm Charlton	.05
417	Eric Davis	.05
418	Rob Dibble	.05
419	John Franco	.05
420	Ken Griffey, Sr.	.05
421	*Chris Hammond*	.15
422	Danny Jackson	.05
423	Barry Larkin	.05
424	Tim Leary	.05
425	Rick Mahler	.05
426	*Joe Oliver*	.05
427	Paul O'Neill	.05
428	Luis Quinones	.05
429	Jeff Reed	.05
430	Jose Rijo	.05
431	Ron Robinson	.05
432	Rolando Roomes	.05
433	Chris Sabo	.05
434	*Scott Scudder*	.05
435	Herm Winningham	.05
436	Steve Balboni	.05
437	Jesse Barfield	.05
438	*Mike Blowers*	.05
439	Tom Brookens	.05
440	Greg Cadaret	.05
441	Alvaro Espinoza	.05
442	*Bob Geren*	.05
443	Lee Guetterman	.05
444	Mel Hall	.05
445	Andy Hawkins	.05
446	Roberto Kelly	.05
447	Don Mattingly	.60
448	Lance McCullers	.05
449	Hensley Meulens	.05
450	Dale Mohorcic	.05
451	Clay Parker	.05
452	Eric Plunk	.05
453	Dave Righetti	.05
454	Deion Sanders	.10
455	Steve Sax	.05
456	Don Slaught	.05
457	Walt Terrell	.05
458	Dave Winfield	.40
459	Jay Bell	.05
460	Rafael Belliard	.05
461	Barry Bonds	.75
462	Bobby Bonilla	.05
463	Sid Bream	.05
464	Benny Distefano	.05
465	Doug Drabek	.05
466	Jim Gott	.05
467	Billy Hatcher	.05
468	Neal Heaton	.05
469	Jeff King	.05
470	Bob Kipper	.05
471	Randy Kramer	.05
472	Bill Landrum	.05
473	Mike LaValliere	.05
474	Jose Lind	.05
475	Junior Ortiz	.05
476	Gary Redus	.05
477	*Rick Reed*	.05
478	R.J. Reynolds	.05
479	Jeff Robinson	.05
480	John Smiley	.05
481	Andy Van Slyke	.05
482	Bob Walk	.05
483	Andy Allanson	.05
484	Scott Bailes	.05

485 Albert Belle .05
486 Bud Black .05
487 Jerry Browne .05
488 Tom Candiotti .05
489 Joe Carter .05
490 David Clark .05
491 John Farrell .05
492 Felix Fermin .05
493 Brook Jacoby .05
494 Dion James .05
495 Doug Jones .05
496 Brad Komminsk .05
497 Rod Nichols .05
498 Pete O'Brien .05
499 *Steve Olin* .05
500 Jesse Orosco .05
501 Joel Skinner .05
502 Cory Snyder .05
503 Greg Swindell .05
504 Rich Yett .05
505 Scott Bankhead .05
506 Scott Bradley .05
507 Greg Briley .05
508 Jay Buhner .05
509 Darnell Coles .05
510 Keith Comstock .05
511 Henry Cotto .05
512 Alvin Davis .05
513 Ken Griffey, Jr. .65
514 Erik Hanson .05
515 Gene Harris .05
516 Brian Holman .05
517 Mike Jackson .05
518 Randy Johnson .40
519 Jeffrey Leonard .05
520 Edgar Martinez .05
521 Dennis Powell .05
522 Jim Presley .05
523 Jerry Reed .05
524 Harold Reynolds .05
525 Mike Schooler .05
526 Bill Swift .05
527 David Valle .05
528 Omar Vizquel .05
529 Ivan Calderon .05
530 Carlton Fisk .40
531 Scott Fletcher .05
532 Dave Gallagher .05
533 Ozzie Guillen .05
534 *Greg Hibbard* .05
535 Shawn Hillegas .05
536 Lance Johnson .05
537 Eric King .05
538 Ron Kittle .05
539 Steve Lyons .05
540 Carlos Martinez .05
541 *Tom McCarthy* .05
542 *Matt Merullo* .05
543 Donn Pall .05
544 Dan Pasqua .05
545 Ken Patterson .05
546 Melido Perez .05
547 Steve Rosenberg .05
548 *Sammy Sosa* 5.00
549 Bobby Thigpen .05
550 Robin Ventura .05
551 Greg Walker .05
552 Don Carman .05
553 *Pat Combs* .05
554 Dennis Cook .05
555 Darren Daulton .05
556 Len Dykstra .05
557 Curt Ford .05
558 Charlie Hayes .05
559 Von Hayes .05
560 Tom Herr .05
561 Ken Howell .05
562 Steve Jeltz .05
563 Ron Jones .05
564 Ricky Jordan .05
565 John Kruk .05
566 Steve Lake .05
567 Roger McDowell .05
568 Terry Mulholland .05
569 Dwayne Murphy .05
570 Jeff Parrett .05
571 Randy Ready .05
572 Bruce Ruffin .05
573 Dickie Thon .05
574 Jose Alvarez .05
575 Geronimo Berroa .05
576 Jeff Blauser .05
577 Joe Boever .05
578 Marty Clary .05
579 Jody Davis .05
580 Mark Eichhorn .05
581 Darrell Evans .05
582 Ron Gant .05
583 Tom Glavine .25
584 *Tommy Greene* .05
585 Tommy Gregg .05
586 *Dave Justice* .40
587 Mark Lemke .05
588 Derek Lilliquist .05
589 Oddibe McDowell .05
590 *Kent Mercker* .05
591 Dale Murphy .20
592 Gerald Perry .05
593 Lonnie Smith .05
594 Pete Smith .05
595 John Smoltz .05
596 *Mike Stanton* .05
597 Andres Thomas .05
598 Jeff Treadway .05
599 Doyle Alexander .05
600 Dave Bergman .05
601 *Brian Dubois* .05
602 Paul Gibson .05
603 Mike Heath .05
604 Mike Henneman .05
605 Guillermo Hernandez .05
606 *Shawn Holman* .05
607 Tracy Jones .05
608 Chet Lemon .05
609 Fred Lynn .05
610 Jack Morris .05
611 Matt Nokes .05
612 Gary Pettis .05
613 *Kevin Ritz* .05
614 Jeff Robinson .05
615 Steve Searcy .05
616 Frank Tanana .05
617 Alan Trammell .05
618 Gary Ward .05
619 Lou Whitaker .05
620 Frank Williams .05
621a George Brett Players of the Decade - 1980 (... 10 .390 hitting ...) 1.00
621b George Brett Players of the Decade - 1980 .25
622 Fernando Valenzuela Players of the Decade - 1981 .05
623 Dale Murphy Players of the Decade - 1982 .05
624a Cal Ripkin, Jr. Players of the Decade - 1983 (Ripken) 1.50
624b Cal Ripken, Jr. Players of the Decade - 1983 .30
625 Ryne Sandberg Players of the Decade - 1984 .25
626 Don Mattingly Players of the Decade - 1985 .30
627 Roger Clemens Players of the Decade - 1986 .30
628 George Bell Players of the Decade - 1987 .05
629 Jose Canseco Players of the Decade - 1988 .10
630a Will Clark Players of the Decade - 1989 (total bases 32) .35
630b Will Clark Players of the Decade - 1989 (total bases 321) .05
631 Mark Davis, Mitch Williams Game Savers .05
632 Wade Boggs, Mike Greenwell Boston Igniters .15
633 Mark Gubicza, Jeff Russell Starter & Stopper .05
634 Tony Fernandez, Cal Ripken Jr. League's Best Shortstops .30
635 Kirby Puckett, Bo Jackson Human Dynamos .20
636 Mike Scott, Nolan Ryan 300 Strikeout Club .30
637 Will Clark, Kevin Mitchell The Dymanic Duo .05
638 Don Mattingly, Mark McGwire A.L. All-Stars .65
639 Howard Johnson, Ryne Sandberg N.L. East Rivals .20
640 *Rudy Seanez, Colin Charland* Major League Prospects .05
641 *George Canale, Kevin Maas* Major League Prospects .10
642 *Kelly Mann, Dave Hansen* Major League Prospects .05
643 *Greg Smith, Stu Tate* Major League Prospects .05
644 *Tom Drees, Dan Howitt* Major League Prospects .05
645 *Mike Roesler, Derrick May* Major League Prospects .05
646 *Scott Hemond, Mark Gardner* Major League Prospects .10
647 *John Orton, Scott Leius* Major League Prospects .10
648 *Rich Monteleone, Dana Williams* Major League Prospects .05
649 *Mike Huff, Steve Frey* Major League Prospects .05
650 *Chuck McElroy, Moises Alou* Major League Prospects .50
651 *Bobby Rose, Mike Hartley* Major League Prospects .10
652 *Matt Kinzer, Wayne Edwards* Major League Prospects .05
653 *Delino DeShields, Jason Grimsley* Major League Prospects .15
654 Athletics, Cubs, Giants & Blue Jays (Checklist) .05
655 Royals, Angels, Padres & Orioles (Checklist) .05
656 Mets, Astros, Cardinals & Red Sox (Checklist) .05
657 Rangers, Brewers, Expos & Twins (Checklist) .05
658 Dodgers, Reds, Yankees & Pirates (Checklist) .05
659 Indians, Mariners, White Sox & Phillies (Checklist) .05
660 Braves, Tigers & Special Cards (Checklist) .05

Update

NM/M

Complete Set (132): 3.00
Common Player: .05
1 Steve Avery .05
2 Francisco Cabrera .05
3 Nick Esasky .05
4 Jim Kremers .05
5 Greg Olson .05
6 Jim Presley .05
7 Shawn Boskie .05
8 Joe Kraemer .05
9 Luis Salazar .05
10 Hector Villanueva .05
11 Glenn Braggs .05
12 Mariano Duncan .05
13 Billy Hatcher .05
14 Tim Layana .05
15 Hal Morris .05
16 Javier Ortiz .05
17 Dave Rohde .05
18 Eric Yelding .05
19 Hubie Brooks .05
20 Kal Daniels .05
21 Dave Hansen .05
22 Mike Hartley .05
23 Stan Javier .05
24 Jose Offerman .05
25 Juan Samuel .05
26 Dennis Boyd .05
27 Delino DeShields .05
28 Steve Frey .05
29 Mark Gardner .05
30 Chris Nabholz .05
31 Bill Sampen .05
32 Dave Schmidt .05
33 Daryl Boston .05
34 Chuck Carr .05
35 John Franco .05
36 *Todd Hundley* .25
37 Julio Machado .05
38 Alejandro Pena .05
39 Darren Reed .05
40 Kelvin Torve .05
41 Darrel Akerfelds .05
42 Jose DeJesus .05
43 Dave Hollins .05
44 Carmelo Martinez .05
45 Brad Moore .05
46 Dale Murphy .15
47 Wally Backman .05
48 Stan Belinda .05
49 Bob Patterson .05
50 Ted Power .05
51 Don Slaught .05
52 Geronimo Pena .05
53 Lee Smith .05
54 John Tudor .05
55 Joe Carter .05
56 Tom Howard .05
57 Craig Lefferts .05
58 Rafael Valdez .05
59 Dave Anderson .05
60 Kevin Bass .05
61 John Burkett .05
62 Gary Carter .40
63 Rick Parker .05
64 Trevor Wilson .05
65 Chris Hoiles .05
66 Tim Hulett .05
67 Dave Johnson .05
68 Curt Schilling .35
69 David Segui .05
70 Tom Brunansky .05
71 Greg Harris .05
72 Dana Kiecker .05
73 Tim Naehring .05
74 Tony Pena .05
75 Jeff Reardon .05
76 Jerry Reed .05
77 Mark Eichhorn .05
78 Mark Langston .05
79 John Orton .05
80 Luis Polonia .05
81 Dave Winfield .40
82 Cliff Young .05
83 Wayne Edwards .05
84 Alex Fernandez .05
85 Craig Grebeck .05
86 Scott Radinsky .05
87 Frank Thomas 2.00
88 Beau Allred .05
89 Sandy Alomar, Jr. .05
90 *Carlos Baerga* .10
91 Kevin Bearse .05
92 Chris James .05
93 Candy Maldonado .05
94 Jeff Manto .05
95 Cecil Fielder .05
96 *Travis Fryman* .25
97 Lloyd Moseby .05
98 Edwin Nunez .05
99 Tony Phillips .05
100 Larry Sheets .05
101 Mark Davis .05
102 Storm Davis .05
103 Gerald Perry .05
104 Terry Shumpert .05
105 Edgar Diaz .05
106 Dave Parker .05
107 Tim Drummond .05
108 Junior Ortiz .05
109 Park Pittman .05
110 Kevin Tapani .05
111 Oscar Azocar .05
112 Jim Leyritz .05
113 Kevin Maas .05
114 Alan Mills .05
115 Matt Nokes .05
116 Pascual Perez .05
117 Ozzie Canseco .05
118 Scott Sanderson .05
119 Tino Martinez .05
120 Jeff Schaefer .05
121 Matt Young .05
122 Brian Bohanon .05
123 Jeff Huson .05
124 Ramon Manon .05
125 Gary Mielke .05
126 Willie Blair .05
127 Glenallen Hill .05
128 *John Olerud* .35
129 Luis Sojo .05
130 Mark Whiten .05
131 Nolan Ryan Three Decades of No Hitters 1.00
132 Checklist .05

1991 FLEER

NM/M

Unopened Factory Set (732): 12.00
Complete Set (720): 10.00
Common Player: .05
Wax Pack (15): .50
Wax Box (36): 12.50

Jumbo Wax Pack (53):		1.25
Jumbo Wax Box (24):		20.00
Cello Pack (30):		1.00
Cello Box (24):		16.00
1	*Troy Afenir*	.05
2	Harold Baines	.05
3	Lance Blankenship	.05
4	Todd Burns	.05
5	Jose Canseco	.30
6	Dennis Eckersley	.35
7	Mike Gallego	.05
8	Ron Hassey	.05
9	Dave Henderson	.05
10	Rickey Henderson	.40
11	Rick Honeycutt	.05
12	Doug Jennings	.05
13	*Joe Klink*	.05
14	Carney Lansford	.05
15	*Darren Lewis*	.05
16	Willie McGee	.05
17a	Mark McGwire (six-line career summary)	.65
17b	Mark McGwire (seven-line career summary)	.65
18	Mike Moore	.05
19	Gene Nelson	.05
20	Dave Otto	.05
21	Jamie Quirk	.05
22	Willie Randolph	.05
23	Scott Sanderson	.05
24	Terry Steinbach	.05
25	Dave Stewart	.05
26	Walt Weiss	.05
27	Bob Welch	.05
28	Curt Young	.05
29	Wally Backman	.05
30	*Stan Belinda*	.05
31	Jay Bell	.05
32	Rafael Belliard	.05
33	Barry Bonds	.75
34	Bobby Bonilla	.05
35	Sid Bream	.05
36	Doug Drabek	.05
37	*Carlos Garcia*	.10
38	Neal Heaton	.05
39	Jeff King	.05
40	Bob Kipper	.05
41	Bill Landrum	.05
42	Mike LaValliere	.05
43	Jose Lind	.05
44	Carmelo Martinez	.05
45	Bob Patterson	.05
46	Ted Power	.05
47	Gary Redus	.05
48	R.J. Reynolds	.05
49	Don Slaught	.05
50	John Smiley	.05
51	Zane Smith	.05
52	*Randy Tomlin*	.10
53	Andy Van Slyke	.05
54	Bob Walk	.05
55	Jack Armstrong	.05
56	Todd Benzinger	.05
57	Glenn Braggs	.05
58	Keith Brown	.05
59	Tom Browning	.05
60	Norm Charlton	.05
61	Eric Davis	.05
62	Rob Dibble	.05
63	Bill Doran	.05
64	Mariano Duncan	.05
65	Chris Hammond	.05
66	Billy Hatcher	.05
67	Danny Jackson	.05
68	Barry Larkin	.05
69	*Tim Layana*	.05
70	*Terry Lee*	.05
71	Rick Mahler	.05
72	Hal Morris	.05
73	Randy Myers	.05
74	Ron Oester	.05
75	Joe Oliver	.05
76	Paul O'Neill	.05
77	Luis Quinones	.05
78	Jeff Reed	.05
79	Jose Rijo	.05
80	Chris Sabo	.05
81	Scott Scudder	.05
82	Herm Winningham	.05
83	Larry Andersen	.05
84	Marty Barrett	.05
85	Mike Boddicker	.05
86	Wade Boggs	.50
87	Tom Bolton	.05
88	Tom Brunansky	.05
89	Ellis Burks	.05
90	Roger Clemens	.55
91	Scott Cooper	.05
92	John Dopson	.05
93	Dwight Evans	.05
94	Wes Gardner	.05
95	*Jeff Gray*	.05
96	Mike Greenwell	.05
97	Greg Harris	.05
98	*Daryl Irvine*	.05
99	*Dana Kiecker*	.05
100	Randy Kutcher	.05
101	Dennis Lamp	.05
102	Mike Marshall	.05
103	John Marzano	.05
104	Rob Murphy	.05
105a	*Tim Naehring* (seven-line career summary)	.05
105b	*Tim Naehring* (nine-line career summary)	.05
106	Tony Pena	.05
107	*Phil Plantier*	.05
108	Carlos Quintana	.05
109	Jeff Reardon	.05
110	Jerry Reed	.05
111	Jody Reed	.05
112	Luis Rivera	.05
113a	Kevin Romine (one-line career summary)	.05
113b	Kevin Romine (two-line career summary)	.05
114	Phil Bradley	.05
115	Ivan Calderon	.05
116	Wayne Edwards	.05
117	Alex Fernandez	.05
118	Carlton Fisk	.40
119	Scott Fletcher	.05
120	*Craig Grebeck*	.05
121	Ozzie Guillen	.05
122	Greg Hibbard	.05
123	Lance Johnson	.05
124	Barry Jones	.05
125a	Ron Karkovice (two-line career summary)	.05
125b	Ron Karkovice (one-line career summary)	.05
126	Eric King	.05
127	Steve Lyons	.05
128	Carlos Martinez	.05
129	Jack McDowell	.05
130	Donn Pall	.05
131	Dan Pasqua	.05
132	Ken Patterson	.05
133	Melido Perez	.05
134	Adam Peterson	.05
135	*Scott Radinsky*	.05
136	Sammy Sosa	.50
137	Bobby Thigpen	.05
138	Frank Thomas	.40
139	Robin Ventura	.05
140	Daryl Boston	.05
141	*Chuck Carr*	.05
142	Mark Carreon	.05
143	David Cone	.05
144	Ron Darling	.05
145	Kevin Elster	.05
146	Sid Fernandez	.05
147	John Franco	.05
148	Dwight Gooden	.05
149	Tom Herr	.05
150	Todd Hundley	.05
151	Gregg Jefferies	.05
152	Howard Johnson	.05
153	Dave Magadan	.05
154	Kevin McReynolds	.05
155	Keith Miller	.05
156	Bob Ojeda	.05
157	Tom O'Malley	.05
158	Alejandro Pena	.05
159	*Darren Reed*	.05
160	Mackey Sasser	.05
161	Darryl Strawberry	.05
162	Tim Teufel	.05
163	Kelvin Torve	.05
164	Julio Valera	.05
165	Frank Viola	.05
166	Wally Whitehurst	.05
167	Jim Acker	.05
168	*Derek Bell*	.10
169	George Bell	.05
170	*Willie Blair*	.05
171	Pat Borders	.05
172	John Cerutti	.05
173	Junior Felix	.05
174	Tony Fernandez	.05
175	Kelly Gruber	.05
176	Tom Henke	.05
177	Glenallen Hill	.05
178	Jimmy Key	.05
179	Manny Lee	.05
180	Fred McGriff	.05
181	Rance Mulliniks	.05
182	Greg Myers	.05
183	John Olerud	.05
184	Luis Sojo	.05
185	Dave Steib	.05
186	Todd Stottlemyre	.05
187	Duane Ward	.05
188	David Wells	.05
189	*Mark Whiten*	.05
190	Ken Williams	.05
191	Frank Wills	.05
192	Mookie Wilson	.05
193	Don Aase	.05
194	Tim Belcher	.05
195	Hubie Brooks	.05
196	Dennis Cook	.05
197	Tim Crews	.05
198	Kal Daniels	.05
199	Kirk Gibson	.05
200	Jim Gott	.05
201	Alfredo Griffin	.05
202	Chris Gwynn	.05
203	Dave Hansen	.05
204	Lenny Harris	.05
205	Mike Hartley	.05
206	Mickey Hatcher	.05
207	*Carlos Hernandez*	.05
208	Orel Hershiser	.05
209	Jay Howell	.05
210	Mike Huff	.05
211	Stan Javier	.05
212	Ramon Martinez	.05
213	Mike Morgan	.05
214	Eddie Murray	.40
215	*Jim Neidlinger*	.05
216	Jose Offerman	.05
217	*Jim Poole*	.05
218	Juan Samuel	.05
219	Mike Scioscia	.05
220	Ray Searage	.05
221	Mike Sharperson	.05
222	Fernando Valenzuela	.05
223	Jose Vizcaino	.05
224	Mike Aldrete	.05
225	*Scott Anderson*	.05
226	Dennis Boyd	.05
227	Tim Burke	.05
228	Delino DeShields	.05
229	Mike Fitzgerald	.05
230	Tom Foley	.05
231	Steve Frey	.05
232	Andres Galarraga	.05
233	Mark Gardner	.05
234	Marquis Grissom	.05
235	Kevin Gross	.05
236	Drew Hall	.05
237	Dave Martinez	.05
238	Dennis Martinez	.05
239	Dale Mohorcic	.05
240	*Chris Nabholz*	.05
241	Otis Nixon	.05
242	Junior Noboa	.05
243	Spike Owen	.05
244	Tim Raines	.05
245	*Mel Rojas*	.10
246	*Scott Ruskin*	.05
247	*Bill Sampen*	.05
248	Nelson Santovenia	.05
249	Dave Schmidt	.05
250	Larry Walker	.05
251	Tim Wallach	.05
252	Dave Anderson	.05
253	Kevin Bass	.05
254	Steve Bedrosian	.05
255	Jeff Brantley	.05
256	John Burkett	.05
257	Brett Butler	.05
258	Gary Carter	.40
259	Will Clark	.05
260	*Steve Decker*	.05
261	Kelly Downs	.05
262	Scott Garrelts	.05
263	Terry Kennedy	.05
264	Mike LaCoss (photo on back actually Ken Oberkfell)	.05
265	*Mark Leonard*	.05
266	Greg Litton	.05
267	Kevin Mitchell	.05
268	Randy O'Neal	.05
269	*Rick Parker*	.05
270	Rick Reuschel	.05
271	Ernest Riles	.05
272	Don Robinson	.05
273	Robby Thompson	.05
274	Mark Thurmond	.05
275	Jose Uribe	.05
276	Matt Williams	.05
277	Trevor Wilson	.05
278	*Gerald Alexander*	.05
279	Brad Arnsberg	.05
280	*Kevin Belcher*	.05
281	*Joe Bitker*	.05
282	Kevin Brown	.05
283	Steve Buechele	.05
284	Jack Daugherty	.05
285	Julio Franco	.05
286	Juan Gonzalez	.20
287	*Bill Haselman*	.05
288	Charlie Hough	.05
289	Jeff Huson	.05
290	Pete Incaviglia	.05
291	Mike Jeffcoat	.05
292	Jeff Kunkel	.05
293	Gary Mielke	.05
294	Jamie Moyer	.05
295	Rafael Palmeiro	.35
296	Geno Petralli	.05
297	Gary Pettis	.05
298	Kevin Reimer	.05
299	Kenny Rogers	.05
300	Jeff Russell	.05
301	John Russell	.05
302a	Nolan Ryan (first horizontal line between 1979/1980)	.75
302b	Nolan Ryan (first horizontal line between 1980/1981)	.75
303	Ruben Sierra	.05
304	Bobby Witt	.05
305	Jim Abbott	.05
306	Kent Anderson	.05
307	Dante Bichette	.05
308	Bert Blyleven	.05
309	Chili Davis	.05
310	Brian Downing	.05
311	Mark Eichhorn	.05
312	Mike Fetters	.05
313	Chuck Finley	.05
314	Willie Fraser	.05
315	Bryan Harvey	.05
316	Donnie Hill	.05
317	Wally Joyner	.05
318	Mark Langston	.05
319	Kirk McCaskill	.05
320	John Orton	.05
321	Lance Parrish	.05
322	Luis Polonia	.05
323	Johnny Ray	.05
324	Bobby Rose	.05
325	Dick Schofield	.05
326	Rick Schu	.05
327a	Lee Stevens (six-line career summary)	.05
327b	Lee Stevens (seven-line career summary)	.05
328	Devon White	.05
329	Dave Winfield	.40
330	*Cliff Young*	.05
331	Dave Bergman	.05
332	*Phil Clark*	.05
333	Darnell Coles	.05
334	Milt Cuyler	.05
335	Cecil Fielder	.05
336	Travis Fryman	.05
337	Paul Gibson	.05
338	Jerry Don Gleaton	.05
339	Mike Heath	.05
340	Mike Henneman	.05
341	Chet Lemon	.05
342	Lance McCullers	.05
343	Jack Morris	.05
344	Lloyd Moseby	.05
345	Edwin Nunez	.05
346	Clay Parker	.05
347	Dan Petry	.05
348	Tony Phillips	.05
349	Jeff Robinson	.05
350	Mark Salas	.05
351	*Mike Schwabe*	.05
352	Larry Sheets	.05
353	John Shelby	.05

354 Frank Tanana .05
355 Alan Trammell .05
356 Gary Ward .05
357 Lou Whitaker .05
358 Beau Allred .05
359 Sandy Alomar,Jr. .05
360 Carlos Baerga .05
361 *Kevin Bearse* .05
362 Tom Brookens .05
363 Jerry Browne .05
364 Tom Candiotti .05
365 Alex Cole .05
366 John Farrell .05
367 Felix Fermin .05
368 Keith Hernandez .05
369 Brook Jacoby .05
370 Chris James .05
371 Dion James .05
372 Doug Jones .05
373 Candy Maldonado .05
374 Steve Olin .05
375 Jesse Orosco .05
376 Rudy Seanez .05
377 Joel Skinner .05
378 Cory Snyder .05
379 Greg Swindell .05
380 Sergio Valdez .05
381 *Mike Walker* .05
382 *Colby Ward* .05
383 *Turner Ward* .05
384 Mitch Webster .05
385 Kevin Wickander .05
386 Darrel Akerfelds .05
387 Joe Boever .05
388a Rod Booker (no 1981 stats) .05
388b Rod Booker (1981 stats included) .05
389 Sil Campusano .05
390 Don Carman .05
391 *Wes Chamberlain* .05
392 Pat Combs .05
393 Darren Daulton .05
394 Jose DeJesus .05
395 Len Dykstra .05
396 Jason Grimsley .05
397 Charlie Hayes .05
398 Von Hayes .05
399 *Dave Hollins* .05
400 Ken Howell .05
401 Ricky Jordan .05
402 John Kruk .05
403 Steve Lake .05
404 *Chuck Malone* .05
405 Roger McDowell .05
406 Chuck McElroy .05
407 *Mickey Morandini* .05
408 Terry Mulholland .05
409 Dale Murphy .15
410 Randy Ready .05
411 Bruce Ruffin .05
412 Dickie Thon .05
413 Paul Assenmacher .05
414 Damon Berryhill .05
415 Mike Bielecki .05
416 *Shawn Boskie* .05
417 Dave Clark .05
418 Doug Dascenzo .05
419a Andre Dawson (no 1976 stats) .25
419b Andre Dawson (1976 stats included) .25
420 Shawon Dunston .05
421 Joe Girardi .05
422 Mark Grace .05
423 Mike Harkey .05
424 Les Lancaster .05
425 Bill Long .05
426 Greg Maddux .50
427 Derrick May .05
428 Jeff Pico .05
429 Domingo Ramos .05
430 Luis Salazar .05
431 Ryne Sandberg .50
432 Dwight Smith .05
433 Greg Smith .05
434 Rick Sutcliffe .05
435 Gary Varsho .05
436 *Hector Villanueva* .05
437 Jerome Walton .05
438 Curtis Wilkerson .05
439 Mitch Williams .05
440 Steve Wilson .05
441 Marvell Wynne .05
442 Scott Bankhead .05
443 Scott Bradley .05
444 Greg Briley .05
445 Mike Brumley .05
446 Jay Buhner .05
447 *Dave Burba* .05
448 Henry Cotto .05
449 Alvin Davis .05
450 Ken Griffey, Jr. .60
451 Erik Hanson .05
452 Gene Harris .05
453 Brian Holman .05
454 Mike Jackson .05
455 Randy Johnson .40
456 Jeffrey Leonard .05
457 Edgar Martinez .05
458 Tino Martinez .05
459 Pete O'Brien .05
460 Harold Reynolds .05
461 Mike Schooler .05
462 Bill Swift .05
463 David Valle .05
464 Omar Vizquel .05
465 Matt Young .05
466 Brady Anderson .05
467 Jeff Ballard .05
468 Juan Bell .05
469a Mike Devereaux ("six" last word in career summary top line) .05
469b Mike Devereaux ("runs" last word in career summary top line) .05
470 Steve Finley .05
471 Dave Gallagher .05
472 *Leo Gomez* .05
473 Rene Gonzales .05
474 Pete Harnisch .05
475 Kevin Hickey .05
476 *Chris Hoiles* .10
477 Sam Horn .05
478 Tim Hulett .05
479 Dave Johnson .05
480 Ron Kittle .05
481 Ben McDonald .05
482 Bob Melvin .05
483 Bob Milacki .05
484 Randy Milligan .05
485 *John Mitchell* .05
486 Gregg Olson .05
487 Joe Orsulak .05
488 Joe Price .05
489 Bill Ripken .05
490 Cal Ripken, Jr. .75
491 Curt Schilling .25
492 *David Segui* .10
493 *Anthony Telford* .05
494 Mickey Tettleton .05
495 Mark Williamson .05
496 Craig Worthington .05
497 Juan Agosto .05
498 Eric Anthony .05
499 Craig Biggio .05
500 Ken Caminiti .05
501 Casey Candaele .05
502 *Andujar Cedeno* .05
503 Danny Darwin .05
504 Mark Davidson .05
505 Glenn Davis .05
506 Jim Deshaies .05
507 *Luis Gonzalez* 1.00
508 Bill Gullickson .05
509 Xavier Hernandez .05
510 Brian Meyer .05
511 Ken Oberkfell .05
512 Mark Portugal .05
513 Rafael Ramirez .05
514 *Karl Rhodes* .10
515 Mike Scott .05
516 *Mike Simms* .05
517 Dave Smith .05
518 Franklin Stubbs .05
519 Glenn Wilson .05
520 Eric Yelding .05
521 Gerald Young .05
522 Shawn Abner .05
523 Roberto Alomar .20
524 Andy Benes .05
525 Joe Carter .05
526 Jack Clark .05
527 Joey Cora .05
528 *Paul Faries* .05
529 Tony Gwynn .50
530 Atlee Hammaker .05
531 Greg Harris .05
532 *Thomas Howard* .05
533 Bruce Hurst .05
534 Craig Lefferts .05
535 Derek Lilliquist .05
536 Fred Lynn .05
537 Mike Pagliarulo .05
538 Mark Parent .05
539 Dennis Rasmussen .05
540 Bip Roberts .05
541 *Richard Rodriguez* .05
542 Benito Santiago .05
543 Calvin Schiraldi .05
544 Eric Show .05
545 Phil Stephenson .05
546 Garry Templeton .05
547 Ed Whitson .05
548 Eddie Williams .05
549 Kevin Appier .05
550 Luis Aquino .05
551 Bob Boone .05
552 George Brett .55
553 *Jeff Conine* .30
554 Steve Crawford .05
555 Mark Davis .05
556 Storm Davis .05
557 Jim Eisenreich .05
558 Steve Farr .05
559 Tom Gordon .05
560 Mark Gubicza .05
561 Bo Jackson .10
562 Mike Macfarlane .05
563 *Brian McRae* .10
564 Jeff Montgomery .05
565 Bill Pecota .05
566 Gerald Perry .05
567 Bret Saberhagen .05
568 *Jeff Schulz* .05
569 Kevin Seitzer .05
570 *Terry Shumpert* .05
571 Kurt Stillwell .05
572 Danny Tartabull .05
573 Gary Thurman .05
574 Frank White .05
575 Willie Wilson .05
576 Chris Bosio .05
577 Greg Brock .05
578 George Canale .05
579 Chuck Crim .05
580 Rob Deer .05
581 *Edgar Diaz* .05
582 *Tom Edens* .05
583 Mike Felder .05
584 Jim Gantner .05
585 Darryl Hamilton .05
586 Ted Higuera .05
587 Mark Knudson .05
588 Bill Krueger .05
589 Tim McIntosh .05
590 Paul Mirabella .05
591 Paul Molitor .40
592 Jaime Navarro .05
593 Dave Parker .05
594 Dan Plesac .05
595 Ron Robinson .05
596 Gary Sheffield .30
597 Bill Spiers .05
598 B.J. Surhoff .05
599 Greg Vaughn .05
600 Randy Veres .05
601 Robin Yount .40
602a Rick Aguilera (five-line career summary) .05
602b Rick Aguilera (four-line career summary) .05
603 Allan Anderson .05
604 Juan Berenguer .05
605 Randy Bush .05
606 Carmen Castillo .05
607 Tim Drummond .05
608 *Scott Erickson* .10
609 Gary Gaetti .05
610a Greg Gagne (horizontal lines under 82 Ft. Lauderdale, 84 Toledo and 87 Twins) .05
610b Greg Gagne (horizontal lines under 82 Orlando, 84 Twins and 88 Twins) .05
611 Dan Gladden .05
612 Mark Guthrie .05
613 Brian Harper .05
614 Kent Hrbek .05
615 Gene Larkin .05
616 Terry Leach .05
617 Nelson Liriano .05
618 Shane Mack .05
619 John Moses .05
620 *Pedro Munoz* .05
621 Al Newman .05
622 Junior Ortiz .05
623 Kirby Puckett .50
624 Roy Smith .05
625 Kevin Tapani .05
626 Gary Wayne .05
627 David West .05
628 Cris Carpenter .05
629 Vince Coleman .05
630 Ken Dayley .05
631 Jose DeLeon .05
632 Frank DiPino .05
633 *Bernard Gilkey* .25
634 Pedro Guerrero .05
635 Ken Hill .05
636 Felix Jose .05
637 *Ray Lankford* .25
638 Joe Magrane .05
639 Tom Niedenfuer .05
640 Jose Oquendo .05
641 Tom Pagnozzi .05
642 Terry Pendleton .05
643 *Mike Perez* .05
644 Bryn Smith .05
645 Lee Smith .05
646 Ozzie Smith .50
647 Scott Terry .05
648 Bob Tewksbury .05
649 Milt Thompson .05
650 John Tudor .05
651 Denny Walling .05
652 *Craig Wilson* .05
653 Todd Worrell .05
654 Todd Zeile .05
655 *Oscar Azocar* .05
656 Steve Balboni .05
657 Jesse Barfield .05
658 Greg Cadaret .05
659 Chuck Cary .05
660 Rick Cerone .05
661 Dave Eiland .05
662a Alvaro Espinoza (no 1979-80 stats) .05
662b Alvaro Espinoza (1979-80 stats included) .05
663 Bob Geren .05
664 Lee Guetterman .05
665 Mel Hall .05
666a Andy Hawkins (no 1978 stats) .05
666b Andy Hawkins (1978 stats included) .05
667 Jimmy Jones .05
668 Roberto Kelly .05
669 Dave LaPoint .05
670 Tim Leary .05
671 *Jim Leyritz* .10
672 Kevin Maas .05
673 Don Mattingly .60
674 Matt Nokes .05
675 Pascual Perez .05
676 Eric Plunk .05
677 Dave Righetti .05
678 Jeff Robinson .05
679 Steve Sax .05
680 Mike Witt .05
681 Steve Avery .05
682 Mike Bell .05
683 Jeff Blauser .05
684 Francisco Cabrera .05
685 Tony Castillo .05
686 Marty Clary .05
687 Nick Esasky .05
688 Ron Gant .05
689 Tom Glavine .25
690 Mark Grant .05
691 Tommy Gregg .05
692 Dwayne Henry .05
693 Dave Justice .05
694 *Jimmy Kremers* .05
695 Charlie Leibrandt .05
696 Mark Lemke .05
697 Oddibe McDowell .05
698 *Greg Olson* .05
699 Jeff Parrett .05
700 Jim Presley .05
701 *Victor Rosario* .05
702 Lonnie Smith .05
703 Pete Smith .05
704 John Smoltz .05
705 Mike Stanton .05
706 Andres Thomas .05
707 Jeff Treadway .05
708 *Jim Vatcher* .05
709 Ryne Sandberg, Cecil Fielder Home Run Kings .10
710 Barry Bonds, Ken Griffey, Jr. Second Generation Superstars .65
711 Bobby Bonilla, Barry Larkin NLCS Team Leaders .05
712 Bobby Thigpen, John Franco Top Game Savers .05
713 Andre Dawson, Ryne Sandberg Chicago's 100 Club .10
714 Athletics, Pirates, Reds, Red Sox Checklists .05
715 Dodgers .05
716 Expos, Giants, Rangers, Angels Checklists .05

717 Tigers, Indians, Phillies, Cubs Checklists .05
718 Checklists (Mariners, Orioles, Astros, Padres) .05
719 Royals, Brewers, Twins, Cardinals Checklists .05
720 Checklists (Yankees, Braves, Super Stars) .05

Update

	NM/M
Complete Set (132):	3.00
Common Player:	.05

1 Glenn Davis .05
2 Dwight Evans .05
3 Jose Mesa .05
4 Jack Clark .05
5 Danny Darwin .05
6 Steve Lyons .05
7 Mo Vaughn .05
8 Floyd Bannister .05
9 Gary Gaetti .05
10 Dave Parker .05
11 Joey Cora .05
12 Charlie Hough .05
13 Matt Merullo .05
14 Warren Newson .05
15 Tim Raines .05
16 Albert Belle .05
17 Glenallen Hill .05
18 Shawn Hillegas .05
19 Mark Lewis .05
20 Charles Nagy .05
21 Mark Whiten .05
22 John Cerutti .05
23 Rob Deer .05
24 Mickey Tettleton .05
25 Warren Cromartie .05
26 Kirk Gibson .05
27 David Howard .05
28 Brent Mayne .05
29 Dante Bichette .05
30 Mark Lee .05
31 Julio Machado .05
32 Edwin Nunez .05
33 Willie Randolph .05
34 Franklin Stubbs .05
35 Bill Wegman .05
36 Chili Davis .05
37 Chuck Knoblauch .05
38 Scott Leius .05
39 Jack Morris .05
40 Mike Pagliarulo .05
41 Lenny Webster .05
42 John Habyan .05
43 Steve Howe .05
44 Jeff Johnson .05
45 Scott Kamieniecki .05
46 Pat Kelly .05
47 Hensley Meulens .05
48 Wade Taylor .05
49 Bernie Williams .20
50 Kirk Dressendorfer .05
51 Ernest Riles .05
52 Rich DeLucia .05
53 Tracy Jones .05
54 Bill Krueger .05
55 Alonzo Powell .05
56 Jeff Schaefer .05
57 Russ Swan .05
58 John Barfield .05
59 Rich Gossage .10
60 Jose Guzman .05
61 Dean Palmer .05
62 *Ivan Rodriguez* 1.50
63 Roberto Alomar .20
64 Tom Candiotti .05
65 Joe Carter .05
66 Ed Sprague .05
67 Pat Tabler .05
68 Mike Timlin .05
69 Devon White .05
70 Rafael Belliard .05
71 Juan Berenguer .05
72 Sid Bream .05
73 Marvin Freeman .05
74 Kent Mercker .05
75 Otis Nixon .05
76 Terry Pendleton .05
77 George Bell .05
78 Danny Jackson .05
79 Chuck McElroy .05
80 Gary Scott .05
81 Heathcliff Slocumb .05
82 Dave Smith .05
83 Rick Wilkins .05
84 Freddie Benavides .05
85 Ted Power .05
86 Mo Sanford .05
87 *Jeff Bagwell* 2.00
88 Steve Finley .05
89 Pete Harnisch .05
90 Darryl Kile .05
91 Brett Butler .05
92 John Candelaria .05
93 Gary Carter .40
94 Kevin Gross .05
95 Bob Ojeda .05
96 Darryl Strawberry .05
97 Ivan Calderon .05
98 Ron Hassey .05
99 Gilberto Reyes .05
100 Hubie Brooks .05
101 Rick Cerone .05
102 Vince Coleman .05
103 Jeff Innis .05
104 Pete Schourek .05
105 Andy Ashby .05
106 Wally Backman .05
107 Darrin Fletcher .05
108 Tommy Greene .05
109 John Morris .05
110 Mitch Williams .05
111 Lloyd McClendon .05
112 Orlando Merced .05
113 Vicente Palacios .05
114 Gary Varsho .05
115 John Wehner .05
116 Rex Hudler .05
117 Tim Jones .05
118 Geronimo Pena .05
119 Gerald Perry .05
120 Larry Andersen .05
121 Jerald Clark .05
122 Scott Coolbaugh .05
123 Tony Fernandez .05
124 Darrin Jackson .05
125 Fred McGriff .05
126 Jose Mota .05
127 Tim Teufel .05
128 Bud Black .05
129 Mike Felder .05
130 Willie McGee .05
131 Dave Righetti .05
132 Checklist .05

1992 FLEER

	NM/M
Unopened Factory Set (732):	17.50
Complete Set (720):	8.00
Common Player:	.05
Wax Pack (15):	.45
Wax Box (36):	10.00
Cello Pack (35):	1.00
Cello Box (24):	16.00

1 Brady Anderson .05
2 Jose Bautista .05
3 Juan Bell .05
4 Glenn Davis .05
5 Mike Devereaux .05
6 Dwight Evans .05
7 Mike Flanagan .05
8 Leo Gomez .05
9 Chris Hoiles .05
10 Sam Horn .05
11 Tim Hulett .05
12 Dave Johnson .05
13 *Chito Martinez* .05
14 Ben McDonald .05
15 Bob Melvin .05
16 *Luis Mercedes* .10
17 Jose Mesa .05
18 Bob Milacki .05
19 Randy Milligan .05
20 Mike Mussina .30
21 Gregg Olson .05
22 Joe Orsulak .05
23 Jim Poole .05
24 *Arthur Rhodes* .10
25 Billy Ripken .05
26 Cal Ripken, Jr. 1.00
27 David Segui .05
28 Roy Smith .05
29 Anthony Telford .05
30 Mark Williamson .05
31 Craig Worthington .05
32 Wade Boggs .55
33 Tom Bolton .05
34 Tom Brunansky .05
35 Ellis Burks .05
36 Jack Clark .05
37 Roger Clemens .60
38 Danny Darwin .05
39 Mike Greenwell .05
40 Joe Hesketh .05
41 Daryl Irvine .05
42 Dennis Lamp .05
43 Tony Pena .05
44 Phil Plantier .05
45 Carlos Quintana .05
46 Jeff Reardon .05
47 Jody Reed .05
48 Luis Rivera .05
49 Mo Vaughn .05
50 Jim Abbott .05
51 Kyle Abbott .05
52 *Ruben Amaro Jr.* .05
53 Scott Bailes .05
54 *Chris Beasley* .05
55 Mark Eichhorn .05
56 Mike Fetters .05
57 Chuck Finley .05
58 Gary Gaetti .05
59 Dave Gallagher .05
60 Donnie Hill .05
61 Bryan Harvey .05
62 Wally Joyner .05
63 Mark Langston .05
64 Kirk McCaskill .05
65 John Orton .05
66 Lance Parrish .05
67 Luis Polonia .05
68 Bobby Rose .05
69 Dick Schofield .05
70 Luis Sojo .05
71 Lee Stevens .05
72 Dave Winfield .50
73 Cliff Young .05
74 Wilson Alvarez .05
75 *Esteban Beltre* .05
76 Joey Cora .05
77 *Brian Drahman* .05
78 Alex Fernandez .05
79 Carlton Fisk .50
80 Scott Fletcher .05
81 Craig Grebeck .05
82 Ozzie Guillen .05
83 Greg Hibbard .05
84 Charlie Hough .05
85 Mike Huff .05
86 Bo Jackson .10
87 Lance Johnson .05
88 Ron Karkovice .05
89 Jack McDowell .05
90 Matt Merullo .05
91 *Warren Newson* .05
92 Donn Pall .05
93 Dan Pasqua .05
94 Ken Patterson .05
95 Melido Perez .05
96 Scott Radinsky .05
97 Tim Raines .05
98 Sammy Sosa .55
99 Bobby Thigpen .05
100 Frank Thomas .50
101 Robin Ventura .05
102 Mike Aldrete .05
103 Sandy Alomar, Jr. .05
104 Carlos Baerga .05
105 Albert Belle .05
106 Willie Blair .05
107 Jerry Browne .05
108 Alex Cole .05
109 Felix Fermin .05
110 Glenallen Hill .05
111 Shawn Hillegas .05
112 Chris James .05
113 Reggie Jefferson .05
114 Doug Jones .05
115 Eric King .05
116 Mark Lewis .05
117 Carlos Martinez .05
118 Charles Nagy .05
119 Rod Nichols .05
120 Steve Olin .05
121 Jesse Orosco .05
122 Rudy Seanez .05
123 Joel Skinner .05
124 Greg Swindell .05
125 Jim Thome .50
126 Mark Whiten .05
127 Scott Aldred .05
128 Andy Allanson .05
129 John Cerutti .05
130 Milt Cuyler .05
131 *Mike Dalton* .05
132 Rob Deer .05
133 Cecil Fielder .05
134 Travis Fryman .05
135 *Dan Gakeler* .05
136 Paul Gibson .05
137 Bill Gullickson .05
138 Mike Henneman .05
139 Pete Incaviglia .05
140 *Mark Leiter* .05
141 *Scott Livingstone* .10
142 Lloyd Moseby .05
143 Tony Phillips .05
144 Mark Salas .05
145 Frank Tanana .05
146 Walt Terrell .05
147 Mickey Tettleton .05
148 Alan Trammell .05
149 Lou Whitaker .05
150 Kevin Appier .05
151 Luis Aquino .05
152 Todd Benzinger .05
153 Mike Boddicker .05
154 George Brett .60
155 Storm Davis .05
156 Jim Eisenreich .05
157 Kirk Gibson .05
158 Tom Gordon .05
159 Mark Gubicza .05
160 *David Howard* .05
161 Mike Macfarlane .05
162 Brent Mayne .05
163 Brian McRae .05
164 Jeff Montgomery .05
165 Bill Pecota .05
166 *Harvey Pulliam* .05
167 Bret Saberhagen .05
168 Kevin Seitzer .05
169 Terry Shumpert .05
170 Kurt Stillwell .05
171 Danny Tartabull .05
172 Gary Thurman .05
173 Dante Bichette .05
174 Kevin Brown .05
175 Chuck Crim .05
176 Jim Gantner .05
177 Darryl Hamilton .05
178 Ted Higuera .05
179 Darren Holmes .05
180 Mark Lee .05
181 Julio Machado .05
182 Paul Molitor .50
183 Jaime Navarro .05
184 Edwin Nunez .05
185 Dan Plesac .05
186 Willie Randolph .05
187 Ron Robinson .05
188 Gary Sheffield .30
189 Bill Spiers .05
190 B.J. Surhoff .05
191 Dale Sveum .05
192 Greg Vaughn .05
193 Bill Wegman .05
194 Robin Yount .50
195 Rick Aguilera .05
196 Allan Anderson .05
197 Steve Bedrosian .05
198 Randy Bush .05
199 Larry Casian .05
200 Chili Davis .05
201 Scott Erickson .05
202 Greg Gagne .05

No.	Player	Price
203	Dan Gladden	.05
204	Brian Harper	.05
205	Kent Hrbek	.05
206	Chuck Knoblauch	.05
207	Gene Larkin	.05
208	Terry Leach	.05
209	Scott Leius	.05
210	Shane Mack	.05
211	Jack Morris	.05
212	Pedro Munoz	.05
213	*Denny Neagle*	.10
214	Al Newman	.05
215	Junior Ortiz	.05
216	Mike Pagliarulo	.05
217	Kirby Puckett	.55
218	Paul Sorrento	.05
219	Kevin Tapani	.05
220	Lenny Webster	.05
221	Jesse Barfield	.05
222	Greg Cadaret	.05
223	Dave Eiland	.05
224	Alvaro Espinoza	.05
225	Steve Farr	.05
226	Bob Geren	.05
227	Lee Guetterman	.05
228	John Habyan	.05
229	Mel Hall	.05
230	Steve Howe	.05
231	*Mike Humphreys*	.05
232	*Scott Kamieniecki*	.10
233	Pat Kelly	.05
234	Roberto Kelly	.05
235	Tim Leary	.05
236	Kevin Maas	.05
237	Don Mattingly	.60
238	Hensley Meulens	.05
239	Matt Nokes	.05
240	Pascual Perez	.05
241	Eric Plunk	.05
242	*John Ramos*	.05
243	Scott Sanderson	.05
244	Steve Sax	.05
245	*Wade Taylor*	.05
246	Randy Velarde	.05
247	Bernie Williams	.05
248	Troy Afenir	.05
249	Harold Baines	.05
250	Lance Blankenship	.05
251	*Mike Bordick*	.10
252	Jose Canseco	.30
253	Steve Chitren	.05
254	Ron Darling	.05
255	Dennis Eckersley	.45
256	Mike Gallego	.05
257	Dave Henderson	.05
258	Rickey Henderson	.50
259	Rick Honeycutt	.05
260	Brook Jacoby	.05
261	Carney Lansford	.05
262	Mark McGwire	.75
263	Mike Moore	.05
264	Gene Nelson	.05
265	Jamie Quirk	.05
266	*Joe Slusarski*	.10
267	Terry Steinbach	.05
268	Dave Stewart	.05
269	Todd Van Poppel	.05
270	Walt Weiss	.05
271	Bob Welch	.05
272	Curt Young	.05
273	Scott Bradley	.05
274	Greg Briley	.05
275	Jay Buhner	.05
276	Henry Cotto	.05
277	Alvin Davis	.05
278	Rich DeLucia	.05
279	Ken Griffey, Jr.	.65
280	Erik Hanson	.05
281	Brian Holman	.05
282	Mike Jackson	.05
283	Randy Johnson	.50
284	Tracy Jones	.05
285	Bill Krueger	.05
286	Edgar Martinez	.05
287	Tino Martinez	.05
288	Rob Murphy	.05
289	Pete O'Brien	.05
290	Alonzo Powell	.05
291	Harold Reynolds	.05
292	Mike Schooler	.05
293	Russ Swan	.05
294	Bill Swift	.05
295	Dave Valle	.05
296	Omar Vizquel	.05
297	Gerald Alexander	.05
298	Brad Arnsberg	.05
299	Kevin Brown	.05
300	Jack Daugherty	.05
301	Mario Diaz	.05
302	Brian Downing	.05
303	Julio Franco	.05
304	Juan Gonzalez	.25
305	Rich Gossage	.10
306	Jose Guzman	.05
307	*Jose Hernandez*	.05
308	Jeff Huson	.05
309	Mike Jeffcoat	.05
310	*Terry Mathews*	.05
311	Rafael Palmeiro	.45
312	Dean Palmer	.05
313	Geno Petralli	.05
314	Gary Pettis	.05
315	Kevin Reimer	.05
316	Ivan Rodriguez	.45
317	Kenny Rogers	.05
318	*Wayne Rosenthal*	.05
319	Jeff Russell	.05
320	Nolan Ryan	1.00
321	Ruben Sierra	.05
322	Jim Acker	.05
323	Roberto Alomar	.20
324	Derek Bell	.05
325	Pat Borders	.05
326	Tom Candiotti	.05
327	Joe Carter	.05
328	Rob Ducey	.05
329	Kelly Gruber	.05
330	*Juan Guzman*	.25
331	Tom Henke	.05
332	Jimmy Key	.05
333	Manny Lee	.05
334	Al Leiter	.05
335	*Bob MacDonald*	.05
336	Candy Maldonado	.05
337	Rance Mulliniks	.05
338	Greg Myers	.05
339	John Olerud	.05
340	*Ed Sprague*	.10
341	Dave Stieb	.05
342	Todd Stottlemyre	.05
343	*Mike Timlin*	.10
344	Duane Ward	.05
345	David Wells	.05
346	Devon White	.05
347	Mookie Wilson	.05
348	Eddie Zosky	.05
349	Steve Avery	.05
350	Mike Bell	.05
351	Rafael Belliard	.05
352	Juan Berenguer	.05
353	Jeff Blauser	.05
354	Sid Bream	.05
355	Francisco Cabrera	.05
356	Marvin Freeman	.05
357	Ron Gant	.05
358	Tom Glavine	.30
359	*Brian Hunter*	.05
360	Dave Justice	.05
361	Charlie Leibrandt	.05
362	Mark Lemke	.05
363	Kent Mercker	.05
364	*Keith Mitchell*	.05
365	Greg Olson	.05
366	Terry Pendleton	.05
367	*Armando Reynoso*	.05
368	Deion Sanders	.10
369	Lonnie Smith	.05
370	Pete Smith	.05
371	John Smoltz	.05
372	Mike Stanton	.05
373	Jeff Treadway	.05
374	*Mark Wohlers*	.05
375	Paul Assenmacher	.05
376	George Bell	.05
377	Shawn Boskie	.05
378	*Frank Castillo*	.05
379	Andre Dawson	.25
380	Shawon Dunston	.05
381	Mark Grace	.05
382	Mike Harkey	.05
383	Danny Jackson	.05
384	Les Lancaster	.05
385	*Cedric Landrum*	.05
386	Greg Maddux	.55
387	Derrick May	.05
388	Chuck McElroy	.05
389	Ryne Sandberg	.55
390	*Heathcliff Slocumb*	.10
391	Dave Smith	.05
392	Dwight Smith	.05
393	Rick Sutcliffe	.05
394	Hector Villanueva	.05
395	*Chico Walker*	.05
396	Jerome Walton	.05
397	*Rick Wilkins*	.15
398	Jack Armstrong	.05
399	*Freddie Benavides*	.05
400	Glenn Braggs	.05
401	Tom Browning	.05
402	Norm Charlton	.05
403	Eric Davis	.05
404	Rob Dibble	.05
405	Bill Doran	.05
406	Mariano Duncan	.05
407	*Kip Gross*	.05
408	Chris Hammond	.05
409	Billy Hatcher	.05
410	*Chris Jones*	.05
411	Barry Larkin	.05
412	Hal Morris	.05
413	Randy Myers	.05
414	Joe Oliver	.05
415	Paul O'Neill	.05
416	Ted Power	.05
417	Luis Quinones	.05
418	Jeff Reed	.05
419	Jose Rijo	.05
420	Chris Sabo	.05
421	Reggie Sanders	.05
422	Scott Scudder	.05
423	Glenn Sutko	.05
424	Eric Anthony	.05
425	Jeff Bagwell	.50
426	Craig Biggio	.05
427	Ken Caminiti	.05
428	Casey Candaele	.05
429	Mike Capel	.05
430	Andujar Cedeno	.05
431	Jim Corsi	.05
432	Mark Davidson	.05
433	Steve Finley	.05
434	Luis Gonzalez	.05
435	Pete Harnisch	.05
436	Dwayne Henry	.05
437	Xavier Hernandez	.05
438	Jimmy Jones	.05
439	*Darryl Kile*	.05
440	*Rob Mallicoat*	.05
441	*Andy Mota*	.05
442	Al Osuna	.05
443	Mark Portugal	.05
444	*Scott Servais*	.10
445	Mike Simms	.05
446	Gerald Young	.05
447	Tim Belcher	.05
448	Brett Butler	.05
449	John Candelaria	.05
450	Gary Carter	.50
451	Dennis Cook	.05
452	Tim Crews	.05
453	Kal Daniels	.05
454	Jim Gott	.05
455	Alfredo Griffin	.05
456	Kevin Gross	.05
457	Chris Gwynn	.05
458	Lenny Harris	.05
459	Orel Hershiser	.05
460	Jay Howell	.05
461	Stan Javier	.05
462	Eric Karros	.05
463	Ramon Martinez	.05
464	Roger McDowell	.05
465	Mike Morgan	.05
466	Eddie Murray	.50
467	Jose Offerman	.05
468	Bob Ojeda	.05
469	Juan Samuel	.05
470	Mike Scioscia	.05
471	Darryl Strawberry	.05
472	*Bret Barberie*	.10
473	Brian Barnes	.05
474	Eric Bullock	.05
475	Ivan Calderon	.05
476	Delino DeShields	.05
477	*Jeff Fassero*	.10
478	Mike Fitzgerald	.05
479	Steve Frey	.05
480	Andres Galarraga	.05
481	Mark Gardner	.05
482	Marquis Grissom	.05
483	*Chris Haney*	.05
484	Barry Jones	.05
485	Dave Martinez	.05
486	Dennis Martinez	.05
487	Chris Nabholz	.05
488	Spike Owen	.05
489	Gilberto Reyes	.05
490	Mel Rojas	.05
491	Scott Ruskin	.05
492	Bill Sampen	.05
493	Larry Walker	.05
494	Tim Wallach	.05
495	Daryl Boston	.05
496	Hubie Brooks	.05
497	Tim Burke	.05
498	Mark Carreon	.05
499	Tony Castillo	.05
500	Vince Coleman	.05
501	David Cone	.05
502	Kevin Elster	.05
503	Sid Fernandez	.05
504	John Franco	.05
505	Dwight Gooden	.05
506	Todd Hundley	.05
507	Jeff Innis	.05
508	Gregg Jefferies	.05
509	Howard Johnson	.05
510	Dave Magadan	.05
511	*Terry McDaniel*	.05
512	Kevin McReynolds	.05
513	Keith Miller	.05
514	Charlie O'Brien	.05
515	Mackey Sasser	.05
516	*Pete Schourek*	.05
517	Julio Valera	.05
518	Frank Viola	.05
519	Wally Whitehurst	.05
520	*Anthony Young*	.05
521	*Andy Ashby*	.10
522	*Kim Batiste*	.05
523	Joe Boever	.05
524	Wes Chamberlain	.05
525	Pat Combs	.05
526	Danny Cox	.05
527	Darren Daulton	.05
528	Jose DeJesus	.05
529	Len Dykstra	.05
530	Darrin Fletcher	.05
531	Tommy Greene	.05
532	Jason Grimsley	.05
533	Charlie Hayes	.05
534	Von Hayes	.05
535	Dave Hollins	.05
536	Ricky Jordan	.05
537	John Kruk	.05
538	Jim Lindeman	.05
539	Mickey Morandini	.05
540	Terry Mulholland	.05
541	Dale Murphy	.20
542	Randy Ready	.05
543	Wally Ritchie	.05
544	Bruce Ruffin	.05
545	Steve Searcy	.05
546	Dickie Thon	.05
547	Mitch Williams	.05
548	Stan Belinda	.05
549	Jay Bell	.05
550	Barry Bonds	1.00
551	Bobby Bonilla	.05
552	Steve Buechele	.05
553	Doug Drabek	.05
554	Neal Heaton	.05
555	Jeff King	.05
556	Bob Kipper	.05
557	Bill Landrum	.05
558	Mike LaValliere	.05
559	Jose Lind	.05
560	Lloyd McClendon	.05
561	Orlando Merced	.05
562	Bob Patterson	.05
563	*Joe Redfield*	.05
564	Gary Redus	.05
565	Rosario Rodriguez	.05
566	Don Slaught	.05
567	John Smiley	.05
568	Zane Smith	.05
569	Randy Tomlin	.05
570	Andy Van Slyke	.05
571	Gary Varsho	.05
572	Bob Walk	.05
573	*John Wehner*	.05
574	Juan Agosto	.05
575	Cris Carpenter	.05
576	Jose DeLeon	.05
577	Rich Gedman	.05
578	Bernard Gilkey	.05
579	Pedro Guerrero	.05
580	Ken Hill	.05
581	Rex Hudler	.05
582	Felix Jose	.05
583	Ray Lankford	.05
584	Omar Olivares	.05
585	Jose Oquendo	.05
586	Tom Pagnozzi	.05
587	Geronimo Pena	.05
588	Mike Perez	.05
589	Gerald Perry	.05
590	Bryn Smith	.05
591	Lee Smith	.05
592	Ozzie Smith	.55
593	Scott Terry	.05
594	Bob Tewksbury	.05
595	Milt Thompson	.05
596	Todd Zeile	.05
597	Larry Andersen	.05
598	Oscar Azocar	.05

599 Andy Benes .05
600 *Ricky Bones* .05
601 Jerald Clark .05
602 Pat Clements .05
603 Paul Faries .05
604 Tony Fernandez .05
605 Tony Gwynn .55
606 Greg Harris .05
607 Thomas Howard .05
608 Bruce Hurst .05
609 Darrin Jackson .05
610 Tom Lampkin .05
611 Craig Lefferts .05
612 *Jim Lewis* .05
613 Mike Maddux .05
614 Fred McGriff .05
615 *Jose Melendez* .05
616 *Jose Mota* .05
617 Dennis Rasmussen .05
618 Bip Roberts .05
619 Rich Rodriguez .05
620 Benito Santiago .05
621 *Craig Shipley* .05
622 Tim Teufel .05
623 *Kevin Ward* .05
624 Ed Whitson .05
625 Dave Anderson .05
626 Kevin Bass .05
627 *Rod Beck* .10
628 Bud Black .05
629 Jeff Brantley .05
630 John Burkett .05
631 Will Clark .05
632 Royce Clayton .05
633 Steve Decker .05
634 Kelly Downs .05
635 Mike Felder .05
636 Scott Garrelts .05
637 Eric Gunderson .05
638 *Bryan Hickerson* .05
639 Darren Lewis .05
640 Greg Litton .05
641 Kirt Manwaring .05
642 *Paul McClellan* .05
643 Willie McGee .05
644 Kevin Mitchell .05
645 Francisco Olivares .05
646 *Mike Remlinger* .10
647 Dave Righetti .05
648 Robby Thompson .05
649 Jose Uribe .05
650 Matt Williams .05
651 Trevor Wilson .05
652 Tom Goodwin (Prospects) .05
653 Terry Bross (Prospects) .05
654 *Mike Christopher* (Prospects) .05
655 Kenny Lofton (Prospects) .05
656 *Chris Cron* (Prospects) .05
657 Willie Banks (Prospects) .05
658 *Pat Rice* (Prospects) .05
659a *Rob Mauer* (Prospects) (last name misspelled) .75
659b *Rob Maurer* (Prospects)(corrected) .05
660 Don Harris (Prospects) .05
661 Henry Rodriguez (Prospects) .05
662 *Cliff Brantley* (Prospects) .05
663 *Mike Linskey* (Prospects) .05
664 Gary Disarcina (Prospects) .05
665 *Gil Heredia* (Prospects) .10
666 *Vinny Castilla* (Prospects) .50
667 Paul Abbott (Prospects) .05
668 Monty Fariss (Prospects) .05
669 *Jarvis Brown* (Prospects) .05
670 *Wayne Kirby* (Prospects) .05
671 *Scott Brosius* (Prospects) .05
672 Bob Hamelin (Prospects) .05
673 *Joel Johnston* (Prospects) .05
674 *Tim Spehr* (Prospects) .05
675 *Jeff Gardner* (Prospects) .05
676 *Rico Rossy* (Prospects) .05
677 *Roberto Hernandez* (Prospects) .20
678 *Ted Wood* (Prospects) .05
679 Cal Eldred (Prospects) .05
680 Sean Berry (Prospects) .05
681 Rickey Henderson (Stolen Base Record) .20
682 Nolan Ryan (Record 7th No-hitter) .25
683 Dennis Martinez (Perfect Game) .05
684 Wilson Alvarez (Rookie No-hitter) .05
685 Joe Carter (3 100 RBI Seasons) .05
686 Dave Winfield (400 Home Runs) .20
687 David Cone(Ties NL Record Strikeouts) .05
688 Jose Canseco (League Leaders) .15
689 Howard Johnson (League Leaders) .05
690 Julio Franco (League Leaders) .05
691 Terry Pendleton (League Leaders) .05
692 Cecil Fielder (League Leaders) .05
693 Scott Erickson (League Leaders) .05
694 Tom Glavine (League Leaders) .05
695 Dennis Martinez (League Leaders) .05
696 Bryan Harvey (League Leaders) .05
697 Lee Smith (League Leaders) .05
698 Roberto & Sandy Alomar, Roberto & Sandy Alomar Super Siblings .10
699 Bobby Bonilla, Will Clark The Indispensables .05
700 Mark Wohlers, Kent Mercker, Alejandro Pena Teamwork .05
701 Chris Jones, Bo Jackson, Gregg Olson, Frank Thomas Tiger Tandems .05
702 Brett Butler, Paul Molitor The Ignitors .10
703 Cal Ripken Jr., Joe Carter The Indispensables II .20
704 Barry Larkin, Kirby Puckett Power Packs .15
705 Mo Vaughn, Cecil Fielder Today and Tomorrow .05
706 Ramon Martinez, Ozzie Guillen Teenage Sensations .05
707 Harold Baines, Wade Boggs Designated Hitters .20
708 Robin Yount (ProVision) .35
709 Ken Griffey, Jr. (ProVision) .60
710 Nolan Ryan (ProVision) .75
711 Cal Ripken, Jr. (ProVision) .75
712 Frank Thomas (ProVision) .50
713 Dave Justice (ProVision) .05
714 Checklist 1-101 .05
715 Checklist 102-194 .05
716 Checklist 195-296 .05
717 Checklist 297-397 .05
718 Checklist 398-494 .05
719 Checklist 495-596 .05
720a Checklist 597-720 (659 Rob Mauer) .05
720b Checklist 597-720 (659 Rob Maurer) .05

All-Stars

NM/M
Complete Set (24): 8.00
Common Player: .10
1 Felix Jose .10
2 Tony Gwynn 1.25
3 Barry Bonds 3.00
4 Bobby Bonilla .10
5 Mike LaValliere .10
6 Tom Glavine .40
7 Ramon Martinez .10
8 Lee Smith .10
9 Mickey Tettleton .10
10 Scott Erickson .10
11 Frank Thomas .75
12 Danny Tartabull .10
13 Will Clark .10
14 Ryne Sandberg 1.25
15 Terry Pendleton .10
16 Barry Larkin .10
17 Rafael Palmeiro .65
18 Julio Franco .10
19 Robin Ventura .10
20 Cal Ripken, Jr. 3.00
21 Joe Carter .10
22 Kirby Puckett 1.25
23 Ken Griffey, Jr. 2.25
24 Jose Canseco .50

Lumber Co.

NM/M
Complete Set (9): 5.00
Common Player: .25
1 Cecil Fielder .25
2 Mickey Tettleton .25
3 Darryl Strawberry .25
4 Ryne Sandberg 1.00
5 Jose Canseco .40
6 Matt Williams .25
7 Cal Ripken, Jr. 2.00
8 Barry Bonds 2.00
9 Ron Gant .25

Rookie Sensations

NM/M
Complete Set (20): 13.50
Common Player: .35
1 Frank Thomas 6.00
2 Todd Van Poppel .35
3 Orlando Merced .35
4 Jeff Bagwell 6.00
5 Jeff Fassero .35
6 Darren Lewis .35
7 Milt Cuyler .35
8 Mike Timlin .35
9 Brian McRae .35
10 Chuck Knoblauch .35
11 Rich DeLucia .35
12 Ivan Rodriguez 4.50
13 Juan Guzman .35
14 Steve Chitren .35
15 Mark Wohlers .35
16 Wes Chamberlain .35
17 Ray Lankford .35
18 Chito Martinez .35
19 Phil Plantier .35
20 Scott Leius .35

Roger Clemens

NM/M
Complete Set (15): 6.00
Common Card: .50
Autographed Card: 40.00
1 Quiet Storm .50
2 Courted by the Mets and Twins .50
3 The Show .50
4 A Rocket Launched .50
5 Time of Trial .50
6 Break Through .50
7 Play it Again Roger .50
8 Business as Usual .50
9 Heee's Back .50
10 Blood, Sweat and Tears .50
11 Prime of Life .50

12 Man for Every Season .50
13 Cooperstown Bound 1.50
14 The Heat of the Moment 1.50
15 Final Words 1.50

Smoke 'N Heat

NM/M
Complete Set (12): 7.50
Common Player: .25
1 Lee Smith .25
2 Jack McDowell .25
3 David Cone .25
4 Roger Clemens 2.00
5 Nolan Ryan 3.00
6 Scott Erickson .25
7 Tom Glavine .50
8 Dwight Gooden .25
9 Andy Benes .25
10 Steve Avery .25
11 Randy Johnson 1.00
12 Jim Abbott .25

Team Leaders

NM/M
Complete Set (20): 10.00
Common Player: .50
1 Don Mattingly 2.00
2 Howard Johnson .50
3 Chris Sabo .50
4 Carlton Fisk 1.25
5 Kirby Puckett 1.50
6 Cecil Fielder .50
7 Tony Gwynn 1.50
8 Will Clark .50
9 Bobby Bonilla .50
10 Len Dykstra .50
11 Tom Glavine .75
12 Rafael Palmeiro 1.00
13 Wade Boggs 1.50
14 Joe Carter .50
15 Ken Griffey, Jr. 2.50
16 Darryl Strawberry .50
17 Cal Ripken, Jr. 3.00
18 Danny Tartabull .50
19 Jose Canseco .75
20 Andre Dawson .50

Update

NM/M
Complete Set (136): 60.00
Common Player: .05
H1 Ken Griffey, Jr. 1992 All-Star Game MVP 1.50
H2 Robin Yount 3000 Career Hits .50
H3 Jeff Reardon Major League Career Saves Record .10

H4	Cecil Fielder Record RBI Performance	.05
1	Todd Frohwirth	.05
2	Alan Mills	.05
3	Rick Sutcliffe	.05
4	*John Valentin*	.25
5	Frank Viola	.05
6	Bob Zupcic	.05
7	Mike Butcher	.05
8	*Chad Curtis*	.50
9	*Damion Easley*	.25
10	Tim Salmon	.50
11	Julio Valera	.05
12	George Bell	.05
13	Roberto Hernandez	.05
14	Shawn Jeter	.05
15	Thomas Howard	.05
16	Jesse Levis	.05
17	Kenny Lofton	.05
18	Paul Sorrento	.05
19	Rico Brogna	.05
20	John Doherty	.05
21	Dan Gladden	.05
22	Buddy Groom	.05
23	Shawn Hare	.05
24	John Kiely	.05
25	Kurt Knudsen	.05
26	Gregg Jefferies	.05
27	Wally Joyner	.05
28	Kevin Koslofski	.05
29	Kevin McReynolds	.05
30	Rusty Meacham	.05
31	Keith Miller	.05
32	Hipolito Pichardo	.05
33	James Austin	.05
34	Scott Fletcher	.05
35	*John Jaha*	.05
36	Pat Listach	.05
37	Dave Nilsson	.05
38	Kevin Seitzer	.05
39	Tom Edens	.05
40	Pat Mahomes	.05
41	John Smiley	.05
42	Charlie Hayes	.05
43	Sam Militello	.05
44	Andy Stankiewicz	.05
45	Danny Tartabull	.05
46	Bob Wickman	.05
47	Jerry Browne	.05
48	Kevin Campbell	.05
49	Vince Horsman	.05
50	Troy Neel	.05
51	Ruben Sierra	.05
52	Bruce Walton	.05
53	Willie Wilson	.05
54	Bret Boone	.50
55	Dave Fleming	.05
56	Kevin Mitchell	.05
57	*Jeff Nelson*	.05
58	Shane Turner	.05
59	Jose Canseco	.65
60	*Jeff Frye*	.05
61	Damilo Leon	.05
62	Roger Pavlik	.05
63	David Cone	.05
64	Pat Hentgen	.05
65	Randy Knorr	.05
66	Jack Morris	.05
67	Dave Winfield	1.00
68	*David Nied*	.05
69	Otis Nixon	.05
70	Alejandro Pena	.05
71	Jeff Reardon	.05
72	Alex Arias	.05
73	Jim Bullinger	.05
74	Mike Morgan	.05
75	Rey Sanchez	.05
76	Bob Scanlan	.05
77	Sammy Sosa	3.00
78	Scott Bankhead	.05
79	Tim Belcher	.05
80	Steve Foster	.05
81	Willie Greene	.05
82	Bip Roberts	.05
83	Scott Ruskin	.05
84	Greg Swindell	.05
85	Juan Guerrero	.05
86	Butch Henry	.05
87	Doug Jones	.05
88	Brian Williams	.05
89	Tom Candiotti	.05
90	Eric Davis	.05
91	Carlos Hernandez	.05
92	*Mike Piazza*	45.00
93	Mike Sharperson	.05
94	Eric Young	.05
95	Moises Alou	.05
96	Greg Colbrunn	.05
97	Wil Cordero	.05
98	Ken Hill	.05
99	John Vander Wal	.05
100	John Wetteland	.05
101	Bobby Bonilla	.05
102	Eric Hilman	.05
103	Pat Howell	.05
104	*Jeff Kent*	10.00
105	Dick Schofield	.05
106	*Ryan Thompson*	.05
107	Chico Walker	.05
108	Juan Bell	.05
109	Mariano Duncan	.05
110	Jeff Grotewold	.05
111	Ben Rivera	.05
112	Curt Schilling	.65
113	Victor Cole	.05
114	Al Martin	.05
115	Roger Mason	.05
116	Blas Minor	.05
117	Tim Wakefield	4.00
118	*Mark Clark*	.05
119	Rheal Cormier	.05
120	Donovan Osborne	.05
121	Todd Worrell	.05
122	Jeremy Hernandez	.05
123	Randy Myers	.05
124	Frank Seminara	.05
125	Gary Sheffield	.75
126	Dan Walters	.05
127	Steve Hosey	.05
128	Mike Jackson	.05
129	Jim Pena	.05
130	Cory Snyder	.05
131	Bill Swift	.05
132	Checklist	.05

1993 FLEER

		NM/M
Complete Set (720):		10.00
Common Player:		.05
Series 1 or 2 Pack (15):		.50
Series 1 or 2 Box (36):		12.50
1	Steve Avery	.05
2	Sid Bream	.05
3	Ron Gant	.05
4	Tom Glavine	.25
5	Brian Hunter	.05
6	Ryan Klesko	.05
7	Charlie Leibrandt	.05
8	Kent Mercker	.05
9	David Nied	.05
10	Otis Nixon	.05
11	Greg Olson	.05
12	Terry Pendleton	.05
13	Deion Sanders	.10
14	John Smoltz	.05
15	Mike Stanton	.05
16	Mark Wohlers	.05
17	Paul Assenmacher	.05
18	Steve Buechele	.05
19	Shawon Dunston	.05
20	Mark Grace	.05
21	Derrick May	.05
22	Chuck McElroy	.05
23	Mike Morgan	.05
24	Rey Sanchez	.05
25	Ryne Sandberg	.60
26	Bob Scanlan	.05
27	Sammy Sosa	.60
28	Rick Wilkins	.05
29	*Bobby Ayala*	.05
30	Tim Belcher	.05
31	*Jeff Branson*	.05
32	Norm Charlton	.05
33	*Steve Foster*	.05
34	Willie Greene	.05
35	Chris Hammond	.05
36	Milt Hill	.05
37	Hal Morris	.05

38	Joe Oliver	.05
39	Paul O'Neill	.05
40	*Tim Pugh*	.05
41	Jose Rijo	.05
42	Bip Roberts	.05
43	Chris Sabo	.05
44	Reggie Sanders	.05
45	Eric Anthony	.05
46	Jeff Bagwell	.50
47	Craig Biggio	.05
48	Joe Boever	.05
49	Casey Candaele	.05
50	Steve Finley	.05
51	Luis Gonzalez	.05
52	Pete Harnisch	.05
53	Xavier Hernandez	.05
54	Doug Jones	.05
55	Eddie Taubensee	.05
56	Brian Williams	.05
57	*Pedro Astacio*	.10
58	Todd Benzinger	.05
59	Brett Butler	.05
60	Tom Candiotti	.05
61	Lenny Harris	.05
62	Carlos Hernandez	.05
63	Orel Hershiser	.05
64	Eric Karros	.05
65	Ramon Martinez	.05
66	Jose Offerman	.05
67	Mike Scioscia	.05
68	Mike Sharperson	.05
69	*Eric Young*	.10
70	Moises Alou	.05
71	Ivan Calderon	.05
72	*Archi Cianfrocco*	.05
73	Wil Cordero	.05
74	Delino DeShields	.05
75	Mark Gardner	.05
76	Ken Hill	.05
77	*Tim Laker*	.05
78	Chris Nabholz	.05
79	Mel Rojas	.05
80	*John Vander Wal*	.10
81	Larry Walker	.05
82	Tim Wallach	.05
83	John Wetteland	.05
84	Bobby Bonilla	.05
85	Daryl Boston	.05
86	Sid Fernandez	.05
87	*Eric Hillman*	.05
88	Todd Hundley	.05
89	Howard Johnson	.05
90	Jeff Kent	.05
91	Eddie Murray	.50
92	Bill Pecota	.05
93	Bret Saberhagen	.05
94	Dick Schofield	.05
95	Pete Schourek	.05
96	Anthony Young	.05
97	Ruben Amaro Jr.	.05
98	Juan Bell	.05
99	Wes Chamberlain	.05
100	Darren Daulton	.05
101	Mariano Duncan	.05
102	Mike Hartley	.05
103	Ricky Jordan	.05
104	John Kruk	.05
105	Mickey Morandini	.05
106	Terry Mulholland	.05
107	*Ben Rivera*	.05
108	Curt Schilling	.25
109	*Keith Shepherd*	.05
110	Stan Belinda	.05
111	Jay Bell	.05
112	Barry Bonds	1.00
113	Jeff King	.05
114	Mike LaValliere	.05
115	Jose Lind	.05
116	Roger Mason	.05
117	Orlando Merced	.05
118	Bob Patterson	.05
119	Don Slaught	.05
120	Zane Smith	.05
121	Randy Tomlin	.05
122	Andy Van Slyke	.05
123	*Tim Wakefield*	.10
124	Rheal Cormier	.05
125	Bernard Gilkey	.05
126	Felix Jose	.05
127	Ray Lankford	.05
128	Bob McClure	.05
129	Donovan Osborne	.05
130	Tom Pagnozzi	.05
131	Geronimo Pena	.05
132	Mike Perez	.05
133	Lee Smith	.05
134	Bob Tewksbury	.05
135	Todd Worrell	.05
136	Todd Zeile	.05

137	Jerald Clark	.05
138	Tony Gwynn	.60
139	Greg Harris	.05
140	Jeremy Hernandez	.05
141	Darrin Jackson	.05
142	Mike Maddux	.05
143	Fred McGriff	.05
144	Jose Melendez	.05
145	Rich Rodriguez	.05
146	Frank Seminara	.05
147	Gary Sheffield	.35
148	Kurt Stillwell	.05
149	*Dan Walters*	.05
150	Rod Beck	.05
151	Bud Black	.05
152	Jeff Brantley	.05
153	John Burkett	.05
154	Will Clark	.05
155	Royce Clayton	.05
156	Mike Jackson	.05
157	Darren Lewis	.05
158	Kirt Manwaring	.05
159	Willie McGee	.05
160	Cory Snyder	.05
161	Bill Swift	.05
162	Trevor Wilson	.05
163	Brady Anderson	.05
164	Glenn Davis	.05
165	Mike Devereaux	.05
166	Todd Frohwirth	.05
167	Leo Gomez	.05
168	Chris Hoiles	.05
169	Ben McDonald	.05
170	Randy Milligan	.05
171	Alan Mills	.05
172	Mike Mussina	.30
173	Gregg Olson	.05
174	Arthur Rhodes	.05
175	David Segui	.05
176	Ellis Burks	.05
177	Roger Clemens	.65
178	Scott Cooper	.05
179	Danny Darwin	.05
180	Tony Fossas	.05
181	*Paul Quantrill*	.10
182	Jody Reed	.05
183	*John Valentin*	.10
184	Mo Vaughn	.05
185	Frank Viola	.05
186	Bob Zupcic	.05
187	Jim Abbott	.05
188	Gary DiSarcina	.05
189	*Damion Easley*	.10
190	Junior Felix	.05
191	Chuck Finley	.05
192	Joe Grahe	.05
193	Bryan Harvey	.05
194	Mark Langston	.05
195	John Orton	.05
196	Luis Polonia	.05
197	Tim Salmon	.05
198	Luis Sojo	.05
199	Wilson Alvarez	.05
200	George Bell	.05
201	Alex Fernandez	.05
202	Craig Grebeck	.05
203	Ozzie Guillen	.05
204	Lance Johnson	.05
205	Ron Karkovice	.05
206	Kirk McCaskill	.05
207	Jack McDowell	.05
208	Scott Radinsky	.05
209	Tim Raines	.05
210	Frank Thomas	.50
211	Robin Ventura	.05
212	Sandy Alomar Jr.	.05
213	Carlos Baerga	.05
214	Dennis Cook	.05
215	Thomas Howard	.05
216	Mark Lewis	.05
217	Derek Lilliquist	.05
218	Kenny Lofton	.05
219	Charles Nagy	.05
220	Steve Olin	.05
221	Paul Sorrento	.05
222	Jim Thome	.40
223	Mark Whiten	.05
224	Milt Cuyler	.05
225	Rob Deer	.05
226	*John Doherty*	.05
227	Cecil Fielder	.05
228	Travis Fryman	.05
229	Mike Henneman	.05
230	*John Kiely*	.05
231	*Kurt Knudsen*	.05
232	Scott Livingstone	.05
233	Tony Phillips	.05
234	Mickey Tettleton	.05
235	Kevin Appier	.05

No.	Player	Price
236	George Brett	.65
237	Tom Gordon	.05
238	Gregg Jefferies	.05
239	Wally Joyner	.05
240	*Kevin Koslofski*	.05
241	Mike Macfarlane	.05
242	Brian McRae	.05
243	Rusty Meacham	.05
244	Keith Miller	.05
245	Jeff Montgomery	.05
246	*Hipolito Pichardo*	.05
247	Ricky Bones	.05
248	Cal Eldred	.05
249	Mike Fetters	.05
250	Darryl Hamilton	.05
251	Doug Henry	.05
252	John Jaha	.05
253	Pat Listach	.05
254	Paul Molitor	.50
255	Jaime Navarro	.05
256	Kevin Seitzer	.05
257	B.J. Surhoff	.05
258	Greg Vaughn	.05
259	Bill Wegman	.05
260	Robin Yount	.50
261	Rick Aguilera	.05
262	Chili Davis	.05
263	Scott Erickson	.05
264	Greg Gagne	.05
265	Mark Guthrie	.05
266	Brian Harper	.05
267	Kent Hrbek	.05
268	Terry Jorgensen	.05
269	Gene Larkin	.05
270	Scott Leius	.05
271	Pat Mahomes	.05
272	Pedro Munoz	.05
273	Kirby Puckett	.60
274	Kevin Tapani	.05
275	Carl Willis	.05
276	Steve Farr	.05
277	John Habyan	.05
278	Mel Hall	.05
279	Charlie Hayes	.05
280	Pat Kelly	.05
281	Don Mattingly	.65
282	Sam Militello	.05
283	Matt Nokes	.05
284	Melido Perez	.05
285	Andy Stankiewicz	.05
286	Danny Tartabull	.05
287	Randy Velarde	.05
288	Bob Wickman	.05
289	Bernie Williams	.05
290	Lance Blankenship	.05
291	Mike Bordick	.05
292	Jerry Browne	.05
293	Dennis Eckersley	.40
294	Rickey Henderson	.50
295	*Vince Horsman*	.05
296	Mark McGwire	.85
297	Jeff Parrett	.05
298	Ruben Sierra	.05
299	Terry Steinbach	.05
300	Walt Weiss	.05
301	Bob Welch	.05
302	Willie Wilson	.05
303	Bobby Witt	.05
304	Bret Boone	.05
305	Jay Buhner	.05
306	Dave Fleming	.05
307	Ken Griffey, Jr.	.75
308	Erik Hanson	.05
309	Edgar Martinez	.05
310	Tino Martinez	.05
311	Jeff Nelson	.05
312	Dennis Powell	.05
313	Mike Schooler	.05
314	Russ Swan	.05
315	Dave Valle	.05
316	Omar Vizquel	.05
317	Kevin Brown	.05
318	Todd Burns	.05
319	Jose Canseco	.35
320	Julio Franco	.05
321	Jeff Frye	.05
322	Juan Gonzalez	.30
323	Jose Guzman	.05
324	Jeff Huson	.05
325	Dean Palmer	.05
326	Kevin Reimer	.05
327	Ivan Rodriguez	.40
328	Kenny Rogers	.05
329	Dan Smith	.05
330	Roberto Alomar	.20
331	Derek Bell	.05
332	Pat Borders	.05
333	Joe Carter	.05
334	Kelly Gruber	.05
335	Tom Henke	.05
336	Jimmy Key	.05
337	Manuel Lee	.05
338	Candy Maldonado	.05
339	John Olerud	.05
340	Todd Stottlemyre	.05
341	Duane Ward	.05
342	Devon White	.05
343	Dave Winfield	.50
344	Edgar Martinez (League Leaders)	.05
345	Cecil Fielder (League Leaders)	.05
346	Kenny Lofton (League Leaders)	.05
347	Jack Morris (League Leaders)	.05
348	Roger Clemens (League Leaders)	.35
349	Fred McGriff (Round Trippers)	.05
350	Barry Bonds (Round Trippers)	.60
351	Gary Sheffield (Round Trippers)	.05
352	Darren Daulton (Round Trippers)	.05
353	Dave Hollins (Round Trippers)	.05
354	Pedro Martinez, Ramon Martinez Brothers In Blue	.25
355	Ivan Rodriguez, Kirby Puckett Power Packs	.25
356	Ryne Sandberg, Gary Sheffield Triple Threats	.20
357	Roberto Alomar, Chuck Knoblauch, Carlos Baerga Infield Trifecta	.05
358	Checklist	.05
359	Checklist	.05
360	Checklist	.05
361	Rafael Belliard	.05
362	Damon Berryhill	.05
363	Mike Bielecki	.05
364	Jeff Blauser	.05
365	Francisco Cabrera	.05
366	Marvin Freeman	.05
367	Dave Justice	.05
368	Mark Lemke	.05
369	Alejandro Pena	.05
370	Jeff Reardon	.05
371	Lonnie Smith	.05
372	Pete Smith	.05
373	Shawn Boskie	.05
374	Jim Bullinger	.05
375	Frank Castillo	.05
376	Doug Dascenzo	.05
377	Andre Dawson	.25
378	Mike Harkey	.05
379	Greg Hibbard	.05
380	Greg Maddux	.60
381	Ken Patterson	.05
382	Jeff Robinson	.05
383	Luis Salazar	.05
384	Dwight Smith	.05
385	Jose Vizcaino	.05
386	Scott Bankhead	.05
387	Tom Browning	.05
388	Darnell Coles	.05
389	Rob Dibble	.05
390	Bill Doran	.05
391	Dwayne Henry	.05
392	Cesar Hernandez	.05
393	Roberto Kelly	.05
394	Barry Larkin	.05
395	Dave Martinez	.05
396	Kevin Mitchell	.05
397	Jeff Reed	.05
398	Scott Ruskin	.05
399	Greg Swindell	.05
400	Dan Wilson	.05
401	Andy Ashby	.05
402	Freddie Benavides	.05
403	Dante Bichette	.05
404	Willie Blair	.05
405	Denis Boucher	.05
406	Vinny Castilla	.05
407	Braulio Castillo	.05
408	Alex Cole	.05
409	Andres Galarraga	.05
410	Joe Girardi	.05
411	Butch Henry	.05
412	Darren Holmes	.05
413	Calvin Jones	.05
414	*Steve Reed*	.05
415	Kevin Ritz	.05
416	*Jim Tatum*	.05
417	Jack Armstrong	.05
418	Bret Barberie	.05
419	Ryan Bowen	.05
420	Cris Carpenter	.05
421	Chuck Carr	.05
422	Scott Chiamparino	.05
423	Jeff Conine	.05
424	Jim Corsi	.05
425	Steve Decker	.05
426	Chris Donnels	.05
427	Monty Fariss	.05
428	Bob Natal	.05
429	*Pat Rapp*	.05
430	Dave Weathers	.05
431	*Nigel Wilson*	.05
432	Ken Caminiti	.05
433	Andujar Cedeno	.05
434	Tom Edens	.05
435	Juan Guerrero	.05
436	Pete Incaviglia	.05
437	Jimmy Jones	.05
438	Darryl Kile	.05
439	Rob Murphy	.05
440	Al Osuna	.05
441	Mark Portugal	.05
442	Scott Servais	.05
443	John Candelaria	.05
444	Tim Crews	.05
445	Eric Davis	.05
446	Tom Goodwin	.05
447	Jim Gott	.05
448	Kevin Gross	.05
449	Dave Hansen	.05
450	Jay Howell	.05
451	Roger McDowell	.05
452	Bob Ojeda	.05
453	Henry Rodriguez	.05
454	Darryl Strawberry	.05
455	Mitch Webster	.05
456	Steve Wilson	.05
457	Brian Barnes	.05
458	Sean Berry	.05
459	Jeff Fassero	.05
460	Darrin Fletcher	.05
461	Marquis Grissom	.05
462	Dennis Martinez	.05
463	Spike Owen	.05
464	Matt Stairs	.05
465	Sergio Valdez	.05
466	Kevin Bass	.05
467	Vince Coleman	.05
468	Mark Dewey	.05
469	Kevin Elster	.05
470	Tony Fernandez	.05
471	John Franco	.05
472	Dave Gallagher	.05
473	Paul Gibson	.05
474	Dwight Gooden	.05
475	Lee Guetterman	.05
476	Jeff Innis	.05
477	Dave Magadan	.05
478	Charlie O'Brien	.05
479	Willie Randolph	.05
480	Mackey Sasser	.05
481	Ryan Thompson	.05
482	Chico Walker	.05
483	Kyle Abbott	.05
484	Bob Ayrault	.05
485	Kim Batiste	.05
486	Cliff Brantley	.05
487	Jose DeLeon	.05
488	Len Dykstra	.05
489	Tommy Greene	.05
490	Jeff Grotewold	.05
491	Dave Hollins	.05
492	Danny Jackson	.05
493	Stan Javier	.05
494	Tom Marsh	.05
495	Greg Matthews	.05
496	Dale Murphy	.15
497	*Todd Pratt*	.05
498	Mitch Williams	.05
499	Danny Cox	.05
500	Doug Drabek	.05
501	Carlos Garcia	.05
502	Lloyd McClendon	.05
503	Denny Neagle	.05
504	Gary Redus	.05
505	Bob Walk	.05
506	John Wehner	.05
507	Luis Alicea	.05
508	Mark Clark	.05
509	Pedro Guerrero	.05
510	Rex Hudler	.05
511	Brian Jordan	.05
512	Omar Olivares	.05
513	Jose Oquendo	.05
514	Gerald Perry	.05
515	Bryn Smith	.05
516	Craig Wilson	.05
517	Tracy Woodson	.05
518	Larry Anderson	.05
519	Andy Benes	.05
520	Jim Deshaies	.05
521	Bruce Hurst	.05
522	Randy Myers	.05
523	Benito Santiago	.05
524	Tim Scott	.05
525	Tim Teufel	.05
526	Mike Benjamin	.05
527	Dave Burba	.05
528	Craig Colbert	.05
529	Mike Felder	.05
530	Bryan Hickerson	.05
531	Chris James	.05
532	Mark Leonard	.05
533	Greg Litton	.05
534	Francisco Oliveras	.05
535	John Patterson	.05
536	Jim Pena	.05
537	Dave Righetti	.05
538	Robby Thompson	.05
539	Jose Uribe	.05
540	Matt Williams	.05
541	Storm Davis	.05
542	Sam Horn	.05
543	Tim Hulett	.05
544	Craig Lefferts	.05
545	Chito Martinez	.05
546	Mark McLemore	.05
547	Luis Mercedes	.05
548	Bob Milacki	.05
549	Joe Orsulak	.05
550	Billy Ripken	.05
551	Cal Ripken, Jr.	1.00
552	Rick Sutcliffe	.05
553	Jeff Tackett	.05
554	Wade Boggs	.60
555	Tom Brunansky	.05
556	Jack Clark	.05
557	John Dopson	.05
558	Mike Gardiner	.05
559	Mike Greenwell	.05
560	Greg Harris	.05
561	Billy Hatcher	.05
562	Joe Hesketh	.05
563	Tony Pena	.05
564	Phil Plantier	.05
565	Luis Rivera	.05
566	Herm Winningham	.05
567	Matt Young	.05
568	Bert Blyleven	.05
569	Mike Butcher	.05
570	Chuck Crim	.05
571	*Chad Curtis*	.15
572	Tim Fortugno	.05
573	Steve Frey	.05
574	Gary Gaetti	.05
575	Scott Lewis	.05
576	Lee Stevens	.05
577	Ron Tingley	.05
578	Julio Valera	.05
579	Shawn Abner	.05
580	Joey Cora	.05
581	Chris Cron	.05
582	Carlton Fisk	.50
583	Roberto Hernandez	.05
584	Charlie Hough	.05
585	Terry Leach	.05
586	Donn Pall	.05
587	Dan Pasqua	.05
588	Steve Sax	.05
589	Bobby Thigpen	.05
590	Albert Belle	.05
591	Felix Fermin	.05
592	Glenallen Hill	.05
593	Brook Jacoby	.05
594	Reggie Jefferson	.05
595	Carlos Martinez	.05
596	Jose Mesa	.05
597	Rod Nichols	.05
598	Junior Ortiz	.05
599	Eric Plunk	.05
600	Ted Power	.05
601	Scott Scudder	.05
602	Kevin Wickander	.05
603	Skeeter Barnes	.05
604	Mark Carreon	.05
605	Dan Gladden	.05
606	Bill Gullickson	.05
607	Chad Kreuter	.05
608	Mark Leiter	.05
609	Mike Munoz	.05
610	Rich Rowland	.05
611	Frank Tanana	.05
612	Walt Terrell	.05
613	Alan Trammell	.05

614 Lou Whitaker .05
615 Luis Aquino .05
616 Mike Boddicker .05
617 Jim Eisenreich .05
618 Mark Gubicza .05
619 David Howard .05
620 Mike Magnante .05
621 Brent Mayne .05
622 Kevin McReynolds .05
623 *Eddie Pierce* .05
624 Bill Sampen .05
625 Steve Shifflett .05
626 Gary Thurman .05
627 Curtis Wikerson .05
628 Chris Bosio .05
629 Scott Fletcher .05
630 Jim Gantner .05
631 Dave Nilsson .05
632 Jesse Orosco .05
633 Dan Plesac .05
634 Ron Robinson .05
635 Bill Spiers .05
636 Franklin Stubbs .05
637 Willie Banks .05
638 Randy Bush .05
639 Chuck Knoblauch .05
640 Shane Mack .05
641 Mike Pagliarulo .05
642 Jeff Reboulet .05
643 John Smiley .05
644 *Mike Trombley* .05
645 Gary Wayne .05
646 Lenny Webster .05
647 Tim Burke .05
648 Mike Gallego .05
649 Dion James .05
650 Jeff Johnson .05
651 Scott Kamieniecki .05
652 Kevin Maas .05
653 Rich Monteleone .05
654 Jerry Nielsen .05
655 Scott Sanderson .05
656 Mike Stanley .05
657 Gerald Williams .05
658 Curt Young .05
659 Harold Baines .05
660 Kevin Campbell .05
661 Ron Darling .05
662 Kelly Downs .05
663 Eric Fox .05
664 Dave Henderson .05
665 Rick Honeycutt .05
666 Mike Moore .05
667 Jamie Quirk .05
668 Jeff Russell .05
669 Dave Stewart .05
670 Greg Briley .05
671 Dave Cochrane .05
672 Henry Cotto .05
673 Rich DeLucia .05
674 Brian Fisher .05
675 Mark Grant .05
676 Randy Johnson .50
677 Tim Leary .05
678 Pete O'Brien .05
679 Lance Parrish .05
680 Harold Reynolds .05
681 Shane Turner .05
682 Jack Daugherty .05
683 *David Hulse* .05
684 Terry Mathews .05
685 Al Newman .05
686 Edwin Nunez .05
687 Rafael Palmeiro .40
688 Roger Pavlik .05
689 Geno Petralli .05
690 Nolan Ryan 1.00
691 David Cone .05
692 Alfredo Griffin .05
693 Juan Guzman .05
694 Pat Hentgen .05
695 Randy Knorr .05
696 Bob MacDonald .05
697 Jack Morris .05
698 Ed Sprague .05
699 Dave Stieb .05
700 Pat Tabler .05
701 Mike Timlin .05
702 David Wells .05
703 Eddie Zosky .05
704 Gary Sheffield (League Leaders) .05
705 Darren Daulton (League Leaders) .05
706 Marquis Grissom (League Leaders) .05
707 Greg Maddux (League Leaders) .10
708 Bill Swift (League Leaders) .05
709 Juan Gonzalez (Round Trippers) .15
710 Mark McGwire (Round Trippers) .50
711 Cecil Fielder (Round Trippers) .05
712 Albert Belle (Round Trippers) .05
713 Joe Carter (Round Trippers) .05
714 Frank Thomas, Cecil Fielder Power Brokers .10
715 Larry Walker, Darren Daulton Unsung Heroes .05
716 Edgar Martinez, Robin Ventura Hot Corner Hammers .05
717 Roger Clemens, Dennis Eckersley Start to Finish .25
718 Checklist .05
719 Checklist .05
720 Checklist .05

All-Stars

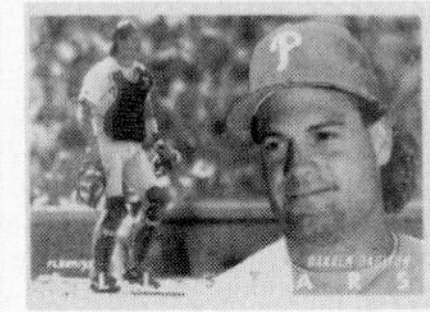

NM/M

Complete Set A.L. (12): 6.00
Complete Set N.L. (12): 3.75
Common Player: .15

AMERICAN LEAGUE
1 Frank Thomas .85
2 Roberto Alomar .40
3 Edgar Martinez .15
4 Pat Listach .15
5 Cecil Fielder .15
6 Juan Gonzalez .40
7 Ken Griffey, Jr. 2.00
8 Joe Carter .15
9 Kirby Puckett 1.00
10 Brian Harper .15
11 Dave Fleming .15
12 Jack McDowell .15

NATIONAL LEAGUE
1 Fred McGriff .15
2 Delino DeShields .15
3 Gary Sheffield .40
4 Barry Larkin .15
5 Felix Jose .15
6 Larry Walker .15
7 Barry Bonds 2.50
8 Andy Van Slyke .15
9 Darren Daulton .15
10 Greg Maddux .75
11 Tom Glavine .25
12 Lee Smith .15

Final Edition

NM/M

Complete Set (310): 7.50
Common Player: .05
1 Steve Bedrosian .05
2 Jay Howell .05
3 Greg Maddux .65
4 *Greg McMichael* .05
5 *Tony Tarasco* .05
6 Jose Bautista .05
7 Jose Guzman .05
8 Greg Hibbard .05
9 Candy Maldonado .05
10 Randy Myers .05
11 *Matt Walbeck* .05
12 Turk Wendell .05
13 Willie Nelson .05
14 Greg Cadaret .05
15 Roberto Kelly .05
16 Randy Milligan .05
17 Kevin Mitchell .05
18 Jeff Reardon .05
19 John Roper .05
20 John Smiley .05
21 Andy Ashby .05
22 Dante Bichette .05
23 Willie Blair .05
24 Pedro Castellano .05
25 Vinny Castilla .05
26 Jerald Clark .05
27 Alex Cole .05
28 *Scott Fredrickson* .05
29 *Jay Gainer* .05
30 Andres Galarraga .05
31 Joe Girardi .05
32 Ryan Hawblitzel .05
33 Charlie Hayes .05
34 Darren Holmes .05
35 Chris Jones .05
36 David Nied .05
37 *J. Owens* .05
38 *Lance Painter* .05
39 Jeff Parrett .05
40 *Steve Reed* .05
41 Armando Reynoso .05
42 Bruce Ruffin .05
43 *Danny Sheaffer* .05
44 Keith Shepherd .05
45 Jim Tatum .05
46 Gary Wayne .05
47 Eric Young .05
48 Luis Aquino .05
49 Alex Arias .05
50 Jack Armstrong .05
51 Bret Barberie .05
52 Geronimo Berroa .05
53 Ryan Bowen .05
54 Greg Briley .05
55 Chris Carpenter .05
56 Chuck Carr .05
57 Jeff Conine .05
58 Jim Corsi .05
59 Orestes Destrade .05
60 Junior Felix .05
61 Chris Hammond .05
62 Bryan Harvey .05
63 Charlie Hough .05
64 Joe Klink .05
65 *Richie Lewis* .05
66 *Mitch Lyden* .05
67 Bob Natal .05
68 *Scott Pose* .05
69 Rich Renteria .05
70 Benito Santiago .05
71 Gary Sheffield .15
72 *Matt Turner* .05
73 Walt Weiss .05
74 *Darrell Whitmore* .05
75 Nigel Wilson .05
76 Kevin Bass .05
77 Doug Drabek .05
78 Tom Edens .05
79 Chris James .05
80 Greg Swindell .05
81 *Omar Daal* .05
82 Raul Mondesi .05
83 Jody Reed .05
84 Cory Snyder .05
85 Rick Trlicek .05
86 Tim Wallach .05
87 Todd Worrell .05
88 Tavo Alvarez .05
89 Frank Bolick .05
90 Kent Bottenfield .05
91 Greg Colbrunn .05
92 Cliff Floyd .05
93 *Lou Frazier* .05
94 Mike Gardiner .05
95 *Mike Lansing* .25
96 Bill Risley .05
97 Jeff Shaw .05
98 Kevin Baez .05
99 *Tim Bogar* .05
100 Jeromy Burnitz .05
101 Mike Draper .05
102 Darrin Jackson .05
103 Mike Maddux .05
104 Joe Orsulak .05
105 Doug Saunders .05
106 Frank Tanana .05
107 Dave Telgheder .05
108 Larry Anderson .05
109 Jim Eisenreich .05
110 Pete Incaviglia .05
111 Danny Jackson .05
112 David West .05
113 Al Martin .05
114 Blas Minor .05
115 Dennis Moeller .05
116 Will Pennyfeather .05
117 Rich Robertson .05
118 Ben Shelton .05
119 Lonnie Smith .05
120 Freddie Toliver .05
121 Paul Wagner .05
122 Kevin Young .05
123 *Rene Arocha* .05
124 Gregg Jefferies .05
125 Paul Kilgus .05
126 Les Lancaster .05
127 Joe Magrane .05
128 Rob Murphy .05
129 Erik Pappas .05
130 Stan Royer .05
131 Ozzie Smith .65
132 Tom Urbani .05
133 Mark Whiten .05
134 Derek Bell .05
135 Doug Brocail .05
136 Phil Clark .05
137 *Mark Ettles* .05
138 Jeff Gardner .05
139 *Pat Gomez* .05
140 Ricky Gutierrez .05
141 Gene Harris .05
142 *Kevin Higgins* .05
143 Trevor Hoffman .05
144 Phil Plantier .05
145 *Kerry Taylor* .05
146 Guillermo Velasquez .05
147 Wally Whitehurst .05
148 *Tim Worrell* .05
149 Todd Benzinger .05
150 Barry Bonds 2.00
151 Greg Brummett .05
152 Mark Carreon .05
153 Dave Martinez .05
154 Jeff Reed .05
155 Kevin Rogers .05
156 Harold Baines .05
157 Damon Buford .05
158 *Paul Carey* .05
159 Jeffrey Hammonds .05
160 Jamie Moyer .05
161 *Sherman Obando* .05
162 *John O'Donoghue* .05
163 Brad Pennington .05
164 Jim Poole .05
165 Harold Reynolds .05
166 Fernando Valenzuela .05
167 *Jack Voight* .05
168 Mark Williamson .05
169 Scott Bankhead .05
170 Greg Blosser .05
171 *Jim Byrd* .05
172 Ivan Calderon .05
173 Andre Dawson .25
174 Scott Fletcher .05
175 Jose Melendez .05
176 Carlos Quintana .05
177 Jeff Russell .05
178 Aaron Sele .05
179 *Rod Correia* .05
180 Chili Davis .05
181 *Jim Edmonds* 3.00
182 Rene Gonzales .05
183 *Hilly Hathaway* .05
184 Torey Lovullo .05
185 Greg Myers .05
186 Gene Nelson .05
187 Troy Percival .05
188 Scott Sanderson .05
189 *Darryl Scott* .05
190 *J.T. Snow* .50
191 Russ Springer .05
192 Jason Bere .05
193 Rodney Bolton .05
194 Ellis Burks .05
195 Bo Jackson .15
196 Mike LaValliere .05
197 Scott Ruffcorn .05
198 *Jeff Schwartz* .05
199 Jerry DiPoto .05
200 Alvaro Espinoza .05
201 Wayne Kirby .05
202 *Tom Kramer* .05
203 Jesse Levis .05
204 Manny Ramirez .50
205 Jeff Treadway .05
206 *Bill Wertz* .05
207 Cliff Young .05

208	Matt Young	.05
209	Kirk Gibson	.05
210	Greg Gohr	.05
211	Bill Krueger	.05
212	Bob MacDonald	.05
213	Mike Moore	.05
214	David Wells	.05
215	*Billy Brewer*	.05
216	David Cone	.05
217	Greg Gagne	.05
218	Mark Gardner	.05
219	Chis Haney	.05
220	Phil Hiatt	.05
221	Jose Lind	.05
222	Juan Bell	.05
223	Tom Brunansky	.05
224	Mike Ignasiak	.05
225	Joe Kmak	.05
226	Tom Lampkin	.05
227	*Graeme Lloyd*	.05
228	Carlos Maldonado	.05
229	Matt Mieske	.05
230	Angel Miranda	.05
231	*Troy O'Leary*	.10
232	Kevin Reimer	.05
233	Larry Casian	.05
234	Jim Deshaies	.05
235	*Eddie Guardado*	.10
236	Chip Hale	.05
237	*Mike Maksudian*	.05
238	David McCarty	.05
239	*Pat Meares*	.05
240	*George Tsamis*	.05
241	Dave Winfield	.50
242	Jim Abbott	.05
243	Wade Boggs	.65
244	*Andy Cook*	.05
245	*Russ Davis*	.10
246	Mike Humphreys	.05
247	Jimmy Key	.05
248	Jim Leyritz	.05
249	Bobby Munoz	.05
250	Paul O'Neill	.05
251	Spike Owen	.05
252	Dave Silvestri	.05
253	*Marcos Armas*	.05
254	Brent Gates	.05
255	Goose Gossage	.25
256	*Scott Lydy*	.05
257	Henry Mercedes	.05
258	*Mike Mohler*	.05
259	Troy Neel	.05
260	Edwin Nunez	.05
261	Craig Paquette	.05
262	Kevin Seitzer	.05
263	Rich Amaral	.05
264	Mike Blowers	.05
265	Chris Bosio	.05
266	Norm Charlton	.05
267	*Jim Converse*	.05
268	*John Cummings*	.05
269	Mike Felder	.05
270	Mike Hampton	.05
271	Bill Haselman	.05
272	Dwayne Henry	.05
273	Greg Litton	.05
274	Mackey Sasser	.05
275	Lee Tinsley	.05
276	David Wainhouse	.05
277	*Jeff Bronkey*	.05
278	Benji Gil	.05
279	Tom Henke	.05
280	Charlie Leibrandt	.05
281	Robb Nen	.05
282	Bill Ripken	.05
283	*Jon Shave*	.05
284	Doug Strange	.05
285	*Matt Whiteside*	.05
286	*Scott Brow*	.05
287	*Willie Canate*	.05
288	Tony Castillo	.05
289	*Domingo Cedeno*	.05
290	Darnell Coles	.05
291	Danny Cox	.05
292	Mark Eichhorn	.05
293	Tony Fernandez	.05
294	Al Leiter	.05
295	Paul Molitor	.50
296	Dave Stewart	.05
297	*Woody Williams*	.05
298	Checklist	.05
299	Checklist	.05
300	Checklist	.05
	DIAMOND TRIBUTE	
1DT	Wade Boggs	.65
2DT	George Brett	.75
3DT	Andre Dawson	.25
4DT	Carlton Fisk	.50
5DT	Paul Molitor	.50
6DT	Nolan Ryan	2.00
7DT	Lee Smith	.05
8DT	Ozzie Smith	.65
9DT	Dave Winfield	.50
10DT	Robin Yount	.50

Golden Moments

		NM/M
Complete Set (6):		4.00
Common Player:		.25
	SERIES 1	2.00
(1)	George Brett	1.50
(2)	Mickey Morandini	.25
(3)	Dave Winfield	.50
	SERIES 2	2.00
(1)	Dennis Eckersley	.40
(2)	Bip Roberts	.25
(3)	Frank Thomas, Juan Gonzalez	1.50

Major League Prospects

		NM/M
Complete Set (36):		7.50
Common Player:		.15
	SERIES 1	5.00
1	Melvin Nieves	.15
2	Sterling Hitchcock	.15
3	Tim Costo	.15
4	Manny Alexander	.15
5	Alan Embree	.15
6	Kevin Young	.15
7	J.T. Snow	.15
8	Russ Springer	.15
9	Billy Ashley	.15
10	Kevin Rogers	.15
11	Steve Hosey	.15
12	Eric Wedge	.15
13	Mike Piazza	3.50
14	Jesse Levis	.15
15	Rico Brogna	.15
16	Alex Arias	.15
17	Rod Brewer	.15
18	Troy Neel	.15
	SERIES 2	2.50
1	Scooter Tucker	.15
2	Kerry Woodson	.15
3	Greg Colbrunn	.15
4	Pedro Martinez	1.50
5	Dave Silvestri	.15
6	Kent Bottenfield	.15
7	Rafael Bournigal	.15
8	J.T. Bruett	.15
9	Dave Mlicki	.15
10	Paul Wagner	.15
11	Mike Williams	.15
12	Henry Mercedes	.15
13	Scott Taylor	.15
14	Dennis Moeller	.15
15	Javier Lopez	.15
16	Steve Cooke	.15
17	Pete Young	.15
18	Ken Ryan	.15

ProVisions

		NM/M
Complete Set (6):		3.00
Common Player:		.40
	SERIES 1	2.00
1	Roberto Alomar	.65
2	Dennis Eckersley	1.00
3	Gary Sheffield	.75
	SERIES 2	1.00
1	Andy Van Slyke	.40
2	Tom Glavine	.75
3	Cecil Fielder	.40

Rookie Sensations

		NM/M
Complete Set (20):		6.25
Common Player:		.25
	SERIES 1	3.00
1	Kenny Lofton	.50
2	Cal Eldred	.25
3	Pat Listach	.25
4	Roberto Hernandez	.25
5	Dave Fleming	.25
6	Eric Karros	.25
7	Reggie Sanders	.25
8	Derrick May	.25
9	Mike Perez	.25
10	Donovan Osborne	.25
	ERIES 2	2.00
1	Moises Alou	.50
2	Pedro Astacio	.25
3	Jim Austin	.25
4	Chad Curtis	.25
5	Gary DiSarcina	.25
6	Scott Livingstone	.25
7	Sam Militello	.25
8	Arthur Rhodes	.25
9	Tim Wakefield	.35
10	Bob Zupcic	.25

Team Leaders

		NM/M
Complete Set (20):		12.50
Common Player:		.40
	SERIES 1	10.00
1	Kirby Puckett	1.25
2	Mark McGwire	3.00
3	Pat Listach	.40
4	Roger Clemens	1.50
5	Frank Thomas	1.00
6	Carlos Baerga	.40
7	Brady Anderson	.40
8	Juan Gonzalez	.50
9	Roberto Alomar	.60
10	Ken Griffey, Jr.	2.00
	SERIES 2	4.00
1	Will Clark	.40
2	Terry Pendleton	.40
3	Ray Lankford	.40
4	Eric Karros	.40
5	Gary Sheffield	.75
6	Ryne Sandberg	1.25
7	Marquis Grissom	.40
8	John Kruk	.40
9	Jeff Bagwell	1.00
10	Andy Van Slyke	.40

Tom Glavine Career Highlights

		NM/M
Complete Set (15):		5.00
Common Card:		.50
Autographed Card:		30.00
1-15	Tom Glavine	.50

1994 FLEER

		NM/M
Complete Set (720):		12.50
Common Player:		.05
Pack (15):		.50
Wax Box (36):		12.50
1	Brady Anderson	.05
2	Harold Baines	.05
3	Mike Devereaux	.05
4	Todd Frohwirth	.05
5	Jeffrey Hammonds	.05
6	Chris Hoiles	.05
7	Tim Hulett	.05
8	Ben McDonald	.05
9	Mark McLemore	.05
10	Alan Mills	.05
11	Jamie Moyer	.05
12	Mike Mussina	.40
13	Gregg Olson	.05
14	Mike Pagliarulo	.05
15	Brad Pennington	.05
16	Jim Poole	.05
17	Harold Reynolds	.05
18	Arthur Rhodes	.05
19	Cal Ripken, Jr.	2.00
20	David Segui	.05
21	Rick Sutcliffe	.05
22	Fernando Valenzuela	.05
23	Jack Voigt	.05
24	Mark Williamson	.05
25	Scott Bankhead	.05
26	Roger Clemens	1.00
27	Scott Cooper	.05
28	Danny Darwin	.05
29	Andre Dawson	.25
30	Rob Deer	.05
31	John Dopson	.05
32	Scott Fletcher	.05
33	Mike Greenwell	.05
34	Greg Harris	.05
35	Billy Hatcher	.05
36	Bob Melvin	.05
37	Tony Pena	.05
38	Paul Quantrill	.05
39	Carlos Quintana	.05
40	Ernest Riles	.05
41	Jeff Russell	.05
42	Ken Ryan	.05
43	Aaron Sele	.05
44	John Valentin	.05
45	Mo Vaughn	.05
46	Frank Viola	.05
47	Bob Zupcic	.05
48	Mike Butcher	.05
49	Rod Correia	.05
50	Chad Curtis	.05
51	Chili Davis	.05
52	Gary DiSarcina	.05
53	Damion Easley	.05
54	Jim Edmonds	.05
55	Chuck Finley	.05
56	Steve Frey	.05
57	Rene Gonzales	.05
58	Joe Grahe	.05
59	Hilly Hathaway	.05
60	Stan Javier	.05
61	Mark Langston	.05
62	Phil Leftwich	.05
63	Torey Lovullo	.05
64	Joe Magrane	.05
65	Greg Myers	.05
66	Ken Patterson	.05
67	Eduardo Perez	.05
68	Luis Polonia	.05
69	Tim Salmon	.20
69a	Tim Salmon (overprinted "PROMOTIONAL SAMPLE")	2.00

No.	Player	Price
70	J.T. Snow	.05
71	Ron Tingley	.05
72	Julio Valera	.05
73	Wilson Alvarez	.05
74	Tim Belcher	.05
75	George Bell	.05
76	Jason Bere	.05
77	Rod Bolton	.05
78	Ellis Burks	.05
79	Joey Cora	.05
80	Alex Fernandez	.05
81	Craig Grebeck	.05
82	Ozzie Guillen	.05
83	Roberto Hernandez	.05
84	Bo Jackson	.10
85	Lance Johnson	.05
86	Ron Karkovice	.05
87	Mike LaValliere	.05
88	Kirk McCaskill	.05
89	Jack McDowell	.05
90	Warren Newson	.05
91	Dan Pasqua	.05
92	Scott Radinsky	.05
93	Tim Raines	.05
94	Steve Sax	.05
95	Jeff Schwarz	.05
96	Frank Thomas	.75
97	Robin Ventura	.05
98	Sandy Alomar, Jr.	.05
99	Carlos Baerga	.05
100	Albert Belle	.05
101	Mark Clark	.05
102	Jerry DiPoto	.05
103	Alvaro Espinoza	.05
104	Felix Fermin	.05
105	Jeremy Hernandez	.05
106	Reggie Jefferson	.05
107	Wayne Kirby	.05
108	Tom Kramer	.05
109	Mark Lewis	.05
110	Derek Lilliquist	.05
111	Kenny Lofton	.05
112	Candy Maldonado	.05
113	Jose Mesa	.05
114	Jeff Mutis	.05
115	Charles Nagy	.05
116	Bob Ojeda	.05
117	Junior Ortiz	.05
118	Eric Plunk	.05
119	Manny Ramirez	.75
120	Paul Sorrento	.05
121	Jim Thome	.60
122	Jeff Treadway	.05
123	Bill Wertz	.05
124	Skeeter Barnes	.05
125	Milt Cuyler	.05
126	Eric Davis	.05
127	John Doherty	.05
128	Cecil Fielder	.05
129	Travis Fryman	.05
130	Kirk Gibson	.05
131	Dan Gladden	.05
132	Greg Gohr	.05
133	Chris Gomez	.05
134	Bill Gullickson	.05
135	Mike Henneman	.05
136	Kurt Knudsen	.05
137	Chad Kreuter	.05
138	Bill Krueger	.05
139	Scott Livingstone	.05
140	Bob MacDonald	.05
141	Mike Moore	.05
142	Tony Phillips	.05
143	Mickey Tettleton	.05
144	Alan Trammell	.05
145	David Wells	.05
146	Lou Whitaker	.05
147	Kevin Appier	.05
148	Stan Belinda	.05
149	George Brett	1.00
150	Billy Brewer	.05
151	Hubie Brooks	.05
152	David Cone	.05
153	Gary Gaetti	.05
154	Greg Gagne	.05
155	Tom Gordon	.05
156	Mark Gubicza	.05
157	Chris Gwynn	.05
158	John Habyan	.05
159	Chris Haney	.05
160	Phil Hiatt	.05
161	Felix Jose	.05
162	Wally Joyner	.05
163	Jose Lind	.05
164	Mike Macfarlane	.05
165	Mike Magnante	.05
166	Brent Mayne	.05
167	Brian McRae	.05
168	Kevin McReynolds	.05
169	Keith Miller	.05
170	Jeff Montgomery	.05
171	Hipolito Pichardo	.05
172	Rico Rossy	.05
173	Juan Bell	.05
174	Ricky Bones	.05
175	Cal Eldred	.05
176	Mike Fetters	.05
177	Darryl Hamilton	.05
178	Doug Henry	.05
179	Mike Ignasiak	.05
180	John Jaha	.05
181	Pat Listach	.05
182	Graeme Lloyd	.05
183	Matt Mieske	.05
184	Angel Miranda	.05
185	Jaime Navarro	.05
186	Dave Nilsson	.05
187	Troy O'Leary	.05
188	Jesse Orosco	.05
189	Kevin Reimer	.05
190	Kevin Seitzer	.05
191	Bill Spiers	.05
192	B.J. Surhoff	.05
193	Dickie Thon	.05
194	Jose Valentin	.05
195	Greg Vaughn	.05
196	Bill Wegman	.05
197	Robin Yount	.75
198	Rick Aguilera	.05
199	Willie Banks	.05
200	Bernardo Brito	.05
201	Larry Casian	.05
202	Scott Erickson	.05
203	Eddie Guardado	.05
204	Mark Guthrie	.05
205	Chip Hale	.05
206	Brian Harper	.05
207	Mike Hartley	.05
208	Kent Hrbek	.05
209	Terry Jorgensen	.05
210	Chuck Knoblauch	.05
211	Gene Larkin	.05
212	Shane Mack	.05
213	David McCarty	.05
214	Pat Meares	.05
215	Pedro Munoz	.05
216	Derek Parks	.05
217	Kirby Puckett	.85
218	Jeff Reboulet	.05
219	Kevin Tapani	.05
220	Mike Trombley	.05
221	George Tsamis	.05
222	Carl Willis	.05
223	Dave Winfield	.75
224	Jim Abbott	.05
225	Paul Assenmacher	.05
226	Wade Boggs	.85
227	Russ Davis	.05
228	Steve Farr	.05
229	Mike Gallego	.05
230	Paul Gibson	.05
231	Steve Howe	.05
232	Dion James	.05
233	Domingo Jean	.05
234	Scott Kamieniecki	.05
235	Pat Kelly	.05
236	Jimmy Key	.05
237	Jim Leyritz	.05
238	Kevin Maas	.05
239	Don Mattingly	1.00
240	Rich Monteleone	.05
241	Bobby Munoz	.05
242	Matt Nokes	.05
243	Paul O'Neill	.05
244	Spike Owen	.05
245	Melido Perez	.05
246	Lee Smith	.05
247	Mike Stanley	.05
248	Danny Tartabull	.05
249	Randy Velarde	.05
250	Bob Wickman	.05
251	Bernie Williams	.20
252	Mike Aldrete	.05
253	Marcos Armas	.05
254	Lance Blankenship	.05
255	Mike Bordick	.05
256	Scott Brosius	.05
257	Jerry Browne	.05
258	Ron Darling	.05
259	Kelly Downs	.05
260	Dennis Eckersley	.60
261	Brent Gates	.05
262	Goose Gossage	.05
263	Scott Hemond	.05
264	Dave Henderson	.05
265	Rick Honeycutt	.05
266	Vince Horsman	.05
267	Scott Lydy	.05
268	Mark McGwire	1.50
269	Mike Mohler	.05
270	Troy Neel	.05
271	Edwin Nunez	.05
272	Craig Paquette	.05
273	Ruben Sierra	.05
274	Terry Steinbach	.05
275	Todd Van Poppel	.05
276	Bob Welch	.05
277	Bobby Witt	.05
278	Rich Amaral	.05
279	Mike Blowers	.05
280	Bret Boone	.05
281	Chris Bosio	.05
282	Jay Buhner	.05
283	Norm Charlton	.05
284	Mike Felder	.05
285	Dave Fleming	.05
286	Ken Griffey, Jr.	1.25
287	Erik Hanson	.05
288	Bill Haselman	.05
289	*Brad Holman*	.05
290	Randy Johnson	.75
291	Tim Leary	.05
292	Greg Litton	.05
293	Dave Magadan	.05
294	Edgar Martinez	.05
295	Tino Martinez	.05
296	Jeff Nelson	.05
297	*Erik Plantenberg*	.05
298	Mackey Sasser	.05
299	*Brian Turang*	.05
300	Dave Valle	.05
301	Omar Vizquel	.05
302	Brian Bohanon	.05
303	Kevin Brown	.05
304	Jose Canseco	.40
305	Mario Diaz	.05
306	Julio Franco	.05
307	Juan Gonzalez	.75
308	Tom Henke	.05
309	David Hulse	.05
310	Manuel Lee	.05
311	Craig Lefferts	.05
312	Charlie Leibrandt	.05
313	Rafael Palmeiro	.75
314	Dean Palmer	.05
315	Roger Pavlik	.05
316	Dan Peltier	.05
317	Geno Petralli	.05
318	Gary Redus	.05
319	Ivan Rodriguez	.65
320	Kenny Rogers	.05
321	Nolan Ryan	2.00
322	Doug Strange	.05
323	Matt Whiteside	.05
324	Roberto Alomar	.30
325	Pat Borders	.05
326	Joe Carter	.05
327	Tony Castillo	.05
328	Darnell Coles	.05
329	Danny Cox	.05
330	Mark Eichhorn	.05
331	Tony Fernandez	.05
332	Alfredo Griffin	.05
333	Juan Guzman	.05
334	Rickey Henderson	.75
335	Pat Hentgen	.05
336	Randy Knorr	.05
337	Al Leiter	.05
338	Paul Molitor	.75
339	Jack Morris	.05
340	John Olerud	.05
341	Dick Schofield	.05
342	Ed Sprague	.05
343	Dave Stewart	.05
344	Todd Stottlemyre	.05
345	Mike Timlin	.05
346	Duane Ward	.05
347	Turner Ward	.05
348	Devon White	.05
349	Woody Williams	.05
350	Steve Avery	.05
351	Steve Bedrosian	.05
352	Rafael Belliard	.05
353	Damon Berryhill	.05
354	Jeff Blauser	.05
355	Sid Bream	.05
356	Francisco Cabrera	.05
357	Marvin Freeman	.05
358	Ron Gant	.05
359	Tom Glavine	.25
360	Jay Howell	.05
361	Dave Justice	.05
362	Ryan Klesko	.05
363	Mark Lemke	.05
364	Javier Lopez	.05
365	Greg Maddux	.85
366	Fred McGriff	.05
367	Greg McMichael	.05
368	Kent Mercker	.05
369	Otis Nixon	.05
370	Greg Olson	.05
371	Bill Pecota	.05
372	Terry Pendleton	.05
373	Deion Sanders	.05
374	Pete Smith	.05
375	John Smoltz	.05
376	Mike Stanton	.05
377	Tony Tarasco	.05
378	Mark Wohlers	.05
379	Jose Bautista	.05
380	Shawn Boskie	.05
381	Steve Buechele	.05
382	Frank Castillo	.05
383	Mark Grace	.10
384	Jose Guzman	.05
385	Mike Harkey	.05
386	Greg Hibbard	.05
387	Glenallen Hill	.05
388	Steve Lake	.05
389	Derrick May	.05
390	Chuck McElroy	.05
391	Mike Morgan	.05
392	Randy Myers	.05
393	Dan Plesac	.05
394	Kevin Roberson	.05
395	Rey Sanchez	.05
396	Ryne Sandberg	.85
397	Bob Scanlan	.05
398	Dwight Smith	.05
399	Sammy Sosa	1.25
400	Jose Vizcaino	.05
401	Rick Wilkins	.05
402	Willie Wilson	.05
403	Eric Yelding	.05
404	Bobby Ayala	.05
405	Jeff Branson	.05
406	Tom Browning	.05
407	Jacob Brumfield	.05
408	Tim Costo	.05
409	Rob Dibble	.05
410	Willie Greene	.05
411	Thomas Howard	.05
412	Roberto Kelly	.05
413	Bill Landrum	.05
414	Barry Larkin	.05
415	*Larry Luebbers*	.05
416	Kevin Mitchell	.05
417	Hal Morris	.05
418	Joe Oliver	.05
419	Tim Pugh	.05
420	Jeff Reardon	.05
421	Jose Rijo	.05
422	Bip Roberts	.05
423	John Roper	.05
424	Johnny Ruffin	.05
425	Chris Sabo	.05
426	Juan Samuel	.05
427	Reggie Sanders	.05
428	Scott Service	.05
429	John Smiley	.05
430	*Jerry Spradlin*	.05
431	Kevin Wickander	.05
432	Freddie Benavides	.05
433	Dante Bichette	.05
434	Willie Blair	.05
435	Daryl Boston	.05
436	Kent Bottenfield	.05
437	Vinny Castilla	.05
438	Jerald Clark	.05
439	Alex Cole	.05
440	Andres Galarraga	.05
441	Joe Girardi	.05
442	Greg Harris	.05
443	Charlie Hayes	.05
444	Darren Holmes	.05
445	Chris Jones	.05
446	Roberto Mejia	.05
447	David Nied	.05
448	J. Owens	.05
449	Jeff Parrett	.05
450	Steve Reed	.05
451	Armando Reynoso	.05
452	Bruce Ruffin	.05
453	Mo Sanford	.05
454	Danny Sheaffer	.05
455	Jim Tatum	.05
456	Gary Wayne	.05
457	Eric Young	.05
458	Luis Aquino	.05
459	Alex Arias	.05
460	Jack Armstrong	.05
461	Bret Barberie	.05
462	Ryan Bowen	.05
463	Chuck Carr	.05
464	Jeff Conine	.05
465	Henry Cotto	.05

466 Orestes Destrade .05
467 Chris Hammond .05
468 Bryan Harvey .05
469 Charlie Hough .05
470 Joe Klink .05
471 Richie Lewis .05
472 *Bob Natal* .05
473 *Pat Rapp* .05
474 *Rich Renteria* .10
475 Rich Rodriguez .05
476 Benito Santiago .05
477 Gary Sheffield .35
478 Matt Turner .05
479 David Weathers .05
480 Walt Weiss .05
481 Darrell Whitmore .05
482 Eric Anthony .05
483 Jeff Bagwell .75
484 Kevin Bass .05
485 Craig Biggio .05
486 Ken Caminiti .05
487 Andujar Cedeno .05
488 Chris Donnels .05
489 Doug Drabek .05
490 Steve Finley .05
491 Luis Gonzalez .25
492 Pete Harnisch .05
493 Xavier Hernandez .05
494 Doug Jones .05
495 Todd Jones .05
496 Darryl Kile .05
497 Al Osuna .05
498 Mark Portugal .05
499 Scott Servais .05
500 Greg Swindell .05
501 Eddie Taubensee .05
502 Jose Uribe .05
503 Brian Williams .05
504 Billy Ashley .05
505 Pedro Astacio .05
506 Brett Butler .05
507 Tom Candiotti .05
508 Omar Daal .05
509 Jim Gott .05
510 Kevin Gross .05
511 Dave Hansen .05
512 Carlos Hernandez .05
513 Orel Hershiser .05
514 Eric Karros .05
515 Pedro Martinez .75
516 Ramon Martinez .05
517 Roger McDowell .05
518 Raul Mondesi .05
519 Jose Offerman .05
520 Mike Piazza 1.25
521 Jody Reed .05
522 Henry Rodriguez .05
523 Mike Sharperson .05
524 Cory Snyder .05
525 Darryl Strawberry .05
526 Rick Trlicek .05
527 Tim Wallach .05
528 Mitch Webster .05
529 Steve Wilson .05
530 Todd Worrell .05
531 Moises Alou .05
532 Brian Barnes .05
533 Sean Berry .05
534 Greg Colbrunn .05
535 Delino DeShields .05
536 Jeff Fassero .05
537 Darrin Fletcher .05
538 Cliff Floyd .05
539 Lou Frazier .05
540 Marquis Grissom .05
541 Butch Henry .05
542 Ken Hill .05
543 Mike Lansing .05
544 *Brian Looney* .05
545 Dennis Martinez .05
546 Chris Nabholz .05
547 Randy Ready .05
548 Mel Rojas .05
549 Kirk Rueter .05
550 Tim Scott .05
551 Jeff Shaw .05
552 Tim Spehr .05
553 John VanderWal .05
554 Larry Walker .05
555 John Wetteland .05
556 Rondell White .05
557 Tim Bogar .05
558 Bobby Bonilla .05
559 Jeromy Burnitz .05
560 Sid Fernandez .05
561 John Franco .05
562 Dave Gallagher .05
563 Dwight Gooden .05
564 Eric Hillman .05
565 Todd Hundley .05
566 Jeff Innis .05
567 Darrin Jackson .05
568 Howard Johnson .05
569 Bobby Jones .05
570 Jeff Kent .05
571 Mike Maddux .05
572 Jeff McKnight .05
573 Eddie Murray .75
574 Charlie O'Brien .05
575 Joe Orsulak .05
576 Bret Saberhagen .05
577 Pete Schourek .05
578 Dave Telgheder .05
579 Ryan Thompson .05
580 Anthony Young .05
581 Ruben Amaro .05
582 Larry Andersen .05
583 Kim Batiste .05
584 Wes Chamberlain .05
585 Darren Daulton .05
586 Mariano Duncan .05
587 Len Dykstra .05
588 Jim Eisenreich .05
589 Tommy Greene .05
590 Dave Hollins .05
591 Pete Incaviglia .05
592 Danny Jackson .05
593 Ricky Jordan .05
594 John Kruk .05
595 Roger Mason .05
596 Mickey Morandini .05
597 Terry Mulholland .05
598 Todd Pratt .05
599 Ben Rivera .05
600 Curt Schilling .25
601 Kevin Stocker .05
602 Milt Thompson .05
603 David West .05
604 Mitch Williams .05
605 Jay Bell .05
606 Dave Clark .05
607 Steve Cooke .05
608 Tom Foley .05
609 Carlos Garcia .05
610 Joel Johnston .05
611 Jeff King .05
612 Al Martin .05
613 Lloyd McClendon .05
614 Orlando Merced .05
615 Blas Minor .05
616 Denny Neagle .05
617 *Mark Petkovsek* .05
618 Tom Prince .05
619 Don Slaught .05
620 Zane Smith .05
621 Randy Tomlin .05
622 Andy Van Slyke .05
623 Paul Wagner .05
624 Tim Wakefield .05
625 Bob Walk .05
626 Kevin Young .05
627 Luis Alicea .05
628 Rene Arocha .05
629 Rod Brewer .05
630 Rheal Cormier .05
631 Bernard Gilkey .05
632 Lee Guetterman .05
633 Gregg Jefferies .05
634 Brian Jordan .05
635 Les Lancaster .05
636 Ray Lankford .05
637 Rob Murphy .05
638 Omar Olivares .05
639 Jose Oquendo .05
640 Donovan Osborne .05
641 Tom Pagnozzi .05
642 Erik Pappas .05
643 Geronimo Pena .05
644 Mike Perez .05
645 Gerald Perry .05
646 Ozzie Smith .85
647 Bob Tewksbury .05
648 Allen Watson .05
649 Mark Whiten .05
650 Tracy Woodson .05
651 Todd Zeile .05
652 Andy Ashby .05
653 Brad Ausmus .05
654 Billy Bean .05
655 Derek Bell .05
656 Andy Benes .05
657 Doug Brocail .05
658 Jarvis Brown .05
659 Archi Cianfrocco .05
660 Phil Clark .05
661 Mark Davis .05
662 Jeff Gardner .05
663 Pat Gomez .05
664 Ricky Gutierrez .05
665 Tony Gwynn .85
666 Gene Harris .05
667 Kevin Higgins .05
668 Trevor Hoffman .05
669 *Pedro A. Martinez* .05
670 Tim Mauser .05
671 Melvin Nieves .05
672 Phil Plantier .05
673 Frank Seminara .05
674 Craig Shipley .05
675 Kerry Taylor .05
676 Tim Teufel .05
677 Guillermo Velasquez .05
678 Wally Whitehurst .05
679 Tim Worrell .05
680 Rod Beck .05
681 Mike Benjamin .05
682 Todd Benzinger .05
683 Bud Black .05
684 Barry Bonds 2.00
685 Jeff Brantley .05
686 Dave Burba .05
687 John Burkett .05
688 Mark Carreon .05
689 Will Clark .10
690 Royce Clayton .05
691 Bryan Hickerson .05
692 Mike Jackson .05
693 Darren Lewis .05
694 Kirt Manwaring .05
695 Dave Martinez .05
696 Willie McGee .05
697 John Patterson .05
698 Jeff Reed .05
699 Kevin Rogers .05
700 Scott Sanderson .05
701 Steve Scarsone .05
702 Billy Swift .05
703 Robby Thompson .05
704 Matt Williams .05
705 Trevor Wilson .05
706 Fred McGriff, Ron Gant, Dave Justice "Brave New World" .10
707 Paul Molitor, John Olerud "1-2 Punch" .10
708 Mike Mussina, Jack McDowell "American Heat" .10
709 Lou Whitaker, Alan Trammell "Together Again" .10
710 Rafael Palmeiro, Juan Gonzalez "Lone Star Lumber" .20
711 Brett Butler, Tony Gwynn "Batmen" .10
712 Kirby Puckett, Chuck Knoblauch "Twin Peaks" .20
713 Mike Piazza, Eric Karros "Back to Back" .25
714 Checklist .05
715 Checklist .05
716 Checklist .05
717 Checklist .05
718 Checklist .05
719 Checklist .05
720 Checklist .05

All-Stars

NM/M

Complete Set (50): 10.00
Common Player: .10
1 Roberto Alomar .20
2 Carlos Baerga .10
3 Albert Belle .10
4 Wade Boggs .75
5 Joe Carter .10
6 Scott Cooper .10
7 Cecil Fielder .10
8 Travis Fryman .10
9 Juan Gonzalez .60
10 Ken Griffey, Jr. 1.50
11 Pat Hentgen .10
12 Randy Johnson .60
13 Jimmy Key .10
14 Mark Langston .10
15 Jack McDowell .10
16 Paul Molitor .60
17 Jeff Montgomery .10
18 Mike Mussina .40
19 John Olerud .10
20 Kirby Puckett .75
21 Cal Ripken, Jr. 2.00
22 Ivan Rodriguez .50
23 Frank Thomas .65
24 Greg Vaughn .10
25 Duane Ward .10
26 Steve Avery .10
27 Rod Beck .10
28 Jay Bell .10
29 Andy Benes .10
30 Jeff Blauser .10
31 Barry Bonds 2.00
32 Bobby Bonilla .10
33 John Burkett .10
34 Darren Daulton .10
35 Andres Galarraga .10
36 Tom Glavine .30
37 Mark Grace .25
38 Marquis Grissom .10
39 Tony Gwynn .75
40 Bryan Harvey .10
41 Dave Hollins .10
42 Dave Justice .10
43 Darryl Kile .10
44 John Kruk .10
45 Barry Larkin .10
46 Terry Mulholland .10
47 Mike Piazza 1.50
48 Ryne Sandberg .75
49 Gary Sheffield .30
50 John Smoltz .10

All-Rookie Team

NM/M

Complete Set (9): 3.00
Common Player: .25
Exchange Card: .25
1 Kurt Abbott .25
2 Rich Becker .25
3 Carlos Delgado 2.00
4 Jorge Fabregas .25
5 Bob Hamelin .25
6 John Hudek .25
7 Tim Hyers .25
8 Luis Lopez .25
9 James Mouton .25

Award Winners

NM/M

Complete Set (6): 4.50
Common Player: .25
1 Frank Thomas .75
2 Barry Bonds 2.00
3 Jack McDowell .25
4 Greg Maddux 1.00

#	Player	NM/M
5	Tim Salmon	.50
6	Mike Piazza	1.50

Golden Moments

		NM/M
Complete Set (10):		5.00
Common Player:		.10
1	Mark Whiten "Four in One"	.10
2	Carlos Baerga "Left and Right"	.10
3	Dave Winfield "3,000 Hit Club"	.50
4	Ken Griffey, Jr. "Eight Straight"	1.50
5	Bo Jackson "Triumphant Return"	.25
6	George Brett "Farewell to Baseball"	1.00
7	Nolan Ryan "Farewell to Baseball"	2.00
8	Fred McGriff "Thirty Times Six"	.10
9	Frank Thomas "Enters 5th Dimension"	.75
10	Chris Bosio, Jim Abbott, Darryl Kile "The No-Hit Parade"	.10

League Leaders

		NM/M
Complete Set (12):		3.00
Common Player:		.10
1	John Olerud	.10
2	Albert Belle	.10
3	Rafael Palmeiro	.75
4	Kenny Lofton	.10
5	Jack McDowell	.10
6	Kevin Appier	.10
7	Andres Galarraga	.10
8	Barry Bonds	2.00
9	Len Dykstra	.10
10	Chuck Carr	.10
11	Tom Glavine	.30
12	Greg Maddux	1.00

Lumber Co.

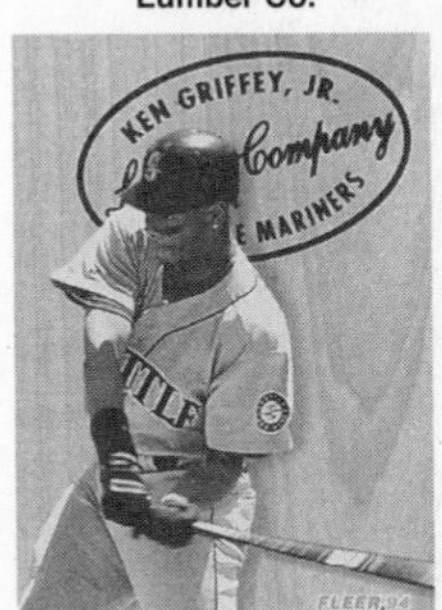

		NM/M
Complete Set (10):		7.50
Common Player:		.40
1	Albert Belle	.40
2	Barry Bonds	2.50
3	Ron Gant	.40
4	Juan Gonzalez	1.00
5	Ken Griffey, Jr.	2.00
6	Dave Justice	.40
7	Fred McGriff	.40
8	Rafael Palmeiro	.75
9	Frank Thomas	1.25
10	Matt Williams	.40

Major League Prospects

		NM/M
Complete Set (35):		4.00
Common Player:		.10
1	Kurt Abbott	.10
2	Brian Anderson	.10
3	Rich Aude	.10
4	Cory Bailey	.10
5	Danny Bautista	.10
6	Marty Cordova	.10
7	Tripp Cromer	.10
8	Midre Cummings	.10
9	Carlos Delgado	1.50
10	Steve Dreyer	.10
11	Steve Dunn	.10
12	Jeff Granger	.10
13	Tyrone Hill	.10
14	Denny Hocking	.10
15	John Hope	.10
16	Butch Huskey	.10
17	Miguel Jimenez	.10
18	Chipper Jones	2.50
19	Steve Karsay	.10
20	Mike Kelly	.10
21	Mike Lieberthal	.20
22	Albie Lopez	.10
23	Jeff McNeely	.10
24	Dan Miceli	.10
25	Nate Minchey	.10
26	Marc Newfield	.10
27	Darren Oliver	.10
28	Luis Ortiz	.10
29	Curtis Pride	.10
30	Roger Salkeld	.10
31	Scott Sanders	.10
32	Dave Staton	.10
33	Salomon Torres	.10
34	Steve Trachsel	.10
35	Chris Turner	.10

ProVisions

		NM/M
Complete Set (9):		4.00
Common Player:		.25
1	Darren Daulton	.25
2	John Olerud	.25
3	Matt Williams	.25
4	Carlos Baerga	.25
5	Ozzie Smith	1.00
6	Juan Gonzalez	.75
7	Jack McDowell	.25
8	Mike Piazza	2.00
9	Tony Gwynn	1.00

Rookie Sensations

		NM/M
Complete Set (20):		6.00
Common Player:		.25
1	Rene Arocha	.25
2	Jason Bere	.25
3	Jeromy Burnitz	.25
4	Chuck Carr	.25
5	Jeff Conine	.25
6	Steve Cooke	.25
7	Cliff Floyd	.25
8	Jeffrey Hammonds	.25
9	Wayne Kirby	.25
10	Mike Lansing	.25
11	Al Martin	.25
12	Greg McMichael	.25
13	Troy Neel	.25
14	Mike Piazza	4.00
15	Armando Reynoso	.25
16	Kirk Rueter	.25
17	Tim Salmon	1.00
18	Aaron Sele	.25
19	J.T. Snow	.25
20	Kevin Stocker	.25

Smoke N' Heat

		NM/M
Complete Set (12):		10.00
Common Player:		.20
1	Roger Clemens	3.50
2	David Cone	.20
3	Juan Guzman	.20
4	Pete Harnisch	.20
5	Randy Johnson	2.00
6	Mark Langston	.20
7	Greg Maddux	2.50
8	Mike Mussina	.75
9	Jose Rijo	.20
10	Nolan Ryan	4.50
11	Curt Schilling	.75
12	John Smoltz	.25

Tim Salmon A.L. Rookie of the Year

		NM/M
Complete Set (15):		12.50
Common Card:		1.00
Autograph/2,000:		15.00
1	Tim Salmon	1.00
2	Tim Salmon	1.00
3	Tim Salmon	1.00
4	Tim Salmon	1.00
5	Tim Salmon	1.00
6	Tim Salmon	1.00
7	Tim Salmon	1.00
8	Tim Salmon	1.00
9	Tim Salmon	1.00
10	Tim Salmon	1.00
11	Tim Salmon	1.00
12	Tim Salmon	1.00
13	Tim Salmon	1.50
14	Tim Salmon	1.50
15	Tim Salmon	1.50

Team Leaders

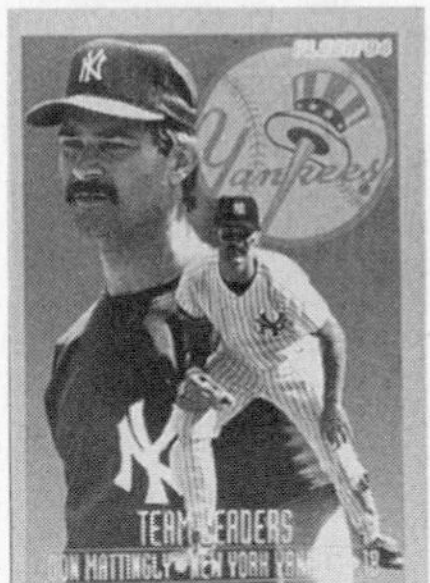

		NM/M
Complete Set (28):		7.50
Common Player:		.10
1	Cal Ripken, Jr.	2.00
2	Mo Vaughn	.10
3	Tim Salmon	.15
4	Frank Thomas	.50
5	Carlos Baerga	.10
6	Cecil Fielder	.10
7	Brian McRae	.10
8	Greg Vaughn	.10
9	Kirby Puckett	.65
10	Don Mattingly	.75
11	Mark McGwire	1.50
12	Ken Griffey, Jr.	1.00
13	Juan Gonzalez	.50
14	Paul Molitor	.50
15	Dave Justice	.10
16	Ryne Sandberg	.65
17	Barry Larkin	.10
18	Andres Galarraga	.10
19	Gary Sheffield	.25
20	Jeff Bagwell	.50
21	Mike Piazza	1.00
22	Marquis Grissom	.10
23	Bobby Bonilla	.10
24	Len Dykstra	.10
25	Jay Bell	.10
26	Gregg Jefferies	.10
27	Tony Gwynn	.65
28	Will Clark	.15

Update

		NM/M
Complete Set (210):		40.00
Common Player:		.05
1	Mark Eichhorn	.05
2	Sid Fernandez	.05
3	Leo Gomez	.05
4	Mike Oquist	.05
5	Rafael Palmeiro	.60
6	Chris Sabo	.05
7	Dwight Smith	.05
8	Lee Smith	.05
9	Damon Berryhill	.05
10	Wes Chamberlain	.05
11	Gar Finnvold	.05
12	Chris Howard	.05
13	Tim Naehring	.05
14	Otis Nixon	.05
15	Brian Anderson	.05
16	Jorge Fabregas	.05
17	Rex Hudler	.05
18	Bo Jackson	.15
19	Mark Leiter	.05
20	Spike Owen	.05
21	Harold Reynolds	.05
22	Chris Turner	.05
23	Dennis Cook	.05
24	Jose DeLeon	.05
25	Julio Franco	.05
26	Joe Hall	.05
27	Darrin Jackson	.05
28	Dane Johnson	.05
29	Norberto Martin	.05
30	Scott Sanderson	.05
31	Jason Grimsley	.05
32	Dennis Martinez	.05
33	Jack Morris	.05
34	Eddie Murray	.75
35	Chad Ogea	.05
36	Tony Pena	.05
37	Paul Shuey	.05
38	Omar Vizquel	.05
39	Danny Bautista	.05
40	Tim Belcher	.05
41	Joe Boever	.05
42	Storm Davis	.05
43	Junior Felix	.05
44	Mike Gardiner	.05
45	Buddy Groom	.05
46	Juan Samuel	.05
47	Vince Coleman	.05
48	Bob Hamelin	.05
49	Dave Henderson	.05
50	Rusty Meacham	.05
51	Terry Shumpert	.05
52	Jeff Bronkey	.05
53	Alex Diaz	.05
54	Brian Harper	.05
55	Jose Mercedes	.05
56	Jody Reed	.05
57	Bob Scanlan	.05
58	Turner Ward	.05
59	Rich Becker	.05
60	Alex Cole	.05
61	Denny Hocking	.05
62	Scott Leius	.05
63	Pat Mahomes	.05

64	Carlos Pulido	.05
65	Dave Stevens	.05
66	Matt Walbeck	.05
67	Xavier Hernandez	.05
68	Sterling Hitchcock	.05
69	Terry Mulholland	.05
70	Luis Polonia	.05
71	Gerald Williams	.05
72	Mark Acre	.05
73	Geronimo Berroa	.05
74	Rickey Henderson	.75
75	Stan Javier	.05
76	Steve Karsay	.05
77	Carlos Reyes	.05
78	Bill Taylor	.05
79	Eric Anthony	.05
80	Bobby Ayala	.05
81	Tim Davis	.05
82	Felix Fermin	.05
83	Reggie Jefferson	.05
84	Keith Mitchell	.05
85	Bill Risley	.05
86	*Alex Rodriguez*	30.00
87	Roger Salkeld	.05
88	Dan Wilson	.05
89	Cris Carpenter	.05
90	Will Clark	.10
91	Jeff Frye	.05
92	Rick Helling	.05
93	Chris James	.05
94	Oddibe McDowell	.05
95	Billy Ripken	.05
96	Carlos Delgado	.60
97	Alex Gonzalez	.05
98	Shawn Green	.50
99	Darren Hall	.05
100	Mike Huff	.05
101	Mike Kelly	.05
102	Roberto Kelly	.05
103	Charlie O'Brien	.05
104	Jose Oliva	.05
105	Gregg Olson	.05
106	Willie Banks	.05
107	Jim Bullinger	.05
108	Chuck Crim	.05
109	Shawon Dunston	.05
110	Karl Rhodes	.05
111	Steve Trachsel	.05
112	Anthony Young	.05
113	Eddie Zambrano	.05
114	Bret Boone	.05
115	Jeff Brantley	.05
116	Hector Carrasco	.05
117	Tony Fernandez	.05
118	Tim Fortugno	.05
119	Erik Hanson	.05
120	Chuck McElroy	.05
121	Deion Sanders	.05
122	Ellis Burks	.05
123	Marvin Freeman	.05
124	Mike Harkey	.05
125	Howard Johnson	.05
126	Mike Kingery	.05
127	Nelson Liriano	.05
128	Marcus Moore	.05
129	Mike Munoz	.05
130	Kevin Ritz	.05
131	Walt Weiss	.05
132	Kurt Abbott	.05
133	Jerry Browne	.05
134	Greg Colbrunn	.05
135	Jeremy Hernandez	.05
136	Dave Magadan	.05
137	Kurt Miller	.05
138	Robb Nen	.05
139	Jesus Taverez	.05
140	Sid Bream	.05
141	Tom Edens	.05
142	Tony Eusebio	.05
143	John Hudek	.05
144	Brian Hunter	.05
145	Orlando Miller	.05
146	James Mouton	.05
147	Shane Reynolds	.05
148	Rafael Bournigal	.05
149	Delino DeShields	.05
150	Garey Ingram	.05
151	Chan Ho Park	.05
152	Wil Cordero	.05
153	Pedro Martinez	.75
154	Randy Milligan	.05
155	Lenny Webster	.05
156	Rico Brogna	.05
157	Josias Manzanillo	.05
158	Kevin McReynolds	.05
159	Mike Remlinger	.05
160	David Segui	.05
161	Pete Smith	.05
162	Kelly Stinnett	.05
163	Jose Vizcaino	.05
164	Billy Hatcher	.05
165	Doug Jones	.05
166	Mike Lieberthal	.05
167	Tony Longmire	.05
168	Bobby Munoz	.05
169	Paul Quantrill	.05
170	Heathcliff Slocumb	.05
171	Fernando Valenzuela	.05
172	Mark Dewey	.05
173	Brian Hunter	.05
174	Jon Lieber	.05
175	Ravelo Manzanillo	.05
176	Dan Miceli	.05
177	Rick White	.05
178	Bryan Eversgerd	.05
179	John Habyan	.05
180	Terry McGriff	.05
181	Vicente Palacios	.05
182	Rich Rodriguez	.05
183	Rick Sutcliffe	.05
184	Donnie Elliott	.05
185	Joey Hamilton	.05
186	Tim Hyers	.05
187	Luis Lopez	.05
188	Ray McDavid	.05
189	Bip Roberts	.05
190	Scott Sanders	.05
191	Eddie Williams	.05
192	Steve Frey	.05
193	Pat Gomez	.05
194	Rich Monteleone	.05
195	Mark Portugal	.05
196	Darryl Strawberry	.05
197	Salomon Torres	.05
198	W. Van Landingham	.05
199	Checklist	.05
200	Checklist	.05
	DIAMOND TRIBUTE	.05
DT1	Barry Bonds	2.00
DT2	Joe Carter	.05
DT3	Will Clark	.10
DT4	Roger Clemens	1.50
DT5	Tony Gwynn	1.00
DT6	Don Mattingly	1.50
DT7	Fred McGriff	.05
DT8	Eddie Murray	.75
DT9	Kirby Puckett	1.00
DT10	Cal Ripken Jr.	2.00

1995 FLEER

	NM/M
Complete Set (600):	15.00
Common Player:	.05
Pack (12):	.75
Wax Box (36):	17.50

1	Brady Anderson	.05
2	Harold Baines	.05
3	Damon Buford	.05
4	Mike Devereaux	.05
5	Mark Eichhorn	.05
6	Sid Fernandez	.05
7	Leo Gomez	.05
8	Jeffrey Hammonds	.05
9	Chris Hoiles	.05
10	Rick Krivda	.05
11	Ben McDonald	.05
12	Mark McLemore	.05
13	Alan Mills	.05
14	Jamie Moyer	.05
15	Mike Mussina	.40
16	Mike Oquist	.05
17	Rafael Palmeiro	.65
18	Arthur Rhodes	.05
19	Cal Ripken, Jr.	2.50
20	Chris Sabo	.05
21	Lee Smith	.05
22	Jack Voight	.05
23	Damon Berryhill	.05
24	Tom Brunansky	.05
25	Wes Chamberlain	.05
26	Roger Clemens	1.25
27	Scott Cooper	.05
28	Andre Dawson	.25
29	Gar Finnvold	.05
30	Tony Fossas	.05
31	Mike Greenwell	.05
32	Joe Hesketh	.05
33	Chris Howard	.05
34	Chris Nabholz	.05
35	Tim Naehring	.05
36	Otis Nixon	.05
37	Carlos Rodriguez	.05
38	Rich Rowland	.05
39	Ken Ryan	.05
40	Aaron Sele	.05
41	John Valentin	.05
42	Mo Vaughn	.05
43	Frank Viola	.05
44	Danny Bautista	.05
45	Joe Boeven	.05
46	Milt Cuyler	.05
47	Storm Davis	.05
48	John Doherty	.05
49	Junior Felix	.05
50	Cecil Fielder	.05
51	Travis Fryman	.05
52	Mike Gardiner	.05
53	Kirk Gibson	.05
54	Chris Gomez	.05
55	Buddy Groom	.05
56	Mike Henneman	.05
57	Chad Kreuter	.05
58	Mike Moore	.05
59	Tony Phillips	.05
60	Juan Samuel	.05
61	Mickey Tettleton	.05
62	Alan Trammell	.05
63	David Wells	.05
64	Lou Whitaker	.05
65	Jim Abbott	.05
66	Joe Ausanio	.05
67	Wade Boggs	1.00
68	Mike Gallego	.05
69	Xavier Hernandez	.05
70	Sterling Hitchcock	.05
71	Steve Howe	.05
72	Scott Kamieniecki	.05
73	Pat Kelly	.05
74	Jimmy Key	.05
75	Jim Leyritz	.05
76	Don Mattingly	1.25
77	Terry Mulholland	.05
78	Paul O'Neill	.05
79	Melido Perez	.05
80	Luis Polonia	.05
81	Mike Stanley	.05
82	Danny Tartabull	.05
83	Randy Velarde	.05
84	Bob Wickman	.05
85	Bernie Williams	.10
86	Gerald Williams	.05
87	Roberto Alomar	.10
88	Pat Borders	.05
89	Joe Carter	.05
90	Tony Castillo	.05
91	Brad Cornett	.05
92	Carlos Delgado	.50
93	Alex Gonzalez	.05
94	Shawn Green	.40
95	Juan Guzman	.05
96	Darren Hall	.05
97	Pat Hentgen	.05
98	Mike Huff	.05
99	Randy Knorr	.05
100	Al Leiter	.05
101	Paul Molitor	.75
102	John Olerud	.05
103	Dick Schofield	.05
104	Ed Sprague	.05
105	Dave Stewart	.05
106	Todd Stottlemyre	.05
107	Devon White	.05
108	Woody Williams	.05
109	Wilson Alvarez	.05
110	Paul Assenmacher	.05
111	Jason Bere	.05
112	Dennis Cook	.05
113	Joey Cora	.05
114	Jose DeLeon	.05
115	Alex Fernandez	.05
116	Julio Franco	.05
117	Craig Graboeck	.05
118	Ozzie Guillen	.05
119	Roberto Hernandez	.05
120	Darrin Jackson	.05
121	Lance Johnson	.05
122	Ron Karkovice	.05
123	Mike LaValliere	.05
124	Norberto Martin	.05
125	Kirk McCaskill	.05
126	Jack McDowell	.05
127	Tim Raines	.05
128	Frank Thomas	.75
129	Robin Ventura	.05
130	Sandy Alomar Jr.	.05
131	Carlos Baerga	.05
132	Albert Belle	.05
133	Mark Clark	.05
134	Alvaro Espinoza	.05
135	Jason Grimsley	.05
136	Wayne Kirby	.05
137	Kenny Lofton	.05
138	Albie Lopez	.05
139	Dennis Martinez	.05
140	Jose Mesa	.05
141	Eddie Murray	.75
142	Charles Nagy	.05
143	Tony Pena	.05
144	Eric Plunk	.05
145	Manny Ramirez	.75
146	Jeff Russell	.05
147	Paul Shuey	.05
148	Paul Sorrento	.05
149	Jim Thome	.65
150	Omar Vizquel	.05
151	Dave Winfield	.75
152	Kevin Appier	.05
153	Billy Brewer	.05
154	Vince Coleman	.05
155	David Cone	.05
156	Gary Gaetti	.05
157	Greg Gagne	.05
158	Tom Gordon	.05
159	Mark Gubicza	.05
160	Bob Hamelin	.05
161	Dave Henderson	.05
162	Felix Jose	.05
163	Wally Joyner	.05
164	Jose Lind	.05
165	Mike Macfarlane	.05
166	Mike Magnante	.05
167	Brent Mayne	.05
168	Brian McRae	.05
169	Rusty Meacham	.05
170	Jeff Montgomery	.05
171	Hipolito Pichardo	.05
172	Terry Shumpert	.05
173	Michael Tucker	.05
174	Ricky Bones	.05
175	*Jeff Cirillo*	.30
176	Alex Diaz	.05
177	Cal Eldred	.05
178	Mike Fetters	.05
179	Darryl Hamilton	.05
180	Brian Harper	.05
181	John Jaha	.05
182	Pat Listach	.05
183	Graeme Lloyd	.05
184	Jose Mercedes	.05
185	Matt Mieske	.05
186	Dave Nilsson	.05
187	Jody Reed	.05
188	Bob Scanlan	.05
189	Kevin Seitzer	.05
190	Bill Spiers	.05
191	B.J. Surhoff	.05
192	Jose Valentin	.05
193	Greg Vaughn	.05
194	Turner Ward	.05
195	Bill Wegman	.05
196	Rick Aguilera	.05
197	Rich Becker	.05
198	Alex Cole	.05
199	Marty Cordova	.05
200	Steve Dunn	.05
201	Scott Erickson	.05
202	Mark Guthrie	.05
203	Chip Hale	.05
204	LaTroy Hawkins	.05
205	Denny Hocking	.05
206	Chuck Knoblauch	.05
207	Scott Leius	.05
208	Shane Mack	.05
209	Pat Mahomes	.05
210	Pat Meares	.05
211	Pedro Munoz	.05
212	Kirby Puckett	1.00
213	Jeff Reboulet	.05
214	Dave Stevens	.05
215	Kevin Tapani	.05
216	Matt Walbeck	.05
217	Carl Willis	.05
218	Brian Anderson	.05
219	Chad Curtis	.05
220	Chili Davis	.05
221	Gary DiSarcina	.05

No.	Player	Price
222	Damion Easley	.05
223	Jim Edmonds	.05
224	Chuck Finley	.05
225	Joe Grahe	.05
226	Rex Hudler	.05
227	Bo Jackson	.10
228	Mark Langston	.05
229	Phil Leftwich	.05
230	Mark Leiter	.05
231	Spike Owen	.05
232	Bob Patterson	.05
233	Troy Percival	.05
234	Eduardo Perez	.05
235	Tim Salmon	.10
236	J.T. Snow	.05
237	Chris Turner	.05
238	Mark Acre	.05
239	Geronimo Berroa	.05
240	Mike Bordick	.05
241	John Briscoe	.05
242	Scott Brosius	.05
243	Ron Darling	.05
244	Dennis Eckersley	.65
245	Brent Gates	.05
246	Rickey Henderson	.75
247	Stan Javier	.05
248	Steve Karsay	.05
249	Mark McGwire	2.00
250	Troy Neel	.05
251	Steve Ontiveros	.05
252	Carlos Reyes	.05
253	Ruben Sierra	.05
254	Terry Steinbach	.05
255	Bill Taylor	.05
256	Todd Van Poppel	.05
257	Bobby Witt	.05
258	Rich Amaral	.05
259	Eric Anthony	.05
260	Bobby Ayala	.05
261	Mike Blowers	.05
262	Chris Bosio	.05
263	Jay Buhner	.05
264	John Cummings	.05
265	Tim Davis	.05
266	Felix Fermin	.05
267	Dave Fleming	.05
268	Goose Gossage	.05
269	Ken Griffey, Jr.	1.50
270	Reggie Jefferson	.05
271	Randy Johnson	.75
272	Edgar Martinez	.05
273	Tino Martinez	.05
274	Greg Pirkl	.05
275	Bill Risley	.05
276	Roger Salkeld	.05
277	Luis Sojo	.05
278	Mac Suzuki	.05
279	Dan Wilson	.05
280	Kevin Brown	.05
281	Jose Canseco	.40
282	Cris Carpenter	.05
283	Will Clark	.10
284	Jeff Frye	.05
285	Juan Gonzalez	.65
286	Rick Helling	.05
287	Tom Henke	.05
288	David Hulse	.05
289	Chris James	.05
290	Manuel Lee	.05
291	Oddibe McDowell	.05
292	Dean Palmer	.05
293	Roger Pavlik	.05
294	Bill Ripken	.05
295	Ivan Rodriguez	.65
296	Kenny Rogers	.05
297	Doug Strange	.05
298	Matt Whiteside	.05
299	Steve Avery	.05
300	Steve Bedrosian	.05
301	Rafael Belliard	.05
302	Jeff Blauser	.05
303	Dave Gallagher	.05
304	Tom Glavine	.30
305	Dave Justice	.05
306	Mike Kelly	.05
307	Roberto Kelly	.05
308	Ryan Klesko	.05
309	Mark Lemke	.05
310	Javier Lopez	.05
311	Greg Maddux	1.00
312	Fred McGriff	.05
313	Greg McMichael	.05
314	Kent Mercker	.05
315	Charlie O'Brien	.05
316	Jose Oliva	.05
317	Terry Pendleton	.05
318	John Smoltz	.05
319	Mike Stanton	.05
320	Tony Tarasco	.05
321	Terrell Wade	.05
322	Mark Wohlers	.05
323	Kurt Abbott	.05
324	Luis Aquino	.05
325	Bret Barberie	.05
326	Ryan Bowen	.05
327	Jerry Browne	.05
328	Chuck Carr	.05
329	Matias Carrillo	.05
330	Greg Colbrunn	.05
331	Jeff Conine	.05
332	Mark Gardner	.05
333	Chris Hammond	.05
334	Bryan Harvey	.05
335	Richie Lewis	.05
336	Dave Magadan	.05
337	Terry Mathews	.05
338	Robb Nen	.05
339	Yorkis Perez	.05
340	Pat Rapp	.05
341	Benito Santiago	.05
342	Gary Sheffield	.40
343	Dave Weathers	.05
344	Moises Alou	.05
345	Sean Berry	.05
346	Wil Cordero	.05
347	Joe Eischen	.05
348	Jeff Fassero	.05
349	Darrin Fletcher	.05
350	Cliff Floyd	.05
351	Marquis Grissom	.05
352	Butch Henry	.05
353	Gil Heredia	.05
354	Ken Hill	.05
355	Mike Lansing	.05
356	Pedro Martinez	.75
357	Mel Rojas	.05
358	Kirk Rueter	.05
359	Tim Scott	.05
360	Jeff Shaw	.05
361	Larry Walker	.05
362	Lenny Webster	.05
363	John Wetteland	.05
364	Rondell White	.05
365	Bobby Bonilla	.05
366	Rico Brogna	.05
367	Jeromy Burnitz	.05
368	John Franco	.05
369	Dwight Gooden	.05
370	Todd Hundley	.05
371	Jason Jacome	.05
372	Bobby Jones	.05
373	Jeff Kent	.05
374	Jim Lindeman	.05
375	Josias Manzanillo	.05
376	Roger Mason	.05
377	Kevin McReynolds	.05
378	Joe Orsulak	.05
379	Bill Pulsipher	.05
380	Bret Saberhagen	.05
381	David Segui	.05
382	Pete Smith	.05
383	Kelly Stinnett	.05
384	Ryan Thompson	.05
385	Jose Vizcaino	.05
386	Toby Borland	.05
387	Ricky Bettalico	.05
388	Darren Daulton	.05
389	Mariano Duncan	.05
390	Len Dykstra	.05
391	Jim Eisenreich	.05
392	Tommy Greene	.05
393	Dave Hollins	.05
394	Pete Incaviglia	.05
395	Danny Jackson	.05
396	Doug Jones	.05
397	Ricky Jordan	.05
398	John Kruk	.05
399	Mike Lieberthal	.05
400	Tony Longmire	.05
401	Mickey Morandini	.05
402	Bobby Munoz	.05
403	Curt Schilling	.25
404	Heathcliff Slocumb	.05
405	Kevin Stocker	.05
406	Fernando Valenzuela	.05
407	David West	.05
408	Willie Banks	.05
409	Jose Bautista	.05
410	Steve Buechele	.05
411	Jim Bullinger	.05
412	Chuck Crim	.05
413	Shawon Dunston	.05
414	Kevin Foster	.05
415	Mark Grace	.10
416	Jose Hernandez	.05
417	Glenallen Hill	.05
418	Brooks Kieschnick	.05
419	Derrick May	.05
420	Randy Myers	.05
421	Dan Plesac	.05
422	Karl Rhodes	.05
423	Rey Sanchez	.05
424	Sammy Sosa	1.50
425	Steve Trachsel	.05
426	Rick Wilkins	.05
427	Anthony Young	.05
428	Eddie Zambrano	.05
429	Bret Boone	.05
430	Jeff Branson	.05
431	Jeff Brantley	.05
432	Hector Carrasco	.05
433	Brian Dorsett	.05
434	Tony Fernandez	.05
435	Tim Fortugno	.05
436	Erik Hanson	.05
437	Thomas Howard	.05
438	Kevin Jarvis	.05
439	Barry Larkin	.05
440	Chuck McElroy	.05
441	Kevin Mitchell	.05
442	Hal Morris	.05
443	Jose Rijo	.05
444	John Roper	.05
445	Johnny Ruffin	.05
446	Deion Sanders	.05
447	Reggie Sanders	.05
448	Pete Schourek	.05
449	John Smiley	.05
450	Eddie Taubensee	.05
451	Jeff Bagwell	.75
452	Kevin Bass	.05
453	Craig Biggio	.05
454	Ken Caminiti	.05
455	Andujar Cedeno	.05
456	Doug Drabek	.05
457	Tony Eusebio	.05
458	Mike Felder	.05
459	Steve Finley	.05
460	Luis Gonzalez	.10
461	Mike Hampton	.05
462	Pete Harnisch	.05
463	John Hudek	.05
464	Todd Jones	.05
465	Darryl Kile	.05
466	James Mouton	.05
467	Shane Reynolds	.05
468	Scott Servais	.05
469	Greg Swindell	.05
470	Dave Veres	.05
471	Brian Williams	.05
472	Jay Bell	.05
473	Jacob Brumfield	.05
474	Dave Clark	.05
475	Steve Cooke	.05
476	Midre Cummings	.05
477	Mark Dewey	.05
478	Tom Foley	.05
479	Carlos Garcia	.05
480	Jeff King	.05
481	Jon Lieber	.05
482	Ravelo Manzanillo	.05
483	Al Martin	.05
484	Orlando Merced	.05
485	Danny Miceli	.05
486	Denny Neagle	.05
487	Lance Parrish	.05
488	Don Slaught	.05
489	Zane Smith	.05
490	Andy Van Slyke	.05
491	Paul Wagner	.05
492	Rick White	.05
493	Luis Alicea	.05
494	Rene Arocha	.05
495	Rheal Cormier	.05
496	Bryan Eversgerd	.05
497	Bernard Gilkey	.05
498	John Habyan	.05
499	Gregg Jefferies	.05
500	Brian Jordan	.05
501	Ray Lankford	.05
502	John Mabry	.05
503	Terry McGriff	.05
504	Tom Pagnozzi	.05
505	Vicente Palacios	.05
506	Geronimo Pena	.05
507	Gerald Perry	.05
508	Rich Rodriguez	.05
509	Ozzie Smith	1.00
510	Bob Tewksbury	.05
511	Allen Watson	.05
512	Mark Whiten	.05
513	Todd Zeile	.05
514	Dante Bichette	.05
515	Willie Blair	.05
516	Ellis Burks	.05
517	Marvin Freeman	.05
518	Andres Galarraga	.05
519	Joe Girardi	.05
520	Greg Harris	.05
521	Charlie Hayes	.05
522	Mike Kingery	.05
523	Nelson Liriano	.05
524	Mike Munoz	.05
525	David Nied	.05
526	Steve Reed	.05
527	Kevin Ritz	.05
528	Bruce Ruffin	.05
529	John Vander Wal	.05
530	Walt Weiss	.05
531	Eric Young	.05
532	Billy Ashley	.05
533	Pedro Astacio	.05
534	Rafael Bournigal	.05
535	Brett Butler	.05
536	Tom Candiotti	.05
537	Omar Daal	.05
538	Delino DeShields	.05
539	Darren Dreifort	.05
540	Kevin Gross	.05
541	Orel Hershiser	.05
542	Garey Ingram	.05
543	Eric Karros	.05
544	Ramon Martinez	.05
545	Raul Mondesi	.05
546	Chan Ho Park	.05
547	Mike Piazza	1.50
548	Henry Rodriguez	.05
549	Rudy Seanez	.05
550	Ismael Valdes	.05
551	Tim Wallach	.05
552	Todd Worrell	.05
553	Andy Ashby	.05
554	Brad Ausmus	.05
555	Derek Bell	.05
556	Andy Benes	.05
557	Phil Clark	.05
558	Donnie Elliott	.05
559	Ricky Gutierrez	.05
560	Tony Gwynn	1.00
561	Joey Hamilton	.05
562	Trevor Hoffman	.05
563	Luis Lopez	.05
564	Pedro Martinez	.05
565	Tim Mauser	.05
566	Phil Plantier	.05
567	Bip Roberts	.05
568	Scott Sanders	.05
569	Craig Shipley	.05
570	Jeff Tabaka	.05
571	Eddie Williams	.05
572	Rod Beck	.05
573	Mike Benjamin	.05
574	Barry Bonds	2.50
575	Dave Burba	.05
576	John Burkett	.05
577	Mark Carreon	.05
578	Royce Clayton	.05
579	Steve Frey	.05
580	Bryan Hickerson	.05
581	Mike Jackson	.05
582	Darren Lewis	.05
583	Kirt Manwaring	.05
584	Rich Monteleone	.05
585	John Patterson	.05
586	J.R. Phillips	.05
587	Mark Portugal	.05
588	Joe Rosselli	.05
589	Darryl Strawberry	.05
590	Bill Swift	.05
591	Robby Thompson	.05
592	William Van Landingham	.05
593	Matt Williams	.05
594	Checklist	.05
595	Checklist	.05
596	Checklist	.05
597	Checklist	.05
598	Checklist	.05
599	Checklist	.05
600	Checklist	.05

All-Fleer 9

		NM/M
Complete Set (9):		4.00
Common Player:		.25
1	Mike Piazza	1.00
2	Frank Thomas	.50
3	Roberto Alomar	.40
4	Cal Ripken Jr.	2.50
5	Matt Williams	.25
6	Barry Bonds	2.50
7	Ken Griffey Jr.	1.00
8	Tony Gwynn	.65
9	Greg Maddux	.65

All-Rookies

		NM/M
Complete Set (9):		1.50
Common Player:		.25
Trade card: 2X		.12
1	Edgardo Alfonzo	.25
2	Jason Bates	.25
3	Brian Boehringer	.25
4	Darren Bragg	.25
5	Brad Clontz	.25
6	Jim Dougherty	.25
7	Todd Hollandsworth	.25
8	Rudy Pemberton	.25
9	Frank Rodriguez	.25

All-Stars

		NM/M
Complete Set (25):		8.00
Common Card:		.20
1	Ivan Rodriguez, Mike Piazza	.75
2	Frank Thomas, Gregg Jefferies	.50
3	Roberto Alomar, Mariano Duncan	.40
4	Wade Boggs, Matt Williams	.65
5	Cal Ripken, Jr., Ozzie Smith	1.50
6	Joe Carter, Barry Bonds	1.50
7	Ken Griffey, Jr., Tony Gwynn	.75
8	Kirby Puckett, Dave Justice	.65
9	Jimmy Key, Greg Maddux	.65
10	Chuck Knoblauch, Wil Cordero	.20
11	Scott Cooper, Ken Caminiti	.20
12	Will Clark, Carlos Garcia	.50
13	Paul Molitor, Jeff Bagwell	.50
14	Travis Fryman, Craig Biggio	.20
15	Mickey Tettleton, Fred McGriff	.20
16	Kenny Lofton, Moises Alou	.20
17	Albert Belle, Marquis Grissom	.20
18	Paul O'Neill, Dante Bichette	.20
19	David Cone, Ken Hill	.20
20	Mike Mussina, Doug Drabek	.50
21	Randy Johnson, John Hudek	.50
22	Pat Hentgen, Danny Jackson	.20
23	Wilson Alvarez, Rod Beck	.20
24	Lee Smith, Randy Myers	.20
25	Jason Bere, Doug Jones	.20

Award Winners

		NM/M
Complete Set (6):		4.00
Common Player:		.25
1	Frank Thomas	1.50
2	Jeff Bagwell	1.50
3	David Cone	.25
4	Greg Maddux	2.00
5	Bob Hamelin	.25
6	Raul Mondesi	.25

League Leaders

		NM/M
Complete Set (10):		4.00
Common Player:		.25
1	Paul O'Neill	.25
2	Ken Griffey, Jr.	1.50
3	Kirby Puckett	.75
4	Jimmy Key	.25
5	Randy Johnson	.65
6	Tony Gwynn	.75
7	Matt Williams	.25
8	Jeff Bagwell	.50
9	Greg Maddux, Ken Hill	.75
10	Andy Benes	.25

Lumber Company

		NM/M
Complete Set (10):		12.00
Common Player:		.40
1	Jeff Bagwell	1.50
2	Albert Belle	.40
3	Barry Bonds	3.50
4	Jose Canseco	.75
5	Joe Carter	.40
6	Ken Griffey, Jr.	2.50
7	Fred McGriff	.40
8	Kevin Mitchell	.40
9	Frank Thomas	1.75
10	Matt Williams	.40

Major League Prospects

		NM/M
Complete Set (10):		6.00
Common Player:		.25
1	Garret Anderson	.50
2	James Baldwin	.25
3	Alan Benes	.25
4	Armando Benitez	.25
5	Ray Durham	.25
6	Brian Hunter	.25
7a	Derek Jeter (no licensor logos on back)	4.00
7b	Derek Jeter (licensor logos on back)	4.00
8	Charles Johnson	.25
9	Orlando Miller	.25
10	Alex Rodriguez	3.00

Pro-Visions

		NM/M
Complete Set (6):		2.00
Common Player:		.25
1	Mike Mussina	.40
2	Raul Mondesi	.25
3	Jeff Bagwell	.75
4	Greg Maddux	1.00
5	Tim Salmon	.25
6	Manny Ramirez	.75

Rookie Sensations

		NM/M
Complete Set (20):		5.00
Common Player:		.25
1	Kurt Abbott	.25
2	Rico Brogna	.25
3	Hector Carrasco	.25
4	Kevin Foster	.25
5	Chris Gomez	.25
6	Darren Hall	.25
7	Bob Hamelin	.25
8	Joey Hamilton	.25
9	John Hudek	.25
10	Ryan Klesko	.25
11	Javier Lopez	.25
12	Matt Mieske	.25
13	Raul Mondesi	.25
14	Manny Ramirez	4.00
15	Shane Reynolds	.25
16	Bill Risley	.25
17	Johnny Ruffin	.25
18	Steve Trachsel	.25
19	William Van Landingham	.25
20	Rondell White	.25

Team Leaders

		NM/M
Complete Set (28):		50.00
Common Card:		.50
1	Cal Ripken, Jr., Mike Mussina	7.50
2	Mo Vaughn, Roger Clemens	4.50
3	Tim Salmon, Chuck Finley	.75
4	Frank Thomas, Jack McDowell	2.50
5	Albert Belle, Dennis Martinez	.50
6	Cecil Fielder, Mike Moore	.50
7	Bob Hamelin, David Cone	.50
8	Greg Vaughn, Ricky Bones	.50
9	Kirby Puckett, Rick Aguilera	3.00
10	Don Mattingly, Jimmy Key	4.50
11	Ruben Sierra, Dennis Eckersley	1.50
12	Ken Griffey, Jr., Randy Johnson	6.00
13	Jose Canseco, Kenny Rogers	1.00
14	Joe Carter, Pat Hentgen	.50
15	Dave Justice, Greg Maddux	3.00
16	Sammy Sosa, Steve Trachsel	5.00
17	Kevin Mitchell, Jose Rijo	.50
18	Dante Bichette, Bruce Ruffin	.50
19	Jeff Conine, Robb Nen	.50
20	Jeff Bagwell, Doug Drabek	2.50
21	Mike Piazza, Ramon Martinez	5.00
22	Moises Alou, Ken Hill	.50
23	Bobby Bonilla, Bret Saberhagen	.50
24	Darren Daulton, Danny Jackson	.50
25	Jay Bell, Zane Smith	.50
26	Gregg Jefferies, Bob Tewksbury	.50
27	Tony Gwynn, Andy Benes	3.00
28	Matt Williams, Rod Beck	.50

Update Diamond Tribute

		NM/M
Complete Set (10):		6.00
Common Player:		.25
1	Jeff Bagwell	.75
2	Albert Belle	.25
3	Barry Bonds	3.00
4	David Cone	.25
5	Dennis Eckersley	.50
6	Ken Griffey Jr.	1.50
7	Rickey Henderson	.60
8	Greg Maddux	1.00
9	Frank Thomas	.75
10	Matt Williams	.25

Update Smooth Leather

		NM/M
Complete Set (10):		7.50
Common Player:		.25
1	Roberto Alomar	.50
2	Barry Bonds	2.50
3	Ken Griffey Jr.	1.50
4	Marquis Grissom	.25
5	Darren Lewis	.25
6	Kenny Lofton	.25
7	Don Mattingly	1.00
8	Cal Ripken Jr.	2.50
9	Ivan Rodriguez	.75
10	Matt Williams	.25

Update Rookie Update

		NM/M
Complete Set (10):		4.00
Common Player:		.10

1	Shane Andrews	.10
2	Ray Durham	.10
3	Shawn Green	.40
4	Charles Johnson	.10
5	Chipper Jones	1.50
6	Esteban Loaiza	.10
7	Hideo Nomo	1.00
8	Jon Nunnally	.10
9	Alex Rodriguez	2.00
10	Julian Tavarez	.10

Update Soaring Stars

		NM/M
Complete Set (9):		3.50
Common Player:		.15
1	Moises Alou	.35
2	Jason Bere	.25
3	Jeff Conine	.25
4	Cliff Floyd	.25
5	Pat Hentgen	.25
6	Kenny Lofton	.25
7	Raul Mondesi	.25
8	Mike Piazza	3.00
9	Tim Salmon	.35

Update Headliners

		NM/M
Complete Set (20):		8.00
Common Player:		.10
1	Jeff Bagwell	.50
2	Albert Belle	.15
3	Barry Bonds	3.00
4	Jose Canseco	.40
5	Joe Carter	.15
6	Will Clark	.25
7	Roger Clemens	2.00
8	Lenny Dykstra	.15
9	Cecil Fielder	.15
10	Juan Gonzalez	.40
11	Ken Griffey Jr.	2.00
12	Kenny Lofton	.15
13	Greg Maddux	.75
14	Fred McGriff	.15
15	Mike Piazza	1.50
16	Kirby Puckett	.75
17	Tim Salmon	.15
18	Frank Thomas	.50
19	Mo Vaughn	.15
20	Matt Williams	.15

Update

		NM/M
Complete Set (200):		7.00
Common Player:		.05
Pack (12):		.50
Wax Box (36):		7.50
1	Manny Alexander	.05
2	Bret Barberie	.05
3	Armando Benitez	.05
4	Kevin Brown	.05
5	Doug Jones	.05
6	Sherman Obando	.05
7	Andy Van Slyke	.05
8	Stan Belinda	.05
9	Jose Canseco	.30
10	Vaughn Eshelman	.05
11	Mike Macfarlane	.05
12	Troy O'Leary	.05
13	Steve Rodriguez	.05
14	Lee Tinsley	.05
15	Tim Vanegmond	.05
16	Mark Whiten	.05
17	Sean Bergman	.05
18	Chad Curtis	.05
19	John Flaherty	.05
20	*Bob Higginson*	.15
21	Felipe Lira	.05
22	Shannon Penn	.05
23	Todd Steverson	.05
24	Sean Whiteside	.05
25	Tony Fernandez	.05
26	Jack McDowell	.05
27	Andy Petitte	.15
28	John Wetteland	.05
29	David Cone	.05
30	Mike Timlin	.05
31	Duane Ward	.05
32	Jim Abbott	.05
33	James Baldwin	.05
34	Mike Devereaux	.05
35	Ray Durham	.05
36	Tim Fortugno	.05
37	Scott Ruffcorn	.05
38	Chris Sabo	.05
39	Paul Assenmacher	.05
40	Bud Black	.05
41	Orel Hershiser	.05
42	Julian Tavarez	.05
43	Dave Winfield	.60
44	Pat Borders	.05
45	*Melvin Bunch*	.05
46	Tom Goodwin	.05
47	Jon Nunnally	.05
48	Joe Randa	.05
49	*Dilson Torres*	.05
50	Joe Vitiello	.05
51	David Hulse	.05
52	Scott Karl	.05
53	Mark Kiefer	.05
54	Derrick May	.05
55	Joe Oliver	.05
56	Al Reyes	.05
57	*Steve Sparks*	.05
58	Jerald Clark	.05
59	Eddie Guardado	.05
60	Kevin Maas	.05
61	David McCarty	.05
62	*Brad Radke*	.50
63	Scott Stahoviak	.05
64	Garret Anderson	.05
65	Shawn Boskie	.05
66	Mike James	.05
67	Tony Phillips	.05
68	Lee Smith	.05
69	Mitch Williams	.05
70	Jim Corsi	.05
71	Mark Harkey	.05
72	Dave Stewart	.05
73	Todd Stottlemyre	.05
74	Joey Cora	.05
75	Chad Kreuter	.05
76	Jeff Nelson	.05
77	Alex Rodriguez	2.00
78	Ron Villone	.05
79	*Bob Wells*	.05
80	*Jose Alberro*	.05
81	Terry Burrows	.05
82	Kevin Gross	.05
83	Wilson Heredia	.05
84	Mark McLemore	.05
85	Otis Nixon	.05
86	Jeff Russell	.05
87	Mickey Tettleton	.05
88	Bob Tewksbury	.05
89	Pedro Borbon	.05
90	Marquis Grissom	.05
91	Chipper Jones	.75
92	Mike Mordecai	.05
93	Jason Schmidt	.15
94	John Burkett	.05
95	Andre Dawson	.25
96	*Matt Dunbar*	.05
97	Charles Johnson	.05
98	Terry Pendleton	.05
99	Rich Scheid	.05
100	Quilvio Veras	.05
101	Bobby Witt	.05
102	Eddie Zosky	.05
103	Shane Andrews	.05
104	Reid Cornelius	.05
105	*Chad Fonville*	.05
106	*Mark Grudzielanek*	.25
107	Roberto Kelly	.05
108	*Carlos Perez*	.05
109	Tony Tarasco	.05
110	Brett Butler	.05
111	Carl Everett	.05
112	Pete Harnisch	.05
113	Doug Henry	.05
114	Kevin Lomon	.05
115	Blas Minor	.05
116	Dave Mlicki	.05
117	*Ricky Otero*	.05
118	Norm Charlton	.05
119	Tyler Green	.05
120	Gene Harris	.05
121	Charlie Hayes	.05
122	Gregg Jefferies	.05
123	*Michael Mimbs*	.05
124	Paul Quantrill	.05
125	Frank Castillo	.05
126	Brian McRae	.05
127	Jaime Navarro	.05
128	Mike Perez	.05
129	Tanyon Sturtze	.05
130	Ozzie Timmons	.05
131	John Courtright	.05
132	Ron Gant	.05
133	Xavier Hernandez	.05
134	Brian Hunter	.05
135	Benito Santiago	.05
136	Pete Smith	.05
137	Scott Sullivan	.05
138	Derek Bell	.05
139	Doug Brocail	.05
140	Ricky Gutierrez	.05
141	Pedro Martinez	.05
142	Orlando Miller	.05
143	Phil Plantier	.05
144	Craig Shipley	.05
145	Rich Aude	.05
146	*Jason Christiansen*	.05
147	*Freddy Garcia*	.25
148	Jim Gott	.05
149	*Mark Johnson*	.05
150	Esteban Loaiza	.05
151	Dan Plesac	.05
152	*Gary Wilson*	.05
153	Allen Battle	.05
154	Terry Bradshaw	.05
155	Scott Cooper	.05
156	Tripp Cromer	.05
157	John Frascatore	.05
158	John Habyan	.05
159	Tom Henke	.05
160	Ken Hill	.05
161	Danny Jackson	.05
162	Donovan Osborne	.05
163	Tom Urbani	.05
164	Roger Bailey	.05
165	*Jorge Brito*	.05
166	Vinny Castilla	.05
167	Darren Holmes	.05
168	Roberto Mejia	.05
169	Bill Swift	.05
170	Mark Thompson	.05
171	Larry Walker	.05
172	Greg Hansell	.05
173	Dave Hansen	.05
174	Carlos Hernandez	.05
175	*Hideo Nomo*	2.00
176	Jose Offerman	.05
177	Antonio Osuna	.05
178	Reggie Williams	.05
179	Todd Williams	.05
180	Andres Berumen	.05
181	Ken Caminiti	.05
182	Andujar Cedeno	.05
183	Steve Finley	.05
184	Bryce Florie	.05
185	Dustin Hermanson	.05
186	Ray Holbert	.05
187	Melvin Nieves	.05
188	Roberto Petagine	.05
189	Jody Reed	.05
190	Fernando Valenzuela	.05
191	Brian Williams	.05
192	Mark Dewey	.05
193	Glenallen Hill	.05
194	*Chris Hook*	.05
195	Terry Mulholland	.05
196	Steve Scarsone	.05
197	Trevor Wilson	.05
198	Checklist	.05
199	Checklist	.05
200	Checklist	.05

1996 FLEER

		NM/M
Complete Set (600):		20.00
Common Player:		.05
Complete Tiffany Set (600):		100.00
Tiffanies:		2X
Pack (11):		.75
Wax Box (36):		16.00
1	Manny Alexander	.05
2	Brady Anderson	.05
3	Harold Baines	.05
4	Armando Benitez	.05
5	Bobby Bonilla	.05
6	Kevin Brown	.05
7	Scott Erickson	.05
8	Curtis Goodwin	.05
9	Jeffrey Hammonds	.05
10	Jimmy Haynes	.05
11	Chris Hoiles	.05
12	Doug Jones	.05
13	Rick Krivda	.05
14	Jeff Manto	.05
15	Ben McDonald	.05
16	Jamie Moyer	.05
17	Mike Mussina	.50
18	Jesse Orosco	.05
19	Rafael Palmeiro	.65
20	Cal Ripken Jr.	2.50
20(p)	Cal Ripken Jr. (overprinted "PROMOTIONAL SAMPLE")	2.50
21	Rick Aguilera	.05
22	Luis Alicea	.05
23	Stan Belinda	.05
24	Jose Canseco	.50
25	Roger Clemens	1.25
26	Vaughn Eshelman	.05
27	Mike Greenwell	.05
28	Erik Hanson	.05
29	Dwayne Hosey	.05
30	Mike Macfarlane	.05
31	Tim Naehring	.05
32	Troy O'Leary	.05
33	Aaron Sele	.05
34	Zane Smith	.05
35	Jeff Suppan	.05
36	Lee Tinsley	.05
37	John Valentin	.05
38	Mo Vaughn	.05
39	Tim Wakefield	.05
40	Jim Abbott	.05
41	Brian Anderson	.05
42	Garret Anderson	.05
43	Chili Davis	.05
44	Gary DiSarcina	.05
45	Damion Easley	.05
46	Jim Edmonds	.05
47	Chuck Finley	.05
48	Todd Greene	.05
49	Mike Harkey	.05
50	Mike James	.05
51	Mark Langston	.05
52	Greg Myers	.05
53	Orlando Palmeiro	.05
54	Bob Patterson	.05
55	Troy Percival	.05
56	Tony Phillips	.05
57	Tim Salmon	.10
58	Lee Smith	.05
59	J.T. Snow	.05
60	Randy Velarde	.05
61	Wilson Alvarez	.05
62	*Luis Andujar*	.05
63	Jason Bere	.05
64	Ray Durham	.05
65	Alex Fernandez	.05
66	Ozzie Guillen	.05
67	Roberto Hernandez	.05

No.	Player	Price
68	Lance Johnson	.05
69	Matt Karchner	.05
70	Ron Karkovice	.05
71	Norberto Martin	.05
72	Dave Martinez	.05
73	Kirk McCaskill	.05
74	Lyle Mouton	.05
75	Tim Raines	.05
76	*Mike Sirotka*	.05
77	Frank Thomas	.75
78	Larry Thomas	.05
79	Robin Ventura	.05
80	Sandy Alomar Jr.	.05
81	Paul Assenmacher	.05
82	Carlos Baerga	.05
83	Albert Belle	.05
84	Mark Clark	.05
85	Alan Embree	.05
86	Alvaro Espinoza	.05
87	Orel Hershiser	.05
88	Ken Hill	.05
89	Kenny Lofton	.05
90	Dennis Martinez	.05
91	Jose Mesa	.05
92	Eddie Murray	.75
93	Charles Nagy	.05
94	Chad Ogea	.05
95	Tony Pena	.05
96	Herb Perry	.05
97	Eric Plunk	.05
98	Jim Poole	.05
99	Manny Ramirez	.75
100	Paul Sorrento	.05
101	Julian Travarez	.05
102	Jim Thome	.60
103	Omar Vizquel	.05
104	Dave Winfield	.75
105	Danny Bautista	.05
106	Joe Boever	.05
107	Chad Curtis	.05
108	John Doherty	.05
109	Cecil Fielder	.05
110	John Flaherty	.05
111	Travis Fryman	.05
112	Chris Gomez	.05
113	Bob Higginson	.05
114	Mark Lewis	.05
115	Jose Lima	.05
116	Felipe Lira	.05
117	Brian Maxcy	.05
118	C.J. Nitkowski	.05
119	Phil Plantier	.05
120	Clint Sodowsky	.05
121	Alan Trammell	.05
122	Lou Whitaker	.05
123	Kevin Appier	.05
124	Johnny Damon	.35
125	Gary Gaetti	.05
126	Tom Goodwin	.05
127	Tom Gordon	.05
128	Mark Gubicza	.05
129	Bob Hamelin	.05
130	David Howard	.05
131	Jason Jacome	.05
132	Wally Joyner	.05
133	Keith Lockhart	.05
134	Brent Mayne	.05
135	Jeff Montgomery	.05
136	Jon Nunnally	.05
137	Juan Samuel	.05
138	*Mike Sweeney*	.50
139	Michael Tucker	.05
140	Joe Vitiello	.05
141	Ricky Bones	.05
142	Chuck Carr	.05
143	Jeff Cirillo	.05
144	Mike Fetters	.05
145	Darryl Hamilton	.05
146	David Hulse	.05
147	John Jaha	.05
148	Scott Karl	.05
149	Mark Kiefer	.05
150	Pat Listach	.05
151	Mark Loretta	.05
152	Mike Matheny	.05
153	Matt Mieske	.05
154	Dave Nilsson	.05
155	Joe Oliver	.05
156	Al Reyes	.05
157	Kevin Seitzer	.05
158	Steve Sparks	.05
159	B.J. Surhoff	.05
160	Jose Valentin	.05
161	Greg Vaughn	.05
162	Fernando Vina	.05
163	Rich Becker	.05
164	Ron Coomer	.05
165	Marty Cordova	.05
166	Chuck Knoblauch	.05
167	*Matt Lawton*	.30
168	Pat Meares	.05
169	Paul Molitor	.75
170	Pedro Munoz	.05
171	Jose Parra	.05
172	Kirby Puckett	1.00
173	Brad Radke	.05
174	Jeff Reboulet	.05
175	Rich Robertson	.05
176	Frank Rodriguez	.05
177	Scott Stahoviak	.05
178	Dave Stevens	.05
179	Matt Walbeck	.05
180	Wade Boggs	1.00
181	David Cone	.05
182	Tony Fernandez	.05
183	Joe Girardi	.05
184	Derek Jeter	2.50
185	Scott Kamieniecki	.05
186	Pat Kelly	.05
187	Jim Leyritz	.05
188	Tino Martinez	.05
189	Don Mattingly	1.25
190	Jack McDowell	.05
191	Jeff Nelson	.05
192	Paul O'Neill	.05
193	Melido Perez	.05
194	Andy Pettitte	.30
195	Mariano Rivera	.15
196	Ruben Sierra	.05
197	Mike Stanley	.05
198	Darryl Strawberry	.05
199	John Wetteland	.05
200	Bob Wickman	.05
201	Bernie Williams	.10
202	Mark Acre	.05
203	Geronimo Berroa	.05
204	Mike Bordick	.05
205	Scott Brosius	.05
206	Dennis Eckersley	.65
207	Brent Gates	.05
208	Jason Giambi	.60
209	Rickey Henderson	.75
210	Jose Herrera	.05
211	Stan Javier	.05
212	Doug Johns	.05
213	Mark McGwire	2.00
214	Steve Ontiveros	.05
215	Craig Paquette	.05
216	Ariel Prieto	.05
217	Carlos Reyes	.05
218	Terry Steinbach	.05
219	Todd Stottlemyre	.05
220	Danny Tartabull	.05
221	Todd Van Poppel	.05
222	John Wasdin	.05
223	George Williams	.05
224	Steve Wojciechowski	.05
225	Rich Amaral	.05
226	Bobby Ayala	.05
227	Tim Belcher	.05
228	Andy Benes	.05
229	Chris Bosio	.05
230	Darren Bragg	.05
231	Jay Buhner	.05
232	Norm Charlton	.05
233	Vince Coleman	.05
234	Joey Cora	.05
235	Russ Davis	.05
236	Alex Diaz	.05
237	Felix Fermin	.05
238	Ken Griffey Jr.	1.75
239	Sterling Hitchcock	.05
240	Randy Johnson	.75
241	Edgar Martinez	.05
242	Bill Risley	.05
243	Alex Rodriquez	2.00
244	Luis Sojo	.05
245	Dan Wilson	.05
246	Bob Wolcott	.05
247	Will Clark	.10
248	Jeff Frye	.05
249	Benji Gil	.05
250	Juan Gonzalez	.65
251	Rusty Greer	.05
252	Kevin Gross	.05
253	Roger McDowell	.05
254	Mark McLemore	.05
255	Otis Nixon	.05
256	Luis Ortiz	.05
257	Mike Pagliarulo	.05
258	Dean Palmer	.05
259	Roger Pavlik	.05
260	Ivan Rodriguez	.65
261	Kenny Rogers	.05
262	Jeff Russell	.05
263	Mickey Tettleton	.05
264	Bob Tewksbury	.05
265	Dave Valle	.05
266	Matt Whiteside	.05
267	Roberto Alomar	.10
268	Joe Carter	.05
269	Tony Castillo	.05
270	Domingo Cedeno	.05
271	Timothy Crabtree	.05
272	Carlos Delgado	.60
273	Alex Gonzalez	.05
274	Shawn Green	.20
275	Juan Guzman	.05
276	Pat Hentgen	.05
277	Al Leiter	.05
278	*Sandy Martinez*	.05
279	Paul Menhart	.05
280	John Olerud	.05
281	Paul Quantrill	.05
282	Ken Robinson	.05
283	Ed Sprague	.05
284	Mike Timlin	.05
285	Steve Avery	.05
286	Rafael Belliard	.05
287	Jeff Blauser	.05
288	Pedro Borbon	.05
289	Brad Clontz	.05
290	Mike Devereaux	.05
291	Tom Glavine	.25
292	Marquis Grissom	.05
293	Chipper Jones	1.00
294	David Justice	.05
295	Mike Kelly	.05
296	Ryan Klesko	.05
297	Mark Lemke	.05
298	Javier Lopez	.05
299	Greg Maddux	1.00
300	Fred McGriff	.05
301	Greg McMichael	.05
302	Kent Mercker	.05
303	Mike Mordecai	.05
304	Charlie O'Brien	.05
305	Eduardo Perez	.05
306	Luis Polonia	.05
307	Jason Schmidt	.05
308	John Smoltz	.05
309	Terrell Wade	.05
310	Mark Wohlers	.05
311	Scott Bullett	.05
312	Jim Bullinger	.05
313	Larry Casian	.05
314	Frank Castillo	.05
315	Shawon Dunston	.05
316	Kevin Foster	.05
317	Matt Franco	.05
318	Luis Gonzalez	.10
319	Mark Grace	.10
320	Jose Hernandez	.05
321	Mike Hubbard	.05
322	Brian McRae	.05
323	Randy Myers	.05
324	Jaime Navarro	.05
325	Mark Parent	.05
326	Mike Perez	.05
327	Rey Sanchez	.05
328	Ryne Sandberg	1.00
329	Scott Servais	.05
330	Sammy Sosa	1.50
331	Ozzie Timmons	.05
332	Steve Trachsel	.05
333	Todd Zeile	.05
334	Bret Boone	.10
335	Jeff Branson	.05
336	Jeff Brantley	.05
337	Dave Burba	.05
338	Hector Carrasco	.05
339	Mariano Duncan	.05
340	Ron Gant	.05
341	Lenny Harris	.05
342	Xavier Hernandez	.05
343	Thomas Howard	.05
344	Mike Jackson	.05
345	Barry Larkin	.05
346	Darren Lewis	.05
347	Hal Morris	.05
348	Eric Owens	.05
349	Mark Portugal	.05
350	Jose Rijo	.05
351	Reggie Sanders	.05
352	Benito Santiago	.05
353	Pete Schourek	.05
354	John Smiley	.05
355	Eddie Taubensee	.05
356	Jerome Walton	.05
357	David Wells	.05
358	Roger Bailey	.05
359	Jason Bates	.05
360	Dante Bichette	.05
361	Ellis Burks	.05
362	Vinny Castilla	.05
363	Andres Galarraga	.05
364	Darren Holmes	.05
365	Mike Kingery	.05
366	Curt Leskanic	.05
367	Quinton McCracken	.05
368	Mike Munoz	.05
369	David Nied	.05
370	Steve Reed	.05
371	Bryan Rekar	.05
372	Kevin Ritz	.05
373	Bruce Ruffin	.05
374	Bret Saberhagen	.05
375	Bill Swift	.05
376	John Vander Wal	.05
377	Larry Walker	.05
378	Walt Weiss	.05
379	Eric Young	.05
380	Kurt Abbott	.05
381	Alex Arias	.05
382	Jerry Browne	.05
383	John Burkett	.05
384	Greg Colbrunn	.05
385	Jeff Conine	.05
386	Andre Dawson	.35
387	Chris Hammond	.05
388	Charles Johnson	.05
389	Terry Mathews	.05
390	Robb Nen	.05
391	Joe Orsulak	.05
392	Terry Pendleton	.05
393	Pat Rapp	.05
394	Gary Sheffield	.45
395	Jesus Tavarez	.05
396	Marc Valdes	.05
397	Quilvio Veras	.05
398	Randy Veres	.05
399	Devon White	.05
400	Jeff Bagwell	.75
401	Derek Bell	.05
402	Craig Biggio	.05
403	John Cangelosi	.05
404	Jim Dougherty	.05
405	Doug Drabek	.05
406	Tony Eusebio	.05
407	Ricky Gutierrez	.05
408	Mike Hampton	.05
409	Dean Hartgraves	.05
410	John Hudek	.05
411	Brian Hunter	.05
412	Todd Jones	.05
413	Darryl Kile	.05
414	Dave Magadan	.05
415	Derrick May	.05
416	Orlando Miller	.05
417	James Mouton	.05
418	Shane Reynolds	.05
419	Greg Swindell	.05
420	Jeff Tabaka	.05
421	Dave Veres	.05
422	Billy Wagner	.05
423	*Donne Wall*	.05
424	Rick Wilkins	.05
425	Billy Ashley	.05
426	Mike Blowers	.05
427	Brett Butler	.05
428	Tom Candiotti	.05
429	Juan Castro	.05
430	John Cummings	.05
431	Delino DeShields	.05
432	Joey Eischen	.05
433	Chad Fonville	.05
434	Greg Gagne	.05
435	Dave Hansen	.05
436	Carlos Hernandez	.05
437	Todd Hollandsworth	.05
438	Eric Karros	.05
439	Roberto Kelly	.05
440	Ramon Martinez	.05
441	Raul Mondesi	.05
442	Hideo Nomo	.65
443	Antonio Osuna	.05
444	Chan Ho Park	.05
445	Mike Piazza	1.75
446	Felix Rodriguez	.05
447	Kevin Tapani	.05
448	Ismael Valdes	.05
449	Todd Worrell	.05
450	Moises Alou	.05
451	Shane Andrews	.05
452	Yamil Benitez	.05
453	Sean Berry	.05
454	Wil Cordero	.05
455	Jeff Fassero	.05
456	Darrin Fletcher	.05
457	Cliff Floyd	.05
458	Mark Grudzielanek	.05
459	Gil Heredia	.05
460	Tim Laker	.05
461	Mike Lansing	.05
462	Pedro Martinez	.75
463	Carlos Perez	.05

464	Curtis Pride	.05
465	Mel Rojas	.05
466	Kirk Rueter	.05
467	*F.P. Santangelo*	.05
468	Tim Scott	.05
469	David Segui	.05
470	Tony Tarasco	.05
471	Rondell White	.05
472	Edgardo Alfonzo	.05
473	Tim Bogar	.05
474	Rico Brogna	.05
475	Damon Buford	.05
476	Paul Byrd	.05
477	Carl Everett	.10
478	John Franco	.05
479	Todd Hundley	.05
480	Butch Huskey	.05
481	Jason Isringhausen	.05
482	Bobby Jones	.05
483	Chris Jones	.05
484	Jeff Kent	.10
485	Dave Mlicki	.05
486	Robert Person	.05
487	Bill Pulsipher	.05
488	Kelly Stinnett	.05
489	Ryan Thompson	.05
490	Jose Vizcaino	.05
491	Howard Battle	.05
492	Toby Borland	.05
493	Ricky Bottalico	.05
494	Darren Daulton	.05
495	Lenny Dykstra	.05
496	Jim Eisenreich	.05
497	Sid Fernandez	.05
498	Tyler Green	.05
499	Charlie Hayes	.05
500	Gregg Jefferies	.05
501	Kevin Jordan	.05
502	Tony Longmire	.05
503	Tom Marsh	.05
504	Michael Mimbs	.05
505	Mickey Morandini	.05
506	Gene Schall	.05
507	Curt Schilling	.25
508	Heathcliff Slocumb	.05
509	Kevin Stocker	.05
510	Andy Van Slyke	.05
511	Lenny Webster	.05
512	Mark Whiten	.05
513	Mike Williams	.05
514	Jay Bell	.05
515	Jacob Brumfield	.05
516	Jason Christiansen	.05
517	Dave Clark	.05
518	Midre Cummings	.05
519	Angelo Encarnacion	.05
520	John Ericks	.05
521	Carlos Garcia	.05
522	Mark Johnson	.05
523	Jeff King	.05
524	Nelson Liriano	.05
525	Esteban Loaiza	.05
526	Al Martin	.05
527	Orlando Merced	.05
528	Dan Miceli	.05
529	Ramon Morel	.05
530	Denny Neagle	.05
531	Steve Parris	.05
532	Dan Plesac	.05
533	Don Slaught	.05
534	Paul Wagner	.05
535	John Wehner	.05
536	Kevin Young	.05
537	Allen Battle	.05
538	David Bell	.05
539	Alan Benes	.05
540	Scott Cooper	.05
541	Tripp Cromer	.05
542	Tony Fossas	.05
543	Bernard Gilkey	.05
544	Tom Henke	.05
545	Brian Jordan	.05
546	Ray Lankford	.05
547	John Mabry	.05
548	T.J. Mathews	.05
549	Mike Morgan	.05
550	Jose Oliva	.05
551	Jose Oquendo	.05
552	Donovan Osborne	.05
553	Tom Pagnozzi	.05
554	Mark Petkovsek	.05
555	Danny Sheaffer	.05
556	Ozzie Smith	1.00
557	Mark Sweeney	.05
558	Allen Watson	.05
559	Andy Ashby	.05
560	Brad Ausmus	.05
561	Willie Blair	.05
562	Ken Caminiti	.05
563	Andujar Cedeno	.05
564	Glenn Dishman	.05
565	Steve Finley	.05
566	Bryce Florie	.05
567	Tony Gwynn	1.00
568	Joey Hamilton	.05
569	Dustin Hermanson	.05
570	Trevor Hoffman	.05
571	Brian Johnson	.05
572	Marc Kroon	.05
573	Scott Livingstone	.05
574	Marc Newfield	.05
575	Melvin Nieves	.05
576	Jody Reed	.05
577	Bip Roberts	.05
578	Scott Sanders	.05
579	Fernando Valenzuela	.05
580	Eddie Williams	.05
581	Rod Beck	.05
582	*Marvin Benard*	.10
583	Barry Bonds	2.50
584	Jamie Brewington	.05
585	Mark Carreon	.05
586	Royce Clayton	.05
587	Shawn Estes	.05
588	Glenallen Hill	.05
589	Mark Leiter	.05
590	Kirt Manwaring	.05
591	David McCarty	.05
592	Terry Mulholland	.05
593	John Patterson	.05
594	J.R. Phillips	.05
595	Deion Sanders	.05
596	Steve Scarsone	.05
597	Robby Thompson	.05
598	Sergio Valdez	.05
599	William VanLandingham	.05
600	Matt Williams	.05

Tiffany

	NM/M
Complete Set (600):	100.00
Common Player:	.15
Stars:	2X

(See 1996 Fleer for checklist and base card values.)

Golden Memories

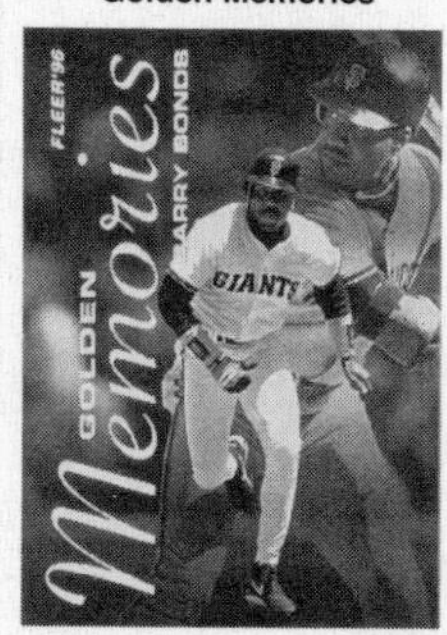

		NM/M
Complete Set (10):		6.00
Common Player:		.10
1	Albert Belle	.10
2	Barry Bonds, Sammy Sosa	1.50
3	Greg Maddux	1.00
4	Edgar Martinez	.10
5	Ramon Martinez	.10
6	Mark McGwire	1.50
7	Eddie Murray	.75
8	Cal Ripken Jr.	2.00
9	Frank Thomas	.75
10	Alan Trammell, Lou Whitaker	.15

LUMBER COMPANY

		NM/M
Complete Set (12):		12.50
Common Player:		.50
1	Albert Belle	.50
2	Dante Bichette	.50
3	Barry Bonds	3.00
4	Ken Griffey Jr.	1.50
5	Mark McGwire	2.00
6	Mike Piazza	1.50
7	Manny Ramirez	1.00
8	Tim Salmon	.60
9	Sammy Sosa	1.25
10	Frank Thomas	1.00
11	Mo Vaughn	.50
12	Matt Williams	.50

Post-Season Glory

		NM/M
Complete Set (5):		1.50
Common Player:		.15
1	Tom Glavine	.25
2	Ken Griffey Jr.	1.00
3	Orel Hershiser	.15
4	Randy Johnson	.50
5	Jim Thome	.50

Prospects

		NM/M
Complete Set (10):		1.00
Common Player:		.15
1	Yamil Benitez	.15
2	Roger Cedeno	.15
3	Tony Clark	.15
4	Micah Franklin	.15
5	Karim Garcia	.30
6	Todd Greene	.15
7	Alex Ochoa	.15
8	Ruben Rivera	.15
9	Chris Snopek	.15
10	Shannon Stewart	.15

Road Warriors

		NM/M
Complete Set (10):		9.00
Common Player:		.35
1	Derek Bell	.40
2	Tony Gwynn	1.25
3	Greg Maddux	1.25
4	Mark McGwire	2.50
5	Mike Piazza	2.00
6	Manny Ramirez	1.00
7	Tim Salmon	.50
8	Frank Thomas	1.00
9	Mo Vaughn	.40
10	Matt Williams	.40

Rookie Sensations

		NM/M
Complete Set (15):		5.00
Common Player:		.25
1	Garret Anderson	.40
2	Marty Cordova	.25
3	Johnny Damon	1.00
4	Ray Durham	.25
5	Carl Everett	.25
6	Shawn Green	.50
7	Brian Hunter	.25
8	Jason Isringhausen	.25
9	Charles Johnson	.25
10	Chipper Jones	2.00
11	John Mabry	.25
12	Hideo Nomo	.50
13	Troy Percival	.25
14	Andy Pettitte	.50
15	Quilvio Veras	.25

Smoke 'N Heat

		NM/M
Complete Set (10):		4.00
Common Player:		.15
1	Kevin Appier	.15
2	Roger Clemens	1.50
3	David Cone	.15
4	Chuck Finley	.15
5	Randy Johnson	.75
6	Greg Maddux	1.00
7	Pedro Martinez	.75
8	Hideo Nomo	.50
9	John Smoltz	.30
10	Todd Stottlemyre	.15

Team Leaders

		NM/M
Complete Set (28):		30.00
Common Player:		.50
1	Cal Ripken Jr.	6.00
2	Mo Vaughn	.50
3	Jim Edmonds	1.00
4	Frank Thomas	2.00
5	Kenny Lofton	.50
6	Travis Fryman	.50
7	Gary Gaetti	.50
8	B.J. Surhoff	.50
9	Kirby Puckett	2.50
10	Don Mattingly	3.00
11	Mark McGwire	4.00
12	Ken Griffey Jr.	3.00
13	Juan Gonzalez	1.00
14	Joe Carter	.50
15	Greg Maddux	2.50
16	Sammy Sosa	3.00
17	Barry Larkin	.50
18	Dante Bichette	.50
19	Jeff Conine	.50
20	Jeff Bagwell	2.00
21	Mike Piazza	3.00
22	Rondell White	.50
23	Rico Brogna	.50
24	Darren Daulton	.50
25	Jeff King	.50
26	Ray Lankford	.50
27	Tony Gwynn	2.50
28	Barry Bonds	6.00

Tomorrow's Legends

		NM/M
Complete Set (10):		3.50
Common Player:		.25
1	Garret Anderson	.25
2	Jim Edmonds	.50
3	Brian Hunter	.25
4	Jason Isringhausen	.25
5	Charles Johnson	.25
6	Chipper Jones	2.00
7	Ryan Klesko	.25
8	Hideo Nomo	1.00
9	Manny Ramirez	1.50
10	Rondell White	.25

Zone

		NM/M
Complete Set (12):		20.00
Common Player:		.75
1	Albert Belle	.75
2	Barry Bonds	6.00
3	Ken Griffey Jr.	4.00
4	Tony Gwynn	3.00
5	Randy Johnson	2.00
6	Kenny Lofton	.75
7	Greg Maddux	3.00
8	Edgar Martinez	.75
9	Mike Piazza	4.00
10	Frank Thomas	2.00
11	Mo Vaughn	.75
12	Matt Williams	.75

Update

		NM/M
Complete Set (250):		12.00
Common Player:		.05
Complete Tiffany Set (250):		40.00
Tiffany Stars:		2X
Pack (11):		1.00
Wax Box (24):		15.00
1	Roberto Alomar	.10
2	Mike Devereaux	.05
3	*Scott McClain*	.05
4	Roger McDowell	.05
5	Kent Mercker	.05
6	Jimmy Myers	.05
7	Randy Myers	.05
8	B.J. Surhoff	.05
9	Tony Tarasco	.05
10	David Wells	.05
11	Wil Cordero	.05
12	Tom Gordon	.05
13	Reggie Jefferson	.05
14	Jose Malave	.05
15	Kevin Mitchell	.05
16	Jamie Moyer	.05
17	Heathcliff Slocumb	.05
18	Mike Stanley	.05
19	George Arias	.05
20	Jorge Fabregas	.05
21	Don Slaught	.05
22	Randy Velarde	.05
23	Harold Baines	.05
24	*Mike Cameron*	.75
25	Darren Lewis	.05
26	Tony Phillips	.05
27	Bill Simas	.05
28	Chris Snopek	.05
29	Kevin Tapani	.05
30	Danny Tartabull	.05
31	Julio Franco	.05
32	Jack McDowell	.05
33	Kimera Bartee	.05
34	Mark Lewis	.05
35	Melvin Nieves	.05
36	Mark Parent	.05
37	Eddie Williams	.05
38	Tim Belcher	.05
39	Sal Fasano	.05
40	Chris Haney	.05
41	Mike Macfarlane	.05
42	Jose Offerman	.05
43	Joe Randa	.05
44	Bip Roberts	.05
45	Chuck Carr	.05
46	Bobby Hughes	.05
47	Graeme Lloyd	.05
48	Ben McDonald	.05
49	Kevin Wickander	.05
50	Rick Aguilera	.05
51	Mike Durant	.05
52	Chip Hale	.05
53	LaTroy Hawkins	.05
54	Dave Hollins	.05
55	Roberto Kelly	.05
56	Paul Molitor	.75
57	*Dan Naulty*	.05
58	Mariano Duncan	.05
59	*Andy Fox*	.05
60	Joe Girardi	.05
61	Dwight Gooden	.05
62	Jimmy Key	.05
63	*Matt Luke*	.05
64	Tino Martinez	.05
65	Jeff Nelson	.05
66	Tim Raines	.05
67	Ruben Rivera	.05
68	Kenny Rogers	.05
69	Gerald Williams	.05
70	*Tony Batista*	.50
71	Allen Battle	.05
72	Jim Corsi	.05
73	Steve Cox	.05
74	Pedro Munoz	.05
75	Phil Plantier	.05
76	Scott Spiezio	.05
77	Ernie Young	.05
78	Russ Davis	.05
79	Sterling Hitchcock	.05
80	Edwin Hurtado	.05
81	*Raul Ibanez*	.05
82	Mike Jackson	.05
83	Ricky Jordan	.05
84	Paul Sorrento	.05
85	Doug Strange	.05
86	Mark Brandenburg	.05
87	Damon Buford	.05
88	Kevin Elster	.05
89	Darryl Hamilton	.05
90	Ken Hill	.05
91	Ed Vosberg	.05
92	Craig Worthington	.05
93	Tilson Brito	.05
94	Giovanni Carrara	.05
95	Felipe Crespo	.05
96	Erik Hanson	.05
97	*Marty Janzen*	.05
98	Otis Nixon	.05
99	Charlie O'Brien	.05
100	Robert Perez	.05
101	Paul Quantrill	.05
102	Bill Risley	.05
103	Juan Samuel	.05
104	Jermaine Dye	.05
105	Wonderful Monds	.05
106	Dwight Smith	.05
107	Jerome Walton	.05
108	Terry Adams	.05
109	Leo Gomez	.05
110	*Robin Jennings*	.05
111	Doug Jones	.05
112	Brooks Kieschnick	.05
113	Dave Magadan	.05
114	*Jason Maxwell*	.05
115	Rodney Myers	.05
116	Eric Anthony	.05
117	Vince Coleman	.05
118	Eric Davis	.05
119	Steve Gibralter	.05
120	Curtis Goodwin	.05
121	Willie Greene	.05
122	Mike Kelly	.05
123	Marcus Moore	.05
124	Chad Mottola	.05
125	Chris Sabo	.05
126	Roger Salkeld	.05
127	Pedro Castellano	.05
128	Trenidad Hubbard	.05
129	Jayhawk Owens	.05
130	Jeff Reed	.05
131	Kevin Brown	.05
132	Al Leiter	.05
133	*Matt Mantei*	.05
134	Dave Weathers	.05
135	Devon White	.05
136	Bob Abreu	.05
137	Sean Berry	.05
138	Doug Brocail	.05
139	Richard Hidalgo	.05
140	Alvin Morman	.05
141	Mike Blowers	.05
142	Roger Cedeno	.05
143	Greg Gagne	.05
144	Karim Garcia	.10
145	*Wilton Guerrero*	.05
146	*Israel Alcantara*	.05
147	Omar Daal	.05
148	Ryan McGuire	.05
149	Sherman Obando	.05
150	Jose Paniagua	.05
151	Henry Rodriguez	.05
152	Andy Stankiewicz	.05
153	Dave Veres	.05
154	Juan Acevedo	.05
155	Mark Clark	.05
156	Bernard Gilkey	.05
157	Pete Harnisch	.05
158	Lance Johnson	.05
159	Brent Mayne	.05
160	Rey Ordonez	.05
161	Kevin Roberson	.05
162	Paul Wilson	.05
163	*David Doster*	.05
164	*Mike Grace*	.05
165	*Rich Hunter*	.05
166	Pete Incaviglia	.05
167	Mike Lieberthal	.05
168	Terry Mulholland	.05
169	Ken Ryan	.05
170	Benito Santiago	.05
171	*Kevin Sefcik*	.05
172	Lee Tinsley	.05
173	Todd Zeile	.05
174	*Francisco Cordova*	.05
175	Danny Darwin	.05
176	Charlie Hayes	.05
177	Jason Kendall	.05
178	Mike Kingery	.05
179	Jon Lieber	.05
180	Zane Smith	.05
181	Luis Alicea	.05
182	Cory Bailey	.05
183	Andy Benes	.05
184	Pat Borders	.05
185	*Mike Busby*	.05
186	Royce Clayton	.05
187	Dennis Eckersley	.65
188	Gary Gaetti	.05
189	Ron Gant	.05
190	Aaron Holbert	.05
191	Willie McGee	.05
192	*Miguel Mejia*	.05
193	Jeff Parrett	.05
194	Todd Stottlemyre	.05
195	Sean Bergman	.05
196	Archi Cianfrocco	.05
197	Rickey Henderson	.75
198	Wally Joyner	.05
199	Craig Shipley	.05
200	Bob Tewksbury	.05
201	Tim Worrell	.05
202	*Rich Aurilia*	.05
203	Doug Creek	.05
204	Shawon Dunston	.05
205	*Osvaldo Fernandez*	.05
206	Mark Gardner	.05
207	Stan Javier	.05
208	Marcus Jensen	.05
209	*Chris Singleton*	.05
210	Allen Watson	.05
211	Jeff Bagwell (Encore)	.75
212	Derek Bell (Encore)	.05
213	Albert Belle (Encore)	.05
214	Wade Boggs (Encore)	1.00
215	Barry Bonds (Encore)	2.00
216	Jose Canseco (Encore)	.50
217	Marty Cordova (Encore)	.05
218	Jim Edmonds (Encore)	.05
219	Cecil Fielder (Encore)	.05
220	Andres Galarraga (Encore)	.05
221	Juan Gonzalez (Encore)	.65
222	Mark Grace (Encore)	.10
223	Ken Griffey Jr. (Encore)	1.50
224	Tony Gwynn (Encore)	1.00
225	Jason Isringhausen (Encore)	.05
226	Derek Jeter (Encore)	2.00
227	Randy Johnson (Encore)	.75
228	Chipper Jones (Encore)	1.00
229	Ryan Klesko (Encore)	.05
230	Barry Larkin (Encore)	.05
231	Kenny Lofton (Encore)	.05
232	Greg Maddux (Encore)	1.00
233	Raul Mondesi (Encore)	.05
234	Hideo Nomo (Encore)	.65
235	Mike Piazza (Encore)	1.50
236	Manny Ramirez (Encore)	.75
237	Cal Ripken Jr. (Encore)	2.00
238	Tim Salmon (Encore)	.10
239	Ryne Sandberg (Encore)	1.00
240	Reggie Sanders (Encore)	.05
241	Gary Sheffield (Encore)	.30
242	Sammy Sosa (Encore)	1.25
243	Frank Thomas (Encore)	.75
244	Mo Vaughn (Encore)	.05
245	Matt Williams (Encore)	.05
246	Checklist	.05
247	Checklist	.05
248	Checklist	.05
249	Checklist	.05
250	Checklist	.05

Update Tiffany

	NM/M
Complete Set (250):	45.00
Common Player:	.15
Glossy Stars:	2X

(See 1996 Fleer Update for checklist and base card values.)

Update Diamond Tribute

		NM/M
Complete Set (10):		50.00
Common Player:		4.00
1	Wade Boggs	6.00
2	Barry Bonds	10.00
3	Ken Griffey Jr.	7.50
4	Tony Gwynn	6.00
5	Rickey Henderson	4.00
6	Greg Maddux	6.00
7	Eddie Murray	4.00
8	Cal Ripken Jr.	10.00
9	Ozzie Smith	6.00
10	Frank Thomas	5.00

Update Headliners

		NM/M
Complete Set (20):		20.00
Common Player:		.25
1	Roberto Alomar	.50
2	Jeff Bagwell	1.00
3	Albert Belle	.25
4	Barry Bonds	3.50
5	Cecil Fielder	.25
6	Juan Gonzalez	.75
7	Ken Griffey Jr.	2.25
8	Tony Gwynn	1.50
9	Randy Johnson	1.00
10	Chipper Jones	1.50
11	Ryan Klesko	.25
12	Kenny Lofton	.25
13	Greg Maddux	1.50
14	Hideo Nomo	.75
15	Mike Piazza	2.25
16	Manny Ramirez	1.00
17	Cal Ripken Jr.	3.50
18	Tim Salmon	.40
19	Frank Thomas	1.00
20	Matt Williams	.25

Update New Horizons

		NM/M
Complete Set (20):		2.00
Common Player:		.25
1	Bob Abreu	.45
2	George Arias	.25
3	Tony Batista	.25
4	Steve Cox	.25
5	David Doster	.25
6	Jermaine Dye	.25
7	Andy Fox	.25
8	Mike Grace	.25
9	Todd Greene	.25
10	Wilton Guerrero	.25
11	Richard Hidalgo	.25
12	Raul Ibanez	.25
13	Robin Jennings	.25
14	Marcus Jensen	.25
15	Jason Kendall	.35
16	Brooks Kieschnick	.25
17	Ryan McGuire	.25
18	Miguel Mejia	.25
19	Rey Ordonez	.25
20	Paul Wilson	.25

Update Rookie Sensations

		NM/M
Complete Set (20):		6.00
Common Player:		.25
1	Jermaine Allensworth	.25
2	James Baldwin	.25
3	Alan Benes	.25
4	Jermaine Dye	.25
5	Darin Erstad	.50
6	Todd Hollandsworth	.25
7	Derek Jeter	2.50
8	Jason Kendall	.25
9	Alex Ochoa	.25
10	Rey Ordonez	.25
11	Edgar Renteria	.25
12	Bob Abreu	.50
13	Nomar Garciaparra	1.50
14	Wilton Guerrero	.25
15	Andruw Jones	1.00
16	Wendell Magee	.25
17	Neifi Perez	.25
18	Scott Rolen	.75
19	Scott Spiezio	.25
20	Todd Walker	.25

Update Smooth Leather

		NM/M
Complete Set (10):		7.00
Common Player:		.40
1	Roberto Alomar	.50
1p	Roberto Alomar (promo)	2.00
2	Barry Bonds	2.50
3	Will Clark	.45
4	Ken Griffey Jr.	1.75
5	Kenny Lofton	.40
6	Greg Maddux	1.00
7	Raul Mondesi	.40
8	Rey Ordonez	.40
9	Cal Ripken Jr.	2.50
9p	Cal Ripken Jr. (promo)	6.00
10	Matt Williams	.40

Update Soaring Stars

		NM/M
Complete Set (10):		6.00
Common Player:		.25
1	Jeff Bagwell	.75
2	Barry Bonds	2.00
3	Juan Gonzalez	.75
4	Ken Griffey Jr.	1.50
5	Chipper Jones	1.00
6	Greg Maddux	1.00
7	Mike Piazza	1.50
8	Manny Ramirez	.75
9	Frank Thomas	.75
10	Matt Williams	.25

1997 FLEER

		NM/M
Complete Set (761):		65.00
Complete Series 1 Set (500):		40.00
Complete Series 2 Set (261):		25.00
Common Player:		.05
Complete Tiffany Set (1-761):		500.00
Tiffany Stars/RCs:		8X
A. Jones Circa AU/200:		35.00
Series 1 or 2 Pack (10):		1.25
Series 1 or 2 Wax Box (36):		30.00
1	Roberto Alomar	.10
2	Brady Anderson	.05
3	Bobby Bonilla	.05
4	Rocky Coppinger	.05
5	Cesar Devarez	.05
6	Scott Erickson	.05
7	Jeffrey Hammonds	.05
8	Chris Hoiles	.05
9	Eddie Murray	1.00
10	Mike Mussina	.40
11	Randy Myers	.05
12	Rafael Palmeiro	.75
13	Cal Ripken Jr.	2.50
14	B.J. Surhoff	.05
15	David Wells	.05
16	Todd Zeile	.05
17	Darren Bragg	.05
18	Jose Canseco	.40
19	Roger Clemens	1.75
20	Wil Cordero	.05
21	Jeff Frye	.05
22	Nomar Garciaparra	1.75
23	Tom Gordon	.05
24	Mike Greenwell	.05
25	Reggie Jefferson	.05
26	Jose Malave	.05
27	Tim Naehring	.05
28	Troy O'Leary	.05
29	Heathcliff Slocumb	.05
30	Mike Stanley	.05
31	John Valentin	.05
32	Mo Vaughn	.05
33	Tim Wakefield	.05
34	Garret Anderson	.05
35	George Arias	.05
36	Shawn Boskie	.05
37	Chili Davis	.05
38	Jason Dickson	.05
39	Gary DiSarcina	.05
40	Jim Edmonds	.05
41	Darin Erstad	.10
42	Jorge Fabregas	.05
43	Chuck Finley	.05
44	Todd Greene	.05
45	*Mike Holtz*	.05
46	Rex Hudler	.05
47	Mike James	.05
48	Mark Langston	.05
49	Troy Percival	.05
50	Tim Salmon	.15
51	Jeff Schmidt	.05
52	J.T. Snow	.05
53	Randy Velarde	.05
54	Wilson Alvarez	.05
55	Harold Baines	.05
56	James Baldwin	.05
57	Jason Bere	.05
58	Mike Cameron	.05
59	Ray Durham	.05
60	Alex Fernandez	.05
61	Ozzie Guillen	.05
62	Roberto Hernandez	.05
63	Ron Karkovice	.05
64	Darren Lewis	.05
65	Dave Martinez	.05
66	Lyle Mouton	.05
67	Greg Norton	.05
68	Tony Phillips	.05
69	Chris Snopek	.05
70	Kevin Tapani	.05
71	Danny Tartabull	.05
72	Frank Thomas	1.00
73	Robin Ventura	.05
74	Sandy Alomar Jr.	.05
75	Albert Belle	.05
76	Mark Carreon	.05
77	Julio Franco	.05
78	*Brian Giles*	1.00
79	Orel Hershiser	.05
80	Kenny Lofton	.05
81	Dennis Martinez	.05
82	Jack McDowell	.05
83	Jose Mesa	.05
84	Charles Nagy	.05
85	Chad Ogea	.05
86	Eric Plunk	.05
87	Manny Ramirez	1.00
88	Kevin Seitzer	.05
89	Julian Tavarez	.05
90	Jim Thome	.65
91	Jose Vizcaino	.05
92	Omar Vizquel	.05
93	Brad Ausmus	.05
94	Kimera Bartee	.05
95	Raul Casanova	.05
96	Tony Clark	.05
97	John Cummings	.05
98	Travis Fryman	.05
99	Bob Higginson	.05
100	Mark Lewis	.05
101	Felipe Lira	.05
102	Phil Nevin	.05
103	Melvin Nieves	.05
104	Curtis Pride	.05
105	A.J. Sager	.05
106	Ruben Sierra	.05
107	Justin Thompson	.05
108	Alan Trammell	.05
109	Kevin Appier	.05
110	Tim Belcher	.05
111	Jaime Bluma	.05
112	Johnny Damon	.35
113	Tom Goodwin	.05
114	Chris Haney	.05
115	Keith Lockhart	.05
116	Mike Macfarlane	.05
117	Jeff Montgomery	.05
118	Jose Offerman	.05
119	Craig Paquette	.05
120	Joe Randa	.05
121	Bip Roberts	.05
122	Jose Rosado	.05
123	Mike Sweeney	.05
124	Michael Tucker	.05
125	Jeromy Burnitz	.05
126	Jeff Cirillo	.05
127	Jeff D'Amico	.05
128	Mike Fetters	.05
129	John Jaha	.05
130	Scott Karl	.05
131	Jesse Levis	.05
132	Mark Loretta	.05
133	Mike Matheny	.05
134	Ben McDonald	.05
135	Matt Mieske	.05
136	Marc Newfield	.05
137	Dave Nilsson	.05
138	Jose Valentin	.05
139	Fernando Vina	.05
140	Bob Wickman	.05
141	Gerald Williams	.05
142	Rick Aguilera	.05
143	Rich Becker	.05
144	Ron Coomer	.05
145	Marty Cordova	.05
146	Roberto Kelly	.05
147	Chuck Knoblauch	.05
148	Matt Lawton	.05
149	Pat Meares	.05
150	Travis Miller	.05
151	Paul Molitor	1.00
152	Greg Myers	.05
153	Dan Naulty	.05
154	Kirby Puckett	1.50
155	Brad Radke	.05
156	Frank Rodriguez	.05
157	Scott Stahoviak	.05
158	Dave Stevens	.05
159	Matt Walbeck	.05
160	Todd Walker	.05
161	Wade Boggs	1.50
162	David Cone	.05
163	Mariano Duncan	.05
164	Cecil Fielder	.05
165	Joe Girardi	.05
166	Dwight Gooden	.05
167	Charlie Hayes	.05
168	Derek Jeter	2.50
169	Jimmy Key	.05
170	Jim Leyritz	.05
171	Tino Martinez	.05
172	*Ramiro Mendoza*	.10
173	Jeff Nelson	.05
174	Paul O'Neill	.05
175	Andy Pettitte	.35
176	Mariano Rivera	.15
177	Ruben Rivera	.05
178	Kenny Rogers	.05
179	Darryl Strawberry	.05
180	John Wetteland	.05
181	Bernie Williams	.10
182	Willie Adams	.05
183	Tony Batista	.05
184	Geronimo Berroa	.05
185	Mike Bordick	.05
186	Scott Brosius	.05
187	Bobby Chouinard	.05
188	Jim Corsi	.05
189	Brent Gates	.05
190	Jason Giambi	.50
191	Jose Herrera	.05
192	*Damon Mashore*	.05
193	Mark McGwire	2.25
194	Mike Mohler	.05
195	Scott Spiezio	.05
196	Terry Steinbach	.05
197	Bill Taylor	.05
198	John Wasdin	.05
199	Steve Wojciechowski	.05
200	Ernie Young	.05
201	Rich Amaral	.05
202	Jay Buhner	.05
203	Norm Charlton	.05
204	Joey Cora	.05
205	Russ Davis	.05
206	Ken Griffey Jr.	2.00
207	Sterling Hitchcock	.05
208	Brian Hunter	.05
209	Raul Ibanez	.05

No.	Player	Price
210	Randy Johnson	1.00
211	Edgar Martinez	.05
212	Jamie Moyer	.05
213	Alex Rodriguez	2.25
214	Paul Sorrento	.05
215	Matt Wagner	.05
216	Bob Wells	.05
217	Dan Wilson	.05
218	Damon Buford	.05
219	Will Clark	.10
220	Kevin Elster	.05
221	Juan Gonzalez	.75
222	Rusty Greer	.05
223	Kevin Gross	.05
224	Darryl Hamilton	.05
225	Mike Henneman	.05
226	Ken Hill	.05
227	Mark McLemore	.05
228	Darren Oliver	.05
229	Dean Palmer	.05
230	Roger Pavlik	.05
231	Ivan Rodriguez	.75
232	Mickey Tettleton	.05
233	Bobby Witt	.05
234	Jacob Brumfield	.05
235	Joe Carter	.05
236	Tim Crabtree	.05
237	Carlos Delgado	.50
238	Huck Flener	.05
239	Alex Gonzalez	.05
240	Shawn Green	.20
241	Juan Guzman	.05
242	Pat Hentgen	.05
243	Marty Janzen	.05
244	Sandy Martinez	.05
245	Otis Nixon	.05
246	Charlie O'Brien	.05
247	John Olerud	.05
248	Robert Perez	.05
249	Ed Sprague	.05
250	Mike Timlin	.05
251	Steve Avery	.05
252	Jeff Blauser	.05
253	Brad Clontz	.05
254	Jermaine Dye	.05
255	Tom Glavine	.30
256	Marquis Grissom	.05
257	Andruw Jones	1.00
258	Chipper Jones	1.50
259	David Justice	.05
260	Ryan Klesko	.05
261	Mark Lemke	.05
262	Javier Lopez	.05
263	Greg Maddux	1.50
264	Fred McGriff	.05
265	Greg McMichael	.05
266	Denny Neagle	.05
267	Terry Pendleton	.05
268	Eddie Perez	.05
269	John Smoltz	.05
270	Terrell Wade	.05
271	Mark Wohlers	.05
272	Terry Adams	.05
273	Brant Brown	.05
274	Leo Gomez	.05
275	Luis Gonzalez	.10
276	Mark Grace	.10
277	Tyler Houston	.05
278	Robin Jennings	.05
279	Brooks Kieschnick	.05
280	Brian McRae	.05
281	Jaime Navarro	.05
282	Ryne Sandberg	1.50
283	Scott Servais	.05
284	Sammy Sosa	1.75
285	*Dave Swartzbaugh*	.05
286	Amaury Telemaco	.05
287	Steve Trachsel	.05
288	*Pedro Valdes*	.05
289	Turk Wendell	.05
290	Bret Boone	.05
291	Jeff Branson	.05
292	Jeff Brantley	.05
293	Eric Davis	.05
294	Willie Greene	.05
295	Thomas Howard	.05
296	Barry Larkin	.05
297	Kevin Mitchell	.05
298	Hal Morris	.05
299	Chad Mottola	.05
300	Joe Oliver	.05
301	Mark Portugal	.05
302	Roger Salkeld	.05
303	Reggie Sanders	.05
304	Pete Schourek	.05
305	John Smiley	.05
306	Eddie Taubensee	.05
307	Dante Bichette	.05
308	Ellis Burks	.05
309	Vinny Castilla	.05
310	Andres Galarraga	.05
311	Curt Leskanic	.05
312	Quinton McCracken	.05
313	Neifi Perez	.05
314	Jeff Reed	.05
315	Steve Reed	.05
316	Armando Reynoso	.05
317	Kevin Ritz	.05
318	Bruce Ruffin	.05
319	Larry Walker	.05
320	Walt Weiss	.05
321	Jamey Wright	.05
322	Eric Young	.05
323	Kurt Abbott	.05
324	Alex Arias	.05
325	Kevin Brown	.05
326	Luis Castillo	.05
327	Greg Colbrunn	.05
328	Jeff Conine	.05
329	Andre Dawson	.25
330	Charles Johnson	.05
331	Al Leiter	.05
332	Ralph Milliard	.05
333	Robb Nen	.05
334	Pat Rapp	.05
335	Edgar Renteria	.05
336	Gary Sheffield	.35
337	Devon White	.05
338	Bob Abreu	.05
339	Jeff Bagwell	1.00
340	Derek Bell	.05
341	Sean Berry	.05
342	Craig Biggio	.05
343	Doug Drabek	.05
344	Tony Eusebio	.05
345	Ricky Gutierrez	.05
346	Mike Hampton	.05
347	Brian Hunter	.05
348	Todd Jones	.05
349	Darryl Kile	.05
350	Derrick May	.05
351	Orlando Miller	.05
352	James Mouton	.05
353	Shane Reynolds	.05
354	Billy Wagner	.05
355	Donne Wall	.05
356	Mike Blowers	.05
357	Brett Butler	.05
358	Roger Cedeno	.05
259	Chad Curtis	.05
360	Delino DeShields	.05
361	Greg Gagne	.05
362	Karim Garcia	.10
363	Wilton Guerrero	.05
364	Todd Hollandsworth	.05
365	Eric Karros	.05
366	Ramon Martinez	.05
367	Raul Mondesi	.05
368	Hideo Nomo	.75
369	Antonio Osuna	.05
370	Chan Ho Park	.05
371	Mike Piazza	2.00
372	Ismael Valdes	.05
373	Todd Worrell	.05
374	Moises Alou	.05
375	Shane Andrews	.05
376	Yamil Benitez	.05
377	Jeff Fassero	.05
378	Darrin Fletcher	.05
379	Cliff Floyd	.05
380	Mark Grudzielanek	.05
381	Mike Lansing	.05
382	Barry Manuel	.05
383	Pedro Martinez	1.00
384	Henry Rodriguez	.05
385	Mel Rojas	.05
386	F.P. Santangelo	.05
387	David Segui	.05
388	Ugueth Urbina	.05
389	Rondell White	.05
390	Edgardo Alfonzo	.05
391	Carlos Baerga	.05
392	Mark Clark	.05
393	Alvaro Espinoza	.05
394	John Franco	.05
395	Bernard Gilkey	.05
396	Pete Harnisch	.05
397	Todd Hundley	.05
398	Butch Huskey	.05
399	Jason Isringhausen	.05
400	Lance Johnson	.05
401	Bobby Jones	.05
402	Alex Ochoa	.05
403	Rey Ordonez	.05
404	Robert Person	.05
405	Paul Wilson	.05
406	Matt Beech	.05
407	Ron Blazier	.05
408	Ricky Bottalico	.05
409	Lenny Dykstra	.05
410	Jim Eisenreich	.05
411	Bobby Estalella	.05
412	Mike Grace	.05
413	Gregg Jefferies	.05
414	Mike Lieberthal	.05
415	Wendell Magee Jr.	.05
416	Mickey Morandini	.05
417	Ricky Otero	.05
418	Scott Rolen	.75
419	Ken Ryan	.05
420	Benito Santiago	.05
421	Curt Schilling	.25
422	Kevin Sefcik	.05
423	Jermaine Allensworth	.05
424	Trey Beamon	.05
425	Jay Bell	.05
426	Francisco Cordova	.05
427	Carlos Garcia	.05
428	Mark Johnson	.05
429	Jason Kendall	.05
430	Jeff King	.05
431	Jon Lieber	.05
432	Al Martin	.05
433	Orlando Merced	.05
434	Ramon Morel	.05
435	Matt Ruebel	.05
436	Jason Schmidt	.05
437	*Marc Wilkins*	.05
438	Alan Benes	.05
439	Andy Benes	.05
440	Royce Clayton	.05
441	Dennis Eckersley	.65
442	Gary Gaetti	.05
443	Ron Gant	.05
444	Aaron Holbert	.05
445	Brian Jordan	.05
446	Ray Lankford	.05
447	John Mabry	.05
448	T.J. Mathews	.05
449	Willie McGee	.05
450	Donovan Osborne	.05
451	Tom Pagnozzi	.05
452	Ozzie Smith	1.50
453	Todd Stottlemyre	.05
454	Mark Sweeney	.05
455	Dmitri Young	.05
456	Andy Ashby	.05
457	Ken Caminiti	.05
458	Archi Cianfrocco	.05
459	Steve Finley	.05
460	John Flaherty	.05
461	Chris Gomez	.05
462	Tony Gwynn	1.50
463	Joey Hamilton	.05
464	Rickey Henderson	1.00
465	Trevor Hoffman	.05
466	Brian Johnson	.05
467	Wally Joyner	.05
468	Jody Reed	.05
469	Scott Sanders	.05
470	Bob Tewksbury	.05
471	Fernando Valenzuela	.05
472	Greg Vaughn	.05
473	Tim Worrell	.05
474	Rich Aurilia	.05
475	Rod Beck	.05
476	Marvin Benard	.05
477	Barry Bonds	2.50
478	Jay Canizaro	.05
479	Shawon Dunston	.05
480	Shawn Estes	.05
481	Mark Gardner	.05
482	Glenallen Hill	.05
483	Stan Javier	.05
484	Marcus Jensen	.05
485	*Bill Mueller*	1.50
486	William VanLandingham	.05
487	Allen Watson	.05
488	Rick Wilkins	.05
489	Matt Williams	.05
489p	Matt Williams ("PROMOTIONAL SAMPLE")	1.50
490	Desi Wilson	.05
491	Albert Belle Checklist	.05
492	Ken Griffey Jr. Checklist	.85
493	Andruw Jones Checklist	.40
494	Chipper Jones Checklist	.60
495	Mark McGwire Checklist	1.00
496	Paul Molitor Checklist	.45
497	Mike Piazza Checklist	.85
498	Cal Ripken Jr. Checklist	1.25
499	Alex Rodriguez Checklist	1.00
500	Frank Thomas Checklist	.45
501	Kenny Lofton	.05
502	Carlos Perez	.05
503	Tim Raines	.05
504	*Danny Patterson*	.05
505	Derrick May	.05
506	Dave Hollins	.05
507	Felipe Crespo	.05
508	Brian Banks	.05
509	Jeff Kent	.05
510	*Bubba Trammell*	.25
511	Robert Person	.05
512	*David Arias* (Ortiz)	30.00
513	Ryan Jones	.05
514	David Justice	.05
515	Will Cunnane	.05
516	Russ Johnson	.05
517	John Burkett	.05
518	*Robinson Checo*	.05
519	*Ricardo Rincon*	.05
520	Woody Williams	.05
521	Rick Helling	.05
522	Jorge Posada	.05
523	Kevin Orie	.05
524	*Fernando Tatis*	.15
525	Jermaine Dye	.05
526	Brian Hunter	.05
527	Greg McMichael	.05
528	Matt Wagner	.05
529	Richie Sexson	.05
530	Scott Ruffcorn	.05
531	Luis Gonzalez	.10
532	Mike Johnson	.05
533	Mark Petkovsek	.05
534	Doug Drabek	.05
535	Jose Canseco	.40
536	Bobby Bonilla	.05
537	J.T. Snow	.05
538	Shawon Dunston	.05
539	John Ericks	.05
540	Terry Steinbach	.05
541	Jay Bell	.05
542	Joe Borowski	.05
543	David Wells	.05
544	*Justin Towle*	.10
545	Mike Blowers	.05
546	Shannon Stewart	.05
547	Rudy Pemberton	.05
548	Bill Swift	.05
549	Osvaldo Fernandez	.05
550	Eddie Murray	1.00
551	Don Wengert	.05
552	Brad Ausmus	.05
553	Carlos Garcia	.05
554	Jose Guillen	.05
555	Rheal Cormier	.05
556	Doug Brocail	.05
557	Rex Hudler	.05
558	Armando Benitez	.05
559	Elieser Marrero	.05
560	*Ricky Ledee*	.25
561	Bartolo Colon	.05
562	Quilvio Veras	.05
563	Alex Fernandez	.05
564	Darren Dreifort	.05
565	Benji Gil	.05
566	Kent Mercker	.05
567	Glendon Rusch	.05
568	*Ramon Tatis*	.05
569	Roger Clemens	1.75
570	Mark Lewis	.05
571	*Emil Brown*	.05
572	Jaime Navarro	.05
573	Sherman Obando	.05
574	John Wasdin	.05
575	Calvin Maduro	.05
576	Todd Jones	.05
577	Orlando Merced	.05
578	Cal Eldred	.05
579	Mark Gubicza	.05
580	Michael Tucker	.05
581	*Tony Saunders*	.05
582	Garvin Alston	.05
583	Joe Roa	.05
584	*Brady Raggio*	.05
585	Jimmy Key	.05
586	*Marc Sagmoen*	.05
587	Jim Bullinger	.05
588	Yorkis Perez	.05
589	*Jose Cruz Jr.*	.75
590	Mike Stanton	.05
591	*Deivi Cruz*	.25
592	Steve Karsay	.05
593	Mike Trombley	.05
594	Doug Glanville	.05
595	Scott Sanders	.05
596	Thomas Howard	.05
597	T.J. Staton	.05
598	Garrett Stephenson	.05
599	Rico Brogna	.05
600	Albert Belle	.05
601	Jose Vizcaino	.05

602	Chili Davis	.05
603	Shane Mack	.05
604	Jim Eisenreich	.05
605	Todd Zeile	.05
606	Brian Boehringer	.05
607	Paul Shuey	.05
608	Kevin Tapani	.05
609	John Wetteland	.05
610	Jim Leyritz	.05
611	Ray Montgomery	.05
612	Doug Bochtler	.05
613	Wady Almonte	.05
614	Danny Tartabull	.05
615	Orlando Miller	.05
616	Bobby Ayala	.05
617	Tony Graffanino	.05
618	Marc Valdes	.05
619	Ron Villone	.05
620	Derrek Lee	.05
621	Greg Colbrunn	.05
622	*Felix Heredia*	.10
623	Carl Everett	.05
624	Mark Thompson	.05
625	Jeff Granger	.05
626	Damian Jackson	.05
627	Mark Leiter	.05
628	Chris Holt	.05
629	*Dario Veras*	.05
630	Dave Burba	.05
631	Darryl Hamilton	.05
632	Mark Acre	.05
633	Fernando Hernandez	.05
634	Terry Mulholland	.05
635	Dustin Hermanson	.05
636	Delino DeShields	.05
637	Steve Avery	.05
638	*Tony Womack*	.10
639	Mark Whiten	.05
640	Marquis Grissom	.05
641	Xavier Hernandez	.05
642	Eric Davis	.05
643	Bob Tewksbury	.05
644	Dante Powell	.05
645	Carlos Castillo	.05
646	Chris Widger	.05
647	Moises Alou	.05
648	Pat Listach	.05
649	Edgar Ramos	.05
650	Deion Sanders	.05
651	John Olerud	.05
652	Todd Dunwoody	.05
653	*Randall Simon*	.10
654	Dan Carlson	.05
655	Matt Williams	.05
656	Jeff King	.05
657	Luis Alicea	.05
658	Brian Moehler	.05
659	Ariel Prieto	.05
660	Kevin Elster	.05
661	Mark Hutton	.05
662	Aaron Sele	.05
663	Graeme Lloyd	.05
664	John Burke	.05
665	Mel Rojas	.05
666	Sid Fernandez	.05
667	Pedro Astacio	.05
668	Jeff Abbott	.05
669	Darren Daulton	.05
670	Mike Bordick	.05
671	Sterling Hitchcock	.05
672	Damion Easley	.05
673	Armando Reynoso	.05
674	Pat Cline	.05
675	*Orlando Cabrera*	.50
676	Alan Embree	.05
677	Brian Bevil	.05
678	David Weathers	.05
679	Cliff Floyd	.05
680	Joe Randa	.05
681	Bill Haselman	.05
682	Jeff Fassero	.05
683	Matt Morris	.05
684	Mark Portugal	.05
685	Lee Smith	.05
686	Pokey Reese	.05
687	Benito Santiago	.05
688	Brian Johnson	.05
689	*Brent Brede*	.05
690	Shigetosi Hasegawa	.05
691	Julio Santana	.05
692	Steve Kline	.05
693	Julian Tavarez	.05
694	John Hudek	.05
695	Manny Alexander	.05
696	Roberto Alomar (Encore)	.10
697	Jeff Bagwell (Encore)	.45
698	Barry Bonds (Encore)	1.25
699	Ken Caminiti (Encore)	.05
700	Juan Gonzalez (Encore)	.35
701	Ken Griffey Jr. (Encore)	.85
702	Tony Gwynn (Encore)	.60
703	Derek Jeter (Encore)	1.25
704	Andruw Jones (Encore)	.45
705	Chipper Jones (Encore)	.60
706	Barry Larkin (Encore)	.05
707	Greg Maddux (Encore)	.60
708	Mark McGwire (Encore)	1.00
709	Paul Molitor (Encore)	.45
710	Hideo Nomo (Encore)	.35
711	Andy Pettitte (Encore)	.30
712	Mike Piazza (Encore)	.85
713	Manny Ramirez (Encore)	.45
714	Cal Ripken Jr. (Encore)	1.25
715	Alex Rodriguez (Encore)	1.00
716	Ryne Sandberg (Encore)	.60
717	John Smoltz (Encore)	.05
718	Frank Thomas (Encore)	.50
719	Mo Vaughn (Encore)	.05
720	Bernie Williams (Encore)	.10
721	Tim Salmon Checklist	.05
722	Greg Maddux Checklist	.60
723	Cal Ripken Jr. Checklist	1.25
724	Mo Vaughn Checklist	.05
725	Ryne Sandberg Checklist	.45
726	Frank Thomas Checklist	.50
727	Barry Larkin Checklist	.05
728	Manny Ramirez Checklist	.45
729	Andres Galarraga Checklist	.05
730	Tony Clark Checklist	.05
731	Gary Sheffield Checklist	.20
732	Jeff Bagwell Checklist	.40
733	Kevin Appier Checklist	.05
734	Mike Piazza Checklist	.85
735	Jeff Cirillo Checklist	.05
736	Paul Molitor Checklist	.40
737	Henry Rodriguez Checklist	.05
738	Todd Hundley Checklist	.05
739	Derek Jeter Checklist	1.25
740	Mark McGwire Checklist	1.00
741	Curt Schilling Checklist	.15
742	Jason Kendall Checklist	.05
743	Tony Gwynn Checklist	.60
744	Barry Bonds Checklist	1.25
745	Ken Griffey Jr. Checklist	.85
746	Brian Jordan Checklist	.05
747	Juan Gonzalez Checklist	.40
748	Joe Carter Checklist	.05
749	Arizona Diamondbacks	.05
750	Tampa Bay Devil Rays	.05
751	*Hideki Irabu*	.15
752	*Jeremi Gonzalez*	.15
753	*Mario Valdez*	.05
754	Aaron Boone	.05
755	Brett Tomko	.05
756	*Jaret Wright*	1.00
757	Ryan McGuire	.05
758	Jason McDonald	.05
759	*Adrian Brown*	.05
760	*Keith Foulke*	.25
761	Checklist	.05

Tiffany

	NM/M
Complete Set (761):	500.00
Common Player:	1.00
Stars/Rcs:	8X

(See 1997 Fleer for checklist and base card values.)

512	David Arias (Ortiz)	140.00

Bleacher Blasters

		NM/M
Complete Set (10):		40.00
Common Player:		1.50
1	Albert Belle	1.50
2	Barry Bonds	10.00
3	Juan Gonzalez	2.00
4	Ken Griffey Jr.	6.00
5	Mark McGwire	8.00
6	Mike Piazza	6.00
7	Alex Rodriguez	8.00
8	Frank Thomas	4.00
9	Mo Vaughn	1.50
10	Matt Williams	1.50

Decade of Excellence

		NM/M
Complete Set (12):		35.00
Common Player:		1.50
Rare Tradition:		12X
1	Wade Boggs	4.50
2	Barry Bonds	9.00
3	Roger Clemens	6.00
4	Tony Gwynn	4.50
5	Rickey Henderson	3.00
6	Greg Maddux	4.50
7	Mark McGwire	6.00
8	Paul Molitor	3.00
9	Eddie Murray	3.00
10	Cal Ripken Jr.	9.00
11	Ryne Sandberg	4.50
12	Matt Williams	1.50

Diamond Tribute

		NM/M
Complete Set (12):		120.00
Common Player:		3.00
1	Albert Belle	3.00
2	Barry Bonds	20.00
3	Juan Gonzalez	5.00
4	Ken Griffey Jr.	12.50
5	Tony Gwynn	10.00
6	Greg Maddux	10.00
7	Mark McGwire	15.00
8	Eddie Murray	8.00
9	Mike Piazza	12.50
10	Cal Ripken Jr.	20.00
11	Alex Rodriguez	15.00
12	Frank Thomas	8.00

Golden Memories

		NM/M
Complete Set (10):		6.00
Common Player:		.25
1	Barry Bonds	2.00
2	Dwight Gooden	.25
3	Todd Hundley	.25
4	Mark McGwire	1.50
5	Paul Molitor	.75
6	Eddie Murray	.75
7	Hideo Nomo	.50
8	Mike Piazza	1.25
9	Cal Ripken Jr.	2.00
10	Ozzie Smith	1.00

Goudey Greats

		NM/M
Complete Set (15):		20.00
Common Player:		.50
Foils:		15X
1	Barry Bonds	4.00
2	Ken Griffey Jr.	3.00
3	Tony Gwynn	2.00
4	Derek Jeter	4.00
5	Chipper Jones	2.00

6	Kenny Lofton	.50
7	Greg Maddux	2.00
8	Mark McGwire	3.50
9	Eddie Murray	1.50
10	Mike Piazza	3.00
11	Cal Ripken Jr.	4.00
12	Alex Rodriguez	3.50
13	Ryne Sandberg	2.00
14	Frank Thomas	1.50
15	Mo Vaughn	.50

Headliners

		NM/M
Complete Set (20):		5.00
Common Player:		.10
1	Jeff Bagwell	.25
2	Albert Belle	.10
3	Barry Bonds	1.00
4	Ken Caminiti	.10
5	Juan Gonzalez	.20
6	Ken Griffey Jr.	.60
7	Tony Gwynn	.40
8	Derek Jeter	1.00
9	Andruw Jones	.25
10	Chipper Jones	.40
11	Greg Maddux	.40
12	Mark McGwire	.75
13	Paul Molitor	.25
14	Eddie Murray	.25
15	Mike Piazza	.60
16	Cal Ripken Jr.	1.00
17	Alex Rodriguez	.75
18	Ryne Sandberg	.40
19	John Smoltz	.20
20	Frank Thomas	.25

Lumber Company

		NM/M
Complete Set (18):		45.00
Common Player:		1.00
1	Brady Anderson	1.00
2	Jeff Bagwell	3.00
3	Albert Belle	1.00
4	Barry Bonds	8.00
5	Jay Buhner	1.00
6	Ellis Burks	1.00
7	Andres Galarraga	1.00
8	Juan Gonzalez	2.00
9	Ken Griffey Jr.	5.00
10	Todd Hundley	1.00
11	Ryan Klesko	1.00
12	Mark McGwire	6.00
13	Mike Piazza	5.00
14	Alex Rodriguez	6.00
15	Gary Sheffield	2.00
16	Sammy Sosa	4.00
17	Frank Thomas	3.00
18	Mo Vaughn	1.00

Night & Day

		NM/M
Complete Set (10):		45.00
Common Player:		1.00
1	Barry Bonds	12.00
2	Ellis Burks	1.00
3	Juan Gonzalez	2.00
4	Ken Griffey Jr.	6.00
5	Mark McGwire	7.50
6	Mike Piazza	6.00
7	Manny Ramirez	4.00

8	Alex Rodriguez	8.00
9	John Smoltz	2.00
10	Frank Thomas	4.00

Soaring Stars

		NM/M
Complete Set (12):		10.00
Common Player:		.25
Glowing:		6X
1	Albert Belle	.25
2	Barry Bonds	2.00
3	Juan Gonzalez	.50
4	Ken Griffey Jr.	1.25
5	Derek Jeter	2.00
6	Andruw Jones	.60
7	Chipper Jones	1.00
8	Greg Maddux	1.00
9	Mark McGwire	1.50
10	Mike Piazza	1.25
11	Alex Rodriguez	1.50
12	Frank Thomas	.75

Team Leaders

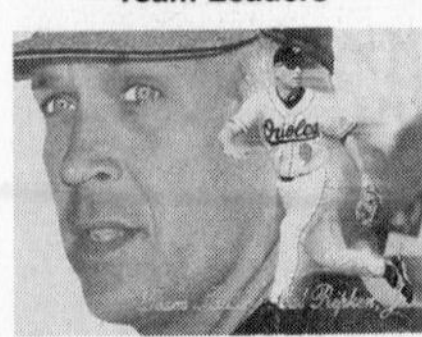

		NM/M
Complete Set (28):		25.00
Common Player:		.25
1	Cal Ripken Jr.	5.00
2	Mo Vaughn	.25
3	Jim Edmonds	.40
4	Frank Thomas	1.50
5	Albert Belle	.25
6	Bob Higginson	.25
7	Kevin Appier	.25
8	John Jaha	.25
9	Paul Molitor	1.50
10	Andy Pettitte	.65
11	Mark McGwire	4.00
12	Ken Griffey Jr.	3.00
13	Juan Gonzalez	.75
14	Pat Hentgen	.25
15	Chipper Jones	2.00
16	Mark Grace	.35
17	Barry Larkin	.25
18	Ellis Burks	.25
19	Gary Sheffield	.60
20	Jeff Bagwell	1.50
21	Mike Piazza	3.00
22	Henry Rodriguez	.25
23	Todd Hundley	.25
24	Curt Schilling	.60
25	Jeff King	.25
26	Brian Jordan	.25
27	Tony Gwynn	1.50
28	Barry Bonds	5.00

Zone

		NM/M
Complete Set (20):		80.00
Common Player:		1.50
1	Jeff Bagwell	5.00
2	Albert Belle	1.50
3	Barry Bonds	15.00
4	Ken Caminiti	1.50
5	Andres Galarraga	1.50
6	Juan Gonzalez	2.50
7	Ken Griffey Jr.	8.00
8	Tony Gwynn	6.00
9	Chipper Jones	6.00
10	Greg Maddux	6.00
11	Mark McGwire	10.00
12	Dean Palmer	1.50
13	Andy Petitte	3.00
14	Mike Piazza	8.00
15	Alex Rodriguez	12.00
16	Gary Sheffield	2.50
17	John Smoltz	2.50
18	Frank Thomas	5.00
19	Jim Thome	4.00
20	Matt Williams	1.50

1998 FLEER

		NM/M
Complete Set (600):		65.00
Complete Series 1 (350):		37.50
Complete Series 2 (250):		27.50
Common Player:		.05
Series 1 or 2 Pack (10):		1.00
Series 1 or 2 Wax Box (36):		20.00
1	Ken Griffey Jr.	1.50
2	Derek Jeter	2.50
3	Gerald Williams	.05
4	Carlos Delgado	.50
5	Nomar Garciaparra	1.50
6	Gary Sheffield	.30
7	Jeff King	.05
8	Cal Ripken Jr.	2.50
9	Matt Williams	.05
10	Chipper Jones	1.00
11	Chuck Knoblauch	.05
12	Mark Grudzielanek	.05
13	Edgardo Alfonzo	.05
14	Andres Galarraga	.05
15	Tim Salmon	.15
16	Reggie Sanders	.05
17	Tony Clark	.05
18	Jason Kendall	.05
19	Juan Gonzalez	.65
20	Ben Grieve	.10
21	Roger Clemens	1.25
22	Raul Mondesi	.05
23	Robin Ventura	.05
24	Derrek Lee	.05
25	Mark McGwire	2.00
26	Luis Gonzalez	.10
27	Kevin Brown	.05
28	Kirk Rueter	.05
29	Bobby Estalella	.05
30	Shawn Green	.35
31	Greg Maddux	1.00
32	Jorge Velandia	.05
33	Larry Walker	.05
34	Joey Cora	.05
35	Frank Thomas	.85
36	*Curtis King*	.05
37	Aaron Boone	.05
38	Curt Schilling	.25
39	Bruce Aven	.05
40	Ben McDonald	.05
41	Andy Ashby	.05
42	Jason McDonald	.05
43	Eric Davis	.05
44	Mark Grace	.10
45	Pedro Martinez	.75
46	Lou Collier	.05
47	Chan Ho Park	.05
48	Shane Halter	.05
49	Brian Hunter	.05
50	Jeff Bagwell	.75
51	Bernie Williams	.10
52	J.T. Snow	.05
53	Todd Greene	.05
54	Shannon Stewart	.05
55	Darren Bragg	.05
56	Fernando Tatis	.05
57	Darryl Kile	.05
58	Chris Stynes	.05
59	Javier Valentin	.05
60	Brian McRae	.05
61	Tom Evans	.05
62	Randall Simon	.05
63	Darrin Fletcher	.05
64	Jaret Wright	.05
65	Luis Ordaz	.05
66	Jose Canseco	.40
67	Edgar Renteria	.05
68	Jay Buhner	.05
69	Paul Konerko	.10
70	Adrian Brown	.05
71	Chris Carpenter	.05
72	Mike Lieberthal	.05
73	Dean Palmer	.05
74	Jorge Fabregas	.05
75	Stan Javier	.05
76	Damion Easley	.05
77	David Cone	.05
78	Aaron Sele	.05
79	Antonio Alfonseca	.05
80	Bobby Jones	.05
81	David Justice	.05
82	Jeffrey Hammonds	.05
83	Doug Glanville	.05
84	Jason Dickson	.05
85	Brad Radke	.05
86	David Segui	.05
87	Greg Vaughn	.05
88	*Mike Cather*	.05
89	Alex Fernandez	.05
90	Billy Taylor	.05
91	Jason Schmidt	.05
92	*Mike DeJean*	.05
93	Domingo Cedeno	.05
94	Jeff Cirillo	.05
95	*Manny Aybar*	.10
96	Jaime Navarro	.05
97	Dennis Reyes	.05
98	Barry Larkin	.05
99	Troy O'Leary	.05
100	Alex Rodriguez	2.00
100p	Alex Rodriguez (overprinted "PROMOTIONAL SAMPLE")	2.00
101	Pat Hentgen	.05
102	Bubba Trammell	.05
103	Glendon Rusch	.05
104	Kenny Lofton	.05
105	Craig Biggio	.05
106	Kelvim Escobar	.05
107	Mark Kotsay	.05
108	Rondell White	.05
109	Darren Oliver	.05
110	Jim Thome	.65
111	Rich Becker	.05
112	Chad Curtis	.05
113	Dave Hollins	.05
114	Bill Mueller	.05
115	Antone Williamson	.05
116	Tony Womack	.05
117	Randy Myers	.05
118	Rico Brogna	.05
119	Pat Watkins	.05
120	Eli Marrero	.05
121	Jay Bell	.05
122	Kevin Tapani	.05
123	*Todd Erdos*	.10
124	Neifi Perez	.05
125	Todd Hundley	.05
126	Jeff Abbott	.05
127	Todd Zeile	.05
128	Travis Fryman	.05
129	Sandy Alomar	.05
130	Fred McGriff	.05
131	Richard Hidalgo	.05
132	Scott Spiezio	.05
133	John Valentin	.05
134	Quilvio Veras	.05
135	Mike Lansing	.05
136	Paul Molitor	.75
137	Randy Johnson	.75
138	Harold Baines	.05
139	Doug Jones	.05
140	Abraham Nunez	.05
141	Alan Benes	.05
142	Matt Perisho	.05
143	Chris Clemons	.05
144	Andy Pettitte	.30
145	Jason Giambi	.40
146	Moises Alou	.05
147	*Chad Fox*	.05
148	Felix Martinez	.05
149	*Carlos Mendoza*	.05
150	Scott Rolen	.65
151	*Jose Cabrera*	.05
152	Justin Thompson	.05
153	Ellis Burks	.05
154	Pokey Reese	.05
155	Bartolo Colon	.05
156	Ray Durham	.05
157	Ugueth Urbina	.05
158	Tom Goodwin	.05
159	*David Dellucci*	.25
160	Rod Beck	.05
161	Ramon Martinez	.05
162	Joe Carter	.05
163	Kevin Orie	.05
164	Trevor Hoffman	.05
165	Emil Brown	.05
166	Robb Nen	.05
167	Paul O'Neill	.05
168	Ryan Long	.05
169	Ray Lankford	.05
170	Ivan Rodriguez	.65
171	Rick Aguilera	.05
172	Deivi Cruz	.05
173	Ricky Bottalico	.05
174	Garret Anderson	.05
175	Jose Vizcaino	.05
176	Omar Vizquel	.05
177	Jeff Blauser	.05
178	Orlando Cabrera	.05
179	Russ Johnson	.05
180	Matt Stairs	.05
181	Will Cunnane	.05
182	Adam Riggs	.05
183	Matt Morris	.05
184	Mario Valdez	.05
185	Larry Sutton	.05
186	*Marc Pisciotta*	.05
187	Dan Wilson	.05
188	John Franco	.05
189	Darren Daulton	.05
190	Todd Helton	.75
191	Brady Anderson	.05
192	Ricardo Rincon	.05
193	Kevin Stocker	.05
194	Jose Valentin	.05
195	Ed Sprague	.05
196	Ryan McGuire	.05
197	*Scott Eyre*	.05
198	Steve Finley	.05
199	T.J. Mathews	.05
200	Mike Piazza	1.50
201	Mark Wohlers	.05
202	Brian Giles	.05
203	Eduardo Perez	.05
204	Shigetosi Hasegawa	.05
205	Mariano Rivera	.15
206	Jose Rosado	.05
207	Michael Coleman	.05
208	James Baldwin	.05
209	Russ Davis	.05
210	Billy Wagner	.05
211	Sammy Sosa	1.50
212	*Frank Catalanotto*	.15
213	Delino DeShields	.05
214	John Olerud	.05
215	Heath Murray	.05
216	Jose Vidro	.05
217	Jim Edmonds	.05
218	Shawon Dunston	.05
219	Homer Bush	.05
220	Midre Cummings	.05
221	Tony Saunders	.05
222	Jeromy Burnitz	.05
223	Enrique Wilson	.05
224	Chili Davis	.05
225	Jerry DiPoto	.05
226	Dante Powell	.05
227	Javier Lopez	.05
228	*Kevin Polcovich*	.10
229	Deion Sanders	.05
230	Jimmy Key	.05
231	Rusty Greer	.05
232	Reggie Jefferson	.05
233	Ron Coomer	.05

#	Player	NM/M
234	Bobby Higginson	.05
235	*Maggio Ordonez*	2.00
236	Miguel Tejada	.25
237	Rick Gorecki	.05
238	Charles Johnson	.05
239	Lance Johnson	.05
240	Derek Bell	.05
241	Will Clark	.10
242	Brady Raggio	.05
243	Orel Hershiser	.05
244	Vladimir Guerrero	.75
245	John LeRoy	.05
246	Shawn Estes	.05
247	Brett Tomko	.05
248	Dave Nilsson	.05
249	Edgar Martinez	.05
250	Tony Gwynn	1.00
251	Mark Bellhorn	.05
252	Jed Hansen	.05
253	Butch Huskey	.05
254	Eric Young	.05
255	Vinny Castilla	.05
256	Hideki Irabu	.05
257	Mike Cameron	.05
258	Juan Encarnacion	.05
259	Brian Rose	.05
260	Brad Ausmus	.05
261	Dan Serafini	.05
262	Willie Greene	.05
263	Troy Percival	.05
264	*Jeff Wallace*	.05
265	Richie Sexson	.05
266	Rafael Palmeiro	.65
267	Brad Fullmer	.05
268	Jeremi Gonzalez	.05
269	*Rob Stanifer*	.05
270	Mickey Morandini	.05
271	Andruw Jones	.75
272	Royce Clayton	.05
273	Takashi Kashiwada	.05
274	*Steve Woodard*	.10
275	Jose Cruz Jr.	.05
276	Keith Foulke	.05
277	Brad Rigby	.05
278	Tino Martinez	.05
279	Todd Jones	.05
280	John Wetteland	.05
281	Alex Gonzalez	.05
282	Ken Cloude	.05
283	Jose Guillen	.05
284	Danny Clyburn	.05
285	David Ortiz	.05
286	John Thomson	.05
287	Kevin Appier	.05
288	Ismael Valdes	.05
289	Gary DiSarcina	.05
290	Todd Dunwoody	.05
291	Wally Joyner	.05
292	Charles Nagy	.05
293	Jeff Shaw	.05
294	*Kevin Millwood*	1.00
295	*Rigo Beltran*	.05
296	Jeff Frye	.05
297	Oscar Henriquez	.05
298	Mike Thurman	.05
299	Garrett Stephenson	.05
300	Barry Bonds	2.50
301	Roger Clemens	.75
302	David Cone	.05
303	Hideki Irabu	.05
304	Randy Johnson	.40
305	Greg Maddux	.50
306	Pedro Martinez	.35
307	Mike Mussina	.25
308	Andy Pettitte	.15
309	Curt Schilling	.10
310	John Smoltz	.05
311	Roger Clemens	1.00
312	Jose Cruz Jr.	.25
313	Nomar Garciaparra	1.00
314	Ken Griffey Jr.	1.00
315	Tony Gwynn	.75
316	Hideki Irabu	.25
317	Randy Johnson	.60
318	Mark McGwire	1.50
319	Curt Schilling	.35
320	Larry Walker	.15
321	Jeff Bagwell	.60
322	Albert Belle	.15
323	Barry Bonds	1.50
324	Jay Buhner	.15
325	Tony Clark	.15
326	Jose Cruz Jr.	.15
327	Andres Galarraga	.15
328	Juan Gonzalez	.30
329	Ken Griffey Jr.	.85
330	Andruw Jones	.60
331	Tino Martinez	.15
332	Mark McGwire	1.00
333	Rafael Palmeiro	.50
334	Mike Piazza	.85
335	Manny Ramirez	.65
336	Alex Rodriguez	1.00
337	Frank Thomas	.65
338	Jim Thome	.65
339	Mo Vaughn	.15
340	Larry Walker	.15
341	Jose Cruz Jr. Checklist	.15
342	Ken Griffey Jr. Checklist	.65
343	Derek Jeter Checklist	1.00
344	Andruw Jones Checklist	.40
345	Chipper Jones Checklist	.50
346	Greg Maddux Checklist	.50
347	Mike Piazza Checklist	.65
348	Cal Ripken Jr. Checklist	1.00
349	Alex Rodriguez Checklist	.75
350	Frank Thomas Checklist	.45
351	Mo Vaughn	.05
352	Andres Galarraga	.05
353	Roberto Alomar	.10
354	Darin Erstad	.10
355	Albert Belle	.05
356	Matt Williams	.05
357	Darryl Kile	.05
358	Kenny Lofton	.05
359	Orel Hershiser	.05
360	Bob Abreu	.05
361	Chris Widger	.05
362	Glenallen Hill	.05
363	Chili Davis	.05
364	Kevin Brown	.05
365	Marquis Grissom	.05
366	Livan Hernandez	.05
367	Moises Alou	.05
368	Matt Lawton	.05
369	Rey Ordonez	.05
370	Kenny Rogers	.05
371	Lee Stevens	.05
372	Wade Boggs	1.00
373	Luis Gonzalez	.05
374	Jeff Conine	.05
375	Esteban Loaiza	.05
376	Jose Canseco	.40
377	Henry Rodriguez	.05
378	Dave Burba	.05
379	Todd Hollandsworth	.05
380	Ron Gant	.05
381	Pedro Martinez	.75
382	Ryan Klesko	.05
383	Derrek Lee	.05
384	Doug Glanville	.05
385	David Wells	.05
386	Ken Caminiti	.05
387	Damon Hollins	.05
388	Manny Ramirez	.75
389	Mike Mussina	.45
390	Jay Bell	.05
391	Mike Piazza	1.50
392	Mike Lansing	.05
393	Mike Hampton	.05
394	Geoff Jenkins	.05
395	Jimmy Haynes	.05
396	Scott Servais	.05
397	Kent Mercker	.05
398	Jeff Kent	.05
399	Kevin Elster	.05
400	*Masato Yoshii*	.50
401	Jose Vizcaino	.05
402	Javier Martinez	.05
403	David Segui	.05
404	Tony Saunders	.05
405	Karim Garcia	.05
406	Armando Benitez	.05
407	Joe Randa	.05
408	Vic Darensbourg	.05
409	Sean Casey	.20
410	Eric Milton	.05
411	Trey Moore	.05
412	Mike Stanley	.05
413	Tom Gordon	.05
414	Hal Morris	.05
415	Braden Looper	.05
416	Mike Kelly	.05
417	John Smoltz	.05
418	Roger Cedeno	.05
419	Al Leiter	.05
420	Chuck Knoblauch	.05
421	Felix Rodriguez	.05
422	Bip Roberts	.05
423	Ken Hill	.05
424	Jermaine Allensworth	.05
425	Esteban Yan	.05
426	Scott Karl	.05
427	Sean Berry	.05
428	Rafael Medina	.05
429	Javier Vazquez	.05
430	Rickey Henderson	.75
431	*Adam Butler*	.05
432	Todd Stottlemyre	.05
433	Yamil Benitez	.05
434	Sterling Hitchcock	.05
435	Paul Sorrento	.05
436	Bobby Ayala	.05
437	Tim Raines	.05
438	Chris Hoiles	.05
439	Rod Beck	.05
440	Donnie Sadler	.05
441	Charles Johnson	.05
442	Russ Ortiz	.05
443	Pedro Astacio	.05
444	Wilson Alvarez	.05
445	Mike Blowers	.05
446	Todd Zeile	.05
447	Mel Rojas	.05
448	F.P. Santangelo	.05
449	Dmitri Young	.05
450	Brian Anderson	.05
451	Cecil Fielder	.05
452	Roberto Hernandez	.05
453	Todd Walker	.05
454	Tyler Green	.05
455	Jorge Posada	.05
456	Geronimo Berroa	.05
457	Jose Silva	.05
458	Bobby Bonilla	.05
459	Walt Weiss	.05
460	Darren Dreifort	.05
461	B.J. Surhoff	.05
462	Quinton McCracken	.05
463	Derek Lowe	.05
464	Jorge Fabregas	.05
465	Joey Hamilton	.05
466	Brian Jordan	.05
467	Allen Watson	.05
468	John Jaha	.05
469	Heathcliff Slocumb	.05
470	Gregg Jefferies	.05
471	Scott Brosius	.05
472	Chad Ogea	.05
473	A.J. Hinch	.05
474	Bobby Smith	.05
475	Brian Moehler	.05
476	DaRond Stovall	.05
477	Kevin Young	.05
478	Jeff Suppan	.05
479	Marty Cordova	.05
480	*John Halama*	.25
481	Bubba Trammell	.05
482	Mike Caruso	.05
483	Eric Karros	.05
484	Jamey Wright	.05
485	Mike Sweeney	.05
486	Aaron Sele	.05
487	Cliff Floyd	.05
488	Jeff Brantley	.05
489	Jim Leyritz	.05
490	Denny Neagle	.05
491	Travis Fryman	.05
492	Carlos Baerga	.05
493	Eddie Taubensee	.05
494	Darryl Strawberry	.05
495	Brian Johnson	.05
496	Randy Myers	.05
497	Jeff Blauser	.05
498	Jason Wood	.05
499	*Rolando Arrojo*	.25
500	Johnny Damon	.05
501	Jose Mercedes	.05
502	Tony Batista	.05
503	Mike Piazza	1.50
504	Hideo Nomo	.65
505	Chris Gomez	.05
506	*Jesus Sanchez*	.05
507	Al Martin	.05
508	Brian Edmondson	.05
509	Joe Girardi	.05
510	Shayne Bennett	.05
511	Joe Carter	.05
512	Dave Mlicki	.05
513	*Rich Butler*	.10
514	Dennis Eckersley	.65
515	Travis Lee	.10
516	John Mabry	.05
517	Jose Mesa	.05
518	Phil Nevin	.05
519	Raul Casanova	.05
520	Mike Fetters	.05
521	Gary Sheffield	.30
522	Terry Steinbach	.05
523	Steve Trachsel	.05
524	Josh Booty	.05
525	Darryl Hamilton	.05
526	Mark McLemore	.05
527	Kevin Stocker	.05
528	Bret Boone	.05
529	Shane Andrews	.05
530	Robb Nen	.05
531	Carl Everett	.05
532	LaTroy Hawkins	.05
533	Fernando Vina	.05
534	Michael Tucker	.05
535	Mark Langston	.05
536	Mickey Mantle	2.00
537	Bernard Gilkey	.05
538	Francisco Cordova	.05
539	Mike Bordick	.05
540	Fred McGriff	.05
541	Cliff Politte	.05
542	Jason Varitek	.05
543	Shawon Dunston	.05
544	Brian Meadows	.05
545	Pat Meares	.05
546	Carlos Perez	.05
547	Desi Relaford	.05
548	Antonio Osuna	.05
549	Devon White	.05
550	Sean Runyan	.05
551	Mickey Morandini	.05
552	Dave Martinez	.05
553	Jeff Fassero	.05
554	*Ryan Jackson*	.05
555	Stan Javier	.05
556	Jaime Navarro	.05
557	Jose Offerman	.05
558	*Mike Lowell*	.50
559	Darrin Fletcher	.05
560	Mark Lewis	.05
561	Dante Bichette	.05
562	Chuck Finley	.05
563	Kerry Wood	.35
564	Andy Benes	.05
565	Freddy Garcia	.05
566	Tom Glavine	.25
567	Jon Nunnally	.05
568	Miguel Cairo	.05
569	Shane Reynolds	.05
570	Roberto Kelly	.05
571	Jose Cruz Jr. Checklist	.25
572	Ken Griffey Jr. Checklist	.65
573	Mark McGwire Checklist	.75
574	Cal Ripken Jr. Checklist	1.00
575	Frank Thomas Checklist	.45
576	Jeff Bagwell	1.00
577	Barry Bonds	3.00
578	Tony Clark	.25
579	Roger Clemens	2.00
580	Jose Cruz Jr.	.25
581	Nomar Garciaparra	1.50
582	Juan Gonzalez	1.00
583	Ben Grieve	.25
584	Ken Griffey Jr.	2.00
585	Tony Gwynn	1.50
586	Derek Jeter	3.00
587	Randy Johnson	1.00
588	Chipper Jones	1.50
589	Greg Maddux	1.50
590	Mark McGwire	2.50
591	Andy Pettitte	.45
592	Paul Molitor	1.00
593	Cal Ripken Jr.	3.00
594	Alex Rodriguez	2.50
595	Scott Rolen	.50
596	Curt Schilling	.50
597	Frank Thomas	1.25
598	Jim Thome	.75
599	Larry Walker	.25
600	Bernie Williams	.30

Decade of Excellence

	NM/M
Complete Set (12):	35.00
Common Player:	1.00
Inserted 1:72	
Rare Traditions:	3X
Inserted 1:720	
1 Roberto Alomar	1.50

2	Barry Bonds	8.00
3	Roger Clemens	5.00
4	David Cone	1.00
5	Andres Galarraga	1.00
6	Mark Grace	1.00
7	Tony Gwynn	4.00
8	Randy Johnson	3.00
9	Greg Maddux	4.00
10	Mark McGwire	6.00
11	Paul O'Neill	1.00
12	Cal Ripken Jr.	8.00

Diamond Standouts

		NM/M
Complete Set (20):		25.00
Common Player:		.50
1	Jeff Bagwell	1.00
2	Barry Bonds	4.00
3	Roger Clemens	2.00
4	Jose Cruz Jr.	.50
5	Andres Galarraga	.50
6	Nomar Garciaparra	2.00
7	Juan Gonzalez	.75
8	Ken Griffey Jr.	2.00
9	Derek Jeter	4.00
10	Randy Johnson	1.00
11	Chipper Jones	1.50
12	Kenny Lofton	.50
13	Greg Maddux	1.50
14	Pedro Martinez	1.00
15	Mark McGwire	3.00
16	Mike Piazza	2.00
17	Alex Rodriguez	3.00
18	Curt Schilling	.75
19	Frank Thomas	1.00
20	Larry Walker	.50

Diamond Tribute

		NM/M
Complete Set (10):		90.00
Common Player:		5.00
DT1	Jeff Bagwell	7.50
DT2	Roger Clemens	10.00
DT3	Nomar Garciaparra	10.00
DT4	Juan Gonzalez	5.00
DT5	Ken Griffey Jr.	12.00
DT6	Mark McGwire	15.00
DT7	Mike Piazza	12.00
DT8	Cal Ripken Jr.	20.00
DT9	Alex Rodriguez	15.00
DT10	Frank Thomas	7.50

In the Clutch

		NM/M
Complete Set (15):		25.00
Common Player:		.40
IC1	Jeff Bagwell	1.00
IC2	Barry Bonds	5.00
IC3	Roger Clemens	2.00
IC4	Jose Cruz Jr.	.40
IC5	Nomar Garciaparra	2.00
IC6	Juan Gonzalez	.75
IC7	Ken Griffey Jr.	2.50
IC8	Tony Gwynn	1.50
IC9	Derek Jeter	5.00
IC10	Chipper Jones	1.50
IC11	Greg Maddux	1.50
IC12	Mark McGwire	4.00
IC13	Mike Piazza	2.50
IC14	Frank Thomas	1.00
IC15	Larry Walker	.40

Lumber Company

		NM/M
Complete Set (15):		50.00
Common Player:		.70
Inserted 1:36 R		
1	Jeff Bagwell	2.50
2	Barry Bonds	8.00
3	Jose Cruz Jr.	.75
4	Nomar Garciaparra	4.00
5	Juan Gonzalez	1.50
6	Ken Griffey Jr.	5.00
7	Tony Gwynn	3.00
8	Chipper Jones	3.00
9	Tino Martinez	.75
10	Mark McGwire	6.00
11	Mike Piazza	5.00
12	Cal Ripken Jr.	8.00
13	Alex Rodriguez	6.00
14	Frank Thomas	2.50
15	Larry Walker	.75

Mickey Mantle Monumental Moments

		NM/M
Complete Set (10):		40.00
Common Card:		5.00
Inserted 1:68		
Gold (51 sets):		3X
1	Armed and Dangerous	5.00
2	Getting Ready in Spring Training	5.00
3	Mantle and Rizzuto Celebrate	5.00
4	Posed for Action	5.00
5	Signed, Sealed and Ready to Deliver	5.00
6	Triple Crown 1956 Season	5.00
7	Number 7 . . .	5.00
8	Mantle's Powerful Swing . . .	5.00
9	Old-Timers Day Introduction	5.00
10	Portrait of Determination	5.00

Promising Forecast

		NM/M
Complete Set (20):		7.00
Common Player:		.25
Inserted 1:12		
PF1	Rolando Arrojo	.25
PF2	Sean Casey	.40
PF3	Brad Fullmer	.25
PF4	Karim Garcia	.35
PF5	Ben Grieve	.25
PF6	Todd Helton	3.00
PF7	Richard Hidalgo	.25
PF8	A.J. Hinch	.25
PF9	Paul Konerko	.35
PF10	Mark Kotsay	.25
PF11	Derrek Lee	1.00
PF12	Travis Lee	.35
PF13	Eric Milton	.25
PF14	Magglio Ordonez	.50
PF15	David Ortiz	.50
PF16	Brian Rose	.25
PF17	Miguel Tejada	.40
PF18	Jason Varitek	.35
PF19	Enrique Wilson	.25
PF20	Kerry Wood	1.00

Rookie Sensations

		NM/M
Complete Set (20):		12.00
Common Player:		.50
Inserted 1:18		
1	Mike Cameron	.50
2	Jose Cruz Jr.	.50
3	Jason Dickson	.50
4	Kelvim Escobar	.50
5	Nomar Garciaparra	3.00
6	Ben Grieve	.50
7	Vladimir Guerrero	3.00
8	Wilton Guerrero	.50
9	Jose Guillen	.50
10	Todd Helton	2.00
11	Livan Hernandez	.50
12	Hideki Irabu	.50
13	Andruw Jones	3.00
14	Matt Morris	.50
15	Magglio Ordonez	1.00
16	Neifi Perez	.50
17	Scott Rolen	2.00
18	Fernando Tatis	.50
19	Brett Tomko	.50
20	Jaret Wright	.50

The Power Game

		NM/M
Complete Set (20):		30.00
Common Player:		.50
Inserted 1:36		
1	Jeff Bagwell	2.00
2	Albert Belle	.50
3	Barry Bonds	6.00
4	Tony Clark	.50
5	Roger Clemens	3.50
6	Jose Cruz Jr.	.50
7	Andres Galarraga	.50
8	Nomar Garciaparra	3.50
9	Juan Gonzalez	1.00
10	Ken Griffey Jr.	4.00
11	Randy Johnson	2.00
12	Greg Maddux	3.00
13	Pedro Martinez	2.00
14	Tino Martinez	.50
15	Mark McGwire	5.00
16	Mike Piazza	4.00
17	Curt Schilling	.75
18	Frank Thomas	2.00
19	Jim Thome	2.00
20	Larry Walker	.50

Vintage '63

		NM/M
Complete Set (126):		20.00
Complete Series 1 (63):		10.00
Complete Series 2 (63):		10.00
Common Player:		.10
1	Jason Dickson	.10
2	Tim Salmon	.25
3	Andruw Jones	.75
4	Chipper Jones	1.00
5	Kenny Lofton	.10
6	Greg Maddux	1.00
7	Rafael Palmeiro	.65
8	Cal Ripken Jr.	2.50
9	Nomar Garciaparra	1.25
10	Mark Grace	.10
11	Sammy Sosa	1.25
12	Frank Thomas	.75
13	Deion Sanders	.10
14	Sandy Alomar	.10
15	David Justice	.10
16	Jim Thome	.75
17	Matt Williams	.10
18	Jaret Wright	.10
19	Vinny Castilla	.10
20	Andres Galarraga	.10
21	Todd Helton	.75
22	Larry Walker	.10
23	Tony Clark	.10
24	Moises Alou	.10
25	Kevin Brown	.10
26	Charles Johnson	.10
27	Edgar Renteria	.10
28	Gary Sheffield	.50
29	Jeff Bagwell	.75
30	Craig Biggio	.10
31	Raul Mondesi	.10
32	Mike Piazza	1.50
33	Chuck Knoblauch	.10
34	Paul Molitor	.75
35	Vladimir Guerrero	.75
36	Pedro Martinez	.75
37	Todd Hundley	.10
38	Derek Jeter	2.50
39	Tino Martinez	.10
40	Paul O'Neill	.10
41	Andy Pettitte	.35
42	Mariano Rivera	.20
43	Bernie Williams	.20
44	Ben Grieve	.10
45	Scott Rolen	.65
46	Curt Schilling	.45
47	Jason Kendall	.10
48	Tony Womack	.10
49	Ray Lankford	.10
50	Mark McGwire	2.00
51	Matt Morris	.10
52	Tony Gwynn	1.00
53	Barry Bonds	2.50
54	Jay Buhner	.10
55	Ken Griffey Jr.	1.50
56	Randy Johnson	.75
57	Edgar Martinez	.10
58	Alex Rodriguez	2.00
59	Juan Gonzalez	.65
60	Rusty Greer	.10
61	Ivan Rodriguez	.65
62	Roger Clemens	1.25
63	Jose Cruz Jr.	.10
	Checklist #1-63	.10
64	Darin Erstad	.20
65	Jay Bell	.10
66	Andy Benes	.10
67	Mickey Mantle	2.00
68	Karim Garcia	.10
69	Travis Lee	.10
70	Matt Williams	.10
71	Andres Galarraga	.10
72	Tom Glavine	.35
73	Ryan Klesko	.10
74	Denny Neagle	.10
75	John Smoltz	.10
76	Roberto Alomar	.20
77	Joe Carter	.10
78	Mike Mussina	.50
79	B.J. Surhoff	.10
80	Dennis Eckersley	.65
81	Pedro Martinez	.75
82	Mo Vaughn	.10
83	Jeff Blauser	.10
84	Henry Rodriguez	.10
85	Albert Belle	.10
86	Sean Casey	.25
87	Travis Fryman	.10
88	Kenny Lofton	.10
89	Darryl Kile	.10
90	Mike Lansing	.10
91	Bobby Bonilla	.10
92	Cliff Floyd	.10
93	Livan Hernandez	.10
94	Derrek Lee	.10
95	Moises Alou	.10
96	Shane Reynolds	.10
97	Jeff Conine	.10
98	Johnny Damon	.35
99	Eric Karros	.10
100	Hideo Nomo	.65
101	Marquis Grissom	.10

102 Matt Lawton .10
103 Todd Walker .10
104 Gary Sheffield .50
105 Bernard Gilkey .10
106 Rey Ordonez .10
107 Chili Davis .10
108 Chuck Knoblauch .10
109 Charles Johnson .10
110 Rickey Henderson .75
111 Bob Abreu .10
112 Doug Glanville .10
113 Gregg Jefferies .10
114 Al Martin .10
115 Kevin Young .10
116 Ron Gant .10
117 Kevin Brown .10
118 Ken Caminiti .10
119 Joey Hamilton .10
120 Jeff Kent .10
121 Wade Boggs 1.00
122 Quinton McCracken .10
123 Fred McGriff .10
124 Paul Sorrento .10
125 Jose Canseco .50
126 Randy Myers .10
Checklist #64-126 .10

Vintage '63 Classic

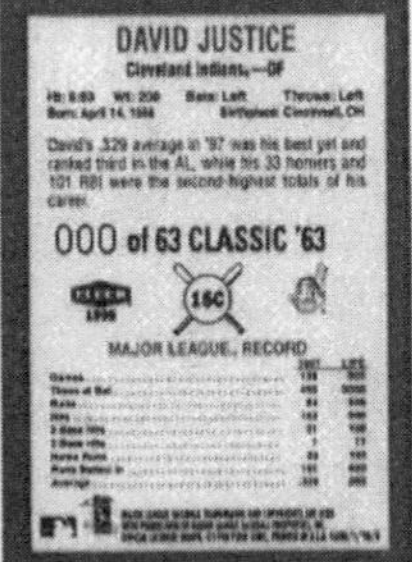

NM/M
Complete Set (128): 650.00
Common Player: 4.00
Stars/RCs: 20X
(See 1998 Fleer Vintage '63 for checklistand base card values.)

Zone

NM/M
Complete Set (15): 130.00
Common Player: 4.00
Inserted 1:288
1 Jeff Bagwell 7.50
2 Barry Bonds 25.00
3 Roger Clemens 10.00
4 Jose Cruz Jr. 4.00
5 Nomar Garciaparra 10.00
6 Juan Gonzalez 6.00
7 Ken Griffey Jr. 12.00
8 Tony Gwynn 9.00
9 Chipper Jones 9.00
10 Greg Maddux 9.00
11 Mark McGwire 15.00
12 Mike Piazza 12.00
13 Alex Rodriguez 20.00
14 Frank Thomas 7.50
15 Larry Walker 4.00

1998 FLEER UPDATE

NM/M
Complete Set (100): 12.50

Common Player: .05
U1 Mark McGwire .75
U2 Sammy Sosa .45
U3 Roger Clemens .45
U4 Barry Bonds 1.00
U5 Kerry Wood .20
U6 Paul Molitor .25
U7 Ken Griffey Jr. .50
U8 Cal Ripken Jr. 1.00
U9 David Wells .05
U10 Alex Rodriguez .75
U11 *Angel Pena* .25
U12 Bruce Chen .05
U13 Craig Wilson .05
U14 *Orlando Hernandez* 1.50
U15 Aramis Ramirez .10
U16 Aaron Boone .05
U17 Bob Henley .05
U18 Juan Guzman .05
U19 Darryl Hamilton .05
U20 Jay Payton .05
U21 *Jeremy Powell* .05
U22 Ben Davis .05
U23 Preston Wilson .10
U24 *Jim Parque* .15
U25 *Odalis Perez* .25
U26 Ron Belliard .05
U27 Royce Clayton .05
U28 George Lombard .05
U29 Tony Phillips .05
U30 *Fernando Seguignol* .15
U31 *Armando Rios* .10
U32 *Jerry Hairston Jr.* .25
U33 *Justin Baughman* .05
U34 Seth Greisinger .05
U35 Alex Gonzalez .05
U36 Michael Barrett .05
U37 Carlos Beltran .35
U38 Ellis Burks .05
U39 Jose Jimenez .05
U40 Carlos Guillen .05
U41 Marlon Anderson .05
U42 Scott Elarton .05
U43 Glenallen Hill .05
U44 Shane Monahan .05
U45 Dennis Martinez .05
U46 *Carlos Febles* .20
U47 Carlos Perez .05
U48 Wilton Guerrero .05
U49 Randy Johnson .45
U50 *Brian Simmons* .05
U51 Carlton Loewer .05
U52 *Mark DeRosa* .50
U53 *Tim Young* .05
U54 Gary Gaetti .05
U55 Eric Chavez .25
U56 Carl Pavano .15
U57 Mike Stanley .05
U58 Todd Stottlemyre .05
U59 *Gabe Kapler* .50
U60 *Mike Jerzembeck* .05
U61 *Mitch Meluskey* .15
U62 Bill Pulsipher .05
U63 Derrick Gibson .05
U64 *John Rocker* .75
U65 Calvin Pickering .05
U66 Blake Stein .05
U67 Fernando Tatis .05
U68 Gabe Alvarez .05
U69 Jeffrey Hammonds .05
U70 Adrian Beltre .25
U71 *Ryan Bradley* .10
U72 *Edgar Clemente* .05
U73 *Rick Croushore* .05
U74 Matt Clement .15
U75 Dermal Brown .05
U76 Paul Bako .05
U77 *Placido Polanco* .50
U78 Jay Tessmer .05
U79 Jarrod Washburn .05
U80 Kevin Witt .05
U81 Mike Metcalfe .05
U82 Daryle Ward .05
U83 *Benj Sampson* .05
U84 *Mike Kinkade* .20
U85 Randy Winn .05
U86 Jeff Shaw .05
U87 *Troy Glaus* 4.00
U88 Hideo Nomo .35
U89 Mark Grudzielanek .05
U90 *Mike Frank* .05
U91 *Bobby Howry* .10
U92 *Ryan Minor* .15
U93 *Corey Koskie* 1.00
U94 *Matt Anderson* .20
U95 Joe Carter .05
U96 Paul Konerko .15
U97 Sidney Ponson .05
U98 *Jeremy Giambi* .25
U99 *Jeff Kubenka* .05
U100 *J.D. Drew* 5.00

1999 FLEER

NM/M
Complete Set (600): 25.00
Common Player: .05
Warning Track: 2X
Inserted 1:1 R
Pack (10): 1.00
Wax Box (36): 25.00
1 Mark McGwire 2.00
2 Sammy Sosa 1.25
3 Ken Griffey Jr. 1.50
4 Kerry Wood .30
5 Derek Jeter 2.50
6 Stan Musial 2.00
7 J.D. Drew .65
7p J.D. Drew (overprinted "PROMOTIONAL SAMPLE") 1.50
8 Cal Ripken Jr. 2.50
9 Alex Rodriguez 2.00
10 Travis Lee .15
11 Andres Galarraga .05
12 Nomar Garciaparra 1.25
13 Albert Belle .05
14 Barry Larkin .05
15 Dante Bichette .05
16 Tony Clark .05
17 Moises Alou .05
18 Rafael Palmeiro .65
19 Raul Mondesi .05
20 Vladimir Guerrero .75
21 John Olerud .05
22 Bernie Williams .10
23 Ben Grieve .05
24 Scott Rolen .65
25 Jeromy Burnitz .05
26 Ken Caminiti .05
27 Barry Bonds 2.50
28 Todd Helton .75
29 Juan Gonzalez .65
30 Roger Clemens 1.25
31 Andruw Jones .75
32 Mo Vaughn .05
33 Larry Walker .05
34 Frank Thomas .75
35 Manny Ramirez .75
36 Randy Johnson .75
37 Vinny Castilla .05
38 Juan Encarnacion .05
39 Jeff Bagwell .75
40 Gary Sheffield .50
41 Mike Piazza 1.50
42 Richie Sexson .05
43 Tony Gwynn 1.00
44 Chipper Jones 1.00
45 Jim Thome .65
46 Craig Biggio .05
47 Carlos Delgado .40
48 Greg Vaughn .05
49 Greg Maddux 1.00
50 Troy Glaus .65
51 Roberto Alomar .10
52 Dennis Eckersley .60
53 Mike Caruso .05
54 Bruce Chen .05
55 Aaron Boone .05
56 Bartolo Colon .05
57 Derrick Gibson .05
58 Brian Anderson .05
59 Gabe Alvarez .05
60 Todd Dunwoody .05
61 Rod Beck .05
62 Derek Bell .05
63 Francisco Cordova .05
64 Johnny Damon .25
65 Adrian Beltre .15
66 Garret Anderson .05
67 Armando Benitez .05
68 Edgardo Alfonzo .05
69 Ryan Bradley .05
70 Eric Chavez .30
71 Bobby Abreu .05
72 Andy Ashby .05
73 Ellis Burks .05
74 Jeff Cirillo .05
75 Jay Buhner .05
76 Ron Gant .05
77 Rolando Arrojo .05
78 Will Clark .10
79 Chris Carpenter .05
80 Jim Edmonds .05
81 Tony Batista .05
82 Shane Andrews .05
83 Mark DeRosa .05
84 Brady Anderson .05
85 Tony Gordon .05
86 Brant Brown .05
87 Ray Durham .05
88 Ron Coomer .05
89 Bret Boone .05
90 Travis Fryman .05
91 Darryl Kile .05
92 Paul Bako .05
93 Cliff Floyd .05
94 Scott Elarton .05
95 Jeremy Giambi .05
96 Darren Dreifort .05
97 Marquis Grissom .05
98 Marty Cordova .05
99 Fernando Seguignol .05
100 Orlando Hernandez .05
101 Jose Cruz Jr. .05
102 Jason Giambi .60
103 Damion Easley .05
104 Freddy Garcia .05
105 Marlon Anderson .05
106 Kevin Brown .05
107 Joe Carter .05
108 Russ Davis .05
109 Brian Jordan .05
110 Wade Boggs 1.00
111 Tom Goodwin .05
112 Scott Brosius .05
113 Darin Erstad .10
114 Jay Bell .05
115 Tom Glavine .25
116 Pedro Martinez .75
117 Mark Grace .10
118 Russ Ortiz .05
119 Magglio Ordonez .10
120 Sean Casey .15
121 *Rafael Roque* .05
122 Brian Giles .05
123 Mike Lansing .05
124 David Cone .05
125 Alex Gonzalez .05
126 Carl Everett .05
127 Jeff King .05
128 Charles Johnson .05
129 Geoff Jenkins .05
130 Corey Koskie .05
131 Brad Fullmer .05
132 Al Leiter .05
133 Rickey Henderson .75
134 Rico Brogna .05
135 Jose Guillen .05
136 Matt Clement .05
137 Carlos Guillen .05
138 Orel Hershiser .05
139 Ray Lankford .05
140 Miguel Cairo .05
141 Chuck Finley .05
142 Rusty Greer .05
143 Kelvim Escobar .05
144 Ryan Klesko .05

No.	Player	Price
145	Andy Benes	.05
146	Eric Davis	.05
147	David Wells	.05
148	Trot Nixon	.05
149	Jose Hernandez	.05
150	Mark Johnson	.05
151	Mike Frank	.05
152	Joey Hamilton	.05
153	David Justice	.05
154	Mike Mussina	.40
155	Neifi Perez	.05
156	Luis Gonzalez	.10
157	Livan Hernandez	.05
158	Dermal Brown	.05
159	Jose Lima	.05
160	Eric Karros	.05
161	Ronnie Belliard	.05
162	Matt Lawton	.05
163	Dustin Hermanson	.05
164	Brian McRae	.05
165	Mike Kinkade	.05
166	A.J. Hinch	.05
167	Doug Glanville	.05
168	Hideo Nomo	.65
169	Jason Kendall	.05
170	Steve Finley	.05
171	Jeff Kent	.05
172	Ben Davis	.05
173	Edgar Martinez	.05
174	Eli Marrero	.05
175	Quinton McCracken	.05
176	Rick Helling	.05
177	Tom Evans	.05
178	Carl Pavano	.10
179	Todd Greene	.05
180	Omar Daal	.05
181	George Lombard	.05
182	Ryan Minor	.05
183	Troy O'Leary	.05
184	Robb Nen	.05
185	Mickey Morandini	.05
186	Robin Ventura	.05
187	Pete Harnisch	.05
188	Kenny Lofton	.05
189	Eric Milton	.05
190	Bobby Higginson	.05
191	Jamie Moyer	.05
192	Mark Kotsay	.05
193	Shane Reynolds	.05
194	Carlos Febles	.05
195	Jeff Kubenka	.05
196	Chuck Knoblauch	.05
197	Kenny Rogers	.05
198	Bill Mueller	.05
199	Shane Monahan	.05
200	Matt Morris	.05
201	Fred McGriff	.05
202	Ivan Rodriguez	.65
203	Kevin Witt	.05
204	Troy Percival	.05
205	David Dellucci	.05
206	Kevin Millwood	.05
207	Jerry Hairston Jr.	.05
208	Mike Stanley	.05
209	Henry Rodriguez	.05
210	Trevor Hoffman	.05
211	Craig Wilson	.05
212	Reggie Sanders	.05
213	Carlton Loewer	.05
214	Omar Vizquel	.05
215	Gabe Kapler	.05
216	Derrek Lee	.05
217	Billy Wagner	.05
218	Dean Palmer	.05
219	Chan Ho Park	.05
220	Fernando Vina	.05
221	Roy Halladay	.05
222	Paul Molitor	.75
223	Ugueth Urbina	.05
224	Rey Ordonez	.05
225	Ricky Ledee	.05
226	Scott Spiezio	.05
227	Wendell Magee Jr.	.05
228	Aramis Ramirez	.05
229	Brian Simmons	.05
230	Fernando Tatis	.05
231	Bobby Smith	.05
232	Aaron Sele	.05
233	Shawn Green	.20
234	Mariano Rivera	.15
235	Tim Salmon	.10
236	Andy Fox	.05
237	Denny Neagle	.05
238	John Valentin	.05
239	Kevin Tapani	.05
240	Paul Konerko	.10
241	Robert Fick	.05
242	Edgar Renteria	.05
243	Brett Tomko	.05
244	Daryle Ward	.05
245	Carlos Beltran	.30
246	Angel Pena	.05
247	Steve Woodard	.05
248	David Ortiz	.05
249	Justin Thompson	.05
250	Rondell White	.05
251	Jaret Wright	.05
252	Ed Sprague	.05
253	Jay Payton	.05
254	Mike Lowell	.05
255	Orlando Cabrera	.05
256	Jason Schmidt	.05
257	David Segui	.05
258	Paul Sorrento	.05
259	John Wetteland	.05
260	Devon White	.05
261	Odalis Perez	.05
262	Calvin Pickering	.05
263	Alex Ramirez	.05
264	Preston Wilson	.05
265	Brad Radke	.05
266	Walt Weiss	.05
267	Tim Young	.05
268	Tino Martinez	.05
269	Matt Stairs	.05
270	Curt Schilling	.25
271	Tony Womack	.05
272	Ismael Valdes	.05
273	Wally Joyner	.05
274	Armando Rios	.05
275	Andy Pettitte	.25
276	Bubba Trammell	.05
277	Todd Zeile	.05
278	Shannon Stewart	.05
279	Matt Williams	.05
280	John Rocker	.05
281	B.J. Surhoff	.05
282	Eric Young	.05
283	Dmitri Young	.05
284	John Smoltz	.05
285	Todd Walker	.05
286	Paul O'Neill	.05
287	Blake Stein	.05
288	Kevin Young	.05
289	Quilvio Veras	.05
290	Kirk Rueter	.05
291	Randy Winn	.05
292	Miguel Tejada	.05
293	J.T. Snow	.05
294	Michael Tucker	.05
295	Jay Tessmer	.05
296	Scott Erickson	.05
297	Tim Wakefield	.05
298	Jeff Abbott	.05
299	Eddie Taubensee	.05
300	Darryl Hamilton	.05
301	Kevin Orie	.05
302	Jose Offerman	.05
303	Scott Karl	.05
304	Chris Widger	.05
305	Todd Hundley	.05
306	Desi Relaford	.05
307	Sterling Hitchcock	.05
308	Delino DeShields	.05
309	Alex Gonzalez	.05
310	Justin Baughman	.05
311	Jamey Wright	.05
312	Wes Helms	.05
313	Dante Powell	.05
314	Jim Abbott	.05
315	Manny Alexander	.05
316	Harold Baines	.05
317	Danny Graves	.05
318	Sandy Alomar	.05
319	Pedro Astacio	.05
320	Jermaine Allensworth	.05
321	Matt Anderson	.05
322	Chad Curtis	.05
323	Antonio Osuna	.05
324	Brad Ausmus	.05
325	Steve Trachsel	.05
326	Mike Blowers	.05
327	Brian Bohanon	.05
328	Chris Gomez	.05
329	Valerio de los Santos	.05
330	Rich Aurilia	.05
331	Michael Barrett	.05
332	Rick Aguilera	.05
333	Adrian Brown	.05
334	Bill Spiers	.05
335	Matt Beech	.05
336	David Bell	.05
337	Juan Acevedo	.05
338	Jose Canseco	.50
339	Wilson Alvarez	.05
340	Luis Alicea	.05
341	Jason Dickson	.05
342	Mike Bordick	.05
343	Ben Ford	.05
344	Keith Lockhart	.05
345	Jason Christiansen	.05
346	Darren Bragg	.05
347	Doug Brocail	.05
348	Jeff Blauser	.05
349	James Baldwin	.05
350	Jeffrey Hammonds	.05
351	Ricky Bottalico	.05
352	Russ Branyon	.05
353	Mark Brownson	.05
354	Dave Berg	.05
355	Sean Bergman	.05
356	Jeff Conine	.05
357	Shayne Bennett	.05
358	Bobby Bonilla	.05
359	Bob Wickman	.05
360	Carlos Baerga	.05
361	Chris Fussell	.05
362	Chili Davis	.05
363	Jerry Spradlin	.05
364	Carlos Hernandez	.05
365	Roberto Hernandez	.05
366	Marvin Benard	.05
367	Ken Cloude	.05
368	Tony Fernandez	.05
369	John Burkett	.05
370	Gary DiSarcina	.05
371	Alan Benes	.05
372	Karim Garcia	.05
373	Carlos Perez	.05
374	Damon Buford	.05
375	Mark Clark	.05
376	*Edgard Clemente*	.05
377	Chad Bradford	.05
378	Frank Catalanotto	.05
379	Vic Darensbourg	.05
380	Sean Berry	.05
381	Dave Burba	.05
382	Sal Fasano	.05
383	Steve Parris	.05
384	Roger Cedeno	.05
385	Chad Fox	.05
386	Wilton Guerrero	.05
387	Dennis Cook	.05
388	Joe Girardi	.05
389	LaTroy Hawkins	.05
390	Ryan Christenson	.05
391	Paul Byrd	.05
392	Lou Collier	.05
393	Jeff Fassero	.05
394	Jim Leyritz	.05
395	Shawn Estes	.05
396	Mike Kelly	.05
397	Rich Croushore	.05
398	Royce Clayton	.05
399	Rudy Seanez	.05
400	Darrin Fletcher	.05
401	Shigetosi Hasegawa	.05
402	Bernard Gilkey	.05
403	Juan Guzman	.05
404	Jeff Frye	.05
405	Marino Santana	.05
406	Alex Fernandez	.05
407	Gary Gaetti	.05
408	Dan Miceli	.05
409	Mike Cameron	.05
410	Mike Remlinger	.05
411	Joey Cora	.05
412	Mark Gardner	.05
413	Aaron Ledesma	.05
414	Jerry Dipoto	.05
415	Ricky Gutierrez	.05
416	John Franco	.05
417	Mendy Lopez	.05
418	Hideki Irabu	.05
419	Mark Grudzielanek	.05
420	Bobby Hughes	.05
421	Pat Meares	.05
422	Jimmy Haynes	.05
423	Bob Henley	.05
424	Bobby Estalella	.05
425	Jon Lieber	.05
426	*Giomar Guevara*	.05
427	Jose Jimenez	.05
428	Deivi Cruz	.05
429	Jonathan Johnson	.05
430	Ken Hill	.05
431	Craig Grebeck	.05
432	Jose Rosado	.05
433	Danny Klassen	.05
434	Bobby Howry	.05
435	Gerald Williams	.05
436	Omar Olivares	.05
437	Chris Hoiles	.05
438	Seth Greisinger	.05
439	Scott Hatteberg	.05
440	Jeremi Gonzalez	.05
441	Wil Cordero	.05
442	Jeff Montgomery	.05
443	Chris Stynes	.05
444	Tony Saunders	.05
445	Einar Diaz	.05
446	Laril Gonzalez	.05
447	Ryan Jackson	.05
448	Mike Hampton	.05
449	Todd Hollandsworth	.05
450	Gabe White	.05
451	John Jaha	.05
452	Bret Saberhagen	.05
453	Otis Nixon	.05
454	Steve Kline	.05
455	Butch Huskey	.05
456	Mike Jerzembeck	.05
457	Wayne Gomes	.05
458	Mike Macfarlane	.05
459	Jesus Sanchez	.05
460	Al Martin	.05
461	Dwight Gooden	.05
462	Ruben Rivera	.05
463	Pat Hentgen	.05
464	Jose Valentin	.05
465	Vladimir Nunez	.05
466	Charlie Hayes	.05
467	Jay Powell	.05
468	Raul Ibanez	.05
469	Kent Mercker	.05
470	John Mabry	.05
471	Woody Williams	.05
472	Roberto Kelly	.05
473	Jim Mecir	.05
474	Dave Hollins	.05
475	Rafael Medina	.05
476	Darren Lewis	.05
477	Felix Heredia	.05
478	Brian Hunter	.05
479	Matt Mantei	.05
480	Richard Hidalgo	.05
481	Bobby Jones	.05
482	Hal Morris	.05
483	Ramiro Mendoza	.05
484	Matt Luke	.05
485	Esteban Loaiza	.05
486	Mark Loretta	.05
487	A.J. Pierzynski	.05
488	Charles Nagy	.05
489	Kevin Sefcik	.05
490	Jason McDonald	.05
491	Jeremy Powell	.05
492	Scott Servais	.05
493	Abraham Nunez	.05
494	Stan Spencer	.05
495	Stan Javier	.05
496	Jose Paniagua	.05
497	Gregg Jefferies	.05
498	Gregg Olson	.05
499	Derek Lowe	.05
500	Willis Otanez	.05
501	Brian Moehler	.05
502	Glenallen Hill	.05
503	Bobby Jones	.05
504	Greg Norton	.05
505	Mike Jackson	.05
506	Kirt Manwaring	.05
507	Eric Weaver	.05
508	Mitch Meluskey	.05
509	Todd Jones	.05
510	Mike Matheny	.05
511	Benj Sampson	.05
512	Tony Phillips	.05
513	Mike Thurman	.05
514	Jorge Posada	.05
515	Bill Taylor	.05
516	Mike Sweeney	.05
517	Jose Silva	.05
518	Mark Lewis	.05
519	Chris Peters	.05
520	Brian Johnson	.05
521	Mike Timlin	.05
522	Mark McLemore	.05
523	Dan Plesac	.05
524	Kelly Stinnett	.05
525	Sidney Ponson	.05
526	Jim Parque	.05
527	Tyler Houston	.05
528	John Thomson	.05
529	Mike Metcalfe	.05
530	Robert Person	.05
531	Marc Newfield	.05
532	Javier Vazquez	.05
533	Terry Steinbach	.05
534	Turk Wendell	.05
535	Tim Raines	.05
536	Brian Meadows	.05
537	Mike Lieberthal	.05
538	Ricardo Rincon	.05
539	Dan Wilson	.05
540	John Johnstone	.05

541	Todd Stottlemyre	.05
542	Kevin Stocker	.05
543	Ramon Martinez	.05
544	Mike Simms	.05
545	Paul Quantrill	.05
546	Matt Walbeck	.05
547	Turner Ward	.05
548	Bill Pulsipher	.05
549	Donnie Sadler	.05
550	Lance Johnson	.05
551	Bill Simas	.05
552	Jeff Reed	.05
553	Jeff Shaw	.05
554	Joe Randa	.05
555	Paul Shuey	.05
556	Mike Redmond	.05
557	Sean Runyan	.05
558	Enrique Wilson	.05
559	Scott Radinsky	.05
560	Larry Sutton	.05
561	Masato Yoshii	.05
562	David Nilsson	.05
563	Mike Trombley	.05
564	Darryl Strawberry	.05
565	Dave Mlicki	.05
566	Placido Polanco	.05
567	Yorkis Perez	.05
568	Esteban Yan	.05
569	Lee Stevens	.05
570	Steve Sinclair	.05
571	Jarrod Washburn	.05
572	Lenny Webster	.05
573	Mike Sirotka	.05
574	Jason Varitek	.05
575	Terry Mulholland	.05
576	Adrian Beltre	.10
577	Eric Chavez	.20
578	J.D. Drew	.35
579	Juan Encarnacion	.05
580	Nomar Garciaparra	.65
581	Troy Glaus	.35
582	Ben Grieve	.05
583	Vladimir Guerrero	.40
584	Todd Helton	.35
585	Derek Jeter	1.25
586	Travis Lee	.10
587	Alex Rodriguez	1.00
588	Scott Rolen	.30
589	Richie Sexson	.05
590	Kerry Wood	.20
591	Ken Griffey Jr.	.75
592	Chipper Jones	.50
593	Alex Rodriguez	1.00
594	Sammy Sosa	.65
595	Mark McGwire	1.00
596	Cal Ripken Jr.	1.25
597	Nomar Garciaparra	.65
598	Derek Jeter	1.25
599	Kerry Wood	.20
600	J.D. Drew	.40

Starting Nine

	NM/M
Common Player:	20.00

(Star and rookie cards valued at 200-250X base versions.)

Warning Track Collection

	NM/M
Complete Set (600):	160.00
Common Player:	.50
Stars:	2X

(See 1999 Fleer for checklist and base card values.)

Date With Destiny

	NM/M
Complete Set (10):	300.00

Common Player: 20.00
Production 100 sets

1	Barry Bonds	60.00
2	Roger Clemens	35.00
3	Ken Griffey Jr.	40.00
4	Tony Gwynn	30.00
5	Greg Maddux	30.00
6	Mark McGwire	50.00
7	Mike Piazza	40.00
8	Cal Ripken Jr.	60.00
9	Alex Rodriguez	50.00
10	Frank Thomas	20.00

Diamond Magic

	NM/M
Complete Set (15):	50.00
Common Player:	1.00

Inserted 1:96

1	Barry Bonds	9.00
2	Roger Clemens	4.50
3	Nomar Garciaparra	4.50
4	Ken Griffey Jr.	5.00
5	Tony Gwynn	3.75
6	Orlando Hernandez	1.00
7	Derek Jeter	9.00
8	Randy Johnson	3.00
9	Chipper Jones	3.75
10	Greg Maddux	3.75
11	Mark McGwire	6.00
12	Alex Rodriguez	7.50
13	Sammy Sosa	4.50
14	Bernie Williams	1.50
15	Kerry Wood	2.00

Going Yard

	NM/M
Complete Set (15):	4.00
Common Player:	.10

Inserted 1:18

1	Moises Alou	.10
2	Albert Belle	.10
3	Jose Canseco	.30
4	Vinny Castilla	.10
5	Andres Galarraga	.10
6	Juan Gonzalez	.20
7	Ken Griffey Jr.	.75
8	Chipper Jones	.50
9	Mark McGwire	1.00
10	Rafael Palmeiro	.35
11	Mike Piazza	.75
12	Alex Rodriguez	1.00
13	Sammy Sosa	.65
14	Greg Vaughn	.10
15	Mo Vaughn	.10

Golden Memories

	NM/M
Complete Set (15):	45.00
Common Player:	.75

Inserted 1:54

1	Albert Belle	.75
2	Barry Bonds	7.50
3	Roger Clemens	4.50
4	Nomar Garciaparra	4.50
5	Juan Gonzalez	1.50
6	Ken Griffey Jr.	3.75
7	Randy Johnson	2.75
8	Greg Maddux	3.25
9	Mark McGwire	5.00
10	Mike Piazza	3.75
11	Cal Ripken Jr.	7.50
12	Alex Rodriguez	6.00
13	Sammy Sosa	4.50
14	David Wells	.75
15	Kerry Wood	2.00

Rookie Flashback

	NM/M
Complete Set (15):	5.00
Common Player:	.25

Inserted 1:6

1	Matt Anderson	.25
2	Rolando Arrojo	.25
3	Adrian Beltre	.50
4	Mike Caruso	.25
5	Eric Chavez	.40
6	J.D. Drew	.75
7	Juan Encarnacion	.25
8	Brad Fullmer	.25
9	Troy Glaus	1.50
10	Ben Grieve	.25
11	Todd Helton	1.50
12	Orlando Hernandez	.25
13	Travis Lee	.40
14	Richie Sexson	.25
15	Kerry Wood	.65

Stan Musial Monumental Moments

	NM/M
Complete Set (10):	15.00
Common Musial:	2.00
Autographed Card:	60.00

1	Life in Donora	2.00
2	Values	2.00
3	In the Beginning	2.00
4	In the Navy	2.00
5	The 1948 Season (w/Red Schoendienst)	2.00
6	Success Stories (w/Pres. Kennedy)	2.00
7	Mr. Cardinal	2.00
8	Most Valuable Player	2.00
9	... baseball's perfect knight	2.00
10	Hall of Fame	2.00

Vintage '61

	NM/M
Complete Set (50):	7.50
Common Player:	.05

Inserted 1:1

1	Mark McGwire	.75
2	Sammy Sosa	.50
3	Ken Griffey Jr.	.60
4	Kerry Wood	.25
5	Derek Jeter	1.00
6	Stan Musial	.75
7	J.D. Drew	.30
8	Cal Ripken Jr.	1.00
9	Alex Rodriguez	.75
10	Travis Lee	.10
11	Andres Galarraga	.05
12	Nomar Garciaparra	.50
13	Albert Belle	.05
14	Barry Larkin	.05
15	Dante Bichette	.05
16	Tony Clark	.05
17	Moises Alou	.05
18	Rafael Palmeiro	.30
19	Raul Mondesi	.05
20	Vladimir Guerrero	.35
21	John Olerud	.05
22	Bernie Williams	.10
23	Ben Grieve	.05
24	Scott Rolen	.30
25	Jeromy Burnitz	.05
26	Ken Caminiti	.05
27	Barry Bonds	1.00
28	Todd Helton	.35
29	Juan Gonzalez	.25
30	Roger Clemens	.50
31	Andruw Jones	.35
32	Mo Vaughn	.05
33	Larry Walker	.05
34	Frank Thomas	.35
35	Manny Ramirez	.35
36	Randy Johnson	.35
37	Vinny Castilla	.05
38	Juan Encarnacion	.05
39	Jeff Bagwell	.35
40	Gary Sheffield	.25
41	Mike Piazza	.60
42	Richie Sexson	.05
43	Tony Gwynn	.45
44	Chipper Jones	.45
45	Jim Thome	.30
46	Craig Biggio	.05
47	Carlos Delgado	.25
48	Greg Vaughn	.05
49	Greg Maddux	.45
50	Troy Glaus	.35

1999 FLEER UPDATE

	NM/M
Complete Set (150):	22.50

Common Player: .10
1 *Rick Ankiel* .25
2 *Peter Bergeron* .25
3 *Pat Burrell* 1.50
4 *Eric Munson* .35
5 *Alfonso Soriano* 3.00
6 *Tim Hudson* 1.50
7 *Erubiel Durazo* .25
8 Chad Hermansen .10
9 Jeff Zimmerman .10
10 *Jesus Pena* .10
11 Ramon Hernandez .10
12 *Trent Durrington* .25
13 Tony Armas Jr. .10
14 *Mike Fyhrie* .10
15 *Danny Kolb* .25
16 *Mike Porzio* .10
17 *Will Brunson* .10
18 *Mike Duvall* .10
19 *Doug Mientkiewicz* .75
20 *Gabe Molina* .15
21 *Luis Vizcaino* .20
22 *Robinson Cancel* .10
23 *Brett Laxton* .10
24 *Joe McEwing* .25
25 *Justin Speier* .20
26 *Kip Wells* .25
27 *Armando Almanza* .10
28 *Joe Davenport* .10
29 *Yamid Haad* .10
30 John Halama .10
31 Adam Kennedy .10
32 *Vicente Padilla* .25
33 *Travis Dawkins* .25
34 *Ryan Rupe* .25
35 *B.J. Ryan* .10
36 *Chance Sanford* .10
37 *Anthony Shumaker* .10
38 *Ryan Glynn* .10
39 *Matt Herges* .20
40 Ben Molina .10
41 Scott Williamson .10
42 *Eric Gagne* 4.00
43 *John McDonald* .10
44 *Scott Sauerbeck* .10
45 *Mike Venafro* .10
46 *Edwards Guzman* .10
47 *Richard Barker* .10
48 Braden Looper .10
49 *Chad Meyers* .10
50 *Scott Strickland* .10
51 Billy Koch .10
52 *Dave Newhan* .10
53 *David Riske* .10
54 Jose Santiago .10
55 *Miguel Del Toro* .10
56 *Orber Moreno* .10
57 Dave Roberts .10
58 *Tim Byrdak* .10
59 *David Lee* .10
60 *Guillermo Mota* .15
61 *Wilton Veras* .15
62 *Joe Mays* .35
63 *Jose Fernandez* .10
64 *Ray King* .10
65 *Chris Petersen* .10
66 Vernon Wells .15
67 Ruben Mateo .10
68 Ben Petrick .10
69 *Chris Tremie* .10
70 Lance Berkman .10
71 Dan Smith .10
72 *Carlos Hernandez* .10
73 *Chad Harville* .25
74 Damaso Marte .10
75 *Aaron Myette* .15
76 *Willis Roberts* .10
77 *Erik Sabel* .10
78 *Hector Almonte* .10
79 Kris Benson .10
80 *Pat Daneker* .10
81 *Freddy Garcia* .50
82 *Byung-Hyun Kim* .25
83 *Wily Pena* 1.00
84 *Dan Wheeler* .15
85 *Tim Harikkala* .10
86 *Derrin Ebert* .10
87 *Horacio Estrada* .10
88 *Liu Rodriguez* .10
89 *Jordan Zimmerman* .10
90 *A.J. Burnett* .40
91 *Doug Davis* .10
92 *Robert Ramsey* .10
93 *Ryan Franklin* .10
94 *Charlie Greene* .10
95 *Bo Porter* .10
96 *Jorge Toca* .10
97 *Casey Blake* .20
98 *Amaury Garcia* .10
99 *Jose Molina* .10

100 *Melvin Mora* 1.00
101 *Joe Nathan* .10
102 *Juan Pena* .25
103 *Dave Borkowski* .10
104 *Eddie Gaillard* .10
105 Rob Radlosky .10
106 *Brett Hinchliffe* .10
107 Carlos Lee .10
108 *Rob Ryan* .10
109 *Jeff Weaver* .50
110 Ed Yarnall .10
111 *Nelson Cruz* .10
112 *Cleatus Davidson* .10
113 *Tim Kubinski* .10
114 *Sean Spencer* .10
115 *Joe Winkelsas* .10
116 *Chris Clapinski* .10
117 *Tom Davey* .10
118 Warren Morris .10
119 *Dan Murray* .10
120 *Jose Nieves* .10
121 *Mark Quinn* .10
122 *Josh Beckett* 6.00
123 *Chad Allen* .10
124 Mike Figga .10
125 *Beiker Graterol* .10
126 *Aaron Scheffer* .10
127 *Wiki Gonzalez* .10
128 Ramon E. Martinez .10
129 *Matt Riley* .25
130 *Chris Woodward* .10
131 Albert Belle .10
132 Roger Cedeno .10
133 Roger Clemens .75
134 Brian Giles .10
135 Rickey Henderson .60
136 Randy Johnson .60
137 Brian Jordan .10
138 Paul Konerko .15
139 Hideo Nomo .50
140 Kenny Rogers .10
141 Wade Boggs .65
142 Jose Canseco .45
143 Roger Clemens .75
144 David Cone .10
145 Tony Gwynn .65
146 Mark McGwire 1.00
147 Cal Ripken Jr. 1.50
148 Alex Rodriguez 1.00
149 Fernando Tatis .10
150 Robin Ventura .10

1999 FLEER BRILLIANTS

NM/M

Complete Set (175): 60.00
Common Player: .25
Common SP (126-175): .50
Blues (1:3): 1.5X
SP Blues (1:6) 1X
Golds: 8X
SP Golds: 3X
Production 99 sets
24 Karat Golds: 40X
SPs: 15X
Production 24 sets
Pack (5): 2.00
Wax Box (24): 32.50
1 Mark McGwire 2.50
2 Derek Jeter 3.00
3 Nomar Garciaparra 1.75
4 Travis Lee .25
5 Jeff Bagwell .75
6 Andres Galarraga .25
7 Pedro Martinez .75
8 Cal Ripken Jr. 3.00
9 Vladimir Guerrero .75
10 Chipper Jones 1.50
11 Rusty Greer .25
12 Omar Vizquel .25
13 Quinton McCracken .25
14 Jaret Wright .25
15 Mike Mussina .50
16 Jason Giambi .60
17 Tony Clark .25
18 Troy O'Leary .25
19 Troy Percival .25
20 Kerry Wood .50
21 Vinny Castilla .25
22 Chris Carpenter .25
23 Richie Sexson .25
24 Ken Griffey Jr. 2.00
25 Barry Bonds 3.00
26 Carlos Delgado .60
27 Frank Thomas .75
28 Manny Ramirez .75
29 Shawn Green .50
30 Mike Piazza 2.00
31 Tino Martinez .25
32 Dante Bichette .25
33 Scott Rolen .65
34 Gabe Alvarez .25
35 Raul Mondesi .25
36 Damion Easley .25
37 Jeff Kent .25
38 Al Leiter .25
39 Alex Rodriguez 2.50
40 Jeff King .25
41 Mark Grace .25
42 Larry Walker .25
43 Moises Alou .25
44 Juan Gonzalez .65
45 Rolando Arrojo .25
46 Tom Glavine .45
47 Johnny Damon .45
48 Livan Hernandez .25
49 Craig Biggio .25
50 Dmitri Young .25
51 Chan Ho Park .25
52 Todd Walker .25
53 Derrek Lee .25
54 Todd Helton .75
55 Ray Lankford .25
56 Jim Thome .65
57 Matt Lawton .25
58 Matt Anderson .25
59 Jose Offerman .25
60 Eric Karros .25
61 Orlando Hernandez .25
62 Ben Grieve .25
63 Bobby Abreu .25
64 Kevin Young .25
65 John Olerud .25
66 Sammy Sosa 1.75
67 Andy Ashby .25
68 Juan Encarnacion .25
69 Shane Reynolds .25
70 Bernie Williams .35
71 Mike Cameron .25
72 Troy Glaus .75
73 Gary Sheffield .60
74 Jeromy Burnitz .25
75 Mike Caruso .25
76 Chuck Knoblauch .25
77 Kenny Rogers .25
78 David Cone .25
79 Tony Gwynn 1.50
80 Aramis Ramirez .25
81 Paul O'Neill .25
82 Charles Nagy .25
83 Javy Lopez .25
84 Scott Erickson .25
85 Trevor Hoffman .25
86 Andruw Jones .75
87 Ray Durham .25
88 Jorge Posada .25
89 Edgar Martinez .25
90 Tim Salmon .35
91 Bobby Higginson .25
92 Adrian Beltre .45
93 Jason Kendall .25
94 Henry Rodriguez .25
95 Greg Maddux 1.50
96 David Justice .25
97 Ivan Rodriguez .65
98 Curt Schilling .45
99 Matt Williams .25
100 Darin Erstad .50
101 Rafael Palmeiro .65
102 David Wells .25
103 Barry Larkin .25
104 Robin Ventura .25
105 Edgar Renteria .25
106 Andy Pettitte .50
107 Albert Belle .25
108 Steve Finley .25
109 Fernando Vina .25
110 Rondell White .25
111 Kevin Brown .25
112 Jose Canseco .50
113 Roger Clemens 1.75
114 Todd Hundley .25
115 Will Clark .35
116 Jim Edmonds .25
117 Randy Johnson .75
118 Denny Neagle .25
119 Brian Jordan .25
120 Dean Palmer .25
121 Roberto Alomar .45
122 Ken Caminiti .25
123 Brian Giles .25
124 Todd Stottlemyre .25
125 Mo Vaughn .25
126 J.D. Drew 1.00
127 Ryan Minor .50
128 Gabe Kapler .50
129 Jeremy Giambi .50
130 Eric Chavez 1.00
131 Ben Davis .50
132 Rob Fick .50
133 George Lombard .50
134 Calvin Pickering .50
135 Preston Wilson .50
136 Corey Koskie .75
137 Russell Branyan .50
138 Bruce Chen .50
139 Matt Clement .75
140 *Pat Burrell* 2.50
141 *Freddy Garcia* 1.00
142 Brian Simmons .50
143 Carlos Febles .50
144 Carlos Guillen .50
145 Fernando Seguignol .50
146 Carlos Beltran 1.00
147 Edgard Clemente .50
148 Mitch Meluskey .50
149 Ryan Bradley .50
150 Marlon Anderson .50
151 *A.J. Burnett* 1.00
152 *Scott Hunter* .50
153 Mark Johnson .50
154 Angel Pena .50
155 Roy Halladay .75
156 *Chad Allen* .50
157 Trot Nixon .75
158 Ricky Ledee .50
159 *Gary Bennett* .50
160 *Micah Bowie* .60
161 Doug Mientkiewicz .60
162 Danny Klassen .50
163 Willis Otanez .50
164 Jin Ho Cho .50
165 Mike Lowell .60
166 Armando Rios .50
167 Tom Evans .50
168 Michael Barrett .50
169 Alex Gonzalez .50
170 *Masao Kida* .60
171 *Peter Tucci* .50
172 Luis Saturria .50
173 Kris Benson .50
174 *Mario Encarnacion* .50
175 *Roosevelt Brown* .50

Illuminators

NM/M

Complete Set (15): 10.00
Common Player: .75
Inserted 1:10
1 Kerry Wood 2.00
2 Ben Grieve .75
3 J.D. Drew 1.50
4 Juan Encarnacion .75
5 Travis Lee .75
6 Todd Helton 3.00
7 Troy Glaus 2.00
8 Ricky Ledee .75
9 Eric Chavez 1.50

10 Ben Davis .75
11 George Lombard .75
12 Jeremy Giambi .75
13 Richie Sexson .75
14 Corey Koskie .75
15 Russell Branyan .75

Shining Stars

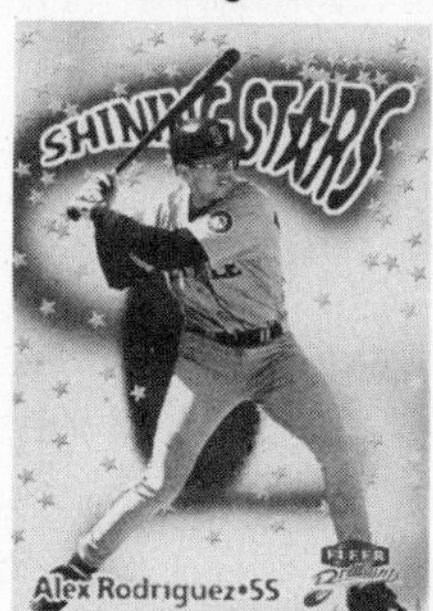

	NM/M
Complete Set (15):	30.00
Common Player:	1.50
Inserted 1:20	
Pulsars:	4X
Inserted 1:400	

1 Ken Griffey Jr. 2.50
2 Mark McGwire 3.00
3 Sammy Sosa 2.25
4 Derek Jeter 4.00
5 Nomar Garciaparra 2.25
6 Alex Rodriguez 3.00
7 Mike Piazza 2.50
8 Juan Gonzalez 1.50
9 Chipper Jones 2.00
10 Cal Ripken Jr. 4.00
11 Frank Thomas 1.50
12 Greg Maddux 2.00
13 Roger Clemens 2.25
14 Vladimir Guerrero 1.50
15 Manny Ramirez 1.50

1999 FLEER MYSTIQUE

	NM/M
Complete Set (160):	125.00
Common Player:	.20
Common SP (1-100):	.75
Common (101-150):	1.00
Production 2,999 sets	
Common (151-160):	2.00
Production 2,500 sets	
Pack (4):	3.00
Wax Box (24):	60.00

1 Ken Griffey Jr. (SP) 2.50
2 Livan Hernandez .20
3 Jeff Kent .20
4 Brian Jordan .20
5 Kevin Young .20
6 Vinny Castilla .20
7 Orlando Hernandez (SP) .75
8 Bobby Abreu .20
9 Vladimir Guerrero (SP) 1.50
10 Chuck Knoblauch .20
11 Nomar Garciaparra (SP) 2.25
12 Jeff Bagwell 1.00
13 Todd Walker .20
14 Johnny Damon .45
15 Mike Caruso .20
16 Cliff Floyd .20
17 Andy Pettitte .35
18 Cal Ripken Jr. (SP) 4.00
19 Brian Giles .20
20 Robin Ventura .20
21 Alex Gonzalez .20
22 Randy Johnson .75
23 Raul Mondesi .20
24 Ken Caminiti .20
25 Tom Glavine .40
26 Derek Jeter (SP) 4.00
27 Carlos Delgado .50
28 Adrian Beltre .35
29 Tino Martinez .20
30 Todd Helton 1.00
31 Juan Gonzalez (SP) 1.25
32 Henry Rodriguez .20
33 Jim Thome .65
34 Paul O'Neill .20
35 Scott Rolen (SP) 1.25
36 Rafael Palmeiro .65
37 Will Clark .25
38 Todd Hundley .20
39 Andruw Jones (SP) 1.50
40 Luis Rolando Arrojo .20
41 Barry Larkin .20
42 Tim Salmon .25
43 Rondell White .20
44 Curt Schilling .40
45 Chipper Jones (SP) 2.00
46 Jeromy Burnitz .20
47 Mo Vaughn .20
48 Tony Clark .20
49 Fernando Tatis .20
50 Dmitri Young .20
51 Wade Boggs 1.50
52 Rickey Henderson .75
53 Manny Ramirez (SP) 1.50
54 Edgar Martinez .20
55 Jason Giambi .65
56 Jason Kendall .20
57 Eric Karros .20
58 Jose Canseco (SP) 1.00
59 Shawn Green .40
60 Ellis Burks .20
61 Derek Bell .20
62 Shannon Stewart .20
63 Roger Clemens (SP) 2.25
64 Sean Casey (SP) .75
65 Jose Offerman .20
66 Sammy Sosa (SP) 2.25
67 Frank Thomas (SP) 1.50
68 Tony Gwynn (SP) 2.00
69 Roberto Alomar .35
70 Mark McGwire (SP) 3.00
71 Troy Glaus 1.00
72 Ray Durham .20
73 Jeff Cirillo .20
74 Alex Rodriguez (SP) 3.00
75 Jose Cruz Jr. .20
76 Juan Encarnacion .20
77 Mark Grace .20
78 Barry Bonds (SP) 4.00
79 Ivan Rodriguez (SP) 1.25
80 Greg Vaughn .20
81 Greg Maddux (SP) 2.00
82 Albert Belle .20
83 John Olerud .20
84 Kenny Lofton .20
85 Bernie Williams .30
86 Matt Williams .20
87 Ray Lankford .20
88 Darin Erstad .40
89 Ben Grieve .20
90 Craig Biggio .20
91 Dean Palmer .20
92 Reggie Sanders .20
93 Dante Bichette .20
94 Pedro Martinez (SP) 1.50
95 Larry Walker .20
96 David Wells .20
97 Travis Lee (SP) .75
98 Mike Piazza (SP) 2.50
99 Mike Mussina .45
100 Kevin Brown .20
101 Ruben Mateo 1.00
102 Roberto Ramirez 1.00
103 *Glen Barker* 1.00
104 *Clay Bellinger* 1.00
105 Carlos Guillen 1.00
106 Scott Schoeneweis 1.00
107 Creighton Gubanich 1.00
108 Scott Williamson 1.00
109 *Edwards Guzman* 1.00
110 *A.J. Burnett* 4.00
111 Jeremy Giambi 1.00
112 Trot Nixon 1.50
113 J.D. Drew 3.00
114 Roy Halladay 1.50
115 *Jose Macias* 2.00
116 Corey Koskie 2.00
117 *Ryan Rupe* 1.50
118 Scott Hunter 1.00
119 Rob Fick 1.00
120 McKay Christensen 1.50
121 Carlos Febles 2.00
122 Gabe Kapler 1.50
123 Jeff Liefer 1.00
124 Warren Morris 1.00
125 Chris Pritchett 1.00
126 Torii Hunter 3.00
127 Armando Rios 1.00
128 Ricky Ledee 1.00
129 *Kelly Dransfeldt* 1.00
130 Jeff Zimmerman 1.50
131 Eric Chavez 2.00
132 Freddy Garcia 3.00
133 Jose Jimenez 1.00
134 *Pat Burrell* 20.00
135 *Joe McEwing* 1.50
136 Kris Benson 1.00
137 *Joe Mays* 2.00
138 Rafael Roque 1.00
139 Cristian Guzman 1.50
140 Michael Barrett 1.50
141 Doug Mientkiewicz 1.50
142 *Jeff Weaver* 4.00
143 Mike Lowell 1.50
144 *Jason Phillips* 2.00
145 Marlon Anderson 1.50
146 *Brett Hinchliffe* 1.00
147 Matt Clement 1.50
148 Terrence Long 1.00
149 Carlos Beltran 2.50
150 Preston Wilson 1.50
151 Ken Griffey Jr. 2.00
152 Mark McGwire 3.00
153 Sammy Sosa 1.50
154 Mike Piazza 2.00
155 Alex Rodriguez 3.00
156 Nomar Garciaparra 1.50
157 Cal Ripken Jr. 4.00
158 Greg Maddux 1.50
159 Derek Jeter 4.00
160 Juan Gonzalez 1.00

Gold

	NM/M
Common Player:	1.00
Stars (1-100):	1.5X
Inserted 1:8	

(See 1999 Fleer Mystique for checklist and base card values.)

Masterpiece

	NM/M
Common Player:	50.00

(Because of their unique nature star Masterpiece values cannot be determined.)

Destiny

	NM/M
Complete Set (10):	35.00
Common Player:	2.00
Production 999 sets	

1 Tony Gwynn 5.00
2 Juan Gonzalez 3.00
3 Scott Rolen 4.00
4 Nomar Garciaparra 6.00
5 Orlando Hernandez 2.00
6 Andruw Jones 4.00
7 Vladimir Guerrero 4.00
8 Darin Erstad 2.00
9 Manny Ramirez 4.00
10 Roger Clemens 6.00

Established

	NM/M
Complete Set (10):	300.00
Common Player:	15.00

Production 100 sets
1 Ken Griffey Jr. 30.00
2 Derek Jeter 60.00
3 Chipper Jones 20.00
4 Greg Maddux 20.00
5 Mark McGwire 45.00
6 Mike Piazza 30.00
7 Cal Ripken Jr. 60.00
8 Alex Rodriguez 45.00
9 Sammy Sosa 25.00
10 Frank Thomas 15.00

Fresh Ink

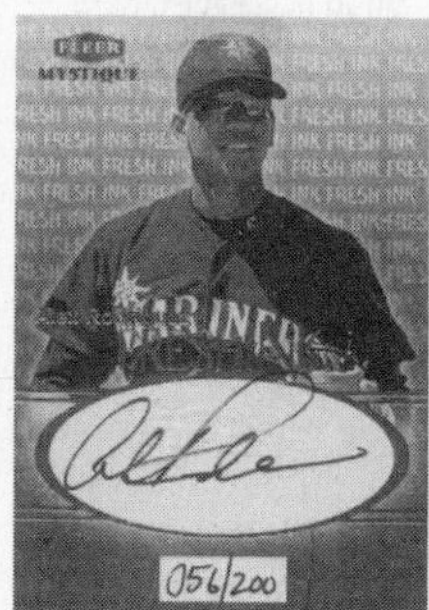

	NM/M
Complete Set (26):	300.00
Common Player:	4.00
Inserted 1:48	
Roberto Alomar (500)	10.00
Michael Barrett (1,000)	6.00
Kris Benson (500)	8.00
Micah Bowie (1,000)	4.00
A.J. Burnett (500)	10.00
Pat Burrell (500)	15.00
Ken Caminiti (250)	10.00
Jose Canseco (250)	25.00
Sean Casey (1,000)	8.00
Edgard Clemente (1,000)	4.00
Bartolo Colon (500)	8.00
J.D. Drew (400)	15.00
Juan Encarnacion (1,000)	4.00
Troy Glaus (400)	15.00
Juan Gonzalez (250)	15.00
Shawn Green (250)	15.00
Tony Gwynn (250)	30.00
Chipper Jones (500)	30.00
Gabe Kapler (750)	6.00
Barry Larkin (250)	25.00
Doug Mientkiewicz (500)	6.00
Alex Rodriguez (200)	80.00
Scott Rolen (140)	30.00
Fernando Tatis (750)	4.00
Robin Ventura (500)	6.00
Todd Walker (1,000)	6.00

Feel the Game

NM/M

Common Player: 10.00
Adrian Beltre (shoe, 430) 15.00
J.D. Drew (jersey, 450) 15.00
Juan Gonzalez (bat glove, 415) 10.00
Tony Gwynn (jersey, 435) 15.00
Kevin Millwood (jersey, 435) 10.00
Alex Rodriguez (bat glove, 345) 30.00
Frank Thomas (jersey, 450) 15.00

Prophetic

NM/M

Complete Set (10): 15.00
Common Player: 1.00
Production 1,999 sets
1 Eric Chavez 1.50
2 J.D. Drew 2.00
3 A.J. Burnett 1.00
4 Ben Grieve 1.00
5 Gabe Kapler 1.00
6 Todd Helton 2.50
7 Troy Glaus 4.00
8 Travis Lee 1.00
9 Pat Burrell 5.00
10 Kerry Wood 1.50

2000 FLEER FOCUS

NM/M

Complete Set (250): 100.00
Common Player: .15
Common Prospect (226-250): 4.00
Production 2,999 sets
Common Portrait (226-250): 8.00
Portraits: 2X
Production 999 sets
Pack: 2.00
Wax Box (24): 35.00
1 Nomar Garciaparra 1.25
2 Adrian Beltre .35
3 Miguel Tejada .35
4 Joe Randa .15
5 Larry Walker .15
6 Jeff Weaver .15
7 Jay Bell .15
8 Ivan Rodriguez .50
9 Edgar Martinez .15
10 Desi Relaford .15
11 Derek Jeter 2.50
12 Delino DeShields .15
13 Craig Biggio .15
14 Chuck Knoblauch .15
15 Chuck Finley .15
16 Brett Tomko .15
17 Bobby Higginson .15
18 Pedro Martinez .75
19 Troy O'Leary .15
20 Rickey Henderson .75
21 Robb Nen .15
22 Rolando Arrojo .15
23 Rondell White .15
24 Royce Clayton .15
25 Rusty Greer .15
26 Stan Spencer .15
27 Steve Finley .15
28 Tom Goodwin .15
29 Troy Percival .15
30 Wilton Guerrero .15
31 Roberto Alomar .30
32 Mike Hampton .15
33 Michael Barrett .15
34 Curt Schilling .40
35 Bill Mueller .15
36 Bernie Williams .30
37 John Smoltz .15
38 B.J. Surhoff .15
39 Pete Harnisch .15
40 Juan Encarnacion .15
41 Derrek Lee .15
42 Jeff Shaw .15
43 David Cone .15
44 Jason Christiansen .15
45 Jeff Kent .15
46 Randy Johnson .75
47 Todd Walker .15
48 Jose Lima .15
49 Jason Giambi .50
50 Ken Griffey Jr. 1.50
51 Bartolo Colon .15
52 Mike Lieberthal .15
53 Shane Reynolds .15
54 Travis Lee .15
55 Travis Fryman .15
56 John Valentin .15
57 Joey Hamilton .15
58 Jay Buhner .15
59 Brad Radke .15
60 A.J. Burnett .15
61 Roy Halladay .25
62 Raul Mondesi .15
63 Matt Mantei .15
64 Mark Grace .15
65 David Justice .15
66 Billy Wagner .15
67 Eric Milton .15
68 Eric Chavez .25
69 Doug Glanville .15
70 Ray Durham .15
71 Mike Sirotka .15
72 Greg Vaughn .15
73 Brian Jordan .15
74 Alex Gonzalez .15
75 Alex Rodriguez 2.00
76 David Nilsson .15
77 Robin Ventura .15
78 Kevin Young .15
79 Wilson Alvarez .15
80 Matt Williams .15
81 Ismael Valdes .15
82 Kenny Lofton .15
83 Carlos Beltran .45
84 Doug Mientkiewicz .15
85 Wally Joyner .15
86 J.D. Drew .35
87 Carlos Delgado .50
88 Tony Womack .15
89 Eric Young .15
90 Manny Ramirez .75
91 Johnny Damon .15
92 Torii Hunter .25
93 Kenny Rogers .15
94 Trevor Hoffman .15
95 John Wetteland .15
96 Ray Lankford .15
97 Tom Glavine .30
98 Carlos Lee .15
99 Richie Sexson .15
100 Carlos Febles .15
101 Chad Allen .15
102 Sterling Hitchcock .15
103 Joe McEwing .15
104 Justin Thompson .15
105 Jim Edmonds .15
106 Kerry Wood .40
107 Jim Thome .65
108 Jeremy Giambi .15
109 Mike Piazza 1.50
110 Darryl Kile .15
111 Darin Erstad .30
112 Kyle Farnsworth .15
113 Omar Vizquel .15
114 Orber Moreno .15
115 Al Leiter .15
116 John Olerud .15
117 Aaron Sele .15
118 Chipper Jones 1.00
119 Paul Konerko .25
120 Chris Singleton .15
121 Fernando Vina .15
122 Andy Ashby .15
123 Eli Marrero .15
124 Edgar Renteria .15
125 Roberto Hernandez .15
126 Andruw Jones .75
127 Magglio Ordonez .25
128 Bob Wickman .15
129 Tony Gwynn 1.00
130 Mark McGwire 2.00
131 Albert Belle .15
132 Pokey Reese .15
133 Tony Clark .15
134 Jeff Bagwell .75
135 Mark Grudzielanek .15
136 Dustin Hermanson .15
137 Reggie Sanders .15
138 Ryan Rupe .15
139 Kevin Millwood .15
140 Bret Saberhagen .15
141 Juan Guzman .15
142 Alex Gonzalez .15
143 Gary Sheffield .30
144 Roger Clemens 1.25
145 Ben Grieve .15
146 Bobby Abreu .15
147 Brian Giles .15
148 Quinton McCracken .15
149 Freddy Garcia .15
150 Erubiel Durazo .15
151 Sidney Ponson .15
152 Scott Williamson .15
153 Ken Caminiti .15
154 Vladimir Guerrero .75
155 Andy Pettitte .25
156 Edwards Guzman .15
157 Shannon Stewart .15
158 Greg Maddux 1.00
159 Mike Stanley .15
160 Sean Casey .25
161 Cliff Floyd .15
162 Devon White .15
163 Scott Brosius .15
164 Marlon Anderson .15
165 Jason Kendall .15
166 Ryan Klesko .15
167 Sammy Sosa 1.25
168 Frank Thomas .75
169 Geoff Jenkins .15
170 Jason Schmidt .15
171 Dan Wilson .15
172 Jose Canseco .40
173 Troy Glaus .75
174 Mariano Rivera .20
175 Scott Rolen .65
176 J.T. Snow .15
177 Rafael Palmeiro .65
178 A.J. Hinch .15
179 Jose Offerman .15
180 Jeff Cirillo .15
181 Dean Palmer .15
182 Jose Rosado .15
183 Armando Benitez .15
184 Brady Anderson .15
185 Cal Ripken Jr. 2.50
186 Barry Larkin .15
187 Damion Easley .15
188 Moises Alou .15
189 Todd Hundley .15
190 Tim Hudson .25
191 Livan Hernandez .15
192 Fred McGriff .15
193 Orlando Hernandez .25
194 Tim Salmon .20
195 Mike Mussina .40
196 Todd Helton .75
197 Juan Gonzalez .50
198 Kevin Brown .15
199 Ugueth Urbina .15
200 Matt Stairs .15
201 Shawn Estes .15
202 Gabe Kapler .15
203 Javy Lopez .15
204 Henry Rodriguez .15
205 Dante Bichette .15
206 Jeromy Burnitz .15
207 Todd Zeile .15
208 Rico Brogna .15
209 Warren Morris .15
210 David Segui .15
211 Vinny Castilla .15
212 Mo Vaughn .15
213 Charles Johnson .15
214 Neifi Perez .15
215 Shawn Green .40
216 Carl Pavano .15
217 Tino Martinez .15
218 Barry Bonds 2.50
219 David Wells .15
220 Paul O'Neill .15
221 Masato Yoshii .15
222 Kris Benson .15
223 Fernando Tatis .15
224 Lee Stevens .15
225 Jose Cruz Jr. .15
226 Rick Ankiel 4.00
227 Matt Riley 4.00
228 Norm Hutchins 4.00
229 Ruben Mateo 4.00
229
230 Ben Petrick 4.00
231 Mario Encarnacion 4.00
232 Nick Johnson 6.00
233 Adam Piatt 6.00
234 Mike Darr 4.00
235 Chad Hermansen 4.00
236 Wily Pena 6.00
237 Octavio Dotel 4.00
238 Vernon Wells 6.00
239 Daryle Ward 4.00
240 Adam Kennedy 4.00
241 Angel Pena 4.00
242 Lance Berkman 6.00
243 Gabe Molina 4.00
244 Steve Lomasney 4.00
245 Jacob Cruz 4.00
246 Mark Quinn 4.00
247 Eric Munson 4.00
248 Alfonso Soriano 6.00
249 Kip Wells 4.00
250 Josh Beckett 6.00
Checklist #171 .05
Checklist #172-25, inserts .05
Checklist inserts .05

Green

NM/M

Common Player: 3.00
Stars: 5-10X
Yng Stars & RCs (226-250): 1-2X
Production 300 sets
(See 2000 Fleer Focus for checklist and base card values.)

Masterpiece

NM/M

Common Player: 100.00
(Values undetermined due to rarity and fluctuating demand. See 2000 Fleer Focusfor checklist.)

Club 3000

NM/M

Complete Set (3): 4.00
Common Player: 1.50
(1) Steve Carlton 1.50
(2) Paul Molitor 1.50
(3) Stan Musial 1.50

Club 3000 Memorabilia

NM/M

Steve Carlton - bat/325 25.00
Steve Carlton - hat/65 75.00
Steve Carlton - jersey/750 20.00
Steve Carlton - bat, hat, jersey/25 200.00
Paul Molitor - bat/355 30.00

Paul Molitor - hat/65	85.00
Paul Molitor - jersey/975	20.00
Paul Molitor - bat, jersey/100	60.00
Stan Musial - bat/325	50.00
Stan Musial - hat/65	125.00
Stan Musial - jersey/975	35.00
Stan Musial - bat, jersey/100	80.00

Feel the Game

	NM/M
Common Player:	5.00
Inserted 1:288	
Adrian Beltre	7.50
Tom Glavine	10.00
Vladimir Guerrero	15.00
Randy Johnson	15.00
Javy Lopez	5.00
Alex Rodriguez	30.00
Scott Rolen	10.00
Cal Ripken Jr.	40.00
Tim Salmon	6.00
Miguel Tejada	10.00

Focal Points

		NM/M
Complete Set (15):		15.00
Common Player:		.75
Inserted 1:6		
1	Mark McGwire	2.50
2	Tony Gwynn	1.00
3	Nomar Garciaparra	2.00
4	Juan Gonzalez	.75
5	Jeff Bagwell	.75
6	Chipper Jones	1.00
7	Cal Ripken Jr.	3.00
8	Alex Rodriguez	2.50
9	Scott Rolen	.75
10	Vladimir Guerrero	.75
11	Mike Piazza	1.50
12	Frank Thomas	.75
13	Ken Griffey Jr.	1.50
14	Sammy Sosa	1.50
15	Derek Jeter	3.00

Focus Pocus

		NM/M
Complete Set (10):		12.00
Common Player:		1.00
Inserted 1:14		
1	Cal Ripken Jr.	3.00
2	Tony Gwynn	1.50
3	Nomar Garciaparra	2.00
4	Juan Gonzalez	1.00
5	Mike Piazza	2.00
6	Mark McGwire	2.50
7	Chipper Jones	1.50
8	Ken Griffey Jr.	2.00
9	Derek Jeter	3.00
10	Alex Rodriguez	2.50

Fresh Ink

	NM/M
Common Player:	5.00
Inserted 1:96	
Chad Allen	5.00
Michael Barrett	5.00
Josh Beckett	20.00
Rob Bell	5.00
Adrian Beltre	15.00
Milton Bradley	8.00
Rico Brogna	5.00
Mike Cameron	8.00
Eric Chavez	15.00
Bruce Chen	5.00
Johnny Damon	20.00

Ben Davis	5.00
J.D. Drew	15.00
Erubiel Durazo	10.00
Jeremy Giambi	6.00
Jason Giambi	25.00
Doug Glanville	6.00
Troy Glaus	25.00
Shawn Green	20.00
Mike Hampton	10.00
Tim Hudson	15.00
John Jaha	5.00
Derek Jeter	150.00
D'Angelo Jimenez	5.00
Nick Johnson	8.00
Andruw Jones	20.00
Jason Kendall	10.00
Adam Kennedy	6.00
Mike Lieberthal	8.00
Edgar Martinez	15.00
Aaron McNeal	5.00
Kevin Millwood	10.00
Mike Mussina	30.00
Magglio Ordonez	15.00
Eric Owens	5.00
Rafael Palmeiro	20.00
Wily Pena	15.00
Adam Piatt	8.00
Cal Ripken Jr.	100.00
Alex Rodriguez	65.00
Scott Rolen	20.00
Tim Salmon	15.00
Chris Singleton	5.00
Mike Sweeney	10.00
Jose Vidro	8.00
Rondell White	8.00
Jaret Wright	5.00

Future Vision

		NM/M
Complete Set (15):		8.00
Common Player:		.40
Inserted 1:9		
1	Rick Ankiel	.40
2	Matt Riley	.40
3	Ruben Mateo	.40
4	Ben Petrick	.40
5	Mario Encarnacion	.40
6	Octavio Dotel	.40
7	Vernon Wells	.65
8	Adam Kennedy	.40
9	Lance Berkman	.40
10	Chad Hermansen	.40
11	Mark Quinn	.40
12	Eric Munson	.40
13	Alfonso Soriano	2.00
14	Kip Wells	.40
15	Josh Beckett	.75

2000 FLEER GAMERS

		NM/M
Complete Set (120):		50.00
Common Player (1-90):		.15
Common (91-110):		1.00
Inserted 1:3		
Common (111-120):		1.50
Inserted 1:8		
Pack:		2.00
Wax Box:		35.00
1	Cal Ripken Jr.	2.00
2	Derek Jeter	2.00
3	Alex Rodriguez	1.50
4	Alex Gonzalez	.15
5	Nomar Garciaparra	1.25
6	Brian Giles	.15
7	Chris Singleton	.15
8	Kevin Brown	.15
9	J.D. Drew	.25
10	Raul Mondesi	.15
11	Sammy Sosa	1.25
12	Carlos Beltran	.50
13	Eric Chavez	.25
14	Gabe Kapler	.15
15	Tim Salmon	.25
16	Manny Ramirez	.75
17	Orlando Hernandez	.15
18	Jeff Kent	.15
19	Juan Gonzalez	.75
20	Moises Alou	.15
21	Jason Giambi	.50
22	Ivan Rodriguez	.60
23	Geoff Jenkins	.15
24	Ken Griffey Jr.	1.25
25	Mark McGwire	1.50
26	Jose Canseco	.40
27	Roberto Alomar	.40
28	Craig Biggio	.15
29	Scott Rolen	.65
30	Vinny Castilla	.15
31	Greg Maddux	1.00
32	Pedro J. Martinez	.75
33	Mike Piazza	1.25
34	Albert Belle	.25
35	Frank Thomas	.75
36	Bobby Abreu	.15
37	Edgar Martinez	.15
38	Pokey Reese	.15
39	Preston Wilson	.15
40	Mike Lieberthal	.15
41	Andruw Jones	.75
42	Damion Easley	.15
43	Mike Cameron	.15
44	Todd Walker	.15
45	Jason Kendall	.15
46	Sean Casey	.25
47	Corey Koskie	.15
48	Warren Morris	.15
49	Andres Galarraga	.15
50	Dean Palmer	.15
51	Jose Vidro	.15
52	Brian Jordan	.15
53	Tony Clark	.15
54	Vladimir Guerrero	.75
55	Mo Vaughn	.15
56	Richie Sexson	.15
57	Tino Martinez	.15
58	Eric Owens	.15
59	Matt Williams	.15
60	Omar Vizquel	.15
61	Rickey Henderson	.75
62	J.T. Snow	.15
63	Mark Grace	.25
64	Carlos Febles	.15
65	Paul O'Neill	.15
66	Randy Johnson	.75
67	Kenny Lofton	.15
68	Roger Cedeno	.15
69	Shawn Green	.35
70	Chipper Jones	1.00
71	Jeff Cirillo	.15
72	Robin Ventura	.15
73	Paul Konerko	.15
74	Jeromy Burnitz	.15
75	Ben Grieve	.15
76	Troy Glaus	.75
77	Jim Thome	.15
78	Bernie Williams	.25
79	Barry Bonds	2.00
80	Ray Durham	.15
81	Adrian Beltre	.15
82	Ray Lankford	.15
83	Carlos Delgado	.50
84	Erubiel Durazo	.15
85	Larry Walker	.15
86	Edgardo Alfonzo	.15
87	Rafael Palmeiro	.65
88	Magglio Ordonez	.25
89	Jeff Bagwell	.75
90	Tony Gwynn	1.00
91	Norm Hutchins	1.00
92	*Derrick Turnbow*	1.50
93	Matt Riley	1.00
94	David Eckstein	1.00
95	Dernell Stenson	1.00
96	Joe Crede	1.00
97	Ben Petrick	1.00
98	Eric Munson	1.00
99	Pablo Ozuna	1.00
100	Josh Beckett	3.00
101	*Aaron McNeal*	1.50
102	Milton Bradley	1.50
103	Alex Escobar	1.50
104	Alfonso Soriano	4.00
105	Wily Pena	1.50
106	Nick Johnson	1.50
107	Adam Piatt	1.00
108	Pat Burrell	2.00
109	Rick Ankiel	1.00
110	Vernon Wells	2.00
111	Alex Rodriguez	3.00
112	Cal Ripken Jr.	4.00
113	Mark McGwire	3.00
114	Ken Griffey Jr.	2.00
115	Mike Piazza	2.00
116	Nomar Garciaparra	3.00
117	Derek Jeter	4.00
118	Chipper Jones	1.50
119	Sammy Sosa	2.00
120	Tony Gwynn	1.50

Extra

	NM/M
Stars (1-90):	5-10X
Inserted 1:24	
Next Gamers (91-110):	1-2X
Inserted 1:36	
Fame Game (110-120):	1-2X
Inserted 1:36	

(See Fleer Gamers for checklist and base card values.)

Cal to Greatness

		NM/M
Complete Set (15):		100.00
Common Ripken (1-5):		3.00
Inserted 1:9		
Common Ripken (6-10):		6.00
Inserted 1:25		
Common Ripken (11-15):		20.00
Inserted 1:144		
1	Cal Ripken Jr.	3.00
2	Cal Ripken Jr.	3.00
3	Cal Ripken Jr.	3.00
4	Cal Ripken Jr.	3.00
5	Cal Ripken Jr.	3.00
6	Cal Ripken Jr.	6.00
7	Cal Ripken Jr.	6.00

8	Cal Ripken Jr.	6.00
9	Cal Ripken Jr.	6.00
10	Cal Ripken Jr.	6.00
11	Cal Ripken Jr.	20.00
12	Cal Ripken Jr.	20.00
13	Cal Ripken Jr.	20.00
14	Cal Ripken Jr.	20.00
15	Cal Ripken Jr.	20.00

Change the Game

		NM/M
Complete Set (15):		50.00
Common Player:		1.50
Inserted 1:24		
1	Alex Rodriguez	6.00
2	Cal Ripken Jr.	7.50
3	Chipper Jones	3.00
4	Derek Jeter	7.50
5	Ken Griffey Jr.	4.00
6	Mark McGwire	6.00
7	Mike Piazza	4.00
8	Nomar Garciaparra	4.00
9	Sammy Sosa	4.00
10	Tony Gwynn	3.00
11	Ivan Rodriguez	1.50
12	Pedro Martinez	2.00
13	Juan Gonzalez	2.00
14	Vladimir Guerrero	2.00
15	Manny Ramirez	2.00

Determined

		NM/M
Complete Set (15):		25.00
Common Player:		.50
Inserted 1:12		
1	Nomar Garciaparra	2.50
2	Chipper Jones	2.00
3	Derek Jeter	4.00
4	Mike Piazza	2.50
5	Jeff Bagwell	1.00
6	Mark McGwire	3.00
7	Greg Maddux	2.00
8	Sammy Sosa	2.50
9	Ken Griffey Jr.	2.50
10	Alex Rodriguez	3.00
11	Tony Gwynn	2.00
12	Cal Ripken Jr.	4.00
13	Barry Bonds	4.00
14	Juan Gonzalez	1.00
15	Sean Casey	.50

Lumber

		NM/M
Common Player:		5.00
Inserted 1:36		
1	Alex Rodriguez	30.00
2	Carlos Delgado	10.00
3	Jose Vidro	5.00
4	Carlos Febles	5.00
5	J.D. Drew	7.50
6	Mike Cameron	5.00
7	Derek Jeter	40.00
8	Eric Chavez	6.00
9	Cal Ripken Jr.	40.00
10	Gabe Kapler	5.00
11	Damion Easley	5.00
12	Frank Thomas	15.00
13	Chris Singleton	5.00
14	Norm Hutchins	5.00
15	Pokey Reese	5.00
16	Rafael Palmeiro	12.00
17	Ray Durham	5.00
18	Ray Lankford	5.00
19	Roger Cedeno	5.00
20	Shawn Green	6.00
21	Wade Boggs	20.00
22	Roberto Alomar	7.50
23	Moises Alou	5.00
24	Adrian Beltre	6.00
25	Barry Bonds	40.00
26	Jason Giambi	10.00
27	Jason Kendall	5.00
28	Paul Konerko	5.00
29	Mike Lieberthal	5.00
30	Edgar Martinez	5.00
31	Raul Mondesi	5.00
32	Scott Rolen	12.00
33	Alfonso Soriano	10.00
34	Ivan Rodriguez	10.00
35	Magglio Ordonez	7.50
36	Chipper Jones	20.00
37	Sean Casey	6.00
38	Edgardo Alfonzo	5.00
39	Robin Ventura	5.00
40	Bernie Williams	6.00
41	Vladimir Guerrero	15.00
42	Tony Clark	5.00
43	Carlos Beltran	10.00
44	Warren Morris	5.00
45	Jim Thome	5.00
46	Jeromy Burnitz	5.00
47	Matt Williams	5.00
48	Erubiel Durazo	5.00

Lumber Autograph

		NM/M
Common Player:		15.00
Inserted 1:287		
1	Derek Jeter	150.00
2	Eric Chavez	20.00
3	Rafael Palmeiro	40.00
4	Shawn Green	35.00
5	Roberto Alomar	45.00
6	Paul Konerko	15.00
7	Sean Casey	15.00
8	Alex Rodriguez	80.00
9	Robin Ventura	20.00
10	Erubiel Durazo	15.00
11	Tony Clark	15.00
12	Alfonso Soriano	60.00

2000 FLEER GREATS OF THE GAME

		NM/M
Complete Set (108):		50.00
Common Player:		.50
Pack (6):		10.00
Wax Box (24):		200.00
1	Mickey Mantle	8.00
2	Gil Hodges	1.00
3	Monte Irvin	1.00
4	Satchel Paige	2.50
5	Roy Campanella	2.00
6	Richie Ashburn	1.00
7	Roger Maris	3.00
8	Ozzie Smith	2.00
9	Reggie Jackson	2.50
10	Eddie Mathews	2.50
11	Dave Righetti	.50
12	Dave Winfield	1.00
13	Lou Whitaker	.50
14	Phil Garner	.50
15	Ron Cey	.50
16	Brooks Robinson	2.50
17	Bruce Sutter	.50
18	Dave Parker	.50
19	Johnny Bench	2.50
20	Fernando Valenzuela	.50
21	George Brett	4.00
22	Paul Molitor	2.00
23	Hoyt Wilhelm	.50
24	Luis Aparicio	.50
25	Frank White	.50
26	Herb Score	.50
27	Kirk Gibson	.50
28	Mike Schmidt	3.00
29	Don Baylor	.50
30	Joe Pepitone	.50
31	Hal McRae	.50
32	Lee Smith	.50
33	Nolan Ryan	7.00
33	Nolan Ryan (overprinted "PROMOTIONAL SAMPLE")	5.00
34	Bill Mazeroski	.75
35	Bobby Doerr	.50
36	Duke Snider	1.00
37	Dick Groat	.50
38	Larry Doby	.50
39	Kirby Puckett	2.00
40	Steve Carlton	1.00
41	Dennis Eckersley	.50
42	Jim Bunning	.50
43	Ron Guidry	.50
44	Alan Trammell	1.00
45	Bob Feller	1.50
46	Dave Concepcion	.50
47	Dwight Evans	.50
48	Enos Slaughter	.50
49	Tom Seaver	2.50
50	Tony Oliva	1.00
51	Mel Stottlemyre	.50
52	Tommy John	.50
53	Willie McCovey	1.00
54	Red Schoendienst	.50
55	Gorman Thomas	.50
56	Ralph Kiner	1.00
57	Robin Yount	2.00
58	Andre Dawson	1.00
59	Al Kaline	2.50
60	Dom DiMaggio	.50
61	Juan Marichal	1.00
62	Jack Morris	.50
63	Warren Spahn	1.50
64	Preacher Roe	.50
65	Darrell Evans	.50
66	Jim Bouton	.50
67	Rocky Colavito	.75
68	Bob Gibson	1.50
69	Whitey Ford	1.50
70	Moose Skowron	.50
71	Boog Powell	1.00
72	Al Lopez	.50
73	Lou Brock	1.00
74	Mickey Lolich	.50
75	Rod Carew	2.00
76	Bob Lemon	.50
77	Frank Howard	.50
78	Phil Rizzuto	1.50
79	Carl Yastrzemski	2.00
80	Rico Carty	.50
81	Jim Kaat	.50
82	Bert Blyleven	.50
83	George Kell	.50
84	Jim Palmer	1.00
85	Maury Wills	1.00
86	Jim Rice	.50
87	Joe Carter	.50
88	Clete Boyer	.50
89	Yogi Berra	2.00
90	Cecil Cooper	.50
91	Davey Johnson	.50
92	Lou Boudreau	.50
93	Orlando Cepeda	1.00
94	Tommy Henrich	.50
95	Hank Bauer	.50
96	Don Larsen	1.50
97	Vida Blue	1.00
98	Ben Oglivie	.50
99	Don Mattingly	5.00
100	Dale Murphy	1.00
101	Ferguson Jenkins	1.00
102	Bobby Bonds	.75
103	Dick Allen	.50
104	Stan Musial	3.00
105	Gaylord Perry	.50
106	Willie Randolph	.50
107	Willie Stargell	1.50
108	Checklist	.50

Autographs

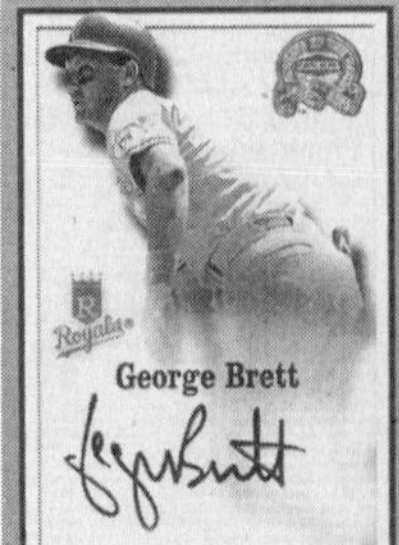

	NM/M
Common Player:	10.00
Inserted 1:6	
Luis Aparicio	20.00
Hank Bauer	10.00
Don Baylor	20.00
Johnny Bench	180.00
Yogi Berra	150.00
Vida Blue	20.00
Bert Blyleven	10.00
Bobby Bonds	10.00
Lou Boudreau	75.00
Jim Bouton	20.00
Clete Boyer	15.00
George Brett (275 or less)	180.00
Lou Brock	20.00
Jim Bunning	30.00
Rod Carew	40.00
Steve Carlton	20.00
Joe Carter/SP	75.00
Orlando Cepeda	15.00
Ron Cey	15.00
Rocky Colavito	30.00
Dave Concepcion (black autograph)	15.00
Dave Concepcion (red autograph)	15.00
Cecil Cooper	10.00
Andre Dawson	15.00
Dom DiMaggio	75.00
Bobby Doerr	15.00
Darrell Evans	15.00
Bob Feller	20.00
Whitey Ford (300 or less)	100.00
Phil Garner	10.00
Bob Gibson	25.00
Kirk Gibson	20.00
Dick Groat	10.00
Ron Guidry	20.00
Tommy Henrich (300 or less)	100.00
Frank Howard	10.00
Reggie Jackson (250 or less)	120.00
Ferguson Jenkins	15.00
Tommy John	10.00
Davey Johnson	10.00
Jim Kaat	15.00
Al Kaline	35.00
George Kell	15.00
Ralph Kiner	20.00
Don Larsen	25.00
Mickey Lolich	10.00
Juan Marichal	40.00
Eddie Mathews	80.00
Don Mattingly (300 or less)	250.00
Bill Mazeroski	20.00
Willie McCovey	80.00
Hal McRae	10.00
Paul Molitor	40.00
Jack Morris	10.00
Dale Murphy	35.00
Stan Musial	100.00
Ben Oglivie	10.00
Tony Oliva	15.00
Jim Palmer/SP	80.00
Dave Parker	15.00
Joe Pepitone	10.00
Gaylord Perry	15.00
Boog Powell	15.00
Kirby Puckett (200 or less)	120.00

Willie Randolph 15.00
Jim Rice 15.00
Dave Righetti 10.00
Phil Rizzuto (200 or less) 140.00
Brooks Robinson 30.00
Preacher Roe 15.00
Nolan Ryan 150.00
Mike Schmidt (175 or less) 250.00
Red Schoendienst 15.00
Herb Score 25.00
Tom Seaver 75.00
Moose Skowron 15.00
Enos Slaughter 20.00
Lee Smith 10.00
Ozzie Smith/SP 150.00
Duke Snider/SP 140.00
Warren Spahn/SP 100.00
Bruce Sutter 12.50
Gorman Thomas 10.00
Alan Trammell 20.00
Frank White 10.00
Hoyt Wilhelm 15.00
Maury Wills 15.00
Dave Winfield 150.00
Carl Yastrzemski 60.00
Robin Yount/SP 125.00

Memorable Moments Auto.

		NM/M
Common Player:		60.00
1	Ron Guidry /78	75.00
2	Nolan Ryan /99	300.00
3	Herb Score /55	40.00
4	Tom Seaver /69	180.00

Retrospection

		NM/M
Complete Set (15):		75.00
Common Player:		4.00
Inserted 1:6		
1	Rod Carew	4.00
2	Stan Musial	8.00
3	Nolan Ryan	15.00
4	Tom Seaver	6.00
5	Brooks Robinson	5.00
6	Al Kaline	6.00
7	Mike Schmidt	10.00
8	Thurman Munson	8.00
9	Steve Carlton	4.00
10	Roger Maris	8.00
11	Duke Snider	5.00
12	Yogi Berra	6.00
13	Carl Yastrzemski	5.00
14	Reggie Jackson	6.00
15	Johnny Bench	8.00

Yankees Clippings

		NM/M
Common Player:		20.00
Inserted 1:48		
1	Mickey Mantle	200.00
2	Ron Guidry	40.00
3	Don Larsen	40.00
4	Elston Howard	40.00
5	Mel Stottlemyre	25.00
6	Don Mattingly	100.00
7	Reggie Jackson	50.00
8	Tommy John	20.00
9	Dave Winfield	25.00
10	Willie Randolph	20.00
11	Tommy Henrich	20.00
12	Billy Martin	50.00
13	Dave Righetti	20.00
14	Joe Pepitone	20.00
15	Thurman Munson	80.00

2000 FLEER IMPACT

		NM/M
Complete Set (200):		15.00
Common Player:		.10
Pack (10):		1.00
Box (36):		20.00
1	Cal Ripken Jr.	1.50
2	Jose Canseco	.25
3	Manny Ramirez	.60
4	Bernie Williams	.30
5	Troy Glaus	.60
6	Jeff Bagwell	.60
7	Corey Koskie	.10
8	Barry Larkin	.10
9	Mark Quinn	.10
10	Russ Ortiz	.10
11	Tim Salmon	.15
12	Preston Wilson	.10
13	Mo Vaughn	.10
14	Ray Lankford	.10
15	Sterling Hitchcock	.10
16	Al Leiter	.10
17	Jim Morris	.10
18	Freddy Garcia	.10
19	Adrian Beltre	.20
20	Eric Chavez	.20
21	Robinson Cancel	.10
22	Edgar Renteria	.10
23	John Jaha	.10
24	Chuck Finley	.10
25	Andres Galarraga	.10
26	Paul Byrd	.10
27	John Halama	.10
28	Eric Karros	.10
29	Mike Piazza	1.00
30	Ryan Rupe	.10
31	Frank Thomas	.60
32	Randy Velarde	.10
33	Bobby Abreu	.10
34	Randy Johnson	.60
35	Matt Williams	.10
36	Tony Gwynn	.75
37	Dean Palmer	.10
38	Aaron Sele	.10
39	Rondell White	.10
40	Erubiel Durazo	.10
41	Curt Schilling	.25
42	Kip Wells	.10
43	Craig Biggio	.10
44	Tom Glavine	.25
45	Trevor Hoffman	.10
46	Greg Vaughn	.10
47	Edgar Martinez	.10
48	Magglio Ordonez	.20
49	Mark Mulder	.10
50	John Rocker	.10
51	Kenny Rogers	.10
52	Gary Sheffield	.25
53	Brian Simmons	.10
54	Tony Womack	.10
55	Ken Caminiti	.10
56	Jeff Cirillo	.10
57	Ray Durham	.10
58	Mike Lieberthal	.10
59	Ruben Mateo	.10
60	Mike Cameron	.10
61	Rusty Greer	.10
62	Alex Rodriguez	1.25
63	Robin Ventura	.10
64	Pokey Reese	.10
65	Jose Lima	.10
66	Neifi Perez	.10
67	Rafael Palmeiro	.50
68	Scott Rolen	.50
69	Mike Hampton	.10
70	Sammy Sosa	1.00
71	Mike Stanley	.10
72	Dan Wilson	.10
73	Kerry Wood	.50
74	Mike Mussina	.30
75	Masato Yoshii	.10
76	Peter Bergeron	.10
77	Carlos Delgado	.50
78	Juan Encarnacion	.10
79	Nomar Garciaparra	1.00
80	Jason Kendall	.10
81	Pedro Martinez	.60
82	Darin Erstad	.40
83	Larry Walker	.10
84	Rick Ankiel	.10
85	Scott Erickson	.10
86	Roger Clemens	.85
87	Matt Lawton	.10
88	Jon Lieber	.10
89	Shane Reynolds	.10
90	Ivan Rodriguez	.50
91	Pat Burrell	.50
92	Kent Bottenfield	.10
93	David Cone	.10
94	Mark Grace	.15
95	Paul Konerko	.10
96	Eric Milton	.10
97	Lee Stevens	.10
98	B.J. Surhoff	.10
99	Billy Wagner	.10
100	Ken Griffey Jr.	1.00
101	Randy Wolf	.10
102	Henry Rodriguez	.10
103	Carlos Beltran	.40
104	Rich Aurilia	.10
105	Chipper Jones	.75
106	Homer Bush	.10
107	Johnny Damon	.10
108	J.D. Drew	.40
109	Orlando Hernandez	.10
110	Brad Radke	.10
111	Wilton Veras	.10
112	Dmitri Young	.10
113	Jermaine Dye	.10
114	Kris Benson	.10
115	Derek Jeter	1.50
116	Cole Liniak	.10
117	Jim Thome	.10
118	Pedro Astacio	.10
119	Carlos Febles	.10
120	Darryl Kile	.10
121	Alfonso Soriano	.50
122	Michael Barrett	.10
123	Ellis Burks	.10
124	Chad Hermansen	.10
125	Trot Nixon	.10
126	Bobby Higginson	.10
127	Rick Helling	.10
128	Chris Carpenter	.10
129	Vinny Castilla	.10
130	Brian Giles	.10
131	Todd Helton	.60
132	Jason Varitek	.10
133	Rob Ducey	.10
134	Octavio Dotel	.10
135	Adam Kennedy	.10
136	Jeff Kent	.10
137	Aaron Boone	.10
138	Todd Walker	.10
139	Jeromy Burnitz	.10
140	Roberto Hernandez	.10
141	Matt LeCroy	.10
142	Ugueth Urbina	.10
143	David Wells	.10
144	Luis Gonzalez	.25
145	Andruw Jones	.50
146	Juan Gonzalez	.60
147	Moises Alou	.10
148	Michael Tejera	.10
149	Brian Jordan	.10
150	Mark McGwire	1.25
151	Shawn Green	.25
152	Jay Bell	.10
153	Fred McGriff	.10
154	Rey Ordonez	.10
155	Matt Stairs	.10
156	A.J. Burnett	.10
157	Omar Vizquel	.10
158	Damion Easley	.10
159	Dante Bichette	.10
160	Javy Lopez	.10
161	Fernando Seguignol	.10
162	Richie Sexson	.10
163	Vladimir Guerrero	.60
164	Kevin Young	.10
165	Josh Beckett	.10
166	Albert Belle	.10
167	Cliff Floyd	.10
168	Gabe Kapler	.10
169	Nick Johnson	.15
170	Raul Mondesi	.10
171	Warren Morris	.10
172	Kenny Lofton	.10
173	Reggie Sanders	.10
174	Mike Sweeney	.10
175	Robert Fick	.10
176	Barry Bonds	1.50
177	Luis Castillo	.10
178	Roger Cedeno	.10
179	Jim Edmonds	.10
180	Geoff Jenkins	.10
181	Adam Piatt	.10
182	Phil Nevin	.10
183	Roberto Alomar	.30
184	Kevin Brown	.10
185	D.T. Cromer	.10
186	Jason Giambi	.50
187	Fernando Tatis	.10
188	Brady Anderson	.10
189	Tony Clark	.10
190	Alex Fernandez	.10
191	Matt Blank	.10
192	Greg Maddux	.75
193	Kevin Millwood	.10
194	Jason Schmidt	.10
195	Shannon Stewart	.10
196	Rolando Arrojo	.10
197	Darren Dreifort	.10
198	Ben Grieve	.10
199	Bartolo Colon	.10
200	Sean Casey	.10

Autographics

		NM/M
Common Player:		5.00
Inserted 1:216		
Silvers:		1-2X
Production 250 sets		
Golds:		1-2X
Production 50 sets		
1	Bobby Abreu	15.00
2	Marlon Anderson	5.00
3	Rick Ankiel	8.00
4	Rob Bell	5.00
5	Carlos Beltran	25.00
6	Wade Boggs	30.00
7	Barry Bonds	200.00
8	Milton Bradley	8.00
9	Pat Burrell	25.00
10	Orlando Cabrera	10.00
11	Chris Carpenter	5.00
12	Sean Casey	8.00
13	Carlos Delgado	20.00
14	J.D. Drew	15.00
15	Ray Durham	8.00
16	Kelvim Escobar	6.00
17	Vladimir Guerrero	30.00
18	Tony Gwynn	35.00
19	Jerry Hairston Jr.	5.00
20	Todd Helton	25.00
21	Nick Johnson	8.00
22	Jason Kendall	8.00
23	Mark Kotsay	8.00
24	Cole Liniak	5.00
25	Jose Macias	5.00
26	Greg Maddux	60.00
27	Ruben Mateo	8.00
28	Ober Moreno	5.00
29	Eric Munson	8.00
30	Joe Nathan	5.00
31	Angel Pena	5.00
32	Adam Piatt	6.00
33	Matt Riley	5.00
34	Cal Ripken Jr.	100.00
35	Alex Rodriguez	75.00
36	Scott Rolen	25.00
37	Jimmy Rollins	8.00
38	B.J. Ryan	5.00
39	Alfonso Soriano	40.00
40	Frank Thomas	25.00
41	Wilton Veras	5.00
42	Billy Wagner	10.00
43	Jeff Weaver	8.00
44	Scott Williamson	6.00

Genuine Coverage

		NM/M
Common Player:		5.00
Inserted 1:720		
1	Alex Rodriguez	65.00
2	Cole Liniak	5.00
3	Barry Bonds	75.00
4	Ben Davis	5.00
5	Bobby Abreu	7.50
6	Mike Sweeney	7.50
7	Rafael Palmeiro	35.00
8	Carlos Lee	5.00
9	Glen Barker	5.00
10	Jason Giambi	30.00
11	Jacque Jones	7.50
12	Joe Nathan	5.00
13	Jason LaRue	5.00
14	Magglio Ordonez	7.50
15	Shannon Stewart	5.00
16	Matt Lawton	5.00
18	Trevor Hoffman	5.00

Mighty Fine in '99

		NM/M
Complete Set (40):		8.00
Common Player:		.15
Inserted 1:1		
1	Clay Bellinger	.15
2	Scott Brosius	.15
3	Roger Clemens	.75
4	David Cone	.15
5	Chad Curtis	.15
6	Chili Davis	.15
7	Joe Girardi	.15
8	Jason Grimsley	.15
9	Orlando Hernandez	.15
10	Hideki Irabu	.15
11	Derek Jeter	2.00
12	Chuck Knoblauch	.15
13	Ricky Ledee	.15
14	Jim Leyritz	.15
15	Tino Martinez	.15
16	Ramiro Mendoza	.15
17	Jeff Nelson	.15
18	Paul O'Neill	.15
19	Andy Pettitte	.25
20	Jorge Posada	.25
21	Mariano Rivera	.25
22	Luis Sojo	.15
23	Mike Stanton	.15
24	Allen Watson	.15
25	Bernie Williams	.30
26	Chipper Jones	.60
27	Ivan Rodriguez	.45
28	Randy Johnson	.50
29	Pedro Martinez	.50
30	Scott Williamson	.15
31	Carlos Beltran	.40
32	Mark McGwire	1.50
33	Ken Griffey Jr.	1.00
34	Robin Ventura	.15
35	Tony Gwynn	.60
36	Wade Boggs	.60
37	Cal Ripken Jr.	2.00
38	Jose Canseco	.40
39	Alex Rodriguez	1.50
40	Fernando Tatis	.15

Point of Impact

		NM/M
Complete Set (10):		20.00
Common Player:		1.00
Inserted 1:30		
1	Ken Griffey Jr.	2.00
2	Mark McGwire	3.00
3	Sammy Sosa	2.00
4	Jeff Bagwell	1.00
5	Derek Jeter	4.00
6	Chipper Jones	1.50
7	Nomar Garciaparra	2.00
8	Cal Ripken Jr.	4.00
9	Barry Bonds	4.00
10	Alex Rodriguez	3.00

2000 FLEER MYSTIQUE

		NM/M
Complete Set (175):		350.00
Common Player:		.20
Common 126-175:		6.00
Production 2,000 sets		
Pack (5):		3.00
Box (20):		50.00
1	Derek Jeter	3.00
2	David Justice	.20
3	Kevin Brown	.20
4	Jason Giambi	.75
5	Jose Canseco	.50
6	Mark Grace	.30
7	Hideo Nomo	.65
8	Edgardo Alfonzo	.20
9	Barry Bonds	3.00
10	Pedro Martinez	1.00
11	Juan Gonzalez	1.00
12	Vladimir Guerrero	1.00
13	Chuck Finley	.20
14	Brian Jordan	.20
15	Richie Sexson	.20
16	Chan Ho Park	.20
17	Tim Hudson	.40
18	Fred McGriff	.20
19	Darin Erstad	.60
20	Chris Singleton	.20
21	Jeff Bagwell	1.00
22	David Cone	.20
23	Edgar Martinez	.20
24	Greg Maddux	1.50
25	Jim Thome	.20
26	Eric Karros	.20
27	Bobby Abreu	.20
28	Greg Vaughn	.20
29	Kevin Millwood	.20
30	Omar Vizquel	.20
31	Marquis Grissom	.20
32	Mike Lieberthal	.20
33	Gabe Kapler	.20
34	Brady Anderson	.20
35	Jeff Cirillo	.20
36	Geoff Jenkins	.20
37	Scott Rolen	.75
38	Rafael Palmeiro	.65
39	Randy Johnson	1.00
40	Barry Larkin	.20
41	Johnny Damon	.40
42	Andy Pettitte	.40
43	Mark McGwire	2.50
44	Albert Belle	.20
45	Derrick Gibson	.20
46	Corey Koskie	.20
47	Curt Schilling	.50
48	Ivan Rodriguez	.65
49	Mike Mussina	.50
50	Todd Helton	1.00
51	Matt Lawton	.20
52	Jason Kendall	.20
53	Kenny Rogers	.20
54	Cal Ripken Jr.	3.00
55	Larry Walker	.20
56	Eric Milton	.20
57	Warren Morris	.20
58	Carlos Delgado	.50
59	Kerry Wood	.65
60	Cliff Floyd	.20
61	Mike Piazza	2.00
62	Jeff Kent	.20
63	Sammy Sosa	2.00
64	Alex Fernandez	.20
65	Mike Hampton	.20
66	Livan Hernandez	.20
67	Matt Williams	.20
68	Roberto Alomar	.45
69	Jermaine Dye	.20
70	Bernie Williams	.35
71	Edgar Renteria	.20
72	Tom Glavine	.40
73	Bartolo Colon	.20
74	Jason Varitek	.20
75	Eric Chavez	.40
76	Fernando Tatis	.20
77	Adrian Beltre	.40
78	Paul Konerko	.20
79	Mike Lowell	.20
80	Robin Ventura	.20
81	Russ Ortiz	.20
82	Troy Glaus	1.00
83	Frank Thomas	1.00
84	Craig Biggio	.20
85	Orlando Hernandez	.20
86	John Olerud	.20
87	Chipper Jones	1.50
88	Manny Ramirez	1.00
89	Shawn Green	.40
90	Ben Grieve	.20
91	Vinny Castilla	.20
92	Tim Salmon	.35
93	Dante Bichette	.20
94	Ken Caminiti	.20
95	Andruw Jones	.75
96	Alex Rodriguez	2.50
97	Erubiel Durazo	.20
98	Sean Casey	.30
99	Carlos Beltran	.50
100	Paul O'Neill	.20
101	Ray Lankford	.20
102	Troy O'Leary	.20
103	Bobby Higginson	.20
104	Rondell White	.20
105	Tony Gwynn	1.50
106	Jim Edmonds	.20
107	Magglio Ordonez	.40
108	Preston Wilson	.20
109	Roger Clemens	1.75
110	Ken Griffey Jr.	2.00
111	Nomar Garciaparra	2.00
112	Juan Encarnacion	.20
113	Michael Barrett	.20
114	Matt Clement	.20
115	David Wells	.20
116	Mo Vaughn	.20
117	Mike Cameron	.20
118	Jose Lima	.20
119	Tino Martinez	.20
120	J.D. Drew	.40
121	Carl Everett	.20
122	Tony Clark	.20
123	Brad Radke	.20
124	Kevin Young	.20
125	Raul Mondesi	.20
126	Cole Liniak	6.00
127	Alfonso Soriano	8.00
128	Lance Berkman	8.00
129	Danny Young	6.00
130	Francisco Cordero	6.00
131	Rob Fick	6.00
132	Matt LeCroy	6.00
133	Adam Piatt	6.00
134	*Derrick Turnbow*	6.00
135	Mark Quinn	6.00
136	Kip Wells	6.00
137	Rob Bell	6.00
138	Brad Penny	6.00
139	Pat Burrell	10.00
140	*Danys Baez*	6.00
141	Chad Hermansen	6.00
142	Steve Lomasney	6.00
143	Peter Bergeron	6.00
144	Jimmy Anderson	6.00
145	Mike Darr	6.00
146	Jacob Cruz	6.00
147	*Kazuhiro Sasaki*	10.00
148	Ben Petrick	6.00
149	Rick Ankiel	6.00
150	*Aaron McNeal*	6.00
152	Octavio Dotel	6.00
152	Juan Pena	6.00
153	Nick Johnson	8.00
154	Wilton Veras	6.00
155	Wily Pena	6.00
156	Mark Mulder	6.00
157	Daryle Ward	6.00
158	*Chad Durbin*	6.00
159	Angel Pena	6.00
160	Dewayne Wise	6.00
161	Tarrik Brock	6.00
162	Marcus Jensen	6.00
163	Kevin Barker	6.00
164	B.J. Ryan	6.00
165	Cesar King	6.00
166	Geoff Blum	6.00
167	Ruben Mateo	6.00
168	Ramon Ortiz	6.00
169	Eric Munson	6.00
170	Josh Beckett	8.00
171	Rafael Furcal	6.00
172	Matt Riley	6.00
173	*Johan Santana*	40.00
174	Mark Johnson	6.00
175	Adam Kennedy	6.00

Gold

Stars (1-125):	4-8X
SPs (126-175):	1X
Inserted 1:20	

(See 2000 Fleer Mystique for checklist and base card values.)

Club 3000

		NM/M
Complete Set (3):		6.00
Common Player:		1.50
Inserted 1:20		
1	Cal Ripken Jr.	5.00
2	Bob Gibson	1.50
3	Dave Winfield	1.50

Club 3000 Memorabilia

	NM/M
Cal Ripken Jr. - jersey/825	40.00
Cal Ripken Jr. - bat/265	75.00
Cal Ripken Jr. - hat/55	120.00
Cal Ripken Jr. - bat, jersey/100	100.00
Cal Ripken bat, hat, jersey/25	
Bob Gibson - jersey/825	20.00
Bob Gibson - bat/265	30.00
Bob Gibson - bat, jersey/100	50.00
Bob Gibson - hat, jersey/100	50.00
Bob Gibson - hat/55	75.00
Bob Gibson bat, hat, jersey/25	
Dave Winfield - jersey/825	15.00
Dave Winfield - bat/270	25.00
Dave Winfield bat, jersey/100	50.00
Dave Winfield - hat/55	60.00
Dave Winfield bat, hat, jersey/25	

Dave Winfield Auto. Memorabilia

		NM/M
Complete Set (2):		
1	Dave Winfield bat/20	140.00
2	Dave Winfield helmet/40	125.00

Diamond Dominators

	NM/M
Complete Set (10):	15.00
Common Player:	.75
Inserted 1:5	

1	Manny Ramirez	1.00
2	Pedro Martinez	1.00
3	Sean Casey	.75
4	Vladimir Guerrero	1.00
5	Sammy Sosa	1.50
6	Nomar Garciaparra	1.50
7	Mark McGwire	2.50
8	Ken Griffey Jr.	1.50
9	Derek Jeter	3.00
10	Alex Rodriguez	2.50

Feel the Game

		NM/M
Common Player:		5.00
Inserted 1:120		
1	Tony Gwynn jersey	20.00
2	Alex Rodriguez jersey	25.00
3	Chipper Jones jersey	20.00
4	Cal Ripken Jr. jersey	40.00
5	Derek Jeter pants	40.00
6	Alex Rodriguez bat	30.00
7	Frank Thomas bat	15.00
8	Barry Bonds bat	40.00
9	Carlos Beltran bat	5.00
10	Shawn Green bat	8.00
11	Michael Barrett bat	5.00
12	Rafael Palmeiro bat	10.00
13	Vladimir Guerrero bat	15.00
14	Pat Burrell bat	12.00

Fresh Ink

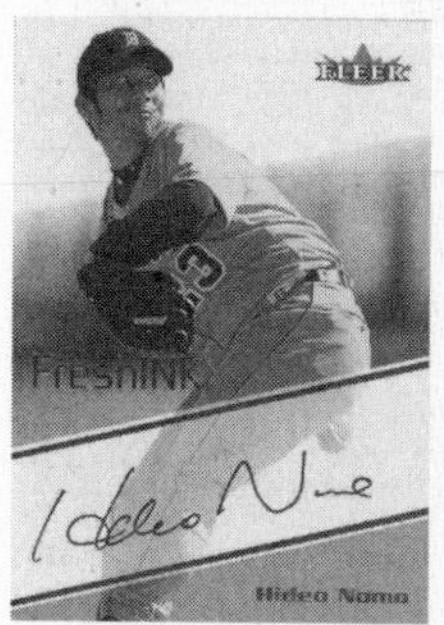

		NM/M
Common Player:		5.00
Inserted 1:40		
1	Chad Allen	5.00
2	Glen Barker	5.00
3	Michael Barrett	5.00
4	Josh Beckett	20.00
5	Rob Bell	5.00
6	Lance Berkman	25.00
7	Kent Bottenfield	5.00
8	Milton Bradley	8.00
9	Orlando Cabrera	10.00
10	Sean Casey	10.00
11	Roger Cedeno	6.00
12	Will Clark	25.00
13	Russ Davis	5.00
14	Carlos Delgado	15.00
15	Einar Diaz	5.00
16	J.D. Drew	10.00
17	Erubiel Durazo	10.00
18	Damion Easley	5.00
19	Carlos Febles	5.00
20	Doug Glanville	6.00
21	Alex Gonzalez	5.00
22	Tony Gwynn	40.00
23	Mike Hampton	8.00
24	Bobby Howry	5.00
25	John Jaha	5.00
26	Nick Johnson	10.00
27	Andruw Jones	20.00
28	Adam Kennedy	8.00
29	Mike Lieberthal	8.00
30	Jose Macias	5.00
31	Ruben Mateo	8.00
32	Raul Mondesi	8.00
33	Heath Murray	5.00
34	Mike Mussina	30.00
35	Hideo Nomo	250.00
36	Magglio Ordonez	15.00
37	Eric Owens	5.00
38	Adam Piatt	5.00
39	Cal Ripken Jr.	100.00
40	Tim Salmon	15.00
41	Chris Singleton	5.00
42	J.T. Snow	8.00
43	Mike Sweeney	10.00
44	Wilton Veras	5.00
45	Jose Vidro	8.00
46	Rondell White	10.00
47	Jaret Wright	5.00

High Praise

		NM/M
Complete Set (10):		18.00
Common Player:		.75
Inserted 1:20		
1	Mark McGwire	3.00
2	Ken Griffey Jr.	2.00
3	Alex Rodriguez	3.00
4	Derek Jeter	4.00
5	Sammy Sosa	2.00
6	Mike Piazza	2.00
7	Nomar Garciaparra	2.00
8	Cal Ripken Jr.	4.00
9	Tony Gwynn	1.50
10	Shawn Green	.75

Rookie I.P.O.

		NM/M
Complete Set (10):		8.00
Common Player:		.50
Inserted 1:10		
1	Josh Beckett	1.00
2	Eric Munson	.50
3	Pat Burrell	2.00
4	Alfonso Soriano	1.50
5	Rick Ankiel	.50
6	Ruben Mateo	.50
7	Mark Quinn	.50
8	Kip Wells	.50
9	Ben Petrick	.50
10	Nick Johnson	.75

Seismic Activity

		NM/M
Complete Set (10):		45.00
Common Player:		3.00
Inserted 1:40		
Richter parallel:		3-5X
Production 100 sets		
1	Ken Griffey Jr.	5.00
2	Sammy Sosa	5.00
3	Derek Jeter	10.00
4	Mark McGwire	8.00
5	Manny Ramirez	3.00
6	Mike Piazza	5.00
7	Vladimir Guerrero	3.00
8	Chipper Jones	4.00
9	Alex Rodriguez	8.00
10	Jeff Bagwell	3.00

Supernaturals

		NM/M
Complete Set (10):		15.00
Common Player:		1.00
Inserted 1:10		
1	Alex Rodriguez	3.00
2	Chipper Jones	1.75
3	Derek Jeter	4.00
4	Ivan Rodriguez	1.00
5	Ken Griffey Jr.	2.00
6	Mark McGwire	3.00
7	Mike Piazza	2.00
8	Nomar Garciaparra	2.00
9	Sammy Sosa	2.00
10	Vladimir Guerrero	1.50

2000 FLEER SHOWCASE

		NM/M
Complete Set (140):		200.00
Common Player (1-100):		.25
Common (101-115):		6.00
Production 1,000 sets		
Common (116-140):		4.00
Production 2,000 sets		
Pack (5):		2.50
Box (24):		50.00
1	Alex Rodriguez	2.50
2	Derek Jeter	3.00
3	Jeromy Burnitz	.25
4	John Olerud	.25
5	Paul Konerko	.25
6	Johnny Damon	.40
7	Curt Schilling	.50
8	Barry Larkin	.25
9	Adrian Beltre	.40
10	Scott Rolen	.75
11	Carlos Delgado	.50
12	Pedro J. Martinez	1.00
13	Todd Helton	1.00
14	Jacque Jones	.25
15	Jeff Kent	.25
16	Darin Erstad	.65
17	Juan Encarnacion	.25
18	Roger Clemens	1.75
19	Tony Gwynn	1.50
20	Nomar Garciaparra	2.00
21	Roberto Alomar	.40
22	Matt Lawton	.25
23	Rich Aurilia	.25
24	Charles Johnson	.25
25	Jim Thome	.25
26	Eric Milton	.25
27	Barry Bonds	3.00
28	Albert Belle	.25
29	Travis Fryman	.25
30	Ken Griffey Jr.	2.00
31	Phil Nevin	.25
32	Chipper Jones	1.50
33	Craig Biggio	.25
34	Mike Hampton	.25
35	Fred McGriff	.25
36	Cal Ripken Jr.	3.00
37	Manny Ramirez	1.00
38	Jose Vidro	.25
39	Trevor Hoffman	.25
40	Tom Glavine	.50
41	Frank Thomas	1.00
42	Chris Widger	.25
43	J.D. Drew	.50
44	Andres Galarraga	.25
45	Pokey Reese	.25
46	Mike Piazza	2.00
47	Kevin Young	.25
48	Sean Casey	.25
49	Carlos Beltran	.60
50	Jason Kendall	.25
51	Vladimir Guerrero	1.00
52	Jermaine Dye	.25
53	Brian Giles	.25
54	Andruw Jones	1.00
55	Richard Hidalgo	.25
56	Robin Ventura	.25
57	Ivan Rodriguez	.65
58	Greg Maddux	1.50
59	Billy Wagner	.25
60	Ruben Mateo	.25
61	Troy Glaus	1.00
62	Dean Palmer	.25
63	Eric Chavez	.40
64	Edgar Martinez	.25
65	Randy Johnson	1.00
66	Preston Wilson	.25
67	Orlando Hernandez	.25
68	Jim Edmonds	.25
69	Carl Everett	.25
70	Larry Walker	.25
71	Ron Belliard	.25
72	Sammy Sosa	2.00
73	Matt Williams	.25
74	Cliff Floyd	.25
75	Bernie Williams	.40
76	Fernando Tatis	.25
77	Steve Finley	.25
78	Jeff Bagwell	1.00
79	Edgardo Alfonzo	.25
80	Jose Canseco	.40
81	Magglio Ordonez	.40
82	Shawn Green	.40
83	Bobby Abreu	.25
84	Tony Batista	.25
85	Mo Vaughn	.25
86	Juan Gonzalez	1.00
87	Paul O'Neill	.25
88	Mark McGwire	2.50
89	Mark Grace	.35
90	Kevin Brown	.25
91	Ben Grieve	.25
92	Shannon Stewart	.25
93	Erubiel Durazo	.25
94	Antonio Alfonseca	.25
95	Jeff Cirillo	.25
96	Greg Vaughn	.25
97	Kerry Wood	.60
98	Geoff Jenkins	.25
99	Jason Giambi	.75
100	Rafael Palmeiro	.65
101	Rafael Furcal	6.00
102	Pablo Ozuna	6.00
103	Brad Penny	6.00
104	Mark Mulder	8.00
105	Adam Piatt	6.00
106	*Mike Lamb*	6.00
107	*Kazuhiro Sasaki*	15.00
108	*Aaron McNeal*	6.00
109	Pat Burrell	8.00
110	Rick Ankiel	6.00
111	Eric Munson	6.00
112	Josh Beckett	8.00
113	Adam Kennedy	6.00
114	Alex Escobar	8.00
115	Chad Hermansen	6.00
116	Kip Wells	4.00
117	Matt LeCroy	4.00
118	Julio Ramirez	4.00
119	Ben Petrick	4.00
120	Nick Johnson	6.00
121	Gookie Dawkins	4.00
122	*Julio Zuleta*	4.00
123	Alfonso Soriano	8.00
124	*Keith McDonald*	4.00
125	Kory DeHaan	4.00
126	Vernon Wells	6.00
127	Dernell Stenson	4.00
128	David Eckstein	4.00
129	Robert Fick	4.00
130	Cole Liniak	4.00
131	Mark Quinn	4.00
132	Eric Gagne	5.00
133	Wily Pena	4.00
134	*Andy Thompson*	4.00
135	*Steve Sisco*	4.00
136	*Paul Rigdon*	6.00
137	Rob Bell	4.00
138	Carlos Guillen	5.00
139	Jimmy Rollins	5.00
140	Jason Conti	4.00

Legacy

Stars (1-100):	30-50X
Prospects (101-140):	3-6X
Production 20 sets	

(See 2000 Fleer Showcase for checklist and base card values.)

2000 FLEER SHOWCASE MASTERPIECE

(Because of each card's unique nature, catalog values cannot be presented.)

Club 3000

		NM/M
Common Player:		3.00
Inserted 1:24		
1	Lou Brock	2.00
2	Nolan Ryan	8.00

Club 3000 Memorabilia

	NM/M
Lou Brock - jersey/680	15.00
Lou Brock - bat/270	25.00
Lou Brock - hat, bat, jersey/25	100.00
Nolan Ryan - jersey/780	40.00
Nolan Ryan - hat/65	120.00
Nolan Ryan - bat/265	60.00
Nolan Ryan - bat, jersey/100	120.00

Consummate Prose

		NM/M
Complete Set (15):		20.00
Common Player:		.50
Inserted 1:6		
1	Jeff Bagwell	1.50
2	Alex Rodriguez	3.00
3	Chipper Jones	2.00
4	Derek Jeter	4.00
5	Manny Ramirez	1.50
6	Tony Gwynn	2.00
7	Sammy Sosa	2.50
8	Ivan Rodriguez	1.00
9	Greg Maddux	2.00
10	Ken Griffey Jr.	2.50
11	Rick Ankiel	.50
12	Cal Ripken Jr.	4.00
13	Pedro Martinez	1.50
14	Mike Piazza	2.50
15	Mark McGwire	3.00

Feel the Game

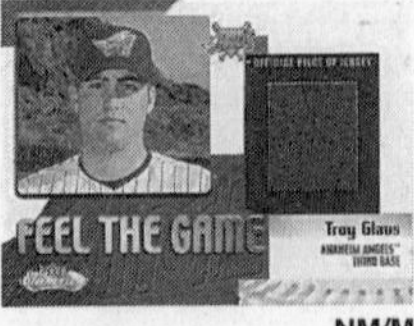

		NM/M
Common Player:		5.00
Inserted 1:72		
1	Barry Bonds	30.00
2	Gookie Dawkins	5.00
3	Darin Erstad	8.00
4	Troy Glaus	10.00
5	Scott Rolen	10.00
6	Alex Rodriguez	25.00
7	Andruw Jones	10.00
8	Robin Ventura	5.00
9	Sean Casey	5.00
10	Cal Ripken Jr.	40.00

Final Answer

		NM/M
Complete Set (10):		20.00
Common Player:		1.00
Inserted 1:10		
1	Alex Rodriguez	3.00
2	Vladimir Guerrero	1.00
3	Cal Ripken Jr.	4.00
4	Sammy Sosa	2.00
5	Barry Bonds	4.00
6	Derek Jeter	4.00
7	Ken Griffey Jr.	2.00
8	Mike Piazza	2.00
9	Nomar Garciaparra	2.00
10	Mark McGwire	3.00

Fresh Ink

		NM/M
Common Player:		5.00
Inserted 1:24		
1	Rick Ankiel	8.00
2	Josh Beckett	20.00
3	Barry Bonds	200.00
4	A.J. Burnett	10.00
5	Pat Burrell	15.00
6	Ken Caminiti	8.00
7	Sean Casey	10.00
8	Jose Cruz Jr.	10.00
9	Gookie Dawkins	5.00
10	Erubiel Durazo	10.00
11	Juan Encarnacion	8.00
12	Darin Erstad	15.00
13	Rafael Furcal	15.00
14	Nomar Garciaparra	100.00
15	Jason Giambi	20.00
16	Jeremy Giambi	6.00
17	Brian Giles	15.00
18	Troy Glaus	20.00
19	Mark Grace	
20	Vladimir Guerrero	30.00
21	Chad Hermansen	5.00
22	Orlando Hernandez	
23	Trevor Hoffman	8.00
24	Randy Johnson	60.00
25	Andruw Jones	15.00
26	Jason Kendall	8.00
27	Paul Konerko	10.00
28	Mike Lowell	10.00
29	Aaron McNeal	5.00
30	Warren Morris	5.00
31	Paul O'Neill	20.00
32	Magglio Ordonez	10.00
33	Pablo Ozuna	5.00
34	Brad Penny	8.00
35	Ben Petrick	5.00
36	Pokey Reese	5.00
37	Cal Ripken Jr.	125.00
38	Alex Rodriguez	75.00
39	Scott Rolen	30.00
40	Jose Vidro	8.00
41	Kip Wells	5.00

License to Skill

		NM/M
Complete Set (10):		25.00
Common Player:		1.50
Inserted 1:20		
1	Vladimir Guerrero	2.00
2	Pedro J. Martinez	2.00
3	Nomar Garciaparra	4.00
4	Ivan Rodriguez	1.50
5	Mark McGwire	5.00
6	Derek Jeter	6.00
7	Ken Griffey Jr.	4.00
8	Randy Johnson	2.00
9	Sammy Sosa	4.00
10	Alex Rodriguez	5.00

Long Gone

		NM/M
Complete Set (10):		25.00
Common Player:		2.00
Inserted 1:20		
1	Sammy Sosa	4.00
2	Derek Jeter	6.00
3	Nomar Garciaparra	4.00
4	Juan Gonzalez	2.00
5	Vladimir Guerrero	2.00
6	Barry Bonds	6.00
7	Jeff Bagwell	2.00
8	Alex Rodriguez	5.00
9	Ken Griffey Jr.	4.00
10	Mark McGwire	5.00

Noise of Summer

		NM/M
Complete Set (10):		15.00
Common Player:		1.00
Inserted 1:10		
1	Chipper Jones	1.50
2	Jeff Bagwell	1.00
3	Manny Ramirez	1.00
4	Mark McGwire	3.00
5	Ken Griffey Jr.	2.00
6	Mike Piazza	2.00
7	Pedro J. Martinez	1.00
8	Alex Rodriguez	3.00
9	Derek Jeter	4.00
10	Randy Johnson	1.00

Prospect Showcase First

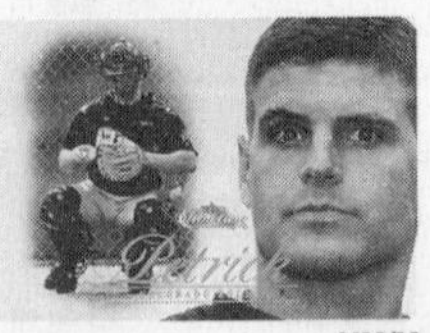

	NM/M
Prospects (101-140):	1-2X
Production 500 sets	

(See Prospects subset in 2000 Fleer Showcase for checklist and base values.)

Sweet Sigs

		NM/M
Common Player:		10.00
Inserted 1:250		
1	Nomar Garciaparra/53	150.00
2	Alex Rodriguez/67	200.00
3	Tony Gwynn	40.00
4	Roger Clemens/79	140.00
5	Scott Rolen	50.00
6	Greg Maddux	80.00
7	Jose Cruz Jr.	15.00
8	Tony Womack	10.00
9	Jay Buhner	10.00
10	Nolan Ryan	125.00

2000 FLEER TRADITION

		NM/M
Complete Set (450):		50.00
Common Player:		.10
Complete Glossy Factory Set (500):		450.00
Complete Glossy Factory Set (455):		90.00
Glossy (1-450):		1-2X
Common Glossy (451-500):		8.00
Five Glossy (451-500) per factory set		
1,000 produced (451-500)		
Pack (10):		1.50
Wax Box:		35.00
1	AL HRs	.50
2	NL HRs	.50
3	AL RBIs	.50
4	NL RBIs	.50
5	AL Avg.	.50
6	NL Avg.	.15
7	AL Wins	.20
8	NL Wins	.40
9	AL ERA	.20
10	NL ERA	.25
11	Matt Mantei	.10
12	John Rocker	.10
13	Kyle Farnsworth	.10
14	Juan Guzman	.10
15	Manny Ramirez	.75
16	Matt Riley-P, Calvin Pickering-1B	.10
17	Tony Clark	.10
18	Brian Meadows	.10
19	Orber Moreno	.10
20	Eric Karros	.10
21	Steve Woodard	.10
22	Scott Brosius	.10
23	Gary Bennett	.10
24	Jason Wood-3B, Dave Borkowski-P	.10
25	Joe McEwing	.10
26	Juan Gonzalez	.75
27	Roy Halladay	.25
28	Trevor Hoffman	.10
29	Arizona Diamondbacks	.10
30	Domingo Guzman-P, Wiki Gonzalez-C	.25
31	Bret Boone	.10
32	Nomar Garciaparra	2.00
33	Bo Porter	.10
34	Eddie Taubensee	.10
35	Pedro Astacio	.10
36	Derek Bell	.10
37	Jacque Jones	.10
38	Ricky Ledee	.10
39	Jeff Kent	.10
40	Matt Williams	.10
41	Alfonso Soriano-SS, D'Angelo Jimenez-3B	.75
42	B.J. Surhoff	.10
43	Denny Neagle	.10
44	Omar Vizquel	.10
45	Jeff Bagwell	.75
46	Mark Grudzielanek	.10
47	LaTroy Hawkins	.10
48	Orlando Hernandez	.10
49	Ken Griffey Jr.	2.00

50 Fernando Tatis .10
51 Quilvio Veras .10
52 Wayne Gomes .10
53 Rick Helling .10
54 Shannon Stewart .10
55 Dermal Brown-OF, Mark Quinn-OF .20
56 Randy Johnson 1.00
57 Greg Maddux 1.50
58 Mike Cameron .10
59 Matt Anderson .10
60 Milwaukee Brewers .10
61 Derrek Lee .10
62 Mike Sweeney .10
63 Fernando Vina .10
64 Orlando Cabrera .20
65 Doug Glanville .10
66 Stan Spencer .10
67 Ray Lankford .10
68 Kelly Dransfeldt .10
69 Alex Gonzalez .10
70 Russell Branyan-3B, Danny Peoples-OF .10
71 Jim Edmonds .10
72 Brady Anderson .10
73 Mike Stanley .10
74 Travis Fryman .10
75 Carlos Febles .10
76 Bobby Higginson .10
77 Carlos Perez .10
78 Steve Cox-1B, Alex Sanchez-OF .10
79 Dustin Hermanson .10
80 Kenny Rogers .10
81 Miguel Tejada .25
82 Ben Davis .10
83 Reggie Sanders .10
84 Eric Davis .10
85 J.D. Drew .45
86 Ryan Rupe .10
87 Bobby Smith .10
88 Jose Cruz Jr. .10
89 Carlos Delgado .50
90 Toronto Blue Jays .10
91 Denny Stark-P, Gil Meche-P .25
92 Randy Velarde .10
93 Aaron Boone .10
94 Javy Lopez .10
95 Johnny Damon .25
96 Jon Lieber .10
97 Montreal Expos .10
98 Mark Kotsay .10
99 Luis Gonzalez .25
100 Larry Walker .10
101 Adrian Beltre .25
102 Alex Ochoa .10
103 Michael Barrett .10
104 Tampa Bay Devil Rays .10
105 Rey Ordonez .10
106 Derek Jeter 3.00
107 Mike Lieberthal .10
108 Ellis Burks .10
109 Steve Finley .10
110 Ryan Klesko .10
111 Steve Avery .10
112 Dave Veres .10
113 Cliff Floyd .10
114 Shane Reynolds .10
115 Kevin Brown .10
116 David Nilsson .10
117 Mike Trombley .10
118 Todd Walker .10
119 John Olerud .10
120 Chuck Knoblauch .10
121 Nomar Garciaparra 2.00
122 Trot Nixon .10
123 Erubiel Durazo .10
124 Edwards Guzman .10
125 Curt Schilling .50
126 Brian Jordan .10
127 Cleveland Indians .10
128 Benito Santiago .10
129 Frank Thomas .75
130 Neifi Perez .10
131 Alex Fernandez .10
132 Jose Lima .10
133 Jorge Toca-1B, Melvin Mora-OF .10
134 Scott Karl .10
135 Brad Radke .10
136 Paul O'Neill .10
137 Kris Benson .10
138 Colorado Rockies .10
139 Jason Phillips .10
140 Robb Nen .10
141 Ken Hill .10
142 Charles Johnson .10
143 Paul Konerko .10
144 Dmitri Young .10
145 Justin Thompson .10
146 Mark Loretta .10
147 Edgardo Alfonzo .10
148 Armando Benitez .10
149 Octavio Dotel .10
150 Wade Boggs 1.50
151 Ramon Hernandez .10
152 Freddy Garcia .10
153 Edgar Martinez .10
154 Ivan Rodriguez .65
155 Kansas City Royals .10
156 Cleatus Davidson-2B, Cristian Guzman-SS .10
157 Andy Benes .10
158 Todd Dunwoody .10
159 Pedro Martinez 1.00
160 Mike Caruso .10
161 Mike Sirotka .10
162 Houston Astros .10
163 Darryl Kile .10
164 Chipper Jones 1.50
165 Carl Everett .10
166 Geoff Jenkins .10
167 Dan Perkins .10
168 Andy Pettitte .25
169 Francisco Cordova .10
170 Jay Buhner .10
171 Jay Bell .10
172 Andruw Jones .75
173 Bobby Howry .10
174 Chris Singleton .10
175 Todd Helton .75
176 A.J. Burnett .10
177 Marquis Grissom .10
178 Eric Milton .10
179 Los Angeles Dodgers .10
180 Kevin Appier .10
181 Brian Giles .10
182 Tom Davey .10
183 Mo Vaughn .10
184 Jose Hernandez .10
185 Jim Parque .10
186 Derrick Gibson .10
187 Bruce Aven .10
188 Jeff Cirillo .10
189 Doug Mientkiewicz .10
190 Eric Chavez .25
191 Al Martin .10
192 Tom Glavine .25
193 Butch Huskey .10
194 Ray Durham .10
195 Greg Vaughn .10
196 Vinny Castilla .10
197 Ken Caminiti .10
198 Joe Mays .10
199 Chicago White Sox .10
200 Mariano Rivera .20
201 Mark McGwire 2.50
202 Pat Meares .10
203 Andres Galarraga .10
204 Tom Gordon .10
205 Henry Rodriguez .10
206 Brett Tomko .10
207 Dante Bichette .10
208 Craig Biggio .10
209 Matt Lawton .10
210 Tino Martinez .10
211 Aaron Myette-P, Josh Paul-C .10
212 Warren Morris .10
213 San Diego Padres .10
214 Ramon E. Martinez .10
215 Troy Percival .10
216 Jason Johnson .10
217 Carlos Lee .10
218 Scott Williamson .10
219 Jeff Weaver .10
220 Ronnie Belliard .10
221 Jason Giambi .65
222 Ken Griffey Jr. 2.00
223 John Halama .10
224 Brett Hinchliffe .10
225 Wilson Alvarez .10
226 Rolando Arrojo .10
227 Ruben Mateo .10
228 Rafael Palmeiro .65
229 David Wells .10
230 Eric Gagne-P, Jeff Williams-P .10
231 Tim Salmon .30
232 Mike Mussina .50
233 Magglio Ordonez .25
234 Ron Villone .10
235 Antonio Alfonseca .10
236 Jeromy Burnitz .10
237 Ben Grieve .10
238 Giomar Guevara .10
239 Garret Anderson .10
240 John Smoltz .10
241 Mark Grace .15
242 Cole Liniak-3B, Jose Molina-C .10
243 Damion Easley .10
244 Jeff Montgomery .10
245 Kenny Lofton .10
246 Masato Yoshii .10
247 Philadelphia Phillies .10
248 Raul Mondesi .10
249 Marlon Anderson .10
250 Shawn Green .40
251 Sterling Hitchcock .10
252 Randy Wolf-P, Anthony Shumaker-P .10
253 Jeff Fassero .10
254 Eli Marrero .10
255 Cincinnati Reds .10
256 Rick Ankiel-P, Adam Kennedy-2B .50
257 Darin Erstad .60
258 Albert Belle .20
259 Bartolo Colon .10
260 Bret Saberhagen .10
261 Carlos Beltran .50
262 Glenallen Hill .10
263 Gregg Jefferies .10
264 Matt Clement .10
265 Miguel Del Toro .10
266 Robinson Cancel-C, Kevin Barker-1B .10
267 San Francisco Giants .10
268 Kent Bottenfield .10
269 Fred McGriff .10
270 Chris Carpenter .10
271 Atlanta Braves .10
272 *Wilton Veras-3B, Tomokazu Ohka-P* .50
273 Will Clark .20
274 Troy O'Leary .10
275 Sammy Sosa 2.00
276 Travis Lee .15
277 Sean Casey .25
278 Ron Gant .10
279 Roger Clemens 1.75
280 Phil Nevin .10
281 Mike Piazza 2.00
282 Mike Lowell .10
283 Kevin Millwood .10
284 Joe Randa .10
285 Jeff Shaw .10
286 Jason Varitek .10
287 Harold Baines .10
288 Gabe Kapler .10
289 Chuck Finley .10
290 Carl Pavano .10
291 Brad Ausmus .10
292 Brad Fullmer .10
293 Boston Red Sox .10
294 Bob Wickman .10
295 Billy Wagner .10
296 Shawn Estes .10
297 Gary Sheffield .40
298 Fernando Seguignol .10
299 Omar Olivares .10
300 Baltimore Orioles .10
301 Matt Stairs .10
302 Andy Ashby .10
303 Todd Greene .10
304 Jesse Garcia .10
305 Kerry Wood .50
306 Roberto Alomar .40
307 New York Mets .10
308 Dean Palmer .10
309 Mike Hampton .10
310 Devon White .10
311 Chad Hermansen-OF, Mike Garcia-P .10
312 Tim Hudson .40
313 John Franco .10
314 Jason Schmidt .10
315 J.T. Snow .10
316 Ed Sprague .10
317 Chris Widger .10
318 *Ben Petrick-C, Luther Hackman-P* .25
319 Jose Mesa .10
320 Jose Canseco .50
321 John Wetteland .10
322 Minnesota Twins .10
323 Jeff DaVanon-OF, Brian Cooper-P .25
324 Tony Womack .10
325 Rod Beck .10
326 Mickey Morandini .10
327 Pokey Reese .10
328 Jaret Wright .10
329 Glen Barker .10
330 Darren Dreifort .10
331 Torii Hunter .15
332 Tony Armas Jr.-P, Peter Bergeron-OF .10
333 Hideki Irabu .10
334 Desi Relaford .10
335 Barry Bonds 3.00
336 Gary DiSarcina .10
337 Gerald Williams .10
338 John Valentin .10
339 David Justice .10
340 Juan Encarnacion .10
341 Jeremy Giambi .10
342 Chan Ho Park .10
343 Vladimir Guerrero 1.00
344 Robin Ventura .10
345 Bobby Abreu .10
346 Tony Gwynn 1.50
347 Jose Jimenez .10
348 Royce Clayton .10
349 Kelvim Escobar .10
350 Chicago Cubs .10
351 Travis Dawkins-SS, Jason LaRue-C .10
352 Barry Larkin .10
353 Cal Ripken Jr. 3.00
353s Cal Ripken Jr. (overpprinted "PROMOTIONAL SAMPLE") 4.00
354 Alex Rodriguez 2.50
355 Todd Stottlemyre .10
356 Terry Adams .10
357 Pittsburgh Pirates .10
358 Jim Thome .10
359 Corey Lee-P, Doug Davis-P .10
360 Moises Alou .10
361 Todd Hollandsworth .10
362 Marty Cordova .10
363 David Cone .10
364 Joe Nathan-P, Wilson Delgado-SS .10
365 Paul Byrd .10
366 Edgar Renteria .10
367 Rusty Greer .10
368 David Segui .10
369 New York Yankees .50
370 Daryle Ward-OF/1B, Carlos Hernandez-2B .10
371 Troy Glaus .75
372 Delino DeShields .10
373 Jose Offerman .10
374 Sammy Sosa 2.00
375 Sandy Alomar Jr. .10
376 Masao Kida .10
377 Richard Hidalgo .10
378 Ismael Valdes .10
379 Ugueth Urbina .10
380 Darryl Hamilton .10
381 John Jaha .10
382 St. Louis Cardinals .10
383 Scott Sauerbeck .10
384 Russ Ortiz .10
385 Jamie Moyer .10
386 Dave Martinez .10
387 Todd Zeile .10
388 Anaheim Angels .10
389 Rob Ryan-OF, Nick Bierbrodt-P .10
390 Rickey Henderson .75
391 Alex Rodriguez 2.50
392 Texas Rangers .10
393 Roberto Hernandez .10
394 Tony Batista .10
395 Oakland Athletics .10
396 *Randall Simon-1B, David Cortes-P* .20
397 Gregg Olson .10
398 Sidney Ponson .10
399 Micah Bowie .10
400 Mark McGwire 2.50
401 Florida Marlins .10
402 Chad Allen .10
403 Casey Blake-3B, Vernon Wells-OF .10
404 Pete Harnisch .10
405 Preston Wilson .10
406 Richie Sexson .10
407 Rico Brogna .10
408 Todd Hundley .10
409 Wally Joyner .10
410 Tom Goodwin .10
411 Joey Hamilton .10
412 Detroit Tigers .10
413 Michael Tejera-P, Ramon Castro-C .25
414 Alex Gonzalez .10
415 Jermaine Dye .10
416 Jose Rosado .10
417 Wilton Guerrero .10
418 Rondell White .10
419 Al Leiter .10
420 Bernie Williams .25
421 A.J. Hinch .10

422 Pat Burrell .50
423 Scott Rolen .65
424 Jason Kendall .10
425 Kevin Young .10
426 Eric Owens .10
427 Derek Jeter 1.00
428 Livan Hernandez .10
429 Russ Davis .10
430 Dan Wilson .10
431 Quinton McCracken .10
432 Homer Bush .10
433 Seattle Mariners .10
434 Chad Harville-P,
Luis Vizcaino-P .10
435 Carlos Beltran .45
436 Scott Williamson .10
437 Pedro Martinez .75
438 Randy Johnson .75
439 Ivan Rodriguez .60
440 Chipper Jones .75
441 Bernie Williams
AL Division .15
442 Pedro Martinez
AL Division .50
443 Derek Jeter AL Champ 1.00
444 Brian Jordan NL Division .10
445 Todd Pratt NL Division .10
446 Kevin Millwood
NL Champ .10
447 Orlando Hernandez
World Series .10
448 Derek Jeter
World Series 1.00
449 Chad Curtis
World Series .10
450 Roger Clemens
World Series .75
451 *Carlos Casimiro* 8.00
452 *Adam Melhuse* 8.00
453 *Adam Bernero* 8.00
454 *Dusty Allen* 8.00
455 *Chan Perry* 8.00
456 *Damian Rolls* 8.00
457 *Josh Phelps* 40.00
458 *Barry Zito* 40.00
459 *Hector Ortiz* 8.00
460 *Juan Pierre* 10.00
461 *Jose Ortiz* 15.00
462 *Chad Zerbe* 8.00
463 *Julio Zuleta* 8.00
464 *Eric Byrnes* 15.00
465 *Wilfredo Rodriguez* 10.00
466 *Wascar Serrano* 8.00
467 *Aaron McNeal* 8.00
468 *Paul Rigdon* 8.00
469 *John Snyder* 8.00
470 *J.C. Romero* 8.00
471 *Talmadge Nunnari* 8.00
472 *Mike Lamb* 8.00
473 *Ryan Kohlmeier* 8.00
474 *Rodney Lindsey* 8.00
475 *Elvis Pena* 8.00
476 *Alex Cabrera* 10.00
477 *Chris Richard* 8.00
478 *Pedro Feliz* 10.00
479 *Ross Gload* 8.00
480 *Timoniel Perez* 8.00
481 *Jason Woolf* 8.00
482 *Kenny Kelly* 8.00
483 *Sang-Hoon Lee* 8.00
484 *John Riedling* 8.00
485 Chris Wakeland 8.00
486 *Britt Reames* 8.00
487 *Greg LaRocca* 8.00
488 *Randy Keisler* 8.00
489 *Xavier Nady* 30.00
490 *Keith Ginter* 10.00
491 *Joey Nation* 8.00
492 *Kazuhiro Sasaki* 15.00
493 *Lesli Brea* 8.00
494 *Jace Brewer* 8.00
495 *Yohanny Valera* 8.00
496 Adam Piatt 10.00
497 Nate Rolison 8.00
498 Aubrey Huff 10.00
499 Jason Tyner 8.00
500 Corey Patterson 12.00

Club 3000

NM/M
Complete Set (3): 5.00
Common Player: 3.00
Inserted 1:36
(1) George Brett 4.00
(2) Rod Carew 2.00
(3) Robin Yount 2.00

Club 3000 Memorabilia

NM/M
George Brett - bat/250 60.00
George Brett - hat/100 75.00
George Brett - jersey/445 30.00
George Brett - bat, jersey/100 90.00
George Brett - bat, hat, jersey/25
Rod Carew - bat/225 30.00
Rod Carew - hat/100 50.00
Rod Carew - jersey/440 20.00
Rod Carew - bat, jersey/100 65.00
Rod Carew - bat, hat, jersey/25
Robin Yount - bat/250 40.00
Robin Yount - hat/100 60.00
Robin Yount - jersey/440 30.00
Robin Yount - bat, jersey/100 75.00
Robin Yount - bat, hat, jersey/25

Dividends

NM/M
Complete Set (15): 15.00
Common Player: .50
Inserted 1:6
1 Alex Rodriguez 2.50
2 Ben Grieve .50
3 Cal Ripken Jr. 3.00
4 Chipper Jones 1.50
5 Derek Jeter 3.00
6 Frank Thomas 1.00
7 Jeff Bagwell 1.00
8 Sammy Sosa 2.00
9 Tony Gwynn 1.50
10 Scott Rolen .75
11 Nomar Garciaparra 2.00
12 Mike Piazza 2.00
13 Mark McGwire 2.50
14 Ken Griffey Jr. 2.00
15 Juan Gonzalez 1.00

Fresh Ink

NM/M
Common Player: 5.00
Inserted 1:144
Rick Ankiel 8.00
Carlos Beltran 25.00
Pat Burrell 15.00
Miguel Cairo 5.00
Sean Casey 8.00
Will Clark 30.00
Mike Darr 5.00
J.D. Drew 10.00
Erubiel Durazo 10.00
Carlos Febles 6.00
Freddy Garcia 8.00
Greg Maddux 80.00
Jason Grilli 5.00
Vladimir Guerrero 35.00
Tony Gwynn 40.00
Jerry Hairston Jr. 8.00
Tim Hudson 15.00
John Jaha 5.00
D'Angelo Jimenez 5.00
Andruw Jones 20.00
Gabe Kapler 6.00
Cesar King 5.00
Jason LaRue 6.00
Mike Lieberthal 8.00
Pedro Martinez 50.00
Gary Matthews Jr. 5.00
Orber Moreno 5.00
Eric Munson 5.00
Rafael Palmeiro 35.00
Jim Parque 6.00
Willi Mo Pena 15.00
Cal Ripken Jr. 100.00
Alex Rodriguez 80.00
Tim Salmon 15.00
Chris Singleton 5.00
Alfonso Soriano 50.00
Ed Yarnall 5.00

Glossy Lumberjacks

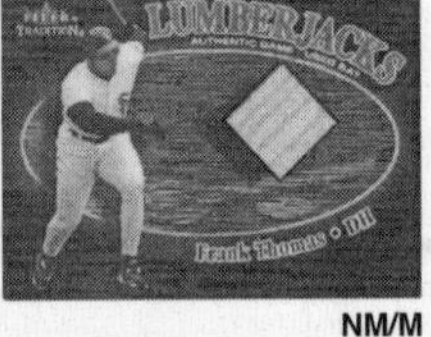

NM/M
Common Player: 8.00
One per Factory set
Production listed
1 Edgardo Alfonzo/145 10.00
2 Roberto Alomar/627 10.00
3 Moises Alou/529 8.00
4 Carlos Beltran/489 8.00
5 Adrian Beltre/127 10.00
6 Wade Boggs/30
7 Barry Bonds/305 40.00
8 Jeromy Burnitz/34
9 Pat Burrell/45 25.00
10 Sean Casey/50 15.00
11 Eric Chavez/259 10.00
12 Tony Clark/70 10.00
13 Carlos Delgado/70 20.00
14 J.D. Drew/135 10.00
15 Erubiel Durazo/70 10.00
16 Ray Durham/35
17 Carlos Febles/120 10.00
18 Jason Giambi/220 15.00
19 Shawn Green/429 10.00
20 Vladimir Guerrero/809 15.00
21 Derek Jeter/180 50.00
22 Chipper Jones/725 15.00
23 Gabe Kapler/160 8.00
24 Jason Kendall/34
25 Paul Konerko/70 10.00
26 Ray Lankford/35
27 Mike Lieberthal/45 10.00
28 Edgar Martinez/211 10.00
29 Raul Mondesi/458 8.00
30 Warren Morris/35 10.00
31 Magglio Ordonez/190 10.00
32 Rafael Palmeiro/49 15.00
33 Pokey Reese/110 8.00
34 Cal Ripken/235 50.00
35 Alex Rodriguez/292 25.00
36 Ivan Rodriguez/602 10.00
37 Scott Rolen/502 10.00
38 Chris Singleton/68 8.00
39 Alfonso Soriano/285 15.00
40 Frank Thomas/489 10.00
41 Jim Thome/479 10.00
42 Robin Ventura/114 10.00
43 Jose Vidro/60 10.00
44 Bernie Williams/215 10.00
45 Matt Williams/152 8.00

Grasskickers

NM/M
Complete Set (15): 50.00
Common Player: 2.00
Inserted 1:30
1 Tony Gwynn 3.00
2 Scott Rolen 2.00
3 Nomar Garciaparra 4.00
4 Mike Piazza 4.00
5 Mark McGwire 6.00
6 Frank Thomas 2.00
7 Cal Ripken Jr. 8.00
8 Chipper Jones 3.00
9 Greg Maddux 3.00
10 Ken Griffey Jr. 4.00
11 Juan Gonzalez 2.00
12 Derek Jeter 8.00
13 Sammy Sosa 4.00
14 Roger Clemens 3.50
15 Alex Rodriguez 6.00

Hall's Well

NM/M
Complete Set (15): 50.00
Common Player: 1.50
Inserted 1:30
1 Mark McGwire 6.00
2 Alex Rodriguez 6.00
3 Cal Ripken Jr. 8.00
4 Chipper Jones 3.00
5 Derek Jeter 8.00
6 Frank Thomas 2.00
7 Greg Maddux 3.00
8 Juan Gonzalez 2.00
9 Ken Griffey Jr. 4.00
10 Mike Piazza 4.00
11 Nomar Garciaparra 4.00
12 Sammy Sosa 4.00
13 Roger Clemens 3.50
14 Ivan Rodriguez 1.50
15 Tony Gwynn 3.00

Ripken Collection

NM/M
Complete Set (10): 50.00
Common Card: 6.00
Inserted 1:30
(Inserted at the rate of 1:30 packs.)

Ten-4

NM/M
Complete Set (10): 20.00
Common Player: 2.00
Inserted 1:18

1	Sammy Sosa	2.00
2	Nomar Garciaparra	2.00
3	Mike Piazza	2.00
4	Mark McGwire	3.00
5	Ken Griffey Jr.	2.00
6	Juan Gonzalez	1.00
7	Derek Jeter	4.00
8	Chipper Jones	1.50
9	Cal Ripken Jr.	4.00
10	Alex Rodriguez	3.00

Who To Watch

		NM/M
Complete Set (15):		5.00
Common Player:		.25
Inserted 1:3		
1	Rick Ankiel	.40
2	Matt Riley	.25
3	Wilton Veras	.25
4	Ben Petrick	.25
5	Chad Hermansen	.25
6	Peter Bergeron	.25
7	Mark Quinn	.25
8	Russell Branyan	.25
9	Alfonso Soriano	1.50
10	Randy Wolf	.50
11	Ben Davis	.25
12	Jeff DaVanon	.25
13	D'Angelo Jimenez	.25
14	Vernon Wells	1.00
15	Adam Kennedy	.40

2000 FLEER TRADITION UPDATE

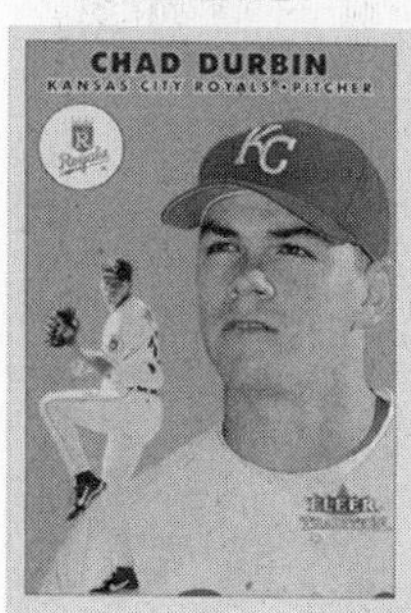

		NM/M
Complete Set (149):		15.00
Common Player:		.15
1	Ken Griffey Jr.	.50
2	Cal Ripken Jr.	1.00
3	Randy Velarde	.15
4	Fred McGriff	.15
5	Derek Jeter	1.00
6	Tom Glavine	.25
7	Brent Mayne	.15
8	Alex Ochoa	.15
9	Scott Sheldon	.15
10	Randy Johnson	.35
11	*Daniel Garibay*	.15
12	Brad Fullmer	.15
13	*Kazuhiro Sasaki*	1.00
14	Andy Tracy	.15
15	Bret Boone	.15
16	*Chad Durbin*	.25
17	*Mark Buehrle*	.75
18	*Julio Zuleta*	.15
19	Jeremy Giambi	.15
20	*Gene Stechschulte*	.15
21	Lou Pote	.15
22	Darrell Einertson	.15
23	Ken Griffey Jr.	.75
24	*Jeff Sparks*	.25
25	*Aaron Fultz*	.15
26	Derek Bell	.15
27	Rob Bell	.15
28	Rob Fick	.15
29	Darryl Kile	.15
30	Clayton Andrews	.15
31	Dave Veres	.15
32	*Hector Mercado*	.15
33	Willie Morales	.15
34	Kelly Wunsch	.15
35	Hideki Irabu	.15
36	Sean DePaula	.15
37	Dewayne Wise	.15
38	Curt Schilling	.25
39	Mark Johnson	.15
40	Mike Cameron	.15
41	Scott Sheldon	.15
42	Brett Tomko	.15
43	*Johan Santana*	8.00
44	Andy Benes	.15
45	Matt LeCroy	.15
46	Ryan Klesko	.15
47	Andy Ashby	.15
48	Octavio Dotel	.15
49	*Eric Byrnes*	1.00
50	Not Issued	
51	Kenny Rogers	.15
52	Ben Weber	.15
53	Matt Blank	.15
54	Tom Goodwin	.15
55	Jim Edmonds	.15
56	*Derrick Turnbow*	.25
57	Mark Mulder	.15
58	Tarrik Brock	.15
59	Danny Young	.15
60	Fernando Vina	.15
61	*Justin Brunette*	.15
62	Jimmy Anderson	.15
63	Reggie Sanders	.15
64	Adam Kennedy	.15
65	Jesse Garcia	.15
66	Al Martin	.15
67	Kevin Walker	.15
68	Brad Penny	.15
69	B.J. Surhoff	.15
70	Geoff Blum	.15
71	Jose Jimenez	.15
72	Chuck Finley	.15
73	Valerio De Los Santos	.15
74	Terry Adams	.15
75	Rafael Furcal	.15
76	Mike Darr	.15
77	Quilvio Veras	.15
78	Armando Almanza	.15
79	Greg Vaughn	.15
80	*Keith McDonald*	.15
81	Eric Cammack	.15
82	Horacio Estrada	.15
83	Kory DeHaan	.15
84	Kevin Hodges	.15
85	*Mike Lamb*	.25
86	Shawn Green	.40
87	Dan Reichert	.15
88	Adam Piatt	.15
89	Mike Garcia	.15
90	*Rodrigo Lopez*	1.00
91	John Olerud	.15
92	Barry Zito	1.00
93	Jimmy Rollins	.15
94	Denny Neagle	.15
95	Rickey Henderson	.50
96	Adam Eaton	.15
97	Brian O'Connor	.15
98	Andy Thompson	.15
99	Jason Boyd	.15
100	Carlos Guillen	.15
101	Raul Gonzalez	.15
102	*Brandon Kolb*	.25
103	Jason Maxwell	.15
104	*Luis Matos*	.75
105	*Morgan Burkhart*	.25
106	Ismael Villegas	.15
107	David Justice	.15
108	Pablo Ozuna	.15
109	Jose Canseco	.40
110	Alex Cora	.15
111	Will Clark	.25
112	Keith Luuloa	.15
113	Bruce Chen	.15
114	Adam Hyzdu	.15
115	Scott Forster	.15
116	Allen McDill	.15
117	Kevin Nicholson	.15
118	Israel Alcantara	.15
119	Juan Alvarez	.15
120	Julio Lugo	.15
121	B.J. Waszgis	.15
122	Jeff D'Amico	.15
123	Ricky Ledee	.15
124	Mark DeRosa	.15
125	*Alex Cabrera*	.50
126	Gary Matthews	.15
127	Richie Sexson	.15
128	Santiago Perez	.15
129	Rondell White	.15
130	*Craig House*	.15
131	Kevin Beirne	.15
132	Wayne Franklin	.15
133	Henry Rodriguez	.15
134	Jay Payton	.15
135	Ron Gant	.15
136	*Paxton Crawford*	.25
137	Kent Bottenfield	.15
138	*Rocky Biddle*	.15
139	Travis Lee	.15
140	Ryan Vogelsong	.15
141	Jason Conti	.15
142	Tim Drew	.15
143	*John Parrish*	.15
144	*Javier Cardona*	.15
145	*Tike Redman*	.15
146	Brian Schneider	.15
147	*Pasqual Coco*	.15
148	*Lorenzo Barcelo*	.15
149	*Jace Brewer*	.25
150	Milton Bradley	.15

Mantle Pieces

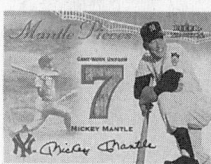

		NM/M
Inserted 1:80 sets		
1	Mickey Mantle	150.00

2001 FLEER AUTHORITY

		NM/M
Complete Set (150):		265.00
Common Player:		.25
Common (101-150):		3.00
Production 2,001		
Pack (5):		6.00
Box (22 + 2 graded packs):		120.00
1	Mark Grace	.35
2	Paul Konerko	.25
3	Sean Casey	.35
4	Jim Thome	.25
5	Todd Helton	.75
6	Tony Clark	.25
7	Jeff Bagwell	.75
8	Mike Sweeney	.25
9	Eric Karros	.25
10	Richie Sexson	.25
11	Doug Mientkiewicz	.25
12	Ryan Klesko	.25
13	John Olerud	.25
14	Mark McGwire	2.00
15	Fred McGriff	.25
16	Rafael Palmeiro	.65
17	Carlos Delgado	.50
18	Roberto Alomar	.40
19	Craig Biggio	.25
20	Jose Vidro	.25
21	Edgardo Alfonzo	.25
22	Jeff Kent	.25
23	Bret Boone	.25
24	Rafael Furcal	.25
25	Nomar Garciaparra	1.50
26	Barry Larkin	.25
27	Cristian Guzman	.25
28	Derek Jeter	2.50
29	Miguel Tejada	.40
30	Jimmy Rollins	.25
31	Rich Aurilia	.25
32	Alex Rodriguez	2.00
33	Cal Ripken Jr.	2.50
34	Troy Glaus	.75
35	Matt Williams	.25
36	Chipper Jones	1.00
37	Jeff Cirillo	.25
38	Robin Ventura	.25
39	Eric Chavez	.35
40	Scott Rolen	.65
41	Phil Nevin	.25
42	Mike Piazza	1.50
43	Jorge Posada	.35
44	Jason Kendall	.25
45	Ivan Rodriguez	.65
46	Frank Thomas	.75
47	Edgar Martinez	.25
48	Darin Erstad	.25
49	Tim Salmon	.35
50	Luis Gonzalez	.35
51	Andruw Jones	.75
52	Carl Everett	.25
53	Manny Ramirez	.75
54	Sammy Sosa	1.50
55	Rondell White	.25
56	Magglio Ordonez	.40
57	Ken Griffey Jr.	1.50
58	Juan Gonzalez	.75
59	Larry Walker	.25
60	Bobby Higginson	.25
61	Cliff Floyd	.25
62	Preston Wilson	.25
63	Moises Alou	.25
64	Lance Berkman	.25
65	Richard Hidalgo	.25
66	Jermaine Dye	.25
67	Mark Quinn	.25
68	Shawn Green	.50
69	Gary Sheffield	.40
70	Jeromy Burnitz	.25
71	Geoff Jenkins	.25
72	Vladimir Guerrero	.75
73	Bernie Williams	.35
74	Johnny Damon	.40
75	Jason Giambi	.60
76	Bobby Abreu	.25
77	Pat Burrell	.50
78	Brian Giles	.25
79	Tony Gwynn	1.00
80	Barry Bonds	2.50
81	J.D. Drew	.40
82	Jim Edmonds	.25
83	Greg Vaughn	.25
84	Raul Mondesi	.25
85	Shannon Stewart	.25
86	Randy Johnson	.75
87	Curt Schilling	.50
88	Tom Glavine	.40
89	Greg Maddux	1.00
90	Pedro Martinez	.75
91	Kerry Wood	.50
92	David Wells	.25
93	Bartolo Colon	.25
94	Mike Hampton	.25
95	Kevin Brown	.25
96	Al Leiter	.25
97	Roger Clemens	1.75
98	Mike Mussina	.50
99	Tim Hudson	.35
100	Kazuhiro Sasaki	.25
101	*Ichiro Suzuki*	35.00
102	*Albert Pujols*	50.00
103	*Drew Henson*	8.00
104	Adam Pettyjohn	3.00
105	*Adrian Hernandez*	3.00
106	Andy Morales	3.00
107	*Tsuyoshi Shinjo*	4.00
108	Juan Uribe	3.00
109	*Jack Wilson*	5.00
110	*Jason Smith*	3.00
111	*Junior Spivey*	6.00
112	*Wilson Betemit*	4.00
113	*Elpidio Guzman*	3.00
114	*Esix Snead*	3.00
115	*Winston Abreu*	3.00
116	*Jeremy Owens*	3.00
117	*Jay Gibbons*	8.00
118	Luis Lopez	3.00
119	*Ryan Freel*	3.00
120	*Rafael Soriano*	5.00
121	*Johnny Estrada*	6.00
122	*Bud Smith*	3.00
123	*Jackson Melian*	3.00
124	*Matt White*	3.00
125	*Travis Hafner*	8.00
126	*Morgan Ensberg*	5.00
127	*Endy Chavez*	3.00
128	*Bret Prinz*	3.00
129	*Juan Diaz*	3.00
130	*Erick Almonte*	4.00
131	*Rob Mackowiak*	3.00
132	*Carlos Valderrama*	3.00
133	*Wilkin Ruan*	3.00
134	*Angel Berroa*	5.00
135	*Henry Mateo*	3.00
136	Bill Ortega	3.00
137	*Billy Sylvester*	3.00
138	*Andres Torres*	3.00
139	Nate Frese	3.00
140	*Casey Fossum*	5.00
141	*Ricardo Rodriguez*	3.00
142	*Brian Roberts*	15.00
143	*Carlos Garcia*	3.00
144	*Brian Lawrence*	5.00

145 *Cory Aldridge* 3.00
146 *Mark Teixeira* 20.00
147 *Juan Cruz* 3.00
148 *Brandon Duckworth* 3.00
149 *Dewon Brazelton* 3.00
150 *Mark Prior* 40.00

Prominence

NM/M

Stars (1-100): 5-10X
Production 125
SP's (101-150): 3-5X
Production 75

(See 2001 Fleer Authority for checklist and base card values.)

Graded

NM/M

Mint: 1-1.5X
NrMt+: .8-1X
NrMt: .4-.6X
No Multipliers for Gem Mint

(See 2001 Fleer Authority for checklist and base card values.)

Authority Figures

NM/M

Complete Set (20): 75.00
Common Card: 2.00
1AF Mark McGwire, Albert Pujols 8.00
2AF Kazuhiro Sasaki, Ichiro Suzuki 8.00
3AF Derek Jeter, Drew Henson 10.00
4AF Ken Griffey Jr., Jackson Melian 6.00
5AF Wilson Betemit, Chipper Jones 4.50
6AF Jeff Bagwell, Morgan Ensberg 4.00
7AF Cal Ripken Jr., Jay Gibbons 10.00
8AF Mike Piazza, Tsuyoshi Shinjo 6.00
9AF Luis Gonzalez, Junior Spivey 2.00
10AF Barry Bonds, Carlos Valderrama 10.00
11AF Todd Helton, Juan Uribe 4.00
12AF Roger Clemens, Adrian Hernandez 5.00
13AF Alex Rodriguez, Travis Hafner 8.00
14AF Scott Rolen, Johnny Estrada 3.00
15AF Brian Giles, Rob Mackowiak 2.00
16AF Randy Johnson, Bret Prinz 4.00
17AF Carlos Delgado, Luis Lopez 3.00
18AF Manny Ramirez, Juan Diaz 4.00
19AF Mike Sweeney, Endy Chavez 2.00
20AF Sammy Sosa, Jaisen Randolph 6.00

Rookie cards are in *Italic*.

Derek Jeter Monumental Moments

NM/M

MM4 Derek Jeter/2000 5.00
MM4AU Derek Jeter/auto/100 100.00

Derek Jeter Reprint Autographs

NM/M

1DJRA Derek Jeter/500 90.00

Diamond Cuts

NM/M

Common Player: 4.00
Inserted 1:10
Rick Ankiel/Shoe 4.00
Jeff Bagwell/Jersey 8.00
Adrian Beltre/Hat 4.00
Craig Biggio/Bat 4.00
Barry Bonds/Hat 35.00
Barry Bonds/Jersey 20.00
Barry Bonds/Pants 20.00
Barry Bonds/Shoe 30.00
Barry Bonds/Wristband/100 50.00
Kevin Brown/Hat 6.00
Kevin Brown/Pants 4.00
Eric Byrnes/Bat 4.00
Sean Casey/Jersey 4.00
Eric Chavez/Hat 6.00
Chipper Jones/Jersey 10.00
Chipper Jones/Bat 10.00
Bartolo Colon/Hat 6.00
Erubiel Durazo/Bat 4.00
Ray Durham/Bat 4.00
Jim Edmonds/Hat 6.00
Jim Edmonds/Shoe 10.00
Darin Erstad/Hat 6.00
Carlos Febles/Bat 4.00
Carlos Febles/Shoe 4.00
Rafael Furcal/Hat 6.00
Juan Gonzalez/Bat Glove 10.00
Juan Gonzalez/Hat 8.00
Luis Gonzalez 6.00
Shawn Green/Bat Glove 10.00
Shawn Green/Bat 6.00
Vladimir Guerrero/Bat 8.00
Tony Gwynn/Bat 8.00
Mike Hampton/Hat 5.00
Mike Hampton/Shoe 5.00
Jerry Hairston Jr./Hat 4.00
Jason Hart/Bat 4.00
Todd Helton/Jersey 8.00
Todd Helton/Pants 8.00
Orlando Hernandez/Bat 4.00
Richard Hidalgo/Bat 4.00
Richard Hidalgo/Bat Glove 15.00
Derek Jeter/Bat 30.00
Derek Jeter/Bat Glove 60.00
Derek Jeter/Jersey 30.00
Derek Jeter/Pants 30.00
Derek Jeter/Shoe 40.00
Randy Johnson/Hat 30.00
Andruw Jones/Bat 6.00
Andruw Jones/Hat 8.00
Jason Kendall/Hat 6.00
Barry Larkin/Jersey 5.00
Matt Lawton/Hat 6.00
Mike Lieberthal/Bat Glove 6.00
Mike Lieberthal/Wristband
Kenny Lofton/Bat 4.00
Edgar Martinez/Bat Glove 8.00
Pedro Martinez/Shoe 10.00
Raul Mondesi/Bat 4.00
Raul Mondesi/Bat Glove 6.00
Hideo Nomo/Bat 15.00
Hideo Nomo/Hat 40.00
Magglio Ordonez/Bat Glove 8.00
Magglio Ordonez/Hat 6.00
David Ortiz/Bat 4.00
Rafael Palmeiro/Bat 8.00
Rafael Palmeiro/Hat 10.00
Chan Ho Park/Hat 5.00
Mike Piazza/Bat 15.00
Mike Piazza/Jersey 15.00
Mike Piazza/Shoe 25.00
Albert Pujols/Pants 30.00
Manny Ramirez/Bat 8.00
Manny Ramirez/Bat Glove 15.00
Manny Ramirez/Hat 15.00
Cal Ripken Jr./Bat Glove 65.00
Cal Ripken Jr./Pants 25.00
Ivan Rodriguez/Bat Glove 10.00
Ivan Rodriguez/Hat 10.00
Ivan Rodriguez/Pants 8.00
Ivan Rodriguez/Shoe 10.00
Scott Rolen/Hat 10.00
Jared Sandberg/Bat 4.00
Deion Sanders/Jersey 4.00
Tsuyoshi Shinjo/Wristband 10.00
Tsuyoshi Shinjo/Bat 6.00
J.T. Snow 4.00
Alfonso Soriano/Hat 20.00
Ichiro Suzuki/Bat 50.00
Ichiro Suzuki/Hat 65.00
Mike Sweeney/Hat 6.00
Miguel Tejada/Hat 6.00
Frank Thomas/Bat 8.00
Frank Thomas/Hat 10.00
Jim Thome/Bat 8.00
Larry Walker/Bat 4.00
Larry Walker/Jersey 4.00
Bernie Williams/Bat 6.00
Brian Giles/Pants 5.00

Seal of Approval

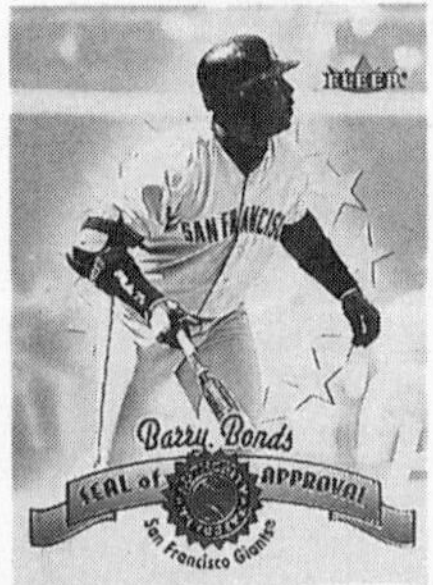

NM/M

Complete Set (15): 45.00
Common Player: 1.50
1SA Derek Jeter 6.00
2SA Alex Rodriguez 5.00
3SA Nomar Garciaparra 4.00
4SA Cal Ripken Jr. 6.00
5SA Mike Piazza 4.00
6SA Mark McGwire 5.00
7SA Tony Gwynn 3.00
8SA Barry Bonds 6.00
9SA Greg Maddux 3.00
10SA Chipper Jones 3.00
11SA Roger Clemens 3.50
12SA Ken Griffey Jr. 4.00
13SA Vladimir Guerrero 2.00
14SA Sammy Sosa 4.00
15SA Todd Helton 1.50

2001 FLEER BOSTON RED SOX 100TH ANNIVERSARY

NM/M

Complete Set (100): 40.00
Common Player: .25
Pack (5): 6.00
Box (24): 125.00
1 Carl Yastrzemski 2.50
2 Mel Parnell .25
3 Birdie Tebbetts .25
4 Tex Hughson .25
5 Nomar Garciaparra 4.00
6 Fred Lynn .50
7 John Valentin .25
8 Rico Petrocelli .25
9 Ted Williams 5.00
10 Roger Clemens 3.00
11 Luis Aparicio .40
12 Cy Young 1.50
13 Carlton Fisk 1.00
14 Pedro Martinez 2.00
15 Joe Dobson .25
16 Babe Ruth 5.00
17 Doc Cramer .25
18 Pete Runnels .25
19 Tony Conigliaro .25
20 Bill Monbouquette .25
21 Boo Ferriss .25
22 Harry Hooper .25
23 Tony Armas .25
24 Joe Cronin 1.00
25 Rick Ferrell .25
26 Wade Boggs 2.25
27 Don Baylor .25
28 Jeff Reardon .25
29 Smokey Joe Wood .25
30 Mo Vaughn .40
31 Walt Dropo .25
32 Vern Stephens .25
33 Bernie Carbo .25
34 George Scott .25
35 Lefty Grove 1.00
36 Dom DiMaggio 1.00
37 Dennis Eckersley .75
38 Johnny Pesky .25
39 Jim Lonborg .25
40 Jimmy Piersall .25
41 Tris Speaker 1.50
42 Frank Malzone .25
43 Bobby Doerr .75
44 Jimmie Foxx 2.00
45 Tony Pena .25
46 Billy Goodman .25
47 Jim Rice .25
48 Reggie Smith .25
49 Bill Buckner .25
50 Earl Wilson .25
51 Rick Burleson .25
52 George Kell .25
53 Dick Radatz .25
54 Dwight Evans .25
55 Luis Tiant .25
56 Elijah "Pumpsie" Green .25
57 Gene Conley .25
58 Jackie Jensen .25
59 Mike Fornieles .25
60 Dutch Leonard .25
61 Jake Stahl .25
62 Don Schwall .25
63 Jimmy Collins .25
64 Herb Pennock .25
65 .25
66 Carney Lansford .25
67 Dick Stuart .25
68 Dave Morehead .25
69 Harry Agganis .25
70 Lou Boudreau .25

71 Joe Morgan .75
72 Don Zimmer .75
73 Tom Yawkey .25
74 Jean Yawkey .25
75 Origin of the Red Sox .25
76 First Season .25
77 World Series History .25
78 Carl Yastrzemski 1.00
79 Carlton Fisk .50
80 Dom DiMaggio .50
81 Wade Boggs .75
82 Nomar Garciaparra 2.00
83 Pedro Martinez 1.00
84 Ted Williams 2.50
85 Jim Rice .25
86 Fred Lynn .25
87 Mo Vaughn .25
88 Bobby Doerr .40
89 Bernie Carbo .25
90 Dennis Eckersley .35
91 Jimmy Piersall .25
92 Luis Tiant .25
93 Jimmy Fund signage .25
94 Green Monster w/Ads .25
95 Green Monster w/All-Star logo .25
96 Ladder shot on Green Monster .25
97 Manual Scoreboard .25
98 Panoramic of Fenway .25
99 Lansdowne St. .25
100 1999 All-Star Game .25

Auto. Caps

NM/M
Complete Set (18): 825.00
Common Player: 15.00
(1) Wade Boggs 75.00
(2) Bill Buckner 20.00
(3) Bernie Carbo 15.00
(4) Roger Clemens 200.00
(5) Dom DiMaggio 30.00
(6) Bobby Doerr 25.00
(7) Dennis Eckersley 50.00
(8) Dwight Evans 40.00
(9) Carlton Fisk 125.00
(10) Nomar Garciaparra 125.00
(11) Jim Lonborg 20.00
(12) Johnny Pesky 15.00
(13) Rico Petrocelli 20.00
(14) Jimmy Piersall 30.00
(15) Jim Rice 40.00
(16) Luis Tiant 30.00
(17) Carl Yastrzemski 200.00
(18) Don Zimmer 30.00

BoSox Sigs

NM/M
Complete Set (16): 1,000
Common Autograph: 15.00
Inserted 1:96
Wade Boggs 80.00
Bill Buckner 20.00
Bernie Carbo 15.00
Roger Clemens/100 200.00
Dom DiMaggio 60.00
Bobby Doerr 40.00
Dwight Evans 35.00
Carlton Fisk 80.00
Nomar Garciaparra 120.00
Jim Lonborg 15.00
Fred Lynn 40.00
Rico Petrocelli 15.00
Jim Rice 40.00
Luis Tiant 30.00
Carl Yastrzemski/200 150.00

Field the Game

NM/M
Complete Set (4): 75.00
(1) Piece of Green Monster outfield wall 20.00
(2) Piece of base from 100th anniver. game 20.00
(3) Piece of baseball from 100th anniv. game 20.00
(4) anniv. game 20.00

Splendid Splinters

NM/M
Complete Set (15): 20.00
Common Player: 1.00
Inserted 1:10
SS1 Babe Ruth 6.00
SS2 Dom DiMaggio 1.50
SS3 Carlton Fisk 2.00
SS4 Carl Yastrzemski 3.00
SS5 Nomar Garciaparra 5.00
SS6 Wade Boggs 2.50
SS7 Ted Williams 5.00
SS8 Jim Rice 1.00
SS9 Mo Vaughn 1.00
SS10 Tris Speaker 2.00
SS11 Dwight Evans 1.00
SS12 Jimmie Foxx 2.50
SS13 Bobby Doerr 1.50
SS14 Fred Lynn 1.00
SS15 Johnny Pesky 1.00

Splendid Splinters Game Bat

NM/M
Complete Set (8): 800.00
Common Player: 15.00
Inserted 1:96
Babe Ruth SP/100 400.00
Carl Yastrzemski 75.00
Nomar Garciaparra 40.00
Wade Boggs 25.00
Ted Williams SP/100 250.00
Jim Rice 15.00
Dwight Evans 15.00
Jimmie Foxx SP/100 200.00

Threads

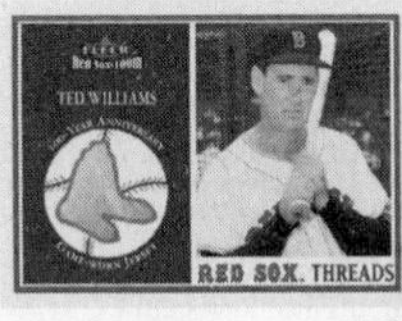

NM/M
Complete Set (9): 400.00
Common Player: 15.00
Inserted 1:96
Wade Boggs 25.00
Roger Clemens 50.00
Dwight Evans 15.00
Carlton Fisk/100 40.00
Pedro Martinez/100 40.00
Jim Rice 20.00
Ted Williams/100 180.00
Carl Yastrzemski 40.00
Don Zimmer 15.00

Yawkey's Heroes

NM/M
Complete Set (20): 15.00
Common Player: .50
Inserted 1:4
1YH Bobby Doerr .75
2YH Dom DiMaggio 1.00
3YH Jim Rice .50
4YH Wade Boggs 1.50
5YH Carlton Fisk 1.00
6YH Nomar Garciaparra 3.00
7YH Dennis Eckersley 1.00
8YH Carl Yastrzemski 2.00
9YH Ted Williams 4.00
10YH Tony Conigliaro .75
11YH Tony Armas .50
12YH Joe Cronin 1.00
13YH Mo Vaughn .50
14YH Johnny Pesky .50
15YH Jim Lonborg .50
16YH Luis Tiant .50
17YH Tony Pena .50
18YH Dwight Evans .50
19YH Fred Lynn .75
20YH Jimmy Piersall .50

2001 FLEER FOCUS

NM/M
Complete Set (240): 140.00
Common Player: .15
Common Prospect (201-224): 3.00
Common Prospect (225-250): 3.00
Pack (10): 2.50
Box (24): 50.00
1 Derek Jeter 2.00
2 Manny Ramirez .75
3 Ken Griffey Jr. 1.25
4 Ken Caminiti .15
5 Joe Randa .15
6 Jason Kendall .15
7 Ron Coomer .15
8 Rondell White .15
9 Tino Martinez .15
10 Nomar Garciaparra 1.25
11 Tony Batista .15
12 Todd Stottlemyre .15
13 Ryan Klesko .15
14 Darin Erstad .50
15 Todd Walker .15
16 Al Leiter .15
17 Carl Everett .15
18 Bobby Abreu .15
19 Raul Mondesi .15
20 Vladimir Guerrero .75
21 Mike Bordick .15
22 Aaron Sele .15
23 Ray Lankford .15
24 Roger Clemens 1.00
25 Kevin Young .15
26 Brad Radke .15
27 Todd Hundley .15
28 Ellis Burks .15
29 Lee Stevens .15
30 Eric Karros .15
31 Darren Dreifort .15
32 Ivan Rodriguez .60
33 Pedro Martinez .75
34 Travis Fryman .15
35 Garret Anderson .15
36 Rafael Palmeiro .60
37 Jason Giambi .50
38 Jeromy Burnitz .15
39 Robin Ventura .15
40 Derek Bell .15
41 Carlos Guillen .15
42 Albert Belle .15
43 Henry Rodriguez .15
44 Brian Jordan .15
45 Mike Sweeney .15
46 Ruben Rivera .15
47 Greg Maddux 1.00
48 Corey Koskie .15
49 Sandy Alomar Jr. .15
50 Mike Mussina .40
51 Tom Glavine .25
52 Aaron Boone .15
53 Frank Thomas .75
54 Kenny Lofton .15
55 Danny Graves .15
56 Jose Valentin .15
57 Travis Lee .15
58 Jim Edmonds .15
59 Jim Thome .15
60 Steve Finley .15
61 Shawn Green .45
62 Lance Berkman .15
63 Mark Quinn .15
64 Randy Johnson .75
65 Dmitri Young .15
66 Andy Pettitte .25
67 Paul O'Neill .15
68 Gil Heredia .15
69 Russell Branyan .15
70 Alex Rodriguez 1.50
71 Geoff Jenkins .15
72 Eric Chavez .25
73 Cal Ripken Jr. 2.00
74 Mark Kotsay .15
75 Jeff D'Amico .15
76 Tony Womack .15
77 Eric Milton .15
78 Joe Girardi .15
79 Peter Bergeron .15
80 Miguel Tejada .25
81 Luis Gonzalez .25
82 Doug Glanville .15
83 Gerald Williams .15
84 Troy O'Leary .15
85 Brian Giles .15
86 Miguel Cairo .15
87 Magglio Ordonez .25
88 Rick Helling .15
89 Bruce Chen .15
90 Jason Varitek .15
91 Mike Lieberthal .15
92 Shawn Estes .15
93 Rick Ankiel .15
94 Tim Salmon .25
95 Jacque Jones .15
96 Johnny Damon .25
97 Larry Walker .15
98 Ruben Mateo .15
99 Brad Fullmer .15
100 Edgardo Alfonzo .15
101 Mark Mulder .15
102 Tony Gwynn 1.00
103 Mike Cameron .15
104 Richie Sexson .15
105 Barry Larkin .15
106 Mike Piazza 1.25
107 Eric Young .15
108 Edgar Renteria .15
109 Todd Zeile .15
110 Luis Castillo .15
111 Sammy Sosa 1.25
112 David Justice .15
113 Delino DeShields .15
114 Mariano Rivera .25
115 Edgar Martinez .15
116 Ray Durham .15
117 Brady Anderson .15
118 Eric Owens .15
119 Alex Gonzalez .15
120 Jay Buhner .15
121 Greg Vaughn .15
122 Mike Lowell .15
123 Marquis Grissom .15
124 Matt Williams .15
125 Dean Palmer .15
126 Troy Glaus .75
127 Bret Boone .15
128 David Ortiz .25
129 Glenallen Hill .15
130 Chipper Jones 1.00
131 Tony Clark .15
132 Terrence Long .15
133 Chuck Finley .15
134 Jeff Bagwell .75
135 J.T. Snow .15
136 Andruw Jones .75
137 Carlos Delgado .50

138 Mo Vaughn .15
139 Derrek Lee .15
140 Bobby Estalella .15
141 Kerry Wood .60
142 Jose Vidro .15
143 Ben Grieve .15
144 Barry Bonds 2.00
145 Javy Lopez .15
146 Adam Kennedy .15
147 Jeff Cirillo .15
148 Cliff Floyd .15
149 Carl Pavano .25
150 Bobby Higginson .15
151 Kevin Brown .15
152 Fernando Tatis .15
153 Matt Lawton .15
154 Damion Easley .15
155 Curt Schilling .25
156 Mark McGwire 1.50
157 Mark Grace .25
158 Adrian Beltre .30
159 Jorge Posada .25
160 Richard Hidalgo .15
161 Vinny Castilla .15
162 Bernie Williams .30
163 John Olerud .15
164 Todd Helton .75
165 Craig Biggio .15
166 David Wells .15
167 Phil Nevin .15
168 Andres Galarraga .15
169 Moises Alou .15
170 Denny Neagle .15
171 Jeffrey Hammonds .15
172 Sean Casey .30
173 Gary Sheffield .40
174 Carlos Lee .15
175 Juan Encarnacion .15
176 Roberto Alomar .40
177 Kenny Rogers .15
178 Charles Johnson .15
179 Shannon Stewart .15
180 B.J. Surhoff .15
181 Paul Konerko .15
182 Jermaine Dye .15
183 Scott Rolen .60
184 Fred McGriff .15
185 Juan Gonzalez .75
186 Carlos Beltran .40
187 Jay Payton .15
188 Chad Hermansen .15
189 Pat Burrell .50
190 Omar Vizquel .15
191 Trot Nixon .15
192 Mike Hampton .15
193 Kris Benson .15
194 Gabe Kapler .15
195 Rickey Henderson .75
196 J.D. Drew .45
197 Pokey Reese .15
198 Jeff Kent .15
199 Jose Cruz Jr. .15
200 Preston Wilson .15
201 Eric Munson 2,499 3.00
202 Alex Cabrera 2,499 3.00
203 Nate Rolison 2,499 3.00
204 Julio Zuleta 2,499 3.00
205 Chris Richard 2,499 3.00
206 Dernell Stenson 2,499 3.00
207 Aaron McNeal 2,499 3.00
208 Aubrey Huff 2,999 5.00
209 Mike Lamb 2,999 3.00
210 Xavier Nady 2,999 4.00
211 Joe Crede 2,999 4.00
212 Ben Petrick 3,499 3.00
213 Morgan Burkhart 3,499 3.00
214 Jason Tyner 1,999 3.00
215 Juan Pierre 1,999 5.00
216 Adam Dunn 1,999 5.00
117 Adam Piatt 1,999 3.00
218 Eric Byrnes 1,999 4.00
219 Corey Patterson 1,999 4.00
220 Kenny Kelly 1,999 3.00
221 Tike Redman 1,999 3.00
222 Luis Matos 1,999 4.00
223 Timoniel Perez 1,999 3.00
224 Vernon Wells 1,999 3.00
225 Barry Zito 4,999 5.00
226 Adam Bernero 4,999 3.00
227 Kazuhiro Sasaki 4,999 6.00
228 Oswaldo Mairena 4,999 3.00
229 Mark Buehrle 4,999 4.00
230 Ryan Dempster 4,999 3.00
231 Tim Hudson 4,999 5.00
232 Scott Downs 4,999 3.00
233 A.J. Burnett 4,999 4.00
234 Adam Eaton 4,999 3.00
235 Paxton Crawford 4,999 3.00
236 Jace Brewer 3,999 3.00
237 Jose Ortiz 3,999 3.00
238 Rafael Furcal 3,999 4.00
239 Julio Lugo 3,999 3.00
240 Tomas de la Rosa 3,999 3.00

Green

NM/M

Common Player: 1.00
Random inserts in packs
Stated print runs listed below

1 Derek Jeter/339 10.00
2 Manny Ramirez/351 4.00
3 Ken Griffey Jr./271 8.00
4 Ken Caminiti/303 1.00
5 Joe Randa/304 1.00
6 Jason Kendall/270 1.50
7 Ron Coomer/270 1.00
8 Rondell White/258 1.50
9 Tino Martinez/258 2.00
10 Nomar Garciaparra/372 10.00
11 Tony Batista/263 1.00
12 Todd Stottlemyre/491 1.00
13 Ryan Klesko/283 1.50
14 Darin Erstad/355 1.50
15 Todd Walker/290 1.00
16 Al Leiter/320 1.00
17 Carl Everett/300 1.00
18 Bobby Abreu/316 1.50
19 Raul Mondesi/271 1.00
20 Vladimir Guerrero/345 5.00
21 Mike Bordick/285 1.00
22 Aaron Sele/451 1.00
23 Ray Lankford/253 1.00
24 Roger Clemens/370 10.00
25 Kevin Young/258 1.00
26 Brad Radke/445 1.00
27 Todd Hundley/284 1.00
28 Ellis Burks/344 1.00
29 Lee Stevens/265 1.00
30 Eric Karros/250 1.00
31 Darren Dreifort/416 1.00
32 Ivan Rodriguez/347 4.00
33 Pedro Martinez/174 5.00
34 Travis Fryman/321 1.50
35 Garret Anderson/286 2.00
36 Rafael Palmeiro/288 3.00
37 Jason Giambi/333 5.00
38 Jeromy Burnitz/232 1.00
39 Robin Ventura/232 1.50
40 Derek Bell/266 1.00
41 Carlos Guillen/257 1.00
42 Albert Belle/281 1.00
43 Henry Rodriguez/256 1.00
44 Brian Jordan/264 1.00
45 Mike Sweeney/333 1.00
46 Ruben Rivera/208 1.00
47 Greg Maddux/300 8.00
48 Corey Koskie/300 1.00
49 Sandy Alomar Jr./289 1.00
50 Mike Mussina/379 3.00
51 Tom Glavine/340 2.00
52 Aaron Boone/285 1.00
53 Frank Thomas/328 4.00
54 Kenny Lofton/278 2.00
55 Danny Graves/256 1.00
56 Jose Valentin/273 1.00
57 Travis Lee/235 1.00
58 Jim Edmonds/295 2.00
59 Jim Thome/269 4.00
60 Steve Finley/280 1.00
61 Shawn Green/269 2.00
62 Lance Berkman/297 2.00
63 Mark Quinn/294 1.00
64 Randy Johnson/264 5.00
65 Dmitri Young/303 1.00
66 Andy Pettitte/435 2.00
67 Paul O'Neill/283 2.00
68 Gil Heredia/412 1.00
69 Russell Branyan/238 1.00
70 Alex Rodriguez/316 10.00
71 Geoff Jenkins/303 1.50
72 Eric Chavez/277 2.00
73 Cal Ripken Jr./256 15.00
74 Mark Kotsay/298 1.00
75 Jeff D'Amico/266 1.00
76 Tony Womack/271 1.00
77 Eric Milton/486 1.00
78 Joe Girardi/278 1.00
79 Peter Bergeron/245 1.00
80 Miguel Tejada/275 2.00
81 Luis Gonzalez/311 2.00
82 Doug Glanville/275 1.00
83 Gerald Williams/274 1.00
84 Troy O'Leary/261 1.00
85 Brian Giles/315 2.00
86 Miguel Cairo/261 1.00
87 Magglio Ordonez/315 2.00
88 Rick Helling/448 1.00
89 Bruce Chen/329 1.00
90 Jason Varitek/248 1.00
91 Mike Lieberthal/278 1.00
92 Shawn Estes/426 1.00
93 Rick Ankiel/350 1.00
94 Tim Salmon/290 2.00
95 Jacque Jones/285 1.00
96 Johnny Damon/327 1.50
97 Larry Walker/309 2.00
98 Ruben Mateo/291 1.00
99 Brad Fullmer/295 1.00
100 Edgardo Alfonzo/324 1.00
101 Mark Mulder/544 2.00
102 Tony Gwynn/323 5.00
103 Mike Cameron/267 1.00
104 Richie Sexson/272 2.00
105 Barry Larkin/313 2.00
106 Mike Piazza/324 8.00
107 Eric Young/297 1.00
108 Edgar Renteria/278 1.00
109 Todd Zeile/268 1.00
110 Luis Castillo/334 1.00
111 Sammy Sosa/320 10.00
112 David Justice/286 1.50
113 Delino DeShields/296 1.00
114 Mariano Rivera/285 1.50
115 Edgar Martinez/324 2.00
116 Ray Durham/280 1.00
117 Brady Anderson/257 1.00
118 Eric Owens/293 1.00
119 Alex Gonzalez/252 1.00
120 Jay Buhner/253 1.00
121 Greg Vaughn/254 1.00
122 Mike Lowell/270 1.00
123 Marquis Grissom/244 1.00
124 Matt Williams/275 1.50
125 Dean Palmer/256 1.00
126 Troy Glaus/284 3.00
127 Bret Boone/251 1.50
128 David Ortiz/282 1.00
129 Glenallen Hill/293 1.00
130 Chipper Jones/311 8.00
131 Tony Clark/274 1.00
132 Terrence Long/288 1.00
133 Chuck Finley/417 1.00
134 Jeff Bagwell/310 4.00
135 J.T. Snow/284 1.00
136 Andruw Jones/303 3.00
137 Carlos Delgado/344 3.00
138 Mo Vaughn/272 1.50
139 Derek Lee/281 1.50
140 Bobby Estalella/234 1.00
141 Kerry Wood/480 3.00
142 Jose Vidro/330 1.00
143 Ben Grieve/279 1.00
144 Barry Bonds/306 12.00
145 Javy Lopez/287 2.00
146 Adam Kennedy/266 1.00
147 Jeff Cirillo/326 1.00
148 Cliff Floyd/300 1.00
149 Carl Pavano/306 1.00
150 Bobby Higginson/300 1.00
151 Kevin Brown/258 2.00
152 Fernando Tatis/253 1.00
153 Matt Lawton/305 1.00
154 Damion Easley/259 1.00
155 Curt Schilling/381 3.00
156 Mark McGwire/305 10.00
157 Mark Grace/280 2.50
158 Adrian Beltre/290 1.50
159 Jorge Posada/287 2.00
160 Richard Hidalgo/314 1.00
161 Vinny Castilla/221 1.00
162 Bernie Williams/307 3.00
163 John Olerud/285 1.50
164 Todd Helton/372 4.00
165 Craig Biggio/268 1.50
166 David Wells/411 1.00
167 Phil Nevin/303 1.00
168 Andres Galarraga/302 1.00
169 Moises Alou/355 2.00
170 Denny Neagle/452 1.00
171 Jeffrey Hammonds/335 1.00
172 Sean Casey/315 1.00
173 Gary Sheffield/325 2.00
174 Carlos Lee/301 1.00
175 Juan Encarnacion/289 1.00
176 Roberto Alomar/310 3.00
177 Kenny Rogers/455 1.00
178 Charles Johnson/304 1.00
179 Shannon Stewart/319 1.00
180 B.J. Surhoff/291 1.00
181 Paul Konerko/298 1.00
182 Jermaine Dye/321 1.00
183 Scott Rolen/298 4.00
184 Fred McGriff/277 2.00
185 Juan Gonzalez/289 4.00
186 Carlos Beltran/247 1.50
187 Jay Payton/291 1.50
188 Chad Hermansen/185 1.00
189 Pat Burrell/260 3.00
190 Omar Vizquel/287 2.00
191 Trot Nixon/276 1.00
192 Mike Hampton/314 1.00
193 Kris Benson/385 1.00
194 Gabe Kapler/302 1.00
195 Rickey Henderson/233 3.00
196 J.D. Drew/295 2.00
197 Pokey Reese/255 1.00
198 Jeff Kent/334 1.50
199 Jose Cruz Jr./242 1.00
200 Preston Wilson/264 1.00
201 Eric Munson/252 1.00
202 Alex Cabrera/263 1.00
203 Nate Rolison/77 1.00
204 Julio Zuleta/294 1.00
205 Chris Richard/265 1.00
206 Dernell Stenson/268 1.00
207 Aaron McNeal/310 1.00
208 Aubrey Huff/287 1.00
209 Mike Lamb/278 1.00
210 Xavier Nady/1
211 Joe Crede/357 2.00
212 Ben Petrick/322 1.00
213 Morgan Burkhart/288 1.00
214 Jason Tyner/226 1.00
215 Juan Pierre/310 3.00
216 Adam Dunn/281 4.00
217 Adam Piatt/299 1.00
218 Eric Byrnes/300 1.00
219 Corey Patterson/167 2.00
220 Kenny Kelly/252 1.00
221 Tike Redman/333 1.00
222 Luis Matos/225 1.00
223 Timo Perez/286 1.00
224 Vernon Wells/243 2.00
225 Barry Zito/272 3.00
226 Adam Bernero/419 1.00
227 Kazuhiro Sasaki/316 2.00
228 Oswaldo Mairena/18 5.00
229 Mark Buehrle/421 1.50
230 Ryan Dempster/366 1.00
231 Tim Hudson/414 2.00
232 Scott Downs/529 1.00
233 A.J. Burnett/479 1.00
234 Adam Eaton/413 1.00
235 Paxton Crawford/341 1.00
236 Jace Brewer/1
237 Jose Ortiz/182 1.00
238 Rafael Furcal/295 2.00
239 Julio Lugo/283 1.00
240 Tomas De La Rosa/288 1.00

Autographics

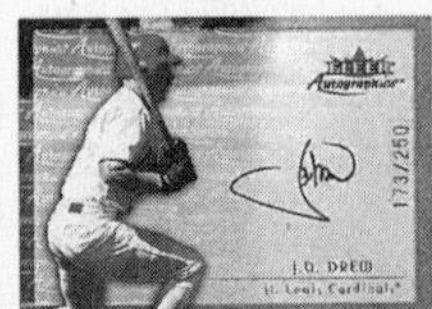

NM/M

Common Player: 5.00
Inserted 1:72
Silvers: 1-1.5X
Production 250 sets
Golds: 1-1.5X
Production 50 sets

Roberto Alomar 30.00
Rick Ankiel 5.00
Albert Belle 5.00
Adrian Beltre 15.00
Lance Berkman 8.00
Barry Bonds 200.00
Jeromy Burnitz 5.00

Pat Burrell 10.00
Sean Casey 8.00
Eric Chavez 10.00
Carlos Delgado 10.00
J.D. Drew 10.00
Jermaine Dye 5.00
Jim Edmonds 10.00
Troy Glaus 15.00
Ben Grieve 5.00
Tony Gwynn 30.00
Randy Johnson 40.00
Chipper Jones 40.00
Mike Lamb 5.00
Mike Lieberthal 5.00
Terrence Long 5.00
Greg Maddux 50.00
Edgar Martinez 15.00
Kevin Millwood 10.00
Mike Mussina 25.00
Corey Patterson 10.00
Jay Payton 8.00
Juan Pierre 8.00
Brad Radke 5.00
Scott Rolen 20.00
Gary Sheffield 15.00
Fernando Tatis 5.00
Robin Ventura 5.00
Kerry Wood 20.00

Bat Company

NM/M
Complete Set (10): 25.00
Common Player: 1.00
Inserted 1:24
1 Barry Bonds 5.00
2 Mark McGwire 4.00
3 Sammy Sosa 3.00
4 Ken Griffey Jr. 3.00
5 Mike Piazza 3.00
6 Derek Jeter 5.00
7 Gary Sheffield 1.00
8 Frank Thomas 1.50
9 Chipper Jones 2.00
10 Alex Rodriguez 4.00

Big Innings

NM/M
Complete Set (25): 15.00
Common Player: .50
Inserted 1:6
VIP: 5-10X
Production 50 sets
1 Rick Ankiel .50
2 Andruw Jones 1.00
3 Brian Giles .50
4 Derek Jeter 4.00
5 Rafael Furcal .50
6 Richie Sexson .50
7 Jay Payton .50
8 Carlos Delgado .75
9 Jermaine Dye .50
10 Darin Erstad .75
11 Pat Burrell .75
12 Richard Hidalgo .50
13 Adrian Beltre .60
14 Todd Helton 1.00
15 Vladimir Guerrero 1.00
16 Nomar Garciaparra 2.00
17 Gabe Kapler .50
18 Carlos Lee .50
19 J.D. Drew .60
20 Troy Glaus 1.00
21 Scott Rolen 1.00
22 Alex Rodriguez 3.00
23 Magglio Ordonez .60
24 Miguel Tejada .60
25 Ruben Mateo .50

Diamond Vision

NM/M
Complete Set (15): 25.00
Common Player: 1.00
Inserted 1:12
1 Derek Jeter 4.00
2 Nomar Garciaparra 2.50
3 Cal Ripken Jr. 4.00
4 Jeff Bagwell 1.50
5 Mark McGwire 3.00
6 Ken Griffey Jr. 2.50
7 Pedro Martinez 1.50
8 Carlos Delgado 1.00
9 Chipper Jones 2.00
10 Barry Bonds 4.00
11 Mike Piazza 2.50
12 Sammy Sosa 2.50
13 Alex Rodriguez 3.00
14 Frank Thomas 1.50
15 Randy Johnson 1.50

Feel the Game

NM/M
Common Player: 5.00
Inserted 1:72
Moises Alou 6.00
Brady Anderson 5.00
Dante Bichette 5.00
Jermaine Dye 5.00
Brian Giles 6.00
Juan Gonzalez 10.00
Rickey Henderson 15.00
Javy Lopez 6.00
Tino Martinez 6.00
Phil Nevin 5.00
Matt Stairs 5.00
Shannon Stewart 5.00
Jose Vidro 5.00

ROY Collection

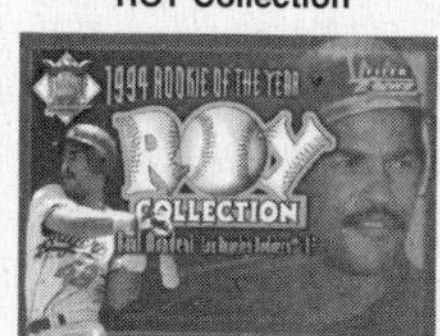

NM/M
Complete Set (25): 75.00
Common Player: 2.00
Inserted 1:24
1 Luis Aparicio 2.00
2 Johnny Bench 3.00
3 Joe Black 2.00
4 Rod Carew 2.00
5 Orlando Cepeda 2.00
6 Carlton Fisk 2.00
7 Ben Grieve 2.00
8 Frank Howard 2.00
9 Derek Jeter 10.00
10 Fred Lynn 2.00
11 Willie Mays 8.00
12 Willie McCovey 2.00
13 Mark McGwire 8.00
14 Raul Mondesi 2.00
15 Thurman Munson 4.00
16 Eddie Murray 2.00
17 Mike Piazza 6.00
18 Cal Ripken Jr. 10.00
19 Frank Robinson 2.00
20 Jackie Robinson 8.00
21 Scott Rolen 3.00
22 Tom Seaver 2.00
23 Fernando Valenzuela 2.00
24 David Justice 2.00
25 Billy Williams 2.00

ROY Collection Memorabilia

NM/M
Common Player: 8.00
Inserted 1:288
1 Luis Aparicio bat 8.00
2 Johnny Bench jersey 15.00
3 Orlando Cepeda bat 8.00
4 Carlton Fisk jersey 10.00
5 Ben Grieve jersey 8.00
6 Frank Howard bat 8.00
7 Derek Jeter jersey 50.00
8 Fred Lynn bat 8.00
9 Willie Mays jersey 60.00
10 Willie McCovey bat 10.00
11 Mark McGwire ball 50.00
12 Raul Mondesi bat 8.00
13 Thurman Munson bat 25.00
14 Eddie Murray jersey 10.00
15 Mike Piazza base 15.00
16 Cal Ripken jersey 50.00
17 Frank Robinson bat 10.00
18 Jackie Robinson jersey 75.00
19 Scott Rolen bat 15.00
20 Tom Seaver jersey 15.00
22 David Justice jersey 8.00

ROY Collection Signed Memorabilia

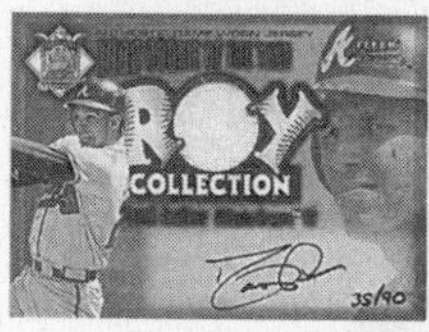

NM/M
Common Player: 25.00
1 Luis Aparicio jsy/56 40.00
2 Johnny Bench/68 85.00
3 Orlando Cepeda/58 25.00
4 Carlton Fisk/72 50.00
5 Ben Grieve/98 25.00
6 Frank Howard/60 25.00
7 Derek Jeter/96 200.00
8 Fred Lynn/75 25.00
9 Willie Mays jsy/51 200.00
10 Willie McCovey bat/59 40.00
11 Raul Mondesi/94 25.00
12 Eddie Murray/77 50.00
13 Cal Ripken/82 275.00
14 Frank Robinson bat/225 50.00
15 Scott Rolen/97 50.00
16 Tom Seaver/67 90.00
18 David Justice/90 25.00

2001 FLEER FUTURES

NM/M
Complete Set (220): 20.00
Common Player: .15
Pack (8): 1.50
Box (28): 30.00
1 Darin Erstad .60
2 Manny Ramirez .75
3 Darryl Kile .15
4 Troy O'Leary .15
5 Mark Quinn .15
6 Brian Giles .15
7 Randy Johnson .75
8 Todd Walker .15
9 Mike Piazza 1.50
10 Fred McGriff .15
11 Sammy Sosa 1.50
12 Chan Ho Park .15
13 John Rocker .15
14 Luis Castillo .15
15 Eric Chavez .25
16 Carlos Delgado .50
17 Sean Casey .25
18 Corey Koskie .15
19 John Olerud .15
20 Nomar Garciaparra 1.50
21 Craig Biggio .15
22 Pat Burrell .40
23 Bengie Molina .15
24 Jim Thome .15
25 Rey Ordonez .15
26 Fernando Tatis .15
27 Eric Young .15
28 Eric Karros .15
29 Adam Eaton .15
30 Brian Jordan .15
31 Jorge Posada .25
32 Gabe Kapler .15
33 Keith Foulke .15
34 Ron Coomer .15
35 Chipper Jones 1.00
36 Miguel Tejada .25
37 David Wells .15
38 Carlos Lee .15
39 Barry Bonds 2.50
40 Derrek Lee .15
41 Tim Hudson .25
42 Billy Koch .15
43 Dmitri Young .15
44 Vladimir Guerrero .75
45 Rickey Henderson .75
46 Jeff Bagwell .75
47 Robert Person .15
48 Brady Anderson .15
49 Lance Berkman .15
50 Mike Lieberthal .15
51 Adam Kennedy .15
52 Russ Branyan .15
53 Robin Ventura .15
54 Mark McGwire 2.00
55 Tony Gwynn 1.00
56 Matt Williams .15
57 Jeff Cirillo .15
58 Roger Clemens 1.25
59 Ivan Rodriguez .65
60 Brad Radke .15
61 Kazuhiro Sasaki .15
62 Cal Ripken Jr. 2.50
63 Ken Caminiti .15
64 Bobby Abreu .15
65 Troy Glaus .75
66 Sandy Alomar Jr. .15
67 Jose Vidro .15
68 Pedro Martinez .75
69 Kevin Young .15
70 Jay Bell .15
71 Larry Walker .15
72 Derek Jeter 2.50
73 Miguel Cairo .15
74 Magglio Ordonez .15
75 Jeromy Burnitz .15
76 J.T. Snow .15
77 Andres Galarraga .15
78 Ryan Dempster .15
79 Ken Griffey Jr. 1.50
80 Aaron Sele .15
81 Tom Glavine .25
82 Hideo Nomo .65
83 Orlando Hernandez .15
84 Tony Batista .15
85 Aaron Boone .15
86 Jacque Jones .15
87 Delino DeShields .15
88 Garret Anderson .15
89 Fernando Seguignol .15
90 Jim Edmonds .15
91 Frank Thomas .75
92 Adrian Beltre .30
93 Ellis Burks .15
94 Andruw Jones .75
95 Tony Clark .15
96 Danny Graves .15
97 Alex Rodriguez 2.00
98 Mike Mussina .40
99 Scott Elarton .15
100 Jason Giambi .50
101 Jay Payton .15
102 Gerald Williams .15
103 Kerry Wood .50
104 Shawn Green .35
105 Greg Maddux 1.00
106 Juan Encarnacion .15
107 Bernie Williams .30
108 Mike Lamb .15
109 Charles Johnson .15
110 Richie Sexson .15
111 Jeff Kent .15
112 Albert Belle .15
113 Cliff Floyd .15
114 Ben Grieve .15
115 Tim Salmon .25
116 Carl Pavano .15
117 Rick Ankiel .15
118 Dante Bichette .15

119 Johnny Damon .30
120 Brian Anderson .15
121 Roberto Alomar .40
122 Mike Hampton .15
123 Greg Vaughn .15
124 Carl Everett .15
125 Moises Alou .15
126 Jason Kendall .15
127 Omar Vizquel .15
128 Mark Grace .25
129 Kevin Brown .15
130 Phil Nevin .15
131 Kevin Millwood .15
132 Bobby Higginson .15
133 Ruben Mateo .15
134 Luis Gonzalez .25
135 Dean Palmer .15
136 Mariano Rivera .25
137 Rick Helling .15
138 Paul Konerko .15
139 Marquis Grissom .15
140 Robb Nen .15
141 Javy Lopez .15
142 Preston Wilson .15
143 Terrence Long .15
144 Shannon Stewart .15
145 Barry Larkin .15
146 Cristian Guzman .15
147 Jay Buhner .15
148 Jermaine Dye .15
149 Kris Benson .15
150 Curt Schilling .40
151 Todd Helton .75
152 Paul O'Neill .15
153 Rafael Palmeiro .65
154 Ray Durham .15
155 Geoff Jenkins .15
156 Livan Hernandez .15
157 Rafael Furcal .15
158 Juan Gonzalez .75
159 Tino Martinez .15
160 Raul Mondesi .15
161 Matt Lawton .15
162 Edgar Martinez .15
163 Richard Hidalgo .15
164 Scott Rolen .65
165 Chuck Finley .15
166 Edgardo Alfonzo .15
167 J.D. Drew .35
168 Trot Nixon .15
169 Carlos Beltran .50
170 Ryan Klesko .15
171 Mo Vaughn .15
172 Kenny Lofton .15
173 Al Leiter .15
174 Rondell White .15
175 Mike Sweeney .15
176 Trevor Hoffman .15
177 Steve Finley .15
178 Jeffrey Hammonds .15
179 David Justice .15
180 Gary Sheffield .40
181 Eric Munson .15
182 Luis Matos .15
183 Alex Cabrera .15
184 Randy Keisler .15
185 Nate Rolison .15
186 Jason Hart .15
187 Timo Perez .15
188 Adam Bernero .15
189 Barry Zito .50
190 Ryan Kohlmeier .15
191 Joey Nation .15
192 Oswaldo Mairena .15
193 Aubrey Huff .15
194 Mark Buehrle .15
195 Jace Brewer .15
196 Julio Zuleta .15
197 Xavier Nady .15
198 Vernon Wells .25
199 Joe Crede .15
200 Scott Downs .15
201 Ben Petrick .15
202 A.J. Burnett .15
203 *Esix Snead* .15
204 Dernell Stenson .15
205 Jose Ortiz .15
206 Paxton Crawford .15
207 Jason Tyner .15
208 Jimmy Rollins .15
209 Juan Pierre .25
210 Keith Ginter .15
211 Adam Dunn .40
212 Larry Barnes .15
213 Adam Piatt .15
214 Rodney Lindsey .15
215 Eric Byrnes .15
216 Julio Lugo .15
217 Corey Patterson .25
218 Reggie Taylor .15
219 Kenny Kelly .15
220 Tike Redman .15

Black Gold

Production 499 sets: 3-6X
(See 2001 Fleer Futures for checklist and base card values.)

Bases Loaded

NM/M
Common Player: 4.00
Inserted 1:134
BL1 Ken Griffey Jr. 10.00
BL2 Mark McGwire 12.00
BL3 Carlos Delgado 4.00
BL4 Chipper Jones 7.50
BL5 Nomar Garciaparra 10.00
BL6 Cal Ripken Jr. 15.00
BL7 Sammy Sosa 10.00
BL8 Jeff Bagwell 6.00
BL9 Vladimir Guerrero 6.00
BL10 Tony Gwynn 7.50
BL11 Frank Thomas 6.00
BL12 Mike Piazza 10.00
BL13 Jason Giambi 5.00
BL14 Troy Glaus 6.00
BL15 Pat Burrell 4.00

Bats to the Future

NM/M
Complete Set (25): 60.00
Common Player: 1.00
Inserted 1:28
1BF Mike Schmidt 6.00
2BF Carlton Fisk 3.00
3BF Paul Molitor 3.00
4BF Vladimir Guerrero 3.00
5BF Dave Parker 1.00
6BF Chipper Jones 5.00
7BF Carlos Delgado 2.00
8BF Tony Gwynn 5.00
9BF Reggie Jackson 5.00
10BF Eddie Murray 1.50
11BF Robin Yount 3.00
12BF Alan Trammell 1.00
13BF Frank Thomas 3.00
14BF Cal Ripken Jr. 8.00
15BF Don Mattingly 6.00
16BF Jim Rice 1.00
17BF Juan Gonzalez 3.00
18BF Todd Helton 3.00
19BF George Brett 6.00
20BF Barry Bonds 8.00
21BF Kirk Gibson 1.00
22BF Matt Williams 1.00
23BF Dave Winfield 1.50
24BF Ryne Sandberg 5.00
25BF Ivan Rodriguez 2.00

Bats to the Future Game Bat

NM/M
Common Player: 5.00
Inserted 1:114
1BF Mike Schmidt 25.00
2BF Carlton Fisk 10.00
3BF Paul Molitor 15.00
4BF Vladimir Guerrero 8.00
5BF Dave Parker 5.00
6BF Chipper Jones 10.00
7BF Chris Delgado 8.00
8BF Tony Gwynn 10.00
9BF Reggie Jackson 10.00
10BF Eddie Murray 8.00
11BF Robin Yount 15.00
12BF Alan Trammell 5.00
13BF Frank Thomas 8.00
14BF Cal Ripken Jr. 30.00
15BF Don Mattingly 30.00
16BF Jim Rice 5.00
17BF Juan Gonzalez 8.00
18BF Todd Helton 8.00
19BF George Brett 25.00
20BF Barry Bonds 25.00
21BF Kirk Gibson 5.00
22BF Matt Williams 5.00
23BF Dave Winfield 8.00
24BF Ryne Sandberg 15.00
25BF Ivan Rodriguez 8.00

Bats to the Future Game Bat Auto.

NM/M
Common Autograph: 40.00
Production 50 sets
1BF Mike Schmidt 150.00
2BF Carlton Fisk 60.00
3BF Paul Molitor 50.00
4BF Vladimir Guerrero 80.00
5BF Dave Parker 40.00
6BF Chipper Jones 75.00
7BF Carlos Delgado 50.00
8BF Tony Gwynn 75.00
9BF Reggie Jackson 70.00
10BF Eddie Murray 70.00
11BF Robin Yount 80.00
12BF Alan Trammell 40.00
13BF Frank Thomas 60.00
14BF Cal Ripken Jr. 200.00
15BF Don Mattingly 150.00
16BF Jim Rice 40.00
17BF Juan Gonzalez 60.00
18BF Todd Helton 60.00
19BF George Brett 150.00
20BF Barry Bonds 200.00
21BF Kirk Gibson 40.00
22BF Matt Williams 40.00
23BF Dave Winfield 60.00
24BF Ryne Sandberg 125.00
25BF Ivan Rodriguez 60.00

Characteristics

NM/M
Complete Set (15): 20.00
Common Player: .75
Inserted 1:9
1C Derek Jeter 4.00
2C Mark McGwire 3.00
3C Nomar Garciaparra 2.50
4C Sammy Sosa 2.50
5C Pedro Martinez 1.50
6C Chipper Jones 2.00
7C Cal Ripken Jr. 4.00
8C Todd Helton 1.50
9C Jim Edmonds .75
10C Ken Griffey Jr. 2.50
11C Alex Rodriguez 3.00
12C Mike Piazza 2.50
13C Vladimir Guerrero 1.50
14C Frank Thomas 1.50
15C Carlos Delgado 1.00

Hot Commodities

NM/M
Complete Set (10): 20.00
Common Player: 1.00
Inserted 1:14
1HC Mark McGwire 3.00
2HC Ken Griffey Jr. 2.50
3HC Derek Jeter 4.00
4HC Cal Ripken Jr. 4.00
5HC Chipper Jones 2.00
6HC Barry Bonds 4.00
7HC Mike Piazza 2.50
8HC Sammy Sosa 2.50
9HC Alex Rodriguez 3.00
10HC Frank Thomas 1.00

September Call-Ups Memorabilia

NM/M
Common Card: 4.00
Production 200 sets
184 Randy Keisler Cap/Cleat 4.00
185 Nate Rolison/Bat 4.00
187 Timoniel Perez/Bat 4.00
191 Joey Nation/Glove 4.00
192 Oswaldo Mairena/Glove 4.00
195 Jace Brewer/Bat 4.00
197 Xavier Nady/Glove 6.00
199 Joe Crede/Bat 6.00
205 Jose Ortiz/Bat 4.00
208 Jimmy Rollins/Glove 6.00
210 Keith Ginter/Bat 4.00
214 Rodney Lindsey/Bat 4.00
217 Corey Patterson/Bat 8.00
218 Reggie Taylor/Bat 4.00
219 Kenny Kelly/Bat 4.00

2001 FLEER GAME TIME

NM/M
Complete Set (121):
Common Player: .15
Common (91-121): 3.00
Production 2,000
Pack (5): 3.00
Box (24): 55.00
1 Derek Jeter 2.00
2 Nomar Garciaparra 1.25
3 Alex Rodriguez 1.50
4 Jason Kendall .15
5 Barry Bonds 2.00
6 David Wells .15
7 Craig Biggio .15
8 Adrian Beltre .30
9 Pat Burrell .40
10 Rafael Palmeiro .60
11 Jim Thome .15
12 Mike Lowell .15
13 Trevor Hoffman .15
14 Pokey Reese .15
15 Juan Encarnacion .15
16 Shawn Green .40
17 Kerry Wood .50
18 Richard Hidalgo .15
19 Scott Rolen .60
20 Jeff Kent .15
21 Alex Gonzalez .15
22 Matt Williams .15
23 Mike Sweeney .15
24 Edgar Martinez .15
25 Sammy Sosa 1.25
26 Bobby Higginson .15
27 Kevin Brown .15
28 Mike Lieberthal .15
29 Pedro J. Martinez .75
30 Jeff Weaver .15
31 Greg Maddux 1.00
32 Mike Hampton .15
33 Vladimir Guerrero .75
34 Greg Vaughn .15
35 Manny Ramirez .75
36 Carlos Beltran .40

37	Eric Chavez	.25
38	Troy Glaus	.75
39	Todd Helton	.75
40	Gary Sheffield	.40
41	Brady Anderson	.15
42	Juan Gonzalez	.75
43	Tim Hudson	.30
44	Kenny Lofton	.15
45	Al Leiter	.15
46	Eric Owens	.15
47	Roberto Alomar	.40
48	Preston Wilson	.15
49	Tony Gwynn	1.00
50	Cal Ripken Jr.	2.00
51	Ben Petrick	.15
52	Jason Giambi	.50
53	Ben Grieve	.15
54	Albert Belle	.15
55	Jose Vidro	.15
56	Barry Zito	.30
57	Ivan Rodriguez	.60
58	Jeff Bagwell	.75
59	Geoff Jenkins	.15
60	Roger Clemens	1.00
61	John Olerud	.15
62	Randy Johnson	.75
63	Matt Lawton	.15
64	Mark McGwire	1.50
65	Brad Radke	.15
66	Frank Thomas	.75
67	Edgardo Alfonzo	.15
68	Brian Giles	.15
69	J.T. Snow	.15
70	Carlos Delgado	.50
71	Chipper Jones	1.00
72	Mark Quinn	.15
73	Mike Mussina	.40
74	Rick Ankiel	.15
75	Rafael Furcal	.15
76	Jim Edmonds	.15
77	Vinny Castilla	.15
78	Sean Casey	.25
79	Derrek Lee	.15
80	Mike Piazza	1.25
81	Warren Morris	.15
82	Tim Salmon	.25
83	Jeromy Burnitz	.15
84	Freddy Garcia	.15
85	Ken Griffey Jr.	1.25
86	Andruw Jones	.75
87	Darryl Kile	.15
88	Magglio Ordonez	.15
89	Bernie Williams	.30
90	Timo Perez	.15
91	*Ichiro Suzuki*	35.00
92	Larry Barnes, Darin Erstad	3.00
93	*Jaisen Randolph*	3.00
94	*Paul Phillips*	3.00
95	*Esix Snead*	3.00
96	*Matt White*	3.00
97	*Ryan Freel*	3.00
98	*Winston Abreu*	3.00
99	*Junior Spivey*	5.00
100	Randy Keisler, Roger Clemens	5.00
101	Brian Cole, Mike Piazza	4.00
102	Aubrey Huff, Chipper Jones	4.00
103	Corey Patterson, Sammy Sosa	5.00
104	Sun-Woo Kim, Pedro Martinez	4.00
105	*Drew Henson*	5.00
106	*Claudio Vargas*	3.00
107	Cesar Izturis, Rafael Furcal	3.00
108	Paxton Crawford, Pedro Martinez	4.00
109	*Adrian Hernandez*	3.00
110	Jace Brewer, Derek Jeter	8.00
111	*Andy Morales*	3.00
112	*Wilson Betemit*	3.00
113	*Juan Diaz*	3.00
114	*Erick Almonte*	4.00
115	*Nick Punto*	3.00
116	*Tsuyoshi Shinjo*	4.00
117	*Jay Gibbons*	5.00
118	*Andres Torres*	3.00
119	*Alexis Gomez*	4.00
120	*Wilken Ruan*	3.00
121	*Albert Pujols*	50.00

Next Game Extra

Cards (91-121): 2-3X
Production 200 sets
(See 2001 Fleer Game Time #91-121 for checklist and base card values.)

Derek Jeter's Monumental Moments

		NM/M
Complete Set (1):		
1JM	Derek Jeter/1996	8.00
1JMS	Derek Jeter Auto/96	80.00

Famers Lumber

		NM/M
Common Player:		8.00
Production 100 sets		
1FL	Luis Aparicio	8.00
2FL	Hank Bauer	8.00
3FL	Paul Blair	8.00
4FL	Bobby Bonds	8.00
5FL	Orlando Cepeda	8.00
6FL	Roberto Clemente	100.00
7FL	Rocky Colavito	10.00
8FL	Bucky Dent	8.00
9FL	Bill Dickey	10.00
10FL	Larry Doby	10.00
11FL	Carlton Fisk	10.00
12FL	Hank Greenberg	25.00
13FL	Elston Howard	8.00
14FL	Frank Howard	8.00
15FL	Reggie Jackson	15.00
16FL	Harmon Killebrew	20.00
17FL	Tony Lazzeri	8.00
18FL	Roger Maris	60.00
19FL	Johnny Mize	10.00
20FL	Thurman Munson	40.00
21FL	Tony Perez	10.00
22FL	Jim Rice	8.00
23FL	Phil Rizzuto	10.00
24FL	Bill Skowron	8.00
25FL	Enos Slaughter	10.00
26FL	Duke Snider	15.00
27FL	Willie Stargell	15.00
28FL	Bill Terry	8.00
29FL	Ted Williams	100.00

Famers Lumber Autograph

		NM/M
Common Player:		40.00
Production 25 sets		
1FLS	Hank Bauer	40.00
2FLS	Bobby Bonds	50.00
3FLS	Orlando Cepeda	50.00
4FLS	Rocky Colavito	50.00
5FLS	Bucky Dent	40.00
6FLS	Larry Doby	50.00
7FLS	Carlton Fisk	65.00
8FLS	Frank Howard	40.00
9FLS	Reggie Jackson	100.00
10FLS	Harmon Killebrew	120.00
11FLS	Tony Perez	40.00
12FLS	Jim Rice	40.00
13FLS	Phil Rizzuto	60.00
14FLS	Bill Skowron	40.00
15FLS	Enos Slaughter	40.00
16FLS	Duke Snider	75.00

Let's Play Two!

		NM/M
Complete Set (15):		30.00
Common Card:		1.50
Inserted 1:24		
1LT	Derek Jeter, Nomar Garciaparra	4.00
2LT	Mark McGwire, Sammy Sosa	3.00
3LT	Pedro J. Martinez, Randy Johnson	1.50
4LT	Vladimir Guerrero, Carlos Delgado	1.50
5LT	Mike Piazza, Roger Clemens	2.50
6LT	Alex Rodriguez, Miguel Tejada	3.00
7LT	Troy Glaus, Chipper Jones	2.00
8LT	Derek Jeter, Alex Rodriguez	4.00
9LT	Cal Ripken Jr., Derek Jeter	4.00
10LT	Jason Giambi, Mark McGwire	3.00
11LT	Jeff Bagwell, Craig Biggio	1.50
12LT	Tom Glavine, Greg Maddux	2.00
13LT	Ken Griffey Jr., Barry Bonds	4.00
14LT	Manny Ramirez, Pedro J. Martinez	1.50
15LT	Alex Rodriguez, Ivan Rodriguez	3.00

Lumber

		NM/M
Common Player:		4.00
Inserted 1:40		
1GL	Roberto Alomar	6.00
2GL	Rick Ankiel	4.00
3GL	Adrian Beltre	6.00
4GL	Barry Bonds	25.00
5GL	Kevin Brown	4.00
7GL	Ken Caminiti	4.00
8GL	Eric Chavez	5.00
9GL	Carlos Delgado	5.00
10GL	J.D. Drew	5.00
11GL	Erubiel Durazo	4.00
12GL	Carl Everett	4.00
13GL	Rafael Furcal	4.00
14GL	Brian Giles	5.00
15GL	Juan Gonzalez	6.00
16GL	Todd Helton	8.00
18GL	Randy Johnson	10.00
19GL	Chipper Jones	10.00
20GL	Pedro J. Martinez	10.00
21GL	Tino Martinez	5.00
23GL	Cal Ripken SP/275	40.00
24GL	Ivan Rodriguez	8.00
25GL	Frank Thomas	8.00
26GL	Jim Thome	8.00
27GL	Bernie Williams	6.00
28GL	Nomar Garciaparra	15.00

New Order

		NM/M
Complete Set (20):		30.00
Common Player:		1.50
Inserted 1:12		
1NO	Derek Jeter	6.00
2NO	Nomar Garciaparra	4.00
3NO	Alex Rodriguez	5.00
4NO	Mark McGwire	5.00
5NO	Sammy Sosa	4.00
6NO	Carlos Delgado	1.50
7NO	Troy Glaus	1.50
8NO	Jason Giambi	1.50
9NO	Mike Piazza	4.00
10NO	Todd Helton	1.50
11NO	Vladimir Guerrero	2.00
12NO	Manny Ramirez	1.50
13NO	Frank Thomas	1.50
14NO	Ken Griffey Jr.	4.00
15NO	Chipper Jones	3.00

Sticktoitness

		NM/M
Complete Set (20):		15.00
Common Player:		.50
Inserted 1:8		
1S	Derek Jeter	4.00
2S	Nomar Garciaparra	3.00
3S	Alex Rodriguez	3.00
4S	Jeff Bagwell	1.00
5S	Bernie Williams	.50
6S	Eric Chavez	.60
7S	Richard Hidalgo	.50
8S	Ichiro Suzuki	2.00
9S	Troy Glaus	.75
10S	Maggiio Ordonez	.50
11S	Corey Patterson	.50
12S	Todd Helton	1.00
13S	Jim Edmonds	.50
14S	Rafael Furcal	.50
15S	Mo Vaughn	.50
16S	Pat Burrell	.65
17S	Adrian Beltre	.60
18S	Andruw Jones	1.00
19S	Manny Ramirez	1.00
20S	Sean Casey	.65

Uniformity

		NM/M
Common Player:		4.00
Inserted 1:25		
1GU	Andres Galarraga	4.00
2GU	Barry Bonds	25.00
3GU	Ben Petrick	4.00
4GU	Brad Radke	4.00
5GU	Brian Jordan	4.00
6GU	Carlos Guillen	4.00
7GU	Fernando Seguignol	4.00
8GU	Fred McGriff	4.00
9GU	Gary Sheffield	5.00
10GU	Greg Maddux	15.00
11GU	Ivan Rodriguez	8.00
12GU	Jay Buhner	4.00
13GU	Jeromy Burnitz	4.00
14GU	John Olerud	4.00
15GU	Kevin Brown	4.00
16GU	Larry Walker	4.00
17GU	Magglio Ordonez	4.00
18GU	Matt Williams	4.00
19GU	Robin Ventura	4.00
20GU	Rondell White	4.00
21GU	Tony Gwynn	15.00
22GU	Troy Glaus	8.00
23GU	Vladimir Guerrero	8.00

2001 FLEER GENUINE

		NM/M
Complete Set (130):		150.00
Common Player:		.25
Common (101-130):		3.00
Production 1,500		
Pack (5):		4.00
Box (24):		80.00
1	Derek Jeter	3.00
2	Nomar Garciaparra	2.00

3 Alex Rodriguez 2.50
4 Frank Thomas 1.00
5 Travis Fryman .25
6 Gary Sheffield .40
7 Jason Giambi .75
8 Trevor Hoffman .25
9 Todd Helton 1.00
10 Ivan Rodriguez .75
11 Roberto Alomar .40
12 Barry Zito .40
13 Kevin Brown .25
14 Shawn Green .40
15 Kenny Lofton .25
16 Jeff Weaver .25
17 Geoff Jenkins .25
18 Carlos Delgado .65
19 Mark Grace .35
20 Ken Griffey Jr. 2.00
21 David Justice .25
22 Brian Giles .25
23 Scott Williamson .25
24 Richie Sexson .25
25 John Olerud .25
26 Sammy Sosa 2.00
27 Bobby Higginson .25
28 Matt Lawton .25
29 Vinny Castilla .25
30 Alex S. Gonzalez .25
31 Manny Ramirez 1.00
32 Brad Radke .25
33 Cal Ripken Jr. 3.00
34 Richard Hidalgo .25
35 Al Leiter .25
36 Freddy Garcia .25
37 Juan Encarnacion .25
38 Corey Koskie .25
39 Greg Vaughn .25
40 Rafael Palmeiro .65
41 Vladimir Guerrero 1.00
42 Troy Glaus .75
43 Mike Hampton .25
44 Jose Vidro .25
45 Ryan Rupe .25
46 Troy O'Leary .25
47 Ben Petrick .25
48 Mike Lieberthal .25
49 Mike Sweeney .25
50 Scott Rolen .75
51 Albert Belle .25
52 Mark Quinn .25
53 Mike Piazza 2.00
54 Mark McGwire 2.50
55 Brady Anderson .25
56 Carlos Beltran .45
57 Michael Barrett .25
58 Jason Kendall .25
59 Jim Edmonds .25
60 Matt Williams .25
61 Pokey Reese .25
62 Bernie Williams .25
63 Barry Bonds 3.00
64 David Wells .25
65 Chipper Jones 1.50
66 Jim Parque .25
67 Derrek Lee .25
68 Darin Erstad .60
69 Edgar Martinez .25
70 Kerry Wood .60
71 Omar Vizquel .25
72 Jeromy Burnitz .25
73 Warren Morris .25
74 Rick Ankiel .25
75 Andruw Jones 1.00
76 Paul Konerko .25
77 Mike Lowell .25
78 Roger Clemens 1.75
79 Tim Hudson .35
80 Rafael Furcal .25
81 Craig Biggio .25
82 Edgardo Alfonzo .25
83 Pat Burrell .50
84 Adrian Beltre .35
85 Tony Gwynn 1.50
86 J.T. Snow .25
87 Randy Johnson 1.00
88 Sean Casey .35
89 Preston Wilson .25
90 Mike Mussina .50
91 Eric Chavez .35
92 Tim Salmon .25
93 Pedro Martinez 1.00
94 Darryl Kile .25
95 Greg Maddux 1.50
96 Magglio Ordonez .25
97 Jeff Bagwell 1.00
98 Timo Perez .25
99 Jeff Kent .25
100 Eric Owens .25
101 *Ichiro Suzuki* 35.00
102 *Elpidio Guzman* 3.00
103 *Tsuyoshi Shinjo* 6.00
104 *Travis Hafner* 8.00
105 Larry Barnes 3.00
106 *Jaisen Randolph* 3.00
107 *Paul Phillips* 3.00
108 *Erick Almonte* 3.00
109 *Nick Punto* 3.00
110 *Jack Wilson* 3.00
111 *Jeremy Owens* 3.00
112 *Esix Snead* 3.00
113 *Jay Gibbons* 8.00
114 *Adrian Hernandez* 4.00
115 *Matt White* 3.00
116 *Ryan Freel* 3.00
117 *Martin Vargas* 3.00
118 *Winston Abreu* 3.00
119 *Junior Spivey* 5.00
120 Paxton Crawford 3.00
121 Randy Keisler 3.00
122 *Juan Diaz* 3.00
123 Aaron Rowand 3.00
124 Toby Hall 3.00
125 Brian Cole 3.00
126 Aubrey Huff 4.00
127 Corey Patterson 4.00
128 Sun-Woo Kim 3.00
129 Jace Brewer 3.00
130 Cesar Izturis 3.00

Final Cut

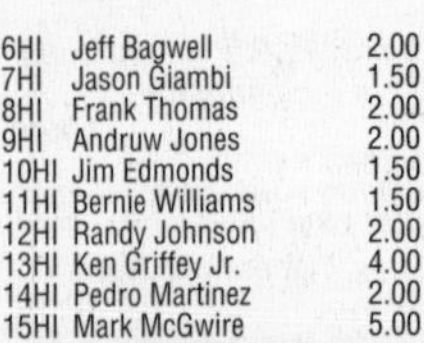

NM/M
Common Player: 4.00
Inserted 1:30
Miguel Tejada SP/170 6.00
Barry Bonds SP/330 40.00
Robin Ventura 4.00
Greg Maddux 15.00
Andruw Jones SP/135 10.00
J.D. Drew SP/75 10.00
Chipper Jones 10.00
Tim Salmon 4.00
Edgar Martinez SP/130 8.00
Troy Glaus 8.00
Frank Thomas 8.00
Pokey Reese 4.00
Larry Walker 4.00
Ivan Rodriguez SP/120 10.00
Scott Rolen 8.00
Cal Ripken Jr. 30.00
Tony Gwynn 10.00
Wade Boggs 10.00
George Brett 30.00
Sean Casey 4.00
Bob Gibson 6.00
Matt Williams 6.00
Robin Yount 8.00
Ron Guidry
(not officially released)
Reggie Jackson
(not officially released)
Don Larsen
(not officially released)

Genuine Coverage PLUS

NM/M
Common Player: 6.00
Production 150 sets
Troy Glaus 8.00
Randy Johnson 10.00
Andruw Jones 8.00
Frank Thomas 8.00
Darin Erstad 6.00
Chipper Jones 15.00
Derek Jeter 35.00
Tony Gwynn 15.00
Barry Bonds 35.00
Cal Ripken Jr. 35.00

High Interest

NM/M
Complete Set (15): 40.00
Common Player: 1.50
Inserted 1:23
1HI Derek Jeter 6.00
2HI Nomar Garciaparra 4.00
3HI Greg Maddux 3.00
4HI Todd Helton 2.00
5HI Sammy Sosa 4.00
6HI Jeff Bagwell 2.00
7HI Jason Giambi 1.50
8HI Frank Thomas 2.00
9HI Andruw Jones 2.00
10HI Jim Edmonds 1.50
11HI Bernie Williams 1.50
12HI Randy Johnson 2.00
13HI Ken Griffey Jr. 4.00
14HI Pedro Martinez 2.00
15HI Mark McGwire 5.00

Material Issue

NM/M
Common Player: 5.00
Inserted 1:30
Randy Johnson 10.00
Scott Rolen 8.00
Robin Ventura 5.00
Tony Gwynn 15.00
Troy Glaus 10.00
Kevin Millwood 5.00
Chipper Jones 15.00
Tom Glavine 5.00
Pedro Martinez SP/60 40.00
Greg Maddux 15.00
Frank Thomas 10.00
Curt Schilling SP/120 10.00
Edgar Martinez 5.00
Darin Erstad 5.00
J.D. Drew 5.00
Cal Ripken Jr. 30.00
Nolan Ryan 40.00
Steve Carlton 5.00

Names of the Game - Game Used

NM/M
Common Player: 10.00
Production 50 sets
Yogi Berra bat 25.00
Orlando Cepeda bat 10.00
Rocky Colavito bat 20.00
Andre Dawson jsy 10.00
Bucky Dent bat 10.00
Rollie Fingers jsy 10.00
Carlton Fisk bat 15.00
Whitey Ford jsy 25.00
Jimmie Foxx bat 80.00
Hank Greenberg bat 50.00
"Catfish" Hunter jsy 10.00
Reggie Jackson jsy 20.00
Randy Johnson jsy 30.00
Chipper Jones bat 30.00
Harmon Killebrew bat 25.00
Tony Lazzeri bat 10.00
Don Mattingly bat 65.00
Willie McCovey bat 20.00
Johnny Mize bat 15.00
Pee Wee Reese jsy 15.00
Cal Ripken Jr. bat 75.00
Phil Rizzuto bat 20.00
Ivan Rodriguez bat 25.00
Preacher Roe jsy 15.00
Babe Ruth bat 300.00
Nolan Ryan jsy 90.00
Tom Seaver jsy 25.00
Bill Skowron bat 10.00
Enos Slaughter bat 10.00
Duke Snider bat 25.00
Willie Stargell bat 15.00
Bill Terry bat 10.00
Ted Williams bat 200.00
Hack Wilson bat 75.00

Names of the Game - Autographs

NM/M
Common Player: 25.00

Yogi Berra 60.00
Orlando Cepeda 20.00
Rocky Colavito 60.00
Andre Dawson 20.00
Bucky Dent 20.00
Rollie Fingers 20.00
Carlton Fisk 40.00
Whitey Ford 40.00
Reggie Jackson 50.00
Randy Johnson 60.00
Chipper Jones 50.00
Harmon Killebrew 60.00
Don Mattingly 90.00
Willie McCovey 25.00
Cal Ripken Jr. 150.00
Ivan Rodriguez 50.00
Preacher Roe 35.00
Nolan Ryan 100.00
Tom Seaver 50.00
Bill Skowron 25.00
Enos Slaughter 30.00
Duke Snider 40.00

Pennant Aggression

NM/M
Complete Set (10): 30.00
Inserted 1:23
1PA Derek Jeter 6.00
2PA Alex Rodriguez 5.00
3PA Nomar Garciaparra 4.00
4PA Mark McGwire 5.00
5PA Ken Griffey Jr. 4.00
6PA Mike Piazza 4.00
7PA Sammy Sosa 4.00
8PA Barry Bonds 6.00
9PA Chipper Jones 3.00
10PA Pedro Martinez 2.00

Tip of the Cap

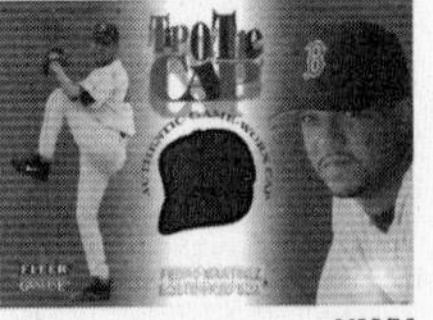

NM/M
Common Player: 8.00
Production 150 sets
Barry Bonds 40.00
Eric Chavez 8.00
Shawn Green 8.00
Vladimir Guerrero 15.00
Randy Johnson 20.00
Andruw Jones 10.00
Javy Lopez 8.00
Rafael Palmeiro 10.00
Ivan Rodriguez 10.00
Miguel Tejada 8.00
Roberto Alomar 10.00
Pedro Martinez 15.00

@ LG (At Large)

NM/M
Complete Set (15): 50.00
Common Player: 1.50
Inserted 1:23
1AL Derek Jeter 7.50
2AL Nomar Garciaparra 4.00
3AL Mark McGwire 6.00
4AL Pedro Martinez 3.00
5AL Tony Gwynn 3.50
6AL Roger Clemens 3.50
7AL Ivan Rodriguez 2.00

8AL Sammy Sosa 4.00
9AL Magglio Ordonez 1.50
10AL Jason Giambi 2.00
11AL Carlos Delgado 2.00
12AL Chipper Jones 3.50
13AL Mike Piazza 4.00
14AL Cal Ripken Jr. 7.50
15AL Ken Griffey Jr. 4.00

2001 FLEER GREATS OF THE GAME

		NM/M
Complete Set (137):		50.00
Common Player:		.25
Hobby Pack (5):		10.00
Hobby Box (24):		200.00
1	Roberto Clemente	2.50
2	George "Sparky" Anderson	.25
3	Babe Ruth	4.00
4	Paul Molitor	1.00
5	Don Larsen	.25
6	Cy Young	1.00
7	Billy Martin	.50
8	Lou Brock	1.00
9	Fred Lynn	.25
10	Johnny Vander Meer	.25
11	Harmon Killebrew	1.00
12	Dave Winfield	1.00
13	Orlando Cepeda	.25
14	Johnny Mize	.75
15	Walter Johnson	1.00
16	Roy Campanella	1.00
17	Monte Irvin	.50
18	Mookie Wilson	.25
19	Elston Howard	.25
20	Walter Alston	.25
21	Rollie Fingers	.25
22	Brooks Robinson	1.00
23	Hank Greenberg	1.00
24	Maury Wills	.25
25	Rich Gossage	.25
26	Leon Day	.25
27	Jimmie Foxx	2.00
28	Alan Trammell	.50
29	Dennis Martinez	.25
30	Don Drysdale	.75
31	Bob Feller	.75
32	Jackie Robinson	3.00
33	Whitey Ford	1.00
34	Enos Slaughter	.25
35	Rod Carew	.75
36	Eddie Mathews	1.00
37	Ron Cey	.25
38	Thurman Munson	1.00
39	Henry Kimbro	.25
40	Ty Cobb	3.00
41	Rocky Colavito	.50
42	Satchel Paige	1.50
43	Andre Dawson	.50
44	Phil Rizzuto	1.00
45	Roger Maris	2.50
46	Bobby Bonds	.25
47	Joe Carter	.25
48	Christy Mathewson	.75
49	Tony Lazzeri	.25
50	Gil Hodges	.25
51	Ray Dandridge	.25
52	Gaylord Perry	.25
53	Ernie Banks	2.00
54	Lou Gehrig	3.00
55	George Kell	.25
56	Wes Parker	.25
57	Sam Jethroe	.25
58	Joe Morgan	.75
59	Steve Garvey	.50
60	Joe Torre	.75
61	Roger Craig	.25
62	Warren Spahn	1.00
63	Willie McCovey	.25
64	Cool Papa Bell	1.00
65	Frank Robinson	1.00
66	Richie Allen	.25
67	Bucky Dent	.25
68	George Foster	.25
69	Hoyt Wilhelm	.25
70	Phil Niekro	.25
71	Buck Leonard	.25
72	Preacher Roe	.25
73	Yogi Berra	1.50
74	Joe Black	.25
75	Nolan Ryan	4.00
76	Pop Lloyd	.25
77	Lester Lockett	.25
78	Paul Blair	.25
79	Ryne Sandberg	2.00
80	Bill Perkins	.25
81	Frank Howard	.25
82	Hack Wilson	1.00
83	Robin Yount	1.00
84	Harry Heilmann	.25
85	Mike Schmidt	3.00
86	Vida Blue	.25
87	George Brett	3.00
88	Juan Marichal	.50
89	Tom Seaver	1.50
90	Bill Skowron	.25
91	Don Mattingly	2.00
92	Jim Bunning	.25
93	Eddie Murray	1.00
94	Tommy Lasorda	.50
95	Pee Wee Reese	.50
96	Bill Dickey	.25
97	Ozzie Smith	1.50
98	Dale Murphy	.25
99	Artie Wilson	.25
100	Bill Terry	.25
101	Jim "Catfish" Hunter	.25
102	Don Sutton	.25
103	Luis Aparicio	.25
104	Reggie Jackson	1.50
105	Ted Radcliffe	.25
106	Carl Erskine	.25
107	Johnny Bench	2.00
108	Carl Furillo	.25
109	Stan Musial	2.00
110	Carlton Fisk	.75
111	Rube Foster	.25
112	Tony Oliva	.25
113	Hank Bauer	.25
114	Jim Rice	.25
115	Willie Mays	3.00
116	Ralph Kiner	.50
117	Al Kaline	1.00
118	Billy Williams	.25
119	Buck O'Neil	.25
120	Tony Perez	.25
121	Dave Parker	.25
122	Kirk Gibson	.25
123	Lou Piniella	.25
124	Ted Williams	4.00
125	Steve Carlton	.75
126	Dizzy Dean	.25
127	Willie Stargell	.50
128	Joe Niekro	.25
129	Lloyd Waner	.25
130	Wade Boggs	2.00
131	Wilmer Fields	.25
132	Bill Mazeroski	.50
133	Duke Snider	1.00
134	Smoky Joe Williams	.25
135	Bob Gibson	1.50
136	Jim Palmer	.75
137	Oscar Charleston	.25

Autographs

		NM/M
Common Player:		10.00
Inserted 1:8		
1	Richie Allen	10.00
2	George "Sparky" Anderson	10.00
3	Luis Aparicio	10.00
4	Ernie Banks SP/250	80.00
5	Hank Bauer	10.00
6	Johnny Bench SP/400	80.00
7	Yogi Berra SP/500	50.00
8	Joe Black	10.00
9	Paul Blair	10.00
9a	Paul Blair double signed	10.00
10	Vida Blue	10.00
11	Wade Boggs	40.00
12	Bobby Bonds	15.00
13	George Brett SP/247	150.00
14	Lou Brock SP/500	40.00
15	Jim Bunning	25.00
16	Rod Carew	20.00
17	Steve Carlton	25.00
18	Joe Carter	10.00
19	Orlando Cepeda	15.00
20	Ron Cey	10.00
21	Rocky Colavito	25.00
22	Roger Craig	10.00
23	Andre Dawson	15.00
24	Bucky Dent	10.00
25	Larry Doby	35.00
26	Carl Erskine	10.00
27	Bob Feller	15.00
28	Wilmer Fields	10.00
29	Rollie Fingers	10.00
30	Carlton Fisk	40.00
31	Whitey Ford	30.00
32	George Foster	10.00
33	Steve Garvey SP/400	40.00
34	Bob Gibson	20.00
35	Kirk Gibson	20.00
36	Rich Gossage	10.00
37	Frank Howard	10.00
38	Monte Irvin	20.00
39	Reggie Jackson SP/400	60.00
40	Sam Jethroe	10.00
41	Al Kaline	30.00
42	George Kell	15.00
43	Harmon Killebrew	30.00
44	Ralph Kiner	20.00
45	Don Larsen	15.00
46	Tommy Lasorda SP/400	40.00
47	Lester Lockett	10.00
48	Fred Lynn	10.00
49	Juan Marichal	20.00
50	Dennis Martinez	10.00
51	Don Mattingly	75.00
52	Willie Mays SP/100	450.00
53	Bill Mazeroski	20.00
54	Willie McCovey	20.00
55	Paul Molitor	25.00
56	Joe Morgan	10.00
57	Dale Murphy	30.00
58	Eddie Murray SP/140	200.00
59	Stan Musial SP/525	75.00
60	Joe Niekro	10.00
61	Phil Niekro	10.00
62	Tony Oliva	10.00
63	Buck O'Neil	20.00
64	Jim Palmer SP/600	20.00
65	Dave Parker	10.00
66	Tony Perez	20.00
67	Gaylord Perry	10.00
68	Lou Piniella	10.00
69	Ted Radcliffe	10.00
70	Jim Rice	10.00
71	Phil Rizzuto SP/425	80.00
72	Brooks Robinson	25.00
73	Frank Robinson	20.00
74	Preacher Roe	20.00
75	Nolan Ryan SP/650	100.00
76	Ryne Sandberg	50.00
77	Mike Schmidt SP/213	175.00
78	Tom Seaver	50.00
79	Bill Skowron	10.00
80	Enos Slaughter	15.00
81	Ozzie Smith	50.00
82	Duke Snider SP/600	50.00
83	Warren Spahn	40.00
84	Willie Stargell (redemption card only, none signed)	10.00
85	Don Sutton	10.00
86	Joe Torre SP/500	40.00
87	Alan Trammell	15.00
88	Hoyt Wilhelm	10.00
89	Billy Williams	10.00
90	Maury Wills	10.00
91	Artie Wilson	10.00
92	Mookie Wilson	10.00
93	Dave Winfield SP/370	60.00
94	Robin Yount SP/400	80.00

Dodger Blues

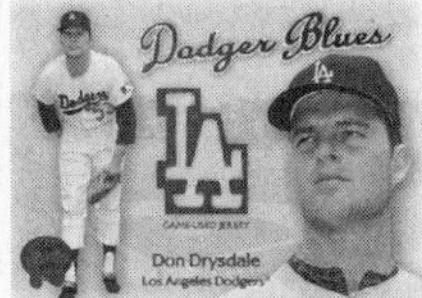

		NM/M
Common Player:		10.00
Inserted 1:36		
(1)	Walter Alston (jersey)	10.00
(2)	Walt Alston (uniform)	10.00
(3)	Roy Campanella (uniform/SP)	75.00
(4)	Roger Craig (jersey)	10.00
(5)	Don Drysdale (jersey)	20.00
(6)	Carl Furillo (jersey)	10.00
(7)	Steve Garvey (jersey)	10.00
(8)	Gil Hodges (uniform)	20.00
(9)	Wes Parker (bat)	10.00
(10)	Wes Parker (jersey)	10.00
(11)	Pee Wee Reese (jersey)	15.00
(12)	Jackie Robinson (uniform/SP)	150.00
(13)	Preacher Roe (jersey)	10.00
(14)	Duke Snider (bat/SP)	75.00
(15)	Don Sutton (jersey)	10.00

Feel the Game Classics

		NM/M
Common Player:		5.00
Inserted 1:72		
1	Luis Aparicio bat	5.00
2	George Brett jersey	30.00
3	Lou Brock jersey	15.00
4	Orlando Cepeda bat	10.00
5	Whitey Ford jersey	15.00
6	Hank Greenberg bat	40.00
7	Elston Howard bat	5.00
8	"Catfish" Hunter jersey	8.00
9	Harmon Killebrew bat	15.00
10	Roger Maris bat	50.00
11	Eddie Mathews bat	15.00
12	W. McCovey bat SP/200	15.00
13	Johnny Mize bat	5.00
14	Paul Molitor jersey	10.00
15	Jim Palmer jersey	10.00
16	Tony Perez bat	5.00
17	Brooks Robinson bat/144	25.00
18	Babe Ruth bat/250	200.00
19	Mike Schmidt jersey	25.00
20	Tom Seaver jersey	20.00
21	Enos Slaughter	10.00
22	Willie Stargell	10.00
23	Hack Wilson	10.00
24	Harry Heilmann	5.00

Retrospection Collection

		NM/M
Complete Set (10):		20.00
Common Player:		1.00
Inserted 1:6		
1	Babe Ruth	5.00
2	Stan Musial	3.00
3	Jimmie Foxx	3.00
4	Roberto Clemente	4.00
5	Ted Williams	4.00
6	Mike Schmidt	4.00
7	Cy Young	1.50

8 Satchel Paige 2.00
9 Hank Greenberg 1.50
10 Jim Bunning 1.00

2001 FLEER LEGACY

NM/M

Complete Set (105):
Common Player: .50
Common (91-105): 8.00
Production 799 sets
Pack (5): 8.00
Box (15 + cap): 140.00
1 Pedro J. Martinez 1.50
2 Andruw Jones 1.50
3 Mike Hampton .50
4 Gary Sheffield .65
5 Barry Zito .65
6 J.D. Drew .75
7 Charles Johnson .50
8 David Wells .50
9 Kazuhiro Sasaki .50
10 Vladimir Guerrero 1.50
11 Pat Burrell .75
12 Ruben Mateo .50
13 Greg Maddux 2.00
14 Sean Casey .65
15 Craig Biggio .50
16 Bernie Williams .65
17 Jeff Kent .50
18 Nomar Garciaparra 2.50
19 Cal Ripken Jr. 4.00
20 Larry Walker .50
21 Adrian Beltre .65
22 Johnny Damon .75
23 Rick Ankiel .50
24 Matt Williams .50
25 Magglio Ordonez .50
26 Richard Hidalgo .50
27 Robin Ventura .50
28 Jason Kendall .50
29 Tony Batista .50
30 Chipper Jones 2.00
31 Jim Thome .50
32 Kevin Brown .50
33 Mike Mussina .65
34 Mark McGwire 3.00
35 Darin Erstad .75
36 Manny Ramirez 1.50
37 Bobby Higginson .50
38 Richie Sexson .50
39 Jason Giambi 1.00
40 Alex Rodriguez 3.00
41 Mark Grace .65
42 Ken Griffey Jr. 2.50
43 Moises Alou .50
44 Edgardo Alfonzo .50
45 Phil Nevin .50
46 Rafael Palmeiro 1.25
47 Javy Lopez .50
48 Juan Gonzalez 1.50
49 Jermaine Dye .50
50 Roger Clemens 2.25
51 Barry Bonds 4.00
52 Carl Everett .50
53 Ben Sheets .50
54 Juan Encarnacion .50
55 Jeromy Burnitz .50
56 Miguel Tejada .65
57 Ben Grieve .50
58 Randy Johnson 1.50
59 Frank Thomas 1.50
60 Preston Wilson .50
61 Mike Piazza 2.50
62 Brian Giles .50
63 Carlos Delgado 1.00
64 Tom Glavine .75
65 Roberto Alomar .65
66 Mike Sweeney .50
67 Orlando Hernandez .50
68 Edgar Martinez .50
69 Tim Salmon .75
70 Kerry Wood 1.00
71 *Jack Wilson* 3.00
72 Matt Lawton .50
73 Scott Rolen 1.25
74 Ivan Rodriguez 1.25
75 Steve Finley .50
76 Barry Larkin .50
77 Jeff Bagwell 1.50
78 Derek Jeter 4.00
79 Tony Gwynn 2.00
80 Raul Mondesi .50
81 Rafael Furcal .50
82 Todd Helton 1.50
83 Shawn Green .75
84 Tim Hudson .65
85 Jim Edmonds .50
86 Troy Glaus 1.50
87 Sammy Sosa 2.50
88 Cliff Floyd .50
89 Jose Vidro .50
90 Bobby Abreu .50
91 *Drew Henson Auto* 40.00
92 *Andy Morales Auto* 8.00
93 *Wilson Betemit Auto* 10.00
94 *Elpidio Guzman* 8.00
95 *Esix Snead* 8.00
96 *Winston Abreu* 8.00
97 *Jeremy Owens* 8.00
99 *Junior Spivey* 15.00
100 *Jaisen Randolph* 8.00
101 *Ichiro Suzuki* 60.00
102 *Albert Pujols/499* 150.00
102 *Albert Pujols Auto/300* 750.00
103 *Tsuyoshi Shinjo* 10.00
104 *Jay Gibbons* 10.00
105 *Juan Uribe* 10.00

Ultimate Legacy

NM/M

Stars (1-90): 3-5X
Rookies (91-100): .3-.75X
Rookies (101-105): .75-1X
Production 250 sets
(See 2001 Fleer Legacy for checklist and base card values.)

Autographed MLB Fitted Cap

NM/M

Common Player: 25.00
Inserted 1:15
Edgardo Alfonzo 25.00
Roberto Alomar 50.00
Ernie Banks/100 100.00
Adrian Beltre 40.00
Johnny Bench/100 125.00
Lance Berkman 30.00
Yogi Berra/200 120.00
Craig Biggio 30.00
Barry Bonds 280.00
Jeromy Burnitz 25.00
Pat Burrell 30.00
Steve Carlton 40.00
Sean Casey 30.00
Orlando Cepeda 30.00
Eric Chavez 25.00
Tony Clark 25.00
Roger Clemens/100 200.00
Johnny Damon 40.00
Dom DiMaggio/200 45.00
J.D. Drew 40.00
Jermaine Dye 25.00
Darin Erstad 40.00
Carlton Fisk/150 80.00
Rafael Furcal 25.00
Nomar Garciaparra/150 150.00
Jason Giambi 50.00
Troy Glaus 35.00
Tom Glavine 50.00
Juan Gonzalez 50.00
Luis Gonzalez 30.00
Tony Gwynn 85.00
Drew Henson 30.00
Derek Jeter 250.00
Andruw Jones 40.00
David Justice 30.00
Paul Konerko 25.00
Don Mattingly 150.00
Willie McCovey 30.00
Paul Molitor 60.00
Stan Musial/200 125.00
Mike Mussina 50.00
Jim Palmer 25.00
Corey Patterson 40.00
Kirby Puckett/200 75.00
Cal Ripken/200 200.00
Brooks Robinson 60.00
Ivan Rodriguez 50.00
Scott Rolen 50.00
Nolan Ryan/150 200.00
Mike Schmidt/150 125.00
Tom Seaver/100 125.00
Ben Sheets 40.00
Ozzie Smith 85.00
Duke Snider 40.00
Miguel Tejada 50.00
Jim Thome 60.00
Matt Williams 25.00
Dave Winfield/150 75.00
Carl Yastrzemski/150 100.00
Robin Yount 100.00
Barry Zito 40.00

Hit Kings

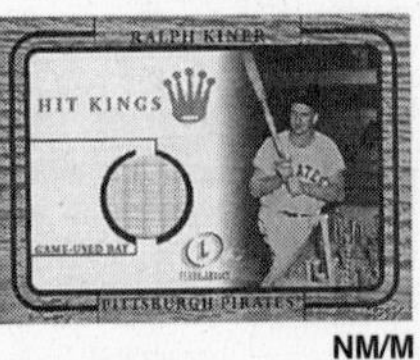

NM/M

Common Player: 5.00
Inserted 1:13
Stan Musial 15.00
Barry Bonds 25.00
Corey Patterson 5.00
Shawn Green 6.00
Ralph Kiner 5.00
Troy O'Leary 5.00
Ivan Rodriguez 6.00
Jose Vidro 5.00
Carlos Beltran 8.00
Jose Canseco 6.00
Juan Encarnacion 5.00
Reggie Jackson 10.00
Ruben Mateo 5.00
Juan Pierre 5.00
Tim Salmon 5.00
Adrian Beltre 6.00
Roger Cedeno 5.00
Troy Glaus 8.00
Jason Kendall 5.00
Rick Ankiel 5.00
Andruw Jones 8.00
Jim Thome 5.00
Tony Batista 5.00
George Brett 20.00
Vladimir Guerrero 10.00
Billy Martin 5.00
Magglio Ordonez 5.00
Johnny Damon 6.00

Hit Kings Short Prints

NM/M

Common Player: 15.00
Production 100 sets
Robin Yount 20.00
Scott Rolen 15.00
Johnny Bench 25.00
Steve Garvey 15.00
Joe Morgan 15.00
Frank Thomas 20.00
Eddie Mathews 20.00
Tony Gwynn 25.00
Roger Clemens 40.00
Wade Boggs 25.00

Hot Gloves

NM/M

Common Player: 15.00

Inserted 1:180
1HG Andruw Jones 15.00
2HG Mike Mussina 15.00
3HG Roberto Alomar 15.00
4HG Tony Gwynn 30.00
5HG Bernie Williams 15.00
6HG Ivan Rodriguez 15.00
7HG Ken Griffey Jr. 40.00
8HG Robin Ventura 15.00
9HG Cal Ripken Jr. 60.00
10HG Jeff Bagwell 20.00
11HG Mark McGwire 50.00
12HG Rafael Palmeiro 15.00
13HG Scott Rolen 15.00
14HG Barry Bonds 60.00
15HG Greg Maddux 30.00

MLB Game Issue - Base

NM/M

Common Player: 4.00
Inserted 1:52
1GI Mark McGwire 15.00
2GI Ken Griffey Jr. 10.00
3GI Sammy Sosa 10.00
4GI Mike Piazza 10.00
5GI Alex Rodriguez 15.00
6GI Derek Jeter 20.00
7GI Cal Ripken Jr. 20.00
8GI Todd Helton 6.00
9GI Tony Gwynn 8.00
10GI Chipper Jones 8.00
11GI Frank Thomas 6.00
12GI Barry Bonds 20.00
13GI Troy Glaus 4.00
14GI Pat Burrell 4.00
15GI Scott Rolen 5.00

MLB Game Issue - Base/Ball

NM/M

Common Player: 10.00
Production 100 sets
Mark McGwire 50.00
Ken Griffey Jr. 40.00
Sammy Sosa 40.00
Mike Piazza 40.00
Alex Rodriguez 50.00
Derek Jeter 60.00
Cal Ripken Jr. 60.00
Todd Helton 15.00
Tony Gwynn 25.00
Chipper Jones 25.00
Frank Thomas 15.00
Barry Bonds 60.00
Troy Glaus 10.00
Pat Burrell 10.00
Scott Rolen 12.50

MLB Game Issue - Base/Ball/Jersey

		NM/M
Common Card:		25.00
Production 50 sets		
	Derek Jeter	100.00
	Cal Ripken Jr.	100.00
	Todd Helton	30.00
	Tony Gwynn	50.00
	Chipper Jones	50.00
	Frank Thomas	30.00
	Barry Bonds	100.00
	Troy Glaus	25.00
	Pat Burrell	25.00
	Scott Rolen	30.00

Tailor Made

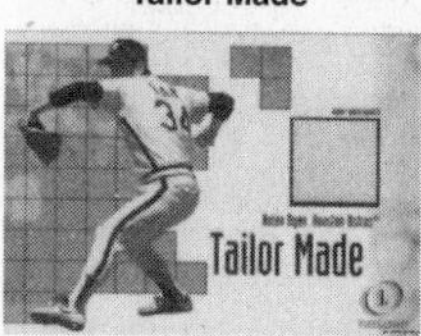

		NM/M
Common Player:		4.00
Inserted 1:15		
2TM	Cal Ripken Jr.	40.00
3TM	Orlando Cepeda	6.00
4TM	Willie McCovey	6.00
5TM	Dave Winfield	6.00
6TM	Don Mattingly	35.00
7TM	Nolan Ryan	40.00
8TM	Manny Ramirez	8.00
9TM	Edgardo Alfonzo	4.00
10TM	Rondell White	4.00
11TM	Lou Piniella	4.00
12TM	Ivan Rodriguez	8.00
13TM	J.D. Drew	4.00
14TM	Barry Bonds	40.00
15TM	Greg Maddux	15.00
16TM	Rick Ankiel	4.00
17TM	Carlos Delgado	8.00
18TM	Kevin Brown	4.00
20TM	Reggie Jackson	10.00
21TM	Shawn Green	6.00
22TM	Jason Kendall	4.00
23TM	Rafael Palmeiro	8.00
24TM	Todd Helton	8.00
25	Curt Schilling	6.00

2001 FLEER PLATINUM

		NM/M
Complete Set (301):		140.00
Common Player:		.15
Common SP (251-300):		1.00
Inserted 1:6		
Card #301 production 1,500		
Pack (10):		5.00
Box (24):		100.00
1	Bobby Abreu	.15
2	Brad Radke	.15
3	Bill Mueller	.15
4	Adam Eaton	.15
5	Antonio Alfonseca	.15
6	Manny Ramirez	.75
7	Adam Kennedy	.15
8	Jose Valentin	.15
9	Jaret Wright	.15
10	Aramis Ramirez	.15
11	Jeff Kent	.15
12	Juan Encarnacion	.15
13	Sandy Alomar Jr.	.15
14	Joe Randa	.15
15	Darryl Kile	.15
16	Darren Dreifort	.15
17	Matt Kinney	.15
18	Pokey Reese	.15
19	Ryan Klesko	.15
20	Shawn Estes	.15
21	Moises Alou	.15
22	Edgar Renteria	.15
23	Chuck Knoblauch	.15
24	Carl Everett	.15
25	Garret Anderson	.15
26	Shane Reynolds	.15
27	Billy Koch	.15
28	Carlos Febles	.15
29	Brian Anderson	.15
30	Armando Rios	.15
31	Ryan Kohlmeier	.15
32	Steve Finley	.15
33	Brady Anderson	.15
34	Cal Ripken Jr.	2.50
35	Paul Konerko	.15
36	Chuck Finley	.15
37	Rick Ankiel	.15
38	Mariano Rivera	.25
39	Corey Koskie	.15
40	Cliff Floyd	.15
41	Kevin Appier	.15
42	Henry Rodriguez	.15
43	Mark Kotsay	.15
44	Brook Fordyce	.15
45	Brad Ausmus	.15
46	Alfonso Soriano	.50
47	Ray Lankford	.15
48	Keith Foulke	.15
49	Rich Aurilia	.15
50	Alex Rodriguez	2.00
51	Eric Byrnes	.15
52	Travis Fryman	.15
53	Jeff Bagwell	.75
54	Scott Rolen	.65
55	Matt Lawton	.15
56	Brad Fullmer	.15
57	Tony Batista	.15
58	Nate Rolison	.15
59	Carlos Lee	.15
60	Rafael Furcal	.15
61	Jay Bell	.15
62	Jimmy Rollins	.15
63	Derrek Lee	.15
64	Andres Galarraga	.15
65	Derek Bell	.15
66	Tim Salmon	.25
67	Travis Lee	.15
68	Kevin Millwood	.15
69	Albert Belle	.15
70	Kazuhiro Sasaki	.15
71	Al Leiter	.15
72	Britt Reames	.15
73	Carlos Beltran	.45
74	Curt Schilling	.50
75	Curtis Leskanic	.15
76	Jeremy Giambi	.15
77	Adrian Beltre	.35
78	David Segui	.15
79	Mike Lieberthal	.15
80	Brian Giles	.15
81	Marvin Benard	.15
82	Aaron Sele	.15
83	Kenny Lofton	.15
84	Doug Glanville	.15
85	Kris Benson	.15
86	Richie Sexson	.15
87	Javy Lopez	.15
88	Doug Mientkiewicz	.15
89	Peter Bergeron	.15
90	Gary Sheffield	.40
91	Derek Lowe	.15
92	Tom Glavine	.40
93	Lance Berkman	.15
94	Chris Singleton	.15
95	Mike Lowell	.25
96	Luis Gonzalez	.30
97	Dante Bichette	.15
98	Mike Sirotka	.15
99	Julio Lugo	.15
100	Juan Gonzalez	.75
101	Craig Biggio	.15
102	Armando Benitez	.15
103	Greg Maddux	1.00
104	Mark Grace	.25
105	John Smoltz	.15
106	J.T. Snow	.15
107	Al Martin	.15
108	Danny Graves	.15
109	Barry Bonds	2.50
110	Lee Stevens	.15
111	Pedro Martinez	.75
112	Shawn Green	.40
113	Bret Boone	.15
114	Matt Stairs	.15
115	Tino Martinez	.15
116	Rusty Greer	.15
117	Mike Bordick	.15
118	Garrett Stephenson	.15
119	Edgar Martinez	.15
120	Ben Grieve	.15
121	Milton Bradley	.15
122	Aaron Boone	.15
123	Ruben Mateo	.15
124	Ken Griffey Jr.	1.50
125	Russell Branyan	.15
126	Shannon Stewart	.15
127	Fred McGriff	.15
128	Ben Petrick	.15
129	Kevin Brown	.15
130	B.J. Surhoff	.15
131	Mark McGwire	2.00
132	Carlos Guillen	.15
133	Adrian Brown	.15
134	Mike Sweeney	.15
135	Eric Milton	.15
136	Cristian Guzman	.15
137	Ellis Burks	.15
138	Fernando Tatis	.15
139	Ben Molina	.15
140	Tony Gwynn	1.00
141	Jeromy Burnitz	.15
142	Miguel Tejada	.25
143	Raul Mondesi	.15
144	Jeffrey Hammonds	.15
145	Pat Burrell	.40
146	Frank Thomas	.75
147	Eric Munson	.15
148	Mike Hampton	.15
149	Mike Cameron	.15
150	Jim Thome	.15
151	Mike Mussina	.50
152	Rick Helling	.15
153	Ken Caminiti	.15
154	John Vander Wal	.15
155	Denny Neagle	.15
156	Robb Nen	.15
157	Jose Canseco	.50
158	Mo Vaughn	.15
159	Phil Nevin	.15
160	Pat Hentgen	.15
161	Sean Casey	.25
162	Greg Vaughn	.15
163	Trot Nixon	.15
164	Roberto Hernandez	.15
165	Vinny Castilla	.15
166	Robin Ventura	.15
167	Alex Ochoa	.15
168	Orlando Hernandez	.15
169	Luis Castillo	.15
170	Quilvio Veras	.15
171	Troy O'Leary	.15
172	Livan Hernandez	.15
173	Roger Cedeno	.15
174	Jose Vidro	.15
175	John Olerud	.15
176	Richard Hidalgo	.15
177	Eric Chavez	.25
178	Fernando Vina	.15
179	Chris Stynes	.15
180	Bobby Higginson	.15
181	Bruce Chen	.15
182	Omar Vizquel	.15
183	Rey Ordonez	.15
184	Trevor Hoffman	.15
185	Jeff Cirillo	.15
186	Billy Wagner	.15
187	David Ortiz	.15
188	Tim Hudson	.40
189	Tony Clark	.15
190	Larry Walker	.15
191	Eric Owens	.15
192	Aubrey Huff	.15
193	Royce Clayton	.15
194	Todd Walker	.15
195	Rafael Palmeiro	.65
196	Todd Hundley	.15
197	Roger Clemens	1.25
198	Jeff Weaver	.15
199	Dean Palmer	.15
200	Geoff Jenkins	.15
201	Matt Clement	.15
202	David Wells	.15
203	Chan Ho Park	.15
204	Hideo Nomo	.65
205	Bartolo Colon	.15
206	John Wetteland	.15
207	Corey Patterson	.15
208	Freddy Garcia	.15
209	David Cone	.15
210	Rondell White	.15
211	Carl Pavano	.15
212	Charles Johnson	.15
213	Ron Coomer	.15
214	Matt Williams	.15
215	Jay Payton	.15
216	Nick Johnson	.15
217	Deivi Cruz	.15
218	Scott Elarton	.15
219	Neifi Perez	.15
220	Jason Isringhausen	.15
221	Jose Cruz	.15
222	Gerald Williams	.15
223	Timo Perez	.15
224	Damion Easley	.15
225	Jeff D'Amico (photo actually Jamey Wright)	.15
226	Preston Wilson	.15
227	Robert Person	.15
228	Jacque Jones	.15
229	Johnny Damon	.25
230	Tony Womack	.15
231	Adam Piatt	.15
232	Brian Jordan	.15
233	Ben Davis	.15
234	Kerry Wood	.50
235	Mike Piazza	1.50
236	David Justice	.15
237	Dave Veres	.15
238	Eric Young	.15
239	Juan Pierre	.15
240	Gabe Kapler	.15
241	Ryan Dempster	.15
242	Dmitri Young	.15
243	Jorge Posada	.35
244	Eric Karros	.15
245	J.D. Drew	.25
246	Todd Zeile	.15
247	Mark Quinn	.15
248	Kenny Kelly	.15
249	Jermaine Dye	.15
250	Barry Zito	.30
251	Jason Hart, Larry Barnes	1.00
252	*Ichiro Suzuki, Elpidio Guzman*	20.00
253	Tsuyoshi Shinjo, Brian Cole	3.00
254	*John Barnes, Adrian Hernandez*	1.00
255	Jason Tyner, Jace Brewer	1.00
256	Brian Buchanan, Luis Rivas	1.00
257	Brent Abernathy, Jose Ortiz	1.00
258	Marcus Giles, Keith Ginter	1.00
259	*Tike Redman, Jaisen Randolph*	1.00
260	Dane Sardinha, David Espinosa	1.00
261	Josh Beckett, Craig House	1.00
262	Jack Cust, Hiram Bocachica	1.00
263	*Alex Escobar, Esix Snead*	1.00
264	Chris Richard, Vernon Wells	1.00
265	Pedro Feliz, Xavier Nady	1.00
266	Brandon Inge, Joe Crede	1.00
267	Ben Sheets, Roy Oswalt	1.00
268	*Drew Henson, Andy Morales*	4.00
269	C.C. Sabathia, Justin Miller	1.00
270	David Eckstein, Jason Gabrowski	1.00
271	Dee Brown, Chris Wakeland	1.00
272	Junior Spivey, Alex Cintron	3.00
273	*Elvis Pena, Juan Uribe*	2.00
274	Carlos Pena, Jason Romano	1.00
275	*Winston Abreu, Wilson Betemit*	1.50
276	Jose Mieses, Nick Neugebauer	1.00
277	Shea Hillenbrand, Dernell Stenson	1.00
278	Jared Sandberg, Toby Hall	1.00
279	Jay Gibbons, Ivanon Coffie	3.00
280	Pablo Ozuna, Santiago Perez	1.00
281	Nomar Garciaparra	6.00
282	Derek Jeter	6.00
283	Jason Giambi	2.50
284	Magglio Ordonez	1.00

285 Ivan Rodriguez 2.00
286 Troy Glaus 2.00
287 Carlos Delgado 2.00
288 Darin Erstad 1.00
289 Bernie Williams 2.00
290 Roberto Alomar 1.50
291 Barry Larkin 1.50
292 Chipper Jones 4.00
293 Vladimir Guerrero 3.00
294 Sammy Sosa 5.00
295 Todd Helton 2.00
296 Randy Johnson 3.00
297 Jason Kendall 1.00
298 Jim Edmonds 1.50
299 Andruw Jones 2.00
300 Edgardo Alfonzo 1.00
301 *Albert Pujols, Donaldo Mendez* 75.00

Platinum Edition

NM/M
Cards (1-250): 4-8X
Production 201 sets
SP's (251-280): 8-20X
SP's (281-300): 5-10X
SP Production 21 sets
(See 2001 Fleer Platinum for checklist and base card values.)

Classic Combinations

NM/M
Common Card: 4.00
#1-10 numbered to 250
11-20 numbered to 500
21-30 numbered to 1,000
31-40 numbered to 2,000
1CC Derek Jeter, Alex Rodriguez 20.00
2CC Willie Mays, Willie McCovey 15.00
3CC Lou Gehrig, Babe Ruth 20.00
4CC Mark McGwire, Ken Griffey Jr. 15.00
5CC Johnny Bench, Roy Campanella 10.00
6CC Ted Williams, Nomar Garciaparra 20.00
7CC Yogi Berra, Mike Piazza 15.00
8CC Ernie Banks, Sammy Sosa 12.00
9CC Nolan Ryan, Randy Johnson 25.00
10CC Roberto Clemente, Vladimir Guerrero 15.00
11CC Lou Gehrig, Stan Musial 15.00
12CC Bill Mazeroski, Roberto Clemente 10.00
13CC Ernie Banks, Alex Rodriguez 10.00
14CC Phil Rizzuto, Derek Jeter 10.00
15CC Mike Piazza, Johnny Bench 8.00
16CC Mark McGwire, Sammy Sosa 10.00
17CC Ted Williams, Tony Gwynn 12.00
18CC Eddie Mathews, Mike Schmidt 10.00
19CC Barry Bonds, Willie Mays 10.00
20CC Nolan Ryan, Pedro Martinez 15.00
21CC Barry Bonds, Ken Griffey Jr. 10.00
22CC Willie McCovey, Reggie Jackson 5.00
23CC Roberto Clemente, Sammy Sosa 8.00
24CC Willie Mays, Ernie Banks 8.00
25CC Eddie Mathews, Chipper Jones 5.00
26CC Mike Schmidt, Brooks Robinson 6.00
27CC Stan Musial, Mark McGwire 8.00
28CC Ted Williams, Roger Maris 8.00
29CC Yogi Berra, Roy Campanella 5.00
30CC Johnny Bench, Tony Perez 5.00
31CC Bill Mazeroski, Joe Carter 3.00
32CC Mike Piazza, Roy Campanella 5.00
33CC Ernie Banks, Craig Biggio 4.00
34CC Frank Robinson, Brooks Robinson 4.00
35CC Mike Schmidt, Scott Rolen 5.00
36CC Roger Maris, Mark McGwire 10.00
37CC Stan Musial, Tony Gwynn 4.00
38CC Ted Williams, Bill Terry 6.00
39CC Derek Jeter, Reggie Jackson 6.00
40CC Yogi Berra, Bill Dickey 4.00

Classic Combinations Memorabilia

NM/M
Production 25 sets
1 Yogi Berra, Bill Dickey 75.00
2 Yogi Berra, Roy Campanella 100.00
3 Roberto Clemente, Vladimir Guerrero 200.00
4 Eddie Mathews, Chipper Jones 80.00
5 Willie McCovey, Reggie Jackson 75.00
6 Phil Rizzuto, Derek Jeter 180.00
7 Brooks Robinson, Frank Robinson 85.00
8 Brooks Robinson, Mike Schmidt 180.00
9 Mike Schmidt, Scott Rolen 160.00
10 Ted Williams, Bill Terry 300.00
11 Ted Williams, Tony Gwynn 375.00

Grandstand Greats

NM/M
Complete Set (20): 25.00
Common Player: 1.00
Inserted 1:12
1GG Chipper Jones 2.00
2GG Alex Rodriguez 3.00
3GG Jeff Bagwell 1.50
4GG Troy Glaus 1.50
5GG Manny Ramirez 1.50
6GG Derek Jeter 4.00
7GG Tony Gwynn 2.00
8GG Greg Maddux 2.00
9GG Nomar Garciaparra 2.50
10GG Sammy Sosa 2.50
11GG Mike Piazza 2.50
12GG Barry Bonds 4.00
13GG Mark McGwire 3.00
14GG Vladimir Guerrero 1.50
15GG Ivan Rodriguez 1.00
16GG Ken Griffey Jr. 2.50
17GG Todd Helton 1.50
18GG Cal Ripken Jr. 4.00
19GG Pedro Martinez 1.50
20GG Frank Thomas 1.50

Nameplates

NM/M
Common Player: 15.00
Inserted 1:12
Cal Ripken /19 200.00
Cal Ripken /21 200.00
Cal Ripken /23 200.00
Cal Ripken /110 100.00
Randy Johnson/99 40.00
Nolan Ryan/40 200.00
Javy Lopez/49 20.00
Frank Thomas/35 40.00
Frank Thomas/75 30.00
Frank Thomas/80 30.00
Jeffrey Hammonds/135 15.00
Larry Walker/79 15.00
Larry Walker/85 15.00
Dave Winfield/80 20.00
Vladimir Guerrero/80 25.00
Vladimir Guerrero/90 25.00
Kevin Millwood/130 15.00
Mike Mussina/91 25.00
Edgar Martinez/87 25.00
Edgar Martinez/120 20.00
Scott Rolen/65 30.00
Ivan Rodriguez/177 25.00
Manny Ramirez/75 25.00
Manny Ramirez/105 25.00
J.D. Drew/170 15.00
Greg Maddux/180 50.00
Chipper Jones/95 40.00
Carlos Beltran/90 15.00
Adrian Beltre 15.00
Matt Williams/175 15.00
Curt Schilling 20.00
Pedro Martinez/120 30.00
Robin Ventura/99 15.00
Tom Glavine/125 15.00
Tony Gwynn/35 75.00
Tony Gwynn/65 40.00
Tony Gwynn/70 40.00
Troy Glaus/85 20.00
Sean Casey/21 35.00
Darin Erstad/39 30.00
Stan Musial/30 150.00

National Patch Time

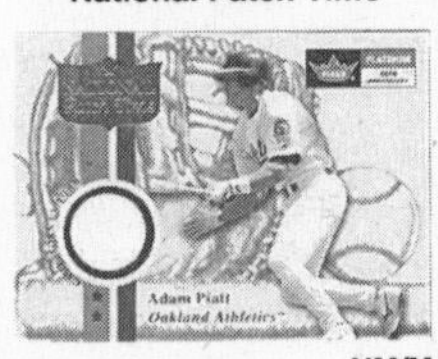

NM/M
Common Player: 4.00
Inserted 1:24 H
Tony Gwynn 8.00
Manny Ramirez 6.00
Freddy Garcia 4.00
Rondell White 4.00
Ivan Rodriguez 5.00
Brady Anderson 4.00
Adam Piatt 4.00
Carl Everett 4.00
Magglio Ordonez 4.00
Edgardo Alfonzo 4.00
Jason Kendall 4.00
Greg Maddux 8.00
Cal Ripken Jr. 30.00
Fred McGriff 4.00
Pedro Martinez 6.00
Roger Clemens 10.00
Wade Boggs 8.00
George Brett 15.00
Ozzie Smith 8.00
Dave Winfield 6.00
Tom Seaver 6.00
Rollie Fingers 4.00
Mike Schmidt 15.00
Eddie Murray 6.00
Nolan Ryan 30.00
Jeff Cirillo 4.00

Mike Mussina 5.00
Carl Yastrzemski (not officially issued)

Rack Pack Autographs

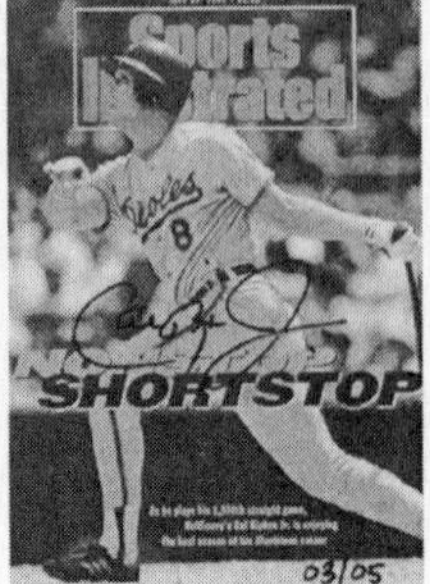

NM/M
Common Player: 5.00
Hank Aaron 1997/90 100.00
Lou Brock 1998/15
Roger Clemens 1998/125 100.00
Jose Cruz Jr. 1997 5.00
J.D. Drew 1999/10
Steve Garvey 1997/15
Bob Gibson 1998/300 25.00
Ben Grieve 100 6.00
Tony Gwynn 1998/125 50.00
Wes Helms 1997 5.00
Harmon Killebrew 1998/300 30.00
Paul Konerko 135 5.00
Willie Mays 1997/115 120.00
Willie Mays 1998/120 120.00
Kirby Puckett 1 997/105 50.00
Cal Ripken Jr. /5
Brooks Robinson 1998/40 75.00
Frank Robinson 1998/115 20.00
Scott Rolen 1998/150 25.00
Alex Rodriguez 1997/94 100.00
Alex Rodriguez 1998/150 70.00

Tickets

No Pricing

20th Anniversary Reprints

NM/M
Complete Set (18): 25.00
Common Player: .50
Inserted 1:8
1AR Cal Ripken Jr. 4.00
2AR Wade Boggs 1.50
3AR Ryne Sandberg 1.50
4AR Tony Gwynn 1.50
5AR Don Mattingly 3.00
6AR Roger Clemens 2.00
7AR Kirby Puckett 1.50
8AR Jose Canseco .75
9AR Barry Bonds 4.00
10AR Ken Griffey Jr. 2.50
11AR Sammy Sosa 2.50
12AR Ivan Rodriguez .75
13AR Jeff Bagwell 1.00
14AR J.D. Drew .75
15AR Troy Glaus 1.00

16AR Rick Ankiel .50
17AR Xavier Nady .50
18AR Jose Ortiz .50

2001 FLEER PLATINUM RC

NM/M
Complete Set (300): 150.00
Common Player: .15
Common (502-601): 1.00
Inserted 1:3 hobby
Pack (10): 5.00
Box (24): 100.00
302 Shawn Wooten .15
303 Todd Walker .15
304 Brian Buchanan .15
305 Jim Edmonds .25
306 Jarrod Washburn .15
307 Jose Rijo .15
308 Tim Raines .15
309 Matt Morris .15
310 Troy Glaus .50
311 Barry Larkin .40
312 Javier Vazquez .15
313 Placido Polanco .15
314 Darin Erstad .25
315 Marty Cordova .15
316 Vladimir Guerrero .75
317 Kerry Robinson .15
318 Byung-Hyun Kim .15
319 C.C. Sabathia .15
320 Edgardo Alfonzo .15
321 Jason Tyner .15
322 Reggie Sanders .15
323 Roberto Alomar .60
324 Matt Lawton .15
325 Brent Abernathy .15
326 Randy Johnson .75
327 Todd Helton .75
328 Andy Pettitte .40
329 Josh Beckett .40
330 Mark DeRosa .15
331 Jose Ortiz .15
332 Derek Jeter 2.00
333 Toby Hall .15
334 Wes Helms .15
335 Jose Macias .15
336 Bernie Williams .60
337 Ivan Rodriguez .75
338 Chipper Jones 1.25
339 Brandon Inge .15
340 Jason Giambi .75
341 Frank Catalanotto .15
342 Andruw Jones .50
343 *Carlos Hernandez* .40
344 Jermaine Dye .15
345 Mike Lamb .15
346 Ken Caminiti .15
347 A.J. Burnett .15
348 Terrence Long .15
349 Ruben Sierra .15
350 Marcus Giles .15
351 Wade Miller .15
352 Mark Mulder .25
353 Carlos Delgado .50
354 Chris Richard .15
355 Daryle Ward .15
356 Brad Penny .15
357 Vernon Wells .25
358 Jason Johnson .15
359 Tim Redding .15
360 Marlon Anderson .15
361 Carlos Pena .15
362 Nomar Garciaparra 2.00
363 Roy Oswalt .40
364 Todd Ritchie .15
365 Jose Mesa .15
366 Shea Hillenbrand .15
367 Dee Brown .15
368 Jason Kendall .25
369 Vinny Castilla .15
370 Fred McGriff .25
371 Neifi Perez .15
372 Xavier Nady .15
373 Abraham Nunez .15
374 Jon Lieber .15
375 Paul LoDuca .15
376 Bubba Trammell .15
377 Brady Clark .15
378 Joel Pineiro .15
379 Mark Grudzielanek .15
380 D'Angelo Jimenez .15
381 Junior Herndon .15
382 Magglio Ordonez .40
383 Ben Sheets .25
384 John Vander Wal .15
385 Pedro Astacio .15
386 Jose Canseco .40
387 Jose Hernandez .15
388 Eric Davis .15
389 Sammy Sosa 1.25
390 Mark Buehrle .15
391 Mark Loretta .15
392 Andres Galarraga .25
393 Scott Spiezio .15
394 Joe Crede .15
395 Luis Rivas .15
396 David Bell .15
397 Einar Diaz .15
398 Adam Dunn .75
399 A.J. Pierzynski .15
400 Jamie Moyer .15
401 Nick Johnson .15
402 Freddy Garcia 4.00
403 Hideo Nomo .50
404 Mark Mulder .25
405 Steve Sparks .15
406 Mariano Rivera .25
407 Mark Buehrle, Mike Mussina .25
408 Randy Johnson .50
409 Randy Johnson .50
410 Curt Schilling, Matt Morris .25
411 Greg Maddux .60
412 Robb Nen .15
413 Randy Johnson .50
414 Barry Bonds 1.00
415 Jason Giambi .40
416 Ichiro Suzuki 2.50
417 Ichiro Suzuki 2.50
418 Alex Rodriguez 1.00
419 Bret Boone .25
420 Ichiro Suzuki 2.50
421 Alex Rodriguez 1.00
422 Jason Giambi .40
423 Alex Rodriguez 1.00
424 Larry Walker .25
425 Rich Aurilia .15
426 Barry Bonds 1.00
427 Sammy Sosa .75
428 Jimmy Rollins, Juan Pierre .15
429 Sammy Sosa .75
430 Lance Berkman .25
431 Sammy Sosa .75
432 Carlos Delgado .25
433 Alex Rodriguez 1.00
434 Greg Vaughn .15
435 Albert Pujols 10.00
436 Ichiro Suzuki 2.50
437 Barry Bonds 1.00
438 Phil Nevin .15
439 Brian Giles .25
440 Bobby Abreu .25
441 Jason Giambi .40
442 Derek Jeter 1.00
443 Mike Piazza .75
444 Vladimir Guerrero .50
445 Corey Koskie .15
446 Richie Sexson .25
447 Shawn Green .25
448 Mike Sweeney .15
449 Jeff Bagwell .40
450 Cliff Floyd .15
451 Roger Cedeno .15
452 Todd Helton .40
453 Juan Gonzalez .30
454 Sean Casey .15
455 Magglio Ordonez .25
456 Sammy Sosa .75
457 Manny Ramirez .40
458 Jeff Conine .15
459 Chipper Jones .60
460 Luis Gonzalez .25
461 Troy Glaus .25
462 Ivan Rodriguez .40
463 Luis Gonzalez, Jack Cust .25
464 Jim Thome, C.C. Sabathia .25
465 Jason Hart, Jason Giambi .25
466 Jeff Bagwell, Roy Oswalt .30
467 Sammy Sosa, Corey Patterson .50
468 Mike Piazza, Alex Escobar .75
469 Ken Griffey Jr., Adam Dunn .75
470 Roger Clemens, Nick Johnson .75
471 Cliff Floyd, Josh Beckett .15
472 Cal Ripken Jr., Jerry Hairston Jr. .75
473 Phil Nevin, Xavier Nady .15
474 Scott Rolen, Jimmy Rollins .25
475 Barry Larkin, David Espinosa .25
476 Larry Walker, Jose Ortiz .15
477 Chipper Jones, Marcus Giles .40
478 Craig Biggio, Keith Ginter .15
479 Magglio Ordonez, Aaron Rowand .25
480 Alex Rodriguez, Carlos Pena .75
481 Derek Jeter, Alfonso Soriano .75
482 Curt Schilling (Post Season Glory) .20
483 (Post Season Glory) .25
484 (Post Season Glory) .25
485 (Post Season Glory) .25
486 (Post Season Glory) .25
487 (Post Season Glory) .25
488 (Post Season Glory) .25
489 Rudolph Giuliani (Post Season Glory) .50
490 George Bush (Post Season Glory) .50
491 (Post Season Glory) .25
492 (Post Season Glory) .25
493 (Post Season Glory) .25
494 Derek Jeter (Post Season Glory) .75
495 (Post Season Glory) .25
496 (Post Season Glory) .25
497 (Post Season Glory) .25
498 (Post Season Glory) .25
499 (Post Season Glory) .25
500 (Post Season Glory) .25
501 (Post Season Glory) .25
502 *Josh Fogg* 1.00
503 Elpidio Guzman 1.00
504 *Corky Miller* 1.00
505 *Cesar Crespo* 1.00
506 *Carlos Garcia* 1.00
507 *Carlos Valderrama* 1.00
508 *Joe Kennedy* 1.00
509 *Henry Mateo* 1.00
510 *Brandon Duckworth* 1.00
511 Ichiro Suzuki 15.00
512 *Zach Day* 2.00
513 *Ryan Freel* 1.00
514 *Brian Lawrence* 2.00
515 *Alexis Gomez* 1.00
516 *Will Ohman* 1.00
517 *Juan Diaz* 1.00
518 *Juan Moreno* 1.00
519 *Rob Mackowiak* 1.00
520 *Horacio Ramirez* 1.50
521 Albert Pujols 50.00
522 Tsuyoshi Shinjo 2.50
523 *Ryan Drese* 1.00
524 *Angel Berroa* 3.00
525 *Josh Towers* 2.50
526 Junior Spivey 1.50
527 *Greg Miller* 1.00
528 *Esix Snead* 1.00
529 *Mark Prior* 15.00
530 Drew Henson 3.00
531 *Brian Reith* 1.00
532 *Andres Torres* 1.00
533 *Casey Fossum* 2.00
534 *Wilmy Caceres* 1.00
535 *Matt White* 1.00
536 *Wilkin Ruan* 1.00
537 *Rick Bauer* 1.00
538 *Morgan Ensberg* 2.00
539 *Geronimo Gil* 1.00
540 *Dewon Brazelton* 1.00
541 *Johnny Estrada* 1.50
542 *Claudio Vargas* 1.00
543 *Donaldo Mendez* 1.00
544 *Kyle Lohse* 2.00
545 *Nate Frese* 1.00
546 *Christian Parker* 1.00
547 *Blaine Neal* 1.00
548 *Travis Hafner* 3.00
549 *Billy Sylvester* 1.00
550 Adam Pettyjohn 1.00
551 Bill Ortega 1.00
552 *Jose Acevedo* 1.00
553 *Steve Green* 1.00
554 *Jay Gibbons* 2.50
555 *Bert Snow* 1.00
556 *Erick Almonte* 1.50
557 *Jeremy Owens* 1.00
558 *Sean Douglass* 1.00
559 *Jason Smith* 1.00
560 *Ricardo Rodriguez* 1.00
561 *Mark Teixeira* 15.00
562 *Tyler Walker* 1.00
563 *Juan Uribe* 1.50
564 *Bud Smith* 1.00
565 *Angel Santos* 1.00
566 *Brandon Lyon* 1.00
567 *Eric Hinske* 2.50
568 *Nick Punto* 1.00
569 *Winston Abreu* 1.00
570 *Jason Phillips* 4.00
571 *Rafael Soriano* 1.50
572 Wilson Betemit 1.00
573 *Endy Chavez* 1.00
574 *Juan Cruz* 1.00
575 *Cory Aldridge* 1.00
576 Adrian Hernandez 1.00
577 *Brandon Larson* 1.50
578 *Bret Prinz* 1.00
579 *Jackson Melian* 1.00
580 *Dave Maurer* 1.00
581 *Jason Michaels* 1.00
582 *Travis Phelps* 1.00
583 *Cody Ransom* 1.00
584 *Benito Baez* 1.00
585 *Brian Roberts* 1.00
586 *Nate Teut* 1.00
587 *Jack Wilson* 1.00
588 *Willie Harris* 1.00
589 *Martin Vargas* 1.00
590 *Steve Torrealba* 1.00
591 *Stubby Clapp* 1.00
592 *Danny Wright* 1.00
593 *Mike Rivera* 1.00
594 *Luis Pineda* 1.00
595 *Lance Davis* 1.00
596 *Ramon Vazquez* 2.00
597 *Dustan Mohr* 1.00
598 *Troy Mattes* 1.00
599 *Grant Balfour* 1.00
600 *Jared Fernandez* 1.00
601 *Jorge Julio* 2.00
E-X
131 *Albert Pujols/499* 200.00
132 *Bud Smith/499* 8.00
133 *Tsuyoshi Shinjo/499* 10.00
134 *Wilson Betemit/499* 8.00
135 *Adrian Hernandez/499* 8.00
136 Jackson Melian/499 8.00
137 *Jay Gibbons/499* 10.00
138 *Johnny Estrada/499* 15.00
139 *Morgan Ensberg/499* 10.00
140 *Drew Henson/499* 20.00
Focus
241 *Tsuyoshi Shinjo/999* 5.00
242 *Wilson Betemit/999* 5.00
243 *Jeremy Owens/999* 5.00
244 *Drew Henson/999* 8.00
245 *Albert Pujols/999* 75.00
246 *Travis Hafner/999* 10.00
247 *Ichiro Suzuki/999* 40.00
248 *Elpidio Guzman/999* 6.00
249 *Matt White/999* 6.00
250 *Junior Spivey/999* 8.00
Futures
221 *Drew Henson/2499* 5.00
222 *Johnny Estrada/2499* 5.00
223 *Elpidio Guzman/2499* 3.00
224 *Albert Pujols/2499* 45.00
225 *Wilson Betemit/2499* 4.00
226 *Mark Teixeira/2499* 15.00
227 *Tsuyoshi Shinjo/2499* 5.00
228 *Matt White/2499* 3.00
229 *Adrian Hernandez/2499* 3.00
230 *Ichiro Suzuki/2499* 30.00
Triple Crown
301 *Elpidio Guzman/2999* 4.00
302 *Drew Henson/2999* 5.00
303 *Bud Smith/2999* 2.00
304 *Carlos Valderrama/2999* 2.00
305 *Tsuyoshi Shinjo/2999* 4.00
306 *Ichiro Suzuki/2999* 30.00
307 Jackson Melian/2999 2.00
308 *Morgan Ensberg/2999* 4.00
309 *Albert Pujols/2999* 50.00
310 *Johnny Estrada/2999* 5.00
Ultra
276 *Junior Spivey, Juan Uribe* 5.00
277 *Albert Pujols, Bud Smith* 50.00
278 *Ichiro Suzuki, Tsuyoshi Shinjo* 25.00
279 Drew Henson, Jackson Melian 5.00
280 *Matt White, Adrian Hernandez* 2.00

Platinum

NM/M
Cards (302-501): 4-8X
Production 201
SPs (502-601):
Production 21 not priced
(See 2001 Fleer Platinum RC for checklist and base card values.)

Lumberjacks Autographs

	NM/M
Production 100 sets	
Barry Bonds	250.00
J.D. Drew	
Adam Dunn	60.00
Luis Gonzalez	40.00
Derek Jeter	150.00
Albert Pujols	500.00
Cal Ripken Jr.	150.00
Mike Sweeney	

Lumberjacks

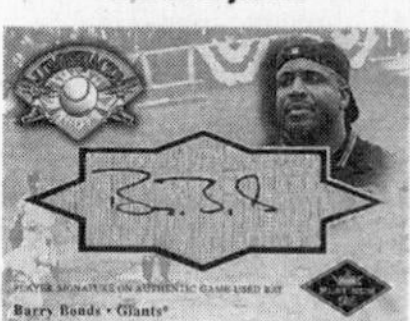

	NM/M
Common Player:	4.00
Inserted 1:1 Rack pack	
Barry Bonds	20.00
Cal Ripken Jr.	
Derek Jeter	20.00
Luis Gonzalez	4.00
Mike Sweeney	4.00
Albert Pujols	15.00
Tony Gwynn	10.00
Adam Dunn	5.00
J.D. Drew	5.00
Brian Giles	4.00
Adrian Beltre	5.00
Bret Boone	4.00
Chipper Jones	10.00
Cliff Floyd	4.00
Darin Erstad	5.00
Gary Sheffield	4.00
Manny Ramirez	8.00
Mike Piazza	12.00
Todd Helton	8.00
Ivan Rodriguez	6.00
Lance Berkman	4.00
Vladimir Guerrero	8.00
Drew Henson	6.00
Cristian Guzman	4.00
Roberto Alomar	5.00
Moises Alou	4.00
Larry Walker	4.00

National Patch Time

	NM/M
Common Player:	4.00
Inserted 1:24 H	
Edgardo Alfonzo	4.00
Brady Anderson	4.00
Adrian Beltre	4.00
Barry Bonds	20.00
Jeromy Burnitz	4.00
Eric Chavez	4.00
Roger Clemens	15.00
J.D. Drew	5.00
Darin Erstad	5.00
Carl Everett	4.00
Freddy Garcia	4.00
Jason Giambi	8.00
Juan Gonzalez	6.00
Mark Grace	6.00
Shawn Green	4.00
Ben Grieve	4.00
Vladimir Guerrero	8.00
Tony Gwynn	10.00
Randy Johnson	8.00
Chipper Jones	10.00
David Justice	4.00
Jeff Kent	4.00
Greg Maddux	10.00
Fred McGriff	4.00
John Olerud	4.00
Magglio Ordonez	4.00
Jorge Posada	5.00
Cal Ripken Jr.	20.00
Mariano Rivera	4.00
Ivan Rodriguez	6.00
Scott Rolen	6.00
Kazuhiro Sasaki	4.00
Aaron Sele	4.00
Gary Sheffield	4.00
John Smoltz	4.00
Frank Thomas	8.00
Mo Vaughn	4.00
Robin Ventura	4.00
Bernie Williams	5.00
Carlos Delgado	6.00
Chan Ho Park	4.00
Todd Helton	8.00
Craig Biggio	4.00
Jeff Bagwell	8.00
Paul LoDuca	4.00

Prime Numbers

		NM/M
Common Player:		8.00
Inserted 1:12 Jumbo pack		
1PN	Jeff Bagwell	15.00
2PN	Cal Ripken Jr.	50.00
3PN	Barry Bonds	50.00
4PN	Todd Helton	15.00
5PN	Derek Jeter	50.00
6PN	Tony Gwynn	20.00
7PN	Kazuhiro Sasaki	8.00
8PN	Chan Ho Park	8.00
9PN	Sean Casey	10.00
10PN	Chipper Jones	20.00
11PN	Pedro Martinez	15.00
12PN	Mike Piazza	30.00
13PN	Carlos Delgado	10.00
14PN	Craig Biggio	
15PN	Roger Clemens	25.00

Winning Combinations

		NM/M
Common Card:		3.00
Varying quantities produced		
1WC	Derek Jeter, Ozzie Smith/2000	8.00
2WC	Barry Bonds, Mark McGwire/500	10.00
3WC	Ichiro Suzuki, Albert Pujols/250	30.00
4WC	Ted Williams, Manny Ramirez/1000	10.00
5WC	Tony Gwynn, Cal Ripken/250	15.00
6WC	Mike Piazza, Derek Jeter/500	10.00
7WC	Dave Winfield, Tony Gwynn/2000	5.00
8WC	Hideo Nomo, Ichiro Suzuki/2000	10.00
9WC	Cal Ripken, Ozzie Smith/1000	10.00
10WC	Mark McGwire, Albert Pujols/2000	10.00
11WC	Jeff Bagwell, Craig Biggio/1000	3.00
12WC	Bobby Bonds, Barry Bonds/250	10.00
13WC	Ted Williams, Stan Musial/250	10.00
14WC	Babe Ruth, Reggie Jackson/500	15.00
15WC	Kazuhiro Sasaki, Ichiro Suzuki/500	10.00
16WC	Nolan Ryan, Roger Clemens/500	15.00
17WC	Roger Clemens, Derek Jeter/250	15.00
18WC	Ivan Rodriguez, Mike Piazza/1000	6.00
19WC	Vladimir Guerrero, Sammy Sosa/2000	6.00
20WC	Barry Bonds, Sammy Sosa/250	10.00
21WC	Roger Clemens, Greg Maddux/1000	8.00
22WC	Juan Gonzalez, Manny Ramirez/2000	3.00
23WC	Todd Helton, Jason Giambi/2000	3.00
24WC	Jeff Bagwell, Lance Berkman/2000	3.00
25WC	Mike Sweeney, George Brett/1000	6.00
26WC	Luis Gonzalez, Babe Ruth/2000	10.00
27WC	Bill Skowron, Don Mattingly/250	10.00
28WC	Yogi Berra, Cal Ripken/2000	10.00
29WC	Pedro Martinez, Nomar Garciaparra/500	8.00
30WC	Ted Kluszewski, Frank Robinson/1000	3.00
31WC	Curt Schilling, Randy Johnson/1000	5.00
32WC	Ken Griffey Jr., Cal Ripken/500	10.00
33WC	Mike Piazza, Johnny Bench/1000	6.00
34WC	Stan Musial, Albert Pujols/500	10.00
35WC	Jackie Robinson, Nellie Fox/500	8.00
36WC	Lefty Grove, Steve Carlton/250	5.00
37WC	Ty Cobb, Tony Gwynn/250	10.00
38WC	Albert Pujols, Frank Robinson/1000	10.00
39WC	Ryne Sandberg, Sammy Sosa/500	10.00
40WC	Cal Ripken Jr., Lou Gehrig/250	20.00

2001 Fleer Premium

		NM/M
Complete Set (235):		
Common Player:		.15
Common SP (201-230):		4.00
Production 1,999		
Cards 231-235 are redemptions		
Hobby Pack (8):		4.00
Hobby Box (24):		80.00
1	Cal Ripken Jr.	2.00
2	Derek Jeter	2.00
3	Edgardo Alfonzo	.15
4	Luis Castillo	.15
5	Mike Lieberthal	.15
6	Kazuhiro Sasaki	.15
7	Jeff Kent	.15
8	Eric Karros	.15
9	Tom Glavine	.40
10	Jeromy Burnitz	.15
11	Travis Fryman	.15
12	Ron Coomer	.15
13	Jeff D'Amico	.15
14	Carlos Febles	.15
15	Kevin Brown	.15
16	Deivi Cruz	.15
17	Tino Martinez	.15
18	Bobby Abreu	.15
19	Roger Clemens	1.00
20	Jeffrey Hammonds	.15
21	Peter Bergeron	.15
22	Ray Lankford	.15
23	Scott Rolen	.60
24	Jermaine Dye	.15
25	Rusty Greer	.15
26	Frank Thomas	.75
27	Jeff Bagwell	.75
28	Cliff Floyd	.15
29	Chris Singleton	.15
30	Steve Finley	.15
31	Orlando Hernandez	.15
32	Tom Goodwin	.15
33	Larry Walker	.15
34	Mike Sweeney	.15
35	Tim Hudson	.30
36	Kerry Wood	.40
37	Mike Lowell	.15
38	Andruw Jones	.75
39	Alex S. Gonzalez	.15
40	Juan Gonzalez	.75
41	J.D. Drew	.25
42	Mark McLemore	.15
43	Royce Clayton	.15
44	Paul O'Neill	.15
45	Carlos Beltran	.45
46	Phil Nevin	.15
47	Rondell White	.15
48	Gerald Williams	.15
49	Geoff Jenkins	.15
50	Marvin Benard	.15
51	Alex Rodriguez	1.50
52	Moises Alou	.15
53	Mike Lansing	.15
54	Omar Vizquel	.15
55	Eric Chavez	.30
56	Mark Quinn	.15
57	Mike Lamb	.15
58	Rick Ankiel	.15
59	Lance Berkman	.15
60	Jeff Conine	.15
61	B.J. Surhoff	.15
62	Todd Helton	.75
63	J.T. Snow	.15
64	John Vander Wal	.15
65	Johnny Damon	.25
66	Bobby Higginson	.15
67	Carlos Delgado	.40
68	Shawn Green	.35
69	Mike Redmond	.15
70	Mike Piazza	1.25
71	Adrian Beltre	.35
72	Juan Encarnacion	.15
73	Chipper Jones	1.00
74	Garret Anderson	.15
75	Paul Konerko	.15
76	Barry Larkin	.15
77	Tony Gwynn	1.00
78	Rafael Palmeiro	.60
79	Randy Johnson	.75
80	Mark Grace	.25
81	Javy Lopez	.15
82	Gabe Kapler	.15
83	Henry Rodriguez	.15
84	Raul Mondesi	.15
85	Adam Piatt	.15
86	Marquis Grissom	.15
87	Charles Johnson	.15
88	Sean Casey	.25
89	Manny Ramirez	.75
90	Curt Schilling	.40
91	Fernando Tatis	.15
92	Derek Bell	.15
93	Tony Clark	.15
94	Homer Bush	.15
95	Nomar Garciaparra	1.25
96	Vinny Castilla	.15
97	Ben Davis	.15
98	Carl Everett	.15
99	Damion Easley	.15
100	Craig Biggio	.15
101	Todd Hollandsworth	.15
102	Jay Payton	.15
103	Gary Sheffield	.35
104	Sandy Alomar Jr.	.15
105	Doug Glanville	.15
106	Barry Bonds	2.00
107	Tim Salmon	.25
108	Terrence Long	.15
109	Jorge Posada	.30
110	Jose Offerman	.15
111	Edgar Martinez	.15
112	Jeremy Giambi	.15
113	Dean Palmer	.15
114	Roberto Alomar	.35
115	Aaron Boone	.15
116	Adam Kennedy	.15
117	Joe Randa	.15
118	Jose Vidro	.15
119	Tony Batista	.15
120	Kevin Young	.15
121	Preston Wilson	.15
122	Jason Kendall	.15
123	Mark Kotsay	.15
124	Timoniel Perez	.15
125	Eric Young	.15
126	Greg Maddux	1.00
127	Richard Hidalgo	.15
128	Brian Giles	.15
129	Fred McGriff	.15
130	Troy Glaus	.75
131	Todd Walker	.15
132	Brady Anderson	.15
133	Jim Edmonds	.15
134	Ben Grieve	.15

135 Greg Vaughn .15
136 Robin Ventura .15
137 Sammy Sosa 1.25
138 Rich Aurilia .15
139 Jose Valentin .15
140 Trot Nixon .15
141 Troy Percival .15
142 Bernie Williams .35
143 Warren Morris .15
144 Jacque Jones .15
145 Danny Bautista .15
146 A.J. Pierzynski .15
147 Mark McGwire 1.50
148 Rafael Furcal .15
149 Ray Durham .15
150 Mike Mussina .40
151 Jay Bell .15
152 David Wells .15
153 Ken Caminiti .15
154 Jim Thome .15
155 Ivan Rodriguez .60
156 Milton Bradley .15
157 Ken Griffey Jr. 1.25
158 Al Leiter .15
159 Corey Koskie .15
160 Shannon Stewart .15
161 Mo Vaughn .15
162 Pedro Martinez .75
163 Todd Hundley .15
164 Darin Erstad .60
165 Ruben Rivera .15
166 Richie Sexson .15
167 Andres Galarraga .15
168 Darryl Kile .15
169 Jose Cruz Jr. .15
170 David Justice .15
171 Vladimir Guerrero .75
172 Jeff Cirillo .15
173 John Olerud .15
174 Devon White .15
175 Ron Belliard .15
176 Pokey Reese .15
177 Mike Hampton .15
178 David Ortiz .15
179 Magglio Ordonez .15
180 Ruben Mateo .15
181 Carlos Lee .15
182 Matt Williams .15
183 Miguel Tejada .25
184 Scott Elarton .15
185 Bret Boone .15
186 Pat Burrell .40
187 Brad Radke .15
188 Brian Jordan .15
189 Matt Lawton .15
190 Al Martin .15
191 Albert Belle .15
192 Tony Womack .15
193 Roger Cedeno .15
194 Travis Lee .15
195 Dmitri Young .15
196 Jay Buhner .15
197 Jason Giambi .50
198 Jason Tyner .15
199 Ben Petrick .15
200 Jose Canseco .40
201 Nick Johnson 4.00
202 Jace Brewer 4.00
203 *Ryan Freel* 4.00
204 *Jaisen Randolph* 4.00
205 Marcus Giles 4.00
206 *Claudio Vargas* 4.00
207 Brian Cole 4.00
208 Scott Hodges 4.00
209 *Winston Abreu* 4.00
210 Shea Hillenbrand 4.00
211 Larry Barnes 4.00
212 *Paul Phillips* 4.00
213 *Pedro Santana* 4.00
214 Ivanon Coffie 4.00
215 *Junior Spivey* 8.00
216 Donzell McDonald 4.00
217 Vernon Wells 5.00
218 Corey Patterson 5.00
219 Sang-Hoon Lee 4.00
220 Jack Cust 4.00
221 Jason Romano 4.00
222 *Jack Wilson* 8.00
223 Adam Everett 4.00
224 *Esix Snead* 4.00
225 Jason Hart 4.00
226 Joe Lawrence 4.00
227 Brandon Inge 4.00
228 Alex Escobar 4.00
229 Abraham Nunez 4.00
230 Jared Sandberg 4.00
231 *Ichiro Suzuki* 50.00
232 *Tsuyoshi Shinjo* 6.00
233 *Albert Pujols* 80.00
234 *Wilson Betemit* 5.00
235 *Drew Henson* 6.00

Star Ruby

Stars (1-200): 5-10X
SPs (201-230): .4-.8X
Production 125 sets
(See 2001 Fleer Premium for checklist and base card values.)

A Time for Heroes

NM/M
Complete Set (20): 30.00
Common Player: 1.00
Inserted 1:20
Darin Erstad 1.00
Alex Rodriguez 4.00
Shawn Green 1.00
Jeff Bagwell 1.50
Sammy Sosa 3.00
Derek Jeter 5.00
Nomar Garciaparra 3.00
Carlos Delgado 1.00
Pat Burrell 1.00
Tony Gwynn 2.50
Chipper Jones 2.50
Jason Giambi 1.00
Magglio Ordonez 1.00
Troy Glaus 1.00
Ivan Rodriguez 1.00
Andruw Jones 1.50
Vladimir Guerrero 2.00
Ken Griffey Jr. 3.00
J.D. Drew 1.00
Todd Helton 1.50

A Time for Heroes Memorabilia

NM/M
Common Player: 4.00
Inserted 1:82
Shawn Green 5.00
Derek Jeter 25.00
Pat Burrell 5.00
Chipper Jones 10.00
Jason Giambi 8.00
Troy Glaus 6.00
Ivan Rodriguez 6.00
Andruw Jones 8.00
J.D. Drew 4.00
Todd Helton 8.00

Brother Wood

NM/M
Common Player: 5.00
Inserted 1:108
1BW Vladimir Guerrero 10.00
2BW Andruw Jones 6.00
3BW Corey Patterson 5.00
4BW Magglio Ordonez 5.00
5BW Jason Giambi 8.00
6BW Rafael Palmeiro 8.00
7BW Eric Chavez 5.00
8BW Pat Burrell 6.00
9BW Adrian Beltre 5.00

Decades of Excellence

NM/M
Complete Set (50): 140.00
Common Player: 1.00
Inserted 1:12
Card #17 does not exist
Babe Ruth, Lou Gehrig 10.00
Lloyd Waner 1.00
Jimmie Foxx 3.00
Hank Greenberg 2.00
Ted Williams 8.00
Johnny Mize 2.00
Enos Slaughter 1.00
Jackie Robinson 6.00
Stan Musial 5.00
Duke Snider 3.00
Eddie Mathews 3.00
Roy Campanella 2.50
Yogi Berra 4.00
Pee Wee Reese 2.00
Phil Rizzuto 2.00
Al Kaline 4.00
Frank Howard 1.00
Roberto Clemente 8.00
Bob Gibson 3.00
Roger Maris 4.00
Don Drysdale 2.50
Maury Wills 1.00
Tom Seaver 2.50
Reggie Jackson 3.00
Johnny Bench 4.00
Carlton Fisk 2.50
Rod Carew 2.00
Steve Carlton 1.00
Mike Schmidt 6.00
Nolan Ryan 10.00
Rickey Henderson 3.00
Roger Clemens 5.00
Don Mattingly 6.00
George Brett 6.00
Greg Maddux 5.00
Cal Ripken Jr. 10.00
Chipper Jones 5.00
Barry Bonds 10.00
Ivan Rodriguez 2.50
Sammy Sosa, Mark McGwire 8.00
Ken Griffey Jr. 6.00
Tony Gwynn 4.00
Vladimir Guerrero 3.00
Shawn Green 1.00
Alex Rodriguez, Derek Jeter, Nomar Garciaparra 8.00
Pat Burrell 2.00
Rick Ankiel 1.00
Eric Chavez 1.00
Troy Glaus 2.00

Decades of Excellence Autograph

NM/M
Common Autograph: 20.00
Production #'s listed
1 Rick Ankiel/99 10.00
2 Johnny Bench/67 65.00
3 Barry Bonds/86 200.00
4 George Brett/73 100.00
5 Rod Carew/67 30.00
6 Steve Carlton/65 30.00
7 Eric Chavez/98 20.00
8 Carlton Fisk/69 50.00
9 Bob Gibson/59 40.00
10 Tony Gwynn/82 50.00
11 Reggie Jackson/67 40.00
12 Chipper Jones/93 60.00
13 Al Kaline/53 80.00
14 Don Mattingly/82 100.00
15 Cal Ripken Jr./82 150.00
16 Nolan Ryan/66 125.00
17 Mike Schmidt/72 80.00
18 Tom Seaver/67 50.00
19 Enos Slaughter/38 40.00
20 Maury Wills/59 20.00

Decades of Excellence Memorabilia

NM/M
Common Player: 8.00
Inserted 1:217 H
1 Rick Ankiel/Jrsy 8.00
2 Barry Bonds/Jrsy
3 Pat Burrell/jrsy 10.00
4 Roy Campanella/bat/50 50.00
5 Eric Chavez/bat 8.00
6 Roberto Clemente/bat/50 125.00
7 Carlton Fisk/uni. 15.00
8 Jimmie Foxx/bat/50 80.00
9 Shawn Green/bat 8.00
10 Tony Gwynn/jrsy 15.00
11 Reggie Jackson/jrsy 15.00
12 Greg Maddux/jrsy 20.00
13 Roger Maris/uni.
14 Pee Wee Reese/jrsy 8.00
15 Cal Ripken /jrsy/50
16 Ivan Rodriguez/bat 8.00
17 Nolan Ryan/jrsy
18 Mike Schmidt/jrsy
19 Tom Seaver/jrsy
20 Duke Snider/bat 15.00
21 Ted Williams/jrsy/50 250.00

Derek Jeter Monumental Moments

NM/M
Numbered to 1,995
Autograph numbered to 95
DJMM Derek Jeter 8.00
DJMM Derek Jeter Auto./95 80.00

Diamond Dominators

NM/M
Common Player: 4.00
Inserted 1:51
1DD Troy Glaus 6.00
2DD Darin Erstad 5.00
3DD J.D. Drew 4.00
4DD Barry Bonds 25.00
5DD Roger Clemens 20.00
6DD Vladimir Guerrero 8.00
7DD Tony Gwynn 10.00
8DD Greg Maddux 10.00
9DD Cal Ripken Jr. 25.00
10DD Ivan Rodriguez 6.00
11DD Frank Thomas 8.00
12DD Bernie Williams 4.00
13DD Jeromy Burnitz 4.00
14DD Juan Gonzalez 6.00

Diamond Dominators Patches

NM/M
Common Player: 15.00
Production 100 sets
1DD Troy Glaus 25.00
2DD Darin Erstad 20.00
3DD J.D. Drew 15.00
4DD Barry Bonds 75.00
5DD Roger Clemens 60.00
6DD Vladimir Guerrero 25.00
7DD Tony Gwynn 50.00
8DD Greg Maddux 50.00
9DD Cal Ripken Jr. 75.00
10DD Ivan Rodriguez 20.00
11DD Frank Thomas 25.00
12DD Bernie Williams 20.00
13DD Jeromy Burnitz 15.00
14DD Juan Gonzalez 25.00

Grip It and Rip It

NM/M
Complete Set (15): 10.00
Common Player: .50
Inserted 1:6
1GRP Roger Clemens, Derek Jeter 2.00
2GRP Scott Rolen, Pat Burrell .50
3GRP Greg Maddux, Andruw Jones 1.00
4GRP Shannon Stewart, Carlos Delgado .50
5GRP Shawn Estes, Barry Bonds 2.00
6GRP Cal Eldred, Frank Thomas .50

7GRP Mark McGwire, Jim Edmonds 2.00
8GRP Jose Vidro, Vladimir Guerrero .75
9GRP Pedro Martinez, Nomar Garciaparra 1.50
10GRP Tom Glavine, Chipper Jones 1.00
11GRP Ken Griffey Jr., Sean Casey 1.00
12GRP Jeff Bagwell, Moises Alou .50
13GRP Troy Glaus, Darin Erstad .50
14GRP Mike Piazza, Robin Ventura 1.00
15GRP Eric Chavez, Jason Giambi .50

Grip It and Rip It Plus

NM/M

Common Card: 8.00
200 Base/Bat Produced
100 Ball/Bat Produced

Roger Clemens, Derek Jeter/100 50.00
Scott Rolen, Pat Burrell/200 8.00
Greg Maddux, Andruw Jones/100 40.00
Shannon Stewart, Carlos Delgado/200 8.00
Shawn Estes, Barry Bonds/100 50.00
Cal Eldred, Frank Thomas/200 15.00
Mark McGwire, Jim Edmonds/100 60.00
Jose Vidro, Vladimir Guerrero/200 15.00
Pedro Martinez, Nomar Garciaparra/100 50.00
Tom Glavine, Chipper Jones/200 15.00
Ken Griffey Jr., Sean Casey/200 20.00
Jeff Bagwell, Moises Alou/200 10.00
Troy Glaus, Darin Erstad/200 10.00
Mike Piazza, Robin Ventura/100 40.00
Eric Chavez, Jason Giambi/200 10.00

Home Field Advantage

NM/M

Complete Set (15): 60.00
Common Player: 2.00
Inserted 1:72

Mike Piazza 6.00
Derek Jeter 10.00
Ken Griffey Jr. 6.00
Carlos Delgado 2.00
Chipper Jones 5.00
Alex Rodriguez 8.00
Sammy Sosa 6.00
Scott Rolen 3.00
Nomar Garciaparra 6.00
Todd Helton 3.00
Vladimir Guerrero 3.00
Jeff Bagwell 3.00
Barry Bonds 10.00
Cal Ripken Jr. 10.00
Mark McGwire 8.00

Home Field Advantage Game Wall

NM/M

Common Player: 6.00
Production 100 sets

Mike Piazza 15.00
Derek Jeter 25.00
Ken Griffey Jr. 15.00
Carlos Delgado 6.00
Chipper Jones 10.00
Alex Rodriguez 20.00
Sammy Sosa 15.00
Scott Rolen 8.00
Nomar Garciaparra 15.00
Todd Helton 8.00
Vladimir Guerrero 8.00
Jeff Bagwell 8.00
Barry Bonds 25.00
Cal Ripken Jr. 25.00
Mark McGwire 20.00

Solid Performers

NM/M

Complete Set (15): 30.00
Common Player: 1.50
Inserted 1:20

1SP Mark McGwire 4.00
2SP Alex Rodriguez 4.00
3SP Nomar Garciaparra 2.50
4SP Derek Jeter 5.00
5SP Vladimir Guerrero 1.50
6SP Todd Helton 1.50
7SP Chipper Jones 2.00
8SP Mike Piazza 2.50
9SP Ivan Rodriguez 1.50
10SP Tony Gwynn 2.00
11SP Cal Ripken Jr. 5.00
12SP Barry Bonds 5.00
13SP Jeff Bagwell 1.50
14SP Ken Griffey Jr. 2.50
15SP Sammy Sosa 2.50

Solid Performers Game Base

NM/M

Common Player: 5.00
Production 150 sets

1SP Mark McGwire 15.00
2SP Alex Rodriguez 15.00
3SP Nomar Garciaparra 12.00
4SP Derek Jeter 20.00
5SP Vladimir Guerrero 8.00
6SP Todd Helton 8.00
7SP Chipper Jones 10.00
8SP Mike Piazza 12.00
9SP Ivan Rodriguez 8.00
10SP Tony Gwynn 10.00
11SP Cal Ripken Jr. 20.00
12SP Barry Bonds 20.00
13SP Jeff Bagwell 8.00
14SP Ken Griffey Jr. 12.00
15SP Sammy Sosa 12.00

2001 FLEER SHOWCASE

NM/M

Complete Set (160):
Common Player: .25
Common SP (116-125): 10.00
Production 500
Common SP (126-145): 4.00
Production 1,500
Common SP (146-160): 4.00
Production 2,000
Pack (5): 5.00
Box (24): 100.00

1 Tony Gwynn 1.50
2 Barry Larkin .25
3 Chan Ho Park .25
4 Darin Erstad .65
5 Rafael Furcal .25
6 Roger Cedeno .25
7 Timo Perez .25
8 Rick Ankiel .25
9 Pokey Reese .25
10 Jeromy Burnitz .25
11 Phil Nevin .25
12 Matt Williams .25
13 Mike Hampton .25
14 Fernando Tatis .25
15 Kazuhiro Sasaki .25
16 Jim Thome .25
17 Geoff Jenkins .25
18 Jeff Kent .25
19 Tom Glavine .40
20 Dean Palmer .25
21 Todd Zeile .25
22 Edgar Renteria .25
23 Andruw Jones 1.00
24 Juan Encarnacion .25
25 Robin Ventura .25
26 J.D. Drew .25
27 Ray Durham .25
28 Richard Hidalgo .25
29 Eric Chavez .35
30 Rafael Palmeiro .75
31 Steve Finley .25
32 Jeff Weaver .25
33 Al Leiter .25
34 Jim Edmonds .25
35 Garret Anderson .25
36 Larry Walker .25
37 Jose Vidro .25
38 Mike Cameron .25
39 Brady Anderson .25
40 Mike Lowell .25
41 Bernie Williams .35
42 Gary Sheffield .40
43 John Smoltz .25
44 Mike Mussina .40
45 Greg Vaughn .25
46 Juan Gonzalez .75
47 Matt Lawton .25
48 Robb Nen .25
49 Brad Radke .25
50 Edgar Martinez .25
51 Mike Bordick .25
52 Shawn Green .40
53 Carl Everett .25
54 Adrian Beltre .40
55 Kerry Wood .50
56 Kevin Brown .25
57 Brian Giles .25
58 Greg Maddux 1.50
59 Preston Wilson .25
60 Orlando Hernandez .25
61 Ben Grieve .25
62 Jermaine Dye .25
63 Travis Lee .25
64 Jose Cruz Jr. .25
65 Rondell White .25
66 Carlos Beltran .45
67 Scott Rolen .75
68 Brad Fullmer .25
69 David Wells .25
70 Mike Sweeney .25
71 Barry Zito .40
72 Tony Batista .25
73 Curt Schilling .40
74 Jeff Cirillo .25
75 Edgardo Alfonzo .25
76 John Olerud .25
77 Carlos Lee .25
78 Moises Alou .25
79 Tim Hudson .35
80 Andres Galarraga .25
81 Roberto Alomar .45
82 Richie Sexson .25
83 Trevor Hoffman .25
84 Omar Vizquel .25
85 Jacque Jones .25
86 J.T. Snow .25
87 Sean Casey .25
88 Craig Biggio .40
89 Mariano Rivera .35
90 Rusty Greer .25
91 Barry Bonds 3.00
92 Pedro Martinez 1.00
93 Cal Ripken Jr. 3.00
94 Pat Burrell .50
95 Chipper Jones 1.50
96 Magglio Ordonez .25
97 Jeff Bagwell 1.00
98 Randy Johnson 1.00
99 Frank Thomas 1.00
100 Jason Kendall .25
101 Nomar Garciaparra 6.00
102 Mark McGwire 8.00
103 Troy Glaus 3.00
104 Ivan Rodriguez 2.50
105 Manny Ramirez 3.00
106 Derek Jeter 10.00
107 Alex Rodriguez 8.00
108 Ken Griffey Jr. 6.00
109 Todd Helton 3.00
110 Sammy Sosa 6.00
111 Vladimir Guerrero 3.00
112 Mike Piazza 6.00
113 Roger Clemens 5.00
114 Jason Giambi 2.50
115 Carlos Delgado 2.00
116 *Ichiro Suzuki* 100.00
117 *Morgan Ensberg* 20.00
118 *Carlos Valderrama* 10.00
119 *Erick Almonte* 10.00
120 *Tsuyoshi Shinjo* 10.00
121 *Albert Pujols* 225.00
122 *Wilson Betemit* 10.00
123 *Adrian Hernandez* 10.00
124 *Jackson Melian* 10.00
125 *Drew Henson* 12.00
126 *Paul Phillips* 4.00
127 *Esix Snead* 4.00
128 *Ryan Freel* 4.00
129 *Junior Spivey* 8.00
130 *Elpidio Guzman* 6.00
131 *Juan Diaz* 4.00
132 *Andres Torres* 4.00
133 *Jay Gibbons* 10.00
134 Bill Ortega 4.00
135 *Alexis Gomez* 4.00
136 *Wilken Ruan* 4.00
137 *Henry Mateo* 4.00
138 *Juan Uribe* 8.00
139 *Johnny Estrada* 10.00
140 *Jaisen Randolph* 4.00
141 *Eric Hinske* 8.00
142 *Jack Wilson* 10.00
143 *Cody Ransom* 4.00
144 *Nate Frese* 4.00
145 *John Grabow* 4.00
146 *Christian Parker* 4.00
147 *Brian Lawrence* 6.00
148 *Brandon Duckworth* 4.00
149 *Winston Abreu* 4.00
150 *Horacio Ramirez* 8.00
151 *Nick Maness* 4.00
152 *Blaine Neal* 4.00
153 *Billy Sylvester* 4.00
154 *David Elder* 4.00
155 *Bert Snow* 4.00
156 *Claudio Vargas* 4.00
157 *Martin Vargas* 4.00
158 *Grant Balfour* 4.00
159 Randy Keisler 4.00
160 *Zach Day* 4.00

Legacy

Stars (1-100): 10-15X
Avant (101-115): 2-4X
RC's (116-125): .75-1.5X
RC's (126-160): 1-2X
Production 50 sets

Autographics

NM/M

Common Player: 5.00
Silvers: 1X
Production 250 sets
Golds: 1-2X
Production 50 sets

Roberto Alomar 30.00
Rick Ankiel 5.00
Albert Belle 8.00
Carlos Beltran 20.00
Adrian Beltre 10.00
Milton Bradley 5.00
Dee Brown 5.00
Jeromy Burnitz 5.00
Pat Burrell 10.00

Sean Casey	8.00
Joseph Crede	5.00
Jose Cruz Jr.	5.00
Ryan Dempster	5.00
J.D. Drew	10.00
Adam Dunn	15.00
Erubiel Durazo	5.00
Jermaine Dye	5.00
David Eckstein	5.00
Alex Escobar	5.00
Seth Etherton	5.00
Adam Everett	5.00
Carlos Febles	5.00
Troy Glaus	15.00
Ben Grieve	5.00
Toby Hall	5.00
Todd Helton	20.00
Shea Hillenbrand	6.00
Aubrey Huff	6.00
D'Angelo Jimenez	5.00
Paul Konerko	8.00
Mike Lamb	5.00
Matt Lawton	5.00
Derrek Lee	8.00
Mike Lieberthal	5.00
Mike Lowell	8.00
Julio Lugo	5.00
Jason Marquis	5.00
Edgar Martinez	15.00
Kevin Millwood	10.00
Eric Milton	5.00
Bengie Molina	5.00
Mike Mussina	25.00
Russ Ortiz	5.00
Corey Patterson	10.00
Jay Payton	5.00
Adam Piatt	5.00
Juan Pierre	5.00
Brad Radke	5.00
John Rocker	5.00
Alex Rodriguez	60.00
Scott Rolen	20.00
Richie Sexson	10.00
Gary Sheffield	10.00
Shannon Stewart	5.00
Miguel Tejada	25.00
Robin Ventura	5.00
Jose Vidro	5.00
Billy Wagner	8.00
Kip Wells	5.00
Rondell White	5.00
Preston Wilson	5.00
Kerry Wood	20.00
Julio Zuleta	5.00

Awards Showcase

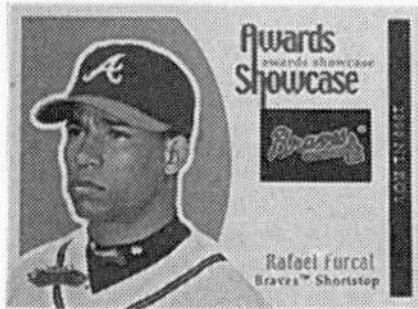

	NM/M
Complete Set (20):	30.00
Common Player:	1.00
Inserted 1:20 Retail	
Derek Jeter	5.00
Derek Jeter	5.00
Jason Giambi	1.50
Jeff Kent	1.00
Pedro Martinez	2.00
Randy Johnson	2.00
Kazuhiro Sasaki	1.00
Rafael Furcal	1.00
Carlos Delgado	1.50
Todd Helton	2.00
Ivan Rodriguez	1.50
Darin Erstad	1.50
Bernie Williams	1.00
Greg Maddux	3.00
Jim Edmonds	1.00
Andruw Jones	2.00
Nomar Garciaparra	4.00
Todd Helton	2.00
Troy Glaus	2.00
Sammy Sosa	4.00

Awards Showcase Memorabilia

	NM/M
Common Player:	10.00
Production 100 sets	
Johnny Bench	20.00
Yogi Berra	15.00

George Brett	40.00
Lou Brock	10.00
Roy Campanella	25.00
Steve Carlton	10.00
Roger Clemens	40.00
Andre Dawson	10.00
Whitey Ford	15.00
Jimmie Foxx	45.00
Kirk Gibson	10.00
Tom Glavine	10.00
Juan Gonzalez	10.00
Elston Howard	10.00
Jim "Catfish" Hunter	10.00
Reggie Jackson	20.00
Randy Johnson	15.00
Chipper Jones	15.00
Harmon Killebrew	20.00
Fred Lynn	
Greg Maddux	25.00
Don Mattingly	75.00
Willie McCovey	10.00
Jim Palmer	10.00
Jim Rice	10.00
Brooks Robinson	20.00
Frank Robinson	15.00
Jackie Robinson	75.00
Ivan Rodriguez	15.00
Mike Schmidt	40.00
Tom Seaver	15.00
Willie Stargell	10.00
Ted Williams	150.00
Robin Yount	25.00

Awards Showcase Autographs

	NM/M
Production 25 sets	
Johnny Bench	100.00
Yogi Berra	90.00
George Brett	200.00
Steve Carlton	60.00
Roger Clemens	180.00
Andre Dawson	40.00
Whitey Ford	80.00
Kirk Gibson	
Tom Glavine	50.00
Juan Gonzalez	50.00
Reggie Jackson	80.00
Randy Johnson	90.00
Chipper Jones	80.00
Harmon Killebrew	75.00
Fred Lynn	25.00
Greg Maddux	150.00
Don Mattingly	175.00
Willie McCovey	40.00
Jim Palmer	40.00
Jim Rice	25.00
Brooks Robinson	75.00
Frank Robinson	50.00
Ivan Rodriguez	50.00
Mike Schmidt	125.00
Tom Seaver	100.00
Robin Yount	

Derek Jeter's Monumental Moments

	NM/M
Production 2,000:	
MM5 Derek Jeter	8.00
Derek Jeter/Auto/100	90.00

Showcase Sticks

	NM/M
Common Player:	4.00
Inserted 1:24	
Roberto Alomar	6.00
Adrian Beltre	5.00

Pat Burrell	6.00
J.D. Drew	4.00
Juan Gonzalez	6.00
Andruw Jones	8.00
Chipper Jones	10.00
Magglio Ordonez	4.00
Ivan Rodriguez	6.00
Scott Rolen	8.00
Frank Thomas	8.00
Roger Cedeno	4.00
Shawn Green	5.00
Richard Hidalgo	4.00
Tony Clark	4.00
Preston Wilson	4.00
Barry Bonds	30.00
Rafael Furcal	4.00
Randy Johnson	8.00
Vladimir Guerrero	8.00
Al Kaline	10.00
George Kell	4.00
Jason Kendall	4.00
Carlos Delgado	5.00
Adam Piatt	4.00
Alex Gonzalez	4.00
Jorge Posada	6.00
Jose Vidro	4.00
Roger Clemens	20.00
Steve Finley	4.00
Reggie Jackson	8.00
Shannon Stewart	4.00
Rick Ankiel	4.00
Jim Thome	8.00
Tsuyoshi Shinjo	6.00
Ichiro Suzuki	25.00

Sweet Sigs

	NM/M
Common Player:	10.00
Inserted 1:24	
Prices for Lumber	
Wall:	1X
Leather:	1-1.5X
Bobby Abreu	15.00
Wilson Betemit	10.00
Russell Branyan	10.00
Pat Burrell	20.00
Eric Chavez	20.00
Rafael Furcal	15.00
Nomar Garciaparra	100.00
Juan Gonzalez	35.00
Elpidio Guzman	10.00
Drew Henson	15.00
Brandon Inge	10.00
Derek Jeter	120.00
Andruw Jones	30.00
Willie Mays	180.00
Jackson Melian	10.00
Xavier Nady	10.00
Jose Ortiz	10.00
Ben Sheets	15.00
Mike Sweeney	15.00
Miguel Tejada	35.00
Albert Pujols	400.00

2001 FLEER TRADITION

		NM/M
Complete Set (450):		35.00
Common Player:		.15
Comp. Factory Set (485):		80.00
Pack (10):		2.00
Box (36):		55.00
1	Andres Galarraga	.15
2	Armando Rios	.15
3	Julio Lugo	.15
4	Darryl Hamilton	.15
5	Dave Veres	.15
6	Edgardo Alfonzo	.15
7	Brook Fordyce	.15
8	Eric Karros	.15
9	Neifi Perez	.15
10	Jim Edmonds	.15
11	Barry Larkin	.15
12	Trot Nixon	.15
13	Andy Pettitte	.35
14	Jose Guillen	.15
15	David Wells	.15
16	Magglio Ordonez	.15
17	David Segui	.15
18	Juan Encarnacion	.15
19	Robert Person	.15
20	Quilvio Veras	.15
21	Mo Vaughn	.15
22	B.J. Surhoff	.15
23	Ken Caminiti	.15
24	Frank Catalanotto	.15
25	Luis Gonzalez	.25
26	Pete Harnisch	.15
27	Alex Gonzalez	.15
28	Mark Quinn	.15
29	Luis Castillo	.15
30	Rick Helling	.15
31	Barry Bonds	2.00
32	Warren Morris	.15
33	Aaron Boone	.15
34	Ricky Gutierrez	.15
35	Preston Wilson	.15
36	Erubiel Durazo	.15
37	Jermaine Dye	.15
38	John Rocker	.15
39	Mark Grudzielanek	.15
40	Pedro Martinez	.75
41	Phil Nevin	.15
42	Luis Matos	.15
43	Orlando Hernandez	.15
44	Steve Cox	.15
45	James Baldwin	.15
46	Rafael Furcal	.15
47	Todd Zeile	.15
48	Elmer Dessens	.15
49	Russell Branyan	.15
50	Juan Gonzalez	.75
51	Mac Suzuki	.15
52	Adam Kennedy	.15
53	Randy Velarde	.15
54	David Bell	.15
55	Royce Clayton	.15
56	Greg Colbrunn	.15
57	Rey Ordonez	.15
58	Kevin Millwood	.15
59	Fernando Vina	.15
60	Eddie Taubensee	.15
61	Enrique Wilson	.15
62	Jay Bell	.15
63	Brian Moehler	.15
64	Brad Fullmer	.15
65	Ben Petrick	.15
66	Orlando Cabrera	.25
67	Shane Reynolds	.15
68	Mitch Meluskey	.15
69	Jeff Shaw	.15
70	Chipper Jones	1.00
71	Tomo Ohka	.15
72	Ruben Rivera	.15
73	Mike Sirotka	.15
74	Scott Rolen	.60
75	Glendon Rusch	.15
76	Miguel Tejada	.35
77	Brady Anderson	.15
78	Bartolo Colon	.15
79	Ron Coomer	.15
80	Gary DiSarcina	.15
81	Geoff Jenkins	.15
82	Billy Koch	.15
83	Mike Lamb	.15
84	Alex Rodriguez	1.50
85	Denny Neagle	.15
86	Michael Tucker	.15
87	Edgar Renteria	.15
88	Brian Anderson	.15
89	Glenallen Hill	.15
90	Aramis Ramirez	.15
91	Rondell White	.15
92	Tony Womack	.15
93	Jeffrey Hammonds	.15
94	Freddy Garcia	.15
95	Bill Mueller	.15
96	Mike Lieberthal	.15

#	Player	Price
97	Michael Barrett	.15
98	Derrek Lee	.15
99	Bill Spiers	.15
100	Derek Lowe	.15
101	Javy Lopez	.15
102	Adrian Beltre	.30
103	Jim Parque	.15
104	Marquis Grissom	.15
105	Eric Chavez	.25
106	Todd Jones	.15
107	Eric Owens	.15
108	Roger Clemens	1.00
109	Denny Hocking	.15
110	Roberto Hernandez	.15
111	Albert Belle	.15
112	Troy Glaus	.75
113	Ivan Rodriguez	.60
114	Carlos Guillen	.15
115	Chuck Finley	.15
116	Dmitri Young	.15
117	Paul Konerko	.15
118	Damon Buford	.15
119	Fernando Tatis	.15
120	Larry Walker	.15
121	Jason Kendall	.15
122	Matt Williams	.15
123	Henry Rodriguez	.15
124	Placido Polanco	.15
125	Bobby Estalella	.15
126	Pat Burrell	.50
127	Mark Loretta	.15
128	Moises Alou	.15
129	Tino Martinez	.15
130	Milton Bradley	.15
131	Todd Hundley	.15
132	Keith Foulke	.15
133	Robert Fick	.15
134	Cristian Guzman	.15
135	Rusty Greer	.15
136	John Olerud	.15
137	Mariano Rivera	.25
138	Jeromy Burnitz	.15
139	Dave Burba	.15
140	Ken Griffey Jr.	1.25
141	Tony Gwynn	1.00
142	Carlos Delgado	.50
143	Edgar Martinez	.15
144	Ramon Hernandez	.15
145	Pedro Astacio	.15
146	Ray Lankford	.15
147	Mike Mussina	.40
148	Ray Durham	.15
149	Lee Stevens	.15
150	Jay Canizaro	.15
151	Adrian Brown	.15
152	Mike Piazza	1.25
153	Cliff Floyd	.15
154	Jose Vidro	.15
155	Jason Giambi	.50
156	Andruw Jones	.75
157	Robin Ventura	.15
158	Gary Sheffield	.40
159	Jeff D'Amico	.15
160	Chuck Knoblauch	.15
161	Roger Cedeno	.15
162	Jim Thome	.15
163	Peter Bergeron	.15
164	Kerry Wood	.50
165	Gabe Kapler	.15
166	Corey Koskie	.15
167	Doug Glanville	.15
168	Brent Mayne	.15
169	Scott Spiezio	.15
170	Steve Karsay	.15
171	Al Martin	.15
172	Fred McGriff	.15
173	Gabe White	.15
174	Alex Gonzalez	.15
175	Mike Darr	.15
176	Bengie Molina	.15
177	Ben Grieve	.15
178	Marlon Anderson	.15
179	Brian Giles	.15
180	Jose Valentin	.15
181	Brian Jordan	.15
182	Randy Johnson	.75
183	Ricky Ledee	.15
184	Russ Ortiz	.15
185	Mike Lowell	.15
186	Curtis Leskanic	.15
187	Bobby Abreu	.15
188	Derek Jeter	2.00
189	Lance Berkman	.15
190	Roberto Alomar	.40
191	Darin Erstad	.60
192	Richie Sexson	.15
193	Alex Ochoa	.15
194	Carlos Febles	.15
195	David Ortiz	.15
196	Shawn Green	.35
197	Mike Sweeney	.15
198	Vladimir Guerrero	.75
199	Jose Jimenez	.15
200	Travis Lee	.15
201	Rickey Henderson	.75
202	Bob Wickman	.15
203	Miguel Cairo	.15
204	Steve Finley	.15
205	Tony Batista	.15
206	Jamey Wright	.15
207	Terrence Long	.15
208	Trevor Hoffman	.15
209	John Vander Wal	.15
210	Greg Maddux	1.00
211	Tim Salmon	.25
212	Herbert Perry	.15
213	Marvin Benard	.15
214	Jose Offerman	.15
215	Jay Payton	.15
216	Jon Lieber	.15
217	Mark Kotsay	.15
218	Scott Brosius	.15
219	Scott Williamson	.15
220	Omar Vizquel	.15
221	Mike Hampton	.15
222	Richard Hidalgo	.15
223	Rey Sanchez	.15
224	Matt Lawton	.15
225	Bruce Chen	.15
226	Ryan Klesko	.15
227	Garret Anderson	.15
228	Kevin Brown	.15
229	Mike Cameron	.15
230	Tony Clark	.15
231	Curt Schilling	.40
232	Vinny Castilla	.15
233	Carl Pavano	.15
234	Eric Davis	.15
235	Darrin Fletcher	.15
236	Matt Stairs	.15
237	Octavio Dotel	.15
238	Mark Grace	.25
239	John Smoltz	.15
240	Matt Clement	.15
241	Ellis Burks	.15
242	Charles Johnson	.15
243	Jeff Bagwell	.75
244	Derek Bell	.15
245	Nomar Garciaparra	1.25
246	Jorge Posada	.35
247	Ryan Dempster	.15
248	J.T. Snow	.15
249	Eric Young	.15
250	Daryle Ward	.15
251	Joe Randa	.15
252	Travis Fryman	.15
253	Mike Williams	.15
254	Jacque Jones	.15
255	Scott Elarton	.15
256	Mark McGwire	1.50
257	Jay Buhner	.15
258	Randy Wolf	.15
259	Sammy Sosa	1.25
260	Chan Ho Park	.15
261	Damion Easley	.15
262	Rick Ankiel	.15
263	Frank Thomas	.75
264	Kris Benson	.15
265	Luis Alicea	.15
266	Jeremy Giambi	.15
267	Geoff Blum	.15
268	Joe Girardi	.15
269	Livan Hernandez	.15
270	Jeff Conine	.15
271	Danny Graves	.15
272	Craig Biggio	.15
273	Jose Canseco	.35
274	Tom Glavine	.30
275	Ruben Mateo	.15
276	Jeff Kent	.15
277	Kevin Young	.15
278	A.J. Burnett	.15
279	Dante Bichette	.15
280	Sandy Alomar Jr.	.15
281	John Wetteland	.15
282	Torii Hunter	.15
283	Jarrod Washburn	.15
284	Rich Aurilia	.15
285	Jeff Cirillo	.15
286	Fernando Seguignol	.15
287	Darren Dreifort	.15
288	Deivi Cruz	.15
289	Pokey Reese	.15
290	Garrett Stephenson	.15
291	Pat Boone	.15
292	Tim Hudson	.35
293	John Flaherty	.15
294	Shannon Stewart	.15
295	Shawn Estes	.15
296	Wilton Guerrero	.15
297	Delino DeShields	.15
298	David Justice	.15
299	Harold Baines	.15
300	Al Leiter	.15
301	Wil Cordero	.15
302	Antonio Alfonseca	.15
303	Sean Casey	.25
304	Carlos Beltran	.40
305	Brad Radke	.15
306	Jason Varitek	.15
307	Shigetosi Hasegawa	.15
308	Todd Stottlemyre	.15
309	Raul Mondesi	.15
310	Mike Bordick	.15
311	Darryl Kile	.15
312	Dean Palmer	.15
313	Johnny Damon	.30
314	Todd Helton	.75
315	Chad Hermansen	.15
316	Kevin Appier	.15
317	Greg Vaughn	.15
318	Robb Nen	.15
319	Jose Cruz Jr.	.15
320	Ron Belliard	.15
321	Bernie Williams	.35
322	Melvin Mora	.15
323	Kenny Lofton	.15
324	Armando Benitez	.15
325	Carlos Lee	.15
326	Damian Jackson	.15
327	Eric Milton	.15
328	J.D. Drew	.30
329	Byung-Hyun Kim	.15
330	Chris Stynes	.15
331	Kazuhiro Sasaki	.15
332	Troy O'Leary	.15
333	Pat Hentgen	.15
334	Brad Ausmus	.15
335	Todd Walker	.15
336	Jason Isringhausen	.15
337	Gerald Williams	.15
338	Aaron Sele	.15
339	Paul O'Neill	.15
340	Cal Ripken Jr.	2.00
341	Manny Ramirez	.75
342	Will Clark	.35
343	Mark Redman	.15
344	Bubba Trammell	.15
345	Troy Percival	.15
346	Chris Singleton	.15
347	Rafael Palmeiro	.60
348	Carl Everett	.15
349	Andy Benes	.15
350	Bobby Higginson	.15
351	Alex Cabrera	.15
352	Barry Zito	.40
353	Jace Brewer	.15
354	Paxton Crawford	.15
355	Oswaldo Mairena	.15
356	Joe Crede	.15
357	A.J. Pierzynski	.15
358	Daniel Garibay	.15
359	Jason Tyner	.15
360	Nate Rolison	.15
361	Scott Downs	.15
362	Keith Ginter	.15
363	Juan Pierre	.15
364	Adam Bernero	.15
365	Chris Richard	.15
366	Joey Nation	.15
367	Aubrey Huff	.15
368	Adam Eaton	.15
369	Jose Ortiz	.15
370	Eric Munson	.15
371	Matt Kinney	.15
372	Eric Byrnes	.15
373	Keith McDonald	.15
374	Matt Wise	.15
375	Timo Perez	.15
376	Julio Zuleta	.15
377	Jimmy Rollins	.15
378	Xavier Nady	.15
379	Ryan Kohlmeier	.15
380	Corey Patterson	.15
381	Todd Helton	.40
382	Moises Alou	.15
383	Vladimir Guerrero	.40
384	Luis Castillo	.15
385	Jeffrey Hammonds	.15
386	Nomar Garciaparra	.75
387	Carlos Delgado	.25
388	Darin Erstad	.15
389	Manny Ramirez	.40
390	Mike Sweeney	.15
391	Sammy Sosa	.75
392	Barry Bonds	1.00
393	Jeff Bagwell	.40
394	Richard Hidalgo	.15
395	Vladimir Guerrero	.40
396	Troy Glaus	.30
397	Frank Thomas	.40
398	Carlos Delgado	.25
399	David Justice	.15
400	Jason Giambi	.25
401	Randy Johnson	.40
402	Kevin Brown	.15
403	Greg Maddux	.50
404	Al Leiter	.15
405	Mike Hampton	.15
406	Pedro Martinez	.40
407	Roger Clemens	.65
408	Mike Sirotka	.15
409	Mike Mussina	.25
410	Bartolo Colon	.15
411	World Series Update	.15
412	World Series Update	.15
413	World Series Update	.15
414	World Series Update	.15
415	World Series Update	.15
416	World Series Update	.15
417	World Series Update	.15
418	World Series Update	.15
419	World Series Update	.15
420	World Series Update	.15
421	Atlanta Braves	.15
422	New York Mets	.15
423	Florida Marlins	.15
424	Philadelphia Phillies	.15
425	Montreal Expos	.15
426	St. Louis Cardinals	.15
427	Cincinnati Reds	.15
428	Chicago Cubs	.15
429	Milwaukee Brewers	.15
430	Houston Astros	.15
431	Pittsburgh Pirates	.15
432	San Francisco Giants	.15
433	Arizona Diamondbacks	.15
434	Los Angeles Dodgers	.15
435	Colorado Rockies	.15
436	San Diego Padres	.15
437	New York Yankees	.15
438	Boston Red Sox	.15
439	Baltimore Orioles	.15
440	Toronto Blue Jays	.15
441	Tampa Bay Devil Rays	.15
442	Chicago White Sox	.15
443	Cleveland Indians	.15
444	Detroit Tigers	.15
445	Kansas City Royals	.15
446	Minnesota Twins	.15
447	Seattle Mariners	.15
448	Oakland Athletics	.15
449	Anaheim Angels	.15
450	Texas Rangers	.15
451	*Albert Pujols*	50.00
452	*Ichiro Suzuki*	15.00
453	*Tsuyoshi Shinjo*	.75
454	*Johnny Estrada*	.75
455	*Elpidio Guzman*	.40
456	*Adrian Hernandez*	.30
457	*Rafael Soriano*	.75
458	*Drew Henson*	1.00
459	*Juan Uribe*	.75
460	*Matt White*	.40
461	*Endy Chavez*	.30
462	*Bud Smith*	.25
463	*Morgan Ensberg*	.75
464	*Jay Gibbons*	2.00
465	*Jackson Melian*	.30
466	*Junior Spivey*	.75
467	*Juan Cruz*	.50
468	*Wilson Betemit*	.40
469	*Alexis Gomez*	.30
470	*Mark Teixeira*	15.00
471	*Erick Almonte*	.30
472	*Travis Hafner*	5.00
473	*Carlos Valderrama*	.30
474	*Brandon Duckworth*	.75
475	*Ryan Freel*	.30
476	*Wilkin Ruan*	.30
477	*Andres Torres*	.30
478	*Josh Towers*	.50
479	*Kyle Lohse*	.75
480	*Jason Michaels*	.30
481	Alfonso Soriano	.50
482	C.C. Sabathia	.15
483	Roy Oswalt	.15
484	Ben Sheets	.15
485	Adam Dunn	.50

Warning Track

	NM/M
Complete Set (23):	120.00
Common Player:	2.00
Inserted 1:72	
1 Josh Gibson	5.00

2 Willie Mays 10.00
3 Mark McGwire 12.00
4 Barry Bonds 15.00
5 Jose Canseco 4.00
6 Ken Griffey Jr. 10.00
7 Cal Ripken Jr. 15.00
8 Rafael Palmeiro 5.00
9 Sammy Sosa 10.00
10 Juan Gonzalez 6.00
11 Frank Thomas 6.00
12 Jeff Bagwell 6.00
13 Gary Sheffield 2.50
14 Larry Walker 2.00
15 Mike Piazza 10.00
16 Larry Doby 4.00
17 Roy Campanella 5.00
18 Manny Ramirez 6.00
19 Chipper Jones 8.00
20 Alex Rodriguez 12.00
21 Ivan Rodriguez 5.00
22 Vladimir Guerrero 6.00
23 Nomar Garciaparra 10.00
24 Andres Galarraga 2.00
25 Jim Thome 2.00

Diamond Tributes

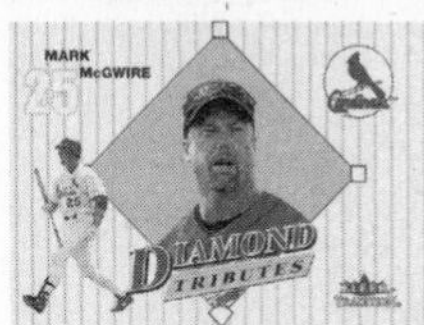

NM/M
Complete Set (30): 35.00
Common Player: .50
Inserted 1:7
1 Jackie Robinson 2.00
2 Mike Piazza 2.00
3 Alex Rodriguez 3.00
4 Barry Bonds 4.00
5 Nomar Garciaparra 2.00
6 Roger Clemens 1.75
7 Ivan Rodriguez .75
8 Cal Ripken Jr. 4.00
9 Manny Ramirez 1.00
10 Chipper Jones 1.50
11 Barry Larkin .50
12 Carlos Delgado .75
13 J.D. Drew .60
14 Carl Everett .50
15 Todd Helton 1.00
16 Greg Maddux 1.50
17 Scott Rolen .75
18 Troy Glaus 1.00
19 Brian Giles .50
20 Jeff Bagwell 1.00
21 Sammy Sosa 2.00
22 Randy Johnson 1.00
23 Andruw Jones 1.00
24 Ken Griffey Jr. 2.00
25 Mark McGwire 3.00
26 Derek Jeter 4.00
27 Vladimir Guerrero 1.00
28 Frank Thomas 1.00
29 Pedro Martinez 1.00
30 Bernie Williams .50

Grass Roots

NM/M
Complete Set (15): 25.00
Common Player: 1.00
Inserted 1:18
1 Derek Jeter 4.00
2 Greg Maddux 2.00
3 Sammy Sosa 2.50
4 Alex Rodriguez 3.00
5 Vladimir Guerrero 1.50
6 Scott Rolen 1.00
7 Frank Thomas 1.50
8 Nomar Garciaparra 2.50
9 Cal Ripken Jr. 4.00
10 Mike Piazza 2.50
11 Ivan Rodriguez 1.00
12 Chipper Jones 2.00
13 Tony Gwynn 2.00
14 Ken Griffey Jr. 2.50
15 Mark McGwire 3.00

Lumber Company

NM/M
Complete Set (20): 25.00
Common Player: .50
Inserted 1:12
1 Vladimir Guerrero 1.50

2 Mo Vaughn .50
3 Ken Griffey Jr. 2.50
4 Juan Gonzalez 1.50
5 Tony Gwynn 2.00
6 Jim Edmonds .50
7 Jason Giambi 1.00
8 Alex Rodriguez 3.00
9 Derek Jeter 4.00
10 Darin Erstad 1.00
11 Andruw Jones 1.50
12 Cal Ripken Jr. 4.00
13 Magglio Ordonez .50
14 Nomar Garciaparra 2.50
15 Chipper Jones 2.00
16 Sean Casey .60
17 Shawn Green .60
18 Mike Piazza 2.50
19 Sammy Sosa 2.50
20 Barry Bonds 4.00

Stitches in Time

NM/M
Complete Set (25): 40.00
Common Player: 1.50
Inserted 1:18
1 Henry Kimbro 1.50
2 Ernie Banks 3.00
3 James "Cool Papa" Bell 2.00
4 Joe Black 1.50
5 Roy Campanella 2.00
6 Ray Dandridge 1.50
7 Leon Day 1.50
8 Larry Doby 2.00
9 Josh Gibson 2.00
10 Elston Howard 2.00
11 Monte Irvin 2.00
12 Buck Leonard 2.00
13 Max Manning 1.50
14 Willie Mays 6.00
15 Buck O'Neil 2.00
16 Satchel Paige 3.00
17 Ted Radcliffe 2.00
18 Jackie Robinson 4.00
19 Bill Perkins 1.50
20 Andrew "Rube" Foster 2.00
21 William "Judy" Johnson 1.50
22 Oscar Charleston 1.50
23 John Henry "Pop" Lloyd 1.50
24 Artie Wilson 1.50
25 Sam Jethroe 1.50

Stitches in Time Game-Used

NM/M
Common Card: 25.00
5 Roy Campanella 60.00
8 Larry Doby bat 25.00
10 Elston Howard bat 25.00
14 Willie Mays jersey 125.00
18 Jackie Robinson jersey 100.00

Stitches in Time Autographs

NM/M
Common Autograph: 20.00
2 Ernie Banks 50.00
4 Joe Black 20.00

11 Monte Irvin 30.00
14 Willie Mays 150.00
15 Buck O'Neil 30.00
17 Ted Radcliffe 25.00
24 Artie Wilson 20.00

Turn Back the Clock

NM/M
Common Card: 8.00
Inserted 1:352
1 Tom Glavine 10.00
2 Greg Maddux 20.00
3 Sean Casey 8.00
4 Pokey Reese 8.00
5 Jason Giambi 15.00
6 Tim Hudson 8.00
7 Larry Walker 8.00
8 Jeffrey Hammonds 8.00
9 Scott Rolen 15.00
10 Pat Burrell 10.00
11 Chipper Jones 20.00
13 Troy Glaus 15.00
14 Tony Gwynn 20.00
15 Cal Ripken Jr. 50.00
16 Tom Glavine, Greg Maddux 75.00
17 Sean Casey, Pokey Reese 30.00
18 Chipper Jones, Greg Maddux 100.00
19 Larry Walker, Jeffrey Hammonds 30.00
20 Scott Rolen, Pat Burrell 40.00
21 Jason Giambi, Tim Hudson 40.00

2001 FLEER TRIPLE CROWN

NM/M
Complete Set (300): 25.00
Common Player: .15
Pack (10): 2.00
Box (24): 40.00
1 Derek Jeter 2.00
2 Vladimir Guerrero .75
3 Henry Rodriguez .15
4 Jason Giambi .50
5 Nomar Garciaparra 1.25
6 Jeff Kent .15
7 Garret Anderson .15
8 Todd Helton .75
9 Barry Bonds 2.00
10 Preston Wilson .15
11 Troy Glaus .75
12 Geoff Jenkins .15
13 Jim Edmonds .15
14 Bobby Higginson .15
15 Mark Quinn .15
16 Barry Larkin .15
17 Richie Sexson .15
18 Fernando Tatis .15
19 John Vander Wal .15
20 Darin Erstad .60
21 Shawn Green .40
22 Scott Rolen .60
23 Tony Batista .15
24 Phil Nevin .15
25 Tim Salmon .25
26 Gary Sheffield .35
27 Ben Grieve .15
28 Jermaine Dye .15
29 Andres Galarraga .15
30 Adrian Beltre .35
31 Rafael Palmeiro .60
32 J.T. Snow .15
33 Edgardo Alfonzo .15
34 Paul Konerko .15
35 Jim Thome .15
36 Andruw Jones .75
37 Mike Sweeney .15
38 Jose Cruz Jr. .15
39 David Ortiz .15
40 Pat Burrell .40
41 Chipper Jones 1.00
42 Jeff Bagwell .75
43 Raul Mondesi .15
44 Rondell White .15
45 Edgar Martinez .15
46 Cal Ripken Jr. 2.00
47 Moises Alou .15
48 Shannon Stewart .15
49 Tino Martinez .15
50 Jason Kendall .15
51 Richard Hidalgo .15
52 Albert Belle .15
53 Jay Payton .15
54 Cliff Floyd .15
55 Rusty Greer .15
56 Matt Williams .15
57 Sammy Sosa 1.25
58 Carl Everett .15
59 Carlos Delgado .50
60 Jeremy Giambi .15
61 Jose Canseco .40
62 David Segui .15
63 Jose Vidro .15
64 Matt Stairs .15
65 Travis Fryman .15
66 Ken Griffey Jr. 1.25
67 Mike Piazza 1.25
68 Mark McGwire 1.50
69 Craig Biggio .15
70 Eric Chavez .25
71 Mo Vaughn .15
72 Matt Lawton .15
73 Miguel Tejada .25
74 Brian Giles .15
75 Sean Casey .25
76 Robin Ventura .15
77 Ivan Rodriguez .60
78 Dean Palmer .15
79 Frank Thomas .75
80 Bernie Williams .30
81 Juan Encarnacion .15
82 John Olerud .15
83 Rich Aurilia .15
84 Juan Gonzalez .75
85 Ray Durham .15
86 Steve Finley .15
87 Ken Caminiti .15
88 Roberto Alomar .40
89 Jeromy Burnitz .15
90 J.D. Drew .15
91 Lance Berkman .15
92 Gabe Kapler .15
93 Larry Walker .15
94 Alex Rodriguez 1.50
95 Jeffrey Hammonds .15
96 Magglio Ordonez .15
97 David Justice .15
98 Eric Karros .15
99 Manny Ramirez .75
100 Paul O'Neill .15
101 Ron Gant .15
102 Erubiel Durazo .15
103 Jason Varitek .15

#	Player	Price
104	Chan Ho Park	.15
105	Corey Koskie	.15
106	Jeff Conine	.15
107	Kevin Tapani	.15
108	Mike Lowell	.15
109	Tim Hudson	.25
110	Bobby Abreu	.15
111	Bret Boone	.15
112	David Wells	.15
113	Brian Jordan	.15
114	Mitch Meluskey	.15
115	Terrence Long	.15
116	Matt Clement	.15
117	Fernando Vina	.15
118	Luis Alicea	.15
119	Jay Bell	.15
120	Mark Grace	.25
121	Carlos Febles	.15
122	Mark Redman	.15
123	Kevin Jordan	.15
124	Pat Meares	.15
125	Mark McLemore	.15
126	Chris Singleton	.15
127	Trot Nixon	.15
128	Carlos Beltran	.40
129	Lee Stevens	.15
130	Kris Benson	.15
131	Jay Buhner	.15
132	Greg Vaughn	.15
133	Eric Young	.15
134	Tony Womack	.15
135	Roger Cedeno	.15
136	Travis Lee	.15
137	Marvin Benard	.15
138	Aaron Sele	.15
139	Rick Ankiel	.15
140	Ruben Mateo	.15
141	Randy Johnson	.75
142	Jason Tyner	.15
143	Mike Redmond	.15
144	Ron Coomer	.15
145	Scott Elarton	.15
146	Javy Lopez	.15
147	Carlos Lee	.15
148	Tony Clark	.15
149	Roger Clemens	1.00
150	Mike Lieberthal	.15
151	Shawn Estes	.15
152	Vinny Castilla	.15
153	Alex Gonzalez	.15
154	Troy Percival	.15
155	Pokey Reese	.15
156	Todd Hollandsworth	.15
157	Marquis Grissom	.15
158	Greg Maddux	1.00
159	Dante Bichette	.15
160	Hideo Nomo	.75
161	Jacque Jones	.15
162	Kevin Young	.15
163	B.J. Surhoff	.15
164	Eddie Taubensee	.15
165	Neifi Perez	.15
166	Orlando Hernandez	.15
167	Francisco Cordova	.15
168	Miguel Cairo	.15
169	Rafael Furcal	.15
170	Sandy Alomar Jr.	.15
171	Jeff Cirillo	.15
172	A.J. Pierzynski	.15
173	Fred McGriff	.15
174	Mike Mussina	.40
175	Aaron Boone	.15
176	Nick Johnson	.15
177	Kent Bottenfield	.15
178	Felipe Crespo	.15
179	Ryan Minor	.15
180	Charles Johnson	.15
181	Damion Easley	.15
182	Michael Barrett	.15
183	Doug Glanville	.15
184	Ben Davis	.15
185	Rickey Henderson	.75
186	Edgard Clemente	.15
187	Dmitri Young	.15
188	Tom Goodwin	.15
189	Mike Hampton	.15
190	Gerald Williams	.15
191	Omar Vizquel	.15
192	Ben Petrick	.15
193	Brad Radke	.15
194	Russ Davis	.15
195	Milton Bradley	.15
196	John Parrish	.15
197	Todd Hundley	.15
198	Carl Pavano	.15
199	Bruce Chen	.15
200	Royce Clayton	.15
201	Homer Bush	.15
202	Mark Grudzielanek	.15
203	Mike Lansing	.15
204	Daryle Ward	.15
205	Jeff D'Amico	.15
206	Ray Lankford	.15
207	Curt Schilling	.40
208	Pedro Martinez	.75
209	Johnny Damon	.30
210	Al Leiter	.15
211	Ruben Rivera	.15
212	Kazuhiro Sasaki	.15
213	Will Clark	.25
214	Rick Helling	.15
215	Adam Piatt	.15
216	Joe Girardi	.15
217	A.J. Burnett	.15
218	Mike Bordick	.15
219	Mike Cameron	.15
220	Tony Gwynn	1.00
221	Deivi Cruz	.15
222	Bubba Trammell	.15
223	Scott Erickson	.15
224	Kerry Wood	.50
225	Derrek Lee	.15
226	Peter Bergeron	.15
227	Chris Gomez	.15
228	Al Martin	.15
229	Brady Anderson	.15
230	Ramon Martinez	.15
231	Darryl Kile	.15
232	Devon White	.15
233	Charlie Hayes	.15
234	Aramis Ramirez	.15
235	Mike Lamb	.15
236	Tom Glavine	.30
237	Troy O'Leary	.15
238	Joe Randa	.15
239	Dustin Hermanson	.15
240	Adam Kennedy	.15
241	Jose Valentin	.15
242	Derek Bell	.15
243	Mark Kotsay	.15
244	Ron Belliard	.15
245	Warren Morris	.15
246	Ozzie Guillen	.15
247	Andy Ashby	.15
248	Jose Offerman	.15
249	Kevin Brown	.15
250	Jorge Posada	.35
251	Alex Cabrera	.15
252	Chan Perry	.15
253	Augie Ojeda	.15
254	Santiago Perez	.15
255	Grant Roberts	.15
256	Dusty Allen	.15
257	Elvis Pena	.15
258	Matt Kinney	.15
259	Timoniel Perez	.15
260	Adam Eaton	.15
261	Geraldo Guzman	.15
262	Damian Rolls	.15
263	Alfonso Soriano	.50
264	Corey Patterson	.15
265	Juan Alvarez	.15
266	Shawn Gilbert	.15
267	Adam Bernero	.15
268	Ben Weber	.15
269	Tike Redman	.15
270	Willie Morales	.15
271	Tomas De La Rosa	.15
272	Rodney Lindsey	.15
273	Carlos Casimiro	.15
274	Jim Mann	.15
275	Pasqual Coco	.15
276	Julio Zuleta	.15
277	Damon Minor	.15
278	Jose Ortiz	.15
279	Eric Munson	.15
280	Andy Thompson	.15
281	Aubrey Huff	.15
282	Chris Richard	.15
283	Ross Gload	.15
284	Travis Dawkins	.15
285	Tim Drew	.15
286	Barry Zito	.40
287	Andy Tracy	.15
288	Julio Lugo	.15
289	Matt DeWitt	.15
290	Keith McDonald	.15
291	J.C. Romero	.15
292	Adam Melhuse	.15
293	Ryan Kohlmeier	.15
294	John Bale	.15
295	Eric Cammack	.15
296	Morgan Burkhart	.15
297	Kory DeHaan	.15
298	Raul Gonzalez	.15
299	Hector Ortiz	.15
300	Talmadge Nunnari	.15

Blue

NM/M

Common Player: 3.00

Produced to # of 2000 HR's

		NM/M
1	Derek Jeter (15)	150.00
2	Vladimir Guerrero (44)	25.00
3	Henry Rodriguez (20)	3.00
4	Jason Giambi (43)	15.00
5	Nomar Garciaparra (21)	25.00
6	Jeff Kent (33)	8.00
7	Garret Anderson (35)	8.00
8	Todd Helton (42)	15.00
9	Barry Bonds (49)	40.00
10	Preston Wilson (31)	3.00
11	Troy Glaus (47)	10.00
12	Geoff Jenkins (34)	8.00
13	Jim Edmonds (42)	10.00
14	Bobby Higginson (30)	3.00
15	Mark Quinn (20)	5.00
16	Barry Larkin (11)	15.00
17	Richie Sexson (30)	10.00
18	Fernando Tatis (18)	3.00
19	John Vander Wal (24)	3.00
20	Darin Erstad (25)	10.00
21	Shawn Green (24)	10.00
22	Scott Rolen (26)	15.00
23	Tony Batista (41)	3.00
24	Phil Nevin (31)	3.00
25	Tim Salmon (34)	5.00
26	Gary Sheffield (43)	8.00
27	Ben Grieve (27)	5.00
28	Jermaine Dye (33)	3.00
29	Andres Galarraga (28)	5.00
30	Adrian Beltre (20)	8.00
31	Rafael Palmeiro (39)	10.00
32	J.T. Snow (19)	5.00
33	Edgardo Alfonzo (25)	5.00
34	Paul Konerko (21)	5.00
35	Jim Thome (37)	15.00
36	Andruw Jones (36)	10.00
37	Mike Sweeney (29)	3.00
38	Jose Cruz Jr. (31)	3.00
39	David Ortiz (10)	8.00
40	Pat Burrell (18)	15.00
41	Chipper Jones (36)	15.00
42	Jeff Bagwell (47)	10.00
43	Raul Mondesi (24)	5.00
44	Rondell White (13)	10.00
45	Edgar Martinez (37)	5.00
46	Cal Ripken Jr. (15)	150.00
47	Moises Alou (30)	5.00
48	Shannon Stewart (21)	3.00
49	Tino Martinez (16)	5.00
50	Jason Kendall (14)	5.00
51	Richard Hidalgo (44)	3.00
52	Albert Belle (23)	3.00
53	Jay Payton (17)	3.00
54	Cliff Floyd (22)	3.00
55	Rusty Greer (8)	8.00
56	Matt Williams (12)	10.00
57	Sammy Sosa (50)	25.00
58	Carl Everett (34)	3.00
59	Carlos Delgado (41)	5.00
60	Jeremy Giambi (10)	5.00
61	Jose Canseco (15)	10.00
62	David Segui (19)	3.00
63	Jose Vidro (24)	3.00
64	Matt Stairs (21)	3.00
65	Travis Fryman (22)	5.00
66	Ken Griffey Jr. (40)	15.00
67	Mike Piazza (38)	15.00
68	Mark McGwire (32)	20.00
69	Craig Biggio (8)	10.00
70	Eric Chavez (26)	10.00
71	Mo Vaughn (36)	5.00
72	Matt Lawton (13)	5.00
73	Miguel Tejada (30)	10.00
74	Brian Giles (35)	5.00
75	Sean Casey (20)	5.00
76	Robin Ventura (24)	5.00
77	Ivan Rodriguez (27)	8.00
78	Dean Palmer (29)	3.00
79	Frank Thomas (43)	10.00
80	Bernie Williams (30)	8.00
81	Juan Encarnacion (14)	5.00
82	John Olerud (14)	5.00
83	Rich Aurilia (20)	3.00
84	Juan Gonzalez (22)	8.00
85	Ray Durham (17)	5.00
86	Steve Finley (35)	3.00
87	Ken Caminiti (15)	5.00
88	Roberto Alomar (19)	15.00
89	Jeromy Burnitz (31)	3.00
90	J.D. Drew (18)	8.00
91	Lance Berkman (21)	8.00
92	Gabe Kapler (14)	8.00
93	Larry Walker (9)	10.00
94	Alex Rodriguez (41)	20.00
95	Jeffrey Hammonds (20)	3.00
96	Magglio Ordonez (32)	5.00
97	David Justice (41)	5.00
98	Eric Karros (31)	3.00
99	Manny Ramirez (38)	10.00
100	Paul O'Neill (18)	8.00

Green

NM/M

Common Player: 1.00

Produced to # of 2000 RBI's

		NM/M
1	Derek Jeter (73)	20.00
2	Vladimir Guerrero (123)	5.00
3	Henry Rodriguez (61)	1.00
4	Jason Giambi (137)	5.00
5	Nomar Garciaparra (96)	10.00
6	Jeff Kent (125)	3.00
7	Garret Anderson (117)	3.00
8	Todd Helton (147)	5.00
9	Barry Bonds (106)	20.00
10	Preston Wilson (121)	1.00
11	Troy Glaus (102)	4.00
12	Geoff Jenkins (94)	3.00
13	Jim Edmonds (108)	4.00
14	Bobby Higginson (102)	1.00
15	Mark Quinn (78)	1.00
16	Barry Larkin (41)	4.00
17	Richie Sexson (91)	4.00
18	Fernando Tatis (64)	1.00
19	John Vander Wal (94)	1.00
20	Darin Erstad (100)	3.00
21	Shawn Green (99)	3.00
22	Scott Rolen (89)	4.00
23	Tony Batista (114)	1.00
24	Phil Nevin (107)	1.00
25	Tim Salmon (97)	3.00
26	Gary Sheffield (109)	3.00
27	Ben Grieve (104)	1.00
28	Jermaine Dye (118)	1.00
29	Andres Galarraga (100)	1.50
30	Adrian Beltre (85)	1.00
31	Rafael Palmeiro (120)	3.00
32	J.T. Snow (96)	1.00
33	Edgardo Alfonzo (94)	1.00
34	Paul Konerko (97)	1.50
35	Jim Thome (106)	4.00
36	Andruw Jones (104)	4.00
37	Mike Sweeney (144)	1.00
38	Jose Cruz Jr. (76)	1.00
39	David Ortiz (63)	1.00
40	Pat Burrell (79)	4.00
41	Chipper Jones (111)	8.00
42	Jeff Bagwell (132)	5.00
43	Raul Mondesi (67)	2.00
44	Rondell White (61)	1.50
45	Edgar Martinez (145)	2.00
46	Cal Ripken Jr. (56)	25.00
47	Moises Alou (114)	1.00
48	Shannon Stewart (69)	1.00
49	Tino Martinez (91)	2.00
50	Jason Kendall (58)	1.00
51	Richard Hidalgo (122)	1.00
52	Albert Belle (103)	1.00
53	Jay Payton (62)	1.00
54	Cliff Floyd (91)	1.00
55	Rusty Greer (65)	1.00
56	Matt Williams (47)	2.00
57	Sammy Sosa (138)	10.00
58	Carl Everett (108)	1.00
59	Carlos Delgado (137)	3.00
60	Jeremy Giambi (50)	1.00
61	Jose Canseco (49)	5.00
62	David Segui (103)	1.00
63	Jose Vidro (97)	1.00
64	Matt Stairs (81)	1.00
65	Travis Fryman (106)	2.00
66	Ken Griffey Jr. (118)	10.00
67	Mike Piazza (113)	10.00
68	Mark McGwire (73)	15.00
69	Craig Biggio (35)	4.00
70	Eric Chavez (86)	4.00
71	Mo Vaughn (117)	3.00
72	Matt Lawton (88)	1.00
73	Miguel Tejada (115)	4.00
74	Brian Giles (123)	3.00
75	Sean Casey (85)	2.00
76	Robin Ventura (84)	2.00
77	Ivan Rodriguez (83)	5.00
78	Dean Palmer (102)	1.00
79	Frank Thomas (143)	5.00
80	Bernie Williams (121)	4.00
81	Juan Encarnacion (72)	1.00
82	John Olerud (103)	3.00
83	Rich Aurilia (79)	1.00
84	Juan Gonzalez (67)	5.00
85	Ray Durham (75)	1.00
86	Steve Finley (96)	1.00
87	Ken Caminiti (45)	1.00
88	Roberto Alomar (89)	5.00

89 Jeromy Burnitz (98) 1.00
90 J.D. Drew (57) 3.00
91 Lance Berkman (67) 2.00
92 Gabe Kapler (66) 2.00
93 Larry Walker (51) 3.00
94 Alex Rodriguez (132) 15.00
95 Jeffrey Hammonds (106) 1.00
96 Magglio Ordonez (126) 3.00
97 David Justice (118) 3.00
98 Eric Karros (106) 1.00
99 Manny Ramirez (122) 5.00
100 Paul O'Neill (100) 2.00

Red

Common Player (1-100):
Stars: 4-8X
Produced to 2000 Bat Avg.
(See 2001 Fleer Triple Crown #1-100 for checklist and base card values.)

Autographics

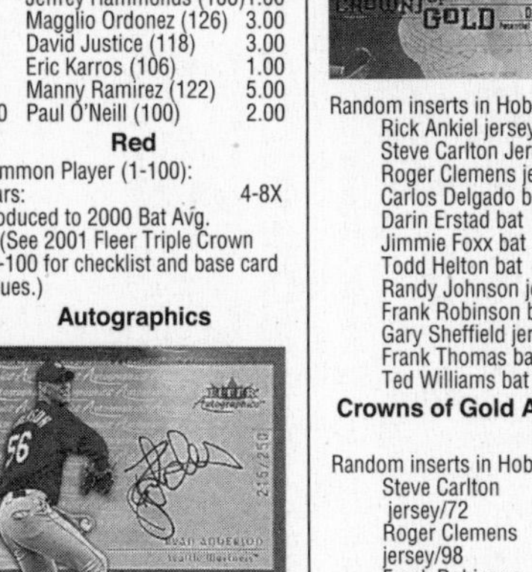

NM/M
Common Autograph: 5.00
Inserted 1:72
Silvers: 1X
Production 250 sets
Golds: 1-2X
Production 50 sets
1 Roberto Alomar 30.00
2 Jimmy Anderson 5.00
3 Ryan Anderson 5.00
4 Rick Ankiel 5.00
5 Adrian Beltre 10.00
6 Peter Bergeron 5.00
7 Lance Berkman 8.00
8 Barry Bonds 200.00
9 Milton Bradley 5.00
10 Dee Brown 5.00
11 Roosevelt Brown 5.00
12 Pat Burrell 10.00
13 Sean Casey 8.00
14 Eric Chavez 10.00
15 Giuseppe Chiaramonte 5.00
16 Joe Crede 5.00
17 Jose Cruz Jr. 5.00
18 Carlos Delgado 10.00
19 Ryan Dempster 5.00
20 Adam Dunn 15.00
21 David Eckstein 5.00
22 Jim Edmonds 10.00
23 Troy Glaus 15.00
24 Chad Green 5.00
25 Tony Gwynn 30.00
26 Todd Helton 20.00
27 Chad Hermansen 5.00
28 Shea Hillenbrand 6.00
29 Aubrey Huff 6.00
30 Randy Johnson 40.00
31 Chipper Jones 40.00
32 Mike Lamb 5.00
33 Corey Lee 5.00
34 Steve Lomasney 5.00
35 Terrence Long 5.00
36 Julio Lugo 5.00
37 Jason Marquis 5.00
38 Bengie Molina 5.00
39 Mike Mussina 25.00
40 Pablo Ozuna 5.00
41 Corey Patterson 10.00
42 Jay Payton 6.00
43 Wily Pena 15.00
44 Josh Phelps 8.00
45 Adam Piatt 5.00
46 Matt Riley 5.00
47 Alex Rodriguez 75.00
48 Alex Sanchez 5.00
49 Gary Sheffield 10.00
50 Alfonso Soriano 40.00
51 Shannon Stewart 6.00
52 Fernando Tatis 5.00
53 Jose Vidro 5.00
54 Preston Wilson 8.00
55 Kerry Wood 25.00
56 Julio Zuleta 5.00

Crowns of Gold

NM/M
Common Player: 4.00

Random inserts in Hobby packs
Rick Ankiel jersey 4.00
Steve Carlton Jersey 10.00
Roger Clemens jersey 40.00
Carlos Delgado bat 8.00
Darin Erstad bat 6.00
Jimmie Foxx bat 100.00
Todd Helton bat 10.00
Randy Johnson jersey 15.00
Frank Robinson bat 10.00
Gary Sheffield jersey 8.00
Frank Thomas bat 10.00
Ted Williams bat 200.00

Crowns of Gold Autograph

NM/M
Random inserts in Hobby packs
Steve Carlton jersey/72 80.00
Roger Clemens jersey/98 200.00
Frank Robinson bat/66 80.00
Ted Williams bat/9

Crowning Achievements

NM/M
Complete Set (15): 15.00
Common Player: .50
Inserted 1:9
1 Troy Glaus 1.00
2 Mark McGwire 2.50
3 Barry Larkin, Craig Biggio .50
4 Ken Griffey Jr. 2.00
5 Rafael Palmeiro .75
6 Alex Rodriguez 2.50
7 Roger Clemens 1.75
8 Mike Piazza 2.00
9 Cal Ripken Jr. 3.00
10 Randy Johnson 1.00
11 Jeff Bagwell 1.00
12 Sammy Sosa 2.00
13 Greg Maddux 1.50
14 Barry Bonds 3.00
15 Fred McGriff .50

Feel the Game

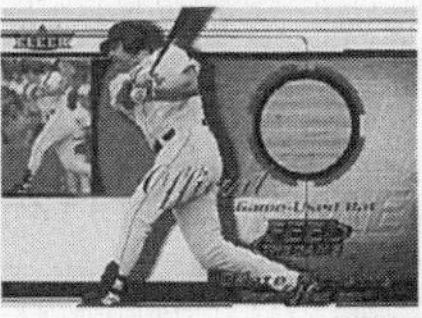

NM/M
Common Player: 4.00
Inserted 1:72
Golds: 1.5-2X
Production 50 sets
Adrian Beltre 6.00
Dante Bichette 4.00
Roger Cedeno 4.00
Ben Davis 4.00
Carlos Delgado 6.00
J.D. Drew 6.00
Jason Giambi 6.00
Brian Giles 4.00
Juan Gonzalez 8.00
Richard Hidalgo 4.00
Chipper Jones 10.00
Eric Karros 4.00
Javy Lopez 4.00
Tino Martinez 4.00
Raul Mondesi 4.00
Phil Nevin 4.00
Chan Ho Park 4.00
Ivan Rodriguez 6.00
Shannon Stewart 4.00
Frank Thomas 8.00
Jose Vidro 4.00
Matt Williams 4.00
Preston Wilson 4.00

Future Threats

NM/M
Complete Set (15): 15.00

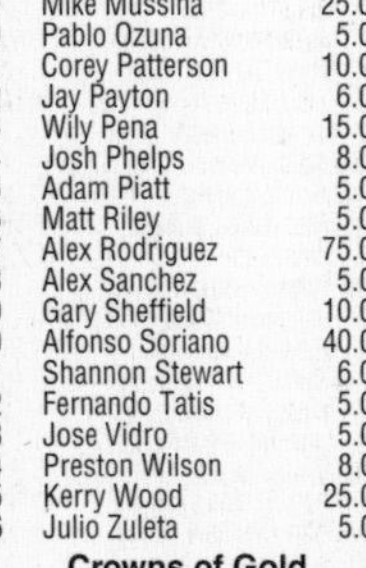

Common Player: .50
Inserted 1:7
1 Derek Jeter 3.00
2 Alex Rodriguez 2.50
3 Magglio Ordonez, Shawn Green .50
4 Larry Walker .50
5 Vladimir Guerrero 1.00
6 Nomar Garciaparra 2.00
7 Ken Griffey Jr. 2.00
8 Barry Bonds 3.00
9 Chipper Jones 1.50
10 Todd Helton 1.00
11 Ivan Rodriguez .75
12 Jeff Bagwell 1.00
13 Frank Thomas 1.00
14 Carlos Delgado .65
15 Mike Piazza 2.00

Glamour Boys

NM/M
Complete Set (15): 40.00
Common Player: 1.50
Inserted 1:24
1 Derek Jeter 6.00
2 Vladimir Guerrero 2.00
3 Scott Rolen, Jeff Bagwell 1.50
4 Sammy Sosa 4.00
5 Ken Griffey Jr. 4.00
6 Mark McGwire 5.00
7 Ivan Rodriguez 1.50
8 Mike Piazza 4.00
9 Nomar Garciaparra 4.00
10 Cal Ripken Jr. 6.00
11 Tony Gwynn 3.00
12 Barry Bonds 6.00
13 Randy Johnson 2.00
14 Alex Rodriguez 5.00
15 Pedro Martinez 2.00

2002 FLEER

NM/M
Complete Set (540): 75.00
Common Player: .15
Pack (10): 2.00
Box (24): 40.00
31 Miguel Tejada .25
32 Todd Hollandsworth .15
33 Marlon Anderson .15
34 Kerry Robinson .15
35 Chris Richard .15
36 Jamey Wright .15
37 Ray Lankford .15
38 Mike Bordick .15
39 Danny Graves .15
40 A.J. Pierzynski .15
41 Shannon Stewart .15
42 Tony Armas Jr. .15
43 Brad Ausmus .15
44 Alfonso Soriano .50
45 Junior Spivey .15
46 Brent Mayne .15
47 Jim Thome .15
48 Dan Wilson .15
49 Geoff Jenkins .15
50 Kris Benson .15
51 Rafael Furcal .15
52 Wiki Gonzalez .15
53 Jeff Kent .15
54 Curt Schilling .40
55 Ken Harvey .15
56 Roosevelt Brown .15
57 David Segui .15
58 Mario Valdez .15
59 Adam Dunn .50
60 Bob Howry .15
61 Michael Barrett .15
62 Garret Anderson .15
63 Kelvim Escobar .15
64 Ben Grieve .15
65 Randy Johnson .75
66 Jose Offerman .15
67 Jason Kendall .15
68 Joel Pineiro .15
69 Alex Escobar .15
70 Chris George .15
71 Bobby Higginson .15
72 Nomar Garciaparra 1.50
73 Pat Burrell .40
74 Lee Stevens .15
75 Felipe Lopez .15
76 Al Leiter .15
77 Jim Edmonds .15
78 Al Levine .15
79 Raul Mondesi .15
80 Jose Valentin .15
81 Matt Clement .15
82 Richard Hidalgo .15
83 Jamie Moyer .15
84 Brian Schneider .15
85 John Franco .15
86 Brian Buchanan .15
87 Roy Oswalt .25
88 Johnny Estrada .15
89 Marcus Giles .15
90 Carlos Valderrama .15
91 Mark Mulder .15
92 Mark Grace .25
93 Andy Ashby .15
94 Woody Williams .15
95 Ben Petrick .15
96 Roy Halladay .30
97 Fred McGriff .15
98 Shawn Green .40
99 Todd Hundley .15
100 Carlos Febles .15
101 Jason Marquis .15
102 Mike Redmond .15
103 Shane Halter .15
104 Trot Nixon .15
105 Jeremy Giambi .15
106 Carlos Delgado .50
107 Richie Sexson .15
108 Russ Ortiz .15
109 David Ortiz .25
110 Curtis Leskanic .15
111 Jay Payton .15
112 Travis Phelps .15
113 J.T. Snow .15
114 Edgar Renteria .15
115 Freddy Garcia .15
116 Cliff Floyd .15
117 Charles Nagy .15
118 Tony Batista .15
119 Rafael Palmeiro .65
120 Darren Dreifort .15
121 Warren Morris .15
122 Augie Ojeda .15
123 Rusty Greer .15
124 Esteban Yan .15
125 Corey Patterson .15
126 Matt Ginter .15
127 Matt Lawton .15
128 Miguel Batista .15
129 Randy Winn .15
130 Eric Milton .15

No.	Player	Price
131	Jack Wilson	.15
132	Sean Casey	.25
133	Mike Sweeney	.15
134	Jason Tyner	.15
135	Carlos Hernandez	.15
136	Shea Hillenbrand	.15
137	Shawn Wooten	.15
138	Peter Bergeron	.15
139	Travis Lee	.15
140	Craig Wilson	.15
141	Carlos Guillen	.15
142	Chipper Jones	1.00
143	Gabe Kapler	.15
144	Raul Ibanez	.15
145	Eric Chavez	.25
146	D'Angelo Jiminez	.15
147	Chad Hermansen	.15
148	Joe Kennedy	.15
149	Mariano Rivera	.25
150	Jeff Bagwell	.75
151	Joe McEwing	.15
152	Ronnie Belliard	.15
153	Desi Relaford	.15
154	Vinny Castilla	.15
155	Tim Hudson	.25
156	Wilton Guerrero	.15
157	Raul Casanova	.15
158	Edgardo Alfonzo	.15
159	Derrek Lee	.15
160	Phil Nevin	.15
161	Roger Clemens	1.25
162	Jason LaRue	.15
163	Brian Lawrence	.15
164	Adrian Beltre	.30
165	Troy Glaus	.75
166	Jeff Weaver	.15
167	B.J. Surhoff	.15
168	Eric Byrnes	.15
169	Mike Sirotka	.15
170	Bill Haselman	.15
171	Javier Vazquez	.15
172	Sidney Ponson	.15
173	Adam Everett	.15
174	Bubba Trammell	.15
175	Robb Nen	.15
176	Barry Larkin	.15
177	Tony Graffanino	.15
178	Rich Garces	.15
179	Juan Uribe	.15
180	Tom Glavine	.25
181	Eric Karros	.15
182	Michael Cuddyer	.15
183	Wade Miller	.15
184	Matt Williams	.15
185	Matt Morris	.15
186	Rickey Henderson	.75
187	Trevor Hoffman	.15
188	Wilson Betemit	.15
189	Steve Karsay	.15
190	Frank Catalanotto	.15
191	Jason Schmidt	.15
192	Roger Cedeno	.15
193	Magglio Ordonez	.15
194	Pat Hentgen	.15
195	Mike Lieberthal	.15
196	Andy Pettitte	.30
197	Jay Gibbons	.15
198	Rolando Arrojo	.15
199	Joe Mays	.15
200	Aubrey Huff	.15
201	Nelson Figueroa	.15
202	Paul Konerko	.25
203	Ken Griffey Jr.	1.50
204	Brandon Duckworth	.15
205	Sammy Sosa	1.50
206	Carl Everett	.15
207	Scott Rolen	.65
208	Orlando Hernandez	.15
209	Todd Helton	.75
210	Preston Wilson	.15
211	Gil Meche	.15
212	Bill Mueller	.15
213	Craig Biggio	.15
214	Dean Palmer	.15
215	Randy Wolf	.15
216	Jeff Suppan	.15
217	Jimmy Rollins	.15
218	Alexis Gomez	.15
219	Ellis Burks	.15
220	Ramon E. Martinez	.15
221	Ramiro Mendoza	.15
222	Einar Diaz	.15
223	Brent Abernathy	.15
224	Darin Erstad	.25
225	Reggie Taylor	.15
226	Jason Jennings	.15
227	Ray Durham	.15
228	John Parrish	.15
229	Kevin Young	.15
230	Xavier Nady	.15
231	Juan Cruz	.15
232	Greg Norton	.15
233	Barry Bonds	2.00
234	Kip Wells	.15
235	Paul LoDuca	.15
236	Javy Lopez	.25
237	Luis Castillo	.15
238	Tom Gordon	.15
239	Mike Mordecai	.15
240	Damian Rolls	.15
241	Julio Lugo	.15
242	Ichiro Suzuki	1.00
243	Tony Womack	.15
244	Matt Anderson	.15
245	Carlos Lee	.15
246	Alex Rodriguez	1.75
247	Bernie Williams	.30
248	Scott Sullivan	.15
249	Mike Hampton	.15
250	Orlando Cabrera	.15
251	Benito Santiago	.15
252	Steve Finley	.15
253	Dave Williams	.15
254	Adam Kennedy	.15
255	Omar Vizquel	.15
256	Garrett Stephenson	.15
257	Fernando Tatis	.15
258	Mike Piazza	1.50
259	Scott Spiezio	.15
260	Jacque Jones	.15
261	Russell Branyan	.15
262	Mark McLemore	.15
263	Mitch Meluskey	.15
264	Marlon Byrd	.15
265	Kyle Farnsworth	.15
266	Billy Sylvester	.15
267	C.C. Sabathia	.15
268	Mark Buehrle	.15
269	Geoff Blum	.15
270	Bret Prinz	.15
271	Placido Polanco	.15
272	John Olerud	.15
273	Pedro J. Martinez	.75
274	Doug Mientkiewicz	.15
275	Jason Bere	.15
276	Bud Smith	.15
277	Terrence Long	.15
278	Troy Percival	.15
279	Derek Jeter	2.00
280	Eric Owens	.15
281	Jay Bell	.15
282	Mike Cameron	.15
283	Joe Randa	.15
284	Brian Roberts	.15
285	Ryan Klesko	.15
286	Ryan Dempster	.15
287	Cristian Guzman	.15
288	Tim Salmon	.25
289	Mark Johnson	.15
290	Brian Giles	.15
291	Jon Lieber	.15
292	Fernando Vina	.15
293	Mike Mussina	.40
294	Juan Pierre	.15
295	Carlos Beltran	.40
296	Vladimir Guerrero	.75
297	Orlando Merced	.15
298	Jose Hernandez	.15
299	Mike Lamb	.15
300	David Eckstein	.15
301	Mark Loretta	.15
302	Greg Vaughn	.15
303	Jose Vidro	.15
304	Jose Ortiz	.15
305	Mark Grudzielanek	.15
306	Rob Bell	.15
307	Elmer Dessens	.15
308	Tomas Perez	.15
309	Jerry Hairston Jr.	.15
310	Mike Stanton	.15
311	Todd Walker	.15
312	Jason Varitek	.15
313	Masato Yoshii	.15
314	Ben Sheets	.15
315	Roberto Hernandez	.15
316	Eli Marrero	.15
317	Josh Beckett	.50
318	Robert Fick	.15
319	Aramis Ramirez	.15
320	Bartolo Colon	.15
321	Kenny Kelly	.15
322	Luis Gonzalez	.25
323	John Smoltz	.15
324	Homer Bush	.15
325	Kevin Millwood	.15
326	Manny Ramirez	.75
327	Armando Benitez	.15
328	Luis Alicea	.15
329	Mark Kotsay	.15
330	Felix Rodriguez	.15
331	Eddie Taubensee	.15
332	John Burkett	.15
333	Ramon Ortiz	.15
334	Daryle Ward	.15
335	Jarrod Washburn	.15
336	Benji Gil	.15
337	Mike Lowell	.15
338	Larry Walker	.15
339	Andruw Jones	.75
340	Scott Elarton	.15
341	Tony McKnight	.15
342	Frank Thomas	.50
343	Kevin Brown	.15
344	Jermaine Dye	.15
345	Luis Rivas	.15
346	Jeff Conine	.15
347	Bobby Kielty	.15
348	Jeffrey Hammonds	.15
349	Keith Foulke	.15
350	Dave Martinez	.15
351	Adam Eaton	.15
352	Brandon Inge	.15
353	Tyler Houston	.15
354	Bobby Abreu	.15
355	Ivan Rodriguez	.65
356	Doug Glanville	.15
357	Jorge Julio	.15
358	Kerry Wood	.50
359	Eric Munson	.15
360	Joe Crede	.15
361	Denny Neagle	.15
362	Vance Wilson	.15
363	Neifi Perez	.15
364	Darryl Kile	.15
365	Jose Macias	.15
366	Michael Coleman	.15
367	Erubiel Durazo	.15
368	Darrin Fletcher	.15
369	Matt White	.15
370	Marvin Benard	.15
371	Brad Penny	.15
372	Chuck Finley	.15
373	Delino DeShields	.15
374	Adrian Brown	.15
375	Corey Koskie	.15
376	Kazuhiro Sasaki	.15
377	Brent Butler	.15
378	Paul Wilson	.15
379	Scott Williamson	.15
380	Mike Young	.15
381	Toby Hall	.15
382	Shane Reynolds	.15
383	Tom Goodwin	.15
384	Seth Etherton	.15
385	Billy Wagner	.15
386	Josh Phelps	.15
387	Kyle Lohse	.15
388	Jeremy Fikac	.15
389	Jorge Posada	.30
390	Bret Boone	.15
391	Angel Berroa	.15
392	Matt Mantei	.15
393	Alex Gonzalez	.15
394	Scott Strickland	.15
395	Charles Johnson	.15
396	Ramon Hernandez	.15
397	Damian Jackson	.15
398	Albert Pujols	1.50
399	Gary Bennett	.15
400	Edgar Martinez	.15
401	Carl Pavano	.15
402	Chris Gomez	.15
403	Jaret Wright	.15
404	Lance Berkman	.15
405	Robert Person	.15
406	Brook Fordyce	.15
407	Adam Pettyjohn	.15
408	Chris Carpenter	.15
409	Rey Ordonez	.15
410	Eric Gagne	.25
411	Damion Easley	.15
412	A.J. Burnett	.15
413	Aaron Boone	.15
414	J.D. Drew	.25
415	Kelly Stinnett	.15
416	Mark Quinn	.15
417	Brad Radke	.15
418	Jose Cruz Jr.	.15
419	Greg Maddux	1.00
420	Steve Cox	.15
421	Torii Hunter	.15
422	Sandy Alomar	.15
423	Barry Zito	.40
424	Bill Hall	.15
425	Marquis Grissom	.15
426	Rich Aurilia	.15
427	Royce Clayton	.15
428	Travis Fryman	.15
429	Pablo Ozuna	.15
430	David Dellucci	.15
431	Vernon Wells	.15
432	Gregg Zaun	.15
433	Alex Gonzalez	.15
434	Hideo Nomo	.40
435	Jeromy Burnitz	.15
436	Gary Sheffield	.25
437	Tino Martinez	.15
438	Tsuyoshi Shinjo	.15
439	Chan Ho Park	.15
440	Tony Clark	.15
441	Brad Fullmer	.15
442	Jason Giambi	.50
443	Billy Koch	.15
444	Mo Vaughn	.15
445	Alex Ochoa	.15
446	Darren Lewis	.15
447	John Rocker	.15
448	Scott Hatteberg	.15
449	Brady Anderson	.15
450	Chuck Knoblauch	.15
451	Pokey Reese	.15
452	Brian Jordan	.15
453	Albie Lopez	.15
454	David Bell	.15
455	Juan Gonzalez	.75
456	Terry Adams	.15
457	Kenny Lofton	.25
458	Shawn Estes	.15
459	Josh Fogg	.15
460	Dmitri Young	.15
461	Johnny Damon	.25
462	Chris Singleton	.15
463	Ricky Ledee	.15
464	Dustin Hermanson	.15
465	Aaron Sele	.15
466	Chris Stynes	.15
467	Matt Stairs	.15
468	Kevin Appier	.15
469	Omar Daal	.15
470	Moises Alou	.15
471	Juan Encarnacion	.15
472	Robin Ventura	.15
473	Eric Hinske	.15
474	Rondell White	.15
475	Carlos Pena	.15
476	Craig Paquette	.15
477	Marty Cordova	.15
478	Brett Tomko	.15
479	Reggie Sanders	.15
480	Roberto Alomar	.15
481	Jeff Cirillo	.15
482	Todd Zeile	.15
483	John Vander Wal	.15
484	Rick Helling	.15
485	Jeff D'Amico	.15
486	David Justice	.15
487	Jason Isringhausen	.15
488	Shigetoshi Hasegawa	.15
489	Eric Young	.15
490	David Wells	.15
491	Ruben Sierra	.15
492	*Aaron Cook*	.50
493	*Takahito Nomura*	.50
494	Austin Kearns	.50
495	*Kazuhisa Ishii*	2.00
496	Mark Teixeira	.50
497	*Rene Reyes*	.50
498	Tim Spooneybarger	.15
499	Ben Broussard	.15
500	*Eric Cyr*	.25
501	*Anastacio Martinez*	.50
502	Morgan Ensberg	.15
503	*Steve Kent*	.25
504	*Franklin Nunez*	.25
505	*Adam Walker*	.25
506	*Anderson Machado*	.50
507	Ryan Drese	.15
508	*Luis Ugueto*	.25
509	*Jorge Nunez*	.25
510	Colby Lewis	.15
511	*Ron Calloway*	.25
512	*Hansel Izquierdo*	.50
513	Jason Lane	.15
514	Rafael Soriano	.15
515	Jackson Melian	.15
516	*Edwin Almonte*	.50
517	*Satoru Komiyama*	.50
518	*Corey Thurman*	.25
519	*Jorge De La Rosa*	.50
520	Victor Martinez	.15
521	Dewan Brazleton	.15
522	Marlon Byrd	.50
523	Jae Weong Seo	.15
524	Orlando Hudson	.15
525	Sean Burroughs	.15
526	Ryan Langerhans	.15

527 David Kelton .15
528 *So Taguchi* .50
529 Tyler Walker .15
530 Hank Blalock .50
531 Mark Prior .75
532 Yankee Stadium .50
533 Fenway Park .50
534 Wrigley Field .50
535 Dodger Stadium .15
536 Camden Yards .15
537 PacBell Park .15
538 Jacobs Field .15
539 SAFECO Field .15
540 Miller Field .15

Barry Bonds Chasing History

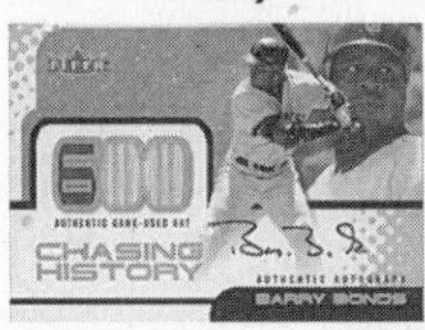

NM/M
Barry Bonds 125.00

Barry Bonds 4X MVP Super

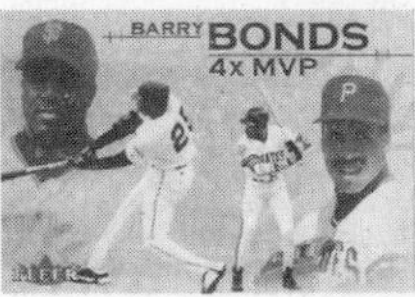

NM/M
Barry Bonds 15.00

Barry Bonds Career Highlights

NM/M
Complete Set (10): 40.00
Common Bonds 1-3: 3.00
Common 4-6 inserted 1:125 H 4.00
7-9 1:250 H 6.00
#10 1:383 6.00
1CH Barry Bonds 3.00
2CH Barry Bonds 3.00
3CH Barry Bonds 3.00
4CH Barry Bonds 4.00
5CH Barry Bonds 4.00
6CH Barry Bonds 4.00
7CH Barry Bonds 6.00
8CH Barry Bonds 6.00
9CH Barry Bonds 6.00
10CH Barry Bonds 6.00

Barry Bonds Career Highlights Autographs

No Pricing
25 sets produced

2002 FLEER BARRY BONDS 600 HR SUPERS

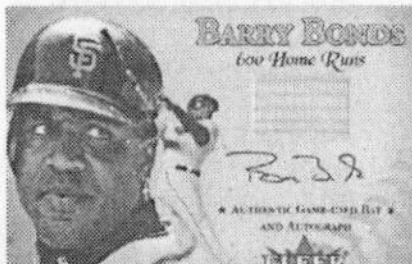

NM/M
Barry Bonds (facsimile signature) 55.00
Barry Bonds (autograph w/bat chip) 250.00

Classic Cuts Autographs

NM/M
Inserted 1:432
LA-A Luis Aparicio 15.00
RC-A Ron Cey 8.00
RF-A Rollie Fingers SP/35
HK-A Harmon Killebrew 35.00
TL-A Tommy Lasorda SP/35
JM-A Juan Marichal 15.00
GP-A Gaylord Perry SP/225 15.00
PR-A Phil Rizzuto SP/125 50.00
BR-A Brooks Robinson SP/200 40.00

Classic Cuts Game Used Autographs

NM/M
Varying quantities produced
LA-B Luis Aparicio Bat/45 25.00
RF-J Rollie Fingers Jsy/35
BR-B Brooks Robinson Bat/45 80.00

Classic Cuts Game Used

NM/M
Common Player: 5.00
Inserted 1:24
SA-P Sparky Anderson Pants 5.00
HB-B Hank Bauer Bat 5.00
JB-B Johnny Bench Bat/100
JB-J Johnny Bench Jsy 15.00
YBB Yogi Berra Bat/72
PB-B Paul Blair Bat 5.00
WB-B Wade Boggs Bat/99 20.00
WB-J Wade Boggs Jsy 10.00
WB-P Wade Boggs Patch/50
BB-B Bobby Bonds Bat 5.00
BB-J Bobby Bonds Jsy 5.00
GB-B George Brett Bat/250 30.00
GB-J George Brett Jsy/250 30.00
RC-B Roy Campanella Bat/7
SC-H Steve Carlton Hat/25
SC-P Steve Carlton Pants 6.00
OC-B Orlando Cepeda Bat/45
OC-P Orlando Cepeda Pants 5.00
AD-J Andre Dawson Jsy 8.00
BD-B Bill Dickey Bat/200 20.00
LD-B Larry Doby Bat/250 10.00
DE-B Dwight Evans Bat/250 10.00
DE-J Dwight Evans Jsy 5.00
RF-J Rollie Fingers Jsy 5.00
CF-B Carlton Fisk Bat 10.00
CF-J Carlton Fisk Jsy/150 20.00
NF-B Nellie Fox Bat/200 20.00
SG-B Steve Garvey Bat 5.00
KG-B Kirk Gibson Bat 5.00
HG-B Hank Greenberg Bat/13
GH-B Gil Hodges Bat/200 15.00
CH-J Jim Hunter Jsy 10.00
BJ-J Bo Jackson Jsy 15.00
RJ-B Reggie Jackson Bat/50
RJ-P Reggie Jackson Pants 10.00
TJ-J Tommy John Jsy/55
TJ-P Tommy John Patch/15
GK-B George Kell Bat/150 15.00
RK-B Ralph Kiner Bat/47
TK-B Ted Kluszewski Bat/200 15.00
TK-P Ted Kluszewski Pants 10.00
TL-B Tony Lazzeri Bat/25
FL-B Fred Lynn Bat/25
RM-P Roger Maris P ants/200 60.00
BM-B Billy Martin Bat/65
EM-B Eddie Mathews Bat/200 20.00
DM-B Don Mattingly Bat/200 50.00
DM-J Don Mattingly Jsy 40.00
DM-P Don Mattingly Patch/50
WM-J Willie McCovey Jsy/300 10.00
PM-B Paul Molitor Bat/250 25.00
PM-P Paul Molitor Patch/110
JM-B Joe Morgan Bat/250 8.00
TM-P Thurman Munson Pants/10
EM-B Eddie Murray Bat 10.00
EM-J Eddie Murray Jsy 10.00
EM-P Eddie Murray Patch/45
JP-J Jim Palmer Jsy/273 8.00
DP-B Dave Parker Bat 5.00
TP-B Tony Perez Bat/250 10.00
TP-J Tony Perez Jsy 8.00
LP-P Lou Piniella Pants 5.00
KP-B Kirby Puckett Bat/25
KP-J Kirby Puckett Jsy 15.00
WR-P Willie Randolph Patch/18
PWR-J Pee Wee Reese Jsy/20
JR-B Jim Rice Bat/225 8.00
JR-J Jim Rice Jsy/90
CR-BG Cal Ripken Jr. Btg Glv/100 75.00
CR-FG Cal Ripken Jr. Fld Glv/50 125.00
CR-J Cal Ripken Jr. Jsy 35.00
CR-P Cal Ripken Jr. Pants/200 40.00
BR-B Brooks Robinson Bat/250 15.00
PR-J Preacher Roe Jsy/19
NR-J Nolan Ryan Jsy 50.00
NR-P Nolan Ryan Pants/200 60.00
RS-B Ryne Sandberg Bat 25.00
OS-J Ozzie Smith Jsy/250 15.00
WS-B Willie Stargell Bat/250 15.00
BT-B Bill Terry Bat/85
JT-J Joe Torre Jsy/125 15.00
AT-B Alan Trammell Bat 10.00
EW-J Earl Weaver Jsy 5.00
HW-P Hoyt Wilhelm Pants/150 15.00
TW-B Ted Williams Bat 85.00
TW-P Ted Williams Pants 120.00
HW-B Hack Wilson Bat/8
DW-B Dave Winfield Bat 8.00
DW-J Dave Winfield Jsy/231 10.00
DW-P Dave Winfield Pants 8.00
DW-P Dave Winfield Patch/25
RY-B Robin Yount Bat 15.00
DZ-J Don Zimmer Jsy/90

Diamond Standouts

NM/M
Complete Set (10): 40.00
Common Player: 2.00
Production 1,200 sets
1DS Mike Piazza 4.00
2DS Derek Jeter 8.00
3DS Ken Griffey Jr. 4.00
4DS Barry Bonds 8.00
5DS Sammy Sosa 4.00
6DS Alex Rodriguez 6.00
7DS Ichiro Suzuki 4.00
8DS Greg Maddux 3.00
9DS Jason Giambi 2.00
10DS Nomar Garciaparra 4.00

2002 FLEER AUTHENTIX

NM/M
Complete Set (170): 85.00
Common Player: .25
Common SP (151-170): 3.00
Production 1,850
Pack (5): 3.00
Box (24): 60.00
1 Derek Jeter 2.00
2 Tim Hudson .35
3 Robert Fick .25
4 Javy Lopez .25
5 Alfonso Soriano .50
6 Ken Griffey Jr. 1.25
7 Rafael Palmeiro .65
8 Bernie Williams .35
9 Adam Dunn .50
10 Ivan Rodriguez .65
11 Vladimir Guerrero .75
12 Pedro J. Martinez .75
13 Bret Boone .25
14 Paul LoDuca .25
15 Tony Batista .25
16 Barry Bonds 2.00
17 Craig Biggio .25
18 Garret Anderson .25
19 Mark Mulder .25
20 Frank Thomas .75
21 Alex Rodriguez 1.50
22 Cristian Guzman .25
23 Sammy Sosa 1.25
24 Ichiro Suzuki 1.25
25 Carlos Beltran .50
26 Edgardo Alfonzo .25
27 Josh Beckett .50
28 Eric Chavez .40
29 Roberto Alomar .40
30 Raul Mondesi .25
31 Mike Piazza 1.25
32 Barry Larkin .25
33 Ruben Sierra .25
34 Tsuyoshi Shinjo .25
35 Magglio Ordonez .25
36 Ben Grieve .25
37 Richie Sexson .25
38 Manny Ramirez .75
39 Jeff Kent .25
40 Shawn Green .40
41 Andruw Jones .75
42 Aramis Ramirez .25
43 Cliff Floyd .25
44 Juan Pierre .25
45 Jose Vidro .25
46 Paul Konerko .25
47 Greg Vaughn .25
48 Geoff Jenkins .25
49 Greg Maddux 1.00
50 Ryan Klesko .25
51 Corey Koskie .25
52 Nomar Garciaparra 1.25
53 Edgar Martinez .25
54 Gary Sheffield .40
55 Randy Johnson .75
56 Bobby Abreu .25
57 Mike Sweeney .25
58 Chipper Jones 1.00
59 Brian Giles .25
60 Charles Johnson .25
61 Ben Sheets .25
62 Jason Giambi .60
63 Todd Helton .75
64 David Eckstein .25
65 Troy Glaus .75
66 Sean Casey .35
67 Gabe Kapler .25
68 Doug Mientkiewicz .25
69 Curt Schilling .40
70 Pat Burrell .40
71 Albert Pujols 1.25
72 Jermaine Dye .25
73 Miguel Tejada .40
74 Jim Thome .25
75 Carlos Delgado .40
76 Fred McGriff .25
77 Mike Cameron .25
78 Jeromy Burnitz .25
79 Jay Gibbons .25
80 Rich Aurilia .25
81 Lance Berkman .25
82 Brian Jordan .25
83 Phil Nevin .25
84 Moises Alou .25
85 Reggie Sanders .25
86 Scott Rolen .65
87 Larry Walker .25
88 Matt Williams .25
89 Roger Clemens 1.00
90 Juan Gonzalez .75
91 Jose Cruz Jr. .25
92 Tino Martinez .25
93 Kerry Wood .65
94 Freddy Garcia .25
95 Jeff Bagwell .75
96 Luis Gonzalez .35
97 Jimmy Rollins .25
98 Bobby Higginson .25
99 Rondell White .25
100 Jorge Posada .35
101 Trot Nixon .25
102 Jason Kendall .25
103 Preston Wilson .25
104 Corey Patterson .25
105 Jose Valentin .25
106 Carlos Lee .25
107 Chris Richard .25
108 Todd Walker .25
109 Ellis Burks .25
110 Brady Anderson .25
111 Kazuhiro Sasaki .25
112 Roy Oswalt .35
113 Kevin Brown .25
114 Jeff Weaver .25
115 Todd Hollandsworth .25
116 Joe Crede .25

117 Tom Glavine .40
118 Mike Lieberthal .25
119 Tim Salmon .35
120 Johnny Damon .40
121 Brad Fullmer .25
122 Mo Vaughn .25
123 Torii Hunter .25
124 Jamie Moyer .25
125 Terrence Long .25
126 Travis Lee .25
127 Jacque Jones .25
128 Lee Stevens .25
129 Russ Ortiz .25
130 Jeremy Giambi .25
131 Mike Mussina .45
132 Orlando Cabrera .25
133 Barry Zito .40
134 Robert Person .25
135 Andy Pettitte .40
136 Drew Henson .40
137 Mark Teixeira .50
138 David Espinosa .25
139 Orlando Hudson .25
140 Colby Lewis .25
141 Bill Hall .25
142 Michael Restovich .25
143 Angel Berroa .40
144 Dewon Brazelton .25
145 Joe Thurston .25
146 Mark Prior .50
147 Dane Sardinha .25
148 Marlon Byrd .25
149 *Jeff Deardorff* .25
150 Austin Kearns .40
151 *Anderson Machado* 5.00
152 *Kazuhisa Ishii* 8.00
153 *Eric Junge* 3.00
154 *Mark Corey* 3.00
155 *So Taguchi* 5.00
156 *Jorge Padilla* 5.00
157 *Steve Kent* 3.00
158 *Jaime Cerda* 3.00
159 *Hansel Izquierdo* 3.00
160 *Rene Reyes* 3.00
161 *Jorge Nunez* 3.00
162 *Corey Thurman* 4.00
163 *Jorge Sosa* 3.00
164 *Franklin Nunez* 3.00
165 *Adam Walker* 3.00
166 *Ryan Baerlocher* 3.00
167 *Ron Calloway* 3.00
168 *Miguel Asencio* 3.00
169 *Luis Ugueto* 3.00
170 *Felix Escalona* 3.00

Front Row

NM/M
Front Row: 4-8X
Front Row SP: 1-2X
Production 150 sets

Second Row

Second Row: 3-5X
Second Row SP: .75-1.5X
Production 250 sets

Autographed AuthenTIX

NM/M
Common Autograph: 10.00
Inserted 1:780
Unripped no pricing
Numbered to 25
Derek Jeter 200.00
Marlon Byrd
Drew Henson
Mark Teixeira/25 35.00
Barry Bonds
Brooks Robinson/145 40.00
Ben Sheets/25 30.00
Mark Prior 80.00
Kazuhisa Ishii 25.00
So Taguchi 15.00
Dane Sardinha 10.00
David Espinosa 10.00

Autographed Jersey AuthenTIX

NM/M
Inserted 1:1,387
Barry Bonds
Chipper Jones
Greg Maddux
Derek Jeter 200.00
Jeff Bagwell 80.00

Ballpark Classics

NM/M
Complete Set (15): 50.00
Common Player: 1.50
Inserted 1:22
1BC Reggie Jackson 3.00
2BC Don Mattingly 6.00
3BC Duke Snider 2.00
4BC Carlton Fisk 2.00
5BC Cal Ripken Jr. 8.00
6BC Willie McCovey 1.50
7BC Robin Yount 3.00
8BC Paul Molitor 3.00
9BC George Brett 6.00
10BC Ryne Sandberg 5.00
11BC Nolan Ryan 8.00
12BC Thurman Munson 4.00
13BC Joe Morgan 1.50
14BC Jim Rice 1.50
15BC Babe Ruth 8.00

Ballpark Classics Memorabilia

NM/M
Common Player: 5.00
Inserted 1:83
Golds: 2X
Production 100
RJ Reggie Jackson 15.00
DM Don Mattingly 30.00
DS Duke Snider 15.00
CF Carlton Fisk 10.00
CR Cal Ripken Jr. 40.00
WC Willie McCovey 15.00
RY Robin Yount 25.00
PM Paul Molitor 15.00
GB George Brett 30.00
RS Ryne Sandberg/SP 75.00
NR Nolan Ryan 30.00
TM Thurman Munson/cap/SP 50.00
JM Joe Morgan 5.00
JR Jim Rice 8.00
BR Babe Ruth/seat 150.00

Bat AuthenTIX

NM/M
Common Player: 5.00
Inserted 1:68
Unripped: 2-3X
Production 50
Pat Burrell 8.00
Ray Durham/SP/52 5.00
Juan Gonzalez 8.00
Drew Henson 5.00
Orlando Hernandez 5.00
Hideo Nomo/SP/41 30.00
Jimmy Rollins 5.00
Manny Ramirez 8.00
Bernie Williams/SP/44 10.00
Derek Jeter/197 40.00
Andruw Jones 8.00
Chipper Jones/SP/37 20.00
Barry Bonds 20.00
Nomar Garciaparra 25.00

Derek Jeter 1996 Autographics

NM/M
Production 100
Derek Jeter 150.00

Jersey AuthenTIX

NM/M
Common Player: 5.00
Inserted 1:12
Unripped: 2-3X
Production 50
Barry Bonds 20.00
Chipper Jones 10.00
Scott Rolen/SP 12.00
Greg Maddux 10.00
Curt Schilling/SP 10.00
Mike Piazza 10.00
Nomar Garciaparra/SP 15.00
Derek Jeter 20.00
Luis Gonzalez/SP 8.00
Jeff Bagwell 8.00
Frank Thomas 8.00
Manny Ramirez/SP 10.00
Shawn Green 5.00
Todd Helton 8.00
Jim Edmonds/SP 10.00
Paul LoDuca 5.00
Alex Rodriguez 10.00
Roberto Alomar 6.00
Andruw Jones/SP 10.00
Barry Zito 8.00
J.D. Drew 5.00
Magglio Ordonez 5.00
Eric Chavez 5.00
Darin Erstad/SP 8.00
Freddy Garcia 5.00
Jim Thome/SP 12.00
Pedro J. Martinez 10.00
Ivan Rodriguez 8.00
Bernie Williams/SP 10.00
Randy Johnson 8.00

Power Alley

NM/M
Complete Set (15): 20.00
Common Player: .50
Inserted 1:11
1PA Sammy Sosa 2.00
2PA Ken Griffey Jr. 2.00
3PA Luis Gonzalez .50
4PA Alex Rodriguez 3.00
5PA Shawn Green .75
6PA Barry Bonds 4.00
7PA Todd Helton 1.00
8PA Jim Thome .50
9PA Troy Glaus 1.00
10PA Manny Ramirez 1.00
11PA Jeff Bagwell 1.00
12PA Jason Giambi .75
13PA Chipper Jones 1.50
14PA Mike Piazza 2.00
15PA Albert Pujols 3.00

2002 FLEER BOX SCORE

NM/M
Complete Set (310):
Common Player: .25
Common (126-150): 3.00
Production 2,499
Complete Rising Star set (40): 30.00
Common (151-190): 1.00
Complete Intl. Set (40): 18.00
Common (191-230): 1.00
Complete All-Star set (40): 20.00
Common (231-270): 1.00
Comp. Cooperstown set (40): 30.00
Common Cooperstown (271-310): 1.00
Print run for all subsets is 2,950
Pack (7): 5.00
Box (18 packs + supp. box): 80.00
1 Derek Jeter 2.00
2 Kevin Brown .25
3 Nomar Garciaparra 1.25
4 Mark Buehrle .25
5 Mike Piazza 1.25
6 David Justice .25
7 Tino Martinez .25
8 Paul Konerko .25
9 Larry Walker .25
10 Ben Sheets .25
11 Mike Cameron .25
12 David Wells .25
13 Barry Zito .35
14 Pat Burrell .45
15 Mike Mussina .50
16 Bud Smith .25
17 Brian Jordan .25
18 Chris Singleton .25
19 Daryle Ward .25
20 Russ Ortiz .25
21 Jason Kendall .25
22 Kerry Wood .65
23 Jeff Weaver .25
24 Tony Armas .25
25 Toby Hall .25
26 Brian Giles .25
27 Juan Pierre .25
28 Ken Griffey Jr. 1.25
29 Mike Sweeney .25
30 John Smoltz .25
31 Sean Casey .35
32 Jeremy Giambi .25
33 Mike Lieberthal .25
34 Rich Aurilia .25
35 Matt Lawton .25
36 Dmitri Young .25
37 Wade Miller .25
38 Jason Giambi .65
39 Jeff Cirillo .25
40 Mark Grace .35
41 Frank Thomas .75
42 Preston Wilson .25
43 Brad Radke .25
44 Greg Maddux 1.00
45 Adam Dunn .50
46 Roy Oswalt .35
47 Troy Glaus .75
48 Edgar Martinez .25
49 Billy Koch .25
50 Chipper Jones 1.00
51 Lance Berkman .25
52 Shannon Stewart .25
53 Eddie Guardado .25
54 C.C. Sabathia .25
55 Craig Biggio .25
56 Roger Clemens 1.00
57 Jimmy Rollins .25
58 Carlos Delgado .50
59 Tony Clark .25
60 Mike Hampton .25
61 Jeromy Burnitz .25
62 Jorge Posada .35
63 Todd Helton .75
64 Richie Sexson .25
65 Ryan Klesko .25
66 Cliff Floyd .25
67 Eric Milton .25
68 Scott Rolen .65
69 Steve Finley .25
70 Ray Durham .25
71 Jeff Bagwell .75
72 Geoff Jenkins .25
73 Jamie Moyer .25
74 David Eckstein .25
75 Johnny Damon .40
76 Pokey Reese .25
77 Mo Vaughn .25
78 Trevor Hoffman .25
79 Albert Pujols 1.50
80 Ben Grieve .25
81 Matt Morris .25
82 Aubrey Huff .25
83 Darin Erstad .60
84 Garret Anderson .25
85 Jacque Jones .25
86 Matt Anderson .25
87 Jose Vidro .25
88 Carlos Lee .25
89 Jeff Suppan .25
90 Al Leiter .25
91 Jeff Kent .25

92	Randy Johnson	.75
93	Moises Alou	.25
94	Bobby Higginson	.25
95	Phil Nevin	.25
96	Alex Rodriguez	1.50
97	Luis Gonzalez	.40
98	A.J. Burnett	.25
99	Torii Hunter	.25
100	Ivan Rodriguez	.60
101	Pedro J. Martinez	.75
102	Brady Anderson	.25
103	Paul LoDuca	.25
104	Eric Chavez	.35
105	Tim Salmon	.35
106	Javier Vazquez	.25
107	Bret Boone	.25
108	Greg Vaughn	.25
109	J.D. Drew	.40
110	Jay Gibbons	.25
111	Jim Thome	.25
112	Shawn Green	.40
113	Tim Hudson	.35
114	John Olerud	.25
115	Raul Mondesi	.25
116	Curt Schilling	.50
117	Corey Patterson	.25
118	Robert Fick	.25
119	Corey Koskie	.25
120	Juan Gonzalez	.75
121	Jerry Hairston Jr.	.25
122	Gary Sheffield	.40
123	Mark Mulder	.25
124	Barry Bonds	2.00
125	Jim Edmonds	.25
126	*Franklyn German*	3.00
127	*Rodrigo Rosario*	3.00
128	Ryan Ludwick	3.00
129	*Jorge de la Rosa*	4.00
130	Jason Lane	3.00
131	*Brian Mallette*	3.00
132	*Chris Baker*	3.00
133	*Kyle Kane*	3.00
134	*Doug Devore*	3.00
135	*Raul Chavez*	3.00
136	*Miguel Asencio*	3.00
137	Luis Garcia	3.00
138	Nick Johnson	3.00
139	*Michael Crudale*	3.00
140	*P.J. Bevis*	3.00
141	*Josh Hancock*	3.00
142	*Jeremy Lambert*	3.00
143	Ben Broussard	3.00
144	*John Ennis*	3.00
145	*Wilson Valdez*	3.00
146	*Eric Good*	3.00
147	*Elio Serrano*	3.00
148	*Jaime Cerda*	3.00
149	Hank Blalock	5.00
150	Brandon Duckworth	3.00
151	Drew Henson	1.50
152	*Kazuhisa Ishii*	3.00
153	*Earl Snyder*	1.00
154	J.M. Gold	1.00
155	*Satoru Komiyama*	1.00
156	Marlon Byrd	1.00
157	*So Taguchi*	2.00
158	Eric Hinske	1.00
159	Mark Prior	4.00
160	*Jorge Padilla*	1.50
161	*Rene Reyes*	1.00
162	*Jorge Nunez*	1.00
163	*Nelson Castro*	1.00
164	*Anderson Machado*	2.00
165	Mark Teixeira	2.00
166	Orlando Hudson	1.00
167	*Edwin Almonte*	1.00
168	*Luis Ugueto*	1.00
169	*Felix Escalona*	1.00
170	*Ron Calloway*	1.00
171	Kevin Mench	1.00
172	*Takahito Nomura*	1.00
173	Sean Burroughs	1.00
174	*Steve Kent*	1.00
175	*Jorge Sosa*	1.00
176	*Mike Moriarty*	1.00
177	Carlos Pena	1.00
178	*Anastacio Martinez*	1.00
179	*Reed Johnson*	1.00
180	*Juan Brito*	1.00
181	Wilson Betemit	1.00
182	Mike Rivera	1.00
183	David Espinosa	1.00
184	*Todd Donovan*	1.00
185	Morgan Ensberg	1.00
186	Dewon Brazelton	1.00
187	*Ben Howard*	1.00
188	Austin Kearns	2.00
189	Josh Beckett	2.00
190	*Brandon Backe*	1.50
191	Ichiro Suzuki	4.00
192	Tsuyoshi Shinjo	1.00
193	Hideo Nomo	2.00
194	Kazuhiro Sasaki	1.00
195	Edgardo Alfonzo	1.00
196	Chan Ho Park	1.00
197	Carlos Hernandez	1.00
198	Byung Kim	1.00
199	Omar Vizquel	1.00
200	Freddy Garcia	1.00
201	Richard Hidalgo	1.00
202	Magglio Ordonez	1.00
203	Bobby Abreu	1.00
204	Roger Cedeno	1.00
205	Andruw Jones	2.00
206	Mariano Rivera	1.50
207	Jose Macias	1.00
208	Orlando Hernandez	1.00
209	Rafael Palmeiro	2.00
210	Danys Baez	1.00
211	Bernie Williams	1.25
212	Carlos Beltran	3.00
213	Roberto Alomar	1.50
214	Jose Cruz Jr.	1.00
215	Ryan Dempster	1.00
216	Erubiel Durazo	1.00
217	Carlos Pena	1.00
218	Sammy Sosa	4.00
219	Adrian Beltre	1.50
220	Aramis Ramirez	1.00
221	Alfonso Soriano	2.00
222	Vladimir Guerrero	2.00
223	Juan Uribe	1.00
224	Cristian Guzman	1.00
225	Manny Ramirez	2.00
226	Juan Cruz	1.00
227	Ramon Ortiz	1.00
228	Juan Encarnacion	1.00
229	Bartolo Colon	1.00
230	Miguel Tejada	1.25
231	Cal Ripken Jr.	6.00
232	Derek Jeter	6.00
233	Pedro J. Martinez	2.00
234	Roberto Alomar	1.50
235	Sandy Alomar	1.00
236	Mike Piazza	4.00
237	Jeff Conine	1.00
238	Fred McGriff	1.00
239	Kirby Puckett	3.00
240	Ken Griffey Jr.	4.00
241	Roger Clemens	3.50
242	Joe Morgan	1.00
243	Willie McCovey	1.00
244	Brooks Robinson	1.00
245	Juan Marichal	1.00
246	Todd Helton	2.00
247	Alex Rodriguez	5.00
248	Barry Bonds	6.00
249	Nomar Garciaparra	4.00
250	Jeff Bagwell	2.00
251	Kenny Lofton	1.00
252	Barry Larkin	1.00
253	Tom Glavine	1.50
254	Magglio Ordonez	1.00
255	Randy Johnson	2.00
256	Chipper Jones	3.00
257	Kevin Brown	1.00
258	Rickey Henderson	2.00
259	Greg Maddux	3.00
260	Jim Thome	1.00
261	Rafael Palmeiro	1.50
262	Frank Thomas	2.00
263	Manny Ramirez	2.00
264	Travis Fryman	1.00
265	Gary Sheffield	1.25
266	Bernie Williams	1.25
267	Matt Williams	1.00
268	Ivan Rodriguez	1.50
269	Mike Mussina	1.25
270	Larry Walker	1.00
271	Jim Palmer	1.00
272	Cal Ripken Jr.	6.00
273	Brooks Robinson	1.00
274	Bobby Doerr	1.00
275	Ernie Banks	2.00
276	Fergie Jenkins	1.00
277	Luis Aparicio	1.00
278	Hoyt Wilhelm	1.00
279	Tom Seaver	1.50
280	Joe Morgan	1.00
281	Lou Boudreau	1.00
282	Larry Doby	1.00
283	Jim Bunning	1.00
284	George Kell	1.00
285	Pee Wee Reese	1.50
286	Eddie Mathews	1.00
287	Robin Yount	2.00
288	Rod Carew	1.00
289	Monte Irvin	1.00
290	Yogi Berra	2.00
291	Whitey Ford	2.00
292	Reggie Jackson	2.00
293	Rollie Fingers	1.00
294	Jim "Catfish" Hunter	1.00
295	Richie Ashburn	1.00
296	Willie Stargell	1.00
297	Ralph Kiner	1.00
298	Orlando Cepeda	1.00
299	Juan Marichal	1.00
300	Gaylord Perry	1.00
301	Willie McCovey	1.00
302	Red Schoendienst	1.00
303	Nolan Ryan	8.00
304	Bob Gibson	1.00
305	Al Kaline	1.00
306	Harmon Killebrew	1.00
307	Stan Musial	3.00
308	Phil Rizzuto	1.00
309	Mike Schmidt	4.00
310	Enos Slaughter	1.00

First Edition

Cards (1-125): 4-8X
Cards (126-150): .5-1X
Cards (151-310): 1-2X
Production 100 sets

All-Star Lineup

NM/M

Common Card: 15.00
1:All-Stars Box

Derek Jeter, Nomar Garciaparra, Alex Rodriguez 50.00
Joe Morgan, Willie McCovey, Brooks Robinson 15.00
Alex Rodriguez, Ivan Rodriguez, Rafael Palmeiro 20.00
Derek Jeter, Mike Mussina, Bernie Williams 35.00
Barry Bonds, Cal Ripken Jr., Frank Thomas 60.00
Cal Ripken Jr., Derek Jeter, Roberto Alomar, Pedro J. Martinez 60.00
Mike Piazza, Barry Bonds, Ken Griffey Jr., Jeff Bagwell 40.00
Roger Clemens, Greg Maddux, Randy Johnson, Pedro J. Martinez 35.00
Todd Helton, Roberto Alomar, Alex Rodriguez, Chipper Jones 25.00
Ken Griffey Jr., Barry Bonds, Larry Walker, Manny Ramirez 35.00

Amazing Greats Patch

NM/M

Common Player: 15.00
Production 150 sets

Derek Jeter	50.00
Barry Bonds	50.00
Mike Piazza	25.00
Ivan Rodriguez	25.00
Nomar Garciaparra	40.00
Bernie Williams	25.00
Kazuhiro Sasaki	15.00
Torii Hunter	25.00
Bret Boone	15.00
Rafael Palmeiro	25.00
Scott Rolen	25.00
Carlos Delgado	20.00
Lance Berkman	15.00
Frank Thomas	25.00
Greg Maddux	30.00

Amazing Greats

NM/M

Complete Set (20): 20.00
Common Player: .50
Inserted 1:5

1AG	Derek Jeter	4.00
2AG	Barry Bonds	4.00
3AG	Mike Piazza	2.50
4AG	Ivan Rodriguez	.75
5AG	Todd Helton	1.00
6AG	Nomar Garciaparra	2.50
7AG	Jim Thome	.50
8AG	Bernie Williams	.50
9AG	Kazuhiro Sasaki	.50
10AG	Torii Hunter	.50
11AG	Bret Boone	.50
12AG	Tim Hudson	.50
13AG	Randy Johnson	1.00
14AG	Rafael Palmeiro	.75
15AG	Scott Rolen	.75
16AG	Carlos Delgado	.75
17AG	Chipper Jones	2.00
18AG	Lance Berkman	.50
19AG	Frank Thomas	1.00
20AG	Greg Maddux	2.00

Amazing Greats Single Swatch

NM/M

Common Player: 5.00
Inserted 1:13
Dual Swatches: 1-2X
Inserted 1:90

Derek Jeter	20.00
Barry Bonds	20.00
Mike Piazza	10.00
Ivan Rodriguez	8.00
Nomar Garciaparra	15.00
Jim Thome/bat	10.00
Bernie Williams	8.00
Kazuhiro Sasaki	5.00
Torii Hunter	6.00
Bret Boone	5.00
Rafael Palmeiro	8.00
Scott Rolen	8.00
Carlos Delgado	8.00
Lance Berkman	5.00
Frank Thomas	8.00
Greg Maddux	10.00

Bat Rack

NM/M

Common Card: 20.00
Production 300 sets

1BR	Derek Jeter, Alfonso Soriano, Bernie Williams	60.00
2BR	Mike Piazza, Roberto Alomar, Mo Vaughn	30.00
3BR	Jeff Bagwell, Lance Berkman, Craig Biggio	30.00
4BR	Eric Chavez, Miguel Tejada, Carlos Pena	15.00
5BR	Alex Rodriguez, Ivan Rodriguez, Rafael Palmeiro	30.00
6BR	Chipper Jones, Gary Sheffield, Andruw Jones	20.00
7BR	Carlos Delgado, Jim Thome, Frank Thomas	20.00
8BR	Derek Jeter, Nomar Garciaparra, Alex Rodriguez	60.00
9BR	Barry Bonds, Adam Dunn, Chipper Jones	35.00
10BR	Magglio Ordonez, Juan Gonzalez, Manny Ramirez	20.00

Bat Rack Quad

NM/M

Common Card 25.00
Production 150 sets

Torii Hunter, Cristian Guzman, Frank Thomas, Maggio Ordonez 25.00
Alex Rodriguez, Ivan Rodriguez, Eric Chavez, Miguel Tejada 40.00
Mike Piazza, Roberto Alomar, Alfonso Soriano, Derek Jeter 80.00
Barry Bonds, Lance Berkman, Alex Rodriguez, Nomar Garciaparra 75.00
Barry Bonds, Chipper Jones, Mike Piazza, Ivan Rodriguez 75.00
Derek Jeter, Miguel Tejada, Nomar Garciaparra, Alex Rodriguez 75.00
Roberto Alomar, Mo Vaughn, Jeff Bagwell, Craig Biggio 25.00
Jim Palmer, Carlos Delgado, Jim Thome, Frank Thomas 25.00

Magglio Ordonez,
Bernie Williams,
Juan Gonzalez,
Manny Ramirez 25.00
Chipper Jones, Adam Dunn,
Jeff Bagwell,
Mo Vaughn 25.00
Alex Rodriguez, Jim Palmer,
Bernie Williams,
Alfonso Soriano 40.00
Carlos Pena, Eric Chavez,
Carlos Delgado,
Juan Gonzalez 20.00
Adam Dunn, Lance Berkman,
Jim Thome,
Manny Ramirez 25.00

Box Score Debuts

NM/M

Complete Set (15): 40.00
Common Player: 2.50
Production 2,002 sets

1	Hank Blalock	6.00
2	Eric Hinske	3.00
3	Kazuhisa Ishii	5.00
4	Sean Burroughs	3.00
5	Andres Torres	2.50
6	Satoru Komiyama	2.50
7	Mark Prior	15.00
8	Kevin Mench	2.50
9	Austin Kearns	3.00
10	Earl Snyder	2.50
11	Jon Rauch	2.50
12	Jason Lane	2.50
13	Ben Howard	2.50
14	Bobby Hill	2.50
15	Dennis Tankersley	2.50

Classic Miniatures

NM/M

Complete Set (40): 25.00
Stars: 1.5-3X base card
Production 2,950 sets
One set per classic mini box
First Editions: 4-8X
Production 100 sets

Classic Miniatures Game-Used

NM/M

Common Player: 6.00
One per Classic Mini box

Derek Jeter/bat	20.00
Mike Piazza/jsy	10.00
Adam Dunn/jsy	6.00
Chipper Jones/bat	10.00
Roger Clemens/jsy	15.00
Alex Rodriguez/jsy	10.00
Pedro Martinez/jsy	10.00
Jim Thome/bat	10.00
Curt Schilling/jsy	8.00
Barry Bonds/bat	20.00

Hall of Fame Material

NM/M

Common Player: 8.00
1:Cooperstown box

Jim Palmer/jsy	8.00
Cal Ripken Jr/jsy	25.00
Brooks Robinson/bat	10.00
Joe Morgan/bat	8.00
Eddie Mathews/bat	10.00
Robin Yount/jsy	15.00
Reggie Jackson/jsy	10.00
"Catfish" Hunter/jsy	8.00
Willie McCovey/jsy	8.00
Nolan Ryan/jsy	30.00

Press Clippings

NM/M

Complete Set (20): 90.00
Common Player: 4.00
Inserted 1:90

1PC	Mark Mulder	4.00
2PC	Curt Schilling	6.00
3PC	Alfonso Soriano	7.50
4PC	Jeff Bagwell	7.50
5PC	J.D. Drew	5.00
6PC	Pedro J. Martinez	7.50
7PC	Bobby Abreu	4.00
8PC	Alex Rodriguez	12.00
9PC	Mike Sweeney	4.00
10PC	Carlos Pena	4.00
11PC	Josh Beckett	6.00
12PC	Roger Clemens	9.00
13PC	Manny Ramirez	7.50
14PC	Adam Dunn	6.00
15PC	Kazuhisa Ishii	4.00
16PC	Ken Griffey Jr.	10.00
17PC	Sammy Sosa	10.00
18PC	Ichiro Suzuki	9.00
19PC	Albert Pujols	15.00
20PC	Troy Glaus	7.50

Press Clippings Game-Used

NM/M

Common Player: 5.00
Inserted 1:13

Mark Mulder/jsy	5.00
Curt Schilling/jsy	8.00
Alfonso Soriano/bat	10.00
Jeff Bagwell/jsy	8.00
J.D. Drew/jsy	5.00
Pedro Martinez/jsy	10.00
Bobby Abreu/jsy	5.00
Alex Rodriguez/jsy	10.00
Mike Sweeney/jsy	5.00
Carlos Pena/jsy	5.00
Josh Beckett/jsy	8.00
Manny Ramirez/jsy	10.00
Adam Dunn/jsy	6.00
Kazuhisa Ishii/jsy	10.00
Ken Griffey Jr/base	10.00
Sammy Sosa/base	15.00
Ichiro Suzuki/base	15.00
Albert Pujols/base	10.00
Troy Glaus/base	5.00
Roger Clemens/jsy/40	

Wave of the Future

NM/M

Common Player: 4.00
1: Rising Stars box

1WF	Drew Henson/bat	5.00
2WF	Kazuhisa Ishii/bat	5.00
3WF	Marlon Byrd/jsy	4.00
4WF	So Taguchi/bat	4.00
5WF	Jorge Padilla/pants/75	10.00
6WF	Rene Reyes/jsy	4.00
7WF	Mark Teixeira/100	10.00
8WF	Carlos Pena/bat	4.00
9WF	Austin Kearns/pants	6.00
10WF	Josh Beckett/jsy/50	15.00

World Piece

NM/M

Common Player: 4.00
1:International box

1WP	Ichiro Suzuki/base	20.00
2WP	Tsuyoshi Shinjo/bat	4.00
3WP	Hideo Nomo/jsy	20.00
4WP	Kazuhiro Sasaki/jsy	4.00
5WP	Chan Ho Park/jsy	4.00
6WP	Magglio Ordonez/jsy	6.00
7WP	Andruw Jones/jsy	8.00
8WP	Rafael Palmeiro/jsy	10.00
9WP	Bernie Williams/jsy	10.00
10WP	Roberto Alomar/bat	6.00

2002 FLEER E-X

NM/M

Complete Set (140):
Common Player: .25
Common SP (101-125): 3.00
Common (126-140): 5.00
Inserted 1:24
Pack (4): 2.50
Box (24): 40.00

1	Alex Rodriguez	1.50
2	Albert Pujols	1.50
3	Ken Griffey Jr.	1.25
4	Vladimir Guerrero	.75
5	Sammy Sosa	1.25
6	Ichiro Suzuki	1.25
7	Jorge Posada	.35
8	Matt Williams	.25
9	Adrian Beltre	.40
10	Pat Burrell	.40
11	Roger Cedeno	.25
12	Tony Clark	.25
13	Steve Finley	.25
14	Rafael Furcal	.25
15	Rickey Henderson	.75
16	Richard Hidalgo	.25
17	Jason Kendall	.25
18	Tino Martinez	.25
19	Scott Rolen	.65
20	Shannon Stewart	.25
21	Jose Vidro	.25
22	Preston Wilson	.25
23	Raul Mondesi	.25
24	Lance Berkman	.25
25	Rick Ankiel	.25
26	Kevin Brown	.25
27	Jeromy Burnitz	.25
28	Jeff Cirillo	.25
29	Carl Everett	.25
30	Eric Chavez	.35
31	Freddy Garcia	.25
32	Mark Grace	.35
33	David Justice	.25
34	Fred McGriff	.25
35	Mike Mussina	.50
36	John Olerud	.25
37	Magglio Ordonez	.25
38	Curt Schilling	.50
39	Aaron Sele	.25
40	Robin Ventura	.25
41	Adam Dunn	.50
42	Jeff Bagwell	.75
43	Barry Bonds	2.00
44	Roger Clemens	1.00
45	Cliff Floyd	.25
46	Jason Giambi	.50
47	Juan Gonzalez	.75
48	Luis Gonzalez	.35
49	Cristian Guzman	.25
50	Todd Helton	.75
51	Derek Jeter	2.00
52	Rafael Palmeiro	.65
53	Mike Sweeney	.25
54	Ben Grieve	.25
55	Phil Nevin	.25
56	Mike Piazza	1.25
57	Moises Alou	.25
58	Ivan Rodriguez	.65
59	Manny Ramirez	.75
60	Brian Giles	.25
61	Jim Thome	.25
62	Larry Walker	.25
63	Bobby Abreu	.25
64	Troy Glaus	.75
65	Garret Anderson	.25
66	Roberto Alomar	.40
67	Bret Boone	.25
68	Marty Cardova	.25
69	Craig Biggio	.25
70	Omar Vizquel	.25
71	Jermaine Dye	.25
72	Darin Erstad	.60
73	Carlos Delgado	.50
74	Nomar Garciaparra	1.25
75	Greg Maddux	1.00
76	Tom Glavine	.40
77	Frank Thomas	.75
78	Shawn Green	.40
79	Bobby Higginson	.25
80	Jeff Kent	.25
81	Chuck Knoblauch	.25
82	Paul Konerko	.25
83	Carlos Lee	.25
84	Jon Lieber	.25
85	Paul LoDuca	.25
86	Mike Lowell	.25
87	Edgar Martinez	.25
88	Doug Mientkiewicz	.25
89	Pedro J. Martinez	.75
90	Randy Johnson	.75
91	Aramis Ramirez	.25
92	J.D. Drew	.40
93	Chris Richard	.25
94	Jimmy Rollins	.25
95	Ryan Klesko	.25
96	Gary Sheffield	.40
97	Chipper Jones	1.00
98	Greg Vaughn	.25
99	Mo Vaughn	.25
100	Bernie Williams	.35
101	*John Foster/2,999*	3.00
102	*Jorge De La Rosa/2,999*	4.00
103	*Edwin Almonte/2,999*	3.00
104	*Chris Booker/2,999*	3.00
105	*Victor Alvarez/2,999*	3.00
106	*Clifford Bartosh2,999*	3.00
107	*Felix Escalona/2,999*	3.00
108	*Corey Thurman/2,999*	3.00
109	*Kazuhisa Ishii/2,999*	6.00
110	*Miguel Ascencio/2,999*	3.00
111	*P.J. Bevis/2,499*	3.00
112	*Gustavo Chacin/2,499*	3.00
113	*Steve Kent/2,499*	3.00
114	*Takahito Nomura/2,499*	3.00
115	*Adam Walker/2,499*	3.00
116	*So Taguchi/2,499*	5.00
117	*Reed Johnson/2,499*	5.00
118	*Rodrigo Rosario/2,499*	3.00
119	*Luis Martinez/2,499*	4.00
120	*Satoru Komiyama/2,499*	3.00
121	Sean Burroughs/1,999	3.00
122	Hank Blalock/1,999	5.00
123	Marlon Byrd/1,999	3.00
124	Nick Johnson/1,999	3.00
125	Mark Teixeira/1,999	5.00
126	David Espinosa	3.00
127	*Adrian Burnside*	3.00
128	*Mark Corey*	3.00
129	Matt Thornton	3.00
130	Dane Sardinha	3.00
131	Juan Rivera	3.00
132	Austin Kearns	5.00
134	Ben Broussard	3.00
135	Orlando Hudson	3.00
136	Carlos Pena	3.00
137	Kenny Kelly	3.00
138	Bill Hall	3.00
139	Ron Chiavacci	3.00
140	Mark Prior	8.00

Essential Credentials Now

Quantity produced listed

19	Scott Rolen Bat/19	45.00
20	Shannon Stewart Bat/20	
21	Jose Vidro Bat/21	
22	Preston Wilson Bat/22	15.00
23	Raul Mondesi Bat/23	
24	Lance Berkman Bat/24	20.00
25	Rick Ankiel Jsy/25	15.00
26	Kevin Brown Jsy/26	20.00
27	Jeromy Burnitz Bat/27	20.00
28	Jeff Cirillo Jsy/28	15.00
29	Carl Everett Jsy/29	15.00
30	Eric Chavez Bat/30	20.00
31	Freddy Garcia Jsy/31	15.00
32	Mark Grace Jsy/32	20.00
33	David Justice Jsy/33	15.00
34	Fred McGriff Jsy/34	15.00
35	Mike Mussina Jsy/35	25.00
36	John Olerud Jsy/36	10.00
37	Magglio Ordonez Jsy/37	15.00
38	Curt Schilling Jsy/38	20.00
39	Aaron Sele Jsy/39	10.00
40	Robin Ventura Jsy/40	10.00
41	Adam Dunn Bat/41	15.00
42	Jeff Bagwell Jsy/42	20.00
43	Barry Bonds Pants/43	75.00
44	Roger Clemens Bat/44	50.00
45	Cliff Floyd Bat/45	10.00
46	Jason Giambi Base/46	15.00
47	Juan Gonzalez Jsy/47	15.00
48	Luis Gonzalez Base/48	10.00
49	Cristian Guzman Bat/49	10.00
50	Todd Helton Base/50	15.00
51	Derek Jeter Bat/51	60.00
52	Rafael Palmeiro Bat/52	20.00
53	Mike Sweeney Bat/53	10.00
54	Ben Grieve Jsy/54	5.00
55	Phil Nevin Bat/55	8.00
56	Mike Piazza Base/56	20.00
57	Moises Alou Bat/57	10.00
58	Ivan Rodriguez Jsy/58	15.00
59	Manny Ramirez Base/59	10.00
60	Brian Giles Bat/60	10.00
61	Jim Thome/61	15.00
62	Larry Walker/62	5.00
63	Bobby Abreu/63	5.00
64	Troy Glaus/64	8.00
65	Garret Anderson/65	8.00
66	Roberto Alomar/66	8.00
67	Bret Boone/67	5.00
68	Marty Cordova/68	4.00
69	Craig Biggio/69	5.00
70	Omar Vizquel/70	4.00
71	Jermaine Dye/71	4.00
72	Darin Erstad/72	5.00
73	Carlos Delgado/73	6.00
74	Nomar Garciaparra/74	15.00
75	Greg Maddux/75	15.00
76	Tom Glavine/76	5.00
77	Frank Thomas/77	8.00
78	Shawn Green/78	6.00
79	Bobby Higginson/79	4.00
80	Jeff Kent/80	5.00
81	Chuck Knoblauch/81	4.00
82	Paul Konerko/82	5.00
83	Carlos Lee/83	5.00

No.	Player	NM/M
84	Jon Lieber/84	5.00
85	Paul LoDuca/85	5.00
86	Mike Lowell/86	6.00
87	Edgar Martinez/87	6.00
88	Doug Mientkiewicz/88	5.00
89	Pedro J. Martinez/89	10.00
90	Randy Johnson/90	10.00
91	Aramis Ramirez/91	6.00
92	J.D. Drew/92	6.00
93	Chris Richard/93	4.00
94	Jimmy Rollins/94	4.00
95	Ryan Klesko/95	6.00
96	Gary Sheffield/96	6.00
97	Chipper Jones/97	10.00
98	Greg Vaughn/98	4.00
99	Mo Vaughn/99	5.00
100	Bernie Williams/100	6.00
101	John Foster NT/101	4.00
102	Jorge De La Rosa NT/102	4.00
103	Edwin Almonte NT/103	4.00
104	Chris Booker NT/104	4.00
105	Victor Alvarez NT/105	4.00
106	Clifford Bartosh NT/106	4.00
107	Felix Escalona NT/107	4.00
108	Corey Thurman NT/108	4.00
109	Kazuhisa Ishii NT/109	10.00
110	Miguel Asencio NT/110	4.00
111	P.J. Bevis NT/111	4.00
112	Gustavo Chacin NT/112	4.00
113	Steve Kent NT/113	4.00
114	Takahito Nomura NT/114	4.00
115	Adam Walker NT/115	4.00
116	So Taguchi NT/116	6.00
117	Reed Johnson NT/117	6.00
118	Rodrigo Rosario NT/118	4.00
119	Luis Martinez NT/119	4.00
120	Satoru Komiyama NT/120	4.00
121	Sean Burroughs NT/121	5.00
122	Hank Blalock NT/122	6.00
123	Marlon Byrd NT/123	4.00
124	Nick Johnson NT/124	4.00
125	Mark Teixeira NT/125	6.00

Essential Credentials Future

Quantity produced listed

No.	Player	NM/M
1	Alex Rodriguez Jsy/60	30.00
2	Albert Pujols Base/59	25.00
3	Ken Griffey Jr. Base/58	20.00
4	Vladimir Guerrero Base/57	15.00
5	Sammy Sosa Base/56	25.00
6	Ichiro Suzuki Base/55	40.00
7	Jorge Posada Bat/54	12.00
8	Matt Williams Bat/53	8.00
9	Adrian Beltre Bat/52	8.00
10	Pat Burrell Bat/51	10.00
11	Roger Cedeno Bat/50	8.00
12	Tony Clark Bat/49	8.00
13	Steve Finley Bat/48	8.00
14	Rafael Furcal Bat/47	12.00
15	Rickey Henderson Bat/46	20.00
16	Richard Hidalgo Bat/45	10.00
17	Jason Kendall Bat/44	10.00
18	Tino Martinez Bat/43	15.00
19	Scott Rolen Bat/42	20.00
20	Shannon Stewart Bat/41	10.00
21	Jose Vidro Bat/40	10.00
22	Preston Wilson Bat/39	10.00
23	Raul Mondesi Bat/38	10.00
24	Lance Berkman Bat/37	10.00
25	Rick Ankiel Jsy/36	8.00
26	Kevin Brown Jsy/35	10.00
27	Jeromy Burnitz Bat/34	8.00
28	Jeff Cirillo Jsy/33	8.00
29	Carl Everett Jsy/32	8.00
30	Eric Chavez Bat/31	10.00
31	Freddy Garcia Jsy/30	10.00
32	Mark Grace Jsy/29	20.00
33	David Justice Jsy/28	15.00
34	Fred McGriff Jsy/27	15.00
35	Mike Mussina Jsy/26	
36	John Olerud Jsy/25	
37	Magglio Ordonez Jsy/24	15.00
38	Curt Schilling Jsy/23	30.00
61	Jim Thome/125	8.00
62	Larry Walker/124	4.00
63	Bobby Abreu/123	4.00
64	Troy Glaus/122	6.00
65	Garret Anderson/121	6.00
66	Roberto Alomar/120	6.00
67	Bret Boone/119	6.00
68	Marty Cordova/118	4.00
69	Craig Biggio/117	4.00
70	Omar Vizquel/116	4.00
71	Jermaine Dye/115	4.00
72	Darin Erstad/114	4.00
73	Carlos Delgado/113	6.00
74	Nomar Garciaparra/112	10.00
75	Greg Maddux/111	10.00
76	Tom Glavine/110	6.00
77	Frank Thomas/109	6.00
78	Shawn Green/108	5.00
79	Bobby Higginson/107	3.00
80	Jeff Kent/106	4.00
81	Chuck Knoblauch/105	3.00
82	Paul Konerko/104	3.00
83	Carlos Lee/103	3.00
84	Jon Lieber/102	3.00
85	Paul LoDuca/101	3.00
86	Mike Lowell/100	4.00
87	Edgar Martinez/99	4.00
88	Doug Mientkiewicz/98	3.00
89	Pedro J. Martinez/97	8.00
90	Randy Johnson/96	8.00
91	Aramis Ramirez/95	4.00
92	J.D. Drew/94	4.00
93	Chris Richard/93	3.00
94	Jimmy Rollins/92	3.00
95	Ryan Klesko/91	4.00
96	Gary Sheffield/90	4.00
97	Chipper Jones/89	8.00
98	Greg Vaughn/88	3.00
99	Mo Vaughn/87	3.00
100	Bernie Williams/86	5.00
101	John Foster NT/85	3.00
102	Jorge De La Rosa NT/84	3.00
103	Edwin Almonte NT/83	3.00
104	Chris Booker NT/82	3.00
105	Victor Alvarez NT/81	3.00
106	Clifford Bartosh NT/80	3.00
107	Felix Escalona NT/79	3.00
108	Corey Thurman NT/78	3.00
109	Kazuhisa Ishii NT/77	12.00
110	Miguel Asencio NT/76	3.00
111	P.J. Bevis NT/75	3.00
112	Gustavo Chacin NT/74	3.00
113	Steve Kent NT/73	3.00
114	Takahito Nomura NT/72	3.00
115	Adam Walker NT/71	3.00
116	So Taguchi NT/70	6.00
117	Reed Johnson NT/69	6.00
118	Rodrigo Rosario NT/68	4.00
119	Luis Martinez NT/67	5.00
120	Satoru Komiyama NT/66	4.00
121	Sean Burroughs NT/65	5.00
122	Hank Blalock NT/64	6.00
123	Marlon Byrd NT/63	4.00
124	Nick Johnson NT/62	4.00
125	Mark Teixeira NT/61	6.00

Barry Bonds 4X MVP

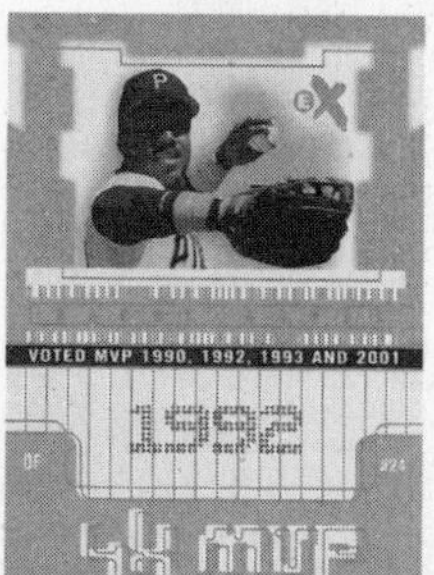

		NM/M
Complete Set (4):		20.00
Common Bonds:		6.00
1BB4X	Barry Bonds/1990	6.00
2BB4X	Barry Bonds/1,992	6.00
3BB4X	Barry Bonds/1,993	6.00
4BB4X	Barry Bonds/2,001	6.00

Behind the Numbers

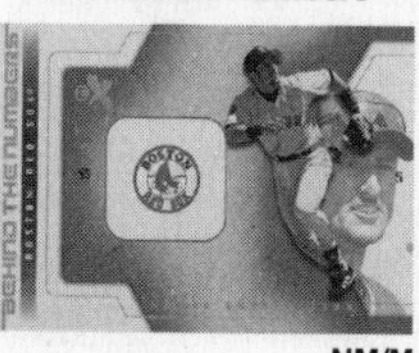

		NM/M
Complete Set (35):		75.00
Common Player:		1.00
Inserted 1:8		
1BTN	Ichiro Suzuki	5.00
2BTN	Jason Giambi	2.50
3BTN	Mike Piazza	5.00
4BTN	Brian Giles	1.00
5BTN	Barry Bonds	8.00
6BTN	Pedro J. Martinez	3.00
7BTN	Nomar Garciaparra	5.00
8BTN	Randy Johnson	3.00
9BTN	Craig Biggio	1.00
10BTN	Manny Ramirez	3.00
11BTN	Mike Mussina	1.50
12BTN	Kerry Wood	2.50
13BTN	Jim Edmonds	1.00
14BTN	Ivan Rodriguez	2.50
15BTN	Jeff Bagwell	3.00
16BTN	Roger Clemens	4.50
17BTN	Chipper Jones	4.00
18BTN	Shawn Green	1.25
19BTN	Albert Pujols	6.00
20BTN	Andruw Jones	3.00
21BTN	Luis Gonzalez	1.00
22BTN	Todd Helton	3.00
23BTN	Jorge Posada	1.25
24BTN	Scott Rolen	2.50
25BTN	Ben Sheets	1.00
26BTN	Alfonso Soriano	2.50
27BTN	Greg Maddux	4.00
28BTN	Gary Sheffield	1.25
29BTN	Barry Zito	1.25
30BTN	Alex Rodriguez	6.00
31BTN	Larry Walker	1.00
32BTN	Derek Jeter	8.00
33BTN	Ken Griffey Jr.	5.00
34BTN	Vladimir Guerrero	3.00
35BTN	Sammy Sosa	5.00

Behind the Numbers Game Jersey

		NM/M
Common Player:		5.00
Inserted 1:24		
1	Jeff Bagwell	10.00
2	Craig Biggio Pants	5.00
3	Barry Bonds SP/50	
4	Roger Clemens	20.00
5	Jim Edmonds	5.00
6	Brian Giles	5.00
7	Luis Gonzalez	5.00
8	Shawn Green	5.00
9	Todd Helton	8.00
10	Derek Jeter SP	30.00
11	Randy Johnson SP	10.00
12	Andruw Jones	8.00
13	Chipper Jones	10.00
14	Greg Maddux	10.00
15	Pedro J. Martinez	10.00
16	Mike Mussina	10.00
17	Mike Piazza Pants	10.00
18	Jorge Posada	8.00
19	Manny Ramirez	8.00
20	Alex Rodriguez	10.00
21	Ivan Rodriguez	8.00
22	Scott Rolen	8.00
23	Alfonso Soriano SP	10.00
24	Barry Zito	6.00

Behind the Numbers Game Jersey Dual

No Pricing
Production 25 sets

1	Craig Biggio, Ivan Rodriguez
2	Barry Bonds, Andruw Jones
3	Jim Edmonds, Shawn Green
4	Brian Giles, Manny Ramirez
5	Greg Maddux, Mike Piazza
6	Scott Rolen, Todd Helton
7	Alfonso Soriano, Larry Walker

Derek Jeter 4X Champ

		NM/M
Complete Set (4):		20.00
Common Jeter:		6.00
1DJFX	Derek Jeter/1,996	6.00
2DJFX	Derek Jeter/1,998	6.00
3DJFX	Derek Jeter/1,999	6.00
4DJFX	Derek Jeter/2,000	6.00

Game Essentials

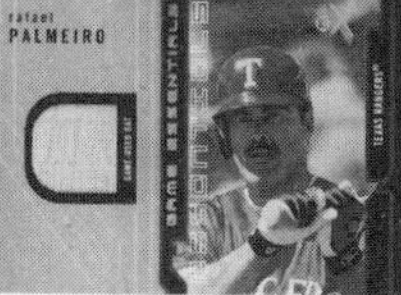

	NM/M
Common Player:	5.00
Carlos Beltran	5.00
Barry Bonds/batting glove	
Barry Bonds/wristband	
Kevin Brown	5.00
Jeromy Burnitz	5.00
Carlos Delgado	8.00
Jason Hart/SP	8.00
Rickey Henderson	20.00
Drew Henson/shoe	5.00
Drew Henson/glove	8.00
Derek Jeter/shoe	40.00
Jason Kendall	5.00
Jeff Kent	10.00
Barry Larkin/glove	20.00
Javy Lopez	8.00
Raul Mondesi/batting glove	8.00
Rafael Palmeiro	10.00
Adam Piatt	5.00
Brad Radke	5.00
Cal Ripken Jr.	30.00
Mariano Rivera	10.00
Alex Rodriguez/batting glove	15.00
Alex Rodriguez/shoe	
Ivan Rodriguez/shoe	10.00
Kazuhiro Sasaki	5.00
J.T. Snow	5.00
Mo Vaughn	5.00
Robin Ventura	8.00
Jose Vidro	5.00
Matt Williams	5.00

HardWear

		NM/M
Complete Set (10):		60.00
Common Player:		4.00
Inserted 1:72 hobby		
1HW	Ivan Rodriguez	4.00
2HW	Mike Piazza	8.00
3HW	Derek Jeter	15.00
4HW	Barry Bonds	15.00
5HW	Todd Helton	4.00
6HW	Roberto Alomar	4.00
7HW	Albert Pujols	10.00
8HW	Ichiro Suzuki	8.00
9HW	Ken Griffey Jr.	8.00
10HW	Jason Giambi	5.00

Hit and Run

		NM/M
Complete Set (30):		50.00
Common Player:		1.00
Inserted 1:12		
1	Adam Dunn	1.00
2	Derek Jeter	6.00
3	Frank Thomas	2.00
4	Albert Pujols	5.00
5	J.D. Drew	1.00
6	Richard Hidalgo	1.00
7	John Olerud	1.00
8	Roberto Alomar	1.00
9	Pat Burrell	1.50
10	Darin Erstad	1.50
11	Mark Grace	1.00
12	Chipper Jones	3.00
13	Jose Vidro	1.00
14	Cliff Floyd	1.00
15	Mo Vaughn	1.00
16	Nomar Garciaparra	4.00
17	Ivan Rodriguez	1.50
18	Luis Gonzalez	1.00
19	Jason Giambi	1.50
20	Bernie Williams	1.00

21 Mike Piazza 4.00
22 Barry Bonds 6.00
23 Jose Ortiz 1.00
24 Magglio Ordonez 1.00
25 Troy Glaus 2.00
26 Alex Rodriguez 5.00
27 Ichiro Suzuki 4.00
28 Sammy Sosa 4.00
29 Ken Griffey Jr. 4.00
30 Vladimir Guerrero 2.00

Hit and Run Game Base

NM/M
Inserted 1:120
1 J.D. Drew 4.00
2 Adam Dunn 6.00
3 Jason Giambi 6.00
4 Troy Glaus 6.00
5 Ken Griffey Jr. 10.00
6 Vladimir Guerrero 8.00
7 Albert Pujols 15.00
8 Sammy Sosa 10.00
9 Ichiro Suzuki 15.00
10 Bernie Williams 6.00

Hit and Run Game Bat and Base

NM/M
Common Player: 10.00
Inserted 1:240
1 Roberto Alomar 15.00
2 Barry Bonds SP 50.00
3 Nomar Garciaparra 30.00
4 Derek Jeter 40.00
5 Chipper Jones 15.00
6 Mike Piazza 20.00
7 Alex Rodriguez 25.00
8 Mo Vaughn 10.00

Hit and Run Game Bat

NM/M
Common Player: 4.00
Inserted 1:24
1 Roberto Alomar 6.00
2 J.D. Drew 4.00
3 Darin Erstad 4.00
4 Cliff Floyd 4.00
5 Nomar Garciaparra 15.00
6 Luis Gonzalez 6.00
7 Richard Hidalgo 4.00
8 Derek Jeter 25.00
9 Chipper Jones 8.00
10 John Olerud 4.00
11 Magglio Ordonez 6.00
12 Jose Ortiz 4.00
13 Mike Piazza 10.00
14 Alex Rodriguez 15.00
15 Ivan Rodriguez 8.00
16 Frank Thomas 8.00
17 Mo Vaughn 4.00
18 Jose Vidro 4.00
19 Bernie Williams 8.00

2002 FLEER FALL CLASSIC

NM/M
Complete Set (100): 30.00
Common Player: .25
Common SP: 3.00
Inserted 1:18 hobby
Pack (5): 5.00
Box (24): 100.00
1 Rabbit Maranville .25
2 Tris Speaker .75
3 Harmon Killebrew 1.00
4 Lou Gehrig 2.00
5 Lou Boudreau .25
6 Al Kaline 1.00
7 Paul Molitor 1.00
7 Paul Molitor/Brewers 4.00
8 Cal Ripken Jr. 3.00
9 Yogi Berra 1.00
10 Phil Rizzuto .75
11 Luis Aparicio .25
11 Luis Aparicio/Orioles 4.00
12 Stan Musial 2.00
13 Mel Ott .75
14 Larry Doby .25
15 Ozzie Smith 1.00
16 Babe Ruth 4.00
16 Babe Ruth/Red Sox 10.00
17 Red Schoendienst .25
17 Red Schoendienst/Cards 3.00
18 Rollie Fingers .25
19 Thurman Munson 1.50
20 Lou Brock .50
21 Paul O'Neill .25
21 Paul O'Neill/Reds 3.00
22 Jim Palmer .50
23 Kirby Puckett 1.00
24 Tony Perez .25
24 Tony Perez/Phila. 3.00
25 Don Larsen .75
26 Steve Garvey .25
26 Steve Garvey/Padres 3.00
27 Jim "Catfish" Hunter .25
27 "Catfish" Hunter/Yanks 4.00
28 Juan Marichal .50
29 Pee Wee Reese .25
30 Orlando Cepeda .25
31 Rich "Goose" Gossage .25
32 Ray Knight .25
33 Eddie Murray .75
34 Nolan Ryan 3.00
35 Alan Trammell .50
36 Grover Alexander .75
37 Joe Carter .25
38 Rogers Hornsby 1.00
39 Jimmie Foxx 1.00
40 Mike Schmidt 1.50
41 Eddie Mathews 1.00
42 Jackie Robinson 1.50
43 Eddie Collins .25
43 Eddie Collins/White Sox 3.00
44 Willie McCovey .25
45 Bob Gibson 1.00
46 Keith Hernandez .50
46 Keith Hernandez/Cards 4.00
47 Brooks Robinson 1.00
48 Mordecai Brown .25
49 Gary Carter .50
50 Kirk Gibson .25
50 Kirk Gibson/Tigers 3.00
51 Johnny Mize .25
52 Johnny Podres .25
53 Darrell Porter .25
54 Willie Stargell .75
55 Lenny Dykstra .25
55 Lenny Dykstra/Phila. 3.00
56 Christy Mathewson .75
57 Walter Johnson 1.00
58 Whitey Ford .75
59 Lefty Grove .50
60 Duke Snider .75
61 Cy Young 1.00
62 Dave Winfield .75
62 Dave Winfield/Yanks 5.00
63 Robin Yount 1.00
64 Fred Lynn .25
65 Ty Cobb 2.00
66 Joe Morgan .25
67 Bill Mazeroski .25
68 Frank Baker .25
69 Chief Bender .25
70 Carlton Fisk .50
71 Jerry Coleman .25
72 Frankie Frisch .25
73 Wade Boggs 1.00
73 Wade Boggs/Yanks 4.00
74 Johnny Bench 1.00
75 Roger Maris 2.00
75 Roger Maris/Cards 8.00
76 Dom DiMaggio .25
77 George Brett 3.00
78 Dave Parker .25
78 Dave Parker/A's 3.00
79 Hank Greenberg .25
80 Pepper Martin .25
81 Graig Nettles .25
81 Graig Nettles/Padres 3.00
82 Dennis Eckersley .50
83 Donn Clendenon .25
84 Tom Seaver 1.00
85 Honus Wagner 1.50
86 Reggie Jackson .75
86 Reggie Jackson/A's 5.00
87 Goose Goslin .25
87 Goose Goslin/Tigers 3.00
88 Tony Kubek .25
89 Roy Campanella 1.00
90 Steve Carlton/Cards 4.00
91 Lou Gehrig, Mel Ott 2.00
92 Eddie Collins, Joe Morgan .25
93 George Brett, Mike Schmidt 2.00
94 Cal Ripken Jr., Ozzie Smith 3.00
95 Thurman Munson, Johnny Bench 1.50
96 Willie Stargell, Stan Musial, Pepper Martin 1.00
97 Babe Ruth, Kirby Puckett, Reggie Jackson 3.00
98 Cy Young, Bob Gibson 1.00
99 Whitey Ford, Steve Carlton 1.00
100 Paul Molitor, Lou Brock .50

Championship Gold

Golds: 5-10X
Gold SP's: 1-2X
Production 50 sets

HOF Plaque

NM/M
Complete Set (30): 90.00
Common Player: 3.00
#'d to HOF induction year
1HOF Babe Ruth 8.00
2HOF Christy Mathewson 3.00
3HOF Honus Wagner 4.00
4HOF Ty Cobb 5.00
5HOF Walter Johnson 4.00
6HOF Cy Young 4.00
7HOF Tris Speaker 3.00
8HOF Eddie Collins 3.00
9HOF Lou Gehrig 6.00
10HOF Jimmie Foxx 4.00
11HOF Jackie Robinson 6.00
12HOF Stan Musial 5.00
13HOF Yogi Berra 4.00
14HOF Duke Snider 4.00
15HOF Juan Marichal 3.00
16HOF Luis Aparicio 3.00
17HOF Pee Wee Reese 3.00
18HOF Willie McCovey 3.00
19HOF Willie Stargell 3.00
20HOF Johnny Bench 5.00
21HOF Joe Morgan 3.00
22HOF Jim Palmer 3.00
23HOF Tom Seaver 5.00
24HOF Reggie Jackson 4.00
25HOF Steve Carlton 3.00
26HOF George Brett 6.00
27HOF Nolan Ryan 8.00
28HOF Robin Yount 4.00
29HOF Kirby Puckett 5.00
30HOF Ozzie Smith 4.00

MVP Collection Game-Used

NM/M
Common Player: 5.00
Inserted 1:100
Golds: .75-2X
Production 100 sets
JB Johnny Bench/200 20.00
DC Donn Clendenon 5.00
RF Rollie Fingers/200 5.00
RJOK Reggie Jackson/50 20.00
RJNY Reggie Jackson 10.00
RK Ray Knight 5.00
PM Paul Molitor/250 15.00
DP Darrell Porter/250 5.00
BR Brooks Robinson/250 20.00
WS Willie Stargell/200 10.00
AT Alan Trammell 10.00

MVP Collection Patch

NM/M
Numbered to MVP Year
JB Johnny Bench/76 45.00
RF Rollie Fingers/74 20.00
RJNY Reggie Jackson/77 40.00
BR Brooks Robinson/70 40.00
AT Alan Trammell/84 30.00

October Legends

NM/M
Common Player: 5.00
Inserted 1:48
Golds: .75-1.5X
Production 100 sets
Joe Morgan 5.00
Wade Boggs/60 20.00
Keith Hernandez/100 15.00
Robin Yount 10.00
Eddie Murray 10.00
Lenny Dykstra/200 8.00
Paul O'Neill 8.00
Red Schoendienst/210 8.00
Pepper Martin/50 15.00
Keith Hernandez/150 20.00
Willie Stargell/225 12.00
Cal Ripken Jr/50
George Brett 20.00
Dave Parker/50 10.00
Tony Perez 5.00
Rollie Fingers 5.00
Gary Carter/200 10.00
Dennis Eckersley 5.00
Juan Marichal 8.00
Pee Wee Reese/200 15.00
Roger Maris 60.00
Frankie Frisch/25
Duke Snider/200 15.00
Darrell Porter/150 5.00
Willie McCovey/150 10.00
Paul Molitor/150 15.00

October Legends Dual

NM/M
Common Card: 10.00
SP's noted
Rollie Fingers, Dennis Eckersley 12.00
Keith Hernandez, Red Schoendienst 12.00
Joe Morgan, Tony Perez 10.00
Wade Boggs, Keith Hernandez 20.00
Lenny Dykstra, Gary Carter 12.00
Robin Yount, Paul Molitor/150 35.00
Roger Maris, Paul O'Neill/200 50.00
Duke Snider, Pee Wee Reese/200 25.00
Juan Marichal, Willie McCovey 15.00
George Brett, Darrell Porter/150 35.00
Willie Stargell, Dave Parker 15.00
Gary Carter, Keith Hernandez 10.00
Cal Ripken Jr., Eddie Murray/200 40.00
Cal Ripken Jr., Eddie Murray/100 50.00
Pepper Martin, Frankie Frisch 15.00

Pennant Chase

	NM/M
Common Player:	10.00
Inserted 1:48 hobby	
Yogi Berra/pants/150	20.00
Carlton Fisk/bat	10.00
Reggie Jackson/jsy	10.00
Fred Lynn/bat	10.00
Thurman Munson/bat	30.00
Wade Boggs/jsy	10.00
Dave Winfield/bat	10.00

Pennant Chase Dual

		NM/M
Production 50 sets		
CFRJ	Carlton Fisk/bat, Reggie Jackson/jsy	30.00
FLTM	Fred Lynn/bat, Thurman Munson/ bat	50.00
WBDW	Wade Boggs/jsy, Dave Winfield/bat	30.00

Rival Factions

		NM/M
Common Card:		2.00
1-24 #'d to 1,000		
25-36 #'d to 500		
37-43 #'d to 50 not priced		
1RF	Carlton Fisk, Thurman Munson	3.00
2RF	Frank Baker, Babe Ruth	8.00
3RF	Jimmie Foxx, Lou Gehrig	6.00
4RF	Steve Carlton, Nolan Ryan	8.00
5RF	Mordecai Brown, Honus Wagner	3.00
6RF	Frankie Frisch, Duke Snider	3.00
7RF	Ozzie Smith, Alan Trammell	3.00
8RF	Larry Doby, Jackie Robinson	5.00
9RF	Steve Garvey, Tony Perez	2.00
10RF	Johnny Bench, Willie Stargell	4.00
11RF	Ty Cobb, Eddie Collins	5.00
12RF	Reggie Jackson, Brooks Robinson	4.00
13RF	Yogi Berra, Roy Campanella	4.00
14RF	Orlando Cepeda, Willie McCovey	2.00
15RF	Al Kaline, Jim Palmer	4.00
16RF	George Brett, Kirby Puckett	6.00
17RF	Bob Gibson, Tom Seaver	4.00
18RF	Cal Ripken Jr., Robin Yount	8.00
19RF	Johnny Mize, Mel Ott	3.00
20RF	Stan Musial, Pee Wee Reese	4.00
21RF	Phil Rizzuto, Ted Williams	8.00
22RF	Hank Greenberg, Lefty Grove	2.00
23RF	Dave Parker, Mike Schmidt	4.00
24RF	Bill Mazeroski, Joe Morgan	2.00
25RF	Johnny Bench, Carlton Fisk	5.00
26RF	George Brett, Mike Schmidt	6.00
27RF	Pee Wee Reese, Phil Rizzuto	4.00
28RF	Stan Musial, Ted Williams	10.00
29RF	Cal Ripken Jr., Alan Trammell	10.00
30RF	Jim "Catfish" Hunter, Tom Seaver	4.00
31RF	Ty Cobb, Honus Wagner	5.00
32RF	Steve Carlton, Lefty Grove	2.00
33RF	Ozzie Smith, Robin Yount	4.00
34RF	Frankie Frisch, Joe Morgan	2.00
35RF	Hank Greenberg, Jackie Robinson	6.00
36RF	Jimmie Foxx, Pepper Martin	4.00
37RF	Lou Gehrig, Cal Ripken Jr.	
38RF	Ozzie Smith, Honus Wagner	
39RF	Reggie Jackson, Dave Winfield	
40RF	Ty Cobb, Rogers Hornsby	
41RF	Babe Ruth, Roger Maris	
42RF	Yogi Berra, Thurman Munson	
43RF	Nolan Ryan, Tom Seaver	
44RF	Joe Morgan, Jackie Robinson	
45RF	Jimmie Foxx, Mel Ott	

Rival Factions Game-Used Dual

	NM/M
Common Card:	12.00
Carlton Fisk, Thurman Munson	30.00
Frank Baker, Babe Ruth/25	
Steve Carlton, Nolan Ryan	40.00
Frankie Frisch, Duke Snider	15.00
Ozzie Smith, Alan Trammell	25.00
Larry Doby, Jackie Robinson/75	60.00
Steve Garvey, Tony Perez	10.00
Johnny Bench, Willie Stargell	20.00
Reggie Jackson, Brooks Robinson	20.00
Orlando Cepeda, Willie McCovey/200	15.00
George Brett, Kirby Puckett	40.00
Cal Ripken Jr., Robin Yount	30.00
Johnny Bench, Carlton Fisk	20.00
Cal Ripken Jr., Alan Trammell	30.00
Jim "Catfish" Hunter, Tom Seaver	15.00
Ozzie Smith, Robin Yount	25.00
Frankie Frisch, Joe Morgan	15.00
Hank Greenberg, Jackie Robinson/50	100.00
Jimmie Foxx, Pepper Martin/200	40.00
Reggie Jackson, Dave Winfield/150	20.00
Babe Ruth, Roger Maris/25	
Yogi Berra, Thurman Munson	40.00
Nolan Ryan, Tom Seaver	45.00
Joe Morgan, Jackie Robinson/50	50.00

Rival Factions Dual Patch

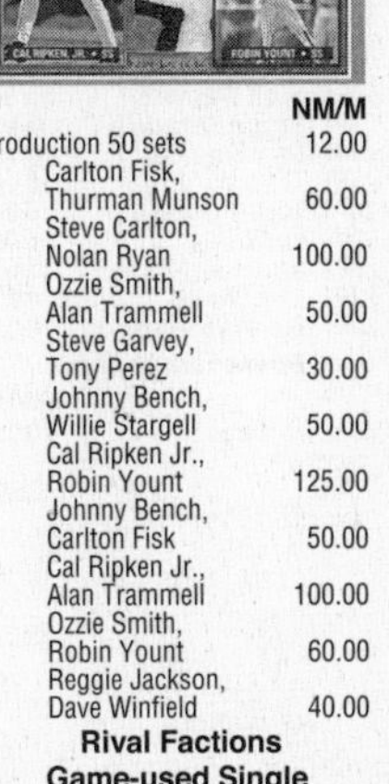

	NM/M
Production 50 sets	12.00
Carlton Fisk, Thurman Munson	60.00
Steve Carlton, Nolan Ryan	100.00
Ozzie Smith, Alan Trammell	50.00
Steve Garvey, Tony Perez	30.00
Johnny Bench, Willie Stargell	50.00
Cal Ripken Jr., Robin Yount	125.00
Johnny Bench, Carlton Fisk	50.00
Cal Ripken Jr., Alan Trammell	100.00
Ozzie Smith, Robin Yount	60.00
Reggie Jackson, Dave Winfield	40.00

Rival Factions Game-used Single

	NM/M
Common Card:	8.00
Inserted 1:32	
Carlton Fisk, Thurman Munson	25.00
Frank Baker, Babe Ruth	25.00
Jimmie Foxx, Lou Gehrig	35.00
Steve Carlton, Nolan Ryan	25.00
Frankie Frisch, Duke Snider	20.00
Ozzie Smith, Alan Trammell	15.00
Larry Doby, Jackie Robinson	15.00
Steve Garvey, Tony Perez	10.00
Johnny Bench, Willie Stargell	10.00
Reggie Jackson, Brooks Robinson	12.00
Orlando Cepeda, Willie McCovey	10.00
Al Kaline, Jim Palmer	10.00
George Brett, Kirby Puckett	25.00
Bob Gibson, Tom Seaver	20.00
Cal Ripken Jr., Robin Yount	30.00
Stan Musial, Pee Wee Reese	25.00
Hank Greenberg, Lefty Grove	20.00
Bill Mazeroski, Joe Morgan	8.00
Johnny Bench, Carlton Fisk	10.00
George Brett, Mike Schmidt	25.00
Pee Wee Reese, Phil Rizzuto	15.00
Cal Ripken Jr., Alan Trammell	35.00
Steve Carlton, Lefty Grove	15.00
Ozzie Smith, Robin Yount	15.00
Frankie Frisch, Joe Morgan	25.00
Hank Greenberg, Jackie Robinson	20.00
Jimmie Foxx, Pepper Martin	30.00
Lou Gehrig, Cal Ripken Jr.	40.00
Reggie Jackson, Dave Winfield	10.00
Babe Ruth, Roger Maris	60.00
Nolan Ryan, Tom Seaver	35.00

Series of Champions

		NM/M
Complete Set (20):		25.00
Common Player:		1.00
Inserted 1:6		
1	Yogi Berra	2.00
2	Wade Boggs	2.00
3	Dave Parker	1.00
4	Joe Carter	1.00
5	Kirk Gibson	1.00
6	Reggie Jackson	2.00
7	Tony Kubek	1.00
8	Don Larsen	1.00
9	Bill Mazeroski	1.00
10	Eddie Murray	1.50
11	Graig Nettles	1.00
12	Tony Perez	1.00
13	Phil Rizzuto	1.50
14	Mike Schmidt	2.50
15	Red Schoendienst	1.00
16	Duke Snider	2.00
17	Ty Cobb	2.50
18	Lou Gehrig	3.00
19	Babe Ruth	4.00

Series of Champions Game-Used

	NM/M
Common Player:	5.00
Inserted 1:36	
Golds:	.75-1.5X
Production 100 sets	
Bat Knob numbered to 10 not priced	
Yogi Berra/bat	15.00
Wade Boggs/jsy	10.00
Dave Parker/bat	5.00
Joe Carter/bat	5.00
Kirk Gibson/bat	5.00
Reggie Jackson/bat	10.00
Tony Kubek/bat	10.00
Eddie Murray/bat	10.00
Graig Nettles/bat	5.00
Tony Perez/bat	5.00
Red Schoendienst/jsy	5.00
Duke Snider/bat	10.00
Babe Ruth/bat/25	180.00

2002 FLEER FLAIR

		NM/M
Complete Set (138):		
Common Player:		.25
Common (101-138):		3.00
Production 1,750		
Pack (5):		4.00
Hobby Box (20):		70.00
1	Scott Rolen	.75
2	Derek Jeter	3.00
3	Sean Casey	.40
4	Hideo Nomo	.75
5	Craig Biggio	.25
6	Randy Johnson	1.00
7	J.D. Drew	.50
8	Greg Maddux	1.50
9	Paul LoDuca	.25
10	John Olerud	.25
11	Barry Larkin	.25
12	Mark Grace	.35
13	Jimmy Rollins	.25
14	Todd Helton	1.00
15	Jim Edmonds	.25
16	Roy Oswalt	.35
17	Phil Nevin	.25
18	Tim Salmon	.35
19	Magglio Ordonez	.25
20	Roger Clemens	1.75
21	Raul Mondesi	.25
22	Edgar Martinez	.25
23	Pedro J. Martinez	1.00
24	Edgardo Alfonzo	.25
25	Bernie Williams	.35
26	Gary Sheffield	.40
27	D'Angelo Jimenez	.25
28	Toby Hall	.25

29 Joe Mays .25
30 Alfonso Soriano .75
31 Mike Piazza 2.00
32 Lance Berkman .25
33 Jim Thome .25
34 Ben Sheets .25
35 Brandon Inge .25
36 Luis Gonzalez .35
37 Jeff Kent .25
38 Ben Grieve .25
39 Carlos Delgado .50
40 Pat Burrell .50
41 Mark Buehrle .25
42 Cristian Guzman .25
43 Shawn Green .40
44 Nomar Garciaparra 2.00
45 Carlos Beltran .60
46 Troy Glaus .75
47 Paul Konerko .25
48 Moises Alou .25
49 Kerry Wood .75
50 Jose Vidro .25
51 Juan Encarnacion .25
52 Bobby Abreu .25
53 C.C. Sabathia .25
54 Alex Rodriguez 2.50
55 Albert Pujols 2.50
56 Bret Boone .25
57 Orlando Hernandez .25
58 Jason Kendall .25
59 Tim Hudson .40
60 Darin Erstad .60
61 Mike Mussina .40
62 Ken Griffey Jr. 2.00
63 Adrian Beltre .35
64 Jeff Bagwell 1.00
65 Vladimir Guerrero 1.00
66 Mike Sweeney .25
67 Sammy Sosa 2.00
68 Andruw Jones .75
69 Richie Sexson .25
70 Matt Morris .25
71 Ivan Rodriguez .75
72 Shannon Stewart .25
73 Barry Bonds 3.00
74 Matt Williams .25
75 Jason Giambi .60
76 Brian Giles .25
77 Cliff Floyd .25
78 Tino Martinez .25
79 Juan Gonzalez 1.00
80 Frank Thomas 1.00
81 Ichiro Suzuki 2.00
82 Barry Zito .35
83 Chipper Jones 1.50
84 Adam Dunn .75
85 Kazuhiro Sasaki .25
86 Mark Quinn .25
87 Rafael Palmeiro .60
88 Jeromy Burnitz .25
89 Curt Schilling .50
90 Chris Richards .25
91 Jon Leiber .25
92 Doug Mientkiewicz .25
93 Roberto Alomar .40
94 Rich Aurilia .25
95 Eric Chavez .35
96 Larry Walker .25
97 Manny Ramirez 1.00
98 Tony Clark .25
99 Tsuyoshi Shinjo .25
100 Josh Beckett .50
101 Dewon Brazelton 3.00
102 *Jeremy Lambert* 3.00
103 Andres Torres 3.00
104 *Matt Childers* 4.00
105 Wilson Betemit 3.00
106 Willie Harris 3.00
107 Drew Henson 4.00
108 Rafael Soriano 3.00
109 Carlos Valderrama 3.00
110 Victor Martinez 6.00
111 Juan Rivera 3.00
112 Felipe Lopez 3.00
113 Brandon Duckworth 3.00
114 Jeremy Owens 3.00
115 *Aaron Cook* 3.00
116 Derrick Lewis 3.00
117 Mark Teixeira 6.00
118 Ken Harvey 5.00
119 Tim Spooneybarger 3.00
120 Bill Hall 3.00
121 Adam Pettyjohn 3.00
122 Ramon Castro 3.00
123 Marlon Byrd 4.00
124 Matt White 3.00
125 *Eric Cyr* 3.00
126 Morgan Ensberg 3.00
127 Horacio Ramirez 4.00
128 *Ron Calloway* 3.00
129 Nick Punto 3.00
130 Joe Kennedy 3.00
131 *So Taguchi* 5.00
132 Austin Kearns 4.00
133 Mark Prior 10.00
134 *Kazuhisa Ishii* 8.00
135 Steve Torrealba 3.00
136 *Adam Walker* 3.00
137 Travis Hafner 4.00
138 Zach Day 3.00

Collection

Collection (1-100): 4-6X
Production 175
Collection (101-138): 1-2X
Production 50

Hot Numbers

NM/M
Common Player: 15.00
Production 100 sets
Manny Ramirez 30.00
Randy Johnson 30.00
Curt Schilling 25.00
Pedro J. Martinez 30.00
Nomar Garciaparra 50.00
Barry Larkin 15.00
Todd Helton 30.00
Larry Walker 15.00
Sean Casey 20.00
Jeff Bagwell 30.00
Craig Biggio 15.00
Shawn Green 20.00
Edgardo Alfonzo 15.00
Mike Piazza 50.00
Derek Jeter 75.00
Roger Clemens
Chipper Jones 40.00
Jim Edmonds 15.00
J.D. Drew 20.00
Ivan Rodriguez 25.00
Rafael Palmeiro 25.00
Alex Rodriguez 60.00
Greg Maddux 40.00
Carlos Delgado 20.00

Jersey Heights

NM/M
Common Player: 4.00
Inserted 1:18 hobby
1JH Edgardo Alfonzo 4.00
2JH Jeff Bagwell 8.00
3JH Craig Biggio 4.00
4JH Barry Bonds 20.00
5JH Sean Casey 4.00
6JH Roger Clemens 15.00
7JH Carlos Delgado 6.00
8JH J.D. Drew 6.00
9JH Jim Edmonds 6.00
10JH Nomar Garciaparra 15.00
11JH Shawn Green 5.00
12JH Todd Helton 8.00
13JH Derek Jeter 20.00
14JH Randy Johnson 8.00
15JH Chipper Jones 8.00
16JH Barry Larkin 6.00
17JH Greg Maddux 10.00
18JH Pedro J. Martinez 8.00
19JH Rafael Palmeiro 8.00
20JH Mike Piazza 10.00
21JH Manny Ramirez 8.00
22JH Alex Rodriguez 15.00
23JH Ivan Rodriguez 6.00
24JH Curt Schilling 6.00
25JH Larry Walker 4.00

Jersey Heights (Dual)

NM/M
Common Card: 15.00
Production 100 sets
Randy Johnson, Curt Schilling 30.00
Pedro J. Martinez, Nomar Garciaparra 50.00
Edgardo Alfonzo, Mike Piazza 30.00
Derek Jeter, Roger Clemens 75.00
Greg Maddux, Chipper Jones 40.00
Jim Edmonds, Jeff Bagwell 20.00
Jeff Bagwell, Craig Biggio 25.00
Rafael Palmeiro, Ivan Rodriguez 25.00
Carlos Delgado, Shawn Green 15.00
Todd Helton, Larry Walker 20.00
Sean Casey, Barry Larkin 25.00
Alex Rodriguez, Manny Ramirez 40.00

Power Tools

NM/M
Common Player: 4.00
Inserted 1:19
Golds: 1-2.5X
Production 100
1PT Roberto Alomar 6.00
2PT Jeff Bagwell/150 8.00
3PT Craig Biggio 4.00
4PT Barry Bonds 15.00
5PT Bret Boone 4.00
6PT Pat Burrell/225 6.00
8PT Eric Chavez 5.00
9PT J.D. Drew/150 8.00
10PT Jim Edmonds 6.00
11PT Juan Gonzalez 6.00
12PT Luis Gonzalez 4.00
13PT Shawn Green 5.00
15PT Derek Jeter 25.00
16PT Doug Mientkiewicz 4.00
17PT Magglio Ordonez 4.00
18PT Rafael Palmeiro/100 8.00
19PT Mike Piazza 10.00
20PT Alex Rodriguez 15.00
21PT Ivan Rodriguez 8.00
22PT Scott Rolen/42 15.00
23PT Reggie Sanders/120 5.00
24PT Gary Sheffield 6.00
25PT Tsuyoshi Shinjo 5.00
26PT Miguel Tejada 6.00
27PT Frank Thomas 8.00
28PT Jim Thome/225 15.00
29PT Larry Walker 4.00
30PT Bernie Williams 6.00

Power Tools Dual

NM/M
Common Card: 10.00
Inserted 1:40
Golds: 1-2.5X
Production 50 sets
1 Eric Chavez, Miguel Tejada 10.00
2 Barry Bonds, Tsuyoshi Shinjo 25.00
3 Jim Edmonds, J.D. Drew 15.00
4 Jeff Bagwell, Craig Biggio 15.00
5 Bernie Williams, Derek Jeter 35.00
6 Roberto Alomar, Mike Piazza 20.00
7 Sean Casey, Jim Thome/40 30.00
8 Pat Burrell, Scott Rolen 15.00
9 Gary Sheffield, Shawn Green 10.00
10 Ivan Rodriguez, Alex Rodriguez 15.00
11 Juan Gonzalez, Rafael Palmeiro 15.00
12 Magglio Ordonez, Frank Thomas 15.00
13 Larry Walker, Todd Helton/225 10.00
14 Luis Gonzalez, Reggie Sanders 10.00
15 Doug Mientkiewicz, Bret Boone 10.00

Sweet Swatch Autographs

NM/M
Common Player: 15.00
Quantity produced listed
Golds: No Pricing
Production 15 sets
Derek Jeter/375 100.00
Barry Bonds/35 250.00
Drew Henson/785 40.00
Mark Teixeira/185 40.00
Dewon Brazelton/185 15.00
Mark Prior/285 80.00
Marlon Byrd/185 15.00
Ozzie Smith/185 65.00
Ron Cey/285 20.00
Paul Molitor/85 50.00
Maury Wills/285 20.00
Dale Murphy/285 60.00
David Espinosa/485 15.00
Dane Sardinha/485 15.00
Ben Sheets/85 50.00
Tony Perez/115 20.00
Brooks Robinson/185 50.00
So Taguchi/335 30.00
Al Kaline/285 50.00
Kazuhisa Ishii/335 30.00
Albert Pujols/50 125.00
Don Mattingly/85 150.00

Sweet Swatch Game-Used

NM/M
Common Player: 8.00
1:hobby box
Jeff Bagwell/490 10.00
Josh Beckett/500 10.00
Darin Erstad/525 8.00
Freddy Garcia/620 8.00
Brian Giles/445 10.00
Juan Gonzalez/505 10.00
Mark Grace/795 15.00
Derek Jeter/525 40.00
Jason Kendall/990 10.00
Paul LoDuca/440 10.00
Greg Maddux/475 15.00
Magglio Ordonez/495 10.00
Rafael Palmeiro/535 10.00
Mike Piazza/1,000 15.00
Alex Rodriguez/550 25.00
Ivan Rodriguez/475 10.00
Tim Salmon/465 8.00
Kazuhiro Sasaki/770 8.00
Alfonso Soriano/775 10.00
Larry Walker/430 8.00
Ted Williams/250 125.00

Sweet Swatch Patch

NM/M
Common Player: 25.00
Random Box Topper
Jeff Bagwell/45 75.00
Josh Beckett/60 55.00
Darin Erstad/50 40.00
Freddy Garcia/50 40.00
Juan Gonzalez/55 75.00
Mark Grace/75 60.00
Derek Jeter/20
Jason Kendall/120 25.00
Paul LoDuca/50 35.00
Greg Maddux/50 90.00
Maggtio Ordonez/55 40.00
Rafael Palmeiro/60 40.00
Mike Piazza/95 100.00
Alex Rodriguez/50 90.00
Ivan Rodriguez/50 60.00
Tim Salmon/40 40.00
Kazuhiro Sasaki/80 50.00
Alfonso Soriano/35 65.00
Larry Walker/60 40.00
Ted Williams/15

2002 FLEER FOCUS JERSEY EDITION

		NM/M
Complete Set (260):		60.00
Common Player:		.15
Common (226-260):		1.00
Inserted 1:4		
Pack (10):		2.00
Box (24):		40.00
1	Mike Piazza	1.50
2	Jason Giambi	.50
3	Jim Thome	.15
4	John Olerud	.15
5	J.D. Drew	.30
6	Richard Hidalgo	.15
7	Rusty Greer	.15
8	Tony Batista	.15
9	Omar Vizquel	.15
10	Randy Johnson	.75
11	Cristian Guzman	.15
12	Mark Grace	.25
13	Jeff Cirillo	.15
14	Mike Cameron	.15
15	Jeromy Burnitz	.15
16	Pokey Reese	.15
17	Richie Sexson	.15
18	Joe Randa	.15
19	Aramis Ramirez	.15
20	Pedro J. Martinez	.75
21	Todd Hollandsworth	.15
22	Rondell White	.15
23	Tsuyoshi Shinjo	.15
24	Melvin Mora	.15
25	Tim Hudson	.30
26	Darrin Fletcher	.15
27	Bill Mueller	.15
28	Jeff Weaver	.15
29	Tony Clark	.15
30	Tom Glavine	.40
31	Jarrod Washburn	.15
32	Greg Vaughn	.15
33	Lee Stevens	.15
34	Charles Johnson	.15
35	Lance Berkman	.15
36	Bud Smith	.15
37	Keith Foulke	.15
38	Ben Davis	.15
39	Daryle Ward	.15
40	Bernie Williams	.30
41	Dean Palmer	.15
42	Mark Mulder	.15
43	Jason LaRue	.15
44	Jay Gibbons	.15
45	Brandon Duckworth	.15
46	Carlos Delgado	.40
47	Barry Zito	.25
48	Matt Morris	.15
49	J.T. Snow	.15
50	Albert Pujols	1.50
51	Brad Fullmer	.15
52	Damion Easley	.15
53	Pat Burrell	.40
54	Kevin Brown	.15
55	Todd Walker	.15
56	Rich Garces	.15
57	Carlos Pena	.15
58	Paul LoDuca	.15
59	Mike Lieberthal	.15
60	Barry Larkin	.15
61	Jon Lieber	.15
62	Jose Cruz	.15
63	Mo Vaughn	.15
64	Ivan Rodriguez	.60
65	Jorge Posada	.25
66	Magglio Ordonez	.15
67	Juan Encarnacion	.15
68	Shawn Estes	.15
69	Kevin Appier	.15
70	Jeff Bagwell	.75
71	Tim Wakefield	.15
72	Shannon Stewart	.15
73	Scott Rolen	.65
74	Bobby Higginson	.15
75	Jim Edmonds	.15
76	Adam Dunn	.50
77	Eric Chavez	.30
78	Adrian Beltre	.30
79	Jason Varitek	.15
80	Barry Bonds	2.50
81	Edgar Renteria	.15
82	Raul Mondesi	.15
83	Eric Karros	.15
84	Ken Griffey Jr.	1.50
85	Jermaine Dye	.15
86	Carlos Beltran	.40
87	Mark Quinn	.15
88	Terrence Long	.15
89	Shawn Green	.40
90	Nomar Garciaparra	1.50
91	Sean Casey	.25
92	Homer Bush	.15
93	Bobby Abreu	.15
94	Jamey Wright	.15
95	Tony Womack	.15
96	Larry Walker	.15
97	Doug Mientkiewicz	.15
98	Jimmy Rollins	.15
99	Brady Anderson	.15
100	Derek Jeter	2.50
101	Kevin Young	.15
102	Juan Pierre	.15
103	Edgar Martinez	.15
104	Corey Koskie	.15
105	Jeffrey Hammonds	.15
106	Luis Gonzalez	.25
107	Travis Fryman	.15
108	Kerry Wood	.50
109	Rafael Palmeiro	.60
110	Ichiro Suzuki	1.00
111	Russ Ortiz	.15
112	Jeff Kent	.15
113	Scott Erickson	.15
114	Bruce Chen	.15
115	Craig Biggio	.15
116	Robin Ventura	.15
117	Alex Rodriguez	2.00
118	Roy Oswalt	.25
119	Fred McGriff	.15
120	Juan Gonzalez	.75
121	David Justice	.15
122	Pat Hentgen	.15
123	Hideo Nomo	.65
124	Ramon Ortiz	.15
125	David Ortiz	.25
126	Phil Nevin	.15
127	Ryan Dempster	.15
128	Toby Hall	.15
129	Vladimir Guerrero	.75
130	Chipper Jones	1.00
131	Russell Branyan	.15
132	Jose Vidro	.15
133	Bubba Trammell	.15
134	Tino Martinez	.15
135	Greg Maddux	1.00
136	Derrek Lee	.15
137	Troy Glaus	.75
138	Joe Crede	.15
139	Steve Cox	.15
140	Sammy Sosa	1.50
141	Corey Patterson	.15
142	Vernon Wells	.15
143	Matt Lawton	.15
144	Gabe Kapler	.15
145	Johnny Damon	.25
146	Marty Cordova	.15
147	Moises Alou	.15
148	Fernando Tatis	.15
149	Tanyon Sturtze	.15
150	Roger Clemens	1.25
151	Paul Konerko	.15
152	Chan Ho Park	.15
153	Marcus Giles	.15
154	David Eckstein	.15
155	Mike Lowell	.15
156	Preston Wilson	.15
157	John Vander Wal	.15
158	Tim Salmon	.25
159	Andy Pettitte	.35
160	Mike Mussina	.40
161	Doug Davis	.15
162	Peter Bergeron	.15
163	Rich Aurilia	.15
164	Eric Milton	.15
165	Geoff Jenkins	.15
166	Todd Helton	.75
167	Bret Boone	.15
168	Kris Benson	.15
169	Brian Anderson	.15
170	Roberto Alomar	.40
171	Javier Vazquez	.15
172	Scott Schoeneweis	.15
173	Ryan Klesko	.15
174	Jacque Jones	.15
175	Andruw Jones	.75
176	Aubrey Huff	.15
177	Mark Buehrle	.15
178	Josh Beckett	.40
179	Ben Sheets	.15
180	Curt Schilling	.40
181	C.C. Sabathia	.15
182	Denny Neagle	.15
183	Jamie Moyer	.15
184	Jason Kendall	.15
185	Dee Brown	.15
186	Frank Thomas	.75
187	Damian Rolls	.15
188	Carlos Lee	.15
189	Kevin Jarvis	.15
190	Manny Ramirez	.75
191	Cliff Floyd	.15
192	Freddy Garcia	.15
193	Orlando Cabrera	.15
194	Mike Sweeney	.15
195	Gary Sheffield	.35
196	Rafael Furcal	.15
197	Esteban Loaiza	.15
198	Mike Hampton	.15
199	Brian Giles	.15
200	Darin Erstad	.60
201	David Wells	.15
202	Kenny Lofton	.15
203	Aaron Sele	.15
204	Jason Schmidt	.15
205	Javy Lopez	.15
206	Dmitri Young	.15
207	Darryl Kile	.15
208	Matt Williams	.15
209	Joe Kennedy	.15
210	Chuck Knoblauch	.15
211	Brian Jordan	.15
212	Roberto Person	.15
213	Alex Ochoa	.15
214	Steve Finley	.15
215	Ben Petrick	.15
216	Al Leiter	.15
217	Mark Kotsay	.15
218	Miguel Tejada	.35
219	David Segui	.15
220	A.J. Burnett	.15
221	Marlon Anderson	.15
222	Wiki Gonzalez	.15
223	Jeff Suppan	.15
224	Dave Roberts	.15
225	Jose Hernandez	.15
226	Angel Berroa	1.00
227	Sean Burroughs	1.00
228	*Luis Martinez*	1.00
229	*Adrian Burnside*	1.00
230	*John Ennis*	1.00
231	*Anastacio Martinez*	1.00
232	Hank Blalock	2.00
233	Eric Hinske	1.00
234	*Chris Booker*	1.00
235	*Colin Young*	1.00
236	*Mark Corey*	1.00
237	*Satoru Komiyama*	1.00
238	*So Taguchi*	2.50
239	*Elio Serrano*	1.00
240	*Reed Johnson*	2.00
241	*Jeremy Lambert*	1.00
242	*Chris Baker*	1.00
243	Orlando Hudson	1.00
244	*Travis Hughes*	1.00
245	*Kevin Frederick*	1.00
246	*Rodrigo Rosario*	1.00
247	*Jeremy Ward*	1.00
248	*Kazuhisa Ishii*	4.00
249	Austin Kearns	1.00
250	*Kyle Kane*	1.00
251	*Cam Esslinger*	1.00
252	*Jeff Austin*	1.00
253	*Brian Mallette*	1.00
254	Mark Prior	5.00
255	Mark Teixeira	2.00
256	Carlos Valderrama	1.00
257	Jason Hart	1.00
258	*Takahito Nomura*	1.00
259	Matt Thornton	1.00
260	Marlon Byrd	1.00

Century

	NM/M
Cards (1-225):	6-10X
Cards (226-260):	.75-1.5X
Production 101-199	

Blue Chips

		NM/M
Complete Set (15):		10.00
Common Player:		.50
Inserted 1:6		
1BC	Albert Pujols	3.00
2BC	Sean Burroughs	.50
3BC	Vernon Wells	.50
4BC	Adam Dunn	1.50
5BC	Pat Burrell	1.00
6BC	Juan Pierre	.50
7BC	Russell Branyan	.50
8BC	Carlos Pena	.50
9BC	Toby Hall	.50
10BC	Hank Blalock	1.00
11BC	Alfonso Soriano	1.50
12BC	Jimmy Rollins	.50
13BC	Jose Ortiz	.50
14BC	Eric Hinske	.50
15BC	Nick Johnson	.50

Blue Chips Game-Used

	NM/M
Inserted 1:96 Hobby	
Russell Branyan/jsy	8.00
Nick Johnson/jsy	10.00
Nick Johnson/patch/100	20.00

International Diamond Co.

		NM/M
Complete Set (25):		25.00
Common Player:		1.00
Inserted 1:8		
1	Bobby Abreu	1.00
2	Adrian Beltre	1.00
3	Jorge Posada	1.00
4	Vladimir Guerrero	3.00
5	Rafael Palmeiro	2.00
6	Sammy Sosa	4.00
7	Larry Walker	1.00
8	Manny Ramirez	3.00
9	Ichiro Suzuki	4.00
10	Jose Cruz	1.00
11	Juan Gonzalez	3.00
12	Bernie Williams	1.00
13	Ivan Rodriguez	2.00
14	Moises Alou	1.00
15	Cristian Guzman	1.00
16	Andruw Jones	3.00
17	Aramis Ramirez	1.00
18	Raul Mondesi	1.00
19	Edgar Martinez	1.00
20	Magglio Ordonez	1.00
21	Roberto Alomar	1.50
22	Chan Ho Park	1.00
23	Kazuhiro Sasaki	1.00
24	Tsuyoshi Shinjo	1.00
25	Hideo Nomo	3.00

Int. Diam. Co. Game-Used

	NM/M
Common Player:	5.00
Inserted 1:144	
Jorge Posada/jsy	15.00
Rafael Palmeiro/jsy	8.00
Manny Ramirez/jsy	10.00
Ivan Rodriguez/jsy	6.00

Andruw Jones/jsy 6.00
Aramis Ramirez/jsy 5.00
Raul Mondesi/jsy 5.00
Edgar Martinez/jsy 6.00
Chan Ho Park/jsy 5.00
Kazuhiro Sasaki/jsy 6.00
Hideo Nomo/jsy 20.00

Int. Diam. Co. Patch

NM/M
Common Player: 15.00
Production 100
Manny Ramirez 25.00
Ivan Rodriguez 25.00
Raul Mondesi 15.00
Edgar Martinez 20.00
Chan Ho Park 20.00
Hideo Nomo 75.00

Jersey Number Parallel

(1-225) print run 26-50: 10-25X
(1-225) p/r 51-75: 8-15X
(1-225) p/r 76-99: 5-10X
Produced to player's jsy #

K Corps

NM/M
Complete Set (15): 20.00
Common Player: 1.00
Inserted 1:12
1KC Roger Clemens 5.00
2KC Randy Johnson 3.00
3KC Tom Glavine 1.50
4KC Josh Beckett 1.50
5KC Matt Morris 1.00
6KC Curt Schilling 1.50
7KC Greg Maddux 4.00
8KC Tim Hudson 1.00
9KC Roy Oswalt 1.00
10KC Kerry Wood 2.00
11KC Barry Zito 1.00
12KC Kevin Brown 1.00
13KC Ryan Dempster 1.00
14KC Ben Sheets 1.00
15KC Pedro J. Martinez 3.00

K Corps Game-Used

NM/M
Common Player: 5.00
Inserted 1:96
2KC Randy Johnson/jsy 15.00
6KC Curt Schilling/jsy 10.00
7KC Greg Maddux/jsy 15.00
11KC Barry Zito/jsy 8.00
12KC Kevin Brown/jsy 5.00
15KC Pedro Martinez/jsy 10.00

K Corps Patch

NM/M
Production 100
Curt Schilling 20.00
Kevin Brown 20.00
Pedro Martinez 30.00

Kings of Swing

NM/M
Complete Set (20): 80.00
Common Player: 2.00
Inserted 1:48
1KS Barry Bonds 10.00
2KS Mike Piazza 6.00
3KS Albert Pujols 8.00
4KS Todd Helton 3.00
5KS Ken Griffey Jr. 6.00
6KS Alex Rodriguez 8.00
7KS Sammy Sosa 6.00
8KS Troy Glaus 3.00
9KS Derek Jeter 10.00
10KS Ichiro Suzuki 6.00
11KS Manny Ramirez 3.00
12KS Roberto Alomar 2.00
13KS Juan Gonzalez 3.00
14KS Shawn Green 2.00
15KS Vladimir Guerrero 3.00
16KS Nomar Garciaparra 6.00
17KS Adam Dunn 2.00
18KS Jason Giambi 2.50
19KS Edgar Martinez 2.00
20KS Chipper Jones 4.00

Kings of Swing Game-Used

NM/M
Common Player: 5.00
Inserted 1:108
Mike Piazza 15.00
Todd Helton 8.00
Alex Rodriguez 15.00
Derek Jeter 30.00
Manny Ramirez 8.00
Shawn Green 5.00
Edgar Martinez 5.00
Chipper Jones 10.00

Kings of Swing Patch

NM/M
Production 100
Todd Helton 25.00
Manny Ramirez 25.00
Shawn Green 20.00
Edgar Martinez 25.00
Mike Piazza 40.00

Larger Than Life

NM/M
Common Player: 4.00
Inserted 1:240
1LL Jason Giambi 6.00
2LL Carlos Delgado 5.00
3LL Alex Rodriguez 20.00
4LL Preston Wilson 4.00
5LL Frank Thomas 9.00
6LL Nomar Garciaparra 15.00
7LL Jim Edmonds 4.00
8LL Jim Thome 4.00
9LL Barry Bonds 25.00
10LL Mo Vaughn 4.00
11LL Ichiro Suzuki 20.00
12LL Ivan Rodriguez 5.00
13LL Gary Sheffield 4.00
14LL Derek Jeter 25.00
15LL Jeff Bagwell 9.00
16LL Mike Piazza 15.00
17LL J.D. Drew 4.00
18LL Sammy Sosa 15.00
19LL Albert Pujols 20.00
20LL Luis Gonzalez 4.00

Larger Than Life Game-Used

NM/M
Common Player: 5.00
Inserted 1:144
Alex Rodriguez/jsy 15.00
Preston Wilson/jsy 5.00
Frank Thomas/jsy 10.00
Jim Edmonds/jsy 6.00
Mo Vaughn/jsy 5.00
Ivan Rodriguez/jsy 8.00
Derek Jeter/jsy 25.00
Jeff Bagwell/jsy/sp/20 25.00
Mike Piazza/jsy 15.00
Luis Gonzalez/jsy 5.00

Larger Than Life Patch

NM/M
Common Player: 15.00
Production 100
Preston Wilson 15.00
Frank Thomas 25.00
Jim Edmonds 15.00
Ivan Rodriguez 25.00
Mike Piazza 40.00
Luis Gonzalez 15.00

Materialistic Away

NM/M
Complete Set (15): 75.00
Common Player: 4.00
Inserted 1:24
Home: 1.5-3X
Production 50 sets
Away Oversized: .5-1X
One per hobby box
Home Oversized: 2-4X
Production 50 sets
1MA Derek Jeter 12.00
2MA Alex Rodriguez 10.00
3MA Mike Piazza 8.00
4MA Ivan Rodriguez 4.00
5MA Chipper Jones 6.00
6MA Todd Helton 5.00
7MA Nomar Garciaparra 8.00
8MA Barry Bonds 12.00
9MA Ichiro Suzuki 8.00
10MA Ken Griffey Jr. 8.00
11MA Jason Giambi 4.00
12MA Sammy Sosa 8.00
13MA Albert Pujols 10.00
14MA Pedro J. Martinez 5.00
15MA Vladimir Guerrero 5.00

2002 FLEER GENUINE

NM/M
Complete Set (140):
Common Player: .15
Common (101-140): 3.00
Production 2,002
Pack (5): 3.00
Box (20): 50.00
1 Alex Rodriguez 2.50
2 Manny Ramirez .75
3 Jim Thome .15
4 Eric Milton .15
5 Todd Helton .75
6 Mike Mussina .50
7 Ichiro Suzuki 1.50
8 Randy Johnson 1.00
9 Mark Mulder .15
10 Johnny Damon .25
11 Sean Casey .25
12 Albert Pujols 2.50
13 Mark Grace .25
14 Moises Alou, Mark Mulder .15
15 Raul Mondesi, Roberto Alomar .15
16 Cliff Floyd, Scott Rolen .30
17 Vladimir Guerrero, Tom Glavine .40
18 Pat Burrell, Bobby Abreu .25
19 Ryan Klesko, Nomar Garciaparra .50
20 Mike Hampton, Darin Erstad .15
21 Shawn Green, Cliff Floyd .15
22 Rich Aurilia, Tim Hudson .15
23 Matt Morris, Jim Thome .15
24 Curt Schilling, Nolan Ryan 1.00
25 Kevin Brown, Reggie Jackson .25
26 Adrian Beltre, Rafael Palmeiro .30
27 Joe Mays, Ken Griffey Jr. .75
28 Luis Gonzalez, Sammy Sosa .75
29 Barry Larkin, Vladimir Guerrero .40
30 A.J. Burnett, Ichiro Suzuki .75
31 Eric Munson .15
32 Juan Gonzalez .75
33 Lance Berkman .15
34 Fred McGriff .15
35 Paul Konerko .15
36 Pedro J. Martinez .75
37 Adam Dunn .50
38 Jeromy Burnitz .15
39 Mike Sweeney .15
40 Bret Boone .15
41 Ken Griffey Jr. 2.00
42 Eric Chavez .25
43 Mark Quinn .15
44 Roberto Alomar .35
45 Bobby Abreu .15
46 Bartolo Colon .15
47 Jimmy Rollins .15
48 Chipper Jones 1.00
49 Ben Sheets .15
50 Freddy Garcia .15
51 Sammy Sosa 2.00
52 Rafael Palmeiro .65
53 Preston Wilson .15
54 Troy Glaus .75
55 Josh Beckett .50
56 C.C. Sabathia .15
57 Magglio Ordonez .15
58 Brian Giles .15
59 Darin Erstad .60
60 Gary Sheffield .35
61 Paul LoDuca .15
62 Derek Jeter 3.00
63 Greg Maddux 1.50
64 Kerry Wood .65
65 Toby Hall .15
66 Barry Bonds 3.00
67 Jeff Bagwell .75
68 Jason Kendall .15
69 Richard Hidalgo .15
70 J.D. Drew .30
71 Tom Glavine .25
72 Javier Vazquez .15
73 Doug Mientkiewicz .15
74 Jason Giambi .50
75 Carlos Delgado .40
76 Aramis Ramirez .15
77 Torii Hunter .15
78 Ivan Rodriguez .65
79 Charles Johnson .15
80 Jeff Kent .15
81 Jacque Jones .15
82 Larry Walker .15
83 Cristian Guzman .15
84 Jermaine Dye .15
85 Roger Clemens 1.75
86 Mike Piazza 2.00
87 Craig Biggio .15
88 Phil Nevin .15
89 Jeff Cirillo .15
90 Barry Zito .25
91 Ryan Dempster .15
92 Mark Buehrle .15
93 Nomar Garciaparra 2.00
94 Frank Thomas .75
95 Jim Edmonds .15
96 Geoff Jenkins .15
97 Scott Rolen .65
98 Tim Hudson .25
99 Shannon Stewart .15
100 Richie Sexson .15
101 Orlando Hudson 3.00
102 *Doug Devore* 3.00
103 *Rene Reyes* 3.00
104 *Steve Bechler* 4.00
105 *Jorge Nunez* 3.00
106 *Mitch Wylie* 3.00
107 *Jaime Cerda* 3.00
108 *Brandon Puffer* 3.00
109 *Tyler Yates* 6.00
110 Bill Hall 3.00
111 *Peter Zamora* 3.00
112 *Jeff Deardorff* 3.00
113 *J.J. Putz* 3.00
114 *Scotty Layfield* 3.00
115 *Brandon Backe* 3.00
116 *Andy Pratt* 3.00
117 Mark Prior 10.00
118 *Franklyn German* 3.00
119 *Todd Donovan* 3.00
120 *Franklin Nunez* 3.00
121 *Adam Walker* 3.00
122 *Ron Calloway* 3.00
123 *Tim Kalita* 3.00
124 *Kazuhisa Ishii* 8.00
125 Mark Teixeira 5.00
126 *Nate Field* 3.00
127 *Nelson Castro* 3.00

128	*So Taguchi*	8.00
129	Marlon Byrd	3.00
130	Drew Henson	3.00
131	Kenny Kelly	3.00
132	*John Ennis*	3.00
133	*Anastacio Martinez*	3.00
134	Matt Guerrier	3.00
135	*Tom Wilson*	3.00
136	*Ben Howard*	4.00
137	*Chris Baker*	3.00
138	*Kevin Frederick*	3.00
159	*Wilson Valdez*	3.00
140	Austin Kearns	4.00

Bat's Incredible

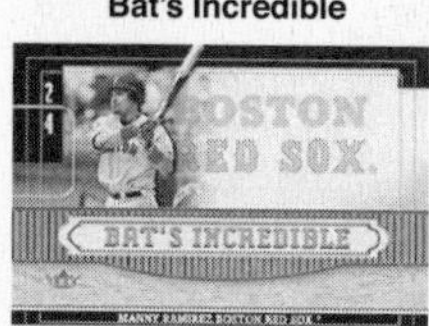

		NM/M
Complete Set (25):		60.00
Common Player:		1.50
Inserted 1:10		
1BI	Todd Helton	2.00
2BI	Chipper Jones	3.00
3BI	Luis Gonzalez	1.50
4BI	Barry Bonds	8.00
5BI	Jason Giambi	2.00
6BI	Alex Rodriguez	6.00
7BI	Manny Ramirez	2.00
8BI	Jeff Bagwell	2.00
9BI	Shawn Green	1.50
10BI	Albert Pujols	6.00
11BI	Paul LoDuca	1.50
12BI	Mike Piazza	5.00
13BI	Derek Jeter	8.00
14BI	Edgar Martinez	1.50
15BI	Juan Gonzalez	2.00
16BI	Magglio Ordonez	1.50
17BI	Jermaine Dye	1.50
18BI	Larry Walker	1.50
19BI	Phil Nevin	1.50
20BI	Ivan Rodriguez	1.50
21BI	Ichiro Suzuki	5.00
22BI	J.D. Drew	1.50
23BI	Vladimir Guerrero	2.00
24BI	Sammy Sosa	5.00
25BI	Ken Griffey Jr.	5.00

Bat's Incredible Game-used

		NM/M
Common Player:		5.00
Inserted 1:20		
	Todd Helton	10.00
	Chipper Jones	10.00
	J.D. Drew	8.00
	Alex Rodriguez	15.00
	Manny Ramirez	10.00
	Shawn Green	6.00
	Derek Jeter	20.00
	Edgar Martinez	8.00
	Juan Gonzalez	8.00
	Jermaine Dye	5.00
	Phil Nevin	5.00
	Ivan Rodriguez	10.00

Genuine Ink

		NM/M
Common Autograph		15.00
Production varies		
	Barry Bonds/150	150.00
	Ron Cey/175	15.00
	Derek Jeter/150	125.00
	Al Kaline/300	60.00
	Don Mattingly/50	100.00
	Paul Molitor	50.00
	Dale Murphy/700	40.00
	Phil Rizzuto/700	30.00
	Brooks Robinson/140	60.00
	Maury Willis/975	15.00

Leaders

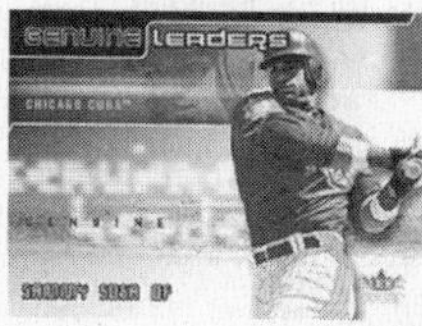

		NM/M
Complete Set (15):		25.00
Common Player:		1.00
Inserted 1:6		
1GL	Sammy Sosa	4.00
2GL	Todd Helton	2.00
3GL	Alex Rodriguez	4.00
4GL	Roger Clemens	3.00
5GL	Barry Bonds	5.00
6GL	Randy Johnson	2.00
7GL	Albert Pujols	4.00
8GL	Curt Schilling	1.00
9GL	Bernie Williams	1.00
10GL	Ken Griffey Jr.	4.00
11GL	Pedro J. Martinez	2.00
12GL	Juan Gonzalez	2.00
13GL	Hideo Nomo	2.00
14GL	Bret Boone	1.00
15GL	Ichiro Suzuki	4.00

Leaders Game-Used

		NM/M
Common Player:		8.00
Inserted 1:16		
	Todd Helton	10.00
	Alex Rodriguez	15.00
	Roger Clemens	15.00
	Barry Bonds	20.00
	Randy Johnson	10.00
	Curt Schilling	8.00
	Bernie Williams	8.00
	Pedro J. Martinez	10.00
	Hideo Nomo	15.00

Names of the Game

		NM/M
Complete Set (30):		60.00
Common Player:		1.00
Inserted 1:10 H, 1:20 R		
1	Mike Piazza	5.00
2	Chipper Jones	4.00
3	Jim Edmonds	1.00
4	Barry Larkin	1.00
5	Frank Thomas	3.00
6	Manny Ramirez	3.00
7	Carlos Delgado	1.50
8	Brian Giles	1.00
9	Kerry Wood	2.00
10	Derek Jeter	8.00
11	Adam Dunn	2.00
12	Gary Sheffield	1.50
13	Luis Gonzalez	1.00
14	Mark Mulder	1.00
15	Roberto Alomar	1.50
16	Scott Rolen	2.50
17	Tom Glavine	1.50
18	Bobby Abreu	1.00
19	Nomar Garciaparra	5.00
20	Darin Erstad	2.00
21	Cliff Floyd	1.00
22	Tim Hudson	1.00
23	Jim Thome	1.00
24	Nolan Ryan	8.00
25	Reggie Jackson	3.00
26	Rafael Palmeiro	2.00
27	Ken Griffey Jr.	5.00
28	Sammy Sosa	5.00
29	Vladimir Guerrero	3.00
30	Ichiro Suzuki	5.00

Names of the Game Memorabilia

		NM/M
Common Player:		5.00
1:24 H, 1:100 R		
1	Roberto Alomar	10.00
2	Carlos Delgado	8.00
3	Jim Edmonds	8.00
4	Darin Erstad	5.00
5	Cliff Floyd	5.00
6	Nomar Garciaparra SP/90	60.00
7	Brian Giles	5.00
8	Luis Gonzalez	5.00
9	Tim Hudson	8.00
10	Derek Jeter	30.00
11	Chipper Jones	10.00
12	Barry Larkin	8.00
13	Mark Mulder	8.00
14	Rafael Palmeiro	10.00
15	Mike Piazza	15.00
16	Manny Ramirez	8.00
17	Scott Rolen	10.00
18	Nolan Ryan	40.00
19	Jim Thome	10.00

Tip of the Cap

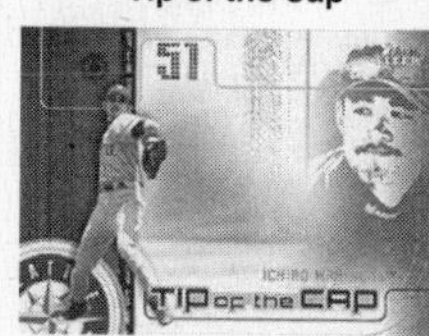

		NM/M
Complete Set (25):		40.00
Common Player:		.50
Inserted 1:6		
1TC	Alex Rodriguez	6.00
2TC	Derek Jeter	8.00
3TC	Kazuhiro Sasaki	.50
4TC	Barry Bonds	8.00
5TC	J.D. Drew	.75
6TC	Tsuyoshi Shinjo	.50
7TC	Alfonso Soriano	1.50
8TC	Albert Pujols	6.00
9TC	Tom Seaver	1.50
10TC	Drew Henson	.75
11TC	Dave Winfield	1.50
12TC	Carlos Delgado	1.00
13TC	Lou Boudreau	.50
14TC	Shawn Green	.75
15TC	Roger Clemens	3.00
16TC	Randy Johnson	1.50
17TC	Sammy Sosa	4.00
18TC	Rafael Palmeiro	1.25
19TC	Ken Griffey Jr.	5.00
20TC	Ichiro Suzuki	5.00
21TC	Eric Chavez	.65
22TC	Andruw Jones	1.50
23TC	Miguel Tejada	.65
24TC	Pedro J. Martinez	1.50
25TC	Tim Salmon	.50

Tip of the Cap Game-Used

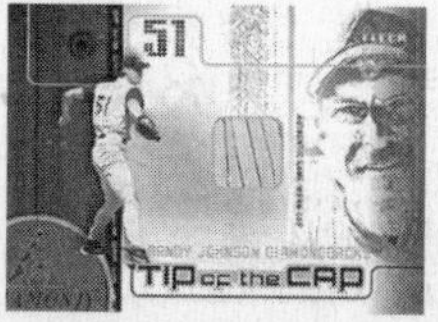

		NM/M
Common Player:		
	Alex Rodriguez/670	20.00
	Barry Bonds/32	75.00
	Tom Seaver/224	25.00
	Drew Henson/361	15.00
	Dave Winfield/363	15.00
	Carlos Delgado/219	15.00
	Lou Boudreau/303	20.00
	Randy Johnson/74	30.00
	Rafael Palmeiro/300	20.00
	Eric Chavez/14	
	Andruw Jones/19	40.00
	Miguel Tejada/225	15.00

Touch 'Em All

		NM/M
Complete Set (25):		60.00
Common Player:		1.50
Inserted 1:10		
1	Derek Jeter	8.00
2	Sammy Sosa	5.00
3	Albert Pujols	6.00
4	Vladimir Guerrero	3.00
5	Ken Griffey Jr.	5.00
6	Nomar Garciaparra	5.00
7	Luis Gonzalez	1.50
8	Barry Bonds	8.00
9	Manny Ramirez	2.50
10	Jason Giambi	2.00
11	Chipper Jones	4.00
12	Ichiro Suzuki	5.00
13	Alex Rodriguez	6.00
14	Juan Gonzalez	2.50
15	Todd Helton	2.50
16	Roberto Alomar	1.50
17	Jeff Bagwell	2.50
18	Mike Piazza	5.00
19	Gary Sheffield	1.50
20	Ivan Rodriguez	2.00
21	Frank Thomas	2.50
22	Bobby Abreu	1.50
23	J.D. Drew	1.50
24	Scott Rolen	2.00
25	Darin Erstad	1.50

Touch 'Em All Base

		NM/M
Common Player:		4.00
Production 350 sets		
	Derek Jeter	15.00
	Sammy Sosa	10.00
	Albert Pujols	15.00
	Vladimir Guerrero	10.00
	Ken Griffey Jr.	10.00
	Nomar Garciaparra	10.00
	Luis Gonzalez	5.00
	Barry Bonds	15.00
	Manny Ramirez	8.00
	Jason Giambi	8.00
	Chipper Jones	8.00
	Ichiro Suzuki	15.00
	Alex Rodriguez	10.00
	Juan Gonzalez	8.00
	Todd Helton	8.00
	Roberto Alomar	6.00
	Jeff Bagwell	8.00
	Mike Piazza	10.00
	Gary Sheffield	6.00
	Ivan Rodriguez	8.00
	Frank Thomas	8.00
	Bobby Abreu	4.00
	J.D. Drew	4.00
	Scott Rolen	8.00
	Darin Erstad	4.00

2002 FLEER GREATS OF THE GAME

		NM/M
Complete Set (100):		45.00
Common Player:		.40
Pack (5):		5.00
Box (24):		100.00
1	Cal Ripken Jr.	6.00
2	Paul Molitor	1.50
3	Roberto Clemente	4.00
4	Cy Young	1.50
5	Tris Speaker	.75
6	Lou Brock	.50
7	Fred Lynn	.40
8	Harmon Killebrew	1.50
9	Ted Williams	6.00
10	Dave Winfield	1.00
11	Orlando Cepeda	.40
12	Johnny Mize	.40
13	Walter Johnson	1.50
14	Roy Campanella	1.50
15	George Sisler	.40
16	Bo Jackson	1.00
17	Rollie Fingers	.40
18	Brooks Robinson	1.50
19	Billy Williams	.40
20	Maury Wills	.40
21	Jimmie Foxx	1.50
22	Alan Trammell	.40
23	Rogers Hornsby	1.50
24	Don Drysdale	1.00
25	Bob Feller	.75
26	Jackie Robinson	5.00
27	Whitey Ford	1.50
28	Enos Slaughter	.40
29	Rod Carew	1.00
30	Eddie Mathews	1.50
31	Ron Cey	.40
32	Thurman Munson	2.00
33	Ty Cobb	3.00
34	Rocky Colavito	.75
35	Satchel Paige	1.50
36	Andre Dawson	.75
37	Phil Rizzuto	.75
38	Roger Maris	3.00
39	Earl Weaver	.40
40	Joe Carter	.40
41	Christy Mathewson	1.50
42	Tony Lazzeri	.40
43	Gil Hodges	.75
44	Gaylord Perry	.40
45	Steve Carlton	1.00
46	George Kell	.40
47	Mickey Cochrane	1.00
48	Joe Morgan	.60
49	Steve Garvey	.40
50	Bob Gibson	1.50
51	Lefty Grove	.40
52	Warren Spahn	1.50
53	Willie McCovey	.75
54	Frank Robinson	1.50
55	Rich "Goose" Gossage	.40
56	Hank Bauer	.40
57	Hoyt Wilhelm	.40
58	Mel Ott	1.00
59	Preacher Roe	.75
60	Yogi Berra	1.50
61	Nolan Ryan	6.00
62	Dizzy Dean	.75
63	Ryne Sandberg	2.00
64	Frank Howard	.40
65	Hack Wilson	.40
66	Robin Yount	1.50
67	Al Kaline	1.50
68	Mike Schmidt	2.00
69	Vida Blue	.40
70	George Brett	3.00
71	Sparky Anderson	.40
72	Tom Seaver	1.50
73	Bill "Moose" Skowron	.40
74	Don Mattingly	2.50
75	Carl Yastrzemski	1.50
76	Eddie Murray	1.00
77	Jim Palmer	1.00
78	Bill Dickey	.75
79	Ozzie Smith	1.50
80	Dale Murphy	.75
81	Nap Lajoie	1.00
82	Jim "Catfish" Hunter	1.00
83	Duke Snider	1.00
84	Luis Aparicio	.40
85	Reggie Jackson	1.50
86	Honus Wagner	1.50
87	Johnny Bench	2.00
88	Stan Musial	3.00
89	Carlton Fisk	.75
90	Tony Oliva	.75
91	Wade Boggs	2.00
92	Jim Rice	.40
93	Bill Mazeroski	.40
94	Ralph Kiner	.40
95	Tony Perez	.40
96	Kirby Puckett	2.00
97	Bobby Bonds	.75
98	Bill Terry	.40
99	Juan Marichal	.75
100	Hank Greenberg	1.00

Autographs

		NM/M
Common Autograph:		10.00
Inserted 1:24		
SA	Sparky Anderson	15.00
LA	Luis Aparicio	15.00
HB	Hank Bauer	10.00
JB	Johnny Bench	50.00
YB	Yogi Berra	40.00
PB	Paul Blair	10.00
VB	Vida Blue	15.00
WB	Wade Boggs	20.00
BB	Bobby Bonds	15.00
GB	George Brett/150	125.00
LB	Lou Brock/250	25.00
RC	Rod Carew/250	40.00
SC	Steve Carlton	25.00
JC	Joe Carter	15.00
OC	Orlando Cepeda	15.00
CE	Ron Cey	10.00
CO	Rocky Colavito	35.00
AD	Andre Dawson	15.00
BF	Bob Feller	15.00
RF	Rollie Fingers	15.00
CF	Carlton Fisk/100	65.00
WF	Whitey Ford	40.00
SG	Steve Garvey	15.00
BG	Bob Gibson/200	30.00
RG	Rich "Goose" Gossage	10.00
FH	Frank Howard	15.00
RJ	Reggie Jackson/150	70.00
AK	Al Kaline	40.00
GK	George Kell	15.00
HK	Harmon Killebrew	30.00
RK	Ralph Kiner/250	25.00
FL	Fred Lynn	15.00
JM	Juan Marichal	15.00
DM	Don Mattingly/300	75.00
BM	Bill Mazeroski/200	20.00
WM	Willie McCovey	25.00
PM	Paul Molitor	25.00
JM	Joe Morgan	15.00
MU	Dale Murphy	40.00
EM	Eddie Murray/250	70.00
SM	Stan Musial/200	75.00
TO	Tony Oliva	15.00
JP	Jim Palmer	20.00
DP	Dave Parker	10.00
TP	Tony Perez	15.00
GP	Gaylord Perry	15.00
KP	Kirby Puckett/250	60.00
JR	Jim Rice	15.00
CR	Cal Ripken Jr./100	180.00
PR	Phil Rizzuto/300	50.00
BR	Brooks Robinson	30.00
FR	Frank Robinson/250	30.00
PR	Preacher Roe	15.00
NR	Nolan Ryan/150	100.00
RS	Ryne Sandberg/200	75.00
MS	Mike Schmidt/150	100.00
TS	Tom Seaver/150	50.00
BS	Bill "Moose" Skowron	10.00
ES	Enos Slaughter	15.00
OS	Ozzie Smith/300	65.00
DS	Duke Snider	25.00
WS	Warren Spahn	50.00
AT	Alan Trammell	20.00
HW	Hoyt Wilhelm	15.00
BW	Billy Williams	15.00
MW	Maury Wills	15.00
DW	Dave Winfield/250	25.00
CY	Carl Yastrzemski/200	75.00
RY	Robin Yount	70.00

Dueling Duos

		NM/M
Complete Set (29):		90.00
Common Player:		2.00
Inserted 1:6		
1DD	Johnny Bench, Carlton Fisk	4.00
2DD	Roy Campanella, Yogi Berra	5.00
3DD	Stan Musial, Ted Williams	8.00
4DD	Carl Yastrzemski, Reggie Jackson	3.00
5DD	Babe Ruth, Jimmie Foxx	8.00
6DD	Steve Carlton, Nolan Ryan	8.00
7DD	Wade Boggs, Don Mattingly	6.00
8DD	Brooks Robinson, Roger Maris	5.00
9DD	Paul Molitor, Don Mattingly	6.00
10DD	Sparky Anderson, Earl Weaver	2.00
11DD	Bob Gibson, Duke Snider	3.00
12DD	Yogi Berra, Gil Hodges	4.00
13DD	Joe Morgan, Ryne Sandberg	3.00
14DD	Tony Perez, Carl Yastrzemski	3.00
15DD	Jimmie Foxx, Bill Dickey	3.00
16DD	Ralph Kiner, Duke Snider	2.00
17DD	Nellie Fox, Rocky Colavito	2.00
18DD	Willie McCovey, Johnny Bench	3.00
19DD	Duke Snider, Eddie Mathews	4.00
20DD	Reggie Jackson, Jim Rice	3.00
21DD	Eddie Murray, Jim Rice	2.00
22DD	Paul Molitor, Dave Winfield	3.00
23DD	Robin Yount, Dave Winfield	3.00
24DD	Enos Slaughter, Ted Kluszewski	2.00
25DD	Wade Boggs, George Brett	4.00
26DD	George Brett, Eddie Murray	4.00
27DD	George Brett, Cal Ripken Jr.	8.00
28DD	Kirby Puckett, Don Mattingly	6.00
29DD	George Brett, Mike Schmidt	5.00

Dueling Duos G-U Single

	NM/M
Common Card:	15.00
Inserted 1:24	
Johnny Bench, Carlton Fisk	20.00
Roy Campanella, Yogi Berra	25.00
Carl Yastrzemski, Reggie Jackson	25.00
Babe Ruth, Jimmie Foxx/75	50.00
Kirby Puckett, Don Mattingly	25.00
Steve Carlton, Nolan Ryan	80.00
Wade Boggs, Don Mattingly	25.00
Brooks Robinson, Roger Maris	25.00
Paul Molitor, Don Mattingly	25.00
Sparky Anderson, Earl Weaver	10.00
Bob Gibson, Duke Snider/200	20.00
Yogi Berra, Gil Hodges	25.00
Joe Morgan, Ryne Sandberg	25.00
Tony Perez, Carl Yastrzemski	25.00
Jimmie Foxx, Bill Dickey	20.00
Ralph Kiner, Duke Snider	20.00
Nellie Fox, Rocky Colavito	20.00
Willie McCovey, Johnny Bench	25.00
Duke Snider, Eddie Mathews	20.00
Reggie Jackson, Jim Rice	20.00
Eddie Murray, Jim Rice	15.00
Paul Molitor, Dave Winfield	15.00
Robin Yount, Dave Winfield	15.00
Enos Slaughter, Ted Kluszewski	10.00
Wade Boggs, George Brett	25.00
George Brett, Eddie Murray	20.00
George Brett, Cal Ripken Jr.	40.00

Dueling Duos Autograph

NM/M

No Pricing
Production 25 sets

1. Johnny Bench, Carlton Fisk
2. Wade Boggs, Don Mattingly
3. George Brett, Mike Schmidt
4. Kirby Puckett, Don Mattingly
5. Duke Snider, Bob Gibson
6. Carl Yastrzemski, Reggie Jackson

Dueling Duos Game Used Dual

No Pricing
Production 25 sets

1DDD	Johnny Bench, Carlton Fisk
2DDD	Roy Campanella, Yogi Berra
3DDD	Carl Yastrzemski, Reggie Jackson
4DDD	Babe Ruth, Jimmie Foxx
5DDD	Kirby Puckett, Don Mattingly
6DDD	Steve Carlton, Nolan Ryan
7DDD	Wade Boggs, Don Mattingly
8DDD	Brooks Robinson, Roger Maris
9DDD	Paul Molitor, Don Mattingly

10DDD Sparky Anderson, Earl Weaver
11DDD Bob Gibson, Duke Snider
12DDD Yogi Berra, Gil Hodges
13DDD Joe Morgan, Ryne Sandberg
14DDD Tony Perez, Carl Yastrzemski
15DDD Jimmie Foxx, Bill Dickey
16DDD Ralph Kiner, Duke Snider
17DDD Nellie Fox, Rocky Colavito
18DDD Willie McCovey, Johnny Bench
19DDD Duke Snider, Eddie Mathews
20DDD Reggie Jackson, Jim Rice
21DDD Eddie Murray, Jim Rice
22DDD Paul Molitor, Dave Winfield
23DDD Robin Yount, Dave Winfield
24DDD Enos Slaughter, Ted Kluszewski
25DDD Wade Boggs, George Brett
26DDD George Brett, Eddie Murray
27DDD George Brett, Cal Ripken Jr.

Through the Years Level 1

NM/M
Common Player: 10.00
Inserted 1:24
George Brett 25.00
Reggie Jackson A's 15.00
Reggie Jackson Angels 15.00
Ted Williams/350 100.00
Robin Yount 20.00
Willie McCovey 10.00
Paul Molitor Brewers 15.00
Paul Molitor Blue Jays 15.00
Jim Palmer 10.00
Brooks Robinson 15.00
Carl Yastrzemski 25.00
Don Mattingly 25.00
Carlton Fisk hitting 15.00
Carlton Fisk fielding 15.00
Nolan Ryan 40.00
Eddie Murray 10.00
Wade Boggs 15.00
Tony Perez 10.00
Ted Kluszewski 10.00
Bo Jackson Royals 15.00
Bo Jackson White Sox 15.00
Johnny Bench 20.00
Jackie Robinson 65.00
Hoyt Wilhelm 10.00
Vida Blue 10.00
Dave Winfield 10.00
Frank Robinson 15.00
Jim Rice 10.00
Jim Rice 10.00
Cal Ripken Hitting 40.00
Cal Ripken Fielding 40.00

Through Years Patch Edition

NM/M
Common Player: 25.00
Production 100 sets
George Brett 80.00
Reggie Jackson A's 30.00
Reggie Jackson Angels 30.00
Ted Williams 120.00
Robin Yount 50.00
Willie McCovey 30.00
Paul Molitor Brewers 40.00
Paul Molitor Blue Jays 40.00
Jim Palmer 25.00
Carl Yastrzemski 75.00
Don Mattingly 60.00
Carlton Fisk 30.00
Carlton Fisk 30.00
Nolan Ryan 75.00
Eddie Murray 25.00
Wade Boggs 30.00
Tony Perez 25.00
Ted Kluszewski 30.00
Bo Jackson Royals 40.00
Bo Jackson White Sox 40.00
Johnny Bench 40.00
Dave Winfield 30.00
Frank Robinson 30.00
Jim Rice 25.00
Jim Rice 25.00
Cal Ripken Jr. 80.00
Cal Ripken Jr. 80.00

Through the Years Level 2

NM/M
Common Player: 25.00
Production 100 sets
George Brett 80.00
Reggie Jackson 30.00
Ted Williams 120.00
Robin Yount 40.00
Willie McCovey 30.00
Paul Molitor 40.00
Jim Palmer 25.00
Carl Yastrzemski 65.00
Don Mattingly 60.00
Carlton Fisk 30.00
Nolan Ryan 75.00
Eddie Murray 25.00
Wade Boggs 30.00
Ted Kluszewski 30.00
Bo Jackson Royals 30.00
Bo Jackson White Sox 30.00
Johnny Bench 40.00
Dave Winfield 25.00
Jim Rice 25.00
Jim Rice 25.00
Cal Ripken Jr. 60.00
Cal Ripken Jr. 60.00

2002 FLEER HOT PROSPECTS

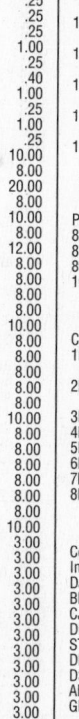

NM/M
Complete Set (125):
Common Player: .25
Common (81-105): 8.00
Production 1,000
Common (106-125): 3.00
Production 1,500
Pack (5): 4.00
Box (18): 50.00
1 Derek Jeter 3.00
2 Garret Anderson .25
3 Scott Rolen .75
4 Bret Boone .25
5 Lance Berkman .25
6 Andruw Jones 1.00
7 Ivan Rodriguez .75
8 Bernie Williams .35
9 Cristian Guzman .25
10 Mo Vaughn .25
11 Troy Glaus 1.00
12 Tim Salmon .35
13 Jason Giambi .65
14 Cliff Floyd .25
15 Tim Hudson .35
16 Curt Schilling .40
17 Sammy Sosa 2.00
18 Alex Rodriguez 2.50
19 Chuck Knoblauch .25
20 Jason Kendall .25
21 Ben Sheets .25
22 Nomar Garciaparra 2.00
23 Ryan Klesko .25
24 Greg Vaughn .25
25 Rafael Palmeiro .75
26 Miguel Tejada .35
27 Shea Hillenbrand .25
28 Jim Thome .25
29 Randy Johnson 1.00
30 Barry Larkin .25
31 Paul LoDuca .25
32 Pedro J. Martinez 1.00
33 Luis Gonzalez .35
34 Carlos Delgado .50
35 Richie Sexson .25
36 Albert Pujols 2.25
37 Bobby Abreu .25
38 Gary Sheffield .40
39 Magglio Ordonez .25
40 Eric Chavez .35
41 Jeff Bagwell 1.00
42 Doug Mientkiewicz .25
43 Moises Alou .25
44 Todd Helton 1.00
45 Ichiro Suzuki 2.00
46 Jose Cruz Jr. .25
47 Freddy Garcia .25
48 Tino Martinez .25
49 Roger Clemens 1.75
50 Greg Maddux 1.50
51 Mike Piazza 2.00
52 Roberto Alomar .50
53 Adam Dunn .50
54 Kerry Wood .75
55 Edgar Martinez .25
56 Ken Griffey Jr. 2.00
57 Juan Gonzalez 1.00
58 Pat Burrell .50
59 Corey Koskie .25
60 Jose Vidro .25
61 Ben Grieve .25
62 Barry Bonds 3.00
63 Raul Mondesi .25
64 Jimmy Rollins .25
65 Mike Sweeney .25
66 Josh Beckett .50
67 Chipper Jones 1.50
68 Jeff Kent .25
69 Tony Batista .25
70 Phil Nevin .25
71 Brian Jordan .25
72 Rich Aurilia .25
73 Brian Giles .25
74 Frank Thomas 1.00
75 Larry Walker .25
76 Shawn Green .40
77 Manny Ramirez 1.00
78 Craig Biggio .25
79 Vladimir Guerrero 1.00
80 Jeromy Burnitz .25
81 Mark Teixeira 10.00
82 *Corey Thurman* 8.00
83 Mark Prior 20.00
84 Marlon Byrd 8.00
85 Austin Kearns 10.00
86 *Satoru Komiyama* 8.00
87 *So Taguchi* 12.00
88 *Jorge Padilla* 8.00
89 *Rene Reyes* 8.00
90 *Jorge Nunez* 8.00
91 *Ron Calloway* 8.00
92 *Kazuhisa Ishii* 10.00
93 Dewon Brazelton 8.00
94 Angel Berroa 8.00
95 *Felix Escalona* 8.00
96 Sean Burroughs 8.00
97 Brandon Duckworth 8.00
98 Hank Blalock 10.00
99 Eric Hinske 8.00
100 Carlos Pena 8.00
101 Morgan Ensberg 8.00
102 Ryan Ludwick 8.00
103 *Chris Snelling* 8.00
104 Jason Lane 8.00
105 Drew Henson 10.00
106 Bobby Kielty 3.00
107 *Earl Snyder* 3.00
108 *Nate Field* 3.00
109 Juan Diaz 3.00
110 Ryan Anderson 3.00
111 Esteban German 3.00
112 *Takahito Nomura* 3.00
113 David Kelton 3.00
114 *Steve Kent* 3.00
115 Colby Lewis 3.00
116 *Jason Simontacchi* 3.00
117 *Rodrigo Rosario* 3.00
118 *Ben Howard* 3.00
119 *Hansel Izquierdo* 3.00
120 *John Ennis* 3.00
121 *Anderson Machado* 3.00
122 *Luis Ugueto* 3.00
123 *Anastacio Martinez* 3.00
124 *Reed Johnson* 6.00
125 Juan Cruz 3.00

Co-Stars

NM/M
Complete Set (15): 25.00
Common Card: 1.00
Inserted 1:6

1CS Barry Bonds, Alex Rodriguez 6.00
2CS Derek Jeter, Nomar Garciaparra 5.00
3CS Andruw Jones, Chipper Jones 3.00
4CS Juan Gonzalez, Jim Thome 2.00
5CS Pedro J. Martinez, Randy Johnson 2.00
6CS Adam Dunn, Pat Burrell 1.50
7CS Frank Thomas, Manny Ramirez 2.00
8CS Jeff Bagwell, Lance Berkman 2.00
9CS So Taguchi, Kazuhisa Ishii 4.00
10CS Jimmy Rollins, Miguel Tejada 1.50
11CS Morgan Ensberg, Carlos Pena 1.00
12CS Adam Dunn, Austin Kearns 2.00
13CS Vladimir Guerrero, Scott Rolen 3.00
14CS Drew Henson, Xavier Nady 1.00
15CS Mike Piazza, Ivan Rodriguez 4.00

Future Swatch Autograph

NM/M
Production 100
83 Mark Prior 75.00
87 So Taguchi 20.00
89 Rene Reyes 10.00
105 Drew Henson 20.00

Inside Barry Bonds

NM/M
Common Bonds: 15.00
1BB Barry Bonds/pants/1,000 20.00
2BB Barry Bonds/pants/900 20.00
3BB Barry Bonds/jsy/800 20.00
4BB Barry Bonds/bat/700 20.00
5BB Barry Bonds/base/600 15.00
6BB Barry Bonds/cleat/500 25.00
7BB Barry Bonds/glove/400 25.00
8BB Barry Bonds/cap/300 30.00

Jerseygraphs

NM/M
Common Player: 10.00
Inserted 1:186
DJ Derek Jeter/108 150.00
BB Barry Bonds/65 250.00
CJ Chipper Jones/100 80.00
DH Drew Henson 30.00
ST So Taguchi/100 25.00
DE David Espinosa 10.00
DS Dane Sardinha 10.00
AB Adrian Beltre/169 35.00
GM Kazuhisa Ishii/40

MLB Hot Materials

NM/M
Common Player: 5.00
Inserted 1:9
Red Hots: 1-2X
Production 50 sets
AD Adam Dunn 8.00
AR Alex Rodriguez 10.00
BB Bret Boone 5.00
BB2 Barry Bonds 20.00
BD Brandon Duckworth 5.00
BG Brian Giles 5.00
BW Bernie Williams 8.00
CD Carlos Delgado 6.00

CG Cristian Guzman 5.00
CP Carlos Pena 8.00
CP Corey Patterson 6.00
CS Curt Schilling 8.00
FT Frank Thomas 10.00
GK Gabe Kapler 5.00
GM Greg Maddux 15.00
GS Gary Sheffield 6.00
IR Ivan Rodriguez 10.00
JB Josh Beckett 8.00
JB2 Jeff Bagwell/108 20.00
JG Juan Gonzalez 8.00
JT Jim Thome 10.00
JU Juan Uribe 5.00
LB Lance Berkman 8.00
MM Mark Mulder 8.00
MA Moises Alou 6.00
MP Mike Piazza 15.00
MS Mike Sweeney 5.00
NJ Nick Johnson 5.00
PL Paul LoDuca 5.00
PM Pedro J. Martinez 10.00
RF Rafael Furcal 5.00
RO Roy Oswalt 5.00
RP Rafael Palmeiro 10.00
SB Sean Burroughs/350 10.00
SG Shawn Green 8.00
TA Tony Armas Jr. 5.00
TH Torii Hunter 5.00
TM Tino Martinez 8.00
VW Vernon Wells 5.00
KI Kazuhisa Ishii/70
TH Todd Helton 8.00
MO Magglio Ordonez 8.00
FG Freddy Garcia 5.00
ST So Taguchi 8.00

MLB Hot Tandems

NM/M

Common Card: 10.00
Production 100 sets
Red Hots 10 sets no pricing
Adam Dunn, Lance Berkman 15.00
Alex Rodriguez, Ivan Rodriguez 30.00
Bret Boone, Freddy Garcia 10.00
Barry Bonds, Kazuhisa Ishii 40.00
Brandon Duckworth, Roy Oswalt 10.00
Bernie Williams, Jorge Posada 15.00
Carlos Delgado, Vernon Wells 10.00
Cristian Guzman, Torii Hunter 10.00
Carlos Pena, Corey Patterson 10.00
Curt Schilling, Greg Maddux 25.00
Frank Thomas, Magglio Ordonez 15.00
Gabe Kapler, Rafael Palmeiro 12.00
Gary Sheffield, Rafael Furcal 10.00
Josh Beckett, Roy Oswalt 10.00
Brandon Duckworth, Josh Beckett 15.00
Jeff Bagwell, Lance Berkman 15.00
Juan Gonzalez, Rafael Palmeiro 15.00
Jim Thome, Shawn Green 15.00
Paul LoDuca, Shawn Green 10.00
Juan Uribe, Miguel Tejada 15.00
Mark Mulder, Miguel Tejada 15.00
Moises Alou, Magglio Ordonez 10.00
Jorge Posada, Mike Piazza 25.00
Mike Sweeney, Todd Helton 15.00
Carlos Pena, Nick Johnson 10.00
Curt Schilling, Pedro J. Martinez 25.00
Tony Armas Jr., Freddy Garcia 10.00
Tino Martinez, Todd Helton 15.00
Barry Bonds, Derek Jeter 60.00
Kazuhisa Ishii, Derek Jeter 40.00
Juan Uribe, Cristian Guzman 10.00
Kazuhisa Ishii, So Taguchi 20.00
Adam Dunn, Corey Patterson 15.00
Bernie Williams, Nick Johnson 10.00
Bret Boone, Torii Hunter 10.00
Greg Maddux, Pedro J. Martinez 20.00
Sean Burroughs, Drew Henson 10.00
Kazuhisa Ishii, Satoru Komiyama 20.00
Kazuhisa Ishii, Mark Prior 25.00
Hank Blalock, Austin Kearns 15.00
Hank Blalock, Mark Teixeira 15.00
Marlon Byrd, Jorge Padilla 10.00
Marlon Byrd, Austin Kearns 10.00
Gabe Kapler, Juan Gonzalez 15.00
Jeff Bagwell, Mike Piazza 25.00

We're Number One

NM/M

Complete Set (10): 35.00
Common Player: 1.50
Inserted 1:15
1WN Derek Jeter 8.00
2WN Barry Bonds 8.00
3WN Ken Griffey Jr. 5.00
4WN Roger Clemens 4.50
5WN Alex Rodriguez 6.00
6WN J.D. Drew 1.50
7WN Chipper Jones 4.00
8WN Manny Ramirez 3.00
9WN Nomar Garciaparra 5.00
10WN Todd Helton 3.00

We're Number One Autograph

NM/M

Common Player:
Derek Jeter/92
Barry Bonds/85 200.00

We're Number One Memorabilia

NM/M

Common Player: 5.00
Inserted 1:25
Derek Jeter/jsy 25.00
Barry Bonds/jsy 20.00
Ken Griffey Jr/base 15.00
Alex Rodriguez/jsy 15.00
J.D. Drew/jsy 5.00
Chipper Jones/jsy 10.00
Manny Ramirez/jsy 10.00
Nomar Garciaparra/jsy 20.00
Todd Helton/jsy 10.00

2002 FLEER MAXIMUM

NM/M

Complete Set (270):
Common Player: .15
Common (201-250): 5.00
Production 500
Common (251-270): .50
Inserted 1:hobby pack
Pack (15): 2.50
Box (16): 35.00
1 Barry Bonds 2.00
2 Alex Rodriguez 1.50
3 Jim Edmonds .15
4 Manny Ramirez .75
5 Jeff Bagwell .75
6 Kazuhiro Sasaki .15
7 Jason Giambi .50
8 J.D. Drew .25
9 Barry Larkin .15
10 Chipper Jones 1.00
11 Rafael Palmeiro .65
12 Roberto Alomar .35
13 Randy Johnson .75
14 Juan Gonzalez .75
15 Gary Sheffield .25
16 Larry Walker .15
17 Todd Helton .75
18 Ivan Rodriguez .65
19 Greg Maddux 1.00
20 Mike Piazza 1.25
21 Tsuyoshi Shinjo .15
22 Luis Gonzalez .25
23 Pedro Martinez .75
24 Albert Pujols 1.50
25 Jose Canseco .35
26 Edgar Martinez .15
27 Moises Alou .15
28 Vladimir Guerrero .75
29 Shawn Green .35
30 Miguel Tejada .25
31 Bernie Williams .30
32 Frank Thomas .75
33 Jim Thome .15
34 Derek Jeter 2.00
35 Julio Lugo .15
36 Mo Vaughn .15
37 Steve Cox .15
38 Brad Radke .15
39 Brian Jordan .15
40 Garret Anderson .15
41 Ichiro Suzuki 1.25
42 Mike Lieberthal .15
43 Preston Wilson .15
44 Bud Smith .15
45 Curt Schilling .40
46 Eric Chavez .25
47 Javier Vazquez .15
48 Jose Ortiz .15
49 Mike Sweeney .15
50 Travis Fryman .15
51 Brady Anderson .15
52 Chan Ho Park .15
53 C.C. Sabathia .15
54 Jack Wilson .25
55 Joe Crede .15
56 Mike Mussina .40
57 Sean Casey .30
58 Bobby Abreu .15
59 Joe Randa .15
60 Jose Vidro .15
61 Juan Uribe .15
62 Mark Grace .25
63 Matt Morris .15
64 Omar Vizquel .15
65 Darryl Kile .15
66 Dee Brown .15
67 Fernando Tatis .15
68 Jeff Cirillo .15
69 Johnny Damon .25
70 Milton Bradley .15
71 Reggie Sanders .15
72 Al Leiter .15
73 Andres Galarraga .15
74 Ellis Burks .15
75 Jermaine Dye .15
76 Juan Pierre .15
77 Junior Spivey .15
78 Mark Quinn .15
79 Ben Sheets .15
80 Brad Fullmer .15
81 Bubba Trammell .15
82 Dante Bichette .15
83 Ken Griffey Jr. 1.25
84 Paul O'Neill .15
85 Robert Fick .15
86 Bret Boone .15
87 Raul Mondesi .15
88 Josh Beckett .40
89 Geoff Jenkins .15
90 Ramon Ortiz .15
91 Robin Ventura .15
92 Tom Glavine .30
93 Jimmy Rollins .15
94 Jamie Moyer .15
95 Magglio Ordonez .15
96 Mike Lowell .15
97 Ryan Dempster .15
98 Scott Schoeneweis .15
99 Todd Zeile .15
100 A.J. Burnett .15
101 Aaron Sele .15
102 Cal Ripken Jr. 2.00
103 Carlos Beltran .45
104 David Eckstein .15
105 Jason Marquis .15
106 Matt Lawton .15
107 Ben Grieve .15
108 Brian Giles .15
109 Josh Towers .15
110 Lance Berkman .15
111 Sammy Sosa 1.25
112 Torii Hunter .15
113 Aubrey Huff .15
114 Craig Biggio .15
115 Doug Mientkiewicz .15
116 Fred McGriff .15
117 Jason Johnson .15
118 Pat Burrell .25
119 Aaron Boone .15
120 Carlos Delgado .50
121 Nomar Garciaparra 1.25
122 Richie Sexson .15
123 Russ Ortiz .15
124 Tim Hudson .25
125 Tony Clark .15
126 Jeromy Burnitz .15
127 Jose Cruz .15
128 Juan Encarnacion .15
129 Mark Mulder .15
130 Mike Hampton .15
131 Rich Aurilia .15
132 Trot Nixon .15
133 Greg Vaughn .15
134 Jacque Jones .15
135 Jason Kendall .15
136 Jay Gibbons .15
137 Mark Buehrle .15
138 Richard Hidalgo .15
139 Rondell White .15
140 Cristian Guzman .15
141 Andy Pettitte .30
142 Chris Richard .15
143 Paul LoDuca .15
144 Phil Nevin .15
145 Ray Durham .15
146 Todd Walker .15
147 Bartolo Colon .15
148 Ben Petrick .15
149 Freddy Garcia .15
150 Jon Lieber .15
151 Jose Hernandez .15
152 Matt Williams .15
153 Shannon Stewart .15
154 Adrian Beltre .30
155 Carlos Lee .15
156 Frank Catalanotto .15
157 Jorge Posada .30
158 Pokey Reese .15
159 Ryan Klesko .15
160 Ugueth Urbina .15
161 Adam Dunn .50
162 Alfonso Soriano .50
163 Ben Davis .15
164 Paul Konerko .25
165 Eric Karros .25
166 Jeff Weaver .15
167 Ruben Sierra .15
168 Bobby Higginson .15
169 Eric Milton .15
170 Kerry Wood .65
171 Roy Oswalt .30
172 Scott Rolen .65
173 Tim Salmon .25
174 Aramis Ramirez .25
175 Jason Tyner .15
176 Juan Cruz .15
177 Keith Foulke .15
178 Kevin Brown .25
179 Roger Clemens 1.00
180 Tony Batista .15
181 Andruw Jones .75
182 Cliff Floyd .15
183 Darin Erstad .25
184 Joe Mays .15
185 Mike Cameron .15
186 Robert Person .15
187 Jeff Kent .25
188 Gabe Kapler .25
189 Jason Jennings .15
190 Jason Varitek .15
191 Barry Zito .25
192 Rickey Henderson .75
193 Tino Martinez .25
194 Brandon Duckworth .15
195 Corey Koskie .15
196 Derrek Lee .25

197 Javy Lopez .25
198 John Olerud .25
199 Terrance Long .15
200 Troy Glaus .75
201 Scott MacRae 5.00
202 Scott Chiasson 5.00
203 Bart Miadich 5.00
204 Brian Bowles 5.00
205 David Williams 5.00
206 Victor Zambrano 5.00
207 Joe Beimel 5.00
208 Scott Stewart 5.00
209 Bob File 5.00
210 Ryan Jensen 5.00
211 Jason Karnuth 5.00
212 Brandon Knight 5.00
213 *Andy Shibilo* 5.00
214 *Chad Ricketts* 5.00
215 Mark Prior 10.00
216 Chad Paronto 5.00
217 Corky Miller 5.00
218 Luis Pineda 5.00
219 Ramon Vazquez 5.00
220 Tony Cogan 5.00
221 Roy Smith 5.00
222 Mark Lukasiewicz 5.00
223 Mike Rivera 5.00
224 Brad Voyles 5.00
225 *Jamie Burke* 5.00
226 Justin Duchscherer 5.00
227 *Eric Cyr* 5.00
228 Mark Lukasiewicz 5.00
229 Marlon Byrd 5.00
230 *Chris Piersoll* 5.00
231 Ramon Vazquez 5.00
232 Tony Cogan 5.00
233 Roy Smith 5.00
234 *Franklin Nunez* 5.00
235 Corky Miller 5.00
236 *Jorge Nunez* 5.00
237 Joe Beimel 5.00
238 Eric Knott 5.00
239 Victor Zambrano 5.00
240 Jason Karnuth 5.00
241 Jason Middlebrook 5.00
242 Scott Stewart 5.00
243 Tim Spooneybarger 5.00
244 David Williams 5.00
245 Bart Miadich 5.00
246 Mike Koplove 5.00
247 Ryan Jensen 5.00
248 Jeremy Fikac 5.00
249 Bob File 5.00
250 Craig Monroe 5.00
251 Albert Pujols 2.00
252 Ichiro Suzuki 2.00
253 Nomar Garciaparra 2.00
254 Barry Bonds 3.00
255 Jason Giambi .75
256 Derek Jeter 3.00
257 Roberto Alomar .75
258 Roger Clemens 2.00
259 Mike Piazza 1.50
260 Vladimir Guerrero 1.00
261 Todd Helton .75
262 Shawn Green .50
263 Chipper Jones 1.00
264 Pedro Martinez 1.00
265 Pat Burrell .50
266 Sammy Sosa 2.00
267 Ken Griffey Jr. 1.50
268 Cal Ripken Jr. 3.00
269 Kerry Wood 1.00
270 Alex Rodriguez 2.50

To The Max

Stars (1-200): 4-6X
Print Run 200-500
Stars (1-200): 4-8X
Print Run 121-199
Stars (1-200): 6-12X
Print Run 75-120
Stars (1-200): 10-25X
Print Run 40-75
Stars (1-200): 15-40X
Print Run 20-39
Rookies (201-250): .5-1X
Production 100
Impact (251-270): 2-4X
Production 200-400

America's Game

NM/M
Complete Set (25): 25.00
Common Player: .50
Inserted 1:10 Retail
1 Pedro Martinez 1.50
2 Miguel Tejada .75
3 Randy Johnson 1.50
4 Barry Bonds 5.00
5 Rafael Palmeiro 1.00
6 Mike Piazza 3.00
7 Greg Maddux 2.50
8 Jeff Bagwell 1.50
9 Edgar Martinez .50
10 Albert Pujols 4.00
11 Todd Helton 1.50
12 Chipper Jones 2.50
13 Luis Gonzalez .50
14 Jason Giambi 1.00
15 Kazuhiro Sasaki .50
16 Dave Winfield 1.00
17 Reggie Jackson 1.50
18 Tom Glavine .75
19 Carlos Delgado .75
20 Bobby Abreu .50
21 Larry Walker .50
22 J.D. Drew .75
23 Alex Rodriguez 4.00
24 Frank Thomas 1.50
25 C.C. Sabathia .50

Americas Game Jersey

NM/M
Common Player: 8.00
Inserted 1:24 H, 1:72 R
1 Jeff Bagwell 10.00
2 Craig Biggio 8.00
3 Barry Bonds 25.00
4 Carlos Delgado 8.00
5 J.D. Drew 5.00
6 Jason Giambi 10.00
7 Tom Glavine 10.00
8 Luis Gonzalez 5.00
9 Todd Helton 10.00
10 Reggie Jackson 10.00
11 Randy Johnson 10.00
12 Chipper Jones 10.00
13 Greg Maddux 10.00
14 Edgar Martinez 8.00
15 Pedro Martinez 10.00
16 Rafael Palmeiro 10.00
17 Chan Ho Park 5.00
18 Mike Piazza 10.00
19 Albert Pujols 20.00
20 Kazuhiro Sasaki 5.00
21 Miguel Tejada 5.00
22 Frank Thomas 10.00
23 Larry Walker 5.00
24 Dave Winfield 5.00

Coverage

NM/M
Common Player: 15.00
Production 100 sets
1 Roberto Alomar Bat 25.00
2 Jeff Bagwell Jsy 20.00
3 Barry Bonds Bat 50.00
4 Jose Canseco Bat 25.00
5 J.D. Drew Bat 25.00
6 Jim Edmonds Bat 20.00
7 Jason Giambi Bat 25.00
8 Juan Gonzalez Bat 25.00
9 Luis Gonzalez Jsy 15.00
10 Todd Helton Jsy 20.00
11 Randy Johnson Jsy 40.00
12 Chipper Jones Bat 25.00
13 Greg Maddux Jsy 40.00
14 Pedro Martinez Jsy 30.00
15 Rafael Palmeiro Pants 25.00
16 Albert Pujols Jsy 50.00
17 Manny Ramirez Bat 20.00
18 Alex Rodriguez Bat 30.00
19 Ivan Rodriguez Bat 25.00
20 Kazuhiro Sasaki Jsy 20.00
21 Gary Sheffield Bat 20.00
22 Tsuyoshi Shinjo Bat 15.00

Coverage Autographs

NM/M
Quantity produced listed
1 Barry Bonds Pants/50 200.00
2 J.D. Drew Bat/100 25.00
3 Jim Edmonds Bat/100 25.00
4 Drew Henson Bat/100 25.00
5 Chipper Jones Bat/50 60.00
6 Albert Pujols Jsy/100 150.00
7 Gary Sheffield Bat/100 30.00

Derek Jeter Legacy Collection

NM/M
Inserted 1:236
DJ Derek Jeter/bat 40.00
DJ Derek Jeter/ Bat Auto/222 150.00
DJ Derek Jeter/jersey 40.00
DJ Derek Jeter/ jersey Auto 200.00

Maximum Power Bat

NM/M
Common Player: 5.00
Inserted 1:24 H
Golds: 3-4X
Production 25 sets
Luis Gonzalez 5.00
Larry Walker 5.00
Frank Thomas 10.00
Manny Ramirez 10.00
Barry Bonds 25.00
Jim Thome 10.00
Tsuyoshi Shinjo 5.00
Bernie Williams/175 25.00
Chipper Jones 10.00
Shawn Green 5.00
Juan Gonzalez 8.00
Jim Edmonds 10.00
Moises Alou 10.00
Roberto Alomar 10.00
Jose Canseco 10.00
Ivan Rodriguez 10.00
Barry Larkin/50 40.00
Mike Piazza 15.00
Gary Sheffield 8.00
J.D. Drew/200 8.00
Alex Rodriguez 15.00
Jason Giambi 10.00
Todd Helton 8.00

Power

NM/M
Complete Set (25): 40.00
Inserted 1:20 Retail
1 Luis Gonzalez 1.00
2 Jimmy Rollins 1.00
3 Larry Walker 1.00
4 Frank Thomas 2.00
5 Manny Ramirez 2.00
6 Barry Bonds 8.00
7 Jim Thome 1.00
8 Tsuyoshi Shinjo 1.00
9 Bernie Williams 1.00
10 Chipper Jones 3.00
11 Shawn Green 1.50
12 Drew Henson 1.00
13 Juan Gonzalez 2.00
14 Jim Edmonds 1.00
15 Moises Alou 1.00
16 Roberto Alomar 1.50
17 Jose Canseco 1.50
18 Ivan Rodriguez 1.50
19 Barry Larkin 1.00
20 Mike Piazza 5.00
21 Gary Sheffield 1.00
22 J.D. Drew 1.00
23 Alex Rodriguez 6.00
24 Jason Giambi 1.50
25 Todd Helton 2.00

2002 FLEER PLATINUM

NM/M
Complete Set (302): 125.00
Common Player: .15
Common (251-260): 2.00
Common (261-302): 1.50
Inserted 1:3 H, 1:6 Retail
Hobby Pack (10): 2.00
Hobby Box (24): 35.00
Rack Box: 70.00
1 Garrett Anderson .15
2 Randy Johnson .65
3 Chipper Jones .75
4 David Cone .15
5 Corey Patterson .15
6 Carlos Lee .15
7 Barry Larkin .15
8 Jim Thome .15
9 Larry Walker .15
10 Randall Simon .15
11 Charles Johnson .15
12 Richard Hidalgo .15
13 Mark Quinn .15
14 Paul LoDuca .15
15 Cristian Guzman .15
16 Orlando Cabrera .15
17 Al Leiter .15
18 Nick Johnson .15
19 Eric Chavez .25
20 Miguel Tejada .25
21 Mike Lieberthal .15
22 Robert Mackowiak .15
23 Ryan Klesko .15
24 Jeff Kent .15
25 Edgar Martinez .15
26 Steve Kline .15
27 Toby Hall .15
28 Rusty Greer .15
29 Jose Cruz Jr. .15
30 Darin Erstad .50
31 Reggie Sanders .15
32 Javy Lopez .15
33 Carl Everett .15
34 Sammy Sosa 1.00
35 Magglio Ordonez .15
36 Todd Walker .15
37 Omar Vizquel .15
38 Matt Anderson .15
39 Jeff Weaver .15
40 Derrek Lee .15
41 Julio Lugo .15
42 Joe Randa .15
43 Chan Ho Park .15
44 Torii Hunter .15
45 Vladimir Guerrero .65
46 Rey Ordonez .15
47 Tino Martinez .15
48 Johnny Damon .25
49 Barry Zito .25
50 Robert Person .15
51 Aramis Ramirez .15
52 Mark Kotsay .15
53 Jason Schmidt .15
54 Jamie Moyer .15
55 David Justice .15
56 Aubrey Huff .15
57 Rick Helling .15
58 Carlos Delgado .40
59 Troy Glaus .65
60 Curt Schilling .40
61 Greg Maddux .75
62 Nomar Garciaparra 1.00
63 Kerry Wood .50
64 Frank Thomas .65

65	Dmitri Young	.15
66	Alex Ochoa	.15
67	Jose Macias	.15
68	Antonio Alfonseca	.15
69	Mike Lowell	.15
70	Wade Miller	.15
71	Mike Sweeney	.15
72	Gary Sheffield	.25
73	Corey Koskie	.15
74	Lee Stevens	.15
75	Jay Payton	.15
76	Mike Mussina	.40
77	Jermaine Dye	.15
78	Bobby Abreu	.15
79	Scott Rolen	.50
80	Todd Ritchie	.15
81	D'Angelo Jimenez	.15
82	Rob Nenn	.15
83	John Olerud	.15
84	Matt Morris	.15
85	Joe Kennedy	.15
86	Gabe Kapler	.15
87	Chris Carpenter	.15
88	David Eckstein	.15
89	Matt Williams	.15
90	John Smoltz	.15
91	Pedro J. Martinez	.65
92	Eric Young	.15
93	Jose Valentin	.15
94	Erubiel Durazo	.15
95	Jeff Cirillo	.15
96	Brandon Inge	.15
97	Josh Beckett	.40
98	Preston Wilson	.15
99	Damian Jackson	.15
100	Adrian Beltre	.25
101	Jeromy Burnitz	.15
102	Joe Mays	.15
103	Michael Barrett	.15
104	Mike Piazza	1.00
105	Brady Anderson	.15
106	Jason Giambi	.40
107	Marlon Anderson	.15
108	Jimmy Rollins	.15
109	Jack Wilson	.15
110	Brian Lawrence	.15
111	Russ Ortiz	.15
112	Kazuhiro Sasaki	.15
113	Placido Polanco	.15
114	Damian Rolls	.15
115	Rafael Palmeiro	.50
116	Brad Fullmer	.15
117	Tim Salmon	.25
118	Tony Womack	.15
119	Tony Batista	.15
120	Trot Nixon	.15
121	Mark Buehrle	.15
122	Derek Jeter	1.50
123	Ellis Burks	.15
124	Mike Hampton	.15
125	Roger Cedeno	.15
126	A.J. Burnett	.15
127	Moises Alou	.15
128	Billy Wagner	.15
129	Kevin Brown	.15
130	Jose Hernandez	.15
131	Doug Mientkiewicz	.15
132	Javier Vazquez	.15
133	Tsuyoshi Shinjo	.15
134	Andy Pettitte	.30
135	Tim Hudson	.25
136	Pat Burrell	.40
137	Brian Giles	.15
138	Kevin Young	.15
139	Xavier Nady	.15
140	J.T. Snow	.15
141	Aaron Sele	.15
142	Albert Pujols	1.25
143	Jason Tyner	.15
144	Ivan Rodriguez	.50
145	Raul Mondesi	.15
146	Matt Lawton	.15
147	Rafael Furcal	.15
148	Jeff Conine	.15
149	Hideo Nomo	.60
150	Jose Canseco	.30
151	Aaron Boone	.15
152	Bartolo Colon	.15
153	Todd Helton	.65
154	Tony Clark	.15
155	Pablo Ozuna	.15
156	Jeff Bagwell	.65
157	Carlos Beltran	.50
158	Shawn Green	.25
159	Geoff Jenkins	.15
160	Eric Milton	.15
161	Jose Vidro	.15
162	Robin Ventura	.15
163	Jorge Posada	.25
164	Terrence Long	.15
165	Brandon Duckworth	.15
166	Chad Hermansen	.15
167	Ben Davis	.15
168	Phil Nevin	.15
169	Bret Boone	.15
170	J.D. Drew	.25
171	Edgar Renteria	.15
172	Randy Winn	.15
173	Alex Rodriguez	1.50
174	Shannon Stewart	.15
175	Steve Finley	.15
176	Marcus Giles	.15
177	Jay Gibbons	.15
178	Manny Ramirez	.65
179	Ray Durham	.15
180	Sean Casey	.25
181	Travis Fryman	.15
182	Denny Neagle	.15
183	Deivi Cruz	.15
184	Luis Castillo	.15
185	Lance Berkman	.15
186	Dee Brown	.15
187	Jeff Shaw	.15
188	Mark Loretta	.15
189	David Ortiz	.25
190	Edgardo Alfonzo	.15
191	Roger Clemens	.75
192	Mariano Rivera	.25
193	Jeremy Giambi	.15
194	Johnny Estrada	.15
195	Craig Wilson	.15
196	Adam Eaton	.15
197	Rich Aurilia	.15
198	Mike Cameron	.15
199	Jim Edmonds	.15
200	Fernando Vina	.15
201	Greg Vaughn	.15
202	Mike Young	.15
203	Vernon Wells	.15
204	Luis Gonzalez	.25
205	Tom Glavine	.30
206	Chris Richard	.15
207	Jon Lieber	.15
208	Keith Foulke	.15
209	Rondell White	.15
210	Bernie Williams	.30
211	Juan Pierre	.15
212	Juan Encarnacion	.15
213	Ryan Dempster	.15
214	Tim Redding	.15
215	Jeff Suppan	.15
216	Mark Grudzielanek	.15
217	Richie Sexson	.15
218	Brad Radke	.15
219	Armando Benitez	.15
220	Orlando Hernandez	.15
221	Alfonso Soriano	.40
222	Mark Mulder	.15
223	Travis Lee	.15
224	Jason Kendall	.15
225	Trevor Hoffman	.15
226	Barry Bonds	1.50
227	Freddy Garcia	.15
228	Darryl Kile	.15
229	Ben Grieve	.15
230	Frank Catalanotto	.15
231	Ruben Sierra	.15
232	Homer Bush	.15
233	Mark Grace	.25
234	Andruw Jones	.60
235	Brian Roberts	.15
236	Fred McGriff	.15
237	Paul Konerko	.15
238	Ken Griffey Jr.	1.00
239	John Burkett	.15
240	Juan Uribe	.15
241	Bobby Higginson	.15
242	Cliff Floyd	.15
243	Craig Biggio	.15
244	Neifi Perez	.15
245	Eric Karros	.15
246	Ben Sheets	.15
247	Tony Armas Jr.	.15
248	Mo Vaughn	.15
249	David Wells	.15
250	Juan Gonzalez	.60
251	Barry Bonds	5.00
252	Sammy Sosa	3.00
253	Ken Griffey Jr.	3.00
254	Roger Clemens	4.00
255	Greg Maddux	2.50
256	Chipper Jones	1.50
257	Alex Rodriguez, Derek Jeter, Nomar Garciaparra	5.00
258	Roberto Alomar	1.50
259	Jeff Bagwell	1.50
260	Mike Piazza	3.00
261	Mark Teixeira	2.00
262	Mark Prior	3.00
263	Alex Escobar	1.50
264	C.C. Sabathia	1.50
265	Drew Henson	1.50
266	Wilson Betemit	1.50
267	Roy Oswalt	1.50
268	Adam Dunn	2.00
269	Bud Smith	1.50
270	Dewon Brazelton	1.50
271	Brandon Backe, Jason Standridge	1.50
272	Wilfredo Rodriguez, Carlos Hernandez	1.50
273	Geronimo Gil, Luis Rivera	1.50
274	Carlos Pena, Jovanny Cedeno	1.50
275	Austin Kearns, Ben Broussard	1.50
276	Jorge De La Rosa, Kenny Kelly	1.50
277	Ryan Drese, Victor Martinez	1.50
278	Joel Pinero, Nate Cornejo	1.50
279	David Kelton, Carlos Zambrano	1.50
281	Donnie Bridges, Wilkin Ruan	1.50
282	Wily Mo Pena, Brandon Claussen	2.00
283	*Jason Jennings, Rene Reyes*	1.50
284	Steve Green, Alfredo Amezaga	1.50
285	Eric Hinske, Felipe Lopez	1.50
286	Anderson Machado, Brad Baisley	1.50
287	Carlos Garcia, Sean Douglass	1.50
288	Pat Strange, Jae Weong Seo	1.50
289	Marcus Thames, Alex Graman	1.50
290	*Matt Childers, Hansel Izquierdo*	1.50
291	*Ron Calloway, Adam Walker*	1.50
292	J.R. House, J.J. Davis	1.50
293	Ryan Anderson, Rafael Soriano	1.50
294	Mike Bynum, Dennis Tankersley	1.50
295	Kurt Ainsworth, Carlos Valderrama	1.50
296	Billy Hall, Cristian Guerrero	1.50
297	Miguel Olivo, Danny Wright	1.50
298	*Marlon Byrd, Jorge Padilla*	1.50
299	Juan Cruz, Ben Christensen	1.50
300	Adam Johnson, Michael Restovich	1.50
301	*So Taguchi*	2.00
302	*Kazuhisa Ishii*	3.00

Edition

Stars (1-250):	4-8X
Production 202	
Cards 251-302:	No Pricing
Production 22	

Barry Bonds RC Autograph

	NM/M
73 cards autographed	
Barry Bonds	450.00

Clubhouse Collection Memorabilia

	NM/M
Common Player:	5.00
Inserted 1:32	
Edgardo Alfonzo/jsy	5.00
Rick Ankiel/jsy	5.00
Craig Biggio/bat	8.00
Adrian Beltre/jsy	5.00
Sean Casey/jsy	8.00
Barry Bonds/jsy	25.00
Scott Rolen/jsy	10.00
Eric Chavez/jsy	8.00
Roger Clemens/jsy	25.00
Carlos Delgado/jsy	8.00
J.D. Drew/jsy	5.00
Darin Erstad/jsy	5.00
Jim Thome/bat	10.00
Juan Gonzalez/bat	8.00
Nomar Garciaparra/jsy	15.00
Todd Helton/jsy	8.00
Derek Jeter/pants	25.00
Randy Johnson/jsy	10.00
Andruw Jones/jsy	8.00
Tim Hudson/jsy	5.00
Jason Kendall/jsy	5.00
Johnny Damon/bat	5.00
Paul LoDuca/jsy	5.00
Greg Maddux/jsy	10.00
Pedro Martinez/jsy	10.00
Raul Mondesi/bat	5.00
Magglio Ordonez/jsy	5.00
Mike Piazza/jsy	10.00
Manny Ramirez/jsy	8.00
Mariano Rivera/jsy	8.00
Ivan Rodriguez/jsy	10.00
Alex Rodriguez/jsy	15.00
Kazuhiro Sasaki/jsy	5.00
Frank Thomas/jsy	10.00
Curt Schilling/jsy	8.00
Gary Sheffield/bat	6.00
Omar Vizquel/jsy	5.00

Clubhouse Collection - Dual

	NM/M
Common Card:	10.00
Inserted 1:96	
Edgardo Alfonzo	10.00
Rick Ankiel	8.00
Craig Biggio	
Adrian Beltre	10.00
Barry Bonds	40.00
Sean Casey	10.00
Eric Chavez	10.00
Roger Clemens	30.00
Carlos Delgado	10.00
J.D. Drew	10.00
Darin Erstad	10.00
Jim Thome	20.00
Juan Gonzalez	15.00
Nomar Garciaparra	30.00
Todd Helton	
Derek Jeter	40.00
Randy Johnson	20.00
Andruw Jones	10.00
Jason Kendall	
Johnny Damon	10.00
Paul LoDuca	10.00
Greg Maddux	20.00
Pedro J. Martinez	20.00
Raul Mondesi	
Magglio Ordonez	10.00
Mike Piazza	30.00
Manny Ramirez	15.00
Mariano Rivera	15.00
Ivan Rodriguez	20.00
Alex Rodriguez	25.00
Scott Rolen	20.00
Kazuhiro Sasaki	10.00
Curt Schilling	20.00
Gary Sheffield	10.00
Frank Thomas	20.00
Jim Thome	20.00
Omar Vizquel	10.00

Cornerstones

	NM/M
Complete Set (40):	120.00

Inserted 1:12 Jumbo
1 Bill Terry, Johnny Mize 1.50
2 Cal Ripken Jr., Eddie Murray 10.00
3 Eddie Mathews, Chipper Jones 3.00
4 Albert Pujols, George Sisler 6.00
5 Sean Casey, Tony Perez 1.50
6 Jimmie Foxx, Scott Rolen 4.00
7 Wade Boggs, George Brett 8.00
8 Rod Carew, Troy Glaus 1.50
9 Jeff Bagwell, Rafael Palmeiro 2.00
10 Willie Stargell, Pie Traynor 2.00
11 Cal Ripken Jr., Brooks Robinson 10.00
12 Tony Perez, Ted Kluszewski 1.50
13 Jason Giambi, Don Mattingly 8.00
14 Hank Greenberg, Jimmie Foxx 4.00
15 Ernie Banks, Willie McCovey 3.00
16 Jim Thome, Travis Fryman 3.00
17 Ted Kluszewski, Sean Casey 1.50
18 Gil Hodges, Johnny Mize 3.00
19 Brooks Robinson, Boog Powell 3.00
20 Bill Terry, George Sisler 2.00
21 Wade Boggs, Don Mattingly 8.00
22 Jason Giambi, Carlos Delgado 2.50
23 Willie Stargell, Bill Madlock 2.00
24 Mark Grace, Matt Williams 2.00
25 Paul Molitor, George Brett 8.00
26 Carlos Delgado, Mo Vaughn 1.50
27 Bill Terry, Willie McCovey 1.50
28 Mike Sweeney, George Brett 8.00
29 Eddie Mathews, Ernie Banks 4.00
30 Eric Karros, Gil Hodges 1.50
31 Paul Molitor, Don Mattingly 8.00
32 Brooks Robinson, Rod Carew 3.00
33 Chipper Jones, Albert Pujols 8.00
34 Harry Heilmann, Hank Greenberg 1.50
35 Frank Thomas, Carlos Delgado 2.50
36 Jeff Bagwell, Todd Helton 2.00
37 Rafael Palmeiro, Fred McGriff 2.00
38 Cal Ripken Jr., Wade Boggs 10.00
39 Orlando Cepeda, Willie McCovey 2.00
40 John Olerud, Mark Grace 2.00

Cornerstones Memorabilia

No Pricing
Production 25 Sets

Cornerstones Numbered

NM/M
Complete Set (40):
#1-10: Production 250
#11-20: Production 250
#21-30: Production 1,000
#31-40: Production 2,000
1 Bill Terry, Johnny Mize 10.00
2 Cal Ripken Jr., Eddie Murray 30.00
3 Eddie Mathews, Chipper Jones 10.00
4 Albert Pujols, George Sisler 20.00
5 Sean Casey, Tony Perez 8.00
6 Jimmie Foxx, Scott Rolen 10.00
7 Wade Boggs, George Brett 20.00
8 Rod Carew, Troy Glaus 10.00
9 Jeff Bagwell, Rafael Palmeiro 10.00
10 Willie Stargell, Pie Traynor 8.00
11 Cal Ripken Jr., Brooks Robinson 20.00
12 Tony Perez, Ted Kluszewski 5.00
13 Jason Giambi, Don Mattingly 15.00
14 Hank Greenberg, Jimmie Foxx 8.00
15 Ernie Banks, Willie McCovey 8.00
16 Jim Thome, Travis Fryman 6.00
17 Ted Kluszewski, Sean Casey 5.00
18 Gil Hodges, Johnny Mize 5.00
19 Brooks Robinson, Boog Powell 8.00
20 Bill Terry, George Sisler 5.00
21 Wade Boggs, Don Mattingly 10.00
22 Jason Giambi Yanks, Carlos Delgado 3.00
23 Willie Stargell, Bill Madlock 4.00
24 Mark Grace, Matt Williams 4.00
25 Paul Molitor, George Brett 10.00
26 Carlos Delgado, Mo Vaughn 3.00
27 Bill Terry, Willie McCovey 4.00
28 Mike Sweeney, George Brett 10.00
29 Eddie Mathews, Ernie Banks 4.00
30 Eric Karros, Gil Hodges 3.00
31 Paul Molitor, Don Mattingly 8.00
32 Brooks Robinson, Rod Carew 3.00
33 Chipper Jones, Albert Pujols 6.00
34 Harry Heilmann, Hank Greenburg 3.00
35 Frank Thomas, Carlos Delgado 3.00
36 Jeff Bagwell, Todd Helton 3.00
37 Rafael Palmeiro, Fred McGriff 3.00
38 Cal Ripken Jr., Wade Boggs 8.00
39 Orlando Cepeda, Willie McCovey 3.00
40 John Olerud, Mark Grace 3.00

Fencebusters

NM/M
Common Player: 5.00
Rack Pack exclusive
Derek Jeter 20.00
J.D. Drew 6.00
Brian Giles 5.00
Moises Alou 5.00
Rafael Palmeiro 6.00
Jeff Bagwell 8.00
Mike Piazza 15.00
Manny Ramirez 8.00
Tino Martinez 5.00
Jim Thome 5.00
Andruw Jones 8.00
Shawn Green 6.00
Frank Thomas 8.00
Miguel Tejada 6.00
Luis Gonzalez 5.00
Alex Rodriguez 12.50
Larry Walker 5.00
Barry Bonds 20.00
Todd Helton 8.00
Chipper Jones 10.00
Roberto Alomar 6.00
Jim Edmonds 5.00

Fencebusters Autographed

NM/M
Numbered to 2001 HR Total
Derek Jeter/21
Jeff Bagwell/39
Miguel Tejada/31
Barry Bonds/73 350.00

National Patch Time

NM/M
Common Player: 20.00
Inserted 1:12 Jumbo
Barry Bonds/75 100.00
Todd Helton/110 40.00
Ivan Rodriguez/225 40.00
Kazuhiro Sasaki/310 20.00
Derek Jeter/65 100.00
Cal Ripken Jr/350 80.00
Darin Erstad/315 20.00
Jose Canseco/150 40.00
Miguel Tejada/55 35.00
Greg Maddux/775 30.00
Juan Gonzalez/50 50.00
J.D. Drew/210 25.00
Manny Ramirez/100 40.00
Pedro Martinez/45 50.00
Carlos Delgado/70 30.00
Magglio Ordonez/85 30.00
Pat Burrell/285 25.00
Adam Dunn/75 40.00
Alex Rodriguez/325 50.00

Wheelhouse

NM/M
Complete Set (20): 40.00
Common Player: 1.00
Inserted 1:12
1WH Derek Jeter 6.00
2WH Barry Bonds 6.00
3WH Luis Gonzalez 1.00
4WH Jason Giambi 1.00
5WH Ivan Rodriguez 1.50
6WH Mike Piazza 4.00
7WH Troy Glaus 1.50
8WH Nomar Garciaparra 4.00
9WH Juan Gonzalez 1.50
10WH Sammy Sosa 4.00
11WH Albert Pujols 5.00
12WH Ken Griffey Jr. 4.00
13WH Scott Rolen 1.00
14WH Jeff Bagwell 1.50
15WH Ichiro Suzuki 4.00
16WH Todd Helton 1.50
17WH Chipper Jones 3.00
18WH Alex Rodriguez 4.00
19WH Vladimir Guerrero 2.00
20WH Manny Ramirez 1.50

2002 FLEER PREMIUM

NM/M
Complete Set (240): 50.00
Common Player: .15
Common SP (201-240): .50
Inserted 1:2
Pack (8): 2.00
Box (24): 35.00
1 Garret Anderson .20
2 Derek Jeter 2.50
3 Ken Griffey Jr. 1.50
4 Luis Castillo .15
5 Richie Sexson .20
6 Mike Mussina .40
7 Ricky Henderson .75
8 Bud Smith .15
9 David Eckstein .15
10 Nomar Garciaparra 1.50
11 Barry Larkin .20
12 Cliff Floyd .15
13 Ben Sheets .20
14 Jorge Posada .30
15 Phil Nevin .15
16 Fernando Vina .15
17 Darin Erstad .65
18 Shea Hillenbrand .15
19 Todd Walker .15
20 Charles Johnson .15
21 Cristian Guzman .15
22 Mariano Rivera .30
23 Bubba Trammell .15
24 Brent Abernathy .15
25 Troy Glaus .75
26 Pedro J. Martinez .75
27 Dmitri Young .15
28 Derrek Lee .20
29 Torii Hunter .20
30 Alfonso Soriano .65
31 Rich Aurilia .15
32 Ben Grieve .15
33 Tim Salmon .30
34 Trot Nixon .15
35 Roberto Alomar .40
36 Mike Lowell .20
37 Jacque Jones .15
38 Bernie Williams .30
39 Barry Bonds 2.50
40 Toby Hall .15
41 Mo Vaughn .20
42 Hideo Nomo .65
43 Travis Fryman .15
44 Preston Wilson .15
45 Corey Koskie .15
46 Eric Chavez .30
47 Andres Galarraga .15
48 Greg Vaughn .15
49 Shawn Wooten .15
50 Manny Ramirez .75
51 Juan Gonzalez .75
52 Moises Alou .20
53 Joe Mays .15
54 Johnny Damon .35
55 Jeff Kent .20
56 Frank Catalanotto .15
57 Steve Finley .15
58 Jason Varitek .15
59 Kenny Lofton .20
60 Jeff Bagwell .75
61 Doug Mientkiewicz .15
62 Jermaine Dye .15
63 John Vander Wal .15
64 Gabe Kapler .15
65 Luis Gonzalez .30
66 Jon Lieber .15
67 C.C. Sabathia .15
68 Lance Berkman .20
69 Eric Milton .15
70 Jason Giambi .50
71 Ichiro Suzuki 1.50
72 Rafael Palmeiro .65
73 Mark Grace .30
74 Fred McGriff .20
75 Jim Thome .20
76 Craig Biggio .20
77 A.J. Pierzynski .15
78 Ramon Hernandez .15
79 Paul Abbott .15
80 Alex Rodriguez 2.00
81 Randy Johnson .75
82 Corey Patterson .20
83 Omar Vizquel .20
84 Richard Hidalgo .15
85 Luis Rivas .15
86 Tim Hudson .30
87 Bret Boone .20
88 Ivan Rodriguez .60
89 Junior Spivey .15
90 Sammy Sosa 1.50
91 Jeff Cirillo .15
92 Roy Oswalt .30
93 Orlando Cabrera .15
94 Terrence Long .15
95 Mike Cameron .15
96 Homer Bush .15
97 Reggie Sanders .15
98 Rondell White .20
99 Mike Hampton .15

No.	Player	Price
100	Carlos Beltran	.50
101	Vladimir Guerrero	.75
102	Miguel Tejada	.30
103	Freddy Garcia	.15
104	Jose Cruz Jr.	.15
105	Curt Schilling	.45
106	Kerry Wood	.65
107	Todd Helton	.75
108	Neifi Perez	.15
109	Javier Vazquez	.15
110	Barry Zito	.30
111	Edgar Martinez	.20
112	Carlos Delgado	.50
113	Matt Williams	.20
114	Eric Young	.15
115	Alex Ochoa	.15
116	Mark Quinn	.15
117	Jose Vidro	.15
118	Bobby Abreu	.20
119	David Bell	.15
120	Brad Fullmer	.15
121	Rafael Furcal	.15
122	Ray Durham	.15
123	Jose Ortiz	.15
124	Joe Randa	.15
125	Edgardo Alfonzo	.15
126	Marlon Anderson	.15
127	Jamie Moyer	.15
128	Alex Gonzalez	.15
129	Marcus Giles	.15
130	Keith Foulke	.15
131	Juan Pierre	.15
132	Mike Sweeney	.15
133	Matt Lawton	.15
134	Pat Burrell	.40
135	John Olerud	.20
136	Raul Mondesi	.20
137	Tom Glavine	.40
138	Paul Konerko	.20
139	Larry Walker	.20
140	Adrian Beltre	.35
141	Al Leiter	.20
142	Mike Lieberthal	.15
143	Kazuhiro Sasaki	.15
144	Shannon Stewart	.15
145	Andruw Jones	.75
146	Carlos Lee	.15
147	Roger Cedeno	.15
148	Kevin Brown	.20
149	Jay Payton	.15
150	Scott Rolen	.65
151	J.D. Drew	.35
152	Chipper Jones	1.00
153	Magglio Ordonez	.20
154	Tony Clark	.15
155	Shawn Green	.35
156	Mike Piazza	1.50
157	Jimmy Rollins	.15
158	Jim Edmonds	.20
159	Javy Lopez	.20
160	Chris Singleton	.15
161	Juan Encarnacion	.15
162	Eric Karros	.15
163	Tsuyoshi Shinjo	.15
164	Brian Giles	.20
165	Darryl Kile	.15
166	Greg Maddux	1.00
167	Frank Thomas	.75
168	Shane Halter	.15
169	Paul LoDuca	.15
170	Robin Ventura	.15
171	Jason Kendall	.15
172	Jason Hart	.15
173	Brady Anderson	.15
174	Jose Valentin	.15
175	Bobby Higginson	.15
176	Gary Sheffield	.40
177	Roger Clemens	1.25
178	Aramis Ramirez	.20
179	Matt Morris	.20
180	Jeff Conine	.15
181	Aaron Boone	.15
182	Jose Macias	.15
183	Jeromy Burnitz	.15
184	Carl Everett	.15
185	Trevor Hoffman	.15
186	Placido Polanco	.15
187	Jay Gibbons	.15
188	Sean Casey	.35
189	Josh Beckett	.40
190	Jeffrey Hammonds	.15
191	Chuck Knoblauch	.15
192	Ryan Klesko	.15
193	Albert Pujols	1.75
194	Chris Richard	.15
195	Adam Dunn	.50
196	A.J. Burnett	.15
197	Geoff Jenkins	.25
198	Tino Martinez	.15
199	Ray Lankford	.15
200	Edgar Renteria	.20
201	*Eric Cyr*	1.00
202	Travis Phelps	.50
203	Rick Bauer	.50
204	Mark Prior	4.00
205	Wilson Betemit	.50
206	Dewon Brazelton	.50
207	Cody Ransom	.50
208	Donnie Bridges	.50
209	Justin Duchscherer	.50
210	Nate Cornejo	.50
211	Jason Romano	.50
212	Juan Cruz	.50
213	Pedro Santana	.50
214	Ryan Drese	.50
215	Bert Snow	.50
216	Nate Frese	.50
217	Rafael Soriano	.50
218	*Franklin Nunez*	.50
219	Tim Spooneybarger	.50
220	Willie Harris	.50
221	Billy Sylvester	.50
222	Carlos Hernandez	.50
223	Mark Teixeira	3.00
224	Adrian Hernandez	.50
225	Andres Torres	.50
226	Marlon Byrd	.50
227	Juan Rivera	.50
228	Adam Johnson	.50
229	Justin Kaye	.50
230	Kyle Kessel	.50
231	Horacio Ramirez	.50
232	Brandon Larson	.50
233	Luis Lopez	.50
234	Robert Mackowiak	.50
235	Henry Mateo	.50
236	Corky Miller	.50
237	Greg Miller	.50
238	Dustan Mohr	.50
239	Bill Ortega	.50
240	Billy Hall	.50

Star Ruby

Stars (1-200):	4-8X
SP's (201-240):	1-2X
Production 125 sets	

Diamond Stars

		NM/M
Complete Set (20):		100.00
Common Player:		2.00
Inserted 1:72		
1DS	Pedro J. Martinez	4.00
2DS	Derek Jeter	15.00
3DS	Sammy Sosa	8.00
4DS	Ken Griffey Jr.	8.00
5DS	Chipper Jones	5.00
6DS	Roger Clemens	10.00
7DS	Ichiro Suzuki	8.00
8DS	Jeff Bagwell	4.00
9DS	Luis Gonzalez	2.00
10DS	Manny Ramirez	4.00
11DS	Alex Rodriguez	12.50
12DS	Kazuhiro Sasaki	2.00
13DS	Mike Piazza	8.00
14DS	Vladimir Guerrero	4.00
15DS	Randy Johnson	4.00
16DS	Ivan Rodriguez	3.00
17DS	Nomar Garciaparra	8.00
18DS	Barry Bonds	15.00
19DS	Todd Helton	4.00
20DS	Greg Maddux	5.00

Diamond Stars Game-Used

	NM/M
Common Player:	5.00
Inserted 1:105	
Barry Bonds/jsy	20.00
Manny Ramirez/jsy	8.00
Ivan Rodriguez/jsy	8.00
Kazuhiro Sasaki/jsy	5.00
Roger Clemens	20.00
Alex Rodriguez	15.00
Derek Jeter	25.00
Chipper Jones	10.00
Todd Helton	8.00
Luis Gonzalez	5.00
Mike Piazza	10.00
Nomar Garciaparra	25.00

Diamond Stars Game-Used Premium

	NM/M
Production 75 sets	
Barry Bonds	60.00
Roger Clemens	60.00
Todd Helton	30.00
Chipper Jones	30.00
Manny Ramirez	25.00
Alex Rodriguez	50.00
Ivan Rodriguez	25.00
Luis Gonzalez	25.00
Mike Piazza	40.00
Kazuhiro Sasaki	20.00

Diamond Stars Dual Game-Used

	NM/M
Numbered to 100	
Barry Bonds	60.00
Todd Helton	20.00
Derek Jeter	60.00
Chipper Jones	30.00
Mike Piazza	35.00
Manny Ramirez	25.00
Alex Rodriguez	40.00

Diamond Stars Autograph

	NM/M
Numbered to 100	
Derek Jeter	125.00

International Pride

		NM/M
Complete Set (15):		10.00
Common Player:		.50
Inserted 1:6		
1IP	Larry Walker	.50
2IP	Albert Pujols	3.00
3IP	Juan Gonzalez	.75
4IP	Ichiro Suzuki	2.00
5IP	Rafael Palmeiro	.65
6IP	Carlos Delgado	.50
7IP	Kazuhiro Sasaki	.50
8IP	Vladimir Guerrero	.75
9IP	Bobby Abreu	.50
10IP	Ivan Rodriguez	.60
11IP	Tsuyoshi Shinjo	.50
12IP	Pedro J. Martinez	.75
13IP	Andruw Jones	.75
14IP	Sammy Sosa	2.00
15IP	Chan Ho Park	.50

International Pride Game-Used

	NM/M
Common Player:	5.00
Inserted 1:90	
Carlos Delgado/jsy	8.00
Juan Gonzalez/jsy	8.00
Andruw Jones/jsy	8.00
Pedro Martinez/jsy	10.00
Rafael Palmeiro/jsy	8.00
Chan Ho Park/jsy	5.00
Albert Pujols/jsy	20.00
Ivan Rodriguez/bat	10.00
Kazuhiro Sasaki/jsy	5.00
Tsuyoshi Shinjo/jsy	5.00

International Pride Premium

	NM/M
Production 75 sets	15.00
Carlos Delgado	25.00
Juan Gonzalez	40.00
Andruw Jones	40.00
Pedro J. Martinez	40.00
Chan Ho Park	15.00
Ivan Rodriguez	25.00
Tsuyoshi Shinjo	15.00
Rafael Palmeiro	25.00
Albert Pujols	75.00
Kazuhiro Sasaki	15.00

Legendary Dynasties

		NM/M
Complete Set (36):		125.00
Common Player:		1.50
Inserted 1:18		
Gold:		1X
Production 300 sets		
1LD	Honus Wagner	4.00
2LD	Christy Mathewson	4.00
3LD	Lou Gehrig	8.00
4LD	Babe Ruth	12.00
5LD	Jimmie Foxx	4.00
6LD	Lefty Grove	2.00
7LD	Al Simmons	1.50
8LD	Bill Dickey	1.50
9LD	Stan Musial	5.00
10LD	Enos Slaughter	1.50
11LD	Johnny Mize	2.00
12LD	Yogi Berra	3.00
13LD	Whitey Ford	3.00
14LD	Jackie Robinson	8.00
15LD	Duke Snider	3.00
16LD	Roger Maris	5.00
17LD	Jim Palmer	2.00
18LD	Don Drysdale	2.00
19LD	Brooks Robinson	3.00
20LD	Rollie Fingers	1.50
21LD	Reggie Jackson	3.00
22LD	Joe Morgan	2.00
23LD	Johnny Bench	5.00
24LD	Thurman Munson	4.00
25LD	Jose Canseco	2.50
26LD	Tom Glavine	2.00
27LD	Chipper Jones	4.00
28LD	Greg Maddux	5.00
29LD	Roberto Alomar	3.00
30LD	David Cone	1.50
31LD	Jim Thome	3.00
32LD	Manny Ramirez	3.00
33LD	Roger Clemens	6.00
34LD	Derek Jeter	8.00
35LD	Bernie Williams	2.50
36LD	Alfonso Soriano	3.00

Legendary Dynasties Game-Used

	NM/M
Common Player:	8.00
Inserted 1:120	
Roberto Alomar/jsy	8.00
Johnny Bench/jsy	15.00
Yogi Berra/bat/SP/75	50.00
Roger Clemens/jsy	25.00
Bill Dickey/bat	25.00
Rollie Fingers/jsy	8.00
Whitey Ford/SP/25	
Reggie Jackson/bat	25.00
Derek Jeter/bat	30.00
Chipper Jones/jsy	10.00
Roger Maris/pants/SP	50.00
Johnny Mize/bat	15.00
Joe Morgan/bat	8.00
Thurman Munson/bat	35.00
Jim Palmer/jsy	10.00
Manny Ramirez/jsy	10.00
Brooks Robinson/bat	30.00
Jackie Robinson/ SP/150	60.00
Babe Ruth/bat	200.00
Duke Snider/bat	30.00
Alfonso Soriano/bat	10.00
Bernie Williams/jsy	8.00

Legendary Dynasties Premium

	NM/M
Numbered to Highest win total	
Rollie Fingers/93	15.00
Roger Clemens/114	50.00
Roger Maris/109	70.00
Roberto Alomar/96	25.00
Reggie Jackson/93	30.00
Manny Ramirez/99	25.00
Johnny Bench/108	35.00

Jim Palmer/109 20.00
Derek Jeter/114 80.00
Alfonso Soriano/99 30.00
Chipper Jones/106 30.00
Bernie Williams/114 20.00

Legendary Dynasties Autographs

NM/M
#'d to World Series Year
Johnny Bench/76 80.00
Yogi Berra/51 60.00
Rollie Fingers/74
Tom Glavine/95
Reggie Jackson/73 60.00
Derek Jeter/96 125.00
Greg Maddux/95
Jim Palmer/70
Brooks Robinson/64

On Base!

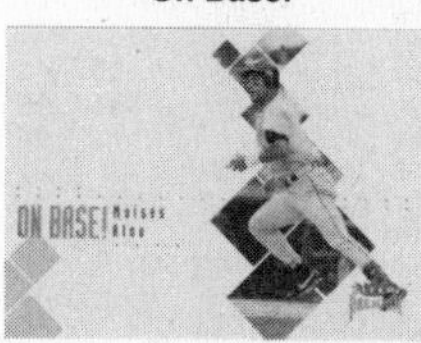

NM/M
Complete Set (30): 125.00
Common Player: 2.00
#'d to 2001 OBP
1OB Frank Thomas/316 5.00
2OB Ivan Rodriguez/347 5.00
3OB Nomar Garciaparra/352 10.00
4OB Ken Griffey Jr/365 8.00
5OB Juan Gonzalez/370 4.00
6OB Shawn Green/372 3.00
7OB Vladimir Guerrero/377 5.00
8OB Derek Jeter/377 15.00
9OB Scott Rolen/378 5.00
10OB Ichiro Suzuki/381 10.00
11OB Mike Piazza/384 10.00
12OB Bernie Williams/395 3.00
13OB Moises Alou/396 3.00
14OB Jeff Bagwell/397 4.00
15OB Alex Rodriguez/399 10.00
16OB Albert Pujols/403 10.00
17OB Manny Ramirez/405 4.00
18OB Carlos Delgado/408 4.00
19OB Jim Edmonds/410 3.00
20OB Roberto Alomar/415 3.00
21OB Jim Thome/416 4.00
22OB Gary Sheffield/417 3.00
23OB Chipper Jones/427 5.00
24OB Luis Gonzalez/429 2.00
25OB Lance Berkman/430 3.00
26OB Todd Helton/432 4.00
27OB Sammy Sosa/437 10.00
28OB Larry Walker/449 2.00
29OB Jason Giambi/477 4.00
30OB Barry Bonds/515 12.00

On Base! Game-Used

NM/M
Common Player: 5.00
Production 100 sets
Roberto Alomar 8.00
Moises Alou 5.00
Jeff Bagwell 8.00
Lance Berkman 5.00
Barry Bonds 20.00
Carlos Delgado 8.00
Jim Edmonds 6.00
Nomar Garciaparra 15.00
Jason Giambi 8.00
Juan Gonzalez 8.00
Luis Gonzalez 5.00
Shawn Green 5.00
Ken Griffey Jr. 20.00
Vladimir Guerrero 8.00
Todd Helton 8.00
Derek Jeter 25.00
Chipper Jones 10.00
Mike Piazza 15.00
Albert Pujols 20.00
Manny Ramirez 10.00
Alex Rodriguez 15.00
Ivan Rodriguez 10.00
Scott Rolen 10.00
Gary Sheffield 6.00
Sammy Sosa 20.00
Ichiro Suzuki 25.00
Frank Thomas 10.00
Jim Thome 8.00
Larry Walker 5.00
Bernie Williams 6.00

2002 FLEER SHOWCASE

NM/M
Complete Set (166): 225.00
Common Player: .25
Common (126-141): 5.00
Production 500
Common (141-166) 4.00
Production 1,500
Pack (5): 3.00
Box (24): 60.00
1 Albert Pujols 2.00
2 Pedro J. Martinez .75
3 Frank Thomas .75
4 Gary Sheffield .40
5 Roberto Alomar .40
6 Luis Gonzalez .35
7 Bobby Abreu .25
8 Carlos Lee .25
9 Preston Wilson .25
10 Todd Helton .75
11 Juan Gonzalez .75
12 Chuck Knoblauch .25
13 Jason Kendall .25
14 Aaron Sele .25
15 Greg Vaughn .25
16 Fred McGriff .25
17 Doug Mientkiewicz .25
18 Richard Hidalgo .25
19 Alfonso Soriano .50
20 Matt Williams .25
21 Bobby Higginson .25
22 Mo Vaughn .25
23 Andruw Jones .75
24 Omar Vizquel .25
25 Bret Boone .25
26 Bernie Williams .35
27 Rafael Furcal .25
28 Jeff Bagwell .75
29 Marty Cardova .25
30 Lance Berkman .25
31 Vernon Wells .25
32 Garret Anderson .25
33 Larry Bigbie .25
34 Steve Finley .25
35 Barry Bonds 3.00
36 Eric Chavez .35
37 Tony Clark .25
38 Roger Clemens 1.50
39 Adam Dunn .50
40 Roger Cedeno .25
41 Carlos Delgado .50
42 Jermaine Dye .25
43 Brian Jordan .25
44 Darin Erstad .65
45 Paul LoDuca .25
46 Jim Edmonds .25
47 Tom Glavine .50
48 Cliff Floyd .25
49 Jon Lieber .25
50 Adrian Beltre .40
51 Joel Pineiro .25
52 Jim Thome .25
53 Jimmy Rollins .25
54 Pat Burrell .40
55 Jeromy Burnitz .25
56 Larry Walker .25
57 Damon Minor .25
58 John Olerud .25
59 Carlos Beltran .50
60 Vladimir Guerrero .75
61 David Justice .25
62 Phil Nevin .25
63 Tino Martinez .25
64 Curt Schilling .75
65 Corey Patterson .25
66 Aubrey Huff .25
67 Mark Grace .35
68 Rafael Palmeiro .65
69 Jorge Posada .35
70 Craig Biggio .25
71 Manny Ramirez .75
72 Mark Quinn .25
73 Raul Mondesi .25
74 Shawn Green .40
75 Brian Giles .25
76 Paul Konerko .25
77 Troy Glaus .75
78 Mike Mussina .40
79 Greg Maddux 1.00
80 Edgar Martinez .25
81 Jose Vidro .25
82 Scott Rolen .65
83 Ben Grieve .25
84 Jeff Kent .25
85 Magglio Ordonez .25
86 Freddy Garcia .25
87 Ivan Rodriguez .65
88 Pokey Reese .25
89 Shannon Stewart .25
90 Randy Johnson .75
91 Cristian Guzman .25
92 Tsuyoshi Shinjo .25
93 Steve Cox .25
94 Mike Sweeney .25
95 Robert Fick .25
96 Sean Casey .40
97 Tim Hudson .35
98 Bud Smith .25
99 Corey Koskie .25
100 Richie Sexson .25
101 Aramis Ramirez .25
102 Barry Larkin .25
103 Rich Aurilia .25
104 Charles Johnson .25
105 Ryan Klesko .25
106 Ben Sheets .25
107 J.D. Drew .40
108 Jay Gibbons .25
109 Kerry Wood .65
110 C.C. Sabathia .25
111 Eric Munson .25
112 Josh Beckett .40
113 Javier Vasquez .25
114 Barry Zito .35
115 Kazuhiro Sasaki .25
116 Bubba Trammell .25
117 Russell Branyan .25
118 Todd Walker .25
119 Mike Hampton .25
120 Jeff Weaver .25
121 Geoff Jenkins .25
122 Edgardo Alfonzo .25
123 Mike Lieberthal .25
124 Mike Lowell .25
125 Kevin Brown .25
126 Derek Jeter 8.00
127 Ichiro Suzuki 5.00
128 Nomar Garciaparra 5.00
129 Ken Griffey Jr. 5.00
130 Jason Giambi 5.00
131 Alex Rodriguez 6.00
132 Chipper Jones 5.00
133 Mike Piazza 5.00
134 Sammy Sosa 5.00
135 Hideo Nomo 5.00
136 *Kazuhisa Ishii* 8.00
137 *Satoru Komiyama* 5.00
138 *So Taguchi* 6.00
139 *Jorge Padilla* 5.00
140 *Rene Reyes* 5.00
141 *Jorge Nunez* 5.00
142 *Nelson Castro* 4.00
143 *Anderson Machado* 4.00
144 *Edwin Almonte* 4.00
145 *Luis Ugueto* 4.00
146 *Felix Escalona* 4.00
147 *Ron Calloway* 4.00
148 *Hansel Izquierdo* 4.00
149 Mark Teixeira 6.00
150 Orlando Hudson 4.00
151 *Aaron Cook* 4.00
152 *Aaron Taylor* 4.00
153 *Takahito Nomura* 4.00
154 Matt Thornton 4.00
155 Mark Prior 10.00
156 *Reed Johnson* 6.00
157 Doug DeVore 4.00
158 *Ben Howard* 4.00
159 *Francis Beltran* 4.00
160 *Brian Mallette* 4.00
161 Sean Burroughs 4.00
162 Michael Restovich 4.00
163 Austin Kearns 4.00
164 Marlon Byrd 4.00
165 Hank Blalock 6.00
166 Mike Rivera 4.00

Legacy

Stars (1-125): 3-5X
Legacy (126-166): 1X
Production 175 sets

Baseball's Best

NM/M
Complete Set (20): 40.00
Common Player: 1.00
Inserted 1:8
1 Derek Jeter 5.00
2 Barry Bonds 5.00
3 Mike Piazza 3.00
4 Alex Rodriguez 4.00
5 Pat Burrell 1.00
6 Rafael Palmeiro 1.00
7 Nomar Garciaparra 3.00
8 Todd Helton 1.50
9 Roger Clemens 2.50
10 Shawn Green 1.00
11 Chipper Jones 2.00
12 Pedro J. Martinez 1.50
13 Luis Gonzalez 1.00
14 Randy Johnson 1.50
15 Ichiro Suzuki 3.00
16 Ken Griffey Jr. 3.00
17 Vladimir Guerrero 1.50
18 Sammy Sosa 3.00
19 Jason Giambi 1.00
20 Albert Pujols 4.00

Baseball's Best Memorabilia

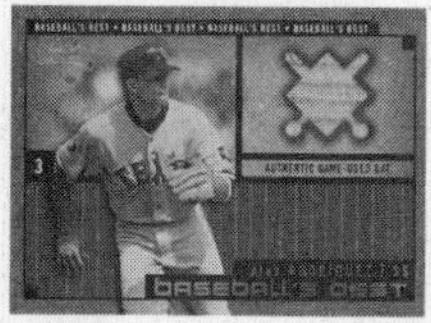

NM/M
Common Player: 5.00
Inserted 1:24
Golds: 1-2X
Production 100 sets
Derek Jeter/jsy 20.00
Barry Bonds/jsy 20.00
Mike Piazza/jsy 10.00
Alex Rodriguez/bat 15.00
Pat Burrell
Rafael Palmeiro/jsy 8.00
Nomar Garciaparra/jsy 10.00
Todd Helton/bat 8.00
Roger Clemens/jsy 15.00
Shawn Green/jsy 5.00
Chipper Jones/jsy 10.00
Pedro Martinez/jsy 8.00
Luis Gonzalez/jsy 5.00
Randy Johnson/jsy 10.00
Ichiro Suzuki/base 15.00
Ken Griffey Jr./base 10.00
Vladimir Guerrero/base 8.00
Sammy Sosa/base 10.00
Jason Giambi/base 8.00
Albert Pujols/base 10.00

Baseball's Best Silver Auto

NM/M
Serial numbered to 400
Derek Jeter 125.00
Barry Bonds 200.00

Baseball's Best Gold Auto

NM/M
Serial numbered to 100
Derek Jeter 150.00
Barry Bonds 225.00

Derek Jeter's Legacy Collection

	NM/M
Complete Set (22):	80.00
Common Jeter:	5.00
Production 1,000 (1-22) sets	

Derek Jeter's Legacy Coll. Memorab.

	NM/M
Quantity produced listed	
Derek Jeter/jsy/300	75.00
Derek Jeter/combo jsy/175	90.00
Derek Jeter/ World Series ball/50	100.00
Derek Jeter/glove/425	60.00

Sweet Sigs Wall

		NM/M
Common Player:		8.00
1	Bobby Abreu/70	20.00
2	Wilson Betemit	
2	Russell Branyan/200	8.00
3	Pat Burrell/35	
4	Sean Casey/35	
5	Eric Chavez/108	15.00
6	Rafael Furcal/207	10.00
7	Nomar Garciaparra/25	
8	Brandon Inge/187	8.00
9	Jackson Melian/146	8.00
9	Elpidio Guzman	
10	Xavier Nady/286	8.00
11	Jose Ortiz/116	8.00
12	Ben Sheets/150	20.00
13	Mike Sweeney/371	10.00

Sweet Sigs Lumber

		NM/M
Common Player:		5.00
1	Bobby Abreu/231	10.00
2	Wilson Betemit	
2	Russell Branyan/425	8.00
3	Pat Burrell/115	10.00
4	Sean Casey/64	20.00
5	Eric Chavez/256	10.00
6	Rafael Furcal/530	10.00
7	Nomar Garciaparra/25	
8	Brandon Inge/528	5.00
9	Jackson Melian/636	5.00
9	Elpidio Guzman	
10	Xavier Nady/589	8.00
11	Jose Ortiz/515	8.00
12	Ben Sheets/458	15.00
13	Mike Sweeney/495	10.00

Sweet Sigs Leather

		NM/M
Common Player:		8.00
1	Bobby Abreu/10	
2	Wilson Betemit	
2	Russell Branyan/90	10.00
3	Pat Burrell/35	
4	Sean Casey/35	
5	Eric Chavez/20	
6	Rafael Furcal/92	15.00
7	Nomar Garciaparra/5	
8	Brandon Inge/122	8.00
9	Jackson Melian/37	
9	Elpidio Guzman	
10	Xavier Nady/301	8.00
11	Jose Ortiz/50	10.00
12	Ben Sheets/60	25.00
13	Mike Sweeney/103	15.00

2002 FLEER TRADITION

		NM/M
Complete Set (500):		175.00
Common Player:		.15
Common SP (1-100):		1.50
Inserted 1:2		
Pack (10):		2.00
Box (36):		50.00
1	Barry Bonds	10.00
2	Cal Ripken Jr.	10.00
3	Tony Gwynn	5.00
4	Brad Radke	1.50
5	Jose Ortiz	1.50
6	Mark Mulder	1.50
7	Jon Lieber	1.50
8	John Olerud	1.50
9	Phil Nevin	1.50
10	Craig Biggio	1.50
11	Pedro Martinez	4.00
12	Fred McGriff	1.50
13	Vladimir Guerrero	4.00
14	Jason Giambi	3.00
15	Mark Kotsay	1.50
16	Bud Smith	1.50
17	Kevin Brown	1.50
18	Darin Erstad	3.00
19	Julio Franco	1.50
20	C.C. Sabathia	1.50
21	Larry Walker	1.50
22	Doug Mientkiewicz	1.50
23	Luis Gonzalez	2.00
24	Albert Pujols	8.00
25	Brian Lawrence	1.50
26	Al Leiter	1.50
27	Mike Sweeney	1.50
28	Jeff Weaver	1.50
29	Matt Morris	1.50
30	Hideo Nomo	4.00
31	Tom Glavine	2.50
32	Magglio Ordonez	1.50
33	Roberto Alomar	2.50
34	Roger Cedeno	1.50
35	Greg Vaughn	1.50
36	Chan Ho Park	1.50
37	Rich Aurilia	1.50
38	Tsuyoshi Shinjo	1.50
39	Eric Young	1.50
40	Bobby Higginson	1.50
41	Marlon Anderson	1.50
42	Mark Grace	2.00
43	Steve Cox	1.50
44	Cliff Floyd	1.50
45	Brian Roberts	1.50
46	Paul Konerko	1.50
47	Brandon Duckworth	1.50
48	Josh Beckett	2.50
49	David Ortiz	2.50
50	Geoff Jenkins	1.50
51	Ruben Sierra	1.50
52	John Franco	1.50
53	Einar Diaz	1.50
54	Luis Castillo	1.50
55	Mark Quinn	1.50
56	Shea Hillenbrand	1.50
57	Rafael Palmeiro	3.00
58	Paul O'Neill	1.50
59	Andruw Jones	4.00
60	Lance Berkman	1.50
61	Jimmy Rollins	1.50
62	Jose Hernandez	1.50
63	Rusty Greer	1.50
64	Wade Miller	1.50
65	David Eckstein	1.50
66	Jose Valentin	1.50
67	Javier Vazquez	1.50
68	Roger Clemens	6.00
69	Omar Vizquel	1.50
70	Roy Oswalt	1.50
71	Shannon Stewart	1.50
72	Byung-Hyun Kim	1.50
73	Jay Gibbons	1.50
74	Barry Larkin	1.50
75	Brian Giles	1.50
76	Andres Galarraga	1.50
77	Sammy Sosa	6.00
78	Manny Ramirez	4.00
79	Carlos Delgado	2.50
80	Jorge Posada	1.50
81	Todd Ritchie	1.50
82	Russ Ortiz	1.50
83	Brent Mayne	1.50
84	Mike Mussina	3.00
85	Raul Mondesi	1.50
86	Mark Loretta	1.50
87	Tim Raines	1.50
88	Ichiro Suzuki	6.00
89	Juan Pierre	1.50
90	Adam Dunn	2.50
91	Jason Tyner	1.50
92	Miguel Tejada	1.50
93	Elpidio Guzman	1.50
94	Freddy Garcia	1.50
95	Marcus Giles	1.50
96	Junior Spivey	1.50
97	Aramis Ramirez	1.50
98	Jose Rijo	1.50
99	Paul LoDuca	1.50
100	Mike Cameron	1.50
101	Alex Hernandez	.15
102	Benji Gil	.15
103	Benito Santiago	.15
104	Bobby Abreu	.15
105	Brad Penny	.15
106	Calvin Murray	.15
107	Chad Durbin	.15
108	Chris Singleton	.15
109	Chris Carpenter	.15
110	David Justice	.15
111	Eric Chavez	.25
112	Fernando Tatis	.15
113	Frank Castillo	.15
114	Jason LaRue	.15
115	Jim Edmonds	.15
116	Joe Kennedy	.15
117	Jose Jimenez	.15
118	Josh Towers	.15
119	Junior Herndon	.15
120	Luke Prokopec	.15
121	Mac Suzuki	.15
122	Mark DeRosa	.15
123	Marty Cordova	.15
124	Michael Tucker	.15
125	Michael Young	.15
126	Robin Ventura	.15
127	Shane Halter	.15
128	Shane Reynolds	.15
129	Tony Womack	.15
130	A.J. Pierzynski	.15
131	Aaron Rowand	.15
132	Antonio Alfonseca	.15
133	Arthur Rhodes	.15
134	Bob Wickman	.15
135	Brady Clark	.15
136	Chad Hermansen	.15
137	Marlon Byrd	.15
138	Dan Wilson	.15
139	David Cone	.15
140	Dean Palmer	.15
141	Denny Neagle	.15
142	Derek Jeter	2.50
143	Erubiel Durazo	.15
144	Felix Rodriguez	.15
145	Jason Hart	.15
146	Jay Bell	.15
147	Jeff Suppan	.15
148	Jeff Zimmerman	.15
149	Kerry Wood	.65
150	Kerry Robinson	.15
151	Kevin Appier	.15
152	Michael Barrett	.15
153	Mo Vaughn	.15
154	Rafael Furcal	.15
155	Sidney Ponson	.15
156	Terry Adams	.15
157	Tim Redding	.15
158	Toby Hall	.15
159	Aaron Sele	.15
160	Bartolo Colon	.15
161	Brad Ausmus	.15
162	Carlos Pena	.15
163	Jace Brewer	.15
164	David Wells	.15
165	David Segui	.15
166	Derek Lowe	.15
167	Derek Bell	.15
168	Jason Grabowski	.15
169	Johnny Damon	.25
170	Jose Mesa	.15
171	Juan Encarnacion	.15
172	Ken Caminiti	.15
173	Ken Griffey Jr.	1.50
174	Luis Rivas	.15
175	Mariano Rivera	.25
176	Mark Grudzielanek	.15
177	Mark McGwire	2.00
178	Mike Bordick	.15
179	Mike Hampton	.15
180	Nick Bierbrodt	.15
181	Paul Byrd	.15
182	Robb Nen	.15
183	Ryan Dempster	.15
184	Ryan Klesko	.15
185	Scott Spiezio	.15
186	Scott Strickland	.15
187	Todd Zeile	.15
188	Tom Gordon	.15
189	Troy Glaus	.75
190	Matt Williams	.15
191	Wes Helms	.15
192	Jerry Hairston Jr.	.15
193	Brook Fordyce	.15
194	Nomar Garciaparra	1.50
195	Kevin Tapani	.15
196	Mark Buehrle	.15
197	Dmitri Young	.15
198	John Rocker	.15
199	Juan Uribe	.15
200	Matt Anderson	.15
201	Alex Gonzalez	.15
202	Julio Lugo	.15
203	Roberto Hernandez	.15
204	Richie Sexson	.15
205	Corey Koskie	.15
206	Tony Armas Jr.	.15
207	Rey Ordonez	.15
208	Orlando Hernandez	.15
209	Pokey Reese	.15
210	Mike Lieberthal	.15
211	Kris Benson	.15
212	Jermaine Dye	.15
213	Livan Hernandez	.15
214	Bret Boone	.15
215	Dustin Hermanson	.15
216	Placido Polanco	.15
217	Jesus Colome	.15
218	Alex Gonzalez	.15
219	Adam Everett	.15
220	Adam Piatt	.15
221	Brad Fullmer	.15
222	Brian Buchanan	.15
223	Chipper Jones	1.00
224	Chuck Finley	.15
225	David Bell	.15
226	Jack Wilson	.25
227	Jason Bere	.15
228	Jeff Conine	.15
229	Jeff Bagwell	.75
230	Joe McEwing	.15
231	Kip Wells	.15
232	Mike Lansing	.15
233	Neifi Perez	.15
234	Omar Daal	.15
235	Reggie Sanders	.15
236	Shawn Wooten	.15
237	Shawn Chacon	.15
238	Shawn Estes	.15
239	Steve Sparks	.15
240	Steve Kline	.15
241	Tino Martinez	.15
242	Tyler Houston	.15
243	Xavier Nady	.15
244	Bengie Molina	.15
245	Ben Davis	.15
246	Casey Fossum	.15
247	Chris Stynes	.15
248	Danny Graves	.15
249	Pedro Feliz	.15
250	Darren Oliver	.15
251	Dave Veres	.15
252	Deivi Cruz	.15
253	Desi Relaford	.15
254	Devon White	.15
255	Edgar Martinez	.15
256	Eric Munson	.15
257	Eric Karros	.15
258	Homer Bush	.15
259	Jason Kendall	.15
260	Javy Lopez	.15
261	Keith Foulke	.15
262	Keith Ginter	.15
263	Nick Johnson	.15
264	Pat Burrell	.35
265	Ricky Gutierrez	.15
266	Russ Johnson	.15
267	Steve Finley	.15
268	Terrence Long	.15
269	Tony Batista	.15
270	Torii Hunter	.15
271	Vinny Castilla	.15
272	A.J. Burnett	.15
273	Adrian Beltre	.35

No.	Player	NM/M
274	Alex Rodriguez	2.00
275	Armando Benitez	.15
276	Billy Koch	.15
277	Brady Anderson	.15
278	Brian Jordan	.15
279	Carlos Febles	.15
280	Daryle Ward	.15
281	Eli Marrero	.15
282	Garret Anderson	.15
283	Jack Cust	.15
284	Jacque Jones	.15
285	Jamie Moyer	.15
286	Jeffrey Hammonds	.15
287	Jim Thome	.15
288	Jon Garland	.15
289	Jose Offerman	.15
290	Matt Stairs	.15
291	Orlando Cabrera	.15
292	Ramiro Mendoza	.15
293	Ray Durham	.15
294	Rickey Henderson	.75
295	Rob Mackowiak	.15
296	Scott Rolen	.65
297	Tim Hudson	.25
298	Todd Helton	.75
299	Tony Clark	.15
300	B.J. Surhoff	.15
301	Bernie Williams	.30
302	Bill Mueller	.15
303	Chris Richard	.15
304	Craig Paquette	.15
305	Curt Schilling	.40
306	Damian Jackson	.15
307	Derrek Lee	.15
308	Eric Milton	.15
309	Frank Catalanotto	.15
310	J.T. Snow	.15
311	Jared Sandberg	.15
312	Jason Varitek	.15
313	Jeff Cirillo	.15
314	Jeromy Burnitz	.15
315	Joe Crede	.15
316	Joel Pineiro	.15
317	Jose Cruz Jr.	.15
318	Kevin Young	.15
319	Marquis Grissom	.15
320	Moises Alou	.15
321	Randall Simon	.15
322	Royce Clayton	.15
323	Tim Salmon	.25
324	Travis Fryman	.15
325	Travis Lee	.15
326	Vance Wilson	.15
327	Jarrod Washburn	.15
328	Ben Petrick	.15
329	Ben Grieve	.15
330	Carl Everett	.15
331	Eric Byrnes	.15
332	Doug Glanville	.15
333	Edgardo Alfonzo	.15
334	Ellis Burks	.15
335	Gabe Kapler	.15
336	Gary Sheffield	.25
337	Greg Maddux	1.00
338	J.D. Drew	.25
339	Jamey Wright	.15
340	Jeff Kent	.15
341	Jeremy Giambi	.15
342	Joe Randa	.15
343	Joe Mays	.15
344	Jose Macias	.15
345	Kazuhiro Sasaki	.15
346	Mike Kinkade	.15
347	Mike Lowell	.15
348	Randy Johnson	.75
349	Randy Wolf	.15
350	Richard Hidalgo	.15
351	Ron Coomer	.15
352	Sandy Alomar	.15
353	Sean Casey	.25
354	Trevor Hoffman	.15
355	Adam Eaton	.15
356	Alfonso Soriano	.50
357	Barry Zito	.25
358	Billy Wagner	.15
359	Brent Abernathy	.15
360	Bret Prinz	.15
361	Carlos Beltran	.40
362	Carlos Guillen	.15
363	Charles Johnson	.15
364	Cristian Guzman	.15
365	Damion Easley	.15
366	Darryl Kile	.15
367	Delino DeShields	.15
368	Eric Davis	.15
369	Frank Thomas	.75
370	Ivan Rodriguez	.65
371	Jay Payton	.15
372	Jeff D'Amico	.15
373	John Burkett	.15
374	Melvin Mora	.15
375	Ramon Ortiz	.15
376	Robert Person	.15
377	Russell Branyan	.15
378	Shawn Green	.25
379	Todd Hollandsworth	.15
380	Tony McKnight	.15
381	Trot Nixon	.15
382	Vernon Wells	.15
383	Troy Percival	.15
384	Albie Lopez	.15
385	Alex Ochoa	.15
386	Andy Pettitte	.25
387	Brandon Inge	.15
388	Bubba Trammell	.15
389	Corey Patterson	.15
390	Damian Rolls	.15
391	Dee Brown	.15
392	Edgar Renteria	.15
393	Eric Gagne	.35
394	Jason Johnson	.15
395	Jeff Nelson	.15
396	John Vander Wal	.15
397	Johnny Estrada	.15
398	Jose Canseco	.40
399	Juan Gonzalez	.75
400	Kevin Millwood	.15
401	Lee Stevens	.15
402	Matt Lawton	.15
403	Mike Lamb	.15
404	Octavio Dotel	.15
405	Ramon Hernandez	.15
406	Ruben Quevedo	.15
407	Todd Walker	.15
408	Troy O'Leary	.15
409	Wascar Serrano	.15
410	Aaron Boone	.15
411	Aubrey Huff	.15
412	Ben Sheets	.15
413	Carlos Lee	.15
414	Chuck Knoblauch	.15
415	Steve Karsay	.15
416	Dante Bichette	.15
417	David Dellucci	.15
418	Esteban Loaiza	.15
419	Fernando Vina	.15
420	Ismael Valdes	.15
421	Jason Isringhausen	.15
422	Jeff Shaw	.15
423	John Smoltz	.15
424	Jose Vidro	.15
425	Kenny Lofton	.15
426	Mark Little	.15
427	Mark McLemore	.15
428	Marvin Benard	.15
429	Mike Piazza	1.50
430	Pat Hentgen	.15
431	Preston Wilson	.15
432	Rick Helling	.15
433	Robert Fick	.15
434	Rondell White	.15
435	Adam Kennedy	.15
436	David Espinosa	.15
437	Dewon Brazelton	.15
438	Drew Henson	.25
439	Juan Cruz	.15
440	Jason Jennings	.15
441	Carlos Garcia	.15
442	Carlos Hernandez	.15
443	Wilkin Ruan	.15
444	Wilson Betemit	.15
445	Horacio Ramirez	.15
446	Danys Baez	.15
447	Abraham Nunez	.15
448	Josh Hamilton	.15
449	Chris George	.15
450	Rick Bauer	.15
451	Donnie Bridges	.15
452	Erick Almonte	.15
453	Cory Aldridge	.15
454	Ryan Drese	.15
455	Jason Romano	.15
456	Corky Miller	.15
457	Rafael Soriano	.15
458	Mark Prior	.75
459	Mark Teixeira	.50
460	Adrian Hernandez	.15
461	Tim Spooneybarger	.15
462	Bill Ortega	.15
463	D'Angelo Jimenez	.15
464	Andres Torres	.15
465	Alexis Gomez	.15
466	Angel Berroa	.15
467	Henry Mateo	.15
468	Endy Chavez	.15
469	Billy Sylvester	.15
470	Nate Frese	.15
471	Luis Gonzalez	.25
472	Barry Bonds	2.50
473	Rich Aurilia	.15
474	Albert Pujols	2.00
475	Todd Helton	.75
476	Moises Alou	.15
477	Lance Berkman	.15
478	Brian Giles	.15
479	Cliff Floyd	.15
480	Sammy Sosa	1.50
481	Shawn Green	.30
482	Jon Lieber	.15
483	Matt Morris	.15
484	Curt Schilling	.40
485	Randy Johnson	.75
486	Manny Ramirez	.75
487	Ichiro Suzuki	1.50
488	Juan Gonzalez	.75
489	Derek Jeter	2.50
490	Alex Rodriguez	2.00
491	Bret Boone	.15
492	Roberto Alomar	.30
493	Jason Giambi	.50
494	Rafael Palmeiro	.65
495	Doug Mientkiewicz	.15
496	Jim Thome	.15
497	Freddy Garcia	.15
498	Mark Buehrle	.15
499	Mark Mulder	.15
500	Roger Clemens	1.25

Diamond Tributes

		NM/M
Complete Set (15):		15.00
Common Player:		.50
Inserted 1:6		
1DT	Cal Ripken Jr.	3.00
2DT	Tony Gwynn	1.00
3DT	Derek Jeter	3.00
4DT	Pedro Martinez	.75
5DT	Mark McGwire	2.50
6DT	Sammy Sosa	2.00
7DT	Barry Bonds	3.00
8DT	Roger Clemens	1.50
9DT	Mike Piazza	2.00
10DT	Alex Rodriguez	2.50
11DT	Randy Johnson	.75
12DT	Chipper Jones	1.00
13DT	Nomar Garciaparra	2.00
14DT	Ichiro Suzuki	2.00
15DT	Jason Giambi	.50

Grass Roots

		NM/M
Complete Set (10):		15.00
Common Player:		.75
Inserted 1:18		
1GR	Barry Bonds	5.00
2GR	Alex Rodriguez	4.00
3GR	Derek Jeter	5.00
4GR	Greg Maddux	2.50
5GR	Ivan Rodriguez	1.00
6GR	Cal Ripken Jr.	5.00
7GR	Bernie Williams	.75
8GR	Jeff Bagwell	1.50
9GR	Scott Rolen	1.00
10GR	Larry Walker	.75

Grass Roots Patch

	NM/M
Production 50 sets	
Barry Bonds	100.00
Alex Rodriguez	75.00
Derek Jeter	
Greg Maddux	50.00
Ivan Rodriguez	25.00
Cal Ripken Jr.	100.00
Bernie Williams	25.00
Jeff Bagwell	40.00
Scott Rolen	30.00
Larry Walker	20.00

Heads Up

		NM/M
Complete Set (10):		45.00
Common Player:		1.00
Inserted 1:36		
1HU	Derek Jeter	8.00
2HU	Ichiro Suzuki	5.00
3HU	Sammy Sosa	5.00
4HU	Mike Piazza	5.00
5HU	Ken Griffey Jr.	5.00
6HU	Alex Rodriguez	6.00
7HU	Barry Bonds	8.00
8HU	Nomar Garciaparra	5.00
9HU	Mark McGwire	6.00
10HU	Cal Ripken Jr.	8.00

Lumber Company

		NM/M
Complete Set (30):		40.00
Common Player:		1.00
Inserted 1:12		
1LC	Moises Alou	1.00
2LC	Luis Gonzalez	1.00
3LC	Todd Helton	2.50
4LC	Mike Piazza	4.00
5LC	J.D. Drew	1.50
6LC	Albert Pujols	5.00
7LC	Chipper Jones	3.00
8LC	Manny Ramirez	2.50
9LC	Miguel Tejada	1.00
10LC	Curt Schilling	1.50
11LC	Alex Rodriguez	5.00
12LC	Barry Larkin	1.00
13LC	Nomar Garciaparra	4.00
14LC	Cliff Floyd	1.00
15LC	Alfonso Soriano	1.50
16LC	Sean Casey	1.00
17LC	Scott Rolen	2.00
18LC	Jose Ortiz	1.00
19LC	Corey Patterson	1.00
20LC	Joe Crede	1.00
21LC	Jace Brewer	1.00
22LC	Derek Jeter	6.00
23LC	Jim Thome	1.00
24LC	Frank Thomas	2.50
25LC	Shawn Green	1.00
26LC	Drew Henson	1.00
27LC	Jimmy Rollins	1.00
28LC	Dave Justice	1.00
29LC	Roberto Alomar	1.50
30LC	Bernie Williams	1.00

Lumber Company Game Used

	NM/M
Common Player:	5.00
Inserted 1:72	
Moises Alou	5.00
Luis Gonzalez	5.00
Todd Helton	8.00
Mike Piazza	12.00
J.D. Drew	6.00
Albert Pujols	15.00
Chipper Jones	10.00
Manny Ramirez	8.00
Miguel Tejada	6.00
Curt Schilling	6.00
Alex Rodriguez	15.00
Barry Larkin	5.00
Nomar Garciaparra	12.00
Cliff Floyd	5.00
Alfonso Soriano	8.00
Sean Casey	6.00
Scott Rolen	8.00
Jose Ortiz	5.00
Corey Patterson	5.00
Joe Crede	5.00
Jace Brewer	5.00
Derek Jeter	25.00
Jim Thome	5.00
Frank Thomas	8.00
Shawn Green	5.00
Drew Henson	5.00
Jimmy Rollins	5.00
Dave Justice	5.00
Roberto Alomar	6.00
Bernie Williams	5.00

This Day in History

		NM/M
Complete Set (29):		120.00
Common Player:		1.50
Inserted 1:18		
1	Cal Ripken Jr.	10.00
2	Barry Bonds	10.00
3	George Brett	4.00
4	Tony Gwynn	3.00

5 Nolan Ryan 10.00
6 Reggie Jackson 3.00
7 Paul Molitor 2.00
8 Ichiro Suzuki 5.00
9 Alex Rodriguez 8.00
10 Don Mattingly 6.00
11 Sammy Sosa 5.00
12 Mark McGwire 8.00
13 Derek Jeter 10.00
14 Roger Clemens 4.00
15 Jim "Catfish" Hunter 1.50
16 Greg Maddux 3.00
17 Ken Griffey Jr. 5.00
18 Gil Hodges 1.50
19 Edgar Martinez 1.50
20 Mike Piazza 5.00
21 Jimmie Foxx 1.50
22 Albert Pujols 6.00
23 Chipper Jones 3.00
24 NOT ISSUED
25 Jeff Bagwell 2.00
26 Nomar Garciaparra 5.00
27 Randy Johnson 2.00
28 Todd Helton 2.00
29 Ted Kluszewski 1.50
30 Ivan Rodriguez 1.75

This Day in History Autographs

NM/M

Common Player:
1 Tony Gwynn/50
2 Reggie Jackson/50
3 Derek Jeter/100 80.00
4 Randy Johnson/75 50.00
5 Don Mattingly/50 90.00
6 Paul Molitor/50
7 Albert Pujols/50 125.00
8 Cal Ripken Jr./50 125.00

This Day in History Game Used

NM/M

Common Player:
Jeff Bagwell Bat/100 15.00
Barry Bonds Jsy/250 40.00
George Brett Jsy/50
Roger Clemens Jsy/150 30.00
Jimmie Foxx Bat/250 40.00
Todd Helton Bat/150 15.00
Gil Hodges Bat/50
Jim "Catfish" Hunter Jsy/250 15.00
Reggie Jackson Bat/50
Reggie Jackson Bat/50
Derek Jeter Jsy/250 40.00
Randy Johnson Jsy/50
Chipper Jones Bat/50
Ted Kluszewski Jsy/50
Greg Maddux Jsy/100 20.00
Don Mattingly Jsy/50
Paul Molitor Bat/50
Mike Piazza Bat/150 20.00
Albert Pujols Jsy/50
Cal Ripken Jr. Jsy/50
Alex Rodriguez Hat/250 30.00
Ivan Rodriguez Jsy/50
Nolan Ryan Pants/50

2002 FLEER TRADITION UPDATE

NM/M

Complete Set (400): 75.00
Common Player: .15
Common SP (1-100): .50
Inserted 1:1
Pack (10): 1.50
Box (36): 35.00
1 *P.J. Bevis* .50
2 *Michael Crudale* .50
3 *Ben Howard* .75
4 *Travis Driskill* .50
5 *Reed Johnson* .50
6 *Kyle Kane* .50
7 Deivis Santos .50
8 *Tim Kalita* .50
9 *Brandon Puffer* .50
10 *Chris Snelling* 1.00
11 *Juan Brito* .50
12 *Tyler Yates* .50
13 *Victor Alvarez* .50
14 *Takahito Nomura* .50
15 *Ron Calloway* .50
16 *Satoru Komiyama* .50
17 *Julius Matos* .50
18 *Jorge Nunez* .50
19 *Anderson Machado* .50
20 *Scotty Layfield* .50
21 *Aaron Cook* .50
22 *Alex Pelaez* .50
23 *Corey Thurman* .50
24 *Nelson Castro* .50
25 *Jeff Austin* .50
26 *Felix Escalona* .50
27 *Luis Ugueto* .50
28 *Jaime Cerda* .50
29 *J.J. Trujillo* .50
30 *Rodrigo Rosario* .50
31 *Jorge Padilla* .50
32 *Shawn Sedlacek* .50
33 *Nate Field* .50
34 *Earl Snyder* .75
35 *Miguel Asencio* .50
36 *Ken Huckaby* .50
37 Valentino Pascucci .50
38 *So Taguchi* 1.00
39 *Brian Mallette* .50
40 *Kazuhisa Ishii* 2.00
41 Matt Thornton .50
42 Mark Corey .50
43 Kirk Saarloos .50
44 Brandon Bracke .50
45 *Hansel Izquierdo* .50
46 *Rene Reyes* .50
47 Luis Garcia .50
48 *Jason Simontacchi* .50
49 *John Ennis* .75
50 *Franklyn German* .50
51 *Aaron Guiel* .50
52 *Howie Clark* .50
53 *David Ross* .50
54 Walt McKeel .50
55 *Francis Beltran* .50
56 *Barry Wesson* .50
57 *Runelvys Hernandez* .50
58 *Oliver Perez* 2.00
59 *Ryan Bukvich* .50
60 *Steve Kent* .50
61 *Julio Mateo* .50
62 Jason Jimenez .50
63 *Jayson Durocher* .75
64 *Kevin Frederick* .50
65 *Kevin Gryboski* .50
66 *Edwin Almonte* .50
67 *John Foster* .50
68 *Doug Devore* 1.00
69 *Tom Shearn* .50
70 *Colin Young* .50
71 *Jon Adkins* .50
72 *Wilbert Nieves* .50
73 Matt Duff .50
74 *Carl Sadler* .50
75 Jason Kershner .50
76 *Brandon Backe* .50
77 *Wilson Valdez* .50
78 *Chris Baker* .50
79 Ryan Jamison .50
80 *Steve Bechler* .75
81 *Allan Simpson* .50
82 *Aaron Taylor* .50
83 *Kevin Cash* .50
84 *Chone Figgins* 1.00
85 *Clay Condrey* .50
86 *Shane Nance* .50
87 *Freddy Sanchez* .50
88 *Jim Rushford* .50
89 *Jeriome Robertson* .50
90 *Trey Lunsford* .50
91 *Cody McKay* .50
92 *Trey Hodges* .50
93 Hee Seop Choi 1.00
94 Joe Borchard .50
95 Orlando Hudson .50
96 Carl Crawford .50
97 Mark Prior 3.00
98 Brett Myers .50
99 Kenny Lofton .50
100 Cliff Floyd .50
101 Randy Winn .15
102 Ryan Dempster .15
103 Josh Phelps .15
104 Marcus Giles .15
105 Rickey Henderson .75
106 Jose Leon .15
107 Tino Martinez .15
108 Greg Norton .15
109 Odalis Perez .15
110 J.C. Romero .15
111 Gary Sheffield .35
112 Ismael Valdes .15
113 Juan Acevedo .15
114 Ben Broussard .15
115 Deivi Cruz .15
116 Geronimo Gil .15
117 Eric Hinske .15
118 Ted Lilly .15
119 Quinton McCracken .15
120 Antonio Alfonseca .15
121 Brent Abernathy .15
122 Johnny Damon .25
123 Francisco Cordova .15
124 Sterling Hitchcock .15
125 Vladimir Nunez .15
126 Andres Galarraga .15
127 Timoniel Perez .15
128 Tsuyoshi Shinjo .15
129 Joe Girardi .15
130 Roberto Alomar .35
131 Ellis Burks .15
132 Mike DeJean .15
133 Alex Gonzalez .15
134 Johan Santana .35
135 Kenny Lofton .15
136 Juan Encarnacion .15
137 Dewon Brazelton .15
138 Jeromy Burnitz .15
139 Elmer Dessens .15
140 Juan Gonzalez .75
141 Todd Hundley .15
142 Tomokazu Ohka .15
143 Robin Ventura .15
144 Rodrigo Lopez .15
145 Ruben Sierra .15
146 Jason Phillips .15
147 Ryan Rupe .15
148 Kevin Appier .15
149 Sean Burroughs .15
150 Masato Yoshii .15
151 Juan Diaz .15
152 Tony Graffanino .15
153 Raul Ibanez .15
154 Kevin Mench .15
155 Pedro Astacio .15
156 Brent Butler .15
157 Kirk Rueter .15
158 Eddie Guardado .15
159 Hideki Irabu .15
160 Wendell Magee .15
161 Antonio Osuna .15
162 Jose Vizcaino .15
163 Danny Bautista .15
164 Vinny Castilla .15
165 Chris Singleton .15
166 Mark Redman .15
167 Olmedo Saenz .15
168 Scott Erickson .15
169 Ty Wigginton .15
170 Jason Isringhausen .15
171 Lou Merloni .15
172 Chris Magruder .15
173 Brandon Berger .15
174 Roger Cedeno .15
175 Kelvim Escobar .15
176 Jose Guillen .15
177 Damian Jackson .15
178 Eric Owens .15
179 Angel Berroa .15
180 Alex Cintron .15
181 Jeff Weaver .15
182 Damon Minor .15
183 Bobby Estalella .15
184 David Justice .15
185 Roy Halladay .25
186 Brian Jordan .15
187 Mike Maroth .15
188 Pokey Reese .15
189 Rey Sanchez .15
190 Hank Blalock .50
191 Jeff Cirillo .15
192 Dmitri Young .15
193 Carl Everett .15
194 Joey Hamilton .15
195 Jorge Julio .15
196 Pablo Ozuna .15
197 Jason Marquis .15
198 Dustan Mohr .15
199 Joe Borowski .15
200 Tony Clark .15
201 David Wells .15
202 Josh Fogg .15
203 Aaron Harang .15
204 John McDonald .15
205 John Stephens .15
206 Chris Reitsma .15
207 Alex Sanchez .15
208 Milton Bradley .15
209 Matt Clement .15
210 Brad Fullmer .15
211 Shigetoshi Hasegawa .15
212 Austin Kearns .50
213 Damaso Marte .15
214 Vicente Padilla .15
215 Raul Mondesi .15
216 Russell Branyan .15
217 Bartolo Colon .15
218 Moises Alou .15
219 Scott Hatteberg .15
220 Bobby Kielty .15
221 Kip Wells .15
222 Scott Stewart .15
223 Victor Martinez .40
224 Marty Cordova .15
225 Desi Relaford .15
226 Reggie Sanders .15
227 Jason Giambi .50
228 Jimmy Haynes .15
229 Billy Koch .15
230 Damian Moss .15
231 Chan Ho Park .15
232 Cliff Floyd .15
233 Todd Zeile .15
234 Jeremy Giambi .15
235 Rick Helling .15
236 Matt Lawton .15
237 Ramon Martinez .15
238 Rondell White .15
239 Scott Sullivan .15
240 Hideo Nomo .60
241 Todd Ritchie .15
242 Ramon Santiago .15
243 Jake Peavy .15
244 Brad Wilkerson .15
245 Reggie Taylor .15
246 Carlos Pena .15
247 Willis Roberts .15
248 Jason Schmidt .15
249 Mike Williams .15
250 Alan Zinter .15
251 Michael Tejera .15
252 Dave Roberts .15
253 Scott Schoeneweis .15
254 Woody Williams .15
255 John Thomson .15
256 Ricardo Rodriguez .15
257 Aaron Sele .15
258 Paul Wilson .15
259 Brett Tomko .15
260 Kenny Rogers .15
261 Mo Vaughn .15
262 John Burkett .15
263 Dennis Stark .15
264 Ray Durham .15
265 Scott Rolen .65
266 Gabe Kapler .15
267 Todd Hollandsworth .15
268 Bud Smith .15
269 Jay Payton .15
270 Tyler Houston .15
271 Brian Moehler .15
272 David Espinosa .15
273 Placido Polanco .15
274 John Patterson .15

275	Adam Hyzdu	.15
276	Albert Pujols	2.00
277	Larry Walker	.15
278	Magglio Ordonez	.15
279	Ryan Klesko	.15
280	Darin Erstad	.60
281	Jeff Kent	.15
282	Paul LoDuca	.15
283	Jim Edmonds	.15
284	Chipper Jones	1.00
285	Bernie Williams	.30
286	Pat Burrell	.40
287	Cliff Floyd	.15
288	Troy Glaus	.75
289	Brian Giles	.15
290	Jim Thome	.15
291	Greg Maddux	1.00
292	Roberto Alomar	.30
293	Jeff Bagwell	.75
294	Rafael Furcal	.15
295	Josh Beckett	.25
296	Carlos Delgado	.35
297	Ken Griffey Jr.	1.50
298	Jason Giambi	.50
299	Paul Konerko	.15
300	Mike Sweeney	.15
301	Alfonso Soriano	.50
302	Shea Hillenbrand	.15
303	Tony Batista	.15
304	Robin Ventura	.15
305	Alex Rodriguez	2.00
306	Nomar Garciaparra	1.50
307	Derek Jeter	2.50
308	Miguel Tejada	.30
309	Omar Vizquel	.15
310	Jorge Posada	.25
311	A.J. Pierzynski	.15
312	Ichiro Suzuki	1.50
313	Manny Ramirez	.75
314	Torii Hunter	.15
315	Garret Anderson	.15
316	Robert Fick	.15
317	Randy Winn	.15
318	Mark Buehrle	.15
319	Freddy Garcia	.15
320	Eddie Guardado	.15
321	Roy Halladay	.25
322	Derek Lowe	.15
323	Pedro J. Martinez	.75
324	Mariano Rivera	.25
325	Kazuhiro Sasaki	.15
326	Barry Zito	.25
327	Johnny Damon	.25
328	Ugueth Urbina	.15
329	Todd Helton	.75
330	Richie Sexson	.15
331	Jose Vidro	.15
332	Luis Castillo	.15
333	Junior Spivey	.15
334	Scott Rolen	.65
335	Mike Lowell	.15
336	Jimmy Rollins	.15
337	Jose Hernandez	.15
338	Mike Piazza	1.50
339	Benito Santiago	.15
340	Sammy Sosa	1.50
341	Barry Bonds	2.50
342	Vladimir Guerrero	.75
343	Lance Berkman	.15
344	Adam Dunn	.40
345	Shawn Green	.25
346	Luis Gonzalez	.25
347	Eric Gagne	.25
348	Tom Glavine	.30
349	Trevor Hoffman	.15
350	Randy Johnson	.75
351	Byung-Hyun Kim	.15
352	Matt Morris	.15
353	Odalis Perez	.15
354	Curt Schilling	.40
355	John Smoltz	.15
356	Mike Williams	.15
357	Andruw Jones	.75
358	Vicente Padilla	.15
359	Mike Remlinger	.15
360	Robb Nen	.15
361	Shawn Green	.25
362	Derek Jeter	2.50
363	Troy Glaus	.75
364	Ken Griffey Jr.	1.50
365	Mike Piazza	1.50
366	Jason Giambi	.50
367	Greg Maddux	1.00
368	Albert Pujols	2.00
369	Pedro J. Martinez	.75
370	Barry Zito	.25
371	Ichiro Suzuki	1.50
372	Nomar Garciaparra	1.50
373	Vladimir Guerrero	.75
374	Randy Johnson	.75
375	Barry Bonds	2.50
376	Sammy Sosa	1.50
377	Hideo Nomo	.75
378	Jeff Bagwell	.75
379	Curt Schilling	.35
380	Jim Thome	.15
381	Todd Helton	.75
382	Roger Clemens	1.25
383	Chipper Jones	1.00
384	Alex Rodriguez	2.00
385	Manny Ramirez	.40
386	Barry Bonds	2.50
387	Jim Thome	.15
388	Adam Dunn	.40
389	Alex Rodriguez	2.00
390	Shawn Green	.25
391	Jason Giambi	.50
392	Lance Berkman	.15
393	Pat Burrell	.40
394	Eric Chavez	.25
395	Mike Piazza	1.50
396	Vladimir Guerrero	.75
397	Paul Konerko	.15
398	Sammy Sosa	1.50
399	Richie Sexson	.15
400	Torii Hunter	.15

Glossy

Stars (1-100): 1-2X
Cards (101-400): 4-8X
Production 200 sets

Diamond Debuts

		NM/M
Complete Set (15):		10.00
Common Player:		.50
Inserted 1:6		
1DD	Mark Prior	2.50
2DD	Eric Hinske	.50
3DD	Kazuhisa Ishii	.50
4DD	Ben Broussard	.50
5DD	Sean Burroughs	.50
6DD	Austin Kearns	1.00
7DD	Hee Seop Choi	1.00
8DD	Kirk Saarloos	.50
9DD	Orlando Hudson	.50
10DD	So Taguchi	.50
11DD	Kevin Mench	.50
12DD	Carl Crawford	.50
13DD	John Patterson	.50
14DD	Hank Blalock	1.50
15DD	Brett Myers	.50

Grass Roots

		NM/M
Complete Set (10):		15.00
Common Player:		1.00
Inserted 1:24		
1GR	Alfonso Soriano	1.50
2GR	Torii Hunter	1.00
3GR	Andruw Jones	1.50
4GR	Jim Edmonds	1.00
5GR	Shawn Green	1.00
6GR	Todd Helton	1.50
7GR	Nomar Garciaparra	4.00
8GR	Roberto Alomar	1.00
9GR	Vladimir Guerrero	1.50
10GR	Ichiro Suzuki	4.00

Grass Patch

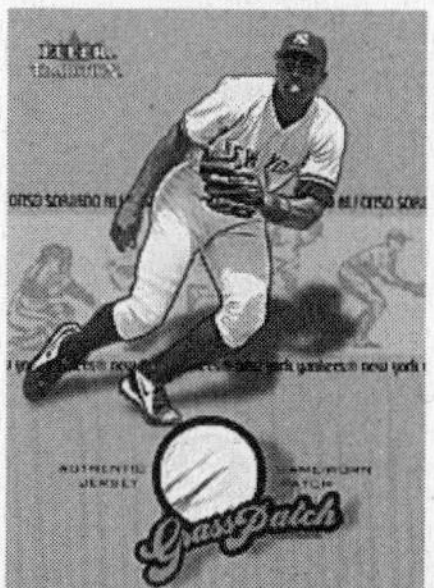

	NM/M
Common Player:	20.00
Production 50 sets	
Alfonso Soriano	30.00
Torii Hunter	20.00
Andruw Jones	30.00
Jim Edmonds	20.00
Shawn Green	20.00
Nomar Garciaparra	50.00
Roberto Alomar	25.00

Heads Up

		NM/M
Complete Set (10):		25.00
Common Player:		2.00
Inserted 1:48		
1HU	Roger Clemens	6.00
2HU	Adam Dunn	2.00
3HU	Kazuhisa Ishii	1.50
4HU	Barry Zito	1.50
5HU	Pedro J. Martinez	4.00
6HU	Alfonso Soriano	3.00
7HU	Mark Prior	3.00
8HU	Chipper Jones	5.00
9HU	Randy Johnson	4.00
10HU	Lance Berkman	1.50

Heads Up Game-Used

	NM/M
Common Player:	5.00
Production 150 sets	
Roger Clemens	25.00
Adam Dunn	10.00
Kazuhisa Ishii	5.00
Barry Zito	5.00
Alfonso Soriano	10.00
Mark Prior	15.00
Chipper Jones	15.00
Randy Johnson	15.00
Lance Berkman	5.00
Mike Piazza	20.00
Barry Bonds	50.00

New York's Finest

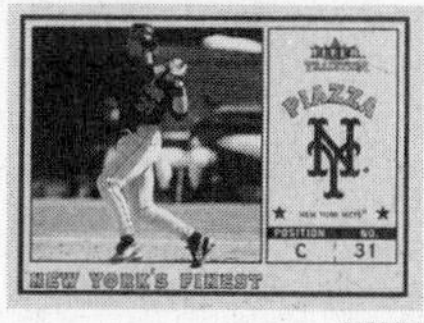

		NM/M
Complete Set (15):		60.00
Common Player:		3.00
Inserted 1:83		
1	Edgardo Alfonzo	3.00
2	Roberto Alomar	4.00
3	Jeromy Burnitz	3.00
4	Satoru Komiyama	3.00
5	Rey Ordonez	3.00
6	Mike Piazza	10.00
7	Mo Vaughn	3.00
8	Roger Clemens	10.00
9	Jason Giambi	5.00
10	Derek Jeter	15.00
11	Mike Mussina	5.00
12	Jorge Posada	3.00
13	Alfonso Soriano	5.00
14	Robin Ventura	3.00
15	Bernie Williams	4.00

N.Y.'s Finest Single Swatch

	NM/M
Common Card:	5.00
Inserted 1:112	

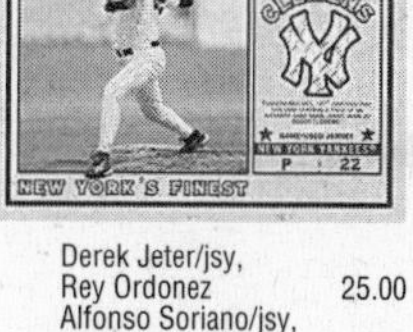

Derek Jeter/jsy, Rey Ordonez	25.00
Alfonso Soriano/jsy, Roberto Alomar	10.00
Roger Clemens/jsy, Mike Piazza	15.00
Mike Mussina/jsy, Mo Vaughn	8.00
Bernie Williams/jsy, Jeromy Burnitz	8.00
Derek Jeter/jsy, Satoru Komiyama	25.00
Robin Ventura/jsy, Edgardo Alfonzo	8.00
Jorge Posada/jsy, Mike Piazza	8.00
Jason Giambi/base, Mo Vaughn	8.00
Alfonso Soriano/jsy, Edgardo Alfonzo	10.00
Derek Jeter, Rey Ordonez/jsy	5.00
Alfonso Soriano, Roberto Alomar/jsy	8.00
Roger Clemens, Mike Piazza/jsy	15.00
Mike Mussina, Mo Vaughn/jsy	6.00
Bernie Williams, Jeromy Burnitz/jsy	5.00
Derek Jeter, Satoru Komiyama/bat	8.00
Robin Ventura, Edgardo Alfonzo/jsy	5.00
Jorge Posada, Mike Piazza/jsy	15.00
Jason Giambi, Mo Vaughn/jsy	6.00
Alfonso Soriano, Edgardo Alfonzo/jsy	5.00

N.Y.'s Finest Dual Swatch

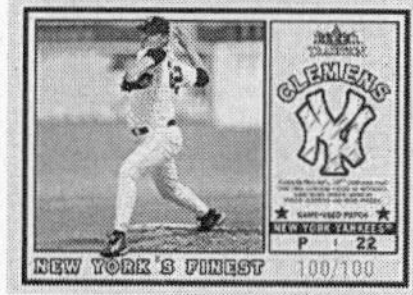

	NM/M
Common Card:	10.00
Production 100 sets	
Derek Jeter, Rey Ordonez	75.00
Alfonso Soriano, Roberto Alomar	40.00
Roger Clemens, Mike Piazza	65.00
Mike Mussina, Mo Vaughn	30.00
Bernie Williams, Jeromy Burnitz	20.00
Robin Ventura, Edgardo Alfonzo	10.00

Plays of the Week

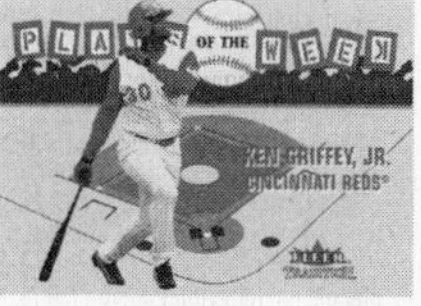

		NM/M
Complete Set (30):		35.00
Common Player:		1.00
Inserted 1:12		
1PW	Troy Glaus	1.50
2PW	Andruw Jones	1.50
3PW	Curt Schilling	1.25
4PW	Manny Ramirez	1.50
5PW	Sammy Sosa	2.50

6PW	Magglio Ordonez	1.00
7PW	Ken Griffey Jr.	2.50
8PW	Jim Thome	1.00
9PW	Larry Walker	1.00
10PW	Robert Fick	1.00
11PW	Josh Beckett	1.00
12PW	Roy Oswalt	1.00
13PW	Mike Sweeney	1.00
14PW	Shawn Green	1.00
15PW	Torii Hunter	1.00
16PW	Vladimir Guerrero	1.50
17PW	Mike Piazza	2.50
18PW	Jason Giambi	1.25
19PW	Eric Chavez	1.00
20PW	Pat Burrell	1.25
21PW	Brian Giles	1.00
22PW	Ryan Klesko	1.00
23PW	Barry Bonds	5.00
24PW	Mike Cameron	1.00
25PW	Albert Pujols	4.00
26PW	Alex Rodriguez	4.00
27PW	Carlos Delgado	1.00
28PW	Richie Sexson	1.00
29PW	Jay Gibbons	1.00
30PW	Randy Winn	1.00

This Day in History

		NM/M
Complete Set (25):		40.00
Common Player:		1.00
1	Shawn Green	1.00
2	Ozzie Smith	2.50
3	Derek Lowe	1.00
4	Ken Griffey Jr.	3.00
5	Barry Bonds	5.00
6	Juan Gonzalez	1.50
7	Wade Boggs	2.00
8	Mark Prior	2.00
9	Thurman Munson	2.00
10	Curt Schilling	1.25
11	Jason Giambi	1.25
12	Cal Ripken Jr.	5.00
13	Craig Biggio	1.00
14	Drew Henson	1.00
15	Steve Carlton	1.00
16	Greg Maddux	2.50
17	Adam Dunn	1.00
18	Vladimir Guerrero	2.00
19	Alex Rodriguez	4.00
20	Carlton Fisk	1.50
21	Ichiro Suzuki	3.00
22	Johnny Bench	2.00
23	Kazuhisa Ishii	1.00
24	Derek Jeter	5.00
25	Jim Thome	1.00

This Day in History Memor.

	NM/M
Common Player:	5.00
Inserted 1:24	
Shawn Green/jsy	5.00
Ozzie Smith/jsy	10.00
Barry Bonds/bat	15.00
Barry Bonds/jsy	15.00
Juan Gonzalez/bat	6.00
Wade Boggs/jsy	6.00
Wade Boggs/pants	6.00
Thurman Munson/jsy/40	
Curt Schilling/jsy	6.00
Craig Biggio/jsy	5.00
Craig Biggio/bat/80	
Adam Dunn/jsy	8.00
Alex Rodriguez/bat	10.00
Alex Rodriguez/jsy	10.00
Carlton Fisk/bat	8.00
Kazuhisa Ishii/jsy	5.00
Derek Jeter/pants	20.00
Jim Thome/bat/120	
Jim Thome/jsy	8.00
Greg Maddux/jsy	10.00

This Day in History Auto.

	NM/M
Inserted 1:582	
Barry Bonds/150	200.00
Mark Prior/64	100.00
Cal Ripken Jr/35	
Drew Henson	20.00
Greg Maddux/99	
Derek Jeter	100.00

2002 FLEER TRIPLE CROWN

		NM/M
Complete Set (270):		30.00
Common Player:		.15
Pack (10):		1.50
Box (24):		30.00
1	Mo Vaughn	.15
2	Derek Jeter	2.00
3	Ken Griffey Jr.	1.25
4	Charles Johnson	.15
5	Geoff Jenkins	.15
6	Chuck Knoblauch	.15
7	Jason Kendall	.15
8	Jim Edmonds	.15
9	David Eckstein	.15
10	Carl Everett	.15
11	Barry Larkin	.15
12	Cliff Floyd	.15
13	Ben Sheets	.15
14	Jeff Conine	.15
15	Brian Giles	.15
16	Darryl Kile	.15
17	Troy Glaus	.65
18	Trot Nixon	.15
19	Jim Thome	.15
20	Preston Wilson	.15
21	Roger Clemens	1.00
22	Chad Hermansen	.15
23	Matt Morris	.15
24	Shawn Wooten	.15
25	Manny Ramirez	.65
26	Roberto Alomar	.30
27	Josh Beckett	.25
28	Jose Hernandez	.15
29	Mike Mussina	.35
30	Jack Wilson	.25
31	Bud Smith	.15
32	Garret Anderson	.15
33	Pedro J. Martinez	.65
34	Travis Fryman	.15
35	Jeff Bagwell	.65
36	Doug Mientkiewicz	.15
37	Andy Pettitte	.25
38	Ryan Klesko	.15
39	Edgar Renteria	.15
40	Mariano Rivera	.25
41	Darin Erstad	.50
42	Hideo Nomo	.50
43	Ellis Burks	.15
44	Craig Biggio	.15
45	Corey Koskie	.15
46	Jason Varitek	.15
47	Xavier Nady	.15
48	Aubrey Huff	.15
49	Tim Salmon	.25
50	Nomar Garciaparra	1.25
51	Juan Gonzalez	.65
52	Moises Alou	.15
53	A.J. Pierzynski	.15
54	Bernie Williams	.30
55	Phil Nevin	.15
56	Ben Grieve	.15
57	Mark Grace	.25
58	Mike Lansing	.15
59	Kenny Lofton	.15
60	Lance Berkman	.15
61	David Ortiz	.25
62	Jason Giambi	.40
63	Mark Kotsay	.15
64	Greg Vaughn	.15
65	Junior Spivey	.15
66	Fred McGriff	.15
67	C.C. Sabathia	.15
68	Richard Hidalgo	.15
69	Torii Hunter	.15
70	Jason Hart	.15
71	Bubba Trammell	.15
72	Jace Brewer	.15
73	Matt Williams	.15
74	Matt Stairs	.15
75	Omar Vizquel	.15
76	Daryle Ward	.15
77	Joe Mays	.15
78	Eric Chavez	.15
79	Andres Galarraga	.15
80	Rafael Palmeiro	.50
81	Steve Finley	.15
82	Eric Young	.15
83	Todd Helton	.65
84	Roy Oswalt	.25
85	Eric Milton	.15
86	Ramon Hernandez	.15
87	Jeff Kent	.15
88	Ivan Rodriguez	.50
89	Luis Gonzalez	.25
90	Corey Patterson	.15
91	Jose Ortiz	.15
92	Mike Sweeney	.15
93	Cristian Guzman	.15
94	Johnny Damon	.25
95	Barry Bonds	2.00
96	Rusty Greer	.15
97	Reggie Sanders	.15
98	Sammy Sosa	1.25
99	Jeff Cirillo	.15
100	Carlos Febles	.15
101	Jose Vidro	.15
102	Jermaine Dye	.15
103	Rich Aurilia	.15
104	Gabe Kapler	.15
105	Randy Johnson	.65
106	Rondell White	.15
107	Ben Petrick	.15
108	Joe Randa	.15
109	Fernando Tatis	.15
110	Tim Hudson	.25
111	John Olerud	.15
112	Alex Rodriguez	1.50
113	Curt Schilling	.40
114	Kerry Wood	.40
115	Alex Ochoa	.15
116	Carlos Beltran	.40
117	Vladimir Guerrero	.65
118	Mark Mulder	.15
119	Bret Boone	.15
120	Carlos Delgado	.35
121	Marcus Giles	.15
122	Paul Konerko	.15
123	Juan Pierre	.15
124	Mark Quinn	.15
125	Edgardo Alfonzo	.15
126	Barry Zito	.25
127	Dan Wilson	.15
128	Jose Cruz Jr.	.15
129	Chipper Jones	.75
130	Ray Durham	.15
131	Larry Walker	.15
132	Neifi Perez	.15
133	Robin Ventura	.15
134	Miguel Tejada	.25
135	Edgar Martinez	.15
136	Raul Mondesi	.15
137	Javy Lopez	.15
138	Jose Canseco	.25
139	Mike Hampton	.15
140	Eric Karros	.15
141	Mike Piazza	1.25
142	Travis Lee	.15
143	Ichiro Suzuki	1.25
144	Shannon Stewart	.15
145	Andruw Jones	.65
146	Frank Thomas	.65
147	Tony Clark	.15
148	Adrian Beltre	.25
149	Matt Lawton	.15
150	Marlon Anderson	.15
151	Freddy Garcia	.15
152	Brian Jordan	.15
153	Carlos Lee	.15
154	Eric Munson	.15
155	Paul LoDuca	.15
156	Jay Payton	.15
157	Scott Rolen	.50
158	Jamie Moyer	.15
159	Tom Glavine	.30
160	Magglio Ordonez	.15
161	Brandon Inge	.15
162	Shawn Green	.25
163	Tsuyoshi Shinjo	.15
164	Mike Lieberthal	.15
165	Kazuhiro Sasaki	.15
166	Greg Maddux	.75
167	Chris Singleton	.15
168	Juan Encarnacion	.15
169	Gary Sheffield	.25
170	Nick Johnson	.15
171	Bobby Abreu	.15
172	Aaron Boone	.15
173	Rafael Furcal	.15
174	Mark Buehrle	.15
175	Bobby Higginson	.15
176	Kevin Brown	.15
177	Tino Martinez	.15
178	Pat Burrell	.30
179	Fernando Vina	.15
180	Jay Gibbons	.15
181	Jose Valentin	.15
182	Derrek Lee	.15
183	Richie Sexson	.15
184	Alfonso Soriano	.50
185	Jimmy Rollins	.15
186	Albert Pujols	1.50
187	Brady Anderson	.15
188	Sean Casey	.25
189	Luis Castillo	.15
190	Jeromy Burnitz	.15
191	Jorge Posada	.25
192	Kevin Young	.15
193	Eli Marrero	.15
194	Shea Hillenbrand	.15
195	Adam Dunn	.40
196	Mike Lowell	.15
197	Jeffrey Hammonds	.15
198	David Justice	.15
199	Aramis Ramirez	.15
200	J.D. Drew	.25
201	Pedro Santana	.15
202	Endy Chavez	.15
203	Donnie Bridges	.15
204	Travis Phelps	.15
205	Drew Henson	.25
206	Angel Berroa	.15
207	George Perez	.15
208	Billy Sylvester	.15
209	Juan Cruz	.15
210	Horacio Ramirez	.15
211	J.J. Davis	.15
212	Cody Ransom	.15
213	Mark Teixeira	.50
214	Nate Frese	.15
215	Brian Rogers	.15
216	Dewon Brazelton	.15
217	Carlos Hernandez	.15
218	Juan Rivera	.15
219	Luis Lopez	.15
220	Benito Baez	.15
221	Bill Ortega	.15
222	Dustan Mohr	.15
223	Corky Miller	.15
224	Tyler Walker	.15
225	Rick Bauer	.15
226	Mark Prior	.65
227	Rafael Soriano	.15
228	Greg Miller	.15
229	Dave Williams	.15
230	Bert Snow	.15
231	Barry Bonds	1.50
232	Rickey Henderson	.50
233	Alex Rodriguez	1.25
234	Luis Gonzalez	.25
235	Derek Jeter	1.50
236	Bud Smith	.15
237	Sammy Sosa	.75
238	Jeff Bagwell	.50
239	Jim Thome	.15
240	Hideo Nomo	.50
241	Greg Maddux	.75
242	Ken Griffey Jr.	1.00
243	Curt Schilling	.25
244	Arizona Diamondbacks	.15
245	Ichiro Suzuki	.75
246	Albert Pujols	1.00
247	Ichiro Suzuki	.75
248	Barry Bonds	1.50
249	Roger Clemens	.65
250	Randy Johnson	.50
251	Todd Helton	.50
252	Rafael Palmeiro	.40
253	Mike Piazza	1.00
254	Alex Rodriguez	1.25
255	Manny Ramirez	.50
256	Ken Griffey Jr.	1.00
257	Jason Giambi	.40

258 Chipper Jones .65
259 Larry Walker .15
260 Sammy Sosa .75
261 Vladimir Guerrero .50
262 Nomar Garciaparra .75
263 Randy Johnson .50
264 Roger Clemens .65
265 Ichiro Suzuki 1.00
266 Barry Bonds 1.50
267 Paul LoDuca .15
268 Albert Pujols 1.00
269 Derek Jeter 1.50
270 Adam Dunn .40

RBI parallel

Stars Print Run 101-200: 4-8X
Stars P/R 76-100: 5-10X
Stars P/R 51-75: 6-12X
Stars P/R 25-50: 10-20X
Numbered to 2001 RBI total
(See 2002 Fleer Triple Crown for checklist and base card values.)

Home Run parallel

Stars Print Run 50-75: 10-20X
Stars P/R 31-50: 15-25X
Stars P/R 21-30: 20-40X
Numbered to 2001 HR total

Batting Average Parallel

Stars: 4-8X
Numbered to 2001 batting avg.
(See 2002 Fleer Triple Crown for checklist and base card values.)

Diamond Immortality

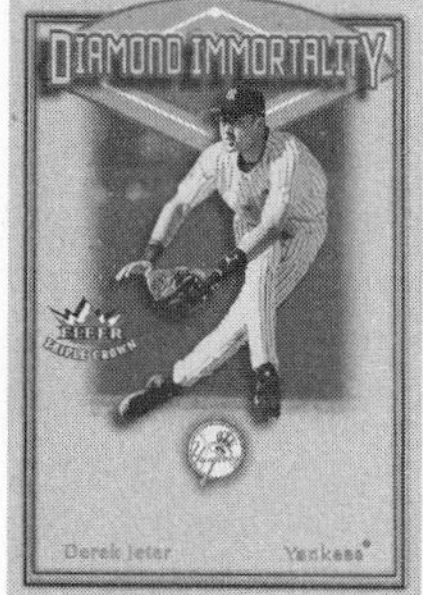

NM/M
Complete Set (10): 25.00
Common Player: 1.00
Inserted 1:12
1DI Derek Jeter 5.00
2DI Barry Bonds 5.00
3DI Ricky Henderson 1.00
4DI Roger Clemens 2.50
5DI Alex Rodriguez 4.00
6DI Albert Pujols 4.00
7DI Nomar Garciaparra 3.00
8DI Ichiro Suzuki 3.00
9DI Chipper Jones 2.00
10DI Ken Griffey Jr. 3.00

Diamond Immortality Game-Used

NM/M
Inserted 1:129
Barry Bonds/jsy 25.00
Roger Clemens/jsy 20.00
Nomar Garciaparra/jsy/sp 40.00
Ricky Henderson/bat 10.00
Derek Jeter/bat 25.00
Chipper Jones/bat 10.00
Albert Pujols/jsy 25.00
Alex Rodriguez/jsy 20.00

Home Run Kings

NM/M
Complete Set (25): 100.00
Common Player: 2.00
Inserted 1:24
1 Ted Williams 10.00
2 Todd Helton 4.00
3 Eddie Murray 2.00
4 Jeff Bagwell 4.00
5 Babe Ruth 15.00
6 Eddie Mathews 5.00
7 Alex Rodriguez 10.00
8 Juan Gonzalez 4.00
9 Chipper Jones 5.00
10 Luis Gonzalez 2.00
11 Johnny Bench 5.00
12 Frank Thomas 4.00
13 Ernie Banks 3.00
14 Jimmie Foxx 4.00
15 Ken Griffey Jr. 8.00
16 Rafael Palmeiro 3.00
17 Sammy Sosa 8.00
18 Reggie Jackson 4.00
19 Barry Bonds 10.00
20 Willie McCovey 2.00
21 Manny Ramirez 4.00
22 Larry Walker 2.00
23 Jason Giambi 4.00
24 Mike Piazza 8.00
25 Jose Canseco 2.00

Home Run Kings Game-Used

NM/M
Common Player: 5.00
Inserted 1:155
Jeff Bagwell/jsy 10.00
Johnny Bench/bat/sp 50.00
Barry Bonds/jsy 25.00
Jimmie Foxx/bat 40.00
Jason Giambi/jsy 10.00
Reggie Jackson/bat 10.00
Eddie Mathews/bat 15.00
Eddie Murray/bat 10.00
Rafael Palmeiro/bat 10.00
Mike Piazza/jsy 15.00
Manny Ramirez/bat/sp 50.00
Todd Helton/bat 10.00
Alex Rodriguez/bat 15.00
Babe Ruth/bat/27
Larry Walker/bat 5.00
Ted Williams/jsy 100.00

Home Run Kings Autograph

NM/M
Common Player:
Johnny Bench/45
Barry Bonds/73 300.00
Alex Rodriguez/52 100.00
Jason Giambi/43
Jose Canseco/46
Jeff Bagwell/47
Reggie Jackson/47
Rafael Palmeiro/47
Larry Walker/49

RBI Kings

NM/M
Complete Set (15): 140.00
Common Player: 4.00
Inserted 1:144
1 Sammy Sosa 15.00
2 Todd Helton 8.00
3 Albert Pujols 20.00
4 Manny Ramirez 8.00
5 Luis Gonzalez 4.00
6 Shawn Green 4.00
7 Barry Bonds 20.00
8 Ken Griffey Jr. 15.00
9 Alex Rodriguez 20.00
10 Jason Giambi 8.00
11 Jeff Bagwell 8.00
12 Vladimir Guerrero 8.00
13 Juan Gonzalez 8.00
14 Chipper Jones 8.00
15 Mike Piazza 15.00

RBI Kings Game-Used

NM/M
Common Player: 5.00
Inserted 1:70
Jeff Bagwell/jsy 10.00
Barry Bonds/jsy 25.00
Jason Giambi/jsy 8.00
Luis Gonzalez/bat 5.00
Juan Gonzalez/bat 8.00
Shawn Green/jsy 6.00
Todd Helton/jsy 10.00
Mike Piazza/jsy 15.00
Albert Pujols/bat/sp 70.00
Manny Ramirez/bat 10.00
Alex Rodriguez/shoe 25.00

Season Crowns

NM/M
Complete Set (10): 25.00
Common Card: 2.00
Inserted 1:12
1SC Barry Bonds, Sammy Sosa, Luis Gonzalez 4.00
2SC Larry Walker, Nomar Garciaparra, Todd Helton 4.00
3SC Sammy Sosa, Todd Helton, Manny Ramirez 4.00
4SC Pedro J. Martinez, Derek Jeter, Cal Ripken Jr. 6.00
5SC Jose Canseco, Barry Bonds, Alex Rodriguez 5.00
6SC Barry Bonds, Jeff Kent, Chipper Jones 4.00
7SC Ichiro Suzuki, Jason Giambi, Ivan Rodriguez 3.00
8SC Curt Schilling, Tom Glavine, Pedro J. Martinez 2.00
9SC Randy Johnson, Pedro J. Martinez, Greg Maddux 3.00
10SC Randy Johnson, Curt Schilling, John Smoltz 2.00

Season Crowns Autograph

NM/M
Jeter #'d to 160
Derek Jeter/160 150.00
Barry Bonds/77 250.00

Season Crowns Game-Used

NM/M
Common Player: 5.00
Inserted 1:90
Barry Bonds/jsy 25.00
Sammy Sosa/base 15.00
Larry Walker/bat 5.00
Nomar Garciaparra/jsy 20.00
Todd Helton/jsy 10.00
Sammy Sosa/base 15.00
Todd Helton/jsy 10.00
Manny Ramirez/jsy 10.00
Pedro Martinez/jsy 10.00
Derek Jeter/pants 25.00
Cal Ripken Jr/bat 60.00
Jose Canseco/jsy 8.00
Barry Bonds/jsy 25.00
Alex Rodriguez/jsy 20.00
Barry Bonds/jsy 25.00
Jeff Kent/jsy 5.00
Ichiro Suzuki/base 25.00
Jason Giambi/jsy 10.00
Ivan Rodriguez/jsy 10.00
Curt Schilling/jsy 10.00
Tom Glavine/jsy 10.00
Pedro Martinez/jsy 10.00
Randy Johnson/jsy 10.00
Pedro Martinez/jsy 10.00
Greg Maddux/jsy 15.00
Randy Johnson/jsy 10.00
Curt Schilling/jsy 10.00
John Smoltz/jsy 5.00

Season Crowns Triple Swatch

NM/M
Production 100 sets
Barry Bonds, Sammy Sosa, Luis Gonzalez 100.00
Larry Walker, Nomar Garciaparra, Todd Helton 40.00
Sammy Sosa, Todd Helton, Manny Ramirez 50.00
Barry Bonds, Jeff Kent, Chipper Jones 80.00
Ichiro Suzuki, Jason Giambi, Ivan Rodriguez 80.00
Curt Schilling, Tom Glavine, Pedro J. Martinez 50.00
Randy Johnson, Pedro J. Martinez, Greg Maddux 50.00
Randy Johnson, Curt Schilling, John Smoltz 50.00

2003 FLEER AUTHENTIX

NM/M
Complete Set (160):
Common Player: .25
Common (111-125): 3.00
Production 1,850
Common (126-160): 1.50
Exclusive to Home Team boxes
Pack (5): 3.00
Box (24): 50.00
1 Derek Jeter 3.00
2 Tom Glavine .40
3 Jason Jennings .25
4 Craig Biggio .25
5 Miguel Tejada .40
6 Barry Bonds 3.00
7 Juan Gonzalez 1.00
8 Luis Gonzalez .40
9 Johnny Damon .40
10 Ellis Burks .25
11 Frank Thomas 1.00
12 Richie Sexson .25
13 Roger Clemens 1.50
14 Matt Morris .25
15 Troy Glaus 1.00
16 Tony Batista .25
17 Magglio Ordonez .25
18 Jose Vidro .25
19 Barry Zito .40
20 Chipper Jones 1.50
21 Moises Alou .25
22 Lance Berkman .25
23 Jacque Jones .25
24 Alfonso Soriano .75
25 Sean Burroughs .25
26 Scott Rolen 1.00
27 Mark Grace .35
28 Manny Ramirez 1.00
29 Ken Griffey Jr. 2.00
30 Josh Beckett .25
31 Kazuhisa Ishii .25
32 Pat Burrell 1.00
33 Edgar Martinez .25
34 Tim Salmon .35
35 Raul Ibanez .25
36 Vladimir Guerrero 1.00
37 Jermaine Dye .25
38 Rich Aurilia .25
39 Rafael Palmeiro .75
40 Kerry Wood .75
41 Omar Vizquel .25
42 Fred McGriff .25
43 Ben Sheets .25
44 Bernie Williams .40
45 Brian Giles .25

46 Jim Edmonds .25
47 Garret Anderson .25
48 Pedro J. Martinez 1.00
49 Adam Dunn .75
50 A.J. Burnett .25
51 Eric Gagne .25
52 Mo Vaughn .25
53 Bobby Abreu .25
54 Bret Boone .25
55 Carlos Delgado .40
56 Gary Sheffield .40
57 Sammy Sosa 2.00
58 Jim Thome .25
59 Jeff Bagwell 1.00
60 David Eckstein .25
61 Jason Kendall .25
62 Albert Pujols 2.50
63 Curt Schilling .40
64 Nomar Garciaparra 2.00
65 Sean Casey .35
66 Shawn Green .40
67 Mike Piazza 2.00
68 Ichiro Suzuki 2.00
69 Eric Hinske .25
70 Greg Maddux 1.50
71 Larry Walker .25
72 Roy Oswalt .40
73 Alex Rodriguez 2.50
74 Austin Kearns .75
75 Cliff Floyd .25
76 Kevin Brown .25
77 Jason Giambi .75
78 Jorge Julio .25
79 Carlos Lee .25
80 Mike Sweeney .25
81 Edgardo Alfonzo .25
82 Eric Chavez .40
83 Andruw Jones 1.00
84 Mark Prior .75
85 Todd Helton 1.00
86 Torii Hunter .25
87 Ryan Klesko .25
88 Aubrey Huff .25
89 Randy Johnson 1.00
90 Barry Larkin .25
91 Mike Lowell .25
92 Jimmy Rollins .25
93 Darin Erstad .65
94 Jay Gibbons .25
95 Paul Konerko .40
96 Bobby Higginson .25
97 Carlos Beltran .60
98 Bartolo Colon .25
99 Jeff Kent .25
100 Ivan Rodriguez .65
101 Joe Borchard .25
102 Mark Teixeira .50
103 Francisco Rodriguez .25
104 Chris Snelling .25
105 Hee Seop Choi .25
106 Hank Blalock .50
107 Marlon Byrd .25
108 Michael Restovich .25
109 Victor Martinez .25
110 Lyle Overbay .25
111 *Brian Stokes* 3.00
112 *Josh Hall* 4.00
113 *Chris Waters* 3.00
114 *Lew Ford* 5.00
115 *Ian Ferguson* 3.00
116 *Josh Willingham* 4.00
117 *Josh Stewart* 3.00
118 *Pete LaForest* 4.00
119 *Jose Contreras* 5.00
120 *Terrmel Sledge* 3.00
121 *Guillermo Quiroz* 4.00
122 *Alejandro Machado* 3.00
123 *Nook Logan* 3.00
124 *Rontrez Johnson* 4.00
125 *Hideki Matsui* 10.00
126 Phil Rizzuto 3.00
127 Robin Ventura 1.50
128 Andy Pettitte 4.00
129 Mike Mussina 3.00
130 Mariano Rivera 3.00
131 Jeff Weaver 1.50
132 David Wells 1.50
133 Tommy Lasorda 2.00
134 Pee Wee Reese 2.00
135 Hideo Nomo 4.00
136 Adrian Beltre 2.00
137 Chin-Feng Chen 4.00
138 Odalis Perez 1.50
139 Dave Roberts 1.50
140 Bobby Doerr 3.00
141 Jason Varitek 1.50
142 Trot Nixon 1.50
143 Tim Wakefield 1.50
144 John Burkett 1.50
145 Jeremy Giambi 1.50
146 Casey Fossum 1.50
147 Phil Niekro 1.50
148 Warren Spahn 4.00
149 Rafael Furcal 2.00
150 Vinny Castilla 1.50
151 Javy Lopez 1.50
152 Jason Marquis 1.50
153 Mike Hampton 1.50
154 Gaylord Perry 1.50
155 Ruben Sierra 1.50
156 Mike Cameron 1.50
157 Freddy Garcia 1.50
158 Joel Pineiro 1.50
159 Jamie Moyer 1.50
160 Carlos Guillen 1.50

Balcony

Stars (1-110): 3-6X
SP's (111-125): .5-1.5X
Production 250 sets
Club Box (1-110): 5-10X
SP's (111-125): .75-2X
Production 100 sets
Standing Room Only: No Pricing
Production 25 sets

Autographed Authentix

NM/M
Quantity produced listed
DJ Derek Jeter/50 150.00
DJ Derek Jeter/150 125.00
DJ Derek Jeter/250 125.00
BB Barry Bonds/50 200.00
BB Barry Bonds/150 200.00
BB Barry Bonds/250 200.00

Autographed Jersey Authentix

NM/M
Quantity Produced listed
DJ Derek Jeter/100 150.00
DJ Derek Jeter/200 150.00
DJ Derek Jeter/300 125.00
NR Nolan Ryan/100 185.00
NR Nolan Ryan/200 150.00
NR Nolan Ryan/300 125.00

Ballpark Classics

NM/M
Complete Set (10): 25.00
Common Player: 1.50
Inserted 1:12
1 Derek Jeter 6.00
2 Randy Johnson 2.00
3 Nomar Garciaparra 4.00
4 Barry Bonds 6.00
5 Alfonso Soriano 2.00
6 Alex Rodriguez 5.00
7 Jim Thome 1.50
8 Chipper Jones 3.00
9 Mike Piazza 4.00
10 Ichiro Suzuki 4.00

Bat Authentix

NM/M
Common Player: 8.00
Inserted 1:78
Unripped: 1.5-3X
Production 50 sets
AD Adam Dunn 8.00
NG Nomar Garciaparra 15.00
JG Jason Giambi 15.00
VG Vladimir Guerrero 10.00
DJ Derek Jeter 30.00
CJ Chipper Jones 10.00
MR Manny Ramirez 10.00
SR Scott Rolen
SS Sammy Sosa 15.00
JT Jim Thome 15.00

Hometown Heroes Memorabilia

NM/M
Common Player: 8.00
Home Team Box exclusive
BB Bret Boone/jsy/200 8.00
KB Kevin Brown/jsy/150 10.00
CC Chin-Feng Chen/jsy/150 35.00
RC Roger Clemens 25.00
JD Johnny Damon/jsy/100 8.00
FG Freddy Garcia/jsy/200 8.00
NG Nomar Garciaparra 25.00
JG Jason Giambi/bat/300 20.00
SG Shawn Green/jsy/100 8.00
KI Kazuhisa Ishii/jsy/100 8.00
DJ Derek Jeter 40.00
AJ Andruw Jones/jsy/150 10.00
CJ Chipper Jones 15.00
GM Greg Maddux/jsy 15.00
EM Edgar Martinez/jsy/200 10.00
PM Pedro Martinez/jsy/100 15.00
MR Manny Ramirez 10.00
GS Gary Sheffield/jsy/100 8.00
AS Alfonso Soriano 15.00
I Ichiro Suzuki/base/100 30.00

Jersey Authentix

NM/M
Common Player: 5.00
Inserted 1:10
Unripped: 1.5-3X
Production 50 sets
JB Jeff Bagwell 8.00
JB2 Josh Beckett 5.00
LB Lance Berkman 5.00
MB Mark Buehrle 5.00
PB Pat Burrell 10.00
SB Sean Burroughs 5.00
RC Roger Clemens 15.00
CD Carlos Delgado 5.00
AD Adam Dunn 8.00
NG Nomar Garciaparra 15.00
VG Vladimir Guerrero 8.00
EH Eric Hinske 5.00
TH Torii Hunter 6.00
DJ Derek Jeter 25.00
RJ Randy Johnson 8.00
CJ Chipper Jones 8.00
GM Greg Maddux 15.00
MP Mike Piazza 12.00
MR Manny Ramirez 8.00
AR Alex Rodriguez 12.00
AS Alfonso Soriano 10.00
SS Sammy Sosa 12.00
MT Miguel Tejada 5.00
KW Kerry Wood 8.00

Jersey Authentix Game of the Week

NM/M
Common Card: 10.00
Inserted 1:240
Unripped: 1.5-3X
Production 50 sets
Derek Jeter, Nomar Garciaparra 45.00
Mike Piazza, Sammy Sosa 25.00
Chipper Jones, Pat Burrell 20.00
Greg Maddux, Randy Johnson 20.00
Alex Rodriguez, Miguel Tejada 20.00
Adam Dunn, Lance Berkman 10.00
Torii Hunter, Alfonso Soriano 15.00
Derek Jeter, Miguel Tejada 25.00
Eric Hinske, Torii Hunter 10.00
Alfonso Soriano, Sammy Sosa 15.00

Ticket Studs

NM/M
Complete Set (15): 25.00
Common Player: 1.00
Inserted 1:6
1TS Curt Schilling 1.00
2TS Greg Maddux 2.50
3TS Torii Hunter 1.00
4TS Mike Piazza 3.00
5TS Pedro J. Martinez 2.00
6TS Nomar Garciaparra 3.00
7TS Derek Jeter 5.00
8TS Alex Rodriguez 4.00
9TS Alfonso Soriano 2.00
10TS Pat Burrell 1.50
11TS Barry Bonds 5.00
12TS Jason Giambi 2.50
13TS Sammy Sosa 2.50
14TS Vladimir Guerrero 1.50
15TS Ichiro Suzuki 3.00

2003 FLEER AVANT

NM/M
Complete Set (90): 240.00
Common Player: .50
Common Retired SP (66-75): 5.00
Production 799
Common Rk (76-90): 3.00
Production 699
Pack (4): 4.00
Box (18): 60.00
1 Adam Dunn .50
2 Barry Zito .50
3 Preston Wilson .50
4 Barry Bonds 4.00
5 Hank Blalock 1.00
6 Omar Vizquel .50
7 Brian Giles .50
8 Kerry Wood .75
9 Miguel Tejada .75
10 Magglio Ordonez .50
11 Randy Johnson 1.00
12 Jeff Bagwell 1.00
13 Pat Burrell .75
14 Jason Giambi .75
15 Mark Prior 1.00
16 Roger Clemens 2.00
17 Sammy Sosa 2.50
18 Jay Gibbons .50
19 Torii Hunter .75
20 Ichiro Suzuki 2.00
21 Derek Jeter 4.00
22 Tom Glavine .50
23 Alfonso Soriano 1.00
24 Manny Ramirez 1.00
25 Frank Thomas 1.00
26 Carlos Pena .50
27 Alex Rodriguez 3.00
28 Edgar Martinez .50
29 Larry Walker .50
30 Rafael Palmeiro .75
31 Mike Piazza 2.00
32 Nomar Garciaparra 2.50
33 Lance Berkman .50
34 Vladimir Guerrero 1.00
35 Troy Glaus .75
36 Ivan Rodriguez .75
37 Mark Mulder .50
38 Curt Schilling .75
39 Mike Sweeney .50
40 Albert Pujols 3.00
41 Tim Hudson .50
42 Greg Maddux 1.50
43 Shawn Green .50
44 Scott Rolen 1.00
45 Gary Sheffield .75
46 Richie Sexson .75
47 Aubrey Huff .50
48 Luis Gonzalez .50
49 Todd Helton 1.00
50 Xavier Nady .50
51 Juan Gonzalez 1.00
52 Pedro J. Martinez 1.00
53 Garret Anderson .50

54	Craig Biggio	.50
55	Bret Boone	.50
56	Ken Griffey Jr.	2.00
57	Kevin Millwood	.50
58	Carlos Delgado	.75
59	Chipper Jones	1.50
60	Hideo Nomo	.50
61	Jim Edmonds	.50
62	Austin Kearns	.75
63	Jim Thome	.50
64	Vernon Wells	.50
65	Mike Lowell	.50
66	Whitey Ford	5.00
67	Bob Gibson	5.00
68	Reggie Jackson	5.00
69	Willie McCovey	5.00
70	Phil Rizzuto	5.00
71	Al Kaline	6.00
72	Brooks Robinson	5.00
73	Nolan Ryan	15.00
74	Mike Schmidt	10.00
75	Tom Seaver	6.00
76	*Hideki Matsui*	15.00
77	Rocco Baldelli	4.00
78	*Jose Contreras*	6.00
79	Hee Seop Choi	3.00
80	Jeremy Bonderman	4.00
81	*Bo Hart*	3.00
82	*Brandon Webb*	5.00
83	Ron Calloway	3.00
84	Jesse Foppert	3.00
85	Kyle Snyder	3.00
86	Mark Teixeira	5.00
87	Jose Reyes	5.00
88	Dontrelle Willis	4.00
89	Reed Johnson	3.00
90	*Rickie Weeks*	10.00

Black/White

	NM/M
Stars (1-65):	4-6X
SP's (66-90):	1-2X
Production 199 sets	

Autographs

		NM/M
Common Autograph:		10.00
Varying quantities produced		
Parallel SP's:		1-1.5X
Production 75 or 150		
DJ	Derek Jeter/75	140.00
MR	Manny Ramirez/100	35.00
VW	Vernon Wells/250	10.00
HB	Hank Blalock/150	25.00
DW	Dontrelle Willis/300	30.00
AK	Al Kaline/200	35.00
BR	Brooks Robinson/300	20.00
BG	Bob Gibson/250	25.00
JR	Jose Reyes/300	25.00
BZ	Barry Zito/150	20.00
EM	Edgar Martinez/246	25.00
BH	Bo Hart/300	15.00
AH	Aubrey Huff/300	15.00
CP	Carlos Pena/150	15.00
MT	Miguel Tejada/150	20.00
ML	Mike Lowell/150	10.00
CB	Craig Biggio/250	15.00
BW	Brandon Webb/300	25.00
RB	Rocco Baldelli/250	30.00

Candid Collection

		NM/M
Complete Set (15):		50.00
Common Player:		2.00
Production 500 sets		
1CC	Derek Jeter	6.00
2CC	Mike Piazza	4.00
3CC	Albert Pujols	6.00
4CC	Randy Johnson	3.00
5CC	Alex Rodriguez	6.00
6CC	Vladimir Guerrero	3.00
7CC	Troy Glaus	2.00
8CC	Ichiro Suzuki	4.00
9CC	Barry Zito	2.00
10CC	Jim Thome	2.00
11CC	Sammy Sosa	5.00
12CC	Greg Maddux	4.00
13CC	Barry Bonds	8.00
14CC	Jason Giambi	3.00
15CC	Nomar Garciaparra	6.00

Candid Collection Memorabilia

	NM/M
Common Player:	
Production 150 sets	
Derek Jeter	30.00
Mike Piazza	12.00
Randy Johnson	8.00
Alex Rodriguez	15.00
Barry Zito	8.00
Jim Thome	15.00
Sammy Sosa	15.00
Greg Maddux	15.00
Jason Giambi	10.00
Nomar Garciaparra	15.00

Hall of Frame

		NM/M
Complete Set (14):		80.00
Common Player:		6.00
Production 299 sets		
1	Richie Ashburn	6.00
2	Rod Carew	8.00
3	Whitey Ford	8.00
4	Bob Gibson	8.00
5	Reggie Jackson	8.00
6	Harmon Killebrew	8.00
7	Willie McCovey	6.00
8	Phil Rizzuto	8.00
9	Al Kaline	10.00
10	Brooks Robinson	8.00
11	Nolan Ryan	15.00
12	Mike Schmidt	10.00
13	Tom Seaver	8.00
14	Warren Spahn	8.00

Hall of Frame Memorabilia

	NM/M
Production 99	
Reggie Jackson	25.00
Willie McCovey	20.00
Al Kaline	35.00
Nolan Ryan	65.00
Mike Schmidt	40.00

Material

		NM/M
Common Player:		
Production 50 sets		
RB	Rocco Baldelli	25.00
AR	Alex Rodriguez	25.00
AS	Alfonso Soriano	20.00
SS	Sammy Sosa	25.00
NG	Nomar Garciaparra	30.00
CJ	Chipper Jones	20.00
RJ	Randy Johnson	15.00
JT	Jim Thome	15.00
GM	Greg Maddux	30.00
JG	Jason Giambi	15.00
VG	Vladimir Guerrero	15.00

On Display

		NM/M
Complete Set (10):		50.00
Common Player:		3.00
Production 399 sets		
1OD	Derek Jeter	6.00
2OD	Barry Bonds	8.00
3OD	Rocco Baldelli	5.00
4OD	Alex Rodriguez	6.00
5OD	Alfonso Soriano	4.00
6OD	Sammy Sosa	6.00
7OD	Nomar Garciaparra	6.00
8OD	Hideki Matsui	20.00
9OD	Miguel Tejada	3.00
10OD	Chipper Jones	5.00

On Display Memorabilia

	NM/M
Common Player:	5.00
Production 250 sets	
Derek Jeter	20.00
Barry Bonds	15.00
Rocco Baldelli	25.00
Alex Rodriguez	10.00
Alfonso Soriano	10.00
Sammy Sosa	12.00
Nomar Garciaparra	15.00
Hideki Matsui	40.00
Miguel Tejada	5.00
Chipper Jones	10.00

2003 FLEER BOX SCORE

		NM/M
Complete Set (245):		
Common Player:		.15
Common Box Score Debut (101-110):		4.00
Production 599		
Common Rookie (111-125):		1.00
Inserted 1:6		
Complete Rising Stars (30):		25.00
Common (126-155):		1.00
Complete All-Stars (30):		20.00
Common (156-185):		.50
Comp. Intl. Road Trip (30):		20.00
Common (186-215):		.50
Comp. Bronx Bombers (30):		30.00
Common (216-245):		.50
Pack (7):		3.00
Box (18 + 1 supplemental box):		40.00
1	Troy Glaus	.75
2	Derek Jeter	3.00
3	Alex Rodriguez	2.50
4	Barry Zito	.40
5	Darin Erstad	.60
6	Tim Hudson	.40
7	Josh Beckett	.15
8	Adam Dunn	.60
9	Tim Salmon	.25
10	Ivan Rodriguez	.50
11	Mark Buehrle	.15
12	Sammy Sosa	2.00
13	Vicente Padilla	.15
14	Randy Johnson	1.00
15	Lance Berkman	.15
16	Jim Thome	.15
17	Luis Gonzalez	.25
18	Craig Biggio	.15
19	Cliff Floyd	.15
20	Pat Burrell	.50
21	Matt Morris	.15
22	Torii Hunter	.15
23	Curt Schilling	.40
24	Paul Konerko	.15
25	Jeff Bagwell	.75
26	Mike Piazza	2.00
27	A.J. Burnett	.15
28	Jimmy Rollins	.15
29	Greg Maddux	1.50
30	Jeff Kent	.15
31	Bobby Abreu	.15
32	Chipper Jones	1.50
33	Mike Sweeney	.15
34	Jason Kendall	.15
35	Gary Sheffield	.30
36	Carlos Beltran	.50
37	Brian Giles	.15
38	Jim Edmonds	.15
39	Roger Clemens	1.75
40	Andruw Jones	.75
41	Paul LoDuca	.15
42	Ryan Klesko	.15
43	Jay Gibbons	.15
44	Shawn Green	.40
45	Sean Burroughs	.15
46	Magglio Ordonez	.15
47	Tony Batista	.15
48	J.D. Drew	.45
49	Hideo Nomo	.50
50	Edgardo Alfonzo	.15
51	Nomar Garciaparra	2.00
52	Frank Thomas	.75
53	Kazuhisa Ishii	.15
54	Rich Aurilia	.15
55	Shea Hillenbrand	.15
56	Tom Glavine	.40
57	Richie Sexson	.15
58	Mo Vaughn	.15
59	Barry Bonds	3.00
60	Carlos Delgado	.50
61	Pedro J. Martinez	1.00
62	Jacque Jones	.15
63	Edgar Martinez	.15
64	Manny Ramirez	.75
65	Bret Boone	.15
66	Kerry Wood	.50
67	Roy Oswalt	.40
68	Cristian Guzman	.15
69	Moises Alou	.15
70	Bartolo Colon	.15
71	Ichiro Suzuki	1.50
72	Jose Vidro	.15
73	Scott Rolen	.75
74	Mark Prior	1.00
75	Vladimir Guerrero	.75
76	Albert Pujols	1.50
77	Aubrey Huff	.15
78	Ken Griffey Jr.	2.00
79	Roberto Alomar	.30
80	Ben Grieve	.15
81	Miguel Tejada	.40
82	Austin Kearns	.50
83	Jason Giambi	.75
84	John Olerud	.15
85	Omar Vizquel	.15
86	Juan Gonzalez	.75
87	Larry Walker	.15
88	Jorge Posada	.25
89	Rafael Palmeiro	.65
90	Todd Helton	.75
91	Bernie Williams	.30
92	Garret Anderson	.15
93	Eric Hinske	.15
94	Mike Lowell	.15
95	Jason Jennings	.15
96	Eric Chavez	.30
97	Alfonso Soriano	1.00
98	David Eckstein	.15
99	Bobby Higginson	.15
100	Roy Halladay	.15
101	*Robby Hammock*	4.00
102	*Hideki Matsui*	12.00
103	Chase Utley	4.00
104	*Oscar Villarreal*	4.00
105	*Jose Contreras*	8.00
106	Rocco Baldelli	4.00
107	*Rontrez Johnson*	4.00
108	Jeremy Bonderman	5.00
109	*Shane Victorino*	4.00
110	Ron Calloway	4.00
111	*Brandon Webb*	4.00
112	*Guillermo Quiroz*	2.00
113	*Clint Barmes*	2.00
114	*Pete LaForest*	1.00
115	*Craig Brazell*	2.00
116	*Todd Wellemeyer*	1.00
117	*Bernie Castro*	1.00
118	*Alejandro Machado*	1.50
119	*Terrmel Sledge*	1.00
120	*Ian Ferguson*	1.00
121	*Lew Ford*	3.00
122	*Nook Logan*	1.50
123	*Mike Nicolas*	1.00
124	*Jeff Duncan*	1.50
125	*Tim Olson*	1.00
126	*Michael Hessman*	1.00

127 *Francisco Rosario* 1.00
128 *Felix Sanchez* 1.00
129 *Andrew Brown* 1.50
130 *Matt Bruback* 2.00
131 *Diegomar Markwell* 2.00
132 *Josh Willingham* 1.00
133 Wes Obermueller 1.50
134 *Phil Seibel* 2.00
135 *Arnie Munoz* 1.00
136 *Matt Kata* 3.00
137 *Joe Valentine* 1.00
138 Ricardo Rodriguez 1.00
139 Lyle Overbay 2.00
140 *Brian Stokes* 1.00
141 *Josh Hall* 1.50
142 Kevin Hooper 1.00
143 *Chien-Ming Wang* 4.00
144 *Prentice Redman* 1.50
145 *Chris Waters* 1.50
146 *Jon Leicester* 1.00
147 *Daniel Cabrera* 3.00
148 *Alfredo Gonzalez* 1.50
149 *Doug Waechter* 1.50
150 Brandon Larson 1.00
151 *Beau Kemp* 1.50
152 *Cory Stewart* 1.00
153 Francisco Rodriguez 1.00
154 Hee Seop Choi 1.50
155 *Mike Neu* 1.00
156 Derek Jeter 3.00
157 Alex Rodriguez 2.50
158 Nomar Garciaparra 2.00
159 Barry Bonds 2.50
160 Sammy Sosa 1.50
161 Vladimir Guerrero .75
162 Roger Clemens 2.00
163 Randy Johnson 1.00
164 Greg Maddux 1.50
165 Ken Griffey Jr. 1.50
166 Mike Piazza 2.00
167 Ichiro Suzuki 1.50
168 Barry Larkin .50
169 Lance Berkman .50
170 Jim Thome .75
171 Jason Giambi 1.00
172 Gary Sheffield .50
173 Ivan Rodriguez .50
174 Miguel Tejada .50
175 Manny Ramirez .75
176 Mike Sweeney .50
177 Larry Walker .50
178 Jeff Bagwell .75
179 Chipper Jones 1.50
180 Craig Biggio .50
181 Curt Schilling .50
182 Pedro J. Martinez 1.00
183 Roberto Alomar .50
184 Bernie Williams .50
185 Magglio Ordonez .50
186 Jose Contreras 1.00
187 Rafael Palmeiro 1.00
188 Andruw Jones .75
189 Bartolo Colon .50
190 Vladimir Guerrero .75
191 Pedro Martinez 1.00
192 Albert Pujols 1.50
193 Manny Ramirez .75
194 Felix Rodriguez .50
195 Alfonso Soriano 1.00
196 Sammy Sosa 1.50
197 Miguel Tejada .50
198 Kazuhisa Ishii .50
199 Hideki Matsui 5.00
200 Hideo Nomo 1.00
201 Tomokazu Ohka .50
202 Kazuhiro Sasaki .50
203 Tsuyoshi Shinjo .50
204 Ichiro Suzuki 1.50
205 Vicente Padilla .50
206 Carlos Beltran .50
207 Jose Cruz Jr. .50
208 Carlos Delgado .50
209 Juan Gonzalez .75
210 Jorge Posada .50
211 Ivan Rodriguez .50
212 Hee Seop Choi .50
213 Bobby Abreu .50
214 Magglio Ordonez .50
215 Francisco Rodriguez .50
216 Juan Acevedo .50
217 Erick Almonte .50
218 Yogi Berra 1.50
219 Brandon Claussen 1.00
220 Roger Clemens 2.00
221 Jose Contreras 1.00
222 Whitey Ford 1.00
223 Jason Giambi 1.00
225 *Michel Hernandez* .50
226 Sterling Hitchcock .50
227 Jim "Catfish" Hunter .75
228 Reggie Jackson 1.00
229 Derek Jeter 3.00
230 Nick Johnson .50
231 Hideki Matsui 5.00
232 Raul Mondesi .50
233 Mike Mussina .75
234 Andy Pettitte .50
235 Jorge Posada .50
236 Mariano Rivera .50
237 Phil Rizzuto 1.00
238 Enos Slaughter .50
239 Alfonso Soriano 1.00
240 Robin Ventura .50
241 Chien-Ming Wang 1.00
242 Jeff Weaver .50
243 David Wells .50
244 Bernie Williams .75
245 Todd Zeile .50

First Edition

Stars (1-100): 4-8X
Rookies (101-125): 1.5-3X
Production 150 sets

All-Star Lineup

NM/M
Common Card: 15.00
Inserted 1:All-Stars set
Derek Jeter, Alex Rodriguez, Nomar Garciaparra 35.00
Barry Bonds, Sammy Sosa, Vladimir Guerrero 15.00
Roger Clemens, Randy Johnson, Greg Maddux 30.00
Jason Giambi, Alfonso Soriano, Derek Jeter 30.00
Craig Biggio, Jeff Bagwell, Lance Berkman 20.00
Chipper Jones, Gary Sheffield, Greg Maddux 30.00
Ivan Rodriguez, Mike Piazza, Randy Johnson, Roger Clemens 40.00
Barry Bonds, Ken Griffey Jr., Manny Ramirez, Ichiro Suzuki
Roberto Alomar, Mike Piazza, Alfonso Soriano, Jason Giambi 45.00
Jim Thome, Roberto Alomar, Alex Rodriguez, Nomar Garciaparra 40.00

Bat Rack

NM/M
Common Card: 20.00
Production 250 sets
Derek Jeter, Alfonso Soriano, Jason Giambi 35.00
Scott Rolen, Miguel Tejada, Troy Glaus 20.00
Jim Thome, Torii Hunter, Mike Piazza 25.00
Troy Glaus, Nomar Garciaparra, Alfonso Soriano 30.00
Lance Berkman, Vladimir Guerrero, Sammy Sosa 20.00
Chipper Jones, Lance Berkman, Vladimir Guerrero 20.00
Torii Hunter, Jason Giambi, Nomar Garciaparra 25.00
Derek Jeter, Miguel Tejada, Alex Rodriguez 25.00
Scott Rolen, Sammy Sosa, Alex Rodriguez 25.00
Torii Hunter, Bernie Williams, Andruw Jones

Bat Rack Quad

NM/M
Production 50 sets
Derek Jeter, Torii Hunter, Troy Glaus, Miguel Tejada 40.00
Derek Jeter, Mike Piazza, Nomar Garciaparra, Chipper Jones 60.00
Vladimir Guerrero, Lance Berkman, Sammy Sosa, Barry Bonds
Jason Giambi, Alfonso Soriano, Alex Rodriguez, Troy Glaus
Alex Rodriguez, Jim Thome, Sammy Sosa, Barry Bonds 50.00

Bronx Bombers Jersey

NM/M
Common Player: 4.00
Inserted 1:Bronx Bombers set
Roger Clemens 15.00
Jason Giambi 12.00
Derek Jeter 20.00
Nick Johnson 4.00
Mike Mussina 10.00
Jorge Posada 8.00
Alfonso Soriano 10.00
Robin Ventura 5.00
Bernie Williams 8.00

Classic Minatures

NM/M
Complete Set (30): 10.00
Common Player: .25
1CM Jim Thome .40
2CM Jason Giambi .50
3CM Miguel Tejada .25
4CM Alfonso Soriano 1.00
5CM Ivan Rodriguez .40
6CM Troy Glaus .40
7CM Mike Piazza 1.00
8CM Barry Bonds 1.50
9CM Sammy Sosa 1.00
10CM Lance Berkman .25
11CM Pat Burrell .25
12CM Chipper Jones .75
13CM Shawn Green .25
14CM Manny Ramirez .50
15CM Ichiro Suzuki .75
16CM Vladimir Guerrero .50
17CM Albert Pujols .75
18CM Ken Griffey Jr. 1.00
19CM Bernie Williams .40
20CM Austin Kearns .40
21CM Randy Johnson .50
22CM Greg Maddux .75
23CM Roger Clemens 1.00
24CM Hideo Nomo .25
25CM Pedro J. Martinez .50
26CM Kerry Wood .40
27CM Mark Prior .50
28CM Derek Jeter 1.50
29CM Alex Rodriguez 1.00
30CM Nomar Garciaparra 1.00

Classic Miniatures Mini Jersey

NM/M
Common Jersey: 4.00
1:Classic Miniatures box
NG Nomar Garciaparra 10.00
JG Jason Giambi 8.00
VG Vladimir Guerrero 5.00
DJ Derek Jeter 15.00
AK Austin Kearns 8.00
GM Greg Maddux 10.00
HN Hideo Nomo 10.00
MP Mark Prior 15.00
MT Miguel Tejada 4.00
JT Jim Thome 8.00

Jersey Rack

NM/M
Common Card: 15.00
Production 350 sets
Derek Jeter, Alfonso Soriano, Jason Giambi 40.00
Curt Schilling, Randy Johnson, Greg Maddux 25.00
Roger Clemens, Pedro J. Martinez, Barry Zito 30.00
Alex Rodriguez, Vladimir Guerrero, Sammy Sosa 25.00
Derek Jeter, Nomar Garciaparra, Alex Rodriguez 30.00
Lance Berkman, Sammy Sosa, Torii Hunter 20.00
Vladimir Guerrero, Jim Thome, Alex Rodriguez 20.00
Derek Jeter, Miguel Tejada, Nomar Garciaparra 30.00
Alfonso Soriano, Eric Chavez, Jim Thome 20.00
Miguel Tejada, Eric Chavez, Barry Zito 15.00

Jersey Rack Quad

NM/M
Common Card:
Production 150 sets
Derek Jeter, Alex Rodriguez, Nomar Garciaparra, Miguel Tejada 60.00
Jim Thome, Jason Giambi, Sammy Sosa, Vladimir Guerrero 50.00
Randy Johnson, Greg Maddux, Roger Clemens, Pedro J. Martinez 60.00
Curt Schilling, Vladimir Guerrero, Randy Johnson, Alex Rodriguez 40.00
Alfonso Soriano, Jim Thome, Sammy Sosa, Eric Chavez 40.00
Eric Chavez, Miguel Tejada, Barry Zito, Nomar Garciaparra 20.00

Press Clippings

NM/M
Complete Set (20): 40.00
Common Player: 1.00
Inserted 1:18
1PC Derek Jeter 6.00
2PC Nomar Garciaparra 5.00
3PC Miguel Tejada 1.00
4PC Barry Bonds 5.00
5PC Alex Rodriguez 5.00
6PC Sammy Sosa 3.00
7PC Lance Berkman 1.00
8PC Torii Hunter 1.00
9PC Troy Glaus 1.50
10PC Eric Chavez 1.00
11PC Tim Hudson 1.00
12PC Randy Johnson 2.00
13PC Mike Piazza 4.00
14PC Roberto Alomar 1.50
15PC Jim Thome 1.50
16PC Alfonso Soriano 3.00
17PC Roger Clemens 4.00
18PC Pedro J. Martinez 2.00
19PC Mark Prior 2.00
20PC Curt Schilling 1.00

Press Clippings Dual

NM/M
Complete Set (10): 35.00
Common Player: 2.00
Production 250 sets
1 Derek Jeter, Nomar Garciaparra 8.00
2 Miguel Tejada, Barry Bonds 6.00

3 Alex Rodriguez, Sammy Sosa 6.00
4 Lance Berkman, Torii Hunter 2.00
5 Troy Glaus, Eric Chavez 2.00
6 Tim Hudson, Randy Johnson 3.00
7 Mike Piazza, Roberto Alomar 5.00
8 Jim Thome, Alfonso Soriano 4.00
9 Roger Clemens, Pedro J. Martinez 5.00
10 Mark Prior, Curt Schilling 3.00

Press Clippings Dual Patch

	NM/M
Common Card:	25.00
Derek Jeter, Nomar Garciaparra/100	60.00
Miguel Tejada, Troy Glaus/150	25.00
Alex Rodriguez, Sammy Sosa/150	80.00
Lance Berkman, Torii Hunter/150	30.00
Troy Glaus, Eric Chavez/150	30.00
Tim Hudson, Randy Johnson/150	30.00
Mike Piazza, Roberto Alomar/150	40.00
Jim Thome, Alfonso Soriano/100	40.00
Roger Clemens, Pedro Martinez/100	50.00
Mark Prior, Curt Schilling/150	40.00

PRESS CLIPPINGS GAME-USED

	NM/M
Common Player:	4.00
Inserted 1:12	
Derek Jeter	15.00
Nomar Garciaparra	15.00
Miguel Tejada	4.00
Alex Rodriguez	10.00
Sammy Sosa	12.00
Lance Berkman	4.00
Torii Hunter	6.00
Troy Glaus	5.00
Eric Chavez	4.00
Tim Hudson	4.00
Randy Johnson	8.00
Mike Piazza	12.00
Roberto Alomar	8.00
Jim Thome	10.00
Alfonso Soriano	10.00
Roger Clemens	12.00
Pedro J. Martinez	8.00
Mark Prior	10.00
Curt Schilling	4.00

Wave of the Future

	NM/M
Common Player:	4.00
Inserted 1:Rising Stars set	
Jeremy Bonderman/bat	12.00
Ron Calloway/jsy	4.00
Hee Seop Choi/jsy	10.00
Brandon Larson/bat	8.00
Lyle Overbay/bat	6.00
Francisco Rodriguez/jsy	6.00
Chase Utley/jsy	6.00

World Piece

	NM/M
Common Player:	4.00
Inserted 1:Intl. Road Trip set	
Vladimir Guerrero	6.00
Pedro Martinez	10.00
Sammy Sosa	12.00
Miguel Tejada	4.00
Hideo Nomo	10.00
Jose Cruz Jr.	4.00
Ivan Rodriguez	6.00
Hee Seop Choi	10.00
Francisco Rodriguez	4.00
Kazuhiro Sasaki	4.00

2003 FLEER DOUBLE HEADER

		NM/M
Complete Set (300):		60.00
Common Player:		.20
Common (181-300):		.40
Pack (8):		2.00
Box (20):		35.00
1	Ramon Vazquez	.20
2	Derek Jeter	2.00
3	Orlando Hudson	.20
4	Miguel Tejada	.30
5	Steve Finley	.20
6	Brad Wilkerson	.20
7	Craig Biggio	.20
8	Marlon Anderson	.20
9	Phil Nevin	.20
10	Hideo Nomo	.50
11	Barry Larkin	.20
12	Alfonso Soriano	.75
13	Rodrigo Lopez	.20
14	Paul Konerko	.25
15	Carlos Beltran	.50
16	Garret Anderson	.20
17	Kazuhisa Ishii	.20
18	Eddie Guardado	.20
19	Juan Gonzalez	.50
20	Mark Mulder	.20
21	Sammy Sosa	1.25
22	Kazuhiro Sasaki	.20
23	Jose Cruz Jr.	.20
24	Tomokazu Ohka	.20
25	Barry Bonds	2.00
26	Carlos Delgado	.50
27	Scott Rolen	.50
28	Steve Cox	.20
29	Mike Sweeney	.20
30	Ryan Klesko	.20
31	Greg Maddux	1.00
32	Derek Lowe	.20
33	David Wells	.20
34	Kerry Wood	.40
35	Randall Simon	.20
36	Ben Howard	.20
37	Jeff Suppan	.20
38	Curt Schilling	.40
39	Eric Gagne	.20
40	Raul Mondesi	.20
41	Jeffrey Hammonds	.20
42	Mo Vaughn	.20
43	Sidney Ponson	.20
44	Adam Dunn	.50
45	Pedro J. Martinez	.75
46	Jason Simontacchi	.20
47	Tom Glavine	.40
48	Torii Hunter	.20
49	Gabe Kapler	.20
50	Andy Van Hekken	.20
51	Ichiro Suzuki	1.25
52	Andruw Jones	.50
53	Bobby Abreu	.20
54	Junior Spivey	.20
55	Ray Durham	.20
56	Mark Buehrle	.20
57	Drew Henson	.20
58	Brandon Duckworth	.20
59	Robert Mackowiak	.20
60	Josh Beckett	.20
61	Chan Ho Park	.20
62	John Smoltz	.20
63	Jimmy Rollins	.20
64	Orlando Cabrera	.20
65	Johnny Damon	.20
66	Austin Kearns	.40
67	Tsuyoshi Shinjo	.20
68	Tim Hudson	.30
69	Coco Crisp	.20
70	Darin Erstad	.60
71	Jacque Jones	.20
72	Vicente Padilla	.20
73	Hee Seop Choi	.20
74	Shea Hillenbrand	.20
75	Edgardo Alfonzo	.20
76	Pat Burrell	.50
77	Ben Sheets	.20
78	Ivan Rodriguez	.40
79	Josh Phelps	.20
80	Adam Kennedy	.20
81	Eric Chavez	.30
82	Bobby Higginson	.20
83	Nomar Garciaparra	1.50
84	J.D. Drew	.30
85	Carl Crawford	.20
86	Matt Morris	.20
87	Chipper Jones	1.00
88	Luis Gonzalez	.30
89	Richie Sexson	.20
90	Eric Milton	.20
91	Andres Galarraga	.20
92	Paul LoDuca	.20
93	Mark Grace	.30
94	Ben Grieve	.20
95	Mike Lowell	.20
96	Roberto Alomar	.35
97	Wade Miller	.20
98	Sean Casey	.20
99	Roger Clemens	1.25
100	Matt Williams	.20
101	Brian Giles	.20
102	Jim Thome	.20
103	Troy Glaus	.75
104	Joe Borchard	.20
105	Vladimir Guerrero	.75
106	Kevin Mench	.20
107	Omar Vizquel	.20
108	Magglio Ordonez	.20
109	Ken Griffey Jr.	1.50
110	Mike Piazza	1.50
111	Mark Teixeira	.40
112	Jason Jennings	.20
113	Ellis Burks	.20
114	Jason Varitek	.20
115	Larry Walker	.20
116	Frank Thomas	.75
117	Ramon Ortiz	.20
118	Mark Quinn	.20
119	Preston Wilson	.20
120	Carlos Lee	.20
121	Brian Lawrence	.20
122	Tim Salmon	.20
123	Shawn Green	.30
124	Randy Johnson	.75
125	Jeff Bagwell	.75
126	C.C. Sabathia	.20
127	Bernie Williams	.35
128	Roy Oswalt	.30
129	Albert Pujols	.75
130	Reggie Sanders	.20
131	Jeff Conine	.20
132	John Olerud	.20
133	Lance Berkman	.20
134	Geoff Jenkins	.20
135	Jim Edmonds	.20
136	Todd Helton	.65
137	Jason Kendall	.20
138	Robin Ventura	.20
139	Randy Winn	.20
140	Carl Everett	.20
141	Jose Vidro	.20
142	Pokey Reese	.20
143	Edgar Renteria	.20
144	Alex Rodriguez	1.75
145	Doug Mientkiewicz	.20
146	Aramis Ramirez	.20
147	Bobby Hill	.20
148	Jorge Posada	.35
149	Sean Burroughs	.20
150	Jeff Kent	.20
151	Tino Martinez	.20
152	Mark Prior	.60
153	Brad Radke	.20
154	Al Leiter	.20
155	Eric Karros	.20
156	Manny Ramirez	.50
157	Jason Lane	.20
158	Mike Lieberthal	.20
159	Shannon Stewart	.20
160	Robert Fick	.20
161	Derrek Lee	.20
162	Jason Giambi	.50
163	Rafael Palmeiro	.65
164	Jay Payton	.20
165	Adrian Beltre	.20
166	Marlon Byrd	.20
167	Bret Boone	.20
168	Roy Halladay	.20
169	Freddy Garcia	.20
170	Rich Aurilia	.20
171	Jared Sandberg	.20
172	Paul Byrd	.20
173	Gary Sheffield	.30
174	Edgar Martinez	.20
175	Eric Hinske	.20
176	Milton Bradley	.20
177	David Eckstein	.20
178	Jay Gibbons	.20
179	Corey Patterson	.20
180	Barry Zito	.20
181-182	Darin Erstad, Troy Glaus	.50
183-184	Curt Schilling, Randy Johnson	.75
185-186	Andruw Jones, Chipper Jones	1.00
187-188	Tony Batista, Jay Gibbons	.40
189-190	Pedro Martinez, Nomar Garciaparra	1.25
191-192	Sammy Sosa, Kerry Wood	1.00
193-194	Paul Konerko, Joe Borchard	.40
195-196	Austin Kearns, Adam Dunn	.50
197-198	Omar Vizquel, Jim Thome	.50
199-200	Larry Walker, Todd Helton	.40
201-202	Josh Beckett, Luis Castillo	.40
203-204	Craig Biggio, Jeff Bagwell	.50
205-206	Paul Byrd, Mike Sweeney	.40
207-208	Adrian Beltre, Shawn Green	.40
209-210	Jose Hernandez, Richie Sexson	.40
211-212	Jacque Jones, Torii Hunter	.40
213-214	Vladimir Guerrero, Jose Vidro	.75
215-216	Edgardo Alfonzo, Mike Piazza	1.50
217-218	Roger Clemens, Derek Jeter	2.00
219-220	Eric Chavez, Miguel Tejada	.40
221-222	Marlon Byrd, Pat Burrell	.50
223-224	Jason Kendall, Brian Giles	.40
225-226	Phil Nevin, Sean Burroughs	.40
227-228	Jeff Kent, Barry Bonds	2.00
229-230	Kazuhiro Sasaki, Ichiro Suzuki	1.25
231-232	Albert Pujols, J.D. Drew	.75
233-234	Juan Gonzalez, Ivan Rodriguez	.50
235-236	Eric Hinske, Orlando Hudson	.40
237-238	Lance Berkman, Chipper Jones	1.00
239-240	Alex Rodriguez, Derek Jeter	2.00
241-242	Ichiro Suzuki, Hideo Nomo	1.25

243-244 Manny Ramirez, Bernie Williams .50
245-246 Tom Glavine, Roger Clemens 1.00
247-248 Ken Griffey Jr., Barry Larkin 1.25
249-250 Mark Teixeira, Mark Prior .40
251-252 Albert Pujols, Drew Henson .75
253-254 Jason Giambi, Todd Helton 1.00
255-256 Jose Vidro, Alfonso Soriano .75
257-258 Shea Hillenbrand, Scott Rolen .50
259-260 Jimmy Rollins, Alex Rodriguez 1.75
261-262 Torii Hunter, Vladimir Guerrero .75
263-264 Ichiro Suzuki, Sammy Sosa 1.25
265-266 Barry Bonds, Manny Ramirez 2.00
267-268 Mike Piazza, Jorge Posada 1.25
269-270 Robin Yount, Ozzie Smith 1.00
271-272 Josh Hancock, Freddy Sanchez .40
273-274 Ryan Bukvich, Shawn Sedlacek .40
275-276 Doug Devore, Rene Reyes .40
277-278 Hank Blalock, Travis Hafner .50
279-280 Eric Junge, Brett Myers .40
281-282 Brad Lidge, Jeriome Robertson .40
283-284 Miguel Asencio, Runelvys Hernandez .40
285-286 Fernando Rodney, Barry Wesson .40
287-288 Victor Alvarez, David Ross .40
289-290 Tony Torcato, Chris Snelling .50
291-292 Kirk Saarloos, Morgan Ensberg .40
293-294 Josh Bard, Wilbert Nieves .40
295-296 Jung Bong, Trey Hodges .40
297-298 Kevin Cash, Reed Johnson .40
299-300 Chone Figgins, John Lackey .40

Flip Card Memorabilia

NM/M

Common Player: 4.00
Inserted 1:20
Golds: .75-2X
Production 100 sets
1 Roberto Alomar/bat/200 10.00
2 Jeff Bagwell/jsy 8.00
3 Adrian Beltre/jsy 4.00
4 Barry Bonds/bat/200 15.00
5 Roger Clemens/jsy/200 12.00
6 J.D. Drew/jsy 6.00
7 Adam Dunn/jsy/200 10.00
8 Nomar Garciaparra/jsy/200 15.00
9 Mark Grace/jsy 8.00
10 Todd Helton/jsy/200 8.00
11 Derek Jeter/jsy/200 20.00
12 Randy Johnson/jsy/200 10.00
13 Chipper Jones/jsy 8.00
14 Eric Karros/jsy 4.00
15 Barry Larkin/jsy/200 8.00
16 Greg Maddux/jsy/200 10.00
17 Hideo Nomo/jsy/200 10.00
18 Kazuhisa Ishii/jsy 6.00
19 Mike Piazza/jsy/200 10.00
20 Jorge Posada/jsy/200 8.00
21 Mark Prior/jsy/200 10.00
22 Alex Rodriguez/jsy 10.00
23 Kazuhiro Sasaki/jsy/200 6.00
24 Curt Schilling/jsy/200 8.00
25 Alfonso Soriano/jsy 8.00
26 Miguel Tejada/jsy 8.00
27 Jim Thome/jsy/200 10.00
28 Robin Ventura/jsy 4.00
29 Bernie Williams/jsy/200 8.00
30 Kerry Wood/jsy/200 10.00

Keystone Combination

NM/M

Complete Set (10): 25.00
Common Card: 1.00
Inserted 1:10
1KC Derek Jeter, Bret Boone 6.00
2KC Miguel Tejada, Jeff Kent 1.00
3KC Nomar Garciaparra, Ray Durham 4.00
4KC Omar Vizquel, Roberto Alomar 1.00
5KC Pee Wee Reese, Joe Morgan 1.00
6KC Alex Rodriguez, Craig Biggio 5.00
7KC Orlando Hudson, Jose Vidro 1.00
8KC Phil Rizzuto, Alfonso Soriano 3.00
9KC Alex Rodriguez, Miguel Tejada 5.00
10KC Nomar Garciaparra, Derek Jeter 6.00

Keystone Combination Memorab.

NM/M

Common Card: 4.00
Inserted 1:40
Derek Jeter, Bret Boone/jsy 8.00
Miguel Tejada, Jeff Kent/jsy 4.00
N.Garciaparra/jsy/175, Ray Durham 12.00
Omar Vizquel, Roberto Alomar/jsy 6.00
Alex Rodriguez, Craig Biggio/jsy 6.00
Orlando Hudson, Jose Vidro/jsy 4.00
Phil Rizzuto, Alfonso Soriano/jsy/75 15.00
Alex Rodriguez/bat, Miguel Tejada 10.00
N.Garciaparra/jsy/175, Derek Jeter 12.00
Derek Jeter/jsy/175, Bret Boone 20.00
Derek Jeter/jsy/175, Nomar Garciaparra 20.00
Alex Rodriguez/jsy/200, Craig Biggio 10.00
Miguel Tejada/jsy, Jeff Kent 8.00
Miguel Tejada/jsy, Alex Rodriguez 8.00

Matinee Idols

NM/M

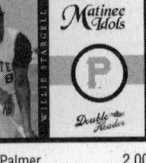

Complete Set (15): 50.00
Common Player: 2.00
Inserted 1:20
1MI Yogi Berra 3.00
2MI Richie Ashburn 3.00
3MI Whitey Ford 3.00
4MI Eddie Mathews 3.00
5MI Jim Palmer 2.00
6MI Al Kaline 6.00
7MI Brooks Robinson 3.00
8MI Willie McCovey 3.00
9MI Billy Williams 2.00
10MI Willie Stargell 3.00
11MI Nolan Ryan 15.00
12MI Rod Carew 3.00
13MI Reggie Jackson 3.00
14MI Tom Seaver 4.00
15MI Mike Schmidt 6.00

Twin Bill

NM/M

Complete Set (20): 45.00
Common Player: 1.00
Inserted 1:10
1a Barry Bonds 5.00
1b Lance Berkman 1.00
2a Derek Jeter 6.00
2b Alex Rodriguez 5.00
3a Roger Clemens 3.00
3b Pedro Martinez 2.00
4a Roberto Alomar 1.25
4b Chipper Jones 3.00
5a Barry Zito 1.00
5b Ichiro Suzuki 4.00
6a Sammy Sosa 3.00
6b Ken Griffey Jr. 4.00
7a Bernie Williams 1.00
7b Manny Ramirez 1.50
8a Nomar Garciaparra 4.00
8b Derek Jeter 6.00
9a Randy Johnson 2.00
9b Greg Maddux 3.00
10a Albert Pujols 2.00
10b Adam Dunn 1.50

Twin Bill Single Swatch

NM/M

Common Player: 1.00
Barry Bonds/cap/100 25.00
Alex Rodriguez/cap/100 15.00
Roger Clemens/cap/100 15.00
Pedro Martinez/cap/100 12.00
Roberto Alomar/cap 10.00
Barry Zito/cap/100 15.00
Bernie Williams/cap/100 10.00
Manny Ramirez/cap/75 12.00
Nomar Garciaparra/cap/100 25.00
Derek Jeter/cap/100 30.00
Randy Johnson/cap/100 15.00
Adam Dunn/cap/100 12.00

Twin Bill Dual Swatch

NM/M

Common Card:
Production 50 sets
Adam Dunn 40.00
Randy Johnson, Barry Zito 35.00

2003 FLEER E-X

NM/M

Complete Set (102): 125.00
Common Player: .50
Common SP (83-102): 3.00
Pack (3): 4.00
Box (20): 60.00
1 Troy Glaus .75
2 Darin Erstad .75
3 Garret Anderson .50
4 Curt Schilling .75
5 Randy Johnson 1.00
6 Luis Gonzalez .50
7 Greg Maddux 1.50
8 Chipper Jones 1.50
9 Andruw Jones 1.00
10 Melvin Mora .50
11 Jay Gibbons .50
12 Nomar Garciaparra 2.00
13 Pedro J. Martinez 1.00
14 Manny Ramirez 1.00
15 Sammy Sosa 2.00
16 Kerry Wood .75
17 Magglio Ordonez .50
18 Frank Thomas 1.00
19 Roberto Alomar .60
20 Barry Larkin .50
21 Adam Dunn 1.00
22 Austin Kearns .75
23 Omar Vizquel .50
24 Larry Walker .50
25 Todd Helton 1.00
26 Preston Wilson .50
27 Dmitri Young .50
28 Ivan Rodriguez .75
29 Mike Lowell .50
30 Jeff Kent .50
31 Jeff Bagwell 1.00
32 Roy Oswalt .75
33 Craig Biggio .50
34 Mike Sweeney .50
35 Carlos Beltran .75
36 Shawn Green .60
37 Kazuhisa Ishii .50
38 Richie Sexson .50
39 Torii Hunter .50
40 Jacque Jones .50
41 Jose Vidro .50
42 Vladimir Guerrero 1.00
43 Mike Piazza 2.00
44 Tom Glavine .60
45 Roger Clemens 1.75
46 Jason Giambi .75
47 Bernie Williams .60
48 Alfonso Soriano 1.00
49 Mike Mussina .60
50 Barry Zito .60
51 Miguel Tejada .60
52 Eric Chavez .60
53 Eric Byrnes .50
54 Jim Thome .50
55 Kevin Millwood .50
56 Brian Giles .50
57 Xavier Nady .50
58 Barry Bonds 3.00
59 Bret Boone .50
60 Edgar Martinez .50
61 Kazuhiro Sasaki .50
62 Edgar Renteria .50
63 J.D. Drew .50
64 Scott Rolen 1.00
65 Jim Edmonds .50
66 Aubrey Huff .50
67 Alex Rodriguez 2.50
68 Juan Gonzalez 1.00
69 Hank Blalock .75
70 Mark Teixeira .75
71 Carlos Delgado .75

72 Vernon Wells .50
73 Shea Hillenbrand .50
74 Gary Sheffield .60
75 Mark Prior .75
76 Ken Griffey Jr. 2.00
77 Lance Berkman .50
78 Hideo Nomo .75
79 Derek Jeter 3.00
80 Ichiro Suzuki 2.00
81 Albert Pujols 2.50
82 Rafael Palmeiro .75
83 Jose Reyes 4.00
84 Rocco Baldelli 4.00
85 Hee Seop Choi 3.00
86 Dontrelle Willis 4.00
87 *Robby Hammock* 3.00
88 *Brandon Webb* 5.00
89 *Matt Kata* 5.00
90 *Todd Wellemeyer* 3.00
91 *Francisco Cruceta* 3.00
92 *Clint Barmes* 6.00
93 Jeremy Bonderman 4.00
94 *Dave Matranga* 4.00
95 *Ryan Wagner* 5.00
96 Jeremy Griffiths 3.00
97 *Hideki Matsui* 15.00
98 *Jose Contreras* 6.00
99 *Chien-Ming Wang* 8.00
100 *Bo Hart* 4.00
101 Dan Haren 5.00
102 *Rickie Weeks* 10.00

X-tra Innings

NM/M
Complete Set (10): 25.00
Common Player: 1.00
Inserted 1:32
1XI Ichiro Suzuki 3.00
2XI Albert Pujols 4.00
3XI Barry Bonds 5.00
4XI Jason Giambi 1.50
5XI Pedro J. Martinez 2.00
6XI Mark Prior 5.00
7XI Derek Jeter 5.00
8XI Curt Schilling 1.00
9XI Jeff Bagwell 1.50
10XI Alex Rodriguez 5.00

Behind the Numbers

NM/M
Complete Set (15): 50.00
Common Player: 1.50
Inserted 1:80
1 Derek Jeter 8.00
2 Alex Rodriguez 8.00
3 Randy Johnson 3.00
4 Chipper Jones 5.00
5 Jim Thome 3.00
6 Alfonso Soriano 4.00
7 Adam Dunn 2.00
8 Nomar Garciaparra 6.00
9 Roger Clemens 6.00
10 Gary Sheffield 1.50
11 Vladimir Guerrero 3.00
12 Greg Maddux 5.00
13 Sammy Sosa 6.00
14 Mike Piazza 5.00
15 Troy Glaus 2.00

Behind the Numbers Game-Used

NM/M
Common Player: 5.00
Inserted 1:10
Patch version: 1.5-2.5X
DJ Derek Jeter 15.00
AR Alex Rodriguez 10.00
RJ Randy Johnson 8.00
CJ Chipper Jones 8.00
JT Jim Thome 8.00
AS Alfonso Soriano 8.00
AD Adam Dunn 6.00
NG Nomar Garciaparra 10.00
RC Roger Clemens 10.00
GS Gary Sheffield 5.00
VG Vladimir Guerrero 8.00
GM Greg Maddux 8.00
SS Sammy Sosa 10.00
MP Mike Piazza 8.00
TG Troy Glaus 5.00
HB Hank Blalock 6.00
TG Tom Glavine 5.00
BM Brett Myers 5.00
LB Lance Berkman 5.00
RB Rocco Baldelli 10.00
BZ Barry Zito 6.00
DW Dontrelle Willis 10.00
RP Rafael Palmeiro 6.00
RA Roberto Alomar 6.00
MB Marlon Byrd 5.00

Behind the Numbers Autograph

No pricing due to scarcity
Numbered to jersey number
Dontrelle Willis
Rocco Baldelli
Marlon Byrd
Hank Blalock
Randy Johnson
Austin Kearns

Diamond Essentials

NM/M
Common Player: 5.00
Inserted 1:480
1DE Randy Johnson 15.00
2DE Ichiro Suzuki 25.00
3DE Albert Pujols 30.00
4DE Barry Bonds 40.00
5DE Hideki Matsui 30.00
6DE Derek Jeter 40.00
7DE Chipper Jones 20.00
8DE Sammy Sosa 25.00
9DE Jeff Bagwell 10.00
10DE Mike Piazza 20.00
11DE Pedro J. Martinez 15.00
12DE Mark Prior 30.00
13DE Jason Giambi 10.00
14DE Jose Reyes 5.00
15DE Alfonso Soriano 15.00

Diamond Essentials Game-Used

NM/M
Common Player: 8.00
Same price for cards #'d 145, 245 & 345
Patch versions: 1.5-2.5X
Production 55
RJ Randy Johnson 8.00
DJ Derek Jeter 15.00
CJ Chipper Jones 8.00
SS Sammy Sosa 12.00
JB Jeff Bagwell 8.00
MP Mike Piazza 10.00
PM Pedro J. Martinez 8.00
MP Mark Prior 20.00
JG Jason Giambi 8.00
JR Jose Reyes 8.00

Diamond Essentials Autograph

NM/M
Common Player:
Dontrelle Willis 30.00
Ryan Wagner 20.00
Rocco Baldelli 25.00
Randy Johnson
Albert Pujols 150.00

Emerald Essentials

NM/M
Complete Set (10): 60.00
Common Player: 4.00
Inserted 1:240
1 Austin Kearns 4.00
2 Alfonso Soriano 8.00
3 Miguel Tejada 4.00
4 Troy Glaus 4.00
5 Adam Dunn 4.00
6 Hideo Nomo 6.00
7 Kerry Wood 6.00
8 Nomar Garciaparra 15.00
9 Roger Clemens 15.00
10 Derek Jeter 15.00

Emerald Essentials Autograph

NM/M
Common Player:
Brandon Webb 20.00
Bo Hart
Hank Blalock 20.00
Marlon Byrd
Austin Kearns

Essential Credentials Now/Future

NM/M
Cards serial numbered 26-50: 6-12X
Cards s/n 51-75: 4-8X
Cards s/n 76-102: 3-5X
SP's (83-102) s/n 83-102: 1-2X
Now is consectutively #'d from 1 to 102
Future is consect. #'d from 102 to 1

Emerald Essentials Game-Used

NM/M
Common Player: 4.00
Same price for levels #'d 175, 250 & 375
Patch versions: 1.5-2.5X
Production 60
AK Austin Kearns 6.00
AS Alfonso Soriano 8.00
MT Miguel Tejada 4.00
TG Troy Glaus 6.00
AD Adam Dunn 6.00
HN Hideo Nomo 15.00
KW Kerry Wood 8.00
NG Nomar Garciaparra 12.00
RC Roger Clemens 12.00
AR Alex Rodriguez 10.00

2003 FLEER FALL CLASSIC

NM/M
Complete Set (87): 30.00
Common Player: .25
Common SP:
Hobby Pack (5): 4.00
Hobby Box (24): 75.00
1 Rod Carew .50
2 Bobby Doerr .25
3 Eddie Mathews 1.00
3 Eddie Mathews/SP/Tigers 4.00
4 Tom Seaver 1.50
5 Lou Brock .75
6 Nolan Ryan 3.00
6 Nolan Ryan/SP/Astros 10.00
7 Pee Wee Reese .25
8 Robin Yount 1.00
9 Bob Feller .50
10 Harmon Killebrew 1.00
11 Hal Newhouser .25
12 Al Kaline 1.00
13 Hoyt Wilhelm .25
14 Early Wynn .25
15 Yogi Berra 1.00
15 Yogi Berra/SP/Mets 4.00
16 Billy Williams .25
17 Rollie Fingers .25
18 Sparky Anderson .25
18 Sparky Anderson/SP/Reds 3.00
19 Lou Boudreau .25
20 Warren Spahn 1.00
21 Enos Slaughter .25
22 Luis Aparicio .50
23 Phil Rizzuto .75
24 Willie McCovey .75
25 Joe Morgan .50
26 Alan Trammell .75
27 Eddie Plank .25
28 Lefty Grove .25
29 Walter Johnson 1.00
30 Roy Campanella 1.00
31 Carlton Fisk .75
32 Bill Dickey .25
33 Rogers Hornsby 1.00
33 Rogers Hornsby/SP/Cubs 5.00
34 Wade Boggs .75
35 Chick Stahl .25
36 Don Drysdale .75
36 Don Drysdale/SP/Dodgers 4.00
37 Jose Canseco .75
38 Roger Maris 2.00
38 Roger Maris/SP/Yankees 8.00
39 Cal Ripken Jr. 3.00
40 Kiki Cuyler .25
40 Kiki Cuyler/SP/Cubs 3.00
41 Hank Greenberg .25
42 Don Larsen .50
43 Eddie Murray .75
43 Eddie Murray/SP/Indians 4.00
44 Jimmy Sebring .25
45 Ozzie Smith 1.50
46 Darryl Strawberry .25
46 Darryl Strawberry/SP/Yankees 3.00
47 Dave Parker .25
48 Gil Hodges .25
48 Gil Hodges/SP/Mets 3.00
49 Joe Carter .50
50 Leo Durocher .25
50 Leo Durocher/SP/Giants 3.00
51 Christy Mathewson .75
52 Elston Howard .25
53 Hughie Jennings .25
54 Nellie Fox .50
55 Carl Yastrzemski 1.00
56 Frank Robinson 1.00
56 Frank Robinson/SP/Reds 4.00
57 Dennis Eckersley .50
58 Grover Alexander .50
58 Grover Alexander/SP/Cards 4.00
59 Carl Hubbell .25
60 Dave Winfield .75
61 Honus Wagner 1.50
62 Duke Snider 1.00
62 Duke Snider/SP/Dodgers 5.00
63 Frankie Frisch .25
63 Frankie Frisch/SP/Cards 3.00
64 Dizzy Dean .75
65 Bob Gibson 1.00
66 Johnny Bench 1.50
67 Ty Cobb 2.00
68 Lou Gehrig 2.50
69 Jim "Catfish" Hunter .50
70 Willie Stargell .75
71 Reggie Jackson 1.00
71 Reggie Jackson/SP/Yankees 5.00
72 George Brett 2.50
73 Babe Ruth 3.00
73 Babe Ruth/SP/Yankees 10.00
74 Cy Young 1.00
75 Jim Palmer .50
76 Mickey Lolich .25
77 Stan Musial 1.50
78 Steve Carlton .75
79 Roberto Clemente 2.50
80 John McGraw .25
81 Paul Molitor .75
82 Red Ruffing .25
83 Connie Mack .25
84 Mike Schmidt 2.00
85 Mickey Cochrane .50
85 Mickey Cochrane/SP/Tigers 4.00

86 Brooks Robinson 1.00
87 Whitey Ford 1.00

Championship Gold

Cards 1-87: 3-6X
Production 50 sets

All-American Collection

NM/M
Common Player: 8.00
OS Ozzie Smith/100 20.00
TS Tom Seaver/100 15.00
SM Stan Musial/100 30.00
CR Cal Ripken Jr/100 60.00
EM Eddie Mathews/100 10.00
NR Nolan Ryan 30.00
YB Yogi Berra 15.00
EM Eddie Murray/100 15.00
FR Frank Robinson 8.00
DS Duke Snider 8.00
RJ Reggie Jackson 8.00
LA Luis Aparicio/100 10.00
GH Gil Hodges 8.00
AK Al Kaline 10.00
BM Bill Mazeroski/100 10.00
BR Brooks Robinson/100 15.00
WB Wade Boggs/100 12.00
AT Alan Trammell/100 12.00

All American Collection Auto

NM/M
Common Autograph:
Varying quantities produced
SP version #'d to 100: 1-1.5X
SP version #'d to 50: 1-2X
LA Luis Aparicio/150 10.00
VB Vida Blue/450 8.00
RB Rick Burleson/250 8.00
SC Steve Carlton/100 20.00
BF Bob Feller/300 15.00
CF Carlton Fisk/75 30.00
AL Al Kaline/325 20.00
HK Harmon Killebrew/150 30.00
FL Fred Lynn/275 8.00
BM Bill Mazeroski/75 20.00
JP Jim Palmer/100 15.00
BR Brooks Robinson/325 20.00
PR Preacher Roe/450 12.00
MS Mike Schmidt/50 60.00
BS "Moose" Skowron/150 10.00
OS Ozzie Smith/50 65.00
DS Duke Snider/100 25.00
WS Warren Spahn/75 40.00
AT Alan Trammell/150 15.00

All Amer. Coll. Jersey Auto.

NM/M
Production 25 sets
LA Luis Aparicio
VB George Brett 160.00
RB Johnny Bench
SC Steve Carlton 50.00
CF Carlton Fisk
AL Al Kaline
HK Harmon Killebrew
FL Fred Lynn
BM Bill Mazeroski
JP Stan Musial
BR Brooks Robinson
PR Nolan Ryan
MS Mike Schmidt
BS "Moose" Skowron
OS Ozzie Smith
DS Duke Snider
AT Alan Trammell

Legendary Collection

NM/M
Common Player:
Inserted 1:Legendary Star Pack
EM Eddie Mathews/SP 15.00
NR Nolan Ryan 30.00
YB Yogi Berra 15.00
EMY Eddie Murray 8.00
FR Frank Robinson 6.00
DS Duke Snider/SP 10.00
DSy Darryl Strawberry 5.00
RJ Reggie Jackson 8.00
RM Roger Maris/SP 30.00
GH Gil Hodges/SP 10.00

Pennant Aggression

NM/M
Complete Set (20): 50.00
Common Player: 3.00
numbered to pennant year
1PA Ty Cobb/1,908 4.00
2PA Honus Wagner/1,909 3.00
3PA Walter Johnson/1,924 3.00
4PA Jimmie Foxx/1,930 4.00
5PA Frankie Frisch/1,931 3.00
6PA Pee Wee Reese/1,947 3.00
7PA Yogi Berra/1,951 4.00
8PA Roy Campanella/1,953 3.00
9PA Whitey Ford/1,961 4.00
10PA Frank Robinson/1,966 3.00
11PA Carl Yastrzemski/1,967 3.00
12PA Brooks Robinson/1,970 3.00
13PA Johnny Bench/1,972 4.00
14PA Reggie Jackson/1,973 3.00
15PA Jim "Catfish" Hunter/1,974 3.00
16PA Joe Morgan/1,975 3.00
17PA Thurman Munson/1,976 4.00
18PA Willie Stargell/1,979 3.00
19PA Mike Schmidt/1,980 4.00
20PA George Brett/1,985 4.00

Pennant Aggression Game-Used

NM/M
Common Player: 8.00
Production 100
Patches: 1.5-2X
Production 50
YB Yogi Berra 15.00
FB Frank Robinson 10.00
CY Carl Yastrzemski 20.00
BR Brooks Robinson 15.00
JB Johnny Bench 15.00
RJ Reggie Jackson 12.00
CH Jim "Catfish" Hunter 8.00
JM Joe Morgan 8.00
TM Thurman Munson 15.00
WS Willie Stargell 10.00
MS Mike Schmidt 25.00
GB George Brett 35.00

Postseason Glory

NM/M
Complete Set (30): 125.00
Common Player: 2.00
#1-15 numbered to 1,500
16-25 numbered to 750
26-30 numbered to 100
1 Carlton Fisk, Carl Yastrzemski 2.00
2 Enos Slaughter, Stan Musial 4.00
3 Reggie Jackson, Thurman Munson 4.00
4 Eddie Plank, Christy Mathewson 3.00
5 Cy Young, Jimmy Sebring 3.00
6 Yogi Berra, Whitey Ford 4.00
7 Mickey Lolich, Alan Trammell 2.00
8 Eddie Mathews, Al Schoendienst 3.00
9 Roy Campanella, Pee Wee Reese 3.00
10 Joe Carter, Bill Mazeroski 2.00
11 Brooks Robinson, Frank Robinson 3.00
12 Tom Seaver, Gil Hodges 3.00
13 Robin Yount, Paul Molitor 2.50
14 Dave Parker, Willie Stargell 2.00
15 Cal Ripken Jr., Jim Palmer 6.00
16 Babe Ruth, Whitey Ford 8.00
18 Lou Brock, Bob Gibson 4.00
19 Mike Schmidt, Brooks Robinson 5.00
20 Johnny Bench, Thurman Munson 5.00
21 Nolan Ryan, Walter Johnson 10.00
22 Don Drysdale, Duke Snider 4.00
23 Joe Carter, Paul Molitor 2.00
24 Hughie Jennings, Ty Cobb 4.00
25 Cal Ripken Jr., Eddie Murray 10.00
26 Mike Schmidt, Steve Carlton 5.00
27 Roberto Clemente, Willie Stargell 15.00
28 Jim Palmer, Nolan Ryan 25.00
29 Joe Morgan, Johnny Bench 10.00
30 Lou Gehrig, Babe Ruth 25.00

Postseason Glory Dual Game-Used

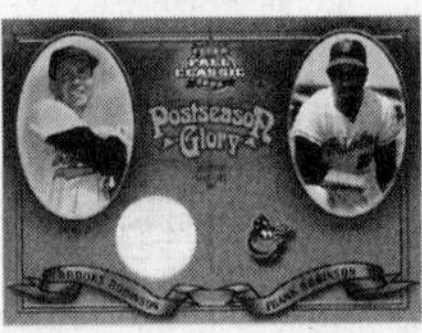

NM/M
Production 100
Single Jerseys: .5X
Production 150
Carlton Fisk, Carl Yastrzemski 25.00
Reggie Jackson, Thurman Munson 25.00
Yogi Berra, Whitey Ford 30.00
Brooks Robinson, Frank Robinson 20.00
Robin Yount, Paul Molitor 25.00
Dave Parker, Willie Stargell/single/150 8.00
Lou Brock, Bob Gibson/single/150 10.00
Joe Carter, Paul Molitor/single/150 8.00
Don Drysdale, Duke Snider 25.00
Cal Ripken Jr., Eddie Murray 50.00
Mike Schmidt, Steve Carlton 25.00
Jim Palmer, Nolan Ryan 40.00
Joe Morgan, Johnny Bench 25.00
Babe Ruth/single/150, Lou Gehrig 125.00

Postseason Glory Dual Patch

NM/M
Production 50
Single Patch: .5-.75X
Production 75
Carlton Fisk, Carl Yastrzemski 70.00
Robin Yount, Paul Molitor 50.00
Lou Brock, Bob Gibson 50.00
Cal Ripken Jr., Eddie Murray 120.00
Mike Schmidt, Steve Carlton 50.00
Jim Palmer, Nolan Ryan 80.00
Joe Morgan, Johnny Bench 50.00
Brooks Robinson, Frank Robinson 40.00

Series Contender

NM/M
Common Player:
Inserted 1:50 Retail
Bat Knobs: Not Priced
Production 9 or 10
SK Al Kaline 15.00
BD Bill Dickey 10.00
DS Darryl Strawberry 5.00
DM Don Mattingly 30.00
PR Phil Rizzuto/SP 10.00
WM Willie McCovey/SP 10.00
HK Harmon Killebrew 25.00
CF Carlton Fisk 6.00
JC Jose Canseco 10.00

Yankee Penstripes

NM/M
Production 100
World Series Edition: No Pricing
Production 26
RJ Reggie Jackson 40.00
BSP Bill "Moose" Skowron 15.00
WB Wade Boggs 50.00
DM Don Mattingly 75.00
DW Dave Winfield 35.00

2003 FLEER FOCUS JERSEY EDITION

NM/M
Complete Set (180): 45.00
Common Player: .15
Common Prospect (161-180): .75
Inserted 1:4
Pack (7): 1.50
Box (24): 30.00
1 Derek Jeter 2.50
2 Preston Wilson .15
3 Trevor Hoffman .15
4 Moises Alou .15
5 Roberto Alomar .35
6 Tim Salmon .25
7 Mike Lowell .15
8 Barry Bonds 2.50
9 Fred McGriff .15
10 Mo Vaughn .15
11 Junior Spivey .15
12 Roy Oswalt .25
13 Ichiro Suzuki 1.50

14	Magglio Ordonez	.25
15	Adam Kennedy	.15
16	Randy Johnson	.75
17	Carlos Beltran	.50
18	John Olerud	.15
19	Joe Borchard	.15
20	Alfonso Soriano	.75
21	Curt Schilling	.50
22	Mike Sweeney	.15
23	Tino Martinez	.15
24	Barry Larkin	.15
25	Miguel Tejada	.40
26	Chipper Jones	1.00
27	Kevin Brown	.15
28	J.D. Drew	.15
29	Sean Casey	.15
30	Bernie Williams	.35
31	Troy Percival	.15
32	Jeff Bagwell	.75
33	Kenny Lofton	.15
34	Kerry Wood	.50
35	Armando Benitez	.15
36	David Eckstein	.15
37	Wade Miller	.15
38	Edgar Martinez	.15
39	Mark Prior	.75
40	Mike Piazza	1.50
41	Shea Hillenbrand	.15
42	Bartolo Colon	.15
43	Darin Erstad	.50
44	A.J. Burnett	.15
45	Jeff Kent	.15
46	Corey Patterson	.15
47	Derek Wigginton	.15
48	Troy Glaus	.75
49	Josh Beckett	.15
50	Brian Lawrence	.15
51	Frank Thomas	.75
52	Jason Giambi	.60
53	Luis Gonzalez	.25
54	Raul Ibanez	.15
55	Kazuhiro Sasaki	.15
56	Mark Buehrle	.15
57	Roger Clemens	1.25
58	Matt Williams	.15
59	Joe Randa	.15
60	Jamie Moyer	.15
61	Paul Konerko	.15
62	Mike Mussina	.50
63	Javy Lopez	.15
64	Brian Jordan	.15
65	Scott Rolen	.75
66	Aaron Boone	.15
67	Eric Chavez	.25
68	Mark Grace	.25
69	Shawn Green	.25
70	Albert Pujols	1.25
71	Sammy Sosa	1.50
72	Edgardo Alfonzo	.15
73	Garret Anderson	.15
74	Lance Berkman	.15
75	Bret Boone	.15
76	Joe Crede	.15
77	Al Leiter	.15
78	Jarrod Washburn	.15
79	Craig Biggio	.15
80	Rich Aurilia	.15
81	Adam Dunn	.60
82	Jermaine Dye	.15
83	Tom Glavine	.40
84	Eric Gagne	.15
85	Jared Sandberg	.15
86	Jim Thome	.15
87	Barry Zito	.35
88	Gary Sheffield	.25
89	Paul LoDuca	.15
90	Matt Morris	.15
91	Juan Pierre	.15
92	Randy Wolf	.15
93	Jay Gibbons	.15
94	Brad Radke	.15
95	Carlos Delgado	.35
96	Carlos Pena	.15
97	Brian Giles	.15
98	Rodrigo Lopez	.15
99	Jacque Jones	.15
100	Juan Gonzalez	.75
101	Randall Simon	.15
102	Mike Williams	.15
103	Derek Lowe	.15
104	Brad Wilkerson	.15
105	Eric Hinske	.15
106	Luis Castillo	.15
107	Phil Nevin	.15
108	Manny Ramirez	.75
109	Vladimir Guerrero	.75
110	Roy Halladay	.15
111	Ellis Burks	.15
112	Bobby Abreu	.15
113	Tony Batista	.15
114	Richie Sexson	.15
115	Rafael Palmeiro	.65
116	Todd Helton	.65
117	Pat Burrell	.60
118	John Smoltz	.15
119	Ben Sheets	.15
120	Aubrey Huff	.15
121	Andruw Jones	.75
122	Kazuhisa Ishii	.15
123	Jim Edmonds	.15
124	Austin Kearns	.60
125	Mark Mulder	.25
126	Greg Maddux	1.00
127	Jose Hernandez	.15
128	Ben Grieve	.15
129	Ken Griffey Jr.	1.50
130	Tim Hudson	.35
131	Jorge Julio	.15
132	Torii Hunter	.15
133	Ivan Rodriguez	.65
134	Jason Jennings	.15
135	Jason Kendall	.15
136	Nomar Garciaparra	1.50
137	Michael Cuddyer	.15
138	Shannon Stewart	.15
139	Larry Walker	.15
140	Aramis Ramirez	.15
141	Johnny Damon	.15
142	Orlando Cabrera	.15
143	Vernon Wells	.15
144	Bobby Higginson	.15
145	Sean Burroughs	.15
146	Pedro J. Martinez	.75
147	Jose Vidro	.15
148	Orlando Hudson	.15
149	Robert Fick	.15
150	Ryan Klesko	.15
151	Kevin Millwood	.15
152	Alex Sanchez	.15
153	Randy Winn	.15
154	Omar Vizquel	.15
155	Mike Lieberthal	.15
156	Marty Cordova	.15
157	Cristian Guzman	.15
158	Alex Rodriguez	2.00
159	C.C. Sabathia	.15
160	Jimmy Rollins	.15
161	*Josh Willingham*	2.00
162	Lance Niekro	.75
163	*Nook Logan*	.75
164	Chase Utley	.75
165	*Pete LaForest*	.75
166	Victor Martinez	.75
167	Adam LaRoche	.75
168	*Ian Ferguson*	.75
169	Mark Teixeira	.75
170	*Chris Waters*	.75
171	*Hideki Matsui*	5.00
172	*Alejandro Machado*	.75
173	*Francisco Rosario*	.75
174	*Terrmel Sledge*	1.00
175	*Guillermo Quiroz*	.75
176	*Lew Ford*	3.00
177	Hank Blalock	.75
178	Lyle Overbay	.75
179	*Matt Bruback*	.75
180	*Jose Contreras*	3.00

Century Jersey Number

Stars (1-160): 5-10X
Prospects (161-180): 2-4X
Numbered to jsy number + 100

Franchise Focus

		NM/M
Complete Set (20):		15.00
Common Player:		.50
Inserted 1:4		
1	Troy Glaus	.75
2	Randy Johnson	1.00
3	Chipper Jones	1.50
4	Nomar Garciaparra	2.00
5	Sammy Sosa	1.50
6	Ken Griffey Jr.	1.50
7	Jeff Bagwell	.75
8	Mike Sweeney	.50
9	Shawn Green	.50
10	Torii Hunter	.50
11	Vladimir Guerrero	1.00
12	Mike Piazza	2.00
13	Jason Giambi	1.00
14	Barry Zito	.50
15	Pat Burrell	.75
16	Barry Bonds	3.00
17	Ichiro Suzuki	1.50
18	Albert Pujols	1.00
19	Alex Rodriguez	2.50
20	Carlos Delgado	.50

Home and Aways

	NM/M
Common Player:	10.00
Inserted 1:288	
Lance Berkman	10.00
J.D. Drew	10.00
Nomar Garciaparra	20.00
Derek Jeter	40.00
Chipper Jones	20.00
Greg Maddux	20.00
Roy Oswalt	10.00
Alex Rodriguez	30.00
Alfonso Soriano	10.00

Materialistic

		NM/M
Common Player:		3.00
Inserted 1:192		
Action Home:		1.5-2.5X
Production 50 sets		
Portrait Away:		.75-1.5X
Inserted 1:576		
Plus (memorabilia):		1.5-2.5X
Production 250 sets		
Portrait Home:		No Pricing
Production One set		
1M	Greg Maddux	5.00
2M	Roger Clemens	5.00
3M	Nomar Garciaparra	6.00
4M	Derek Jeter	10.00
5M	Mike Piazza	6.00
6M	Pat Burrell	3.00
7M	Alfonso Soriano	5.00
8M	Chipper Jones	5.00
9M	Adam Dunn	3.00
10M	Alex Rodriguez	8.00
11M	Jason Giambi	4.00
12M	Sammy Sosa	5.00
13M	Albert Pujols	4.00
14M	Ken Griffey Jr.	5.00
15M	Ichiro Suzuki	5.00

Materialistic Oversize Autographs

		NM/M
Complete Set (3):		200.00
(1)	Reggie Jackson/360	50.00
(2)	Derek Jeter/360	100.00
(3)	Chipper Jones/80	75.00

Shirtified

		NM/M
Complete Set (15):		35.00
Common Player:		1.00
Inserted 1:24		
1	Manny Ramirez	2.00
2	Jarrod Washburn	1.00
3	Greg Maddux	4.00
4	Austin Kearns	2.00
5	Jim Thome	2.00
6	Kazuhisa Ishii	1.00
7	Mike Piazza	5.00
8	Alfonso Soriano	3.00
9	Pat Burrell	2.00
10	Derek Jeter	8.00
11	Miguel Tejada	1.50
12	Roger Clemens	4.00
13	Alex Rodriguez	6.00
14	Barry Bonds	8.00
15	Scott Rolen	2.00

Shirtified Game-Used

	NM/M
Common Player:	
Inserted 1:35	
Patches:	2-3X
Production 200	
Manny Ramirez	8.00
Greg Maddux	12.00
Mike Piazza	10.00
Alfonso Soriano	15.00
Derek Jeter	25.00
Miguel Tejada	6.00
Roger Clemens	12.00
Alex Rodriguez	12.00

Team Colors

		NM/M
Complete Set (20):		20.00
Common Player:		.50
Inserted 1:12		
1TC	Alex Rodriguez	3.50
2TC	Mark Prior	1.50
3TC	Derek Jeter	4.00
4TC	Curt Schilling	1.00
5TC	Pat Burrell	1.00
6TC	Josh Beckett	.50
7TC	Sean Burroughs	.50
8TC	Troy Glaus	1.00
9TC	Torii Hunter	.75
10TC	Jeff Bagwell	1.00
11TC	Pedro J. Martinez	1.50
12TC	Mike Piazza	3.00
13TC	Lance Berkman	.75
14TC	Nomar Garciaparra	2.50
15TC	Chipper Jones	2.00
16TC	Eric Chavez	.75
17TC	Barry Zito	.75
18TC	Barry Bonds	4.00
19TC	Adam Dunn	1.00
20TC	Randy Johnson	1.50

Team Colors Game Used

	NM/M
Common Player:	4.00
Inserted 1:28	
Multi-Color:	1.5X
Production 250	
Derek Jeter	25.00
Curt Schilling	5.00
Josh Beckett	4.00
Troy Glaus	8.00
Jeff Bagwell	8.00
Pedro J. Martinez	8.00
Lance Berkman	8.00
Nomar Garciaparra	15.00
Chipper Jones	10.00
Eric Chavez	6.00
Barry Bonds	
Adam Dunn	8.00
Randy Johnson	8.00

2003 FLEER GENUINE

	NM/M
Complete Set (130):	150.00
Common Player:	.25

Common Gen. Upside (101-130): 3.00
Production 799
Pack (5): 2.00
Box (24): 40.00

1 Derek Jeter 3.00
2 Mo Vaughn .25
3 Adam Dunn .75
4 Aubrey Huff .25
5 Jacque Jones .25
6 Kerry Wood .60
7 Barry Bonds 3.00
8 Kevin Brown .25
9 Sammy Sosa 2.00
10 Ray Durham .25
11 Carlos Beltran .50
12 Tony Batista .25
13 Bobby Abreu .25
14 Craig Biggio .25
15 Gary Sheffield .45
16 Jermaine Dye .25
17 Carlos Pena .25
18 Tim Salmon .35
19 Mike Piazza 2.00
20 Moises Alou .25
21 Edgardo Alfonzo .25
22 Mike Sweeney .25
23 Jay Gibbons .25
24 Kevin Millwood .25
25 A.J. Burnett .25
26 Austin Kearns .75
27 Rafael Palmeiro .75
28 Vladimir Guerrero 1.00
29 Paul Konerko .25
30 Scott Rolen .75
31 Fred McGriff .25
32 Frank Thomas 1.00
33 John Olerud .25
34 Eric Gagne .25
35 Nomar Garciaparra 2.00
36 Ryan Klesko .25
37 Lance Berkman .25
38 Andruw Jones .75
39 Pat Burrell .60
40 Juan Encarnacion .25
41 Curt Schilling .50
42 Jason Giambi .65
43 Barry Larkin .25
44 Alex Rodriguez 2.50
45 Kazuhisa Ishii .25
46 Pedro J. Martinez 1.00
47 Sean Burroughs .25
48 Roy Oswalt .40
49 Chipper Jones 1.50
50 Barry Zito .40
51 Jeff Kent .25
52 Rodrigo Lopez .25
53 Jim Thome .25
54 Ivan Rodriguez .60
55 Luis Gonzalez .40
56 Alfonso Soriano 1.00
57 Josh Beckett .25
58 Junior Spivey .25
59 Bernie Williams .40
60 Omar Vizquel .25
61 Eric Hinske .25
62 Jose Vidro .25
63 Bartolo Colon .25
64 Jim Edmonds .25
65 Ben Sheets .25
66 Mark Prior 1.00
67 Edgar Martinez .25
68 Raul Ibanez .25
69 Darin Erstad .40
70 Roger Clemens 1.75
71 C.C. Sabathia .25
72 Carlos Delgado .50
73 Tom Glavine .40
74 Magglio Ordonez .40
75 Ichiro Suzuki 1.50
76 Johnny Damon .40
77 Brian Giles .25
78 Jeff Bagwell 1.00
79 Greg Maddux 1.50
80 Eric Chavez .40
81 Larry Walker .25
82 Randy Johnson 1.00
83 Miguel Tejada .40
84 Todd Helton .75
85 Jarrod Washburn .25
86 Troy Glaus .75
87 Ken Griffey Jr. 2.00
88 Albert Pujols 2.00
89 Torii Hunter .25
90 Joe Crede .25
91 Matt Morris .25
92 Shawn Green .40
93 Manny Ramirez 1.00
94 Jason Kendall .25
95 Preston Wilson .25
96 Garret Anderson .25
97 Cliff Floyd .25
98 Sean Casey .25
99 Juan Gonzalez .75
100 Richie Sexson .25
101 Joe Borchard 3.00
102 *Josh Stewart* 3.00
103 Francisco Rodriguez 4.00
104 Jeremy Bonderman 4.00
105 Walter Young 3.00
106 *Brandon Webb* 5.00
107 Lyle Overbay 4.00
108 *Jose Contreras* 6.00
109 Victor Martinez 4.00
110 *Hideki Matsui* 10.00
111 *Brian Stokes* 3.00
112 *Daniel Cabrera* 6.00
113 *Josh Willingham* 3.00
114 Mark Teixeira 4.00
115 *Pete LaForest* 3.00
116 *Chris Waters* 3.00
117 *Chien-Ming Wang* 5.00
118 *Ian Ferguson* 3.00
119 Rocco Baldelli 4.00
120 *Terrmel Sledge* 4.00
121 Hank Blalock 4.00
122 *Alejandro Machado* 3.00
123 Hee Seop Choi 4.00
124 *Guillermo Quiroz* 4.00
125 Chase Utley 4.00
126 *Nook Logan* 3.00
127 *Josh Hall* 3.00
128 Ryan Church 3.00
129 *Lew Ford* 6.00
130 *Francisco Rosario* 3.00

Reflection

NM/M

Cards 1-100 print run 25-50: 8-15X
Cards 101-130 p/r 101-130: .5-1.5X
Cards 1-100 p/r 51-80: 4-8X
Cards 1-100 p/r 81-130: 3-5X
Ascending consecutively #'d from 1-130
Descending consecutively #'d from 130-1

Article Insider

NM/M

Common Player: 4.00
Inserted 1:24

Adam Dunn 5.00
Andruw Jones 6.00
Alex Rodriguez 10.00
Alfonso Soriano 8.00
Chipper Jones 8.00
Curt Schilling 5.00
Derek Jeter 15.00
Don Mattingly 25.00
Greg Maddux 10.00
Jeff Bagwell 6.00
Jason Giambi 10.00
Lance Berkman 4.00
Magglio Ordonez 4.00
Mike Piazza 10.00
Miguel Tejada 4.00
Nomar Garciaparra 15.00
Pat Burrell 4.00
Pedro J. Martinez 8.00
Randy Johnson 6.00
Shawn Green 4.00
Sammy Sosa 10.00
Troy Glaus 5.00
Torii Hunter 5.00
Todd Helton 6.00
Vladimir Guerrero 6.00

Article Insider Autograph

NM/M

Quantity produced listed

Lance Berkman/165 25.00
Lance Berkman/100 25.00
Lance Berkman/50 40.00
Derek Jeter/100 125.00
Don Mattingly/170 85.00
Don Mattingly/100 100.00

Long Ball Threats

NM/M

Complete Set (15): 15.00
Common Card: .50
Inserted 1:8

1 Derek Jeter, Nomar Garciaparra 3.00
2 Jim Thome, Pat Burrell 1.00
3 Alex Rodriguez, Rafael Palmeiro 3.00
4 Alfonso Soriano, Hideki Matsui 3.00
5 Torii Hunter, Vladimir Guerrero 1.00
6 Mike Sweeney, Phil Nevin .50
7 Mike Piazza, Sammy Sosa 2.00
8 Shawn Green, Jason Giambi 1.00
9 Magglio Ordonez, Andruw Jones 1.00
10 Eric Chavez, Carlos Delgado .75
11 Manny Ramirez, Jeff Bagwell 1.00
12 Scott Rolen, Troy Glaus 1.00
13 Barry Bonds, Miguel Tejada 3.00
14 Albert Pujols, Lance Berkman 2.00
15 Chipper Jones, Todd Helton 1.50

Long Ball Threats Dual Jersey

NM/M

Common Card: 5.00
Inserted 1:72

Derek Jeter, Nomar Garciaparra 30.00
Jim Thome, Pat Burrell 15.00
Alex Rodriguez, Rafael Palmeiro 15.00
Torii Hunter, Vladimir Guerrero 10.00
Mike Sweeney, Phil Nevin 5.00
Mike Piazza, Sammy Sosa 20.00
Magglio Ordonez, Andruw Jones 10.00
Scott Rolen, Troy Glaus 10.00
Chipper Jones, Todd Helton 12.00

Long Ball Threats Single Jersey

NM/M

Common Player: 3.00
Inserted 1:13

Derek Jeter/jsy, Nomar Garciaparra 15.00
Derek Jeter, Nomar Garciaparra/jsy 10.00
Jim Thome/jsy, Pat Burrell 6.00
Jim Thome, Pat Burrell/jsy 6.00
Alfonso Soriano/jsy, Hideki Matsui 8.00
Torii Hunter/jsy, Vladimir Guerrero 6.00
Torii Hunter, Vladimir Guerrero/jsy 6.00
Mike Sweeney/jsy, Phil Nevin 3.00
Mike Sweeney, Phil Nevin/jsy 3.00
Mike Piazza/jsy, Sammy Sosa 8.00
Mike Piazza, Sammy Sosa/jsy 10.00
Shawn Green/jsy, Jason Giambi 4.00
Magglio Ordonez/jsy, Andruw Jones 4.00
Eric Chavez, Carlos Delgado/jsy 5.00
Manny Ramirez/jsy, Jeff Bagwell 8.00
Manny Ramirez, Jeff Bagwell/jsy 8.00
Scott Rolen/jsy, Troy Glaus 6.00
Scott Rolen, Troy Glaus/jsy 6.00
Barry Bonds, Miguel Tejada/jsy 5.00
Albert Pujols, Lance Berkman/jsy 4.00
Chipper Jones/jsy, Todd Helton 8.00
Chipper Jones, Todd Helton/jsy 6.00

Long Ball Threats Dual Patch

NM/M

#'d to combined 2002 HR total

Derek Jeter, Nomar Garciaparra/42 80.00
Jim Thome, Pat Burrell/89 30.00
Alex Rodriguez, Rafael Palmeiro/100 50.00
Mike Piazza, Sammy Sosa/82 75.00
Shawn Green, Jason Giambi/83 40.00
Magglio Ordonez, Andruw Jones/73 40.00
Manny Ramirez, Jeff Bagwell/64 40.00
Scott Rolen, Troy Glaus/61 50.00

Tools of the Game 1-Piece

NM/M

Common Player:
Inserted 1:42
2-Piece: 1.5-3X
Production 250
3-Piece: 3-6X
Production 100

Adam Dunn 6.00
Mike Piazza 8.00
Derek Jeter 15.00
Alex Rodriguez 10.00
Alfonso Soriano 10.00
Jason Giambi 8.00
Sammy Sosa 10.00
Vladimir Guerrero 6.00

Tools of the Game

NM/M

Complete Set (15): 20.00

Common Player: .75
Inserted 1:20
1 Adam Dunn 1.00
2 Chipper Jones 2.00
3 Torii Hunter .75
4 Mike Piazza 1.50
5 Hideki Matsui 8.00
6 Nomar Garciaparra 3.00
7 Derek Jeter 4.00
8 Alex Rodriguez 3.00
9 Alfonso Soriano 2.00
10 Pat Burrell .75
11 Barry Bonds 4.00
12 Jason Giambi 1.50
13 Sammy Sosa 2.00
14 Vladimir Guerrero 1.00
15 Ichiro Suzuki 2.00

2003 FLEER HARDBALL

NM/M
Complete Set (280): 85.00
Common Player: .15
Common (241-280): .75
Inserted 1:2 hobby
Pack (7): 1.75
Box (24): 30.00
1 Barry Bonds 2.00
2 Derek Jeter 2.00
3 Jason Varitek .15
4 Magglio Ordonez .25
5 Ryan Dempster .15
6 Adam Everett .15
7 Paul LoDuca .15
8 Brad Wilkerson .15
9 Al Leiter .15
10 Jermaine Dye .15
11 Robert Mackowiak .15
12 J.T. Snow .15
13 Juan Gonzalez .60
14 Eric Hinske .15
15 Greg Maddux 1.00
16 Moises Alou .15
17 Carlos Lee .15
18 Richard Hidalgo .15
19 Jorge Posada .25
20 Mike Lieberthal .15
21 Jeff Cirillo .15
22 Corey Patterson .15
23 C.C. Sabathia .15
24 Brian Giles .15
25 Edgar Martinez .15
26 Trot Nixon .15
27 Kerry Wood .50
28 Austin Kearns .40
29 Lance Berkman .15
30 Hideo Nomo .50
31 Brad Radke .15
32 John Valentin .15
33 Tim Hudson .35
34 Aramis Ramirez .15
35 Kevin Mench .15
36 Kevin Appier .15
37 Chris Richard .15
38 Ruben Mateo .15
39 Juan Pierre .15
40 Nick Neugebauer .15
41 Mike Mussina .40
42 Rich Aurilia .15
43 Albert Pujols 1.00
44 Carlos Delgado .50
45 Junior Spivey .15
46 Marcus Giles .15
47 Johnny Damon .25
48 Mark Prior .50
49 Omar Vizquel .15
50 Craig Biggio .15
51 Chuck Knoblauch .15
52 Eric Milton .15
53 Jeromy Burnitz .15
54 Jim Thome .15
55 Steve Finley .15
56 Kevin Millwood .15
57 Alex Gonzalez .15
58 Ben Broussard .15
59 Derrek Lee .15
60 Joe Randa .15
61 Doug Mientkiewicz .15
62 Jason L. Phillips .15
63 Brett Myers .15
64 Josh Fogg .15
65 Reggie Sanders .15
66 Chipper Jones 1.00
67 Roosevelt Brown .15
68 Matt Lawton .15
69 Charles Johnson .15
70 Mark Quinn .15
71 Jacque Jones .15
72 Armando Benitez .15
73 Bobby Abreu .15
74 Jason Kendall .15
75 Jeff Kent .15
76 Mark Teixeira .50
77 Garret Anderson .15
78 Jerry Hairston Jr. .15
79 Tony Graffanino .15
80 Josh Beckett .15
81 Eric Gagne .15
82 Fernando Tatis .15
83 Brett Tomko .15
84 Fernando Vina .15
85 Rafael Palmeiro .65
86 Luis Gonzalez .35
87 Javy Lopez .15
88 Shea Hillenbrand .15
89 Hee Seop Choi .15
90 Preston Wilson .15
91 Neifi Perez .15
92 Ray Lankford .15
93 Tsuyoshi Shinjo .15
94 Ben Grieve .15
95 Jarrod Washburn .15
96 Gary Sheffield .35
97 Derek Lowe .15
98 Tony Womack .15
99 Milton Bradley .15
100 Brad Penny .15
101 Mike Sweeney .15
102 A.J. Pierzynski .15
103 Edgardo Alfonzo .15
104 Marlon Byrd .15
105 Sean Burroughs .15
106 Kazuhiro Sasaki .15
107 Damian Rolls .15
108 Troy Glaus .60
109 Rafael Furcal .15
110 Nomar Garciaparra 1.25
111 Josh Bard .15
112 Alex Gonzalez .15
113 Cristian Guzman .15
114 Roger Cedeno .15
115 Freddy Garcia .15
116 Travis Phelps .15
117 Juan Cruz .15
118 Frank Thomas .60
119 Jaret Wright .15
120 Carlos Beltran .45
121 Ronnie Belliard .15
122 Roger Clemens 1.00
123 Vicente Padilla .15
124 Joel Pineiro .15
125 Jared Sandberg .15
126 Tom Glavine .35
127 Matt Clement .15
128 Aaron Rowand .15
129 Alex Escobar .15
130 Randy Wolf .15
131 Ichiro Suzuki 1.00
132 Toby Hall .15
133 Scott Spiezio .15
134 Bobby Higginson .15
135 A.J. Burnett .15
136 Cesar Izturis .15
137 Roberto Alomar .40
138 Trevor Hoffman .15
139 Edgar Renteria .15
140 Rusty Greer .15
141 David Eckstein .15
142 Pedro J. Martinez .75
143 Joe Crede .15
144 Robert Fick .15
145 Mike Lowell .15
146 Brian Jordan .15
147 Mark Mulder .25
148 Scott Rolen .60
149 Ivan Rodriguez .60
150 Adam Kennedy .15
151 Ken Griffey Jr. 1.25
152 Larry Walker .15
153 Carlos Pena .15
154 Geoff Jenkins .15
155 Bartolo Colon .15
156 Mariano Rivera .25
157 Robb Nen .15
158 Bret Boone .15
159 Shannon Stewart .15
160 Chris Singleton .15
161 Todd Walker .15
162 Jay Payton .15
163 Zach Day .15
164 Bernie Williams .40
165 Bubba Trammell .15
166 Matt Morris .15
167 Jose Cruz Jr. .15
168 Mark Grace .40
169 Andruw Jones .75
170 Cliff Floyd .15
171 Antonio Alfonseca .15
172 Jeff Bagwell .75
173 Shawn Green .40
174 Joe Mays .15
175 Mike Piazza 1.25
176 Adam Piatt .15
177 Pokey Reese .15
178 Carl Everett .15
179 Tim Salmon .35
180 Rodrigo Lopez .15
181 Brandon Inge .15
182 Kazuhisa Ishii .15
183 Jose Vidro .15
184 Barry Zito .40
185 Phil Nevin .15
186 J.D. Drew .35
187 Vernon Wells .15
188 Darin Erstad .50
189 Barry Larkin .15
190 Jason Jennings .15
191 Luis Castillo .15
192 Adrian Beltre .35
193 Tony Armas .15
194 Terrence Long .15
195 Mark Kotsay .15
196 Tino Martinez .15
197 Jayson Werth .15
198 Eric Chavez .25
199 Matt Williams .15
200 Jon Lieber .15
201 Eddie Taubensee .15
202 Shane Reynolds .15
203 Alex Sanchez .15
204 Jason Giambi .60
205 Jimmy Rollins .15
206 Jamie Moyer .15
207 Francisco Rodriguez .15
208 Marty Cordova .15
209 Aaron Boone .15
210 Mike Hampton .15
211 Mark Redman .15
212 Richie Sexson .15
213 Andy Pettitte .40
214 Livan Hernandez .15
215 Jason Isringhausen .15
216 Curt Schilling .40
217 Manny Ramirez .75
218 Jose Valentin .15
219 Brent Butler .15
220 Billy Wagner .15
221 Ben Sheets .15
222 Jeff Weaver .15
223 Brent Abernathy .15
224 Jay Gibbons .15
225 Sean Casey .15
226 Greg Norton .15
227 Andy Van Hekken .15
228 Kevin Brown .15
229 Orlando Cabrera .15
230 Scott Hatteberg .15
231 Ryan Klesko .15
232 Roy Halladay .15
233 Randy Johnson .75
234 Mark Buehrle .15
235 Todd Helton .60
236 Jeffrey Hammonds .15
237 Sidney Ponson .15
238 Kip Wells .15
239 John Olerud .15
240 Aubrey Huff .15
241 Derek Jeter 4.00
242 Barry Bonds 4.00
243 Ichiro Suzuki 2.00
244 Troy Glaus 1.00
245 Alex Rodriguez 3.00
246 Sammy Sosa 2.00
247 Lance Berkman .75
248 Jason Giambi 2.00
249 Nomar Garciaparra 2.50
250 Miguel Tejada .75
251 Albert Pujols 1.50
252 Mike Piazza 2.50
253 Vladimir Guerrero 1.50
254 Shawn Green .75
255 Todd Helton .75
256 Ken Griffey Jr. 2.00
257 Torii Hunter .75
258 Chipper Jones 2.00
259 Alfonso Soriano 1.50
260 Luis Gonzalez .75
261 Pedro J. Martinez 1.50
262 Tim Hudson .75
263 Roger Clemens 2.00
264 Greg Maddux 2.00
265 Randy Johnson 1.50
266 Vinnie Chulk .50
267 Jose Castillo 1.50
268 *Craig Brazell* 1.50
269 *Felix Sanchez* .50
270 John Webb .50
271 *Josh Hall* .50
272 Alexis Rios .50
273 *Phil Seibel* .50
274 *Prentice Redman* 1.50
275 Walter Young 1.00
276 Nic Jackson .50
277 Adam Morrissey .50
278 Bobby Jenks .75
279 Rodrigo Rosario .50
280 Chin-Feng Chen 1.00

Gold

Gold (1-240): 2-3X
Gold (241-280): 1-2X
Inserted 1:4 hobby

Platinum

Cards (1-240): 8-15X
Cards (241-280): 3-5X
Production 50 sets

Discs

NM/M
Complete Set (20): 50.00
Common Player: 1.00
Inserted 1:24
1D Derek Jeter 8.00
2D Barry Bonds 8.00
3D Ichiro Suzuki 4.00
4D Sammy Sosa 4.00
5D Nomar Garciaparra 5.00
6D Lance Berkman 1.50
7D Jason Giambi 4.00
8D Mike Piazza 5.00
9D Shawn Green 1.50
10D Barry Zito 1.50
11D Albert Pujols 3.00
12D Alex Rodriguez 6.00
13D Tim Salmon 1.00
14D Eric Chavez 1.00
15D Ken Griffey Jr. 4.00
16D Alfonso Soriano 3.00
17D Vladimir Guerrero 2.50
18D Francisco Rodriguez 1.00
19D Miguel Tejada 1.50
20D Randy Johnson 2.50

On the Ball

NM/M
Complete Set (15): 20.00
Common Player: 1.00
Inserted 1:12
1 Derek Jeter 4.00
2 Barry Bonds 4.00
3 Nomar Garciaparra 2.50
4 Alfonso Soriano 1.50
5 Mike Piazza 2.50
6 Alex Rodriguez 3.00

7 Chipper Jones 2.00
8 Randy Johnson 1.50
9 Pedro J. Martinez 1.50
10 Albert Pujols 1.50
11 Vladimir Guerrero 1.50
12 Sammy Sosa 2.00
13 Ichiro Suzuki 2.00
14 Troy Glaus 1.00
15 Jason Giambi 2.00

On the Ball Memorabilia

NM/M

Common Player: 5.00
Inserted 1:18
Derek Jeter/bat 15.00
Barry Bonds/jsy 15.00
Nomar Garciaparra/jsy 10.00
Alfonso Soriano/jsy 10.00
Mike Piazza/jsy 10.00
Alex Rodriguez/jsy 10.00
Chipper Jones/bat 8.00
Randy Johnson/jsy 8.00
Pedro J. Martinez/jsy 8.00
Troy Glaus/jsy 5.00

Round Numbers

NM/M

Complete Set (14): 50.00
Common Player: 3.00
Production 1,000 sets
1 Nolan Ryan 10.00
2 Al Kaline 6.00
3 Mike Schmidt 6.00
4 Yogi Berra 4.00
5 Brooks Robinson 4.00
6 Tom Seaver 4.00
7 Willie McCovey 3.00
8 Harmon Killebrew 4.00
9 Richie Ashburn 3.00
10 Lou Brock 3.00
11 Jim Palmer 3.00
12 Willie Stargell 4.00
13 Whitey Ford 4.00
14 Robin Yount 5.00

Round Numbers Memorabilia

NM/M

Inserted 1:288
Al Kaline/jsy 20.00
Mike Schmidt/jsy 15.00
Harmon Killebrew/bat 30.00
Lou Brock/jsy 30.00

Round Trippers

NM/M

Complete Set (20): 15.00
Common Player: .50
Inserted 1:8
1 Alfonso Soriano 1.50
2 Alex Rodriguez 3.00
3 Lance Berkman .75
4 Shawn Green .75
5 Pat Burrell 1.00
6 Andruw Jones .75
7 Garret Anderson .50
8 Miguel Tejada .75
9 Mike Piazza 2.50
10 Eric Chavez .50
11 Rafael Palmeiro .75
12 Chipper Jones 2.00
13 Manny Ramirez 1.00
14 Jeff Bagwell 1.00
15 Torii Hunter .75
16 Nomar Garciaparra 2.50
17 Sammy Sosa 2.00
18 Vladimir Guerrero 1.50
19 Troy Glaus 1.00
20 Jason Giambi 2.00

Round Trippers Rounding First

NM/M

Common Player: 5.00
Quantity produced listed
Rounding Second: No Pricing
Production 10 sets
Rounding Third: No Pricing
Production 3 sets
Alfonso Soriano/jsy/228 10.00
Alex Rodriguez/jsy/536 12.00
Lance Berkman/jsy/557 5.00
Shawn Green/bat/249 5.00
Pat Burrell/bat/502 10.00
Andruw Jones/jsy/569 5.00
Garret Anderson/bat/40 20.00
Miguel Tejada/jsy/524 5.00
Mike Piazza/bat/289 12.00
Eric Chavez/jsy/572 5.00
Rafael Palmeiro/jsy/515 6.00
Chipper Jones/jsy/570 10.00
Manny Ramirez/jsy/530 8.00
Jeff Bagwell/bat/344 6.00
Nomar Garciaparra/bat/529 12.00

Signatures

NM/M

Bonds 600 HR inscription: 1-1.5X
Barry Bonds/255 200.00
Derek Jeter 110.00
Barry Bonds/25

2003 FLEER HOT PROSPECTS

NM/M

Complete Set (120):
Common Player: .25
Common SP (81-120): 5.00
Production 1,250 unless noted
Pack (5): 4.00
Box (15): 50.00
1 Derek Jeter 3.00
2 Ryan Klesko .25
3 Troy Glaus .75
4 Jeff Kent .40
5 Frank Thomas .75
6 Gary Sheffield .50
7 Jim Edmonds .40
8 Pat Burrell .50
9 Jacque Jones .25
10 Jason Jennings .25
11 Pedro J. Martinez 1.00
12 Rafael Palmeiro .50
13 Jason Kendall .25
14 Tom Glavine .40
15 Josh Beckett .25
16 Luis Gonzalez .40
17 Edgar Martinez .25
18 Miguel Tejada .50
19 Fred McGriff .40
20 Adam Dunn .50
21 Lance Berkman .50
22 Maggio Ordonez .40
23 Darin Erstad .40
24 Rich Aurilia .25
25 Mike Piazza 1.50
26 Shawn Green .50
27 Larry Walker .40
28 Manny Ramirez .75
29 Juan Gonzalez .75
30 Eric Chavez .50
31 Torii Hunter .50
32 A.J. Burnett .25
33 Sammy Sosa 1.50
34 Eric Hinske .25
35 Brian Giles .50
36 Mike Sweeney .25
37 Sean Casey .25
38 Chipper Jones 1.50
39 Scott Rolen .75
40 Jason Giambi 1.00
41 Mo Vaughn .25
42 Roy Oswalt .25
43 Paul Konerko .25
44 Tim Salmon .40
45 Edgardo Alfonzo .25
46 Jermaine Dye .25
47 Ben Sheets .25
48 Todd Helton .75
49 Greg Maddux 1.50
50 Albert Pujols 2.00
51 Jim Thome .75
52 Vladimir Guerrero .75
53 Ivan Rodriguez .50
54 Nomar Garciaparra 2.00
55 Alex Rodriguez 2.50
56 Alfonso Soriano 1.50
57 Kazuhisa Ishii .25
58 Austin Kearns .50
59 Curt Schilling .50
60 Bret Boone .40
61 Mark Prior 1.50
62 Garret Anderson .40
63 Barry Bonds 2.50
64 Roger Clemens 2.00
65 Jeff Bagwell .75
66 Omar Vizquel .40
67 Jay Gibbons .25
68 Aubrey Huff .25
69 Bobby Abreu .25
70 Richie Sexson .50
71 Bobby Higginson .25
72 Kerry Wood .50
73 Carlos Delgado .50
74 Sean Burroughs .25
75 Jose Vidro .25
76 Ken Griffey Jr. 1.50
77 Randy Johnson 1.00
78 Ichiro Suzuki 1.50
79 Barry Zito .50
80 Carlos Beltran .25
81 Joe Borchard 5.00
82 Mark Teixeira 5.00
83 *Brandon Webb* 8.00
84 *Shane Victorino/auto/400* 8.00
85 Hee Seop Choi 5.00
86 Hank Blalock 6.00
87 Brett Myers 6.00
88 *Mike Ryan* 5.00
89 Jesse Foppert 8.00
90 Lyle Overbay 6.00
91 *Brian Stokes/auto/400* 10.00
92 *Josh Hall/auto/400* 10.00
93 *Chris Waters/auto/400* 10.00
94 *Lew Ford/auto/400* 25.00
95 *Ian Ferguson/auto/500* 8.00
96 *Josh Willingham* 5.00
97 *Josh Stewart/auto/500* 8.00
98 *Pete LaForest/auto/500* 8.00
99 *J.Contreras/auto/jsy/300* 40.00
100 *Termel Sledge/auto/500* 8.00
101 *Guillermo Quiroz/auto/500* 15.00
102 *Alejandro Machado/auto/500* 8.00
103 *Nook Logan/auto/jsy/400* 10.00
104 *Robby Hammock/auto/jsy/400* 10.00
105 *Hideki Matsui/base* 15.00
106 *Wilfredo Ledezma* 5.00
107 Rocco Baldelli/jsy 8.00
108 *Oscar Villarreal* 5.00
109 *Todd Wellemeyer/auto/400* 8.00
110 *Michael Hessman/auto/400* 8.00
111 Jeremy Bonderman/auto/jsy/400 20.00
112 *Craig Brazell/auto/jsy/400* 10.00
113 *Francisco Rosario/auto/jsy/400* 10.00
114 *Jeff Duncan/auto/jsy/400* 10.00
115 *Daniel Cabrera/auto/jsy/400* 25.00
116 Dontrelle Willis/auto/jsy/400 40.00
117 *Cory Stewart/auto/500* 10.00
118 *Tim Olson/auto/jsy/400* 10.00
119 *Chien-Ming Wang/auto/jsy/500* 120.00

Class Of...

NM/M

Common Duo: 10.00
Inserted 1:15
Barry Zito, Josh Beckett 10.00
Pat Burrell, J.D. Drew 12.00
Mark Prior, Mark Teixeira 25.00
Austin Kearns, Sean Burroughs 10.00
Troy Glaus, Lance Berkman 10.00
Darin Erstad, Todd Helton 10.00
Manny Ramirez, Shawn Green 10.00
Matt Morris, Kerry Wood 10.00
Nomar Garciaparra, Paul Konerko 15.00
Alex Rodriguez, Torii Hunter 20.00

Cream of the Crop

NM/M

Complete Set (15): 35.00
Common Player: 1.50
Inserted 1:5
1 Barry Bonds 5.00
2 Derek Jeter 5.00
3 Ichiro Suzuki 3.00
4 Nomar Garciaparra 3.00
5 Roger Clemens 3.00
6 Alex Rodriguez 4.00
7 Greg Maddux 2.50
8 Mike Piazza 2.50

9 Sammy Sosa 2.50
10 Jason Giambi 2.00
11 Hideki Matsui 6.00
12 Albert Pujols 4.00
13 Vladimir Guerrero 1.50
14 Jim Thome 1.50
15 Pedro J. Martinez 1.50

Hot Triple Patch

NM/M

Production 50 sets
Some not priced yet
Derek Jeter, Nomar Garciaparra, Alex Rodriguez 125.00
Torii Hunter, Sammy Sosa, Vladimir Guerrero
Mark Prior, Josh Beckett, Greg Maddux 125.00
Rafael Palmeiro, Hee Seop Choi, Mark Teixeira
Mike Piazza, Pat Burrell, Jim Thome 50.00
Lance Berkman, Troy Glaus, Chipper Jones 50.00
Jason Giambi, Miguel Tejada, Adam Dunn
Randy Johnson, Alfonso Soriano, Shawn Green 50.00
Derek Jeter, Torii Hunter, Mark Prior 100.00
Nomar Garciaparra, Sammy Sosa, Mike Piazza 90.00
Pat Burrell, Jim Thome, Lance Berkman 40.00
Vladimir Guerrero, Troy Glaus, Chipper Jones 60.00
Jason Giambi, Alex Rodriguez, Miguel Tejada
Adam Dunn, Randy Johnson, Josh Beckett
Alfonso Soriano, Greg Maddux, Shawn Green 60.00

Hot Materials

NM/M

Common Player: 5.00
Production 499 sets
Red-Hots: 1-2X
Production 50
1HM Derek Jeter 20.00
2HM Torii Hunter 8.00
3HM Mark Prior 15.00
4HM Nomar Garciaparra 15.00
5HM Sammy Sosa 15.00
6HM Rafael Palmeiro 6.00
7HM Hee Seop Choi 10.00
8HM Mark Teixeira 5.00
9HM Mike Piazza 10.00
10HM Pat Burrell 8.00
11HM Jim Thome 8.00
12HM Lance Berkman 5.00
13HM Vladimir Guerrero 6.00
14HM Troy Glaus 5.00
15HM Chipper Jones 8.00
16HM Lyle Overbay 5.00
17HM Jason Giambi 8.00
18HM Alex Rodriguez 10.00
19HM Miguel Tejada 5.00
20HM Adam Dunn 6.00
21HM Randy Johnson 8.00
22HM Josh Beckett 5.00
23HM Alfonso Soriano 10.00
24HM Greg Maddux 10.00
25HM Shawn Green 5.00
26HM Carlos Delgado 5.00
27HM Todd Helton 6.00
28HM Mike Sweeney 5.00
29HM Manny Ramirez 6.00
30HM Tom Glavine 5.00

Hot Tandems

NM/M

Common Duo: 8.00

Production 100 sets
Red-Hots numbered to 10
Derek Jeter, Chipper Jones 25.00
Derek Jeter, Mike Piazza 25.00
Derek Jeter, Miguel Tejada 25.00
Torii Hunter, Lance Berkman 10.00
Mark Prior, Sammy Sosa 30.00
Sammy Sosa, Pat Burrell 20.00
Rafael Palmeiro, Mark Teixeira 10.00
Hee Seop Choi, Lyle Overbay 15.00
Alex Rodriguez, Mark Teixeira 20.00
Mike Piazza, Chipper Jones 15.00
Pat Burrell, Jim Thome 10.00
Lance Berkman, Adam Dunn 8.00
Nomar Garciaparra, Miguel Tejada 15.00
Randy Johnson, Greg Maddux 12.00
Mark Prior, Josh Beckett 15.00
Miguel Tejada, Alex Rodriguez 15.00
Jason Giambi, Jim Thome 10.00

Playergraphs

NM/M

Common Player: 10.00
Production 400 sets
Red-Hots: 1-1.5X
Production 100
Hank Blalock 20.00
Brett Myers 10.00
Mark Prior 50.00
Carlos Zambrano 20.00
Mark Teixeira 20.00
Francisco Rodriguez 10.00
Roy Oswalt 15.00
Xavier Nady 10.00
Jose Reyes 25.00
Aubrey Huff 10.00

2003 FLEER MYSTIQUE

NM/M

Complete Set (130):
Common Player: .25
Common SP (81-130): 3.00
Production 699
Pack (4): 3.00
Box (20): 40.00
1 Alex Rodriguez 2.50
2 Derek Jeter 3.00
3 Jose Vidro .25
4 Miguel Tejada .40
5 Albert Pujols 2.50
6 Rocco Baldelli .25
7 Jose Reyes .50
8 Hideo Nomo .75
9 Hank Blalock .75
10 Chipper Jones 1.50
11 Barry Larkin .25
12 Alfonso Soriano 1.00
13 Aramis Ramirez .25
14 Darin Erstad .65
15 Jim Edmonds .25
16 Garret Anderson .25
17 Todd Helton 1.00
18 Jason Kendall .25
19 Aubrey Huff .25
20 Troy Glaus .75
21 Sammy Sosa 2.00
22 Roger Clemens 1.75
23 Mark Teixeira .50
24 Barry Bonds 3.00
25 Jim Thome .25
26 Carlos Delgado .50
27 Vladimir Guerrero 1.00
28 Austin Kearns .50
29 Pat Burrell .75
30 Ken Griffey Jr. 2.00
31 Greg Maddux 1.50
32 Corey Patterson .25
33 Larry Walker .25
34 Kerry Wood .65
35 Frank Thomas 1.00
36 Dontrelle Willis .25
37 Randy Johnson 1.00
38 Curt Schilling .40
39 Jay Gibbons .25
40 Dmitri Young .25
41 Edgar Martinez .25
42 Kevin Brown .25
43 Scott Rolen 1.00
44 Adam Dunn .75
45 Pedro J. Martinez 1.00
46 Corey Koskie .25
47 Tom Glavine .40
48 Torii Hunter .25
49 Shawn Green .40
50 Nomar Garciaparra 2.00
51 Bernie Williams .40
52 Milton Bradley .25
53 Jason Giambi .75
54 Mike Lieberthal .25
55 Jeff Bagwell 1.00
56 Carlos Pena .25
57 Lance Berkman .25
58 Jose Cruz Jr. .25
59 Josh Beckett .25
60 Mark Mulder .40
61 Mike Piazza 2.00
62 Mark Prior 1.00
63 Sean Burroughs .25
64 Angel Berroa .25
65 Geoff Jenkins .25
66 Magglio Ordonez .25
67 Craig Biggio .25
68 Roberto Alomar .40
69 Hee Seop Choi .25
70 J.D. Drew .25
71 Richie Sexson .25
72 Brian Giles .25
73 Gary Sheffield .50
74 Manny Ramirez 1.00
75 Barry Zito .45
76 Andruw Jones 1.00
77 Ivan Rodriguez .65
78 Ichiro Suzuki 2.00
79 Mike Sweeney .25
80 Vernon Wells .25
81 *Craig Brazell* 5.00
82 *Wilfredo Ledezma* 3.00
83 *Josh Willingham* 6.00
84 *Chien-Ming Wang* 8.00
85 *Mike Ryan* 3.00
86 *Mike Gallo* 3.00
87 *Rickie Weeks* 15.00
88 *Brian Stokes* 3.00
89 *Humberto Quintero* 3.00
90 *Ramon Nivar* 3.00
91 Jeremy Griffiths 3.00
92 *Terrmel Sledge* 4.00
93 *Brandon Webb* 6.00
94 *David DeJesus* 5.00
95 *Doug Waechter* 3.00
96 Jeremy Bonderman 6.00
97 *Felix Sanchez* 3.00
98 *Colin Porter* 3.00
99 *Francisco Cruceta* 3.00
100 *Hideki Matsui* 15.00
101 *Chris Waters* 6.00
102 Dan Haren 5.00
103 *Lew Ford* 6.00
104 *Oscar Villarreal* 3.00
105 *Ryan Wagner* 6.00
106 *Prentice Redman* 3.00
107 *Josh Stewart* 6.00
108 *Carlos Mendez* 3.00
109 *Michael Hessman* 6.00
110 *Josh Hall* 6.00
111 *Daniel Garcia* 6.00
112 *Matt Kata* 6.00
113 *Michel Hernandez* 3.00
114 *Sergio Mitre* 6.00
115 *Pete LaForest* 6.00
116 *Edwin Jackson* 10.00
117 *Matt Diaz* 6.00
118 *Greg Aquino* 3.00
119 *Jose Contreras* 8.00
120 *Jeff Duncan* 6.00
121 *Richard Fischer* 3.00
122 *Todd Wellemeyer* 6.00
123 *Robby Hammock* 6.00
124 *Delmon Young* 15.00
125 *Clint Barmes* 8.00
126 *Phil Seibel* 3.00
127 *Bo Hart* 6.00
128 *Jon Leicester* 6.00
129 *Chad Gaudin* 6.00
130 *Guillermo Quiroz* 6.00

Gold

Stars (1-80): 4-8X
Production 150
SP's (81-130): 1-2X
Production 50

Awe Pairs

NM/M

Complete Set (20): 60.00
Common Duo: 2.00
Production 250 sets
Golds: 1.5X
#'d to team win total for 2003
1 Nomar Garciaparra, Pedro J. Martinez 8.00
2 Derek Jeter, Alfonso Soriano 8.00
3 Rocco Baldelli, Aubrey Huff 2.00
4 Carlos Delgado, Vernon Wells 2.00
5 Troy Glaus, Garret Anderson 2.00
6 Ichiro Suzuki, Bret Boone 5.00
7 Alex Rodriguez, Hank Blalock 8.00
8 Chipper Jones, Andruw Jones 5.00
9 Dontrelle Willis, Mike Lowell 3.00
10 Vladimir Guerrero, Orlando Cabrera 4.00
11 Tom Glavine, Mike Piazza 5.00
12 Jim Thome, Mike Lieberthal 3.00
13 Sammy Sosa, Corey Patterson 6.00
14 Jeff Bagwell, Lance Berkman 3.00
15 Geoff Jenkins, Richie Sexson 2.00
16 Albert Pujols, Jim Edmonds 6.00

17 Todd Helton, Larry Walker 3.00
18 Paul LoDuca, Shawn Green 2.00
19 Ryan Klesko, Sean Burroughs 2.00
20 Barry Bonds, Rich Aurilia 8.00

Awe Pairs Game-Used

NM/M
Common Duo: 10.00
Production 100 sets
Golds: No Pricing
Production 10 sets
Nomar Garciaparra, Pedro J. Martinez 25.00
Derek Jeter, Alfonso Soriano 30.00
Rocco Baldelli, Aubrey Huff 15.00
Carlos Delgado, Vernon Wells 10.00
Troy Glaus, Garret Anderson 10.00
Alex Rodriguez, Hank Blalock
Chipper Jones, Andruw Jones 15.00
Dontrelle Willis, Mike Lowell 25.00
Vladimir Guerrero, Orlando Cabrera 10.00
Tom Glavine, Mike Piazza 20.00
Jim Thome, Mike Lieberthal 15.00
Sammy Sosa, Corey Patterson 20.00
Jeff Bagwell, Lance Berkman 15.00
Geoff Jenkins, Richie Sexson 10.00
Albert Pujols, Jim Edmonds 20.00
Todd Helton, Larry Walker 10.00
Paul LoDuca, Shawn Green 10.00
Ryan Klesko, Sean Burroughs 10.00

Diamond Dominators

NM/M
Complete Set (10): 50.00
Common Player: 3.00
Production 100 sets
1 Mike Piazza 8.00
2 Greg Maddux 8.00
3 Alfonso Soriano 5.00
4 Barry Zito 3.00
5 Alex Rodriguez 10.00
6 Roger Clemens 10.00
7 Sammy Sosa 10.00
8 Adam Dunn 3.00
9 Randy Johnson 5.00
10 Pedro J. Martinez 5.00

Diamond Dominators Game-Used

NM/M
Common Player: 6.00
Production 75 sets
Golds: No Pricing
Production 10 sets
RC Roger Clemens 20.00
AD Adam Dunn 6.00
RJ Randy Johnson 10.00
GM Greg Maddux 25.00
PM Pedro Martinez 12.00
MP Mike Piazza 15.00
AR Alex Rodriguez 15.00
AS Alfonso Soriano 12.00
SS Sammy Sosa 20.00
BZ Barry Zito 8.00

Diamond Dominators Gold

NM/M
Some not priced due to scarcity
Numbered to jersey number
1DD Mike Piazza/31 25.00
2DD Greg Maddux/31 25.00
3DD Alfonso Soriano/12
4DD Barry Zito/75 5.00
5DD Alex Rodriguez/3
6DD Roger Clemens/22
7DD Sammy Sosa/21
8DD Adam Dunn/44 6.00
9DD Randy Johnson/51 8.00
10DD Pedro Martinez/45 10.00

Ink Appeal Autographs

NM/M
Common Player: 15.00
Production 50 sets
RB Rocco Baldelli 40.00
HB Hank Blalock 35.00
BH Bo Hart 25.00
AH Aubrey Huff 15.00
TH Torii Hunter 20.00
CP Corey Patterson 15.00
JR Jose Reyes 25.00
MR Mike Ryan 15.00
JW Josh Willingham 15.00

Ink Appeal Gold Autographs

NM/M
Numbered to Jersey number
Some not priced due to scarcity
RB Rocco Baldelli/5
HB Hank Blalock/9
BH Bo Hart/31 50.00
AH Aubrey Huff/19
TH Torii Hunter/48 20.00
CP Corey Patterson/20
JR Jose Reyes/7
MR Mike Ryan/54 15.00
RW Rickie Weeks/2
JW Josh Willingham/70 12.00
DW Dontrelle Willis/35

Ink Appeal Dual Autographs

NM/M
No pricing due to scarcity
Production 20 sets
Golds: No Pricing
Production 5 sets

Rare Finds Single Swatch

NM/M
Common Player: 6.00
Production 150 sets
Golds: No Pricing
Production 15 sets
JG Jason Giambi, Roger Clemens, Derek Jeter 10.00
RC Jason Giambi, Roger Clemens, Derek Jeter 15.00
DJ Jason Giambi, Roger Clemens, Derek Jeter 20.00
RJ Randy Johnson, Curt Schilling, Brandon Webb 8.00
BW Randy Johnson, Curt Schilling, Brandon Webb 10.00
NG Nomar Garciaparra, Pedro J. Martinez, Manny Ramirez 15.00
PM Nomar Garciaparra, Pedro J. Martinez, Manny Ramirez 8.00
MP Mark Prior, Kerry Wood, Sammy Sosa 15.00
SS Mark Prior, Kerry Wood, Sammy Sosa 12.00
JB Jeff Bagwell, Craig Biggio, Lance Berkman 6.00
AK Austin Kearns, Adam Dunn, Barry Larkin 6.00
BL Austin Kearns, Adam Dunn, Barry Larkin 6.00
SR Jim Edmonds, Scott Rolen, J.D. Drew 10.00
JD Jim Edmonds, Scott Rolen, J.D. Drew 6.00
CJ Chipper Jones, Andruw Jones, Greg Maddux 10.00
GM Chipper Jones, Andruw Jones, Greg Maddux 15.00
MT Barry Zito, Miguel Tejada, Mark Mulder 6.00
MM Barry Zito, Miguel Tejada, Mark Mulder 6.00
AR Alex Rodriguez, Mark Teixeira, Rafael Palmeiro 15.00
MT Alex Rodriguez, Mark Teixeira, Rafael Palmeiro 8.00

Rare Finds Dual Swatch

NM/M
Common Dual: 10.00
Production 75 sets
Golds: No Pricing
Production 10 sets
Jason Giambi, Roger Clemens, Derek Jeter 35.00
Jason Giambi, Roger Clemens, Derek Jeter 40.00
Randy Johnson, Curt Schilling, Brandon Webb 15.00
Randy Johnson, Curt Schilling, Brandon Webb 10.00
Nomar Garciaparra, Pedro J. Martinez, Manny Ramirez 20.00
Nomar Garciaparra, Pedro J. Martinez, Manny Ramirez 15.00
Mark Prior, Kerry Wood, Sammy Sosa 25.00
Mark Prior, Kerry Wood, Sammy Sosa 30.00
Jeff Bagwell, Craig Biggio, Lance Berkman 10.00
Austin Kearns, Adam Dunn, Barry Larkin 10.00
Jim Edmonds, Scott Rolen, J.D. Drew 15.00
Chipper Jones, Andruw Jones, Greg Maddux 20.00
Chipper Jones, Andruw Jones, Greg Maddux 20.00
Barry Zito, Miguel Tejada, Mark Mulder 10.00
Alex Rodriguez, Mark Teixeira, Rafael Palmeiro 20.00

Rare Finds Triple Swatch

NM/M
Production 50 sets
Golds: No Pricing
Production 5 sets
Jason Giambi, Roger Clemens, Derek Jeter 50.00
Randy Johnson, Curt Schilling, Brandon Webb 25.00
Nomar Garciaparra, Pedro J. Martinez, Manny Ramirez 60.00
Mark Prior, Kerry Wood, Sammy Sosa 50.00
Jeff Bagwell, Craig Biggio, Lance Berkman 20.00
Austin Kearns, Adam Dunn, Barry Larkin 20.00
Jim Edmonds, Scott Rolen, J.D. Drew 25.00
Chipper Jones, Andruw Jones, Greg Maddux 40.00
Barry Zito, Miguel Tejada, Mark Mulder 15.00
Alex Rodriguez, Mark Teixeira, Rafael Palmeiro 40.00

Secret Weapons

NM/M
Complete Set (10): 25.00
Common Player: 2.00
Production 250 sets
Golds: 1X
#'d to career batting average
1 Hank Blalock 3.00
2 Dontrelle Willis 3.00
3 Jose Reyes 3.00
4 Bo Hart 4.00
5 Corey Patterson 2.00
6 Hideki Matsui 8.00
7 Mark Teixeira 3.00
8 Brandon Webb 3.00
9 Rocco Baldelli 3.00
10 Mark Prior 8.00

Shining Stars

NM/M
Complete Set (15): 50.00
Common Player: 2.00
Production 300 sets
1SS Derek Jeter 8.00
2SS Barry Bonds 8.00
3SS Nomar Garciaparra 6.00
4SS Austin Kearns 2.00
5SS Vladimir Guerrero 3.00
6SS Jim Thome 3.00
7SS Ichiro Suzuki 5.00
8SS Jason Giambi 3.00
9SS Albert Pujols 6.00
10SS Ken Griffey Jr. 5.00
11SS Chipper Jones 5.00
12SS Scott Rolen 3.00
13SS Manny Ramirez 3.00
14SS Jeff Bagwell 3.00
15SS Torii Hunter 2.00

Shining Stars Game-Used

NM/M
Common Player: 6.00
Production 100 sets
Patch: 1.5X
Production 50 sets
JB Jeff Bagwell 8.00
CD Carlos Delgado 6.00
NG Nomar Garciaparra 15.00
JG Jason Giambi 8.00
VG Vladimir Guerrero
TH Todd Helton 8.00
TH Torii Hunter 8.00
DJ Derek Jeter 20.00
AJ Andruw Jones 6.00
CJ Chipper Jones 10.00
AK Austin Kearns 6.00
AP Albert Pujols 15.00
MR Manny Ramirez 8.00
SR Scott Rolen 10.00
JT Jim Thome 8.00

Shining Stars Gold

NM/M
Numbered to career HR total
1SS Derek Jeter/127 10.00
2SS Barry Bonds/658 5.00
3SS Nomar Garciaparra/173 10.00
4SS Austin Kearns/28 10.00
5SS Vladimir Guerrero/234 4.00
6SS Jim Thome/381 3.00
7SS Ichiro Suzuki/29 30.00
8SS Jason Giambi/269 3.00
9SS Albert Pujols/114 8.00
10SS Ken Griffey Jr./481 4.00
11SS Chipper Jones/280 5.00
12SS Scott Rolen/192 4.00
13SS Manny Ramirez/347 3.00
14SS Jeff Bagwell/419 3.00
15SS Torii Hunter/96 4.00

2003 FLEER PATCHWORKS

NM/M
Complete Set (115):

Common Player: .15
Common Prospect (91-115): 3.00
Production 1,500
Pack (5): 3.00
Box (24): 60.00
1 Luis Castillo .15
2 Derek Jeter 2.00
3 Vladimir Guerrero .75
4 Bobby Higginson .15
5 Pat Burrell .40
6 Ivan Rodriguez .60
7 Craig Biggio .15
8 Troy Glaus .60
9 Barry Bonds 2.00
10 Hideo Nomo .60
11 Barry Larkin .15
12 Roberto Alomar .35
13 Rodrigo Lopez .15
14 Eric Chavez .25
15 Shawn Green .25
16 Joe Randa .15
17 Mark Grace .25
18 Jason Kendall .15
19 Hee Seop Choi .15
20 Luis Gonzalez .25
21 Sammy Sosa 1.25
22 Larry Walker .15
23 Phil Nevin .15
24 Manny Ramirez .75
25 Jim Thome .15
26 Randy Johnson .75
27 Jose Vidro .15
28 Austin Kearns .35
29 Mike Sweeney .15
30 Magglio Ordonez .15
31 Mike Piazza 1.25
32 Eric Hinske .15
33 Alex Rodriguez 1.50
34 Kerry Wood .60
35 Matt Morris .15
36 Lance Berkman .15
37 Michael Cuddyer .15
38 Curt Schilling .40
39 Sean Burroughs .15
40 Ken Griffey Jr. 1.25
41 Edgardo Alfonzo .15
42 Carlos Pena .15
43 Adam Dunn .50
44 Pedro J. Martinez .75
45 Miguel Tejada .35
46 Tom Glavine .35
47 Torii Hunter .15
48 Jason Giambi .50
49 Tony Batista .15
50 Ben Grieve .15
51 Ichiro Suzuki 1.25
52 Bobby Abreu .15
53 Todd Helton .75
54 Kazuhiro Sasaki .15
55 Nomar Garciaparra 1.25
56 Francisco Rodriguez .15
57 Ellis Burks .15
58 Frank Thomas .75
59 Greg Maddux 1.00
60 Josh Beckett .25
61 Brad Wilkerson .15
62 Joe Borchard .15
63 Carlos Delgado .40
64 Alfonso Soriano .75
65 Chipper Jones 1.00
66 J.D. Drew .25
67 Mark Prior .75
68 Rafael Palmeiro .60
69 Jeff Kent .15
70 Adrian Beltre .25
71 Marlon Byrd .15
72 Orlando Hudson .15
73 Junior Spivey .15
74 Jeff Bagwell .75
75 Barry Zito .35
76 Roger Clemens 1.00
77 Aubrey Huff .15
78 Geoff Jenkins .15
79 Andruw Jones .75
80 Scott Rolen .75
81 Omar Vizquel .15
82 Darin Erstad .50
83 Bernie Williams .35
84 Freddy Garcia .15
85 Richie Sexson .15
86 Josh Phelps .15
87 Albert Pujols 1.50
88 Aramis Ramirez .15
89 Shea Hillenbrand .15
90 Cristian Guzman .15
91 Adam LaRoche 3.00
92 *David Pember* 3.00
93 *Termel Sledge* 3.00
94 *Hideki Matsui* 10.00
95 *Nook Logan* 4.00
96 *Jose Contreras* 4.00
97 *Pete LaForest* 3.00
98 *Richard Fischer* 3.00
99 *Francisco Rosario* 3.00
100 *Josh Willingham* 4.00
101 *Alejandro Machado* 3.00
102 *Lew Ford* 4.00
103 *Joe Valentine* 3.00
104 *Guillermo Quiroz* 4.00
105 *Chien-Ming Wang* 4.00
106 Jhonny Peralta 4.00
107 *Shane Victorino* 3.00
108 *Prentice Redman* 3.00
109 *Matt Bruback* 3.00
110 Lance Niekro 3.00
111 Travis Hughes 3.00
112 Nic Jackson 3.00
113 *Hector Luna* 4.00
114 Cliff Lee 3.00
115 *Tim Olson* 4.00

Star Ruby

Stars (1-90): 4-8X
Prospects (91-115): 1-3X
Production 100 sets

Diamond Ink

NM/M
Quantity Signed Listed
Derek Jeter/210 90.00
Derek Jeter/101 125.00
Derek Jeter/50 175.00
Mark Prior/88 75.00
Troy Glaus/351 25.00
Mike Schmidt/194 75.00

Licensed Apparel - jersey

NM/M
Common Player: 4.00
Production 500 sets
J.D. Drew 8.00
Magglio Ordonez 6.00
Todd Helton 8.00
Paul Konerko 4.00
Shawn Green 6.00
Carlos Beltran 4.00
Kevin Brown 4.00
Shannon Stewart 4.00
Mike Mussina 8.00
Adam Dunn 10.00
Jimmy Rollins 4.00
Darin Erstad 6.00
Chipper Jones 10.00
Mike Piazza 10.00
Derek Jeter 20.00

Licensed Apparel - patch

NM/M
Common Player: 10.00
Production 300 sets
J.D. Drew 12.00
Magglio Ordonez 15.00
Todd Helton 20.00
Paul Konerko 10.00
Shawn Green 15.00
Carlos Beltran 10.00
Kevin Brown 10.00
Shannon Stewart 10.00
Mike Mussina 15.00
Adam Dunn 20.00
Jimmy Rollins 15.00
Darin Erstad 25.00
Chipper Jones 20.00
Mike Piazza 25.00
Derek Jeter 40.00

National Pastime

NM/M
Complete Set (25): 40.00
Common Player: 1.00

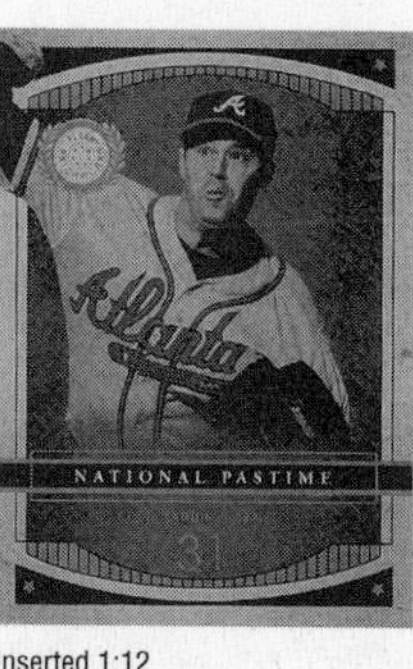

Inserted 1:12
1NP Barry Bonds 6.00
2NP Kazuhiro Sasaki 1.00
3NP Mike Piazza 4.00
4NP Barry Zito 1.50
5NP Sammy Sosa 3.00
6NP Pedro J. Martinez 2.00
7NP Craig Biggio 1.00
8NP Rafael Palmeiro 1.50
9NP Greg Maddux 3.00
10NP Manny Ramirez 2.00
11NP Adam Dunn 1.50
12NP Omar Vizquel 1.00
13NP Hideo Nomo 1.00
14NP Alex Rodriguez 5.00
15NP Pat Burrell 1.00
16NP Nomar Garciaparra 4.00
17NP Randy Johnson 2.00
18NP Juan Gonzalez 1.50
19NP Chipper Jones 3.00
20NP Frank Thomas 1.50
21NP Vladimir Guerrero 2.00
22NP Troy Glaus 2.00
23NP Albert Pujols 3.00
24NP Ichiro Suzuki 3.00
25NP Ken Griffey Jr. 3.00

National Patchtime - trim

NM/M
Common Player: 12.00
Production 200 sets
Vladimir Guerrero 12.00
Manny Ramirez 15.00
Rafael Palmeiro 12.00
Nomar Garciaparra 25.00
Greg Maddux 20.00
Mike Piazza 20.00
Pedro J. Martinez 20.00
Hideo Nomo 20.00
Alex Rodriguez 25.00
Chipper Jones 20.00
Frank Thomas 20.00

National Patchtime - team name

NM/M
Common Player: 15.00
Production 100 sets
Vladimir Guerrero 15.00
Rafael Palmeiro 20.00
Nomar Garciaparra 35.00
Sammy Sosa 40.00
Mike Piazza 30.00
Barry Zito 20.00
Hideo Nomo 30.00
Alex Rodriguez 30.00
Pat Burrell 20.00
Randy Johnson 45.00
Chipper Jones 35.00
Troy Glaus 30.00
Omar Vizquel 20.00

National Patchtime - number

NM/M
Common Player: 15.00
Production 75 sets
Vladimir Guerrero 20.00
Manny Ramirez 25.00
Craig Biggio 15.00
Rafael Palmeiro 20.00
Nomar Garciaparra 40.00
Greg Maddux 25.00
Sammy Sosa 45.00
Mike Piazza 30.00
Pedro J. Martinez 25.00
Hideo Nomo 25.00
Alex Rodriguez 30.00
Pat Burrell 20.00
Randy Johnson 45.00
Juan Gonzalez
Chipper Jones 35.00
Frank Thomas 30.00
Troy Glaus
Omar Vizquel

National Patchtime - nameplate

NM/M
Production 50 sets
Vladimir Guerrero 40.00
Rafael Palmeiro 25.00
Nomar Garciaparra 40.00
Greg Maddux 30.00
Sammy Sosa 60.00
Mike Piazza 35.00
Barry Zito 40.00
Hideo Nomo 50.00
Alex Rodriguez 50.00
Pat Burrell 25.00
Randy Johnson 50.00
Chipper Jones 35.00
Frank Thomas 40.00
Troy Glaus 30.00
Omar Vizquel

National Pastime - MLB logo

Production One Set

Numbers Game

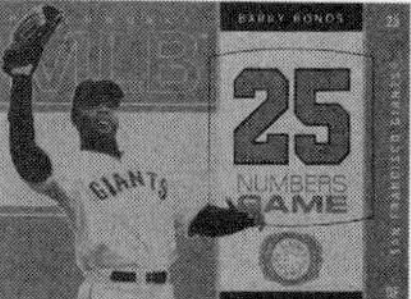

NM/M
Complete Set (15): 30.00
Common Player: 1.00
Inserted 1:24
1 Ichiro Suzuki 3.00
2 Derek Jeter 6.00
3 Alex Rodriguez 5.00
4 Miguel Tejada 1.00
5 Nomar Garciaparra 4.00
6 Jason Giambi 3.00
7 J.D. Drew 1.00
8 Barry Bonds 6.00
9 Alfonso Soriano 2.00
10 Jeff Bagwell 1.50
11 Barry Larkin 1.00
12 Roberto Alomar 1.00
13 Larry Walker 1.00
14 Roger Clemens 3.00
15 Ken Griffey Jr. 3.00

Numbers Game - jersey

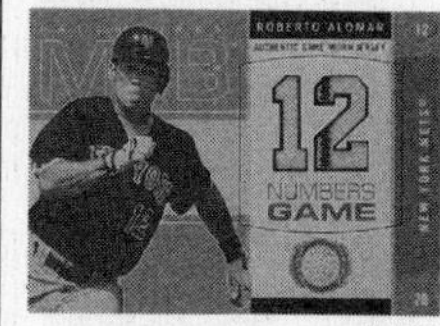

NM/M
Common Player: 4.00
Inserted 1:25
Barry Larkin 6.00
Roberto Alomar 4.00
Jeff Bagwell 8.00
Jason Giambi 8.00
Larry Walker 4.00
Derek Jeter 15.00
Alex Rodriguez 10.00
Alfonso Soriano 10.00
Roger Clemens 12.00
Miguel Tejada 4.00

Numbers Game - patch

NM/M
Common Player: 10.00
Production 300 sets
Barry Larkin 15.00
Roberto Alomar 15.00
Jeff Bagwell 25.00
Jason Giambi 15.00
Larry Walker 10.00
Derek Jeter 40.00
Alex Rodriguez 25.00
Alfonso Soriano 25.00

Roger Clemens 30.00
Miguel Tejada 10.00

Past, Present, Future

NM/M
Complete Set (10): 40.00
Common Card: 4.00
Inserted 1:72
1 Eddie Mathews, Rafael Palmeiro, Alex Rodriguez 5.00
2 Phil Rizzuto, Derek Jeter, Alfonso Soriano 5.00
3 Reggie Jackson, Barry Bonds, Sammy Sosa 6.00
4 Billy Williams, Sammy Sosa, Hee Seop Choi 4.00
5 Joe Morgan, Roberto Alomar, Alfonso Soriano 3.00
6 Yogi Berra, Mike Piazza, Josh Phelps 4.00
7 Nolan Ryan, Roger Clemens, Kerry Wood 6.00
8 Mike Schmidt, Scott Rolen, Eric Hinske 4.00
9 Barry Bonds, Alex Rodriguez, Alfonso Soriano 5.00
10 Yogi Berra, Derek Jeter, Hideki Matsui 6.00

Patch, Present, Future single

NM/M
Common Player: 10.00
Production 200 sets
Rafael Palmeiro 15.00
Alex Rodriguez 20.00
Derek Jeter 50.00
Alfonso Soriano 50.00
Barry Bonds 50.00
Sammy Sosa 25.00
Sammy Sosa 25.00
Roberto Alomar 25.00
Alfonso Soriano 50.00
Mike Piazza 25.00
Roger Clemens 40.00
Kerry Wood 40.00
Scott Rolen
Eric Hinske 10.00
Alex Rodriguez 20.00
Alfonso Soriano 50.00
Derek Jeter 50.00

Patch, Present, Future dual

Production 100 sets
Rafael Palmeiro, Alex Rodriguez
Derek Jeter, Alfonso Soriano
Sammy Sosa, Hee Seop Choi
Roberto Alomar, Alfonso Soriano
Mike Piazza, Josh Phelps
Roger Clemens, Kerry Wood
Scott Rolen, Eric Hinske
Alex Rodriguez, Alfonso Soriano

Patchworks

NM/M
Common Player: 8.00
Production 250 sets
2 Frank Thomas 12.00
8 Lance Berkman 15.00
9 Kazuhiro Sasaki 15.00
10 Roy Oswalt 15.00
11 Bernie Williams 15.00
12PW Bob Abreu 15.00
14PW Greg Maddux 20.00
15PW Josh Beckett 8.00
16PW Mark Grace 20.00
17PW Eric Chavez 10.00
18PW Andruw Jones 15.00
19PW Adrian Beltre 8.00

Patchworks - dual color

NM/M
Common Player: 10.00
Production 100 sets
Alex Rodriguez 35.00
Frank Thomas 20.00
Vladimir Guerrero 20.00
Roberto Alomar 20.00
Kerry Wood 35.00
Curt Schilling 15.00
Lance Berkman 20.00
Kazuhiro Sasaki 35.00
Roy Oswalt 20.00
Bernie Williams 25.00
Bob Abreu 10.00
Carlos Delgado 12.00
Greg Maddux 25.00
Josh Beckett 10.00
Mark Grace 15.00
Eric Chavez 15.00
Andruw Jones 15.00
Adrian Beltre 10.00

Patchworks - multi-color

NM/M
Common Player: 20.00
Production 50 sets
Alex Rodriguez 60.00
Frank Thomas 30.00
Vladimir Guerrero 35.00
Roberto Alomar 35.00
Kerry Wood 40.00
Curt Schilling 20.00
Lance Berkman 25.00
Kazuhiro Sasaki 50.00
Roy Oswalt 40.00
Bernie Williams 35.00
Bob Abreu 25.00
Carlos Delgado 20.00
Greg Maddux 35.00
Josh Beckett 20.00
Mark Grace 30.00
Eric Chavez 30.00
Andruw Jones 30.00
Adrian Beltre 20.00

2003 FLEER PLATINUM

NM/M
Complete Set (250): 40.00
Common Player: .15
Common SP (221-250): .50
Hobby Pack (10): 1.50
Hobby Box (14 + 4 jumbo + 1 Rack): 35.00
Jumbo Pack: 3.00
Rack Pack: 5.00
1 Barry Bonds 2.50
2 Sean Casey .25
3 Todd Walker .15
4 Tony Batista .15
5 Todd Zeile .15
6 Ruben Sierra .15
7 Jose Cruz Jr. .15
8 Ben Grieve .15
9 Robert Mackowiak .15
10 Gary Sheffield .25
11 Armando Benitez .15
12 Tim Hudson .25
13 Eric Milton .15
14 Andy Pettitte .40
15 Jeff Bagwell .75
16 Jeff Kent .15
17 Joe Randa .15
18 Benito Santiago .15
19 Russell Branyan .15
20 Cliff Floyd .15
21 Chris Richard .15
22 Randy Winn .15
23 Freddy Garcia .15
24 Derek Lowe .15
25 Ben Sheets .15
26 Fred McGriff .15
27 Bret Boone .15
28 Jose Hernandez .15
29 Phil Nevin .15
30 Mike Piazza 1.50
31 Bobby Abreu .15
32 Darin Erstad .50
33 Andruw Jones .75
34 Brad Wilkerson .15
35 Brian Lawrence .15
36 Vladimir Nunez .15
37 Kazuhiro Sasaki .15
38 Carlos Delgado .45
39 Steve Cox .15
40 Adrian Beltre .25
41 Josh Bard .15
42 Randall Simon .15
43 Johnny Damon .25
44 Ken Griffey Jr. 1.50
45 Sammy Sosa 1.50
46 Kevin Brown .15
47 Kazuhisa Ishii .15
48 Matt Morris .15
49 Mark Prior .75
50 Kip Wells .15
51 Hee Seop Choi .15
52 Craig Biggio .15
53 Derek Jeter 2.50
54 Albert Pujols 1.25
55 Joe Borchard .15
56 Robert Fick .15
57 Jacque Jones .15
58 Juan Pierre .15
59 Bernie Williams .35
60 Elmer Dessens .15
61 Al Leiter .15
62 Curt Schilling .40
63 Carlos Pena .15
64 Tino Martinez .15
65 Fernando Vina .15
66 Aaron Boone .15
67 Michael Barrett .15
68 Frank Thomas .75
69 J.D. Drew .25
70 Vladimir Guerrero .75
71 Shannon Stewart .15
72 Mark Buehrle .15
73 Jamie Moyer .15
74 Brad Radke .15
75 Mike Williams .15
76 Ryan Klesko .15
77 Roberto Alomar .35
78 Edgardo Alfonzo .15
79 Matt Williams .15
80 Edgar Martinez .15
81 Shawn Green .25
82 Kenny Lofton .15
83 Josh Beckett .15
84 Trevor Hoffman .15
85 Kevin Millwood .15
86 Odalis Perez .15
87 Jarrod Washburn .15
88 Jason Giambi .60
89 Eric Young .15
90 Barry Larkin .15
91 Aramis Ramirez .15
92 Ivan Rodriguez .50
93 Steve Finley .15
94 Brian Jordan .15
95 Manny Ramirez .75
96 Preston Wilson .15
97 Rodrigo Lopez .15
98 Ramon Ortiz .15
99 Jim Thome .15
100 Luis Castillo .15
101 Alex Rodriguez 2.00
102 Jared Sandberg .15
103 Ellis Burks .15
104 Pat Burrell .60
105 Brian Giles .15
106 Mark Kotsay .15
107 Dave Roberts .15
108 Roy Halladay .15
109 Chan Ho Park .15
110 Erubiel Durazo .15
111 Bobby Hill .15
112 Cristian Guzman .15
113 Troy Glaus .60
114 Lance Berkman .15
115 Juan Encarnacion .15
116 Chipper Jones 1.00
117 Corey Patterson .15
118 Vernon Wells .15
119 Matt Clement .15
120 Billy Koch .15
121 Hideo Nomo .50
122 Derrek Lee .15
123 Todd Helton .75
124 Sean Burroughs .15
125 Jason Kendall .15
126 Dmitri Young .15
127 Adam Dunn .60
128 Bobby Higginson .15
129 Raul Mondesi .15
130 Bubba Trammell .15
131 A.J. Burnett .15
132 Randy Johnson .75
133 Mark Mulder .15
134 Mariano Rivera .25
135 Kerry Wood .50
136 Mo Vaughn .15
137 Jimmy Rollins .15
138 Jose Valentin .15
139 Brad Fullmer .15
140 Mike Cameron .15
141 Luis Gonzalez .25
142 Kevin Appier .15
143 Mike Hampton .15
144 Pedro J. Martinez .75
145 Javier Vazquez .15
146 Doug Mientkiewicz .15
147 Adam Kennedy .15
148 Rafael Furcal .15
149 Eric Chavez .25
150 Mike Lieberthal .15
151 Moises Alou .15
152 Jermaine Dye .15
153 Torii Hunter .15
154 Trot Nixon .15
155 Larry Walker .15
156 Jorge Julio .15
157 Mike Mussina .40
158 Kirk Rueter .15
159 Rafael Palmeiro .65
160 Pokey Reese .15
161 Miguel Tejada .35
162 Robin Ventura .15
163 Raul Ibanez .15
164 Roger Cedeno .15
165 Juan Gonzalez .65
166 Carlos Lee .15
167 Tim Salmon .25
168 Orlando Hernandez .15
169 Wade Miller .15
170 Troy Percival .15
171 Billy Wagner .15
172 Jeff Conine .15
173 Junior Spivey .15
174 Edgar Renteria .15
175 Scott Rolen .65
176 Jason Varitek .15
177 Ben Broussard .15
178 Jeremy Giambi .15
179 Gabe Kapler .15
180 Armando Rios .15
181 Ichiro Suzuki 2.00
182 Tom Glavine .35
183 Greg Maddux 1.00
184 Roy Oswalt .25
185 John Smoltz .15
186 Eric Karros .15
187 Alfonso Soriano .75
188 Nomar Garciaparra 1.50
189 Joe Crede .15
190 Javy Lopez .15
191 Carlos Beltran .50
192 Jim Edmonds .15
193 Geoff Jenkins .15
194 Magglio Ordonez .25
195 Daryle Ward .15
196 Roger Clemens 1.25
197 Byung-Hyun Kim .15
198 Robb Nen .15
199 C.C. Sabathia .15
200 Barry Zito .35
201 Mark Grace .25
202 Paul Konerko .25
203 Mike Sweeney .15
204 John Olerud .15
205 Jose Vidro .15
206 Ray Durham .15
207 Omar Vizquel .15
208 Shea Hillenbrand .15
209 Mike Lowell .15
210 Aubrey Huff .15
211 Eric Hinske .15
212 Paul LoDuca .15
213 Jay Gibbons .15
214 Austin Kearns .50
215 Richie Sexson .15
216 Garret Anderson .15
217 Eric Gagne .15
218 Jason Jennings .15
219 Damian Moss .15
220 David Eckstein .15
221 Mark Teixeira 1.00
222 Bill Hall .50
223 Bobby Jenks .75
224 Adam Morrisey .50
225 Rodrigo Rosario .50
226 Brett Myers .75

227 Tony Alvarez .50
228 Willie Bloomquist 2.00
229 Ben Howard .50
230 Nic Jackson .50
231 Carl Crawford .50
232 Omar Infante .50
233 Francisco Rodriguez 1.00
234 Andy Van Hekken .50
235 Kirk Saarloos .50
236 *Dusty Wathan* .75
237 Jamey Carroll 1.50
238 Jason L. Phillips 1.50
239 Jose Castillo 4.00
240 *Arnaldo Munoz* 2.00
241 Orlando Hudson .50
242 Drew Henson .75
243 Jason Lane .75
244 Vinnie Chulk 1.50
245 *Prentice Redman* 2.00
246 Marlon Byrd 1.00
247 Chin-Feng Chen 1.00
248 *Craig Brazell* 2.00
249 John Webb 1.50
250 Adam LaRoche 1.00

Platinum Finish

Stars (1-220): 5-10X
SP (221-250): 2-4X
Production 100 sets

Barry Bonds Chasing History

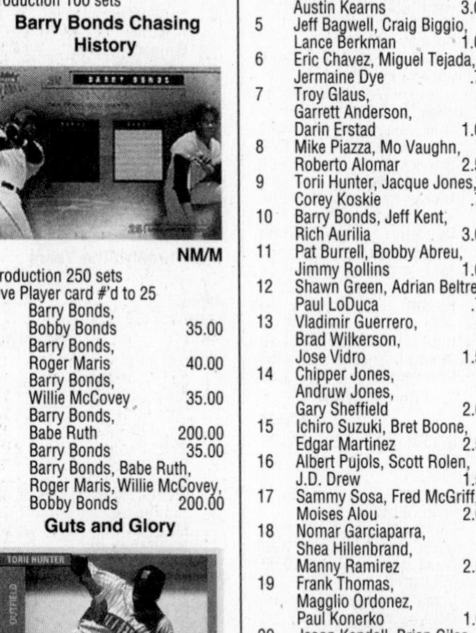

NM/M

Production 250 sets
Five Player card #'d to 25
Barry Bonds, Bobby Bonds 35.00
Barry Bonds, Roger Maris 40.00
Barry Bonds, Willie McCovey 35.00
Barry Bonds, Babe Ruth 200.00
Barry Bonds 35.00
Barry Bonds, Babe Ruth, Roger Maris, Willie McCovey, Bobby Bonds 200.00

Guts and Glory

NM/M

Complete Set (20): 12.00
Common Player: .40
Inserted 1:4
1GG Jason Giambi 1.00
2GG Alfonso Soriano .75
3GG Scott Rolen .50
4GG Ivan Rodriguez .50
5GG Barry Bonds 1.50
6GG Jim Edmonds .40
7GG Darin Erstad .40
8GG Brian Giles .40
9GG Luis Gonzalez .40
10GG Adam Dunn .50
11GG Torii Hunter .40
12GG Andruw Jones .40
13GG Sammy Sosa 1.00
14GG Ichiro Suzuki 1.50
15GG Miguel Tejada .40
16GG Roger Clemens 1.00
17GG Curt Schilling .40
18GG Nomar Garciaparra 1.50
19GG Derek Jeter 2.00
20GG Alex Rodriguez 1.50

Heart of the Order

NM/M

Complete Set (20): 20.00
Common Card: .75
Inserted 1:12
1 Jason Giambi, Derek Jeter, Alfonso Soriano 3.00
2 Todd Helton, Preston Wilson, Larry Walker .75
3 Rafael Palmeiro, Alex Rodriguez, Ivan Rodriguez 3.00
4 Adam Dunn, Ken Griffey Jr., Austin Kearns 3.00
5 Jeff Bagwell, Craig Biggio, Lance Berkman 1.00
6 Eric Chavez, Miguel Tejada, Jermaine Dye .75
7 Troy Glaus, Garrett Anderson, Darin Erstad 1.00
8 Mike Piazza, Mo Vaughn, Roberto Alomar 2.50
9 Torii Hunter, Jacque Jones, Corey Koskie .75
10 Barry Bonds, Jeff Kent, Rich Aurilia 3.00
11 Pat Burrell, Bobby Abreu, Jimmy Rollins 1.00
12 Shawn Green, Adrian Beltre, Paul LoDuca .75
13 Vladimir Guerrero, Brad Wilkerson, Jose Vidro 1.50
14 Chipper Jones, Andruw Jones, Gary Sheffield 2.00
15 Ichiro Suzuki, Bret Boone, Edgar Martinez 2.50
16 Albert Pujols, Scott Rolen, J.D. Drew 1.50
17 Sammy Sosa, Fred McGriff, Moises Alou 2.00
18 Nomar Garciaparra, Shea Hillenbrand, Manny Ramirez 2.50
19 Frank Thomas, Magglio Ordonez, Paul Konerko 1.00
20 Jason Kendall, Brian Giles, Aramis Ramirez .75

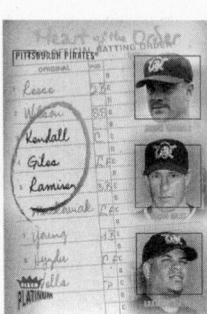

Heart of the Order Memorabilia

NM/M

Common Card: 5.00
Production 400 sets
Jason Giambi, Derek Jeter, Alfonso Soriano/bat 15.00
Todd Helton/jsy, Preston Wilson, Larry Walker 8.00
Rafael Palmeiro/jsy, Alex Rodriguez, Ivan Rodriguez 6.00
Adam Dunn, Ken Griffey Jr., Austin Kearns/pants 12.00
Jeff Bagwell, Craig Biggio, Lance Berkman
Eric Chavez, Miguel Tejada, Jermaine Dye
Troy Glaus, Garrett Anderson, Darin Erstad/jsy 8.00
Mike Piazza/jsy, Mo Vaughn, Roberto Alomar 10.00
Torii Hunter, Jacque Jones, Corey Koskie
Barry Bonds, Jeff Kent/jsy, Rich Aurilia 6.00
Pat Burrell, Bobby Abreu, Jimmy Rollins/jsy 6.00
Shawn Green, Adrian Beltre/jsy, Paul LoDuca 5.00
Vladimir Guerrero, Brad Wilkerson, Jose Vidro/jsy 5.00
Chipper Jones/jsy, Andruw Jones, Gary Sheffield 10.00
Ichiro Suzuki, Bret Boone/jsy, Edgar Martinez 5.00
Albert Pujols, Scott Rolen, J.D. Drew/jsy 8.00
Sammy Sosa/jsy, Fred McGriff, Moises Alou 12.00
Nomar Garciaparra, Shea Hillenbrand, Manny Ramirez/jsy 8.00
Frank Thomas, Magglio Ordonez/jsy, Paul Konerko 5.00
Jason Kendall, Brian Giles/bat, Aramis Ramirez 5.00

MLB Scouting Report

NM/M

Complete Set (32): 55.00
Common Player: 1.00
Production 400 sets
1 Jason Giambi 3.00
2 Paul Konerko 1.00
3 Jim Thome 1.50
4 Alfonso Soriano 2.00
5 Troy Glaus 1.50
6 Eric Hinske 1.00
7 Paul LoDuca 1.00
8 Mike Piazza 4.00
9 Marlon Byrd 1.00
10 Garrett Anderson 1.00
11 Barry Bonds 5.00
12 Pat Burrell 1.50
13 Joe Crede 1.00
14 J.D. Drew 1.00
15 Ken Griffey Jr. 4.00
16 Vladimir Guerrero 2.00
17 Torii Hunter 1.00
18 Chipper Jones 3.00
19 Austin Kearns 1.00
20 Albert Pujols 2.00
21 Manny Ramirez 1.50
22 Gary Sheffield 1.00
23 Sammy Sosa 3.00
24 Ichiro Suzuki 4.00
25 Bernie Williams 1.25
26 Randy Johnson 2.00
27 Greg Maddux 3.00
28 Hideo Nomo 1.00
29 Nomar Garciaparra 4.00
30 Derek Jeter 6.00
31 Alex Rodriguez 5.00
32 Miguel Tejada 1.00

MLB Scouting Report Game Used

NM/M

Common Player: 6.00
Production 250 sets
3 Jim Thome Jsy 10.00
4 Alfonso Soriano Bat 10.00
8 Mike Piazza Jsy 15.00
11 Barry Bonds Jsy 20.00
14 J.D. Drew Jsy 6.00
18 Chipper Jones Jsy 10.00
19 Austin Kearns Pants 10.00
21 Manny Ramirez Jsy 8.00
23 Sammy Sosa Jsy 15.00
26 Randy Johnson Jsy 10.00
27 Greg Maddux Jsy 10.00
28 Hideo Nomo Jsy 20.00
30 Derek Jeter Jsy 20.00

Nameplates

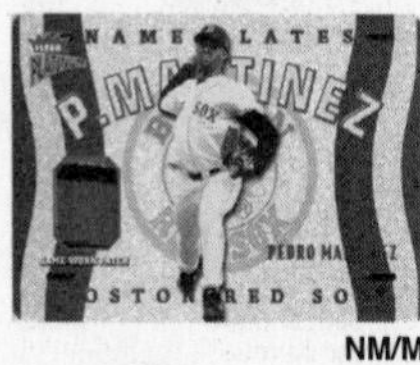

NM/M

Common Player:
Jumbo Pack Exclusive
Barry Larkin/97 30.00
Kazuhiro Sasaki/82 20.00
Greg Maddux/248 25.00
Craig Biggio/152 25.00
Pedro J. Martinez/244 35.00
Barry Zito/248 25.00
Nomar Garciaparra/258 40.00
Rickey Henderson
John Olerud/180 25.00
Ivan Rodriguez/189 20.00
Jeff Bagwell/121 45.00
Chipper Jones/251 40.00
Frank Thomas/58 45.00
Roger Clemens/141 40.00
Mike Piazza/200 35.00
Mark Prior/123 40.00
Manny Ramirez/94 30.00
Kerry Wood/49 45.00
Rafael Palmeiro/245 20.00
Jimmy Rollins/74 20.00
Barry Bonds/251 50.00
Adam Dunn/117 25.00
Alex Rodriguez/248 40.00
Miguel Tejada/225 20.00
Chin-Feng Chen/110 100.00

Portraits

NM/M

Complete Set (20): 25.00
Common Player: .75
Inserted 1:20
1 Josh Beckett .75
2 Roberto Alomar 1.00
3 Alfonso Soriano 2.00
4 Mike Piazza 3.00
5 Ivan Rodriguez 1.00
6 Edgar Martinez .75
7 Barry Bonds 4.00
8 Adam Dunn 1.25
9 Juan Gonzalez 1.00
10 Chipper Jones 2.50
11 Albert Pujols 1.50
12 Magglio Ordonez .75
13 Shea Hillenbrand .75
14 Larry Walker .75
15 Pedro J. Martinez 1.50
16 Kerry Wood 1.00
17 Barry Zito 1.00
18 Nomar Garciaparra 3.00
19 Derek Jeter 5.00
20 Alex Rodriguez 4.00

Portraits Game Jersey

NM/M

Common Player: 5.00
Inserted 1:86
4 Mike Piazza 10.00
5 Ivan Rodriguez 6.00
7 Barry Bonds 15.00
8 Adam Dunn 8.00
10 Chipper Jones 8.00
15 Pedro J. Martinez 8.00
16 Kerry Wood 8.00
17 Barry Zito 5.00
18 Nomar Garciaparra 10.00
19 Derek Jeter SP/150 25.00

Portraits Game Patch

NM/M

Common Player: 25.00
Production 100 sets
4 Mike Piazza 35.00
5 Ivan Rodriguez 25.00
7 Barry Bonds 40.00
8 Adam Dunn 25.00
10 Chipper Jones 25.00
15 Pedro J. Martinez 25.00
16 Kerry Wood 25.00
17 Barry Zito 25.00
18 Nomar Garciaparra 40.00
19 Derek Jeter 45.00

2003 FLEER ROOKIES & GREATS

NM/M
Complete Set (75): 30.00
Common Player: .25
Pack (5): 6.00
Box (20): 100.00
1 Troy Glaus .65
2 Gary Sheffield .40
3 Sammy Sosa 2.00
4 Mark Prior .75
5 Dontrelle Willis .25
6 Shawn Green .50
7 Vladimir Guerrero .75
8 Jose Reyes .25
9 Miguel Tejada .40
10 Bret Boone .25
11 Rocco Baldelli .40
12 Rafael Palmeiro .65
13 Ichiro Suzuki 1.50
14 Carlos Delgado .50
15 Garret Anderson .25
16 Richie Sexson .25
17 Roger Clemens 1.75
18 Barry Zito .40
19 Jim Thome .25
20 Alex Rodriguez 2.50
21 Randy Johnson .75
22 Chipper Jones 1.00
23 Kerry Wood .60
24 Ken Griffey Jr. 1.50
25 Ivan Rodriguez .60
26 Jeff Kent .25
27 Todd Helton .75
28 Jeff Bagwell .75
29 Hideo Nomo .60
30 Torii Hunter .25
31 Brian Giles .25
32 Albert Pujols 2.00
33 Vernon Wells .25
34 Nomar Garciaparra 2.00
35 Maggilo Ordonez .25
36 C.C. Sabathia .25
37 Preston Wilson .25
38 Mike Sweeney .25
39 Jose Vidro .25
40 Jason Giambi .60
41 Derek Jeter 3.00
42 Mike Piazza 1.50
43 Rich Harden .25
44 Jason Kendall .25
45 Barry Bonds 3.00
46 Barry Larkin .25
47 Dmitri Young .25
48 Craig Biggio .25
49 Angel Berroa .25
50 Alfonso Soriano .75
51 Kevin Millwood .25
52 Edgar Martinez .25
53 Jim Edmonds .25
54 Curt Schilling .40
55 Jay Gibbons .25
56 Pedro J. Martinez .75
57 Greg Maddux 1.00
58 Manny Ramirez .75
59 Frank Thomas .75
60 Adam Dunn .60
61 Babe Ruth 3.00
62 Bob Gibson 1.00
63 Willie Stargell .75
64 Mike Schmidt 2.00
65 Nolan Ryan 3.00
66 Tom Seaver 1.00
67 Brooks Robinson 1.00
68 Willie McCovey .50
69 Harmon Killebrew 1.00
70 Al Kaline 1.00
71 Reggie Jackson 1.00
72 Eddie Mathews .75
73 Ralph Kiner .25
74 Cal Ripken Jr. 3.00
75 Phil Rizzuto .25
Ultra
Production 1,500
U-251 *Chien-Ming Wang* 3.00
U-252 *Rickie Weeks* 6.00
U-253 *Brandon Webb* 4.00
U-254 *Hideki Matsui* 8.00
U-255 *Michael Hessman* 2.00
U-256 *Ryan Wagner* 3.00
U-257 *Matt Kata* 3.00
U-258 *Edwin Jackson* 6.00
U-259 *Jose Contreras* 3.00
U-260 *Delmon Young* 8.00
U-261 *Bo Hart* 3.00
U-262 *Jeff Duncan* 3.00
U-263 *Robby Hammock* 2.00
U-264 Jeremy Bonderman 3.00
U-265 *Clint Barmes* 2.00
Authentix
Production 1,250
A-161 *Chien-Ming Wang* 4.00
A-162 *Rickie Weeks* 8.00
A-163 *Brandon Webb* 4.00
A-164 *Craig Brazell* 3.00
A-165 *Michael Hessman* 3.00
A-166 *Ryan Wagner* 5.00
A-167 *Matt Kata* 4.00
A-168 *Edwin Jackson* 8.00
A-169 *Mike Ryan* 3.00
A-170 *Delmon Young* 10.00
A-171 *Bo Hart* 4.00
A-172 *Jeff Duncan* 4.00
A-173 *Robby Hammock* 3.00
A-174 Jeremy Bonderman 3.00
A-175 *Clint Barmes* 3.00
Genuine
Production 1,000
G-131 Dan Haren 5.00
G-132 *Rickie Weeks* 8.00
G-133 *Prentice Redman* 4.00
G-134 *Craig Brazell* 4.00
G-135 *Jon Leicester* 4.00
G-136 *Ryan Wagner* 6.00
G-137 *Matt Kata* 5.00
G-138 *Edwin Jackson* 8.00
G-139 *Mike Ryan* 5.00
G-140 *Delmon Young* 10.00
G-141 *Bo Hart* 5.00
G-142 *Jeff Duncan* 5.00
G-143 *Robby Hammock* 4.00
G-144 *Michael Hessman* 4.00
G-145 *Clint Barmes* 4.00
Showcase
Production 750
S-136 *Chien-Ming Wang* 6.00
S-137 *Rickie Weeks* 10.00
S-138 *Brandon Webb* 5.00
S-139 *Hideki Matsui* 10.00
S-140 *Michael Hessman* 4.00
S-141 *Ryan Wagner* 6.00
S-142 *Bo Hart* 5.00
S-143 *Edwin Jackson* 8.00
S-144 *Jose Contreras* 6.00
S-145 *Delmon Young* 10.00
Flair
Production 500
F-126 *Jeff Duncan* 6.00
F-127 *Rickie Weeks* 12.00
F-128 *Brandon Webb* 10.00
F-129 *Robby Hammock* 5.00
F-130 *Jon Leicester* 5.00
F-131 *Ryan Wagner* 8.00
F-132 *Bo Hart* 6.00
F-133 *Edwin Jackson* 10.00
F-134 *Sergio Mitre* 5.00
F-135 *Delmon Young* 15.00
Hot Prospects
Production 250
H-120 *Josh Willingham* 10.00
H-121 *Rickie Weeks* 15.00
H-122 *Prentice Redman* 8.00
H-123 *Mike Ryan* 8.00
H-124 *Oscar Villarreal* 8.00
H-125 *Ryan Wagner* 10.00
H-126 *Bo Hart* 10.00
H-127 *Edwin Jackson* 12.00

Boyhood Idols

NM/M
Common Player: 5.00
Production 615 sets
Carlton Fisk 8.00
Joe Carter 5.00
Cal Ripken Jr. 20.00
Mike Schmidt 15.00
Robin Yount 8.00
Joe Morgan 5.00
Jim Palmer 5.00
Harmon Killebrew 8.00
Brooks Robinson 8.00
Frank Howard 5.00
Bill "Moose" Skowron 5.00
Bob Feller
Bucky Dent 5.00
Nolan Ryan 20.00
Don Mattingly 20.00

Boyhood Idols Auto

NM/M
Production 50 unless noted
Carlton Fisk 30.00
Joe Carter
Jim Palmer
Harmon Killebrew/40
Brooks Robinson 35.00
Frank Howard
Bill "Moose" Skowron
Bucky Dent 20.00

Dynamic Debuts

NM/M
Complete Set (10): 10.00
Common Player: .50
Inserted 1:10
1DD Rickie Weeks 4.00
2DD Brandon Webb 1.00
3DD Jose Reyes 1.00
4DD Bo Hart 1.00
5DD Dontrelle Willis 1.00
6DD Rich Harden .50
7DD Ryan Wagner .50
8DD Rocco Baldelli 1.00
9DD Mark Teixeira 1.00
10DD Hideki Matsui 5.00

Dynamic Debuts Autograph

NM/M
Common Player: 10.00
Production 100
Rickie Weeks 50.00
Jose Reyes 30.00
Bo Hart 10.00
Dontrelle Willis 30.00
Ryan Wagner 10.00

Looming Large

NM/M
Complete Set (15): 30.00
Common Player: 1.50
Production 500 sets
Uncommon: 1-2X
Production 150
Rare: No Pricing
Production 15
1LL Chien-Ming Wang 4.00
2LL Rickie Weeks 6.00
3LL Brandon Webb 3.00
4LL Hideki Matsui 6.00
5LL Michael Hessman 1.50
6LL Ryan Wagner 1.50
7LL Matt Kata 1.50
8LL Edwin Jackson 1.50
9LL Jose Contreras 1.50
10LL Delmon Young 6.00
11LL Bo Hart 3.00
12LL Jeff Duncan 1.50
13LL Robby Hammock 1.50
14LL Jeremy Bonderman 1.50
15LL Clint Barmes 1.50

The Naturals

NM/M
Complete Set (25): 45.00
Common Player: .50
Inserted 1:5
Uncommons: 2-4X
Production 75 sets
1 Cal Ripken Jr. 5.00
2 Mike Schmidt 3.00
3 Derek Jeter 5.00
4 Joe Carter .50
5 Nomar Garciaparra 3.00
6 Frank Howard .50
7 Al Kaline 2.00
8 Albert Pujols 4.00
9 Nolan Ryan 5.00
10 Duke Snider 1.50
11 Alex Rodriguez 4.00
12 Brooks Robinson 1.50
13 Roger Clemens 4.00
14 Sammy Sosa 3.00
15 Jim Palmer 1.00
16 Alfonso Soriano 2.00
17 Don Mattingly 3.00
18 Harmon Killebrew 1.50
19 Bob Feller .50
20 Reggie Jackson 1.50
21 Ichiro Suzuki 2.50
22 Barry Bonds 5.00
23 Hideki Matsui 4.00
24 Willie Stargell .50
25 Pee Wee Reese .50

The Naturals Memorabilia

NM/M
Common Player: 5.00
Production 250 unless noted
CR Cal Ripken Jr. 30.00
MS Mike Schmidt 15.00
DJ Derek Jeter 20.00
JC Joe Carter 5.00
NG Nomar Garciaparra 15.00
FH Frank Howard/400 5.00
AK Al Kaline 15.00
AP Albert Pujols 12.00
NR Nolan Ryan/400 25.00
DS Duke Snider 10.00
AR Alex Rodriguez 10.00
BR Brooks Robinson/400 10.00
RC Roger Clemens/400 15.00
SS Sammy Sosa
JP Jim Palmer 8.00
AS Alfonso Soriano 8.00
DM Don Mattingly 20.00
HK Harmon Killebrew/400 10.00
BF Bob Feller
RJ Reggie Jackson/400 10.00

The Naturals Autograph

NM/M
Common Player:
Production 50
Joe Carter 15.00
Bob Feller 25.00
Frank Howard 25.00
Al Kaline 40.00
Harmon Killebrew 35.00
Jim Palmer 15.00
Cal Ripken Jr. 140.00
Brooks Robinson 35.00
Nolan Ryan 100.00
Duke Snider 25.00

The Naturals Jersey Auto

NM/M
Common Player:
Production 30
Joe Carter 25.00
Frank Howard 25.00
Al Kaline 60.00
Harmon Killebrew 50.00
Jim Palmer 25.00
Cal Ripken Jr. 150.00
Brooks Robinson 50.00
Nolan Ryan 120.00
Duke Snider 40.00

The Naturals Patch

NO Pricing
Production 25
Patch Autos: No Pricing
Production 5

Through the Years

NM/M
Common Duo: 10.00
Production 360
Patches: No Pricing
Production 25
Sammy Sosa, Mark Prior 25.00
Mark Prior, Jose Reyes 15.00
Nolan Ryan, Hank Blalock 25.00
Roger Clemens, Chien-Ming Wang 35.00
Jim Thome, Mike Schmidt 25.00
Alex Rodriguez, Mark Teixeira 25.00
Randy Johnson, Brandon Webb 15.00
Phil Rizzuto, Jose Reyes 15.00
Nomar Garciaparra, Bobby Doerr 20.00
Jason Giambi, Reggie Jackson 15.00
Derek Jeter, Phil Rizzuto 45.00
Barry Larkin, Joe Morgan 10.00
Harmon Killebrew, Torii Hunter 20.00
Willie McCovey, Barry Bonds 15.00
Bo Hart, Lou Brock 15.00
Jose Contreras, Mike Mussina 10.00
Michael Hessman, Chipper Jones 12.00
Steve Carlton, Kevin Millwood 12.00
Robin Yount, Scott Podsednik 20.00
Eddie Mathews, Chipper Jones 15.00

2003 FLEER SHOWCASE

NM/M
Complete Set (135): 50.00
Common Player: .25
Common SP (106-135): 1.00
Inserted 1:4
Pack (5): 3.00
Box (24): 60.00
1 David Eckstein .25
2 Curt Schilling .75

3	Jay Gibbons	.25
4	Kerry Wood	.75
5	Jeff Bagwell	1.00
6	Hideo Nomo	.75
7	Tim Hudson	.40
8	J.D. Drew	.50
9	Josh Phelps	.25
10	Bartolo Colon	.25
11	Bobby Abreu	.25
12	Matt Morris	.25
13	Kazuhiro Sasaki	.25
14	Sean Burroughs	.25
15	Vicente Padilla	.25
16	Jorge Posada	.35
17	Torii Hunter	.25
18	Richie Sexson	.25
19	Lance Berkman	.25
20	Todd Helton	1.00
21	Paul Konerko	.25
22	Pedro J. Martinez	1.00
23	Rodrigo Lopez	.25
24	Gary Sheffield	.35
25	Darin Erstad	.50
26	Nomar Garciaparra	2.50
27	Adam Dunn	.75
28	Jason Giambi	.75
29	Miguel Tejada	.40
30	Chipper Jones	1.50
31	Alex Rodriguez	3.00
32	Barry Bonds	4.00
33	Roger Clemens	2.00
34	Sammy Sosa	2.50
35	Randy Johnson	1.00
36	Tim Salmon	.35
37	Shea Hillenbrand	.25
38	Larry Walker	.25
39	A.J. Burnett	.25
40	Shawn Green	.50
41	Cristian Guzman	.25
42	Bernie Williams	.35
43	Mark Mulder	.25
44	Brian Giles	.25
45	Bret Boone	.25
46	Juan Gonzalez	.75
47	Roy Halladay	.25
48	Wade Miller	.25
49	Jeff Kent	.25
50	Carlos Delgado	.50
51	Mike Lowell	.25
52	Jim Edmonds	.25
53	Ivan Rodriguez	.75
54	Aubrey Huff	.25
55	Ryan Klesko	.25
56	Paul LoDuca	.25
57	Roy Oswalt	.50
58	Omar Vizquel	.25
59	Manny Ramirez	1.00
60	Andruw Jones	1.00
61	Troy Glaus	1.00
62	Ichiro Suzuki	2.50
63	Albert Pujols	2.50
64	Derek Jeter	4.00
65	Mark Prior	1.00
66	Ken Griffey Jr.	2.50
67	Vladimir Guerrero	1.00
68	Mike Piazza	2.50
69	Alfonso Soriano	1.00
70	Greg Maddux	1.50
71	Adam Kennedy	.25
72	Junior Spivey	.25
73	Tom Glavine	.40
74	Derek Lowe	.25
75	Magglio Ordonez	.25
76	Jim Thome	.25
77	Robert Fick	.25
78	Josh Beckett	.25
79	Mike Sweeney	.25
80	Kazuhisa Ishii	.25
81	Roberto Alomar	.40
82	Barry Zito	.40
83	Pat Burrell	.65
84	Scott Rolen	1.00
85	John Olerud	.25
86	Eric Hinske	.25
87	Rafael Palmeiro	.75
88	Edgar Martinez	.25
89	Eric Chavez	.40
90	Jose Vidro	.25
91	Craig Biggio	.25
92	Rich Aurilia	.25
93	Austin Kearns	.75
94	Luis Gonzalez	.40
95	Garrett Anderson	.25
96	Yogi Berra	1.50
97	Al Kaline	1.50
98	Robin Yount	1.00
99	Reggie Jackson	1.00
100	Harmon Killebrew	1.50
101	Eddie Mathews	1.50
102	Willie McCovey	.50
103	Nolan Ryan	4.00
104	Mike Schmidt	2.50
105	Tom Seaver	1.00
106	Francisco Rodriguez	1.00
107	Carl Crawford	1.00
108	Ben Howard	1.00
109	Hank Blalock	2.00
110	Hee Seop Choi	2.00
111	Kirk Saarloos	1.00
112	*Lew Ford*	3.00
113	Andy Van Hekken	1.00
114	Drew Henson	1.50
115	Marlon Byrd	1.00
116	Jayson Werth	1.00
117	Willie Bloomquist	1.00
118	Joe Borchard	1.00
119	Mark Teixeira	2.00
120	Bobby Hill	1.00
121	Jason Lane	1.00
122	Omar Infante	1.00
123	Victor Martinez	1.50
124	Jorge Padilla	1.00
125	John Lackey	1.00
126	Anderson Machado	1.00
127	Rodrigo Rosario	1.00
128	Freddy Sanchez	1.00
129	Tony Alvarez	1.00
130	Matt Thornton	1.00
131	Joe Thurston	1.00
132	Brett Myers	1.00
133	Antonio Perez	1.00
134	Chris Snelling	1.00
135	*Terrmel Sledge*	2.00

Legacy

Legacy Stars (1-105): 3-6X
SP's (106-135): 1-3X
Production 150 sets
Masterpiece 1 of 1 also exists

Baseball's Best

		NM/M
Complete Set (15):		40.00
Common Player:		1.50
Inserted 1:24		
1	Curt Schilling	2.00
2	Barry Zito	2.00
3	Torii Hunter	2.00
4	Pedro J. Martinez	4.00
5	Bernie Williams	2.00
6	Magglio Ordonez	1.50
7	Alfonso Soriano	4.00
8	Hideo Nomo	2.00
9	Jason Giambi	5.00
10	Sammy Sosa	5.00
11	Vladimir Guerrero	4.00
12	Ken Griffey Jr.	5.00
13	Troy Glaus	3.00
14	Ichiro Suzuki	6.00
15	Albert Pujols	4.00

Baseball's Best Memorabilia

		NM/M
Common Player:		5.00
Inserted 1:24		
CS	Curt Schilling	6.00
BZ	Barry Zito	6.00
TH	Torii Hunter	8.00
PM	Pedro J. Martinez	10.00
BW	Bernie Williams	8.00
MO	Magglio Ordonez	5.00
AS	Alfonso Soriano	15.00
HN	Hideo Nomo	8.00
JG	Jason Giambi	8.00
SS	Sammy Sosa	15.00

Hot Gloves

		NM/M
Complete Set (10):		15.00
Common Player:		1.00
Inserted 1:8		
1	Greg Maddux	2.00
2	Ivan Rodriguez	1.00
3	Derek Jeter	4.00
4	Mike Piazza	2.50
5	Nomar Garciaparra	2.50
6	Andruw Jones	1.00
7	Scott Rolen	1.00
8	Barry Bonds	3.00
9	Roger Clemens	2.00
10	Alex Rodriguez	3.00

Hot Gloves Memorabilia

		NM/M
Common Player:		5.00
Production 350 sets		
GM	Greg Maddux	12.00
IR	Ivan Rodriguez	5.00
DJ	Derek Jeter	25.00
MP	Mike Piazza	15.00
NG	Nomar Garciaparra	15.00
AJ	Andruw Jones	6.00
SR	Scott Rolen	15.00
BB	Barry Bonds	25.00
RC	Roger Clemens	15.00
AR	Alex Rodriguez	15.00

Sweet Sigs

		NM/M
Quantity produced listed		
DJ	Derek Jeter/250	130.00
DJ	Derek Jeter/50/red	185.00
BB	Barry Bonds/ 90 MVP/150	200.00
BB	Barry Bonds/ 92 MVP/100	200.00
BB	Barry Bonds/ 93 MVP/75	200.00
BB	Barry Bonds/02 MVP/25	

Sweet Stitch

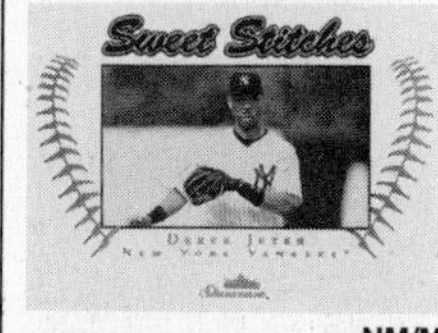

		NM/M
Complete Set (10):		12.00
Common Player:		.75
Inserted 1:8		
1SS	Derek Jeter	4.00
2SS	Randy Johnson	1.50
3SS	Jeff Bagwell	1.00
4SS	Nomar Garciaparra	2.50
5SS	Roger Clemens	2.00
6SS	Todd Helton	.75
7SS	Barry Bonds	3.00
8SS	Alfonso Soriano	1.50
9SS	Miguel Tejada	.75
10SS	Mark Prior	.75

Sweet Stitch Patch

		NM/M
Common Player:		20.00
DJ	Derek Jeter/50	60.00
RJ	Randy Johnson/150	40.00
JB	Jeff Bagwell/150	35.00
NG	Nomar Garciaparra/ 150	45.00
RC	Roger Clemens/50	45.00
TH	Todd Helton/50	30.00
BB	Barry Bonds/150	75.00
AS	Alfonso Soriano/50	40.00
MT	Miguel Tejada/150	20.00
MP	Mark Prior/150	40.00

Sweet Stitch Memorabilia

		NM/M
Varying quantities produced		
DJ	Derek Jeter	25.00
RJ	Randy Johnson	8.00
JB	Jeff Bagwell	8.00
NG	Nomar Garciaparra	12.00
RC	Roger Clemens	12.00
TH	Todd Helton	5.00
BB	Barry Bonds	20.00
AS	Alfonso Soriano	12.00
MT	Miguel Tejada	5.00
MP	Mark Prior	15.00

Thundersticks

		NM/M
Complete Set (10):		12.00
Common Player:		.75
Inserted 1:8		
1TS	Adam Dunn	1.00
2TS	Alex Rodriguez	3.00
3TS	Barry Bonds	4.00
4TS	Jim Thome	1.00
5TS	Chipper Jones	2.00
6TS	Manny Ramirez	1.00
7TS	Carlos Delgado	.75
8TS	Mike Piazza	2.50
9TS	Shawn Green	.75
10TS	Pat Burrell	1.00

Thundersticks Bat

		NM/M
Common Player:		5.00
Golds:		1-2.5X
Production 99 sets		
AD	Adam Dunn	10.00
AR	Alex Rodriguez	15.00
BB	Barry Bonds	20.00
JT	Jim Thome	8.00
CJS	Chipper Jones	8.00
MR	Manny Ramirez	8.00
SG	Shawn Green	5.00
PB	Pat Burrell	10.00

2003 FLEER SPLENDID SPLINTERS

		NM/M
Complete Set (150):		
Common Player:		.20
Common Wood (91-110):		6.00
Production 499		
Common SP (111-140):		1.50
Inserted 1:6		
Common (141-150):		3.00
Production 999		
Pack (5):		3.00
Box (24):		50.00
1	David Eckstein	.20
2	Barry Larkin	.40
3	Edgardo Alfonzo	.20
4	Darin Erstad	.50

5	Ellis Burks	.20
6	Omar Vizquel	.40
7	Bartolo Colon	.20
8	Roberto Alomar	.50
9	Garret Anderson	.40
10	Al Leiter	.20
11	Tim Salmon	.40
12	Larry Walker	.40
13	Jorge Posada	.50
14	Curt Schilling	.50
15	Jason Jennings	.20
16	Jason Giambi	1.00
17	Robert Fick	.20
18	Kazuhiro Sasaki	.20
19	Bernie Williams	.50
20	Junior Spivey	.20
21	Mike Lowell	.20
22	Luis Gonzalez	.40
23	Josh Beckett	.20
24	John Smoltz	.20
25	Mike Mussina	.50
26	Gary Sheffield	.40
27	Tom Glavine	.40
28	Tim Hudson	.40
29	Austin Kearns	.75
30	Andruw Jones	.50
31	Roger Clemens	1.50
32	Mark Mulder	.40
33	Jay Gibbons	.20
34	Jeff Kent	.40
35	Barry Zito	.40
36	Rodrigo Lopez	.20
37	Jeff Bagwell	.75
38	Eric Chavez	.40
39	Pedro J. Martinez	1.00
40	Lance Berkman	.50
41	Bobby Abreu	.40
42	Wade Miller	.20
43	Bret Boone	.20
44	Vicente Padilla	.20
45	Shea Hillenbrand	.20
46	Roy Oswalt	.40
47	Pat Burrell	.75
48	Manny Ramirez	.75
49	Craig Biggio	.40
50	Randy Wolf	.20
51	Kerry Wood	.50
52	Mike Sweeney	.20
53	Brian Giles	.40
54	Kazuhisa Ishii	.20
55	Jason Kendall	.20
56	Hideo Nomo	.40
57	Josh Phelps	.20
58	Sean Burroughs	.20
59	Paul Konerko	.20
60	Shawn Green	.40
61	Ryan Klesko	.40
62	Magglio Ordonez	.40
63	Paul LoDuca	.20
64	Edgar Martinez	.20
65	J.D. Drew	.30
66	Phil Nevin	.20
67	Jim Edmonds	.40
68	Matt Morris	.40
69	Aubrey Huff	.20
70	Adam Dunn	.75
71	John Olerud	.40
72	Juan Gonzalez	.50
73	Scott Rolen	.50
74	Rafael Palmeiro	.50
75	Roy Halladay	.20
76	Kevin Brown	.20
77	Ivan Rodriguez	.50
78	Eric Hinske	.20
79	Frank Thomas	.75
80	Carlos Delgado	.40
81	Bobby Higginson	.20
82	Trevor Hoffman	.20
83	Cliff Floyd	.20
84	Derek Lowe	.20
85	Richie Sexson	.50
86	Rich Aurilia	.20
87	Sean Casey	.20
88	Cristian Guzman	.20
89	Randy Winn	.20
90	Jose Vidro	.20
91	Mark Prior	7.50
92	Derek Jeter	15.00
93	Alex Rodriguez	12.00
94	Greg Maddux	9.00
95	Troy Glaus	7.50
96	Vladimir Guerrero	7.50
97	Todd Helton	7.50
98	Albert Pujols	10.00
99	Torii Hunter	6.00
100	Mike Piazza	10.00
101	Ichiro Suzuki	10.00
102	Sammy Sosa	10.00
103	Ken Griffey Jr.	10.00
104	Nomar Garciaparra	10.00
105	Barry Bonds	15.00
106	Chipper Jones	9.00
107	Jim Thome	6.00
108	Miguel Tejada	6.00
109	Randy Johnson	7.50
110	Alfonso Soriano	7.50
111	*Guillermo Quiroz*	3.00
112	*Josh Willingham*	3.00
113	*Alejandro Machado*	1.50
114	*Chris Waters*	2.00
115	Adam LaRoche	1.50
116	*Prentice Redman*	3.00
117	Jhonny Peralta	4.00
118	*Francisco Rosario*	1.50
119	*Shane Victorino*	2.00
120	*Chien-Ming Wang*	5.00
121	*Matt Bruback*	2.00
122	*Rontrez Johnson*	3.00
123	*Josh Hall*	2.00
124	*Matt Kata*	3.00
125	*Hector Luna*	2.00
126	*Josh Stewart*	2.00
127	*Craig Brazell*	2.00
128	*Tim Olson*	2.00
129	*Michel Hernandez*	1.50
130	*Michael Hessman*	2.00
131	*Clint Barmes*	5.00
132	Justin Morneau	1.50
133	Chris Snelling	1.50
134	Bobby Jenks	1.50
135	*Tim Hummel*	1.50
136	Adam Morrissey	1.50
137	Carl Crawford	1.50
138	Garrett Atkins	1.50
139	Jung Bong	1.50
140	Ken Harvey	1.50
141	Chin-Feng Chen	2.00
142	Hee Seop Choi	2.00
143	Lance Niekro	2.00
144	Mark Teixeira	2.00
145	*Nook Logan*	3.00
146	*Terrmel Sledge*	3.00
147	*Lew Ford*	6.00
148	*Ian Ferguson*	3.00
149	*Hideki Matsui/499*	15.00
150	*Jose Contreras*	6.00

Bat Chips

		NM/M
Common Player:		4.00
Production 425 sets		
1	Jason Giambi	8.00
2	Jeff Bagwell	8.00
3	Manny Ramirez	8.00
4	Adam Dunn	8.00
5	Derek Jeter	25.00
6	Alex Rodriguez	15.00
7	Troy Glaus	5.00
8	Mike Piazza	15.00
9	Sammy Sosa	12.00
10	Nomar Garciaparra	18.00
11	Barry Bonds	18.00
12	Jim Thome	10.00
13	Miguel Tejada	5.00
14	Alfonso Soriano	10.00
15	Ryan Klesko	4.00
16	Sean Casey	4.00
17	Bernie Williams	8.00
18	Vladimir Guerrero	8.00
19	Gary Sheffield	5.00

Family Tree

		NM/M
Complete Set (10):		10.00
Common Player:		.50
Inserted 1:8		
1	Lance Niekro, Phil Niekro	.50
2	Bob Boone, Bret Boone	.50
3	Sandy Alomar Jr., Roberto Alomar	.50
4	Ken Griffey Sr., Ken Griffey Jr.	2.00
5	Jason Giambi, Jeremy Giambi	1.50
6	Bobby Bonds, Barry Bonds	3.00
7	Tony Perez, Eduardo Perez	.50
8	Brian Giles, Marcus Giles	.75
9	Felipe Alou, Moises Alou	.75
10	Pedro J. Martinez, Ramon Martinez	1.50

Home Run Club

		NM/M
Complete Set (12):		50.00
Common Player:		2.00
Inserted 1:72		
1	Barry Bonds	10.00
2	Jason Giambi	5.00
3	Sammy Sosa	6.00
4	Jim Thome	4.00
5	Lance Berkman	2.00
6	Alfonso Soriano	5.00
7	Vladimir Guerrero	4.00
8	Shawn Green	2.00
9	Troy Glaus	3.00
10	Pat Burrell	3.00
11	Alex Rodriguez	10.00
12	Mike Piazza	8.00

Home Run Club Autographs

		NM/M
Quantity produced listed		
BB1	Barry Bonds/ black ink/150	150.00
CR1	Cal Ripken Jr/ black ink/300	100.00
CR2	Cal Ripken Jr/ blue ink/150	125.00
CR3	Cal Ripken Jr/ Red ink/50	200.00
DJ1	Derek Jeter/ black ink/400	80.00
DJ2	Derek Jeter/ blue ink/250	100.00
DJ3	Derek Jeter/ Red ink/50	125.00

Home Run Club Memorabilia

	NM/M
Common Player:	5.00
Production 599 sets	
Barry Bonds/jsy	20.00
Jason Giambi/bat	8.00
Sammy Sosa/jsy	12.00
Jim Thome/bat	8.00
Lance Berkman/bat	5.00
Alfonso Soriano/jsy	15.00
Vladimir Guerrero/jsy	8.00
Shawn Green/jsy	5.00
Troy Glaus/bat	6.00
Pat Burrell/bat	10.00
Alex Rodriguez/jsy	15.00
Mike Piazza/jsy	12.00
Todd Helton/jsy	8.00
Rafael Palmeiro/jsy	6.00

Knot Hole Gang

		NM/M
Complete Set (15):		40.00
Common Player:		1.00
Inserted 1:24		
1	Derek Jeter	6.00
2	Barry Bonds	6.00
3	Sammy Sosa	3.00
4	Jason Giambi	3.00
5	Alfonso Soriano	2.00
6	Roger Clemens	3.00
7	Miguel Tejada	1.00
8	Greg Maddux	3.00
9	Randy Johnson	2.00
10	Chipper Jones	3.00
11	Nomar Garciaparra	4.00
12	Alex Rodriguez	5.00
13	Ichiro Suzuki	4.00
14	Vladimir Guerrero	2.00
15	Albert Pujols	2.00

Knot Hole Gang Game-Used

	NM/M
Common Player:	4.00
Inserted 1:40	
Derek Jeter	20.00
Barry Bonds	15.00
Sammy Sosa	10.00
Vladimir Guerrero	8.00
Alfonso Soriano	8.00
Roger Clemens	10.00
Miguel Tejada	5.00
Greg Maddux	10.00
Randy Johnson	8.00
Chipper Jones	8.00
Nomar Garciaparra	12.00
Alex Rodriguez	12.00
Magglio Ordonez	4.00
Lance Berkman	6.00

Knot Hole Gang Patch

	NM/M
Common Player:	15.00
Production 99 sets	
Derek Jeter	45.00
Barry Bonds	45.00
Sammy Sosa	35.00
Vladimir Guerrero	25.00
Alfonso Soriano	25.00
Roger Clemens	25.00
Miguel Tejada	15.00
Greg Maddux	30.00
Randy Johnson	20.00

	Player	NM/M
	Chipper Jones	30.00
	Nomar Garciaparra	35.00
	Alex Rodriguez	35.00

Splendid Splinters

		NM/M
Complete Set (10):		15.00
Common Player:		1.00
Inserted 1:12		
1	Derek Jeter	4.00
2	Barry Bonds	4.00
3	Scott Rolen	1.00
4	Nomar Garciaparra	2.50
5	Sammy Sosa	2.00
6	Alfonso Soriano	1.50
7	Alex Rodriguez	3.00
8	Mike Piazza	2.50
9	Manny Ramirez	1.00
10	Jeff Bagwell	1.00

Splendid Splinters G-U

		NM/M
Common Player:		8.00
Production 349 sets		
	Derek Jeter	20.00
	Barry Bonds	20.00
	Nomar Garciaparra	15.00
	Sammy Sosa	10.00
	Alfonso Soriano	10.00
	Alex Rodriguez	12.00
	Mike Piazza	12.00
	Manny Ramirez	8.00
	Jeff Bagwell	8.00

Splendid Splinters Dual

		NM/M
Production 99 sets		
	Derek Jeter, Alfonso Soriano	40.00
	Barry Bonds, Sammy Sosa	50.00
	Alex Rodriguez, Nomar Garciaparra	40.00
	Mike Piazza, Jeff Bagwell	25.00

2003 FLEER TRADITION

		NM/M
Complete Set (485):		150.00
Common Player:		.15
Common SP (1-100):		1.00
Inserted 1:1		
Hobby Pack (10):		1.50
Hobby Box (40):		40.00
1	Jarrod Washburn, Troy Glaus, Garret Anderson, Ramon Ortiz	1.50
2	Luis Gonzalez, Randy Johnson, Andruw Jones	1.50
3	Andruw Jones, Chipper Jones, Tom Glavine, Kevin Millwood	2.00
4	Tony Batista, Rodrigo Lopez	1.00
5	Manny Ramirez, Nomar Garciaparra, Derek Lowe, Pedro J. Martinez	3.00
6	Sammy Sosa, Matt Clement, Kerry Wood	3.00
7	Mark Buehrle, Magglio Ordonez, Danny Wright	1.00
8	Adam Dunn, Aaron Boone, Jimmy Haynes	1.00
9	C.C. Sabathia, Jim Thome	1.50
10	Todd Helton, Jason Jennings	1.50
11	Randall Simon, Steve Sparks, Mark Redman	1.00
12	Derrek Lee, Mike Lowell, A.J. Burnett	1.00
13	Lance Berkman, Roy Oswalt	1.50
14	Paul Byrd, Carlos Beltran	1.00
15	Shawn Green, Hideo Nomo	1.50
16	Richie Sexson, Ben Sheets	1.00
17	Torii Hunter, Kyle Lohse, Johan Santana	1.00
18	Vladimir Guerrero, Tomokazu Ohka, Javier Vazquez	2.00
19	Mike Piazza, Al Leiter	3.00
20	Jason Giambi, David Wells, Roger Clemens	4.00
21	Eric Chavez, Miguel Tejada, Barry Zito	1.50
22	Pat Burrell, Vicente Padilla, Randy Wolf	1.50
23	Brian Giles, Josh Fogg, Kip Wells	1.00
24	Ryan Klesko, Brian Lawrence	1.00
25	Barry Bonds, Russ Ortiz, Jason Schmidt	5.00
26	Mike Cameron, Bret Boone, Freddy Garcia	1.00
27	Albert Pujols, Matt Morris	3.00
28	Aubrey Huff, Randy Winn, Joe Kennedy, Tanyon Sturtze	1.00
29	Alex Rodriguez, Kenny Rogers, Chan Ho Park	5.00
30	Carlos Delgado, Roy Halladay	1.00
31	Greg Maddux	6.00
32	Nick Neugebauer	1.00
33	Larry Walker	1.50
34	Freddy Garcia	1.00
35	Rich Aurilia	1.00
36	Craig Wilson	1.00
37	Jeff Suppan	1.00
38	Joel Pineiro	1.00
39	Pedro Feliz	1.00
40	Bartolo Colon	1.50
41	Pete Walker	1.00
42	Mo Vaughn	1.50
43	Sidney Ponson	1.00
44	Jason Isringhausen	1.00
45	Hideki Irabu	1.00
46	Pedro J. Martinez	4.00
47	Tom Glavine	2.50
48	Matt Lawton	1.00
49	Kyle Lohse	1.00
50	Corey Patterson	1.00
51	Ichiro Suzuki	6.00
52	Wade Miller	1.00
53	Ben Diggins	1.00
54	Jayson Werth	1.00
55	Masato Yoshii	1.00
56	Mark Buehrle	1.00
57	Drew Henson	1.50
58	Dave Williams	1.00
59	Juan Rivera	1.00
60	Scott Schoeneweis	1.00
61	Josh Beckett	1.50
62	Vinny Castilla	1.00
63	Barry Zito	2.00
64	Jose Valentin	1.00
65	Jon Lieber	1.00
66	Jorge Padilla	1.00
67	Luis Aparicio	1.00
68	Boog Powell	1.00
69	Dick Radatz	1.00
70	Frank Malzone	1.00
71	Lou Brock	1.50
72	Billy Williams	1.00
73	Early Wynn	1.00
74	Jim Bunning	1.00
75	Al Kaline	5.00
76	Eddie Mathews	3.00
77	Harmon Killebrew	5.00
78	Gil Hodges	1.00
79	Duke Snider	3.00
80	Yogi Berra	4.00
81	Whitey Ford	3.00
82	Willie Stargell	1.50
83	Willie McCovey	1.50
84	Gaylord Perry	1.00
85	Red Schoendienst	1.00
86	Luis Castillo	1.00
87	Derek Jeter	8.00
88	Orlando Hudson	1.00
89	Bobby Higginson	1.00
90	Brent Butler	1.00
91	Brad Wilkerson	1.00
92	Craig Biggio	1.50
93	Marlon Anderson	1.00
94	Ty Wigginton	1.00
95	Hideo Nomo	3.00
96	Barry Larkin	2.00
97	Roberto Alomar	3.00
98	Omar Vizquel	1.50
99	Andres Galarraga	1.00
100	Shawn Green	1.50
101	Rafael Furcal	.15
102	Bill Selby	.15
103	Brent Abernathy	.15
104	Nomar Garciaparra	1.50
105	Michael Barrett	.15
106	Travis Hafner	.15
107	Carl Crawford	.15
108	Jeff Cirillo	.15
109	Mike Hampton	.15
110	Kip Wells	.15
111	Luis Alicea	.15
112	Ellis Burks	.15
113	Matt Anderson	.15
114	Carlos Beltran	.50
115	Paul LoDuca	.15
116	Lance Berkman	.15
117	Moises Alou	.15
118	Roger Cedeno	.15
119	Brad Fullmer	.15
120	Sean Burroughs	.15
121	Eric Byrnes	.15
122	Milton Bradley	.15
123	Jason Giambi	.75
124	Brook Fordyce	.15
125	Kevin Appier	.15
126	Steve Cox	.15
127	Danny Bautista	.15
128	Edgardo Alfonzo	.15
129	Matt Clement	.15
130	Robb Nen	.15
131	Roy Halladay	.15
132	Brian Jordan	.15
133	A.J. Burnett	.15
134	Aaron Cook	.15
135	Paul Byrd	.15
136	Ramon Ortiz	.15
137	Adam Hyzdu	.15
138	Rafael Soriano	.15
139	Marty Cordova	.15
140	Nelson Cruz	.15
141	Jamie Moyer	.15
142	Raul Mondesi	.15
143	Josh Bard	.15
144	Elmer Dessens	.15
145	Rickey Henderson	.75
146	Joe McEwing	.15
147	Luis Rivas	.15
148	Armando Benitez	.15
149	Keith Foulke	.15
150	Zach Day	.15
151	Troy Lunsford	.15
152	Bobby Abreu	.15
153	Juan Cruz	.15
154	Ramon Hernandez	.15
155	Brandon Duckworth	.15
156	Matt Ginter	.15
157	Robert Mackowiak	.15
158	Josh Pearce	.15
159	Marlon Byrd	.15
160	Todd Walker	.15
161	Chad Hermansen	.15
162	Felix Escalona	.15
163	Ruben Mateo	.15
164	Mark Johnson	.15
165	Juan Pierre	.15
166	Gary Sheffield	.30
167	Edgar Martinez	.15
168	Randy Winn	.15
169	Pokey Reese	.15
170	Kevin Mench	.15
171	Albert Pujols	1.50
172	J.T. Snow	.15
173	Dean Palmer	.15
174	Jay Payton	.15
175	Abraham Nunez	.15
176	Richie Sexson	.15
177	Jose Vidro	.15
178	Geoff Jenkins	.15
179	Dan Wilson	.15
180	John Olerud	.15
181	Javy Lopez	.15
182	Carl Everett	.15
183	Vernon Wells	.15
184	Juan Gonzalez	.75
185	Jorge Posada	.35
186	Mike Sweeney	.15
187	Cesar Izturis	.15
188	Jason Schmidt	.15
189	Chris Richard	.15
190	Jason Phillips	.15
191	Fred McGriff	.15
192	Shea Hillenbrand	.15
193	Ivan Rodriguez	.50
194	Mike Lowell	.15
195	Neifi Perez	.15
196	Kenny Lofton	.15
197	A.J. Pierzynski	.15
198	Larry Bigbie	.15
199	Juan Uribe	.15
200	Jeff Bagwell	.75
201	Timoniel Perez	.15
202	Jeremy Giambi	.15
203	Deivi Cruz	.15
204	Marquis Grissom	.15
205	Chipper Jones	1.00
206	Alex Gonzalez	.15
207	Steve Finley	.15
208	Ben Davis	.15
209	Mike Bordick	.15
210	Casey Fossum	.15
211	Aramis Ramirez	.15
212	Aaron Boone	.15
213	Orlando Cabrera	.15
214	Hee Seop Choi	.15
215	Jeromy Burnitz	.15
216	Todd Hollandsworth	.15
217	Rey Sanchez	.15
218	Jose Cruz Jr.	.15
219	Roosevelt Brown	.15
220	Odalis Perez	.15
221	Carlos Delgado	.40
222	Orlando Hernandez	.15
223	Adam Everett	.15
224	Adrian Beltre	.25
225	Ken Griffey Jr.	1.50
226	Brad Penny	.15
227	Carlos Lee	.15
228	J.C. Romero	.15
229	Ramon Martinez	.15
230	Matt Morris	.15
231	Ben Howard	.15
232	Damon Minor	.15
233	Jason Marquis	.15
234	Paul Wilson	.15
235	Ryan Dempster	.15
236	Jeffrey Hammonds	.15
237	Jaret Wright	.15
238	Carlos Pena	.15
239	Toby Hall	.15
240	Rick Helling	.15
241	Alex Escobar	.15
242	Trevor Hoffman	.15
243	Bernie Williams	.35
244	Jorge Julio	.15
245	Byung-Hyun Kim	.15
246	Mike Redmond	.15
247	Tony Armas	.15
248	Aaron Rowand	.15
249	Rusty Greer	.15
250	Aaron Harang	.15
251	Jeremy Fikac	.15
252	Jay Gibbons	.15
253	Brandon Puffer	.15
254	Dewayne Wise	.15
255	Chan Ho Park	.15
256	David Bell	.15
257	Kenny Rogers	.15
258	Mark Quinn	.15
259	Greg LaRocca	.15
260	Reggie Taylor	.15
261	Brett Tomko	.15
262	Jack Wilson	.15
263	Billy Wagner	.15
264	Greg Norton	.15
265	Tim Salmon	.25
266	Joe Randa	.15
267	Geronimo Gil	.15
268	Johnny Damon	.25
269	Robin Ventura	.15
270	Frank Thomas	.75
271	Terrence Long	.15
272	Mark Redman	.15
273	Mark Kotsay	.15
274	Ben Sheets	.15
275	Reggie Sanders	.15
276	Mark Grace	.25
277	Eddie Guardado	.15
278	Julio Mateo	.15
279	Bengie Molina	.15
280	Bill Hall	.15
281	Eric Chavez	.30
282	Joe Kennedy	.15
283	John Valentin	.15
284	Ray Durham	.15
285	Trot Nixon	.15

286 Rondell White .15
287 Alex Gonzalez .15
288 Tomas Perez .15
289 Jared Sandberg .15
290 Jacque Jones .15
291 Cliff Floyd .15
292 Ryan Klesko .15
293 Morgan Ensberg .15
294 Jerry Hairston Jr. .15
295 Doug Mientkiewicz .15
296 Darin Erstad .50
297 Jeff Conine .15
298 Johnny Estrada .15
299 Mark Mulder .15
300 Jeff Kent .15
301 Roger Clemens 1.25
302 Endy Chavez .15
303 Joe Crede .15
304 J.D. Drew .30
305 David Dellucci .15
306 Eli Marrero .15
307 Josh Fogg .15
308 Mike Crudale .15
309 Bret Boone .15
310 Mariano Rivera .30
311 Mike Piazza 1.50
312 Jason Jennings .15
313 Jason Varitek .15
314 Vicente Padilla .15
315 Kevin Millwood .15
316 Nick Johnson .15
317 Shane Reynolds .15
318 Joe Thurston .15
319 Mike Lamb .15
320 Aaron Sele .15
321 Fernando Tatis .15
322 Randy Wolf .15
323 David Justice .15
324 Andy Pettitte .30
325 Freddy Sanchez .15
326 Scott Spiezio .15
327 Randy Johnson .75
328 Karim Garcia .15
329 Eric Milton .15
330 Jermaine Dye .15
331 Kevin Brown .15
332 Adam Pettyjohn .15
333 Jason Lane .15
334 Mark Prior .60
335 Mike Lieberthal .15
336 Matt White .15
337 John Patterson .15
338 Marcus Giles .15
339 Kazuhisa Ishii .15
340 Willie Harris .15
341 Travis Phelps .15
342 Randall Simon .15
343 Manny Ramirez .75
344 Kerry Wood .60
345 Shannon Stewart .15
346 Mike Mussina .40
347 Joe Borchard .15
348 Tyler Walker .15
349 Preston Wilson .15
350 Damian Moss .15
351 Eric Karros .15
352 Bobby Kielty .15
353 Jason LaRue .15
354 Phil Nevin .15
355 Tony Graffanino .15
356 Antonio Alfonseca .15
357 Eddie Taubensee .15
358 Luis Ugueto .15
359 Greg Vaughn .15
360 Corey Thurman .15
361 Omar Infante .15
362 Alex Cintron .15
363 Esteban Loaiza .15
364 Tino Martinez .15
365 David Eckstein .15
366 *David Pember* .15
367 Damian Rolls .15
368 Richard Hidalgo .15
369 Brad Radke .15
370 Alex Sanchez .15
371 Ben Grieve .15
372 Brandon Inge .15
373 Adam Piatt .15
374 Charles Johnson .15
375 Rafael Palmeiro .65
376 Joe Mays .15
377 Derrek Lee .15
378 Fernando Vina .15
379 Andruw Jones .75
380 Troy Glaus .75
381 Bobby Hill .15
382 C.C. Sabathia .15
383 Jose Hernandez .15
384 Al Leiter .15
385 Jarrod Washburn .15
386 Cody Ransom .15
387 Matt Stairs .15
388 Edgar Renteria .15
389 Tsuyoshi Shinjo .15
390 Matt Williams .15
391 Bubba Trammell .15
392 Jason Kendall .15
393 Scott Rolen .65
394 Chuck Knoblauch .15
395 Jimmy Rollins .15
396 Gary Bennett .15
397 David Wells .15
398 Ronnie Belliard .15
399 Austin Kearns .50
400 Tim Hudson .30
401 Andy Van Hekken .15
402 Ray Lankford .15
403 Todd Helton .75
404 Jeff Weaver .15
405 Gabe Kapler .15
406 Luis Gonzalez .40
407 Sean Casey .15
408 Kazuhiro Sasaki .15
409 Mark Teixeira .50
410 Brian Giles .15
411 Robert Fick .15
412 Wilkin Ruan .15
413 Jose Rijo .15
414 Ben Broussard .15
415 Aubrey Huff .15
416 Magglio Ordonez .25
417 Barry Bonds 2.00
418 Miguel Tejada .40
419 Randy Johnson .75
420 Barry Zito .30
421 Jason Jennings .15
422 Eric Hinske .15
423 Benito Santiago .15
424 Adam Kennedy .15
425 Troy Glaus .65
426 Brandon Phillips .15
427 Jake Peavy .15
428 Jason Romano .15
429 Jeriome Robertson .15
430 Aaron Guiel .15
431 Hank Blalock .15
432 Brad Lidge .15
433 Francisco Rodriguez .15
434 Jaime Cerda .15
435 Jung Bong .15
436 Reed Johnson .15
437 Rene Reyes .15
438 Chris Snelling .15
439 Miguel Olivo .15
440 Brian Banks .15
441 Eric Junge .15
442 Kirk Saarloos .15
443 Jamey Carroll .15
444 Josh Hancock .15
445 Michael Restovich .15
446 William Bloomquist .15
447 John Lackey .15
448 Marcus Thames .15
449 Victor Martinez .15
450 Brett Myers .15
451 Wes Obermueller .15
452 Hansel Izquierdo .15
453 Brian Tallet .15
454 Craig Monroe .15
455 Doug Devore .15
456 John Buck .15
457 Tony Alvarez .15
458 Wily Mo Pena .15
459 John Stephens .15
460 Tony Torcato .15
461 Adam Kennedy .15
462 Alex Rodriguez .15
463 Derek Lowe .15
464 Garret Anderson .15
465 Pat Burrell .50
466 Eric Gagne .15
467 Tomokazu Ohka .15
468 Josh Phelps .15
469 Sammy Sosa 1.50
470 Jim Thome .15
471 Vladimir Guerrero .75
472 Jason Simontacchi .15
473 Adam Dunn .50
474 Jim Edmonds .15
475 Barry Bonds 2.00
476 Paul Konerko .25
477 Alfonso Soriano .75
478 Curt Schilling .40
479 John Smoltz .15
480 Torii Hunter .15
481 Rodrigo Lopez .15
482 Miguel Tejada .35
483 Eric Hinske .15
484 Roy Oswalt .25
485 Junior Spivey .15

B/W Goudey

NM/M
Complete Set (25): 80.00
Common Player: 1.50
Production 1,936 sets
Golds: 4-8X
Production 36 sets
1BWG Jim Thome 2.50
2BWG Derek Jeter 10.00
3BWG Alex Rodriguez 8.00
4BWG Mark Prior 1.50
5BWG Nomar Garciaparra 6.00
6BWG Curt Schilling 2.00
7BWG Pat Burrell 2.00
8BWG Frank Thomas 2.50
9BWG Roger Clemens 5.00
10BWG Chipper Jones 5.00
11BWG Barry Larkin 1.50
12BWG Hideo Nomo 2.00
13BWG Pedro J. Martinez 3.00
14BWG Jeff Bagwell 2.50
15BWG Greg Maddux 5.00
16BWG Vladimir Guerrero 3.00
17BWG Ichiro Suzuki 6.00
18BWG Mike Piazza 8.00
19BWG Drew Henson 1.50
20BWG Albert Pujols 3.00
21BWG Sammy Sosa 5.00
22BWG Jason Giambi 5.00
23BWG Randy Johnson 3.00
24BWG Ken Griffey Jr. 6.00
25BWG Barry Bonds 8.00

Glossy

SP's (1-100): 1-2X
Cards (101-485): 5-10X
Production 100 sets
Randomly inserted in Update packs

Game-used Parallel

NM/M
Common Player: 5.00
Inserted 1:35
Golds: 1-2X
Production 100 sets
Derek Jeter/jsy/150 35.00
Craig Biggio/bat 8.00
Hideo Nomo/jsy/200 20.00
Barry Larkin/jsy/200 10.00
Kazuhiro Sasaki/jsy/200 10.00
Greg Maddux/jsy 15.00
Mo Vaughn/jsy/60 10.00
Pedro Martinez/jsy/200 12.00
Barry Zito/jsy 10.00
Luis Aparicio/jsy/150 10.00
Willie Stargell/pants/150 15.00
Nomar Garciaparra/jsy/200 20.00
Edgardo Alfonzo/jsy/200 8.00
John Olerud/jsy 6.00
Juan Gonzalez/bat/200 10.00
Jorge Posada/bat 8.00
Shea Hillenbrand/bat 10.00
Ivan Rodriguez/jsy 8.00
Mike Lowell/bat 5.00
Jeff Bagwell/jsy/200 12.00
Chipper Jones/jsy 15.00
Jeromy Burnitz/jsy/200 6.00
Adrian Beltre/jsy 6.00
Robin Ventura/jsy 8.00
Frank Thomas/jsy 10.00
Mark Grace/jsy 10.00
Darin Erstad/jsy 8.00
Roger Clemens/jsy/150 20.00
J.D. Drew/jsy 8.00
Mike Piazza/jsy/150 20.00
Randy Johnson/jsy/150 12.00
Mark Prior/jsy/200 20.00
Kazuhisa Ishii/jsy 10.00
Manny Ramirez/jsy/150 10.00
Kerry Wood/jsy/200 15.00
Mike Mussina/jsy 10.00
Eric Karros/jsy 5.00
Rafael Palmeiro/jsy 8.00
Andruw Jones/bat/150 10.00
Jason Kendall/jsy 6.00
Jimmy Rollins/jsy 8.00
Barry Bonds/jsy/50 40.00
Miguel Tejada/bat/150 8.00
Jason Jennings/jsy 6.00

Hardball Preview

NM/M
Complete Set (10): 125.00
Common Player: 5.00
Inserted 1:400
1 Miguel Tejada 5.00
2 Derek Jeter 25.00
3 Mike Piazza 20.00
4 Barry Bonds 20.00
5 Mark Prior 5.00
6 Ichiro Suzuki 20.00
7 Alex Rodriguez 20.00
8 Nomar Garciaparra 15.00
9 Alfonso Soriano 12.00
10 Ken Griffey Jr. 15.00

Lumber Company

NM/M
Complete Set (30): 70.00
Common Player: 1.00
Inserted 1:10
1 Mike Piazza 6.00
2 Derek Jeter 8.00
3 Alex Rodriguez 6.00
4 Miguel Tejada 1.00
5 Nomar Garciaparra 5.00
6 Andruw Jones 1.50
7 Pat Burrell 1.50
8 Albert Pujols 3.00
9 Jeff Bagwell 2.00
10 Chipper Jones 4.00
11 Ichiro Suzuki 6.00
12 Alfonso Soriano 3.00
13 Eric Chavez 1.50
14 Brian Giles 1.00
15 Shawn Green 1.50
16 Jim Thome 2.00
17 Lance Berkman 1.50
18 Bernie Williams 1.50
19 Manny Ramirez 2.00
20 Vladimir Guerrero 3.00
21 Carlos Delgado 1.25
22 Scott Rolen 1.50
23 Sammy Sosa 4.00
24 Ken Griffey Jr. 5.00
25 Barry Bonds 6.00
26 Todd Helton 1.50
27 Jason Giambi 4.00
28 Austin Kearns 1.50
29 Jeff Kent 1.00
30 Magglio Ordonez 1.00

Lumber Company Bat

NM/M
Common Player: 6.00

Inserted 1:108
Jeff Bagwell/200 15.00
Lance Berkman/200 10.00
Barry Bonds/150 25.00
Pat Burrell/75 25.00
Eric Chavez/125 8.00
Carlos Delgado/200 6.00
Nomar Garciaparra/200 25.00
Brian Giles/200 8.00
Shawn Green/200 8.00
Todd Helton 8.00
Derek Jeter/96 35.00
Andruw Jones 8.00
Chipper Jones 15.00
Austin Kearns/75 18.00
Jeff Kent/200 6.00
Magglio Ordonez 6.00
Mike Piazza/200 20.00
Manny Ramirez 10.00
Alex Rodriguez 15.00
Scott Rolen/80 25.00
Alfonso Soriano/200 12.00
Miguel Tejada 10.00
Jim Thome/200 12.00
Bernie Williams 10.00

Lumber Company Bat Gold

NM/M
Numbered to 2002 HR total
Jeff Bagwell/31
Lance Berkman/42 25.00
Barry Bonds/46 70.00
Pat Burrell/37 50.00
Eric Chavez/34 20.00
Carlos Delgado/33 35.00
Nomar Garciaparra/24 60.00
Brian Giles/38 25.00
Shawn Green/42 35.00
Todd Helton/30 35.00
Derek Jeter/18 200.00
Andruw Jones/35 25.00
Chipper Jones/26 45.00
Austin Kearns/13 35.00
Jeff Kent/37 20.00
Magglio Ordonez/38 25.00
Mike Piazza/33 65.00
Manny Ramirez/33
Alex Rodriguez/57 40.00
Scott Rolen/31
Alfonso Soriano/39
Miguel Tejada/34 35.00
Jim Thome/52 30.00
Bernie Williams/19

Milestones

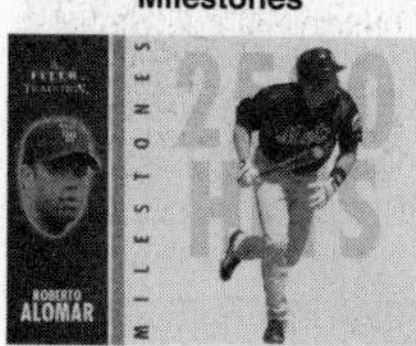

NM/M
Complete Set (25): 40.00
Common Player: 1.00
Inserted 1:5
1 Eddie Mathews 1.50
2 Rickey Henderson 1.50
3 Harmon Killebrew 1.50
4 Al Kaline 2.50
5 Willie McCovey 1.00
6 Tom Seaver 2.00
7 Reggie Jackson 2.00
8 Mike Schmidt 3.00
9 Nolan Ryan 5.00
10 Mike Piazza 4.00
11 Randy Johnson 2.00
12 Bernie Williams 1.50
13 Rafael Palmeiro 1.50
14 Juan Gonzalez 1.50
15 Ken Griffey Jr. 3.00
16 Derek Jeter 5.00
17 Roger Clemens 3.00
18 Roberto Alomar 1.50
19 Manny Ramirez 1.50
20 Luis Gonzalez 1.00
21 Barry Bonds 4.00
22 Nomar Garciaparra 3.00
23 Fred McGriff 1.00
24 Greg Maddux 2.50
25 Barry Bonds 4.00

Milestones Game-used

NM/M
Common Player: 8.00

Inserted 1:143
Golds: 1-2X
Production 100 sets
Roberto Alomar/bat/200 8.00
Barry Bonds/600 HR/bat/100 30.00
Barry Bonds/5 MVP/jsy/200 25.00
Roger Clemens/jsy/150 20.00
Nomar Garciaparra/jsy/200 20.00
Juan Gonzalez/bat/250 10.00
Luis Gonzalez
Derek Jeter/jsy/150 35.00
Randy Johnson/jsy/100 15.00
Greg Maddux 20.00
Fred McGriff 5.00
Rafael Palmeiro/jsy/200 8.00
Mike Piazza/jsy/100 20.00
Manny Ramirez/jsy/150 10.00
Bernie Williams/jsy/200 10.00

Standouts

NM/M
Complete Set (15): 60.00
Common Player: 1.50
Inserted 1:40
1SO Greg Maddux 5.00
2SO Derek Jeter 10.00
3SO Alex Rodriguez 8.00
4SO Miguel Tejada 2.00
5SO Nomar Garciaparra 6.00
6SO Barry Bonds 8.00
7SO Pat Burrell 2.00
8SO Ken Griffey Jr. 6.00
9SO Alfonso Soriano 4.00
10SO Mike Piazza 8.00
11SO Sammy Sosa 5.00
12SO Ichiro Suzuki 6.00
13SO Vladimir Guerrero 3.00
14SO Roger Clemens 5.00
15SO Adam Dunn 2.50

2003 FLEER TRADITION UPDATE

NM/M
Complete Set (398): 175.00
Common Player: .15
Common Rookie (286-398): .50
Cards (286-299):
Inserted 1:4
Pack (10): 2.00
Box (32 + 25 c
ount update box): 50.00
1 Aaron Boone .15
2 Carl Everett .15
3 Eduardo Perez .15
4 Jason Michaels .15
5 Karim Garcia .15
6 Rainier Olmedo .15
7 Scott Williamson .15
8 Adam Kennedy .15
9 Carl Pavano .15
10 Eli Marrero .15
11 Jason Simontacchi .15
12 Keith Foulke .15
13 Preston Wilson .15
14 Scott Hatteberg .15
15 Adam Dunn .50
16 Carlos Baerga .15
17 Elmer Dessens .15
18 Javier Vazquez .15
19 Kenny Rogers .15
20 Quinton McCracken .15
21 Shane Reynolds .15
22 Adam Eaton .15
23 Carlos Zambrano .15
24 Enrique Wilson .15
25 Jeff DaVanon .15
26 Kenny Lofton .25
27 Ramon Castro .15
28 Shannon Stewart .15
29 Al Martin .15
30 Carlos Guillen .15
31 Eric Karros .15
32 Tim Worrell .15
33 Kevin Millwood .25
34 Randall Simon .15
35 Shawn Chacon .15
36 Alex Rodriguez 1.50
37 Casey Blake .15
38 Eric Munson .15
39 Jeff Kent .25
40 Kris Benson .15
41 Randy Winn .15
42 Shea Hillenbrand .15
43 Alfonso Soriano 1.00
44 Chris George .15
45 Eric Bruntlett .15
46 Jeromy Burnitz .15
47 Kyle Farnsworth .15
48 Torii Hunter .40
49 Sidney Ponson .15
50 Andres Galarraga .25
51 Chris Singleton .15
52 Eric Gagne .25
53 Jesse Foppert .15
54 Lance Carter .15
55 Ray Durham .15
56 Tanyon Sturtze .15
57 Andy Ashby .15
58 Cliff Floyd .15
59 Eric Young .15
60 Jhonny Peralta .50
61 Livan Hernandez .15
62 Reggie Sanders .15
63 Tim Spooneybarger .15
64 Angel Berroa .15
65 Coco Crisp .15
66 Eric Hinske .15
67 Jim Edmonds .25
68 Luis Matos .15
69 Rickey Henderson .40
70 Todd Walker .15
71 Antonio Alfonseca .15
72 Corey Koskie .15
73 Erubiel Durazo .15
74 Jim Thome .50
75 Lyle Overbay .15
76 Robert Fick .15
77 Todd Hollandsworth .15
78 Aramis Ramirez .15
79 Cristian Guzman .15
80 Esteban Loaiza .15
81 Jody Gerut .15
82 Mark Grudzielanek .15
83 Roberto Alomar .40
84 Todd Hundley .15
85 Mike Hampton .15
86 Curt Schilling .40
87 Francisco Rodriguez .15
88 John Lackey .15
89 Mark Redman .15
90 Robin Ventura .25
91 Todd Zeile .15
92 B.J. Surhoff .15
93 Raul Mondesi .25
94 Frank Catalanotto .15
95 John Smoltz .25
96 Mark Ellis .15
97 Rocco Baldelli .50
98 Todd Pratt .15
99 Barry Bonds 2.00
100 Danny Graves .15
101 Fred McGriff .25
102 John Burkett .15
103 Marquis Grissom .15
104 Rocky Biddle .15
105 Tom Glavine .25
106 Bartolo Colon .25
107 Darren Bragg .15
108 Gabe Kapler .15
109 John Franco .15
110 Matt Mantei .15
111 Rod Beck .15
112 Tomokazu Ohka .15
113 Ben Petrick .15
114 Darren Dreifort .15
115 Garret Anderson .25
116 John Vander Wal .15
117 Melvin Mora .15
118 Rodrigo Lopez .15
119 Raul Ibanez .15
120 Benito Santiago .15
121 David Ortiz .15
122 Gary Bennett .15
123 Jon Garland .15
124 Michael Young .15
125 Rodrigo Rosario .15
126 Travis Lee .15
127 Bill Mueller .15
128 Derek Lowe .15
129 Gil Meche .15
130 Jose Guillen .15
131 Miguel Cabrera .40
132 Ron Calloway .15
133 Troy Percival .15
134 Billy Koch .15
135 Dmitri Young .15
136 Glendon Rusch .15
137 Jose Jimenez .15
138 Miguel Tejada .40
139 John Thomson .15
140 Troy O'Leary .15
141 Bobby Kielty .15
142 Dontrelle Willis .50
143 Greg Myers .15
144 Jose Vizcaino .15
145 Mike MacDougal .15
146 Ronnie Belliard .15
147 Tyler Houston .15
148 Brady Clark .15
149 Edgardo Alfonzo .15
150 Guillermo Mota .15
151 Jose Lima .15
152 Mike Williams .15
153 Roy Oswalt .25
154 Scott Podsednik .25
155 Brandon Lyon .15
156 Henry Mateo .15
157 Jose Macias .15
158 Mike Bordick .15
159 Royce Clayton .15
160 Vance Wilson .15
161 Brent Abernathy .15
162 Horacio Ramirez .15
163 Jose Reyes .40
164 Nick Punto .15
165 Ruben Sierra .15
166 Victor Zambrano .15
167 Brett Tomko .15
168 Ivan Rodriguez .75
169 Jose Mesa .15
170 Octavio Dotel .15
171 Russ Ortiz .15
172 Vladimir Guerrero .75
173 Brian Lawrence .15
174 Jae Weong Seo .15
175 Jose Cruz Jr. .15
176 Pat Burrell .40
177 Russell Branyan .15
178 Warren Morris .15
179 Brian Boehringer .15
180 Jason Johnson .15
181 Josh Phelps .15
182 Paul Konerko .15
183 Ryan Franklin .15
184 Wes Helms .15
185 Brooks Kieschnick .15
186 Jason Davis .15
187 Juan Pierre .15
188 Paul Wilson .15
189 Sammy Sosa 1.50
190 Wil Cordero .15
191 Byung-Hyun Kim .15
192 Juan Encarnacion .15
193 Placido Polanco .15
194 Sandy Alomar .15
195 Julio Lugo .15
196 Junior Spivey .15
197 Woody Williams .15
198 Xavier Nady .15
199 Mark Loretta .15
200 Deivi Cruz .15
201 Jorge Posada .25
202 Carlos Delgado .25
203 Alfonso Soriano .50
204 Alex Rodriguez 1.00
205 Troy Glaus .25
206 Garret Anderson .15
207 Hideki Matsui 2.00

No.	Player	Price
208	Ichiro Suzuki	.75
209	Esteban Loaiza	.15
210	Manny Ramirez	.25
211	Roger Clemens	.75
212	Roy Halladay	.15
213	Jason Giambi	.25
214	Edgar Martinez	.15
215	Bret Boone	.15
216	Hank Blalock	.15
217	Nomar Garciaparra	.75
218	Vernon Wells	.15
219	Melvin Mora	.15
220	Magglio Ordonez	.15
221	Mike Sweeney	.15
222	Barry Zito	.25
223	Carl Everett	.15
224	Shigetoshi Hasegawa	.15
225	Jamie Moyer	.15
226	Mark Mulder	.15
227	Eddie Guardado	.15
228	Ramon Hernandez	.15
229	Keith Foulke	.15
230	Javy Lopez	.15
231	Todd Helton	.25
232	Marcus Giles	.15
233	Edgar Renteria	.15
234	Scott Rolen	.25
235	Barry Bonds	1.00
236	Albert Pujols	.75
237	Gary Sheffield	.25
238	Jim Edmonds	.25
239	Jason Schmidt	.15
240	Mark Prior	1.00
241	Dontrelle Willis	.25
242	Kerry Wood	.25
243	Kevin Brown	.15
244	Woody Williams	.15
245	Paul LoDuca	.15
246	Richie Sexson	.15
247	Jose Vidro	.15
248	Luis Castillo	.15
249	Aaron Boone	.15
250	Mike Lowell	.15
251	Rafael Furcal	.15
252	Andruw Jones	.25
253	Preston Wilson	.15
254	John Smoltz	.15
255	Eric Gagne	.15
256	Randy Wolf	.15
257	Billy Wagner	.15
258	Luis Gonzalez	.15
259	Russ Ortiz	.15
260	Jim Thome, Pedro J. Martinez	.40
261	Alfonso Soriano, Jeff Bagwell	.50
262	Dontrelle Willis, Rocco Baldelli	.15
263	Carlos Delgado, Vladimir Guerrero	.25
264	Sammy Sosa, Magglio Ordonez	.50
265	Jason Giambi, Adam Dunn	.25
266	Mike Sweeney, Albert Pujols	.50
267	Barry Bonds, Torii Hunter	.75
268	Ichiro Suzuki, Andruw Jones	.50
269	Chipper Jones, Hank Blalock	.50
270	Mark Prior, Vernon Wells	.75
271	Nomar Garciaparra, Scott Rolen	.75
272	Alex Rodriguez, Lance Berkman	.75
273	Roger Clemens, Kerry Wood	.75
274	Derek Jeter, Jose Reyes	.75
275	Greg Maddux, Barry Zito	.50
276	Carlos Delgado	.25
277	J.D. Drew	.15
278	Barry Bonds	1.00
279	Albert Pujols	.75
280	Jim Thome	.25
281	Sammy Sosa	.75
282	Alfonso Soriano	.50
283	Hideki Matsui	1.00
284	Mike Piazza	.50
285	Vladimir Guerrero	.40
286	Rich Harden	.50
287	Chin-Hui Tsao	.50
288	*Edwin Jackson*	4.00
289	*Chien-Ming Wang*	3.00
290	*Josh Willingham*	2.00
291	*Matt Kata*	2.00
292	*Jose Contreras*	2.00
293	Chris Bootcheck	.50
294	Javier Lopez	1.00
295	*Delmon Young*	8.00
296	Pedro Liriano	.50
297	Noah Lowry	.50
298	Khalil Greene	3.00
299	Rob Bowen	.50
300	*Bo Hart*	2.00
301	*Beau Kemp*	.25
302	Gerald Laird	.15
303	*Miguel Ojeda*	.40
304	*Todd Wellemeyer*	.75
305	*Ryan Wagner*	2.00
306	*Jeff Duncan*	1.50
307	*Wilfredo Ledezma*	1.50
308	Wes Obermueller	.15
309	*Bernie Castro*	.25
310	*Tim Olson*	.25
311	*Colin Porter*	2.00
312	*Francisco Cruceta*	1.50
313	*Guillermo Quiroz*	1.50
314	*Brian Stokes*	.50
315	*Robby Hammock*	.50
316	*Lew Ford*	2.00
317	Todd Linden	.15
318	*Mike Gallo*	.50
319	*Francisco Rosario*	1.50
320	*Rosman Garcia*	.50
321	*Felix Sanchez*	.50
322	*Chad Gaudin*	1.00
323	*Phil Seibel*	.50
324	*Jason Gilfillan*	.50
325	*Terrmel Sledge*	.75
326	*Alfredo Gonzalez*	.50
327	*Josh Stewart*	1.00
328	Jeremy Griffiths	.15
329	*Cory Stewart*	.50
330	*Josh Hall*	1.00
331	*Arnie Munoz*	.50
332	Garrett Atkins	.15
333	Neal Cotts	.15
334	Dan Haren	2.00
335	*Shane Victorino*	.50
336	*David Sanders*	.50
337	*Oscar Villarreal*	.50
338	*Michael Hessman*	.50
339	*Andrew Brown*	.50
340	Kevin Hooper	.15
341	*Prentice Redman*	.50
342	*Brandon Webb*	3.00
343	Jimmy Gobble	.15
344	*Pete LaForest*	.50
345	*Chris Waters*	.75
346	*Hideki Matsui*	8.00
347	*Chris Capuano*	.75
348	*Jon Leicester*	.50
349	*Mike Nicolas*	.50
350	*Nook Logan*	.50
351	*Craig Brazell*	1.00
352	*Aaron Looper*	.50
353	*D.J. Carrasco*	.50
354	*Clint Barmes*	1.00
355	*Doug Waechter*	.75
356	*Julio Manon*	.50
357	*Jeremy Bonderman*	2.00
358	*Diegomar Markwell*	.50
359	*Dave Matranga*	.75
360	*Luis Ayala*	.50
361	Jason Stanford	.15
362	*Roger Deago*	.50
363	*Geoff Geary*	1.00
364	*Edgar Gonzalez*	.50
365	*Michel Hernandez*	.50
366	*Aquilino Lopez*	.50
367	*David Manning*	1.00
368	*Carlos Mendez*	.50
369	Matt Miller	.15
370	*Micheal Nakamura*	1.00
371	*Mike Neu*	.50
372	*Ramon Nivar*	.50
373	*Kevin Ohme*	.50
374	*Alex Prieto*	1.00
375	*Stephen Randolph*	.50
376	*Brian Sweeney*	1.00
377	*Matt Diaz*	.50
378	Mike Gonzalez	.15
379	*Daniel Cabrera*	2.00
380	*Fernando Cabrera*	.50
381	*David DeJesus*	.50
382	*Mike Ryan*	1.00
383	*Rick Roberts*	.50
384	Seung Jun Song	.15
385	*Rickie Weeks*	6.00
386	*Humberto Quintero*	.50
387	Alexis Rios	.15
388	*Aaron Miles*	2.00
389	*Tom Gregorio*	.50
390	*Anthony Ferrari*	.75
391	*Kevin Correia*	.75
392	*Rafael Betancourt*	.75
393	*Rett Johnson*	.50
394	*Richard Fischer*	.50
395	*Greg Aquino*	.50
396	*Daniel Garcia*	1.00
397	*Sergio Mitre*	1.00
398	Edwin Almonte	.15

Glossy

Stars (1-285): 5-10X
Rookies (286-398): .5-1.5X
Production 100 sets

Diamond Debuts

		NM/M
Complete Set (25):		40.00
Common Player:		1.00
Inserted 1:10		
1	Dontrelle Willis	4.00
2	Bo Hart	1.00
3	Jose Reyes	4.00
4	Chin-Hui Tsao	1.00
5	Brandon Webb	3.00
6	Rich Harden	2.00
7	Jesse Foppert	1.00
8	Rocco Baldelli	2.00
9	Hideki Matsui	5.00
10	Ron Calloway	1.00
11	Jeremy Bonderman	1.50
12	Mark Teixeira	3.00
13	Ryan Wagner	2.00
14	Jose Contreras	2.00
15	Miguel Cabrera	4.00
16	Lew Ford	1.00
17	Jeff Duncan	1.50
18	Matt Kata	1.00
19	Jeremy Griffiths	1.00
20	Todd Wellemeyer	1.00
21	Robby Matranga	1.00
22	Dave Matranga	1.00
23	Laynce Nix	1.00
24	Jhonny Peralta	1.00
25	Oscar Villarreal	1.00

Long GONE!

		NM/M
Complete Set (20):		60.00
Common Player:		2.00
Quantity produced listed		
1	Barry Bonds/475	8.00
2	Jason Giambi/440	2.00
3	Albert Pujols/452	6.00
4	Chipper Jones/420	4.00
5	Manny Ramirez/430	2.00
6	Sammy Sosa/536	5.00
7	Alfonso Soriano/440	3.00
8	Alex Rodriguez/430	6.00
9	Jim Thome/445	3.00
10	Vladimir Guerrero/502	3.00
11	Austin Kearns/430	2.00
12	Jeff Bagwell/420	2.00
13	Andruw Jones/430	2.00
14	Carlos Delgado/451	2.00
15	Nomar Garciaparra/440	6.00
16	Adam Dunn/464	2.00
17	Mike Piazza/450	4.00
18	Derek Jeter/410	6.00
19	Ken Griffey Jr./420	4.00
20	Hank Blalock/424	2.00

Milestones

		NM/M
Complete Set (20):		25.00
Common Player:		1.00
Inserted 1:8		
1	Roger Clemens	3.00
2	Rafael Palmeiro	1.00
3	Jeff Bagwell	1.00
4	Barry Bonds	4.00
5	Sammy Sosa	2.50
6	Albert Pujols	3.00
7	Ichiro Suzuki	2.00
8	Alfonso Soriano	1.50
9	Alex Rodriguez	3.00
10	Randy Johnson	1.50
11	Manny Ramirez	1.00
12	Chipper Jones	2.00
13	Todd Helton	1.00
14	Ken Griffey Jr.	2.00
15	Jim Thome	1.00
16	Frank Thomas	1.00
17	Pedro J. Martinez	1.50
18	Hideo Nomo	1.00
19	Jason Schmidt	1.00
20	Carlos Delgado	1.00

Turn Back the Clock

		NM/M
Complete Set (10):		75.00
Common Player:		4.00
Inserted 1:160		
1	Yogi Berra	8.00
2	Mike Schmidt	15.00
3	Tom Seaver	6.00
4	Reggie Jackson	5.00
5	Pee Wee Reese	4.00
6	Phil Rizzuto	4.00
7	Jim Palmer	4.00
8	Robin Yount	15.00
9	Nolan Ryan	20.00
10	Al Kaline	10.00

Throwback Threads

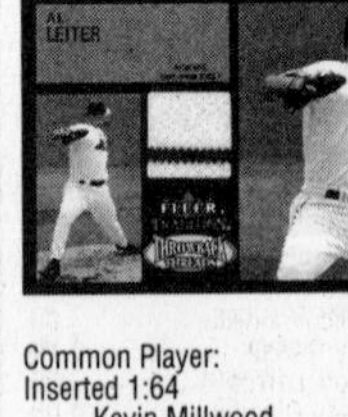

	NM/M
Common Player:	4.00
Inserted 1:64	
Kevin Millwood	6.00
Vladimir Guerrero	8.00
Troy Glaus	6.00
Mike Piazza	10.00
Al Leiter	4.00

Throwback Threads Patch

	NM/M
Common Player:	10.00
Production 100 sets	
Kevin Millwood	15.00
Vladimir Guerrero	20.00
Troy Glaus	15.00
Mike Piazza	25.00
Al Leiter	10.00

Throwback Threads Dual

	NM/M
Production 100	
Vladimir Guerrero, Troy Glaus	15.00
Mike Piazza, Al Leiter	15.00

Milestones Memorabilia

	NM/M
Common Player:	5.00
Inserted 1:20	
Golds:	1-2X
Production 100 sets	
Roger Clemens	15.00
Rafael Palmeiro	5.00
Jeff Bagwell	8.00
Sammy Sosa	10.00
Alfonso Soriano	10.00
Alex Rodriguez	10.00
Randy Johnson	8.00
Manny Ramirez	5.00
Chipper Jones	8.00
Todd Helton	6.00
Jim Thome	8.00
Frank Thomas	8.00
Pedro J. Martinez	8.00
Hideo Nomo	8.00
Jason Schmidt	8.00
Carlos Delgado	5.00

2004 FLEER AMERICA'S NATIONAL PASTIME

		NM/M
Common Player (1-60):		.25
Minor Stars (1-60):		.60
Common Card (61-90):		3.00
Production 699 Sets		
Pack (5):		10.00
Box (10):		100.00
1	Hideki Matsui	2.50
2	Khalil Greene	1.00
3	Pedro J. Martinez	1.00
4	Sammy Sosa	2.00
5	Mark Teixeira	.40
6	Orlando Cabrera	.25
7	Scott Podsednik	.25
8	Miguel Tejada	.60
9	Andruw Jones	.75
10	Manny Ramirez	.75
11	Jose Reyes	.25
12	Bobby Abreu	.40
13	Alex Rodriguez	2.50
14	Ivan Rodriguez	.60
15	Jason Schmidt	.40
16	Mike Piazza	1.50
17	Eric Chavez	.40
18	Mark Prior	2.50
19	Adam Dunn	.60
20	Richard Hidalgo	.25
21	Todd Helton	.75
22	Rocco Baldelli	.60
23	Roy Oswalt	.40
24	Angel Berroa	.25
25	Jason Giambi	1.00
26	Jim Thome	1.00
27	Javy Lopez	.40
28	Derek Jeter	3.00
29	Tom Glavine	.40
30	Magglio Ordonez	.40
31	Austin Kearns	.60
32	Scott Rolen	1.00
33	Miguel Cabrera	.75
34	Vernon Wells	.40
35	Frank Thomas	.75
36	Jeff Bagwell	.75
37	Shannon Stewart	.25
38	Richie Sexson	.60
39	Hideo Nomo	.40
40	Nomar Garciaparra	2.50
41	C.C. Sabathia	.25
42	Albert Pujols	2.50
43	Barry Zito	.60
44	Hank Blalock	.60
45	Carlos Delgado	.75
46	Greg Maddux	1.50
47	Randy Johnson	1.00
48	Josh Beckett	.75
49	Kerry Wood	.75
50	Roger Clemens	1.50
51	Garret Anderson	.40
52	Ichiro Suzuki	2.00
53	Kip Wells	.25
54	Vladimir Guerrero	1.00
55	Shawn Green	.40
56	Chipper Jones	1.50
57	Aubrey Huff	.25
58	Ken Griffey Jr.	1.50
59	Torii Hunter	.60
60	Alfonso Soriano	1.00
61	*Chris Shelton*	8.00
62	Graham Koonce	4.00
63	*Kazuo Matsui*	8.00
64	*Alfredo Simon*	4.00
65	Mike Gosling	3.00
66	Mike Rouse	4.00
67	*Mariano Gomez*	3.00
68	*Justin Leone*	3.00
69	*Jose Capellan*	3.00
70	*Donald Kelly*	4.00
71	*Merkin Valdez*	4.00
72	*Greg Dobbs*	4.00
73	*Shingo Takatsu*	4.00
74	*Chris Aguila*	3.00
75	*Jerome Gamble*	4.00
76	*Onil Joseph*	4.00
77	*Ramon Ramirez*	4.00
78	*Angel Chavez*	3.00
79	*Hector Gimenez*	3.00
80	*Ivan Ochoa*	4.00
81	*Aarom Baldiris*	4.00
82	*Akinori Otsuka*	4.00
83	*Ruddy Yan*	3.00
84	*Jerry Gil*	3.00
85	*Shawn Hill*	3.00
86	*John Gall*	4.00
87	*Jason Bartlett*	4.00
88	*Jorge Sequea*	4.00
89	*Luis Gonzalez*	4.00
90	Sean Henn	3.00

Red

(1-60):	1X-4X
(61-90):	.75X-1.25X
Production 150 Sets	

White

(1-60):	2X-6X
(61-90):	.75X-2X
Production 50 Sets	

Blue

No Pricing
Production 1 Set

American GAME

		NM/M
Common Player:		1.00
Inserted 1:10 (hobby)		
Inserted 1:12 (retail)		
1	Greg Maddux	2.50
2	Randy Johnson	2.00
3	Roger Clemens	4.00
4	Mark Prior	4.00
5	Mike Piazza	2.50
6	Alex Rodriguez	4.00
7	Adam Dunn	1.00
8	Jim Thome	2.00
9	Derek Jeter	5.00
10	Scott Rolen	2.00
11	Nomar Garciaparra	4.00
12	Kerry Wood	1.50
13	Chipper Jones	2.50
14	Frank Thomas	1.50
15	Jeff Bagwell	1.50

American Game Jersey

		NM/M
Common Player:		8.00
Inserted 1:96		
Patch #'d between 25 & 50:		2X-6X
Patch #'d less than 25:		No Pricing
Masterpiece:		No Pricing
Production 1 Set		
AM-JB	Jeff Bagwell/50	8.00
AM-RCL	Roger Clemens/47	10.00
AM-AD	Adam Dunn/30	8.00
AM-DJ	Derek Jeter/10	15.00
AM-RJO	Randy Johnson/42	8.00
AM-CJ	Chipper Jones/37	10.00
AM-GM	Greg Maddux/46	12.00
AM-MP	Mike Piazza/29	10.00
AM-MPR	Mark Prior/45	15.00
AM-AR	Alex Rodriguez/13	15.00
AM-SR	Scott Rolen/49	8.00
AM-FT	Frank Thomas/35	8.00
AM-JT	Jim Thome/47	8.00
AM-KW	Kerry Wood/43	8.00

America Game Retired - Single

Numbered between 6 & 31
No Pricing

AM-GB	George Brett/5
AM-RC	Roberto Clemente/25
AM-CF	Carlton Fisk/20
AM-AK	Al Kaline/6
AM-DM	Don Mattingly/23
AM-TM	Thurman Munson/15
AM-CR	Cal Ripken Jr./25
AM-BR	Babe Ruth/25
AM-MS	Mike Schmidt/25
AM-DW	Dave Winfield/31

History in the Making

		NM/M
Common Player:		.75
Inserted 1:5 (hobby)		
Inserted 1:4 (retail)		
1	Pedro J. Martinez	1.50
2	Alex Rodriguez	3.00
3	Sammy Sosa	2.50
4	Mike Piazza	2.00
5	Jason Giambi	1.50
6	Jim Thome	1.50
7	Derek Jeter	4.00
8	Hideo Nomo	.75
9	Nomar Garciaparra	3.00
10	Albert Pujols	3.00
11	Greg Maddux	2.00
12	Randy Johnson	1.50
13	Roger Clemens	2.00
14	Ichiro Suzuki	2.50
15	Vladimir Guerrero	1.50
16	Chipper Jones	2.00
17	Ken Griffey Jr.	2.00
18	Manny Ramirez	1.00
19	Ivan Rodriguez	.75
20	Mark Prior	3.00
21	Austin Kearns	.75
22	Alfonso Soriano	1.50
23	Barry Zito	.75
24	Josh Beckett	1.00
25	Angel Berroa	.75
26	Jose Reyes	.75
27	Adam Dunn	.75
28	Todd Helton	1.00
29	Hank Blalock	.75
30	Kazuo Matsui	6.00

Box Topper

No Pricing
Numbered to indicated quantity

Red

	NM/M
Peter Gammons/50	20.00
Ernie Harwell/50	20.00
Ralph Kiner/50	20.00

White

	NM/M
Red Barber/1	
Leo Durocher/2	
Peter Gammons/22	
Ernie Harwell/30	15.00
Ralph Kiner/23	
Billy Martin/2	

Masterpiece

No Pricing

National Treasures

	NM/M
Common Card:	3.00
Production 500 Sets	

Gold:	Numbered to notable year	
#75-99:		1X-3X
#25-74:		1X-5X
less than 25:		No Pricing
2NT	Kenesaw Landis	3.00
5NT	Leo Durocher	3.00
9NT	Peter Gammons	3.00
10NT	Ernie Harwell	3.00
11NT	Billy Martin	4.00
12NT	John McGraw	3.00
13NT	Red Barber	3.00
15NT	Casey Stengel	3.00
16NT	Sparky Anderson	3.00
17NT	Harry Caray	4.00
18NT	Ban Johnson	3.00
20NT	Ralph Kiner	3.00

Ted Williams Reprint Set

	NM/M
Ted Williams Card (1-81):	6.00
Production 406 Sets	
Masterpiece:	No Pricing
Production 1 Set	

History In The Making - Jersey

		NM/M
Common Player:		5.00
Inserted 1:36		
Patch:		2X-6X
Numbered between 20 & 50		
Masterpiece:		No Pricing
Production 1 Set		
HM-JB	Josh Beckett/45	8.00
HM-AB	Angel Berroa/20	5.00
HM-MB	Hank Blalock/48	8.00
HM-RC	Roger Clemens/26	10.00
HM-AD	Adam Dunn/49	8.00
HM-JG	Jason Giambi/24	8.00
HM-VG	Vladimir Guerrero/50	8.00
HM-TH	Todd Helton/32	8.00
HM-DJ	Derek Jeter/22	15.00
HM-RJ	Randy Johnson/50	8.00
HM-CJ	Chipper Jones/48	10.00
HM-AK	Austin Kearns/41	8.00
HM-GM	Greg Maddux/47	12.00
HM-PM	Pedro J. Martinez/45	8.00
HM-KM	Kazuo Matsui/20	20.00
HM-HN	Hideo Nomo/50	5.00
HM-MP	Mike Piazza/42	10.00
HM-MPR	Mark Prior/49	15.00
HM-AP	Albert Pujols/46	15.00
HM-MR	Manny Ramirez/46	8.00
HM-JR	Jose Reyes/37	5.00
HM-AR	Alex Rodriguez/21	15.00
HM-IR	Ivan Rodriguez/43	8.00
HM-AS	Alfonso Soriano/48	8.00
HM-SS	Sammy Sosa/39	12.00
HM-JT	Jim Thome/49	8.00
HM-BZ	Barry Zito/44	8.00

Game-Used

No Pricing
Production 9 Sets

Signature Swing

	NM/M
Numbered to indicated quantity	

Carlos Beltran/176 25.00
Lance Berkman/173 15.00
Hank Blalock/265 15.00
Joe Carter/95 12.00
Sean Casey/169 12.00
Eric Chavez/138 15.00
Bucky Dent/21
David Eckstein/161 10.00
Jim Edmonds/10
Carlton Fisk/36 40.00
Lew Ford/183 20.00
Luis Gonzalez/61 15.00
Vladimir Guerrero/4
Frank Howard/60 20.00
Derek Jeter/35 125.00
Andruw Jones/23
Chipper Jones/116 40.00
Al Kaline/79 40.00
Austin Kearns/20
Javy Lopez/220 15.00
Edgar Martinez/85 20.00
Don Mattingly/15
Bill Mazeroski/61 25.00
Stan Musial/15
Jim Palmer/33 25.00
Dave Parker/57 15.00
Corey Patterson/8
Mike Piazza/64 100.00
Albert Pujols/110 125.00
Cal Ripken Jr./6
Gary Sheffield/25 60.00
Warren Spahn/188 30.00
Miguel Tejada/3
Alan Trammell/138 10.00

Numbered to indicated quantity
Carlos Beltran/109 25.00
Lance Berkman/98 20.00
Hank Blalock/109 20.00
George Brett/42 120.00
Joe Carter/22
Sean Casey/108 15.00
Eric Chavez/85 20.00
Bucky Dent/35 20.00
David Eckstein/76 15.00
Jim Edmonds/22
Carlton Fisk/51 40.00
Lew Ford/109 20.00
Jay Gibbons/33 20.00
Luis Gonzalez/109 10.00
Frank Howard/24
Derek Jeter/22
Chipper Jones/88 40.00
Al Kaline/43 50.00
Javy Lopez/65 20.00
Edgar Martinez/22
Don Mattingly/73 50.00
Bill Mazeroski/56 30.00
Stan Musial/36 60.00
Jim Palmer/25 25.00
Dave Parker/79 15.00
Mike Piazza/31 125.00
Juan Pierre/52
Albert Pujols/76 150.00
Gary Sheffield/26 60.00
Bill "Moose" Skowron/59 15.00
Warren Spahn/106 40.00
Alan Trammell/89 15.00

Signature Swing - White

NM/M

Numbered to indicated quantity
Carlos Beltran/29 25.00
Lance Berkman/42 25.00
Hank Blalock/29 30.00
George Brett/30 120.00
Joe Carter/35 20.00
Sean Casey/25 20.00
Eric Chavez/34 25.00
Bucky Dent/8
David Eckstein/8
Jim Edmonds/42 20.00
Carlton Fisk/37 40.00
Lew Ford/3
Jay Gibbons/28 20.00
Luis Gonzalez/57 20.00
Vladimir Guerrero/44 30.00
Frank Howard/48 25.00
Aubrey Huff/34 15.00
Derek Jeter/24
Chipper Jones/45 50.00
Al Kaline/29 50.00
Javy Lopez/43 20.00
Edgar Martinez/37 30.00
Don Mattingly/35 80.00
Bill Mazeroski/19
Stan Musial/39 60.00
Rafael Palmeiro/47 50.00
Jim Palmer/1
Dave Parker/34 15.00
Corey Patterson/14
Mike Piazza/40 125.00
Juan Pierce/2
Scott Podsednik/2
Albert Pujols/43 175.00
Cal Ripken Jr./25 200.00
Ivan Rodriguez/35 50.00
Scott Rolen/28 80.00
Gary Sheffield/43 60.00
Bill "Moose" Skowron/28 20.00
Warren Spahn/4
Frank Thomas/43 80.00
Alan Trammell/28 20.00

Signature Swing - Blue

NM/M

Numbered to indicated quantity
Sean Casey/37 40.00
Adam Dunn/31 20.00
David Eckstein/44 15.00
Jim Edmonds/37 20.00
Lew Ford/44 40.00
Bill Mazeroski/39 50.00
Jim Palmer/44 25.00
Dave Parker/29 15.00
Scott Podsednik/38 20.00
Warren Spahn/26 50.00

Signs of the Future - Gold

NM/M

Numbered to indicated quantity
Jeremy Bonderman/300 8.00
Miguel Cabrera/300 20.00
Bobby Crosby/299 20.00
Adam Everett/285 10.00
Luis Gonzalez/264 8.00
Mike Gosling/195 8.00
Khalil Greene/300 50.00
Rich Harden/304 10.00
Sean Henn/300 8.00
Koyie Hill/340 8.00
Ryan Howard/53 25.00
Tim Hudson/72 20.00
Adam LaRoche/78 8.00
Micheal Nakamura/231 8.00
Alexis Rios/45 15.00
Alfredo Simon/258 8.00
Javier Vazquez/21 20.00
Ryan Wagner/251 10.00
Dontrelle Willis/47 40.00
Kevin Youkilis/317 15.00

Signs of the Future - Red

NM/M

Numbered to indicated quantity
Aarom Baldiris/64 10.00
Jeremy Bonderman/120 10.00
A.J. Burnett/58 20.00
Miguel Cabrera/133 25.00
Bobby Crosby/114 20.00
Adam Everett/106 12.00
Luis Gonzalez/132 10.00
Mike Gosling/132 10.00
Khalil Greene/121 50.00
Rich Harden/133 15.00
Sean Henn/128 10.00
Koyie Hill/58 12.00
Edwin Jackson/52 15.00
Graham Koonce/55 10.00
Josh Labandeira/55 8.00
Adam LaRoche/124 8.00
Justin Leone/68 20.00
Micheal Nakamura/133 10.00
Bubba Nelson/99 10.00
Jose Reyes/93 12.00
Mike Rouse/124 8.00
Alfredo Simon/112 10.00
Ryan Wagner/98 12.00
Kerry Wood/55 30.00
Kevin Youkilis/133 20.00

Signs Of The Future - White

NM/M

Numbered to indicated quantity
Garrett Atkins/25 15.00
Miguel Cabrera/34 40.00
Bobby Crosby/52 30.00
Adam Everett/36 15.00
Luis Gonzalez/50 15.00
Mike Gosling/41 12.00
Khalil Greene/52 80.00
Rich Harden/52 20.00
Sean Henn/48 12.00
Koyie Hill/27 15.00
Tim Hudson/28 40.00
Adam LaRoche/50 12.00
Micheal Nakamura/33 15.00
Jose Reyes/52 20.00
Alexis Rios/39 15.00
Mike Rouse/40 10.00
Alfredo Simon/28 15.00
Ryan Wagner/46 15.00
Kevin Youkilis/52 25.00

2004 FLEER AUTHENTIX

NM/M

Complete Set (130):
Common Player: .25
Common SP (101-130): 2.50
Production 999
Pack (5): 4.00
Box (24): 80.00
1 Albert Pujols 2.50
2 Derek Jeter 3.00
3 Jody Gerut .25
4 Mark Teixeira .40
5 Tom Glavine .50
6 Kerry Wood 1.00
7 Ichiro Suzuki 1.50
8 Jose Vidro .25
9 Mark Prior 2.00
10 Jim Edmonds .50
11 Richie Sexson .50
12 Jay Gibbons .25
13 Jason Kendall .25
14 Lance Berkman .50
15 Andruw Jones .75
16 Jim Thome 1.00
17 Josh Beckett .75
18 Troy Glaus .50
19 Jason Giambi 1.00
20 Sammy Sosa 2.00
21 Bret Boone .40
22 Eric Gagne .40
23 Nomar Garciaparra 2.00
24 Geoff Jenkins .50
25 Ivan Rodriguez .50
26 Preston Wilson .40
27 Alex Rodriguez 2.50
28 Jorge Posada .50
29 Ken Griffey Jr. 1.50
30 Rocco Baldelli .50
31 Shannon Stewart .25
32 Frank Thomas .75
33 Edgar Renteria .25
34 Torii Hunter .50
35 Corey Patterson .25
36 Edgar Martinez .40
37 Jeff Bagwell .75
38 Greg Maddux 1.50
39 Mike Lieberthal .25
40 Craig Biggio .40
41 Randy Johnson 1.00
42 Marlon Byrd .25
43 Jay Payton .25
44 Carlos Delgado .75
45 Scott Podsednik .50
46 Pedro J. Martinez 1.00
47 Carlos Beltran .40
48 Mike Sweeney .25
49 Gary Sheffield .50
50 Pat Burrell .50
51 Shawn Green .40
52 Tony Batista .25
53 Brian Giles .40
54 Roy Oswalt .40
55 Brandon Webb .40
56 Miguel Tejada .50
57 Miguel Cabrera .75
58 Luis Gonzalez .40
59 Billy Wagner .25
60 Craig Monroe .25
61 Vernon Wells .40
62 Bernie Williams .50
63 Austin Kearns .50
64 Aubrey Huff .25
65 Mike Piazza 1.50
66 Magglio Ordonez .50
67 Bo Hart .25
68 Hideo Nomo .50
69 Curt Schilling .50
70 Barry Zito .50
71 Todd Helton .75
72 Roy Halladay .50
73 Alfonso Soriano 1.00
74 Roberto Alomar .50
75 Scott Rolen 1.00
76 Manny Ramirez .75
77 Sean Burroughs .25
78 Angel Berroa .25
79 Javy Lopez .40
80 Reggie Sanders .25
81 Juan Pierre .25
82 Chipper Jones 1.50
83 Bobby Abreu .40
84 Dontrelle Willis .40
85 Tim Salmon .40
86 Eric Chavez .40
87 Adam Dunn .50
88 Rafael Palmeiro .75
89 Hideki Matsui 2.50
90 Esteban Loaiza .25
91 Darin Erstad .40
92 Vladimir Guerrero 1.00
93 David Ortiz .25
94 Jason Schmidt .40
95 Dmitri Young .25
96 Garret Anderson .50
97 Mark Mulder .25
98 Omar Vizquel .25
99 Hank Blalock .50
100 Jose Reyes .25
101 Rickie Weeks 8.00
102 Chad Gaudin 2.50
103 Ryan Wagner 3.00
104 Koyie Hill 2.50
105 Rich Harden 2.50
106 Edwin Jackson 4.00
107 Khalil Greene 3.00
108 Chien-Ming Wang 3.00
109 Matt Kata 2.50
110 Chin-Hui Tsao 2.50
111 Dan Haren 2.50
112 Delmon Young 8.00
113 Mike Hessman 2.50
114 Bobby Crosby 2.50
115 *Cory Sullivan* 2.50
116 Brandon Watson 2.50
117 Aaron Miles 2.50
118 Jonny Gomes 2.50
119 Graham Koonce 2.50
120 *Shawn Hill* 2.50
121 Garrett Atkins 2.50
122 *John Gall* 2.50
123 *Chad Bentz* 2.50
124 *Alfredo Simon* 2.50
125 *Josh Labandeira* 3.00
126 Ryan Howard 3.00
127 *Jason Bartlett* 2.50
128 Dallas McPherson 2.50
129 *Greg Dobbs* 2.50
130 *Jerry Gil* 2.50

Balcony

Stars (1-100): 4-8X
SP's (101-130): 1-2X
Production 100 sets

Club Box

Stars (1-100): 10-15X
SP's (101-130): 2-4X
Production 25 sets

Standing Room Only

No Pricing
Production 5 sets

Autographed Authentix

NM/M

Common Autograph: 15.00
Production 75
Championship: No Pricing
Production 25
Rocco Baldelli 40.00
Angel Berroa 15.00

Marlon Byrd 15.00
Miguel Cabrera 40.00
Eric Gagne 40.00
Roy Halladay 20.00
Trot Nixon 35.00
Juan Pierre 15.00
Albert Pujols 120.00
Vernon Wells 20.00

Ballpark Classics

NM/M
Complete Set (10): 15.00
Common Player: 1.00
Inserted 1:12
1BC Nomar Garciaparra 3.00
2BC Alfonso Soriano 1.50
3BC Chipper Jones 1.50
4BC Albert Pujols 3.00
5BC Jason Giambi 1.00
6BC Mark Prior 3.00
7BC Sammy Sosa 2.50
8BC Derek Jeter 4.00
9BC Greg Maddux 2.00
10BC Alex Rodriguez 3.00

Ballpar Classics Game-Used

NM/M
Common Player: 8.00
Inserted 1:37
Nomar Garciaparra 10.00
Jason Giambi 8.00
Derek Jeter 15.00
Chipper Jones 8.00
Greg Maddux 10.00
Mark Prior 15.00
Albert Pujols 15.00
Alex Rodriguez 10.00
Alfonso Soriano 8.00
Sammy Sosa 12.00

Jersey Authentix Autograph

NM/M
Common Autograph: 15.00
Production 100
All-Star Autographs: 1-1.25X
Production 50
Championship Autos.: No Pricing
Production 10
Albert Pujols 125.00
Juan Pierre 15.00
Miguel Cabrera 40.00
Eric Gagne 40.00
Marlon Byrd 15.00
Rocco Baldelli 40.00
Roy Halladay 25.00
Vernon Wells 20.00
Trot Nixon 35.00

Jersey Authentix Ripped

NM/M
Common Player: 4.00
Inserted 1:16
Unripped: 2-3X
Production 50 sets
All-Star Unripped: No Pricing
Production one set
Jeff Bagwell 8.00
Josh Beckett 6.00
Miguel Cabrera 8.00
Hee Seop Choi 4.00
Nomar Garciaparra 10.00
Jason Giambi 8.00
Torii Hunter 5.00
Derek Jeter 15.00
Randy Johnson 8.00
Chipper Jones 8.00
Austin Kearns 6.00
Greg Maddux 8.00
Juan Pierre 4.00
Mark Prior 15.00
Albert Pujols 15.00
Jose Reyes 8.00
Alex Rodriguez 10.00
Ivan Rodriguez 6.00
Alfonso Soriano 8.00
Sammy Sosa 12.00
Mark Teixeira 6.00
Jim Thome 8.00

Dontrelle Willis 6.00
Kerry Wood 8.00
Barry Zito 6.00

Jersey Authentix Game of the Week

NM/M
Common Duo: 10.00
Inserted 1:120
Unripped: 1-1.5X
Production 50
1 Dontrelle Willis, Kerry Wood 20.00
2 Miguel Cabrera, Mark Teixeira 15.00
3 Nomar Garciaparra, Alfonso Soriano 15.00
4 Jim Thome, Ivan Rodriguez 10.00
5 Josh Beckett, Mark Prior 25.00
6 Alex Rodriguez, Derek Jeter 35.00
7 Jeff Bagwell, Austin Kearns 15.00
8 Jason Giambi, Barry Zito 10.00
9 Jose Reyes, Juan Pierre 10.00
10 Chipper Jones, Albert Pujols 20.00

Ticket for Four

NM/M
Common Quad Jersey: 20.00
Production 100 sets
1 Dontrelle Willis, Josh Beckett, Mark Prior, Kerry Wood 30.00
2 Nomar Garciaparra, Alex Rodriguez, Derek Jeter, Jose Reyes 50.00
3 Ivan Rodriguez, Miguel Cabrera, Hee Seop Choi, Juan Pierre
4 Jason Giambi, Jim Thome, Mark Teixeira, Jeff Bagwell 25.00
5 Chipper Jones, Albert Pujols, Sammy Sosa, Torii Hunter 40.00
6 Greg Maddux, Randy Johnson, Kerry Wood, Barry Zito 20.00
7 Nomar Garciaparra, Alfonso Soriano, Chipper Jones, Albert Pujols 40.00
8 Sammy Sosa, Derek Jeter, Alex Rodriguez, Jim Thome 50.00
9 Mark Prior, Greg Maddux, Austin Kearns, Ivan Rodriguez 25.00
10 Jason Giambi, Randy Johnson, Jeff Bagwell, Torii Hunter 20.00

Ticket Studs

NM/M
Complete Set (15): 20.00
Common Player: .75
Inserted 1:6
1TS Nomar Garciaparra 3.00
2TS Josh Beckett 1.00
3TS Derek Jeter 4.00
4TS Mark Prior 3.00
5TS Albert Pujols 3.00
6TS Alfonso Soriano 1.50
7TS Jim Thome 1.50
8TS Ichiro Suzuki 2.00
9TS Hideki Matsui 3.00
10TS Dontrelle Willis .75
11TS Mike Schmidt 2.00
12TS Nolan Ryan 4.00
13TS Reggie Jackson 1.00
14TS Tom Seaver 1.00
15TS Brooks Robinson 1.00

2004 FLEER CLASSIC CLIPPINGS

NM/M
Common Player (1-75): .25
Minor Stars (1-75): .40
Common Player (76-110): 5.00
Production 500 Sets
Pack (5): 5.00
Box (18): 90.00
1 Juan Pierre .25

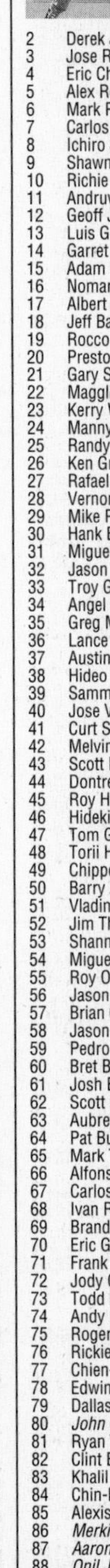

2 Derek Jeter 3.00
3 Jose Reyes .40
4 Eric Chavez .40
5 Alex Rodriguez 2.50
6 Mark Prior 2.50
7 Carlos Beltran .40
8 Ichiro Suzuki 2.00
9 Shawn Green .40
10 Richie Sexson .60
11 Andruw Jones .75
12 Geoff Jenkins .40
13 Luis Gonzalez .40
14 Garret Anderson .40
15 Adam Dunn .60
16 Nomar Garciaparra 2.50
17 Albert Pujols 2.50
18 Jeff Bagwell .75
19 Rocco Baldelli .60
20 Preston Wilson .25
21 Gary Sheffield .60
22 Magglio Ordonez .40
23 Kerry Wood .75
24 Manny Ramirez .75
25 Randy Johnson 1.00
26 Ken Griffey Jr. 1.50
27 Rafael Palmeiro .40
28 Vernon Wells .25
29 Mike Piazza 1.50
30 Hank Blalock .60
31 Miguel Cabrera .75
32 Jason Giambi 1.00
33 Troy Glaus .60
34 Angel Berroa .25
35 Greg Maddux 1.50
36 Lance Berkman .40
37 Austin Kearns .60
38 Hideo Nomo .40
39 Sammy Sosa 2.00
40 Jose Vidro .25
41 Curt Schilling .60
42 Melvin Mora .25
43 Scott Podsednik .40
44 Dontrelle Willis .40
45 Roy Halladay .40
46 Hideki Matsui 2.50
47 Tom Glavine .40
48 Torii Hunter .60
49 Chipper Jones 1.50
50 Barry Zito .60
51 Vladimir Guerrero 1.00
52 Jim Thome 1.00
53 Shannon Stewart .25
54 Miguel Tejada .60
55 Roy Oswalt .40
56 Jason Kendall .40
57 Brian Giles .40
58 Jason Schmidt .40
59 Pedro J. Martinez 1.00
60 Bret Boone .40
61 Josh Beckett .75
62 Scott Rolen 1.00
63 Aubrey Huff .25
64 Pat Burrell .40
65 Mark Teixeira .40
66 Alfonso Soriano 1.00
67 Carlos Delgado .75
68 Ivan Rodriguez .60
69 Brandon Webb .25
70 Eric Gagne .40
71 Frank Thomas .75
72 Jody Gerut .25
73 Todd Helton .75
74 Andy Pettitte .60
75 Roger Clemens 1.50
76 Rickie Weeks 8.00
77 Chien-Ming Wang 8.00
78 Edwin Jackson 6.00
79 Dallas McPherson 8.00
80 *John Gall* 5.00
81 Ryan Wagner 6.00
82 Clint Barmes 8.00
83 Khalil Greene 6.00
84 Chin-Hui Tsao 6.00
85 Alexis Rios 6.00
86 *Merkin Valdez* 5.00
87 *Aarom Baldiris* 5.00
88 *Onil Joseph* 5.00
89 *Ruddy Yan* 5.00
90 *Chad Bentz* 5.00
91 *Shawn Hill* 5.00
92 Delmon Young 8.00
93 *Hector Gimenez* 5.00
94 *William Bergolla* 5.00
95 *Ronny Cedeno* 5.00
96 *Angel Chavez* 5.00
97 *Justin Leone* 5.00
98 *Ivan Ochoa* 5.00
99 *Ian Snell* 8.00
100 Rich Harden 6.00
101 Joe Mauer 10.00
102 *Akinori Otsuka* 10.00
103 Bobby Crosby 6.00
104 Garrett Atkins 5.00
105 Dan Haren 5.00
106 Koyie Hill 5.00
107 *Kazuo Matsui* 20.00
108 Adam LaRoche 5.00
109 Terrmel Sledge 5.00
110 *Shingo Takatsu* 5.00

First Edition

(1-75): 1X-5X
(76-110): .5X-1.25X
Production 150 Sets

Press Proof Cyan

(1-100): No Pricing
Production 1 Set

Press Proof Magenta

(1-100): No Pricing
Production 1 Set

Press Proof Yellow

(1-100): No Pricing
Production 1 Set

Press Proof Black

(1-100): No Pricing
Production 1 Set

Press Clippings

NM/M
Common Player: 1.25
Inserted 1:6
1PC Josh Beckett 1.75
2PC Albert Pujols 4.00
3PC Derek Jeter 5.00
4PC Alex Rodriguez 5.00
5PC Jim Thome 2.00
6PC Angel Berroa 1.00
7PC Dontrelle Willis 1.25
8PC Roy Halladay 1.25
9PC Kerry Wood 1.75
10PC Mark Prior 4.00
11PC Roger Clemens 3.00
12PC Hideki Matsui 4.00
13PC Ichiro Suzuki 3.50
14PC Eric Gagne 1.25
15PC Miguel Cabrera 1.75
16PC Nomar Garciaparra 4.00
17PC Hank Blalock 1.25
18PC Chipper Jones 3.00
19PC Sammy Sosa 3.50
20PC Alfonso Soriano 2.00

Classic Clippings

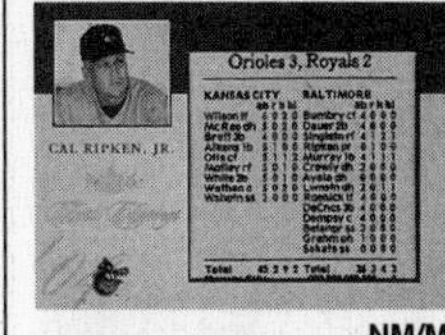

NM/M
Common Player (1-20): 4.00
Production 750 Sets
Common Player (21-25): 8.00
Production 100 Sets
1CC Nolan Ryan 15.00
2CC Mike Schmidt 6.00
3CC Cal Ripken Jr. 10.00
4CC Don Mattingly 8.00
5CC Roger Clemens 5.00
6CC Randy Johnson 4.00
7CC Mark Prior 4.00
8CC Jim Thome 5.00
9CC Sammy Sosa 5.00
10CC Pedro J. Martinez 4.00
11CC Chipper Jones 4.00
12CC Vladimir Guerrero 4.00
13CC Albert Pujols 6.00
14CC Ichiro Suzuki 6.00
15CC Derek Jeter 10.00
16CC Alex Rodriguez 8.00

17CC Greg Maddux 5.00
18CC Nomar Garciaparra 8.00
19CC Mike Piazza 6.00
20CC Ken Griffey Jr. 8.00
21CC Pie Traynor 8.00
22CC Bill Dickey 8.00
23CC George Sisler 10.00
24CC Ted Williams 20.00
25CC Enos Slaughter 8.00

All-Star Lineup Triple Jersey Silver

NM/M
Common Card: 15.00
Production 75 Sets
Gold Triple Patch: 2X-4X
Production 25 Sets
No Gold Card For ASL-SMA

S/C/G Alfonso Soriano, Roger Clemens, Jason Giambi 25.00
R/G/R Alex Rodriguez, Nomar Garciaparra, Manny Ramirez 25.00
W/P/W Kerry Wood, Mark Prior, Dontrelle Willis 30.00
S/P/W Gary Sheffield, Albert Pujols, Preston Wilson 20.00
C/H/R Luis Castillo, Todd Helton, Scott Rolen 15.00
D/S/G Carlos Delgado, Alfonso Soriano, Troy Glaus 15.00
W/D/H Vernon Wells, Carlos Delgado, Roy Halladay 15.00
S/M/A Ichiro Suzuki, Hideki Matsui, Garret Anderson 30.00
R/R/P Edgar Renteria, Scott Rolen, Albert Pujols 50.00
S/J/L Gary Sheffield, Andruw Jones, Javy Lopez 15.00
C/Z/H Roger Clemens, Barry Zito, Roy Halladay 20.00
C/W/L Luis Castillo, Dontrelle Willis, Mike Lowell 10.00
O/B/G Magglio Ordonez, Hank Blalock, Troy Glaus 15.00
G/R/G Nomar Garciaparra, Alex Rodriguez, Jason Giambi 40.00
H/S/P Todd Helton, Richie Sexson, Albert Pujols 20.00

Bat Rack (3 bat) - Green

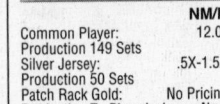

NM/M
Common Card: 10.00
Production 175 Sets
Red: .5X-1.5X
Production 50 Sets
Gold: 1X-2X
Production 25 Sets

Derek Jeter, Alex Rodriguez, Gary Sheffield 40.00
Sammy Sosa, Derek Lee, Mark Prior 30.00
Miguel Cabrera, Juan Pierre, Josh Beckett 15.00
Nomar Garciaparra, Manny Ramirez, Curt Schilling 20.00
Alfonso Soriano, Hank Blalock, Mark Teixeira 15.00
Mike Piazza, Jose Reyes, Kazuo Matsui 20.00
Richie Sexson, Brandon Webb, Roberto Alomar 10.00
Mark Prior, Josh Beckett, Curt Schilling 15.00
Carlos Delgado, Aubrey Huff, Jason Giambi 10.00
Albert Pujols, Scott Rolen, Jim Edmonds 30.00
Rocco Baldelli, Aubrey Huff, Carlos Delgado 10.00
Jeff Bagwell, Jim Thome, Todd Helton 15.00
Gary Sheffield, Manny Ramirez, Rocco Baldelli 10.00
Troy Glaus, Scott Rolen, Hank Blalock 15.00
Roberto Alomar, Jose Reyes, Alfonso Soriano 15.00
Alex Rodriguez, Miguel Tejada, Miguel Cabrera 15.00
Vladimir Guerrero, Juan Pierre, Chipper Jones 10.00
Jason Giambi, Jim Thome, Todd Helton 15.00
Vladimir Guerrero, Albert Pujols, Sammy Sosa 25.00
Derek Jeter, Hideki Matsui, Nomar Garciaparra 40.00

Bat Rack (4 bat) - Green

NM/M
Common Card: 15.00
Production 75 Sets
Red: 1X-2X
Production 25 Sets
Gold: No Pricing
Production 10 Sets

Derek Jeter, Alex Rodriguez, Gary Sheffield, Jason Giambi 50.00
Sammy Sosa, Mark Prior, Miguel Cabrera, Josh Beckett 40.00
Derek Jeter, Alex Rodriguez, Kazuo Matsui, Nomar Garciaparra 60.00
Juan Pierre, Gary Sheffield, Miguel Cabrera, Rocco Baldelli 15.00
Jim Thome, Jeff Bagwell, Mark Teixeira, Carlos Delgado 20.00
Albert Pujols, Mark Prior, Alex Rodriguez, Curt Schilling 50.00
Todd Helton, Jose Reyes, Kazuo Matsui, Scott Rolen 40.00
Sammy Sosa, Vladimir Guerrero, Jim Edmonds, Chipper Jones 25.00
Alfonso Soriano, Roberto Alomar, Hank Blalock, Troy Glaus 15.00
Rocco Baldelli, Chipper Jones, Juan Pierre, Manny Ramirez 20.00
Jim Thome, Jeff Bagwell, Todd Helton, Derek Lee 20.00
Curt Schilling, Nomar Garciaparra, Brandon Webb, Richie Sexson 25.00
Mike Piazza, Jose Reyes, Albert Pujols, Scott Rolen 30.00
Vladimir Guerrero, Miguel Tejada, Jason Giambi, Mike Piazza 25.00
Jeff Bagwell, Derrek Lee, Aubrey Huff, Carlos Delgado 20.00

Bat Rack Autographs-Bronze

NM/M
Common Player: 12.00
Production 75 Sets
Roberto Alomar 40.00
Josh Beckett 30.00
Hank Blalock 30.00
Miguel Cabrera 40.00
Jim Edmonds 30.00
Aubrey Huff 12.00
Edgar Martinez 20.00
Jose Reyes 25.00
Gary Sheffield 30.00
Mark Teixeira 20.00

Jersey Rack (3 jersey)-Blue

NM/M
Common Card: 15.00
Production 225 Sets
Bronze Jersey: .5X-1.25X
Production 99 Sets
Silver Jersey: .75X-1.5X
Production To Player's Jersey No.
Patch Pack Gold: No Pricing
Production 125 Sets

Derek Jeter, Alex Rodriguez, Jason Giambi 50.00
Sammy Sosa, Kerry Wood, Mark Prior 30.00
Miguel Cabrera, Dontrelle Willis, Josh Beckett 15.00
Nomar Garciaparra, Pedro J. Martinez, Curt Schilling 15.00
Alex Rodriguez, Derek Jeter, Nomar Garciaparra 40.00
Mike Piazza, Ivan Rodriguez, Javy Lopez 20.00
Roger Clemens, Mark Prior, Josh Beckett 20.00
Roger Clemens, Andy Pettitte, Roy Oswalt 40.00
Dontrelle Willis, Kerry Wood, Curt Schilling 20.00
Albert Pujols, Sammy Sosa, Manny Ramirez 20.00
Rocco Baldelli, Miguel Cabrera, Albert Pujols 20.00
Barry Zito, Tim Hudson, Mark Mulder 15.00
Randy Johnson, Richie Sexson, Brandon Webb 15.00
Dontrelle Willis, Brandon Webb, Angel Berroa 15.00
Carlos Delgado, Miguel Tejada, Alfonso Soriano 15.00

Jersey Rack Auto. - Bronze

NM/M
Common Player: 12.00
Production 149 Sets
Silver Jersey: .5X-1.5X
Production 50 Sets
Patch Rack Gold: No Pricing
Production To Player's Jersey No.
Garret Anderson 15.00
Garrett Atkins 12.00
Rocco Baldelli 20.00
Josh Beckett 20.00
Angel Berroa 15.00
Marlon Byrd 12.00
Miguel Cabrera 40.00
Carlos Delgado 20.00
Jody Gerut 12.00
Roy Halladay 15.00
Dan Haren 12.00
Torii Hunter 15.00
Edwin Jackson 20.00
Barry Larkin 40.00
Mark Mulder 15.00
Mike Mussina 30.00
Andy Pettitte 40.00
Albert Pujols 120.00
Ivan Rodriguez 50.00
Scott Rolen 50.00
Ryan Wagner 12.00
Brandon Webb 15.00
Dontrelle Willis 20.00
Kerry Wood 30.00

Phenom Lineup Auto. - Red

NM/M
Common Card: 10.00
Production 150 Sets
Silver: .5X-1.25X
Production 99 Sets
Gold: .5X-1.5X
Production 50 Sets
Cards contain autograph of the first player listed.

Ryan Howard, Jim Thome, Todd Helton 10.00
John Gall, Albert Pujols, Scott Rolen 10.00
Jose Reyes, Kazuo Matsui, Rickie Weeks 20.00
Hank Blalock, Troy Glaus, Alex Rodriguez 20.00
Rich Harden, Roy Halladay, Barry Zito 10.00
Alexis Rios, Carlos Delgado, Vernon Wells 10.00
Laynce Nix, Alex Rodriguez, Garret Anderson 10.00
Khalil Greene, Edgar Renteria, Mike Lowell 25.00
Dontrelle Willis, Mark Prior, Kerry Wood 20.00
Rickie Weeks, Luis Castillo, Jose Reyes 20.00
Dallas McPherson, Troy Glaus, Garret Anderson 15.00
Chien-Ming Wang, Hideki Matsui, Jason Giambi 20.00
Scott Podsednik, Albert Pujols, Andruw Jones 15.00
Bobby Crosby, Nomar Garciaparra, Alex Rodriguez 18.00
Ryan Wagner, Dontrelle Willis, Mark Prior 10.00
Delmon Young, Ichiro Suzuki, Hideki Matsui 30.00
Grady Sizemore, Manny Ramirez, Garret Anderson 20.00
Adam LaRoche, Albert Pujols, Jim Thome 10.00
Edwin Jackson, Mark Prior, Kerry Wood 15.00
Miguel Cabrera, Luis Castillo, Mike Lowell 40.00
Merkin Valdez, Edwin Jackson, Dontrelle Willis 10.00
Angel Berroa, Nomar Garciaparra, Alex Rodriguez 10.00

C.C. Signature Edition

NM/M
Common Player: 15.00
Production 50 Sets
Masterpiece: No Pricing
Production 1 Set
1 Nolan Ryan 125.00
2 Mike Schmidt 75.00
3 Cal Ripken Jr. 175.00
4 Don Mattingly 75.00

5 Albert Pujols 125.00
6 Randy Johnson 60.00
7 Khalil Greene 40.00
8 Rickie Weeks 30.00
9 Edwin Jackson 15.00
10 Rich Harden 15.00
16 Vladimir Guerrero 40.00
17 Mark Prior 75.00

2004 FLEER EX

NM/M
Common Player (1-40): 1.50
Minor Stars (1-40): 2.00
Common Player (41-65): 5.00
Production 500 Sets
Die-Cuts (41-65): .75X-1.25X
First 150 seq. #'d cards are die-cut
1 Vladimir Guerrero 3.50
2 Randy Johnson 3.50
3 Chipper Jones 4.00
4 Miguel Tejada 2.50
5 Pedro J. Martinez 3.50
6 Nomar Garciaparra 6.00
7 Sammy Sosa 5.00
8 Greg Maddux 4.00
9 Frank Thomas 3.00
10 Ken Griffey Jr. 4.00
11 Omar Vizquel 2.00
12 Todd Helton 3.00
13 Ivan Rodriguez 2.50
14 Miguel Cabrera 3.00
15 Dontrelle Willis 2.00
16 Jeff Bagwell 3.00
17 Roger Clemens 4.00
18 Carlos Beltran 2.00
19 Hideo Nomo 2.00
20 Scott Podsednik 1.50
21 Torii Hunter 2.50
22 Jose Vidro 1.50
23 Mike Piazza 4.00
24 Hideki Matsui 6.00
25 Alex Rodriguez 6.00
26 Derek Jeter 8.00
27 Tim Hudson 2.00
28 Jim Thome 3.50
29 Craig Wilson 1.50
30 Brian Giles 2.00
31 Jason Schmidt 2.00
32 Ichiro Suzuki 5.00
33 Scott Rolen 3.50
34 Albert Pujols 6.00
35 Rocco Baldelli 2.50
36 Alfonso Soriano 3.50
37 Carlos Delgado 3.00
38 Curt Schilling 2.50
39 Mark Prior 6.00
40 Josh Beckett 3.00
41 *Merkin Valdez* 5.00
42 *Akinori Otsuka* 8.00
43 *Ian Snell* 5.00
44 *Kazuo Matsui* 10.00
45 *Jason Bartlett* 8.00
46 *Dennis Sarfate* 5.00
47 Sean Henn 5.00
48 David Aardsma 5.00
49 Casey Kotchman 8.00
50 *John Gall* 5.00
51 *William Bergolla* 5.00
52 *Angel Chavez* 5.00
53 *Hector Gimenez* 5.00
54 *Aarom Baldiris* 5.00
55 *Justin Leone* 8.00
56 *Onil Joseph* 5.00
57 *Freddy Guzman* 5.00
58 *Andres Blanco* 5.00
59 *Greg Dobbs* 5.00
60 Joe Mauer 5.00
61 *Luis Gonzalez* 8.00
62 *Chris Saenz* 5.00
63 Zack Greinke 5.00
64 *Jose Capellan* 8.00
65 *Brad Halsey* 10.00

Essential Credentials Now

Cards 51-65: 1X-2X
Cards 41-50: 1.25X-2.25X
Cards 25-40: 3X-5X
Cards 1-24: No Pricing
Production 65 - 1 Sets

Essential Credentials Future

Cards 1-25: .75X-2X
Cards 26-40: 2X-4X
Cards 41-65: No Pricing
Production 65 - 1 Sets

Clearly Authentics Black Patch

NM/M
Common Player: 10.00
Production 75 Sets
Jeff Bagwell 20.00
Rocco Baldelli 15.00
Josh Beckett 20.00
Lance Berkman 15.00
Hank Blalock 15.00
Pat Burrell 15.00
Miguel Cabrera 20.00
Rod Carew 30.00
Roger Clemens 30.00
Adam Dunn 15.00
Eric Gagne 15.00
Jason Giambi 25.00
Brian Giles 15.00
Troy Glaus 15.00
Shawn Green 15.00
Vladimir Guerrero 25.00
Tony Gwynn 30.00
Todd Helton 20.00
Rickey Henderson 30.00
Tim Hudson 15.00
Torii Hunter 15.00
Randy Johnson 25.00
Andruw Jones 20.00
Chipper Jones 30.00
Greg Maddux 30.00
Pedro J. Martinez 25.00
Hideki Matsui 40.00
Kazuo Matsui 40.00
Don Mattingly 40.00
Paul Molitor 30.00
Eddie Murray 50.00
Hideo Nomo 15.00
Magglio Ordonez 15.00
Rafael Palmeiro 20.00
Mike Piazza 30.00
Mark Prior 40.00
Albert Pujols 40.00
Manny Ramirez 20.00
Cal Ripken Jr. 75.00
Alex Rodriguez 40.00
Ivan Rodriguez 15.00
Scott Rolen 25.00
Curt Schilling 15.00
Ozzie Smith 25.00
Alfonso Soriano 25.00
Sammy Sosa 35.00
Mark Teixeira 15.00
Miguel Tejada 15.00
Frank Thomas 20.00
Jim Thome 25.00
Rickie Weeks 15.00
Dontrelle Willis 15.00
Kerry Wood 20.00
Barry Zito 15.00

Clearly Authentics Turquoise Nameplate

No Pricing
Sequentially #'d to varying quantities

Clearly Authentics Tan Double Patch

No Pricing
Production 22 Sets

Clearly Authentics Tan Double Patches

No Pricing
Production 22 Sets

Clearly Authentics Burgundy Triple Patch

No Pricing
Production 13 Sets

Clearly Authentics Royal Patch/Bat/Jersey

No Pricing
Production 8 Sets

Clearly Authentics - Double MLB Logo

No Pricing
Production 1 Set

Clearly Authentics Signature Black Jersey

NM/M
Sequentially #'d to varying quantities
Burgundy Buttons: No Pricing
Production 6 Sets
Emerald MLB Logo: No Pricing
Production 1 Set
Josh Beckett/50 30.00
Hank Blalock/50 50.00
Miguel Cabrera/50 30.00
Roger Clemens/50 150.00
J.D. Drew 30.00
Adam Dunn/49
Troy Glaus/50 25.00
Vladimir Guerrero/50 50.00
Todd Helton/50 40.00
Randy Johnson/17
Chipper Jones/50 60.00
Greg Maddux/37
Pedro J. Martinez/23
Roy Oswalt/49 30.00
Rafael Palmeiro/43 60.00
Mike Piazza/37
Mark Prior/46
Albert Pujols/50 225.00
Manny Ramirez/50 60.00
Mariano Rivera/50 80.00
Ivan Rodriguez/50
Scott Rolen/50
Gary Sheffield/50 50.00
Frank Thomas/50 60.00
Jim Thome/50
Bernie Williams/42 75.00
Dontrelle Willis/50 25.00
Kerry Wood/34 50.00
Barry Zito/18

ConnEXions

NM/M
Production 25 or 50 Sets
1 Adrian Beltre/25, Carlos Beltran/25
2 Rickie Weeks/25, Delmon Young/25
3 Bo Jackson/25, Deion Sanders/25
4 Bill Buckner/50, Mookie Wilson/50
5 Joe Niekro/50, Phil Niekro/50
6 Casey Kotchman/50, Joe Mauer/50 100.00
7 Shannon Stewart/25, Torii Hunter/25 90.00
8 Craig Wilson/25, Jack Wilson/25
9 Johnny Damon/25, Trot Nixon/25 90.00
10 Carlos Lee/25, Magglio Ordonez/25 30.00
11 Eric Gagne/25, Billy Wagner/25
12 Scott Podsednik/25, Lyle Overbay/25 60.00
13 Barry Zito/25, Tim Hudson/25 125.00
14 Bucky Dent/50, Mike Torrez/50 40.00
15 Brian Giles/25, Marcus Giles/25 60.00
16 Kirk Gibson/25, Dennis Eckersley/25
17 Dontrelle Willis/25, Miguel Cabrera/25 60.00
18 Michael Young/50, Khalil Greene/50 80.00
19 Mark Teixeira/25, Hank Blalock/25 100.00

Classic ConnEXions Doubles

No Pricing
Production 22 Sets
Emerald: No Pricing
Production 1 Set

Classic ConnEXions Triples

No Pricing
Production 13 Sets
Emerald: No Pricing
Production 1 Set

Check Mates

NM/M
Production 1 or 25 Sets
1 Albert Pujols/25, Stan Musial/25 500.00
2 Eddie Murray/25, Rafael Palmeiro/25 200.00
3 Tom Seaver/25, Nolan Ryan/25
4 Ernie Banks/25, Ryne Sandberg/25 300.00
5 George Brett/25, Mike Schmidt/25
6 Yogi Berra/25, Johnny Bench/25
7 Mark Prior/25, Kerry Wood/25
8 Randy Johnson/25, Greg Maddux/25
9 Manny Ramirez/25, Pedro J. Martinez/25 300.00
10 Wade Boggs/25, Tony Gwynn/25 175.00
11 Reggie Jackson/25, Don Mattingly/25 200.00
12 Cal Ripken Jr./25, Ozzie Smith/25
13 Carl Yastrzemski/25, Duke Snider/25
14 Robin Yount/25, Kirby Puckett/25 150.00
15 Rickey Henderson/25, Jose Canseco/25
16 Honus Wagner/1, Ty Cobb/1
17 Babe Ruth/1, Lou Gehrig/1

Double Barrel

No Pricing
Production 1 Set

Signings of the Times Best Year

NM/M
Sequentially #'d to Player's Best Year
Emerald: No Pricing
Production 1 Set
Ernie Banks/58 (bat) 60.00
Johnny Bench/72 (jersey) 60.00
Yogi Berra/54 (bat)
Wade Boggs/87 (bat) 40.00
George Brett/80 (jersey) 80.00
Jose Canseco/88 (jersey) 30.00
Will Clark/91 (jersey) 40.00

Tony Gwynn/94 (jersey) 50.00
Rickey Henderson/90 (jersey) 75.00
Bo Jackson/89 (jersey) 60.00
Reggie Jackson/73 (jersey)
Don Mattingly/85 (jersey) 80.00
Eddie Murray/83 (jersey) 60.00
Stan Musial/48 (bat) 75.00
Kirby Puckett/88 (bat)
Cal Ripken Jr./91 (jersey)
Nolan Ryan/73 (jersey) 150.00
Ryne Sandberg/90 (bat) 60.00
Deion Sanders/92 (jersey)
Mike Schmidt/80 (jersey) 80.00
Tom Seaver/69 (jersey) 75.00
Ozzie Smith/87 (jersey) 50.00
Duke Snider/55 (bat) 50.00
Carl Yastrzemski/67 (bat) 60.00
Robin Yount/82 (jersey)

Signings of the Times HOF Year

NM/M

Sequentially #'d to Player's HOF Year
Ernie Banks/77 (bat) 60.00
Johnny Bench/89 (jersey) 60.00
Yogi Berra/72 (bat) 50.00
George Brett/99 (jersey) 80.00
Reggie Jackson/93 (jersey) 50.00
Eddie Murray/3 (jersey)
Stan Musial/69 (bat) 75.00
Kirby Puckett/1 (bat)
Nolan Ryan/99 (jersey)
Mike Schmidt/95 (jersey) 75.00
Tom Seaver/92 (jersey) 50.00
Ozzie Smith/2 (jersey)
Duke Snider/80 (bat) 30.00
Carl Yastrzemski/89 (bat) 60.00
Robin Yount/99 (jersey)

Signings of the Times Debut Year

NM/M

Sequentially #'d to Player's Debut Year
Ernie Banks/53 (bat) 60.00
Johnny Bench/67 (jersey) 60.00
Yogi Berra/46 (bat) 60.00
Wade Boggs/82 (bat) 40.00
George Brett/73 (jersey)
Jose Canseco/85 (jersey) 30.00
Will Clark/86 (jersey) 40.00
Tony Gwynn/82 (jersey) 50.00
Rickey Henderson/79 (jersey) 75.00
Bo Jackson/86 (jersey) 60.00
Reggie Jackson/67 (jersey) 50.00
Don Mattingly/82 (jersey) 80.00
Eddie Murray/77 (jersey) 60.00
Stan Musial/41 (bat) 75.00
Kirby Puckett/84 (bat) 50.00
Cal Ripken Jr./81 (jersey)
Nolan Ryan/66 (jersey) 150.00
Ryne Sandberg/81 (bat) 60.00
Deion Sanders/89 (jersey) 40.00
Mike Schmidt/72 (jersey) 80.00
Tom Seaver/67 (jersey)
Ozzie Smith/78 (jersey) 50.00
Duke Snider/47 (bat) 50.00
Carl Yastrzemski/61 (bat) 75.00
Robin Yount/74 (jersey) 40.00

Signings of the Times Pewter

NM/M

Sequentially #'d to varying quantities
Ernie Banks/21 (bat)
Yogi Berra/32 (bat)
Wade Boggs/32 (bat) 50.00
Jose Canseco/27 (jersey) 75.00
Will Clark/44 (jersey)
Tony Gwynn/21 (jersey)
Rickey Henderson/32 (jersey) 75.00
Bo Jackson/60 (jersey) 50.00
Don Mattingly/33 (jersey) 80.00
Eddie Murray/50 (jersey) 80.00
Stan Musial/51 (bat) 80.00
Kirby Puckett/31 (bat) 50.00
Cal Ripken Jr./32 (jersey)
Ryne Sandberg/28 (bat) 60.00
Deion Sanders/44 (jersey)
Duke Snider/21 (bat)
Ozzie Smith/36 (jersey) 80.00

2004 FLEER FLAIR

NM/M

Common Player (1-60): 1.00
Minor Star (1-60): 1.25
Unlisted Star (1-60): 1.75
Common Rookie (61-82): 5.00
Rookie Production 799 Sets
Collection Row (1-60): 1X-3X
Collection Row (61-82): .5X-2X
Row 1 Production 125 Sets
Collection Row 2: No Pricing
Production 1 Set
Box (1): 100.00

1 Brandon Webb 1.00
2 Todd Helton 2.00
3 Jeff Bagwell 2.00
4 Shawn Green 1.25
5 Vladimir Guerrero 3.00
6 Tom Glavine 1.25
7 Jason Giambi 3.00
8 Barry Zito 1.75
9 Jason Kendall 1.25
10 Carlos Delgado 2.00
11 Curt Schilling 1.75
12 Ken Griffey Jr. 3.50
13 Mike Piazza 3.50
14 Alfonso Soriano 3.00
15 Albert Pujols 5.00
16 Chipper Jones 3.50
17 Alex Rodriguez 5.00
18 Miguel Tejada 1.75
19 Pedro J. Martinez 3.00
20 Mark Prior 5.00
21 Magglio Ordonez 1.25
22 Scott Podsednik 1.75
23 Shannon Stewart 1.00
24 Rocco Baldelli 1.75
25 Darin Erstad 1.25
26 Omar Vizquel 1.00
27 Angel Berroa 1.00
28 Jose Vidro 1.00
29 Rich Harden 1.00
30 Andruw Jones 2.00
31 Troy Glaus 1.75
32 Sammy Sosa 4.00
33 Dontrelle Willis 1.25
34 Ivan Rodriguez 1.75
35 Nomar Garciaparra 5.00
36 Josh Beckett 2.00
37 Jose Reyes 1.00
38 Scott Rolen 3.00
39 Greg Maddux 3.50
40 Andy Pettitte 1.75
41 Jason Schmidt 1.25
42 Edgar Martinez 1.25
43 Manny Ramirez 2.00
44 Torii Hunter 1.75
45 Mark Teixeira 1.25
46 Hideo Nomo 1.00
47 Brian Giles 1.25
48 Adam Dunn 1.75
49 Fernando Vina 1.00
50 Hideki Matsui 5.00
51 Jim Thome 3.00
52 Hank Blalock 1.75
53 Miguel Cabrera 2.00
54 Randy Johnson 3.00
55 Javy Lopez 1.25
56 Frank Thomas 2.00
57 Roger Clemens 3.50
58 Marlon Byrd 1.00
59 Derek Jeter 6.00
60 Ichiro Suzuki 4.00
61 *Kazuo Matsui* 25.00
62 *Chad Bentz* 8.00
63 *Greg Dobbs* 5.00
64 *John Gall* 5.00
65 *Cory Sullivan* 5.00
66 *Hector Gimenez* 5.00
67 Graham Koonce 5.00
68 *Jason Bartlett* 5.00
69 *Angel Chavez* 5.00
70 *Ronny Cedeno* 5.00
71 *Donald Kelly* 5.00
72 *Ivan Ochoa* 5.00
73 *Ruddy Yan* 5.00
74 Mike Gosling 5.00
75 *Alfredo Simon* 5.00
76 *Jerome Gamble* 5.00
77 *Chris Aguila* 5.00
78 Mike Rouse 5.00
79 *Justin Leone* 5.00
80 *Merkin Valdez* 5.00
81 *Aarom Baldiris* 5.00
82 *Chris Shelton* 8.00

Autograph Collection

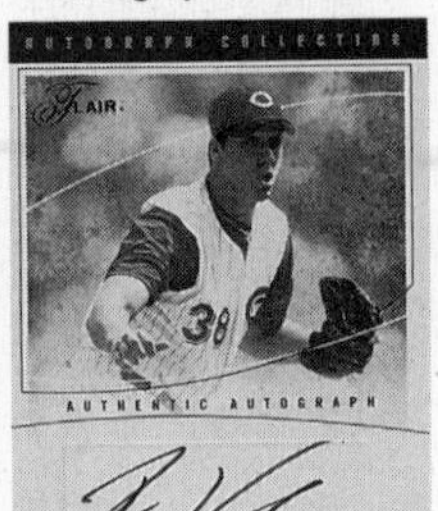

NM/M

Common Player: 10.00
Production between 65-200 Sets
Crown: .5X-1X
Production 100 Sets
Parchment: 1X-1.75X
Production 25 Sets
Platinum: No Pricing
Production 10 Sets
Masterpiece: No Pricing
Production 1 Set
Garrett Atkins/195 10.00
Rocco Baldelli/180 25.00
Aarom Baldiris/180 10.00
Jason Bartlett/95 15.00
Josh Beckett/65 40.00
Angel Berroa/178 15.00
Miguel Cabrera/172 40.00
Bobby Crosby/87 30.00
Jim Edmonds/73 25.00
John Gall/94 30.00
Khalil Greene/40 195.00
Dan Haren/195 15.00
Ryan Howard/185 15.00
Edwin Jackson/183 15.00
Andruw Jones/163 25.00
Graham Koonce/175 10.00
Josh Labandeira/166 10.00
Adam LaRoche/280 15.00
Justin Leone/180 15.00
Ryan Meaux/180 10.00
Mike Mussina/69 50.00
Micheal Nakamura/180 10.00
Bubba Nelson/185 10.00
Corey Patterson/172 15.00
Juan Pierre/94 15.00
Scott Podsednik/96 25.00
Mark Prior/60 100.00
Alexis Rios/185 20.00
Michael Rouse/195 10.00
Chris Shelton/170 10.00
Grady Sizemore/197 20.00
Alfonso Soriano
Merkin Valdez/179 10.00
Javier Vazquez/187 30.00
Ryan Wagner/175 15.00
Chien-Ming Wang/178 30.00
Brandon Webb/122 15.00
Rickie Weeks/169 30.00
Dontrelle Willis/73 30.00
Kerry Wood/73 40.00
Delmon Young/177 25.00

Cuts and Glory

NM/M

Common Player: 25.00
Production 100 Sets
Silver: .75X-1.25X
Production 50 Sets
Gold: No Pricing
Production 15 Sets
Platinum: No Pricing
Production 3 Sets
Masterpiece: No Pricing
Production 1 Set
Garret Anderson 30.00
Hank Blalock 25.00
Marlon Byrd 25.00
Carlos Delgado 30.00
Adam Dunn 40.00
Eric Gagne 40.00
Luis Gonzalez 25.00
Vladimir Guerrero 50.00
Ricky Henderson 100.00
Torii Hunter 25.00
Randy Johnson 60.00
Chipper Jones 60.00
Austin Kearns 25.00
Greg Maddux 75.00
Edgar Martinez 40.00
Magglio Ordonez 25.00
Albert Pujols 150.00
Jose Reyes 30.00
Scott Rolen 40.00
Mark Teixeira 25.00
Frank Thomas 75.00

Diamond Cuts Game-Used Blue

NM/M

Common Player: 5.00
Production 250 Sets
Blue Die-Cut: 1X-3X
Production 25 Sets
Red: .5X-1.25X
Production 175 Sets
Red Die-Cut: No Pricing
Production 18 Sets
Pewter: .5X-1.5X
Production 125 Sets
Pewter Die-Cut: No Pricing
Production 13 Sets
Copper: .5X-1.5X
Production 75 Sets
Die-Cut Copper: No Pricing
Production 8 Sets
Silver: .5X-1.5X
Production 50 Sets
Silver Die-Cut: No Pricing
Production 5 Sets
Gold: 1X-5X
Numbered to player's jersey No.

Gold Die-Cut: No Pricing
Production 3 Sets
Platinum: 2X-5X
Numbered to 2003 HR/Win total
Platinum Die-Cut: No Pricing
Production 1 Set
Purple: No Pricing
Production 1 Set

JB	Josh Beckett	8.00
HB	Hank Blalock	5.00
RC	Roger Clemens	10.00
NG	Nomar Garciaparra	12.00
DJ	Derek Jeter	15.00
AJ	Andruw Jones	8.00
CJ	Chipper Jones	8.00
PM	Pedro J. Martinez	8.00
HM	Hideki Matsui	12.00
ANP	Andy Pettitte	8.00
MIP	Mike Piazza	8.00
MAP	Mark Prior	12.00
ALP	Albert Pujols	12.00
JR	Jose Reyes	5.00
SR	Scott Rolen	8.00
SS	Curt Schilling	5.00
SS	Sammy Sosa	10.00
IS	Ichiro Suzuki	10.00
MT	Mark Teixeira	5.00
DW	Dontrelle Willis	5.00

Dual Patch

No Pricing
Production 10 Sets

Hot Numbers Game-Used Blue

NM/M
Common Player: 5.00
Production 250 Sets
Blue Die-Cut: 1X-3X
Production 25 Sets
Red: .5X-1.25X
Production 175 Sets
Red Die-Cut: No Pricing
Production 18 Sets
Pewter: .5X-1.5X
Production 125 Sets
Pewter Die-Cut: No Pricing
Production 13 Sets
Copper: .5X-1.5X
Production 75 Sets
Die-Cut Copper: No Pricing
Production 8 Sets
Silver: .5X-1.5X
Production 50 Sets
Silver Die-Cut: No Pricing
Production 5 Sets
Gold: 1X-5X
Numbered to player's jersey No.
Gold Die-Cut: No Pricing
Production 3 Sets
Platinum: 2X-5X
Numbered to 2003 HR/Win total
Platinum Die-Cut: No Pricing
Production 1 Set
Purple: No Pricing
Production 1 Set

Jeff Bagwell	8.00
Rocco Baldelli	5.00
Josh Beckett	8.00
Hank Blalock	5.00
Nomar Garciaparra	12.00
Jason Giambi	8.00
Troy Glaus	5.00
Tom Glavine	5.00
Vladimir Guerrero	8.00
Todd Helton	8.00
Derek Jeter	15.00
Randy Johnson	8.00
Chipper Jones	8.00
Barry Larkin	5.00
Greg Maddux	8.00
Pedro J. Martinez	8.00
Mike Mussina	5.00
Hideo Nomo	5.00
Mike Piazza	8.00
Mark Prior	12.00
Albert Pujols	12.00
Manny Ramirez	8.00
Alex Rodriguez	12.00
Curt Schilling	5.00
Sammy Sosa	10.00
Mark Teixeira	5.00
Frank Thomas	8.00
Jim Thome	8.00
Brandon Webb	5.00
Kerry Wood	8.00

Lettermen

No Pricing
Numbered to number of letters in player's last name

Power Tools Game-Used Blue

NM/M
Common Player: 5.00
Production 250 Sets
Blue Die-Cut: 1X-3X
Production 25 Sets
Red: .5X-1.25X
Production 175 Sets
Red Die-Cut: No Pricing
Production 18 Sets
Pewter: .5X-1.5X
Production 125 Sets
Pewter Die-Cut: No Pricing
Production 13 Sets
Copper: .5X-1.5X
Production 75 Sets
Die-Cut Copper: No Pricing
Production 8 Sets
Silver: .5X-1.5X
Production 50 Sets
Silver Die-Cut: No Pricing
Production 5 Sets
Gold: 1X-5X
Numbered to player's jersey No.
Gold Die-Cut: No Pricing
Production 3 Sets
Platinum: 2X-5X
Numbered to 2003 HR total
Platinum Die-Cut No Pricing
Production 1 Set
Purple: No Pricing
Production 1 Set

Rocco Baldelli	5.00
Adam Dunn	5.00
Nomar Garciaparra	12.00
Jason Giambi	8.00
Vladimir Guerrero	8.00
Derek Jeter	15.00
Chipper Jones	8.00
Mike Piazza	10.00
Jorge Posada	8.00
Albert Pujols	12.00
Manny Ramirez	8.00
Alex Rodriguez	12.00
Alfonso Soriano	8.00
Sammy Sosa	10.00
Jim Thome	8.00

SIGnificant Cuts

NM/M
Serially Numbered

RA	Roberto Alomar/50	60.00
JB1	Josh Beckett/10	
JB2	Johnny Bench/25	100.00
VC	Vince Carter/200	50.00
TC	Ty Cobb	2,650
DE	Dennis Eckersley/75	30.00
FF	Frank Frisch/1	
CG	Charlie Gehringer/2	
RH	Roy Halladay/50	40.00
CJ	Chipper Jones/22	
BL	Barry Larkin/75	30.00
DM	Don Mattingly/25	
PM	Paul Molitor/75	50.00
TO	Tomokazu Ohka	
RP	Rafael Palmeiro/25	
AP1	Andy Pettitte/50	40.00
AP2	Albert Pujols/20	
JR	Jose Reyes/25	40.00
CR	Cal Ripken Jr./25	
MR	Mariano Rivera/50	75.00
IR	Ivan Rodriguez/50	50.00
BR	Babe Ruth/1	
NR	Nolan Ryan/25	200.00
MS	Mike Schmidt/25	125.00
GS	Gary Sheffield/50	50.00
ES	Enos Slaughter/3	
JS	John Smoltz/75	
MT	Miguel Tejada/25	
BT	Bill Terry/3	

2004 FLEER GENUINE INSIDER

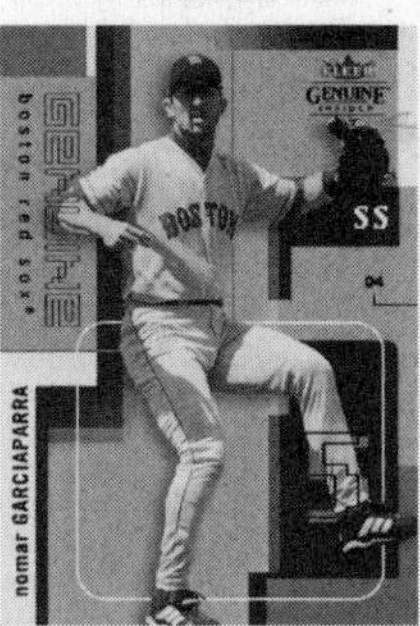

NM/M
Common Player (1-90): .25
Minor Stars: .40
Common Rookie Insider (91-100): 4.00
Production 499 Sets
Common Upside (101-120): 4.00
Production 799 Sets
Common Mini Rookie: 4.00
Production 350 Sets
Pack (5): 4.00
Box (18): 75.00

1	Troy Glaus	.60
2	Eric Chavez	.40
3	Lance Berkman	.40
4	Pedro J. Martinez	1.00
5	Jim Edmonds	.40
6	Tom Glavine	.40
7	Ken Griffey Jr.	1.50
8	Vernon Wells	.40
9	Hideki Matsui	2.50
10	Jeff Bagwell	.75
11	Rafael Palmeiro	.40
12	Edgar Martinez	.40
13	Bernie Williams	.60
14	Josh Beckett	.75
15	Javy Lopez	.40
16	Ichiro Suzuki	2.00
17	Scott Podsednik	.40
18	Sammy Sosa	2.00
19	Mark Teixeira	.40
20	Jorge Posada	.60
21	Miguel Cabrera	.75
22	Chipper Jones	1.50
23	Sean Burroughs	.25
24	Dmitri Young	.25
25	Brandon Webb	.25
26	Bobby Abreu	.40
27	Hideo Nomo	.40
28	Frank Thomas	.75
29	Alex Rodriguez	2.50
30	Derek Jeter	3.00
31	Todd Helton	.75
32	Andruw Jones	.75
33	Jason Kendall	.40
34	Eric Gagne	.40
35	Omar Vizquel	.40
36	Vladimir Guerrero	1.00
37	Jim Thome	1.00
38	Mike Sweeney	.25
39	Manny Ramirez	.75
40	Scott Rolen	1.00
41	Jose Vidro	.25
42	Adam Dunn	.60
43	Garret Anderson	.40
44	Mike Lieberthal	.25
45	Roy Oswalt	.40
46	Geoff Jenkins	.40
47	Magglio Ordonez	.40
48	Hank Blalock	.60
49	Barry Zito	.60
50	Dontrelle Willis	.40
51	Greg Maddux	1.50
52	Brian Giles	.40
53	Shawn Green	.40
54	Carlos Lee	.25
55	Carlos Delgado	.75
56	Alfonso Soriano	1.00
57	Angel Berroa	.25
58	Kerry Wood	.75
59	Rocco Baldelli	.60
60	Gary Sheffield	.60
61	Ivan Rodriguez	.60
62	Richie Sexson	.60
63	Marlon Byrd	.25
64	Carlos Beltran	.40
65	Mark Prior	2.50
66	Aubrey Huff	.25
67	Jason Giambi	1.00
68	Curt Schilling	.60
69	Reggie Sanders	.25
70	Mike Piazza	1.50
71	Craig Monroe	.25
72	Randy Johnson	1.00
73	Pat Burrell	.40
74	Craig Biggio	.40
75	Nomar Garciaparra	2.50
76	Albert Pujols	2.50
77	Jose Reyes	.25
78	Preston Wilson	.25
79	Miguel Tejada	.60
80	Bret Boone	.40
81	Shannon Stewart	.25
82	Jody Gerut	.25
83	Tim Salmon	.25
84	Tim Hudson	.40
85	Juan Pierre	.25
86	Jay Gibbons	.40
87	Jason Schmidt	.40
88	Torii Hunter	.60
89	Austin Kearns	.25
90	Roy Halladay	.40
91	*John Gall*	8.00
92	*Hideki Matsui*	25.00
93	*Merkin Valdez*	4.00
94	*William Bergolla*	8.00
95	*Angel Chavez*	4.00
96	*Hector Gimenez*	4.00
97	*Aarom Baldiris*	4.00
98	*Justin Leone*	6.00
99	*Onil Joseph*	5.00
100	*Freddy Guzman*	4.00
101	Rickie Weeks	6.00
102	*Chad Bentz*	5.00
103	Bobby Crosby	6.00
104	Dallas McPherson	5.00
105	Brandon Watson	4.00
106	Garrett Atkins	6.00
107	Graham Koonce	4.00
108	Chien-Ming Wang	4.00
109	Jonny Gomes	4.00
110	Edwin Jackson	4.00
111	*Alfredo Simon*	5.00
112	Delmon Young	6.00
113	Angel Guzman	4.00
114	Ryan Howard	4.00
115	Scott Hairston	10.00
116	Edwin Encarnacion	5.00
117	Byron Gettis	4.00
118	Kevin Youkilis	8.00
119	Grady Sizemore	4.00
120	Corey Hart	4.00
121	*Greg Dobbs*	4.00
122	*Jerry Gil*	4.00
123	*Shawn Hill*	4.00
124	*John Labandeira*	4.00
125	*Jason Bartlett*	4.00
126	*Ronny Cedeno*	4.00
127	*Donald Kelly*	8.00
128	*Ivan Ochoa*	5.00
129	*Mariano Gomez*	5.00
130	*Ruddy Yan*	5.00

Autograph Insider

NM/M
Common Player: 10.00
Production As Indicated

RA	Roberto Alomar/150	30.00
MB	Marlon Byrd/550	10.00
MC	Miguel Cabrera/250	40.00
DE	David Eckstein/350	10.00
JG	Jody Gerut/550	10.00
JG2	Jay Gibbons/350	10.00
VG	Vladimir Guerrero/27	
OH	Orlando Hudson/550	15.00
AH	Aubrey Huff/550	10.00
RJ	Randy Johnson/51	
CJ	Chipper Jones/50	
AK	Austin Kearns/350	10.00
MO	Magglio Ordonez/250	20.00
RP	Rafael Palmeiro/150	50.00
SP	Scott Podsednik/550	15.00
JR	Jose Reyes/350	20.00
MR	Mariano Rivera/150	60.00

IR	Ivan Rodriguez/150	40.00
JR2	Jimmy Rollins/350	10.00
JS	Jason Schmidt/300	300.00
JS2	John Smoltz/150	30.00
MT	Mark Teixeira/350	20.00
BW	Brandon Webb/450	10.00

Autograph Insider - Jersey

		NM/M
Common Player:		10.00
Production 100 Sets		
RA	Roberto Alomar	30.00
MB	Marlon Byrd	10.00
MC	Miguel Cabrera	40.00
DE	David Eckstein	15.00
JG	Jody Gerut	25.00
JG2	Jay Gibbons	20.00
OH	Orlando Hudson	10.00
AH	Aubrey Huff	10.00
AK	Austin Kearns	20.00
MO	Magglio Ordonez	40.00
RP	Rafael Palmeiro	50.00
SP	Scott Podsednik	25.00
AP	Albert Pujols	100.00
JR	Jose Reyes	30.00
MR	Mariano Rivera	75.00
IR	Ivan Rodriguez	50.00
JR2	Jimmy Rollins	15.00
JS	Jason Schmidt	20.00
JS2	John Smoltz	50.00
MT	Mark Teixeira	25.00
BW	Brandon Webb	10.00

Autograph Insider - Bat

		NM/M
Common Card:		20.00
Production 50 Sets		
RA	Roberto Alomar	40.00
MB	Marlon Byrd	20.00
MC	Miguel Cabrera	60.00
DE	David Eckstein	30.00
JG	Jody Gerut	25.00
JG2	Jay Gibbons	20.00
OH	Orlando Hudson	20.00
AH	Aubrey Huff	25.00
AK	Austin Kearns	20.00
RP	Rafael Palmeiro	50.00
SP	Scott Podsednik	25.00
JR	Jose Reyes	30.00
IR	Ivan Rodriguez	50.00
JR2	Jimmy Rollins	25.00
MT	Mark Teixeira	25.00

Autograph Insider - Ball

No Pricing
Production 10 Sets

Autograph Insider-Cut Sigs

No Pricing

RM	Roger Maris/1
CS	Casey Stengel/3
BT	Bill Terry/10
PT	Pie Traynor/1
ZW	Zack Wheat/1

Classic Confrontations

		NM/M
Common Card:		3.00
Inserted 1:18		
1CC	Mike Piazza, Roger Clemens	4.00
2CC	Pedro J. Martinez, Derek Jeter	6.00
3CC	Randy Johnson, Jeff Bagwell	3.00
4CC	Mark Prior, A lbert Pujols	5.00
5CC	Josh Beckett, Sammy Sosa	4.00
6CC	Eric Gagne, Hank Blalock	3.00
7CC	Mariano Rivera, Nomar Garciaparra	5.00
8CC	Curt Schilling, Chipper Jones	4.00
9CC	Kerry Wood, Jim Edmonds	3.00
10CC	Barry Zito, Alfonso Soriano	3.00
11CC	Randy Johnson, Ken Griffey Jr.	4.00
12CC	Derek Jeter, John Smoltz	6.00
13CC	Roy Oswalt, Ken Griffey Jr.	4.00
14CC	Dontrelle Willis, Hideki Matsui	4.00
15CC	Hideo Nomo, Ichiro Suzuki	4.00

Cl. Confrontations Jersey

		NM/M
Common Card:		5.00
Production 400 Sets		
JB	Jeff Bagwell with Randy Johnson	6.00
JB2	Josh Beckett with Sammy Sosa	6.00
HB	Hank Blalock with Eric Gagne	8.00
RC	Roger Clemens with Mike Piazza	15.00
JE	Jim Edmonds with Kerry Wood	5.00
EG	Eric Gagne with Hank Blalock	5.00
NG	Nomar Garciaparra with Mariano Rivera	8.00
DJ	Derek Jeter with Pedro J. Martinez	15.00
RJ1	Randy Johnson with Jeff Bagwell	8.00
RJ2	Randy Johnson with Ken Griffey Jr.	8.00
CJ	Chipper Jones with Curt Schilling	8.00
PM	Pedro J. Martinez with Derek Jeter	10.00
HN	Hideo Nomo with Ichiro Suzuki	12.00
RO	Roy Oswalt with Ken Griffey Jr.	5.00
MP	Mike Piazza with Roger Clemens	8.00
MP2	Mark Prior with Albert Pujols	12.00
AP	Albert Pujols with Mark Prior	12.00
MR	Mariano Rivera with Nomar Garciaparra	8.00
CS	Curt Schilling with Chipper Jones	5.00
JS	John Smoltz with Derek Jeter	5.00
AS	Alfonso Soriano with Barry Zito	8.00
SS	Sammy Sosa with Josh Beckett	8.00
DW	Dontrelle Willis with Matsui	5.00
KW	Kerry Wood with Jim Edmonds	8.00
BZ	Barry Zito with Alfonso Soriano	5.00

Classic Conf. Dual Jersey

	NM/M
Common Card:	12.00
Production 100 Sets	
Dual Patch:	No Pricing
Production 10 Sets	
Barry Zito, Alfonso Soriano	12.00
Curt Schilling, Chipper Jones	12.00
Eric Gagne, Hank Blalock	12.00
Josh Beckett, Sammy Sosa	12.00
Kerry Wood, Jim Edmonds	15.00
Mark Prior, Albert Pujols	25.00
Mike Piazza, Roger Clemens	15.00
Mariano Rivera, Nomar Garciaparra	20.00
Pedro J. Martinez, Derek Jeter	20.00
Randy Johnson, Jeff Bagwell	12.00

Genuine Reflection

(1-90):	.5X-2X
(101-120):	.5X-1.25X
Production 99 Sets	

Gen. Article Insider-Jersey

		NM/M
Common Player:		5.00
Production 250 Sets		
Bat:		.75X-1.25X
Production 100 Sets		
Jersey/Bat:		.75X-1.5X
Production 50 Sets		
Jersey Tags:		No Pricing
Production 5 Sets		
RB	Rocco Baldelli	5.00
LB	Lance Berkman	5.00
HB	Hank Blalock	5.00
MC	Miguel Cabrera	8.00
CD	Carlos Delgado	6.00
AD	Adam Dunn	5.00
NG	Nomar Garciaparra	12.00
JG	Jason Giambi	6.00
TG	Troy Glaus	5.00
VG	Vladimir Guerrero	8.00
TH	Todd Helton	8.00
DJ	Derek Jeter	18.00
CJ	Chipper Jones	8.00
MO	Magglio Ordonez	5.00
RP	Rafael Palmeiro	5.00
MP	Mike Piazza	8.00
AP	Albert Pujols	12.00
MR	Manny Ramirez	6.00
JR	Jose Reyes	6.00
AR	Alex Rodriguez	15.00
CS	Gary Sheffield	6.00
AS	Alfonso Soriano	8.00
SS	Sammy Sosa	10.00
MT	Mark Teixeira	5.00
JT	Jim Thome	6.00

Tools of the Game

		NM/M
Common Player:		1.00
Inserted 1:6		
1TG	Jason Giambi	1.50
2TG	Torii Hunter	1.00
3TG	Derek Jeter	4.00
4TG	Nomar Garciaparra	3.00
5TG	Albert Pujols	3.00
6TG	Jim Thome	1.50
7TG	Alex Rodriguez	4.00
8TG	Chipper Jones	2.00
9TG	Sammy Sosa	2.50
10TG	Jose Reyes	1.00
11TG	Pedro J. Martinez	1.50
12TG	Greg Maddux	2.00
13TG	Randy Johnson	1.50
14TG	Curt Schilling	1.00
15TG	Mark Prior	3.00
16TG	Ichiro Suzuki	2.50
17TG	Hideki Matsui	3.00
18TG	Kazuo Matsui	2.50
19TG	Ken Griffey Jr.	2.00
20TG	Josh Beckett	1.00

Tools of Game-Game Jersey

		NM/M
Common Player:		5.00
Production 250 Sets		
Jersey/Bat:		.75X-2X
Production 125		
Jersey/Bat/Cap:		1X-2.5X
Production 75		
NG	Nomar Garciaparra	12.00
JG	Jason Giambi	8.00
TH	Torii Hunter	5.00
DJ	Derek Jeter	15.00
RJ	Randy Johnson	6.00
CJ	Chipper Jones	8.00
GM	Greg Maddux	6.00
PM	Pedro J. Martinez	6.00
MP	Mark Prior	15.00
AP	Albert Pujols	12.00
JR	Jose Reyes	8.00
AR	Alex Rodriguez	15.00
CS	Curt Schilling	5.00
SS	Sammy Sosa	10.00
JT	Jim Thome	6.00

2004 FLEER GREATS OF THE GAME

		NM/M
Common Player:		.40
Pack (5):		10.00
Box (15):		130.00
1	Lou Gehrig	4.00
2	Ty Cobb	3.00
3	Dizzy Dean	1.50
4	Jimmie Foxx	1.50
5	Hank Greenberg	1.00
6	Babe Ruth	6.00
7	Honus Wagner	1.50
8	Mickey Cochrane	1.50
9	Pepper Martin	.40
10	Charlie Gehringer	.75
11	Carl Hubbell	.40
12	Bill Terry	.40
13	Mel Ott	.75
14	Bill Dickey	1.50
15	Ted Williams	6.00
16	Roger Maris	3.00
17	Thurman Munson	2.00
18	Phil Rizzuto	2.00
19	Stan Musial	3.00
20	Duke Snider	2.50
21	Reggie Jackson	1.50
22	Don Mattingly	1.50
23	Vida Blue	.75
24	Harmon Killebrew	1.50
25	Lou Brock	.75
26	Al Kaline	1.00
27	Dave Parker	.40
28	Nolan Ryan	6.00
29	Jim Rice	.40
30	Paul Molitor	2.00
31	Dwight Evans	.40
32	Brooks Robinson	1.50
33	Jose Canseco	.40
34	Alan Trammell	.40
35	Johnny Bench	2.00
36	Carlton Fisk	1.00
37	Jim Palmer	1.50
38	George Brett	2.00
39	Mike Schmidt	2.00
40	Tony Perez	.75
41	Paul Blair	.40
42	Fred Lynn	.40
43	Carl Yastrzemski	1.50
44	Steve Carlton	1.00
45	Dennis Eckersley	1.50
46	Tom Seaver	1.50
47	Juan Marichal	.75
48	Tony Gwynn	2.00
49	Bill "Moose" Skowron	.75
50	Bob Gibson	1.50
51	Luis Tiant	.75
52	Eddie Murray	1.00
53	Frank Robinson	2.00

54 Rocky Colavito .75
55 Bobby Shantz .40
56 Ernie Banks 2.00
57 Rod Carew 1.00
58 Gorman Thomas .40
59 Bernie Carbo .40
60 Joe Rudi .40
61 Graig Nettles .75
62 Ron Guidry .75
63 Whitey Ford 1.50
64 George Kell 1.00
65 Cal Ripken Jr. 6.00
66 Willie McCovey .75
67 Bo Jackson 1.00
68 Kirby Puckett 2.00
69 Ted Kluszewski .75
70 Johnny Podres .40
71 Davey Lopes .40
72 Chris Short .40
73 Jeff Torborg .40
74 Bill Freehan .40
75 Frank Tanana .40
76 Jack Morris .75
77 Rick Dempsey .40
78 Yogi Berra 1.50
79 Tim McCarver .40
80 Rusty Staub .40
81 Tony Lazzeri .40
82 Al Rosen .40
83 Willie McGee .75
84 Preacher Roe .75
85 Dave Kingman .40
86 Luis Aparicio 1.00
87 John Kruk .40
88 Bing Miller .40
89 Joe Charboneau .40
90 Mark Fidrych .40
91 Jim "Catfish" Hunter 2.00
92 Nap Lajoie 2.00
93 Eddie Murray 2.00
94 Johnny Pesky 1.00
95 Tom Seaver 2.00
96 Frank Robinson 2.00
97 Enos Slaughter 1.00
98 Cecil Travis .40
99 Robin Yount 2.00
100 Don Zimmer .75
101 Babe Herman .40
102 Ron Santo .40
103 Willie Stargell 2.00
104 Paul Molitor
105 Jimmy Piersall .75
106 Johnny Sain .40
107 Joe Pepitone .75
108 Ryne Sandberg 3.00
109 Jim Thorpe 3.00
110 Steve Garvey 1.50
111 Ray Knight .75
112 Fernando Valenzuela 1.00
113 Will Clark 1.00
114 Tony Kubek .75
115 Jim Bouton .40
116 Jerry Koosman .75
117 Steve Carlton 3.00
118 Richie Ashburn .75
119 Roberto Clemente 6.00
120 Paul O'Neill .40
121 Reggie Jackson 3.00
122 Andre Dawson 1.50
123 Hoyt Wilhelm 1.00
124 Dale Murphy 1.50
125 Dwight Gooden 1.50
126 Roger Maris 1.00
127 Bill Mazeroski 1.00
128 Don Newcombe .75
129 Robin Roberts .75
130 Duke Snider 2.00
131 Eddie Mathews 3.00
132 Wade Boggs 2.00
133 Rollie Fingers 1.50
134 Frankie Frisch .40
135 Billy Williams .75
136 Rod Carew 1.50
137 Dom DiMaggio .75
138 Orel Hershiser .40
139 Gary Carter 1.00
140 Keith Hernandez .75
141 Bob Lemon .75
142 Nolan Ryan 6.00
143 Ozzie Smith 1.50
144 Rick Sutcliffe .40
145 Carlton Fisk 1.50

Blue

Cards 81-145
Cards #'d to 51-96: 3X-5X
Cards #'d to 26-50: 5X-10X
Cards #'d to less than 25: No Pricing

Gold Border Autographs

NM/M
Common Player: 10.00
Randomly Inserted
Ernie Banks 60.00
Johnny Bench 60.00
Yogi Berra 80.00
Paul Blair 10.00
Vida Blue 10.00
George Brett 125.00
Lou Brock 20.00
Jose Canseco 30.00
Bernie Carbo 10.00
Rod Carew 30.00
Steve Carlton 30.00
Rocky Colavito 100.00
Rick Dempsey 15.00
Dennis Eckersley 50.00
Dwight Evans 15.00
Carlton Fisk 40.00
Whitey Ford 40.00
Bill Freehan 10.00
Bob Gibson 25.00
Ron Guidry 20.00
Tony Gwynn 50.00
Bo Jackson 50.00
Reggie Jackson 100.00
Al Kaline 25.00
George Kell 15.00
Harmon Killebrew 30.00
Davey Lopes 10.00
Fred Lynn 10.00
Juan Marichal 20.00
Don Mattingly 80.00
Tim McCarver 15.00
Willie McCovey 40.00
Paul Molitor 40.00
Jack Morris 10.00
Eddie Murray 80.00
Stan Musial 100.00
Graig Nettles 15.00
Jim Palmer 20.00
Dave Parker 10.00
Tony Perez 30.00
Johnny Podres 10.00
Kirby Puckett 80.00
Jim Rice 20.00
Cal Ripken Jr. 150.00
Phil Rizzuto 40.00
Brooks Robinson 20.00
Frank Robinson 30.00
Joe Rudi 10.00
Nolan Ryan 150.00
Mike Schmidt 60.00
Tom Seaver 80.00
Bobby Shantz 10.00
Bill "Moose" Skowron 10.00
Duke Snider 30.00
Rusty Staub 10.00
Frank Tanana 10.00
Gorman Thomas 10.00
Luis Tiant 10.00
Jeff Torborg 10.00
Alan Trammell 10.00
Carl Yastrzemski 60.00

Gold Border Auto. Series 2

NM/M
Common Player: 15.00
Inserted 1:75
LA Luis Aparicio 20.00
WB Wade Boggs 40.00
JBO Jim Bouton 15.00
RC2 Rod Carew Twins 40.00
SC2 Steve Carlton Cards 30.00
GC Gary Carter 25.00
JCH Joe Charboneau 15.00
WC Will Clark 40.00

DC David Cone 40.00
AD Andre Dawson 20.00
DD Dom DiMaggio 50.00
RF Rollie Fingers 15.00
CF2 Carlton Fisk White Sox 40.00
SG Steve Garvey 15.00
DG Dwight Gooden 20.00
KH Keith Hernandez 15.00
OH Orel Hershiser 15.00
RJ2 Reggie Jackson Angels 60.00
DK Dave Kingman 15.00
RK Ray Knight 15.00
JK Jerry Koosman 20.00
JKR John Kruk 15.00
TK Tony Kubek 25.00
BM Bill Mazeroski 30.00
WMG Willie McGee 25.00
PM2 Paul Molitor Jays 40.00
DMU Dale Murphy 25.00
DN Don Newcombe 15.00
PO Paul O'Neill 30.00
JPP Joe Pepitone 15.00
JPS Johnny Pesky 25.00
JPI Jimmy Piersall 20.00
RR Robin Roberts 25.00
FR2 Frank Robinson O's 30.00
PRO Preacher Roe 20.00
AR Al Rosen 15.00
NR2 Nolan Ryan Angels 120.00
RS Ryne Sandberg 75.00
DS Deion Sanders 30.00
RST Ron Santo 20.00
TS2 Tom Seaver Reds 75.00
OS Ozzie Smith 40.00
DS2 Duke Snider 40.00
BW Billy Williams 20.00
RY Robin Yount 40.00
DZ Don Zimmer 25.00

Announcing Greats

NM/M
Common Card: 6.00
Inserted 1:12 Retail
1AG Harry Kalas, Mike Schmidt 8.00
2AG Vin Scully, Steve Garvey 12.00
3AG Harry Caray, Ryne Sandberg 12.00
4AG Ned Martin, Carlton Fisk 6.00
5AG Ernie Harwell, Kirk Gibson 6.00
6AG Ken Harrelson, Carl Yastrzemski 8.00
7AG Don Mattingly, Phil Rizzuto 10.00
8AG Yogi Berra, Mel Allen 10.00
9AG Jonathan Miller, Cal Ripken Jr. 10.00
10AG Marty Brennaman, Johnny Bench 8.00

Announcing Greats Autographs

NM/M
Sequentially #'d between 1 & 50
Harry Kalas, Mike Schmidt/25
Harry Caray, Ryne Sandberg/2
Ernie Harwell, Kirk Gibson/48
Ken Harrelson, Carl Yastrzemski/50 75.00
Phil Rizzuto, Don Mattingly/26 225.00
Mel Allen, Yogi Berra/1
Cal Ripken Jr., Jonathan Miller/8
Johnny Bench, Marty Brennaman/50 60.00

Battery Mates

NM/M
Common Card: 5.00
Serially Numbered
1BM Steve Carlton, Tim McCarver/1972 5.00
2BM Don Drysdale, Roy Campanella/1957 5.00
3BM Tom Seaver, Johnny Bench/1979 8.00
4BM Whitey Ford, Yogi Berra/1956 8.00
5BM Ron Guidry, Thurman Munson/1978 8.00
6BM Nolan Ryan, Jeff Torborg/1973 10.00
7BM Denny McLain, Bill Freehan/1968 5.00
8BM Lefty Gomez, Bill Dickey/1934 5.00
9BM Jim Palmer, Rick Dempsey/1977 5.00
10BM Luis Tiant, Carlton Fisk 5.00

Single Panel: Battery Mates

NM/M
Common Card: 15.00
Serially Numbered
TM Steve Carlton, Tim McCarver/72 30.00
TS-JB Tom Seaver, Johnny Bench/79 60.00
WF-YB Whitey Ford, Yogi Berra/56 40.00
RG-TM Ron Guidry, Thurman Munson/78 25.00
NR-JT Nolan Ryan, Jeff Torborg/73 15.00
DM-BF Denny McLain, Bill Freehan/68 60.00
JP-RD Jim Palmer, Rick Dempsey/77 25.00

Dual Panel: Battery Mates

No Pricing
Production 10 Sets

Single Cuts: Etched in Time

NM/M
No Pricing

Etched In Time Series 2

NM/M
Sequentially #'d to indicated quantity
Cards #'d 25 or less: No Pricing
EA Ethan Allen/75 150.00
LA Luke Appling/23
RA Richie Ashburn/2
EAV Earl Averill/50 125.00
GB George H. Burns/4
DC Dolph Camilli/40 250.00
MC Max Carey/1
EC Earle Combs/1
TCN Tony Conigliaro/1
WC Walker Cooper/20
JC Joe Cronin/5
RF Rick Ferrell/50
NF Nellie Fox/2
BG Bob Grim/5
BGR Burleigh Grimes/5
GH Gabby Hartnett/5
BH Babe Herman/35 250.00
GIL Gil Hodges/2
CAT Jim "Catfish" Hunter/5
GK George Kelly/3
HK Harvey Kuenn/32 120.00
NL Nap Lajoie/1
BL Bob Lemon/10
FL Freddie Lindstrom/5
SM Sal Maglie/40 100.00
JM Joe Medwick/8
BUD Buddy Myer/3
LOD Lefty O'Doul/3
ER Edd Roush/95 100.00

RR Red Ruffing/5
CR Chico Ruiz/5
PR Pete Runnels/35 200.00
CS Chris Short/30 120.00
WS Willie Stargell/16
JT Jim Thorpe/1
PT Pie Traynor/1
ZW Zack Wheat/4
HWI Hoyt Wilhelm/10
TW2 Ted Williams/1
EW Early Wynn/5

Forever

NM/M
Common Player: 4.00
Sequentially #'d to player's rookie year
1 Fernando Valenzuela/1980 4.00
2 Steve Garvey/1969 4.00
3 Zach Wheat/1909 4.00
4 Orel Hershiser/1983 4.00
5 Duke Snider/1947 6.00
6 Jim Rice/1974 5.00
7 Carlton Fisk/1969 6.00
8 Wade Boggs/1982 6.00
9 Ted Williams/1939 10.00
10 Carl Yastrzemski/1961 8.00
11 Dom DiMaggio/1940 5.00
12 Ron Santo/1960 4.00
13 Billy Williams/1959 5.00
14 Ryne Sandberg/1981 8.00
15 Ernie Banks/1953 8.00
16 Gabby Hartnett/1922 4.00
17 Hack Wilson/1923 6.00
18 Dwight Gooden/1984 5.00
19 Ray Knight/1974 4.00
20 Tom Seaver/1967 8.00
21 Nolan Ryan/1966 10.00
22 Keith Hernandez/1974 5.00
23 Darryl Strawberry/1983 5.00
24 Bob Gibson/1959 8.00
25 Pepper Martin/1928 4.00
26 Stan Musial/1941 8.00
27 Frankie Frisch/1919 4.00
28 Steve Carlton/1965 8.00
29 Ozzie Smith/1978 6.00

Forever Game-Used Jersey

NM/M
Common Player: 10.00
Production 149 Sets
Jersey: .75X-1.5X
Production 99 Sets
Patch Number: 1X-2X
Production 49 Sets
Patch Logo: No Pricing
Production 10 Sets
EB Ernie Banks 20.00
WB Wade Boggs 12.00
SC Steve Carlton 12.00
DD Dom DiMaggio 20.00
CF Carlton Fisk 15.00
SG Steve Garvey 10.00
BG Bob Gibson 15.00
DG Dwight Gooden 10.00
KH Keith Hernandez 10.00
OH Orel Hershiser 10.00
RK Ray Knight 10.00
SM Stan Musial 30.00
JR Jim Rice 12.00
NR Nolan Ryan 50.00
RS Ryne Sandberg 25.00
RST Ron Santo 10.00
TS Tom Seaver 15.00
OS Ozzie Smith 15.00
DS Darryl Strawberry 12.00
FV Fernando Valenzuela 10.00
BW Billy Williams 10.00

TW Ted Williams 75.00
CY Carl Yastrzemski 20.00

Comparison Cuts: Dual Cut

No Pricing
Production 1 Set

Personality Cuts

No Pricing
Production 1 Set

Personality Cuts Series 2

No Pricing
Production 1 or 2 Sets

The Glory/Time: G-U Patch

No Pricing
Production 25 Sets

The Glory of Their Time

NM/M
Common Player: 4.00
Serially Numbered
1GOT Harmon Killebrew/1961 4.00
2GOT Johnny Bench/1974 5.00
3GOT George Brett/1980 8.00
4GOT Tony Gwynn/1987 4.00
5GOT Paul Molitor/1987 5.00
6GOT Don Mattingly/1986 8.00
7GOT Reggie Jackson/1980 8.00
8GOT Carlton Fisk/1985 5.00
9GOT Cal Ripken Jr./1983 10.00
10GOT Brooks Robinson/1964 4.00
11GOT Eddie Murray/1980 5.00
12GOT Bill "Moose" Skowron/1960 4.00
13GOT Lou Brock/1974 5.00
14GOT Don Drysdale/1962 5.00
15GOT Tony Gwynn/1997 4.00
16GOT Mike Schmidt/1980 8.00
17GOT Carl Yastrzemski/1967 8.00
18GOT Babe Ruth/1927 10.00
19GOT Nolan Ryan/1989 10.00
20GOT Yogi Berra/1950 8.00
21GOT Al Kaline/1955 5.00
22GOT Ty Cobb/1911 5.00
23GOT Duke Snider/1955 5.00
24GOT Stan Musial/1948 8.00
25GOT Jose Canseco/1988 5.00
26GOT Rocky Colavito/1958 5.00
27GOT Dave Winfield/1979 4.00
28GOT Nolan Ryan/1982 10.00
29GOT Thurman Munson/1977 8.00
30GOT Jackie Robinson/1949 8.00
31GOT Kirby Puckett/1988 8.00
32GOT Ted Kluszewski/1954 5.00
33GOT Warren Spahn/1953 5.00
34GOT Willie McCovey/1969 4.00
35GOT Phil Rizzuto/1950 5.00

The Glory/ Time: Game-Used

NM/M
Common Player: 10.00
Production 250 Sets
Hobby Only
Gold: 1.5X-2X
Retail Only (Not Numbered)
No Rizzuto Retail Version
JB Johnny Bench/jersey 15.00
YB Yogi Berra/pants 15.00
GB George Brett/jersey 15.00
LB Lou Brock/jersey 15.00
JC1 Jose Canseco/jersey 10.00
JC2 Jose Canseco/bat 10.00

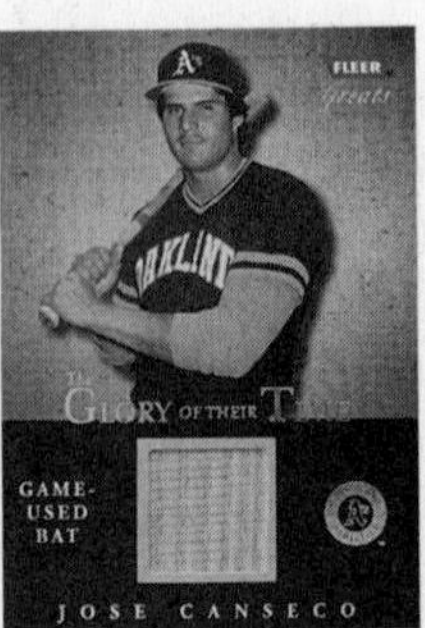

RC Rocky Colavito/bat 25.00
DD Don Drysdale/jersey 15.00
CF1 Carlton Fisk/jersey 10.00
CF2 Carlton Fisk/bat 10.00
TG1 Tony Gwynn/jersey 10.00
TG2 Tony Gwynn/jersey 10.00
RJ Reggie Jackson/pants 20.00
AK Al Kaline/pants 15.00
HK Harmon Killebrew/bat 10.00
TK Ted Kluszewski/pants 15.00
DM Don Mattingly/pants 20.00
WM Willie McCovey/pants 10.00
PM Paul Molitor/jersey 15.00
TM Thurman Munson/pants 15.00
EM Eddie Murray/jersey 10.00
KP Kirby Puckett/bat 20.00
CR Cal Ripken Jr./jersey 25.00
PR Phil Rizzuto/pants 15.00
BR Brooks Robinson/jersey 10.00
NR1 Nolan Ryan/jersey 20.00
NR2 Nolan Ryan/bat 20.00
MS Mike Schmidt/jersey 15.00
MS Bill "Moose" Skowron/pants 10.00
WS Warren Spahn/jersey 20.00
DW Dave Winfield/jersey 10.00
CY Carl Yastrzemski/jersey 20.00

Yankee Clippings

NM/M
Common Player: 25.00
Inserted 1:45
YB Yogi Berra 60.00
WB Wade Boggs 40.00
RJ Reggie Jackson 40.00
LG Roger Maris 400.00
DM Don Mattingly 100.00
PO Paul O'Neill 30.00
PR Phil Rizzuto 325.00
BS Bill "Moose" Skowron 25.00

Yankee Clippings Autographs

No Pricing
Sequentially #'d between 3 & 26
YB Yogi Berra/15
WB Wade Boggs/26
RJ Reggie Jackson/15
LG Roger Maris/3
DM Don Mattingly/15
PO Paul O'Neill/26
PR Phil Rizzuto/26
BS Bill "Moose" Skowron/26

2004 FLEER HOT PROSPECTS DRAFT EDITION

NM/M
Common Player (1-60): .25
Common Rookie (61-70): 3.00
Common Rookie (71-120): 15.00
Production 1,000 Sets
Cards 112 & 113 do not exist
Production 299 Sets
Pack (5): 8.00
Box (15): 100.00
1 Miguel Tejada .60
2 Jose Vidro .25
3 Hideki Matsui 2.50
4 Roger Clemens 2.50
5 Craig Wilson .25
6 Bobby Crosby .25
7 Pat Burrell .40
8 Mike Sweeney .25
9 Craig Biggio .40
10 Scott Rolen 1.00
11 Roy Halladay .40
12 Lyle Overbay .25
13 Rocco Baldelli .60
14 Mike Piazza 1.50
15 Rafael Palmeiro .75
16 Hank Blalock .60
17 Sammy Sosa 2.00
18 Dontrelle Willis .40
19 Alfonso Soriano 1.00
20 Gary Sheffield .60
21 Jim Thome 1.00
22 Ivan Rodriguez .60
23 Adam Dunn .60
24 Kerry Wood .75
25 Khalil Greene .75
26 Richie Sexson .60
27 Nomar Garciaparra 2.50
28 Andruw Jones .75
29 Tom Glavine .40
30 Carlos Beltran .60
31 Chipper Jones 1.50
32 Jeff Bagwell .75
33 Tim Hudson .40
34 Alex Rodriguez 2.50
35 Omar Vizquel .40
36 Albert Pujols 2.50
37 Frank Thomas .75
38 Ben Sheets .40
39 Jason Schmidt .40
40 Miguel Cabrera .75
41 Carlos Delgado .75
42 Ichiro Suzuki 2.00
43 Curt Schilling .60
44 Todd Helton .75
45 Ken Griffey Jr. 1.50
46 Mark Prior 2.50
47 Vladimir Guerrero 1.00
48 Pedro Martinez 1.00
49 Manny Ramirez .75
50 Joe Mauer .40
51 Jorge Posada .60
52 Troy Glaus .60
53 Randy Johnson 1.00
54 Adrian Beltre .40
55 Eric Gagne .40
56 Josh Beckett .75
57 Jason Giambi 1.00
58 Barry Zito .60
59 Lance Berkman .40
60 Derek Jeter 3.00
61 *Kazuo Matsui* 5.00
62 *Jason Bartlett* 5.00
63 *John Gall* 3.00
64 *Chris Saenz* 3.00
65 *Merkin Valdez* 5.00
66 *Akinori Otsuka* 3.00
67 *Joey Gathright* 5.00
68 *Brad Halsey* 5.00
69 David Aardsma 4.00
70 Scott Kazmir 8.00
71 *Matt Bush AU* 50.00
72 *John Bowker AU* 30.00
73 *Mike Ferris AU* 15.00
74 *Brian Bixler AU* 15.00
75 *Scott Elbert AU* 25.00
76 *Josh Fields AU* 40.00
77 *Bill Bray AU* 15.00
78 *Greg Golson AU* 30.00
79 *Neil Walker AU* 30.00
80 *Phillip Hughes AU* 30.00
81 *Chris Nelson AU* 60.00
82 *Mark Rogers AU* 40.00
83 *Trevor Plouffe AU* 30.00
84 *Christian Garcia AU* 15.00
85 *Thomas Diamond AU* 50.00
86 *B.J. Szymanski AU* 30.00
87 *Richie Robnett AU* 25.00
88 *Seth Smith AU* 25.00
89 *Kyle Waldrop AU* 30.00
90 *Curtis Thigpen AU* 15.00

91 *J.P. Howell AU* 15.00
92 *Blake DeWitt AU* 50.00
93 *Taylor Tankersley AU* 20.00
94 *Zach Jackson AU* 20.00
95 *Justin Orenduff AU* 15.00
96 *Tyler Lumsden AU* 20.00
97 *Danny Putnam* 20.00
98 *Jon Poterson AU* 30.00
99 *Matt Fox AU* 15.00
100 *Gio Gonzalez AU* 15.00
101 *Huston Street AU* 60.00
102 *Jay Rainville AU* 30.00
103 *Matt Durkin AU* 20.00
104 *Brett Smith AU* 20.00
105 *Justin Hoyman AU* 20.00
106 *Erick San Pedro AU* 15.00
107 *Jeff Marquez AU* 15.00
108 *Hunter Pence AU* 60.00
109 *Dustin Pedroia AU* 60.00
110 *Kurt Suzuki AU* 60.00
111 *Billy Buckner AU* 20.00
114 *J.C. Holt AU* 15.00
115 *Homer Bailey AU* 40.00
116 *David Purcey AU* 20.00
117 *Jeremy Sowers AU* 40.00
118 *Chris Lambert AU* 15.00
119 *Eric Hurley AU* 25.00
120 *Grant Johnson AU* 20.00

Red Hot

Veterans (1-60): 2X-4X
Rookies (61-70): 1X-2X
Production 150
Rookies (71-120): No Pricing
Production 25 Sets

White Hot

Cards (1-120): No Pricing
Production 1 Set

Alumni Ink

No Pricing
Production 15 Sets
Red Hot: No Pricing
Production 5 Sets
White Hot: No Pricing
Production 1 Set
TG Mark Teixeira, Nomar Garciaparra
HS J.P. Howell, Huston Street
PJ Mark Prior, Randy Johnson

Double Team Jersey

NM/M
Common Player: 10.00
Production 100 Sets
Red Hot: No Pricing
Production 25 Sets
White Hot: No Pricing
Production 1 Set
Patch: .75X-1.5X
Production 50 Sets
Patch Red Hot: No Pricing
Production 10 Sets
Patch White Hot: No Pricing
Production 1 Set
CB Carlos Beltran 15.00
RCA Rod Carew 20.00
RCL Roger Clemens 20.00
JG Jason Giambi 12.00
TG Tom Glavine 10.00
VG Vladimir Guerrero 15.00
RH Rickey Henderson 20.00
RJ Reggie Jackson 25.00
GM Greg Maddux 15.00
PM Pedro Martinez 15.00
EM Eddie Murray 20.00
HN Hideo Nomo 15.00
RP Rafael Palmeiro 12.00
MP Mike Piazza 20.00
MR Manny Ramirez 15.00
IR Ivan Rodriguez 10.00
SR Scott Rolen 15.00
NR Nolan Ryan 50.00
AS Alfonso Soriano 12.00
MT Miguel Tejada 10.00

Draft Rewind

NM/M
Common Player: 2.00
Inserted 1:5
1 Joe Mauer 2.00
2 Derek Jeter 6.00
3 Chipper Jones 3.50
4 Greg Maddux 3.50
5 Alex Rodriguez 5.00
6 Nomar Garciaparra 5.00
7 Curt Schilling 3.00
8 Kerry Wood 3.00
9 Troy Glaus 3.00
10 Pat Burrell 2.00
11 Mark Mulder 2.00
12 Josh Beckett 3.00
13 Barry Zito 3.00
14 Mark Prior 5.00
15 Rickie Weeks 2.00
16 Khalil Greene 3.00
17 Ken Griffey Jr. 3.50
18 Gary Sheffield 3.00
19 Todd Helton 3.00
20 Barry Larkin 2.00
21 Kevin Brown 2.00
22 Frank Thomas 3.00
23 Manny Ramirez 3.00
24 Roger Clemens 5.00
25 Lance Berkman 2.00
26 Randy Johnson 3.00
27 Jason Giambi 3.00
28 Ben Sheets 2.00
29 Scott Rolen 3.00
30 Tom Glavine 2.00

Draft Rewind Jersey

NM/M
Common Player: 8.00
Sequentially #'d to indicated quantity
Red Hot: No Pricing
Production 10 Sets
White Hot: No Pricing
Production 1 Set
Patch
Cards #'d 41-68: .75X-1.5X
Cards #'d 29 or less: No Pricing
Patch Red Hot: No Pricing
Production 5 Sets
Patch White Hot: No Pricing
Production 1 Set
RB Rocco Baldelli/119 8.00
JB Josh Beckett/102 10.00
LB Lance Berkman/116 8.00
KB Kevin Brown/104 8.00
PB Pat Burrell/101 8.00
EC Eric Chavez/110 8.00
RC Roger Clemens/119 15.00
JG Jason Giambi/158 8.00
TG Troy Glaus/103 8.00
TG Tom Glavine/147 8.00
KG Khalil Greene/113 15.00
ZG Zack Greinke/106 8.00
TH Todd Helton/108 10.00
RJ Randy Johnson/136 10.00
CJ Chipper Jones/101 12.00
CK Casey Kotchman/113 8.00
BL Barry Larkin/104 10.00
GM Greg Maddux/131 12.00
JM Joe Mauer/101 10.00
MM Mark Mulder/102 8.00
MP Mark Prior/102 12.00
MR Manny Ramirez/113 10.00
SR Scott Rolen/146 10.00
CS Curt Schilling/139 10.00
BS Ben Sheets/110 8.00
GS Gary Sheffield/106 8.00
FT Frank Thomas/107 15.00
RW Rickie Weeks/102 8.00
KW Kerry Wood/104 10.00
BZ Barry Zito/109 8.00

Hot Tandems

NM/M
Common Card: 3.00
Inserted 1:15
1HT Mark Prior, Greg Maddux 6.00
2HT Jim Thome, Pat Burrell 3.50
3HT Ken Griffey Jr., Adam Dunn 4.00
4HT Mike Piazza, Tom Glavine 4.00
5HT Alex Rodriguez, Derek Jeter 10.00
6HT Roger Clemens, Andy Pettitte 6.00
7HT Hideki Matsui, Jason Giambi 6.00
8HT Hank Blalock, Alfonso Soriano 3.50
9HT Manny Ramirez, David Ortiz 3.50
10HT Miguel Cabrera, Dontrelle Willis 3.50
11HT Hideki Matsui, Ichiro Suzuki 6.00
12HT Albert Pujols, Scott Rolen 6.00
13HT Curt Schilling, Pedro J. Martinez 3.50
14HT Nomar Garciaparra, Sammy Sosa 5.00
15HT Kazuo Matsui, Derek Jeter 8.00

Hot Materials

NM/M
Common Player: 5.00
Production 325 Sets
Red Hot: 1X-2X
Production 50 Sets
White Hot Patch: No Pricing
Production 1 Set
JB Jeff Bagwell Jsy 6.00
LB Lance Berkman Jsy 5.00
HB Hank Blalock Jsy 6.00
MC Miguel Cabrera Jsy 8.00
RC Roger Clemens Jsy 12.00
CD Carlos Delgado Jsy 6.00
JD J.D. Drew Jsy 6.00
AD Adam Dunn Jsy 6.00
JE Jim Edmonds Jsy 5.00
EG Eric Gagne Jsy 6.00
VG Vladimir Guerrero Jsy 8.00
THE Todd Helton Jsy 6.00
THU Tim Hudson Jsy 5.00
THN Torii Hunter Jsy 6.00
RJ Randy Johnson Jsy 8.00
AJ Andruw Jones Jsy 6.00
CJ Chipper Jones Jsy 8.00
HM Hideki Matsui Jsy 20.00
KM Kazuo Matsui Jsy 10.00
JM Joe Mauer Jsy 8.00
MM Mike Mussina Jsy 6.00
HN Hideo Nomo Jsy 8.00
LO Lyle Overbay Jsy 5.00
APE Andy Pettitte Jsy 6.00
MPI Mike Piazza Jsy 8.00
JP Jorge Posada Jsy 6.00
MPR Mark Prior Jsy 12.00
APU Albert Pujols Jsy 12.00
MR Manny Ramirez Jsy 8.00
IR Ivan Rodriguez Jsy 6.00
CS Curt Schilling Jsy 8.00
JS Jason Schmidt Jsy 5.00
AS Alfonso Soriano Jsy 8.00
SS Sammy Sosa Jsy 10.00
MTX Mark Teixeira Jsy 6.00
MTJ Miguel Tejada Jsy 5.00
FT Frank Thomas Jsy 8.00
JT Jim Thome Jsy 8.00
DW Dontrelle Willis Jsy 5.00
KW Kerry Wood Jsy 8.00

Past, Present, Future Triple Auto.

NM/M
Production 33 Sets
Red Hot: No Pricing
Production 3 Sets
White Hot: No Pricing
Production 1 Set
Matt Durkin, Mookie Wilson, Mike Piazza 150.00
Hideo Nomo, Scott Elbert, Kirk Gibson 250.00
Josh Fields, Carlton Fisk, Ryan Meaux 80.00
Greg Golson, Steve Carlton, Jim Thome 100.00
Jack Wilson, Neil Walker, Ralph Kiner 80.00
Phillip Hughes, Yogi Berra, Mike Mussina
Ryne Sandberg, Mark Prior, Grant Johnson 250.00
Homer Bailey, Johnny Bench, Adam Dunn 150.00
Rickie Weeks, Mark Rogers, Robin Yount
Trevor Plouffe, Harmon Killebrew, Lew Ford
Joe Carter, Alexis Rios, David Purcey
Thomas Diamond, Nolan Ryan, Michael Young
Albert Pujols, Chris Lambert, Stan Musial 300.00
Richie Robnett, Reggie Jackson, Eric Chavez 80.00
Gary Sheffield, Miguel Cabrera, Taylor Tankersley
Dustin Pedroia, Bill Buckner, Manny Ramirez 60.00

2004 FLEER INSCRIBED

NM/M
Common Player (1-75): .25
Common Player (76-85): 3.00
Production 1,000 Sets
Numbered to 750 3.00
Not all 750 of each card not released
Pack (5): 10.00
Box (12): 85.00
1 Vladimir Guerrero 1.00
2 Bartolo Colon .40
3 Troy Glaus .60
4 Richie Sexson .60
5 Randy Johnson 1.00
6 Luis Gonzalez .40
7 J.D. Drew .40
8 Chipper Jones 1.50
9 Andruw Jones .75
10 Melvin Mora .25
11 Miguel Tejada .60
12 Curt Schilling .60
13 Pedro J. Martinez 1.00
14 Nomar Garciaparra 2.50
15 Kerry Wood .75
16 Mark Prior 2.50
17 Sammy Sosa 2.00
18 Frank Thomas .75
19 Magglio Ordonez .40
20 Sean Casey .25
21 Ken Griffey Jr. 1.50
22 Adam Dunn .60
23 Jody Gerut .25
24 Omar Vizquel .25
25 Todd Helton .75
26 Vinny Castilla .25
27 Alex Sanchez .25
28 Ivan Rodriguez .60
29 Dontrelle Willis .40
30 Josh Beckett .75
31 Miguel Cabrera .75
32 Roger Clemens 1.50
33 Andy Pettitte .60
34 Jeff Bagwell .75
35 Ken Harvey .25
36 Carlos Beltran .60
37 Shawn Green .40
38 Hideo Nomo .40
39 Scott Podsednik .25
40 Ben Sheets .40
41 Torii Hunter .60
42 Jacque Jones .25
43 Jose Vidro .25
44 Mike Piazza 1.50
45 Tom Glavine .40

46 Derek Jeter 3.00
47 Alex Rodriguez 2.50
48 Jason Giambi 1.00
49 Hideki Matsui 2.50
50 Eric Chavez .40
51 Barry Zito .60
52 Tim Hudson .40
53 Mark Mulder .40
54 Jim Thome 1.00
55 Pat Burrell .40
56 Chase Utley .25
57 Jason Kendall .40
58 Jack Wilson .25
59 Khalil Greene .75
60 Brian Giles .40
61 Jason Schmidt .40
62 Marquis Grissom .25
63 Ichiro Suzuki 2.00
64 Bret Boone .40
65 Albert Pujols 2.50
66 Scott Rolen 1.00
67 Jim Edmonds .40
68 Tino Martinez .25
69 Rocco Baldelli .60
70 Alfonso Soriano 1.00
71 Michael Young .25
72 Hank Blalock .40
73 Roy Halladay .40
74 Carlos Delgado .75
75 Vernon Wells .40
76 Johnny Bench 3.00
77 Reggie Jackson 5.00
78 Al Kaline 3.00
79 Nolan Ryan 10.00
80 Tom Seaver 3.00
81 Robin Yount 6.00
82 Mike Schmidt 5.00
83 Jim Palmer 3.00
84 Harmon Killebrew 5.00
85 Joe Morgan 3.00
86 *Kazuo Matsui* 5.00
87 *Luis Gonzalez* 3.00
88 *Yadier Molina* 4.00
89 *Jon Knott* 3.00
90 Kevin Youkilis 5.00
91 *Chris Saenz* 3.00
92 *Andres Blanco* 3.00
93 David Aardsma 3.00
94 *Merkin Valdez* 3.00
95 *Jason Bartlett* 3.00
96 *John Gall* 3.00
97 Zack Greinke 3.00
98 Scott Hairston 3.00
99 Matt Holliday 4.00
100 Casey Kotchman 5.00

Red

No Pricing
Production 5 Sets

Gold

Veterans (1-75): 2X-5X
Rookies (76-100): .75X-2X
Production 199 Sets

Autographs Silver

NM/M
Common Player: 10.00
Numbered to indicated quantity
Red: No Pricing
Production 25 Sets
Purple: .5X-2X
Numbered to jersey number
RB Rocco Baldelli/34 25.00
CB Carlos Beltran/296 25.00
AB Angel Berroa/11
JB Jeremy Bonderman/287 10.00
EC Eric Chavez/322 15.00
EG Eric Gagne/57 40.00
BG Brian Giles/134 15.00
LG Luis Gonzalez/55 15.00
RHL Roy Halladay/139 15.00
RHR Rich Harden/235 10.00
TH Trevor Hoffman/174 15.00
RJ Randy Johnson/20
BL Barry Larkin/140 20.00
JL Javy Lopez/257 15.00
WM Wade Miller/195 10.00
TN Trot Nixon/318 10.00
LO Lyle Overbay/240 10.00
SP Scott Podsednik/280 10.00
AP Albert Pujols/5
BR Brad Radke/168 15.00
DW Dontrelle Willis/290

Award Winners

NM/M
Common Player:
Production 150 Sets
1 Alex Rodriguez 10.00
2 Eric Gagne 3.00
3 Miguel Tejada 4.00
4 Roy Halladay 3.00
5 Randy Johnson 5.00
6 Barry Zito 4.00
7 Chipper Jones 3.00
8 Ivan Rodriguez 4.00
9 Pedro J. Martinez 5.00
10 Barry Larkin 3.00
11 Dontrelle Willis 3.00
12 Angel Berroa 3.00
13 Kerry Wood 5.00
14 Albert Pujols 8.00
15 Hideo Nomo 3.00

Award Winners Autographs

NM/M
Common Player: 15.00
Numbered to Award Year
All cards not released for some cards
AB Angel Berroa/103 15.00
RH Roy Halladay/102 20.00
CJ Chipper Jones 99/35
BL Barry Larkin 95/50 30.00
HN Hideo Nomo 95/15
IR Ivan Rodriguez 99/35
DW Dontrelle Willis/103 25.00
BZ Barry Zito 99/35

Award Winners Jersey Silver

NM/M
Common Player:
Production 175 Sets
Copper: .75X-1.5X
Production 99 Sets
Purple: 1X-3X
Production 49 Sets
AB Angel Berroa 5.00
EG Eric Gagne 8.00
RH Roy Halladay 5.00
RJ Randy Johnson 10.00
CJ Chipper Jones 10.00
BL Barry Larkin 5.00
PM Pedro J. Martinez 10.00
HN Hideo Nomo 5.00
AP Albert Pujols 15.00
IR Ivan Rodriguez 8.00
MT Miguel Tejada 8.00
DW Dontrelle Willis 5.00
KW Kerry Wood 10.00
BZ Barry Zito 8.00

Facsimile Signature Gold

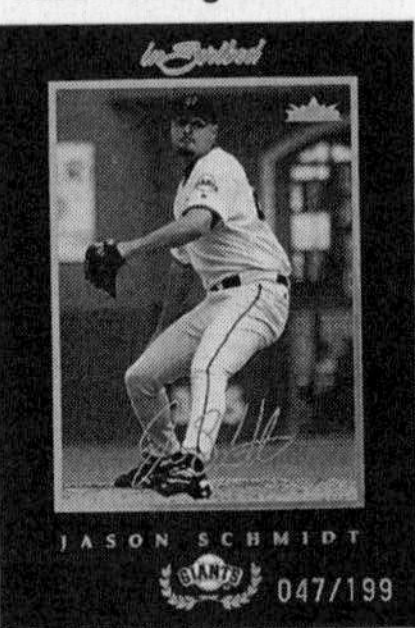

Current (1-75): 3X-5X
Retired (76-85): 1X-2X
Rookies (86-100): .75X-1.5X
Production 199 Sets

Induction Ceremony

NM/M
Common Player: 6.00
Numbered to Year of Induction
1 Carlton Fisk/100 8.00
2 Tony Perez/100 6.00
3 Nolan Ryan/99 20.00
4 Robin Yount/99 10.00
5 Orlando Cepeda/99 8.00
6 Bill Mazeroski/101 8.00
7 Larry Doby/98 6.00
8 Phil Niekro/97 6.00
9 Jim Bunning/96 6.00
10 Sparky Anderson/100 6.00
11 Phil Rizzuto/94 8.00
12 Rollie Fingers/92 6.00
13 Hal Newhouser/92 6.00
14 Rod Carew/91 8.00
15 Reggie Jackson/93 8.00
16 Tom Seaver/92 8.00
17 Bob Gibson/81 8.00
18 Jim Palmer/90 6.00
19 Joe Morgan/90 6.00
20 Al Kaline/80 10.00

Induction Ceremony Auto. Bronze

NM/M
Common Player: 20.00
Numbered to 50
Silver: No Pricing
Production 15 Sets
Gold: No Pricing
Production 5 Sets
JB Jim Bunning 20.00
OC Orlando Cepeda/40 20.00
RF Rollie Fingers 30.00
CF Carlton Fisk 30.00
BG Bob Gibson 40.00
RJ Reggie Jackson/30
AK Al Kaline 50.00
JM Joe Morgan
PN Phil Niekro/35
JP Jim Palmer
TP Tony Perez 30.00
NR Nolan Ryan/35
TS Tom Seaver/30
RY Robin Yount/40

Induction Ceremony Material Silver

NM/M
Common Player: 10.00
Numbered (2-digit) to Induction Year
Masterpiece: No Pricing
Production 1 Set
SA Sparky Anderson/100 10.00
RC Rod Carew/91 15.00
OC Orlando Cepeda/99 10.00
LD Larry Doby/98 20.00
RF Rollie Fingers/92 10.00
CF Carlton Fisk/100 15.00
RJ Reggie Jackson/93 10.00
AK Al Kaline/80 20.00
BM Bill Mazeroski/101 10.00
JM Joe Morgan/90 15.00
PN Phil Niekro/97 10.00
JP Jim Palmer/90 10.00
TP Tony Perez/100 15.00
PR Phil Rizzuto/94 20.00
NR Nolan Ryan/99 25.00
TS Tom Seaver/92 10.00
RY Robin Yount/99 10.00

Names of the Game

NM/M
Common Player: 2.00
Production 299 Sets
1 Nomar Garciaparra 8.00
2 Randy Johnson 3.00
3 Hideki Matsui 8.00
4 Frank Thomas 2.00
5 Ivan Rodriguez 2.00
6 Roger Clemens 5.00
7 Chipper Jones 5.00
8 Dontrelle Willis 2.00
9 Luis Gonzalez 2.00
10 Alex Rodriguez 8.00
11 Eric Gagne 2.00
12 Juan Gonzalez 2.00
13 Hideo Nomo 2.00
14 Sean Casey 2.00
15 Greg Maddux 5.00
16 Cal Ripken Jr. 15.00
17 Carl Yastrzemski 5.00
18 Tony Perez 3.00
19 Joe Morgan 3.00
20 Carlton Fisk 3.00
21 Willie McCovey 5.00
22 Al Kaline 5.00
23 Dennis Eckersley 3.00
24 Ted Williams 10.00
25 Willie Stargell 5.00
26 Rollie Fingers 3.00
27 Yogi Berra 2.00
28 Reggie Jackson 5.00
29 Harmon Killebrew 5.00
30 Nolan Ryan 10.00

Names of the Game Autograph Silver

NM/M
Common Player: 15.00
Stated Production 99 Sets
All 99 not released for some cards
Gold: No Pricing
Stated Production 25 Sets
All 25 not released for some cards
SC Sean Casey 20.00
DE Dennis Eckersley/90 25.00
RF Rollie Fingers/90 25.00
CF Carlton Fisk/50 30.00
LG Luis Gonzalez/75 15.00
RJ Reggie Jackson/35
CJ Chipper Jones/40 40.00
AK Al Kaline/90 40.00
JM Joe Morgan/40
TP Tony Perez/40
CR Cal Ripken Jr./20
IR Ivan Rodriguez/40
NR Nolan Ryan/35
DW Dontrelle Willis 25.00
CY Carl Yastrzemski/30

Names of the Game Material Copper

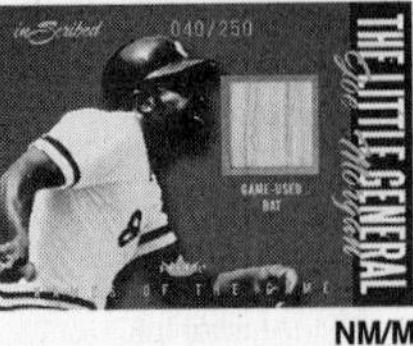

NM/M
Common Player: 5.00
Production 250 Sets
Gold: .5X-1.25X
Production 150 Sets
Red: .75X-1.5X
Production 79 Sets
Purple: 1X-2X
Production 33 Sets
YB Yogi Berra 10.00
SC Sean Casey 5.00
RC Roger Clemens 10.00
DE Dennis Eckersley 8.00
RF Rollie Fingers 8.00
CF Carlton Fisk 8.00
EG Eric Gagne 10.00
JG Juan Gonzalez 5.00
LG Luis Gonzalez 5.00
RJA Reggie Jackson 10.00
RJO Randy Johnson 8.00
CJ Chipper Jones 8.00
AK Al Kaline 10.00
HK Harmon Killebrew 10.00
GM Greg Maddux 10.00
HM Hideki Matsui 15.00
WM Willie McCovey 10.00
JM Joe Morgan 8.00
HN Hideo Nomo 5.00
TP Tony Perez 8.00
CR Cal Ripken Jr. 30.00
IR Ivan Rodriguez 5.00
NR Nolan Ryan 20.00
WS Willie Stargell 10.00
FT Frank Thomas 5.00
TW Ted Williams 25.00
DW Dontrelle Willis 5.00
CY Carl Yastrzemski 10.00

Rookie Autographs Notation

NM/M
Common Player: 15.00
Stated Production 750 Sets
75 Notation Cards for each player
87 Luis A. Gonzalez 4/6/04 15.00
89 Jon Knott 5/30/04 15.00
90 Kevin Youkilis 5/15/04 20.00
91 Chris Saenz 4/24/04 15.00
92 Andres Blanco 4/17/04 15.00
94 Merkin Valdez Go Giants 20.00
95 Jason Bartlett Go Twins 20.00
96A John Gall Gall-Star/25
96B John Gall Go Cards/50 20.00
98 Scott Hairston 5/17/04 15.00
100 Casey Kotchman 5/9/04 25.00

2004 FLEER LEGACY

		NM/M
Common Player (1-60):		1.50
Common Rookie (61-75):		4.00
Production 599 Sets		
Box (1 pack, 1 autographed baseball):		150.00
1	Angel Berroa	1.50
2	Derek Jeter	8.00
3	Jody Gerut	1.50
4	Curt Schilling	2.50
5	Khalil Greene	3.00
6	Manny Ramirez	3.00
7	Rocco Baldelli	2.50
8	Sammy Sosa	5.00
9	Shawn Green	2.00
10	Austin Kearns	2.50
11	Frank Thomas	3.00
12	Alfonso Soriano	3.50
13	Alex Rodriguez	6.00
14	Carlos Delgado	3.00
15	Chipper Jones	4.00
16	Edgar Martinez	2.00
17	Ivan Rodriguez	2.50
18	Mark Prior	6.00
19	Mike Piazza	4.00
20	Orlando Cabrera	1.50
21	Adam Dunn	2.50
22	Andruw Jones	3.00
23	Eric Chavez	2.00
24	Mark Teixeira	2.00
25	Scott Podsednik	1.50
26	Torii Hunter	2.50
27	Miguel Cabrera	3.00
28	Hideki Matsui	6.00
29	Jose Reyes	1.50
30	Vladimir Guerrero	3.50
31	Albert Pujols	6.00
32	Greg Maddux	4.00
33	Jason Giambi	3.50
34	Randy Johnson	3.50
35	Roger Clemens	6.00
36	Casey Kotchman	2.00
37	Ken Griffey Jr.	4.00
38	Todd Helton	3.00
39	Javy Lopez	1.50
40	Jim Thome	3.50
41	Josh Beckett	3.00
42	Kerry Wood	3.00
43	Scott Rolen	3.50
44	Pat Burrell	2.00
45	Pedro J. Martinez	3.50
46	Barry Zito	2.50
47	Hank Blalock	2.50
48	Hideo Nomo	2.00
49	Jeff Bagwell	3.00
50	Magglio Ordonez	2.00
51	Ichiro Suzuki	5.00
52	Joe Mauer	2.00
53	Richie Sexson	2.50
54	Shannon Stewart	1.50
55	Craig Wilson	1.50
56	Miguel Tejada	2.50
57	Sean Casey	1.50
58	Tom Glavine	2.00
59	Jason Schmidt	2.00
60	Nomar Garciaparra	6.00
61	*Kazuo Matsui*	8.00
62	*Justin Leone*	4.00
63	*Merkin Valdez*	6.00
64	*Shingo Takatsu*	6.00
65	*Andres Blanco*	4.00
66	*Angel Chavez*	4.00
67	*Hector Gimenez*	4.00
68	*Akinori Otsuka*	4.00
69	*Jason Bartlett*	4.00
70	*Luis Gonzalez*	4.00
71	Sean Henn	4.00
72	Mike Rouse	4.00
73	*Chris Aguila*	4.00
74	*Aarom Baldiris*	4.00
75	*Jerry Gil*	4.00

Rookie cards are in *Italic.*

Gold Legacy

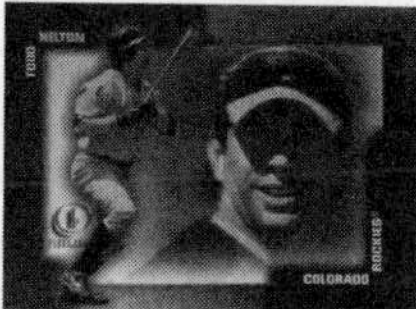

Veterans (1-60):	2X-4X
Rookies (61-75):	.75X-1.5X
Production 50 Sets	

Ultimate Legacy

No Pricing
Production 1 Set

Franchise Legacy Patch

		NM/M
Common Player:		10.00
Production 99 Sets		
Patch 50:		.5X-1.5X
Production 50 Sets		
Patch 25:		No Pricing
Production 25 Sets		
Masterpiece:		No Pricing
Production 1 Set		
JBA	Jeff Bagwell	15.00
JBE	Josh Beckett	15.00
JB	Johnny Bench	
RC	Roger Clemens	25.00
VG	Vladimir Guerrero	15.00
RJ	Randy Johnson	20.00
CJ	Chipper Jones	20.00
JL	Javy Lopez	10.00
GM	Greg Maddux	30.00
PM	Pedro Martinez	15.00
HM	Hideki Matsui	60.00
KM	Kazuo Matsui	20.00
DM	Don Mattingly	40.00
HN	Hideo Nomo	20.00
MP	Mike Piazza	20.00
MPR	Mark Prior	15.00
AP	Albert Pujols	50.00
CR	Cal Ripken Jr.	60.00
IR	Ivan Rodriguez	15.00
NR	Nolan Ryan	50.00
SS	Sammy Sosa	15.00
MT	Miguel Tejada	10.00
JT	Jim Thome	15.00
KW	Kerry Wood	15.00

Franchise Legacy Quad Patch

NM/M

No Pricing
Sequentially #'d between 2 & 22

Franchise Dual Patch

No Pricing
Sequentially #'d between 5 & 31

Hit Kings Patch Silver

		NM/M
Common Player:		15.00
Production 99 Sets		
Gold:		.5X-1.5X
Production 50 Sets		
Masterpiece:		No Pricing
Production 1 Set		
JB	Jeff Bagwell	15.00
LB	Lance Berkman	15.00
HB	Hank Blalock	20.00
MC	Miguel Cabrera	20.00
CD	Carlos Delgado	20.00
AD	Adam Dunn	30.00
JG	Jason Giambi	15.00
VG	Vladimir Guerrero	20.00
CJ	Chipper Jones	20.00
AK	Austin Kearns	15.00
HM	Hideki Matsui	50.00
MP	Mike Piazza	25.00
AP	Albert Pujols	50.00
MR	Manny Ramirez	25.00
SR	Scott Rolen	20.00
MS	Mike Schmidt	40.00
RS	Richie Sexson	15.00
GS	Gary Sheffield	20.00
SS	Sammy Sosa	20.00
MT	Mark Teixeira	15.00
FT	Frank Thomas	15.00
JT	Jim Thome	25.00

Hit Kings Dual Patch

NM/M

No Pricing
Sequentially numbered between 7 & 21

2004 FLEER PATCHWORKS

		NM/M
Common Player (1-90):		.15
Common Rookie (91-110):		2.00
Minor Rookies:		3.00
Unlisted Rookies:		5.00
Production 799 Sets		
Pack (5):		4.00
Box (18):		70.00
1	Kerry Wood	1.00
2	Brian Giles	.40
3	Tino Martinez	.15
4	Mark Mulder	.40
5	Andy Pettitte	.60
6	Gary Sheffield	.60
7	Mark Teixeira	.40
8	Garret Anderson	.40
9	Craig Biggio	.40
10	Alfonso Soriano	1.50
11	Bret Boone	.40
12	Mike Piazza	2.00
13	Todd Helton	1.00
14	Jay Gibbons	.40
15	Eric Chavez	.40
16	Andruw Jones	1.00
17	Adam Dunn	.60
18	Corey Koskie	.15
19	Rafael Palmeiro	1.00
20	Ivan Rodriguez	.60
21	Tom Glavine	.40
22	Luis Gonzalez	.40
23	Miguel Tejada	.60
24	Jose Vidro	.15
25	Richie Sexson	.60
26	Roy Halladay	.40
27	Vladimir Guerrero	1.50
28	Randy Johnson	1.50
29	Vernon Wells	.40
30	Pat Burrell	.40
31	Jason Schmidt	.40
32	Casey Blake	.15
33	Greg Maddux	2.00
34	Mike Lowell	.15
35	Hideo Nomo	.40
36	Carlos Delgado	1.00
37	Dontrelle Willis	.40
38	Shawn Green	.40
39	Pedro Martinez	1.50
40	Josh Beckett	1.00
41	Eric Gagne	.40
42	Manny Ramirez	1.00
43	Jim Edmonds	.40
44	Curt Schilling	.60
45	Mike Sweeney	.15
46	Albert Pujols	3.00
47	Nomar Garciaparra	3.00
48	Alex Rodriguez	3.00
49	Angel Berroa	.15
50	Jim Thome	1.50
51	Edgardo Alfonzo	.15
52	Jeremy Bonderman	.15
53	Miguel Cabrera	1.00
54	Bobby Higginson	.15
55	John Smoltz	.40
56	Jason Kendall	.40
57	Torii Hunter	.60
58	Troy Glaus	.60
59	Rafael Furcal	.40
60	Austin Kearns	.60
61	Esteban Loaiza	.15
62	Darin Erstad	.40
63	Jose Reyes	.15
64	Preston Wilson	.15
65	Rocco Baldelli	.60
66	Barry Zito	.60
67	Ken Griffey Jr.	2.00
68	Frank Thomas	1.00
69	Roger Clemens	2.00
70	Brett Myers	.15
71	Billy Wagner	.15
72	Scott Podsednik	.15
73	Jody Gerut	.15
74	Bartolo Colon	.40
75	Jeff Bagwell	1.00
76	Jason Giambi	1.50
77	Edgar Martinez	.40
78	Chipper Jones	2.00
79	Jason Bay	.15
80	Doug Mientkiewicz	.15
81	Hank Blalock	.60
82	Sammy Sosa	2.00
83	Derek Jeter	4.00
84	Ichiro Suzuki	2.00
85	Ben Sheets	.40
86	Magglio Ordonez	.40
87	Carlos Beltran	.40
88	Mark Prior	3.00
89	Sean Burroughs	.15
90	Tim Hudson	.40
91	*Hector Gimenez*	8.00
92	*Khalil Greene*	5.00
93	Rickie Weeks	8.00
94	Delmon Young	10.00
95	*Donald Kelly*	3.00
96	*Chad Bentz*	5.00
97	*Greg Dobbs*	3.00
98	*John Gall*	5.00
99	*Cory Sullivan*	3.00
100	*Kazuo Matsui*	25.00
101	Graham Koonce	3.00
102	*Jason Bartlett*	8.00
103	*Angel Chavez*	2.00
104	*Ronny Cedeno*	3.00
105	*Jerry Gil*	3.00
106	*Ivan Ochoa*	3.00
107	*Ruddy Yan*	8.00
108	Mike Gosling	2.00
109	*Alfredo Simon*	2.00
110	*Koyie Hill*	2.00

Ruby

Ruby (1-90):	3X-10X
Ruby (91-110):	.5X-2X
Production 50 Sets	

Autoworks

		NM/M
Common Player:		10.00
Inserted 1:54		
Parallel:		.5X-1.25X
Production 100 Sets		
Patch		
Production 10 Sets		
1	Garret Anderson/145	15.00
2	Josh Beckett/148	25.00
3	Angel Berroa/145	10.00
4	Eric Gagne/193	20.00
5	Jody Gerut/376	10.00
6	Roy Halladay/286	10.00
7	Mark Mulder/190	15.00
8	Andy Pettitte/148	30.00
9	Scott Podsednik/146	20.00
10	Albert Pujols/193	120.00
11	Grady Sizemore/263	15.00
12	Miguel Tejada/164	20.00

By The Numbers

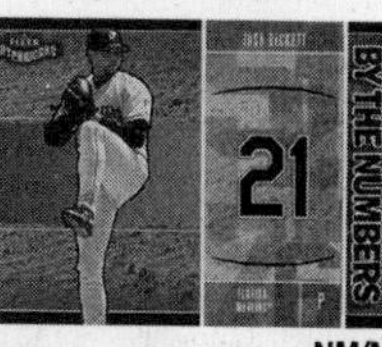

		NM/M
Common Player:		3.00
Inserted 1:24		
Patch:		3X-8X
Production 100 Sets		
1	Albert Pujols	8.00
2	Derek Jeter	10.00
3	Mike Piazza	6.00
4	Nomar Garciaparra	8.00
5	Eric Gagne	4.00
6	Sammy Sosa	6.00
7	Josh Beckett	4.00
8	Vladimir Guerrero	5.00
9	Jose Reyes	3.00
10	Bret Boone	3.00
11	Alex Rodriguez	8.00
12	Randy Johnson	6.00

13	Chipper Jones	6.00
14	Tim Hudson	4.00
15	Rocco Baldelli	4.00

Game-Used Level 1

		NM/M
Common Player:		6.00
Production 200 Sets		
Level 2:		1X-1.5X
Production 100 Sets		
Patch:		1X-2X
Production 50 Sets		
1	Albert Pujols	15.00
2	Andy Pettitte	6.00
3	Dontrelle Willis	6.00
4	Mike Piazza	10.00
5	Barry Zito	6.00
6	Troy Glaus	6.00
7	Carlos Delgado	8.00
8	Torii Hunter	6.00
9	Roy Halladay	6.00
10	Andruw Jones	8.00
11	Garret Anderson	6.00
12	Larry Walker	6.00
13	Shawn Green	6.00
14	Bernie Williams	6.00
15	Alfonso Soriano	10.00
16	Bret Boone	6.00
17	Hank Blalock	6.00
18	Jose Reyes	6.00
19	Mark Prior	15.00

Licensed Apparel

		NM/M
Common Player:		5.00
Production 300 Sets		
Team Name:		1X-2X
Production 150 Sets		
Number:		1X-2X
Production 100 Sets		
Nameplate:		1X-3X
Production 50 Sets		
Jersey Tags:		
Production 10 Sets		
MLB Logo		
Production 1 Set		
1	Albert Pujols	15.00
2	Derek Jeter	18.00
3	Alex Rodriguez	15.00
4	Jim Thome	8.00
5	Mike Piazza	10.00
6	Dontrelle Willis	5.00
7	Torii Hunter	5.00
8	Tim Hudson	5.00
9	Sammy Sosa	12.00
10	Troy Glaus	5.00
11	Andruw Jones	8.00
12	Austin Kearns	5.00
13	Jeff Bagwell	8.00
14	Mark Prior	15.00
15	Bret Boone	5.00

National Pastime

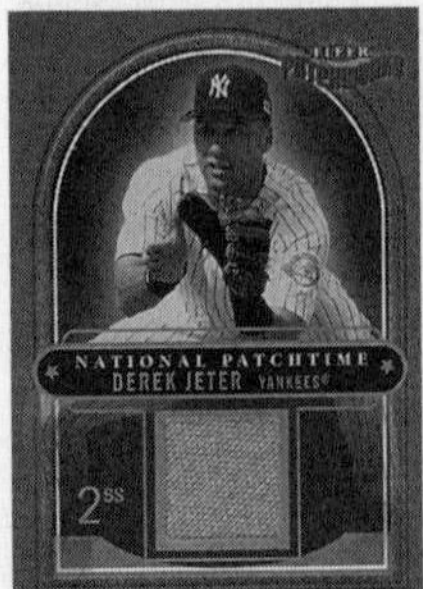

		NM/M
Common Player:		5.00
Production 250 Sets		
Jersey:		1X-1.5X
Production 350 Sets		
Gold Jersey:		1X-2X
Production 200 Sets		
Patch:		1X-3X
Production 100 Sets		
1	Albert Pujols	15.00
2	Alex Rodriguez	15.00
3	Derek Jeter	18.00
4	Nomar Garciaparra	15.00
5	Jim Thome	8.00
6	Chipper Jones	10.00
7	Mark Prior	15.00
8	Ichiro Suzuki	12.00
9	Jeff Bagwell	6.00
10	Troy Glaus	5.00
11	Randy Johnson	8.00
12	Sammy Sosa	12.00
13	Austin Kearns	5.00
14	Miguel Cabrera	6.00
15	Vladimir Guerrero	8.00

Stitches In Time

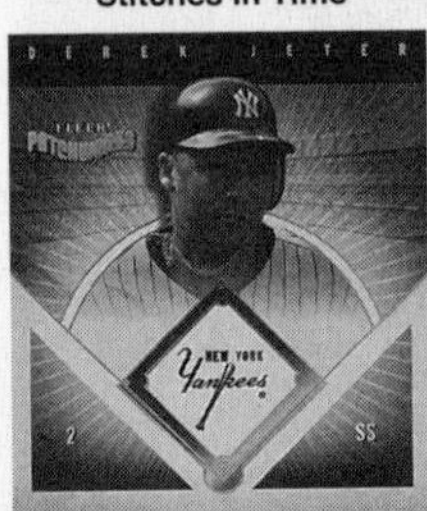

		NM/M
Common Player:		2.00
Inserted 1:12		
Jersey:		
Production 350 Sets		
Patch:		
Production 150 Sets		
1	Albert Pujols	5.00
2	Alex Rodriguez	5.00
3	Derek Jeter	6.00
4	Nomar Garciaparra	5.00
5	Jim Thome	3.00
6	Chipper Jones	3.00
7	Mark Prior	5.00
8	Eric Gagne	2.00
9	Jeff Bagwell	3.00
10	Troy Glaus	2.00
11	Randy Johnson	3.00
12	Sammy Sosa	4.00
13	Austin Kearns	2.00
14	Miguel Cabrera	2.00
15	Vladimir Guerrero	3.00
16	Mike Piazza	3.00
17	Jason Giambi	3.00
18	Tim Hudson	2.00
19	Carlos Delgado	3.00
20	Rocco Baldelli	2.00
21	Ichiro Suzuki	4.00
22	Barry Zito	2.00
23	Pedro Martinez	3.00
24	Torii Hunter	2.00
25	Andruw Jones	3.00

2004 FLEER PLATINUM

		NM/M
Complete Set (200):		35.00
Common Player:		.15
Common SP:		.50
Inserted 1:3		
Pack (7):		2.00
Jumbo Pack (20):		5.00
Box (18 + 4 jumbo):		55.00
1	Luis Castillo	.15
2	Preston Wilson	.15
3	Johan Santana	.15
4	Fred McGriff	.25
5	Albert Pujols	1.50
6	Reggie Sanders	.15
7	Ivan Rodriguez	.40
8	Roy Halladay	.25
9	Brian Giles	.25
10	Bernie Williams	.40
11	Barry Larkin	.25
12	Marlon Anderson	.15
13	Ramon Ortiz	.15
14	Luis Matos	.15
15	Esteban Loaiza	.15
16	Orlando Cabrera	.15
17	Jamie Moyer	.15
18	Tino Martinez	.15
19	Josh Beckett	.50
20	Derek Jeter	2.00
21	Derek Lowe	.15
22	Jack Wilson	.15
23	Bret Boone	.25
24	Matt Morris	.15
25	Javier Vazquez	.25
26	Joe Crede	.15
27	Jose Vidro	.15
28	Mike Piazza	1.00
29	Curt Schilling	.40
30	Alex Rodriguez	1.50
31	John Olerud	.25
32	Dontrelle Willis	.25
33	Larry Walker	.25
34	Joe Randa	.15
35	Paul LoDuca	.15
36	Marlon Byrd	.15
37	Bo Hart	.15
38	Rafael Palmeiro	.50
39	Garret Anderson	.40
40	Tom Glavine	.25
41	Ichiro Suzuki	1.25
42	Derek Lee	.25
43	Lance Berkman	.25
44	Nomar Garciaparra	1.50
45	Mike Sweeney	.15
46	A.J. Burnett	.15
47	Sean Casey	.15
48	Eric Gagne	.25
49	Joel Pineiro	.15
50	Russ Ortiz	.15
51	Placido Polanco	.15
52	Sammy Sosa	1.25
53	Mark Teixeira	.25
54	Randy Wolf	.15
55	Vladimir Guerrero	.75
56	Tim Hudson	.25
57	Lew Ford	.15
58	Carlos Delgado	.50
59	Darin Erstad	.25
60	Mike Lieberthal	.15
61	Craig Biggio	.25
62	Ryan Klesko	.25
63	C.C. Sabathia	.15
64	Carlos Lee	.15
65	Al Leiter	.15
66	Brandon Webb	.15
67	Jacque Jones	.15
68	Kerry Wood	.50
69	Omar Vizquel	.25
70	Jeremy Bonderman	.15
71	Kevin Brown	.25
72	Richie Sexson	.40
73	Zach Day	.15
74	Mike Mussina	.40
75	Sidney Ponson	.15
76	Andruw Jones	.50
77	Woody Williams	.15
78	Kazuhiro Sasaki	.15
79	Matt Clement	.15
80	Shea Hillenbrand	.15
81	Bartolo Colon	.25
82	Ken Griffey Jr.	1.00
83	Todd Helton	.50
84	Dmitri Young	.15
85	Richard Hidalgo	.15
86	Carlos Beltran	.25
87	Brad Wilkerson	.15
88	Andy Pettitte	.40
89	Miguel Tejada	.40
90	Edgar Martinez	.25
91	Vernon Wells	.25
92	Magglio Ordonez	.25
93	Tony Batista	.15
94	Jose Reyes	.15
95	Matt Stairs	.15
96	Manny Ramirez	.50
97	Carlos Pena	.15
98	A.J. Pierzynski	.15
99	Jim Thome	.75
100	Aubrey Huff	.15
101	Roberto Alomar	.40
102	Luis Gonzalez	.25
103	Chipper Jones	1.00
104	Jay Gibbons	.25
105	Adam Dunn	.40
106	Jay Payton	.15
107	Scott Podsednik	.40
108	Roy Oswalt	.25
109	Milton Bradley	.15
110	Shawn Green	.25
111	Ryan Wagner	.15
112	Eric Chavez	.25
113	Pat Burrell	.25
114	Frank Thomas	.50
115	Jason Kendall	.25
116	Jake Peavy	.15
117	Mike Cameron	.15
118	Jim Edmonds	.25
119	Hank Blalock	.40
120	Troy Glaus	.40
121	Jeff Kent	.25
122	Jason Schmidt	.25
123	Corey Patterson	.15
124	Austin Kearns	.40
125	Edwin Jackson	.15
126	Alfonso Soriano	.75
127	Bobby Abreu	.25
128	Scott Rolen	.75
129	Jeff Bagwell	.50
130	Shannon Stewart	.15
131	Rich Aurilia	.15
132	Ty Wigginton	.15
133	Randy Johnson	.75
134	Rocco Baldelli	.40
135	Hideo Nomo	.25
136	Greg Maddux	1.00
137	Johnny Damon	.25
138	Mark Prior	1.50
139	Corey Koskie	.15
140	Miguel Cabrera	.50
141	Hideki Matsui	1.50
142	Jose Cruz	.15
143	Barry Zito	.40
144	Javy Lopez	.25
145	Jason Varitek	.15
146	Moises Alou	.25
147	Torii Hunter	.40
148	Juan Encarnacion	.15
149	Jorge Posada	.40
150	Marquis Grissom	.15
151	Rich Harden	.15
152	Gary Sheffield	.40
153	Pedro J. Martinez	.75
154	Brad Radke	.15
155	Mike Lowell	.15
156	Jason Giambi	.75
157	Mark Mulder	.25
158	Ben Weber	.15
159	Mark DeRosa	.15
160	Melvin Mora	.15
161	Bill Mueller	.15
162	Jon Garland	.15
163	Jody Gerut	.15
164	Javier Lopez	.15
165	Craig Monroe	.15
166	Juan Pierre	.15
167	Morgan Ensberg	.15
168	Angel Berroa	.15
169	Geoff Jenkins	.25
170	Matt LeCroy	.15
171	Livan Hernandez	.15
172	Jason L. Phillips	.15
173	Mariano Rivera	.25
174	Erubiel Durazo	.15
175	Jason Michaels	.15
176	Kip Wells	.15
177	Ray Durham	.15
178	Randy Winn	.15
179	Edgar Renteria	.15
180	Carl Crawford	.15
181	Laynce Nix	.15
182	Greg Myers	.15
183	Delmon Young, Chad Gaudin	1.00
184	Humberto Quintero, Bernie Castro	.50
185	Craig Brazell, Daniel Garcia	.50
186	Ryan Wing, Francisco Cruceta	.50
187	William Bergolla, Josh Hall	.50
188	Clint Barmes, Garrett Atkins	.50
189	Chris Bootcheck, Richard Fischer	.50

190 Edgar Gonzalez, Matt Kata .50
191 Andrew Brown, Koyie Hill .50
192 John Gall, Dan Haren .50
193 Chad Bentz, Luis Ayala .50
194 Hector Gimenez, Eric Bruntlett .50
195 Boof Bonser, Rob Bowen .50
196 Chris Snelling, Rett Johnson .50
197 Rickie Weeks, Adam Morrissey 1.00
198 Noah Lowry, Todd Linden .50
199 Chris Waters, Brett Evert .50
200 Jorge DePaula, Chien-Ming Wang .50

Finish

Stars (1-200): 4-6X
Production 100 sets

Big Signs

NM/M
Complete Set (15): 25.00
Common Player: .75
Inserted 1:9
1 Albert Pujols 3.00
2 Derek Jeter 4.00
3 Mike Piazza 2.00
4 Jason Giambi 1.50
5 Ichiro Suzuki 2.50
6 Nomar Garciaparra 3.00
7 Mark Prior 3.00
8 Randy Johnson 1.50
9 Greg Maddux 2.00
10 Sammy Sosa 2.50
11 Ken Griffey Jr. 2.00
12 Dontrelle Willis .75
13 Alex Rodriguez 3.00
14 Chipper Jones 2.00
15 Hank Blalock .75

Big Signs Autographs

NM/M
Production 100
Hank Blalock 25.00
Mark Prior
Albert Pujols 150.00
Dontrelle Willis 25.00

Classic Combinations

NM/M
Complete Set (10): 50.00
Common Player: 3.00
Inserted 1:108
1 Ivan Rodriguez, Mike Piazza 6.00
2 Alex Rodriguez, Sammy Sosa 8.00
3 Dontrelle Willis, Angel Berroa 3.00
4 Nomar Garciaparra, Derek Jeter 10.00
5 Ichiro Suzuki, Hideo Nomo 6.00
6 Josh Beckett, Kerry Wood 4.00
7 Albert Pujols, Carlos Delgado 8.00
8 Alfonso Soriano, Joe Morgan 4.00
9 Jason Giambi, Reggie Jackson 4.00
10 Nolan Ryan, Tom Seaver 10.00

Clubhouse Memorabilia

NM/M
Common Player: 5.00
Inserted 1:24
Rocco Baldelli 10.00
Josh Beckett 8.00
Hank Blalock 6.00
Nomar Garciaparra 12.00
Jason Giambi 8.00
Vladimir Guerrero 8.00
Rich Harden
Todd Helton 6.00
Torii Hunter 5.00
Derek Jeter 15.00
Chipper Jones 8.00
Austin Kearns 6.00
Mike Lowell
Greg Maddux 10.00
Hideo Nomo 8.00
Mike Piazza 8.00
Mark Prior 15.00
Albert Pujols 12.00
Alex Rodriguez 10.00
Richie Sexson 5.00
Alfonso Soriano 6.00
Sammy Sosa 12.00
Miguel Tejada 5.00
Jim Thome 8.00
Dontrelle Willis 8.00

Clubhouse Memorabilia Dual

NM/M
Common Player: 10.00
Production 50 sets
Hank Blalock 15.00
Nomar Garciaparra 30.00
Jason Giambi 15.00
Vladimir Guerrero 20.00
Todd Helton 20.00
Torii Hunter 15.00
Derek Jeter 35.00
Chipper Jones 15.00
Austin Kearns 10.00
Greg Maddux 30.00
Hideo Nomo 25.00
Mark Prior 35.00
Albert Pujols 30.00
Alex Rodriguez 25.00
Sammy Sosa 20.00
Jim Thome 20.00

Nameplates

NM/M
Common Player: 8.00
Inserted 1:4 Jumbo
Varying quantities produced
1 Austin Kearns 10.00
2 Juan Pierre 10.00
3 Albert Pujols 30.00
4 Manny Ramirez 15.00
5 Kerry Wood 20.00
6 Alex Rodriguez 20.00
7 Angel Berroa
8 Barry Zito 10.00
9 Hee Seop Choi 8.00
10 Kevin Brown 10.00
11 Jose Reyes 15.00
12 Marlon Byrd 10.00
13 Nomar Garciaparra 20.00
14 Josh Beckett 15.00
16 Hideo Nomo 15.00
19 Randy Johnson 15.00
20 Hank Blalock 12.00
21 Tom Glavine/25 25.00
22 Luis Castillo 8.00
23 Mark Teixeira 12.00
24 Gary Sheffield 10.00
25 Richie Sexson 10.00
26 Miguel Cabrera 20.00
27 Sammy Sosa 25.00
28 Curt Schilling 10.00
30 Chipper Jones 20.00

Portraits

NM/M
Complete Set (10): 25.00
Common Player: 1.50
Inserted 1:18
1 Jason Giambi 1.50
2 Nomar Garciaparra 4.00
3 Vladimir Guerrero 1.50
4 Mark Prior 4.00
5 Jim Thome 1.50
6 Derek Jeter 5.00
7 Sammy Sosa 3.00
8 Alex Rodriguez 4.00
9 Greg Maddux 2.50
10 Albert Pujols 4.00

Portraits Jersey

NM/M
Common Player: 8.00
Inserted 1:48
Nomar Garciaparra 15.00
Jason Giambi 8.00
Vladimir Guerrero 8.00
Derek Jeter 15.00
Greg Maddux 8.00
Mark Prior 8.00
Albert Pujols 15.00
Alex Rodriguez 10.00
Sammy Sosa 12.00
Jim Thome 8.00

Portraits Patch

NM/M
Common Player: 10.00
Production 100 sets
Nomar Garciaparra 20.00
Jason Giambi 10.00
Vladimir Guerrero 10.00
Derek Jeter 25.00
Greg Maddux
Mark Prior 25.00
Albert Pujols 30.00
Alex Rodriguez 15.00
Sammy Sosa 20.00
Jim Thome 12.00

Scouting Report

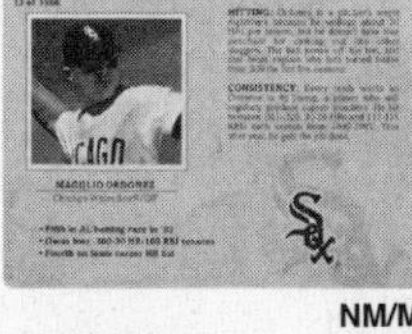

NM/M
Complete Set (15): 35.00
Common Player: 1.50
Production 400 sets
1 Josh Beckett 2.00
2 Todd Helton 2.00
3 Rocco Baldelli 2.00
4 Pedro J. Martinez 3.00
5 Jeff Bagwell 2.00
6 Mark Prior 6.00
7 Ichiro Suzuki 4.00
8 Barry Zito 2.00
9 Manny Ramirez 2.00
10 Miguel Cabrera 2.00
11 Richie Sexson 1.50
12 Hideki Matsui 8.00
13 Magglio Ordonez 1.50
14 Brandon Webb 1.50
15 Kerry Wood 2.00

Scouting Report Memorabilia

NM/M
Common Player: 6.00
Production 250 sets
Jeff Bagwell 8.00
Rocco Baldelli 8.00
Josh Beckett 8.00
Miguel Cabrera
Todd Helton 6.00
Pedro J. Martinez 8.00
Mark Prior 15.00
Manny Ramirez 6.00
Brandon Webb 6.00
Kerry Wood 8.00

2004 FLEER SHOWCASE

NM/M
Complete Set (130):
Common Player: .25
Common SP (101-130): 1.00
Inserted 1:6
Pack (5): 4.50
Box (24): 90.00
1 Corey Patterson .25
2 Ken Griffey Jr. 1.50
3 Preston Wilson .40
4 Juan Pierre .25
5 Jose Reyes .50
6 Jason Schmidt .40
7 Rocco Baldelli .50
8 Carlos Delgado .75
9 Hideki Matsui 2.50
10 Nomar Garciaparra 2.00
11 Brian Giles .40
12 Darin Erstad .40
13 Larry Walker .40
14 Bernie Williams .50
15 Laynce Nix .25
16 Manny Ramirez .75
17 Magglio Ordonez .50
18 Khalil Greene .25
19 Jim Edmonds .40
20 Troy Glaus .50
21 Curt Schilling .50
22 Chipper Jones 1.50
23 Sammy Sosa 2.00
24 Frank Thomas .75
25 Todd Helton .75
26 Craig Biggio .40
27 Shannon Stewart .25
28 Mark Mulder .40
29 Mike Lieberthal .25
30 Reggie Sanders .25
31 Edgar Martinez .25
32 Bo Hart .25
33 Mark Teixeira .40
34 Jay Gibbons .25
35 Roberto Alomar .50
36 Kip Wells .25
37 J.D. Drew .25
38 Jason Varitek .25
39 Craig Monroe .25
40 Roy Oswalt .40
41 Edgardo Alfonzo .25
42 Roy Halladay .50
43 Gary Sheffield .50
44 Lance Berkman .50
45 Torii Hunter .50
46 Vladimir Guerrero 1.00
47 Marlon Byrd .25
48 Austin Kearns .50
49 Angel Berroa .25
50 Geoff Jenkins .50
51 Aubrey Huff .25
52 Dontrelle Willis .50
53 Tony Batista .25
54 Shawn Green .40
55 Jason Kendall .25
56 Garret Anderson .50
57 Andruw Jones .75
58 Dmitri Young .25
59 Richie Sexson .50
60 Jorge Posada .50
61 Bobby Abreu .40
62 Vernon Wells .40
63 Javy Lopez .40
64 Josh Beckett .75
65 Eric Chavez .40
66 Tim Salmon .40
67 Brandon Webb .40
68 Pedro J. Martinez 1.00
69 Kerry Wood 1.00
70 Jose Vidro .25
71 Alfonso Soriano 1.00

72	Barry Zito	.50
73	Sean Burroughs	.25
74	Jamie Moyer	.25
75	Luis Gonzalez	.40
76	Adam Dunn	.50
77	Mike Piazza	1.50
78	Pat Burrell	.50
79	Scott Rolen	1.00
80	Milton Bradley	.25
81	Mike Sweeney	.25
82	Hank Blalock	.50
83	Esteban Loaiza	.25
84	Hideo Nomo	.50
85	Derek Jeter	3.00
86	Albert Pujols	2.50
87	Greg Maddux	1.50
88	Mark Prior	2.00
89	Mike Lowell	.25
90	Jeff Bagwell	.75
91	Scott Podsednik	.50
92	Tom Glavine	.50
93	Jason Giambi	1.00
94	Jim Thome	1.00
95	Ichiro Suzuki	2.00
96	Randy Johnson	1.00
97	Omar Vizquel	.25
98	Ivan Rodriguez	.50
99	Miguel Tejada	.50
100	Alex Rodriguez	2.50
101	Rickie Weeks	3.00
102	Chad Gaudin	1.00
103	Rich Harden	1.00
104	Edwin Jackson	1.50
105	Chien-Ming Wang	1.00
106	Matt Kata	1.00
107	Delmon Young	3.00
108	Ryan Wagner	1.00
109	Jeff Duncan	1.00
110	Prentice Redman	1.00
111	Clint Barmes	1.00
112	Jeremy Guthrie	1.00
113	Brian Stokes	1.00
114	David DeJesus	1.00
115	Felix Sanchez	1.00
116	Josh Stewart	1.00
117	Daniel Garcia	1.00
118	Jon Leicester	1.00
119	Francisco Cruceta	1.00
120	Oscar Villarreal	1.00
121	Michael Hessman	1.00
122	Michel Hernandez	1.00
123	Richard Fischer	1.00
124	Robby Hammock	1.00
125	Guillermo Quiroz	1.00
126	Craig Brazell	1.00
127	Wilfredo Ledezma	1.00
128	Josh Willingham	1.00
129	Ramon Nivar	1.00
130	Matt Diaz	1.00

Legacy

Stars (1-100):	4-8X
SP's (101-130):	1-3X

Production 99 sets

Masterpiece

No Pricing
Production one set

Albert Pujols Legacy Collection

	NM/M
Complete Set (10):	60.00
Common Pujols:	8.00

Production 1,000 sets

1	Albert Pujols	8.00
2	Albert Pujols	8.00
3	Albert Pujols	8.00
4	Albert Pujols	8.00
5	Albert Pujols	8.00
6	Albert Pujols	8.00
7	Albert Pujols	8.00
8	Albert Pujols	8.00
9	Albert Pujols	8.00
10	Albert Pujols	8.00

Albert Pujols Legacy Coll. Jersey

NM/M

Varying quantities produced

1	Albert Pujols/10	
2	Albert Pujols/20	
3	Albert Pujols/30	40.00
4	Albert Pujols/40	30.00
5	Albert Pujols/50	30.00
6	Albert Pujols/60	30.00
7	Albert Pujols/70	25.00
8	Albert Pujols/80	25.00
9	Albert Pujols/90	25.00
10	Albert Pujols/100	25.00

Albert Pujols Legacy Coll. Auto.

Varying quantities produced
No Pricing

Baseball's Best

		NM/M
Complete Set (15):		20.00
Common Player:		.75
Inserted 1:24		
1	Derek Jeter	4.00
2	Mark Prior	3.00
3	Mike Piazza	2.50
4	Jeff Bagwell	1.00
5	Kerry Wood	1.00
6	Ivan Rodriguez	1.00
7	Albert Pujols	3.00
8	Jim Thome	1.50
9	Sammy Sosa	2.50
10	Vladimir Guerrero	1.50
11	Eric Gagne	.75
12	Randy Johnson	1.50
13	Todd Helton	1.00
14	Chipper Jones	2.00
15	Alex Rodriguez	4.00

Baseball's Best Memorabilia

	NM/M
Common Player:	5.00
Inserted 1:72	
Parallel 150:	.75-1.5X
Production 150	
Parallel 50:	1.5-2X
Patch versions:	2-4X
Production 50	
Derek Jeter	15.00
Mark Prior	15.00
Mike Piazza	10.00
Jeff Bagwell	8.00
Kerry Wood	8.00
Ivan Rodriguez	5.00
Albert Pujols	15.00
Jim Thome	8.00
Sammy Sosa	10.00
Vladimir Guerrero	8.00
Eric Gagne	8.00
Randy Johnson	8.00
Todd Helton	8.00
Chipper Jones	8.00
Alex Rodriguez	10.00

Grace

		NM/M
Complete Set (20):		20.00
Common Player:		.75
Inserted 1:12		
1	Kerry Wood	1.50
2	Derek Jeter	4.00
3	Nomar Garciaparra	3.00
4	Mike Piazza	2.50
5	Mark Prior	3.00
6	Jose Reyes	1.00
7	Dontrelle Willis	.75
8	Pedro J. Martinez	1.50
9	Tim Hudson	.75
10	Troy Glaus	.75
11	Hank Blalock	1.00
12	Albert Pujols	3.00
13	Juan Pierre	.75
14	Angel Berroa	.75
15	Rocco Baldelli	1.00
16	Carlos Delgado	1.00
17	Manny Ramirez	1.00
18	Alex Rodriguez	3.00
19	Andruw Jones	1.00
20	Luis Gonzalez	.75

Grace Memorabilia

	NM/M
Common Player:	5.00
Inserted 1:48	
Parallel 150:	1-1.5X
Production 150	
Patch:	1.5-2.5X
Production 50	
Derek Jeter	15.00
Nomar Garciaparra	10.00
Mike Piazza	10.00
Mark Prior	15.00
Dontrelle Willis	5.00
Pedro J. Martinez	8.00
Albert Pujols	15.00
Rocco Baldelli	8.00
Manny Ramirez	8.00
Alex Rodriguez	10.00

Hot Gloves Memorabilia

	NM/M
Common Player:	20.00
All Jerseys unless noted	
Production 50 sets	
Derek Jeter	60.00
Nomar Garciaparra	50.00
Alex Rodriguez	40.00
Chipper Jones	40.00
Ichiro Suzuki/base	65.00
Mark Prior	40.00
Vladimir Guerrero	30.00
Albert Pujols	50.00
Ivan Rodriguez	20.00
Hideki Matsui/base	60.00
Sammy Sosa	40.00
Jim Thome	20.00
Rocco Baldelli	20.00
Jeff Bagwell	20.00

Hot Gloves

		NM/M
Common Player:		8.00
Inserted 1:288		
1	Derek Jeter	40.00
2	Nomar Garciaparra	30.00
3	Alex Rodriguez	30.00
4	Chipper Jones	15.00
5	Torii Hunter	8.00
6	Ichiro Suzuki	35.00
7	Mark Prior	30.00
8	Vladimir Guerrero	15.00
9	Albert Pujols	30.00
10	Ivan Rodriguez	10.00
11	Hideki Matsui	30.00
12	Sammy Sosa	25.00
13	Jim Thome	15.00
14	Rocco Baldelli	10.00
15	Jeff Bagwell	10.00

Sweet Sigs

	NM/M
Common Player:	6.00
Inserted 1:24	
Sweet Sigs Game-Used: No Pricing	
Production 5	
Hank Blalock/824	20.00
Taylor Bucholz/redemp.	6.00
John Gall/redemp.	8.00
Bo Hart/667	15.00
Torii Hunter/294	15.00
Austin Kearns/224	20.00
Wilfredo Ledezma/376	6.00
Mike Lowell/44	15.00
Chien-Ming Wang/35	
Corey Patterson/176	15.00
Carlos Pena/48	10.00
Albert Pujols/redemp.	120.00
Jose Reyes/115	35.00
Scott Rolen/200	25.00
Michael Ryan/288	12.00
Miguel Tejada/52	20.00
Ryan Wagner/redemp.	10.00
Brandon Webb/1,000	15.00
Rickie Weeks/416	30.00
Josh Willingham/180	6.00
Dontrelle Willis/26	60.00
Delmon Young/1,000	25.00
Barry Zito/248	25.00

2004 FLEER SWEET SIGS

		NM/M
Common Player (1-75):		.20
Unlisted Star (1-75):		.60
Common Future Sig-cess (76-100):		3.00
Future Sig-cess Production 999 Sets		
Pack (6):		5.00
Box (12):		80.00
1	Manny Ramirez	1.00
2	Frank Thomas	1.00
3	Josh Beckett	1.00
4	Shawn Green	.40
5	Tom Glavine	.40
6	Marquis Grissom	.20
7	Nomar Garciaparra	3.00
8	Magglio Ordonez	.40
9	Alex 1odriguez	3.00
10	Chipper Jones	2.00
11	Jody Gerut	.20
12	Dontrelle Willis	.40
13	Lance Berkman	.40
14	Jose Vidro	.20
15	Barry Zito	.60
16	Jason Kendall	.40
17	Scott Rolen	1.50
18	Troy Glaus	.60
19	Brandon Webb	.20
20	Tim Hudson	.40
21	Shannon Stewart	.20
22	Darin Erstad	.40
23	Curt Schilling	.60
24	Bret Boone	.40
25	Richie Sexson	.60
26	Hideki Matsui	3.00
27	Albert Pujols	3.00
28	Greg Maddux	2.00
29	Austin Kearns	.60
30	Todd Helton	1.00
31	Miguel Cabrera	1.00
32	Jeff Bagwell	1.00
33	Marlon Byrd	.20
34	Ichiro Suzuki	2.50
35	Rocco Baldelli	.60
36	Garret Anderson	.40
37	Javy Lopez	.40
38	Kerry Wood	1.00
39	Adam Dunn	.60
40	Geoff Jenkins	.40
41	Derek Jeter	4.00
42	Rich Harden	.20
43	Alfonso Soriano	1.50
44	Ken Griffey Jr.	2.00
45	Ivan Rodriguez	.60
46	Pedro J. Martinez	1.50
47	Andy Pettitte	.60
48	Gary Sheffield	.60
49	Brian Giles	.40
50	Carlos Delgado	1.00
51	Mike Piazza	2.00
52	Hank Blalock	.60
53	Roger Clemens	2.00
54	Scott Podsednik	.20
55	Torii Hunter	.60
56	Jose Reyes	.20
57	Jim Thome	1.50
58	Jason Schmidt	.40
59	Jose Cruz	.20
60	Mark Teixeira	.40

61 Randy Johnson 1.50
62 Miguel Tejada .60
63 Sammy Sosa 2.50
64 Larry Walker .40
65 Carl Everett .20
66 Luis Castillo .20
67 Jason Giambi 1.50
68 Mike Sweeney .20
69 Andruw Jones 1.00
70 Vladimir Guerrero 1.50
71 J.D. Drew .40
72 Mark Prior 3.00
73 Angel Berroa .20
74 Hideo Nomo .40
75 Roy Halladay .40
76 *John Gall* 3.00
77 *Angel Chavez* 3.00
78 *Alfredo Simon* 3.00
79 *Merkin Valdez* 3.00
80 *Chad Bentz* 3.00
81 *Justin Leone* 6.00
82 Mike Rouse 3.00
83 *Aarom Baldiris* 3.00
84 *Chris Shelton* 5.00
85 *Akinori Otsuka* 6.00
86 *Ruddy Yan* 3.00
87 *Ramon Ramirez* 3.00
88 *Hector Gimenez* 6.00
89 Mike Gosling 3.00
90 *Greg Dobbs* 3.00
91 *Kazuo Matsui* 8.00
92 *Donald Kelly* 6.00
93 *Shingo Takatsu* 6.00
94 *Ivan Ochoa* 5.00
95 *Chris Aguila* 5.00
96 *Jason Bartlett* 3.00
97 Graham Koonce 5.00
98 *Ronny Cedeno* 3.00
99 *Jerome Gamble* 3.00
100 *Onil Joseph* 3.00

Gold

(1-75): 1X-5X
(76-100): .5X-2X
Production 99 Sets

Black

(1-100): No Pricing
Production 5 Sets

Sweet Sigs Copper

NM/M
Common Player: 10.00
Sequentially Numbered
Gold: .75X-1.5X
Production 30 Sets
Hideo Nomo #'d to 10
No Roger Clemens or Ted Williams Gold card
Masterpiece: No Pricing
Production 1 Set
GA Garret Anderson/100 20.00
RB Rocco Baldelli/75 25.00
JB Josh Beckett/75 30.00
CB Carlos Beltran/75 20.00
LB Lance Berkman/150 20.00
AB Angel Berroa/75 20.00
JB Jeremy Bonderman/150 15.00
MC Miguel Cabrera/150 30.00
MC Mike Cameron/150 20.00
RC Roger Clemens/52 400.00
CC Carl Crawford/150 15.00
JD Johnny Damon/100 30.00
JD J.D. Drew/98 40.00
DE Dennis Eckersley/75 40.00
AE Adam Everett/150 10.00
JF Julio Franco/150 30.00
LG Luis Gonzalez/150 15.00
KG Khalil Greene/150 40.00
VG Vladimir Guerrero/75 75.00
TH Torii Hunter/150 25.00
EJ Edwin Jackson/75 15.00
RJ Randy Johnson/28 150.00
CJ Chipper Jones/50 100.00
MK Matt Kata/150 10.00
BL Barry Larkin/50 50.00
CL Carlos Lee/150 15.00
AL Al Leiter/75 25.00
KL Kenny Lofton/50 50.00
JL Javy Lopez/75 25.00
GM Greg Maddux/50 75.00
PM Pedro J. Martinez/75 125.00
JM Joe Mauer/150 40.00
WM Wade Miller/150 20.00
KM Kevin Millwood/100 15.00
PM Paul Molitor/75 40.00
SM Stan Musial/25 80.00
MM Mike Mussina/50 40.00
LN Lance Niekro/150 10.00
HN Hideo Nomo/5
JO John Olerud/75 30.00
MO Magglio Ordonez/150 20.00
RO Russ Ortiz/150 15.00
RO Roy Oswalt/150 20.00
AO Akinori Otsuka/150 20.00
BP Brad Penny/150 10.00
AP Andy Pettitte/50 40.00
MP Mike Piazza/50 120.00
AP Albert Pujols/73 300.00
BR Brad Radke/100 20.00
JR Jose Reyes/163 20.00
AR Alexis Rios/150 15.00
NR Nolan Ryan/50 300.00
CS C.C. Sabathia/150 20.00
TS Tim Salmon/100 40.00
DS Deion Sanders/50 50.00
JS Johan Santana/150 80.00
MS Mike Schmidt/50 60.00
SS Shannon Stewart/75 20.00
FT Frank Thomas/75 75.00
MV Merkin Valdez/150
JV Jason Varitek/75 40.00
OV Omar Vizquel/100
TW Tim Wakefield/150 30.00
VW Vernon Wells/150 20.00
BW Bernie Williams/50 80.00
TW Ted Williams
DW Dontrelle Willis/150 20.00
KW Kerry Wood/75 60.00
CY Carl Yastrzemski/50 100.00
BZ Barry Zito/44 30.00

Ballpark Heroes

NM/M
Common Player: 1.25
Inserted 1:6
1 Rocco Baldelli 1.75
2 Adam Dunn 1.75
3 Nomar Garciaparra 5.00
4 Ken Griffey Jr. 3.50
5 Vladimir Guerrero 3.00
6 Torii Hunter 1.75
7 Andruw Jones 2.00
8 Mike Piazza 3.50
9 Alfonso Soriano 3.00
10 Frank Thomas 2.00
11 Dontrelle Willis 1.25
12 Barry Zito 1.75
13 Javy Lopez 1.25
14 Miguel Cabrera 2.00
15 Kazuo Matsui 3.50
16 Josh Beckett 2.00
17 Derek Jeter 6.00
18 Greg Maddux 3.50
19 Pedro J. Martinez 3.00
20 Hideo Nomo 1.25
21 Mark Prior 5.00
22 Albert Pujols 5.00
23 Alex Rodriguez 5.00
24 Scott Rolen 3.00
25 Ichiro Suzuki 4.00

Ballpark Heroes Silver Jersey

NM/M
Common Player: 4.00
Sequentially Numbered
RB Rocco Baldelli/250 4.00
JB Josh Beckett/225
MC Miguel Cabrera/196 5.00
AD Adam Dunn/215 4.00
VG Vladimir Guerrero/200 6.00
GM Greg Maddux/224 8.00
PM Pedro J. Martinez/239 6.00
KM Kazuo Matsui/39
HN Hideo Nomo/210 4.00
MP Mike Piazza/163 8.00
MP Mark Prior/176
AP Albert Pujols/199 12.00
AR Alex Rodriguez/35
SR Scott Rolen/221 6.00
AS Alfonso Soriano/235 6.00
FT Frank Thomas/242 5.00
DW Dontrelle Willis/186 4.00
BZ Barry Zito/195 4.00

Ballpark Heroes Copper Jersey

NM/M
Common Player: 5.00
Production 110 Sets
Gold Patch: 1X-3X
Production 50 Sets
Masterpiece Patch: No Pricing
Production 1 Set
RB Rocco Baldelli/110 5.00
JB Josh Beckett/110
MC Miguel Cabrera/110 6.00
AD Adam Dunn/110 5.00
VG Vladimir Guerrero/110 8.00
GM Greg Maddux/110 10.00
PM Pedro J. Martinez/110 8.00
KM Kazuo Matsui/110
HN Hideo Nomo/110 5.00
MP Mike Piazza/110 10.00
MP Mark Prior/110
AP Albert Pujols/110 15.00
AR Alex Rodriguez/110
SR Scott Rolen/110 8.00
AS Alfonso Soriano/110 8.00
FT Frank Thomas/110 6.00
DW Dontrelle Willis/110 5.00
BZ Barry Zito/110 5.00

Ballpark Heroes Black Patch

NM/M
Sequentially Numbered
RB Rocco Baldelli/5
JB Josh Beckett/21
MC Miguel Cabrera/24
AD Adam Dunn/44
VG Vladimir Guerrero/27
GM Greg Maddux/31
PM Pedro J. Martinez/45
KM Kazuo Matsui/25
HN Hideo Nomo/10
MP Mike Piazza/31 50.00
MP Mark Prior/22
AP Albert Pujols/5
AR Alex Rodriguez/13
SR Scott Rolen/27
AS Alfonso Soriano/12
FT Frank Thomas/35
DW Dontrelle Willis/35
BZ Barry Zito/75

Ballpark Heroes Duals

No Pricing
Sequentially Numbered

Ballpark Heroes Quad

NM/M
Sequentially Numbered
1 Josh Beckett/42, Greg Maddux/42, Pedro J. Martinez/42, Mark Prior/42 150.00
2 Dontrelle Willis/26, Kazuo Matsui/26, Miguel Cabrera/26, Rocco Baldelli/26 75.00
4 Dontrelle Willis/32, Josh Beckett/32, Derek Jeter/32, Alex Rodriguez/32 150.00
5 Albert Pujols/37, Vladimir Guerrero/37, Mike Piazza/37, Alex Rodriguez/37 150.00

Sweet Swing

NM/M
Common Player: 2.50
Inserted 1:12
1SS Sammy Sosa 5.00
2SS Vladimir Guerrero 3.50
3SS Jason Giambi 3.50
4SS Chipper Jones 4.00
5SS Alfonso Soriano 3.50
6SS Manny Ramirez 3.00
7SS Todd Helton 3.00
8SS Alex Rodriguez 6.00
9SS Albert Pujols 6.00
10SS Jeff Bagwell 3.00
11SS Mike Piazza 4.00
12SS Hank Blalock 2.50

13SS Jim Thome 3.50
14SS Carlos Delgado 3.00
15SS Nomar Garciaparra 6.00

Sweet Swing Silver Bat

NM/M
Common Player: 5.00
Sequentially Numbered
HB Hank Blalock/15
JG Jason Giambi/247 6.00
VG Vladimir Guerrero/250 6.00
CJ Chipper Jones/235 8.00
MP Mike Piazza/231 8.00
AP Albert Pujols/237 12.00
MR Manny Ramirez/224 5.00
AR Alex Rodriguez/213 12.00
AS Alfonso Soriano/216 6.00
SS Sammy Sosa/221 10.00
JT Jim Thome/245 6.00

Sweet Swing Copper Jersey

NM/M
Common Player: 4.00
Production 200 Sets
Gold Bat/Jersey: 1.5X-4X
Production 50 Sets
Masterpiece Bat/Patch
Production 1 Set
HB Hank Blalock/200 4.00
JG Jason Giambi/200 6.00
VG Vladimir Guerrero/200 6.00
CJ Chipper Jones/200 8.00
MP Mike Piazza/200 8.00
AP Albert Pujols/200 12.00
MR Manny Ramirez/200 5.00
AR Alex Rodriguez/200 12.00
AS Alfonso Soriano/200 6.00
SS Sammy Sosa/200 10.00
JT Jim Thome/200 6.00

Sweet Swing Quad

NM/M
Sequentially Numbered
1 Jason Giambi/35, Alex Rodriguez/35, Jeff Bagwell/35, Manny Ramirez/35 80.00
3 Mike Piazza/32, Alfonso Soriano/32, Todd Helton/32, Hank Blalock/32 125.00

Sweet Stitches Silver Jersey

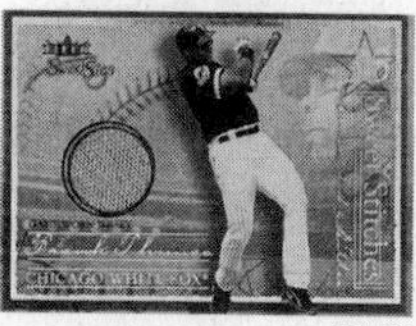

NM/M
Common Player: 5.00
Sequentially Numbered
RB Rocco Baldelli/23
JB Josh Beckett/153
HB Hank Blalock/166 5.00
MC Miguel Cabrera/169 8.00
RC Roger Clemens/165 8.00
JG Jason Giambi/125 8.00
VG Vladimir Guerrero/172 8.00
RJ Randy Johnson/10
AJ Andruw Jones/175 8.00
GM Greg Maddux/156 8.00
KM Kazuo Matsui/175

HN Hideo Nomo/110
MO Magglio Ordonez/113 5.00
MP Mike Piazza/174 8.00
MP Mark Prior/172 12.00
AP Albert Pujols/170 12.00
MR Manny Ramirez/163 8.00
JR Jose Reyes/171 5.00
AR Alex Rodriguez/8
SR Scott Rolen/166 8.00
GS Gary Sheffield/88 8.00
AS Alfonso Soriano/162 8.00
SS Sammy Sosa/158 10.00
MT Mark Teixeira/158 5.00
MT Miguel Tejada/162 5.00
FT Frank Thomas/159 8.00
JT Jim Thome/8 8.00
KW Kerry Wood/134 8.00

Sweet Stitches Copper Jersey

NM/M
Common Player: 5.00
Production 125 Sets
Gold Patch: 1X-3X
Production 50 Sets
Masterpiece Patch: No Pricing
Production 1 Set
RB Rocco Baldelli/125
JB Josh Beckett/125
HB Hank Blalock/125 5.00
MC Miguel Cabrera/125 8.00
RC Roger Clemens/125 8.00
JG Jason Giambi/125 8.00
VG Vladimir Guerrero/125 8.00
RJ Randy Johnson/125
AJ Andruw Jones/125 10.00
GM Greg Maddux/125 8.00
KM Kazuo Matsui/125
HN Hideo Nomo/125
MO Magglio Ordonez/125 5.00
MP Mike Piazza/125 8.00
MP Mark Prior/125 12.00
AP Albert Pujols/125 15.00
MR Manny Ramirez/125 8.00
JR Jose Reyes/125 5.00
AR Alex Rodriguez/125
SR Scott Rolen/125 8.00
GS Gary Sheffield/125 8.00
AS Alfonso Soriano/125 8.00
SS Sammy Sosa/125 10.00
MT Mark Teixeira/125 5.00
MT Miguel Tejada/125 5.00
FT Frank Thomas/125 8.00
JT Jim Thome/125 8.00
KW Kerry Wood/125 8.00

Sweet Stitches Quad Patches

NM/M
Sequentially Numbered
No pricing for quantities less than 25
4 Andruw Jones/31, Miguel Cabrera/31, Albert Pujols/31, Sammy Sosa/31 80.00
10 Greg Maddux/33, Sammy Sosa/33, Mark Prior/33, Kerry Wood/33 150.00

2004 FLEER TRADITION

NM/M
Complete Set (500): 100.00
Common Player: .15
Common SP (401-500): .25
Pack (10): 1.75
Hobby Box (36): 50.00
1 Juan Pierre .15
2 Josh Beckett .50
3 Ivan Rodriguez .50
4 Miguel Cabrera .50
5 Dontrelle Willis .25
6 Derek Jeter 2.00
7 Jason Giambi .75
8 Bernie Williams .40
9 Alfonso Soriano .75
10 Hideki Matsui 2.00
11 Garret Anderson, Ramon Ortiz, John Lackey .15
12 Luis Gonzalez, Brandon Webb, Curt Schilling .25
13 Javy Lopez, Gary Sheffield, Russ Ortiz .25
14 Tony Batista, Jay Gibbons, Sidney Ponson, Jason Johnson .15
15 Manny Ramirez, Nomar Garciaparra, Derek Lowe, Pedro J. Martinez .50
16 Sammy Sosa, Mark Prior, Kerry Wood .75
17 Frank Thomas, Carlos Lee, Esteban Loaiza .25
18 Adam Dunn, Sean Casey, Chris Reitsma, Paul Wilson .25
19 Jody Gerut, C.C. Sabathia .15
20 Preston Wilson, Darren Oliver, Jason Jennings .15
21 Dmitri Young, Mike Maroth, Jeremy Bonderman .15
22 Mike Lowell, Dontrelle Willis, Josh Beckett .25
23 Jeff Bagwell, Jeriome Robertson, Wade Miller .25
24 Carlos Beltran, Darrell May .15
25 Adrian Beltre, Shawn Green, Hideo Nomo, Kevin Brown .15
26 Richie Sexson, B en Sheets .15
27 Torii Hunter, Brad Radke, Johan Santana .15
28 Vladimir Guerrero, Orlando Cabrera, Livan Hernandez, Javier Vazquez .25
29 Cliff Floyd, Ty Wigginton, Steve Trachsel, Al Leiter .15
30 Jason Giambi, Andy Pettitte, Mike Mussina .40
31 Eric Chavez, Miguel Tejada, Tim Hudson .25
32 Jim Thome, Randy Wolf .25
33 Reggie Sanders, Josh Fogg, Kip Wells .15
34 Ryan Klesko, Mark Loretta, Jake Peavy .15
35 Jose Cruz, Edgardo Alfonzo, Jason Schmidt .15
36 Bret Boone, Jamie Moyer, Joel Pineiro .15
37 Albert Pujols, Woody Williams .75
38 Aubrey Huff, Victor Zambrano .15
39 Alex Rodriguez, John Thomson .75
40 Carlos Delgado, Roy Halladay .25
41 Greg Maddux 1.00
42 Ben Grieve .15
43 Darin Erstad .25
44 Ruben Sierra .15
45 Byung-Hyun Kim .15
46 Freddy Garcia .15
47 Richard Hidalgo .15
48 Tike Redman .15
49 Kevin Millwood .25
50 Marquis Grissom .15
51 Jae Weong Seo .15
52 Wil Cordero .15
53 LaTroy Hawkins .15
54 Jolbert Cabrera .15
55 Kevin Appier .15
56 John Lackey .15
57 Garret Anderson .25
58 R.A. Dickey .15
59 David Segui .15
60 Erubiel Durazo .15
61 Bobby Abreu .25
62 Travis Hafner .15
63 Victor Zambrano .15
64 Randy Johnson .75
65 Bernie Williams .40
66 J.T. Snow .15
67 Sammy Sosa 1.50
68 Al Leiter .15
69 Jason Jennings .15
70 Matt Morris .15
71 Mike Hampton .15
72 Juan Encarnacion .15
73 Alex Gonzalez .15
74 Bartolo Colon .25
75 Brett Myers .15
76 Michael Young .15
77 Ichiro Suzuki 1.50
78 Jason Johnson .15
79 Brad Ausmus .15
80 Ted Lilly .15
81 Ken Griffey Jr. 1.00
82 Chone Figgins .15
83 Edgar Martinez .25
84 Adam Eaton .15
85 Ken Harvey .15
86 Francisco Rodriguez .15
87 Bill Mueller .15
88 Mike Maroth .15
89 Charles Johnson .15
90 Jhonny Peralta .15
91 Kip Wells .15
92 Cesar Izturis .15
93 Matt Clement .15
94 Lyle Overbay .15
95 Kirk Rueter .15
96 Cristian Guzman .15
97 Garrett Stephenson .15
98 Lance Berkman .25
99 Brett Tomko .15
100 Chris Stynes .15
101 Nate Cornejo .15
102 Aaron Rowand .15
103 Javier Vazquez .15
104 Jason Kendall .25
105 Mark Redman .15
106 Benito Santiago .15
107 C.C. Sabathia .15
108 David Wells .15
109 Mark Ellis .15
110 Casey Blake .15
111 Sean Burroughs .15
112 Carlos Beltran .25
113 Ramon Hernandez .15
114 Eric Hinske .15
115 Luis Gonzalez .25
116 Jarrod Washburn .15
117 Ronnie Belliard .15
118 Troy Percival .15
119 Jose Valentine .15
120 Chase Utley .15
121 Odalis Perez .15
122 Steve Finley .15
123 Bret Boone .25
124 Jeff Conine .15
125 Jason Fogg .15
126 Neifi Perez .15
127 Ben Sheets .25
128 Randy Winn .15
129 Matt Stairs .15
130 Carlos Delgado .50
131 Morgan Ensberg .15
132 Vinny Castilla .15
133 Matt Mantei .15
134 Alex Rodriguez 1.50
135 Matthew LeCroy .15
136 Woody Williams .15
137 Frank Catalanotto .15
138 Rondell White .15
139 Scott Rolen .75
140 Cliff Floyd .15
141 Chipper Jones .75
142 Robin Ventura .15
143 Mariano Rivera .25
144 Brady Clark .15
145 Ramon Ortiz .15
146 Omar Infante .15
147 Mike Matheny .15
148 Pedro J. Martinez .75
149 Carlos Baerga .15
150 Shannon Stewart .15
151 Travis Lee .15
152 Eric Byrnes .15
153 Rafael Furcal .25
154 B.J. Surhoff .15
155 Zach Day .15
156 Marlon Anderson .15
157 Mark Hendrickson .15
158 Mike Mussina .50
159 Randall Simon .15
160 Jeff DaVanon .15
161 Joel Pineiro .15
162 Vernon Wells .25
163 Adam Kennedy .15
164 Trot Nixon .15
165 Rodrigo Lopez .15
166 Curt Schilling .50
167 Horacio Ramirez .15
168 Gerald Laird .15
169 Magglio Ordonez .25
170 Scott Schoeneweis .15
171 Andruw Jones .50
172 Tino Martinez .25
173 Moises Alou .25
174 Kelvim Escobar .15
175 Xavier Nady .15
176 Ramon Martinez .15
177 Pat Hentgen .15
178 Austin Kearns .40
179 D'Angelo Jimenez .15
180 Deivi Cruz .15
181 John Smoltz .25
182 Toby Hall .15
183 Mark Buehrle .15
184 Howie Clark .15
185 David Ortiz .15
186 Raul Mondesi .15
187 Milton Bradley .15
188 Jorge Julio .15
189 Victor Martinez .15
190 Gabe Kapler .15
191 Julio Franco .15
192 Ryan Freel .15
193 Brad Fullmer .15
194 Joe Borowski .15
195 Darren Oliver .15
196 Jason Varitek .15
197 Greg Myers .15
198 Eric Munson .15
199 Tim Wakefield .15
200 Kyle Farnsworth .15
201 John Vander Wal .15
202 Alex Escobar .15
203 Sean Casey .15
204 John Thomson .15
205 Carlos Zambrano .15
206 Kenny Lofton .15
207 Marcus Giles .15
208 Wade Miller .15
209 Geoff Blum .15
210 Jason LaRue .15
211 Omar Vizquel .25
212 Carlos Pena .15
213 Adam Dunn .40
214 Oscar Villarreal .15
215 Paul Konerko .15
216 Hideo Nomo .40
217 Mike Sweeney .15
218 Coco Crisp .15
219 Shawn Chacon .15
220 Brook Fordyce .15
221 Josh Beckett .50
222 Paul Wilson .15
223 Josh Towers .15
224 Geoff Jenkins .25
225 Shawn Green .25
226 Derek Lee .15
227 Karim Garcia .15
228 Preston Wilson .15
229 Dane Sardinha .15
230 Aramis Ramirez .15
231 Doug Mientkiewicz .15
232 Jay Gibbons .15
233 Adam Everett .15
234 Brooks Kieschnick .15
235 Dmitri Young .15
236 Brad Penny .15
237 Todd Zeile .15
238 Eric Gagne .25
239 Esteban Loaiza .15
240 Billy Wagner .15
241 Nomar Garciaparra 1.50
242 Desi Relaford .15
243 Luis Rivas .15
244 Andy Pettitte .40
245 Ty Wigginton .15
246 Edgar Gonzalez .15
247 Brian Anderson .15
248 Richie Sexson .40
249 Russell Branyan .15
250 Jose Guillen .15
251 Chin-Hui Tsao .15
252 Jose Hernandez .15
253 Kevin Brown .25
254 Pete LaForest .15
255 Adrian Beltre .15
256 Jacque Jones .15
257 Jimmy Rollins .15
258 Brandon Phillips .15
259 Derek Jeter 2.00

260 Carl Everett .15
261 Wes Helms .15
262 Kyle Lohse .15
263 Jason L. Phillips .15
264 Jake Peavy .15
265 Orlando Hernandez .15
266 Keith Foulke .15
267 Brad Wilkerson .15
268 Corey Koskie .15
269 Josh Hall .15
270 Bobby Higginson .15
271 Andres Galarraga .15
272 Alfonso Soriano .75
273 Carlos Rivera .15
274 Steve Trachsel .15
275 David Bell .15
276 Endy Chavez .15
277 Jay Payton .15
278 Mark Mulder .25
279 Terrence Long .15
280 A.J. Burnett .15
281 Pokey Reese .15
282 Phil Nevin .15
283 Jose Contreras .25
284 Jim Thome .75
285 Pat Burrell .40
286 Luis Castillo .15
287 Juan Uribe .15
288 Raul Ibanez .25
289 Sidney Ponson .15
290 Shane Hatteberg .15
291 Jack Wilson .15
292 Reggie Sanders .15
293 Brian Giles .25
294 Craig Biggio .25
295 Kazuhisa Ishii .15
296 Jim Edmonds .25
297 Trevor Hoffman .15
298 Ray Durham .15
299 Mike Lieberthal .15
300 Todd Worrell .15
301 Chris George .15
302 Jamie Moyer .15
303 Mike Cameron .15
304 Matt Kinney .15
305 Aubrey Huff .15
306 Brian Lawrence .15
307 Carlos Guillen .15
308 J.D. Drew .15
309 Paul LoDuca .15
310 Tim Salmon .25
311 Jason Schmidt .15
312 A.J. Pierzynski .15
313 Lance Carter .15
314 Julio Lugo .15
315 Johan Santana .15
316 Laynce Nix .15
317 John Olerud .25
318 Robb Quinlan .15
319 Scott Spiezio .15
320 Tony Clark .15
321 Jose Vidro .15
322 Shea Hillenbrand .15
323 Doug Glanville .15
324 Orlando Palmeiro .15
325 Juan Gonzalez .40
326 Jason Giambi .75
327 Junior Spivey .15
328 Tom Glavine .25
329 Reed Johnson .15
330 David Eckstein .15
331 Damian Jackson .15
332 Orlando Hudson .15
333 Barry Zito .40
334 Robert Fick .15
335 Aaron Boone .15
336 Rafael Palmeiro .50
337 Bobby Kielty .15
338 Tony Batista .15
339 Ryan Dempster .15
340 Derek Lowe .25
341 Alex Cintron .15
342 Jermaine Dye .15
343 John Burkett .15
344 Javy Lopez .25
345 Eric Karros .15
346 Corey Patterson .25
347 Josh Phelps .15
348 Ryan Klesko .25
349 Craig Wilson .15
350 Brian Roberts .15
351 Roberto Alomar .40
352 Frank Thomas .50
353 Gary Sheffield .40
354 Alex Gonzalez .15
355 Jose Cruz .15
356 Jerome Williams .15
357 Mark Kotsay .15
358 Chris Reitsma .15
359 Carlos Lee .15
360 Todd Helton .50
361 Gil Meche .15
362 Ryan Franklin .15
363 Josh Bard .15
364 Juan Pierre .15
365 Barry Larkin .25
366 Edgar Renteria .15
367 Alex Sanchez .15
368 Jeff Bagwell .50
369 Ben Broussard .15
370 Chan Ho Park .15
371 Darrell May .15
372 Roy Oswalt .25
373 Craig Monroe .15
374 Fred McGriff .25
375 Bengie Molina .15
376 Aaron Guiel .15
377 Jeriome Robertson .15
378 Kenny Rogers .15
379 Colby Lewis .15
380 Jeromy Burnitz .15
381 Orlando Cabrera .15
382 Joe Randa .15
383 Miguel Batista .15
384 Brad Radke .15
385 Jason Giambi .75
386 Vladimir Guerrero .75
387 Melvin Mora .15
388 Royce Clayton .15
389 Danny Garcia .15
390 Manny Ramirez .50
391 Dave McCarty .15
392 Mark Grudzielanek .15
393 Mike Piazza 1.00
394 Jorge Posada .40
395 Tim Hudson .25
396 Placido Polanco .15
397 Mark Loretta .15
398 Jesse Foppert .15
399 Albert Pujols 1.50
400 Jeremi Gonzalez .15
401 Paul Bako .25
402 Luis Matos .25
403 Johnny Damon .50
404 Kerry Wood 1.00
405 Joe Crede .25
406 Jason Davis .25
407 Larry Walker .50
408 Ivan Rodriguez 1.00
409 Nick Johnson .25
410 Jose Lima .25
411 Brian Jordan .25
412 Eddie Guardado .25
413 Ron Calloway .25
414 Aaron Heilman .25
415 Eric Chavez .50
416 Randy Wolf .25
417 Jason Bay .25
418 Edgardo Alfonzo .25
419 Kazuhiro Sasaki .25
420 Eduardo Perez .25
421 Carl Crawford .25
422 Troy Glaus 1.00
423 Joaquin Benoit .25
424 Russ Ortiz .25
425 Larry Bigbie .25
426 Todd Walker .25
427 Kris Benson .25
428 Sandy Alomar .25
429 Jody Gerut .25
430 Rene Reyes .25
431 Mike Lowell .25
432 Jeff Kent .25
433 Mike MacDougal .25
434 Dave Roberts .25
435 Torii Hunter .75
436 Tomokazu Ohka .25
437 Jeremy Griffiths .25
438 Miguel Tejada .75
439 Vicente Padilla .25
440 Bobby Hill .25
441 Rich Aurilia .25
442 Shigetoshi Hasegawa .25
443 So Taguchi .25
444 Damian Rolls .25
445 Roy Halladay .75
446 Rocco Baldelli .75
447 Dontrelle Willis .75
448 Mark Prior 3.00
449 Jason Lane .25
450 Angel Berroa .25
451 Jose Reyes .75
452 Ryan Wagner .25
453 Marlon Byrd .25
454 Hee Seop Choi .25
455 Brandon Webb .50
456 Bo Hart .75
457 Hank Blalock 1.00
458 Mark Teixeira .75
459 Hideki Matsui 4.00
460 Scott Podsednik .25
461 Miguel Cabrera 1.00
462 Josh Beckett 1.00
463 Mariano Rivera .50
464 Ivan Rodriguez 1.00
465 Alex Rodriguez 3.00
466 Albert Pujols 3.00
467 Roy Halladay .75
468 Eric Gagne .50
469 Angel Berroa .25
470 Dontrelle Willis .50
471 Chris Bootcheck, Tom Gregorio, Richard Fischer .25
472 Matt Kata, Tim Olson, Robby Hammock .25
473 Michael Hessman, Chris Waters, Humberto Quintero .25
474 Carlos Mendez, Daniel Cabrera, Jeremy Guthrie .25
475 Edwin Almonte, Phil Seibel, Felix Sanchez .25
476 Todd Wellemeyer, Jon Leicester, Sergio Mitre .25
477 Josh Stewart, Neal Cotts, Aaron Miles .25
478 Terrmel Sledge, Josh Hall, Brandon Claussen .25
479 Francisco Cruceta, Jason Stanford, Rafael Betancourt .25
480 Javier Lopez, Garrett Atkins, Clint Barmes .25
481 Wilfredo Ledezma, Nook Logan, Jeremy Bonderman .25
482 Josh Willingham, Kevin Hooper, Rick Roberts .25
483 Colin Porter, Mike Gallo, Dave Matranga .25
484 David DeJesus, Jason Gilfillan, Jimmy Gobble .25
485 Koyie Hill, Alfredo Gonzalez, Andrew Brown .25
486 Rickie Weeks, Pedro Liriano, Wes Obermueller 1.00
487 Alex Prieto, Mike Ryan, Lew Ford .25
488 Julio Manon, Luis Ayala, Seung Jun Song .25
489 Jeff Duncan, Prentice Redman, Craig Brazell .25
490 Chien-Ming Wang, Michel Hernandez, Mike Gonzalez .25
491 Rich Harden, Mike Neu, Geoff Geary .25
492 Diegomar Markwell, Chad Gaudin, David Sanders .25
493 Beau Kemp, Micheal Nakamura, D.J. Carrasco .25
494 Khalil Greene, Miguel Ojeda, Bernie Castro .25
495 Noah Lowry, Todd Linden, Kevin Correia .25
496 Aaron Looper, Brian Sweeney, Rett Johnson .25
497 Bo Hart, Dan Haren, Kevin Ohme .50
498 Delmon Young, Doug Waechter, Matt Diaz 1.00
499 Gerald Laird, Rosman Garcia, Ramon Nivar .25
500 Alexis Rios, Guillermo Quiroz, Francisco Rosario .25

Career Tributes

NM/M

Complete Set (10): 30.00
Common Player: 3.00
Numbered to last season.
Die-Cuts: 2-3X.
#'d to last two digits of last season.
1CT Mike Schmidt/1,989. 5.00
2CT Nolan Ryan/1,993. 6.00
3CT Tom Seaver/1,986. 4.00
4CT Reggie Jackson/1,987 3.00
5CT Bob Gibson/1,975 4.00
6CT Harmon Killebrew/1,975 4.00
7CT Phil Rizzuto/1,956 3.00
8CT Lou Brock/1,979 3.00
9CT Eddie Mathews/1,968 3.00
10CT Al Kaline/1,974 4.00

Diamond Tributes

NM/M

Complete Set (20): 18.00
Common Player: .50
Inserted 1:6
1DT Derek Jeter 3.00
2DT Chipper Jones 1.50
3DT Vladimir Guerrero 1.00
4DT Kerry Wood .75
5DT Jim Thome 1.00
6DT Nomar Garciaparra 2.00
7DT Alex Rodriguez 3.00
8DT Mike Piazza 1.50
9DT Jason Giambi 1.00
10DT Barry Zito .50
11DT Dontrelle Willis .50
12DT Albert Pujols 2.50
13DT Todd Helton .75
14DT Richie Sexson .50
15DT Randy Johnson 1.00
16DT Pedro J. Martinez 1.00
17DT Josh Beckett .75
18DT Manny Ramirez .75
19DT Roy Halladay .50
20DT Mark Prior 2.00

Diamond Tributes Game-Used

NM/M

Common Player: 5.00
Inserted 1:36
Patch versions: 2-3X
Production 50 sets
Josh Beckett 8.00
Nomar Garciaparra 10.00
Jason Giambi 8.00
Vladimir Guerrero 8.00
Roy Halladay 5.00
Todd Helton 8.00
Derek Jeter 15.00
Randy Johnson 8.00
Chipper Jones 8.00
Pedro J. Martinez 10.00
Mike Piazza 8.00
Mark Prior 15.00
Albert Pujols 15.00
Manny Ramirez 8.00
Alex Rodriguez 10.00
Richie Sexson 6.00
Jim Thome 8.00

Dontrelle Willis 8.00
Kerry Wood 8.00
Barry Zito 8.00

Retrospection Collection

NM/M
Complete Set (10): 60.00
Common Player: 4.00
Inserted 1:360
1RC Rickie Weeks 10.00
2RC Delmon Young 12.00
3RC Torii Hunter 5.00
4RC Aubrey Huff 4.00
5RC Rocco Baldelli 6.00
6RC Mike Lowell 4.00
7RC Dontrelle Willis 6.00
8RC Albert Pujols 10.00
9RC Bo Hart 8.00
10RC Brandon Webb 4.00

Retrospection Collection Autograph

NM/M
Common Autograph: 10.00
Production 60
Hank Blalock 25.00
Bo Hart 25.00
Aubrey Huff 10.00
Torii Hunter 30.00
Austin Kearns 20.00
Corey Patterson 25.00
Albert Pujols 75.00
Jose Reyes 20.00
Scott Rolen 30.00
Mike Ryan 15.00
Ryan Wagner 15.00
Brandon Webb 20.00
Rickie Weeks 50.00
Josh Willingham 20.00
Dontrelle Willis 35.00
Delmon Young 50.00

Standouts Game-Used

NM/M
Common Player: 4.00
Inserted 1:41
Rocco Baldelli 8.00
Angel Berroa 5.00
Hank Blalock 6.00
Marlon Byrd 5.00
Miguel Cabrera 8.00
Hee Seop Choi 4.00
Bo Hart 8.00
Scott Podsednik
Jose Reyes 8.00
Mark Teixeira 6.00
Brandon Webb 5.00
Dontrelle Willis 6.00

This Day in History

NM/M
Complete Set (15): 12.00
Common Player: .50
Inserted 1:18
1 Josh Beckett 1.00
2 Carlos Delgado 1.00
3 Javy Lopez .50
4 Greg Maddux 2.00
5 Rafael Palmeiro 1.00
6 Sammy Sosa 2.50
7 Jeff Bagwell 1.00
8 Frank Thomas 1.00
9 Kevin Millwood .50
10 Jose Reyes .50
11 Rafael Furcal .50
12 Alfonso Soriano 1.50
13 Eric Gagne .50
14 Hideki Matsui 4.00
15 Hank Blalock .75

This Day in History Memorabilia

NM/M
Common Player: 5.00
Inserted 1:288
Jeff Bagwell 8.00
Carlos Delgado 5.00
Javy Lopez 5.00
Greg Maddux 15.00
Rafael Palmeiro 8.00
Jose Reyes
Alfonso Soriano 8.00
Sammy Sosa 12.00
Frank Thomas 8.00

This Day/History Dual Memorabilia

NM/M
Production 25 sets
Roger Clemens, Greg Maddux
Rafael Palmeiro, Sammy Sosa
Frank Thomas, Jeff Bagwell 25.00
Carlos Delgado, Jose Reyes
Javy Lopez, Alfonso Soriano

2005 FLEER

NM/M
Common Player (1-50): 1.00
Common Class '05 (51-80): 3.00
Minor Class '05 (51-80): 4.00
Production 699 Sets
Common Veteran (81-90): 3.00
Production 699 Sets
Box (1): 90.00
1 Curt Schilling 1.75
2 Jim Thome 3.00
3 Miguel Cabrera 2.00
4 Randy Johnson 3.50
5 David Ortiz 1.75
6 Vladimir Guerrero 3.00
7 Nomar Garciaparra 5.00
8 Ivan Rodriguez 1.75
9 Jason Schmidt 1.25
10 Khalil Greene 2.00
11 Jose Vidro 1.00
12 Lyle Overbay 1.00
13 Todd Helton 2.00
14 Vernon Wells 1.25
15 B.J. Upton 1.25
16 Hideki Matsui 5.00
17 Pedro Martinez 3.00
18 Victor Martinez 1.00
19 Adam Dunn 1.75
20 Andruw Jones 2.00
21 Jeff Bagwell 2.00
22 Mike Sweeney 1.00
23 Mike Piazza 3.50
24 Ben Sheets 1.25
25 Adrian Beltre 1.25
26 Chipper Jones 3.50
27 Greg Maddux 3.50
28 Manny Ramirez 2.00
29 Roger Clemens 5.00
30 Johan Santana 1.25
31 Derek Jeter 6.00
32 Jason Bay 1.00
33 Ken Griffey Jr. 3.50
34 Miguel Tejada 1.75
35 Richie Sexson 1.75
36 Scott Rolen 3.00
37 Alfonso Soriano 3.00
38 Ichiro Suzuki 4.00
39 Sammy Sosa 4.00
40 Barry Zito 1.75
41 Kazuo Matsui 3.00
42 Mark Teixeira 1.25
43 Carlos Beltran 1.75
44 Mark Prior 5.00
45 Travis Hafner 1.00
46 Alex Rodriguez 5.00
47 Lew Ford 1.00
48 Albert Pujols 5.00
49 Frank Thomas 2.00
50 Juan Pierre 1.00
51 David Aardsma 5.00
52 J.D. Durbin 3.00
53 Zack Greinke 4.00
54 Dioner Navarro 4.00
55 Edwin Encarnacion 4.00
56 *Luis Hernandez* 4.00
57 Jeff Baker 4.00
58 Victor Diaz 5.00
59 Joey Gathright 3.00
60 Casey Kotchman 4.00
61 David Wright 5.00
62 Jon Knott 3.00
63 Charlton Jimerson 4.00
64 Nick Swisher 5.00
65 Ryan Raburn 3.00
66 Josh Kroeger 3.00
67 Kelly Johnson 4.00
68 *Justin Verlander* 6.00
69 Taylor Buchholz 3.00
70 *Ubaldo Jimenez* 5.00
71 Russ Adams 4.00
72 Ronny Cedeno 4.00
73 Bobby Jenks 5.00
74 Dan Meyer 4.00
75 Jeff Francis 3.00
76 Scott Kazmir 5.00
77 Sean Burnett 3.00
78 Jose Lopez 4.00
79 Andres Blanco 3.00
80 Gavin Floyd 4.00
81 Tom Seaver 3.00
82 Steve Carlton 3.00
83 Al Kaline 4.00
84 Cal Ripken Jr. 10.00
85 Willie McCovey 5.00
86 Johnny Bench 5.00
87 Nolan Ryan 10.00
88 Mike Schmidt 4.00
89 Carlton Fisk 3.00
90 Don Mattingly 4.00

Raw 1

Stars (1-50):
Class of '05 (51-80): .5X-2X
Veterans: .5X-2X
Production 100 Sets

Row 2

Cards 1-90: No Pricing
Production 1 Set

Cuts and Glory Jersey

NM/M
Common Card: 15.00
Production 100 Sets
Patch: 2X-4X
Production 50 Sets
Jersey and Patch: No Pricing
Production 15 Sets
Masterpiece Logo: No Pricing
Production 1 Set
HA Hank Aaron
JB Johnny Bench 60.00
CC Carl Crawford 20.00
JL Javy Lopez 20.00
JP Josh Phelps 15.00
BS Ben Sheets 20.00
SS Shannon Stewart 20.00

Cust and Glory Dual Patch

Production 35 Sets
HA Hank Aaron
SS Shannon Stewart

Diamond Cuts Jersey

NM/M
Common Player: 5.00
Production 150 Sets
Die-Cut: .75X-1.5X
Production 75 Sets
Patch: 1X-3X
Production 50 Sets
Super Patch: No Pricing
Production 20 Sets
Die-Cut Patch: No Pricing
Production 10 Sets
MLB Logo Masterpiece: No Pricing
Production 1 Set
JB Jeff Bagwell 8.00
CB Carlos Beltran 6.00
HB Hank Blalock 6.00
MC Miguel Cabrera 8.00
RC Roger Clemens 12.00
AD Adam Dunn 6.00
VG Vladimir Guerrero 8.00
TH Todd Helton 8.00
RJ Randy Johnson 8.00
AJ Andruw Jones 8.00
CJ Chipper Jones 8.00
AK Austin Kearns 6.00
PM Pedro Martinez 8.00
VM Victor Martinez 5.00
HM Hideki Matsui 15.00
HN Hideo Nomo 8.00
DO David Ortiz 6.00
MP Mike Piazza 8.00
MP2 Mark Prior 12.00
AP Albert Pujols 12.00
MR Manny Ramirez 8.00
SR Scott Rolen 8.00
CS Curt Schilling 6.00
GS Gary Sheffield 6.00
AS Alfonso Soriano 8.00
SS Sammy Sosa 10.00
MT Mark Teixeira 5.00
JT Jim Thome 8.00
BU B.J. Upton 5.00
KW Kerry Wood 8.00

Diamond Cuts Dual Jersey

NM/M
Common Card: 8.00
Production 99 Sets
Die-Cut: .5X-1.5X
Production 50 Sets
Patch: No Pricing
Production 15 Sets
Patch Die-Cut: No Pricing
Production 5 Sets
BC Jeff Bagwell, Roger Clemens 15.00
BM Carlos Beltran, Pedro Martinez 10.00
BS Hank Blalock, Alfonso Soriano 10.00
CH Miguel Cabrera, Todd Helton 10.00
DK Adam Dunn, Austin Kearns 8.00
JJ Chipper Jones, Andruw Jones 12.00
JS Randy Johnson, Curt Schilling 10.00
MS Hideki Matsui, Gary Sheffield 20.00
MT Victor Martinez, Mark Teixeira 8.00
NU Hideo Nomo, B.J. Upton 10.00
OR David Ortiz, Manny Ramirez 10.00
PR Albert Pujols, Scott Rolen 15.00
PT Mike Piazza, Jim Thome 12.00
PW Mark Prior, Kerry Wood 15.00
SG Sammy Sosa, Vladimir Guerrero 15.00

Dynasty Foundations

NM/M
Common Card: 6.00
Production 500 Sets
1DF Rod Carew, Nolan Ryan, Vladimir Guerrero, Garret Anderson, Darin Erstad 8.00
2DF Cal Ripken Jr., Brooks Robinson, Miguel Tejada, Javy Lopez, Jim Palmer 15.00
3DF Ted Williams, Manny Ramirez, Johnny Damon, Carl Yastrzemski, David Ortiz 15.00
4DF Ryne Sandberg, Sammy Sosa, Ernie Banks, Greg Maddux, Mark Prior 10.00
5DF Adam Dunn, Johnny Bench, Tony Perez, Austin Kearns, Joe Morgan 8.00
6DF Victor Martinez, Travis Hafner, Bob Feller, C.C. Sabathia, Larry Doby 6.00
7DF Aaron Miles, Matt Holliday, Todd Helton, Garrett Atkins, Preston Wilson 6.00
8DF Miguel Cabrera, Dontrelle Willis, Juan Pierre, Al Leiter, Josh Beckett 6.00
9DF Lance Berkman, Jeff Bagwell, Craig Biggio, Roger Clemens, Roy Oswalt 8.00
10DF Ben Sheets, Lyle Overbay, Robin Yount, Geoff Jenkins, Paul Molitor 8.00

11DF Johan Santana, Shannon Stewart, Harmon Killebrew, Torii Hunter, Lee Ford 6.00
12DF Tom Glavine, Mike Piazza, Tom Seaver, Nolan Ryan, Pedro Martinez 8.00
13DF Eric Chavez, Reggie Jackson, Bobby Crosby, Dennis Eckersley, Barry Zito 6.00
14DF Jim Thome, Bobby Abreu, Gavin Floyd, Robin Roberts, Mike Schmidt 6.00
15DF Craig Wilson, Willie Stargell, Bill Mazeroski, Jason Bay, Jack Wilson 6.00
16DF Willie McCovey, Jason Schmidt, Juan Marichal, Orlando Cepeda, Ray Durham 6.00
17DF Scott Rolen, Mark Mulder, Albert Pujols, Jim Edmonds, Stan Musial 10.00
18DF Rocco Baldelli, Scott Kazmir, Aubrey Huff, B.J. Upton, Carl Crawford 6.00
19DF Alfonso Soriano, Mark Teixeira, Hank Blalock, Nolan Ryan, Michael Young 10.00
20DF Alexis Rios, Paul Molitor, Roy Halladay, Vernon Wells, Orlando Hudson 6.00

Dynasty Cornerstones Dual Signatures

Sequentially numbered
BV Jeremy Bonderman, Justin Verlander/30
GS Dwight Gooden, Darryl Strawberry/15
PM Albert Pujols, Stan Musial/2
PS Mike Piazza, Tom Seaver/3
VO Jason Varitek, David Ortiz/2

Dynasty Foundations Dual Player Jersey

NM/M
Common Card: 10.00
Production 150 Sets
Patch: 1X-3X
Production 50 Sets
BO Miguel Tejada, Javy Lopez 15.00
BR Manny Ramirez, David Ortiz 10.00
CI Victor Martinez, Travis Hafner 10.00
CR1 Adam Dunn, Austin Kearns 12.00
CR2 Todd Helton, Preston Wilson 12.00
FM Miguel Cabrera, Juan Pierre 10.00
HA Jeff Bagwell, Lance Berkman 12.00
LA Vladimir Guerrero, Garret Anderson 12.00
MT Johan Santana, Torii Hunter 12.00
NM Mike Piazza, Tom Glavine 10.00
OA Barry Zito, Eric Chavez 10.00
PP Jim Thome, Bobby Abreu 10.00
SC Scott Rolen, Albert Pujols 25.00
TD B.J. Upton, Scott Kazmir 10.00
TR Mark Teixeira, Michael Young 10.00

Dynasty Foundations Three Player Jersey

NM/M
Common Card: 15.00
Production 99 Sets
Patch: No Pricing
Production 25 Sets
BO Cal Ripken Jr., Miguel Tejada, Javy Lopez
CR1 Adam Dunn, Austin Kearns, Joe Morgan 15.00
FM Miguel Cabrera, Josh Beckett, Juan Pierre 15.00
HA Jeff Bagwell, Lance Berkman, Roger Clemens 40.00
LA Vladimir Guerrero, Garret Anderson, Darin Erstad 20.00
MT Johan Santana, Torii Hunter, Shannon Stewart 15.00
NM Mike Piazza, Pedro Martinez, Tom Glavine 20.00
SC Scott Rolen, Albert Pujols, Jim Edmonds 40.00
TR Alfonso Soriano, Mark Teixeira, Michael Young 15.00

Dynasty Cornerstones Signatures

NM/M
Sequentially Numbered
JB Jeremy Bonderman/75 20.00
DG Dwight Gooden/25 30.00
SM Stan Musial/3
DO David Ortiz/75 40.00

Dynasty Foundations Four Player Jersey

NM/M
Production 40 Sets
Patch: No Pricing
Production 15 Sets
NM Mike Piazza, Nolan Ryan, Pedro Martinez, Tom Glavine 100.00

Head of the Class Triple Player Jersey

NM/M
Common Card: 15.00
Numbered to Debut Year
No pricing for quantities 3 or less
Patch: 1X-3X
Production 33 Sets
MLB Logo Masterpiece: No Pricing
Production 1 Set
AGJ Bobby Abreu, Vladimir Guerrero, Andruw Jones/96 20.00
BGB Carlos Beltran, Troy Glaus, Adrian Beltre/98 15.00
BTR Jeff Bagwell, Jim Thome, Ivan Rodriguez/91 15.00
GBH Eric Gagne, A.J. Burnett, Tim Hudson/99 15.00
JDR Chipper Jones, Carlos Delgado, Manny Ramirez/93 20.00
OHS David Ortiz, Torii Hunter, Richie Sexson/97 15.00
SNP Jason Schmidt, Hideo Nomo, Andy Pettitte/95 20.00

Letterman

Sequentially numbered between 4-8
No Pricing

Significant Signings Blue

NM/M
Common Player: 10.00
Sequentially #'d to indicated quantity
Silver Die-Cut: 1X-3X
Cards #'d 50 or less: .25X-1X
Production 50 Sets
Gold Jersey: No Pricing
Production 25 Sets
Patch: No Pricing
Production 15 Sets
Masterpiece Jersey Tag: No Pricing
Production 1 Set
JB Jason Bay/250 15.00
CB Carlos Beltran/4
AB Adrian Beltre/30 50.00
MC Miguel Cabrera/250 20.00
SC Steve Carlton/59 30.00
RC Roger Clemens/43
BC Bobby Crosby/93 15.00
GF Gavin Floyd/221 10.00
LF Lew Ford/230 10.00
ZG Zack Greinke/250 10.00
TH Travis Hafner/250 10.00
SK Scott Kazmir/250 10.00
CK Casey Kotchman/250 10.00
PM Pedro Martinez/101 40.00
VM Victor Martinez/224 10.00
DM Don Mattingly/103 40.00
JM Justin Morneau/225 20.00
JP Jake Peavy/200
JR Jeremy Reed/250 40.00
CR Cal Ripken Jr./16
NR Nolan Ryan/92 100.00
MS Mike Schmidt/20
MT Mark Teixeira/160
BU B.J. Upton/250 10.00
KW Kerry Wood/200 25.00
DW David Wright/250 30.00

Significant Dual

NM/M
Common Player: 30.00
Production 40 Sets
Dual Jersey: No Pricing
Production 15 Sets
Dual Patch: No Pricing
Production 5 Sets
BR Adrian Beltre, Jeremy Reed 60.00
CF Steve Carlton, Gavin Floyd 40.00
FM Lew Ford, Justin Morneau 40.00
MH Victor Martinez, Travis Hafner 30.00
RC Nolan Ryan, Roger Clemens
SR Mike Schmidt, Cal Ripken Jr. 250.00
UK B.J. Upton, Scott Kazmir

2005 FLEER AMERICA'S NATIONAL PASTIME

NM/M
Common Player (1-50): .25
Common Player (51-70): 3.00
Production 699 Sets
Common Player (71-80): 3.00
Production 699 Sets
Pack (5):
Box (10):
1 Khalil Greene .75
2 Pedro Martinez 1.00
3 Mark Teixeira .40
4 Jim Thome 1.00
5 Jack Wilson .25
6 Johan Santana .40
7 Jason Bay .25
8 Adam Dunn .60
9 Lyle Overbay .25
10 Jason Schmidt .40
11 Bobby Crosby .25
12 J.D. Drew .40
13 Ken Griffey Jr. 1.50
14 Sammy Sosa 2.00
15 Hank Blalock .60
16 Victor Martinez .25
17 Randy Johnson 1.00
18 Vernon Wells .40
19 Todd Helton .75
20 Javy Lopez .40
21 Kazuo Matsui .60
22 Ben Sheets .40
23 Brad Wilkerson .25
24 Miguel Cabrera .75
25 Mike Sweeney .25
26 Roger Clemens 2.50
27 Chipper Jones 1.50
28 Hideki Matsui 2.50
29 Manny Ramirez .75
30 Scott Rolen 1.00
31 Lance Berkman .40
32 Jim Edmonds .40
33 Derek Jeter 3.00
34 B.J. Upton .40
35 Carlos Delgado .75
36 Ichiro Suzuki 2.00
37 Nomar Garciaparra 2.50
38 Albert Pujols 2.50
39 Ivan Rodriguez .60
40 Gary Sheffield .60
41 Alfonso Soriano 1.00
42 Carlos Beltran .60
43 Magglio Ordonez .40
44 Alex Rodriguez 2.50
45 Curt Schilling .60
46 Greg Maddux 1.50
47 Vladimir Guerrero 1.00
48 Mike Piazza 1.50
49 Miguel Tejada .60
50 Adrian Beltre .40
51 Scott Kazmir 5.00
52 Gavin Floyd 4.00
53 Zack Greinke 4.00
54 David Wright 5.00
55 David Aardsma 4.00
56 Ryan Raburn 3.00
57 Joey Gathright 3.00
58 J.D. Durbin 3.00
59 Sean Burnett 3.00
60 Jose Lopez 3.00
61 Nick Swisher 4.00
62 Bobby Jenks 3.00
63 Kelly A. Johnson 3.00
65 Ronny Cedeno 4.00
66 Edwin Encarnacion 3.00
67 Jeff Baker 3.00
68 Taylor Buchholz 3.00
69 *Justin Verlander* 5.00
70 *Luis Hernandez* 5.00
71 Mike Schmidt 5.00
72 Al Kaline 3.00
73 Yogi Berra 4.00
74 Robin Yount 4.00
75 Nolan Ryan 6.00
76 Johnny Bench 5.00
77 Eddie Murray 4.00
78 Tom Seaver 4.00
79 Willie McCovey 3.00
80 Cal Ripken Jr. 6.00

Red Foil

Cards 1-50: 1X-3X
Cards 51-70: .75X-1.5X
Cards 71-80: .75X-1.5X
Production 150 Sets

White Foil

NM/M
Cards 1-50 #'d to 41-57: 2X-6X
Cards 1-50 #'d to 26-40: 4X-8X
Cards 1-50 #'d 25 or less: No Pricing
Cards 71-80 #'d to 26-44: 1X-3X
Cards 71-80 #'d 25 or less: No Pricing
Numbered to player's jersey number

Blue Foil

No Pricing
Production 1 Set

Grand Old Gamers

NM/M
Common Player: .75
Inserted 1:5
1 Pedro Martinez 1.50
2 Jim Thome 1.50
3 Ken Griffey Jr. 2.00
4 Sammy Sosa 2.50
5 Hank Blalock 1.00
6 Randy Johnson 1.50
7 Roger Clemens 3.00
8 Chipper Jones 2.00
9 Hideki Matsui 3.00
10 Manny Ramirez 1.25
11 Derek Jeter 4.00
12 Ichiro Suzuki 2.50
13 Nomar Garciaparra 3.00
14 Albert Pujols 3.00
15 Gary Sheffield 1.00
16 Alfonso Soriano 1.50
17 Alex Rodriguez 3.00
18 Curt Schilling 1.00
19 Vladimir Guerrero 1.50
20 Mike Piazza 2.00
21 Greg Maddux 2.00
22 Frank Thomas 1.25
23 Adrian Beltre .75
24 Barry Larkin .75
25 Todd Helton 1.25
26 Kerry Wood 1.25
27 Kazuo Matsui 1.00
28 Scott Rolen 1.50
29 Ivan Rodriguez 1.00
30 Miguel Tejada 1.00
31 Mark Teixeira .75
32 Rafael Palmeiro 1.25
33 Andruw Jones 1.25
34 Carlos Beltran 1.00
35 Jeff Bagwell 1.25

Grand Old Gamers Jersey

NM/M
Common Player: 6.00
Inserted 1:36 Retail
JB Jeff Bagwell 8.00
CB Carlos Beltran 8.00
AB Adrian Beltre 6.00
HB Hank Blalock 8.00
RC Roger Clemens SP/50 15.00
VG Vladimir Guerrero 8.00
TH Todd Helton 8.00
RJ Randy Johnson 8.00
AJ Andruw Jones 8.00
CJ Chipper Jones 8.00
BL Barry Larkin 6.00
GM Greg Maddux SP/75 12.00
PM Pedro Martinez 8.00
HM Hideki Matsui SP/50 15.00
KM Kazuo Matsui 8.00
RP Rafael Palmeiro 8.00
MP Mike Piazza 8.00

AP Albert Pujols 12.00
MR Manny Ramirez 8.00
IR Ivan Rodriguez 8.00
SR Scott Rolen 8.00
CS Curt Schilling 8.00
GS Gary Sheffield 8.00
AS Alfonso Soriano 8.00
SS Sammy Sosa 12.00
MT Mark Teixeira 6.00
FT Frank Thomas 8.00
JT Jim Thome 8.00
KW Kerry Wood 8.00

Gamers Patch Blue

NM/M
Numbered to player's jersey number
Cards numbered
25 or less: No Pricing
Masterpiece: No Pricing
Production 1 Set
JB Jeff Bagwell/5
CB Carlos Beltran/15
AB Adrian Beltre/5
HB Hank Blalock/9
RC Roger Clemens/22
VG Vladimir Guerrero/27 25.00
TH Todd Helton/17
RJ Randy Johnson/51 20.00
AJ Andruw Jones/25
CJ Chipper Jones/10
BL Barry Larkin/11
GM Greg Maddux/31 25.00
PM Pedro Martinez/45 20.00
HM Hideki Matsui/55 50.00
KM Kazuo Matsui/25
RP Rafael Palmeiro/25
MP Mike Piazza/31 25.00
AP Albert Pujols/5
MR Manny Ramirez/24
IR Ivan Rodriguez/7
SR Scott Rolen/27 25.00
CS Curt Schilling/38 15.00
GS Gary Sheffield/11
AS Alfonso Soriano/12
SS Sammy Sosa/21
MT Mark Teixeira/23
FT Frank Thomas/35 15.00
JT Jim Thome/25
KW Kerry Wood/34 20.00

Gamers Dual Patch

NM/M
Cards #'d to 25 or less: No Pricing
Production 5-33 Sets
Ivan Rodriguez, Mike Piazza/31 75.00
Hank Blalock, Mark Teixeira/33 30.00

Historical Record

NM/M
Common Card: 2.00
Inserted 1:6
1 Ichiro Suzuki/2004 2.50
2 Greg Maddux/2004 2.00
3 Alex Rodriguez/1998 3.00
4 Mike Piazza/2004 2.00
5 Nolan Ryan/1991 5.00
6 Albert Pujols/2001 3.00
7 Mike Schmidt/1987 4.00
8 Randy Johnson/2004 2.00
9 Sammy Sosa/2003 2.50
10 Cal Ripken Jr./1996 5.00
11 Roger Clemens/2004 3.00
12 Hideki Matsui/2003 3.00
13 Hideo Nomo/1994 2.00
14 Gene Autry/1961 2.00
15 Walter O'Malley/1944 2.00

Historical Record Jersey

NM/M
Common Player: 6.00
Inserted 1:96 Retail
RC Roger Clemens 10.00
RJ Randy Johnson 8.00
GM Greg Maddux 8.00
HM Hideki Matsui 12.00
HN Hideo Nomo 6.00
MP Mike Piazza 8.00
AP Albert Pujols 10.00
CR Cal Ripken Jr. 30.00
NR0 Nolan Ryan 20.00
MS Mike Schmidt 25.00
SS Sammy Sosa 10.00

Historical Record Dual Patch

No Pricing
Production 8-25 Sets

Historical Record Patch Blue

No Pricing
Numbered to player's jersey number
Masterpiece: No Pricing
Production 1 Set

Beltway Baseball

NM/M
Common Card: 6.00
Production 202 Sets
1 Ed Delahanty 8.00
2 Benjamin Harrison 8.00
3 William Howard Taft 6.00
4 Clark Griffith 6.00
5 Bobby Burke 8.00
6 Roy Seivers 8.00
7 Tom Cheney 8.00
8 Woodrow Wilson 8.00
9 Franklin D. Roosevelt 8.00
10 John F. Kennedy 10.00
11 Frank Howard 8.00
12 Griffith Stadium 10.00
13 RFK Stadium 8.00
14 All-Star Game 6.00
15 Ted Williams 15.00
16 Harmon Killebrew 12.00
17 Jeff Burroughs 8.00
18 All-Star Game 6.00
19 Unveiling the Nationals 10.00
20 New Logo 8.00

Bases Auto Silver

NM/M
Sequentially #'d to indicated quantity
Blue: No Pricing
Production 1 Set
AB Adrian Beltre/19
MCAM Mike Cameron/375 10.00
SH Shea Hillenbrand/316 10.00
JL Javy Lopez/158 15.00
HN Hideo Nomo/10
AP Albert Pujols/2
CR Cal Ripken Jr./8
MT Mark Teixeira/225 20.00
JV Justin Verlander/401 15.00

First Name Bases Auto Red

NM/M
Cards #'d 25 or less: No Pricing
Sequentially #'d to indicated quantity
AB Adrian Beltre/22
MCAM Mike Cameron/90 15.00
SH Shea Hillenbrand/41
BL Barry Larkin/27 40.00
JL Javy Lopez/25
HN Hideo Nomo/22
AP Albert Pujols/15
CR Cal Ripken Jr./25
MT Mark Teixeira/95 30.00
JV Justin Verlander/99 20.00

First Name Bases Auto Gold

NM/M
Cards #'d 25 or less: No Pricing
Sequentially #'d to indicated quantity
AB Adrian Beltre/96 25.00
MCAM Mike Cameron/126 15.00
SH Shea Hillenbrand/99 15.00
JL Javy Lopez/73 15.00
HN Hideo Nomo/73
AP Albert Pujols/73 200.00
CR Cal Ripken Jr./73
MT Mark Teixeira/147 25.00
JV Justin Verlander/149 20.00

Signature Swings Silver

NM/M
Common Player: 10.00
Gold: .75X-1.5X
Sequentially #'d between 50 & 199
BAY Jason Bay 20.00
JB Johnny Bench
LB Lance Berkman
CC Carl Crawford 10.00
JE Johnny Estrada
AE Adam Everett 10.00
CF Chone Figgins 10.00
LF Lew Ford 10.00
JG Joey Gathright 10.00
KG Khalil Greene 30.00
TH Travis Hafner 10.00
AH Aubrey Huff 10.00
RJ Reggie Jackson
CK Casey Kotchman 10.00
JK Josh Kroeger
KUB Jason Kubel
VAL Val Majewski 10.00
VM Victor Martinez
JM Joe Mauer 25.00
DM Dallas McPherson 15.00
JMO Justin Morneau 40.00
DO David Ortiz
WMP Wily Mo Pena 25.00
JP Josh Phelps 10.00
MP Mike Piazza
RR Ryan Raburn 10.00
BR Brooks Robinson
MS Mike Schmidt
SS Shannon Stewart 10.00
NS Nick Swisher 15.00
BJU B.J. Upton 15.00
CU Chase Utley 12.00
DW David Wright 40.00
MY Michael Young 10.00

Signature Swings Bat Red

NM/M
Common Player: 20.00
Production 30-99 Sets
BAY Jason Bay/99 20.00
JB Johnny Bench/42 80.00
LB Lance Berkman/99 20.00
WB Wade Boggs/45
CC Carl Crawford/99 20.00
LF Lew Ford/76 20.00
RJ Reggie Jackson/30
CK Casey Kotchman/99 20.00
MP Mike Piazza/30
BR Brooks Robinson/64 40.00
MS Mike Schmidt/30 100.00
SS Shannon Stewart/99 20.00
BJU B.J. Upton/99
DW David Wright/99 60.00

Signature Swings Jersey White

NM/M
Production 3-29 Sets
Cards #'d less than 25: No Pricing
LB Lance Berkman/29 30.00
CC Carl Crawford/29 30.00
JP Josh Phelps/27 15.00

Signature Swings Patch Blue

NM/M
Numbered to player's jersey number
Cards #'d less than 25: No Pricing
Masterpiece: No Pricing
Production 1 Set
BAY Jason Bay/38 60.00
JP Josh Phelps/45 20.00

2005 FLEER AUTHENTIX

NM/M
Common Player (1-100): .25
Common Player Autograph
(101-125): 10.00
Production 250 Sets
Pack (5):
Box ( ):
1 Albert Pujols 2.50
2 Bernie Williams .60
3 Vinny Castilla .25
4 Rocco Baldelli .60
5 Mike Piazza 1.50
6 Sean Casey .25
7 Oliver Perez .25
8 Tony Batista .25
9 Paul Konerko .25
10 Scott Rolen 1.00
11 Justin Morneau .25
12 Nomar Garciaparra 2.50
13 Lance Berkman .40
14 Mike Sweeney .25
15 Miguel Tejada .75
16 Craig Wilson .25
17 Craig Biggio .40
18 Shea Hillenbrand .25
19 Mark Mulder .40
20 Juan Pierre .25
21 Troy Glaus .60
22 Eric Chavez .40
23 Jeromy Burnitz .25
24 Carl Crawford .25
25 Kazuo Matsui .75
26 Ivan Rodriguez .60
27 Aubrey Huff .25
28 Derek Jeter 3.00
29 Casey Blake .25
30 Mark Teixeira .40
31 Brad Wilkerson .25
32 Austin Kearns .60
33 Jim Edmonds .40
34 Johan Santana .40
35 Kerry Wood .75
36 Ichiro Suzuki 2.00
37 Lyle Overbay .25
38 Melvin Mora .25
39 Jason Bay .25
40 Jake Westbrook .25
41 Andruw Jones .75
42 Chase Utley .25
43 Carl Pavano .25
44 Luis Gonzalez .40
45 Bobby Crosby .25
46 Carlos Guillen .25
47 Carlos Delgado .75
48 Alex Rodriguez 2.50
49 Todd Helton .75
50 Michael Young .25
51 Geoff Jenkins .40
52 Pedro Martinez 1.00
53 Brian Giles .40
54 Ken Harvey .25
55 Johnny Estrada .25
56 Billy Wagner .25
57 Roger Clemens 2.50
58 Chipper Jones 1.50
59 Jim Thome 1.00
60 Miguel Cabrera .75
61 Vladimir Guerrero 1.00
62 Gary Sheffield .60
63 Travis Hafner .25
64 Alfonso Soriano 1.00
65 Richard Hidalgo .25
66 Adam Dunn .60
67 Garret Anderson .40
68 Lew Ford .25
69 Mark Prior 2.50
70 Bret Boone .40
71 Ben Sheets .40
72 David Ortiz .60
73 Mark Loretta .25
74 Eric Gagne .40
75 Curt Schilling .60
76 Jason Schmidt .40
77 Adrian Beltre .40
78 Javy Lopez .40
79 Jack Wilson .25
80 Carlos Beltran .60
81 J.D. Drew .40
82 Bobby Abreu .40
83 Jeff Bagwell .75
84 Randy Johnson 1.00
85 Tim Hudson .40
86 Carlos Pena .25
87 Vernon Wells .40
88 Tom Glavine .40
89 Victor Martinez .25
90 Hank Blalock .60
91 Jose Vidro .25
92 Magglio Ordonez .40
93 Jake Peavy .25
94 Torii Hunter .60
95 Sammy Sosa 2.00
96 Hideki Matsui 2.50
97 Shawn Green .40
98 Manny Ramirez .75
99 Khalil Greene .75
100 Jason Marquis .25
101 B.J. Upton Auto 20.00
102 Scott Kazmir Auto 20.00
103 Gavin Floyd Auto 20.00
104 Jeff Francis Auto 20.00
105 Russ Adams Auto Exch 10.00
106 Zack Greinke Auto 15.00
107 David Wright Auto 60.00
108 David Aardsma Auto 20.00
109 Josh Kroeger Auto 10.00
110 Ryan Raburn Auto 30.00
111 Jason Kubel Auto 10.00
112 Casey Kotchman Auto 20.00
113 Joey Gathright Auto 15.00
114 Jon Knott Auto 10.00
115 J.D. Durbin Auto 25.00
116 Andres Blanco Auto 10.00

117 Charlton Jimerson Auto 10.00
118 Sean Burnett Auto 15.00
119 Joe Mauer Auto 30.00
120 *Justin Verlander Auto* 30.00
121 Mike Gosling Auto 10.00
122 Jeff Keppinger Auto 10.00
123 David Krynzel Auto 10.00
124 Jose Lopez Auto 15.00
125 Ruben Gotay Auto 15.00

General Admission

Cards 1-100: 1X-2.5X
Cards 101-125: .75X-1.5X
Production 100 Sets

Mezzanine

Cards 1-100: 1X-3X
Cards 101-125: .75X-2X
Production 75 Sets

Club Box

Cards 1-100: 1X-3.25X
Cards 101-125: 1X-2X
Production 50 Sets

Standing Room Only

Cards 1-125: No Pricing
Production 10 Sets

Autographed General Admission

NM/M
Common Player: 15.00
Production 100 Sets
Mezzanine: 1X-2X
Production 40 Sets
Club Box: No Pricing
Production 5 Sets
Standing Room Only: No Pricing
Production 1 Set
AA-JB Jason Bay 15.00
AA-JE Johnny Estrada 15.00
AA-CF Chone Figgins 20.00
AA-LF Lew Ford 15.00
AA-KG Khalil Greene 50.00
AA-TH Travis Hafner 15.00
AA-JM Justin Morneau 40.00
AA-JS Johan Santana 25.00
AA-BS Ben Sheets 20.00
AA-CU Chase Utley 15.00
AA-JW Jack Wilson 15.00

Auto. Jersey General Admission

NM/M
Common Player: 20.00
Production 75 Sets
Mezzanine: No Pricing
Production 15 Sets
Club Box: No Pricing
Production 5 Sets
Standing Room Only: No Pricing
Production 1 Set
AJA-JB Jason Bay 20.00
AJA-MC Miguel Cabrera 30.00
AJA-JE Johnny Estrada 20.00
AJA-CF Chone Figgins 25.00
AJA-LF Lew Ford 20.00
AJA-KG Khalil Greene 60.00
AJA-TH Travis Hafner 20.00
AJA-JM Justin Morneau 50.00
AJA-JS Johan Santana 30.00
AJA-MS Mike Schmidt 75.00
AJA-BS Ben Sheets 25.00
AJA-CU Chase Utley 20.00
AJA-JW Jack Wilson 20.00

Auto. Patch General Admission

NM/M
Production 40 Sets
Mezzanine: No Pricing
Production 10 Sets
Club Box: No Pricing
Production 5 Sets
Standing Room Only
Production 1 Set
APA-CF Chone Figgins 25.00
APA-MP Mike Piazza 150.00
APA-CR Cal Ripken Jr. 400.00
APA-MS Mike Schmidt 150.00
APA-JT Jim Thome 80.00

Hot Ticket

NM/M
Common Player: 2.00
Inserted 1:12
1 Derek Jeter 6.00
2 Roger Clemens 5.00
3 Vladimir Guerrero 3.00
4 Manny Ramirez 2.00
5 Alex Rodriguez 5.00
6 Albert Pujols 5.00
7 Mike Piazza 3.50
8 Hideki Matsui 5.00
9 Sammy Sosa 4.00
10 Chipper Jones 3.50

Hot Ticket Jersey

NM/M
Common Player: 8.00
Inserted 1:87
Patch
Cards #'d to 55: 1X-3X
Cards #'d to 27: 2X-4X
Cards #'d to 25 or less: No Pricing
Sequentially #'d to player's jersey #
MLB Logo: No Pricing
Production 1 Set
HT-RC Roger Clemens 15.00
HT-VG Vladimir Guerrero 8.00
HT-CJ Chipper Jones 10.00
HT-HM Hideki Matsui 25.00
HT-MP Mike Piazza 10.00
HT-AP Albert Pujols 20.00
HT-MR Manny Ramirez 8.00
HT-SS Sammy Sosa 12.00

Jersey General Admission

NM/M
Common Player: 5.00
Inserted 1:16
Jersey Mezzanine: 1X-3X
Production 75 Sets
Jersey Club Box: No Pricing
Production 25 Sets
Jersey Standing Room Only: No Pricing
Production 1 Set
Patch General Admission: 2X-4X
Production 75 Sets
Patch Mezzanine: No Pricing
Production 15 Sets
Patch Club Box: No Pricing
Production 5 Sets
Patch Standing Room Only: No Pricing
Production 1 Set
JA-CB Carlos Beltran 10.00
JA-AB Adrian Beltre 5.00
JA-LB Lance Berkman 5.00
JA-HB Hank Blalock 5.00
JA-MC Miguel Cabrera 8.00
JA-RC Roger Clemens 12.00
JA-AD Adam Dunn 5.00
JA-EG Eric Gagne 5.00
JA-KG Khalil Greene 10.00
JA-VG Vladimir Guerrero 8.00
JA-TH Todd Helton 5.00
JA-RJ Randy Johnson 8.00
JA-CJ Chipper Jones 8.00
JA-PM Pedro Martinez 8.00
JA-HM Hideki Matsui 20.00
JA-KM Kazuo Matsui 10.00
JA-JM Joe Mauer 8.00
JA-HN Hideo Nomo 8.00
JA-DO David Ortiz 10.00
JA-MP Mike Piazza 8.00
JA-AP Albert Pujols 15.00
JA-MR Manny Ramirez 8.00
JA-MR2 Mariano Rivera 5.00
JA-IR Ivan Rodriguez 5.00
JA-SR Scott Rolen 8.00
JA-JS Johan Santana 5.00
JA-CS Curt Schilling 5.00
JA-GS Gary Sheffield 5.00
JA-AS Alfonso Soriano 8.00
JA-SS Sammy Sosa 10.00
JA-JT Jim Thome 8.00
JA-BU B.J. Upton 8.00
JA-BW Bernie Williams 5.00
JA-KW Kerry Wood 8.00
JA-DW David Wright 15.00

Jersey Game of the Week

NM/M
Common Player: 10.00
Sequentially #'d between 10 & 200
No pricing for cards #'d to 20 or less
Patch: No Pricing
Production 10 Sets
JAGW-BR Carlos Beltran, Scott Rolen/120 15.00
JAGW-BT Tony Batista, Miguel Tejada/170 10.00
JAGW-CG Eric Chavez, Troy Glaus/150 12.00
JAGW-CJ Roger Clemens, Randy Johnson/70 15.00
JAGWCJ2 Miguel Cabrera, Chipper Jones/90 12.00
JAGW-CP Carl Crawford, Juan Pierre/190 10.00
JAGW-DT Adam Dunn, Jim Thome/110 20.00
JAGW-GG Shawn Green, Vladimir Guerrero/180 12.00
JAGW-GS Vladimir Guerrero, Alfonso Soriano/100 15.00
JAGW-KG Scott Kazmir, Zack Greinke/80 10.00
JAGW-MM Kazuo Matsui, Hideki Matsui/30 100.00
JAGWMM2 Joe Mauer, Victor Martinez/130 10.00
JAGW-MR Pedro Martinez, Mariano Rivera/60 12.00
JAGW-OP David Ortiz, Albert Pujols/200 15.00
JAGW-OS Magglio Ordonez, Sammy Sosa/160 15.00
JAGW-PS Albert Pujols, Sammy Sosa/10
JAGWPS2 Mike Piazza, Gary Sheffield/20
JAGW-RH Manny Ramirez, Torii Hunter/140 10.00
JAGW-SS Johan Santana, Curt Schilling/40 30.00
JAGW-WO Kerry Wood, Roy Oswalt/50 30.00

Showstoppers

NM/M
Common Player: 2.00
Inserted 1:8
1 Nomar Garciaparra 4.00
2 Ichiro Suzuki 3.50
3 Ken Griffey Jr. 3.00
4 Alex Rodriguez 4.00
5 Albert Pujols 4.00
6 Derek Jeter 5.00
7 Roger Clemens 4.00
8 Randy Johnson 2.50
9 Hideo Nomo 2.00
10 Jim Thome 2.50
11 Mike Piazza 3.00
12 Hideki Matsui 4.00
13 Sammy Sosa 3.50
14 Kerry Wood 2.00
15 Eric Gagne 2.00

Teammate Trios

NM/M
Common Card: 12.00
Production 75 Sets
Hometown 1: 2X-3X
Production 25 Sets
Hometown 2: No Pricing
Production 5 Sets
TT-BR David Ortiz, Manny Ramirez, Pedro Martinez 25.00
TT-NY Hideki Matsui, Bernie Williams, Gary Sheffield 30.00
TT-AB J.D. Drew, Chipper Jones, Andruw Jones 15.00
TT-CC Sammy Sosa, Mark Prior, Nomar Garciaparra 25.00
TT-CI Victor Martinez, Travis Hafner, Casey Blake 12.00
TT-HA Lance Berkman, Roger Clemens, Carlos Beltran 25.00
TT-MT Johan Santana, Torii Hunter, Corey Koskie 12.00
TT-WN Tony Batista, Jose Vidro, Brad Wilkerson 12.00
TT-NM Mike Piazza, David Wright, Kazuo Matsui 40.00
TT-OA Barry Zito, Tim Hudson, Mark Mulder 12.00
TT-PP Bobby Abreu, Jim Thome, Pat Burrell 15.00
TT-SC Scott Rolen, Albert Pujols, Jim Edmonds 30.00
TT-TD Scott Kazmir, Rocco Baldelli, B.J. Upton 25.00
TT-TR Hank Blalock, Mark Teixeira, Alfonso Soriano 15.00
TT-LD Shawn Green, Adrian Beltre, Steve Finley 12.00

2005 FLEER CLASSIC CLIPPINGS

NM/M
Common Player (1-75): .25
Common Legends (76-105): 2.00
Production 999 Sets
Common Player (106-125): 3.00
Inserted 1:6
1 Frank Thomas .75
2 Vladimir Guerrero 1.00
3 Ken Griffey Jr. 1.50
4 Derek Jeter 3.00
5 Rafael Palmeiro .75
6 Adrian Beltre .40
7 Khalil Greene .75
8 Richie Sexson .60
9 Roger Clemens 2.50
10 Mike Piazza 1.50
11 Chipper Jones 1.50
12 Juan Pierre .25
13 Todd Helton .75

14 Ben Sheets .40
15 John Smoltz .40
16 Steve Finley .25
17 Jim Thome 1.00
18 Vernon Wells .40
19 Melvin Mora .25
20 Dontrelle Willis .40
21 Eric Gagne .40
22 Craig Wilson .25
23 Curt Schilling .60
24 Justin Morneau .25
25 Jason Schmidt .40
26 Kerry Wood .75
27 Ivan Rodriguez .60
28 Rocco Baldelli .60
29 Mark Prior 2.50
30 Josh Beckett .75
31 Scott Rolen 1.00
32 Nomar Garciaparra 2.50
33 Carl Crawford .25
34 Paul Konerko .40
35 Miguel Cabrera .75
36 Hank Blalock .60
37 Sammy Sosa 2.00
38 Jim Edmonds .40
39 David Ortiz .60
40 Lance Berkman .40
41 Ichiro Suzuki 2.00
42 Adam Dunn .60
43 Carlos Guillen .25
44 Alfonso Soriano 1.00
45 Victor Martinez .25
46 Torii Hunter .60
47 Kazuo Matsui .60
48 Andruw Jones .75
49 Matt Holliday .25
50 Eric Chavez .40
51 Randy Johnson 1.00
52 Lew Ford .25
53 Hideki Matsui 2.50
54 Manny Ramirez .75
55 Mark Teixeira .40
56 Jose Vidro .25
57 Mike Sweeney .25
58 Jack Wilson .25
59 Greg Maddux 1.50
60 Tony Batista .25
61 Albert Pujols 2.50
62 Miguel Tejada .60
63 Carlos Beltran .60
64 Bobby Abreu .40
65 Carlos Delgado .75
66 Travis Hafner .25
67 Scott Podsednik .25
68 Gary Sheffield .60
69 Johan Santana .40
70 Barry Zito .60
71 Pedro Martinez 1.00
72 Brian Giles .40
73 Garret Anderson .40
74 Jeff Bagwell .75
75 Alex Rodriguez 2.50
76 Johnny Bench 4.00
77 Yogi Berra 3.00
78 Lou Brock 3.00
79 Rod Carew 3.00
80 Orlando Cepeda 2.00
81 Carlton Fisk 5.00
82 Bob Gibson 3.00
83 Reggie Jackson 5.00
84 Al Kaline 4.00
85 Harmon Killebrew 3.00
86 Ralph Kiner 4.00
87 Willie McCovey 2.00
88 Eddie Murray 4.00
89 Phil Rizzuto 4.00
90 Brooks Robinson 3.00
91 Nolan Ryan 5.00
92 Mike Schmidt 4.00
93 Tom Seaver 3.00
94 Willie Stargell 2.00
95 Rollie Fingers 2.00
96 Dennis Eckersley 2.00
97 Enos Slaughter 2.00
98 Jim Palmer 2.00
99 Warren Spahn 3.00
100 Joe Morgan 2.00
101 Richie Ashburn 3.00
102 Robin Yount 3.00
103 Bob Feller 3.00
104 Pee Wee Reese 2.00
105 Eddie Mathews 3.00
106 David Wright 6.00
107 David Aardsma 3.00
108 B.J. Upton 3.00
109 Scott Kazmir 4.00
110 Gavin Floyd 3.00
111 Jeff Francis 3.00
112 Dioner Navarro 3.00
113 Zack Greinke 3.00
114 Nick Swisher 5.00
115 Josh Kroeger 3.00
116 Ryan Raburn 3.00
117 Victor Diaz 4.00
118 Casey Kotchman 4.00
119 Joey Gathright 3.00
120 Jon Knott 3.00
121 J.D. Durbin 3.00
122 Andres Blanco 3.00
123 *Charlton Jimerson* 3.00
124 Russ Adams 3.00
125 *Justin Verlander* 5.00

First Edition

(1-75): 2X-5X
(76-105): 1X-1.5X
(106-125): 1X-2X
Production 150 Sets

Final Edition

No Pricing
Production 1 Set

Classic Clippings

NM/M
Common Player: 3.00
Gold: 2X-5X
Production 51-95 Sets
1 Nolan Ryan/1991 6.00
2 Cal Ripken Jr./1995 8.00
3 Joe Carter/1993 3.00
4 Bucky Dent/1978 3.00
5 Kirk Gibson/1988 3.00
6 Reggie Jackson/1977 5.00
7 Carlton Fisk/1975 4.00
8 Bobby Thomson/1951 3.00
9 Bill Mazeroski/1960 3.00
10 Don Larsen/1956 4.00

Bat Rack Quad Blue

NM/M
Inserted 1:118
Silver: No Pricing
Production 10 Sets
Purple: No Pricing
Production 1 Set
Manny Ramirez, Wade Boggs, Carl Yastrzemski, Bobby Doerr 50.00
Kirby Puckett, Jacque Jones, Harmon Killebrew, Torii Hunter 40.00
Brandon Webb, Randy Johnson, Curt Schilling, Roger Clemens 40.00
Al Kaline, Tony Gwynn, Frank Howard, Rocky Colavito 50.00
Jose Reyes, Gary Carter, Mike Piazza, Kazuo Matsui 30.00
Bobby Abreu, Adam Dunn, Rocco Baldelli, Hideki Matsui 30.00
Jim Thome, Albert Pujols, Jeff Bagwell, Todd Helton 40.00
Hank Blalock, Miguel Tejada, Troy Glaus, Ivan Rodriguez 25.00
Carlos Delgado, Jason Giambi, Rafael Palmeiro, Mark Teixeira 25.00

Cut of History Single Jersey Blue

NM/M
Common Player: 6.00
Inserted 1:21
Silver Patch: No Pricing
Production 25 Sets
Purple Patch: No Pricing
Production 1 Set
SA Sparky Anderson 6.00
JB Johnny Bench 15.00
OC Orlando Cepeda 8.00
CF Carlton Fisk 10.00
BG Bob Gibson 8.00
DG Dwight Gooden 6.00
RJ Reggie Jackson 12.00
DM Don Mattingly 15.00
WM Willie McCovey 6.00
JM Joe Morgan SP/82
EM Eddie Murray 10.00
CR Cal Ripken Jr. 20.00
BR Brooks Robinson 8.00
NR Nolan Ryan 20.00
MS Mike Schmidt 12.00
TS Tom Seaver 10.00
OS Ozzie Smith 15.00
WS Willie Stargell 10.00
DS Darryl Strawberry 6.00
CY Carl Yastrzemski 10.00

Cut of History Single Autograph Blue

NM/M
Common Player: 20.00
Inserted 1:161
Silver: No Pricing
Production 25 Sets
Purple: No Pricing
Production 1 Set
JB Johnny Bench 50.00
BB Bill Buckner 20.00
BF Bob Feller 20.00
KG Kirk Gibson 20.00
DG Dwight Gooden 30.00
DL Don Larsen 20.00
DM Don Mattingly 50.00
JP Jim Palmer 30.00
BR Brooks Robinson 40.00
DS Darryl Strawberry 25.00
MW Mookie Wilson 20.00

Cut of History Dual Autograph Blue

NM/M
Production 49 Sets
Silver: No Pricing
Production 22 Sets
Purple: No Pricing
Production 1 Set
GE Kirk Gibson, Dennis Eckersley 50.00
GS Dwight Gooden, Darryl Strawberry 40.00
WB Mookie Wilson, Bill Buckner 40.00

Cut of History Triple Autograph Blue

No Pricing
Production 15 Sets
Silver: No Pricing
Production 5 Sets
Purple: No Pricing
Production 1 Set

Cut of History Dual Jersey Blue

NM/M
Common Card: 15.00
Inserted 1:112
Silver Patch: No Pricing
Production 15 Sets
Purple Patch: No Pricing
Production 1 Set
BF Johnny Bench, Carlton Fisk 20.00
BS Lou Brock, Mike Schmidt 25.00
CM Orlando Cepeda, Willie McCovey 15.00
GS Dwight Gooden, Darryl Strawberry 15.00
JY Reggie Jackson, Carl Yastrzemski 20.00
RS Cal Ripken Jr., Ozzie Smith 30.00
RS Nolan Ryan, Tom Seaver 30.00
SJ Willie Stargell, Reggie Jackson 20.00

Cut of History Triple Jersey Blue

NM/M
Inserted 1:67
Silver Patch: No Pricing
Production 25 Sets
Purple Patch: No Pricing
Production 1 Set
ACW Hank Aaron, Roberto Clemente, Ted Williams 300.00
BSG Lou Brock, Kirk Gibson, Ozzie Smith 50.00
JKM Reggie Jackson, Harmon Killebrew, Willie McCovey 40.00
MMC Eddie Murray, Orlando Cepeda, Willie McCovey 25.00
MRS Don Mattingly, Cal Ripken Jr., Mike Schmidt 75.00
OJM Paul O'Neill, Don Mattingly, Reggie Jackson 50.00
RCJ Nolan Ryan, Roger Clemens, Randy Johnson 80.00

Jersey Rack Dual Jersey Blue

NM/M
Common Card: 10.00
Inserted 1:100
Silver Patch: No Pricing
Production 25 Sets
Purple Patch: No Pricing
Production 1 Set
BW Josh Beckett, Kerry Wood 12.00
CJ Miguel Cabrera, Andruw Jones 12.00
DB Adam Dunn, Lance Berkman 10.00
GS Vladimir Guerrero, Sammy Sosa 15.00
GT Khalil Greene, Miguel Tejada 15.00
HB Todd Helton, Jeff Bagwell 12.00
HE Torii Hunter, Jim Edmonds 10.00
JC Randy Johnson, Roger Clemens 20.00
JW Chipper Jones, David Wright 15.00
MM Hideki Matsui, Kazuo Matsui 25.00
OG David Ortiz, Jason Giambi 12.00
RB Scott Rolen, Adrian Beltre 12.00
RS Manny Ramirez, Gary Sheffield 12.00
SG John Smoltz, Eric Gagne 12.00
SM Jason Schmidt, Pedro Martinez 12.00
SM1 Alfonso Soriano, Kazuo Matsui 10.00
SP Curt Schilling, Mark Prior 12.00
TP Jim Thome, Mike Piazza 12.00
WS Dontrelle Willis, Johan Santana 12.00

Triple Jersey Blue

NM/M
Common Card: 12.00
Inserted 1:54
Silver Patch: No Pricing
Production 25 Sets
Purple Patch: No Pricing
CJS Roger Clemens, Randy Johnson, Jason Schmidt 20.00
CSJ Roger Clemens, Curt Schilling, Randy Johnson 20.00
EHJ Jim Edmonds, Torii Hunter, Andruw Jones 12.00
GRS Vladimir Guerrero, Manny Ramirez, Gary Sheffield 15.00
GSR Eric Gagne, John Smoltz, Mariano Rivera 15.00
HSB Todd Helton, Alfonso Soriano, Adrian Beltre 12.00
MGT Kazuo Matsui, Khalil Greene, Miguel Tejada 15.00
MRG Hideki Matsui, Mariano Rivera, Jason Giambi 25.00
ORM David Ortiz, Manny Ramirez, Pedro Martinez 15.00
PRE Albert Pujols, Scott Rolen, Jim Edmonds 25.00
PTB Albert Pujols, Jim Thome, Jeff Bagwell 20.00

RBJ Scott Rolen, Adrian Beltre, Chipper Jones 15.00
SDC Sammy Sosa, Adam Dunn, Miguel Cabrera 12.00
SJJ John Smoltz, Chipper Jones, Andruw Jones 20.00
SPB Jason Schmidt, Mark Prior, Josh Beckett 15.00
STB Sammy Sosa, Miguel Tejada, Adrian Beltre 15.00
WPM David Wright, Mike Piazza, Kazuo Matsui 20.00
WSW Dontrelle Willis, Johan Santana, Kerry Wood 15.00

Diamond Signings Single Blue

NM/M

Inserted 1:29
Silver: No Pricing
Production 25 Sets
Purple: No Pricing
Production 1 Set
JB Jason Bay 20.00
AB Andres Blanco 15.00
CF Chone Figgins 15.00
GF Gavin Floyd 20.00
KG Khalil Greene 30.00
ZG Zack Greinke 15.00
TH Travis Hafner 10.00
CJ Charlton Jimerson 10.00
SK Scott Kazmir 20.00
CK Casey Kotchman 10.00
BL Brad Lidge 40.00
JM Justin Morneau 20.00
DN Dioner Navarro 10.00
JP Jake Peavy 20.00
NS Nick Swisher 15.00
BU B.J. Upton 15.00
JV Justin Verlander 20.00
DW David Wright 50.00

Diamond Signings Triple Blue

NM/M

Sequentially Numbered
Silver: No Pricing
Production 5 Sets
Purple: No Pricing
Production 1 Set
Khalil Greene, B.J. Upton, Bobby Crosby 60.00
Justin Verlander, Gavin Floyd, Scott Kazmir 75.00
Nick Swisher, Charlton Jimerson, Chone Figgins 30.00
Casey Kotchman, Justin Morneau, Jason Bay 60.00

Diamond Signings Dual Blue

NM/M

Production 49 Sets
Silver: No Pricing
Production 22 Sets
Purple: No Pricing
Production 1 Set
BC Jason Bay, B. Crosby Exch 30.00
FU Gavin Floyd, Chase Utley 40.00
KM Casey Kotchman, Justin Morneau

Press Clippings

NM/M

Common Player: 2.00
Inserted 1:6
Gold: No Pricing
Production 4 Sets
1 Ichiro Suzuki 4.00
2 Manny Ramirez 2.00
3 Albert Pujols 5.00
4 David Ortiz 2.00
5 Greg Maddux 3.00
6 Ken Griffey Jr. 3.00
7 Vladimir Guerrero 3.00
8 Randy Johnson 3.00
9 Johan Santana 2.00
10 Roger Clemens 5.00
11 Bobby Crosby 2.00
12 Jason Bay 2.00

2005 FLEER PLATINUM

NM/M

Common Players (1-100): .25
Minor Players (1-100): .40
Common Players (101-125): 3.00
Production 1,000 Sets
1 Nomar Garciaparra 1.50
2 Matt Holliday .25
3 Rickie Weeks .25
4 Jim Thome .75
5 Roy Halladay .40
6 Paul Konerko .25
7 Lance Berkman .40
8 Ichiro Suzuki 1.25
9 Kerry Wood .60
10 Lew Ford .25
11 Omar Vizquel .40
12 Manny Ramirez .60
13 Carlos Beltran .50
14 Lyle Overbay .25
15 Billy Wagner .40
16 Jose Vidro .25
17 Vladimir Guerrero .75
18 Miguel Tejada .50
19 Alex Rodriguez 1.50
20 Rocco Baldelli .50
21 David Ortiz .50
22 Victor Martinez .25
23 Shawn Green .40
24 Jason Bay .25
25 Pedro Martinez .75
26 Travis Hafner .25
27 Eric Gagne .40
28 Jack Wilson .25
29 Ivan Rodriguez .50
30 Jody Gerut .25
31 Adrian Beltre .40
32 Craig Wilson .25
33 J.D. Drew .40
34 Craig Biggio .40
35 Mark Mulder .40
36 Mark Teixeira .50
37 Melvin Mora .25
38 Ken Griffey Jr. 1.00
39 Mike Sweeney .25
40 Khalil Greene .60
41 Rafael Palmeiro .60
42 Austin Kearns .50
43 Garret Anderson .40
44 Trevor Hoffman .25
45 Andruw Jones .60
46 Adam Dunn .50
47 Angel Berroa .25
48 Ryan Klesko .40
49 Sean Casey .25
50 Kazuo Matsui .50
51 Jim Edmonds .40
52 Magglio Ordonez .40
53 Tom Glavine .40
54 Larry Walker .40
55 Johnny Estrada .25
56 Brad Lidge .25
57 Barry Zito .50
58 Michael Young .40
59 Chipper Jones 1.00
60 Andy Pettitte .50
61 Eric Chavez .40
62 Carlos Delgado .60
63 David Eckstein .25
64 Dmitri Young .25
65 Mike Piazza 1.00
66 Albert Pujols 1.50
67 Luis Gonzalez .40
68 Hideki Matsui 1.50
69 Gary Sheffield .50
70 Carl Crawford .25
71 Curt Schilling .50
72 Todd Helton .60
73 Ben Sheets .40
74 Bobby Abreu .40
75 Jose Guillen .25
76 Richie Sexson .50
77 Miguel Cabrera .60
78 Bernie Williams .50
79 Aubrey Huff .25
80 John Smoltz .40
81 Jeff Bagwell .60
82 Tim Hudson .40
83 Alfonso Soriano .75
84 Freddy Garcia .25
85 Johan Santana .40
86 Bret Boone .40
87 Troy Glaus .50
88 Carlos Guillen .25
89 Derek Jeter 2.00
90 Scott Rolen .75
91 Sammy Sosa 1.25
92 Jacque Jones .25
93 Jason Schmidt .40
94 Randy Johnson .75
95 Dontrelle Willis .40
96 Mariano Rivera .40
97 Hank Blalock .50
98 Mark Prior 1.50
99 Torii Hunter .50
100 Roger Clemens 1.50
101 David Wright 6.00
102 Justin Morneau 4.00
103 Scott Kazmir 4.00
104 Gavin Floyd 3.00
105 *Justin Verlander* 8.00
106 Zack Greinke 4.00
107 David Aardsma 3.00
108 Ryan Raburn 4.00
109 Joey Gathright 3.00
110 J.D. Durbin 3.00
111 Sean Burnett 3.00
112 Jose Lopez 5.00
113 Nick Swisher 4.00
114 Bobby Jenks 3.00
115 Kelly Johnson 8.00
116 B.J. Upton 5.00
117 Ronny Cedeno 3.00
118 Edwin Encarnacion 6.00
119 Jeff Baker 3.00
120 Taylor Buchholz 3.00
121 *Livan Hernandez* 4.00
122 Dioner Navarro 4.00
123 Victor Diaz 4.00
124 Jon Knott 4.00
125 Russ Adams 3.00

Finish

Cards 1-100: 3X-6X
Cards 101-125: .75X-1.25X
Production 199 Sets

Extreme

Cards 1-125: No Pricing
Production 20 Sets

Autograph Die Cuts

NM/M

Numbered to indicated quantities
1 Lew Ford/99 12.00
3 Jason Bay/50 15.00
4 Travis Hafner/99
6 Brad Lidge/99 30.00
7 Michael Young/99
8 David Eckstein/99 15.00
9 Carl Crawford/50
10 Miguel Cabrera/50
11 David Wright/50 30.00
12 Justin Morneau/99
13 Scott Kazmir/99
14 Gavin Floyd/99
15 Justin Verlander/99
16 David Aardsma/10
18 Joey Gathright/50 10.00
22 Russ Adams/20

Decade of Excellence

NM/M

Common Player: 2.00
Inserted 1:199
1 Albert Pujols 6.00
2 Derek Jeter 8.00
3 Randy Johnson 4.00
4 Ichiro Suzuki 5.00
5 Alex Rodriguez 6.00
6 Mike Piazza 4.00
7 Greg Maddux 4.00
8 Curt Schilling 3.00
9 Frank Thomas 3.00
10 Torii Hunter 3.00
11 Al Kaline 6.00
12 Travis Hafner 2.00
13 Ivan Rodriguez 3.00
14 Rafael Palmeiro 3.00
15 Mike Schmidt 8.00
16 Johnny Bench 8.00
17 Jim Edmonds 2.00
18 Pedro Martinez 4.00
19 Robin Yount 6.00
20 Sammy Sosa 5.00

Decade of Excellence Jersey Silver

NM/M

Common Player: 5.00
Inserted 1:54
Gold: .75X-1.25X
Production 99 Sets
Patch Platinum: No Pricing
Production 10 Sets
JB Johnny Bench 15.00
JE Jim Edmonds 5.00
TF Travis Hafner 5.00
TH Torii Hunter 5.00
RJ Randy Johnson 8.00
AK Al Kaline 10.00
GM Greg Maddux 8.00
PM Pedro Martinez 8.00
RP Rafael Palmeiro 8.00
MP Mike Piazza 8.00
AP Albert Pujols 12.00
IR Ivan Rodriguez 5.00
CS Curt Schilling 5.00
MS Mike Schmidt 15.00
SS Sammy Sosa 10.00
FT Frank Thomas 8.00
RY Robin Yount 10.00

Decade of Ex. Auto. Jersey Platinum

No Pricing
Production 5 Sets

Diamond Dominators Jersey Silver

NM/M

Common Player:
Inserted 1:45
Gold: .75X-1.25X
Production 199 Sets (Hobby)
Red: .5X-1X
Inserted 1:50 (Retail)
RB Rocco Baldelli 5.00
AB Adrian Beltre 5.00
MC Miguel Cabrera 8.00
EG Eric Gagne 5.00
JG Jason Giambi 8.00
KG Khalil Greene 8.00
VG Vladimir Guerrero 8.00
TH Tim Hudson 5.00
RJ Randy Johnson 8.00
CJ Chipper Jones 4.00
KM Kazuo Matsui 5.00
DO David Ortiz 5.00
MP Mike Piazza 8.00
AP Albert Pujols 12.00
IR Ivan Rodriguez 5.00
SR Scott Rolen 8.00
CS Curt Schilling 5.00
AS Alfonso Soriano 8.00
SS Sammy Sosa 10.00

Diamond Dominators

NM/M

Common Player: 2.00
Inserted 1:12 Retail
1 Albert Pujols 6.00
2 Curt Schilling 3.00
3 Adrian Beltre 2.00
4 Randy Johnson 4.00
5 Ivan Rodriguez 3.00
6 Mike Piazza 4.00
7 Chipper Jones 4.00
8 Sammy Sosa 5.00
9 Tim Hudson 2.00
10 Rocco Baldelli 3.00
11 Alfonso Soriano 4.00
12 David Ortiz 3.00
13 Mariano Rivera 2.00
14 Kazuo Matsui 3.00
15 Khalil Greene 3.00
16 Eric Gagne 2.00
17 Vladimir Guerrero 4.00
18 Jason Giambi 4.00
19 Scott Rolen 4.00
20 Miguel Cabrera 3.00

Diamond Dominators Metal

NM/M

Common Player: 2.00
Inserted 1:18 Hobby
1 Albert Pujols 6.00
2 Curt Schilling 3.00
3 Adrian Beltre 2.00
4 Randy Johnson 4.00
5 Ivan Rodriguez 3.00
6 Mike Piazza 4.00
7 Chipper Jones 4.00
8 Sammy Sosa 5.00
9 Tim Hudson 2.00
10 Rocco Baldelli 3.00
11 Alfonso Soriano 4.00
12 David Ortiz 3.00
13 Kazuo Matsui 3.00
14 Khalil Greene 3.00
15 Eric Gagne 2.00
16 Vladimir Guerrero 4.00
17 Jason Giambi 4.00
18 Scott Rolen 4.00
19 Miguel Cabrera 3.00

Diamond Dominators Metal Patch

1X-2X Diamond Dominators Jersey Silver
Sequentially #'d to 30
HA Hank Aaron 100.00

Diamond Dominators Metal Autograph

No Pricing
Production 10 Sets

Lumberjacks

NM/M

Common Player: .75
Inserted 1:6
Bat Silver: 2X-3X
Inserted 1:9
Bat Gold: 2X-4X
Production 250 Sets
Bat Patch: No Pricing
Production 20 Sets

1 Albert Pujols 2.50
2 Jim Thome 1.25
3 Andruw Jones 1.00
4 Kazuo Matsui .75
5 Adam Dunn .75
6 Bernie Williams .75
7 Hank Blalock .75
8 Bobby Abreu .75
9 Rocco Baldelli .75
10 Jacque Jones .75
11 Mark Teixeira .75
12 Ichiro Suzuki 2.00
13 Gary Sheffield .75
14 Sean Casey .75
15 Carl Crawford .75

Lumberjacks Autograph Platinum

No Pricing
Production 20 Sets

Nameplates Dual Patch Platinum

NM/M

No Pricing
Production 25 Sets
Masterpiece: No Pricing
Production 1 Set

Nameplates Dual Patch Auto Platinum

No Pricing
Production 1 Set
SKJR Scott Kazmir, Jose Reyes
SRMB Scott Rolen, Marlon Byrd

2005 FLEER SHOWCASE

NM/M

Common Player (1-100): .25
Common Showcasing Talent (101-110): 2.00
Inserted 1:5
Common Showcasing History (111-135): .40
Inserted 1:20
Pack (5):
Box (20):

1 Albert Pujols 2.50
2 Rocco Baldelli .60
3 Bernie Williams .60
4 Shawn Green .40
5 Garret Anderson .40
6 Paul Konerko .25
7 Mike Sweeney .25
8 Jim Thome 1.00
9 Mark Teixeira .40
10 Mark Prior 2.50
11 Angel Berroa .25
12 Barry Zito .60
13 Carlos Delgado .75
14 Troy Glaus .60
15 Travis Hafner .25
16 Lyle Overbay .25
17 David Ortiz .60
18 Ivan Rodriguez .60
19 Jack Wilson .25
20 Jason Schmidt .40
21 Mike Piazza 1.50
22 David Eckstein .25
23 Ben Sheets .40
24 Randy Johnson 1.00
25 Jacque Jones .25
26 Jody Gerut .25
27 Kris Benson .25
28 Luis Gonzalez .40
29 Victor Martinez .25
30 Torii Hunter .60
31 Gary Sheffield .60
32 Miguel Tejada .60
33 Dontrelle Willis .60
34 Bret Boone .40
35 Hideki Matsui .60
36 Shea Hillenbrand .25
37 Wily Mo Pena .25
38 Johan Santana .40
39 Derek Jeter 3.00
40 Chipper Jones 1.50
41 Sean Casey .25
42 Corey Koskie .25
43 Alex Rodriguez 2.50
44 Andruw Jones .75
45 Austin Kearns .60
46 Jose Vidro .25
47 Adam Dunn .60
48 Adrian Beltre .40
49 Bobby Abreu .40
50 Michael Young .25
51 Freddy Garcia .25
52 Eric Gagne .40
53 Chase Utley .25
54 Alfonso Soriano 1.00
55 Nick Johnson .25
56 Johnny Estrada .25
57 Jeff Bagwell .75
58 Randy Winn .25
59 Roy Halladay .40
60 J.D. Drew .40
61 Craig Biggio .40
62 Scott Rolen 1.00
63 Nomar Garciaparra 2.50
64 Matt Holliday .25
65 Billy Wagner .25
66 Carl Crawford .25
67 Pedro J. Martinez 1.00
68 Jeremy Bonderman .25
69 Jason Bay .25
70 A.J. Pierzynski .25
71 Vladimir Guerrero 1.00
72 Rickie Weeks .60
73 Mark Loretta .25
74 Todd Helton .75
75 Manny Ramirez .75
76 Carlos Guillen .25
77 Khalil Greene .75
78 Javy Lopez .40
79 Josh Beckett .75
80 Ichiro Suzuki 2.00
81 Magglio Ordonez .40
82 Ken Harvey .25
83 Mark Mulder .40
84 Hank Blalock .60
85 Richard Hidalgo .25
86 Curt Schilling .60
87 Jeromy Burnitz .25
88 Craig Wilson .25
89 Aubrey Huff .25
90 Kerry Wood .75
91 Andy Pettitte .60
92 Tim Hudson .40
93 Jim Edmonds .40
94 Melvin Mora .25
95 Miguel Cabrera .75
96 Trevor Hoffman .25
97 J.T. Snow .25
98 Sammy Sosa 2.00
99 Roger Clemens 2.50
100 Eric Chavez 4.00
101 B.J. Upton 5.00
102 Gavin Floyd 3.00
103 Casey Kotchman 3.00
104 David Wright 5.00
105 Dioner Navarro 3.00
106 Scott Kazmir 3.00
107 Andres Blanco 2.00
108 Joey Gathright 2.00
109 Jon Knott 2.00
110 Charlton Jimerson 3.00
111 Larry Doby .75
112 Reggie Jackson 2.00
113 Enos Slaughter .60
114 Bill "Moose" Skowron .60
115 Duke Snider .75
116 Harmon Killebrew 1.00
117 Willie McCovey .75
118 Rollie Fingers 1.00
119 Preacher Roe .40
120 Carlton Fisk .60
121 Andre Dawson .60
122 Orlando Cepeda .60
123 Bucky Dent .40
124 Cal Ripken Jr. 1.50
125 Nolan Ryan 3.00
126 Tony Perez .60
127 Mike Schmidt 1.50
128 Johnny Bench 1.50
129 Sparky Anderson .40
130 Ted Williams 2.50
131 Al Kaline .75
132 Carl Yastrzemski 1.00
133 Eddie Murray .75
134 Roberto Clemente 1.50
135 Yogi Berra 1.50

Masterpiece Legacy

Cards (1-135): No Pricing
Production 1 Set

Masterpiece Showpiece Patch

Cards (1-135): No Pricing
Production 1 Set
Autograph Patch: No Pricing
Production 1 Set
Patch Showdown: No Pricing
Production 1 Set
Patch Showtime: No Pricing
Production 1 Set

Autographed Legacy

NM/M

Common Player: 15.00
Sequentially numbered

1 Albert Pujols/11
6 Paul Konerko/299
8 Jim Thome/34 60.00
9 Mark Teixeira/102
10 Mark Prior/43
12 Barry Zito/45
15 Travis Hafner/299
16 Lyle Overbay/450
18 Ivan Rodriguez/217 40.00
19 Jack Wilson/298 15.00
20 Jason Schmidt/127
21 Mike Piazza/26 150.00
22 David Eckstein/40
23 Ben Sheets/427 15.00
26 Jody Gerut/299
40 Chipper Jones/41 60.00
45 Austin Kearns/460 10.00
46 Jose Vidro/300
47 Adam Dunn/52 50.00
48 Adrian Beltre/180 25.00
50 Michael Young/80 15.00
52 Eric Gagne/310 30.00
53 Chase Utley/446
55 Nick Johnson/300
59 Roy Halladay/99 15.00
60 J.D. Drew/14
65 Billy Wagner/12
66 Carl Crawford/290
68 Jeremy Bonderman/97 15.00
72 Rickie Weeks/453 20.00
75 Manny Ramirez/31 75.00
77 Khalil Greene/299 40.00
81 Magglio Ordonez/300
88 Craig Wilson/40 20.00
89 Aubrey Huff/453 15.00
90 Kerry Wood/28
92 Tim Hudson/183 30.00
95 Miguel Cabrera/32
99 Roger Clemens/64 15.00
100 Eric Chavez/204 15.00
101 B.J. Upton/299
103 Casey Kotchman/454 15.00
104 David Wright/298
106 Scott Kazmir/458 20.00
107 Andres Blanco/23
109 Jon Knott/402 15.00
111 Larry Doby/25
112 Reggie Jackson/17
114 Bill "Moose" Skowron/64 15.00
119 Preacher Roe/304 15.00
120 Carlton Fisk/86 30.00
122 Orlando Cepeda/19
123 Bucky Dent/99 15.00
124 Cal Ripken Jr./53
125 Nolan Ryan/13
131 Al Kaline/7
132 Carl Yastrzemski/14
135 Yogi Berra/25

Measures of Greatness

NM/M

Common Player: .75
Inserted 1:5
Jersey Red: 2X-4X
Production 340 Sets
Patch: No Pricing
Production 10 Sets
Masterpiece: No Pricing
Production 1 Set

1 Albert Pujols 4.00
2 Mike Piazza 2.50
3 Vladimir Guerrero 2.00
4 Jim Thome 2.00
5 Pedro J. Martinez 2.00
6 Rafael Palmeiro .75
7 Adrian Beltre .75
8 Sammy Sosa 3.00
9 Todd Helton 1.50
10 Randy Johnson 2.00
11 Jeff Bagwell 1.50
12 Jason Giambi 2.00
13 Scott Rolen 2.00
14 Greg Maddux 2.50
15 Alfonso Soriano 2.00
16 Mariano Rivera .75
17 Curt Schilling 1.00
18 Derek Jeter 5.00
19 Chipper Jones 2.50
20 Roger Clemens 4.00

Showtime

Veterans (1-100): 3X-6X
Showcasing Talent (101-110): 2X-4X
Showcasing History (111-135): 1X-3X
Production 99 Sets
Masterpiece: No Pricing
Production 1 Set

Showdown

Cards (1-135): No Pricing
Production 15 Sets
Masterpiece: No Pricing
Production 1 Set

Swing Time

NM/M

Common Player: 2.50
Inserted 1:45
Jersey Red: 1X-3X
Production 610 Sets
Patch: 2X-5X
Production 50 Sets
Masterpiece: No Pricing
Production 1 Set

1 Ivan Rodriguez 2.50
2 Gary Sheffield 2.50
3 Bernie Williams 2.50
4 Vladimir Guerrero 3.50
5 Jim Edmonds 2.50
6 Manny Ramirez 3.00
7 Todd Helton 3.00
8 Hank Blalock 2.50
9 Hideki Matsui 6.00
10 David Ortiz 2.50
11 Albert Pujols 6.00
12 Miguel Tejada 2.50
13 Miguel Cabrera 3.00
14 Alex Rodriguez 6.00
15 Ichiro Suzuki 5.00

Timepiece Extreme

No Pricing
Production 1 Set

Timepiece Ink

No Pricing
Production 10 Sets

Timepiece Unique

No Pricing
Production 5 Sets

Wave of the Future

		NM/M
Common Player:		1.00
Inserted 1:15		
Jersey Red:		1X-3X
Production 610 Sets		
Patch:		2X-5X
Production 50 Sets		
Masterpiece:		No Pricing
Production 1 Set		
1	Kazuo Matsui	5.00
2	Johan Santana	1.50
3	Khalil Greene	2.00
4	Dontrelle Willis	1.50
5	Mark Teixeira	1.50
6	Travis Hafner	1.00
7	Jason Bay	1.50
8	Angel Berroa	1.00
9	Miguel Cabrera	2.00
10	Joe Mauer	1.50
11	Adam Dunn	2.00
12	B.J. Upton	3.00
13	Victor Martinez	1.00
14	Michael Young	1.00
15	David Wright	3.00

2005 FLEER TRADITION

		NM/M
Common Player (1-300):		.15
Common Card (301-330):		3.00
Unlisted Card (301-330):		4.00
Inserted 1:2		
Common Player (331-350):		.15
Cards 1-12; 331-350 Inserted 1:2		
Pack (10):		
Box (36):		
1	Johan Santana, Curt Schilling, Jake Westbrook	.40
2	Ben Sheets, Jake Peavy, Randy Johnson	.75
3	Johan Santana, Bartolo Colon, Curt Schilling	.40
4	Carl Pavano, Roy Oswalt, Roger Clemens	1.50
5	Johan Santana, Pedro Martinez, Curt Schilling	.75
6	Jason Schmidt, Randy Johnson, Ben Sheets	.75
7	Melvin Mora, Vladimir Guerrero, Ichiro Suzuki	1.25
8	Adrian Beltre, Todd Helton, Mark Loretta	.50
9	Manny Ramirez, Paul Konerko, David Ortiz	.50
10	Albert Pujols, Adrian Beltre, Adam Dunn	1.50
11	David Ortiz, Manny Ramirez, Miguel Tejada	.50
12	Albert Pujols, Vinny Castilla, Scott Rolen	1.50
13	Jason Bay	.15
14	Greg Maddux	1.00
15	Melvin Mora	.15
16	Matt Stairs	.15
17	Scott Podsednik	.25
18	Bartolo Colon	.25
19	Roger Clemens	1.50
20	Eric Hinske	.15
21	Johnny Estrada	.15
22	Brett Tomko	.15
23	John Buck	.15
24	Nomar Garciaparra	1.50
25	Milton Bradley	.15
26	Craig Biggio	.25
27	Kyle Denney	.50
28	Brad Penny	.15
29	Todd Helton	.50
30	Luis Gonzalez	.25
31	Bill Hall	.15
32	Ruben Sierra	.15
33	Zack Greinke	.15
34	Sandy Alomar Jr.	.15
35	Jason Giambi	.75
36	Ben Sheets	.25
37	Edgardo Alfonzo	.15
38	Kenny Rogers	.15
39	Coco Crisp	.15
40	Randy Choate	.50
41	Braden Looper	.15
42	Adam Dunn	.40
43	Adam Eaton	.15
44	Luis Castillo	.25
45	Casey Fossum	.15
46	Mike Piazza	1.00
47	Juan Pierre	.15
48	Doug Davis	.15
49	Manny Ramirez	.50
50	Travis Hafner	.15
51	Jack Wilson	.15
52	Mike Maroth	.15
53	Ken Harvey	.15
54	Brooks Kieschnick	.15
55	Brad Fullmer	.15
56	Octavio Dotel	.15
57	Mike Matheny	.15
58	Andruw Jones	.50
59	Alfonso Soriano	.75
60	Royce Clayton	.15
61	Jon Garland	.15
62	John Mabry	.15
63	Rafael Palmeiro	.25
64	Garrett Atkins	.15
65	Brian Meadows	.15
66	Tony Armas Jr.	.15
67	Toby Hall	.15
68	Carlos Baerga	.15
69	Barry Larkin	.25
70	Jody Gerut	.15
71	Brent Mayne	.15
72	Shigetoshi Hasegawa	.15
73	Jose Cruz Jr.	.15
74	Dan Wilson	.15
75	Sidney Ponson	.15
76	Jason Jennings	.15
77	A.J. Burnett	.15
78	Tony Batista	.15
79	Kris Benson	.15
80	Sean Burroughs	.15
81	Eric Young	.15
82	Casey Kotchman	.40
83	Derrek Lee	.25
84	Mariano Rivera	.25
85	Julio Franco	.15
86	Corey Patterson	.15
87	Carlos Beltran	.40
88	Trevor Hoffman	.15
89	Danny Garcia	.15
90	Marco Scutaro	.15
91	Marquis Grissom	.15
92	Aubrey Huff	.15
93	Tony Womack	.15
94	Placido Polanco	.15
95	Bengie Molina	.15
96	Roger Cedeno	.15
97	Geoff Jenkins	.25
98	Kip Wells	.15
99	Derek Jeter	2.00
100	Omar Infante	.15
101	Phil Nevin	.15
102	Edgar Renteria	.15
103	B.J. Surhoff	.15
104	David DeJesus	.15
105	Raul Ibanez	.15
106	Hank Blalock	.40
107	Shawn Estes	.15
108	Wily Mo Pena	.15
109	Shawn Green	.25
110	David Wright	.50
111	Kenny Lofton	.15
112	Matt Clement	.15
113	Cesar Izturis	.15
114	John Lackey	.15
115	Torii Hunter	.40
116	Charles Johnson	.15
117	Ray Durham	.15
118	Luke Hudson	.15
119	Jeremy Bonderman	.15
120	Sean Casey	.15
121	Johnny Damon	.25
122	Eric Milton	.15
123	Shea Hillenbrand	.15
124	Jim Edmonds	.25
125	Jim Edmonds	.25
126	Javier Vazquez	.15
127	Jon Adkins	.15
128	Mike Lowell	.15
129	Khalil Greene	.50
130	Quinton McCracken	.15
131	Edgar Martinez	.25
132	Matt Lawton	.15
133	Jeff Weaver	.15
134	Marlon Byrd	.15
135	John Smoltz	.25
136	Grady Sizemore	.15
137	Brian Roberts	.15
138	Dee Brown	.15
139	Joel Pineiro	.15
140	David Dellucci	.15
141	Bobby Higginson	.15
142	Ryan Madson	.15
143	Scott Hatteberg	.15
144	Greg Zaun	.15
145	Brian Jordan	.15
146	Jason Isringhausen	.15
147	Vinnie Chulk	.15
148	Al Leiter	.15
149	Pedro Martinez	.15
150	Carlos Guillen	.15
151	Randy Wolf	.15
152	Vernon Wells	.25
153	Barry Zito	.40
154	Pedro Feliz	.15
155	Omar Vizquel	.15
156	Chone Figgins	.15
157	David Ortiz	.40
158	*Sun-Woo Kim*	1.00
159	Adam Kennedy	.15
160	Carlos Lee	.15
161	Rick Ankiel	.15
162	Roy Oswalt	.25
163	Armando Benitez	.15
164	Erubiel Durazo	.15
165	Adam Hyzdu	.15
166	Esteban Yan	.15
167	Victor Santos	.15
168	Kevin Millwood	.15
169	Andy Pettitte	.60
170	Mike Cameron	.15
171	Scott Rolen	.75
172	Trot Nixon	.15
173	Eric Munson	.15
174	Roy Halladay	.25
175	Juan Encarnacion	.15
176	Eric Chavez	.25
177	Terrmel Sledge	.15
178	Jason Schmidt	.25
179	Endy Chavez	.15
180	Carlos Zambrano	.15
181	Carlos Delgado	.50
182	Dewon Brazelton	.15
183	J.D. Drew	.25
184	Orlando Cabrera	.15
185	Craig Wilson	.15
186	Chin-Hui Tsao	.15
187	Jolbert Cabrera	.15
188	Rod Barajas	.15
189	Craig Monroe	.15
190	Dave Berg	.15
191	Carlos Silva	.15
192	Eric Gagne	.25
193	Marcus Giles	.15
194	Nick Johnson	.15
195	Kelvim Escobar	.15
196	Wade Miller	.15
197	David Bell	.15
198	Rondell White	.15
199	Brian Giles	.25
200	Jeromy Burnitz	.15
201	Carl Pavano	.15
202	Alex Rios	.15
203	Ryan Freel	.15
204	R.A. Dickey	.15
205	Miguel Cairo	.15
206	Kerry Wood	.50
207	C.C. Sabathia	.15
208	Jaime Cerda	.15
209	Jerome Williams	.15
210	Ryan Wagner	.15
211	Javy Lopez	.25
212	Tike Redman	.15
213	Richie Sexson	.40
214	Shannon Stewart	.15
215	Ben Davis	.15
216	Jeff Bagwell	.50
217	David Wells	.15
218	Justin Leone	.15
219	Brad Radke	.15
220	Ramon Santiago	.15
221	Richard Hidalgo	.15
222	Aaron Miles	.15
223	Mark Loretta	.15
224	Aaron Boone	.15
225	Steve Trachsel	.15
226	Geoff Blum	.15
227	Shingo Takatsu	.15
228	Kevin Youkilis	.15
229	Laynce Nix	.15
230	Daniel Cabrera	.15
231	Kyle Lohse	.15
232	Todd Pratt	.15
233	Reed Johnson	.15
234	Lance Berkman	.25
235	Hideki Matsui	1.50
236	Randy Winn	.15
237	Joe Randa	.15
238	Bob Howry	.15
239	Jason LaRue	.15
240	Jose Valentin	.15
241	Livan Hernandez	.15
242	Jamie Moyer	.15
243	Garret Anderson	.25
244	Brad Ausmus	.15
245	Russell Branyan	.15
246	Paul Wilson	.15
247	Tim Wakefield	.15
248	Roberto Alomar	.40
249	Kazuhisa Ishii	.15
250	Tino Martinez	.15
251	Tomokazu Ohka	.15
252	Mark Redman	.15
253	Paul Byrd	.15
254	Greg Aquino	.15
255	Adrian Beltre	.25
256	Ricky Ledee	.15
257	Josh Fogg	.15
258	Derek Lowe	.15
259	Lew Ford	.15
260	Bobby Crosby	.15
261	Jim Thome	.75
262	Jaret Wright	.15
263	Chin-Feng Chen	.15
264	Troy Glaus	.40
265	Jorge Sosa	.15
266	Mike Lamb	.15
267	Russ Ortiz	.15
268	Reggie Sanders	.15
269	Orlando Hudson	.15
270	Rodrigo Lopez	.15
271	Jose Vidro	.15
272	Akinori Otsuka	.15
273	Victor Martinez	.15
274	Carl Crawford	.15
275	Roberto Novoa	.25
276	Brian Lawrence	.15
277	Angel Berroa	.15
278	Josh Beckett	.50
279	Lyle Overbay	.15
280	Dustin Hermanson	.15
281	Jeff Conine	.15
282	Mark Prior	1.50
283	Kevin Brown	.25
284	Magglio Ordonez	.25
285	Dontrelle Willis	.25
286	Dallas McPherson	.25
287	Rafael Furcal	.25
288	Ty Wigginton	.15
289	Moises Alou	.25
290	A.J. Pierzynski	.15
291	Todd Walker	.15
292	Hideo Nomo	.15
293	Larry Walker	.25
294	Choo Freeman	.15
295	Eduardo Perez	.15
296	Miguel Tejada	.40
297	Corey Koskie	.15
298	Jermaine Dye	.15
299	John Riedling	.15

300 John Olerud .25
301 Tim Bittner, Jake Woods, Bobby Jenks 5.00
302 Josh Kroeger, Casey Daigle, Brandon Medders 5.00
303 Kelly Johnson, Charles Thomas, Dan Meyer 4.00
304 Eddy Rodriguez, Ryan Hannaman, John Maine 6.00
305 Anastacio Martinez, Jerome Gamble, Lenny Dinardo 8.00
306 Ronny Cedeno, Carlos Vasquez, Renyel Pinto 6.00
307 Arnie Munoz, Ryan Wing, Felix Diaz 6.00
308 William Bergolla, Ray Olmedo, Edwin Encarnacion 4.00
309 Mariano Gomez, Ivan Ochoa, Kazuhito Tadano 3.00
310 Toby Miller, Jeff Baker, Matt Holliday 6.00
311 Preston Larrison, Curtis Granderson, Ryan Raburn 8.00
312 Josh Wilson, Logan Kensing, Kevin Cave 5.00
313 Hector Gimenez, Willy Taveras, Taylor Buchholz 3.00
314 Ruben Gotay, Brian Bass, Andres Blanco 4.00
315 Joel Hanrahan, Willy Ayber, Yhency Brazoban 3.00
316 David Krynzel, Ben Hendrickson, Corey Hart 3.00
317 Colby Miller, Jason Kubel, J.D. Durban 5.00
318 Maicer Izturis, Chad Cordero, Brandon Watson 3.00
319 Victor Diaz, Aarom Baldiris, Wayne Lydon 8.00
320 Edwardo Sierra, Dioner Navarro, Sean Henn 3.00
321 Nick Swisher, Joe Blanton, Dan Johnson 6.00
322 Ryan Howard, Gavin Floyd, Keith Bucktrot 6.00
323 Ryan Doumit, Sean Burnett, Bobby Bradley 6.00
324 Justin Germano, Rusty Tucker, Freddy Guzman 6.00
325 David Aardsma, Justin Knoedler, Alfredo Simon 4.00
326 Jose Lopez, Rene Rivera, Cha Sueng Baek 4.00
327 Yadier Molina, Evan Rust, Adam Wainwright 4.00
328 Jorge Cantu, Scott Kazmir, B.J. Upton 5.00
329 Adrian Gonzalez, Ramon Nivar, Jason Bourgeois 6.00
330 Russ Adams, Dustin McGowan, Gustavo Chacin 8.00
331 Alfonso Soriano .75
332 Albert Pujols 1.50
333 David Ortiz .40
334 Manny Ramirez .50
335 Jason Bay .15
336 Bobby Crosby .15
337 Roger Clemens 1.50
338 Johan Santana .25
339 Jim Thome .75
340 Vladimir Guerrero .75
341 David Ortiz .40
342 Alex Rodriguez 1.50
343 Albert Pujols 1.50
344 Carlos Beltran .40
345 Johnny Damon .25
346 Scott Rolen .75
347 Larry Walker .25
348 Curt Schilling .40
349 Pedro Martinez .75
350 David Ortiz .40

Gray Backs

Cards 13-300: .75X-1.5X
Cards 1-10; 301-350: .5X-1.25X
Inserted 1:2

Club 3,000/500/300

NM/M

Inserted 1:360
1 Ernie Banks 500 40.00
2 Stan Musial 3000 60.00
3 Steve Carlton 3000 40.00
4 Greg Maddux 300 60.00
5 Dave Winfield 3000 60.00
6 Rafael Palmeiro 500 70.00
7 Rickey Henderson 3000 50.00
8 Roger Clemens 3000 30.00
9 Don Sutton 300
10 George Brett 3000
11 Reggie Jackson 500 30.00
12 Wade Boggs 3000
13 Bob Gibson 3000 40.00
14 Eddie Murray 3000 30.00
15 Tom Seaver 3000 40.00
16 Willie McCovey 500 25.00
17 Rod Carew 3000 60.00
18 Fergie Jenkins 300
19 Phil Niekro 300
20 Frank Robinson 500 40.00

Cooperstown Tribute

NM/M

Common Player: 4.00
Sequentially #'d to HOF Induction Year
Gold: .5X-1X
Inserted 1:24
Jersey: 1X-2X
Inserted 1:200
There are 20 total jersey cards for Joe Morgan & Yogi Berra
No pricing for Morgan & Berra jers. card
Patch: No Pricing
Production 10 Sets
1 Mike Schmidt/1995 5.00
2 Al Kaline/1980 4.00
3 Yogi Berra/1972 6.00
4 Robin Yount/1999 4.00
5 Joe Morgan/1990 4.00
6 Willie Stargell/1988 4.00
7 Harmon Killebrew/1984 5.00
8 Nolan Ryan/1999 10.00
9 Carlton Fisk/2000 5.00
10 Johnny Bench/1989 6.00

Diamond Tributes

NM/M

Common Player: 2.00
Inserted 1:6
1 Albert Pujols 5.00
2 Alex Rodriguez 5.00
3 Ken Griffey Jr. 3.50
4 Sammy Sosa 4.00
5 Chipper Jones 3.50
6 Johan Santana 2.00
7 Roger Clemens 5.00
8 Pedro Martinez 3.00
9 Jim Thome 3.00
10 Greg Maddux 3.50
11 Alfonso Soriano 3.00
12 Derek Jeter 6.00
13 Randy Johnson 3.00
14 Miguel Cabrera 2.00
15 Adrian Beltre 2.00
16 Ivan Rodriguez 2.00
17 Manny Ramirez 2.00
18 Mark Teixeira 2.00
19 Adam Dunn 2.00
20 Scott Rolen 3.00
21 Mike Piazza 3.50
22 J.D. Drew 2.00
23 Hideki Matsui 5.00
24 Nomar Garciaparra 5.00
25 Kazuo Matsui 3.00

Diamond Tribute Jersey

NM/M

Common Player: 6.00
Inserted 1:30
Patch: 1X-3X
Production 50 Sets
AB Adrian Beltre Bat 6.00
MC Miguel Cabrera Bat/30
RC Roger Clemens Jsy 12.00
JD J.D. Drew Bat 6.00
NG Nomar Garciaparra Bat 12.00
RJ Randy Johnson Jsy 8.00
CJ Chipper Jones Bat 10.00
GM Greg Maddux Jsy 10.00
PM Pedro Martinez Jsy 8.00
HM Hideki Matsui Bat 15.00
KM Kazuo Matsui Bat 8.00
MP Mike Piazza Bat 10.00
AP Albert Pujols Bat 15.00
MR Manny Ramirez Bat 6.00
SR Scott Rolen Bat/27
JS Johan Santana Jsy 8.00
AS Alfonso Soriano Bat 8.00
SS Sammy Sosa Bat 10.00
MT Mark Teixeira Bat 6.00
JT Jim Thome Bat 8.00

Diamond Tributes Dual Patch

NM/M

Common Player: 75.00
Production 50 Sets
APSR Albert Pujols, Scott Rolen 100.00
ASMT Alfonso Soriano, Mark Teixeira 75.00
CJJD Chipper Jones, J.D. Drew 80.00
HMKM Hideki Matsui, Kazuo Matsui 125.00
JTAB Jim Thome, Adrian Beltre 75.00
MPIR Mike Piazza, Ivan Rodriguez 75.00
PMMR Pedro Martinez, Manny Ramirez 120.00
RCJS Roger Clemens, Johan Santana 100.00
RJGM Randy Johnson, Greg Maddux 75.00
SSMC Miguel Cabrera, Sammy Sosa 80.00

Standouts

NM/M

Common Player: 3.50
Inserted 1:18
1 Albert Pujols 6.00
2 Ichiro Suzuki 5.00
3 Derek Jeter 8.00
4 Randy Johnson 3.50
5 Greg Maddux 4.00
6 Hideki Matsui 6.00
7 Mike Piazza 4.00
8 Vladimir Guerrero 3.50
9 Sammy Sosa 5.00
10 Jim Thome 3.50
11 Chipper Jones 4.00
12 Alex Rodriguez 6.00
13 Roger Clemens 6.00
14 Nomar Garciaparra 6.00
15 Lance Berkman 3.50

Standouts Jersey

NM/M

Common Player: 10.00
Inserted 1:18
Patch: 1X-3X
Production 50 Sets

LB Lance Berkman 6.00
RC Roger Clemens 18.00
VG Vladimir Guerrero 10.00
RJ Randy Johnson 10.00
CJ Chipper Jones 12.00
GM Greg Maddux 12.00
HM Hideki Matsui 20.00
MP Mike Piazza 12.00
AP Albert Pujols 18.00
SS Sammy Sosa 15.00
JT Jim Thome 10.00

1990 LEAF

BOB TEWKSBURY P

NM/M

Complete Set (528): 80.00
Series 1 (264): 50.00
Series 2 (264): 25.00
Common Player: .10
Series 1 Foil Pack (15): 6.50
Series 1 Foil Box (36): 160.00
Series 2 Foil Pack (15): 2.50
Series 2 Foil Box (36): 60.00
1 Introductory card .10
2 Mike Henneman .10
3 Steve Bedrosian .10
4 Mike Scott .10
5 Allan Anderson .10
6 Rick Sutcliffe .10
7 Gregg Olson .10
8 Kevin Elster .10
9 Pete O'Brien .10
10 Carlton Fisk 1.00
11 Joe Magrane .10
12 Roger Clemens 2.50
13 Tom Glavine .35
14 Tom Gordon .10
15 Todd Benzinger .10
16 Hubie Brooks .10
17 Roberto Kelly .10
18 Barry Larkin .10
19 Mike Boddicker .10
20 Roger McDowell .10
21 Nolan Ryan 5.00
22 John Farrell .10
23 Bruce Hurst .10
24 Wally Joyner .10
25 Greg Maddux 2.00
26 Chris Bosio .10
27 John Cerutti .10
28 Tim Burke .10
29 Dennis Eckersley .75
30 Glenn Davis .10
31 Jim Abbott .10
32 Mike LaValliere .10

No.	Player	Price
33	Andres Thomas	.10
34	Lou Whitaker	.10
35	Alvin Davis	.10
36	Melido Perez	.10
37	Craig Biggio	.10
38	Rick Aguilera	.10
39	Pete Harnisch	.10
40	David Cone	.10
41	Scott Garrelts	.10
42	Jay Howell	.10
43	Eric King	.10
44	Pedro Guerrero	.10
45	Mike Bielecki	.10
46	Bob Boone	.10
47	Kevin Brown	.10
48	Jerry Browne	.10
49	Mike Scioscia	.10
50	Chuck Cary	.10
51	Wade Boggs	2.00
52	Von Hayes	.10
53	Tony Fernandez	.10
54	Dennis Martinez	.10
55	Tom Candiotti	.10
56	Andy Benes	.10
57	Rob Dibble	.10
58	Chuck Crim	.10
59	John Smoltz	.10
60	Mike Heath	.10
61	Kevin Gross	.10
62	Mark McGwire	3.50
63	Bert Blyleven	.10
64	Bob Walk	.10
65	Mickey Tettleton	.10
66	Sid Fernandez	.10
67	Terry Kennedy	.10
68	Fernando Valenzuela	.10
69	Don Mattingly	2.50
70	Paul O'Neill	.10
71	Robin Yount	1.00
72	Bret Saberhagen	.10
73	Geno Petralli	.10
74	Brook Jacoby	.10
75	Roberto Alomar	.25
76	Devon White	.10
77	Jose Lind	.10
78	Pat Combs	.10
79	Dave Steib	.10
80	Tim Wallach	.10
81	Dave Stewart	.10
82	*Eric Anthony*	.10
83	Randy Bush	.10
84	Checklist	.10
85	Jaime Navarro	.10
86	Tommy Gregg	.10
87	Frank Tanana	.10
88	Omar Vizquel	.10
89	Ivan Calderon	.10
90	Vince Coleman	.10
91	Barry Bonds	5.00
92	Randy Milligan	.10
93	Frank Viola	.10
94	Matt Williams	.10
95	Alfredo Griffin	.10
96	Steve Sax	.10
97	Gary Gaetti	.10
98	Ryne Sandberg	2.00
99	Danny Tartabull	.10
100	Rafael Palmeiro	1.00
101	Jesse Orosco	.10
102	Garry Templeton	.10
103	Frank DiPino	.10
104	Tony Pena	.10
105	Dickie Thon	.10
106	Kelly Gruber	.10
107	*Marquis Grissom*	2.00
108	Jose Canseco	.60
109	Mike Blowers	.10
110	Tom Browning	.10
111	Greg Vaughn	.10
112	Oddibe McDowell	.10
113	Gary Ward	.10
114	Jay Buhner	.10
115	Eric Show	.10
116	Bryan Harvey	.10
117	Andy Van Slyke	.10
118	Jeff Ballard	.10
119	Barry Lyons	.10
120	Kevin Mitchell	.10
121	Mike Gallego	.10
122	Dave Smith	.10
123	Kirby Puckett	2.00
124	Jerome Walton	.10
125	Bo Jackson	.20
126	Harold Baines	.10
127	Scott Bankhead	.10
128	Ozzie Guillen	.10
129	Jose Oquendo	.10
130	John Dopson	.10
131	Charlie Hayes	.10
132	Fred McGriff	.10
133	Chet Lemon	.10
134	Gary Carter	1.00
135	Rafael Ramirez	.10
136	Shane Mack	.10
137	Mark Grace	.10
138	Phil Bradley	.10
139	Dwight Gooden	.10
140	Harold Reynolds	.10
141	Scott Fletcher	.10
142	Ozzie Smith	2.00
143	Mike Greenwell	.10
144	Pete Smith	.10
145	Mark Gubicza	.10
146	Chris Sabo	.10
147	Ramon Martinez	.10
148	Tim Leary	.10
149	Randy Myers	.10
150	Jody Reed	.10
151	Bruce Ruffin	.10
152	Jeff Russell	.10
153	Doug Jones	.10
154	Tony Gwynn	2.00
155	Mark Langston	.10
156	Mitch Williams	.10
157	Gary Sheffield	.60
158	Tom Henke	.10
159	Oil Can Boyd	.10
160	Rickey Henderson	1.00
161	Bill Doran	.10
162	Chuck Finley	.10
163	Jeff King	.10
164	Nick Esasky	.10
165	Cecil Fielder	.10
166	Dave Valle	.10
167	Robin Ventura	.10
168	Jim Deshaies	.10
169	Juan Berenguer	.10
170	Craig Worthington	.10
171	Gregg Jefferies	.10
172	Will Clark	.10
173	Kirk Gibson	.10
174	Checklist	.10
175	Bobby Thigpen	.10
176	John Tudor	.10
177	Andre Dawson	.35
178	George Brett	2.50
179	Steve Buechele	.10
180	Albert Belle	.10
181	Eddie Murray	1.00
182	Bob Geren	.10
183	Rob Murphy	.10
184	Tom Herr	.10
185	George Bell	.10
186	Spike Owen	.10
187	Cory Snyder	.10
188	Fred Lynn	.10
189	Eric Davis	.10
190	Dave Parker	.10
191	Jeff Blauser	.10
192	Matt Nokes	.10
193	*Delino DeShields*	.50
194	Scott Sanderson	.10
195	Lance Parrish	.10
196	Bobby Bonilla	.10
197	Cal Ripken, Jr.	5.00
198	Kevin McReynolds	.10
199	Robby Thompson	.10
200	Tim Belcher	.10
201	Jesse Barfield	.10
202	Mariano Duncan	.10
203	Bill Spiers	.10
204	Frank White	.10
205	Julio Franco	.10
206	Greg Swindell	.10
207	Benito Santiago	.10
208	Johnny Ray	.10
209	Gary Redus	.10
210	Jeff Parrett	.10
211	Jimmy Key	.10
212	Tim Raines	.10
213	Carney Lansford	.10
214	Gerald Young	.10
215	Gene Larkin	.10
216	Dan Plesac	.10
217	Lonnie Smith	.10
218	Alan Trammell	.10
219	Jeffrey Leonard	.10
220	*Sammy Sosa*	30.00
221	Todd Zeile	.10
222	Bill Landrum	.10
223	Mike Devereaux	.10
224	Mike Marshall	.10
225	Jose Uribe	.10
226	Juan Samuel	.10
227	Mel Hall	.10
228	Kent Hrbek	.10
229	Shawon Dunston	.10
230	Kevin Seitzer	.10
231	Pete Incaviglia	.10
232	Sandy Alomar	.10
233	Bip Roberts	.10
234	Scott Terry	.10
235	Dwight Evans	.10
236	Ricky Jordan	.10
237	*John Olerud*	5.00
238	Zane Smith	.10
239	Walt Weiss	.10
240	Alvaro Espinoza	.10
241	Billy Hatcher	.10
242	Paul Molitor	1.00
243	Dale Murphy	.30
244	Dave Bergman	.10
245	Ken Griffey, Jr.	3.00
246	Ed Whitson	.10
247	Kirk McCaskill	.10
248	Jay Bell	.10
249	*Ben McDonald*	.50
250	Darryl Strawberry	.10
251	Brett Butler	.10
252	Terry Steinbach	.10
253	Ken Caminiti	.10
254	Dan Gladden	.10
255	Dwight Smith	.10
256	Kurt Stillwell	.10
257	Ruben Sierra	.10
258	Mike Schooler	.10
259	Lance Johnson	.10
260	Terry Pendleton	.10
261	Ellis Burks	.10
262	Len Dykstra	.10
263	Mookie Wilson	.10
264	Checklist (Nolan Ryan)	.10
265	Nolan Ryan (No-Hit King)	2.00
266	Brian DuBois	.10
267	Don Robinson	.10
268	Glenn Wilson	.10
269	*Kevin Tapani*	.25
270	Marvell Wynne	.10
271	Billy Ripken	.10
272	Howard Johnson	.10
273	Brian Holman	.10
274	Dan Pasqua	.10
275	Ken Dayley	.10
276	Jeff Reardon	.10
277	Jim Presley	.10
278	Jim Eisenreich	.10
279	Danny Jackson	.10
280	Orel Hershiser	.10
281	Andy Hawkins	.10
282	Jose Rijo	.10
283	Luis Rivera	.10
284	John Kruk	.10
285	Jeff Huson	.10
286	Joel Skinner	.10
287	Jack Clark	.10
288	Chili Davis	.10
289	Joe Girardi	.10
290	B.J. Surhoff	.10
291	Luis Sojo	.10
292	Tom Foley	.10
293	Mike Moore	.10
294	Ken Oberkfell	.10
295	Luis Polonia	.10
296	Doug Drabek	.10
297	*Dave Justice*	2.00
298	Paul Gibson	.10
299	Edgar Martinez	.10
300	*Frank Thomas*	12.00
301	Eric Yelding	.10
302	Greg Gagne	.10
303	Brad Komminsk	.10
304	Ron Darling	.10
305	Kevin Bass	.10
306	Jeff Hamilton	.10
307	Ron Karkovice	.10
308	Milt Thompson	.10
309	Mike Harkey	.10
310	Mel Stottlemyre	.10
311	Kenny Rogers	.10
312	Mitch Webster	.10
313	Kal Daniels	.10
314	Matt Nokes	.10
315	Dennis Lamp	.10
316	Ken Howell	.10
317	Glenallen Hill	.10
318	Dave Martinez	.10
319	Chris James	.10
320	Mike Pagliarulo	.10
321	Hal Morris	.10
322	Rob Deer	.10
323	Greg Olson	.10
324	Tony Phillips	.10
325	*Larry Walker*	8.00
326	Ron Hassey	.10
327	Jack Howell	.10
328	John Smiley	.10
329	Steve Finley	.10
330	Dave Magadan	.10
331	Greg Litton	.10
332	Mickey Hatcher	.10
333	Lee Guetterman	.10
334	Norm Charlton	.10
335	Edgar Diaz	.10
336	Willie Wilson	.10
337	Bobby Witt	.10
338	Candy Maldonado	.10
339	Craig Lefferts	.10
340	Dante Bichette	.10
341	Wally Backman	.10
342	Dennis Cook	.10
343	Pat Borders	.10
344	Wallace Johnson	.10
345	Willie Randolph	.10
346	Danny Darwin	.10
347	Al Newman	.10
348	Mark Knudson	.10
349	Joe Boever	.10
350	Larry Sheets	.10
351	Mike Jackson	.10
352	Wayne Edwards	.10
353	*Bernard Gilkey*	.50
354	Don Slaught	.10
355	Joe Orsulak	.10
356	John Franco	.10
357	Jeff Brantley	.10
358	Mike Morgan	.10
359	Deion Sanders	.10
360	Terry Leach	.10
361	Les Lancaster	.10
362	Storm Davis	.10
363	Scott Coolbaugh	.10
364	Checklist	.10
365	Cecilio Guante	.10
366	Joey Cora	.10
367	Willie McGee	.10
368	Jerry Reed	.10
369	Darren Daulton	.10
370	Manny Lee	.10
371	Mark Gardner	.10
372	Rick Honeycutt	.10
373	Steve Balboni	.10
374	Jack Armstrong	.10
375	Charlie O'Brien	.10
376	Ron Gant	.10
377	Lloyd Moseby	.10
378	Gene Harris	.10
379	Joe Carter	.10
380	Scott Bailes	.10
381	R.J. Reynolds	.10
382	Bob Melvin	.10
383	Tim Teufel	.10
384	John Burkett	.10
385	Felix Jose	.10
386	Larry Andersen	.10
387	David West	.10
388	Luis Salazar	.10
389	Mike Macfarlane	.10
390	Charlie Hough	.10
391	Greg Briley	.10
392	Donn Pall	.10
393	Bryn Smith	.10
394	Carlos Quintana	.10
395	Steve Lake	.10
396	*Mark Whiten*	.15
397	Edwin Nunez	.10
398	Rick Parker	.10
399	Mark Portugal	.10
400	Roy Smith	.10
401	Hector Villanueva	.10
402	Bob Milacki	.10
403	Alejandro Pena	.10
404	Scott Bradley	.10
405	Ron Kittle	.10
406	Bob Tewksbury	.10
407	Wes Gardner	.10
408	Ernie Whitt	.10
409	Terry Shumpert	.10
410	Tim Layana	.10
411	Chris Gwynn	.10
412	Jeff Robinson	.10
413	Scott Scudder	.10
414	Kevin Romine	.10
415	Jose DeJesus	.10
416	Mike Jeffcoat	.10
417	Rudy Seanez	.10
418	Mike Dunne	.10
419	Dick Schofield	.10
420	Steve Wilson	.10
421	Bill Krueger	.10
422	Junior Felix	.10
423	Drew Hall	.10
424	Curt Young	.10
425	Franklin Stubbs	.10
426	Dave Winfield	1.00
427	Rick Reed	.10

428	Charlie Leibrandt	.10
429	Jeff Robinson	.10
430	Erik Hanson	.10
431	Barry Jones	.10
432	Alex Trevino	.10
433	John Moses	.10
434	Dave Johnson	.10
435	Mackey Sasser	.10
436	Rick Leach	.10
437	Lenny Harris	.10
438	Carlos Martinez	.10
439	Rex Hudler	.10
440	Domingo Ramos	.10
441	Gerald Perry	.10
442	John Russell	.10
443	*Carlos Baerga*	.50
444	Checklist	.10
445	Stan Javier	.10
446	*Kevin Maas*	.10
447	Tom Brunansky	.10
448	Carmelo Martinez	.10
449	*Willie Blair*	.10
450	Andres Galarraga	.10
451	Bud Black	.10
452	Greg Harris	.10
453	Joe Oliver	.10
454	Greg Brock	.10
455	Jeff Treadway	.10
456	Lance McCullers	.10
457	Dave Schmidt	.10
458	Todd Burns	.10
459	Max Venable	.10
460	Neal Heaton	.10
461	Mark Williamson	.10
462	Keith Miller	.10
463	Mike LaCoss	.10
464	*Jose Offerman*	.25
465	*Jim Leyritz*	.50
466	Glenn Braggs	.10
467	Ron Robinson	.10
468	Mark Davis	.10
469	Gary Pettis	.10
470	Keith Hernandez	.10
471	Dennis Rasmussen	.10
472	Mark Eichhorn	.10
473	Ted Power	.10
474	Terry Mulholland	.10
475	Todd Stottlemyre	.10
476	Jerry Goff	.10
477	Gene Nelson	.10
478	Rich Gedman	.10
479	Brian Harper	.10
480	Mike Felder	.10
481	Steve Avery	.10
482	Jack Morris	.10
483	Randy Johnson	1.00
484	Scott Radinsky	.10
485	Jose DeLeon	.10
486	*Stan Belinda*	.10
487	Brian Holton	.10
488	Mark Carreon	.10
489	Trevor Wilson	.10
490	Mike Sharperson	.10
491	*Alan Mills*	.10
492	John Candelaria	.10
493	Paul Assenmacher	.10
494	Steve Crawford	.10
495	Brad Arnsberg	.10
496	Sergio Valdez	.10
497	Mark Parent	.10
498	Tom Pagnozzi	.10
499	Greg Harris	.10
500	Randy Ready	.10
501	Duane Ward	.10
502	Nelson Santovenia	.10
503	Joe Klink	.10
504	Eric Plunk	.10
505	Jeff Reed	.10
506	Ted Higuera	.10
507	Joe Hesketh	.10
508	Dan Petry	.10
509	Matt Young	.10
510	Jerald Clark	.10
511	*John Orton*	.10
512	Scott Ruskin	.10
513	*Chris Hoiles*	.50
514	Daryl Boston	.10
515	Francisco Oliveras	.10
516	Ozzie Canseco	.10
517	*Xavier Hernandez*	.10
518	Fred Manrique	.10
519	Shawn Boskie	.10
520	Jeff Montgomery	.10
521	Jack Daugherty	.10
522	Keith Comstock	.10
523	*Greg Hibbard*	.10
524	Lee Smith	.10
525	Dana Kiecker	.10
526	Darrel Akerfelds	.10
527	Greg Myers	.10
528	Checklist	.10

1991 LEAF

		NM/M
Complete Set (528):		8.00
Common Player:		.05
Series 1 or 2 Pack (15):		.50
Series 1 or 2 Box (36):		12.50
1	The Leaf Card	.05
2	Kurt Stillwell	.05
3	Bobby Witt	.05
4	Tony Phillips	.05
5	Scott Garrelts	.05
6	Greg Swindell	.05
7	Billy Ripken	.05
8	Dave Martinez	.05
9	Kelly Gruber	.05
10	Juan Samuel	.05
11	Brian Holman	.05
12	Craig Biggio	.05
13	Lonnie Smith	.05
14	Ron Robinson	.05
15	Mike LaValliere	.05
16	Mark Davis	.05
17	Jack Daugherty	.05
18	Mike Henneman	.05
19	Mike Greenwell	.05
20	Dave Magadan	.05
21	Mark Williamson	.05
22	Marquis Grissom	.05
23	Pat Borders	.05
24	Mike Scioscia	.05
25	Shawon Dunston	.05
26	Randy Bush	.05
27	John Smoltz	.05
28	Chuck Crim	.05
29	Don Slaught	.05
30	Mike Macfarlane	.05
31	Wally Joyner	.05
32	Pat Combs	.05
33	Tony Pena	.05
34	Howard Johnson	.05
35	Leo Gomez	.05
36	Spike Owen	.05
37	Eric Davis	.05
38	Roberto Kelly	.05
39	Jerome Walton	.05
40	Shane Mack	.05
41	Kent Mercker	.05
42	B.J. Surhoff	.05
43	Jerry Browne	.05
44	Lee Smith	.05
45	Chuck Finley	.05
46	Terry Mulholland	.05
47	Tom Bolton	.05
48	Tom Herr	.05
49	Jim Deshaies	.05
50	Walt Weiss	.05
51	Hal Morris	.05
52	Lee Guetterman	.05
53	Paul Assenmacher	.05
54	Brian Harper	.05
55	Paul Gibson	.05
56	John Burkett	.05
57	Doug Jones	.05
58	Jose Oquendo	.05
59	Dick Schofield	.05
60	Dickie Thon	.05
61	Ramon Martinez	.05
62	Jay Buhner	.05
63	Mark Portugal	.05
64	Bob Welch	.05
65	Chris Sabo	.05
66	Chuck Cary	.05
67	Mark Langston	.05
68	Joe Boever	.05
69	Jody Reed	.05
70	Alejandro Pena	.05
71	Jeff King	.05
72	Tom Pagnozzi	.05
73	Joe Oliver	.05
74	Mike Witt	.05
75	Hector Villanueva	.05
76	Dan Gladden	.05
77	Dave Justice	.05
78	Mike Gallego	.05
79	Tom Candiotti	.05
80	Ozzie Smith	.60
81	Luis Polonia	.05
82	Randy Ready	.05
83	Greg Harris	.05
84	Dave Justice Checklist	.05
85	Kevin Mitchell	.05
86	Mark McLemore	.05
87	Terry Steinbach	.05
88	Tom Browning	.05
89	Matt Nokes	.05
90	Mike Harkey	.05
91	Omar Vizquel	.05
92	Dave Bergman	.05
93	Matt Williams	.05
94	Steve Olin	.05
95	Craig Wilson	.05
96	Dave Stieb	.05
97	Ruben Sierra	.05
98	Jay Howell	.05
99	Scott Bradley	.05
100	Eric Yelding	.05
101	Rickey Henderson	.45
102	Jeff Reed	.05
103	Jimmy Key	.05
104	Terry Shumpert	.05
105	Kenny Rogers	.05
106	Cecil Fielder	.05
107	Robby Thompson	.05
108	Alex Cole	.05
109	Randy Milligan	.05
110	Andres Galarraga	.05
111	Bill Spiers	.05
112	Kal Daniels	.05
113	Henry Cotto	.05
114	Casy Candaele	.05
115	Jeff Blauser	.05
116	Robin Yount	.45
117	Ben McDonald	.05
118	Bret Saberhagen	.05
119	Juan Gonzalez	.35
120	Lou Whitaker	.05
121	Ellis Burks	.05
122	Charlie O'Brien	.05
123	John Smiley	.05
124	Tim Burke	.05
125	John Olerud	.05
126	Eddie Murray	.45
127	Greg Maddux	.60
128	Kevin Tapani	.05
129	Ron Gant	.05
130	Jay Bell	.05
131	Chris Hoiles	.05
132	Tom Gordon	.05
133	Kevin Seitzer	.05
134	Jeff Huson	.05
135	Jerry Don Gleaton	.05
136	Jeff Brantley	.05
137	Felix Fermin	.05
138	Mike Devereaux	.05
139	Delino DeShields	.05
140	David Wells	.05
141	Tim Crews	.05
142	Erik Hanson	.05
143	Mark Davidson	.05
144	Tommy Gregg	.05
145	Jim Gantner	.05
146	Jose Lind	.05
147	Danny Tartabull	.05
148	Geno Petralli	.05
149	Travis Fryman	.05
150	Tim Naehring	.05
151	Kevin McReynolds	.05
152	Joe Orsulak	.05
153	Steve Frey	.05
154	Duane Ward	.05
155	Stan Javier	.05
156	Damon Berryhill	.05
157	Gene Larkin	.05
158	Greg Olson	.05
159	Mark Knudson	.05
160	Carmelo Martinez	.05
161	Storm Davis	.05
162	Jim Abbott	.05
163	Len Dykstra	.05
164	Tom Brunansky	.05
165	Dwight Gooden	.05
166	Jose Mesa	.05
167	Oil Can Boyd	.05
168	Barry Larkin	.05
169	Scott Sanderson	.05
170	Mark Grace	.05
171	Mark Guthrie	.05
172	Tom Glavine	.15
173	Gary Sheffield	.30
174	Roger Clemens Checklist	.25
175	Chris James	.05
176	Milt Thompson	.05
177	Donnie Hill	.05
178	Wes Chamberlain	.05
179	John Marzano	.05
180	Frank Viola	.05
181	Eric Anthony	.05
182	Jose Canseco	.30
183	Scott Scudder	.05
184	Dave Eiland	.05
185	Luis Salazar	.05
186	Pedro Munoz	.05
187	Steve Searcy	.05
188	Don Robinson	.05
189	Sandy Alomar	.05
190	Jose DeLeon	.05
191	John Orton	.05
192	Darren Daulton	.05
193	Mike Morgan	.05
194	Greg Briley	.05
195	Karl Rhodes	.05
196	Harold Baines	.05
197	Bill Doran	.05
198	Alvaro Espinoza	.05
199	Kirk McCaskill	.05
200	Jose DeJesus	.05
201	Jack Clark	.05
202	Daryl Boston	.05
203	Randy Tomlin	.05
204	Pedro Guerrero	.05
205	Billy Hatcher	.05
206	Tim Leary	.05
207	Ryne Sandberg	.60
208	Kirby Puckett	.60
209	Charlie Leibrandt	.05
210	Rick Honeycutt	.05
211	Joel Skinner	.05
212	Rex Hudler	.05
213	Bryan Harvey	.05
214	Charlie Hayes	.05
215	Matt Young	.05
216	Terry Kennedy	.05
217	Carl Nichols	.05
218	Mike Moore	.05
219	Paul O'Neill	.05
220	Steve Sax	.05
221	Shawn Boskie	.05
222	Rich DeLucia	.05
223	Lloyd Moseby	.05
224	Mike Kingery	.05
225	Carlos Baerga	.05
226	Bryn Smith	.05
227	Todd Stottlemyre	.05
228	Julio Franco	.05
229	Jim Gott	.05
230	Mike Schooler	.05
231	Steve Finley	.05
232	Dave Henderson	.05
233	Luis Quinones	.05
234	Mark Whiten	.05
235	Brian McRae	.05
236	Rich Gossage	.05
237	Rob Deer	.05
238	Will Clark	.10
239	Albert Belle	.05
240	Bob Melvin	.05
241	Larry Walker	.05
242	Dante Bichette	.05
243	Orel Hershiser	.05
244	Pete O'Brien	.05
245	Pete Harnisch	.05
246	Jeff Treadway	.05
247	Julio Machado	.05
248	Dave Johnson	.05
249	Kirk Gibson	.05
250	Kevin Brown	.05
251	Milt Cuyler	.05
252	Jeff Reardon	.05
253	David Cone	.05
254	Gary Redus	.05
255	Junior Noboa	.05
256	Greg Myers	.05
257	Dennis Cook	.05
258	Joe Girardi	.05
259	Allan Anderson	.05
260	Paul Marak	.05
261	Barry Bonds	2.00
262	Juan Bell	.05
263	Russ Morman	.05
264	George Brett Checklist	.25
265	Jerald Clark	.05
266	Dwight Evans	.05
267	Roberto Alomar	.15
268	Danny Jackson	.05

#	Player	Price
269	Brian Downing	.05
270	John Cerutti	.05
271	Robin Ventura	.05
272	Gerald Perry	.05
273	Wade Boggs	.60
274	Dennis Martinez	.05
275	Andy Benes	.05
276	Tony Fossas	.05
277	Franklin Stubbs	.05
278	John Kruk	.05
279	Kevin Gross	.05
280	Von Hayes	.05
281	Frank Thomas	.45
282	Rob Dibble	.05
283	Mel Hall	.05
284	Rick Mahler	.05
285	Dennis Eckersley	.35
286	Bernard Gilkey	.05
287	Dan Plesac	.05
288	Jason Grimsley	.05
289	Mark Lewis	.05
290	Tony Gwynn	.60
291	Jeff Russell	.05
292	Curt Schilling	.25
293	Pascual Perez	.05
294	Jack Morris	.05
295	Hubie Brooks	.05
296	Alex Fernandez	.05
297	Harold Reynolds	.05
298	Craig Worthington	.05
299	Willie Wilson	.05
300	Mike Maddux	.05
301	Dave Righetti	.05
302	Paul Molitor	.45
303	Gary Gaetti	.05
304	Terry Pendleton	.05
305	Kevin Elster	.05
306	Scott Fletcher	.05
307	Jeff Robinson	.05
308	Jesse Barfield	.05
309	Mike LaCoss	.05
310	Andy Van Slyke	.05
311	Glenallen Hill	.05
312	Bud Black	.05
313	Kent Hrbek	.05
314	Tim Teufel	.05
315	Tony Fernandez	.05
316	Beau Allred	.05
317	Curtis Wilkerson	.05
318	Bill Sampen	.05
319	Randy Johnson	.45
320	Mike Heath	.05
321	Sammy Sosa	1.00
322	Mickey Tettleton	.05
323	Jose Vizcaino	.05
324	John Candelaria	.05
325	David Howard	.05
326	Jose Rijo	.05
327	Todd Zeile	.05
328	Gene Nelson	.05
329	Dwayne Henry	.05
330	Mike Boddicker	.05
331	Ozzie Guillen	.05
332	Sam Horn	.05
333	Wally Whitehurst	.05
334	Dave Parker	.05
335	George Brett	.75
336	Bobby Thigpen	.05
337	Ed Whitson	.05
338	Ivan Calderon	.05
339	Mike Pagliarulo	.05
340	Jack McDowell	.05
341	Dana Kiecker	.05
342	Fred McGriff	.05
343	Mark Lee	.05
344	Alfredo Griffin	.05
345	Scott Bankhead	.05
346	Darrin Jackson	.05
347	Rafael Palmeiro	.35
348	Steve Farr	.05
349	Hensley Meulens	.05
350	Danny Cox	.05
351	Alan Trammell	.05
352	Edwin Nunez	.05
353	Joe Carter	.05
354	Eric Show	.05
355	Vance Law	.05
356	Jeff Gray	.05
357	Bobby Bonilla	.05
358	Ernest Riles	.05
359	Ron Hassey	.05
360	Willie McGee	.05
361	Mackey Sasser	.05
362	Glenn Braggs	.05
363	Mario Diaz	.05
364	Barry Bonds Checklist	.35
365	Kevin Bass	.05
366	Pete Incaviglia	.05
367	Luis Sojo	.05
368	Lance Parrish	.05
369	Mark Leonard	.05
370	Heathcliff Slocumb	.05
371	Jimmy Jones	.05
372	Ken Griffey, Jr.	1.00
373	Chris Hammond	.05
374	Chili Davis	.05
375	Joey Cora	.05
376	Ken Hill	.05
377	Darryl Strawberry	.05
378	Ron Darling	.05
379	Sid Bream	.05
380	Bill Swift	.05
381	Shawn Abner	.05
382	Eric King	.05
383	Mickey Morandini	.05
384	Carlton Fisk	.45
385	Steve Lake	.05
386	Mike Jeffcoat	.05
387	Darren Holmes	.05
388	Tim Wallach	.05
389	George Bell	.05
390	Craig Lefferts	.05
391	Ernie Whitt	.05
392	Felix Jose	.05
393	Kevin Maas	.05
394	Devon White	.05
395	Otis Nixon	.05
396	Chuck Knoblauch	.05
397	Scott Coolbaugh	.05
398	Glenn Davis	.05
399	Manny Lee	.05
400	Andre Dawson	.20
401	Scott Chiamparino	.05
402	Bill Gullickson	.05
403	Lance Johnson	.05
404	Juan Agosto	.05
405	Danny Darwin	.05
406	Barry Jones	.05
407	Larry Andersen	.05
408	Luis Rivera	.05
409	Jaime Navarro	.05
410	Roger McDowell	.05
411	Brett Butler	.05
412	Dale Murphy	.15
413	Tim Raines	.05
414	Norm Charlton	.05
415	Greg Cadaret	.05
416	Chris Nabholz	.05
417	Dave Stewart	.05
418	Rich Gedman	.05
419	Willie Randolph	.05
420	Mitch Williams	.05
421	Brook Jacoby	.05
422	Greg Harris	.05
423	Nolan Ryan	2.00
424	Dave Rohde	.05
425	Don Mattingly	.75
426	Greg Gagne	.05
427	Vince Coleman	.05
428	Dan Pasqua	.05
429	Alvin Davis	.05
430	Cal Ripken, Jr.	2.00
431	Jamie Quirk	.05
432	Benito Santiago	.05
433	Jose Uribe	.05
434	Candy Maldonado	.05
435	Junior Felix	.05
436	Deion Sanders	.05
437	John Franco	.05
438	Greg Hibbard	.05
439	Floyd Bannister	.05
440	Steve Howe	.05
441	Steve Decker	.05
442	Vicente Palacios	.05
443	Pat Tabler	.05
444	Darryl Strawberry Checklist	.05
445	Mike Felder	.05
446	Al Newman	.05
447	Chris Donnels	.05
448	Rich Rodriguez	.05
449	Turner Ward	.05
450	Bob Walk	.05
451	Gilberto Reyes	.05
452	Mike Jackson	.05
453	Rafael Belliard	.05
454	Wayne Edwards	.05
455	Andy Allanson	.05
456	Dave Smith	.05
457	Gary Carter	.45
458	Warren Cromartie	.05
459	Jack Armstrong	.05
460	Bob Tewksbury	.05
461	Joe Klink	.05
462	Xavier Hernandez	.05
463	Scott Radinsky	.05
464	Jeff Robinson	.05
465	Gregg Jefferies	.05
466	Denny Neagle	.05
467	Carmelo Martinez	.05
468	Donn Pall	.05
469	Bruce Hurst	.05
470	Eric Bullock	.05
471	Rick Aguilera	.05
472	Charlie Hough	.05
473	Carlos Quintana	.05
474	Marty Barrett	.05
475	Kevin Brown	.05
476	Bobby Ojeda	.05
477	Edgar Martinez	.05
478	Bip Roberts	.05
479	Mike Flanagan	.05
480	John Habyan	.05
481	Larry Casian	.05
482	Wally Backman	.05
483	Doug Dascenzo	.05
484	Rick Dempsey	.05
485	Ed Sprague	.05
486	Steve Chitren	.05
487	Mark McGwire	1.50
488	Roger Clemens	.75
489	Orlando Merced	.05
490	Rene Gonzales	.05
491	Mike Stanton	.05
492	Al Osuna	.05
493	Rick Cerone	.05
494	Mariano Duncan	.05
495	Zane Smith	.05
496	John Morris	.05
497	Frank Tanana	.05
498	Junior Ortiz	.05
499	Dave Winfield	.45
500	Gary Varsho	.05
501	Chico Walker	.05
502	Ken Caminiti	.05
503	Ken Griffey, Sr.	.05
504	Randy Myers	.05
505	Steve Bedrosian	.05
506	Cory Snyder	.05
507	Cris Carpenter	.05
508	Tim Belcher	.05
509	Jeff Hamilton	.05
510	Steve Avery	.05
511	Dave Valle	.05
512	Tom Lampkin	.05
513	Shawn Hillegas	.05
514	Reggie Jefferson	.05
515	Ron Karkovice	.05
516	Doug Drabek	.05
517	Tom Henke	.05
518	Chris Bosio	.05
519	Gregg Olson	.05
520	Bob Scanlan	.05
521	Alonzo Powell	.05
522	Jeff Ballard	.05
523	Ray Lankford	.05
524	Tommy Greene	.05
525	Mike Timlin	.05
526	Juan Berenguer	.05
527	Scott Erickson	.05
528	Sandy Alomar Jr. Checklist	.05

Gold Rookies

		NM/M
Complete Set (26):		10.00
Common Player:		.10
1	Scott Leius	.10
2	Luis Gonzalez	.40
3	Wil Cordero	.10
4	Gary Scott	.10
5	Willie Banks	.10
6	Arthur Rhodes	.10
7	Mo Vaughn	.25
8	Henry Rodriguez	.10
9	Todd Van Poppel	.10
10	Reggie Sanders	.10
11	Rico Brogna	.10
12	Mike Mussina	2.00
13	Kirk Dressendorfer	.10
14	Jeff Bagwell	6.00
15	Pete Schourek	.10
16	Wade Taylor	.10
17	Pat Kelly	.10
18	Tim Costo	.10
19	Roger Salkeld	.10
20	Andujar Cedeno	.10
21	Ryan Klesko	.10
22	Mike Huff	.10
23	Anthony Young	.10
24	Eddie Zosky	.10
25	Nolan Ryan (7th no-hitter)	.50
26	Rickey Henderson (record steal)	.25
	Babe Ruth Plooey	.01
265	Scott Leius	4.00
266	Luis Gonzalez	6.00
267	Wil Cordero	4.00
268	Gary Scott	4.00
269	Willie Banks	4.00
270	Arthur Rhodes	4.00
271	Mo Vaughn	10.00
272	Henry Rodriguez	4.00
273	Todd Van Poppel	4.00
274	Reggie Sanders	4.00
275	Rico Brogna	4.00
276	Mike Mussina	30.00

1992 LEAF

		NM/M
Complete Set (528):		7.50
Common Player:		.05
Series 1 or 2 Pack:		.40
Series 1 or 2 Wax Box:		7.50
1	Jim Abbott	.05
2	Cal Eldred	.05
3	Bud Black	.05
4	Dave Howard	.05
5	Luis Sojo	.05
6	Gary Scott	.05
7	Joe Oliver	.05
8	Chris Gardner	.05
9	Sandy Alomar	.05
10	Greg Harris	.05
11	Doug Drabek	.05
12	Darryl Hamilton	.05
13	Mike Mussina	.30
14	Kevin Tapani	.05
15	Ron Gant	.05
16	Mark McGwire	1.00
17	Robin Ventura	.05
18	Pedro Guerrero	.05
19	Roger Clemens	.65
20	Steve Farr	.05
21	Frank Tanana	.05
22	Joe Hesketh	.05
23	Erik Hanson	.05
24	Greg Cadaret	.05
25	Rex Hudler	.05
26	Mark Grace	.05
27	Kelly Gruber	.05
28	Jeff Bagwell	.45
29	Darryl Strawberry	.05
30	Dave Smith	.05
31	Kevin Appier	.05
32	Steve Chitren	.05
33	Kevin Gross	.05
34	Rick Aguilera	.05
35	Juan Guzman	.05
36	Joe Orsulak	.05
37	Tim Raines	.05
38	Harold Reynolds	.05
39	Charlie Hough	.05
40	Tony Phillips	.05
41	Nolan Ryan	1.50

No.	Player	Price
42	Vince Coleman	.05
43	Andy Van Slyke	.05
44	Tim Burke	.05
45	Luis Polonia	.05
46	Tom Browning	.05
47	Willie McGee	.05
48	Gary DiSarcina	.05
49	Mark Lewis	.05
50	Phil Plantier	.05
51	Doug Dascenzo	.05
52	Cal Ripken, Jr.	1.50
53	Pedro Munoz	.05
54	Carlos Hernandez	.05
55	Jerald Clark	.05
56	Jeff Brantley	.05
57	Don Mattingly	.65
58	Roger McDowell	.05
59	Steve Avery	.05
60	John Olerud	.05
61	Bill Gullickson	.05
62	Juan Gonzalez	.30
63	Felix Jose	.05
64	Robin Yount	.45
65	Greg Briley	.05
66	Steve Finley	.05
67	Checklist	.05
68	Tom Gordon	.05
69	Rob Dibble	.05
70	Glenallen Hill	.05
71	Calvin Jones	.05
72	Joe Girardi	.05
73	Barry Larkin	.05
74	Andy Benes	.05
75	Milt Cuyler	.05
76	Kevin Bass	.05
77	Pete Harnisch	.05
78	Wilson Alvarez	.05
79	Mike Devereaux	.05
80	Doug Henry	.05
81	Orel Hershiser	.05
82	Shane Mack	.05
83	Mike Macfarlane	.05
84	Thomas Howard	.05
85	Alex Fernandez	.05
86	Reggie Jefferson	.05
87	Leo Gomez	.05
88	Mel Hall	.05
89	Mike Greenwell	.05
90	Jeff Russell	.05
91	Steve Buechele	.05
92	David Cone	.05
93	Kevin Reimer	.05
94	Mark Lemke	.05
95	Bob Tewksbury	.05
96	Zane Smith	.05
97	Mark Eichhorn	.05
98	Kirby Puckett	.60
99	Paul O'Neill	.05
100	Dennis Eckersley	.35
101	Duane Ward	.05
102	Matt Nokes	.05
103	Mo Vaughn	.05
104	Pat Kelly	.05
105	Ron Karkovice	.05
106	Bill Spiers	.05
107	Gary Gaetti	.05
108	Mackey Sasser	.05
109	Robby Thompson	.05
110	Marvin Freeman	.05
111	Jimmy Key	.05
112	Dwight Gooden	.05
113	Charlie Leibrandt	.05
114	Devon White	.05
115	Charles Nagy	.05
116	Rickey Henderson	.45
117	Paul Assenmacher	.05
118	Junior Felix	.05
119	Julio Franco	.05
120	Norm Charlton	.05
121	Scott Servais	.05
122	Gerald Perry	.05
123	Brian McRae	.05
124	Don Slaught	.05
125	Juan Samuel	.05
126	Harold Baines	.05
127	Scott Livingstone	.05
128	Jay Buhner	.05
129	Darrin Jackson	.05
130	Luis Mercedes	.05
131	Brian Harper	.05
132	Howard Johnson	.05
133	Checklist	.05
134	Dante Bichette	.05
135	Dave Righetti	.05
136	Jeff Montgomery	.05
137	Joe Grahe	.05
138	Delino DeShields	.05
139	Jose Rijo	.05
140	Ken Caminiti	.05
141	Steve Olin	.05
142	Kurt Stillwell	.05
143	Jay Bell	.05
144	Jaime Navarro	.05
145	Ben McDonald	.05
146	Greg Gagne	.05
147	Jeff Blauser	.05
148	Carney Lansford	.05
149	Ozzie Guillen	.05
150	Milt Thompson	.05
151	Jeff Reardon	.05
152	Scott Sanderson	.05
153	Cecil Fielder	.05
154	Greg Harris	.05
155	Rich DeLucia	.05
156	Roberto Kelly	.05
157	Bryn Smith	.05
158	Chuck McElroy	.05
159	Tom Henke	.05
160	Luis Gonzalez	.25
161	Steve Wilson	.05
162	Shawn Boskie	.05
163	Mark Davis	.05
164	Mike Moore	.05
165	Mike Scioscia	.05
166	Scott Erickson	.05
167	Todd Stottlemyre	.05
168	Alvin Davis	.05
169	Greg Hibbard	.05
170	David Valle	.05
171	Dave Winfield	.45
172	Alan Trammell	.05
173	Kenny Rogers	.05
174	John Franco	.05
175	Jose Lind	.05
176	Pete Schourek	.05
177	Von Hayes	.05
178	Chris Hammond	.05
179	John Burkett	.05
180	Dickie Thon	.05
181	Joel Skinner	.05
182	Scott Cooper	.05
183	Andre Dawson	.25
184	Billy Ripken	.05
185	Kevin Mitchell	.05
186	Brett Butler	.05
187	Tony Fernandez	.05
188	Cory Snyder	.05
189	John Habyan	.05
190	Dennis Martinez	.05
191	John Smoltz	.05
192	Greg Myers	.05
193	Rob Deer	.05
194	Ivan Rodriguez	.45
195	Ray Lankford	.05
196	Bill Wegman	.05
197	Edgar Martinez	.05
198	Darryl Kile	.05
199	Checklist	.05
200	Brent Mayne	.05
201	Larry Walker	.05
202	Carlos Baerga	.05
203	Russ Swan	.05
204	Mike Morgan	.05
205	Hal Morris	.05
206	Tony Gwynn	.60
207	Mark Leiter	.05
208	Kirt Manwaring	.05
209	Al Osuna	.05
210	Bobby Thigpen	.05
211	Chris Hoiles	.05
212	B.J. Surhoff	.05
213	Lenny Harris	.05
214	Scott Leius	.05
215	Gregg Jefferies	.05
216	Bruce Hurst	.05
217	Steve Sax	.05
218	Dave Otto	.05
219	Sam Horn	.05
220	Charlie Hayes	.05
221	Frank Viola	.05
222	Jose Guzman	.05
223	Gary Redus	.05
224	Dave Gallagher	.05
225	Dean Palmer	.05
226	Greg Olson	.05
227	Jose DeLeon	.05
228	Mike LaValliere	.05
229	Mark Langston	.05
230	Chuck Knoblauch	.05
231	Bill Doran	.05
232	Dave Henderson	.05
233	Roberto Alomar	.20
234	Scott Fletcher	.05
235	Tim Naehring	.05
236	Mike Gallego	.05
237	Lance Johnson	.05
238	Paul Molitor	.45
239	Dan Gladden	.05
240	Willie Randolph	.05
241	Will Clark	.10
242	Sid Bream	.05
243	Derek Bell	.05
244	Bill Pecota	.05
245	Terry Pendleton	.05
246	Randy Ready	.05
247	Jack Armstrong	.05
248	Todd Van Poppel	.05
249	Shawon Dunston	.05
250	Bobby Rose	.05
251	Jeff Huson	.05
252	Bip Roberts	.05
253	Doug Jones	.05
254	Lee Smith	.05
255	George Brett	.65
256	Randy Tomlin	.05
257	Todd Benzinger	.05
258	Dave Stewart	.05
259	Mark Carreon	.05
260	Pete O'Brien	.05
261	Tim Teufel	.05
262	Bob Milacki	.05
263	Mark Guthrie	.05
264	Darrin Fletcher	.05
265	Omar Vizquel	.05
266	Chris Bosio	.05
267	Jose Canseco	.30
268	Mike Boddicker	.05
269	Lance Parrish	.05
270	Jose Vizcaino	.05
271	Chris Sabo	.05
272	Royce Clayton	.05
273	Marquis Grissom	.05
274	Fred McGriff	.05
275	Barry Bonds	1.50
276	Greg Vaughn	.05
277	Gregg Olson	.05
278	Dave Hollins	.05
279	Tom Glavine	.25
280	Bryan Hickerson	.05
281	Scott Radinsky	.05
282	Omar Olivares	.05
283	Ivan Calderon	.05
284	Kevin Maas	.05
285	Mickey Tettleton	.05
286	Wade Boggs	.60
287	Stan Belinda	.05
288	Bret Barberie	.05
289	Jose Oquendo	.05
290	Frank Castillo	.05
291	Dave Stieb	.05
292	Tommy Greene	.05
293	Eric Karros	.05
294	Greg Maddux	.60
295	Jim Eisenreich	.05
296	Rafael Palmeiro	.35
297	Ramon Martinez	.05
298	Tim Wallach	.05
299	Jim Thome	.45
300	Chito Martinez	.05
301	Mitch Williams	.05
302	Randy Johnson	.45
303	Carlton Fisk	.45
304	Travis Fryman	.05
305	Bobby Witt	.05
306	Dave Magadan	.05
307	Alex Cole	.05
308	Bobby Bonilla	.05
309	Bryan Harvey	.05
310	Rafael Belliard	.05
311	Mariano Duncan	.05
312	Chuck Crim	.05
313	John Kruk	.05
314	Ellis Burks	.05
315	Craig Biggio	.05
316	Glenn Davis	.05
317	Ryne Sandberg	.60
318	Mike Sharperson	.05
319	Rich Rodriguez	.05
320	Lee Guetterman	.05
321	Benito Santiago	.05
322	Jose Offerman	.05
323	Tony Pena	.05
324	Pat Borders	.05
325	Mike Henneman	.05
326	Kevin Brown	.05
327	Chris Nabholz	.05
328	Franklin Stubbs	.05
329	Tino Martinez	.05
330	Mickey Morandini	.05
331	Checklist	.05
332	Mark Gubicza	.05
333	Bill Landrum	.05
334	Mark Whiten	.05
335	Darren Daulton	.05
336	Rick Wilkins	.05
337	*Brian Jordan*	.25
338	Kevin Ward	.05
339	Ruben Amaro	.05
340	Trevor Wilson	.05
341	Andujar Cedeno	.05
342	Michael Huff	.05
343	Brady Anderson	.05
344	Craig Grebeck	.05
345	Bobby Ojeda	.05
346	Mike Pagliarulo	.05
347	Terry Shumpert	.05
348	Dann Bilardello	.05
349	Frank Thomas	.45
350	Albert Belle	.05
351	Jose Mesa	.05
352	Rich Monteleone	.05
353	Bob Walk	.05
354	Monty Fariss	.05
355	Luis Rivera	.05
356	Anthony Young	.05
357	Geno Petralli	.05
358	Otis Nixon	.05
359	Tom Pagnozzi	.05
360	Reggie Sanders	.05
361	Lee Stevens	.05
362	Kent Hrbek	.05
363	Orlando Merced	.05
364	Mike Bordick	.05
365	Dion James	.05
366	Jack Clark	.05
367	Mike Stanley	.05
368	Randy Velarde	.05
369	Dan Pasqua	.05
370	Pat Listach	.05
371	Mike Fitzgerald	.05
372	Tom Foley	.05
373	Matt Williams	.05
374	Brian Hunter	.05
375	Joe Carter	.05
376	Bret Saberhagen	.05
377	Mike Stanton	.05
378	Hubie Brooks	.05
379	Eric Bell	.05
380	Walt Weiss	.05
381	Danny Jackson	.05
382	Manuel Lee	.05
383	Ruben Sierra	.05
384	Greg Swindell	.05
385	Ryan Bowen	.05
386	Kevin Ritz	.05
387	Curtis Wilkerson	.05
388	Gary Varsho	.05
389	Dave Hansen	.05
390	Bob Welch	.05
391	Lou Whitaker	.05
392	Ken Griffey, Jr.	.75
393	Mike Maddux	.05
394	Arthur Rhodes	.05
395	Chili Davis	.05
396	Eddie Murray	.45
397	Checklist	.05
398	Dave Cochrane	.05
399	Kevin Seitzer	.05
400	Ozzie Smith	.60
401	Paul Sorrento	.05
402	Les Lancaster	.05
403	Junior Noboa	.05
404	Dave Justice	.05
405	Andy Ashby	.05
406	Danny Tartabull	.05
407	Bill Swift	.05
408	Craig Lefferts	.05
409	Tom Candiotti	.05
410	Lance Blankenship	.05
411	Jeff Tackett	.05
412	Sammy Sosa	.65
413	Jody Reed	.05
414	Bruce Ruffin	.05
415	Gene Larkin	.05
416	John Vanderwal	.05
417	Tim Belcher	.05
418	Steve Frey	.05
419	Dick Schofield	.05
420	Jeff King	.05
421	Kim Batiste	.05
422	Jack McDowell	.05
423	Damon Berryhill	.05
424	Gary Wayne	.05
425	Jack Morris	.05
426	Moises Alou	.05
427	Mark McLemore	.05
428	Juan Guerrero	.05
429	Scott Scudder	.05
430	Eric Davis	.05
431	Joe Slusarski	.05
432	Todd Zeile	.05
433	Dwayne Henry	.05
434	Cliff Brantley	.05
435	Butch Henry	.05
436	Todd Worrell	.05
437	Bob Scanlan	.05

438 Wally Joyner .05
439 John Flaherty .05
440 Brian Downing .05
441 Darren Lewis .05
442 Gary Carter .45
443 Wally Ritchie .05
444 Chris Jones .05
445 Jeff Kent .05
446 Gary Sheffield .30
447 Ron Darling .05
448 Deion Sanders .05
449 Andres Galarraga .05
450 Chuck Finley .05
451 Derek Lilliquist .05
452 Carl Willis .05
453 Wes Chamberlain .05
454 Roger Mason .05
455 Spike Owen .05
456 Thomas Howard .05
457 Dave Martinez .05
458 Pete Incaviglia .05
459 Keith Miller .05
460 Mike Fetters .05
461 Paul Gibson .05
462 George Bell .05
463 Checklist .05
464 Terry Mulholland .05
465 Storm Davis .05
466 Gary Pettis .05
467 Randy Bush .05
468 Ken Hill .05
469 Rheal Cormier .05
470 Andy Stankiewicz .05
471 Dave Burba .05
472 Henry Cotto .05
473 Dale Sveum .05
474 Rich Gossage .05
475 William Suero .05
476 Doug Strange .05
477 Bill Krueger .05
478 John Wetteland .05
479 Melido Perez .05
480 Lonnie Smith .05
481 Mike Jackson .05
482 Mike Gardiner .05
483 David Wells .05
484 Barry Jones .05
485 Scott Bankhead .05
486 Terry Leach .05
487 Vince Horsman .05
488 Dave Eiland .05
489 Alejandro Pena .05
490 Julio Valera .05
491 Joe Boever .05
492 Paul Miller .05
493 *Arci Cianfrocco* .05
494 Dave Fleming .05
495 Kyle Abbott .05
496 Chad Kreuter .05
497 Chris James .05
498 Donnie Hill .05
499 Jacob Brumfield .05
500 Ricky Bones .05
501 Terry Steinbach .05
502 Bernard Gilkey .05
503 Dennis Cook .05
504 Len Dykstra .05
505 Mike Bielecki .05
506 Bob Kipper .05
507 Jose Melendez .05
508 Rick Sutcliffe .05
509 Ken Patterson .05
510 Andy Allanson .05
511 Al Newman .05
512 Mark Gardner .05
513 Jeff Schaefer .05
514 Jim McNamara .05
515 Peter Hoy .05
516 Curt Schilling .30
517 Kirk McCaskill .05
518 Chris Gwynn .05
519 Sid Fernandez .05
520 Jeff Parrett .05
521 Scott Ruskin .05
522 Kevin McReynolds .05
523 Rick Cerone .05
524 Jesse Orosco .05
525 Troy Afenir .05
526 John Smiley .05
527 Dale Murphy .25
528 Leaf Set Card .05

1992 LEAF GOLD PREVIEWS

NM/M
Complete Set (33): 30.00
Common Player: .50
1 Steve Avery .50
2 Ryne Sandberg 2.00

3 Chris Sabo .50
4 Jeff Bagwell 1.50
5 Darryl Strawberry .50
6 Bret Barbarie .50
7 Howard Johnson .50
8 John Kruk .50
9 Andy Van Slyke .50
10 Felix Jose .50
11 Fred McGriff .50
12 Will Clark .60
13 Cal Ripken, Jr. 4.00
14 Phil Plantier .50
15 Lee Stevens .50
16 Frank Thomas 1.50
17 Mark Whiten .50
18 Cecil Fielder .50
19 George Brett 2.50
20 Robin Yount 1.50
21 Scott Erickson .50
22 Don Mattingly 2.50
23 Jose Canseco 1.00
24 Ken Griffey, Jr. 3.00
25 Nolan Ryan 4.00
26 Joe Carter .50
27 Deion Sanders .50
28 Dean Palmer .50
29 Andy Benes .50
30 Gary DiSarcina .50
31 Chris Hoiles .50
32 Mark McGwire 3.00
33 Reggie Sanders .50

1992 LEAF GOLD EDITION

NM/M
Complete Set (528): 35.00
Common Player: .10
Stars/Rookies: 3X
(See 1992 Leaf for checklist and base card values)

Gold Rookies

NM/M
Complete Set (24): 4.00
Common Player: .25
Jumbo: 1.5X
1 Chad Curtis .25
2 Brent Gates .25
3 Pedro Martinez 3.00
4 Kenny Lofton .35
5 Turk Wendell .25
6 Mark Hutton .25
7 Todd Hundley .25
8 Matt Stairs .25
9 Ed Taubensee .25
10 David Nied .25
11 Salomon Torres .25
12 Bret Boone .50
13 John Ruffin .25
14 Ed Martel .25
15 Rick Trlicek .25
16 Raul Mondesi .25
17 Pat Mahomes .25
18 Dan Wilson .25
19 Donovan Osborne .25
20 Dave Silvestri .25
21 Gary DiSarcina .25
22 Denny Neagle .25
23 Steve Hosey .25
24 John Doherty .25

1993 LEAF

NM/M
Complete Set (550): 12.50
Common Player: .05
Series 1 or 2 Pack (14): .65
Series 1 or 2 Box (36): 12.50
Update Pack (14): 1.50
Update Box (36): 25.00
1 Ben McDonald .05
2 Sid Fernandez .05
3 Juan Guzman .05
4 Curt Schilling .40
5 Ivan Rodriguez .65
6 Don Slaught .05
7 Terry Steinbach .05
8 Todd Zeile .05
9 Andy Stankiewicz .05
10 Tim Teufel .05
11 Marvin Freeman .05
12 Jim Austin .05
13 Bob Scanlan .05
14 Rusty Meacham .05
15 Casey Candaele .05
16 Travis Fryman .05
17 Jose Offerman .05
18 Albert Belle .05
19 John Vander Wahl (Vander Wal) .05
20 Dan Pasqua .05
21 Frank Viola .05
22 Terry Mulholland .05
23 Gregg Olson .05
24 Randy Tomlin .05
25 Todd Stottlemyre .05
26 Jose Oquendo .05
27 Julio Franco .05
28 Tony Gwynn 1.00
29 Ruben Sierra .05
30 Bobby Thigpen .05
31 Jim Bullinger .05
32 Rick Aguilera .05
33 Scott Servais .05
34 Cal Eldred .05
35 Mike Piazza 1.50
36 Brent Mayne .05
37 Wil Cordero .05
38 Milt Cuyler .05
39 Howard Johnson .05
40 Kenny Lofton .05
41 Alex Fernandez .05
42 Denny Neagle .05
43 Tony Pena .05
44 Bob Tewksbury .05
45 Glenn Davis .05
46 Fred McGriff .05
47 John Olerud .05
48 Steve Hosey .05
49 Rafael Palmeiro .65
50 Dave Justice .05
51 Pete Harnisch .05
52 Sam Militello .05
53 Orel Hershiser .05
54 Pat Mahomes .05
55 Greg Colbrunn .05
56 Greg Vaughn .05
57 Vince Coleman .05
58 Brian McRae .05
59 Len Dykstra .05
60 Dan Gladden .05
61 Ted Power .05
62 Donovan Osborne .05
63 Ron Karkovice .05
64 Frank Seminara .05
65 Bob Zupcic .05
66 Kirt Manwaring .05
67 Mike Devereaux .05
68 Mark Lemke .05
69 Devon White .05
70 Sammy Sosa 1.25
71 Pedro Astacio .05
72 Dennis Eckersley .60
73 Chris Nabholz .05
74 Melido Perez .05
75 Todd Hundley .05
76 Kent Hrbek .05
77 Mickey Morandini .05
78 Tim McIntosh .05
79 Andy Van Slyke .05
80 Kevin McReynolds .05
81 Mike Henneman .05
82 Greg Harris .05
83 Sandy Alomar Jr. .05
84 Mike Jackson .05
85 Ozzie Guillen .05
86 Jeff Blauser .05
87 John Valentin .05
88 Rey Sanchez .05
89 Rick Sutcliffe .05
90 Luis Gonzalez .25
91 Jeff Fassero .05
92 Kenny Rogers .05
93 Bret Saberhagen .05
94 Bob Welch .05
95 Darren Daulton .05
96 Mike Gallego .05
97 Orlando Merced .05
98 Chuck Knoblauch .05
99 Bernard Gilkey .05
100 Billy Ashley .05
101 Kevin Appier .05
102 Jeff Brantley .05
103 Bill Gullickson .05
104 John Smoltz .05
105 Paul Sorrento .05
106 Steve Buechele .05
107 Steve Sax .05
108 Andujar Cedeno .05
109 Billy Hatcher .05
110 Checklist .05
111 Alan Mills .05
112 John Franco .05
113 Jack Morris .05
114 Mitch Williams .05
115 Nolan Ryan 2.50
116 Jay Bell .05
117 Mike Bordick .05
118 Geronimo Pena .05
119 Danny Tartabull .05
120 Checklist .05
121 Steve Avery .05
122 Ricky Bones .05
123 Mike Morgan .05
124 Jeff Montgomery .05
125 Jeff Bagwell .75
126 Tony Phillips .05
127 Lenny Harris .05
128 Glenallen Hill .05
129 Marquis Grissom .05
130 Gerald Williams (photo, stats actually Bernie Williams) .20
131 Greg Harris .05
132 Tommy Greene .05
133 Chris Hoiles .05
134 Bob Walk .05
135 Duane Ward .05
136 Tom Pagnozzi .05
137 Jeff Huson .05
138 Kurt Stillwell .05
139 Dave Henderson .05
140 Darrin Jackson .05
141 Frank Castillo .05
142 Scott Erickson .05
143 Darryl Kile .05
144 Bill Wegman .05
145 Steve Wilson .05
146 George Brett 1.25
147 Moises Alou .05
148 Lou Whitaker .05
149 Chico Walker .05
150 Jerry Browne .05
151 Kirk McCaskill .05
152 Zane Smith .05
153 Matt Young .05
154 Lee Smith .05
155 Leo Gomez .05

No.	Player	Value
156	Dan Walters	.05
157	Pat Borders	.05
158	Matt Williams	.05
159	Dean Palmer	.05
160	John Patterson	.05
161	Doug Jones	.05
162	John Habyan	.05
163	Pedro Martinez	.75
164	Carl Willis	.05
165	Darrin Fletcher	.05
166	B.J. Surhoff	.05
167	Eddie Murray	.75
168	Keith Miller	.05
169	Ricky Jordan	.05
170	Juan Gonzalez	.65
171	Charles Nagy	.05
172	Mark Clark	.05
173	Bobby Thigpen	.05
174	Tim Scott	.05
175	Scott Cooper	.05
176	Royce Clayton	.05
177	Brady Anderson	.05
178	Sid Bream	.05
179	Derek Bell	.05
180	Otis Nixon	.05
181	Kevin Gross	.05
182	Ron Darling	.05
183	John Wetteland	.05
184	Mike Stanley	.05
185	Jeff Kent	.05
186	Brian Harper	.05
187	Mariano Duncan	.05
188	Robin Yount	.75
189	Al Martin	.05
190	Eddie Zosky	.05
191	Mike Munoz	.05
192	Andy Benes	.05
193	Dennis Cook	.05
194	Bill Swift	.05
195	Frank Thomas	.75
196	Damon Berryhill	.05
197	Mike Greenwell	.05
198	Mark Grace	.05
199	Darryl Hamilton	.05
200	Derrick May	.05
201	Ken Hill	.05
202	Kevin Brown	.05
203	Dwight Gooden	.05
204	Bobby Witt	.05
205	Juan Bell	.05
206	Kevin Maas	.05
207	Jeff King	.05
208	Scott Leius	.05
209	Rheal Cormier	.05
210	Darryl Strawberry	.05
211	Tom Gordon	.05
212	Bud Black	.05
213	Mickey Tettleton	.05
214	Pete Smith	.05
215	Felix Fermin	.05
216	Rick Wilkins	.05
217	George Bell	.05
218	Eric Anthony	.05
219	Pedro Munoz	.05
220	Checklist	.05
221	Lance Blankenship	.05
222	Deion Sanders	.10
223	Craig Biggio	.05
224	Ryne Sandberg	1.00
225	Ron Gant	.05
226	Tom Brunansky	.05
227	Chad Curtis	.05
228	Joe Carter	.05
229	Brian Jordan	.05
230	Brett Butler	.05
231	Frank Bolick	.05
232	Rod Beck	.05
233	Carlos Baerga	.05
234	Eric Karros	.05
235	Jack Armstrong	.05
236	Bobby Bonilla	.05
237	Don Mattingly	1.25
238	Jeff Gardner	.05
239	Dave Hollins	.05
240	Steve Cooke	.05
241	Jose Canseco	.35
242	Ivan Calderon	.05
243	Tim Belcher	.05
244	Freddie Benavides	.05
245	Roberto Alomar	.25
246	Rob Deer	.05
247	Will Clark	.10
248	Mike Felder	.05
249	Harold Baines	.05
250	David Cone	.05
251	Mark Guthrie	.05
252	Ellis Burks	.05
253	Jim Abbott	.05
254	Chili Davis	.05
255	Chris Bosio	.05
256	Bret Barberie	.05
257	Hal Morris	.05
258	Dante Bichette	.05
259	Storm Davis	.05
260	Gary DiSarcina	.05
261	Ken Caminiti	.05
262	Paul Molitor	.75
263	Joe Oliver	.05
264	Pat Listach	.05
265	Gregg Jefferies	.05
266	Jose Guzman	.05
267	Eric Davis	.05
268	Delino DeShields	.05
269	Barry Bonds	2.50
270	Mike Bielecki	.05
271	Jay Buhner	.05
272	*Scott Pose*	.05
273	Tony Fernandez	.05
274	Chito Martinez	.05
275	Phil Plantier	.05
276	Pete Incaviglia	.05
277	Carlos Garcia	.05
278	Tom Henke	.05
279	Roger Clemens	1.25
280	Rob Dibble	.05
281	Daryl Boston	.05
282	Greg Gagne	.05
283	Cecil Fielder	.05
284	Carlton Fisk	.75
285	Wade Boggs	1.00
286	Damion Easley	.05
287	Norm Charlton	.05
288	Jeff Conine	.05
289	Roberto Kelly	.05
290	Jerald Clark	.05
291	Rickey Henderson	.75
292	Chuck Finley	.05
293	Doug Drabek	.05
294	Dave Stewart	.05
295	Tom Glavine	.35
296	Jaime Navarro	.05
297	Ray Lankford	.05
298	Greg Hibbard	.05
299	Jody Reed	.05
300	Dennis Martinez	.05
301	Dave Martinez	.05
302	Reggie Jefferson	.05
303	*John Cummings*	.05
304	Orestes Destrade	.05
305	Mike Maddux	.05
306	David Segui	.05
307	Gary Sheffield	.35
308	Danny Jackson	.05
309	Criag Lefferts	.05
310	Andre Dawson	.20
311	Barry Larkin	.05
312	Alex Cole	.05
313	Mark Gardner	.05
314	Kirk Gibson	.05
315	Shane Mack	.05
316	Bo Jackson	.10
317	Jimmy Key	.05
318	Greg Myers	.05
319	Ken Griffey, Jr.	1.50
320	Monty Fariss	.05
321	Kevin Mitchell	.05
322	Andres Galarraga	.05
323	Mark McGwire	2.00
324	Mark Langston	.05
325	Steve Finley	.05
326	Greg Maddux	1.00
327	Dave Nilsson	.05
328	Ozzie Smith	1.00
329	Candy Maldonado	.05
330	Checklist	.05
331	*Tim Pugh*	.05
332	Joe Girardi	.05
333	Junior Feliz	.05
334	Greg Swindell	.05
335	Ramon Martinez	.05
336	Sean Berry	.05
337	Joe Orsulak	.05
338	Wes Chamberlain	.05
339	Stan Belinda	.05
340	Checklist	.05
341	Bruce Hurst	.05
342	John Burkett	.05
343	Mike Mussina	.40
344	Scott Fletcher	.05
345	Rene Gonzales	.05
346	Roberto Hernandez	.05
347	Carlos Martinez	.05
348	Bill Krueger	.05
349	Felix Jose	.05
350	John Jaha	.05
351	Willie Banks	.05
352	Matt Nokes	.05
353	Kevin Seitzer	.05
354	Erik Hanson	.05
355	*David Hulse*	.05
356	*Domingo Martinez*	.05
357	Greg Olson	.05
358	Randy Myers	.05
359	Tom Browning	.05
360	Charlie Hayes	.05
361	Bryan Harvey	.05
362	Eddie Taubensee	.05
363	Tim Wallach	.05
364	Mel Rojas	.05
365	Frank Tanana	.05
366	John Kruk	.05
367	*Tim Laker*	.05
368	Rich Rodriguez	.05
369	Darren Lewis	.05
370	Harold Reynolds	.05
371	Jose Melendez	.05
372	Joe Grahe	.05
373	Lance Johnson	.05
374	Jose Mesa	.05
375	Scott Livingstone	.05
376	Wally Joyner	.05
377	Kevin Reimer	.05
378	Kirby Puckett	1.00
379	Paul O'Neill	.05
380	Randy Johnson	.75
381	Manuel Lee	.05
382	Dick Schofield	.05
383	Darren Holmes	.05
384	Charlie Hough	.05
385	John Orton	.05
386	Edgar Martinez	.05
387	Terry Pendleton	.05
388	Dan Plesac	.05
389	Jeff Reardon	.05
390	David Nied	.05
391	Dave Magadan	.05
392	Larry Walker	.05
393	Ben Rivera	.05
394	Lonnie Smith	.05
395	Craig Shipley	.05
396	Willie McGee	.05
397	Arthur Rhodes	.05
398	Mike Stanton	.05
399	Luis Polonia	.05
400	Jack McDowell	.05
401	Mike Moore	.05
402	Jose Lind	.05
403	Bill Spiers	.05
404	Kevin Tapani	.05
405	Spike Owen	.05
406	Tino Martinez	.05
407	Charlie Leibrandt	.05
408	Ed Sprague	.05
409	Bryn Smith	.05
410	Benito Santiago	.05
411	Jose Rijo	.05
412	Pete O'Brien	.05
413	Willie Wilson	.05
414	Bip Roberts	.05
415	Eric Young	.05
416	Walt Weiss	.05
417	Milt Thompson	.05
418	Chris Sabo	.05
419	Scott Sanderson	.05
420	Tim Raines	.05
421	Alan Trammell	.05
422	Mike Macfarlane	.05
423	Dave Winfield	.75
424	Bob Wickman	.05
425	David Valie	.05
426	Gary Redus	.05
427	Turner Ward	.05
428	Reggie Sanders	.05
429	Todd Worrell	.05
430	Julio Valera	.05
431	Cal Ripken, Jr.	2.50
432	Mo Vaughn	.05
433	John Smiley	.05
434	Omar Vizquel	.05
435	Billy Ripken	.05
436	Cory Snyder	.05
437	Carlos Quintana	.05
438	Omar Olivares	.05
439	Robin Ventura	.05
440	Checklist	.05
441	Kevin Higgins	.05
442	Carlos Hernandez	.05
443	Dan Peltier	.05
444	Derek Lilliquist	.05
445	Tim Salmon	.05
446	*Sherman Obando*	.05
447	Pat Kelly	.05
448	Todd Van Poppel	.05
449	Mark Whiten	.05
450	Checklist	.05
451	Pat Meares	.05
452	*Tony Tarasco*	.05
453	Chris Gwynn	.05
454	Armando Reynoso	.05
455	Danny Darwin	.05
456	Willie Greene	.05
457	Mike Blowers	.05
458	*Kevin Roberson*	.05
459	*Graeme Lloyd*	.05
460	David West	.05
461	Joey Cora	.05
462	Alex Arias	.05
463	Chad Kreuter	.05
464	Mike Lansing	.05
465	Mike Timlin	.05
466	Paul Wagner	.05
467	Mark Portugal	.05
468	Jim Leyritz	.05
469	Ryan Klesko	.05
470	Mario Diaz	.05
471	Guillermo Velasquez	.05
472	Fernando Valenzuela	.05
473	Raul Mondesi	.05
474	Mike Pagliarulo	.05
475	Chris Hammond	.05
476	Torey Lovullo	.05
477	Trevor Wilson	.05
478	*Marcos Armas*	.05
479	Dave Gallagher	.05
480	Jeff Treadway	.05
481	Jeff Branson	.05
482	Dickie Thon	.05
483	Eduardo Perez	.05
484	David Wells	.05
485	Brian Williams	.05
486	Domingo Cedeno	.05
487	Tom Candiotti	.05
488	Steve Frey	.05
489	Greg McMichael	.05
490	Marc Newfield	.05
491	Larry Andersen	.05
492	Damon Buford	.05
493	Ricky Gutierrez	.05
494	Jeff Russell	.05
495	Vinny Castilla	.05
496	Wilson Alvarez	.05
497	Scott Bullett	.05
498	Larry Casian	.05
499	Jose Vizcaino	.05
500	*J.T. Snow*	.75
501	Bryan Hickerson	.05
502	Jeremy Hernandez	.05
503	Jeromy Burnitz	.05
504	Steve Farr	.05
505	J. Owens	.05
506	Craig Paquette	.05
507	Jim Eisenreich	.05
508	Matt Whiteside	.05
509	Luis Aquino	.05
510	Mike LaValliere	.05
511	Jim Gott	.05
512	Mark McLemore	.05
513	Randy Milligan	.05
514	Gary Gaetti	.05
515	Lou Frazier	.05
516	Rich Amaral	.05
517	Gene Harris	.05
518	Aaron Sele	.05
519	Mark Wohlers	.05
520	Scott Kamieniecki	.05
521	Kent Mercker	.05
522	Jim Deshaies	.05
523	Kevin Stocker	.05
524	Jason Bere	.05
525	Tim Bogar	.05
526	Brad Pennington	.05
527	*Curt Leskanic*	.05
528	Wayne Kirby	.05
529	Tim Costo	.05
530	Doug Henry	.05
531	Trevor Hoffman	.05
532	Kelly Gruber	.05
533	Mike Harkey	.05
534	John Doherty	.05
535	Erik Pappas	.05
536	Brent Gates	.05
537	Roger McDowell	.05
538	Chris Haney	.05
539	Blas Minor	.05
540	Pat Hentgen	.05
541	Chuck Carr	.05
542	Doug Strange	.05
543	Xavier Hernandez	.05
544	Paul Quantrill	.05
545	Anthony Young	.05
546	Bret Boone	.05
547	Dwight Smith	.05
548	Bobby Munoz	.05
549	Russ Springer	.05
550	Roger Pavlik	.05
----	Dave Winfield (3000 Hits)	2.00

Fasttrack

		NM/M
Complete Set (20):		15.00
Common Player:		.60
1	Frank Thomas	3.00
2	Tim Wakefield	.60
3	Kenny Lofton	.60
4	Mike Mussina	1.00
5	Juan Gonzalez	2.50
6	Chuck Knoblauch	.60
7	Eric Karros	.60
8	Ray Lankford	.60
9	Juan Guzman	.60
10	Pat Listach	.60
11	Carlos Baerga	.60
12	Felix Jose	.60
13	Steve Avery	.60
14	Robin Ventura	.60
15	Ivan Rodriguez	2.50
16	Cal Eldred	.60
17	Jeff Bagwell	3.00
18	Dave Justice	.60
19	Travis Fryman	.60
20	Marquis Grissom	.60

Gold All-Stars

		NM/M
Complete Set (20):		15.00
Common Player:		.25
1	Ivan Rodriguez, Darren Daulton	.75
2	Don Mattingly, Fred McGriff	1.50
3	Cecil Fielder, Jeff Bagwell	.75
4	Carlos Baerga, Ryne Sandberg	1.00
5	Chuck Knoblauch, Delino DeShields	.25
6	Robin Ventura, Terry Pendleton	.25
7	Ken Griffey, Jr., Andy Van Slyke	2.00
8	Joe Carter, Dave Justice	.25
9	Jose Canseco, Tony Gwynn	1.00
10	Dennis Eckersley, Rob Dibble	.60
11	Mark McGwire, Will Clark	2.50
12	Frank Thomas, Mark Grace	.75
13	Roberto Alomar, Craig Biggio	.50
14	Barry Larkin, Cal Ripken, Jr.	3.00
15	Gary Sheffield, Edgar Martinez	.50
16	Juan Gonzalez, Barry Bonds	3.00
17	Kirby Puckett, Marquis Grissom	1.00
18	Jim Abbott, Tom Glavine	.40
19	Nolan Ryan, Greg Maddux	3.00
20	Roger Clemens, Doug Drabek	1.50

Gold Rookies

		NM/M
Complete Set (20):		5.00
Common Player:		.25
1	Kevin Young	.25
2	Wil Cordero	.25
3	Mark Kiefer	.25
4	Gerald Williams	.25
5	Brandon Wilson	.25
6	Greg Gohr	.25
7	Ryan Thompson	.25
8	Tim Wakefield	.25
9	Troy Neel	.25
10	Tim Salmon	.50
11	Kevin Rogers	.25
12	Rod Bolton	.25
13	Ken Ryan	.25
14	Phil Hiatt	.25
15	Rene Arocha	.25
16	Nigel Wilson	.25
17	J.T. Snow	.50
18	Benji Gil	.25
19	Chipper Jones	3.00
20	Darrell Sherman	.25

Heading for the Hall

		NM/M
Complete Set (10):		10.00
Common Player:		.75
1	Nolan Ryan	2.50
2	Tony Gwynn	1.00
3	Robin Yount	1.00
4	Eddie Murray	1.00
5	Cal Ripken, Jr.	2.50
6	Roger Clemens	2.00
7	George Brett	2.00
8	Ryne Sandberg	1.00
9	Kirby Puckett	1.00
10	Ozzie Smith	1.00

Frank Thomas

		NM/M
Complete Set (10):		4.50
Common Card:		.75
Autographed Card:		30.00
1	Frank Thomas Aggressive	.75
2	Frank Thomas Serious	.75
3	Frank Thomas Intense	.75
4	Frank Thomas Confident	.75
5	Frank Thomas Assertive	.75
6	Frank Thomas Power	.75
7	Frank Thomas Control	.75
8	Frank Thomas Strength	.75
9	Frank Thomas Concentration	.75
10	Frank Thomas Preparation	.75

Update Gold All-Stars

		NM/M
Complete Set (10):		7.50
Common Player:		.25
1	Mark Langston, Terry Mulholland	.25
2	Ivan Rodriguez, Darren Daulton	.50
3	John Olerud, John Kruk	.25
4	Roberto Alomar, Ryne Sandberg	1.00
5	Wade Boggs, Gary Sheffield	.75
6	Cal Ripken, Jr., Barry Larkin	3.00
7	Kirby Puckett, Barry Bonds	2.50
8	Marquis Grissom, Ken Griffey Jr.	2.00
9	Joe Carter, Dave Justice	.25
10	Mark Grace, Paul Molitor	.75

Update Gold Rookies

		NM/M
Complete Set (5):		3.50
Common Player:		.25
Jumbos:		1.5X
1	Allen Watson	.25
2	Jeffrey Hammonds	.25
3	David McCarty	.25
4	Mike Piazza	3.00
5	Roberto Meija	.25

Update Frank Thomas Super

		NM/M
Complete Set (10):		17.50
Common Card:		2.00
1	Frank Thomas Aggressive	2.00
2	Frank Thomas Serious	2.00
3	Frank Thomas Intense	2.00
4	Frank Thomas Confident	2.00
5	Frank Thomas Assertive	2.00
6	Frank Thomas Power	2.00
7	Frank Thomas Control	2.00
8	Frank Thomas Strength	2.00
9	Frank Thomas Concentration	2.00
10	Frank Thomas Preparation	2.00

Update Frank Thomas Autograph

		NM/M
FT	Frank Thomas	35.00

1994 LEAF

		NM/M
Complete Set (440):		10.00
Common Player:		.05
Series 1 or 2 Pack (12):		.75
Series 1 or 2 Box (36):		12.50
1	Cal Ripken, Jr.	2.50
2	Tony Tarasco	.05
3	Joe Girardi	.05
4	Bernie Williams	.20
5	Chad Kreuter	.05
6	Troy Neel	.05
7	Tom Pagnozzi	.05
8	Kirk Rueter	.05
9	Chris Bosio	.05
10	Dwight Gooden	.05
11	Mariano Duncan	.05
12	Jay Bell	.05
13	Lance Johnson	.05
14	Richie Lewis	.05
15	Dave Martinez	.05
16	Orel Hershiser	.05
17	Rob Butler	.05
18	Glenallen Hill	.05
19	Chad Curtis	.05
20	Mike Stanton	.05
21	Tim Wallach	.05
22	Milt Thompson	.05
23	Kevin Young	.05
24	John Smiley	.05
25	Jeff Montgomery	.05
26	Robin Ventura	.05
27	Scott Lydy	.05
28	Todd Stottlemyre	.05
29	Mark Whiten	.05
30	Robby Thompson	.05
31	Bobby Bonilla	.05
32	Andy Ashby	.05
33	Greg Myers	.05
34	Billy Hatcher	.05
35	Brad Holman	.05
36	Mark McLemore	.05
37	Scott Sanders	.05
38	Jim Abbott	.05
39	David Wells	.05
40	Roberto Kelly	.05
41	Jeff Conine	.05
42	Sean Berry	.05
43	Mark Grace	.05
44	Eric Young	.05
45	Rick Aguilera	.05
46	Chipper Jones	1.00
47	Mel Rojas	.05
48	Ryan Thompson	.05
49	Al Martin	.05
50	Cecil Fielder	.05
51	Pat Kelly	.05
52	Kevin Tapani	.05
53	Tim Costo	.05
54	Dave Hollins	.05
55	Kirt Manwaring	.05
56	Gregg Jefferies	.05
57	Ron Darling	.05
58	Bill Haselman	.05
59	Phil Plantier	.05
60	Frank Viola	.05
61	Todd Zeile	.05
62	Bret Barberie	.05
63	Roberto Mejia	.05
64	Chuck Knoblauch	.05
65	Jose Lind	.05
66	Brady Anderson	.05
67	Ruben Sierra	.05
68	Jose Vizcaino	.05
69	Joe Grahe	.05
70	Kevin Appier	.05
71	Wilson Alvarez	.05
72	Tom Candiotti	.05
73	John Burkett	.05
74	Anthony Young	.05
75	Scott Cooper	.05
76	Nigel Wilson	.05
77	John Valentin	.05
78	Dave McCarty	.05
79	Archi Cianfrocco	.05
80	Lou Whitaker	.05
81	Dante Bichette	.05
82	Mark Dewey	.05
83	Danny Jackson	.05
84	Harold Baines	.05

#	Player	NM/M
85	Todd Benzinger	.05
86	Damion Easley	.05
87	Danny Cox	.05
88	Jose Bautista	.05
89	Mike Lansing	.05
90	Phil Hiatt	.05
91	Tim Pugh	.05
92	Tino Martinez	.05
93	Raul Mondesi	.05
94	Greg Maddux	1.00
95	Al Leiter	.05
96	Benito Santiago	.05
97	Len Dykstra	.05
98	Sammy Sosa	1.25
99	Tim Bogar	.05
100	Checklist	.05
101	Deion Sanders	.10
102	Bobby Witt	.05
103	Wil Cordero	.05
104	Rich Amaral	.05
105	Mike Mussina	.50
106	Reggie Sanders	.05
107	Ozzie Guillen	.05
108	Paul O'Neill	.05
109	Tim Salmon	.05
110	Rheal Cormier	.05
111	Billy Ashley	.05
112	Jeff Kent	.05
113	Derek Bell	.05
114	Danny Darwin	.05
115	Chip Hale	.05
116	Tim Raines	.05
117	Ed Sprague	.05
118	Darrin Fletcher	.05
119	Darren Holmes	.05
120	Alan Trammell	.05
121	Don Mattingly	1.25
122	Greg Gagne	.05
123	Jose Offerman	.05
124	Joe Orsulak	.05
125	Jack McDowell	.05
126	Barry Larkin	.05
127	Ben McDonald	.05
128	Mike Bordick	.05
129	Devon White	.05
130	Mike Perez	.05
131	Jay Buhner	.05
132	Phil Leftwich	.05
133	Tommy Greene	.05
134	Charlie Hayes	.05
135	Don Slaught	.05
136	Mike Gallego	.05
137	Dave Winfield	.75
138	Steve Avery	.05
139	Derrick May	.05
140	Bryan Harvey	.05
141	Wally Joyner	.05
142	Andre Dawson	.20
143	Andy Benes	.05
144	John Franco	.05
145	Jeff King	.05
146	Joe Oliver	.05
147	Bill Gullickson	.05
148	Armando Reynoso	.05
149	Dave Fleming	.05
150	Checklist	.05
151	Todd Van Poppel	.05
152	Bernard Gilkey	.05
153	Kevin Gross	.05
154	Mike Devereaux	.05
155	Tim Wakefield	.05
156	Andres Galarraga	.05
157	Pat Meares	.05
158	Jim Leyritz	.05
159	Mike Macfarlane	.05
160	Tony Phillips	.05
161	Brent Gates	.05
162	Mark Langston	.05
163	Allen Watson	.05
164	Randy Johnson	.75
165	Doug Brocail	.05
166	Rob Dibble	.05
167	Roberto Hernandez	.05
168	Felix Jose	.05
169	Steve Cooke	.05
170	Darren Daulton	.05
171	Eric Karros	.05
172	Geronimo Pena	.05
173	Gary DiSarcina	.05
174	Marquis Grissom	.05
175	Joey Cora	.05
176	Jim Eisenreich	.05
177	Brad Pennington	.05
178	Terry Steinbach	.05
179	Pat Borders	.05
180	Steve Buechele	.05
181	Jeff Fassero	.05
182	Mike Greenwell	.05
183	Mike Henneman	.05
184	Ron Karkovice	.05
185	Pat Hentgen	.05
186	Jose Guzman	.05
187	Brett Butler	.05
188	Charlie Hough	.05
189	Terry Pendleton	.05
190	Melido Perez	.05
191	Orestes Destrade	.05
192	Mike Morgan	.05
193	Joe Carter	.05
194	Jeff Blauser	.05
195	Chris Hoiles	.05
196	Ricky Gutierrez	.05
197	Mike Moore	.05
198	Carl Willis	.05
199	Aaron Sele	.05
200	Checklist	.05
201	Tim Naehring	.05
202	Scott Livingstone	.05
203	Luis Alicea	.05
204	*Torey Lovullo*	.05
205	Jim Gott	.05
206	Bob Wickman	.05
207	Greg McMichael	.05
208	Scott Brosius	.05
209	Chris Gwynn	.05
210	Steve Sax	.05
211	Dick Schofield	.05
212	Robb Nen	.05
213	Ben Rivera	.05
214	Vinny Castilla	.05
215	Jamie Moyer	.05
216	Wally Whitehurst	.05
217	Frank Castillo	.05
218	Mike Blowers	.05
219	Tim Scott	.05
220	Paul Wagner	.05
221	Jeff Bagwell	.75
222	Ricky Bones	.05
223	Sandy Alomar Jr.	.05
224	Rod Beck	.05
225	Roberto Alomar	.20
226	Jack Armstrong	.05
227	Scott Erickson	.05
228	Rene Arocha	.05
229	Eric Anthony	.05
230	Jeromy Burnitz	.05
231	Kevin Brown	.05
232	Tim Belcher	.05
233	Bret Boone	.05
234	Dennis Eckersley	.60
235	Tom Glavine	.30
236	Craig Biggio	.05
237	Pedro Astacio	.05
238	Ryan Bowen	.05
239	Brad Ausmus	.05
240	Vince Coleman	.05
241	Jason Bere	.05
242	Ellis Burks	.05
243	Wes Chamberlain	.05
244	Ken Caminiti	.05
245	Willie Banks	.05
246	Sid Fernandez	.05
247	Carlos Baerga	.05
248	Carlos Garcia	.05
249	Jose Canseco	.50
250	Alex Diaz	.05
251	Albert Belle	.05
252	Moises Alou	.05
253	Bobby Ayala	.05
254	Tony Gwynn	1.00
255	Roger Clemens	1.25
256	Eric Davis	.05
257	Wade Boggs	1.00
258	Chili Davis	.05
259	Rickey Henderson	.75
260	Andujar Cedeno	.05
261	Cris Carpenter	.05
262	Juan Guzman	.05
263	Dave Justice	.05
264	Barry Bonds	2.50
265	Pete Incaviglia	.05
266	Tony Fernandez	.05
267	Cal Eldred	.05
268	Alex Fernandez	.05
269	Kent Hrbek	.05
270	Steve Farr	.05
271	Doug Drabek	.05
272	Brian Jordan	.05
273	Xavier Hernandez	.05
274	David Cone	.05
275	Brian Hunter	.05
276	Mike Harkey	.05
277	Delino DeShields	.05
278	David Hulse	.05
279	Mickey Tettleton	.05
280	Kevin McReynolds	.05
281	Darryl Hamilton	.05
282	Ken Hill	.05
283	Wayne Kirby	.05
284	Chris Hammond	.05
285	Mo Vaughn	.05
286	Ryan Klesko	.05
287	Rick Wilkins	.05
288	Bill Swift	.05
289	Rafael Palmeiro	.65
290	Brian Harper	.05
291	Chris Turner	.05
292	Luis Gonzalez	.25
293	Kenny Rogers	.05
294	Kirby Puckett	1.00
295	Mike Stanley	.05
296	Carlos Reyes	.05
297	Charles Nagy	.05
298	Reggie Jefferson	.05
299	Bip Roberts	.05
300	Darrin Jackson	.05
301	Mike Jackson	.05
302	Dave Nilsson	.05
303	Ramon Martinez	.05
304	Bobby Jones	.05
305	Johnny Ruffin	.05
306	Brian McRae	.05
307	Bo Jackson	.10
308	Dave Stewart	.05
309	John Smoltz	.05
310	Dennis Martinez	.05
311	Dean Palmer	.05
312	David Nied	.05
313	Eddie Murray	.75
314	Darryl Kile	.05
315	Rick Sutcliffe	.05
316	Shawon Dunston	.05
317	John Jaha	.05
318	Salomon Torres	.05
319	Gary Sheffield	.45
320	Curt Schilling	.30
321	Greg Vaughn	.05
322	Jay Howell	.05
323	Todd Hundley	.05
324	Chris Sabo	.05
325	Stan Javier	.05
326	Willie Greene	.05
327	Hipolito Pichardo	.05
328	Doug Strange	.05
329	Dan Wilson	.05
330	Checklist	.05
331	Omar Vizquel	.05
332	Scott Servais	.05
333	Bob Tewksbury	.05
334	Matt Williams	.05
335	Tom Foley	.05
336	Jeff Russell	.05
337	Scott Leius	.05
338	Ivan Rodriguez	.65
339	Kevin Seitzer	.05
340	Jose Rijo	.05
341	Eduardo Perez	.05
342	Kirk Gibson	.05
343	Randy Milligan	.05
344	Edgar Martinez	.05
345	Fred McGriff	.05
346	Kurt Abbott	.05
347	John Kruk	.05
348	Mike Felder	.05
349	Dave Staton	.05
350	Kenny Lofton	.05
351	Graeme Lloyd	.05
352	David Segui	.05
353	Danny Tartabull	.05
354	Bob Welch	.05
355	Duane Ward	.05
356	Tuffy Rhodes	.05
357	Lee Smith	.05
358	Chris James	.05
359	Walt Weiss	.05
360	Pedro Munoz	.05
361	Paul Sorrento	.05
362	Todd Worrell	.05
363	Bob Hamelin	.05
364	Julio Franco	.05
365	Roberto Petagine	.05
366	Willie McGee	.05
367	Pedro Martinez	.75
368	Ken Griffey, Jr.	1.50
369	B.J. Surhoff	.05
370	Kevin Mitchell	.05
371	John Doherty	.05
372	Manuel Lee	.05
373	Terry Mulholland	.05
374	Zane Smith	.05
375	Otis Nixon	.05
376	Jody Reed	.05
377	Doug Jones	.05
378	John Olerud	.05
379	Greg Swindell	.05
380	Checklist	.05
381	Royce Clayton	.05
382	Jim Thome	.65
383	Steve Finley	.05
384	Ray Lankford	.05
385	Henry Rodriguez	.05
386	Dave Magadan	.05
387	Gary Redus	.05
388	Orlando Merced	.05
389	Tom Gordon	.05
390	Luis Polonia	.05
391	Mark McGwire	2.00
392	Mark Lemke	.05
393	Doug Henry	.05
394	Chuck Finley	.05
395	Paul Molitor	.75
396	Randy Myers	.05
397	Larry Walker	.05
398	Pete Harnisch	.05
399	Darren Lewis	.05
400	Frank Thomas	.75
401	Jack Morris	.05
402	Greg Hibbard	.05
403	Jeffrey Hammonds	.05
404	Will Clark	.10
405	Travis Fryman	.05
406	Scott Sanderson	.05
407	Gene Harris	.05
408	Chuck Carr	.05
409	Ozzie Smith	1.00
410	Kent Mercker	.05
411	Andy Van Slyke	.05
412	Jimmy Key	.05
413	Pat Mahomes	.05
414	John Wetteland	.05
415	Todd Jones	.05
416	Greg Harris	.05
417	Kevin Stocker	.05
418	Juan Gonzalez	.65
419	Pete Smith	.05
420	Pat Listach	.05
421	Trevor Hoffman	.05
422	Scott Fletcher	.05
423	Mark Lewis	.05
424	Mickey Morandini	.05
425	Ryne Sandberg	1.00
426	Erik Hanson	.05
427	Gary Gaetti	.05
428	Harold Reynolds	.05
429	Mark Portugal	.05
430	David Valle	.05
431	Mitch Williams	.05
432	Howard Johnson	.05
433	Hal Morris	.05
434	Tom Henke	.05
435	Shane Mack	.05
436	Mike Piazza	1.50
437	Bret Saberhagen	.05
438	Jose Mesa	.05
439	Jaime Navarro	.05
440	Checklist	.05

Clean-Up Crew

		NM/M
Complete Set (12):		8.00
Common Player:		1.00
1	Larry Walker	1.00
2	Andres Galarraga	1.00
3	Dave Hollins	1.00
4	Bobby Bonilla	1.00
5	Cecil Fielder	1.00
6	Danny Tartabull	1.00
7	Juan Gonzalez	2.00
8	Joe Carter	1.00
9	Fred McGriff	1.00
10	Matt Williams	1.00
11	Albert Belle	1.00
12	Harold Baines	1.00

5th Anniversary

		NM/M
300	Frank Thomas	2.50

Gamers

		NM/M
Complete Set (12):		30.00
Common Player:		1.00
1	Ken Griffey, Jr.	6.00
2	Len Dykstra	1.00
3	Juan Gonzalez	3.00
4	Don Mattingly	6.00
5	Dave Justice	1.00
6	Mark Grace	1.00
7	Frank Thomas	4.00
8	Barry Bonds	7.50
9	Kirby Puckett	4.50
10	Will Clark	1.00
11	John Kruk	1.00
12	Mike Piazza	6.00

Gold Rookies

		NM/M
Complete Set (20):		6.00
Common Player:		.25
1	Javier Lopez	.25
2	Rondell White	.25
3	Butch Huskey	.25
4	Midre Cummings	.25
5	Scott Ruffcorn	.25
6	Manny Ramirez	3.50
7	Danny Bautista	.25
8	Russ Davis	.25
9	Steve Karsay	.25
10	Carlos Delgado	2.50
11	Bob Hamelin	.25
12	Marcus Moore	.25
13	Miguel Jimenez	.25
14	Matt Walbeck	.25
15	James Mouton	.25
16	Rich Becker	.25
17	Brian Anderson	.25
18	Cliff Floyd	.25
19	Steve Trachsel	.25
20	Hector Carrasco	.25

Gold Stars

		NM/M
Complete Set (15):		60.00
Common Player:		3.00
1	Roberto Alomar	4.00
2	Barry Bonds	12.00
3	Dave Justice	3.00
4	Ken Griffey, Jr.	9.00
5	Len Dykstra	3.00
6	Don Mattingly	7.50
7	Andres Galarraga	3.00
8	Greg Maddux	6.00
9	Carlos Baerga	3.00
10	Paul Molitor	5.00
11	Frank Thomas	5.00
12	John Olerud	3.00
13	Juan Gonzalez	4.00
14	Fred McGriff	3.00
15	Jack McDowell	3.00

MVP Contenders

		NM/M
Complete Set, Silver (30):		20.00
Complete Set, Gold (30):		40.00
Common Player, Silver:		.25
Common Player, Gold:		.50
AMERICAN LEAGUE		2.00
1a	Albert Belle (silver)	.25
1b	Albert Belle (gold)	.50
2a	Jose Canseco (silver)	1.25
2b	Jose Canseco (gold)	2.00
3a	Joe Carter (silver)	.25
3b	Joe Carter (gold)	.50
4a	Will Clark (silver)	.35
4b	Will Clark (gold)	.60
5a	Cecil Fielder (silver)	.25
5b	Cecil Fielder (gold)	.50
6a	Juan Gonzalez (silver)	1.50
6b	Juan Gonzalez (gold)	2.50
7a	Ken Griffey, Jr. (silver)	4.00
7b	Ken Griffey, Jr. (gold)	7.50
8a	Paul Molitor (silver)	2.00
8b	Paul Molitor (gold)	4.00
9a	Rafael Palmeiro (silver)	1.50
9b	Rafael Palmeiro (gold)	2.50
10a	Kirby Puckett (silver)	2.50
10b	Kirby Puckett (gold)	5.00
11a	Cal Ripken, Jr. (silver)	6.00
11b	Cal Ripken, Jr. (gold)	12.50
12a	Frank Thomas (silver)	2.00
12b	Frank Thomas (gold)	4.00
13a	Mo Vaughn (silver)	.25
13b	Mo Vaughn (gold)	.50
14a	Carlos Baerga (silver)	.25
14b	Carlos Baerga (gold)	.50
15	AL Bonus Card (silver)	.25
NATIONAL LEAGUE		.60
1a	Gary Sheffield (silver)	.35
1b	Gary Sheffield (gold)	.65
2a	Jeff Bagwell (silver)	2.00
2b	Jeff Bagwell (gold)	4.00
3a	Dante Bichette (silver)	.25
3b	Dante Bichette (gold)	.50
4a	Barry Bonds (silver)	6.00
4b	Barry Bonds (gold)	12.50
5a	Darren Daulton (silver)	.25
5b	Darren Daulton (gold)	.50
6a	Andres Galarraga (silver)	.25
6b	Andres Galarraga (gold)	.50
7a	Gregg Jefferies (silver)	.25
7b	Gregg Jefferies (gold)	.50
8a	Dave Justice (silver)	.25
8b	Dave Justice (gold)	.50
9a	Ray Lankford (silver)	.25
9b	Ray Lankford (gold)	.50
10a	Fred McGriff (silver)	.25
10b	Fred McGriff (gold)	.50
11a	Barry Larkin (silver)	.25
11b	Barry Larkin (gold)	.50
12a	Mike Piazza (silver)	4.00
12b	Mike Piazza (gold)	7.50
13a	Deion Sanders (silver)	.25
13b	Deion Sanders (gold)	.50
14a	Matt Williams (silver)	.25
14b	Matt Williams (gold)	.50
15	NL Bonus Card (silver)	.25

Power Brokers

		NM/M
Complete Set (10):		8.00
Common Player:		.40
1	Frank Thomas	.75
2	Dave Justice	.40
3	Barry Bonds	3.00
4	Juan Gonzalez	.65
5	Ken Griffey, Jr.	2.00
6	Mike Piazza	2.00
7	Cecil Fielder	.40
8	Fred McGriff	.40
9	Joe Carter	.40
10	Albert Belle	.40

Slide Show

		NM/M
Complete Set (10):		9.00
Common Player:		.25
1	Frank Thomas	1.00
2	Mike Piazza	2.00
3	Darren Daulton	.25
4	Ryne Sandberg	1.50
5	Roberto Alomar	.50
6	Barry Bonds	3.00
7	Juan Gonzalez	.75
8	Tim Salmon	.25
9	Ken Griffey, Jr.	2.00
10	Dave Justice	.25

Statistical Standouts

		NM/M
Complete Set (10):		10.00
Common Player:		.40
1	Frank Thomas	.75
2	Barry Bonds	2.50
3	Juan Gonzalez	.65
4	Mike Piazza	2.00
5	Greg Maddux	1.00
6	Ken Griffey, Jr.	2.00
7	Joe Carter	.40
8	Dave Winfield	.75
9	Tony Gwynn	1.00
10	Cal Ripken, Jr.	2.50

1994 LEAF/LIMITED

		NM/M
Complete Set (160):		35.00
Common Player:		.25
Pack (5):		2.50
Wax Box (20):		40.00
1	Jeffrey Hammonds	.25
2	Ben McDonald	.25
3	Mike Mussina	.75
4	Rafael Palmeiro	1.50
5	Cal Ripken, Jr.	6.00
6	Lee Smith	.25
7	Roger Clemens	3.00
8	Scott Cooper	.25
9	Andre Dawson	.40
10	Mike Greenwell	.25
11	Aaron Sele	.25
12	Mo Vaughn	.25
13	*Brian Anderson*	.25
14	Chad Curtis	.25
15	Chili Davis	.25
16	Gary DiSarcina	.25
17	Mark Langston	.25
18	Tim Salmon	.25
19	Wilson Alvarez	.25
20	Jason Bere	.25
21	Julio Franco	.25
22	Jack McDowell	.25
23	Tim Raines	.25
24	Frank Thomas	2.00
25	Robin Ventura	.25
26	Carlos Baerga	.25
27	Albert Belle	.25
28	Kenny Lofton	.25
29	Eddie Murray	2.00
30	Manny Ramirez	2.00
31	Cecil Fielder	.25
32	Travis Fryman	.25
33	Mickey Tettleton	.25
34	Alan Trammell	.25
35	Lou Whitaker	.25
36	David Cone	.25
37	Gary Gaetti	.25
38	Greg Gagne	.25
39	Bob Hamelin	.25
40	Wally Joyner	.25
41	Brian McRae	.25
42	Ricky Bones	.25
43	Brian Harper	.25
44	John Jaha	.25
45	Pat Listach	.25
46	Dave Nilsson	.25
47	Greg Vaughn	.25
48	Kent Hrbek	.25
49	Chuck Knoblauch	.25
50	Shane Mack	.25
51	Kirby Puckett	2.50
52	Dave Winfield	2.00
53	Jim Abbott	.25
54	Wade Boggs	2.50
55	Jimmy Key	.25
56	Don Mattingly	3.00
57	Paul O'Neill	.25
58	Danny Tartabull	.25
59	Dennis Eckersley	1.50
60	Rickey Henderson	2.00
61	Mark McGwire	5.00
62	Troy Neel	.25
63	Ruben Sierra	.25
64	Eric Anthony	.25
65	Jay Buhner	.25
66	Ken Griffey, Jr.	4.00
67	Randy Johnson	2.00
68	Edgar Martinez	.25
69	Tino Martinez	.25
70	Jose Canseco	.75
71	Will Clark	.35
72	Juan Gonzalez	1.50
73	Dean Palmer	.25
74	Ivan Rodriguez	1.50
75	Roberto Alomar	.40
76	Joe Carter	.25
77	Carlos Delgado	1.00
78	Paul Molitor	2.00
79	John Olerud	.25
80	Devon White	.25
81	Steve Avery	.25
82	Tom Glavine	.50
83	Dave Justice	.25
84	Roberto Kelly	.25
85	Ryan Klesko	.25
86	Javier Lopez	.25
87	Greg Maddux	2.50
88	Fred McGriff	.25
89	Shawon Dunston	.25
90	Mark Grace	.25
91	Derrick May	.25
92	Sammy Sosa	3.00
93	Rick Wilkins	.25
94	Bret Boone	.25
95	Barry Larkin	.25
96	Kevin Mitchell	.25
97	Hal Morris	.25
98	Deion Sanders	.25
99	Reggie Sanders	.25
100	Dante Bichette	.25
101	Ellis Burks	.25
102	Andres Galarraga	.25
103	Joe Girardi	.25
104	Charlie Hayes	.25
105	Chuck Carr	.25
106	Jeff Conine	.25
107	Bryan Harvey	.25
108	Benito Santiago	.25
109	Gary Sheffield	.60
110	Jeff Bagwell	2.00
111	Craig Biggio	.25
112	Ken Caminiti	.25
113	Andujar Cedeno	.25

114	Doug Drabek	.25
115	Luis Gonzalez	.40
116	Brett Butler	.25
117	Delino DeShields	.25
118	Eric Karros	.25
119	Raul Mondesi	.25
120	Mike Piazza	4.00
121	Henry Rodriguez	.25
122	Tim Wallach	.25
123	Moises Alou	.25
124	Cliff Floyd	.25
125	Marquis Grissom	.25
126	Ken Hill	.25
127	Larry Walker	.25
128	John Wetteland	.25
129	Bobby Bonilla	.25
130	John Franco	.25
131	Jeff Kent	.25
132	Bret Saberhagen	.25
133	Ryan Thompson	.25
134	Darren Daulton	.25
135	Mariano Duncan	.25
136	Len Dykstra	.25
137	Danny Jackson	.25
138	John Kruk	.25
139	Jay Bell	.25
140	Jeff King	.25
141	Al Martin	.25
142	Orlando Merced	.25
143	Andy Van Slyke	.25
144	Bernard Gilkey	.25
145	Gregg Jefferies	.25
146	Ray Lankford	.25
147	Ozzie Smith	2.50
148	Mark Whiten	.25
149	Todd Zeile	.25
150	Derek Bell	.25
151	Andy Benes	.25
152	Tony Gwynn	2.50
153	Phil Plantier	.25
154	Bip Roberts	.25
155	Rod Beck	.25
156	Barry Bonds	6.00
157	John Burkett	.25
158	Royce Clayton	.25
159	Bill Swift	.25
160	Matt Williams	.25

Gold

		NM/M
Complete Set (18):		20.00
Common Player:		.25
1	Frank Thomas	1.50
2	Gregg Jefferies	.25
3	Roberto Alomar	.50
4	Mariano Duncan	.25
5	Wade Boggs	2.00
6	Matt Williams	.25
7	Cal Ripken, Jr.	4.00
8	Ozzie Smith	2.00
9	Kirby Puckett	2.00
10	Barry Bonds	4.00
11	Ken Griffey, Jr.	3.00
12	Tony Gwynn	2.00
13	Joe Carter	.25
14	Dave Justice	.25
15	Ivan Rodriguez	1.25
16	Mike Piazza	3.00
17	Jimmy Key	.25
18	Greg Maddux	2.00

Rookies

		NM/M
Complete Set (80):		17.50
Common Player:		.25
Pack (5):		3.00
Box (20):		60.00
1	Charles Johnson	.25
2	Rico Brogna	.25
3	Melvin Nieves	.25
4	Rich Becker	.25
5	Russ Davis	.25
6	Matt Mieske	.25
7	Paul Shuey	.25
8	Hector Carrasco	.25
9	J.R. Phillips	.25
10	Scott Ruffcorn	.25
11	Kurt Abbott	.25
12	Danny Bautista	.25
13	Rick White	.25
14	Steve Dunn	.25
15	Joe Ausanio	.25
16	Salomon Torres	.25
17	Rick Bottalico	.25
18	Johnny Ruffin	.25
19	Kevin Foster	.25
20	*W. Van Landingham*	.25
21	Troy O'Leary	.25
22	Mark Acre	.25
23	Norberto Martin	.25
24	*Jason Jacome*	.25
25	Steve Trachsel	.25
26	Denny Hocking	.25
27	Mike Lieberthal	.25
28	Gerald Williams	.25
29	John Mabry	.25
30	Greg Blosser	.25
31	Carl Everett	.25
32	Steve Karsay	.25
33	Jose Valentin	.25
34	Jon Lieber	.25
35	Chris Gomez	.25
36	Jesus Tavarez	.25
37	Tony Longmire	.25
38	Luis Lopez	.25
39	Matt Walbeck	.25
40	Rikkert Faneyte	.25
41	Shane Reynolds	.25
42	Joey Hamilton	.25
43	Ismael Valdes	.25
44	Danny Miceli	.25
45	Darren Bragg	.25
46	Alex Gonzalez	.25
47	Rick Helling	.25
48	Jose Oliva	.25
49	Jim Edmonds	4.00
50	Miguel Jimenez	.25
51	Tony Eusebio	.25
52	Shawn Green	4.00
53	Billy Ashley	.25
54	Rondell White	.25
55	Cory Bailey	.25
56	Tim Davis	.25
57	John Hudek	.25
58	Darren Hall	.25
59	Darren Dreifort	.25
60	Mike Kelly	.25
61	Marcus Moore	.25
62	Garret Anderson	.25
63	Brian Hunter	.25
64	Mark Smith	.25
65	Garey Ingram	.25
66	*Rusty Greer*	.25
67	Marc Newfield	.25
68	Gar Finnvold	.25
69	Paul Spoljaric	.25
70	Ray McDavid	.25
71	Orlando Miller	.25
72	Jorge Fabregas	.25
73	Ray Holbert	.25
74	Armando Benitez	.25
75	Ernie Young	.25
76	James Mouton	.25
77	*Robert Perez*	.25
78	*Chan Ho Park*	1.00
79	Roger Salkeld	.25
80	Tony Tarasco	.25

Rookies Rookie Phenoms

		NM/M
Complete Set (10):		260.00
Common Player:		1.00
Production 5,000 sets		
1	Raul Mondesi	1.00
2	Bob Hamelin	1.00
3	Midre Cummings	1.00
4	Carlos Delgado	8.00
5	Cliff Floyd	1.00
6	Jeffrey Hammonds	1.00
7	Ryan Klesko	1.00
8	Javier Lopez	1.00
9	Manny Ramirez	10.00
10	Alex Rodriguez	250.00

1995 LEAF

		NM/M
Complete Set (400):		12.50
Common Player:		.05
Series 1 or 2 Pack (12):		.75
Series 1 or 2 Wax Box (36):		15.00
1	Frank Thomas	.75
2	Carlos Garcia	.05
3	Todd Hundley	.05
4	Damion Easley	.05
5	Roberto Mejia	.05
6	John Mabry	.05
7	Aaron Sele	.05
8	Kenny Lofton	.05
9	John Doherty	.05
10	Joe Carter	.05
11	Mike Lansing	.05
12	John Valentin	.05
13	Ismael Valdes	.05
14	Dave McCarty	.05
15	Melvin Nieves	.05
16	Bobby Jones	.05
17	Trevor Hoffman	.05
18	John Smoltz	.05
19	Leo Gomez	.05
20	Roger Pavlik	.05
21	Dean Palmer	.05
22	Rickey Henderson	.75
23	Eddie Taubensee	.05
24	Damon Buford	.05
25	Mark Wohlers	.05
26	Jim Edmonds	.05
27	Wilson Alvarez	.05
28	Matt Williams	.05
29	Jeff Montgomery	.05
30	Shawon Dunston	.05
31	Tom Pagnozzi	.05
32	Jose Lind	.05
33	Royce Clayton	.05
34	Cal Eldred	.05
35	Chris Gomez	.05
36	Henry Rodriguez	.05
37	Dave Fleming	.05
38	Jon Lieber	.05
39	Scott Servais	.05
40	Wade Boggs	1.00
41	John Olerud	.05
42	Eddie Williams	.05
43	Paul Sorrento	.05
44	Ron Karkovice	.05
45	Kevin Foster	.05
46	Miguel Jimenez	.05
47	Reggie Sanders	.05
48	Rondell White	.05
49	Scott Leius	.05
50	Jose Valentin	.05
51	William Van Landingham	.05
52	Denny Hocking	.05
53	Jeff Fassero	.05
54	Chris Hoiles	.05
55	Walt Weiss	.05
56	Geronimo Berroa	.05
57	Rich Rowland	.05
58	Dave Weathers	.05
59	Sterling Hitchcock	.05
60	Raul Mondesi	.05
61	Rusty Greer	.05
62	Dave Justice	.05
63	Cecil Fielder	.05
64	Brian Jordan	.05
65	Mike Lieberthal	.05
66	Rick Aguilera	.05
67	Chuck Finley	.05
68	Andy Ashby	.05
69	Alex Fernandez	.05
70	Ed Sprague	.05
71	Steve Buechele	.05
72	Willie Greene	.05
73	Dave Nilsson	.05
74	Bret Saberhagen	.05
75	Jimmy Key	.05
76	Darren Lewis	.05
77	Steve Cooke	.05
78	Kirk Gibson	.05
79	Ray Lankford	.05
80	Paul O'Neill	.05
81	Mike Bordick	.05
82	Wes Chamberlain	.05
83	Rico Brogna	.05
84	Kevin Appier	.05
85	Juan Guzman	.05
86	Kevin Seitzer	.05
87	Mickey Morandini	.05
88	Pedro Martinez	.75
89	Matt Mieske	.05
90	Tino Martinez	.05
91	Paul Shuey	.05
92	Bip Roberts	.05
93	Chili Davis	.05
94	Deion Sanders	.05
95	Darrell Whitmore	.05
96	Joe Orsulak	.05
97	Bret Boone	.05
98	Kent Mercker	.05
99	Scott Livingstone	.05
100	Brady Anderson	.05
101	James Mouton	.05
102	Jose Rijo	.05
103	Bobby Munoz	.05
104	Ramon Martinez	.05
105	Bernie Williams	.10
106	Troy Neel	.05
107	Ivan Rodriguez	.65
108	Salomon Torres	.05
109	Johnny Ruffin	.05
110	Darryl Kile	.05
111	Bobby Ayala	.05
112	Ron Darling	.05
113	Jose Lima	.05
114	Joey Hamilton	.05
115	Greg Maddux	1.00
116	Greg Colbrunn	.05
117	Ozzie Guillen	.05
118	Brian Anderson	.05
119	Jeff Bagwell	.75
120	Pat Listach	.05
121	Sandy Alomar	.05
122	Jose Vizcaino	.05
123	Rick Helling	.05
124	Allen Watson	.05
125	Pedro Munoz	.05
126	Craig Biggio	.05
127	Kevin Stocker	.05
128	Wil Cordero	.05
129	Rafael Palmeiro	.65
130	Gar Finnvold	.05
131	Darren Hall	.05
132	Heath Slocumb	.05
133	Darrin Fletcher	.05
134	Cal Ripken Jr.	2.50
135	Dante Bichette	.05
136	Don Slaught	.05
137	Pedro Astacio	.05
138	Ryan Thompson	.05
139	Greg Gohr	.05
140	Javier Lopez	.05
141	Lenny Dykstra	.05
142	Pat Rapp	.05
143	Mark Kiefer	.05
144	Greg Gagne	.05
145	Eduardo Perez	.05
146	Felix Fermin	.05
147	Jeff Frye	.05
148	Terry Steinbach	.05
149	Jim Eisenreich	.05
150	Brad Ausmus	.05
151	Randy Myers	.05
152	Rick White	.05
153	Mark Portugal	.05
154	Delino DeShields	.05
155	Scott Cooper	.05
156	Pat Hentgen	.05
157	Mark Gubicza	.05

#	Player	NM/M
158	Carlos Baerga	.05
159	Joe Girardi	.05
160	Rey Sanchez	.05
161	Todd Jones	.05
162	Luis Polonia	.05
163	Steve Trachsel	.05
164	Roberto Hernandez	.05
165	John Patterson	.05
166	Rene Arocha	.05
167	Will Clark	.10
168	Jim Leyritz	.05
169	Todd Van Poppel	.05
170	Robb Nen	.05
171	Midre Cummings	.05
172	Jay Buhner	.05
173	Kevin Tapani	.05
174	Mark Lemke	.05
175	Marcus Moore	.05
176	Wayne Kirby	.05
177	Rich Amaral	.05
178	Lou Whitaker	.05
179	Jay Bell	.05
180	Rick Wilkins	.05
181	Paul Molitor	.75
182	Gary Sheffield	.35
183	Kirby Puckett	1.00
184	Cliff Floyd	.05
185	Darren Oliver	.05
186	Tim Naehring	.05
187	John Hudek	.05
188	Eric Young	.05
189	Roger Salkeld	.05
190	Kirt Manwaring	.05
191	Kurt Abbott	.05
192	David Nied	.05
193	Todd Zeile	.05
194	Wally Joyner	.05
195	Dennis Martinez	.05
196	Billy Ashley	.05
197	Ben McDonald	.05
198	Bob Hamelin	.05
199	Chris Turner	.05
200	Lance Johnson	.05
201	Willie Banks	.05
202	Juan Gonzalez	.50
203	Scott Sanders	.05
204	Scott Brosius	.05
205	Curt Schilling	.25
206	Alex Gonzalez	.05
207	Travis Fryman	.05
208	Tim Raines	.05
209	Steve Avery	.05
210	Hal Morris	.05
211	Ken Griffey Jr.	1.50
212	Ozzie Smith	1.00
213	Chuck Carr	.05
214	Ryan Klesko	.05
215	Robin Ventura	.05
216	Luis Gonzalez	.20
217	Ken Ryan	.05
218	Mike Piazza	1.50
219	Matt Walbeck	.05
220	Jeff Kent	.05
221	Orlando Miller	.05
222	Kenny Rogers	.05
223	J.T. Snow	.05
224	Alan Trammell	.05
225	John Franco	.05
226	Gerald Williams	.05
227	Andy Benes	.05
228	Dan Wilson	.05
229	Dave Hollins	.05
230	Vinny Castilla	.05
231	Devon White	.05
232	Fred McGriff	.05
233	Quilvio Veras	.05
234	Tom Candiotti	.05
235	Jason Bere	.05
236	Mark Langston	.05
237	Mel Rojas	.05
238	Chuck Knoblauch	.05
239	Bernard Gilkey	.05
240	Mark McGwire	2.00
241	Kirk Rueter	.05
242	Pat Kelly	.05
243	Ruben Sierra	.05
244	Randy Johnson	.75
245	Shane Reynolds	.05
246	Danny Tartabull	.05
247	Darryl Hamilton	.05
248	Danny Bautista	.05
249	Tom Gordon	.05
250	Tom Glavine	.25
251	Orlando Merced	.05
252	Eric Karros	.05
253	Benji Gil	.05
254	Sean Bergman	.05
255	Roger Clemens	1.25
256	Roberto Alomar	.20
257	Benito Santiago	.05
258	Robby Thompson	.05
259	Marvin Freeman	.05
260	Jose Offerman	.05
261	Greg Vaughn	.05
262	David Segui	.05
263	Geronimo Pena	.05
264	Tim Salmon	.05
265	Eddie Murray	.75
266	Mariano Duncan	.05
267	*Hideo Nomo*	2.50
268	Derek Bell	.05
269	Mo Vaughn	.05
270	Jeff King	.05
271	Edgar Martinez	.05
272	Sammy Sosa	1.25
273	Scott Ruffcorn	.05
274	Darren Daulton	.05
275	John Jaha	.05
276	Andres Galarraga	.05
277	Mark Grace	.05
278	Mike Moore	.05
279	Barry Bonds	2.50
280	Manny Ramirez	.75
281	Ellis Burks	.05
282	Greg Swindell	.05
283	Barry Larkin	.05
284	Albert Belle	.05
285	Shawn Green	.35
286	John Roper	.05
287	Scott Erickson	.05
288	Moises Alou	.05
289	Mike Blowers	.05
290	Brent Gates	.05
291	Sean Berry	.05
292	Mike Stanley	.05
293	Jeff Conine	.05
294	Tim Wallach	.05
295	Bobby Bonilla	.05
296	Bruce Ruffin	.05
297	Chad Curtis	.05
298	Mike Greenwell	.05
299	Tony Gwynn	1.00
300	Russ Davis	.05
301	Danny Jackson	.05
302	Pete Harnisch	.05
303	Don Mattingly	1.25
304	Rheal Cormier	.05
305	Larry Walker	.05
306	Hector Carrasco	.05
307	Jason Jacome	.05
308	Phil Plantier	.05
309	Harold Baines	.05
310	Mitch Williams	.05
311	Charles Nagy	.05
312	Ken Caminiti	.05
313	Alex Rodriguez	2.00
314	Chris Sabo	.05
315	Gary Gaetti	.05
316	Andre Dawson	.25
317	Mark Clark	.05
318	Vince Coleman	.05
319	Brad Clontz	.05
320	Steve Finley	.05
321	Doug Drabek	.05
322	Mark McLemore	.05
323	Stan Javier	.05
324	Ron Gant	.05
325	Charlie Hayes	.05
326	Carlos Delgado	.50
327	Ricky Bottalico	.05
328	Rod Beck	.05
329	Mark Acre	.05
330	Chris Bosio	.05
331	Tony Phillips	.05
332	Garret Anderson	.05
333	Pat Meares	.05
334	Todd Worrell	.05
335	Marquis Grissom	.05
336	Brent Mayne	.05
337	Lee Tinsley	.05
338	Terry Pendleton	.05
339	David Cone	.05
340	Tony Fernandez	.05
341	Jim Bullinger	.05
342	Armando Benitez	.05
343	John Smiley	.05
344	Dan Miceli	.05
345	Charles Johnson	.05
346	Lee Smith	.05
347	Brian McRae	.05
348	Jim Thome	.65
349	Jose Oliva	.05
350	Terry Mulholland	.05
351	Tom Henke	.05
352	Dennis Eckersley	.65
353	Sid Fernandez	.05
354	Paul Wagner	.05
355	John Dettmer	.05
356	John Wetteland	.05
357	John Burkett	.05
358	Marty Cordova	.05
359	Norm Charlton	.05
360	Mike Devereaux	.05
361	Alex Cole	.05
362	Brett Butler	.05
363	Mickey Tettleton	.05
364	Al Martin	.05
365	Tony Tarasco	.05
366	Pat Mahomes	.05
367	Gary DiSarcina	.05
368	Bill Swift	.05
369	Chipper Jones	1.00
370	Orel Hershiser	.05
371	Kevin Gross	.05
372	Dave Winfield	.75
373	Andujar Cedeno	.05
374	Jim Abbott	.05
375	Glenallen Hill	.05
376	Otis Nixon	.05
377	Roberto Kelly	.05
378	Chris Hammond	.05
379	Mike Macfarlane	.05
380	J.R. Phillips	.05
381	Luis Alicea	.05
382	Bret Barberie	.05
383	Tom Goodwin	.05
384	Mark Whiten	.05
385	Jeffrey Hammonds	.05
386	Omar Vizquel	.05
387	Mike Mussina	.35
388	Rickey Bones	.05
389	Steve Ontiveros	.05
390	Jeff Blauser	.05
391	Jose Canseco	.35
392	Bob Tewksbury	.05
393	Jacob Brumfield	.05
394	Doug Jones	.05
395	Ken Hill	.05
396	Pat Borders	.05
397	Carl Everett	.05
398	Gregg Jefferies	.05
399	Jack McDowell	.05
400	Denny Neagle	.05

Cornerstones

		NM/M
Complete Set (6):		3.50
Common Player:		.40
1	Frank Thomas, Robin Ventura	.75
2	Cecil Fielder, Travis Fryman	.40
3	Don Mattingly, Wade Boggs	2.00
4	Jeff Bagwell, Ken Caminiti	.75
5	Will Clark, Dean Palmer	.40
6	J.R. Phillips, Matt Williams	.40

Frank Thomas

		NM/M
Complete Set (6):		7.50
Common Card:		1.50
1	The Rookie	1.50
2	Sophomore Stardom	1.50
3	Super Star	1.50
4	AL MVP	1.50
5	Back-To-Back	1.50
6	The Big Hurt	1.50

Gold Stars

		NM/M
Complete Set (14):		35.00
Common Player:		1.00
1	Jeff Bagwell	2.50
2	Albert Belle	1.00
3	Tony Gwynn	3.50
4	Ken Griffey Jr.	4.50
5	Barry Bonds	6.00
6	Don Mattingly	4.00
7	Raul Mondesi	1.00
8	Joe Carter	1.00
9	Greg Maddux	3.50
10	Frank Thomas	2.50
11	Mike Piazza	4.50
12	Jose Canseco	1.50
13	Kirby Puckett	3.50
14	Matt Williams	1.00

Gold Rookies

		NM/M
Complete Set (16):		3.00
Common Player:		.10
1	Alex Rodriguez	2.50
2	Garret Anderson	.10
3	Shawn Green	.50
4	Armando Benitez	.10
5	Darren Dreifort	.10
6	Orlando Miller	.10
7	Jose Oliva	.10
8	Ricky Bottalico	.10
9	Charles Johnson	.10
10	Brian Hunter	.10
11	Ray McDavid	.10
12	Chan Ho Park	.10
13	Mike Kelly	.10
14	Cory Bailey	.10
15	Alex Gonzalez	.10
16	Andrew Lorraine	.10

Great Gloves

		NM/M
Complete Set (16):		3.00
Common Player:		.15
1	Jeff Bagwell	.35
2	Roberto Alomar	.20
3	Barry Bonds	1.00
4	Wade Boggs	.45
5	Andres Galarraga	.15
6	Ken Griffey Jr.	.60
7	Marquis Grissom	.15
8	Kenny Lofton	.15
9	Barry Larkin	.15
10	Don Mattingly	.50
11	Greg Maddux	.45

12	Kirby Puckett	.45
13	Ozzie Smith	.45
14	Cal Ripken Jr.	1.00
15	Matt Williams	.15
16	Ivan Rodriguez	.30

Heading for the Hall

		NM/M
Complete Set (8):		50.00
Common Player:		4.50
1	Frank Thomas	4.50
2	Ken Griffey Jr.	9.00
3	Jeff Bagwell	4.50
4	Barry Bonds	15.00
5	Kirby Puckett	6.00
6	Cal Ripken Jr.	15.00
7	Tony Gwynn	6.00
8	Paul Molitor	4.50

Slideshow

		NM/M
Complete Set (16):		35.00
Complete Series 1 (1a-8a):		20.00
Complete Series 2 (1b-8b):		20.00
Same CL and prices for both series		
Common Player:		1.50
1a	Raul Mondesi	1.50
1b	Raul Mondesi	1.50
2a	Frank Thomas	3.00
2b	Frank Thomas	3.00
3a	Fred McGriff	1.50
3b	Fred McGriff	1.50
4a	Cal Ripken Jr.	6.00
4b	Cal Ripken Jr.	6.00
5a	Jeff Bagwell	3.00
5b	Jeff Bagwell	3.00
6a	Will Clark	1.50
6b	Will Clark	1.50
7a	Matt Williams	1.50
7b	Matt Williams	1.50
8a	Ken Griffey Jr.	4.50
8b	Ken Griffey Jr.	4.50

Statistical Standouts

		NM/M
Complete Set (9):		95.00
Common Player:		3.00
Promos:		25-50%
1	Joe Carter	3.00
2	Ken Griffey Jr.	25.00
3	Don Mattingly	15.00
4	Fred McGriff	3.00
5	Paul Molitor	9.00
6	Kirby Puckett	12.50
7	Cal Ripken Jr.	30.00
8	Frank Thomas	9.00
9	Matt Williams	3.00

300 Club

		NM/M
Complete Set (18):		12.50
Common Player:		.25
1	Frank Thomas	1.00
2	Paul Molitor	1.00
3	Mike Piazza	3.00
4	Moises Alou	.25
5	Mike Greenwell	.25
6	Will Clark	.25
7	Hal Morris	.25
8	Edgar Martinez	.25
9	Carlos Baerga	.25
10	Ken Griffey Jr.	3.00
11	Wade Boggs	1.50
12	Jeff Bagwell	1.00
13	Tony Gwynn	1.50
14	John Kruk	.25
15	Don Mattingly	2.00
16	Mark Grace	.25
17	Kirby Puckett	1.50
18	Kenny Lofton	.25

1995 LEAF/LIMITED

		NM/M
Complete Set (192):		20.00
Common Player:		.10
Series 1 or 2 Pack (5):		2.00
Series 1 or 2 Wax Box (20):		30.00
1	Frank Thomas	.75
2	Geronimo Berroa	.10
3	Tony Phillips	.10
4	Roberto Alomar	.25
5	Steve Avery	.10
6	Darryl Hamilton	.10
7	Scott Cooper	.10
8	Mark Grace	.10
9	Billy Ashley	.10
10	Wil Cordero	.10
11	Barry Bonds	5.00
12	Kenny Lofton	.10
13	Jay Buhner	.10
14	Alex Rodriguez	3.00
15	Bobby Bonilla	.10
16	Brady Anderson	.10
17	Ken Caminiti	.10
18	Charlie Hayes	.10
19	Jay Bell	.10
20	Will Clark	.15
21	Jose Canseco	.35
22	Bret Boone	.10
23	Dante Bichette	.10
24	Kevin Appier	.10
25	Chad Curtis	.10
26	Marty Cordova	.10
27	Jason Bere	.10
28	Jimmy Key	.10
29	Rickey Henderson	.75
30	Tim Salmon	.10
31	Joe Carter	.10
32	Tom Glavine	.35
33	Pat Listach	.10
34	Brian Jordan	.10
35	Brian McRae	.10
36	Eric Karros	.10
37	Pedro Martinez	.75
38	Royce Clayton	.10
39	Eddie Murray	.75
40	Randy Johnson	.75
41	Jeff Conine	.10
42	Brett Butler	.10
43	Jeffrey Hammonds	.10
44	Andujar Cedeno	.10
45	Dave Hollins	.10
46	Jeff King	.10
47	Benji Gil	.10
48	Roger Clemens	2.00
49	Barry Larkin	.10
50	Joe Girardi	.10
51	Bob Hamelin	.10
52	Travis Fryman	.10
53	Chuck Knoblauch	.10
54	Ray Durham	.10
55	Don Mattingly	2.00
56	Ruben Sierra	.10
57	J.T. Snow	.10
58	Derek Bell	.10
59	David Cone	.10
60	Marquis Grissom	.10
61	Kevin Seitzer	.10
62	Ozzie Smith	1.50
63	Rick Wilkins	.10
64	*Hideo Nomo*	3.00
65	Tony Tarasco	.10
66	Manny Ramirez	.75
67	Charles Johnson	.10
68	Craig Biggio	.10
69	Bobby Jones	.10
70	Mike Mussina	.60
71	Alex Gonzalez	.10
72	Gregg Jefferies	.10
73	Rusty Greer	.10
74	Mike Greenwell	.10
75	Hal Morris	.10
76	Paul O'Neill	.10
77	Luis Gonzalez	.25
78	Chipper Jones	1.50
79	Mike Piazza	2.50
80	Rondell White	.10
81	Glenallen Hill	.10
82	Shawn Green	.50
83	Bernie Williams	.10
84	Jim Thome	.65
85	Terry Pendleton	.10
86	Rafael Palmeiro	.65
87	Tony Gwynn	1.50
88	Mickey Tettleton	.10
89	John Valentin	.10
90	Deion Sanders	.10
91	Larry Walker	.10
92	Michael Tucker	.10
93	Alan Trammell	.10
94	Tim Raines	.10
95	Dave Justice	.10
96	Tino Martinez	.10
97	Cal Ripken Jr.	5.00
98	Deion Sanders	.10
99	Darren Daulton	.10
100	Paul Molitor	.75
101	Randy Myers	.10
102	Wally Joyner	.10
103	Carlos Perez	.10
104	Brian Hunter	.10
105	Wade Boggs	1.50
106	*Bobby Higginson*	.50
107	Jeff Kent	.10
108	Jose Offerman	.10
109	Dennis Eckersley	.65
110	Dave Nilsson	.10
111	Chuck Finley	.10
112	Devon White	.10
113	Bip Roberts	.10
114	Ramon Martinez	.10
115	Greg Maddux	1.50
116	Curtis Goodwin	.10
117	John Jaha	.10
118	Ken Griffey Jr.	2.50
119	Geronimo Pena	.10
120	Shawon Dunston	.10
121	Ariel Prieto	.10
122	Kirby Puckett	1.50
123	Carlos Baerga	.10
124	Todd Hundley	.10
125	Tim Naehring	.10
126	Gary Sheffield	.45
127	Dean Palmer	.10
128	Rondell White	.10
129	Greg Gagne	.10
130	Jose Rijo	.10
131	Ivan Rodriguez	.65
132	Jeff Bagwell	.75
133	Greg Vaughn	.10
134	Chili Davis	.10
135	Al Martin	.10
136	Kenny Rogers	.10
137	Aaron Sele	.10
138	Raul Mondesi	.10
139	Cecil Fielder	.10
140	Tim Wallach	.10
141	Andres Galarraga	.10
142	Lou Whitaker	.10
143	Jack McDowell	.10
144	Matt Williams	.10
145	Ryan Klesko	.10
146	Carlos Garcia	.10
147	Albert Belle	.10
148	Ryan Thompson	.10
149	Roberto Kelly	.10
150	Edgar Martinez	.10
151	Robby Thompson	.10
152	Mo Vaughn	.10
153	Todd Zeile	.10
154	Harold Baines	.10
155	Phil Plantier	.10
156	Mike Stanley	.10
157	Ed Sprague	.10
158	Moises Alou	.10
159	Quilvio Veras	.10
160	Reggie Sanders	.10
161	Delino DeShields	.10
162	Rico Brogna	.10
163	Greg Colbrunn	.10
164	Steve Finley	.10
165	Orlando Merced	.10
166	Mark McGwire	3.00
167	Garret Anderson	.10
168	Paul Sorrento	.10
169	Mark Langston	.10
170	Danny Tartabull	.10
171	Vinny Castilla	.10
172	Javier Lopez	.10
173	Bret Saberhagen	.10
174	Eddie Williams	.10
175	Scott Leius	.10
176	Juan Gonzalez	.50
177	Gary Gaetti	.10
178	Jim Edmonds	.10
179	John Olerud	.10
180	Lenny Dykstra	.10
181	Ray Lankford	.10
182	Ron Gant	.10
183	Doug Drabek	.10
184	Fred McGriff	.10
185	Andy Benes	.10
186	Kurt Abbott	.10
187	Bernard Gilkey	.10
188	Sammy Sosa	2.00
189	Lee Smith	.10
190	Dennis Martinez	.10
191	Ozzie Guillen	.10
192	Robin Ventura	.10

Gold

		NM/M
Complete Set (24):		10.00
Common Player:		.25
1	Frank Thomas	.60
2	Jeff Bagwell	.60
3	Raul Mondesi	.25
4	Barry Bonds	1.50
5	Albert Belle	.25
6	Ken Griffey Jr.	1.00
7	Cal Ripkin (Ripken) Jr.	1.50
8	Will Clark	.25
9	Jose Canseco	.45
10	Larry Walker	.25
11	Kirby Puckett	.75
12	Don Mattingly	1.00
13	Tim Salmon	.25
14	Roberto Alomar	.35
15	Greg Maddux	.75
16	Mike Piazza	1.00
17	Matt Williams	.25
18	Kenny Lofton	.25
19	Alex Rodriquez (Rodriguez)	1.25
20	Tony Gwynn	.75
21	Mo Vaughn	.25
22	Chipper Jones	.75
23	Manny Ramirez	.60
24	Deion Sanders	.25

Lumberjacks

		NM/M
Complete Set (16):		55.00
Common Player:		2.00
1	Albert Belle	2.00
2	Barry Bonds	12.00
3	Juan Gonzalez	3.50
4	Ken Griffey Jr.	7.50
5	Fred McGriff	2.00
6	Mike Piazza	7.50
7	Kirby Puckett	6.00
8	Mo Vaughn	2.00
9	Frank Thomas	4.50
10	Jeff Bagwell	4.50
11	Matt Williams	2.00
12	Jose Canseco	3.00

13	Raul Mondesi	2.00
14	Manny Ramirez	4.50
15	Cecil Fielder	2.00
16	Cal Ripken Jr.	12.00

Bat Patrol

		NM/M
Complete Set (24):		7.50
Common Player:		.15
1	Frank Thomas	.75
2	Tony Gwynn	1.00
3	Wade Boggs	1.00
4	Larry Walker	.25
5	Ken Griffey Jr.	1.50
6	Jeff Bagwell	.75
7	Manny Ramirez	.75
8	Mark Grace	.25
9	Kenny Lofton	.15
10	Mike Piazza	1.50
11	Will Clark	.25
12	Mo Vaughn	.25
13	Carlos Baerga	.15
14	Rafael Palmeiro	.65
15	Barry Bonds	2.50
16	Kirby Puckett	1.00
17	Roberto Alomar	.35
18	Barry Larkin	.15
19	Eddie Murray	.75
20	Tim Salmon	.25
21	Don Mattingly	1.25
22	Fred McGriff	.15
23	Albert Belle	.25
24	Dante Bichette	.15

1996 LEAF

		NM/M
Complete Set (220):		10.00
Common Player:		.05
Pack (12):		1.00
Wax Box (30):		25.00
1	John Smoltz	.10
2	Dennis Eckersley	.60
3	Delino DeShields	.05
4	Cliff Floyd	.05
5	Chuck Finley	.05
6	Cecil Fielder	.05
7	Tim Naehring	.05
8	Carlos Perez	.05
9	Brad Ausmus	.05
10	*Matt Lawton*	.15
11	Alan Trammell	.05
12	Steve Finley	.05
13	Paul O'Neill	.05
14	Gary Sheffield	.40
15	Mark McGwire	1.50
16	Bernie Williams	.05
17	Jeff Montgomery	.05
18	Chan Ho Park	.05
19	Greg Vaughn	.05
20	Jeff Kent	.05
21	Cal Ripken Jr.	2.00
22	Charles Johnson	.05
23	Eric Karros	.05
24	Alex Rodriguez	1.50
25	Chris Snopek	.05
26	Jason Isringhausen	.05
27	Chili Davis	.05
28	Chipper Jones	.75
29	Bret Saberhagen	.05
30	Tony Clark	.05
31	Marty Cordova	.05
32	Dwayne Hosey	.05
33	Fred McGriff	.05
34	Deion Sanders	.05
35	Orlando Merced	.05
36	Brady Anderson	.05
37	Ray Lankford	.05
38	Manny Ramirez	.65
39	Alex Fernandez	.05
40	Greg Colbrunn	.05
41	Ken Griffey Jr.	1.00
42	Mickey Morandini	.05
43	Chuck Knoblauch	.05
44	Quinton McCracken	.05
45	Tim Salmon	.05
46	Jose Mesa	.05
47	Marquis Grissom	.05
48	Checklist	.05
49	Raul Mondesi	.05
50	Mark Grudzielanek	.05
51	Ray Durham	.05
52	Matt Williams	.05
53	Bob Hamelin	.05
54	Lenny Dykstra	.05
55	Jeff King	.05
56	LaTroy Hawkins	.05
57	Terry Pendleton	.05
58	Kevin Stocker	.05
59	Ozzie Timmons	.05
60	David Justice	.05
61	Ricky Bottalico	.05
62	Andy Ashby	.05
63	Larry Walker	.05
64	Jose Canseco	.40
65	Bret Boone	.05
66	Shawn Green	.35
67	Chad Curtis	.05
68	Travis Fryman	.05
69	Roger Clemens	1.00
70	David Bell	.05
71	Rusty Greer	.05
72	Bob Higginson	.05
73	Joey Hamilton	.05
74	Kevin Seitzer	.05
75	Julian Tavarez	.05
76	Troy Percival	.05
77	Kirby Puckett	.75
78	Barry Bonds	2.00
79	Michael Tucker	.05
80	Paul Molitor	.65
81	Carlos Garcia	.05
82	Johnny Damon	.35
83	Mike Hampton	.05
84	Ariel Prieto	.05
85	Tony Tarasco	.05
86	Pete Schourek	.05
87	Tom Glavine	.30
88	Rondell White	.05
89	Jim Edmonds	.05
90	Robby Thompson	.05
91	Wade Boggs	.75
92	Pedro Martinez	.65
93	Gregg Jefferies	.05
94	Albert Belle	.05
95	Benji Gil	.05
96	Denny Neagle	.05
97	Mark Langston	.05
98	Sandy Alomar	.05
99	Tony Gwynn	.75
100	Todd Hundley	.05
101	Dante Bichette	.05
102	Eddie Murray	.65
103	Lyle Mouton	.05
104	John Jaha	.05
105	Checklist	.05
106	Jon Nunnally	.05
107	Juan Gonzalez	.50
108	Kevin Appier	.05
109	Brian McRae	.05
110	Lee Smith	.05
111	Tim Wakefield	.05
112	Sammy Sosa	1.00
113	Jay Buhner	.05
114	Garret Anderson	.05
115	Edgar Martinez	.05
116	Edgardo Alfonzo	.05
117	Billy Ashley	.05
118	Joe Carter	.05
119	Javy Lopez	.05
120	Bobby Bonilla	.05
121	Ken Caminiti	.05
122	Barry Larkin	.05
123	Shannon Stewart	.05
124	Orel Hershiser	.05
125	Jeff Conine	.05
126	Mark Grace	.05
127	Kenny Lofton	.05
128	Luis Gonzalez	.25
129	Rico Brogna	.05
130	Mo Vaughn	.05
131	Brad Radke	.05
132	Jose Herrera	.05
133	Rick Aguilera	.05
134	Gary DiSarcina	.05
135	Andres Galarraga	.05
136	Carl Everett	.05
137	Steve Avery	.05
138	Vinny Castilla	.05
139	Dennis Martinez	.05
140	John Wetteland	.05
141	Alex Gonzalez	.05
142	Brian Jordan	.05
143	Todd Hollandsworth	.05
144	Terrell Wade	.05
145	Wilson Alvarez	.05
146	Reggie Sanders	.05
147	Will Clark	.10
148	Hideo Nomo	.50
149	J.T. Snow	.05
150	Frank Thomas	.65
151	Ivan Rodriguez	.60
152	Jay Bell	.05
153	Checklist	.05
154	David Cone	.05
155	Roberto Alomar	.20
156	Carlos Delgado	.40
157	Carlos Baerga	.05
158	Geronimo Berroa	.05
159	Joe Vitiello	.05
160	Terry Steinbach	.05
161	Doug Drabek	.05
162	David Segui	.05
163	Ozzie Smith	.75
164	Kurt Abbott	.05
165	Randy Johnson	.65
166	John Valentin	.05
167	Mickey Tettleton	.05
168	Ruben Sierra	.05
169	Jim Thome	.60
170	Mike Greenwell	.05
171	Quilvio Veras	.05
172	Robin Ventura	.05
173	Bill Pulsipher	.05
174	Rafael Palmeiro	.60
175	Hal Morris	.05
176	Ryan Klesko	.05
177	Eric Young	.05
178	Shane Andrews	.05
179	Brian Hunter	.05
180	Brett Butler	.05
181	John Olerud	.05
182	Moises Alou	.05
183	Glenallen Hill	.05
184	Ismael Valdes	.05
185	Andy Pettitte	.25
186	Yamil Benitez	.05
187	Jason Bere	.05
188	Dean Palmer	.05
189	Jimmy Haynes	.05
190	Trevor Hoffman	.05
191	Mike Mussina	.40
192	Greg Maddux	.75
193	Ozzie Guillen	.05
194	Pat Listach	.05
195	Derek Bell	.05
196	Darren Daulton	.05
197	John Mabry	.05
198	Ramon Martinez	.05
199	Jeff Bagwell	.65
200	Mike Piazza	1.00
201	Al Martin	.05
202	Aaron Sele	.05
203	Ed Sprague	.05
204	Rod Beck	.05
205	Checklist	.05
206	Mike Lansing	.05
207	Craig Biggio	.05
208	Jeffrey Hammonds	.05
209	Dave Nilsson	.05
210	Dante Bichette, Albert Belle Checklist, Inserts	.05
211	Derek Jeter	2.00
212	Alan Benes	.05
213	Jason Schmidt	.05
214	Alex Ochoa	.05
215	Ruben Rivera	.05
216	Roger Cedeno	.05
217	Jeff Suppan	.05
218	Billy Wagner	.05
219	Mark Loretta	.05
220	Karim Garcia	.10

Press Proofs

	NM/M
Complete Set, Gold (220):	200.00
Complete Set, Silver (220):	100.00
Complete Set, Bronze (220):	75.00
Common Player, Gold:	1.00
Common Player, Silver:	.50
Common Player, Bronze:	.25

(Press Proof stars valued as follows in comparison to regular-issue '96 Leaf: Gold - 15X; Silver - 6X; Bronze - 4X.)

All-Star MVP Contenders

		NM/M
Complete Set (20):		12.50
Common Card:		.25
Golds:		1.5X
1	Frank Thomas	.75
2	Mike Piazza	1.50
2c	Mike Piazza (redeemed and punch-cancelled)	1.00
3	Sammy Sosa	1.50
4	Cal Ripken Jr.	2.00
5	Jeff Bagwell	.75
6	Reggie Sanders	.25
7	Mo Vaughn	.25
8	Tony Gwynn	1.00
9	Dante Bichette	.25
10	Tim Salmon	.25
11	Chipper Jones	1.00
12	Kenny Lofton	.25
13	Manny Ramirez	.75
14	Barry Bonds	2.00
15	Raul Mondesi	.25
16	Kirby Puckett	1.00
17	Albert Belle	.25
18	Ken Griffey Jr.	1.50
19	Greg Maddux	1.00
20	Bonus card	.10

Frank Thomas' Greatest Hits

		NM/M
Complete Set (8):		12.50
Common Card:		2.00
1	1990	2.00
2	1991	2.00
3	1992	2.00
4	1993	2.00
5	1994	2.00
6	1995	2.00
7	Career	2.00
8	MVP	2.00

Frank Thomas The Big Heart

		NM/M
Complete Set (4):		35.00
Common Card:		10.00
(1)	Frank Thomas (bat on shoulder)	10.00
(2)	Frank Thomas (holding glove)	10.00

(3)	Frank Thomas (horizontal)	10.00
(4)	Frank Thomas (seated)	10.00

Gold Leaf Stars

		NM/M
Complete Set (15):		125.00
Common Player:		3.00
1	Frank Thomas	9.00
2	Dante Bichette	3.00
3	Sammy Sosa	15.00
4	Ken Griffey Jr.	15.00
5	Mike Piazza	15.00
6	Tim Salmon	3.00
7	Hideo Nomo	6.00
8	Cal Ripken Jr.	20.00
9	Chipper Jones	12.00
10	Albert Belle	3.00
11	Tony Gwynn	12.00
12	Mo Vaughn	3.00
13	Barry Larkin	3.00
14	Manny Ramirez	9.00
15	Greg Maddux	12.00

Hats Off

		NM/M
Complete Set (8):		30.00
Common Player:		3.00
1	Cal Ripken Jr.	12.00
2	Barry Larkin	3.00
3	Frank Thomas	4.50
4	Mo Vaughn	3.00
5	Ken Griffey Jr.	7.50
6	Hideo Nomo	4.00
7	Albert Belle	3.00
8	Greg Maddux	6.00

Picture Perfect

		NM/M
Complete Set (12):		22.50
Common Player:		1.00
Promos:		2X
1	Frank Thomas	2.00
2	Cal Ripken Jr.	5.00
3	Greg Maddux	2.50
4	Manny Ramirez	2.00
5	Chipper Jones	2.50
6	Tony Gwynn	2.50
7	Ken Griffey Jr.	3.00
8	Albert Belle	1.00
9	Jeff Bagwell	2.00
10	Mike Piazza	3.00
11	Mo Vaughn	1.00
12	Barry Bonds	5.00

Statistical Standouts

		NM/M
Complete Set (8):		60.00
Common Player:		3.00

1	Cal Ripken Jr.	20.00
2	Tony Gwynn	10.00
3	Frank Thomas	7.50
4	Ken Griffey Jr.	13.50
5	Hideo Nomo	6.00
6	Greg Maddux	10.00
7	Albert Belle	3.00
8	Chipper Jones	10.00

Total Bases

		NM/M
Complete Set (12):		25.00
Common Player:		1.00
Promos:		2X
1	Frank Thomas	2.50
2	Albert Belle	1.00
3	Rafael Palmeiro	2.00
4	Barry Bonds	6.00
5	Kirby Puckett	3.00
6	Joe Carter	1.00
7	Paul Molitor	2.50
8	Fred McGriff	1.00
9	Ken Griffey Jr.	4.00
10	Carlos Baerga	1.00
11	Juan Gonzalez	2.00
12	Cal Ripken Jr.	6.00

1996 LEAF/LIMITED

		NM/M
Complete Set (90):		15.00
Common Player:		.10
Gold Set (90):		50.00
Gold Stars/Rookies:		3X
Pack (5):		1.50
Wax Box (14):		20.00
1	Ivan Rodriguez	.60
2	Roger Clemens	1.50
3	Gary Sheffield	.40
4	Tino Martinez	.10
5	Sammy Sosa	1.50
6	Reggie Sanders	.10
7	Ray Lankford	.10
8	Manny Ramirez	.75
9	Jeff Bagwell	.75
10	Greg Maddux	1.00
11	Ken Griffey Jr.	1.50
12	Rondell White	.10
13	Mike Piazza	1.50
14	Marc Newfield	.10
15	Cal Ripken Jr.	3.00
16	Carlos Delgado	.40
17	Tim Salmon	.10
18	Andres Galarraga	.10
19	Chuck Knoblauch	.10
20	Matt Williams	.10
21	Mark McGwire	2.00
22	Ben McDonald	.10
23	Frank Thomas	.75
24	Johnny Damon	.35
25	Gregg Jefferies	.10
26	Travis Fryman	.10
27	Chipper Jones	1.00
28	David Cone	.10
29	Kenny Lofton	.10
30	Mike Mussina	.30
31	Alex Rodriguez	2.00
32	Carlos Baerga	.10
33	Brian Hunter	.10
34	Juan Gonzalez	.60
35	Bernie Williams	.10
36	Wally Joyner	.10
37	Fred McGriff	.10
38	Randy Johnson	.75
39	Marty Cordova	.10
40	Garret Anderson	.10
41	Albert Belle	.10
42	Edgar Martinez	.10
43	Barry Larkin	.10
44	Paul O'Neill	.10
45	Cecil Fielder	.10
46	Rusty Greer	.10
47	Mo Vaughn	.10
48	Dante Bichette	.10
49	Ryan Klesko	.10
50	Roberto Alomar	.25
51	Raul Mondesi	.10
52	Robin Ventura	.10
53	Tony Gwynn	1.00
54	Mark Grace	.10
55	Jim Thome	.60
56	Jason Giambi	.50
57	Tom Glavine	.25
58	Jim Edmonds	.10
59	Pedro Martinez	.75
60	Charles Johnson	.10
61	Wade Boggs	1.00
62	Orlando Merced	.10
63	Craig Biggio	.10
64	Brady Anderson	.10
65	Hideo Nomo	.60
66	Ozzie Smith	1.00
67	Eddie Murray	.75
68	Will Clark	.15
69	Jay Buhner	.10
70	Kirby Puckett	1.00
71	Barry Bonds	3.00
72	Ray Durham	.10
73	Sterling Hitchcock	.10
74	John Smoltz	.10
75	Andre Dawson	.35
76	Joe Carter	.10
77	Ryne Sandberg	1.00
78	Rickey Henderson	.75
79	Brian Jordan	.10
80	Greg Vaughn	.10
81	Andy Pettitte	.25
82	Dean Palmer	.10
83	Paul Molitor	.75
84	Rafael Palmeiro	.60
85	Henry Rodriguez	.10
86	Larry Walker	.10
87	Ismael Valdes	.10
88	Derek Bell	.10
89	J.T. Snow	.10
90	Jack McDowell	.10

Lumberjacks

		NM/M
Complete Set (10):		40.00
Common Player:		1.50
Lumberjack Blacks (500):		2X
Promos:		2X
1	Ken Griffey Jr.	5.00
2	Sammy Sosa	5.00
3	Cal Ripken Jr.	7.50
4	Frank Thomas	3.00
5	Alex Rodriguez	6.00
6	Mo Vaughn	1.50
7	Chipper Jones	4.00
8	Mike Piazza	5.00
9	Jeff Bagwell	3.00
10	Mark McGwire	6.00

Pennant Craze

		NM/M
Complete Set (10):		20.00
Common Player:		1.00
Promos:		2X
1	Juan Gonzalez	1.25
2	Cal Ripken Jr.	4.00
3	Frank Thomas	1.50
4	Ken Griffey Jr.	2.50
5	Albert Belle	1.00
6	Greg Maddux	2.00
7	Paul Molitor	1.50
8	Alex Rodriguez	3.00
9	Barry Bonds	4.00
10	Chipper Jones	2.00

Rookies

		NM/M
Complete Set (10):		7.50
Common Player:		.50
Limited Gold:		3X
1	Alex Ochoa	.50
2	Darin Erstad	1.00
3	Ruben Rivera	.50
4	Derek Jeter	5.00
5	Jermaine Dye	.50
6	Jason Kendall	.50
7	Mike Grace	.50
8	Andruw Jones	2.50
9	Rey Ordonez	.50
10	George Arias	.50

1996 LEAF/ PREFERRED

		NM/M
Complete Set (150):		15.00
Common Player:		.05
Pack (6):		1.00
Wax Box (24):		20.00
1	Ken Griffey Jr.	1.25
2	Rico Brogna	.05
3	Gregg Jefferies	.05
4	Reggie Sanders	.05
5	Manny Ramirez	.75
6	Shawn Green	.40
7	Tino Martinez	.05
8	Jeff Bagwell	.75
9	Marc Newfield	.05
10	Ray Lankford	.05
11	Jay Bell	.05
12	Greg Maddux	1.00
13	Frank Thomas	.75
14	Travis Fryman	.05
15	Mark McGwire	1.50
16	Chuck Knoblauch	.05
17	Sammy Sosa	1.25
18	Matt Williams	.05
19	Roger Clemens	1.25
20	Rondell White	.05
21	Ivan Rodriguez	.65
22	Cal Ripken Jr.	2.00
23	Ben McDonald	.05
24	Kenny Lofton	.05
25	Mike Piazza	1.25

26 David Cone .05
27 Gary Sheffield .40
28 Tim Salmon .05
29 Andres Galarraga .05
30 Johnny Damon .35
31 Ozzie Smith 1.00
32 Carlos Baerga .05
33 Raul Mondesi .05
34 Moises Alou .05
35 Alex Rodriguez 1.50
36 Mike Mussina .40
37 Jason Isringhausen .05
38 Barry Larkin .05
39 Bernie Williams .05
40 Chipper Jones 1.00
41 Joey Hamilton .05
42 Charles Johnson .05
43 Juan Gonzalez .50
44 Greg Vaughn .05
45 Robin Ventura .05
46 Albert Belle .05
47 Rafael Palmeiro .65
48 Brian Hunter .05
49 Mo Vaughn .05
50 Paul O'Neill .05
51 Mark Grace .05
52 Randy Johnson .75
53 Pedro Martinez .75
54 Marty Cordova .05
55 Garret Anderson .05
56 Joe Carter .05
57 Jim Thome .60
58 Edgardo Alfonzo .05
59 Dante Bichette .05
60 Darryl Hamilton .05
61 Roberto Alomar .20
62 Fred McGriff .05
63 Kirby Puckett 1.00
64 Hideo Nomo .60
65 Alex Fernandez .05
66 Ryan Klesko .05
67 Wade Boggs 1.00
68 Eddie Murray .75
69 Eric Karros .05
70 Jim Edmonds .05
71 Edgar Martinez .05
72 Andy Pettitte .30
73 Mark Grudzielanek .05
74 Tom Glavine .25
75 Ken Caminiti .05
76 Will Clark .10
77 Craig Biggio .05
78 Brady Anderson .05
79 Tony Gwynn 1.00
80 Larry Walker .05
81 Brian Jordan .05
82 Lenny Dykstra .05
83 Butch Huskey .05
84 Jack McDowell .05
85 Cecil Fielder .05
86 Jose Canseco .40
87 Jason Giambi .50
88 Rickey Henderson .75
89 Kevin Seitzer .05
90 Carlos Delgado .40
91 Ryne Sandberg 1.00
92 Dwight Gooden .05
93 Michael Tucker .05
94 Barry Bonds 2.00
95 Eric Young .05
96 Dean Palmer .05
97 Henry Rodriguez .05
98 John Mabry .05
99 J.T. Snow .05
100 Andre Dawson .25
101 Ismael Valdes .05
102 Charles Nagy .05
103 Jay Buhner .05
104 Derek Bell .05
105 Paul Molitor .75
106 Hal Morris .05
107 Ray Durham .05
108 Bernard Gilkey .05
109 John Valentin .05
110 Melvin Nieves .05
111 John Smoltz .05
112 Terrell Wade .05
113 Chad Mottola .05
114 Tony Clark .05
115 John Wasdin .05
116 Derek Jeter 2.00
117 Rey Ordonez .05
118 Jason Thompson .05
119 *Robin Jennings* .05
120 *Rocky Coppinger* .05
121 Billy Wagner .05
122 Steve Gibralter .05
123 Jermaine Dye .05
124 Jason Kendall .05
125 *Mike Grace* .05
126 Jason Schmidt .05
127 Paul Wilson .05
128 Alan Benes .05
129 Justin Thompson .05
130 Brooks Kieschnick .05
131 George Arias .05
132 *Osvaldo Fernandez* .20
133 Todd Hollandsworth .05
134 Eric Owens .05
135 Chan Ho Park .05
136 Mark Loretta .05
137 Ruben Rivera .05
138 Jeff Suppan .05
139 Ugueth Urbina .05
140 LaTroy Hawkins .05
141 Chris Snopek .05
142 Edgar Renteria .05
143 Raul Casanova .05
144 Jose Herrera .05
145 *Matt Lawton* .05
146 *Ralph Milliard* .05
147 Frank Thomas Checklist .05
148 Jeff Bagwell Checklist .05
149 Ken Griffey Jr. Checklist .05
150 Mike Piazza Checklist .05

Press Proofs

NM/M
Complete Set (150): 100.00
Common Player: .50
Stars/Rookies: 12X
(See 1996 Leaf Preferred for checklist and base card values.)

Leaf Steel

NM/M
Complete Set (77): 25.00
Common Player: .15
Gold: 2X
1 Frank Thomas 1.00
2 Paul Molitor 1.00
3 Kenny Lofton .15
4 Travis Fryman .15
5 Jeff Conine .15
6 Barry Bonds 3.00
7 Gregg Jefferies .15
8 Alex Rodriguez 2.50
9 Wade Boggs 1.50
10 David Justice .15
11 Hideo Nomo .75
12 Roberto Alomar .30
13 Todd Hollandsworth .15
14 Mark McGwire 2.50
15 Rafael Palmeiro .75
16 Will Clark .25
17 Cal Ripken Jr. 3.00
18 Derek Bell .15
19 Gary Sheffield .50
20 Juan Gonzalez .65
21 Garret Anderson .15
22 Mo Vaughn .15
23 Robin Ventura .15
24 Carlos Baerga .15
25 Tim Salmon .15
26 Matt Williams .15
27 Fred McGriff .15
28 Rondell White .15
29 Ray Lankford .15
30 Lenny Dykstra .15
31 J.T. Snow .15
32 Sammy Sosa 2.00
33 Chipper Jones 1.50
34 Bobby Bonilla .15
35 Paul Wilson .15
36 Darren Daulton .15
37 Larry Walker .15
38 Raul Mondesi .15
39 Jeff Bagwell 1.00
40 Derek Jeter 3.00
41 Kirby Puckett 1.50
42 Jason Isringhausen .15
43 Vinny Castilla .15
44 Jim Edmonds .15
45 Ron Gant .15
46 Carlos Delgado .50
47 Jose Canseco .40
48 Tony Gwynn 1.50
49 Mike Mussina .50
50 Charles Johnson .15
51 Mike Piazza 2.00
52 Ken Griffey Jr. 2.00
53 Greg Maddux 1.50
54 Mark Grace .15
55 Ryan Klesko .15
56 Dennis Eckersley .75
57 Rickey Henderson 1.00
58 Michael Tucker .15
59 Joe Carter .15
60 Randy Johnson 1.00
61 Brian Jordan .15
62 Shawn Green .50
63 Roger Clemens 2.00
64 Andres Galarraga .15
65 Johnny Damon .40
66 Ryne Sandberg 1.50
67 Alan Benes .15
68 Albert Belle .15
69 Barry Larkin .15
70 Marty Cordova .15
71 Dante Bichette .15
72 Craig Biggio .15
73 Reggie Sanders .15
74 Moises Alou .15
75 Chuck Knoblauch .15
76 Cecil Fielder .15
77 Manny Ramirez 1.00

Staremaster

NM/M
Complete Set (12): 50.00
Common Player: 3.00
1 Chipper Jones 5.00
2 Alex Rodriguez 7.50
3 Derek Jeter 10.00
4 Tony Gwynn 5.00
5 Frank Thomas 4.00
6 Ken Griffey Jr. 6.00
7 Cal Ripken Jr. 10.00
8 Greg Maddux 5.00
9 Albert Belle 3.00
10 Barry Bonds 10.00
11 Jeff Bagwell 4.00
12 Mike Piazza 6.00

Steel Power

NM/M
Complete Set (8): 17.50
Common Player: 1.00
1 Albert Belle 1.00
2 Mo Vaughn 1.00
3 Ken Griffey Jr. 3.50
4 Cal Ripken Jr. 5.00
5 Mike Piazza 3.50
6 Barry Bonds 5.00
7 Jeff Bagwell 2.50
8 Frank Thomas 2.50

1996 LEAF/ SIGNATURE SERIES

NM/M
Complete Set (150): 30.00
Complete 1st Series (100): 20.00
Complete Extended Series (50): 10.00
Common Player: .05
Pack (4): 3.50
Wax Box (12): 35.00
1 Mike Piazza 1.25

2 Juan Gonzalez .65
3 Greg Maddux 1.00
4 Marc Newfield .05
5 Wade Boggs 1.00
6 Ray Lankford .05
7 Frank Thomas .75
8 Rico Brogna .05
9 Tim Salmon .05
10 Ken Griffey Jr. 1.25
11 Manny Ramirez .75
12 Cecil Fielder .05
13 Gregg Jefferies .05
14 Rondell White .05
15 Cal Ripken Jr. 2.00
16 Alex Rodriguez 1.50
17 Bernie Williams .05
18 Andres Galarraga .05
19 Mike Mussina .50
20 Chuck Knoblauch .05
21 Joe Carter .05
22 Jeff Bagwell .75
23 Mark McGwire 1.50
24 Sammy Sosa 1.00
25 Reggie Sanders .05
26 Chipper Jones 1.00
27 Jeff Cirillo .05
28 Roger Clemens 1.25
29 Craig Biggio .05
30 Gary Sheffield .45
31 Paul O'Neill .05
32 Johnny Damon .35
33 Jason Isringhausen .05
34 Jay Bell .05
35 Henry Rodriguez .05
36 Matt Williams .05
37 Randy Johnson .75
38 Fred McGriff .05
39 Jason Giambi .60
40 Ivan Rodriguez .65
41 Raul Mondesi .05
42 Barry Larkin .05
43 Ryan Klesko .05
44 Joey Hamilton .05
45 Todd Hundley .05
46 Jim Edmonds .05
47 Dante Bichette .05
48 Roberto Alomar .20
49 Mark Grace .05
50 Brady Anderson .05
51 Hideo Nomo .65
52 Ozzie Smith 1.00
53 Robin Ventura .05
54 Andy Pettitte .35
55 Kenny Lofton .05
56 John Mabry .05
57 Paul Molitor .75
58 Rey Ordonez .05
59 Albert Belle .05
60 Charles Johnson .05
61 Edgar Martinez .05
62 Derek Bell .05
63 Carlos Delgado .50
64 Raul Casanova .05
65 Ismael Valdes .05
66 J.T. Snow .05
67 Derek Jeter 2.00
68 Jason Kendall .05
69 John Smoltz .05
70 Chad Mottola .05
71 Jim Thome .60
72 Will Clark .10
73 Mo Vaughn .05
74 John Wasdin .05
75 Rafael Palmeiro .65
76 Mark Grudzielanek .05
77 Larry Walker .05
78 Alan Benes .05
79 Michael Tucker .05
80 Billy Wagner .05

81	Paul Wilson	.05
82	Greg Vaughn	.05
83	Dean Palmer	.05
84	Ryne Sandberg	1.00
85	Eric Young	.05
86	Jay Buhner	.05
87	Tony Clark	.05
88	Jermaine Dye	.05
89	Barry Bonds	2.00
90	Ugueth Urbina	.05
91	Charles Nagy	.05
92	Ruben Rivera	.05
93	Todd Hollandsworth	.05
94	*Darin Erstad*	1.50
95	Brooks Kieschnick	.05
96	Edgar Renteria	.05
97	Lenny Dykstra	.05
98	Tony Gwynn	1.00
99	Kirby Puckett	1.00
100	Checklist	.05
101	Andruw Jones	.75
102	Alex Ochoa	.05
103	David Cone	.05
104	Rusty Greer	.05
105	Jose Canseco	.45
106	Ken Caminiti	.05
107	Mariano Rivera	.15
108	Ron Gant	.05
109	Darryl Strawberry	.05
110	Vladimir Guerrero	.75
111	George Arias	.05
112	Jeff Conine	.05
113	Bobby Higginson	.05
114	Eric Karros	.05
115	Brian Hunter	.05
116	Eddie Murray	.75
117	Todd Walker	.05
118	Chan Ho Park	.05
119	John Jaha	.05
120	David Justice	.05
121	Makoto Suzuki	.05
122	Scott Rolen	.65
123	Tino Martinez	.05
124	Kimera Bartee	.05
125	Garret Anderson	.05
126	Brian Jordan	.05
127	Andre Dawson	.30
128	Javier Lopez	.05
129	Bill Pulsipher	.05
130	Dwight Gooden	.05
131	Al Martin	.05
132	Terrell Wade	.05
133	Steve Gibralter	.05
134	Tom Glavine	.35
135	Kevin Appier	.05
136	Tim Raines	.05
137	Curtis Pride	.05
138	Todd Greene	.05
139	Bobby Bonilla	.05
140	Trey Beamon	.05
141	Marty Cordova	.05
142	Rickey Henderson	.75
143	Ellis Burks	.05
144	Dennis Eckersley	.65
145	Kevin Brown	.05
146	Carlos Baerga	.05
147	Brett Butler	.05
148	Marquis Grissom	.05
149	Karim Garcia	.05
150	Checklist	.05

Press Proofs

	NM/M
Common Gold:	2.00
Gold Stars:	8X
Common Platinum:	4.00
Platinum Stars:	20X

(See 1996 Leaf/Signature Series for checklist and base card values.)

Autographs

	NM/M
Common Bronze Player:	3.00
Silver:	1.5X
Gold:	2X

SPs: 100 Gold, 200 Silver, 700 Bronze

(1)	Kurt Abbott	3.00
(2)	Juan Acevedo	3.00
(3)	Terry Adams	3.00
(4)	Manny Alexander	3.00
(5)	Roberto Alomar (SP)	35.00
(6)	Moises Alou	12.00
(7)	Wilson Alvarez	3.00
(8)	Garret Anderson	10.00
(9)	Shane Andrews	3.00
(10)	Andy Ashby	3.00
(11)	Pedro Astacio	3.00
(12)	Brad Ausmus	3.00
(13)	Bobby Ayala	3.00
(14)	Carlos Baerga	3.00
(15)	Harold Baines	10.00
(16)	Jason Bates	3.00
(17)	Allen Battle	3.00
(18)	Rich Becker	3.00
(19)	David Bell	3.00
(20)	Rafael Belliard	3.00
(21)	Andy Benes	3.00
(22)	Armando Benitez	3.00
(23)	Jason Bere	3.00
(24)	Geronimo Berroa	3.00
(25)	Willie Blair	3.00
(26)	Mike Blowers	3.00
(27)	Wade Boggs (SP)	45.00
(28)	Ricky Bones	3.00
(29)	Mike Bordick	3.00
(30)	Toby Borland	3.00
(31)	Ricky Bottalico	3.00
(32)	Darren Bragg	3.00
(33)	Jeff Branson	3.00
(34)	Tilson Brito	3.00
(35)	Rico Brogna	3.00
(36)	Scott Brosius	7.50
(37)	Damon Buford	3.00
(38)	Mike Busby	3.00
(39)	Tom Candiotti	3.00
(40)	Frank Castillo	3.00
(41)	Andujar Cedeno	3.00
(42)	Domingo Cedeno	3.00
(43)	Roger Cedeno	3.00
(44)	Norm Charlton	3.00
(45)	Jeff Cirillo	3.00
(46)	Will Clark	9.00
(47)	Jeff Conine	3.00
(48)	Steve Cooke	3.00
(49)	Joey Cora	3.00
(50)	Marty Cordova	3.00
(51)	Rheal Cormier	3.00
(52)	Felipe Crespo	3.00
(53)	Chad Curtis	3.00
(54)	Johnny Damon	15.00
(55)	Russ Davis	3.00
(56)	Andre Dawson	10.00
(57a)	Carlos Delgado (black autograph)	15.00
(57b)	Carlos Delgado (blue autograph)	15.00
(58)	Doug Drabek	3.00
(59)	Darren Dreifort	3.00
(60)	Shawon Dunston	3.00
(61)	Ray Durham	3.00
(62)	Jim Edmonds	10.00
(63)	Joey Eischen	3.00
(64)	Jim Eisenreich	3.00
(65)	Sal Fasano	3.00
(66)	Jeff Fassero	3.00
(67)	Alex Fernandez	3.00
(68)	Darrin Fletcher	3.00
(69)	Chad Fonville	3.00
(70)	Kevin Foster	3.00
(71)	John Franco	4.00
(72)	Julio Franco	5.00
(73)	Marvin Freeman	3.00
(74)	Travis Fryman	3.00
(75)	Gary Gaetti	3.00
(76)	Carlos Garcia	3.00
(77)	Jason Giambi	10.00
(78)	Benji Gil	3.00
(79)	Greg Gohr	3.00
(80)	Chris Gomez	3.00
(81)	Leo Gomez	3.00
(82)	Tom Goodwin	3.00
(83)	Mike Grace	3.00
(84)	Mike Greenwell	3.00
(85)	Rusty Greer	3.00
(86)	Mark Grudzielanek	4.00
(87)	Mark Gubicza	3.00
(88)	Juan Guzman	4.00
(89)	Darryl Hamilton	3.00
(90)	Joey Hamilton	3.00
(91)	Chris Hammond	3.00
(92)	Mike Hampton	7.50
(93)	Chris Haney	3.00
(94)	Todd Haney	3.00
(95)	Erik Hanson	3.00
(96)	Pete Harnisch	3.00
(97)	LaTroy Hawkins	3.00
(98)	Charlie Hayes	3.00
(99)	Jimmy Haynes	3.00
(100)	Roberto Hernandez	3.00
(101)	Bobby Higginson	4.00
(102)	Glenallen Hill	3.00
(103)	Ken Hill	3.00
(104)	Sterling Hitchcock	3.00
(105)	Trevor Hoffman	10.00
(106)	Dave Hollins	3.00
(107)	Dwayne Hosey	3.00
(108)	Thomas Howard	3.00
(109)	Steve Howe	6.00
(110)	John Hudek	3.00
(111)	Rex Hudler	3.00
(112)	Brian Hunter	3.00
(113)	Butch Huskey	3.00
(114)	Mark Hutton	3.00
(115)	Jason Jacome	3.00
(116)	John Jaha	3.00
(117)	Reggie Jefferson	3.00
(118)	Derek Jeter (SP)	150.00
(119)	Bobby Jones	3.00
(120)	Todd Jones	3.00
(121)	Brian Jordan	5.00
(122)	Kevin Jordan	3.00
(123)	Jeff Juden	3.00
(124)	Ron Karkovice	3.00
(125)	Roberto Kelly	3.00
(126)	Mark Kiefer	3.00
(127)	Brooks Kieschnick	3.00
(128)	Jeff King	3.00
(129)	Mike Lansing	4.00
(130)	Matt Lawton	7.50
(131)	Al Leiter	6.00
(132)	Mark Leiter	3.00
(133)	Curtis Leskanic	3.00
(134)	Darren Lewis	3.00
(135)	Mark Lewis	3.00
(136)	Felipe Lira	3.00
(137)	Pat Listach	3.00
(138)	Keith Lockhart	3.00
(139)	Kenny Lofton (SP)	25.00
(140)	John Mabry	3.00
(141)	Mike Macfarlane	3.00
(142)	Kirt Manwaring	3.00
(143)	Al Martin	3.00
(144)	Norberto Martin	3.00
(145)	Dennis Martinez	5.00
(146)	Pedro Martinez	40.00
(147)	Sandy Martinez	3.00
(148)	Mike Matheny	3.00
(149)	T.J. Mathews	3.00
(150)	David McCarty	3.00
(151)	Ben McDonald	3.00
(152)	Pat Meares	3.00
(153)	Orlando Merced	3.00
(154)	Jose Mesa	3.00
(155)	Matt Mieske	3.00
(156)	Orlando Miller	3.00
(157)	Mike Mimbs	3.00
(158)	Paul Molitor (SP)	50.00
(159)	Raul Mondesi (SP)	20.00
(160)	Jeff Montgomery	3.00
(161)	Mickey Morandini	3.00
(162)	Lyle Mouton	3.00
(163)	James Mouton	3.00
(164)	Jamie Moyer	3.00
(165)	Rodney Myers	3.00
(166)	Denny Neagle	3.00
(167)	Robb Nen	3.00
(168)	Marc Newfield	3.00
(169)	Dave Nilsson	3.00
(170)	Jon Nunnally	3.00
(171)	Chad Ogea	3.00
(172)	Troy O'Leary	3.00
(173)	Rey Ordonez	3.00
(174)	Jayhawk Owens	3.00
(175)	Tom Pagnozzi	3.00
(176)	Dean Palmer	3.00
(177)	Roger Pavlik	3.00
(178)	Troy Percival	4.00
(179)	Carlos Perez	3.00
(180)	Robert Perez	3.00
(181)	Andy Pettitte	30.00
(182)	Phil Plantier	3.00
(183)	Mike Potts	3.00
(184)	Curtis Pride	3.00
(185)	Ariel Prieto	3.00
(186)	Bill Pulsipher	3.00
(187)	Brad Radke	4.00
(188)	Manny Ramirez (SP)	35.00
(189)	Joe Randa	3.00
(190)	Pat Rapp	3.00
(191)	Bryan Rekar	3.00
(192)	Shane Reynolds	3.00
(193)	Arthur Rhodes	3.00
(194)	Mariano Rivera	45.00
(195a)	Alex Rodriguez (SP, black autograph)	120.00
(195b)	Alex Rodriguez (SP, blue autograph)	120.00
(196)	Frank Rodriguez	3.00
(197)	Mel Rojas	3.00
(198)	Ken Ryan	3.00
(199)	Bret Saberhagen	3.00
(200)	Tim Salmon	5.00
(201)	Rey Sanchez	3.00
(202)	Scott Sanders	3.00
(203)	Steve Scarsone	3.00
(204)	Curt Schilling	30.00
(205)	Jason Schmidt	20.00
(206)	David Segui	3.00
(207)	Kevin Seitzer	3.00
(208)	Scott Servais	3.00
(209)	Don Slaught	3.00
(210)	Zane Smith	3.00
(211)	Paul Sorrento	3.00
(212)	Scott Stahoviak	3.00
(213)	Mike Stanley	3.00
(214)	Terry Steinbach	3.00
(215)	Kevin Stocker	3.00
(216)	Jeff Suppan	3.00
(217)	Bill Swift	3.00
(218)	Greg Swindell	3.00
(219)	Kevin Tapani	3.00
(220)	Danny Tartabull	3.00
(221)	Julian Tavarez	3.00
(222a)	Frank Thomas (SP) (blue autograph)	50.00
(222b)	Frank Thomas (SP) (black autograph)	50.00
(223)	Jim Thome (SP) (Silver)	40.00
(224)	Ozzie Timmons	3.00
(225a)	Michael Tucker (black autograph)	3.00
(225b)	Michael Tucker (blue autograph)	3.00
(226)	Ismael Valdez	3.00
(227)	Jose Valentin	3.00
(228)	Todd Van Poppel	3.00
(229)	Mo Vaughn (SP)	15.00
(230)	Quilvio Veras	3.00
(231)	Fernando Vina	3.00
(232)	Joe Vitiello	3.00
(233)	Jose Vizcaino	3.00
(234)	Omar Vizquel	10.00
(235)	Terrell Wade	3.00
(236)	Paul Wagner	3.00
(237)	Matt Walbeck	3.00
(238)	Jerome Walton	3.00
(239)	Turner Ward	3.00
(240)	Allen Watson	3.00
(241)	David Weathers	3.00
(242)	Walt Weiss	3.00
(244)	Turk Wendell	3.00
(244)	Rondell White	5.00
(245)	Brian Williams	3.00
(246)	George Williams	3.00
(247)	Paul Wilson	3.00
(248)	Bobby Witt	3.00
(249)	Bob Wolcott	3.00
(250)	Eric Young	3.00
(251)	Ernie Young	3.00
(252)	Greg Zaun	3.00
---	Frank Thomas (Autographed jumbo edition of 1,500)	25.00

Extended Autographs

	NM/M
Common Player:	2.00

Extended Pack:		20.00
Extended Box:		150.00
(1)	Scott Aldred	2.00
(2)	Mike Aldrete	2.00
(3)	Rich Amaral	2.00
(4)	Alex Arias	2.00
(5)	Paul Assenmacher	2.00
(6)	Roger Bailey	2.00
(7)	Erik Bennett	2.00
(8)	Sean Bergman	2.00
(9)	Doug Bochtler	2.00
(10)	Tim Bogar	2.00
(11)	Pat Borders	2.00
(12)	Pedro Borbon	2.00
(13)	Shawn Boskie	2.00
(14)	Rafael Bournigal	2.00
(15)	Mark Brandenburg	2.00
(16)	John Briscoe	2.00
(17)	Jorge Brito	2.00
(18)	Doug Brocail	2.00
(19)	Jay Buhner (SP, 1000)	15.00
(20)	Scott Bullett	2.00
(21)	Dave Burba	2.00
(22)	Ken Caminiti (SP, 1000)	25.00
(23)	John Cangelosi	2.00
(24)	Cris Carpenter	2.00
(25)	Chuck Carr	2.00
(26)	Larry Casian	2.00
(27)	Tony Castillo	2.00
(28)	Jason Christiansen	2.00
(29)	Archi Cianfrocco	2.00
(30)	Mark Clark	2.00
(31)	Terry Clark	2.00
(32)	Roger Clemens (SP, 1000)	150.00
(33)	Jim Converse	2.00
(34)	Dennis Cook	2.00
(35)	Francisco Cordova	2.00
(36)	Jim Corsi	2.00
(37)	Tim Crabtree	2.00
(38)	Doug Creek (SP, 1950)	2.00
(39)	John Cummings	2.00
(40)	Omar Daal	2.00
(41)	Rich DeLucia	2.00
(42)	Mark Dewey	2.00
(43)	Alex Diaz	2.00
(44)	Jermaine Dye (SP, 2500)	12.50
(45)	Ken Edenfield	2.00
(46)	Mark Eichhorn	2.00
(47)	John Ericks	2.00
(48)	Darin Erstad	10.00
(49)	Alvaro Espinoza	2.00
(50)	Jorge Fabregas	2.00
(51)	Mike Fetters	2.00
(52)	John Flaherty	2.00
(53)	Bryce Florie	2.00
(54)	Tony Fossas	2.00
(55)	Lou Frazier	2.00
(56)	Mike Gallego	2.00
(57)	Karim Garcia (SP, 2500)	5.00
(58)	Jason Giambi	10.00
(59)	Ed Giovanola	2.00
(60)	Tom Glavine (SP, 1250)	40.00
(61)	Juan Gonzalez (SP, 1000)	40.00
(61)	Juan Gonzalez (redemption card)	5.00
(62)	Craig Grebeck	2.00
(63)	Buddy Groom	2.00
(64)	Kevin Gross	2.00
(65)	Eddie Guardado	4.00
(66)	Mark Guthrie	2.00
(67)	Tony Gwynn (SP, 1000)	80.00
(68)	Chip Hale	2.00
(69)	Darren Hall	2.00
(70)	Lee Hancock	2.00
(71)	Dave Hansen	2.00
(72)	Bryan Harvey	2.00
(73)	Bill Haselman	2.00
(74)	Mike Henneman	2.00
(75)	Doug Henry	2.00
(76)	Gil Heredia	2.00
(77)	Carlos Hernandez	2.00
(78)	Jose Hernandez	2.00
(79)	Darren Holmes	2.00
(80)	Mark Holzemer	2.00
(81)	Rick Honeycutt	2.00
(82)	Chris Hook	2.00
(83)	Chris Howard	2.00
(84)	Jack Howell	2.00
(85)	David Hulse	2.00
(86)	Edwin Hurtado	2.00
(87)	Jeff Huson	2.00
(88)	Mike James	2.00
(89)	Derek Jeter (SP, 1000)	160.00
(90)	Brian Johnson	2.00
(91)	Randy Johnson (SP, 1000)	125.00
(92)	Mark Johnson	2.00
(93)	Andruw Jones (SP, 2000)	25.00
(93)	Andruw Jones (redemption card)	5.00
(94)	Chris Jones	2.00
(95)	Ricky Jordan	2.00
(96)	Matt Karchner	2.00
(97)	Scott Karl	2.00
(98)	Jason Kendall (SP, 2500)	10.00
(99)	Brian Keyser	2.00
(100)	Mike Kingery	2.00
(101)	Wayne Kirby	2.00
(102)	Ryan Klesko (SP, 1000)	10.00
(103)	Chuck Knoblauch (SP, 1000)	8.00
(104)	Chad Kreuter	2.00
(105)	Tom Lampkin	2.00
(106)	Scott Leius	2.00
(107)	Jon Lieber	4.00
(108)	Nelson Liriano	2.00
(109)	Scott Livingstone	2.00
(110)	Graeme Lloyd	2.00
(111)	Kenny Lofton (SP, 1000)	15.00
(112)	Luis Lopez	2.00
(113)	Torey Lovullo	2.00
(114)	Greg Maddux (SP, 500)	175.00
(115)	Mike Maddux	2.00
(116)	Dave Magadan	2.00
(117)	Mike Magnante	2.00
(118)	Joe Magrane	2.00
(119)	Pat Mahomes	2.00
(120)	Matt Mantei	2.00
(121)	John Marzano	2.00
(122)	Terry Matthews	2.00
(123)	Chuck McElroy	2.00
(124)	Fred McGriff (SP, 1000)	30.00
(125)	Mark McLemore	2.00
(126)	Greg McMichael	2.00
(127)	Blas Minor	2.00
(128)	Dave Mlicki	2.00
(129)	Mike Mohler	2.00
(130)	Paul Molitor (SP, 1000)	30.00
(131)	Steve Montgomery	2.00
(132)	Mike Mordecai	2.00
(133)	Mike Morgan	2.00
(134)	Mike Munoz	2.00
(135)	Greg Myers	2.00
(136)	Jimmy Myers	2.00
(137)	Mike Myers	2.00
(138)	Bob Natal	2.00
(139)	Dan Naulty	2.00
(140)	Jeff Nelson	4.00
(141)	Warren Newson	2.00
(142)	Chris Nichting	2.00
(143)	Melvin Nieves	2.00
(144)	Charlie O'Brien	2.00
(145)	Alex Ochoa	2.00
(146)	Omar Olivares	2.00
(147)	Joe Oliver	2.00
(148)	Lance Painter	2.00
(149)	Rafael Palmeiro (SP, 2000)	35.00
(150)	Mark Parent	2.00
(151)	Steve Parris (SP, 1800)	5.00
(152)	Bob Patterson	2.00
(153)	Tony Pena	3.00
(154)	Eddie Perez	2.00
(155)	Yorkis Perez	2.00
(156)	Robert Person	2.00
(157)	Mark Petkovsek	2.00
(158)	Andy Pettitte (SP, 1000)	125.00
(159)	J.R. Phillips	2.00
(160)	Hipolito Pichardo	2.00
(161)	Eric Plunk	2.00
(162)	Jimmy Poole	2.00
(163)	Kirby Puckett (SP, 1000)	80.00
(164)	Paul Quantrill	2.00
(165)	Tom Quinlan	2.00
(166)	Jeff Reboulet	2.00
(167)	Jeff Reed	2.00
(168)	Steve Reed	2.00
(169)	Carlos Reyes	2.00
(170)	Bill Risley	2.00
(171)	Kevin Ritz	2.00
(172)	Kevin Roberson	2.00
(173)	Rich Robertson	2.00
(174)	Alex Rodriguez (SP, 500)	180.00
(174)	Alex Rodriguez (redemption card)	15.00
(175)	Ivan Rodriguez (SP, 1250)	40.00
(176)	Bruce Ruffin	2.00
(177)	Juan Samuel	2.00
(178)	Tim Scott	2.00
(179)	Kevin Sefcik	2.00
(180)	Jeff Shaw	4.00
(181)	Danny Sheaffer	2.00
(182)	Craig Shipley	2.00
(183)	Dave Silvestri	2.00
(184)	Aaron Small	2.00
(185)	John Smoltz (SP, 1000)	140.00
(186)	Luis Sojo	2.00
(187)	Sammy Sosa (SP, 1000)	160.00
(188)	Steve Sparks	2.00
(189)	Tim Spehr	2.00
(190)	Russ Springer	2.00
(191)	Matt Stairs	2.00
(192)	Andy Stankiewicz	2.00
(193)	Mike Stanton	2.00
(194)	Kelly Stinnett	2.00
(195)	Doug Strange	2.00
(196)	Mark Sweeney	2.00
(197)	Jeff Tabaka	2.00
(198)	Jesus Tavarez	2.00
(199)	Frank Thomas (SP, 1000)	45.00
(200)	Larry Thomas	2.00
(201)	Mark Thompson	2.00
(202)	Mike Timlin	4.00
(203)	Steve Trachsel	2.00
(204)	Tom Urbani	2.00
(205)	Julio Valera	2.00
(206)	Dave Valle	2.00
(207)	William VanLandingham	2.00
(208)	Mo Vaughn (SP, 1000)	10.00
(209)	Dave Veres	2.00
(210)	Ed Vosberg	2.00
(211)	Don Wengert	2.00
(212)	Matt Whiteside	2.00
(213)	Bob Wickman	2.00
(214)	Matt Williams (SP, 1250)	10.00
(215)	Mike Williams	2.00
(216)	Woody Williams	4.00
(217)	Craig Worthington	2.00
---	Frank Thomas (Autographed jumbo edition of 1,500)	30.00

Extended Autographs - Century Marks

		NM/M
Common Player:		15.00
(1)	Jay Buhner	30.00
(2)	Ken Caminiti	30.00
(3)	Roger Clemens	250.00
(4)	Jermaine Dye	30.00
(5)	Darin Erstad	45.00
(6)	Karim Garcia	30.00
(7)	Jason Giambi	75.00
(8)	Tom Glavine	90.00
(9)	Juan Gonzalez	90.00
(9)	Juan Gonzalez (redemption card)	7.50
(10)	Tony Gwynn	150.00
(11)	Derek Jeter	350.00
(11)	Derek Jeter (redemption card)	15.00
(12)	Randy Johnson	185.00
(13)	Andruw Jones	150.00
(13)	Andruw Jones (redemption card)	7.50
(14)	Jason Kendall	30.00
(15)	Ryan Klesko	30.00
(16)	Chuck Knoblauch	30.00
(17)	Kenny Lofton	30.00
(18)	Greg Maddux	200.00
(19)	Fred McGriff	30.00
(20)	Paul Molitor	110.00
(21)	Alex Ochoa	15.00
(22)	Rafael Palmeiro	110.00
(22)	Rafael Palmeiro (redemption card)	7.50
(23)	Andy Pettitte	75.00
(24)	Kirby Puckett	185.00
(25)	Alex Rodriguez	350.00
(25)	Alex Rodriguez (redemption card)	15.00
(26)	Ivan Rodriguez	100.00
(27)	John Smoltz	100.00
(28)	Sammy Sosa	350.00
(29)	Frank Thomas	135.00
(30)	Mo Vaughn	30.00
(31)	Matt Williams	30.00

1997 LEAF

		NM/M
Complete Set (400):		25.00
Common Player:		.05
Jackie Robinson 1948 Leaf Reprint:		10.00
Series 1 Pack (12):		2.00
Series 1 Wax Box (18):		30.00
Series 2 Pack (12):		1.50
Series 2 Wax Box (24):		30.00
1	Wade Boggs	1.50
2	Brian McRae	.05
3	Jeff D'Amico	.05
4	George Arias	.05
5	Billy Wagner	.05
6	Ray Lankford	.05
7	Will Clark	.10
8	Edgar Renteria	.05
9	Alex Ochoa	.05
10	Roberto Hernandez	.05
11	Joe Carter	.05
12	Gregg Jefferies	.05
13	Mark Grace	.05
14	Roberto Alomar	.10
15	Joe Randa	.05
16	Alex Rodriguez	2.50
17	Tony Gwynn	1.50
18	Steve Gibralter	.05
19	Scott Stahoviak	.05
20	Matt Williams	.05
21	Quinton McCracken	.05
22	Ugueth Urbina	.05
23	Jermaine Allensworth	.05
24	Paul Molitor	.75
25	Carlos Delgado	.50
26	Bob Abreu	.05
27	John Jaha	.05
28	Rusty Greer	.05
29	Kimera Bartee	.05
30	Ruben Rivera	.05
31	Jason Kendall	.05
32	Lance Johnson	.05
33	Robin Ventura	.05
34	Kevin Appier	.05
35	John Mabry	.05
36	Ricky Otero	.05
37	Mike Lansing	.05
38	Mark McGwire	2.50
39	Tim Naehring	.05
40	Tom Glavine	.30
41	Rey Ordonez	.05
42	Tony Clark	.05
43	Rafael Palmeiro	.65

44 Pedro Martinez .75
45 Keith Lockhart .05
46 Dan Wilson .05
47 John Wetteland .05
48 Chan Ho Park .05
49 Gary Sheffield .40
50 Shawn Estes .05
51 Royce Clayton .05
52 Jaime Navarro .05
53 Raul Casanova .05
54 Jeff Bagwell 1.00
55 Barry Larkin .05
56 Charles Nagy .05
57 Ken Caminiti .05
58 Todd Hollandsworth .05
59 Pat Hentgen .05
60 Jose Valentin .05
61 Frank Rodriguez .05
62 Mickey Tettleton .05
63 Marty Cordova .05
64 Cecil Fielder .05
65 Barry Bonds 3.00
66 Scott Servais .05
67 Ernie Young .05
68 Wilson Alvarez .05
69 Mike Grace .05
70 Shane Reynolds .05
71 Henry Rodriguez .05
72 Eric Karros .05
73 Mark Langston .05
74 Scott Karl .05
75 Trevor Hoffman .05
76 Orel Hershiser .05
77 John Smoltz .05
78 Raul Mondesi .05
79 Jeff Brantley .05
80 Donne Wall .05
81 Joey Cora .05
82 Mel Rojas .05
83 Chad Mottola .05
84 Omar Vizquel .05
85 Greg Maddux 1.50
86 Jamey Wright .05
87 Chuck Finley .05
88 Brady Anderson .05
89 Alex Gonzalez .05
90 Andy Benes .05
91 Reggie Jefferson .05
92 Paul O'Neill .05
93 Javier Lopez .05
94 Mark Grudzielanek .05
95 Marc Newfield .05
96 Kevin Ritz .05
97 Fred McGriff .05
98 Dwight Gooden .05
99 Hideo Nomo .65
100 Steve Finley .05
101 Juan Gonzalez .65
102 Jay Buhner .05
103 Paul Wilson .05
104 Alan Benes .05
105 Manny Ramirez 1.00
106 Kevin Elster .05
107 Frank Thomas 1.00
108 Orlando Miller .05
109 Ramon Martinez .05
110 Kenny Lofton .05
111 Bernie Williams .05
112 Robby Thompson .05
113 Bernard Gilkey .05
114 Ray Durham .05
115 Jeff Cirillo .05
116 Brian Jordan .05
117 Rich Becker .05
118 Al Leiter .05
119 Mark Johnson .05
120 Ellis Burks .05
121 Sammy Sosa 2.00
122 Willie Greene .05
123 Michael Tucker .05
124 Eddie Murray .75
125 Joey Hamilton .05
126 Antonio Osuna .05
127 Bobby Higginson .05
128 Tomas Perez .05
129 Tim Salmon .05
130 Mark Wohlers .05
131 Charles Johnson .05
132 Randy Johnson .75
133 Brooks Kieschnick .05
134 Al Martin .05
135 Dante Bichette .05
136 Andy Pettitte .30
137 Jason Giambi .60
138 James Baldwin .05
139 Ben McDonald .05
140 Shawn Green .35
141 Geronimo Berroa .05
142 Jose Offerman .05
143 Curtis Pride .05
144 Terrell Wade .05
145 Ismael Valdes .05
146 Mike Mussina .40
147 Mariano Rivera .15
148 Ken Hill .05
149 Darin Erstad .25
150 Jay Bell .05
151 Mo Vaughn .05
152 Ozzie Smith 1.50
153 Jose Mesa .05
154 Osvaldo Fernandez .05
155 Vinny Castilla .05
156 Jason Isringhausen .05
157 B.J. Surhoff .05
158 Robert Perez .05
159 Ron Coomer .05
160 Darren Oliver .05
161 Mike Mohler .05
162 Russ Davis .05
163 Bret Boone .05
164 Ricky Bottalico .05
165 Derek Jeter 3.00
166 Orlando Merced .05
167 John Valentin .05
168 Andruw Jones 1.00
169 Angel Echevarria .05
170 Todd Walker .05
171 Desi Relaford .05
172 Trey Beamon .05
173 *Brian Giles* .75
174 Scott Rolen .60
175 Shannon Stewart .05
176 Dmitri Young .05
177 Justin Thompson .05
178 Trot Nixon .05
179 Josh Booty .05
180 Robin Jennings .05
181 Marvin Benard .05
182 Luis Castillo .05
183 Wendell Magee .05
184 Vladimir Guerrero 1.00
185 Nomar Garciaparra 2.00
186 Ryan Hancock .05
187 Mike Cameron .05
188 Cal Ripken Jr. (Legacy) 1.50
189 Chipper Jones (Legacy) .75
190 Albert Belle (Legacy) .05
191 Mike Piazza (Legacy) 1.00
192 Chuck Knoblauch (Legacy) .05
193 Ken Griffey Jr. (Legacy) 1.00
194 Ivan Rodriguez (Legacy) .30
195 Jose Canseco (Legacy) .25
196 Ryne Sandberg (Legacy) .75
197 Jim Thome (Legacy) .30
198 Andy Pettitte (Checklist) .05
199 Andruw Jones (Checklist) .50
200 Derek Jeter (Checklist) 1.50
201 Chipper Jones 1.50
202 Albert Belle .05
203 Mike Piazza 2.00
204 Ken Griffey Jr. 2.00
205 Ryne Sandberg 1.50
206 Jose Canseco .40
207 Chili Davis .05
208 Roger Clemens 2.00
209 Deion Sanders .05
210 Darryl Hamilton .05
211 Jermaine Dye .05
212 Matt Williams .05
213 Kevin Elster .05
214 John Wetteland .05
215 Garret Anderson .05
216 Kevin Brown .05
217 Matt Lawton .05
218 Cal Ripken Jr. 3.00
219 Moises Alou .05
220 Chuck Knoblauch .05
221 Ivan Rodriguez .65
222 Travis Fryman .05
223 Jim Thome .65
224 Eddie Murray .75
225 Eric Young .05
226 Ron Gant .05
227 Tony Phillips .05
228 Reggie Sanders .05
229 Johnny Damon .35
230 Bill Pulsipher .05
231 Jim Edmonds .05
232 Melvin Nieves .05
233 Ryan Klesko .05
234 David Cone .05
235 Derek Bell .05
236 Julio Franco .05
237 Juan Guzman .05
238 Larry Walker .05
239 Delino DeShields .05
240 Troy Percival .05
241 Andres Galarraga .05
242 Rondell White .05
243 John Burkett .05
244 J.T. Snow .05
245 Alex Fernandez .05
246 Edgar Martinez .05
247 Craig Biggio .05
248 Todd Hundley .05
249 Jimmy Key .05
250 Cliff Floyd .05
251 Jeff Conine .05
252 Curt Schilling .35
253 Jeff King .05
254 Tino Martinez .05
255 Carlos Baerga .05
256 Jeff Fassero .05
257 Dean Palmer .05
258 Robb Nen .05
259 Sandy Alomar Jr. .05
260 Carlos Perez .05
261 Rickey Henderson .75
262 Bobby Bonilla .05
263 Darren Daulton .05
264 Jim Leyritz .05
265 Dennis Martinez .05
266 Butch Huskey .05
267 Joe Vitiello .05
268 Steve Trachsel .05
269 Glenallen Hill .05
270 Terry Steinbach .05
271 Mark McLemore .05
272 Devon White .05
273 Jeff Kent .05
274 Tim Raines .05
275 Carlos Garcia .05
276 Hal Morris .05
277 Gary Gaetti .05
278 John Olerud .05
279 Wally Joyner .05
280 Brian Hunter .05
281 Steve Karsay .05
282 Denny Neagle .05
283 Jose Herrera .05
284 Todd Stottlemyre .05
285 Bip Roberts .05
286 Kevin Seitzer .05
287 Benji Gil .05
288 Dennis Eckersley .65
289 Brad Ausmus .05
290 Otis Nixon .05
291 Darryl Strawberry .05
292 Marquis Grissom .05
293 Darryl Kile .05
294 Quilvio Veras .05
295 Tom Goodwin .05
296 Benito Santiago .05
297 Mike Bordick .05
298 Roberto Kelly .05
299 David Justice .05
300 Carl Everett .05
301 Mark Whiten .05
302 Aaron Sele .05
303 Darren Dreifort .05
304 Bobby Jones .05
305 Fernando Vina .05
306 Ed Sprague .05
307 Andy Ashby .05
308 Tony Fernandez .05
309 Roger Pavlik .05
310 Mark Clark .05
311 Mariano Duncan .05
312 Tyler Houston .05
313 Eric Davis .05
314 Greg Vaughn .05
315 David Segui .05
316 Dave Nilsson .05
317 F.P. Santangelo .05
318 Wilton Guerrero .05
319 Jose Guillen .05
320 Kevin Orie .05
321 Derrek Lee .05
322 *Bubba Trammell* .50
323 Pokey Reese .05
324 *Hideki Irabu* .25
325 Scott Spiezio .05
326 Bartolo Colon .05
327 Damon Mashore .05
328 Ryan McGuire .05
329 Chris Carpenter .05
330 *Jose Cruz Jr.* .50
331 Todd Greene .05
332 Brian Moehler .05
333 Mike Sweeney .05
334 Neifi Perez .05
335 Matt Morris .05
336 Marvin Benard .05
337 Karim Garcia .05
338 Jason Dickson .05
339 Brant Brown .05
340 Jeff Suppan .05
341 *Deivi Cruz* .25
342 Antone Williamson .05
343 Curtis Goodwin .05
344 Brooks Kieschnick .05
345 *Tony Womack* .25
346 Rudy Pemberton .05
347 Todd Dunwoody .05
348 Frank Thomas (Legacy) .50
349 Andruw Jones (Legacy) .50
350 Alex Rodriguez (Legacy) 1.25
351 Greg Maddux (Legacy) .75
352 Jeff Bagwell (Legacy) .50
353 Juan Gonzalez (Legacy) .35
354 Barry Bonds (Legacy) 1.50
355 Mark McGwire (Legacy) 1.25
356 Tony Gwynn (Legacy) .75
357 Gary Sheffield (Legacy) .25
358 Derek Jeter (Legacy) 1.50
359 Manny Ramirez (Legacy) .50
360 Hideo Nomo (Legacy) .30
361 Sammy Sosa (Legacy) 1.00
362 Paul Molitor (Legacy) .40
363 Kenny Lofton (Legacy) .05
364 Eddie Murray (Legacy) .40
365 Barry Larkin (Legacy) .05
366 Roger Clemens (Legacy) 1.00
367 John Smoltz (Legacy) .05
368 Alex Rodriguez (Gamers) 1.50
369 Frank Thomas (Gamers) .40
370 Cal Ripken Jr. (Gamers) 1.50
371 Ken Griffey Jr. (Gamers) 1.50
372 Greg Maddux (Gamers) 1.00
373 Mike Piazza (Gamers) 1.25
374 Chipper Jones (Gamers) 1.00
375 Albert Belle (Gamers) .05
376 Chuck Knoblauch (Gamers) .05
377 Brady Anderson (Gamers) .05
378 David Justice (Gamers) .05
379 Randy Johnson (Gamers) .40
380 Wade Boggs (Gamers) .75
381 Kevin Brown (Gamers) .05
382 Tom Glavine (Gamers) .05
383 Raul Mondesi (Gamers) .05
384 Ivan Rodriguez (Gamers) .30
385 Larry Walker (Gamers) .05
386 Bernie Williams (Gamers) .05
387 Rusty Greer (Gamers) .05
388 Rafael Palmeiro (Gamers) .05
389 Matt Williams (Gamers) .05
390 Eric Young (Gamers) .05
391 Fred McGriff (Gamers) .05
392 Ken Caminiti (Gamers) .05
393 Roberto Alomar (Gamers) .05
394 Brian Jordan (Gamers) .05
395 Mark Grace (Gamers) .05
396 Jim Edmonds (Gamers) .05
397 Deion Sanders (Gamers) .05
398 Vladimir Guerrero Checklist .50
399 Darin Erstad Checklist .10
400 Nomar Garciaparra Checklist 1.00

Dress for Success

		NM/M
Complete Set (18):		17.50
Common Player:		.25
1	Greg Maddux	1.50
2	Cal Ripken Jr.	3.00
3	Albert Belle	.25
4	Frank Thomas	1.00
5	Dante Bichette	.25
6	Gary Sheffield	.50
7	Jeff Bagwell	1.00

8 Mike Piazza 2.00
9 Mark McGwire 2.25
10 Ken Caminiti .25
11 Alex Rodriguez 2.50
12 Ken Griffey Jr. 2.00
13 Juan Gonzalez .75
14 Brian Jordan .25
15 Mo Vaughn .25
16 Ivan Rodriguez .75
17 Andruw Jones 1.00
18 Chipper Jones 1.50

Fractal Matrix

NM/M
Common Bronze: .35
Common Silver: .50
Common Gold: 1.25
1 Wade Boggs G/Y 8.00
2 Brian McRae B/Y .35
3 Jeff D'Amico B/Y .35
4 George Arias S/Y .50
5 Billy Wagner S/Y .50
6 Ray Lankford B/Z .35
7 Will Clark S/Y .60
8 Edgar Renteria S/Y .50
9 Alex Ochoa S/Y .50
10 Roberto Hernandez B/X .35
11 Joe Carter S/Y .50
12 Gregg Jefferies B/Y .35
13 Mark Grace S/Y .75
14 Roberto Alomar G/Y 2.00
15 Joe Randa B/X .35
16 Alex Rodriguez G/Z 10.00
17 Tony Gwynn G/Z 6.00
18 Steve Gibralter B/Y .35
19 Scott Stahoviak B/X .35
20 Matt Williams S/Z .50
21 Quinton McCracken B/Y .35
22 Ugueth Urbina B/X .35
23 Jermaine Allensworth S/X .50
24 Paul Molitor G/X 5.00
25 Carlos Delgado S/Y 1.00
26 Bob Abreu S/Y .50
27 John Jaha S/Y .50
28 Rusty Greer S/Z .50
29 Kimera Bartee B/X .35
30 Ruben Rivera S/Y .50
31 Jason Kendall S/Y .50
32 Lance Johnson B/X .35
33 Robin Ventura B/Y .35
34 Kevin Appier S/X .50
35 John Mabry S/Y .50
36 Ricky Otero B/X .35
37 Mike Lansing B/X .35
38 Mark McGwire G/Z 10.00
39 Tim Naehring B/X .35
40 Tom Glavine S/Z 1.00
41 Rey Ordonez S/Y .50
42 Tony Clark S/Y .50
43 Rafael Palmeiro S/Z 2.00
44 Pedro Martinez B/X 2.00
45 Keith Lockhart B/X .35
46 Dan Wilson B/Y .35
47 John Wetteland B/Y .35
48 Chan Ho Park B/X .35
49 Gary Sheffield G/Z 3.00
50 Shawn Estes B/X .35
51 Royce Clayton B/X .35
52 Jaime Navarro B/X .35
53 Raul Casanova B/X .35
54 Jeff Bagwell G/Z 5.00
55 Barry Larkin G/X 1.25
56 Charles Nagy B/Y .35
57 Ken Caminiti G/Y 1.25
58 Todd Hollandsworth S/Z .50
59 Pat Hentgen S/X .50
60 Jose Valentin B/X .35
61 Frank Rodriguez B/X .35
62 Mickey Tettleton B/X .35
63 Marty Cordova G/X 1.25
64 Cecil Fielder S/X .50
65 Barry Bonds G/Z 13.50
66 Scott Servais B/X .35
67 Ernie Young B/X .35
68 Wilson Alvarez B/X .35
69 Mike Grace B/X .35
70 Shane Reynolds S/X .50
71 Henry Rodriguez S/Y .50
72 Eric Karros B/X .35
73 Mark Langston B/X .35
74 Scott Karl B/X .35
75 Trevor Hoffman B/X .35
76 Orel Hershiser S/X .50
77 John Smoltz G/Y 1.50
78 Raul Mondesi G/Z 1.25
79 Jeff Brantley B/X .35
80 Donne Wall B/X .35
81 Joey Cora B/X .35
82 Mel Rojas B/X .35
83 Chad Mottola B/X .35
84 Omar Vizquel B/X .35
85 Greg Maddux G/Z 6.00
86 Jamey Wright S/Y .50
87 Chuck Finley B/X .35
88 Brady Anderson G/Y 1.25
89 Alex Gonzalez S/X .50
90 Andy Benes B/X .35
91 Reggie Jefferson B/X .35
92 Paul O'Neill B/Y .35
93 Javier Lopez S/X .50
94 Mark Grudzielanek S/X .50
95 Marc Newfield B/X .35
96 Kevin Ritz B/X .35
97 Fred McGriff G/Y 1.25
98 Dwight Gooden S/X .50
99 Hideo Nomo S/Y 1.50
100 Steve Finley B/X .35
101 Juan Gonzalez G/Z 4.00
102 Jay Buhner S/Z .50
103 Paul Wilson S/Y .50
104 Alan Benes B/Y .35
105 Manny Ramirez G/Z 5.00
106 Kevin Elster B/X .35
107 Frank Thomas G/Z 5.00
108 Orlando Miller B/X .35
109 Ramon Martinez B/X .35
110 Kenny Lofton G/Z 1.25
111 Bernie Williams G/Y 1.25
112 Robby Thompson B/X .35
113 Bernard Gilkey B/Z .35
114 Ray Durham B/X .35
115 Jeff Cirillo S/Z .50
116 Brian Jordan G/Z 1.25
117 Rich Becker S/Y .50
118 Al Leiter B/X .35
119 Mark Johnson B/X .35
120 Ellis Burks B/Y .35
121 Sammy Sosa G/Z 7.50
122 Willie Greene B/X .35
123 Michael Tucker B/X .35
124 Eddie Murray G/Y 6.00
125 Joey Hamilton S/Y .50
126 Antonio Osuna B/X .35
127 Bobby Higginson S/Y .50
128 Tomas Perez B/X .35
129 Tim Salmon G/Z 1.25
130 Mark Wohlers B/X .35
131 Charles Johnson S/X .50
132 Randy Johnson S/Y 2.00
133 Brooks Kieschnick S/X .50
134 Al Martin S/Y .50
135 Dante Bichette B/X .35
136 Andy Pettitte G/Z 2.00
137 Jason Giambi G/Y 4.00
138 James Baldwin S/X .50
139 Ben McDonald B/X .35
140 Shawn Green S/X 1.00
141 Geronimo Berroa B/Y .35
142 Jose Offerman B/X .35
143 Curtis Pride B/X .35
144 Terrell Wade B/X .35
145 Ismael Valdes S/X .50
146 Mike Mussina S/Y 1.25
147 Mariano Rivera S/X .75
148 Ken Hill B/Y .35
149 Darin Erstad G/Z 4.00
150 Jay Bell B/X .35
151 Mo Vaughn G/Z 1.25
152 Ozzie Smith G/Y 8.00
153 Jose Mesa B/X .35
154 Osvaldo Fernandez B/X .35
155 Vinny Castilla B/Y .35
156 Jason Isringhausen S/Y .50
157 B.J. Surhoff B/X .35
158 Robert Perez B/X .35
159 Ron Coomer B/X .35
160 Darren Oliver B/X .35
161 Mike Mohler B/X .35
162 Russ Davis B/X .35
163 Bret Boone B/X .35
164 Ricky Bottalico B/X .35
165 Derek Jeter G/Z 13.50
166 Orlando Merced B/X .35
167 John Valentin B/X .35
168 Andruw Jones G/Z 5.00
169 Angel Echevarria B/X .35
170 Todd Walker G/Z 1.25
171 Desi Relaford B/Y .35
172 Trey Beamon S/X .50
173 Brian Giles S/Y .50
174 Scott Rolen G/Z 3.50
175 Shannon Stewart S/Z .50
176 Dmitri Young G/Z 1.25
177 Justin Thompson B/X .35
178 Trot Nixon S/Y .50
179 Josh Booty S/Y .50
180 Robin Jennings B/X .35
181 Marvin Benard B/X .35
182 Luis Castillo B/Y .35
183 Wendell Magee B/X .35
184 Vladimir Guerrero G/X 5.00
185 Nomar Garciaparra G/X 12.50
186 Ryan Hancock B/X .35
187 Mike Cameron S/X .50
188 Cal Ripken Jr. B/Z (Legacy) 5.00
189 Chipper Jones S/Z (Legacy) 4.00
190 Albert Belle S/Z (Legacy) 1.00
191 Mike Piazza B/Z (Legacy) 4.00
192 Chuck Knoblauch S/Y (Legacy) .50
193 Ken Griffey Jr. B/Z (Legacy) 3.50
194 Ivan Rodriguez G/Z (Legacy) 4.00
195 Jose Canseco S/X (Legacy) 1.25
196 Ryne Sandberg S/X (Legacy) 3.00
197 Jim Thome G/Y (Legacy) 1.50
198 Andy Pettitte B/Y Checklist .75
199 Andruw Jones B/Y Checklist 2.00
200 Derek Jeter S/Y Checklist 2.00
201 Chipper Jones G/X 10.00
202 Albert Belle G/Y 1.25
203 Mike Piazza G/Y 12.00
204 Ken Griffey Jr. G/X 15.00
205 Ryne Sandberg G/Z 6.00
206 Jose Canseco S/Y .75
207 Chili Davis B/X .35
208 Roger Clemens G/Z 6.50
209 Deion Sanders G/Z 1.50
210 Darryl Hamilton B/X .35
211 Jermaine Dye S/X .50
212 Matt Williams G/Y 1.25
213 Kevin Elster B/X .35
214 John Wetteland S/X .50
215 Garret Anderson G/Z 1.25
216 Kevin Brown G/Y 1.25
217 Matt Lawton S/Y .50
218 Cal Ripken Jr. G/X 16.50
219 Moises Alou G/Y 1.25
220 Chuck Knoblauch G/Z 1.25
221 Ivan Rodriguez G/Y 5.50
222 Travis Fryman B/Y .35
223 Jim Thome G/Z 2.00
224 Eddie Murray S/Z 3.00
225 Eric Young G/Z 1.25
226 Ron Gant S/X .50
227 Tony Phillips B/X .35
228 Reggie Sanders B/Y .35
229 Johnny Damon S/Z 1.00
230 Bill Pulsipher B/X .35
231 Jim Edmonds G/Z 1.25
232 Melvin Nieves B/X .35
233 Ryan Klesko G/Z 1.25
234 David Cone S/X .50
235 Derek Bell B/Y .35
236 Julio Franco S/X .50
237 Juan Guzman B/X .35
238 Larry Walker G/Z 1.25
239 Delino DeShields B/X .35
240 Troy Percival B/Y .35
241 Andres Galarraga G/Z 1.25
242 Rondell White G/Z 1.25
243 John Burkett B/X .35
244 J.T. Snow B/Y .35
245 Alex Fernandez S/Y .50
246 Edgar Martinez G/Z 1.25
247 Craig Biggio G/Z 1.25
248 Todd Hundley G/Y 1.25
249 Jimmy Key S/X .50
250 Cliff Floyd B/Y .35
251 Jeff Conine B/Y .35
252 Curt Schilling B/X .65
253 Jeff King B/X .35
254 Tino Martinez G/Z 1.25
255 Carlos Baerga S/Y .50
256 Jeff Fassero B/Y .35
257 Dean Palmer S/Y .50
258 Robb Nen B/X .35
259 Sandy Alomar Jr. S/Y .50
260 Carlos Perez B/X .35
261 Rickey Henderson S/Y 2.00
262 Bobby Bonilla S/Y .50
263 Darren Daulton B/X .35
264 Jim Leyritz B/X .35
265 Dennis Martinez B/X .35
266 Butch Huskey B/X .35
267 Joe Vitiello S/Y .50
268 Steve Trachsel B/X .35
269 Glenallen Hill B/X .35
270 Terry Steinbach B/X .35
271 Mark McLemore B/X .35
272 Devon White B/X .35
273 Jeff Kent B/X .35
274 Tim Raines B/X .35
275 Carlos Garcia B/X .35
276 Hal Morris B/X .35
277 Gary Gaetti B/X .35
278 John Olerud S/Y .50
279 Wally Joyner B/X .35
280 Brian Hunter S/X .50
281 Steve Karsay B/X .35
282 Denny Neagle S/X .50
283 Jose Herrera B/X .35
284 Todd Stottlemyre B/X .35
285 Bip Roberts S/X .50
286 Kevin Seitzer B/X .35
287 Benji Gil B/X .35
288 Dennis Eckersley S/X .50
289 Brad Ausmus B/X .35
290 Otis Nixon B/X .35
291 Darryl Strawberry B/X .35
292 Marquis Grissom S/Y .50
293 Darryl Kile B/X .35
294 Quilvio Veras B/X .35
295 Tom Goodwin B/X .35
296 Benito Santiago B/X .35
297 Mike Bordick B/X .35
298 Roberto Kelly B/X .35
299 David Justice G/Z 1.25
300 Carl Everett B/X .35
301 Mark Whiten B/X .35
302 Aaron Sele B/X .35
303 Darren Dreifort B/X .35
304 Bobby Jones B/X .35
305 Fernando Vina B/X .35
306 Ed Sprague B/X .35
307 Andy Ashby S/X .50
308 Tony Fernandez B/X .35
309 Roger Pavlik B/X .35
310 Mark Clark B/X .35
311 Mariano Duncan B/X .35
312 Tyler Houston B/X .35
313 Eric Davis S/Y .50
314 Greg Vaughn B/Y .35
315 David Segui S/Y .50
316 Dave Nilsson S/X .50
317 F.P. Santangelo S/X .50
318 Wilton Guerrero G/Z 1.25
319 Jose Guillen G/Z 1.25
320 Kevin Orie S/Y .50
321 Derrek Lee G/Z 2.50
322 Bubba Trammell S/Y .50
323 Pokey Reese G/Z 1.25
324 Hideki Irabu G/X 1.25
325 Scott Spiezio S/Z .50
326 Bartolo Colon G/Z 1.25
327 Damon Mashore S/Y .50
328 Ryan McGuire S/Y .50
329 Chris Carpenter B/X .35
330 Jose Cruz, Jr. G/X 1.25
331 Todd Greene S/Z .50
332 Brian Moehler B/X .35
333 Mike Sweeney B/Y .35
334 Neifi Perez G/Z 1.25
335 Matt Morris S/Y .50
336 Marvin Benard B/Y .35
337 Karim Garcia S/Z .75
338 Jason Dickson S/Y .50
339 Brant Brown S/Y .50
340 Jeff Suppan S/Z .50
341 Deivi Cruz B/X .35
342 Antone Williamson G/Z 1.25
343 Curtis Goodwin B/X .35
344 Brooks Kieschnick S/Y .50
345 Tony Womack B/X .35

#	Player	Price
346	Rudy Pemberton B/X	.35
347	Todd Dunwoody B/X	.35
348	Frank Thomas S/Y (Legacy)	2.25
349	Andruw Jones S/X (Legacy)	2.00
350	Alex Rodriguez B/Y (Legacy)	4.00
351	Greg Maddux S/Y (Legacy)	3.00
352	Jeff Bagwell B/Y (Legacy)	2.25
353	Juan Gonzalez S/Y (Legacy)	1.50
354	Barry Bonds B/Y (Legacy)	5.00
355	Mark McGwire B/Y (Legacy)	4.00
356	Tony Gwynn B/Y (Legacy)	3.00
357	Gary Sheffield B/X (Legacy)	.75
358	Derek Jeter S/X (Legacy)	4.00
359	Manny Ramirez S/Y (Legacy)	2.00
360	Hideo Nomo G/Z (Legacy)	4.00
361	Sammy Sosa B/X (Legacy)	3.50
362	Paul Molitor S/Z (Legacy)	3.00
363	Kenny Lofton B/Y (Legacy)	.35
364	Eddie Murray B/X (Legacy)	2.00
365	Barry Larkin S/Z (Legacy)	.50
366	Roger Clemens S/Y (Legacy)	3.50
367	John Smoltz B/Z (Legacy)	.35
368	Alex Rodriguez S/X (Gamers)	3.25
369	Frank Thomas B/X (Gamers)	2.25
370	Cal Ripken Jr. S/Y (Gamers)	4.00
371	Ken Griffey Jr. S/Y (Gamers)	3.25
372	Greg Maddux B/X (Gamers)	3.00
373	Mike Piazza S/X (Gamers)	3.25
374	Chipper Jones B/Y (Gamers)	3.00
375	Albert Belle B/X (Gamers)	.50
376	Chuck Knoblauch B/X (Gamers)	.35
377	Brady Anderson B/Z (Gamers)	.35
378	David Justice S/X (Gamers)	.50
379	Randy Johnson B/Z (Gamers)	2.00
380	Wade Boggs B/X (Gamers)	3.00
381	Kevin Brown B/X (Gamers)	.35
382	Tom Glavine G/Y (Gamers)	3.00
383	Raul Mondesi S/X (Gamers)	.50
384	Ivan Rodriguez S/X (Gamers)	1.25
385	Larry Walker B/Y (Gamers)	.35
386	Bernie Williams B/Z (Gamers)	.45
387	Rusty Greer G/Y (Gamers)	1.25
388	Rafael Palmeiro G/Y (Gamers)	4.50
389	Matt Williams B/X (Gamers)	.35
390	Eric Young B/X (Gamers)	.35
391	Fred McGriff B/X (Gamers)	.35
392	Ken Caminiti B/X (Gamers)	.35
393	Roberto Alomar B/Z (Gamers)	.75
394	Brian Jordan B/X (Gamers)	.35
395	Mark Grace G/Z (Gamers)	1.25
396	Jim Edmonds B/Y (Gamers)	.35
397	Deion Sanders S/Y (Gamers)	.50
398	Vladimir Guerrero S/Z Checklist	1.25
399	Darin Erstad S/Y Checklist	1.00
400	Nomar Garciaparra S/Z Checklist	2.00

Banner Season

		NM/M
Complete Set (15):		30.00
Common Player:		.50
1	Jeff Bagwell	2.50
2	Ken Griffey Jr.	5.00
3	Juan Gonzalez	1.50
4	Frank Thomas	2.50
5	Alex Rodriguez	6.00
6	Kenny Lofton	.50
7	Chuck Knoblauch	.50
8	Mo Vaughn	.50
9	Chipper Jones	4.00
10	Ken Caminiti	.50
11	Craig Biggio	.50
12	John Smoltz	.50
13	Pat Hentgen	.50
14	Derek Jeter	7.50
15	Todd Hollandsworth	.50

Get-A-Grip

		NM/M
Complete Set (16):		30.00
Common Card:		1.00
1	Ken Griffey Jr., Greg Maddux	3.00
2	John Smoltz, Frank Thomas	1.50
3	Mike Piazza, Andy Pettitte	3.00
4	Randy Johnson, Chipper Jones	2.50
5	Tom Glavine, Alex Rodriguez	4.00
6	Pat Hentgen, Jeff Bagwell	1.50
7	Kevin Brown, Juan Gonzalez	1.25
8	Barry Bonds, Mike Mussina	5.00
9	Hideo Nomo, Albert Belle	1.25
10	Troy Percival, Andruw Jones	1.50
11	Roger Clemens, Brian Jordan	3.00
12	Paul Wilson, Ivan Rodriguez	1.25
13	Andy Benes, Mo Vaughn	1.00
14	Al Leiter, Derek Jeter	5.00
15	Bill Pulsipher, Cal Ripken Jr.	5.00
16	Mariano Rivera, Ken Caminiti	1.00

Knot-Hole Gang

		NM/M
Complete Set (12):		18.00
Common Player:		.50
Promos:		2X
1	Chuck Knoblauch	.50
2	Ken Griffey Jr.	3.50
3	Frank Thomas	1.50
4	Tony Gwynn	2.50
5	Mike Piazza	3.50
6	Jeff Bagwell	1.50
7	Rusty Greer	.50
8	Cal Ripken Jr.	5.00
9	Chipper Jones	2.50
10	Ryan Klesko	.50
11	Barry Larkin	.50
12	Paul Molitor	1.50

Leagues of the Nation

		NM/M
Complete Set (15):		60.00
Common Card:		1.50
1	Juan Gonzalez, Barry Bonds	10.00
2	Cal Ripken Jr., Chipper Jones	10.00
3	Mark McGwire, Ken Caminiti	7.00
4	Derek Jeter, Kenny Lofton	10.00
5	Ivan Rodriguez, Mike Piazza	6.00
6	Ken Griffey Jr., Larry Walker	6.00
7	Frank Thomas, Sammy Sosa	5.00
8	Paul Molitor, Barry Larkin	3.00
9	Albert Belle, Deion Sanders	1.50
10	Matt Williams, Jeff Bagwell	3.00
11	Mo Vaughn, Gary Sheffield	1.50
12	Alex Rodriguez, Tony Gwynn	7.50
13	Tino Martinez, Scott Rolen	2.00
14	Darin Erstad, Wilton Guerrero	2.00
15	Tony Clark, Vladimir Guerrero	3.00

Statistical Standouts

		NM/M
Complete Set (15):		175.00
Common Player:		4.00
1	Albert Belle	4.00
2	Juan Gonzalez	9.00
3	Ken Griffey Jr.	20.00
4	Alex Rodriguez	25.00
5	Frank Thomas	12.00
6	Chipper Jones	15.00
7	Greg Maddux	15.00
8	Mike Piazza	20.00
9	Cal Ripken Jr.	30.00
10	Mark McGwire	25.00
11	Barry Bonds	30.00
12	Derek Jeter	30.00
13	Ken Caminiti	4.00
14	John Smoltz	4.00
15	Paul Molitor	12.00

Thomas Collection

		NM/M
Complete Set (6):		360.00
Common Card:		60.00
1	Frank Thomas Hat	60.00
2	Frank Thomas Home Jersey	80.00
3	Frank Thomas Batting Glove	60.00
4	Frank Thomas Bat	60.00
5	Frank Thomas Sweatband	60.00
6	Frank Thomas Away Jersey	80.00

Warning Track

		NM/M
Complete Set (18):		40.00
Common Player:		1.00
1	Ken Griffey Jr.	6.00
2	Albert Belle	1.00
3	Barry Bonds	7.50
4	Andruw Jones	4.00
5	Kenny Lofton	1.00
6	Tony Gwynn	5.00
7	Manny Ramirez	4.00
8	Rusty Greer	1.00
9	Bernie Williams	1.00
10	Gary Sheffield	2.00
11	Juan Gonzalez	2.50
12	Raul Mondesi	1.00
13	Brady Anderson	1.00
14	Rondell White	1.00
15	Sammy Sosa	6.00
16	Deion Sanders	1.00
17	David Justice	1.00
18	Jim Edmonds	1.00

22kt Gold Stars

		NM/M
Complete Set (36):		115.00
Common Player:		1.00
1	Frank Thomas	4.00
2	Alex Rodriguez	8.00
3	Ken Griffey Jr.	6.50
4	Andruw Jones	4.00
5	Chipper Jones	5.50
6	Jeff Bagwell	4.00
7	Derek Jeter	10.00
8	Deion Sanders	1.00
9	Ivan Rodriguez	3.50
10	Juan Gonzalez	3.00
11	Greg Maddux	5.50
12	Andy Pettitte	2.50
13	Roger Clemens	6.00
14	Hideo Nomo	3.00
15	Tony Gwynn	5.50
16	Barry Bonds	10.00
17	Kenny Lofton	1.00

No.	Player	NM/M
18	Paul Molitor	4.00
19	Jim Thome	3.00
20	Albert Belle	1.00
21	Cal Ripken Jr.	10.00
22	Mark McGwire	8.00
23	Barry Larkin	1.00
24	Mike Piazza	6.50
25	Darin Erstad	2.00
26	Chuck Knoblauch	1.00
27	Vladimir Guerrero	4.00
28	Tony Clark	1.00
29	Scott Rolen	3.00
30	Nomar Garciaparra	6.50
31	Eric Young	1.00
32	Ryne Sandberg	5.50
33	Roberto Alomar	2.00
34	Eddie Murray	4.00
35	Rafael Palmeiro	3.50
36	Jose Guillen	1.00

1998 LEAF

		NM/M
Complete Set (200):		40.00
Common Player:		.05
Common SP (#148-197):		.40
Pack (10):		2.00
Wax Box (24):		40.00
1	Rusty Greer	.05
2	Tino Martinez	.05
3	Bobby Bonilla	.05
4	Jason Giambi	.50
5	Matt Morris	.05
6	Craig Counsell	.05
7	Reggie Jefferson	.05
8	Brian Rose	.05
9	Ruben Rivera	.05
10	Shawn Estes	.05
11	Tony Gwynn	1.00
12	Jeff Abbott	.05
13	Jose Cruz Jr.	.05
14	Francisco Cordova	.05
15	Ryan Klesko	.05
16	Tim Salmon	.05
17	Brett Tomko	.05
18	Matt Williams	.05
19	Joe Carter	.05
20	Harold Baines	.05
21	Gary Sheffield	.50
22	Charles Johnson	.05
23	Aaron Boone	.05
24	Eddie Murray	.75
25	Matt Stairs	.05
26	David Cone	.05
27	Jon Nunnally	.05
28	Chris Stynes	.05
29	Enrique Wilson	.05
30	Randy Johnson	.75
31	Garret Anderson	.05
32	Manny Ramirez	.75
33	Jeff Suppan	.05
34	Rickey Henderson	.75
35	Scott Spiezio	.05
36	Rondell White	.05
37	Todd Greene	.05
38	Delino DeShields	.05
39	Kevin Brown	.05
40	Chili Davis	.05
41	Jimmy Key	.05
42	NOT ISSUED	
43	Mike Mussina	.40
44	Joe Randa	.05
45	Chan Ho Park	.05
46	Brad Radke	.05
47	Geronimo Berroa	.05
48	Wade Boggs	1.00
49	Kevin Appier	.05
50	Moises Alou	.05
51	David Justice	.05
52	Ivan Rodriguez	.65
53	J.T. Snow	.05
54	Brian Giles	.05
55	Will Clark	.10
56	Justin Thompson	.05
57	Javier Lopez	.05
58	Hideki Irabu	.05
59	Mark Grudzielanek	.05
60	Abraham Nunez	.05
61	Todd Hollandsworth	.05
62	Jay Bell	.05
63	Nomar Garciaparra	1.25
64	Vinny Castilla	.05
65	Lou Collier	.05
66	Kevin Orie	.05
67	John Valentin	.05
68	Robin Ventura	.05
69	Denny Neagle	.05
70	Tony Womack	.05
71	Dennis Reyes	.05
72	Wally Joyner	.05
73	Kevin Brown	.05
74	Ray Durham	.05
75	Mike Cameron	.05
76	Dante Bichette	.05
77	Jose Guillen	.05
78	Carlos Delgado	.50
79	Paul Molitor	.75
80	Jason Kendall	.05
81	Mark Belhorn	.05
82	Damian Jackson	.05
83	Bill Mueller	.05
84	Kevin Young	.05
85	Curt Schilling	.25
86	Jeffrey Hammonds	.05
87	Sandy Alomar Jr.	.05
88	Bartolo Colon	.05
89	Wilton Guerrero	.05
90	Bernie Williams	.05
91	Deion Sanders	.05
92	Mike Piazza	1.25
93	Butch Huskey	.05
94	Edgardo Alfonzo	.05
95	Alan Benes	.05
96	Craig Biggio	.05
97	Mark Grace	.05
98	Shawn Green	.25
99	Derrek Lee	.60
100	Ken Griffey Jr.	1.25
101	Tim Raines	.05
102	Pokey Reese	.05
103	Lee Stevens	.05
104	Shannon Stewart	.05
105	John Smoltz	.05
106	Frank Thomas	.75
107	Jeff Fassero	.05
108	Jay Buhner	.05
109	Jose Canseco	.50
110	Omar Vizquel	.05
111	Travis Fryman	.05
112	Dave Nilsson	.05
113	John Olerud	.05
114	Larry Walker	.05
115	Jim Edmonds	.05
116	Bobby Higginson	.05
117	Todd Hundley	.05
118	Paul O'Neill	.05
119	Bip Roberts	.05
120	Ismael Valdes	.05
121	Pedro Martinez	.75
122	Jeff Cirillo	.05
123	Andy Benes	.05
124	Bobby Jones	.05
125	Brian Hunter	.05
126	Darryl Kile	.05
127	Pat Hentgen	.05
128	Marquis Grissom	.05
129	Eric Davis	.05
130	Chipper Jones	1.00
131	Edgar Martinez	.05
132	Andy Pettitte	.20
133	Cal Ripken Jr.	2.00
134	Scott Rolen	.65
135	Ron Coomer	.05
136	Luis Castillo	.05
137	Fred McGriff	.05
138	Neifi Perez	.05
139	Eric Karros	.05
140	Alex Fernandez	.05
141	Jason Dickson	.05
142	Lance Johnson	.05
143	Ray Lankford	.05
144	Sammy Sosa	1.25
145	Eric Young	.05
146	Bubba Trammell	.05
147	Todd Walker	.05
148	Mo Vaughn	.40
149	Jeff Bagwell	1.00
150	Kenny Lofton	.40
151	Raul Mondesi	.40
152	Mike Piazza	2.00
153	Chipper Jones	1.50
154	Larry Walker	.40
155	Greg Maddux	1.50
156	Ken Griffey Jr.	2.00
157	Frank Thomas	1.00
158	Darin Erstad	.75
159	Roberto Alomar	.60
160	Albert Belle	.40
161	Jim Thome	.75
162	Tony Clark	.40
163	Chuck Knoblauch	.40
164	Derek Jeter	3.00
165	Alex Rodriguez	2.50
166	Tony Gwynn	1.50
167	Roger Clemens	2.00
168	Barry Larkin	.40
169	Andres Galarraga	.40
170	Vladimir Guerrero	1.00
171	Mark McGwire	2.50
172	Barry Bonds	3.00
173	Juan Gonzalez	.75
174	Andruw Jones	1.00
175	Paul Molitor	1.00
176	Hideo Nomo	.75
177	Cal Ripken Jr.	3.00
178	Brad Fullmer	.40
179	Jaret Wright	.40
180	Bobby Estalella	.40
181	Ben Grieve	.40
182	Paul Konerko	.60
183	David Ortiz	.75
184	Todd Helton	1.00
185	Juan Encarnacion	.40
186	Miguel Tejada	.60
187	Jacob Cruz	.40
188	Mark Kotsay	.40
189	Fernando Tatis	.40
190	Ricky Ledee	.40
191	Richard Hidalgo	.40
192	Richie Sexson	.40
193	Luis Ordaz	.40
194	Eli Marrero	.40
195	Livan Hernandez	.40
196	Homer Bush	.40
197	Raul Ibanez	.40
198	Nomar Garciaparra Checklist	.60
199	Scott Rolen Checklist	.30
200	Jose Cruz Jr. Checklist	.05
201	Al Martin	.05

Crusade

		NM/M
Complete Set (30):		400.00
Common Player:		6.00
Purples:		3X
Reds:		12X
3	Jim Edmonds	7.50
4	Darin Erstad	7.50
11	Mike Mussina	15.00
15	Albert Belle	6.00
18	Manny Ramirez	25.00
19	Jim Thome	20.00
24	Bubba Trammell	6.00
26	Bobby Higginson	6.00
28	Paul Molitor	25.00
30	Todd Walker	6.00
34	Andy Pettitte	10.00
35	Wade Boggs	30.00
40	Alex Rodriguez	60.00
41	Randy Johnson	25.00
46	Ivan Rodriguez	20.00
48	Roger Clemens	40.00
54	John Smoltz	6.00
56	Andruw Jones	25.00
58	Javier Lopez	6.00
59	Fred McGriff	6.00
64	Pokey Reese	6.00
66	Andres Galarraga	6.00
70	Eric Young	6.00
73	Moises Alou	6.00
76	Ben Grieve	6.00
79	Mike Piazza	50.00
91	Jason Kendall	6.00
95	Alan Benes	6.00
97	Tony Gwynn	30.00
98	Ken Caminiti	6.00

Heading for the Hall

		NM/M
Complete Set (20):		35.00
Common Player:		.75
Samples:		1X
1	Roberto Alomar	1.00
2	Jeff Bagwell	1.50
3	Albert Belle	.75
4	Wade Boggs	2.00
5	Barry Bonds	5.00
6	Roger Clemens	2.50
7	Juan Gonzalez	1.50
8	Ken Griffey Jr.	3.00
9	Tony Gwynn	2.00
10	Barry Larkin	.75
11	Kenny Lofton	.75
12	Greg Maddux	2.00
13	Mark McGwire	4.00
14	Paul Molitor	1.50
15	Eddie Murray	1.50
16	Mike Piazza	3.00
17	Cal Ripken Jr.	5.00
18	Ivan Rodriguez	1.25
19	Ryne Sandberg	2.00
20	Frank Thomas	1.50

Statistical Standouts

		NM/M
Complete Set (24):		55.00
Common Player:		1.00
Die-Cuts:		2X
1	Frank Thomas	2.50
2	Ken Griffey Jr.	4.00
3	Alex Rodriguez	5.00
4	Mike Piazza	4.00
5	Greg Maddux	3.00
6	Cal Ripken Jr.	6.00
7	Chipper Jones	3.00
8	Juan Gonzalez	2.00
9	Jeff Bagwell	2.50
10	Mark McGwire	5.00
11	Tony Gwynn	3.00
12	Mo Vaughn	1.00
13	Nomar Garciaparra	4.00
14	Jose Cruz Jr.	1.00
15	Vladimir Guerrero	2.50
16	Scott Rolen	2.00
17	Andy Pettitte	1.50
18	Randy Johnson	2.50
19	Larry Walker	1.00
20	Kenny Lofton	1.00
21	Tony Clark	1.00
22	David Justice	1.00
23	Derek Jeter	6.00
24	Barry Bonds	6.00

Fractal Matrix

		NM/M
Complete Set (200):		250.00

Common Bronze:		.25
Common Silver:		.75
Common Gold:		2.00
1	Rusty Greer G/Z	2.00
2	Tino Martinez G/Z	2.00
3	Bobby Bonilla S/Y	.75
4	Jason Giambi S/Y	1.25
5	Matt Morris S/Y	.75
6	Craig Counsell B/X	.25
7	Reggie Jefferson B/X	.25
8	Brian Rose S/Y	.75
9	Ruben Rivera B/X	.25
10	Shawn Estes S/Y	.75
11	Tony Gwynn G/Z	10.00
12	Jeff Abbott B/Y	.25
13	Jose Cruz Jr. G/Z	2.00
14	Francisco Cordova B/X	.25
15	Ryan Klesko B/X	.25
16	Tim Salmon G/Y	2.00
17	Brett Tomko B/X	.25
18	Matt Williams S/Y	.75
19	Joe Carter B/X	.25
20	Harold Baines B/X	.25
21	Gary Sheffield S/Z	1.25
22	Charles Johnson S/X	.75
23	Aaron Boone B/X	.25
24	Eddie Murray G/Y	7.50
25	Matt Stairs B/X	.25
26	David Cone B/X	.25
27	Jon Nunnally B/X	.25
28	Chris Stynes B/X	.25
29	Enrique Wilson B/Y	.25
30	Randy Johnson S/Z	2.00
31	Garret Anderson S/Y	.75
32	Manny Ramirez G/Z	7.50
33	Jeff Suppan S/X	.75
34	Rickey Henderson B/X	1.00
35	Scott Spiezio B/X	.25
36	Rondell White S/Y	.75
37	Todd Greene S/Z	.75
38	Delino DeShields B/X	.25
39	Kevin Brown S/X	.75
40	Chili Davis B/X	.25
41	Jimmy Key B/X	.25
42	NOT ISSUED	
43	Mike Mussina G/Y	5.00
44	Joe Randa B/X	.25
45	Chan Ho Park S/Z	.75
46	Brad Radke B/X	.25
47	Geronimo Berroa B/X	.25
48	Wade Boggs S/Y	2.50
49	Kevin Appier B/X	.25
50	Moises Alou S/Y	.75
51	David Justice G/Y	2.00
52	Ivan Rodriguez G/Z	6.00
53	J.T. Snow B/X	.25
54	Brian Giles B/X	.25
55	Will Clark B/Y	.25
56	Justin Thompson S/Y	.75
57	Javier Lopez S/X	.75
58	Hideki Irabu B/Z	.25
59	Mark Grudzielanek B/X	.25
60	Abraham Nunez S/X	.75
61	Todd Hollandsworth B/X	.25
62	Jay Bell B/X	.25
63	Nomar Garciaparra G/Z	10.00
64	Vinny Castilla B/Y	.25
65	Lou Collier B/Y	.25
66	Kevin Orie S/X	.75
67	John Valentin B/X	.25
68	Robin Ventura B/X	.25
69	Denny Neagle B/X	.25
70	Tony Womack S/Y	.75
71	Dennis Reyes S/Y	.75
72	Wally Joyner B/X	.25
73	Kevin Brown B/Y	.25
74	Ray Durham B/X	.25
75	Mike Cameron S/Z	.75
76	Dante Bichette B/X	.25
77	Jose Guillen G/Y	2.00
78	Carlos Delgado B/Y	.50
79	Paul Molitor G/Z	7.50
80	Jason Kendall B/X	.25
81	Mark Belhorn B/X	.25
82	Damian Jackson B/X	.25
83	Bill Mueller B/X	.25
84	Kevin Young B/X	.25
85	Curt Schilling B/X	.40
86	Jeffrey Hammonds B/X	.25
87	Sandy Alomar Jr. S/Y	.75
88	Bartolo Colon B/Y	.50
89	Wilton Guerrero B/Y	.25
90	Bernie Williams G/Y	2.00
91	Deion Sanders S/Y	.75
92	Mike Piazza G/X	12.50
93	Butch Huskey B/X	.25
94	Edgardo Alfonzo S/X	.75
95	Alan Benes S/Y	.75
96	Craig Biggio S/Y	.75
97	Mark Grace S/Y	.75
98	Shawn Green S/Y	1.50
99	Derrek Lee S/Y	2.00
100	Ken Griffey Jr. G/Z	12.50
101	Tim Raines B/X	.25
102	Pokey Reese S/X	.75
103	Lee Stevens B/X	.25
104	Shannon Stewart S/Y	.75
105	John Smoltz S/Y	.75
106	Frank Thomas G/X	7.50
107	Jeff Fassero B/X	.25
108	Jay Buhner B/Y	.25
109	Jose Canseco B/X	.50
110	Omar Vizquel B/X	.25
111	Travis Fryman B/X	.25
112	Dave Nilsson B/X	.25
113	John Olerud B/X	.25
114	Larry Walker G/Z	2.00
115	Jim Edmonds S/Y	.75
116	Bobby Higginson S/X	.75
117	Todd Hundley S/X	.75
118	Paul O'Neill B/X	.25
119	Bip Roberts B/X	.25
120	Ismael Valdes B/X	.25
121	Pedro Martinez S/Y	2.00
122	Jeff Cirillo B/X	.25
123	Andy Benes B/X	.25
124	Bobby Jones B/X	.25
125	Brian Hunter B/X	.25
126	Darryl Kile B/X	.25
127	Pat Hentgen B/X	.25
128	Marquis Grissom B/X	.25
129	Eric Davis B/X	.25
130	Chipper Jones G/Z	10.00
131	Edgar Martinez S/Z	.75
132	Andy Pettitte G/Z	3.00
133	Cal Ripken Jr. G/X	20.00
134	Scott Rolen G/Z	6.00
135	Ron Coomer B/X	.25
136	Luis Castillo B/Y	.25
137	Fred McGriff B/Y	.25
138	Neifi Perez S/Y	.75
139	Eric Karros B/X	.25
140	Alex Fernandez B/X	.25
141	Jason Dickson B/X	.25
142	Lance Johnson B/X	.25
143	Ray Lankford B/Y	.25
144	Sammy Sosa G/Y	10.00
145	Eric Young B/Y	.25
146	Bubba Trammell S/Y	.75
147	Todd Walker S/Y	.75
148	Mo Vaughn S/X	.75
149	Jeff Bagwell S/X	2.00
150	Kenny Lofton S/X	.75
151	Raul Mondesi S/X	.75
152	Mike Piazza S/X	4.00
153	Chipper Jones S/X	3.00
154	Larry Walker S/X	.75
155	Greg Maddux S/X	3.00
156	Ken Griffey Jr. S/X	4.00
157	Frank Thomas S/X	2.00
158	Darin Erstad B/Z	.50
159	Roberto Alomar B/Y	.35
160	Albert Belle G/Y	2.00
161	Jim Thome G/Y	4.00
162	Tony Clark G/Y	2.00
163	Chuck Knoblauch B/Y	.25
164	Derek Jeter G/Z	20.00
165	Alex Rodriguez G/Z	15.00
166	Tony Gwynn B/X	1.25
167	Roger Clemens G/Z	12.00
168	Barry Larkin B/Y	.25
169	Andres Galarraga B/Y	.25
170	Vladimir Guerrero G/Z	7.50
171	Mark McGwire B/Z	2.00
172	Barry Bonds B/Z	3.00
173	Juan Gonzalez G/Z	4.00
174	Andruw Jones G/Z	7.50
175	Paul Molitor B/X	1.00
176	Hideo Nomo B/Z	.75
177	Cal Ripken Jr. B/X	2.25
178	Brad Fullmer S/Z	.75
179	Jaret Wright G/Z	2.00
180	Bobby Estalella B/Y	.25
181	Ben Grieve G/X	2.00
182	Paul Konerko G/Z	3.00
183	David Ortiz G/Z	6.00
184	Todd Helton G/X	5.00
185	Juan Encarnacion G/Z	2.00
186	Miguel Tejada G/Z	4.00
187	Jacob Cruz B/Y	.25
188	Mark Kotsay G/Z	2.00
189	Fernando Tatis S/Z	.75
190	Ricky Ledee S/Y	.75
191	Richard Hidalgo S/Y	.75
192	Richie Sexson S/Y	.75
193	Luis Ordaz B/X	.25
194	Eli Marrero S/Z	.75
195	Livan Hernandez S/Z	.75
196	Homer Bush B/X	.25
197	Raul Ibanez B/X	.25
198	Nomar Garciaparra B/X Checklist	.75
199	Scott Rolen B/X Checklist	.35
200	Jose Cruz Jr. B/X Checklist	.25
201	Al Martin B/X	.25

Fractal Matrix Diamond Axis

	NM/M
Common Player:	7.50
Stars/Rookies:	20X
SP (148-177):	12X

(See 1998 Leaf for checklist and base card values.)

1998 LEAF FRACTAL FOUNDATION

		NM/M
Complete Set (200):		60.00
Common Player:		.20
Semistars:		.60
Pack (3):		2.00
Wax Box (18):		35.00
1	Rusty Greer	.20
2	Tino Martinez	.20
3	Bobby Bonilla	.20
4	Jason Giambi	.60
5	Matt Morris	.20
6	Craig Counsell	.20
7	Reggie Jefferson	.20
8	Brian Rose	.20
9	Ruben Rivera	.20
10	Shawn Estes	.20
11	Tony Gwynn	1.50
12	Jeff Abbott	.20
13	Jose Cruz Jr.	.20
14	Francisco Cordova	.20
15	Ryan Klesko	.20
16	Tim Salmon	.20
17	Brett Tomko	.20
18	Matt Williams	.20
19	Joe Carter	.20
20	Harold Baines	.20
21	Gary Sheffield	.50
22	Charles Johnson	.20
23	Aaron Boone	.20
24	Eddie Murray	1.00
25	Matt Stairs	.20
26	David Cone	.20
27	Jon Nunnally	.20
28	Chris Stynes	.20
29	Enrique Wilson	.20
30	Randy Johnson	1.00
31	Garret Anderson	.20
32	Manny Ramirez	1.00
33	Jeff Suppan	.20
34	Rickey Henderson	1.00
35	Scott Spiezio	.20
36	Rondell White	.20
37	Todd Greene	.20
38	Delino DeShields	.20
39	Kevin Brown	.20
40	Chili Davis	.20
41	Jimmy Key	.20
42	NOT ISSUED	
43	Mike Mussina	.40
44	Joe Randa	.20
45	Chan Ho Park	.20
46	Brad Radke	.20
47	Geronimo Berroa	.20
48	Wade Boggs	1.50
49	Kevin Appier	.20
50	Moises Alou	.20
51	David Justice	.20
52	Ivan Rodriguez	.75
53	J.T. Snow	.20
54	Brian Giles	.20
55	Will Clark	.20
56	Justin Thompson	.20
57	Javier Lopez	.20
58	Hideki Irabu	.20
59	Mark Grudzielanek	.20
60	Abraham Nunez	.20
61	Todd Hollandsworth	.20
62	Jay Bell	.20
63	Nomar Garciaparra	1.75
64	Vinny Castilla	.20
65	Lou Collier	.20
66	Kevin Orie	.20
67	John Valentin	.20
68	Robin Ventura	.20
69	Denny Neagle	.20
70	Tony Womack	.20
71	Dennis Reyes	.20
72	Wally Joyner	.20
73	Kevin Brown	.20
74	Ray Durham	.20
75	Mike Cameron	.20
76	Dante Bichette	.20
77	Jose Guillen	.20
78	Carlos Delgado	.50
79	Paul Molitor	1.00
80	Jason Kendall	.20
81	Mark Belhorn	.20
82	Damian Jackson	.20
83	Bill Mueller	.20
84	Kevin Young	.20
85	Curt Schilling	.40
86	Jeffrey Hammonds	.20
87	Sandy Alomar Jr.	.20
88	Bartolo Colon	.20
89	Wilton Guerrero	.20
90	Bernie Williams	.20
91	Deion Sanders	.20
92	Mike Piazza	2.00
93	Butch Huskey	.20
94	Edgardo Alfonzo	.20
95	Alan Benes	.20
96	Craig Biggio	.20
97	Mark Grace	.20
98	Shawn Green	.40
99	Derrek Lee	.50
100	Ken Griffey Jr.	2.00
101	Tim Raines	.20
102	Pokey Reese	.20
103	Lee Stevens	.20
104	Shannon Stewart	.20
105	John Smoltz	.20
106	Frank Thomas	1.00
107	Jeff Fassero	.20
108	Jay Buhner	.20
109	Jose Canseco	.40
110	Omar Vizquel	.20
111	Travis Fryman	.20
112	Dave Nilsson	.20
113	John Olerud	.20
114	Larry Walker	.20
115	Jim Edmonds	.20
116	Bobby Higginson	.20
117	Todd Hundley	.20
118	Paul O'Neill	.20
119	Bip Roberts	.20
120	Ismael Valdes	.20
121	Pedro Martinez	1.00
122	Jeff Cirillo	.20
123	Andy Benes	.20
124	Bobby Jones	.20
125	Brian Hunter	.20
126	Darryl Kile	.20
127	Pat Hentgen	.20
128	Marquis Grissom	.20
129	Eric Davis	.20
130	Chipper Jones	1.50
131	Edgar Martinez	.20

132 Andy Pettitte .35
133 Cal Ripken Jr. 3.00
134 Scott Rolen .75
135 Ron Coomer .20
136 Luis Castillo .20
137 Fred McGriff .20
138 Neifi Perez .20
139 Eric Karros .20
140 Alex Fernandez .20
141 Jason Dickson .20
142 Lance Johnson .20
143 Ray Lankford .20
144 Sammy Sosa 1.75
145 Eric Young .20
146 Bubba Trammell .20
147 Todd Walker .20
148 Mo Vaughn .20
149 Jeff Bagwell 1.00
150 Kenny Lofton .20
151 Raul Mondesi .20
152 Mike Piazza 2.00
153 Chipper Jones 1.50
154 Larry Walker .20
155 Greg Maddux 1.50
156 Ken Griffey Jr. 2.00
157 Frank Thomas 1.00
158 Darin Erstad .50
159 Roberto Alomar .40
160 Albert Belle .20
161 Jim Thome .75
162 Tony Clark .20
163 Chuck Knoblauch .20
164 Derek Jeter 3.00
165 Alex Rodriguez 2.50
166 Tony Gwynn 1.50
167 Roger Clemens 1.75
168 Barry Larkin .20
169 Andres Galarraga .20
170 Vladimir Guerrero 1.00
171 Mark McGwire 2.50
172 Barry Bonds 3.00
173 Juan Gonzalez .75
174 Andruw Jones 1.00
175 Paul Molitor 1.00
176 Hideo Nomo .75
177 Cal Ripken Jr. 3.00
178 Brad Fullmer .20
179 Jaret Wright .20
180 Bobby Estalella .20
181 Ben Grieve .20
182 Paul Konerko .40
183 David Ortiz .75
184 Todd Helton 1.00
185 Juan Encarnacion .20
186 Miguel Tejada .40
187 Jacob Cruz .20
188 Mark Kotsay .20
189 Fernando Tatis .20
190 Ricky Ledee .20
191 Richard Hidalgo .20
192 Richie Sexson .20
193 Luis Ordaz .20
194 Eli Marrero .20
195 Livan Hernandez .20
196 Homer Bush .20
197 Raul Ibanez .20
198 Nomar Garciaparra Checklist 1.00
199 Scott Rolen Checklist .30
200 Jose Cruz Jr. Checklist .20

Fractal Materials

NM/M
Complete Set (200): 375.00
Complete Plastic Set (100): 65.00
Common Plastic (3,250): .35
Complete Leather Set (50): 55.00
Common Leather (1,000): .75
Complete Nylon Set (30): 60.00
Common Nylon (500): 1.25
Complete Wood Set (20): 200.00
Common Wood (250): 5.00
Wax Box: 120.00
1 Rusty Greer N 1.25
2 Tino Martinez W 5.00
3 Bobby Bonilla N 1.25
4 Jason Giambi N 4.00
5 Matt Morris L .75
6 Craig Counsell P .35
7 Reggie Jefferson P .35
8 Brian Rose P .35
9 Ruben Rivera L .75
10 Shawn Estes L .75
11 Tony Gwynn W 20.00
12 Jeff Abbott P .35
13 Jose Cruz Jr. W 5.00
14 Francisco Cordova P .35
15 Ryan Klesko L .75
16 Tim Salmon W 5.00
17 Brett Tomko L .75
18 Matt Williams N 1.25
19 Joe Carter P .35
20 Harold Baines P .35
21 Gary Sheffield N 2.50
22 Charles Johnson L .75
23 Aaron Boone P .35
24 Eddie Murray N 5.00
25 Matt Stairs P .35
26 David Cone P .35
27 Jon Nunnally P .35
28 Chris Stynes P .35
29 Enrique Wilson P .35
30 Randy Johnson W 15.00
31 Garret Anderson N 1.25
32 Manny Ramirez W 15.00
33 Jeff Suppan L .75
34 Rickey Henderson N 5.00
35 Scott Spiezio P .35
36 Rondell White L .75
37 Todd Greene N 1.25
38 Delino DeShields P .35
39 Kevin Brown L .75
40 Chili Davis P .35
41 Jimmy Key P .35
42 NOT ISSUED
43 Mike Mussina N 4.00
44 Joe Randa P .35
45 Chan Ho Park N 1.25
46 Brad Radke P .35
47 Geronimo Berroa P .35
48 Wade Boggs N 6.00
49 Kevin Appier P .35
50 Moises Alou N 1.25
51 David Justice N 1.25
52 Ivan Rodriguez W 12.50
53 J.T. Snow L .75
54 Brian Giles P .35
55 Will Clark L .75
56 Justin Thompson N 1.25
57 Javier Lopez P .35
58 Hideki Irabu L .75
59 Mark Grudzielanek P .35
60 Abraham Nunez P .35
61 Todd Hollandsworth P .35
62 Jay Bell P .35
63 Nomar Garciaparra W 20.00
64 Vinny Castilla P .35
65 Lou Collier P .35
66 Kevin Orie L .75
67 John Valentin P .35
68 Robin Ventura P .35
69 Denny Neagle P .35
70 Tony Womack L .75
71 Dennis Reyes L .75
72 Wally Joyner P .35
73 Kevin Brown P .35
74 Ray Durham P .35
75 Mike Cameron N 1.25
76 Dante Bichette L .75
77 Jose Guillen N 1.25
78 Carlos Delgado L 1.50
79 Paul Molitor W 15.00
80 Jason Kendall P .35
81 Mark Belhorn L .75
82 Damian Jackson P .35
83 Bill Mueller P .35
84 Kevin Young P .35
85 Curt Schilling P .60
86 Jeffrey Hammonds P .35
87 Sandy Alomar Jr. L .75
88 Bartolo Colon P .35
89 Wilton Guerrero L .75
90 Bernie Williams N 1.25
91 Deion Sanders N 1.25
92 Mike Piazza W 25.00
93 Butch Huskey L .75
94 Edgardo Alfonzo L .75
95 Alan Benes L .75
96 Craig Biggio N 1.25
97 Mark Grace L .75
98 Shawn Green L 1.25
99 Derrek Lee L 2.00
100 Ken Griffey Jr. W 25.00
101 Tim Raines P .35
102 Pokey Reese P .35
103 Lee Stevens P .35
104 Shannon Stewart N 1.25
105 John Smoltz L .75
106 Frank Thomas W 15.00
107 Jeff Fassero P .35
108 Jay Buhner L .75
109 Jose Canseco L 1.50
110 Omar Vizquel P .35
111 Travis Fryman P .35
112 Dave Nilsson P .35
113 John Olerud P .35
114 Larry Walker W 5.00
115 Jim Edmonds N 1.25
116 Bobby Higginson L .75
117 Todd Hundley L .75
118 Paul O'Neill P .35
119 Bip Roberts P .35
120 Ismael Valdes P .35
121 Pedro Martinez N 5.00
122 Jeff Cirillo P .35
123 Andy Benes P .35
124 Bobby Jones P .35
125 Brian Hunter P .35
126 Darryl Kile P .35
127 Pat Hentgen P .35
128 Marquis Grissom P .35
129 Eric Davis P .35
130 Chipper Jones W 20.00
131 Edgar Martinez N 1.25
132 Andy Pettitte W 10.00
133 Cal Ripken Jr. W 35.00
134 Scott Rolen W 12.50
135 Ron Coomer P .35
136 Luis Castillo L .75
137 Fred McGriff L .75
138 Neifi Perez L .75
139 Eric Karros P .35
140 Alex Fernandez P .35
141 Jason Dickson P .35
142 Lance Johnson P .35
143 Ray Lankford P .35
144 Sammy Sosa N 7.00
145 Eric Young P .35
146 Bubba Trammell L .75
147 Todd Walker L .75
148 Mo Vaughn P .35
149 Jeff Bagwell P 3.00
150 Kenny Lofton P .35
151 Raul Mondesi P .35
152 Mike Piazza P 5.00
153 Chipper Jones P 4.00
154 Larry Walker P .35
155 Greg Maddux P 4.00
156 Ken Griffey Jr. P 5.00
157 Frank Thomas P 3.00
158 Darin Erstad L 2.00
159 Roberto Alomar P .65
160 Albert Belle L .75
161 Jim Thome L 2.00
162 Tony Clark L .75
163 Chuck Knoblauch L .75
164 Derek Jeter P 7.50
165 Alex Rodriguez P 6.00
166 Tony Gwynn P 4.00
167 Roger Clemens L 5.00
168 Barry Larkin P .35
169 Andres Galarraga P .35
170 Vladimir Guerrero L 4.00
171 Mark McGwire L 6.00
172 Barry Bonds L 7.50
173 Juan Gonzalez P 2.00
174 Andruw Jones P 3.00
175 Paul Molitor P 3.00
176 Hideo Nomo L 2.00
177 Cal Ripken Jr. P 7.50
178 Brad Fullmer P .35
179 Jaret Wright N 1.25
180 Bobby Estalella P .35
181 Ben Grieve W 5.00
182 Paul Konerko W 6.00
183 David Ortiz N 2.50
184 Todd Helton W 10.00
185 Juan Encarnacion N 1.25
186 Miguel Tejada N 1.50
187 Jacob Cruz P .35
188 Mark Kotsay N 1.25
189 Fernando Tatis L .75
190 Ricky Ledee P .35
191 Richard Hidalgo P .35
192 Richie Sexson P .35
193 Luis Ordaz P .35
194 Eli Marrero L .75
195 Livan Hernandez L (Gold Leaf Rookies) .75
196 Homer Bush P (Gold Leaf Rookies) .35
197 Raul Ibanez P (Gold Leaf Rookies) .35
198 Nomar Garciaparra P Checklist 3.00
199 Scott Rolen P Checklist .40
200 Jose Cruz Jr. P Checklist .35
201 Al Martin L .75

2001 LEAF ROOKIES & STARS

NM/M
Complete Set (300):
Common Player: .15
Common (101-200): 1.50
Inserted 1:4
Common (201-300): 4.00
Inserted 1:24 8.00
Pack (5): 6.00
Box (24): 120.00
1 Alex Rodriguez 2.50
2 Derek Jeter 3.00
3 Aramis Ramirez .15
4 Cliff Floyd .15
5 Nomar Garciaparra 2.00
6 Craig Biggio .15
7 Ivan Rodriguez .75
8 Cal Ripken Jr. 3.00
9 Fred McGriff .15
10 Chipper Jones 1.50
11 Roberto Alomar .50
12 Moises Alou .15
13 Freddy Garcia .15
14 Bobby Abreu .15
15 Shawn Green .50
16 Jason Giambi .50
17 Todd Helton 1.00
18 Robert Fick .15
19 Tony Gwynn 1.50
20 Luis Gonzalez .35
21 Sean Casey .25
22 Roger Clemens 1.75
23 Brian Giles .15
24 Manny Ramirez 1.00
25 Barry Bonds 3.00
26 Richard Hidalgo .15
27 Vladimir Guerrero 1.00
28 Kevin Brown .15
29 Mike Sweeney .15
30 Ken Griffey Jr. 2.00
31 Mike Piazza 2.00
32 Richie Sexson .15
33 Matt Morris .15
34 Jorge Posada .25
35 Eric Chavez .25
36 Mark Buehrle .15
37 Jeff Bagwell 1.00
38 Curt Schilling .35
39 Bartolo Colon .15
40 Mark Quinn .15
41 Tony Clark .15
42 Brad Radke .15
43 Gary Sheffield .35
44 Doug Mientkiewicz .15
45 Pedro Martinez 1.00
46 Carlos Lee .15
47 Troy Glaus 1.00
48 Preston Wilson .15
49 Phil Nevin .15
50 Chan Ho Park .15
51 Randy Johnson 1.00
52 Jermaine Dye .15
53 Terrence Long .15
54 Joe Mays .15
55 Scott Rolen .75
56 Miguel Tejada .25

#	Player	Price
57	Jim Thome	.15
58	Jose Vidro	.15
59	Gabe Kapler	.15
60	Darin Erstad	.75
61	Jim Edmonds	.15
62	Jarrod Washburn	.15
63	Tom Glavine	.40
64	Adrian Beltre	.50
65	Sammy Sosa	2.00
66	Juan Gonzalez	1.00
67	Rafael Furcal	.15
68	Mike Mussina	.50
69	Mark McGwire	2.50
70	Ryan Klesko	.15
71	Raul Mondesi	.15
72	Trot Nixon	.15
73	Barry Larkin	.15
74	Rafael Palmeiro	.75
75	Mark Mulder	.25
76	Carlos Delgado	.60
77	Mike Hampton	.15
78	Carl Everett	.15
79	Paul Konerko	.15
80	Larry Walker	.15
81	Kerry Wood	.60
82	Frank Thomas	1.00
83	Andruw Jones	1.00
84	Eric Milton	.15
85	Ben Grieve	.15
86	Carlos Beltran	.50
87	Tim Hudson	.25
88	Hideo Nomo	1.00
89	Greg Maddux	1.50
90	Edgar Martinez	.15
91	Lance Berkman	.15
92	Pat Burrell	.45
93	Jeff Kent	.15
94	Maggio Ordonez	.15
95	Cristian Guzman	.15
96	Jose Canseco	.30
97	J.D. Drew	.60
98	Bernie Williams	.40
99	Kazuhiro Sasaki	.15
100	Rickey Henderson	1.00
101	*Wilson Guzman*	1.50
102	Nick Neugebauer	1.50
103	*Lance Davis*	1.50
104	Felipe Lopez	1.50
105	Toby Hall	1.50
106	Jack Cust	1.50
107	Jason Kamuth	1.50
108	*Bart Miadich*	1.50
109	*Brian Roberts*	10.00
110	*Brandon Larson*	2.00
111	*Sean Douglass*	1.50
112	Joe Crede	1.50
113	Tim Redding	1.50
114	Adam Johnson	1.50
115	Marcus Giles	1.50
116	Jose Ortiz	1.50
117	*Jose Mieses*	1.50
118	*Nick Maness*	1.50
119	*Les Walrond*	1.50
120	*Travis Phelps*	1.50
121	*Troy Mattes*	1.50
122	Carlos Garcia	1.50
123	Bill Ortega	1.50
124	*Gene Altman*	1.50
125	Nate Frese	1.50
126	Alfonso Soriano	1.00
127	Jose Nunez	1.50
128	*Bob File*	1.50
129	Dan Wright	1.50
130	Nick Johnson	1.50
131	Brent Abernathy	1.50
132	*Steve Green*	1.50
133	*Billy Sylvester*	1.50
134	*Scott MacRae*	1.50
135	*Kris Keller*	1.50
136	*Scott Stewart*	1.50
137	*Henry Mateo*	1.50
138	Timoniel Perez	1.50
139	*Nate Teut*	1.50
140	*Jason Michaels*	1.50
141	*Junior Spivey*	4.00
142	Carlos Pena	1.50
143	*Wilmy Caceres*	1.50
144	David Lundquist	1.50
145	*Jack Wilson*	4.00
146	*Jeremy Fikac*	1.50
147	Alex Escobar	1.50
148	Abraham Nunez	1.50
149	Xavier Nady	1.50
150	Michael Cuddyer	1.50
151	*Greg Miller*	1.50
152	Eric Munson	1.50
153	Aubrey Huff	1.50
154	*Tim Christman*	1.50
155	*Erick Almonte*	1.50
156	Mike Penny	1.50
157	*Delvin James*	1.50
158	Ben Sheets	1.50
159	Jason Hart	1.50
160	*Jose Acevedo*	1.50
161	*Will Ohman*	1.50
162	*Erik Hiljus*	1.50
163	*Juan Moreno*	1.50
164	*Mike Koplove*	1.50
165	*Pedro Santana*	1.50
166	Jimmy Rollins	1.50
167	*Matt White*	1.50
168	*Cesar Crespo*	1.50
169	Carlos Hernandez	1.50
170	Chris George	1.50
171	*Brad Voyles*	1.50
172	*Luis Pineda*	1.50
173	Carlos Zambrano	1.50
174	Nate Comejo	1.50
175	*Jason Smith*	1.50
176	*Craig Monroe*	1.50
177	*Cody Ransom*	1.50
178	*John Grabow*	1.50
179	Pedro Feliz	1.50
180	*Jeremy Owens*	1.50
181	Kurt Ainsworth	1.50
182	Luis Lopez	1.50
183	*Stubby Clapp*	1.50
184	*Ryan Freel*	1.50
185	*Duaner Sanchez*	1.50
186	Jason Jennings	1.50
187	*Kyle Lohse*	3.00
188	*Jerrod Riggan*	1.50
189	*Joe Beimel*	1.50
190	*Nick Punto*	1.50
191	*Willie Harris*	1.50
192	*Ryan Jensen*	1.50
193	*Adam Pettyjohn*	1.50
194	*Donaldo Mendez*	1.50
195	*Bret Prinz*	1.50
196	*Paul Phillips*	1.50
197	*Brian Lawrence*	2.00
198	Cesar Izturis	1.50
199	*Blaine Neal*	1.50
200	*Josh Fogg*	1.50
201	*Josh Towers*	4.00
202	*Tim Spooneybarger*	4.00
203	*Mike Rivera*	4.00
204	*Juan Cruz*	6.00
205	*Albert Pujols*	150.00
206	Josh Beckett	4.00
207	Roy Oswalt	4.00
208	*Elpidio Guzman*	4.00
209	*Horacio Ramirez*	8.00
210	Corey Patterson	4.00
211	*Geronimo Gil*	4.00
212	*Jay Gibbons*	10.00
213	Orlando Woodwards	4.00
214	David Espinosa	4.00
215	*Angel Berroa*	8.00
216	*Brandon Duckworth*	6.00
217	*Brian Reith*	4.00
218	*David Brous*	4.00
219	*Bud Smith*	4.00
220	*Ramon Vazquez*	4.00
221	*Mark Teixeira*	50.00
222	*Justin Atchley*	4.00
223	*Tony Cogan*	4.00
224	*Grant Balfour*	4.00
225	*Ricardo Rodriguez*	4.00
226	*Brian Rogers*	4.00
227	Adam Dunn	4.00
228	*Wilson Betemit*	4.00
229	*Juan Diaz*	4.00
230	*Jackson Melian*	4.00
231	*Claudio Vargas*	4.00
232	*Wilkin Ruan*	4.00
233	*Justin Duchscherer*	6.00
234	*Kevin Olsen*	4.00
235	Tony Fiore	4.00
236	*Jeremy Affeldt*	4.00
237	*Mike Maroth*	4.00
238	C.C. Sabathia	4.00
239	*Cory Aldridge*	4.00
240	*Zach Day*	6.00
241	*Brett Jodie*	4.00
242	*Winston Abreu*	4.00
243	*Travis Hafner*	15.00
244	*Joe Kennedy*	4.00
245	*Rick Bauer*	4.00
246	Mike Young	8.00
247	*Ken Vining*	4.00
248	*Doug Nickle*	4.00
249	Pablo Ozuno	4.00
250	*Dustan Mohr*	4.00
251	*Ichiro Suzuki*	50.00
252	*Ryan Drese*	4.00
253	*Morgan Ensberg*	15.00
254	*George Perez*	4.00
255	*Roy Smith*	4.00
256	*Juan Uribe*	6.00
257	*Dewon Brazelton*	4.00
258	*Endy Chavez*	4.00
259	*Kris Foster*	4.00
260	*Eric Knott*	4.00
261	*Corky Miller*	4.00
262	Larry Bigbie	4.00
263	*Andres Torres*	4.00
264	*Adrian Hernandez*	4.00
265	*Johnny Estrada*	6.00
266	*David Williams*	4.00
267	Steve Lomasney	4.00
268	*Victor Zambrano*	6.00
269	Keith Ginter	4.00
270	*Casey Fossum*	6.00
271	*Josue Perez*	4.00
272	Josh Phelps	4.00
273	*Mark Prior*	40.00
274	*Brandon Berger*	4.00
275	*Scott Podsednik*	15.00
276	*Jorge Julio*	6.00
277	*Esix Snead*	4.00
278	*Brandon Knight*	4.00
279	*Saul Rivera*	4.00
280	*Benito Baez*	4.00
281	*Robert Mackowiak*	4.00
282	*Eric Hinske*	8.00
283	Juan Rivera	4.00
284	*Kevin Joseph*	4.00
285	Juan Pena	4.00
286	*Brandon Lyon*	4.00
287	Adam Everett	4.00
288	Eric Valent	4.00
289	Ken Harvey	4.00
290	*Bert Snow*	4.00
291	*Wily Mo Pena*	4.00
292	*Rafael Soriano*	4.00
293	*Carlos Valderrama*	4.00
294	*Christian Parker*	4.00
295	*Tsuyoshi Shinjo*	4.00
296	*Martin Vargas*	4.00
297	*Luke Hudson*	4.00
298	Dee Brown	4.00
299	*Alexis Gomez*	4.00
300	*Angel Santos*	4.00

Longevity

Stars (1-100): 10-20X
Production 50
#'s 101-300 production 25

Autographs

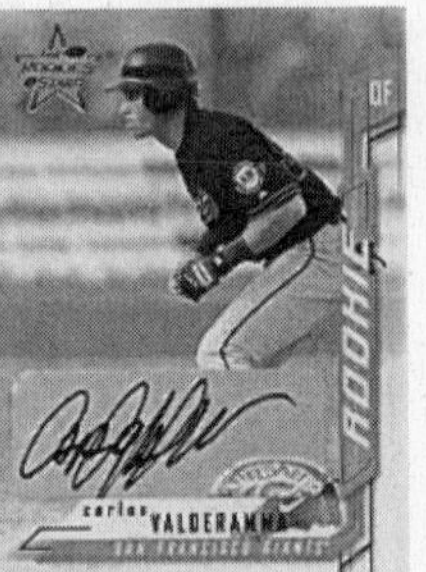

		NM/M
	Common Player:	8.00
107	Jason Karnuth	8.00
110	Brandon Larson/100	10.00
117	Jose Mieses	8.00
118	Nick Maness	8.00
119	Les Walrond	8.00
122	Carlos Garcia	8.00
123	Bill Ortega	8.00
124	Gene Altman	8.00
125	Nate Frese	8.00
130	Nick Johnson/100	8.00
133	Billy Sylvester	8.00
135	Kris Keller	8.00
139	Nate Teut	8.00
140	Jason Michaels	8.00
143	Wilmy Caceres	8.00
145	Jack Wilson/100	25.00
151	Greg Miller	8.00
155	Erick Almonte	8.00
156	Mike Penney	8.00
157	Delvin James	8.00
161	Will Ohman	8.00
167	Matt White	8.00
180	Jeremy Owens	8.00
184	Ryan Freel	10.00
185	Duaner Sanchez	8.00
193	Adam Pettyjohn/100	8.00
194	Donaldo Mendez/100	10.00
196	Paul Phillips	8.00
197	Brian Lawrence/100	8.00
199	Blaine Neal	8.00
201	Josh Towers/100	15.00
203	Michael Rivera	8.00
204	Juan Cruz/100	10.00
205	Albert Pujols SP	
207	Roy Oswalt SP	40.00
208	Elpidio Guzman/100	8.00
209	Horacio Ramirez	15.00
210	Corey Patterson SP	25.00
211	Geronimo Gil	8.00
212	Jay Gibbons/100	30.00
213	Orlando Woodards	8.00
215	Angel Berroa/100	25.00
216	Brandon Duckworth/100	10.00
218	David Brous	8.00
219	Bud Smith SP	8.00
221	Mark Teixeira/100	350.00
223	Tony Cogan	8.00
225	Ricardo Rodriguez	8.00
226	Brian Rogers	8.00
227	Adam Dunn SP	50.00
228	Wilson Betemit/100	10.00
231	Claudio Vargas	8.00
232	Wilkin Ruan	8.00
234	Kevin Olsen	8.00
236	Jeremy Affeldt	10.00
237	Mike Maroth	8.00
238	C.C. Sabathia SP	
239	Cory Aldridge	8.00
240	Zach Day	10.00
243	Travis Hafner	40.00
244	Joe Kennedy/100	15.00
254	George Perez	8.00
256	Juan Uribe	10.00
257	Dewon Brazelton/100	10.00
261	Corky Miller/100	8.00
263	Andres Torres/100	8.00
265	Johnny Estrada/100	30.00
266	David Williams	10.00
270	Casey Fossum	8.00
273	Mark Prior/100	275.00
274	Brandon Berger	8.00
277	Esix Snead	8.00
282	Eric Hinske	15.00
292	Rafael Soriano	15.00
293	Carlos Valderrama	8.00
299	Alexis Gomez	8.00

Dress For Success

		NM/M
	Common Player:	8.00
	Inserted 1:96	
	Prime Cuts:	2X
	Numbered to 50 each	
1	Cal Ripken Jr.	40.00
2	Mike Piazza	35.00
3	Barry Bonds	40.00
4	Frank Thomas	20.00
5	Nomar Garciaparra	35.00
6	Richie Sexson	8.00
7	Brian Giles	8.00
8	Todd Helton	20.00
9	Ivan Rodriguez	15.00
10	Andruw Jones	20.00
11	Juan Gonzalez	20.00
12	Vladimir Guerrero	20.00
13	Greg Maddux	25.00
14	Tony Gwynn	25.00
15	Randy Johnson	20.00
16	Jeff Bagwell	20.00
17	Kerry Wood	15.00
18	Roberto Alomar	8.00
19	Chipper Jones	25.00
20	Pedro Martinez	20.00

21 Shawn Green 10.00
22 Magglio Ordonez 10.00
23 Darin Erstad 12.00
24 Rafael Palmeiro 15.00
25 Edgar Martinez 8.00

Freshman Orientation

NM/M
Common Player: 8.00
Inserted 1:96
Class Officers: 2X
Numbered to 50 each
1 Adam Dunn 15.00
2 Josh Towers 8.00
3 Vernon Wells 10.00
4 Corey Patterson 10.00
5 Albert Pujols
6 Ben Sheets 8.00
7 Pedro Feliz 8.00
8 Keith Ginter 8.00
9 Luis Rivas 8.00
10 Andres Torres 8.00
11 Carlos Valderrama 8.00
12 Brandon Inge 8.00
13 Jay Gibbons 15.00
14 Cesar Izturis 8.00
15 Marcus Giles 8.00
16 Tsuyoshi Shinjo 12.00
17 Eric Valent 8.00
18 David Espinosa 8.00
19 Aubrey Huff 8.00
20 Wilmy Caceres 8.00
21 Bud Smith 8.00
22 Ricardo Rodriguez 8.00
23 Wes Helms 8.00
24 Jason Hart 8.00
25 Dee Brown 8.00

Great American Treasures

NM/M
Inserted 1:1,120
1 Barry Bonds (jersey) 100.00
2 Magglio Ordonez (bat) 40.00
3 Derek Jeter (ball) 150.00
4 Nolan Ryan (ball) 600.00
5 Sammy Sosa (ball) 125.00
6 Tom Glavine (jersey) 50.00
7 Ivan Rodriguez (bat) 30.00
8 Pedro Martinez (ball) 100.00
9 Mark McGwire (ball) 250.00
10 Ted Williams (ball) 350.00
11 Ryne Sandberg (bat) 60.00
12 Barry Bonds (ball) 300.00
13 Hideo Nomo (ball) 450.00
14 Roger Maris (ball) 300.00
15 Ty Cobb (ball) 750.00
16 Harmon Killebrew (bat) 150.00
17 Magglio Ordonez (cap) 30.00
18 Wade Boggs (bat) 40.00
19 Hank Aaron (cap) 400.00
20 David Cone (ball) 100.00

Great American Treasures Auto

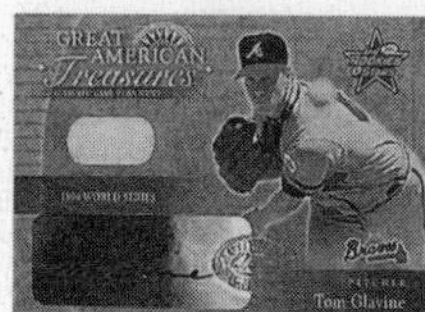

NM/M
GT-6 Tom Glavine 96 WS Jsy 125.00
GT-11 Ryne Sandberg 91 AS Bat 300.00
GT-16 Harmon Killebrew 570 HR Bat 200.00
GT-18 Wade Boggs WS Bat 150.00

Player's Collection

NM/M
Singles #'d to 100
1 Tony Gwynn bat 30.00
2 Tony Gwynn jsy 30.00
3 Tony Gwynn pants 30.00
4 Tony Gwynn shoe 30.00
5 Tony Gwynn quad/25
6 Cal Ripken jsy 75.00
7 Cal Ripken bat 75.00
8 Cal Ripken glove 75.00
9 Cal Ripken jsy 75.00
10 Cal Ripken quad/25
11 Barry Bonds jsy 60.00
12 Barry Bonds shoe 60.00
13 Barry Bonds pants 60.00
14 Barry Bonds bat 60.00
15 Barry Bonds quad/25

Player's Collection Auto.

VALUES UNDETERMINED
PC-1 Tony Gwynn Bat
PC-6 Cal Ripken Jr. Jsy
PC-7 Cal Ripken Jr. Bat

Slideshow

NM/M
Common Player: 10.00
Production 100 sets
View Masters: 1.5X
Numbered to 25 each
1 Cal Ripken Jr. 60.00
2 Chipper Jones 35.00
3 Jeff Bagwell 25.00
4 Larry Walker 10.00
5 Greg Maddux 35.00
6 Ivan Rodriguez 20.00
7 Andruw Jones 25.00
8 Lance Berkman 10.00
9 Luis Gonzalez 10.00
10 Tony Gwynn 35.00
11 Troy Glaus 25.00
12 Todd Helton 25.00
13 Roberto Alomar 10.00
14 Barry Bonds 60.00
15 Vladimir Guerrero 25.00
16 Sean Casey 10.00
17 Curt Schilling 15.00
18 Frank Thomas 25.00
19 Pedro Martinez 25.00
20 Juan Gonzalez 25.00
21 Randy Johnson 25.00
22 Kerry Wood 15.00
23 Mike Sweeney 10.00
24 Magglio Ordonez 10.00
25 Kazuhiro Sasaki 10.00
26 Manny Ramirez 25.00
27 Roger Clemens 40.00
28 Albert Pujols 50.00
29 Hideo Nomo 25.00
30 Miguel Tejada 10.00

Slideshow Autographs

VALUES UNDETERMINED

Statistical Standouts

NM/M
Common Player: 5.00
Inserted 1:96
1 Ichiro Suzuki 35.00
2 Barry Bonds 40.00
3 Ivan Rodriguez 10.00
4 Jeff Bagwell 10.00
5 Vladimir Guerrero 10.00
6 Mike Sweeney 5.00
7 Miguel Tejada 5.00
8 Mike Piazza 30.00
9 Darin Erstad 5.00
10 Alex Rodriguez 35.00
11 Jason Giambi 8.00
12 Cal Ripken Jr. 40.00
13 Albert Pujols 35.00
14 Carlos Delgado 8.00
15 Rafael Palmeiro 8.00
16 Lance Berkman 5.00
17 Luis Gonzalez 5.00
18 Sammy Sosa 30.00
19 Andruw Jones 10.00
20 Derek Jeter 40.00
21 Edgar Martinez 5.00
22 Troy Glaus 10.00
23 Magglio Ordonez 5.00
24 Mark McGwire 35.00
25 Manny Ramirez 10.00

Statistical Standouts Auto.

VALUES UNDETERMINED

Triple Threads

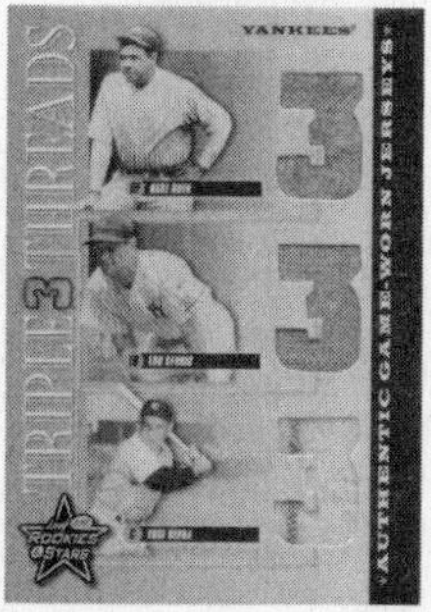

NM/M
Common Card: 50.00
Numbered to 100
TT-1 Pedro Martinez, Manny Ramirez, Nomar Garciaparra 100.00
TT-2 Frank Robinson, Cal Ripken Jr., Brooks Robinson 200.00
TT-3 Yogi Berra, Lou Gehrig, Babe Ruth 500.00
TT-4 Andre Dawson, Ryne Sandberg, Ernie Banks 140.00
TT-5 Warren Spahn, Hank Aaron, Eddie Mathews 150.00
TT-6 Greg Maddux, Chipper Jones, Andruw Jones 75.00
TT-7 Nolan Ryan, Ivan Rodriguez, Juan Gonzalez 100.00
TT-8 Lance Berkman, Jeff Bagwell, Craig Biggio 50.00
TT-9 Rod Carew, Harmon Killebrew, Kirby Puckett 75.00
TT-10 Luis Gonzalez, Curt Schilling, Randy Johnson 60.00

2002 LEAF

NM/M
Complete Set (1-200): 80.00
Common Player: .15
Common (151-200): 1.50
Inserted 1:6
Pack (4): 1.50
Box (24): 30.00
1 Tim Salmon .25
2 Troy Glaus .65
3 Curt Schilling .40
4 Luis Gonzalez .25
5 Mark Grace .25
6 Matt Williams .15
7 Randy Johnson .65
8 Tom Glavine .40
9 Brady Anderson .15
10 Hideo Nomo .65
11 Pedro Martinez .65
12 Corey Patterson .15
13 Paul Konerko .25
14 Jon Lieber .15
15 Carlos Lee .15
16 Magglio Ordonez .15
17 Adam Dunn .40
18 Ken Griffey Jr. 1.00
19 C.C. Sabathia .15
20 Jim Thome .50
21 Juan Gonzalez .65
22 Kenny Lofton .15
23 Juan Encarnacion .15
24 Tony Clark .15
25 A.J. Burnett .15
26 Josh Beckett .25
27 Lance Berkman .15
28 Eric Karros .15
29 Shawn Green .30
30 Brad Radke .15
31 Joe Mays .15
32 Javier Vazquez .15
33 Alfonso Soriano .50
34 Jorge Posada .25
35 Eric Chavez .25
36 Mark Mulder .15
37 Miguel Tejada .25
38 Tim Hudson .25
39 Bobby Abreu .15
40 Pat Burrell .40
41 Ryan Klesko .15
42 NOT ISSUED
43 John Olerud .15
44 Ellis Burks .15
45 Mike Cameron .15
46 Jim Edmonds .15
47 Ben Grieve .15
48 Carlos Pena .15
49 Alex Rodriguez 1.50
50 Raul Mondesi .15
51 Billy Koch .15
52 Manny Ramirez .65
53 Darin Erstad .25
54 Troy Percival .15
55 Andruw Jones .65
56 Chipper Jones .75
57 David Segui .15
58 Chris Stynes .15
59 Trot Nixon .15
60 Sammy Sosa 1.00
61 Kerry Wood .50
62 Frank Thomas .65
63 Barry Larkin .15
64 Bartolo Colon .15

65 Kazuhiro Sasaki .15
66 Roberto Alomar .35
67 Mike Hampton .15
68 Roger Cedeno .15
69 Cliff Floyd .15
70 Mike Lowell .15
71 Billy Wagner .15
72 Craig Biggio .15
73 Jeff Bagwell .65
74 Carlos Beltran .50
75 Mark Quinn .15
76 Mike Sweeney .15
77 Gary Sheffield .25
78 Kevin Brown .15
79 Paul LoDuca .15
80 Ben Sheets .15
81 Jeromy Burnitz .15
82 Richie Sexson .15
83 Corey Koskie .15
84 Eric Milton .15
85 Jose Vidro .15
86 Mike Piazza 1.00
87 Robin Ventura .15
88 Andy Pettitte .25
89 Mike Mussina .40
90 Orlando Hernandez .15
91 Roger Clemens .85
92 Barry Zito .25
93 Jermaine Dye .15
94 Jimmy Rollins .15
95 Jason Kendall .15
96 Rickey Henderson .65
97 Andres Galarraga .15
98 Bret Boone .15
99 Freddy Garcia .15
100 J.D. Drew .25
101 Jose Cruz Jr. .15
102 Greg Maddux .75
103 Javy Lopez .15
104 Nomar Garciaparra 1.00
105 Fred McGriff .15
106 Keith Foulke .15
107 Ray Durham .15
108 Sean Casey .25
109 Todd Walker .15
110 Omar Vizquel .15
111 Travis Fryman .15
112 Larry Walker .15
113 Todd Helton .65
114 Bobby Higginson .15
115 Charles Johnson .15
116 Moises Alou .15
117 Richard Hidalgo .15
118 Roy Oswalt .25
119 Neifi Perez .15
120 Adrian Beltre .30
121 Chan Ho Park .15
122 Geoff Jenkins .15
123 Doug Mientkiewicz .15
124 Torii Hunter .15
125 Vladimir Guerrero .65
126 Matt Lawton .15
127 Tsuyoshi Shinjo .15
128 Bernie Williams .40
129 Derek Jeter 2.00
130 Mariano Rivera .25
131 Tino Martinez .15
132 Jason Giambi .45
133 Scott Rolen .50
134 Brian Giles .15
135 Phil Nevin .15
136 Trevor Hoffman .15
137 Barry Bonds 2.00
138 Jeff Kent .15
139 Shannon Stewart .15
140 Shawn Estes .15
141 Edgar Martinez .15
142 Ichiro Suzuki 1.00
143 Albert Pujols 1.50
144 Bud Smith .15
145 Matt Morris .15
146 Frank Catalanotto .15
147 Gabe Kapler .15
148 Ivan Rodriguez .45
149 Rafael Palmeiro .45
150 Carlos Delgado .40
151 Marlon Byrd 2.00
152 Alex Herrera 1.50
153 *Brandon Backe* 2.00
154 *Jorge De La Rosa* 2.00
155 Corky Miller 1.50
156 Dennis Tankersley 1.50
157 *Kyle Kane* 2.00
158 Justin Duchscherer 1.50
159 *Brian Mallette* 2.00
160 Eric Hinske 1.50
161 Jason Lane 1.50
162 Hee Seop Choi 3.00
163 Juan Cruz 1.50
164 *Rodrigo Rosario* 2.00
165 Matt Guerrier 1.50
166 *Anderson Machado* 2.00
167 Geronimo Gil 1.50
168 Dewon Brazelton 1.50
169 Mark Prior 6.00
170 Bill Hall 1.50
171 *Jorge Padilla* 2.00
172 Josh Pearce 1.50
173 *Allan Simpson* 2.00
174 *Doug Devore* 2.00
175 Morgan Ensberg 1.50
176 Angel Berroa 1.50
177 *Steve Bechler* 2.00
178 Antonio Perez 1.50
179 Mark Teixeira 3.00
180 Mark Ellis 1.50
181 Michael Cuddyer 1.50
182 Mike Rivera 1.50
183 *Raul Chavez* 2.00
184 Juan Pena 1.50
185 Austin Kearns 2.00
186 Ryan Ludwick 1.50
187 Ed Rogers 1.50
188 Wilson Betemit 1.50
189 Nick Neugebauer 1.50
190 *Tom Shearn* 2.00
191 *Eric Cyr* 2.00
192 Victor Martinez 1.50
193 Brandon Berger 1.50
194 Erik Bedard 1.50
195 *Franklin German* 2.00
196 Joe Thurston 1.50
197 John Buck 1.50
198 *Jeff Deardorff* 2.00
199 *Ryan Jamison* 2.00
200 Alfredo Amezaga 1.50
201 *So Taguchi/500* 8.00
202 *Kazuhisa Ishii/250* 15.00

Press Proof Blue

Stars (1-150): 5-10X
Inserted 1:24 Retail

Press Proof Red

Stars (1-150): 4-6X
Inserted 1:12 Retail

Autograph

Quantity produced listed
201 So Taguchi/50
202 Kazuhisa Ishii/25

Burn n' Turn

NM/M
Complete Set (10): 50.00
Common Player: 4.00
Inserted 1:96
1 Fernando Vina, Edgar Renteria 4.00
2 Alex Rodriguez, Mike Young 10.00
3 Derek Jeter, Alfonso Soriano 15.00
4 Carlos Guillen, Bret Boone 4.00
5 Jose Vidro, Orlando Cabrera 4.00
6 Barry Larkin, Todd Walker 4.00
7 Carlos Febles, Neifi Perez 4.00
8 Jeff Kent, Rich Aurilia 4.00
9 Craig Biggio, Julio Lugo 5.00
10 Miguel Tejada, Mark Ellis 4.00

Clean Up Crew

NM/M
Complete Set (15): 90.00
Common Player: 4.00
Inserted 1:192
1 Barry Bonds 20.00
2 Sammy Sosa 12.00
3 Luis Gonzalez 4.00
4 Richie Sexson 4.00
5 Jim Thome 6.00
6 Chipper Jones 8.00
7 Alex Rodriguez 15.00
8 Troy Glaus 6.00
9 Rafael Palmeiro 5.00
10 Lance Berkman 4.00
11 Mike Piazza 12.00
12 Jason Giambi 5.00
13 Todd Helton 6.00
14 Shawn Green 5.00
15 Carlos Delgado 5.00

Clubhouse Signatures Bronze

NM/M
Common Player: 5.00
(1) Wilson Betemit/150 6.00
(2) Marlon Byrd/200 6.00
(3) Joe Crede/200 8.00
(4) Andre Dawson/100 30.00
(5) J.D. Drew/25 35.00
(6) Adam Dunn/200 25.00
(7) Jermaine Dye/125 10.00
(8) Mark Ellis/300 8.00
(9) Johnny Estrada/250 8.00
(10) Bob Feller/250 15.00
(11) Robert Fick/300 5.00
(12) Steve Garvey/200 15.00
(13) Austin Kearns/300 10.00
(14) Jason Lane/250 5.00
(15) Paul LoDuca/300 8.00
(16) Terrence Long/250 5.00
(17) Edgar Martinez/50 30.00
(18) Don Mattingly/25 100.00
(19) Joe Mays/200 6.00
(20) Mark Mulder/50 25.00
(21) Xavier Nady/200 8.00
(22) Roy Oswalt/300 10.00
(23) Aramis Ramirez/250 15.00
(24) Tim Redding/300 5.00
(25) Phil Rizzuto/25 45.00
(26) Ryne Sandberg/25 100.00
(27) Ron Santo/300 15.00
(28) Bud Smith/200 5.00
(29) Ozzie Smith/25 85.00
(30) Alfonso Soriano/75 30.00
(31) Alan Trammell/75 15.00
(32) Billy Williams/150 10.00
(33) Barry Zito/100 25.00

Clubhouse Signatures Silver

NM/M
Common Player: 10.00
(1) Rich Aurilia/100 15.00
(2) Wilson Betemit/100 15.00
(3) Marlon Byrd/100 15.00
(4) Sean Casey/50 20.00
(5) Eric Chavez/100 20.00
(6) Roger Clemens/25 150.00
(7) Joe Crede/50 20.00
(8) Andre Dawson/100 30.00
(9) Adam Dunn/75 40.00
(10) Jermaine Dye/100 15.00
(11) Mark Ellis/100 10.00
(12) Johnny Estrada/100 15.00
(13) Bob Feller/100 20.00
(14) Robert Fick/100 15.00
(15) Steve Garvey/100 20.00
(16) Vladimir Guerrero/25 60.00
(17) Todd Helton/25 50.00
(18) Austin Kearns/100 20.00
(19) Jason Lane/100 15.00
(20) Paul LoDuca/100 15.00
(21) Terrence Long/100 10.00
(22) Edgar Martinez/100 25.00
(23) Joe Mays/50 20.00
(24) Mark Mulder/100 30.00
(25) Xavier Nady/100 10.00
(26) Roy Oswalt/100 20.00
(27) Aramis Ramirez/100 20.00
(28) Tim Redding/100 10.00
(29) Cal Ripken Jr./25 225.00
(30) Phil Rizzuto/25 50.00
(31) Ron Santo/100 40.00
(32) Mike Schmidt/75 75.00
(33) Bud Smith/100 10.00
(34) Miguel Tejada/100 30.00
(35) Javier Vazquez/100 15.00
(36) Billy Williams/100 20.00
(37) Barry Zito/100 30.00

Clubhouse Signatures Gold

NM/M
Common Player: 15.00
Numbered to 25
(1) Rich Aurilia 15.00
(2) Josh Beckett 60.00
(3) Wilson Betemit 15.00
(4) Marlon Byrd 15.00
(5) Sean Casey 25.00
(6) Eric Chavez 30.00
(7) Roger Clemens 150.00
(8) Joe Crede 50.00
(9) Andre Dawson 40.00
(10) J.D. Drew 40.00
(11) Adam Dunn 65.00
(12) Jermaine Dye 20.00
(13) Mark Ellis 15.00
(14) Johnny Estrada 20.00
(15) Bob Feller 45.00
(16) Robert Fick 15.00
(17) Steve Garvey 40.00
(18) Luis Gonzalez 35.00
(19) Vladimir Guerrero 75.00
(20) Todd Helton 50.00
(21) Orel Hershiser 35.00
(22) Austin Kearns 50.00
(23) Jason Lane 15.00
(24) Paul LoDuca 25.00
(25) Terrence Long 15.00
(26) Edgar Martinez 30.00
(27) Don Mattingly 125.00
(28) Joe Mays 25.00
(29) Mark Mulder 40.00
(30) Xavier Nady 20.00
(31) Roy Oswalt 30.00
(32) Chan Ho Park 15.00
(33) Kirby Puckett 125.00
(34) Aramis Ramirez 40.00
(35) Tim Redding 15.00
(36) Cal Ripken Jr. 225.00
(37) Phil Rizzuto 60.00
(38) Ryne Sandberg 125.00
(39) Ron Santo 65.00
(40) Mike Schmidt 90.00
(41) Bud Smith 20.00
(42) Ozzie Smith 100.00
(43) Alfonso Soriano 80.00
(44) Miguel Tejada 30.00
(45) Alan Trammell 25.00
(46) Javier Vazquez 20.00
(47) Billy Williams 35.00
(48) Barry Zito 50.00

Cornerstones

NM/M
Production 50 sets
Some not priced yet
1 Andruw Jones, Chipper Jones 40.00
4 Curt Schilling, Randy Johnson 40.00
6 Larry Walker, Todd Helton 25.00
7 Carlos Delgado, Shannon Stewart 25.00
10 Bernie Williams, Roger Clemens 60.00

Future 500 Club

NM/M
Complete Set (10): 40.00
Common Player: 2.00
Inserted 1:64
1 Sammy Sosa 8.00
2 Mike Piazza 8.00
3 Alex Rodriguez 10.00
4 Chipper Jones 6.00
5 Jeff Bagwell 4.00
6 Carlos Delgado 2.00
7 Shawn Green 2.00
8 Ken Griffey Jr. 8.00
9 Rafael Palmeiro 3.00
10 Vladimir Guerrero 4.00

Game Collection

NM/M
Common Player: 5.00
Inserted 1:62 R
SPs indicated
AB B Adrian Beltre (bat) 5.00
AD BG Adam Dunn (batting glove/25) 25.00
AG B Andres Galarraga (bat) 5.00
AJ B Andruw Jones (bat/300) 8.00

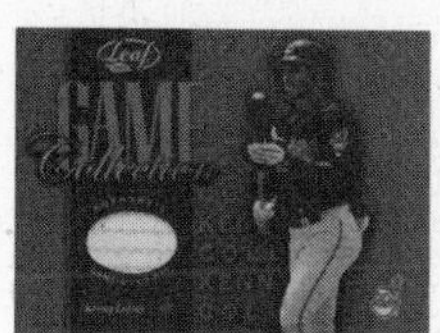

BG B Brian Giles (bat) 5.00
BH B Bobby Higginson (bat) 5.00
BS H Ben Sheets (hat/25) 35.00
BW S Bernie Williams (shoe/25) 30.00
BZ FG Barry Zito (fielding glove/25) 25.00
CB B Carlos Beltran (bat) 8.00
CBI B Craig Biggio (bat) 6.00
CF B Carlton Fisk (bat) 10.00
CK B Chuck Knoblauch (bat) 5.00
CP S Corey Patterson (shoe/25) 25.00
EM B Eddie Murray (bat/250) 15.00
GJ P Geoff Jenkins (pants) 5.00
IR BG Ivan Rodriguez (batting glove/25) 30.00
JB B Jeff Bagwell (bat/100) 15.00
JD H Johnny Damon (hat/25) 25.00
JE B Juan Encarnacion (bat) 5.00
JG B Juan Gonzalez (bat) 8.00
KL B Kenny Lofton (bat) 5.00
KW S Kerry Wood (shoe/25) 40.00
LB BG Lance Berkman (batting glove/25) 25.00
LW B Larry Walker (bat/50) 15.00
MB BG Marlon Byrd (batting glove/25) 20.00
MG B Mark Grace (bat/200) 8.00
MM FG Mike Mussina (fielding glove/25) 55.00
MO B Magglio Ordonez (bat/150) 6.00
MP B Mike Piazza (bat/100) 15.00
PB B Pat Burrell (bat/100) 15.00
RA B Roberto Alomar (bat) 8.00
RD B Ray Durham (bat) 5.00
RG B Rusty Greer (bat) 5.00
RJ FG Randy Johnson (fielding glove) 80.00
RP B Rafael Palmeiro (bat) 10.00
RP BG Rafael Palmeiro (batting glove/25) 30.00
RV B Robin Ventura (bat) 5.00
SC B Sean Casey (bat) 5.00
SR B Scott Rolen (bat/250) 15.00
SS H Shannon Stewart (hat/25) 20.00
TC B Tony Clark (bat) 5.00
TG BG Tony Gwynn (batting glove/25) 90.00
TH B Todd Helton (bat) 10.00
TN B Trot Nixon (bat) 5.00
WB B Wade Boggs (bat) 8.00

Gold Leaf Rookies

NM/M
Complete Set (10): 20.00
Common Player: 2.00
Inserted 1:24
1 Josh Beckett 4.00
2 Marlon Byrd 2.00
3 Dennis Tankersley 2.00
4 Jason Lane 2.00
5 Dewon Brazelton 2.00
6 Mark Prior 5.00
7 Bill Hall 2.00
8 Angel Berroa 2.00
9 Mark Teixeira 4.00
10 John Buck 2.00

Heading for the Hall

NM/M
Complete Set (10): 40.00
Common Player: 2.00
Inserted 1:64
1 Greg Maddux 4.00
2 Ozzie Smith 4.00
3 Andre Dawson 2.00
4 Dennis Eckersley 2.00
5 Roberto Alomar 2.00
6 Cal Ripken Jr. 10.00
7 Roger Clemens 5.00
8 Tony Gwynn 4.00
9 Alex Rodriguez 8.00
10 Jeff Bagwell 3.00

League of Nations

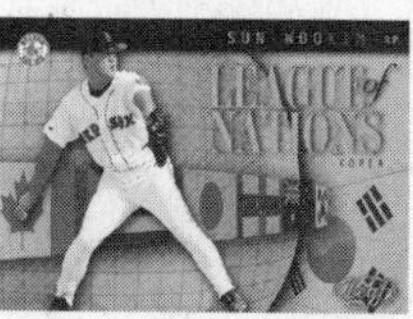

NM/M
Complete Set (10): 20.00
Common Player: 2.00
Inserted 1:60
1 Ichiro Suzuki 8.00
2 Tsuyoshi Shinjo 2.00
3 Chan Ho Park 2.00
4 Larry Walker 2.00
5 Andruw Jones 4.00
6 Hideo Nomo 4.00
7 Byung-Hyun Kim 2.00
8 Sun-Woo Kim 2.00
9 Orlando Hernandez 2.00
10 Luke Prokopec 2.00

Heading for the Hall Autographs

NM/M
Common Player: 25.00
Production 50 each
1 Greg Maddux 125.00
2 Ozzie Smith 100.00
3 Andre Dawson 40.00
4 Dennis Eckersley 45.00
5 Roberto Alomar 25.00
6 Cal Ripken Jr. 200.00
7 Roger Clemens 150.00
8 Tony Gwynn 100.00
9 Alex Rodriguez 150.00
10 Jeff Bagwell 40.00

Retired Numbers

#'d to jersey number
Values Undetermined

Rookie Reprints

NM/M
Complete Set (6): 35.00
Common Player: 3.00
#'d to year of issue
1 Roger Clemens/1,985 10.00
2 Kirby Puckett/1,985 9.00
3 Andres Galarraga/1,986 3.00
4 Fred McGriff/1,986 3.00
5 Sammy Sosa/1,990 10.00
6 Frank Thomas/1,990 8.00

Shirt Off My Back

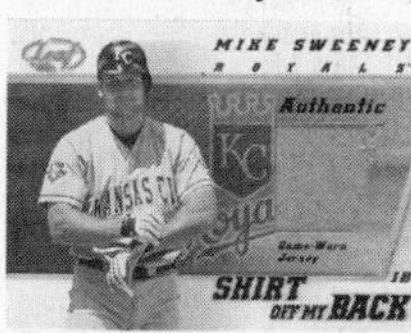

NM/M
Common Player: 5.00
Inserted 1:29
Patch variations: 2-4X
RA Roberto Alomar 8.00
JB Jeff Bagwell/SP 20.00
MB Michael Barrett 5.00
CB Carlos Beltran 15.00
LB Lance Berkman 5.00
GB George Brett/SP 50.00
KB Kevin Brown 5.00
MB Mark Buehrle 5.00
AB A.J. Burnett 5.00
JBU Jeromy Burnitz 5.00
CD Carlos Delgado 8.00
RD Ryan Dempster 5.00
DE Darin Erstad/SP 15.00
CF Cliff Floyd 5.00
FG Freddy Garcia/SP 8.00
NG Nomar Garciaparra/SP 40.00
TGL Troy Glaus/SP 20.00
TGL Tom Glavine 8.00
LG Luis Gonzalez 5.00
TG Tony Gwynn 25.00
MH Mike Hampton 5.00
TH Todd Helton 20.00
THU Tim Hudson 6.00
BJA Bo Jackson/SP 25.00
RJ Randy Johnson 20.00
CJ Chipper Jones/SP 30.00
AK Al Kaline/SP 20.00
EK Eric Karros 5.00
BL Barry Larkin 5.00
CL Carlos Lee 5.00
JL Javy Lopez 5.00
GM Greg Maddux/SP 30.00
EM Edgar Martinez/SP 8.00
PM Pedro Martinez/SP 20.00
DM Don Mattingly/SP 50.00
KM Kevin Millwood 5.00
HN Hideo Nomo/SP 25.00
JO John Olerud 5.00
MO Magglio Ordonez 5.00
RP Rafael Palmeiro 10.00
CHP Chan Ho Park/SP 8.00
TP Troy Percival 5.00
AP Andy Pettitte/SP 12.00
MP Mike Piazza 30.00
KP Kirby Puckett 25.00
BR Brad Radke 5.00
MR Manny Ramirez 20.00
CR Cal Ripken Jr./SP/50 100.00
AR Alex Rodriguez 35.00
SR Scott Rolen/SP 15.00
KS Kazuhiro Sasaki/SP 8.00
CS Curt Schilling/SP 15.00
RS Richie Sexson 5.00
TS Tsuyoshi Shinjo/SP 8.00
JS John Smoltz 5.00
MS Mike Sweeney 5.00
MT Miguel Tejada 6.00
LW Larry Walker/SP 8.00
MW Matt Williams 5.00
DW Dave Winfield/SP 20.00

2002 LEAF CERTIFIED

NM/M
Complete Set (200):
Common Player: .50
Common (151-200): 5.00
Production 500
Pack (5): 6.00
Box (16): 75.00
1 Alex Rodriguez 4.00
2 Luis Gonzalez .65
3 Javier Vazquez .50

4 Juan Uribe .50
5 Ben Sheets .50
6 George Brett 4.00
7 Magglio Ordonez .50
8 Randy Johnson 1.00
9 Joe Kennedy .50
10 Richie Sexson .50
11 Larry Walker .50
12 Lance Berkman .50
13 Jose Cruz Jr. .50
14 Doug Davis .50
15 Cliff Floyd .50
16 Ryan Klesko .50
17 Troy Glaus 1.00
18 Robert Person .50
19 Bartolo Colon .50
20 Adam Dunn .75
21 Kevin Brown .50
22 John Smoltz .50
23 Edgar Martinez .50
24 Eric Karros .50
25 Tony Gwynn 2.00
26 Mark Mulder .50
27 Don Mattingly 4.00
28 Brandon Duckworth .50
29 C.C. Sabathia .50
30 Nomar Garciaparra 3.00
31 Adam Johnson .50
32 Miguel Tejada .65
33 Ryne Sandberg 2.00
34 Roger Clemens 2.50
35 Edgardo Alfonzo .50
36 Jason Jennings .50
37 Todd Helton 1.00
38 Nolan Ryan 5.00
39 Paul LoDuca .50
40 Cal Ripken Jr. 5.00
41 Terrence Long .50
42 Mike Sweeney .50
43 Carlos Lee .50
44 Ben Grieve .50
45 Tony Armas Jr. .50
46 Joe Mays .50
47 Jeff Kent .50
48 Andy Pettitte .65
49 Kirby Puckett 2.00
50 Aramis Ramirez .50
51 Tim Redding .50
52 Freddy Garcia .50
53 Javy Lopez .50
54 Mike Schmidt 4.00
55 Wade Miller .50
56 Ramon Ortiz .50
57 Ray Durham .50
58 J.D. Drew .75
59 Bret Boone .50
60 Mark Buehrle .50
61 Geoff Jenkins .50
62 Greg Maddux 2.00
63 Mark Grace .65
64 Toby Hall .50
65 A.J. Burnett .50
66 Bernie Williams .65
67 Roy Oswalt .65
68 Shannon Stewart .50
69 Barry Zito .65
70 Juan Pierre .50
71 Preston Wilson .50
72 Rafael Furcal .50
73 Sean Casey .65
74 John Olerud .50
75 Paul Konerko .75
76 Vernon Wells .50
77 Juan Gonzalez 1.00
78 Ellis Burks .50
79 Jim Edmonds .75
80 Robert Fick .50
81 Michael Cuddyer .50
82 Tim Hudson .65

83	Phil Nevin	.50
84	Curt Schilling	.75
85	Juan Cruz	.50
86	Jeff Bagwell	1.00
87	Raul Mondesi	.50
88	Bud Smith	.50
89	Omar Vizquel	.50
90	Vladimir Guerrero	1.00
91	Garret Anderson	.50
92	Mike Piazza	3.00
93	Josh Beckett	.65
94	Carlos Delgado	1.00
95	Kazuhiro Sasaki	.50
96	Chipper Jones	2.00
97	Jacque Jones	.50
98	Pedro J. Martinez	1.00
99	Marcus Giles	.50
100	Craig Biggio	.50
101	Orlando Cabrera	.50
102	Al Leiter	.50
103	Michael Barrett	.50
104	Hideo Nomo	1.00
105	Mike Mussina	.75
106	Jeremy Giambi	.50
107	Cristian Guzman	.50
108	Frank Thomas	1.00
109	Carlos Beltran	1.00
110	Jorge Posada	.65
111	Roberto Alomar	.65
112	Bobby Abreu	.50
113	Robin Ventura	.50
114	Pat Burrell	.75
115	Kenny Lofton	.50
116	Adrian Beltre	.75
117	Gary Sheffield	.75
118	Jermaine Dye	.50
119	Manny Ramirez	1.00
120	Brian Giles	.50
121	Tsuyoshi Shinjo	.50
122	Rafael Palmeiro	.85
123	Mo Vaughn	.50
124	Kerry Wood	.75
125	Moises Alou	.50
126	Rickey Henderson	1.00
127	Corey Patterson	.50
128	Jim Thome	1.00
129	Richard Hidalgo	.50
130	Darin Erstad	.75
131	Johnny Damon	.75
132	Juan Encarnacion	.50
133	Scott Rolen	1.00
134	Tom Glavine	.75
135	Ivan Rodriguez	.85
136	Jay Gibbons	.50
137	Trot Nixon	.50
138	Nick Neugebauer	.50
139	Barry Larkin	.50
140	Andruw Jones	1.00
141	Shawn Green	.75
142	Jose Vidro	.50
143	Derek Jeter	5.00
144	Ichiro Suzuki	3.00
145	Ken Griffey Jr.	3.00
146	Barry Bonds	5.00
147	Albert Pujols	4.00
148	Sammy Sosa	3.00
149	Jason Giambi	.75
150	Alfonso Soriano	.75
151	Drew Henson/bat	8.00
152	Luis Garcia/bat	5.00
153	Geronimo Gil/jsy	5.00
154	Corky Miller/jsy	5.00
155	Mike Rivera/bat	5.00
156	Mark Ellis/jsy	5.00
157	Josh Pearce/bat	5.00
158	Ryan Ludwick/bat	5.00
159	*So Taguchi/bat*	12.00
160	Cody Ransom/jsy	5.00
161	*Jeff Deardorff/bat*	5.00
162	*Franklyn German/bat*	5.00
163	Ed Rogers/jsy	5.00
164	*Eric Cyr/jsy*	5.00
165	*Victor Alvarez/jsy*	5.00
166	Victor Martinez/jsy	15.00
167	Brandon Berger/jsy	5.00
168	Juan Diaz/jsy	5.00
169	*Kevin Frederick/jsy*	5.00
170	*Earl Snyder/bat*	5.00
171	Morgan Ensberg/bat	8.00
172	*Ryan Jamison/jsy*	5.00
173	*Rodrigo Rosario/jsy*	5.00
174	Willie Harris/bat	5.00
175	Ramon Vazquez/bat	5.00
176	*Kazuhisa Ishii/bat*	12.00
177	Hank Blalock/jsy	10.00
178	Mark Prior/bat	20.00
179	Dewon Brazelton/jsy	5.00
180	*Doug Devore/jsy*	5.00
181	*Jorge Padilla/bat*	5.00
182	Mark Teixeira/jsy	10.00
183	Orlando Hudson/bat	5.00
184	John Buck/jsy	5.00
185	Erik Bedard/jsy	5.00
186	*Allan Simpson/jsy*	5.00
187	Travis Hafner/jsy	10.00
188	Jason Lane/jsy	5.00
189	Marlon Byrd/jsy	5.00
190	Joe Thurston/jsy	5.00
191	*Brandon Backe/jsy*	5.00
192	Josh Phelps/jsy	5.00
193	Bill Hall/bat	5.00
194	*Chris Snelling/bat*	8.00
195	Austin Kearns/jsy	8.00
196	Antonio Perez/bat	5.00
197	Angel Berroa/bat	8.00
198	*Anderson Machado/jsy*	5.00
199	Alfredo Amezaga/jsy	5.00
200	Eric Hinske/bat	8.00

Mirror Red

NM/M

Common (1-200): 5.00
Cards (151-200): .5-1X base
Production 150 sets
Mirror Blues (1-200): .5-1.5X
Production 75 sets
Mirror Golds not priced
Production 25 sets
Mirror Emerald five sets produced
Mirror Black one set produced

1	Alex Rodriguez/jsy	25.00
2	Luis Gonzalez/jsy	5.00
3	Javier Vazquez/bat	5.00
4	Juan Uribe/jsy	5.00
5	Ben Sheets/jsy	8.00
6	George Brett/jsy	40.00
7	Magglio Ordonez/jsy	8.00
8	Randy Johnson/jsy	15.00
9	Joe Kennedy/jsy	5.00
10	Richie Sexson/jsy	10.00
11	Larry Walker/jsy	8.00
12	Lance Berkman/jsy	8.00
13	Jose Cruz Jr/jsy	5.00
14	Doug Davis/jsy	5.00
15	Cliff Floyd/jsy	5.00
16	Ryan Klesko/bat	5.00
17	Troy Glaus/jsy	10.00
18	Robert Person/jsy	5.00
19	Bartolo Colon/jsy	5.00
20	Adam Dunn/jsy	15.00
21	Kevin Brown/jsy	8.00
22	John Smoltz/jsy	8.00
23	Edgar Martinez/jsy	8.00
24	Eric Karros/jsy	5.00
25	Tony Gwynn/jsy	20.00
26	Mark Mulder/jsy	8.00
27	Don Mattingly/jsy	40.00
28	Brandon Duckworth/jsy	5.00
29	C.C. Sabathia/jsy	5.00
30	Nomar Garciaparra/jsy	20.00
31	Adam Johnson/jsy	5.00
32	Miguel Tejada/jsy	8.00
33	Ryne Sandberg/jsy	40.00
34	Roger Clemens/jsy	25.00
35	Edgardo Alfonzo/jsy	5.00
36	Jason Jennings/jsy	5.00
37	Todd Helton/jsy	10.00
38	Nolan Ryan/jsy	60.00
39	Paul LoDuca/jsy	5.00
40	Cal Ripken Jr/jsy	55.00
41	Terrence Long/jsy	5.00
42	Mike Sweeney/jsy	5.00
43	Carlos Lee/jsy	5.00
44	Ben Grieve/jsy	5.00
45	Tony Armas Jr/jsy	5.00
46	Joe Mays/jsy	5.00
47	Jeff Kent/jsy	8.00
48	Andy Pettitte/jsy	8.00
49	Kirby Puckett/jsy	15.00
50	Aramis Ramirez/jsy	8.00
51	Tim Redding/jsy	5.00
52	Freddy Garcia/jsy	5.00
53	Javy Lopez/jsy	6.00
54	Mike Schmidt/jsy	35.00
55	Wade Miller/jsy	5.00
56	Ramon Ortiz/jsy	5.00
57	Ray Durham/jsy	5.00
58	J.D. Drew/jsy	5.00
59	Bret Boone/jsy	5.00
60	Mark Buehrle/jsy	5.00
61	Geoff Jenkins/jsy	5.00
62	Greg Maddux/jsy	20.00
63	Mark Grace/jsy	10.00
64	Toby Hall/jsy	5.00
65	A.J. Burnett/jsy	5.00
66	Bernie Williams/jsy	8.00
67	Roy Oswalt/jsy	8.00
68	Shannon Stewart/jsy	5.00
69	Barry Zito/jsy	8.00
70	Juan Pierre/jsy	5.00
71	Preston Wilson/jsy	5.00
72	Rafael Furcal/jsy	5.00
73	Sean Casey/jsy	5.00
74	John Olerud/jsy	5.00
75	Paul Konerko/jsy	5.00
76	Vernon Wells/jsy	5.00
77	Juan Gonzalez/jsy	8.00
78	Ellis Burks/jsy	5.00
79	Jim Edmonds/jsy	8.00
80	Robert Fick/jsy	5.00
81	Michael Cuddyer/jsy	5.00
82	Tim Hudson/jsy	5.00
83	Phil Nevin/jsy	5.00
84	Curt Schilling/jsy	8.00
85	Juan Cruz/jsy	5.00
86	Jeff Bagwell/jsy	10.00
87	Raul Mondesi/jsy	5.00
88	Bud Smith/jsy	5.00
89	Omar Vizquel/jsy	5.00
90	Vladimir Guerrero/jsy	20.00
91	Garret Anderson/jsy	8.00
92	Mike Piazza/jsy	15.00
93	Josh Beckett/jsy	8.00
94	Carlos Delgado/jsy	8.00
95	Kazuhiro Sasaki/jsy	5.00
96	Chipper Jones/jsy	10.00
97	Jacque Jones/jsy	5.00
98	Pedro Martinez/jsy	15.00
99	Marcus Giles/jsy	5.00
100	Craig Biggio/jsy	6.00
101	Orlando Cabrera/jsy	5.00
102	Al Leiter/jsy	5.00
103	Michael Barrett/jsy	5.00
104	Hideo Nomo/jsy	15.00
105	Mike Mussina/jsy	12.00
106	Jeremy Giambi/jsy	5.00
107	Cristian Guzman/jsy	5.00
108	Frank Thomas/jsy	10.00
109	Carlos Beltran/bat	8.00
110	Jorge Posada/bat	8.00
111	Roberto Alomar/bat	12.00
112	Bobby Abreu/bat	6.00
113	Robin Ventura/bat	10.00
114	Pat Burrell/bat	18.00
115	Kenny Lofton/bat	6.00
116	Adrian Beltre/bat	8.00
117	Gary Sheffield/bat	6.00
118	Jermaine Dye/bat	5.00
119	Manny Ramirez/bat	8.00
120	Brian Giles/bat	5.00
121	Tsuyoshi Shinjo/bat	5.00
122	Rafael Palmeiro/bat	10.00
123	Mo Vaughn/bat	5.00
124	Kerry Wood/bat	15.00
125	Moises Alou/bat	8.00
126	Rickey Henderson/bat	15.00
127	Corey Patterson/bat	8.00
128	Jim Thome/bat	15.00
129	Richard Hidalgo/bat	5.00
130	Darin Erstad/jsy	5.00
131	Johnny Damon/bat	5.00
132	Juan Encarnacion/bat	5.00
133	Scott Rolen/bat	10.00
134	Tom Glavine/bat	8.00
135	Ivan Rodriguez/bat	10.00
136	Jay Gibbons/bat	5.00
137	Trot Nixon/bat	5.00
138	Nick Neugebauer/bat	5.00
139	Barry Larkin/jsy	10.00
140	Andruw Jones/bat	8.00
141	Shawn Green/bat	8.00
142	Jose Vidro/jsy	5.00
143	Derek Jeter/base	25.00
144	Ichiro Suzuki/base	20.00
145	Ken Griffey Jr/base	15.00
146	Barry Bonds/base	20.00
147	Albert Pujols/base	15.00
148	Sammy Sosa/base	15.00
149	Jason Giambi/base	8.00
150	Alfonso Soriano/jsy	10.00
151	Drew Henson/bat	5.00
152	Luis Garcia/bat	5.00
153	Geronimo Gil/jsy	5.00
154	Corky Miller/jsy	5.00
155	Mike Rivera/bat	5.00
156	Mark Ellis/jsy	5.00
157	Josh Pearce/bat	5.00
158	Ryan Ludwick/bat	5.00
159	So Taguchi/bat	12.00
160	Cody Ransom/jsy	5.00
161	Jeff Deardorff/bat	5.00
162	Franklyn German/bat	5.00
163	Ed Rogers/jsy	5.00
164	Eric Cyr/jsy	5.00
165	Victor Alvarez/jsy	5.00
166	Victor Martinez/jsy	10.00
167	Brandon Berger/jsy	5.00
168	Juan Diaz/jsy	5.00
169	Kevin Frederick/jsy	5.00
170	Earl Snyder/bat	5.00
171	Morgan Ensberg/bat	5.00
172	Ryan Jamison/jsy	5.00
173	Rodrigo Rosario/jsy	5.00
174	Willie Harris/bat	5.00
175	Ramon Vazquez/bat	5.00
176	Kazuhisa Ishii/bat	15.00
177	Hank Blalock/jsy	10.00
178	Mark Prior/bat	15.00
179	Dewon Brazelton/jsy	5.00
180	Doug Devore/jsy	5.00
181	Jorge Padilla/bat	5.00
182	Mark Teixeira/jsy	10.00
183	Orlando Hudson/bat	5.00
184	John Buck/jsy	5.00
185	Erik Bedard/jsy	5.00
186	Allan Simpson/jsy	5.00
187	Travis Hafner/jsy	8.00
188	Jason Lane/jsy	5.00
189	Marlon Byrd/jsy	5.00
190	Joe Thurston/jsy	5.00
191	Brandon Backe/jsy	5.00
192	Josh Phelps/jsy	5.00
193	Bill Hall/bat	5.00
194	Chris Snelling/bat	5.00
195	Austin Kearns/jsy	8.00
196	Antonio Perez/bat	5.00
197	Angel Berroa/bat	6.00
198	Anderson Machado/jsy	5.00
199	Alfredo Amezaga/jsy	5.00
200	Eric Hinske/bat	6.00

All Certified Team

NM/M

Complete Set (25): 75.00
Common Player: 1.50
Inserted 1:17
Mirror Blues: 2-4X
Production 50 sets
Mirror Reds: 1.5-3X
Production 75 sets
Golds not priced 25 sets produced

1	Ichiro Suzuki	5.00
2	Alex Rodriguez	6.00
3	Sammy Sosa	5.00
4	Jeff Bagwell	3.00
5	Greg Maddux	4.00
6	Todd Helton	3.00
7	Nomar Garciaparra	5.00
8	Ken Griffey Jr.	5.00
9	Roger Clemens	4.50
10	Adam Dunn	2.00
11	Chipper Jones	4.00
12	Hideo Nomo	3.00
13	Lance Berkman	1.50
14	Barry Bonds	8.00
15	Manny Ramirez	3.00

16 Jason Giambi 2.00
17 Rickey Henderson 3.00
18 Randy Johnson 3.00
19 Derek Jeter 8.00
20 Kazuhisa Ishii 1.50
21 Frank Thomas 3.00
22 Mike Piazza 5.00
23 Albert Pujols 6.00
24 Pedro J. Martinez 3.00
25 Vladimir Guerrero 3.00

Certified Skills

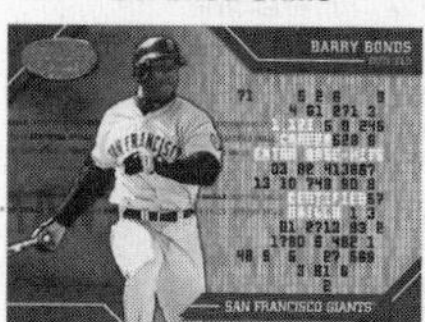

NM/M
Complete Set (20): 65.00
Common Player: 2.00
Inserted 1:17
Mirror Blues: 1.5-2.5X
Production 75 sets
Mirror Reds: 1-2X
Production 150 sets
Mirror Golds not priced 25 sets
1 Barry Bonds 8.00
2 Greg Maddux 4.00
3 Rickey Henderson 2.00
4 Ichiro Suzuki 5.00
5 Pedro J. Martinez 2.00
6 Kazuhisa Ishii 1.50
7 Alex Rodriguez 6.00
8 Mike Piazza 5.00
9 Sammy Sosa 5.00
10 Derek Jeter 8.00
11 Albert Pujols 6.00
12 Roger Clemens 4.50
13 Mark Prior 2.00
14 Chipper Jones 3.00
15 Ken Griffey Jr. 5.00
16 Frank Thomas 2.00
17 Randy Johnson 2.00
18 Vladimir Guerrero 2.00
19 Nomar Garciaparra 5.00
20 Jeff Bagwell 2.00

Fabric of the Game

NM/M
Common Player:
1 Bobby Doerr/10
1 Bobby Doerr/37 20.00
1 Bobby Doerr HOF 86/4
1 Bobby Doerr/1
1 Bobby Doerr/25
1 Bobby Doerr HOF 86 AU/1
2 Ozzie Smith/15
2 Ozzie Smith/78 40.00
2 Ozzie Smith/1
2 Ozzie Smith/15
2 Ozzie Smith HOF 02 AU/5
3 Pee Wee Reese/5
3 Pee Wee Reese/40 35.00
3 Pee Wee Reese HOF 84/5
3 Pee Wee Reese/1
3 Pee Wee Reese/10
4 Tommy Lasorda/80 8.00
4 Tommy Lasorda/54 15.00
4 Tommy Lasorda HOF 97/20
4 Tommy Lasorda/2
4 Tommy Lasorda/50 15.00
5 Red Schoendienst/5
5 Red Schoendienst/45 20.00
5 Red Schoendienst HOF 89/5
5 Red Schoendienst/2
5 Red Schoendienst/10
6 Lou Gehrig/5
6 Lou Gehrig/23
6 Lou Gehrig HOF 39/5
6 Lou Gehrig/4
6 Lou Gehrig/10
7 Harmon Killebrew/10
7 Harmon Killebrew/54 35.00
7 Harmon Killebrew/3
7 Harmon Killebrew/20
7 Harmon Killebrew HOF 84 AU/5
8 Roger Maris A's/10
8 Roger Maris A's/57 75.00
8 Roger Maris A's/3
8 Roger Maris A's/10
9 Babe Ruth/5
9 Babe Ruth/14
9 Babe Ruth HOF 36/5
9 Babe Ruth/4
9 Babe Ruth/10
10 Mel Ott/5
10 Mel Ott/26 75.00
10 Mel Ott HOF 5/15
10 Mel Ott/4
10 Mel Ott/10
11 Paul Molitor/100 20.00
11 Paul Molitor/78 20.00
11 Paul Molitor/4
11 Paul Molitor/50 30.00
12 Duke Snider/5
12 Duke Snider/47 40.00
12 Duke Snider/4
12 Duke Snider/10
12 Duke Snider HOF 80 AU/5
13 Brooks Robinson/5
13 Brooks Robinson/55 40.00
13 Brooks Robinson/5
13 Brooks Robinson/10
13 Brooks Robinson HOF 83 AU/5
14 George Brett/40 75.00
14 George Brett/73 50.00
14 George Brett HOF 99/5
14 George Brett/5
14 George Brett/25
14 George Brett HOF 99 AU/5
15 Johnny Bench/80 20.00
15 Johnny Bench/67 30.00
15 Johnny Bench HOF 89/15
15 Johnny Bench/5
15 Johnny Bench/50 30.00
15 Johnny Bench HOF 89 AU/5
16 Lou Boudreau/5
16 Lou Boudreau/38 20.00
16 Lou Boudreau HOF 70/5
16 Lou Boudreau/5
16 Lou Boudreau/10
17 Stan Musial/5
17 Stan Musial/41 60.00
17 Stan Musial/6
17 Stan Musial/10
17 Stan Musial HOF 69 AU/5
18 Al Kaline/5
18 Al Kaline/53 30.00
18 Al Kaline/6
18 Al Kaline/10
18 Al Kaline HOF 80 AU/5
19 Steve Garvey/100 8.00
19 Steve Garvey/69 15.00
19 Steve Garvey/6
19 Steve Garvey/45 15.00
20 Nomar Garciaparra/100 25.00
20 Nomar Garciaparra/96 25.00
20 Nomar Garciaparra/50 35.00
20 Nomar Garciaparra AU/5
21 Joe Morgan/80 10.00
21 Joe Morgan/63 20.00
21 Joe Morgan HOF 90/15
21 Joe Morgan/8
21 Joe Morgan/50 20.00
21 Joe Morgan HOF 90 AU/5
22 Willie Stargell/5
22 Willie Stargell/62 25.00
22 Willie Stargell HOF 88/5
22 Willie Stargell/8
22 Willie Stargell/10
23 Andre Dawson/80 15.00
23 Andre Dawson/76 15.00
23 Andre Dawson Hawk/15
23 Andre Dawson/8
23 Andre Dawson/50 20.00
23 Andre Dawson Hawk AU/50
24 Gary Carter/100 10.00
24 Gary Carter/74 20.00
24 Gary Carter/8
24 Gary Carter/50 20.00
25 Reggie Jackson A's/10
25 Reggie Jackson A's/67 30.00
25 Reggie Jackson A's/9
25 Reggie Jackson A's/25
25 Reggie Jackson A's HOF 93 AU/5
26 Ted Williams/5
26 Ted Williams/39
26 Ted Williams HOF 66/5
26 Ted Williams/9
26 Ted Williams/10
27 Phil Rizzuto/5
27 Phil Rizzuto/41 30.00
27 Phil Rizzuto/10
27 Phil Rizzuto/10
27 Phil Rizzuto HOF 94 AU/5
28 Luis Aparicio/5
28 Luis Aparicio/56 20.00
28 Luis Aparicio/11
28 Luis Aparicio/10
28 Luis Aparicio HOF 84 AU/5
29 Robin Yount/80 30.00
29 Robin Yount/74 30.00
29 Robin Yount HOF 99/15
29 Robin Yount/19
29 Robin Yount/50 40.00
29 Robin Yount HOF 99 AU/5
30 Tony Gwynn/100 20.00
30 Tony Gwynn/82 20.00
30 Tony Gwynn/14
30 Tony Gwynn/50 30.00
30 Tony Gwynn AU/5
31 Ernie Banks/5
31 Ernie Banks/53 40.00
31 Ernie Banks/14
31 Ernie Banks/10
31 Ernie Banks HOF 77 AU/5
32 Joe Torre/50 15.00
32 Joe Torre/60 15.00
32 Joe Torre/15
32 Joe Torre/25
33 Bo Jackson/100 20.00
33 Bo Jackson/86 20.00
33 Bo Jackson/16
33 Bo Jackson/35 50.00
34 Alfonso Soriano/80 20.00
34 Alfonso Soriano/99 20.00
34 Alfonso Soriano/12
34 Alfonso Soriano/50 25.00
35 Cal Ripken Jr./80 60.00
35 Cal Ripken Jr./81 60.00
35 Cal Ripken Jr. Iron Man/15
35 Cal Ripken Jr./8
35 Cal Ripken Jr./50 80.00
35 Cal Ripken Jr. Iron Man AU/5
36 Miguel Tejada/100 10.00
36 Miguel Tejada/97 10.00
36 Miguel Tejada/4
36 Miguel Tejada/50 20.00
37 Alex Rodriguez M's/100 20.00
37 Alex Rodriguez M's/94 20.00
37 Alex Rodriguez M's/3
37 Alex Rodriguez M's/50 35.00
38 Mike Schmidt/80 40.00
38 Mike Schmidt/72 40.00
38 Mike Schmidt HOF 95/15
38 Mike Schmidt/20
38 Mike Schmidt/50 50.00
38 Mike Schmidt HOF 95 AU/5
39 Lou Brock/5
39 Lou Brock/61 25.00
39 Lou Brock/20
39 Lou Brock/10
39 Lou Brock HOF 85 AU/5
40 Don Sutton/80 8.00
40 Don Sutton/66 10.00
40 Don Sutton HOF 98/15
40 Don Sutton/20
40 Don Sutton/50 15.00
40 Don Sutton HOF 98 AU/5
41 Roberto Clemente/5
41 Roberto Clemente/55 125.00
41 Roberto Clemente HOF 73/5
41 Roberto Clemente/21
41 Roberto Clemente/10
42 Jim Palmer/20
42 Jim Palmer/65 20.00
42 Jim Palmer/22
42 Jim Palmer/15
42 Jim Palmer HOF 90 AU/5
43 Don Mattingly/40 75.00
43 Don Mattingly/82 50.00
43 Don Mattingly Donnie BB/5
43 Don Mattingly/23
43 Don Mattingly/25
43 Don Mattingly Donnie BB AU/5
44 Ryne Sandberg/40 60.00
44 Ryne Sandberg/81 40.00
44 Ryne Sandberg Ryno/5
44 Ryne Sandberg/23
44 Ryne Sandberg/25
44 Ryne Sandberg Ryno AU/5
45 Early Wynn/5
45 Early Wynn/39 20.00
45 Early Wynn HOF 72/5
45 Early Wynn/24
45 Early Wynn/10
46 Mike Piazza Dodgers/100 20.00
46 Mike Piazza Dodgers/92 20.00
46 Mike Piazza Dodgers/31 40.00
46 Mike Piazza Dodgers/50 25.00
47 Wade Boggs/100 15.00
47 Wade Boggs/82 15.00
47 Wade Boggs/26 40.00
47 Wade Boggs/45 30.00
48 Jim "Catfish" Hunter/10
48 Jim "Catfish" Hunter/65 25.00
48 Jim "Catfish" Hunter HOF 87/5
48 Jim "Catfish" Hunter/27 40.00
48 Jim "Catfish" Hunter/25
49 Juan Marichal/20
49 Juan Marichal/60 20.00
49 Juan Marichal/27 40.00
49 Juan Marichal/15
49 Juan Marichal HOF 83 AU/5
50 Carlton Fisk Red Sox/80 25.00
50 Carlton Fisk Red Sox/69 40.00
50 Carlton Fisk Red Sox HOF 00/15
50 Carlton Fisk Red Sox/27 50.00
50 Carlton Fisk Red Sox/50 30.00
50 Carlton Fisk Red Sox HOF 00 AU/5
51 Curt Schilling/100 15.00
51 Curt Schilling/88 15.00
51 Curt Schilling/38 25.00
51 Curt Schilling/50 20.00
52 Rod Carew Angels/80 15.00
52 Rod Carew Angels/67 25.00
52 Rod Carew Angels HOF 91/15
52 Rod Carew Angels/29
52 Rod Carew Angels/50 25.00
52 Rod Carew Angels HOF 91 AU/5
53 Rod Carew Twins/10
53 Rod Carew Twins/67 25.00
53 Rod Carew Twins/29
53 Rod Carew Twins/25
53 Rod Carew Twins HOF 91 AU/5
54 Joe Carter/100 8.00
54 Joe Carter/83 8.00
54 Joe Carter/29 15.00
54 Joe Carter/50 10.00
55 Nolan Ryan Angels/5
55 Nolan Ryan Angels/66 60.00
55 Nolan Ryan Angels HOF 99/5
55 Nolan Ryan Angels/30
55 Nolan Ryan Angels/10
55 Nolan Ryan Angels HOF 99 AU/5
56 Orlando Cepeda/80 8.00
56 Orlando Cepeda/55 10.00
56 Orlando Cepeda HOF 99/15
56 Orlando Cepeda/30 25.00
56 Orlando Cepeda/50 15.00
56 Orlando Cepeda HOF 99 AU/5
57 Dave Winfield/80 15.00
57 Dave Winfield/73 20.00
57 Dave Winfield HOF 01/15
57 Dave Winfield/31 30.00
57 Dave Winfield/50 20.00
57 Dave Winfield HOF 01 AU/5
58 Hoyt Wilhelm/80 8.00
58 Hoyt Wilhelm/52 10.00
58 Hoyt Wilhelm HOF 85/15
58 Hoyt Wilhelm/31 20.00
58 Hoyt Wilhelm/50 15.00
58 Hoyt Wilhelm HOF 85 AU/5
59 Steve Carlton/80 15.00
59 Steve Carlton/65 20.00
59 Steve Carlton HOF 94/15
59 Steve Carlton/32 30.00
59 Steve Carlton/50 20.00
59 Steve Carlton HOF 94 AU/5
60 Eddie Murray/100 15.00
60 Eddie Murray/77 15.00
60 Eddie Murray/33 30.00
60 Eddie Murray/50 20.00
61 Nolan Ryan Rangers/40 75.00
61 Nolan Ryan Rangers/66 60.00
61 Nolan Ryan Rangers HOF 99/5
61 Nolan Ryan Rangers/34 75.00
61 Nolan Ryan Rangers/25
61 Nolan Ryan Ranges HOF 99 AU/5

62 Nolan Ryan Astros/40 75.00
62 Nolan Ryan Astros/66 60.00
62 Nolan Ryan Astros HOF 99/5
62 Nolan Ryan Astros/34 75.00
62 Nolan Ryan Astros/25
62 Nolan Ryan Astros HOF 99 AU/5
63 Kirby Puckett/40 40.00
63 Kirby Puckett/84 20.00
63 Kirby Puckett HOF 01/5
63 Kirby Puckett/34 40.00
63 Kirby Puckett/25
63 Kirby Puckett HOF 01 AU/5
64 Yogi Berra/5
64 Yogi Berra/46 40.00
64 Yogi Berra/35 40.00
64 Yogi Berra/10
64 Yogi Berra HOF 72 AU/5
65 Phil Niekro/80 8.00
65 Phil Niekro/64 10.00
65 Phil Niekro HOF 95/15
65 Phil Niekro/35 15.00
65 Phil Niekro/50 10.00
65 Phil Niekro HOF 97 AU/5
66 Gaylord Perry/80 8.00
66 Gaylord Perry/62 10.00
66 Gaylord Perry HOF 91/20
66 Gaylord Perry/36 15.00
66 Gaylord Perry/50 10.00
67 Pedro Martinez Expos/100 15.00
67 Pedro Martinez Expos/92 15.00
67 Pedro Martinez Expos/45 25.00
67 Pedro Martinez Expos/50 20.00
68 Alex Rodriguez Rgr/100 20.00
68 Alex Rodriguez Rgr/94 20.00
68 Alex Rodriguez Rgr/50 30.00
68 Alex Rodriguez Rgr AU/3
69 Dave Parker/100 8.00
69 Dave Parker/73 10.00
69 Dave Parker/39 15.00
69 Dave Parker/50 10.00
70 Darin Erstad/100 8.00
70 Darin Erstad/96 8.00
70 Darin Erstad/17
70 Darin Erstad/50 15.00
71 Eddie Matthews/5
71 Eddie Matthews/52 30.00
71 Eddie Matthews HOF 78/5
71 Eddie Matthews/41 35.00
71 Eddie Matthews/10
72 Tom Seaver Mets/5
72 Tom Seaver Mets/67 30.00
72 Tom Seaver Mets/41 40.00
72 Tom Seaver Mets/10
72 Tom Seaver Mets HOF 92 AU/5
73 Tom Seaver Reds/10
73 Tom Seaver Reds/67 30.00
73 Tom Seaver Reds/41 40.00
73 Tom Seaver Reds/25
73 Tom Seaver Reds HOF 92 AU/5
74 Jackie Robinson/5
74 Jackie Robinson/47 100.00
74 Jackie Robinson HOF 62/5
74 Jackie Robinson/42 100.00
74 Jackie Robinson/10
75 Randy Johnson M's/80 15.00
75 Randy Johnson M's/88 15.00
75 Randy Johnson M's Big Unit/20
75 Randy Johnson M's/51 25.00
75 Randy Johnson M's/50 25.00
76 Reggie Jackson Yanks/10
76 Reggie Jackson Yanks/57 30.00
76 Reggie Jackson Yanks/44 40.00
76 Reggie Jackson Yanks/25
76 Reggie Jackson Yanks HOF 93 AU/5
77 Reggie Jackson Angels/80 20.00
77 Reggie Jackson Angels/67 30.00
77 Reggie Jackson Angels HOF 93/15
77 Reggie Jackson Angels/44 40.00
77 Reggie Jackson Angels/50 40.00
77 Reggie Jackson Angels HOF 93 AU/5
78 Willie McCovey/80 10.00
78 Willie McCovey/59 15.00
78 Willie McCovey HOF 86/15
78 Willie McCovey/44 20.00
78 Willie McCovey/50 20.00
78 Willie McCovey HOF 86 AU/5
79 Eric Davis/100 5.00
79 Eric Davis/84 5.00
79 Eric Davis/34 10.00
79 Eric Davis/50 8.00
79 Eric Davis AU/10
80 Carlos Delgado/95 6.00
80 Carlos Delgado/93 6.00
80 Carlos Delgado/25
80 Carlos Delgado/25
81 Dale Murphy/100 20.00
81 Dale Murphy/76 20.00
81 Dale Murphy/50 30.00
81 Dale Murphy AU/3
82 Brian Giles/100 5.00
82 Brian Giles/95 5.00
82 Brian Giles/24
82 Brian Giles/50 8.00
83 Kazuhiro Sasaki/100 8.00
83 Kazuhiro Sasaki/100 8.00
83 Kazuhiro Sasaki/22
83 Kazuhiro Sasaki/50 10.00
84 Phil Nevin/100 5.00
84 Phil Nevin/95 5.00
84 Phil Nevin/23
84 Phil Nevin/50 8.00
85 Frank Thomas/80 15.00
85 Frank Thomas/90 15.00
85 Frank Thomas Big Hurt/15
85 Frank Thomas/35 25.00
85 Frank Thomas/50 15.00
85 Frank Thomas Big Hurt AU/5
86 Raul Mondesi/100 5.00
86 Raul Mondesi/93 5.00
86 Raul Mondesi/43 8.00
86 Raul Mondesi/50 8.00
87 Don Drysdale/5
87 Don Drysdale/56 25.00
87 Don Drysdale HOF 84/5
87 Don Drysdale/53 25.00
87 Don Drysdale/10
88 Gary Sheffield/100 6.00
88 Gary Sheffield/88 6.00
88 Gary Sheffield/10
88 Gary Sheffield/50 10.00
89 Andy Pettitte/100 15.00
89 Andy Pettitte/95 15.00
89 Andy Pettitte/46 30.00
89 Andy Pettitte/50 20.00
90 Lance Berkman/45 20.00
90 Lance Berkman/99 10.00
90 Lance Berkman/12
90 Lance Berkman/25
90 Lance Berkman AU/5
91 Paul LoDuca/100 5.00
91 Paul LoDuca/98 5.00
91 Paul LoDuca/16
91 Paul LoDuca/50 8.00
92 Kevin Brown/25
92 Kevin Brown/86 5.00
92 Kevin Brown/27 15.00
92 Kevin Brown/25
93 Jim Thome/100 15.00
93 Jim Thome/91 15.00
93 Jim Thome/20
93 Jim Thome/50 25.00
93 Jim Thome AU/5
94 Mike Sweeney/100 5.00
94 Mike Sweeney/95 5.00
94 Mike Sweeney/29 15.00
94 Mike Sweeney/50 10.00
95 Pedro J. Martinez Red Sox/100 15.00
95 Pedro J. Martinez Red Sox/92 15.00
95 Pedro J. Martinez Red Sox/45 25.00
95 Pedro J. Martinez Red Sox/45 25.00
96 Cliff Floyd/100 5.00
96 Cliff Floyd/93 5.00
96 Cliff Floyd/30 15.00
96 Cliff Floyd/50 10.00
97 Larry Walker/100 8.00
97 Larry Walker/89 8.00
97 Larry Walker/33 30.00
97 Larry Walker/50 10.00
98 Ivan Rodriguez/80 10.00
98 Ivan Rodriguez/91 10.00
98 Ivan Rodriguez/15
98 Ivan Rodriguez/7
98 Ivan Rodriguez/50 20.00
98 Ivan Rodriguez AU/5
99 Aramis Ramirez/100 8.00
99 Aramis Ramirez/98 8.00
99 Aramis Ramirez/16
99 Aramis Ramirez/50 12.00
100 Roberto Alomar/100 10.00
100 Roberto Alomar/88 10.00
100 Roberto Alomar/12
100 Roberto Alomar/50 15.00
101 Ben Sheets/100 8.00
101 Ben Sheets/101 8.00
101 Ben Sheets/15
101 Ben Sheets/50 15.00
102 Adam Dunn/5
102 Adam Dunn/101 20.00
102 Adam Dunn/39 40.00
102 Adam Dunn/5
102 Adam Dunn AU/5
103 Hideo Nomo/15
103 Hideo Nomo/95 30.00
103 Hideo Nomo/11
103 Hideo Nomo/20
104 C.C. Sabathia/50 10.00
104 C.C. Sabathia/101 5.00
104 C.C. Sabathia/52 10.00
104 C.C. Sabathia/50 10.00
105 Rickey Henderson A's/100 20.00
105 Rickey Henderson A's/79 20.00
105 Rickey Henderson A's/30 50.00
105 Rickey Henderson A's/50 30.00
105 Rickey Henderson A's AU/5
106 Carlton Fisk White Sox/80 20.00
106 Carlton Fisk White Sox/69 30.00
106 Carlton Fisk White Sox HOF 00/15
106 Carlton Fisk White Sox/72 30.00
106 Carlton Fisk White Sox/50 30.00
106 Carlton Fisk White Sox HOF 00 AU/5
107 Chan Ho Park/100 5.00
107 Chan Ho Park/94 5.00
107 Chan Ho Park/61 8.00
107 Chan Ho Park/50 8.00
108 Mike Mussina/100 20.00
108 Mike Mussina/91 20.00
108 Mike Mussina/35 50.00
108 Mike Mussina/50 30.00
109 Mark Mulder/100 8.00
109 Mark Mulder/100 8.00
109 Mark Mulder/20 20.00
109 Mark Mulder/35 20.00
110 Tsuyoshi Shinjo/100 5.00
110 Tsuyoshi Shinjo/101 5.00
110 Tsuyoshi Shinjo/5
110 Tsuyoshi Shinjo/30 20.00
111 Pat Burrell/100 10.00
111 Pat Burrell/100 10.00
111 Pat Burrell/5
111 Pat Burrell/50 15.00
112 Edgar Martinez/100 10.00
112 Edgar Martinez/87 10.00
112 Edgar Martinez/11
112 Edgar Martinez/50 15.00
113 Barry Larkin/100 10.00
113 Barry Larkin/86 10.00
113 Barry Larkin/11
113 Barry Larkin/50 15.00
114 Jeff Kent/100 6.00
114 Jeff Kent/92 6.00
114 Jeff Kent/21
114 Jeff Kent/50 8.00
115 Chipper Jones/100 15.00
115 Chipper Jones/93 15.00
115 Chipper Jones/10
115 Chipper Jones/50 30.00
116 Maggio Ordonez/100 8.00
116 Maggio Ordonez/97 8.00
116 Maggio Ordonez/30 30.00
116 Maggio Ordonez/50 15.00
117 Jim Edmonds/100 8.00
117 Jim Edmonds/93 8.00
117 Jim Edmonds/15
117 Jim Edmonds/50 15.00
118 Andruw Jones/100 10.00
118 Andruw Jones/96 10.00
118 Andruw Jones/25
118 Andruw Jones/45 20.00
119 Jose Canseco/100 15.00
119 Jose Canseco/85 15.00
119 Jose Canseco/23
119 Jose Canseco/50 30.00
119 Jose Canseco AU/10
120 Manny Ramirez/100 10.00
120 Manny Ramirez/93 10.00
120 Manny Ramirez/24
120 Manny Ramirez/50 20.00
121 Sean Casey/100 10.00
121 Sean Casey/97 10.00
121 Sean Casey/21
121 Sean Casey/50 15.00
122 Bret Boone/100 6.00
122 Bret Boone/92 6.00
122 Bret Boone/29 15.00
122 Bret Boone/50 10.00
123 Tim Hudson/100 8.00
123 Tim Hudson/99 8.00
123 Tim Hudson/15
123 Tim Hudson/50 15.00
124 Craig Biggio/100 10.00
124 Craig Biggio/88 10.00
124 Craig Biggio/7
124 Craig Biggio/50 15.00
125 Mike Piazza Mets/100 20.00
125 Mike Piazza Mets/92 20.00
125 Mike Piazza Mets/31 40.00
125 Mike Piazza Mets/51 25.00
126 Jack Morris/100 5.00
126 Jack Morris/77 5.00
126 Jack Morris/47 10.00
126 Jack Morris/25
127 Roy Oswalt/100 8.00
127 Roy Oswalt/101 8.00
127 Roy Oswalt/39 15.00
127 Roy Oswalt/50 15.00
127 Roy Oswalt AU/5
128 Shawn Green/100 8.00
128 Shawn Green/93 8.00
128 Shawn Green/15
128 Shawn Green/50 15.00
129 Carlos Beltran/100 8.00
129 Carlos Beltran/98 8.00
129 Carlos Beltran/15
129 Carlos Beltran/50 10.00
130 Todd Helton/100 10.00
130 Todd Helton/97 10.00
130 Todd Helton/17
130 Todd Helton/50 20.00
131 Barry Zito/75 15.00
131 Barry Zito/100 10.00
131 Barry Zito/75 15.00
131 Barry Zito/30 30.00
132 J.D. Drew/100 15.00
132 J.D. Drew/98 15.00
132 J.D. Drew/7
132 J.D. Drew/50 20.00
133 Mark Grace/100 10.00
133 Mark Grace/88 10.00
133 Mark Grace/17
133 Mark Grace/50 20.00
134 Rickey Henderson Mets/100 20.00
134 Rickey Henderson Mets/79 20.00
134 Rickey Henderson/24
134 Rickey Henderson Mets/50 30.00
135 Greg Maddux/100 20.00
135 Greg Maddux/86 20.00
135 Greg Maddux/31
135 Greg Maddux/50 30.00
136 Garret Anderson/100 8.00
136 Garret Anderson/94 8.00
136 Garret Anderson/16
136 Garret Anderson/50 15.00
137 Rafael Palmeiro/100 15.00
137 Rafael Palmeiro/86 15.00
137 Rafael Palmeiro/20
137 Rafael Palmeiro/50 20.00
137 Rafael Palmeiro AU/5
138 Luis Gonzalez/50 10.00
138 Luis Gonzalez/90 8.00
138 Luis Gonzalez/20
138 Luis Gonzalez/45 15.00
139 Nick Johnson/100 5.00
139 Nick Johnson/101 5.00
139 Nick Johnson/26 20.00
139 Nick Johnson/50 10.00
139 Nick Johnson AU/10
140 Vladimir Guerrero/80 15.00
140 Vladimir Guerrero/96 15.00
140 Vladimir Guerrero/22
140 Vladimir Guerrero/50 25.00
140 Vladimir Guerrero AU/5
141 Mark Buehrle/20
141 Mark Buehrle/100 5.00
141 Mark Buehrle/56 8.00
141 Mark Buehrle/20
142 Troy Glaus/100 15.00
142 Troy Glaus/98 15.00
142 Troy Glaus/25
142 Troy Glaus/50 25.00
143 Juan Gonzalez/100 10.00
143 Juan Gonzalez/89 10.00
143 Juan Gonzalez/22

143	Juan Gonzalez/50	15.00
144	Kerry Wood/100	15.00
144	Kerry Wood/98	15.00
144	Kerry Wood/34	40.00
144	Kerry Wood/50	30.00
145	Roger Clemens/80	25.00
145	Roger Clemens/84	25.00
145	Roger Clemens Rocket/15	
145	Roger Clemens/20	
145	Roger Clemens/50	40.00
145	Roger Clemens Rocket AU/5	
146	Bob Abreu/100	8.00
146	Bob Abreu/96	8.00
146	Bob Abreu/53	15.00
146	Bob Abreu/50	15.00
147	Bernie Williams/95	10.00
147	Bernie Williams/91	10.00
147	Bernie Williams/51	20.00
147	Bernie Williams/25	
148	Tom Glavine/100	10.00
148	Tom Glavine/87	10.00
148	Tom Glavine/47	25.00
148	Tom Glavine/50	25.00
149	Jorge Posada/100	10.00
149	Jorge Posada/95	10.00
149	Jorge Posada/20	
149	Jorge Posada/50	25.00
150	Randy Johnson D'Backs/80	15.00
150	Randy Johnson D'Backs/88	15.00
150	Randy Johnson D'Backs Big Unit/20	
150	Randy Johnson D'Backs/51	30.00
150	Randy Johnson D'Backs/50	30.00

2002 LEAF ROOKIES & STARS

		NM/M
	Complete Set (400):	
	Common Player:	.15
	Common SP (1-300):	.75
	Common (301-400):	.40
	Inserted 1:2	
	Pack (6):	1.50
	Box (24):	30.00
1	Darin Erstad	.25
2	Garret Anderson	.15
3	Troy Glaus	.40
4	David Eckstein	.15
5	Adam Kennedy	.15
6	Kevin Appier	.15
6	Kevin Appier/SP/Mets	.75
6	Kevin Appier/SP/Royals	.75
7	Jarrod Washburn	.15
8	David Segui	.15
9	Jay Gibbons	.15
10	Tony Batista	.15
11	Scott Erickson	.15
12	Jeff Conine	.15
13	Melvin Mora	.15
14	Shea Hillenbrand	.15
15	Manny Ramirez	.65
15	Manny Ramirez/SP/Indians	2.00
16	Pedro J. Martinez	.65
16	Pedro J. Martinez/SP/Dodgers	2.50
16	Pedro J. Martinez/SP/Expos	2.50
17	Nomar Garciaparra	1.00
18	Rickey Henderson	.65
18	Rickey Henderson/SP/Angels	3.00
18	Rickey Henderson/SP/A's	3.00
18	Rickey Henderson/SP/Blue Jays	3.00
18	Rickey Henderson/SP/M's	3.00
18	Rickey Henderson/SP/Mets	3.00
18	Rickey Henderson/SP/Padres	3.00
18	Rickey Henderson/SP/Yankees	3.00
19	Johnny Damon	.25
19	Johnny Damon/SP/A's	1.00
19	Johnny Damon/SP/Royals	1.00
20	Trot Nixon	.15
21	Derek Lowe	.15
22	Jason Varitek	.15
23	Tim Wakefield	.15
24	Frank Thomas	.65
25	Kenny Lofton	.15
25	Kenny Lofton/SP/Indians	.75
26	Magglio Ordonez	.15
27	Ray Durham	.15
28	Mark Buehrle	.15
29	Paul Konerko	.25
29	Paul Konerko/SP/Dodgers	1.00
29	Paul Konerko/SP/Reds	1.00
30	Jose Valentin	.15
31	C.C. Sabathia	.15
32	Ellis Burks	.15
32	Ellis Burks/SP/Giants	.75
32	Ellis Burks/SP/Red Sox	.75
32	Ellis Burks/SP/Rockies	.75
33	Omar Vizquel	.15
33	Omar Vizquel/SP/Mariners	1.00
34	Jim Thome	.50
35	Matt Lawton	.15
36	Travis Fryman	.15
36	Travis Fryman/SP/Tigers	.75
37	Robert Fick	.15
38	Bobby Higginson	.15
39	Steve Sparks	.15
40	Mike Rivera	.15
41	Wendell Magee	.15
42	Randall Simon	.15
43	Carlos Pena	.15
43	Carlos Pena/SP/A's	.75
43	Carlos Pena/SP/Rangers	.75
44	Mike Sweeney	.15
45	Chuck Knoblauch	.15
46	Carlos Beltran	.50
47	Joe Randa	.15
48	Paul Byrd	.15
49	Mac Suzuki	.15
50	Torii Hunter	.15
51	Jacque Jones	.15
52	David Ortiz	.35
53	Corey Koskie	.15
54	Brad Radke	.15
55	Doug Mientkiewicz	.15
56	A.J. Pierzynski	.15
57	Dustan Mohr	.15
58	Derek Jeter	2.00
59	Bernie Williams	.30
60	Roger Clemens	.85
60	Roger Clemens/SP/Blue Jays	4.00
60	Roger Clemens/SP/Red Sox	4.00
61	Mike Mussina	.40
61	Mike Mussina/SP/Orioles	1.50
62	Jorge Posada	.25
63	Alfonso Soriano	.50
64	Jason Giambi	.40
64	Jason Giambi/SP/A's	2.50
65	Robin Ventura	.15
65	Robin Ventura/SP/Mets	.75
65	Robin Ventura/SP/White Sox	.75
66	Andy Pettitte	.25
67	David Wells	.15
67	David Wells/SP/Blue Jays	.75
67	David Wells/SP/Tigers	.75
68	Nick Johnson	.15
69	Jeff Weaver	.15
69	Jeff Weaver/SP/Tigers	.75
70	Raul Mondesi	.15
70	Raul Mondesi/SP/Blue Jays	.75
70	Raul Mondesi/SP/Dodgers	.75
71	Tim Hudson	.25
72	Barry Zito	.25
73	Mark Mulder	.25
74	Miguel Tejada	.25
75	Eric Chavez	.25
76	Billy Koch	.15
76	Billy Koch/SP/Blue Jays	.75
77	Jermaine Dye	.15
77	Jermaine Dye/SP/Royals	.75
78	Scott Hatteberg	.15
79	Ichiro Suzuki	1.00
80	Edgar Martinez	.15
81	Mike Cameron	.15
81	Mike Cameron/SP/White Sox	.75
82	John Olerud	.15
82	John Olerud/SP/Blue Jays	.75
82	John Olerud/SP/Mets	.75
83	Bret Boone	.15
84	Dan Wilson	.15
85	Freddy Garcia	.15
86	Jamie Moyer	.15
87	Carlos Guillen	.15
88	Ruben Sierra	.15
89	Kazuhiro Sasaki	.15
90	Mark McLemore	.15
91	Ben Grieve	.15
92	Aubrey Huff	.15
93	Steve Cox	.15
94	Toby Hall	.15
95	Randy Winn	.15
96	Brent Abernathy	.15
97	Chan Ho Park	.15
97	Chan Ho Park/SP/Dodgers	.75
98	Alex Rodriguez	1.50
98	Alex Rodriguez/SP/Mariners	4.00
99	Juan Gonzalez	.40
99	Juan Gonzalez/SP/Indians	1.50
99	Juan Gonzalez/SP/Tigers	1.50
100	Rafael Palmeiro	.60
100	Rafael Palmeiro/SP/Cubs	1.00
100	Rafael Palmeiro/SP/Orioles	1.00
101	Ivan Rodriguez	.50
102	Rusty Greer	.15
103	Kenny Rogers	.15
103	Kenny Rogers/SP/A's	.75
103	Kenny Rogers/SP/Yankees	.75
104	Hank Blalock	.40
105	Mark Teixeira	.25
106	Carlos Delgado	.40
107	Shannon Stewart	.15
108	Eric Hinske	.15
109	Roy Halladay	.25
110	Felipe Lopez	.15
111	Vernon Wells	.15
112	Curt Schilling	.40
112	Curt Schilling/SP/Phillies	1.50
113	Randy Johnson	.65
113	Randy Johnson/SP/Astros	3.00
113	Randy Johnson/SP/Expos	3.00
113	Randy Johnson/SP/Mariners	3.00
114	Luis Gonzalez	.25
114	Luis Gonzalez/SP/Astros	1.00
114	Luis Gonzalez/SP/Cubs	1.00
115	Mark Grace	.25
115	Mark Grace/SP/Cubs	1.50
116	Junior Spivey	.15
117	Tony Womack	.15
118	Matt Williams	.15
118	Matt Williams/SP/Giants	1.00
118	Matt Williams/SP/Indians	1.00
119	Danny Bautista	.15
120	Byung-Hyun Kim	.15
121	Craig Counsell	.15
122	Greg Maddux	.75
122	Greg Maddux/SP/Cubs	4.00
123	Tom Glavine	.25
124	John Smoltz	.15
124	John Smoltz/SP/Tigers	.75
125	Chipper Jones	.75
126	Gary Sheffield	.25
127	Andruw Jones	.65
128	Vinny Castilla	.15
129	Damian Moss	.15
130	Rafael Furcal	.15
131	Kerry Wood	.50
132	Fred McGriff	.15
132	Fred McGriff/SP/Blue Jays	1.00
132	Fred McGriff/SP/Braves	1.00
132	Fred McGriff/SP/Devil Rays	1.00
132	Fred McGriff/SP/Padres	1.00
133	Sammy Sosa	1.00
133	Sammy Sosa/SP/Rangers	4.00
133	Sammy Sosa/SP/White Sox	4.00
134	Alex Gonzalez	.15
135	Corey Patterson	.15
136	Moises Alou	.15
137	Mark Prior	.65
138	Jon Lieber	.15
139	Matt Clement	.15
140	Ken Griffey Jr.	1.00
140	Ken Griffey Jr./SP/Mariners	4.00
141	Barry Larkin	.15
142	Adam Dunn	.40
143	Sean Casey	.15
143	Sean Casey/SP/Indians	.75
144	Jose Rijo	.15
145	Elmer Dessens	.15
146	Austin Kearns	.15
147	Corky Miller	.15
148	Todd Walker	.15
148	Todd Walker/SP/Rockies	.75
148	Todd Walker/SP/Expos	.75
149	Chris Reitsma	.15
150	Ryan Dempster	.15
151	Larry Walker	.15
152	Todd Helton	.65
153	Juan Uribe	.15
154	Juan Pierre	.15
155	Mike Hampton	.15
156	Todd Zeile	.15
157	Josh Beckett	.25
158	Mike Lowell	.15
158	Mike Lowell/SP/Yankees	.75
159	Derrek Lee	.15
160	A.J. Burnett	.15
161	Luis Castillo	.15
162	Tim Raines	.15
163	Preston Wilson	.15
164	Juan Encarnacion	.15
165	Jeff Bagwell	.65
166	Craig Biggio	.15
167	Lance Berkman	.15
168	Wade Miller	.15
169	Roy Oswalt	.25
170	Richard Hidalgo	.15
171	Carlos Hernandez	.15
172	Daryle Ward	.15
173	Shawn Green	.30
173	Shawn Green/SP/Blue Jays	1.00
174	Adrian Beltre	.35
175	Paul LoDuca	.15
176	Eric Karros	.15
177	Kevin Brown	.15
178	Hideo Nomo	.65
178	Hideo Nomo/SP/Brewers	1.50
178	Hideo Nomo/SP/Mets	1.50
178	Hideo Nomo/SP/Red Sox	1.50
178	Hideo Nomo/SP/Tigers	1.50
179	Odalis Perez	.15
180	Eric Gagne	.35
181	Brian Jordan	.15
182	Cesar Izturis	.15
183	Geoff Jenkins	.15
184	Richie Sexson	.15
184	Richie Sexson/SP/Indians	1.00
185	Jose Hernandez	.15
186	Ben Sheets	.15
187	Ruben Quevedo	.15
188	Jeffrey Hammonds	.15
189	Alex Sanchez	.15
190	Vladimir Guerrero	.65
191	Jose Vidro	.15
192	Orlando Cabrera	.15
193	Michael Barrett	.15
194	Javier Vazquez	.15
195	Tony Armas Jr.	.15
196	Andres Galarraga	.15
197	Tomokazu Ohka	.15
198	Bartolo Colon	.15
198	Bartolo Colon/SP/Indians	.75
199	Cliff Floyd	.15
199	Cliff Floyd/SP/Marlins	.75
200	Mike Piazza	1.00
200	Mike Piazza/SP/Dodgers	4.00
200	Mike Piazza/SP/Marlins	4.00
201	Jeromy Burnitz	.15
202	Roberto Alomar	.35
202	Roberto Alomar/SP/Blue Jays	1.50

202 Roberto Alomar/SP/Indians 1.50
202 Roberto Alomar/SP/Orioles 1.50
202 Roberto Alomar/SP/Padres 1.50
203 Mo Vaughn .15
203 Mo Vaughn/SP/Angels 1.00
203 Mo Vaughn/SP/Red Sox 1.00
204 Al Leiter .15
204 Al Leiter/SP/Blue Jays .75
205 Pedro Astacio .15
206 Edgardo Alfonzo .15
207 Armando Benitez .15
208 Scott Rolen .50
209 Pat Burrell .35
210 Bobby Abreu .15
210 Bobby Abreu/SP/Astros 1.00
211 Mike Lieberthal .15
212 Brandon Duckworth .15
213 Jimmy Rollins .15
214 Jeremy Giambi .15
215 Vicente Padilla .15
216 Travis Lee .15
217 Jason Kendall .15
218 Brian Giles .15
218 Brian Giles/SP/Indians 1.00
219 Aramis Ramirez .15
220 Pokey Reese .15
221 Kip Wells .15
222 Josh Fogg .15
222 Josh Fogg/SP/White Sox .75
223 Mike Williams .15
224 Ryan Klesko .15
224 Ryan Klesko/SP/Braves .75
225 Phil Nevin .15
225 Phil Nevin/SP/Tigers .75
226 Brian Lawrence .15
227 Mark Kotsay .15
228 Brett Tomko .15
229 Trevor Hoffman .15
229 Trevor Hoffman/SP/Marlins .75
230 Barry Bonds 2.00
230 Barry Bonds/SP/Pirates 6.00
231 Jeff Kent .15
231 Jeff Kent/SP/Blue Jays 1.00
232 Rich Aurilia .15
233 Tsuyoshi Shinjo .15
233 Tsuyoshi Shinjo/SP/Mets 1.00
234 Benito Santiago .15
234 Benito Santiago/SP/Padres .75
235 Kirk Rueter .15
236 Kurt Ainsworth .15
237 Livan Hernandez .15
238 Russ Ortiz .15
239 David Bell .15
240 Jason Schmidt .15
241 Reggie Sanders .15
242 Jim Edmonds .25
242 Jim Edmonds/SP/Angels 1.00
243 J.D. Drew .25
244 Albert Pujols 1.50
245 Fernando Vina .15
246 Tino Martinez .15
246 Tino Martinez/SP/Mariners 1.00
246 Tino Martinez/SP/Yankees 1.00
247 Edgar Renteria .15
248 Matt Morris .15
249 Woody Williams .15
250 Jason Isringhausen .15
250 Jason Isringhausen/SP/A's .75
251 Cal Ripken Jr. 2.00
252 Cal Ripken Jr. 2.00
253 Cal Ripken Jr. 2.00
254 Cal Ripken Jr. 2.00
255 Ryne Sandberg .75
256 Don Mattingly 1.00
257 Don Mattingly 1.00
258 Roger Clemens .85
259 Roger Clemens .85
260 Roger Clemens .85
261 Roger Clemens .85
262 Roger Clemens .85
263 Roger Clemens .85
264 Roger Clemens .85
265 Rickey Henderson .65
266 Rickey Henderson .65
267 Jose Canseco .40
268 Barry Bonds 2.00
269 Barry Bonds 2.00
270 Barry Bonds 2.00
271 Barry Bonds 2.00
272 Jeff Bagwell .65
273 Kirby Puckett .75
274 Kirby Puckett .75
275 Greg Maddux .75
276 Greg Maddux .75
277 Greg Maddux .75
278 Greg Maddux .75
279 Ken Griffey Jr. 1.00
280 Mike Piazza 1.00
281 Kirby Puckett .75
282 Mike Piazza 1.00
283 Frank Thomas .65
284 Hideo Nomo .65
285 Randy Johnson .65
286 Juan Gonzalez .65
287 Derek Jeter 2.00
288 Derek Jeter 2.00
289 Derek Jeter 2.00
290 Nomar Garciaparra 1.00
291 Pedro J. Martinez .65
292 Kerry Wood .50
293 Sammy Sosa 1.00
294 Chipper Jones .75
295 Ivan Rodriguez .50
296 Ivan Rodriguez .50
297 Albert Pujols 1.50
298 Ichiro Suzuki 1.00
299 Ichiro Suzuki 1.00
300 Ichiro Suzuki 1.00
301 *So Taguchi* 1.00
302 *Kazuhisa Ishii* 2.00
303 *Jeremy Lambert* .50
304 Sean Burroughs .40
305 *P.J. Bevis* .50
306 Jon Rauch .40
307 *Scotty Layfield* .50
308 Miguel Ascencio .40
309 *Franklyn German* .50
310 *Luis Ugueto* .50
311 *Jorge Sosa* .50
312 *Felix Escalona* .50
313 *Jose Valverde* .50
314 *Jeremy Ward* .50
315 *Kevin Gryboski* .50
316 *Francis Beltran* .50
317 Joe Thurston .40
318 *Cliff Lee* 1.00
319 *Takahito Nomura* .50
320 Bill Hall .40
321 Marlon Byrd .50
322 *Andy Shibilo* .50
323 *Edwin Almonte* .50
324 *Brandon Backe* .40
325 *Chone Figgins* 1.50
326 *Brian Mallette* .50
327 *Rodrigo Rosario* .50
328 *Anderson Machado* .50
329 *Jorge Padilla* .50
330 *Allan Simpson* .50
331 *Doug Devore* .50
332 Drew Henson .50
333 *Raul Chavez* .50
334 *Tom Shearn* .50
335 *Ben Howard* .50
336 *Chris Baker* .50
337 *Travis Hughes* .50
338 Kevin Mench .40
339 Brian Tallet .40
340 *Mike Moriarty* .50
341 *Corey Thurman* .50
342 *Terry Pearson* .50
343 *Steve Kent* .50
344 *Satoru Komiyama* .50
345 Jason Lane .40
346 *Freddy Sanchez* .50
347 *Brandon Puffer* .50
348 *Clay Condrey* .50
349 *Rene Reyes* .50
350 Hee Seop Choi .50
351 Rodrigo Lopez .40
352 *Colin Young* .50
353 *Jason Simontacchi* .50
354 *Oliver Perez* 2.00
355 Kirk Saarloos .50
356 Marcus Thames .40
357 *Jeff Austin* .50
358 Justin Kaye .40
359 *Julio Mateo* .50
360 *Mike Smith* .50
361 *Chris Snelling* .75
362 Dennis Tankersley .40
363 *Runelvys Hernandez* .50
364 *Aaron Cook* .50
365 Joe Borchard .40
366 *Earl Snyder* .50
367 *Shane Nance* .50
368 *Aaron Guiel* .50
369 *Steve Bechler* .50
370 *Tim Kalita* .50
371 *Shawn Sedlacek* .50
372 *Eric Good* .50
373 *Eric Junge* .50
374 Matt Thornton .40
375 *Travis Driskill* .50
376 *Mitch Wylie* .50
377 *John Ennis* .50
378 *Reed Johnson* .75
379 *Juan Brito* .50
380 *Ron Calloway* .50
381 *Adrian Burnside* .50
382 *Josh Bard* .50
383 *Matt Childers* .50
384 *Gustavo Chacin* .50
385 *Luis Martinez* .50
386 *Trey Hodges* .50
387 *Hansel Izquierdo* .50
388 *Jeriome Robertson* .50
389 *Victor Alvarez* .50
390 *David Ross* .50
391 Ron Chiavacci .40
392 *Adam Walker* .50
393 *Mike Gonzalez* .50
394 *John Foster* .50
395 *Kyle Kane* .50
396 *Cam Esslinger* .50
397 *Kevin Frederick* .50
398 *Franklin Nunez* .50
399 *Todd Donovan* .50
400 *Kevin Cash* .50

Longevity

Stars (1-300): 5-10X
SP's (1-300): 1-3X
Production 100
Rookies (301-400): Not Priced
Production 25

BLC Homers

NM/M

Common Player: 20.00
Production 25 sets
1 Luis Gonzalez 20.00
2 Luis Gonzalez 20.00
3 Luis Gonzalez 20.00
4 Todd Helton 35.00
5 Todd Helton 35.00
6 Todd Helton 35.00
7 Todd Helton 35.00
8 Todd Helton 35.00
9 Todd Helton 35.00
10 Todd Helton 35.00
11 Todd Helton 35.00
12 Jim Thome 35.00
13 Jim Thome 35.00
14 Jim Thome 35.00
15 Rafael Palmeiro 30.00
16 Rafael Palmeiro 30.00
17 Rafael Palmeiro 30.00
18 Rafael Palmeiro 30.00
19 Rafael Palmeiro 30.00
20 Troy Glaus 35.00
21 Troy Glaus 35.00
22 Troy Glaus 35.00
23 Gary Sheffield 20.00
24 Gary Sheffield 20.00
25 Gary Sheffield 20.00
26 Mike Piazza 50.00
27 Mike Piazza 50.00
28 Mike Piazza 50.00
29 Mike Piazza 50.00
30 Mike Piazza 50.00

Dress For Success

NM/M

Common Player: 5.00
Production 250 sets
Prime Cuts: Not Priced
Production 25 sets
1 Mike Piazza 25.00
2 Cal Ripken Jr. 40.00
3 Carlos Delgado 8.00
4 Chipper Jones 20.00
5 Bernie Williams 8.00
6 Carlos Beltran 10.00
7 Curt Schilling 10.00
8 Greg Maddux 20.00
9 Ivan Rodriguez 12.00
10 Alex Rodriguez 20.00
11 Roger Clemens 20.00
12 Todd Helton 15.00
13 Jim Edmonds 8.00
14 Manny Ramirez 15.00
15 Mark Buehrle 8.00

Freshman Orientation

NM/M

Common Player: 5.00
Inserted 1:142
Class Officer parallel: 1.5X
Production 50 sets
1 Andres Torres/bat 8.00
2 Mark Ellis/jsy 8.00
3 Erik Bedard/bat 8.00
4 Delvin James/jsy 5.00
5 Austin Kearns/bat 10.00
6 Josh Pearce/bat 5.00
7 Rafael Soriano/jsy 8.00
8 Jason Lane/bat 8.00
9 Mark Prior/jsy 20.00
10 Alfredo Amezaga/bat 5.00
11 Ryan Ludwick/bat 5.00
12 So Taguchi/bat 10.00
13 Duaner Sanchez/bat 5.00
14 Kazuhisa Ishii/jsy 15.00
15 Zach Day/jsy 8.00
16 Eric Cyr/bat 5.00
17 Francis Beltran/jsy 5.00
18 Joe Borchard/jsy 10.00
19 Jeremy Affeldt/shoe 10.00
20 Alexis Gomez/jsy 5.00

Great American Signings

NM/M

Common Autograph: 5.00
Inserted 1:56
Brent Abernathy/175 5.00
Bobby Abreu/25
Brandon Backe/175 5.00
Chris Baker/175 5.00
Francis Beltran/175 5.00
Raul Chavez/175 5.00
Roger Clemens/10
Doug Devore/175 5.00
Adam Dunn/25
Felix Escalona/100 8.00
Franklyn German/175 5.00
Jay Gibbons/150 10.00
Geronimo Gil
Vladimir Guerrero/15
Bill Hall/175 8.00
Rickey Henderson/20
Drew Henson/50 35.00
Eric Hinske/175 8.00
Ben Howard/175 5.00
Aubrey Huff/175 8.00

Travis Hughes/175	5.00
Kazuhisa Ishii/25	
Cesar Izturis/175	8.00
Nick Johnson/175	8.00
Austin Kearns/75	10.00
Satoru Komiyama/75	20.00
Jason Lane/150	8.00
Barry Larkin/25	
Brian Lawrence/175	5.00
Anderson Machado/175	5.00
Don Mattingly/25	
Roy Oswalt/100	15.00
Jorge Padilla/175	5.00
Oliver Perez/175	25.00
Albert Pujols/25	
Rene Reyes/175	5.00
Mike Rivera/175	5.00
Rodrigo Rosario/175	5.00
Tom Shearn/175	5.00
Chris Snelling/175	10.00
Alfonso Soriano/25	
Mac Suzuki/100	30.00
So Taguchi/50	40.00
Dennis Tankersley/175	8.00
Corey Thurman/175	5.00
Luis Ugueto/175	5.00
Kip Wells/175	5.00
Bernie Williams/15	
Kerry Wood/25	

Statistical Standouts

		NM/M
Complete Set (50):		120.00
Common Player:		1.50
Inserted 1:12		
1	Adam Dunn	2.50
2	Alex Rodriguez	8.00
3	Andruw Jones	4.00
4	Brian Giles	1.50
5	Chipper Jones	5.00
6	Cliff Floyd	1.50
7	Craig Biggio	1.50
8	Frank Thomas	4.00
9	Fred McGriff	1.50
10	Garret Anderson	1.50
11	Greg Maddux	5.00
12	Luis Gonzalez	1.50
13	Magglio Ordonez	1.50
14	Ivan Rodriguez	3.00
15	Ken Griffey Jr.	6.00
16	Ichiro Suzuki	6.00
17	Jason Giambi	2.50
18	Derek Jeter	10.00
19	Sammy Sosa	6.00
20	Albert Pujols	8.00
21	J.D. Drew	1.50
22	Jeff Bagwell	4.00
23	Jim Edmonds	1.50
24	Jose Vidro	1.50
25	Juan Encarnacion	1.50
26	Kerry Wood	3.00
27	Al Leiter	1.50
28	Curt Schilling	2.50
29	Manny Ramirez	4.00
30	Lance Berkman	1.50
31	Miguel Tejada	1.50
32	Mike Piazza	6.00
33	Nomar Garciaparra	6.00
34	Omar Vizquel	1.50
35	Pat Burrell	2.00
36	Paul Konerko	1.50
37	Rafael Palmeiro	3.00
38	Randy Johnson	4.00
39	Richie Sexson	1.50
40	Roger Clemens	5.50
41	Shawn Green	2.00
42	Todd Helton	4.00
43	Tom Glavine	1.50
44	Troy Glaus	4.00
45	Vladimir Guerrero	4.00
46	Mike Sweeney	1.50
47	Alfonso Soriano	3.00
48	Barry Zito	1.50
49	John Smoltz	1.50
50	Ellis Burks	1.50

Stat. Standouts Materials

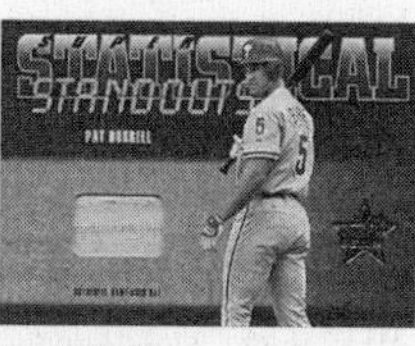

		NM/M
Common Player:		5.00
Inserted 1:69		
Super Materials:		2-3X
Production 25 sets		
1	Adam Dunn/bat/200	15.00
2	Alex Rodriguez/bat/200	15.00
3	Andruw Jones/bat/200	10.00
4	Brian Giles/bat	8.00
5	Chipper Jones/bat/200	15.00
6	Cliff Floyd/jsy	5.00
7	Craig Biggio/jsy	8.00
8	Frank Thomas/jsy/125	12.00
9	Fred McGriff/bat	10.00
10	Garret Anderson/bat	8.00
11	Greg Maddux/jsy/200	20.00
12	Luis Gonzalez/jsy	8.00
13	Magglio Ordonez/ bat/150	10.00
14	Ivan Rodriguez/jsy/100	15.00
15	Ken Griffey Jr/base/100	15.00
16	Ichiro Suzuki/base/100	30.00
17	Jason Giambi/base	10.00
18	Derek Jeter/base/100	25.00
19	Sammy Sosa/base/100	15.00
20	Albert Pujols/base/100	15.00
21	J.D. Drew/bat/150	10.00
22	Jeff Bagwell/jsy/150	15.00
23	Jim Edmonds/bat	8.00
24	Jose Vidro/bat	5.00
25	Juan Encarnacion/bat	5.00
26	Kerry Wood/jsy/200	15.00
27	Al Leiter/jsy	8.00
28	Curt Schilling/jsy/225	12.00
29	Manny Ramirez/ bat/100	15.00
30	Lance Berkman/ bat/150	10.00
31	Miguel Tejada/jsy	10.00
32	Mike Piazza/bat/200	20.00
33	Nomar Garciaparra/ bat/200	20.00
34	Omar Vizquel/jsy	8.00
35	Pat Burrell/bat	10.00
36	Paul Konerko/jsy	6.00
37	Rafael Palmeiro/bat	10.00
38	Randy Johnson/ jsy/200	15.00
39	Richie Sexson/jsy	10.00
40	Roger Clemens/ jsy/200	20.00
41	Shawn Green/jsy	10.00
42	Todd Helton/jsy/175	15.00
43	Tom Glavine/jsy/125	10.00
44	Troy Glaus/jsy	10.00
45	Vladimir Guerrero/jsy	15.00
46	Mike Sweeney/bat	5.00
47	Alfonso Soriano/ jsy/200	15.00
48	Barry Zito/jsy/100	8.00
49	John Smoltz/jsy	8.00
50	Ellis Burks/jsy	5.00

Triple Threads

		NM/M
Common Card:		25.00
Production 100 sets		
1	Reggie Jackson, Alfonso Soriano, Don Mattingly	80.00
2	Alex Rodriguez, Rafael Palmeiro, Ivan Rodriguez	30.00
3	Mike Piazza, Gary Carter, Rickey Henderson	40.00
4	Dale Murphy, Andruw Jones, Chipper Jones	40.00
5	Mike Schmidt, Steve Carlton, Scott Rolen	85.00
6	Rickey Henderson	40.00
7	Johnny Bench, Joe Morgan, Tom Seaver	50.00
8	Randy Johnson, Pedro J. Martinez, Vladimir Guerrero	35.00
9	Nolan Ryan, Rod Carew, Troy Glaus	75.00
10	Lou Brock, J.D. Drew, Stan Musial	65.00

2003 LEAF

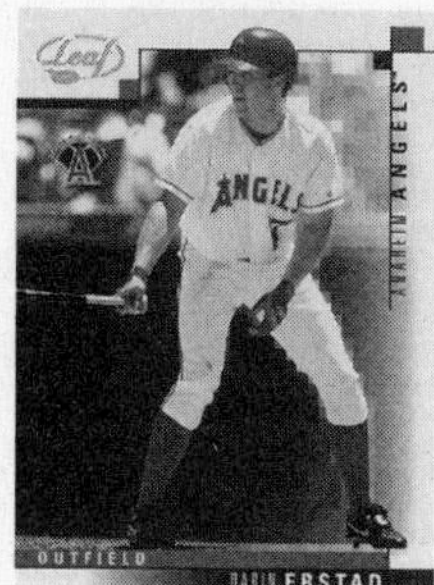

		NM/M
Complete Set (320):		40.00
Common Player:		.15
Pack (10):		1.50
Box (24):		30.00
1	Brad Fullmer	.15
2	Darin Erstad	.25
3	David Eckstein	.15
4	Garret Anderson	.15
5	Jarrod Washburn	.15
6	Kevin Appier	.15
7	Tim Salmon	.25
8	Troy Glaus	.75
9	Troy Percival	.15
10	Buddy Groom	.15
11	Jay Gibbons	.15
12	Jeff Conine	.15
13	Marty Cordova	.15
14	Melvin Mora	.15
15	Rodrigo Lopez	.15
16	Tony Batista	.15
17	Jorge Julio	.15
18	Cliff Floyd	.15
19	Derek Lowe	.15
20	Jason Varitek	.15
21	Johnny Damon	.25
22	Manny Ramirez	.75
23	Nomar Garciaparra	1.25
24	Pedro J. Martinez	.75
25	Rickey Henderson	.75
26	Shea Hillenbrand	.15
27	Trot Nixon	.15
28	Carlos Lee	.15
29	Frank Thomas	.75
30	Jose Valentin	.15
31	Magglio Ordonez	.15
32	Mark Buehrle	.15
33	Paul Konerko	.25
34	C.C. Sabathia	.15
35	Danys Baez	.15
36	Ellis Burks	.15
37	Jim Thome	.75
38	Omar Vizquel	.15
39	Ricky Gutierrez	.15
40	Travis Fryman	.15
41	Bobby Higginson	.15
42	Carlos Pena	.15
43	Juan Acevedo	.15
44	Mark Redman	.15
45	Randall Simon	.15
46	Robert Fick	.15
47	Steve Sparks	.15
48	Carlos Beltran	.50
49	Joe Randa	.15
50	Michael Tucker	.15
51	Mike Sweeney	.15
52	Paul Byrd	.15
53	Raul Ibanez	.15
54	Runelvys Hernandez	.15
55	A.J. Pierzynski	.15
56	Brad Radke	.15
57	Corey Koskie	.15
58	Cristian Guzman	.15
59	David Ortiz	.50
60	Doug Mientkiewicz	.15
61	Dustan Mohr	.15
62	Eddie Guardado	.15
63	Jacque Jones	.15
64	Torii Hunter	.15
65	Alfonso Soriano	.50
66	Andy Pettitte	.35
67	Bernie Williams	.30
68	David Wells	.15
69	Derek Jeter	2.00
70	Jason Giambi	.40
71	Jeff Weaver	.15
72	Jorge Posada	.25
73	Mike Mussina	.30
74	Nick Johnson	.15
75	Raul Mondesi	.15
76	Robin Ventura	.15
77	Roger Clemens	1.00
78	Barry Zito	.25
79	Billy Koch	.15
80	David Justice	.15
81	Eric Chavez	.25
82	Jermaine Dye	.15
83	Mark Mulder	.15
84	Miguel Tejada	.30
85	Ray Durham	.15
86	Scott Hatteberg	.15
87	Ted Lilly	.15
88	Tim Hudson	.25
89	Bret Boone	.15
90	Carlos Guillen	.15
91	Chris Snelling	.15
92	Dan Wilson	.15
93	Edgar Martinez	.15
94	Freddy Garcia	.15
95	Ichiro Suzuki	1.25
96	Jamie Moyer	.15
97	Joel Pineiro	.15
98	John Olerud	.15
99	Mark McLemore	.15
100	Mike Cameron	.15
101	Kazuhiro Sasaki	.15
102	Aubrey Huff	.15
103	Ben Grieve	.15
104	Joe Kennedy	.15
105	Paul Wilson	.15
106	Randy Winn	.15
107	Steve Cox	.15
108	Alex Rodriguez	1.50
109	Chan Ho Park	.15
110	Hank Blalock	.50
111	Herbert Perry	.15
112	Ivan Rodriguez	.65
113	Juan Gonzalez	.75
114	Kenny Rogers	.15
115	Kevin Mench	.15
116	Rafael Palmeiro	.65
117	Carlos Delgado	.40
118	Eric Hinske	.15
119	Jose Cruz	.15
120	Josh Phelps	.15
121	Roy Halladay	.25
122	Shannon Stewart	.15
123	Vernon Wells	.15
124	Curt Schilling	.40
125	Junior Spivey	.15
126	Luis Gonzalez	.25
127	Mark Grace	.25
128	Randy Johnson	.75
129	Steve Finley	.15
130	Tony Womack	.15
131	Andruw Jones	.75
132	Chipper Jones	1.00
133	Gary Sheffield	.30
134	Greg Maddux	1.00
135	John Smoltz	.25
136	Kevin Millwood	.15
137	Rafael Furcal	.15
138	Tom Glavine	.40
139	Alex Gonzalez	.15
140	Corey Patterson	.15
141	Fred McGriff	.15
142	Jon Lieber	.15
143	Kerry Wood	.65
144	Mark Prior	.75
145	Matt Clement	.15
146	Moises Alou	.15
147	Sammy Sosa	1.25
148	Aaron Boone	.15
149	Adam Dunn	.50
150	Austin Kearns	.15
151	Barry Larkin	.15
152	Danny Graves	.15

153 Elmer Dessens .15
154 Ken Griffey Jr. 1.25
155 Sean Casey .25
156 Todd Walker .15
157 Gabe Kapler .15
158 Jason Jennings .15
159 Jay Payton .15
160 Larry Walker .15
161 Mike Hampton .15
162 Todd Helton .75
163 Todd Zeile .15
164 A.J. Burnett .15
165 Derrek Lee .15
166 Josh Beckett .50
167 Juan Encarnacion .15
168 Luis Castillo .15
169 Mike Lowell .15
170 Preston Wilson .15
171 Billy Wagner .15
172 Craig Biggio .25
173 Daryle Ward .15
174 Jeff Bagwell .75
175 Lance Berkman .15
176 Octavio Dotel .15
177 Richard Hidalgo .15
178 Roy Oswalt .25
179 Adrian Beltre .40
180 Eric Gagne .40
181 Eric Karros .15
182 Hideo Nomo .65
183 Kazuhisa Ishii .15
184 Kevin Brown .15
185 Mark Grudzielanek .15
186 Odalis Perez .15
187 Paul LoDuca .15
188 Shawn Green .40
189 Alex Sanchez .15
190 Ben Sheets .15
191 Jeffrey Hammonds .15
192 Jose Hernandez .15
193 Takahito Nomura .15
194 Richie Sexson .15
195 Andres Galarraga .15
196 Bartolo Colon .15
197 Brad Wilkerson .15
198 Javier Vazquez .15
199 Jose Vidro .15
200 Michael Barrett .15
201 Tomokazu Ohka .15
202 Vladimir Guerrero .75
203 Al Leiter .15
204 Armando Benitez .15
205 Edgardo Alfonzo .15
206 Mike Piazza 1.25
207 Mo Vaughn .15
208 Pedro Astacio .15
209 Roberto Alomar .35
210 Roger Cedeno .15
211 Timoniel Perez .15
212 Bobby Abreu .15
213 Jimmy Rollins .15
214 Mike Lieberthal .15
215 Pat Burrell .25
216 Randy Wolf .15
217 Travis Lee .15
218 Vicente Padilla .15
219 Aramis Ramirez .15
220 Brian Giles .15
221 Craig Wilson .15
222 Jason Kendall .15
223 Josh Fogg .15
224 Kevin Young .15
225 Kip Wells .15
226 Mike Williams .15
227 Brett Tomko .15
228 Brian Lawrence .15
229 Mark Kotsay .15
230 Oliver Perez .15
231 Phil Nevin .15
232 Ryan Klesko .15
233 Sean Burroughs .15
234 Trevor Hoffman .15
235 Barry Bonds 2.00
236 Benito Santiago .15
237 Jeff Kent .15
238 Kirk Rueter .15
239 Livan Hernandez .15
240 Kenny Lofton .15
241 Rich Aurilia .15
242 Russ Ortiz .15
243 Albert Pujols 1.50
244 Edgar Renteria .15
245 J.D. Drew .40
246 Jason Isringhausen .15
247 Jim Edmonds .40
248 Matt Morris .15
249 Tino Martinez .15
250 Scott Rolen .75
251 Curt Schilling .25
252 Ivan Rodriguez .35
253 Mike Piazza .75
254 Sammy Sosa .75
255 Matt Williams .15
256 Frank Thomas .25
257 Barry Bonds 1.00
258 Roger Clemens .65
259 Rickey Henderson .25
260 Ken Griffey Jr. .60
261 Greg Maddux .50
262 Randy Johnson .40
263 Jeff Bagwell .25
264 Roberto Alomar .25
265 Tom Glavine .25
266 Juan Gonzalez .25
267 Mark Grace .25
268 Mike Mussina .25
269 Ryan Klesko .15
270 Fred McGriff .15
271 Joe Borchard .15
272 Chris Snelling .15
273 Brian Tallet .15
274 Cliff Lee .15
275 Freddy Sanchez .15
276 Chone Figgins .15
277 Kevin Cash .15
278 Josh Bard .15
279 Jeriome Robertson .15
280 Jeremy Hill .15
281 Shane Nance .15
282 Jeff Baker .15
283 Trey Hodges .15
284 Eric Eckenstahler .15
285 Jim Rushford .15
286 Carlos Rivera .15
287 Josh Bonifay .15
288 Garrett Atkins .15
289 Nic Jackson .15
290 Corwin Malone .15
291 Jimmy Gobble .15
292 Josh Wilson .15
293 *Clint Barmes* .50
294 Jon Adkins .15
295 Tim Kalita .15
296 Nelson Castro .15
297 Colin Young .15
298 Adrian Burnside .15
299 Luis Martinez .15
300 *Termel Sledge* .50
301 Todd Donovan .15
302 Jeremy Ward .15
303 Wilson Valdez .15
304 *Jose Contreras* .75
305 Marshall McDougall .15
306 Mitch Wylie .15
307 Ron Calloway .15
308 Jose Valverde .15
309 Jason Davis .15
310 Scotty Layfield .15
311 Matt Thornton .15
312 Adam Walker .15
313 Gustavo Chacin .15
314 Ron Chiavacci .15
315 Wilbert Nieves .15
316 Clifford Bartosh .15
317 Mike Gonzalez .15
318 Jeremy Guthrie .15
319 Eric Junge .15
320 Ben Kozlowski .15

Red Press Proofs

Stars: 3-5X
Inserted 1:12

Blue Press Proofs

Stars: 8-15X
Production 50 sets

Green

No Pricing
Production 25 sets

Clean Up Crew

NM/M
Complete Set (10): 30.00
Common Card: 1.50
Inserted 1:49
1 Alex Rodriguez, Rafael Palmeiro, Ivan Rodriguez 6.00
2 Nomar Garciaparra, Manny Ramirez, Cliff Floyd 5.00
3 Jason Giambi, Bernie Williams, Jorge Posada 4.00
4 Rich Aurilia, Jeff Kent, Barry Bonds 6.00
5 Larry Walker, Todd Helton, Jay Payton 1.50
6 Lance Berkman, Jeff Bagwell, Daryle Ward 2.00
7 Scott Rolen, Albert Pujols, Jim Edmonds 5.00
8 Gary Sheffield, Chipper Jones, Andruw Jones 4.00
9 Miguel Tejada, Eric Chavez, Jermaine Dye 1.50
10 Sammy Sosa, Moises Alou, Fred McGriff 4.00

Clean Up Crew Memorabilia

NM/M
Production 50 sets
1 Alex Rodriguez, Rafael Palmeiro, Ivan Rodriguez 30.00
2 Nomar Garciaparra, Manny Ramirez, Cliff Floyd 25.00
3 Jason Giambi, Bernie Williams, Jorge Posada 25.00
4 Rich Aurilia, Jeff Kent, Barry Bonds 35.00
5 Larry Walker, Todd Helton, Jay Payton 20.00
6 Lance Berkman, Jeff Bagwell, Daryle Ward 25.00
7 Scott Rolen, Albert Pujols, Jim Edmonds 40.00
8 Gary Sheffield, Chipper Jones, Andruw Jones 30.00
9 Miguel Tejada, Eric Chavez, Jermaine Dye 20.00
10 Sammy Sosa, Moises Alou, Fred McGriff 30.00

Clubhouse Signatures Bronze

NM/M
Common Bronze Auto: 8.00
Inserted 1:300
Silvers: 1-2X
Production 100 sets
Golds: No Pricing
Production 25 sets
Edwin Almonte 8.00
Jeff Baker 10.00
Josh Bard 10.00
Angel Berroa 8.00
Joe Crede/SP/25 15.00
Andre Dawson/SP/50 25.00
Bobby Doerr/SP/100 20.00
Adam Dunn/SP/10
Dwight "Doc" Gooden 25.00
Drew Henson/SP/50 20.00
Eric Hinske 10.00
Torii Hunter/SP/75 35.00
Omar Infante 8.00
Brian Lawrence 8.00
Kevin Mench 8.00
Jack Morris/SP/100 15.00
Franklin Nunez 8.00
Magglio Ordonez/SP/50 25.00
Corey Patterson/SP/100 15.00
Jhonny Peralta 20.00
J.C. Romero 10.00
Chris Snelling/SP/100 10.00
Alfonso Soriano/SP/25 40.00
Brian Tallet/SP/100 8.00

Game Collection

NM/M
Common Player: 8.00
Production 150 sets
1 Miguel Tejada/cap 10.00
2 Shannon Stewart/cap 6.00
3 Mike Schmidt/jacket 40.00
4 Nolan Ryan/jacket 75.00
5 Rafael Palmeiro/glove 15.00
6 Andruw Jones/shoe 10.00
7 Bernie Williams/shoe 15.00
8 Ivan Rodriguez/shoe 10.00
9 Lance Berkman/shoe 10.00
10 Magglio Ordonez/shoe 10.00
11 Roy Oswalt/glove 10.00
12 Andy Pettitte/shoe 10.00
13 Vladimir Guerrero/glove 30.00
14 Jason Jennings/glove 8.00
15 Mike Sweeney/shoe 8.00
16 Joe Borchard/shoe 10.00
17 Mark Prior/shoe 15.00
18 Gary Carter/jacket 10.00
19 Austin Kearns/glove 10.00
20 Ryan Klesko/glove 10.00

Gold Leaf Rookies

NM/M
Complete Set (10): 10.00
Common Player: 1.00
Inserted 1:24
Mirror Golds: 10-20X
Production 25 sets
1 Joe Borchard 1.00
2 Chone Figgins 1.00
3 Alexis Gomez 1.00
4 Chris Snelling 1.00
5 Cliff Lee 1.00
6 Victor Martinez 2.00
7 Hee Seop Choi 1.50
8 Michael Restovich 1.00
9 Anderson Machado 1.00
10 Drew Henson 2.00

Hard Hats

NM/M
Complete Set (12): 15.00
Common Player: 1.00
Inserted 1:13
1 Alex Rodriguez 4.00
2 Bernie Williams 1.00
3 Ivan Rodriguez 1.25
4 Jeff Bagwell 1.50
5 Rafael Furcal 1.00
6 Rafael Palmeiro 1.50
7 Tony Gwynn 2.00
8 Vladimir Guerrero 1.50
9 Adrian Beltre 1.00
10 Shawn Green 1.00
11 Andruw Jones 1.50
12 George Brett 4.00

Hard Hats Batting Helmets

NM/M
Common Player: 15.00
Production 100 sets
1 Alex Rodriguez 50.00
2 Bernie Williams 35.00
3 Ivan Rodriguez 30.00
4 Jeff Bagwell 40.00
5 Rafael Furcal 15.00
6 Rafael Palmeiro 35.00
7 Tony Gwynn 35.00
8 Vladimir Guerrero 35.00
9 Adrian Beltre 20.00
10 Shawn Green 20.00
11 Andruw Jones 20.00
12 George Brett 100.00

Home / Away

NM/M
Complete Set (20): 40.00
Common Player: 1.00

Home inserted 1:34
1 Andruw Jones/Home 1.50
2 Cal Ripken Jr./Home 6.00
3 Edgar Martinez/Home 1.00
4 Jim Thome/Home 1.50
5 Larry Walker/Home 1.00
6 Nomar Garciaparra/Home 4.00
7 Mark Prior/Home 1.50
8 Mike Piazza/Home 4.00
9 Vladimir Guerrero/Home 1.50
10 Chipper Jones/Home 3.00
Away inserted 1:34
1 Andruw Jones 1.50
2 Cal Ripken Jr. 6.00
3 Edgar Martinez 1.00
4 Jim Thome 2.00
5 Larry Walker 1.00
6 Nomar Garciaparra 4.00
7 Mark Prior 1.50
8 Mike Piazza 4.00
9 Vladimir Guerrero 2.00
10 Chipper Jones 3.00

Home / Away Memorabilia

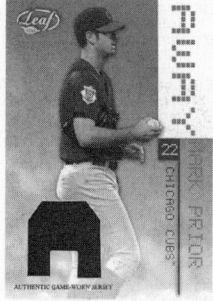

NM/M
Common Player: 6.00
Home Production 250
1 Andruw Jones/Home 8.00
2 Cal Ripken Jr./Home 45.00
3 Edgar Martinez/Home 8.00
4 Jim Thome/Home 10.00
5 Larry Walker/Home 8.00
6 Nomar Garciaparra/Home 20.00
7 Mark Prior/Home 15.00
8 Mike Piazza/Home 15.00
9 Vladimir Guerrero/Home 12.00
10 Chipper Jones/Home 15.00
Away Production 250
1 Andruw Jones 8.00
2 Cal Ripken Jr. 45.00
3 Edgar Martinez 8.00
4 Jim Thome 10.00
5 Larry Walker 6.00
6 Nomar Garciaparra 20.00
7 Mark Prior 15.00
8 Mike Piazza 15.00
9 Vladimir Guerrero 12.00
10 Chipper Jones 15.00

Maple & Ash

NM/M
Common Player: 6.00
Production 400 sets
1 Jorge Posada 8.00
2 Mike Piazza 12.00
3 Alex Rodriguez 15.00
4 Jeff Bagwell 10.00
5 Joe Borchard 6.00
6 Miguel Tejada 6.00
7 Adam Dunn 8.00
8 Jim Thome 8.00
9 Lance Berkman 6.00
10 Torii Hunter 6.00
11 Carlos Delgado 6.00
12 Reggie Jackson 10.00
13 Juan Gonzalez 6.00
14 Vladimir Guerrero 10.00
15 Richie Sexson 6.00

Number Off My Back

NM/M
Production 50 sets
1 Carlos Delgado 15.00
2 Don Mattingly 100.00
3 Todd Helton 30.00
4 Vernon Wells 10.00
5 Bernie Williams 20.00
6 Luis Gonzalez 20.00
7 Kerry Wood 30.00
8 Eric Chavez 10.00
9 Shawn Green 15.00
10 Roy Oswalt 15.00
11 Nomar Garciaparra 40.00
12 Robin Yount 60.00
13 Troy Glaus 20.00
14 C.C. Sabathia 10.00
15 Alex Rodriguez 50.00
16 Mark Mulder 10.00
17 Will Clark 60.00
18 Alfonso Soriano 30.00
19 Andy Pettitte 20.00
20 Curt Schilling 25.00

Shirt Off My Back

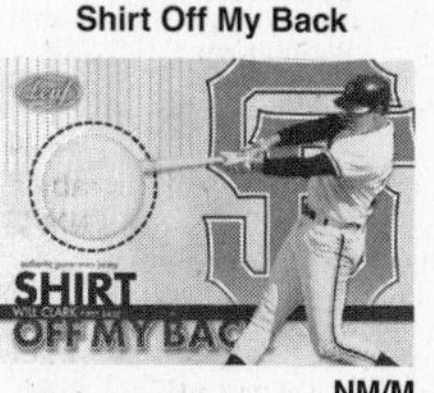

NM/M
Common Player: 5.00
Production 500 sets
Number Off My Back: 2-4X
Production 50 sets
1 Carlos Delgado 6.00
2 Don Mattingly 25.00
3 Todd Helton 10.00
4 Vernon Wells 5.00
5 Bernie Williams 6.00
6 Luis Gonzalez 6.00
7 Kerry Wood 8.00
8 Eric Chavez 6.00
9 Shawn Green 6.00
10 Roy Oswalt 5.00
11 Nomar Garciaparra 12.00
12 Robin Yount 15.00
13 Troy Glaus 8.00
14 C.C. Sabathia 5.00
15 Alex Rodriguez 15.00
16 Mark Mulder 5.00
17 Will Clark 10.00
18 Alfonso Soriano 10.00
19 Andy Pettitte 8.00
20 Curt Schilling 8.00

Slick Leather

NM/M
Complete Set (15): 20.00
Common Player: 1.00
Inserted 1:21
1 Omar Vizquel 1.00
2 Roberto Alomar 1.50
3 Ivan Rodriguez 2.00
4 Greg Maddux 3.00
5 Scott Rolen 2.00
6 Todd Helton 2.00
7 Andruw Jones 2.00
8 Jim Edmonds 1.50
9 Barry Bonds 6.00
10 Eric Chavez 1.00
11 Ichiro Suzuki 5.00
12 Mike Mussina 1.50
13 John Olerud 1.00
14 Torii Hunter 1.00
15 Larry Walker 1.00

60

NM/M
Complete Set (50): 80.00
Common Player: .75
Inserted 1:8
Foil Parallels: 3-5X
Production 60 sets
1 Troy Glaus 3.00
2 Curt Schilling 2.00
3 Randy Johnson 3.00
4 Andruw Jones 3.00
5 Chipper Jones 4.00
6 Greg Maddux 4.00
7 Tom Glavine 1.00
8 Manny Ramirez 3.00
9 Nomar Garciaparra 5.00
10 Pedro J. Martinez 3.00
11 Rickey Henderson 3.00
12 Sammy Sosa 5.00
13 Frank Thomas 3.00
14 Magglio Ordonez .75
15 Mark Buehrle .75
16 Adam Dunn 1.50
17 Ken Griffey Jr. 5.00
18 Jim Thome 2.00
19 Omar Vizquel .75
20 Larry Walker .75
21 Todd Helton 3.00
22 Lance Berkman .75
23 Roy Oswalt .75
24 Mike Sweeney .75
25 Hideo Nomo 3.00
26 Kazuhisa Ishii 1.00
27 Shawn Green 1.00
28 Torii Hunter .75
29 Vladimir Guerrero 3.00
30 Mike Piazza 5.00
31 Alfonso Soriano 3.00
32 Bernie Williams 1.00
33 Derek Jeter 8.00
34 Jason Giambi 2.00
35 Roger Clemens 4.00
36 Barry Zito .75
37 Miguel Tejada .75
38 Pat Burrell 1.00
39 Ryan Klesko .75
40 Barry Bonds 8.00
41 Jeff Kent .75
42 Ichiro Suzuki 5.00
43 John Olerud .75
44 Albert Pujols 5.00
45 Jim Edmonds 1.00
46 Scott Rolen 2.50
47 Alex Rodriguez 6.00
48 Ivan Rodriguez 2.50
49 Rafael Palmeiro 2.50
50 Roy Halladay .75

2003 LEAF CERTIFIED MATERIALS

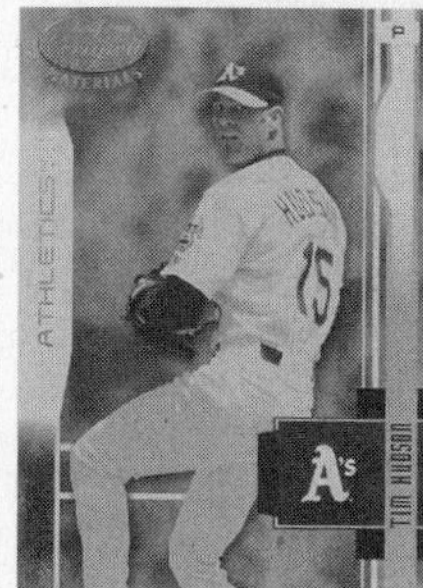

NM/M
Complete Set (250):
Common Player: .50
Common SP Auto. (206-250): 6.00
Production 400 unless noted
Mirror Red Auto SP's (06-250): 1-1.5X
Production 100
Mirror Blue Auto SP's (206-250): 1-2X
Production 50
Mirror Gold Autos (206-250): No Pricing
Production 25
Pack (5): 20.00
Box (10): 150.00
1 Troy Glaus 1.00
2 Alfredo Amezaga .50
3 Garret Anderson 1.00
4 Nolan Ryan 6.00
5 Darin Erstad .75
6 Junior Spivey .50
7 Randy Johnson 2.00
8 Curt Schilling 1.50
9 Luis Gonzalez .75
10 Steve Finley .50
11 Matt Williams .75
12 Greg Maddux 3.00
13 Chipper Jones 2.00
14 Gary Sheffield 1.00
15 Adam LaRoche .50
16 Andruw Jones 1.00
17 Robert Fick .50
18 John Smoltz 1.00
19 Javy Lopez .75
20 Jay Gibbons .50
21 Geronimo Gil .50
22 Cal Ripken Jr. 6.00
23 Nomar Garciaparra 4.00
24 Pedro J. Martinez 2.00
25 Freddy Sanchez .50
26 Rickey Henderson 1.00
27 Manny Ramirez 1.50
28 Casey Fossum .50
29 Sammy Sosa 3.00
30 Kerry Wood 2.00
31 Corey Patterson 1.00
32 Nic Jackson .50
33 Mark Prior 2.00
34 Juan Cruz .50
35 Steve Smyth .50
36 Magglio Ordonez .75
37 Joe Borchard .50
38 Frank Thomas 1.50
39 Mark Buehrle .50
40 Joe Crede .50
41 Carlos Lee .50
42 Paul Konerko .50
43 Adam Dunn 1.50
44 Corky Miller .50
45 Brandon Larson .50
46 Ken Griffey Jr. 3.00
47 Barry Larkin 1.00
48 Sean Casey .50
49 Wily Mo Pena 1.00
50 Austin Kearns .75
51 Victor Martinez 1.00
52 Brian Tallet .50
53 Cliff Lee .50
54 Jeremy Guthrie .50
55 C.C. Sabathia .50
56 Ricardo Rodriguez .50
57 Omar Vizquel 1.00
58 Travis Hafner .50
59 Todd Helton 1.50
60 Jason Jennings .50
61 Jeff Baker .50
62 Larry Walker 1.00
63 Travis Chapman .50
64 Mike Maroth .50
65 Josh Beckett 1.00
66 Ivan Rodriguez 1.50
67 Brad Penny .50
68 A.J. Burnett .50
69 Craig Biggio 1.00
70 Roy Oswalt 1.00
71 Jason Lane .50
72 Nolan Ryan 6.00
73 Wade Miller .50
74 Richard Hidalgo .50
75 Jeff Bagwell 1.50
76 Lance Berkman 1.00
77 Rodrigo Rosario .50
78 Jeff Kent 1.00
79 John Buck .50
80 Angel Berroa .50
81 Mike Sweeney .50
82 Mac Suzuki .50
83 Alexis Gomez .50
84 Carlos Beltran 1.50
85 Runelvys Hernandez .50
86 Hideo Nomo 1.00
87 Paul LoDuca .50
88 Cesar Izturis .50
89 Kazuhisa Ishii .50
90 Shawn Green 1.00
91 Joe Thurston .50
92 Adrian Beltre 1.00
93 Kevin Brown 1.00
94 Richie Sexson 1.00
95 Ben Sheets 1.00
96 Takahito Nomura .50
97 Geoff Jenkins .50
98 Bill Hall .50
99 Torii Hunter 1.00
100 A.J. Pierzynski .50
101 Michael Cuddyer .50
102 Jose Morban .50
103 Brad Radke .50
104 Jacque Jones .50
105 Eric Milton .50
106 Joe Mays .50

No.	Player	Price
107	Adam Johnson	.50
108	Javier Vazquez	.50
109	Vladimir Guerrero	2.00
110	Jose Vidro	.50
111	Michael Barrett	.50
112	Orlando Cabrera	.50
113	Tom Glavine	1.00
114	Roberto Alomar	1.00
115	Tsuyoshi Shinjo	.50
116	Cliff Floyd	.50
117	Mike Piazza	3.00
118	Al Leiter	.50
119	Don Mattingly	4.00
120	Roger Clemens	4.00
121	Derek Jeter	6.00
122	Alfonso Soriano	2.00
123	Drew Henson	.50
124	Brandon Claussen	.50
125	Christian Parker	.50
126	Jason Giambi	1.00
127	Mike Mussina	1.00
128	Bernie Williams	1.00
129	Jason Anderson	.50
130	Nick Johnson	.50
131	Jorge Posada	1.00
132	Andy Pettitte	1.00
133	Barry Zito	1.00
134	Miguel Tejada	1.00
135	Eric Chavez	1.00
136	Tim Hudson	1.00
137	Mark Mulder	.75
138	Terrence Long	.50
139	Mark Ellis	.50
140	Jim Thome	1.50
141	Pat Burrell	.75
142	Marlon Byrd	.50
143	Bobby Abreu	.75
144	Brandon Duckworth	.50
145	Robert Person	.50
146	Anderson Machado	.50
147	Aramis Ramirez	1.00
148	Jack Wilson	.50
149	Carlos Rivera	.50
150	Jose Castillo	.50
151	Walter Young	.50
152	Brian Giles	.75
153	Jason Kendall	.50
154	Ryan Klesko	.75
155	Mike Rivera	.50
156	Sean Burroughs	.50
157	Brian Lawrence	.50
158	Xavier Nady	.50
159	Dennis Tankersley	.50
160	Phil Nevin	.50
161	Barry Bonds	6.00
162	Kenny Lofton	.50
163	Rich Aurilia	.50
164	Ichiro Suzuki	4.00
165	Edgar Martinez	.75
166	Chris Snelling	.50
167	Rafael Soriano	.50
168	John Olerud	.75
169	Bret Boone	.75
170	Freddy Garcia	.50
171	Aaron Sele	.50
172	Kazuhiro Sasaki	.50
173	Albert Pujols	4.00
174	Scott Rolen	2.00
175	So Taguchi	.50
176	Jim Edmonds	1.00
177	Edgar Renteria	1.00
178	J.D. Drew	1.00
179	Antonio Perez	.50
180	Dewon Brazelton	.50
181	Aubrey Huff	.50
182	Toby Hall	.50
183	Ben Grieve	.50
184	Joe Kennedy	.50
185	Alex Rodriguez	5.00
186	Rafael Palmeiro	1.50
187	Hank Blalock	1.50
188	Mark Teixeira	1.00
189	Juan Gonzalez	1.50
190	Kevin Mench	.50
191	Nolan Ryan	6.00
192	Doug Davis	.50
193	Eric Hinske	.50
194	Vinnie Chulk	.50
195	Alexis Rios	.50
196	Carlos Delgado	1.00
197	Shannon Stewart	.50
198	Josh Phelps	.50
199	Vernon Wells	.75
200	Roy Halladay	.75
201	Babe Ruth	8.00
202	Lou Gehrig	6.00
203	Jackie Robinson	6.00
204	Ty Cobb	6.00
205	Thurman Munson	4.00
206	*Prentice Redman*	8.00
207	*Craig Brazell*	10.00
208	*Nook Logan*	15.00
209	Hong-Chih Huo	30.00
210	*Matt Kata*	10.00
211	*Chien-Ming Wang*	60.00
212	*Alejandro Machado*	6.00
213	*Michael Hessman*	8.00
214	*Francisco Rosario*	8.00
215	Pedro Liriano	8.00
216	Jeremy Bonderman	25.00
217	*Oscar Villarreal*	10.00
218	*Arnie Munoz*	6.00
219	*Tim Olson*	10.00
220	*Jose Contreras/100*	40.00
221	*Francisco Cruceta*	10.00
222	John Webb	10.00
223	*Phil Seibel*	6.00
224	*Aaron Looper*	10.00
225	*Brian Stokes*	10.00
226	*Guillermo Quiroz*	10.00
227	*Fernando Cabrera*	10.00
228	*Josh Hall*	10.00
229	*Diegomar Markwell*	8.00
230	*Andrew Brown*	10.00
231	*Doug Waechter*	10.00
232	*Felix Sanchez*	10.00
233	Gerardo Garcia	8.00
234	*Matt Bruback*	8.00
235	*Michel Hernandez*	8.00
236	*Rett Johnson*	10.00
237	*Ryan Cameron*	8.00
238	*Rob Hammock*	10.00
239	*Clint Barmes*	20.00
240	*Brandon Webb*	20.00
241	*Jon Leicester*	6.00
242	*Shane Bazzell*	10.00
243	*Joe Valentine*	10.00
244	*Josh Stewart*	10.00
245	*Pete LaForest*	8.00
246	*Shane Victorino*	8.00
247	*Terrmel Sledge*	10.00
248	*Lew Ford*	25.00
249	*Todd Wellemeyer*	10.00
250	*Hideki Matsui/No Auto.*	15.00

Mirror Red

Stars (1-205):	2-5X
SP's (206-250):	.2-.4X
Production 100 sets	
Mirror Blues (1-205):	4-10X
SP's (206-250):	.3-.5X
Production 50 sets	
Mirror Golds:	No Pricing
Production 25 sets	
Mirror Emeralds:	No Pricing
Production 5 sets	
Mirror Blacks:	One set produced

Mirror Red Materials

		NM/M
	Common Player:	4.00
	Production 250 unless noted	
	Mirror Red SP's (206-250):	.5X
	Mirror Blues:	1-1.5X
	Production 100	
	Mirror Golds:	No Pricing
	Production 25 sets	
	Mirror Emeralds:	No Pricing
	Production 5 sets	
	Mirror Blacks:	One set produced
1	Troy Glaus	6.00
2	Alfredo Amezaga	4.00
3	Garret Anderson	6.00
4	Nolan Ryan/35	65.00
5	Darin Erstad	5.00
6	Junior Spivey	4.00
7	Randy Johnson	8.00
8	Curt Schilling	8.00
9	Luis Gonzalez	5.00
10	Steve Finley	4.00
11	Matt Williams	5.00
12	Greg Maddux	10.00
13	Chipper Jones	10.00
14	Gary Sheffield/125	6.00
15	Adam LaRoche	4.00
16	Andruw Jones	6.00
17	Robert Fick	4.00
18	John Smoltz	6.00
19	Javy Lopez	6.00
20	Jay Gibbons	4.00
21	Geronimo Gil	4.00
22	Cal Ripken Jr/35	75.00
23	Nomar Garciaparra	15.00
24	Pedro J. Martinez	10.00
25	Freddy Sanchez	4.00
26	Rickey Henderson	10.00
27	Manny Ramirez	8.00
28	Casey Fossum	4.00
29	Sammy Sosa	15.00
30	Kerry Wood	10.00
31	Corey Patterson	6.00
32	Nic Jackson	4.00
33	Mark Prior	10.00
34	Juan Cruz	4.00
35	Steve Smyth	4.00
36	Magglio Ordonez	6.00
37	Joe Borchard	4.00
38	Frank Thomas	10.00
39	Mark Buehrle	5.00
40	Joe Crede/100	8.00
41	Carlos Lee	4.00
42	Paul Konerko	6.00
43	Adam Dunn	8.00
45	Brandon Larson/150	6.00
46	Ken Griffey Jr.	12.00
47	Barry Larkin	8.00
48	Sean Casey	6.00
49	Wily Mo Pena	6.00
50	Austin Kearns	6.00
51	Victor Martinez/100	8.00
55	C.C. Sabathia	4.00
56	Ricardo Rodriguez	4.00
57	Omar Vizquel	6.00
58	Travis Hafner	6.00
59	Todd Helton	8.00
60	Jason Jennings	4.00
61	Jeff Baker/100	
62	Larry Walker	6.00
63	Travis Chapman	6.00
64	Mike Maroth	4.00
65	Josh Beckett	6.00
66	Ivan Rodriguez	8.00
67	Brad Penny	4.00
68	A.J. Burnett	4.00
69	Craig Biggio	6.00
70	Roy Oswalt	6.00
71	Jason Lane	4.00
72	Nolan Ryan/35	65.00
73	Wade Miller	5.00
74	Richard Hidalgo	4.00
75	Jeff Bagwell	10.00
76	Lance Berkman	6.00
77	Rodrigo Rosario	4.00
78	Jeff Kent	6.00
79	John Buck	4.00
80	Angel Berroa	4.00
81	Mike Sweeney	6.00
84	Carlos Beltran	8.00
86	Hideo Nomo	15.00
87	Paul LoDuca	6.00
88	Cesar Izturis	4.00
89	Kazuhisa Ishii	5.00
90	Shawn Green	6.00
91	Joe Thurston	4.00
92	Adrian Beltre	6.00
93	Kevin Brown	6.00
94	Richie Sexson	6.00
95	Ben Sheets	6.00
97	Geoff Jenkins	5.00
98	Bill Hall	4.00
99	Torii Hunter	8.00
101	Michael Cuddyer	4.00
102	Jose Morban	4.00
103	Brad Radke	6.00
104	Jacque Jones	6.00
105	Eric Milton	4.00
106	Joe Mays	5.00
107	Adam Johnson	5.00
108	Javier Vazquez	5.00
109	Vladimir Guerrero	10.00
110	Jose Vidro	4.00
111	Michael Barrett/50	6.00
112	Orlando Cabrera	5.00
113	Tom Glavine	8.00
114	Roberto Alomar	10.00
115	Tsuyoshi Shinjo	4.00
116	Cliff Floyd	5.00
117	Mike Piazza	10.00
118	Al Leiter	5.00
119	Don Mattingly/35	60.00
120	Roger Clemens	25.00
121	Derek Jeter	20.00
122	Alfonso Soriano	8.00
123	Drew Henson	6.00
124	Brandon Claussen/50	10.00
125	Christian Parker	4.00
126	Jason Giambi	6.00
127	Mike Mussina	10.00
128	Bernie Williams	8.00
130	Nick Johnson	4.00
131	Jorge Posada	8.00
132	Andy Pettitte	10.00
133	Barry Zito	6.00
134	Miguel Tejada	6.00
135	Eric Chavez	6.00
136	Tim Hudson	6.00
137	Mark Mulder	6.00
138	Terrence Long	4.00
139	Mark Ellis	4.00
140	Jim Thome	8.00
141	Pat Burrell	6.00
142	Marlon Byrd	4.00
143	Bobby Abreu	6.00
144	Brandon Duckworth	4.00
145	Robert Person	4.00
146	Anderson Machado	4.00
147	Aramis Ramirez	6.00
148	Jack Wilson	4.00
150	Jose Castillo	4.00
151	Walter Young	4.00
152	Brian Giles	6.00
153	Jason Kendall	5.00
154	Ryan Klesko/25	
155	Mike Rivera	4.00
157	Brian Lawrence	4.00
158	Xavier Nady/60	8.00
159	Dennis Tankersley	4.00
160	Phil Nevin	4.00
161	Barry Bonds	20.00
162	Kenny Lofton	6.00
163	Rich Aurilia	5.00
164	Ichiro Suzuki	25.00
165	Edgar Martinez/100	8.00
166	Chris Snelling	4.00
167	Rafael Soriano	4.00
168	John Olerud	4.00
169	Bret Boone	5.00
170	Freddy Garcia	4.00
171	Aaron Sele	4.00
172	Kazuhiro Sasaki	4.00
173	Albert Pujols	25.00
174	Scott Rolen	10.00
175	So Taguchi	4.00
176	Jim Edmonds	6.00
177	Edgar Renteria	8.00
178	J.D. Drew	6.00
179	Antonio Perez	4.00
180	Dewon Brazelton	4.00
181	Aubrey Huff/50	8.00
182	Toby Hall	4.00
183	Ben Grieve	4.00
184	Joe Kennedy	4.00
185	Alex Rodriguez	15.00
186	Rafael Palmeiro	8.00
187	Hank Blalock	8.00
188	Mark Teixeira	8.00
189	Juan Gonzalez	8.00
190	Kevin Mench	4.00
191	Nolan Ryan/35	65.00
192	Doug Davis	4.00
193	Eric Hinske	8.00
196	Carlos Delgado	6.00
197	Shannon Stewart	5.00
198	Josh Phelps	4.00
199	Vernon Wells	5.00
200	Roy Halladay	8.00
201	Babe Ruth/15	

202 Lou Gehrig/15
203 Jackie Robinson/15
204 Ty Cobb/15
205 Thurman Munson/15

Mirror Red Signatures

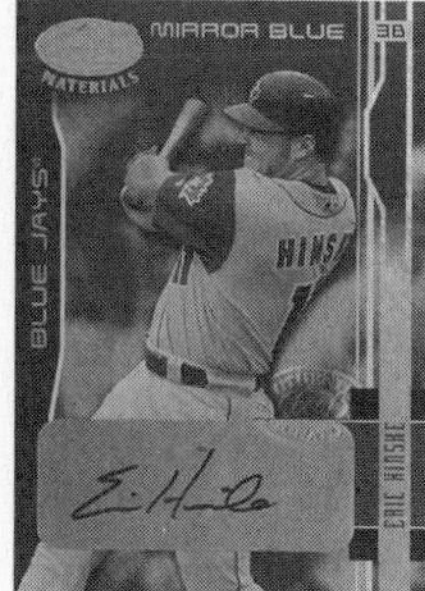

NM/M
Common Player:
Production 100 unless noted
Mirror Blues: 1-1.5X
Production 50
Mirror Golds: 1.5-2X
Production 25 sets
Mirror Emeralds: No Pricing
Production 5 sets
Mirror Blacks: One set produced
2 Alfredo Amezaga 6.00
3 Garret Anderson/10
4 Nolan Ryan/5
6 Junior Spivey/15
15 Adam LaRoche 10.00
17 Robert Fick/15 20.00
20 Jay Gibbons 15.00
21 Geronimo Gil/15 15.00
22 Cal Ripken Jr./5
25 Freddy Sanchez 10.00
28 Casey Fossum/50 10.00
31 Corey Patterson/6
32 Nic Jackson 10.00
33 Mark Prior/15
34 Juan Cruz/15 15.00
35 Steve Smyth/94 8.00
37 Joe Borchard/50 15.00
39 Mark Buehrle/50 20.00
40 Joe Crede/30 15.00
45 Brandon Larson 10.00
49 Wily Mo Pena 20.00
51 Victor Martinez/50 25.00
52 Brian Tallet/15
53 Cliff Lee/50 15.00
54 Jeremy Guthrie/50 15.00
56 Ricardo Rodriguez 8.00
60 Jason Jennings/50 12.00
61 Jeff Baker/50 8.00
63 Travis Chapman 10.00
64 Mike Maroth 10.00
70 Roy Oswalt/50 20.00
71 Jason Lane 10.00
72 Nolan Ryan/5
73 Wade Miller/50 15.00
74 Richard Hidalgo/10
77 Rodrigo Rosario 10.00
79 John Buck/15
80 Angel Berroa/50 15.00
81 Mike Sweeney/10
82 Mac Suzuki/15
83 Alexis Gomez/15
85 Runelvys Hernandez 10.00
86 Hideo Nomo/16
87 Paul LoDuca/15
88 Cesar Izturis 6.00
89 Kazuhisa Ishii/5
91 Joe Thurston 8.00
94 Richie Sexson/10
95 Ben Sheets/10
96 Takahito Nomura/15
98 Bill Hall 10.00
100 A.J. Pierzynski/10
102 Jose Morban 8.00
106 Joe Mays/9
107 Adam Johnson/50 10.00
108 Javier Vazquez/15
110 Jose Vidro/15
116 Cliff Floyd/10
117 Mike Piazza/20 150.00
119 Don Mattingly/5
122 Alfonso Soriano/15
123 Drew Henson/10
124 Brandon Claussen/60 15.00
125 Christian Parker/50 10.00
129 Jason Anderson 10.00
130 Nick Johnson/15
133 Barry Zito/10
134 Miguel Tejada/10
135 Eric Chavez/10
136 Tim Hudson/10
138 Terrence Long/50 15.00
141 Pat Burrell/6
142 Marlon Byrd 10.00
143 Bobby Abreu/10
144 Brandon Duckworth/50 10.00
145 Robert Person/50 10.00
146 Anderson Machado 8.00
148 Jack Wilson/15
149 Carlos Rivera 8.00
150 Jose Castillo 8.00
151 Walter Young 8.00
152 Brian Giles/15
154 Ryan Klesko/10
155 Mike Rivera 8.00
157 Brian Lawrence 8.00
158 Xavier Nady/15
159 Dennis Tankersley/15
165 Edgar Martinez/10
166 Chris Snelling 10.00
167 Rafael Soriano/50 12.00
170 Freddy Garcia/15
173 Albert Pujols/10
176 Jim Edmonds/10
179 Antonio Perez/50 8.00
180 Dewon Brazelton/50 8.00
181 Aubrey Huff/50 15.00
182 Toby Hall/50 10.00
184 Joe Kennedy/50 12.00
187 Hank Blalock/50 40.00
188 Mark Teixeira/50 40.00
189 Juan Gonzalez/10
190 Kevin Mench 10.00
191 Nolan Ryan/5
193 Eric Hinske 15.00
194 Vinnie Chulk 8.00
195 Alexis Rios 25.00
197 Shannon Stewart/15

Fabric of the Game

NM/M
Common Player: 4.00
Quantity produced listed
1BA Bobby Doerr/50 15.00
1JY Bobby Doerr/39 15.00
1PS Bobby Doerr/50 15.00
2BA Ozzie Smith/100 25.00
2IN Ozzie Smith/50 30.00
2JY Ozzie Smith/88 20.00
2PS Ozzie Smith/50 30.00
3DY Pee Wee Reese/32 30.00
3JY Pee Wee Reese/58 15.00
4BA Jeff Bagwell/100 10.00
4DY Jeff Bagwell/65 10.00
4IN Jeff Bagwell/50 12.00
4JY Jeff Bagwell/98 10.00
4PS Jeff Bagwell/50 12.00
5BA Tommy Lasorda/100 8.00
5DY Tommy Lasorda/58 10.00
5JY Tommy Lasorda/84 8.00
5PS Tommy Lasorda/50 10.00
6JY Red Schoendienst/55 10.00
7BA Harmon Killebrew/50 15.00
7DY Harmon Killebrew/61 15.00
7IN Harmon Killebrew/50 15.00
7JY Harmon Killebrew/71 15.00
7PS Harmon Killebrew/50 15.00
8DY Roger Maris/55 40.00
8JY Roger Maris/58 40.00
8PS Roger Maris/50 40.00
9BA Alex Rodriguez/100 15.00
9DY Alex Rodriguez/77 15.00
9IN Alex Rodriguez/50 15.00
9JY Alex Rodriguez/99 15.00
9PS Alex Rodriguez/50 15.00
10BA Alex Rodriguez/100 15.00
10DY Alex Rodriguez/72 15.00
10IN Alex Rodriguez/50 15.00
10JY Alex Rodriguez/101 15.00
10PS Alex Rodriguez/50 15.00
11BA Dale Murphy/50 15.00
11DY Dale Murphy/66 15.00
11IN Dale Murphy/50 15.00
11JY Dale Murphy/85 15.00
11PS Dale Murphy/50 15.00
12BA Alan Trammell/100 10.00
12IN Alan Trammell/50 10.00
12JY Alan Trammell/90 10.00
12PS Alan Trammell/50 10.00
13BA Babe Ruth/10 250.00
13DY Babe Ruth/13 250.00
13IN Babe Ruth/10 250.00
13JY Babe Ruth/30 200.00
13PS Babe Ruth/10 250.00
14BA Lou Gehrig/10
14DY Lou Gehrig/13
14IN Lou Gehrig/10
14JY Lou Gehrig/38 200.00
15BA Babe Ruth/10
15DY Babe Ruth/13
15IN Babe Ruth/10
15JY Babe Ruth/30 250.00
16BA Mel Ott/10
16JY Mel Ott/46 30.00
17BA Paul Molitor/100 15.00
17DY Paul Molitor/70 15.00
17IN Paul Molitor/50 15.00
17JY Paul Molitor/84 15.00
17PS Paul Molitor/50 15.00
18BA Duke Snider/15
18DY Duke Snider/58 15.00
18JY Duke Snider/62 15.00
19BA Miguel Tejada/50 10.00
19DY Miguel Tejada/68 8.00
19IN Miguel Tejada/50 10.00
19JY Miguel Tejada/99 5.00
19PS Miguel Tejada/50 10.00
20BA Lou Gehrig/10
20DY Lou Gehrig/13
20IN Lou Gehrig/10
20JY Lou Gehrig/38 200.00
21BA Brooks Robinson/15
21DY Brooks Robinson/54 15.00
21JY Brooks Robinson/66 15.00
22BA George Brett/50 30.00
22DY George Brett/69 25.00
22IN George Brett/50 30.00
22JY George Brett/91 25.00
22PS George Brett/50 30.00
23BA Johnny Bench/50 15.00
23DY Johnny Bench/59 15.00
23IN Johnny Bench/50 15.00
23JY Johnny Bench/81 15.00
23PS Johnny Bench/50 15.00
24JY Lou Boudreau/48 15.00
25BA Nomar Garciaparra/100 20.00
25IN Nomar Garciaparra/50 25.00
25JY Nomar Garciaparra/100 20.00
25PS Nomar Garciaparra/50 25.00
26BA Tsuyoshi Shinjo/50 8.00
26DY Tsuyoshi Shinjo/62 8.00
26JY Tsuyoshi Shinjo/101 5.00
27BA Pat Burrell/100 8.00
27DY Pat Burrell/46 10.00
27JY Pat Burrell/101 8.00
28BA Albert Pujols/100 20.00
28IN Albert Pujols/50 25.00
28JY Albert Pujols/101 20.00
28JN Albert Pujols/5
28PS Albert Pujols/50 25.00
29BA Stan Musial/10
29JY Stan Musial/43 30.00
29PS Stan Musial/10
30BA Al Kaline/20
30IN Al Kaline/15
30JY Al Kaline/64 15.00
31BA Ivan Rodriguez/100 8.00
31DY Ivan Rodriguez/72 8.00
31IN Ivan Rodriguez/50 10.00
31JY Ivan Rodriguez/101 5.00
32BA Craig Biggio/100 6.00
32DY Craig Biggio/65 8.00
32JY Craig Biggio/101 6.00
32PS Craig Biggio/50 10.00
33BA Joe Morgan/10
33IN Joe Morgan/10
33DY Joe Morgan/59 10.00
33JY Joe Morgan/74 8.00
34BA Willie Stargell/50 15.00
34IN Willie Stargell/15
34JY Willie Stargell/68 15.00
34PS Willie Stargell/50 15.00
35BA Andre Dawson/100 8.00
35IN Andre Dawson/50 10.00
35JY Andre Dawson/87 8.00
35PS Andre Dawson/50 10.00
36BA Gary Carter/100 10.00
36DY Gary Carter/62 10.00
36IN Gary Carter/50 10.00
36JY Gary Carter/85 8.00
36PS Gary Carter/50 10.00
37BA Cal Ripken Jr./50 50.00
37DY Cal Ripken Jr./54 50.00
37IN Cal Ripken Jr./50 50.00
37JY Cal Ripken Jr./101 40.00
37PS Cal Ripken Jr./50 50.00
38BA Enos Slaughter/15
38IN Enos Slaughter/15
38JY Enos Slaughter/53 20.00
38PS Enos Slaughter/25
39BA Reggie Jackson/50 15.00
39DY Reggie Jackson/68 15.00
39IN Reggie Jackson/25
39JY Reggie Jackson/75 15.00
39PS Reggie Jackson/50 15.00
40BA Phil Rizzuto/20
40IN Phil Rizzuto/15
40JY Phil Rizzuto/47 15.00
41BA Chipper Jones/100 10.00
41DY Chipper Jones/66 15.00
41IN Chipper Jones/50 15.00
41JY Chipper Jones/101 10.00
41PS Chipper Jones/50 15.00
42BA Hideo Nomo/100 10.00
42DY Hideo Nomo/58 15.00
42IN Hideo Nomo/50 15.00
42JY Hideo Nomo/95 10.00
42PS Hideo Nomo/50 15.00
43BA Luis Aparicio/25
43IN Luis Aparicio/15
43JY Luis Aparicio/69 10.00
43PS Luis Aparicio/20
44BA Hideo Nomo/100 10.00
44IN Hideo Nomo/50 15.00
44JY Hideo Nomo/101 10.00
44PS Hideo Nomo/50 15.00
45BA Edgar Martinez/100 8.00
45DY Edgar Martinez/77 8.00
45JY Edgar Martinez/100 8.00
45PS Edgar Martinez/50 10.00
46BA Barry Larkin/100 6.00
46DY Barry Larkin/59 10.00
46JY Barry Larkin/100 6.00
46PS Barry Larkin/50 10.00
47BA Alfonso Soriano/100 10.00
47IN Alfonso Soriano/50 15.00
47JY Alfonso Soriano/102 10.00
47PS Alfonso Soriano/50 15.00
48BA Wade Boggs/100 8.00
48DY Wade Boggs/98 8.00
48IN Wade Boggs/50 10.00
48JY Wade Boggs/99 8.00
48PS Wade Boggs/50 10.00
49BA Wade Boggs/50 10.00
49IN Wade Boggs/50 10.00
49JY Wade Boggs/94 8.00
49PS Wade Boggs/50 10.00
50BA Ernie Banks/15
50IN Ernie Banks/15
50JN Ernie Banks/14
50JY Ernie Banks/68 15.00
51BA Joe Torre/50 10.00
51DY Joe Torre/66 10.00
51IN Joe Torre/50 10.00
51JY Joe Torre/66 10.00
51PS Joe Torre/50 10.00
52BA Tim Hudson/100 4.00
52DY Tim Hudson/68 6.00
52JY Tim Hudson/101 4.00
52PS Tim Hudson/50 6.00
53BA Shawn Green/100 4.00
53DY Shawn Green/58 6.00
53JY Shawn Green/102 4.00
53PS Shawn Green/50 6.00
54BA Carlos Beltran/100 6.00
54DY Carlos Beltran/69 8.00
54JY Carlos Beltran/101 6.00
54PS Carlos Beltran/50 8.00
55BA Bo Jackson/50 15.00
55DY Bo Jackson/69 15.00
55IN Bo Jackson/25
55JY Bo Jackson/90 10.00
55PS Bo Jackson/50 15.00
56BA Hal Newhouser/50 8.00
56JY Hal Newhouser/55 8.00
56PS Hal Newhouser/50 8.00
57BA Jason Giambi/100 6.00
57DY Jason Giambi/68 8.00
57IN Jason Giambi/50 8.00
57JY Jason Giambi/101 6.00
57PS Jason Giambi/50 8.00
58BA Lance Berkman/100 6.00
58DY Lance Berkman/65 8.00
58IN Lance Berkman/50 8.00
58JY Lance Berkman/102 6.00
58PS Lance Berkman/50 8.00
59BA Todd Helton/100 6.00

59DY Todd Helton/93 6.00
59JY Todd Helton/100 6.00
59PS Todd Helton/50 8.00
60BA Mark Grace/100 8.00
60IN Mark Grace/25
60JY Mark Grace/95 8.00
60PS Mark Grace/50 15.00
61BA Fred Lynn/100 6.00
61JY Fred Lynn/75 8.00
61PS Fred Lynn/50 8.00
62BA Bob Feller/10
62DY Bob Feller/15
62JN Bob Feller/19
62JY Bob Feller/52 15.00
63BA Robin Yount/100 20.00
63DY Robin Yount/70 20.00
63IN Robin Yount/50 25.00
63JN Robin Yount/19
63JY Robin Yount/88 20.00
63PS Robin Yount/50 25.00
64BA Tony Gwynn/100 15.00
64DY Tony Gwynn/69 20.00
64IN Tony Gwynn/50 20.00
64JN Tony Gwynn/19
64JY Tony Gwynn/99 20.00
64PS Tony Gwynn/50 20.00
65BA Tony Gwynn/100 15.00
65DY Tony Gwynn/69 15.00
65IN Tony Gwynn/50 15.00
65JY Tony Gwynn/99 15.00
65PS Tony Gwynn/50 15.00
66BA Frank Robinson/10
66DY Frank Robinson/54 10.00
66JN Frank Robinson/20
66JY Frank Robinson/70 10.00
67BA Mike Schmidt/50 20.00
67DY Mike Schmidt/46 20.00
67IN Mike Schmidt/50 20.00
67JY Mike Schmidt/81 20.00
67PS Mike Schmidt/50 20.00
68BA Lou Brock/20
68IN Lou Brock/15
68JY Lou Brock/66 15.00
69BA Don Sutton/50 8.00
69DY Don Sutton/58 8.00
69JY Don Sutton/72 8.00
70BA Mark Mulder/100 4.00
70DY Mark Mulder/68 6.00
70JY Mark Mulder/101 4.00
70PS Mark Mulder/50 6.00
71BA Luis Gonzalez/100 4.00
71DY Luis Gonzalez/98 4.00
71JY Luis Gonzalez/101 4.00
71PS Luis Gonzalez/50 6.00
72BA Jorge Posada/100 6.00
72DY Jorge Posada/13
72IN Jorge Posada/25
72JY Jorge Posada/101 6.00
72PS Jorge Posada/50 8.00
73BA Sammy Sosa/100 20.00
73IN Sammy Sosa/50 25.00
73JY Sammy Sosa/101 20.00
73PS Sammy Sosa/50 25.00
74BA Roberto Alomar/100 8.00
74DY Roberto Alomar/62 10.00
74IN Roberto Alomar/25
74JY Roberto Alomar/102 8.00
74PS Roberto Alomar/50 10.00
75BA Roberto Clemente/10
75JN Roberto Clemente/21
75JY Roberto Clemente/69 80.00
75PS Roberto Clemente/10
76BA Jeff Kent/100 4.00
76DY Jeff Kent/58 6.00
76IN Jeff Kent/25
76JY Jeff Kent/101 4.00
76PS Jeff Kent/50 6.00
77BA Sean Casey/20
77DY Sean Casey/59 8.00
77JN Sean Casey/21
77JY Sean Casey/100 4.00
77PS Sean Casey/25
78BA Roger Clemens/50 25.00
78DY Roger Clemens/7
78IN Roger Clemens/50 25.00
78JN Roger Clemens/21
78JY Roger Clemens/95 20.00
78PS Roger Clemens/50 20.00
79BA Warren Spahn/20
79DY Warren Spahn/53 15.00
79JN Warren Spahn/21
79JY Warren Spahn/58 15.00
79PS Warren Spahn/15
80BA Roger Clemens/100 20.00
80DY Roger Clemens/13
80IN Roger Clemens/50 25.00
80JN Roger Clemens/22
80JY Roger Clemens/102 25.00
80PS Roger Clemens/50 25.00
81BA Jim Palmer/50 10.00
81DY Jim Palmer/54 10.00
81JN Jim Palmer/22
81JY Jim Palmer/69 10.00
81PS Jim Palmer/50 10.00
82BA Juan Gonzalez/50 10.00
82DY Juan Gonzalez/15
82JN Juan Gonzalez/22
82JY Juan Gonzalez/101 6.00
82PS Juan Gonzalez/50 10.00
83BA Will Clark/100 15.00
83DY Will Clark/58 15.00
83JN Will Clark/22
83JY Will Clark/88 15.00
83PS Will Clark/50 15.00
84BA Don Mattingly/50 25.00
84DY Don Mattingly/13
84IN Don Mattingly/50 25.00
84JN Don Mattingly/23
84JY Don Mattingly/93 25.00
84PS Don Mattingly/50 25.00
85BA Ryne Sandberg/40 30.00
85IN Ryne Sandberg/50 30.00
85JN Ryne Sandberg/23
85JY Ryne Sandberg/85 30.00
85PS Ryne Sandberg/50 30.00
86BA Early Wynn/20
86JN Early Wynn/24
86JY Early Wynn/55 8.00
86PS Early Wynn/15
87BA Manny Ramirez/50 8.00
87JN Manny Ramirez/24
87JY Manny Ramirez/102 6.00
87PS Manny Ramirez/50 8.00
88BA Rickey Henderson/100 10.00
88DY Rickey Henderson/62 15.00
88IN Rickey Henderson/50 15.00
88JN Rickey Henderson/24
88JY Rickey Henderson/99 10.00
88PS Rickey Henderson/50 15.00
89BA Rickey Henderson/100 10.00
89DY Rickey Henderson/69 15.00
89PS Rickey Henderson/50 15.00
90BA Jason Giambi/100 8.00
90IN Jason Giambi/50 10.00
90JN Jason Giambi/25
90JY Jason Giambi/102 8.00
90PS Jason Giambi/50 10.00
91BA Carlos Delgado/100 4.00
91DY Carlos Delgado/77 4.00
91JN Carlos Delgado/25
91JY Carlos Delgado/100 4.00
91PS Carlos Delgado/50 6.00
92BA Jim Thome/100 8.00
92JN Jim Thome/25
92JY Jim Thome/102 10.00
92PS Jim Thome/50 10.00
93BA Andruw Jones/100 6.00
93DY Andruw Jones/66 8.00
93JN Andruw Jones/25
93JY Andruw Jones/101 6.00
93PS Andruw Jones/50 8.00
94BA Rafael Palmeiro/100 8.00
94DY Rafael Palmeiro/72 8.00
94JN Rafael Palmeiro/25
94JY Rafael Palmeiro/102 8.00
94PS Rafael Palmeiro/50 8.00
95BA Troy Glaus/100 6.00
95DY Troy Glaus/97 6.00
95IN Troy Glaus/50 6.00
95JN Troy Glaus/25
95JY Troy Glaus/100 6.00
95PS Troy Glaus/50 8.00
96BA Wade Boggs/100 8.00
96IN Wade Boggs/50 10.00
96JN Wade Boggs/26 25.00
96JY Wade Boggs/86 8.00
96PS Wade Boggs/50 10.00
97BA Jim "Catfish" Hunter/50 10.00
97DY Jim "Catfish" Hunter/68 10.00
97JN Jim "Catfish" Hunter/27 15.00
97JY Jim "Catfish" Hunter/68 10.00
97PS Jim "Catfish" Hunter/50 10.00
98BA Juan Marichal/50 10.00
98DY Juan Marichal/58 10.00
98JN Juan Marichal/27 20.00
98JY Juan Marichal/67 10.00
98PS Juan Marichal/50 10.00
99BA Carlton Fisk/50 15.00
99IN Carlton Fisk/25
99JN Carlton Fisk/27 25.00
99JY Carlton Fisk/80 10.00
99PS Carlton Fisk/50 15.00
100BA Vladimir Guerrero/100 8.00
100DY Vladimir Guerrero/69 15.00
100IN Vladimir Guerrero/25
100JN Vladimir Guerrero/27 30.00
100JY Vladimir Guerrero/101 8.00
100PS Vladimir Guerrero/50 15.00
101BA Rod Carew/100 10.00
101DY Rod Carew/65 15.00
101JN Rod Carew/29 20.00
101JY Rod Carew/85 10.00
101PS Rod Carew/50 15.00
102BA Rod Carew/50 15.00
102DY Rod Carew/61 15.00
102JN Rod Carew/29 20.00
102JY Rod Carew/71 10.00
102PS Rod Carew/50 15.00
103BA Joe Carter/50 6.00
103DY Joe Carter/77 8.00
103IN Joe Carter/25
103JN Joe Carter/29 15.00
103JY Joe Carter/94 6.00
103PS Joe Carter/25
104BA Mike Sweeney/100 4.00
104DY Mike Sweeney/69 6.00
104IN Mike Sweeney/25
104JN Mike Sweeney/29 15.00
104JY Mike Sweeney/101 4.00
104PS Mike Sweeney/50 6.00
105BA Nolan Ryan/25
105DY Nolan Ryan/65 40.00
105IN Nolan Ryan/25
105JN Nolan Ryan/30 50.00
105JY Nolan Ryan/70 40.00
105PS Nolan Ryan/50 40.00
106BA Orlando Cepeda/50 8.00
106DY Orlando Cepeda/58 8.00
106IN Orlando Cepeda/50 8.00
106JN Orlando Cepeda/30 15.00
106JY Orlando Cepeda/65 8.00
106PS Orlando Cepeda/50 8.00
107BA Magglio Ordonez/100 4.00
107IN Magglio Ordonez/25
107JN Magglio Ordonez/30 15.00
107JY Magglio Ordonez/100 4.00
107PS Magglio Ordonez/50 6.00
108BA Hoyt Wilhelm/50 8.00
108IN Hoyt Wilhelm/25
108JN Hoyt Wilhelm/31 15.00
108JY Hoyt Wilhelm/68 8.00
108PS Hoyt Wilhelm/50 8.00
109BA Mike Piazza/100 15.00
109DY Mike Piazza/62 20.00
109IN Mike Piazza/50 25.00
109JN Mike Piazza/31 30.00
109JY Mike Piazza/100 15.00
109PS Mike Piazza/50 20.00
110BA Greg Maddux/100 10.00
110DY Greg Maddux/66 15.00
110IN Greg Maddux/50 15.00
110JN Greg Maddux/31 30.00
110JY Greg Maddux/102 10.00
110PS Greg Maddux/50 15.00
111BA Mark Prior/100 10.00
111DY Mark Prior/7
111IN Mark Prior/50 15.00
111JN Mark Prior/22
111JY Mark Prior/102 10.00
111PS Mark Prior/50 15.00
112BA Torii Hunter/100 6.00
112DY Torii Hunter/61 8.00
112IN Torii Hunter/50 8.00
112JN Torii Hunter/48 10.00
112JY Torii Hunter/101 6.00
112PS Torii Hunter/50 8.00
113BA Steve Carlton/100 8.00
113DY Steve Carlton/46 15.00
113IN Steve Carlton/50 10.00
113JN Steve Carlton/32 15.00
113JY Steve Carlton/81 8.00
113PS Steve Carlton/50 10.00
114BA Jose Canseco/100 10.00
114DY Jose Canseco/68 10.00
114IN Jose Canseco/50 15.00
114JN Jose Canseco/33 15.00
114JY Jose Canseco/89 10.00
114PS Jose Canseco/50 15.00
115BA Nolan Ryan/50 30.00
115DY Nolan Ryan/72 30.00
115IN Nolan Ryan/50 30.00
115JN Nolan Ryan/34 40.00
115JY Nolan Ryan/90 30.00
115PS Nolan Ryan/50 30.00
116BA Nolan Ryan/50 30.00
116DY Nolan Ryan/65 30.00
116JN Nolan Ryan/34 40.00
116JY Nolan Ryan/84 30.00
116PS Nolan Ryan/50 30.00
117BA Ty Cobb/25
117IN Ty Cobb/25
117JY Ty Cobb/27
117PS Ty Cobb/10
118BA Kerry Wood/100 10.00
118IN Kerry Wood/25
118JN Kerry Wood/34 25.00
118JY Kerry Wood/101 10.00
118PS Kerry Wood/50 15.00
119BA Mike Mussina/50 10.00
119IN Mike Mussina/25
119JN Mike Mussina/35 25.00
119JY Mike Mussina/101 8.00
119PS Mike Mussina/50 15.00
120BA Yogi Berra/10
120DY Yogi Berra/13
120JN Yogi Berra/35 25.00
120JY Yogi Berra/47 25.00
120PS Yogi Berra/10
121BA Thurman Munson/25
121IN Thurman Munson/25
121JY Thurman Munson/79 25.00
121PS Thurman Munson/5
122BA Frank Thomas/100 8.00
122IN Frank Thomas/25
122JN Frank Thomas/35 15.00
122JY Frank Thomas/94 6.00
122PS Frank Thomas/50 8.00
123BA Rickey Henderson/50 15.00
123DY Rickey Henderson/68 10.00
123JN Rickey Henderson/35 20.00
123JY Rickey Henderson/80 10.00
123PS Rickey Henderson/50 15.00
124BA Mike Mussina/100 6.00
124DY Mike Mussina/54 10.00
124IN Mike Mussina/25
124JN Mike Mussina/35 20.00
124JY Mike Mussina/97 6.00
124PS Mike Mussina/50 10.00
125BA Gaylord Perry/100 6.00
125DY Gaylord Perry/77 6.00
125JN Gaylord Perry/36 10.00
125JY Gaylord Perry/82 6.00
125PS Gaylord Perry/50 8.00
126BA Nick Johnson/100 4.00
126JN Nick Johnson/36 6.00
126JY Nick Johnson/102 4.00
126PS Nick Johnson/50 8.00
127BA Curt Schilling/100 8.00
127DY Curt Schilling/98 8.00
127JN Curt Schilling/38 15.00
127JY Curt Schilling/102 8.00
127PS Curt Schilling/50 8.00
128BA Dave Parker/100 6.00
128IN Dave Parker/25
128JN Dave Parker/39 10.00
128JY Dave Parker/80 8.00
128PS Dave Parker/50 8.00
129BA Eddie Mathews/15
129DY Eddie Mathews/53 15.00
129IN Eddie Mathews/15
129JN Eddie Mathews/41 25.00
129JY Eddie Mathews/59 20.00
130BA Tom Seaver/10
130DY Tom Seaver/62 15.00
130JN Tom Seaver/41 20.00
130JY Tom Seaver/69 15.00
131BA Tom Seaver/10
131DY Tom Seaver/59 15.00
131JN Tom Seaver/41 25.00
131JY Tom Seaver/78 15.00
131PS Tom Seaver/22
132BA Jackie Robinson/10
132DY Jackie Robinson/32
132JN Jackie Robinson/42 80.00
132JY Jackie Robinson/52 60.00
133BA Reggie Jackson/100 10.00
133DY Reggie Jackson/65 15.00
133IN Reggie Jackson/50 15.00
133JN Reggie Jackson/44 20.00
133JY Reggie Jackson/80 10.00
133PS Reggie Jackson/50 15.00
134BA Willie McCovey/100 8.00
134DY Willie McCovey/58 10.00
134JN Willie McCovey/44 10.00
134JY Willie McCovey/77 8.00
134PS Willie McCovey/50 10.00
135BA Eric Davis/100 6.00
135DY Eric Davis/59 8.00
135JN Eddie Davis/44 10.00
135JY Eric Davis/89 6.00

135PS Eric Davis/50 8.00
136BA Adam Dunn/100 8.00
136DY Adam Dunn/59 10.00
136JN Adam Dunn/44 15.00
136JY Adam Dunn/102 8.00
136PS Adam Dunn/50 10.00
137BA Roy Oswalt/100 4.00
137DY Roy Oswalt/65 6.00
137IN Roy Oswalt/50 6.00
137JN Roy Oswalt/44 8.00
137JY Roy Oswalt/102 4.00
137PS Roy Oswalt/50 6.00
138BA Pedro J. Martinez/50 15.00
138DY Pedro J. Martinez/69 15.00
138JN Pedro J. Martinez/45 20.00
138JY Pedro J. Martinez/95 6.00
138PS Pedro J. Martinez/50 10.00
139BA Pedro J. Martinez/100 8.00
139IN Pedro J. Martinez/50 10.00
139JN Pedro J. Martinez/45 15.00
139JY Pedro J. Martinez/102 8.00
139PS Pedro J. Martinez/50 10.00
140BA Andy Pettitte/100 6.00
140JN Andy Pettitte/46 10.00
140JY Andy Pettitte/97 6.00
140PS Andy Pettitte/50 8.00
141BA Jack Morris/100 6.00
141IN Jack Morris/50 8.00
141JN Jack Morris/47 10.00
141JY Jack Morris/85 6.00
141PS Jack Morris/50 8.00
142BA Tom Glavine/100 6.00
142DY Tom Glavine/66 10.00
142JN Tom Glavine/47 15.00
142JY Tom Glavine/100 6.00
142PS Tom Glavine/50 10.00
143BA Randy Johnson/100 10.00
143DY Randy Johnson/77 15.00
143IN Randy Johnson/50 15.00
143JN Randy Johnson/51 15.00
143JY Randy Johnson/98 10.00
143PS Randy Johnson/50 15.00
144BA Bernie Williams/100 8.00
144IN Bernie Williams/50 10.00
144JN Bernie Williams/51 10.00
144JY Bernie Williams/100 8.00
144PS Bernie Williams/50 10.00
145BA Randy Johnson/50 15.00
145DY Randy Johnson/98 10.00
145IN Randy Johnson/50 15.00
145JN Randy Johnson/51 15.00
145JY Randy Johnson/102 15.00
145PS Randy Johnson/50 15.00
146BA Don Drysdale/15
146DY Don Drysdale/58 10.00
146JN Don Drysdale/53 10.00
146JY Don Drysdale/64 10.00
147BA Mark Buehrle/100 4.00
147JN Mark Buehrle/56 6.00
147JY Mark Buehrle/101 4.00
147PS Mark Buehrle/50 6.00
148BA Chan Ho Park/100 4.00
148DY Chan Ho Park/58 6.00
148JN Chan Ho Park/61 6.00
148JY Chan Ho Park/101 4.00
148PS Chan Ho Park/50 6.00
149BA Carlton Fisk/100 8.00
149IN Carlton Fisk/50 15.00
149JN Carlton Fisk/72 15.00
149JY Carlton Fisk/92 15.00
149PS Carlton Fisk/50 15.00
150BA Barry Zito/100 6.00
150DY Barry Zito/68 8.00
150JN Barry Zito/75 8.00
150JY Barry Zito/101 6.00
150PS Barry Zito/50 8.00

2003 LEAF LIMITED

NM/M

Complete Set (170):
Common Player (1-151): 1.50
Production 999
Common (152-170): 4.00
Production 399
Common Auto Memor. (171-200): 15.00
Production 99
Common Auto. (171-200): 8.00
Pack (4): 75.00
Box (4): 250.00

1 Derek Jeter 6.00
2 Eric Chavez 1.50
3 Alex Rodriguez 5.00
4 Miguel Tejada 1.50
5 Nomar Garciaparra 4.00
6 Jeff Bagwell 3.00
7 Jim Thome 2.00
8 Pat Burrell 1.50
9 Albert Pujols 5.00
10 Juan Gonzalez 3.00
11 Shawn Green 1.50
12 Craig Biggio 1.50
13 Chipper Jones 3.00
14 Hideo Nomo 2.00
15 Vernon Wells 1.50
16 Gary Sheffield 2.00
17 Barry Larkin 1.50
18 Josh Beckett 1.50
19 Edgar Martinez 1.50
20 Ivan Rodriguez 2.00
21 Jeff Kent 1.50
22 Roberto Alomar 1.50
23 Alfonso Soriano 3.00
24 Jim Thome 2.00
25 Juan Gonzalez 3.00
26 Carlos Beltran 2.00
27 Shawn Green 1.50
28 Tim Hudson 1.50
29 Deion Sanders 1.50
30 Rafael Palmeiro 2.00
31 Todd Helton 3.00
32 Lance Berkman 1.50
33 Mike Mussina 2.00
34 Kazuhisa Ishii 1.50
35 Bill Burrell 1.50
36 Miguel Tejada 1.50
37 Juan Gonzalez 2.00
38 Roberto Alomar 1.50
39 Roberto Alomar 1.50
40 Luis Gonzalez 1.50
41 Jorge Posada 1.50
42 Mark Mulder 1.50
43 Sammy Sosa 4.00
44 Mark Prior 3.00
45 Roger Clemens 4.00
46 Tom Glavine 1.50
47 Mark Teixeira 1.50
48 Manny Ramirez 2.00
49 Frank Thomas 2.00
50 Troy Glaus 3.00
51 Andruw Jones 3.00
52 Jason Giambi 2.00
53 Jim Thome 2.00
54 Barry Bonds 6.00
55 Rafael Palmeiro 2.00
56 Edgar Martinez 1.50
57 Vladimir Guerrero 3.00
58 Roberto Alomar 1.50
59 Mike Sweeney 1.50
60 Magglio Ordonez 1.50
61 Ken Griffey Jr. 4.00
62 Craig Biggio 1.50
63 Greg Maddux 4.00
64 Mike Piazza 4.00
65 Tom Glavine 1.50
66 Kerry Wood 2.00
67 Frank Thomas 3.00
68 Mike Mussina 2.00
69 Nick Johnson 1.50
70 Bernie Williams 1.50
71 Scott Rolen 2.00
72 Curt Schilling 2.00
73 Adam Dunn 2.00
74 Roy Oswalt 1.50
75 Pedro J. Martinez 3.00
76 Tom Glavine 1.50
77 Torii Hunter 1.50
78 Austin Kearns 1.50
79 Randy Johnson 3.00
80 Bernie Williams 1.50
81 Ichiro Suzuki 4.00
82 Kerry Wood 2.00
83 Kazuhisa Ishii 1.50
84 Randy Johnson 3.00
85 Nick Johnson 1.50
86 Josh Beckett 1.50
87 Curt Schilling 2.00
88 Mike Mussina 2.00
89 Pedro J. Martinez 3.00
90 Barry Zito 1.50
91 Jim Edmonds 1.50
92 Rickey Henderson 3.00
93 Rickey Henderson 3.00
94 Rickey Henderson 3.00
95 Rickey Henderson 3.00
96 Rickey Henderson 3.00
97 Randy Johnson 3.00
98 Mark Grace 1.50
99 Pedro J. Martinez 3.00
100 Hee Seop Choi 1.50
101 Ivan Rodriguez 2.00
102 Jeff Kent 1.50
103 Hideo Nomo 3.00
104 Hideo Nomo 3.00
105 Mike Piazza 4.00
106 Tom Glavine 1.50
107 Roberto Alomar 1.50
108 Roger Clemens 5.00
109 Jason Giambi 2.00
110 Jim Thome 2.00
111 Alex Rodriguez 5.00
112 Juan Gonzalez 2.00
113 Torii Hunter 1.50
114 Roy Oswalt 1.50
115 Curt Schilling 2.00
116 Magglio Ordonez 1.50
117 Rafael Palmeiro 2.00
118 Andruw Jones 3.00
119 Manny Ramirez 3.00
120 Mark Teixeira 1.50
121 Mark Mulder 1.50
122 Garret Anderson 1.50
123 Tim Hudson 1.50
124 Todd Helton 3.00
125 Troy Glaus 3.00
126 Derek Jeter 6.00
127 Barry Bonds 6.00
128 Greg Maddux 4.00
129 Roger Clemens 5.00
130 Nomar Garciaparra 4.00
131 Mike Piazza 4.00
132 Alex Rodriguez 5.00
133 Ichiro Suzuki 4.00
134 Randy Johnson 3.00
135 Sammy Sosa 4.00
136 Ken Griffey Jr. 4.00
137 Alfonso Soriano 3.00
138 Jason Giambi 2.00
139 Albert Pujols 5.00
140 Chipper Jones 3.00
141 Adam Dunn 2.00
142 Pedro J. Martinez 3.00
143 Vladimir Guerrero 3.00
144 Mark Prior 3.00
145 Barry Zito 1.50
146 Jeff Bagwell 3.00
147 Lance Berkman 1.50
148 Shawn Green 1.50
149 Jason Giambi 2.00
150 Randy Johnson 3.00
151 Alex Rodriguez 5.00
152 Babe Ruth 10.00
153 Ty Cobb 6.00
154 Jackie Robinson 6.00
155 Lou Gehrig 8.00
156 Thurman Munson 6.00
157 Roberto Clemente 8.00
158 Nolan Ryan 10.00
159 Nolan Ryan 10.00
160 Nolan Ryan 10.00
161 Cal Ripken Jr. 10.00
162 Don Mattingly 8.00
163 Stan Musial 6.00
164 Tony Gwynn 3.00
165 Yogi Berra 3.00
166 Johnny Bench 5.00
167 Mike Schmidt 8.00
168 George Brett 8.00
169 Ryne Sandberg 4.00
170 Ernie Banks 5.00
171 J. Bonderman/auto/jsy 75.00
172 *Jose Contreras/auto* 40.00
173 *Chien-Ming Wang/auto* 120.00
174 *Hideki Matsui/base* 40.00
175 *Hong-Chih Kuo/auto/bat* 30.00
176 *Brandon Webb/auto/bat* 40.00
177 Richard Fischer/auto 8.00
178 Robby Hammock/auto/bat 20.00
179 *Todd Wellemeyer/auto/49* 15.00
180 *Prentice Redman/auto/bat* 10.00
181 *Nook Logan/auto* 20.00
182 *Craig Brazell/auto* 15.00
183 *Tim Olson/auto/bat* 15.00
184 *Matt Kata/auto/bat* 20.00
185 A. Machado/auto 8.00
186 *Michael Hessman/auto* 10.00
187 *Oscar Villarreal/auto* 8.00
188 *Guillermo Quiroz/auto/bat* 20.00
189 *Michel Hernandez/auto* 10.00
190 *Clint Barmes/auto/bat* 40.00
191 *Pete LaForest/auto/bat* 20.00
192 *Adam Loewen/auto* 25.00
193 *Terrmel Sledge/auto/bat* 15.00
194 *Lew Ford/auto/bat* 40.00
195 *Todd Wellemeyer/auto/49* 15.00
196 *Clint Barmes/auto/bat* 40.00
197 J. Bonderman/auto/jsy 50.00
198 *Brandon Webb/auto/jsy* 40.00
199 *Hideki Matsui/base* 30.00
200 *Jose Contreras/auto* 40.00

Gold Spotlight

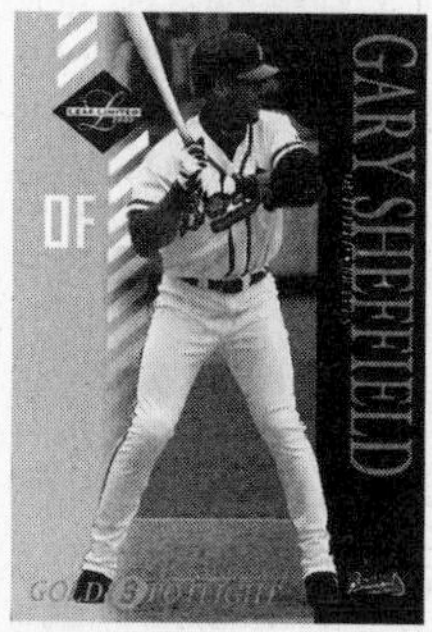

Golds (1-151): 2-4X
Golds (152-170): 1.5-3X
Production 50
Golds (171-200): No Pricing
Production 10 to 25

Silver Spotlight

Silvers (1-170): 1-2X
Production 100
Silver Auto Memor. (171-200): 1X
Silver Memor. (171-200): 1X
Silver Auto: 1X
Production 29 to 50

Jersey Numbers

NM/M

Common Player:
Production 5-100
Some not priced due to scarcity

1 Rod Carew/50 20.00
2 Nolan Ryan/50 40.00
3 Reggie Jackson/50 20.00
4 Brooks Robinson/50 25.00
5 Frank Robinson/50 15.00
6 Cal Ripken Jr./100 40.00
7 Carlton Fisk/50 15.00
8 Roger Clemens/100 15.00
9 Carlton Fisk/5
10 Lou Boudreau/50 10.00
11 Bob Feller/25 30.00
12 Al Kaline/10
13 Alan Trammell/50 10.00
14 Harmon Killebrew/50 25.00
15 Rod Carew/50 20.00
16 Kirby Puckett/50 20.00
17 Babe Ruth/5
18 Lou Gehrig/5
19 Yogi Berra/50 30.00
20 Thurman Munson/50 30.00
21 Don Mattingly/100 25.00
22 Roger Maris/10
23 Rickey Henderson/5
24 Reggie Jackson/5
25 Alex Rodriguez/100 10.00
26 Randy Johnson/50 10.00
27 Nolan Ryan/100 30.00
28 Dale Murphy/50 20.00
29 Warren Spahn/50 20.00
30 Eddie Mathews/50 25.00
31 Ernie Banks/5
32 Ryne Sandberg/100 30.00
33 Johnny Bench/50 30.00
34 Joe Morgan/50 10.00
35 Randy Johnson/50 10.00

36 Nolan Ryan/100 30.00
37 Pee Wee Reese/50 15.00
38 Duke Snider/50 25.00
39 Jackie Robinson/25 65.00
40 Robin Yount/50 30.00
41 Paul Molitor/50 20.00
42 Pedro Martinez/50 10.00
43 Randy Johnson/50 10.00
44 Tom Seaver/25 25.00
45 Gary Carter/50 10.00
46 Mike Schmidt/50 30.00
47 Steve Carlton/50 10.00
48 Willie Stargell/50 20.00
50 Ozzie Smith/50 35.00
51 Stan Musial/100 30.00
52 Enos Slaughter/50 10.00
53 Orlando Cepeda/50 10.00
54 Willie McCovey/50 15.00
57 Harmon Killebrew, Rod Carew/25 50.00
58 Harmon Killebrew, Kirby Puckett/25 50.00
68 Thurman Munson, Yogi Berra/25 50.00
69 Don Mattingly, Yogi Berra/25 60.00
71 Dale Murphy, Warren Spahn/25 50.00
72 Dale Murphy, Eddie Mathews/25 45.00
73 Eddie Mathews, Warren Spahn/25 60.00
74 Joe Morgan, Johnny Bench/25 40.00
75 Duke Snider, Pee Wee Reese/25 40.00
78 Paul Molitor, Robin Yount/25 75.00
81 Ozzie Smith, Stan Musial/25 60.00
82 Enos Slaughter, Stan Musial/25 60.00
83 Orlando Cepeda, Willie McCovey/25 40.00
84 Nolan Ryan, Reggie Jackson/25 60.00
90 Alex Rodriguez, Randy Johnson/25 25.00
91 Pedro J. Martinez, Randy Johnson/25 35.00
94 Reggie Jackson/25 35.00
95 Nolan Ryan/25 60.00
96 Nolan Ryan/25 60.00
97 Nolan Ryan/25 60.00
98 Nolan Ryan/25 60.00
99 Cal Ripken Jr., Rafael Palmeiro/25 90.00
100 Dale Murphy, Deion Sanders/25 50.00

Jersey Numbers Retired

NM/M

Many not priced due to scarcity
1 Rod Carew/29 30.00
2 Nolan Ryan/30 50.00
5 Frank Robinson/20 20.00
7 Carlton Fisk/27 30.00
9 Carlton Fisk/27 15.00
16 Kirby Puckett/34 35.00
21 Don Mattingly/23 50.00
27 Nolan Ryan/34 50.00
30 Eddie Mathews/41 20.00
36 Nolan Ryan/34 50.00
39 Jackie Robinson/42 50.00
44 Tom Seaver/41 20.00
46 Mike Schmidt/20 50.00
47 Steve Carlton/32 15.00
49 Roberto Clemente/21 100.00
53 Orlando Cepeda/30 15.00
54 Willie McCovey/44 10.00

Leather

NM/M

Common Player:
Production 10-25
Golds: No Pricing
Production 5-10
Leather & Lace: No Pricing
Production 10
Leather & Lace Gold: No Pricing
Production 5
1 Alex Rodriguez/25 40.00
2 Chipper Jones/25 30.00
3 Jimmie Foxx/25 65.00
4 Kirby Puckett/25 25.00
5 Mike Schmidt/25 65.00
6 Roger Clemens/25 45.00
7 Steve Carlton/10
8 Tony Gwynn/25 40.00
9 Nolan Ryan/10
10 Vladimir Guerrero/25 25.00
11 Adam Dunn/25 20.00
12 Andruw Jones/25 25.00
13 Curt Schilling/25 20.00
14 Randy Johnson/25 25.00
15 Mark Prior/25 65.00

Lineups - Jerseys

NM/M

Production 5-50
1 Paul Molitor, Robin Yount/50 35.00
2 Bernie Williams, Don Mattingly/50 40.00
3 Hee Seop Choi, Sammy Sosa/50 30.00
4 Derek Jeter, Hideki Matsui/50/base 30.00
5 Andre Dawson, Ryne Sandberg/50 35.00
6 Bo Jackson, George Brett/50 50.00
7 Jose Canseco, Reggie Jackson/50 25.00
8 Mark Grace, Ryne Sandberg/50 35.00
9 Jose Canseco, Rickey Henderson/50 25.00
10 Hideo Nomo, Mike Piazza/50 25.00

Lineups - Bats

NM/M

Common Player:
Production 25-50
1 Paul Molitor, Robin Yount/50 35.00
2 Bernie Williams, Don Mattingly/50 40.00
4 Derek Jeter, Hideki Matsui/25 60.00
5 Andre Dawson, Ryne Sandberg/50 40.00
6 Bo Jackson, George Brett/50 40.00
7 Jose Canseco, Reggie Jackson/50 25.00
8 Mark Grace, Ryne Sandberg/50 40.00
9 Jose Canseco, Rickey Henderson/50 30.00
10 Hideo Nomo, Mike Piazza/50 30.00

Lineups - Buttons

No Pricing
Production one set

Lumberjacks

NM/M

Some not priced due to scarcity
Production 1-25
Black: No Pricing
Production 1-5
Silver: No Pricing
Production 1-10
1 Babe Ruth/25 200.00
2 Lou Gehrig/25 150.00
3 Roberto Clemente/25 120.00
4 Stan Musial/25 40.00
5 Rogers Hornsby/25 50.00
6 Don Mattingly/25 50.00
7 Rickey Henderson/25 20.00
8 Cal Ripken Jr./25 75.00
9 Yogi Berra/25 30.00
10 Reggie Jackson/25 35.00
11 George Brett/25 60.00
12 Mel Ott/25 40.00
13 Roger Maris/25 60.00
14 Ryne Sandberg/25 50.00
15 Eddie Mathews/15
16 Richie Ashburn/25 40.00
17 Mike Schmidt/25 40.00
18 Tony Gwynn/25 25.00
19 Ty Cobb/25 110.00
20 Thurman Munson/25 35.00
21 Jimmie Foxx/25 60.00
22 Duke Snider/25 25.00
23 Ernie Banks/1
24 Alex Rodriguez/25 30.00
25 Nomar Garciaparra/25 30.00
26 Hideki Matsui/25/base 50.00
27 Ichiro Suzuki/25/base 35.00
28 Barry Bonds/25/base 35.00
29 Mike Piazza/25 30.00
30 Alfonso Soriano/25 25.00
31 Al Kaline/25 30.00
32 Harmon Killebrew/5
33 Dale Murphy/25 30.00
34 Orlando Cepeda/25 30.00
35 Willie McCovey/25 30.00
36 Willie Stargell/5
37 Brooks Robinson/25 30.00

Lumberjacks Combos

NM/M

Production 1-25
Black: No Pricing
Production 1-5
Silver: No Pricing
Production 1-10
38 Hideki Matsui, Ichiro Suzuki/25/base 80.00
40 Don Mattingly, Lou Gehrig/25 240.00
41 Thurman Munson, Yogi Berra/25 50.00
42 Mike Schmidt, Richie Ashburn/25 60.00
43 Rogers Hornsby, Stan Musial/25 80.00
44 Don Mattingly, Roger Maris/25 100.00

Lumberjacks - Jerseys/Bats

NM/M

Production 1-25
Some not priced due to scarcity
Black: No Pricing
Production 1-5
Silver: No Pricing
Production 1-10
4 Stan Musial/25 60.00
6 Don Mattingly/25 75.00
8 Cal Ripken Jr./25 140.00
9 Yogi Berra/25 30.00
11 George Brett/25 80.00
13 Roger Maris/25 100.00
14 Ryne Sandberg/25 65.00
15 Eddie Mathews/25 40.00
17 Mike Schmidt/25 65.00
18 Tony Gwynn/25 40.00
20 Thurman Munson/25 40.00
24 Alex Rodriguez/25 40.00
25 Nomar Garciaparra/25 40.00
26 Hideki Matsui/25/base/ball 65.00
27 Ichiro Suzuki/25/base/ball 60.00
28 Barry Bonds/25/base/ball 60.00
29 Mike Piazza/25 40.00
30 Alfonso Soriano/25 25.00
33 Dale Murphy/25 40.00
35 Willie McCovey/25 35.00
36 Willie Stargell/25 30.00
37 Brooks Robinson/25 30.00

Lumberjacks - Jerseys

NM/M

Production 1-25
Black: No Pricing
Production 1-5
Silver: No Pricing
Production 1-10
4 Stan Musial/25 40.00
6 Don Mattingly/25 50.00
8 Cal Ripken Jr./25 80.00
9 Yogi Berra/25 25.00
11 George Brett/25 60.00
12 Mel Ott/25 40.00
14 Ryne Sandberg/25 50.00
15 Eddie Mathews/25 25.00
17 Mike Schmidt/25 50.00
18 Tony Gwynn/25 25.00
20 Thurman Munson/25 25.00
22 Duke Snider/25 20.00
24 Alex Rodriguez/25 30.00
25 Nomar Garciaparra/25 30.00
26 Hideki Matsui/25/ball 50.00
27 Ichiro Suzuki/25/ball 30.00
28 Barry Bonds/25/ball 40.00
29 Mike Piazza/25 25.00
30 Alfonso Soriano/25 25.00
32 Harmon Killebrew/25 25.00
33 Dale Murphy/25 25.00
34 Orlando Cepeda/25 15.00
35 Willie McCovey/25 20.00
36 Willie Stargell/25 30.00
37 Brooks Robinson/25 20.00

Lumberjacks Combos - Jerseys

NM/M

Production 1-25
Some not priced due to scarcity
Black: No Pricing
Production 1-5
Silver: No Pricing
Production 1-10
38 Hideki Matsui, Ichiro Suzuki/25/ball 100.00
39 Ernie Banks, Ryne Sandberg/5
40 Don Mattingly, Lou Gehrig/15
41 Thurman Munson, Yogi Berra/25 60.00
44 Don Mattingly, Roger Maris/5
45 Babe Ruth, Lou Gehrig/5

Lumberjacks Combos - Jerseys/Bats

NM/M

Production 1-25
Some not priced due to scarcity
Black: No Pricing
Production 1-5
Silver: No Pricing
Production 1-10
38 Hideki Matsui, Ichiro Suzuki/25/ball 100.00
41 Thurman Munson, Yogi Berra/25 50.00
42 Mike Schmidt, Richie Ashburn/25 60.00

Lumberjacks - Barrel

No pricing due to scarcity

Material Monikers Jerseys

NM/M

Common Player:
2 Eric Chavez/25 25.00
4 Miguel Tejada/25 35.00
12 Craig Biggio/25 35.00
15 Vernon Wells/25 25.00
19 Edgar Martinez/25 40.00
26 Carlos Beltran/25 50.00
28 Tim Hudson/25 25.00
44 Mark Prior/25 65.00
47 Mark Teixeira/25 30.00
69 Nick Johnson/25 20.00
73 Adam Dunn/25 40.00
74 Roy Oswalt/25 25.00
77 Torii Hunter/25 25.00
85 Nick Johnson/25 20.00
113 Torii Hunter/25 25.00
114 Roy Oswalt/25 25.00
120 Mark Teixeira/25 40.00

Material Monikers Jersey Numbers

NM/M

Production 1-25
Many not priced due to scarcity
2 Eric Chavez/25 25.00
4 Miguel Tejada/25 30.00
12 Craig Biggio/25 35.00
15 Vernon Wells/25 20.00
19 Edgar Martinez/25 30.00
26 Carlos Beltran/25 50.00
28 Tim Hudson/25 25.00
44 Mark Prior/25 65.00
47 Mark Teixeira/25 40.00
69 Nick Johnson/25 15.00
73 Adam Dunn/25 40.00
74 Roy Oswalt/25 20.00
77 Torii Hunter/25 25.00
85 Nick Johnson/25 15.00
113 Torii Hunter/25 25.00
114 Roy Oswalt/25 20.00
120 Mark Teixeira/25 40.00

Material Monikers Bats

NM/M

Production 1-25
No pricing for many, due to scarcity
2 Eric Chavez/25 35.00
12 Craig Biggio/25 40.00
15 Vernon Wells/25 30.00
19 Edgar Martinez/25 50.00
26 Carlos Beltran/25 40.00

28 Tim Hudson/25 40.00
44 Mark Prior/25 80.00
47 Mark Teixeira/25 40.00
69 Nick Johnson/25 25.00
73 Adam Dunn/25 40.00
74 Roy Oswalt/25 30.00
77 Torii Hunter/25 30.00
85 Nick Johnson/25 25.00
113 Torii Hunter/25 30.00
114 Roy Oswalt/25 30.00
120 Mark Teixeira/25 40.00

Material Monikers Jersey Position

NM/M
Production 1-25
Many not priced due to scarcity
2 Eric Chavez/25 25.00
4 Miguel Tejada/25 30.00
12 Craig Biggio/25 35.00
15 Vernon Wells/25 20.00
19 Edgar Martinez/25 40.00
26 Carlos Beltran/25 50.00
28 Tim Hudson/25 25.00
29 Deion Sanders/25 50.00
44 Mark Prior/25 65.00
47 Mark Teixeira/25 40.00
69 Nick Johnson/25 20.00
73 Adam Dunn/25 40.00
74 Roy Oswalt/25 25.00
77 Torii Hunter/25 25.00
85 Nick Johnson/25 20.00
113 Torii Hunter/25 25.00
114 Roy Oswalt/25 25.00
120 Mark Teixeira/25 40.00

Player Threads

NM/M
Production 5-50
Some not priced due to scarcity
Primes: No Pricing
Production 5-10
1 Roger Clemens/50 15.00
2 Alex Rodriguez/50 15.00
3 Pedro Martinez/50 10.00
4 Randy Johnson/50 10.00
5 Curt Schilling/50 8.00
7 Nolan Ryan/50 35.00
8 Hideo Nomo/50 12.00
9 Mike Piazza/50 15.00
11 Rickey Henderson/50 15.00
12 Ivan Rodriguez/50 10.00
13 Gary Sheffield/50 8.00
14 Jeff Kent/50 8.00
15 Roberto Alomar/50 10.00
16 Rafael Palmeiro/50 10.00
17 Juan Gonzalez/50 8.00
18 Shawn Green/50 8.00
19 Jason Giambi/50 8.00
20 Jim Thome/50 10.00
21 Scott Rolen/50 12.00
22 Mike Mussina/50 10.00
23 Tom Glavine/50 8.00
24 Sammy Sosa/50 15.00

Player Threads Double

NM/M
Production 5-50
Some not priced due to scarcity
Double Primes: No Pricing
Production 5-10
1 Roger Clemens/50 25.00
2 Alex Rodriguez/50 25.00
3 Pedro Martinez/50 20.00
4 Randy Johnson/50 15.00
5 Curt Schilling/50 10.00
7 Nolan Ryan/50 50.00
8 Hideo Nomo/50 20.00
9 Mike Piazza/50 25.00
11 Rickey Henderson/50 20.00
12 Ivan Rodriguez/50 15.00
13 Gary Sheffield/50 10.00
14 Jeff Kent/50 10.00
15 Roberto Alomar/50 15.00
16 Rafael Palmeiro/50 15.00
17 Juan Gonzalez/50 15.00
18 Shawn Green/50 10.00
19 Jason Giambi/50 15.00
20 Jim Thome/50 15.00
21 Scott Rolen/50 20.00
22 Mike Mussina/50 15.00
23 Tom Glavine/50 10.00
24 Sammy Sosa/50 25.00

Player Threads Triple

NM/M
Production 50
Some not priced due to scarcity
Triple Primes: No Pricing
Production 5-10
4 Randy Johnson/50 20.00
7 Nolan Ryan/50 75.00
8 Hideo Nomo/50 60.00
11 Rickey Henderson/50 30.00
13 Gary Sheffield/50 15.00
14 Jeff Kent/50 15.00
15 Roberto Alomar/50 25.00

Team Threads

NM/M
Production 10-50
Some not priced due to scarcity
Primes: No Pricing
Production 5-10
26 Alex Rodriguez, Nolan Ryan/50 50.00
27 Hideo Nomo, Mike Piazza/50 20.00
28 Cal Ripken Jr., Mike Mussina/50 50.00
29 Hideo Nomo, Kazuhisa Ishii/50 15.00
30 Nolan Ryan, Randy Johnson/50 40.00

Team Trademarks Threads Jersey Number

NM/M
Some not priced due to scarcity
Primes: 1-1.5X
Production 1-25
Some not priced due to scarcity
3 Jim Palmer/22 20.00
12 Eric Davis/44 8.00
15 Jack Morris/47 8.00
17 Deion Sanders/24 25.00
19 Orlando Cepeda/30 10.00
23 Rod Carew/29 20.00
24 Will Clark/22 50.00
25 Willie McCovey/44 10.00
27 Nolan Ryan/34 50.00
31 Rod Carew/29 20.00
32 Nolan Ryan/34 50.00
34 Nolan Ryan/30 50.00
37 Greg Maddux/31 30.00

Team Trademarks Autographs

NM/M
Some not priced due to scarcity
1 Alan Trammell/25 40.00
3 Jim Palmer/25 30.00
5 Gary Carter/25 40.00
6 Andre Dawson/25 30.00
8 Dale Murphy/25 50.00
10 Bobby Doerr/25 35.00
11 Brooks Robinson/25 50.00
12 Eric Davis/25 35.00
13 Fred Lynn/25 30.00
15 Jack Morris/25 25.00
16 Al Kaline/25 60.00
17 Deion Sanders/25 50.00
18 Luis Aparicio/25 35.00
20 Phil Rizzuto/25 40.00
24 Will Clark/25 70.00

Team Trademarks Jersey Autograph

NM/M
Some not priced due to scarcity
12 Eric Davis/44 30.00
15 Jack Morris/47 25.00
23 Rod Carew/29 50.00
25 Willie McCovey/44 25.00
27 Nolan Ryan/34 140.00
31 Rod Carew/29 50.00
32 Nolan Ryan/34 140.00
34 Nolan Ryan/30 140.00
37 Greg Maddux/31 150.00

Threads

NM/M
Common Player: 8.00
Varying quantities produced
1 Derek Jeter/base/50 20.00
2 Eric Chavez/25 10.00
3 Alex Rodriguez/100 15.00
4 Miguel Tejada/50 8.00
5 Nomar Garciaparra/100 15.00
6 Jeff Bagwell/50 10.00
7 Jim Thome/50 10.00
8 Pat Burrell/50 10.00
9 Albert Pujols/100 20.00
10 Juan Gonzalez/25 20.00
11 Shawn Green/50 10.00
12 Craig Biggio/25 10.00
13 Chipper Jones/50 20.00
14 Hideo Nomo/100 12.00
15 Vernon Wells/25 10.00
16 Gary Sheffield/25 10.00
17 Barry Larkin/25 15.00
18 Josh Beckett/25 15.00
19 Edgar Martinez/25 15.00
20 Ivan Rodriguez/25 20.00
21 Jeff Kent/25 10.00
22 Roberto Alomar/25 15.00
23 Alfonso Soriano/100 8.00
24 Jim Thome/50 10.00
25 Juan Gonzalez/25 10.00
26 Carlos Beltran/25 20.00
27 Shawn Green/50 8.00
28 Tim Hudson/25 10.00
29 Deion Sanders/25 20.00
30 Rafael Palmeiro/25 20.00
31 Todd Helton/50 10.00
32 Lance Berkman/25 10.00
33 Mike Mussina/50 10.00
34 Kazuhisa Ishii/50 8.00
35 Pat Burrell/25 10.00
36 Miguel Tejada/50 8.00
37 Juan Gonzalez/25 10.00
38 Roberto Alomar/25 15.00
39 Roberto Alomar/25 15.00
40 Luis Gonzalez/25 10.00
41 Jorge Posada/50 15.00
42 Mark Mulder/25 10.00
43 Sammy Sosa/100 15.00
44 Mark Prior/50 20.00
45 Roger Clemens/100 10.00
46 Tom Glavine/25 15.00
47 Mark Teixeira/25 10.00
48 Manny Ramirez/50 12.00
49 Frank Thomas/25 15.00
50 Troy Glaus/50 8.00
51 Andruw Jones/50 8.00
52 Jason Giambi/100 8.00
53 Jim Thome/50 10.00
54 Barry Bonds/50/base 25.00
55 Rafael Palmeiro/25 15.00
56 Edgar Martinez/25 10.00
57 Vladimir Guerrero/50 10.00
58 Roberto Alomar/25 15.00
59 Mike Sweeney/25 10.00
60 Maggio Ordonez/25 10.00
62 Craig Biggio/25 10.00
63 Greg Maddux/100 10.00
64 Mike Piazza/100 10.00
65 Tom Glavine/25 15.00
66 Kerry Wood/25 20.00
67 Frank Thomas/25 20.00
68 Mike Mussina/50 10.00
69 Nick Johnson/25 8.00
70 Bernie Williams/50 10.00
71 Scott Rolen/25 20.00
72 Curt Schilling/25 15.00
73 Adam Dunn/50 10.00
74 Roy Oswalt/25 10.00
75 Pedro Martinez/25 20.00
76 Tom Glavine/25 15.00
77 Torii Hunter/25 10.00
78 Austin Kearns/25 10.00
79 Randy Johnson/100 8.00
80 Bernie Williams/50 10.00
81 Ichiro Suzuki/50 25.00
82 Kerry Wood/25 20.00
83 Kazuhisa Ishii/50 8.00
84 Randy Johnson/50 8.00
85 Nick Johnson/25 8.00
86 Josh Beckett/25 10.00
87 Curt Schilling/25 15.00
88 Mike Mussina/50 10.00
89 Pedro Martinez/25 15.00
90 Barry Zito/75 8.00
91 Jim Edmonds/100 6.00
92 Rickey Henderson/100 8.00
93 Rickey Henderson/50 12.00
94 Rickey Henderson/50 12.00
95 Rickey Henderson/50 12.00
96 Rickey Henderson/50 12.00
97 Randy Johnson/50 8.00
98 Mark Grace/50 10.00
99 Pedro Martinez/25 15.00
100 Hee Seop Choi/25 8.00
101 Ivan Rodriguez/25 15.00
102 Jeff Kent/25 10.00
103 Hideo Nomo/5
104 Hideo Nomo/50 10.00
105 Mike Piazza/100 10.00
106 Tom Glavine/25 15.00
107 Roberto Alomar/25 15.00
108 Roger Clemens/100 10.00
109 Jason Giambi/25 10.00
110 Jim Thome/25 15.00
111 Alex Rodriguez/100 10.00
112 Juan Gonzalez/25 10.00
113 Torii Hunter/25 10.00
114 Roy Oswalt/25 10.00
115 Curt Schilling/25 15.00
116 Magglio Ordonez/25 10.00
117 Rafael Palmeiro/25 15.00
118 Andruw Jones/50 8.00
119 Manny Ramirez/50 12.00
120 Mark Teixeira/25 10.00
121 Mark Mulder/25 10.00
123 Tim Hudson/25 10.00
124 Todd Helton/50 10.00
125 Troy Glaus/50 6.00
126 Derek Jeter/base/50 20.00
127 Barry Bonds/base/50 25.00
128 Greg Maddux/100 10.00
129 Roger Clemens/100 10.00
130 Nomar Garciaparra/100 10.00
131 Mike Piazza/100 10.00
132 Alex Rodriguez/100 10.00
133 Ichiro Suzuki/base/50 25.00
134 Randy Johnson/100 8.00
135 Sammy Sosa/100 15.00
137 Alfonso Soriano/100 8.00
138 Jason Giambi/100 6.00
139 Albert Pujols/100 20.00
140 Chipper Jones/25 20.00
141 Adam Dunn/50 8.00
142 Pedro Martinez/50 10.00
143 Vladimir Guerrero/50 10.00
144 Mark Prior/50 20.00
145 Barry Zito/50 8.00
146 Jeff Bagwell/50 12.00
147 Lance Berkman/socks/25 10.00
148 Shawn Green/25 10.00
149 Jason Giambi/25 10.00
150 Randy Johnson/25 20.00
151 Alex Rodriguez/100 10.00
152 Babe Ruth/5
153 Ty Cobb/100 100.00
154 Jackie Robinson/50 50.00
155 Lou Gehrig/5
156 Thurman Munson/100 15.00
157 Roberto Clemente/10
158 Nolan Ryan/100 30.00
159 Nolan Ryan/100 30.00
160 Nolan Ryan/100 30.00
161 Cal Ripken Jr./100 60.00
162 Don Mattingly/100 25.00
163 Stan Musial/100 25.00
164 Tony Gwynn/100 12.00
165 Yogi Berra/100 12.00
166 Johnny Bench/100 12.00
167 Mike Schmidt/100 25.00
168 George Brett/100 30.00
169 Ryne Sandberg/100 25.00
170 Ernie Banks/50 30.00

Threads Double

NM/M
Common Player:
Production 5 to 25
Some not priced due to scarcity
Primes: No Pricing
Production 1 to 10
3 Alex Rodriguez/25 40.00
4 Miguel Tejada/25 25.00
9 Albert Pujols/15
10 Juan Gonzalez/25 20.00
12 Craig Biggio/25 25.00
14 Hideo Nomo/25 40.00
15 Vernon Wells/25 15.00
26 Carlos Beltran/25 25.00
28 Tim Hudson/25 20.00
31 Todd Helton/25 25.00
32 Lance Berkman/25 15.00
34 Kazuhisa Ishii/25 20.00
37 Juan Gonzalez/25 20.00
43 Sammy Sosa/25 50.00
44 Mark Prior/25 30.00
47 Mark Teixeira/10
51 Andruw Jones/25 20.00
54 Barry Bonds/25 60.00

55 Rafael Palmeiro/25 30.00
60 Magglio Ordonez/25 20.00
66 Kerry Wood/5
73 Adam Dunn/25 20.00
75 Pedro Martinez/25 30.00
78 Austin Kearns/25 20.00
81 Ichiro Suzuki/25 60.00
90 Barry Zito/25 20.00
94 Rickey Henderson/25 25.00
101 Ivan Rodriguez/25 25.00
109 Jason Giambi/25 25.00
116 Magglio Ordonez/25 20.00
117 Rafael Palmeiro/25 30.00
118 Andruw Jones/25 20.00
120 Mark Teixeira/25 20.00
123 Tim Hudson/25 20.00
124 Todd Helton/25 25.00
127 Barry Bonds/25 50.00
132 Alex Rodriguez/25 40.00
133 Ichiro Suzuki/25 60.00
135 Sammy Sosa/25 50.00
141 Adam Dunn/25 30.00
142 Pedro Martinez/25 35.00
144 Mark Prior/25 60.00
145 Barry Zito/25 20.00
146 Jeff Bagwell/25 30.00
147 Lance Berkman/25 15.00
149 Jason Giambi/25 20.00
152 Babe Ruth/5
155 Lou Gehrig/5
157 Roberto Clemente/5
158 Nolan Ryan/25 80.00
162 Don Mattingly/25 65.00
164 Tony Gwynn/25 40.00
165 Mike Schmidt/25 65.00
168 George Brett/25 75.00
169 Ryne Sandberg/25 65.00

Threads Position

NM/M

Common (2-151): 8.00
#'s 2-151
Production 25
#'s 152-170
Production 5-25
Primes: 1-1.5X
Production 25 for #'s 2-151
2 Eric Chavez 8.00
3 Alex Rodriguez 25.00
4 Miguel Tejada 10.00
5 Nomar Garciaparra 30.00
6 Jeff Bagwell 15.00
7 Jim Thome 15.00
8 Pat Burrell 10.00
9 Albert Pujols 35.00
10 Juan Gonzalez 10.00
11 Shawn Green 10.00
12 Craig Biggio 8.00
13 Chipper Jones 25.00
14 Hideo Nomo 30.00
15 Vernon Wells 8.00
16 Gary Sheffield 10.00
17 Barry Larkin 10.00
18 Josh Beckett 15.00
19 Edgar Martinez 15.00
20 Ivan Rodriguez 15.00
21 Jeff Kent 8.00
22 Roberto Alomar 15.00
23 Alfonso Soriano 20.00
25 Juan Gonzalez 15.00
26 Carlos Beltran 8.00
27 Shawn Green 10.00
28 Tim Hudson 10.00
29 Deion Sanders 30.00
30 Rafael Palmeiro 15.00
31 Todd Helton 15.00
32 Lance Berkman 10.00
33 Mike Mussina 15.00
34 Kazuhisa Ishii 10.00
35 Pat Burrell 10.00
36 Miguel Tejada 10.00
37 Juan Gonzalez 15.00
38 Roberto Alomar 15.00
39 Roberto Alomar 15.00
40 Luis Gonzalez 10.00
41 Jorge Posada 15.00
42 Mark Mulder 10.00
43 Sammy Sosa 40.00
44 Mark Prior 40.00
45 Roger Clemens 40.00
46 Tom Glavine 15.00
47 Mark Teixeira 10.00
48 Manny Ramirez 15.00
49 Frank Thomas 15.00
50 Troy Glaus 10.00
51 Andruw Jones 15.00
52 Jason Giambi 15.00
53 Jim Thome 15.00
55 Rafael Palmeiro 15.00
56 Edgar Martinez 15.00
57 Vladimir Guerrero 15.00
58 Roberto Alomar 15.00
60 Magglio Ordonez 10.00
62 Craig Biggio 10.00
63 Greg Maddux 30.00
64 Mike Piazza 25.00
65 Tom Glavine 15.00
66 Kerry Wood 15.00
67 Frank Thomas 15.00
68 Mike Mussina 15.00
69 Nick Johnson 10.00
70 Bernie Williams 15.00
71 Scott Rolen 15.00
72 Curt Schilling 15.00
73 Adam Dunn 15.00
74 Roy Oswalt 8.00
75 Pedro J. Martinez 15.00
76 Tom Glavine 15.00
77 Torii Hunter 15.00
78 Austin Kearns 15.00
79 Randy Johnson 15.00
80 Bernie Williams 15.00
82 Kerry Wood 15.00
83 Kazuhisa Ishii 10.00
84 Randy Johnson 15.00
85 Nick Johnson 10.00
86 Josh Beckett 15.00
87 Curt Schilling 15.00
88 Mike Mussina 15.00
89 Pedro J. Martinez 15.00
90 Barry Zito 15.00
91 Jim Edmonds 15.00
93 Rickey Henderson 25.00
94 Rickey Henderson 25.00
95 Rickey Henderson 25.00
96 Rickey Henderson 25.00
97 Randy Johnson 15.00
98 Mark Grace 15.00
99 Pedro J. Martinez 15.00
100 Hee Seop Choi 10.00
101 Ivan Rodriguez 15.00
102 Jeff Kent 10.00
104 Hideo Nomo 30.00
105 Mike Piazza 25.00
106 Tom Glavine 15.00
107 Roberto Alomar 15.00
108 Roger Clemens 40.00
109 Jason Giambi 15.00
110 Jim Thome 15.00
111 Alex Rodriguez 25.00
112 Juan Gonzalez 15.00
113 Torii Hunter 15.00
114 Roy Oswalt 10.00
115 Curt Schilling 15.00
116 Magglio Ordonez 10.00
117 Rafael Palmeiro 15.00
118 Andruw Jones 15.00
119 Manny Ramirez 15.00
120 Mark Teixeira 15.00
121 Mark Mulder 10.00
123 Tim Hudson 10.00
124 Todd Helton 15.00
125 Troy Glaus 10.00
128 Greg Maddux 30.00
129 Roger Clemens 40.00
130 Nomar Garciaparra 30.00
131 Mike Piazza 25.00
132 Alex Rodriguez 25.00
134 Randy Johnson 15.00
135 Sammy Sosa 40.00
137 Alfonso Soriano 20.00
138 Jason Giambi 15.00
139 Albert Pujols 35.00
140 Chipper Jones 25.00
141 Adam Dunn 15.00
142 Pedro J. Martinez 15.00
143 Vladimir Guerrero 15.00
144 Mark Prior 40.00
145 Barry Zito 15.00
146 Jeff Bagwell 15.00
147 Lance Berkman 10.00
148 Shawn Green 10.00
149 Jason Giambi 15.00
150 Randy Johnson 15.00
151 Alex Rodriguez 25.00
152 Babe Ruth/5
153 Ty Cobb 125.00
154 Jackie Robinson/10
155 Lou Gehrig/5
156 Thurman Munson 30.00
157 Roberto Clemente/5
158 Nolan Ryan 50.00
159 Nolan Ryan 50.00
160 Nolan Ryan 50.00
161 Cal Ripken Jr. 85.00
162 Don Mattingly 60.00
163 Stan Musial 60.00
164 Tony Gwynn 30.00
165 Yogi Berra 30.00
168 George Brett 60.00
169 Ryne Sandberg 60.00
170 Ernie Banks/5

Threads Number

NM/M

Common Player:
7 Jim Thome/25 20.00
18 Josh Beckett/61 10.00
24 Jim Thome/25 20.00
29 Deion Sanders/21 35.00
30 Rafael Palmeiro/25 20.00
33 Mike Mussina/35 15.00
40 Luis Gonzalez/20 15.00
41 Jorge Posada/20 25.00
42 Mark Mulder/20 15.00
43 Sammy Sosa/21 50.00
44 Mark Prior/22 40.00
45 Roger Clemens/22 50.00
46 Tom Glavine/47 8.00
47 Mark Teixeira/23 15.00
48 Manny Ramirez/24 30.00
49 Frank Thomas/35 15.00
50 Troy Glaus/25 10.00
51 Andruw Jones/25 15.00
52 Jason Giambi/52 10.00
53 Jim Thome/25 20.00
55 Rafael Palmeiro/25 20.00
57 Vladimir Guerrero/27 20.00
59 Mike Sweeney/29 10.00
60 Magglio Ordonez/30 10.00
63 Greg Maddux/31 25.00
64 Mike Piazza/31 30.00
65 Tom Glavine/47 8.00
66 Kerry Wood/52 15.00
67 Frank Thomas/35 15.00
68 Mike Mussina/35 15.00
69 Nick Johnson/36 8.00
70 Bernie Williams/51 10.00
71 Scott Rolen/27 20.00
72 Curt Schilling/38 10.00
73 Adam Dunn/44 8.00
74 Roy Oswalt/44 6.00
75 Pedro Martinez/45 10.00
76 Tom Glavine/47 8.00
77 Torii Hunter/48 8.00
78 Austin Kearns/28 10.00
79 Randy Johnson/51 10.00
80 Bernie Williams/51 10.00
82 Kerry Wood/34 20.00
84 Randy Johnson/51 10.00
85 Nick Johnson/36 8.00
86 Josh Beckett/61 8.00
87 Curt Schilling/38 10.00
88 Mike Mussina/35 15.00
89 Pedro Martinez/45 10.00
90 Barry Zito/75 8.00
93 Rickey Henderson/24 25.00
94 Rickey Henderson/35 20.00
95 Rickey Henderson/24 25.00
96 Rickey Henderson/24 25.00
97 Randy Johnson/51 10.00
99 Pedro Martinez/45 10.00
105 Mike Piazza/31 30.00
106 Tom Glavine/47 8.00
108 Roger Clemens/21 50.00
110 Jim Thome/25 15.00
112 Juan Gonzalez/22 20.00
113 Torii Hunter/48 8.00
114 Roy Oswalt/44 6.00
115 Curt Schilling/38 10.00
116 Magglio Ordonez/30 8.00
117 Rafael Palmeiro/25 20.00
118 Andruw Jones/25 10.00
119 Manny Ramirez/24 25.00
120 Mark Teixeira/23 20.00
121 Mark Mulder/20 15.00
125 Troy Glaus/25 12.00
128 Greg Maddux/31 25.00
129 Roger Clemens/22 50.00
131 Mike Piazza/31 30.00
134 Randy Johnson/51 12.00
135 Sammy Sosa/21 50.00
138 Jason Giambi/25 10.00
141 Adam Dunn/44 8.00
142 Pedro Martinez/45 10.00
143 Vladimir Guerrero/27 20.00
144 Mark Prior/22 40.00
145 Barry Zito/75 8.00
150 Randy Johnson/51 10.00
154 Jackie Robinson/42 50.00
157 Roberto Clemente/21 140.00
158 Nolan Ryan/34 50.00
159 Nolan Ryan/30 50.00
160 Nolan Ryan/34 50.00
162 Don Mattingly/23 50.00
165 Yogi Berra/42 15.00
167 Mike Schmidt/20 60.00
169 Ryne Sandberg/23 60.00

Timber

NM/M

Common Player: 10.00
Production 25 sets
2 Eric Chavez 10.00
3 Alex Rodriguez 25.00
4 Miguel Tejada 10.00
5 Nomar Garciaparra 30.00
6 Jeff Bagwell 15.00
7 Jim Thome 15.00
8 Pat Burrell 15.00
9 Albert Pujols 35.00
10 Juan Gonzalez 15.00
11 Shawn Green 10.00
12 Craig Biggio 10.00
13 Chipper Jones 25.00
14 Hideo Nomo 30.00
15 Vernon Wells 10.00
16 Gary Sheffield 10.00
17 Barry Larkin 15.00
18 Josh Beckett 15.00
19 Edgar Martinez 15.00
20 Ivan Rodriguez 15.00
21 Jeff Kent 10.00
22 Roberto Alomar 15.00
23 Alfonso Soriano 20.00
24 Jim Thome 15.00
25 Juan Gonzalez 15.00
26 Carlos Beltran 10.00
27 Shawn Green 10.00
28 Tim Hudson 10.00
30 Rafael Palmeiro 15.00
31 Todd Helton 15.00
32 Lance Berkman 10.00
33 Mike Mussina 15.00
34 Kazuhisa Ishii 10.00
35 Pat Burrell 15.00
36 Miguel Tejada 10.00
37 Juan Gonzalez 15.00
38 Roberto Alomar 15.00
39 Roberto Alomar 15.00
40 Luis Gonzalez 10.00
41 Jorge Posada 15.00
42 Mark Mulder 10.00
43 Sammy Sosa 40.00
44 Mark Prior 40.00
45 Roger Clemens 40.00
46 Tom Glavine 15.00
47 Mark Teixeira 15.00
48 Manny Ramirez 15.00
49 Frank Thomas 15.00
50 Troy Glaus 10.00
51 Andruw Jones 15.00
52 Jason Giambi 15.00
53 Jim Thome 15.00
55 Rafael Palmeiro 15.00
56 Edgar Martinez 15.00
57 Vladimir Guerrero 15.00
58 Roberto Alomar 15.00
59 Mike Sweeney 10.00
60 Magglio Ordonez 10.00
62 Craig Biggio 10.00
63 Greg Maddux 30.00
64 Mike Piazza 25.00
65 Tom Glavine 15.00
66 Kerry Wood 15.00
67 Frank Thomas 15.00
68 Mike Mussina 15.00
69 Nick Johnson 10.00
70 Bernie Williams 15.00
71 Scott Rolen 15.00
72 Curt Schilling 15.00
73 Adam Dunn 15.00
74 Roy Oswalt 10.00
75 Pedro J. Martinez 15.00
76 Tom Glavine 15.00
77 Torii Hunter 15.00
78 Austin Kearns 15.00
79 Randy Johnson 15.00
80 Bernie Williams 15.00
82 Kerry Wood 15.00
83 Kazuhisa Ishii 10.00
84 Randy Johnson 15.00
85 Nick Johnson 10.00
86 Josh Beckett 15.00
87 Curt Schilling 15.00
88 Mike Mussina 15.00
89 Pedro J. Martinez 15.00
90 Barry Zito 15.00
91 Jim Edmonds 10.00
92 Rickey Henderson 15.00
93 Rickey Henderson 15.00
94 Rickey Henderson 15.00
95 Rickey Henderson 15.00
96 Rickey Henderson 15.00
97 Randy Johnson 15.00
98 Mark Grace 15.00
99 Pedro J. Martinez 15.00
101 Ivan Rodriguez 15.00

102 Jeff Kent 10.00
103 Hideo Nomo 30.00
104 Hideo Nomo 30.00
105 Mike Piazza 25.00
106 Tom Glavine 15.00
107 Roberto Alomar 15.00
108 Roger Clemens 40.00
109 Jason Giambi 15.00
110 Jim Thome 15.00
111 Alex Rodriguez 25.00
112 Juan Gonzalez 15.00
113 Torii Hunter 15.00
114 Roy Oswalt 10.00
115 Curt Schilling 15.00
116 Magglio Ordonez 10.00
117 Rafael Palmeiro 15.00
118 Andruw Jones 15.00
119 Manny Ramirez 15.00
120 Mark Teixeira 15.00
121 Mark Mulder 10.00
122 Garret Anderson 10.00
123 Tim Hudson 10.00
124 Todd Helton 15.00
125 Troy Glaus 10.00
128 Greg Maddux 30.00
129 Roger Clemens 40.00
130 Nomar Garciaparra 30.00
131 Mike Piazza 25.00
132 Alex Rodriguez 25.00
134 Randy Johnson 15.00
135 Sammy Sosa 40.00
137 Alfonso Soriano 20.00
138 Jason Giambi 15.00
139 Albert Pujols 35.00
140 Chipper Jones 25.00
141 Adam Dunn 15.00
142 Pedro J. Martinez 15.00
143 Vladimir Guerrero 15.00
144 Mark Prior 40.00
145 Barry Zito 15.00
146 Jeff Bagwell 15.00
147 Lance Berkman 10.00
148 Shawn Green 10.00
149 Jason Giambi 15.00
150 Randy Johnson 15.00
151 Alex Rodriguez 25.00
152 Babe Ruth 180.00
153 Ty Cobb 125.00
155 Lou Gehrig 150.00
156 Thurman Munson 30.00
157 Roberto Clemente 140.00
158 Nolan Ryan 50.00
159 Nolan Ryan 50.00
160 Nolan Ryan 50.00
161 Cal Ripken Jr. 85.00
162 Don Mattingly 60.00
163 Stan Musial 60.00
164 Tony Gwynn 30.00
165 Yogi Berra 30.00
166 Johnny Bench 35.00
167 Mike Schmidt 60.00
168 George Brett 60.00
169 Ryne Sandberg 60.00
170 Ernie Banks/1 10.00

TNT

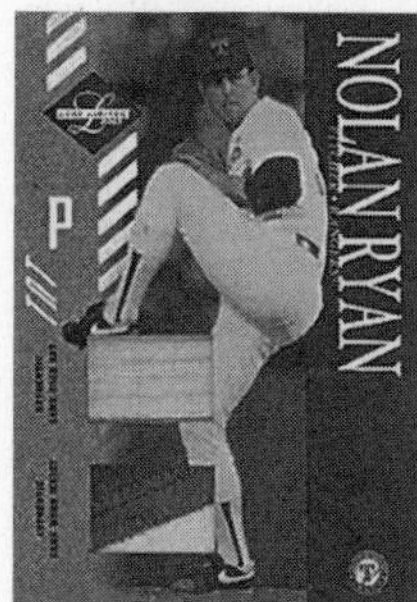

NM/M

Production 25 unless noted
Some not priced due to scarcity
Primes: 1X
Production 1-25
No pricing production 15 or less

2 Eric Chavez 15.00
3 Alex Rodriguez 45.00
4 Miguel Tejada 15.00
5 Nomar Garciaparra 45.00
6 Jeff Bagwell 25.00
7 Jim Thome 30.00
8 Pat Burrell 30.00
9 Albert Pujols 60.00
10 Juan Gonzalez 25.00
11 Shawn Green 15.00
12 Craig Biggio 15.00
13 Chipper Jones 40.00
14 Hideo Nomo 50.00
15 Vernon Wells 15.00
16 Gary Sheffield 25.00
17 Barry Larkin 20.00
18 Josh Beckett 25.00
19 Edgar Martinez 25.00
20 Ivan Rodriguez 20.00
21 Jeff Kent 10.00
22 Roberto Alomar 20.00
23 Alfonso Soriano 30.00
24 Jim Thome 30.00
25 Juan Gonzalez 25.00
26 Carlos Beltran 20.00
27 Shawn Green 15.00
28 Tim Hudson 20.00
30 Rafael Palmeiro 20.00
31 Todd Helton 20.00
32 Lance Berkman 20.00
33 Mike Mussina 25.00
34 Kazuhisa Ishii 10.00
35 Pat Burrell 30.00
36 Miguel Tejada 15.00
37 Juan Gonzalez 25.00
38 Roberto Alomar 20.00
39 Roberto Alomar 20.00
40 Luis Gonzalez 15.00
41 Jorge Posada 25.00
42 Mark Mulder 20.00
43 Sammy Sosa 40.00
44 Mark Prior 40.00
45 Roger Clemens 50.00
46 Tom Glavine 20.00
47 Mark Teixeira 20.00
48 Manny Ramirez 25.00
49 Frank Thomas 35.00
50 Troy Glaus 15.00
51 Andruw Jones 20.00
52 Jason Giambi 15.00
53 Jim Thome 30.00
55 Rafael Palmeiro 25.00
56 Edgar Martinez 20.00
57 Vladimir Guerrero 30.00
58 Mike Sweeney 10.00
60 Magglio Ordonez 15.00
62 Craig Biggio 20.00
63 Greg Maddux 40.00
64 Mike Piazza 40.00
65 Tom Glavine 20.00
66 Kerry Wood 30.00
67 Frank Thomas 35.00
68 Mike Mussina 25.00
69 Nick Johnson 15.00
70 Bernie Williams 15.00
71 Scott Rolen 30.00
72 Curt Schilling 20.00
73 Adam Dunn 25.00
74 Roy Oswalt 15.00
75 Pedro J. Martinez 35.00
76 Tom Glavine 20.00
77 Torii Hunter 15.00
78 Austin Kearns 15.00
79 Randy Johnson 30.00
80 Bernie Williams 20.00
82 Kerry Wood 30.00
83 Kazuhisa Ishii 10.00
84 Randy Johnson 30.00
85 Nick Johnson 15.00
86 Josh Beckett 20.00
87 Curt Schilling 25.00
88 Mike Mussina 25.00
89 Pedro J. Martinez 35.00
90 Barry Zito 15.00
91 Jim Edmonds 20.00
92 Rickey Henderson 35.00
93 Rickey Henderson 35.00
94 Rickey Henderson 35.00
95 Rickey Henderson 35.00
96 Rickey Henderson 35.00
97 Randy Johnson 30.00
98 Mark Grace 20.00
99 Pedro J. Martinez 35.00
101 Ivan Rodriguez 20.00
102 Jeff Kent 10.00
103 Hideo Nomo 40.00
104 Hideo Nomo 40.00
105 Mike Piazza 40.00
106 Tom Glavine 20.00
107 Roberto Alomar 25.00
108 Roger Clemens 50.00
109 Jason Giambi 20.00
110 Jim Thome 30.00
111 Alex Rodriguez 45.00
112 Juan Gonzalez 25.00
113 Torii Hunter 15.00
114 Roy Oswalt 15.00
115 Curt Schilling 25.00
116 Magglio Ordonez 15.00
117 Rafael Palmeiro 25.00
118 Andruw Jones 15.00
119 Manny Ramirez 30.00
120 Mark Teixeira 25.00
121 Mark Mulder 20.00
123 Tim Hudson 20.00
124 Todd Helton 20.00
125 Troy Glaus 15.00
128 Greg Maddux 40.00
129 Roger Clemens 50.00
130 Nomar Garciaparra 40.00
131 Mike Piazza 40.00
132 Alex Rodriguez 40.00
134 Randy Johnson 30.00
135 Sammy Sosa 40.00
137 Alfonso Soriano 30.00
138 Jason Giambi 20.00
139 Albert Pujols 60.00
140 Chipper Jones 30.00
141 Adam Dunn 25.00
142 Pedro J. Martinez 35.00
143 Vladimir Guerrero 30.00
144 Mark Prior 40.00
145 Barry Zito 15.00
146 Jeff Bagwell 25.00
147 Lance Berkman 20.00
148 Shawn Green 15.00
149 Jason Giambi 20.00
150 Randy Johnson 30.00
151 Alex Rodriguez 40.00
152 Babe Ruth/5
153 Ty Cobb/10
155 Lou Gehrig/5
156 Thurman Munson 50.00
157 Roberto Clemente/5
158 Nolan Ryan 65.00
159 Nolan Ryan 65.00
160 Nolan Ryan 65.00
161 Cal Ripken Jr. 100.00
162 Don Mattingly 65.00
163 Stan Musial 65.00
164 Tony Gwynn 40.00
165 Yogi Berra 40.00
166 Johnny Bench 40.00
167 Mike Schmidt 65.00
168 George Brett 75.00
169 Ryne Sandberg 65.00
170 Ernie Banks/1

7th Inning Stretch

NM/M

Production 50 unless noted
1 Alex Rodriguez 20.00
3 Sammy Sosa 25.00
4 Juan Gonzalez 10.00
5 Albert Pujols 30.00
6 Chipper Jones 15.00
7 Alfonso Soriano/40 15.00
8 Jim Thome 15.00
9 Mike Piazza 20.00
10 Rafael Palmeiro 15.00

2004 LEAF

NM/M

Complete Set (300): 50.00
Common Player: .15
Common (202-301): .25
Pack (8): 5.00
Box (24): 90.00

1 Darin Erstad .25
2 Garret Anderson .25
3 Jarrod Washburn .15
4 Kevin Appier .15
5 Tim Salmon .25
6 Troy Glaus .40
7 Troy Percival .15
8 Jason Johnson .15
9 Jay Gibbons .25
10 Melvin Mora .15
11 Sidney Ponson .15
12 Tony Batista .15
13 Derek Lowe .25
14 Robert Person .15
15 Manny Ramirez .50
16 Nomar Garciaparra 1.50
17 Pedro J. Martinez .75
18 Jorge de la Rosa .15
19 Bartolo Colon .25
20 Carlos Lee .15
21 Esteban Loaiza .15
22 Frank Thomas .50
23 Joe Crede .15
24 Magglio Ordonez .25
25 Ryan Ludwick .15
26 Luis Garcia .15
27 Brandon Phillips .15
28 C.C. Sabathia .15
29 Jhonny Peralta .15
30 Josh Bard .15
31 Omar Vizquel .25
32 Fernando Rodney .15
33 Mike Maroth .15
34 Bobby Higginson .15
35 Omar Infante .15
36 Dmitri Young .15
37 Eric Munson .15
38 Jeremy Bonderman .15
39 Carlos Beltran .25
40 Jeremy Affeldt .15
41 Dee Brown .15
42 .15
43 Mike Sweeney .15
44 Brent Abernathy .15
45 Runelvys Hernandez .15
46 A.J. Pierzynski .15
47 Corey Koskie .15
48 Cristian Guzman .15
49 Jacque Jones .15
50 Kenny Rogers .15
51 J.C. Romero .15
52 Torii Hunter .40
53 Alfonso Soriano .75
54 Bernie Williams .50
55 David Wells .15
56 Derek Jeter 2.00
57 Hideki Matsui 1.50
58 Jason Giambi .75
59 Jorge Posada .40
60 Jose Contreras .25
61 Mike Mussina .50
62 Nick Johnson .15
63 Roger Clemens 1.50
64 Barry Zito .40
65 Justin Duchscherer .15
66 Eric Chavez .25
67 Erubiel Durazo .15
68 Miguel Tejada .40
69 Mark Mulder .25
70 Terrence Long .15
71 Tim Hudson .25
72 Bret Boone .25
73 Dan Wilson .15
74 Edgar Martinez .25
75 Freddy Garcia .15
76 Rafael Soriano .15
77 Ichiro Suzuki 1.25
78 Jamie Moyer .15
79 John Olerud .25
80 Kazuhiro Sasaki .15
81 Aubrey Huff .15
82 Carl Crawford .15
83 Joe Kennedy .15
84 Rocco Baldelli .40
85 Toby Hall .15
86 Alex Rodriguez 1.50
87 Kevin Mench .15
88 Hank Blalock .25
89 Juan Gonzalez .50
90 Mark Teixeira .25
91 Rafael Palmeiro .50
92 Carlos Delgado .50
93 Eric Hinske .15
94 Josh Phelps .15
95 Brian Bowles .15
96 Roy Halladay .40
97 Shannon Stewart .15
98 Vernon Wells .25
99 Curt Schilling .40
100 Junior Spivey .15
101 Luis Gonzalez .25
102 Lyle Overbay .15
103 Mark Grace .40
104 Randy Johnson .75
105 Shea Hillenbrand .15
106 Andruw Jones .50

107	Chipper Jones	.75
108	Gary Sheffield	.40
109	Greg Maddux	1.00
110	Javy Lopez	.25
111	John Smoltz	.25
112	Marcus Giles	.15
113	Rafael Furcal	.25
114	Corey Patterson	.15
115	Juan Cruz	.15
116	Kerry Wood	.50
117	Mark Prior	1.50
118	Moises Alou	.25
119	Sammy Sosa	1.00
120	Aaron Boone	.15
121	Adam Dunn	.50
122	Austin Kearns	.50
123	Barry Larkin	.40
124	Ken Griffey Jr.	1.00
125	Brian Reith	.15
126	Wily Mo Pena	.15
127	Jason Jennings	.15
128	Jay Payton	.15
129	Larry Walker	.25
130	Preston Wilson	.15
131	Todd Helton	.50
132	Dontrelle Willis	.40
133	Ivan Rodriguez	.50
134	Josh Beckett	.50
135	Juan Encarnacion	.15
136	Mike Lowell	.15
137	Craig Biggio	.25
138	Jeff Bagwell	.50
139	Jeff Kent	.25
140	Lance Berkman	.25
141	Richard Hidalgo	.15
142	Roy Oswalt	.25
143	Eric Gagne	.25
144	Fred McGriff	.25
145	Hideo Nomo	.40
146	Kazuhisa Ishii	.15
147	Kevin Brown	.25
148	Paul LoDuca	.15
149	Shawn Green	.25
150	Ben Sheets	.25
151	Geoff Jenkins	.25
152	Rey Sanchez	.15
153	Richie Sexson	.40
154	Wes Helms	.15
155	Shane Nance	.15
156	Fernando Tatis	.15
157	Javier Vazquez	.15
158	Jose Vidro	.15
159	Orlando Cabrera	.15
160	Henry Mateo	.15
161	Vladimir Guerrero	.75
162	Zach Day	.15
163	Edwin Almonte	.15
164	Al Leiter	.15
165	Cliff Floyd	.15
166	Jae Weong Seo	.15
167	Mike Piazza	1.00
168	Roberto Alomar	.50
169	Tom Glavine	.25
170	Bobby Abreu	.25
171	Brandon Duckworth	.15
172	Jim Thome	.75
173	Kevin Millwood	.25
174	Pat Burrell	.25
175	Aramis Ramirez	.15
176	Jack Wilson	.15
177	Brian Giles	.25
178	Jason Kendall	.25
179	Kenny Lofton	.25
180	Kip Wells	.15
181	Kris Benson	.15
182	Albert Pujols	1.50
183	J.D. Drew	.15
184	Jim Edmonds	.25
185	Matt Morris	.15
186	Scott Rolen	.75
187	Woody Williams	.15
188	Clifford Bartosh	.15
189	Brian Lawrence	.15
190	Ryan Klesko	.25
191	Sean Burroughs	.15
192	Xavier Nady	.15
193	Dennis Tankersley	.15
194	Donaldo Mendez	.15
195	Barry Bonds	2.00
196	Benito Santiago	.15
197	Edgardo Alfonzo	.15
198	Cody Ransom	.15
199	Jason Schmidt	.15
200	Rich Aurilia	.15
201	Ken Harvey	.15
202	Adam Loewen	.25
203	Alfredo Gonzalez	.25
204	Arnie Munoz	.25
205	Andrew Brown	.25
206	Josh Hall	.25
207	Josh Stewart	.25
208	Clint Barmes	.25
209	Brandon Webb	.25
210	Chien-Ming Wang	.25
211	Edgar Gonzalez	.25
212	Alejandro Machado	.25
213	Jeremy Griffiths	.25
214	Craig Brazell	.25
215	Daniel Cabrera	.25
216	Fernando Cabrera	.25
217	Terrmel Sledge	.25
218	Rob Hammock	.25
219	Francisco Rosario	.25
220	Francisco Cruceta	.25
221	Rett Johnson	.25
222	Guillermo Quiroz	.25
223	Hong-Chih Kuo	.25
224	Ian Ferguson	.25
225	Tim Olson	.25
226	Todd Wellemeyer	.25
227	Rich Fischer	.25
228	Phil Seibel	.25
229	Joe Valentine	.25
230	Matt Kata	.25
231	Michael Hessman	.25
232	Michel Hernandez	.25
233	Doug Waechter	.25
234	Prentice Redman	.25
235	Nook Logan	.25
236	Oscar Villarreal	.25
237	Pete LaForest	.25
238	Matt Bruback	.25
239	Josh Willingham	.25
240	Greg Aquino	.25
241	Lew Ford	.25
242	Jeff Duncan	.25
243	Chris Waters	.25
244	Miguel Ojeda	.25
245	Rosman Garcia	.25
246	Felix Sanchez	.25
247	Jon Leicester	.25
248	Roger Deago	.25
249	Mike Ryan	.25
250	Chris Capuano	.25
251	Matt White	.25
252	Bernie Williams	.50
253	Mark Grace	.50
254	Chipper Jones	1.00
255	Greg Maddux	1.50
256	Sammy Sosa	2.00
257	Mike Mussina	.75
258	Tim Salmon	.50
259	Barry Larkin	.50
260	Randy Johnson	1.00
261	Jeff Bagwell	.75
262	Roberto Alomar	.50
263	Tom Glavine	.50
264	Roger Clemens	2.50
265	Barry Bonds	3.00
266	Ivan Rodriguez	.75
267	Pedro J. Martinez	1.00
268	Ken Griffey Jr.	1.50
269	Jim Thome	1.00
270	Frank Thomas	.75
271	Mike Piazza	1.50
272	Troy Glaus	.40
273	Melvin Mora	.25
274	Nomar Garciaparra	2.00
275	Magglio Ordonez	.40
276	Omar Vizquel	.40
277	Dmitri Young	.25
278	Mike Sweeney	.25
279	Torii Hunter	.50
280	Derek Jeter	2.00
281	Barry Zito	.50
282	Ichiro Suzuki	1.50
283	Rocco Baldelli	.50
284	Alex Rodriguez	2.00
285	Carlos Delgado	.50
286	Randy Johnson	.75
287	Greg Maddux	1.00
288	Sammy Sosa	1.50
289	Ken Griffey Jr.	1.00
290	Todd Helton	.50
291	Ivan Rodriguez	.50
292	Jeff Bagwell	.50
293	Hideo Nomo	.50
294	Richie Sexson	.50
295	Vladimir Guerrero	.75
296	Mike Piazza	1.00
297	Jim Thome	.75
298	Jason Kendall	.40
299	Albert Pujols	1.50
300	Ryan Klesko	.40
301	Barry Bonds	2.00

Red Press Proof

Stars (1-301): 1-2X
Inserted 1:8

Blue Press Proof

Stars (1-301): 4-8X
Production 100 sets

Gold Press Proof

Cards (1-301): 12-25X
Production 25 sets

Black Press Proof

Stars (1-301): 5-10X
Production 50 sets
Hot Pack exclusive

Away

NM/M

Complete Set (10): 20.00
Common Player: 1.00
Inserted 1:35

1	Greg Maddux	2.50
2	Sammy Sosa	3.00
3	Alex Rodriguez	4.00
4	Albert Pujols	4.00
5	Jason Giambi	1.50
6	Chipper Jones	2.00
7	Vladimir Guerrero	1.50
8	Mike Piazza	2.50
9	Nomar Garciaparra	3.00
10	Austin Kearns	1.00

Away Jersey

NM/M

Common Player: 5.00
Inserted 1:119
Prime: 1.5-2X
Production 50

1	Greg Maddux	8.00
2	Sammy Sosa	12.00
3	Alex Rodriguez	10.00
4	Albert Pujols	15.00
5	Jason Giambi	8.00
6	Chipper Jones	8.00
7	Vladimir Guerrero	8.00
8	Mike Piazza	10.00
9	Nomar Garciaparra	12.00
10	Austin Kearns	5.00

Autographs

NM/M

Common Autograph 6.00

14	Robert Person	6.00
18	Jorge De La Rosa	6.00
25	Ryan Ludwick	8.00
26	Luis Garcia	6.00
29	Jhonny Peralta	6.00
30	Josh Bard	6.00
32	Fernando Rodney	6.00
33	Mike Maroth	6.00
35	Omar Infante	6.00
37	Eric Munson/9	
41	Dee Brown	6.00
44	Brent Abernathy/SP	10.00
51	J.C. Romero	6.00
65	Justin Duchscherer	10.00
70	Terrence Long/SP	15.00
76	Rafael Soriano	8.00
85	Toby Hall/SP	10.00
87	Kevin Mench	6.00
95	Brian Bowles	6.00
115	Juan Cruz	6.00
125	Brian Reith	6.00
126	Wily Mo Pena	8.00
127	Jason Jennings	6.00
150	Ben Sheets/17	
155	Shane Nance	6.00
160	Henry Mateo/SP	8.00
163	Edwin Almonte	6.00
171	Brandon Duckworth	6.00
176	Jack Wilson	6.00
180	Kip Wells	6.00
188	Clifford Bartosh	6.00
189	Brian Lawrence	6.00
193	Dennis Tankersley	6.00
194	Donaldo Mendez	6.00
198	Cody Ransom/SP	8.00
247	Jon Leicester/SP	8.00

Clean Up Crew

NM/M

Complete Set (10): 20.00
Common Player: 1.00
Inserted 1:49

1	Sammy Sosa, Moises Alou, Hee Seop Choi	3.00
2	Jason Giambi, Alfonso Soriano, Hideki Matsui	5.00
3	Vernon Wells, Carlos Delgado, Josh Phelps	1.00
4	Alex Rodriguez, Juan Gonzalez, Hank Blalock	4.00
5	Gary Sheffield, Andruw Jones, Chipper Jones	2.50
6	Ken Griffey Jr., Austin Kearns, Aaron Boone	3.00
7	Albert Pujols, Jim Edmonds, Scott Rolen	4.00
8	Jeff Bagwell, Jeff Kent, Lance Berkman	1.50
9	Todd Helton, Preston Wilson, Larry Walker	1.50
10	Miguel Tejada, Erubiel Durazo, Eric Chavez	1.00

Clean Up Crew Materials

NM/M

Common Card: 15.00
Production 50 sets

1	Sammy Sosa, Moises Alou, Hee Seop Choi	35.00
2	Jason Giambi, Alfonso Soriano, Hideki Matsui	60.00
3	Vernon Wells, Carlos Delgado, Josh Phelps	15.00
4	Alex Rodriguez, Juan Gonzalez, Hank Blalock	35.00
5	Gary Sheffield, Andruw Jones, Chipper Jones	20.00
6	Ken Griffey Jr., Austin Kearns, Aaron Boone	25.00
7	Albert Pujols, Jim Edmonds, Scott Rolen	40.00
8	Jeff Bagwell, Jeff Kent, Lance Berkman	25.00
9	Todd Helton, Preston Wilson, Larry Walker	20.00
10	Miguel Tejada, Erubiel Durazo, Eric Chavez	15.00

Cornerstones

NM/M

Complete Set (10): 20.00
Common Player: 1.00
Inserted 1:78

1	Alex Rodriguez, Hank Blalock	4.00
2	Kerry Wood, Mark Prior	4.00
3	Roger Clemens, Alfonso Soriano	4.00

4 Nomar Garciaparra, Manny Ramirez 4.00
5 Austin Kearns, Adam Dunn 1.00
6 Tom Glavine, Mike Piazza 2.50
7 Andruw Jones, Chipper Jones 2.50
8 Albert Pujols, Scott Rolen 4.00
9 Curt Schilling, Randy Johnson 2.00
10 Hideo Nomo, Kazuhisa Ishii 1.00

Cornerstones Materials

NM/M
Common Duo: 15.00
Production 50 sets
1 Alex Rodriguez, Hank Blalock 25.00
2 Kerry Wood, Mark Prior 60.00
3 Roger Clemens, Alfonso Soriano 40.00
4 Nomar Garciaparra, Manny Ramirez 30.00
5 Austin Kearns, Adam Dunn 15.00
6 Tom Glavine, Mike Piazza
7 Andruw Jones, Chipper Jones 20.00
8 Albert Pujols, Scott Rolen 40.00
9 Curt Schilling, Randy Johnson 20.00
10 Hideo Nomo, Kazuhisa Ishii 20.00

Exhibits

NM/M
Common Player: 2.50
Production 66 sets
Variations #'d to 63: 1X
Variations #'d to 46: 1X
Variations #'d 21 to 27: 1.5X
1 Adam Dunn 2.50
2 Albert Pujols 8.00
3 Alex Rodriguez 8.00
4 Alfonso Soriano 4.00
5 Andruw Jones 3.00
6 Barry Bonds 10.00
7 Barry Larkin 2.50
8 Barry Zito 2.50
9 Cal Ripken Jr. 10.00
10 Chipper Jones 5.00
11 Dale Murphy 2.50
12 Derek Jeter 10.00
13 Don Mattingly 8.00
14 Ernie Banks 5.00
15 Frank Thomas 4.00
16 George Brett 6.00
17 Greg Maddux 5.00
18 Hank Blalock 2.50
19 Hideo Nomo 2.50
20 Ichiro Suzuki 6.00
21 Jason Giambi 3.00
22 Jim Thome 4.00
23 Juan Gonzalez 2.50
24 Ken Griffey Jr. 5.00
25 Kirby Puckett 4.00
26 Mark Prior 8.00
27 Mike Mussina 2.50
28 Mike Piazza 5.00
29 Mike Schmidt 6.00
30 Nolan Ryan 8.00
31 Nolan Ryan 8.00
32 Nolan Ryan 8.00
33 Nomar Garciaparra 8.00
34 Ozzie Smith 2.50
35 Pedro J. Martinez 4.00
36 Randy Johnson 3.00
37 Reggie Jackson 2.50
38 Reggie Jackson 2.50
39 Rickey Henderson 2.50
40 Roberto Alomar 2.50
41 Roberto Clemente 8.00
42 Rod Carew 3.00
43 Roger Clemens 8.00
44 Sammy Sosa 6.00
45 Stan Musial 6.00
46 Tom Glavine 2.50
47 Tom Seaver 4.00
48 Tony Gwynn 4.00
49 Vladimir Guerrero 4.00
50 Yogi Berra 4.00

Gamers

NM/M
Complete Set (20): 40.00

Common Player: 1.00
Quantum: 2-4X
Production 100 sets
1 Albert Pujols 4.00
2 Alex Rodriguez 4.00
3 Alfonso Soriano 1.50
4 Barry Bonds 5.00
5 Barry Zito 1.00
6 Chipper Jones 2.00
7 Derek Jeter 5.00
8 Greg Maddux 2.50
9 Ichiro Suzuki 3.00
10 Jason Giambi 1.50
11 Jeff Bagwell 1.50
12 Ken Griffey Jr. 2.50
13 Manny Ramirez 1.50
14 Mark Prior 4.00
15 Mike Piazza 2.50
16 Nomar Garciaparra 3.00
17 Pedro J. Martinez 2.00
18 Randy Johnson 2.00
19 Roger Clemens 3.00
20 Sammy Sosa 3.00

Gold Leaf Rookies

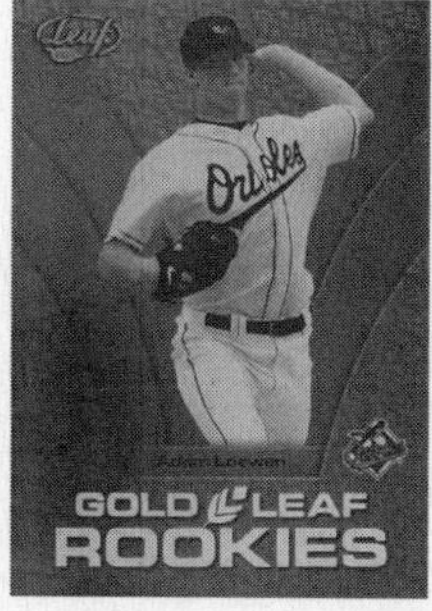

NM/M
Complete Set (10): 6.00
Common Player: .50
Inserted 1:23
Mirror Gold: No Pricing
Production 25 sets
1 Adam Loewen 2.00
2 Rickie Weeks 5.00
3 Khalil Greene .50
4 Chad Tracy .50
5 Alexis Rios .50
6 Craig Brazell .50
7 Clint Barmes .50
8 Pete LaForest .50
9 Alfredo Gonzalez .50
10 Arnie Munoz .50

Home

NM/M
Complete Set (10): 20.00
Common Player: 1.00
Inserted 1:35
1 Greg Maddux 2.50
2 Sammy Sosa 3.00
3 Alex Rodriguez 4.00
4 Albert Pujols 4.00
5 Jason Giambi 1.50
6 Chipper Jones 2.00
7 Vladimir Guerrero 1.50
8 Mike Piazza 2.50
9 Nomar Garciaparra 3.00

10 Austin Kearns 1.00

Home Jersey

NM/M
Common Player: 5.00
Inserted 1:119
Primes: 1.5-2X
Production 50
1 Greg Maddux 8.00
2 Sammy Sosa 12.00
3 Alex Rodriguez 10.00
4 Albert Pujols 15.00
5 Jason Giambi 8.00
6 Chipper Jones 8.00
7 Vladimir Guerrero 8.00
8 Mike Piazza 10.00
9 Nomar Garciaparra 12.00
10 Austin Kearns 5.00

MVP Winners

NM/M
Complete Set (20): 50.00
Common Player: 1.00
Gold: 1-2X
Production 500 sets
1 Stan Musial - 1948 NL 3.00
2 Ernie Banks - 1958 NL 2.00
3 Roberto Clemente - 1966 NL 4.00
4 George Brett - 1980 AL 4.00
5 Mike Schmidt - 1980 NL 4.00
6 Cal Ripken Jr. - 1983 AL 5.00
7 Dale Murphy - 1983 NL 1.50
8 Ryne Sandberg - 1984 NL 3.00
9 Don Mattingly - 1985 AL 3.00
10 Roger Clemens - 1986 AL 4.00
11 Rickey Henderson - 1990 AL 1.00
12 Cal Ripken Jr. - 1991 AL 5.00
13 Barry Bonds - 1992 NL 5.00
14 Barry Bonds - 1993 NL 5.00
15 Frank Thomas - 1994 AL 1.50
16 Ken Griffey Jr. - 1997 AL 2.50
17 Sammy Sosa - 1998 NL 3.00
18 Chipper Jones - 1999 NL 2.00
19 Jason Giambi - 2000 AL 1.50
20 Ichiro Suzuki - 2001 AL 3.00

Picture Perfect

NM/M
Complete Set (15): 25.00
Common Player: 1.00
Inserted 1:37

1 Albert Pujols 5.00
2 Alex Rodriguez 5.00
3 Alfonso Soriano 2.00
4 Austin Kearns 1.00
5 Carlos Delgado 1.50
6 Chipper Jones 2.50
7 Hank Blalock 1.50
8 Jason Giambi 2.00
9 Jeff Bagwell 1.50
10 Jim Thome 2.00
11 Manny Ramirez 1.50
12 Mike Piazza 3.00
13 Nomar Garciaparra 4.00
14 Sammy Sosa 4.00
15 Todd Helton 1.50

Picture Perfect Materials

NM/M
Common Player: 6.00
Inserted 1:437
1 Albert Pujols 15.00
2 Alex Rodriguez 10.00
3 Alfonso Soriano 8.00
4 Austin Kearns 6.00
5 Carlos Delgado 6.00
6 Chipper Jones 8.00
7 Hank Blalock 6.00
8 Jason Giambi 8.00
9 Jeff Bagwell 8.00
10 Jim Thome 10.00
11 Manny Ramirez 6.00
12 Mike Piazza 10.00
13 Nomar Garciaparra 10.00
14 Sammy Sosa 10.00
15 Todd Helton 8.00

Shirt Off My Back

NM/M
Common Player: 4.00
Inserted 1:47
1 Shawn Green 4.00
2 Andruw Jones 6.00
3 Ivan Rodriguez 6.00
4 Hideo Nomo 6.00
5 Don Mattingly 20.00
6 Mark Prior 15.00
7 Alfonso Soriano 6.00
8 Richie Sexson 5.00
9 Vernon Wells 4.00
10 Nomar Garciaparra 8.00
11 Jason Giambi 6.00
12 Austin Kearns 5.00
13 Chipper Jones 6.00
14 Rickey Henderson 6.00
15 Alex Rodriguez 12.00
16 Garret Anderson 4.00
17 Vladimir Guerrero 4.00
18 Sammy Sosa 10.00
19 Mike Piazza 8.00
20 David Wells 4.00
21 Scott Rolen 6.00
22 Adam Dunn 5.00
23 Carlos Delgado 5.00
24 Greg Maddux 8.00
25 Hank Blalock 5.00

Shirt Off My Back Team Logo Patch

NM/M
Common Player: 10.00
Autographs: No Pricing
Production 5 sets
Jersey Number Patch: .75-1X
Production 50 sets
Sosa #'d to 42
Jersey Number Patch Auto: No Pricing
Production 5 sets
1 Shawn Green/41 15.00
2 Andruw Jones/75 15.00
3 Ivan Rodriguez/75 15.00
4 Hideo Nomo/74 20.00
5 Don Mattingly/7
6 Mark Prior/46 30.00
7 Alfonso Soriano/28 25.00
8 Richie Sexson/38 15.00
9 Vernon Wells/74 10.00
10 Nomar Garciaparra/75 25.00
11 Jason Giambi/26 20.00

12 Austin Kearns/32 10.00
13 Chipper Jones/75 20.00
14 Rickey Henderson/40 20.00
15 Alex Rodriguez/75 30.00
16 Garret Anderson/71 10.00
17 Vladimir Guerrero/55 20.00
18 Sammy Sosa/39 25.00
19 Mike Piazza/75 20.00
20 David Wells/74 10.00
21 Scott Rolen/29 30.00
22 Adam Dunn/32 15.00
23 Carlos Delgado/56 15.00
24 Greg Maddux/75 20.00
25 Hank Blalock/62 15.00

Sunday Dress

NM/M
Complete Set (10): 10.00
Common Player: .75
Inserted 1:17
1 Frank Thomas 1.00
2 Barry Zito .75
3 Mike Piazza 2.00
4 Mark Prior 3.00
5 Jeff Bagwell 1.00
6 Roy Oswalt .75
7 Todd Helton 1.00
8 Magglio Ordonez .75
9 Alex Rodriguez 3.00
10 Manny Ramirez 1.00

Sunday Dress Jersey

NM/M
Common Player: 5.00
Inserted 1:119
Prime Jersey: 1-1.5X
Production 100
1 Frank Thomas 8.00
2 Barry Zito 6.00
3 Mike Piazza 10.00
4 Mark Prior 15.00
5 Jeff Bagwell 8.00
6 Roy Oswalt 5.00
7 Todd Helton 8.00
8 Magglio Ordonez 6.00
9 Alex Rodriguez 10.00
10 Manny Ramirez 6.00

2004 LEAF CERTIFIED CUTS

NM/M
Complete Set (300):
Common Player (1-200): .75
Common (201-250): 2.00
Production 599
Common (251-300): 5.00
Production 499
Auto. production 99-499
Pack (5): 20.00
Box (10): 160.00
1 Vladimir Guerrero 1.50
2 Garret Anderson .75
3 John Lackey .75
4 Bartolo Colon .75
5 Troy Glaus .75
6 Tim Salmon .75
7 Shea Hillenbrand .75
8 Brandon Webb .75
9 Roberto Alomar .75
10 Randy Johnson 2.00
11 Alex Cintron .75
12 Richie Sexson .75
13 Luis Gonzalez .75
14 Adam LaRoche .75
15 Rafael Furcal .75
16 Chipper Jones 2.00
17 Marcus Giles .75
18 Andruw Jones 1.00
19 Russ Ortiz .75
20 Rafael Palmeiro 1.00
21 Melvin Mora .75
22 Luis Matos .75
23 Jay Gibbons .75
24 Adam Loewen .75
25 Larry Bigbie .75
26 Rodrigo Lopez .75
27 Javy Lopez .75
28 Miguel Tejada 1.00
29 Trot Nixon .75
30 Curt Schilling 1.00
31 Jason Varitek .75
32 Manny Ramirez 1.00
33 Keith Foulke .75
34 Derek Lowe .75
35 Pedro J. Martinez 1.50
36 Nomar Garciaparra 2.50
37 Bill Mueller .75
38 Johnny Damon .75
39 David Ortiz 1.50
40 Mark Prior 1.50
41 Kerry Wood 1.50
42 Sammy Sosa 2.50
43 Derrek Lee .75
44 Greg Maddux 2.00
45 Aramis Ramirez .75
46 Matt Clement .75
47 Carlos Zambrano .75
48 Todd Walker .75
49 Moises Alou .75
50 Corey Patterson .75
51 Frank Thomas 1.00
52 Magglio Ordonez .75
53 Carlos Lee .75
54 Mark Buehrle .75
55 Esteban Loaiza .75
56 Joe Crede .75
57 Paul Konerko .75
58 Adam Dunn 1.00
59 Austin Kearns .75
60 Barry Larkin .75
61 Ryan Wagner .75
62 Danny Graves .75
63 Sean Casey .75
64 Ken Griffey Jr. 2.00
65 Jody Gerut .75
66 Cliff Lee .75
67 Victor Martinez .75
68 C.C. Sabathia .75
69 Omar Vizquel .75
70 Travis Hafner .75
71 Todd Helton 1.00
72 Preston Wilson .75
73 Jeromy Burnitz .75
74 Larry Walker .75
75 Ivan Rodriguez 1.00
76 Rondell White .75
77 Miguel Cabrera 1.50
78 Luis Castillo .75
79 Josh Beckett .75
80 Mike Lowell .75
81 Dontrelle Willis .75
82 Brad Penny .75
83 Hee Seop Choi .75
84 Juan Pierre .75
85 Andy Pettitte .75
86 Jeff Bagwell 1.00
87 Roy Oswalt .75
88 Lance Berkman .75
89 Morgan Ensberg .75
90 Craig Biggio .75
91 Octavio Dotel .75
92 Wade Miller .75
93 Jeff Kent .75
94 Richard Hidalgo .75
95 Roger Clemens 3.00
96 Carlos Beltran 1.00
97 Angel Berroa .75
98 Jeremy Affeldt .75
99 Juan Gonzalez .75
100 Mike Sweeney .75
101 Kazuhisa Ishii .75
102 Shawn Green .75
103 Milton Bradley .75
104 Paul LoDuca .75
105 Hideo Nomo .75
106 Eric Gagne .75
107 Adrian Beltre .75
108 Scott Podsednik .75
109 Rickie Weeks .75
110 Ben Sheets .75
111 Geoff Jenkins .75
112 Jacque Jones .75
113 Johan Santana 1.00
114 Shannon Stewart .75
115 Corey Koskie .75
116 Lew Ford .75
117 Torii Hunter .75
118 Chad Cordero .75
119 Orlando Cabrera .75
120 Jose Vidro .75
121 Nick Johnson .75
122 Brad Wilkerson .75
123 Mike Piazza 2.00
124 Jae Weong Seo .75
125 Jose Reyes .75
126 Tom Glavine .75
127 Jorge Posada .75
128 Gary Sheffield 1.00
129 Bernie Williams .75
130 Mike Mussina 1.00
131 Mariano Rivera .75
132 Bubba Crosby .75
133 Kevin Brown .75
134 Javier Vazquez .75
135 Jason Giambi .75
136 Derek Jeter 4.00
137 Alex Rodriguez 4.00
138 Hideki Matsui 3.00
139 Mark Mulder .75
140 Jermaine Dye .75
141 Tim Hudson .75
142 Barry Zito .75
143 Eric Chavez .75
144 Bobby Crosby .75
145 Eric Byrnes .75
146 Marlon Byrd .75
147 Billy Wagner .75
148 Mike Lieberthal .75
149 Jimmy Rollins .75
150 Jim Thome 1.50
151 Bobby Abreu .75
152 Pat Burrell .75
153 Jose Castillo .75
154 Craig Wilson .75
155 Jason Bay .75
156 Jason Kendall .75
157 Raul Mondesi .75
158 Jay Payton .75
159 Trevor Hoffman .75
160 Jake Peavy .75
161 Sean Burroughs .75
162 Phil Nevin .75
163 Brian Giles .75
164 Ryan Klesko .75
165 Todd Linden .75
166 Jerome Williams .75
167 Jason Schmidt 1.00
168 Ray Durham .75
169 Marquis Grissom .75
170 Shigetoshi Hasegawa .75
171 Edgar Martinez .75
172 Freddy Garcia .75
173 Bret Boone .75
174 Raul Ibanez .75
175 Ichiro Suzuki 3.00
176 Randy Winn .75
177 Scott Rolen 1.50
178 Jim Edmonds .75
179 Albert Pujols 3.00
180 Matt Morris .75
181 Edgar Renteria .75
182 Aubrey Huff .75
183 Delmon Young .75
184 Dewon Brazelton .75
185 Rocco Baldelli .75
186 Carl Crawford .75
187 Mark Teixeira .75
188 Hank Blalock 1.00
189 Michael Young .75
190 Laynce Nix .75
191 Alfonso Soriano 1.50
192 Kevin Mench .75
193 Adrian Gonzalez .75
194 Alexis Rios .75
195 Roy Halladay .75
196 Vernon Wells .75
197 Carlos Delgado .75
198 Bill Hall .75
199 Jose Guillen .75
200 Jeremy Bonderman .75
201 Roger Clemens Yanks SP 6.00
202 Alex Rodriguez Rgr SP 6.00
203 Greg Maddux Braves SP 4.00
204 Miguel Tejada A's SP 2.00
205 Alfonso Soriano Yanks SP 3.00
206 Andy Pettitte Yanks SP 2.00
207 Curt Schilling D'backs SP 2.00
208 Gary Sheffield Braves SP 2.00
209 Ivan Rodriguez Marlins SP 2.00
210 Jim Thome Indians SP 2.00
211 Mike Mussina O's SP 2.00
212 Mike Piazza Dodgers SP 4.00
213 Randy Johnson M's SP 3.00
214 Roger Clemens Sox SP 6.00
215 Sammy Sosa Sox SP 4.00
216 Alex Rodriguez M's SP 6.00
217 Randy Johnson Astros SP 3.00
218 Vladimir Guerrero Expos SP 3.00
219 Rafael Palmeiro Rgr SP 2.00
220 Manny Ramirez Indians SP 2.00
221 Mike Piazza Marlins SP 4.00
222 Cal Ripken Jr. LGD 10.00
223 Ted Williams LGD 8.00
224 Duke Snider LGD 2.00
225 Ernie Banks LGD 4.00
226 Ryne Sandberg LGD 8.00
227 Mark Grace LGD 2.00
228 Andre Dawson LGD 2.00
229 Bob Feller LGD 2.00
230 Bob Feller LGD 6.00
231 George Brett LGD 8.00
232 Bo Jackson LGD 3.00
233 Robin Yount LGD 4.00
234 Harmon Killebrew LGD 4.00
235 Gary Carter LGD 2.00
236 Don Mattingly LGD 8.00
237 Phil Rizzuto LGD 2.00
238 Babe Ruth LGD 8.00
239 Lou Gehrig LGD 8.00
240 Reggie Jackson LGD 3.00
241 Rickey Henderson LGD 3.00
242 Mike Schmidt LGD 8.00
243 Roberto Clemente LGD 8.00
244 Tony Gwynn LGD 3.00
245 Will Clark LGD 3.00
246 Lou Brock LGD 2.00
247 Bob Gibson LGD 3.00
248 Stan Musial LGD 5.00
249 Nolan Ryan LGD 10.00
250 Dale Murphy LGD 2.00
251 *Aarom Baldiris Auto/499* 8.00
252 *Akinori Otsuka Auto/99* 40.00
253 *Andres Blanco Auto/499* 8.00
254 *Angel Chavez Auto/499* 5.00
255 *Carlos Hines Auto/199* 8.00
256 *Carlos Vasquez Auto/499* 10.00
257 *Casey Daigle/499* 10.00
258 *Chris Oxspring Auto/499* 8.00
259 *Colby Miller Auto/499* 5.00
260 *David Crouthers Auto/199* 8.00
261 *Donald Kelly Auto/499* 5.00
262 *Eddy Rodriguez Auto/499* 10.00
263 *Edwardo Sierra Auto/299* 8.00
264 *Edwin Moreno Auto/499* 10.00
265 *Fernando Nieve Auto/499* 5.00
266 *Freddy Guzman Auto/499* 5.00
267 *Greg Dobbs Auto/499* 5.00
268 *Brad Halsey Auto/499* 5.00
269 *Hector Gimenez Auto/499* 8.00
270 *Ivan Ochoa Auto/499* 5.00
271 *Jake Woods Auto/499* 8.00
272 *Jamie Brown Auto/499* 5.00
273 *Jason Bartlett Auto/499* 8.00
274 *Jason Szuminski Auto/499* 5.00
275 *John Gall/499* 5.00
276 *Jorge Vasquez Auto/499* 5.00
277 *Josh Labandeira Auto/499* 8.00
278 *Justin Hampson Auto/499* 5.00
279 *Kazuo Matsui/499* 15.00
280 *Kevin Cave Auto/499* 8.00
281 *Lance Cormier Auto/499* 5.00
282 *Lincoln Holdzkom Auto/199* 8.00
283 *Merkin Valdez Auto/199* 15.00
284 *Mike Wuertz Auto/499* 8.00
285 *Mike Johnston Auto/499* 5.00

286 Mike Rouse Auto/329 8.00
287 *Onil Joseph Auto/499* 5.00
288 *Phil Stockman Auto/499* 5.00
289 *Roberto Novoa Auto/499* 8.00
290 *Ronald Belisario Auto/499* 5.00
291 *Ronny Cedeno Auto/499* 5.00
292 *Ryan Meaux Auto/499* 5.00
293 *Scott Proctor/499* 5.00
294 Sean Henn Auto/199 10.00
295 *Shawn Camp Auto/499* 5.00
296 *Shawn Hill Auto/499* 5.00
297 *Shingo Takatsu Auto/99* 40.00
298 *Tim Bittner Auto/199* 8.00
299 *William Bergolla/499* 5.00
300 *Yadier Molina Auto/499* 15.00

Marble Black

No Pricing
Production one set

Marble Blue

Blue 1-200: 3-5X
Blue 201-250: 2-3X
Blue 251-300: .5-1X
Production 50 sets

Marble Emerald

NM/M
No Pricing
Production 5 sets

Marble Gold

Gold 1-200: 6-8X
Gold 201-250: 2-4X
Gold 251-300: No Pricing
Production 25 sets

Marble Red

NM/M
Red 1-200: 2-3X
Red 201-250: 1-2X
Red 251-300: .4-1X
Production 100 sets

Marble Material Black

No Pricing
Production one set

Marble Material Emerald Prime

No Pricing
Production 5 sets

Marble Signature Black

No Pricing
Production one set

Marble Signature Emerald

No Pricing
Production 1-5

Marble Signature Gold

No Pricing
Production 1-25

Check Signature Green

No Pricing
Production 1-15

Check Signature Red

No Pricing

Check Signature Material Red

NM/M
Quantity Produced Listed
4 Bob Gibson Hat/25 50.00
5 Bobby Doerr Jsy/25 30.00
6 Brooks Robinson Bat/25 65.00
7 Cal Ripken Jr. Jsy/10
8 Cal Ripken Jr. Jsy/10
9 Cal Ripken Jr. Bat/10
10 Cal Ripken Jr. Jkt/10
11 Carl Yastrzemski Jsy/6
12 Carl Yastrzemski Bat/6
13 Carlton Fisk Jkt/25 50.00
14 Carlton Fisk Jsy/25 50.00
16 Dale Murphy Jsy/25 40.00
17 Dale Murphy Jsy/25 40.00
18 Don Mattingly Jsy/10
19 Don Mattingly Jsy/10
20 Don Mattingly Bat/10
21 Don Mattingly Jkt/10
22 Duke Snider Pants/50 40.00
23 Ozzie Smith Jsy/12
24 Ozzie Smith Jsy/12
25 Ozzie Smith Bat/12
26 Frank Robinson Bat/25 40.00
27 George Brett Jsy/15 100.00
28 George Brett Jsy/15 100.00
29 George Brett Bat/15 100.00
33 Harmon Killebrew Shoe/25 65.00
34 Harmon Killebrew Bat/25 65.00
38 Kirby Puckett Fld Glv/10
39 Kirby Puckett Bat/10
41 Lou Brock Jsy/25 40.00
43 Luis Aparicio Pants/25 25.00
44 Mark Grace Fld Glve/25 40.00
46 Mike Schmidt Fld Glv/10
47 Mike Schmidt Jsy/10
48 Mike Schmidt Jkt/10
49 Mike Schmidt Bat/10
50 Nolan Ryan Jkt/15
51 Nolan Ryan Pants/15
52 Nolan Ryan Jkt/15
53 Paul Molitor Bat/25 40.00
57 Red Schoendienst Bat/25 25.00
63 Ron Santo Bat/14
65 Ryne Sandberg Jsy/25 75.00
67 Stan Musial Jsy/14
68 Stan Musial Jsy/14
69 Stan Musial Bat/14
70 Steve Carlton Pants/10
71 Steve Carlton Jsy/10
73 Tony Gwynn Jsy/25 70.00
74 Tony Gwynn Jsy/25 70.00
77 Whitey Ford Pants/25 60.00
78 Will Clark Jsy/25 40.00
79 Will Clark Bat/25 40.00

Check Signature Material Green

NM/M
Quantity Produced Listed
1 Al Kaline Bat/33 65.00
2 Andre Dawson Jsy/33 25.00
4 Bob Gibson Hat/15 50.00
6 Brooks Robinson Bat/15 80.00
22 Duke Snider Pants/25 50.00
26 Frank Robinson Bat/15 50.00
41 Lou Brock Jsy/15 50.00
43 Luis Aparicio Pants/15 30.00
44 Mark Grace Fld Glv/15 50.00
53 Paul Molitor Bat/15 40.00
77 Whitey Ford Pants/15 75.00

Check Signature Blue

NM/M
Quantity produced listed
1 Al Kaline/22 60.00
2 Andre Dawson/22 25.00
22 Duke Snider/20 40.00
31 George Kell/60 35.00

Check Signature Material Blue

NM/M
Quantity produced listed
1 Al Kaline Bat/50 50.00
2 Andre Dawson Jsy/50 20.00
4 Bob Gibson Hat/50 30.00
5 Bobby Doerr Jsy/50 20.00
6 Brooks Robinson Bat/50 50.00
7 Cal Ripken Jr. Jsy/25 200.00
8 Cal Ripken Jr. Jsy/25 200.00
9 Cal Ripken Jr. Bat/25 200.00
10 Cal Ripken Jr. Jkt/25 200.00
13 Carlton Fisk Jkt/35 40.00
14 Carlton Fisk Jsy/35 40.00
16 Dale Murphy Jsy/50 30.00
17 Dale Murphy Jsy/50 30.00
18 Don Mattingly Jsy/25 80.00
19 Don Mattingly Gray Jsy/25 80.00
20 Don Mattingly Bat/25 80.00
21 Don Mattingly Jkt/25 80.00
22 Duke Snider Pants/100 40.00
23 Ozzie Smith Jsy/40 60.00
24 Ozzie Smith Jsy/40 60.00
25 Ozzie Smith Bat/40 60.00
26 Frank Robinson Bat/50 30.00
27 George Brett White Jsy/30 80.00
28 George Brett Blue Jsy/30 80.00
29 George Brett Bat/30 80.00
32 Hal Newhouser Jsy/15 30.00
33 Harmon Killebrew Shoe/35 60.00
34 Harmon Killebrew Bat/35 60.00
38 Kirby Puckett Fld Glv/25 60.00
39 Kirby Puckett Bat/25 60.00
40 Lou Boudreau Jsy/15 100.00
41 Lou Brock Jsy/50 30.00
43 Luis Aparicio Pants/50 20.00
44 Mark Grace Fld Glv/50 30.00
46 Mike Schmidt Fld Glv/25 80.00
47 Mike Schmidt Jsy/25 80.00
48 Mike Schmidt Jkt/25 80.00
49 Mike Schmidt Bat/25 80.00
50 Nolan Ryan Astros Jkt/30 150.00
51 Nolan Ryan Rgr Pants/30 150.00
52 Nolan Ryan Angels Jkt/30 150.00
53 Paul Molitor Bat/50 35.00
57 Red Schoendienst Bat/50 20.00
63 Ron Santo Bat/25 40.00
65 Ryne Sandberg Jsy/50 65.00
67 Stan Musial White Jsy/30 80.00
68 Stan Musial Gray Jsy/30 80.00
69 Stan Musial Bat/30 80.00
70 Steve Carlton Pants/25 40.00
71 Steve Carlton Jsy/25 40.00
73 Tony Gwynn White Jsy/50 50.00
74 Tony Gwynn Navy Jsy/50 50.00
77 Whitey Ford Pants/50 30.00
78 Will Clark Jsy/50 50.00
79 Will Clark Bat/50 50.00

Hall of Fame Souvenirs

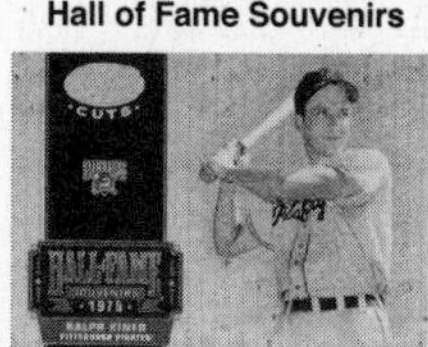

NM/M
Quantity produced listed
1 Ernie Banks/84 8.00
2 Stan Musial/93 15.00
3 Nolan Ryan/99 25.00
4 Duke Snider/87 8.00
5 Bob Feller/94 8.00
6 George Brett/98 20.00
7 Robin Yount/78 15.00
8 Harmon Killebrew/83 10.00
9 Gary Carter/78 4.00
10 Phil Rizzuto/75 8.00
11 Reggie Jackson/94 8.00
12 Mike Schmidt/97 20.00
13 Lou Brock/80 6.00
14 Bob Gibson/84 8.00
15 Bobby Doerr/75 6.00
16 Tony Perez/77 4.00
17 Whitey Ford/78 8.00
18 Juan Marichal/84 4.00
19 Monte Irvin/75 4.00
20 Fergie Jenkins/75 4.00
21 Ralph Kiner/75 8.00
22 Eddie Murray/85 10.00
23 George Kell/75 4.00
24 Hoyt Wilhelm/84 4.00
25 Carlton Fisk/80 6.00
26 Rod Carew/91 8.00
27 Frank Robinson/89 6.00
28 Gaylord Perry/77 4.00
29 Red Schoendienst/75 4.00
30 Brooks Robinson/92 8.00
31 Al Kaline/88 10.00
32 Orlando Cepeda/75 4.00
33 Steve Carlton/96 4.00
34 Luis Aparicio/85 4.00
35 Warren Spahn/83 8.00
36 Kirby Puckett/82 10.00
37 Phil Niekro/80 4.00
38 Jim Bunning/75 4.00
39 Tom Seaver/99 8.00
40 Paul Molitor/85 8.00
41 Johnny Bench/96 8.00
42 Don Sutton/82 4.00
43 Robin Roberts/87 6.00
44 Jim Palmer/93 6.00
45 Joe Morgan/82 4.00
46 Roberto Clemente/93 25.00
47 Lou Gehrig/100 10.00
48 Babe Ruth/95 20.00
49 Ty Cobb/98 10.00
50 Ted Williams/94 20.00

HOF Souvenirs Material

NM/M
Production 25 Sets
1 Ernie Banks Jsy 30.00
2 Stan Musial Jsy 50.00
3 Nolan Ryan Jsy 60.00
4 Duke Snider Pants 20.00
5 Bob Feller Jsy 20.00
6 George Brett Jsy 50.00
7 Robin Yount Jsy 40.00
8 Harmon Killebrew Jsy 25.00
9 Gary Carter Jkt 15.00
10 Phil Rizzuto Pants 20.00
11 Reggie Jackson Jsy 25.00
12 Mike Schmidt Jsy 50.00
13 Lou Brock Jsy 20.00
14 Bob Gibson Jsy 20.00
15 Bobby Doerr Jsy 15.00
16 Tony Perez Bat 10.00
17 Whitey Ford Pants 25.00
18 Juan Marichal Jsy 15.00
20 Fergie Jenkins Pants 10.00
21 Ralph Kiner Bat 25.00
22 Eddie Murray Jsy 25.00
24 Hoyt Wilhelm Jsy 10.00
25 Carlton Fisk Jsy 20.00
26 Rod Carew Jsy 20.00
27 Frank Robinson Jsy 15.00
29 Red Schoendienst Jsy 15.00
30 Brooks Robinson Bat 30.00
31 Al Kaline Pants 30.00
32 Orlando Cepeda Bat 10.00
33 Steve Carlton Pants 15.00
34 Luis Aparicio Pants 10.00
35 Warren Spahn Pants 25.00
36 Kirby Puckett Jsy 25.00
37 Phil Niekro Jsy 10.00
39 Tom Seaver Jsy 25.00
40 Paul Molitor Bat 20.00
41 Johnny Bench Jsy 25.00
42 Don Sutton Jsy 10.00
43 Robin Roberts Hat 15.00
44 Jim Palmer Jsy 15.00
45 Joe Morgan Jsy 15.00
46 Roberto Clemente Jsy 80.00
47 Lou Gehrig Pants 150.00
48 Babe Ruth Pants 275.00
49 Ty Cobb Pants 150.00
50 Ted Williams Jsy 125.00

Hall of Fame Souvenirs Sign.

NM/M
Quantity produced listed
3 Nolan Ryan/34 150.00
4 Duke Snider/50 30.00
5 Bob Feller/50 30.00
6 George Brett/5
8 Harmon Killebrew/25 50.00
9 Gary Carter/50 15.00
10 Phil Rizzuto/50 25.00
11 Reggie Jackson/9
12 Mike Schmidt/20 60.00
13 Lou Brock/50 25.00
14 Bob Gibson/45 25.00
15 Bobby Doerr/50 15.00
16 Tony Perez/50 15.00
17 Whitey Ford/16 40.00
18 Juan Marichal/50 15.00
19 Monte Irvin/50 25.00
20 Fergie Jenkins/50 15.00
21 Ralph Kiner/50 25.00
22 Eddie Murray/33 60.00
23 George Kell/50 15.00
24 Hoyt Wilhelm/49 15.00
25 Carlton Fisk/27 30.00
26 Rod Carew/29 30.00
28 Gaylord Perry/50 15.00
29 Red Schoendienst/50 15.00
30 Brooks Robinson/50 40.00
31 Al Kaline/50 40.00
32 Orlando Cepeda/50 15.00
33 Steve Carlton/50 25.00
34 Luis Aparicio/50 15.00
35 Warren Spahn/21 50.00

36 Kirby Puckett/34 50.00
37 Phil Niekro/50 15.00
38 Jim Bunning/50 15.00
40 Paul Molitor/25 30.00
41 Johnny Bench/5
42 Don Sutton/50 15.00
43 Robin Roberts/50 15.00
44 Jim Palmer/22 20.00
45 Joe Morgan/25 20.00

HOF Souvenirs Sign. Material

NM/M

Quantity Produced Listed
3 Nolan Ryan Jsy/34 180.00
5 Bob Feller Jsy/19 50.00
12 Mike Schmidt Jsy/20 80.00
13 Lou Brock Jsy/20 40.00
14 Bob Gibson Jsy/45 30.00
16 Tony Perez Bat/24 25.00
17 Whitey Ford Pants/16 50.00
18 Juan Marichal Jsy/27 30.00
20 Fergie Jenkins Pants/31 30.00
22 Eddie Murray Jsy/33 85.00
25 Carlton Fisk Jsy/27 50.00
26 Rod Carew Jsy/29 50.00
32 Orlando Cepeda Bat/30 30.00
33 Steve Carlton Pants/32 40.00
35 Warren Spahn Pants/2175.00
36 Kirby Puckett Jsy/34 65.00
37 Phil Niekro Jsy/35 25.00
42 Don Sutton Jsy/40 20.00
43 Robin Roberts Hat/36 25.00
44 Jim Palmer Jsy/22 30.00
45 Joe Morgan Jsy/16 35.00

K-Force

NM/M

Quantity Produced Listed
1 Nolan Ryan/500 8.00
2 Steve Carlton/500 2.00
3 Roger Clemens/500 6.00
4 Randy Johnson/500 3.00
5 Bert Blyleven/500 1.50
6 Tom Seaver/500 3.00
7 Don Sutton/500 1.50
8 Gaylord Perry/500 1.50
9 Phil Niekro/500 1.50
10 Fergie Jenkins/500 1.50
11 Bob Gibson/500 3.00
12 Nolan Ryan/383 8.00
13 Randy Johnson/308 3.00
14 Bob Feller/348 3.00
15 Curt Schilling/319 3.00
16 Pedro J. Martinez/313 3.00
17 Dwight Gooden/276 1.50
18 John Smoltz/276 2.00
19 Curt Schilling/316 3.00
20 Randy Johnson/319 3.00
21 Pedro Martinez/305 3.00
22 Roger Clemens/291 6.00
23 Roger Clemens/292 6.00
24 Tom Seaver/289 3.00
25 Hal Newhouser/275 2.00
26 Jim Bunning/201 2.00
27 Robin Roberts/198 3.00
28 Warren Spahn/191 4.00
29 Jack Morris/232 2.00
30 Nolan Ryan/270 8.00
31 Hideo Nomo/236 3.00
32 Barry Zito/205 2.00
33 Mike Mussina/214 3.00
34 Roy Oswalt/208 2.00
35 Mark Prior/245 4.00
36 Kerry Wood/266 4.00
37 Roy Halladay/204 2.00
38 Esteban Loaiza/207 1.50
39 Whitey Ford/94 6.00
40 Bob Gibson/17 12.00
41 Ben Sheets/18 8.00
42 Hoyt Wilhelm/139 3.00
43 Satchel Paige/91 10.00
44 Burleigh Grimes/136 3.00
45 Mark Prior, Kerry Wood/500 4.00
46 Nolan Ryan, Roger Clemens/500 10.00
47 Steve Carlton, Randy Johnson/500 3.00
48 Nolan Ryan, Roger Clemens/500 8.00
49 Nolan Ryan, Steve Carlton/500 8.00
50 Kerry Wood, Roger Clemens/20 30.00

K-Force Material

NM/M

Quantity Produced Listed
1 Nolan Ryan Jsy/100 25.00
2 Steve Carlton Jsy/32 12.00
3 Roger Clemens Jsy/25 25.00
4 Randy Johnson Jsy/51 15.00
5 Bert Blyleven Jsy/28 10.00
6 Tom Seaver Jsy/25 25.00
8 Gaylord Perry Jsy/36 8.00
9 Phil Niekro Jsy/35 10.00
10 Fergie Jenkins Pants/31 10.00
11 Bob Gibson Jsy/45 15.00
12 Nolan Ryan Jkt/100 25.00
13 Randy Johnson Jsy/51 15.00
14 Bob Feller Jsy/25 20.00
15 Curt Schilling Jsy/25 12.00
16 Pedro J. Martinez Jsy/45 15.00
17 Dwight Gooden Jsy/25 10.00
18 John Smoltz Jsy/25 15.00
19 Curt Schilling Jsy/25 12.00
20 Randy Johnson Jsy/51 15.00
21 Pedro Martinez Jsy/45 15.00
22 Roger Clemens Jsy/100 15.00
25 Hal Newhouser Jsy/25 20.00
28 Warren Spahn Jsy/50 15.00
29 Jack Morris Jsy/47 8.00
30 Nolan Ryan Jkt/100 25.00
31 Hideo Nomo Jsy/25 20.00
32 Barry Zito Jsy/25 10.00
33 Mike Mussina Jsy/25 20.00
34 Roy Oswalt Jsy/44 6.00
35 Mark Prior Jsy/50 15.00
36 Kerry Wood Jsy/34 20.00
39 Whitey Ford Jsy/50 15.00
40 Bob Gibson Jsy/50 10.00
41 Ben Sheets Jsy/25 10.00
43 Satchel Paige Jsy/100 60.00
44 Burleigh Grimes Pants/100 75.00
45 Mark Prior Jsy, Kerry Wood Pants/50 20.00
46 Nolan Ryan Jsy, Roger Clemens Jsy/50 40.00
47 Steve Carlton Jsy, Randy Johnson Jsy/50 25.00
48 Nolan Ryan Pants, Roger Clemens Jsy/50 40.00
49 Nolan Ryan Jsy, Carlton Fisk Pants/50 35.00
50 Kerry Wood Jsy, Roger Clemens Jsy/50 25.00

K-Force Signature

NM/M

Quantity Produced Listed
2 Steve Carlton/50 30.00
5 Bert Blyleven/50 15.00
7 Don Sutton/50 15.00
8 Gaylord Perry/50 15.00
9 Phil Niekro/50 25.00
10 Fergie Jenkins/50 15.00
14 Bob Feller/50 30.00
17 Dwight Gooden/50 20.00
26 Jim Bunning/50 25.00
27 Robin Roberts/50 20.00
29 Jack Morris/50 15.00
34 Roy Oswalt/50 15.00
38 Esteban Loaiza/50 10.00

K-Force Signature Material

NM/M

Quantity Produced Listed
1 Nolan Ryan Jsy/34 150.00
2 Steve Carlton Jsy/32 50.00
5 Bert Blyleven Jsy/28 25.00
8 Gaylord Perry Jsy/36 25.00
9 Phil Niekro Jsy/35 40.00
10 Fergie Jenkins Pants/31 25.00
11 Bob Gibson Jsy/45 40.00
12 Nolan Ryan Jkt/34 150.00
14 Bob Feller Jsy/19 50.00
17 Dwight Gooden Jsy/16 30.00
28 Warren Spahn Jsy/21 65.00
29 Jack Morris Jsy/47 20.00
30 Nolan Ryan Jkt/34 150.00
34 Roy Oswalt Jsy/44 20.00
36 Kerry Wood Jsy/34 50.00
37 Roy Halladay Jsy/32 15.00
39 Whitey Ford Jsy/16 50.00
40 Bob Gibson Jsy/45 30.00

Marble Material Red Position

NM/M

Quantity Produced Listed
1 Vladimir Guerrero Jsy/100 10.00
2 Garret Anderson Jsy/100 4.00
5 Troy Glaus Jsy/75 4.00
6 Tim Salmon Jsy/75 6.00
8 Brandon Webb Jsy/10
10 Randy Johnson Jsy/100 8.00
12 Richie Sexson Jsy/10
13 Luis Gonzalez Jsy/100 4.00
15 Rafael Furcal Jsy/100 4.00
16 Chipper Jones Jsy/100 8.00
17 Marcus Giles Jsy/100 4.00
18 Andruw Jones Jsy/100 6.00
20 Rafael Palmeiro Jsy/100 8.00
21 Melvin Mora Jsy/50 6.00
22 Luis Matos Jsy/50 6.00
23 Jay Gibbons Jsy/100 4.00
25 Larry Bigbie Jsy/50 6.00
26 Rodrigo Lopez Jsy/50 1,000,006
27 Javy Lopez Jsy/25 10.00
28 Miguel Tejada Jsy/100 6.00
30 Curt Schilling Jsy/50 8.00
31 Jason Varitek Jsy/100 4.00
32 Manny Ramirez Jsy/100 8.00
35 Pedro J. Martinez Jsy/100 10.00
39 David Ortiz Jsy/100 8.00
40 Mark Prior Jsy/100 10.00
41 Kerry Wood Pants/100 10.00
42 Sammy Sosa Jsy/100 10.00
44 Greg Maddux Jsy/50 15.00
45 Aramis Ramirez Jsy/100 6.00
49 Moises Alou Jsy/10
51 Frank Thomas Jsy/100 8.00
52 Maggio Ordonez Jsy/100 4.00
53 Carlos Lee Jsy/100 4.00
54 Mark Buehrle Jsy/100 4.00
57 Paul Konerko Jsy/50 6.00
58 Adam Dunn Jsy/100 8.00
59 Austin Kearns Jsy/100 4.00
60 Barry Larkin Jsy/100 6.00
63 Sean Casey Jsy/10
65 Jody Gerut Jsy/100 4.00
66 Cliff Lee Jsy/100 4.00
67 Victor Martinez Jsy/100 6.00
68 C.C. Sabathia Jsy/100 4.00
69 Omar Vizquel Jsy/100 4.00
70 Travis Hafner Jsy/100 4.00
71 Todd Helton Jsy/100 8.00
72 Preston Wilson Jsy/100 4.00
73 Jeromy Burnitz Jsy/10
74 Larry Walker Jsy/10
75 Ivan Rodriguez Jsy/50 10.00
77 Miguel Cabrera Jsy/100 8.00
79 Josh Beckett Jsy/100 6.00
81 Dontrelle Willis Jsy/100 4.00
82 Brad Penny Jsy/100 4.00
85 Andy Pettitte Jsy/10
86 Jeff Bagwell Jsy/100 8.00
87 Roy Oswalt Jsy/100 4.00
88 Lance Berkman Jsy/100 4.00
89 Morgan Ensberg Jsy/100 4.00
90 Craig Biggio Jsy/100 6.00
93 Jeff Kent Jsy/100 4.00
94 Richard Hidalgo Pants/100 4.00
95 Roger Clemens Jsy/25 30.00
96 Carlos Beltran Jsy/100 6.00
97 Angel Berroa Pants/100 4.00
100 Mike Sweeney Jsy/100 4.00
101 Kazuhisa Ishii Jsy/100 4.00
102 Shawn Green Jsy/100 4.00
104 Paul LoDuca Jsy/100 4.00
105 Hideo Nomo Jsy/100 8.00
107 Adrian Beltre Jsy/100 8.00
110 Ben Sheets Jsy/100 6.00
111 Geoff Jenkins Jsy/100 4.00
112 Jacque Jones Jsy/100 4.00
113 Johan Santana Jsy/100 8.00
114 Shannon Stewart Jsy/100 4.00
117 Torii Hunter Jsy/75 4.00
119 Orlando Cabrera Jsy/10
120 Jose Vidro Jsy/10
123 Mike Piazza Jsy/100 10.00
124 Jae Weong Seo Jsy/10
125 Jose Reyes Jsy/75 4.00
126 Tom Glavine Jsy/75 6.00
127 Jorge Posada Jsy/100 8.00
129 Bernie Williams Jsy/100 6.00
130 Mike Mussina Jsy/25 20.00
131 Mariano Rivera Jsy/100 8.00
135 Jason Giambi Jsy/10
138 Hideki Matsui Jsy/100 25.00
139 Mark Mulder Jsy/100 4.00
141 Tim Hudson Jsy/10
142 Barry Zito Jsy/100 4.00
143 Eric Chavez Jsy/100 4.00
146 Marlon Byrd Jsy/100 4.00
150 Jim Thome Jsy/100 8.00
151 Bobby Abreu Jsy/100 4.00
152 Pat Burrell Jsy/100 4.00
154 Craig Wilson Jsy/100 4.00
156 Jason Kendall Jsy/100 4.00
161 Sean Burroughs Jsy/100 4.00
163 Brian Giles Jsy/10
164 Ryan Klesko Jsy/100 4.00
166 Jerome Williams Jsy/25 10.00
171 Edgar Martinez Jsy/100 6.00
172 Freddy Garcia Jsy/100 4.00
177 Scott Rolen Jsy/100 10.00
178 Jim Edmonds Jsy/100 6.00
179 Albert Pujols Jsy/100 20.00
180 Matt Morris Jsy/75 4.00
181 Edgar Renteria Jsy/25 10.00
182 Aubrey Huff Jsy/100 4.00
184 Dewon Brazelton Jsy/10
185 Rocco Baldelli Jsy/100 4.00
186 Carl Crawford Jsy/100 4.00
187 Mark Teixeira Jsy/25 8.00
188 Hank Blalock Jsy/100 8.00
191 Alfonso Soriano Jsy/100 8.00
192 Kevin Mench Jsy/100 4.00
195 Roy Halladay Jsy/100 4.00
196 Vernon Wells Jsy/100 4.00
197 Carlos Delgado Jsy/100 4.00
200 Jeremy Bonderman Jsy/100 4.00
201 Roger Clemens Jsy/100 10.00
202 Alex Rodriguez Jsy/100 10.00
203 Greg Maddux Jsy/100 10.00
204 Miguel Tejada Jsy/100 4.00
205 Alfonso Soriano Jsy/100 8.00
206 Andy Pettitte Jsy/100 6.00
207 Curt Schilling Jsy/100 8.00
208 Gary Sheffield Jsy/50 8.00
209 Ivan Rodriguez Jsy/100 8.00
210 Jim Thome Jsy/25 20.00
211 Mike Mussina Jsy/50 10.00
212 Mike Piazza Jsy/100 10.00
213 Randy Johnson Jsy/100 8.00
214 Roger Clemens Jsy/100 10.00
215 Sammy Sosa Jsy/50 15.00
216 Alex Rodriguez Jsy/100 10.00
217 Randy Johnson Jsy/100 8.00
218 Vladimir Guerrero Jsy/100 8.00
219 Rafael Palmeiro Jsy/100 8.00
221 Mike Piazza Jsy/100 10.00
222 Cal Ripken Jr. Jsy/50 50.00
223 Ted Williams Jsy/25 100.00
225 Ernie Banks Jsy/50 15.00
226 Ryne Sandberg Jsy/100 15.00

227 Mark Grace Jsy/25 20.00
228 Andre Dawson Jsy/100 6.00
229 Bob Feller Jsy/25 20.00
230 Ty Cobb Pants/1
231 George Brett Jsy/100 15.00
232 Bo Jackson Jsy/100 10.00
233 Robin Yount Jsy/100 12.00
234 Harmon Killebrew Jsy/25 25.00
235 Gary Carter Jkt/100 6.00
236 Don Mattingly Jsy/50 25.00
237 Phil Rizzuto Pants/25 20.00
238 Babe Ruth Pants/50 200.00
239 Lou Gehrig Pants/50 150.00
240 Reggie Jackson Jsy/100 8.00
241 Rickey Henderson Jsy/100 10.00
242 Mike Schmidt Jsy/50 25.00
243 Roberto Clemente Jsy/50 75.00
244 Tony Gwynn Jsy/100 10.00
245 Will Clark Jsy/100 10.00
246 Lou Brock Jsy/25 20.00
247 Bob Gibson Jsy/25 20.00
248 Stan Musial Jsy/25 60.00
249 Nolan Ryan Jsy/50 40.00
250 Dale Murphy Jsy/100 10.00

Marble Signature Blue

NM/M

Quantity Produced Listed
2 Garret Anderson/50 20.00
3 John Lackey/75 15.00
7 Shea Hillenbrand/75 15.00
8 Brandon Webb/75 10.00
11 Alex Cintron/75 10.00
14 Adam LaRoche/75 15.00
15 Rafael Furcal/50 20.00
17 Marcus Giles/50 15.00
19 Russ Ortiz/75 10.00
21 Melvin Mora/75 15.00
22 Luis Matos/75 10.00
23 Jay Gibbons/75 15.00
24 Adam Loewen/50 10.00
25 Larry Bigbie/75 15.00
26 Rodrigo Lopez/75 10.00
29 Trot Nixon/50 35.00
33 Keith Foulke/75 8.00
39 David Ortiz/50 40.00
40 Mark Prior/25 60.00
41 Kerry Wood/25 50.00
43 Derrek Lee/25 30.00
45 Aramis Ramirez/75 20.00
46 Matt Clement/25 15.00
47 Carlos Zambrano/75 35.00
48 Todd Walker/75 10.00
52 Magglio Ordonez/25 20.00
53 Carlos Lee/75 15.00
54 Mark Buehrle/50 15.00
55 Esteban Loaiza/25 15.00
58 Adam Dunn/25 40.00
59 Austin Kearns/25 20.00
63 Sean Casey/25 25.00
65 Jody Gerut/75 8.00
66 Cliff Lee/75 10.00
67 Victor Martinez/75 20.00
68 C.C. Sabathia/75 15.00
70 Travis Hafner/75 15.00
72 Preston Wilson/75 15.00
77 Miguel Cabrera/50 35.00
80 Mike Lowell/25 20.00
82 Brad Penny/75 10.00
87 Roy Oswalt/50 15.00
89 Morgan Ensberg/75 12.00
90 Craig Biggio/25 30.00
91 Octavio Dotel/75 15.00
92 Wade Miller/75 10.00
96 Carlos Beltran/50 50.00
97 Angel Berroa/50 10.00
98 Jeremy Affeldt/75 10.00
103 Milton Bradley/75 15.00
104 Paul LoDuca/50 15.00
108 Scott Podsednik/75 15.00
109 Rickie Weeks/25 25.00
112 Jacque Jones/75 10.00
113 Johan Santana/50 50.00
114 Shannon Stewart/50 15.00
116 Lew Ford/75 15.00
117 Torii Hunter/25 25.00
118 Chad Cordero/75 10.00
119 Orlando Cabrera/75 20.00
120 Jose Vidro/50 10.00
125 Jose Reyes/25 20.00
132 Bubba Crosby/75 10.00
139 Mark Mulder/25 25.00
140 Jermaine Dye/75 10.00
144 Bobby Crosby/75 40.00
145 Eric Byrnes/75 10.00
146 Marlon Byrd/75 10.00
148 Mike Lieberthal/75 15.00
153 Jose Castillo/75 10.00
154 Craig Wilson/75 10.00
155 Jason Bay/75 25.00
158 Jay Payton/75 10.00
161 Sean Burroughs/25 15.00
165 Todd Linden/75 8.00
170 Shigetoshi Hasegawa/50 40.00
171 Edgar Martinez/25 40.00
174 Raul Ibanez/75 10.00
177 Scott Rolen/50 35.00
182 Aubrey Huff/75 10.00
183 Delmon Young/25 25.00
184 Dewon Brazelton/75 10.00
186 Carl Crawford/75 20.00
187 Mark Teixeira/25 40.00
188 Hank Blalock/50 25.00
189 Michael Young/75 15.00
190 Laynce Nix/75 15.00
191 Alfonso Soriano/25 50.00
193 Adrian Gonzalez/75 10.00
194 Alexis Rios/75 20.00
196 Vernon Wells/50 15.00
198 Bill Hall/75 10.00
199 Jose Guillen/75 15.00
200 Jeremy Bonderman/75 10.00
218 Vladimir Guerrero/5 5.00
222 Cal Ripken Jr./25 150.00
224 Duke Snider/35 35.00
228 Andre Dawson/50 20.00
229 Bob Feller/50 30.00
235 Gary Carter/25 20.00
237 Phil Rizzuto/25 40.00
245 Will Clark/25 50.00
246 Lou Brock/25 35.00
247 Bob Gibson/25 40.00
248 Stan Musial/25 75.00
249 Nolan Ryan/25 150.00
250 Dale Murphy/50 30.00
251 Aarom Baldiris/75 10.00
252 Akinori Otsuka/25 50.00
253 Andres Blanco/75 10.00
254 Angel Chavez/75 8.00
255 Carlos Hines/75 8.00
256 Carlos Vasquez/75 12.00
258 Chris Oxspring/75 10.00
259 Colby Miller/75 8.00
261 Donald Kelly/75 8.00
262 Eddy Rodriguez/75 8.00
263 Edwardo Sierra/65 10.00
264 Edwin Moreno/75 12.00
265 Fernando Nieve/75 8.00
266 Freddy Guzman/75 8.00
267 Greg Dobbs/75 8.00
268 Brad Halsey/75 8.00
269 Hector Gimenez/75 8.00
270 Ivan Ochoa/75 8.00
271 Jake Woods/75 10.00
272 Jamie Brown/75 8.00
273 Jason Bartlett/75 15.00
274 Jason Szuminski/75 8.00
275 John Gall/75 10.00
276 Jorge Vasquez/75 8.00
277 Josh Labandeira/75 8.00
278 Justin Hampson/75 8.00
280 Kevin Cave/75 10.00
281 Lance Cormier/75 8.00
283 Merkin Valdez/75 15.00
284 Mike Wuertz/75 10.00
285 Mike Johnston/75 8.00
287 Onil Joseph/75 8.00
288 Phil Stockman/75 8.00
289 Roberto Novoa/75 10.00
290 Ronald Belisario/75 8.00
291 Ronny Cedeno/75 8.00
292 Ryan Meaux/75 8.00
293 Scott Proctor/75 10.00
295 Shawn Camp/75 8.00
296 Shawn Hill/75 8.00
297 Shingo Takatsu/25 60.00
299 William Bergolla/75 8.00
300 Yadier Molina/75 25.00

Marble Signature Red

NM/M

Quantity Produced Listed
2 Garret Anderson/50 20.00
3 John Lackey/100 15.00
7 Shea Hillenbrand/100 15.00
8 Brandon Webb/100 10.00
9 Roberto Alomar/1
11 Alex Cintron/100 10.00
14 Adam LaRoche/100 15.00
15 Rafael Furcal/50 20.00
16 Chipper Jones/1
17 Marcus Giles/50 15.00
18 Andruw Jones/1
19 Russ Ortiz/100 10.00
21 Melvin Mora/100 15.00
22 Luis Matos/100 10.00
23 Jay Gibbons/100 15.00
25 Larry Bigbie/100 15.00
26 Rodrigo Lopez/100 10.00
29 Trot Nixon/50 35.00
33 Keith Foulke/100 8.00
39 David Ortiz/50 40.00
40 Mark Prior/25 60.00
43 Derrek Lee/50 25.00
45 Aramis Ramirez/100 20.00
46 Matt Clement/25 15.00
47 Carlos Zambrano/100 35.00
48 Todd Walker/100 10.00
53 Carlos Lee/100 15.00
54 Mark Buehrle/50 15.00
55 Esteban Loaiza/100 10.00
58 Adam Dunn/25 40.00
59 Austin Kearns/25 20.00
63 Sean Casey/25 25.00
65 Jody Gerut/100 8.00
66 Cliff Lee/100 10.00
67 Victor Martinez/100 20.00
68 C.C. Sabathia/100 15.00
70 Travis Hafner/100 15.00
72 Preston Wilson/100 15.00
77 Miguel Cabrera/50 35.00
80 Mike Lowell/25 20.00
82 Brad Penny/100 10.00
89 Morgan Ensberg/100 10.00
90 Craig Biggio/25 30.00
91 Octavio Dotel/100 15.00
92 Wade Miller/100 10.00
96 Carlos Beltran/50 50.00
97 Angel Berroa/50 10.00
98 Jeremy Affeldt/100 10.00
103 Milton Bradley/100 15.00
104 Paul LoDuca/50 15.00
108 Scott Podsednik/100 15.00
109 Rickie Weeks/25 25.00
112 Jacque Jones/100 10.00
113 Johan Santana/50 50.00
114 Shannon Stewart/50 15.00
116 Lew Ford/100 15.00
117 Torii Hunter/25 25.00
118 Chad Cordero/100 10.00
119 Orlando Cabrera/100 20.00
120 Jose Vidro/50 10.00
132 Bubba Crosby/100 10.00
139 Mark Mulder/25 25.00
140 Jermaine Dye/100 10.00
144 Bobby Crosby/100 40.00
145 Eric Byrnes/100 10.00
146 Marlon Byrd/100 10.00
148 Mike Lieberthal/100 15.00
153 Jose Castillo/100 10.00
154 Craig Wilson/100 10.00
155 Jason Bay/100 25.00
158 Jay Payton/100 10.00
161 Sean Burroughs/25 15.00
165 Todd Linden/100 8.00
170 Shigetoshi Hasegawa/50 40.00
171 Edgar Martinez/25 40.00
174 Raul Ibanez/100 10.00
177 Scott Rolen/50 35.00
182 Aubrey Huff/100 10.00
183 Delmon Young/25 25.00
184 Dewon Brazelton/100 10.00
186 Carl Crawford/100 20.00
187 Mark Teixeira/25 40.00
188 Hank Blalock/50 25.00
189 Michael Young/100 15.00
190 Laynce Nix/100 15.00
191 Alfonso Soriano/25 50.00
193 Adrian Gonzalez/100 10.00
194 Alexis Rios/100 20.00
196 Vernon Wells/50 15.00
198 Bill Hall/100 10.00
199 Jose Guillen/100 15.00
200 Jeremy Bonderman/100 10.00
222 Cal Ripken Jr./25 150.00
224 Duke Snider/25 40.00
228 Andre Dawson/100 20.00
229 Bob Feller/100 25.00
235 Gary Carter/25 20.00
237 Phil Rizzuto/25 40.00
245 Will Clark/25 50.00
247 Bob Gibson/25 40.00
248 Stan Musial/25 75.00
249 Nolan Ryan/25 150.00
250 Dale Murphy/50 30.00
251 Aarom Baldiris/100 10.00
252 Akinori Otsuka/25 50.00
253 Andres Blanco/100 10.00
254 Angel Chavez/100 8.00
255 Carlos Hines/100 8.00
256 Carlos Vasquez/100 12.00
258 Chris Oxspring/100 10.00
259 Colby Miller/100 8.00
260 David Crouthers/50 8.00
261 Donald Kelly/100 8.00
262 Eddy Rodriguez/100 8.00
263 Edwardo Sierra/100 10.00
264 Edwin Moreno/100 10.00
266 Freddy Guzman/100 8.00
267 Greg Dobbs/100 8.00
268 Brad Halsey/100 8.00
269 Hector Gimenez/100 8.00
270 Ivan Ochoa/100 8.00
271 Jake Woods/100 10.00
272 Jamie Brown/100 8.00
273 Jason Bartlett/100 15.00
274 Jason Szuminski/100 8.00
275 John Gall/100 10.00
276 Jorge Vasquez/100 8.00
277 Josh Labandeira/100 8.00
280 Kevin Cave/100 10.00
281 Lance Cormier/100 8.00
283 Merkin Valdez/100 15.00
284 Mike Wuertz/100 10.00
285 Mike Johnston/100 8.00
287 Onil Joseph/100 8.00
288 Phil Stockman/100 8.00
289 Roberto Novoa/100 10.00
291 Ronny Cedeno/100 8.00
292 Ryan Meaux/100 8.00
293 Scott Proctor/100 10.00
295 Shawn Camp/100 8.00
297 Shingo Takatsu/25 60.00
299 William Bergolla/100 8.00
300 Yadier Molina/100 25.00

Stars

NM/M

Production 599 Sets
1 Ryne Sandberg 6.00
2 Mark Prior 3.00
3 Andre Dawson 2.00
4 Don Mattingly 6.00
5 Vladimir Guerrero 3.00
6 Garret Anderson 2.00
7 Dale Murphy 2.00
8 Cal Ripken Jr. 10.00
9 Mark Grace 3.00
10 Kerry Wood 3.00
11 Frank Thomas 3.00
12 Magglio Ordonez 2.00
13 Adam Dunn 3.00
14 Preston Wilson 2.00
15 Bo Jackson 3.00
16 Carlos Beltran 3.00
17 Tony Gwynn 4.00
18 Will Clark 3.00
19 Edgar Martinez 2.00
20 Scott Rolen 3.00
21 Alfonso Soriano 3.00
22 Randy Johnson 3.00
23 Chipper Jones 3.00
24 Andruw Jones 2.00
25 Javy Lopez 3.00
26 Curt Schilling 3.00
27 Manny Ramirez 5.00
28 Sammy Sosa 4.00
29 Greg Maddux 2.00
30 Todd Helton 3.00
31 Jeff Bagwell 3.00
32 Shawn Green 2.00
33 Mike Piazza 5.00
34 Jorge Posada 2.00
35 Gary Sheffield 3.00
36 Mike Mussina 3.00
37 Miguel Cabrera 3.00
38 Rickey Henderson 3.00
39 Albert Pujols 8.00
40 Vernon Wells 2.00
41 Fred Lynn 2.00
42 Alan Trammell 2.00
43 Lenny Dykstra 2.00
44 Dwight Gooden 2.00
45 Keith Hernandez 2.00
46 Luis Tiant 2.00
47 Orel Hershiser 2.00
48 George Foster 2.00
49 Darryl Strawberry 2.00
50 Marty Marion 2.00

Stars Signature

Quantity Produced Listed		NM/M
3	Andre Dawson/50	20.00
4	Don Mattingly/25	65.00
6	Garret Anderson/50	20.00
7	Dale Murphy/50	30.00
12	Magglio Ordonez/25	20.00
13	Adam Dunn/25	40.00
14	Preston Wilson/50	15.00
16	Carlos Beltran/50	40.00
18	Will Clark/25	40.00
19	Edgar Martinez/25	40.00
20	Scott Rolen/25	40.00
37	Miguel Cabrera/50	40.00
40	Vernon Wells/25	20.00
41	Fred Lynn/50	10.00
42	Alan Trammell/50	20.00
43	Lenny Dykstra/50	20.00
44	Dwight Gooden/50	20.00
45	Keith Hernandez/50	20.00
46	Luis Tiant/50	15.00
47	Orel Hershiser/50	25.00
48	George Foster/50	10.00
49	Darryl Strawberry/50	20.00

Stars Signature Jersey

Quantity Produced Listed		NM/M
1	Ryne Sandberg/23	75.00
2	Mark Prior/22	65.00
4	Don Mattingly/23	75.00
5	Vladimir Guerrero/27	60.00
6	Garret Anderson/16	35.00
9	Mark Grace/17	50.00
10	Kerry Wood/34	50.00
11	Frank Thomas/35	50.00
12	Magglio Ordonez/30	25.00
13	Adam Dunn/44	50.00
14	Preston Wilson/44	20.00
15	Bo Jackson/16	125.00
16	Carlos Beltran/15	75.00
17	Tony Gwynn/19	75.00
18	Will Clark/22	65.00
20	Scott Rolen/27	60.00
24	Andruw Jones/25	40.00
28	Sammy Sosa/21	150.00
29	Greg Maddux/31	100.00
30	Todd Helton/17	50.00
34	Jorge Posada/20	50.00
37	Miguel Cabrera/24	50.00
41	Fred Lynn/19	20.00
45	Keith Hernandez/37	20.00
46	Luis Tiant/25	25.00
48	George Foster/15	25.00
49	Darryl Strawberry/18	35.00
50	Marty Marion/25	25.00

Marble Sig. Material Gold Position

Quantity Produced Listed		NM/M
2	Garret Anderson Jsy/50	20.00
8	Brandon Webb Jsy/50	15.00
15	Rafael Furcal Jsy/50	20.00
17	Marcus Giles Jsy/50	20.00
21	Melvin Mora Jsy/50	20.00
22	Luis Matos Jsy/50	15.00
23	Jay Gibbons Jsy/50	15.00
25	Larry Bigbie Jsy/50	15.00
26	Rodrigo Lopez Jsy/50	10.00
45	Aramis Ramirez Jsy/50	30.00
53	Carlos Lee Jsy/50	20.00
54	Mark Buehrle Jsy/50	20.00
59	Austin Kearns Jsy/50	20.00
65	Jody Gerut Jsy/50	10.00
66	Cliff Lee Jsy/50	15.00
67	Victor Martinez Jsy/50	25.00
68	C.C. Sabathia Jsy/50	20.00
70	Travis Hafner Jsy/50	20.00
72	Preston Wilson Jsy/50	20.00
82	Brad Penny Jsy/50	10.00
89	Morgan Ensberg Jsy/50	10.00
90	Craig Biggio Jsy/10	
96	Carlos Beltran Jsy/50	50.00
97	Angel Berroa Pants/50	10.00
104	Paul LoDuca Jsy/25	25.00
112	Jacque Jones Jsy/50	20.00
113	Johan Santana Jsy/50	50.00
114	Shannon Stewart Jsy/50	20.00
117	Torii Hunter Jsy/25	25.00
119	Orlando Cabrera Jsy/50	20.00
120	Jose Vidro Jsy/50	10.00
139	Mark Mulder Jsy/25	25.00
146	Marlon Byrd Jsy/50	15.00
154	Craig Wilson Jsy/50	15.00
161	Sean Burroughs Jsy/50	15.00
171	Edgar Martinez Jsy/25	50.00
182	Aubrey Huff Jsy/50	20.00
186	Carl Crawford Jsy/50	30.00
188	Hank Blalock Jsy/25	50.00
200	Jeremy Bonderman Jsy/50	10.00
228	Andre Dawson Jsy/50	20.00
229	Bob Feller Jsy/50	35.00
234	Harmon Killebrew Jsy/25	65.00

Marble Sig. Mat. Gold Number

Quantity Produced Listed		NM/M
1	Vladimir Guerrero Jsy/27	60.00
8	Brandon Webb Jsy/55	10.00
18	Andruw Jones Jsy/25	40.00
22	Luis Matos Jsy/32	15.00
23	Jay Gibbons Jsy/31	25.00
32	Manny Ramirez Jsy/24	75.00
39	David Ortiz Jsy/34	50.00
40	Mark Prior Jsy/22	75.00
41	Kerry Wood Pants/34	50.00
42	Sammy Sosa Jsy/21	150.00
44	Greg Maddux Jsy/31	100.00
51	Frank Thomas Jsy/35	50.00
52	Magglio Ordonez Jsy/30	25.00
53	Carlos Lee Jsy/45	20.00
54	Mark Buehrle Jsy/56	20.00
58	Adam Dunn Jsy/44	40.00
59	Austin Kearns Jsy/28	25.00
66	Cliff Lee Jsy/34	15.00
67	Victor Martinez Jsy/41	25.00
68	C.C. Sabathia Jsy/52	20.00
70	Travis Hafner Jsy/48	20.00
71	Todd Helton Jsy/17	60.00
72	Preston Wilson Jsy/44	20.00
81	Dontrelle Willis Jsy/35	30.00
82	Brad Penny Jsy/31	15.00
85	Andy Pettitte Jsy/21	50.00
104	Paul LoDuca Jsy/16	35.00
113	Johan Santana Jsy/57	50.00
114	Shannon Stewart Jsy/23	25.00
117	Torii Hunter Jsy/48	20.00
119	Orlando Cabrera Jsy/18	30.00
123	Mike Piazza Jsy/31	100.00
124	Jae Weong Seo Jsy/26	20.00
125	Jose Reyes Jsy/7	
127	Jorge Posada Jsy/20	40.00
130	Mike Mussina Jsy/35	40.00
139	Mark Mulder Jsy/20	25.00
141	Tim Hudson Jsy/15	30.00
146	Marlon Byrd Jsy/29	15.00
177	Scott Rolen Jsy/27	50.00
182	Aubrey Huff Jsy/19	30.00
184	Dewon Brazelton Jsy/45	15.00
186	Carl Crawford Jsy/13	
187	Mark Teixeira Jsy/23	50.00
195	Roy Halladay Jsy/32	15.00
200	Jeremy Bonderman Jsy/38	10.00
236	Don Mattingly Jsy/23	85.00
240	Reggie Jackson Jsy/44	50.00
241	Rickey Henderson Jsy/35	50.00
242	Mike Schmidt Pants/20	100.00
244	Tony Gwynn Jsy/19	75.00
245	Will Clark Jsy/22	50.00
246	Lou Brock Jsy/20	40.00
247	Bob Gibson Jsy/45	40.00
249	Nolan Ryan Jsy/34	150.00

Marble Material Blue Number

Quanity Produced Listed		NM/M
1	Vladimir Guerrero Jsy/27	25.00
2	Garret Anderson Jsy/16	15.00
5	Troy Glaus Jsy/25	10.00
6	Tim Salmon Jsy/15	20.00
8	Brandon Webb Jsy/55	5.00
10	Randy Johnson Jsy/51	12.00
13	Luis Gonzalez Jsy/20	10.00
17	Marcus Giles Jsy/22	10.00
18	Andruw Jones Jsy/25	10.00
20	Rafael Palmeiro Jsy/25	15.00
22	Luis Matos Jsy/32	10.00
23	Jay Gibbons Jsy/31	10.00
26	Rodrigo Lopez Jsy/19	10.00
27	Javy Lopez Jsy/18	15.00
30	Curt Schilling Jsy/38	12.00
31	Jason Varitek Jsy/33	10.00
32	Manny Ramirez Jsy/24	20.00
35	Pedro Martinez Jsy/45	15.00
39	David Ortiz Jsy/34	20.00
40	Mark Prior Jsy/22	20.00
41	Kerry Wood Pants/34	20.00
42	Sammy Sosa Jsy/21	30.00
44	Greg Maddux Jsy/31	25.00
45	Aramis Ramirez Jsy/16	15.00
49	Moises Alou Jsy/18	15.00
51	Frank Thomas Jsy/35	20.00
52	Magglio Ordonez Jsy/30	10.00
53	Carlos Lee Jsy/45	5.00
54	Mark Buehrle Jsy/56	5.00
58	Adam Dunn Jsy/44	12.00
59	Austin Kearns Jsy/28	10.00
63	Sean Casey Jsy/21	10.00
66	Cliff Lee Jsy/34	8.00
67	Victor Martinez Jsy/41	8.00
68	C.C. Sabathia Jsy/52	5.00
70	Travis Hafner Jsy/48	8.00
71	Todd Helton Jsy/17	20.00
72	Preston Wilson Jsy/44	5.00
73	Jeromy Burnitz Jsy/35	5.00
74	Larry Walker Jsy/33	10.00
77	Miguel Cabrera Jsy/24	20.00
79	Josh Beckett Jsy/21	12.00
81	Dontrelle Willis Jsy/35	10.00
82	Brad Penny Jsy/31	8.00
85	Andy Pettitte Jsy/21	15.00
87	Roy Oswalt Jsy/44	5.00
88	Lance Berkman Jsy/17	10.00
95	Roger Clemens Jsy/22	25.00
100	Mike Sweeney Jsy/29	10.00
101	Kazuhisa Ishii Jsy/17	15.00
107	Adrian Beltre Jsy/29	15.00
113	Johan Santana Jsy/57	15.00
114	Shannon Stewart Jsy/23	10.00
117	Torii Hunter Jsy/48	5.00
119	Orlando Cabrera Jsy/18	20.00
120	Jose Vidro Jsy/3	
123	Mike Piazza Jsy/31	30.00
124	Jae Weong Seo Jsy/26	10.00
126	Tom Glavine Jsy/47	10.00
127	Jorge Posada Jsy/20	15.00
129	Bernie Williams Jsy/51	10.00
130	Mike Mussina Jsy/35	15.00
131	Mariano Rivera Jsy/42	10.00
135	Jason Giambi Jsy/25	10.00
138	Hideki Matsui Jsy/55	40.00
139	Mark Mulder Jsy/20	10.00
142	Barry Zito Jsy/75	5.00
146	Marlon Byrd Jsy/29	10.00
150	Jim Thome Jsy/25	20.00
151	Bobby Abreu Jsy/53	5.00
154	Craig Wilson Jsy/36	5.00
161	Sean Burroughs Jsy/32	10.00
163	Brian Giles Jsy/24	8.00
164	Ryan Klesko Jsy/30	10.00
166	Jerome Williams Jsy/57	5.00
172	Freddy Garcia Jsy/34	8.00
177	Scott Rolen Jsy/27	20.00
178	Jim Edmonds Jsy/15	15.00
180	Matt Morris Jsy/35	10.00
181	Edgar Renteria Jsy/15	15.00
182	Aubrey Huff Jsy/19	10.00
184	Dewon Brazelton Jsy/45	5.00
187	Mark Teixeira Jsy/23	15.00
192	Kevin Mench Jsy/28	8.00
195	Roy Halladay Jsy/32	10.00
197	Carlos Delgado Jsy/25	10.00
200	Jeremy Bonderman Jsy/38	5.00
201	Roger Clemens Jsy/22	30.00
203	Greg Maddux Jsy/31	25.00
206	Andy Pettitte Jsy/46	10.00
207	Curt Schilling Jsy/38	12.00
210	Jim Thome Jsy/25	20.00
211	Mike Mussina Jsy/35	15.00
212	Mike Piazza Jsy/31	30.00
213	Randy Johnson Jsy/51	15.00
214	Roger Clemens Jsy/21	30.00
215	Sammy Sosa Jsy/21	30.00
217	Randy Johnson Jsy/51	15.00
218	Vladimir Guerrero Jsy/27	25.00
219	Rafael Palmeiro Jsy/25	15.00
221	Mike Piazza Jsy/25	30.00
226	Ryne Sandberg Jsy/23	40.00
227	Mark Grace Jsy/17	25.00
229	Bob Feller Jsy/19	20.00
232	Bo Jackson Jsy/16	40.00
233	Robin Yount Jsy/19	40.00
236	Don Mattingly Jsy/23	40.00
241	Rickey Henderson Jsy/35	25.00
242	Mike Schmidt Jsy/20	40.00
243	Roberto Clemente Jsy/21	100.00
245	Will Clark Jsy/22	30.00
246	Lou Brock Jsy/20	20.00
247	Bob Gibson Jsy/45	15.00
249	Nolan Ryan Jsy/34	40.00

2004 LEAF CERTIFIED MATERIALS

		NM/M
Complete Set (300):		
Common Player:		.50
Common (201-211):		4.00
Common (212-240):		4.00
Production 500		
Common Auto (241-300):		8.00
Pack (5):		10.00
Box (10):		85.00
1	A.J. Burnett	.50
2	Adam Dunn	1.00
3	Adam LaRoche	.50
4	Adam Loewen	.50
5	Adrian Beltre	.75
6	Al Leiter	.50
7	Albert Pujols	3.00
8	Alex Rodriguez	3.00
9	Alexis Rios	.50
10	Alfonso Soriano	1.50
11	Andruw Jones	1.00
12	Andy Pettitte	.75
13	Angel Berroa	.50
14	Aramis Ramirez	.75
15	Aubrey Huff	.50
16	Austin Kearns	.50
17	Barry Larkin	.75
18	Barry Zito	.75
19	Ben Sheets	.75
20	Bernie Williams	.75
21	Bobby Abreu	.75
22	Brad Penny	.50
23	Brad Wilkerson	.50
24	Brandon Webb	.50
25	Brendan Harris	.50
26	Bret Boone	.50
27	Brett Myers	.50
28	Bubba Crosby	.50
29	Brian Giles	.50
30	Chad Cordero	.50
31	Bubba Nelson	.50
32	Byron Gettis	.50
33	C.C. Sabathia	.50
34	Carl Crawford	.50
35	Carl Everett	.50
36	Carlos Beltran	.75
37	Carlos Delgado	.75
38	Carlos Lee	.50
39	Chad Gaudin	.50
40	Cliff Lee	.50
41	Chipper Jones	1.50
42	Cliff Floyd	.50

43	Clint Barmes	.50
44	Corey Patterson	.75
45	Craig Biggio	.75
46	Curt Schilling	1.00
47	Dan Haren	.50
48	Darin Erstad	.50
49	David Ortiz	1.00
50	Delmon Young	.50
51	Derek Jeter	4.00
52	Dewon Brazelton	.50
53	Dontrelle Willis	.75
54	Edgar Martinez	.75
55	Edgar Renteria	.75
56	Edwin Almonte	.50
57	Edwin Jackson	.50
58	Eric Chavez	.75
59	Eric Hinske	.50
60	Eric Munson	.50
61	Erubiel Durazo	.50
62	Frank Thomas	1.00
63	Fred McGriff	.50
64	Freddy Garcia	.50
65	Garret Anderson	.75
66	Garrett Atkins	.50
67	Gary Sheffield	.75
68	Geoff Jenkins	.50
69	Greg Maddux	2.00
70	Hank Blalock	1.00
71	Hee Seop Choi	.50
72	Hideki Matsui	2.50
73	Hideo Nomo	.75
74	Craig Wilson	.50
75	Ichiro Suzuki	2.50
76	Ivan Rodriguez	1.00
77	J.D. Drew	.50
78	John Lackey	.50
79	Jacque Jones	.50
80	Jae Weong Seo	.50
81	Jamie Moyer	.50
82	Jason Giambi	1.00
83	Jason Jennings	.50
84	Jason Kendall	.50
85	Melvin Mora	.50
86	Jason Varitek	.75
87	Javier Vazquez	.75
88	Javy Lopez	.75
89	Jay Gibbons	.50
90	Jay Payton	.50
91	Jeff Bagwell	1.00
92	Jeff Baker	.50
93	Jeff Kent	.50
94	Jeremy Bonderman	.50
95	Milton Bradley	.50
96	Jerome Williams	.50
97	Jim Edmonds	.75
98	Jim Thome	1.50
99	Jody Gerut	.50
100	Joe Borchard	.50
101	Joe Crede	.50
102	Johan Santana	.50
103	John Olerud	.50
104	John Smoltz	.75
105	Johnny Damon	.75
106	Jorge Posada	.75
107	Jose Castillo	.50
108	Jose Reyes	.50
109	Jose Vidro	.50
110	Josh Beckett	1.00
111	Josh Phelps	.50
112	Juan Encarnacion	.50
113	Juan Gonzalez	1.00
114	Junior Spivey	.50
115	Kazuhisa Ishii	.50
116	Kenny Lofton	.50
117	Kerry Wood	1.50
118	Kevin Millwood	.50
119	Kevin Youkilis	.50
120	Lance Berkman	.50
121	Larry Bigbie	.50
122	Larry Walker	.75
123	Luis Castillo	.50
124	Luis Gonzalez	.50
125	Luis Matos	.50
126	Lyle Overbay	.50
127	Magglio Ordonez	.75
128	Manny Ramirez	1.00
129	Marcus Giles	.50
130	Mariano Rivera	.75
131	Mark Buehrle	.50
132	Mark Mulder	.75
133	Mark Prior	1.50
134	Mark Teixeira	.75
135	Marlon Byrd	.50
136	Matt Morris	.50
137	Miguel Cabrera	1.00
138	Mike Lowell	.50
139	Mike Mussina	.75
140	Mike Piazza	2.00
141	Mike Sweeney	.50
142	Morgan Ensberg	.50
143	Nick Johnson	.50
144	Nomar Garciaparra	2.00
145	Omar Vizquel	.50
146	Orlando Cabrera	.50
147	Orlando Hudson	.50
148	Pat Burrell	.50
149	Paul Konerko	.50
150	Paul LoDuca	.50
151	Pedro J. Martinez	1.50
152	Jermaine Dye	.50
153	Preston Wilson	.50
154	Rafael Furcal	.50
155	Rafael Palmeiro	1.00
156	Randy Johnson	1.50
157	Rich Aurilia	.50
158	Rich Harden	.50
159	Richard Hidalgo	.50
160	Richie Sexson	.75
161	Rickie Weeks	.75
162	Roberto Alomar	.75
163	Rocco Baldelli	.50
164	Roger Clemens	3.00
165	Roy Halladay	.50
166	Roy Oswalt	.75
167	Ryan Howard	.75
168	Ryan Klesko	.50
169	Rodrigo Lopez	.50
170	Sammy Sosa	2.50
171	Scott Podsednik	.50
172	Scott Rolen	1.50
173	Sean Burroughs	.50
174	Sean Casey	.50
175	Shannon Stewart	.50
176	Shawn Green	.75
177	Shea Hillenbrand	.50
178	Shigetoshi Hasegawa	.50
179	Steve Finley	.50
180	Tim Hudson	.75
181	Todd Helton	1.00
182	Tom Glavine	.75
183	Torii Hunter	.75
184	Trot Nixon	.50
185	Troy Glaus	.75
186	Vernon Wells	.50
187	Victor Martinez	.75
188	Vladimir Guerrero	1.50
189	Wade Miller	.50
190	Brandon Larson	.50
191	Travis Hafner	.75
192	Tim Salmon	.75
193	Tim Redding	.50
194	Runelvys Hernandez	.50
195	Ramon Nivar	.50
196	Moises Alou	.75
197	Michael Young	.50
198	Laynce Nix	.50
199	Tino Martinez	.50
200	Randall Simon	.50
201	Roger Clemens SP	8.00
202	Greg Maddux SP	8.00
203	Vladimir Guerrero SP	6.00
204	Miguel Tejada SP	4.00
205	Kevin Brown SP	4.00
206	Jason Giambi SP	5.00
207	Curt Schilling SP	5.00
208	Alex Rodriguez SP	8.00
209	Alfonso Soriano SP	6.00
210	Ivan Rodriguez SP	6.00
211	Rafael Palmeiro SP	6.00
212	Gary Carter LGD	4.00
213	Duke Snider LGD	5.00
214	Whitey Ford LGD	4.00
215	Bob Feller LGD	4.00
216	Reggie Jackson LGD	5.00
217	Ryne Sandberg LGD	10.00
218	Dale Murphy LGD	4.00
219	Tony Gwynn LGD	6.00
220	Don Mattingly LGD	10.00
221	Mike Schmidt LGD	10.00
222	Rickey Henderson LGD	5.00
223	Cal Ripken Jr. LGD	20.00
224	Nolan Ryan LGD	15.00
225	George Brett LGD	10.00
226	Bob Gibson LGD	5.00
227	Lou Brock LGD	4.00
228	Andre Dawson LGD	4.00
229	Rod Carew LGD	4.00
230	Wade Boggs LGD	4.00
231	Roberto Clemente LGD	12.00
232	Roy Campanella LGD	5.00
233	Babe Ruth LGD	15.00
234	Lou Gehrig LGD	10.00
235	Ty Cobb LGD	8.00
236	Roger Maris LGD	6.00
237	Satchel Paige LGD	6.00
238	Ernie Banks LGD	6.00
239	Ted Williams LGD	10.00
240	Stan Musial LGD	6.00
241	*Hector Gimenez/ auto/500*	8.00
242	*Justin Germano/ auto/500*	8.00
243	*Ian Snell/auto/500*	8.00
244	Graham Koonce/ auto/500	8.00
245	*Jose Capellan/ auto/500*	30.00
246	*Onil Joseph/auto/500*	8.00
247	*Shingo Takatsu/ auto/200*	40.00
248	*Carlos Hines/auto/500*	8.00
249	*Lincoln Holdzkom/ auto/500*	8.00
250	Mike Gosling/auto/500	8.00
251	*Edwardo Sierra/ auto/500*	10.00
252	*Renyel Pinto/auto/500*	10.00
253	*Merkin Valdez/ auto/500*	12.00
254	*Angel Chavez/auto/500*	8.00
255	*Ivan Ochoa/auto/1000*	8.00
256	*Greg Dobbs/auto/300*	8.00
257	*William Bergolla/ auto/500*	8.00
258	*Aarom Baldiris/ auto/500*	10.00
259	Kazuo Matsui/500	12.00
260	*Carlos Vasquez/ auto/500*	8.00
261	*Freddy Guzman/ auto/500*	8.00
262	*Akinori Otsuka/ auto/200*	40.00
263	*Mariano Gomez/ auto/200*	8.00
264	*Nick Regilio/auto/500*	8.00
265	*Jamie Brown/auto/500*	8.00
266	*Shawn Hill/auto/500*	8.00
267	*Roberto Novoa/ auto/500*	8.00
268	Sean Henn/auto/500	10.00
269	*Ramon Ramirez/ auto/500*	8.00
270	*Ronny Cedeno/ auto/1000*	8.00
271	Ryan Wing/auto/400	8.00
272	*Ruddy Yan/auto/500*	8.00
273	*Fernando Nieve/ auto/500*	8.00
274	*Rusty Tucker/auto/500*	8.00
275	*Jason Bartlett/auto/500*	8.00
276	Mike Rouse/auto/500	8.00
277	*Dennis Sarfate/ auto/500*	8.00
278	*Cory Sullivan/auto/500*	8.00
279	*Casey Daigle/auto/250*	8.00
280	*Chris Shelton/auto/400*	35.00
281	*Jesse Harper/auto/400*	8.00
282	*Mike Wuertz/auto/500*	12.00
283	*Tim Bausher/auto/400*	8.00
284	*Jorge Sequea/auto/500*	8.00
285	*Josh Labandeira/ auto/100*	12.00
286	*Justin Leone/auto/500*	12.00
287	*Tim Bittner/auto/500*	8.00
288	*Andres Blanco/auto/500*	8.00
289	*Kevin Cave/auto/1000*	8.00
290	*Mike Johnston/ auto/1000*	8.00
291	*Jason Szuminski/ auto/500*	8.00
292	*Shawn Camp/500*	8.00
293	*Colby Miller/auto/500*	8.00
294	Jake Woods/auto/500	8.00
295	*Ryan Meaux/auto/500*	8.00
296	*Donald Kelly/auto/500*	8.00
297	*Edwin Moreno/auto/500*	8.00
298	*Phil Stockman/auto/500*	8.00
299	*Jorge Vasquez/500*	8.00
300	*Kazuhito Tadano/ auto/500*	25.00

Mirror Black

No Pricing
Production one set

Mirror Blue

Stars (1-200):	3-5X
Mirror Blue (201-240):	1-2X
Auto. (241-300):	.5X
No Auto. (241-300):	1X

Production 50 sets

Mirror Emerald

No Pricing
Production 5 sets

Mirror Gold

Mirror Gold (1-200):	4-8X
Mirror Gold (201-240):	1.5-2X
Mirror Gold (241-300):	No Pricing

Production 25 sets

Mirror Red

Mirror Red (1-200):	2-4X
Mirror Red (201-240):	.5-1X
Mirror Red (241-300):	.5X

Production 100 sets

Mirror White

Mirror White (1-200):	2-4X
Mirror White (201-240):	.5-1X
Mirror White (241-300):	.5X

Production 100 sets

Mirror Autograph Black

No Pricing
Production one set

Mirror Autograph Blue

Mirror Auto Blue:.5-1.5X Red Auto.
Production 1-100
No pricing 25 or less

Mirror Autograph Red

NM/M

Quantity produced listed

3	Adam LaRoche/250	8.00
4	Adam Loewen/250	8.00
9	Alexis Rios/250	15.00
10	Alfonso Soriano Rgr/25	50.00
11	Andruw Jones/25	25.00
12	Andy Pettitte/25	35.00
13	Angel Berroa/100	10.00
14	Aramis Ramirez/100	25.00
15	Aubrey Huff/250	10.00
16	Austin Kearns/200	12.00
17	Barry Larkin/25	40.00
22	Brad Penny/25	15.00
24	Brandon Webb/250	8.00
25	Brendan Harris/50	10.00
27	Brett Myers/100	8.00
28	Bubba Crosby/250	8.00
30	Chad Cordero/250	8.00
31	Bubba Nelson/250	8.00
32	Byron Gettis/250	8.00
36	Carlos Beltran/100	25.00
38	Carlos Lee/250	10.00
39	Chad Gaudin/100	8.00
40	Cliff Lee/250	10.00
43	Clint Barmes/100	15.00
47	Dan Haren/250	8.00
49	David Ortiz/250	40.00
50	Delmon Young/50	30.00
52	Dewon Brazelton/250	8.00
53	Dontrelle Willis/100	20.00
56	Edwin Almonte/250	8.00
57	Edwin Jackson/250	8.00
58	Eric Chavez/25	30.00
62	Frank Thomas/50	50.00
65	Garret Anderson/250	15.00
67	Gary Sheffield/50	30.00
70	Hank Blalock/100	30.00
74	Craig Wilson/250	10.00
78	John Lackey/250	8.00
79	Jacque Jones/250	8.00
80	Jae Weong Seo/100	15.00
85	Melvin Mora/250	15.00
86	Jason Varitek/100	40.00
89	Jay Gibbons/250	8.00
90	Jay Payton/250	8.00
91	Jeff Bagwell/50	50.00
92	Jeff Baker/25	20.00
96	Jerome Williams/100	15.00
97	Jim Edmonds/25	35.00
99	Jody Gerut/250	10.00
100	Joe Borchard/250	10.00
101	Joe Crede/50	15.00
102	Johan Santana/250	25.00
106	Jorge Posada/25	50.00
107	Jose Castillo/250	8.00
109	Jose Vidro/250	10.00
110	Josh Beckett/25	50.00
113	Juan Gonzalez/25	40.00
114	Junior Spivey/25	15.00

117 Kerry Wood/50 50.00
119 Kevin Youkilis/250 10.00
120 Lance Berkman/25 30.00
121 Larry Bigbie/250 12.00
123 Luis Castillo/25 15.00
125 Luis Matos/250 8.00
127 Magglio Ordonez/250 15.00
129 Marcus Giles/250 12.00
131 Mark Buehrle/250 12.00
132 Mark Mulder/250 20.00
133 Mark Prior/100 50.00
134 Mark Teixeira/100 25.00
135 Marlon Byrd/250 8.00
137 Miguel Cabrera/250 30.00
140 Mike Piazza/25 125.00
142 Morgan Ensberg/250 8.00
146 Orlando Cabrera/25 20.00
150 Paul LoDuca/25 25.00
152 Jermaine Dye/250 10.00
153 Preston Wilson/250 10.00
154 Rafael Furcal/100 12.00
157 Rich Aurilia/25 15.00
158 Rich Harden/203 15.00
165 Roy Halladay/50 15.00
166 Roy Oswalt/50 15.00
167 Ryan Howard/100 30.00
169 Rodrigo Lopez/250 8.00
170 Sammy Sosa/50 100.00
171 Scott Podsednik/250 15.00
172 Scott Rolen/100 40.00
175 Shannon Stewart/100 8.00
176 Shawn Green/25 30.00
177 Shea Hillenbrand/250 10.00
178 Shigetoshi Hasegawa/250 40.00
179 Steve Finley/100 20.00
183 Torii Hunter/250 15.00
184 Trot Nixon/250 20.00
187 Victor Martinez/250 20.00
188 Vladimir Guerrero Angels/50 75.00
190 Brandon Larson/200 10.00
191 Travis Hafner/250 15.00
197 Michael Young/250 15.00
212 Gary Carter LGD/250 15.00
213 Duke Snider LGD/250 25.00
214 Whitey Ford LGD/50 40.00
215 Bob Feller LGD/250 20.00
216 Reggie Jackson LGD/50 50.00
217 Ryne Sandberg LGD/50 60.00
218 Dale Murphy LGD/50 30.00
219 Tony Gwynn LGD/50 50.00
220 Don Mattingly LGD/50 75.00
221 Mike Schmidt LGD/50 75.00
222 Rickey Henderson LGD/50 50.00
223 Cal Ripken Jr. LGD/50 180.00
224 Nolan Ryan LGD/50 100.00
225 George Brett LGD/50 75.00
226 Bob Gibson LGD/100 25.00
227 Lou Brock LGD/100 25.00
228 Andre Dawson LGD/250 15.00
229 Rod Carew LGD/50 25.00
230 Wade Boggs LGD/50 25.00
238 Ernie Banks LGD/50 60.00
240 Stan Musial LGD/100 60.00
241 Hector Gimenez NG/200 8.00
242 Justin Germano NG/100 8.00
243 Ian Snell NG/100 8.00
244 Graham Koonce NG/200 8.00
245 Jose Capellan NG/100 40.00
246 Onil Joseph NG/200 8.00
247 Shingo Takatsu NG/50 50.00
248 Carlos Hines NG/200 8.00
249 Lincoln Holdzkom NG/100 8.00
250 Mike Gosling NG/100 10.00
251 Edwardo Sierra NG/200 10.00
252 Renyel Pinto NG/100 10.00
253 Merkin Valdez NG/200 12.00
254 Angel Chavez NG/200 8.00
255 Ivan Ochoa NG/200 8.00
257 William Bergolla NG/200 8.00
258 Aarom Baldiris NG/100 10.00
260 Carlos Vasquez NG/200 8.00
261 Freddy Guzman NG/200 8.00
262 Akinori Otsuka NG/50 50.00
264 Nick Regilio NG/200 8.00
266 Shawn Hill NG/200 8.00
268 Sean Henn NG/200 10.00
269 Ramon Ramirez NG/200 8.00
270 Ronny Cedeno NG/100 8.00
273 Fernando Nieve NG/200 8.00
274 Rusty Tucker NG/200 8.00
275 Jason Bartlett NG/200 8.00
276 Mike Rouse NG/200 8.00
277 Dennis Sarfate NG/200 8.00
278 Cory Sullivan NG/200 8.00
282 Mike Wuertz NG/200 8.00
284 Jorge Sequea NG/100 8.00
287 Tim Bittner NG/250 8.00
288 Andres Blanco NG/100 12.00
289 Kevin Cave NG/100 10.00
290 Mike Johnston NG/100 8.00
293 Colby Miller NG/100 8.00
294 Jake Woods NG/100 10.00
295 Ryan Meaux NG/200 8.00
296 Donald Kelly NG/100 8.00
297 Edwin Moreno NG/100 8.00
298 Phil Stockman NG/100 8.00

Mirror Autograph Emerald

No Pricing
Production 1-5

Mirror Autograph Gold

No Pricing
Production 1-25

Mirror Autograph White

White Auto. (1-240): .75-1.5X Red Auto
White Auto (241-300): .5-1X Red Auto
Production 1-100
No pricing 25 or less

Mirror Bat Blue

NM/M
Blue Bat: 1-1.5X Red price
Production 25-100
Cards listed don't have a red version
217 Ryne Sandberg/50 40.00
219 Tony Gwynn/50 20.00
221 Mike Schmidt/50 25.00
223 Cal Ripken Jr./50 50.00
224 Nolan Ryan/50 35.00
225 George Brett/50 30.00

Mirror Bat Red

NM/M
Common Player: 4.00
Quantity produced listed
Black: No Pricing
Production one set
Emerald: No Pricing
Production 5 sets
2 Adam Dunn/150 6.00
3 Adam LaRoche/250 4.00
5 Adrian Beltre/150 4.00
7 Albert Pujols/150 15.00
8 Alex Rodriguez Yanks/250 10.00
9 Alexis Rios/250 4.00
10 Alfonso Soriano Rgr/150 8.00
11 Andruw Jones/150 8.00
12 Andy Pettitte/250 6.00
13 Angel Berroa/150 4.00
15 Aubrey Huff/150 4.00
16 Austin Kearns/150 4.00
17 Barry Larkin/150 6.00
20 Bernie Williams/150 6.00
21 Bobby Abreu/150 6.00
24 Brandon Webb/150 4.00
25 Brendan Harris/250 4.00
26 Bret Boone/150 4.00
29 Brian Giles/250 4.00
35 Carl Everett/250 4.00
36 Carlos Beltran/150 6.00
37 Carlos Delgado/150 6.00
38 Carlos Lee/150 4.00
41 Chipper Jones/150 8.00
42 Cliff Floyd/250 4.00
43 Clint Barmes/250 4.00
44 Corey Patterson/250 6.00
45 Craig Biggio/150 4.00
47 Dan Haren/150 4.00
48 Darin Erstad/150 4.00
49 David Ortiz/250 8.00
50 Delmon Young/250 6.00
51 Derek Jeter/150 20.00
54 Edgar Martinez/150 6.00
55 Edgar Renteria/150 6.00
59 Eric Hinske/150 4.00
60 Eric Munson/250 4.00
61 Erubiel Durazo/250 4.00
62 Frank Thomas/150 8.00
63 Fred McGriff/150 4.00
65 Garret Anderson/150 6.00
67 Gary Sheffield/250 6.00
68 Geoff Jenkins/150 4.00
70 Hank Blalock/150 8.00
71 Hee Seop Choi/250 4.00
73 Hideo Nomo/150 8.00
76 Ivan Rodriguez Tigers/250 8.00
77 J.D. Drew/250 6.00
79 Jacque Jones/150 4.00
82 Jason Giambi Yanks/150 6.00
83 Jason Jennings/150 4.00
86 Jason Varitek/150 6.00
88 Javy Lopez/250 6.00
89 Jay Gibbons/150 4.00
91 Jeff Bagwell/150 8.00
92 Jeff Baker/250 4.00
93 Jeff Kent/150 4.00
97 Jim Edmonds/150 6.00
98 Jim Thome/150 8.00
100 Joe Borchard/150 4.00
101 Joe Crede/250 4.00
103 John Olerud/150 4.00
105 Johnny Damon/250 4.00
106 Jorge Posada/150 6.00
107 Jose Castillo/250 4.00
108 Jose Reyes/150 4.00
109 Jose Vidro/150 4.00
110 Josh Beckett/150 6.00
111 Josh Phelps/150 4.00
112 Juan Encarnacion/250 4.00
113 Juan Gonzalez/250 6.00
114 Junior Spivey/250 4.00
115 Kazuhisa Ishii/150 4.00
116 Kenny Lofton/250 4.00
117 Kerry Wood/150 8.00
119 Kevin Youkilis/250 4.00
120 Lance Berkman/150 4.00
122 Larry Walker/150 4.00
123 Luis Castillo/150 4.00
124 Luis Gonzalez/150 4.00
126 Lyle Overbay/250 4.00
127 Magglio Ordonez/150 4.00
128 Manny Ramirez/150 8.00
129 Marcus Giles/250 4.00
131 Mark Buehrle/150 4.00
132 Mark Mulder/150 6.00
133 Mark Prior/150 10.00
134 Mark Teixeira/150 6.00
135 Marlon Byrd/150 4.00
137 Miguel Cabrera/250 8.00
138 Mike Lowell/150 4.00
140 Mike Piazza/150 10.00
141 Mike Sweeney/150 4.00
143 Nick Johnson/250 4.00
144 Nomar Garciaparra/150 10.00
145 Omar Vizquel/150 4.00
146 Orlando Cabrera/250 4.00
147 Orlando Hudson/150 4.00
148 Pat Burrell/150 4.00
149 Paul Konerko/150 4.00
150 Paul LoDuca/150 4.00
152 Jermaine Dye/250 4.00
153 Preston Wilson/150 4.00
154 Rafael Furcal/150 4.00
155 Rafael Palmeiro O's/150 8.00
157 Rich Aurilia/250 4.00
159 Richard Hidalgo/150 4.00
160 Richie Sexson/250 6.00
161 Rickie Weeks/250 6.00
162 Roberto Alomar/250 6.00
163 Rocco Baldelli/150 4.00
164 Roger Clemens Astros/250 12.00
168 Ryan Klesko/150 4.00
170 Sammy Sosa/150 12.00
174 Sean Casey/250 4.00
175 Shannon Stewart/150 4.00
176 Shawn Green/150 4.00
181 Todd Helton/150 8.00
183 Torii Hunter/150 6.00
184 Trot Nixon/150 6.00
185 Troy Glaus/150 6.00
186 Vernon Wells/150 4.00
187 Victor Martinez/250 4.00
188 Vladimir Guerrero Angels/250 8.00
189 Wade Miller/250 4.00
190 Brandon Larson/175 4.00
191 Travis Hafner/150 6.00
192 Tim Salmon/150 4.00
195 Ramon Nivar/150 4.00
196 Moises Alou/250 6.00
197 Michael Young/250 4.00
198 Laynce Nix/150 4.00
199 Tino Martinez/250 4.00
200 Randall Simon/250 4.00
201 Roger Clemens Yanks/150 12.00
203 Vladimir Guerrero Expos/150 8.00
204 Miguel Tejada/150 6.00
206 Jason Giambi A's/150 6.00
208 Alex Rodriguez Rgr/150 10.00
209 Alfonso Soriano Yanks/150 8.00
210 Ivan Rodriguez Marlins/150 8.00
211 Rafael Palmeiro Rgr/150 8.00
212 Gary Carter LGD/150 8.00
216 Reggie Jackson LGD/150 10.00
220 Don Mattingly LGD/150 20.00
222 Rickey Henderson LGD/150 8.00
227 Lou Brock LGD/150 6.00
228 Andre Dawson LGD/150 6.00
229 Rod Carew LGD/150 8.00
230 Wade Boggs LGD/150 6.00
240 Stan Musial LGD/100 25.00

Mirror Bat Gold

NM/M
Gold Bat: 1.5-3X Red price
Production 25 sets
Cards listed don't have a red version
69 Greg Maddux 25.00
217 Ryne Sandberg 50.00
219 Tony Gwynn 25.00
221 Mike Schmidt 40.00
223 Cal Ripken Jr. 90.00
224 Nolan Ryan 60.00
225 George Brett 40.00
231 Roberto Clemente 90.00
233 Babe Ruth 200.00
234 Lou Gehrig 150.00
235 Ty Cobb 125.00
236 Roger Maris 40.00
239 Ted Williams 80.00

Mirror Bat White

NM/M
White Bat: .75-1X Red price
Production 25-200
Cards listed don't have a red version
219 Tony Gwynn/100 15.00
221 Mike Schmidt/100 20.00
223 Cal Ripken Jr./100 40.00
224 Nolan Ryan/100 30.00
225 George Brett/100 20.00
231 Roberto Clemente/50 65.00
233 Babe Ruth/25 200.00
234 Lou Gehrig/25 150.00
235 Ty Cobb/25 125.00
236 Roger Maris/25 40.00
239 Ted Williams/25 80.00

Mirror Combo Red

NM/M
Common (2-211): 6.00
Production 250
Common (212-239): 8.00
Production 50-250
Black Prime: No Pricing
Production one set
2 Adam Dunn Bat-Jsy 8.00
5 Adrian Beltre Bat-Jsy 6.00
7 Albert Pujols Bat-Jsy 25.00
11 Andruw Jones Bat-Jsy 8.00
13 Angel Berroa Bat-Pants 6.00
15 Aubrey Huff Bat-Jsy 6.00
16 Austin Kearns Bat-Jsy 6.00
17 Barry Larkin Bat-Jsy 8.00
18 Barry Zito Bat-Jsy 6.00
19 Ben Sheets Bat-Jsy 6.00
20 Bernie Williams Bat-Jsy 10.00

21 Bobby Abreu Bat-Jsy 8.00
22 Brad Penny Bat-Jsy 6.00
24 Brandon Webb Bat-Jsy 6.00
26 Bret Boone Bat-Jsy 6.00
36 Carlos Beltran Bat-Jsy 8.00
37 Carlos Delgado Bat-Jsy 8.00
38 Carlos Lee Bat-Jsy 6.00
41 Chipper Jones Bat-Jsy 10.00
45 Craig Biggio Bat-Pants 6.00
47 Dan Haren Bat-Jsy 6.00
51 Derek Jeter Bat-Jsy 30.00
52 Dewon Brazelton Glv-Jsy 6.00
54 Edgar Martinez Bat-Jsy 8.00
55 Edgar Renteria Bat-Jsy 8.00
58 Eric Chavez Bat-Jsy 8.00
59 Eric Hinske Bat-Jsy 6.00
62 Frank Thomas Bat-Jsy 10.00
63 Fred McGriff Bat-Jsy 6.00
65 Garret Anderson Bat-Jsy 8.00
68 Geoff Jenkins Bat-Jsy 6.00
70 Hank Blalock Bat-Jsy 10.00
73 Hideo Nomo Bat-Jsy 10.00
79 Jacque Jones Bat-Jsy 6.00
82 Jason Giambi Bat-Jsy 10.00
83 Jason Jennings Bat-Jsy 6.00
86 Jason Varitek Bat-Jsy 10.00
89 Jay Gibbons Bat-Jsy 6.00
91 Jeff Bagwell Bat-Jsy 10.00
93 Jeff Kent Bat-Jsy 6.00
97 Jim Edmonds Bat-Jsy 8.00
98 Jim Thome Bat-Jsy 10.00
100 Joe Borchard Bat-Jsy 6.00
103 John Olerud Bat-Jsy 6.00
106 Jorge Posada Bat-Jsy 8.00
108 Jose Reyes Bat-Jsy 6.00
109 Jose Vidro Bat-Jsy 6.00
110 Josh Beckett Bat-Jsy 8.00
111 Josh Phelps Bat-Jsy 6.00
115 Kazuhisa Ishii Bat-Jsy 6.00
117 Kerry Wood Bat-Jsy 12.00
120 Lance Berkman Bat-Jsy 6.00
122 Larry Walker Bat-Jsy 6.00
123 Luis Castillo Bat-Jsy 6.00
124 Luis Gonzalez Bat-Jsy 6.00
127 Magglio Ordonez Bat-Jsy 6.00
128 Manny Ramirez Bat-Jsy 10.00
131 Mark Buehrle Bat-Jsy 6.00
132 Mark Mulder Bat-Jsy 8.00
133 Mark Prior Bat-Jsy 12.00
134 Mark Teixeira Bat-Jsy 8.00
135 Marlon Byrd Bat-Jsy 6.00
138 Mike Lowell Bat-Jsy 6.00
140 Mike Piazza Bat-Jsy 12.00
141 Mike Sweeney Bat-Jsy 6.00
142 Morgan Ensberg Bat-Jsy 6.00
144 Nomar Garciaparra Bat-Jsy 12.00
145 Omar Vizquel Bat-Jsy 6.00
147 Orlando Hudson Bat-Jsy 6.00
148 Pat Burrell Bat-Jsy 6.00
149 Paul Konerko Bat-Jsy 6.00
150 Paul LoDuca Bat-Jsy 6.00
151 Pedro J. Martinez Bat-Jsy 10.00
153 Preston Wilson Bat-Jsy 6.00
154 Rafael Furcal Bat-Jsy 6.00
155 Rafael Palmeiro O's Bat-Jsy 10.00
156 Randy Johnson Bat-Jsy 12.00
159 Richard Hidalgo Bat-Pants 6.00
163 Rocco Baldelli Bat-Jsy 6.00
166 Roy Oswalt Bat-Jsy 6.00
168 Ryan Klesko Bat-Jsy 6.00
170 Sammy Sosa Bat-Jsy 15.00
172 Scott Rolen Bat-Jsy 10.00
175 Shannon Stewart Bat-Jsy 6.00
176 Shawn Green Bat-Jsy 6.00
180 Tim Hudson Bat-Jsy 8.00
181 Todd Helton Bat-Jsy 10.00
182 Tom Glavine Bat-Jsy 8.00
183 Torii Hunter Bat-Jsy 8.00
184 Trot Nixon Bat-Jsy 8.00
185 Troy Glaus Bat-Jsy 8.00
186 Vernon Wells Bat-Jsy 6.00
191 Travis Hafner Bat-Jsy 8.00
192 Tim Salmon Bat-Jsy 6.00
195 Ramon Nivar Bat-Jsy 6.00
201 Roger Clemens Bat-Jsy 15.00
203 Vladimir Guerrero Bat-Jsy 12.00
204 Miguel Tejada Bat-Jsy 8.00
206 Jason Giambi Bat-Jsy 8.00
207 Curt Schilling Bat-Jsy 8.00
208 Alex Rodriguez Bat-Jsy 12.00
209 Alfonso Soriano Bat-Jsy 10.00
210 Ivan Rodriguez Bat-Jsy 10.00
211 Rafael Palmeiro Bat-Jsy 10.00
212 Gary Carter LGD Bat-Pants/250 8.00
216 Reggie Jackson LGD Bat-Jsy/250 12.00
217 Ryne Sandberg LGD Bat-Jsy/250 25.00
218 Dale Murphy LGD Bat-Jsy/250 10.00
219 Tony Gwynn LGD Bat-Jsy/250 12.00
220 Don Mattingly LGD Bat-Jsy/250 25.00
221 Mike Schmidt LGD Bat-Pants/250 25.00
222 Rickey Henderson LGD Bat-Jsy/250 10.00
223 Cal Ripken Jr. LGD Bat-Jsy/250 35.00
224 Nolan Ryan LGD Bat-Jsy/250 35.00
225 George Brett LGD Bat-Jsy/250 25.00
227 Lou Brock LGD Bat-Jsy/250 8.00
228 Andre Dawson LGD Bat-Jsy/250 8.00
229 Rod Carew LGD Bat-Jkt/250 10.00
230 Wade Boggs LGD Bat-Jsy/250 8.00
231 Roberto Clemente LGD Bat-Jsy/100 100.00
232 Roy Campanella LGD Bat-Pants/100 15.00
233 Babe Ruth LGD Bat-Pants/50 350.00
234 Lou Gehrig LGD Bat-Pants/50 200.00
235 Ty Cobb LGD Bat-Pants/50 200.00
236 Roger Maris LGD Bat-Pants/100 50.00
238 Ernie Banks LGD Bat-Pants/100 15.00
239 Ted Williams LGD Bat-Jkt/100 85.00

Mirror Fabric Blue

NM/M
Blue: 1-1.5X Red price
Production 25-100
Cards listed don't have red version
217 Ryne Sandberg/100 25.00
219 Tony Gwynn/100 15.00
220 Don Mattingly/100 25.00
221 Mike Schmidt/100 20.00
223 Cal Ripken Jr./100 35.00
224 Nolan Ryan/100 25.00
225 George Brett/100 15.00
231 Roberto Clemente/25 90.00
233 Babe Ruth/25 240.00
234 Lou Gehrig/25 150.00
235 Ty Cobb/25 140.00
236 Roger Maris/25 50.00
237 Satchel Paige/25 90.00
239 Ted Williams/25 100.00

Mirror Fabric Red

NM/M
Common Player: 4.00
Quantity produced listed
1 A.J. Burnett Jsy/250 4.00
2 Adam Dunn Jsy/150 6.00
5 Adrian Beltre Jsy/150 6.00
6 Al Leiter Jsy/250 4.00
7 Albert Pujols Jsy/150 15.00
11 Andruw Jones Jsy/150 6.00
13 Angel Berroa Pants/150 4.00
15 Aubrey Huff Jsy/150 4.00
16 Austin Kearns Jsy/150 4.00
17 Barry Larkin Jsy/150 6.00
18 Barry Zito Jsy/150 5.00
19 Ben Sheets Jsy/150 4.00
20 Bernie Williams Jsy/150 6.00
21 Bobby Abreu Jsy/150 6.00
22 Brad Penny Jsy/150 4.00
27 Brett Myers Jsy/250 4.00
33 C.C. Sabathia Jsy/250 4.00
34 Carl Crawford Jsy/250 4.00
36 Carlos Beltran Jsy/150 6.00
38 Carlos Lee Jsy/150 4.00
39 Chad Gaudin Jsy/250 4.00
41 Chipper Jones Jsy/150 8.00
45 Craig Biggio Pants/150 4.00
47 Dan Haren Jsy/150 4.00
48 Darin Erstad Jsy/250 4.00
51 Derek Jeter Jsy/150 20.00
53 Dontrelle Willis Jsy/250 6.00
54 Edgar Martinez Jsy/150 6.00
55 Edgar Renteria Jsy/150 6.00
58 Eric Chavez Jsy/150 4.00
59 Eric Hinske Jsy/150 4.00
62 Frank Thomas Jsy/150 8.00
64 Freddy Garcia Jsy/250 4.00
66 Garrett Atkins Jsy/250 4.00
68 Geoff Jenkins Jsy/150 4.00
70 Hank Blalock Jsy/150 6.00
72 Hideki Matsui Base/250 15.00
73 Hideo Nomo Jsy/150 8.00
75 Ichiro Suzuki Base/250 15.00
79 Jacque Jones Jsy/150 4.00
81 Jamie Moyer Jsy/250 4.00
82 Jason Giambi Jsy/150 6.00
83 Jason Jennings Jsy/150 4.00
84 Jason Kendall Jsy/250 4.00
86 Jason Varitek Jsy/150 6.00
89 Jay Gibbons Jsy/150 4.00
91 Jeff Bagwell Jsy/150 8.00
93 Jeff Kent Jsy/150 4.00
96 Jerome Williams Jsy/250 4.00
97 Jim Edmonds Jsy/150 6.00
98 Jim Thome Jsy/150 8.00
102 Jose Santana Jsy/250 4.00
103 John Olerud Jsy/150 4.00
104 John Smoltz Jsy/250 4.00
108 Jose Reyes Jsy/150 4.00
109 Jose Vidro Jsy/150 4.00
110 Josh Beckett Jsy/150 6.00
111 Josh Phelps Jsy/150 4.00
115 Kazuhisa Ishii Jsy/150 4.00
117 Kerry Wood Jsy/150 8.00
118 Kevin Millwood Jsy/250 4.00
120 Lance Berkman Jsy/150 4.00
121 Larry Bigbie Jsy/250 4.00
122 Larry Walker Jsy/150 4.00
123 Luis Castillo Jsy/150 4.00
124 Luis Gonzalez Jsy/150 4.00
130 Mariano Rivera Jsy/250 6.00
131 Mark Buehrle Jsy/150 4.00
133 Mark Prior Jsy/150 10.00
135 Marlon Byrd Jsy/150 4.00
136 Matt Morris Jsy/250 4.00
139 Mike Mussina Jsy/250 6.00
140 Mike Piazza Jsy/150 10.00
141 Mike Sweeney Jsy/150 4.00
142 Morgan Ensberg Jsy/150 4.00
144 Nomar Garciaparra Jsy/150 10.00
145 Omar Vizquel Jsy/150 4.00
147 Orlando Hudson Jsy/150 4.00
148 Pat Burrell Jsy/150 4.00
151 Pedro J. Martinez Jsy/150 8.00
153 Preston Wilson Jsy/150 4.00
154 Rafael Furcal Jsy/150 4.00
156 Randy Johnson Jsy/150 8.00
158 Rich Harden Jsy/250 4.00
159 Richard Hidalgo Pants/150 4.00
163 Rocco Baldelli Jsy/150 4.00
165 Roy Halladay Jsy/250 4.00
168 Ryan Klesko Jsy/150 4.00
170 Sammy Sosa Jsy/150 12.00
172 Scott Rolen Jsy/150 8.00
173 Sean Burroughs Jsy/250 4.00
175 Shannon Stewart Jsy/150 4.00
176 Shawn Green Jsy/150 4.00
179 Steve Finley Jsy/250 4.00
180 Tim Hudson Jsy/150 6.00
181 Todd Helton Jsy/150 8.00
182 Tom Glavine Jsy/150 6.00
185 Troy Glaus Jsy/150 6.00
186 Vernon Wells Jsy/150 4.00
191 Travis Hafner Jsy/150 6.00
192 Tim Salmon Jsy/150 6.00
193 Tim Redding Jsy/250 4.00
194 Runelvys Hernandez Jsy/250 4.00
195 Ramon Nivar Jsy/150 4.00
201 Roger Clemens Jsy/150 15.00
202 Greg Maddux Jsy/250 10.00
203 Vladimir Guerrero Jsy/150 8.00
204 Miguel Tejada Jsy/150 6.00
205 Kevin Brown Jsy/250 4.00
206 Jason Giambi Jsy/150 6.00
207 Curt Schilling Jsy/150 6.00
208 Alex Rodriguez Jsy/150 10.00
209 Alfonso Soriano Jsy/150 8.00
210 Ivan Rodriguez Jsy/150 8.00
212 Gary Carter LGD Pants/150 6.00
226 Bob Gibson LGD Jsy/250 10.00
237 Satchel Paige LGD CO Jsy/100 50.00

Mirror Fabric Gold

NM/M
Gold: 2-3X Red price
Production 10-25
No pricing 20 or less
Cards listed don't have red version
217 Ryne Sandberg/25 45.00
219 Tony Gwynn/25 30.00
220 Don Mattingly/25 60.00
221 Mike Schmidt/25 40.00
223 Cal Ripken Jr./25 90.00
224 Nolan Ryan/25 60.00
225 George Brett/25 50.00

Mirror Fabric White

NM/M
White: .5-1.5X Red price
Production 25-200
Cards listed don't have red version
217 Ryne Sandberg/25 45.00
219 Tony Gwynn/25 25.00
220 Don Mattingly/25 50.00
221 Mike Schmidt/25 40.00
223 Cal Ripken Jr./25 90.00
224 Nolan Ryan/25 60.00
225 George Brett/25 50.00
231 Roberto Clemente/25 90.00
233 Babe Ruth/25 240.00
234 Lou Gehrig/25 150.00
235 Ty Cobb/25 140.00
236 Roger Maris/25 50.00
237 Satchel Paige/25 90.00
239 Ted Williams/25 100.00

Fabric of the Game

NM/M
Common Player: 6.00
Quantity produced listed
AL/NL: .75-1.5X
Production 1-100
Jersey Number: .75-2X
Production 1-72
Position: .75-2X

Production 1-100		
Prime:		No Pricing
Production one set		
Game Reward:		.75-2X
Production 1-50		
Jersey Year:		.75-2X
Production 1-99		
Game Stats:		.75-2X
Production 1-66		
No Pricing production 20 or less		
1	Ozzie Smith Jsy/100	20.00
2	Al Kaline Pants/100	15.00
3	Alan Trammell Jsy/100	10.00
4	Albert Pujols Jsy/100	20.00
5	Alex Rodriguez Jsy/100	12.00
6	Alex Rodriguez Jsy/100	12.00
7	Andre Dawson Jsy/100	8.00
8	Andre Dawson Pants/100	8.00
9	Babe Ruth Jsy/10	
10	Babe Ruth Pants/10	
11	Billy Williams Jsy/100	10.00
12	Bo Jackson Jsy/100	20.00
13	Bob Feller Jsy/50	15.00
14	Bob Gibson Jsy/50	15.00
15	Bobby Doerr Jsy/100	8.00
16	Brooks Robinson Jsy/25	25.00
17	Cal Ripken Jr. Jsy/100	30.00
18	Carl Yastrzemski Jsy/100	20.00
19	Carlton Fisk Jsy/100	10.00
20	Dale Murphy Jsy/100	12.00
21	Darryl Strawberry Pants/100	10.00
22	Darryl Strawberry Jsy/100	10.00
23	Dave Parker Jsy/100	10.00
24	Dave Parker Jsy/100	10.00
25	Dave Winfield Jsy/50	10.00
26	Dave Winfield Jsy/100	10.00
27	Deion Sanders Jsy/25	25.00
28	Derek Jeter Jsy/100	20.00
29	Don Drysdale Jsy/100	15.00
30	Don Mattingly Jsy/100	20.00
31	Don Mattingly Jkt/100	20.00
32	Don Sutton Jsy/100	8.00
33	Duke Snider Jsy/100	12.00
34	Dwight Gooden Jsy/100	8.00
35	Early Wynn Jsy/100	10.00
36	Eddie Mathews Jsy/50	20.00
37	Eddie Murray Jsy/100	15.00
38	Eddie Murray Jsy/100	15.00
39	Enos Slaughter Jsy/100	10.00
40	Eric Davis Jsy/50	10.00
41	Ernie Banks Jsy/100	15.00
42	Fergie Jenkins Pants/100	10.00
43	Frank Robinson Jsy/100	10.00
44	Fred Lynn Jsy/10	
45	Gary Carter Jsy/100	10.00
46	Gaylord Perry Jsy/25	15.00
47	George Brett White Jsy/100	20.00
48	George Foster Jsy/100	8.00
49	Hal Newhouser Jsy/100	8.00
50	Harmon Killebrew Jsy/25	30.00
51	Harmon Killebrew Pants/25	30.00
52	Harold Baines Jsy/100	10.00
53	Hoyt Wilhelm Jsy/50	10.00
54	Jack Morris Jsy/100	8.00
55	Jackie Robinson Jsy/10	
56	Jim "Catfish" Hunter Jsy/100	10.00
57	Jim Palmer Jsy/100	10.00
58	Jim Rice Jsy/100	10.00
59	Joe Carter Jsy/100	8.00
60	Joe Morgan Jsy/100	10.00
61	Tommy Lasorda Jsy/100	8.00
62	Johnny Mize Pants/100	12.00
63	Johnny Bench Jsy/100	15.00
64	Jose Canseco Jsy/100	10.00
65	Juan Marichal Jsy/100	10.00
66	Kirby Puckett Jsy/100	15.00
67	Lou Boudreau Jsy/100	10.00
68	Lou Brock Jsy/100	10.00
69	Lou Gehrig Jsy/10	
70	Lou Gehrig Pants/10	
71	Luis Aparicio Jsy/100	10.00
72	Luis Aparicio Pants/100	10.00
73	Mariano Rivera Jsy/100	10.00
74	Mark Grace Jsy/100	12.00
75	Mark Prior Jsy/100	12.00
76	Mel Ott Jsy/25	60.00
77	Mel Ott Pants/25	60.00
78	Mike Schmidt Jsy/100	20.00
79	Mike Schmidt Pants/100	20.00
80	Mike Schmidt Jkt/100	20.00
81	Nolan Ryan Angels Jsy/100	25.00
82	Nolan Ryan Angels Jkt/100	25.00
83	Nolan Ryan Astros Jsy/100	25.00
84	Nolan Ryan Astros Jkt/100	25.00
85	Nolan Ryan Rgr Jsy/100	25.00
86	Nolan Ryan Rgr Pants/100	25.00
87	Ty Cobb Pants/10	
88	Ozzie Smith Jsy/100	15.00
89	Paul Molitor Jsy/100	12.00
90	Pee Wee Reese Jsy/100	15.00
91	Phil Niekro Jsy/100	8.00
92	Phil Rizzuto Jsy/100	15.00
93	Phil Rizzuto Pants/100	15.00
94	Red Schoendienst Jsy/100	10.00
95	Reggie Jackson Jkt/100	15.00
96	Reggie Jackson Jsy/100	15.00
97	Richie Ashburn Jsy/100	20.00
98	Rickey Henderson Jsy/50	15.00
99	Roberto Clemente Jsy/50	75.00
100	Robin Yount Jsy/100	15.00
101	Rod Carew Jsy/100	10.00
102	Rod Carew Pants/100	10.00
103	Rod Carew Jkt/100	10.00
104	Rod Carew Jsy/100	10.00
105	Roger Clemens Jsy/100	15.00
106	Roger Clemens Jsy/100	15.00
107	Roger Maris Jsy/100	30.00
108	Roger Maris Pants/100	30.00
109	Roger Maris Jsy/100	30.00
110	Roy Campanella Pants/100	15.00
111	Ryne Sandberg Jsy/100	25.00
112	Stan Musial Jsy/50	30.00
113	Steve Carlton Jsy/100	10.00
114	Ted Williams Jsy/100	75.00
115	Ted Williams Jkt/100	75.00
116	Thurman Munson Jsy/100	25.00
117	Thurman Munson Pants/100	25.00
118	Tony Gwynn Jsy/100	15.00
119	Wade Boggs Jsy/100	10.00
120	Wade Boggs Jsy/100	10.00
121	Warren Spahn Jsy/100	15.00
122	Warren Spahn Pants/100	15.00
123	Whitey Ford Jsy/100	15.00
124	Whitey Ford Pants/100	15.00
125	Will Clark Jsy/100	15.00
126	Willie McCovey Jsy/100	10.00
127	Willie Stargell Jsy/100	15.00
128	Yogi Berra Jsy/25	35.00
129	Frankie Frisch Jkt/100	15.00
130	Marty Marion Jsy/100	10.00
131	Tommy John Pants/100	8.00
132	Chipper Jones Jsy/100	10.00
133	Sammy Sosa Jsy/100	15.00
134	Rickey Henderson Jsy/100	10.00
135	Mike Piazza Jsy/100	12.00
136	Mike Piazza Jsy/100	12.00
137	Nomar Garciaparra Jsy/100	15.00
138	Hideo Nomo Jsy/100	10.00
139	Hideo Nomo Jsy/50	15.00
140	Randy Johnson Jsy/100	10.00
141	Randy Johnson Jsy/100	10.00
142	Randy Johnson Jsy/100	10.00
143	Jason Giambi Jsy/100	6.00
144	Jason Giambi Jsy/100	6.00
145	Curt Schilling Jsy/100	6.00
146	Dennis Eckersley Jsy/100	10.00
147	Carlton Fisk Jkt/100	10.00
148	Tom Seaver Jsy/25	30.00
149	Joe Torre Jsy/100	10.00
150	Pedro Martinez Jsy/100	10.00
151	Albert Pujols Jsy/100	20.00
152	Andre Dawson Jsy/50	10.00
153	Bert Blyleven Jsy/100	8.00
154	Bo Jackson Jsy/100	15.00
155	Cal Ripken Jr. Pants/100	35.00
156	Carlton Fisk Jsy/100	10.00
157	Curt Schilling Jsy/100	6.00
158	Darryl Strawberry Jsy/100	8.00
159	Dave Concepcion Jsy/100	8.00
160	Dwight Evans Jsy/100	8.00
161	Ernie Banks Pants/100	15.00
162	Fred McGriff Jsy/1	
163	Gary Carter Pants/100	8.00
164	Gary Sheffield Jsy/100	6.00
165	George Brett Jsy/100	20.00
166	Greg Maddux Jsy/100	10.00
167	Ivan Rodriguez Jsy/100	10.00
168	Joe Morgan Jsy/100	10.00
169	Jose Canseco Jsy/100	10.00
170	Juan Gonzalez Jsy/100	8.00
171	Juan Gonzalez Jsy/100	8.00
172	Keith Hernandez Jsy/100	10.00
173	Ken Boyer Jsy/100	20.00
174	Kerry Wood Jsy/100	10.00
175	Lee Smith Jsy/100	8.00
176	Luis Tiant Jsy/100	8.00
177	Manny Ramirez Jsy/100	8.00
178	Mark Grace Jsy/100	12.00
179	Matt Williams Jsy/100	8.00
180	Miguel Tejada Jsy/100	6.00
181	Mike Mussina Jsy/100	10.00
182	Mike Piazza Jsy/100	12.00
183	Nomar Garciaparra Jsy/100	15.00
184	Pedro Martinez Jsy/100	10.00
185	Rafael Palmeiro Jsy/100	8.00
186	Reggie Jackson Pants/100	12.00
187	Rickey Henderson Jsy/100	10.00
188	Rickey Henderson Pants/100	10.00
189	Rickey Henderson Jsy/100	10.00
190	Sammy Sosa Jsy/100	15.00
191	Satchel Paige Jsy/100	60.00
192	Shawn Green Jsy/100	6.00
193	Stan Musial Jsy/50	35.00
194	Steve Carlton Jsy/100	10.00
195	Steve Garvey Jsy/100	8.00
196	Tom Seaver Jsy/100	12.00
197	Tony Gwynn Pants/100	12.00
198	Vladimir Guerrero Jsy/100	10.00
199	Wade Boggs Jsy/100	10.00
200	Willie Stargell Jsy/100	10.00

Fabric of the Game Auto

	NM/M
No Pricing	
Production 1-10	
AL/NL Auto:	No Pricing
Production 1-25	
Jersey Number Auto.:	No Pricing
Production 1-8	
Jersey Year Auto.:	No Pricing
Production 1-8	
Position Auto.:	No Pricing
Production 1-8	
Reward Auto.:	No Pricing
Production 1-8	
Stats Auto.:	No Pricing
Production 1-8	

2004 LEAF LIMITED

		NM/M
Complete Set (275):		
Common Player (1-200):		1.50
Common SP (201-229):		3.00
Production 499		
Common SP (251-275):		10.00
Production 99		
Pack (4):		60.00
Box (4):		200.00
1	Adam Dunn	2.00
2	Adrian Beltre	2.00
3	Albert Pujols	6.00
4	Alex Rodriguez	6.00
5	Alfonso Soriano	2.50
6	Andruw Jones	1.50
7	Andy Pettitte	1.50
8	Angel Berroa	1.50
9	Aramis Ramirez	1.50
10	Aubrey Huff	1.50
11	Aubrey Huff	1.50
12	Barry Larkin	1.50
13	Barry Zito	1.50
14	Bartolo Colon	1.50
15	Ben Sheets	1.50
16	Bernie Williams	1.50
17	Bobby Abreu	1.50
18	Brandon Webb	1.50
19	Brian Giles	1.50
20	C.C. Sabathia	1.50
21	Carlos Beltran	2.00
22	Carlos Delgado	1.50
23	Chipper Jones	3.00
24	Craig Biggio	1.50
25	Curt Schilling	3.00
26	Darin Erstad	1.50
27	Delmon Young	1.50
28	Derek Jeter	6.00
29	Derek Lee	1.50
30	Dontrelle Willis	1.50
31	Edgar Renteria	1.50
32	Eric Chavez	1.50
33	Esteban Loaiza	1.50
34	Frank Thomas	2.00
35	Fred McGriff	1.50
36	Garret Anderson	1.50
37	Gary Sheffield	1.50
38	Geoff Jenkins	1.50
39	Greg Maddux	3.00
40	Hank Blalock	2.00
41	Hideki Matsui	5.00
42	Hideo Nomo	1.50
43	Ichiro Suzuki	5.00
44	Ivan Rodriguez	2.00
45	J.D. Drew	1.50
46	Jacque Jones	1.50
47	Jae Weong Seo	1.50
48	Jake Peavy	1.50
49	Jamie Moyer	1.50
50	Jason Giambi	1.50
51	Jason Kendall	1.50
52	Jason Schmidt	1.50
53	Jason Varitek	1.50
54	Javier Vazquez	1.50
55	Javy Lopez	1.50
56	Jay Gibbons	1.50
57	Jay Payton	1.50
58	Jeff Bagwell	1.50
59	Jeff Kent	1.50
60	Jeremy Bonderman	1.50
61	Jermaine Dye	1.50
62	Jeromy Burnitz	1.50
63	Jim Edmonds	2.00
64	Jim Thome	1.50
65	Jimmy Rollins	1.50
66	Jody Gerut	1.50
67	Johan Santana	2.00
68	John Olerud	1.50

69	John Smoltz	1.50
70	Johnny Damon	2.00
71	Jorge Posada	1.50
72	Jose Contreras	1.50
73	Jose Reyes	1.50
74	Jose Vidro	1.50
75	Josh Beckett	1.50
76	Juan Gonzalez	1.50
77	Juan Pierre	1.50
78	Junior Spivey	1.50
79	Kazuhisa Ishii	1.50
80	Keith Foulke	1.50
81	Ken Griffey Jr.	3.00
82	Ken Harvey	1.50
83	Kenny Rogers	1.50
84	Kerry Wood	2.50
85	Kevin Brown	1.50
86	Kevin Millwood	1.50
87	Kip Wells	1.50
88	Lance Berkman	1.50
89	Larry Bigbie	1.50
90	Larry Walker	1.50
91	Laynce Nix	1.50
92	Luis Castillo	1.50
93	Luis Gonzalez	1.50
94	Luis Matos	1.50
95	Lyle Overbay	1.50
96	Magglio Ordonez	1.50
97	Manny Ramirez	2.00
98	Marcus Giles	1.50
99	Mark Buehrle	1.50
100	Mark Mulder	1.50
101	Mark Prior	3.00
102	Mark Teixeira	1.50
103	Marlon Byrd	1.50
104	Matt Morris	1.50
105	Melvin Mora	1.50
106	Michael Young	1.50
107	Miguel Cabrera	3.00
108	Miguel Tejada	2.00
109	Mike Lowell	1.50
110	Mike Mussina	2.00
111	Mike Piazza	4.00
112	Mike Sweeney	1.50
113	Milton Bradley	1.50
114	Moises Alou	1.50
115	Morgan Ensberg	1.50
116	Nick Johnson	1.50
117	Nomar Garciaparra	4.00
118	Omar Vizquel	1.50
119	Orlando Cabrera	1.50
120	Pat Burrell	1.50
121	Paul Konerko	1.50
122	Paul LoDuca	1.50
123	Pedro J. Martinez	3.00
124	Preston Wilson	1.50
125	Rafael Furcal	1.50
126	Rafael Palmeiro	2.00
127	Randy Johnson	3.00
128	Rich Harden	1.50
129	Richard Hidalgo	1.50
130	Richie Sexson	1.50
131	Rickie Weeks	1.50
132	Roberto Alomar	1.50
133	Robin Ventura	1.50
134	Rocco Baldelli	1.50
135	Roger Clemens	6.00
136	Roy Halladay	1.50
137	Roy Oswalt	1.50
138	Russ Ortiz	1.50
139	Ryan Klesko	1.50
140	Sammy Sosa	5.00
141	Scott Podsednik	1.50
142	Scott Rolen	3.00
143	Sean Burroughs	1.50
144	Sean Casey	1.50
145	Shannon Stewart	1.50
146	Shawn Green	1.50
147	Shigetoshi Hasegawa	1.50
148	Sidney Ponson	1.50
149	Steve Finley	1.50
150	Tim Hudson	1.50
151	Tim Salmon	1.50
152	Tino Martinez	1.50
153	Todd Helton	2.00
154	Tom Glavine	2.00
155	Torii Hunter	1.50
156	Trot Nixon	1.50
157	Troy Glaus	1.50
158	Vernon Wells	1.50
159	Victor Martinez	1.50
160	Vinny Castilla	1.50
161	Vladimir Guerrero	3.00
162	Alex Rodriguez	6.00
163	Alfonso Soriano	2.50
164	Andy Pettitte	1.50
165	Curt Schilling	3.00
166	Gary Sheffield	1.50
167	Greg Maddux	3.00
168	Hideo Nomo	1.50
169	Ivan Rodriguez	2.00
170	Jason Giambi	1.50
171	Jim Thome	2.00
172	Juan Gonzalez	1.50
173	Ken Griffey Jr.	3.00
174	Kevin Brown	1.50
175	Manny Ramirez	2.00
176	Miguel Tejada	2.00
177	Mike Mussina	1.50
178	Mike Piazza	4.00
179	Pedro Martinez	3.00
180	Rafael Palmeiro	2.00
181	Randy Johnson	3.00
182	Roger Clemens	6.00
183	Scott Rolen	3.00
184	Shawn Green	1.50
185	Tom Glavine	1.50
186	Vladimir Guerrero	3.00
187	Alex Rodriguez	6.00
188	Mike Piazza	4.00
189	Randy Johnson	3.00
190	Roger Clemens	6.00
191	Albert Pujols	6.00
192	Barry Zito	1.50
193	Chipper Jones	3.00
194	Garret Anderson	1.50
195	Jeff Bagwell	2.00
196	Josh Beckett	1.50
197	Magglio Ordonez	1.50
198	Mark Prior	3.00
199	Sammy Sosa	5.00
200	Todd Helton	2.00
201	Andre Dawson	3.00
202	Babe Ruth	8.00
203	Bob Feller	4.00
204	Bob Gibson	4.00
205	Bobby Doerr	3.00
206	Cal Ripken Jr.	10.00
207	Dale Murphy	4.00
208	Don Mattingly	8.00
209	Gary Carter	3.00
210	George Brett	8.00
211	Jackie Robinson	5.00
212	Lou Brock	4.00
213	Lou Gehrig	6.00
214	Mark Grace	4.00
215	Maury Wills	3.00
216	Mike Schmidt	8.00
217	Nolan Ryan	8.00
218	Orel Hershiser	3.00
219	Paul Molitor	4.00
220	Roberto Clemente	8.00
221	Rod Carew	4.00
222	Roy Campanella	4.00
223	Ryne Sandberg	8.00
224	Stan Musial	6.00
225	Ted Williams	8.00
226	Tony Gwynn	6.00
227	Ty Cobb	5.00
228	Whitey Ford	4.00
229	Yogi Berra	4.00
230	Carlos Beltran	3.00
231	David Ortiz	3.00
232	David Ortiz	3.00
233	Carlos Zambrano	1.50
234	Carlos Lee	1.50
235	Travis Hafner	1.50
236	Brad Penny	1.50
237	Wade Miller	1.50
238	Edgar Martinez	1.50
239	Carl Crawford	1.50
240	Roy Oswalt	1.50
241	Kazuo Matsui	8.00
242	Carlos Beltran	3.00
243	Carlos Beltran	3.00
244	Miguel Cabrera	2.00
245	Scott Rolen	3.00
246	Hank Blalock	2.00
247	Vernon Wells	1.50
248	Adam Dunn	2.00
249	Preston Wilson	1.50
250	Victor Martinez	1.50
251	*Aarom Baldiris*	10.00
252	*Akinori Otsuka*	35.00
253	*Andres Blanco*	10.00
254	*Brad Halsey*	10.00
255	*Joey Gathright*	25.00
256	*Colby Miller*	10.00
257	*Fernando Nieve*	10.00
258	*Freddy Guzman*	15.00
259	*Hector Gimenez*	10.00
260	*Jake Woods*	10.00
261	*Jason Bartlett*	10.00
262	*John Gall*	15.00
263	*Jose Capellan*	35.00
264	*Josh Labandeira*	10.00
265	*Justin Germano*	10.00
266	*Kazuhito Tadano*	40.00
267	*Lance Cormier*	10.00
268	*Merkin Valdez*	20.00
269	*Mike Gosling*	10.00
270	*Ramon Ramirez*	10.00
271	*Rusty Tucker*	10.00
272	*Shawn Hill*	10.00
273	*Shingo Takatsu*	40.00
274	*William Bergolla*	10.00
275	*Yadier Molina*	20.00

Bronze Spotlight

Bronze: 1-2X
Production 100 sets

Gold Spotlight

Golds (1-250): 3-5X
Production 25 sets

Platinum Spotlight

No Pricing
Production one set

Silver Spotlight

Silver (1-250): 2-3X
Production 50 sets

Barrels

No Pricing
Production 1-5

Cuts

NM/M

Quantity produced listed

1	Nolan Ryan/100	125.00
2	Bob Gibson/50	40.00
3	Harmon Killebrew/100	40.00
4	Duke Snider/100	30.00
5	George Brett/100	75.00
6	Stan Musial/100	80.00
7	Alan Trammell/100	20.00
8	Cal Ripken Jr./100	180.00
9	Steve Carlton/50	40.00
10	Phil Rizzuto/100	30.00
11	Mark Prior/50	65.00
12	Will Clark/100	40.00
13	Lou Brock/100	30.00
14	Ozzie Smith/100	60.00
15	Bob Feller/100	30.00
16	Gary Carter/50	25.00
17	Al Kaline/100	40.00
18	Brooks Robinson/100	40.00
19	Tony Gwynn/100	50.00
20	Mike Schmidt/100	75.00
21	Ralph Kiner/50	40.00
22	Jim Palmer/50	40.00
23	Don Mattingly/100	75.00
24	Paul Molitor/50	40.00
25	Dale Murphy/100	30.00

Cuts Gold

NM/M

Quantity produced listed

1	Nolan Ryan/34	200.00
2	Bob Gibson/45	40.00
9	Steve Carlton/32	50.00
11	Mark Prior/22	85.00
12	Will Clark/22	65.00
13	Lou Brock/20	50.00
15	Bob Feller/28	50.00
19	Tony Gwynn/19	100.00
20	Mike Schmidt/20	100.00
22	Jim Palmer/22	50.00
23	Don Mattingly/23	100.00

Legends Material Autographs Number

NM/M

Quanity produced listed

1	Al Kaline Pants/50	50.00
3	Bob Feller Jsy/50	30.00
4	Bob Gibson Jsy/50	30.00
7	Carl Yastrzemski Jsy/25	80.00
8	Harmon Killebrew Jsy/25	65.00
9	Hoyt Wilhelm Jsy/25	40.00
12	Lou Brock Jsy/50	30.00
13	Luis Aparicio Pants/50	20.00
15	Reggie Jackson Jsy/50	50.00
16	Red Schoendienst Jsy/50	30.00
19	Stan Musial Jsy/50	75.00
23	Whitey Ford Pants/25	50.00
24	Yogi Berra Jsy/25	75.00

Legends Material Autographs Position

NM/M

Quantity produced listed

1	Al Kaline Pants/50	50.00
3	Bob Feller Jsy/50	30.00
4	Bob Gibson Jsy/50	30.00
5	Brooks Robinson Jsy/5	
7	Carl Yastrzemski Jsy/25	80.00
8	Harmon Killebrew Jsy/25	65.00
9	Hoyt Wilhelm Jsy/25	40.00
12	Lou Brock Jsy/50	30.00
13	Luis Aparicio Pants/50	20.00
15	Reggie Jackson Jsy/50	50.00
16	Red Schoendienst Jsy/50	30.00
19	Stan Musial Jsy/50	75.00
22	Warren Spahn Jsy/10	
23	Whitey Ford Pants/25	50.00
24	Yogi Berra Jsy/25	75.00

Legends Material Number

NM/M

Quantity produced listed

1	Al Kaline Pants/50	15.00
2	Babe Ruth Pants/50	160.00
3	Bob Feller Jsy/50	10.00
4	Bob Gibson Jsy/50	10.00
5	Brooks Robinson Jsy/5	
6	Burleigh Grimes Pants/100	40.00
7	Carl Yastrzemski Jsy/100	15.00
8	Harmon Killebrew Jsy/25	25.00
9	Hoyt Wilhelm Jsy/100	5.00
10	Johnny Mize Pants/100	10.00
11	Ernie Banks Pants/50	15.00
12	Lou Brock Jsy/50	10.00
13	Luis Aparicio Pants/100	5.00
14	Pee Wee Reese Jsy/50	10.00
15	Reggie Jackson Jsy/100	10.00
16	Red Schoendienst Jsy/50	8.00
17	Roberto Clemente Jsy/25	80.00
18	Roger Maris Pants/100	25.00
19	Stan Musial Jsy/100	20.00
20	Ted Williams Jsy/50	75.00
21	Ty Cobb Pants/50	80.00
22	Warren Spahn Jsy/100	10.00
23	Whitey Ford Pants/100	10.00
24	Yogi Berra Jsy/50	15.00
25	Satchel Paige CO Jsy/100	50.00

Legends Material Position

NM/M

Quantity produced listed

1	Al Kaline Pants/50	15.00
2	Babe Ruth Pants/50	160.00
3	Bob Feller Jsy/50	10.00
4	Bob Gibson Jsy/50	10.00
6	Burleigh Grimes Pants/100	40.00
7	Carl Yastrzemski Jsy/100	15.00
8	Harmon Killebrew Jsy/25	25.00

9 Hoyt Wilhelm Jsy/100 5.00
10 Johnny Mize Pants/100 10.00
11 Ernie Banks Pants/50 15.00
12 Lou Brock Jsy/50 10.00
13 Luis Aparicio Pants/100 5.00
14 Pee Wee Reese Jsy/50 10.00
15 Reggie Jackson Jsy/100 10.00
16 Red Schoendienst Jsy/50 8.00
17 Roberto Clemente Jsy/25 80.00
18 Roger Maris Pants/100 25.00
19 Stan Musial Jsy/100 20.00
20 Ted Williams Jsy/50 75.00
21 Ty Cobb Pants/50 80.00
22 Warren Spahn Jsy/100 10.00
23 Whitey Ford Pants/100 10.00
24 Yogi Berra Jsy/50 15.00
25 Satchel Paige CO Jsy/100 50.00

Lumberjacks

NM/M
Common Player: 2.00
Quantity produced listed
Black: 1X-3X
Production 16-100
1 Al Kaline/399 4.00
2 Albert Pujols/114 15.00
3 Andre Dawson/438 2.00
4 Babe Ruth/714 8.00
5 Bo Jackson/141 5.00
6 Bobby Doerr/223 3.00
7 Brooks Robinson/268 4.00
8 Cal Ripken Jr./431 10.00
9 Carlton Fisk/376 2.00
10 Dale Murphy/398 2.00
11 Darryl Strawberry/335 2.00
12 Don Mattingly/222 6.00
13 Duke Snider/407 3.00
14 Eddie Mathews/512 3.00
15 Eddie Murray/504 3.00
16 Frank Robinson/586 3.00
17 Frank Thomas/418 3.00
18 Gary Carter/324 2.00
19 George Brett/317 6.00
20 Harmon Killebrew/573 4.00
21 Hideki Matsui/16
22 Lou Gehrig/493 5.00
23 Mark Grace/173 2.00
24 Mike Piazza/358 4.00
25 Mike Schmidt/548 5.00
26 Orlando Cepeda/379 2.00
27 Rafael Palmeiro/528 2.00
28 Ralph Kiner/369 2.00
29 Reggie Jackson/563 3.00
30 Rickey Henderson/297 3.00
31 Roger Maris/275 5.00
32 Ryne Sandberg/282 4.00
33 Sammy Sosa/539 4.00
34 Scott Rolen/192 4.00
35 Stan Musial/475 4.00
36 Ted Williams/521 6.00
37 Thurman Munson/113 5.00
38 Vladimir Guerrero/234 4.00
39 Willie McCovey/521 2.00
40 Willie Stargell/475 2.00
41 Roberto Clemente, Stan Musial 6.00
42 Cal Ripken Jr., Ernie Banks 10.00
43 Babe Ruth, Lou Gehrig 8.00
44 George Brett, Mike Schmidt 8.00
45 Frank Robinson, Jackie Robinson 4.00
46 Don Mattingly, Roger Maris 8.00
47 Nomar Garciaparra, Ted Williams 8.00
48 Johnny Bench, Mike Piazza 4.00
49 Reggie Jackson, Sammy Sosa 4.00
50 Mel Ott, Willie McCovey 4.00

Lumberjacks Autographs Bat

NM/M
Quantity produced listed
1 Al Kaline/100 40.00
3 Andre Dawson/50 20.00
5 Bo Jackson/25 70.00
6 Bobby Doerr/50 25.00
7 Brooks Robinson/50 60.00
8 Cal Ripken Jr./25 200.00
9 Carlton Fisk/25 40.00
10 Dale Murphy/100 25.00
11 Darryl Strawberry/25 25.00
12 Don Mattingly/25 80.00
17 Frank Thomas/25 70.00
18 Gary Carter/50 20.00
19 George Brett/25 80.00
20 Harmon Killebrew/50 50.00
23 Mark Grace/17 50.00
25 Mike Schmidt/25 80.00
28 Ralph Kiner/100 25.00
29 Reggie Jackson/25 60.00
32 Ryne Sandberg/25 90.00
34 Scott Rolen/25 50.00
35 Stan Musial/50 75.00
39 Willie McCovey/25 40.00

Lumberjacks Autographs

NM/M
Quantity produced listed
1 Al Kaline/100 30.00
3 Andre Dawson/100 15.00
5 Bo Jackson/25 60.00
6 Bobby Doerr/100 20.00
7 Brooks Robinson/100 50.00
8 Cal Ripken Jr./25 180.00
9 Carlton Fisk/25 30.00
10 Dale Murphy/100 20.00
11 Darryl Strawberry/100 15.00
12 Don Mattingly/25 70.00
13 Duke Snider/100 20.00
16 Frank Robinson/100 20.00
17 Frank Thomas/50 50.00
18 Gary Carter/100 15.00
19 George Brett/25 70.00
20 Harmon Killebrew/100 40.00
23 Mark Grace/25 40.00
25 Mike Schmidt/50 65.00
28 Ralph Kiner/100 20.00
29 Reggie Jackson/25 50.00
30 Rickey Henderson/25 50.00
32 Ryne Sandberg/25 90.00
34 Scott Rolen/25 40.00
35 Stan Musial/50 65.00
39 Willie McCovey/25 30.00

Lumberjacks Autographs Jersey

NM/M
Quantity produced listed
1 Al Kaline Pants/100 40.00
3 Andre Dawson/50 20.00
5 Bo Jackson/25 70.00
6 Bobby Doerr/100 15.00
7 Brooks Robinson/25 75.00
8 Cal Ripken Jr./25 200.00
9 Carlton Fisk/50 30.00
10 Dale Murphy/100 25.00
11 Darryl Strawberry Pants/25 25.00
12 Don Mattingly/25 80.00
15 Eddie Murray/25 70.00
16 Frank Robinson/50 30.00
17 Frank Thomas/25 70.00
18 Gary Carter/50 20.00
19 George Brett/25 80.00
20 Harmon Killebrew/25 60.00
23 Mark Grace/17 50.00
25 Mike Schmidt/25 80.00
26 Orlando Cepeda Pants/50 20.00
29 Reggie Jackson/25 60.00
32 Ryne Sandberg/25 90.00
34 Scott Rolen/25 50.00
35 Stan Musial/50 75.00
39 Willie McCovey/25 40.00

Lumberjacks Barrel

Quantity produced listed
No Pricing
Production 1-5

Lumberjacks Bat

NM/M
Quantity produced listed
1 Al Kaline/100 15.00
2 Albert Pujols/100 15.00
3 Andre Dawson/25 15.00
4 Babe Ruth/100 125.00
5 Bo Jackson/50 15.00
6 Bobby Doerr/25 12.00
7 Brooks Robinson/100 20.00
8 Cal Ripken Jr./100 40.00
9 Carlton Fisk/100 10.00
10 Dale Murphy/50 15.00
11 Darryl Strawberry/25 15.00
12 Don Mattingly/100 20.00
14 Eddie Mathews/100 10.00
15 Eddie Murray/100 15.00
16 Frank Robinson/100 8.00
17 Frank Thomas/25 20.00
18 Gary Carter/50 10.00
19 George Brett/100 20.00
20 Harmon Killebrew/100 15.00
21 Hideki Matsui/100 25.00
22 Lou Gehrig/100 100.00
23 Mark Grace/25 15.00
24 Mike Piazza/50 15.00
25 Mike Schmidt/100 15.00
26 Orlando Cepeda/50 8.00
27 Rafael Palmeiro/50 10.00
28 Ralph Kiner/100 8.00
29 Reggie Jackson/100 10.00
30 Rickey Henderson/100 10.00
31 Roger Maris/100 25.00
32 Ryne Sandberg/100 15.00
33 Sammy Sosa/100 10.00
34 Scott Rolen/25 15.00
35 Stan Musial/100 25.00
36 Ted Williams/100 50.00
37 Thurman Munson/100 20.00
38 Vladimir Guerrero/25 15.00
39 Willie McCovey/100 10.00
40 Willie Stargell/50 10.00
41 Roberto Clemente, Stan Musial/100 85.00
42 Cal Ripken Jr., Ernie Banks/50 100.00
43 Babe Ruth, Lou Gehrig/25 250.00
44 George Brett, Mike Schmidt/50 50.00
46 Don Mattingly, Roger Maris/50 40.00
47 Nomar Garciaparra, Ted Williams/100 75.00
48 Johnny Bench, Mike Piazza/25 35.00
49 Reggie Jackson, Sammy Sosa/50 20.00
50 Mel Ott, Willie McCovey/100 40.00

Lumberjacks Combos

NM/M
Quantity produced listed
1 Al Kaline Bat-Pants/100 20.00
2 Albert Pujols Bat-Jsy/100 20.00
3 Andre Dawson Bat-Jsy/50 15.00
4 Babe Ruth Bat-Jsy/25 400.00
5 Bo Jackson Bat-Jsy/50 20.00
6 Bobby Doerr Bat-Jsy/50 12.00
7 Brooks Robinson Bat-Jsy/25 40.00
8 Cal Ripken Jr. Bat-Jsy/100 50.00
9 Carlton Fisk Bat-Jsy/50 15.00
10 Dale Murphy Bat-Jsy/100 15.00
11 Darryl Strawberry Bat-Pants/25 15.00
12 Don Mattingly Bat-Jsy/100 25.00
14 Eddie Mathews Bat-Jsy/50 15.00
15 Eddie Murray Bat-Jsy/50 20.00
16 Frank Robinson Bat-Jsy/100 15.00
17 Frank Thomas Bat-Jsy/50 20.00
18 Gary Carter Bat-Jsy/50 10.00
19 George Brett Bat-Jsy/100 25.00
20 Harmon Killebrew Bat-Jsy/50 30.00
21 Hideki Matsui Bat-Jsy/100 30.00
22 Lou Gehrig Bat-Jsy/25 250.00
23 Mark Grace Bat-Jsy/17 30.00
24 Mike Piazza Bat-Jsy/100 15.00
25 Mike Schmidt Bat-Jsy/100 20.00
26 Orlando Cepeda Bat-Pants/50 10.00
27 Rafael Palmeiro Bat-Jsy/50 15.00
29 Reggie Jackson Bat-Jsy/100 15.00
30 Rickey Henderson Bat-Jsy/100 15.00
31 Roger Maris Bat-Jsy/50 40.00
32 Ryne Sandberg Bat-Jsy/50 25.00
33 Sammy Sosa Bat-Jsy/100 15.00
34 Scott Rolen Bat-Jsy/25 20.00
35 Stan Musial Bat-Jsy/100 30.00
36 Ted Williams Bat-Jsy/50 75.00
37 Thurman Munson Bat-Jsy/100 25.00
38 Vladimir Guerrero Bat-Jsy/50 15.00
39 Willie McCovey Bat-Jsy/100 15.00
40 Willie Stargell Bat-Jsy/100 12.00

Lumberjacks Jersey

NM/M
Quantity produced listed
1 Al Kaline Pants/50 20.00
2 Albert Pujols/100 15.00
3 Andre Dawson/25 15.00
4 Babe Ruth/25 300.00
5 Bo Jackson/100 10.00
6 Bobby Doerr/100 5.00
7 Brooks Robinson/25 30.00
8 Cal Ripken Jr./100 40.00
9 Carlton Fisk/100 10.00
10 Dale Murphy/100 10.00
11 Darryl Strawberry Pants/50 8.00
12 Don Mattingly/100 20.00
13 Duke Snider/4
14 Eddie Mathews/100 10.00
15 Eddie Murray/50 20.00
16 Frank Robinson/50 10.00
17 Frank Thomas/100 10.00
18 Gary Carter/50 10.00
19 George Brett/100 20.00
20 Harmon Killebrew/25 30.00
21 Hideki Matsui/100 25.00
22 Lou Gehrig/25 180.00
23 Mark Grace/100 8.00
24 Mike Piazza/100 10.00
25 Mike Schmidt/100 15.00
26 Orlando Cepeda Pants/100 5.00
27 Rafael Palmeiro/50 10.00
29 Reggie Jackson/100 10.00
30 Rickey Henderson/100 10.00
31 Roger Maris/100 25.00

32 Ryne Sandberg/100 15.00
33 Sammy Sosa/100 10.00
34 Scott Rolen/50 10.00
35 Stan Musial/50 30.00
36 Ted Williams/100 50.00
37 Thurman Munson/100 20.00
38 Vladimir Guerrero/50 10.00
39 Willie McCovey/100 10.00
40 Willie Stargell/100 8.00
41 Roberto Clemente, Stan Musial/50 120.00
42 Cal Ripken Jr., Ernie Banks Pants/100 65.00
43 Babe Ruth, Lou Gehrig/25 400.00
44 George Brett, Mike Schmidt Jkt/100 30.00
45 Frank Robinson, Jackie Robinson/25 30.00
46 Don Mattingly, Roger Maris Pants/100 25.00
47 Johnny Bench, Mike Piazza/100 10.00
49 Reggie Jackson, Sammy Sosa/100 15.00
50 Mel Ott Pants, Willie McCovey/25 80.00

Matching Numbers

NM/M

Quantity produced listed
Prime: No Pricing
Production One Set
1 Bobby Doerr Jsy, Pee Wee Reese Jsy/100 10.00
2 Lou Gehrig Pants, Mel Ott Jsy/50 160.00
3 Albert Pujols Jsy, George Brett Jsy/100 30.00
4 Cal Ripken Jr. Jsy, Carl Yastrzemski Jsy/100 50.00
5 Dwight Gooden Jsy, Whitey Ford Pants/50 15.00
6 Mark Grace Jsy, Todd Helton Jsy/25 25.00
7 Robin Yount Jsy, Tony Gwynn Jsy/50 40.00
8 Frank Robinson Jsy, Mike Schmidt Jsy/100 25.00
9 Roberto Clemente Jsy, Sammy Sosa Jsy/100 75.00
10 Roger Clemens Jsy, Warren Spahn Pant/100 25.00
11 Mark Prior Jsy, Roger Clemens Jsy/50 25.00
12 Don Mattingly Jkt, Ryne Sandberg Jsy/100 30.00
13 Billy Williams Jsy, Wade Boggs Jsy/100 10.00
14 Jim "Catfish" Hunter Jsy, Juan Marichal Jsy/50 10.00
15 Fergie Jenkins Pants, Greg Maddux Jsy/50 20.00
16 Kerry Wood Pants, Nolan Ryan Jsy/100 35.00
17 Rickey Henderson Jsy, Roger Maris Pants/100 40.00
18 Dontrelle Willis Jsy, Mike Mussina Jsy/50 15.00
19 Reggie Jackson Jsy, Willie McCovey Jsy/100 15.00
20 Bob Gibson Jsy, Pedro Martinez Jsy/50 15.00
21 Duke Snider Jsy, Paul Molitor Jsy/100 10.00
22 Johnny Bench Jsy, Lou Boudreau Jsy/100 15.00
23 Andre Dawson Jsy, Chipper Jones Jsy/100 15.00
24 Ernie Banks Jsy, Boyer Jsy/100 15.00
25 Manny Ramirez Jsy, Rickey Henderson Jsy/100 15.00
26 Carlton Fisk Jsy, Scott Rolen Jsy/100 15.00
27 Nolan Ryan Jsy, Orlando Cepeda Pant/100 25.00
28 Roy Halladay Jsy, Steve Carlton Jsy/100 8.00
29 Eddie Mathews Jsy, Tom Seaver Jsy/100 15.00
30 Brandon Webb Jsy, Orel Hershiser Jsy/100 10.00

Moniker Bat

NM/M

Quanity produced listed
1 Adam Dunn/50 30.00
5 Alfonso Soriano/25 50.00
6 Andruw Jones/25 40.00
8 Angel Berroa/25 15.00
9 Aramis Ramirez/25 25.00
10 Aubrey Huff/25 25.00
15 Ben Sheets/25 25.00
21 Carlos Beltran/50 40.00
24 Craig Biggio/25 40.00
27 Delmon Young/50 30.00
30 Dontrelle Willis/25 30.00
31 Edgar Renteria/25 25.00
34 Frank Thomas/25 70.00
35 Fred McGriff/50 30.00
36 Garret Anderson/50 20.00
37 Gary Sheffield/25 40.00
40 Hank Blalock/50 35.00
61 Jermaine Dye/25 25.00
71 Jorge Posada/25 50.00
84 Kerry Wood/25 50.00
88 Lance Berkman/25 40.00
100 Mark Mulder/50 20.00
101 Mark Prior/50 50.00
102 Mark Teixeira/25 40.00
106 Michael Young/50 15.00
107 Miguel Cabrera/40 40.00
109 Mike Lowell/25 25.00
122 Paul LoDuca/25 25.00
124 Preston Wilson/25 20.00
131 Rickie Weeks/25 25.00
137 Roy Oswalt/25 20.00
144 Sean Casey/50 20.00
145 Shannon Stewart/25 25.00
155 Torii Hunter/25 25.00
156 Trot Nixon/25 25.00
158 Vernon Wells/50 20.00
159 Victor Martinez/50 25.00
163 Alfonso Soriano/25 50.00
166 Gary Sheffield/25 35.00
194 Garret Anderson/50 20.00
198 Mark Prior/50 50.00
201 Andre Dawson/50 20.00
205 Bobby Doerr/25 25.00
207 Dale Murphy/100 25.00
208 Don Mattingly/50 75.00
209 Gary Carter/100 15.00
212 Lou Brock/50 30.00
214 Mark Grace/25 30.00
216 Mike Schmidt/50 75.00
217 Nolan Ryan/50 150.00
219 Paul Molitor/50 30.00
221 Rod Carew/50 35.00
223 Ryne Sandberg/25 80.00
224 Stan Musial/50 75.00
226 Tony Gwynn/50 50.00
230 Carlos Beltran/50 40.00
231 David Ortiz/50 60.00
232 David Ortiz/50 60.00
234 Carlos Lee/50 20.00
235 Travis Hafner/25 25.00
238 Edgar Martinez/25 40.00
240 Roy Oswalt/25 30.00
242 Carlos Beltran/50 45.00
243 Carlos Beltran/50 45.00
244 Miguel Cabrera/50 40.00
246 Hank Blalock/50 35.00
247 Vernon Wells/50 20.00
248 Adam Dunn/50 35.00
249 Preston Wilson/25 25.00
250 Victor Martinez/25 25.00

Moniker Bronze

NM/M

Quanity produced listed
Silver: .5X-1.5X
Production 1-50
No pricing 15 or less
Platinum: No Pricing
Production One Set
1 Adam Dunn/50 30.00
3 Albert Pujols/25 180.00
5 Alfonso Soriano/100 30.00
6 Andruw Jones/50 30.00
8 Angel Berroa/25 15.00
11 Austin Kearns/50 20.00
18 Brandon Webb/21 15.00
21 Carlos Beltran/50 40.00
23 Chipper Jones/25 65.00
24 Craig Biggio/5 40.00
30 Dontrelle Willis/25 30.00
31 Edgar Renteria/25 25.00
34 Frank Thomas/50 60.00
36 Garret Anderson/50 20.00
37 Gary Sheffield/50 25.00
39 Greg Maddux/25 85.00
40 Hank Blalock/50 35.00
46 Jacque Jones/25 25.00
58 Jeff Bagwell/25 75.00
71 Jorge Posada/25 50.00
76 Juan Gonzalez/25 30.00
79 Kazuhisa Ishii/25 35.00
84 Kerry Wood/25 50.00
88 Lance Berkman/50 30.00
98 Marcus Giles/25 25.00
100 Mark Mulder/100 15.00
101 Mark Prior/50 50.00
102 Mark Teixeira/50 30.00
106 Michael Young/50 15.00
107 Miguel Cabrera/50 40.00
109 Mike Lowell/25 25.00
122 Paul LoDuca/25 25.00
131 Rickie Weeks/25 25.00
137 Roy Oswalt/10 20.00
140 Sammy Sosa/25 85.00
142 Scott Rolen/25 60.00
144 Sean Casey/25 25.00
145 Shannon Stewart/25 25.00
153 Todd Helton/25 40.00
155 Torii Hunter/50 20.00
156 Trot Nixon/25 25.00
158 Vernon Wells/25 25.00
163 Alfonso Soriano/100 30.00
166 Gary Sheffield/10 30.00
167 Greg Maddux/5 80.00
172 Juan Gonzalez/25 40.00
183 Scott Rolen/25 50.00
191 Albert Pujols/5 180.00
193 Chipper Jones/5 65.00
194 Garret Anderson/10 20.00
195 Jeff Bagwell/25 75.00
198 Mark Prior/50 50.00
199 Sammy Sosa/25 80.00
200 Todd Helton/25 40.00
201 Andre Dawson/100 15.00
203 Bob Feller/100 20.00
204 Bob Gibson/100 20.00
205 Bobby Doerr/100 15.00
206 Cal Ripken Jr./25 180.00
207 Dale Murphy/100 25.00
208 Don Mattingly/100 60.00
209 Gary Carter/100 15.00
210 George Brett/25 75.00
212 Lou Brock/100 20.00
214 Mark Grace/100 20.00
215 Maury Wills/100 15.00
216 Mike Schmidt/100 60.00
217 Nolan Ryan/100 120.00
218 Orel Hershiser/25 40.00
219 Paul Molitor/100 25.00
221 Rod Carew/100 25.00
223 Ryne Sandberg/100 50.00
224 Stan Musial/100 60.00
226 Tony Gwynn/100 40.00
230 Carlos Beltran/50 45.00
231 David Ortiz/50 60.00
232 David Ortiz/50 60.00
233 Carlos Zambrano/25 30.00
234 Carlos Lee/25 20.00
238 Edgar Martinez/25 40.00
240 Roy Oswalt/50 20.00
242 Carlos Beltran/50 40.00
243 Carlos Beltran/50 40.00
244 Miguel Cabrera/50 40.00
245 Scott Rolen/25 50.00
246 Hank Blalock/50 35.00
247 Vernon Wells/25 25.00
248 Adam Dunn/50 35.00

Moniker Gold

NM/M

Quanity produced listed
5 Alfonso Soriano/25 40.00
21 Carlos Beltran/25 50.00
100 Mark Mulder/25 25.00
163 Alfonso Soriano/25 40.00
201 Andre Dawson/25 20.00
203 Bob Feller/25 35.00
204 Bob Gibson/25 40.00
205 Bobby Doerr/25 25.00
207 Dale Murphy/25 40.00
208 Don Mattingly/25 90.00
209 Gary Carter/25 25.00
212 Lou Brock/25 30.00
214 Mark Grace/25 30.00
215 Maury Wills/25 25.00
216 Mike Schmidt/25 85.00
217 Nolan Ryan/25 150.00
219 Paul Molitor/25 40.00
221 Rod Carew/25 35.00
223 Ryne Sandberg/25 75.00
224 Stan Musial/25 100.00
226 Tony Gwynn/25 50.00

Moniker Jersey

NM/M

Quanity produced listed
Prime: No Pricing
Production One Set
1 Adam Dunn/50 30.00
5 Alfonso Soriano/50 40.00
6 Andruw Jones/25 40.00
8 Angel Berroa Pants/25 15.00
9 Aramis Ramirez/25 25.00
10 Aubrey Huff/25 25.00
11 Austin Kearns/25 25.00
15 Ben Sheets/25 25.00
18 Brandon Webb/25 15.00
20 C.C. Sabathia/25 25.00
21 Carlos Beltran/50 40.00
23 Chipper Jones/25 65.00
24 Craig Biggio/25 40.00
30 Dontrelle Willis/25 30.00
32 Eric Chavez/50 20.00
34 Frank Thomas/25 70.00
35 Fred McGriff/25 40.00
36 Garret Anderson/50 20.00
40 Hank Blalock/50 35.00
46 Jacque Jones/25 25.00
63 Jim Edmonds/25 40.00
66 Jody Gerut/25 15.00
67 Johan Santana/25 40.00
71 Jorge Posada/25 50.00
74 Jose Vidro/25 15.00
84 Kerry Wood/25 50.00
88 Lance Berkman/25 40.00
89 Larry Bigbie/25 20.00
98 Marcus Giles/25 25.00
99 Mark Buehrle/25 25.00
100 Mark Mulder/75 15.00
101 Mark Prior/50 50.00
102 Mark Teixeira/25 40.00
105 Melvin Mora/25 25.00
107 Miguel Cabrera/38 40.00
109 Mike Lowell/25 25.00
115 Morgan Ensberg/25 15.00
122 Paul LoDuca/25 25.00
124 Preston Wilson/25 25.00
137 Roy Oswalt/25 25.00
142 Scott Rolen/50 50.00
143 Sean Burroughs/25 25.00
144 Sean Casey/25 25.00
145 Shannon Stewart/25 25.00
149 Steve Finley/25 25.00
153 Todd Helton/25 40.00
154 Tom Glavine/25 40.00
155 Torii Hunter/25 25.00
156 Trot Nixon/25 25.00
158 Vernon Wells/50 20.00
159 Victor Martinez/50 20.00
163 Alfonso Soriano/50 40.00
166 Gary Sheffield/25 40.00
172 Juan Gonzalez/25 40.00
183 Scott Rolen/50 40.00
185 Tom Glavine/25 40.00
193 Chipper Jones/25 65.00
194 Garret Anderson/50 20.00
200 Todd Helton/25 40.00
201 Andre Dawson/50 20.00
204 Bob Gibson/50 30.00
205 Bobby Doerr/50 20.00
207 Dale Murphy/100 25.00
208 Don Mattingly/50 70.00
209 Gary Carter/100 15.00
216 Mike Schmidt/50 75.00
217 Nolan Ryan/100 120.00
218 Orel Hershiser/50 30.00
219 Paul Molitor/50 30.00
221 Rod Carew/50 30.00
223 Ryne Sandberg/25 100.00
224 Stan Musial/25 100.00
226 Tony Gwynn/100 40.00
228 Whitey Ford Pants/25 40.00
229 Yogi Berra/25 75.00
230 Carlos Beltran/50 40.00
231 David Ortiz/50 60.00
232 David Ortiz/50 60.00
234 Carlos Lee/50 20.00
235 Travis Hafner/25 25.00
236 Brad Penny/25 15.00
237 Wade Miller/25 15.00
238 Edgar Martinez/50 40.00
239 Carl Crawford/25 25.00
240 Roy Oswalt/25 25.00
242 Carlos Beltran/50 45.00
243 Carlos Beltran/50 45.00

244 Miguel Cabrera/50 40.00
245 Scott Rolen/50 40.00
246 Hank Blalock/50 35.00
247 Vernon Wells/50 20.00
248 Adam Dunn/50 35.00
249 Preston Wilson/25 25.00

Moniker Jersey Number

NM/M

Quanity produced listed
Prime: No Pricing
Production One Set

1 Adam Dunn/50 30.00
5 Alfonso Soriano/50 40.00
6 Andruw Jones/25 40.00
8 Angel Berroa Pants/25 15.00
9 Aramis Ramirez/25 25.00
10 Aubrey Huff/25 25.00
11 Austin Kearns/25 25.00
15 Ben Sheets/25 25.00
18 Brandon Webb/25 15.00
20 C.C. Sabathia/25 25.00
21 Carlos Beltran/50 40.00
23 Chipper Jones/25 65.00
24 Craig Biggio/25 40.00
30 Dontrelle Willis/25 30.00
32 Eric Chavez/50 20.00
34 Frank Thomas/25 70.00
35 Fred McGriff/25 40.00
36 Garret Anderson/50 20.00
40 Hank Blalock/50 35.00
46 Jacque Jones/25 25.00
63 Jim Edmonds/25 40.00
66 Jody Gerut/25 15.00
67 Johan Santana/25 40.00
71 Jorge Posada/25 50.00
74 Jose Vidro/25 15.00
84 Kerry Wood/25 50.00
88 Lance Berkman/25 40.00
90 Larry Walker/25 20.00
98 Marcus Giles/25 25.00
99 Mark Buehrle/25 25.00
100 Mark Mulder/75 15.00
101 Mark Prior/50 50.00
102 Mark Teixeira/25 40.00
105 Melvin Mora/25 25.00
107 Miguel Cabrera/50 30.00
109 Mike Lowell/25 25.00
115 Morgan Ensberg/25 15.00
122 Paul LoDuca/25 25.00
124 Preston Wilson/25 25.00
137 Roy Oswalt/25 25.00
140 Sammy Sosa/25 120.00
142 Scott Rolen/25 50.00
143 Sean Burroughs/25 25.00
145 Shannon Stewart/25 25.00
149 Steve Finley/25 25.00
153 Todd Helton/25 40.00
154 Tom Glavine/25 40.00
155 Torii Hunter/25 25.00
156 Trot Nixon/25 25.00
158 Vernon Wells/50 20.00
159 Victor Martinez/50 20.00
163 Alfonso Soriano/50 40.00
166 Gary Sheffield/25 40.00
172 Juan Gonzalez/25 40.00
183 Scott Rolen/50 40.00
185 Tom Glavine/25 40.00
193 Chipper Jones/25 65.00
194 Garret Anderson/50 20.00
199 Sammy Sosa/25 120.00
200 Todd Helton/25 40.00
201 Andre Dawson/50 20.00
204 Bob Gibson/25 40.00
205 Bobby Doerr/50 20.00
207 Dale Murphy/100 25.00
208 Don Mattingly/50 70.00
209 Gary Carter/100 15.00
216 Mike Schmidt/50 75.00
217 Nolan Ryan/100 120.00
218 Orel Hershiser/50 30.00
219 Paul Molitor/50 30.00
221 Rod Carew/50 30.00
223 Ryne Sandberg/25 100.00
224 Stan Musial/25 100.00
226 Tony Gwynn/100 40.00
228 Whitey Ford Pants/25 40.00
229 Yogi Berra/25 75.00
230 Carlos Beltran/50 40.00
231 David Ortiz/50 60.00
232 David Ortiz/50 60.00
234 Carlos Lee/50 20.00
235 Travis Hafner/25 25.00
236 Brad Penny/25 15.00
237 Wade Miller/25 15.00
238 Edgar Martinez/50 40.00
239 Carl Crawford/25 25.00
240 Roy Oswalt/25 25.00
242 Carlos Beltran/50 45.00
243 Carlos Beltran/50 45.00
244 Miguel Cabrera/50 40.00
245 Scott Rolen/50 40.00
246 Hank Blalock/50 35.00
247 Vernon Wells/50 20.00
248 Adam Dunn/50 35.00
249 Preston Wilson/25 25.00
250 Victor Martinez/50 20.00

Player Threads Double

NM/M

Quantity produced listed

1 Mike Piazza/100 15.00
2 Roger Clemens/100 20.00
3 Nolan Ryan/100 30.00
4 Reggie Jackson/100 15.00
5 Wade Boggs/100 10.00
6 Steve Carlton/100 10.00
7 Ivan Rodriguez/100 10.00
8 Pedro Martinez/100 10.00
9 Rickey Henderson/50 25.00
10 Rickey Henderson/100 20.00
11 Randy Johnson/50 20.00
12 Curt Schilling/100 10.00
13 Roger Maris/100 40.00
14 Sammy Sosa/100 15.00
15 Gary Carter/100 8.00
16 Gary Sheffield/50 10.00
17 Eddie Murray/50 20.00
18 Hideo Nomo/50 15.00
19 Rafael Palmeiro/100 10.00
20 Andre Dawson/50 10.00

Player Threads Jersey Number

NM/M

Quantity produced listed
Prime: No Pricing
Production One Set

1 Mike Piazza/100 10.00
3 Nolan Ryan Jkt/100 20.00
4 Reggie Jackson/100 10.00
5 Wade Boggs/50 10.00
6 Steve Carlton Pants/100 5.00
7 Ivan Rodriguez/25 15.00
8 Pedro Martinez/50 12.00
10 Rickey Henderson Pants/100 10.00
11 Randy Johnson/50 10.00
12 Curt Schilling/25 20.00
13 Roger Maris/50 50.00
14 Sammy Sosa/100 10.00
15 Gary Carter Pants/50 8.00
16 Gary Sheffield/25 10.00
17 Eddie Murray/50 15.00
18 Hideo Nomo/50 10.00
19 Rafael Palmeiro/50 10.00
20 Andre Dawson/50 8.00

Player Threads Triple

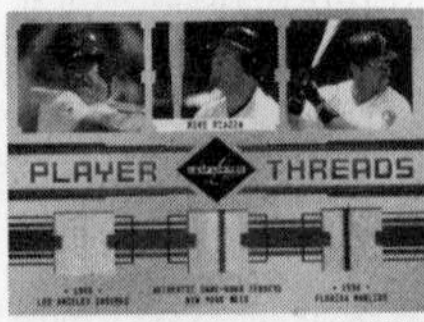

NM/M

Quantity produced listed

1 Mike Piazza/50 30.00
2 Roger Clemens/25 50.00
3 Nolan Ryan/50 70.00
4 Reggie Jackson/25 40.00
5 Wade Boggs/25 30.00
6 Steve Carlton/25 25.00
7 Ivan Rodriguez/25 30.00
8 Pedro Martinez/25 30.00
10 Rickey Henderson/25 50.00
12 Curt Schilling/25 30.00
13 Roger Maris/25 120.00
14 Sammy Sosa/25 40.00
15 Gary Carter/25 20.00
17 Eddie Murray/25 40.00
18 Hideo Nomo/25 30.00
19 Rafael Palmeiro/50 20.00
20 Andre Dawson/25 20.00

Team Threads Jersey Number

NM/M

Common Card: 15.00
Production 100 Sets
Prime: No Pricing
Production One Set

1 Stan Musial, Albert Pujols 40.00
2 Cal Ripken Jr. Jkt, Mike Mussina 40.00
3 Carlton Fisk, Roger Clemens 25.00
4 Dale Murphy, Chipper Jones 15.00
5 Tony Gwynn, Dave Winfield 25.00
6 Don Mattingly, Hideki Matsui 50.00
7 Lou Boudreau, Early Wynn 15.00
8 Ernie Banks, Sammy Sosa 30.00
9 Nolan Ryan Jkt, Jeff Bagwell 50.00
10 Mike Schmidt, Jim Thome 25.00

Team Trademarks

NM/M

Common Player: 5.00
Production 100 Sets
Gold: No Pricing
Production 10 Sets

1 Bob Gibson 8.00
2 Cal Ripken Jr. 30.00
3 Carl Yastrzemski 10.00
4 Dale Murphy 8.00
5 Gary Carter 5.00
6 George Brett 15.00
7 Tom Seaver 8.00
8 Kerry Wood 8.00
9 Lou Brock 8.00
10 Luis Aparicio 5.00
11 Mike Piazza 10.00
12 Nolan Ryan 15.00
13 Nolan Ryan 15.00
14 Randy Johnson 8.00
15 Reggie Jackson 8.00
16 Ricky Henderson 8.00
17 Robin Yount 10.00
18 Rod Carew 8.00
19 Ryne Sandberg 15.00
20 Steve Carlton 5.00
21 Steve Garvey 5.00
22 Johnny Bench 8.00
23 Tony Gwynn 10.00
24 Whitey Ford 8.00
25 Will Clark 8.00

Team Trademarks Autographs

NM/M

Quantity produced listed

1 Bob Gibson/100 20.00
2 Cal Ripken Jr./25 150.00
3 Carl Yastrzemski/25 60.00
4 Dale Murphy/100 20.00
5 Gary Carter/100 15.00
6 George Brett/25 65.00
7 Tom Seaver/25 50.00
8 Kerry Wood/25 40.00
9 Lou Brock/100 20.00
10 Luis Aparicio/100 15.00
11 Mike Piazza/5
12 Nolan Ryan Astros/25 100.00
13 Nolan Ryan Rgr/25 100.00
14 Randy Johnson/5
15 Reggie Jackson/25 50.00
16 Ricky Henderson/10
17 Robin Yount/50 50.00
18 Rod Carew/50 25.00
19 Ryne Sandberg/25 65.00
20 Steve Carlton/100 20.00
21 Steve Garvey/50 15.00
22 Johnny Bench/25 50.00
23 Tony Gwynn/100 30.00
24 Whitey Ford/25 30.00
25 Will Clark/34 50.00

Team Trademarks Auto. Jersey Numbers

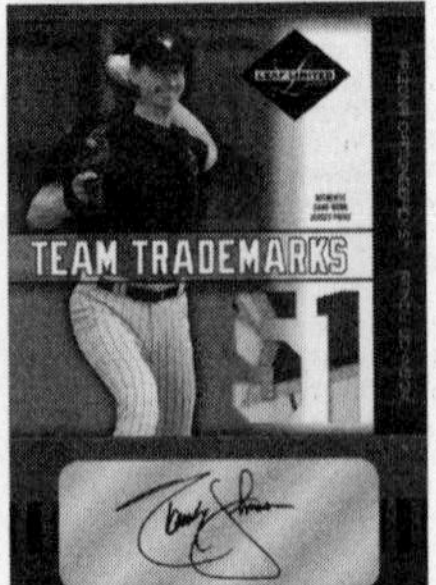

NM/M

Quantity produced listed
Prime: No Pricing
Production One Set

1 Bob Gibson/100 25.00
2 Cal Ripken Jr. Pants/25 200.00
3 Carl Yastrzemski/25 75.00
4 Dale Murphy/100 25.00
5 Gary Carter/100 15.00
6 George Brett/25 80.00
7 Tom Seaver/25 65.00
8 Kerry Wood Pants/25 50.00
9 Lou Brock/100 25.00
10 Luis Aparicio Pants/100 15.00
12 Nolan Ryan Astros/25 120.00
13 Nolan Ryan Rgr/25 120.00
15 Reggie Jackson Pants/25 60.00
17 Robin Yount/50 75.00
18 Rod Carew Jkt/50 30.00
19 Ryne Sandberg/50 65.00
20 Steve Carlton/25 40.00
22 Johnny Bench/50 50.00
23 Tony Gwynn/50 50.00
24 Whitey Ford/50 30.00
25 Will Clark/84 40.00

Team Trademarks Jersey Number

NM/M

Quantity produced listed
Prime: No Pricing
Production One Set

1 Bob Gibson/100 10.00
2 Cal Ripken Jr. Pants/100 40.00
3 Carl Yastrzemski/100 15.00
4 Dale Murphy/100 10.00
5 Gary Carter/100 5.00
6 George Brett/100 15.00
7 Tom Seaver/100 10.00
8 Kerry Wood Pants/50 10.00
9 Lou Brock/100 10.00
10 Luis Aparicio Pants/100 5.00
11 Mike Piazza/50 15.00
12 Nolan Ryan Astros/100 20.00
13 Nolan Ryan Rgr/100 20.00
14 Randy Johnson/50 10.00
15 Reggie Jackson Pants/100 8.00
16 Ricky Henderson/100 10.00
17 Robin Yount/100 10.00
18 Rod Carew Jkt/100 8.00
19 Ryne Sandberg/100 15.00
20 Steve Carlton/50 5.00
22 Johnny Bench/100 10.00
23 Tony Gwynn/100 10.00
24 Whitey Ford/100 10.00
25 Will Clark/50 15.00

Threads Jersey

NM/M

Quanity produced listed
Prime: No Pricing
Production One Set
Button: No Pricing
Production 1-6

1 Adam Dunn/25 15.00
3 Albert Pujols/50 20.00
5 Alfonso Soriano/25 15.00
6 Andruw Jones/25 10.00
11 Austin Kearns/25 10.00
12 Barry Larkin/25 15.00
13 Barry Zito/25 8.00
16 Bernie Williams/50 8.00

21 Carlos Beltran/25 15.00
22 Carlos Delgado/25 8.00
23 Chipper Jones/50 10.00
24 Craig Biggio/25 15.00
25 Curt Schilling/25 20.00
30 Dontrelle Willis/25 8.00
31 Edgar Renteria/25 10.00
32 Eric Chavez/25 8.00
34 Frank Thomas/25 20.00
36 Garret Anderson/25 10.00
39 Greg Maddux/50 15.00
40 Hank Blalock/25 10.00
41 Hideki Matsui/50 40.00
42 Hideo Nomo/50 10.00
44 Ivan Rodriguez/25 15.00
50 Jason Giambi/50 5.00
55 Javy Lopez/25 10.00
58 Jeff Bagwell/50 10.00
59 Jeff Kent/50 5.00
63 Jim Edmonds/25 10.00
64 Jim Thome/50 10.00
69 John Smoltz/25 15.00
71 Jorge Posada/25 15.00
75 Josh Beckett/25 10.00
76 Juan Gonzalez/25 15.00
84 Kerry Wood/50 12.00
88 Lance Berkman/50 5.00
90 Larry Walker/25 15.00
93 Luis Gonzalez/25 8.00
96 Magglio Ordonez/25 8.00
97 Manny Ramirez/50 10.00
100 Mark Mulder/25 10.00
101 Mark Prior/50 12.00
107 Miguel Cabrera/25 15.00
108 Miguel Tejada/25 10.00
110 Mike Mussina/50 10.00
111 Mike Piazza/50 15.00
112 Mike Sweeney/25 10.00
123 Pedro J. Martinez/50 12.00
126 Rafael Palmeiro/25 15.00
127 Randy Johnson/25 20.00
137 Roy Oswalt/25 10.00
140 Sammy Sosa/50 15.00
142 Scott Rolen/25 20.00
146 Shawn Green/25 8.00
150 Tim Hudson/25 10.00
153 Todd Helton/50 10.00
154 Tom Glavine/25 15.00
155 Torii Hunter/25 10.00
157 Troy Glaus/25 10.00
158 Vernon Wells/25 8.00
161 Vladimir Guerrero/25 20.00
162 Alex Rodriguez/100 10.00
163 Alfonso Soriano/25 10.00
164 Andy Pettitte/25 15.00
165 Curt Schilling/25 10.00
166 Gary Sheffield/25 10.00
167 Greg Maddux/50 15.00
168 Hideo Nomo/25 20.00
169 Ivan Rodriguez/50 12.00
170 Jason Giambi/25 8.00
172 Juan Gonzalez/25 15.00
174 Kevin Brown/25 8.00
176 Miguel Tejada/25 10.00
177 Mike Mussina/50 10.00
178 Mike Piazza/25 25.00
179 Pedro Martinez/25 20.00
180 Rafael Palmeiro/25 15.00
181 Randy Johnson/50 10.00
182 Roger Clemens/100 10.00
183 Scott Rolen/25 20.00
184 Shawn Green/25 8.00
185 Tom Glavine/25 15.00
186 Vladimir Guerrero/25 20.00
187 Alex Rodriguez/100 10.00
189 Randy Johnson/50 10.00
190 Roger Clemens/100 10.00
191 Albert Pujols/50 20.00
192 Barry Zito/25 10.00
193 Chipper Jones/50 10.00
194 Garret Anderson/25 10.00
195 Jeff Bagwell/50 10.00
196 Josh Beckett/25 10.00
197 Magglio Ordonez/25 10.00
198 Mark Prior/50 12.00
199 Sammy Sosa/50 15.00
200 Todd Helton/50 10.00
201 Andre Dawson/50 5.00
202 Babe Ruth/25 350.00
203 Bob Feller/25 20.00
205 Bobby Doerr/50 8.00
206 Cal Ripken Jr./100 40.00
207 Dale Murphy/100 10.00
208 Don Mattingly/50 25.00
209 Gary Carter/50 8.00
210 George Brett/100 15.00
211 Jackie Robinson/50 40.00
212 Lou Brock/25 20.00
213 Lou Gehrig/25 140.00
214 Mark Grace/25 15.00
215 Maury Wills/50 5.00
216 Mike Schmidt/100 15.00
217 Nolan Ryan/100 20.00
218 Orel Hershiser/25 15.00
219 Paul Molitor/50 10.00
220 Roberto Clemente/25 80.00
221 Rod Carew/100 10.00
222 Roy Campanella Pants/50 15.00
223 Ryne Sandberg/50 25.00
224 Stan Musial/25 40.00
225 Ted Williams/50 75.00
226 Tony Gwynn/100 10.00
227 Ty Cobb Pants/100 75.00
228 Whitey Ford Pants/25 20.00
229 Yogi Berra/25 25.00
230 Carlos Beltran/25 15.00
231 David Ortiz/25 20.00
232 David Ortiz/25 20.00
238 Edgar Martinez/25 10.00
240 Roy Oswalt/25 8.00
242 Carlos Beltran/25 15.00
243 Carlos Beltran/25 15.00
244 Miguel Cabrera/25 15.00
245 Scott Rolen/25 20.00
246 Hank Blalock/25 12.00
247 Vernon Wells/25 8.00
248 Adam Dunn/25 15.00
249 Preston Wilson/5

Threads Jersey Number

NM/M

Quanity produced listed
Prime: No Pricing
Production One Set
MLB Logo: No Pricing
Production One Set
1 Adam Dunn/25 15.00
3 Albert Pujols/50 20.00
5 Alfonso Soriano/25 15.00
6 Andruw Jones/25 10.00
11 Austin Kearns/25 8.00
12 Barry Larkin/25 15.00
13 Barry Zito/25 8.00
16 Bernie Williams/50 10.00
21 Carlos Beltran/25 15.00
22 Carlos Delgado/25 8.00
23 Chipper Jones/50 10.00
24 Craig Biggio/25 10.00
25 Curt Schilling/25 20.00
30 Dontrelle Willis/25 8.00
31 Edgar Renteria/25 10.00
32 Eric Chavez/25 8.00
34 Frank Thomas/25 15.00
36 Garret Anderson/25 10.00
39 Greg Maddux/50 15.00
40 Hank Blalock/25 12.00
41 Hideki Matsui/50 40.00
42 Hideo Nomo/50 10.00
44 Ivan Rodriguez/25 20.00
50 Jason Giambi/50 5.00
55 Javy Lopez/25 8.00
58 Jeff Bagwell/50 10.00
59 Jeff Kent/25 10.00
63 Jim Edmonds/25 10.00
64 Jim Thome/50 15.00
69 John Smoltz/25 15.00
71 Jorge Posada/25 15.00
75 Josh Beckett/25 10.00
76 Juan Gonzalez/25 15.00
84 Kerry Wood/50 12.00
88 Lance Berkman/50 5.00
90 Larry Walker/25 10.00
93 Luis Gonzalez/25 8.00
96 Magglio Ordonez/25 8.00
97 Manny Ramirez/50 12.00
100 Mark Mulder/25 10.00
101 Mark Prior/50 12.00
107 Miguel Cabrera/25 15.00
108 Miguel Tejada/25 10.00
110 Mike Mussina/50 10.00
111 Mike Piazza/50 15.00
112 Mike Sweeney/25 10.00
123 Pedro J. Martinez/50 12.00
126 Rafael Palmeiro/25 15.00
127 Randy Johnson/25 20.00
137 Roy Oswalt/25 10.00
140 Sammy Sosa/50 15.00
142 Scott Rolen/25 20.00
146 Shawn Green/25 8.00
150 Tim Hudson/25 10.00
153 Todd Helton/50 10.00
154 Tom Glavine/25 15.00
155 Torii Hunter/25 10.00
157 Troy Glaus/25 8.00
158 Vernon Wells/25 8.00
161 Vladimir Guerrero/25 20.00
162 Alex Rodriguez/100 10.00
163 Alfonso Soriano/50 10.00
164 Andy Pettitte/25 15.00
165 Curt Schilling/25 10.00
166 Gary Sheffield/25 10.00
167 Greg Maddux/50 15.00
168 Hideo Nomo/25 20.00
169 Ivan Rodriguez/50 12.00
170 Jason Giambi/25 8.00
172 Juan Gonzalez/25 12.00
174 Kevin Brown/25 8.00
176 Miguel Tejada/25 10.00
177 Mike Mussina/50 10.00
178 Mike Piazza/25 25.00
179 Pedro Martinez/25 20.00
180 Rafael Palmeiro/25 15.00
181 Randy Johnson/50 10.00
182 Roger Clemens/100 10.00
183 Scott Rolen/25 20.00
184 Shawn Green/25 8.00
185 Tom Glavine/25 15.00
186 Vladimir Guerrero/25 20.00
187 Alex Rodriguez/100 10.00
189 Randy Johnson/50 10.00
190 Roger Clemens/100 10.00
191 Albert Pujols/50 20.00
192 Barry Zito/25 8.00
193 Chipper Jones/50 10.00
194 Garret Anderson/25 10.00
195 Jeff Bagwell/50 10.00
196 Josh Beckett/25 10.00
197 Magglio Ordonez/25 8.00
198 Mark Prior/50 12.00
199 Sammy Sosa/50 15.00
200 Todd Helton/50 10.00
201 Andre Dawson/50 8.00
202 Babe Ruth/25 300.00
203 Bob Feller/25 20.00
205 Bobby Doerr/50 8.00
206 Cal Ripken Jr./100 40.00
207 Dale Murphy/100 10.00
208 Don Mattingly/50 25.00
209 Gary Carter/50 8.00
210 George Brett/100 15.00
211 Jackie Robinson/100 40.00
212 Lou Brock/25 20.00
213 Lou Gehrig/25 150.00
214 Mark Grace/25 15.00
215 Maury Wills/50 8.00
216 Mike Schmidt/100 15.00
217 Nolan Ryan/100 20.00
218 Orel Hershiser/25 15.00
219 Paul Molitor/50 10.00
220 Roberto Clemente/25 80.00
221 Rod Carew/100 10.00
222 Roy Campanella Pants/50 15.00
223 Ryne Sandberg/50 25.00
224 Stan Musial/25 40.00
225 Ted Williams/50 75.00
226 Tony Gwynn/100 10.00
227 Ty Cobb Pants/100 60.00
228 Whitey Ford Pants/25 20.00
229 Yogi Berra/25 25.00
230 Carlos Beltran/25 15.00
231 David Ortiz/25 20.00
232 David Ortiz/25 20.00
238 Edgar Martinez/25 10.00
240 Roy Oswalt H/25 10.00
242 Carlos Beltran/25 15.00
243 Carlos Beltran/25 15.00
244 Miguel Cabrera/25 15.00
245 Scott Rolen/25 20.00
246 Hank Blalock/25 10.00
247 Vernon Wells/25 10.00
248 Adam Dunn/25 15.00

Timber

NM/M

Quanity produced listed
1 Adam Dunn/25 15.00
4 Alex Rodriguez/100 10.00
5 Alfonso Soriano/25 15.00
6 Andruw Jones/25 10.00
7 Andy Pettitte/25 15.00
11 Austin Kearns/25 8.00
12 Barry Larkin/25 15.00
13 Barry Zito/25 8.00
16 Bernie Williams/25 12.00
21 Carlos Beltran/25 15.00
22 Carlos Delgado/25 10.00
23 Chipper Jones/25 20.00
24 Craig Biggio/25 12.00
25 Curt Schilling/25 20.00
30 Dontrelle Willis/25 8.00
32 Eric Chavez/25 8.00
34 Frank Thomas/25 20.00
35 Fred McGriff/25 12.00
36 Garret Anderson/25 8.00
37 Gary Sheffield/25 10.00
39 Greg Maddux/25 25.00
40 Hank Blalock/25 10.00
41 Hideki Matsui/25 60.00
42 Hideo Nomo/25 20.00
44 Ivan Rodriguez/25 20.00
50 Jason Giambi/25 8.00
55 Javy Lopez/25 8.00
58 Jeff Bagwell/25 15.00
59 Jeff Kent/25 8.00
63 Jim Edmonds/25 10.00
64 Jim Thome/25 20.00
71 Jorge Posada/25 15.00
75 Josh Beckett/25 10.00
76 Juan Gonzalez/25 15.00
84 Kerry Wood/25 20.00
85 Kevin Brown/25 8.00
88 Lance Berkman/25 8.00
90 Larry Walker/25 10.00
93 Luis Gonzalez/25 8.00
96 Magglio Ordonez/25 8.00
97 Manny Ramirez/25 15.00
100 Mark Mulder/25 8.00
101 Mark Prior/25 20.00
102 Mark Teixeira/25 10.00
106 Michael Young/25 8.00
107 Miguel Cabrera/25 15.00
108 Miguel Tejada/25 10.00
109 Mike Lowell/25 8.00
110 Mike Mussina/25 15.00
111 Mike Piazza/25 25.00
112 Mike Sweeney/25 8.00
116 Nick Johnson/25 8.00
117 Nomar Garciaparra/25 20.00
122 Paul LoDuca/25 8.00
123 Pedro J. Martinez/25 20.00
126 Rafael Palmeiro/25 15.00
127 Randy Johnson/25 20.00
130 Richie Sexson/25 10.00
134 Rocco Baldelli/25 8.00
135 Roger Clemens/25 25.00
137 Roy Oswalt/25 8.00
140 Sammy Sosa/50 15.00
142 Scott Rolen/25 20.00
146 Shawn Green/25 8.00
150 Tim Hudson/25 8.00
153 Todd Helton/25 15.00
154 Tom Glavine/25 15.00
155 Torii Hunter/25 8.00
156 Trot Nixon/25 10.00
157 Troy Glaus/25 8.00
158 Vernon Wells/25 8.00
161 Vladimir Guerrero/25 20.00
162 Alex Rodriguez/100 10.00
163 Alfonso Soriano/25 15.00
164 Andy Pettitte/25 15.00
165 Curt Schilling/25 10.00
166 Gary Sheffield/25 10.00
167 Greg Maddux/25 25.00
168 Hideo Nomo/25 15.00
169 Ivan Rodriguez/25 15.00
170 Jason Giambi/25 8.00
171 Jim Thome/25 15.00
172 Juan Gonzalez/25 10.00
174 Kevin Brown/25 8.00
175 Manny Ramirez/25 15.00
176 Miguel Tejada/25 10.00
177 Mike Mussina/25 15.00
178 Mike Piazza/25 25.00
179 Pedro Martinez/25 20.00
180 Rafael Palmeiro/25 15.00
181 Randy Johnson/25 20.00
182 Roger Clemens/25 25.00
183 Scott Rolen/25 20.00
184 Shawn Green/25 8.00
185 Tom Glavine/25 15.00
186 Vladimir Guerrero/25 20.00
187 Alex Rodriguez/100 10.00
188 Mike Piazza/25 25.00
189 Randy Johnson/25 20.00
190 Roger Clemens/25 25.00
191 Albert Pujols/50 20.00
192 Barry Zito/25 8.00
193 Chipper Jones/25 20.00
194 Garret Anderson/25 8.00
195 Jeff Bagwell/25 15.00
196 Josh Beckett/25 8.00
197 Magglio Ordonez/25 8.00
198 Mark Prior/25 20.00
199 Sammy Sosa/50 15.00
200 Todd Helton/25 15.00
201 Andre Dawson/50 8.00
202 Babe Ruth/100 120.00
206 Cal Ripken Jr./100 40.00
207 Dale Murphy/50 15.00
208 Don Mattingly/50 25.00
209 Gary Carter/25 10.00
210 George Brett/50 25.00
212 Lou Brock/25 15.00
213 Lou Gehrig/100 100.00
214 Mark Grace/25 15.00

216 Mike Schmidt/50 25.00
217 Nolan Ryan/50 30.00
219 Paul Molitor/50 10.00
220 Roberto Clemente/100 75.00
221 Rod Carew/25 25.00
222 Roy Campanella/100 10.00
223 Ryne Sandberg/50 25.00
224 Stan Musial/100 20.00
225 Ted Williams/100 50.00
226 Tony Gwynn/50 20.00
227 Ty Cobb/100 75.00
229 Yogi Berra/100 10.00
230 Carlos Beltran/25 15.00
231 David Ortiz/25 20.00
232 David Ortiz/25 20.00
238 Edgar Martinez/25 15.00
240 Roy Oswalt/25 10.00
242 Carlos Beltran/25 15.00
243 Carlos Beltran/25 15.00
244 Miguel Cabrera/25 15.00
245 Scott Rolen/25 20.00
246 Hank Blalock/25 10.00
248 Adam Dunn/25 15.00

TNT

NM/M

Quanity produced listed
Prime: No Pricing
Production One Set
1 Adam Dunn Bat-Jsy/50 10.00
3 Albert Pujols Bat-Jsy/100 15.00
5 Alfonso Soriano Bat-Jsy/50 10.00
6 Andruw Jones Bat-Jsy/50 8.00
11 Austin Kearns Bat-Jsy/50 5.00
12 Barry Larkin Bat-Jsy/25 20.00
13 Barry Zito Bat-Jsy/50 5.00
16 Bernie Williams Bat-Jsy/50 10.00
21 Carlos Beltran Bat-Jsy/50 10.00
22 Carlos Delgado Bat-Jsy/50 5.00
23 Chipper Jones Bat-Jsy/50 15.00
24 Craig Biggio Bat-Jsy/50 8.00
25 Curt Schilling Bat-Jsy/25 25.00
32 Eric Chavez Bat-Jsy/25 10.00
34 Frank Thomas Bat-Jsy/25 20.00
36 Garret Anderson Bat-Jsy/25 10.00
39 Greg Maddux Bat-Jsy/50 20.00
40 Hank Blalock Bat-Jsy/50 8.00
41 Hideki Matsui Bat-Jsy/50 50.00
42 Hideo Nomo Bat-Jsy/25 20.00
44 Ivan Rodriguez Bat-Jsy/25 20.00
50 Jason Giambi Bat-Jsy/50 8.00
55 Javy Lopez Bat-Jsy/25 10.00
56 Jay Gibbons Bat-Jsy/5
58 Jeff Bagwell Bat-Jsy/50 10.00
59 Jeff Kent Bat-Jsy/25 10.00
63 Jim Edmonds Bat-Jsy/25 10.00
64 Jim Thome Bat-Jsy/50 15.00
71 Jorge Posada Bat-Jsy/25 20.00
75 Josh Beckett Bat-Jsy/25 10.00
76 Juan Gonzalez Bat-Jsy/25 20.00
84 Kerry Wood Bat-Jsy/50 15.00
88 Lance Berkman Bat-Jsy/50 5.00
90 Larry Walker Bat-Jsy/25 20.00
93 Luis Gonzalez Bat-Jsy/25 10.00
96 Magglio Ordonez Bat-Jsy/25 10.00
97 Manny Ramirez Bat-Jsy/50 15.00
100 Mark Mulder Bat-Jsy/25 10.00
101 Mark Prior Bat-Jsy/50 15.00
102 Mark Teixeira Bat-Jsy/25 10.00
107 Miguel Cabrera Bat-Jsy/25 20.00
108 Miguel Tejada Bat-Jsy/25 10.00
109 Mike Lowell Bat-Jsy/25 10.00
110 Mike Mussina Bat-Jsy/50 10.00
111 Mike Piazza Bat-Jsy/50 20.00
112 Mike Sweeney Bat-Jsy/25 10.00
123 Pedro J. Martinez Bat-Jsy/50 15.00
126 Rafael Palmeiro Bat-Jsy/25 20.00
127 Randy Johnson Bat-Jsy/50 15.00
137 Roy Oswalt Bat-Jsy/25 10.00
140 Sammy Sosa Bat-Jsy/50 20.00
142 Scott Rolen Bat-Jsy/25 25.00
146 Shawn Green Bat-Jsy/25 10.00
150 Tim Hudson Bat-Jsy/25 10.00
153 Todd Helton Bat-Jsy/50 10.00
154 Tom Glavine Bat-Jsy/25 20.00
155 Torii Hunter Bat-Jsy/25 10.00
156 Trot Nixon Bat-Jsy/10
157 Troy Glaus Bat-Jsy/25 10.00
158 Vernon Wells Bat-Jsy/25 10.00
161 Vladimir Guerrero Bat-Jsy/25 25.00
162 Alex Rodriguez Bat-Jsy/100 10.00
163 Alfonso Soriano Bat-Jsy/50 10.00
164 Andy Pettitte Bat-Jsy/25 20.00
165 Curt Schilling Bat-Jsy/25 10.00
166 Gary Sheffield Bat-Jsy/25 10.00
167 Greg Maddux Bat-Jsy/50 20.00
168 Hideo Nomo Bat-Jsy/25 20.00
169 Ivan Rodriguez Bat-Jsy/50 15.00
170 Jason Giambi Bat-Jsy/25 10.00
172 Juan Gonzalez Bat-Jsy/25 15.00
174 Kevin Brown Bat-Jsy/25 10.00
176 Miguel Tejada Bat-Jsy/25 10.00
177 Mike Mussina Bat-Jsy/50 10.00
178 Mike Piazza Bat-Jsy/50 20.00
179 Pedro Martinez Bat-Jsy/50 15.00
180 Rafael Palmeiro Bat-Jsy/50 10.00
181 Randy Johnson Bat-Jsy/50 15.00
182 Roger Clemens Bat-Jsy/100 10.00
183 Scott Rolen Bat-Jsy/25 25.00
184 Shawn Green Bat-Jsy/25 10.00
185 Tom Glavine Bat-Jsy/25 20.00
186 Vladimir Guerrero Bat-Jsy/25 25.00
187 Alex Rodriguez Bat-Jsy/100 10.00
189 Randy Johnson Bat-Jsy/50 15.00
190 Roger Clemens Bat-Jsy/100 10.00
191 Albert Pujols Bat-Jsy/50 25.00
192 Barry Zito Bat-Jsy/25 10.00
193 Chipper Jones Bat-Jsy/50 15.00
194 Garret Anderson Bat-Jsy/25 10.00
195 Jeff Bagwell Bat-Jsy/50 10.00
196 Josh Beckett Bat-Jsy/25 10.00
197 Magglio Ordonez Bat-Jsy/25 10.00
198 Mark Prior Bat-Jsy/50 15.00
199 Sammy Sosa Bat-Jsy/50 20.00
200 Todd Helton Bat-Jsy/50 10.00
201 Andre Dawson Bat-Jsy/50 8.00
202 Babe Ruth Bat-Jsy/25 425.00
206 Cal Ripken Jr. Bat-Jsy/100 60.00
207 Dale Murphy Bat-Jsy/100 10.00
208 Don Mattingly Bat-Jsy/100 20.00
209 Gary Carter Bat-Jsy/50 10.00
210 George Brett Bat-Jsy/100 20.00
212 Lou Brock Bat-Jsy/25 25.00
213 Lou Gehrig Bat-Jsy/25 250.00
214 Mark Grace Bat-Jsy/25 20.00
216 Mike Schmidt Bat-Jsy/50 30.00
217 Nolan Ryan Bat-Jsy/100 25.00
219 Paul Molitor Bat-Jsy/25 20.00
221 Rod Carew Bat-Jsy/50 15.00
222 Roy Campanella Bat-Pants/50 20.00
223 Ryne Sandberg Bat-Jsy/50 30.00
224 Stan Musial Bat-Jsy/25 50.00
225 Ted Williams Bat-Jsy/50 100.00
226 Tony Gwynn Bat-Jsy/100 15.00
227 Ty Cobb Bat-Pants/50 120.00
230 Carlos Beltran Bat-Jsy/25 20.00
231 David Ortiz Bat-Jsy/25 25.00
232 David Ortiz Bat-Jsy/25 25.00
238 Edgar Martinez Bat-Jsy/25 15.00
240 Roy Oswalt Bat-Jsy/25 10.00
242 Carlos Beltran Bat-Jsy/25 20.00
243 Carlos Beltran Bat-Jsy/25 20.00
244 Miguel Cabrera Bat-Jsy/25 20.00
245 Scott Rolen Bat-Jsy/25 20.00
246 Hank Blalock Bat-Jsy/25 10.00
247 Vernon Wells Bat-Jsy/25 10.00
248 Adam Dunn Bat-Jsy/25 20.00

2005 LEAF

NM/M

Complete Set (300):
Common Player (1-200): .15
Common SP (201-250): 1.00
Inserted 1:3
Common SP (251-300): 1.00
#251-270 inserted 1:6
271-300 inserted 1:4
Hobby pack (8): 4.00
Hobby box (24): 80.00
1 Bartolo Colon .25
2 Casey Kotchman .15
3 Chone Figgins .15
4 Darin Erstad .25
5 Francisco Rodriguez .25
6 Garret Anderson .25
7 Jarrod Washburn .15
8 Troy Glaus .25
9 Vladimir Guerrero .50
10 Brandon Webb .15
11 Casey Fossum .15
12 Luis Gonzalez .25
13 Randy Johnson .50
14 Richie Sexson .25
15 Andruw Jones .25
16 Chipper Jones .50
17 J.D. Drew .25
18 John Smoltz .25
19 Johnny Estrada .15
20 Marcus Giles .15
21 Rafael Furcal .25
22 Russ Ortiz .15
23 Javy Lopez .25
24 Jay Gibbons .15
25 Melvin Mora .15
26 Miguel Tejada .40
27 Rafael Palmeiro .40
28 Sidney Ponson .15
29 Bill Mueller .15
30 Curt Schilling .40
31 David Ortiz .50
32 Doug Mientkiewicz .15
33 Jason Varitek .25
34 Johnny Damon .40
35 Manny Ramirez .50
36 Pedro J. Martinez .50
37 Trot Nixon .15
38 Aramis Ramirez .25
39 Corey Patterson .25
40 Derrek Lee .25
41 Greg Maddux .75
42 Kerry Wood .50
43 Mark Prior .50
44 Moises Alou .25
45 Nomar Garciaparra 1.00
46 Sammy Sosa 1.00
47 Carlos Lee .15
48 Kip Wells .15
49 Magglio Ordonez .25
50 Mark Buehrle .15
51 Paul Konerko .25
52 Roberto Alomar .25
53 Adam Dunn .40
54 Austin Kearns .15
55 Barry Larkin .25
56 Danny Graves .15
57 Ken Griffey Jr. 1.00
58 Sean Casey .15
59 C.C. Sabathia .15
60 Cliff Lee .15
61 Jody Gerut .15
62 Omar Vizquel .25
63 Travis Hafner .15
64 Victor Martinez .25
65 Charles Johnson .15
66 Jason Jennings .15
67 Jeromy Burnitz .15
68 Preston Wilson .15
69 Todd Helton .40
70 Bobby Higginson .15
71 Dmitri Young .15
72 Eric Munson .15
73 Ivan Rodriguez .40
74 Jeremy Bonderman .15
75 Rondell White .15
76 A.J. Burnett .15
77 Carl Pavano .25
78 Dontrelle Willis .25
79 Hee Seop Choi .15
80 Josh Beckett .25
81 Juan Pierre .15
82 Miguel Cabrera .50
83 Mike Lowell .15
84 Paul LoDuca .15
85 Andy Pettitte .25
86 Carlos Beltran .40
87 Craig Biggio .25
88 Jeff Bagwell .40
89 Jeff Kent .25
90 Lance Berkman .25
91 Roger Clemens 1.50
92 Roy Oswalt .25
93 Andres Blanco .15
94 Jeremy Affeldt .15
95 Juan Gonzalez .25
96 Ken Harvey .15
97 Mike Sweeney .15
98 Zack Greinke .15
99 Adrian Beltre .25
100 Brad Penny .15
101 Eric Gagne .25
102 Kazuhisa Ishii .15
103 Milton Bradley .15
104 Shawn Green .25

#	Player	Price
105	Steve Finley	.15
106	Ben Sheets	.25
107	Bill Hall	.15
108	Danny Kolb	.15
109	Geoff Jenkins	.15
110	Junior Spivey	.15
111	Lyle Overbay	.15
112	Scott Podsednik	.15
113	A.J. Pierzynski	.15
114	Brad Radke	.15
115	Corey Koskie	.15
116	Jacque Jones	.15
117	Joe Mauer	.25
118	Joe Nathan	.15
119	Shannon Stewart	.15
120	Torii Hunter	.25
121	Brad Wilkerson	.15
122	Jeff Fassero	.15
123	Jose Vidro	.15
124	Livan Hernandez	.15
125	Nick Johnson	.15
126	Al Leiter	.25
127	Jose Reyes	.15
128	Kazuo Matsui	.25
129	Mike Cameron	.15
130	Mike Piazza	1.00
131	Richard Hidalgo	.15
132	Tom Glavine	.25
133	Alex Rodriguez	1.50
134	Bernie Williams	.25
135	Derek Jeter	1.50
136	Gary Sheffield	.40
137	Jason Giambi	.25
138	Javier Vazquez	.25
139	Jorge Posada	.25
140	Kevin Brown	.15
141	Mariano Rivera	.25
142	Mike Mussina	.25
143	Barry Zito	.25
144	Bobby Crosby	.25
145	Eric Chavez	.25
146	Erubiel Durazo	.15
147	Jermaine Dye	.15
148	Mark Mulder	.25
149	Tim Hudson	.25
150	Bobby Abreu	.25
151	Eric Milton	.15
152	Jim Thome	.50
153	Kevin Millwood	.15
154	Mike Lieberthal	.15
155	Pat Burrell	.25
156	Randy Wolf	.15
157	Craig Wilson	.15
158	Jack Wilson	.15
159	Jason Bay	.25
160	Jason Kendall	.15
161	Kris Benson	.15
162	Brian Giles	.15
163	Jake Peavy	.25
164	Jay Payton	.15
165	Khalil Greene	.25
166	Mark Loretta	.15
167	Ryan Klesko	.15
168	Sean Burroughs	.15
169	David Aardsma	.15
170	Edgardo Alfonzo	.15
171	Jason Schmidt	.25
172	Merkin Valdez	.15
173	Ray Durham	.15
174	Bret Boone	.15
175	Dan Wilson	.15
176	Ichiro Suzuki	1.25
177	Jamie Moyer	.15
178	Rich Aurilia	.15
179	Albert Pujols	1.50
180	Edgar Renteria	.25
181	Jason Isringhausen	.15
182	Jeff Suppan	.15
183	Jim Edmonds	.25
184	Scott Rolen	.50
185	Woody Williams	.15
186	Aubrey Huff	.15
187	Carl Crawford	.15
188	Dewon Brazelton	.15
189	Jose Cruz Jr.	.15
190	Rocco Baldelli	.25
191	Alfonso Soriano	.40
192	Hank Blalock	.40
193	Kenny Rogers	.15
194	Laynce Nix	.15
195	Mark Teixeira	.25
196	Michael Young	.15
197	Alexis Rios	.15
198	Carlos Delgado	.25
199	Roy Halladay	.15
200	Vernon Wells	.15
201	Josh Kroeger	1.00
202	Angel Guzman	1.00
203	Brad Halsey	1.00
204	Bucky Jacobsen	1.00
205	Carlos Hines	1.00
206	Carlos Vasquez	1.00
207	Billy Traber	1.00
208	Bubba Crosby	1.00
209	Chris Oxspring	1.00
210	Chris Shelton	1.00
211	Colby Miller	1.00
212	David Crouthers	1.00
213	Dennis Sarfate	1.00
214	Donald Kelly	1.00
215	Edwardo Sierra	1.00
216	Edwin Moreno	1.00
217	Fernando Nieve	1.00
218	Freddy Guzman	1.00
219	Greg Dobbs	1.00
220	Hector Gimenez	1.00
221	Andy Green	1.00
222	Jason Bartlett	1.00
223	Jerry Gil	1.00
224	Jesse Crain	2.00
225	Joey Gathright	1.00
226	John Gall	1.00
227	Jorge Sequea	1.00
228	Jorge Vasquez	1.00
229	Josh Labandeira	1.00
230	Justin Leone	1.00
231	Lance Cormier	1.00
232	Lincoln Holdzkom	1.00
233	Miguel Olivo	1.00
234	Mike Rouse	1.00
235	Onil Joseph	1.00
236	Phil Stockman	1.00
237	Ramon Ramirez	1.00
238	Robb Quinlan	1.00
239	Roberto Novoa	1.00
240	Ronald Belisario	1.00
241	Ronny Cedeno	1.00
242	Ruddy Yan	1.00
243	Ryan Meaux	1.00
244	Ryan Wing	1.00
245	Scott Proctor	1.00
246	Sean Henn	1.00
247	Tim Bausher	1.00
248	Tim Bittner	1.00
249	William Bergolla	1.00
250	Yadier Molina	1.00
251	Bernie Williams	1.00
252	Craig Biggio	1.00
253	Chipper Jones	2.00
254	Greg Maddux	3.00
255	Sammy Sosa	3.00
256	Mike Mussina	1.50
257	Tim Salmon	1.00
258	Barry Larkin	1.00
259	Randy Johnson	2.00
260	Jeff Bagwell	1.50
261	Roberto Alomar	1.50
262	Tom Glavine	1.00
263	Roger Clemens	4.00
264	Alex Rodriguez	4.00
265	Ivan Rodriguez	1.50
266	Pedro J. Martinez	2.00
267	Ken Griffey Jr.	3.00
268	Jim Thome	2.00
269	Frank Thomas	1.50
270	Mike Piazza	3.00
271	Garret Anderson	1.00
272	Luis Gonzalez	1.00
273	John Smoltz	1.00
274	Rafael Palmeiro	1.50
275	Curt Schilling	1.50
276	Mark Prior	2.00
277	Magglio Ordonez	1.00
278	Adam Dunn	1.50
279	Travis Hafner	1.00
280	Jeromy Burnitz	1.00
281	Carlos Guillen	1.00
282	Dontrelle Willis	1.00
283	Carlos Beltran	1.50
284	Zack Greinke	1.00
285	Adrian Beltre	1.00
286	Ben Sheets	1.00
287	Johan Santana	1.00
288	Livan Hernandez	1.00
289	Kazuo Matsui	1.00
290	Derek Jeter	4.00
291	Tim Hudson	1.00
292	Eric Milton	1.00
293	Jason Kendall	1.00
294	Jake Peavy	1.00
295	Ray Durham	1.00
296	Ichiro Suzuki	3.00
297	Scott Rolen	2.00
298	Carl Crawford	1.00
299	Hank Blalock	1.50
300	Roy Halladay	1.00

Press Proofs Blue

Blue (1-200): 5-10X
Blue (201-250): 1-2X
Blue (251-300): 2-4X
Production 75 sets

Press Proofs Gold

Gold (1-200): 10-20X
Gold (201-250): 2-4X
Blue (251-300): 4-8X
Production 25 sets

Press Proofs Red

Red (1-200): 2-4X
Red (201-250): .5-1X
Red (251-300): 1-2X
Inserted 1:8

4 Star Staffs

NM/M

Common Card: 2.00
Inserted 1:48
Die-cut: 1X
Production 250 Sets

#	Players	Price
1	Greg Maddux, John Smoltz, Kevin Millwood, Tom Glavine	4.00
2	A.J. Burnett, Carl Pavano, Dontrelle Willis, Josh Beckett	2.00
3	Andy Pettitte, David Wells, Mike Mussina, Roger Clemens	6.00
4	Carlos Zambrano, Greg Maddux, Kerry Wood, Mark Prior	6.00
5	Andy Pettitte, Mariano Rivera, Mike Mussina, Roger Clemens	3.00
6	Curt Schilling, Derek Lowe, Pedro J. Martinez, Tim Wakefield	4.00
7	Barry Zito, Mark Mulder, Rich Harden, Tim Hudson	2.00
8	Brandon Webb, Byung-Hyun Kim, Curt Schilling, Randy Johnson	3.00
9	Jamie Moyer, Kenny Rogers, Kevin Brown, Nolan Ryan	8.00
10	Kelvim Escobar, Roger Clemens, Roy Halladay, Woody Williams	6.00
11	Andy Pettitte, Roger Clemens, Roy Oswalt, Wade Miller	6.00
12	Barry Zito, Billy Koch, Mark Mulder, Tim Hudson	2.00
13	Eric Gagne, Hideo Nomo, Kazuhisa Ishii, Kevin Brown	3.00
14	Greg Maddux, Jason Schmidt, John Smoltz, Tom Glavine	5.00
15	Derek Lowe, Hideo Nomo, Pedro Martinez, Tim Wakefield	4.00

Alternate Threads

NM/M

Complete Set (25): 30.00
Common Player: 1.00
Inserted 1:18
Holo: 1X-2X
Production 150 Sets
Holo Die-cut: 2X-4X
Production 50 Sets

#	Player	Price
1	Adam Dunn	1.50
2	C.C. Sabathia	1.00
3	Curt Schilling	1.50
4	Dontrelle Willis	1.00
5	Greg Maddux	3.00
6	Hank Blalock	1.50
7	Ichiro Suzuki	4.00
8	Jeff Bagwell	1.50
9	Ken Griffey Jr.	3.00
10	Ken Harvey	1.00
11	Magglio Ordonez	1.00
12	Mark Mulder	1.00
13	Mark Teixeira	1.00
14	Michael Young	1.00
15	Miguel Tejada	1.50
16	Mike Piazza	4.00
17	Pedro Martinez	2.00
18	Randy Johnson	2.00
19	Roger Clemens	6.00
20	Sammy Sosa	4.00
21	Tim Hudson	1.00
22	Todd Helton	1.50
23	Torii Hunter	1.00
24	Travis Hafner	1.00
25	Vernon Wells	1.00

Autographs

NM/M

Common Autograph: 5.00

#	Player	Price
201	Josh Kroeger	5.00
202	Angel Guzman	15.00
203	Brad Halsey	5.00
204	Bucky Jacobsen	10.00
205	Carlos Hines	5.00
207	Bill Tucker	5.00
208	Bubba Crosby	10.00
210	Chris Shelton	8.00
211	Colby Miller	5.00
212	David Crouthers	5.00
217	Fernando Nieve	10.00
220	Hector Gimenez	5.00
221	Andy Green	5.00
222	Jason Bartlett	5.00
227	Jorge Sequea/84	10.00
228	Jorge Vasquez	8.00
232	Lincoln Holdzkom	8.00
233	Miguel Olivo	8.00
234	Mike Rouse	8.00
236	Phil Stockman	8.00
237	Ramon Ramirez	8.00
242	Ruddy Yan	5.00
245	Scott Proctor	8.00
247	Tim Bausher	8.00
249	William Bergolla	10.00

Autographs Blue

NM/M

No Pricing
Production 15-25
Golds: No Pricing

Autographs Red

NM/M

Common Autograph:

#	Player	Price
3	Chone Figgins/100	8.00
19	Johnny Estrada/100	15.00
24	Jay Gibbons/100	10.00
47	Carlos Lee/100	10.00
56	Danny Graves/100	8.00
60	Cliff Lee/100	10.00
63	Travis Hafner/50	15.00
74	Jeremy Bonderman/100	10.00
94	Jeremy Affeldt/100	8.00
96	Ken Harvey/100	8.00
103	Milton Bradley/100	10.00
111	Lyle Overbay/50	15.00
118	Joe Nathan/100	10.00
144	Bobby Crosby/100	25.00
154	Mike Lieberthal/50	15.00
157	Craig Wilson/50	15.00
158	Jack Wilson/100	12.00
163	Jake Peavy/50	25.00
172	Merkin Valdez/100	8.00
182	Jeff Suppan/100	10.00
187	Carl Crawford/50	15.00
188	Dewon Brazelton/50	10.00
194	Laynce Nix/100	10.00

201 Josh Kroeger/100 8.00
202 Angel Guzman/100 15.00
203 Brad Halsey/100 8.00
204 Bucky Jacobsen/100 10.00
205 Carlos Hines/100 8.00
207 Billy Traber/100 8.00
208 Bubba Crosby/100 10.00
210 Chris Shelton/100 8.00
211 Colby Miller/100 8.00
212 David Crouthers/100 8.00
217 Fernando Nieve/100 10.00
218 Freddy Guzman/100 10.00
220 Hector Gimenez/100 8.00
221 Andy Green/100 8.00
222 Jason Bartlett/100 8.00
224 Josh Crain/100 15.00
227 Jorge Sequea/84 10.00
228 Jorge Vasquez/100 8.00
233 Miguel Olivo/100 8.00
234 Mike Rouse/100 8.00
236 Phil Stockman/100 10.00
237 Ramon Ramirez/100 8.00
238 Robb Quinlan/100 8.00
241 Ronny Cedeno/65 10.00
242 Ruddy Yan/100 8.00
243 Ryan Meaux/93 8.00
247 Tim Bausher/100 8.00
249 William Bergolla/100 10.00
250 Yadier Molina/100 15.00

Clean Up Crew

NM/M
Complete Set (15): 45.00
Common Card:
Inserted 1:49
Die-cut: 1X
Production 250 Sets
1 Albert Pujols, Jim Edmonds, Scott Rolen 6.00
2 Melvin Mora, Miguel Tejada, Rafael Palmeiro 3.00
3 Alfonso Soriano, Michael Young, Hank Blalock 3.00
4 Gary Sheffield, Alex Rodriguez, Hideki Matsui 5.00
5 Moises Alou, Sammy Sosa, Nomar Garciaparra 5.00
6 Paul LoDuca, Mike Lowell, Miguel Cabrera 3.00
7 Carlos Beltran, Lance Berkman, Jeff Bagwell 3.00
8 Paul Konerko, Magglio Ordonez, Frank Thomas 3.00
9 Sean Casey, Ken Griffey Jr., Adam Dunn 5.00
10 Vladimir Guerrero, Garret Anderson, Troy Glaus 3.00
11 Joe Morgan, Johnny Bench, Tony Perez 3.00
12 Keith Hernandez, Darryl Strawberry, Gary Carter 2.00
13 Jim Rice, Carl Yastrzemski, Dwight Evans 5.00
14 Ryne Sandberg, Andre Dawson, Mark Grace 6.00
15 Cal Ripken Jr., Eddie Murray, Rafael Palmeiro 10.00

Cornerstones

NM/M
Complete Set (20): 50.00
Common Card: 1.50
Inserted 1:37
1 Albert Pujols, Scott Rolen 6.00
2 Hideki Matsui, Jorge Posada 5.00
3 Nomar Garciaparra, Sammy Sosa 4.00
4 David Ortiz, Manny Ramirez 3.00
5 Miguel Cabrera, Mike Lowell 3.00
6 Hank Blalock, Mark Teixeira 2.00
7 Chipper Jones, J.D. Drew 3.00
8 Craig Biggio, Jeff Bagwell 3.00
9 Kazuo Matsui, Mike Piazza 4.00
10 Shawn Green, Adrian Beltre 1.50
11 Bobby Abreu, Jim Thome 3.00
12 Mike Schmidt, Steve Carlton 6.00
13 Cal Ripken Jr., Eddie Murray 10.00
14 Carl Yastrzemski, Dwight Evans 5.00
15 Joe Morgan, Johnny Bench 3.00
16 Dale Murphy, Phil Niekro 2.00
17 Alan Trammell, Kirk Gibson 2.00
18 Jose Canseco, Rickey Henderson 3.00
19 Paul Molitor, Robin Yount 4.00
20 Bo Jackson, George Brett 6.00

Cornerstones Bats

NM/M
Common Dual Bat: 8.00
1 Albert Pujols, Scott Rolen 20.00
2 Hideki Matsui, Jorge Posada 35.00
3 Sammy Sosa, Nomar Garciaparra 15.00
4 Manny Ramirez, David Ortiz 20.00
5 Miguel Cabrera, Mike Lowell 10.00
6 Hank Blalock, Mark Teixeira 10.00
7 Chipper Jones, J.D. Drew 15.00
8 Craig Biggio, Jeff Bagwell 10.00
9 Mike Piazza, Kazuo Matsui 15.00
10 Shawn Green, Adrian Beltre 8.00

Cornerstones Jerseys

NM/M
Common Dual Jersey: 8.00
1 Albert Pujols, Scott Rolen 20.00
2 Hideki Matsui, Jorge Posada 35.00
4 Manny Ramirez, David Ortiz 20.00
5 Miguel Cabrera, Mike Lowell 10.00
6 Hank Blalock, Mark Teixeira 10.00
8 Craig Biggio, Jeff Bagwell 10.00
9 Mike Piazza, Kazuo Matsui 15.00
10 Shawn Green, Adrian Beltre 8.00

Cy Young Winners

NM/M
Complete Set (15): 30.00
Common Player: 1.50
Inserted 1:31
Gold: 1X
Production 350 Sets
Gold Die-cut: 1.5X-2X
Production 100 Sets
1 Warren Spahn 3.00
2 Whitey Ford 3.00
3 Bob Gibson 3.00
4 Tom Seaver 3.00
5 Steve Carlton 2.00
6 Jim Palmer 2.00
7 Rollie Fingers 1.50
8 Dwight Gooden 1.50
9 Roger Clemens 6.00
10 Orel Hershiser 1.50
11 Greg Maddux 4.00
12 Dennis Eckersley 2.00
13 Randy Johnson 3.00
14 Pedro Martinez 3.00
15 Eric Gagne 2.00

Fans of the Game

NM/M
Common Card: 1.50
Inserted 1:24
1 Sean Astin 1.50
2 Tony Danza 1.50
3 Taye Diggs 1.50

Fans of the Game Autograph

NM/M
1 Sean Astin 30.00
2 Tony Danza SP/50
3 Taye Diggs 30.00

Game Collection

NM/M
Inserted 1:118
1 Cal Ripken Jr. Bat 30.00
2 Carl Crawford Jsy 5.00
3 Dale Murphy Bat 20.00
4 Don Mattingly Bat 25.00
5 George Brett Jsy 25.00
6 Victor Martinez Bat 8.00
7 Sean Casey Bat 5.00
8 Torii Hunter Bat 5.00
9 Magglio Ordonez Bat 5.00
10 Lance Berkman Bat 5.00
11 Mike Schmidt Bat 25.00
12 Nolan Ryan Jkt 40.00
13 Paul LoDuca Bat 5.00
14 Preston Wilson Bat 5.00
15 Rod Carew Jkt 10.00
16 Reggie Jackson Bat 10.00
17 Ivan Rodriguez Bat 8.00
18 Larry Walker Cards Bat 10.00
19 Miguel Tejada Bat 8.00
20 Vladimir Guerrero Bat 10.00

Game Collection Autograph

NM/M
Production 5-200
2 Carl Crawford Jsy/200 15.00
6 Victor Martinez Bat/200 20.00
7 Sean Casey Bat/200 20.00
8 Torii Hunter Bat/50 25.00
13 Paul LoDuca Bat/100 20.00

Gamers

NM/M
Complete Set (15): 20.00
Common Player: 1.00
Inserted 1:13
Quantum: 2X-3X
Production 175 Sets
Quantum Die-cut: 3X-5X
Production 50 Sets
1 Albert Pujols 4.00
2 Alex Rodriguez 3.00
3 Alfonso Soriano 1.50
4 Chipper Jones 1.50
5 Derek Jeter 4.00
6 Greg Maddux 2.00
7 Ichiro Suzuki 3.00
8 Jim Thome 1.50
9 Ken Griffey Jr. 2.00
10 Lance Berkman 1.00
11 Miguel Tejada 1.00
12 Mike Piazza 2.50
13 Roger Clemens 4.00
14 Scott Rolen 1.50
15 Vladimir Guerrero 1.50

Gold Rookies

NM/M
Complete Set (10): 15.00
Common Player: 2.00
Inserted 1:24
Mirror: 3X-5X
Production 25 Sets
1 Dennis Sarfate 2.00
2 Donnie Kelly 2.00
3 Eddy Rodriguez 2.00
4 Edwin Moreno 2.00
5 Greg Dobbs 2.00
6 Josh Labandeira 2.00
7 Kevin Cave 2.00
8 Mariano Gomez 2.00
9 Ronald Belisario 2.00
10 Ruddy Yan 2.00

Gold Rookies Autograph

NM/M
Common Autograph:
Mirror: No Pricing
Production 25 Sets
1 Dennis Sarfate 10.00
2 Donnie Kelly 8.00
5 Greg Dobbs 8.00
7 Kevin Cave 10.00
9 Ronald Belisario 8.00
10 Ruddy Yan 8.00

Gold Stars

NM/M
Complete Set (20): 40.00
Common Player: .75
Inserted 1:27
Mirror: 4X-6X
Production 25 Sets
1 Albert Pujols 4.00
2 Ichiro Suzuki 3.00
3 Derek Jeter 4.00

4	Alex Rodriguez	3.00
5	Scott Rolen	1.50
6	Randy Johnson	1.50
7	Roger Clemens	4.00
8	Greg Maddux	2.00
9	Alfonso Soriano	1.50
10	Mark Mulder	.75
11	Sammy Sosa	3.00
12	Mike Piazza	3.00
13	Rafael Palmeiro	.75
14	Ivan Rodriguez	.75
15	Miguel Cabrera	.75
16	Stan Musial	3.00
17	Nolan Ryan	6.00
18	Don Mattingly	4.00
19	George Brett	4.00
20	Cal Ripken Jr.	6.00

Home/Road

NM/M

Common Player: 1.00
Inserted 1:22
Home & Road price is identical

1H	Albert Pujols H	4.00
1R	Albert Pujols R	4.00
2H	Alfonso Soriano H	1.50
2R	Alfonso Soriano R	1.50
3H	Carlos Beltran H	1.00
3R	Carlos Beltran R	1.00
4H	Chipper Jones H	1.50
4R	Chipper Jones R	1.50
5H	Frank Thomas H	1.50
5R	Frank Thomas R	1.50
6H	Hank Blalock H	1.00
6R	Hank Blalock R	1.00
7H	Ivan Rodriguez H	1.50
7R	Ivan Rodriguez R	1.50
8H	Manny Ramirez H	1.50
8R	Manny Ramirez R	1.50
9H	Mark Prior H	1.50
9R	Mark Prior R	1.50
10H	Miguel Cabrera H	1.50
10R	Miguel Cabrera R	1.50
11H	Miguel Tejada H	1.00
11R	Miguel Tejada R	1.00
12H	Mike Piazza H	2.50
12R	Mike Piazza R	2.50
13H	Roger Clemens H	4.00
13R	Roger Clemens R	4.00
14H	Todd Helton H	1.50
14R	Todd Helton R	1.50
15H	Vladimir Guerrero H	1.50
15R	Vladimir Guerrero R	1.50

Home/Road Jersey

NM/M

Common Player:

1H	Albert Pujols H	20.00
1R	Albert Pujols R	20.00
2H	Alfonso Soriano H	8.00
3H	Carlos Beltran H	8.00
3R	Carlos Beltran R	8.00
4R	Chipper Jones R	8.00
5H	Frank Thomas H	8.00
5R	Frank Thomas R	8.00
6H	Hank Blalock H	8.00
7H	Ivan Rodriguez H	8.00
7R	Ivan Rodriguez R	8.00
8R	Manny Ramirez R	8.00
9H	Mark Prior H	10.00
11H	Miguel Tejada H	5.00
11R	Miguel Tejada R	5.00
12H	Mike Piazza H	12.00
13H	Roger Clemens H	15.00
13R	Roger Clemens R	15.00
14H	Todd Helton H	8.00
14R	Todd Helton R	8.00
15H	Vladimir Guerrero H	8.00

Patch Off My Back

NM/M

Common Patch: 15.00
Production 50 Sets

1	Adam Dunn	25.00
2	Aubrey Huff	15.00
3	Austin Kearns	15.00
4	Bobby Crosby	25.00
5	C.C. Sabathia	15.00
7	David Ortiz	25.00
8	Dewon Brazelton	15.00
9	Edgar Martinez	20.00
10	Frankie Francisco	15.00
11	Garret Anderson	20.00
12	Hideki Matsui	50.00
13	Hideo Nomo	20.00
14	Jack Wilson	15.00
15	Javy Lopez	15.00
16	Jay Gibbons	15.00
17	Jim Edmonds	20.00
18	Jody Gerut	15.00
19	Joey Gathright	15.00
20	Johan Santana	20.00
21	Jose Reyes	15.00
22	Jose Vidro	15.00
23	Lance Berkman	15.00
24	Mariano Rivera	20.00
25	Mark Teixeira	20.00
26	Michael Young	15.00
27	Mike Cameron	15.00
28	Mike Sweeney	15.00
29	Omar Vizquel	15.00
30	Preston Wilson	15.00
31	Rocco Baldelli	15.00
32	Scott Rolen	25.00
33	Sean Burroughs	15.00
34	Sean Casey	15.00
35	Tim Hudson	20.00
36	Torii Hunter	20.00
37	Trevor Hoffman	20.00
38	Troy Glaus	20.00
39	Vernon Wells	15.00
40	Victor Martinez	20.00

Patch Off My Back Autograph

NM/M

Production 10-75

1	Adam Dunn/10	
2	Aubrey Huff/50	35.00
4	Bobby Crosby/75	50.00
5	C.C. Sabathia/75	30.00
7	David Ortiz/50	100.00
8	Dewon Brazelton/75	25.00
11	Garret Anderson/25	
14	Jack Wilson/75	30.00
16	Jay Gibbons/50	25.00
18	Jody Gerut/75	20.00
20	Johan Santana/50	60.00
22	Jose Vidro/75	25.00
25	Mark Teixeira/10	
26	Michael Young/75	35.00
29	Omar Vizquel/10	
33	Sean Burroughs/25	25.00
34	Sean Casey/10	
36	Torii Hunter/10	
39	Vernon Wells/10	
40	Victor Martinez/75	35.00

Picture Perfect

NM/M

Complete Set (20): 30.00
Common Player: 1.00
Inserted 1:20
Die-cut: 2X-3X
Production 100 Sets

1	Albert Pujols	4.00
2	Alex Rodriguez	3.00
3	Alfonso Soriano	1.50
4	Derek Jeter	4.00
5	Greg Maddux	2.00
6	Hideki Matsui	3.00
7	Ichiro Suzuki	3.00
8	Ivan Rodriguez	1.00
9	Jim Thome	1.50
10	Mark Mulder	1.00
11	Mark Prior	1.50
12	Miguel Tejada	1.00
13	Mike Mussina	1.00
14	Mike Piazza	2.50
15	Nomar Garciaparra	2.50
16	Randy Johnson	1.50
17	Roger Clemens	4.00
18	Sammy Sosa	2.50
19	Scott Rolen	1.50
20	Vladimir Guerrero	1.50

Shirt Off My Back

NM/M

Common Player: 5.00
Inserted 1:48

1	Adam Dunn	15.00
4	Bobby Crosby	15.00
5	C.C. Sabathia	8.00
7	David Ortiz	15.00
8	Dewon Brazelton	5.00
9	Edgar Martinez	5.00
10	Frankie Francisco	5.00
11	Garret Anderson	5.00
12	Hideki Matsui	25.00
13	Hideo Nomo	8.00
14	Jack Wilson	5.00
15	Javy Lopez	8.00
16	Jay Gibbons	5.00
17	Jim Edmonds	15.00
18	Jody Gerut SP	5.00
19	Joey Gathright	5.00
20	Johan Santana	10.00
21	Jose Reyes	5.00
22	Jose Vidro	5.00
23	Lance Berkman	5.00
25	Mark Teixeira	5.00
26	Michael Young	5.00
27	Mike Cameron	5.00
28	Mike Sweeney	5.00
29	Omar Vizquel	8.00
30	Preston Wilson	5.00
31	Rocco Baldelli	8.00
32	Scott Rolen	10.00
33	Sean Burroughs	5.00
34	Sean Casey	5.00
35	Tim Hudson	5.00
36	Torii Hunter	5.00
37	Trevor Hoffman	5.00
38	Troy Glaus	5.00
39	Vernon Wells	5.00
40	Victor Martinez	8.00

Sportscasters 70 Green

NM/M

Common Player: 2.00
Production 70 Sets
Variations #'d 35-65: 1X
Variations #'d 20-30: 1.5X
No pricing 15 or less

1	Adam Dunn	3.00
2	Al Kaline	5.00
3	Albert Pujols	8.00
4	Alex Rodriguez	8.00
5	Alfonso Soriano	3.00
6	Bob Gibson	3.00
7	Cal Ripken Jr.	25.00
8	Carl Yastrzemski	8.00
9	Dale Murphy	3.00
10	Derek Jeter	10.00
11	Don Mattingly	10.00
12	Duke Snider	4.00
13	Eric Gagne	3.00
14	Ernie Banks	6.00
15	Frank Robinson	3.00
16	George Brett	10.00
17	Greg Maddux	6.00
18	Harmon Killebrew	5.00
19	Ichiro Suzuki	8.00
20	Ivan Rodriguez	4.00
21	Jim Edmonds	2.00
22	Jim Palmer	2.00
23	Jim Thome	4.00
24	Johnny Bench	5.00
25	Ken Griffey Jr.	6.00
26	Larry Walker	3.00
27	Mark Mulder	2.00
28	Mark Prior	4.00
29	Miguel Tejada	3.00
30	Mike Mussina	3.00
31	Mike Piazza	6.00
32	Mike Schmidt	10.00
33	Nolan Ryan	15.00
34	Nomar Garciaparra	6.00
35	Pedro Martinez	4.00
36	Rafael Palmeiro	3.00
37	Randy Johnson	4.00
38	Reggie Jackson	3.00
39	Rickey Henderson	4.00
40	Roberto Clemente	15.00
41	Rod Carew	3.00
42	Roger Clemens	8.00
43	Ryne Sandberg	8.00
44	Sammy Sosa	6.00
45	Stan Musial	8.00
46	Steve Carlton	2.00
47	Tony Gwynn	5.00
48	Vladimir Guerrero	4.00
49	Warren Spahn	4.00
50	Willie McCovey	3.00

2005 LEAF CENTURY

NM/M

Complete Set (200): 40.00
Common Player: .25
Pack (5): 12.00
Box (10): 100.00

1	Brian Roberts	.25
2	Derek Jeter	2.00
3	Harmon Killebrew	1.00
4	Angel Berroa	.25

5 George Brett 2.00
6 Stan Musial 1.50
7 Ivan Rodriguez .50
8 Cal Ripken Jr. 3.00
9 Hank Blalock .50
10 Miguel Tejada .50
11 Barry Larkin .40
12 Alfonso Soriano .75
13 Alex Rodriguez 2.00
14 Paul Konerko .25
15 Jim Edmonds .40
16 Garret Anderson .40
17 Todd Helton .50
18 Moises Alou .40
19 Tony Gwynn .75
20 Mike Schmidt 2.00
21 Sammy Sosa 1.25
22 Roger Clemens 2.00
23 Tony Perez .25
24 Manny Ramirez .75
25 Jim Thome .75
26 Chase Utley .25
27 Scott Rolen .75
28 Austin Kearns .25
29 John Smoltz .40
30 Ken Griffey Jr. 1.00
31 Mike Piazza 1.00
32 Steve Carlton .50
33 Larry Walker .40
34 Nolan Ryan 2.50
35 Mike Mussina .40
36 Joe Nathan .25
37 Kenny Rogers .25
38 Eric Gagne .40
39 Brett Myers .25
40 Rich Harden .25
41 Victor Martinez .40
42 Mariano Rivera .40
43 Dennis Eckersley .50
44 Roy Oswalt .25
45 Pedro Martinez .75
46 Jason Bay .40
47 Tom Glavine .40
48 Torii Hunter .25
49 Larry Bigbie .25
50 Nomar Garciaparra 1.50
51 Ichiro Suzuki 1.50
52 C.C. Sabathia .25
53 Bobby Abreu .40
54 Doug Mientkiewicz .25
55 Hideki Matsui 1.50
56 Mark Buehrle .25
57 Johan Santana .50
58 Johnny Damon .75
59 Edgar Martinez .40
60 Preston Wilson .25
61 Livan Hernandez .25
62 Eric Chavez .25
63 Lyle Overbay .40
64 Jason Schmidt .50
65 Cliff Lee .25
66 Shingo Takatsu .25
67 Jeff Bagwell .50
68 Danny Graves .25
69 Kip Wells .25
70 Steve Finley .25
71 Lew Ford .25
72 Chone Figgins .25
73 Delmon Young .40
74 Esteban Loaiza .25
75 Barry Zito .40
76 Carlos Delgado .40
77 Joe Mauer .40
78 Ryan Wagner .25
79 John Lackey .25
80 Adrian Beltre .40
81 Vernon Wells .25
82 Sean Burroughs .25
83 Francisco Cordero .25
84 Carlos Guillen .25
85 Eric Byrnes .25
86 Jose Reyes .25
87 Rocco Baldelli .25
88 Josh Beckett .40
89 Casey Kotchman .40
90 Scott Podsednik .25
91 Mike Sweeney .25
92 Khalil Greene .50
93 Trot Nixon .25
94 Chad Cordero .25
95 Derek Lowe .25
96 Jason Giambi .40
97 Jose Guillen .25
98 Craig Biggio .40
99 Pat Burrell .40
100 Kazuo Matsui .25
101 Rafael Furcal .25
102 Jack Wilson .25
103 Edgar Renteria .50
104 Carlos Beltran .75
105 Albert Pujols 2.00
106 Melvin Mora .25
107 J.D. Drew .40
108 Andre Dawson .50
109 Jody Gerut .25
110 Michael Young .25
111 Gary Sheffield .50
112 Wade Boggs .50
113 Carl Crawford .25
114 Paul LoDuca .25
115 Tim Hudson .40
116 Aramis Ramirez .40
117 Lance Berkman .40
118 Javy Lopez .40
119 Robin Yount 1.00
120 Mark Mulder .25
121 Sean Casey .25
122 Will Clark .50
123 Don Mattingly 2.00
124 Miguel Cabrera .75
125 Rafael Palmeiro .50
126 David Ortiz .75
127 Vladimir Guerrero .75
128 Ken Harvey .25
129 Rod Carew .50
130 Magglio Ordonez .25
131 Greg Maddux 1.00
132 Roy Halladay .25
133 Javier Vazquez .25
134 Kerry Wood .75
135 Frank Thomas .50
136 Tom Gordon .25
137 Jake Peavy .25
138 Curt Schilling .75
139 Dewon Brazelton .25
140 Jae Weong Seo .25
141 Danny Kolb .25
142 Jeff Kent .40
143 Juan Encarnacion .25
144 Adam Dunn .50
145 Carlos Lee .25
146 Matt Clement .25
147 Guillermo Mota .25
148 Travis Hafner .40
149 Brad Wilkerson .25
150 Eric Milton .25
151 Randy Johnson .75
152 Joe Crede .25
153 Mark Kotsay .25
154 Jason Varitek .40
155 David Wright .75
156 Brad Penny .25
157 Francisco Rodriguez .25
158 Gary Carter .50
159 Adrian Gonzalez .25
160 Derrek Lee .40
161 Mark Prior .75
162 Carlos Zambrano .40
163 Bobby Crosby .40
164 Jermaine Dye .25
165 Kris Benson .25
166 Dontrelle Willis .40
167 Dallas McPherson .40
168 Johnny Estrada .40
169 Milton Bradley .25
170 Shannon Stewart .25
171 Ben Sheets .40
172 Richard Hidalgo .25
173 Laynce Nix .25
174 B.J. Upton .50
175 Craig Wilson .25
176 Hideo Nomo .40
177 Troy Glaus .40
178 Akinori Otsuka .25
179 Rickie Weeks .40
180 Mike Lowell .40
181 Marcus Giles .25
182 Randy Wolf .25
183 A.J. Burnett .25
184 Aubrey Huff .25
185 Billy Ripken .25
186 Octavio Dotel .25
187 Kazuhisa Ishii .25
188 Mark Teixeira .50
189 Todd Walker .25
190 Dale Murphy .50
191 Alexis Rios .25
192 Reggie Sanders .25
193 Orlando Cabrera .25
194 Shawn Green .40
195 Andy Pettitte .40
196 Chipper Jones .75
197 Jose Vidro .25
198 Jacque Jones .25
199 Brian Giles .25
200 Andruw Jones .40

Post Marks Gold

Golds: 4-8X
Production 50 sets

Post Marks Silver

Silvers: 3-6X
Production 100 sets

Post Marks Platinum

No Pricing
Production one set

Air Mail Bat

NM/M

Production 50-250
1 Babe Ruth/50 150.00
2 Frank Robinson/250 12.00
3 Harmon Killebrew/100 20.00
4 Sammy Sosa/100 10.00
5 Reggie Jackson/250 15.00
6 Mike Schmidt/100 20.00
7 Rafael Palmeiro/100 8.00
8 Ted Williams/50 80.00
9 Willie McCovey/250 10.00
10 Ernie Banks/100 20.00

Air Mail Bat Signature

NM/M

Production 1-25
2 Frank Robinson/25 40.00
3 Harmon Killebrew/25 60.00
9 Willie McCovey/25 35.00

Material Bat

NM/M

Common Player: 5.00
3 Harmon Killebrew/250 12.00
4 Angel Berroa/50 5.00
5 George Brett/250 15.00
6 Stan Musial/250 15.00
7 Ivan Rodriguez/100 8.00
8 Cal Ripken Jr./250 25.00
9 Hank Blalock/100 8.00
10 Miguel Tejada/100 6.00
11 Barry Larkin/100 6.00
12 Alfonso Soriano/100 8.00
14 Paul Konerko/50 5.00
15 Jim Edmonds/100 8.00
16 Garret Anderson/100 5.00
17 Todd Helton/100 8.00
18 Moises Alou/50 6.00
19 Tony Gwynn/250 10.00
20 Mike Schmidt/250 15.00
21 Sammy Sosa/100 10.00
22 Roger Clemens/100 15.00
23 Tony Perez/100 8.00
24 Manny Ramirez/100 10.00
25 Jim Thome/100 12.00
27 Scott Rolen/100 10.00
28 Austin Kearns/50 5.00
31 Mike Piazza/100 12.00
32 Steve Carlton/250 8.00
33 Larry Walker/100 8.00
34 Nolan Ryan/250 20.00
35 Mike Mussina/100 8.00
41 Victor Martinez/50 8.00
44 Roy Oswalt/100 5.00
45 Pedro Martinez/100 8.00
47 Tom Glavine/100 6.00
48 Torii Hunter/100 6.00
50 Nomar Garciaparra/100 15.00
53 Bobby Abreu/25 10.00
54 Doug Mientkiewicz/50 5.00
55 Hideki Matsui/100 25.00
56 Mark Buehrle/50 6.00
58 Johnny Damon/100 12.00
59 Edgar Martinez/100 6.00
60 Preston Wilson/50 6.00
62 Eric Chavez/100 5.00
63 Lyle Overbay/50 8.00
67 Jeff Bagwell/100 8.00
71 Lew Ford/50 5.00
73 Delmon Young/100 8.00
75 Barry Zito/100 5.00
76 Carlos Delgado/100 5.00
80 Adrian Beltre/100 8.00
81 Vernon Wells/100 5.00
86 Jose Reyes/50 8.00
87 Rocco Baldelli/100 5.00
88 Josh Beckett/100 5.00
91 Mike Sweeney/50 5.00
93 Trot Nixon/50 6.00
96 Jason Giambi/100 5.00
98 Craig Biggio/100 6.00
99 Pat Burrell/50 8.00
100 Kazuo Matsui/100 8.00
101 Rafael Furcal/50 6.00
102 Jack Wilson/50 8.00
103 Edgar Renteria/100 6.00
104 Carlos Beltran/100 8.00
105 Albert Pujols/100 15.00
106 Melvin Mora/50 5.00
107 J.D. Drew/100 5.00
108 Andre Dawson/250 6.00
109 Jody Gerut/50 6.00
110 Michael Young/250 5.00
111 Gary Sheffield/100 6.00
112 Wade Boggs/250 8.00
114 Paul LoDuca/100 10.00
115 Tim Hudson/100 5.00
116 Aramis Ramirez/50 8.00
117 Lance Berkman/250 5.00
118 Javy Lopez/100 5.00
119 Robin Yount/250 10.00
120 Mark Mulder/100 5.00
121 Sean Casey/50 5.00
122 Will Clark/250 8.00
123 Don Mattingly/250 15.00
124 Miguel Cabrera/50 12.00
125 Rafael Palmeiro/250 8.00
126 David Ortiz/250 12.00
127 Vladimir Guerrero/250 8.00
128 Ken Harvey/50 5.00
129 Rod Carew/250 8.00
130 Magglio Ordonez/250 5.00
131 Greg Maddux/100 10.00
134 Kerry Wood/100 8.00
135 Frank Thomas/100 8.00
138 Curt Schilling/100 8.00
142 Jeff Kent/250 5.00
143 Juan Encarnacion/50 5.00
144 Adam Dunn/250 8.00
145 Carlos Lee/250 5.00
148 Travis Hafner/50 6.00
149 Brad Wilkerson/100 5.00
151 Randy Johnson/100 10.00
152 Joe Crede/50 6.00
154 Jason Varitek/250 10.00
156 Brad Penny/50 5.00
158 Gary Carter/250 8.00
160 Derrek Lee/250 5.00
161 Mark Prior/100 10.00
164 Jermaine Dye/50 5.00
166 Dontrelle Willis/100 6.00
168 Johnny Estrada/50 6.00
170 Shannon Stewart/100 5.00
171 Ben Sheets/50 8.00
172 Richard Hidalgo/50 5.00
173 Laynce Nix/50 5.00
174 B.J. Upton/50 8.00
175 Craig Wilson/100 5.00
176 Hideo Nomo/100 8.00
177 Troy Glaus/250 5.00
179 Rickie Weeks/25 8.00
180 Mike Lowell/100 5.00
181 Marcus Giles/5
183 A.J. Burnett/100 5.00
184 Aubrey Huff/50 5.00
187 Kazuhisa Ishii/100 5.00
188 Mark Teixeira/250 5.00
190 Dale Murphy/250 8.00

191 Alexis Rios/50 5.00
193 Orlando Cabrera/50 6.00
194 Shawn Green/250 5.00
195 Andy Pettitte/100 6.00
196 Chipper Jones/100 8.00
197 Jose Vidro/250 5.00
198 Jacque Jones/100 5.00
199 Brian Giles/250 5.00
200 Andruw Jones/250 6.00

Material Fabric Number

NM/M

Common Player: 5.00
20 Mike Schmidt Jsy/20 50.00
21 Sammy Sosa Jsy/21 20.00
22 Roger Clemens Jsy/22 40.00
23 Tony Perez Jsy/24 15.00
24 Manny Ramirez Jsy/24 20.00
25 Jim Thome Jsy/25 20.00
27 Scott Rolen Jsy/27 20.00
28 Austin Kearns Jsy/28 15.00
29 John Smoltz Jsy/29 20.00
31 Mike Piazza Jsy/31 25.00
32 Steve Carlton Pants/32 15.00
34 Nolan Ryan Jsy/34 50.00
35 Mike Mussina Jsy/35 15.00
39 Brett Myers Jsy/39 8.00
41 Victor Martinez Jsy/41 8.00
42 Mariano Rivera Jsy/42 15.00
43 Dennis Eckersley Jsy/43 10.00
44 Roy Oswalt Jsy/44 8.00
45 Pedro Martinez Jsy/45 10.00
47 Tom Glavine Jsy/47 10.00
48 Torii Hunter Jsy/48 8.00
52 C.C. Sabathia Jsy/52 8.00
53 Bobby Abreu Jsy/53 8.00
55 Hideki Matsui Jsy/55 35.00
56 Mark Buehrle Jsy/56 8.00
57 Johan Santana Jsy/57 15.00
60 Preston Wilson Jsy/44 8.00
61 Livan Hernandez Jsy/61 5.00
65 Cliff Lee Jsy/34 8.00
71 Lew Ford Jsy/20 10.00
75 Barry Zito Jsy/75 5.00
76 Carlos Delgado Jsy/25 10.00
78 Ryan Wagner Jsy/38 5.00
80 Adrian Beltre Jsy/29 15.00
82 Sean Burroughs Jsy/32 8.00
83 Francisco Cordero Jsy/31 8.00
85 Eric Byrnes Jsy/22 8.00
91 Mike Sweeney Jsy/29 8.00
96 Jason Giambi Jsy/25 10.00
100 Kazuo Matsui Jsy/25 12.00
118 Javy Lopez Jsy/18 15.00
119 Robin Yount Jsy/19 30.00
120 Mark Mulder Jsy/20 12.00
121 Sean Casey Jsy/21 10.00
122 Will Clark Jsy/22 20.00
123 Don Mattingly Pants/23 40.00
124 Miguel Cabrera Jsy/24 20.00
125 Rafael Palmeiro Jsy/25 15.00
126 David Ortiz Jsy/34 20.00
127 Vladimir Guerrero Jsy/27 20.00
128 Ken Harvey Jsy/28 10.00
129 Rod Carew Jsy/29 20.00
130 Magglio Ordonez Jsy/30 10.00
131 Greg Maddux Jsy/31 25.00
132 Roy Halladay Jsy/32 10.00
134 Kerry Wood Jsy/34 20.00
135 Frank Thomas Jsy/35 20.00
138 Curt Schilling Jsy/34 15.00
139 Dewon Brazelton Jsy/45 5.00
140 Jae Weong Seo Jsy/40 5.00
141 Danny Kolb Jsy/41 5.00
144 Adam Dunn Jsy/44 15.00
145 Carlos Lee Jsy/45 8.00
146 Matt Clement Jsy/30 10.00
148 Travis Hafner Jsy/48 8.00
151 Randy Johnson Pants/51 15.00
154 Jason Varitek Jsy/33 20.00
157 Francisco Rodriguez Jsy/57 5.00
162 Carlos Zambrano Jsy/38 8.00
164 Jermaine Dye Jsy/24 10.00
166 Dontrelle Willis Jsy/35 12.00
168 Johnny Estrada Jsy/23 10.00
170 Shannon Stewart Jsy/23 10.00
175 Craig Wilson Jsy/36 5.00
177 Troy Glaus Jsy/25 15.00
180 Mike Lowell Jsy/19 20.00
183 A.J. Burnett Jsy/34 10.00
188 Mark Teixeira Jsy/23 15.00
195 Andy Pettitte Jsy/21 20.00
200 Andruw Jones Jsy/5 15.00

Material Fabric Position

NM/M

Common Player: 4.00
Prime: No Pricing
Production 1 set
1 Brian Roberts Jsy/250 4.00
3 Harmon Killebrew Jsy/250 12.00
4 Angel Berroa Jsy/250 4.00
5 George Brett Jsy/250 15.00
6 Stan Musial Pants/100 15.00
7 Ivan Rodriguez Jsy/250 6.00
8 Cal Ripken Jr. Jkt/250 25.00
9 Hank Blalock Jsy/250 8.00
10 Miguel Tejada Jsy/250 6.00
11 Barry Larkin Jsy/100 6.00
12 Alfonso Soriano Jsy/250 4.00
14 Paul Konerko Jsy/250 4.00
15 Jim Edmonds Jsy/250 6.00
16 Garret Anderson Jsy/250 4.00
17 Todd Helton Jsy/250 6.00
19 Tony Gwynn Jsy/250 10.00
20 Mike Schmidt Jsy/250 15.00
21 Sammy Sosa Jsy/250 10.00
22 Roger Clemens Jsy/250 12.00
23 Tony Perez Jsy/250 6.00
24 Manny Ramirez Jsy/250 8.00
25 Jim Thome Jsy/250 8.00
27 Scott Rolen Jsy/250 8.00
28 Austin Kearns Jsy/250 4.00
29 John Smoltz Jsy/250 6.00
31 Mike Piazza Jsy/250 10.00
32 Steve Carlton Pants/250 6.00
34 Nolan Ryan Jsy/250 20.00
35 Mike Mussina Jsy/250 6.00
39 Brett Myers Jsy/250 4.00
40 Rich Harden Jsy/1
41 Victor Martinez Jsy/250 4.00
42 Mariano Rivera Jsy/250 6.00
43 Dennis Eckersley Jsy/250 6.00
44 Roy Oswalt Jsy/250 4.00
45 Pedro Martinez Jsy/250 8.00
46 Jason Bay Jsy/250 4.00
47 Tom Glavine Jsy/250 6.00
48 Torii Hunter Jsy/250 4.00
49 Larry Bigbie Jsy/250 4.00
52 C.C. Sabathia Jsy/250 4.00
53 Bobby Abreu Jsy/250 4.00
55 Hideki Matsui Jsy/250 20.00
56 Mark Buehrle Jsy/250 4.00
57 Johan Santana Jsy/250 8.00
59 Edgar Martinez Jsy/250 6.00
60 Preston Wilson Jsy/250 4.00
61 Livan Hernandez Jsy/250 4.00
62 Eric Chavez Jsy/250 6.00
63 Lyle Overbay Jsy/250 4.00
65 Cliff Lee Jsy/250 4.00
67 Jeff Bagwell Jsy/250 8.00
71 Lew Ford Jsy/250 4.00
72 Chone Figgins Jsy/250 4.00
75 Barry Zito Jsy/250 4.00
76 Carlos Delgado Jsy/250 4.00
78 Ryan Wagner Jsy/250 4.00
80 Adrian Beltre Jsy/250 8.00
81 Vernon Wells Jsy/250 4.00
82 Sean Burroughs Jsy/250 4.00
83 Francisco Cordero Jsy/250 4.00
85 Eric Byrnes Jsy/250 10.00
86 Jose Reyes Jsy/250 4.00
87 Rocco Baldelli Jsy/250 4.00
88 Josh Beckett Jsy/250 4.00
90 Scott Podsednik Jsy/250 4.00
91 Mike Sweeney Jsy/250 4.00
93 Trot Nixon Jsy/250 4.00
96 Jason Giambi Jsy/250 4.00
98 Craig Biggio Jsy/250 6.00
99 Pat Burrell Jsy/250 4.00
100 Kazuo Matsui Jsy/250 4.00
101 Rafael Furcal Jsy/250 4.00
102 Jack Wilson Jsy/250 4.00
103 Edgar Renteria Jsy/250 6.00
104 Carlos Beltran Jsy/250 8.00
105 Albert Pujols Jsy/250 15.00
106 Melvin Mora Jsy/100 4.00
108 Andre Dawson Jsy/250 6.00
109 Jody Gerut Jsy/250 4.00
110 Michael Young Jsy/250 4.00
111 Gary Sheffield Jsy/250 6.00
112 Wade Boggs Jsy/100 8.00
113 Carl Crawford Jsy/250 4.00
115 Tim Hudson Jsy/250 4.00
116 Aramis Ramirez Jsy/250 6.00
117 Lance Berkman Jsy/250 4.00
118 Javy Lopez Jsy/250 4.00
119 Robin Yount Jsy/250 10.00
120 Mark Mulder Jsy/250 4.00
121 Sean Casey Jsy/250 4.00
122 Will Clark Jsy/250 6.00
123 Don Mattingly Pants/250 15.00
124 Miguel Cabrera Jsy/250 8.00
125 Rafael Palmeiro Jsy/250 8.00
126 David Ortiz Jsy/250 8.00
127 Vladimir Guerrero Jsy/250 8.00
128 Ken Harvey Jsy/250 4.00
129 Rod Carew Jsy/250 8.00
130 Magglio Ordonez Jsy/250 4.00
131 Greg Maddux Jsy/250 10.00
132 Roy Halladay Jsy/250 4.00
134 Kerry Wood Jsy/250 8.00
135 Frank Thomas Jsy/250 8.00
138 Curt Schilling Jsy/250 8.00
139 Dewon Brazelton Jsy/100 4.00
140 Jae Weong Seo Jsy/100 4.00
141 Danny Kolb Jsy/250 4.00
142 Jeff Kent Jsy/100 6.00
144 Adam Dunn Jsy/250 6.00
145 Carlos Lee Jsy/250 4.00
146 Matt Clement Jsy/250 4.00
148 Travis Hafner Jsy/250 4.00
151 Randy Johnson Pants/250 8.00
154 Jason Varitek Jsy/100 15.00
157 Francisco Rodriguez Jsy/100 4.00
158 Gary Carter Jsy/250 6.00
161 Mark Prior Jsy/250 8.00
162 Carlos Zambrano Jsy/100 6.00
163 Bobby Crosby Jsy/250 8.00
164 Jermaine Dye Jsy/100 4.00
166 Dontrelle Willis Jsy/250 4.00
168 Johnny Estrada Jsy/100 4.00
170 Shannon Stewart Jsy/100 4.00
171 Ben Sheets Jsy/250 6.00
173 Laynce Nix Jsy/100 4.00
175 Craig Wilson Jsy/100 4.00
176 Hideo Nomo Jsy/250 8.00
177 Troy Glaus Jsy/250 4.00
180 Mike Lowell 4.00
181 Marcus Giles Jsy/5
183 A.J. Burnett Jsy/100 4.00
184 Aubrey Huff Jsy/250 4.00
187 Kazuhisa Ishii Jsy/250 4.00
188 Mark Teixeira Jsy/250 6.00
190 Dale Murphy Jsy/250 8.00
194 Shawn Green Jsy/250 4.00
195 Andy Pettitte Jsy/250 6.00
196 Chipper Jones Jsy/250 8.00
197 Jose Vidro Jsy/100 4.00
198 Jacque Jones Jsy/250 4.00
199 Brian Giles Jsy/5
200 Andruw Jones Jsy/250 6.00

Pennant Patches

NM/M

Production 5-25
1 Ozzie Smith/25 40.00
2 Keith Hernandez/25 20.00
3 Rickey Henderson/25 30.00
4 Paul Molitor/25 25.00
5 George Brett/25 50.00
6 Steve Garvey/25 20.00
7 Randy Johnson/25 25.00
8 Cal Ripken Jr./25 90.00
9 Darryl Strawberry/25 20.00
10 Chipper Jones/25 30.00
11 Steve Carlton/25 20.00
12 Orel Hershiser/25 20.00
13 Carlton Fisk/25 25.00
14 Dave Parker/25 20.00
15 Rollie Fingers/25 20.00
16 Dwight Gooden/25 20.00
17 Mark Grace/10
18 Dontrelle Willis/25 15.00
19 Dave Righetti/25 15.00
20 Brooks Robinson/5

Pennant Patches Signature

NM/M

Production 5-25
2 Keith Hernandez/25 40.00
6 Steve Garvey/25 35.00
9 Darryl Strawberry/25 40.00
11 Steve Carlton/25 40.00
15 Rollie Fingers/25 35.00
16 Dwight Gooden/25 40.00

Shirts

NM/M

Production 25-100
1 Rod Carew/100 10.00
2 Red Schoendienst/50 8.00
3 Harmon Killebrew/50 20.00
4 Joe Cronin/50 35.00
5 Early Wynn/50 8.00
6 Gaylord Perry/100 8.00
7 Willie McCovey/100 10.00
8 Carl Yastrzemski/100 20.00
9 Reggie Jackson/100 10.00
10 Duke Snider/50 15.00
11 Luis Aparicio/100 8.00
12 Bob Gibson/50 15.00
13 Maury Wills/50 8.00
14 Ernie Banks/50 20.00
15 Enos Slaughter/100 10.00
16 Whitey Ford/100 15.00
17 Warren Spahn/100 15.00
18 Roger Maris/100 35.00
19 Hal Newhouser/100 10.00
20 Marty Marion/25 12.00

Shirts Signature

NM/M

Production 5-50
Prime: No Pricing
Production one set
2 Red Schoendienst/25 25.00
6 Gaylord Perry/50 20.00
7 Willie McCovey/50 30.00
11 Luis Aparicio/50 25.00
13 Maury Wills/50 20.00

Signature Post Marks Gold

NM/M

Production 1-50
36 Joe Nathan/50 20.00
39 Brett Myers/50 12.00
40 Rich Harden/50 15.00
49 Larry Bigbie/50 15.00
61 Livan Hernandez/50 15.00
63 Lyle Overbay/50 15.00
65 Cliff Lee/50 12.00
68 Danny Graves/25 20.00
71 Lew Ford/50 15.00
72 Chone Figgins/50 20.00
74 Esteban Loaiza/50 20.00
78 Ryan Wagner/50 10.00
79 John Lackey/50 15.00
83 Francisco Cordero/25 15.00
85 Eric Byrnes/25 20.00
89 Casey Kotchman/50 25.00
90 Scott Podsednik/50 15.00
94 Chad Cordero/25 15.00
97 Jose Guillen/25 20.00
102 Jack Wilson/50 15.00
106 Melvin Mora/25 20.00
109 Jody Gerut/50 10.00
128 Ken Harvey/50 10.00
136 Tom Gordon/50 15.00
137 Jake Peavy/25 25.00
139 Dewon Brazelton/50 10.00
140 Jae Weong Seo/25 20.00
141 Danny Kolb/50 20.00
145 Carlos Lee/25 20.00
147 Guillermo Mota/50 10.00
148 Travis Hafner/25 20.00
156 Brad Penny/50 10.00
159 Adrian Gonzalez/50 15.00
163 Bobby Crosby/25 30.00

164 Jermaine Dye/25 20.00
166 Dontrelle Willis/1
168 Johnny Estrada/25 25.00
169 Milton Bradley/25 20.00
170 Shannon Stewart/25 15.00
171 Ben Sheets/1
173 Laynce Nix/50 20.00
174 B.J. Upton/5
175 Craig Wilson/50 15.00
176 Hideo Nomo/1
178 Akinori Otsuka/1
179 Rickie Weeks/1
180 Mike Lowell/1
181 Marcus Giles/10
182 Randy Wolf/50 15.00
184 Aubrey Huff/25 20.00
185 Billy Ripken/50 10.00
186 Octavio Dotel/50 15.00
187 Kazuhisa Ishii/1
188 Mark Teixeira/1
189 Todd Walker/25 20.00
190 Dale Murphy/1
191 Alexis Rios/50 15.00
193 Orlando Cabrera/10
194 Shawn Green/1
195 Andy Pettitte/1
196 Chipper Jones/1
197 Jose Vidro/10
198 Jacque Jones/25 15.00
200 Andruw Jones/1

Signature Post Marks Silver

NM/M

Production 1-250
Platinum: No Pricing
Production one set
1 Brian Roberts/250 8.00
4 Angel Berroa/25 15.00
36 Joe Nathan/250 15.00
39 Brett Myers/250 8.00
40 Rich Harden/100 15.00
49 Larry Bigbie/250 10.00
52 C.C. Sabathia/25 20.00
56 Mark Buehrle/50 15.00
61 Livan Hernandez/100 10.00
63 Lyle Overbay/100 15.00
65 Cliff Lee/250 8.00
68 Danny Graves/100 10.00
71 Lew Ford/100 10.00
72 Chone Figgins/250 10.00
74 Esteban Loaiza/250 10.00
78 Ryan Wagner/250 10.00
79 John Lackey/250 10.00
82 Sean Burroughs/25 15.00
83 Francisco Cordero/100 8.00
85 Eric Byrnes/100 10.00
89 Casey Kotchman/250 20.00
90 Scott Podsednik/100 10.00
93 Trot Nixon/25 25.00
94 Chad Cordero/250 8.00
97 Jose Guillen/100 10.00
102 Jack Wilson/100 10.00
106 Melvin Mora/100 10.00
108 Andre Dawson/25 25.00
109 Jody Gerut/250 8.00
116 Aramis Ramirez/25 25.00
128 Ken Harvey/250 8.00
136 Tom Gordon/250 10.00
137 Jake Peavy/100 20.00
139 Dewon Brazelton/250 8.00
140 Jae Weong Seo/100 10.00
141 Danny Kolb/250 12.00
145 Carlos Lee/100 12.00
147 Guillermo Mota/250 8.00
148 Travis Hafner/100 15.00
155 David Wright/25 80.00
156 Brad Penny/250 8.00
157 Francisco Rodriguez/100 15.00
159 Adrian Gonzalez/250 10.00
160 Derrek Lee/25 30.00
162 Carlos Zambrano/25 25.00
163 Bobby Crosby/100 25.00
164 Jermaine Dye/250 10.00
168 Johnny Estrada/200 15.00
169 Milton Bradley/100 15.00
170 Shannon Stewart/50 15.00
173 Laynce Nix/250 10.00
175 Craig Wilson/100 15.00
181 Marcus Giles/25 20.00
182 Randy Wolf/250 12.00
184 Aubrey Huff/100 10.00
185 Billy Ripken/250 8.00
186 Octavio Dotel/250 10.00
189 Todd Walker/100 15.00
191 Alexis Rios/200 10.00
193 Orlando Cabrera/25 20.00
197 Jose Vidro/25 15.00
198 Jacque Jones/100 10.00

Stamps Masterpiece Signature Centenni

No Pricing
Production 1-2

Stamps Material Centennial

NM/M

Production 1-39
1 Pee Wee Reese Bat/39 20.00
3 Babe Ruth Jsy/39 275.00
4 George Brett Jsy/39 40.00
5 Stan Musial Bat/39 40.00
6 Bob Feller Pants/39 15.00
7 Cal Ripken Jr. Pants/39 100.00
8 Ted Williams Jsy/39 100.00
11 Dwight Evans Jsy/39 25.00
12 Dave Concepcion Jsy/39 20.00
13 Ernie Banks Jsy/39 25.00
14 Pedro J. Martinez Jsy/39 20.00
16 Scott Rolen Jsy/39 25.00
17 Tony Gwynn Jsy/39 30.00
18 Mike Schmidt Jsy/39 60.00
19 Roberto Clemente Hat/21 200.00
20 Roger Clemens Jsy/39 35.00
21 Don Mattingly Jsy/39 50.00
22 Tony Perez Bat/39 15.00
23 Roger Maris Jsy/39 75.00
24 Billy Williams Jsy/39 15.00
25 Juan Marichal Pants/39 20.00
26 Hank Blalock Jsy/39 20.00
27 Maury Wills Jsy/39 15.00
28 Fergie Jenkins Pants/39 20.00
29 Steve Carlton Jsy/39 15.00
30 Dale Murphy Jsy/39 20.00
31 Kerry Wood Jsy/39 20.00
32 Gaylord Perry Jsy/39 15.00
33 Fred Lynn Jsy/39 20.00
34 Tom Seaver Bat/39 20.00
36 Reggie Jackson Pants/39 25.00
37 Bob Gibson Jsy/39 20.00
38 Jack Morris Jsy/39 20.00
39 Torii Hunter Jsy/39 15.00
40 Andre Dawson Jsy/39 20.00
41 Dave Righetti Jsy/39 15.00
42 Hideki Matsui Pants/39 65.00
43 Lou Brock Jkt/39 25.00
44 Yogi Berra Bat/39 30.00
45 Frankie Frisch Jkt/39 25.00
46 Sean Casey Jsy/39 15.00
47 Sammy Sosa Jsy/39 30.00
48 Ralph Kiner Bat/39 30.00
49 Hoyt Wilhelm Jsy/39 15.00
50 Jim Rice Jsy/39 20.00
51 Duke Snider Pants/39 25.00
52 Harold Baines Jsy/39 20.00
53 Willie Stargell Jsy/39 20.00
54 Johnny Bench Pants/39 25.00
55 Carlton Fisk Jsy/39 25.00
56 Jim Palmer Jsy/39 20.00
57 Bobby Doerr Jsy/39 20.00
58 Mark Prior Jsy/39 30.00
60 Lou Boudreau Jsy/39 25.00
61 Alan Trammell Bat/39 20.00
62 Al Kaline Bat/39 25.00
63 Warren Spahn Pants/39 30.00
64 Bert Blyleven Jsy/39 20.00
65 Miguel Cabrera Jsy/39 25.00
66 Luis Tiant Jsy/39 15.00
67 Harmon Killebrew Jsy/39 30.00
68 Richie Ashburn Pants/39 25.00
69 Michael Young Jsy/39 15.00
70 Tony Oliva Jsy/39 20.00
71 Mark Mulder Jsy/39 15.00
72 Nolan Ryan Jsy/39 75.00
73 Willie McCovey Jsy/39 25.00
74 Kirk Gibson Jsy/39 20.00
75 Carl Yastrzemski Pants/39 40.00

Stamps Material Legendary Fields

NM/M

Production 1-34
1 Pee Wee Reese Bat/34 30.00
11 Dwight Evans Jsy/34 25.00
12 Dave Concepcion Jsy/34 20.00
13 Ernie Banks Jsy/34 40.00
14 Pedro J. Martinez Jsy/34 25.00
15 Whitey Ford Jsy/34 35.00
19 Roberto Clemente Hat/21 200.00
21 Don Mattingly Jsy/34 50.00
22 Tony Perez Bat/34 20.00
23 Roger Maris Jsy/34 85.00
24 Billy Williams Jsy/34 30.00
28 Fergie Jenkins Pants/34 20.00
29 Steve Carlton Jsy/34 25.00
31 Kerry Wood Jsy/34 30.00
33 Fred Lynn Jsy/34 20.00
36 Reggie Jackson Pants/34 25.00
38 Jack Morris Jsy/34 25.00
40 Andre Dawson Jsy/34 20.00
41 Dave Righetti Jsy/34 20.00
42 Hideki Matsui Pants/34 80.00
44 Yogi Berra Bat/34 40.00
47 Sammy Sosa Jsy/34 40.00
48 Ralph Kiner Bat/34 20.00
49 Hoyt Wilhelm Jsy/34 15.00
50 Jim Rice Jsy/34 20.00
51 Duke Snider Pants/34 40.00
52 Harold Baines Jsy/34 15.00
53 Willie Stargell Jsy/34 30.00
54 Johnny Bench Pants/34 40.00
55 Carlton Fisk Jsy/34 25.00
57 Bobby Doerr Jsy/34 25.00
58 Mark Prior Jsy/34 40.00
61 Alan Trammell Bat/34 30.00
62 Al Kaline Bat/34 40.00
66 Luis Tiant Jsy/34 25.00
74 Kirk Gibson Jsy/34 30.00
75 Carl Yastrzemski Pants/34 50.00

Stamps Material Legendary Players 20

NM/M

3 Babe Ruth Jsy/19
19 Roberto Clemente Hat/21 200.00

Stamps Material Legendary Players 33

NM/M

3 Babe Ruth Jsy/19
19 Roberto Clemente Hat/21 200.00

Stamps Material Olympic

NM/M

Production 1-92
1 Pee Wee Reese Bat/92 15.00
4 George Brett Jsy/92 30.00
5 Stan Musial Bat/92 30.00
6 Bob Feller Pants/92 15.00
7 Cal Ripken Jr. Pants/92 60.00
11 Dwight Evans Jsy/24 20.00
12 Dave Concepcion Jsy/13
13 Ernie Banks Jsy/92 25.00
14 Pedro J. Martinez Jsy/45 20.00
16 Scott Rolen Jsy/27 30.00
17 Tony Gwynn Jsy/92 30.00
18 Mike Schmidt Jsy/92 40.00
19 Roberto Clemente Hat/21 200.00
20 Roger Clemens Jsy/92 30.00
21 Don Mattingly Jsy/23 40.00
22 Tony Perez Bat/24 30.00
23 Roger Maris Jsy/9
24 Billy Williams Jsy/26 20.00
25 Juan Marichal Pants/92 15.00
26 Hank Blalock Jsy/92 15.00
27 Maury Wills Jsy/30 20.00
28 Fergie Jenkins Pants/92 15.00
29 Steve Carlton Jsy/92 15.00
30 Dale Murphy Jsy/92 20.00
31 Kerry Wood Jsy/92 20.00
32 Gaylord Perry Jsy/92 15.00
33 Fred Lynn Jsy/92 15.00
34 Tom Seaver Bat/92 20.00
36 Reggie Jackson Pants/44 20.00
37 Bob Gibson Jsy/45 25.00
38 Jack Morris Jsy/92 15.00
39 Torii Hunter Jsy/48 15.00
41 Dave Righetti Jsy/92 15.00
42 Hideki Matsui Pants/92 40.00
43 Lou Brock Jkt/92 15.00
44 Yogi Berra Bat/92 25.00
45 Frankie Frisch Jkt/92 15.00
46 Sean Casey Jsy/21 25.00
47 Sammy Sosa Jsy/92 25.00
48 Ralph Kiner Bat/92 15.00
49 Hoyt Wilhelm Jsy/92 15.00
50 Jim Rice Jsy/92 15.00
51 Duke Snider Pants/92 20.00
52 Harold Baines Jsy/92 15.00
53 Willie Stargell Jsy/92 20.00
54 Johnny Bench Pants/92 20.00
55 Carlton Fisk Jsy/92 25.00
56 Jim Palmer Jsy/92 15.00
57 Bobby Doerr Jsy/92 15.00
58 Mark Prior Jsy/92 20.00
60 Lou Boudreau Jsy/92 20.00
61 Alan Trammell Bat/92 15.00
62 Al Kaline Bat/92 20.00
63 Warren Spahn Pants/92 25.00
65 Miguel Cabrera Jsy/92 20.00
66 Luis Tiant Jsy/23 20.00
67 Harmon Killebrew Jsy/92 30.00
68 Richie Ashburn Pants/92 20.00
70 Tony Oliva Jsy/92 15.00
71 Mark Mulder Jsy/20 20.00
72 Nolan Ryan Jsy/30 100.00
73 Willie McCovey Jsy/92 20.00
74 Kirk Gibson Jsy/92 15.00
75 Carl Yastrzemski Pants/92 30.00

Stamps Material Pro Ball

NM/M

Production 1-69
1 Pee Wee Reese Bat/69 20.00
4 George Brett Jsy/69 40.00
5 Stan Musial Bat/69 30.00
6 Bob Feller Pants/69 20.00
7 Cal Ripken Jr. Pants/69 60.00
11 Dwight Evans Jsy/24 30.00
13 Ernie Banks Jsy/69 30.00
14 Pedro J. Martinez Jsy/45 25.00
16 Scott Rolen Jsy/27 40.00
17 Tony Gwynn Jsy/69 35.00
18 Mike Schmidt Jsy/69 60.00
19 Roberto Clemente Hat/21 200.00
20 Roger Clemens Jsy/69 30.00
21 Don Mattingly Jsy/23 50.00
22 Tony Perez Bat/24 20.00
24 Billy Williams Jsy/69 15.00
25 Juan Marichal Pants/69 15.00
26 Hank Blalock Jsy/69 15.00
27 Maury Wills Jsy/69 15.00
28 Fergie Jenkins Pants/69 20.00
29 Steve Carlton Jsy/69 15.00
30 Dale Murphy Jsy/69 15.00
31 Kerry Wood Jsy/69 20.00
32 Gaylord Perry Jsy/69 15.00
33 Fred Lynn Jsy/69 15.00
34 Tom Seaver Bat/69 20.00
36 Reggie Jackson Pants/69 15.00
37 Bob Gibson Jsy/45 25.00
38 Jack Morris Jsy/69 15.00
39 Torii Hunter Jsy/48 15.00
40 Andre Dawson Jsy/69 15.00
41 Dave Righetti Jsy/69 15.00
42 Hideki Matsui Pants/69 40.00
43 Lou Brock Jkt/69 15.00
44 Yogi Berra Bat/69 25.00
45 Frankie Frisch Jkt/69 20.00
46 Sean Casey Jsy/69 15.00
47 Sammy Sosa Jsy/69 20.00
48 Ralph Kiner Bat/69 15.00
49 Hoyt Wilhelm Jsy/69 15.00
50 Jim Rice Jsy/69 15.00
51 Duke Snider Pants/69 20.00
52 Harold Baines Jsy/69 15.00
53 Willie Stargell Jsy/69 20.00
54 Johnny Bench Pants/69 20.00
55 Carlton Fisk Jsy/69 15.00
56 Jim Palmer Jsy/69 15.00
57 Bobby Doerr Jsy/69 15.00
58 Mark Prior Jsy/69 20.00
60 Lou Boudreau Jsy/69 25.00
61 Alan Trammell Bat/69 15.00
62 Al Kaline Bat/69 20.00

#	Card	NM/M
63	Warren Spahn Pants/69	25.00
65	Miguel Cabrera Jsy/69	15.00
66	Luis Tiant Jsy/69	15.00
67	Harmon Killebrew Jsy/69	35.00
68	Richie Ashburn Pants/69	20.00
69	Michael Young Jsy/69	15.00
70	Tony Oliva Jsy/69	20.00
71	Mark Mulder Jsy/20	25.00
72	Nolan Ryan Jsy/69	60.00
73	Willie McCovey Jsy/69	25.00
74	Kirk Gibson Jsy/69	15.00
75	Carl Yastrzemski Pants/69	30.00

Stamps Material USA Flag

Production 1-100

#	Card	NM/M
1	Pee Wee Reese Bat/100	15.00
4	George Brett Jsy/100	35.00
5	Stan Musial Bat/100	25.00
6	Bob Feller Pants/100	15.00
7	Cal Ripken Jr. Pants/100	65.00
11	Dwight Evans Jsy/24	30.00
13	Ernie Banks Jsy/100	30.00
14	Pedro J. Martinez Jsy/45	25.00
16	Scott Rolen Jsy/27	40.00
17	Tony Gwynn Jsy/100	30.00
18	Mike Schmidt Jsy/100	50.00
19	Roberto Clemente Hat/21	200.00
20	Roger Clemens Jsy/100	25.00
21	Don Mattingly Jsy/100	30.00
22	Tony Perez Bat/100	15.00
24	Billy Williams Jsy/100	10.00
25	Juan Marichal Pants/100	15.00
26	Hank Blalock Jsy/100	15.00
27	Maury Wills Jsy/100	10.00
28	Fergie Jenkins Pants/100	15.00
29	Steve Carlton Jsy/100	15.00
30	Dale Murphy Jsy/100	15.00
31	Kerry Wood Jsy/100	20.00
32	Gaylord Perry Jsy/100	10.00
33	Fred Lynn Jsy/100	10.00
34	Tom Seaver Bat/100	15.00
36	Reggie Jackson Pants/44	20.00
37	Bob Gibson Jsy/100	20.00
38	Jack Morris Jsy/100	10.00
39	Torii Hunter Jsy/48	15.00
40	Andre Dawson	15.00
41	Dave Righetti Jsy/100	10.00
42	Hideki Matsui Pants/100	40.00
43	Lou Brock Jkt/100	15.00
44	Yogi Berra Bat/100	20.00
45	Frankie Frisch Jkt/100	15.00
46	Sean Casey Jsy/100	10.00
47	Sammy Sosa Jsy/100	15.00
48	Ralph Kiner Bat/100	15.00
49	Hoyt Wilhelm Jsy/100	10.00
50	Jim Rice Jsy/100	12.00
51	Duke Snider Pants/100	15.00
52	Harold Baines Jsy/100	10.00
53	Willie Stargell Jsy/100	15.00
54	Johnny Bench Pants/100	20.00
55	Carlton Fisk Jsy/72	15.00
56	Jim Palmer Jsy/100	15.00
57	Bobby Doerr Jsy/100	15.00
58	Mark Prior Jsy/100	15.00
62	Al Kaline Bat/100	15.00
63	Warren Spahn Pants/100	20.00
64	Bert Blyleven Jsy/28	20.00
65	Miguel Cabrera Jsy/24	25.00
66	Luis Tiant Jsy/23	20.00
67	Harmon Killebrew Jsy/100	30.00
68	Richie Ashburn Pants/100	15.00
70	Tony Oliva Jsy/100	15.00
71	Mark Mulder Jsy/20	25.00
72	Nolan Ryan Jsy/100	50.00
73	Willie McCovey Jsy/44	25.00
74	Kirk Gibson Jsy/100	10.00
75	Carl Yastrzemski Pants/100	25.00

Stamps Centennial Autograph

Production 1-40

#	Card	NM/M
2	Red Schoendienst/39	40.00
6	Bob Feller/39	40.00
11	Dwight Evans/39	30.00
15	Whitey Ford/27	50.00
22	Tony Perez/24	40.00
24	Billy Williams/39	30.00
25	Juan Marichal/39	30.00
27	Maury Wills/39	25.00
28	Fergie Jenkins/39	30.00
29	Steve Carlton/39	30.00
30	Dale Murphy/39	50.00
32	Gaylord Perry/39	25.00
33	Fred Lynn/39	30.00
35	Ron Guidry/39	40.00
38	Jack Morris/39	25.00
39	Torii Hunter/39	25.00
40	Andre Dawson/39	30.00
41	Dave Righetti/39	20.00
43	Lou Brock/20	40.00
46	Sean Casey/21	40.00
48	Ralph Kiner/39	30.00
50	Jim Rice/39	35.00
51	Duke Snider/25	50.00
52	Harold Baines/39	25.00
56	Jim Palmer/45	40.00
57	Bobby Doerr/59	30.00
59	Monte Irvin/39	35.00
61	Alan Trammell/40	30.00
62	Al Kaline/39	50.00
64	Bert Blyleven/39	25.00
65	Miguel Cabrera/39	30.00
66	Luis Tiant/39	25.00
69	Michael Young/39	25.00
70	Tony Oliva/39	35.00
71	Mark Mulder/25	40.00

Stamps Legendary Fields Autograph

Production 1-34

#	Card	NM/M
11	Dwight Evans/34	30.00
22	Tony Perez/34	35.00
24	Billy Williams/34	30.00
28	Fergie Jenkins/34	30.00
29	Steve Carlton/34	30.00
33	Fred Lynn/34	30.00
35	Ron Guidry/34	50.00
36	Reggie Jackson/1	
38	Jack Morris/34	25.00
40	Andre Dawson/34	30.00
41	Dave Righetti/34	20.00
48	Ralph Kiner/34	30.00
50	Jim Rice/34	35.00
52	Harold Baines/34	25.00
57	Bobby Doerr/34	35.00
59	Monte Irvin/34	35.00
66	Luis Tiant/23	30.00

Stamps Material Centennial Autograph

Production 1-39

#	Card	NM/M
2	Red Schoendienst Jsy/39	40.00
6	Bob Feller Pants/39	40.00
11	Dwight Evans Jsy/39	30.00
22	Tony Perez Bat/24	40.00
24	Billy Williams Jsy/39	35.00
25	Juan Marichal Pants/39	30.00
27	Maury Wills Jsy/39	30.00
28	Fergie Jenkins Pants/39	35.00
29	Steve Carlton Jsy/39	30.00
30	Dale Murphy Jsy/39	50.00
32	Gaylord Perry Jsy/39	30.00
33	Fred Lynn Jsy/39	30.00
37	Bob Gibson Jsy/39	40.00
38	Jack Morris Jsy/39	25.00
40	Andre Dawson Jsy/39	35.00
43	Lou Brock Jkt/39	30.00
46	Sean Casey Jsy/39	30.00
48	Ralph Kiner Bat/39	30.00
50	Jim Rice Jsy/39	35.00
51	Duke Snider Pants/39	50.00
52	Harold Baines Jsy/39	25.00
56	Jim Palmer Jsy/22	50.00
57	Bobby Doerr Jsy/39	35.00
61	Alan Trammell Bat/39	30.00
62	Al Kaline Bat/39	50.00
64	Bert Blyleven Jsy/39	25.00
65	Miguel Cabrera Jsy/39	50.00
66	Luis Tiant Jsy/39	30.00
67	Harmon Killebrew Jsy/39	60.00
69	Michael Young Jsy/10	
70	Tony Oliva Jsy/39	35.00
71	Mark Mulder Jsy/20	40.00
72	Nolan Ryan Jsy/10	
74	Kirk Gibson Jsy/39	30.00
75	Carl Yastrzemski Pants/8	

Stamps Material Legendary Fields Auto

Production 1-34

#	Card	NM/M
11	Dwight Evans Jsy/34	30.00
22	Tony Perez Bat/34	40.00
24	Billy Williams Jsy/34	30.00
28	Fergie Jenkins Pants/34	35.00
29	Steve Carlton Jsy/34	35.00
33	Fred Lynn Jsy/34	30.00
38	Jack Morris Jsy/34	30.00
40	Andre Dawson Jsy/34	30.00
41	Dave Righetti Jsy/34	20.00
50	Jim Rice Jsy/33	40.00
66	Luis Tiant Jsy/23	35.00
74	Kirk Gibson Jsy/23	30.00

Stamps Material Olympic Autograph

Production 1-29

#	Card	NM/M
6	Bob Feller Pants/29	45.00
11	Dwight Evans Jsy/24	35.00
22	Tony Perez Bat/29	40.00
24	Billy Williams Jsy/29	35.00
25	Juan Marichal Pants/29	35.00
27	Maury Wills Jsy/29	30.00
28	Fergie Jenkins Pants/29	35.00
29	Steve Carlton Jsy/29	35.00
30	Dale Murphy Jsy/29	50.00
32	Gaylord Perry Jsy/29	30.00
33	Fred Lynn Jsy/29	35.00
37	Bob Gibson Jsy/29	40.00
38	Jack Morris Jsy/29	30.00
40	Andre Dawson Jsy/25	35.00
43	Lou Brock Jkt/20	40.00
46	Sean Casey Jsy/21	40.00
56	Jim Palmer Jsy/22	50.00
64	Bert Blyleven Jsy/28	30.00
65	Miguel Cabrera Jsy/24	60.00
66	Luis Tiant Jsy/23	30.00
71	Mark Mulder Jsy/20	40.00
74	Kirk Gibson Jsy/23	30.00

Stamps Material Pro Ball Autograph

Production 1-69

#	Card	NM/M
6	Bob Feller Pants/69	30.00
11	Dwight Evans Jsy/24	30.00
22	Tony Perez Bat/24	40.00
24	Billy Williams Jsy/26	35.00
25	Juan Marichal Pants/27	35.00
27	Maury Wills Jsy/69	20.00
28	Fergie Jenkins Pants/69	25.00
29	Steve Carlton Jsy/69	30.00
30	Dale Murphy Jsy/69	40.00
32	Gaylord Perry Jsy/69	20.00
33	Fred Lynn Jsy/69	25.00
37	Bob Gibson Jsy/45	35.00
43	Lou Brock Jkt/20	40.00
46	Sean Casey Jsy/21	40.00
57	Bobby Doerr Jsy/48	30.00
65	Miguel Cabrera Jsy/24	50.00
66	Luis Tiant Jsy/23	30.00
71	Mark Mulder Jsy/20	40.00
74	Kirk Gibson Jsy/23	30.00

Stamps Material USA Flag Autograph

Production 1-37

#	Card	NM/M
2	Red Schoendienst Jsy/37	40.00
6	Bob Feller Pants/8	40.00
11	Dwight Evans Jsy/37	30.00
22	Tony Perez Bat/37	35.00
24	Billy Williams Jsy/37	30.00
25	Juan Marichal Pants/37	30.00
27	Maury Wills Jsy/37	25.00
28	Fergie Jenkins Pants/37	30.00
29	Steve Carlton Jsy/37	30.00
30	Dale Murphy Jsy/37	50.00
32	Gaylord Perry Jsy/37	25.00
33	Fred Lynn Jsy/37	30.00
37	Bob Gibson Jsy/37	40.00
38	Jack Morris Jsy/37	25.00
41	Dave Righetti Jsy/37	20.00
43	Lou Brock Jkt/37	30.00
46	Sean Casey Jsy/37	30.00
48	Ralph Kiner Bat/37	30.00
50	Jim Rice Jsy/37	30.00
51	Duke Snider Pants/37	40.00
52	Harold Baines Jsy/37	25.00
56	Jim Palmer Jsy/37	35.00
57	Bobby Doerr Jsy/37	40.00
61	Alan Trammell Bat/37	30.00
62	Al Kaline Bat/37	50.00
64	Bert Blyleven Jsy/37	25.00
65	Miguel Cabrera Jsy/37	50.00
66	Luis Tiant Jsy/37	25.00
67	Harmon Killebrew Jsy/37	60.00
70	Tony Oliva Jsy/37	35.00
71	Mark Mulder Jsy/37	30.00
74	Kirk Gibson Jsy/23	30.00

Stamps Olympic Autograph

Production 1-92

#	Card	NM/M
2	Red Schoendienst/92	25.00
6	Bob Feller/92	25.00
11	Dwight Evans/92	20.00
22	Tony Perez/24	40.00
24	Billy Williams/26	35.00
25	Juan Marichal/27	35.00
27	Maury Wills/92	20.00
28	Fergie Jenkins/92	25.00
29	Steve Carlton/92	20.00
30	Dale Murphy/92	30.00
32	Gaylord Perry/92	20.00
33	Fred Lynn/92	20.00
35	Ron Guidry/48	35.00
38	Jack Morris/92	20.00
39	Torii Hunter/48	25.00
40	Andre Dawson/92	25.00
43	Lou Brock/20	40.00
46	Sean Casey/21	40.00
50	Jim Rice/92	25.00
52	Harold Baines/92	20.00
56	Jim Palmer/22	50.00
57	Bobby Doerr/92	25.00
59	Monte Irvin/92	40.00
61	Alan Trammell/92	25.00
62	Al Kaline/92	40.00
64	Bert Blyleven/92	20.00
65	Miguel Cabrera/24	60.00
66	Luis Tiant/92	20.00
70	Tony Oliva/91	20.00
71	Mark Mulder/20	40.00

Stamps Pro Ball Autograph

Production 1-69

#	Card	NM/M
6	Bob Feller/69	30.00
11	Dwight Evans/69	25.00
22	Tony Perez/24	40.00
24	Billy Williams/26	35.00
25	Juan Marichal/27	35.00
27	Maury Wills/69	20.00
28	Fergie Jenkins/69	25.00
29	Steve Carlton/69	30.00
30	Dale Murphy/69	40.00
32	Gaylord Perry/69	20.00
33	Fred Lynn/69	25.00
35	Ron Guidry/49	40.00
38	Jack Morris/47	20.00
39	Torii Hunter/48	25.00
43	Lou Brock/20	40.00
46	Sean Casey/21	40.00
57	Bobby Doerr/69	30.00
59	Monte Irvin/20	40.00
64	Bert Blyleven/28	25.00
65	Miguel Cabrera/24	50.00
66	Luis Tiant/23	30.00
71	Mark Mulder/20	40.00

Stamps USA Flag Autograph

Production 1-100

#	Card	NM/M
2	Red Schoendienst/100	25.00
6	Bob Feller/100	25.00
11	Dwight Evans/24	35.00
22	Tony Perez/24	40.00
24	Billy Williams/26	35.00
25	Juan Marichal/27	35.00
27	Maury Wills/100	20.00
28	Fergie Jenkins/100	25.00
29	Steve Carlton/100	20.00
30	Dale Murphy/100	30.00
32	Gaylord Perry/100	20.00
33	Fred Lynn/100	20.00
35	Ron Guidry/49	35.00
38	Jack Morris/100	20.00

39 Torii Hunter/48 25.00
40 Andre Dawson/100 25.00
43 Lou Brock/20 40.00
46 Sean Casey/21 40.00
48 Ralph Kiner/100 25.00
51 Duke Snider/25 45.00
52 Harold Baines/100 20.00
56 Jim Palmer/22 50.00
57 Bobby Doerr/100 25.00
59 Monte Irvin/100 40.00
61 Alan Trammell/100 25.00
62 Al Kaline/100 40.00
64 Bert Blyleven/100 20.00
65 Miguel Cabrera/24 60.00
66 Luis Tiant/100 20.00
70 Tony Oliva/100 20.00
71 Mark Mulder/20 40.00

Timeline Threads Jersey Number

NM/M
Production 1-43
6 Orlando Cepeda Pants/30 10.00
9 Tony Perez Jsy/24 15.00
11 Tommy John Jsy/25 15.00
15 Carlton Fisk Jsy/27 20.00
17 Bert Blyleven Jsy/28 10.00
20 Lou Brock Jsy/20 20.00
21 Sammy Sosa Jsy/21 20.00
22 Roger Clemens Jsy/22 40.00
23 Don Mattingly Jsy/23 40.00
24 Rickey Henderson Jsy/35 15.00
26 Wade Boggs Jsy/26 20.00
29 Jim "Catfish" Hunter Jsy/29 15.00
30 Maury Wills Jsy/30 10.00
31 Hoyt Wilhelm Jsy/31 10.00
33 Eddie Murray Pants/33 30.00
34 Nolan Ryan Pants/34 50.00
35 Phil Niekro Jsy/35 10.00
38 Curt Schilling Jsy/38 15.00
40 Sandy Koufax Jsy/32 500.00
41 Don Sutton Jsy/20 15.00
42 Randy Johnson Jsy/51 15.00
43 Dennis Eckersley Jsy/43 10.00
44 Frank Thomas Jsy/35 20.00
45 Mike Mussina Jsy/35 15.00
46 Greg Maddux Jsy/31 25.00
47 Jim Palmer Pants/22 15.00
49 Mike Piazza Jsy/31 25.00

Timeline Threads Position

NM/M
Common Player: 4.00
1 Bobby Doerr Jsy/39 10.00
2 Burleigh Grimes Pants/26 50.00
3 Babe Ruth Pants/30 200.00
4 Joe Cronin Pants/38 20.00
5 Johnny Bench Pants/71 15.00
6 Orlando Cepeda Pants/62 8.00
7 Ivan Rodriguez Jsy/103 8.00
8 Cal Ripken Jr. Jsy/78 40.00
9 Tony Perez Jsy/78 8.00
10 Andre Dawson Jsy/86 8.00
11 Tommy John Jsy/86 4.00
12 Alfonso Soriano Jsy/102 8.00
13 Ozzie Smith Jsy/78 15.00
14 Ernie Banks Jsy/70 15.00
15 Carlton Fisk Jsy/80 8.00
16 Bo Jackson Jsy/89 10.00
17 Bert Blyleven Jsy/83 4.00
18 Darryl Strawberry Jsy/88 6.00
19 Bob Feller Pants/36 8.00
20 Lou Brock Jsy/74 8.00
21 Sammy Sosa Jsy/103 12.00
22 Roger Clemens Jsy/101 15.00
23 Don Mattingly Jsy/94 20.00
24 Rickey Henderson Jsy/83 10.00
25 Albert Pujols Jsy/103 15.00
26 Wade Boggs Jsy/87 10.00
27 Joe Morgan Jsy/82 8.00
28 Gary Carter Jsy/86 8.00
29 Jim "Catfish" Hunter Jsy/78 6.00
30 Maury Wills Jsy/65 4.00
31 Hoyt Wilhelm Jsy/68 4.00
32 Matt Williams Jsy/95 4.00
33 Eddie Murray Pants/88 8.00
34 Nolan Ryan Pants/90 25.00
35 Phil Niekro Jsy/80 6.00
36 Paul Molitor Jsy/96 10.00
37 Dale Murphy Jsy/83 8.00
38 Curt Schilling Jsy/99 8.00
39 Fred Lynn Jsy/75 4.00
40 Sandy Koufax Jsy/64 260.00
41 Don Sutton Jsy/76 4.00
42 Randy Johnson Jsy/98 8.00
43 Dennis Eckersley Jsy/97 6.00
44 Frank Thomas Jsy/94 8.00
45 Mike Mussina Jsy/100 6.00
46 Greg Maddux Jsy/96 10.00
47 Jim Palmer Pants/76 6.00
48 Harmon Killebrew Jsy/62 20.00
49 Mike Piazza Jsy/99 10.00
50 Billy Martin Jsy/83 15.00

Timeline Threads Number Autograph

Production 1-19
Position Autograph: No Pricing
Production 1-19
Prime: No Pricing
Production one set

2005 LEAF CERTIFIED MATERIALS

NM/M
Complete Set (250):
Common Player: .50
Common Auto. (201-250): 6.00
Production 499 unless noted
Hobby Pack (5): 10.00
Hobby Box (10): 90.00
1 A.J. Burnett .50
2 Adam Dunn .75
3 Adrian Beltre .75
4 Bret Boone .50
5 Albert Pujols 2.50
6 Alex Rodriguez 2.50
7 Alfonso Soriano 1.00
8 Andruw Jones 1.00
9 Andy Pettitte .75
10 Aramis Ramirez .75
11 Aubrey Huff .50
12 Austin Kearns .50
13 B.J. Upton .50
14 Brandon Webb .50
15 Barry Zito .50
16 Tim Salmon .50
17 Bobby Abreu .50
18 Bobby Crosby .50
19 Brad Penny .50
20 Preston Wilson .50
21 C.C. Sabathia .50
22 Carl Crawford .50
23 Keith Foulke .50
24 Carlos Beltran .75
25 Casey Kotchman .50
26 Chipper Jones 1.00
27 Chone Figgins .50
28 Craig Biggio .75
29 Craig Wilson .50
30 Curt Schilling 1.00
31 Danny Kolb .50
32 David Ortiz 1.00
33 Orlando Hudson .50
34 David Wright 1.50
35 Derek Jeter 2.50
36 Jake Peavy .50
37 Derrek Lee .75
38 Dontrelle Willis .75
39 Edgar Renteria .50
40 Angel Berroa .50
41 Eric Chavez .50
42 Akinori Otsuka .50
43 Francisco Rodriguez .50
44 Garret Anderson .50
45 Gary Sheffield .75
46 Greg Maddux 1.50
47 Hideki Matsui 2.00
48 Hideo Nomo .75
49 Ichiro Suzuki 2.00
50 Ivan Rodriguez .75
51 J.D. Drew .50
52 J.T. Snow .50
53 Jack Wilson .50
54 Jamie Moyer .50
55 Jason Bay .50
56 Jason Giambi .75
57 Trot Nixon .50
58 Jason Schmidt .50
59 Jason Varitek .50
60 Roy Oswalt .50
61 Javy Lopez .50
62 Eric Byrnes .50
63 Jeff Bagwell .75
64 Jeff Kent .50
65 Jeff Suppan .50
66 Jeremy Bonderman .50
67 Jermaine Dye .50
68 Kazuhito Tadano .50
69 Jim Edmonds .75
70 Jim Thome .75
71 Johan Santana 1.00
72 John Smoltz .75
73 Johnny Damon 1.00
74 Johnny Estrada .50
75 Brett Myers .50
76 Jose Guillen .50
77 Jose Vidro .50
78 Josh Beckett .50
79 Edwin Jackson .50
80 Raul Ibanez .50
81 Rich Harden .50
82 Justin Morneau .50
83 Kazuhisa Ishii .50
84 Kazuo Matsui .50
85 Ken Griffey Jr. 1.50
86 Ken Harvey .50
87 Frank Thomas .75
88 Kerry Wood .75
89 Wade Miller .50
90 Kevin Millwood .50
91 Jeremy Affeldt .50
92 Francisco Cordero .50
93 Lance Berkman .50
94 Larry Walker .50
95 Laynce Nix .50
96 Luis Gonzalez .50
97 Lyle Overbay .50
98 Carlos Zambrano .75
99 Manny Ramirez 1.00
100 Marcus Giles .50
101 Mark Buehrle .50
102 Mark Loretta .50
103 Mark Mulder .50
104 Mark Prior 1.00
105 Mark Teixeira .75
106 Marlon Byrd .50
107 Rafael Furcal .50
108 Melvin Mora .50
109 Michael Young .50
110 Miguel Cabrera 1.00
111 Miguel Tejada .75
112 Mike Lowell .50
113 Mike Mussina .75
114 Mike Piazza 1.50
115 Moises Alou .50
116 Livan Hernandez .50
117 Nomar Garciaparra 1.50
118 Omar Vizquel .50
119 Orlando Cabrera .50
120 Pat Burrell .50
121 Paul Konerko .50
122 Paul LoDuca .50
123 Pedro Martinez 1.00
124 Rafael Palmeiro .75
125 Randy Johnson 1.00
126 Richard Hidalgo .50
127 Richie Sexson .50
128 Magglio Ordonez .50
129 Roger Clemens 2.50
130 Russ Ortiz .50
131 Sammy Sosa 1.50
132 Scott Podsednik .50
133 Scott Rolen 1.00
134 Sean Burroughs .50
135 Sean Casey .50
136 Shawn Green .50
137 Jorge Posada .75
138 Roy Halladay .50
139 Steve Finley .50
140 Tim Hudson .75
141 Todd Helton .75
142 Tom Glavine .75
143 Torii Hunter .50
144 Travis Hafner .50
145 Trevor Hoffman .50
146 Troy Glaus .50
147 Vernon Wells .50
148 Victor Martinez .50
149 Vladimir Guerrero 1.00
150 Sammy Sosa 1.50
151 Hank Blalock .75
152 Danny Graves .50
153 Rocco Baldelli .50
154 Carlos Delgado .50
155 Bubba Nelson .50
156 Kevin Youkilis .50
157 Jacque Jones .50
158 Mike Lieberthal .50
159 Ben Sheets .50
160 Lew Ford .50
161 Ervin Santana .50
162 Jody Gerut .50
163 Nick Johnson .50
164 Brian Roberts .50
165 Joe Nathan .50
166 Mike Sweeney .50
167 Ryan Wagner .50
168 David Dellucci .50
169 Jae Weong Seo .50
170 Tom Gordon .50
171 Carlos Lee .50
172 Octavio Dotel .50
173 Jose Castillo .50
174 Troy Percival .50
175 Carlos Delgado .50
176 Curt Schilling 1.00
177 David Ortiz 1.00
178 Greg Maddux 1.50
179 Ivan Rodriguez .75
180 Jeff Kent .50
181 Larry Walker .50
182 Miguel Tejada .75
183 Pedro J. Martinez 1.00
184 Rafael Palmeiro .75
185 Roger Clemens 2.50
186 Shawn Green .50
187 Tim Hudson .75
188 Tom Glavine .75
189 Troy Glaus .50
190 Vladimir Guerrero 1.00
191 Cal Ripken Jr. 4.00
192 Don Mattingly 2.00
193 George Brett 2.00
194 Harmon Killebrew 1.50
195 Mike Schmidt 2.00
196 Nolan Ryan 3.00
197 Stan Musial 2.00
198 Tony Gwynn 1.00
199 Wade Boggs 1.00
200 Willie Mays 2.00
201 *Ambiorix Concepcion/auto* 10.00
202 *Agustin Montero/auto* 8.00
203 *Carlos Ruiz/auto* 8.00
204 *Casey Rogowski/auto* 6.00
205 *Chris Resop/auto* 8.00
206 *Chris Roberson/auto* 6.00
207 *Colter Bean* 2.00
208 *Danny Rueckel/auto* 6.00
209 *David Gassner/auto* 8.00
210 *Devon Lowery/auto* 8.00
211 *Norihiro Nakamura/auto/115* 40.00
212 *Erick Threets/auto/299* 6.00
213 *Garrett Jones/auto/299* 8.00
214 *Geovany Soto/auto* 6.00
215 *Jared Gothreaux/auto/299* 6.00
216 *Jason Hammel/auto/299* 10.00
217 *Jeff Miller/auto/299* 6.00
218 *Jeff Niemann/auto/299* 15.00
219 Huston Street 2.00
220 *John Hattig Jr./auto* 6.00
221 *Justin Verlander/auto/299* 25.00
222 *Justin Wechsler/auto* 6.00
223 *Luke Scott/auto* 10.00
224 *Mark McLemore/auto* 8.00
225 *Mark Woodyard/auto/299* 6.00
226 *Matt Lindstrom/auto/299* 8.00
227 *Miguel Negron/auto* 6.00
228 *Mike Morse/auto* 15.00
229 *Nate McLouth/auto* 8.00
230 *Paulino Reynoso/auto/299* 6.00
231 *Philip Humber/auto/299* 15.00
232 *Tony Pena/auto* 6.00

233 *Randy Messenger/auto* 6.00
234 *Raul Tablado/auto* 8.00
235 *Russel Rohlicek/auto* 6.00
236 *Ryan Speier/auto* 8.00
237 *Scott Munter/auto* 8.00
238 *Sean Thompson/auto* 6.00
239 *Sean Tracey/auto/299* 6.00
240 *Marcos Carvajal* 1.50
241 *Travis Bowyer/auto* 10.00
242 *Ubaldo Jimenez/auto* 6.00
243 *Wladimir Balentien/ auto* 12.00
244 *Eude Brito* 8.00
245 *Ambiorix Burgos* 2.00
246 *Tadahito Iguchi* 5.00
247 *Dae-Sung Koo* 1.00
248 *Chris Seddon* 2.00
249 *Keiichi Yabu/auto* 15.00
250 *Yunieskv Betancourt/ auto* 25.00

Mirror Black

No Pricing
Production one set

Mirror Blue

Mirror Blue (1-200): 3-6X
Auto. (201-250): .5X
No Auto. (201-250): 1-2X
Production 50 sets

Mirror Emerald

No Pricing
Production 5 sets

Mirror Gold

Mirror Gold (1-200): 5-10X
Mirror Gol (201-250): No Pricing
Production 25 sets

Mirror Red

Mirror Red (1-200): 2-4X
Auto. (201-250): .4X
No Auto. (201-250): 1X
Production 100 sets

Mirror White

Mirror White (1-200): 2-4X
Auto. (201-250): .4X
No Auto. (201-250): 1X
Production 100 sets

Cuts Blue

NM/M

Production 1-80
2 Hank Aaron/1
3 Willie Mays/26 150.00
5 Cal Ripken Jr./8
6 Nolan Ryan/7
7 Jim Palmer/50 25.00
8 Tony Gwynn/5
9 Rod Carew/5
10 Ryne Sandberg/5
12 Steve Carlton/50 25.00
14 Mike Schmidt/5
15 Maury Wills/80 20.00
16 Harmon Killebrew/3
18 Duke Snider/10
19 Don Mattingly/5
20 Dale Murphy/50 30.00

Cuts Green

NM/M

Production 3-50
2 Hank Aaron/5
3 Willie Mays/11
5 Cal Ripken Jr./8
6 Nolan Ryan/7
7 Jim Palmer/50 25.00
8 Tony Gwynn/5
9 Rod Carew/5
10 Ryne Sandberg/5
12 Steve Carlton/50 25.00
14 Mike Schmidt/5
15 Maury Wills/80 20.00
16 Harmon Killebrew/3
18 Duke Snider/10
19 Don Mattingly/5
20 Dale Murphy/50 30.00

Cuts Materials Blue

NM/M

Production 4-43
2 Hank Aaron Bat/43 275.00
3 Willie Mays Pants/24 175.00
4 Sandy Koufax Jsy/32 400.00
5 Cal Ripken Jr. Pants/8
6 Nolan Ryan Jsy/34 100.00
7 Jim Palmer Hat/22
8 Tony Gwynn Pants/19
9 Rod Carew Jsy/29 25.00
10 Ryne Sandberg Jsy/23 120.00
12 Steve Carlton Pants/32 25.00
14 Mike Schmidt Jsy/20 65.00
16 Harmon Killebrew Jsy/5
18 Duke Snider Pants/4
19 Don Mattingly Jsy/23 75.00
20 Dale Murphy Jsy/7

Cuts Materials Green

NM/M

Production 4-32
2 Hank Aaron Bat/5
3 Willie Mays Pants/24 175.00
4 Sandy Koufax Jsy/10
5 Cal Ripken Jr. Pants/8
6 Nolan Ryan Jsy/7
7 Jim Palmer Hat/22
8 Tony Gwynn Pants/19
9 Rod Carew Jsy/29 25.00
10 Ryne Sandberg Jsy/23 120.00
12 Steve Carlton Pants/32 25.00
14 Mike Schmidt Jsy/20 65.00
16 Harmon Killebrew Jsy/5
18 Duke Snider Pants/4
19 Don Mattingly Jsy/5
20 Dale Murphy Jsy/8

Cuts Materials Red

NM/M

Production 4-32
2 Hank Aaron Bat/5
3 Willie Mays Pants/24 175.00
4 Sandy Koufax Jsy/10
5 Cal Ripken Jr. Pants/8
6 Nolan Ryan Jsy/7
7 Jim Palmer Hat/22
8 Tony Gwynn Pants/19
9 Rod Carew Jsy/29 25.00
10 Ryne Sandberg Jsy/23 120.00
12 Steve Carlton Pants/32 25.00
14 Mike Schmidt Jsy/20 65.00
16 Harmon Killebrew Jsy/3
18 Duke Snider Pants/4
19 Don Mattingly Jsy/5
20 Dale Murphy Jsy/8

Cuts Red

NM/M

Production 1-60
2 Hank Aaron/5
3 Willie Mays/1
5 Cal Ripken Jr./8
6 Nolan Ryan/7
7 Jim Palmer/50 25.00
8 Tony Gwynn/5
9 Rod Carew/5
10 Ryne Sandberg/5
12 Steve Carlton/50 25.00
14 Mike Schmidt/5
15 Maury Wills/60 20.00
16 Harmon Killebrew/3
18 Duke Snider/10
19 Don Mattingly/5
20 Dale Murphy/50 30.00

Fabric of the Game

NM/M

Common Player:
Production 5-100
1 Al Oliver Jsy/50 6.00
2 Alan Trammell Jsy/100 6.00
3 Andres Galarraga Jsy/100 4.00
4 Andres Galarraga Jsy/100 4.00
5 Babe Ruth Jsy/10
6 Babe Ruth Pants/25 240.00
7 Billy Martin Pants/100 15.00
8 Billy Williams Jsy/50 6.00
9 Bo Jackson Jsy/100 10.00
10 Bo Jackson Jsy/100 10.00
11 Bob Feller Pants/5
12 Bob Gibson Jsy/25 12.00
13 Bobby Doerr Pants/50 10.00
14 Burleigh Grimes Pants/25 50.00
15 Cal Ripken Jr. Jsy/50 30.00
16 Cal Ripken Jr. Jsy/50 30.00
17 Carl Yastrzemski Pants/50 15.00
18 Carlton Fisk Jkt/50 10.00
19 Jim "Catfish" Hunter Pants/50 8.00
20 Darryl Strawberry Jsy/25 8.00
21 Darryl Strawberry Jsy/100 4.00
22 Dave Concepcion Jsy/50 6.00
23 Dave Righetti Jsy/50 8.00
24 Dave Winfield Pants/100 8.00
25 David Cone Jsy/100 4.00
26 David Justice Jsy/100 4.00
27 Deion Sanders Jsy/50 8.00
28 Deion Sanders Jsy/50 8.00
29 Dennis Eckersley Jsy/50 8.00
30 Dennis Eckersley Pants/50 8.00
31 Don Mattingly Jsy/100 15.00
32 Don Sutton Jsy/25 8.00
33 Don Sutton Jsy/50 6.00
34 Duke Snider Jsy/10
35 Duke Snider Jsy/10
36 Dwight Evans Jsy/5
37 Dwight Gooden Jsy/100 6.00
38 Eddie Murray Jsy/25 15.00
39 Eddie Murray Pants/50 10.00
40 Edgar Martinez Jsy/100 4.00
41 Ernie Banks Jsy/25 15.00
42 Fergie Jenkins Jsy/50 8.00
43 Frankie Frisch Jkt/50 20.00
44 Fred Lynn Jsy/50 4.00
45 Fred McGriff Jsy/100 6.00
46 Gary Carter Jsy/50 6.00
47 Gary Carter Jsy/50 6.00
48 Gaylord Perry Jsy/50 6.00
49 Gaylord Perry Jsy/50 6.00
50 George Brett Jsy/25 20.00
51 Hal Newhouser Jsy/50 8.00
52 Hank Aaron Jsy/5
53 Hank Aaron Jsy/5
54 Harmon Killebrew Jsy/25 15.00
55 Harmon Killebrew Jsy/50 12.00
56 Harold Baines Jsy/50 8.00
57 Hoyt Wilhelm Jsy/100 6.00
58 Jack Morris Jsy/100 4.00
59 Jim Thorpe Jsy/25 300.00
60 Jose Cruz Jsy/100 4.00
61 Jim Rice Jsy/50 8.00
62 Joe Cronin Jsy/50 15.00
63 Joe Cronin Pants/100 15.00
64 Joe Morgan Jsy/50 8.00
65 Joe Torre Jsy/50 10.00
66 John Kruk Jsy/100 10.00
67 Johnny Bench Jsy/50 10.00
68 Juan Marichal Pants/100 6.00
69 Keith Hernandez Jsy/10
70 Kirby Puckett Jsy/10
71 Kirk Gibson Jsy/100 4.00
72 Lee Smith Jsy/100 4.00
73 Lenny Dykstra Jsy/100 6.00
74 Lou Boudreau Jsy/25 15.00
75 Luis Aparicio Jsy/50 6.00
76 Luis Tiant Pants/100 4.00
77 Mark Grace Jsy/50 8.00
78 Hoyt Wilhelm Jsy/100 6.00
79 Matt Williams Jsy/100 6.00
80 Matt Williams Jsy/50 6.00
81 Mike Schmidt Jkt/5
82 Nolan Ryan Jsy/50 20.00
83 Nolan Ryan Jsy/15
84 Nolan Ryan Jsy/25 25.00
85 Nolan Ryan Jsy/25 25.00
86 Orlando Cepeda Pants/50 8.00
87 Ozzie Smith Pants/25 15.00
88 Paul Molitor Jsy/50 8.00
89 Paul Molitor Jsy/50 8.00
90 Paul Molitor Pants/50 8.00
91 Phil Niekro Jsy/50 8.00
92 Reggie Jackson Pants/100 8.00
93 Reggie Jackson Jkt/100 8.00
94 Reggie Jackson Jsy/50 8.00
95 Reggie Jackson Jsy/50 8.00
96 Rickey Henderson Jkt/100 10.00
97 Rickey Henderson Jsy/50 10.00
98 Rickey Henderson Jsy/50 10.00
99 Rickey Henderson Jsy/50 10.00
100 Rickey Henderson Jsy/50 10.00
101 Rickey Henderson Pants/50 10.00
102 Robin Ventura Jsy/100 6.00
103 Robin Ventura Jsy/100 6.00
104 Robin Yount Jsy/50 12.00
105 Rod Carew Jsy/100 8.00
106 Rod Carew Jsy/100 8.00
107 Roger Maris Pants/50 40.00
108 Ron Cey Jsy/50 8.00
109 Ron Guidry Pants/100 6.00
110 Ryne Sandberg Jsy/50 15.00
111 Sandy Koufax Jsy/25 180.00
112 Stan Musial Jsy/25 25.00
113 Stan Musial Pants/25 25.00
114 Steve Garvey Jsy/100 6.00
115 Ted Williams Jkt/50 50.00
116 Ted Williams Jsy/25 50.00
117 Tom Seaver Jsy/50 10.00
118 Tom Seaver Pants/50 10.00
119 Tommy John Jsy/100 4.00
120 Tommy John Pants/100 4.00
121 Tommy Lasorda Jsy/100 6.00
122 Tony Gwynn Jsy/100 10.00
123 Tony Gwynn Pants/100 10.00
124 Tony Perez Jsy/50 8.00
125 Wade Boggs Jsy/100 8.00
126 Warren Spahn Jsy/25 15.00
127 Whitey Ford Jsy/25 15.00
128 Will Clark Jsy/50 8.00
129 Willie Mays Pants/50 40.00
130 Willie McCovey Pants/100 10.00
131 Roger Clemens Jsy/50 15.00
132 Roger Clemens Jsy/50 15.00
133 Roger Clemens Jsy/50 15.00
134 Randy Johnson Jsy/50 8.00
135 Randy Johnson Jsy/50 8.00
136 Cal Ripken Jr. Jsy/50 30.00
137 Don Mattingly Jsy/100 15.00
138 George Brett Jsy/25 20.00
139 Harmon Killebrew Jsy/25 15.00
140 Mike Schmidt Jsy/50 20.00
141 Nolan Ryan Jkt/25 25.00
142 Stan Musial Jsy/5
143 Tony Gwynn Jsy/100 10.00
144 Wade Boggs Jsy/50 10.00
145 Willie Mays Jsy/25 50.00
146 Hideo Nomo Jsy/100 10.00
147 Dale Murphy Jsy/100 10.00
148 Dale Murphy Jsy/100 10.00
149 Bo Jackson Jsy/50 12.00
150 Darryl Strawberry Jsy/506.00
151 Deion Sanders Jsy/50 8.00
152 Deion Sanders Pants/50 8.00
153 Dennis Eckersley Jsy/50 8.00
154 Dwight Gooden Jsy/100 6.00
155 Edgar Martinez Jsy/100 4.00
156 Lou Brock Jsy/50 8.00
157 Steve Carlton Pants/50 6.00
158 Albert Pujols Jsy/50 20.00
159 Tom Glavine Jsy/100 8.00
160 Hideki Matsui Pants/50 20.00
161 Babe Ruth Pants, Jim Thorpe Jsy/25 500.00
162 Ted Williams Jkt, Bob Gibson Jsy/50 50.00
163 Willie Mays Jsy, Bob Gibson Jsy/10
164 Whitey Ford Jsy, Sandy Koufax Jsy/25 150.00
165 Roger Maris Pants, Don Mattingly Jsy/25 50.00
166 Nolan Ryan Jsy, Tom Seaver Jsy/50 25.00
167 Cal Ripken Jr. Jsy, George Brett Jsy/100 40.00
168 Ryne Sandberg Jsy, Mike Schmidt Jsy/50 30.00
169 Tony Gwynn Jsy, Wade Boggs Jsy/50 15.00
170 Carlton Fisk Jsy, Johnny Bench Pants/50 15.00

171 Duke Snider Pants, Harmon Killebrew Jsy/10
172 Reggie Jackson Pants, Darryl Strawberry Jsy/50 10.00
173 Robin Yount Jsy, Paul Molitor Jsy/50 20.00
174 Warren Spahn Pants, Juan Marichal Jsy/50 15.00
175 Bo Jackson Jsy, Deion Sanders Pants/100 15.00
176 Tony Gwynn Jsy, Rickey Henderson Jsy/100 15.00
177 Hideki Matsui Jsy, Jim Edmonds Jsy/100 20.00
178 Rickey Henderson Pants, Lou Brock Jsy/100 15.00
179 Roger Clemens Jsy, Albert Pujols Jsy/100 25.00
180 Hideo Nomo Jsy, Kazuhisa Ishii Jsy/100 12.00

Fabric of the Game Auto.

No Pricing
Production One Set

Fabric of the Game Reward

NM/M

Production 3-50
1 Al Oliver Jsy/50 6.00
2 Alan Trammell Jsy/50 8.00
3 Andres Galarraga Jsy/50 6.00
4 Andres Galarraga Jsy/50 6.00
7 Billy Martin Pants/50 15.00
9 Bo Jackson Jsy/50 12.00
10 Bo Jackson Jsy/50 12.00
13 Bobby Doerr Pants/25 12.00
17 Carl Yastrzemski Pants/25 15.00
19 Jim "Catfish" Hunter Pants/50 8.00
21 Darryl Strawberry Jsy/50 6.00
23 Dave Righetti Jsy/25 8.00
44 Fred Lynn Jsy/50 4.00
45 Fred McGriff Jsy/5
46 Gary Carter Jsy/50 6.00
47 Gary Carter Jsy/25 8.00
48 Gaylord Perry Jsy/50 6.00
49 Gaylord Perry Jsy/25 8.00
51 Hal Newhouser Jsy/25 8.00
58 Jack Morris Jsy/50 6.00
61 Jim Rice Jsy/50 8.00
62 Joe Cronin Jsy/25 20.00
63 Joe Cronin Pants/25 20.00
64 Joe Morgan Jsy/25 10.00
66 John Kruk Jsy/50 10.00
68 Juan Marichal Pants/25 10.00
71 Kirk Gibson Jsy/25 8.00
72 Lee Smith Jsy/50 4.00
75 Luis Aparicio Jsy/25 8.00
76 Luis Tiant Pants/25 6.00
78 Hoyt Wilhelm Jsy/25 10.00
79 Matt Williams Jsy/25 8.00
82 Nolan Ryan Jsy/25 25.00
85 Nolan Ryan Jsy/25 25.00
86 Orlando Cepeda Pants/25 10.00
87 Ozzie Smith Pants/25 15.00
88 Paul Molitor Jsy/50 8.00
89 Paul Molitor Jsy/50 8.00
90 Paul Molitor Pants/25 10.00
91 Phil Niekro Jsy/25 8.00
92 Reggie Jackson Pants/50 10.00
93 Reggie Jackson Jkt/25 10.00
95 Reggie Jackson Jsy/25 10.00
96 Rickey Henderson Jkt/50 10.00
97 Rickey Henderson Jsy/50 10.00
99 Rickey Henderson Jsy/25 12.00
102 Robin Ventura Jsy/50 6.00
103 Robin Ventura Jsy/50 6.00
104 Robin Yount Jsy/50 12.00
105 Rod Carew Jsy/25 10.00
106 Rod Carew Jsy/50 10.00
108 Ron Cey Jsy/50 8.00
109 Ron Guidry Pants/50 8.00
110 Ryne Sandberg Jsy/50 15.00
111 Sandy Koufax Jsy/25 180.00
113 Stan Musial Pants/25 25.00
114 Steve Garvey Jsy/25 8.00
115 Ted Williams Jkt/25 50.00
118 Tom Seaver Pants/50 10.00
119 Tommy John Jsy/50 4.00
120 Tommy John Pants/50 4.00
121 Tommy Lasorda Jsy/50 6.00
122 Tony Gwynn Jsy/50 10.00
123 Tony Gwynn Pants/50 10.00
124 Tony Perez Jsy/50 8.00
125 Wade Boggs Jsy/50 10.00
126 Warren Spahn Pants/50 12.00
128 Will Clark Jsy/50 8.00
129 Willie Mays Pants/25 50.00
130 Willie McCovey Pants/50 10.00
131 Roger Clemens Jsy/25 20.00
132 Roger Clemens Jsy/50 15.00
133 Roger Clemens Jsy/50 15.00
134 Randy Johnson Jsy/50 10.00
135 Randy Johnson Jsy/50 10.00
136 Cal Ripken Jr. Jsy/50 30.00
137 Don Mattingly Jsy/50 15.00
138 George Brett Jsy/25 20.00
139 Harmon Killebrew Jsy/25 15.00
140 Mike Schmidt Jsy/25 20.00
143 Tony Gwynn Jsy/50 10.00
144 Wade Boggs Jsy/25 10.00
145 Willie Mays Jsy/25 50.00
146 Hideo Nomo Jsy/50 10.00
147 Dale Murphy Jsy/50 10.00
148 Dale Murphy Jsy/50 10.00
150 Darryl Strawberry Jsy/50 6.00
151 Deion Sanders Jsy/50 8.00
152 Deion Sanders Pants/50 8.00
153 Dennis Eckersley Jsy/50 8.00
154 Dwight Gooden Jsy/50 6.00
155 Edgar Martinez Jsy/50 4.00
156 Lou Brock Jsy/50 8.00
157 Steve Carlton Pants/50 6.00
158 Albert Pujols Jsy/50 20.00
159 Tom Glavine Jsy/50 8.00
160 Hideki Matsui Pants/50 20.00
161 Babe Ruth Pants, Jim Thorpe Jsy/25 500.00
162 Ted Williams Jkt, Stan Musial Jsy/25 50.00
163 Willie Mays Jsy, Bob Gibson Jsy/25 50.00
164 Whitey Ford Jsy, Sandy Koufax Jsy/25 150.00
165 Roger Maris Pants, Don Mattingly Jsy/25 50.00
166 Nolan Ryan Jsy, Tom Seaver Jsy/50 25.00
167 Cal Ripken Jr. Jsy, George Brett Jsy/50 40.00
168 Ryne Sandberg Jsy, Mike Schmidt Jsy/50 30.00
169 Tony Gwynn Jsy, Wade Boggs Jsy/50 15.00
170 Carlton Fisk Jsy, Johnny Bench Pants/25 20.00
172 Reggie Jackson Pants, Darryl Strawberry Jsy/50 10.00
173 Robin Yount Jsy, Paul Molitor Jsy/25 20.00
174 Warren Spahn Pants, Juan Marichal Jsy/25 20.00
175 Bo Jackson Jsy, Deion Sanders Pants/50 15.00
176 Tony Gwynn Jsy, Rickey Henderson Jsy/50 20.00
177 Hideki Matsui Jsy, Jim Edmonds Jsy/50 20.00
178 Rickey Henderson Pants, Lou Brock Jsy/50 20.00
179 Roger Clemens Jsy, Albert Pujols Jsy/50 25.00
180 Hideo Nomo Jsy, Kazuhisa Ishii Jsy/50 15.00

Fabric of the Game Stats

NM/M

Production 3-75
1 Al Oliver Jsy/75 6.00
2 Alan Trammell Jsy/5
3 Andres Galarraga Jsy/75 6.00
4 Andres Galarraga Jsy/75 6.00
7 Billy Martin Pants/75 15.00
8 Billy Williams Jsy/75 6.00
9 Bo Jackson Jsy/75 10.00
10 Bo Jackson Jsy/75 10.00
13 Bobby Doerr Jsy/25 12.00
14 Burleigh Grimes Pants/25 50.00
15 Cal Ripken Jr. Jsy/75 30.00
16 Cal Ripken Jr. Jsy/75 30.00
17 Carl Yastrzemski Pants/25 15.00
18 Carlton Fisk Jkt/75 10.00
19 Jim "Catfish" Hunter Pants/75 8.00
21 Darryl Strawberry Jsy/75 6.00
22 Dave Concepcion Jsy/75 4.00
23 Dave Righetti Jsy/25 8.00
24 Dave Winfield Pants/75 8.00
25 David Cone Jsy/75 4.00
26 David Justice Jsy/75 4.00
27 Deion Sanders Jsy/75 8.00
28 Deion Sanders Jsy/75 8.00
29 Dennis Eckersley Jsy/75 8.00
30 Dennis Eckersley Pants/75 8.00
39 Eddie Murray Pants/75 12.00
40 Edgar Martinez Jsy/75 4.00
43 Frankie Frisch Jkt/75 15.00
44 Fred Lynn Jsy/50 4.00
45 Fred McGriff Jsy/75 6.00
46 Gary Carter Jsy/50 6.00
47 Gary Carter Jsy/25 8.00
48 Gaylord Perry Jsy/50 6.00
49 Gaylord Perry Jsy/25 8.00
51 Hal Newhouser Jsy/25 10.00
54 Harmon Killebrew Jsy/25 15.00
55 Harmon Killebrew Jsy/50 12.00
56 Harold Baines Jsy/50 8.00
57 Hoyt Wilhelm Jsy/50 6.00
62 Joe Cronin Jsy/25 20.00
63 Joe Cronin Pants/25 20.00
64 Joe Morgan Jsy/25 10.00
66 John Kruk Jsy/75 10.00
71 Kirk Gibson Jsy/25 8.00
72 Lee Smith Jsy/75 4.00
73 Lenny Dykstra Jsy/75 6.00
75 Luis Aparicio Jsy/25 8.00
76 Luis Tiant Pants/25 6.00
78 Hoyt Wilhelm Jsy/25 10.00
79 Matt Williams Jsy/25 8.00
82 Nolan Ryan Jsy/25 25.00
85 Nolan Ryan Jsy/25 25.00
86 Orlando Cepeda Pants/25 10.00
87 Ozzie Smith Pants/25 15.00
88 Paul Molitor Jsy/50 8.00
89 Paul Molitor Jsy/50 8.00
90 Paul Molitor Pants/25 10.00
91 Phil Niekro Jsy/25 8.00
92 Reggie Jackson Pants/50 10.00
93 Reggie Jackson Jkt/25 10.00
94 Reggie Jackson Jsy/75 10.00
95 Reggie Jackson Jsy/50 10.00
96 Rickey Henderson Jkt/75 10.00
97 Rickey Henderson Jsy/75 10.00
98 Rickey Henderson Jsy/50 10.00
101 Rickey Henderson Pants/75 10.00
102 Robin Ventura Jsy/50 6.00
103 Robin Ventura Jsy/50 6.00
104 Robin Yount Jsy/50 12.00
105 Rod Carew Jsy/25 10.00
106 Rod Carew Jsy/75 8.00
107 Roger Maris Pants/50 40.00
108 Ron Cey Jsy/50 8.00
109 Ron Guidry Pants/50 8.00
111 Sandy Koufax Jsy/25 180.00
113 Stan Musial Pants/25 25.00
114 Steve Garvey Jsy/25 8.00
115 Ted Williams Jkt/25 50.00
117 Tom Seaver Jsy/75 10.00
118 Tom Seaver Pants/50 10.00
119 Tommy John Jsy/25 6.00
120 Tommy John Pants/25 6.00
121 Tommy Lasorda Jsy/75 6.00
124 Tony Perez Jsy/75 8.00
125 Wade Boggs Jsy/75 10.00
126 Warren Spahn Pants/75 12.00
128 Will Clark Jsy/50 8.00
129 Willie Mays Pants/25 50.00
130 Willie McCovey Pants/75 10.00
131 Roger Clemens Jsy/25 20.00
140 Mike Schmidt Jsy/25 20.00
144 Wade Boggs Jsy/50 10.00
145 Willie Mays Jsy/25 25.00
146 Hideo Nomo Jsy/75 10.00
147 Dale Murphy Jsy/25 10.00
148 Dale Murphy Jsy/75 10.00
153 Dennis Eckersley Jsy/75 8.00
154 Dwight Gooden Jsy/75 6.00
155 Edgar Martinez Jsy/75 4.00
156 Lou Brock Jsy/75 8.00
157 Steve Carlton Pants/75 6.00
159 Tom Glavine Jsy/75 8.00
160 Hideki Matsui Pants/75 20.00
161 Babe Ruth Pants, Jim Thorpe Jsy/25 500.00
162 Ted Williams Jkt, Stan Musial Jsy/25 50.00
163 Willie Mays Jsy, Bob Gibson Jsy/25 50.00
164 Whitey Ford Jsy, Sandy Koufax Jsy/25 150.00
165 Roger Maris Pants, Don Mattingly Jsy/25 50.00
166 Nolan Ryan Jsy, Tom Seaver Jsy/50 25.00
167 Cal Ripken Jr. Jsy, George Brett Jsy/50 40.00
168 Ryne Sandberg Jsy, Mike Schmidt Jsy/50 30.00
169 Tony Gwynn Jsy, Wade Boggs Jsy/50 15.00
170 Carlton Fisk Jsy, Johnny Bench Pants/25 20.00
172 Reggie Jackson Pants, Darryl Strawberry Jsy/50 10.00
173 Robin Yount Jsy, Paul Molitor Jsy/25 20.00
174 Warren Spahn Pants, Juan Marichal Jsy/25 20.00
175 Bo Jackson Jsy, Deion Sanders Pants/50 15.00
176 Tony Gwynn Jsy, Rickey Henderson Jsy/50 20.00
177 Hideki Matsui Jsy, Jim Edmonds Jsy/50 20.00
178 Rickey Henderson Pants, Lou Brock Jsy/50 20.00
179 Roger Clemens Jsy, Albert Pujols Jsy/50 25.00
180 Hideo Nomo Jsy, Kazuhisa Ishii Jsy/50 15.00

Gold Team

NM/M

Complete Set (25):
Common Player: 1.00
Inserted 1:7
Mirror: 2X-3X
1 Albert Pujols 4.00
2 Alex Rodriguez 3.00
3 Carlos Beltran 1.00
4 Chipper Jones 1.50
5 Curt Schilling 1.50
6 Derek Jeter 4.00
7 Greg Maddux 2.50
8 Hank Blalock 1.00
9 Ichiro Suzuki 3.00
10 Ivan Rodriguez 1.00
11 Jim Thome 1.00
12 Ken Griffey Jr. 3.00
13 Lyle Overbay 1.00
14 Manny Ramirez 1.50
15 Mark Mulder 1.00
16 Mark Prior 1.50
17 Michael Young 1.00
18 Miguel Cabrera 1.50
19 Mike Piazza 2.00
20 Pedro Martinez 1.50
21 Randy Johnson 1.50
22 Roger Clemens 4.00
23 Sammy Sosa 2.00
24 Tim Hudson 1.00
25 Todd Helton 1.50

Gold Team Autograph

No Pricing
Production 5-10

Gold Team Jersey Number

NM/M

Production 100-250
1 Albert Pujols/100 20.00
3 Carlos Beltran/200 5.00
4 Chipper Jones/100 8.00

5 Curt Schilling/250 8.00
7 Greg Maddux/100 10.00
8 Hank Blalock/250 4.00
10 Ivan Rodriguez/120 6.00
11 Jim Thome/250 6.00
13 Lyle Overbay/250 4.00
14 Manny Ramirez/250 8.00
15 Mark Mulder/250 4.00
16 Mark Prior/100 4.00
17 Michael Young/250 4.00
18 Miguel Cabrera/100 8.00
19 Mike Piazza/250 10.00
20 Pedro Martinez/100 8.00
21 Randy Johnson/250 8.00
22 Roger Clemens/250 10.00
23 Sammy Sosa/250 8.00
24 Tim Hudson/100 4.00
25 Todd Helton/100 6.00

Mirror Autograph Blue

NM/M

Production 1-100
Black: No Pricing
Production One Set
Emerald: No Pricing
Production 1-5
18 Bobby Crosby/25 25.00
25 Casey Kotchman/25 15.00
33 Orlando Hudson/100 10.00
53 Jack Wilson/25 15.00
62 Eric Byrnes/25 12.00
66 Jeremy Bonderman/25 20.00
67 Jermaine Dye/25 15.00
68 Kazuhito Tadano/50 15.00
79 Edwin Jackson/100 8.00
80 Raul Ibanez/25 15.00
86 Ken Harvey/100 8.00
89 Wade Miller/100 10.00
91 Jeremy Affeldt/100 8.00
95 Laynce Nix/50 10.00
106 Marlon Byrd/100 8.00
155 Bubba Nelson/100 8.00
156 Kevin Youkilis/25 25.00
160 Lew Ford/25 15.00
161 Ervin Santana/100 10.00
165 Joe Nathan/25 20.00
167 Ryan Wagner/25 10.00
168 David Dellucci/25 20.00
169 Jae Weong Seo/25 15.00
173 Jose Castillo/100 10.00
223 Luke Scott/49 15.00
229 Nate McLouth/49 15.00
234 Raul Tablado/49 10.00
243 Wladimir Balentien/49 25.00

Mirror Autograph Gold

NM/M

Production 1-25
2 Adam Dunn/25 35.00
11 Aubrey Huff/25 15.00
12 Austin Kearns/25 10.00
13 B.J. Upton/25 15.00
14 Brandon Webb/25 15.00
16 Tim Salmon/25 30.00
18 Bobby Crosby/25 25.00
19 Brad Penny/25 15.00
21 C.C. Sabathia/25 15.00
23 Keith Foulke/25 25.00
25 Casey Kotchman/25 15.00
27 Chone Figgins/25 12.00
29 Craig Wilson/25 10.00
31 Danny Kolb/25 10.00
33 Orlando Hudson/25 10.00
34 David Wright/25 60.00
36 Jake Peavy/25 35.00
37 Derrek Lee/25 40.00
39 Edgar Renteria/25 20.00
40 Angel Berroa/25 10.00
41 Eric Chavez/25 20.00
42 Akinori Otsuka/25 25.00
43 Francisco Rodriguez/25 25.00
44 Garret Anderson/25 20.00
53 Jack Wilson/25 15.00
54 Jamie Moyer/25 15.00
55 Jason Bay/25 25.00
57 Trot Nixon/25 20.00
60 Roy Oswalt/25 25.00
62 Eric Byrnes/25 12.00
63 Jeff Bagwell/25 40.00
65 Jeff Suppan/25 15.00
66 Jeremy Bonderman/25 20.00
67 Jermaine Dye/25 15.00
68 Kazuhito Tadano/25 15.00
75 Brett Myers/25 20.00
76 Jose Guillen/25 15.00
77 Jose Vidro/25 15.00
79 Edwin Jackson/25 10.00
80 Raul Ibanez/25 15.00
81 Rich Harden/25 20.00
86 Ken Harvey/25 10.00
89 Wade Miller/25 15.00
91 Jeremy Affeldt/25 12.00
92 Francisco Cordero/25 15.00
95 Laynce Nix/25 12.00
97 Lyle Overbay/25 15.00
98 Carlos Zambrano/25 30.00
101 Mark Buehrle/25 25.00
102 Mark Loretta/25 15.00
106 Marlon Byrd/25 10.00
107 Rafael Furcal/25 25.00
109 Michael Young/25 25.00
110 Miguel Cabrera/25 40.00
128 Magglio Ordonez/25 15.00
134 Sean Burroughs/25 10.00
135 Sean Casey/25 15.00
139 Steve Finley/25 15.00
143 Torii Hunter/25 20.00
144 Travis Hafner/25 20.00
147 Vernon Wells/25 15.00
152 Danny Graves/25 12.00
155 Bubba Nelson/25 10.00
156 Kevin Youkilis/25 25.00
157 Jacque Jones/25 15.00
158 Mike Lieberthal/25 15.00
160 Lew Ford/25 15.00
161 Ervin Santana/25 15.00
162 Jody Gerut/25 15.00
163 Nick Johnson/25 20.00
164 Brian Roberts/25 30.00
165 Joe Nathan/25 20.00
167 Ryan Wagner/25 10.00
168 David Dellucci/25 20.00
169 Jae Weong Seo/25 15.00
170 Tom Gordon/25 15.00
171 Carlos Lee/25 20.00
172 Octavio Dotel/25 12.00
173 Jose Castillo/25 15.00
174 Troy Percival/25 15.00
194 Harmon Killebrew/25 40.00

Mirror Autograph Red

NM/M

Production 1-250
16 Tim Salmon/25 30.00
18 Bobby Crosby/50 25.00
25 Casey Kotchman/50 12.00
33 Orlando Hudson/250 8.00
53 Jack Wilson/50 12.00
62 Eric Byrnes/50 10.00
66 Jeremy Bonderman/50 15.00
67 Jermaine Dye/50 15.00
68 Kazuhito Tadano/100 12.00
79 Edwin Jackson/250 8.00
80 Raul Ibanez/50 12.00
86 Ken Harvey/250 8.00
89 Wade Miller/250 10.00
91 Jeremy Affeldt/250 8.00
92 Francisco Cordero/25 15.00
95 Laynce Nix/100 8.00
106 Marlon Byrd/250 8.00
155 Bubba Nelson/250 6.00
156 Kevin Youkilis/50 20.00
160 Lew Ford/50 12.00
161 Ervin Santana/250 10.00
162 Jody Gerut/50 15.00
164 Brian Roberts/25 30.00
165 Joe Nathan/50 15.00
167 Ryan Wagner/50 10.00
168 David Dellucci/50 15.00
169 Jae Weong Seo/25 15.00
173 Jose Castillo/250 10.00
202 Agustin Montero/99 10.00
211 Norihiro Nakamura/99 50.00
212 Erick Threets/49 10.00
218 Jeff Niemann/49 25.00
221 Justin Verlander/49 30.00
223 Luke Scott/99 15.00
229 Nate McLouth/25 15.00
230 Paulino Reynoso/49 10.00
231 Philip Humber/49 25.00
234 Raul Tablado/99 12.00
239 Sean Tracey/49 10.00
243 Wladimir Balentien/99 15.00

Mirror Bat Blue

NM/M

Production 75-100
Black: No Pricing
Production One Set
Emerald: No Pricing
Production 5 Sets
2 Adam Dunn/100 6.00
5 Albert Pujols/100 20.00
8 Andruw Jones/100 8.00
11 Aubrey Huff/100 4.00
13 B.J. Upton/100 6.00
14 Brandon Webb/100 4.00
16 Tim Salmon/100 4.00
25 Casey Kotchman/100 4.00
26 Chipper Jones/100 8.00
32 David Ortiz/100 10.00
37 Derrek Lee/100 8.00
38 Dontrelle Willis/100 6.00
44 Garret Anderson/100 4.00
45 Gary Sheffield/100 6.00
59 Jason Varitek/100 8.00
61 Javy Lopez/100 4.00
63 Jeff Bagwell/100 6.00
77 Jose Vidro/100 4.00
93 Lance Berkman/100 4.00
99 Manny Ramirez/100 8.00
105 Mark Teixeira/100 6.00
109 Michael Young/100 4.00
110 Miguel Cabrera/5 8.00
111 Miguel Tejada/100 8.00
117 Nomar Garciaparra/100 8.00
121 Paul Konerko/100 4.00
124 Rafael Palmeiro/100 6.00
128 Magglio Ordonez/100 4.00
136 Shawn Green/100 4.00
141 Todd Helton/100 6.00
142 Tom Glavine/100 4.00
143 Torii Hunter/100 4.00
144 Travis Hafner/100 4.00
148 Victor Martinez/100 4.00
149 Vladimir Guerrero/100 8.00
150 Sammy Sosa/100 8.00
153 Rocco Baldelli/100 4.00
160 Lew Ford/100 4.00
166 Mike Sweeney/75 4.00
184 Rafael Palmeiro/100 6.00
188 Tom Glavine/100 4.00
190 Vladimir Guerrero/100 8.00

Mirror Bat Red

NM/M

Production 100-250
Gold: 1X-2X
Production 25 Sets
2 Adam Dunn/250 6.00
5 Albert Pujols/250 15.00
8 Andruw Jones/250 6.00
11 Aubrey Huff/250 4.00
13 B.J. Upton/250 4.00
14 Brandon Webb/100 4.00
16 Tim Salmon/250 4.00
25 Casey Kotchman/250 4.00
26 Chipper Jones/250 6.00
28 Craig Biggio/50 6.00
29 Craig Wilson/250 4.00
34 David Wright/250 10.00
38 Dontrelle Willis/250 4.00
44 Garret Anderson/250 4.00
45 Gary Sheffield/250 6.00
59 Jason Varitek/250 6.00
61 Javy Lopez/250 4.00
63 Jeff Bagwell/250 6.00
77 Jose Vidro/250 4.00
93 Lance Berkman/250 4.00
99 Manny Ramirez/250 8.00
105 Mark Teixeira/250 6.00
109 Michael Young/250 4.00
110 Miguel Cabrera/250 8.00
111 Miguel Tejada/250 8.00
121 Paul Konerko/250 4.00
124 Rafael Palmeiro/250 6.00
128 Magglio Ordonez/250 4.00
136 Shawn Green/250 4.00
141 Todd Helton/250 6.00
142 Tom Glavine/250 4.00
143 Torii Hunter/200 4.00
148 Victor Martinez/250 4.00
149 Vladimir Guerrero/250 8.00
150 Sammy Sosa/250 8.00
153 Rocco Baldelli/250 4.00
160 Lew Ford/250 4.00
166 Mike Sweeney/100 4.00
184 Rafael Palmeiro/100 6.00
188 Tom Glavine/250 4.00
190 Vladimir Guerrero/250 8.00

Mirror Fabric Blue

NM/M

Production 50-100
Black: No Pricing
Production One Set
Emerald: No Pricing
Production 5 Sets
2 Adam Dunn Jsy/100 6.00
5 Albert Pujols Jsy/100 15.00
7 Alfonso Soriano Jsy/100 6.00
8 Andruw Jones Jsy/100 6.00
10 Aramis Ramirez Jsy/100 6.00
11 Aubrey Huff Jsy/100 4.00
13 B.J. Upton Jsy/100 4.00
14 Brandon Webb Pants/100 4.00
15 Barry Zito Jsy/100 4.00
17 Bobby Abreu Jsy/100 4.00
18 Bobby Crosby Jsy/50 6.00
25 Casey Kotchman Jsy/100 4.00
26 Chipper Jones Jsy/100 8.00
28 Craig Biggio Jsy/100 4.00
30 Curt Schilling Jsy/100 8.00
32 David Ortiz Jsy/100 8.00
37 Derrek Lee Jsy/100 8.00
38 Dontrelle Willis Jsy/100 4.00
41 Eric Chavez Jsy/100 4.00
43 Francisco Rodriguez Jsy/100 4.00
44 Garret Anderson Jsy/100 4.00
46 Greg Maddux Jsy/100 10.00
47 Hideki Matsui Pants/100 15.00
48 Hideo Nomo Jsy/100 6.00
50 Ivan Rodriguez Jsy/100 4.00
57 Trot Nixon Jsy/100 4.00
60 Roy Oswalt Jsy/50 4.00
61 Javy Lopez Jsy/100 4.00
63 Jeff Bagwell Jsy/100 6.00
69 Jim Edmonds Jsy/100 6.00
70 Jim Thome Jsy/100 6.00
71 Johan Santana Jsy/100 6.00
73 Johnny Damon Jsy/100 8.00
78 Josh Beckett Jsy/100 4.00
82 Justin Morneau Jsy/100 4.00
84 Kazuo Matsui Jsy/100 4.00
87 Frank Thomas Jsy/100 6.00
88 Kerry Wood Jsy/100 6.00
92 Francisco Cordero Jsy/100 4.00
93 Lance Berkman Jsy/100 4.00
94 Larry Walker Jsy/100 6.00
96 Luis Gonzalez Jsy/100 4.00
97 Lyle Overbay Jsy/100 4.00
98 Carlos Zambrano Jsy/100 6.00
99 Manny Ramirez Jsy/100 8.00
104 Mark Prior Jsy/100 8.00
109 Michael Young Jsy/100 4.00
110 Miguel Cabrera Jsy/100 8.00
111 Miguel Tejada Jsy/100 6.00
113 Mike Mussina Jsy/50 6.00
114 Mike Piazza Jsy/100 8.00
121 Paul Konerko Jsy/100 4.00
124 Rafael Palmeiro Jsy/100 6.00
129 Roger Clemens Jsy/100 10.00
131 Sammy Sosa Jsy/100 8.00
133 Scott Rolen Jsy/100 6.00
135 Sean Casey Jsy/100 4.00
138 Roy Halladay Jsy/100 4.00
141 Todd Helton Jsy/100 6.00
144 Travis Hafner Jsy/100 4.00
147 Vernon Wells Jsy/100 4.00
148 Victor Martinez Jsy/100 4.00
149 Vladimir Guerrero Jsy/100 8.00
151 Hank Blalock Jsy/100 4.00
153 Rocco Baldelli Jsy/100 4.00
159 Ben Sheets Jsy/100 4.00
160 Lew Ford Jsy/100 4.00
166 Mike Sweeney Jsy/100 4.00
178 Greg Maddux Jsy/100 10.00
179 Ivan Rodriguez Jsy/100 4.00
183 Pedro J. Martinez Jsy/100 8.00
184 Rafael Palmeiro Pants/100 6.00
185 Roger Clemens Jsy/100 10.00
188 Tom Glavine Jsy/100 4.00
190 Vladimir Guerrero Jsy/100 8.00

Mirror Fabric Red

NM/M

Production 100-250
Gold: 1X-2X
Production 25 Sets
2 Adam Dunn Jsy/250 6.00
5 Albert Pujols Jsy/250 15.00
7 Alfonso Soriano Jsy/250 6.00
8 Andruw Jones Jsy/250 6.00
10 Aramis Ramirez Jsy/250 4.00
11 Aubrey Huff Jsy/250 4.00
13 B.J. Upton Jsy/250 4.00
14 Brandon Webb Pants/100 4.00
15 Barry Zito Jsy/250 4.00
17 Bobby Abreu Jsy/250 4.00
20 Preston Wilson Jsy/250 4.00

25 Casey Kotchman Jsy/250 4.00
26 Chipper Jones Jsy/250 8.00
28 Craig Biggio Jsy/250 4.00
30 Curt Schilling Jsy/250 8.00
32 David Ortiz Jsy/250 8.00
37 Derrek Lee Jsy/250 8.00
38 Dontrelle Willis Jsy/225 4.00
41 Eric Chavez Jsy/250 4.00
43 Francisco Rodriguez Jsy/250 4.00
44 Garret Anderson Jsy/250 4.00
45 Gary Sheffield Jsy/250 6.00
46 Greg Maddux Jsy/250 10.00
47 Hideki Matsui Jsy/250 15.00
48 Hideo Nomo Jsy/250 6.00
50 Ivan Rodriguez Jsy/250 4.00
57 Trot Nixon Jsy/250 4.00
60 Roy Oswalt Jsy/250 4.00
61 Javy Lopez Jsy/250 4.00
63 Jeff Bagwell Jsy/250 6.00
69 Jim Edmonds Jsy/250 6.00
70 Jim Thome Jsy/250 6.00
71 Johan Santana Jsy/250 6.00
82 Justin Morneau Jsy/250 4.00
84 Kazuo Matsui Jsy/250 4.00
87 Frank Thomas Jsy/250 6.00
88 Kerry Wood Jsy/250 6.00
92 Francisco Cordero Jsy/250 4.00
93 Lance Berkman Jsy/250 4.00
94 Larry Walker Jsy/250 6.00
96 Luis Gonzalez Jsy/250 4.00
97 Lyle Overbay Jsy/250 4.00
98 Carlos Zambrano Jsy/250 4.00
99 Manny Ramirez Jsy/250 8.00
104 Mark Prior Jsy/250 8.00
109 Michael Young Jsy/250 4.00
110 Miguel Cabrera Jsy/250 8.00
111 Miguel Tejada Jsy/250 6.00
114 Mike Piazza Jsy/250 8.00
121 Paul Konerko Jsy/250 4.00
124 Rafael Palmeiro Jsy/250 6.00
129 Roger Clemens Jsy/250 10.00
131 Sammy Sosa Jsy/250 8.00
133 Scott Rolen Jsy/250 6.00
135 Sean Casey Jsy/250 4.00
138 Roy Halladay Jsy/250 4.00
141 Todd Helton Jsy/250 6.00
144 Travis Hafner Jsy/250 4.00
147 Vernon Wells Jsy/250 4.00
148 Victor Martinez Jsy/250 4.00
149 Vladimir Guerrero Jsy/250 8.00
153 Rocco Baldelli Jsy/250 4.00
159 Ben Sheets Jsy/250 4.00
160 Lew Ford Jsy/250 4.00
166 Mike Sweeney Jsy/250 4.00
178 Greg Maddux Jsy/250 10.00
179 Ivan Rodriguez Jsy/250 4.00
183 Pedro J. Martinez Jsy/250 8.00
184 Rafael Palmeiro Jsy/250 6.00
185 Roger Clemens Jsy/250 10.00
188 Tom Glavine Jsy/250 4.00
190 Vladimir Guerrero Jsy/100 8.00

Mirror Fabric White

NM/M

Production 50-250
2 Adam Dunn Jsy/250 6.00
5 Albert Pujols Jsy/100 15.00
7 Alfonso Soriano Jsy/100 6.00
8 Andruw Jones Jsy/100 6.00
10 Aramis Ramirez Jsy/100 6.00
11 Aubrey Huff Jsy/150 4.00
13 B.J. Upton Jsy/250 4.00
15 Barry Zito Jsy/100 4.00
26 Chipper Jones Jsy/250 8.00
28 Craig Biggio Pants/250 4.00
30 Curt Schilling Jsy/100 8.00
32 David Ortiz Jsy/100 8.00
34 David Wright Jsy/100 10.00
38 Dontrelle Willis Jsy/50 4.00
41 Eric Chavez Jsy/100 4.00
44 Garret Anderson Jsy/100 4.00
45 Gary Sheffield Jsy/50 6.00
46 Greg Maddux Jsy/50 10.00
47 Hideki Matsui Pants/100 15.00
48 Hideo Nomo Jsy/100 6.00
57 Trot Nixon Jsy/100 4.00
60 Roy Oswalt Jsy/25 6.00
63 Jeff Bagwell Jsy/100 6.00
69 Jim Edmonds Jsy/100 6.00
70 Jim Thome Jsy/100 6.00
71 Johan Santana Jsy/100 6.00
78 Josh Beckett Jsy/250 4.00
82 Justin Morneau Jsy/100 4.00
84 Kazuo Matsui Jsy/250 4.00
88 Kerry Wood Jsy/50 6.00
93 Lance Berkman Jsy/250 4.00
94 Larry Walker Jsy/100 6.00
95 Laynce Nix Jsy/100 4.00
96 Luis Gonzalez Jsy/250 4.00
98 Carlos Zambrano Jsy/100 6.00
99 Manny Ramirez Jsy/100 8.00
104 Mark Prior Jsy/100 8.00
109 Michael Young Jsy/100 4.00
110 Miguel Cabrera Jsy/150 8.00
111 Miguel Tejada Jsy/100 8.00
113 Mike Mussina Jsy/100 6.00
114 Mike Piazza Jsy/100 8.00
121 Paul Konerko Jsy/150 4.00
124 Rafael Palmeiro Jsy/150 6.00
129 Roger Clemens Jsy/100 10.00
131 Sammy Sosa Jsy/150 8.00
133 Scott Rolen Jsy/100 6.00
135 Sean Casey Jsy/100 4.00
138 Roy Halladay Jsy/100 4.00
141 Todd Helton Jsy/100 6.00
144 Travis Hafner Jsy/100 4.00
147 Vernon Wells Jsy/250 4.00
148 Victor Martinez Jsy/250 4.00
149 Vladimir Guerrero Jsy/250 8.00
151 Hank Blalock Jsy/100 4.00
159 Ben Sheets Jsy/100 4.00
166 Mike Sweeney Jsy/50 4.00
178 Greg Maddux Jsy/200 10.00
179 Ivan Rodriguez Jsy/250 4.00
184 Rafael Palmeiro Jsy/250 6.00
185 Roger Clemens Jsy/100 10.00
188 Tom Glavine Jsy/250 4.00

Skills

NM/M

Common: 1.50
Inserted 1:7
Mirror: 2X-3X
1 Andy Pettitte 1.50
2 Barry Zito 1.50
3 Bobby Crosby 2.00
4 Brandon Webb 1.50
5 Craig Biggio 2.00
6 David Ortiz 3.00
7 Dontrelle Willis 2.00
8 Francisco Rodriguez 1.50
9 Gary Sheffield 2.00
10 Jack Wilson 1.50
11 Jason Bay 1.50
12 Jeff Bagwell 2.00
13 Jim Edmonds 2.00
14 Josh Beckett 1.50
15 Kerry Wood 2.00
16 Lance Berkman 1.50
17 Mark Buehrle 1.50
18 Mark Teixeira 2.00
19 Miguel Tejada 2.00
20 Paul Konerko 1.50
21 Scott Rolen 2.00
22 Sean Burroughs 1.50
23 Vernon Wells 1.50
24 Victor Martinez 1.50
25 Vladimir Guerrero 3.00

Skills Autographs

NM/M

Production 5-25
3 Bobby Crosby/25 25.00
11 Jason Bay/25 25.00

Skills Jersey Position

NM/M

Production 100-250
Prime: No Pricing
Production 5-25
1 Andy Pettitte/250 4.00
2 Barry Zito/250 4.00
3 Bobby Crosby/100 6.00
4 Brandon Webb Pants/100 4.00
5 Craig Biggio/250 4.00
6 David Ortiz/250 8.00
7 Dontrelle Willis/100 4.00
8 Francisco Rodriguez/250 4.00
9 Gary Sheffield/50 6.00
10 Jack Wilson/50 4.00
11 Jason Bay/100 4.00
12 Jeff Bagwell/250 6.00
13 Jim Edmonds/250 6.00
14 Josh Beckett/250 4.00
15 Kerry Wood/50 6.00
16 Lance Berkman/250 4.00
17 Mark Buehrle/150 4.00
19 Miguel Tejada/250 8.00
20 Paul Konerko/100 4.00
21 Scott Rolen/100 6.00
22 Sean Burroughs/100 4.00
23 Vernon Wells/250 4.00
24 Victor Martinez/250 4.00
25 Vladimir Guerrero/250 8.00

2005 LEAF LIMITED

NM/M

Complete Set (205):
Common Player (1-150): 1.00
Production 699
Common (151-175, 197): 4.00
Production 99
Commmon Auto (176-196, 198-200): 12.00
Production 99
Pack (4): 60.00
1 Roger Clemens 5.00
2 Roger Clemens 5.00
3 Ichiro Suzuki 4.00
4 Ichiro Suzuki 4.00
5 Todd Helton 1.50
6 Todd Helton 1.50
7 Vladimir Guerrero 2.00
8 Vladimir Guerrero 2.00
9 Miguel Cabrera 2.00
10 Miguel Cabrera 2.00
11 Albert Pujols 5.00
12 Albert Pujols 5.00
13 Mark Prior 2.00
14 Mark Prior 2.00
15 Chipper Jones 2.00
16 Chipper Jones 2.00
17 Jeff Bagwell 1.50
18 Jeff Bagwell 1.50
19 Kerry Wood 1.00
20 Kerry Wood 1.00
21 Gary Sheffield 1.50
22 Carl Crawford 1.00
23 Mariano Rivera 1.50
24 Curt Schilling 2.00
25 Ben Sheets 1.00
26 Jimmy Rollins 1.00
27 Melvin Mora 1.00
28 Corey Patterson 1.00
29 Rafael Furcal 1.00
30 Jim Thome 1.50
31 Derek Jeter 5.00
32 Jake Peavy 1.50
33 Francisco Cordero 1.00
34 Aramis Ramirez 1.50
35 Javy Lopez 1.00
36 Aaron Rowand 1.00
37 Jason Bay 1.00
38 Michael Young 1.00
39 Ivan Rodriguez 1.50
40 Joe Nathan 1.00
41 Oliver Perez 1.00
42 Adam Dunn 1.50
43 Eric Chavez 1.00
44 Pedro Martinez 2.00
45 Roy Oswalt 1.00
46 Carlos Delgado 1.00
47 Jeff Kent 1.00
48 Johnny Damon 2.00
49 Edgar Renteria 1.00
50 Mark Buehrle 1.00
51 Carl Pavano 1.00
52 J.D. Drew 1.00
53 Hank Blalock 1.00
54 Moises Alou 1.00
55 Brad Radke 1.00
56 Brad Wilkerson 1.00
57 Sean Casey 1.00
58 Mike Lowell 1.00
59 Octavio Dotel 1.00
60 Francisco Rodriguez 1.00
61 Jose Guillen 1.00
62 Greg Maddux 3.00
63 A.J. Burnett 1.00
64 Chris Carpenter 1.00
65 Jose Reyes 1.00
66 Travis Hafner 1.00
67 Rich Harden 1.00
68 Bret Boone 1.00
69 Scott Podsednik 1.00
70 Andruw Jones 1.50
71 Milton Bradley 1.00
72 Zack Greinke 1.00
73 Torii Hunter 1.00
74 Paul Konerko 1.50
75 David Wells 1.00
76 Tim Hudson 1.50
77 Sammy Sosa 2.50
78 Jason Varitek 1.50
79 Lance Berkman 1.00
80 Justin Morneau 1.00
81 Troy Glaus 1.00
82 Jose Vidro 1.00
83 Joe Mauer 1.50
84 Josh Beckett 1.00
85 Craig Biggio 1.00
86 Luis Gonzalez 1.00
87 Larry Walker 1.00
88 Barry Zito 1.00
89 Jacque Jones 1.00
90 Lyle Overbay 1.00
91 Roy Halladay 1.50
92 Orlando Cabrera 1.00
93 Magglio Ordonez 1.00
94 Mike Sweeney 1.00
95 Rafael Palmeiro 1.50
96 Brandon Webb 1.00
97 Preston Wilson 1.00
98 Shannon Stewart 1.00
99 Trot Nixon 1.00
100 Mike Piazza 2.50
101 Dontrelle Willis 1.50
102 Ken Griffey Jr. 3.00
103 Andy Pettitte 1.00
104 Kazuo Matsui 1.00
105 Bobby Crosby 1.00
106 Shawn Green 1.00
107 Alfonso Soriano 2.00
108 Carlos Zambrano 1.00
109 Keith Foulke 1.00
110 Aubrey Huff 1.00
111 Adrian Beltre 1.00
112 Mark Teixeira 1.50
113 Randy Johnson 2.00
114 Miguel Tejada 1.50
115 Alex Rodriguez 4.00
116 Carlos Beltran 1.50
117 Bobby Abreu 1.50
118 Johan Santana 1.50
119 Manny Ramirez 2.00
120 Juan Pierre 1.00
121 Scott Rolen 1.50
122 Livan Hernandez 1.00
123 Carlos Lee 1.00
124 Derrek Lee 1.50
125 Brian Giles 1.00
126 Nomar Garciaparra 2.00
127 John Smoltz 1.50
128 Jim Edmonds 1.50
129 Bartolo Colon 1.00
130 Garret Anderson 1.00
131 Austin Kearns 1.00
132 Shingo Takatsu 1.00
133 Omar Vizquel 1.00
134 Tom Glavine 1.00
135 Mark Mulder 1.50
136 Bernie Williams 1.00
137 Richie Sexson 1.00
138 Mike Mussina 1.50
139 Mark Loretta 1.00
140 Vernon Wells 1.00
141 David Wright 2.00
142 Marcus Giles 1.00
143 David Ortiz 2.00
144 Victor Martinez 1.00
145 Hideki Matsui 4.00
146 C.C. Sabathia 1.00
147 Angel Berroa 1.00
148 Troy Percival 1.00
149 Paul LoDuca 1.00
150 Jorge Posada 1.50
151 Willie Mays 8.00
152 Ryne Sandberg 8.00
153 Rickey Henderson 4.00
154 Ted Williams 10.00
155 Roberto Clemente 10.00
156 George Brett 8.00
157 Whitey Ford 4.00
158 Duke Snider 4.00
159 Don Mattingly 10.00
160 Bob Gibson 4.00
161 Hank Aaron 8.00
162 Al Kaline 6.00
163 Nolan Ryan 10.00
164 Stan Musial 6.00
165 George Kell 4.00
166 Harmon Killebrew 6.00
167 Cal Ripken Jr. 15.00
168 Babe Ruth 10.00
169 Roger Clemens SP 8.00
170 Curt Schilling SP 4.00
171 Rafael Palmeiro SP 4.00
172 Randy Johnson SP 5.00

173 Mike Piazza SP 5.00
174 Greg Maddux SP 6.00
175 Sammy Sosa SP 5.00
176 *Hayden Penn Auto* 15.00
177 *Ambiorix Concepcion Auto* 15.00
178 *Casey Rogowski Auto* 12.00
179 Prince Fielder Auto 85.00
180 *Geovany Soto Auto* 15.00
181 *Wladimir Balentien Auto* 25.00
182 *Jason Hammel Auto* 15.00
183 *Keiichi Yabu Auto* 25.00
184 *Brandon McCarthy Auto* 50.00
185 *Ubaldo Jimenez Auto* 15.00
186 *Keiichi Yabu Auto* 25.00
187 *Miguel Negron Auto* 15.00
188 *Mike Morse Auto* 25.00
189 *Nate McLouth Auto* 15.00
190 *Norihiro Nakamura Auto* 40.00
191 *Bill McCarthy Auto* 50.00
192 *Tony Pena Auto* 12.00
193 *Ambiorix Concepcion Auto* 15.00
194 *Raul Tablado Auto* 15.00
195 *Hayden Penn Auto* 15.00
196 *Sean Thompson Auto* 15.00
197 *Tadahito Iguchi* 15.00
198 *Ubaldo Jimenez Auto* 15.00
199 *Wladimir Balentien Auto* 25.00
200 *Prince Fielder Auto* 85.00
201 *Philip Humber Auto/99* 40.00
202 *Jeff Niemann Auto/95* 40.00
203 *Justin Verlander Auto/70* 50.00
205 *Yuniesky Betancourt Auto/99* 50.00

Bronze Spotlight

Bronze (1-150): 1-1.5X
Bronze (151-175): 1X
Bronze (176-200): .25X
Production 99 Sets

Gold Spotlight

Gold (1-150): 2-4X
Gold (151-175): 2-3X
Production 25 Sets
Gold (176-205): No Pricing
Production 5-25

Platinum Spotlight

No Pricing
Production One Set

Silver Spotlight

Silver (1-150): 1-2X
Silver (151-175): 1-1.5X
Silver (176-200): .25X
Production 50 Sets

Cuts Silver

NM/M

Production 7-99
Platinum: No Pricing
Production One Set
1 Orlando Cepeda/30 35.00
2 Hank Aaron/44 275.00
3 Willie Mays/24 175.00
4 Sandy Koufax/32 400.00
5 Cal Ripken Jr./25 150.00
6 Nolan Ryan/34 120.00
7 Jim Palmer/22 30.00
8 Tony Gwynn/19 60.00
9 Rod Carew/29 40.00
10 Ryne Sandberg/23 70.00
11 Stan Musial/28 70.00
12 Steve Carlton/32 30.00
14 Mike Schmidt/20 60.00
15 Harmon Killebrew/25 40.00
17 Duke Snider/53 30.00
18 Don Mattingly/25 50.00
19 Dale Murphy/25 35.00
20 Craig Biggio/7
21 Juan Marichal/99 25.00
22 Greg Maddux/37 10.00
23 Lou Brock/20
24 Paul Molitor/25 35.00
25 Wade Boggs/26 40.00
26 Mark Prior/27 40.00
28 Al Kaline/28 40.00

Cuts Gold

Production 3-30
No Pricing

Legends

NM/M

Common Player:
Production 50 Sets
Foil: No Pricing
Production 10 Sets
1 Billy Martin 4.00
2 Bobby Doerr 3.00
3 Carlton Fisk 4.00
4 Harmon Killebrew 5.00
5 Duke Snider 5.00
6 George Brett 6.00
7 Johnny Bench 5.00
8 Lou Boudreau 3.00
9 Brooks Robinson 4.00
10 Al Kaline 4.00
11 Stan Musial 5.00
12 Burleigh Grimes 3.00
13 Cal Ripken Jr. 10.00
14 Carl Yastrzemski 6.00
15 Willie Stargell 3.00
16 Yogi Berra 4.00
17 Enos Slaughter 3.00
18 Phil Rizzuto 3.00
19 Luis Aparicio 3.00
20 Ernie Banks 5.00
21 Hal Newhouser 3.00
22 Whitey Ford 4.00
23 Tony Gwynn 4.00
24 Bob Feller 4.00
25 Don Sutton 3.00
26 Lou Brock 3.00
27 Jim Palmer 3.00
28 Billy Williams 2.00
29 Juan Marichal 3.00
30 Rod Carew 3.00
31 Jim "Catfish" Hunter 2.00
32 Maury Wills 2.00
33 Joe Cronin 2.00
34 Fergie Jenkins 2.00
35 Sandy Koufax 5.00
36 Steve Carlton 3.00
37 Eddie Murray 3.00
38 Roger Maris 4.00
39 Gaylord Perry 2.00
40 Bob Gibson 3.00
41 Tom Seaver 3.00
42 Dennis Eckersley 2.00
43 Reggie Jackson 3.00
44 Willie McCovey 3.00
45 Willie Mays 6.00
46 Willie Mays 6.00
47 Rickey Henderson 3.00
48 Rickey Henderson 3.00
49 Nolan Ryan 6.00
50 Nolan Ryan 6.00

Legends Jersey Number

NM/M

Production 1-45
3 Carlton Fisk/50 10.00
25 Don Sutton/20 8.00
26 Lou Brock/20 10.00
27 Jim Palmer/22 8.00
28 Billy Williams/26 8.00
29 Juan Marichal/27 8.00
30 Rod Carew/29 10.00
31 Jim "Catfish" Hunter Pants/29 8.00
34 Fergie Jenkins/31 6.00
35 Sandy Koufax/32 250.00
36 Steve Carlton/32 8.00
37 Eddie Murray/33 12.00
39 Gaylord Perry/36 6.00
40 Bob Gibson/45 10.00
41 Tom Seaver/41 10.00
42 Dennis Eckersley/45 5.00
43 Reggie Jackson Pants/44 8.00
44 Willie McCovey/44 10.00
45 Willie Mays/24 40.00
46 Willie Mays/24 40.00
49 Nolan Ryan/30 25.00
50 Nolan Ryan/30 25.00

Legends Jersey Number Prime

NM/M

Production 1-25
3 Carlton Fisk/25 12.00
6 George Brett/25 20.00
13 Cal Ripken Jr./25 50.00
15 Willie Stargell/25 20.00
23 Tony Gwynn/25 25.00
26 Lou Brock/25 20.00
40 Bob Gibson/25 20.00
42 Dennis Eckersley/25 15.00
47 Rickey Henderson/25 20.00
48 Rickey Henderson/25 20.00

Legends Signature

NM/M

Production 2-50
2 Bobby Doerr/50 15.00
4 Harmon Killebrew/50 30.00
5 Duke Snider/25 35.00
9 Brooks Robinson/50 25.00
10 Al Kaline/50 40.00
18 Phil Rizzuto/50 35.00
19 Luis Aparicio/50 20.00
24 Bob Feller/50 25.00
25 Don Sutton/50 15.00
26 Lou Brock/50 30.00
27 Jim Palmer/50 20.00
28 Billy Williams/25 20.00
29 Juan Marichal/50 25.00
30 Rod Carew/25 35.00
32 Maury Wills/50 15.00
34 Fergie Jenkins/50 15.00
36 Steve Carlton/50 25.00
39 Gaylord Perry/50 15.00
40 Bob Gibson/25 40.00
42 Dennis Eckersley/50 20.00

Legends Signature Jersey Number Prime

NM/M

42 Dennis Eckersley/25 30.00

Legends Signature Jersey Number

NM/M

Production 5-30
2 Bobby Doerr Pants/25 25.00
4 Harmon Killebrew/25 40.00
11 Stan Musial/25 65.00
13 Cal Ripken Jr./25 150.00
18 Phil Rizzuto Pants/25 40.00
19 Luis Aparicio/25 25.00
23 Tony Gwynn/25 40.00
25 Don Sutton/20 20.00
27 Jim Palmer/22 25.00
34 Fergie Jenkins/25 20.00
36 Steve Carlton/25 30.00
39 Gaylord Perry/25 20.00
40 Bob Gibson/25 40.00
42 Dennis Eckersley/25 25.00
44 Willie McCovey/25 40.00
45 Willie Mays/24 160.00
46 Willie Mays/24 160.00
49 Nolan Ryan/30 90.00
50 Nolan Ryan/30 90.00

Lettermen

NM/M

Production 4-21
DU-H Dale Murphy H/20 150.00
DU-M Dale Murphy M/20 150.00
DU-P Dale Murphy P/20 150.00
DU-R Dale Murphy R/20 150.00
DU-U Dale Murphy U/20 150.00
DU-Y Dale Murphy Y/20 150.00
NR-A Nolan Ryan A/21 200.00
NR-N Nolan Ryan N/21 200.00
NR-R Nolan Ryan R/21 200.00
NR-Y Nolan Ryan Y/21 200.00

Lumberjacks

NM/M

Common Player:
Production 50 Sets
Foil: No Pricing
1 Al Kaline 4.00
2 Albert Pujols 8.00
3 Andre Dawson 3.00
4 Babe Ruth 8.00
5 Cal Ripken Jr. 15.00
6 Chipper Jones 4.00
7 Dale Murphy 3.00
8 Dave Winfield 3.00
9 Don Mattingly 6.00
10 Duke Snider 4.00
11 Eddie Murray 3.00
12 Frank Robinson 4.00
13 Frank Thomas 4.00
14 Gary Carter 3.00
15 Hack Wilson 3.00
16 Hank Aaron 10.00
17 Harmon Killebrew 4.00
18 Joe Morgan 3.00
19 Johnny Bench 4.00
20 Kirby Puckett 4.00
21 Kirk Gibson 3.00
22 Manny Ramirez 4.00
23 Mark Grace 3.00
24 Mike Piazza 5.00
25 Mike Schmidt 6.00
26 Orlando Cepeda 3.00
27 Paul Molitor 4.00
28 Rafael Palmeiro 4.00
29 Ralph Kiner 3.00
30 Reggie Jackson 4.00
31 Richie Ashburn 3.00
32 Rickey Henderson 4.00
33 Robin Yount 5.00
34 Rod Carew 4.00
35 Ryne Sandberg 6.00
36 Stan Musial 5.00
37 Ted Williams 8.00
38 Tony Gwynn 4.00
39 Vladimir Guerrero 4.00
40 Willie Mays 8.00
41 Ernie Banks, Bernie Williams 6.00
42 Ted Williams, Joe Cronin 10.00
43 George Brett, Bo Jackson 8.00
44 John Kruk, Jim Thome 3.00
45 Willie Mays, Jim Thorpe 8.00
46 Wade Boggs, Johnny Damon 6.00
47 M. Williams, W. Clark 3.00
48 Willie Stargell, D. Parker 4.00
49 Ichiro Suzuki, Edgar Martinez 6.00
50 Carl Yastrzemski, Carlton Fisk 6.00

Lumberjacks Barrel

No Pricing
Production 1-5

Lumberjacks Bat

NM/M

Production 1-50
1 Al Kaline/50 10.00
4 Babe Ruth/25 180.00
8 Dave Winfield/50 10.00
11 Eddie Murray/25 15.00
12 Frank Robinson/50 15.00
14 Gary Carter/25 10.00
15 Hack Wilson/50 40.00
16 Hank Aaron/50 40.00
18 Joe Morgan/25 8.00
19 Johnny Bench/50 10.00
20 Kirby Puckett/50 10.00
25 Mike Schmidt/50 15.00
26 Orlando Cepeda/25 8.00
27 Paul Molitor/50 8.00
29 Ralph Kiner/25 15.00
31 Richie Ashburn/25 15.00
33 Robin Yount/25 20.00
35 Ryne Sandberg/25 20.00
36 Stan Musial/50 20.00
37 Ted Williams/50 40.00
40 Willie Mays/50 30.00
43 George Brett, Bo Jackson/50 25.00
47 M. Williams, W. Clark/50 15.00
48 Willie Stargell, D. Parker/50 15.00
50 Carl Yastrzemski, Carlton Fisk/50 20.00

Lumberjacks Combos

NM/M

Production 1-50
2 Albert Pujols Bat-Jsy/50 30.00
5 Cal Ripken Jr. Bat-Jsy/50 35.00
6 Chipper Jones Bat-Jsy/25 15.00
7 Dale Murphy Bat-Jsy/50 12.00
8 Dave Winfield Bat-Pants/50 8.00
11 Eddie Murray Bat-Jsy/25 20.00
13 Frank Thomas Bat-Jsy/25 15.00
16 Hank Aaron Bat-Jsy/25 60.00
19 Johnny Bench Bat-Jsy/25 15.00
20 Kirby Puckett Bat-Jsy/25 15.00
21 Kirk Gibson Bat-Jsy/50 8.00
22 Manny Ramirez Bat-Jsy/50 12.00
23 Mark Grace Bat-Jsy/50 12.00
24 Mike Piazza Bat-Jsy/50 15.00
25 Mike Schmidt Bat-Jsy/25 25.00
26 Orlando Cepeda Bat-Pants/50 8.00
27 Paul Molitor Bat-Jsy/50 12.00
31 Richie Ashburn Bat-Jsy/25 15.00

33 Robin Yount Bat-Jsy/50 15.00
34 Rod Carew Bat-Jsy/5
36 Stan Musial Bat-Jsy/25 35.00
40 Willie Mays Bat-Jsy/25 50.00

Lumberjacks Combos Prime

NM/M

Production 1-50
2 Albert Pujols Bat-Jsy/50 35.00
3 Andre Dawson Bat-Jsy/50 8.00
5 Cal Ripken Jr. Bat-Jsy/25 50.00
6 Chipper Jones Bat-Jsy/50 15.00
11 Eddie Murray Bat-Jsy/25 25.00
12 Frank Robinson Bat-Jsy/50 12.00
13 Frank Thomas Bat-Jsy/50 15.00
14 Gary Carter Bat-Jsy/50 10.00
18 Joe Morgan Bat-Jsy/25 15.00
21 Kirk Gibson Bat-Jsy/50 8.00
22 Manny Ramirez Bat-Jsy/25 20.00
24 Mike Piazza Bat-Jsy/50 15.00
28 Rafael Palmeiro Bat-Jsy/50 12.00
32 Rickey Henderson Bat-Jsy/25 15.00
33 Robin Yount Bat-Jsy/50 25.00
34 Rod Carew Bat-Jsy/50 12.00
39 Vladimir Guerrero Bat-Jsy/50 15.00

Lumberjacks Jersey

NM/M

Production 1-50
4 Babe Ruth/25 250.00
8 Dave Winfield Pants/50 6.00
10 Duke Snider Pants/50 10.00
11 Eddie Murray/25 15.00
14 Gary Carter/50 5.00
16 Hank Aaron/25 40.00
19 Johnny Bench/25 15.00
20 Kirby Puckett/25 15.00
27 Paul Molitor/50 8.00
30 Reggie Jackson/50 10.00
31 Richie Ashburn/50 10.00
33 Robin Yount/50 12.00
35 Ryne Sandberg/50 12.00
36 Stan Musial/25 25.00
37 Ted Williams/25 50.00
40 Willie Mays/25 35.00
41 Ernie Banks, Bernie Williams/25 30.00
42 Ted Williams, Joe Cronin/25 60.00
43 George Brett, Bo Jackson/50 30.00
44 John Kruk, Jim Thome/25 20.00
45 Willie Mays, Jim Thorpe/25 200.00
46 Wade Boggs, Johnny Damon/50 20.00
47 M. Williams, W. Clark/50 20.00
48 Willie Stargell, D. Parker/25 25.00

Lumberjacks Jersey Prime

NM/M

2 Albert Pujols/25 40.00
3 Andre Dawson/50 10.00
5 Cal Ripken Jr./25 50.00
6 Chipper Jones/50 20.00
11 Eddie Murray/25 25.00
12 Frank Robinson/25 10.00
13 Frank Thomas/50 15.00
14 Gary Carter/50 10.00
21 Kirk Gibson/50 10.00
24 Mike Piazza/50 15.00
25 Mike Schmidt/25 30.00
28 Rafael Palmeiro/50 15.00
32 Rickey Henderson/25 20.00
33 Robin Yount/50 25.00
34 Rod Carew/50 15.00
35 Ryne Sandberg/25 30.00
38 Tony Gwynn/50 20.00
39 Vladimir Guerrero/25 20.00

Lumberjacks Signature

NM/M

Production 1-50
1 Al Kaline/50 40.00
3 Andre Dawson/25 20.00
5 Cal Ripken Jr./21 120.00
9 Don Mattingly/50 50.00
10 Duke Snider/50 25.00
12 Frank Robinson/50 30.00
13 Frank Thomas/25 50.00
14 Gary Carter/50 20.00
17 Harmon Killebrew/50 35.00
18 Joe Morgan/25 25.00
19 Johnny Bench/50 40.00
20 Kirby Puckett/25 40.00
23 Mark Grace/25 35.00
25 Mike Schmidt/50 40.00
27 Paul Molitor/50 30.00
29 Ralph Kiner/50 30.00
34 Rod Carew/50 25.00
35 Ryne Sandberg/50 40.00
36 Stan Musial/50 50.00
38 Tony Gwynn/50 35.00
40 Willie Mays/25 140.00

Lumberjacks Signature Combos Prime

Production 1-25
No Pricing

Lumberjacks Signature Jersey Prime

NM/M

Production 1-25
3 Andre Dawson/25 30.00
5 Cal Ripken Jr./25 160.00
7 Dale Murphy/25 50.00
12 Frank Robinson/25 35.00
14 Gary Carter/25 30.00

Lumberjacks Signature Bat

NM/M

Production 1-100
1 Al Kaline/50 40.00
3 Andre Dawson/100 20.00
5 Cal Ripken Jr./25 140.00
7 Dale Murphy/100 25.00
9 Don Mattingly/50 50.00
12 Frank Robinson/100 35.00
13 Frank Thomas/25 50.00
14 Gary Carter/25 25.00
18 Joe Morgan/50 25.00
19 Johnny Bench/25 50.00
21 Kirk Gibson/25 25.00
23 Mark Grace/25 40.00
26 Orlando Cepeda/100 20.00
27 Paul Molitor/25 40.00
29 Ralph Kiner/100 30.00
33 Robin Yount/25 50.00
34 Rod Carew/25 30.00
36 Stan Musial/25 65.00
38 Tony Gwynn/50 40.00

Lumberjacks Signature Combos

NM/M

Production 1-100
3 Andre Dawson Bat-Jsy/100 20.00
5 Cal Ripken Jr. Bat-Jsy/25 140.00
7 Dale Murphy Bat-Jsy/100 25.00
9 Don Mattingly Bat-Jsy/50 50.00
13 Frank Thomas Bat-Jsy/25 50.00
14 Gary Carter Bat-Jsy/25 25.00
23 Mark GraceBat-Jsy/25 40.00
38 Tony Gwynn Bat-Jsy/25 45.00

Lumberjacks Signature Jersey

NM/M

Production 1-100
3 Andre Dawson/100 20.00
5 Cal Ripken Jr./25 140.00
7 Dale Murphy/100 25.00
9 Don Mattingly/50 50.00
10 Duke Snider Pants/50 30.00
13 Frank Thomas/25 50.00
14 Gary Carter/50 25.00
17 Harmon Killebrew/25 40.00
19 Johnny Bench/25 50.00
23 Mark Grace/25 40.00
27 Paul Molitor/25 40.00
30 Reggie Jackson/25 40.00
33 Robin Yount/25 50.00
38 Tony Gwynn/50 40.00

Matching Numbers

NM/M

Production 5-50
Prime: No Pricing
Production 1-5
1 Ted Williams, Roger Maris/25 160.00
2 Nolan Ryan, Kerry Wood/50 35.00
3 Cal Ripken Jr., Gary Carter/50 40.00
4 Willie Mays, Rickey Henderson/25
5 Johnny Bench, Albert Pujols/50 40.00
6 Roger Clemens, W. Clark/50 35.00
7 Willie McCovey, Reggie Jackson/25 20.00
8 Ryne Sandberg, Don Mattingly/50 35.00
9 Duke Snider, Joe Cronin/25 25.00

Monikers Bronze

NM/M

Production 1-100
9 Miguel Cabrera/100 25.00
10 Miguel Cabrera/100 25.00
13 Mark Prior/50 35.00
14 Mark Prior/50 35.00
25 Ben Sheets/100 15.00
27 Melvin Mora/50 15.00
29 Rafael Furcal/25 20.00
32 Jake Peavy/50 25.00
33 Francisco Cordero/25 15.00
38 Michael Young/25 25.00
40 Joe Nathan/25 20.00
43 Eric Chavez/25 25.00
45 Roy Oswalt/50 25.00
49 Edgar Renteria/25 20.00
50 Mark Buehrle/25 30.00
57 Sean Casey/50 15.00
59 Octavio Dotel/25 12.00
60 Francisco Rodriguez/25 30.00
61 Jose Guillen/25 20.00
66 Travis Hafner/50 15.00
67 Rich Harden/50 15.00
71 Milton Bradley/25 15.00
73 Torii Hunter/25 25.00
74 Paul Konerko/50 30.00
76 Tim Hudson/25 25.00
80 Justin Morneau/100 15.00
82 Jose Vidro/25 15.00
84 Josh Beckett/25 30.00
85 Craig Biggio/25 30.00
89 Jacque Jones/50 15.00
91 Roy Halladay/25 15.00
93 Magglio Ordonez/100 15.00
96 Brandon Webb/50 15.00
97 Preston Wilson/50 15.00
98 Shannon Stewart/50 10.00
99 Trot Nixon/50 20.00
105 Bobby Crosby/40 15.00
107 Alfonso Soriano/25 30.00
108 Carlos Zambrano/50 25.00
109 Keith Foulke/25 30.00
110 Aubrey Huff/50 15.00
112 Mark Teixeira/100 25.00
116 Carlos Beltran/25 30.00
118 Johan Santana/100 30.00
121 Scott Rolen/25 30.00
123 Carlos Lee/50 20.00
124 Derrek Lee/50 25.00
130 Garret Anderson/100 15.00
131 Austin Kearns/100 15.00
133 Omar Vizquel/50 20.00
135 Mark Mulder/50 20.00
139 Mark Loretta/25 20.00
141 David Wright/50 50.00
144 Victor Martinez/25 15.00
151 Willie Mays/25 175.00
152 Ryne Sandberg/25 50.00
158 Duke Snider/50 25.00
159 Don Mattingly/25 50.00
160 Bob Gibson/50 50.00
162 Al Kaline/50 30.00
163 Nolan Ryan/25 80.00
164 Stan Musial/25 60.00
165 George Kell/50 15.00
166 Harmon Killebrew/50 30.00
167 Cal Ripken Jr./25 120.00
176 Hayden Penn/50 20.00
177 Ambiorix Concepcion/50 15.00
179 Prince Fielder/50 100.00
181 Wladimir Balentien/50 30.00
182 Jason Hammel/50 15.00
183 Keiichi Yabu/50 25.00
184 Brandon McCarthy/50 50.00
185 Ubaldo Jimenez/50 15.00
186 Keiichi Yabu/50 25.00
187 Miguel Negron/50 10.00
188 Mike Morse/50 30.00
189 Nate McLouth/50 15.00
190 Norihiro Nakamura/50 50.00
191 Brandon McCarthy/50 50.00
192 Tony Pena/50 10.00
193 Ambiorix Concepcion/50 15.00
194 Raul Tablado/50 15.00
195 Hayden Penn/50 20.00
196 Sean Thompson/50 12.00
198 Ubaldo Jimenez/50 15.00
199 Wladimir Balentien/50 30.00
200 Prince Fielder/50 100.00

Monikers Material Bat Bronze

NM/M

Production 1-100
Platinum: No Pricing
Production One Set
9 Miguel Cabrera/50 35.00
10 Miguel Cabrera/50 35.00
13 Mark Prior/25 40.00
14 Mark Prior/25 40.00
29 Rafael Furcal/75 15.00
34 Aramis Ramirez/100 20.00
37 Jason Bay/100 20.00
38 Michael Young/100 20.00
43 Eric Chavez/50 20.00
45 Roy Oswalt/50 25.00
50 Mark Buehrle/50 25.00
57 Sean Casey/25 15.00
66 Travis Hafner/100 15.00
73 Torii Hunter/50 20.00
74 Paul Konerko/50 30.00
80 Justin Morneau/100 15.00
82 Jose Vidro/100 10.00
85 Craig Biggio/25 30.00
93 Magglio Ordonez/50 20.00
97 Preston Wilson/50 15.00
98 Shannon Stewart/50 10.00
107 Alfonso Soriano/25 30.00
110 Aubrey Huff/100 12.00
111 Adrian Beltre/25 20.00
112 Mark Teixeira/50 30.00
116 Carlos Beltran/25 30.00
121 Scott Rolen/25 30.00
123 Carlos Lee/100 15.00
124 Derrek Lee/100 20.00
130 Garret Anderson/100 15.00
131 Austin Kearns/100 15.00
140 Vernon Wells/50 15.00
141 David Wright/50 60.00
143 David Ortiz/50 50.00
144 Victor Martinez/100 15.00
147 Angel Berroa/100 10.00

Monikers Material Button Gold

NM/M

No Pricing
Production 1-5
Platinum: No Pricing
Production One Set

Monikers Mat. Jersey Number Silver

NM/M

Production 1-75
Prime Platinum: No Pricing
Production One Set
9 Miguel Cabrera/50 35.00
10 Miguel Cabrera/50 35.00
13 Mark Prior/25 40.00
25 Ben Sheets Pants/50 20.00
33 Francisco Cordero/25 25.00
34 Aramis Ramirez/75 20.00
38 Michael Young/50 25.00
43 Eric Chavez/75 20.00
45 Roy Oswalt/75 25.00
57 Sean Casey/75 15.00
60 Francisco Rodriguez/75 25.00
66 Travis Hafner/50 20.00
70 Andruw Jones/25 40.00
85 Craig Biggio/25 30.00
89 Jacque Jones/25 15.00
90 Lyle Overbay/75 10.00
98 Shannon Stewart/75 10.00
99 Trot Nixon/50 35.00
101 Dontrelle Willis/24 30.00
107 Alfonso Soriano/50 30.00
112 Mark Teixeira/50 30.00
117 Bobby Abreu/75 20.00

121	Scott Rolen/25	30.00
124	Derrek Lee/25	25.00
128	Jim Edmonds/25	35.00
130	Garret Anderson/50	20.00
131	Austin Kearns/75	15.00
140	Vernon Wells/50	15.00
141	David Wright/75	60.00
143	David Ortiz/75	50.00
144	Victor Martinez/75	15.00
152	Ryne Sandberg/50	40.00
158	Duke Snider/25	40.00
159	Don Mattingly/50	60.00
160	Bob Gibson/50	30.00
163	Nolan Ryan/25	100.00
164	Stan Musial/25	80.00
166	Harmon Killebrew/50	35.00
167	Cal Ripken Jr./25	140.00

Monikers Material Jersey Prime Gold

NM/M

Production 1-100

Platinum: No Pricing

Production One Set

9	Miguel Cabrera/50	40.00
10	Miguel Cabrera/50	40.00
13	Mark Prior/25	65.00
14	Mark Prior/25	65.00
25	Ben Sheets/50	25.00
34	Aramis Ramirez/100	25.00
38	Michael Young/100	25.00
43	Eric Chavez/75	25.00
45	Roy Oswalt/100	30.00
57	Sean Casey/30	20.00
60	Francisco Rodriguez/75	30.00
66	Travis Hafner/100	25.00
70	Andruw Jones/50	40.00
84	Josh Beckett/25	40.00
88	Barry Zito/25	30.00
89	Jacque Jones/50	15.00
98	Shannon Stewart/75	15.00
107	Alfonso Soriano/50	40.00
112	Mark Teixeira/20	50.00
117	Bobby Abreu/100	25.00
121	Scott Rolen/50	35.00
128	Jim Edmonds/25	40.00
130	Garret Anderson/50	25.00
131	Austin Kearns/75	20.00
140	Vernon Wells/50	20.00
152	Ryne Sandberg/25	75.00
159	Don Mattingly/25	85.00
160	Bob Gibson/25	50.00
163	Nolan Ryan/25	120.00
167	Cal Ripken Jr./25	175.00

Monikers Silver

NM/M

Production 1-50

9	Miguel Cabrera/50	30.00
10	Miguel Cabrera/50	30.00
13	Mark Prior/25	40.00
14	Mark Prior/25	40.00
25	Ben Sheets/50	20.00
27	Melvin Mora/25	20.00
29	Rafael Furcal/25	20.00
32	Jake Peavy/50	25.00
33	Francisco Cordero/25	15.00
38	Michael Young/25	25.00
40	Joe Nathan/25	20.00
43	Eric Chavez/25	25.00
45	Roy Oswalt/25	30.00
49	Edgar Renteria/25	25.00
50	Mark Buehrle/25	30.00
57	Sean Casey/25	20.00
59	Octavio Dotel/25	12.00
60	Francisco Rodriguez/25	30.00
61	Jose Guillen/25	20.00
66	Travis Hafner/50	15.00
67	Rich Harden/50	15.00
71	Milton Bradley/25	15.00
80	Justin Morneau/50	15.00
89	Jacque Jones/25	15.00
93	Magglio Ordonez/50	15.00
96	Brandon Webb/25	20.00
97	Preston Wilson/25	20.00
98	Shannon Stewart/25	15.00
99	Trot Nixon/25	25.00
105	Bobby Crosby/29	20.00
108	Carlos Zambrano/50	25.00
109	Keith Foulke/25	30.00
110	Aubrey Huff/25	20.00
112	Mark Teixeira/50	35.00
118	Johan Santana/50	35.00
123	Carlos Lee/50	20.00
130	Garret Anderson/50	20.00
131	Austin Kearns/50	15.00
133	Omar Vizquel/25	25.00
135	Mark Mulder/50	20.00
139	Mark Loretta/25	20.00
141	David Wright/25	60.00
144	Victor Martinez/25	15.00
151	Willie Mays/25	175.00
152	Ryne Sandberg/25	50.00
158	Duke Snider/25	30.00
159	Don Mattingly/25	50.00
162	Al Kaline/25	35.00
163	Nolan Ryan/25	80.00
164	Stan Musial/25	60.00
165	George Kell/50	15.00
166	Harmon Killebrew/25	40.00
167	Cal Ripken Jr./25	120.00

Team Trademarks

NM/M

Common Player: 3.00

Production 50 Sets

Foil: No Pricing

Production 10 Sets

1	Ryne Sandberg	8.00
2	George Brett	8.00
3	Steve Carlton	3.00
4	Reggie Jackson	4.00
5	Edgar Martinez	3.00
6	Barry Larkin	4.00
7	Ozzie Smith	6.00
8	Carlton Fisk	4.00
9	Wade Boggs	5.00
10	Will Clark	4.00
11	Nolan Ryan	8.00
12	Gary Carter	3.00
13	Don Mattingly	8.00
14	Willie Stargell	4.00
15	Don Sutton	3.00
16	Kirk Gibson	3.00
17	Kirby Puckett	5.00
18	Dale Murphy	4.00
19	Rickey Henderson	4.00
20	Willie Mays	8.00
21	Cal Ripken Jr.	10.00
22	Paul Molitor	4.00
23	Tony Gwynn	5.00
24	Andre Dawson	3.00
25	Bob Feller	4.00
26	Alan Trammell	3.00
27	Dave Parker	3.00
28	Dave Righetti	3.00
29	Dwight Gooden	3.00
30	Harold Baines	3.00
31	Jack Morris	3.00
32	John Kruk	3.00
33	Lee Smith	3.00
34	Lenny Dykstra	3.00
35	Luis Tiant	3.00
36	Matt Williams	3.00
37	Ron Guidry	3.00
38	Tony Oliva	3.00

Team Trademarks Jersey Number

NM/M

Production 1-50

1	Ryne Sandberg/23	20.00
3	Steve Carlton Pants/32	8.00
4	Reggie Jackson/44	10.00
8	Carlton Fisk/50	8.00
9	Wade Boggs/26	10.00
11	Nolan Ryan Pants/34	25.00
20	Willie Mays/24	40.00

Team Trademarks Jersey Number Prime

NM/M

1	Ryne Sandberg/50	25.00
2	George Brett/50	25.00
3	Steve Carlton/50	10.00
4	Reggie Jackson/50	15.00
5	Edgar Martinez/50	15.00
6	Barry Larkin/50	15.00
7	Ozzie Smith/50	20.00
8	Carlton Fisk/50	15.00
9	Wade Boggs/50	15.00
10	Will Clark/50	15.00
11	Nolan Ryan/50	25.00
12	Gary Carter/50	12.00
13	Don Mattingly/40	25.00
14	Willie Stargell/50	15.00
15	Don Sutton/25	12.00
16	Kirk Gibson/50	12.00
18	Dale Murphy/50	15.00
19	Rickey Henderson/50	15.00
21	Cal Ripken Jr./25	50.00
23	Tony Gwynn/50	20.00
24	Andre Dawson/25	15.00
26	Alan Trammell/25	12.00
27	Dave Parker/50	10.00
29	Dwight Gooden/50	15.00
30	Harold Baines/25	15.00
31	Jack Morris/47	10.00
32	John Kruk/25	15.00
33	Lee Smith/47	10.00
34	Lenny Dykstra/25	15.00
38	Tony Oliva/26	15.00

Team Trademarks Signature

NM/M

Production 5-50

1	Ryne Sandberg/25	50.00
2	George Brett/5	
3	Steve Carlton/25	25.00
4	Reggie Jackson/25	30.00
5	Edgar Martinez/50	20.00
6	Barry Larkin/50	25.00
7	Ozzie Smith/50	35.00
8	Carlton Fisk/50	25.00
9	Wade Boggs/25	35.00
10	Will Clark/50	25.00
11	Nolan Ryan/50	75.00
12	Gary Carter/50	15.00
13	Don Mattingly/25	50.00
15	Don Sutton/100	12.00
16	Kirk Gibson/50	20.00
17	Kirby Puckett/25	40.00
18	Dale Murphy/100	20.00
20	Willie Mays/25	160.00
21	Cal Ripken Jr./50	90.00
22	Paul Molitor/25	25.00
23	Tony Gwynn/25	40.00
24	Andre Dawson/100	15.00
25	Bob Feller/50	20.00
26	Alan Trammell/25	25.00
27	Dave Parker/50	15.00
28	Dave Righetti/25	20.00
29	Dwight Gooden/50	15.00
30	Harold Baines/50	15.00
31	Jack Morris/50	12.00
32	John Kruk/25	20.00
33	Lee Smith/50	15.00
34	Lenny Dykstra/25	20.00
35	Luis Tiant/50	15.00
36	Matt Williams/50	20.00
37	Ron Guidry/25	25.00
38	Tony Oliva/50	15.00

Team Trade. Sig. Jersey Number Prime

NM/M

3	Steve Carlton/25	30.00
24	Andre Dawson/25	30.00
27	Dave Parker/39	20.00
31	Jack Morris/47	20.00
33	Lee Smith/47	25.00
38	Tony Oliva/26	35.00

Team Trademarks Sign. Jersey Number

NM/M

Production 1-72

4	Reggie Jackson/44	50.00
8	Carlton Fisk/72	35.00
9	Wade Boggs/26	50.00
11	Nolan Ryan Pants/34	90.00
17	Kirby Puckett/34	60.00
27	Dave Parker/39	25.00
31	Jack Morris/47	20.00
33	Lee Smith/47	20.00
37	Ron Guidry Pants/49	20.00

Threads Button

No Pricing

Production 1-7

Threads Jersey Number

Production 1-50

Logo: No Pricing

Production One Set

152	Ryne Sandberg/50	15.00
154	Ted Williams/25	60.00
157	Whitey Ford/50	12.00
158	Duke Snider/25	15.00
164	Stan Musial/25	25.00
166	Harmon Killebrew/50	20.00

Timber Barrel

No Pricing

Production 1-3

TNT

NM/M

Production 1-50

Prime: .50X-1.5X

Production 5-100

7	Vladimir Guerrero Bat-Jsy/30	15.00
10	Miguel Cabrera Bat-Jsy/25	12.00
11	Albert Pujols Bat-Jsy/50	25.00
12	Albert Pujols Bat-Jsy/50	25.00
13	Mark Prior Bat-Jsy/50	10.00
14	Mark Prior Bat-Jsy/50	10.00
15	Chipper Jones Bat-Jsy/50	12.00
16	Chipper Jones Bat-Jsy/50	12.00
39	Ivan Rodriguez Bat-Jsy/25	12.00
42	Adam Dunn Bat-Jsy/50	5.00
62	Greg Maddux Bat-Jsy/25	20.00
100	Mike Piazza Bat-Jsy/50	12.00
107	Alfonso Soriano Bat-Jsy/50	12.00
112	Mark Teixeira Bat-Jsy/50	10.00
119	Manny Ramirez Bat-Jsy/50	12.00
121	Scott Rolen Bat-Jsy/50	10.00
124	Derrek Lee Bat-Jsy/50	8.00
143	David Ortiz Bat-Jsy/50	15.00
151	Willie Mays Bat-Jsy/25	50.00
153	Rickey Henderson Bat-Jsy/50	15.00
154	Ted Williams Bat-Jsy/25	85.00
159	Don Mattingly Bat-Jsy/50	20.00
161	Hank Aaron Bat-Jsy/25	50.00
163	Nolan Ryan Bat-Jsy/50	25.00
164	Stan Musial Bat-Jsy/25	30.00
166	Harmon Killebrew Bat-Jsy/25	20.00
167	Cal Ripken Jr. Bat-Jsy/50	30.00
169	Roger Clemens Bat-Jsy/50	15.00
171	Rafael Palmeiro Bat-Jsy/50	10.00
172	Randy Johnson Bat-Jsy/25	15.00
174	Greg Maddux Bat-Jsy/50	15.00
175	Sammy Sosa Bat-Jsy/50	15.00

M

1996 METAL UNIVERSE

NM/M

Complete Set (250):	17.50
Common Player:	.10
Pack (8):	1.50
Wax Box (24):	17.50

1	Roberto Alomar	.20
2	Brady Anderson	.10
3	Bobby Bonilla	.10
4	Chris Hoiles	.10
5	Ben McDonald	.10
6	Mike Mussina	.40
7	Randy Myers	.10
8	Rafael Palmeiro	.60
9	Cal Ripken Jr.	2.50
10	B.J. Surhoff	.10
11	Luis Alicea	.10
12	Jose Canseco	.50
13	Roger Clemens	1.25
14	Wil Cordero	.10
15	Tom Gordon	.10
16	Mike Greenwell	.10
17	Tim Naehring	.10
18	Troy O'Leary	.10
19	Mike Stanley	.10
20	John Valentin	.10

No.	Player	Price
21	Mo Vaughn	.10
22	Tim Wakefield	.10
23	Garret Anderson	.10
24	Chili Davis	.10
25	Gary DiSarcina	.10
26	Jim Edmonds	.10
27	Chuck Finley	.10
28	Todd Greene	.10
29	Mark Langston	.10
30	Troy Percival	.10
31	Tony Phillips	.10
32	Tim Salmon	.10
33	Lee Smith	.10
34	J.T. Snow	.10
35	Ray Durham	.10
36	Alex Fernandez	.10
37	Ozzie Guillen	.10
38	Roberto Hernandez	.10
39	Lyle Mouton	.10
40	Frank Thomas	.75
41	Robin Ventura	.10
42	Sandy Alomar	.10
43	Carlos Baerga	.10
44	Albert Belle	.10
45	Orel Hershiser	.10
46	Kenny Lofton	.10
47	Dennis Martinez	.10
48	Jack McDowell	.10
49	Jose Mesa	.10
50	Eddie Murray	.75
51	Charles Nagy	.10
52	Manny Ramirez	.75
53	Julian Tavarez	.10
54	Jim Thome	.60
55	Omar Vizquel	.10
56	Chad Curtis	.10
57	Cecil Fielder	.10
58	John Flaherty	.10
59	Travis Fryman	.10
60	Chris Gomez	.10
61	Felipe Lira	.10
62	Kevin Appier	.10
63	Johnny Damon	.35
64	Tom Goodwin	.10
65	Mark Gubicza	.10
66	Jeff Montgomery	.10
67	Jon Nunnally	.10
68	Ricky Bones	.10
69	Jeff Cirillo	.10
70	John Jaha	.10
71	Dave Nilsson	.10
72	Joe Oliver	.10
73	Kevin Seitzer	.10
74	Greg Vaughn	.10
75	Marty Cordova	.10
76	Chuck Knoblauch	.10
77	Pat Meares	.10
78	Paul Molitor	.75
79	Pedro Munoz	.10
80	Kirby Puckett	1.00
81	Brad Radke	.10
82	Scott Stahoviak	.10
83	Matt Walbeck	.10
84	Wade Boggs	1.00
85	David Cone	.10
86	Joe Girardi	.10
87	Derek Jeter	2.50
88	Jim Leyritz	.10
89	Tino Martinez	.10
90	Don Mattingly	1.50
91	Paul O'Neill	.10
92	Andy Pettitte	.25
93	Tim Raines	.10
94	Kenny Rogers	.10
95	Ruben Sierra	.10
96	John Wetteland	.10
97	Bernie Williams	.10
98	Geronimo Berroa	.10
99	Dennis Eckersley	.65
100	Brent Gates	.10
101	Mark McGwire	2.00
102	Steve Ontiveros	.10
103	Terry Steinbach	.10
104	Jay Buhner	.10
105	Vince Coleman	.10
106	Joey Cora	.10
107	Ken Griffey Jr.	1.50
108	Randy Johnson	.75
109	Edgar Martinez	.10
110	Alex Rodriguez	2.00
111	Paul Sorrento	.10
112	Will Clark	.10
113	Juan Gonzalez	.50
114	Rusty Greer	.10
115	Dean Palmer	.10
116	Ivan Rodriguez	.65
117	Mickey Tettleton	.10
118	Joe Carter	.10
119	Alex Gonzalez	.10
120	Shawn Green	.30
121	Erik Hanson	.10
122	Pat Hentgen	.10
123	*Sandy Martinez*	.10
124	Otis Nixon	.10
125	John Olerud	.10
126	Steve Avery	.10
127	Tom Glavine	.40
128	Marquis Grissom	.10
129	Chipper Jones	1.00
130	David Justice	.10
131	Ryan Klesko	.10
132	Mark Lemke	.10
133	Javier Lopez	.10
134	Greg Maddux	1.00
135	Fred McGriff	.10
136	John Smoltz	.10
137	Mark Wohlers	.10
138	Frank Castillo	.10
139	Shawon Dunston	.10
140	Luis Gonzalez	.20
141	Mark Grace	.10
142	Brian McRae	.10
143	Jaime Navarro	.10
144	Rey Sanchez	.10
145	Ryne Sandberg	1.00
146	Sammy Sosa	1.25
147	Bret Boone	.10
148	Curtis Goodwin	.10
149	Barry Larkin	.10
150	Hal Morris	.10
151	Reggie Sanders	.10
152	Pete Schourek	.10
153	John Smiley	.10
154	Dante Bichette	.10
155	Vinny Castilla	.10
156	Andres Galarraga	.10
157	Bret Saberhagen	.10
158	Bill Swift	.10
159	Larry Walker	.10
160	Walt Weiss	.10
161	Kurt Abbott	.10
162	John Burkett	.10
163	Greg Colbrunn	.10
164	Jeff Conine	.10
165	Chris Hammond	.10
166	Charles Johnson	.10
167	Al Leiter	.10
168	Pat Rapp	.10
169	Gary Sheffield	.40
170	Quilvio Veras	.10
171	Devon White	.10
172	Jeff Bagwell	.75
173	Derek Bell	.10
174	Sean Berry	.10
175	Craig Biggio	.10
176	Doug Drabek	.10
177	Tony Eusebio	.10
178	Brian Hunter	.10
179	Orlando Miller	.10
180	Shane Reynolds	.10
181	Mike Blowers	.10
182	Roger Cedeno	.10
183	Eric Karros	.10
184	Ramon Martinez	.10
185	Raul Mondesi	.10
186	Hideo Nomo	.60
187	Mike Piazza	1.50
188	Moises Alou	.10
189	Yamil Benitez	.10
190	Darrin Fletcher	.10
191	Cliff Floyd	.10
192	Pedro Martinez	.75
193	Carlos Perez	.10
194	David Segul	.10
195	Tony Tarasco	.10
196	Rondell White	.10
197	Edgardo Alfonzo	.10
198	Rico Brogna	.10
199	Carl Everett	.10
200	Todd Hundley	.10
201	Jason Isringhausen	.10
202	Lance Johnson	.10
203	Bobby Jones	.10
204	Jeff Kent	.10
205	Bill Pulsipher	.10
206	Jose Vizcaino	.10
207	Ricky Bottalico	.10
208	Darren Daulton	.10
209	Lenny Dykstra	.10
210	Jim Eisenreich	.10
211	Gregg Jefferies	.10
212	Mickey Morandini	.10
213	Heathcliff Slocumb	.10
214	Jay Bell	.10
215	Carlos Garcia	.10
216	Jeff King	.10
217	Al Martin	.10
218	Orlando Merced	.10
219	Dan Miceli	.10
220	Denny Neagle	.10
221	Andy Benes	.10
222	Royce Clayton	.10
223	Gary Gaetti	.10
224	Ron Gant	.10
225	Bernard Gilkey	.10
226	Brian Jordan	.10
227	Ray Lankford	.10
228	John Mabry	.10
229	Ozzie Smith	1.00
230	Todd Stottlemyre	.10
231	Andy Ashby	.10
232	Brad Ausmus	.10
233	Ken Caminiti	.10
234	Steve Finley	.10
235	Tony Gwynn	1.00
236	Joey Hamilton	.10
237	Rickey Henderson	.75
238	Trevor Hoffman	.10
239	Wally Joyner	.10
240	Rod Beck	.10
241	Barry Bonds	2.50
242	Glenallen Hill	.10
243	Stan Javier	.10
244	Mark Leiter	.10
245	Deion Sanders	.10
246	William VanLandingham	.10
247	Matt Williams	.10
248	Checklist	.10
249	Checklist	.10
250	Checklist	.10

Platinum Edition

		NM/M
Complete Set (247):		75.00
Common Player:		.25
Stars:		5X

(See 1996 Metal Universe for checklist and base card values.)

Heavy Metal

		NM/M
Complete Set (10):		5.00
Common Player:		.35
1	Albert Belle	.35
2	Barry Bonds	1.50
3	Juan Gonzalez	.50
4	Ken Griffey Jr.	1.00
5	Mark McGwire	1.25
6	Mike Piazza	1.00
7	Sammy Sosa	.90
8	Frank Thomas	.60
9	Mo Vaughn	.35
10	Matt Williams	.35

Mining for Gold

		NM/M
Complete Set (12):		12.50
Common Player:		.75
1	Yamil Benitez	.75
2	Marty Cordova	.75
3	Shawn Green	2.00
4	Todd Greene	.75
5	Brian Hunter	.75
6	Derek Jeter	7.50
7	Charles Johnson	.75
8	Chipper Jones	3.50
9	Hideo Nomo	2.50
10	Alex Ochoa	.75
11	Andy Pettitte	1.00
12	Quilvio Veras	.75

Mother Lode

		NM/M
Complete Set (12):		15.00
Common Player:		.75
1	Barry Bonds	4.50
2	Jim Edmonds	.75
3	Ken Griffey Jr.	3.50
4	Kenny Lofton	.75
5	Raul Mondesi	.75
6	Rafael Palmeiro	1.50
7	Manny Ramirez	2.00
8	Cal Ripken Jr.	4.50
9	Tim Salmon	.75
10	Ryne Sandberg	3.00
11	Frank Thomas	2.00
12	Matt Williams	.75

Platinum Portraits

		NM/M
Complete Set (10):		4.00
Common Player:		.40
1	Garret Anderson	.40
2	Marty Cordova	.40
3	Jim Edmonds	.40
4	Jason Isringhausen	.40
5	Chipper Jones	2.25
6	Ryan Klesko	.40
7	Hideo Nomo	1.00
8	Carlos Perez	.40
9	Manny Ramirez	1.50
10	Rondell White	.40

Titanium

	NM/M
Complete Set (10):	15.00

Common Player: .50
1 Albert Belle .50
2 Barry Bonds 4.00
3 Ken Griffey Jr. 2.50
4 Tony Gwynn 1.50
5 Greg Maddux 1.50
6 Mike Piazza 2.50
7 Cal Ripken Jr. 4.00
8 Frank Thomas 1.00
9 Mo Vaughn .50
10 Matt Williams .50

1997 METAL UNIVERSE

NM/M
Complete Set (250): 17.50
Common Player: .10
Pack (8): 1.50
Wax Box (24): 18.00
1 Roberto Alomar .20
2 Brady Anderson .10
3 Rocky Coppinger .10
4 Chris Hoiles .10
5 Eddie Murray .60
6 Mike Mussina .40
7 Rafael Palmeiro .50
8 Cal Ripken Jr. 2.00
9 B.J. Surhoff .10
10 Brant Brown .10
11 Mark Grace .10
12 Brian McRae .10
13 Jaime Navarro .10
14 Ryne Sandberg .75
15 Sammy Sosa 1.00
16 Amaury Telemaco .10
17 Steve Trachsel .10
18 Darren Bragg .10
19 Jose Canseco .40
20 Roger Clemens 1.00
21 Nomar Garciaparra 1.00
22 Tom Gordon .10
23 Tim Naehring .10
24 Mike Stanley .10
25 John Valentin .10
26 Mo Vaughn .10
27 Jermaine Dye .10
28 Tom Glavine .30
29 Marquis Grissom .10
30 Andruw Jones .60
31 Chipper Jones .75
32 Ryan Klesko .10
33 Greg Maddux .75
34 Fred McGriff .10
35 John Smoltz .10
36 Garret Anderson .10
37 George Arias .10
38 Gary DiSarcina .10
39 Jim Edmonds .10
40 Darin Erstad .25
41 Chuck Finley .10
42 Troy Percival .10
43 Tim Salmon .10
44 Bret Boone .10
45 Jeff Brantley .10
46 Eric Davis .10
47 Barry Larkin .10
48 Hal Morris .10
49 Mark Portugal .10
50 Reggie Sanders .10
51 John Smiley .10
52 Wilson Alvarez .10
53 Harold Baines .10
54 James Baldwin .10
55 Albert Belle .10
56 Mike Cameron .10
57 Ray Durham .10
58 Alex Fernandez .10
59 Roberto Hernandez .10
60 Tony Phillips .10
61 Frank Thomas .60
62 Robin Ventura .10
63 Jeff Cirillo .10
64 Jeff D'Amico .10
65 John Jaha .10
66 Scott Karl .10
67 Ben McDonald .10
68 Marc Newfield .10
69 Dave Nilsson .10
70 Jose Valentin .10
71 Dante Bichette .10
72 Ellis Burks .10
73 Vinny Castilla .10
74 Andres Galarraga .10
75 Kevin Ritz .10
76 Larry Walker .10
77 Walt Weiss .10
78 Jamey Wright .10
79 Eric Young .10
80 Julio Franco .10
81 Orel Hershiser .10
82 Kenny Lofton .10
83 Jack McDowell .10
84 Jose Mesa .10
85 Charles Nagy .10
86 Manny Ramirez .60
87 Jim Thome .50
88 Omar Vizquel .10
89 Matt Williams .10
90 Kevin Appier .10
91 Johnny Damon .35
92 Chili Davis .10
93 Tom Goodwin .10
94 Keith Lockhart .10
95 Jeff Montgomery .10
96 Craig Paquette .10
97 Jose Rosado .10
98 Michael Tucker .10
99 Wilton Guerrero .10
100 Todd Hollandsworth .10
101 Eric Karros .10
102 Ramon Martinez .10
103 Raul Mondesi .10
104 Hideo Nomo .60
105 Mike Piazza 1.25
106 Ismael Valdes .10
107 Todd Worrell .10
108 Tony Clark .10
109 Travis Fryman .10
110 Bob Higginson .10
111 Mark Lewis .10
112 Melvin Nieves .10
113 Justin Thompson .10
114 Wade Boggs .75
115 David Cone .10
116 Cecil Fielder .10
117 Dwight Gooden .10
118 Derek Jeter 2.00
119 Tino Martinez .10
120 Paul O'Neill .10
121 Andy Pettitte .20
122 Mariano Rivera .20
123 Darryl Strawberry .10
124 John Wetteland .10
125 Bernie Williams .10
126 Tony Batista .10
127 Geronimo Berroa .10
128 Scott Brosius .10
129 Jason Giambi .50
130 Jose Herrera .10
131 Mark McGwire 1.50
132 John Wasdin .10
133 Bob Abreu .10
134 Jeff Bagwell .60
135 Derek Bell .10
136 Craig Biggio .10
137 Brian Hunter .10
138 Darryl Kile .10
139 Orlando Miller .10
140 Shane Reynolds .10
141 Billy Wagner .10
142 Donne Wall .10
143 Jay Buhner .10
144 Jeff Fassero .10
145 Ken Griffey Jr. 1.25
146 Sterling Hitchcock .10
147 Randy Johnson .60
148 Edgar Martinez .10
149 Alex Rodriguez 1.50
149p Alex Rodriguez ("PROMOTIONAL SAMPLE") 1.50
150 Paul Sorrento .10
151 Dan Wilson .10
152 Moises Alou .10
153 Darrin Fletcher .10
154 Cliff Floyd .10
155 Mark Grudzielanek .10
156 Vladimir Guerrero .60
157 Mike Lansing .10
158 Pedro Martinez .60
159 Henry Rodriguez .10
160 Rondell White .10
161 Will Clark .10
162 Juan Gonzalez .50
163 Rusty Greer .10
164 Ken Hill .10
165 Mark McLemore .10
166 Dean Palmer .10
167 Roger Pavlik .10
168 Ivan Rodriguez .50
169 Mickey Tettleton .10
170 Bobby Bonilla .10
171 Kevin Brown .10
172 Greg Colbrunn .10
173 Jeff Conine .10
174 Jim Eisenreich .10
175 Charles Johnson .10
176 Al Leiter .10
177 Robb Nen .10
178 Edgar Renteria .10
179 Gary Sheffield .40
180 Devon White .10
181 Joe Carter .10
182 Carlos Delgado .40
183 Alex Gonzalez .10
184 Shawn Green .35
185 Juan Guzman .10
186 Pat Hentgen .10
187 Orlando Merced .10
188 John Olerud .10
189 Robert Perez .10
190 Ed Sprague .10
191 Mark Clark .10
192 John Franco .10
193 Bernard Gilkey .10
194 Todd Hundley .10
195 Lance Johnson .10
196 Bobby Jones .10
197 Alex Ochoa .10
198 Rey Ordonez .10
199 Paul Wilson .10
200 Ricky Bottalico .10
201 Gregg Jefferies .10
202 Wendell Magee Jr. .10
203 Mickey Morandini .10
204 Ricky Otero .10
205 Scott Rolen .50
206 Benito Santiago .10
207 Curt Schilling .25
208 Rich Becker .10
209 Marty Cordova .10
210 Chuck Knoblauch .10
211 Pat Meares .10
212 Paul Molitor .60
213 Frank Rodriguez .10
214 Terry Steinbach .10
215 Todd Walker .10
216 Andy Ashby .10
217 Ken Caminiti .10
218 Steve Finley .10
219 Tony Gwynn .75
220 Joey Hamilton .10
221 Rickey Henderson .60
222 Trevor Hoffman .10
223 Wally Joyner .10
224 Scott Sanders .10
225 Fernando Valenzuela .10
226 Greg Vaughn .10
227 Alan Benes .10
228 Andy Benes .10
229 Dennis Eckersley .50
230 Ron Gant .10
231 Brian Jordan .10
232 Ray Lankford .10
233 John Mabry .10
234 Tom Pagnozzi .10
235 Todd Stottlemyre .10
236 Jermaine Allensworth .10
237 Francisco Cordova .10
238 Jason Kendall .10
239 Jeff King .10
240 Al Martin .10
241 Rod Beck .10
242 Barry Bonds 2.00
243 Shawn Estes .10
244 Mark Gardner .10
245 Glenallen Hill .10
246 Bill Mueller .10
247 J.T. Snow .10
248 Checklist .10
249 Checklist .10
250 Checklist .10

Blast Furnace

NM/M
Complete Set (12): 40.00
Common Player: 1.50
1 Jeff Bagwell 4.00

2 Albert Belle 1.50
3 Barry Bonds 7.50
4 Andres Galarraga 1.50
5 Juan Gonzalez 2.50
6 Ken Griffey Jr. 5.00
7 Todd Hundley 1.50
8 Mark McGwire 6.00
9 Mike Piazza 5.00
10 Alex Rodriguez 6.00
11 Frank Thomas 4.00
12 Mo Vaughn 1.50

Emerald Autographs

NM/M
Complete Set (6): 75.00
Common Autograph: 4.00
1 Darin Erstad 6.00
2 Todd Hollandsworth 4.00
3 Alex Ochoa 4.00
4 Alex Rodriguez 60.00
5 Scott Rolen 10.00
6 Todd Walker 4.00

Magnetic Field

NM/M
Complete Set (10): 15.00
Common Player: .75
1 Roberto Alomar .75
2 Jeff Bagwell 1.25
3 Barry Bonds 3.00
4 Ken Griffey Jr. 2.00
5 Derek Jeter 3.00
6 Kenny Lofton .75
7 Edgar Renteria .75
8 Cal Ripken Jr. 3.00
9 Alex Rodriguez 2.50
10 Matt Williams .75

Mining for Gold

NM/M
Complete Set (10): 12.00
Common Player: .75
1 Bob Abreu .75
2 Kevin Brown .75
3 Nomar Garciaparra 3.50
4 Vladimir Guerrero 3.00
5 Wilton Guerrero .75
6 Andruw Jones 3.00

7	Curt Lyons	.75
8	Neifi Perez	.75
9	Scott Rolen	2.00
10	Todd Walker	.75

Mother Lode

		NM/M
Complete Set (12):		80.00
Common Player:		2.00
1	Roberto Alomar	2.50
2	Jeff Bagwell	6.00
3	Barry Bonds	15.00
4	Ken Griffey Jr.	10.00
5	Andruw Jones	6.00
6	Chipper Jones	8.00
7	Kenny Lofton	2.00
8	Mike Piazza	10.00
9	Cal Ripken Jr.	15.00
10	Alex Rodriguez	12.50
11	Frank Thomas	6.00
12	Matt Williams	2.00

Platinum Portraits

		NM/M
Complete Set (10):		10.00
Common Player:		.60
1	James Baldwin	.60
2	Jermaine Dye	.60
3	Todd Hollandsworth	.60
4	Derek Jeter	5.00
5	Chipper Jones	2.00
6	Jason Kendall	.60
7	Rey Ordonez	.60
8	Andy Pettitte	1.00
9	Edgar Renteria	.60
10	Alex Rodriguez	3.25

Titanium

		NM/M
Complete Set (10):		24.00
Common Player:		1.50
1	Jeff Bagwell	2.00
2	Albert Belle	1.50
3	Ken Griffey Jr.	3.00
4	Chipper Jones	2.50
5	Greg Maddux	2.50
6	Mark McGwire	4.00
7	Mike Piazza	3.00
8	Cal Ripken Jr.	5.00
9	Alex Rodriguez	4.00
10	Frank Thomas	2.00

1998 METAL UNIVERSE

		NM/M
Complete Set (220):		15.00
Common Player:		.10
Pack (8):		1.50
Wax Box (24):		20.00
1	Jose Cruz Jr.	.10
2	Jeff Abbott	.10
3	Rafael Palmeiro	.65
4	Ivan Rodriguez	.65
5	Jaret Wright	.10
6	Derek Bell	.10
7	Chuck Finley	.10
8	Travis Fryman	.10
9	Randy Johnson	.75
10	Derrek Lee	.50
11	Bernie Williams	.10
12	Carlos Baerga	.10
13	Ricky Bottalico	.10
14	Ellis Burks	.10
15	Russ Davis	.10
16	Nomar Garciaparra	1.00
17	Joey Hamilton	.10
18	Jason Kendall	.10
19	Darryl Kile	.10
20	Edgardo Alfonzo	.10
21	Moises Alou	.10
22	Bobby Bonilla	.10
23	Jim Edmonds	.10
24	Jose Guillen	.10
25	Chuck Knoblauch	.10
26	Javy Lopez	.10
27	Billy Wagner	.10
28	Kevin Appier	.10
29	Joe Carter	.10
30	Todd Dunwoody	.10
31	Gary Gaetti	.10
32	Juan Gonzalez	.60
33	Jeffrey Hammonds	.10
34	Roberto Hernandez	.10
35	Dave Nilsson	.10
36	Manny Ramirez	.75
37	Robin Ventura	.10
38	Rondell White	.10
39	Vinny Castilla	.10
40	Will Clark	.10
41	Scott Hatteberg	.10
42	Russ Johnson	.10
43	Ricky Ledee	.10
44	Kenny Lofton	.10
45	Paul Molitor	.75
46	Justin Thompson	.10
47	Craig Biggio	.10
48	Damion Easley	.10
49	Brad Radke	.10
50	Ben Grieve	.10
51	Mark Bellhorn	.10
52	*Henry Blanco*	.10
53	Mariano Rivera	.20
54	Reggie Sanders	.10
55	Paul Sorrento	.10
56	Terry Steinbach	.10
57	Mo Vaughn	.10
58	Brady Anderson	.10
59	Tom Glavine	.40
60	Sammy Sosa	1.25
61	Larry Walker	.10
62	Rod Beck	.10
63	Jose Canseco	.45
64	Steve Finley	.10
65	Pedro Martinez	.75
66	John Olerud	.10
67	Scott Rolen	.60
68	Ismael Valdes	.10
69	Andrew Vessel	.10
70	Mark Grudzielanek	.10
71	Eric Karros	.10
72	Jeff Shaw	.10
73	Lou Collier	.10
74	Edgar Martinez	.10
75	Vladimir Guerrero	.75
76	Paul Konerko	.25
77	Kevin Orie	.10
78	Kevin Polcovich	.10
79	Brett Tomko	.10
80	Jeff Bagwell	.75
81	Barry Bonds	2.50
82	David Justice	.10
83	Hideo Nomo	.60
84	Ryne Sandberg	1.00
85	Shannon Stewart	.10
86	Derek Wallace	.10
87	Tony Womack	.10
88	Jason Giambi	.50
89	Mark Grace	.10
90	Pat Hentgen	.10
91	Raul Mondesi	.10
92	Matt Morris	.10
93	Matt Perisho	.10
94	Tim Salmon	.10
95	Jeremi Gonzalez	.10
96	Shawn Green	.25
97	Todd Greene	.10
98	Ruben Rivera	.10
99	Deion Sanders	.10
100	Alex Rodriguez	2.00
101	Will Cunnane	.10
102	Ray Lankford	.10
103	Ryan McGuire	.10
104	Charles Nagy	.10
105	Rey Ordonez	.10
106	Mike Piazza	1.50
107	Tony Saunders	.10
108	Curt Schilling	.25
109	Fernando Tatis	.10
110	Mark McGwire	2.00
111	*David Dellucci*	.10
112	Garret Anderson	.10
113	Shane Bowers	.10
114	David Cone	.10
115	Jeff King	.10
116	Matt Williams	.10
117	Aaron Boone	.10
118	Dennis Eckersley	.65
119	Livan Hernandez	.10
120	Richard Hidalgo	.10
121	Bobby Higginson	.10
122	Tino Martinez	.10
123	Tim Naehring	.10
124	Jose Vidro	.10
125	John Wetteland	.10
126	Jay Bell	.10
127	Albert Belle	.10
128	Marty Cordova	.10
129	Chili Davis	.10
130	Jason Dickson	.10
131	Rusty Greer	.10
132	Hideki Irabu	.10
133	Greg Maddux	1.00
134	Billy Taylor	.10
135	Jim Thome	.60
136	Gerald Williams	.10
137	Jeff Cirillo	.10
138	Delino DeShields	.10
139	Andres Galarraga	.10
140	Willie Greene	.10
141	John Jaha	.10
142	Charles Johnson	.10
143	Ryan Klesko	.10
144	Paul O'Neill	.10
145	Robinson Checo	.10
146	Roberto Alomar	.20
147	Wilson Alvarez	.10
148	Bobby Jones	.10
149	Raul Casanova	.10
150	Andruw Jones	.75
151	Mike Lansing	.10
152	Mickey Morandini	.10
153	Neifi Perez	.10
154	Pokey Reese	.10
155	Edgar Renteria	.10
156	Eric Young	.10
157	Darin Erstad	.20
158	Kelvim Escobar	.10
159	Carl Everett	.10
160	Tom Gordon	.10
161	Ken Griffey Jr.	1.50
162	Al Martin	.10
163	Bubba Trammell	.10
164	Carlos Delgado	.30
165	Kevin Brown	.10
166	Ken Caminiti	.10
167	Roger Clemens	1.25
168	Ron Gant	.10
169	Jeff Kent	.10
170	Mike Mussina	.40
171	Dean Palmer	.10
172	Henry Rodriguez	.10
173	Matt Stairs	.10
174	Jay Buhner	.10
175	Frank Thomas	.75
176	Mike Cameron	.10
177	Johnny Damon	.35
178	Tony Gwynn	1.00
179	John Smoltz	.10
180	B.J. Surhoff	.10
181	Antone Williamson	.10
182	Alan Benes	.10
183	Jeromy Burnitz	.10
184	Tony Clark	.10
185	Shawn Estes	.10
186	Todd Helton	.65
187	Todd Hundley	.10
188	Chipper Jones	1.00
189	Mark Kotsay	.10
190	Barry Larkin	.10
191	Mike Lieberthal	.10
192	Andy Pettitte	.25
193	Gary Sheffield	.35
194	Jeff Suppan	.10
195	Mark Wohlers	.10
196	Dante Bichette	.10
197	Trevor Hoffman	.10
198	J.T. Snow	.10
199	Derek Jeter	2.50
200	Cal Ripken Jr.	2.50
201	*Steve Woodard*	.25
202	Ray Durham	.10
203	Barry Bonds	1.50
204	Tony Clark	.10
205	Roger Clemens	.65
206	Ken Griffey Jr.	.75
207	Tony Gwynn	.50
208	Derek Jeter	1.50
209	Randy Johnson	.40
210	Mark McGwire	1.00
211	Hideo Nomo	.30
212	Mike Piazza	.75
213	Cal Ripken Jr.	1.50
214	Alex Rodriguez	1.00
215	Frank Thomas	.40
216	Mo Vaughn	.10
217	Larry Walker	.10
218	Ken Griffey Jr. Checklist	.50
219	Alex Rodriguez Checklist	.60
220	Frank Thomas Checklist	.30

Precious Metal Gems

	NM/M
Common Player:	3.00
Stars:	25X

Production 50 sets
(See 1998 Metal Universe for checklist and base card values.)

All-Galactic Team

		NM/M
Complete Set (18):		140.00
Common Player:		3.00
Inserted 1:192		
1	Ken Griffey Jr.	12.50
2	Frank Thomas	7.50
3	Chipper Jones	10.00
4	Albert Belle	3.00
5	Juan Gonzalez	5.00
6	Jeff Bagwell	7.50
7	Andruw Jones	7.50
8	Cal Ripken Jr.	20.00
9	Derek Jeter	20.00
10	Nomar Garciaparra	10.00
11	Darin Erstad	4.00
12	Greg Maddux	10.00
13	Alex Rodriguez	15.00
14	Mike Piazza	12.50
15	Vladimir Guerrero	7.50
16	Jose Cruz Jr.	3.00
17	Mark McGwire	15.00
18	Scott Rolen	5.00

Diamond Heroes

	NM/M
Complete Set (6):	8.00
Common Player:	.50

Inserted 1:18

1	Ken Griffey Jr.	2.00
2	Frank Thomas	1.50
3	Andruw Jones	1.50
4	Alex Rodriguez	2.50
5	Jose Cruz Jr.	.50
6	Cal Ripken Jr.	3.00

Platinum Portraits

		NM/M
Complete Set (12):		90.00
Common Player:		4.00
Inserted 1:360		
1	Ken Griffey Jr.	12.00
2	Frank Thomas	7.50
3	Chipper Jones	9.00
4	Jose Cruz Jr.	4.00
5	Andruw Jones	7.50
6	Cal Ripken Jr.	17.50
7	Derek Jeter	17.50
8	Darin Erstad	4.00
9	Greg Maddux	9.00
10	Alex Rodriguez	15.00
11	Mike Piazza	12.00
12	Vladimir Guerrero	7.50

Universal Language

		NM/M
Complete Set (20):		16.00
Common Player:		.40
Inserted 1:6		
1	Ken Griffey Jr.	1.25
2	Frank Thomas	.75
3	Chipper Jones	1.00
4	Albert Belle	.40
5	Juan Gonzalez	.60
6	Jeff Bagwell	.75
7	Andruw Jones	.75
8	Cal Ripken Jr.	2.00
9	Derek Jeter	2.00
10	Nomar Garciaparra	1.00
11	Darin Erstad	.50
12	Greg Maddux	1.00
13	Alex Rodriguez	1.50
14	Mike Piazza	1.25
15	Vladimir Guerrero	.75
16	Jose Cruz Jr.	.40
17	Hideo Nomo	.60
18	Kenny Lofton	.40
19	Tony Gwynn	1.00
20	Scott Rolen	.60

Titanium

		NM/M
Complete Set (15):		50.00
Common Player:		2.00
Inserted 1:96		
1	Ken Griffey Jr.	5.00
2	Frank Thomas	3.00
3	Chipper Jones	4.00
4	Jose Cruz Jr.	2.00
5	Juan Gonzalez	2.50
6	Scott Rolen	2.50
7	Andruw Jones	3.00
8	Cal Ripken Jr.	7.50
9	Derek Jeter	7.50
10	Nomar Garciaparra	4.00
11	Darin Erstad	2.50
12	Greg Maddux	4.00
13	Alex Rodriguez	6.00
14	Mike Piazza	5.00
15	Vladimir Guerrero	3.00

1999 METAL UNIVERSE

		NM/M
Complete Set (300):		15.00
Common Player:		.10
Pack (8):		1.00
Wax Box (24):		20.00
1	Mark McGwire	1.50
2	Jim Edmonds	.10
3	Travis Fryman	.10
4	Tom Gordon	.10
5	Jeff Bagwell	.65
6	Rico Brogna	.10
7	Tom Evans	.10
8	John Franco	.10
9	Juan Gonzalez	.50
10	Paul Molitor	.65
11	Roberto Alomar	.20
12	Mike Hampton	.10
13	Orel Hershiser	.10
14	Todd Stottlemyre	.10
15	Robin Ventura	.10
16	Todd Walker	.10
17	Bernie Williams	.10
18	Shawn Estes	.10
19	Richie Sexson	.10
20	Kevin Millwood	.10
21	David Ortiz	.50
22	Mariano Rivera	.15
23	Ivan Rodriguez	.60
24	Mike Sirotka	.10
25	David Justice	.10
26	Carl Pavano	.10
27	Albert Belle	.10
28	Will Clark	.10
29	Jose Cruz Jr.	.10
30	Trevor Hoffman	.10
31	Dean Palmer	.10
32	Edgar Renteria	.10
33	David Segui	.10
34	B.J. Surhoff	.10
35	Miguel Tejada	.15
36	Bob Wickman	.10
37	Charles Johnson	.10
38	Andruw Jones	.65
39	Mike Lieberthal	.10
40	Eli Marrero	.10
41	Neifi Perez	.10
42	Jim Thome	.50
43	Barry Bonds	2.00
44	Carlos Delgado	.30
45	Chuck Finley	.10
46	Brian Meadows	.10
47	Tony Gwynn	.75
48	Jose Offerman	.10
49	Cal Ripken Jr.	2.00
50	Alex Rodriguez	1.50
51	Esteban Yan	.10
52	Matt Stairs	.10
53	Fernando Vina	.10
54	Rondell White	.10
55	Kerry Wood	.30
56	Dmitri Young	.10
57	Ken Caminiti	.10
58	Alex Gonzalez	.10
59	Matt Mantei	.10
60	Tino Martinez	.10
61	Hal Morris	.10
62	Rafael Palmeiro	.60
63	Troy Percival	.10
64	Bobby Smith	.10
65	Ed Sprague	.10
66	Brett Tomko	.10
67	Steve Trachsel	.10
68	Ugueth Urbina	.10
69	Jose Valentin	.10
70	Kevin Brown	.10
71	Shawn Green	.30
72	Dustin Hermanson	.10
73	Livan Hernandez	.10
74	Geoff Jenkins	.10
75	Jeff King	.10
76	Chuck Knoblauch	.10
77	Edgar Martinez	.10
78	Fred McGriff	.10
79	Mike Mussina	.40
80	Dave Nilsson	.10
81	Kenny Rogers	.10
82	Tim Salmon	.10
83	Reggie Sanders	.10
84	Wilson Alvarez	.10
85	Rod Beck	.10
86	Jose Guillen	.10
87	Bob Higginson	.10
88	Gregg Olson	.10
89	Jeff Shaw	.10
90	Masato Yoshii	.10
91	Todd Helton	.50
92	David Dellucci	.10
93	Johnny Damon	.35
94	Cliff Floyd	.10
95	Ken Griffey Jr.	1.00
96	Juan Guzman	.10
97	Derek Jeter	2.00
98	Barry Larkin	.10
99	Quinton McCracken	.10
100	Sammy Sosa	.85
101	Kevin Young	.10
102	Jay Bell	.10
103	Jay Buhner	.10
104	Jeff Conine	.10
105	Ryan Jackson	.10
106	Sidney Ponson	.10
107	Jeromy Burnitz	.10
108	Roberto Hernandez	.10
109	A.J. Hinch	.10
110	Hideki Irabu	.10
111	Paul Konerko	.20
112	Henry Rodriguez	.10
113	Shannon Stewart	.10
114	Tony Womack	.10
115	Wilton Guerrero	.10
116	Andy Benes	.10
117	Jeff Cirillo	.10
118	Chili Davis	.10
119	Eric Davis	.10
120	Vladimir Guerrero	.65
121	Dennis Reyes	.10
122	Rickey Henderson	.65
123	Mickey Morandini	.10
124	Jason Schmidt	.10
125	J.T. Snow	.10
126	Justin Thompson	.10
127	Billy Wagner	.10
128	Armando Benitez	.10
129	Sean Casey	.15
130	Brad Fullmer	.10
131	Ben Grieve	.10
132	Robb Nen	.10
133	Shane Reynolds	.10
134	Todd Zeile	.10
135	Brady Anderson	.10
136	Aaron Boone	.10
137	Orlando Cabrera	.10
138	Jason Giambi	.50
139	Randy Johnson	.65
140	Jeff Kent	.10
141	John Wetteland	.10
142	Rolando Arrojo	.10
143	Scott Brosius	.10
144	Mark Grace	.10
145	Jason Kendall	.10
146	Travis Lee	.10
147	Gary Sheffield	.40
148	David Cone	.10
149	Jose Hernandez	.10
150	Todd Jones	.10
151	Al Martin	.10
152	Ismael Valdes	.10
153	Wade Boggs	.75
154	Garret Anderson	.10
155	Bobby Bonilla	.10
156	Darryl Kile	.10
157	Ryan Klesko	.10
158	Tim Wakefield	.10
159	Kenny Lofton	.10
160	Jose Canseco	.40
161	Doug Glanville	.10
162	Todd Hundley	.10
163	Brian Jordan	.10
164	Steve Finley	.10
165	Tom Glavine	.25
166	Al Leiter	.10
167	Raul Mondesi	.10
168	Desi Relaford	.10
169	Bret Saberhagen	.10
170	Omar Vizquel	.10
171	Larry Walker	.10
172	Bobby Abreu	.10
173	Moises Alou	.10
174	Mike Caruso	.10
175	Royce Clayton	.10
176	Bartolo Colon	.10
177	Marty Cordova	.10
178	Darin Erstad	.30
179	Nomar Garciaparra	.75
180	Andy Ashby	.10
181	Dan Wilson	.10
182	Larry Sutton	.10
183	Tony Clark	.10
184	Andres Galarraga	.10
185	Ray Durham	.10
186	Hideo Nomo	.60
187	Steve Woodard	.10
188	Scott Rolen	.35
189	Mike Stanley	.10
190	Jaret Wright	.10
191	Vinny Castilla	.10
192	Jason Christiansen	.10
193	Paul Bako	.10
194	Carlos Perez	.10
195	Mike Piazza	1.00
196	Fernando Tatis	.10
197	Mo Vaughn	.10
198	Devon White	.10
199	Ricky Gutierrez	.10
200	Charlie Hayes	.10
201	Brad Radke	.10
202	Rick Helling	.10
203	John Smoltz	.10
204	Frank Thomas	.65
205	David Wells	.10
206	Roger Clemens	.85
207	Mark Grudzielanek	.10
208	Chipper Jones	.75
209	Ray Lankford	.10
210	Pedro Martinez	.65
211	Manny Ramirez	.65
212	Greg Vaughn	.10
213	Craig Biggio	.10
214	Rusty Greer	.10
215	Greg Maddux	.75
216	Rick Aguilera	.10
217	Andy Pettitte	.20
218	Dante Bichette	.10
219	Damion Easley	.10
220	Matt Morris	.10
221	John Olerud	.10
222	Chan Ho Park	.10
223	Curt Schilling	.25
224	John Valentin	.10
225	Matt Williams	.10
226	Ellis Burks	.10
227	Tom Goodwin	.10
228	Javy Lopez	.10
229	Eric Milton	.10
230	Paul O'Neill	.10
231	Magglio Ordonez	.15
232	Derrek Lee	.45
233	Ken Griffey Jr.	.60
234	Randy Johnson	.30
235	Alex Rodriguez	.75
236	Darin Erstad	.15
237	Juan Gonzalez	.20
238	Derek Jeter	1.00
239	Tony Gwynn	.40
240	Kerry Wood	.20
241	Cal Ripken Jr.	1.00
242	Sammy Sosa	.50
243	Greg Maddux	.40
244	Mark McGwire	.75
245	Chipper Jones	.40
246	Barry Bonds	1.00
247	Ben Grieve	.10
248	Ben Davis	.10
249	Robert Fick	.10
250	Carlos Guillen	.10
251	Mike Frank	.10
252	Ryan Minor	.10
253	Troy Glaus	.65
254	Matt Anderson	.10
255	Josh Booty	.10
256	Gabe Alvarez	.10

257	Gabe Kapler	.10
258	Enrique Wilson	.10
259	Alex Gonzalez	.10
260	Preston Wilson	.10
261	Eric Chavez	.20
262	Adrian Beltre	.30
263	Corey Koskie	.10
264	*Robert Machado*	.10
265	Orlando Hernandez	.10
266	Matt Clement	.10
267	Luis Ordaz	.10
268	Jeremy Giambi	.10
269	J.D. Drew	.50
269a	J.D. Drew	30.00
270	Cliff Politte	.10
271	Carlton Loewer	.10
272	Aramis Ramirez	.10
273	Ken Griffey Jr.	.60
274	Randy Johnson	.30
275	Alex Rodriguez	.75
276	Darin Erstad	.20
277	Scott Rolen	.25
278	Juan Gonzalez	.20
279	Jeff Bagwell	.30
280	Mike Piazza	.65
281	Derek Jeter	1.00
282	Travis Lee	.10
283	Tony Gwynn	.40
284	Kerry Wood	.20
285	Albert Belle	.10
286	Sammy Sosa	.50
287	Mo Vaughn	.10
288	Nomar Garciaparra	.45
289	Frank Thomas	.30
290	Cal Ripken Jr.	1.00
291	Greg Maddux	.40
292	Chipper Jones	.40
293	Ben Grieve	.10
294	Andruw Jones	.30
295	Mark McGwire	.75
296	Roger Clemens	.50
297	Barry Bonds	1.00
298	Ken Griffey Jr.-Checklist	.60
299	Kerry Wood-Checklist	.20
300	Alex Rodriguez-Checklist	.75

Precious Metal Gems

	NM/M
Common Player:	3.00
Stars:	25X

Gem Master 1 of 1:
(Value undetermined)
(See 1999 Metal Universe for checklist and base card values.)

Neophytes

		NM/M
Complete Set (15):		7.50
Common Player:		.35
Inserted 1:6		
1	Troy Glaus	3.00
2	Travis Lee	.75
3	Scott Elarton	.35
4	Ricky Ledee	.35
5	Richard Hidalgo	.35
6	J.D. Drew	1.50
7	Paul Konerko	.75
8	Orlando Hernandez	.75
9	Mike Caruso	.35
10	Mike Frank	.35
11	Miguel Tejada	.50
12	Matt Anderson	.35
13	Kerry Wood	1.00
14	Gabe Alvarez	.35
15	Adrian Beltre	.50

Diamond Soul

		NM/M
Complete Set (15):		60.00
Common Player:		1.50
Inserted 1:72		
1	Cal Ripken Jr.	12.00
2	Alex Rodriguez	9.00
3	Chipper Jones	6.00
4	Derek Jeter	12.00
5	Frank Thomas	4.00
6	Greg Maddux	6.00
7	Juan Gonzalez	3.00
8	Ken Griffey Jr.	7.50
9	Kerry Wood	3.00
10	Mark McGwire	9.00
11	Mike Piazza	7.50
12	Nomar Garciaparra	6.00
13	Scott Rolen	2.50
14	Tony Gwynn	6.00
15	Travis Lee	1.50

Boyz With The Wood

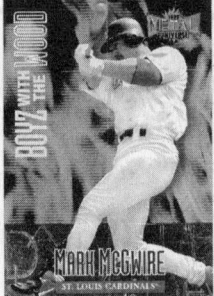

		NM/M
Complete Set (15):		17.50
Common Player:		.60
Inserted 1:18		
1	Ken Griffey Jr.	2.00
2	Frank Thomas	1.00
3	Jeff Bagwell	1.00
4	Juan Gonzalez	.75
5	Mark McGwire	2.50
6	Scott Rolen	.60
7	Travis Lee	.60
8	Tony Gwynn	2.00
9	Mike Piazza	2.00
10	Chipper Jones	2.00
11	Nomar Garciaparra	2.00
12	Derek Jeter	3.00
13	Cal Ripken Jr.	3.00
14	Andruw Jones	1.00
15	Alex Rodriguez	2.50

Linchpins

		NM/M
Complete Set (10):		75.00
Common Player:		5.00
Inserted 1:360		
1	Mike Piazza	10.00
2	Mark McGwire	12.50
3	Kerry Wood	5.00
4	Ken Griffey Jr.	10.00
5	Greg Maddux	7.50
6	Frank Thomas	6.00
7	Derek Jeter	15.00
8	Chipper Jones	7.50
9	Cal Ripken Jr.	15.00
10	Alex Rodriguez	12.50

Planet Metal

		NM/M
Complete Set (15):		45.00
Common Player:		1.50
Inserted 1:36		
1	Alex Rodriguez	9.00
2	Andruw Jones	3.50
3	Cal Ripken Jr.	12.00
4	Chipper Jones	5.00
5	Darin Erstad	2.00
6	Derek Jeter	12.00
7	Frank Thomas	3.50
8	Travis Lee	1.50
9	Scott Rolen	2.50
10	Nomar Garciaparra	5.00
11	Mike Piazza	6.50
12	Mark McGwire	9.00
13	Ken Griffey Jr.	6.50
14	Juan Gonzalez	2.50
15	Jeff Bagwell	3.50

2000 METAL

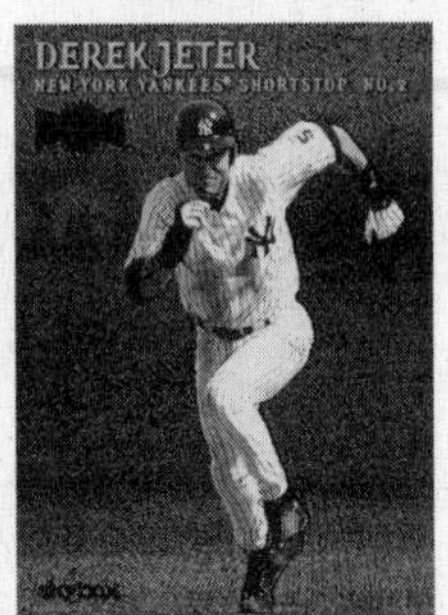

		NM/M
Complete Set (250):		20.00
Common Player:		.10
Common Prospect (201-250):		.50
Inserted 1:2		
Pack (10):		1.50
Wax Box (28):		25.00
1	Tony Gwynn	1.00
2	Derek Jeter	2.50
3	Johnny Damon	.35
4	Javy Lopez	.10
5	Preston Wilson	.10
6	Derek Bell	.10
7	Richie Sexson	.10
8	Vinny Castilla	.10
9	Billy Wagner	.10
10	Carlos Beltran	.50
11	Chris Singleton	.10
12	Nomar Garciaparra	1.00
13	Carlos Febles	.10
14	Jason Varitek	.10
15	Luis Gonzalez	.20
16	Jon Lieber	.10
17	Mo Vaughn	.10
18	Dave Burba	.10
19	Brady Anderson	.10
20	Carlos Lee	.20
21	Chuck Finley	.10
22	Alex Gonzalez	.10
23	Matt Williams	.10
24	Chipper Jones	1.00
25	Pokey Reese	.10
26	Todd Helton	.65
27	Mike Mussina	.40
28	Butch Huskey	.10
29	Jeff Bagwell	.75
30	Juan Encarnacion	.10
31	A.J. Burnett	.10
32	Micah Bowie	.10
33	Brian Jordan	.10
34	Scott Erickson	.10
35	Sean Casey	.25
36	John Smoltz	.10
37	Edgard Clemente	.10
38	Mike Hampton	.10
39	Tom Glavine	.35
40	Albert Belle	.10
41	Jim Thome	.60
42	Jermaine Dye	.10
43	Sammy Sosa	1.25
44	Pedro Martinez	.75
45	Paul Konerko	.20
46	Damion Easley	.10
47	Cal Ripken Jr.	2.50
48	Jose Lima	.10
49	Mike Lowell	.10
50	Randy Johnson	.75
51	Dean Palmer	.10
52	Tim Salmon	.10
53	Kevin Millwood	.10
54	Mark Grace	.10
55	Aaron Boone	.10
56	Omar Vizquel	.10
57	Moises Alou	.10
58	Travis Fryman	.10
59	Erubiel Durazo	.10
60	Carl Everett	.10
61	Charles Johnson	.10
62	Trot Nixon	.10
63	Andres Galarraga	.10
64	Magglio Ordonez	.10
65	Pedro Astacio	.10
66	Roberto Alomar	.20
67	Pete Harnisch	.10
68	Scott Williamson	.10
69	Alex Fernandez	.10
70	Robin Ventura	.10
71	Chad Allen	.10
72	Darin Erstad	.20
73	Ron Coomer	.10
74	Ellis Burks	.10
75	Kent Bottenfield	.10
76	Ken Griffey Jr.	1.50
77	Mike Piazza	1.50
78	Jorge Posada	.20
79	Dante Bichette	.10
80	Adrian Beltre	.25
81	Andruw Jones	.75
82	Wilson Alvarez	.10
83	Edgardo Alfonzo	.10
84	Brian Giles	.10
85	Gary Sheffield	.25
86	Matt Stairs	.10
87	Bret Boone	.10
88	Kenny Rogers	.10
89	Barry Bonds	2.50
90	Scott Rolen	.60
91	Edgar Renteria	.10
92	Larry Walker	.10
93	Roger Cedeno	.10
94	Kevin Brown	.10
95	Lee Stevens	.10
96	Brad Radke	.10
97	Andy Pettitte	.25
98	Bobby Higginson	.10
99	Eric Chavez	.25
100	Alex Rodriguez	2.00
100s	Alex Rodriguez (overprinted "PROMOTIONAL SAMPLE")	2.00
101	Shannon Stewart	.10
102	Ryan Rupe	.10
103	Freddy Garcia	.10
104	John Jaha	.10
105	Greg Maddux	1.00
106	Hideki Irabu	.10
107	Rey Ordonez	.10
108	Troy O'Leary	.10
109	Frank Thomas	.75
110	Corey Koskie	.10
111	Bernie Williams	.10
112	Barry Larkin	.10
113	Kevin Appier	.10
114	Curt Schilling	.35
115	Bartolo Colon	.10
116	Edgar Martinez	.10
117	Ray Lankford	.10
118	Todd Walker	.10
119	John Wetteland	.10

120 David Nilsson .10
121 Tino Martinez .10
122 Phil Nevin .10
123 Ben Grieve .10
124 Ron Gant .10
125 Jeff Kent .10
126 Rick Helling .10
127 Russ Ortiz .10
128 Troy Glaus .65
129 Chan Ho Park .10
130 Jeromy Burnitz .10
131 Aaron Sele .10
132 Mike Sirotka .10
133 Brad Ausmus .10
134 Jose Rosado .10
135 Mariano Rivera .25
136 Jason Giambi .50
137 Mike Lieberthal .10
138 Chris Carpenter .10
139 Henry Rodriguez .10
140 Mike Sweeney .10
141 Vladimir Guerrero .75
142 Charles Nagy .10
143 Jason Kendall .10
144 Matt Lawton .10
145 Michael Barrett .10
146 David Cone .10
147 Bobby Abreu .10
148 Fernando Tatis .10
149 Jose Canseco .40
150 Craig Biggio .10
151 Matt Mantei .10
152 Jacque Jones .10
153 John Halama .10
154 Trevor Hoffman .10
155 Rondell White .10
156 Reggie Sanders .10
157 Steve Finley .10
158 Roberto Hernandez .10
159 Geoff Jenkins .10
160 Chris Widger .10
161 Orel Hershiser .10
162 Tim Hudson .20
163 Kris Benson .10
164 Kevin Young .10
165 Rafael Palmeiro .60
166 David Wells .10
167 Ben Davis .10
168 Jamie Moyer .10
169 Randy Wolf .10
170 Jeff Cirillo .10
171 Warren Morris .10
172 Billy Koch .10
173 Marquis Grissom .10
174 Geoff Blum .10
175 Octavio Dotel .10
176 Orlando Hernandez .20
177 J.D. Drew .25
178 Carlos Delgado .40
179 Sterling Hitchcock .10
180 Shawn Green .25
181 Tony Clark .10
182 Joe McEwing .10
183 Fred McGriff .10
184 Tony Batista .10
185 Al Leiter .10
186 Roger Clemens 1.25
187 Al Martin .10
188 Eric Milton .10
189 Bobby Smith .10
190 Rusty Greer .10
191 Shawn Estes .10
192 Ken Caminiti .10
193 Eric Karros .10
194 Manny Ramirez .75
195 Jim Edmonds .10
196 Paul O'Neill .10
197 Rico Brogna .10
198 Ivan Rodriguez .60
199 Doug Glanville .10
200 Mark McGwire 2.00
201 Mark Quinn .50
202 Norm Hutchins .50
203 Ramon Ortiz .50
204 Brett Laxton .50
205 Jimmy Anderson .50
206 Calvin Murray .50
207 Wilton Veras .50
208 Chad Hermansen .50
209 Nick Johnson .50
210 Kevin Barker .50
211 Casey Blake .50
212 Chad Meyers .50
213 Kip Wells .50
214 Eric Munson .50
215 Lance Berkman .50
216 Wily Pena .50
217 Gary Matthews Jr. .50
218 Travis Dawkins .50
219 Josh Beckett .75
220 Tony Armas Jr. .50
221 Alfonso Soriano 1.00
222 Pat Burrell 1.00
223 *Danys Baez* .50
224 Adam Kennedy .50
225 Ruben Mateo .50
226 Vernon Wells .75
227 Brian Cooper .50
228 *Jeff DaVanon* .50
229 Glen Barker .50
230 Robinson Cancel .50
231 D'Angelo Jimenez .50
232 Adam Piatt .50
233 Buddy Carlyle .50
234 Chad Hutchinson .50
235 Matt Riley .50
236 Cole Liniak .50
237 Ben Petrick .50
238 Peter Bergeron .50
239 Cesar King .50
240 Aaron Myette .50
241 Eric Gagne .60
242 Joe Nathan .50
243 Bruce Chen .50
244 Rob Bell .50
245 *Juan Sosa* .60
246 Julio Ramirez .50
247 Wade Miller .50
248 *Trace Coquillette* .50
249 Robert Ramsay .50
250 Rick Ankiel .60

Emerald

NM/M

Complete Set (250): 100.00
Common Player: .25
Stars: 2.5X
Inserted 1:4
Prospects (201-250): 2.5X
Inserted 1:8

Autographics

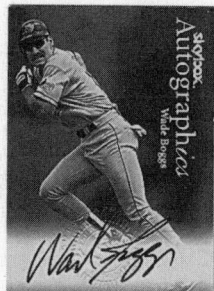

NM/M

Common Player: 4.00
Bobby Abreu 8.00
Chad Allen 4.00
Marlon Anderson 4.00
Rick Ankiel 6.00
Glen Barker 4.00
Rob Bell 4.00
Mark Bellhorn 5.00
Peter Bergeron 4.00
Lance Berkman 8.00
Wade Boggs 25.00
Barry Bonds 150.00
Kent Bottenfield 4.00
Pat Burrell 10.00
Miguel Cairo 4.00
Mike Cameron 6.00
Chris Carpenter 6.00
Roger Cedeno 4.00
Mike Darr 6.00
Einar Diaz 4.00
J.D. Drew 15.00
Erubiel Durazo 6.00
Ray Durham 6.00
Damion Easley 4.00
Scott Elarton 4.00
Jeremy Giambi 4.00
Doug Glanville 4.00
Shawn Green 10.00
Jerry Hairston Jr. 4.00
Bob Howry 4.00
Norm Hutchins 4.00
Randy Johnson 40.00
Jacque Jones 4.00
Gabe Kapler 6.00
Cesar King 4.00
Mark Kotsay 4.00
Cole Liniak 4.00
Greg Maddux 50.00
Pedro Martinez 30.00
Ruben Mateo 4.00
Warren Morris 4.00
Heath Murray 4.00
Joe Nathan 4.00
Jim Parque 4.00
Angel Pena 4.00
Cal Ripken Jr. 100.00
Alex Rodriguez 60.00
Ryan Rupe 4.00
Randall Simon 4.00
Chris Singleton 4.00
Mike Sweeney 6.00
Wilton Veras 4.00
Scott Williamson 4.00
Randy Wolf 6.00
Tony Womack 6.00

Base Shredders

NM/M

Complete Set (18): 160.00
Common Player: 5.00
Inserted 1:288
(1) Roberto Alomar 7.50
(2) Michael Barrett 5.00
(3) Tony Clark 5.00
(4) Ben Davis 5.00
(5) Erubiel Durazo 5.00
(6) Troy Glaus 12.50
(7) Ben Grieve 5.00
(8) Vladimir Guerrero 15.00
(9) Tony Gwynn 25.00
(10) Todd Helton 12.50
(11) Eric Munson 5.00
(12) Rafael Palmeiro 10.00
(13) Manny Ramirez 20.00
(14) Ivan Rodriguez 10.00
(15) Miguel Tejada 7.50
(16) Mo Vaughn 5.00
(17) Larry Walker 5.00
(18) Matt Williams 5.00

Fusion

NM/M

Complete Set (15): 12.50
Common Player: .50
Inserted 1:4
1 Ken Griffey Jr., Alex Rodriguez 2.00
2 Mark McGwire, Rick Ankiel 2.00
3 Scott Rolen, Curt Schilling .50
4 Pedro Martinez, Nomar Garciaparra 1.25
5 Carlos Beltran, Carlos Febles .60
6 Sammy Sosa, Mark Grace 1.50
7 Vladimir Guerrero, Ugueth Urbina 1.00
8 Roger Clemens, Derek Jeter 3.00
9 Jeff Bagwell, Craig Biggio 1.00
10 Chipper Jones, Andruw Jones 1.50
11 Cal Ripken Jr., Mike Mussina 2.50
12 Manny Ramirez, Roberto Alomar 1.00
13 Sean Casey, Barry Larkin .50
14 Ivan Rodriguez, Rafael Palmeiro .75
15 Mike Piazza, Robin Ventura 1.50

Heavy Metal

NM/M

Complete Set (10): 15.00
Common Player: 1.50
Inserted 1:20
1 Sammy Sosa 2.25
2 Mark McGwire 3.00
3 Ken Griffey Jr. 2.50
4 Mike Piazza 2.50
5 Nomar Garciaparra 2.00
6 Alex Rodriguez 3.00
7 Manny Ramirez 1.50
8 Jeff Bagwell 1.50
9 Chipper Jones 2.00
10 Vladimir Guerrero 1.50

Hit Machines

NM/M

Complete Set (10): 20.00
Common Player: 1.00
Inserted 1:20
1 Ken Griffey Jr. 3.00
2 Mark McGwire 4.00
3 Frank Thomas 1.50
4 Tony Gwynn 2.00
5 Rafael Palmeiro 1.25
6 Bernie Williams 1.00
7 Derek Jeter 6.00
8 Sammy Sosa 2.50
9 Mike Piazza 3.00
10 Chipper Jones 2.00

Platinum Portraits

NM/M

Complete Set (10): 6.00
Common Player: .25
Inserted 1:8
1 Carlos Beltran .50
2 Vladimir Guerrero .75
3 Manny Ramirez .75
4 Ivan Rodriguez .65
5 Sean Casey .40
6 Alex Rodriguez 1.50
7 Derek Jeter 2.00
8 Nomar Garciaparra 1.00
9 Vernon Wells .25
10 Shawn Green .50

Talent Show

		NM/M
Complete Set (15):		6.00
Common Player:		.30
Inserted 1:4		
1	Rick Ankiel	.45
2	Matt Riley	.30
3	Chad Hermansen	.30
4	Ruben Mateo	.30
5	Eric Munson	.30
6	Alfonso Soriano	1.50
7	Wilton Veras	.30
8	Vernon Wells	.75
9	Erubiel Durazo	.30
10	Pat Burrell	1.50
11	Ben Davis	.30
12	A.J. Burnett	.30
13	Peter Bergeron	.30
14	Mark Quinn	.30
15	Ben Petrick	.30

P

1993 PACIFIC

		NM/M
Complete Set (660):		20.00
Common Player:		.05
1	Rafael Belliard	.05
2	Sid Bream	.05
3	Francisco Cabrera	.05
4	Marvin Freeman	.05
5	Ron Gant	.05
6	Tom Glavine	.25
7	Brian Hunter	.05
8	Dave Justice	.05
9	Ryan Klesko	.05
10	Melvin Nieves	.05
11	Deion Sanders	.05
12	John Smoltz	.05
13	Mark Wohlers	.05
14	Brady Anderson	.05
15	Glenn Davis	.05
16	Mike Devereaux	.05
17	Leo Gomez	.05
18	Chris Hoiles	.05
19	Chito Martinez	.05
20	Ben McDonald	.05
21	Mike Mussina	.40
22	Gregg Olson	.05
23	Joe Orsulak	.05
24	Cal Ripken, Jr.	1.50
25	David Segui	.05
26	Rick Sutcliffe	.05
27	Wade Boggs	.65
28	Tom Brunansky	.05
29	Ellis Burks	.05
30	Roger Clemens	.75
31	John Dopson	.05
32	John Flaherty	.05
33	Mike Greenwell	.05
34	Tony Pena	.05
35	Carlos Quintana	.05
36	Luis Rivera	.05
37	Mo Vaughn	.05
38	Frank Viola	.05
39	Matt Young	.05
40	Scott Bailes	.05
41	Bert Blyleven	.05
42	Chad Curtis	.05
43	Gary DiSarcina	.05
44	Chuck Finley	.05
45	Mike Fitzgerald	.05
46	Gary Gaetti	.05
47	Rene Gonzales	.05
48	Mark Langston	.05
49	Scott Lewis	.05
50	Luis Polonia	.05
51	Tim Salmon	.05
52	Lee Stevens	.05
53	Steve Buechele	.05
54	Frank Castillo	.05
55	Doug Dascenzo	.05
56	Andre Dawson	.25
57	Shawon Dunston	.05
58	Mark Grace	.05
59	Mike Morgan	.05
60	Luis Salazar	.05
61	Rey Sanchez	.05
62	Ryne Sandberg	.65
63	Dwight Smith	.05
64	Jerome Walton	.05
65	Rick Wilkins	.05
66	Wilson Alvarez	.05
67	George Bell	.05
68	Joey Cora	.05
69	Alex Fernandez	.05
70	Carlton Fisk	.50
71	Craig Grebeck	.05
72	Ozzie Guillen	.05
73	Jack McDowell	.05
74	Scott Radinsky	.05
75	Tim Raines	.05
76	Bobby Thigpen	.05
77	Frank Thomas	.50
78	Robin Ventura	.05
79	Tom Browning	.05
80	Jacob Brumfield	.05
81	Rob Dibble	.05
82	Bill Doran	.05
83	Billy Hatcher	.05
84	Barry Larkin	.05
85	Hal Morris	.05
86	Joe Oliver	.05
87	Jeff Reed	.05
88	Jose Rijo	.05
89	Bip Roberts	.05
90	Chris Sabo	.05
91	Sandy Alomar, Jr.	.05
92	Brad Arnsberg	.05
93	Carlos Baerga	.05
94	Albert Belle	.05
95	Felix Fermin	.05
96	Mark Lewis	.05
97	Kenny Lofton	.05
98	Carlos Martinez	.05
99	Rod Nicholos	.05
100	Dave Rohde	.05
101	Scott Scudder	.05
102	Paul Sorrento	.05
103	Mark Whiten	.05
104	Mark Carreon	.05
105	Milt Cuyler	.05
106	Rob Deer	.05
107	Cecil Fielder	.05
108	Travis Fryman	.05
109	Dan Gladden	.05
110	Bill Gullickson	.05
111	Les Lancaster	.05
112	Mark Leiter	.05
113	Tony Phillips	.05
114	Mickey Tettleton	.05
115	Alan Trammell	.05
116	Lou Whitaker	.05
117	Jeff Bagwell	.50
118	Craig Biggio	.05
119	Joe Boever	.05
120	Casey Candaele	.05
121	Andujar Cedeno	.05
122	Steve Finley	.05
123	Luis Gonzalez	.05
124	Pete Harnisch	.05
125	Jimmy Jones	.05
126	Mark Portugal	.05
127	Rafael Ramirez	.05
128	Mike Simms	.05
129	Eric Yelding	.05
130	Luis Aquino	.05
131	Kevin Appier	.05
132	Mike Boddicker	.05
133	George Brett	.75
134	Tom Gordon	.05
135	Mark Gubicza	.05
136	David Howard	.05
137	Gregg Jefferies	.05
138	Wally Joyner	.05
139	Brian McRae	.05
140	Jeff Montgomery	.05
141	Terry Shumpert	.05
142	Curtis Wilkerson	.05
143	Brett Butler	.05
144	Eric Davis	.05
145	Kevin Gross	.05
146	Dave Hansen	.05
147	Lenny Harris	.05
148	Carlos Hernandez	.05
149	Orel Hershiser	.05
150	Jay Howell	.05
151	Eric Karros	.05
152	Ramon Martinez	.05
153	Jose Offerman	.05
154	Mike Sharperson	.05
155	Darryl Strawberry	.05
156	Jim Gantner	.05
157	Darryl Hamilton	.05
158	Doug Henry	.05
159	John Jaha	.05
160	Pat Listach	.05
161	Jaime Navarro	.05
162	Dave Nilsson	.05
163	Jesse Orosco	.05
164	Kevin Seitzer	.05
165	B.J. Surhoff	.05
166	Greg Vaughn	.05
167	Robin Yount	.50
168	Rick Aguilera	.05
169	Scott Erickson	.05
170	Mark Guthrie	.05
171	Kent Hrbek	.05
172	Chuck Knoblauch	.05
173	Gene Larkin	.05
174	Shane Mack	.05
175	Pedro Munoz	.05
176	Mike Pagliarulo	.05
177	Kirby Puckett	.65
178	Kevin Tapani	.05
179	Gary Wayne	.05
180	Moises Alou	.05
181	Brian Barnes	.05
182	Archie Cianfrocco	.05
183	Delino DeShields	.05
184	Darrin Fletcher	.05
185	Marquis Grissom	.05
186	Ken Hill	.05
187	Dennis Martinez	.05
188	Bill Sampen	.05
189	John VanderWal	.05
190	Larry Walker	.05
191	Tim Wallach	.05
192	Bobby Bonilla	.05
193	Daryl Boston	.05
194	Vince Coleman	.05
195	Kevin Elster	.05
196	Sid Fernandez	.05
197	John Franco	.05
198	Dwight Gooden	.05
199	Howard Johnson	.05
200	Willie Randolph	.05
201	Bret Saberhagen	.05
202	Dick Schofield	.05
203	Pete Schourek	.05
204	Greg Cadaret	.05
205	John Habyan	.05
206	Pat Kelly	.05
207	Kevin Maas	.05
208	Don Mattingly	.75
209	Matt Nokes	.05
210	Melido Perez	.05
211	Scott Sanderson	.05
212	Andy Stankiewicz	.05
213	Danny Tartabull	.05
214	Randy Velarde	.05
215	Bernie Williams	.05
216	Harold Baines	.05
217	Mike Bordick	.05
218	Scott Brosius	.05
219	Jerry Browne	.05
220	Ron Darling	.05
221	Dennis Eckersley	.40
222	Rickey Henderson	.50
223	Rick Honeycutt	.05
224	Mark McGwire	1.25
225	Ruben Sierra	.05
226	Terry Steinbach	.05
227	Bob Welch	.05
228	Willie Wilson	.05
229	Ruben Amaro	.05
230	Kim Batiste	.05
231	Juan Bell	.05
232	Wes Chamberlain	.05
233	Darren Daulton	.05
234	Mariano Duncan	.05
235	Len Dykstra	.05
236	Dave Hollins	.05
237	Stan Javier	.05
238	John Kruk	.05
239	Mickey Morandini	.05
240	Terry Mulholland	.05
241	Mitch Williams	.05
242	Stan Belinda	.05
243	Jay Bell	.05
244	Carlos Garcia	.05
245	Jeff King	.05
246	Mike LaValliere	.05
247	Lloyd McClendon	.05
248	Orlando Merced	.05
249	Paul Miller	.05
250	Gary Redus	.05
251	Don Slaught	.05
252	Zane Smith	.05
253	Andy Van Slyke	.05
254	Tim Wakefield	.05
255	Andy Benes	.05
256	Dann Bilardello	.05
257	Tony Gwynn	.65
258	Greg Harris	.05
259	Darrin Jackson	.05
260	Mike Maddux	.05
261	Fred McGriff	.05
262	Rich Rodriguez	.05
263	Benito Santiago	.05
264	Gary Sheffield	.35
265	Kurt Stillwell	.05
266	Tim Teufel	.05
267	Bud Black	.05
268	John Burkett	.05
269	Will Clark	.05
270	Royce Calyton	.05
271	Bryan Hickerson	.05
272	Chris James	.05
273	Darren Lewis	.05
274	Willie McGee	.05
275	Jim McNamara	.05
276	Francisco Oliveras	.05
277	Robby Thompson	.05
278	Matt Williams	.05
279	Trevor Wilson	.05
280	Bret Boone	.05
281	Greg Briley	.05
282	Jay Buhner	.05
283	Henry Cotto	.05
284	Rich DeLucia	.05
285	Dave Fleming	.05
286	Ken Griffey, Jr.	1.00
287	Erik Hanson	.05
288	Randy Johnson	.50
289	Tino Martinez	.05
290	Edgar Martinez	.05
291	Dave Valle	.05
292	Omar Vizquel	.05
293	Luis Alicea	.05
294	Bernard Gilkey	.05
295	Felix Jose	.05
296	Ray Lankford	.05
297	Omar Olivares	.05
298	Jose Oquendo	.05
299	Tom Pagnozzi	.05
300	Geronimo Pena	.05
301	Gerald Perry	.05
302	Ozzie Smith	.65
303	Lee Smith	.05
304	Bob Tewksbury	.05
305	Todd Zeile	.05
306	Kevin Brown	.05
307	Todd Burns	.05
308	Jose Canseco	.35
309	Hector Fajardo	.05
310	Julio Franco	.05
311	Juan Gonzalez	.25
312	Jeff Huson	.05
313	Rob Maurer	.05
314	Rafael Palmeiro	.45
315	Dean Palmer	.05
316	Ivan Rodriguez	.45
317	Nolan Ryan	1.50
318	Dickie Thon	.05
319	Roberto Alomar	.20
320	Derek Bell	.05
321	Pat Borders	.05
322	Joe Carter	.05
323	Kelly Gruber	.05
324	Juan Guzman	.05
325	Manny Lee	.05
326	Jack Morris	.05
327	John Olerud	.05
328	Ed Sprague	.05
329	Todd Stottlemyre	.05
330	Duane Ward	.05
331	Steve Avery	.05
332	Damon Berryhill	.05
333	Jeff Blauser	.05
334	Mark Lemke	.05
335	Greg Maddux	.65
336	Kent Mercker	.05
337	Otis Nixon	.05
338	Greg Olson	.05
339	Bill Pecota	.05
340	Terry Pendleton	.05
341	Mike Stanton	.05
342	Todd Frohwirth	.05
343	Tim Hulett	.05
344	Mark McLemore	.05
345	Luis Mercedes	.05

346 Alan Mills .05
347 Sherman Obando .05
348 Jim Poole .05
349 Harold Reynolds .05
350 Arthur Rhodes .05
351 Jeff Tackett .05
352 Fernando Valenzuela .05
353 Scott Bankhead .05
354 Ivan Calderon .05
355 Scott Cooper .05
356 Danny Darwin .05
357 Scott Fletcher .05
358 Tony Fossas .05
359 Greg Harris .05
360 Joe Hesketh .05
361 Jose Melendez .05
362 Paul Quantrill .05
363 John Valentin .05
364 Mike Butcher .05
365 Chuck Crim .05
366 Chili Davis .05
367 Damion Easley .05
368 Steve Frey .05
369 Joe Grahe .05
370 Greg Myers .05
371 John Orton .05
372 J.T. Snow .05
373 Ron Tingley .05
374 Julio Valera .05
375 Paul Assenmacher .05
376 Jose Bautista .05
377 Jose Guzman .05
378 Greg Hibbard .05
379 Candy Maldonado .05
380 Derrick May .05
381 Dan Plesac .05
382 Tommy Shields .05
383 Sammy Sosa .75
384 Jose Vizcaino .05
385 Greg Walbeck .05
386 Ellis Burks .05
387 Roberto Hernandez .05
388 Mike Huff .05
389 Bo Jackson .10
390 Lance Johnson .05
391 Ron Karkovice .05
392 Kirk McCaskill .05
393 Donn Pall .05
394 Dan Pasqua .05
395 Steve Sax .05
396 Dave Stieb .05
397 Bobby Ayala .05
398 Tim Belcher .05
399 Jeff Branson .05
400 Cesar Hernandez .05
401 Roberto Kelly .05
402 Randy Milligan .05
403 Kevin Mitchell .05
404 Juan Samuel .05
405 Reggie Sanders .05
406 John Smiley .05
407 Dan Wilson .05
408 Mike Christopher .05
409 Dennis Cook .05
410 Alvaro Espinoza .05
411 Glenallen Hill .05
412 Reggie Jefferson .05
413 Derek Lilliquist .05
414 Jose Mesa .05
415 Charles Nagy .05
416 Junior Ortiz .05
417 Eric Plunk .05
418 Ted Power .05
419 Scott Aldred .05
420 Andy Ashby .05
421 Freddie Benavides .05
422 Dante Bichette .05
423 Willie Blair .05
424 Vinny Castilla .05
425 Jerald Clark .05
426 Alex Cole .05
427 Andres Galarraga .05
428 Joe Girardi .05
429 Charlie Hayes .05
430 Butch Henry .05
431 Darren Holmes .05
432 Dale Murphy .20
433 David Nied .05
434 Jeff Parrett .05
435 *Steve Reed* .05
436 Armando Reynoso .05
437 Bruce Ruffin .05
438 Bryn Smith .05
439 Jim Tatum .05
440 Eric Young .05
441 Skeeter Barnes .05
442 Tom Bolton .05
443 Kirk Gibson .05
444 Chad Krueter .05
445 Bill Krueger .05
446 Scott Livingstone .05
447 Bob MacDonald .05
448 Mike Moore .05
449 Mike Munoz .05
450 Gary Thurman .05
451 David Wells .05
452 Alex Arias .05
453 Jack Armstrong .05
454 Bret Barberie .05
455 Ryan Bowen .05
456 Cris Carpenter .05
457 Chuck Carr .05
458 Jeff Conine .05
459 Steve Decker .05
460 Orestes Destrade .05
461 Monty Fariss .05
462 Junior Felix .05
463 Bryan Harvey .05
464 Trevor Hoffman .05
465 Charlie Hough .05
466 Dave Magadan .05
467 Bob McClure .05
468 Rob Natal .05
469 Scott Pose .05
470 Rich Renteria .05
471 Benito Santiago .05
472 Matt Turner .05
473 Walt Weiss .05
474 Eric Anthony .05
475 Chris Donnels .05
476 Doug Drabek .05
477 Xavier Hernandez .05
478 Doug Jones .05
479 Darryl Kile .05
480 Scott Servais .05
481 Greg Swindell .05
482 Eddie Taubensee .05
483 Jose Uribe .05
484 Brian Williams .05
485 Billy Brewer .05
486 David Cone .05
487 Greg Gagne .05
488 Phil Hiatt .05
489 Jose Lind .05
490 Brent Mayne .05
491 Kevin McReynolds .05
492 Keith Miller .05
493 Hipolito Pichardo .05
494 Harvey Pulliam .05
495 Rico Rossay .05
496 Pedro Astacio .05
497 Tom Candiotti .05
498 Tom Goodwin .05
499 Jim Gott .05
500 Pedro Martinez .50
501 Roger McDowell .05
502 Mike Piazza .75
503 Jody Reed .05
504 Rick Trlicek .05
505 Mitch Weber .05
506 Steve Wilson .05
507 James Austin .05
508 Ricky Bones .05
509 Alex Diaz .05
510 Mike Fetters .05
511 Teddy Higuera .05
512 Graeme Lloyd .05
513 Carlos Maldonado .05
514 Josias Manzanillo .05
515 Kevin Reimer .05
516 Bill Spiers .05
517 Bill Wegman .05
518 Willie Banks .05
519 J.T. Bruett .05
520 Brian Harper .05
521 Terry Jorgensen .05
522 Scott Leius .05
523 Pat Mahomes .05
524 Dave McCarty .05
525 Jeff Reboulet .05
526 Mike Trombley .05
527 Carl Willis .05
528 Dave Winfield .50
529 Sean Berry .05
530 Frank Bolick .05
531 Kent Bottenfield .05
532 Wil Cordero .05
533 Jeff Fassero .05
534 Tim Laker .05
535 Mike Lansing .05
536 Chris Nabholz .05
537 Mel Rojas .05
538 John Wetteland .05
539 Ted Wood (Front photo actually Frank Bollick) .05
540 Mike Draper .05
541 Tony Fernandez .05
542 Todd Hundley .05
543 Jeff Innis .05
544 Jeff McKnight .05
545 Eddie Murray .50
546 Charlie O'Brien .05
547 Frank Tanana .05
548 Ryan Thompson .05
549 Chico Walker .05
550 Anthony Young .05
551 Jim Abbott .05
552 Wade Boggs .75
553 Steve Farr .05
554 Neal Heaton .05
555 Steve Howe .05
556 Dion James .05
557 Scott Kamieniecki .05
558 Jimmy Key .05
559 Jim Leyritz .05
560 Paul O'Neill .05
561 Spike Owen .05
562 Lance Blankenship .05
563 Joe Boever .05
564 Storm Davis .05
565 Kelly Downs .05
566 Eric Fox .05
567 Rich Gossage .05
568 Dave Henderson .05
569 Shawn Hillegas .05
570 *Mike Mohler* .05
571 Troy Neel .05
572 Dale Sveum .05
573 Larry Anderson .05
574 Bob Ayrault .05
575 Jose DeLeon .05
576 Jim Eisenreich .05
577 Pete Incaviglia .05
578 Danny Jackson .05
579 Ricky Jordan .05
580 Ben Rivera .05
581 Curt Schilling .25
582 Milt Thompson .05
583 David West .05
584 John Candelaria .05
585 Steve Cooke .05
586 Tom Foley .05
587 Al Martin .05
588 Blas Minor .05
589 Dennis Moeller .05
590 Denny Neagle .05
591 Tom Prince .05
592 Randy Tomlin .05
593 Bob Walk .05
594 Kevin Young .05
595 Pat Gomez .05
596 Ricky Gutierrez .05
597 Gene Harris .05
598 Jeremy Hernandez .05
599 Phil Plantier .05
600 Tim Scott .05
601 Frank Seminara .05
602 Darrell Sherman .05
603 Craig Shipley .05
604 Guillermo Velasquez .05
605 Dan Walters .05
606 Mike Benjamin .05
607 Barry Bonds 1.50
608 Jeff Brantley .05
609 Dave Burba .05
610 Craig Colbert .05
611 Mike Jackson .05
612 Kirt Manwaring .05
613 Dave Martinez .05
614 Dave Righetti .05
615 Kevin Rogers .05
616 Bill Swift .05
617 Rich Amaral .05
618 Mike Blowers .05
619 Chris Bosio .05
620 Norm Charlton .05
621 John Cummings .05
622 Mike Felder .05
623 Bill Haselman .05
624 Tim Leary .05
625 Pete O'Brien .05
626 Russ Swan .05
627 Fernando Vina .05
628 Rene Arocha .05
629 Rod Brewer .05
630 Ozzie Canseco .05
631 Rheal Cormier .05
632 Brian Jordan .05
633 Joe Magrane .05
634 Donovan Osborne .05
635 Mike Perez .05
636 Stan Royer .05
637 Hector Villanueva .05
638 Tracy Woodson .05
639 Benji Gil .05
640 Tom Henke .05
641 David Hulse .05
642 Charlie Leibrandt .05
643 Robb Nen .05
644 Dan Peltier .05
645 Billy Ripken .05
646 Kenny Rogers .05
647 John Russell .05
648 Dan Smith .05
649 Matt Whiteside .05
650 William Canate .05
651 Darnell Coles .05
652 Al Leiter .05
653 Dominigo Martinez .05
654 Paul Molitor .50
655 Luis Sojo .05
656 Dave Stewart .05
657 Mike Timlin .05
658 Turner Ward .05
659 Devon White .05
660 Eddie Zosky .05

Insert

NM/M

Complete Set (20): 60.00
Common Player: 3.00
1 Francisco Cabrera 3.00
2 Jose Lind 3.00
3 Dennis Martinez 3.00
4 Ramon Martinez 3.00
5 Jose Rijo 3.00
6 Benito Santiago 3.00
7 Roberto Alomar 9.00
8 Sandy Alomar Jr. 3.00
9 Carlos Baerga 3.00
10 George Bell 3.00
11 Jose Canseco 6.00
12 Alex Fernandez 3.00
13 Julio Franco 3.00
14 Igor (Juan) Gonzalez 12.00
15 Ozzie Guillen 3.00
16 Teddy Higuera 3.00
17 Edgar Martinez 3.00
18 Hipolito Pichardo 3.00
19 Luis Polonia 3.00
20 Ivan Rodriguez 7.50

1994 PACIFIC CROWN

NM/M

Complete Set (660): 20.00
Common Player: .05
Pack (12): 1.00
Wax Box (36): 20.00
1 Steve Avery .05
2 Steve Bedrosian .05
3 Damon Beryhill .05
4 Jeff Blauser .05
5 Sid Bream .05
6 Francisco Cabrera .05
7 Ramon Caraballo .05
8 Ron Gant .05
9 Tom Glavine .25
10 Chipper Jones .75
11 Dave Justice .05
12 Ryan Klesko .05
13 Mark Lemke .05
14 Javier Lopez .05
15 Greg Maddux .75
16 Fred McGriff .05
17 Greg McMichael .05
18 Kent Mercker .05
19 Otis Nixon .05
20 Terry Pendleton .05
21 Deion Sanders .05
22 John Smoltz .05
23 Tony Tarasco .05
24 Manny Alexander .05
25 Brady Anderson .05
26 Harold Baines .05
27 Damion Buford (Damon) .05
28 Paul Carey .05

No.	Player	Value
29	Mike Devereaux	.05
30	Todd Frohwirth	.05
31	Leo Gomez	.05
32	Jeffrey Hammonds	.05
33	Chris Hoiles	.05
34	Tim Hullett	.05
35	Ben McDonald	.05
36	Mark McLemore	.05
37	Alan Mills	.05
38	Mike Mussina	.35
39	Sherman Obando	.05
40	Gregg Olson	.05
41	Mike Pagliarulo	.05
42	Jim Poole	.05
43	Harold Reynolds	.05
44	Cal Ripken, Jr.	2.00
45	David Segui	.05
46	Fernando Valenzuela	.05
47	Jack Voight	.05
48	Scott Bankhead	.05
49	Roger Clemens	1.00
50	Scott Cooper	.05
51	Danny Darwin	.05
52	Andre Dawson	.20
53	John Dopson	.05
54	Scott Fletcher	.05
55	Tony Fossas	.05
56	Mike Greenwell	.05
57	Billy Hatcher	.05
58	Jeff McNeely	.05
59	Jose Melendez	.05
60	Tim Naehring	.05
61	Tony Pena	.05
62	Carlos Quintana	.05
63	Paul Quantrill	.05
64	Luis Rivera	.05
65	Jeff Russell	.05
66	Aaron Sele	.05
67	John Valentin	.05
68	Mo Vaughn	.05
69	Frank Viola	.05
70	Bob Zupcic	.05
71	Mike Butcher	.05
72	Ron Correia	.05
73	Chad Curtis	.05
74	Chili Davis	.05
75	Gary DiSarcina	.05
76	Damion Easley	.05
77	John Farrell	.05
78	Chuck Finley	.05
79	Joe Grahe	.05
80	Stan Javier	.05
81	Mark Langston	.05
82	Phil Leftwich	.05
83	Torey Lovullo	.05
84	Joe Magrane	.05
85	Greg Myers	.05
86	Eduardo Perez	.05
87	Luis Polonia	.05
88	Tim Salmon	.05
89	J.T. Snow	.05
90	Kurt Stillwell	.05
91	Ron Tingley	.05
92	Chris Turner	.05
93	Julio Valera	.05
94	Jose Bautista	.05
95	Shawn Boskie	.05
96	Steve Buechele	.05
97	Frank Castillo	.05
98	Mark Grace	.05
99	Jose Guzman	.05
100	Mike Harkey	.05
101	Greg Hibbard	.05
102	Doug Jennings	.05
103	Derrick May	.05
104	Mike Morgan	.05
105	Randy Myers	.05
106	Karl Rhodes	.05
107	Kevin Robinson	.05
108	Rey Sanchez	.05
109	Ryne Sandberg	.75
110	Tommy Shields	.05
111	Dwight Smith	.05
112	Sammy Sosa	.75
113	Jose Vizcaino	.05
114	Turk Wendell	.05
115	Rick Wilkins	.05
116	Willie Wilson	.05
117	Eddie Zambrano	.05
118	Wilson Alvarez	.05
119	Tim Belcher	.05
120	Jason Bere	.05
121	Rodney Bolton	.05
122	Ellis Burks	.05
123	Joey Cora	.05
124	Alex Fernandez	.05
125	Ozzie Guillen	.05
126	Craig Grebeck	.05
127	Roberto Hernandez	.05
128	Bo Jackson	.10
129	Lance Johnson	.05
130	Ron Karkovice	.05
131	Mike Lavalliere	.05
132	Norberto Martin	.05
133	Kirk McCaskill	.05
134	Jack McDowell	.05
135	Scott Radinsky	.05
136	Tim Raines	.05
137	Steve Sax	.05
138	Frank Thomas	.60
139	Dan Pasqua	.05
140	Robin Ventura	.05
141	Jeff Branson	.05
142	Tom Browning	.05
143	Jacob Brumfield	.05
144	Tim Costo	.05
145	Rob Dibble	.05
146	Brian Dorsett	.05
147	Steve Foster	.05
148	Cesar Hernandez	.05
149	Roberto Kelly	.05
150	Barry Larkin	.05
151	Larry Luebbers	.05
152	Kevin Mitchell	.05
153	Joe Oliver	.05
154	Tim Pugh	.05
155	Jeff Reardon	.05
156	Jose Rijo	.05
157	Bip Roberts	.05
158	Chris Sabo	.05
159	Juan Samuel	.05
160	Reggie Sanders	.05
161	John Smiley	.05
162	Jerry Spradlin	.05
163	Gary Varsho	.05
164	Sandy Alomar Jr.	.05
165	Carlos Baerga	.05
166	Albert Belle	.05
167	Mark Clark	.05
168	Alvaro Espinoza	.05
169	Felix Fermin	.05
170	Reggie Jefferson	.05
171	Wayne Kirby	.05
172	Tom Kramer	.05
173	Jesse Levis	.05
174	Kenny Lofton	.05
175	Candy Maldonado	.05
176	Carlos Martinez	.05
177	Jose Mesa	.05
178	Jeff Mutis	.05
179	Charles Nagy	.05
180	Bob Ojeda	.05
181	Junior Ortiz	.05
182	Eric Plunk	.05
183	Manny Ramirez	.60
184	Paul Sorrento	.05
185	Jeff Treadway	.05
186	Bill Wertz	.05
187	Freddie Benavides	.05
188	Dante Bichette	.05
189	Willie Blair	.05
190	Daryl Boston	.05
191	Pedro Castellano	.05
192	Vinny Castilla	.05
193	Jerald Clark	.05
194	Alex Cole	.05
195	Andres Galarraga	.05
196	Joe Girardi	.05
197	Charlie Hayes	.05
198	Darren Holmes	.05
199	Chris Jones	.05
200	Curt Leskanic	.05
201	Roberto Mejia	.05
202	David Nied	.05
203	J. Owens	.05
204	Steve Reed	.05
205	Armando Reynoso	.05
206	Bruce Ruffin	.05
207	Keith Shepherd	.05
208	Jim Tatum	.05
209	Eric Young	.05
210	Skeeter Barnes	.05
211	Danny Bautista	.05
212	Tom Bolton	.05
213	Eric Davis	.05
214	Storm Davis	.05
215	Cecil Fielder	.05
216	Travis Fryman	.05
217	Kirk Gibson	.05
218	Dan Gladden	.05
219	John Doherty	.05
220	Chris Gomez	.05
221	David Haas	.05
222	Bill Krueger	.05
223	Chad Kreuter	.05
224	Mark Leiter	.05
225	Bob MacDonald	.05
226	Mike Moore	.05
227	Tony Phillips	.05
228	Rich Rowland	.05
229	Mickey Tettleton	.05
230	Alan Trammell	.05
231	David Wells	.05
232	Lou Whitaker	.05
233	Luis Aquino	.05
234	Alex Arias	.05
235	Jack Armstrong	.05
236	Ryan Bowen	.05
237	Chuck Carr	.05
238	Matias Carrillo	.05
239	Jeff Conine	.05
240	Henry Cotto	.05
241	Orestes Destrade	.05
242	Chris Hammond	.05
243	Bryan Harvey	.05
244	Charlie Hough	.05
245	Richie Lewis	.05
246	Mitch Lyden	.05
247	Dave Magadan	.05
248	Bob Natal	.05
249	Benito Santiago	.05
250	Gary Sheffield	.30
251	Matt Turner	.05
252	David Weathers	.05
253	Walt Weiss	.05
254	Darrell Whitmore	.05
255	Nigel Wilson	.05
256	Eric Anthony	.05
257	Jeff Bagwell	.60
258	Kevin Bass	.05
259	Craig Biggio	.05
260	Ken Caminiti	.05
261	Andujar Cedeno	.05
262	Chris Donnels	.05
263	Doug Drabek	.05
264	Tom Edens	.05
265	Steve Finley	.05
266	Luis Gonzalez	.05
267	Pete Harnisch	.05
268	Xavier Hernandez	.05
269	Todd Jones	.05
270	Darryl Kile	.05
271	Al Osuna	.05
272	Rick Parker	.05
273	Mark Portugal	.05
274	Scott Servais	.05
275	Greg Swindell	.05
276	Eddie Taubensee	.05
277	Jose Uribe	.05
278	Brian Williams	.05
279	Kevin Appier	.05
280	Billy Brewer	.05
281	David Cone	.05
282	Greg Gagne	.05
283	Tom Gordon	.05
284	Chris Gwynn	.05
285	John Habyan	.05
286	Chris Haney	.05
287	Phil Hiatt	.05
288	David Howard	.05
289	Felix Jose	.05
290	Wally Joyner	.05
291	Kevin Koslofski	.05
292	Jose Lind	.05
293	Brent Mayne	.05
294	Mike Mcfarlane	.05
295	Brian McRae	.05
296	Kevin McReynolds	.05
297	Keith Miller	.05
298	Jeff Montgomery	.05
299	Hipolito Pichardo	.05
300	Rico Rossy	.05
301	Curtis Wilkerson	.05
302	Pedro Astacio	.05
303	Rafael Bournigal	.05
304	Brett Butler	.05
305	Tom Candiotti	.05
306	Omar Daal	.05
307	Jim Gott	.05
308	Kevin Gross	.05
309	Dave Hansen	.05
310	Carlos Hernandez	.05
311	Orel Hershiser	.05
312	Eric Karros	.05
313	Pedro Martinez	.60
314	Ramon Martinez	.05
315	Roger McDowell	.05
316	Raul Mondesi	.05
317	Jose Offerman	.05
318	Mike Piazza	1.00
319	Jody Reed	.05
320	Henry Rodriguez	.05
321	Cory Snyder	.05
322	Darryl Strawberry	.05
323	Tim Wallach	.05
324	Steve Wilson	.05
325	Juan Bell	.05
326	Ricky Bones	.05
327	Alex Diaz	.05
328	Cal Eldred	.05
329	Darryl Hamilton	.05
330	Doug Henry	.05
331	John Jaha	.05
332	Pat Listach	.05
333	Graeme Lloyd	.05
334	Carlos Maldonado	.05
335	Angel Miranda	.05
336	Jaime Navarro	.05
337	Dave Nilsson	.05
338	Rafael Novoa	.05
339	Troy O'Leary	.05
340	Jesse Orosco	.05
341	Kevin Seitzer	.05
342	Bill Spiers	.05
343	William Suero	.05
344	B.J. Surhoff	.05
345	Dickie Thon	.05
346	Jose Valentin	.05
347	Greg Vaughn	.05
348	Robin Yount	.60
349	Willie Banks	.05
350	Bernardo Brito	.05
351	Scott Erickson	.05
352	Mark Guthrie	.05
353	Chip Hale	.05
354	Brian Harper	.05
355	Kent Hrbek	.05
356	Terry Jorgenson	.05
357	Chuck Knoblauch	.05
358	Gene Larkin	.05
359	Scott Leius	.05
360	Shane Mack	.05
361	David McCarty	.05
362	Pat Meares	.05
363	Pedro Munoz	.05
364	Derek Parks	.05
365	Kirby Puckett	.75
366	Jeff Reboulet	.05
367	Kevin Tapani	.05
368	Mike Trombley	.05
369	George Tsamis	.05
370	Carl Willis	.05
371	Dave Winfield	.60
372	Moises Alou	.05
373	Brian Barnes	.05
374	Sean Berry	.05
375	Frank Bolick	.05
376	Wil Cordero	.05
377	Delino DeShields	.05
378	Jeff Fassero	.05
379	Darren Fletcher	.05
380	Cliff Floyd	.05
381	Lou Frazier	.05
382	Marquis Grissom	.05
383	Gil Heredia	.05
384	Mike Lansing	.05
385	Oreste Marrero	.05
386	Dennis Martinez	.05
387	Curtis Pride	.05
388	Mel Rojas	.05
389	Kirk Rueter	.05
390	Joe Siddall	.05
391	John Vander Wal	.05
392	Larry Walker	.05
393	John Wetteland	.05
394	Rondell White	.05
395	Tom Bogar	.05
396	Bobby Bonilla	.05
397	Jeromy Burnitz	.05
398	Mike Draper	.05
399	Sid Fernandez	.05
400	John Franco	.05
401	Dave Gallagher	.05
402	Dwight Gooden	.05
403	Eric Hillman	.05
404	Todd Hundley	.05
405	Butch Huskey	.05
406	Jeff Innis	.05
407	Howard Johnson	.05
408	Jeff Kent	.05
409	Ced Landrum	.05
410	Mike Maddux	.05
411	Josias Manzanillo	.05
412	Jeff McKnight	.05
413	Eddie Murray	.60
414	Tito Navarro	.05
415	Joe Orsulak	.05
416	Bret Saberhagen	.05
417	Dave Telgheder	.05
418	Ryan Thompson	.05
419	Chico Walker	.05
420	Jim Abbott	.05
421	Wade Boggs	.75
422	Mike Gallego	.05
423	Mark Hutton	.05
424	Dion James	.05

425 Domingo Jean .05
426 Pat Kelly .05
427 Jimmy Key .05
428 Jim Leyritz .05
429 Kevin Maas .05
430 Don Mattingly 1.00
431 Bobby Munoz .05
432 Matt Nokes .05
433 Paul O'Neill .05
434 Spike Owen .05
435 Melido Perez .05
436 Lee Smith .05
437 Andy Stankiewicz .05
438 Mike Stanley .05
439 Danny Tartabull .05
440 Randy Velarde .05
441 Bernie Williams .05
442 Gerald Williams .05
443 Mike Witt .05
444 Marcos Armas .05
445 Lance Blankenship .05
446 Mike Bordick .05
447 Ron Darling .05
448 Dennis Eckersley .45
449 Brent Gates .05
450 Goose Gossage .05
451 Scott Hemond .05
452 Dave Henderson .05
453 Shawn Hillegas .05
454 Rick Honeycutt .05
455 Scott Lydy .05
456 Mark McGwire 1.50
457 Henry Mercedes .05
458 Mike Mohler .05
459 Troy Neel .05
460 Edwin Nunez .05
461 Craig Paquette .05
462 Ruben Sierra .05
463 Terry Steinbach .05
464 Todd Van Poppel .05
465 Bob Welch .05
466 Bobby Witt .05
467 Ruben Amaro .05
468 Larry Anderson .05
469 Kim Batiste .05
470 Wes Chamberlain .05
471 Darren Daulton .05
472 Mariano Duncan .05
473 Len Dykstra .05
474 Jim Eisenreich .05
475 Tommy Greene .05
476 Dave Hollins .05
477 Pete Incaviglia .05
478 Danny Jackson .05
479 John Kruk .05
480 Tony Longmire .05
481 Jeff Manto .05
482 Mike Morandini .05
483 Terry Mulholland .05
484 Todd Pratt .05
485 Ben Rivera .05
486 Curt Schilling .25
487 Kevin Stocker .05
488 Milt Thompson .05
489 David West .05
490 Mitch Williams .05
491 Jeff Ballard .05
492 Jay Bell .05
493 Scott Bullett .05
494 Dave Clark .05
495 Steve Cooke .05
496 Midre Cummings .05
497 Mark Dewey .05
498 Carlos Garcia .05
499 Jeff King .05
500 Al Martin .05
501 Lloyd McClendon .05
502 Orlando Merced .05
503 Blas Minor .05
504 Denny Neagle .05
505 Tom Prince .05
506 Don Slaught .05
507 Zane Smith .05
508 Randy Tomlin .05
509 Andy Van Slyke .05
510 Paul Wagner .05
511 Tim Wakefield .05
512 Bob Walk .05
513 John Wehner .05
514 Kevin Young .05
515 Billy Bean .05
516 Andy Benes .05
517 Derek Bell .05
518 Doug Brocail .05
519 Jarvis Brown .05
520 Phil Clark .05
521 Mark Davis .05
522 Jeff Gardner .05
523 Pat Gomez .05
524 Ricky Gutierrez .05
525 Tony Gwynn .75
526 Gene Harris .05
527 Kevin Higgins .05
528 Trevor Hoffman .05
529 Luis Lopez .05
530 Pedro A. Martinez .05
531 Melvin Nieves .05
532 Phil Plantier .05
533 Frank Seminara .05
534 Craig Shipley .05
535 Tim Tuefel .05
536 Guillermo Velasquez .05
537 Wally Whitehurst .05
538 Rod Beck .05
539 Todd Benzinger .05
540 Barry Bonds 2.00
541 Jeff Brantley .05
542 Dave Burba .05
543 John Burkett .05
544 Will Clark .05
545 Royce Clayton .05
546 Brian Hickerson (Bryan) .05
547 Mike Jackson .05
548 Darren Lewis .05
549 Kirt Manwaring .05
550 Dave Martinez .05
551 Willie McGee .05
552 Jeff Reed .05
553 Dave Righetti .05
554 Kevin Rogers .05
555 Steve Scarsone .05
556 Bill Swift .05
557 Robby Thompson .05
558 Salomon Torres .05
559 Matt Williams .05
560 Trevor Wilson .05
561 Rich Amaral .05
562 Mike Blowers .05
563 Chris Bosio .05
564 Jay Buhner .05
565 Norm Charlton .05
566 Jim Converse .05
567 Rich DeLucia .05
568 Mike Felder .05
569 Dave Fleming .05
570 Ken Griffey, Jr. 1.00
571 Bill Haselman .05
572 Dwayne Henry .05
573 Brad Holman .05
574 Randy Johnson .60
575 Greg Litton .05
576 Edgar Martinez .05
577 Tino Martinez .05
578 Jeff Nelson .05
579 Mark Newfield .05
580 Roger Salkeld .05
581 Mackey Sasser .05
582 Brian Turang .05
583 Omar Vizquel .05
584 Dave Valle .05
585 Luis Alicea .05
586 Rene Arocha .05
587 Rheal Cormier .05
588 Tripp Cromer .05
589 Bernard Gilkey .05
590 Lee Guetterman .05
591 Gregg Jefferies .05
592 Tim Jones .05
593 Paul Kilgus .05
594 Les Lancaster .05
595 Omar Olivares .05
596 Jose Oquendo .05
597 Donovan Osborne .05
598 Tom Pagnozzi .05
599 Erik Pappas .05
600 Geronimo Pena .05
601 Mike Perez .05
602 Gerald Perry .05
603 Stan Royer .05
604 Ozzie Smith .75
605 Bob Tewksbury .05
606 Allen Watson .05
607 Mark Whiten .05
608 Todd Zeile .05
609 Jeff Bronkey .05
610 Kevin Brown .05
611 Jose Canseco .35
612 Doug Dascenzo .05
613 Butch Davis .05
614 Mario Diaz .05
615 Julio Franco .05
616 Benji Gil .05
617 Juan Gonzalez .30
618 Tom Henke .05
619 Jeff Huson .05
620 David Hulse .05
621 Craig Lefferts .05
622 Rafael Palmeiro .50
623 Dean Palmer .05
624 Bob Patterson .05
625 Roger Pavlik .05
626 Gary Redus .05
627 Ivan Rodriguez .50
628 Kenny Rogers .05
629 Jon Shave .05
630 Doug Strange .05
631 Matt Whiteside .05
632 Roberto Alomar .15
633 Pat Borders .05
634 Scott Brow .05
635 Rob Butler .05
636 Joe Carter .05
637 Tony Castillo .05
638 Mark Eichhorn .05
639 Tony Fernandez .05
640 *Huck Flener* .05
641 Alfredo Griffin .05
642 Juan Guzman .05
643 Rickey Henderson .60
644 Pat Hentgen .05
645 Randy Knorr .05
646 Al Leiter .05
647 Dominigo Martinez .05
648 Paul Molitor .60
649 Jack Morris .05
650 John Olerud .05
651 Ed Sprague .05
652 Dave Stewart .05
653 Devon White .05
654 Woody Williams .05
655 Barry Bonds (MVP) 1.00
656 Greg Maddux (CY) .40
657 Jack McDowell (CY) .05
658 Mike Piazza (ROY) .65
659 Tim Salmon (ROY) .05
660 Frank Thomas (MVP) .25

All Latino All-Star Team

		NM/M
Complete Set (20):		4.00
Common Player:		.25
1	Benito Santiago	.25
2	Dave Magadan	.25
3	Andres Galarraga	.25
4	Luis Gonzalez	.25
5	Jose Offerman	.25
6	Bobby Bonilla	.25
7	Dennis Martinez	.25
8	Mariano Duncan	.25
9	Orlando Merced	.25
10	Jose Rijo	.25
11	Danny Tartabull	.25
12	Ruben Sierra	.25
13	Ivan Rodriguez	1.00
14	Juan Gonzalez	1.00
15	Jose Canseco	.50
16	Rafael Palmeiro	1.00
17	Roberto Alomar	.50
18	Eduardo Perez	.25
19	Alex Fernandez	.25
20	Omar Vizquel	.25

Jewels of the Crown

		NM/M
Complete Set (36):		40.00
Common Player:		1.00
1	Robin Yount	2.50
2	Juan Gonzalez	1.25
3	Rafael Palmeiro	2.00
4	Paul Molitor	2.50
5	Roberto Alomar	1.25
6	John Olerud	1.00
7	Randy Johnson	2.50
8	Ken Griffey, Jr.	4.00
9	Wade Boggs	3.00
10	Don Mattingly	3.50
11	Kirby Puckett	3.00

12	Tim Salmon	1.00
13	Frank Thomas	2.50
14	Fernando Valenzuela (Comeback Player)	1.00
15	Cal Ripken, Jr.	6.00
16	Carlos Baerga	1.00
17	Kenny Lofton	1.00
18	Cecil Fielder	1.00
19	John Burkett	1.00
20	Andres Galarraga (Comeback Player)	1.00
21	Charlie Hayes	1.00
22	Orestes Destrade	1.00
23	Jeff Conine	1.00
24	Jeff Bagwell	2.50
25	Mark Grace	1.00
26	Ryne Sandberg	3.00
27	Gregg Jefferies	1.00
28	Barry Bonds	6.00
29	Mike Piazza	3.50
30	Greg Maddux	3.00
31	Darren Daulton	1.00
32	John Kruk	1.00
33	Len Dykstra	1.00
34	Orlando Merced	1.00
35	Tony Gwynn	3.00
36	Robby Thompson	1.00

Homerun Leaders

		NM/M
Complete Set (20):		25.00
Common Player:		1.00
1	Juan Gonzalez	1.50
2	Ken Griffey, Jr.	3.00
3	Frank Thomas	2.50
4	Albert Belle	1.00
5	Rafael Palmeiro	1.50
6	Joe Carter	1.00
7	Dean Palmer	1.00
8	Mickey Tettleton	1.00
9	Tim Salmon	1.00
10	Danny Tartabull	1.00
11	Barry Bonds	5.00
12	Dave Justice	1.00
13	Matt Williams	1.00
14	Fred McGriff	1.00
15	Ron Gant	1.00
16	Mike Piazza	3.00
17	Bobby Bonilla	1.00
18	Phil Plantier	1.00
19	Sammy Sosa	3.00
20	Rick Wilkins	1.00

Jewels of the Crown - Retail

		NM/M
Complete Set (36):		40.00
Common Player:		.75
1	Robin Yount	2.50
2	Juan Gonzalez	1.25
3	Rafael Palmeiro	1.25
4	Paul Molitor	2.50
5	Roberto Alomar	1.00
6	John Olerud	.75
7	Randy Johnson	2.50
8	Ken Griffey, Jr.	4.00
9	Wade Boggs	3.00
10	Don Mattingly	3.50
11	Kirby Puckett	3.00
12	Tim Salmon	.75
13	Frank Thomas	2.50
14	Fernando Valenzuela (Comeback Player)	.75
15	Cal Ripken, Jr.	5.00
16	Carlos Baerga	.75
17	Kenny Lofton	.75
18	Cecil Fielder	.75
19	John Burkett	.75
20	Andres Galarraga (Comeback Player)	.75

21	Charlie Hayes	.75
22	Orestes Destrade	.75
23	Jeff Conine	.75
24	Jeff Bagwell	2.50
25	Mark Grace	.75
26	Ryne Sandberg	3.00
27	Gregg Jefferies	.75
28	Barry Bonds	5.00
29	Mike Piazza	3.50
30	Greg Maddux	3.00
31	Darren Daulton	.75
32	John Kruk	.75
33	Len Dykstra	.75
34	Orlando Merced	.75
35	Tony Gwynn	3.00
36	Robby Thompson	.75

1995 PACIFIC PRISM

		NM/M
Complete Set (144):		65.00
Common Player:		.25
Pack (2):		.60
Wax Box (36):		12.50
1	Dave Justice	.25
2	Ryan Klesko	.25
3	Javier Lopez	.25
4	Greg Maddux	2.00
5	Fred McGriff	.25
6	Tony Tarasco	.25
7	Jeffrey Hammonds	.25
8	Mike Mussina	.75
9	Rafael Palmeiro	1.25
10	Cal Ripken Jr.	5.00
11	Lee Smith	.25
12	Roger Clemens	2.50
13	Scott Cooper	.25
14	Mike Greenwell	.25
15	Carlos Rodriguez	.25
16	Mo Vaughn	.25
17	Chili Davis	.25
18	Jim Edmonds	.25
19	Jorge Fabregas	.25
20	Bo Jackson	.35
21	Tim Salmon	.25
22	Mark Grace	.25
23	Jose Guzman	.25
24	Randy Myers	.25
25	Rey Sanchez	.25
26	Sammy Sosa	2.50
27	Wilson Alvarez	.25
28	Julio Franco	.25
29	Ozzie Guillen	.25
30	Jack McDowell	.25
31	Frank Thomas	1.50
32	Bret Boone	.25
33	Barry Larkin	.25
34	Hal Morris	.25
35	Jose Rijo	.25
36	Deion Sanders	.25
37	Carlos Baerga	.25
38	Albert Belle	.25
39	Kenny Lofton	.25
40	Dennis Martinez	.25
41	Manny Ramirez	1.50
42	Omar Vizquel	.25
43	Dante Bichette	.25
44	Marvin Freeman	.25
45	Andres Galarraga	.25
46	Mike Kingery	.25
47	Danny Bautista	.25
48	Cecil Fielder	.25
49	Travis Fryman	.25
50	Tony Phillips	.25
51	Alan Trammell	.25
52	Lou Whitaker	.25
53	Alex Arias	.25
54	Bret Barberie	.25
55	Jeff Conine	.25
56	Charles Johnson	.25
57	Gary Sheffield	.65
58	Jeff Bagwell	1.50
59	Craig Biggio	.25
60	Doug Drabek	.25
61	Tony Eusebio	.25
62	Luis Gonzalez	.25
63	David Cone	.25
64	Bob Hamelin	.25
65	Felix Jose	.25
66	Wally Joyner	.25
67	Brian McRae	.25
68	Brett Butler	.25
69	Garey Ingram	.25
70	Ramon Martinez	.25
71	Raul Mondesi	.25
72	Mike Piazza	2.50
73	Henry Rodriguez	.25
74	Ricky Bones	.25
75	Pat Listach	.25
76	Dave Nilsson	.25
77	Jose Valentin	.25
78	Rick Aguilera	.25
79	Denny Hocking	.25
80	Shane Mack	.25
81	Pedro Munoz	.25
82	Kirby Puckett	2.00
83	Dave Winfield	1.50
84	Moises Alou	.25
85	Wil Cordero	.25
86	Cliff Floyd	.25
87	Marquis Grissom	.25
88	Pedro Martinez	1.50
89	Larry Walker	.25
90	Bobby Bonilla	.25
91	Jeromy Burnitz	.25
92	John Franco	.25
93	Jeff Kent	.25
94	Jose Vizcaino	.25
95	Wade Boggs	2.00
96	Jimmy Key	.25
97	Don Mattingly	2.50
98	Paul O'Neill	.25
99	Luis Polonia	.25
100	Danny Tartabull	.25
101	Geronimo Berroa	.25
102	Rickey Henderson	1.50
103	Ruben Sierra	.25
104	Terry Steinbach	.25
105	Darren Daulton	.25
106	Mariano Duncan	.25
107	Lenny Dykstra	.25
108	Mike Lieberthal	.25
109	Tony Longmire	.25
110	Tom Marsh	.25
111	Jay Bell	.25
112	Carlos Garcia	.25
113	Orlando Merced	.25
114	Andy Van Slyke	.25
115	Derek Bell	.25
116	Tony Gwynn	2.00
117	Luis Lopez	.25
118	Bip Roberts	.25
119	Rod Beck	.25
120	Barry Bonds	5.00
121	Darryl Strawberry	.25
122	Bill Van Landingham	.25
123	Matt Williams	.25
124	Jay Buhner	.25
125	Felix Fermin	.25
126	Ken Griffey Jr.	3.00
127	Randy Johnson	1.50
128	Edgar Martinez	.25
129	Alex Rodriguez	4.00
130	Rene Arocha	.25
131	Gregg Jefferies	.25
132	Mike Perez	.25
133	Ozzie Smith	2.00
134	Jose Canseco	.65
135	Will Clark	.25
136	Juan Gonzalez	1.00
137	Ivan Rodriguez	1.25
138	Roberto Alomar	.50
139	Joe Carter	.25
140	Carlos Delgado	.75
141	Alex Gonzalez	.25
142	Juan Guzman	.25
143	Paul Molitor	1.50
144	John Olerud	.25

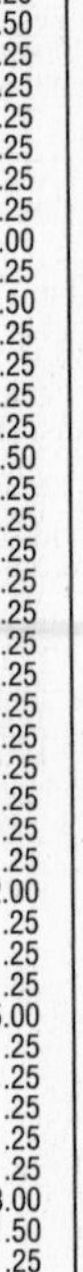

1995 PACIFIC

		NM/M
Complete Set (450):		20.00
Common Player:		.05
Pack (12):		1.00
Wax Box (36):		20.00
1	Steve Avery	.05
2	Rafael Belliard	.05
3	Jeff Blauser	.05
4	Tom Glavine	.25

5	Dave Justice	.05
6	Mike Kelly	.05
7	Roberto Kelly	.05
8	Ryan Klesko	.05
9	Mark Lemke	.05
10	Javier Lopez	.05
11	Greg Maddux	.75
12	Fred McGriff	.05
13	Greg McMichael	.05
14	Jose Oliva	.05
15	John Smoltz	.05
16	Tony Tarasco	.05
17	Brady Anderson	.05
18	Harold Baines	.05
19	Armando Benitez	.05
20	Mike Devereaux	.05
21	Leo Gomez	.05
22	Jeffrey Hammonds	.05
23	Chris Hoiles	.05
24	Ben McDonald	.05
25	Mark McLemore	.05
26	Jamie Moyer	.05
27	Mike Mussina	.40
28	Rafael Palmeiro	.50
29	Jim Poole	.05
30	Cal Ripken Jr.	2.00
31	Lee Smith	.05
32	Mark Smith	.05
33	Jose Canseco	.35
34	Roger Clemens	1.00
35	Scott Cooper	.05
36	Andre Dawson	.25
37	Tony Fossas	.05
38	Mike Greenwell	.05
39	Chris Howard	.05
40	Jose Melendez	.05
41	Nate Minchey	.05
42	Tim Naehring	.05
43	Otis Nixon	.05
44	Carlos Rodriguez	.05
45	Aaron Sele	.05
46	Lee Tinsley	.05
47	Sergio Valdez	.05
48	John Valentin	.05
49	Mo Vaughn	.05
50	Brian Anderson	.05
51	Garret Anderson	.05
52	Rod Correia	.05
53	Chad Curtis	.05
54	Mark Dalesandro	.05
55	Chili Davis	.05
56	Gary DiSarcina	.05
57	Damion Easley	.05
58	Jim Edmonds	.05
59	Jorge Fabregas	.05
60	Chuck Finley	.05
61	Bo Jackson	.10
62	Mark Langston	.05
63	Eduardo Perez	.05
64	Tim Salmon	.05
65	J.T. Snow	.05
66	Willie Banks	.05
67	Jose Bautista	.05
68	Shawon Dunston	.05
69	Kevin Foster	.05
70	Mark Grace	.05
71	Jose Guzman	.05
72	Jose Hernandez	.05
73	Blaise Ilsley	.05
74	Derrick May	.05
75	Randy Myers	.05
76	Karl Rhodes	.05
77	Kevin Roberson	.05
78	Rey Sanchez	.05
79	Sammy Sosa	.75
80	Steve Trachsel	.05
81	Eddie Zambrano	.05
82	Wilson Alvarez	.05
83	Jason Bere	.05
84	Joey Cora	.05
85	Jose DeLeon	.05
86	Alex Fernandez	.05
87	Julio Franco	.05
88	Ozzie Guillen	.05
89	Joe Hall	.05
90	Roberto Hernandez	.05
91	Darrin Jackson	.05
92	Lance Johnson	.05
93	Norberto Martin	.05
94	Jack McDowell	.05
95	Tim Raines	.05
96	Olmedo Saenz	.05
97	Frank Thomas	.60
98	Robin Ventura	.05
99	Bret Boone	.05
100	Jeff Brantley	.05
101	Jacob Brumfield	.05
102	Hector Carrasco	.05
103	Brian Dorsett	.05
104	Tony Fernandez	.05
105	Willie Greene	.05
106	Erik Hanson	.05
107	Kevin Jarvis	.05
108	Barry Larkin	.05
109	Kevin Mitchell	.05
110	Hal Morris	.05
111	Jose Rijo	.05
112	Johnny Ruffin	.05
113	Deion Sanders	.05
114	Reggie Sanders	.05
115	Sandy Alomar Jr.	.05
116	Ruben Amaro	.05
117	Carlos Baerga	.05
118	Albert Belle	.05
119	Alvaro Espinoza	.05
120	Rene Gonzales	.05
121	Wayne Kirby	.05
122	Kenny Lofton	.05
123	Candy Maldonado	.05
124	Dennis Martinez	.05
125	Eddie Murray	.60
126	Charles Nagy	.05
127	Tony Pena	.05
128	Manny Ramirez	.60
129	Paul Sorrento	.05
130	Jim Thome	.40
131	Omar Vizquel	.05
132	Dante Bichette	.05
133	Ellis Burks	.05
134	Vinny Castilla	.05
135	Marvin Freeman	.05
136	Andres Galarraga	.05
137	Joe Girardi	.05
138	Charlie Hayes	.05
139	Mike Kingery	.05
140	Nelson Liriano	.05
141	Roberto Mejia	.05
142	David Nied	.05
143	Steve Reed	.05
144	Armando Reynoso	.05
145	Bruce Ruffin	.05
146	John Vander Wal	.05
147	Walt Weiss	.05
148	Skeeter Barnes	.05
149	Tim Belcher	.05
150	Junior Felix	.05
151	Cecil Fielder	.05
152	Travis Fryman	.05
153	Kirk Gibson	.05
154	Chris Gomez	.05
155	Buddy Groom	.05
156	Chad Kreuter	.05
157	Mike Moore	.05
158	Tony Phillips	.05
159	Juan Samuel	.05
160	Mickey Tettleton	.05
161	Alan Trammell	.05
162	David Wells	.05
163	Lou Whitaker	.05
164	Kurt Abbott	.05
165	Luis Aquino	.05
166	Alex Arias	.05
167	Bret Barberie	.05
168	Jerry Browne	.05
169	Chuck Carr	.05
170	Matias Carrillo	.05
171	Greg Colbrunn	.05
172	Jeff Conine	.05
173	Carl Everett	.05
174	Robb Nen	.05
175	Yorkis Perez	.05
176	Pat Rapp	.05
177	Benito Santiago	.05
178	Gary Sheffield	.35
179	Darrell Whitmore	.05
180	Jeff Bagwell	.60
181	Kevin Bass	.05
182	Craig Biggio	.05

183 Andujar Cedeno .05
184 Doug Drabek .05
185 Tony Eusebio .05
186 Steve Finley .05
187 Luis Gonzalez .05
188 Pete Harnisch .05
189 John Hudek .05
190 Orlando Miller .05
191 James Mouton .05
192 Roberto Petagine .05
193 Shane Reynolds .05
194 Greg Swindell .05
195 Dave Veres .05
196 Kevin Appier .05
197 Stan Belinda .05
198 Vince Coleman .05
199 David Cone .05
200 Gary Gaetti .05
201 Greg Gagne .05
202 Mark Gubicza .05
203 Bob Hamelin .05
204 Dave Henderson .05
205 Felix Jose .05
206 Wally Joyner .05
207 Jose Lind .05
208 Mike Macfarlane .05
209 Brian McRae .05
210 Jeff Montgomery .05
211 Hipolito Pichardo .05
212 Pedro Astacio .05
213 Brett Butler .05
214 Omar Daal .05
215 Delino DeShields .05
216 Darren Dreifort .05
217 Carlos Hernandez .05
218 Orel Hershiser .05
219 Garey Ingram .05
220 Eric Karros .05
221 Ramon Martinez .05
222 Raul Mondesi .05
223 Jose Offerman .05
224 Mike Piazza 1.00
225 Henry Rodriguez .05
226 Ismael Valdes .05
227 Tim Wallach .05
228 Jeff Cirillo .05
229 Alex Diaz .05
230 Cal Eldred .05
231 Mike Fetters .05
232 Brian Harper .05
233 Ted Higuera .05
234 John Jaha .05
235 Graeme Lloyd .05
236 Jose Mercedes .05
237 Jaime Navarro .05
238 Dave Nilsson .05
239 Jesse Orosco .05
240 Jody Reed .05
241 Jose Valentin .05
242 Greg Vaughn .05
243 Turner Ward .05
244 Rick Aguilera .05
245 Rich Becker .05
246 Jim Deshaies .05
247 Steve Dunn .05
248 Scott Erickson .05
249 Kent Hrbek .05
250 Chuck Knoblauch .05
251 Scott Leius .05
252 David McCarty .05
253 Pat Meares .05
254 Pedro Munoz .05
255 Kirby Puckett .75
256 Carlos Pulido .05
257 Kevin Tapani .05
258 Matt Walbeck .05
259 Dave Winfield .60
260 Moises Alou .05
261 Juan Bell .05
262 Freddie Benavides .05
263 Sean Berry .05
264 Wil Cordero .05
265 Jeff Fassero .05
266 Darrin Fletcher .05
267 Cliff Floyd .05
268 Marquis Grissom .05
269 Gil Heredia .05
270 Ken Hill .05
271 Pedro Martinez .60
272 Mel Rojas .05
273 Larry Walker .05
274 John Wetteland .05
275 Rondell White .05
276 Tim Bogar .05
277 Bobby Bonilla .05
278 Rico Brogna .05
279 Jeromy Burnitz .05
280 John Franco .05
281 Eric Hillman .05
282 Todd Hundley .05
283 Jeff Kent .05
284 Mike Maddux .05
285 Joe Orsulak .05
286 Luis Rivera .05
287 Bret Saberhagen .05
288 David Segui .05
289 Ryan Thompson .05
290 Fernando Vina .05
291 Jose Vizcaino .05
292 Jim Abbott .05
293 Wade Boggs .75
294 Russ Davis .05
295 Mike Gallego .05
296 Xavier Hernandez .05
297 Steve Howe .05
298 Jimmy Key .05
299 Don Mattingly 1.00
300 Terry Mulholland .05
301 Paul O'Neill .05
302 Luis Polonia .05
303 Mike Stanley .05
304 Danny Tartabull .05
305 Randy Velarde .05
306 Bob Wickman .05
307 Bernie Williams .05
308 Mark Acre .05
309 Geronimo Berroa .05
310 Mike Bordick .05
311 Dennis Eckersley .50
312 Rickey Henderson .60
313 Stan Javier .05
314 Miguel Jimenez .05
315 Francisco Matos .05
316 Mark McGwire 1.50
317 Troy Neel .05
318 Steve Ontiveros .05
319 Carlos Reyes .05
320 Ruben Sierra .05
321 Terry Steinbach .05
322 Bob Welch .05
323 Bobby Witt .05
324 Larry Andersen .05
325 Kim Batiste .05
326 Darren Daulton .05
327 Mariano Duncan .05
328 Lenny Dykstra .05
329 Jim Eisenreich .05
330 Danny Jackson .05
331 John Kruk .05
332 Tony Longmire .05
333 Tom Marsh .05
334 Mickey Morandini .05
335 Bobby Munoz .05
336 Todd Pratt .05
337 Tom Quinlan .05
338 Kevin Stocker .05
339 Fernando Valenzuela .05
340 Jay Bell .05
341 Dave Clark .05
342 Steve Cooke .05
343 Carlos Garcia .05
344 Jeff King .05
345 Jon Lieber .05
346 Ravelo Manzanillo .05
347 Al Martin .05
348 Orlando Merced .05
349 Denny Neagle .05
350 Alejandro Pena .05
351 Don Slaught .05
352 Zane Smith .05
353 Andy Van Slyke .05
354 Rick White .05
355 Kevin Young .05
356 Andy Ashby .05
357 Derek Bell .05
358 Andy Benes .05
359 Phil Clark .05
360 Donnie Elliott .05
361 Ricky Gutierrez .05
362 Tony Gwynn .75
363 Trevor Hoffman .05
364 Tim Hyers .05
365 Luis Lopez .05
366 Jose Martinez .05
367 Pedro A. Martinez .05
368 Phil Plantier .05
369 Bip Roberts .05
370 A.J. Sager .05
371 Jeff Tabaka .05
372 Todd Benzinger .05
373 Barry Bonds 2.00
374 John Burkett .05
375 Mark Carreon .05
376 Royce Clayton .05
377 Pat Gomez .05
378 Erik Johnson .05
379 Darren Lewis .05
380 Kirt Manwaring .05
381 Dave Martinez .05
382 John Patterson .05
383 Mark Portugal .05
384 Darryl Strawberry .05
385 Salomon Torres .05
386 Bill Van Landingham .05
387 Matt Williams .05
388 Rich Amaral .05
389 Bobby Ayala .05
390 Mike Blowers .05
391 Chris Bosio .05
392 Jay Buhner .05
393 Jim Converse .05
394 Tim Davis .05
395 Felix Fermin .05
396 Dave Fleming .05
397 Goose Gossage .05
398 Ken Griffey Jr. 1.00
399 Randy Johnson .60
400 Edgar Martinez .05
401 Tino Martinez .05
402 Alex Rodriguez 1.50
403 Dan Wilson .05
404 Luis Alicea .05
405 Rene Arocha .05
406 Bernard Gilkey .05
407 Gregg Jefferies .05
408 Ray Lankford .05
409 Terry McGriff .05
410 Omar Olivares .05
411 Jose Oquendo .05
412 Vicente Palacios .05
413 Geronimo Pena .05
414 Mike Perez .05
415 Gerald Perry .05
416 Ozzie Smith .75
417 Bob Tewksbury .05
418 Mark Whiten .05
419 Todd Zeile .05
420 Esteban Beltre .05
421 Kevin Brown .05
422 Cris Carpenter .05
423 Will Clark .05
424 Hector Fajardo .05
425 Jeff Frye .05
426 Juan Gonzalez .30
427 Rusty Greer .05
428 Rick Honeycutt .05
429 David Hulse .05
430 Manny Lee .05
431 Junior Ortiz .05
432 Dean Palmer .05
433 Ivan Rodriguez .50
434 Dan Smith .05
435 Roberto Alomar .15
436 Pat Borders .05
437 Scott Brow .05
438 Rob Butler .05
439 Joe Carter .05
440 Tony Castillo .05
441 Domingo Cedeno .05
442 Brad Cornett .05
443 Carlos Delgado .35
444 Alex Gonzalez .05
445 Juan Guzman .05
446 Darren Hall .05
447 Paul Molitor .60
448 John Olerud .05
449 Robert Perez .05
450 Devon White .05

Gold Crown Die-cut

NM/M

Complete Set (20): 30.00
Common Player: .45
1 Greg Maddux 2.50
2 Fred McGriff .45
3 Rafael Palmeiro 1.50
4 Cal Ripken Jr. 4.50
5 Jose Canseco 1.00
6 Frank Thomas 2.00
7 Albert Belle .45
8 Manny Ramirez 2.00
9 Andres Galarraga .45
10 Jeff Bagwell 2.00
11 Chan Ho Park .45
12 Raul Mondesi .45
13 Mike Piazza 3.00
14 Kirby Puckett 2.50
15 Barry Bonds 4.50
16 Ken Griffey Jr. 3.00
17 Alex Rodriguez 3.50
18 Juan Gonzalez 1.00
19 Roberto Alomar 1.00
20 Carlos Delgado 1.25

Hot Hispanics

NM/M

Complete Set (36): 20.00
Common Player: .25
1 Roberto Alomar 1.25
2 Moises Alou .25
3 Wilson Alvarez .25
4 Carlos Baerga .25
5 Geronimo Berroa .25
6 Jose Canseco 1.00
7 Hector Carrasco .25
8 Wil Cordero .25
9 Carlos Delgado 1.50
10 Damion Easley .25
11 Tony Eusebio .25
12 Hector Fajardo .25
13 Andres Galarraga .25
14 Carlos Garcia .25
15 Chris Gomez .25
16 Alex Gonzalez .25
17 Juan Gonzalez 1.25
18 Luis Gonzalez .25
19 Felix Jose .25
20 Javier Lopez .25
21 Luis Lopez .25
22 Dennis Martinez .25
23 Orlando Miller .25
24 Raul Mondesi .25
25 Jose Oliva .25
26 Rafael Palmeiro 2.00
27 Yorkis Perez .25
28 Manny Ramirez 2.50
29 Jose Rijo .25
30 Alex Rodriguez 4.00
31 Ivan Rodriguez 2.00
32 Carlos Rodriguez .25
33 Sammy Sosa 3.00
34 Tony Tarasco .25
35 Ismael Valdes .25
36 Bernie Williams .25

Marquee Prism

		NM/M
Complete Set (36):		22.50
Common Player:		.35
1	Jose Canseco	.65
2	Gregg Jefferies	.35
3	Fred McGriff	.35
4	Joe Carter	.35
5	Tim Salmon	.35
6	Wade Boggs	1.25
7	Dave Winfield	1.00
8	Bob Hamelin	.35
9	Cal Ripken Jr.	3.00
10	Don Mattingly	1.50
11	Juan Gonzalez	.50
12	Carlos Delgado	.65
13	Barry Bonds	3.00
14	Albert Belle	.35
15	Raul Mondesi	.35
16	Jeff Bagwell	1.00
17	Mike Piazza	1.50
18	Rafael Palmeiro	.75
19	Frank Thomas	1.00
20	Matt Williams	.35
21	Ken Griffey Jr.	2.00
22	Will Clark	.35
23	Bobby Bonilla	.35
24	Kenny Lofton	.35
25	Paul Molitor	1.00
26	Kirby Puckett	1.25
27	Dave Justice	.35
28	Jeff Conine	.35
29	Bret Boone	.35
30	Larry Walker	.35
31	Cecil Fielder	.35
32	Manny Ramirez	1.00
33	Javier Lopez	.35
34	Jimmy Key	.35
35	Andres Galarraga	.35
36	Tony Gwynn	1.25

1996 PACIFIC CROWN COLLECTION

		NM/M
Complete Set (450):		17.50
Common Player:		.05
Pack (12):		1.00
Wax Box (36):		25.00
1	Steve Avery	.05
2	Ryan Klesko	.05
3	Pedro Borbon	.05
4	Chipper Jones	1.00
5	Kent Mercker	.05
6	Greg Maddux	1.00
7	Greg McMichael	.05
8	Mark Wohlers	.05
9	Fred McGriff	.05
10	John Smoltz	.05
11	Rafael Belliard	.05
12	Mark Lemke	.05
13	Tom Glavine	.30
14	Javier Lopez	.05
15	Jeff Blauser	.05
16	Dave Justice	.05
17	Marquis Grissom	.05
18	Greg Maddux (NL Cy Young)	.50
19	Randy Myers	.05
20	Scott Servais	.05
21	Sammy Sosa	1.00
22	Kevin Foster	.05
23	Jose Hernandez	.05
24	Jim Bullinger	.05
25	Mike Perez	.05
26	Shawon Dunston	.05
27	Rey Sanchez	.05
28	Frank Castillo	.05
29	Jaime Navarro	.05
30	Brian McRae	.05
31	Mark Grace	.05
32	Roberto Rivera	.05
33	Luis Gonzalez	.05
34	Hector Carrasco	.05
35	Bret Boone	.05
36	Thomas Howard	.05
37	Hal Morris	.05
38	John Smiley	.05
39	Jeff Brantley	.05
40	Barry Larkin	.05
41	Mariano Duncan	.05
42	Xavier Hernandez	.05
43	Pete Schourek	.05
44	Reggie Sanders	.05
45	Dave Burba	.05
46	Jeff Branson	.05
47	Mark Portugal	.05
48	Ron Gant	.05
49	Benito Santiago	.05
50	Barry Larkin (NL MVP)	.05
51	Steve Reed	.05
52	Kevin Ritz	.05
53	Dante Bichette	.05
54	Darren Holmes	.05
55	Ellis Burks	.05
56	Walt Weiss	.05
57	Armando Reynoso	.05
58	Vinny Castilla	.05
59	Jason Bates	.05
60	Mike Kingery	.05
61	Bryan Rekar	.05
62	Curtis Leskanic	.05
63	Bret Saberhagen	.05
64	Andres Galarraga	.05
65	Larry Walker	.05
66	Joe Girardi	.05
67	Quilvio Veras	.05
68	Robb Nen	.05
69	Mario Diaz	.05
70	Chuck Carr	.05
71	Alex Arias	.05
72	Pat Rapp	.05
73	Rich Garces	.05
74	Kurt Abbott	.05
75	Andre Dawson	.25
76	Greg Colbrunn	.05
77	John Burkett	.05
78	Terry Pendleton	.05
79	Jesus Tavarez	.05
80	Charles Johnson	.05
81	Yorkis Perez	.05
82	Jeff Conine	.05
83	Gary Sheffield	.45
84	Brian Hunter	.05
85	Derrick May	.05
86	Greg Swindell	.05
87	Derek Bell	.05
88	Dave Veres	.05
89	Jeff Bagwell	.75
90	Todd Jones	.05
91	Orlando Miller	.05
92	Pedro A. Martinez	.05
93	Tony Eusebio	.05
94	Craig Biggio	.05
95	Shane Reynolds	.05
96	James Mouton	.05
97	Doug Drabek	.05
98	Dave Magadan	.05
99	Ricky Gutierrez	.05
100	Hideo Nomo	.50
101	Delino DeShields	.05
102	Tom Candiotti	.05
103	Mike Piazza	1.50
104	Ramon Martinez	.05
105	Pedro Astacio	.05
106	Chad Fonville	.05
107	Raul Mondesi	.05
108	Ismael Valdes	.05
109	Jose Offerman	.05
110	Todd Worrell	.05
111	Eric Karros	.05
112	Brett Butler	.05
113	Juan Castro	.05
114	Roberto Kelly	.05
115	Omar Daal	.05
116	Antonio Osuna	.05
117	Hideo Nomo (NL Rookie of Year)	.50
118	Mike Lansing	.05
119	Mel Rojas	.05
120	Sean Berry	.05
121	David Segui	.05
122	Tavo Alvarez	.05
123	Pedro Martinez	.75
124	*F.P. Santangelo*	.05
125	Rondell White	.05
126	Cliff Floyd	.05
127	Henry Rodriguez	.05
128	Tony Tarasco	.05
129	Yamil Benitez	.05
130	Carlos Perez	.05
131	Wil Cordero	.05
132	Jeff Fassero	.05
133	Moises Alou	.05
134	John Franco	.05
135	Rico Brogna	.05
136	Dave Mlicki	.05
137	Bill Pulsipher	.05
138	Jose Vizcaino	.05
139	Carl Everett	.05
140	Edgardo Alfonzo	.05
141	Bobby Jones	.05
142	Alberto Castillo	.05
143	Joe Orsulak	.05
144	Jeff Kent	.05
145	Ryan Thompson	.05
146	Jason Isringhausen	.05
147	Todd Hundley	.05
148	Alex Ochoa	.05
149	Charlie Hayes	.05
150	Michael Mimbs	.05
151	Darren Daulton	.05
152	Toby Borland	.05
153	Andy Van Slyke	.05
154	Mickey Morandini	.05
155	Sid Fernandez	.05
156	Tom Marsh	.05
157	Kevin Stocker	.05
158	Paul Quantrill	.05
159	Gregg Jefferies	.05
160	Ricky Bottalico	.05
161	Lenny Dykstra	.05
162	Mark Whiten	.05
163	Tyler Green	.05
164	Jim Eisenreich	.05
165	Heathcliff Slocumb	.05
166	Esteban Loaiza	.05
167	Rich Aude	.05
168	Jason Christiansen	.05
169	Ramon Morel	.05
170	Orlando Merced	.05
171	Paul Wagner	.05
172	Jeff King	.05
173	Jay Bell	.05
174	Jacob Brumfield	.05
175	Nelson Liriano	.05
176	Dan Miceli	.05
177	Carlos Garcia	.05
178	Denny Neagle	.05
179	Angelo Encarnacion	.05
180	Al Martin	.05
181	Midre Cummings	.05
182	Eddie Williams	.05
183	Roberto Petagine	.05
184	Tony Gwynn	1.00
185	Andy Ashby	.05
186	Melvin Nieves	.05
187	Phil Clark	.05
188	Brad Ausmus	.05
189	Bip Roberts	.05
190	Fernando Valenzuela	.05
191	Marc Newfield	.05
192	Steve Finley	.05
193	Trevor Hoffman	.05
194	Andujar Cedeno	.05
195	Jody Reed	.05
196	Ken Caminiti	.05
197	Joey Hamilton	.05
198	Tony Gwynn (NL Batting Champ)	.50
199	Shawn Barton	.05
200	Deion Sanders	.05
201	Rikkert Faneyte	.05
202	Barry Bonds	2.50
203	Matt Williams	.05
204	Jose Bautista	.05
205	Mark Leiter	.05
206	Mark Carreon	.05
207	Robby Thompson	.05
208	Terry Mulholland	.05
209	Rod Beck	.05
210	Royce Clayton	.05
211	J.R. Phillips	.05
212	Kirt Manwaring	.05
213	Glenallen Hill	.05
214	William Van Landingham	.05
215	Scott Cooper	.05
216	Bernard Gilkey	.05
217	Allen Watson	.05
218	Donovan Osborne	.05
219	Ray Lankford	.05
220	Tony Fossas	.05
221	Tom Pagnozzi	.05
222	John Mabry	.05
223	Tripp Cromer	.05
224	Mark Petkovsek	.05
225	Mike Morgan	.05
226	Ozzie Smith	1.00
227	Tom Henke	.05
228	Jose Oquendo	.05
229	Brian Jordan	.05
230	Cal Ripken Jr.	2.50
231	Scott Erickson	.05
232	Harold Baines	.05
233	Jeff Manto	.05
234	Jesse Orosco	.05
235	Jeffrey Hammonds	.05
236	Brady Anderson	.05
237	Manny Alexander	.05
238	Chris Hoiles	.05
239	Rafael Palmeiro	.60
240	Ben McDonald	.05
241	Curtis Goodwin	.05
242	Bobby Bonilla	.05
243	Mike Mussina	.60
244	Kevin Brown	.05
245	Armando Benitez	.05
246	Jose Canseco	.50
247	Erik Hanson	.05
248	Mo Vaughn	.05
249	Tim Naehring	.05
250	Vaughn Eshelman	.05
251	Mike Greenwell	.05
252	Troy O'Leary	.05
253	Tim Wakefield	.05
254	Dwayne Hosey	.05
255	John Valentin	.05
256	Rick Aguilera	.05
257	Mike MacFarlane	.05
258	Roger Clemens	1.50
259	Luis Alicea	.05
260	Mo Vaughn (AL MVP)	.05
261	Mark Langston	.05
262	Jim Edmonds	.05
263	Rod Correia	.05
264	Tim Salmon	.05
265	J.T. Snow	.05
266	Orlando Palmeiro	.05
267	Jorge Fabregas	.05
268	Jim Abbott	.05
269	Eduardo Perez	.05
270	Lee Smith	.05
271	Gary DiSarcina	.05
272	Damion Easley	.05
273	Tony Phillips	.05
274	Garret Anderson	.05
275	Chuck Finley	.05
276	Chili Davis	.05
277	Lance Johnson	.05
278	Alex Fernandez	.05
279	Robin Ventura	.05
280	Chris Snopek	.05
281	Brian Keyser	.05
282	Lyle Mouton	.05
283	*Luis Andujar*	.05
284	Tim Raines	.05
285	Larry Thomas	.05
286	Ozzie Guillen	.05
287	Frank Thomas	.75
288	Roberto Hernandez	.05
289	Dave Martinez	.05
290	Ray Durham	.05
291	Ron Karkovice	.05
292	Wilson Alvarez	.05
293	Omar Vizquel	.05
294	Eddie Murray	.75
295	Sandy Alomar	.05
296	Orel Hershiser	.05
297	Jose Mesa	.05
298	Julian Tavarez	.05
299	Dennis Martinez	.05
300	Carlos Baerga	.05
301	Manny Ramirez	.75
302	Jim Thome	.60
303	Kenny Lofton	.05
304	Tony Pena	.05
305	Alvaro Espinoza	.05
306	Paul Sorrento	.05
307	Albert Belle	.05
308	Danny Bautista	.05
309	Chris Gomez	.05
310	Jose Lima	.05
311	Phil Nevin	.05
312	Alan Trammell	.05
313	Chad Curtis	.05
314	John Flaherty	.05
315	Travis Fryman	.05
316	Todd Steverson	.05
317	Brian Bohanon	.05
318	Lou Whitaker	.05
319	Bobby Higginson	.05
320	Steve Rodriguez	.05
321	Cecil Fielder	.05
322	Felipe Lira	.05
323	Juan Samuel	.05
324	Bob Hamelin	.05
325	Tom Goodwin	.05

326 Johnny Damon .25
327 Hipolito Pichardo .05
328 Dilson Torres .05
329 Kevin Appier .05
330 Mark Gubicza .05
331 Jon Nunnally .05
332 Gary Gaetti .05
333 Brent Mayne .05
334 Brent Cookson .05
335 Tom Gordon .05
336 Wally Joyner .05
337 Greg Gagne .05
338 Fernando Vina .05
339 Joe Oliver .05
340 John Jaha .05
341 Jeff Cirillo .05
342 Pat Listach .05
343 Dave Nilsson .05
344 Steve Sparks .05
345 Ricky Bones .05
346 David Hulse .05
347 Scott Karl .05
348 Darryl Hamilton .05
349 B.J. Surhoff .05
350 Angel Miranda .05
351 Sid Roberson .05
352 Matt Mieske .05
353 *Jose Valentin* .05
354 *Matt Lawton* .25
355 Eddie Guardado .05
356 Brad Radke .05
357 Pedro Munoz .05
358 Scott Stahoviak .05
359 Erik Schullstrom .05
360 Pat Meares .05
361 Marty Cordova .05
362 Scott Leius .05
363 Matt Walbeck .05
364 Rich Becker .05
365 Kirby Puckett 1.00
366 Oscar Munoz .05
367 Chuck Knoblauch .05
368 Marty Cordova (AL Rookie of Year) .05
369 Bernie Williams .05
370 Mike Stanley .05
371 Andy Pettitte .25
372 Jack McDowell .05
373 Sterling Hitchcock .05
374 David Cone .05
375 Randy Velarde .05
376 Don Mattingly 1.50
377 Melido Perez .05
378 Wade Boggs 1.00
379 Ruben Sierra .05
380 Tony Fernandez .05
381 John Wetteland .05
382 Mariano Rivera .15
383 Derek Jeter 2.50
384 Paul O'Neill .05
385 Mark McGwire 2.00
386 Scott Brosius .05
387 Don Wengert .05
388 Terry Steinbach .05
389 Brent Gates .05
390 Craig Paquette .05
391 Mike Bordick .05
392 Ariel Prieto .05
393 Dennis Eckersley .65
394 Carlos Reyes .05
395 Todd Stottlemyre .05
396 Rickey Henderson .75
397 Geronimo Berroa .05
398 Steve Ontiveros .05
399 Mike Gallego .05
400 Stan Javier .05
401 Randy Johnson .75
402 Norm Charlton .05
403 Mike Blowers .05
404 Tino Martinez .05
405 Dan Wilson .05
406 Andy Benes .05
407 Alex Diaz .05
408 Edgar Martinez .05
409 Chris Bosio .05
410 Ken Griffey Jr. 1.50
411 Luis Sojo .05
412 Bob Wolcott .05
413 Vince Coleman .05
414 Rich Amaral .05
415 Jay Buhner .05
416 Alex Rodriguez 2.00
417 Joey Cora .05
418 Randy Johnson (AL Cy Young) .25
419 Edgar Martinez (AL Batting Champ) .05
420 Ivan Rodriguez .65
421 Mark McLemore .05
422 Mickey Tettleton .05
423 Juan Gonzalez .40
424 Will Clark .05
425 Kevin Gross .05
426 Dean Palmer .05
427 Kenny Rogers .05
428 Bob Tewksbury .05
429 Benji Gil .05
430 Jeff Russell .05
431 Rusty Greer .05
432 Roger Pavlik .05
433 Esteban Beltre .05
434 Otis Nixon .05
435 Paul Molitor .75
436 Carlos Delgado .50
437 Ed Sprague .05
438 Juan Guzman .05
439 Domingo Cedeno .05
440 Pat Hentgen .05
441 Tomas Perez .05
442 John Olerud .05
443 Shawn Green .25
444 Al Leiter .05
445 Joe Carter .05
446 Robert Perez .05
447 Devon White .05
448 Tony Castillo .05
449 Alex Gonzalez .05
450 Roberto Alomar .20
450p Roberto Alomar (unmarked promo card, "Games: 128" on back) 1.50

Cramer's Choice

		NM/M
Complete Set (10):		150.00
Common Player:		6.00
1	Roberto Alomar	7.50
2	Wade Boggs	15.00
3	Cal Ripken Jr.	30.00
4	Greg Maddux	15.00
5	Frank Thomas	12.50
6	Tony Gwynn	15.00
7	Mike Piazza	20.00
8	Ken Griffey Jr.	25.00
9	Manny Ramirez	12.50
10	Edgar Martinez	6.00

Latinas

		NM/M
Complete Set (36):		16.00
Common Player:		.25
1	Roberto Alomar	.50
2	Moises Alou	.25
3	Carlos Baerga	.25
4	Geronimo Berroa	.25
5	Ricky Bones	.25
6	Bobby Bonilla	.25
7	Jose Canseco	.65
8	Vinny Castilla	.25
9	Pedro Martinez	1.50
10	John Valentin	.25
11	Andres Galarraga	.25
12	Juan Gonzalez	.75
13	Ozzie Guillen	.25
14	Esteban Loaiza	.25
15	Javier Lopez	.25
16	Dennis Martinez	.25
17	Edgar Martinez	.25
18	Tino Martinez	.25
19	Orlando Merced	.25
20	Jose Mesa	.25
21	Raul Mondesi	.25
22	Jaime Navarro	.25
23	Rafael Palmeiro	.75
24	Carlos Perez	.25
25	Manny Ramirez	1.50
26	Alex Rodriguez	3.50
27	Ivan Rodriguez	1.25
28	David Segui	.25
29	Ruben Sierra	.25
30	Sammy Sosa	2.00
31	Julian Tavarez	.25
32	Ismael Valdes	.25
33	Fernando Valenzuela	.25
34	Quilvio Veras	.25
35	Omar Vizquel	.25
36	Bernie Williams	.25

Die-Cuts

		NM/M
Complete Set (36):		45.00
Common Player:		.75
1	Roberto Alomar	1.00
2	Will Clark	.75
3	Johnny Damon	1.00
4	Don Mattingly	2.50
5	Edgar Martinez	.75
6	Manny Ramirez	1.50
7	Mike Piazza	2.50
8	Quilvio Veras	.75
9	Rickey Henderson	1.50
10	Jeff Bagwell	1.50
11	Andres Galarraga	.75
12	Tim Salmon	.75
13	Ken Griffey Jr.	2.50
14	Sammy Sosa	2.00
15	Cal Ripken Jr.	4.50
16	Raul Mondesi	.75
17	Jose Canseco	1.00
18	Frank Thomas	1.50
19	Hideo Nomo	1.00
20	Wade Boggs	2.00
21	Reggie Sanders	.75
22	Carlos Baerga	.75
23	Mo Vaughn	.75
24	Ivan Rodriguez	1.25
25	Kirby Puckett	2.00
26	Albert Belle	.75
27	Vinny Castilla	.75
28	Greg Maddux	2.00
29	Dante Bichette	.75
30	Deion Sanders	.75
31	Chipper Jones	2.00
32	Cecil Fielder	.75
33	Randy Johnson	1.50
34	Mark McGwire	3.50
35	Tony Gwynn	2.00
36	Barry Bonds	4.50

Hometown of the Players

		NM/M
Complete Set (20):		15.00
Common Player:		.50
1	Mike Piazza	1.50
2	Greg Maddux	1.00
3	Tony Gwynn	1.00
4	Carlos Baerga	.50

5	Don Mattingly	1.50
6	Cal Ripken Jr.	2.50
7	Chipper Jones	1.00
8	Andres Galarraga	.50
9	Manny Ramirez	.75
10	Roberto Alomar	.60
11	Ken Griffey Jr.	1.50
12	Jose Canseco	.60
13	Frank Thomas	.75
14	Vinny Castilla	.50
15	Roberto Kelly	.50
16	Dennis Martinez	.50
17	Kirby Puckett	1.00
18	Raul Mondesi	.50
19	Hideo Nomo	.60
20	Edgar Martinez	.50

October Moments

		NM/M
Complete Set (20):		30.00
Common Player:		.60
1	Carlos Baerga	.60
2	Albert Belle	.75
3	Dante Bichette	.60
4	Jose Canseco	1.25
5	Tom Glavine	1.00
6	Ken Griffey Jr.	5.00
7	Randy Johnson	2.50
8	Chipper Jones	3.50
9	Dave Justice	.60
10	Ryan Klesko	.60
11	Kenny Lofton	.60
12	Javier Lopez	.60
13	Greg Maddux	3.50
14	Edgar Martinez	.60
15	Don Mattingly	4.00
16	Hideo Nomo	1.25
17	Mike Piazza	4.00
18	Manny Ramirez	2.50
19	Reggie Sanders	.60
20	Jim Thome	1.50

Milestones

		NM/M
Complete Set (10):		12.50
Common Player:		.50
1	Albert Belle	.50
2	Don Mattingly	2.25
3	Tony Gwynn	2.00
4	Jose Canseco	1.00
5	Marty Cordova	.50
6	Wade Boggs	2.00
7	Greg Maddux	2.00
8	Eddie Murray	1.50
9	Ken Griffey Jr.	2.50
10	Cal Ripken Jr.	3.00

1996 PACIFIC PRISM

		NM/M
Complete Set (144):		50.00
Common Player:		.35
Golds:		1.5X
Pack (2):		.65
Wax Box (36):		20.00
1	Tom Glavine	.75
2	Chipper Jones	2.00
3	David Justice	.35
4	Ryan Klesko	.35
5	Javier Lopez	.35
6	Greg Maddux	2.00
7	Fred McGriff	.35
8	Frank Castillo	.35
9	Luis Gonzalez	.35
10	Mark Grace	.35
11	Brian McRae	.35
12	Jaime Navarro	.35
13	Sammy Sosa	2.00
14	Bret Boone	.35
15	Ron Gant	.35
16	Barry Larkin	.35
17	Reggie Sanders	.35
18	Benito Santiago	.35
19	Dante Bichette	.35
20	Vinny Castilla	.35
21	Andres Galarraga	.35
22	Bryan Rekar	.35
23	Roberto Alomar	1.00
23p	Roberto Alomar ("Azulejos" rather than "Los Azulajos" on back, unmarked promo card)	1.00
24	Jeff Conine	.35
25	Andre Dawson	.50
26	Charles Johnson	.35
27	Gary Sheffield	1.00
28	Quilvio Veras	.35
29	Jeff Bagwell	1.50
30	Derek Bell	.35
31	Craig Biggio	.35
32	Tony Eusebio	.35
33	Karim Garcia	.35
34	Eric Karros	.35
35	Ramon Martinez	.35
36	Raul Mondesi	.35
37	Hideo Nomo	1.00
38	Mike Piazza	3.00
39	Ismael Valdes	.35
40	Moises Alou	.35
41	Wil Cordero	.35
42	Pedro Martinez	1.50
43	Mel Rojas	.35
44	David Segui	.35
45	Edgardo Alfonzo	.35
46	Rico Brogna	.35
47	John Franco	.35
48	Jason Isringhausen	.35
49	Jose Vizcaino	.35
50	Ricky Bottalico	.35
51	Darren Daulton	.35
52	Lenny Dykstra	.35
53	Tyler Green	.35
54	Gregg Jefferies	.35
55	Jay Bell	.35
56	Jason Christiansen	.35
57	Carlos Garcia	.35
58	Esteban Loaiza	.35
59	Orlando Merced	.35
60	Andujar Cedeno	.35
61	Tony Gwynn	2.00
62	Melvin Nieves	.35
63	Phil Plantier	.35
64	Fernando Valenzuela	.35
65	Barry Bonds	4.50
66	J.R. Phillips	.35
67	Deion Sanders	.35
68	Matt Williams	.35
69	Bernard Gilkey	.35
70	Tom Henke	.35
71	Brian Jordan	.35
72	Ozzie Smith	2.00
73	Manny Alexander	.35
74	Bobby Bonilla	.35
75	Mike Mussina	1.00
76	Rafael Palmeiro	1.00
77	Cal Ripken Jr.	4.50
78	Jose Canseco	1.00
79	Roger Clemens	2.50
80	John Valentin	.35
81	Mo Vaughn	.35
82	Tim Wakefield	.35
83	Garret Anderson	.35
84	Damion Easley	.35
85	Jim Edmonds	.35
86	Tim Salmon	.35
87	Wilson Alvarez	.35
88	Alex Fernandez	.35
89	Ozzie Guillen	.35
90	Roberto Hernandez	.35
91	Frank Thomas	1.50
92	Robin Ventura	.35
93	Carlos Baerga	.35
94	Albert Belle	.35
95	Kenny Lofton	.35
96	Dennis Martinez	.35
97	Eddie Murray	1.50
98	Manny Ramirez	1.50
99	Omar Vizquel	.35
100	Chad Curtis	.35
101	Cecil Fielder	.35
102	Felipe Lira	.35
103	Alan Trammell	.35
104	Kevin Appier	.35
105	Johnny Damon	.35
106	Gary Gaetti	.35
107	Wally Joyner	.35
108	Ricky Bones	.35
109	John Jaha	.35
110	B.J. Surhoff	.35
111	Jose Valentin	.35
112	Fernando Vina	.35
113	Marty Cordova	.35
114	Chuck Knoblauch	.35
115	Scott Leius	.35
116	Pedro Munoz	.35
117	Kirby Puckett	2.00
118	Wade Boggs	2.00
119	Don Mattingly	2.50
120	Jack McDowell	.35
121	Paul O'Neill	.35
122	Ruben Rivera	.35
123	Bernie Williams	.35
124	Geronimo Berroa	.35
125	Rickey Henderson	1.50
126	Mark McGwire	3.50
127	Terry Steinbach	.35
128	Danny Tartabull	.35
129	Jay Buhner	.35
130	Joey Cora	.35
131	Ken Griffey Jr.	3.00
132	Randy Johnson	1.50
133	Edgar Martinez	.35
134	Tino Martinez	.35
135	Will Clark	.35
136	Juan Gonzalez	.75
137	Dean Palmer	.35
138	Ivan Rodriguez	1.25
139	Mickey Tettleton	.35
140	Larry Walker	.35
141	Joe Carter	.35
142	Carlos Delgado	1.00
143	Alex Gonzalez	.35
144	Paul Molitor	1.50

Gold

	NM/M
Complete Set (144):	100.00
Common Player:	.50
Stars:	1.5X

(See 1996 Pacific Prism for checklist and base card values.)

Fence Busters

		NM/M
Complete Set (19):		50.00
Common Player:		1.50
1	Albert Belle	1.50
2	Dante Bichette	1.50
3	Barry Bonds	7.50
4	Jay Buhner	1.50
5	Jose Canseco	2.25
6	Ken Griffey Jr.	5.00
7	Chipper Jones	4.00
8	David Justice	1.50
9	Eric Karros	1.50
10	Edgar Martinez	1.50
11	Mark McGwire	6.00
12	Eddie Murray	3.00
13	Mike Piazza	5.00
14	Kirby Puckett	4.00
15	Cal Ripken Jr.	7.50
16	Tim Salmon	1.50
17	Sammy Sosa	4.00
18	Frank Thomas	3.00
19	Mo Vaughn	1.50

Flame Throwers

		NM/M
Complete Set (10):		25.00
Common Player:		1.50
1	Roger Clemens	6.50
2	David Cone	1.50
3	Tom Glavine	2.50
4	Randy Johnson	4.50
5	Greg Maddux	6.00
6	Ramon Martinez	1.50
7	Jose Mesa	1.50
8	Mike Mussina	2.50
9	Hideo Nomo	3.00
10	Jose Rijo	1.50

Red Hot Stars

		NM/M
Complete Set (20):		25.00
Common Player:		.50
1	Roberto Alomar	.75
2	Jeff Bagwell	1.50
3	Albert Belle	.50
4	Wade Boggs	2.00
5	Barry Bonds	4.00
6	Jose Canseco	1.00
7	Ken Griffey Jr.	2.50
8	Tony Gwynn	2.00
9	Randy Johnson	1.50
10	Chipper Jones	2.00
11	Greg Maddux	2.00
12	Edgar Martinez	.50
13	Don Mattingly	2.50
14	Mike Piazza	2.50
15	Kirby Puckett	2.00
16	Manny Ramirez	1.50
17	Cal Ripken Jr.	4.00
18	Tim Salmon	.50
19	Frank Thomas	1.50
20	Mo Vaughn	.50

1997 PACIFIC CROWN

		NM/M
Complete Set (450):		30.00
Common Player:		.05
Pack (12):		1.25
Wax Box (36):		32.50
1	Garret Anderson	.05
2	George Arias	.05
3	Chili Davis	.05
4	Gary DiSarcina	.05
5	Jim Edmonds	.05
6	Darin Erstad	.15
7	Jorge Fabregas	.05
8	Chuck Finley	.05
9	Rex Hudler	.05
10	Mark Langston	.05
11	Orlando Palmeiro	.05
12	Troy Percival	.05
13	Tim Salmon	.05
14	J.T. Snow	.05
15	Randy Velarde	.05
16	Manny Alexander	.05
17	Roberto Alomar	.25
18	Brady Anderson	.05
19	Armando Benitez	.05
20	Bobby Bonilla	.05
21	Rocky Coppinger	.05
22	Scott Erickson	.05
23	Jeffrey Hammonds	.05
24	Chris Hoiles	.05
25	Eddie Murray	.75
26	Mike Mussina	.60
27	Randy Myers	.05
28	Rafael Palmeiro	.65
29	Cal Ripken Jr.	2.50
30	B.J. Surhoff	.05
31	Tony Tarasco	.05
32	Esteban Beltre	.05
33	Darren Bragg	.05
34	Jose Canseco	.60
35	Roger Clemens	1.50
36	Wil Cordero	.05
37	Alex Delgado	.05
38	Jeff Frye	.05
39	Nomar Garciaparra	1.00
40	Tom Gordon	.05
41	Mike Greenwell	.05
42	Reggie Jefferson	.05
43	Tim Naehring	.05
44	Troy O'Leary	.05
45	Heathcliff Slocumb	.05
46	Lee Tinsley	.05
47	John Valentin	.05
48	Mo Vaughn	.05
49	Wilson Alvarez	.05
50	Harold Baines	.05
51	Ray Durham	.05
52	Alex Fernandez	.05
53	Ozzie Guillen	.05
54	Roberto Hernandez	.05
55	Ron Karkovice	.05
56	Darren Lewis	.05
57	Norberto Martin	.05
58	Dave Martinez	.05
59	Lyle Mouton	.05
60	Jose Munoz	.05
61	Tony Phillips	.05
62	Rich Sauveur	.05
63	Danny Tartabull	.05
64	Frank Thomas	.75
65	Robin Ventura	.05
66	Sandy Alomar Jr.	.05
67	Albert Belle	.05
68	Julio Franco	.05
69	*Brian Giles*	.50
70	Danny Graves	.05
71	Orel Hershiser	.05
72	Jeff Kent	.05
73	Kenny Lofton	.05
74	Dennis Martinez	.05
75	Jack McDowell	.05
76	Jose Mesa	.05
77	Charles Nagy	.05
78	Manny Ramirez	.75
79	Julian Tavarez	.05
80	Jim Thome	.60
81	Jose Vizcaino	.05

82 Omar Vizquel .05
83 Brad Ausmus .05
84 Kimera Bartee .05
85 Raul Casanova .05
86 Tony Clark .05
87 Travis Fryman .05
88 Bobby Higginson .05
89 Mark Lewis .05
90 Jose Lima .05
91 Felipe Lira .05
92 Phil Nevin .05
93 Melvin Nieves .05
94 Curtis Pride .05
95 Ruben Sierra .05
96 Alan Trammell .05
97 Kevin Appier .05
98 Tim Belcher .05
99 Johnny Damon .35
100 Tom Goodwin .05
101 Bob Hamelin .05
102 David Howard .05
103 Jason Jacome .05
104 Keith Lockhart .05
105 Mike Macfarlane .05
106 Jeff Montgomery .05
107 Jose Offerman .05
108 Hipolito Pichardo .05
109 Joe Randa .05
110 Bip Roberts .05
111 Chris Stynes .05
112 Mike Sweeney .05
113 Joe Vitiello .05
114 Jeromy Burnitz .05
115 Chuck Carr .05
116 Jeff Cirillo .05
117 Mike Fetters .05
118 David Hulse .05
119 John Jaha .05
120 Scott Karl .05
121 Jesse Levis .05
122 Mark Loretta .05
123 Mike Matheny .05
124 Ben McDonald .05
125 Matt Mieske .05
126 Angel Miranda .05
127 Dave Nilsson .05
128 Jose Valentin .05
129 Fernando Vina .05
130 Ron Villone .05
131 Gerald Williams .05
132 Rick Aguilera .05
133 Rich Becker .05
134 Ron Coomer .05
135 Marty Cordova .05
136 Eddie Guardado .05
137 Denny Hocking .05
138 Roberto Kelly .05
139 Chuck Knoblauch .05
140 Matt Lawton .05
141 Pat Meares .05
142 Paul Molitor .75
143 Greg Myers .05
144 Jeff Reboulet .05
145 Scott Stahoviak .05
146 Todd Walker .05
147 Wade Boggs 1.00
148 David Cone .05
149 Mariano Duncan .05
150 Cecil Fielder .05
151 Dwight Gooden .05
152 Derek Jeter 2.50
153 Jim Leyritz .05
154 Tino Martinez .05
155 Paul O'Neill .05
156 Andy Pettitte .25
157 Tim Raines .05
158 Mariano Rivera .15
159 Ruben Rivera .05
160 Kenny Rogers .05
161 Darryl Strawberry .05
162 John Wetteland .05
163 Bernie Williams .05
164 Tony Batista .05
165 Geronimo Berroa .05
166 Mike Bordick .05
167 Scott Brosius .05
168 Brent Gates .05
169 Jason Giambi .65
170 Jose Herrera .05
171 Brian Lesher .05
172 *Damon Mashore* .05
173 Mark McGwire 2.00
174 Ariel Prieto .05
175 Carlos Reyes .05
176 Matt Stairs .05
177 Terry Steinbach .05
178 John Wasdin .05
179 Ernie Young .05
180 Rich Amaral .05
181 Bobby Ayala .05
182 Jay Buhner .05
183 Rafael Carmona .05
184 Norm Charlton .05
185 Joey Cora .05
186 Ken Griffey Jr. 1.50
187 Sterling Hitchcock .05
188 Dave Hollins .05
189 Randy Johnson .75
190 Edgar Martinez .05
191 Jamie Moyer .05
192 Alex Rodriguez 2.00
193 Paul Sorrento .05
194 Salomon Torres .05
195 Bob Wells .05
196 Dan Wilson .05
197 Will Clark .05
198 Kevin Elster .05
199 Rene Gonzales .05
200 Juan Gonzalez .40
201 Rusty Greer .05
202 Darryl Hamilton .05
203 Mike Henneman .05
204 Ken Hill .05
205 Mark McLemore .05
206 Darren Oliver .05
207 Dean Palmer .05
208 Roger Pavlik .05
209 Ivan Rodriguez .65
210 Kurt Stillwell .05
211 Mickey Tettleton .05
212 Bobby Witt .05
213 Tilson Brito .05
214 Jacob Brumfield .05
215 Miguel Cairo .05
216 Joe Carter .05
217 Felipe Crespo .05
218 Carlos Delgado .60
219 Alex Gonzalez .05
220 Shawn Green .15
221 Juan Guzman .05
222 Pat Hentgen .05
223 Charlie O'Brien .05
224 John Olerud .05
225 Robert Perez .05
226 Tomas Perez .05
227 Juan Samuel .05
228 Ed Sprague .05
229 Mike Timlin .05
230 Rafael Belliard .05
231 Jermaine Dye .05
232 Tom Glavine .25
233 Marquis Grissom .05
234 Andruw Jones .75
235 Chipper Jones 1.00
236 David Justice .05
237 Ryan Klesko .05
238 Mark Lemke .05
239 Javier Lopez .05
240 Greg Maddux 1.00
241 Fred McGriff .05
242 Denny Neagle .05
243 Eddie Perez .05
244 John Smoltz .05
245 Mark Wohlers .05
246 Brant Brown .05
247 Scott Bullett .05
248 Leo Gomez .05
249 Luis Gonzalez .05
250 Mark Grace .05
251 Jose Hernandez .05
252 Brooks Kieschnick .05
253 Brian McRae .05
254 Jaime Navarro .05
255 Mike Perez .05
256 Rey Sanchez .05
257 Ryne Sandberg 1.00
258 Scott Servais .05
259 Sammy Sosa 1.00
260 *Pedro Valdes* .05
261 Turk Wendell .05
262 Bret Boone .05
263 Jeff Branson .05
264 Jeff Brantley .05
265 Dave Burba .05
266 Hector Carrasco .05
267 Eric Davis .05
268 Willie Greene .05
269 Lenny Harris .05
270 Thomas Howard .05
271 Barry Larkin .05
272 Hal Morris .05
273 Joe Oliver .05
274 Eric Owens .05
275 Jose Rijo .05
276 Reggie Sanders .05
277 Eddie Taubensee .05
278 Jason Bates .05
279 Dante Bichette .05
280 Ellis Burks .05
281 Vinny Castilla .05
282 Andres Galarraga .05
283 Quinton McCracken .05
284 Jayhawk Owens .05
285 Jeff Reed .05
286 Bryan Rekar .05
287 Armando Reynoso .05
288 Kevin Ritz .05
289 Bruce Ruffin .05
290 John Vander Wal .05
291 Larry Walker .05
292 Walt Weiss .05
293 Eric Young .05
294 Kurt Abbott .05
295 Alex Arias .05
296 Miguel Batista .05
297 Kevin Brown .05
298 Luis Castillo .05
299 Greg Colbrunn .05
300 Jeff Conine .05
301 Charles Johnson .05
302 Al Leiter .05
303 Robb Nen .05
304 Joe Orsulak .05
305 Yorkis Perez .05
306 Edgar Renteria .05
307 Gary Sheffield .30
308 Jesus Tavarez .05
309 Quilvio Veras .05
310 Devon White .05
311 Jeff Bagwell .75
312 Derek Bell .05
313 Sean Berry .05
314 Craig Biggio .05
315 Doug Drabek .05
316 Tony Eusebio .05
317 Ricky Gutierrez .05
318 Xavier Hernandez .05
319 Brian L. Hunter .05
320 Darryl Kile .05
321 Derrick May .05
322 Orlando Miller .05
323 James Mouton .05
324 Bill Spiers .05
325 Pedro Astacio .05
326 Brett Butler .05
327 Juan Castro .05
328 Roger Cedeno .05
329 Delino DeShields .05
330 Karim Garcia .10
331 Todd Hollandsworth .05
332 Eric Karros .05
333 Oreste Marrero .05
334 Ramon Martinez .05
335 Raul Mondesi .05
336 Hideo Nomo .50
337 Antonio Osuna .05
338 Chan Ho Park .05
339 Mike Piazza 1.50
340 Ismael Valdes .05
341 Moises Alou .05
342 Omar Daal .05
343 Jeff Fassero .05
344 Cliff Floyd .05
345 Mark Grudzielanek .05
346 Mike Lansing .05
347 Pedro Martinez .75
348 Sherman Obando .05
349 Jose Paniagua .05
350 Henry Rodriguez .05
351 Mel Rojas .05
352 F.P. Santangelo .05
353 Dave Segui .05
354 Dave Silvestri .05
355 Ugueth Urbina .05
356 Rondell White .05
357 Edgardo Alfonzo .05
358 Carlos Baerga .05
359 Tim Bogar .05
360 Rico Brogna .05
361 Alvaro Espinoza .05
362 Carl Everett .05
363 John Franco .05
364 Bernard Gilkey .05
365 Todd Hundley .05
366 Butch Huskey .05
367 Jason Isringhausen .05
368 Bobby Jones .05
369 Lance Johnson .05
370 Brent Mayne .05
371 Alex Ochoa .05
372 Rey Ordonez .05
373 Ron Blazier .05
374 Ricky Bottalico .05
375 David Doster .05
376 Lenny Dykstra .05
377 Jim Eisenreich .05
378 Bobby Estalella .05
379 Gregg Jefferies .05
380 Kevin Jordan .05
381 Ricardo Jordan .05
382 Mickey Morandini .05
383 Ricky Otero .05
384 Benito Santiago .05
385 Gene Schall .05
386 Curt Schilling .25
387 Kevin Sefcik .05
388 Kevin Stocker .05
389 Jermaine Allensworth .05
390 Jay Bell .05
391 Jason Christiansen .05
392 Francisco Cordova .05
393 Mark Johnson .05
394 Jason Kendall .05
395 Jeff King .05
396 Jon Lieber .05
397 Nelson Liriano .05
398 Esteban Loaiza .05
399 Al Martin .05
400 Orlando Merced .05
401 Ramon Morel .05
402 Luis Alicea .05
403 Alan Benes .05
404 Andy Benes .05
405 Terry Bradshaw .05
406 Royce Clayton .05
407 Dennis Eckersley .65
408 Gary Gaetti .05
409 Mike Gallego .05
410 Ron Gant .05
411 Brian Jordan .05
412 Ray Lankford .05
413 John Mabry .05
414 Willie McGee .05
415 Tom Pagnozzi .05
416 Ozzie Smith 1.00
417 Todd Stottlemyre .05
418 Mark Sweeney .05
419 Andy Ashby .05
420 Ken Caminiti .05
421 Archi Cianfrocco .05
422 Steve Finley .05
423 Chris Gomez .05
424 Tony Gwynn 1.00
425 Joey Hamilton .05
426 Rickey Henderson .75
427 Trevor Hoffman .05
428 Brian Johnson .05
429 Wally Joyner .05
430 Scott Livingstone .05
431 Jody Reed .05
432 Craig Shipley .05
433 Fernando Valenzuela .05
434 Greg Vaughn .05
435 Rich Aurilia .05
436 Kim Batiste .05
437 Jose Bautista .05
438 Rod Beck .05
439 Marvin Benard .05
440 Barry Bonds 2.50
441 Shawon Dunston .05
442 Shawn Estes .05
443 Osvaldo Fernandez .05
444 Stan Javier .05
445 David McCarty .05
446 *Bill Mueller* .15
447 Steve Scarsone .05
448 Robby Thompson .05
449 Rick Wilkins .05
450 Matt Williams .05

Silver

	NM/M
Common Player:	1.00
Stars/Rookies:	12X

(See 1997 Pacific Crown for checklist andbase card values.)

Light Blue

	NM/M
Complete Set (450):	60.00
Common Player:	.25
Stars:	1X

(See 1997 Pacific Crown for checklist andbase card values.)

Card-Supials

		NM/M
Complete Set (72):		80.00
Complete Large Set (36):		60.00
Complete Small Set (36):		45.00
Common Large:		.75
Small Cards:		75%
1	Roberto Alomar	1.00
2	Brady Anderson	.75
3	Eddie Murray	2.00
4	Cal Ripken Jr.	5.00
5	Jose Canseco	1.00
6	Mo Vaughn	.75
7	Frank Thomas	2.00
8	Albert Belle	.75
9	Omar Vizquel	.75
10	Chuck Knoblauch	.75
11	Paul Molitor	2.00
12	Wade Boggs	2.50
13	Derek Jeter	5.00
14	Andy Pettitte	1.00
15	Mark McGwire	3.50
16	Jay Buhner	.75
17	Ken Griffey Jr.	3.00
18	Alex Rodriguez	3.50
19	Juan Gonzalez	1.00
20	Ivan Rodriguez	1.50
21	Andruw Jones	2.00
22	Chipper Jones	2.50
23	Ryan Klesko	.75
24	Greg Maddux	2.50
25	Ryne Sandberg	2.50
26	Andres Galarraga	.75
27	Gary Sheffield	1.00
28	Jeff Bagwell	2.00
29	Todd Hollandsworth	.75
30	Hideo Nomo	1.00
31	Mike Piazza	3.00
32	Todd Hundley	.75
33	Dennis Eckersley	1.50
34	Ken Caminiti	.75
35	Tony Gwynn	2.50
36	Barry Bonds	5.00

Cramer's Choice Awards

		NM/M
Complete Set (10):		75.00
Common Player:		4.50
1	Roberto Alomar	5.00
2	Frank Thomas	9.00
3	Albert Belle	4.50
4	Andy Pettitte	4.50
5	Ken Griffey Jr.	17.50
6	Alex Rodriguez	25.00
7	Chipper Jones	12.00
8	John Smoltz	4.50
9	Mike Piazza	15.00
10	Tony Gwynn	12.00

Gold Crown Die-Cuts

		NM/M
Complete Set (36):		65.00
Common Player:		1.00
1	Roberto Alomar	1.25
2	Brady Anderson	1.00
3	Mike Mussina	1.50
4	Eddie Murray	2.75
5	Cal Ripken Jr.	8.50
6	Jose Canseco	2.00
7	Frank Thomas	2.75
8	Albert Belle	1.00
9	Omar Vizquel	1.00
10	Wade Boggs	3.50
11	Derek Jeter	8.50
12	Andy Pettitte	1.25
13	Mariano Rivera	1.25
14	Bernie Williams	1.00
15	Mark McGwire	6.50
16	Ken Griffey Jr.	5.00
17	Edgar Martinez	1.00
18	Alex Rodriquez	6.50
19	Juan Gonzalez	1.50
20	Ivan Rodriguez	2.50
21	Andruw Jones	2.75
22	Chipper Jones	3.50
23	Ryan Klesko	1.00
24	John Smoltz	1.00
25	Ryne Sandberg	3.50
26	Andres Galarraga	1.00
27	Edgar Renteria	1.00
28	Jeff Bagwell	2.75
29	Todd Hollandsworth	1.00
30	Hideo Nomo	1.50
31	Mike Piazza	5.00
32	Todd Hundley	1.00
33	Brian Jordan	1.00
34	Ken Caminiti	1.00
35	Tony Gwynn	3.50
36	Barry Bonds	8.50

Fireworks Die-Cuts

		NM/M
Complete Set (20):		40.00
Common Player:		.75
1	Roberto Alomar	1.00
2	Brady Anderson	.75
3	Eddie Murray	2.50
4	Cal Ripken Jr.	7.50
5	Frank Thomas	2.50
6	Albert Belle	.75
7	Derek Jeter	7.50
8	Andy Pettitte	1.00
9	Bernie Williams	.75
10	Mark McGwire	6.50
11	Ken Griffey Jr.	5.00
12	Alex Rodriguez	6.50
13	Juan Gonzalez	1.25
14	Andruw Jones	2.50
15	Chipper Jones	3.50
16	Hideo Nomo	1.25
17	Mike Piazza	5.00
18	Henry Rodriguez	.75
19	Tony Gwynn	3.50
20	Barry Bonds	7.50

Latinos of the Major Leagues

		NM/M
Complete Set (36):		45.00
Common Player:		1.00
1	George Arias	1.00
2	Roberto Alomar	1.50
3	Rafael Palmeiro	2.50
4	Bobby Bonilla	1.00
5	Jose Canseco	2.00
6	Wilson Alvarez	1.00
7	Dave Martinez	1.00
8	Julio Franco	1.00
9	Manny Ramirez	3.00
10	Omar Vizquel	1.00
11	Marty Cordova	1.00
12	Roberto Kelly	1.00
13	Tino Martinez	1.00
14	Mariano Rivera	1.50
15	Ruben Rivera	1.00
16	Bernie Williams	1.00
17	Geronimo Berroa	1.00
18	Joey Cora	1.00
19	Edgar Martinez	1.00
20	Alex Rodriguez	6.00
21	Juan Gonzalez	2.00
22	Ivan Rodriguez	2.50
23	Andruw Jones	3.00
24	Javier Lopez	1.00
25	Sammy Sosa	4.50
26	Vinny Castilla	1.00
27	Andres Galarraga	1.00
28	Ramon Martinez	1.00
29	Raul Mondesi	1.00
30	Ismael Valdes	1.00
31	Pedro Martinez	3.00
32	Henry Rodriguez	1.00
33	Carlos Baerga	1.00
34	Rey Ordonez	1.00
35	Fernando Valenzuela	1.00
36	Osvaldo Fernandez	1.00

Triple Crown Die-Cuts

		NM/M
Complete Set (20):		75.00
Common Player:		2.00
1	Brady Anderson	2.00
2	Rafael Palmeiro	4.00
3	Mo Vaughn	2.00
4	Frank Thomas	5.00
5	Albert Belle	2.00
6	Jim Thome	4.00
7	Cecil Fielder	2.00
8	Mark McGwire	10.00
9	Ken Griffey Jr.	7.50
10	Alex Rodriguez	10.00
11	Juan Gonzalez	3.00
12	Andruw Jones	5.00
13	Chipper Jones	6.00
14	Dante Bichette	2.00
15	Ellis Burks	2.00
16	Andres Galarraga	2.00
17	Jeff Bagwell	5.00
18	Mike Piazza	7.50
19	Ken Caminiti	2.00
20	Barry Bonds	12.50

1997 PACIFIC INVINCIBLE

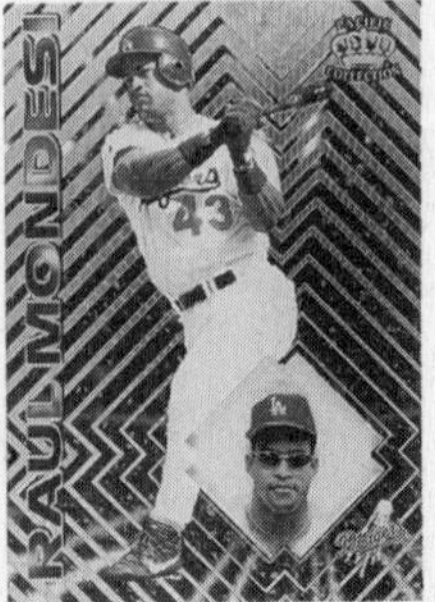

		NM/M
Complete Set (150):		30.00
Common Player:		.25
Light Blues:		1X
Platinums:		2X
Pack (3):		1.00
Wax Box (36):		25.00
1	Chili Davis	.25
2	Jim Edmonds	.25
3	Darin Erstad	.50
4	Orlando Palmeiro	.25
5	Tim Salmon	.25
6	J.T. Snow	.25
7	Roberto Alomar	.50
8	Brady Anderson	.25
9	Eddie Murray	1.50
10	Mike Mussina	1.00
11	Rafael Palmeiro	1.25
12	Cal Ripken Jr.	4.00
13	Jose Canseco	1.00
14	Roger Clemens	2.50
15	Nomar Garciaparra	2.00
16	Reggie Jefferson	.25
17	Mo Vaughn	.25
18	Wilson Alvarez	.25
19	Harold Baines	.25
20	Alex Fernandez	.25
21	Danny Tartabull	.25
22	Frank Thomas	1.50
23	Robin Ventura	.25
24	Sandy Alomar Jr.	.25
25	Albert Belle	.25
26	Kenny Lofton	.25
27	Jim Thome	.75
28	Omar Vizquel	.25
29	Raul Casanova	.25
30	Tony Clark	.25
31	Travis Fryman	.25
32	Bobby Higginson	.25
33	Melvin Nieves	.25
34	Justin Thompson	.25
35	Johnny Damon	.50
36	Tom Goodwin	.25
37	Jeff Montgomery	.25
38	Jose Offerman	.25
39	John Jaha	.25
40	Jeff Cirillo	.25
41	Dave Nilsson	.25
42	Jose Valentin	.25
43	Fernando Vina	.25
44	Marty Cordova	.25
45	Roberto Kelly	.25
46	Chuck Knoblauch	.25
47	Paul Molitor	1.50
48	Todd Walker	.25
49	Wade Boggs	2.00
50	Cecil Fielder	.25
51	Derek Jeter	4.00
52	Tino Martinez	.25
53	Andy Pettitte	.40
54	Mariano Rivera	.40
55	Bernie Williams	.25
56	Tony Batista	.25
57	Geronimo Berroa	.25
58	Jason Giambi	.75
59	Mark McGwire	3.00
60	Terry Steinbach	.25
61	Jay Buhner	.25
62	Joey Cora	.25
63	Ken Griffey Jr.	2.50
64	Edgar Martinez	.25
65	Alex Rodriguez	3.00
66	Paul Sorrento	.25
67	Will Clark	.25
68	Juan Gonzalez	.75
69	Rusty Greer	.25
70	Dean Palmer	.25
71	Ivan Rodriguez	1.25
72	Joe Carter	.25
73	Carlos Delgado	.75
74	Juan Guzman	.25
75	Pat Hentgen	.25
76	Ed Sprague	.25
77	Jermaine Dye	.25
78	Andruw Jones	1.50
79	Chipper Jones	2.00
80	Ryan Klesko	.25
81	Javier Lopez	.25
82	Greg Maddux	2.00
83	John Smoltz	.25
84	Mark Grace	.25
85	Luis Gonzalez	.25
86	Brooks Kieschnick	.25
87	Jaime Navarro	.25
88	Ryne Sandberg	2.00
89	Sammy Sosa	2.00
90	Bret Boone	.25
91	Jeff Brantley	.25
92	Eric Davis	.25
93	Barry Larkin	.25
94	Reggie Sanders	.25
95	Ellis Burks	.25
96	Dante Bichette	.25
97	Vinny Castilla	.25
98	Andres Galarraga	.25
99	Eric Young	.25
100	Kevin Brown	.25
101	Jeff Conine	.25
102	Charles Johnson	.25
103	Edgar Renteria	.25

104	Gary Sheffield	.75
105	Jeff Bagwell	1.50
106	Derek Bell	.25
107	Sean Berry	.25
108	Craig Biggio	.25
109	Shane Reynolds	.25
110	Karim Garcia	.25
111	Todd Hollandsworth	.25
112	Ramon Martinez	.25
113	Raul Mondesi	.25
114	Hideo Nomo	.75
115	Mike Piazza	2.50
116	Ismael Valdes	.25
117	Moises Alou	.25
118	Mark Grudzielanek	.25
119	Pedro Martinez	1.50
120	Henry Rodriguez	.25
121	F.P. Santangelo	.25
122	Carlos Baerga	.25
123	Bernard Gilkey	.25
124	Todd Hundley	.25
125	Lance Johnson	.25
126	Alex Ochoa	.25
127	Rey Ordonez	.25
128	Lenny Dykstra	.25
129	Gregg Jefferies	.25
130	Ricky Otero	.25
131	Benito Santiago	.25
132	Jermaine Allensworth	.25
133	Francisco Cordova	.25
134	Carlos Garcia	.25
135	Jason Kendall	.25
136	Al Martin	.25
137	Dennis Eckersley	1.25
138	Ron Gant	.25
139	Brian Jordan	.25
140	John Mabry	.25
141	Ozzie Smith	2.00
142	Ken Caminiti	.25
143	Steve Finley	.25
144	Tony Gwynn	2.00
145	Wally Joyner	.25
146	Fernando Valenzuela	.25
147	Barry Bonds	4.00
148	Jacob Cruz	.25
149	Osvaldo Fernandez	.25
150	Matt Williams	.25

Gate Attractions

		NM/M
Complete Set (32):		80.00
Common Player:		1.00
1	Roberto Alomar	1.00
2	Brady Anderson	1.00
3	Cal Ripken Jr.	8.00
4	Frank Thomas	2.50
5	Kenny Lofton	1.00
6	Omar Vizquel	1.00
7	Paul Molitor	2.50
8	Wade Boggs	3.00
9	Derek Jeter	8.00
10	Andy Pettitte	1.50
11	Bernie Williams	1.00
12	Geronimo Berroa	1.00
13	Mark McGwire	6.00
14	Ken Griffey Jr.	4.50
15	Alex Rodriguez	6.00
16	Juan Gonzalez	1.50
17	Andruw Jones	2.50
18	Chipper Jones	3.00
19	Greg Maddux	3.00
20	Ryne Sandberg	3.00
21	Sammy Sosa	3.00
22	Andres Galarraga	1.00
23	Jeff Bagwell	2.50
24	Todd Hollandsworth	1.00
25	Hideo Nomo	1.50
26	Mike Piazza	4.50
27	Todd Hundley	1.00
28	Lance Johnson	1.00
29	Ozzie Smith	3.00
30	Ken Caminiti	1.00
31	Tony Gwynn	3.00
32	Barry Bonds	8.00

Sizzling Lumber

		NM/M
Complete Set (36):		50.00
Common Player:		.50
1A	Cal Ripken Jr.	6.50
1B	Rafael Palmeiro	2.50
1C	Roberto Alomar	1.00
2A	Frank Thomas	3.00
2B	Robin Ventura	.50
2C	Harold Baines	.50
3A	Albert Belle	.50
3B	Manny Ramirez	3.00
3C	Kenny Lofton	.50
4A	Derek Jeter	6.50
4B	Bernie Williams	.50
4C	Wade Boggs	3.50
5A	Mark McGwire	5.00
5B	Jason Giambi	2.00
5C	Geronimo Berroa	.50
6A	Ken Griffey Jr.	4.00
6B	Alex Rodriguez	5.00
6C	Jay Buhner	.50
7A	Juan Gonzalez	1.50
7B	Dean Palmer	.50
7C	Ivan Rodriguez	2.50
8A	Ryan Klesko	.50
8B	Chipper Jones	3.50
8C	Andruw Jones	3.00
9A	Dante Bichette	.50
9B	Andres Galarraga	.50
9C	Vinny Castilla	.50
10A	Jeff Bagwell	3.00
10B	Craig Biggio	.50
10C	Derek Bell	.50
11A	Mike Piazza	4.00
11B	Raul Mondesi	.50
11C	Karim Garcia	.50
12A	Tony Gwynn	3.50
12B	Ken Caminiti	.50
12C	Greg Vaughn	.50

Sluggers & Hurlers

		NM/M
Complete Set (24):		80.00
Common Player:		2.00
SH-1a	Cal Ripken Jr.	10.00
SH-1b	Mike Mussina	2.50
SH-2a	Jose Canseco	2.50
SH-2b	Roger Clemens	6.00
SH-3a	Frank Thomas	3.50
SH-3b	Wilson Alvarez	2.00
SH-4a	Kenny Lofton	2.00
SH-4b	Orel Hershiser	2.00
SH-5a	Derek Jeter	10.00
SH-5b	Andy Pettitte	2.00
SH-6a	Ken Griffey Jr.	6.00
SH-6b	Randy Johnson	3.50
SH-7a	Alex Rodriguez	7.50
SH-7b	Jamie Moyer	2.00
SH-8a	Andruw Jones	3.50
SH-8b	Greg Maddux	4.50
SH-9a	Chipper Jones	4.50
SH-9b	John Smoltz	2.00
SH-10a	Jeff Bagwell	3.50
SH-10b	Shane Reynolds	2.00
SH-11a	Mike Piazza	6.00
SH-11b	Hideo Nomo	2.50
SH-12a	Tony Gwynn	4.50
SH-12b	Fernando Valenzuela	2.00

1998 PACIFIC

		NM/M
Complete Set (450):		40.00
Common Player:		.05
Pack (12):		1.00
Wax Box (36):		20.00
1	Luis Alicea	.05
2	Garret Anderson	.05
3	Jason Dickson	.05
4	Gary DiSarcina	.05
5	Jim Edmonds	.05
6	Darin Erstad	.15
7	Chuck Finley	.05
8	Shigetosi Hasegawa	.05
9	Rickey Henderson	.75
10	Dave Hollins	.05
11	Mark Langston	.05
12	Orlando Palmeiro	.05
13	Troy Percival	.05
14	Tony Phillips	.05
15	Tim Salmon	.05
16	Allen Watson	.05
17	Roberto Alomar	.25
18	Brady Anderson	.05
19	Harold Baines	.05
20	Armando Benitez	.05
21	Geronimo Berroa	.05
22	Mike Bordick	.05
23	Eric Davis	.05
24	Scott Erickson	.05
25	Chris Hoiles	.05
26	Jimmy Key	.05
27	Aaron Ledesma	.05
28	Mike Mussina	.50
29	Randy Myers	.05
30	Jesse Orosco	.05
31	Rafael Palmeiro	.65
32	Jeff Reboulet	.05
33	Cal Ripken Jr.	2.00
34	B.J. Surhoff	.05
35	Steve Avery	.05
36	Darren Bragg	.05
37	Wil Cordero	.05
38	Jeff Frye	.05
39	Nomar Garciaparra	1.00
40	Tom Gordon	.05
41	Bill Haselman	.05
42	Scott Hatteberg	.05
43	Butch Henry	.05
44	Reggie Jefferson	.05
45	Tim Naehring	.05
46	Troy O'Leary	.05
47	Jeff Suppan	.05
48	John Valentin	.05
49	Mo Vaughn	.05
50	Tim Wakefield	.05
51	James Baldwin	.05
52	Albert Belle	.05
53	Tony Castillo	.05
54	Doug Drabek	.05
55	Ray Durham	.05
56	Jorge Fabregas	.05
57	Ozzie Guillen	.05
58	Matt Karchner	.05
59	Norberto Martin	.05
60	Dave Martinez	.05
61	Lyle Mouton	.05
62	Jaime Navarro	.05
63	Frank Thomas	.75
64	Mario Valdez	.05
65	Robin Ventura	.05
66	Sandy Alomar Jr.	.05
67	Paul Assenmacher	.05
68	Tony Fernandez	.05
69	Brian Giles	.05
70	Marquis Grissom	.05
71	Orel Hershiser	.05
72	Mike Jackson	.05
73	David Justice	.05
74	Albie Lopez	.05
75	Jose Mesa	.05
76	Charles Nagy	.05
77	Chad Ogea	.05
78	Manny Ramirez	.75
79	Jim Thome	.60
80	Omar Vizquel	.05
81	Matt Williams	.05
82	Jaret Wright	.05
83	Willie Blair	.05
84	Raul Casanova	.05
85	Tony Clark	.05
86	Deivi Cruz	.05
87	Damion Easley	.05
88	Travis Fryman	.05
89	Bobby Higginson	.05
90	Brian Hunter	.05
91	Todd Jones	.05
92	Dan Miceli	.05
93	Brian Moehler	.05
94	Melvin Nieves	.05
95	Jody Reed	.05
96	Justin Thompson	.05
97	Bubba Trammell	.05
98	Kevin Appier	.05
99	Jay Bell	.05
100	Yamil Benitez	.05
101	Johnny Damon	.35
102	Chili Davis	.05
103	Jermaine Dye	.05
104	Jed Hansen	.05
105	Jeff King	.05
106	Mike Macfarlane	.05
107	Felix Martinez	.05
108	Jeff Montgomery	.05
109	Jose Offerman	.05
110	Dean Palmer	.05
111	Hipolito Pichardo	.05
112	Jose Rosado	.05
113	Jeromy Burnitz	.05
114	Jeff Cirillo	.05
115	Cal Eldred	.05
116	John Jaha	.05
117	Doug Jones	.05
118	Scott Karl	.05
119	Jesse Levis	.05
120	Mark Loretta	.05
121	Ben McDonald	.05
122	Jose Mercedes	.05
123	Matt Mieske	.05
124	Dave Nilsson	.05
125	Jose Valentin	.05
126	Fernando Vina	.05
127	Gerald Williams	.05
128	Rick Aguilera	.05
129	Rich Becker	.05
130	Ron Coomer	.05
131	Marty Cordova	.05
132	Eddie Guardado	.05
133	LaTroy Hawkins	.05
134	Denny Hocking	.05
135	Chuck Knoblauch	.05
136	Matt Lawton	.05
137	Pat Meares	.05
138	Paul Molitor	.75
139	David Ortiz	.50
140	Brad Radke	.05
141	Terry Steinbach	.05
142	Bob Tewksbury	.05
143	Javier Valentin	.05
144	Wade Boggs	1.00
145	David Cone	.05
146	Chad Curtis	.05
147	Cecil Fielder	.05
148	Joe Girardi	.05
149	Dwight Gooden	.05
150	Hideki Irabu	.05
151	Derek Jeter	2.00
152	Tino Martinez	.05
153	Ramiro Mendoza	.05
154	Paul O'Neill	.05
155	Andy Pettitte	.20

No.	Player	NM/M
156	Jorge Posada	.05
157	Mariano Rivera	.15
158	Rey Sanchez	.05
159	Luis Sojo	.05
160	David Wells	.05
161	Bernie Williams	.05
162	Rafael Bournigal	.05
163	Scott Brosius	.05
164	Jose Canseco	.50
165	Jason Giambi	.60
166	Ben Grieve	.05
167	Dave Magadan	.05
168	Brent Mayne	.05
169	Jason McDonald	.05
170	Izzy Molina	.05
171	Ariel Prieto	.05
172	Carlos Reyes	.05
173	Scott Spiezio	.05
174	Matt Stairs	.05
175	Bill Taylor	.05
176	Dave Telgheder	.05
177	Steve Wojciechowski	.05
178	Rich Amaral	.05
179	Bobby Ayala	.05
180	Jay Buhner	.05
181	Rafael Carmona	.05
182	Ken Cloude	.05
183	Joey Cora	.05
184	Russ Davis	.05
185	Jeff Fassero	.05
186	Ken Griffey Jr.	1.25
187	Raul Ibanez	.05
188	Randy Johnson	.75
189	Roberto Kelly	.05
190	Edgar Martinez	.05
191	Jamie Moyer	.05
192	Omar Olivares	.05
193	Alex Rodriguez	1.50
194	Heathcliff Slocumb	.05
195	Paul Sorrento	.05
196	Dan Wilson	.05
197	Scott Bailes	.05
198	John Burkett	.05
199	Domingo Cedeno	.05
200	Will Clark	.05
201	*Hanley Frias*	.05
202	Juan Gonzalez	.40
203	Tom Goodwin	.05
204	Rusty Greer	.05
205	Wilson Heredia	.05
206	Darren Oliver	.05
207	Billy Ripken	.05
208	Ivan Rodriguez	.65
209	Lee Stevens	.05
210	Fernando Tatis	.05
211	John Wetteland	.05
212	Bobby Witt	.05
213	Jacob Brumfield	.05
214	Joe Carter	.05
215	Roger Clemens	1.25
216	Felipe Crespo	.05
217	Jose Cruz Jr.	.05
218	Carlos Delgado	.50
219	Mariano Duncan	.05
220	Carlos Garcia	.05
221	Alex Gonzalez	.05
222	Juan Guzman	.05
223	Pat Hentgen	.05
224	Orlando Merced	.05
225	Tomas Perez	.05
226	Paul Quantrill	.05
227	Benito Santiago	.05
228	Woody Williams	.05
229	Rafael Belliard	.05
230	Jeff Blauser	.05
231	Pedro Borbon	.05
232	Tom Glavine	.25
233	Tony Graffanino	.05
234	Andruw Jones	.75
235	Chipper Jones	1.00
236	Ryan Klesko	.05
237	Mark Lemke	.05
238	Kenny Lofton	.05
239	Javier Lopez	.05
240	Fred McGriff	.05
241	Greg Maddux	1.00
242	Denny Neagle	.05
243	John Smoltz	.05
244	Michael Tucker	.05
245	Mark Wohlers	.05
246	Manny Alexander	.05
247	Miguel Batista	.05
248	Mark Clark	.05
249	Doug Glanville	.05
250	Jeremi Gonzalez	.05
251	Mark Grace	.05
252	Jose Hernandez	.05
253	Lance Johnson	.05
254	Brooks Kieschnick	.05
255	Kevin Orie	.05
256	Ryne Sandberg	1.00
257	Scott Servais	.05
258	Sammy Sosa	1.00
259	Kevin Tapani	.05
260	Ramon Tatis	.05
261	Bret Boone	.05
262	Dave Burba	.05
263	Brook Fordyce	.05
264	Willie Greene	.05
265	Barry Larkin	.05
266	Pedro A. Martinez	.05
267	Hal Morris	.05
268	Joe Oliver	.05
269	Eduardo Perez	.05
270	Pokey Reese	.05
271	Felix Rodriguez	.05
272	Deion Sanders	.05
273	Reggie Sanders	.05
274	Jeff Shaw	.05
275	Scott Sullivan	.05
276	Brett Tomko	.05
277	Roger Bailey	.05
278	Dante Bichette	.05
279	Ellis Burks	.05
280	Vinny Castilla	.05
281	Frank Castillo	.05
282	*Mike DeJean*	.05
283	Andres Galarraga	.05
284	Darren Holmes	.05
285	Kirt Manwaring	.05
286	Quinton McCracken	.05
287	Neifi Perez	.05
288	Steve Reed	.05
289	John Thomson	.05
290	Larry Walker	.05
291	Walt Weiss	.05
292	Kurt Abbott	.05
293	Antonio Alfonseca	.05
294	Moises Alou	.05
295	Alex Arias	.05
296	Bobby Bonilla	.05
297	Kevin Brown	.05
298	Craig Counsell	.05
299	Darren Daulton	.05
300	Jim Eisenreich	.05
301	Alex Fernandez	.05
302	Felix Heredia	.05
303	Livan Hernandez	.05
304	Charles Johnson	.05
305	Al Leiter	.05
306	Robb Nen	.05
307	Edgar Renteria	.05
308	Gary Sheffield	.45
309	Devon White	.05
310	Bob Abreu	.10
311	Brad Ausmus	.05
312	Jeff Bagwell	.75
313	Derek Bell	.05
314	Sean Berry	.05
315	Craig Biggio	.05
316	Ramon Garcia	.05
317	Luis Gonzalez	.05
318	Ricky Gutierrez	.05
319	Mike Hampton	.05
320	Richard Hidalgo	.05
321	Thomas Howard	.05
322	Darryl Kile	.05
323	Jose Lima	.05
324	Shane Reynolds	.05
325	Bill Spiers	.05
326	Tom Candiotti	.05
327	Roger Cedeno	.05
328	Greg Gagne	.05
329	Karim Garcia	.05
330	Wilton Guerrero	.05
331	Todd Hollandsworth	.05
332	Eric Karros	.05
333	Ramon Martinez	.05
334	Raul Mondesi	.05
335	Otis Nixon	.05
336	Hideo Nomo	.40
337	Antonio Osuna	.05
338	Chan Ho Park	.05
339	Mike Piazza	1.25
340	Dennis Reyes	.05
341	Ismael Valdes	.05
342	Todd Worrell	.05
343	Todd Zeile	.05
344	Darrin Fletcher	.05
345	Mark Grudzielanek	.05
346	Vladimir Guerrero	.75
347	Dustin Hermanson	.05
348	Mike Lansing	.05
349	Pedro Martinez	.75
350	Ryan McGuire	.05
351	Jose Paniagua	.05
352	Carlos Perez	.05
353	Henry Rodriguez	.05
354	F.P. Santangelo	.05
355	David Segui	.05
356	Ugueth Urbina	.05
357	Marc Valdes	.05
358	Jose Vidro	.05
359	Rondell White	.05
360	Juan Acevedo	.05
361	Edgardo Alfonzo	.05
362	Carlos Baerga	.05
363	Carl Everett	.05
364	John Franco	.05
365	Bernard Gilkey	.05
366	Todd Hundley	.05
367	Butch Huskey	.05
368	Bobby Jones	.05
369	Takashi Kashiwada	.05
370	Greg McMichael	.05
371	Brian McRae	.05
372	Alex Ochoa	.05
373	John Olerud	.05
374	Rey Ordonez	.05
375	Turk Wendell	.05
376	Ricky Bottalico	.05
377	Rico Brogna	.05
378	Lenny Dykstra	.05
379	Bobby Estalella	.05
380	Wayne Gomes	.05
381	Tyler Green	.05
382	Gregg Jefferies	.05
383	Mark Leiter	.05
384	Mike Lieberthal	.05
385	Mickey Morandini	.05
386	Scott Rolen	.60
387	Curt Schilling	.25
388	Kevin Stocker	.05
389	Danny Tartabull	.05
390	Jermaine Allensworth	.05
391	Adrian Brown	.05
392	Jason Christiansen	.05
393	Steve Cooke	.05
394	Francisco Cordova	.05
395	Jose Guillen	.05
396	Jason Kendall	.05
397	Jon Lieber	.05
398	Esteban Loaiza	.05
399	Al Martin	.05
400	*Kevin Polcovich*	.05
401	Joe Randa	.05
402	Ricardo Rincon	.05
403	Tony Womack	.05
404	Kevin Young	.05
405	Andy Benes	.05
406	Royce Clayton	.05
407	Delino DeShields	.05
408	Mike Difelice	.05
409	Dennis Eckersley	.60
410	John Frascatore	.05
411	Gary Gaetti	.05
412	Ron Gant	.05
413	Brian Jordan	.05
414	Ray Lankford	.05
415	Willie McGee	.05
416	Mark McGwire	1.50
417	Matt Morris	.05
418	Luis Ordaz	.05
419	Todd Stottlemyre	.05
420	Andy Ashby	.05
421	Jim Bruske	.05
422	Ken Caminiti	.05
423	Will Cunnane	.05
424	Steve Finley	.05
425	John Flaherty	.05
426	Chris Gomez	.05
427	Tony Gwynn	1.00
428	Joey Hamilton	.05
429	Carlos Hernandez	.05
430	Sterling Hitchcock	.05
431	Trevor Hoffman	.05
432	Wally Joyner	.05
433	Greg Vaughn	.05
434	Quilvio Veras	.05
435	Wilson Alvarez	.05
436	Rod Beck	.05
437	Barry Bonds	2.00
438	Jacob Cruz	.05
439	Shawn Estes	.05
440	Darryl Hamilton	.05
441	Roberto Hernandez	.05
442	Glenallen Hill	.05
443	Stan Javier	.05
444	Brian Johnson	.05
445	Jeff Kent	.05
446	Bill Mueller	.05
447	Kirk Rueter	.05
448	J.T. Snow	.05
449	Julian Tavarez	.05
450	Jose Vizcaino	.05

Red/Silver/Blue

	NM/M
Common Red:	1.50
Red Stars:	6X
Common Silver:	.75
Silver Stars:	3X
Common Platinum Blue:	3.00
Platinum Blue Stars:	15X

(See 1998 Pacific for checklist and base card values.)

Cramer's Choice

		NM/M
Complete Set (10):		150.00
Common Player:		7.50
Inserted 1:721		
1	Greg Maddux	15.00
2	Roberto Alomar	7.50
3	Cal Ripken Jr.	30.00
4	Nomar Garciaparra	15.00
5	Larry Walker	7.50
6	Mike Piazza	17.50
7	Mark McGwire	25.00
8	Tony Gwynn	15.00
9	Ken Griffey Jr.	20.00
10	Roger Clemens	17.50

Gold Crown Die-Cuts

		NM/M
Complete Set (36):		85.00
Common Player:		1.50
1	Chipper Jones	4.00
2	Greg Maddux	4.00
3	Denny Neagle	1.50
4	Roberto Alomar	2.00
5	Rafael Palmeiro	2.50
6	Cal Ripken Jr.	8.00
7	Nomar Garciaparra	4.00
8	Mo Vaughn	1.50
9	Frank Thomas	3.00
10	Sandy Alomar Jr.	1.50
11	David Justice	1.50
12	Manny Ramirez	3.00
13	Andres Galarraga	1.50
14	Larry Walker	1.50
15	Moises Alou	1.50
16	Livan Hernandez	1.50
17	Gary Sheffield	2.00
18	Jeff Bagwell	3.00
19	Raul Mondesi	1.50
20	Hideo Nomo	2.00
21	Mike Piazza	4.50
22	Derek Jeter	8.00
23	Tino Martinez	1.50
24	Bernie Williams	1.50
25	Ben Grieve	1.50
26	Mark McGwire	6.50
27	Tony Gwynn	4.00
28	Barry Bonds	8.00
29	Ken Griffey Jr.	5.00
30	Randy Johnson	3.00
31	Edgar Martinez	1.50
32	Alex Rodriguez	6.50
33	Juan Gonzalez	2.00
34	Ivan Rodriguez	2.50
35	Roger Clemens	4.50
36	Jose Cruz Jr.	1.50

Home Run Hitters

	NM/M
Complete Set (20):	50.00
Common Player:	1.00

1	Rafael Palmeiro	3.00
2	Mo Vaughn	1.00
3	Sammy Sosa	4.00
4	Albert Belle	1.00
5	Frank Thomas	3.50
6	David Justice	1.00
7	Jim Thome	3.00
8	Matt Williams	1.00
9	Vinny Castilla	1.00
10	Andres Galarraga	1.00
11	Larry Walker	1.00
12	Jeff Bagwell	3.50
13	Mike Piazza	4.50
14	Tino Martinez	1.00
15	Mark McGwire	6.00
16	Barry Bonds	7.50
17	Jay Buhner	1.00
18	Ken Griffey Jr.	5.00
19	Alex Rodriguez	6.00
20	Juan Gonzalez	2.00

In the Cage

		NM/M
Complete Set (20):		175.00
Common Player:		4.00
1	Chipper Jones	12.00
2	Roberto Alomar	4.00
3	Cal Ripken Jr.	25.00
4	Nomar Garciaparra	12.00
5	Frank Thomas	10.00
6	Sandy Alomar Jr.	4.00
7	David Justice	4.00
8	Larry Walker	4.00
9	Bobby Bonilla	4.00
10	Mike Piazza	16.00
11	Tino Martinez	4.00
12	Bernie Williams	4.00
13	Mark McGwire	20.00
14	Tony Gwynn	12.00
15	Barry Bonds	25.00
16	Ken Griffey Jr.	16.00
17	Edgar Martinez	4.00
18	Alex Rodriguez	20.00
19	Juan Gonzalez	6.00
20	Ivan Rodriguez	7.50

Latinos of the Major Leagues

		NM/M
Complete Set (36):		30.00
Common Player:		.50
Inserted 2:37		
1	Andruw Jones	2.50
2	Javier Lopez	.50
3	Roberto Alomar	1.25
4	Geronimo Berroa	.50
5	Rafael Palmeiro	2.00
6	Nomar Garciaparra	3.00
7	Sammy Sosa	3.00
8	Ozzie Guillen	.50
9	Sandy Alomar Jr.	.50
10	Manny Ramirez	2.50
11	Omar Vizquel	.50
12	Vinny Castilla	.50
13	Andres Galarraga	.50
14	Moises Alou	.50
15	Bobby Bonilla	.50
16	Livan Hernandez	.50
17	Edgar Renteria	.50
18	Wilton Guerrero	.50
19	Raul Mondesi	.50
20	Ismael Valdes	.50
21	Fernando Vina	.50
22	Pedro Martinez	2.50
23	Edgardo Alfonzo	.50
24	Carlos Baerga	.50
25	Rey Ordonez	.50
26	Tino Martinez	.50
27	Mariano Rivera	1.00
28	Bernie Williams	.50
29	Jose Canseco	1.50
30	Joey Cora	.50
31	Roberto Kelly	.50
32	Edgar Martinez	.50
33	Alex Rodriguez	3.50
34	Juan Gonzalez	1.50
35	Ivan Rodriguez	2.00
36	Jose Cruz Jr.	.50

Team Checklists

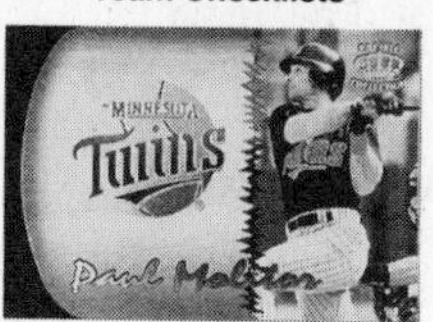

		NM/M
Complete Set (30):		60.00
Common Player:		.50
1	Tim Salmon, Jim Edmonds	.50
2	Cal Ripken Jr., Roberto Alomar	6.00
3	Nomar Garciaparra, Mo Vaughn	3.50
4	Frank Thomas, Albert Belle	2.50
5	Sandy Alomar Jr., Manny Ramirez	2.50
6	Justin Thompson, Tony Clark	.50
7	Johnny Damon, Jermaine Dye	.75
8	Dave Nilsson, Jeff Cirillo	.50
9	Paul Molitor, Chuck Knoblauch	2.50
10	Tino Martinez, Derek Jeter	6.00
11	Ben Grieve, Jose Canseco	1.00
12	Ken Griffey Jr., Alex Rodriguez	5.00
13	Juan Gonzalez, Ivan Rodriguez	2.00
14	Jose Cruz Jr., Roger Clemens	4.00
15	Greg Maddux, Chipper Jones	3.50
16	Sammy Sosa, Mark Grace	3.50
17	Barry Larkin, Deion Sanders	.50
18	Larry Walker, Andres Galarraga	.50
19	Moises Alou, Bobby Bonilla	.50
20	Jeff Bagwell, Craig Biggio	2.50
21	Mike Piazza, Hideo Nomo	4.00
22	Pedro Martinez, Henry Rodriguez	2.50
23	Rey Ordonez, Carlos Baerga	.50
24	Curt Schilling, Scott Rolen	1.50
25	Al Martin, Tony Womack	.50
26	Mark McGwire, Dennis Eckersley	5.00
27	Tony Gwynn, Wally Joyner	3.50
28	Barry Bonds, J.T. Snow	6.00
29	Matt Williams, Jay Bell	.50
30	Fred McGriff, Roberto Hernandez	.50

1998 PACIFIC AURORA

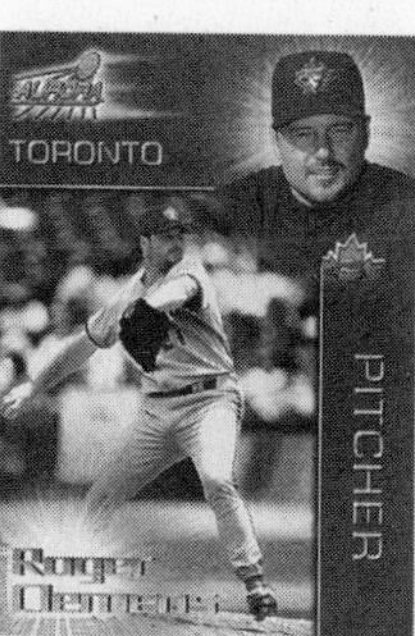

		NM/M
Complete Set (200):		20.00
Common Player:		.05
Pack (6):		1.00
Wax Box (36):		20.00
1	Garret Anderson	.05
2	Jim Edmonds	.05
3	Darin Erstad	.15
4	Cecil Fielder	.05
5	Chuck Finley	.05
6	Todd Greene	.05
7	Ken Hill	.05
8	Tim Salmon	.05
9	Roberto Alomar	.20
10	Brady Anderson	.05
11	Joe Carter	.05
12	Mike Mussina	.35
13	Rafael Palmeiro	.65
14	Cal Ripken Jr.	2.50
15	B.J. Surhoff	.05
16	Steve Avery	.05
17	Nomar Garciaparra	1.00
18	Pedro Martinez	.75
19	John Valentin	.05
20	Jason Varitek	.05
21	Mo Vaughn	.05
22	Albert Belle	.05
23	Ray Durham	.05
24	*Magglio Ordonez*	1.50
25	Frank Thomas	.75
26	Robin Ventura	.05
27	Sandy Alomar Jr.	.05
28	Travis Fryman	.05
29	Dwight Gooden	.05
30	David Justice	.05
31	Kenny Lofton	.05
32	Manny Ramirez	.75
33	Jim Thome	.60
34	Omar Vizquel	.05
35	Enrique Wilson	.05
36	Jaret Wright	.05
37	Tony Clark	.05
38	Bobby Higginson	.05
39	Brian Hunter	.05
40	Bip Roberts	.05
41	Justin Thompson	.05
42	Jeff Conine	.05
43	Johnny Damon	.35
44	Jermaine Dye	.05
45	Jeff King	.05
46	Jeff Montgomery	.05
47	Hal Morris	.05
48	Dean Palmer	.05
49	Terry Pendleton	.05
50	Rick Aguilera	.05
51	Marty Cordova	.05
52	Paul Molitor	.75
53	Otis Nixon	.05
54	Brad Radke	.05
55	Terry Steinbach	.05
56	Todd Walker	.05
57	Chili Davis	.05
58	Derek Jeter	2.50
59	Chuck Knoblauch	.05
60	Tino Martinez	.05
61	Paul O'Neill	.05
62	Andy Pettitte	.20
63	Mariano Rivera	.15
64	Bernie Williams	.05
65	Jason Giambi	.50
66	Ben Grieve	.05
67	Rickey Henderson	.75
68	A.J. Hinch	.05
69	Kenny Rogers	.05
70	Jay Buhner	.05
71	Joey Cora	.05
72	Ken Griffey Jr.	1.50
73	Randy Johnson	.75
74	Edgar Martinez	.05
75	Jamie Moyer	.05
76	Alex Rodriguez	2.00
77	David Segui	.05
78	*Rolando Arrojo*	.35
79	Wade Boggs	1.00
80	Roberto Hernandez	.05
81	Dave Martinez	.05
82	Fred McGriff	.05
83	Paul Sorrento	.05
84	Kevin Stocker	.05
85	Will Clark	.05
86	Juan Gonzalez	.40
87	Tom Goodwin	.05
88	Rusty Greer	.05
89	Ivan Rodriguez	.65
90	John Wetteland	.05
91	Jose Canseco	.40
92	Roger Clemens	1.25
93	Jose Cruz Jr.	.05
94	Carlos Delgado	.50
95	Pat Hentgen	.05
96	Jay Bell	.05
97	Andy Benes	.05
98	Karim Garcia	.05
99	Travis Lee	.05
100	Devon White	.05
101	Matt Williams	.05
102	Andres Galarraga	.05
103	Tom Glavine	.30
104	Andruw Jones	.75
105	Chipper Jones	1.00
106	Ryan Klesko	.05
107	Javy Lopez	.05
108	Greg Maddux	1.00
109	Walt Weiss	.05
110	Rod Beck	.05
111	Jeff Blauser	.05
112	Mark Grace	.05
113	Lance Johnson	.05
114	Mickey Morandini	.05
115	Henry Rodriguez	.05
116	Sammy Sosa	1.00
117	Kerry Wood	.35
118	Lenny Harris	.05
119	Damian Jackson	.05
120	Barry Larkin	.05
121	Reggie Sanders	.05
122	Brett Tomko	.05
123	Dante Bichette	.05
124	Ellis Burks	.05
125	Vinny Castilla	.05
126	Todd Helton	.75
127	Darryl Kile	.05
128	Larry Walker	.05
129	Bobby Bonilla	.05
130	Livan Hernandez	.05
131	Charles Johnson	.05
132	Derrek Lee	.50
133	Edgar Renteria	.05
134	Gary Sheffield	.35
135	Moises Alou	.05
136	Jeff Bagwell	.75
137	Derek Bell	.05
138	Craig Biggio	.05
139	*John Halama*	.15
140	Mike Hampton	.05
141	Richard Hidalgo	.05
142	Wilton Guerrero	.05
143	Todd Hollandsworth	.05
144	Eric Karros	.05
145	Paul Konerko	.05
146	Raul Mondesi	.05
147	Hideo Nomo	.40
148	Chan Ho Park	.05
149	Mike Piazza	1.25
150	Jeromy Burnitz	.05
151	Todd Dunn	.05
152	Marquis Grissom	.05
153	John Jaha	.05
154	Dave Nilsson	.05
155	Fernando Vina	.05
156	Mark Grudzielanek	.05
157	Vladimir Guerrero	.75
158	F.P. Santangelo	.05
159	Jose Vidro	.05
160	Rondell White	.05
161	Edgardo Alfonzo	.05
162	Carlos Baerga	.05
163	John Franco	.05
164	Todd Hundley	.05
165	Brian McRae	.05
166	John Olerud	.05
167	Rey Ordonez	.05
168	*Masato Yoshii*	.25
169	Ricky Bottalico	.05
170	Doug Glanville	.05
171	Gregg Jefferies	.05
172	Desi Relaford	.05
173	Scott Rolen	.60
174	Curt Schilling	.30
175	Jose Guillen	.05
176	Jason Kendall	.05
177	Al Martin	.05
178	Abraham Nunez	.05

179 Kevin Young .05
180 Royce Clayton .05
181 Delino DeShields .05
182 Gary Gaetti .05
183 Ron Gant .05
184 Brian Jordan .05
185 Ray Lankford .05
186 Willie McGee .05
187 Mark McGwire 2.00
188 Kevin Brown .05
189 Ken Caminiti .05
190 Steve Finley .05
191 Tony Gwynn 1.00
192 Wally Joyner .05
193 Ruben Rivera .05
194 Quilvio Veras .05
195 Barry Bonds 2.50
196 Shawn Estes .05
197 Orel Hershiser .05
198 Jeff Kent .05
199 Robb Nen .05
200 J.T. Snow .05

Cubes

NM/M
Complete Set (20): 75.00
Common Player: 1.50
Inserted 1:box
1 Travis Lee 1.50
2 Chipper Jones 4.00
3 Greg Maddux 4.00
4 Cal Ripken Jr. 10.00
5 Nomar Garciaparra 4.00
6 Frank Thomas 3.00
7 Manny Ramirez 3.00
8 Larry Walker 1.50
9 Hideo Nomo 2.00
10 Mike Piazza 5.00
11 Derek Jeter 10.00
12 Ben Grieve 1.50
13 Mark McGwire 7.50
14 Tony Gwynn 4.00
15 Barry Bonds 10.00
16 Ken Griffey Jr. 6.00
17 Alex Rodriguez 7.50
18 Wade Boggs 4.00
19 Juan Gonzalez 2.00
20 Jose Cruz Jr. 1.50

Hardball Cel-Fusion

NM/M
Complete Set (20): 60.00
Common Player: 2.00
Inserted 1:73
1 Travis Lee 2.00
2 Chipper Jones 6.00
3 Greg Maddux 6.00
4 Cal Ripken Jr. 15.00
5 Nomar Garciaparra 6.00
6 Frank Thomas 4.50
7 David Justice 2.00
8 Jeff Bagwell 4.50
9 Hideo Nomo 3.00
10 Mike Piazza 7.50
11 Derek Jeter 15.00
12 Ben Grieve 2.00
13 Scott Rolen 3.00
14 Mark McGwire 12.00
15 Tony Gwynn 6.00
16 Ken Griffey Jr. 9.00
17 Alex Rodriguez 12.00
18 Ivan Rodriguez 3.50
19 Roger Clemens 7.50
20 Jose Cruz Jr. 2.00

Kings of the Major Leagues

NM/M
Complete Set (10): 75.00
Common Player: 7.50
Inserted 1:361
1 Chipper Jones 9.00
2 Greg Maddux 9.00
3 Cal Ripken Jr. 20.00
4 Nomar Garciaparra 9.00
5 Frank Thomas 7.50
6 Mike Piazza 10.00
7 Mark McGwire 15.00
8 Tony Gwynn 9.00
9 Ken Griffey Jr. 12.00
10 Alex Rodriguez 15.00

On Deck Laser-Cut

NM/M
Complete Set (20): 30.00
Common Player: .60
Inserted 1:9
1 Travis Lee .60
2 Chipper Jones 2.25
3 Greg Maddux 2.25
4 Cal Ripken Jr. 6.00
5 Nomar Garciaparra 2.25
6 Frank Thomas 1.50
7 Manny Ramirez 1.50
8 Larry Walker .60
9 Hideo Nomo 1.00
10 Mike Piazza 2.50
11 Derek Jeter 6.00
12 Ben Grieve .60
13 Mark McGwire 4.50
14 Tony Gwynn 2.25
15 Barry Bonds 6.00
16 Ken Griffey Jr. 3.00
17 Alex Rodriguez 4.50
18 Wade Boggs 2.25
19 Juan Gonzalez 1.00
20 Jose Cruz Jr. .60

Pennant Fever

NM/M
Complete Set (50): 25.00
Common Player: .20
Inserted 1:1
Reds (1:4 Retail): 2X
Silvers (250 sets): 4X
Platinum Blues (100 sets): 12X
Coppers (20 sets): 40X
1 Tony Gwynn 1.00
2 Derek Jeter 2.00
3 Alex Rodriguez 1.50
4 Paul Molitor .75
5 Nomar Garciaparra 1.00
6 Jeff Bagwell .75
7 Ivan Rodriguez .65
8 Cal Ripken Jr. 2.00
9 Matt Williams .20
10 Chipper Jones 1.00
11 Edgar Martinez .20
12 Wade Boggs 1.00
13 Paul Konerko .30
14 Ben Grieve .20
15 Sandy Alomar Jr. .20
16 Travis Lee .20
17 Scott Rolen .65
18 Ryan Klesko .20
19 Juan Gonzalez .40
20 Albert Belle .20
21 Roger Clemens 1.25
22 Javy Lopez .20
23 Jose Cruz Jr. .20
24 Ken Griffey Jr. 1.25
25 Mark McGwire 1.50
26 Brady Anderson .20
27 Jaret Wright .20
28 Roberto Alomar .30
29 Joe Carter .20
30 Hideo Nomo .40
31 Mike Piazza 1.25
32 Andres Galarraga .20
33 Larry Walker .20
34 Tim Salmon .20
35 Frank Thomas .75
36 Moises Alou .20
37 David Justice .20
38 Manny Ramirez .75
39 Jim Edmonds .20
40 Barry Bonds 2.00
41 Jim Thome .65
42 Mo Vaughn .20
43 Rafael Palmeiro .65
44 Darin Erstad .30
45 Pedro Martinez .75
46 Greg Maddux 1.00
47 Jose Canseco .45
48 Vladimir Guerrero .75
49 Bernie Williams .20
50 Randy Johnson .75

1998 PACIFIC CROWN ROYALE

NM/M
Complete Set (144): 60.00
Common Player: .20
Pack (6): 1.00
Wax Box (24): 20.00
1 Garret Anderson .20
2 Jim Edmonds .20
3 Darin Erstad .50
4 Tim Salmon .20
5 Jarrod Washburn .20
6 David Dellucci .20
7 Travis Lee .20
8 Devon White .20
9 Matt Williams .20
10 Andres Galarraga .20
11 Tom Glavine .35
12 Andruw Jones 2.00
13 Chipper Jones 3.00
14 Ryan Klesko .20
15 Javy Lopez .20
16 Greg Maddux 3.00
17 Walt Weiss .20
18 Roberto Alomar .75
19 Harold Baines .20
20 Eric Davis .20
21 Mike Mussina 1.00
22 Rafael Palmeiro 1.50
23 Cal Ripken Jr. 5.00
24 Nomar Garciaparra 3.00
25 Pedro Martinez 2.00
26 Troy O'Leary .20
27 Mo Vaughn .20
28 Tim Wakefield .20
29 Mark Grace .20
30 Mickey Morandini .20
31 Sammy Sosa 3.00
32 Kerry Wood .50
33 Albert Belle .20
34 Mike Caruso .20
35 Ray Durham .20
36 Frank Thomas 2.00
37 Robin Ventura .20
38 Bret Boone .20
39 Sean Casey .25
40 Barry Larkin .20
41 Reggie Sanders .20
42 Sandy Alomar Jr. .20
43 David Justice .20
44 Kenny Lofton .20
45 Manny Ramirez 2.00
46 Jim Thome 1.00
47 Omar Vizquel .20
48 Jaret Wright .20
49 Dante Bichette .20
50 Ellis Burks .20
51 Vinny Castilla .20
52 Todd Helton 2.00
53 Larry Walker .20
54 Tony Clark .20
55 Damion Easley .20
56 Bobby Higginson .20
57 Cliff Floyd .20
58 Livan Hernandez .20
59 Derrek Lee .75
60 Edgar Renteria .20
61 Moises Alou .20
62 Jeff Bagwell 2.00
63 Derek Bell .20
64 Craig Biggio .20
65 Johnny Damon .35
66 Jeff King .20
67 Hal Morris .20
68 Dean Palmer .20
69 Bobby Bonilla .20
70 Eric Karros .20
71 Raul Mondesi .20
72 Gary Sheffield .75
73 Jeromy Burnitz .20
74 Jeff Cirillo .20
75 Marquis Grissom .20
76 Fernando Vina .20
77 Marty Cordova .20
78 Pat Meares .20
79 Paul Molitor 2.00
80 Terry Steinbach .20
81 Todd Walker .20
82 Brad Fullmer .20
83 Vladimir Guerrero 2.00
84 Carl Pavano .20
85 Rondell White .20
86 Carlos Baerga .20
87 Hideo Nomo 1.00
88 John Olerud .20
89 Rey Ordonez .20
90 Mike Piazza 3.00
91 *Masato Yoshii* .75
92 *Orlando Hernandez* .75
93 Hideki Irabu .20
94 Derek Jeter 5.00
95 Chuck Knoblauch .20
96 Ricky Ledee .20
97 Tino Martinez .20
98 Paul O'Neill .20
99 Bernie Williams .20
100 Jason Giambi 1.25
101 Ben Grieve .20
102 Rickey Henderson 2.00
103 Matt Stairs .20
104 Bob Abreu .25
105 Doug Glanville .20
106 Scott Rolen 1.50
107 Curt Schilling .35
108 Jose Guillen .20
109 Jason Kendall .20
110 Jason Schmidt .20
111 Kevin Young .20
112 Delino DeShields .20
113 Brian Jordan .20
114 Ray Lankford .20
115 Mark McGwire 4.00
116 Tony Gwynn 3.00
117 Wally Joyner .20
118 Ruben Rivera .20
119 Greg Vaughn .20
120 Rich Aurilia .20
121 Barry Bonds 5.00
122 Bill Mueller .20
123 Robb Nen .20
124 Jay Buhner .20
125 Ken Griffey Jr. 3.50
126 Edgar Martinez .20
127 Shane Monahan .20
128 Alex Rodriguez 4.00
129 David Segui .20
130 *Rolando Arrojo* .75
131 Wade Boggs 3.00
132 Quinton McCracken .20

133	Fred McGriff	.20
134	Bobby Smith	.20
135	Will Clark	.20
136	Juan Gonzalez	1.00
137	Rusty Greer	.20
138	Ivan Rodriguez	1.50
139	Aaron Sele	.20
140	John Wetteland	.20
141	Jose Canseco	1.00
142	Roger Clemens	3.50
143	Carlos Delgado	1.25
144	Shawn Green	.50

All-Stars

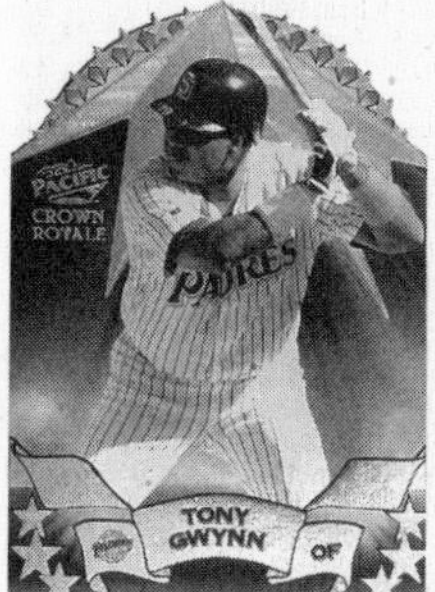

		NM/M
Complete Set (20):		110.00
Common Player:		1.50
Inserted 1:25		
1	Roberto Alomar	2.00
2	Cal Ripken Jr.	15.00
3	Kenny Lofton	1.50
4	Jim Thome	5.00
5	Derek Jeter	15.00
6	David Wells	1.50
7	Ken Griffey Jr.	10.00
8	Alex Rodriguez	12.00
9	Juan Gonzalez	4.00
10	Ivan Rodriguez	5.00
11	Gary Sheffield	2.50
12	Chipper Jones	7.50
13	Greg Maddux	7.50
14	Walt Weiss	1.50
15	Larry Walker	1.50
16	Craig Biggio	1.50
17	Mike Piazza	10.00
18	Mark McGwire	12.00
19	Tony Gwynn	7.50
20	Barry Bonds	15.00

Cramer's Choice Awards

		NM/M
Complete Set (10):		65.00
Common Player:		4.00
Inserted 1:box		
1	Cal Ripken Jr.	15.00
2	Ken Griffey Jr.	9.00
3	Alex Rodriguez	12.00
4	Juan Gonzalez	5.00
5	Travis Lee	4.00
6	Chipper Jones	7.50
7	Greg Maddux	7.50
8	Kerry Wood	5.00
9	Mark McGwire	12.00
10	Tony Gwynn	7.50

Firestone on Baseball

		NM/M
Complete Set (26):		50.00
Common Player:		.35
Firestone Auto. Card:		18.00
Inserted 1:12		
1	Travis Lee	.35
2	Chipper Jones	3.00
3	Greg Maddux	3.00
4	Cal Ripken Jr.	6.00
5	Nomar Garciaparra	3.00
6	Mo Vaughn	.35
7	Kerry Wood	1.00
8	Frank Thomas	2.25
9	Manny Ramirez	2.25
10	Larry Walker	.35
11	Gary Sheffield	1.00
12	Paul Molitor	2.25
13	Hideo Nomo	1.50
14	Mike Piazza	3.50
15	Ben Grieve	.35
16	Mark McGwire	5.00
17	Tony Gwynn	3.00
18	Barry Bonds	6.00
19	Ken Griffey Jr.	4.00
20	Randy Johnson	2.25
21	Alex Rodriquez	5.00
22	Wade Boggs	3.00
23	Juan Gonzalez	1.50
24	Ivan Rodriguez	1.75
25	Roger Clemens	3.50
26	Roy Firestone	.35

Home Run Fever

		NM/M
Complete Set (10):		30.00
Common Player:		1.50
Inserted 1:73		
1	Andres Galarraga	1.50
2	Sammy Sosa	4.50
3	Albert Belle	1.50
4	Jim Thome	3.00
5	Mark McGwire	7.50
6	Greg Vaughn	1.50
7	Ken Griffey Jr.	6.00
8	Alex Rodriguez	7.50
9	Juan Gonzalez	2.50
10	Jose Canseco	2.50

Pillars of the Game

		NM/M
Complete Set (25):		20.00
Common Player:		.35
Inserted 1:1		
1	Jim Edmonds	.35
2	Travis Lee	.35
3	Chipper Jones	1.00
4	Tom Glavine, John Smoltz, Greg Maddux	1.00
5	Cal Ripken Jr.	2.50
6	Nomar Garciaparra	1.00
7	Mo Vaughn	.35
8	Sammy Sosa	1.00
9	Kerry Wood	.40
10	Frank Thomas	.75
11	Jim Thome	.65
12	Larry Walker	.35
13	Moises Alou	.35
14	Raul Mondesi	.35
15	Mike Piazza	1.25
16	Hideki Irabu	.35
17	Bernie Williams	.35
18	Ben Grieve	.35
19	Scott Rolen	.65
20	Mark McGwire	2.00
21	Tony Gwynn	1.00
22	Ken Griffey Jr.	1.50
23	Alex Rodriguez	2.00
24	Juan Gonzalez	.40
25	Roger Clemens	1.25

1998 PACIFIC INVINCIBLE

		NM/M
Complete Set (150):		60.00
Common Player:		.20
Silvers:		4X
Inserted 2:37		
Platinum Blues:		6X
Inserted 1:73		
Pack (5):		1.25
Wax Box (36):		32.50
1	Garret Anderson	.20
2	Jim Edmonds	.20
3	Darin Erstad	.35
4	Chuck Finley	.20
5	Tim Salmon	.20
6	Roberto Alomar	.35
7	Brady Anderson	.20
8	Geronimo Berroa	.20
9	Eric Davis	.20
10	Mike Mussina	.50
11	Rafael Palmeiro	1.00
12	Cal Ripken Jr.	6.00
13	Steve Avery	.20
14	Nomar Garciaparra	2.50
15	John Valentin	.20
16	Mo Vaughn	.20
17	Albert Belle	.20
18	Ozzie Guillen	.20
19	Norberto Martin	.20
20	Frank Thomas	1.50
21	Robin Ventura	.20
22	Sandy Alomar Jr.	.20
23	David Justice	.20
24	Kenny Lofton	.20
25	Manny Ramirez	1.50
26	Jim Thome	1.00
27	Omar Vizquel	.20
28	Matt Williams	.20
29	Jaret Wright	.20
30	Raul Casanova	.20
31	Tony Clark	.20
32	Deivi Cruz	.20
33	Bobby Higginson	.20
34	Justin Thompson	.20
35	Yamil Benitez	.20
36	Johnny Damon	.35
37	Jermaine Dye	.20
38	Jed Hansen	.20
39	Larry Sutton	.20
40	Jeromy Burnitz	.20
41	Jeff Cirillo	.20
42	Dave Nilsson	.20
43	Jose Valentin	.20
44	Fernando Vina	.20
45	Marty Cordova	.20
46	Chuck Knoblauch	.20
47	Paul Molitor	1.50
48	Brad Radke	.20
49	Terry Steinbach	.20
50	Wade Boggs	2.50
51	Hideki Irabu	.20
52	Derek Jeter	6.00
53	Tino Martinez	.20
54	Andy Pettitte	.30
55	Mariano Rivera	.30
56	Bernie Williams	.20
57	Jose Canseco	.75
58	Jason Giambi	.75
59	Ben Grieve	.20
60	Aaron Small	.20
61	Jay Buhner	.20
62	Ken Cloude	.20
63	Joey Cora	.20
64	Ken Griffey Jr.	3.50
65	Randy Johnson	1.50
66	Edgar Martinez	.20
67	Alex Rodriguez	5.00
68	Will Clark	.20
69	Juan Gonzalez	.75
70	Rusty Greer	.20
71	Ivan Rodriguez	1.00
72	Joe Carter	.20
73	Roger Clemens	3.00
74	Jose Cruz Jr.	.20
75	Carlos Delgado	.75
76	Andruw Jones	1.50
77	Chipper Jones	2.50
78	Ryan Klesko	.20
79	Javier Lopez	.20
80	Greg Maddux	2.50
81	Miguel Batista	.20
82	Jeremi Gonzalez	.20
83	Mark Grace	.20
84	Kevin Orie	.20
85	Sammy Sosa	2.50
86	Barry Larkin	.20
87	Deion Sanders	.20
88	Reggie Sanders	.20
89	Chris Stynes	.20
90	Dante Bichette	.20
91	Vinny Castilla	.20
92	Andres Galarraga	.20
93	Neifi Perez	.20
94	Larry Walker	.20
95	Moises Alou	.20
96	Bobby Bonilla	.20
97	Kevin Brown	.20
98	Craig Counsell	.20
99	Livan Hernandez	.20
100	Edgar Renteria	.20
101	Gary Sheffield	.60
102	Jeff Bagwell	1.50
103	Craig Biggio	.20
104	Luis Gonzalez	.20
105	Darryl Kile	.20
106	Wilton Guerrero	.20
107	Eric Karros	.20
108	Ramon Martinez	.20
109	Raul Mondesi	.20
110	Hideo Nomo	.75
111	Chan Ho Park	.20
112	Mike Piazza	3.00
113	Mark Grudzielanek	.20
114	Vladimir Guerrero	1.50
115	Pedro Martinez	1.50
116	Henry Rodriguez	.20
117	David Segui	.20
118	Edgardo Alfonzo	.20
119	Carlos Baerga	.20
120	John Franco	.20
121	John Olerud	.20
122	Rey Ordonez	.20
123	Ricky Bottalico	.20
124	Gregg Jefferies	.20
125	Mickey Morandini	.20
126	Scott Rolen	1.00
127	Curt Schilling	.45
128	Jose Guillen	.20
129	Esteban Loaiza	.20
130	Al Martin	.20
131	Tony Womack	.20
132	Dennis Eckersley	1.00
133	Gary Gaetti	.20
134	Curtis King	.20
135	Ray Lankford	.20
136	Mark McGwire	5.00
137	Ken Caminiti	.20
138	Steve Finley	.20
139	Tony Gwynn	2.50
140	Carlos Hernandez	.20
141	Wally Joyner	.20
142	Barry Bonds	6.00
143	Jacob Cruz	.20
144	Shawn Estes	.20
145	Stan Javier	.20
146	J.T. Snow	.20
147	Nomar Garciaparra (ROY)	1.00
148	Scott Rolen (ROY)	.60
149	Ken Griffey Jr. (MVP)	1.75
150	Larry Walker (MVP)	.20

Cramer's Choice

	NM/M
Complete Green Set (10):	200.00
Common Green (99 sets):	10.00
Dark Blues (80 sets):	1X

Light Blues (50 sets):		1.5X
Reds (25 sets):		2X
Golds (15 sets):		3X
Purples (10 sets):		5X
1	Greg Maddux	20.00
2	Roberto Alomar	10.00
3	Cal Ripken Jr.	40.00
4	Nomar Garciaparra	20.00
5	Larry Walker	10.00
6	Mike Piazza	22.50
7	Mark McGwire	30.00
8	Tony Gwynn	20.00
9	Ken Griffey Jr.	25.00
10	Roger Clemens	22.50

Interleague Players

		NM/M
Complete Set (30):		120.00
Common Player:		1.50
Inserted 1:73		
1A	Roberto Alomar	2.50
1N	Craig Biggio	1.50
2A	Cal Ripken Jr.	12.00
2N	Chipper Jones	6.00
3A	Nomar Garciaparra	6.00
3N	Scott Rolen	3.50
4A	Mo Vaughn	1.50
4N	Andres Galarraga	1.50
5A	Frank Thomas	4.50
5N	Tony Gwynn	6.00
6A	Albert Belle	1.50
6N	Barry Bonds	12.00
7A	Hideki Irabu	1.50
7N	Hideo Nomo	2.50
8A	Derek Jeter	12.00
8N	Rey Ordonez	1.50
9A	Tino Martinez	1.50
9N	Mark McGwire	10.00
10A	Alex Rodriguez	10.00
10N	Edgar Renteria	1.50
11A	Ken Griffey Jr.	7.50
11N	Larry Walker	1.50
12A	Randy Johnson	4.50
12N	Greg Maddux	6.00
13A	Ivan Rodriguez	3.50
13N	Mike Piazza	6.50
14A	Roger Clemens	6.50
14N	Pedro Martinez	4.50
15A	Jose Cruz Jr.	1.50
15N	Wilton Guerrero	1.50

Moments in Time

		NM/M
Complete Set (20):		100.00
Common Player:		3.00
Inserted 1:145		
1	Chipper Jones	10.00
2	Cal Ripken Jr.	17.50
3	Frank Thomas	7.50
4	David Justice	3.00
5	Andres Galarraga	3.00
6	Larry Walker	3.00
7	Livan Hernandez	3.00
8	Wilton Guerrero	3.00
9	Hideo Nomo	4.50
10	Mike Piazza	12.00
11	Pedro Martinez	7.50
12	Bernie Williams	3.00
13	Ben Grieve	3.00
14	Scott Rolen	6.00
15	Mark McGwire	15.00
16	Tony Gwynn	10.00
17	Ken Griffey Jr.	13.50
18	Alex Rodriguez	15.00
19	Juan Gonzalez	4.50
20	Jose Cruz Jr.	3.00

Photoengravings

		NM/M
Complete Set (18):		50.00
Common Player:		1.00
Inserted 1:37		
1	Greg Maddux	3.50
2	Cal Ripken Jr.	7.50
3	Nomar Garciaparra	3.50
4	Frank Thomas	2.50
5	Larry Walker	1.00
6	Mike Piazza	4.00
7	Hideo Nomo	2.00
8	Pedro Martinez	2.50
9	Derek Jeter	7.50
10	Tino Martinez	1.00
11	Mark McGwire	6.00
12	Tony Gwynn	3.50
13	Barry Bonds	7.50
14	Ken Griffey Jr.	5.00
15	Alex Rodriguez	6.00
16	Ivan Rodriguez	2.25
17	Roger Clemens	4.00
18	Jose Cruz Jr.	1.00

1998 PACIFIC OMEGA

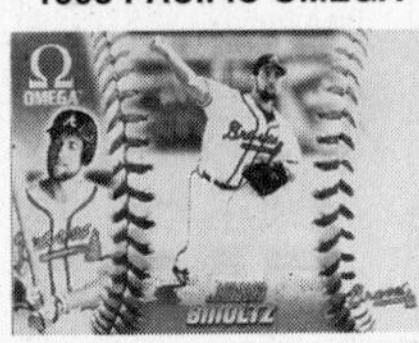

		NM/M
Complete Set (250):		25.00
Common Player:		.10
Reds:		4X
Pack (6):		1.00
Wax Box (36):		15.00
1	Garret Anderson	.10
2	Gary DiSarcina	.10
3	Jim Edmonds	.10
4	Darin Erstad	.20
5	Cecil Fielder	.10
6	Chuck Finley	.10
7	Shigetosi Hasegawa	.10
8	Tim Salmon	.10
9	Brian Anderson	.10
10	Jay Bell	.10
11	Andy Benes	.10
12	Yamil Benitez	.10
13	Jorge Fabregas	.10
14	Travis Lee	.10
15	Devon White	.10
16	Matt Williams	.10
17	Andres Galarraga	.10
18	Tom Glavine	.35
19	Andruw Jones	.75
20	Chipper Jones	1.00
21	Ryan Klesko	.10
22	Javy Lopez	.10
23	Greg Maddux	1.00
24	*Kevin Millwood*	.50
25	Denny Neagle	.10
26	John Smoltz	.10
27	Roberto Alomar	.20
28	Brady Anderson	.10
29	Joe Carter	.10
30	Eric Davis	.10
31	Jimmy Key	.10
32	Mike Mussina	.40
33	Rafael Palmeiro	.65
34	Cal Ripken Jr.	2.50
35	B.J. Surhoff	.10
36	Dennis Eckersley	.65
37	Nomar Garciaparra	1.00
38	Reggie Jefferson	.10
39	Derek Lowe	.10
40	Pedro Martinez	.75
41	Brian Rose	.10
42	John Valentin	.10
43	Jason Varitek	.10
44	Mo Vaughn	.10
45	Jeff Blauser	.10
46	Jeremi Gonzalez	.10
47	Mark Grace	.10
48	Lance Johnson	.10
49	Kevin Orie	.10
50	Henry Rodriguez	.10
51	Sammy Sosa	1.00
52	Kerry Wood	.35
53	Albert Belle	.10
54	Mike Cameron	.10
55	Mike Caruso	.10
56	Ray Durham	.10
57	Jaime Navarro	.10
58	Greg Norton	.10
59	*Magglio Ordonez*	1.50
60	Frank Thomas	.75
61	Robin Ventura	.10
62	Bret Boone	.10
63	Willie Greene	.10
64	Barry Larkin	.10
65	Jon Nunnally	.10
66	Eduardo Perez	.10
67	Reggie Sanders	.10
68	Brett Tomko	.10
69	Sandy Alomar Jr.	.10
70	Travis Fryman	.10
71	David Justice	.10
72	Kenny Lofton	.10
73	Charles Nagy	.10
74	Manny Ramirez	.75
75	Jim Thome	.65
76	Omar Vizquel	.10
77	Enrique Wilson	.10
78	Jaret Wright	.10
79	Dante Bichette	.10
80	Ellis Burks	.10
81	Vinny Castilla	.10
82	Todd Helton	.75
83	Darryl Kile	.10
84	Mike Lansing	.10
85	Neifi Perez	.10
86	Larry Walker	.10
87	Raul Casanova	.10
88	Tony Clark	.10
89	Luis Gonzalez	.10
90	Bobby Higginson	.10
91	Brian Hunter	.10
92	Bip Roberts	.10
93	Justin Thompson	.10
94	Josh Booty	.10
95	Craig Counsell	.10
96	Livan Hernandez	.10
97	*Ryan Jackson*	.10
98	Mark Kotsay	.10
99	Derrek Lee	.50
100	Mike Piazza	1.25
101	Edgar Renteria	.10
102	Cliff Floyd	.10
103	Moises Alou	.10
104	Jeff Bagwell	.75
105	Derrick Bell	.10
106	Sean Berry	.10
107	Craig Biggio	.10
108	*John Halama*	.15
109	Richard Hidalgo	.10
110	Shane Reynolds	.10
111	Tim Belcher	.10
112	Brian Bevil	.10
113	Jeff Conine	.10
114	Johnny Damon	.25
115	Jeff King	.10
116	Jeff Montgomery	.10
117	Dean Palmer	.10
118	Terry Pendleton	.10
119	Bobby Bonilla	.10
120	Wilton Guerrero	.10
121	Todd Hollandsworth	.10
122	Charles Johnson	.10
123	Eric Karros	.10
124	Paul Konerko	.20
125	Ramon Martinez	.10
126	Raul Mondesi	.10
127	Hideo Nomo	.40
128	Gary Sheffield	.45
129	Ismael Valdes	.10
130	Jeromy Burnitz	.10
131	Jeff Cirillo	.10
132	Todd Dunn	.10
133	Marquis Grissom	.10
134	John Jaha	.10
135	Scott Karl	.10
136	Dave Nilsson	.10
137	Jose Valentin	.10
138	Fernando Vina	.10
139	Rick Aguilera	.10
140	Marty Cordova	.10
141	Pat Meares	.10
142	Paul Molitor	.75
143	David Ortiz	.50
144	Brad Radke	.10
145	Terry Steinbach	.10
146	Todd Walker	.10
147	Shane Andrews	.10
148	Brad Fullmer	.10
149	Mark Grudzielanek	.10
150	Vladimir Guerrero	.75
151	F.P. Santangelo	.10
152	Jose Vidro	.10
153	Rondell White	.10
154	Carlos Baerga	.10
155	Bernard Gilkey	.10
156	Todd Hundley	.10
157	Butch Huskey	.10
158	Bobby Jones	.10
159	Brian McRae	.10
160	John Olerud	.10
161	Rey Ordonez	.10
162	*Masato Yoshii*	.25
163	David Cone	.10
164	Hideki Irabu	.10
165	Derek Jeter	2.50
166	Chuck Knoblauch	.10
167	Tino Martinez	.10
168	Paul O'Neill	.10
169	Andy Pettitte	.30
170	Mariano Rivera	.15
171	Darryl Strawberry	.10
172	David Wells	.10
173	Bernie Williams	.10
174	*Ryan Christenson*	.15
175	Jason Giambi	.60
176	Ben Grieve	.10
177	Rickey Henderson	.75
178	A.J. Hinch	.10
179	Kenny Rogers	.10
180	Ricky Bottalico	.10
181	Rico Brogna	.10
182	Doug Glanville	.10
183	Gregg Jefferies	.10
184	Mike Lieberthal	.10
185	Scott Rolen	.65
186	Curt Schilling	.35
187	Jermaine Allensworth	.10
188	Lou Collier	.10
189	Jose Guillen	.10
190	Jason Kendall	.10
191	Al Martin	.10
192	Tony Womack	.10
193	Kevin Young	.10
194	Royce Clayton	.10
195	Delino DeShields	.10
196	Gary Gaetti	.10
197	Ron Gant	.10
198	Brian Jordan	.10
199	Ray Lankford	.10
200	Mark McGwire	2.00
201	Todd Stottlemyre	.10
202	Kevin Brown	.10
203	Ken Caminiti	.10
204	Steve Finley	.10
205	Tony Gwynn	1.00
206	Carlos Hernandez	.10
207	Wally Joyner	.10
208	Greg Vaughn	.10
209	Barry Bonds	2.50
210	Shawn Estes	.10
211	Orel Hershiser	.10
212	Stan Javier	.10
213	Jeff Kent	.10
214	Bill Mueller	.10
215	Robb Nen	.10
216	J.T. Snow	.10
217	Jay Buhner	.10
218	Ken Cloude	.10
219	Joey Cora	.10
220	Ken Griffey Jr.	1.50
221	Glenallen Hill	.10
222	Randy Johnson	.75
223	Edgar Martinez	.10
224	Jamie Moyer	.10
225	Alex Rodriguez	2.00
226	David Segui	.10
227	Dan Wilson	.10
228	*Rolando Arrojo*	.25

229 Wade Boggs 1.00
230 Miguel Cairo .10
231 Roberto Hernandez .10
232 Quinton McCracken .10
233 Fred McGriff .10
234 Paul Sorrento .10
235 Kevin Stocker .10
236 Will Clark .10
237 Juan Gonzalez .40
238 Rusty Greer .10
239 Rick Helling .10
240 Roberto Kelly .10
241 Ivan Rodriguez .65
242 Aaron Sele .10
243 John Wetteland .10
244 Jose Canseco .50
245 Roger Clemens 1.25
246 Jose Cruz Jr. .10
247 Carlos Delgado .50
248 Alex Gonzalez .10
249 Ed Sprague .10
250 Shannon Stewart .10

EO Portraits

NM/M
Complete Set (20): 70.00
Common Player: 1.25
Inserted 1:73
1 Cal Ripken Jr. 10.00
2 Nomar Garciaparra 5.00
3 Mo Vaughn 1.25
4 Frank Thomas 4.00
5 Manny Ramirez 4.00
6 Ben Grieve 1.25
7 Ken Griffey Jr. 6.50
8 Alex Rodriguez 7.50
9 Juan Gonzalez 2.00
10 Ivan Rodriguez 3.50
11 Travis Lee 1.25
12 Greg Maddux 5.00
13 Chipper Jones 5.00
14 Kerry Wood 2.00
15 Larry Walker 1.25
16 Jeff Bagwell 4.00
17 Mike Piazza 6.00
18 Mark McGwire 7.50
19 Tony Gwynn 5.00
20 Barry Bonds 10.00

Face to Face

NM/M
Complete Set (10): 50.00
Common Player: 2.00
Inserted 1:145
1 Alex Rodriguez, Nomar Garciaparra 9.00
2 Mark McGwire, Ken Griffey Jr. 9.00
3 Mike Piazza, Sandy Alomar Jr. 6.00
4 Kerry Wood, Roger Clemens 6.00
5 Cal Ripken Jr., Paul Molitor 10.00
6 Tony Gwynn, Wade Boggs 5.00
7 Frank Thomas, Chipper Jones 5.00
8 Travis Lee, Ben Grieve 2.00
9 Hideo Nomo, Hideki Irabu 3.50
10 Juan Gonzalez, Manny Ramirez 3.50

Prism

NM/M
Complete Set (20): 30.00
Common Player: .75
Inserted 1:37
1 Cal Ripken Jr. 4.50
2 Nomar Garciaparra 2.50
3 Pedro Martinez 1.50
4 Frank Thomas 1.50
5 Manny Ramirez 1.50
6 Brian Giles .75
7 Derek Jeter 4.50
8 Ben Grieve .75
9 Ken Griffey Jr. 3.00
10 Alex Rodriguez 3.50
11 Juan Gonzalez 1.00
12 Travis Lee .75
13 Chipper Jones 2.50
14 Greg Maddux 2.50
15 Kerry Wood 1.00
16 Larry Walker .75
17 Hideo Nomo 1.00
18 Mike Piazza 3.00
19 Mark McGwire 3.50
20 Tony Gwynn 2.50

Online

NM/M
Complete Set (36): 35.00
Common Player: .45
Inserted 1:9
1 Cal Ripken Jr. 5.00
2 Nomar Garciaparra 2.00
3 Pedro Martinez 1.50
4 Mo Vaughn .45
5 Frank Thomas 1.50
6 Sandy Alomar Jr. .45
7 Manny Ramirez 1.50
8 Jaret Wright .45
9 Paul Molitor 1.50
10 Derek Jeter 5.00
11 Bernie Williams .45
12 Ben Grieve .45
13 Ken Griffey Jr. 3.00
14 Edgar Martinez .45
15 Alex Rodriguez 4.00
16 Wade Boggs 2.00
17 Juan Gonzalez .75
18 Ivan Rodriguez 1.00
19 Roger Clemens 2.50
20 Travis Lee .45
21 Matt Williams .45
22 Andres Galarraga .45
23 Chipper Jones 2.00
24 Greg Maddux 2.00
25 Sammy Sosa 2.00
26 Kerry Wood .75
27 Barry Larkin .45
28 Larry Walker .45
29 Derrek Lee 1.00
30 Jeff Bagwell 1.50
31 Hideo Nomo .75
32 Mike Piazza 2.50
33 Scott Rolen 1.00
34 Mark McGwire 4.00
35 Tony Gwynn 2.00
36 Barry Bonds 5.00

1998 PACIFIC ONLINE

NM/M
Complete Set (800): 60.00
Common Player: .05
Web Stars/RCs: 2X
Inserted 1:1
Pack (9): .75
Wax Box (36): 20.00
1 Garret Anderson .05
2 *Rich DeLucia* .05
3 Jason Dickson .05
4 Gary DiSarcina .05
5 Jim Edmonds .05
6 Darin Erstad .15

7 Cecil Fielder .05
8 Chuck Finley .05
9 Carlos Carcia .05
10 Shigetosi Hasegawa .05
11 Ken Hill .05
12 Dave Hollins .05
13 Mike Holtz .05
14 Mike James .05
15 Norberto Martin .05
16 Damon Mashore .05
17 Jack McDowell .05
18 Phil Nevin .05
19 Omar Olivares .05
20 Troy Percival .05
21 Rich Robertson .05
22 Tim Salmon .05
23 Craig Shipley .05
24 Matt Walbeck .05
25 Allen Watson .05
26 Jim Edmonds (Angels checklist) .05
27 Brian Anderson .05
28 Tony Batista .05
29 Jay Bell .05
30 Andy Benes .05
31 Yamil Benitez .05
32 Willie Blair .05
33 Brent Brede .05
34 Scott Brow .05
35 Omar Daal .05
36 David Dellucci .05
37 Edwin Diaz .05
38 Jorge Fabregas .05
39 Andy Fox .05
40 Karim Garcia .05
41a Travis Lee (batting) .05
41b Travis Lee (fielding) .05
42 Barry Manuel .05
43 Gregg Olson .05
44 Felix Rodriguez .05
45 Clint Sodowsky .05
46 Russ Springer .05
47 Andy Stankiewicz .05
48 Kelly Stinnett .05
49 Jeff Suppan .05
50 Devon White .05
51 Matt Williams .05
52 Travis Lee (Diamondbacks checklist) .05
53 Danny Bautista .05
54 Rafael Belliard .05
55 *Adam Butler* .10
56 Mike Cather .05
57 Brian Edmondson .05
58 Alan Embree .05
59 Andres Galarraga .05
60 Tom Glavine .35
61 Tony Graffanino .05
62 Andruw Jones .65
63a Chipper Jones (batting) .75
63b Chipper Jones (fielding) .75
64 Ryan Klesko .05
65 Keith Lockhart .05
66 Javy Lopez .05
67a Greg Maddux (batting) .75
67b Greg Maddux (pitching) .75
68 Dennis Martinez .05
69 *Kevin Millwood* .50
70 Denny Neagle .05
71 Eddie Perez .05
72 Curtis Pride .05
73 John Smoltz .05
74 Michael Tucker .05
75 Walt Weiss .05
76 Gerald Williams .05
77 Mark Wohlers .05
78 Chipper Jones (Braves checklist) .40
79 Roberto Alomar .15
80 Brady Anderson .05
81 Harold Baines .05
82 Armando Benitez .05
83 Mike Bordick .05
84 Joe Carter .05
85 Norm Charlton .05
86 Eric Davis .05
87 Doug Drabek .05
88 Scott Erickson .05
89 Jeffrey Hammonds .05
90 Chris Hoiles .05
91 Scott Kamieniecki .05
92 Jimmy Key .05
93 Terry Mathews .05
94 Alan Mills .05
95 Mike Mussina .25
96 Jesse Orosco .05
97 Rafael Palmeiro .60
98 Sidney Ponson .05
99 Jeff Reboulet .05
100 Arthur Rhodes .05
101a Cal Ripken Jr. (batting) 2.00
101b Cal Ripken Jr. (batting, close-up) 2.00
102 Nerio Rodriguez .05
103 B.J. Surhoff .05
104 Lenny Webster .05
105 Cal Ripken Jr. (Orioles checklist) 1.00
106 Steve Avery .05
107 Mike Benjamin .05
108 Darren Bragg .05
109 Damon Buford .05
110 Jim Corsi .05
111 Dennis Eckersley .60
112 Rich Garces .05
113a Nomar Garciaparra (batting) .75
113b Nomar Garciaparra (fielding) .75
114 Tom Gordon .05
115 Scott Hatteberg .05
116 Butch Henry .05
117 Reggie Jefferson .05
118 Mark Lemke .05
119 Darren Lewis .05
120 Jim Leyritz .05
121 Derek Lowe .05
122 Pedro Martinez .65
123 Troy O'Leary .05
124 Brian Rose .05
125 Bret Saberhagen .05
126 Donnie Sadler .05
127 Brian Shouse .05
128 John Valentin .05
129 Jason Varitek .05
130 Mo Vaughn .05
131 Tim Wakefield .05
132 John Wasdin .05
133 Nomar Garciaparra (Red Sox checklist) .45
134 Terry Adams .05
135 Manny Alexander .05
136 Rod Beck .05
137 Jeff Blauser .05
138 Brant Brown .05
139 Mark Clark .05
140 Jeremi Gonzalez .05
141 Mark Grace .05
142 Jose Hernandez .05
143 Tyler Houston .05
144 Lance Johnson .05
145 Sandy Martinez .05
146 Matt Mieske .05
147 Mickey Morandini .05
148 Terry Mulholland .05
149 Kevin Orie .05
150 Bob Patterson .05
151 Marc Pisciotta .05
152 Henry Rodriguez .05
153 Scott Servais .05
154 Sammy Sosa .75
155 Kevin Tapani .05
156 Steve Trachsel .05
157a Kerry Wood (pitching) .30
157b Kerry Wood (pitching, close-up) .30
158 Kerry Wood (Cubs checklist) .20
159 Jeff Abbott .05
160 James Baldwin .05
161 Albert Belle .05
162 Jason Bere .05
163 Mike Cameron .05
164 Mike Caruso .05
165 Carlos Castillo .05
166 Tony Castillo .05
167 Ray Durham .05
168 Scott Eyre .05

No.	Player	Value
169	Tom Fordham	.05
170	Keith Foulke	.05
171	Lou Frazier	.05
172	Matt Karchner	.05
173	Chad Kreuter	.05
174	Jaime Navarro	.05
175	Greg Norton	.05
176	Charlie O'Brien	.05
177	Maggilo Ordonez	.15
178	Ruben Sierra	.05
179	Bill Simas	.05
180	Mike Sirotka	.05
181	Chris Snopek	.05
182a	Frank Thomas (in batter's box)	.65
182b	Frank Thomas (swinging)	.65
183	Robin Ventura	.05
184	Frank Thomas (White Sox checklist)	.40
185	Stan Belinda	.05
186	Aaron Boone	.05
187	Bret Boone	.05
188	Brook Fordyce	.05
189	Willie Greene	.05
190	Pete Harnisch	.05
191	Lenny Harris	.05
192	Mark Hutton	.05
193	Damian Jackson	.05
194	Ricardo Jordan	.05
195	Barry Larkin	.05
196	Eduardo Perez	.05
197	Pokey Reese	.05
198	Mike Remlinger	.05
199	Reggie Sanders	.05
200	Jeff Shaw	.05
201	Chris Stynes	.05
202	Scott Sullivan	.05
203	Eddie Taubensee	.05
204	Brett Tomko	.05
205	Pat Watkins	.05
206	David Weathers	.05
207	Gabe White	.05
208	Scott Winchester	.05
209	Barry Larkin (Reds checklist)	.05
210	Sandy Alomar Jr.	.05
211	Paul Assenmacher	.05
212	Geronimo Berroa	.05
213	Pat Borders	.05
214	Jeff Branson	.05
215	Dave Burba	.05
216	Bartolo Colon	.05
217	Shawon Dunston	.05
218	Travis Fryman	.05
219	Brian Giles	.05
220	Dwight Gooden	.05
221	Mike Jackson	.05
222	David Justice	.05
223	Kenny Lofton	.05
224	Jose Mesa	.05
225	Alvin Morman	.05
226	Charles Nagy	.05
227	Chad Ogea	.05
228	Eric Plunk	.05
229	Manny Ramirez	.65
230	Paul Shuey	.05
231	Jim Thome	.65
232	Ron Villone	.05
233	Omar Vizquel	.05
234	Enrique Wilson	.05
235	Jaret Wright	.05
236	Manny Ramirez (Indians checklist)	.40
237	Pedro Astacio	.05
238	Jason Bates	.05
239	Dante Bichette	.05
240	Ellis Burks	.05
241	Vinny Castilla	.05
242	Greg Colbrunn	.05
243	Mike DeJean	.05
244	Jerry Dipoto	.05
245	Curtis Goodwin	.05
246	Todd Helton	.65
247	Bobby Jones	.05
248	Darryl Kile	.05
249	Mike Lansing	.05
250	Curtis Leskanic	.05
251	Nelson Liriano	.05
252	Kirt Manwaring	.05
253	Chuck McElroy	.05
254	Mike Munoz	.05
255	Neifi Perez	.05
256	Jeff Reed	.05
257	Mark Thompson	.05
258	John Vander Wal	.05
259	Dave Veres	.05
260a	Larry Walker (batting)	.05
260b	Larry Walker (batting, close-up)	.05
261	Jamey Wright	.05
262	Larry Walker (Rockies checklist)	.05
263	Kimera Bartee	.05
264	Doug Brocail	.05
265	Raul Casanova	.05
266	Frank Castillo	.05
267	Frank Catalanotto	.05
268	Tony Clark	.05
269	Deivi Cruz	.05
270	Roberto Duran	.05
271	Damion Easley	.05
272	Bryce Florie	.05
273	Luis Gonzalez	.05
274	Bob Higginson	.05
275	Brian Hunter	.05
276	Todd Jones	.05
277	Greg Keagle	.05
278	Jeff Manto	.05
279	Brian Moehler	.05
280	Joe Oliver	.05
281	Joe Randa	.05
282	Billy Ripken	.05
283	Bip Roberts	.05
284	Sean Runyan	.05
285	A.J. Sager	.05
286	Justin Thompson	.05
287	Tony Clark (Tigers checklist)	.05
288	Antonio Alfonseca	.05
289	Dave Berg	.05
290	Josh Booty	.05
291	John Cangelosi	.05
292	Craig Counsell	.05
293	Vic Darensbourg	.05
294	Cliff Floyd	.05
295	Oscar Henriquez	.05
296	Felix Heredia	.05
297	*Ryan Jackson*	.05
298	Mark Kotsay	.05
299	Andy Larkin	.05
300	Derrek Lee	.60
301	Brian Meadows	.05
302	Rafael Medina	.05
303	Jay Powell	.05
304	Edgar Renteria	.05
305	*Jesus Sanchez*	.05
306	Rob Stanifer	.05
307	Greg Zaun	.05
308	Derrek Lee (Marlins checklist)	.30
309	Moises Alou	.05
310	Brad Ausmus	.05
311a	Jeff Bagwell (batting)	.65
311b	Jeff Bagwell (fielding)	.65
312	Derek Bell	.05
313	Sean Bergman	.05
314	Sean Berry	.05
315	Craig Biggio	.05
316	Tim Bogar	.05
317	Jose Cabrera	.05
318	Dave Clark	.05
319	Tony Eusebio	.05
320	Carl Everett	.05
321	Ricky Gutierrez	.05
322	John Halama	.05
323	Mike Hampton	.05
324	Doug Henry	.05
325	Richard Hidalgo	.05
326	Jack Howell	.05
327	Jose Lima	.05
328	Mike Magnante	.05
329	Trever Miller	.05
330	C.J. Nitkowski	.05
331	Shane Reynolds	.05
332	Bill Spiers	.05
333	Billy Wagner	.05
334	Jeff Bagwell (Astros checklist)	.40
335	Tim Belcher	.05
336	Brian Bevil	.05
337	Johnny Damon	.35
338	Jermaine Dye	.05
339	Sal Fasano	.05
340	Shane Halter	.05
341	Chris Haney	.05
342	Jed Hansen	.05
343	Jeff King	.05
344	Jeff Montgomery	.05
345	Hal Morris	.05
346	Jose Offerman	.05
347	Dean Palmer	.05
348	Terry Pendleton	.05
349	Hipolito Pichardo	.05
350	Jim Pittsley	.05
351	Pat Rapp	.05
352	Jose Rosado	.05
353	Glendon Rusch	.05
354	Scott Service	.05
355	Larry Sutton	.05
356	Mike Sweeney	.05
357	Joe Vitiello	.05
358	Matt Whisenant	.05
359	Ernie Young	.05
360	Jeff King (Royals checklist)	.05
361	Bobby Bonilla	.05
362	Jim Bruske	.05
363	Juan Castro	.05
364	Roger Cedeno	.05
365	Mike Devereaux	.05
366	Darren Dreifort	.05
367	Jim Eisenreich	.05
368	Wilton Guerrero	.05
369	Mark Guthrie	.05
370	Darren Hall	.05
371	Todd Hollandsworth	.05
372	Thomas Howard	.05
373	Trenidad Hubbard	.05
374	Charles Johnson	.05
375	Eric Karros	.05
376	Paul Konerko	.20
377	Matt Luke	.05
378	Ramon Martinez	.05
379	Raul Mondesi	.05
380	Hideo Nomo	.35
381	Antonio Osuna	.05
382	Chan Ho Park	.05
383	Tom Prince	.05
384	Scott Radinsky	.05
385	Gary Sheffield	.40
386	Ismael Valdes	.05
387	Jose Vizcaino	.05
388	Eric Young	.05
389	Gary Sheffield (Dodgers checklist)	.10
390	Jeromy Burnitz	.05
391	Jeff Cirillo	.05
392	Cal Eldred	.05
393	Chad Fox	.05
394	Marquis Grissom	.05
395	Bob Hamelin	.05
396	Bobby Hughes	.05
397	Darrin Jackson	.05
398	John Jaha	.05
399	Geoff Jenkins	.05
400	Doug Jones	.05
401	Jeff Juden	.05
402	Scott Karl	.05
403	Jesse Levis	.05
404	Mark Loretta	.05
405	Mike Matheny	.05
406	Jose Mercedes	.05
407	Mike Myers	.05
408	Marc Newfield	.05
409	Dave Nilsson	.05
410	Al Reyes	.05
411	Jose Valentin	.05
412	Fernando Vina	.05
413	Paul Wagner	.05
414	Bob Wickman	.05
415	Steve Woodard	.05
416	Marquis Grissom (Brewers checklist)	.05
417	Rick Aguilera	.05
418	Ron Coomer	.05
419	Marty Cordova	.05
420	Brent Gates	.05
421	Eddie Guardado	.05
422	Denny Hocking	.05
423	Matt Lawton	.05
424	Pat Meares	.05
425	Orlando Merced	.05
426	Eric Milton	.05
427	Paul Molitor	.65
428	Mike Morgan	.05
429	Dan Naulty	.05
430	Otis Nixon	.05
431	Alex Ochoa	.05
432	David Ortiz	.40
433	Brad Radke	.05
434	Todd Ritchie	.05
435	Frank Rodriguez	.05
436	Terry Steinbach	.05
437	Greg Swindell	.05
438	Bob Tewksbury	.05
439	Mike Trombley	.05
440	Javier Valentin	.05
441	Todd Walker	.05
442	Paul Molitor (Twins checklist)	.40
443	Shane Andrews	.05
444	Miguel Batista	.05
445	Shayne Bennett	.05
446	Rick DeHart	.05
447	Brad Fullmer	.05
448	Mark Grudzielanek	.05
449	Vladimir Guerrero	.65
450	Dustin Hermanson	.05
451	Steve Kline	.05
452	Scott Livingstone	.05
453	Mike Maddux	.05
454	Derrick May	.05
455	Ryan McGuire	.05
456	Trey Moore	.05
457	Mike Mordecai	.05
458	Carl Pavano	.05
459	Carlos Perez	.05
460	F.P. Santangelo	.05
461	DaRond Stovall	.05
462	Anthony Telford	.05
463	Ugueth Urbina	.05
464	Marc Valdes	.05
465	Jose Vidro	.05
466	Rondell White	.05
467	Chris Widger	.05
468	Vladimir Guerrero (Expos checklist)	.40
469	Edgardo Alfonzo	.05
470	Carlos Baerga	.05
471	Rich Becker	.05
472	Brian Bohanon	.05
473	Alberto Castillo	.05
474	Dennis Cook	.05
475	John Franco	.05
476	Matt Franco	.05
477	Bernard Gilkey	.05
478	John Hudek	.05
479	Butch Huskey	.05
480	Bobby Jones	.05
481	Al Leiter	.05
482	Luis Lopez	.05
483	Brian McRae	.05
484	Dave Mlicki	.05
485	John Olerud	.05
486	Rey Ordonez	.05
487	Craig Paquette	.05
488a	Mike Piazza (batting)	1.00
488b	Mike Piazza (batting, close-up)	1.00
489	Todd Pratt	.05
490	Mel Rojas	.05
491	Tim Spehr	.05
492	Turk Wendell	.05
493	*Masato Yoshii*	.25
494	Mike Piazza (Mets checklist)	.45
495	Willie Banks	.05
496	Scott Brosius	.05
497	Mike Buddie	.05
498	Homer Bush	.05
499	David Cone	.05
500	Chad Curtis	.05
501	Chili Davis	.05
502	Joe Girardi	.05
503	Darren Holmes	.05
504	Hideki Irabu	.05
505a	Derek Jeter (batting)	2.00
505b	Derek Jeter (fielding)	2.00
506	Chuck Knoblauch	.05
507	Graeme Lloyd	.05
508	Tino Martinez	.05
509	Ramiro Mendoza	.05
510	Jeff Nelson	.05
511	Paul O'Neill	.05
512	Andy Pettitte	.20
513	Jorge Posada	.05
514	Tim Raines	.05
515	Mariano Rivera	.15
516	Luis Sojo	.05
517	Mike Stanton	.05
518	Darryl Strawberry	.05
519	Dale Sveum	.05
520	David Wells	.05
521	Bernie Williams	.05
522	Bernie Williams (Yankees checklist)	.05
523	Kurt Abbott	.05
524	Mike Blowers	.05
525	Rafael Bournigal	.05
526	Tom Candiotti	.05
527	Ryan Christenson	.05
528	Mike Fetters	.05
529	Jason Giambi	.50
530a	Ben Grieve (batting)	.05
530b	Ben Grieve (running)	.05
531	Buddy Groom	.05
532	Jimmy Haynes	.05
533	Rickey Henderson	.65
534	A.J. Hinch	.05
535	Mike Macfarlane	.05
536	Dave Magadan	.05
537	T.J. Mathews	.05
538	Jason McDonald	.05
539	Kevin Mitchell	.05
540	Mike Mohler	.05
541	Mike Oquist	.05

542 Ariel Prieto .05
543 Kenny Rogers .05
544 Aaron Small .05
545 Scott Spiezio .05
546 Matt Stairs .05
547 Bill Taylor .05
548 Dave Telgheder .05
549 Jack Voigt .05
550 Ben Grieve (A's checklist) .05
551 Bob Abreu .10
552 Ruben Amaro .05
553 Alex Arias .05
554 Matt Beech .05
555 Ricky Bottalico .05
556 Billy Brewer .05
557 Rico Brogna .05
558 Doug Glanville .05
559 Wayne Gomes .05
560 Mike Grace .05
561 Tyler Green .05
562 Rex Hudler .05
563 Gregg Jefferies .05
564 Kevin Jordan .05
565 Mark Leiter .05
566 Mark Lewis .05
567 Mike Lieberthal .05
568 Mark Parent .05
569 Yorkis Perez .05
570 Desi Relaford .05
571 Scott Rolen .50
572 Curt Schilling .35
573 Kevin Sefcik .05
574 Jerry Spradlin .05
575 Garrett Stephenson .05
576 Darrin Winston .05
577 Scott Rolen (Phillies checklist) .20
578 Jermaine Allensworth .05
579 Jason Christiansen .05
580 Lou Collier .05
581 Francisco Cordova .05
582 Elmer Dessens .05
583 Freddy Garcia .05
584 Jose Guillen .05
585 Jason Kendall .05
586 Jon Lieber .05
587 Esteban Loaiza .05
588 Al Martin .05
589 Javier Martinez .05
590 *Chris Peters* .05
591 Kevin Polcovich .05
592 Ricardo Rincon .05
593 Jason Schmidt .05
594 Jose Silva .05
595 Mark Smith .05
596 Doug Strange .05
597 Turner Ward .05
598 Marc Wilkins .05
599 Mike Williams .05
600 Tony Womack .05
601 Kevin Young .05
602 Tony Womack (Pirates checklist) .05
603 Manny Aybar .05
604 Kent Bottenfield .05
605 Jeff Brantley .05
606 Mike Busby .05
607 Royce Clayton .05
608 Delino DeShields .05
609 John Frascatore .05
610 Gary Gaetti .05
611 Ron Gant .05
612 David Howard .05
613 Brian Hunter .05
614 Brian Jordan .05
615 Tom Lampkin .05
616 Ray Lankford .05
617 Braden Looper .05
618 John Mabry .05
619 Eli Marrero .05
620 Willie McGee .05
621a Mark McGwire (batting) 1.50
621b Mark McGwire (fielding) 1.50
622 Kent Mercker .05
623 Matt Morris .05
624 Donovan Osborne .05
625 Tom Pagnozzi .05
626 Lance Painter .05
627 Mark Petkovsek .05
628 Todd Stottlemyre .05
629 Mark McGwire (Cardinals checklist) .75
630 Andy Ashby .05
631 Brian Boehringer .05
632 Kevin Brown .05
633 Ken Caminiti .05
634 Steve Finley .05
635 Ed Giovanola .05
636 Chris Gomez .05
637a Tony Gwynn (blue jersey) .75
637b Tony Gwynn (white jersey) .75
SAMPLE
Tony Gwynn (SAMPLE overprint on back) 1.00
638 Joey Hamilton .05
639 Carlos Hernandez .05
640 Sterling Hitchcock .05
641 Trevor Hoffman .05
642 Wally Joyner .05
643 Dan Miceli .05
644 James Mouton .05
645 Greg Myers .05
646 Carlos Reyes .05
647 Andy Sheets .05
648 Pete Smith .05
649 Mark Sweeney .05
650 Greg Vaughn .05
651 Quilvio Veras .05
652 Tony Gwynn (Padres checklist) .40
653 Rich Aurilia .05
654 Marvin Benard .05
655a Barry Bonds (batting) 2.00
655b Barry Bonds (batting, close-up) 2.00
656 Danny Darwin .05
657 Shawn Estes .05
658 Mark Gardner .05
659 Darryl Hamilton .05
660 Charlie Hayes .05
661 Orel Hershiser .05
662 Stan Javier .05
663 Brian Johnson .05
664 John Johnstone .05
665 Jeff Kent .05
666 Brent Mayne .05
667 Bill Mueller .05
668 Robb Nen .05
669 Jim Poole .05
670 Steve Reed .05
671 Rich Rodriguez .05
672 Kirk Rueter .05
673 Rey Sanchez .05
674 J.T. Snow .05
675 Julian Tavarez .05
676 Barry Bonds (Giants checklist) 1.00
677 Rich Amaral .05
678 Bobby Ayala .05
679 Jay Buhner .05
680 Ken Cloude .05
681 Joey Cora .05
682 Russ Davis .05
683 Rob Ducey .05
684 Jeff Fassero .05
685 Tony Fossas .05
686a Ken Griffey Jr. (batting) 1.25
686b Ken Griffey Jr. (fielding) 1.25
687 Glenallen Hill .05
688 Jeff Huson .05
689 Randy Johnson .65
690 Edgar Martinez .05
691 John Marzano .05
692 Jamie Moyer .05
693a Alex Rodriguez (batting) 1.50
693b Alex Rodriguez (fielding) 1.50
694 David Segui .05
695 Heathcliff Slocumb .05
696 Paul Spoljaric .05
697 Bill Swift .05
698 Mike Timlin .05
699 Bob Wells .05
700 Dan Wilson .05
701 Ken Griffey Jr. (Mariners checklist) .50
702 Wilson Alvarez .05
703 *Rolando Arrojo* .30
704a Wade Boggs (batting) .75
704b Wade Boggs (fielding) .75
705 Rich Butler .05
706 Miguel Cairo .05
707 Mike Difelice .05
708 John Flaherty .05
709 Roberto Hernandez .05
710 Mike Kelly .05
711 Aaron Ledesma .05
712 Albie Lopez .05
713 Dave Martinez .05
714 Quinton McCracken .05
715 Fred McGriff .05
716 Jim Mecir .05
717 Tony Saunders .05
718 Bobby Smith .05
719 Paul Sorrento .05
720 Dennis Springer .05
721 Kevin Stocker .05
722 Ramon Tatis .05
723 Bubba Trammell .05
724 Esteban Yan .05
725 Wade Boggs (Devil Rays checklist) .40
726 Luis Alicea .05
727 Scott Bailes .05
728 John Burkett .05
729 Domingo Cedeno .05
730 Will Clark .05
731 Kevin Elster .05
732a Juan Gonzalez (bat) .35
732b Juan Gonzalez (no bat) .35
733 Tom Goodwin .05
734 Rusty Greer .05
735 Eric Gunderson .05
736 Bill Haselman .05
737 Rick Helling .05
738 Roberto Kelly .05
739 Mark McLemore .05
740 Darren Oliver .05
741 Danny Patterson .05
742 Roger Pavlik .05
743a Ivan Rodriguez (batting) .60
743b Ivan Rodriguez (fielding) .60
744 Aaron Sele .05
745 Mike Simms .05
746 Lee Stevens .05
747 Fernando Tatis .05
748 John Wetteland .05
749 Bobby Witt .05
750 Juan Gonzalez (Rangers checklist) .20
751 Carlos Almanzar .05
752 Kevin Brown .05
753 Jose Canseco .40
754 Chris Carpenter .05
755 Roger Clemens 1.00
756 Felipe Crespo .05
757 Jose Cruz Jr. .05
758 Mark Dalesandro .05
759 Carlos Delgado .50
760 Kelvim Escobar .05
761 Tony Fernandez .05
762 Darrin Fletcher .05
763 Alex Gonzalez .05
764 Craig Grebeck .05
765 Shawn Green .35
766 Juan Guzman .05
767 Erik Hanson .05
768 Pat Hentgen .05
769 Randy Myers .05
770 Robert Person .05
771 Dan Plesac .05
772 Paul Quantrill .05
773 Bill Risley .05
774 Juan Samuel .05
775 Steve Sinclair .05
776 Ed Sprague .05
777 Mike Stanley .05
778 Shannon Stewart .05
779 Woody Williams .05
780 Roger Clemens (Blue Jays checklist) .45

1998 PACIFIC ONLINE WEB CARDS

Web Stars/RCs: 2X
Inserted 1:1
(See 1998 Pacific Online for checklist and base card values.)

1998 PACIFIC PARAMOUNT

NM/M
Complete Set (250): 20.00
Common Player: .10
Pack (6): 1.00
Wax Box (36): 15.00
1 Garret Anderson .10
2 Gary DiSarcina .10
3 Jim Edmonds .10
4 Darin Erstad .20
5 Cecil Fielder .10
6 Chuck Finley .10
7 Todd Greene .10
8 Shigetosi Hasegawa .10
9 Tim Salmon .10
10 Roberto Alomar .20
11 Brady Anderson .10
12 Joe Carter .10
13 Eric Davis .10
14 Ozzie Guillen .10
15 Mike Mussina .40
16 Rafael Palmeiro .65
17 Cal Ripken Jr. 2.50
18 B.J. Surhoff .10
19 Steve Avery .10
20 Nomar Garciaparra 1.00
21 Reggie Jefferson .10
22 Pedro Martinez .75
23 Tim Naehring .10
24 John Valentin .10
25 Mo Vaughn .10
26 James Baldwin .10
27 Albert Belle .10
28 Ray Durham .10
29 Benji Gil .10
30 Jaime Navarro .10
31 *Magglio Ordonez* 1.50
32 Frank Thomas .75
33 Robin Ventura .10
34 Sandy Alomar Jr. .10
35 Geronimo Berroa .10
36 Travis Fryman .10
37 David Justice .10
38 Kenny Lofton .10
39 Charles Nagy .10
40 Manny Ramirez .75
41 Jim Thome .65
42 Omar Vizquel .10
43 Jaret Wright .10
44 Raul Casanova .10
45 *Frank Catalanotto* .20
46 Tony Clark .10
47 Bobby Higginson .10
48 Brian Hunter .10
49 Todd Jones .10
50 Bip Roberts .10
51 Justin Thompson .10
52 Kevin Appier .10
53 Johnny Damon .35
54 Jermaine Dye .10
55 Jeff King .10
56 Jeff Montgomery .10
57 Dean Palmer .10
58 Jose Rosado .10
59 Larry Sutton .10
60 Rick Aguilera .10
61 Marty Cordova .10
62 Pat Meares .10
63 Paul Molitor .75
64 Otis Nixon .10
65 Brad Radke .10
66 Terry Steinbach .10
67 Todd Walker .10
68 Hideki Irabu .10
69 Derek Jeter 2.50
70 Chuck Knoblauch .10
71 Tino Martinez .10
72 Paul O'Neill .10
73 Andy Pettitte .20
74 Mariano Rivera .15
75 Bernie Williams .10
76 Mark Bellhorn .10
77 Tom Candiotti .10
78 Jason Giambi .50
79 Ben Grieve .10
80 Rickey Henderson .75
81 Jason McDonald .10
82 Aaron Small .10
83 Miguel Tejada .20
84 Jay Buhner .10
85 Joey Cora .10
86 Jeff Fassero .10
87 Ken Griffey Jr. 1.50
88 Randy Johnson .75
89 Edgar Martinez .10
90 Alex Rodriguez 2.00
91 David Segui .10
92 Dan Wilson .10
93 Wilson Alvarez .10
94 Wade Boggs 1.00
95 Miguel Cairo .10
96 John Flaherty .10
97 Dave Martinez .10
98 Quinton McCracken .10

99	Fred McGriff	.10
100	Paul Sorrento	.10
101	Kevin Stocker	.10
102	John Burkett	.10
103	Will Clark	.10
104	Juan Gonzalez	.40
105	Rusty Greer	.10
106	Roberto Kelly	.10
107	Ivan Rodriguez	.65
108	Fernando Tatis	.10
109	John Wetteland	.10
110	Jose Canseco	.40
111	Roger Clemens	1.25
112	Jose Cruz Jr.	.10
113	Carlos Delgado	.50
114	Alex Gonzalez	.10
115	Pat Hentgen	.10
116	Ed Sprague	.10
117	Shannon Stewart	.10
118	Brian Anderson	.10
119	Jay Bell	.10
120	Andy Benes	.10
121	Yamil Benitez	.10
122	Jorge Fabregas	.10
123	Travis Lee	.10
124	Devon White	.10
125	Matt Williams	.10
126	Bob Wolcott	.10
127	Andres Galarraga	.10
128	Tom Glavine	.35
129	Andruw Jones	.75
130	Chipper Jones	1.00
131	Ryan Klesko	.10
132	Javy Lopez	.10
133	Greg Maddux	1.00
134	Denny Neagle	.10
135	John Smoltz	.10
136	Rod Beck	.10
137	Jeff Blauser	.10
138	Mark Grace	.10
139	Lance Johnson	.10
140	Mickey Morandini	.10
141	Kevin Orie	.10
142	Sammy Sosa	1.00
143	Aaron Boone	.10
144	Bret Boone	.10
145	Dave Burba	.10
146	Lenny Harris	.10
147	Barry Larkin	.10
148	Reggie Sanders	.10
149	Brett Tomko	.10
150	Pedro Astacio	.10
151	Dante Bichette	.10
152	Ellis Burks	.10
153	Vinny Castilla	.10
154	Todd Helton	.75
155	Darryl Kile	.10
156	Jeff Reed	.10
157	Larry Walker	.10
158	Bobby Bonilla	.10
159	Todd Dunwoody	.10
160	Livan Hernandez	.10
161	Charles Johnson	.10
162	Mark Kotsay	.10
163	Derrek Lee	.60
164	Edgar Renteria	.10
165	Gary Sheffield	.50
166	Moises Alou	.10
167	Jeff Bagwell	.75
168	Derek Bell	.10
169	Craig Biggio	.10
170	Mike Hampton	.10
171	Richard Hidalgo	.10
172	Chris Holt	.10
173	Shane Reynolds	.10
174	Wilton Guerrero	.10
175	Eric Karros	.10
176	Paul Konerko	.20
177	Ramon Martinez	.10
178	Raul Mondesi	.10
179	Hideo Nomo	.40
180	Chan Ho Park	.10
181	Mike Piazza	1.25
182	Ismael Valdes	.10
183	Jeromy Burnitz	.10
184	Jeff Cirillo	.10
185	Todd Dunn	.10
186	Marquis Grissom	.10
187	John Jaha	.10
188	Doug Jones	.10
189	Dave Nilsson	.10
190	Jose Valentin	.10
191	Fernando Vina	.10
192	Orlando Cabrera	.10
193	Steve Falteisek	.10
194	Mark Grudzielanek	.10
195	Vladimir Guerrero	.75
196	Carlos Perez	.10
197	F.P. Santangelo	.10
198	Jose Vidro	.10
199	Rondell White	.10
200	Edgardo Alfonzo	.10
201	Carlos Baerga	.10
202	John Franco	.10
203	Bernard Gilkey	.10
204	Todd Hundley	.10
205	Butch Huskey	.10
206	Bobby Jones	.10
207	Brian McRae	.10
208	John Olerud	.10
209	Rey Ordonez	.10
210	Ricky Bottalico	.10
211	Bobby Estalella	.10
212	Doug Glanville	.10
213	Gregg Jefferies	.10
214	Mike Lieberthal	.10
215	Desi Relaford	.10
216	Scott Rolen	.65
217	Curt Schilling	.35
218	Adrian Brown	.10
219	Emil Brown	.10
220	Francisco Cordova	.10
221	Jose Guillen	.10
222	Al Martin	.10
223	Abraham Nunez	.10
224	Tony Womack	.10
225	Kevin Young	.10
226	Alan Benes	.10
227	Royce Clayton	.10
228	Gary Gaetti	.10
229	Ron Gant	.10
230	Brian Jordan	.10
231	Ray Lankford	.10
232	Mark McGwire	2.00
233	Todd Stottlemyre	.10
234	Kevin Brown	.10
235	Ken Caminiti	.10
236	Steve Finley	.10
237	Tony Gwynn	1.00
238	Wally Joyner	.10
239	Ruben Rivera	.10
240	Greg Vaughn	.10
241	Quilvio Veras	.10
242	Barry Bonds	2.50
243	Jacob Cruz	.10
244	Shawn Estes	.10
245	Orel Hershiser	.10
246	Stan Javier	.10
247	Brian Johnson	.10
248	Jeff Kent	.10
249	Robb Nen	.10
250	J.T. Snow	.10

Holographic Silver

	NM/M
Common Player:	1.00
Holographic Silver Stars:	20X
Production 99 sets	

(See 1998 Pacific Paramount for checklist and base card values.)

Gold/Copper/Red

	NM/M
Common Gold/Copper Player:	.25
Gold/Copper Stars:	1X
Inserted 1:1	
Common Red Player:	.30
Red Stars:	2X

(See 1998 Pacific Paramount for checklist and base card values.)

Platinum Blue

	NM/M
Common Platinum Blue Player:	1.00
Platinum Blue Stars:	4X
Inserted 1:73	

(See 1998 Pacific Paramount for checklist and base card values.)

Cooperstown Bound

		NM/M
Complete Set (10):		60.00
Common Player:		5.25
Inserted 1:361		
Pacific Proofs:		6X
Production 20 sets		
1	Greg Maddux	6.50
2	Cal Ripken Jr.	13.50
3	Frank Thomas	5.00
4	Mike Piazza	7.50
5	Paul Molitor	5.00
6	Mark McGwire	12.00
7	Tony Gwynn	6.50
8	Barry Bonds	13.50
9	Ken Griffey Jr.	9.00
10	Wade Boggs	6.50

Fielder's Choice

		NM/M
Complete Set (20):		45.00
Common Player:		.75
Inserted 1:73		
1	Chipper Jones	3.00
2	Greg Maddux	3.00
3	Cal Ripken Jr.	6.00
4	Nomar Garciaparra	3.00
5	Frank Thomas	2.50
6	David Justice	.75
7	Larry Walker	.75
8	Jeff Bagwell	2.50
9	Hideo Nomo	1.25
10	Mike Piazza	3.50
11	Derek Jeter	6.00
12	Ben Grieve	.75
13	Mark McGwire	4.50
14	Tony Gwynn	3.00
15	Barry Bonds	6.00
16	Ken Griffey Jr.	4.00
17	Alex Rodriguez	4.50
18	Wade Boggs	3.00
19	Ivan Rodriguez	2.00
20	Jose Cruz Jr.	.75

Inaugural Issue

	NM/M
Common Player:	3.00

(Stars and rookies valued at 50-75X regular Paramount version.)

Special Delivery

		NM/M
Complete Set (20):		30.00
Common Player:		.50
Inserted 1:37		
1	Chipper Jones	2.50
2	Greg Maddux	2.50
3	Cal Ripken Jr.	5.00
4	Nomar Garciaparra	2.50
5	Pedro Martinez	2.00
6	Frank Thomas	2.00
7	David Justice	.50
8	Larry Walker	.50
9	Jeff Bagwell	2.00
10	Hideo Nomo	1.00
11	Mike Piazza	3.00
12	Vladimir Guerrero	2.00
13	Derek Jeter	5.00
14	Ben Grieve	.50
15	Mark McGwire	4.00
16	Tony Gwynn	2.50
17	Barry Bonds	5.00
18	Ken Griffey Jr.	3.50
19	Alex Rodriguez	4.00
20	Jose Cruz Jr.	.50

Team Checklists

		NM/M
Complete Set (30):		25.00
Common Player:		.25
Inserted 1:18		
1	Tim Salmon	.25
2	Cal Ripken Jr.	4.00
3	Nomar Garciaparra	1.50
4	Frank Thomas	1.00
5	Manny Ramirez	1.00
6	Tony Clark	.25
7	Dean Palmer	.25
8	Paul Molitor	1.00
9	Derek Jeter	4.00
10	Ben Grieve	.25
11	Ken Griffey Jr.	2.50
12	Wade Boggs	1.50
13	Ivan Rodriguez	.75
14	Roger Clemens	2.00
15	Matt Williams	.25
16	Chipper Jones	1.50
17	Sammy Sosa	1.50
18	Barry Larkin	.25
19	Larry Walker	.25
20	Livan Hernandez	.25
21	Jeff Bagwell	1.00
22	Mike Piazza	2.00
23	John Jaha	.25
24	Vladimir Guerrero	1.00
25	Todd Hundley	.25
26	Scott Rolen	.75
27	Kevin Young	.25
28	Mark McGwire	3.00
29	Tony Gwynn	1.50
30	Barry Bonds	4.00

1998 PACIFIC REVOLUTION

		NM/M
Complete Set (150):		65.00
Common Player:		.25
Pack (3):		1.00
Wax Box (24):		20.00
1	Garret Anderson	.25
2	Jim Edmonds	.25
3	Darin Erstad	.40
4	Chuck Finley	.25
5	Tim Salmon	.25
6	Jay Bell	.25
7	Travis Lee	.25

8	Devon White	.25
9	Matt Williams	.25
10	Andres Galarraga	.25
11	Tom Glavine	.45
12	Andruw Jones	2.50
13	Chipper Jones	3.50
14	Ryan Klesko	.25
15	Javy Lopez	.25
16	Greg Maddux	3.50
17	Walt Weiss	.25
18	Roberto Alomar	.40
19	Joe Carter	.25
20	Mike Mussina	1.25
21	Rafael Palmeiro	2.00
22	Cal Ripken Jr.	6.00
23	B.J. Surhoff	.25
24	Nomar Garciaparra	3.00
25	Reggie Jefferson	.25
26	Pedro Martinez	2.50
27	Troy O'Leary	.25
28	Mo Vaughn	.25
29	Mark Grace	.25
30	Mickey Morandini	.25
31	Henry Rodriguez	.25
32	Sammy Sosa	3.00
33	Kerry Wood	1.25
34	Albert Belle	.25
35	Ray Durham	.25
36	*Magglio Ordonez*	2.00
37	Frank Thomas	2.50
38	Robin Ventura	.25
39	Bret Boone	.25
40	Barry Larkin	.25
41	Reggie Sanders	.25
42	Brett Tomko	.25
43	Sandy Alomar	.25
44	David Justice	.25
45	Kenny Lofton	.25
46	Manny Ramirez	2.50
47	Jim Thome	2.00
48	Omar Vizquel	.25
49	Jaret Wright	.25
50	Dante Bichette	.25
51	Ellis Burks	.25
52	Vinny Castilla	.25
53	Todd Helton	2.50
54	Larry Walker	.25
55	Tony Clark	.25
56	Deivi Cruz	.25
57	Damion Easley	.25
58	Bobby Higginson	.25
59	Brian Hunter	.25
60	Cliff Floyd	.25
61	Livan Hernandez	.25
62	Derrek Lee	1.50
63	Edgar Renteria	.25
64	Moises Alou	.25
65	Jeff Bagwell	2.50
66	Derek Bell	.25
67	Craig Biggio	.25
68	Richard Hidalgo	.25
69	Johnny Damon	.40
70	Jeff King	.25
71	Hal Morris	.25
72	Dean Palmer	.25
73	Bobby Bonilla	.25
74	Charles Johnson	.25
75	Paul Konerko	.35
76	Raul Mondesi	.25
77	Gary Sheffield	.75
78	Jeromy Burnitz	.25
79	Marquis Grissom	.25
80	Dave Nilsson	.25
81	Fernando Vina	.25
82	Marty Cordova	.25
83	Pat Meares	.25
84	Paul Molitor	2.50
85	Brad Radke	.25
86	Terry Steinbach	.25
87	Todd Walker	.25
88	Brad Fullmer	.25
89	Vladimir Guerrero	2.50
90	Carl Pavano	.25
91	Rondell White	.25
92	Bernard Gilkey	.25
93	Hideo Nomo	1.25
94	John Olerud	.25
95	Rey Ordonez	.25
96	Mike Piazza	4.00
97	*Masato Yoshii*	.65
98	Hideki Irabu	.25
99	Derek Jeter	6.00
100	Chuck Knoblauch	.25
101	Tino Martinez	.25
102	Paul O'Neill	.25
103	Darryl Strawberry	.25
104	Bernie Williams	.25
105	Jason Giambi	1.50
106	Ben Grieve	.25
107	Rickey Henderson	2.50
108	Matt Stairs	.25
109	Doug Glanville	.25
110	Desi Relaford	.25
111	Scott Rolen	1.50
112	Curt Schilling	.45
113	Jason Kendall	.25
114	Al Martin	.25
115	Jason Schmidt	.25
116	Kevin Young	.25
117	Delino DeShields	.25
118	Gary Gaetti	.25
119	Brian Jordan	.25
120	Ray Lankford	.25
121	Mark McGwire	5.00
122	Kevin Brown	.25
123	Steve Finley	.25
124	Tony Gwynn	3.50
125	Wally Joyner	.25
126	Greg Vaughn	.25
127	Barry Bonds	6.00
128	Orel Hershiser	.25
129	Jeff Kent	.25
130	Bill Mueller	.25
131	Jay Buhner	.25
132	Ken Griffey Jr.	4.50
133	Randy Johnson	2.50
134	Edgar Martinez	.25
135	Alex Rodriguez	5.00
136	David Segui	.25
137	*Rolando Arrojo*	.75
138	Wade Boggs	3.50
139	Quinton McCracken	.25
140	Fred McGriff	.25
141	Will Clark	.25
142	Juan Gonzalez	1.25
143	Tom Goodwin	.25
144	Ivan Rodriguez	2.00
145	Aaron Sele	.25
146	John Wetteland	.25
147	Jose Canseco	.50
148	Roger Clemens	4.00
149	Jose Cruz Jr.	.25
150	Carlos Delgado	.65

Shadows

		NM/M
Common Player:		2.00
Stars/Rookies:		6X

(See 1998 Pacific Revolution for checklist and base card values.)

Foul Pole

		NM/M
Complete Set (20):		100.00
Common Player:		2.00
Inserted 1:49		
1	Cal Ripken Jr.	15.00
2	Nomar Garciaparra	7.50
3	Mo Vaughn	2.00
4	Frank Thomas	6.00
5	Manny Ramirez	6.00
6	Bernie Williams	2.00
7	Ben Grieve	2.00
8	Ken Griffey Jr.	10.00
9	Alex Rodriguez	12.00
10	Juan Gonzalez	3.00
11	Ivan Rodriguez	5.00
12	Travis Lee	2.00
13	Chipper Jones	7.50
14	Sammy Sosa	7.50
15	Vinny Castilla	2.00
16	Moises Alou	2.00
17	Gary Sheffield	3.00
18	Mike Piazza	9.00
19	Mark McGwire	12.00
20	Barry Bonds	15.00

Major League Icons

		NM/M
Complete Set (10):		50.00
Common Player:		4.50
Inserted 1:121		
1	Cal Ripken Jr.	15.00
2	Nomar Garciaparra	7.50
3	Frank Thomas	6.00
4	Ken Griffey Jr.	10.00
5	Alex Rodriguez	12.50
6	Chipper Jones	7.50
7	Kerry Wood	4.50
8	Mike Piazza	9.00
9	Mark McGwire	12.50
10	Tony Gwynn	7.50

Prime Time Performers

		NM/M
Complete Set (20):		25.00
Common Player:		.50
Inserted 1:25		
1	Cal Ripken Jr.	4.50
2	Nomar Garciaparra	2.00
3	Frank Thomas	1.50
4	Jim Thome	1.25
5	Hideki Irabu	.50
6	Derek Jeter	4.50
7	Ben Grieve	.50
8	Ken Griffey Jr.	3.00
9	Alex Rodriguez	3.50
10	Juan Gonzalez	.75
11	Ivan Rodriguez	1.25
12	Travis Lee	.50
13	Chipper Jones	2.00
14	Greg Maddux	2.00
15	Kerry Wood	.75
16	Larry Walker	.50
17	Jeff Bagwell	1.50
18	Mike Piazza	2.50
19	Mark McGwire	3.50
20	Tony Gwynn	2.00

Rookies and Hardball Heroes

		NM/M
Complete Set (30):		20.00
Common Player:		.25
Inserted 1:6		
Gold (1-20):		10X
Production 50 sets		
1	Justin Baughman	.25
2	Jarrod Washburn	.25
3	Travis Lee	.25
4	Kerry Wood	.50
5	Magglio Ordonez	.50
6	Todd Helton	1.00
7	Derrek Lee	.25
8	Richard Hidalgo	.25
9	Mike Caruso	.25
10	David Ortiz	.75
11	Brad Fullmer	.25
12	Masato Yoshii	.25
13	Orlando Hernandez	.25
14	Ricky Ledee	.25
15	Ben Grieve	.25
16	Carlton Loewer	.25
17	Desi Relaford	.25
18	Ruben Rivera	.25
19	Rolando Arrojo	.25
20	Matt Perisho	.25
21	Chipper Jones	2.00
22	Greg Maddux	2.00
23	Cal Ripken Jr.	5.00
24	Nomar Garciaparra	2.00
25	Frank Thomas	1.00
26	Mark McGwire	4.00
27	Tony Gwynn	2.00
28	Ken Griffey Jr.	3.00
29	Alex Rodriguez	4.00
30	Juan Gonzalez	.50

Showstoppers

		NM/M
Complete Set (36):		30.00
Common Player:		.45
Inserted 1:12		
1	Cal Ripken Jr.	5.00
2	Nomar Garciaparra	2.50
3	Pedro Martinez	2.00
4	Mo Vaughn	.45
5	Frank Thomas	2.00
6	Manny Ramirez	2.00
7	Jim Thome	1.75
8	Jaret Wright	.45
9	Paul Molitor	2.00
10	Orlando Hernandez	.60
11	Derek Jeter	5.00
12	Bernie Williams	.45
13	Ben Grieve	.45
14	Ken Griffey Jr.	3.50
15	Alex Rodriguez	4.00
16	Wade Boggs	2.50
17	Juan Gonzalez	1.00
18	Ivan Rodriguez	1.75
19	Jose Canseco	.75
20	Roger Clemens	3.00
21	Travis Lee	.45
22	Andres Galarraga	.45
23	Chipper Jones	2.50
24	Greg Maddux	2.50
25	Sammy Sosa	2.50
26	Kerry Wood	.75
27	Vinny Castilla	.45
28	Larry Walker	.45
29	Moises Alou	.45
30	Raul Mondesi	.45
31	Gary Sheffield	.75
32	Hideo Nomo	1.00
33	Mike Piazza	3.00
34	Mark McGwire	4.00
35	Tony Gwynn	2.50
36	Barry Bonds	5.00

1999 PACIFIC

		NM/M
Complete Set (500):		30.00
Common Player:		.10
Platinum Blues (1:73):		15X
Reds (1:1R):		2.5X
Pack (10):		1.00
Wax Box (36):		35.00
1	Garret Anderson	.10
2	Jason Dickson	.10
3	Gary DiSarcina	.10
4	Jim Edmonds	.10
5	Darin Erstad	.25

6 Chuck Finley .10
7 Shigetosi Hasegawa .10
8 Ken Hill .10
9 Dave Hollins .10
10 Phil Nevin .10
11 Troy Percival .10
12a Tim Salmon (action) .10
12b Tim Salmon (portrait) .10
13 Brian Anderson .10
14 Tony Batista .10
15 Jay Bell .10
16 Andy Benes .10
17 Yamil Benitez .10
18 Omar Daal .10
19 David Dellucci .10
20 Karim Garcia .10
21 Bernard Gilkey .10
22a Travis Lee (action) .10
22b Travis Lee (portrait) .10
23 Aaron Small .10
24 Kelly Stinnett .10
25 Devon White .10
26 Matt Williams .10
27a Bruce Chen (action) .10
27b Bruce Chen (portrait) .10
28a Andres Galarraga (action) .10
28b Andres Galarraga (portrait) .10
29 Tom Glavine .35
30 Ozzie Guillen .10
31 Andruw Jones 1.00
32a Chipper Jones (action) 1.50
32b Chipper Jones (portrait) 1.50
33 Ryan Klesko .10
34 George Lombard .10
35 Javy Lopez .10
36a Greg Maddux (action) 1.50
36b Greg Maddux (portrait) 1.50
37a Marty Malloy (action) .10
37b Marty Malloy (portrait) .10
38 Dennis Martinez .10
39 Kevin Millwood .10
40a Alex Rodriguez (action) 2.50
40b Alex Rodriguez (portrait) 2.50
41 Denny Neagle .10
42 John Smoltz .10
43 Michael Tucker .10
44 Walt Weiss .10
45a Roberto Alomar (action) .25
45b Roberto Alomar (portrait) .25
46 Brady Anderson .10
47 Harold Baines .10
48 Mike Bordick .10
49a Danny Clyburn (action) .10
49b Danny Clyburn (portrait) .10
50 Eric Davis .10
51 Scott Erickson .10
52 Chris Hoiles .10
53 Jimmy Key .10
54a Ryan Minor (action) .10
54b Ryan Minor (portrait) .10
55 Mike Mussina .40
56 Jesse Orosco .10
57a Rafael Palmeiro (action) .75
57b Rafael Palmeiro (portrait) .75
58 Sidney Ponson .10
59 Arthur Rhodes .10
60a Cal Ripken Jr. (action) 3.00
60b Cal Ripken Jr. (portrait) 3.00
61 B.J. Surhoff .10
62 Steve Avery .10
63 Darren Bragg .10
64 Dennis Eckersley .75
65a Nomar Garciaparra (action) 1.50
65b Nomar Garciaparra (portrait) 1.50
66a Sammy Sosa (action) 1.50
66b Sammy Sosa (portrait) 1.50
67 Tom Gordon .10
68 Reggie Jefferson .10
69 Darren Lewis .10
70a Mark McGwire (action) 2.50
70b Mark McGwire (portrait) 2.50
71 Pedro Martinez 1.00
72 Troy O'Leary .10
73 Bret Saberhagen .10
74 Mike Stanley .10
75 John Valentin .10
76 Jason Varitek .10
77 Mo Vaughn .10
78 Tim Wakefield .10
79 Manny Alexander .10
80 Rod Beck .10
81 Brant Brown .10
82 Mark Clark .10
83 Gary Gaetti .10
84 Mark Grace .10
85 Jose Hernandez .10
86 Lance Johnson .10
87a Jason Maxwell (action) .10
87b Jason Maxwell (portrait) .10
88 Mickey Morandini .10
89 Terry Mulholland .10
90 Henry Rodriguez .10
91 Scott Servais .10
92 Kevin Tapani .10
93 Pedro Valdes .10
94 Kerry Wood .40
95 Jeff Abbott .10
96 James Baldwin .10
97 Albert Belle .10
98 Mike Cameron .10
99 Mike Caruso .10
100 Wil Cordero .10
101 Ray Durham .10
102 Jaime Navarro .10
103 Greg Norton .10
104 Magglio Ordonez .25
105 Mike Sirotka .10
106a Frank Thomas (action) 1.00
106b Frank Thomas (portrait) 1.00
107 Robin Ventura .10
108 Craig Wilson .10
109 Aaron Boone .10
110 Bret Boone .10
111 Sean Casey .15
112 Pete Harnisch .10
113 John Hudek .10
114 Barry Larkin .10
115 Eduardo Perez .10
116 Mike Remlinger .10
117 Reggie Sanders .10
118 Chris Stynes .10
119 Eddie Taubensee .10
120 Brett Tomko .10
121 Pat Watkins .10
122 Dmitri Young .10
123 Sandy Alomar Jr. .10
124 Dave Burba .10
125 Bartolo Colon .10
126 Joey Cora .10
127 Brian Giles .10
128 Dwight Gooden .10
129 Mike Jackson .10
130 David Justice .10
131 Kenny Lofton .10
132 Charles Nagy .10
133 Chad Ogea .10
134a Manny Ramirez (action) 1.00
134b Manny Ramirez (portrait) 1.00
135 Richie Sexson .10
136a Jim Thome (action) .75
136b Jim Thome (portrait) .75
137 Omar Vizquel .10
138 Jaret Wright .10
139 Pedro Astacio .10
140 Jason Bates .10
141a Dante Bichette (action) .10
141b Dante Bichette (portrait) .10
142a Vinny Castilla (action) .10
142b Vinny Castilla (portrait) .10
143a Edgar Clemente (action) .10
143b Edgar Clemente (portrait) .10
144a Derrick Gibson (action) .10
144b Derrick Gibson (portrait) .10
145 Curtis Goodwin .10
146a Todd Helton (action) 1.00
146b Todd Helton (portrait) 1.00
147 Bobby Jones .10
148 Darryl Kile .10
149 Mike Lansing .10
150 Chuck McElroy .10
151 Neifi Perez .10
152 Jeff Reed .10
153 John Thomson .10
154a Larry Walker (action) .10
154b Larry Walker (portrait) .10
155 Jamey Wright .10
156 Kimera Bartee .10
157 Geronimo Berroa .10
158 Raul Casanova .10
159 Frank Catalanotto .10
160 Tony Clark .10
161 Deivi Cruz .10
162 Damion Easley .10
163 Juan Encarnacion .10
164 Luis Gonzalez .10
165 Seth Greisinger .10
166 Bob Higginson .10
167 Brian Hunter .10
168 Todd Jones .10
169 Justin Thompson .10
170 Antonio Alfonseca .10
171 Dave Berg .10
172 John Cangelosi .10
173 Craig Counsell .10
174 Todd Dunwoody .10
175 Cliff Floyd .10
176 Alex Gonzalez .10
177 Livan Hernandez .10
178 Ryan Jackson .10
179 Mark Kotsay .10
180 Derrek Lee .65
181 Matt Mantei .10
182 Brian Meadows .10
183 Edgar Renteria .10
184a Moises Alou (action) .10
184b Moises Alou (portrait) .10
185 Brad Ausmus .10
186a Jeff Bagwell (action) 1.00
186b Jeff Bagwell (portrait) 1.00
187 Derek Bell .10
188 Sean Berry .10
189 Craig Biggio .10
190 Carl Everett .10
191 Ricky Gutierrez .10
192 Mike Hampton .10
193 Doug Henry .10
194 Richard Hidalgo .10
195 Randy Johnson 1.00
196a Russ Johnson (action) .10
196b Russ Johnson (portrait) .10
197 Shane Reynolds .10
198 Bill Spiers .10
199 Kevin Appier .10
200 Tim Belcher .10
201 Jeff Conine .10
202 Johnny Damon .35
203 Jermaine Dye .10
204a Jeremy Giambi (batting stance) .10
204b Jeremy Giambi (follow-through) .10
205 Jeff King .10
206 Shane Mack .10
207 Jeff Montgomery .10
208 Hal Morris .10
209 Jose Offerman .10
210 Dean Palmer .10
211 Jose Rosado .10
212 Glendon Rusch .10
213 Larry Sutton .10
214 Mike Sweeney .10
215 Bobby Bonilla .10
216 Alex Cora .10
217 Darren Dreifort .10
218 Mark Grudzielanek .10
219 Todd Hollandsworth .10
220 Trenidad Hubbard .10
221 Charles Johnson .10
222 Eric Karros .10
223 Matt Luke .10
224 Ramon Martinez .10
225 Raul Mondesi .10
226 Chan Ho Park .10
227 Jeff Shaw .10
228 Gary Sheffield .40
229 Eric Young .10
230 Jeromy Burnitz .10
231 Jeff Cirillo .10
232 Marquis Grissom .10
233 Bobby Hughes .10
234 John Jaha .10
235 Geoff Jenkins .10
236 Scott Karl .10
237 Mark Loretta .10
238 Mike Matheny .10
239 Mike Myers .10
240 Dave Nilsson .10
241 Bob Wickman .10
242 Jose Valentin .10
243 Fernando Vina .10
244 Rick Aguilera .10
245 Ron Coomer .10
246 Marty Cordova .10
247 Denny Hocking .10
248 Matt Lawton .10
249 Pat Meares .10
250a Paul Molitor (action) 1.00
250b Paul Molitor (portrait) 1.00
251 Otis Nixon .10
252 Alex Ochoa .10
253 David Ortiz .65
254 A.J. Pierzynski .10
255 Brad Radke .10
256 Terry Steinbach .10
257 Bob Tewksbury .10
258 Todd Walker .10
259 Shane Andrews .10
260 Shayne Bennett .10
261 Orlando Cabrera .10
262 Brad Fullmer .10
263 Vladimir Guerrero 1.00
264 Wilton Guerrero .10
265 Dustin Hermanson .10
266 Terry Jones .10
267 Steve Kline .10
268 Carl Pavano .10
269 F.P. Santangelo .10
270a Fernando Seguignol (action) .10
270b Fernando Seguignol (portrait) .10
271 Ugueth Urbina .10
272 Jose Vidro .10
273 Chris Widger .10
274 Edgardo Alfonzo .10
275 Carlos Baerga .10
276 John Franco .10
277 Todd Hundley .10
278 Butch Huskey .10
279 Bobby Jones .10
280 Al Leiter .10
281 Greg McMichael .10
282 Brian McRae .10
283 Hideo Nomo .50
284 John Olerud .10
285 Rey Ordonez .10
286a Mike Piazza (action) 1.75
286b Mike Piazza (portrait) 1.75
287 Turk Wendell .10
288 Masato Yoshii .10
289 David Cone .10
290 Chad Curtis .10
291 Joe Girardi .10
292 Orlando Hernandez .10
293a Hideki Irabu (action) .10
293b Hideki Irabu (portrait) .10
294a Derek Jeter (action) 3.00
294b Derek Jeter (portrait) 3.00
295 Chuck Knoblauch .10
296a Mike Lowell (action) .10
296b Mike Lowell (portrait) .10
297 Tino Martinez .10
298 Ramiro Mendoza .10
299 Paul O'Neill .10
300 Andy Pettitte .25
301 Jorge Posada .10
302 Tim Raines .10
303 Mariano Rivera .15
304 David Wells .10
305a Bernie Williams (action) .10
305b Bernie Williams (portrait) .10
306 Mike Blowers .10
307 Tom Candiotti .10
308a Eric Chavez (action) .15
308b Eric Chavez (portrait) .15
309 Ryan Christenson .10
310 Jason Giambi .65
311a Ben Grieve (action) .10
311b Ben Grieve (portrait) .10
312 Rickey Henderson 1.00
313 A.J. Hinch .10
314 Jason McDonald .10
315 Bip Roberts .10
316 Kenny Rogers .10
317 Scott Spiezio .10
318 Matt Stairs .10
319 Miguel Tejada .20
320 Bob Abreu .20
321 Alex Arias .10
322a *Gary Bennett* (action) .10
322b *Gary Bennett* (portrait) .10
323 Ricky Bottalico .10
324 Rico Brogna .10
325 Bobby Estalella .10
326 Doug Glanville .10
327 Kevin Jordan .10
328 Mark Leiter .10
329 Wendell Magee .10
330 Mark Portugal .10
331 Desi Relaford .10

332	Scott Rolen	.65
333	Curt Schilling	.35
334	Kevin Sefcik	.10
335	Adrian Brown	.10
336	Emil Brown	.10
337	Lou Collier	.10
338	Francisco Cordova	.10
339	Freddy Garcia	.10
340	Jose Guillen	.10
341	Jason Kendall	.10
342	Al Martin	.10
343	Abraham Nunez	.10
344	Aramis Ramirez	.10
345	Ricardo Rincon	.10
346	Jason Schmidt	.10
347	Turner Ward	.10
348	Tony Womack	.10
349	Kevin Young	.10
350	Juan Acevedo	.10
351	Delino DeShields	.10
352a	J.D. Drew (action)	.40
352b	J.D. Drew (portrait)	.40
353	Ron Gant	.10
354	Brian Jordan	.10
355	Ray Lankford	.10
356	Eli Marrero	.10
357	Kent Mercker	.10
358	Matt Morris	.10
359	Luis Ordaz	.10
360	Donovan Osborne	.10
361	Placido Polanco	.10
362	Fernando Tatis	.10
363	Andy Ashby	.10
364	Kevin Brown	.10
365	Ken Caminiti	.10
366	Steve Finley	.10
367	Chris Gomez	.10
368a	Tony Gwynn (action)	1.50
368b	Tony Gwynn (portrait)	1.50
369	Joey Hamilton	.10
370	Carlos Hernandez	.10
371	Trevor Hoffman	.10
372	Wally Joyner	.10
373	Jim Leyritz	.10
374	Ruben Rivera	.10
375	Greg Vaughn	.10
376	Quilvio Veras	.10
377	Rich Aurilia	.10
378a	Barry Bonds (action)	3.00
378b	Barry Bonds (portrait)	3.00
379	Ellis Burks	.10
380	Joe Carter	.10
381	Stan Javier	.10
382	Brian Johnson	.10
383	Jeff Kent	.10
384	Jose Mesa	.10
385	Bill Mueller	.10
386	Robb Nen	.10
387a	Armando Rios (action)	.10
387b	Armando Rios (portrait)	.10
388	Kirk Rueter	.10
389	Rey Sanchez	.10
390	J.T. Snow	.10
391	David Bell	.10
392	Jay Buhner	.10
393	Ken Cloude	.10
394	Russ Davis	.10
395	Jeff Fassero	.10
396a	Ken Griffey Jr. (action)	2.00
396b	Ken Griffey Jr. (portrait)	2.00
397	*Giomar Guevara*	.10
398	Carlos Guillen	.10
399	Edgar Martinez	.10
400	Shane Monahan	.10
401	Jamie Moyer	.10
402	David Segui	.10
403	Makoto Suzuki	.10
404	Mike Timlin	.10
405	Dan Wilson	.10
406	Wilson Alvarez	.10
407	Rolando Arrojo	.10
408	Wade Boggs	1.50
409	Miguel Cairo	.10
410	Roberto Hernandez	.10
411	Mike Kelly	.10
412	Aaron Ledesma	.10
413	Albie Lopez	.10
414	Dave Martinez	.10
415	Quinton McCracken	.10
416	Fred McGriff	.10
417	Bryan Rekar	.10
418	Paul Sorrento	.10
419	Randy Winn	.10
420	John Burkett	.10
421	Will Clark	.10
422	Royce Clayton	.10
423a	Juan Gonzalez (action)	.50
423b	Juan Gonzalez (portrait)	.50
424	Tom Goodwin	.10
425	Rusty Greer	.10
426	Rick Helling	.10
427	Roberto Kelly	.10
428	Mark McLemore	.10
429a	Ivan Rodriguez (action)	.75
429b	Ivan Rodriguez (portrait)	.75
430	Aaron Sele	.10
431	Lee Stevens	.10
432	Todd Stottlemyre	.10
433	John Wetteland	.10
434	Todd Zeile	.10
435	Jose Canseco	.50
436a	Roger Clemens (action)	1.75
436b	Roger Clemens (portrait)	1.75
437	Felipe Crespo	.10
438a	Jose Cruz Jr. (action)	.10
438b	Jose Cruz Jr. (portrait)	.10
439	Carlos Delgado	.50
440a	Tom Evans (action)	.10
440b	Tom Evans (portrait)	.10
441	Tony Fernandez	.10
442	Darrin Fletcher	.10
443	Alex Gonzalez	.10
444	Shawn Green	.30
445	Roy Halladay	.10
446	Pat Hentgen	.10
447	Juan Samuel	.10
448	Benito Santiago	.10
449	Shannon Stewart	.10
450	Woody Williams	.10

Cramer's Choice

		NM/M
Complete Set (10):		65.00
Common Player:		7.50
Inserted 1:721		
1	Cal Ripken Jr.	20.00
2	Nomar Garciaparra	12.50
3	Frank Thomas	10.00
4	Ken Griffey Jr.	15.00
5	Alex Rodriguez	17.50
6	Greg Maddux	12.50
7	Sammy Sosa	12.50
8	Kerry Wood	7.50
9	Mark McGwire	17.50
10	Tony Gwynn	12.50

Dynagon Diamond

		NM/M
Complete Set (20):		20.00
Common Player:		.40
Inserted 1:9		
Titanium (99 Sets):		8X
1	Cal Ripken Jr.	2.50
2	Nomar Garciaparra	1.00
3	Frank Thomas	.75
4	Derek Jeter	2.50
5	Ben Grieve	.40
6	Ken Griffey Jr.	1.50
7	Alex Rodriguez	2.00
8	Juan Gonzalez	.50
9	Travis Lee	.40
10	Chipper Jones	1.00
11	Greg Maddux	1.00
12	Sammy Sosa	1.00
13	Kerry Wood	.50
14	Jeff Bagwell	.75
15	Hideo Nomo	.50
16	Mike Piazza	12.50
17	J.D. Drew	.50
18	Mark McGwire	2.00
19	Tony Gwynn	1.00
20	Barry Bonds	2.50

Gold Crown Die-Cuts

		NM/M
Complete Set (36):		75.00
Common Player:		.75
Inserted 1:37		
1	Darin Erstad	1.00
2	Cal Ripken Jr.	7.50
3	Nomar Garciaparra	4.00
4	Pedro Martinez	3.00
5	Mo Vaughn	.75
6	Frank Thomas	3.00
7	Kenny Lofton	.75
8	Manny Ramirez	3.00
9	Paul Molitor	3.00
10	Derek Jeter	7.50
11	Bernie Williams	.75
12	Ben Grieve	.75
13	Ken Griffey Jr.	5.00
14	Alex Rodriguez	6.00
15	Wade Boggs	4.00
16	Juan Gonzalez	1.50
17	Ivan Rodriguez	2.50
18	Jose Canseco	1.50
19	Roger Clemens	4.50
20	Travis Lee	.75
21	Chipper Jones	4.00
22	Greg Maddux	4.00
23	Sammy Sosa	4.00
24	Kerry Wood	1.50
25	Todd Helton	3.00
26	Larry Walker	.75
27	Jeff Bagwell	3.00
28	Craig Biggio	.75
29	Raul Mondesi	.75
30	Vladimir Guerrero	3.00
31	Mike Piazza	4.50
32	Scott Rolen	2.00
33	J.D. Drew	1.50
34	Mark McGwire	6.00
35	Tony Gwynn	4.00
36	Barry Bonds	7.50

Timelines

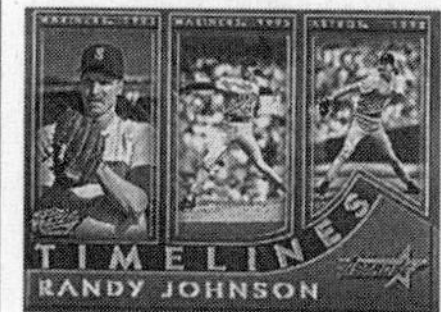

		NM/M
Complete Set (20):		200.00
Common Player:		6.00
Inserted 1:181 H		
1	Cal Ripken Jr.	30.00
2	Frank Thomas	12.00
3	Jim Thome	10.00
4	Paul Molitor	12.00
5	Bernie Williams	6.00
6	Derek Jeter	30.00
7	Ken Griffey Jr.	20.00
8	Alex Rodriguez	25.00
9	Wade Boggs	15.00
10	Jose Canseco	9.00
11	Roger Clemens	17.50
12	Andres Galarraga	6.00
13	Chipper Jones	15.00
14	Greg Maddux	15.00
15	Sammy Sosa	15.00
16	Larry Walker	6.00
17	Randy Johnson	12.00
18	Mike Piazza	17.50
19	Mark McGwire	25.00
20	Tony Gwynn	15.00

Hot Cards

		NM/M
Complete Set (10):		75.00
Common Player:		3.00

1	Alex Rodriguez	12.50
2	Tony Gwynn	7.50
3	Ken Griffey Jr.	10.00
4	Sammy Sosa	7.50
5	Ivan Rodriguez	6.00
6	Derek Jeter	15.00
7	Cal Ripken Jr.	15.00
8	Mark McGwire	12.50
9	J.D. Drew	4.50
10	Bernie Williams	3.00

Team Checklists

		NM/M
Complete Set (30):		30.00
Common Player:		.30
Inserted 1:18		
1	Darin Erstad	.50
2	Cal Ripken Jr.	3.00
3	Nomar Garciaparra	1.50
4	Frank Thomas	1.00
5	Manny Ramirez	1.00
6	Damion Easley	.30
7	Jeff King	.30
8	Paul Molitor	1.00
9	Derek Jeter	3.00
10	Ben Grieve	.30
11	Ken Griffey Jr.	2.00
12	Wade Boggs	1.50
13	Juan Gonzalez	.60
14	Roger Clemens	1.75
15	Travis Lee	.30
16	Chipper Jones	1.50
17	Sammy Sosa	1.50
18	Barry Larkin	.30
19	Todd Helton	1.00
20	Mark Kotsay	.30
21	Jeff Bagwell	1.00
22	Raul Mondesi	.30
23	Jeff Cirillo	.30
24	Vladimir Guerrero	1.00
25	Mike Piazza	1.75
26	Scott Rolen	.75
27	Jason Kendall	.30
28	Mark McGwire	2.50
29	Tony Gwynn	1.50
30	Barry Bonds	3.00

1999 PACIFIC AURORA

		NM/M
Complete Set (200):		20.00
Common Player:		.10
Opening Days:		20X
Production 31 sets		
Reds:		2X
Retail Only (1:6)		
Pack (6):		1.50
Wax Box (36):		22.50
1	Garret Anderson	.10

2	Jim Edmonds	.10
3	Darin Erstad	.30
4	Matt Luke	.10
5	Tim Salmon	.10
6	Mo Vaughn	.10
7	Jay Bell	.10
8	David Dellucci	.10
9	Steve Finley	.10
10	Bernard Gilkey	.10
11	Randy Johnson	1.00
12	Travis Lee	.10
13	Matt Williams	.10
14	Andres Galarraga	.10
15	Tom Glavine	.35
16	Andruw Jones	1.00
17	Chipper Jones	1.50
18	Brian Jordan	.10
19	Javy Lopez	.10
20	Greg Maddux	1.50
21	Albert Belle	.10
22	Will Clark	.10
23	Scott Erickson	.10
24	Mike Mussina	.40
25	Cal Ripken Jr.	3.00
26	B.J. Surhoff	.10
27	Nomar Garciaparra	1.50
28	Reggie Jefferson	.10
29	Darren Lewis	.10
30	Pedro Martinez	1.00
31	John Valentin	.10
32	Rod Beck	.10
33	Mark Grace	.10
34	Lance Johnson	.10
35	Mickey Morandini	.10
36	Sammy Sosa	1.50
37	Kerry Wood	.40
38	James Baldwin	.10
39	Mike Caruso	.10
40	Ray Durham	.10
41	Magglio Ordonez	.25
42	Frank Thomas	1.00
43	Aaron Boone	.10
44	Sean Casey	.20
45	Barry Larkin	.10
46	Hal Morris	.10
47	Denny Neagle	.10
48	Greg Vaughn	.10
49	Pat Watkins	.10
50	Roberto Alomar	.25
51	Sandy Alomar Jr.	.10
52	David Justice	.10
53	Kenny Lofton	.10
54	Manny Ramirez	1.00
55	Richie Sexson	.10
56	Jim Thome	.75
57	Omar Vizquel	.10
58	Dante Bichette	.10
59	Vinny Castilla	.10
60	*Edgard Clemente*	.10
61	Derrick Gibson	.10
62	Todd Helton	1.00
63	Darryl Kile	.10
64	Larry Walker	.10
65	Tony Clark	.10
66	Damion Easley	.10
67	Bob Higginson	.10
68	Brian Hunter	.10
69	Dean Palmer	.10
70	Justin Thompson	.10
71	Craig Counsell	.10
72	Todd Dunwoody	.10
73	Cliff Floyd	.10
74	Alex Gonzalez	.10
75	Livan Hernandez	.10
76	Mark Kotsay	.10
77	Derrek Lee	.65
78	Moises Alou	.10
79	Jeff Bagwell	1.00
80	Derek Bell	.10
81	Craig Biggio	.10
82	Ken Caminiti	.10
83	Richard Hidalgo	.10
84	Shane Reynolds	.10
85	Jeff Conine	.10
86	Johnny Damon	.35
87	Jermaine Dye	.10
88	Jeff King	.10
89	Jeff Montgomery	.10
90	Mike Sweeney	.10
91	Kevin Brown	.10
92	Mark Grudzielanek	.10
93	Eric Karros	.10
94	Raul Mondesi	.10
95	Chan Ho Park	.10
96	Gary Sheffield	.40
97	Jeromy Burnitz	.10
98	Jeff Cirillo	.10
99	Marquis Grissom	.10
100	Geoff Jenkins	.10
101	Dave Nilsson	.10
102	Jose Valentin	.10
103	Fernando Vina	.10
104	Marty Cordova	.10
105	Matt Lawton	.10
106	David Ortiz	.60
107	Brad Radke	.10
108	Todd Walker	.10
109	Shane Andrews	.10
110	Orlando Cabrera	.10
111	Brad Fullmer	.10
112	Vladimir Guerrero	1.00
113	Wilton Guerrero	.10
114	Carl Pavano	.10
115	Fernando Seguignol	.10
116	Ugueth Urbina	.10
117	Edgardo Alfonzo	.10
118	Bobby Bonilla	.10
119	Rickey Henderson	1.00
120	Hideo Nomo	.60
121	John Olerud	.10
122	Rey Ordonez	.10
123	Mike Piazza	2.00
124	Masato Yoshii	.10
125	Scott Brosius	.10
126	Orlando Hernandez	.10
127	Hideki Irabu	.10
128	Derek Jeter	3.00
129	Chuck Knoblauch	.10
130	Tino Martinez	.10
131	Jorge Posada	.10
132	Bernie Williams	.10
133	Eric Chavez	.20
134	Ryan Christenson	.10
135	Jason Giambi	.65
136	Ben Grieve	.10
137	A.J. Hinch	.10
138	Matt Stairs	.10
139	Miguel Tejada	.20
140	Bob Abreu	.20
141	*Gary Bennett*	.10
142	Desi Relaford	.10
143	Scott Rolen	.75
144	Curt Schilling	.35
145	Kevin Sefcik	.10
146	Brian Giles	.10
147	Jose Guillen	.10
148	Jason Kendall	.10
149	Aramis Ramirez	.10
150	Tony Womack	.10
151	Kevin Young	.10
152	Eric Davis	.10
153	J.D. Drew	.50
154	Ray Lankford	.10
155	Eli Marrero	.10
156	Mark McGwire	2.50
157	Luis Ordaz	.10
158	Edgar Renteria	.10
159	Andy Ashby	.10
160	Tony Gwynn	1.50
161	Trevor Hoffman	.10
162	Wally Joyner	.10
163	Jim Leyritz	.10
164	Ruben Rivera	.10
165	Reggie Sanders	.10
166	Quilvio Veras	.10
167	Rich Aurilia	.10
168	Marvin Benard	.10
169	Barry Bonds	3.00
170	Ellis Burks	.10
171	Jeff Kent	.10
172	Bill Mueller	.10
173	J.T. Snow	.10
174	Jay Buhner	.10
175	Jeff Fassero	.10
176	Ken Griffey Jr.	2.25
177	Carlos Guillen	.10
178	Edgar Martinez	.10
179	Alex Rodriguez	2.50
180	David Segui	.10
181	Dan Wilson	.10
182	Rolando Arrojo	.10
183	Wade Boggs	1.50
184	Jose Canseco	.40
185	Aaron Ledesma	.10
186	Dave Martinez	.10
187	Quinton McCracken	.10
188	Fred McGriff	.10
189	Juan Gonzalez	.60
190	Tom Goodwin	.10
191	Rusty Greer	.10
192	Roberto Kelly	.10
193	Rafael Palmeiro	.75
194	Ivan Rodriguez	.75
195	Roger Clemens	2.00
196	Jose Cruz Jr.	.10
197	Carlos Delgado	.60
198	Alex Gonzalez	.10
199	Roy Halladay	.10
200	Pat Hentgen	.10

Complete Players

		NM/M
Complete Set (10):		40.00
Common Player:		3.00
Production 299 sets		
1	Cal Ripken Jr.	9.00
2	Nomar Garciaparra	4.50
3	Sammy Sosa	4.50
4	Kerry Wood	3.00
5	Frank Thomas	4.00
6	Mike Piazza	5.00
7	Mark McGwire	7.50
8	Tony Gwynn	4.50
9	Ken Griffey Jr.	6.00
10	Alex Rodriguez	7.50

Kings of the Major Leagues

		NM/M
Complete Set (10):		80.00
Common Player:		5.00
Inserted 1:361		
1	Cal Ripken Jr.	17.50
2	Nomar Garciaparra	9.00
3	Sammy Sosa	9.00
4	Kerry Wood	5.00
5	Frank Thomas	7.50
6	Mike Piazza	10.00
7	Mark McGwire	15.00
8	Tony Gwynn	9.00
9	Ken Griffey Jr.	12.50
10	Alex Rodriguez	15.00

On Deck

		NM/M
Complete Set (20):		17.50
Common Player:		.50
Inserted 1:9		
1	Chipper Jones	1.00
2	Cal Ripken Jr.	3.00
3	Nomar Garciaparra	1.00
4	Sammy Sosa	1.00
5	Frank Thomas	.75
6	Manny Ramirez	.75
7	Todd Helton	.75
8	Larry Walker	.50
9	Jeff Bagwell	.75
10	Vladimir Guerrero	.75
11	Mike Piazza	1.50
12	Derek Jeter	3.00
13	Bernie Williams	.50
14	J.D. Drew	.50
15	Mark McGwire	2.50
16	Tony Gwynn	1.00
17	Ken Griffey Jr.	2.00
18	Alex Rodriguez	2.50
19	Juan Gonzalez	.50
20	Ivan Rodriguez	.65

Pennant Fever

		NM/M
Complete Set (20):		30.00
Common Player:		.75
Silver (250 Sets):		2X
Platinum Blue (100):		6X
Copper (20):		20X
Tony Gwynn Autograph:		25.00
1	Chipper Jones	2.00
2	Greg Maddux	2.00
3	Cal Ripken Jr.	5.00
4	Nomar Garciaparra	2.00
5	Sammy Sosa	2.00
6	Kerry Wood	.75
7	Frank Thomas	1.50
8	Manny Ramirez	1.50
9	Todd Helton	1.50
10	Jeff Bagwell	1.50
11	Mike Piazza	2.50
12	Derek Jeter	5.00
13	Bernie Williams	.75
14	J.D. Drew	.75
15	Mark McGwire	4.00
16	Tony Gwynn	2.00
17	Ken Griffey Jr.	3.00
18	Alex Rodriguez	4.00
19	Juan Gonzalez	.75
20	Ivan Rodriguez	1.25

Styrotechs

		NM/M
Complete Set (20):		35.00
Common Player:		1.00
Inserted 1:37		
1	Chipper Jones	3.00
2	Greg Maddux	3.00
3	Cal Ripken Jr.	6.00
4	Nomar Garciaparra	3.00
5	Sammy Sosa	3.00
6	Kerry Wood	1.25
7	Frank Thomas	2.00
8	Manny Ramirez	2.00
9	Larry Walker	1.00
10	Jeff Bagwell	2.00
11	Mike Piazza	4.00
12	Derek Jeter	6.00
13	Bernie Williams	1.00
14	J.D. Drew	1.25
15	Mark McGwire	5.00
16	Tony Gwynn	3.00
17	Ken Griffey Jr.	4.50
18	Alex Rodriguez	5.00
19	Juan Gonzalez	1.25
20	Ivan Rodriguez	1.50

1999 PACIFIC CROWN COLLECTION

	NM/M
Complete Set (300):	20.00

Common Player:		.10
Red Stars:		6X
Inserted 1:9		
Platinum Blue Stars:		30X
Inserted 1:73		
Pack (12):		1.00
Wax Box (36):		22.50
1	Garret Anderson	.10
2	Gary DiSarcina	.10
3	Jim Edmonds	.10
4	Darin Erstad	.25
5	Shigetosi Hasegawa	.10
6	Norberto Martin	.10
7	Omar Olivares	.10
8	Orlando Palmeiro	.10
9	Tim Salmon	.10
10	Randy Velarde	.10
11	Tony Batista	.10
12	Jay Bell	.10
13	Yamil Benitez	.10
14	Omar Daal	.10
15	David Dellucci	.10
16	Karim Garcia	.10
17	Travis Lee	.10
18	Felix Rodriguez	.10
19	Devon White	.10
20	Matt Williams	.10
21	Andres Galarraga	.10
22	Tom Glavine	.35
23	Ozzie Guillen	.10
24	Andruw Jones	1.00
25	Chipper Jones	1.50
26	Ryan Klesko	.10
27	Javy Lopez	.10
28	Greg Maddux	1.50
29	Dennis Martinez	.10
30	Odaliz Perez	.10
31	Rudy Seanez	.10
32	John Smoltz	.10
33	Roberto Alomar	.25
34	Armando Benitez	.10
35	Scott Erickson	.10
36	Juan Guzman	.10
37	Mike Mussina	.35
38	Jesse Orosco	.10
39	Rafael Palmeiro	.75
40	Sidney Ponson	.10
41	Cal Ripken Jr.	3.00
42	B.J. Surhoff	.10
43	Lenny Webster	.10
44	Dennis Eckersley	.75
45	Nomar Garciaparra	1.50
46	Darren Lewis	.10
47	Pedro Martinez	1.00
48	Troy O'Leary	.10
49	Bret Saberhagen	.10
50	John Valentin	.10
51	Mo Vaughn	.10
52	Tim Wakefield	.10
53	Manny Alexander	.10
54	Rod Beck	.10
55	Gary Gaetti	.10
56	Mark Grace	.10
57	Felix Heredia	.10
58	Jose Hernandez	.10
59	Henry Rodriguez	.10
60	Sammy Sosa	1.50
61	Kevin Tapani	.10
62	Kerry Wood	.45
63	James Baldwin	.10
64	Albert Belle	.10
65	Mike Caruso	.10
66	Carlos Castillo	.10
67	Wil Cordero	.10
68	Jaime Navarro	.10
69	Magglio Ordonez	.25
70	Frank Thomas	1.00
71	Robin Ventura	.10
72	Bret Boone	.10
73	Sean Casey	.20
74	*Guillermo Garcia*	.10
75	Barry Larkin	.10
76	Melvin Nieves	.10
77	Eduardo Perez	.10
78	Roberto Petagine	.10
79	Reggie Sanders	.10
80	Eddie Taubensee	.10
81	Brett Tomko	.10
82	Sandy Alomar Jr.	.10
83	Bartolo Colon	.10
84	Joey Cora	.10
85	Einar Diaz	.10
86	David Justice	.10
87	Kenny Lofton	.10
88	Manny Ramirez	1.00
89	Jim Thome	.75
90	Omar Vizquel	.10
91	Enrique Wilson	.10
92	Pedro Astacio	.10
93	Dante Bichette	.10
94	Vinny Castilla	.10
95	*Edgard Clemente*	.10
96	Todd Helton	1.00
97	Darryl Kile	.10
98	Mike Munoz	.10
99	Neifi Perez	.10
100	Jeff Reed	.10
101	Larry Walker	.10
102	Gabe Alvarez	.10
103	Kimera Bartee	.10
104	Frank Castillo	.10
105	Tony Clark	.10
106	Deivi Cruz	.10
107	Damion Easley	.10
108	Luis Gonzalez	.10
109	Marino Santana	.10
110	Justin Thompson	.10
111	Antonio Alfonseca	.10
112	Alex Fernandez	.10
113	Cliff Floyd	.10
114	Alex Gonzalez	.10
115	Livan Hernandez	.10
116	Mark Kotsay	.10
117	Derrek Lee	.65
118	Edgar Renteria	.10
119	Jesus Sanchez	.10
120	Moises Alou	.10
121	Jeff Bagwell	1.00
122	Derek Bell	.10
123	Craig Biggio	.10
124	Tony Eusebio	.10
125	Ricky Gutierrez	.10
126	Richard Hidalgo	.10
127	Randy Johnson	1.00
128	Jose Lima	.10
129	Shane Reynolds	.10
130	Johnny Damon	.40
131	Carlos Febles	.10
132	Jeff King	.10
133	Mendy Lopez	.10
134	Hal Morris	.10
135	Jose Offerman	.10
136	Jose Rosado	.10
137	Jose Santiago	.10
138	Bobby Bonilla	.10
139	Roger Cedeno	.10
140	Alex Cora	.10
141	Eric Karros	.10
142	Raul Mondesi	.10
143	Antonio Osuna	.10
144	Chan Ho Park	.10
145	Gary Sheffield	.30
146	Ismael Valdes	.10
147	Jeromy Burnitz	.10
148	Jeff Cirillo	.10
149	Valerio de los Santos	.10
150	Marquis Grissom	.10
151	Scott Karl	.10
152	Dave Nilsson	.10
153	Al Reyes	.10
154	Rafael Roque	.10
155	Jose Valentin	.10
156	Fernando Vina	.10
157	Rick Aguilera	.10
158	Hector Carrasco	.10
159	Marty Cordova	.10
160	Eddie Guardado	.10
161	Paul Molitor	1.00
162	Otis Nixon	.10
163	Alex Ochoa	.10
164	David Ortiz	.45
165	Frank Rodriguez	.10
166	Todd Walker	.10
167	Miguel Batista	.10
168	Orlando Cabrera	.10
169	Vladimir Guerrero	1.00
170	Wilton Guerrero	.10
171	Carl Pavano	.10
172	Robert Perez	.10
173	F.P. Santangelo	.10
174	Fernando Seguignol	.10
175	Ugueth Urbina	.10
176	Javier Vazquez	.10
177	Edgardo Alfonzo	.10
178	Carlos Baerga	.10
179	John Franco	.10
180	Luis Lopez	.10
181	Hideo Nomo	.50
182	John Olerud	.10
183	Rey Ordonez	.10
184	Mike Piazza	1.75
185	Armando Reynoso	.10
186	Masato Yoshii	.10
187	David Cone	.10
188	Orlando Hernandez	.10
189	Hideki Irabu	.10
190	Derek Jeter	3.00
191	Ricky Ledee	.10
192	Tino Martinez	.10
193	Ramiro Mendoza	.10
194	Paul O'Neill	.10
195	Jorge Posada	.10
196	Mariano Rivera	.15
197	Luis Sojo	.10
198	Bernie Williams	.10
199	Rafael Bournigal	.10
200	Eric Chavez	.20
201	Ryan Christenson	.10
202	Jason Giambi	.60
203	Ben Grieve	.10
204	Rickey Henderson	1.00
205	A.J. Hinch	.10
206	Kenny Rogers	.10
207	Miguel Tejada	.20
208	Jorge Velandia	.10
209	Bobby Abreu	.20
210	Marlon Anderson	.10
211	Alex Arias	.10
212	Bobby Estalella	.10
213	Doug Glanville	.10
214	Scott Rolen	.65
215	Curt Schilling	.35
216	Kevin Sefcik	.10
217	Adrian Brown	.10
218	Francisco Cordova	.10
219	Freddy Garcia	.10
220	Jose Guillen	.10
221	Jason Kendall	.10
222	Al Martin	.10
223	Abraham Nunez	.10
224	Aramis Ramirez	.10
225	Ricardo Rincon	.10
226	Kevin Young	.10
227	J.D. Drew	.40
228	Ron Gant	.10
229	Jose Jimenez	.10
230	Brian Jordan	.10
231	Ray Lankford	.10
232	Eli Marrero	.10
233	Mark McGwire	2.50
234	Luis Ordaz	.10
235	Placido Polanco	.10
236	Fernando Tatis	.10
237	Andy Ashby	.10
238	Kevin Brown	.10
239	Ken Caminiti	.10
240	Steve Finley	.10
241	Chris Gomez	.10
242	Tony Gwynn	1.50
243	Carlos Hernandez	.10
244	Trevor Hoffman	.10
245	Wally Joyner	.10
246	Ruben Rivera	.10
247	Greg Vaughn	.10
248	Quilvio Veras	.10
249	Rich Aurilia	.10
250	Barry Bonds	3.00
251	Stan Javier	.10
252	Jeff Kent	.10
253	Ramon Martinez	.10
254	Jose Mesa	.10
255	Armando Rios	.10
256	Rich Rodriguez	.10
257	Rey Sanchez	.10
258	J.T. Snow	.10
259	Julian Tavarez	.10
260	Jeff Fassero	.10
261	Ken Griffey Jr.	2.00
262	*Giomar Guevara*	.10
263	Carlos Guillen	.10
264	Raul Ibanez	.10
265	Edgar Martinez	.10
266	Jamie Moyer	.10
267	Alex Rodriguez	2.50
268	David Segui	.10
269	Makoto Suzuki	.10
270	Wilson Alvarez	.10
271	Rolando Arrojo	.10
272	Wade Boggs	1.50
273	Miguel Cairo	.10
274	Roberto Hernandez	.10
275	Aaron Ledesma	.10
276	Albie Lopez	.10
277	Quinton McCracken	.10
278	Fred McGriff	.10
279	Esteban Yan	.10
280	Luis Alicea	.10
281	Will Clark	.10
282	Juan Gonzalez	.50
283	Rusty Greer	.10
284	Rick Helling	.10
285	Xavier Hernandez	.10
286	Roberto Kelly	.10
287	Esteban Loaiza	.10
288	Ivan Rodriguez	.75
289	Aaron Sele	.10
290	John Wetteland	.10
291	Jose Canseco	.40
292	Roger Clemens	1.75
293	Felipe Crespo	.10
294	Jose Cruz Jr.	.10
295	Carlos Delgado	.60
296	Kelvim Escobar	.10
297	Tony Fernandez	.10
298	Alex Gonzalez	.10
299	Tomas Perez	.10
300	Juan Samuel	.10

In The Cage

		NM/M
Complete Set (20):		80.00
Common Player:		2.00
Inserted 1:145		
1	Chipper Jones	7.50
2	Cal Ripken Jr.	15.00
3	Nomar Garciaparra	7.50
4	Sammy Sosa	7.50
5	Frank Thomas	5.00
6	Manny Ramirez	5.00
7	Todd Helton	5.00
8	Moises Alou	2.00
9	Vladimir Guerrero	5.00
10	Mike Piazza	9.00
11	Derek Jeter	15.00
12	Ben Grieve	2.00
13	J.D. Drew	3.00
14	Mark McGwire	12.00
15	Tony Gwynn	7.50
16	Ken Griffey Jr.	10.00
17	Edgar Martinez	2.00
18	Alex Rodriguez	12.00
19	Juan Gonzalez	2.50
20	Ivan Rodriguez	4.00

Latinos/Major Leagues

		NM/M
Complete Set (36):		25.00
Common Player:		.30
Inserted 1:18		
1	Roberto Alomar	.60
2	Rafael Palmeiro	2.00
3	Nomar Garciaparra	3.50
4	Pedro Martinez	2.50
5	Magglio Ordonez	1.50
6	Sandy Alomar Jr.	.30
7	Bartolo Colon	.30
8	Manny Ramirez	2.50
9	Omar Vizquel	.30
10	Enrique Wilson	.30
11	David Ortiz	1.50
12	Orlando Hernandez	.30
13	Tino Martinez	.30
14	Mariano Rivera	.45
15	Bernie Williams	.30
16	Edgar Martinez	.30
17	Alex Rodriguez	5.00
18	David Segui	.30
19	Rolando Arrojo	.30
20	Juan Gonzalez	1.25
21	Ivan Rodriguez	2.00
22	Jose Canseco	1.00
23	Jose Cruz Jr.	.30
24	Andres Galarraga	.30
25	Andruw Jones	2.50
26	Javy Lopez	.30
27	Sammy Sosa	3.50
28	Vinny Castilla	.30
29	Alex Gonzalez	.30
30	Moises Alou	.30
31	Bobby Bonilla	.30
32	Raul Mondesi	.30
33	Fernando Vina	.30
34	Vladimir Guerrero	2.50
35	Carlos Baerga	.30
36	Rey Ordonez	.30

Pacific Cup

		NM/M
Complete Set (10):		80.00
Common Player:		5.00
Inserted 1:721		
1	Cal Ripken Jr.	20.00
2	Nomar Garciaparra	8.00
3	Frank Thomas	6.00
4	Ken Griffey Jr.	12.00
5	Alex Rodriguez	16.00
6	Greg Maddux	8.00
7	Sammy Sosa	8.00
8	Kerry Wood	5.00
9	Mark McGwire	16.00
10	Tony Gwynn	8.00

Players Choice

		NM/M
Complete Set (6):		55.00
Common Player:		5.00
10	Randy Velarde	5.00
41	Cal Ripken Jr.	30.00
47	Pedro Martinez	12.00
88	Manny Ramirez	12.00
112	Alex Fernandez	5.00
128	Jose Lima	5.00

Tape Measure

		NM/M
Complete Set (20):		20.00
Common Player:		.60
Inserted 1:73		
1	Andres Galarraga	.60
2	Chipper Jones	2.50
3	Nomar Garciaparra	2.50
4	Sammy Sosa	2.50
5	Frank Thomas	1.50
6	Manny Ramirez	1.50
7	Vinny Castilla	.60
8	Moises Alou	.60
9	Jeff Bagwell	1.50
10	Raul Mondesi	.60
11	Vladimir Guerrero	1.50
12	Mike Piazza	2.75
13	J.D. Drew	1.00
14	Mark McGwire	3.50
15	Greg Vaughn	.60
16	Ken Griffey Jr.	3.00
17	Alex Rodriguez	3.50
18	Juan Gonzalez	1.00
19	Ivan Rodriguez	1.25
20	Jose Canseco	1.00

Team Checklists

		NM/M
Complete Set (30):		25.00
Common Player:		.50
Inserted 1:37		
1	Darin Erstad	.60
2	Travis Lee	.50
3	Chipper Jones	1.75
4	Cal Ripken Jr.	4.00
5	Nomar Garciaparra	1.75
6	Sammy Sosa	1.75
7	Frank Thomas	1.25
8	Barry Larkin	.50
9	Manny Ramirez	1.25
10	Larry Walker	.50
11	Bob Higginson	.50
12	Livan Hernandez	.50
13	Moises Alou	.50
14	Jeff King	.50
15	Raul Mondesi	.50
16	Marquis Grissom	.50
17	David Ortiz	1.00
18	Vladimir Guerrero	1.25
19	Mike Piazza	2.00
20	Derek Jeter	4.00
21	Ben Grieve	.50
22	Scott Rolen	.75
23	Jason Kendall	.50
24	Mark McGwire	3.00
25	Tony Gwynn	1.75
26	Barry Bonds	4.00
27	Ken Griffey Jr.	2.50
28	Wade Boggs	1.75
29	Juan Gonzalez	.75
30	Jose Canseco	.60

1999 PACIFIC CROWN ROYALE

		NM/M
Complete Set (144):		75.00
Common Player:		.25
Common SP:		.50
Limited Series (99 Sets):		6X
SPs:		2X
Opening Day (72 Sets):		12X
SPs:		2X
Pack (6):		2.00
Wax Box (24):		35.00
1	Jim Edmonds	.25
2	Darin Erstad	.50
3	Troy Glaus	2.00
4	Tim Salmon	.25
5	Mo Vaughn	.25
6	Jay Bell	.25
7	Steve Finley	.25
8	Randy Johnson	2.00
9	Travis Lee	.25
10	Matt Williams	.25
11	Andruw Jones	2.00
12	Chipper Jones	3.00
13	Brian Jordan	.25
14	Ryan Klesko	.25
15	Javy Lopez	.25
16	Greg Maddux	3.00
17	Randall Simon (SP)	.50
18	Albert Belle	.25
19	Will Clark	.25
20	Delino DeShields	.25
21	Mike Mussina	.50
22	Cal Ripken Jr.	6.00
23	Nomar Garciaparra	3.00
24	Pedro Martinez	2.00
25	Jose Offerman	.25
26	John Valentin	.25
27	Mark Grace	.25
28	Lance Johnson	.25
29	Henry Rodriguez	.25
30	Sammy Sosa	3.00
31	Kerry Wood	1.00
32	Mike Caruso	.25
33	Ray Durham	.25
34	Magglio Ordonez	.40
35	Brian Simmons (SP)	.50
36	Frank Thomas	2.00
37	Mike Cameron	.25
38	Barry Larkin	.25
39	Greg Vaughn	.25
40	Dmitri Young	.25
41	Roberto Alomar	.40
42	Sandy Alomar Jr.	.25
43	David Justice	.25
44	Kenny Lofton	.25
45	Manny Ramirez	2.00
46	Jim Thome	1.50
47	Dante Bichette	.25
48	Vinny Castilla	.25
49	Todd Helton	2.00
50	Larry Walker	.25
51	Tony Clark	.25
52	Damion Easley	.25
53	Bob Higginson	.25
54	Brian Hunter	.25
55	Gabe Kapler (SP)	.50
56	*Jeff Weaver* (SP)	2.50
57	Cliff Floyd	.25
58	Alex Gonzalez (SP)	.50
59	Mark Kotsay	.25
60	Derrek Lee	1.00
61	Preston Wilson (SP)	.75
62	Moises Alou	.25
63	Jeff Bagwell	2.00
64	Derek Bell	.25
65	Craig Biggio	.25
66	Ken Caminiti	.25
67	Carlos Beltran (SP)	2.00
68	Johnny Damon	.45
69	Carlos Febles (SP)	.65
70	Jeff King	.25
71	Kevin Brown	.25
72	Todd Hundley	.25
73	Eric Karros	.25
74	Raul Mondesi	.25
75	Gary Sheffield	.75
76	Jeromy Burnitz	.25
77	Jeff Cirillo	.25
78	Marquis Grissom	.25
79	Fernando Vina	.25
80	*Chad Allen* (SP)	.50
81	Matt Lawton	.25
82	Doug Mientkiewicz (SP)	.75
83	Brad Radke	.25
84	Todd Walker	.25
85	Michael Barrett (SP)	.50
86	Brad Fullmer	.25
87	Vladimir Guerrero	2.00
88	Wilton Guerrero	.25
89	Ugueth Urbina	.25
90	Bobby Bonilla	.25
91	Rickey Henderson	2.00
92	Rey Ordonez	.25
93	Mike Piazza	3.50
94	Robin Ventura	.25
95	Roger Clemens	3.50
96	Orlando Hernandez	.25
97	Derek Jeter	6.00
98	Chuck Knoblauch	.25
99	Tino Martinez	.25
100	Bernie Williams	.25
101	Eric Chavez (SP)	1.50
102	Jason Giambi	1.00
103	Ben Grieve	.25
104	Tim Raines	.25
105	Marlon Anderson (SP)	.65
106	Doug Glanville	.25
107	Scott Rolen	1.25
108	Curt Schilling	.40
109	Brian Giles	.25
110	Jose Guillen	.25
111	Jason Kendall	.25
112	Kevin Young	.25
113	J.D. Drew (SP)	2.00
114	Jose Jimenez (SP)	.50
115	Ray Lankford	.25
116	Mark McGwire	5.00
117	Fernando Tatis	.25
118	Matt Clement (SP)	.75
119	Tony Gwynn	3.00
120	Trevor Hoffman	.25
121	Wally Joyner	.25
122	Reggie Sanders	.25
123	Barry Bonds	6.00
124	Ellis Burks	.25
125	Jeff Kent	.25
126	J.T. Snow	.25
127	*Freddy Garcia* (SP)	1.00
128	Ken Griffey Jr.	4.00
129	Edgar Martinez	.25
130	Alex Rodriguez	5.00
131	David Segui	.25
132	Rolando Arrojo	.25
133	Wade Boggs	3.00
134	Jose Canseco	.65
135	Quinton McCracken	.25
136	Fred McGriff	.25
137	Juan Gonzalez	1.00
138	Rusty Greer	.25
139	Rafael Palmeiro	1.50
140	Ivan Rodriguez	1.50
141	Jose Cruz Jr.	.25
142	Carlos Delgado	.75
143	Shawn Green	.75
144	Roy Halladay (SP)	1.00

Century 21

		NM/M
Complete Set (10):		30.00
Common Player:		2.00
Inserted 1:25		
1	Cal Ripken Jr.	7.50
2	Nomar Garciaparra	4.00
3	Sammy Sosa	4.00
4	Frank Thomas	3.00
5	Mike Piazza	4.50
6	J.D. Drew	2.00
7	Mark McGwire	6.00
8	Tony Gwynn	4.00
9	Ken Griffey Jr.	5.00
10	Alex Rodriguez	6.00

Cramer's Choice Premiums

		NM/M
Complete Set (10):		20.00
Common Player:		2.00
Inserted 1:box		
Dark Blue (35 Sets):		5X
Green (30):		6X
Red (25):		8X
Light Blue (20):		10X
Gold (10):		15X
Purple (1):		Value Undetermined
1	Cal Ripken Jr.	6.50
2	Nomar Garciaparra	3.00
3	Sammy Sosa	3.00
4	Frank Thomas	2.50
5	Mike Piazza	3.50
6	Derek Jeter	6.50
7	J.D. Drew	2.00
8	Mark McGwire	5.00
9	Tony Gwynn	3.00
10	Ken Griffey Jr.	4.00

Gold Crown Die-Cut Premiums

		NM/M
Complete Set (6):		15.00
Common Player:		2.50
Inserted 6:10 boxes		
1	Cal Ripken Jr.	7.00
2	Mike Piazza	4.50
3	Ken Griffey Jr.	5.00
4	Tony Gwynn	3.00
5	Mark McGwire	6.00
6	J.D. Drew	2.50

Living Legends

		NM/M
Complete Set (10):		100.00
Common Player:		7.50
Production 375 sets		
1	Greg Maddux	10.00
2	Cal Ripken Jr.	20.00

3 Nomar Garciaparra 10.00
4 Sammy Sosa 10.00
5 Frank Thomas 7.50
6 Mike Piazza 12.00
7 Mark McGwire 15.00
8 Tony Gwynn 10.00
9 Ken Griffey Jr. 13.50
10 Alex Rodriguez 15.00

Master Performers

NM/M
Complete Set (20): 40.00
Common Player: 1.00
Inserted 2:25
1 Chipper Jones 2.50
2 Greg Maddux 2.50
3 Cal Ripken Jr. 5.00
4 Nomar Garciaparra 2.50
5 Sammy Sosa 2.50
6 Frank Thomas 2.00
7 Raul Mondesi 1.00
8 Vladimir Guerrero 2.00
9 Mike Piazza 3.00
10 Roger Clemens 3.00
11 Derek Jeter 5.00
12 Scott Rolen 1.75
13 J.D. Drew 1.50
14 Mark McGwire 4.00
15 Tony Gwynn 2.50
16 Barry Bonds 5.00
17 Ken Griffey Jr. 3.50
18 Alex Rodriguez 4.00
19 Juan Gonzalez 1.50
20 Ivan Rodriguez 1.75

Pillars of the Game

NM/M
Complete Set (25): 30.00
Common Player: .50
Inserted 1:1
1 Mo Vaughn .50
2 Chipper Jones 2.00
3 Greg Maddux 2.00
4 Albert Belle .50
5 Cal Ripken Jr. 4.00
6 Nomar Garciaparra 2.00
7 Sammy Sosa 2.00
8 Frank Thomas 1.50
9 Manny Ramirez 1.50
10 Jeff Bagwell 1.50
11 Raul Mondesi .50
12 Vladimir Guerrero 1.50
13 Mike Piazza 2.25
14 Roger Clemens 2.25
15 Derek Jeter 4.00
16 Bernie Williams .50
17 Ben Grieve .50
18 J.D. Drew 1.00
19 Mark McGwire 3.00
20 Tony Gwynn 2.00
21 Barry Bonds 4.00
22 Ken Griffey Jr. 2.50
23 Alex Rodriguez 3.00
24 Juan Gonzalez 1.00
25 Ivan Rodriguez 1.25

Pivotal Players

NM/M
Complete Set (25): 20.00
Common Player: .50
Inserted 1:1
1 Mo Vaughn .50
2 Chipper Jones 2.00
3 Greg Maddux 2.00
4 Albert Belle .50
5 Cal Ripken Jr. 4.00
6 Nomar Garciaparra 2.00
7 Sammy Sosa 2.00
8 Frank Thomas 1.50
9 Manny Ramirez 1.50
10 Craig Biggio .50
11 Raul Mondesi .50
12 Vladimir Guerrero 1.50
13 Mike Piazza 2.25
14 Roger Clemens 2.50
15 Derek Jeter 4.00
16 Bernie Williams .50
17 Ben Grieve .50
18 Scott Rolen .60
19 J.D. Drew .75
20 Mark McGwire 3.00
21 Tony Gwynn 2.00
22 Ken Griffey Jr. 2.50
23 Alex Rodriguez 3.00
24 Juan Gonzalez .75
25 Ivan Rodriguez 1.00

Pivotal Players Show Cards

NM/M
Common Card: 5.00
Stars: 6-8X
(See 1999 Pacific Crown Royale Pivotal Players for checklist and base values.)

1999 PACIFIC INVINCIBLE

NM/M
Complete Set (150): 60.00
Common Player: .25
Opening Day (69 Sets): 6X
Platinum Blues (67): 6X
Pack (3): 1.50
Wax Box (24): 35.00
1 Jim Edmonds .25
2 Darin Erstad .50
3 Troy Glaus 2.50
4 Tim Salmon .25
5 Mo Vaughn .25
6 Steve Finley .25
7 Randy Johnson 2.50
8 Travis Lee .25
9 Dante Powell .25
10 Matt Williams .25
11 Bret Boone .25
12 Andruw Jones 2.50
13 Chipper Jones 3.00
14 Brian Jordan .25
15 Ryan Klesko .25
16 Javy Lopez .25
17 Greg Maddux 3.00
18 Brady Anderson .25
19 Albert Belle .25
20 Will Clark .25
21 Mike Mussina .75
22 Cal Ripken Jr. 6.00
23 Nomar Garciaparra 3.00
24 Pedro Martinez 2.50
25 Trot Nixon .25
26 Jose Offerman .25
27 Donnie Sadler .25
28 John Valentin .25
29 Mark Grace .25
30 Lance Johnson .25
31 Henry Rodriguez .25
32 Sammy Sosa 3.00
33 Kerry Wood 1.25
34 McKay Christensen .25
35 Ray Durham .25
36 Jeff Liefer .25
37 Frank Thomas 2.50
38 Mike Cameron .25
39 Barry Larkin .25
40 Greg Vaughn .25
41 Dmitri Young .25
42 Roberto Alomar .50
43 Sandy Alomar Jr. .25
44 David Justice .25
45 Kenny Lofton .25
46 Manny Ramirez 2.50
47 Jim Thome 2.25
48 Dante Bichette .25
49 Vinny Castilla .25
50 Darryl Hamilton .25
51 Todd Helton 2.50
52 Neifi Perez .25
53 Larry Walker .25
54 Tony Clark .25
55 Damion Easley .25
56 Bob Higginson .25
57 Brian Hunter .25
58 Gabe Kapler .25
59 Cliff Floyd .25
60 Alex Gonzalez .25
61 Mark Kotsay .25
62 Derrek Lee 2.00
63 Braden Looper .25
64 Moises Alou .25
65 Jeff Bagwell 2.50
66 Craig Biggio .25
67 Ken Caminiti .25
68 Scott Elarton .25
69 Mitch Meluskey .25
70 Carlos Beltran .65
71 Johnny Damon .50
72 Carlos Febles .25
73 Jeremy Giambi .25
74 Kevin Brown .25
75 Todd Hundley .25
76 Paul LoDuca .25
77 Raul Mondesi .25
78 Gary Sheffield 1.00
79 Geoff Jenkins .25
80 Jeromy Burnitz .25
81 Marquis Grissom .25
82 Jose Valentin .25
83 Fernando Vina .25
84 Corey Koskie .25
85 Matt Lawton .25
86 Christian Guzman .25
87 Torii Hunter .25
88 Doug Mientkiewicz .25
89 Michael Barrett .25
90 Brad Fullmer .25
91 Vladimir Guerrero 2.50
92 Fernando Seguignol .25
93 Ugueth Urbina .25
94 Bobby Bonilla .25
95 Rickey Henderson 2.50
96 Rey Ordonez .25
97 Mike Piazza 3.50
98 Robin Ventura .25
99 Roger Clemens 3.50
100 Derek Jeter 6.00
101 Chuck Knoblauch .25
102 Tino Martinez .25
103 Paul O'Neill .25
104 Bernie Williams .25
105 Eric Chavez .50
106 Ryan Christenson .25
107 Jason Giambi 1.25
108 Ben Grieve .25
109 Miguel Tejada .50
110 Marlon Anderson .25
111 Doug Glanville .25
112 Scott Rolen 2.25
113 Curt Schilling .50
114 Brian Giles .25
115 Warren Morris .25
116 Jason Kendall .25
117 Kris Benson .25
118 J.D. Drew 1.25
119 Ray Lankford .25
120 Mark McGwire 5.00
121 Matt Clement .25
122 Tony Gwynn 3.00
123 Trevor Hoffman .25
124 Wally Joyner .25
125 Reggie Sanders .25
126 Barry Bonds 6.00
127 Ellis Burks .25
128 Jeff Kent .25
129 Stan Javier .25
130 J.T. Snow .25
131 Jay Buhner .25
132 *Freddy Garcia* 2.00
133 Ken Griffey Jr. 4.00
134 Russ Davis .25
135 Edgar Martinez .25
136 Alex Rodriguez 5.00
137 David Segui .25
138 Rolando Arrojo .25
139 Wade Boggs 3.00
140 Jose Canseco 1.00
141 Quinton McCracken .25
142 Fred McGriff .25
143 Juan Gonzalez 1.25
144 Tom Goodwin .25
145 Rusty Greer .25
146 Ivan Rodriguez 2.25
147 Jose Cruz Jr. .25
148 Carlos Delgado 1.00
149 Shawn Green .75
150 Roy Halladay .25

Diamond Magic

NM/M
Complete Set (10): 35.00

Common Player: 3.00
Inserted 1:49
1 Cal Ripken Jr. 7.50
2 Nomar Garciaparra 4.00
3 Sammy Sosa 4.00
4 Frank Thomas 3.50
5 Mike Piazza 4.50
6 J.D. Drew 3.00
7 Mark McGwire 6.00
8 Tony Gwynn 4.00
9 Ken Griffey Jr. 5.00
10 Alex Rodriguez 6.00

Flash Point

NM/M
Complete Set (20): 50.00
Common Player: 1.25
Inserted 1:25
1 Mo Vaughn 1.25
2 Chipper Jones 3.50
3 Greg Maddux 3.50
4 Cal Ripken Jr. 9.00
5 Nomar Garciaparra 3.50
6 Sammy Sosa 3.50
7 Frank Thomas 2.50
8 Manny Ramirez 2.50
9 Vladimir Guerrero 2.50
10 Mike Piazza 4.00
11 Roger Clemens 4.00
12 Derek Jeter 9.00
13 Ben Grieve 1.25
14 Scott Rolen 2.00
15 J.D. Drew 1.50
16 Mark McGwire 7.50
17 Tony Gwynn 3.50
18 Ken Griffey Jr. 5.00
19 Alex Rodriguez 7.50
20 Juan Gonzalez 1.50

Giants of the Game

NM/M
Complete Set (10): 300.00
Common Player: 25.00
Production 10 sets
1 Cal Ripken Jr. 75.00
2 Nomar Garciaparra 35.00
3 Sammy Sosa 35.00
4 Frank Thomas 30.00
5 Mike Piazza 40.00
6 J.D. Drew 25.00
7 Mark McGwire 60.00
8 Tony Gwynn 35.00
9 Ken Griffey Jr. 50.00
10 Alex Rodriguez 60.00

Sandlot Heroes

NM/M
Complete Set (20): 15.00
Common Player: .50
Inserted 1:1
SportsFest (10 Sets): 25X
1 Mo Vaughn .50
2 Chipper Jones 1.00
3 Greg Maddux 1.00
4 Cal Ripken Jr. 3.00
5 Nomar Garciaparra 1.00
6 Sammy Sosa 1.00
7 Frank Thomas .75
8 Manny Ramirez .75
9 Vladimir Guerrero .75
10 Mike Piazza 1.25
11 Roger Clemens 1.25
12 Derek Jeter 3.00
13 Eric Chavez .50
14 Ben Grieve .50
15 J.D. Drew .60
16 Mark McGwire 2.00
17 Tony Gwynn 1.00
18 Ken Griffey Jr. 1.50

19 Alex Rodriguez 2.00
20 Juan Gonzalez .60

Seismic Force

NM/M
Complete Set (20): 15.00
Common Player: .50
Inserted 1:1
SportsFest (20 Sets): 15X
1 Mo Vaughn .50
2 Chipper Jones 1.00
3 Greg Maddux 1.00
4 Cal Ripken Jr. 3.00
5 Nomar Garciaparra 1.00
6 Sammy Sosa 1.00
7 Frank Thomas .75
8 Manny Ramirez .75
9 Vladimir Guerrero .75
10 Mike Piazza 1.25
11 Bernie Williams .50
12 Derek Jeter 3.00
13 Ben Grieve .50
14 J.D. Drew .60
15 Mark McGwire 2.00
16 Tony Gwynn 1.00
17 Ken Griffey Jr. 1.50
18 Alex Rodriguez 2.00
19 Juan Gonzalez .50
20 Ivan Rodriguez .65

Thunder Alley

NM/M
Complete Set (20): 75.00
Common Player: 2.50
Inserted 1:121
1 Mo Vaughn 2.50
2 Chipper Jones 6.00
3 Cal Ripken Jr. 12.00
4 Nomar Garciaparra 6.00
5 Sammy Sosa 6.00
6 Frank Thomas 5.00
7 Manny Ramirez 5.00
8 Todd Helton 5.00
9 Vladimir Guerrero 5.00
10 Mike Piazza 7.50
11 Derek Jeter 12.00
12 Ben Grieve 2.50
13 Scott Rolen 4.50
14 J.D. Drew 3.00
15 Mark McGwire 10.00
16 Tony Gwynn 6.00
17 Ken Griffey Jr. 9.00
18 Alex Rodriguez 10.00
19 Juan Gonzalez 3.00
20 Ivan Rodriguez 4.50

1999 PACIFIC OMEGA

NM/M
Complete Set (250): 20.00
Common Player: .10
Gold (299 Sets): 4X
Copper (99): 10X
Platinum Blue (75): 15X
Premire Date (50): 20X
Wax Pack (6): 1.50
Wax Box (36): 35.00
1 Garret Anderson .10
2 Jim Edmonds .10
3 Darin Erstad .20
4 Chuck Finley .10
5 Troy Glaus .75
6 Troy Percival .10
7 Chris Pritchett .10
8 Tim Salmon .10
9 Mo Vaughn .10
10 Jay Bell .10
11 Steve Finley .10
12 Luis Gonzalez .10
13 Randy Johnson .75
14 *Byung-Hyun Kim* .75
15 Travis Lee .10
16 Matt Williams .10
17 Tony Womack .10
18 Bret Boone .10
19 Mark DeRosa .10
20 Tom Glavine .35
21 Andruw Jones .75
22 Chipper Jones 1.00
23 Brian Jordan .10
24 Ryan Klesko .10
25 Javy Lopez .10
26 Greg Maddux 1.00
27 John Smoltz .10
28 Bruce Chen, Odalis Perez .10
29 Brady Anderson .10
30 Harold Baines .10
31 Albert Belle .10
32 Will Clark .10
33 Delino DeShields .10
34 Jerry Hairston Jr. .10
35 Charles Johnson .10
36 Mike Mussina .40
37 Cal Ripken Jr. 2.50
38 B.J. Surhoff .10
39 Jin Ho Cho .10
40 Nomar Garciaparra 1.00
41 Pedro Martinez .75
42 Jose Offerman .10
43 Troy O'Leary .10
44 John Valentin .10
45 Jason Varitek .10
46 Juan Pena, Brian Rose .10
47 Mark Grace .10
48 Glenallen Hill .10
49 Tyler Houston .10
50 Mickey Morandini .10
51 Henry Rodriguez .10
52 Sammy Sosa 1.00
53 Kevin Tapani .10
54 Mike Caruso .10
55 Ray Durham .10
56 Paul Konerko .20
57 Carlos Lee .10
58 Magglio Ordonez .20
59 Mike Sirotka .10
60 Frank Thomas .75
61 Mark L. Johnson, Chris Singleton .10
62 Mike Cameron .10
63 Sean Casey .20
64 Pete Harnisch .10
65 Barry Larkin .10
66 Pokey Reese .10
67 Greg Vaughn .10
68 Scott Williamson .10
69 Dmitri Young .10
70 Roberto Alomar .25
71 Sandy Alomar Jr. .10
72 Travis Fryman .10
73 David Justice .10
74 Kenny Lofton .10
75 Manny Ramirez .75
76 Richie Sexson .10
77 Jim Thome .65
78 Omar Vizquel .10
79 Jaret Wright .10
80 Dante Bichette .10
81 Vinny Castilla .10
82 Todd Helton .75
83 Darryl Hamilton .10
84 Darryl Kile .10
85 Neifi Perez .10
86 Larry Walker .10
87 Tony Clark .10
88 Damion Easley .10
89 Juan Encarnacion .10
90 Bobby Higginson .10
91 Gabe Kapler .10
92 Dean Palmer .10
93 Justin Thompson .10
94 *Masao Kida, Jeff Weaver* 1.00
95 Bruce Aven .10
96 Luis Castillo .10
97 Alex Fernandez .10
98 Cliff Floyd .10
99 Alex Gonzalez .10
100 Mark Kotsay .10
101 Preston Wilson .10
102 Moises Alou .10
103 Jeff Bagwell .75
104 Derek Bell .10
105 Craig Biggio .10
106 Mike Hampton .10
107 Richard Hidalgo .10
108 Jose Lima .10
109 Billy Wagner .10
110 Russ Johnson, Daryle Ward .10
111 Carlos Beltran .50
112 Johnny Damon .35
113 Jermaine Dye .10
114 Carlos Febles .10
115 Jeremy Giambi .10
116 Joe Randa .10
117 Mike Sweeney .10
118 Orber Moreno, Jose Santiago .10
119 Kevin Brown .10
120 Todd Hundley .10
121 Eric Karros .10
122 Raul Mondesi .10
123 Chan Ho Park .10
124 Angel Pena .10
125 Gary Sheffield .45
126 Devon White .10
127 Eric Young .10
128 Ron Belliard .10
129 Jeromy Burnitz .10
130 Jeff Cirillo .10
131 Marquis Grissom .10
132 Geoff Jenkins .10
133 David Nilsson .10
134 Hideo Nomo .40
135 Fernando Vina .10
136 Ron Coomer .10
137 Marty Cordova .10
138 Corey Koskie .10
139 Brad Radke .10
140 Todd Walker .10
141 Chad Allen, Torii Hunter .10
142 Cristian Guzman, Jacque Jones .10
143 Michael Barrett .10
144 Orlando Cabrera .10
145 Vladimir Guerrero .75
146 Wilton Guerrero .10
147 Ugueth Urbina .10
148 Rondell White .10
149 Chris Widger .10
150 Edgardo Alfonzo .10
151 Roger Cedeno .10
152 Octavio Dotel .10
153 Rickey Henderson .75
154 John Olerud .10
155 Rey Ordonez .10
156 Mike Piazza 1.25
157 Robin Ventura .10
158 Scott Brosius .10
159 Roger Clemens 1.25
160 David Cone .10
161 Chili Davis .10
162 Orlando Hernandez .10
163 Derek Jeter 2.50
164 Chuck Knoblauch .10
165 Tino Martinez .10
166 Paul O'Neill .10
167 Bernie Williams .10
168 Jason Giambi .60
169 Ben Grieve .10
170 *Chad Harville* .10
171 *Tim Hudson* 2.00
172 Tony Phillips .10
173 Kenny Rogers .10
174 Matt Stairs .10
175 Miguel Tejada .25
176 Eric Chavez .25
177 Bobby Abreu .20
178 Ron Gant .10
179 Doug Glanville .10
180 Mike Lieberthal .10
181 Desi Relaford .10
182 Scott Rolen .65
183 Curt Schilling .35
184 Marlon Anderson, Randy Wolf .10
185 Brant Brown .10
186 Brian Giles .10
187 Jason Kendall .10
188 Al Martin .10
189 Ed Sprague .10
190 Kevin Young .10
191 Kris Benson, Warren Morris .10
192 Kent Bottenfield .10
193 Eric Davis .10
194 J.D. Drew .45
195 Ray Lankford .10
196 *Joe McEwing* .25
197 Mark McGwire 2.00
198 Edgar Renteria .10
199 Fernando Tatis .10
200 Andy Ashby .10
201 Ben Davis .10
202 Tony Gwynn 1.00
203 Trevor Hoffman .10
204 Wally Joyner .10
205 Gary Matthews Jr. .10
206 Ruben Rivera .10
207 Reggie Sanders .10
208 Rich Aurilia .10
209 Marvin Benard .10
210 Barry Bonds 2.50
211 Ellis Burks .10
212 Stan Javier .10
213 Jeff Kent .10
214 Robb Nen .10
215 J.T. Snow .10
216 David Bell .10
217 Jay Buhner .10
218 *Freddy Garcia* .50
219 Ken Griffey Jr. 1.50
220 Brian Hunter .10
221 Butch Huskey .10
222 Edgar Martinez .10
223 Jamie Moyer .10
224 Alex Rodriguez 2.00
225 David Segui .10
226 Rolando Arrojo .10
227 Wade Boggs 1.00
228 Miguel Cairo .10
229 Jose Canseco .60
230 Dave Martinez .10
231 Fred McGriff .10
232 Kevin Stocker .10
233 Mike Duvall, David Lamb .10
234 Royce Clayton .10
235 Juan Gonzalez .40
236 Rusty Greer .10
237 Ruben Mateo .10
238 Rafael Palmeiro .65
239 Ivan Rodriguez .65
240 John Wetteland .10
241 Todd Zeile .10
242 Jeff Zimmerman .10
243 Homer Bush .10
244 Jose Cruz Jr. .10
245 Carlos Delgado .60
246 Tony Fernandez .10
247 Shawn Green .35
248 Shannon Stewart .10
249 David Wells .10
250 Roy Halladay, Billy Koch .10

Debut Duos

NM/M
Complete Set (10): 45.00
Common Player: 2.50
Inserted 1:145
1 Nomar Garciaparra, Vladimir Guerrero 6.00
2 Derek Jeter, Andy Pettitte 12.00
3 Garret Anderson, Alex Rodriguez 9.00
4 Chipper Jones, Raul Mondesi 6.00
5 Pedro Martinez, Mike Piazza 6.50
6 Mo Vaughn, Bernie Williams 2.50
7 Juan Gonzalez, Ken Griffey Jr. 7.50
8 Sammy Sosa, Larry Walker 6.00
9 Barry Bonds, Mark McGwire 12.00
10 Wade Boggs, Tony Gwynn 6.00

Diamond Masters

NM/M
Complete Set (36): 27.50
Common Player: .25
Inserted 1:9
1 Darin Erstad .35

2	Mo Vaughn	.25
3	Matt Williams	.25
4	Andruw Jones	.75
5	Chipper Jones	1.00
6	Greg Maddux	1.00
7	Cal Ripken Jr.	3.00
8	Nomar Garciaparra	1.00
9	Pedro Martinez	.75
10	Sammy Sosa	1.00
11	Frank Thomas	.75
12	Kenny Lofton	.25
13	Manny Ramirez	.75
14	Larry Walker	.25
15	Gabe Kapler	.25
16	Jeff Bagwell	.75
17	Craig Biggio	.25
18	Raul Mondesi	.25
19	Vladimir Guerrero	.75
20	Mike Piazza	1.25
21	Roger Clemens	1.25
22	Derek Jeter	3.00
23	Bernie Williams	.25
24	Scott Rolen	.65
25	J.D. Drew	.60
26	Mark McGwire	2.00
27	Fernando Tatis	.25
28	Tony Gwynn	1.00
29	Barry Bonds	3.00
30	Ken Griffey Jr.	1.50
31	Alex Rodriguez	2.00
32	Jose Canseco	.60
33	Juan Gonzalez	.40
34	Ruben Mateo	.25
35	Ivan Rodriguez	.65
36	Rusty Greer	.25

EO Portraits

		NM/M
Complete Set (20):		60.00
Common Player:		1.00
Inserted 1:73		
1-of-1 Numbered Parallels Exist		
1	Mo Vaughn	1.00
2	Chipper Jones	5.00
3	Greg Maddux	5.00
4	Cal Ripken Jr.	10.00
5	Nomar Garciaparra	5.00
6	Sammy Sosa	5.00
7	Frank Thomas	4.00
8	Manny Ramirez	4.00
9	Jeff Bagwell	4.00
10	Mike Piazza	5.50
11	Roger Clemens	5.50
12	Derek Jeter	10.00
13	Scott Rolen	3.00
14	Mark McGwire	8.00
15	Tony Gwynn	5.00
16	Barry Bonds	10.00
17	Ken Griffey Jr.	6.00
18	Alex Rodriguez	8.00
19	Jose Canseco	2.50
20	Juan Gonzalez	2.00

Hit Machine 3000

		NM/M
Complete Set (20):		24.00
Common Card:		1.50
1	The Hitting Machine	1.50
2	The Eyes Have It	1.50
3	The Art of Hitting	1.50
4	Solid as a Rock	1.50
5	Seeing Doubles	1.50
6	Pithcer's Worst Nightmare	1.50
7	Portrait of an All-Star	1.50
8	An American Hero	1.50
9	Fan Favorite	1.50
10	Mr. Batting Title	1.50

11	4-for-5!	1.50
12	Mission Accomplished	1.50
13	One Hit Away	1.50
14	A Tip of the Hat	1.50
15	It's a Base Hit!	1.50
16	2997th - Grand Slam!	1.50
17	2998th Hit	1.50
18	2999th Hit - 2-Run Double	1.50
19	3000th Hit!	1.50
20	3000 Hits, 8874 At-Bats, 18 Years	1.50

HR '99

		NM/M
Complete Set (20):		20.00
Common Player:		.25
Inserted 1:37		
1	Mo Vaughn	.25
2	Matt Williams	.25
3	Chipper Jones	2.00
4	Albert Belle	.25
5	Nomar Garciaparra	2.00
6	Sammy Sosa	2.00
7	Frank Thomas	1.25
8	Manny Ramirez	1.25
9	Jeff Bagwell	1.25
10	Raul Mondesi	.25
11	Vladimir Guerrero	1.25
12	Mike Piazza	2.25
13	Derek Jeter	4.00
14	Mark McGwire	3.00
15	Fernando Tatis	.25
16	Barry Bonds	4.00
17	Ken Griffey Jr.	2.50
18	Alex Rodriguez	3.00
19	Jose Canseco	.75
20	Juan Gonzalez	.65

5-Tool Talents

		NM/M
Complete Set (30):		40.00
Common Player:		.40
Inserted 4:37		
1	Randy Johnson	1.50
2	Greg Maddux	2.00
3	Pedro Martinez	1.50
4	Kevin Brown	.40
5	Roger Clemens	2.50
6	Carlos Lee	.40
7	Gabe Kapler	.40
8	Carlos Beltran	.75
9	J.D. Drew	.75
10	Ruben Mateo	.40
11	Chipper Jones	2.00
12	Sammy Sosa	2.00
13	Manny Ramirez	1.50
14	Vladimir Guerrero	1.50
15	Mark McGwire	4.00
16	Ken Griffey Jr.	3.00
17	Jose Canseco	.75
18	Nomar Garciaparra	2.00
19	Frank Thomas	1.50
20	Larry Walker	.40
21	Jeff Bagwell	1.50
22	Mike Piazza	2.50
23	Tony Gwynn	2.00
24	Juan Gonzalez	.75
25	Cal Ripken Jr.	5.00
26	Derek Jeter	5.00
27	Scott Rolen	1.25
28	Barry Bonds	5.00
29	Alex Rodriguez	4.00
30	Ivan Rodriguez	1.25

5-Tool Talents Tiered

		NM/M
	TIER 1 (BLUE, 100 SETS)	
1	Randy Johnson	4.00
6	Carlos Lee	2.00
11	Chipper Jones	5.00
18	Nomar Garciaparra	5.00
21	Jeff Bagwell	4.00
28	Barry Bonds	7.50
	TIER 2 (RED, 75 SETS)	
2	Greg Maddux	7.50
7	Gabe Kapler	2.00
13	Manny Ramirez	6.00
16	Ken Griffey Jr.	10.00
19	Frank Thomas	6.00
30	Ivan Rodriguez	5.00
	TIER 3 (GREEN, 50 SETS)	
3	Pedro Martinez	12.50
8	Carlos Beltran	6.00
15	Mark McGwire	20.00
20	Larry Walker	2.00
25	Cal Ripken Jr.	30.00
26	Derek Jeter	30.00
	TIER 4 (PURPLE, 25 SETS)	
4	Kevin Brown	7.50
9	J.D. Drew	15.00
12	Sammy Sosa	25.00
17	Jose Canseco	20.00
23	Tony Gwynn	25.00
29	Alex Rodriguez	35.00

1999 PACIFIC PARAMOUNT

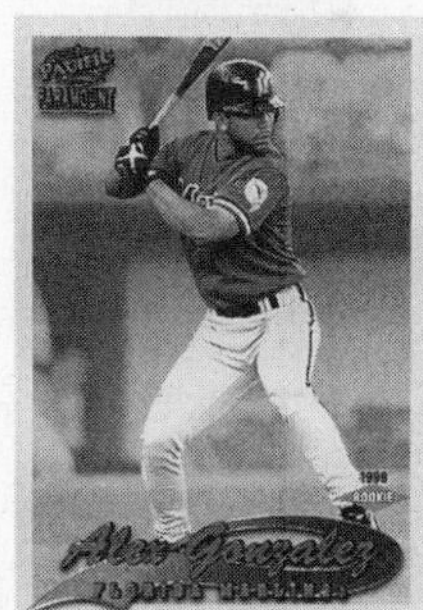

		NM/M
Complete Set (250):		25.00
Common Player:		.10
Copper (1:1H):		2X
Red (1:1R):		2X
Gold (1:1R):		2X
Platinum Blue (1:73):		4X
Holographic Gold (199):		10X
Holographic Silver (99 Sets):		15X
Opening Day (74):		15X
Pack (6):		1.00
Wax Box (36):		25.00
1	Garret Anderson	.10
2	Gary DiSarcina	.10
3	Jim Edmonds	.10
4	Darin Erstad	.25
5	Chuck Finley	.10
6	Troy Glaus	.75
7	Troy Percival	.10
8	Tim Salmon	.10
9	Mo Vaughn	.10
10	Tony Batista	.10
11	Jay Bell	.10
12	Andy Benes	.10
13	Steve Finley	.10
14	Luis Gonzalez	.10
15	Randy Johnson	.75
16	Travis Lee	.10
17	Todd Stottlemyre	.10
18	Matt Williams	.10
19	David Dellucci	.10
20	Bret Boone	.10
21	Andres Galarraga	.10
22	Tom Glavine	.35
23	Andruw Jones	.75
24	Chipper Jones	1.50
25	Brian Jordan	.10
26	Ryan Klesko	.10
27	Javy Lopez	.10
28	Greg Maddux	1.50
29	John Smoltz	.10
30	Brady Anderson	.10
31	Albert Belle	.10
32	Will Clark	.10
33	Delino DeShields	.10
34	Charles Johnson	.10
35	Mike Mussina	.40
36	Cal Ripken Jr.	3.00
37	B.J. Surhoff	.10
38	Nomar Garciaparra	1.50
39	Reggie Jefferson	.10
40	Darren Lewis	.10
41	Pedro Martinez	.75
42	Troy O'Leary	.10
43	Jose Offerman	.10
44	Donnie Sadler	.10
45	John Valentin	.10
46	Rod Beck	.10
47	Gary Gaetti	.10
48	Mark Grace	.10
49	Lance Johnson	.10
50	Mickey Morandini	.10
51	Henry Rodriguez	.10
52	Sammy Sosa	1.50
53	Kerry Wood	.40
54	Mike Caruso	.10
55	Ray Durham	.10
56	Paul Konerko	.20
57	Jaime Navarro	.10
58	Greg Norton	.10
59	Magglio Ordonez	.30
60	Frank Thomas	.75
61	Aaron Boone	.10
62	Mike Cameron	.10
63	Barry Larkin	.10
64	Hal Morris	.10
65	Pokey Reese	.10
66	Brett Tomko	.10
67	Greg Vaughn	.10
68	Dmitri Young	.10
69	Roberto Alomar	.25
70	Sandy Alomar Jr.	.10
71	Bartolo Colon	.10
72	Travis Fryman	.10
73	David Justice	.10
74	Kenny Lofton	.10
75	Manny Ramirez	.75
76	Richie Sexson	.10
77	Jim Thome	.65
78	Omar Vizquel	.10
79	Dante Bichette	.10
80	Vinny Castilla	.10
81	Darryl Hamilton	.10
82	Todd Helton	.75
83	Darryl Kile	.10
84	Mike Lansing	.10
85	Neifi Perez	.10
86	Larry Walker	.10
87	Tony Clark	.10
88	Damion Easley	.10
89	Bob Higginson	.10
90	Brian Hunter	.10
91	Dean Palmer	.10
92	Justin Thompson	.10
93	Todd Dunwoody	.10
94	Cliff Floyd	.10
95	Alex Gonzalez	.10
96	Livan Hernandez	.10
97	Mark Kotsay	.10
98	Derrek Lee	.60
99	Kevin Orie	.10
100	Moises Alou	.10
101	Jeff Bagwell	.75
102	Derek Bell	.10
103	Craig Biggio	.10
104	Ken Caminiti	.10
105	Ricky Gutierrez	.10
106	Richard Hidalgo	.10
107	Billy Wagner	.10
108	Jeff Conine	.10
109	Johnny Damon	.35
110	Carlos Febles	.10
111	Jeremy Giambi	.10
112	Jeff King	.10
113	Jeff Montgomery	.10
114	Joe Randa	.10
115	Kevin Brown	.10
116	Mark Grudzielanek	.10
117	Todd Hundley	.10

118 Eric Karros .10
119 Raul Mondesi .10
120 Chan Ho Park .10
121 Gary Sheffield .40
122 Devon White .10
123 Eric Young .10
124 Jeromy Burnitz .10
125 Jeff Cirillo .10
126 Marquis Grissom .10
127 Geoff Jenkins .10
128 Dave Nilsson .10
129 Jose Valentin .10
130 Fernando Vina .10
131 Rick Aguilera .10
132 Ron Coomer .10
133 Marty Cordova .10
134 Matt Lawton .10
135 David Ortiz .50
136 Brad Radke .10
137 Terry Steinbach .10
138 Javier Valentin .10
139 Todd Walker .10
140 Orlando Cabrera .10
141 Brad Fullmer .10
142 Vladimir Guerrero .75
143 Wilton Guerrero .10
144 Carl Pavano .10
145 Ugueth Urbina .10
146 Rondell White .10
147 Chris Widger .10
148 Edgardo Alfonzo .10
149 Bobby Bonilla .10
150 Rickey Henderson .75
151 Brian McRae .10
152 Hideo Nomo .40
153 John Olerud .10
154 Rey Ordonez .10
155 Mike Piazza 1.75
156 Robin Ventura .10
157 Masato Yoshii .10
158 Roger Clemens 1.75
159 David Cone .10
160 Orlando Hernandez .10
161 Hideki Irabu .10
162 Derek Jeter 3.00
163 Chuck Knoblauch .10
164 Tino Martinez .10
165 Paul O'Neill .10
166 Darryl Strawberry .10
167 Bernie Williams .10
168 Eric Chavez .20
169 Ryan Christenson .10
170 Jason Giambi .50
171 Ben Grieve .10
172 Tony Phillips .10
173 Tim Raines .10
174 Scott Spiezio .10
175 Miguel Tejada .20
176 Bobby Abreu .20
177 Rico Brogna .10
178 Ron Gant .10
179 Doug Glanville .10
180 Desi Relaford .10
181 Scott Rolen .65
182 Curt Schilling .35
183 Brant Brown .10
184 Brian Giles .10
185 Jose Guillen .10
186 Jason Kendall .10
187 Al Martin .10
188 Ed Sprague .10
189 Kevin Young .10
190 Eric Davis .10
191 J.D. Drew .40
192 Ray Lankford .10
193 Eli Marrero .10
194 Mark McGwire 2.50
195 Edgar Renteria .10
196 Fernando Tatis .10
197 Andy Ashby .10
198 Tony Gwynn 1.50
199 Carlos Hernandez .10
200 Trevor Hoffman .10
201 Wally Joyner .10
202 Jim Leyritz .10
203 Ruben Rivera .10
204 Matt Clement .10
205 Quilvio Veras .10
206 Rich Aurilia .10
207 Marvin Benard .10
208 Barry Bonds 3.00
209 Ellis Burks .10
210 Jeff Kent .10
211 Bill Mueller .10
212 Robb Nen .10
213 J.T. Snow .10
214 Jay Buhner .10
215 Jeff Fassero .10
216 Ken Griffey Jr. 2.00
217 Carlos Guillen .10
218 Butch Huskey .10
219 Edgar Martinez .10
220 Alex Rodriguez 2.50
221 David Segui .10
222 Dan Wilson .10
223 Rolando Arrojo .10
224 Wade Boggs 1.50
225 Jose Canseco .50
226 Roberto Hernandez .10
227 Dave Martinez .10
228 Quinton McCracken .10
229 Fred McGriff .10
230 Kevin Stocker .10
231 Randy Winn .10
232 Royce Clayton .10
233 Juan Gonzalez .40
234 Tom Goodwin .10
235 Rusty Greer .10
236 Rick Helling .10
237 Rafael Palmeiro .65
238 Ivan Rodriguez .65
239 Aaron Sele .10
240 John Wetteland .10
241 Todd Zeile .10
242 Jose Cruz Jr. .10
243 Carlos Delgado .50
244 Tony Fernandez .10
245 Cecil Fielder .10
246 Alex Gonzalez .10
247 Shawn Green .35
248 Roy Halladay .10
249 Shannon Stewart .10
250 David Wells .10

Cooperstown Bound

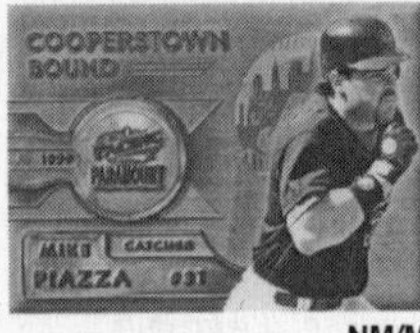

NM/M
Complete Set (10): 35.00
Common Player: 3.00
Inserted 1:361
1 Greg Maddux 4.00
2 Cal Ripken Jr. 10.00
3 Nomar Garciaparra 4.00
4 Sammy Sosa 4.00
5 Frank Thomas 3.00
6 Mike Piazza 5.00
7 Mark McGwire 10.00
8 Tony Gwynn 4.00
9 Ken Griffey Jr. 6.00
10 Alex Rodriguez 8.00

Fielder's Choice

NM/M
Complete Set (20): 60.00
Common Player: 2.50
Inserted 1:73
1 Chipper Jones 5.00
2 Greg Maddux 5.00
3 Cal Ripken Jr. 10.00
4 Nomar Garciaparra 5.00
5 Sammy Sosa 5.00
6 Kerry Wood 3.00
7 Frank Thomas 4.00
8 Manny Ramirez 4.00
9 Todd Helton 4.00
10 Jeff Bagwell 4.00
11 Mike Piazza 5.50
12 Derek Jeter 10.00
13 Bernie Williams 2.50
14 J.D. Drew 3.00
15 Mark McGwire 7.50
16 Tony Gwynn 5.00
17 Ken Griffey Jr. 6.00
18 Alex Rodriguez 7.50
19 Juan Gonzalez 2.50
20 Ivan Rodriguez 3.50

Personal Bests

NM/M
Complete Set (36): 45.00
Common Player: .50
Inserted 1:37
1 Darin Erstad .65
2 Mo Vaughn .50
3 Travis Lee .50
4 Chipper Jones 3.00
5 Greg Maddux 3.00
6 Albert Belle .50
7 Cal Ripken Jr. 6.00
8 Nomar Garciaparra 3.00
9 Sammy Sosa 3.00
10 Kerry Wood 1.00
11 Frank Thomas 2.00
12 Greg Vaughn .50
13 Manny Ramirez 2.00
14 Todd Helton 2.00
15 Larry Walker .50
16 Jeff Bagwell 2.00
17 Craig Biggio .50
18 Raul Mondesi .50
19 Vladimir Guerrero 2.00
20 Hideo Nomo 1.00
21 Mike Piazza 3.50
22 Roger Clemens 3.50
23 Derek Jeter 6.00
24 Bernie Williams .50
25 Eric Chavez .75
26 Ben Grieve .50
27 Scott Rolen 1.50
28 J.D. Drew 1.25
29 Mark McGwire 4.50
30 Tony Gwynn 3.00
31 Barry Bonds 6.00
32 Ken Griffey Jr. 4.00
33 Alex Rodriguez 4.50
34 Jose Canseco 1.25
35 Juan Gonzalez 1.00
36 Ivan Rodriguez 1.50

Team Checklists

NM/M
Complete Set (30): 40.00
Common Player: .50
Inserted 2:37
1 Mo Vaughn .50
2 Travis Lee .50
3 Chipper Jones 3.00
4 Cal Ripken Jr. 6.00
5 Nomar Garciaparra 3.00
6 Sammy Sosa 3.00
7 Frank Thomas 2.50
8 Greg Vaughn .50
9 Manny Ramirez 2.50
10 Larry Walker .50
11 Damion Easley .50
12 Mark Kotsay .50
13 Jeff Bagwell 2.50
14 Jeremy Giambi .50
15 Raul Mondesi .50
16 Marquis Grissom .50
17 Brad Radke .50
18 Vladimir Guerrero 2.50
19 Mike Piazza 3.50
20 Roger Clemens 3.50
21 Ben Grieve .50
22 Scott Rolen 2.00
23 Brian Giles .50
24 Mark McGwire 5.00
25 Tony Gwynn 3.00
26 Barry Bonds 6.00
27 Ken Griffey Jr. 4.00
28 Jose Canseco 1.25
29 Juan Gonzalez 1.25
30 Jose Cruz Jr. .50

1999 PACIFIC PRISM

NM/M
Complete Set (150): 50.00
Common Player: .15
Red (2:25R): 3X
HoloGold (480 Sets): 3X
HoloPurple (320): 4X
HoloMirror (160): 8X
HoloBlue (80): 15X
Retail Pack (3): 1.00
Hobby Pack (5): 1.50
1 Garret Anderson .15
2 Jim Edmonds .15
3 Darin Erstad .30
4 Chuck Finley .15
5 Tim Salmon .15
6 Jay Bell .15
7 David Dellucci .15
8 Travis Lee .15
9 Matt Williams .15
10 Andres Galarraga .15
11 Tom Glavine .40
12 Andruw Jones 1.50
13 Chipper Jones 2.00
14 Ryan Klesko .15
15 Javy Lopez .15
16 Greg Maddux 2.00
17 Roberto Alomar .50
18 Ryan Minor .15
19 Mike Mussina .40
20 Rafael Palmeiro 1.25
21 Cal Ripken Jr. 4.00
22 Nomar Garciaparra 2.00
23 Pedro Martinez 1.50
24 John Valentin .15
25 Mo Vaughn .15
26 Tim Wakefield .15
27 Rod Beck .15
28 Mark Grace .15
29 Lance Johnson .15
30 Sammy Sosa 2.00
31 Kerry Wood .50
32 Albert Belle .15
33 Mike Caruso .15
34 Magglio Ordonez .30
35 Frank Thomas 1.50
36 Robin Ventura .15
37 Aaron Boone .15
38 Barry Larkin .15
39 Reggie Sanders .15
40 Brett Tomko .15
41 Sandy Alomar Jr. .15
42 Bartolo Colon .15
43 David Justice .15
44 Kenny Lofton .15
45 Manny Ramirez 1.50
46 Richie Sexson .15
47 Jim Thome 1.00
48 Omar Vizquel .15
49 Dante Bichette .15
50 Vinny Castilla .15
51 *Edgard Clemente* .15
52 Todd Helton 1.50
53 Quinton McCracken .15
54 Larry Walker .15
55 Tony Clark .15
56 Damion Easley .15
57 Luis Gonzalez .15
58 Bob Higginson .15
59 Brian Hunter .15
60 Cliff Floyd .15
61 Alex Gonzalez .15
62 Livan Hernandez .15

No.	Player	Price
63	Derrek Lee	.65
64	Edgar Renteria	.15
65	Moises Alou	.15
66	Jeff Bagwell	1.50
67	Derek Bell	.15
68	Craig Biggio	.15
69	Randy Johnson	1.50
70	Johnny Damon	.35
71	Jeff King	.15
72	Hal Morris	.15
73	Dean Palmer	.15
74	Eric Karros	.15
75	Raul Mondesi	.15
76	Chan Ho Park	.15
77	Gary Sheffield	.50
78	Jeromy Burnitz	.15
79	Jeff Cirillo	.15
80	Marquis Grissom	.15
81	Jose Valentin	.15
82	Fernando Vina	.15
83	Paul Molitor	1.50
84	Otis Nixon	.15
85	David Ortiz	.65
86	Todd Walker	.15
87	Vladimir Guerrero	1.50
88	Carl Pavano	.15
89	Fernando Seguignol	.15
90	Ugueth Urbina	.15
91	Carlos Baerga	.15
92	Bobby Bonilla	.15
93	Hideo Nomo	.75
94	John Olerud	.15
95	Rey Ordonez	.15
96	Mike Piazza	2.25
97	David Cone	.15
98	Orlando Hernandez	.15
99	Hideki Irabu	.15
100	Derek Jeter	4.00
101	Tino Martinez	.15
102	Bernie Williams	.15
103	Eric Chavez	.25
104	Jason Giambi	1.00
105	Ben Grieve	.15
106	Rickey Henderson	1.50
107	Bob Abreu	.25
108	Doug Glanville	.15
109	Scott Rolen	1.00
110	Curt Schilling	.40
111	Emil Brown	.15
112	Jose Guillen	.15
113	Jason Kendall	.15
114	Al Martin	.15
115	Aramis Ramirez	.15
116	Kevin Young	.15
117	J.D. Drew	.75
118	Ron Gant	.15
119	Brian Jordan	.15
120	Eli Marrero	.15
121	Mark McGwire	3.00
122	Kevin Brown	.15
123	Tony Gwynn	2.00
124	Trevor Hoffman	.15
125	Wally Joyner	.15
126	Greg Vaughn	.15
127	Barry Bonds	4.00
128	Ellis Burks	.15
129	Jeff Kent	.15
130	Robb Nen	.15
131	J.T. Snow	.15
132	Jay Buhner	.15
133	Ken Griffey Jr.	2.50
134	Edgar Martinez	.15
135	Alex Rodriguez	3.00
136	David Segui	.15
137	Rolando Arrojo	.15
138	Wade Boggs	2.00
139	Aaron Ledesma	.15
140	Fred McGriff	.15
141	Will Clark	.15
142	Juan Gonzalez	.75
143	Rusty Greer	.15
144	Ivan Rodriguez	1.25
145	Aaron Sele	.15
146	Jose Canseco	.40
147	Roger Clemens	2.25
148	Jose Cruz Jr.	.15
149	Carlos Delgado	.50
150	Alex Gonzalez	.15

Ahead of the Game

		NM/M
Complete Set (20):		40.00
Common Player:		1.00
Inserted 1:49		
1	Darin Erstad	1.25
2	Travis Lee	1.00
3	Chipper Jones	3.00
4	Cal Ripken Jr.	6.00
5	Nomar Garciaparra	3.00
6	Sammy Sosa	3.00
7	Kerry Wood	1.25
8	Frank Thomas	2.00
9	Manny Ramirez	2.00
10	Todd Helton	2.00
11	Jeff Bagwell	2.00
12	Mike Piazza	3.50
13	Derek Jeter	6.00
14	Bernie Williams	1.00
15	J.D. Drew	1.25
16	Mark McGwire	5.00
17	Tony Gwynn	3.00
18	Ken Griffey Jr.	4.00
19	Alex Rodriguez	5.00
20	Ivan Rodriguez	1.50

Diamond Glory

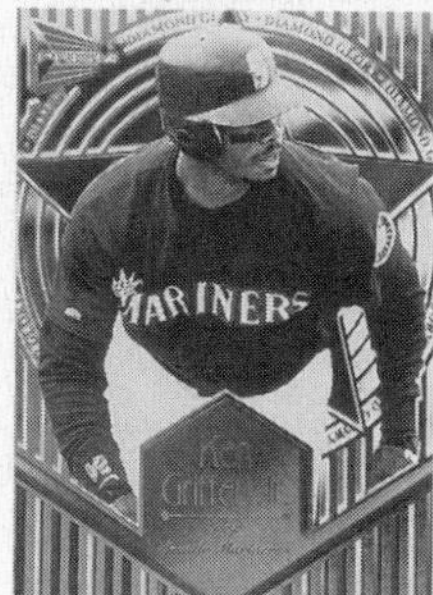

		NM/M
Complete Set (20):		25.00
Common Player:		.60
Inserted 2:25		
1	Darin Erstad	.60
2	Travis Lee	.60
3	Chipper Jones	2.00
4	Greg Maddux	2.00
5	Cal Ripken Jr.	3.50
6	Nomar Garciaparra	2.00
7	Sammy Sosa	2.00
8	Kerry Wood	.75
9	Frank Thomas	1.50
10	Todd Helton	1.50
11	Jeff Bagwell	1.50
12	Mike Piazza	2.25
13	Derek Jeter	3.50
14	Bernie Williams	.60
15	J.D. Drew	.75
16	Mark McGwire	3.00
17	Tony Gwynn	2.00
18	Ken Griffey Jr.	2.50
19	Alex Rodriguez	3.00
20	Juan Gonzalez	.75

Ballpark Legends

		NM/M
Complete Set (10):		40.00
Common Player:		2.50
Inserted 1:193		
1	Cal Ripken Jr.	10.00
2	Nomar Garciaparra	5.00
3	Frank Thomas	4.00
4	Ken Griffey Jr.	6.00
5	Alex Rodriguez	7.50
6	Greg Maddux	5.00
7	Sammy Sosa	5.00
8	Kerry Wood	2.50
9	Mark McGwire	7.50
10	Tony Gwynn	5.00

Epic Performers

		NM/M
Complete Set (10):		60.00
Common Player:		4.00
Inserted 1:97 H		
1	Cal Ripken Jr.	15.00
2	Nomar Garciaparra	7.50
3	Frank Thomas	6.00
4	Ken Griffey Jr.	10.00
5	Alex Rodriguez	12.50
6	Greg Maddux	7.50
7	Sammy Sosa	7.50
8	Kerry Wood	4.00
9	Mark McGwire	12.50
10	Tony Gwynn	7.50

1999 PACIFIC PRIVATE STOCK

		NM/M
Complete Set (150):		25.00
Common Player:		.10
Pack (6):		1.50
Wax Box (24):		20.00
Wax Box (36):		25.00
1	Jeff Bagwell	1.00
2	Roger Clemens	1.75
3	J.D. Drew	.60
4	Nomar Garciaparra	1.50
5	Juan Gonzalez	.50
6	Ken Griffey Jr.	2.00
7	Tony Gwynn	1.50
8	Derek Jeter	3.00
9	Chipper Jones	1.50
10	Travis Lee	.10
11	Greg Maddux	1.50
12	Mark McGwire	2.50
13	Mike Piazza	1.75
14	Manny Ramirez	1.00
15	Cal Ripken Jr.	3.00
16	Alex Rodriguez	2.50
17	Ivan Rodriguez	.75
18	Sammy Sosa	1.50
19	Frank Thomas	1.00
20	Kerry Wood	.40
21	Roberto Alomar	.25
22	Moises Alou	.10
23	Albert Belle	.10
24	Craig Biggio	.10
25	Wade Boggs	1.50
26	Barry Bonds	3.00
27	Jose Canseco	.50
28	Jim Edmonds	.10
29	Darin Erstad	.25
30	Andres Galarraga	.10
31	Tom Glavine	.35
32	Ben Grieve	.10
33	Vladimir Guerrero	1.00
34	Wilton Guerrero	.10
35	Todd Helton	1.00
36	Andruw Jones	1.00
37	Ryan Klesko	.10
38	Kenny Lofton	.10
39	Javy Lopez	.10
40	Pedro Martinez	1.00
41	Paul Molitor	1.00
42	Raul Mondesi	.10
43	Rafael Palmeiro	.75
44	Tim Salmon	.10
45	Jim Thome	.75
46	Mo Vaughn	.10
47	Larry Walker	.10
48	David Wells	.10
49	Bernie Williams	.10
50	Jaret Wright	.10
51	Bobby Abreu	.15
52	Garret Anderson	.10
53	Rolando Arrojo	.10
54	Tony Batista	.10
55	Rod Beck	.10
56	Derek Bell	.10
57	Marvin Benard	.10
58	Dave Berg	.10
59	Dante Bichette	.10
60	Aaron Boone	.10
61	Bret Boone	.10
62	Scott Brosius	.10
63	Brant Brown	.10
64	Kevin Brown	.10
65	Jeromy Burnitz	.10
66	Ken Caminiti	.10
67	Mike Caruso	.10
68	Sean Casey	.20
69	Vinny Castilla	.10
70	Eric Chavez	.20
71	Ryan Christenson	.10
72	Jeff Cirillo	.10
73	Tony Clark	.10
74	Will Clark	.10
75	*Edgard Clemente*	.10
76	David Cone	.10
77	Marty Cordova	.10
78	Jose Cruz Jr.	.10
79	Eric Davis	.10
80	Carlos Delgado	.50
81	David Dellucci	.10
82	Delino DeShields	.10
83	Gary DiSarcina	.10
84	Damion Easley	.10
85	Dennis Eckersley	.65
86	Cliff Floyd	.10
87	Jason Giambi	.65
88	Doug Glanville	.10
89	Alex Gonzalez	.10
90	Mark Grace	.10
91	Rusty Greer	.10
92	Jose Guillen	.10
93	Carlos Guillen	.10
94	Jeffrey Hammonds	.10
95	Rick Helling	.10
96	Bob Henley	.10
97	Livan Hernandez	.10
98	Orlando Hernandez	.10
99	Bob Higginson	.10
100	Trevor Hoffman	.10
101	Randy Johnson	1.00
102	Brian Jordan	.10
103	Wally Joyner	.10
104	Eric Karros	.10
105	Jason Kendall	.10
106	Jeff Kent	.10
107	Jeff King	.10
108	Mark Kotsay	.10
109	Ray Lankford	.10
110	Barry Larkin	.10
111	Mark Loretta	.10
112	Edgar Martinez	.10
113	Tino Martinez	.10
114	Quinton McCracken	.10
115	Fred McGriff	.10
116	Ryan Minor	.10
117	Hal Morris	.10
118	Bill Mueller	.10
119	Mike Mussina	.40
120	Dave Nilsson	.10
121	Otis Nixon	.10
122	Hideo Nomo	.50
123	Paul O'Neill	.10
124	Jose Offerman	.10
125	John Olerud	.10
126	Rey Ordonez	.10
127	David Ortiz	.50
128	Dean Palmer	.10
129	Chan Ho Park	.10
130	Aramis Ramirez	.10
131	Edgar Renteria	.10
132	Armando Rios	.10
133	Henry Rodriguez	.10
134	Scott Rolen	.75
135	Curt Schilling	.35
136	David Segui	.10
137	Richie Sexson	.10
138	Gary Sheffield	.45
139	John Smoltz	.10
140	Matt Stairs	.10
141	Justin Thompson	.10
142	Greg Vaughn	.10
143	Omar Vizquel	.10
144	Tim Wakefield	.10
145	Todd Walker	.10
146	Devon White	.10
147	Rondell White	.10
148	Matt Williams	.10
149	*Enrique Wilson*	.25
150	Kevin Young	.10

Exclusive Series

		NM/M
Complete Set (20):		50.00
Common Player:		1.00
Production:		299 sets H
1	Jeff Bagwell	2.00
2	Roger Clemens	3.50
3	J.D. Drew	1.25
4	Nomar Garciaparra	3.00
5	Juan Gonzalez	1.25
6	Ken Griffey Jr.	4.00
7	Tony Gwynn	3.00
8	Derek Jeter	6.00
9	Chipper Jones	3.00

10	Travis Lee	1.00
11	Greg Maddux	3.00
12	Mark McGwire	5.00
13	Mike Piazza	3.50
14	Manny Ramirez	2.00
15	Cal Ripken Jr.	6.00
16	Alex Rodriguez	5.00
17	Ivan Rodriguez	1.50
18	Sammy Sosa	3.00
19	Frank Thomas	2.00
20	Kerry Wood	1.25

Vintage Series

		NM/M
Complete Set (50):		375.00
Common Player:		2.50
Production:		99 sets
1	Jeff Bagwell	12.50
2	Roger Clemens	17.50
3	J.D. Drew	7.50
4	Nomar Garciaparra	15.00
5	Juan Gonzalez	6.00
6	Ken Griffey Jr.	20.00
7	Tony Gwynn	15.00
8	Derek Jeter	30.00
9	Chipper Jones	15.00
10	Travis Lee	2.50
11	Greg Maddux	15.00
12	Mark McGwire	25.00
13	Mike Piazza	17.50
14	Manny Ramirez	12.50
15	Cal Ripken Jr.	30.00
16	Alex Rodriguez	25.00
17	Ivan Rodriguez	10.00
18	Sammy Sosa	15.00
19	Frank Thomas	12.50
20	Kerry Wood	6.00
21	Roberto Alomar	3.50
22	Moises Alou	2.50
23	Albert Belle	2.50
24	Craig Biggio	2.50
25	Wade Boggs	15.00
26	Barry Bonds	30.00
27	Jose Canseco	5.00
28	Jim Edmonds	2.50
29	Darin Erstad	3.50
30	Andres Galarraga	2.50
31	Tom Glavine	5.00
32	Ben Grieve	2.50
33	Vladimir Guerrero	12.50
34	Wilton Guerrero	2.50
35	Todd Helton	12.50
36	Andruw Jones	12.50
37	Ryan Klesko	2.50
38	Kenny Lofton	2.50
39	Javy Lopez	2.50
40	Pedro Martinez	12.50
41	Paul Molitor	12.50
42	Raul Mondesi	2.50
43	Rafael Palmeiro	10.00
44	Tim Salmon	2.50
45	Jim Thome	10.00
46	Mo Vaughn	2.50
47	Larry Walker	2.50
48	David Wells	2.50
49	Bernie Williams	2.50
50	Jaret Wright	2.50

Platinum Series

		NM/M
Complete Set (50):		160.00
Common Player:		.75
Production 199 sets		
1	Jeff Bagwell	5.00
2	Roger Clemens	6.50
3	J.D. Drew	3.00
4	Nomar Garciaparra	6.00
5	Juan Gonzalez	2.50
6	Ken Griffey Jr.	8.00
7	Tony Gwynn	6.00
8	Derek Jeter	12.00
9	Chipper Jones	6.00
10	Travis Lee	.75
11	Greg Maddux	6.00
12	Mark McGwire	10.00
13	Mike Piazza	6.50
14	Manny Ramirez	5.00
15	Cal Ripken Jr.	12.00
16	Alex Rodriguez	10.00
17	Ivan Rodriguez	4.00
18	Sammy Sosa	6.00
19	Frank Thomas	5.00
20	Kerry Wood	2.00
21	Roberto Alomar	1.50
22	Moises Alou	.75
23	Albert Belle	.75
24	Craig Biggio	.75
25	Wade Boggs	6.00
26	Barry Bonds	12.00
27	Jose Canseco	3.00
28	Jim Edmonds	.75
29	Darin Erstad	1.50
30	Andres Galarraga	.75
31	Tom Glavine	2.00
32	Ben Grieve	.75
33	Vladimir Guerrero	5.00
34	Wilton Guerrero	.75
35	Todd Helton	5.00
36	Andruw Jones	5.00
37	Ryan Klesko	.75
38	Kenny Lofton	.75
39	Javy Lopez	.75
40	Pedro Martinez	5.00
41	Paul Molitor	5.00
42	Raul Mondesi	.75
43	Rafael Palmeiro	4.00
44	Tim Salmon	.75
45	Jim Thome	3.50
46	Mo Vaughn	.75
47	Larry Walker	.75
48	David Wells	.75
49	Bernie Williams	.75
50	Jaret Wright	.75

Preferred Series

		NM/M
Complete Set (20):		37.50
Common Player:		.60
Production:		399 sets
1	Jeff Bagwell	1.50
2	Roger Clemens	2.25
3	J.D. Drew	.75
4	Nomar Garciaparra	2.00
5	Juan Gonzalez	.75
6	Ken Griffey Jr.	2.50
7	Tony Gwynn	2.00
8	Derek Jeter	5.00
9	Chipper Jones	2.00
10	Travis Lee	.60
11	Greg Maddux	2.00
12	Mark McGwire	3.50
13	Mike Piazza	2.25
14	Manny Ramirez	1.50
15	Cal Ripken Jr.	5.00
16	Alex Rodriguez	3.50
17	Ivan Rodriguez	1.25
18	Sammy Sosa	2.00
19	Frank Thomas	1.50
20	Kerry Wood	.75

Homerun History

		NM/M
Complete Set (22):		25.00
Common McGwire:		1.50
Common Sosa:		1.00
Inserted 1:12		
1	Mark McGwire Home Run #61	3.00
2	Sammy Sosa Home Run #59	1.00
3	Mark McGwire Home Run #62	1.50
4	Sammy Sosa Home Run #60	1.00
5	Mark McGwire Home Run #63	1.50
6	Sammy Sosa Home Run #61	3.00
7	Mark McGwire Home Run #64	1.50
8	Sammy Sosa Home Run #62	1.00
9	Mark McGwire Home Run #65	1.50
10	Sammy Sosa Home Run #63	1.00
11	Mark McGwire Home Run #67	1.50
12	Sammy Sosa Home Run #64	1.00
13	Mark McGwire Home Run #68	1.50
14	Sammy Sosa Home Run #65	1.00
15	Mark McGwire Home Run #70	5.00
16	Sammy Sosa Home Run #66	3.00
17	Mark McGwire A Season of Celebration	1.50
18	Sammy Sosa A Season of Celebration	1.00
19	Sammy Sosa, Mark McGwire Awesome Power	1.50
20	Mark McGwire, Sammy Sosa Transcending Sports	1.50
21	Mark McGwire Crown Die-Cut	1.50
22	Cal Ripken Jr. Crown Die-Cut	1.00

PS-206

		NM/M
Complete Set (150):		20.00
Common Player:		.15
Inserted 1:1		
Red Parallels:		4X
Inserted 1:25		
1	Jeff Bagwell	.75
2	Roger Clemens	1.25
3	J.D. Drew	.50
4	Nomar Garciaparra	1.00
5	Juan Gonzalez	.40
6	Ken Griffey Jr.	1.50
7	Tony Gwynn	1.00
8	Derek Jeter	3.00
9	Chipper Jones	1.00
10	Travis Lee	.15
11	Greg Maddux	1.00
12	Mark McGwire	2.00
13	Mike Piazza	1.25
14	Manny Ramirez	.75
15	Cal Ripken Jr.	3.00
16	Alex Rodriguez	2.00
17	Ivan Rodriguez	.65
18	Sammy Sosa	1.00
19	Frank Thomas	.75
20	Kerry Wood	.40
21	Roberto Alomar	.30
22	Moises Alou	.15
23	Albert Belle	.15
24	Craig Biggio	.15
25	Wade Boggs	1.00
26	Barry Bonds	3.00
27	Jose Canseco	.50
28	Jim Edmonds	.15
29	Darin Erstad	.30
30	Andres Galarraga	.15
31	Tom Glavine	.35
32	Ben Grieve	.15
33	Vladimir Guerrero	.75
34	Wilton Guerrero	.15
35	Todd Helton	.75
36	Andruw Jones	.75
37	Ryan Klesko	.15
38	Kenny Lofton	.15
39	Javy Lopez	.15
40	Pedro Martinez	.75
41	Paul Molitor	.75
42	Raul Mondesi	.15
43	Rafael Palmeiro	.65
44	Tim Salmon	.15
45	Jim Thome	.65
46	Mo Vaughn	.15
47	Larry Walker	.15
48	David Wells	.15
49	Bernie Williams	.15
50	Jaret Wright	.15
51	Bobby Abreu	.15
52	Garret Anderson	.15
53	Rolando Arrojo	.15
54	Tony Batista	.15
55	Rod Beck	.15
56	Derek Bell	.15
57	Marvin Benard	.15
58	Dave Berg	.15
59	Dante Bichette	.15
60	Aaron Boone	.15
61	Bret Boone	.15
62	Scott Brosius	.15
63	Brant Brown	.15
64	Kevin Brown	.15
65	Jeromy Burnitz	.15
66	Ken Caminiti	.15
67	Mike Caruso	.15
68	Sean Casey	.25
69	Vinny Castilla	.15
70	Eric Chavez	.25
71	Ryan Christenson	.15
72	Jeff Cirillo	.15
73	Tony Clark	.15
74	Will Clark	.15
75	Edgard Clemente	.15
76	David Cone	.15
77	Marty Cordova	.15
78	Jose Cruz Jr.	.15
79	Eric Davis	.15
80	Carlos Delgado	.60
81	David Dellucci	.15
82	Delino DeShields	.15
83	Gary DiSarcina	.15
84	Damion Easley	.15
85	Dennis Eckersley	.65
86	Cliff Floyd	.15
87	Jason Giambi	.60
88	Doug Glanville	.15
89	Alex Gonzalez	.15
90	Mark Grace	.15
91	Rusty Greer	.15
92	Jose Guillen	.15
93	Carlos Guillen	.15
94	Jeffrey Hammonds	.15
95	Rick Helling	.15
96	Bob Henley	.15
97	Livan Hernandez	.15
98	Orlando Hernandez	.15
99	Bob Higginson	.15
100	Trevor Hoffman	.15
101	Randy Johnson	.75
102	Brian Jordan	.15
103	Wally Joyner	.15
104	Eric Karros	.15
105	Jason Kendall	.15
106	Jeff Kent	.15
107	Jeff King	.15
108	Mark Kotsay	.15
109	Ray Lankford	.15
110	Barry Larkin	.15
111	Mark Loretta	.15
112	Edgar Martinez	.15
113	Tino Martinez	.15
114	Quinton McCracken	.15
115	Fred McGriff	.15
116	Ryan Minor	.15
117	Hal Morris	.15
118	Bill Mueller	.15
119	Mike Mussina	.40
120	Dave Nilsson	.15
121	Otis Nixon	.15
122	Hideo Nomo	.40
123	Paul O'Neill	.15
124	Jose Offerman	.15
125	John Olerud	.15
126	Rey Ordonez	.15
127	David Ortiz	.50
128	Dean Palmer	.15
129	Chan Ho Park	.15
130	Aramis Ramirez	.15
131	Edgar Renteria	.15
132	Armando Rios	.15
133	Henry Rodriguez	.15
134	Scott Rolen	.60
135	Curt Schilling	.35
136	David Segui	.15
137	Richie Sexson	.15
138	Gary Sheffield	.50
139	John Smoltz	.15
140	Matt Stairs	.15
141	Justin Thompson	.15
142	Greg Vaughn	.15
143	Omar Vizquel	.15
144	Tim Wakefield	.15
145	Todd Walker	.15
146	Devon White	.15
147	Rondell White	.15
148	Matt Williams	.15
149	Enrique Wilson	.15
150	Kevin Young	.15

1999 PACIFIC REVOLUTION

	NM/M
Complete Set (150):	60.00
Common Player:	.15
Red (299 R):	2X
SP:	1.5X
Premiere Date (49 H):	12X
SP:	6X
Wax Pack (3):	2.00
Wax Box (24):	35.00

#	Player	Price
1	Jim Edmonds	.15
2	Darin Erstad	.30
3	Troy Glaus	1.00
4	Tim Salmon	.15
5	Mo Vaughn	.15
6	Steve Finley	.15
7	Luis Gonzalez	.15
8	Randy Johnson	1.00
9	Travis Lee	.15
10	Matt Williams	.15
11	Andruw Jones	1.00
12	Chipper Jones	1.50
13	Brian Jordan	.15
14	Javy Lopez	.15
15	Greg Maddux	1.50
16	*Kevin McGlinchy* (SP)	1.00
17	John Smoltz	.15
18	Brady Anderson	.15
19	Albert Belle	.15
20	Will Clark	.15
21	*Willis Otanez* (SP)	.25
22	*Calvin Pickering* (SP)	.25
23	Cal Ripken Jr.	4.00
24	Nomar Garciaparra	1.50
25	Pedro Martinez	1.00
26	Troy O'Leary	.15
27	Jose Offerman	.15
28	Mark Grace	.15
29	Mickey Morandini	.15
30	Henry Rodriguez	.15
31	Sammy Sosa	1.50
32	Ray Durham	.15
33	Carlos Lee (SP)	.50
34	*Jeff Liefer* (SP)	.35
35	Magglio Ordonez	.30
36	Frank Thomas	1.00
37	Mike Cameron	.15
38	Sean Casey	.35
39	Barry Larkin	.15
40	Greg Vaughn	.15
41	Roberto Alomar	.35
42	Sandy Alomar Jr.	.15
43	David Justice	.15
44	Kenny Lofton	.15
45	Manny Ramirez	1.00
46	Richie Sexson	.15
47	Jim Thome	.65
48	Dante Bichette	.15
49	Vinny Castilla	.15
50	Darryl Hamilton	.15
51	Todd Helton	1.00
52	Larry Walker	.15
53	Tony Clark	.15
54	Damion Easley	.15
55	Bob Higginson	.15
56	Gabe Kapler (SP)	.25
57	*Alex Gonzalez* (SP)	.35
58	Mark Kotsay	.15
59	Kevin Orie	.15
60	Preston Wilson (SP)	1.00
61	Jeff Bagwell	1.00
62	Derek Bell	.15
63	Craig Biggio	.15
64	Ken Caminiti	.15
65	Carlos Beltran (SP)	.65
66	Johnny Damon	.35
67	Jermaine Dye	.15
68	Carlos Febles (SP)	.35
69	Kevin Brown	.15
70	Todd Hundley	.15
71	Eric Karros	.15
72	Raul Mondesi	.15
73	Gary Sheffield	.45
74	Jeromy Burnitz	.15
75	Jeff Cirillo	.15
76	Marquis Grissom	.15
77	Fernando Vina	.15
78	*Chad Allen* (SP)	.25
79	*Corey Koskie* (SP)	1.50
80	*Doug Mientkiewicz* (SP)	1.00
81	Brad Radke	.15
82	Todd Walker	.15
83	*Michael Barrett* (SP)	.35
84	Vladimir Guerrero	1.00
85	Wilton Guerrero	.15
86	*Guillermo Mota* (SP)	.35
87	Rondell White	.15
88	Edgardo Alfonzo	.15
89	Rickey Henderson	1.00
90	John Olerud	.15
91	Mike Piazza	2.00
92	Robin Ventura	.15
93	Roger Clemens	2.00
94	Chili Davis	.15
95	Derek Jeter	4.00
96	Chuck Knoblauch	.15
97	Tino Martinez	.15
98	Paul O'Neill	.15
99	Bernie Williams	.15
100	Eric Chavez (SP)	.35
101	Jason Giambi	.65
102	Ben Grieve	.15
103	John Jaha	.15
104	*Olmedo Saenz* (SP)	.25
105	Bobby Abreu	.25
106	Doug Glanville	.15
107	Desi Relaford	.15
108	Scott Rolen	.75
109	Curt Schilling	.35
110	Brian Giles	.15
111	Jason Kendall	.15
112	Pat Meares	.15
113	Kevin Young	.15
114	J.D. Drew (SP)	1.00
115	Ray Lankford	.15
116	Eli Marrero	.15
117	*Joe McEwing* (SP)	.35
118	Mark McGwire	3.00
119	Fernando Tatis	.15
120	Tony Gwynn	1.50
121	Trevor Hoffman	.15
122	Wally Joyner	.15
123	Reggie Sanders	.15
124	Barry Bonds	4.00
125	Ellis Burks	.15
126	Jeff Kent	.15
127	*Ramon Martinez* (SP)	.25
128	*Joe Nathan* (SP)	.25
129	*Freddy Garcia* (SP)	1.00
130	Ken Griffey Jr.	2.50
131	Brian Hunter	.15
132	Edgar Martinez	.15
133	Alex Rodriguez	3.00
134	David Segui	.15
135	Wade Boggs	1.50
136	Jose Canseco	.45
137	Quinton McCracken	.15
138	Fred McGriff	.15
139	*Kelly Dransfeldt* (SP)	.25
140	Juan Gonzalez	.50
141	Rusty Greer	.15
142	Rafael Palmeiro	.75
143	Ivan Rodriguez	.75
144	Lee Stevens	.15
145	Jose Cruz Jr.	.15
146	Carlos Delgado	.60
147	Shawn Green	.50
148	*Roy Halladay* (SP)	1.50
149	Shannon Stewart	.15
150	*Kevin Witt* (SP)	.35

Shadow

	NM/M
Common Player:	4.00
Stars:	6X
SPs:	3X

(See 1999 Pacific Revolution for checklist and base card values.)

Diamond Legacy

	NM/M
Complete Set (36):	60.00
Common Player:	.50
Inserted 2:25	

#	Player	Price
1	Troy Glaus	2.00
2	Mo Vaughn	.50
3	Matt Williams	.50
4	Chipper Jones	3.00
5	Andruw Jones	2.00
6	Greg Maddux	3.00
7	Albert Belle	.50
8	Cal Ripken Jr.	6.00
9	Nomar Garciaparra	3.00
10	Sammy Sosa	3.00
11	Frank Thomas	2.00
12	Manny Ramirez	2.00
13	Todd Helton	2.00
14	Larry Walker	.50
15	Gabe Kapler	.50
16	Jeff Bagwell	2.00
17	Craig Biggio	.50
18	Raul Mondesi	.50
19	Vladimir Guerrero	2.00
20	Mike Piazza	3.50
21	Roger Clemens	3.50
22	Derek Jeter	6.00
23	Bernie Williams	.50
24	Ben Grieve	.50
25	Scott Rolen	1.75
26	J.D. Drew	1.50
27	Mark McGwire	5.00
28	Fernando Tatis	.50
29	Tony Gwynn	3.00
30	Barry Bonds	6.00
31	Ken Griffey Jr.	4.00
32	Alex Rodriguez	5.00
33	Jose Canseco	1.25
34	Juan Gonzalez	1.00
35	Ivan Rodriguez	1.75
36	Shawn Green	1.50

Foul Pole

	NM/M
Complete Set (20):	100.00
Common Player:	1.50
Inserted 1:49	

#	Player	Price
1	Chipper Jones	8.00
2	Andruw Jones	6.00
3	Cal Ripken Jr.	16.00
4	Nomar Garciaparra	8.00
5	Sammy Sosa	8.00
6	Frank Thomas	6.00
7	Manny Ramirez	6.00
8	Jeff Bagwell	6.00
9	Raul Mondesi	1.50
10	Vladimir Guerrero	6.00
11	Mike Piazza	9.00
12	Derek Jeter	16.00
13	Bernie Williams	1.50
14	Scott Rolen	5.00
15	J.D. Drew	3.00
16	Mark McGwire	12.00
17	Tony Gwynn	8.00
18	Ken Griffey Jr.	10.00
19	Alex Rodriguez	12.00
20	Juan Gonzalez	3.00

Icons

	NM/M
Complete Set (10):	50.00
Common Player:	4.00
Inserted 1:121	

#	Player	Price
1	Cal Ripken Jr.	10.00
2	Nomar Garciaparra	5.00
3	Sammy Sosa	5.00
4	Frank Thomas	4.00
5	Mike Piazza	6.50
6	Derek Jeter	10.00
7	Mark McGwire	8.00
8	Tony Gwynn	5.00
9	Ken Griffey Jr.	7.50
10	Alex Rodriguez	8.00

Thorn in the Side

	NM/M
Complete Set (20):	35.00
Common Player:	1.00
Inserted 1:25	

#	Player	Price
1	Mo Vaughn	1.00
2	Chipper Jones	3.00
3	Greg Maddux	3.00
4	Cal Ripken Jr.	6.00
5	Nomar Garciaparra	3.00
6	Sammy Sosa	3.00
7	Frank Thomas	2.25
8	Manny Ramirez	2.25
9	Jeff Bagwell	2.25
10	Mike Piazza	3.50
11	Derek Jeter	6.00
12	Bernie Williams	1.00
13	J.D. Drew	1.50
14	Mark McGwire	4.50
15	Tony Gwynn	3.00
16	Barry Bonds	6.00
17	Ken Griffey Jr.	4.00
18	Alex Rodriguez	4.50
19	Juan Gonzalez	1.50
20	Ivan Rodriguez	2.00

Tripleheader

	NM/M
Complete Set (30):	30.00
Common Player:	.25
Inserted 4:25 H	
Tier 1 (1-10)	
Production 99 sets H	
Tier 2 (11-20)	
Production 199 sets H	
Tier 3 (21-30)	
Production 299 sets H	

#	Player	Price
1	Greg Maddux	1.50
2	Cal Ripken Jr.	3.00
3	Nomar Garciaparra	1.50
4	Sammy Sosa	1.50
5	Frank Thomas	1.00
6	Mike Piazza	1.75
7	Mark McGwire	2.50
8	Tony Gwynn	1.50
9	Ken Griffey Jr.	2.00
10	Alex Rodriguez	2.50
11	Mo Vaughn	.25
12	Chipper Jones	1.50
13	Manny Ramirez	1.00
14	Larry Walker	.25
15	Jeff Bagwell	1.00
16	Vladimir Guerrero	1.00
17	Derek Jeter	3.00
18	J.D. Drew	.60
19	Barry Bonds	3.00
20	Juan Gonzalez	.50
21	Troy Glaus	1.00
22	Andruw Jones	1.00
23	Matt Williams	.25

24 Craig Biggio .25
25 Raul Mondesi .25
26 Roger Clemens 1.75
27 Bernie Williams .25
28 Scott Rolen .75
29 Jose Canseco .50
30 Ivan Rodriguez .75

2000 PACIFIC

	NM/M
Complete Set (500):	60.00
Common Player:	.10
Pack (12):	1.50
Wax Box (24):	25.00

1 Garret Anderson .15
2 Tim Belcher .10
3 Gary DiSarcina .10
4 Trent Durrington .10
5 Jim Edmonds .15
6a Darin Erstad (action) .35
6b Darin Erstad (portrait) .35
7 Chuck Finley .10
8 Troy Glaus .75
9 Todd Greene .10
10 Bret Hemphill .10
11 Ken Hill .10
12 Ramon Ortiz .10
13 Troy Percival .10
14 Mark Petkovsek .10
15 Tim Salmon .20
16a Mo Vaughn .15
16b Mo Vaughn (portrait) .15
17 Jay Bell .10
18 Omar Daal .10
19 Erubiel Durazo .10
20 Steve Finley .10
21 Bernard Gilkey .10
22 Luis Gonzalez .20
23 Randy Johnson .75
24 Byung-Hyun Kim .10
25 Travis Lee .10
26 Matt Mantei .10
27 Armando Reynoso .10
28 Rob Ryan .10
29 Kelly Stinnett .10
30 Todd Stottlemyre .10
31a Matt Williams (action) .15
31b Matt Williams (portrait) .15
32 Tony Womack .10
33 Bret Boone .10
34 Andres Galarraga .15
35 Tom Glavine .35
36 Ozzie Guillen .10
37a Andruw Jones (action) .75
37b Andruw Jones (portrait) .75
38a Chipper Jones (action) 1.00
38b Chipper Jones (portrait) 1.00
39 Brian Jordan .10
40 Ryan Klesko .15
41 Javy Lopez .15
42a Greg Maddux (action) 1.00
42b Greg Maddux (portrait) 1.00
43 Kevin Millwood .15
44 John Rocker .10
45 Randall Simon .10
46 John Smoltz .15
47 Gerald Williams .10
48 Brady Anderson .15
49a Albert Belle (action) .15
49b Albert Belle (portrait) .15
50 Mike Bordick .10
51 Will Clark .25
52 Jeff Conine .10
53 Delino DeShields .10
54 Jerry Hairston Jr. .10
55 Charles Johnson .10
56 Eugene Kingsale .10
57 Ryan Minor .10
58 Mike Mussina .35
59 Sidney Ponson .10
60a Cal Ripken Jr. (action) 2.50
60b Cal Ripken Jr. (portrait) 2.50
61 B.J. Surhoff .10
62 Mike Timlin .10
63 Rod Beck .10
64a Nomar Garciaparra (action) 1.50
64b Nomar Garciaparra (portrait) 1.50
65 Tom Gordon .10
66 Butch Huskey .10
67 Derek Lowe .10
68a Pedro Martinez (action) .75
68b Pedro Martinez (portrait) .75
69 Trot Nixon .10
70 Jose Offerman .10
71 Troy O'Leary .10
72 Pat Rapp .10
73 Donnie Sadler .10
74 Mike Stanley .10
75 John Valentin .10
76 Jason Varitek .10
77 Wilton Veras .15
78 Tim Wakefield .10
79 Rick Aguilera .10
80 Manny Alexander .10
81 Roosevelt Brown .10
82 Mark Grace .20
83 Glenallen Hill .10
84 Lance Johnson .10
85 Jon Lieber .10
86 Cole Liniak .10
87 Chad Meyers .10
88 Mickey Morandini .10
89 Jose Nieves .10
90 Henry Rodriguez .10
91a Sammy Sosa (action) 1.50
91b Sammy Sosa (portrait) 1.50
92 Kevin Tapani .10
93 Kerry Wood .50
94 Mike Caruso .10
95 Ray Durham .10
96 Brook Fordyce .10
97 Bobby Howry .10
98 Paul Konerko .25
99 Carlos Lee .10
100 Aaron Myette .10
101 Greg Norton .10
102 Magglio Ordonez .25
103 Jim Parque .10
104 Liu Rodriguez .10
105 Chris Singleton .10
106 Mike Sirotka .10
107a Frank Thomas (action) .75
107b Frank Thomas (portrait) .75
108 Kip Wells .10
109 Aaron Boone .10
110 Mike Cameron .10
111a Sean Casey (action) .20
111b Sean Casey (portrait) .20
112 Jeffrey Hammonds .10
113 Pete Harnisch .10
114a Barry Larkin (portrait) .15
114b Barry Larkin (portrait) .15
115 Jason LaRue .10
116 Denny Neagle .10
117 Pokey Reese .10
118 Scott Sullivan .10
119 Eddie Taubensee .10
120 Greg Vaughn .10
121 Scott Williamson .10
122 Dmitri Young .10
123a Roberto Alomar (action) .35
123b Roberto Alomar (portrait) .35
124 Sandy Alomar Jr. .10
125 Harold Baines .10
126 Russell Branyan .10
127 Dave Burba .10
128 Bartolo Colon .10
129 Travis Fryman .15
130 Mike Jackson .10
131 David Justice .15
132a Kenny Lofton (action) .15
132b Kenny Lofton (portrait) .15
133 Charles Nagy .10
134a Manny Ramirez (action) .75
134b Manny Ramirez (portrait) .75
135 Dave Roberts .10
136 Richie Sexson .15
137 Jim Thome .60
138 Omar Vizquel .15
139 Jaret Wright .10
140 Pedro Astacio .10
141 Dante Bichette .10
142 Brian Bohanon .10
143a Vinny Castilla (action) .10
143b Vinny Castilla (portrait) .10
144 Edgard Clemente .10
145 Derrick Gibson .10
146 Todd Helton .75
147 Darryl Kile .10
148 Mike Lansing .10
149 Kirt Manwaring .10
150 Neifi Perez .10
151 Ben Petrick .10
152 *Juan Sosa* .20
153 Dave Veres .10
154a Larry Walker (action) .15
154b Larry Walker (portrait) .15
155 Brad Ausmus .10
156 Dave Borkowski .10
157 Tony Clark .10
158 Francisco Cordero .10
159 Deivi Cruz .10
160 Damion Easley .10
161 Juan Encarnacion .10
162 Robert Fick .10
163 Bobby Higginson .10
164 Gabe Kapler .15
165 Brian Moehler .10
166 Dean Palmer .10
167 Luis Polonia .10
168 Justin Thompson .10
169 Jeff Weaver .10
170 Antonio Alfonseca .10
171 Bruce Aven .10
172 A.J. Burnett .15
173 Luis Castillo .10
174 Ramon Castro .10
175 Ryan Dempster .10
176 Alex Fernandez .10
177 Cliff Floyd .10
178 Amaury Garcia .10
179 Alex Gonzalez .10
180 Mark Kotsay .10
181 Mike Lowell .15
182 Brian Meadows .10
183 Kevin Orie .10
184 Julio Ramirez .10
185 Preston Wilson .15
186 Moises Alou .15
187a Jeff Bagwell (action) .75
187b Jeff Bagwell (portrait) .75
188 Glen Barker .10
189 Derek Bell .10
190a Craig Biggio (action) .15
190b Craig Biggio (portrait) .15
191 Ken Caminiti .10
192 Scott Elarton .10
193 Carl Everett .10
194 Mike Hampton .10
195 Carlos Hernandez .10
196 Richard Hidalgo .10
197 Jose Lima .10
198 Shane Reynolds .15
199 Bill Spiers .15
200 Billy Wagner .15
201a Carlos Beltran (action) .50
201b Carlos Beltran (portrait) .50
202 Dermal Brown .10
203 Johnny Damon .25
204 Jermaine Dye .10
205 Carlos Febles .10
206 Jeremy Giambi .10
207 Mark Quinn .10
208 Joe Randa .10
209 Dan Reichert .10
210 Jose Rosado .10
211 Rey Sanchez .10
212 Jeff Suppan .10
213 Mike Sweeney .10
214a Kevin Brown (action) .15
214b Kevin Brown (portrait) .15
215 Darren Dreifort .10
216 Eric Gagne .10
217 Mark Grudzielanek .10
218 Todd Hollandsworth .10
219 Todd Hundley .10
220 Eric Karros .15
221 Raul Mondesi .15
222 Chan Ho Park .10
223 Jeff Shaw .10
224a Gary Sheffield (action) .30
224b Gary Sheffield (portrait) .30
225 Ismael Valdes .10
226 Devon White .10
227 Eric Young .10
228 Kevin Barker .10
229 Ron Belliard .10
230a Jeromy Burnitz (action) .10
230b Jeromy Burnitz (portrait) .10
231 Jeff Cirillo .10
232 Marquis Grissom .10
233 Geoff Jenkins .10
234 Mark Loretta .10
235 David Nilsson .10
236 Hideo Nomo .75
237 Alex Ochoa .10
238 Kyle Peterson .10
239 Fernando Vina .10
240 Bob Wickman .10
241 Steve Woodard .10
242 Chad Allen .10
243 Ron Coomer .10
244 Marty Cordova .10
245 Cristian Guzman .10
246 Denny Hocking .10
247 Jacque Jones .10
248 Corey Koskie .10
249 Matt Lawton .10
250 Joe Mays .10
251 Eric Milton .10
252 Brad Radke .10
253 Mark Redman .10
254 Terry Steinbach .10
255 Todd Walker .10
256 Tony Armas Jr. .10
257 Michael Barrett .10
258 Peter Bergeron .10
259 Geoff Blum .10
260 Orlando Cabrera .10
261 *Trace Coquillette* .15
262 Brad Fullmer .10
263a Vladimir Guerrero (action) .75
263b Vladimir Guerrero (portrait) .75
264 Wilton Guerrero .10
265 Dustin Hermanson .10
266 Manny Martinez .10
267 Ryan McGuire .10
268 Ugueth Urbina .10
269 Jose Vidro .10
270 Rondell White .15
271 Chris Widger .10
272 Edgardo Alfonzo .15
273 Armando Benitez .10
274 Roger Cedeno .10
275 Dennis Cook .10
276 Octavio Dotel .10
277 John Franco .10
278 Darryl Hamilton .10
279 Rickey Henderson .75
280 Orel Hershiser .10
281 Al Leiter .15
282a John Olerud (action) .15
282b John Olerud (portrait) .15
283 Rey Ordonez .10
284a Mike Piazza (action) 1.50
284b Mike Piazza (portrait) 1.50
285 Kenny Rogers .10
286 Jorge Toca .10
287 Robin Ventura .15
288 Scott Brosius .10
289a Roger Clemens (action) 1.25
289b Roger Clemens (portrait) 1.25
290 David Cone .15
291 Chili Davis .10
292 Orlando Hernandez .15
293 Hideki Irabu .10
294a Derek Jeter (action) 2.50
294b Derek Jeter (portrait) 2.50
295 Chuck Knoblauch .10
296 Ricky Ledee .10
297 Jim Leyritz .10
298 Tino Martinez .15
299 Paul O'Neill .15
300 Andy Pettitte .25
301 Jorge Posada .15
302 Mariano Rivera .25
303 Alfonso Soriano .75
304a Bernie Williams (action) .20
304b Bernie Williams (portrait) .20
305 Ed Yarnall .10
306 Kevin Appier .10
307 Rich Becker .10
308 Eric Chavez .25
309 Jason Giambi .60
310 Ben Grieve .10
311 Ramon Hernandez .10
312 Tim Hudson .25
313 John Jaha .10
314 Doug Jones .10
315 Omar Olivares .10
316 Mike Oquist .10
317 Matt Stairs .10
318 Miguel Tejada .25
319 Randy Velarde .10
320 Bobby Abreu .15
321 Marlon Anderson .10
322 Alex Arias .10
323 Rico Brogna .10
324 Paul Byrd .10
325 Ron Gant .10
326 Doug Glanville .10

327 Wayne Gomes .10
328 Mike Lieberthal .10
329 Robert Person .10
330 Desi Relaford .10
331a Scott Rolen (action) .60
331b Scott Rolen (portrait) .60
332a Curt Schilling (action) .35
332b Curt Schilling (portrait) .35
333 Kris Benson .10
334 Adrian Brown .10
335 Brant Brown .10
336 Brian Giles .15
337 Chad Hermansen .10
338 Jason Kendall .15
339 Al Martin .10
340 Pat Meares .10
341a Warren Morris (action) .10
341b Warren Morris (portrait) .10
342 Todd Ritchie .10
343 Jason Schmidt .10
344 Ed Sprague .10
345 Mike Williams .10
346 Kevin Young .10
347 Rick Ankiel .15
348 Ricky Bottalico .10
349 Kent Bottenfield .10
350 Darren Bragg .10
351 Eric Davis .15
352a J.D. Drew (action) .35
352b J.D. Drew (portrait) .35
353 Adam Kennedy .10
354 Ray Lankford .10
355 Joe McEwing .10
356a Mark McGwire (action) 2.00
356b Mark McGwire (portrait) 2.00
357 Matt Morris .10
358 Darren Oliver .10
359 Edgar Renteria .10
360 Fernando Tatis .10
361 Andy Ashby .10
362 Ben Davis .10
363a Tony Gwynn (action) 1.00
363b Tony Gwynn (portrait) 1.00
364 Sterling Hitchcock .10
365 Trevor Hoffman .10
366 Damian Jackson .10
367 Wally Joyner .10
368 Dave Magadan .10
369 Gary Matthews Jr. .10
370 Phil Nevin .10
371 Eric Owens .10
372 Ruben Rivera .10
373a Reggie Sanders (action) .10
373b Reggie Sanders (portrait) .10
374 Quilvio Veras .10
375 Rich Aurilia .10
376 Marvin Benard .10
377a Barry Bonds (action) 2.50
377b Barry Bonds (portrait) 2.50
378 Ellis Burks .10
379 Shawn Estes .10
380 Livan Hernandez .10
381a Jeff Kent (action) .15
381b Jeff Kent (portrait) .15
382 Brent Mayne .10
383 Bill Mueller .10
384 Calvin Murray .10
385 Robb Nen .10
386 Russ Ortiz .10
387 Kirk Rueter .10
388 J.T. Snow .10
389 David Bell .10
390 Jay Buhner .15
391 Russ Davis .10
392a Freddy Garcia (action) .10
392b Freddy Garcia (portrait) .10
393a Ken Griffey Jr. (action) 1.50
393b Ken Griffey Jr. (portrait) 1.50
394 Carlos Guillen .10
395 John Halama .10
396 Brian Hunter .10
397 Ryan Jackson .10
398 Edgar Martinez .10
399 Gil Meche .10
400 Jose Mesa .10
401 Jamie Moyer .10
402a Alex Rodriguez (action) 2.00
402b Alex Rodriguez (portrait) 2.00
403 Dan Wilson .10
404 Wilson Alvarez .10
405 Rolando Arrojo .10
406a Wade Boggs (action) 1.00
406b Wade Boggs (portrait) 1.00
407 Miguel Cairo .10
408a Jose Canseco (action) .40
408b Jose Canseco (portrait) .40
409 John Flaherty .10
410 Jose Guillen .10
411 Roberto Hernandez .10
412 Terrell Lowery .10
413 Dave Martinez .10
414 Quinton McCracken .10
415a Fred McGriff (action) .15
415b Fred McGriff (portrait) .15
416 Ryan Rupe .10
417 Kevin Stocker .10
418 Bubba Trammell .10
419 Royce Clayton .10
420a Juan Gonzalez (action) .75
420b Juan Gonzalez (portrait) .75
421 Tom Goodwin .10
422 Rusty Greer .10
423 Rick Helling .10
424 Roberto Kelly .10
425 Ruben Mateo .10
426 Mark McLemore .10
427 Mike Morgan .10
428 Rafael Palmeiro .65
429a Ivan Rodriguez (action) .65
429b Ivan Rodriguez (portrait) .65
430 Aaron Sele .10
431 Lee Stevens .10
432 John Wetteland .10
433 Todd Zeile .10
434 Jeff Zimmerman .10
435 Tony Batista .10
436 Casey Blake .10
437 Homer Bush .10
438 Chris Carpenter .10
439 Jose Cruz Jr. .10
440a Carlos Delgado (action) .50
440b Carlos Delgado (portrait) .50
441 Tony Fernandez .10
442 Darrin Fletcher .10
443 Alex Gonzalez .10
444a Shawn Green (action) .35
444b Shawn Green (portrait) .35
445 Roy Halladay .20
446 Billy Koch .10
447 David Segui .10
448 Shannon Stewart .10
449 David Wells .10
450 Vernon Wells .15

Copper

NM/M
Common Copper: 5.00
Stars: 4-8X
Production 99 sets

Platinum Blue

NM/M
Common Player: 8.00
Stars: 6X to 10X
Production 75 sets

Premiere Date

NM/M
Common Player: 15.00
Stars: 8X to 15X
Production 37 sets

2000 PACIFIC RUBY RED (SEVEN-11)

NM/M
Complete Set (500): 65.00
Common Player: .15
Stars/Rookies 1.5X
(See 2000 Pacific for checklist and base card values.)

Cramer's Choice Awards

NM/M
Complete Set (10): 300.00
Common Player: 25.00
Inserted 1:721
1 Chipper Jones 25.00
2 Cal Ripken Jr. 50.00
3 Nomar Garciaparra 30.00
4 Sammy Sosa 30.00
5 Mike Piazza 30.00
6 Derek Jeter 50.00
7 Mark McGwire 40.00
8 Tony Gwynn 25.00

9 Ken Griffey Jr. 30.00
10 Alex Rodriguez 40.00

Command Performers

NM/M
Complete Set (20): 45.00
Common Player: 1.00
Inserted 1:24 Retail
1 Chipper Jones 3.00
2 Greg Maddux 3.00
3 Cal Ripken Jr. 6.00
4 Nomar Garciaparra 4.00
5 Sammy Sosa 4.00
6 Sean Casey 1.00
7 Manny Ramirez 2.00
8 Larry Walker 1.00
9 Jeff Bagwell 2.00
10 Vladimir Guerrero 2.00
11 Mike Piazza 4.00
12 Roger Clemens 3.50
13 Derek Jeter 6.00
14 Mark McGwire 5.00
15 Tony Gwynn 3.00
16 Barry Bonds 6.00
17 Ken Griffey Jr. 4.00
18 Alex Rodriguez 5.00
19 Ivan Rodriguez 1.50
20 Shawn Green 1.25

Diamond Leaders

NM/M
Complete Set (30): 25.00
Common Card: .50
Inserted 2:25
1 Garret Anderson, Chuck Finley, Troy Percival, Mo Vaughn
Anaheim Angels .50
2 Albert Belle, Mike Mussina, B.J. Surhoff
Baltimore Orioles .50
3 Nomar Garciaparra, Pedro J. Martinez, Troy O'Leary
Boston Red Sox 3.00
4 Ray Durham, Magglio Ordonez, Frank Thomas
Chicago White Sox 1.50
5 Bartolo Colon, Manny Ramirez, Omar Vizquel
Cleveland Indians 1.50
6 Deivi Cruz, Dave Mlicki, David Palmer
Detroit Tigers .50
7 Johnny Damon, Jermaine Dye, Jose Rosado, Mike Sweeney
Kansas City Royals .50
8 Corey Koskie, Eric Milton, Brad Radke
Minnesota Twins .50
9 Orlando Hernandez, Derek Jeter, Mariano Rivera, Bernie Williams
New York Yankees 4.00
10 Jeremy Giambi, Tim Hudson, Matt Stairs
Oakland Athletics 1.00
11 Freddy Garcia, Ken Griffey Jr., Edgar Martinez
Seattle Mariners 3.00
12 Jose Canseco, Roberto Hernandez, Fred McGriff
Tampa Bay Devil Rays .75
13 Rafael Palmeiro, Ivan Rodriguez, John Wetteland
Texas Rangers 1.00
14 Carlos Delgado, Shannon Stewart, David Wells
Toronto Blue Jays 1.00
15 Luis Gonzalez, Randy Johnson, Matt Williams Arizona
Diamondbacks 1.50
16 Chipper Jones, Brian Jordan, Greg Maddux
Atlanta Braves 2.00
17 Mark Grace, Jon Lieber, Sammy Sosa
Chicago Cubs 3.00
18 Sean Casey, Pete Harnisch, Greg Vaughn
Cincinnati Reds .50
19 Pedro Astacio, Dante Bichette, Larry Walker
Colorado Rockies .50
20 Luis Castillo, Alex Fernandez, Preston Wilson
Florida Marlins .50
21 Jeff Bagwell, Mike Hampton, Billy Wagner
Houston Astros 1.50
22 Kevin Brown, Mark Grudzielanek, Eric Karros
Los Angeles Dodgers .50
23 Jeromy Burnitz, Jeff Cirillo, Marquis Grissom, Hideo Nomo
Milwaukee Brewers 1.00
24 Vladimir Guerrero, Dustin Hermanson, Ugueth Urbina
Montreal Expos 1.50
25 Roger Cedeno, Rickey Henderson, Mike Piazza
New York Mets 3.00
26 Bobby Abreu, Mike Lieberthal, Curt Schilling
Philadelphia Phillies .75
27 Brian Giles, Jason Kendall, Kevin Young
Pittsburgh Pirates .50
28 Kent Bottenfield, Ray Lankford, Mark McGwire
St. Louis Cardinals 3.50
29 Tony Gwynn, Trevor Hoffman, Reggie Sanders
San Diego Padres 2.00
30 Barry Bonds, Jeff Kent, Russ Ortiz
San Francisco Giants 4.00

Gold Crown Die-Cuts

NM/M
Complete Set (36): 150.00
Common Player: 1.50
Inserted 1:25
1 Mo Vaughn 1.50
2 Matt Williams 1.50

3 Andruw Jones 6.00
4 Chipper Jones 8.00
5 Greg Maddux 8.00
6 Cal Ripken Jr. 15.00
7 Nomar Garciaparra 10.00
8 Pedro Martinez 6.00
9 Sammy Sosa 10.00
10 Magglio Ordonez 2.50
11 Frank Thomas 6.00
12 Sean Casey 1.50
13 Roberto Alomar 2.50
14 Manny Ramirez 6.00
15 Larry Walker 1.50
16 Jeff Bagwell 6.00
17 Craig Biggio 1.50
18 Carlos Beltran 4.00
19 Vladimir Guerrero 6.00
20 Mike Piazza 10.00
21 Roger Clemens 9.00
22 Derek Jeter 15.00
23 Bernie Williams 2.00
24 Scott Rolen 5.00
25 Warren Morris 1.50
26 J.D. Drew 2.00
27 Mark McGwire 12.00
28 Tony Gwynn 8.00
29 Barry Bonds 15.00
30 Ken Griffey Jr. 10.00
31 Alex Rodriguez 12.00
32 Jose Canseco 2.00
33 Juan Gonzalez 6.00
34 Rafael Palmeiro 5.00
35 Ivan Rodriguez 5.00
36 Shawn Green 3.00

Ornaments

NM/M
Complete Set (20): 40.00
Common Player: 1.00
Inserted 2:25
1 Mo Vaughn 1.00
2 Chipper Jones 3.00
3 Greg Maddux 3.00
4 Cal Ripken Jr. 6.00
5 Nomar Garciaparra 4.00
6 Sammy Sosa 4.00
7 Frank Thomas 2.00
8 Manny Ramirez 2.00
9 Larry Walker 1.00
10 Jeff Bagwell 2.00
11 Mike Piazza 4.00
12 Roger Clemens 3.50
13 Derek Jeter 6.00
14 Scott Rolen 1.50
15 J.D. Drew 1.25
16 Mark McGwire 5.00
17 Tony Gwynn 3.00
18 Ken Griffey Jr. 4.00
19 Alex Rodriguez 5.00
20 Ivan Rodriguez 1.50

Past & Present

NM/M
Complete Set (20): 80.00
Common Player: 1.50
Inserted 1:49 H
1 Chipper Jones 5.00
2 Greg Maddux 5.00
3 Cal Ripken Jr. 10.00
4 Nomar Garciaparra 6.00
5 Pedro Martinez 4.00
6 Sammy Sosa 6.00
7 Frank Thomas 4.00
8 Manny Ramirez 4.00
9 Larry Walker 1.50
10 Jeff Bagwell 4.00
11 Mike Piazza 6.00
12 Roger Clemens 5.50
13 Derek Jeter 10.00
14 Mark McGwire 8.00

15 Tony Gwynn 5.00
16 Barry Bonds 10.00
17 Ken Griffey Jr. 6.00
18 Alex Rodriguez 8.00
19 Wade Boggs 5.00
20 Ivan Rodriguez 3.00

Reflections

NM/M
Common Player: 3.00
Inserted 1:97
1 Andruw Jones 6.00
2 Chipper Jones 8.00
3 Cal Ripken Jr. 20.00
4 Nomar Garciaparra 12.00
5 Sammy Sosa 12.00
6 Frank Thomas 6.00
7 Manny Ramirez 6.00
8 Jeff Bagwell 6.00
9 Vladimir Guerrero 6.00
10 Mike Piazza 12.00
11 Derek Jeter 20.00
12 Bernie Williams 3.00
13 Scott Rolen 5.00
14 J.D. Drew 3.00
15 Mark McGwire 15.00
16 Tony Gwynn 8.00
17 Ken Griffey Jr. 12.00
18 Alex Rodriguez 15.00
19 Juan Gonzalez 6.00
20 Ivan Rodriguez 5.00

2000 PACIFIC AURORA

NM/M
Complete Set (151): 25.00
Common Player: .15
Pack (10): 2.00
Wax Box (24): 30.00
1 Darin Erstad .25
2 Troy Glaus .75
3 Tim Salmon .25
4 Mo Vaughn .15
5 Jay Bell .15
6 Erubiel Durazo .15
7 Luis Gonzalez .25
8 Randy Johnson .75
9 Matt Williams .15
10 Tom Glavine .35
11 Andruw Jones .75
12 Chipper Jones 1.00
13 Brian Jordan .15
14 Greg Maddux 1.00
15 Kevin Millwood .15
16 Albert Belle .15
17 Will Clark .25
18 Mike Mussina .35
19 Cal Ripken Jr. 2.50
20 B.J. Surhoff .15
21 Nomar Garciaparra 1.50
22 Pedro Martinez .75
23 Troy O'Leary .15
24 Wilton Veras .15
25 Mark Grace .25
26 Henry Rodriguez .15
27 Sammy Sosa 1.50
28 Kerry Wood .50
29 Ray Durham .15
30 Paul Konerko .25
31 Carlos Lee .15
32 Magglio Ordonez .25
33 Chris Singleton .15
34 Frank Thomas .75
35 Mike Cameron .15
36 Sean Casey .25
37 Barry Larkin .15
38 Pokey Reese .15
39 Eddie Taubensee .15
40 Roberto Alomar .40
41 David Justice .15
42 Kenny Lofton .15
43 Manny Ramirez .75
44 Richie Sexson .15
45 Jim Thome .60
46 Omar Vizquel .15
47 Todd Helton .75
48 Mike Lansing .15
49 Neifi Perez .15
50 Ben Petrick .15
51 Larry Walker .15
52 Tony Clark .15
53 Damion Easley .15
54 Juan Encarnacion .15
55 Juan Gonzalez .75
56 Dean Palmer .15
57 Luis Castillo .15
58 Cliff Floyd .15
59 Alex Gonzalez .15
60 Mike Lowell .15
61 Preston Wilson .15
62 Jeff Bagwell .75
63 Craig Biggio .15
64 Ken Caminiti .15
65 Jose Lima .15
66 Billy Wagner .15
67 Carlos Beltran .50
68 Johnny Damon .25
69 Jermaine Dye .15
70 Mark Quinn .15
71 Mike Sweeney .15
72 Kevin Brown .15
73 Shawn Green .35
74 Eric Karros .15
75 Chan Ho Park .15
76 Gary Sheffield .40
77 Ron Belliard .15
78 Jeromy Burnitz .15
79 Marquis Grissom .15
80 Geoff Jenkins .15
81 David Nilsson .15
82 Ron Coomer .15
83 Jacque Jones .15
84 Brad Radke .15
85 Todd Walker .15
86 Michael Barrett .15
87 Peter Bergeron .15
88 Vladimir Guerrero .75
89 Jose Vidro .15
90 Rondell White .15
91 Edgardo Alfonzo .15
92 Darryl Hamilton .15
93 Rey Ordonez .15
94 Mike Piazza 1.50
95 Robin Ventura .15
96 Roger Clemens 1.25
97 Orlando Hernandez .15
98 Derek Jeter 2.50
99 Tino Martinez .15
100 Mariano Rivera .25
101 Bernie Williams .25
102 Eric Chavez .25
103 Jason Giambi .60
104 Ben Grieve .15
105 Tim Hudson .25
106 John Jaha .15
107 Matt Stairs .15
108 Bobby Abreu .15
109 Doug Glanville .15
110 Mike Lieberthal .15
111 Scott Rolen .60
112 Curt Schilling .40
113 Brian Giles .15
114 Chad Hermansen .15
115 Jason Kendall .15
116 Warren Morris .15
117 Kevin Young .15
118 Rick Ankiel .25
119 J.D. Drew .25
120 Ray Lankford .15
121 Mark McGwire 2.00
122 Edgar Renteria .15
123 Fernando Tatis .15
124 Ben Davis .15
125 Tony Gwynn 1.00
126 Trevor Hoffman .15
127 Phil Nevin .15
128 Barry Bonds 2.50
129 Ellis Burks .15
130 Jeff Kent .15
131 J.T. Snow .15
132 Freddy Garcia .15
133 Ken Griffey Jr. 1.50
133a Ken Griffey Jr. Reds 2.00
134 Edgar Martinez .15
135 Alex Rodriguez 2.00
136 Dan Wilson .15
137 Jose Canseco .40
138 Roberto Hernandez .15
139 Dave Martinez .15
140 Fred McGriff .15
141 Rusty Greer .15
142 Ruben Mateo .15
143 Rafael Palmeiro .65
144 Ivan Rodriguez .65
145 Jeff Zimmerman .15
146 Homer Bush .15
147 Carlos Delgado .50
148 Raul Mondesi .15
149 Shannon Stewart .15
150 Vernon Wells .15

Copper

Stars: 2X-4X
Production 399 sets

Silver

Stars: 3-6X
Production 199 sets

Platinum Blue

Stars: 5-10X
Production 67 sets

Pinstripes

NM/M
Complete Set (50): 30.00
Common Player: .25
Premiere Date: 3-6X
Production 51 sets
4 Mo Vaughn .25
8 Randy Johnson 1.50
9 Matt Williams .25
11 Andruw Jones 1.50
12 Chipper Jones 2.00
14 Greg Maddux 2.00
19 Cal Ripken Jr. 4.00
21 Nomar Garciaparra 2.50
22 Pedro Martinez 1.50
27 Sammy Sosa 2.50
32 Magglio Ordonez .35
34 Frank Thomas 1.50
36 Sean Casey .35
37 Barry Larkin .25
42 Kenny Lofton .25
43 Manny Ramirez 1.50
45 Jim Thome 1.50
47 Todd Helton 1.50
51 Larry Walker .25
55 Juan Gonzalez 1.50
62 Jeff Bagwell 1.50
63 Craig Biggio .25
67 Carlos Beltran .50
73 Shawn Green .40
76 Gary Sheffield .40
78 Jeromy Burnitz .25
88 Vladimir Guerrero 1.50
91 Edgardo Alfonzo .25
94 Mike Piazza 2.50
96 Roger Clemens 2.25
97 Orlando Hernandez .25
98 Derek Jeter 4.00
101 Bernie Williams .35
102 Eric Chavez .35
105 Tim Hudson .35
111 Scott Rolen 1.25
112 Curt Schilling .50
113 Brian Giles .25
114 Rick Ankiel .25

#	Player	NM/M
121	Mark McGwire	3.00
125	Tony Gwynn	2.00
128	Barry Bonds	4.00
130	Jeff Kent	.25
133	Ken Griffey Jr.	2.50
135	Alex Rodriguez	3.00
137	Jose Canseco	.50
140	Fred McGriff	.25
143	Rafael Palmeiro	.75
144	Ivan Rodriguez	.75
147	Carlos Delgado	1.00

At-Bat Styrotechs

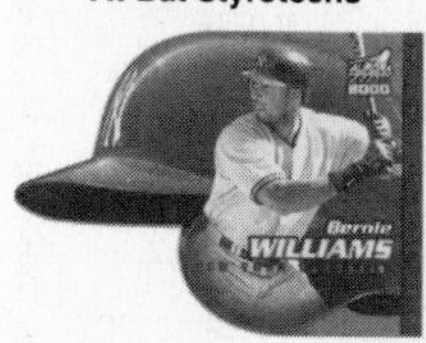

		NM/M
Complete Set (20):		125.00
Common Player:		2.00
Production 299 sets		
1	Chipper Jones	7.50
2	Cal Ripken Jr.	15.00
3	Nomar Garciaparra	10.00
4	Sammy Sosa	10.00
5	Frank Thomas	6.00
6	Manny Ramirez	6.00
7	Larry Walker	2.00
8	Jeff Bagwell	6.00
9	Carlos Beltran	2.00
10	Vladimir Guerrero	6.00
11	Mike Piazza	10.00
12	Derek Jeter	15.00
13	Bernie Williams	2.00
14	Mark McGwire	12.00
15	Tony Gwynn	7.50
16	Barry Bonds	15.00
17	Ken Griffey Jr.	10.00
18	Alex Rodriguez	12.00
19	Jose Canseco	3.00
20	Ivan Rodriguez	5.00

Dugout View Net-Fusions

		NM/M
Complete Set (20):		110.00
Common Player:		2.50
Inserted 1:37		
1	Mo Vaughn	2.50
2	Chipper Jones	8.00
3	Cal Ripken Jr.	15.00
4	Nomar Garciaparra	10.00
5	Sammy Sosa	10.00
6	Manny Ramirez	6.00
7	Larry Walker	2.50
8	Juan Gonzalez	6.00
9	Jeff Bagwell	6.00
10	Craig Biggio	2.50
11	Shawn Green	3.00
12	Vladimir Guerrero	6.00
13	Mike Piazza	10.00
14	Derek Jeter	15.00
15	Scott Rolen	5.00
16	Mark McGwire	12.00
17	Tony Gwynn	8.00
18	Ken Griffey Jr.	10.00
19	Alex Rodriguez	12.00
20	Rafael Palmeiro	4.00

Pennant Fever

		NM/M
Complete Set (20):		25.00
Common Player:		1.00
T. Gwynn Auto./147		75.00
Inserted 4:37		
1	Andruw Jones	1.50
2	Chipper Jones	2.00
3	Greg Maddux	2.00
4	Cal Ripken Jr.	4.00
5	Nomar Garciaparra	2.50
6	Pedro Martinez	1.50
7	Sammy Sosa	2.50
8	Manny Ramirez	1.50
9	Jim Thome	1.50
10	Jeff Bagwell	1.50
11	Mike Piazza	2.50
12	Roger Clemens	2.25
13	Derek Jeter	4.00
14	Bernie Williams	1.00
15	Mark McGwire	3.00
16	Tony Gwynn	2.00
17	Ken Griffey Jr.	2.50
18	Alex Rodriguez	3.00
19	Rafael Palmeiro	1.00
20	Ivan Rodriguez	1.00

Star Factor

		NM/M
Complete Set (10):		200.00
Common Player:		20.00
Inserted 1:361		
1	Chipper Jones	20.00
2	Cal Ripken Jr.	40.00
3	Nomar Garciaparra	25.00
4	Sammy Sosa	25.00
5	Mike Piazza	25.00
6	Derek Jeter	40.00
7	Mark McGwire	30.00
8	Tony Gwynn	20.00
9	Ken Griffey Jr.	25.00
10	Alex Rodriguez	30.00

2000 PACIFIC CROWN COLLECTION

		NM/M
Complete Set (300):		25.00
Common Player:		.10
Pack (10):		1.50
Wax Box (36):		30.00
1	Garret Anderson	.10
2	Darin Erstad	.25
3	Ben Molina	.10
4	Ramon Ortiz	.10
5	Orlando Palmeiro	.10
6	Troy Percival	.10
7	Tim Salmon	.15
8	Mo Vaughn	.10
9	Mo Vaughn Checklist	.10
10	Jay Bell	.10
11	Omar Daal	.10
12	Erubiel Durazo	.10
13	Steve Finley	.10
14	Hanley Frias	.10
15	Luis Gonzalez	.25
16	Randy Johnson	.75
17	Matt Williams	.10
18	Matt Williams Checklist	.10
19	Andres Galarraga	.10
20	Tom Glavine	.35
21	Andruw Jones	.75
22	Chipper Jones	1.00
23	Brian Jordan	.10
24	Javy Lopez	.10
25	Greg Maddux	1.00
26	Kevin Millwood	.10
27	Eddie Perez	.10
28	John Smoltz	.10
29	Chipper Jones Checklist	.50
30	Albert Belle	.15
31	Jesse Garcia	.10
32	Jerry Hairston Jr.	.10
33	Charles Johnson	.10
34	Mike Mussina	.30
35	Sidney Ponson	.10
36	Cal Ripken Jr.	2.50
37	B.J. Surhoff	.10
38	Cal Ripken Jr. Checklist	1.00
39	Nomar Garciaparra	1.50
40	Pedro Martinez	.75
41	Ramon Martinez	.10
42	Trot Nixon	.10
43	Jose Offerman	.10
44	Troy O'Leary	.10
45	John Valentin	.10
46	Wilton Veras	.10
47	Nomar Garciaparra Checklist	.75
48	Mark Grace	.15
49	Felix Heredia	.10
50	Jose Molina	.10
51	Jose Nieves	.10
52	Henry Rodriguez	.10
53	Sammy Sosa	1.50
54	Kerry Wood	.65
55	Sammy Sosa Checklist	.60
56	Mike Caruso	.10
57	Carlos Castillo	.10
58	Jason Dellaero	.10
59	Carlos Lee	.10
60	Magglio Ordonez	.25
61	Jesus Pena	.10
62	Liu Rodriguez	.10
63	Frank Thomas	.75
64	Magglio Ordonez Checklist	.15
65	Aaron Boone	.10
66	Mike Cameron	.10
67	Sean Casey	.20
68	Juan Guzman	.10
69	Barry Larkin	.10
70	Pokey Reese	.10
71	Eddie Taubensee	.10
72	Greg Vaughn	.10
73	Sean Casey Checklist	.15
74	Roberto Alomar	.25
75	Sandy Alomar Jr.	.10
76	Bartolo Colon	.10
77	Jacob Cruz	.10
78	Einar Diaz	.10
79	David Justice	.10
80	Kenny Lofton	.10
81	Manny Ramirez	.75
82	Richie Sexson	.10
83	Jim Thome	.75
84	Omar Vizquel	.10
85	Enrique Wilson	.10
86	Manny Ramirez Checklist	.40
87	Pedro Astacio	.10
88	Henry Blanco	.10
89	Vinny Castilla	.10
90	Edgard Clemente	.10
91	Todd Helton	.75
92	Neifi Perez	.10
93	Terry Shumpert	.10
94	*Juan Sosa*	.20
95	Larry Walker	.10
96	Vinny Castilla Checklist	.10
97	Tony Clark	.10
98	Deivi Cruz	.10
99	Damion Easley	.10
100	Juan Encarnacion	.10
101	Karim Garcia	.10
102	Luis Garcia	.10
103	Juan Gonzalez	.75
104	Jose Macias	.10
105	Dean Palmer	.10
106	Juan Encarnacion Checklist	.10
107	Antonio Alfonseca	.10
108	Armando Almanza	.10
109	Bruce Aven	.10
110	Luis Castillo	.10
111	Ramon Castro	.10
112	Alex Fernandez	.10
113	Cliff Floyd	.10
114	Alex Gonzalez	.10
115	*Michael Tejera*	.10
116	Preston Wilson	.10
117	Luis Castillo Checklist	.10
118	Jeff Bagwell	.75
119	Craig Biggio	.10
120	Jose Cabrera	.10
121	Tony Eusebio	.10
122	Carl Everett	.10
123	Ricky Gutierrez	.10
124	Mike Hampton	.10
125	Richard Hidalgo	.10
126	Jose Lima	.10
127	Billy Wagner	.10
128	Jeff Bagwell Checklist	.40
129	Carlos Beltran	.50
130	Johnny Damon	.25
131	Jermaine Dye	.10
132	Carlos Febles	.10
133	Jeremy Giambi	.10
134	Jose Rosado	.10
135	Rey Sanchez	.10
136	Jose Santiago	.10
137	Carlos Beltran Checklist	.10
138	Kevin Brown	.10
139	Craig Counsell	.10
140	Shawn Green	.40
141	Eric Karros	.10
142	Angel Pena	.10
143	Gary Sheffield	.25
144	Ismael Valdes	.10
145	Jose Vizcaino	.10
146	Devon White	.10
147	Eric Karros Checklist	.10
148	Ron Belliard	.10
149	Jeromy Burnitz	.10
150	Jeff Cirillo	.10
151	Marquis Grissom	.10
152	Geoff Jenkins	.10
153	Dave Nilsson	.10
154	Rafael Roque	.10
155	Jose Valentin	.10
156	Fernando Vina	.10
157	Jeromy Burnitz	.10
158	Chad Allen	.10
159	Ron Coomer	.10
160	Eddie Guardado	.10
161	Cristian Guzman	.10
162	Jacque Jones	.10
163	Javier Valentin	.10
164	Todd Walker	.10
165	Ron Coomer Checklist	.10
166	Michael Barrett	.10
167	Miguel Batista	.10
168	Vladimir Guerrero	.75
169	Wilton Guerrero	.10
170	Fernando Seguignol	.10
171	Ugueth Urbina	.10
172	Javier Vazquez	.10
173	Jose Vidro	.10
174	Rondell White	.10
175	Vladimir Guerrero Checklist	.25
176	Edgardo Alfonzo	.10
177	Armando Benitez	.10
178	Roger Cedeno	.10
179	Octavio Dotel	.10
180	Melvin Mora	.10
181	Rey Ordonez	.10
182	Mike Piazza	1.50
183	Jorge Toca	.10
184	Robin Ventura	.10
185	Edgardo Alfonzo Checklist	.10
186	Roger Clemens	1.25
187	David Cone	.10
188	Orlando Hernandez	.10
189	Derek Jeter	2.50
190	Ricky Ledee	.10
191	Tino Martinez	.10
192	Ramiro Mendoza	.10
193	Jorge Posada	.10
194	Mariano Rivera	.15
195	Alfonso Soriano	.75
196	Bernie Williams	.30
197	Derek Jeter Checklist	1.00
198	Eric Chavez	.15
199	Jason Giambi	.60
200	Ben Grieve	.10
201	Ramon Hernandez	.10
202	Tim Hudson	.25
203	John Jaha	.10
204	Omar Olivares	.10
205	Olmedo Saenz	.10
206	Matt Stairs	.10
207	Miguel Tejada	.20
208	Tim Hudson Checklist	.20
209	Rico Brogna	.10
210	Bobby Abreu	.10
211	Marlon Anderson	.10
212	Alex Arias	.10
213	Doug Glanville	.10
214	Robert Person	.10
215	Scott Rolen	.60
216	Curt Schilling	.35
217	Scott Rolen Checklist	.25
218	Francisco Cordova	.10
219	Brian Giles	.10
220	Jason Kendall	.10
221	Warren Morris	.10
222	Abraham Nunez	.10
223	Aramis Ramirez	.10
224	Jose Silva	.10
225	Kevin Young	.10
226	Brian Giles Checklist	.10
227	Rick Ankiel	.15
228	Ricky Bottalico	.10

229	J.D. Drew	.25
230	Ray Lankford	.10
231	Mark McGwire	2.00
232	Eduardo Perez	.10
233	Placido Polanco	.10
234	Edgar Renteria	.10
235	Fernando Tatis	.10
236	Mark McGwire Checklist	.85
237	Carlos Almanzar	.10
238	Wiki Gonzalez	.10
239	Tony Gwynn	1.00
240	Trevor Hoffman	.10
241	Damian Jackson	.10
242	Wally Joyner	.10
243	Ruben Rivera	.10
244	Reggie Sanders	.10
245	Quilvio Veras	.10
246	Tony Gwynn Checklist	.50
247	Rich Aurilia	.10
248	Marvin Benard	.10
249	Barry Bonds	2.50
250	Ellis Burks	.10
251	Miguel Del Toro	.10
252	Edwards Guzman	.10
253	Livan Hernandez	.10
254	Jeff Kent	.10
255	Russ Ortiz	.10
256	Armando Rios	.10
257	Barry Bonds Checklist	1.00
258	Rafael Bournigal	.10
259	Freddy Garcia	.10
260	Ken Griffey Jr.	15.00
261	Carlos Guillen	.10
262	Raul Ibanez	.10
263	Edgar Martinez	.10
264	Jose Mesa	.10
265	Jamie Moyer	.10
266	John Olerud	.10
267	Jose Paniagua	.10
268	Alex Rodriguez	2.00
269	Alex Rodriguez Checklist	1.00
270	Wilson Alvarez	.10
271	Rolando Arrojo	.10
272	Wade Boggs	1.00
273	Miguel Cairo	.10
274	Jose Canseco	.40
275	Jose Guillen	.10
276	Roberto Hernandez	.10
277	Albie Lopez	.10
278	Fred McGriff	.10
279	Esteban Yan	.10
280	Jose Canseco Checklist	.20
281	Rusty Greer	.10
282	Roberto Kelly	.10
283	Esteban Loaiza	.10
284	Ruben Mateo	.10
285	Rafael Palmeiro	.65
286	Ivan Rodriguez	.65
287	Aaron Sele	.10
288	John Wetteland	.10
289	Ivan Rodriguez Checklist	.25
290	Tony Batista	.10
291	Jose Cruz Jr.	.10
292	Carlos Delgado	.50
293	Kelvim Escobar	.10
294	Tony Fernandez	.10
295	Billy Koch	.10
296	Raul Mondesi	.10
297	Willis Otanez	.10
298	David Segui	.10
299	David Wells	.10
300	Carlos Delgado Checklist	.20

Holographic Purple

Stars: 4-8X
Production 199 sets

Platinum Blue

Stars: 8-15X
Production 67 sets

In The Cage

		NM/M
Complete Set (20):		250.00
Common Player:		5.00
Inserted 1:145		
1	Mo Vaughn	5.00
2	Chipper Jones	15.00
3	Cal Ripken Jr.	30.00
4	Nomar Garciaparra	20.00
5	Sammy Sosa	20.00
6	Frank Thomas	10.00
7	Roberto Alomar	6.00
8	Manny Ramirez	10.00
9	Larry Walker	5.00
10	Jeff Bagwell	10.00
11	Vladimir Guerrero	10.00
12	Mike Piazza	20.00
13	Derek Jeter	30.00
14	Bernie Williams	5.00
15	Mark McGwire	25.00
16	Tony Gwynn	15.00
17	Ken Griffey Jr.	20.00
18	Alex Rodriguez	25.00
19	Rafael Palmeiro	8.00
20	Ivan Rodriguez	8.00

Latinos of the Major Leagues

		NM/M
Complete Set (36):		20.00
Common Player:		.25
Inserted 2:37		
Parallel:		2-4X
Production 99 sets		
1	Erubiel Durazo	.25
2	Luis Gonzalez	.25
3	Andruw Jones	1.00
4	Nomar Garciaparra	2.00
5	Pedro Martinez	1.00
6	Sammy Sosa	2.00
7	Carlos Lee	.25
8	Magglio Ordonez	.25
9	Roberto Alomar	.65
10	Manny Ramirez	1.00
11	Omar Vizquel	.25
12	Vinny Castilla	.25
13	Juan Gonzalez	1.00
14	Luis Castillo	.25
15	Jose Lima	.25
16	Carlos Beltran	.75
17	Vladimir Guerrero	1.00
18	Edgardo Alfonzo	.25
19	Roger Cedeno	.25
20	Rey Ordonez	.25
21	Orlando Hernandez	.25
22	Tino Martinez	.25
23	Mariano Rivera	.35
24	Bernie Williams	.50
25	Miguel Tejada	.50
26	Bobby Abreu	.25
27	Fernando Tatis	.25
28	Freddy Garcia	.25
29	Edgar Martinez	.25
30	Alex Rodriguez	3.00
31	Jose Canseco	.65
32	Ruben Mateo	.25
33	Rafael Palmeiro	.75
34	Ivan Rodriguez	.75
35	Carlos Delgado	.65
36	Raul Mondesi	.25

Moment of Truth

		NM/M
Complete Set (30):		50.00
Common Player:		.50
Inserted 1:37		
1	Mo Vaughn	.50
2	Chipper Jones	3.00
3	Greg Maddux	3.00
4	Albert Belle	.50
5	Cal Ripken Jr.	6.00
6	Nomar Garciaparra	4.00
7	Pedro Martinez	2.00
8	Sammy Sosa	4.00
9	Frank Thomas	2.00
10	Barry Larkin	.50
11	Kenny Lofton	.50
12	Manny Ramirez	2.00
13	Larry Walker	.50
14	Juan Gonzalez	2.00
15	Jeff Bagwell	2.00
16	Craig Biggio	.50
17	Carlos Beltran	1.00
18	Vladimir Guerrero	2.00
19	Mike Piazza	4.00
20	Roger Clemens	3.50
21	Derek Jeter	6.00
22	Bernie Williams	.75
23	Mark McGwire	5.00
24	Tony Gwynn	3.00
25	Barry Bonds	6.00
26	Ken Griffey Jr.	4.00
27	Alex Rodriguez	5.00
28	Rafael Palmeiro	1.50
29	Ivan Rodriguez	1.50
30	Carlos Delgado	1.00

Pacific Cup

		NM/M
Complete Set (10):		220.00
Inserted 1:721		
1	Cal Ripken Jr.	40.00
2	Nomar Garciaparra	25.00
3	Pedro Martinez	15.00
4	Sammy Sosa	25.00
5	Vladimir Guerrero	15.00
6	Derek Jeter	40.00
7	Mark McGwire	35.00
8	Tony Gwynn	20.00
9	Ken Griffey Jr.	25.00
10	Alex Rodriguez	35.00

Timber 2000

		NM/M
Complete Set (20):		100.00
Common Player:		2.00
Inserted 1:73		
1	Chipper Jones	8.00
2	Nomar Garciaparra	10.00
3	Sammy Sosa	10.00
4	Magglio Ordonez	2.00
5	Manny Ramirez	6.00
6	Vinny Castilla	2.00
7	Juan Gonzalez	6.00
8	Jeff Bagwell	6.00
9	Shawn Green	3.00
10	Vladimir Guerrero	6.00
11	Mike Piazza	10.00
12	Derek Jeter	15.00
13	Bernie Williams	2.00
14	Mark McGwire	12.00
15	Ken Griffey Jr.	10.00
16	Alex Rodriguez	12.00
17	Jose Canseco	3.00
18	Rafael Palmeiro	5.00
19	Ivan Rodriguez	5.00
20	Carlos Delgado	4.00

2000 PACIFIC CROWN ROYALE

		NM/M
Complete Set (144):		40.00
Common Player:		.25
Common SP:		1.00
Pack (6):		2.50
Box (24):		45.00
1	Darin Erstad	.40
2	Troy Glaus	1.00
3	Adam Kennedy SP	1.00
4	*Derrick Turnbow SP*	1.00
5	Mo Vaughn	.25
6	Erubiel Durazo	.25
7	Steve Finley	.25
8	Randy Johnson	1.00
9	Travis Lee	.25
10	Matt Williams	.25
11	Rafael Furcal SP	1.00
12	Andres Galarraga	.25
13	Andruw Jones	1.00
14	Chipper Jones	1.50
15	Javy Lopez	.25
16	Greg Maddux	1.50
17	Albert Belle	.25
18	Will Clark	.35
19	Mike Mussina	.40
20	Cal Ripken Jr.	3.00
21	Carl Everett	.25
22	Nomar Garciaparra	2.00
23	Pedro Martinez	1.00
24	Jason Varitek	.25
25	*Scott Downs SP*	1.00
26	Mark Grace	.35
27	Sammy Sosa	2.00
28	Kerry Wood	.65
29	Ray Durham	.25
30	Paul Konerko	.25
31	Carlos Lee	.25
32	Magglio Ordonez	.40
33	Frank Thomas	1.00
34	Rob Bell SP	1.00
35	Sean Casey	.25
36	Ken Griffey Jr.	2.00
37	Barry Larkin	.25
38	Pokey Reese	.25
39	Roberto Alomar	.40
40	David Justice	.25
41	Kenny Lofton	.25
42	Manny Ramirez	1.00
43	Richie Sexson	.25
44	Jim Thome	.75
45	Rolando Arrojo	.25
46	Jeff Cirillo	.25
47	Tom Goodwin	.25
48	Todd Helton	1.00
49	Larry Walker	.25
50	Tony Clark	.25
51	Juan Encarnacion	.25
52	Juan Gonzalez	1.00
53	Hideo Nomo	1.00
54	Dean Palmer	.25
55	Cliff Floyd	.25
56	Alex Gonzalez	.25
57	Mike Lowell	.25
58	Brad Penny SP	1.00
59	Preston Wilson	.25
60	Moises Alou	.25
61	Jeff Bagwell	1.00
62	Craig Biggio	.25
63	Roger Cedeno	.25
64	Julio Lugo SP	1.00
65	Carlos Beltran	.60
66	Johnny Damon	.40
67	Jermaine Dye	.25
68	Carlos Febles	.25
69	Mark Quinn SP	1.00
70	Kevin Brown	.25
71	Shawn Green	.50
72	Eric Karros	.25
73	Gary Sheffield	.50
74	Kevin Barker SP	1.00
75	Ron Belliard	.25
76	Jeromy Burnitz	.25
77	Geoff Jenkins	.25
78	Jacque Jones	.25
79	Corey Koskie	.25
80	Matt LeCroy SP	1.00
81	Brad Radke	.25
82	Peter Bergeron SP	1.00
83	Matt Blank SP	1.00
84	Vladimir Guerrero	1.00
85	Hideki Irabu	.25
86	Rondell White	.25
87	Edgardo Alfonzo	.25
88	Mike Hampton	.25
89	Rickey Henderson	1.00
90	Rey Ordonez	.25
91	Jay Payton SP	1.00
92	Mike Piazza	2.00
93	Roger Clemens	1.75
94	Orlando Hernandez	.25
95	Derek Jeter	3.00
96	Tino Martinez	.25
97	Alfonso Soriano SP	2.50
98	Bernie Williams	.40
99	Eric Chavez	.40
100	Jason Giambi	.75

101	Ben Grieve	.25
102	Tim Hudson	.50
103	Terrence Long SP	1.00
104	Mark Mulder SP	1.00
105	Adam Piatt SP	1.00
106	Bobby Abreu	.25
107	Doug Glanville	.25
108	Mike Lieberthal	.25
109	Scott Rolen	.75
110	Brian Giles	.25
111	Chad Hermansen SP	1.00
112	Jason Kendall	.25
113	Warren Morris	.25
114	Rick Ankiel SP	1.00
115	*Justin Brunette SP*	1.00
116	J.D. Drew	.40
117	Mark McGwire	2.50
118	Fernando Tatis	.25
119	Wiki Gonzalez SP	1.00
120	Tony Gwynn	1.50
121	Trevor Hoffman	.25
122	Ryan Klesko	.25
123	Barry Bonds	3.00
124	Ellis Burks	.25
125	Jeff Kent	.25
126	Calvin Murray SP	1.00
127	J.T. Snow	.25
128	Freddy Garcia	.25
129	John Olerud	.25
130	Alex Rodriguez	2.50
131	*Kazuhiro Sasaki SP*	3.00
132	Jose Canseco	.50
133	Vinny Castilla	.25
134	Fred McGriff	.25
135	Greg Vaughn	.25
136	Gabe Kapler	.25
137	*Mike Lamb SP*	1.00
138	Ruben Mateo SP	1.00
139	Rafael Palmeiro	.75
140	Ivan Rodriguez	.75
141	Tony Batista	.25
142	Carlos Delgado	.75
143	Raul Mondesi	.25
144	Shannon Stewart	.25

Platinum Blue

Stars:	3-6X
Production 75 sets	

Limited Series

Stars:	2-4X
Production 144 sets	

Premiere Date

Stars:	2-4X
Production 121 sets	

Red

All singles:	1X
base cards in retail packs	

Card-Supials

		NM/M
Complete Set (20):		40.00
Common Card:		1.00
Inserted 2:25		
1	Randy Johnson, Erubiel Durazo	2.00
2	Chipper Jones, Andruw Jones	3.00
3	Cal Ripken Jr., Matt Riley	6.00
4	Nomar Garciaparra, Jason Varitek	4.00
5	Sammy Sosa, Kerry Wood	4.00
6	Frank Thomas, Magglio Ordonez	2.00
7	Ken Griffey Jr., Sean Casey	4.00
8	Manny Ramirez, Richie Sexson	2.00
9	Larry Walker, Ben Petrick	1.00
10	Juan Gonzalez, Juan Encarnacion	2.00
11	Jeff Bagwell, Lance Berkman	2.00
12	Shawn Green, Eric Gagne	1.00
13	Vladimir Guerrero, Peter Bergeron	2.00
14	Mike Piazza, Edgardo Alfonzo	4.00
15	Derek Jeter, Alfonso Soriano	5.00
16	Scott Rolen, Bobby Abreu	1.50
17	Mark McGwire, Rick Ankiel	5.00
18	Tony Gwynn, Ben Davis	3.00
19	Alex Rodriguez, Freddy Garcia	5.00
20	Ivan Rodriguez, Ruben Mateo	1.50

Cramer's Choice Jumbo

		NM/M
Complete Set (10):		35.00
Common Player:		1.00
Inserted 1:box H		
Aqua:		5-10X
Production 20 sets		
Blue:		2-5X
Production 35 sets		
Gold:		10-20X
Production 10 sets		
Green:		3-6X
Production 30 sets		
Red:		4-8X
Production 25 sets		
1	Cal Ripken Jr.	6.00
2	Nomar Garciaparra	4.00
3	Ken Griffey Jr.	4.00
4	Sammy Sosa	4.00
5	Mike Piazza	4.00
6	Derek Jeter	6.00
7	Rick Ankiel	1.00
8	Mark McGwire	5.00
9	Tony Gwynn	2.00
10	Alex Rodriguez	5.00

Feature Attractions

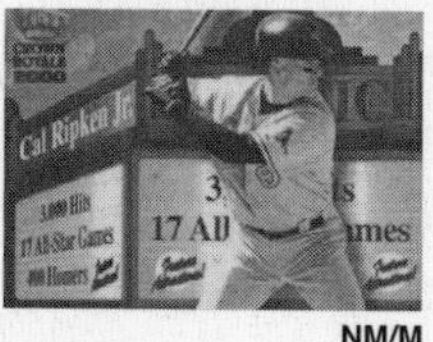

		NM/M
Complete Set (25):		10.00
Common Player:		.25
Inserted 1:1		
Exclusive Showing:		30-50X
Production 20 sets		
1	Erubiel Durazo	.25
2	Chipper Jones	1.00
3	Greg Maddux	1.00
4	Cal Ripken Jr.	2.50
5	Nomar Garciaparra	1.50
6	Pedro Martinez	.75
7	Sammy Sosa	1.50
8	Frank Thomas	.75
9	Ken Griffey Jr.	1.50
10	Manny Ramirez	.75
11	Larry Walker	.25
12	Juan Gonzalez	.75
13	Jeff Bagwell	.75
14	Carlos Beltran	.50
15	Shawn Green	.50
16	Vladimir Guerrero	.75
17	Mike Piazza	1.50
18	Roger Clemens	1.25
19	Derek Jeter	2.50
20	Ben Grieve	.25
21	Rick Ankiel	.35
22	Mark McGwire	2.00
23	Tony Gwynn	1.00
24	Alex Rodriguez	2.00
25	Ivan Rodriguez	.65

Final Numbers

		NM/M
Complete Set (25):		10.00
Common Player:		.25
Inserted 1:1		
1	Randy Johnson	.75
2	Andruw Jones	.75
3	Chipper Jones	1.00
4	Cal Ripken Jr.	2.50
5	Nomar Garciaparra	1.50
6	Pedro Martinez	.75
7	Sammy Sosa	1.50
8	Ken Griffey Jr.	1.50
9	Sean Casey	.35
10	Manny Ramirez	.75
11	Larry Walker	.25
12	Jeff Bagwell	.75
13	Craig Biggio	.25
14	Shawn Green	.50
15	Vladimir Guerrero	.75
16	Mike Piazza	1.50
17	Derek Jeter	2.50
18	Bernie Williams	.35
19	Scott Rolen	.65
20	Mark McGwire	2.00
21	Tony Gwynn	1.00
22	Barry Bonds	2.50
23	Alex Rodriguez	2.00
24	Jose Canseco	.40
25	Ivan Rodriguez	.65

Jumbo

		NM/M
Complete Set (6):		25.00
Inserted 6:10 boxes H		
1	Cal Ripken Jr.	6.00
2	Nomar Garciaparra	4.00
3	Ken Griffey Jr.	4.00
4	Derek Jeter	6.00
5	Mark McGwire	5.00
6	Alex Rodriguez	5.00

Proofs

		NM/M
Complete Set (36):		90.00
Common Player:		1.00
Inserted 1:25		
Proofs:		2-3X
1	Erubiel Durazo	1.50
2	Randy Johnson	3.00
3	Chipper Jones	5.00
4	Greg Maddux	5.00
5	Cal Ripken Jr.	10.00
6	Nomar Garciaparra	8.00
7	Pedro Martinez	3.00
8	Sammy Sosa	5.00
9	Frank Thomas	2.50
10	Sean Casey	1.50
11	Ken Griffey Jr.	5.00
12	Manny Ramirez	2.50
13	Jim Thome	2.50
14	Larry Walker	1.50
15	Juan Gonzalez	2.50
16	Jeff Bagwell	2.50
17	Craig Biggio	1.50
18	Carlos Beltran	2.00
19	Shawn Green	2.00
20	Vladimir Guerrero	2.50
21	Edgardo Alfonzo	1.00
22	Mike Piazza	5.00
23	Roger Clemens	6.00
24	Derek Jeter	10.00
25	Alfonso Soriano	4.00
26	Bernie Williams	2.00
27	Ben Grieve	1.00
28	Rick Ankiel	1.00
29	Mark McGwire	8.00
30	Tony Gwynn	3.00
31	Barry Bonds	8.00
32	Alex Rodriguez	8.00
33	Jose Canseco	2.00
34	Vinny Castilla	1.00
35	Ivan Rodriguez	2.00
36	Rafael Palmeiro	2.00

Sweet Spot Signatures

		NM/M
Common Player:		5.00
1	Adam Kennedy	5.00
2	Trot Nixon	8.00
3	Magglio Ordonez	10.00
4	Sean Casey	8.00
5	Travis Dawkins	5.00
6	Todd Helton	25.00
7	Ben Petrick	5.00
8	Jeff Weaver	6.00
9	Preston Wilson	5.00
10	Lance Berkman	10.00
11	Roger Cedeno	5.00
12	Eric Gagne	10.00
13	Kevin Barker	5.00
14	Kyle Peterson	5.00
15	Tony Armas Jr.	5.00
16	Peter Bergeron	5.00
17	Alfonso Soriano	40.00
18	Ben Grieve	5.00
19	Ramon Hernandez	5.00
20	Brian Giles	8.00
21	Chad Hermansen	5.00
22	Warren Morris	5.00
23	Ben Davis	5.00
24	Rick Ankiel	5.00
25	Chad Hutchinson	5.00
26	Freddy Garcia	10.00
27	Gabe Kapler	5.00
28	Ruben Mateo	5.00
29	Billy Koch	5.00
30	Vernon Wells	5.00

2000 PACIFIC INVINCIBLE

		NM/M
Complete Set (150):		75.00
Common Player:		.25
Pack (3):		2.00
Box (36):		50.00
1	Darin Erstad	.50
2	Troy Glaus	1.50
3	Ramon Ortiz	.25
4	Tim Salmon	.35
5	Mo Vaughn	.25
6	Erubiel Durazo	.25
7	Luis Gonzalez	.35
8	Randy Johnson	1.50
9	Matt Williams	.25
10	Rafael Furcal	.25
11	Andres Galarraga	.25
12	Tom Glavine	.40
13	Andruw Jones	1.50
14	Chipper Jones	2.00
15	Greg Maddux	2.00
16	Kevin Millwood	.25
17	Albert Belle	.25
18	Will Clark	.35
19	Mike Mussina	.40
20	Matt Riley	.25
21	Cal Ripken Jr.	4.00
22	Carl Everett	.25
23	Nomar Garciaparra	2.50
24	Steve Lomasney	.25
25	Pedro Martinez	1.50
26	*Tomo Ohka*	.75

27	Wilton Veras	.25
28	Mark Grace	.35
29	Sammy Sosa	2.50
30	Kerry Wood	.75
31	Eric Young	.25
32	*Julio Zuleta*	.25
33	Paul Konerko	.35
34	Carlos Lee	.25
35	Magglio Ordonez	.35
36	Josh Paul	.25
37	Frank Thomas	1.50
38	Rob Bell	.25
39	Dante Bichette	.25
40	Sean Casey	.35
41	Ken Griffey Jr.	2.50
42	Barry Larkin	.25
43	Pokey Reese	.25
44	Roberto Alomar	.40
45	Manny Ramirez	1.50
46	Richie Sexson	.25
47	Jim Thome	1.50
48	Omar Vizquel	.25
49	Jeff Cirillo	.25
50	Todd Helton	1.50
51	Neifi Perez	.25
52	Larry Walker	.25
53	Tony Clark	.25
54	Juan Encarnacion	.25
55	Juan Gonzalez	1.50
56	Hideo Nomo	1.00
57	Luis Castillo	.25
58	Alex Gonzalez	.25
59	Brad Penny	.25
60	Preston Wilson	.25
61	Moises Alou	.25
62	Jeff Bagwell	1.50
63	Lance Berkman	.25
64	Craig Biggio	.25
65	Roger Cedeno	.25
66	Jose Lima	.25
67	Carlos Beltran	.50
68	Johnny Damon	.35
69	*Chad Durbin*	.50
70	Jermaine Dye	.25
71	Carlos Febles	.25
72	Mark Quinn	.25
73	Kevin Brown	.25
74	Eric Gagne	.25
75	Shawn Green	.50
76	Eric Karros	.25
77	Gary Sheffield	.40
78	Kevin Barker	.25
79	Ron Belliard	.25
80	Jeromy Burnitz	.25
81	Geoff Jenkins	.25
82	Jacque Jones	.25
83	Corey Koskie	.25
84	Matt LeCroy	.25
85	David Ortiz	.35
86	*Johan Santana*	20.00
87	Todd Walker	.25
88	Peter Bergeron	.25
89	Vladimir Guerrero	1.50
90	Jose Vidro	.25
91	Rondell White	.25
92	Edgardo Alfonzo	.25
93	Derek Bell	.25
94	Mike Hampton	.25
95	Rey Ordonez	.25
96	Mike Piazza	2.50
97	Robin Ventura	.25
98	Roger Clemens	2.25
99	Orlando Hernandez	.25
100	Derek Jeter	4.00
101	Alfonso Soriano	.75
102	Bernie Williams	.35
103	Eric Chavez	.40
104	Jason Giambi	.75
105	Ben Grieve	.25
106	Tim Hudson	.40
107	Miguel Tejada	.40
108	Bobby Abreu	.25
109	Doug Glanville	.25
110	Mike Lieberthal	.25
111	Scott Rolen	.75
112	Brian Giles	.25
113	Chad Hermansen	.25
114	Jason Kendall	.25
115	Warren Morris	.25
116	Aramis Ramirez	.25
117	Rick Ankiel	.25
118	J.D. Drew	.40
119	Mark McGwire	3.00
120	Fernando Tatis	.25
121	Fernando Vina	.25
122	Bret Boone	.25
123	Ben Davis	.25
124	Tony Gwynn	2.00
125	Trevor Hoffman	.25
126	Ryan Klesko	.25
127	Rich Aurilia	.25
128	Barry Bonds	4.00
129	Ellis Burks	.25
130	Jeff Kent	.25
131	Freddy Garcia	.25
132	Carlos Guillen	.25
133	Edgar Martinez	.25
134	John Olerud	.25
135	Robert Ramsay	.25
136	Alex Rodriguez	3.00
137	*Kazuhiro Sasaki*	3.00
138	Jose Canseco	.50
139	Vinny Castilla	.25
140	Fred McGriff	.25
141	Greg Vaughn (front photois Mo Vaughn)	.25
142	Dan Wheeler	.25
143	Gabe Kapler	.25
144	Ruben Mateo	.25
145	Rafael Palmeiro	.75
146	Ivan Rodriguez	.75
147	Tony Batista	.25
148	Carlos Delgado	.65
149	Raul Mondesi	.25
150	Vernon Wells	.25

Platinum Blue

Stars: 4-8X
Production 67 sets

Holographic Purple

Stars: 2-3X
Production 299 sets

Diamond Aces

		NM/M
Complete Set (20):		5.00
Common Player:		.25
Inserted 1:1		
Edition of 399 Parallel:		2-3X
1	Randy Johnson	.75
2	Greg Maddux	1.00
3	Tom Glavine	.40
4	John Smoltz	.25
5	Mike Mussina	.50
6	Pedro Martinez	.75
7	Kerry Wood	.60
8	Bartolo Colon	.25
9	Brad Penny	.25
10	Billy Wagner	.25
11	Kevin Brown	.25
12	Mike Hampton	.25
13	Roger Clemens	1.50
14	David Cone	.25
15	Orlando Hernandez	.25
16	Mariano Rivera	.40
17	Tim Hudson	.40
18	Trevor Hoffman	.25
19	Rick Ankiel	.25
20	Freddy Garcia	.25

Eyes of the World

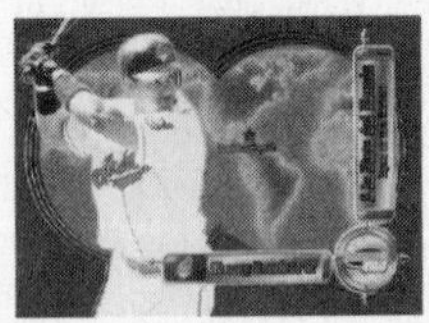

		NM/M
Complete Set (20):		30.00
Common Player:		.75
Inserted 1:25		
1	Erubiel Durazo	.75
2	Andruw Jones	2.00
3	Cal Ripken Jr.	6.00
4	Nomar Garciaparra	4.00
5	Pedro Martinez	2.00
6	Sammy Sosa	4.00
7	Ken Griffey Jr.	4.00
8	Manny Ramirez	2.00
9	Larry Walker	.75
10	Juan Gonzalez	2.00
11	Carlos Beltran	1.25
12	Vladimir Guerrero	2.00
13	Orlando Hernandez	.75
14	Derek Jeter	6.00
15	Mark McGwire	5.00
16	Tony Gwynn	3.00
17	Freddy Garcia	.75
18	Alex Rodriguez	5.00
19	Jose Canseco	1.25
20	Ivan Rodriguez	1.50

Game Gear

		NM/M
Common Card:		4.00
1	Jeff Bagwell Jsy/1000	8.00
2	Tom Glavine Jsy/1000	6.00
3	Mark Grace Jsy/1000	8.00
4	Eric Karros Jsy/1000	4.00
5	Edgar Martinez Jsy/800	6.00
6	Manny Ramirez Jsy/975	8.00
7	Cal Ripken Jr. Jsy/1000	25.00
8	Alex Rodriguez Jsy/900	15.00
9	Ivan Rodriguez Jsy/675	6.00
10	Mo Vaughn Jsy/1000	4.00
11	Edgar Martinez Bat-Jsy/200	8.00
12	Manny Ramirez Jsy/145	15.00
13	Alex Rodriguez Bat-Jsy/200	25.00
14	Ivan Rodriguez Bat-Jsy/200	10.00
15	Edgar Martinez Bat/200	10.00
16	Manny Ramirez Bat/200	15.00
17	Ivan Rodriguez Bat/200	8.00
18	Alex Rodriguez Bat/200	20.00
19	Jeff Bagwell Patch/125	30.00
20	Tom Glavine Patch/110	25.00
21	Mark Grace Patch/125	25.00
22	Tony Gwynn Patch/65	40.00
23	Chipper Jones Patch/80	40.00
24	Eric Karros Patch/125	15.00
25	Greg Maddux Patch/80	50.00
26	Edgar Martinez Patch/125	20.00
27	Manny Ramirez Patch/125	30.00
28	Cal Ripken Jr. Patch/125	65.00
29	Alex Rodriguez Patch/125	50.00
30	Ivan Rodriguez Patch/125	25.00
31	Frank Thomas Patch/125	25.00
32	Mo Vaughn Patch/125	15.00

Kings of the Diamond

		NM/M
Complete Set (30):		10.00
Common Player:		.20
Inserted 1:1		
1	Mo Vaughn	.20
2	Erubiel Durazo	.20
3	Andruw Jones	.65
4	Chipper Jones	.75
5	Cal Ripken Jr.	1.50
6	Nomar Garciaparra	1.00
7	Sammy Sosa	1.00
8	Frank Thomas	.65
9	Sean Casey	.25
10	Ken Griffey Jr.	1.00
11	Manny Ramirez	.65
12	Larry Walker	.20
13	Juan Gonzalez	.65
14	Jeff Bagwell	.65
15	Craig Biggio	.20
16	Carlos Beltran	.50
17	Shawn Green	.35
18	Vladimir Guerrero	.65
19	Mike Piazza	1.00
20	Derek Jeter	1.50
21	Bernie Williams	.40
22	Ben Grieve	.20
23	Scott Rolen	.40
24	Mark McGwire	1.25
25	Tony Gwynn	.75
26	Barry Bonds	1.50
27	Alex Rodriguez	1.25
28	Jose Canseco	.25
29	Rafael Palmeiro	.50
30	Ivan Rodriguez	.50

Lighting The Fire

		NM/M
Complete Set (20):		120.00
Common Player:		3.00
Inserted 1:49		
1	Chipper Jones	8.00
2	Greg Maddux	8.00
3	Cal Ripken Jr.	15.00
4	Nomar Garciaparra	10.00
5	Pedro Martinez	6.00
6	Ken Griffey Jr.	10.00
7	Sammy Sosa	10.00
8	Manny Ramirez	6.00
9	Juan Gonzalez	6.00
10	Jeff Bagwell	6.00
11	Shawn Green	3.00
12	Vladimir Guerrero	6.00
13	Mike Piazza	10.00
14	Roger Clemens	9.00
15	Derek Jeter	15.00
16	Mark McGwire	12.00
17	Tony Gwynn	8.00
18	Alex Rodriguez	12.00
19	Jose Canseco	3.00
20	Ivan Rodriguez	5.00

Ticket To Stardom

		NM/M
Complete Set (20):		250.00
Common Player:		5.00
Inserted 1:121		
1	Andruw Jones	10.00
2	Chipper Jones	15.00
3	Cal Ripken Jr.	30.00
4	Nomar Garciaparra	20.00
5	Pedro Martinez	10.00
6	Ken Griffey Jr.	20.00
7	Sammy Sosa	20.00
8	Manny Ramirez	10.00
9	Jeff Bagwell	10.00
10	Shawn Green	5.00
11	Vladimir Guerrero	10.00
12	Mike Piazza	20.00
13	Derek Jeter	30.00
14	Alfonso Soriano	8.00
15	Scott Rolen	6.00
16	Rick Ankiel	5.00
17	Mark McGwire	25.00
18	Tony Gwynn	15.00
19	Alex Rodriguez	25.00
20	Ivan Rodriguez	8.00

2000 PACIFIC OMEGA

	NM/M
Complete Set (255):	300.00
Common Player:	.10
Common (151-255):	4.00
Production 999 sets	

1 Garret Anderson .10
2 Darin Erstad .25
3 Troy Glaus .75
4 Tim Salmon .20
5 Mo Vaughn .10
6 Jay Bell .10
7 Steve Finley .10
8 Luis Gonzalez .20
9 Randy Johnson .75
10 Matt Williams .10
11 Andres Galarraga .10
12 Andruw Jones .75
13 Chipper Jones 1.00
14 Brian Jordan .10
15 Greg Maddux 1.00
16 B.J. Surhoff .10
17 Brady Anderson .10
18 Albert Belle .10
19 Mike Mussina .40
20 Cal Ripken Jr. 2.50
21 Carl Everett .10
22 Nomar Garciaparra 1.50
23 Pedro Martinez .75
24 Jason Varitek .10
25 Mark Grace .20
26 Sammy Sosa 1.50
27 Rondell White .10
28 Kerry Wood .35
29 Eric Young .10
30 Ray Durham .10
31 Carlos Lee .10
32 Magglio Ordonez .25
33 Frank Thomas .75
34 Sean Casey .20
35 Ken Griffey Jr. 1.50
36 Barry Larkin .10
37 Pokey Reese .10
38 Roberto Alomar .40
39 Kenny Lofton .10
40 Manny Ramirez .75
41 David Segui .10
42 Jim Thome .60
43 Omar Vizquel .10
44 Jeff Cirillo .10
45 Jeffrey Hammonds .10
46 Todd Helton .75
47 Todd Hollandsworth .10
48 Larry Walker .10
49 Tony Clark .10
50 Juan Encarnacion .10
51 Juan Gonzalez .75
52 Bobby Higginson .10
53 Hideo Nomo .75
54 Dean Palmer .10
55 Luis Castillo .10
56 Cliff Floyd .10
57 Derrek Lee .10
58 Mike Lowell .10
59 Henry Rodriguez .10
60 Preston Wilson .10
61 Moises Alou .10
62 Jeff Bagwell .75
63 Craig Biggio .10
64 Ken Caminiti .10
65 Richard Hidalgo .10
66 Carlos Beltran .40
67 Johnny Damon .25
68 Jermaine Dye .10
69 Joe Randa .10
70 Mike Sweeney .10
71 Adrian Beltre .20
72 Kevin Brown .10
73 Shawn Green .35
74 Eric Karros .10
75 Chan Ho Park .10
76 Gary Sheffield .30
77 Ron Belliard .10
78 Jeromy Burnitz .10
79 Geoff Jenkins .10
80 Richie Sexson .10
81 Ron Coomer .10
82 Jacque Jones .10
83 Corey Koskie .10
84 Matt Lawton .10
85 Vladimir Guerrero .75
86 Lee Stevens .10
87 Jose Vidro .10
88 Edgardo Alfonzo .10
89 Derek Bell .10
90 Mike Bordick .10
91 Mike Piazza 1.50
92 Robin Ventura .10
93 Jose Canseco .40
94 Roger Clemens 1.25
95 Orlando Hernandez .10
96 Derek Jeter 2.50
97 David Justice .10
98 Tino Martinez .10
99 Jorge Posada .10
100 Bernie Williams .40
101 Eric Chavez .20
102 Jason Giambi .50
103 Ben Grieve .10
104 Miguel Tejada .25
105 Bobby Abreu .10
106 Doug Glanville .10
107 Travis Lee .10
108 Mike Lieberthal .10
109 Scott Rolen .65
110 Brian S. Giles .10
111 Jason Kendall .10
112 Warren Morris .10
113 Kevin Young .10
114 Will Clark .20
115 J.D. Drew .20
116 Jim Edmonds .10
117 Mark McGwire 2.00
118 Edgar Renteria .10
119 Fernando Tatis .10
120 Fernando Vina .10
121 Bret Boone .10
122 Tony Gwynn 1.00
123 Trevor Hoffman .10
124 Phil Nevin .10
125 Eric Owens .10
126 Barry Bonds 2.50
127 Ellis Burks .10
128 Jeff Kent .10
129 J.T. Snow .10
130 Jay Buhner .10
131 Mike Cameron .10
132 Rickey Henderson .75
133 Edgar Martinez .10
134 John Olerud .10
135 Alex Rodriguez 2.00
136 *Kazuhiro Sasaki* 1.00
137 Fred McGriff .10
138 Greg Vaughn .10
139 Gerald Williams .10
140 Rusty Greer .10
141 Gabe Kapler .10
142 Ricky Ledee .10
143 Rafael Palmeiro .65
144 Ivan Rodriguez .65
145 Tony Batista .10
146 Jose Cruz Jr. .10
147 Carlos Delgado .50
148 Brad Fullmer .10
149 Shannon Stewart .10
150 David Wells .10
151 Juan Alvarez, Jeff DaVanon 6.00
152 Seth Etherton, Adam Kennedy 4.00
153 Ramon Ortiz, Lou Pote 4.00
154 Derrick Turnbow, Eric Weaver 4.00
155 Rod Barajas, Jason Conti 4.00
156 Byung-Hyun Kim, Rob Ryan 4.00
157 David Cortes, George Lombard 4.00
158 Ivanon Coffie, Melvin Mora 4.00
159 *Ryan Kohlmeier, Luis Matos* 6.00
160 *Willie Morales, John Parrish* 4.00
161 *Chris Richard, Jay Spurgeon* 5.00
162 *Israel Alcantara, Tomokazu Ohka* 5.00
163 *Paxton Crawford, Sang-Hoon Lee* 4.00
164 Mike Mahoney, Wilton Veras 4.00
165 *Daniel Garibay, Ross Gload* 4.00
166 Gary Matthews Jr., Phil Norton 4.00
167 Roosevelt Brown, Ruben Quevedo 4.00
168 *Lorenzo Barcelo, Rocky Biddle* 4.00
169 Mark Buehrle, John Garland 8.00
170 Aaron Myette, Josh Paul 4.00
171 Kip Wells, Kelly Wunsch 4.00
172 Rob Bell, Travis Dawkins 4.00
173 *Hector Mercado, John Riedling* 4.00
174 Russell Branyan, Sean DePaula 4.00
175 Tim Drew, Mark Watson 4.00
176 Craig House, Ben Petrick 5.00
177 Robert Fick, Jose Macias 4.00
178 Javier Cardona, Brandon Villafuerte 4.00
179 Armando Almanza, A.J. Burnett 4.00
180 Ramon Castro, Pablo Ozuna 4.00
181 Lance Berkman, Jason Green 4.00
182 Julio Lugo, Tony McKnight 4.00
183 Mitch Meluskey, Wade Miller 4.00
184 *Chad Durbin, Hector Ortiz* 5.00
185 Dermal Brown, Mark Quinn 4.00
186 Eric Gagne, Mike Judd 4.00
187 Kane Davis, Valerio de los Santos 4.00
188 *Santiago Perez, Paul Rigdon* 4.00
189 Matt Kinney, Matt LeCroy 4.00
190 Jason Maxwell, A.J. Pierzynski 4.00
191 *J.C. Romero, Johan Santana* 50.00
192 Tony Armas Jr., Peter Bergeron 4.00
193 Matt Blank, Milton Bradley 4.00
194 Tomas De La Rossa, Scott Forster 4.00
195 *Yovanny Lara, Talmadge Nunnari* 4.00
196 Brian Schneider, Andy Tracy 4.00
197 Scott Strickland, T.J. Tucker 4.00
198 *Eric Cammack, Jim Mann* 4.00
199 Grant Roberts, Jorge Toca 4.00
200 Alfonso Soriano, Jay Tessmer 8.00
201 Terrence Long, Mark Mulder 4.00
202 Pat Burrell, Cliff Politte 4.00
203 Jimmy Anderson, Bronson Arroyo 4.00
204 Mike Darr, Kory DeHaan 4.00
205 Adam Eaton, Wiki Gonzalez 4.00
206 Brandon Kolb, Kevin Walker 4.00
207 Damon Minor, Calvin Murray 4.00
208 *Kevin Hodges, Joel Pineiro* 40.00
209 *Rob Ramsay, Kazuhiro Sasaki* 8.00
210 Rick Ankiel, Mike Matthews 4.00
211 Steve Cox, Travis Harper 4.00
212 *Kenny Kelly, Damian Rolls* 4.00
213 Doug Davis, Scott Sheldon 4.00
214 Brian Sikorski, Pedro Valdes 4.00
215 Francisco Cordero, B.J. Waszgis 4.00
216 *Matt DeWitt, Josh Phelps* 8.00
217 Vernon Wells, Dewayne Wise 4.00
218 Geraldo Guzman, Jason Marquis 4.00
219 *Rafael Furcal, Steve Sisco* 4.00
220 B.J. Ryan, Kevin Beirne 4.00
221 Matt Ginter, Brad Penny 4.00
222 Julio Zuleta, Eric Munson 5.00
223 Dan Reichert, Jeff Williams 4.00
224 Jason LaRue, Danny Ardoin 4.00
225 Ray King, Mark Redman 4.00
226 Joe Crede, Mike Bell 4.00
227 Juan Pierre, Jay Payton 6.00
228 *Wayne Franklin, Randy Choate* 4.00
229 Chris Truby, Adam Piatt 4.00
230 Kevin Nicholson, Chris Woodward 4.00
231 Barry Zito, Jason Boyd 15.00
232 Brian O'Connor, Miguel Del Toro 4.00
233 Carlos Guillen, Aubrey Huff 4.00
234 Chad Hermansen, Jason Tyner 4.00
235 Aaron Fultz, Ryan Vogelsong 4.00
236 Shawn Wooten, Vance Wilson 4.00
237 *Danny Klassen, Mike Lamb* 4.00
238 *Chad Bradford, Gene Stechschulte* 4.00
239 Ismael Villegas, Hector Ramirez, Matt T. Williams, Luis Vizcaino 4.00
240 *Mike Garcia, Domingo Guzman, Justin Brunette, Pasqual Coco* 4.00
241 *Frank Charles, Keith McDonald* 4.00
242 *Carlos Casimiro, Morgan Burkhart* 4.00
243 Raul Gonzalez, Shawn Gilbert 4.00
244 *Darrell Einertson, Jeff Sparks* 4.00
245 *Augie Ojeda, Brady Clark, Todd Belitz, Eric Byrnes* 6.00
246 Leo Estrella, Charlie Greene 4.00
247 *Trace Coquillette, Pedro Feliz* 6.00
248 Tike Redman, David Newhan 4.00
249 Rodrigo Lopez, John Bales 6.00
250 *Corey Patterson, Jose Ortiz* 6.00
251 *Britt Reames, Oswaldo Mairena* 4.00
252 *Xavier Nady, Timoniel Perez* 6.00
253 Tom Jacquez, Vicente Padilla 4.00
254 *Elvis Pena, Adam Melhuse* 4.00
255 *Ben Weber, Alex Cabrera* 6.00

Copper

Stars (1-150): 8-15X
Production 45 sets

Platinum Blue

Stars (1-150): 6-10X
Production 55 sets

Premiere Date

Stars (1-150): 4-8X
Production 77 sets

AL Contenders

NM/M

Complete Set (18): 20.00
Common Player: .50
Inserted 2:37

1 Darin Erstad .75
2 Troy Glaus 1.50
3 Mo Vaughn .50
4 Albert Belle .50
5 Cal Ripken Jr. 4.00
6 Nomar Garciaparra 3.00
7 Pedro Martinez 1.50
8 Frank Thomas 1.50
9 Manny Ramirez 1.50
10 Jim Thome 1.25
11 Juan Gonzalez 1.50
12 Roger Clemens 2.50
13 Derek Jeter 4.00
14 Bernie Williams .75

15	Jason Giambi	1.00
16	Alex Rodriguez	3.50
17	Edgar Martinez	.50
18	Carlos Delgado	1.00

NL Contenders

		NM/M
Complete Set (18):		20.00
Common Player:		.50
Inserted 2:37		
1	Randy Johnson	1.50
2	Chipper Jones	2.00
3	Greg Maddux	2.00
4	Sammy Sosa	2.50
5	Sean Casey	.50
6	Ken Griffey Jr.	2.50
7	Todd Helton	1.50
8	Jeff Bagwell	1.50
9	Shawn Green	.50
10	Gary Sheffield	.75
11	Vladimir Guerrero	1.50
12	Mike Piazza	2.50
13	Scott Rolen	1.00
14	Barry Bonds	4.00
15	Rick Ankiel	.50
16	J.D. Drew	.50
17	Jim Edmonds	.50
18	Mark McGwire	3.00

EO Portraits

		NM/M
Complete Set (20):		125.00
Common Player:		3.00
Inserted 1:73		
1-of-1 Die-Cut Parallels Exist		
1	Chipper Jones	8.00
2	Greg Maddux	8.00
3	Cal Ripken Jr.	15.00
4	Pedro Martinez	6.00
5	Nomar Garciaparra	10.00
6	Sammy Sosa	10.00
7	Frank Thomas	6.00
8	Ken Griffey Jr.	10.00
9	Gary Sheffield	4.00
10	Vladimir Guerrero	6.00
11	Mike Piazza	10.00
12	Roger Clemens	9.00
13	Derek Jeter	15.00
14	Pat Burrell	4.00
15	Tony Gwynn	8.00
16	Barry Bonds	15.00
17	Alex Rodriguez	12.00
18	Rick Ankiel	3.00
19	Mark McGwire	12.00
20	Ivan Rodriguez	5.00

MLB Generations

		NM/M
Complete Set (20):		100.00
Common Card:		3.00
Inserted 1:145		
1	Mark McGwire, Pat Burrell	12.00
2	Cal Ripken Jr., Alex Rodriguez	15.00
3	Randy Johnson, Rick Ankiel	6.00
4	Tony Gwynn, Darin Erstad	8.00
5	Barry Bonds, Magglio Ordonez	15.00
6	Frank Thomas, Jason Giambi	6.00
7	Roger Clemens, Kerry Wood	9,000,008
8	Mike Piazza, Mitch Meluskey	10.00
9	Ken Griffey Jr., Andruw Jones	10.00
10	Bernie Williams, J.D. Drew	4.00
11	Chipper Jones, Troy Glaus	8.00
12	Andres Galarraga, Todd Helton	6.00
13	Juan Gonzalez, Vladimir Guerrero	6.00
14	Craig Biggio, Rafael Furcal	3.00
15	Sammy Sosa, Jermaine Dye	10.00
16	Larry Walker, Richard Hidalgo	3.00
17	Greg Maddux, Adam Eaton	8.00
18	Barry Larkin, Derek Jeter	15.00
19	Roberto Alomar, Jose Vidro	4.00
20	Jeff Kent, Edgardo Alfonzo	3.00

Full Court

		NM/M
Complete Set (36):		30.00
Common Player:		.50
Inserted 4:37 H		
1	Magglio Ordonez	.50
2	Manny Ramirez	1.50
3	Todd Helton	1.50
4	David Justice	.50
5	Bernie Williams	.50
6	Jason Giambi	1.00
7	Scott Rolen	1.00
8	Jeff Kent	.50
9	Edgar Martinez	.50
10	Randy Johnson	1.50
11	Greg Maddux	2.00
12	Mike Mussina	.60
13	Pedro Martinez	1.50
14	Chuck Finley	.50
15	Kevin Brown	.50
16	Roger Clemens	2.25
17	Tim Hudson	.50
18	Rick Ankiel	.50
19	Troy Glaus	1.50
20	Chipper Jones	2.00
21	Nomar Garciaparra	2.50
22	Jeff Bagwell	1.50
23	Shawn Green	.60
24	Vladimir Guerrero	1.50
25	Mike Piazza	2.50
26	Jim Edmonds	.50
27	Rafael Palmeiro	.75
28	Cal Ripken Jr.	4.00
29	Sammy Sosa	2.50
30	Frank Thomas	1.50
31	Ken Griffey Jr.	2.50
32	Gary Sheffield	.50
33	Barry Bonds	4.00
34	Alex Rodriguez	3.00
35	Mark McGwire	3.00
36	Carlos Delgado	1.00

Signatures

		NM/M
Common Player:		5.00
1	Darin Erstad	10.00
2	Nomar Garciaparra	125.00
3	Cal Eldred	5.00
4	Magglio Ordonez	10.00
5	Frank Thomas	30.00
6	Brady Clark	5.00
7	Richard Hidalgo	5.00
8	Gary Sheffield	10.00
9	Pat Burrell	15.00
10	Jim Edmonds	10.00

Stellar Performers

		NM/M
Complete Set (20):		50.00
Common Player:		1.00
Inserted 1:37		
1	Darin Erstad	1.00
2	Chipper Jones	3.00
3	Greg Maddux	3.00
4	Cal Ripken Jr.	6.00
5	Pedro Martinez	2.00
6	Nomar Garciaparra	4.00
7	Sammy Sosa	4.00
8	Frank Thomas	2.00
9	Ken Griffey Jr.	4.00
10	Todd Helton	2.00
11	Jeff Bagwell	2.00
12	Vladimir Guerrero	2.00
13	Mike Piazza	4.00
14	Derek Jeter	6.00
15	Roger Clemens	3.50
16	Tony Gwynn	3.00
17	Barry Bonds	6.00
18	Alex Rodriguez	5.00
19	Mark McGwire	5.00
20	Ivan Rodriguez	1.50

2000 PACIFIC PARAMOUNT

		NM/M
Complete Set (250):		25.00
Common Player:		.10
Pack (6):		1.50
Wax Box (36):		40.00
1	Garret Anderson	.10
2	Jim Edmonds	.10
3	Darin Erstad	.25
4	Chuck Finley	.10
5	Troy Glaus	.75
6	Troy Percival	.10
7	Tim Salmon	.20
8	Mo Vaughn	.10
9	Jay Bell	.10
10	Erubiel Durazo	.10
11	Steve Finley	.10
12	Luis Gonzalez	.20
13	Randy Johnson	.75
14	Travis Lee	.10
15	Matt Mantei	.10
16	Matt Williams	.10
17	Tony Womack	.10
18	Bret Boone	.10
19	Tom Glavine	.35
20	Andruw Jones	.75
21	Chipper Jones	1.00
22	Brian Jordan	.10
23	Javy Lopez	.10
24	Greg Maddux	1.00
25	Kevin Millwood	.10
26	John Rocker	.10
27	John Smoltz	.10
28	Brady Anderson	.10
29	Albert Belle	.10
30	Will Clark	.20
31	Charles Johnson	.10
32	Mike Mussina	.35
33	Cal Ripken Jr.	2.00
34	B.J. Surhoff	.10
35	Nomar Garciaparra	1.25
36	Derek Lowe	.10
37	Pedro Martinez	.75
38	Trot Nixon	.10
39	Troy O'Leary	.10
40	Jose Offerman	.10
41	John Valentin	.10
42	Jason Varitek	.10
43	Mark Grace	.20
44	Glenallen Hill	.10
45	Jon Lieber	.10
46	Cole Liniak	.10
47	Jose Nieves	.10
48	Henry Rodriguez	.10
49	Sammy Sosa	1.25
50	Kerry Wood	.65
51	Jason Dellaero	.10
52	Ray Durham	.10
53	Paul Konerko	.10
54	Carlos Lee	.10
55	Greg Norton	.10
56	Magglio Ordonez	.10
57	Chris Singleton	.10
58	Frank Thomas	.75
59	Aaron Boone	.10
60	Mike Cameron	.10
61	Sean Casey	.20
62	Pete Harnisch	.10
63	Barry Larkin	.10
64	Pokey Reese	.10
65	Greg Vaughn	.10
66	Scott Williamson	.10
67	Roberto Alomar	.35
68	*Sean DePaula*	.20
69	Travis Fryman	.10
70	David Justice	.10
71	Kenny Lofton	.10
72	Manny Ramirez	.75
73	Richie Sexson	.10
74	Jim Thome	.65
75	Omar Vizquel	.10
76	Pedro Astacio	.10
77	Vinny Castilla	.10
78	Derrick Gibson	.10
79	Todd Helton	.75
80	Neifi Perez	.10
81	Ben Petrick	.10
82	Larry Walker	.10
83	Brad Ausmus	.10
84	Tony Clark	.10
85	Deivi Cruz	.10
86	Damion Easley	.10
87	Juan Encarnacion	.10
88	Juan Gonzalez	.75
89	Bobby Higginson	.10
90	Dave Mlicki	.10
91	Dean Palmer	.10
92	Bruce Aven	.10
93	Luis Castillo	.10
94	Ramon Castro	.10
95	Cliff Floyd	.10
96	Alex Gonzalez	.10
97	Mike Lowell	.10
98	Preston Wilson	.10
99	Jeff Bagwell	.75
100	Derek Bell	.10
101	Craig Biggio	.10
102	Ken Caminiti	.10
103	Carl Everett	.10
104	Mike Hampton	.10
105	Jose Lima	.10
106	Billy Wagner	.10
107	Daryle Ward	.10
108	Carlos Beltran	.40
109	Johnny Damon	.25
110	Jermaine Dye	.10
111	Carlos Febles	.10
112	Mark Quinn	.10
113	Joe Randa	.10
114	Jose Rosado	.10
115	Mike Sweeney	.10
116	Kevin Brown	.10
117	Shawn Green	.35
118	Mark Grudzielanek	.10
119	Todd Hollandsworth	.10
120	Eric Karros	.10
121	Chan Ho Park	.10
122	Gary Sheffield	.35
123	Devon White	.10
124	Eric Young	.10
125	Kevin Barker	.10
126	Ron Belliard	.10
127	Jeromy Burnitz	.10
128	Jeff Cirillo	.10
129	Marquis Grissom	.10
130	Geoff Jenkins	.10
131	David Nilsson	.10
132	Chad Allen	.10
133	Ron Coomer	.10

134 Jacque Jones .10
135 Corey Koskie .10
136 Matt Lawton .10
137 Brad Radke .10
138 Todd Walker .10
139 Michael Barrett .10
140 Peter Bergeron .10
141 Brad Fullmer .10
142 Vladimir Guerrero .75
143 Ugueth Urbina .10
144 Jose Vidro .10
145 Rondell White .10
146 Edgardo Alfonzo .10
147 Armando Benitez .10
148 Roger Cedeno .10
149 Rickey Henderson .75
150 Melvin Mora .10
151 John Olerud .10
152 Rey Ordonez .10
153 Mike Piazza 1.25
154 Jorge Toca .10
155 Robin Ventura .10
156 Roger Clemens 1.00
157 David Cone .10
158 Orlando Hernandez .10
159 Derek Jeter 2.00
160 Chuck Knoblauch .10
161 Ricky Ledee .10
162 Tino Martinez .10
163 Paul O'Neill .10
164 Mariano Rivera .20
165 Alfonso Soriano .75
166 Bernie Williams .25
167 Eric Chavez .25
168 Jason Giambi .50
169 Ben Grieve .10
170 Tim Hudson .25
171 John Jaha .10
172 Matt Stairs .10
173 Miguel Tejada .25
174 Randy Velarde .10
175 Bobby Abreu .10
176 Marlon Anderson .10
177 Rico Brogna .10
178 Ron Gant .10
179 Doug Glanville .10
180 Mike Lieberthal .10
181 Scott Rolen .65
182 Curt Schilling .35
183 Brian Giles .10
184 Chad Hermansen .10
185 Jason Kendall .10
186 Al Martin .10
187 Pat Meares .10
188 Warren Morris .10
189 Ed Sprague .10
190 Kevin Young .10
191 Rick Ankiel .20
192 Kent Bottenfield .10
193 Eric Davis .10
194 J.D. Drew .25
195 Adam Kennedy .10
196 Ray Lankford .10
197 Joe McEwing .10
198 Mark McGwire 1.50
199 Edgar Renteria .10
200 Fernando Tatis .10
201 Mike Darr .10
202 Ben Davis .10
203 Tony Gwynn 1.00
204 Trevor Hoffman .10
205 Damian Jackson .10
206 Phil Nevin .10
207 Reggie Sanders .10
208 Quilvio Veras .10
209 Rich Aurilia .10
210 Marvin Benard .10
211 Barry Bonds 2.00
212 Ellis Burks .10
213 Livan Hernandez .10
214 Jeff Kent .10
215 Russ Ortiz .10
216 J.T. Snow .10
217 Paul Abbott .10
218 David Bell .10
219 Freddy Garcia .10
220 Ken Griffey Jr. 1.50
221 Carlos Guillen .10
222 Brian Hunter .10
223 Edgar Martinez .10
224 Jamie Moyer .10
225 Alex Rodriguez 1.50
226 Wade Boggs 1.00
227 Miguel Cairo .10
228 Jose Canseco .40
229 Roberto Hernandez .10
230 Dave Martinez .10
231 Quinton McCracken .10
232 Fred McGriff .10
233 Kevin Stocker .10
234 Royce Clayton .10
235 Rusty Greer .10
236 Ruben Mateo .10
237 Rafael Palmeiro .65
238 Ivan Rodriguez .65
239 Aaron Sele .10
240 John Wetteland .10
241 Todd Zeile .10
242 Tony Batista .10
243 Homer Bush .10
244 Carlos Delgado .50
245 Tony Fernandez .10
246 Billy Koch .10
247 Raul Mondesi .10
248 Shannon Stewart .10
249 David Wells .10
250 Vernon Wells .10

Holographic Gold

Stars: 3-6X
Production 199 sets

Emerald

Stars: 1-2X
Yng Stars & RCs: 1X
Inserted 1:1 7-11 pack
Inserted 1:1 R
Stars: 1-2X
Yng Stars & Rcs: 1X

Holographic Green

Stars: 6-10X
Production 99 sets, 7-11 insert

Ruby Red

Stars: 1-2X
RCs: 1X
Inserted 9 per 7-11 pack

Premiere Date

Stars: 8-15X
Production 50 sets

Copper

Stars: 2X
Inserted 1:1 H

Holographic Silver

Stars: 5-10X
Production 99 sets

Platinum Blue

Stars: 6-12X
Production 67 sets

Cooperstown Bound

NM/M
Complete Set (10): 220.00
Common Player: 20.00
Inserted 1:361
Proofs: 2X
Production 20 sets, hobby only
Canvas Proofs:
VALUES UNDETERMINED
Production 1 set
1 Greg Maddux 20.00
2 Cal Ripken Jr. 40.00
3 Nomar Garciaparra 25.00
4 Sammy Sosa 25.00
5 Roger Clemens 30.00
6 Derek Jeter 40.00
7 Mark McGwire 30.00
8 Tony Gwynn 20.00
9 Ken Griffey Jr. 25.00
10 Alex Rodriguez 30.00

Double Vision

NM/M
Complete Set (36): 220.00
Common Player: 3.00
Inserted 1:37
1 Chipper Jones 8.00

2 Cal Ripken Jr. 15.00
3 Nomar Garciaparra 10.00
4 Pedro Martinez 6.00
5 Sammy Sosa 10.00
6 Manny Ramirez 6.00
7 Jeff Bagwell 6.00
8 Craig Biggio 3.00
9 Vladimir Guerrero 6.00
10 Mike Piazza 10.00
11 Roger Clemens 9.00
12 Derek Jeter 15.00
13 Mark McGwire 12.00
14 Tony Gwynn 8.00
15 Ken Griffey Jr. 10.00
16 Alex Rodriguez 12.00
17 Rafael Palmeiro 5.00
18 Ivan Rodriguez 5.00
19 Chipper Jones 8.00
20 Cal Ripken Jr. 15.00
21 Nomar Garciaparra 10.00
22 Pedro Martinez 6.00
23 Sammy Sosa 10.00
24 Manny Ramirez 6.00
25 Jeff Bagwell 6.00
26 Craig Biggio 3.00
27 Vladimir Guerrero 6.00
28 Mike Piazza 10.00
29 Roger Clemens 9.00
30 Derek Jeter 15.00
31 Mark McGwire 12.00
32 Tony Gwynn 8.00
33 Ken Griffey Jr. 10.00
34 Alex Rodriguez 12.00
35 Rafael Palmeiro 5.00
36 Ivan Rodriguez 5.00

Fielder's Choice

NM/M
Complete Set (20): 150.00
Common Player: 3.00
Inserted 1:73
Gold Parallel (10 sets issued): 6-8X
1 Andruw Jones 5.00
2 Chipper Jones 8.00
3 Greg Maddux 8.00
4 Cal Ripken Jr. 20.00
5 Nomar Garciaparra 10.00
6 Sammy Sosa 10.00
7 Sean Casey 3.00
8 Manny Ramirez 5.00
9 Larry Walker 3.00
10 Jeff Bagwell 5.00
11 Mike Piazza 10.00
12 Derek Jeter 20.00
13 Bernie Williams 3.00
14 Scott Rolen 4.00
15 Mark McGwire 15.00
16 Tony Gwynn 8.00
17 Barry Bonds 20.00
18 Ken Griffey Jr. 10.00
19 Alex Rodriguez 15.00
20 Ivan Rodriguez 4.00

Maximum Impact

NM/M
Complete Set (20): 25.00
Common Player: .50
Inserted 2:25 7-11 packs
1 Chipper Jones 2.00
2 Cal Ripken Jr. 4.00
3 Nomar Garciaparra 2.50
4 Pedro Martinez 1.50
5 Sammy Sosa 2.50
6 Manny Ramirez 1.50
7 Larry Walker .50
8 Jeff Bagwell 1.50
9 Carlos Beltran .75
10 Vladimir Guerrero 1.50
11 Mike Piazza 2.50
12 Derek Jeter 4.00
13 Roger Clemens 2.25
14 Mark McGwire 3.00
15 Tony Gwynn 2.00
16 Barry Bonds 4.00
17 Ken Griffey Jr. 2.50
18 Alex Rodriguez 3.00
19 Ivan Rodriguez 1.00
20 Carlos Delgado .75

Season in Review

NM/M
Complete Set (30): 25.00
Common Player: .50
Inserted 2:37
1 Randy Johnson 1.50
2 Matt Williams .50
3 Chipper Jones 2.00
4 Greg Maddux 2.00
5 Cal Ripken Jr. 4.00
6 Nomar Garciaparra 2.50
7 Pedro Martinez 1.50
8 Sammy Sosa 2.50
9 Manny Ramirez 1.50
10 Larry Walker .50
11 Jeff Bagwell 1.50
12 Craig Biggio .50
13 Carlos Beltran .75
14 Mark Quinn .50
15 Vladimir Guerrero 1.50
16 Mike Piazza 2.50
17 Robin Ventura .50
18 Roger Clemens 2.25
19 David Cone .50
20 Derek Jeter 4.00
21 Mark McGwire 3.00
22 Fernando Tatis .50
23 Tony Gwynn 2.00
24 Barry Bonds 4.00
25 Ken Griffey Jr. 2.50
26 Alex Rodriguez 3.00
27 Wade Boggs 2.00
28 Jose Canseco .65
29 Rafael Palmeiro 1.00
30 Ivan Rodriguez 1.00

2000 PACIFIC PARAMOUNT UPDATE

NM/M
Complete Set (100): 10.00
Common Player: .10
Production 12,500 sets; retail exclusive
1-U Adam Kennedy .10
2-U Bengie Molina .10
3-U Derrick Turnbow .10
4-U Randy Johnson .75
5-U Danny Klassen .10

6-U	Vicente Padilla	.10
7-U	Rafael Furcal	.10
8-U	Andres Galarraga	.10
9-U	Chipper Jones	1.00
10-U	Fernando Lunar	.10
11-U	Willie Morales	.10
12-U	Cal Ripken Jr.	2.00
13-U	B.J. Ryan	.10
14-U	Carl Everett	.10
15-U	Nomar Garciaparra	1.25
16-U	Pedro Martinez	.75
17-U	Wilton Veras	.10
18-U	Scott Downs	.10
19-U	Daniel Garibay	.10
20-U	Sammy Sosa	1.25
21-U	Julio Zuleta	.10
22-U	Josh Paul	.10
23-U	Frank Thomas	.75
24-U	Rob Bell	.10
25-U	Dante Bichette	.10
26-U	Travis Dawkins	.10
27-U	Ken Griffey Jr.	1.25
28-U	Chuck Finley	.10
29-U	Manny Ramirez	.75
30-U	Paul Rigdon	.10
31-U	Jeff Cirillo	.10
32-U	Larry Walker	.10
33-U	Masato Yoshii	.10
34-U	Robert Fick	.10
35-U	Jose Macias	.10
36-U	Juan Gonzalez	.75
37-U	Hideo Nomo	.75
38-U	Jason Grilli	.10
39-U	Pablo Ozuna	.10
40-U	Brad Penny	.10
41-U	Jeff Bagwell	.75
42-U	Lance Berkman	.10
43-U	Roger Cedeno	.10
44-U	Octavio Dotel	.10
45-U	Chad Durbin	.10
46-U	Eric Gagne	.10
47-U	Shawn Green	.35
48-U	Jose Hernandez	.10
49-U	Matt LeCroy	.10
50-U	Johan Santana	.10
51-U	Vladimir Guerrero	.75
52-U	Hideki Irabu	.10
53-U	Andrew Tracy	.10
54-U	Derek Bell	.10
55-U	Eric Cammack	.10
56-U	Mike Hampton	.10
57-U	Jay Payton	.10
58-U	Mike Piazza	1.25
59-U	Todd Zeile	.10
60-U	Roger Clemens	1.00
61-U	Darrell Einertson	.10
62-U	Derek Jeter	2.00
63-U	Jason Giambi	.60
64-U	Terrence Long	.10
65-U	Mark Mulder	.10
66-U	Adam Piatt	.10
67-U	Luis Vizcaino	.10
68-U	Pat Burrell	.35
69-U	Scott Rolen	.65
70-U	Chad Hermansen	.10
71-U	Rick Ankiel	.15
72-U	Jim Edmonds	.10
73-U	Mark McGwire	1.50
74-U	Gene Stechschulte	.10
75-U	Fernando Vina	.10
76-U	Bret Boone	.10
77-U	Tony Gwynn	1.00
78-U	Ryan Klesko	.10
79-U	David Newhan	.10
80-U	Kevin Walker	.10
81-U	Barry Bonds	2.00
82-U	Aaron Fultz	.10
83-U	Ben Weber	.10
84-U	Rickey Henderson	.75
85-U	Kevin Hodges	.10
86-U	John Olerud	.10
87-U	Robert Ramsay	.10
88-U	Alex Rodriguez	1.50
89-U	Kazuhiro Sasaki	.15
90-U	Vinny Castilla	.10
91-U	Jeff Sparks	.10
92-U	Greg Vaughn	.10
93-U	Francisco Cordero	.10
94-U	Gabe Kapler	.10
95-U	Mike Lamb	.10
96-U	Ivan Rodriguez	.65
97-U	Clayton Andrews	.10
98-U	Brad Fullmer	.10
99-U	Raul Mondesi	.10
100-U	Dewayne Wise	.10

2000 PACIFIC PRISM

	NM/M
Complete Set (150):	10.00
Common Player:	.10
Pack (5):	1.50
Wax Box (24):	15.00

1	*Jeff DaVanon*	.10
2	Troy Glaus	.50
3	Tim Salmon	.15
4	Mo Vaughn	.10
5	Jay Bell	.10
6	Erubiel Durazo	.10
7	Luis Gonzalez	.20
8	Randy Johnson	.50
9	Matt Williams	.10
10	Andres Galarraga	.10
11	Andruw Jones	.50
12	Chipper Jones	.65
13	Brian Jordan	.10
14	Greg Maddux	.65
15	Kevin Millwood	.10
16	John Smoltz	.10
17	Albert Belle	.15
18	Mike Mussina	.25
19	Calvin Pickering	.10
20	Cal Ripken Jr.	1.50
21	B.J. Surhoff	.10
22	Nomar Garciaparra	1.00
23	Pedro Martinez	.50
24	Troy O'Leary	.10
25	John Valentin	.10
26	Jason Varitek	.10
27	Mark Grace	.15
28	Henry Rodriguez	.10
29	Sammy Sosa	1.00
30	Kerry Wood	.25
31	Ray Durham	.10
32	Carlos Lee	.10
33	Magglio Ordonez	.10
34	Chris Singleton	.10
35	Frank Thomas	.50
36	Sean Casey	.15
37	Travis Dawkins	.10
38	Barry Larkin	.10
39	Pokey Reese	.10
40	Scott Williamson	.10
41	Roberto Alomar	.20
42	Bartolo Colon	.10
43	David Justice	.10
44	Manny Ramirez	.50
45	Richie Sexson	.10
46	Jim Thome	.50
47	Omar Vizquel	.10
48	Pedro Astacio	.10
49	Todd Helton	.50
50	Neifi Perez	.10
51	Ben Petrick	.10
52	Larry Walker	.10
53	Tony Clark	.10
54	Damion Easley	.10
55	Juan Gonzalez	.50
56	Dean Palmer	.10
57	A.J. Burnett	.10
58	Luis Castillo	.10
59	Cliff Floyd	.10
60	Alex Gonzalez	.10
61	Preston Wilson	.10
62	Jeff Bagwell	.50
63	Craig Biggio	.10
64	Ken Caminiti	.10
65	Jose Lima	.10
66	Billy Wagner	.10
67	Carlos Beltran	.30
68	Johnny Damon	.25
69	Jermaine Dye	.10
70	Carlos Febles	.10
71	Mike Sweeney	.10
72	Kevin Brown	.10
73	Shawn Green	.25
74	Eric Karros	.10
75	Chan Ho Park	.10
76	Gary Sheffield	.30
77	Ron Belliard	.10
78	Jeromy Burnitz	.10
79	Marquis Grissom	.10
80	Geoff Jenkins	.10
81	Mark Loretta	.10
82	Ron Coomer	.10
83	Jacque Jones	.10
84	Corey Koskie	.10
85	Brad Radke	.10
86	Todd Walker	.10
87	Michael Barrett	.10
88	Peter Bergeron	.10
89	Vladimir Guerrero	.50
90	Jose Vidro	.10
91	Rondell White	.10
92	Edgardo Alfonzo	.10
93	Rickey Henderson	.50
94	Rey Ordonez	.10
95	Mike Piazza	1.00
96	Robin Ventura	.10
97	Roger Clemens	.75
98	Orlando Hernandez	.10
99	Derek Jeter	1.50
100	Tino Martinez	.10
101	Mariano Rivera	.15
102	Alfonso Soriano	.50
103	Bernie Williams	.20
104	Eric Chavez	.15
105	Jason Giambi	.30
106	Ben Grieve	.10
107	Tim Hudson	.20
108	John Jaha	.10
109	Bobby Abreu	.10
110	Doug Glanville	.10
111	Mike Lieberthal	.10
112	Scott Rolen	.40
113	Curt Schilling	.25
114	Brian Giles	.10
115	Jason Kendall	.10
116	Warren Morris	.10
117	Kevin Young	.10
118	Rick Ankiel	.10
119	J.D. Drew	.15
120	Chad Hutchinson	.10
121	Ray Lankford	.10
122	Mark McGwire	1.25
123	Fernando Tatis	.10
124	Bret Boone	.10
125	Ben Davis	.10
126	Tony Gwynn	.65
127	Trevor Hoffman	.10
128	Barry Bonds	1.50
129	Ellis Burks	.10
130	Jeff Kent	.10
131	J.T. Snow	.10
132	Freddy Garcia	.10
133	Ken Griffey Jr.	1.00
134	Edgar Martinez	.10
135	John Olerud	.10
136	Alex Rodriguez	1.25
137	Jose Canseco	.20
138	Vinny Castilla	.10
139	Roberto Hernandez	.10
140	Fred McGriff	.10
141	Rusty Greer	.10
142	Ruben Mateo	.10
143	Rafael Palmeiro	.40
144	Ivan Rodriguez	.40
145	Lee Stevens	.10
146	Tony Batista	.10
147	Carlos Delgado	.35
148	Shannon Stewart	.10
149	David Wells	.10
150	Vernon Wells	.10

Holographic Blue

	NM/M
Common Player:	1.00
Stars:	4-6X
Production 80 sets	

Holographic Mirror

	NM/M
Common Player:	1.50
Stars:	4-6X
Production 160 sets	

Holographic Gold

	NM/M
Common Player:	.50
Stars:	2-4X
Production 480 sets	

Holographic Purple

	NM/M
Common Player:	1.00
Stars:	6-8X
Production 99 sets	

Premiere Date

	NM/M
Common Player:	1.50
Stars:	8-10X
Production 61 sets	

Drops Silver

	NM/M
Complete Set (150):	50.00
Common Player:	.50
Stars:	2-4X

Rapture Gold

	NM/M
Complete Set (150):	50.00
Common Player:	.50
Stars:	2-3X

(See 2000 Prism for checklist and base card values.)

A.L. Legends

		NM/M
Complete Set (10):		15.00
Common Player:		.50
Inserted 1:25		
1	Mo Vaughn	.50
2	Cal Ripken Jr.	4.00
3	Nomar Garciaparra	2.50
4	Manny Ramirez	1.50
5	Roger Clemens	2.00
6	Derek Jeter	4.00
7	Ken Griffey Jr.	2.50
8	Alex Rodriguez	3.00
9	Jose Canseco	.75
10	Rafael Palmeiro	1.00

N.L. Legends

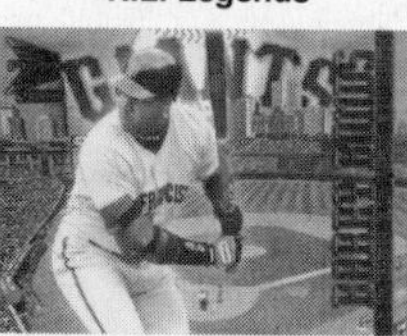

		NM/M
Complete Set (10):		15.00
Common Player:		.50
Inserted 1:25		
1	Chipper Jones	2.00
2	Greg Maddux	2.00
3	Sammy Sosa	2.50
4	Larry Walker	.50
5	Jeff Bagwell	1.00
6	Vladimir Guerrero	1.00
7	Mike Piazza	2.50
8	Mark McGwire	3.00
9	Tony Gwynn	2.00
10	Barry Bonds	4.00

Center Stage

		NM/M
Complete Set (20):		40.00
Common Player:		1.00
Inserted 1:25		
1	Chipper Jones	3.00
2	Cal Ripken Jr.	6.00
3	Nomar Garciaparra	4.00
4	Pedro Martinez	2.00
5	Sammy Sosa	4.00
6	Sean Casey	1.00
7	Manny Ramirez	2.00
8	Jim Thome	1.50
9	Jeff Bagwell	2.00
10	Carlos Beltran	1.50
11	Vladimir Guerrero	2.00
12	Mike Piazza	4.00
13	Derek Jeter	6.00
14	Bernie Williams	1.00
15	Scott Rolen	1.50
16	Mark McGwire	5.00
17	Tony Gwynn	3.00
18	Ken Griffey Jr.	4.00
19	Alex Rodriguez	5.00
20	Ivan Rodriguez	1.50

Diamond Dial-A-Stats

		NM/M
Complete Set (10):		90.00
Common Player:		8.00
Inserted 1:193		
1	Chipper Jones	8.00
2	Greg Maddux	8.00
3	Cal Ripken Jr.	20.00
4	Sammy Sosa	10.00
5	Mike Piazza	10.00
6	Roger Clemens	9.00
7	Mark McGwire	15.00
8	Tony Gwynn	8.00
9	Ken Griffey Jr.	10.00
10	Alex Rodriguez	15.00

Prospects

		NM/M
Complete Set (10):		12.00
Common Player:		1.00
Inserted 1:97		
1	Erubiel Durazo	1.00
2	Wilton Veras	1.00
3	Ben Petrick	1.00
4	Mark Quinn	1.00
5	Peter Bergeron	1.00
6	Alfonso Soriano	5.00
7	Tim Hudson	2.00
8	Chad Hermansen	1.00
9	Rick Ankiel	1.50
10	Ruben Mateo	1.00

2000 PACIFIC PRIVATE STOCK

		NM/M
Complete Set (150):		50.00
Common Player:		.15
Common SP Prospect:		1.00
Inserted 1:4		
Pack (7):		2.00
Wax Box (24):		35.00
1	Darin Erstad	.25
2	Troy Glaus	.75
3	Tim Salmon	.25
4	Mo Vaughn	.15
5	Jay Bell	.15
6	Luis Gonzalez	.25
7	Randy Johnson	.75
8	Matt Williams	.15
9	Andruw Jones	.75
10	Chipper Jones	1.00
11	Brian Jordan	.15
12	Greg Maddux	1.00
13	Kevin Millwood	.15
14	Albert Belle	.20
15	Mike Mussina	.35
16	Cal Ripken Jr.	2.00
17	B.J. Surhoff	.15
18	Nomar Garciaparra	1.25
19	Butch Huskey	.15
20	Pedro Martinez	.75
21	Troy O'Leary	.15
22	Mark Grace	.25
23	Bo Porter (SP)	1.00
24	Henry Rodriguez	.15
25	Sammy Sosa	1.25
26	Kerry Wood	.40
27	Jason Dellaero (SP)	1.00
28	Ray Durham	.15
29	Paul Konerko	.20
30	Carlos Lee	.15
31	Magglio Ordonez	.25
32	Frank Thomas	.75
33	Mike Cameron	.15
34	Sean Casey	.25
35	Barry Larkin	.15
36	Greg Vaughn	.15
37	Roberto Alomar	.40
38	Russell Branyan (SP)	1.00
39	Kenny Lofton	.15
40	Manny Ramirez	.75
41	Richie Sexson	.15
42	Jim Thome	.75
43	Omar Vizquel	.15
44	Dante Bichette	.15
45	Vinny Castilla	.15
46	Todd Helton	.75
47	Ben Petrick (SP)	1.00
48	Juan Sosa (SP)	1.00
49	Larry Walker	.15
50	Tony Clark	.15
51	Damion Easley	.15
52	Juan Encarnacion	.15
53	Robert Fick (SP)	1.00
54	Dean Palmer	.15
55	A.J. Burnett (SP)	1.00
56	Luis Castillo	.15
57	Alex Gonzalez	.15
58	Julio Ramirez (SP)	1.00
59	Preston Wilson	.15
60	Jeff Bagwell	.75
61	Craig Biggio	.15
62	Ken Caminiti	.15
63	Carl Everett	.15
64	Mike Hampton	.15
65	Billy Wagner	.15
66	Carlos Beltran	.50
67	Dermal Brown (SP)	1.00
68	Jermaine Dye	.15
69	Carlos Febles	.15
70	Mark Quinn (SP)	1.00
71	Mike Sweeney	.15
72	Kevin Brown	.15
73	Eric Gagne (SP)	1.50
74	Eric Karros	.15
75	Raul Mondesi	.15
76	Gary Sheffield	.40
77	Jeromy Burnitz	.15
78	Jeff Cirillo	.15
79	Geoff Jenkins	.15
80	David Nilsson	.15
81	Ron Coomer	.15
82	Jacque Jones	.15
83	Corey Koskie	.15
84	Brad Radke	.15
85	Tony Armas Jr. (SP)	1.50
86	Peter Bergeron (SP)	1.00
87	Vladimir Guerrero	.75
88	Jose Vidro	.15
89	Rondell White	.15
90	Edgardo Alfonzo	.15
91	Roger Cedeno	.15
92	Rickey Henderson	.75
93	Jay Payton (SP)	1.00
94	Mike Piazza	1.25
95	Jorge Toca (SP)	1.00
96	Robin Ventura	.15
97	Roger Clemens	1.00
98	David Cone	.15
99	Derek Jeter	2.00
100	D'Angelo Jimenez (SP)	1.00
101	Tino Martinez	.15
102	Alfonso Soriano (SP)	3.00
103	Bernie Williams	.25
104	Jason Giambi	.50
105	Ben Grieve	.15
106	Tim Hudson	.25
107	Matt Stairs	.15
108	Bobby Abreu	.15
109	Doug Glanville	.15
110	Scott Rolen	.65
111	Curt Schilling	.40
112	Brian Giles	.15
113	Chad Hermansen (SP)	1.00
114	Jason Kendall	.15
115	Warren Morris	.15
116	Rick Ankiel (SP)	1.00
117	J.D. Drew	.25
118	Adam Kennedy (SP)	1.00
119	Ray Lankford	.15
120	Mark McGwire	1.50
121	Fernando Tatis	.15
122	Mike Darr (SP)	1.00
123	Ben Davis	.15
124	Tony Gwynn	1.00
125	Trevor Hoffman	.15
126	Reggie Sanders	.15
127	Barry Bonds	2.00
128	Ellis Burks	.15
129	Jeff Kent	.15
130	J.T. Snow	.15
131	Freddy Garcia	.15
132	Ken Griffey Jr.	1.25
133	Carlos Guillen (SP)	1.00
134	Edgar Martinez	.15
135	Alex Rodriguez	1.50
136	Miguel Cairo	.15
137	Jose Canseco	.40
138	Steve Cox (SP)	1.00
139	Roberto Hernandez	.15
140	Fred McGriff	.15
141	Juan Gonzalez	.75
142	Rusty Greer	.15
143	Ruben Mateo (SP)	1.00
144	Rafael Palmeiro	.65
145	Ivan Rodriguez	.65
146	Carlos Delgado	.50
147	Tony Fernandez	.15
148	Shawn Green	.35
149	Shannon Stewart	.15
150	Vernon Wells (SP)	1.00

Gold Portraits

Stars:	5-10X
Prospects:	1-2X
Production 99 sets	

Premiere Date

Stars:	5-10X
Prospects:	1-2X
Inserted 1:24	

Silver Portraits

Stars:	3-6X
Prospects:	1-2X
Production 199 sets	

Canvas

		NM/M
Complete Set (20):		120.00
Common Player:		2.00
Inserted 1:49		
1	Chipper Jones	8.00
2	Greg Maddux	8.00
3	Cal Ripken Jr.	15.00
4	Nomar Garciaparra	10.00
5	Sammy Sosa	10.00
6	Frank Thomas	6.00
7	Manny Ramirez	6.00
8	Larry Walker	2.00
9	Jeff Bagwell	6.00
10	Vladimir Guerrero	6.00
11	Mike Piazza	10.00
12	Roger Clemens	9.00
13	Derek Jeter	15.00
14	Mark McGwire	12.00
15	Tony Gwynn	8.00
16	Barry Bonds	15.00
17	Ken Griffey Jr.	10.00
18	Alex Rodriguez	12.00
19	Juan Gonzalez	6.00
20	Ivan Rodriguez	5.00

Extreme Action

		NM/M
Complete Set (20):		25.00
Common Player:		.50
Inserted 2:25		
1	Andruw Jones	1.50
2	Chipper Jones	2.00
3	Cal Ripken Jr.	4.00
4	Nomar Garciaparra	2.50
5	Sammy Sosa	2.50
6	Frank Thomas	1.50
7	Roberto Alomar	.60
8	Manny Ramirez	1.50
9	Larry Walker	.50
10	Jeff Bagwell	1.50
11	Vladimir Guerrero	1.50
12	Mike Piazza	2.50
13	Derek Jeter	4.00
14	Bernie Williams	.50
15	Scott Rolen	1.00
16	Mark McGwire	3.00
17	Tony Gwynn	2.00
18	Ken Griffey Jr.	2.50
19	Alex Rodriguez	3.00
20	Ivan Rodriguez	1.00

PS-2000

		NM/M
Complete Set (60):		15.00
Common Player:		.15
Inserted 2:pack		
1	Mo Vaughn	.15
2	Greg Maddux	1.00
3	Andruw Jones	.75
4	Chipper Jones	1.00

5 Cal Ripken Jr. 2.50
6 Nomar Garciaparra 1.50
7 Pedro Martinez .75
8 Sammy Sosa 1.50
9 Jason Dellaero .15
10 Magglio Ordonez .15
11 Frank Thomas .75
12 Sean Casey .25
13 Russell Branyan .15
14 Manny Ramirez .75
15 Richie Sexson .15
16 Ben Petrick .15
17 Juan Sosa .15
18 Larry Walker .15
19 Robert Fick .15
20 Craig Biggio .15
21 Jeff Bagwell .75
22 Carlos Beltran .50
23 Dermal Brown .15
24 Mark Quinn .15
25 Eric Gagne .15
26 Jeromy Burnitz .15
27 Tony Armas Jr. .15
28 Peter Bergeron .15
29 Vladimir Guerrero .75
30 Edgardo Alfonzo .15
31 Mike Piazza 1.50
32 Jorge Toca .15
33 Roger Clemens 1.25
34 Alfonso Soriano .65
35 Bernie Williams .25
36 Derek Jeter 2.50
37 Tim Hudson .25
38 Bobby Abreu .15
39 Scott Rolen .65
40 Brian Giles .15
41 Chad Hermansen .15
42 Warren Morris .15
43 Rick Ankiel .15
44 J.D. Drew .25
45 Adam Kennedy .15
46 Mark McGwire 2.00
47 Mike Darr .15
48 Tony Gwynn 1.00
49 Barry Bonds 2.50
50 Ken Griffey Jr. 1.50
51 Carlos Guillen .15
52 Alex Rodriguez 1.50
53 Juan Gonzalez .75
54 Ruben Mateo .15
55 Ivan Rodriguez .65
56 Rafael Palmeiro .65
57 Jose Canseco .40
58 Steve Cox .15
59 Shawn Green .30
60 Vernon Wells .15

PS-2000 Stars

NM/M
Complete Set (20): 40.00
Common Player: 1.00
Production 299 sets
1 Mo Vaughn 1.00
2 Greg Maddux 4.00
3 Cal Ripken Jr. 8.00
4 Pedro Martinez 3.00
5 Sammy Sosa 5.00
6 Frank Thomas 3.00
7 Larry Walker 1.00
8 Craig Biggio 1.00
9 Jeff Bagwell 3.00
10 Mike Piazza 5.00
11 Roger Clemens 4.50
12 Bernie Williams 1.00
13 Mark McGwire 6.00
14 Tony Gwynn 4.00
15 Barry Bonds 8.00
16 Ken Griffey Jr. 5.00
17 Juan Gonzalez 3.00
18 Ivan Rodriguez 2.00
19 Rafael Palmeiro 2.00
20 Jose Canseco 1.50

PS-2000 New Wave

NM/M
Complete Set (20): 40.00
Common Player: 1.00
Production 199 sets
1 Andruw Jones 3.50
2 Chipper Jones 5.00
3 Nomar Garciaparra 6.00
4 Magglio Ordonez 1.00
5 Sean Casey 1.00
6 Manny Ramirez 3.50
7 Richie Sexson 1.00
8 Carlos Beltran 2.00
9 Jeromy Burnitz 1.00
10 Vladimir Guerrero 3.50
11 Edgardo Alfonzo 1.00
12 Derek Jeter 10.00
13 Tim Hudson 1.00
14 Bobby Abreu 1.00
15 Scott Rolen 2.50
16 Brian Giles 1.00
17 Warren Morris 1.00
18 J.D. Drew 1.25
19 Alex Rodriguez 8.00
20 Shawn Green 1.25

PS-2000 Rookies

NM/M
Complete Set (20): 20.00
Common Player: 1.00
Inserted 99 sets
1 Jason Dellaero 1.00
2 Russell Branyan 1.00
3 Ben Petrick 1.00
4 Juan Sosa 1.00
5 Robert Fick 1.00
6 Dermal Brown 1.00
7 Mark Quinn 1.00
8 Eric Gagne 1.50
9 Tony Armas Jr. 1.00
10 Peter Bergeron 1.00
11 Jorge Toca 1.00
12 Alfonso Soriano 6.00
13 Chad Hermansen 1.00
14 Rick Ankiel 1.00
15 Adam Kennedy 1.50
16 Mike Darr 1.00
17 Carlos Guillen 1.00
18 Steve Cox 1.00
19 Ruben Mateo 1.00
20 Vernon Wells 1.50

Reserve

NM/M
Complete Set (20): 50.00
Common Player: 1.00
Inserted 1:25
1 Chipper Jones 3.00
2 Greg Maddux 3.00
3 Cal Ripken Jr. 6.00
4 Nomar Garciaparra 4.00
5 Sammy Sosa 4.00
6 Frank Thomas 2.00
7 Manny Ramirez 2.00
8 Larry Walker 1.00
9 Jeff Bagwell 2.00
10 Vladimir Guerrero 2.00
11 Mike Piazza 4.00
12 Roger Clemens 3.50
13 Derek Jeter 6.00
14 Mark McGwire 5.00
15 Tony Gwynn 3.00
16 Barry Bonds 6.00
17 Ken Griffey Jr. 4.00
18 Alex Rodriguez 5.00
19 Ivan Rodriguez 1.50
20 Shawn Green 1.25

2000 PACIFIC VANGUARD

NM/M
Complete Set (100): 30.00
Common Player: .15
Pack (4): 2.00
Wax Box (24): 35.00
1 Troy Glaus 1.00
2 Tim Salmon .25
3 Mo Vaughn .15
4 Albert Belle .15
5 Mike Mussina .35
6 Cal Ripken Jr. 3.00
7 Nomar Garciaparra 2.00
8 Pedro Martinez 1.00
9 Troy O'Leary .15
10 Wilton Veras .15
11 Magglio Ordonez .15
12 Chris Singleton .15
13 Frank Thomas 1.00
14 Roberto Alomar .40
15 Russell Branyan .15
16 Manny Ramirez 1.00
17 Jim Thome .75
18 Omar Vizquel .15
19 Tony Clark .15
20 Juan Gonzalez 1.00
21 Dean Palmer .15
22 Carlos Beltran .50
23 Johnny Damon .30
24 Jermaine Dye .15
25 Mark Quinn .15
26 Jacque Jones .15
27 Corey Koskie .15
28 Brad Radke .15
29 Roger Clemens 1.75
30 Derek Jeter 3.00
31 Alfonso Soriano .75
32 Bernie Williams .30
33 Eric Chavez .30
34 Jason Giambi .75
35 Ben Grieve .15
36 Tim Hudson .30
37 Mike Cameron .15
38 Freddy Garcia .15
39 Edgar Martinez .15
40 Alex Rodriguez 2.50
41 Jose Canseco .50
42 Vinny Castilla .15
43 Fred McGriff .15
44 Rusty Greer .15
45 Ruben Mateo .15
46 Rafael Palmeiro .75
47 Ivan Rodriguez .65
48 Carlos Delgado .75
49 Shannon Stewart .15
50 Vernon Wells .15
51 Erubiel Durazo .15
52 Randy Johnson 1.00
53 Matt Williams .15
54 Andruw Jones 1.00
55 Chipper Jones 1.50
56 Greg Maddux 1.50
57 Mark Grace .25
58 Sammy Sosa 2.00
59 Kerry Wood .50
60 Sean Casey .25
61 Ken Griffey Jr. 2.00
62 Barry Larkin .15
63 Todd Helton 1.00
64 Ben Petrick .15
65 Larry Walker .15
66 Luis Castillo .15
67 Alex Gonzalez .15
68 Preston Wilson .15
69 Jeff Bagwell 1.00
70 Craig Biggio .15
71 Billy Wagner .15
72 Kevin Brown .15
73 Shawn Green .40
74 Gary Sheffield .40
75 Kevin Barker .15
76 Ron Belliard .15
77 Jeromy Burnitz .15
78 Michael Barrett .15
79 Peter Bergeron .15
80 Vladimir Guerrero 1.00
81 Edgardo Alfonzo .15
82 Rey Ordonez .15
83 Mike Piazza 2.00
84 Robin Ventura .15
85 Bobby Abreu .15
86 Mike Lieberthal .15
87 Scott Rolen .75
88 Brian Giles .15
89 Chad Hermansen .15
90 Jason Kendall .15
91 Rick Ankiel .15
92 J.D. Drew .25
93 Mark McGwire 2.50
94 Fernando Tatis .15
95 Ben Davis .15
96 Tony Gwynn 1.50
97 Trevor Hoffman .15
98 Barry Bonds 3.00
99 Ellis Burks .15
100 Jeff Kent .15

Green

A.L. (1-50): 3-6X
Production 99 sets
N.L. (51-100): 2-4X
Production 199 sets

Gold

A.L. (1-50): 2-4X
Production 199 sets R
N.L. (51-100): 3-6X
Production 99 sets R

Premiere Date

Stars: 3-5X
Production 135 sets H

Purple

Production 10 sets
(VALUES UNDETERMINED)

A.L. Vanguard Press

NM/M
Complete Set (10): 10.00
Common Player: .65
Inserted 2:25
1 Cal Ripken Jr. 3.00
2 Nomar Garciaparra 2.00
3 Pedro Martinez 1.00
4 Manny Ramirez 1.00
5 Carlos Beltran .65
6 Roger Clemens 1.50
7 Derek Jeter 3.00
8 Alex Rodriguez 2.50
9 Rafael Palmeiro .75
10 Ivan Rodriguez .75

N.L. Vanguard Press

NM/M
Complete Set (10): 10.00
Common Player: .50
Inserted 2:37
1 Chipper Jones 1.50
2 Greg Maddux 1.50
3 Sammy Sosa 2.00
4 Ken Griffey Jr. 2.00
5 Larry Walker .50
6 Jeff Bagwell 1.00
7 Vladimir Guerrero 1.00
8 Mike Piazza 2.00
9 Mark McGwire 2.50
10 Tony Gwynn 1.50

Cosmic Force

NM/M
Complete Set (10): 30.00
Common Player: 3.00
Inserted 1:73
1 Chipper Jones 3.00
2 Cal Ripken Jr. 6.00
3 Nomar Garciaparra 4.00
4 Sammy Sosa 4.00
5 Ken Griffey Jr. 4.00
6 Mike Piazza 4.00
7 Derek Jeter 6.00
8 Mark McGwire 5.00
9 Tony Gwynn 3.00
10 Alex Rodriguez 5.00

Game Worn Jersey

NM/M

Inserted 1:120
1 Greg Maddux 10.00
2 Tony Gwynn 10.00
3 Alex Rodriguez 20.00
4 Frank Thomas 8.00
5 Chipper Jones 10.00

Diamond Architects

NM/M

Complete Set (20): 25.00
Common Player: .50
Inserted 1:25
1 Chipper Jones 2.00
2 Greg Maddux 2.00
3 Cal Ripken Jr. 4.00
4 Nomar Garciaparra 2.50
5 Sammy Sosa 2.50
6 Ken Griffey Jr. 2.50
7 Manny Ramirez 1.50
8 Larry Walker .50
9 Jeff Bagwell 1.50
10 Vladimir Guerrero 1.50
11 Mike Piazza 2.50
12 Roger Clemens 2.25
13 Derek Jeter 4.00
14 Bernie Williams .50
15 Scott Rolen 1.00
16 Mark McGwire 3.00
17 Tony Gwynn 2.00
18 Alex Rodriguez 3.00
19 Rafael Palmeiro 1.00
20 Ivan Rodriguez .75

High Voltage

NM/M

Complete Set (36): 10.00
Common Player: .15
Inserted 1:1
1 Mo Vaughn .15
2 Erubiel Durazo .15
3 Randy Johnson .60
4 Andruw Jones .60
5 Chipper Jones .75
6 Greg Maddux .75
7 Cal Ripken Jr. 2.00
8 Nomar Garciaparra 1.25
9 Pedro Martinez .60
10 Sammy Sosa 1.25
11 Frank Thomas .60
12 Sean Casey .25
13 Ken Griffey Jr. 1.25
14 Barry Larkin .15
15 Manny Ramirez .60
16 Jim Thome .50
17 Larry Walker .15
18 Jeff Bagwell .60
19 Craig Biggio .15
20 Carlos Beltran .40
21 Shawn Green .25
22 Vladimir Guerrero .60
23 Edgardo Alfonzo .15
24 Mike Piazza 1.50
25 Roger Clemens 1.00
26 Derek Jeter 2.00
27 Bernie Williams .25
28 Scott Rolen .60
29 Brian Giles .15
30 Rick Ankiel .15
31 Mark McGwire 1.50
32 Tony Gwynn .75
33 Barry Bonds 2.00
34 Alex Rodriguez 1.50
35 Rafael Palmeiro .60
36 Ivan Rodriguez .60

2000 PACIFIC REVOLUTION

NM/M

Complete Set (150): 60.00
Common Player: .25
Common SP: 1.00
Pack (3): 2.00
Box: 35.00
1 Darin Erstad .50
2 Troy Glaus 1.00
3 Adam Kennedy SP 1.50
4 Mo Vaughn .25
5 Erubiel Durazo .25
6 Steve Finley .25
7 Luis Gonzalez .35
8 Randy Johnson 1.00
9 Travis Lee .25
10 Vicente Padilla SP 1.00
11 Matt Williams .25
12 Rafael Furcal SP 1.00
13 Andres Galarraga .25
14 Andruw Jones 1.00
15 Chipper Jones 1.50
16 Greg Maddux 1.50
17 Luis Rivera SP 1.00
18 Albert Belle .25
19 Mike Bordick .25
20 Will Clark .35
21 Mike Mussina .40
22 Cal Ripken Jr. 3.00
23 B.J. Surhoff .25
24 Carl Everett .25
25 Nomar Garciaparra 2.00
26 Pedro Martinez 1.00
27 Jason Varitek .25
28 Wilton Veras SP 1.00
29 Shane Andrews .25
30 *Scott Downs SP* 1.00
31 Mark Grace .35
32 Sammy Sosa 2.00
33 Kerry Wood .50
34 Ray Durham .25
35 Paul Konerko .35
36 Carlos Lee .25
37 Magglio Ordonez .25
38 Frank Thomas 1.00
39 Rob Bell SP 1.00
40 Sean Casey .40
41 Ken Griffey Jr. 2.00
42 Barry Larkin .25
43 Pokey Reese .25
44 Roberto Alomar .40
45 David Justice .25
46 Kenny Lofton .25
47 Manny Ramirez 1.00
48 Richie Sexson .25
49 Jim Thome 1.00
50 Jeff Cirillo .25
51 Jeffrey Hammonds .25
52 Todd Helton 1.00
53 Larry Walker .25
54 Tony Clark .25
55 Juan Gonzalez 1.00
56 Hideo Nomo 1.00
57 Dean Palmer .25
58 Alex Gonzalez .25
59 Mike Lowell .25
60 Pablo Ozuna SP 1.00
61 Brad Penny SP 1.00
62 Preston Wilson .25
63 Moises Alou .25
64 Jeff Bagwell 1.00
65 Craig Biggio .25
66 Ken Caminiti .25
67 Julio Lugo SP 1.00
68 Carlos Beltran .60
69 Johnny Damon .40
70 Jermaine Dye .25
71 Carlos Febles .25
72 Mark Quinn SP 1.00
73 Kevin Brown .25
74 Shawn Green .65
75 Chan Ho Park .50
76 Gary Sheffield .50
77 Kevin Barker SP 1.00
78 Ron Belliard .25
79 Jeromy Burnitz .25
80 Geoff Jenkins .25
81 Cristian Guzman .25
82 Jacque Jones .25
83 Corey Koskie .25
84 Matt Lawton .25
85 Peter Bergeron SP 1.00
86 Vladimir Guerrero 1.00
87 Andy Tracy SP 1.00
88 Jose Vidro .25
89 Rondell White .25
90 Edgardo Alfonzo .25
91 Derek Bell .25
92 Eric Cammack SP 1.00
93 Mike Piazza 2.00
94 Robin Ventura .25
95 Roger Clemens 1.75
96 Orlando Hernandez .25
97 Derek Jeter 3.00
98 Tino Martinez .25
99 Alfonso Soriano SP 3.00
100 Bernie Williams .35
101 Eric Chavez .35
102 Jason Giambi .75
103 Ben Grieve .25
104 Terrence Long SP 1.00
105 Mark Mulder SP 1.00
106 Adam Piatt SP 1.00
107 Bobby Abreu .25
108 Rico Brogna .25
109 Doug Glanville .25
110 Mike Lieberthal .25
111 Scott Rolen .75
112 Brian Giles .25
113 Chad Hermansen SP 1.00
114 Jason Kendall .25
115 Warren Morris .25
116 Rick Ankiel SP 1.00
117 J.D. Drew .40
118 Jim Edmonds .25
119 Mark McGwire 2.50
120 Fernando Tatis .25
121 Fernando Vina .25
122 Tony Gwynn 1.50
123 Trevor Hoffman .25
124 Ryan Klesko .25
125 Eric Owens .25
126 Barry Bonds 3.00
127 Ellis Burks .25
128 Bobby Estalella .25
129 Jeff Kent .25
130 *Scott Linebrink SP* 1.00
131 Jay Buhner .25
132 Stan Javier .25
133 Edgar Martinez .25
134 John Olerud .25
135 Alex Rodriguez 2.50
136 *Kazuhiro Sasaki SP* 2.00
137 Jose Canseco .40
138 Vinny Castilla .25
139 Fred McGriff .25
140 Greg Vaughn .25
141 Gabe Kapler .25
142 *Mike Lamb SP* 1.00
143 Ruben Mateo .25
144 Rafael Palmeiro .75
145 Ivan Rodriguez .75
146 Tony Batista .25
147 Jose Cruz Jr. .25
148 Carlos Delgado .75
149 Brad Fullmer .25
150 Raul Mondesi .25

Red

Stars: 1-2X
SPs: 1X
Production 299 sets

Shadow

Stars: 3-6X
SPs: 1-2X
Production 99 sets

Foul Pole Net-Fusions

NM/M

Complete Set (20): 110.00
Common Player: 2.00
Inserted 1:49
1 Chipper Jones 8.00
2 Cal Ripken Jr. 15.00
3 Nomar Garciaparra 10.00
4 Pedro Martinez 6.00
5 Sammy Sosa 10.00
6 Frank Thomas 6.00
7 Ken Griffey Jr. 10.00
8 Manny Ramirez 6.00
9 Jeff Bagwell 6.00
10 Shawn Green 3.00
11 Vladimir Guerrero 6.00
12 Mike Piazza 10.00
13 Derek Jeter 15.00
14 Bernie Williams 2.00
15 Rick Ankiel 2.00
16 Mark McGwire 12.00
17 Tony Gwynn 8.00
18 Barry Bonds 15.00
19 Alex Rodriguez 12.00
20 Ivan Rodriguez 5.00

Game-Ball Signatures

NM/M

Common Player: 5.00
1 Randy Johnson 40.00
2 Greg Maddux 90.00
3 Rafael Furcal 7.50
4 Shane Andrews 5.00
5 Sean Casey 10.00
6 Travis Dawkins 5.00
7 Alex Gonzalez 5.00
8 Shane Reynolds 5.00
9 Eric Gagne 10.00
10 Kevin Barker 5.00
11 Eric Milton 5.00
12 Mark Quinn 5.00
13 Alfonso Soriano 40.00
14 Brian Giles 6.00
15 Mark Mulder 10.00
16 Adam Piatt 5.00
17 Warren Morris 5.00
18 Rick Ankiel 6.00
19 Adam Kennedy 6.00
20 Fernando Tatis 5.00
21 Barry Bonds 100.00
22 Alex Rodriguez 75.00
23 Ruben Mateo 5.00
24 Billy Koch 5.00
25 Brad Penny 5.00

Icons

NM/M

Complete Set (20): 250.00
Common Player: 8.00
Inserted 1:121
1 Randy Johnson 10.00
2 Chipper Jones 15.00
3 Greg Maddux 15.00
4 Cal Ripken Jr. 30.00
5 Nomar Garciaparra 20.00
6 Pedro Martinez 10.00
7 Sammy Sosa 20.00
8 Frank Thomas 10.00
9 Ken Griffey Jr. 20.00
10 Juan Gonzalez 10.00
11 Jeff Bagwell 10.00

12	Vladimir Guerrero	10.00
13	Mike Piazza	20.00
14	Roger Clemens	17.50
15	Derek Jeter	30.00
16	Mark McGwire	25.00
17	Tony Gwynn	15.00
18	Barry Bonds	30.00
19	Alex Rodriguez	25.00
20	Ivan Rodriguez	8.00

On Deck

		NM/M
Complete Set (20):		40.00
Common Player:		1.00
Inserted 1:25		
1	Chipper Jones	3.00
2	Cal Ripken Jr.	6.00
3	Nomar Garciaparra	4.00
4	Sammy Sosa	4.00
5	Frank Thomas	2.00
6	Ken Griffey Jr.	4.00
7	Manny Ramirez	2.00
8	Larry Walker	1.00
9	Juan Gonzalez	2.00
10	Jeff Bagwell	2.00
11	Shawn Green	1.50
12	Vladimir Guerrero	2.00
13	Mike Piazza	4.00
14	Derek Jeter	6.00
15	Scott Rolen	1.50
16	Mark McGwire	5.00
17	Tony Gwynn	3.00
18	Alex Rodriguez	5.00
19	Jose Canseco	1.50
20	Ivan Rodriguez	1.75

Season Opener

		NM/M
Complete Set (36):		35.00
Common Player:		.50
Inserted 2:25		
1	Erubiel Durazo	.50
2	Randy Johnson	1.50
3	Andruw Jones	1.50
4	Chipper Jones	2.00
5	Greg Maddux	2.00
6	Cal Ripken Jr.	4.00
7	Nomar Garciaparra	3.00
8	Pedro Martinez	1.50
9	Sammy Sosa	2.50
10	Frank Thomas	1.50
11	Magglio Ordonez	.50
12	Ken Griffey Jr.	2.50
13	Barry Larkin	.50
14	Kenny Lofton	.50
15	Manny Ramirez	1.50
16	Jim Thome	1.50
17	Larry Walker	.50
18	Juan Gonzalez	1.50
19	Jeff Bagwell	1.50
20	Craig Biggio	.50
21	Carlos Beltran	.75
22	Shawn Green	.75
23	Vladimir Guerrero	1.50
24	Mike Piazza	2.50
25	Orlando Hernandez	.50
26	Derek Jeter	4.00
27	Bernie Williams	.50
28	Eric Chavez	.50
29	Scott Rolen	1.00
30	Jim Edmonds	.50
31	Tony Gwynn	2.00
32	Barry Bonds	4.00
33	Alex Rodriguez	3.00
34	Jose Canseco	.65
35	Ivan Rodriguez	1.00
36	Rafael Palmeiro	1.00

Triple Header

		NM/M
Complete Set (30):		25.00
Common Player:		.25
Inserted 4:25		
Parallel (1-10):		3-6X
99 sets produced		
Parallel (11-20):		3-6X
99 sets produced		
Parallel (21-30):		1-2X
599 sets produced		
1	Chipper Jones	1.50
2	Cal Ripken Jr.	3.00
3	Nomar Garciaparra	2.00
4	Frank Thomas	1.00
5	Larry Walker	.25
6	Vladimir Guerrero	1.00
7	Mike Piazza	2.00
8	Derek Jeter	3.00
9	Tony Gwynn	1.50
10	Ivan Rodriguez	.75
11	Sammy Sosa	2.00
12	Ken Griffey Jr.	2.00
13	Manny Ramirez	1.00
14	Jeff Bagwell	1.00
15	Shawn Green	.40
16	Mark McGwire	2.50
17	Barry Bonds	3.00
18	Alex Rodriguez	2.50
19	Jose Canseco	.50
20	Rafael Palmeiro	.75
21	Randy Johnson	1.00
22	Tom Glavine	.40
23	Greg Maddux	1.50
24	Mike Mussina	.40
25	Pedro Martinez	1.00
26	Kerry Wood	.60
27	Chuck Finley	.25
28	Kevin Brown	.25
29	Roger Clemens	1.75
30	Rick Ankiel	.25

2001 PACIFIC

		NM/M
Complete Set (500):		40.00
Common Player:		.10
Pack (12):		1.00
Box (36):		25.00
1	Garret Anderson	.10
2	Gary DiSarcina	.10
3	Darin Erstad	.25
4	Seth Etherton	.10
5	Ron Gant	.10
6	Troy Glaus	.75
7	Shigetosi Hasegawa	.10
8	Adam Kennedy	.10
9	Ben Molina	.10
10	Ramon Ortiz	.10
11	Troy Percival	.10
12	Tim Salmon	.20
13	Scott Schoeneweis	.10
14	Mo Vaughn	.10
15	Jarrod Washburn	.10
16	Brian Anderson	.10
17	Danny Bautista	.10
18	Jay Bell	.10
19	Greg Colbrunn	.10
20	Erubiel Durazo	.10
21	Steve Finley	.10
22	Luis Gonzalez	.20
23	Randy Johnson	.75
24	Byung-Hyun Kim	.10
25	Matt Mantei	.10
26	Armando Reynoso	.10
27	Todd Stottlemyre	.10
28	Matt Williams	.10
29	Tony Womack	.10
30	Andy Ashby	.10
31	Bobby Bonilla	.10
32	Rafael Furcal	.10
33	Andres Galarraga	.10
34	Tom Glavine	.35
35	Andruw Jones	.75
36	Chipper Jones	1.00
37	Brian Jordan	.10
38	Wally Joyner	.10
39	Keith Lockhart	.10
40	Javy Lopez	.10
41	Greg Maddux	1.00
42	Kevin Millwood	.10
43	John Rocker	.10
44	Reggie Sanders	.10
45	John Smoltz	.10
46	B.J. Surhoff	.10
47	Quilvio Veras	.10
48	Walt Weiss	.10
49	Brady Anderson	.10
50	Albert Belle	.15
51	Jeff Conine	.10
52	Delino DeShields	.10
53	Brook Fordyce	.10
54	Jerry Hairston Jr.	.10
55	Mark Lewis	.10
56	Luis Matos	.10
57	Melvin Mora	.10
58	Mike Mussina	.35
59	Chris Richard	.10
60	Cal Ripken Jr.	2.00
61	Manny Alexander	.10
62	Rolando Arrojo	.10
63	Midre Cummings	.10
64	Carl Everett	.10
65	Nomar Garciaparra	1.25
66	Mike Lansing	.10
67	Darren Lewis	.10
68	Derek Lowe	.10
69	Pedro Martinez	.75
70	Ramon Martinez	.10
71	Trot Nixon	.10
72	Troy O'Leary	.10
73	Jose Offerman	.10
74	Tomo Ohka	.10
75	Jason Varitek	.10
76	Rick Aguilera	.10
77	Shane Andrews	.10
78	Brant Brown	.10
79	Damon Buford	.10
80	Joe Girardi	.10
81	Mark Grace	.20
82	Willie Greene	.10
83	Ricky Gutierrez	.10
84	Jon Lieber	.10
85	Sammy Sosa	1.25
86	Kevin Tapani	.10
87	Rondell White	.10
88	Kerry Wood	.50
89	Eric Young	.10
90	Harold Baines	.10
91	James Baldwin	.10
92	Ray Durham	.10
93	Cal Eldred	.10
94	Keith Foulke	.10
95	Charles Johnson	.10
96	Paul Konerko	.20
97	Carlos Lee	.10
98	Magglio Ordonez	.10
99	Jim Parque	.10
100	Herbert Perry	.10
101	Chris Singleton	.10
102	Mike Sirotka	.10
103	Frank Thomas	.75
104	Jose Valentin	.10
105	Rob Bell	.10
106	Aaron Boone	.10
107	Sean Casey	.20
108	Danny Graves	.10
109	Ken Griffey Jr.	1.25
110	Pete Harnisch	.10
111	Brian L. Hunter	.10
112	Barry Larkin	.10
113	Pokey Reese	.10
114	Benito Santiago	.10
115	Chris Stynes	.10
116	Michael Tucker	.10
117	Ron Villone	.10
118	Scott Williamson	.10
119	Dmitri Young	.10
120	Roberto Alomar	.35
121	Sandy Alomar Jr.	.10
122	Russell Branyan	.10
123	Dave Burba	.10
124	Bartolo Colon	.10
125	Wil Cordero	.10
126	Einar Diaz	.10
127	Chuck Finley	.10
128	Travis Fryman	.10
129	Kenny Lofton	.10
130	Charles Nagy	.10
131	Manny Ramirez	.75
132	David Segui	.10
133	Jim Thome	.65
134	Omar Vizquel	.10
135	Brian Bohanon	.10
136	Jeff Cirillo	.10
137	Jeff Frye	.10
138	Jeffrey Hammonds	.10
139	Todd Helton	.75
140	Todd Hollandsworth	.10
141	Jose Jimenez	.10
142	Brent Mayne	.10
143	Neifi Perez	.10
144	Ben Petrick	.10
145	Juan Pierre	.10
146	Larry Walker	.10
147	Todd Walker	.10
148	Masato Yoshii	.10
149	Brad Ausmus	.10
150	Rich Becker	.10
151	Tony Clark	.10
152	Deivi Cruz	.10
153	Damion Easley	.10
154	Juan Encarnacion	.10
155	Robert Fick	.10
156	Juan Gonzalez	.75
157	Bobby Higginson	.10
158	Todd Jones	.10
159	Wendell Magee Jr.	.10
160	Brian Moehler	.10
161	Hideo Nomo	.75
162	Dean Palmer	.10
163	Jeff Weaver	.10
164	Antonio Alfonseca	.10
165	David Berg	.10
166	A.J. Burnett	.10
167	Luis Castillo	.10
168	Ryan Dempster	.10
169	Cliff Floyd	.10
170	Alex Gonzalez	.10
171	Mark Kotsay	.10
172	Derrek Lee	.10
173	Mike Lowell	.10
174	Mike Redmond	.10
175	Henry Rodriguez	.10
176	Jesus Sanchez	.10
177	Preston Wilson	.10
178	Moises Alou	.10
179	Jeff Bagwell	.75
180	Glen Barker	.10
181	Lance Berkman	.10
182	Craig Biggio	.10
183	Tim Bogar	.10
184	Ken Caminiti	.10
185	Roger Cedeno	.10
186	Scott Elarton	.10
187	Tony Eusebio	.10
188	Richard Hidalgo	.10
189	Jose Lima	.10
190	Mitch Meluskey	.10
191	Shane Reynolds	.10
192	Bill Spiers	.10
193	Billy Wagner	.10
194	Daryle Ward	.10
195	Carlos Beltran	.40
196	Ricky Bottalico	.10
197	Johnny Damon	.25
198	Jermaine Dye	.10
199	Jorge Fabregas	.10
200	David McCarty	.10
201	Mark Quinn	.10
202	Joe Randa	.10
203	Jeff Reboulet	.10
204	Rey Sanchez	.10
205	Blake Stein	.10
206	Jeff Suppan	.10
207	Mac Suzuki	.10
208	Mike Sweeney	.10
209	Greg Zaun	.10
210	Adrian Beltre	.25
211	Kevin Brown	.10
212	Alex Cora	.10
213	Darren Dreifort	.10
214	Tom Goodwin	.10
215	Shawn Green	.30
216	Mark Grudzielanek	.10
217	Todd Hundley	.10
218	Eric Karros	.10
219	Chad Kreuter	.10
220	Jim Leyritz	.10
221	Chan Ho Park	.10
222	Jeff Shaw	.10
223	Gary Sheffield	.25
224	Devon White	.10
225	Ron Belliard	.10
226	Henry Blanco	.10
227	Jeromy Burnitz	.10
228	Jeff D'Amico	.10
229	Marquis Grissom	.10
230	Charlie Hayes	.10
231	Jimmy Haynes	.10
232	Tyler Houston	.10
233	Geoff Jenkins	.10
234	Mark Loretta	.10
235	James Mouton	.10
236	Richie Sexson	.10
237	Jamey Wright	.10
238	Jay Canizaro	.10
239	Ron Coomer	.10

#	Player	Price
240	Cristian Guzman	.10
241	Denny Hocking	.10
242	Torii Hunter	.10
243	Jacque Jones	.10
244	Corey Koskie	.10
245	Matt Lawton	.10
246	Matt LeCroy	.10
247	Eric Milton	.10
248	David Ortiz	.25
249	Brad Radke	.10
250	Mark Redman	.10
251	Michael Barrett	.10
252	Peter Bergeron	.10
253	Milton Bradley	.10
254	Orlando Cabrera	.10
255	Vladimir Guerrero	.75
256	Wilton Guerrero	.10
257	Dustin Hermanson	.10
258	Hideki Irabu	.10
259	Fernando Seguignol	.10
260	Lee Stevens	.10
261	Andy Tracy	.10
262	Javier Vazquez	.10
263	Jose Vidro	.10
264	Edgardo Alfonzo	.10
265	Derek Bell	.10
266	Armando Benitez	.10
267	Mike Bordick	.10
268	John Franco	.10
269	Darryl Hamilton	.10
270	Mike Hampton	.10
271	Lenny Harris	.10
272	Al Leiter	.10
273	Joe McEwing	.10
274	Rey Ordonez	.10
275	Jay Payton	.10
276	Mike Piazza	1.25
277	Glendon Rusch	.10
278	Bubba Trammell	.10
279	Robin Ventura	.10
280	Todd Zeile	.10
281	Scott Brosius	.10
282	Jose Canseco	.25
283	Roger Clemens	1.00
284	David Cone	.10
285	Dwight Gooden	.10
286	Orlando Hernandez	.10
287	Glenallen Hill	.10
288	Derek Jeter	2.00
289	David Justice	.10
290	Chuck Knoblauch	.10
291	Tino Martinez	.10
292	Denny Neagle	.10
293	Paul O'Neill	.10
294	Andy Pettitte	.20
295	Jorge Posada	.10
296	Mariano Rivera	.20
297	Luis Sojo	.10
298	Jose Vizcaino	.10
299	Bernie Williams	.25
300	Kevin Appier	.10
301	Eric Chavez	.20
302	Ryan Christenson	.10
303	Jason Giambi	.50
304	Jeremy Giambi	.10
305	Ben Grieve	.10
306	Gil Heredia	.10
307	Ramon Hernandez	.10
308	Tim Hudson	.20
309	Jason Isringhausen	.10
310	Terrence Long	.10
311	Mark Mulder	.10
312	Adam Piatt	.10
313	Matt Stairs	.10
314	Miguel Tejada	.25
315	Randy Velarde	.10
316	Alex Arias	.10
317	Pat Burrell	.25
318	Omar Daal	.10
319	Travis Lee	.10
320	Mike Lieberthal	.10
321	Randy Wolf	.10
322	Bobby Abreu	.10
323	Jeff Brantley	.10
324	Bruce Chen	.10
325	Doug Glanville	.10
326	Kevin Jordan	.10
327	Robert Person	.10
328	Scott Rolen	.65
329	Jimmy Anderson	.10
330	Mike Benjamin	.10
331	Kris Benson	.10
332	Adam Brown	.10
333	Brian Giles	.10
334	Jason Kendall	.10
335	Pat Meares	.10
336	Warren Morris	.10
337	Aramis Ramirez	.10
338	Todd Ritchie	.10
339	Jason Schmidt	.10
340	John Vander Wal	.10
341	Mike Williams	.10
342	Enrique Wilson	.10
343	Kevin Young	.10
344	Rick Ankiel	.10
345	Andy Benes	.10
346	Will Clark	.15
347	Eric Davis	.10
348	J.D. Drew	.20
349	Shawon Dunston	.10
350	Jim Edmonds	.10
351	Pat Hentgen	.10
352	Darryl Kile	.10
353	Ray Lankford	.10
354	Mike Matheny	.10
355	Mark McGwire	1.50
356	Craig Paquette	.10
357	Edgar Renteria	.10
358	Garrett Stephenson	.10
359	Fernando Tatis	.10
360	Dave Veres	.10
361	Fernando Vina	.10
362	Bret Boone	.10
363	Matt Clement	.10
364	Ben Davis	.10
365	Adam Eaton	.10
366	Wiki Gonzalez	.10
367	Tony Gwynn	1.00
368	Damian Jackson	.10
369	Ryan Klesko	.10
370	John Mabry	.10
371	Dave Magadan	.10
372	Phil Nevin	.10
373	Eric Owens	.10
374	Desi Relaford	.10
375	Ruben Rivera	.10
376	Woody Williams	.10
377	Rich Aurilia	.10
378	Marvin Bernard	.10
379	Barry Bonds	2.00
380	Ellis Burks	.10
381	Bobby Estalella	.10
382	Shawn Estes	.10
383	Mark Gardner	.10
384	Livan Hernandez	.10
385	Jeff Kent	.10
386	Bill Mueller	.10
387	Robb Nen	.10
388	Russ Ortiz	.10
389	Armando Rios	.10
390	Kirk Rueter	.10
391	J.T. Snow	.10
392	David Bell	.10
393	Jay Buhner	.10
394	Mike Cameron	.10
395	Freddy Garcia	.10
396	Carlos Guillen	.10
397	John Halama	.10
398	Rickey Henderson	.75
399	Al Martin	.10
400	Edgar Martinez	.10
401	Mark McLemore	.10
402	Jamie Moyer	.10
403	John Olerud	.10
404	Joe Oliver	.10
405	Alex Rodriguez	1.50
406	Kazuhiro Sasaki	.15
407	Aaron Sele	.10
408	Dan Wilson	.10
409	Miguel Cairo	.10
410	Vinny Castilla	.10
411	Steve Cox	.10
412	John Flaherty	.10
413	Jose Guillen	.10
414	Roberto Hernandez	.10
415	Russ Johnson	.10
416	Felix Martinez	.10
417	Fred McGriff	.10
418	Greg Vaughn	.10
419	Gerald Williams	.10
420	Luis Alicea	.10
421	Frank Catalanotto	.10
422	Royce Clayton	.10
423	Chad Curtis	.10
424	Rusty Greer	.10
425	Bill Haselman	.10
426	Rick Helling	.10
427	Gabe Kapler	.10
428	Mike Lamb	.10
429	Ricky Ledee	.10
430	Ruben Mateo	.10
431	Rafael Palmeiro	.65
432	Ivan Rodriguez	.65
433	Kenny Rogers	.10
434	John Wetteland	.10
435	Jeff Zimmerman	.10
436	Tony Batista	.10
437	Homer Bush	.10
438	Chris Carpenter	.10
439	Marty Cordova	.10
440	Jose Cruz Jr.	.10
441	Carlos Delgado	.40
442	Darrin Fletcher	.10
443	Brad Fullmer	.10
444	Alex S. Gonzalez	.10
445	Billy Koch	.10
446	Raul Mondesi	.10
447	Mickey Morandini	.10
448	Shannon Stewart	.10
449	Steve Trachsel	.10
450	David Wells	.10
451	Juan Alvarez	.10
452	Shawn Wooten	.10
453	Ismael Villegas	.10
454	Carlos Casimiro	.10
455	Morgan Burkhart	.10
456	Paxton Crawford	.10
457	Dernell Stenson	.10
458	Ross Gload	.10
459	Raul Gonzalez	.10
460	Corey Patterson	.10
461	Julio Zuleta	.10
462	Rocky Biddle	.10
463	Joe Crede	.10
464	Matt Ginter	.10
465	Aaron Myette	.10
466	Mike Bell	.10
467	Travis Dawkins	.10
468	Mark Watson	.10
469	Elvis Pena	.10
470	Eric Munson	.10
471	Pablo Ozuna	.10
472	Frank Charles	.10
473	Mike Judd	.10
474	Hector Ramirez	.10
475	Jack Cressend	.10
476	Talmadge Nunnari	.10
477	Jorge Toca	.10
478	Alfonso Soriano	.65
479	Jay Tessmer	.10
480	Jake Westbrook	.10
481	Todd Belitz	.10
482	Eric Byrnes	.10
483	Jose Ortiz	.10
484	Tike Redman	.10
485	Domingo Guzman	.10
486	Rodrigo Lopez	.10
487	Pedro Feliz	.10
488	Damon Minor	.10
489	Ryan Vogelsong	.10
490	Joel Pineiro	.10
491	Justin Brunette	.10
492	Keith McDonald	.10
493	Aubrey Huff	.10
494	Kenny Kelly	.10
495	Damian Rolls	.10
496	John Bale	.10
497	Pasqual Coco	.10
498	Matt DeWitt	.10
499	Leo Estrella	.10
500	Josh Phelps	.10

Hobby Limited

Stars: 8-15X
Production 70 sets

Premiere Date

Stars: 20-30X
Production 35 sets

Extreme

Stars: 15-25X
Production 45 sets

Cramer's Choice Awards

		NM/M
Complete Set (10):		275.00
Common Player:		15.00
Inserted 1:721		
Styrene & Canvas pricing unavailable		
1	Cal Ripken Jr.	50.00
2	Nomar Garciaparra	30.00
3	Sammy Sosa	30.00
4	Frank Thomas	15.00
5	Ken Griffey Jr.	30.00
6	Mike Piazza	30.00
7	Derek Jeter	50.00
8	Mark McGwire	40.00
9	Barry Bonds	50.00
10	Alex Rodriguez	40.00

Gold Crown Die-Cuts

		NM/M
Complete Set (36):		100.00
Common Player:		1.50
Inserted 1:73		
1	Darin Erstad	1.50
2	Troy Glaus	4.00
3	Randy Johnson	4.00
4	Rafael Furcal	1.50
5	Andruw Jones	4.00
6	Chipper Jones	5.00
7	Greg Maddux	5.00
8	Cal Ripken Jr.	10.00
9	Nomar Garciaparra	8.00
10	Pedro Martinez	4.00
11	Sammy Sosa	8.00
12	Kerry Wood	2.50
13	Frank Thomas	4.00
14	Ken Griffey Jr.	8.00
15	Manny Ramirez	4.00
16	Todd Helton	4.00
17	Jeff Bagwell	4.00
18	Shawn Green	1.50
19	Gary Sheffield	1.50
20	Vladimir Guerrero	4.00
21	Mike Piazza	8.00
22	Jose Canseco	2.00
23	Roger Clemens	6.00
24	Derek Jeter	10.00
25	Jason Giambi	2.50
26	Pat Burrell	2.00
27	Rick Ankiel	1.50
28	Jim Edmonds	1.50
29	Mark McGwire	9.00
30	Tony Gwynn	5.00
31	Barry Bonds	10.00
32	Rickey Henderson	4.00
33	Edgar Martinez	1.50
34	Alex Rodriguez	9.00
35	Ivan Rodriguez	3.00
36	Carlos Delgado	2.00

On The Horizon

		NM/M
Complete Set (10):		20.00
Common Player:		2.00
Inserted 1:145		
1	Rafael Furcal	2.00
2	Corey Patterson	2.50
3	Russell Branyan	2.00
4	Juan Pierre	2.50
5	Mark Quinn	2.00
6	Alfonso Soriano	6.00
7	Adam Piatt	2.00
8	Pat Burrell	4.50
9	Kazuhiro Sasaki	2.50
10	Aubrey Huff	2.00

Ornaments

		NM/M
Complete Set (24):		25.00
Common Player:		.50
Inserted 2:37		
1	Rafael Furcal	.50
2	Chipper Jones	2.00
3	Greg Maddux	2.00
4	Cal Ripken Jr.	4.00

5	Nomar Garciaparra	2.50
6	Pedro Martinez	1.50
7	Sammy Sosa	2.50
8	Frank Thomas	1.50
9	Ken Griffey Jr.	2.50
10	Manny Ramirez	1.50
11	Todd Helton	1.50
12	Vladimir Guerrero	1.50
13	Mike Piazza	2.50
14	Roger Clemens	2.25
15	Derek Jeter	4.00
16	Pat Burrell	1.00
17	Rick Ankiel	.50
18	Mark McGwire	3.00
19	Barry Bonds	4.00
20	Alex Rodriguez	3.00
21	Troy Glaus	1.50
22	Tom Glavine	.50
23	Jim Edmonds	.50
24	Ivan Rodriguez	1.00

AL Decade's Best

		NM/M
Complete Set (18):		20.00
Common Player:		.50
Inserted 2:37		
1	Rickey Henderson	1.50
2	Rafael Palmeiro	1.00
3	Cal Ripken Jr.	4.00
4	Jose Canseco	.75
5	Juan Gonzalez	1.50
6	Frank Thomas	1.50
7	Albert Belle	.50
8	Edgar Martinez	.50
9	Mo Vaughn	.50
10	Derek Jeter	4.00
11	Mark McGwire	3.00
12	Alex Rodriguez	3.00
13	Ken Griffey Jr.	2.50
14	Nomar Garciaparra	2.50
15	Roger Clemens	2.00
16	Bernie Williams	.50
17	Ivan Rodriguez	1.00
18	Pedro Martinez	1.50

NL Decade's Best

		NM/M
Complete Set (18):		15.00
Common Player:		.50
Inserted 2:37		
1	Barry Bonds	4.00
2	Jeff Bagwell	1.00
3	Tom Glavine	.65
4	Gary Sheffield	.65
5	Fred McGriff	.50
6	Greg Maddux	1.50
7	Mike Piazza	2.00
8	Tony Gwynn	1.50
9	Hideo Nomo	1.00
10	Andres Galarraga	.50
11	Larry Walker	.50
12	Scott Rolen	.75
13	Pedro Martinez	1.00
14	Sammy Sosa	2.00
15	Mark McGwire	3.00
16	Kerry Wood	.75
17	Chipper Jones	1.50
18	Mark Grace	.75

2001 PACIFIC PRIVATE STOCK

		NM/M
Complete Set (150):		50.00
Common Player:		.25
Common (126-150):		1.00
Inserted 1:4		
Hobby Pack (7):		10.00
Hobby Box (10):		75.00
1	Darin Erstad	.50
2	Troy Glaus	1.00
3	Tim Salmon	.35
4	Mo Vaughn	.25
5	Steve Finley	.25
6	Luis Gonzalez	.35
7	Randy Johnson	1.00
8	Matt Williams	.25
9	Rafael Furcal	.25
10	Andres Galarraga	.25
11	Tom Glavine	.45
12	Andruw Jones	1.00
13	Chipper Jones	1.50
14	Greg Maddux	1.50
15	B.J. Surhoff	.25
16	Brady Anderson	.25
17	Albert Belle	.25
18	Mike Mussina	.45
19	Cal Ripken Jr.	3.00
20	Carl Everett	.25
21	Nomar Garciaparra	2.00
22	Pedro Martinez	1.00
23	Mark Grace	.35
24	Sammy Sosa	2.00
25	Kerry Wood	.50
26	Carlos Lee	.25
27	Magglio Ordonez	.25
28	Frank Thomas	1.00
29	Sean Casey	.35
30	Ken Griffey Jr.	2.00
31	Barry Larkin	.25
32	Pokey Reese	.25
33	Roberto Alomar	.40
34	Kenny Lofton	.25
35	Manny Ramirez	1.00
36	Jim Thome	.75
37	Omar Vizquel	.25
38	Jeff Cirillo	.25
39	Jeffrey Hammonds	.25
40	Todd Helton	1.00
41	Larry Walker	.25
42	Tony Clark	.25
43	Juan Encarnacion	.25
44	Juan Gonzalez	1.00
45	Hideo Nomo	1.00
46	Cliff Floyd	.25
47	Derrek Lee	.25
48	Henry Rodriguez	.25
49	Preston Wilson	.25
50	Jeff Bagwell	1.00
51	Craig Biggio	.25
52	Richard Hidalgo	.25
53	Moises Alou	.25
54	Carlos Beltran	.50
55	Johnny Damon	.40
56	Jermaine Dye	.25
57	Mac Suzuki	.25
58	Mike Sweeney	.25
59	Adrian Beltre	.40
60	Kevin Brown	.25
61	Shawn Green	.50
62	Eric Karros	.25
63	Chan Ho Park	.25
64	Gary Sheffield	.40
65	Jeromy Burnitz	.25
66	Geoff Jenkins	.25
67	Richie Sexson	.25
68	Jacque Jones	.25
69	Matt Lawton	.25
70	Eric Milton	.25
71	Vladimir Guerrero	1.00
72	Jose Vidro	.25
73	Edgardo Alfonzo	.25
74	Mike Hampton	.25
75	Mike Piazza	2.00
76	Robin Ventura	.25
77	Jose Canseco	.50
78	Roger Clemens	1.75
79	Derek Jeter	3.00
80	David Justice	.25
81	Jorge Posada	.25
82	Bernie Williams	.35
83	Jason Giambi	.65
84	Ben Grieve	.25
85	Tim Hudson	.35
86	Terrence Long	.25
87	Miguel Tejada	.35
88	Bobby Abreu	.25
89	Pat Burrell	.50
90	Mike Lieberthal	.25
91	Scott Rolen	.75
92	Kris Benson	.25
93	Brian Giles	.25
94	Jason Kendall	.25
95	Aramis Ramirez	.25
96	Rick Ankiel	.25
97	Will Clark	.35
98	J.D. Drew	.25
99	Jim Edmonds	.25
100	Mark McGwire	2.50
101	Fernando Tatis	.25
102	Adam Eaton	.25
103	Tony Gwynn	1.50
104	Phil Nevin	.25
105	Eric Owens	.25
106	Barry Bonds	3.00
107	Jeff Kent	.25
108	J.T. Snow	.25
109	Rickey Henderson	1.00
110	Edgar Martinez	.25
111	John Olerud	.25
112	Alex Rodriguez	2.50
113	Kazuhiro Sasaki	.25
114	Vinny Castilla	.25
115	Fred McGriff	.25
116	Greg Vaughn	.25
117	Gabe Kapler	.25
118	Ruben Mateo	.25
119	Rafael Palmeiro	.75
120	Ivan Rodriguez	.75
121	Tony Batista	.25
122	Jose Cruz Jr.	.25
123	Carlos Delgado	.75
124	Shannon Stewart	.25
125	David Wells	.25
126	Shawn Wooten	1.00
127	George Lombard	1.00
128	Morgan Burkhart	1.00
129	Ross Gload	1.00
130	Corey Patterson	1.00
131	Julio Zuleta	1.00
132	Joe Crede	1.00
133	Matt Ginter	1.00
134	Travis Dawkins	1.00
135	Eric Munson	1.00
136	Dee Brown	1.00
137	Luke Prokopec	1.00
138	Timoniel Perez	1.00
139	Alfonso Soriano	2.00
140	Jake Westbrook	1.00
141	Eric Byrnes	1.00
142	Adam Hyzdu	1.00
143	Jimmy Rollins	1.50
144	Xavier Nady	1.00
145	Ryan Vogelsong	1.00
146	Joel Pineiro	2.00
147	Aubrey Huff	1.00
148	Kenny Kelly	1.00
149	Josh Phelps	1.00
150	Vernon Wells	1.00

Silver

Stars:	.5-1.5X
SP's:	.5-1X

Base cards in retail

Premiere Date

Stars:	4-8X
SP's:	1-2X

Production 90 sets

Silver Portraits

Stars:	2-5X
SP's:	1X

Production 290 sets R

Gold Portraits

Stars:	6-10X
SP's (126-150):	1-2X

Production 75 sets H

Artist's Canvas

		NM/M
Complete Set (20):		50.00
Common Player:		1.00
Inserted 1:21		
1	Randy Johnson	2.50
2	Chipper Jones	4.00
3	Greg Maddux	4.00
4	Cal Ripken Jr.	8.00
5	Nomar Garciaparra	5.00

6	Pedro Martinez	2.50
7	Sammy Sosa	5.00
8	Frank Thomas	2.50
9	Ken Griffey Jr.	5.00
10	Manny Ramirez	2.50
11	Vladimir Guerrero	2.50
12	Mike Piazza	5.00
13	Roger Clemens	4.50
14	Derek Jeter	6.00
15	Jason Giambi	2.50
16	Rick Ankiel	1.00
17	Mark McGwire	6.00
18	Barry Bonds	8.00
19	Alex Rodriguez	6.00
20	Ivan Rodriguez	2.00

Extreme Action

		NM/M
Complete Set (20):		20.00
Common Player:		2.00
Inserted 1:11		
1	Troy Glaus	1.00
2	Rafael Furcal	.50
3	Chipper Jones	1.50
4	Cal Ripken Jr.	3.00
5	Nomar Garciaparra	2.00
6	Sammy Sosa	2.00
7	Ken Griffey Jr.	2.00
8	Manny Ramirez	1.00
9	Todd Helton	1.00
10	Jeff Bagwell	1.00
11	Vladimir Guerrero	1.00
12	Derek Jeter	3.00
13	Mike Piazza	2.00
14	Pat Burrell	.75
15	Jim Edmonds	.50
16	Mark McGwire	2.50
17	Barry Bonds	3.00
18	Alex Rodriguez	2.50
19	Ivan Rodriguez	.75
20	Carlos Delgado	.75

Game Gear

		NM/M
Common Player:		4.00
Inserted 1:1 H		
1	Garret Anderson Bat	6.00
2	Darin Erstad Jsy	5.00

3 Ron Gant Bat 4.00
4 Troy Glaus Jsy 8.00
5 Tim Salmon Bat 5.00
6 Mo Vaughn Jsy Grey 4.00
7 Mo Vaughn Jsy White 4.00
8 Mo Vaughn Bat 4.00
9 Jay Bell Jsy 4.00
10 Jay Bell Bat 4.00
11 Erubiel Durazo Jsy Black 4.00
12 Erubiel Durazo Jsy White 4.00
13 Erubiel Durazo Bat 4.00
14 Steve Finley Bat 4.00
15 Randy Johnson Jsy 10.00
16 Byung-Hyun Kim Jsy White 4.00
17 Byung-Hyun Kim Jsy Grey 4.00
18 Matt Williams Jsy Grey 4.00
19 Matt Williams Jsy White 4.00
20 Matt Williams Jsy Purple 4.00
21 Bobby Bonilla Jsy 4.00
22 Rafael Furcal Bat 5.00
23 Andruw Jones Bat 8.00
24 Chipper Jones Jsy 10.00
25 Chipper Jones Bat 10.00
26 Brian Jordan Jsy 4.00
27 Javier Lopez Bat 4.00
28 Greg Maddux Jsy 15.00
29 Greg Maddux Bat 15.00
30 Brady Anderson Bat 4.00
31 Albert Belle Bat 4.00
32 Nomar Garciaparra Bat 15.00
33 Pedro Martinez Bat 10.00
34 Jose Offerman Bat 4.00
35 Damon Buford Jsy 4.00
36 Jose Nieves Bat 4.00
38 Kerry Wood Bat 8.00
39 James Baldwin Jsy 4.00
40 Ray Durham Jsy 4.00
41 Ray Durham Bat 4.00
42 Carlos Lee Bat 4.00
43 Magglio Ordonez Jsy 6.00
44 Magglio Ordonez Bat 6.00
45 Chris Singleton Jsy 4.00
46 Aaron Boone Bat 4.00
47 Sean Casey Bat 4.00
48 Barry Larkin Jsy 6.00
49 Pokey Reese Jsy 4.00
50 Pokey Reese Bat 4.00
51 Dmitri Young Bat 4.00
52 Roberto Alomar Bat 8.00
53 Einar Diaz Bat 4.00
54 Kenny Lofton Jsy 4.00
55 David Segui Bat 4.00
56 Omar Vizquel Jsy 5.00
57 Luis Castillo Jsy 4.00
58 Jeff Cirillo Jsy 4.00
59 Jeff Frye Bat 4.00
60 Todd Helton Jsy 8.00
61 Todd Helton Bat 8.00
62 Neifi Perez Bat 4.00
63 Larry Walker Jsy 4.00
64 Larry Walker Bat 4.00
65 Masato Yoshii Jsy 4.00
66 Brad Ausmus Jsy 4.00
67 Rich Becker Bat 4.00
68 Tony Clark Bat 4.00
69 Deivi Cruz Bat 4.00
70 Juan Gonzalez Bat 6.00
71 Dean Palmer Bat 4.00
72 Cliff Floyd Jsy White 4.00
73 Cliff Floyd Jsy Teal 4.00
74 Cliff Floyd Bat 4.00
75 Alex Gonzalez Jsy 4.00
76 Alex Gonzalez Marlins Bat 4.00
77 Mark Kotsay Bat 4.00
78 Derrek Lee Bat 4.00
79 Pablo Ozuna Jsy 4.00
80 Craig Biggio Bat 4.00
81 Ken Caminiti Bat 4.00
82 Roger Cedeno Bat 4.00
83 Ricky Bottalico Bat 4.00
84 Dee Brown Bat 4.00
85 Jermaine Dye Bat 4.00
86 David McCarty Bat 4.00
87 Hector Ortiz Bat 4.00
88 Joe Randa Bat 4.00
89 Adrian Beltre Jsy 4.00
90 Kevin Brown Jsy 6.00
91 Alex Cora Bat 4.00
92 Darren Dreifort Bat 4.00
93 Shawn Green Jsy White 6.00
94 Shawn Green Jsy Grey 6.00
95 Shawn Green Bat 6.00
96 Todd Hundley Jsy 4.00
97 Eric Karros Bat 4.00
98 Chan Ho Park Jsy 4.00
99 Chan Ho Park Bat 4.00
101 Gary Sheffield Bat 6.00
102 Ismael Valdes Bat 4.00
103 Jeromy Burnitz Bat 4.00
104 Marquis Grissom Bat 4.00
105 Matt Lawton Bat 4.00
106 Fernando Seguignol Bat 4.00
107 Edgardo Alfonzo White Swing 4.00
108 Edgardo Alfonzo Jsy White Drop 4.00
109 Edgardo Alfonzo Jsy Black 4.00
110 Derek Bell Jsy White 4.00
111 Derek Bell Jsy Black 4.00
112 Armando Benitez Bat 4.00
113 Al Leiter Bat 4.00
114 Rey Ordonez Jsy Grey Field 4.00
115 Rey Ordonez Jsy White 4.00
116 Rey Ordonez Jsy Grey Bunt 4.00
117 Rey Ordonez Bat 4.00
118 Jay Payton Bat 4.00
119 Mike Piazza Jsy 10.00
120 Robin Ventura Jsy Black Hit 4.00
121 Robin Ventura Jsy Black Field 4.00
122 Robin Ventura Jsy White 4.00
123 Luis Polonia Bat 4.00
124 Bernie Williams Bat 6.00
125 Eric Chavez Jsy 4.00
126 Jason Giambi Jsy 8.00
127 Jason Giambi Bat 8.00
128 Ben Grieve Jsy 4.00
129 Ben Grieve Bat 4.00
130 Ramon Hernandez Bat 4.00
131 Tim Hudson Jsy 6.00
132 Terrence Long Bat 4.00
133 Mark Mulder Jsy 6.00
134 Adam Piatt Jsy 4.00
135 Olmedo Saenz Bat 4.00
136 Matt Stairs Bat 4.00
137 Mike Stanley Bat 4.00
138 Miguel Tejada Bat 6.00
139 Travis Lee Bat 4.00
140 Brian Giles Bat 5.00
141 Jason Kendall Jsy 4.00
142 Will Clark Bat 6.00
143 J.D. Drew Bat 4.00
144 Jim Edmonds Bat 6.00
145 Mark McGwire Bat 50.00
146 Edgar Renteria Bat 4.00
147 Garrett Stephenson Jsy 4.00
148 Tony Gwynn Jsy 10.00
149 Ruben Rivera Bat 4.00
150 Barry Bonds Jsy 40.00
151 Barry Bonds Bat 40.00
152 Ellis Burks Jsy 4.00
153 J.T. Snow Bat 4.00
154 Jay Buhner Jsy 4.00
155 Jay Buhner Bat 4.00
156 Carlos Guillen Jsy 4.00
157 Carlos Guillen Bat 4.00
158 Rickey Henderson Bat 15.00
159 Edgar Martinez Bat 6.00
160 Gil Meche Jsy 4.00
161 John Olerud Bat 5.00
162 Joe Oliver Bat 4.00
163 Alex Rodriguez Jsy 30.00
164 Kazuhiro Sasaki Jsy 4.00
165 Dan Wilson Jsy 4.00
166 Dan Wilson Bat 4.00
167 Vinny Castilla Bat 4.00
168 Jose Guillen Bat 4.00
169 Fred McGriff Jsy 5.00
170 Rusty Greer Bat 4.00
171 Mike Lamb Bat 4.00
172 Ruben Mateo Jsy 4.00
173 Ruben Mateo Bat 4.00
174 Rafael Palmeiro Jsy 8.00
175 Rafael Palmeiro Bat 8.00
178 Tony Batista Bat 4.00
179 Marty Cordova Bat 4.00
180 Jose Cruz Jr. Bat 4.00
181 Alex Gonzalez Blue Jays Bat 4.00
182 Raul Mondesi Bat 4.00

Game Jersey Patch

NM/M

Common Player: 8.00
2 Darin Erstad 8.00
4 Troy Glaus 15.00
6 Mo Vaughn Grey 8.00
7 Mo Vaughn White 8.00
9 Jay Bell 8.00
11 Erubiel Durazo Black 8.00
12 Erubiel Durazo White 8.00
15 Randy Johnson 40.00
16 Byung-Hyun Kim White 8.00
17 Byung-Hyun Kim Grey 8.00
18 Matt Williams Grey 8.00
19 Matt Williams White 8.00
20 Matt Williams Purple 8.00
21 Bobby Bonilla 8.00
24 Chipper Jones 25.00
26 Brian Jordan 8.00
28 Greg Maddux 80.00
35 Damon Buford 8.00
39 James Baldwin 8.00
40 Ray Durham 8.00
43 Magglio Ordonez 20.00
45 Chris Singleton 8.00
48 Barry Larkin 15.00
49 Pokey Reese 8.00
54 Kenny Lofton 10.00
56 Omar Vizquel 10.00
57 Luis Castillo 8.00
58 Jeff Cirillo 8.00
60 Todd Helton 20.00
63 Larry Walker 10.00
65 Masato Yoshii 8.00
66 Brad Ausmus 8.00
72 Cliff Floyd White 8.00
73 Cliff Floyd Teal 8.00
75 Alex Gonzalez 8.00
79 Pablo Ozuna 8.00
89 Adrian Beltre 8.00
90 Kevin Brown 15.00
93 Shawn Green White 15.00
94 Shawn Green Grey 15.00
96 Todd Hundley 8.00
98 Chan Ho Park 8.00
107 Edgardo Alfonzo White Swing 8.00
108 Edgardo Alfonzo White Drop 8.00
109 Edgardo Alfonzo Black 8.00
110 Derek Bell White 8.00
111 Derek Bell Black 8.00
114 Rey Ordonez Grey Field 8.00
115 Rey Ordonez White 8.00
116 Rey Ordonez Grey Bunt 8.00
119 Mike Piazza 75.00
120 Robin Ventura Black Hit 10.00
121 Robin Ventura Black Field 10.00
122 Robin Ventura White 10.00
125 Eric Chavez 15.00
126 Jason Giambi 15.00
128 Ben Grieve 8.00
131 Tim Hudson 15.00
133 Mark Mulder 15.00
134 Adam Piatt 8.00
141 Jason Kendall 10.00
147 Garrett Stephenson 8.00
148 Tony Gwynn 40.00
150 Barry Bonds 90.00
152 Ellis Burks 8.00
154 Jay Buhner 8.00
156 Carlos Guillen 8.00
160 Gil Meche 8.00
163 Alex Rodriguez
164 Kazuhiro Sasaki 15.00
165 Dan Wilson 8.00
169 Fred McGriff 10.00
172 Ruben Mateo 8.00
174 Rafael Palmeiro 25.00

PS-206 Stars

NM/M

Complete Set (20): 50.00
Common Player: 1.00
Inserted 3:hobby case
1 Chipper Jones 3.00
2 Greg Maddux 3.00
3 Cal Ripken Jr. 6.00
4 Nomar Garciaparra 4.00
5 Pedro Martinez 2.00
6 Sammy Sosa 4.00
7 Frank Thomas 2.00
8 Ken Griffey Jr. 4.00
9 Manny Ramirez 2.00
10 Jeff Bagwell 2.00
11 Gary Sheffield 1.00
12 Mike Piazza 4.00
13 Roger Clemens 3.50
14 Derek Jeter 6.00
15 Rick Ankiel 1.00
16 Mark McGwire 5.00
17 Tony Gwynn 3.00
18 Barry Bonds 6.00
19 Alex Rodriguez 5.00
20 Ivan Rodriguez 1.50

PS-206 Action

NM/M

Complete Set (60): 20.00
Common Player: .15
Inserted 2:pack
1 Darin Erstad .25
2 Troy Glaus .65
3 Randy Johnson .65
4 Rafael Furcal .15
5 Tom Glavine .40
6 Andruw Jones .65
7 Chipper Jones .75
8 Greg Maddux .75
9 Albert Belle .15
10 Mike Mussina .40
11 Cal Ripken Jr. 1.50
12 Nomar Garciaparra 1.00
13 Pedro Martinez .65
14 Mark Grace .25
15 Sammy Sosa 1.00
16 Kerry Wood .35
17 Magglio Ordonez .15
18 Frank Thomas .65
19 Ken Griffey Jr. 1.00
20 Barry Larkin .15
21 Roberto Alomar .35
22 Manny Ramirez .65
23 Jim Thome .60
24 Jeff Cirillo .15
25 Todd Helton .65
26 Larry Walker .15
27 Juan Gonzalez .65
28 Hideo Nomo .65
29 Preston Wilson .15
30 Jeff Bagwell .65
31 Craig Biggio .15
32 Johnny Damon .25
33 Jermaine Dye .15
34 Shawn Green .30
35 Gary Sheffield .25
36 Vladimir Guerrero .65
37 Mike Piazza 1.00
38 Jose Canseco .40
39 Roger Clemens .85
40 Derek Jeter 1.50
41 Bernie Williams .30
42 Jason Giambi .50
43 Ben Grieve .15
44 Pat Burrell .40
45 Scott Rolen .50
46 Rick Ankiel .15
47 J.D. Drew .25
48 Jim Edmonds .15
49 Mark McGwire 1.25
50 Tony Gwynn .75
51 Barry Bonds 1.50
52 Jeff Kent .15
53 Edgar Martinez .15
54 Alex Rodriguez 1.25
55 Kazuhiro Sasaki .15
56 Fred McGriff .15
57 Rafael Palmeiro .50
58 Ivan Rodriguez .50
59 Tony Batista .15
60 Carlos Delgado .45

PS-206 New Wave

NM/M

Complete Set (20): 30.00
Common Player: 1.00
Inserted 2:hobby case
1 Darin Erstad 1.50
2 Troy Glaus 5.00
3 Rafael Furcal 1.00
4 Andruw Jones 5.00
5 Magglio Ordonez 1.00
6 Carlos Lee 1.00
7 Todd Helton 5.00
8 Johnny Damon 1.50
9 Jermaine Dye 1.00
10 Vladimir Guerrero 5.00
11 Jason Giambi 4.00
12 Ben Grieve 1.00
13 Pat Burrell 3.00
14 Rick Ankiel 1.00
15 J.D. Drew 1.50
16 Adam Eaton 1.00

17	Kazuhiro Sasaki	1.00
18	Ruben Mateo	1.00
19	Tony Batista	1.00
20	Carlos Delgado	3.00

PS-206 Rookies

		NM/M
Complete Set (20):		50.00
Common Player:		3.00
Inserted 1:case		
1	George Lombard	3.00
2	Morgan Burkhart	3.00
3	Corey Patterson	5.00
4	Julio Zuleta	3.00
5	Joe Crede	3.00
6	Matt Ginter	3.00
7	Aaron Myette	3.00
8	Travis Dawkins	3.00
9	Eric Munson	3.00
10	Dee Brown	3.00
11	Luke Prokopec	3.00
12	Jorge Toca	3.00
13	Alfonso Soriano	7.50
14	Eric Byrnes	3.00
15	Adam Hyzdu	3.00
16	Jimmy Rollins	4.00
17	Joel Pineiro	5.00
18	Aubrey Huff	4.00
19	Kenny Kelly	3.00
20	Vernon Wells	3.00

Reserve

		NM/M
Complete Set (20):		25.00
Common Player:		.50
Inserted 1:21 H		
1	Randy Johnson	1.50
2	Chipper Jones	2.00
3	Greg Maddux	2.00
4	Cal Ripken Jr.	4.00
5	Nomar Garciaparra	2.50
6	Pedro Martinez	1.50
7	Sammy Sosa	2.50
8	Frank Thomas	1.50
9	Ken Griffey Jr.	2.50
10	Todd Helton	1.50
11	Vladimir Guerrero	1.50
12	Mike Piazza	2.50
13	Roger Clemens	2.25
14	Derek Jeter	4.00
15	Rick Ankiel	.50
16	Mark McGwire	3.00
17	Tony Gwynn	2.00
18	Barry Bonds	4.00
19	Alex Rodriguez	3.00
20	Ivan Rodriguez	1.00

1992 PINNACLE

		NM/M
Complete Set (620):		15.00
Common Player:		.05
Foil Pack (16):		.75
Foil Box (36):		17.50
Jumbo Pack (24+3):		1.50
Jumbo Box (12):		22.50
1	Frank Thomas	.75
2	Benito Santiago	.05
3	Carlos Baerga	.05
4	Cecil Fielder	.05
5	Barry Larkin	.05
6	Ozzie Smith	1.00
7	Willie McGee	.05
8	Paul Molitor	.75
9	Andy Van Slyke	.05
10	Ryne Sandberg	1.00
11	Kevin Seitzer	.05
12	Len Dykstra	.05
13	Edgar Martinez	.05
14	Ruben Sierra	.05
15	Howard Johnson	.05
16	Dave Henderson	.05
17	Devon White	.05
18	Terry Pendleton	.05
19	Steve Finley	.05
20	Kirby Puckett	1.00
21	Orel Hershiser	.05
22	Hal Morris	.05
23	Don Mattingly	1.25
24	Delino DeShields	.05
25	Dennis Eckersley	.60
26	Ellis Burks	.05
27	Jay Buhner	.05
28	Matt Williams	.05
29	Lou Whitaker	.05
30	Alex Fernandez	.05
31	Albert Belle	.05
32	Todd Zeile	.05
33	Tony Pena	.05
34	Jay Bell	.05
35	Rafael Palmeiro	.65
36	Wes Chamberlain	.05
37	George Bell	.05
38	Robin Yount	.75
39	Vince Coleman	.05
40	Bruce Hurst	.05
41	Harold Baines	.05
42	Chuck Finley	.05
43	Ken Caminiti	.05
44	Ben McDonald	.05
45	Roberto Alomar	.15
46	Chili Davis	.05
47	Bill Doran	.05
48	Jerald Clark	.05
49	Jose Lind	.05
50	Nolan Ryan	2.00
51	Phil Plantier	.05
52	Gary DiSarcina	.05
53	Kevin Bass	.05
54	Pat Kelly	.05
55	Mark Wohlers	.05
56	Walt Weiss	.05
57	Lenny Harris	.05
58	Ivan Calderon	.05
59	Harold Reynolds	.05
60	George Brett	1.25
61	Gregg Olson	.05
62	Orlando Merced	.05
63	Steve Decker	.05
64	John Franco	.05
65	Greg Maddux	1.00
66	Alex Cole	.05
67	Dave Hollins	.05
68	Kent Hrbek	.05
69	Tom Pagnozzi	.05
70	Jeff Bagwell	.75
71	Jim Gantner	.05
72	Matt Nokes	.05
73	Brian Harper	.05
74	Andy Benes	.05
75	Tom Glavine	.35
76	Terry Steinbach	.05
77	Dennis Martinez	.05
78	John Olerud	.05
79	Ozzie Guillen	.05
80	Darryl Strawberry	.05
81	Gary Gaetti	.05
82	Dave Righetti	.05
83	Chris Hoiles	.05
84	Andujar Cedeno	.05
85	Jack Clark	.05
86	David Howard	.05
87	Bill Gullickson	.05
88	Bernard Gilkey	.05
89	Kevin Elster	.05
90	Kevin Maas	.05
91	Mark Lewis	.05
92	Greg Vaughn	.05
93	Bret Barberie	.05
94	Dave Smith	.05
95	Roger Clemens	1.25
96	Doug Drabek	.05
97	Omar Vizquel	.05
98	Jose Guzman	.05
99	Juan Samuel	.05
100	Dave Justice	.05
101	Tom Browning	.05
102	Mark Gubicza	.05
103	Mickey Morandini	.05
104	Ed Whitson	.05
105	Lance Parrish	.05
106	Scott Erickson	.05
107	Jack McDowell	.05
108	Dave Stieb	.05
109	Mike Moore	.05
110	Travis Fryman	.05
111	Dwight Gooden	.05
112	Fred McGriff	.05
113	Alan Trammell	.05
114	Roberto Kelly	.05
115	Andre Dawson	.25
116	Bill Landrum	.05
117	Brian McRae	.05
118	B.J. Surhoff	.05
119	Chuck Knoblauch	.05
120	Steve Olin	.05
121	Robin Ventura	.05
122	Will Clark	.05
123	Tino Martinez	.05
124	Dale Murphy	.25
125	Pete O'Brien	.05
126	Ray Lankford	.05
127	Juan Gonzalez	.40
128	Ron Gant	.05
129	Marquis Grissom	.05
130	Jose Canseco	.50
131	Mike Greenwell	.05
132	Mark Langston	.05
133	Brett Butler	.05
134	Kelly Gruber	.05
135	Chris Sabo	.05
136	Mark Grace	.05
137	Tony Fernandez	.05
138	Glenn Davis	.05
139	Pedro Munoz	.05
140	Craig Biggio	.05
141	Pete Schourek	.05
142	Mike Boddicker	.05
143	Robby Thompson	.05
144	Mel Hall	.05
145	Bryan Harvey	.05
146	Mike LaValliere	.05
147	John Kruk	.05
148	Joe Carter	.05
149	Greg Olson	.05
150	Julio Franco	.05
151	Darryl Hamilton	.05
152	Felix Fermin	.05
153	Jose Offerman	.05
154	Paul O'Neill	.05
155	Tommy Greene	.05
156	Ivan Rodriguez	.65
157	Dave Stewart	.05
158	Jeff Reardon	.05
159	Felix Jose	.05
160	Doug Dascenzo	.05
161	Tim Wallach	.05
162	Dan Plesac	.05
163	Luis Gonzalez	.05
164	Mike Henneman	.05
165	Mike Devereaux	.05
166	Luis Polonia	.05
167	Mike Sharperson	.05
168	Chris Donnels	.05
169	Greg Harris	.05
170	Deion Sanders	.05
171	Mike Schooler	.05
172	Jose DeJesus	.05
173	Jeff Montgomery	.05
174	Milt Cuyler	.05
175	Wade Boggs	1.00
176	Kevin Tapani	.05
177	Bill Spiers	.05
178	Tim Raines	.05
179	Randy Milligan	.05
180	Rob Dibble	.05
181	Kirt Manwaring	.05
182	Pascual Perez	.05
183	Juan Guzman	.05
184	John Smiley	.05
185	David Segui	.05
186	Omar Olivares	.05
187	Joe Slusarski	.05
188	Erik Hanson	.05
189	Mark Portugal	.05
190	Walt Terrell	.05
191	John Smoltz	.05
192	Wilson Alvarez	.05
193	Jimmy Key	.05
194	Larry Walker	.05
195	Lee Smith	.05
196	Pete Harnisch	.05
197	Mike Harkey	.05
198	Frank Tanana	.05
199	Terry Mulholland	.05
200	Cal Ripken, Jr.	2.00
201	Dave Magadan	.05
202	Bud Black	.05
203	Terry Shumpert	.05
204	Mike Mussina	.40
205	Mo Vaughn	.05
206	Steve Farr	.05
207	Darrin Jackson	.05
208	Jerry Browne	.05
209	Jeff Russell	.05
210	Mike Scioscia	.05
211	Rick Aguilera	.05
212	Jaime Navarro	.05
213	Randy Tomlin	.05
214	Bobby Thigpen	.05
215	Mark Gardner	.05
216	Norm Charlton	.05
217	Mark McGwire	1.75
218	Skeeter Barnes	.05
219	Bob Tewksbury	.05
220	Junior Felix	.05
221	Sam Horn	.05
222	Jody Reed	.05
223	Luis Sojo	.05
224	Jerome Walton	.05
225	Darryl Kile	.05
226	Mickey Tettleton	.05
227	Dan Pasqua	.05
228	Jim Gott	.05
229	Bernie Williams	.05
230	Shane Mack	.05
231	Steve Avery	.05
232	Dave Valle	.05
233	Mark Leonard	.05
234	Spike Owen	.05
235	Gary Sheffield	.20
236	Steve Chitren	.05
237	Zane Smith	.05
238	Tom Gordon	.05
239	Jose Oquendo	.05
240	Todd Stottlemyre	.05
241	Darren Daulton	.05
242	Tim Naehring	.05
243	Tony Phillips	.05
244	Shawon Dunston	.05
245	Manuel Lee	.05
246	Mike Pagliarulo	.05
247	Jim Thome	.65
248	Luis Mercedes	.05
249	Cal Eldred	.05
250	Derek Bell	.05
251	Arthur Rhodes	.05
252	Scott Cooper	.05
253	Roberto Hernandez	.05
254	Mo Sanford	.05
255	Scott Servais	.05
256	Eric Karros	.05
257	Andy Mota	.05
258	Keith Mitchell	.05
259	Joel Johnston	.05
260	John Wehner	.05
261	Gino Minutelli	.05
262	Greg Gagne	.05
263	Stan Royer	.05
264	Carlos Garcia	.05
265	Andy Ashby	.05
266	Kim Batiste	.05
267	Julio Valera	.05
268	Royce Clayton	.05
269	Gary Scott	.05
270	Kirk Dressendorfer	.05
271	Sean Berry	.05
272	Lance Dickson	.05
273	Rob Maurer	.05
274	Scott Brosius	.05
275	Dave Fleming	.05
276	Lenny Webster	.05
277	Mike Humphreys	.05
278	Freddie Benavides	.05
279	Harvey Pulliam	.05
280	Jeff Carter	.05
281	Jim Abbott, Nolan Ryan	.25
282	Wade Boggs, George Brett	.25
283	Ken Griffey Jr., Rickey Henderson	.50
284	Dale Murphy, Wally Joyner	.10
285	Chuck Knoblauch, Ozzie Smith	.20
286	Robin Ventura, Lou Gehrig	.20
287	Robin Yount	.30
288	Bob Tewksbury	.05
289	Kirby Puckett	.50
290	Kenny Lofton	.05
291	Jack McDowell	.05
292	John Burkett	.05
293	Dwight Smith	.05
294	Nolan Ryan	1.00
295	*Manny Ramirez*	2.50
296	*Cliff Floyd*	.50
297	*Al Shirley*	.05
298	*Brian Barber*	.05
299	*Jon Farrell*	.05
300	*Scott Ruffcorn*	.05
301	*Tyrone Hill*	.05
302	*Benji Gil*	.05
303	*Tyler Green*	.05
304	Allen Watson	.05
305	Jay Buhner	.05
306	Roberto Alomar	.05

#	Player	Value
307	Chuck Knoblauch	.05
308	Darryl Strawberry	.05
309	Danny Tartabull	.05
310	Bobby Bonilla	.05
311	Mike Felder	.05
312	Storm Davis	.05
313	Tim Teufel	.05
314	Tom Brunansky	.05
315	Rex Hudler	.05
316	Dave Otto	.05
317	Jeff King	.05
318	Dan Gladden	.05
319	Bill Pecota	.05
320	Franklin Stubbs	.05
321	Gary Carter	.75
322	Melido Perez	.05
323	Eric Davis	.05
324	Greg Myers	.05
325	Pete Incaviglia	.05
326	Von Hayes	.05
327	Greg Swindell	.05
328	Steve Sax	.05
329	Chuck McElroy	.05
330	Gregg Jefferies	.05
331	Joe Oliver	.05
332	Paul Faries	.05
333	David West	.05
334	Craig Grebeck	.05
335	Chris Hammond	.05
336	Billy Ripken	.05
337	Scott Sanderson	.05
338	Dick Schofield	.05
339	Bob Milacki	.05
340	Kevin Reimer	.05
341	Jose DeLeon	.05
342	Henry Cotto	.05
343	Daryl Boston	.05
344	Kevin Gross	.05
345	Milt Thompson	.05
346	Luis Rivera	.05
347	Al Osuna	.05
348	Rob Deer	.05
349	Tim Leary	.05
350	Mike Stanton	.05
351	Dean Palmer	.05
352	Trevor Wilson	.05
353	Mark Eichhorn	.05
354	Scott Aldred	.05
355	Mark Whiten	.05
356	Leo Gomez	.05
357	Rafael Belliard	.05
358	Carlos Quintana	.05
359	Mark Davis	.05
360	Chris Nabholz	.05
361	Carlton Fisk	.75
362	Joe Orsulak	.05
363	Eric Anthony	.05
364	Greg Hibbard	.05
365	Scott Leius	.05
366	Hensley Meulens	.05
367	Chris Bosio	.05
368	Brian Downing	.05
369	Sammy Sosa	1.00
370	Stan Belinda	.05
371	Joe Grahe	.05
372	Luis Salazar	.05
373	Lance Johnson	.05
374	Kal Daniels	.05
375	Dave Winfield	.75
376	Brook Jacoby	.05
377	Mariano Duncan	.05
378	Ron Darling	.05
379	Randy Johnson	.75
380	Chito Martinez	.05
381	Andres Galarraga	.05
382	Willie Randolph	.05
383	Charles Nagy	.05
384	Tim Belcher	.05
385	Duane Ward	.05
386	Vicente Palacios	.05
387	Mike Gallego	.05
388	Rich DeLucia	.05
389	Scott Radinsky	.05
390	Damon Berryhill	.05
391	Kirk McCaskill	.05
392	Pedro Guerrero	.05
393	Kevin Mitchell	.05
394	Dickie Thon	.05
395	Bobby Bonilla	.05
396	Bill Wegman	.05
397	Dave Martinez	.05
398	Rick Sutcliffe	.05
399	Larry Andersen	.05
400	Tony Gwynn	1.00
401	Rickey Henderson	.75
402	Greg Cadaret	.05
403	Keith Miller	.05
404	Bip Roberts	.05
405	Kevin Brown	.05
406	Mitch Williams	.05
407	Frank Viola	.05
408	Darren Lewis	.05
409	Bob Walk	.05
410	Bob Walk	.05
411	Todd Frohwirth	.05
412	Brian Hunter	.05
413	Ron Karkovice	.05
414	Mike Morgan	.05
415	Joe Hesketh	.05
416	Don Slaught	.05
417	Tom Henke	.05
418	Kurt Stillwell	.05
419	Hector Villanueva	.05
420	Glenallen Hill	.05
421	Pat Borders	.05
422	Charlie Hough	.05
423	Charlie Leibrandt	.05
424	Eddie Murray	.75
425	Jesse Barfield	.05
426	Mark Lemke	.05
427	Kevin McReynolds	.05
428	Gilberto Reyes	.05
429	Ramon Martinez	.05
430	Steve Buechele	.05
431	David Wells	.05
432	Kyle Abbott	.05
433	John Habyan	.05
434	Kevin Appier	.05
435	Gene Larkin	.05
436	Sandy Alomar, Jr.	.05
437	Mike Jackson	.05
438	Todd Benzinger	.05
439	Teddy Higuera	.05
440	Reggie Sanders	.05
441	Mark Carreon	.05
442	Bret Saberhagen	.05
443	Gene Nelson	.05
444	Jay Howell	.05
445	Roger McDowell	.05
446	Sid Bream	.05
447	Mackey Sasser	.05
448	Bill Swift	.05
449	Hubie Brooks	.05
450	David Cone	.05
451	Bobby Witt	.05
452	Brady Anderson	.05
453	Lee Stevens	.05
454	Luis Aquino	.05
455	Carney Lansford	.05
456	Carlos Hernandez	.05
457	Danny Jackson	.05
458	Gerald Young	.05
459	Tom Candiotti	.05
460	Billy Hatcher	.05
461	John Wetteland	.05
462	Mike Bordick	.05
463	Don Robinson	.05
464	Jeff Johnson	.05
465	Lonnie Smith	.05
466	Paul Assenmacher	.05
467	Alvin Davis	.05
468	Jim Eisenreich	.05
469	Brent Mayne	.05
470	Jeff Brantley	.05
471	Tim Burke	.05
472	*Pat Mahomes*	.05
473	Ryan Bowen	.05
474	Bryn Smith	.05
475	Mike Flanagan	.05
476	Reggie Jefferson	.05
477	Jeff Blauser	.05
478	Craig Lefferts	.05
479	Todd Worrell	.05
480	Scott Scudder	.05
481	Kirk Gibson	.05
482	Kenny Rogers	.05
483	Jack Morris	.05
484	Russ Swan	.05
485	Mike Huff	.05
486	Ken Hill	.05
487	Geronimo Pena	.05
488	Charlie O'Brien	.05
489	Mike Maddux	.05
490	Scott Livingstone	.05
491	Carl Willis	.05
492	Kelly Downs	.05
493	Dennis Cook	.05
494	Joe Magrane	.05
495	Bob Kipper	.05
496	Jose Mesa	.05
497	Charlie Hayes	.05
498	Joe Girardi	.05
499	Doug Jones	.05
500	Barry Bonds	2.00
501	Bill Krueger	.05
502	Glenn Braggs	.05
503	Eric King	.05
504	Frank Castillo	.05
505	Mike Gardiner	.05
506	Cory Snyder	.05
507	Steve Howe	.05
508	Jose Rijo	.05
509	Sid Fernandez	.05
510	*Archi Cianfrocco*	.05
511	Mark Guthrie	.05
512	Bob Ojeda	.05
513	John Doherty	.05
514	Dante Bichette	.05
515	Juan Berenguer	.05
516	Jeff Robinson	.05
517	Mike MacFarlane	.05
518	Matt Young	.05
519	Otis Nixon	.05
520	Brian Holman	.05
521	Chris Haney	.05
522	*Jeff Kent*	.75
523	*Chad Curtis*	.25
524	Vince Horsman	.05
525	Rod Nichols	.05
526	*Peter Hoy*	.05
527	Shawn Boskie	.05
528	Alejandro Pena	.05
529	Dave Burba	.05
530	Ricky Jordan	.05
531	David Silvestri	.05
532	John Patterson	.05
533	Jeff Branson	.05
534	Derrick May	.05
535	Esteban Beltre	.05
536	Jose Melendez	.05
537	Wally Joyner	.05
538	Eddie Taubensee	.05
539	Jim Abbott	.05
540	*Brian Williams*	.05
541	Donovan Osborne	.05
542	Patrick Lennon	.05
543	*Mike Groppuso*	.05
544	*Jarvis Brown*	.05
545	*Shawn Livesy*	.05
546	Jeff Ware	.05
547	Danny Tartabull	.05
548	*Bobby Jones*	.05
549	Ken Griffey, Jr.	1.50
550	*Rey Sanchez*	.05
551	*Pedro Astacio*	.10
552	*Juan Guerrero*	.05
553	*Jacob Brumfield*	.05
554	*Ben Rivera*	.05
555	*Brian Jordan*	.40
556	Denny Neagle	.05
557	Cliff Brantley	.05
558	Anthony Young	.05
559	*John VanderWal*	.05
560	*Monty Fariss*	.05
561	*Russ Springer*	.05
562	*Pat Listach*	.05
563	Pat Hentgen	.05
564	Andy Stankiewicz	.05
565	Mike Perez	.05
566	Mike Bielecki	.05
567	Butch Henry	.05
568	*Dave Nilsson*	.05
569	*Scott Hatteberg*	.05
570	Ruben Amaro Jr.	.05
571	Todd Hundley	.05
572	Moises Alou	.05
573	Hector Fajardo	.05
574	Todd Van Poppel	.05
575	Willie Banks	.05
576	Bob Zupcic	.05
577	*J.J. Johnson*	.05
578	John Burkett	.05
579	Trever Miller	.05
580	Scott Bankhead	.05
581	Rich Amaral	.05
582	Kenny Lofton	.05
583	Matt Stairs	.05
584	Don Mattingly, Rod Carew	.25
585	Jack Morris, Steve Avery	.05
586	Roberto Alomar, Sandy Alomar	.10
587	Scott Sanderson, Catfish Hunter	.05
588	Dave Justice, Willie Stargell	.05
589	Rex Hudler, Roger Staubach	.05
590	David Cone, Jackie Gleason	.05
591	Willie Davis, Tony Gwynn	.15
592	Orel Hershiser	.05
593	John Wetteland	.05
594	Tom Glavine	.05
595	Randy Johnson	.25
596	Jim Gott	.05
597	Donald Harris	.05
598	*Shawn Hare*	.05
599	Chris Gardner	.05
600	Rusty Meacham	.05
601	Benito Santiago	.05
602	Eric Davis	.05
603	Jose Lind	.05
604	Dave Justice	.05
605	Tim Raines	.05
606	Randy Tomlin	.05
607	Jack McDowell	.05
608	Greg Maddux	.30
609	Charles Nagy	.05
610	Tom Candiotti	.05
611	David Cone	.05
612	Steve Avery	.05
613	*Rod Beck*	.10
614	Rickey Henderson	.25
615	Benito Santiago	.05
616	Ruben Sierra	.05
617	Ryne Sandberg	.50
618	Nolan Ryan	1.00
619	Brett Butler	.05
620	Dave Justice	.05

Rookies

		NM/M
Complete Set (30):		2.00
Common Player:		.05
1	Luis Mercedes	.05
2	Scott Cooper	.05
3	Kenny Lofton	.25
4	John Doherty	.05
5	Pat Listach	.05
6	Andy Stankiewicz	.05
7	Derek Bell	.25
8	Gary DiSarcina	.05
9	Roberto Hernandez	.15
10	Joel Johnston	.05
11	Pat Mahomes	.05
12	Todd Van Poppel	.05
13	Dave Fleming	.05
14	Monty Fariss	.05
15	Gary Scott	.05
16	Moises Alou	.25
17	Todd Hundley	.25
18	Kim Batiste	.05
19	Denny Neagle	.05
20	Donovan Osborne	.05
21	Mark Wohlers	.05
22	Reggie Sanders	.10
23	Brian Williams	.05
24	Eric Karros	.25
25	Frank Seminara	.05
26	Royce Clayton	.05
27	Dave Nilsson	.05
28	Matt Stairs	.25
29	Chad Curtis	.25
30	Carlos Hernandez	.25

Rookie Idols

		NM/M
Complete Set (18):		17.50
Common Player:		.50
1	Reggie Sanders, Eric Davis	.50
2	Hector Fajardo, Jim Abbott	.50
3	Gary Cooper, George Brett	3.50
4	Mark Wohlers, Roger Clemens	3.50
5	Luis Mercedes, Julio Franco	.50
6	Willie Banks, Dwight Gooden	.50
7	Kenny Lofton, Rickey Henderson	1.50
8	Keith Mitchell, Dave Henderson	.50
9	Kim Batiste, Barry Larkin	.50
10	Thurman Munson, Todd Hundley	1.00
11	Eddie Zosky, Cal Ripken Jr.	4.50
12	Todd Van Poppel, Nolan Ryan	4.50

13	Ryne Sandberg, Jim Thome	2.50
14	Dave Fleming, Bobby Murcer	.50
15	Royce Clayton, Ozzie Smith	2.50
16	Don Harris, Darryl Strawberry	.50
17	Alan Trammell, Chad Curtis	.50
18	Derek Bell, Dave Winfield	1.50

Slugfest

		NM/M
Complete Set (15):		15.00
Common Player:		.30
1	Cecil Fielder	.30
2	Mark McGwire	2.50
3	Jose Canseco	.65
4	Barry Bonds	3.00
5	Dave Justice	.30
6	Bobby Bonilla	.30
7	Ken Griffey, Jr.	2.00
8	Ron Gant	.30
9	Ryne Sandberg	1.50
10	Ruben Sierra	.30
11	Frank Thomas	1.00
12	Will Clark	.30
13	Kirby Puckett	1.50
14	Cal Ripken, Jr.	3.00
15	Jeff Bagwell	1.00

Team Pinnacle

		NM/M
Complete Set (12):		20.00
Common Player:		1.00
1	Roger Clemens, Ramon Martinez	4.00
2	Jim Abbott, Steve Avery	1.00
3	Benito Santiago, Ivan Rodriguez	2.00
4	Frank Thomas, Will Clark	2.50
5	Roberto Alomar, Ryne Sandberg	3.00
6	Robin Ventura, Matt Williams	1.00
7	Cal Ripken, Jr., Barry Larkin	5.00
8	Danny Tartabull, Barry Bonds	5.00
9	Brett Butler, Ken Griffey Jr.	4.50
10	Ruben Sierra, Dave Justice	1.00
11	Dennis Eckersley, Rob Dibble	1.50
12	Scott Radinsky, John Franco	1.00

Team 2000

		NM/M
Complete Set (80):		3.00
Common Player:		.05
1	Mike Mussina	.30
2	Phil Plantier	.05
3	Frank Thomas	.50
4	Travis Fryman	.05
5	Kevin Appier	.05
6	Chuck Knoblauch	.05
7	Pat Kelly	.05
8	Ivan Rodriguez	.40
9	Dave Justice	.05
10	Jeff Bagwell	.50
11	Marquis Grissom	.05
12	Andy Benes	.05
13	Gregg Olson	.05
14	Kevin Morton	.05
15	Tim Naehring	.05
16	Dave Hollins	.05
17	Sandy Alomar Jr.	.05
18	Albert Belle	.05
19	Charles Nagy	.05
20	Brian McRae	.05
21	Larry Walker	.05
22	Delino DeShields	.05
23	Jeff Johnson	.05
24	Bernie Williams	.05
25	Jose Offerman	.05
26	Juan Gonzalez	.25
27	Juan Guzman	.05
28	Eric Anthony	.05
29	Brian Hunter	.05
30	John Smoltz	.05
31	Deion Sanders	.05
32	Greg Maddux	.75
33	Andujar Cedeno	.05
34	Royce Clayton	.05
35	Kenny Lofton	.05
36	Cal Eldred	.05
37	Jim Thome	.50
38	Gary DiSarcina	.05
39	Brian Jordan	.05
40	Chad Curtis	.05
41	Ben McDonald	.05
42	Jim Abbott	.05
43	Robin Ventura	.05
44	Milt Cuyler	.05
45	Gregg Jefferies	.05
46	Scott Radinsky	.05
47	Ken Griffey, Jr.	1.00
48	Roberto Alomar	.15
49	Ramon Martinez	.05
50	Bret Barberie	.05
51	Ray Lankford	.05
52	Leo Gomez	.05
53	Tommy Greene	.05
54	Mo Vaughn	.05
55	Sammy Sosa	.75
56	Carlos Baerga	.05
57	Mark Lewis	.05
58	Tom Gordon	.05
59	Gary Sheffield	.25
60	Scott Erickson	.05
61	Pedro Munoz	.05
62	Tino Martinez	.05
63	Darren Lewis	.05
64	Dean Palmer	.05
65	John Olerud	.05
66	Steve Avery	.05
67	Pete Harnisch	.05
68	Luis Gonzalez	.05
69	Kim Batiste	.05
70	Reggie Sanders	.05
71	Luis Mercedes	.05
72	Todd Van Poppel	.05
73	Gary Scott	.05
74	Monty Fariss	.05
75	Kyle Abbott	.05
76	Eric Karros	.05
77	Mo Sanford	.05
78	Todd Hundley	.05
79	Reggie Jefferson	.05
80	Pat Mahomes	.05

1993 PINNACLE

		NM/M
Complete Set (620):		17.50
Common Player:		.05
Series 1 Pack (15):		.35
Series 1 Box (36):		8.00
Series 2 Pack (15):		.75
Series 2 Box (36):		20.00
1	Gary Sheffield	.30
2	Cal Eldred	.05
3	Larry Walker	.05
4	Deion Sanders	.05
5	Dave Fleming	.05
6	Carlos Baerga	.05
7	Bernie Williams	.05
8	John Kruk	.05
9	Jimmy Key	.05
10	Jeff Bagwell	.60
11	Jim Abbott	.05
12	Terry Steinbach	.05
13	Bob Tewksbury	.05
14	Eric Karros	.05
15	Ryne Sandberg	.75
16	Will Clark	.05
17	Edgar Martinez	.05
18	Eddie Murray	.60
19	Andy Van Slyke	.05
20	Cal Ripken, Jr.	2.00
21	Ivan Rodriguez	.50
22	Barry Larkin	.05
23	Don Mattingly	.85
24	Gregg Jefferies	.05
25	Roger Clemens	.85
26	Cecil Fielder	.05
27	Kent Hrbek	.05
28	Robin Ventura	.05
29	Rickey Henderson	.60
30	Roberto Alomar	.15
31	Luis Polonia	.05
32	Andujar Cedeno	.05
33	Pat Listach	.05
34	Mark Grace	.05
35	Otis Nixon	.05
36	Felix Jose	.05
37	Mike Sharperson	.05
38	Dennis Martinez	.05
39	Willie McGee	.05
40	Kenny Lofton	.05
41	Randy Johnson	.60
42	Andy Benes	.05
43	Bobby Bonilla	.05
44	Mike Mussina	.50
45	Len Dykstra	.05
46	Ellis Burks	.05
47	Chris Sabo	.05
48	Jay Bell	.05
49	Jose Canseco	.40
50	Craig Biggio	.05
51	Wally Joyner	.05
52	Mickey Tettleton	.05
53	Tim Raines	.05
54	Brian Harper	.05
55	Rene Gonzales	.05
56	Mark Langston	.05
57	Jack Morris	.05
58	Mark McGwire	1.50
59	Ken Caminiti	.05
60	Terry Pendleton	.05
61	Dave Nilsson	.05
62	Tom Pagnozzi	.05
63	Mike Morgan	.05
64	Darryl Strawberry	.05
65	Charles Nagy	.05
66	Ken Hill	.05
67	Matt Williams	.05
68	Jay Buhner	.05
69	Vince Coleman	.05
70	Brady Anderson	.05
71	Fred McGriff	.05
72	Ben McDonald	.05
73	Terry Mulholland	.05
74	Randy Tomlin	.05
75	Nolan Ryan	2.00
76	Frank Viola	.05
77	Jose Rijo	.05
78	Shane Mack	.05
79	Travis Fryman	.05
80	Jack McDowell	.05
81	Mark Gubicza	.05
82	Matt Nokes	.05
83	Bert Blyleven	.05
84	Eric Anthony	.05
85	Mike Bordick	.05
86	John Olerud	.05
87	B.J. Surhoff	.05
88	Bernard Gilkey	.05
89	Shawon Dunston	.05
90	Tom Glavine	.30
91	Brett Butler	.05
92	Moises Alou	.05
93	Albert Belle	.05
94	Darren Lewis	.05
95	Omar Vizquel	.05
96	Dwight Gooden	.05
97	Gregg Olson	.05
98	Tony Gwynn	.75
99	Darren Daulton	.05
100	Dennis Eckersley	.50
101	Rob Dibble	.05
102	Mike Greenwell	.05
103	Jose Lind	.05
104	Julio Franco	.05
105	Tom Gordon	.05
106	Scott Livingstone	.05
107	Chuck Knoblauch	.05
108	Frank Thomas	.60
109	Melido Perez	.05
110	Ken Griffey, Jr.	1.00
111	Harold Baines	.05
112	Gary Gaetti	.05
113	Pete Harnisch	.05
114	David Wells	.05
115	Charlie Leibrandt	.05
116	Ray Lankford	.05
117	Kevin Seitzer	.05
118	Robin Yount	.60
119	Lenny Harris	.05
120	Chris James	.05
121	Delino DeShields	.05
122	Kirt Manwaring	.05
123	Glenallen Hill	.05
124	Hensley Meulens	.05
125	Darrin Jackson	.05
126	Todd Hundley	.05
127	Dave Hollins	.05
128	Sam Horn	.05
129	Roberto Hernandez	.05
130	Vicente Palacios	.05
131	George Brett	.85
132	Dave Martinez	.05
133	Kevin Appier	.05
134	Pat Kelly	.05
135	Pedro Munoz	.05
136	Mark Carreon	.05
137	Lance Johnson	.05
138	Devon White	.05
139	Julio Valera	.05
140	Eddie Taubensee	.05
141	Willie Wilson	.05
142	Stan Belinda	.05
143	John Smoltz	.05
144	Darryl Hamilton	.05
145	Sammy Sosa	.75
146	Carlos Hernandez	.05
147	Tom Candiotti	.05
148	Mike Felder	.05
149	Rusty Meacham	.05
150	Ivan Calderon	.05
151	Pete O'Brien	.05
152	Erik Hanson	.05
153	Billy Ripken	.05
154	Kurt Stillwell	.05
155	Jeff Kent	.05
156	Mickey Morandini	.05
157	Randy Milligan	.05
158	Reggie Sanders	.05
159	Luis Rivera	.05
160	Orlando Merced	.05
161	Dean Palmer	.05
162	Mike Perez	.05
163	Scott Erikson	.05
164	Kevin McReynolds	.05
165	Kevin Maas	.05
166	Ozzie Guillen	.05
167	Rob Deer	.05
168	Danny Tartabull	.05
169	Lee Stevens	.05
170	Dave Henderson	.05
171	Derek Bell	.05
172	Steve Finley	.05
173	Greg Olson	.05

174 Geronimo Pena .05
175 Paul Quantrill .05
176 Steve Buechele .05
177 Kevin Gross .05
178 Tim Wallach .05
179 Dave Valle .05
180 Dave Silvestri .05
181 Bud Black .05
182 Henry Rodriguez .05
183 Tim Teufel .05
184 Mark McLemore .05
185 Bret Saberhagen .05
186 Chris Hoiles .05
187 Ricky Jordan .05
188 Don Slaught .05
189 Mo Vaughn .05
190 Joe Oliver .05
191 Juan Gonzalez .30
192 Scott Leius .05
193 Milt Cuyler .05
194 Chris Haney .05
195 Ron Karkovice .05
196 Steve Farr .05
197 John Orton .05
198 Kelly Gruber .05
199 Ron Darling .05
200 Ruben Sierra .05
201 Chuck Finley .05
202 Mike Moore .05
203 Pat Borders .05
204 Sid Bream .05
205 Todd Zeile .05
206 Rick Wilkins .05
207 Jim Gantner .05
208 Frank Castillo .05
209 Dave Hansen .05
210 Trevor Wilson .05
211 Sandy Alomar, Jr. .05
212 Sean Berry .05
213 Tino Martinez .05
214 Chito Martinez .05
215 Dan Walters .05
216 John Franco .05
217 Glenn Davis .05
218 Mariano Duncan .05
219 Mike LaValliere .05
220 Rafael Palmeiro .50
221 Jack Clark .05
222 Hal Morris .05
223 Ed Sprague .05
224 John Valentin .05
225 Sam Militello .05
226 Bob Wickman .05
227 Damion Easley .05
228 John Jaha .05
229 Bob Ayrault .05
230 Mo Sanford .05
231 Walt Weiss .05
232 Dante Bichette .05
233 Steve Decker .05
234 Jerald Clark .05
235 Bryan Harvey .05
236 Joe Girardi .05
237 Dave Magadan .05
238 David Nied .05
239 *Eric Wedge* .05
240 Rico Brogna .05
241 J.T. Bruett .05
242 Jonathan Hurst .05
243 Bret Boone .05
244 Manny Alexander .05
245 Scooter Tucker .05
246 Troy Neel .05
247 Eddie Zosky .05
248 Melvin Nieves .05
249 Ryan Thompson .05
250 Shawn Barton .05
251 Ryan Klesko .05
252 Mike Piazza 1.00
253 Steve Hosey .05
254 Shane Reynolds .05
255 Dan Wilson .05
256 Tom Marsh .05
257 Barry Manuel .05
258 Paul Miller .05
259 Pedro Martinez .60
260 Steve Cooke .05
261 Johnny Guzman .05
262 Mike Butcher .05
263 Bien Figueroa .05
264 Rich Rowland .05
265 Shawn Jeter .05
266 Gerald Williams .05
267 Derek Parks .05
268 Henry Mercedes .05
269 *David Hulse* .05
270 *Tim Pugh* .05
271 William Suero .05
272 Ozzie Canseco .05
273 Fernando Ramsey .05
274 Bernardo Brito .05
275 Dave Mlicki .05
276 Tim Salmon .05
277 Mike Raczka .05
278 *Ken Ryan* .05
279 Rafael Bournigal .05
280 Wil Cordero .05
281 Billy Ashley .05
282 Paul Wagner .05
283 Blas Minor .05
284 Rick Trlicek .05
285 Willie Greene .05
286 Ted Wood .05
287 Phil Clark .05
288 Jesse Levis .05
289 Tony Gwynn .40
290 Nolan Ryan 1.00
291 Dennis Martinez .05
292 Eddie Murray .30
293 Robin Yount .30
294 George Brett .45
295 Dave Winfield .30
296 Bert Blyleven .05
297 Jeff Bagwell .30
298 John Smoltz .05
299 Larry Walker .05
300 Gary Sheffield .15
301 Ivan Rodriguez .30
302 Delino DeShields .05
303 Tim Salmon .05
304 Bernard Gilkey .05
305 Cal Ripken, Jr. 1.00
306 Barry Larkin .05
307 Kent Hrbek .05
308 Rickey Henderson .30
309 Darryl Strawberry .05
310 John Franco .05
311 Todd Stottlemyre .05
312 Luis Gonzalez .05
313 Tommy Greene .05
314 Randy Velarde .05
315 Steve Avery .05
316 Jose Oquendo .05
317 Rey Sanchez .05
318 Greg Vaughn .05
319 Orel Hershiser .05
320 Paul Sorrento .05
321 Royce Clayton .05
322 John Vander Wal .05
323 Henry Cotto .05
324 Pete Schourek .05
325 David Segui .05
326 Arthur Rhodes .05
327 Bruce Hurst .05
328 Wes Chamberlain .05
329 Ozzie Smith .75
330 Scott Cooper .05
331 Felix Fermin .05
332 Mike Macfarlane .05
333 Dan Gladden .05
334 Kevin Tapani .05
335 Steve Sax .05
336 Jeff Montgomery .05
337 Gary DiSarcina .05
338 Lance Blankenship .05
339 Brian Williams .05
340 Duane Ward .05
341 Chuck McElroy .05
342 Joe Magrane .05
343 Jaime Navarro .05
344 Dave Justice .05
345 Jose Offerman .05
346 Marquis Grissom .05
347 Bill Swift .05
348 Jim Thome .50
349 Archi Cianfrocco .05
350 Anthony Young .05
351 Leo Gomez .05
352 Bill Gullickson .05
353 Alan Trammell .05
354 Dan Pasqua .05
355 Jeff King .05
356 Kevin Brown .05
357 Tim Belcher .05
358 Bip Roberts .05
359 Brent Mayne .05
360 Rheal Cormier .05
361 Mark Guthrie .05
362 Craig Grebeck .05
363 Andy Stankiewicz .05
364 Juan Guzman .05
365 Bobby Witt .05
366 Mark Portugal .05
367 Brian McRae .05
368 Mark Lemke .05
369 Bill Wegman .05
370 Donovan Osborne .05
371 Derrick May .05
372 Carl Willis .05
373 Chris Nabholz .05
374 Mark Lewis .05
375 John Burkett .05
376 Luis Mercedes .05
377 Ramon Martinez .05
378 Kyle Abbott .05
379 Mark Wohlers .05
380 Bob Walk .05
381 Kenny Rogers .05
382 Tim Naehring .05
383 Alex Fernandez .05
384 Keith Miller .05
385 Mike Henneman .05
386 Rick Aguilera .05
387 George Bell .05
388 Mike Gallego .05
389 Howard Johnson .05
390 Kim Batiste .05
391 Jerry Browne .05
392 Damon Berryhill .05
393 Ricky Bones .05
394 Omar Olivares .05
395 Mike Harkey .05
396 Pedro Astacio .05
397 John Wetteland .05
398 Rod Beck .05
399 Thomas Howard .05
400 Mike Devereaux .05
401 Tim Wakefield .05
402 Curt Schilling .30
403 Zane Smith .05
404 Bob Zupcic .05
405 Tom Browning .05
406 Tony Phillips .05
407 John Doherty .05
408 Pat Mahomes .05
409 John Habyan .05
410 Steve Olin .05
411 Chad Curtis .05
412 Joe Grahe .05
413 John Patterson .05
414 Brian Hunter .05
415 Doug Henry .05
416 Lee Smith .05
417 Bob Scanlan .05
418 Kent Mercker .05
419 Mel Rojas .05
420 Mark Whiten .05
421 Carlton Fisk .60
422 Candy Maldonado .05
423 Doug Drabek .05
424 Wade Boggs .75
425 Mark Davis .05
426 Kirby Puckett .75
427 Joe Carter .05
428 Paul Molitor .60
429 Eric Davis .05
430 Darryl Kile .05
431 Jeff Parrett .05
432 Jeff Blauser .05
433 Dan Plesac .05
434 Andres Galarraga .05
435 Jim Gott .05
436 Jose Mesa .05
437 Ben Rivera .05
438 Dave Winfield .60
439 Norm Charlton .05
440 Chris Bosio .05
441 Wilson Alvarez .05
442 Dave Stewart .05
443 Doug Jones .05
444 Jeff Russell .05
445 Ron Gant .05
446 Paul O'Neill .05
447 Charlie Hayes .05
448 Joe Hesketh .05
449 Chris Hammond .05
450 Hipolito Pichardo .05
451 Scott Radinsky .05
452 Bobby Thigpen .05
453 Xavier Hernandez .05
454 Lonnie Smith .05
455 *Jamie Arnold* .05
456 B.J. Wallace .05
457 *Derek Jeter* 6.00
458 *Jason Kendall* .75
459 Rick Helling .05
460 *Derek Wallace* .05
461 *Sean Lowe* .05
462 *Shannon Stewart* .60
463 *Benji Grigsby* .05
464 *Todd Steverson* .05
465 *Dan Serafini* .05
466 Michael Tucker .05
467 Chris Roberts .05
468 *Pete Janicki* .05
469 *Jeff Schmidt* .05
470 Don Mattingly .45
471 Cal Ripken, Jr. 1.00
472 Jack Morris .05
473 Terry Pendleton .05
474 Dennis Eckersley .25
475 Carlton Fisk .30
476 Wade Boggs .35
477 Len Dykstra .05
478 Danny Tartabull .05
479 Jeff Conine .10
480 Gregg Jefferies .05
481 Paul Molitor .30
482 John Valentin .05
483 Alex Arias .10
484 Barry Bonds 1.00
485 Doug Drabek .05
486 Dave Winfield .30
487 Brett Butler .05
488 Harold Baines .05
489 David Cone .05
490 Willie McGee .05
491 Robby Thompson .05
492 Pete Incaviglia .05
493 Manuel Lee .05
494 Rafael Belliard .05
495 Scott Fletcher .05
496 Jeff Frye .05
497 Andre Dawson .25
498 Mike Scioscia .05
499 Spike Owen .05
500 Sid Fernandez .05
501 Joe Orsulak .05
502 Benito Santiago .05
503 Dale Murphy .25
504 Barry Bonds 2.00
505 Jose Guzman .05
506 Tony Pena .05
507 Greg Swindell .05
508 Mike Pagliarulo .05
509 Lou Whitaker .05
510 Greg Gagne .05
511 Butch Henry .05
512 Jeff Brantley .05
513 Jack Armstrong .05
514 Danny Jackson .05
515 Junior Felix .05
516 Milt Thompson .05
517 Greg Maddux .75
518 Eric Young .05
519 Jody Reed .05
520 Roberto Kelly .05
521 Darren Holmes .05
522 Craig Lefferts .05
523 Charlie Hough .05
524 Bo Jackson .10
525 Bill Spiers .05
526 Orestes Destrade .05
527 Greg Hibbard .05
528 Roger McDowell .05
529 Cory Snyder .05
530 Harold Reynolds .05
531 Kevin Reimer .05
532 Rick Sutcliffe .05
533 Tony Fernandez .05
534 Tom Brunansky .05
535 Jeff Reardon .05
536 Chili Davis .05
537 Bob Ojeda .05
538 Greg Colbrunn .05
539 Phil Plantier .05
540 Brian Jordan .05
541 Pete Smith .05
542 Frank Tanana .05
543 John Smiley .05
544 David Cone .05
545 Daryl Boston .05
546 Tom Henke .05
547 Bill Krueger .05
548 Freddie Benavides .05
549 Randy Myers .05
550 Reggie Jefferson .05
551 Kevin Mitchell .05
552 Dave Stieb .05
553 Bret Barberie .05
554 Tim Crews .05
555 Doug Dascenzo .05
556 Alex Cole .05
557 Jeff Innis .05
558 Carlos Garcia .05
559 Steve Howe .05
560 Kirk McCaskill .05
561 Frank Seminara .05
562 Cris Carpenter .05
563 Mike Stanley .05
564 Carlos Quintana .05
565 Mitch Williams .05
566 Juan Bell .05
567 Eric Fox .05
568 Al Leiter .05
569 Mike Stanton .05

570	Scott Kamieniecki	.05
571	Ryan Bowen	.05
572	Andy Ashby	.05
573	Bob Welch	.05
574	Scott Sanderson	.05
575	Joe Kmak	.05
576	Scott Pose	.05
577	Ricky Gutierrez	.05
578	Mike Trombley	.05
579	*Sterling Hitchcock*	.10
580	Rodney Bolton	.05
581	Tyler Green	.05
582	Tim Costo	.05
583	*Tim Laker*	.05
584	*Steve Reed*	.05
586	Robb Nen	.05
587	*Jim Tatum*	.05
588	Frank Bolick	.05
589	Kevin Young	.05
590	*Matt Whiteside*	.05
591	Cesar Hernandez	.05
592	*Mike Mohler*	.05
593	Alan Embree	.05
594	Terry Jorgensen	.05
595	*John Cummings*	.05
596	Domingo Martinez	.05
597	Benji Gil	.05
598	*Todd Pratt*	.05
599	*Rene Arocha*	.05
600	Dennis Moeller	.05
601	Jeff Conine	.05
602	Trevor Hoffman	.05
603	Daniel Smith	.05
604	Lee Tinsley	.05
605	Dan Peltier	.05
606	Billy Brewer	.05
607	*Matt Walbeck*	.05
608	Richie Lewis	.05
609	*J.T. Snow*	.40
610	*Pat Gomez*	.05
611	Phil Hiatt	.05
612	Alex Arias	.05
613	Kevin Rogers	.05
614	Al Martin	.05
615	Greg Gohr	.05
616	*Grame Lloyd*	.05
617	Kent Bottenfield	.05
618	Chuck Carr	.05
619	*Darrell Sherman*	.05
620	*Mike Lansing*	.15

Cooperstown

		NM/M
Complete Set (30):		7.50
Common Player:		.25
Dufex:		25X
Promo:		30X
1	Nolan Ryan	2.00
2	George Brett	.85
3	Robin Yount	.65
4	Carlton Fisk	.65
5	Dale Murphy	.35
6	Dennis Eckersley	.50
7	Rickey Henderson	.65
8	Ryne Sandberg	.75
9	Ozzie Smith	.75
10	Dave Winfield	.65
11	Andre Dawson	.35
12	Kirby Puckett	.75
13	Wade Boggs	.75
14	Don Mattingly	.85
15	Barry Bonds	2.00
16	Will Clark	.25
17	Cal Ripken, Jr.	2.00
18	Roger Clemens	.85
19	Dwight Gooden	.25
20	Tony Gwynn	.75
21	Joe Carter	.25
22	Ken Griffey, Jr.	1.00
23	Paul Molitor	.60
24	Frank Thomas	.60
25	Juan Gonzalez	.35
26	Barry Larkin	.25
27	Eddie Murray	.60
28	Cecil Fielder	.25
29	Roberto Alomar	.35
30	Mark McGwire	1.50

Joe DiMaggio Autographs

		NM/M
Complete Set (5):		850.00
1-5	Joe DiMaggio	175.00

Rookie Team Pinnacle

		NM/M
Complete Set (10):		20.00
Common Player:		1.50
1	Pedro Martinez, Mike Trombley	6.00
2	Kevin Rogers, Sterling Hitchcock	1.50
3	Mike Piazza, Jesse Levis	10.00
4	Ryan Klesko, J.T. Snow	1.50
5	John Patterson, Bret Boone	1.50
6	Domingo Martinez, Kevin Young	1.50
7	Wil Cordero, Manny Alexander	1.50
8	Steve Hosey, Tim Salmon	1.50
9	Ryan Thompson, Gerald Williams	1.50
10	Melvin Nieves, David Hulse	1.50

Slugfest

		NM/M
Complete Set (30):		12.50
Common Player:		.25
1	Juan Gonzalez	.50
2	Mark McGwire	2.00
3	Cecil Fielder	.25
4	Joe Carter	.25
5	Fred McGriff	.25
6	Barry Bonds	2.50
7	Gary Sheffield	.50
8	Dave Hollins	.25
9	Frank Thomas	1.00
10	Danny Tartabull	.25
11	Albert Belle	.25
12	Ruben Sierra	.25
13	Larry Walker	.25
14	Jeff Bagwell	1.00
15	Dave Justice	.25
16	Kirby Puckett	1.25
17	John Kruk	.25
18	Howard Johnson	.25
19	Darryl Strawberry	.25
20	Will Clark	.25
21	Kevin Mitchell	.25
22	Mickey Tettleton	.25
23	Don Mattingly	1.50
24	Jose Canseco	.75
25	Sam Militello	.25
26	Andre Dawson	.50
27	Ryne Sandberg	1.25
28	Ken Griffey, Jr.	1.75
29	Carlos Baerga	.25
30	Travis Fryman	.25

Team Pinnacle

		NM/M
Complete Set (11):		15.00
Common Player:		.60
1	Greg Maddux, Mike Mussina	3.50
2	Tom Glavine, John Smiley	1.00
3	Darren Daulton, Ivan Rodriguez	1.50
4	Fred McGriff, Frank Thomas	2.50
5	Delino DeShields, Carlos Baerga	.60
6	Gary Sheffield, Edgar Martinez	.75
7	Ozzie Smith, Pat Listach	3.50
8	Barry Bonds, Juan Gonzalez	4.50
9	Kirby Puckett, Andy Van Slyke	3.50
10	Larry Walker, Joe Carter	.60
11	Rick Aguilera, Rob Dibble	.60

Team 2001

		NM/M
Complete Set (30):		5.00
Common Player:		.05
1	Wil Cordero	.05
2	Cal Eldred	.05
3	Mike Mussina	.60
4	Chuck Knoblauch	.05
5	Melvin Nieves	.05
6	Tim Wakefield	.05
7	Carlos Baerga	.05
8	Bret Boone	.05
9	Jeff Bagwell	1.00
10	Travis Fryman	.05
11	Royce Clayton	.05
12	Delino DeShields	.05
13	Juan Gonzalez	.50
14	Pedro Martinez	1.00
15	Bernie Williams	.05
16	Billy Ashley	.05
17	Marquis Grissom	.05
18	Kenny Lofton	.05
19	Ray Lankford	.05
20	Tim Salmon	.05
21	Steve Hosey	.05
22	Charles Nagy	.05
23	Dave Fleming	.05
24	Reggie Sanders	.05
25	Sam Militello	.05
26	Eric Karros	.05
27	Ryan Klesko	.05
28	Dean Palmer	.05
29	Ivan Rodriguez	.75
30	Sterling Hitchcock	.05

Tribute

		NM/M
Complete Set (10):		10.00
George Brett Card (1-5):		1.00
Nolan Ryan Card (6-10):		1.50
1	George Brett Kansas City Royalty	1.00
2	George Brett The Chase for .400	1.00
3	Pine Tar Pandemonium - "The Bat"	1.00
4	George Brett MVP and a World Series, Too	1.00
5	George Brett 3,000 or Bust	1.00
6	Nolan Ryan The Rookie	1.50
7	Nolan Ryan Angel of No Mercy	1.50
8	Nolan Ryan Astronomical Success	1.50
9	Nolan Ryan 5,000 Ks	1.50
10	Nolan Ryan No-Hitter No. 7	1.50

1994 PINNACLE

		NM/M
Complete Set (540):		15.00
Common Player:		.05
Series 1 or 2 Pack (14):		.75
Series 1 or 2 Box (24):		12.50
1	Frank Thomas	.65
2	Carlos Baerga	.05
3	Sammy Sosa	.75
4	Tony Gwynn	.75
5	John Olerud	.05
6	Ryne Sandberg	.75
7	Moises Alou	.05
8	Steve Avery	.05
9	Tim Salmon	.05
10	Cecil Fielder	.05
11	Greg Maddux	.75
12	Barry Larkin	.05
13	Mike Devereaux	.05
14	Charlie Hayes	.05
15	Albert Belle	.05
16	Andy Van Slyke	.05
17	Mo Vaughn	.05
18	Brian McRae	.05
19	Cal Eldred	.05
20	Craig Biggio	.05
21	Kirby Puckett	.75
22	Derek Bell	.05
23	Don Mattingly	.85
24	John Burkett	.05
25	Roger Clemens	.85
26	Barry Bonds	2.00
27	Paul Molitor	.65
28	Mike Piazza	1.00

29 Robin Ventura .05
30 Jeff Conine .05
31 Wade Boggs .75
32 Dennis Eckersley .50
33 Bobby Bonilla .05
34 Len Dykstra .05
35 Manny Alexander .05
36 Ray Lankford .05
37 Greg Vaughn .05
38 Chuck Finley .05
39 Todd Benzinger .05
40 Dave Justice .05
41 Rob Dibble .05
42 Tom Henke .05
43 David Nied .05
44 Sandy Alomar Jr. .05
45 Pete Harnisch .05
46 Jeff Russell .05
47 Terry Mulholland .05
48 Kevin Appier .05
49 Randy Tomlin .05
50 Cal Ripken, Jr. 2.00
51 Andy Benes .05
52 Jimmy Key .05
53 Kirt Manwaring .05
54 Kevin Tapani .05
55 Jose Guzman .05
56 Todd Stottlemyre .05
57 Jack McDowell .05
58 Orel Hershiser .05
59 Chris Hammond .05
60 Chris Nabholz .05
61 Ruben Sierra .05
62 Dwight Gooden .05
63 John Kruk .05
64 Omar Vizquel .05
65 Tim Naehring .05
66 Dwight Smith .05
67 Mickey Tettleton .05
68 J.T. Snow .05
69 Greg McMichael .05
70 Kevin Mitchell .05
71 Kevin Brown .05
72 Scott Cooper .05
73 Jim Thome .60
74 Joe Girardi .05
75 Eric Anthony .05
76 Orlando Merced .05
77 Felix Jose .05
78 Tommy Greene .05
79 Bernard Gilkey .05
80 Phil Plantier .05
81 Danny Tartabull .05
82 Trevor Wilson .05
83 Chuck Knoblauch .05
84 Rick Wilkins .05
85 Devon White .05
86 Lance Johnson .05
87 Eric Karros .05
88 Gary Sheffield .35
89 Wil Cordero .05
90 Ron Darling .05
91 Darren Daulton .05
92 Joe Orsulak .05
93 Steve Cooke .05
94 Darryl Hamilton .05
95 Aaron Sele .05
96 John Doherty .05
97 Gary DiSarcina .05
98 Jeff Blauser .05
99 John Smiley .05
100 Ken Griffey, Jr. 1.00
101 Dean Palmer .05
102 Felix Fermin .05
103 Jerald Clark .05
104 Doug Drabek .05
105 Curt Schilling .30
106 Jeff Montgomery .05
107 Rene Arocha .05
108 Carlos Garcia .05
109 Wally Whitehurst .05
110 Jim Abbott .05
111 Royce Clayton .05
112 Chris Hoiles .05
113 Mike Morgan .05
114 Joe Magrane .05
115 Tom Candiotti .05
116 Ron Karkovice .05
117 Ryan Bowen .05
118 Rod Beck .05
119 John Wetteland .05
120 Terry Steinbach .05
121 Dave Hollins .05
122 Jeff Kent .05
123 Ricky Bones .05
124 Brian Jordan .05
125 Chad Kreuter .05
126 John Valentin .05
127 Billy Hathaway .05
128 Wilson Alvarez .05
129 Tino Martinez .05
130 Rodney Bolton .05
131 David Segui .05
132 Wayne Kirby .05
133 Eric Young .05
134 Scott Servais .05
135 Scott Radinsky .05
136 Bret Barberie .05
137 John Roper .05
138 Ricky Gutierrez .05
139 Bernie Williams .05
140 Bud Black .05
141 Jose Vizcaino .05
142 Gerald Williams .05
143 Duane Ward .05
144 Danny Jackson .05
145 Allen Watson .05
146 Scott Fletcher .05
147 Delino DeShields .05
148 Shane Mack .05
149 Jim Eisenreich .05
150 Troy Neel .05
151 Jay Bell .05
152 B.J. Surhoff .05
153 Mark Whiten .05
154 Mike Henneman .05
155 Todd Hundley .05
156 Greg Myers .05
157 Ryan Klesko .05
158 Dave Fleming .05
159 Mickey Morandini .05
160 Blas Minor .05
161 Reggie Jefferson .05
162 David Hulse .05
163 Greg Swindell .05
164 Roberto Hernandez .05
165 Brady Anderson .05
166 Jack Armstrong .05
167 Phil Clark .05
168 Melido Perez .05
169 Darren Lewis .05
170 Sam Horn .05
171 Mike Harkey .05
172 Juan Guzman .05
173 Bob Natal .05
174 Deion Sanders .05
175 Carlos Quintana .05
176 Mel Rojas .05
177 Willie Banks .05
178 Ben Rivera .05
179 Kenny Lofton .05
180 Leo Gomez .05
181 Roberto Mejia .05
182 Mike Perez .05
183 Travis Fryman .05
184 Ben McDonald .05
185 Steve Frey .05
186 Kevin Young .05
187 Dave Magadan .05
188 Bobby Munoz .05
189 Pat Rapp .05
190 Jose Offerman .05
191 Vinny Castilla .05
192 Ivan Calderon .05
193 Ken Caminiti .05
194 Benji Gil .05
195 Chuck Carr .05
196 Derrick May .05
197 Pat Kelly .05
198 Jeff Brantley .05
199 Jose Lind .05
200 Steve Buechele .05
201 Wes Chamberlain .05
202 Eduardo Perez .05
203 Bret Saberhagen .05
204 Gregg Jefferies .05
205 Darrin Fletcher .05
206 Kent Hrbek .05
207 Kim Batiste .05
208 Jeff King .05
209 Donovan Osborne .05
210 Dave Nilsson .05
211 Al Martin .05
212 Mike Moore .05
213 Sterling Hitchcock .05
214 Geronimo Pena .05
215 Kevin Higgins .05
216 Norm Charlton .05
217 Don Slaught .05
218 Mitch Williams .05
219 Derek Lilliquist .05
220 Armando Reynoso .05
221 Kenny Rogers .05
222 Doug Jones .05
223 Luis Aquino .05
224 Mike Oquist .05
225 Darryl Scott .05
226 Kurt Abbott .05
227 Andy Tomberlin .05
228 Norberto Martin .05
229 Pedro Castellano .05
230 *Curtis Pride* .05
231 Jeff McNeely .05
232 Scott Lydy .05
233 Darren Oliver .05
234 Danny Bautista .05
235 Butch Huskey .05
236 Chipper Jones .75
237 Eddie Zambrano .05
238 Jean Domingo .05
239 Javier Lopez .05
240 Nigel Wilson .05
241 *Drew Denson* .05
242 Raul Mondesi .05
243 Luis Ortiz .05
244 Manny Ramirez .65
245 Greg Blosser .05
246 Rondell White .05
247 Steve Karsay .05
248 Scott Stahoviak .05
249 Jose Valentin .05
250 Marc Newfield .05
251 Keith Kessinger .05
252 Carl Everett .05
253 John O'Donoghue .05
254 Turk Wendell .05
255 Scott Ruffcorn .05
256 Tony Tarasco .05
257 Andy Cook .05
258 Matt Mieske .05
259 Luis Lopez .05
260 Ramon Caraballo .05
261 Salomon Torres .05
262 *Brooks Kieschnick* .05
263 *Daron Kirkreit* .05
264 *Bill Wagner* .10
265 *Matt Drews* .05
266 Scott Christman .05
267 *Torii Hunter* 1.00
268 *Jamey Wright* .05
269 Jeff Granger .05
270 *Trot Nixon* 1.00
271 Randy Myers .05
272 Trevor Hoffman .05
273 Bob Wickman .05
274 Willie McGee .05
275 Hipolito Pichardo .05
276 Bobby Witt .05
277 Gregg Olson .05
278 Randy Johnson .65
279 Robb Nen .05
280 Paul O'Neill .05
281 Lou Whitaker .05
282 Chad Curtis .05
283 Doug Henry .05
284 Tom Glavine .30
285 Mike Greenwell .05
286 Roberto Kelly .05
287 Roberto Alomar .15
288 Charlie Hough .05
289 Alex Fernandez .05
290 Jeff Bagwell .65
291 Wally Joyner .05
292 Andujar Cedeno .05
293 Rick Aguilera .05
294 Darryl Strawberry .05
295 Mike Mussina .35
296 Jeff Gardner .05
297 Chris Gwynn .05
298 Matt Williams .05
299 Brent Gates .05
300 Mark McGwire 1.50
301 Jim Deshaies .05
302 Edgar Martinez .05
303 Danny Darwin .05
304 Pat Meares .05
305 Benito Santiago .05
306 Jose Canseco .40
307 Jim Gott .05
308 Paul Sorrento .05
309 Scott Kamieniecki .05
310 Larry Walker .05
311 Mark Langston .05
312 John Jaha .05
313 Stan Javier .05
314 Hal Morris .05
315 Robby Thompson .05
316 Pat Hentgen .05
317 Tom Gordon .05
318 Joey Cora .05
319 Luis Alicea .05
320 Andre Dawson .25
321 Darryl Kile .05
322 Jose Rijo .05
323 Luis Gonzalez .05
324 Billy Ashley .05
325 David Cone .05
326 Bill Swift .05
327 Phil Hiatt .05
328 Craig Paquette .05
329 Bob Welch .05
330 Tony Phillips .05
331 Archi Cianfrocco .05
332 Dave Winfield .65
333 David McCarty .05
334 Al Leiter .05
335 Tom Browning .05
336 Mark Grace .05
337 Jose Mesa .05
338 Mike Stanley .05
339 Roger McDowell .05
340 Damion Easley .05
341 Angel Miranda .05
342 John Smoltz .05
343 Jay Buhner .05
344 Bryan Harvey .05
345 Joe Carter .05
346 Dante Bichette .05
347 Jason Bere .05
348 Frank Viola .05
349 Ivan Rodriguez .60
350 Juan Gonzalez .35
351 Steve Finley .05
352 Mike Felder .05
353 Ramon Martinez .05
354 Greg Gagne .05
355 Ken Hill .05
356 Pedro Munoz .05
357 Todd Van Poppel .05
358 Marquis Grissom .05
359 Milt Cuyler .05
360 Reggie Sanders .05
361 Scott Erickson .05
362 Billy Hatcher .05
363 Gene Harris .05
364 Rene Gonzales .05
365 Kevin Rogers .05
366 Eric Plunk .05
367 Todd Zeile .05
368 John Franco .05
369 Brett Butler .05
370 Bill Spiers .05
371 Terry Pendleton .05
372 Chris Bosio .05
373 Orestes Destrade .05
374 Dave Stewart .05
375 Darren Holmes .05
376 Doug Strange .05
377 Brian Turang .05
378 Carl Willis .05
379 Mark McLemore .05
380 Bobby Jones .05
381 Scott Sanders .05
382 Kirk Rueter .05
383 Randy Velarde .05
384 Fred McGriff .05
385 Charles Nagy .05
386 Rich Amaral .05
387 Geronimo Berroa .05
388 Eric Davis .05
389 Ozzie Smith .75
390 Alex Arias .05
391 Brad Ausmus .05
392 Cliff Floyd .05
393 Roger Salkeld .05
394 Jim Edmonds .05
395 Jeromy Burnitz .05
396 Dave Staton .05
397 Rob Butler .05
398 Marcos Armas .05
399 Darrell Whitmore .05
400 Ryan Thompson .05
401 *Ross Powell* .05
402 Joe Oliver .05
403 Paul Carey .05
404 Bob Hamelin .05
405 Chris Turner .05
406 Nate Minchey .05
407 *Lonnie Maclin* .05
408 Harold Baines .05
409 Brian Williams .05
410 Johnny Ruffin .05
411 *Julian Tavarez* .05
412 Mark Hutton .05
413 Carlos Delgado .50
414 Chris Gomez .05
415 Mike Hampton .05
416 Alex Diaz .05
417 Jeffrey Hammonds .05
418 Jayhawk Owens .05
419 J.R. Phillips .05
420 *Cory Bailey* .05
421 Denny Hocking .05
422 Jon Shave .05
423 Damon Buford .05
424 Troy O'Leary .05

425 Tripp Cromer .05
426 Albie Lopez .05
427 Tony Fernandez .05
428 Ozzie Guillen .05
429 Alan Trammell .05
430 *John Wasdin* .05
431 Marc Valdes .05
432 *Brian Anderson* .20
433 *Matt Brunson* .05
434 *Wayne Gomes* .05
435 *Jay Powell* .05
436 *Kirk Presley* .05
437 *Jon Ratliff* .05
438 *Derrek Lee* 2.00
439 Tom Pagnozzi .05
440 Kent Mercker .05
441 *Phil Leftwich* .05
442 Jamie Moyer .05
443 John Flaherty .05
444 Mark Wohlers .05
445 Jose Bautista .05
446 Andres Galarraga .05
447 Mark Lemke .05
448 Tim Wakefield .05
449 Pat Listach .05
450 Rickey Henderson .65
451 Mike Gallego .05
452 Bob Tewksbury .05
453 Kirk Gibson .05
454 Pedro Astacio .05
455 Mike Lansing .05
456 Sean Berry .05
457 Bob Walk .05
458 Chili Davis .05
459 Ed Sprague .05
460 Kevin Stocker .05
461 Mike Stanton .05
462 Tim Raines .05
463 Mike Bordick .05
464 David Wells .05
465 Tim Laker .05
466 Cory Snyder .05
467 Alex Cole .05
468 Pete Incaviglia .05
469 Roger Pavlik .05
470 Greg W. Harris .05
471 Xavier Hernandez .05
472 Erik Hanson .05
473 Jesse Orosco .05
474 Greg Colbrunn .05
475 Harold Reynolds .05
476 Greg Harris .05
477 Pat Borders .05
478 Melvin Nieves .05
479 Mariano Duncan .05
480 Greg Hibbard .05
481 Tim Pugh .05
482 Bobby Ayala .05
483 Sid Fernandez .05
484 Tim Wallach .05
485 Randy Milligan .05
486 Walt Weiss .05
487 Matt Walbeck .05
488 Mike Macfarlane .05
489 Jerry Browne .05
490 Chris Sabo .05
491 Tim Belcher .05
492 Spike Owen .05
493 Rafael Palmeiro .60
494 Brian Harper .05
495 Eddie Murray .65
496 Ellis Burks .05
497 Karl Rhodes .05
498 Otis Nixon .05
499 Lee Smith .05
500 Bip Roberts .05
501 Pedro Martinez .65
502 Brian L. Hunter .05
503 Tyler Green .05
504 Bruce Hurst .05
505 Alex Gonzalez .05
506 Mark Portugal .05
507 Bob Ojeda .05
508 Dave Henderson .05
509 Bo Jackson .10
510 Bret Boone .05
511 Mark Eichhorn .05
512 Luis Polonia .05
513 Will Clark .05
514 Dave Valle .05
515 Dan Wilson .05
516 Dennis Martinez .05
517 Jim Leyritz .05
518 Howard Johnson .05
519 Jody Reed .05
520 Julio Franco .05
521 Jeff Reardon .05
522 Willie Greene .05
523 Shawon Dunston .05
524 Keith Mitchell .05
525 Rick Helling .05
526 Mark Kiefer .05
527 *Chan Ho Park* .75
528 Tony Longmire .05
529 Rich Becker .05
530 Tim Hyers .05
531 Darrin Jackson .05
532 Jack Morris .05
533 Rick White .05
534 Mike Kelly .05
535 James Mouton .05
536 Steve Trachsel .05
537 Tony Eusebio .05
538 Kelly Stinnett .05
539 Paul Spoljaric .05
540 Darren Dreifort .05

Artist's Proof

NM/M
Complete Set (540): 250.00
Common Player: 1.50
Stars/Rookies: 20X
(See 1994 Pinnacle for checklist and base card values.)

Museum Collection

NM/M
Complete Set (540): 225.00
Common Player: 1.00
Stars/Rookies: 6X
(See 1994 Pinnacle for checklist and base card values.)

1994 PINNACLE NEW GENERATION

NM/M
Complete Set (25): 5.00
Common Player: .25
1 Tim Salmon .25
2 Mike Piazza 2.00
3 Jason Bere .25
4 Jeffrey Hammonds .25
5 Aaron Sele .25
6 Salomon Torres .25
7 Wil Cordero .25
8 Allen Watson .25
9 J.T. Snow .25
10 Cliff Floyd .25
10a Cliff Floyd (overprinted "SAMPLE" card) .50
11 Jeff McNeely .25
12 Butch Huskey .25
13 J.R. Phillips .25
14 Bobby Jones .25
15 Javier Lopez .25
16 Scott Ruffcorn .25
17 Manny Ramirez 1.25
18 Carlos Delgado 1.00
19 Rondell White .25
20 Chipper Jones 1.50
21 Billy Ashley .25
22 Nigel Wilson .25
23 Jeromy Burnitz .25
24 Danny Bautista .25
25 Darrell Whitmore .25

1994 PINNACLE POWER SURGE

NM/M
Complete Set (25): 4.00
Common Player: .25
1 Dave Justice .25
2 Chris Hoiles .25
3 Mo Vaughn .25
4 Tim Salmon .25
5 J.T. Snow .25
6 Frank Thomas .65
7 Sammy Sosa .75

8 Rick Wilkins .25
9 Robin Ventura .25
10 Reggie Sanders .25
11 Albert Belle .25
12 Carlos Baerga .25
12a Carlos Baerga (overprinted "SAMPLE" card) .50
13 Manny Ramirez .65
14 Travis Fryman .25
15 Gary Sheffield .35
16 Jeff Bagwell .65
17 Mike Piazza 1.00
18 Eric Karros .25
19 Cliff Floyd .25
20 Mark Whiten .25
21 Phil Plantier .25
22 Derek Bell .25
23 Ken Griffey Jr. 1.00
24 Juan Gonzalez .35
25 Dean Palmer .25

Rookie Team Pinnacle

NM/M
Complete Set (9): 12.00
Common Player: .75
1 Carlos Delgado, Javier Lopez 2.50
2 Bob Hamelin, J.R. Phillips .75
3 Jon Shave, Keith Kessinger .75
4 Butch Huskey, Luis Ortiz .75
5 Chipper Jones, Kurt Abbott 5.00
6 Rondell White, Manny Ramirez 3.00
7 Cliff Floyd, Jeffrey Hammonds .75
8 Marc Newfield, Nigel Wilson .75
9 Salomon Torres, Mark Hutton .75

Run Creators

NM/M
Complete Set (44): 17.50
Common Player: .25
1 John Olerud .25
2 Frank Thomas 1.00
3 Ken Griffey, Jr. 3.00
4 Paul Molitor 1.00
5 Rafael Palmeiro .75
6 Roberto Alomar .35
7 Juan Gonzalez .50
8 Albert Belle .25
9 Travis Fryman .25
10 Rickey Henderson 1.00
11 Tony Phillips .25
12 Mo Vaughn .25
13 Tim Salmon .25
14 Kenny Lofton .25
15 Carlos Baerga .25
16 Greg Vaughn .25
17 Jay Buhner .25
18 Chris Hoiles .25
19 Mickey Tettleton .25
20 Kirby Puckett 1.50
21 Danny Tartabull .25
22 Devon White .25
23 Barry Bonds 4.00
24 Lenny Dykstra .25
25 John Kruk .25
26 Fred McGriff .25
27 Gregg Jefferies .25
28 Mike Piazza 3.00
29 Jeff Blauser .25
30 Andres Galarraga .25
31 Darren Daulton .25
32 Dave Justice .25
33 Craig Biggio .25
34 Mark Grace .25
35 Tony Gwynn 1.50
36 Jeff Bagwell 1.00
37 Jay Bell .25
38 Marquis Grissom .25
39 Matt Williams .25
40 Charlie Hayes .25
41 Dante Bichette .25
42 Bernard Gilkey .25
43 Brett Butler .25
44 Rick Wilkins .25

Team Pinnacle

NM/M
Complete Set (9): 20.00
Common Player: .75
1 Jeff Bagwell, Frank Thomas 2.00
2 Carlos Baerga, Robby Thompson .75
3 Matt Williams, Dean Palmer .75
4 Cal Ripken, Jr., Jay Bell 6.00
5 Ivan Rodriguez, Mike Piazza 4.00
6 Len Dykstra, Ken Griffey, Jr. 4.00
7 Juan Gonzalez, Barry Bonds 6.00
8 Tim Salmon, Dave Justice .75
9 Greg Maddux, Jack McDowell 3.00

1994 PINNACLE THE NATURALS

NM/M
Complete Set (25): 6.00
Common Player: .15
1 Frank Thomas .50
2 Barry Bonds 1.50
3 Ken Griffey, Jr. 1.00
4 Juan Gonzalez .25
5 Dave Justice .15
6 Albert Belle .15
7 Kenny Lofton .15
8 Roberto Alomar .35
9 Tim Salmon .15
10 Randy Johnson .50
11 Kirby Puckett .65
12 Tony Gwynn .65
13 Fred McGriff .15
14 Ryne Sandberg .65
15 Greg Maddux .65
16 Matt Williams .15
17 Lenny Dykstra .15
18 Gary Sheffield .35
18a Gary Sheffield (overprinted "SAMPLE") .50

19	Mike Piazza	1.00
20	Dean Palmer	.15
21	Travis Fryman	.15
22	Carlos Baerga	.15
23	Cal Ripken, Jr.	1.50
24	John Olerud	.15
25	Roger Clemens	.75

Tribute

		NM/M
Complete Set (18):		15.00
Common Player:		.25
1	Paul Molitor	1.00
2	Jim Abbott	.25
3	Dave Winfield	1.00
4	Bo Jackson	.35
5	Dave Justice	.25
6	Len Dykstra	.25
7	Mike Piazza	2.50
8	Barry Bonds	4.50
9	Randy Johnson	1.00
10	Ozzie Smith	1.50
11	Mark Whiten	.25
12	Greg Maddux	1.50
13	Cal Ripken, Jr.	4.50
14	Frank Thomas	1.00
15	Juan Gonzalez	.45
16	Roberto Alomar	.25
17	Ken Griffey, Jr.	3.00
18	Lee Smith	.25

1995 PINNACLE

		NM/M
Complete Set (450):		15.00
Common Player:		.10
Hobby Pack (12):		1.00
Hobby Wax Box (24):		15.00
Retail Pack (12):		1.00
Retail Wax Box (36):		20.00
1	Jeff Bagwell	.75
2	Roger Clemens	1.25
3	Mark Whiten	.10
4	Shawon Dunston	.10
5	Bobby Bonilla	.10
6	Kevin Tapani	.10
7	Eric Karros	.10
8	Cliff Floyd	.10
9	Pat Kelly	.10
10	Jeffrey Hammonds	.10
11	Jeff Conine	.10
12	Fred McGriff	.10
13	Chris Bosio	.10
14	Mike Mussina	.40
15	Danny Bautista	.10
16	Mickey Morandini	.10
17	Chuck Finley	.10
18	Jim Thome	.65
19	Luis Ortiz	.10
20	Walt Weiss	.10
21	Don Mattingly	1.25
22	Bob Hamelin	.10
23	Melido Perez	.10
24	Kevin Mitchell	.10
25	John Smoltz	.10
26	Hector Carrasco	.10
27	Pat Hentgen	.10
28	Derrick May	.10
29	Mike Kingery	.10
30	Chuck Carr	.10
31	Billy Ashley	.10
32	Todd Hundley	.10
33	Luis Gonzalez	.10
34	Marquis Grissom	.10
35	Jeff King	.10
36	Eddie Williams	.10
37	Tom Pagnozzi	.10
38	Chris Hoiles	.10
39	Sandy Alomar	.10
40	Mike Greenwell	.10
41	Lance Johnson	.10
42	Junior Felix	.10
43	Felix Jose	.10
44	Scott Leius	.10
45	Ruben Sierra	.10
46	Kevin Seitzer	.10
47	Wade Boggs	1.00
48	Reggie Jefferson	.10
49	Jose Canseco	.40
50	Dave Justice	.10
51	John Smiley	.10
52	Joe Carter	.10
53	Rick Wilkins	.10
54	Ellis Burks	.10
55	Dave Weathers	.10
56	Pedro Astacio	.10
57	Ryan Thompson	.10
58	James Mouton	.10
59	Mel Rojas	.10
60	Orlando Merced	.10
61	Matt Williams	.10
62	Bernard Gilkey	.10
63	J.R. Phillips	.10
64	Lee Smith	.10
65	Jim Edmonds	.10
66	Darrin Jackson	.10
67	Scott Cooper	.10
68	Ron Karkovice	.10
69	Chris Gomez	.10
70	Kevin Appier	.10
71	Bobby Jones	.10
72	Doug Drabek	.10
73	Matt Mieske	.10
74	Sterling Hitchcock	.10
75	John Valentin	.10
76	Reggie Sanders	.10
77	Wally Joyner	.10
78	Turk Wendell	.10
79	Wendell Hayes	.10
80	Bret Barberie	.10
81	Troy Neel	.10
82	Ken Caminiti	.10
83	Milt Thompson	.10
84	Paul Sorrento	.10
85	Trevor Hoffman	.10
86	Jay Bell	.10
87	Mark Portugal	.10
88	Sid Fernandez	.10
89	Charles Nagy	.10
90	Jeff Montgomery	.10
91	Chuck Knoblauch	.10
92	Jeff Frye	.10
93	Tony Gwynn	1.00
94	John Olerud	.10
95	David Nied	.10
96	Chris Hammond	.10
97	Edgar Martinez	.10
98	Kevin Stocker	.10
99	Jeff Fassero	.10
100	Curt Schilling	.30
101	Dave Clark	.10
102	Delino DeShields	.10
103	Leo Gomez	.10
104	Dave Hollins	.10
105	Tim Naehring	.10
106	Otis Nixon	.10
107	Ozzie Guillen	.10
108	Jose Lind	.10
109	Stan Javier	.10
110	Greg Vaughn	.10
111	Chipper Jones	1.00
112	Ed Sprague	.10
113	Mike Macfarlane	.10
114	Steve Finley	.10
115	Ken Hill	.10
116	Carlos Garcia	.10
117	Lou Whitaker	.10
118	Todd Zeile	.10
119	Gary Sheffield	.40
120	Ben McDonald	.10
121	Pete Harnisch	.10
122	Ivan Rodriguez	.65
123	Wilson Alvarez	.10
124	Travis Fryman	.10
125	Pedro Munoz	.10
126	Mark Lemke	.10
127	Jose Valentin	.10
128	Ken Griffey Jr.	1.50
129	Omar Vizquel	.10
130	Milt Cuyler	.10
131	Steve Traschel	.10
132	Alex Rodriguez	2.00
133	Garret Anderson	.10
134	Armando Benitez	.10
135	Shawn Green	.35
136	Jorge Fabregas	.10
137	Orlando Miller	.10
138	Rikkert Faneyte	.10
139	Ismael Valdes	.10
140	Jose Oliva	.10
141	Aaron Small	.10
142	Tim Davis	.10
143	Ricky Bottalacio	.10
144	Mike Matheny	.10
145	Roberto Petagine	.10
146	Fausto Cruz	.10
147	Bryce Florie	.10
148	Jose Lima	.10
149	John Hudek	.10
150	Duane Singleton	.10
151	John Mabry	.10
152	Robert Eenhoorn	.10
153	Jon Lieber	.10
154	Garey Ingram	.10
155	Paul Shuey	.10
156	Mike Lieberthal	.10
157	Steve Dunn	.10
158	Charles Johnson	.10
159	Ernie Young	.10
160	Jose Martinez	.10
161	Kurt Miller	.10
162	Joey Eischen	.10
163	Dave Stevens	.10
164	Brian Hunter	.10
165	Jeff Cirillo	.10
166	Mark Smith	.10
167	*McKay Christensen*	.10
168	C.J. Nitkowski	.10
169	*Antone Williamson*	.10
170	Paul Konerko	.15
171	*Scott Elarton*	.15
172	Jacob Shumate	.10
173	Terrence Long	.10
174	*Mark Johnson*	.10
175	Ben Grieve	.10
176	*Jayson Peterson*	.10
177	Checklist	.10
178	Checklist	.10
179	Checklist	.10
180	Checklist	.10
181	Brian Anderson	.10
182	Steve Buechele	.10
183	Mark Clark	.10
184	Cecil Fielder	.10
185	Steve Avery	.10
186	Devon White	.10
187	Craig Shipley	.10
188	Brady Anderson	.10
189	Kenny Lofton	.10
190	Alex Cole	.10
191	Brent Gates	.10
192	Dean Palmer	.10
193	Alex Gonzalez	.10
194	Steve Cooke	.10
195	Ray Lankford	.10
196	Mark McGwire	2.00
197	Marc Newfield	.10
198	Pat Rapp	.10
199	Darren Lewis	.10
200	Carlos Baerga	.10
201	Rickey Henderson	.75
202	Kurt Abbott	.10
203	Kirt Manwaring	.10
204	Cal Ripken Jr.	2.50
205	Darren Daulton	.10
206	Greg Colbrunn	.10
207	Darryl Hamilton	.10
208	Bo Jackson	.15
209	Tony Phillips	.10
210	Geronimo Berroa	.10
211	Rich Becker	.10
212	Tony Tarasco	.10
213	Karl Rhodes	.10
214	Phil Plantier	.10
215	J.T. Snow	.10
216	Mo Vaughn	.10
217	Greg Gagne	.10
218	Rickey Bones	.10
219	Mike Bordick	.10
220	Chad Curtis	.10
221	Royce Clayton	.10
222	Roberto Alomar	.15
223	Jose Rijo	.10
224	Ryan Klesko	.10
225	Mark Langston	.10
226	Frank Thomas	.75
227	Juan Gonzalez	.40
228	Ron Gant	.10
229	Javier Lopez	.10
230	Sammy Sosa	1.00
231	Kevin Brown	.10
232	Gary DiSarcina	.10
233	Albert Belle	.10
234	Jay Buhner	.10
235	Pedro Martinez	.75
236	Bob Tewksbury	.10
237	Mike Piazza	1.50
238	Darryl Kile	.10
239	Bryan Harvey	.10
240	Andres Galarraga	.10
241	Jeff Blauser	.10
242	Jeff Kent	.10
243	Bobby Munoz	.10
244	Greg Maddux	1.00
245	Paul O'Neill	.10
246	Lenny Dykstra	.10
247	Todd Van Poppel	.10
248	Bernie Williams	.05
249	Glenallen Hill	.10
250	Duane Ward	.10
251	Dennis Eckersley	.60
252	Pat Mahomes	.10
253	Rusty Greer (photo actually Jeff Frye)	.10
254	Roberto Kelly	.10
255	Randy Myers	.10
256	Scott Ruffcorn	.10
257	Robin Ventura	.10
258	Eduardo Perez	.10
259	Aaron Sele	.10
260	Paul Molitor	.75
261	Juan Guzman	.10
262	Darren Oliver	.10
263	Mike Stanley	.10
264	Tom Glavine	.30
265	Rico Brogna	.10
266	Craig Biggio	.10
267	Darrell Whitmore	.10
268	Jimmy Key	.10
269	Will Clark	.10
270	David Cone	.10
271	Brian Jordan	.10
272	Barry Bonds	2.50
273	Danny Tartabull	.10
274	Ramon Martinez	.10
275	Al Martin	.10
276	Fred McGriff (Swing Men)	.10
277	Carlos Delgado (Swing Men)	.25
278	Juan Gonzalez (Swing Men)	.20
279	Shawn Green (Swing Men)	.20
280	Carlos Baerga (Swing Men)	.10
281	Cliff Floyd (Swing Men)	.10
282	Ozzie Smith (Swing Men)	.50
283	Alex Rodriguez (Swing Men)	1.00
284	Kenny Lofton (Swing Men)	.10
285	Dave Justice (Swing Men)	.10
286	Tim Salmon (Swing Men)	.10
287	Manny Ramirez (Swing Men)	.40
288	Will Clark (Swing Men)	.10
289	Garret Anderson (Swing Men)	.10
290	Billy Ashley (Swing Men)	.10
291	Tony Gwynn (Swing Men)	.50
292	Raul Mondesi (Swing Men)	.10
293	Rafael Palmeiro (Swing Men)	.30
294	Matt Williams (Swing Men)	.10
295	Don Mattingly (Swing Men)	.60
296	Kirby Puckett (Swing Men)	.50
297	Paul Molitor (Swing Men)	.40
298	Albert Belle (Swing Men)	.10

No.	Player	Price
299	Barry Bonds (Swing Men)	1.25
300	Mike Piazza (Swing Men)	.85
301	Jeff Bagwell (Swing Men)	.40
302	Frank Thomas (Swing Men)	.40
303	Chipper Jones (Swing Men)	.50
304	Ken Griffey Jr. (Swing Men)	.75
305	Cal Ripken Jr. (Swing Men)	1.25
306	Eric Anthony	.10
307	Todd Benzinger	.10
308	Jacob Brumfield	.10
309	Wes Chamberlain	.10
310	Tino Martinez	.10
311	Roberto Mejia	.10
312	Jose Offerman	.10
313	David Segui	.10
314	Eric Young	.10
315	Rey Sanchez	.10
316	Raul Mondesi	.10
317	Bret Boone	.10
318	Andre Dawson	.30
319	Brian McRae	.10
320	Dave Nilsson	.10
321	Moises Alou	.10
322	Don Slaught	.10
323	Dave McCarty	.10
324	Mike Huff	.10
325	Rick Aguilera	.10
326	Rod Beck	.10
327	Kenny Rogers	.10
328	Andy Benes	.10
329	Allen Watson	.10
330	Randy Johnson	.75
331	Willie Greene	.10
332	Hal Morris	.10
333	Ozzie Smith	1.00
334	Jason Bere	.10
335	Scott Erickson	.10
336	Dante Bichette	.10
337	Willie Banks	.10
338	Eric Davis	.10
339	Rondell White	.10
340	Kirby Puckett	1.00
341	Deion Sanders	.10
342	Eddie Murray	.75
343	Mike Harkey	.10
344	Joey Hamilton	.10
345	Roger Salkeld	.10
346	Wil Cordero	.10
347	John Wetteland	.10
348	Geronimo Pena	.10
349	Kirk Gibson	.10
350	Manny Ramirez	.75
351	William Van Landingham	.10
352	B.J. Surhoff	.10
353	Ken Ryan	.10
354	Terry Steinbach	.10
355	Bret Saberhagen	.10
356	John Jaha	.10
357	Joe Girardi	.10
358	Steve Karsay	.10
359	Alex Fernandez	.10
360	Salomon Torres	.10
361	John Burkett	.10
362	Derek Bell	.10
363	Tom Henke	.10
364	Gregg Jefferies	.10
365	Jack McDowell	.10
366	Andujar Cedeno	.10
367	Dave Winfield	.75
368	Carl Everett	.10
369	Danny Jackson	.10
370	Jeromy Burnitz	.10
371	Mark Grace	.10
372	Larry Walker	.10
373	Bill Swift	.10
374	Dennis Martinez	.10
375	Mickey Tettleton	.10
376	Mel Nieves	.10
377	Cal Eldred	.10
378	Orel Hershiser	.10
379	David Wells	.10
380	Gary Gaetti	.10
381	Tim Raines	.10
382	Barry Larkin	.10
383	Jason Jacome	.10
384	Tim Wallach	.10
385	Robby Thompson	.10
386	Frank Viola	.10
387	Dave Stewart	.10
388	Bip Roberts	.10
389	Ron Darling	.10
390	Carlos Delgado	.45
391	Tim Salmon	.10
392	Alan Trammell	.10
393	Kevin Foster	.10
394	Jim Abbott	.10
395	John Kruk	.10
396	Andy Van Slyke	.10
397	Dave Magadan	.10
398	Rafael Palmeiro	.65
399	Mike Devereaux	.10
400	Benito Santiago	.10
401	Brett Butler	.10
402	John Franco	.10
403	Matt Walbeck	.10
404	Terry Pendleton	.10
405	Chris Sabo	.10
406	Andrew Lorraine	.10
407	Dan Wilson	.10
408	Mike Lansing	.10
409	Ray McDavid	.10
410	Shane Andrews	.10
411	Tom Gordon	.10
412	Chad Ogea	.10
413	James Baldwin	.10
414	Russ Davis	.10
415	Ray Holbert	.10
416	Ray Durham	.10
417	Matt Nokes	.10
418	Rodney Henderson	.10
419	Gabe White	.10
420	Todd Hollandsworth	.10
421	Midre Cummings	.10
422	Harold Baines	.10
423	Troy Percival	.10
424	Joe Vitiello	.10
425	Andy Ashby	.10
426	Michael Tucker	.10
427	Mark Gubicza	.10
428	Jim Bullinger	.10
429	Jose Malave	.10
430	Pete Schourek	.10
431	Bobby Ayala	.10
432	Marvin Freeman	.10
433	Pat Listach	.10
434	Eddie Taubensee	.10
435	Steve Howe	.10
436	Kent Mercker	.10
437	Hector Fajardo	.10
438	Scott Kamieniecki	.10
439	Robb Nen	.10
440	Mike Kelly	.10
441	Tom Candiotti	.10
442	Albie Lopez	.10
443	Jeff Granger	.10
444	Rich Aude	.10
445	Luis Polonia	.10
446	Frank Thomas A.L. Checklist	.40
447	Ken Griffey Jr. A.L. Checklist	.65
448	Mike Piazza N.L. Checklist	.75
449	Jeff Bagwell N.L. Checklist	.40
450	Frank Thomas, Ken Griffey Jr., Mike Piazza, Jeff Bagwell Insert Checklist	.40

Artist's Proof

	NM/M
Complete Set (450):	300.00
Common Player:	1.00
Stars/Rookies:	10X

(See 1995 Pinnacle for checklist and base card values.)

Museum Collection

	NM/M
Complete Set (450):	200.00
Common Player:	.50
Stars/Rookies:	4X

(See 1995 Pinnacle for checklist and base card values.)

Redemption card .25

E.T.A. '95

No.	Player	NM/M
	Complete Set (6):	5.00
	Common Player:	.70
1	Ben Grieve	.75
2	Alex Ochoa	.75
3	Joe Vitiello	.75
4	Johnny Damon	3.00
5	Trey Beamon	.75
6	Brooks Kieschnick	.75

Gate Attraction

No.	Player	NM/M
	Complete Set (18):	25.00
	Common Player:	.50
1	Ken Griffey Jr.	3.50
2	Frank Thomas	1.50
3	Cal Ripken Jr.	5.00
4	Jeff Bagwell	1.50
5	Mike Piazza	3.50
6	Barry Bonds	5.00
7	Kirby Puckett	2.00
8	Albert Belle	.50
9	Tony Gwynn	2.00
10	Raul Mondesi	.50
11	Will Clark	.50
12	Don Mattingly	2.75
13	Roger Clemens	2.75
14	Paul Molitor	1.50
15	Matt Williams	.50
16	Greg Maddux	2.00
17	Kenny Lofton	.50
18	Cliff Floyd	.50

Performers

No.	Player	NM/M
	Complete Set (18):	15.00
	Common Player:	.35
1	Frank Thomas	2.00
2	Albert Belle	.35
3	Barry Bonds	3.50
4	Juan Gonzalez	1.00
5	Andres Galarraga	.35
6	Raul Mondesi	.35
7	Paul Molitor	2.00
8	Tim Salmon	.35
9	Mike Piazza	2.50
10	Gregg Jefferies	.35
11	Will Clark	.35
12	Greg Maddux	2.25
13	Manny Ramirez	2.00
14	Kirby Puckett	2.25
15	Shawn Green	1.25
16	Rafael Palmeiro	1.75
17	Paul O'Neill	.35
18	Jason Bere	.35

New Blood

No.	Player	NM/M
	Complete Set (9):	10.00
	Common Player:	.70
1	Alex Rodriguez	5.00
2	Shawn Green	1.50
3	Brian Hunter	.75
4	Garret Anderson	.75
5	Charles Johnson	.75
6	Chipper Jones	3.00
7	Carlos Delgado	1.50
8	Billy Ashley	.75
9	J.R. Phillips	.75

Red Hot

No.	Player	NM/M
	Complete Set (25):	35.00
	Common Player:	.75
1	Cal Ripken Jr.	5.50
2	Ken Griffey Jr.	4.00
3	Frank Thomas	1.50
4	Jeff Bagwell	1.50
5	Mike Piazza	4.00
6	Barry Bonds	5.50
7	Albert Belle	.75
8	Tony Gwynn	2.00
9	Kirby Puckett	2.00
10	Don Mattingly	2.50
11	Matt Williams	.75
12	Greg Maddux	2.00
13	Raul Mondesi	.75
14	Paul Molitor	1.50
15	Manny Ramirez	1.50
16	Joe Carter	.75
17	Will Clark	.75
18	Roger Clemens	2.50
19	Tim Salmon	.75
20	Dave Justice	.75
21	Kenny Lofton	.75
22	Deion Sanders	.75
23	Roberto Alomar	1.00
24	Cliff Floyd	.75
25	Carlos Baerga	.75

Team Pinnacle

		NM/M
	Complete Set (9):	30.00
	Common Player:	.70
1	Mike Mussina, Greg Maddux	5.00
2	Carlos Delgado, Mike Piazza	6.00
3	Frank Thomas, Jeff Bagwell	4.00
4	Roberto Alomar, Craig Biggio	1.00
5	Cal Ripken Jr., Ozzie Smith	10.00
6	Travis Fryman, Matt Williams	.75
7	Ken Griffey Jr., Barry Bonds	10.00
8	Albert Belle, Dave Justice	.75
9	Kirby Puckett, Tony Gwynn	5.00

Upstarts

No.	Player	NM/M
	Complete Set (30):	10.00
	Common Player:	.15
1	Frank Thomas	1.50
2	Roberto Alomar	.30
3	Mike Piazza	2.50
4	Javier Lopez	.15
5	Albert Belle	.15
6	Carlos Delgado	.75
7	Rusty Greer	.15
8	Tim Salmon	.15
9	Raul Mondesi	.15
10	Juan Gonzalez	.75
11	Manny Ramirez	1.50
12	Sammy Sosa	2.00
13	Jeff Kent	.15
14	Melvin Nieves	.15
15	Rondell White	.15
16	Shawn Green	.75
17	Bernie Williams	.15
18	Aaron Sele	.15
19	Jason Bere	.15
20	Joey Hamilton	.15
21	Mike Kelly	.15
22	Wil Cordero	.15
23	Moises Alou	.15
24	Roberto Kelly	.15
25	Deion Sanders	.15
26	Steve Karsay	.15
27	Bret Boone	.15
28	Willie Greene	.15
29	Billy Ashley	.15
30	Brian Anderson	.15

White Hot

		NM/M
Complete Set (25):		140.00
Common Player:		2.50
1	Cal Ripken Jr.	16.00
2	Ken Griffey Jr.	13.50
3	Frank Thomas	8.00
4	Jeff Bagwell	8.00
5	Mike Piazza	13.50
6	Barry Bonds	16.00
7	Albert Belle	2.50
8	Tony Gwynn	10.00
9	Kirby Puckett	10.00
10	Don Mattingly	12.00
11	Matt Williams	2.50
12	Greg Maddux	10.00
13	Raul Mondesi	2.50
14	Paul Molitor	8.00
15	Manny Ramirez	8.00
16	Joe Carter	2.50
17	Will Clark	2.50
18	Roger Clemens	12.00
19	Tim Salmon	2.50
20	Dave Justice	2.50
21	Kenny Lofton	2.50
22	Deion Sanders	2.50
23	Roberto Alomar	3.50
24	Cliff Floyd	2.50
25	Carlos Baerga	2.50

1996 PINNACLE

		NM/M
Complete Set (400):		15.00
Common Player:		.10
Series 1 or 2 Pack (10):		.75
Series 1 or 2 Box (24):		15.00
1	Greg Maddux	1.00
2	Bill Pulsipher	.10
3	Dante Bichette	.10
4	Mike Piazza	1.50
5	Garret Anderson	.10
6	Steve Finley	.10
7	Andy Benes	.10
8	Chuck Knoblauch	.10
9	Tom Gordon	.10
10	Jeff Bagwell	.75
11	Wil Cordero	.10
12	John Mabry	.10
13	Jeff Frye	.10
14	Travis Fryman	.10
15	John Wetteland	.10
16	Jason Bates	.10
17	Danny Tartabull	.10
18	Charles Nagy	.10
19	Robin Ventura	.10
20	Reggie Sanders	.10
21	Dave Clark	.10
22	Jaime Navarro	.10
23	Joey Hamilton	.10
24	Al Leiter	.10
25	Deion Sanders	.10
26	Tim Salmon	.10
27	Tino Martinez	.10
28	Mike Greenwell	.10
29	Phil Plantier	.10
30	Bobby Bonilla	.10
31	Kenny Rogers	.10
32	Chili Davis	.10
33	Joe Carter	.10
34	Mike Mussina	.40
35	Matt Mieske	.10
36	Jose Canseco	.40
37	Brad Radke	.10
38	Juan Gonzalez	.40
39	David Segui	.10
40	Alex Fernandez	.10
41	Jeff Kent	.10
42	Todd Zeile	.10
43	Darryl Strawberry	.10
44	Jose Rijo	.10
45	Ramon Martinez	.10
46	Manny Ramirez	.75
47	Gregg Jefferies	.10
48	Bryan Rekar	.10
49	Jeff King	.10
50	John Olerud	.10
51	Marc Newfield	.10
52	Charles Johnson	.10
53	Robby Thompson	.10
54	Brian Hunter	.10
55	Mike Blowers	.10
56	Keith Lockhart	.10
57	Ray Lankford	.10
58	Tim Wallach	.10
59	Ivan Rodriguez	.65
60	Ed Sprague	.10
61	Paul Molitor	.75
62	Eric Karros	.10
63	Glenallen Hill	.10
64	Jay Bell	.10
65	Tom Pagnozzi	.10
66	Greg Colbrunn	.10
67	Edgar Martinez	.10
68	Paul Sorrento	.10
69	Kirt Manwaring	.10
70	Pete Schourek	.10
71	Orlando Merced	.10
72	Shawon Dunston	.10
73	Ricky Bottalico	.10
74	Brady Anderson	.10
75	Steve Ontiveros	.10
76	Jim Abbott	.10
77	Carl Everett	.10
78	Mo Vaughn	.10
79	Pedro Martinez	.75
80	Harold Baines	.10
81	Alan Trammell	.10
82	Steve Avery	.10
83	Jeff Cirillo	.10
84	John Valentin	.10
85	Bernie Williams	.10
86	Andre Dawson	.30
87	Dave Winfield	.75
88	B.J. Surhoff	.10
89	Jeff Blauser	.10
90	Barry Larkin	.10
91	Cliff Floyd	.10
92	Sammy Sosa	1.00
93	Andres Galarraga	.10
94	Dave Nilsson	.10
95	James Mouton	.10
96	Marquis Grissom	.10
97	Matt Williams	.10
98	John Jaha	.10
99	Don Mattingly	1.25
100	Tim Naehring	.10
101	Kevin Appier	.10
102	Bobby Higginson	.10
103	Andy Pettitte	.25
104	Ozzie Smith	1.00
105	Kenny Lofton	.10
106	Ken Caminiti	.10
107	Walt Weiss	.10
108	Jack McDowell	.10
109	Brian McRae	.10
110	Gary Gaetti	.10
111	Curtis Goodwin	.10
112	Dennis Martinez	.10
113	Omar Vizquel	.10
114	Chipper Jones	1.00
115	Mark Gubicza	.10
116	Ruben Sierra	.10
117	Eddie Murray	.75
118	Chad Curtis	.10
119	Hal Morris	.10
120	Ben McDonald	.10
121	Marty Cordova	.10
122	Ken Griffey Jr.	1.50
123	Gary Sheffield	.40
124	Charlie Hayes	.10
125	Shawn Green	.40
126	Jason Giambi	.50
127	Mark Langston	.10
128	Mark Whiten	.10
129	Greg Vaughn	.10
130	Mark McGwire	1.75
131	Hideo Nomo	.40
132	Eric Karros, Raul Mondesi, Hideo Nomo, Mike Piazza	.50
133	Jason Bere	.10
134	Ken Griffey Jr.	.65
135	Frank Thomas	.40
136	Cal Ripken Jr.	1.00
137	Albert Belle	.10
138	Mike Piazza	.65
139	Dante Bichette	.10
140	Sammy Sosa	.50
141	Mo Vaughn	.10
142	Tim Salmon	.10
143	Reggie Sanders	.10
144	Cecil Fielder	.10
145	Jim Edmonds	.10
146	Rafael Palmeiro	.10
147	Edgar Martinez	.10
148	Barry Bonds	1.00
149	Manny Ramirez	.35
150	Larry Walker	.10
151	Jeff Bagwell	.35
152	Ron Gant	.10
153	Andres Galarraga	.10
154	Eddie Murray	.35
155	Kirby Puckett	.50
156	Will Clark	.10
157	Don Mattingly	.60
158	Mark McGwire	.75
159	Dean Palmer	.10
160	Matt Williams	.10
161	Fred McGriff	.10
162	Joe Carter	.10
163	Juan Gonzalez	.15
164	Alex Ochoa	.10
165	Ruben Rivera	.10
166	Tony Clark	.10
167	Brian Barber	.10
168	Matt Lawton	.10
169	Terrell Wade	.10
170	Johnny Damon	.30
171	Derek Jeter	2.00
172	Phil Nevin	.10
173	Robert Perez	.10
174	C.J. Nitkowski	.10
175	Joe Vitiello	.10
176	Roger Cedeno	.10
177	Ron Coomer	.10
178	Chris Widger	.10
179	Jimmy Haynes	.10
180	*Mike Sweeney*	.50
181	Howard Battle	.10
182	John Wasdin	.10
183	Jim Pittsley	.10
184	Bob Wolcott	.10
185	LaTroy Hawkins	.10
186	Nigel Wilson	.10
187	Dustin Hermanson	.10
188	Chris Snopek	.10
189	Mariano Rivera	.15
190	Jose Herrera	.10
191	Chris Stynes	.10
192	Larry Thomas	.10
193	David Bell	.10
194	Frank Thomas	.40
195	Ken Griffey Jr.	.65
196	Cal Ripken Jr.	.75
197	Jeff Bagwell	.35
198	Mike Piazza	.60
199	Barry Bonds	.75
200	Garret Anderson, Chipper Jones	.25
201	Frank Thomas	.75
202	Michael Tucker	.10
203	Kirby Puckett	1.00
204	Alex Gonzalez	.10
205	Tony Gwynn	1.00
206	Moises Alou	.10
207	Albert Belle	.10
208	Barry Bonds	2.00
209	Fred McGriff	.10
210	Dennis Eckersley	.65
211	Craig Biggio	.10
212	David Cone	.10
213	Will Clark	.10
214	Cal Ripken Jr.	2.00
215	Wade Boggs	1.00
216	Pete Schourek	.10
217	Darren Daulton	.10
218	Carlos Baerga	.10
219	Larry Walker	.10
220	Denny Neagle	.10
221	Jim Edmonds	.10
222	Lee Smith	.10
223	Jason Isringhausen	.10
224	Jay Buhner	.10
225	John Olerud	.10
226	Jeff Conine	.10
227	Dean Palmer	.10
228	Jim Abbott	.10
229	Raul Mondesi	.10
230	Tom Glavine	.35
231	Kevin Seitzer	.10
232	Lenny Dykstra	.10
233	Brian Jordan	.10
234	Rondell White	.10
235	Bret Boone	.10
236	Randy Johnson	.75
237	Paul O'Neill	.10
238	Jim Thome	.65
239	Edgardo Alfonzo	.10
240	Terry Pendleton	.10
241	Harold Baines	.10
242	Roberto Alomar	.20
243	Mark Grace	.10
244	Derek Bell	.10
245	Vinny Castilla	.10
246	Cecil Fielder	.10
247	Roger Clemens	1.25
248	Orel Hershiser	.10
249	J.T. Snow	.10
250	Rafael Palmeiro	.65
251	Bret Saberhagen	.10
252	Todd Hollandsworth	.10
253	Ryan Klesko	.10
254	Greg Maddux	.50
255	Ken Griffey Jr.	.65
256	Hideo Nomo	.15
257	Frank Thomas	.40
258	Cal Ripken Jr.	1.00
259	Jeff Bagwell	.35
260	Barry Bonds	1.00
261	Mo Vaughn	.10
262	Albert Belle	.10
263	Sammy Sosa	.50
264	Reggie Sanders	.10
265	Mike Piazza	.65
266	Chipper Jones	.50
267	Tony Gwynn	.50
268	Kirby Puckett	.50
269	Wade Boggs	.45
270	Will Clark	.10
271	Gary Sheffield	.10
272	Dante Bichette	.10
273	Randy Johnson	.35
274	Matt Williams	.10
275	Alex Rodriguez	.75
276	Tim Salmon	.10
277	Johnny Damon	.10
278	Manny Ramirez	.35
279	Derek Jeter	1.00
280	Eddie Murray	.35
281	Ozzie Smith	.50
282	Garret Anderson	.10
283	Raul Mondesi	.10
284	Terry Steinbach	.10
285	Carlos Garcia.	.10
286	Dave Justice.	.10
287	Eric Anthony.	.10
288	Benji Gil.	.10
289	Bob Hamelin.	.10
290	Dwayne Hosey.	.10
291	Andy Pettitte.	.25
292	Rod Beck.	.10
293	Shane Andrews.	.10
294	Julian Tavarez.	.10
295	Willie Greene.	.10
296	Ismael Valdes.	.10
297	Glenallen Hill.	.10
298	Troy Percival.	.10
299	Ray Durham.	.10
300	Jeff Conine .	.10
301.8	Ken Griffey Jr.	.75
302	Will Clark.	.10
303	Mike Greenwell .	.10
304.9	Carlos Baerga.	.10
305.3	Paul Molitor .	.35
305.6	Jeff Bagwell.	.35
306	Mark Grace.	.10
307	Don Mattingly .	.60
308	Hal Morris.	.10
309	Butch Huskey.	.10
310	Ozzie Guillen.	.10
311	Erik Hanson.	.10
312	Kenny Lofton .	.10
313	Edgar Martinez .	.10
314	Kurt Abbott.	.10
315	John Smoltz.	.10
316	Ariel Prieto	.10

317 Mark Carreon .10
318 Kirby Puckett .50
319 Carlos Perez .10
320 Gary DiSarcina .10
321 Trevor Hoffman .10
322 Mike Piazza .65
323 Frank Thomas .40
324 Juan Acevedo .10
325 Bip Roberts .10
326 Javier Lopez .10
327 Benito Santiago .10
328 Mark Lewis .10
329 Royce Clayton .10
330 Tom Gordon .10
331 Ben McDonald .10
332 Dan Wilson .10
333 Ron Gant .10
334 Wade Boggs .45
335 Paul Molitor .75
336 Tony Gwynn .50
337 Sean Berry .10
338 Rickey Henderson .75
339 Wil Cordero .10
340 Kent Mercker .10
341 Kenny Rogers .10
342 Ryne Sandberg 1.00
343 Charlie Hayes .10
344 Andy Benes .10
345 Sterling Hitchcock .10
346 Bernard Gilkey .10
347 Julio Franco .10
348 Ken Hill .10
349 Russ Davis .10
350 Mike Blowers .10
351 B.J. Surhoff .10
352 Lance Johnson .10
353 Darryl Hamilton .10
354 Shawon Dunston .10
355 Rick Aguilera .10
356 Danny Tartabull .10
357 Todd Stottlemyre .10
358 Mike Bordick .10
359 Jack McDowell .10
360 Todd Zeile .10
361 Tino Martinez .10
362 Greg Gagne .10
363 Mike Kelly .10
364 Tim Raines .10
365 Ernie Young .10
366 Mike Stanley .10
367 Wally Joyner .10
368 Karim Garcia .10
369 Paul Wilson .10
370 Sal Fasano .10
371 Jason Schmidt .10
372 *Livan Hernandez* .25
373 George Arias .10
374 Steve Gibralter .10
375 Jermaine Dye .10
376 Jason Kendall .10
377 Brooks Kieschnick .10
378 Jeff Ware .10
379 Alan Benes .10
380 Rey Ordonez .10
381 Jay Powell .10
382 *Osvaldo Fernandez* .15
383 *Wilton Guerrero* .10
384 Eric Owens .10
385 George Williams .10
386 Chan Ho Park .10
387 Jeff Suppan .10
388 *F.P. Santangelo* .10
389 Terry Adams .10
390 Bob Abreu .10
391 *Quinton McCracken* .10
392 *Mike Busby* .10
393 Cal Ripken Jr. .75
394 Ken Griffey Jr. .60
395 Frank Thomas .40
396 Chipper Jones .50
397 Greg Maddux .50
398 Mike Piazza .65
399 Ken Griffey Jr., Frank Thomas, Cal Ripken Jr., Greg Maddux, Chipper Jones, Mike Piazza .50

Starburst

NM/M
Complete Set (200): 150.00
Common Player: .40
Common Artist's Proof: .75
Artist's Proofs: 2X
1 Greg Maddux 3.00
2 Bill Pulsipher .40
3 Dante Bichette .40
4 Mike Piazza 4.00
5 Garret Anderson .40 
6 Chuck Knoblauch .40
7 Jeff Bagwell 2.25
8 Wil Cordero .40
9 Travis Fryman .40
10 Reggie Sanders .40
11 Deion Sanders .40
12 Tim Salmon .40
13 Tino Martinez .40
14 Bobby Bonilla .40
15 Joe Carter .40
16 Mike Mussina 1.25
17 Jose Canseco 1.25
18 Manny Ramirez 2.25
19 Gregg Jefferies .40
20 Charles Johnson .40
21 Brian Hunter .40
22 Ray Lankford .40
23 Ivan Rodriguez 2.00
24 Paul Molitor 2.25
25 Eric Karros .40
26 Edgar Martinez .40
27 Shawon Dunston .40
28 Mo Vaughn .40
29 Pedro Martinez 2.25
30 Marty Cordova .40
31 Ken Caminiti .40
32 Gary Sheffield .75
33 Shawn Green .75
34 Cliff Floyd .40
35 Andres Galarraga .40
36 Matt Williams .40
37 Don Mattingly 3.50
38 Kevin Appier .40
39 Ozzie Smith 3.00
40 Kenny Lofton .40
41 Ken Griffey Jr. 4.00
42 Jack McDowell .40
43 Gary Gaetti .40
44 Dennis Martinez .40
45 Chipper Jones 3.00
46 Eddie Murray 2.25
47 Bernie Williams .40
48 Andre Dawson .60
49 Dave Winfield 2.25
50 B.J. Surhoff .40
51 Barry Larkin .40
52 Alan Trammell .40
53 Sammy Sosa 3.00
54 Hideo Nomo 1.00
55 Mark McGwire 4.50
56 Jay Bell .40
57 Juan Gonzalez 1.00
58 Chili Davis .40
59 Robin Ventura .40
60 John Mabry .40
61 Ken Griffey Jr. 2.00
62 Frank Thomas 1.25
63 Cal Ripken Jr. 3.00
64 Albert Belle .40
65 Mike Piazza 2.00
66 Dante Bichette .40
67 Sammy Sosa 1.50
68 Mo Vaughn .40
69 Tim Salmon .40
70 Reggie Sanders .40
71 Cecil Fielder .40
72 Jim Edmonds .40
73 Rafael Palmeiro .75
74 Edgar Martinez .40
75 Barry Bonds 3.00
76 Manny Ramirez 1.25
77 Larry Walker .40
78 Jeff Bagwell 1.25
79 Ron Gant .40
80 Andres Galarraga .40
81 Eddie Murray 1.25
82 Kirby Puckett 1.50
83 Will Clark .40
84 Don Mattingly 1.75
85 Mark McGwire 2.25
86 Dean Palmer .40
87 Matt Williams .40
88 Fred McGriff .40
89 Joe Carter .40
90 Juan Gonzalez .65
91 Alex Ochoa .40
92 Ruben Rivera .40
93 Tony Clark .40
94 Pete Schourek .40
95 Terrell Wade .40
96 Johnny Damon .65
97 Derek Jeter 6.00
98 Phil Nevin .40
99 Robert Perez .40
100 Dustin Hermanson .40
101 Frank Thomas 2.25
102 Michael Tucker .40
103 Kirby Puckett 3.00
104 Alex Gonzalez .40
105 Tony Gwynn 3.00
106 Moises Alou .40
107 Albert Belle .40
108 Barry Bonds 6.00
109 Fred McGriff .40
110 Dennis Eckersley 1.50
111 Craig Biggio .40
112 David Cone .40
113 Will Clark .40
114 Cal Ripken Jr. 6.00
115 Wade Boggs 3.00
116 Pete Schourek .40
117 Darren Daulton .40
118 Carlos Baerga .40
119 Larry Walker .40
120 Denny Neagle .40
121 Jim Edmonds .40
122 Lee Smith .40
123 Jason Isringhausen .40
124 Jay Buhner .40
125 John Olerud .40
126 Jeff Conine .40
127 Dean Palmer .40
128 Jim Abbott .40
129 Raul Mondesi .40
130 Tom Glavine .60
131 Kevin Seitzer .40
132 Lenny Dykstra .40
133 Brian Jordan .40
134 Rondell White .40
135 Bret Boone .40
136 Randy Johnson 2.25
137 Paul O'Neill .40
138 Jim Thome .75
139 Edgardo Alfonzo .40
140 Terry Pendleton .40
141 Harold Baines .40
142 Roberto Alomar .45
143 Mark Grace .40
144 Derek Bell .40
145 Vinny Castilla .40
146 Cecil Fielder .40
147 Roger Clemens 3.50
148 Orel Hershiser .40
149 J.T. Snow .40
150 Rafael Palmeiro 1.75
151 Bret Saberhagen .40
152 Todd Hollandsworth .40
153 Ryan Klesko .40
154 Greg Maddux 1.50
155 Ken Griffey Jr. 2.00
156 Hideo Nomo .65
157 Frank Thomas 1.25
158 Cal Ripken Jr. 3.00
159 Jeff Bagwell 1.25
160 Barry Bonds 3.00
161 Mo Vaughn .40
162 Albert Belle .40
163 Sammy Sosa 1.50
164 Reggie Sanders .40
165 Mike Piazza 2.00
166 Chipper Jones 1.50
167 Tony Gwynn 1.50
168 Kirby Puckett 1.50
169 Wade Boggs 1.25
170 Will Clark .40
171 Gary Sheffield .45
172 Dante Bichette .40
173 Randy Johnson 1.25
174 Matt Williams .40
175 Alex Rodriguez 4.50
176 Tim Salmon .40
177 Johnny Damon .40
178 Manny Ramirez 1.25
179 Derek Jeter 3.00
180 Eddie Murray 1.25
181 Ozzie Smith 1.50
182 Garret Anderson .40
183 Raul Mondesi .40
184 Jeff Conine .40
185 Ken Griffey Jr. 2.00
186 Will Clark .40
187 Mike Greenwell .40
188 Carlos Baerga .40
189 Paul Molitor 1.25
190 Jeff Bagwell 1.25
191 Mark Grace .40
192 Don Mattingly 1.75
193 Hal Morris .40
194 Kenny Lofton .40
195 Edgar Martinez .40
196 Kirby Puckett 1.50
197 Mike Piazza 2.00
198 Frank Thomas 1.25
199 Wade Boggs 1.25
200 Tony Gwynn 1.50

Artist's Proof

NM/M
Common Artist's Proof: 2.00
Stars: 3X
(See 1996 Pinnacle Starburst for checklist and base card values.)

Foil Series 2

NM/M
Complete Set (200): 15.00
Common Player: .20
Stars: 1.5X
(See 1996 Pinnacle #201-399 for checklistand base card values.)

Cal Ripken Tribute

NM/M
1 of 1 Cal Ripken Jr. 5.00

Christie Brinkley Collection

NM/M
Complete Set (16): 15.00
Common Player: .80
1 Greg Maddux 3.50
2 Ryan Klesko .75
3 Dave Justice .75
4 Tom Glavine 1.50
5 Chipper Jones 3.50
6 Fred McGriff .75
7 Javier Lopez .75
8 Marquis Grissom .75
9 Jason Schmidt .75
10 Albert Belle .75
11 Manny Ramirez 2.25
12 Carlos Baerga .75
13 Sandy Alomar .75
14 Jim Thome 2.25
15 Julio Franco .75
16 Kenny Lofton .75

Essence of the Game

		NM/M
Complete Set (18):		35.00
Common Player:		.70
1	Cal Ripken Jr.	6.00
2	Greg Maddux	3.00
3	Frank Thomas	2.50
4	Matt Williams	.75
5	Chipper Jones	3.00
6	Reggie Sanders	.75
7	Ken Griffey Jr.	4.00
8	Kirby Puckett	3.00
9	Hideo Nomo	1.50
10	Mike Piazza	4.00
11	Jeff Bagwell	2.50
12	Mo Vaughn	.75
13	Albert Belle	.75
14	Tim Salmon	.75
15	Don Mattingly	3.50
16	Will Clark	.75
17	Eddie Murray	2.50
18	Barry Bonds	6.00

First Rate

		NM/M
Complete Set (18):		40.00
Common Player:		1.25
1	Ken Griffey Jr.	5.00
2	Frank Thomas	2.50
3	Mo Vaughn	1.25
4	Chipper Jones	3.50
5	Alex Rodriguez	6.50
6	Kirby Puckett	3.50
7	Gary Sheffield	1.75
8	Matt Williams	1.25
9	Barry Bonds	7.50
10	Craig Biggio	1.25
11	Robin Ventura	1.25
12	Michael Tucker	1.25
13	Derek Jeter	7.50
14	Manny Ramirez	2.50
15	Barry Larkin	1.25
16	Shawn Green	1.75
17	Will Clark	1.25
18	Mark McGwire	6.50

Pinnacle Power

		NM/M
Complete Set (20):		40.00
Common Player:		1.25
1	Frank Thomas	2.50
2	Mo Vaughn	1.25
2p	Mo Vaughn (promo)	1.50
3	Ken Griffey Jr.	4.50
4	Matt Williams	1.25
5	Barry Bonds	6.00
6	Reggie Sanders	1.25
7	Mike Piazza	4.50
8	Jim Edmonds	1.25
9	Dante Bichette	1.25
10	Sammy Sosa	3.50
11	Jeff Bagwell	2.50
12	Fred McGriff	1.25
13	Albert Belle	1.25
14	Tim Salmon	1.25
15	Joe Carter	1.25
16	Manny Ramirez	2.50
17	Eddie Murray	2.50
18	Cecil Fielder	1.25
19	Larry Walker	1.25
20	Juan Gonzalez	1.75

Project Stardom

		NM/M
Complete Set (18):		35.00
Common Player:		1.00
1	Paul Wilson	1.00
2	Derek Jeter	8.50
3	Karim Garcia	1.00
4	Johnny Damon	2.75
5	Alex Rodriguez	7.50
6	Chipper Jones	6.50
7	Charles Johnson	1.00
8	Bob Abreu	1.25
9	Alan Benes	1.00
10	Richard Hidalgo	1.00
11	Brooks Kieschnick	1.00
12	Garret Anderson	1.00
13	Livan Hernandez	1.00
14	Manny Ramirez	5.00
15	Jermaine Dye	1.00
16	Todd Hollandsworth	1.00
17	Raul Mondesi	1.00
18	Ryan Klesko	1.00

Skylines

		NM/M
Complete Set (18):		375.00
Common Player:		10.00
1	Ken Griffey Jr.	50.00
2	Frank Thomas	30.00
3	Greg Maddux	40.00
4	Cal Ripken Jr.	65.00
5	Albert Belle	10.00
6	Mo Vaughn	10.00
7	Mike Piazza	50.00
8	Wade Boggs	40.00
9	Will Clark	10.00
10	Barry Bonds	65.00
11	Gary Sheffield	10.00
12	Hideo Nomo	25.00
13	Tony Gwynn	40.00
14	Kirby Puckett	40.00
15	Chipper Jones	40.00
16	Jeff Bagwell	30.00
17	Manny Ramirez	30.00
18	Raul Mondesi	10.00

Slugfest

		NM/M
Complete Set (18):		40.00
Common Player:		1.25
1	Frank Thomas	2.75
2	Ken Griffey Jr.	4.00
3	Jeff Bagwell	2.75
4	Barry Bonds	5.00
5	Mo Vaughn	1.25
6	Albert Belle	1.25
7	Mike Piazza	4.00
8	Matt Williams	1.25
9	Dante Bichette	1.25
10	Sammy Sosa	3.00
11	Gary Sheffield	2.00
12	Reggie Sanders	1.25
13	Manny Ramirez	2.75
14	Eddie Murray	2.75
15	Juan Gonzalez	2.25
16	Dean Palmer	1.25
17	Rafael Palmeiro	2.75
18	Cecil Fielder	1.25

Team Pinnacle

		NM/M
Complete Set (9):		30.00
Common Player:		1.50
1	Frank Thomas, Jeff Bagwell	3.00
2	Chuck Knoblauch, Craig Biggio	1.50
3	Jim Thome, Matt Williams	3.00
4	Barry Larkin, Cal Ripken Jr.	7.50
5	Barry Bonds, Tim Salmon	7.50
6	Ken Griffey Jr., Reggie Sanders	6.00
7	Albert Belle, Sammy Sosa	4.00
8	Ivan Rodriguez, Mike Piazza	6.00
9	Greg Maddux, Randy Johnson	4.00

Team Spirit

		NM/M
Complete Set (12):		45.00
Common Player:		1.25
1	Greg Maddux	4.00
2	Ken Griffey Jr.	5.00
3	Derek Jeter	8.00
4	Mike Piazza	5.00
5	Cal Ripken Jr.	8.00
6	Frank Thomas	2.75
7	Jeff Bagwell	2.75
8	Mo Vaughn	1.25
9	Albert Belle	1.25
10	Chipper Jones	4.00
11	Johnny Damon	1.50
12	Barry Bonds	8.00

Team Tomorrow

		NM/M
Complete Set (10):		20.00
Common Player:		.50
1	Ruben Rivera	.50
2	Johnny Damon	1.00
3	Raul Mondesi	.50
4	Manny Ramirez	3.00
5	Hideo Nomo	1.50
6	Chipper Jones	4.00
7	Garret Anderson	.50
8	Alex Rodriguez	5.00
9	Derek Jeter	6.00
10	Karim Garcia	.50

1996 PINNACLE/ AFICIONADO

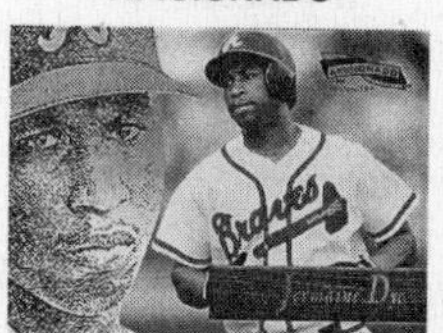

		NM/M
Complete Set (200):		20.00
Common Player:		.10
Common Artist's Proof:		.50
Artist's Proof Stars:		8X
Pack (5):		1.50
Wax Box (16):		30.00
1	Jack McDowell	.10
2	Jay Bell	.10
3	Rafael Palmeiro	1.25
4	Wally Joyner	.10
5	Ozzie Smith	2.00
6	Mark McGwire	3.00
7	Kevin Seitzer	.10
8	Fred McGriff	.10
9	Roger Clemens	2.25
9s	Roger Clemens (marked "SAMPLE")	4.00
10	Randy Johnson	1.50
11	Cecil Fielder	.10
12	David Cone	.10
13	Chili Davis	.10
14	Andres Galarraga	.10
15	Joe Carter	.10
16	Ryne Sandberg	2.00
17	Paul O'Neill	.10
18	Cal Ripken Jr.	4.00
19	Wade Boggs	2.00
20	Greg Gagne	.10
21	Edgar Martinez	.10
22	Greg Maddux	2.00
23	Ken Caminiti	.10
24	Kirby Puckett	2.00
25	Craig Biggio	.10
26	Will Clark	.10
27	Ron Gant	.10
28	Eddie Murray	1.50
29	Lance Johnson	.10
30	Tony Gwynn	2.00
31	Dante Bichette	.10
32	Darren Daulton	.10
33	Danny Tartabull	.10
34	Jeff King	.10
35	Tom Glavine	.40
36	Rickey Henderson	1.50
37	Jose Canseco	1.00
38	Barry Larkin	.10
39	Dennis Martinez	.10
40	Ruben Sierra	.10
41	Bobby Bonilla	.10
42	Jeff Conine	.10
43	Lee Smith	.10
44	Charlie Hayes	.10
45	Walt Weiss	.10
46	Jay Buhner	.10
47	Kenny Rogers	.10
48	Paul Molitor	1.50
49	Hal Morris	.10
50	Todd Stottlemyre	.10
51	Mike Stanley	.10
52	Mark Grace	.10
53	Lenny Dykstra	.10
54	Andre Dawson	.25
55	Dennis Eckersley	1.25
56	Ben McDonald	.10
57	Ray Lankford	.10
58	Mo Vaughn	.10
59	Frank Thomas	1.50
60	Julio Franco	.10
61	Jim Abbott	.10
62	Greg Vaughn	.10
63	Marquis Grissom	.10
64	Tino Martinez	.10
65	Kevin Appier	.10
66	Matt Williams	.10
67	Sammy Sosa	2.00
68	Larry Walker	.10
69	Ivan Rodriguez	1.25
70	Eric Karros	.10
71	Bernie Williams	.10
72	Carlos Baerga	.10
73	Jeff Bagwell	1.50
74	Pete Schourek	.10
75	Ken Griffey Jr.	2.50
76	Bernard Gilkey	.10
77	Albert Belle	.10
78	Chuck Knoblauch	.10
79	John Smoltz	.10
80	Barry Bonds	4.00
81	Vinny Castilla	.10
82	John Olerud	.10
83	Mike Mussina	1.00
84	Alex Fernandez	.10
85	Shawon Dunston	.10
86	Travis Fryman	.10
87	Moises Alou	.10
88	Dean Palmer	.10
89	Gregg Jefferies	.10
90	Jim Thome	1.25
91	Dave Justice	.10
92	B.J. Surhoff	.10
93	Ramon Martinez	.10
94	Gary Sheffield	.40
95	Andy Benes	.10
96	Reggie Sanders	.10
97	Roberto Alomar	.35
98	Omar Vizquel	.10
99	Juan Gonzalez	.75
100	Robin Ventura	.10
101	Jason Isringhausen	.10
102	Greg Colbrunn	.10
103	Brian Jordan	.10
104	Shawn Green	.40
105	Brian Hunter	.10
106	Rondell White	.10
107	Ryan Klesko	.10
107s	Ryan Klesko (marked "SAMPLE")	1.00
108	Sterling Hitchcock	.10
109	Manny Ramirez	1.50
110	Bret Boone	.10
111	Michael Tucker	.10
112	Julian Tavarez	.10
113	Benji Gil	.10
114	Kenny Lofton	.10
115	Mike Kelly	.10
116	Ray Durham	.10
117	Trevor Hoffman	.10
118	Butch Huskey	.10
119	Phil Nevin	.10
120	Pedro Martinez	1.50
121	Wil Cordero	.10
122	Tim Salmon	.10

123 Jim Edmonds .10
124 Mike Piazza 2.50
125 Rico Brogna .10
126 John Mabry .10
127 Chipper Jones 2.00
128 Johnny Damon .35
129 Raul Mondesi .10
130 Denny Neagle .10
131 Marc Newfield .10
132 Hideo Nomo .75
133 Joe Vitiello .10
134 Garret Anderson .10
135 Dave Nilsson .10
136 Alex Rodriguez 3.00
137 Russ Davis .10
138 Frank Rodriguez .10
139 Royce Clayton .10
140 John Valentin .10
141 Marty Cordova .10
142 Alex Gonzalez .10
143 Carlos Delgado .75
144 Willie Greene .10
145 Cliff Floyd .10
146 Bobby Higginson .10
147 J.T. Snow .10
148 Derek Bell .10
149 Edgardo Alfonzo .10
150 Charles Johnson .10
151 Hideo Nomo (Global Reach) .60
152 Larry Walker (Global Reach) .10
153 Bob Abreu (Global Reach) .10
154 Karim Garcia (Global Reach) .10
155 Dave Nilsson (Global Reach) .10
156 Chan Ho Park (Global Reach) .10
157 Dennis Martinez (Global Reach) .10
158 Sammy Sosa (Global Reach) 1.25
159 Rey Ordonez (Global Reach) .10
160 Roberto Alomar (Global Reach) .10
161 George Arias .10
162 Jason Schmidt .10
163 Derek Jeter 4.00
164 Chris Snopek .10
165 Todd Hollandsworth .10
166 Sal Fasano .10
167 Jay Powell .10
168 Paul Wilson .10
169 Jim Pittsley .10
170 LaTroy Hawkins .10
171 Bob Abreu .10
172 *Mike Grace* .10
173 Karim Garcia .10
174 Richard Hidalgo .10
175 Felipe Crespo .10
176 Terrell Wade .10
177 Steve Gibralter .10
178 Jermaine Dye .10
179 Alan Benes .10
180 *Wilton Guerrero* .10
181 Brooks Kieschnick .10
182 Roger Cedeno .10
183 *Osvaldo Fernandez* .10
184 *Matt Lawton* .50
185 George Williams .10
186 Jimmy Haynes .10
187 *Mike Busby* .10
188 Chan Ho Park .10
189 Marc Barcelo .10
190 Jason Kendall .10
191 Rey Ordonez .10
192 Tyler Houston .10
193 John Wasdin .10
194 Jeff Suppan .10
195 Jeff Ware .10
196 Checklist .10
197 Checklist .10
198 Checklist .10
199 Checklist .10
200 Checklist .10

Magic Numbers

NM/M
Complete Set (10): 15.50
Common Player: .75
Samples: 1X
1 Ken Griffey Jr. 3.25
2 Greg Maddux 2.50
3 Frank Thomas 1.50
4 Mo Vaughn .75
5 Jeff Bagwell 1.50

6 Chipper Jones 2.50
7 Albert Belle .75
8 Cal Ripken Jr. 4.50
9 Matt Williams .75
10 Sammy Sosa 2.50

Rivals

NM/M
Complete Set (24): 65.00
Common Player: 2.00
1 Ken Griffey Jr., Frank Thomas 4.00
2 Frank Thomas, Cal Ripken Jr. 4.50
3 Cal Ripken Jr., Mo Vaughn 4.00
4 Mo Vaughn, Ken Griffey Jr. 2.50
5 Ken Griffey Jr., Cal Ripken Jr. 5.00
6 Frank Thomas, Mo Vaughn 2.00
7 Cal Ripken Jr., Ken Griffey Jr. 5.00
8 Mo Vaughn, Frank Thomas 2.00
9 Ken Griffey Jr., Mo Vaughn 2.50
10 Frank Thomas, Ken Griffey Jr. 4.00
11 Cal Ripken Jr., Frank Thomas 4.50
12 Mo Vaughn, Cal Ripken Jr. 4.00
13 Mike Piazza, Jeff Bagwell 2.50
14 Jeff Bagwell, Barry Bonds 4.50
15 Jeff Bagwell, Mike Piazza 2.50
16 Tony Gwynn, Mike Piazza 3.00
17 Mike Piazza, Barry Bonds 5.00
18 Jeff Bagwell, Tony Gwynn 2.00
19 Barry Bonds, Mike Piazza 5.00
20 Tony Gwynn, Jeff Bagwell 2.00
21 Mike Piazza, Tony Gwynn 3.00
22 Barry Bonds, Jeff Bagwell 4.50
23 Tony Gwynn, Barry Bonds 4.50
24 Barry Bonds, Tony Gwynn 4.50

Slick Picks

NM/M
Complete Set (32): 40.00
Common Player: .50
1 Mike Piazza 2.50
2 Cal Ripken Jr. 4.00
3 Ken Griffey Jr. 2.50
4 Paul Wilson .50
5 Frank Thomas 1.50
6 Mo Vaughn .50
7 Barry Bonds 4.00
8 Albert Belle .50
9 Jeff Bagwell 1.50
10 Dante Bichette .50
11 Hideo Nomo .75
12 Raul Mondesi .50
13 Manny Ramirez 1.50
14 Greg Maddux 2.00
15 Tony Gwynn 2.00
16 Ryne Sandberg 2.00
17 Reggie Sanders .50
18 Derek Jeter 4.00
19 Johnny Damon .75
20 Alex Rodriguez 3.00
21 Ryan Klesko .50
22 Jim Thome 1.50
23 Kenny Lofton .50
24 Tino Martinez .50
25 Randy Johnson 1.50
26 Wade Boggs 2.00
27 Juan Gonzalez .75
28 Kirby Puckett 2.00
29 Tim Salmon .50
30 Chipper Jones 2.00
31 Garret Anderson .50
32 Eddie Murray 1.50

1997 PINNACLE

NM/M
Complete Set (200): 10.00
Common Player: .05
Pack (10): 1.00
Wax Box (24): 12.50
Wax Retail Box (16): 10.00
1 Cecil Fielder .05
2 Garret Anderson .05
3 Charles Nagy .05
4 Darryl Hamilton .05
5 Greg Myers .05
6 Eric Davis .05
7 Jeff Frye .05
8 Marquis Grissom .05
9 Curt Schilling .35
10 Jeff Fassero .05
11 Alan Benes .05
12 Orlando Miller .05
13 Alex Fernandez .05
14 Andy Pettitte .25
15 Andre Dawson .25
16 Mark Grudzielanek .05
17 Joe Vitiello .05
18 Juan Gonzalez .40
19 Mark Whiten .05
20 Lance Johnson .05
21 Trevor Hoffman .05
22 Marc Newfield .05
23 Jim Eisenreich .05
24 Joe Carter .05
25 Jose Canseco .30
26 Bill Swift .05
27 Ellis Burks .05
28 Ben McDonald .05
29 Edgar Martinez .05
30 Jamie Moyer .05
31 Chan Ho Park .05
32 Carlos Delgado .50
33 Kevin Mitchell .05
34 Carlos Garcia .05
35 Darryl Strawberry .05
36 Jim Thome .60
37 Jose Offerman .05
38 Ryan Klesko .05
39 Ruben Sierra .05
40 Devon White .05
41 Brian Jordan .05
42 Tony Gwynn .75
43 Rafael Palmeiro .50
44 Dante Bichette .05
45 Scott Stahoviak .05
46 Roger Cedeno .05
47 Ivan Rodriguez .50
48 Bob Abreu .05
49 Darryl Kile .05
50 Darren Dreifort .05
51 Shawon Dunston .05
52 Mark McGwire 1.50
53 Tim Salmon .05
54 Gene Schall .05
55 Roger Clemens .85
56 Rondell White .05
57 Ed Sprague .05
58 Craig Paquette .05
59 David Segui .05
60 Jaime Navarro .05
61 Tom Glavine .35
62 Jeff Brantley .05
63 Kimera Bartee .05
64 Fernando Vina .05
65 Eddie Murray .65
66 Lenny Dykstra .05
67 Kevin Elster .05
68 Vinny Castilla .05
69 Todd Greene .05
70 Brett Butler .05
71 Robby Thompson .05
72 Reggie Jefferson .05
73 Todd Hundley .05
74 Jeff King .05
75 Ernie Young .05
76 Jeff Bagwell .65
77 Dan Wilson .05
78 Paul Molitor .65
79 Kevin Seitzer .05
80 Kevin Brown .05
81 Ron Gant .05
82 Dwight Gooden .05
83 Todd Stottlemyre .05
84 Ken Caminiti .05
85 James Baldwin .05
86 Jermaine Dye .05
87 Harold Baines .05
88 Pat Hentgen .05
89 Frank Rodriguez .05
90 Mark Johnson .05
91 Jason Kendall .05
92 Alex Rodriguez 1.50
93 Alan Trammell .05
94 Scott Brosius .05
95 Delino DeShields .05
96 Chipper Jones .75
97 Barry Bonds 2.00
98 Brady Anderson .05
99 Ryne Sandberg .75
100 Albert Belle .05
101 Jeff Cirillo .05
102 Frank Thomas .65
103 Mike Piazza 1.00
104 Rickey Henderson .65
105 Rey Ordonez .05
106 Mark Grace .05
107 Terry Steinbach .05
108 Ray Durham .05
109 Barry Larkin .05
110 Tony Clark .05
111 Bernie Williams .05
112 John Smoltz .05
113 Moises Alou .05
114 Alex Gonzalez .05
115 Rico Brogna .05
116 Eric Karros .05
117 Jeff Conine .05
118 Todd Hollandsworth .05
119 Troy Percival .05
120 Paul Wilson .05
121 Orel Hershiser .05
122 Ozzie Smith .75
123 Dave Hollins .05

124	Ken Hill	.05
125	Rick Wilkins	.05
126	Scott Servais	.05
127	Fernando Valenzuela	.05
128	Mariano Rivera	.15
129	Mark Loretta	.05
130	Shane Reynolds	.05
131	Darren Oliver	.05
132	Steve Trachsel	.05
133	Darren Bragg	.05
134	Jason Dickson	.05
135	Darren Fletcher	.05
136	Gary Gaetti	.05
137	Joey Cora	.05
138	Terry Pendleton	.05
139	Derek Jeter	2.00
140	Danny Tartabull	.05
141	John Flaherty	.05
142	B.J. Surhoff	.05
143	Mark Sweeney	.05
144	Chad Mottola	.05
145	Andujar Cedeno	.05
146	Tim Belcher	.05
147	Mark Thompson	.05
148	Rafael Bournigal	.05
149	Marty Cordova	.05
150	Osvaldo Fernandez	.05
151	Mike Stanley	.05
152	Ricky Bottalico	.05
153	Donnie Wall	.05
154	Omar Vizquel	.05
155	Mike Mussina	.30
156	Brant Brown	.05
157	F.P. Santangelo	.05
158	Ryan Hancock	.05
159	Jeff D'Amico	.05
160	Luis Castillo	.05
161	Darin Erstad	.10
162	Ugueth Urbina	.05
163	Andruw Jones	.65
164	Steve Gibralter	.05
165	Robin Jennings	.05
166	Mike Cameron	.05
167	George Arias	.05
168	Chris Stynes	.05
169	Justin Thompson	.05
170	Jamey Wright	.05
171	Todd Walker	.05
172	Nomar Garciaparra	.75
173	Jose Paniagua	.05
174	Marvin Benard	.05
175	Rocky Coppinger	.05
176	Quinton McCracken	.05
177	Amaury Telemaco	.05
178	Neifi Perez	.05
179	Todd Greene	.05
180	Jason Thompson	.05
181	Wilton Guerrero	.05
182	Edgar Renteria	.05
183	Billy Wagner	.05
184	Alex Ochoa	.05
185	Billy McMillon	.05
186	Kenny Lofton	.05
187	Andres Galarraga	.05
188	Chuck Knoblauch	.05
189	Greg Maddux	.75
190	Mo Vaughn	.05
191	Cal Ripken Jr.	2.00
192	Hideo Nomo	.40
193	Ken Griffey Jr.	1.00
194	Sammy Sosa	.75
195	Jay Buhner	.05
196	Manny Ramirez	.65
197	Matt Williams	.05
198	Andruw Jones	.30
199	Darin Erstad	.05
200	Trey Beamon	.05

Museum Collection

	NM/M
Complete Set (200):	100.00
Common Player:	1.00
Stars/Rookies:	6X

(See 1997 Pinnacle for checklist and regular-issue card values.)

Artist's Proofs

	NM/M
Common Bronze (125):	1.00
Bronze Stars:	30X
Common Silver (50):	2.50
Silver Stars:	12X
Common Gold (25):	4.00
Gold Stars:	10X

(See 1997 Pinnacle for checklist and base card values.)

Cardfrontations

		NM/M
	Complete Set (20):	35.00
	Common Player:	.50
1	Greg Maddux, Mike Piazza	3.00
2	Tom Glavine, Ken Caminiti	.75
3	Randy Johnson, Cal Ripken Jr.	5.00
4	Kevin Appier, Mark McGwire	4.00
5	Andy Pettitte, Juan Gonzalez	1.00
6	Pat Hentgen, Albert Belle	.50
7	Hideo Nomo, Chipper Jones	2.00
8	Ismael Valdes, Sammy Sosa	2.50
9	Mike Mussina, Manny Ramirez	1.50
10	David Cone, Jay Buhner	.50
11	Mark Wohlers, Gary Sheffield	.75
12	Alan Benes, Barry Bonds	5.00
13	Roger Clemens, Ivan Rodriguez	2.50
14	Mariano Rivera, Ken Griffey Jr.	3.00
15	Dwight Gooden, Frank Thomas	1.50
16	John Wetteland, Darin Erstad	.50
17	John Smoltz, Brian Jordan	.50
18	Kevin Brown, Jeff Bagwell	1.50
19	Jack McDowell, Alex Rodriguez	4.00
20	Charles Nagy, Bernie Williams	.50

Home/Away

		NM/M
	Complete Set (24):	65.00
	Common Player:	2.00
1	Chipper Jones	5.00
2	Ken Griffey Jr.	6.00
3	Mike Piazza	6.00
4	Frank Thomas	4.00
5	Jeff Bagwell	4.00
6	Alex Rodriguez	8.00
7	Barry Bonds	10.00
8	Mo Vaughn	2.00
9	Derek Jeter	10.00
10	Mark McGwire	8.00
11	Cal Ripken Jr.	10.00
12	Albert Belle	2.00

Passport to the Majors

		NM/M
	Complete Set (25):	55.00
	Common Player:	1.00
1	Greg Maddux	4.00
1s	Greg Maddux ("SAMPLE" overprint)	4.00
2	Ken Griffey Jr.	6.00
3	Frank Thomas	3.00
4	Cal Ripken Jr.	10.00
5	Mike Piazza	6.00
6	Alex Rodriguez	7.50
7	Mo Vaughn	1.00
8	Chipper Jones	4.00
9	Roberto Alomar	1.00
10	Edgar Martinez	1.00
11	Javier Lopez	1.00
12	Ivan Rodriguez	2.50
13	Juan Gonzalez	1.50
14	Carlos Baerga	1.00
15	Sammy Sosa	4.00
16	Manny Ramirez	3.00
17	Raul Mondesi	1.00
18	Henry Rodriguez	1.00
19	Rafael Palmeiro	2.50
20	Rey Ordonez	1.00
21	Hideo Nomo	1.50
22	Makoto Suzuki	1.00
23	Chan Ho Park	1.00
24	Larry Walker	1.00
25	Ruben Rivera	1.00

Shades

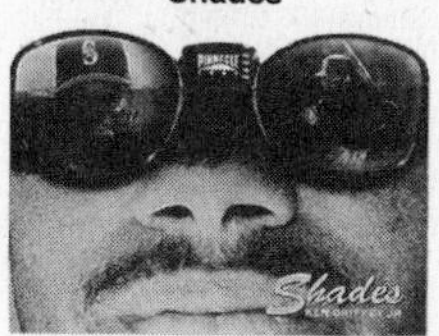

		NM/M
	Complete Set (10):	15.00
	Common Player:	.75
1	Ken Griffey Jr.	3.00
2	Juan Gonzalez	1.50
3	John Smoltz	.75
4	Gary Sheffield	1.00
5	Cal Ripken Jr.	5.00
6	Mo Vaughn	.75
7	Brian Jordan	.75
8	Mike Piazza	3.00
9	Frank Thomas	2.25
10	Alex Rodriguez	4.00

Team Pinnacle

		NM/M
	Complete Set (10):	22.00
	Common Player:	1.00
1	Frank Thomas, Jeff Bagwell	3.00
2	Chuck Knoblauch, Eric Young	1.00
3	Ken Caminiti, Jim Thome	2.00
4	Alex Rodriguez, Chipper Jones	5.00
5	Mike Piazza, Ivan Rodriguez	4.00
6	Albert Belle, Barry Bonds	6.00
7	Ken Griffey Jr., Ellis Burks	4.00
8	Juan Gonzalez, Gary Sheffield	1.75
9	John Smoltz, Andy Pettitte	1.50
10	All Players	1.00

1997 PINNACLE CERTIFIED

		NM/M
	Complete Set (150):	30.00
	Common Player:	.15
	Jose Cruz Jr. Redemption:	2.00
	Pack (6):	2.00
	Wax Box (20):	35.00
1	Barry Bonds	3.00
2	Mo Vaughn	.15
3	Matt Williams	.15
4	Ryne Sandberg	1.25
5	Jeff Bagwell	1.00
6	Alan Benes	.15
7	John Wetteland	.15
8	Fred McGriff	.15
9	Craig Biggio	.15
10	Bernie Williams	.15
11	Brian L. Hunter	.15
12	Sandy Alomar Jr.	.15
13	Ray Lankford	.15
14	Ryan Klesko	.15
15	Jermaine Dye	.15
16	Andy Benes	.15
17	Albert Belle	.15
18	Tony Clark	.15
19	Dean Palmer	.15
20	Bernard Gilkey	.15
21	Ken Caminiti	.15
22	Alex Rodriguez	2.25
23	Tim Salmon	.15
24	Larry Walker	.15
25	Barry Larkin	.15
26	Mike Piazza	1.50
27	Brady Anderson	.15
28	Cal Ripken Jr.	3.00
29	Charles Nagy	.15
30	Paul Molitor	1.00
31	Darin Erstad	.25
32	Rey Ordonez	.15
33	Wally Joyner	.15
34	David Cone	.15
35	Sammy Sosa	1.25
36	Dante Bichette	.15
37	Eric Karros	.15
38	Omar Vizquel	.15
39	Roger Clemens	1.25
40	Joe Carter	.15
41	Frank Thomas	1.00
42	Javier Lopez	.15
43	Mike Mussina	.45
44	Gary Sheffield	.60
45	Tony Gwynn	1.25
46	Jason Kendall	.15
47	Jim Thome	.75
48	Andres Galarraga	.15
49	Mark McGwire	2.25
50	Troy Percival	.15
51	Derek Jeter	3.00
52	Todd Hollandsworth	.15
53	Ken Griffey Jr.	1.50
54	Randy Johnson	1.00
55	Pat Hentgen	.15
56	Rusty Greer	.15
57	John Jaha	.15
58	Kenny Lofton	.15
59	Chipper Jones	1.25
60	Robb Nen	.15
61	Rafael Palmeiro	.75
62	Mariano Rivera	.30
63	Hideo Nomo	.50
64	Greg Vaughn	.15
65	Ron Gant	.15
66	Eddie Murray	1.00
67	John Smoltz	.15
68	Manny Ramirez	1.00
69	Juan Gonzalez	.50
70	F.P. Santangelo	.15
71	Moises Alou	.15
72	Alex Ochoa	.15
73	Chuck Knoblauch	.15
74	Raul Mondesi	.15
75	J.T. Snow	.15
76	Rickey Henderson	1.00

77	Bobby Bonilla	.15
78	Wade Boggs	1.25
79	Ivan Rodriguez	.75
80	Brian Jordan	.15
81	Al Leiter	.15
82	Jay Buhner	.15
83	Greg Maddux	1.25
84	Edgar Martinez	.15
85	Kevin Brown	.15
86	Eric Young	.15
87	Todd Hundley	.15
88	Ellis Burks	.15
89	Marquis Grissom	.15
90	Jose Canseco	.60
91	Henry Rodriguez	.15
92	Andy Pettitte	.45
93	Mark Grudzielanek	.15
94	Dwight Gooden	.15
95	Roberto Alomar	.50
96	Paul Wilson	.15
97	Will Clark	.15
98	Rondell White	.15
99	Charles Johnson	.15
100	Jim Edmonds	.15
101	Jason Giambi	.60
102	Billy Wagner	.15
103	Edgar Renteria	.15
104	Johnny Damon	.45
105	Jason Isringhausen	.15
106	Andruw Jones	1.00
107	Jose Guillen	.15
108	Kevin Orie	.15
109	*Brian Giles*	1.25
110	Danny Patterson	.15
111	Vladimir Guerrero	1.00
112	Scott Rolen	.75
113	Damon Mashore	.15
114	Nomar Garciaparra	1.25
115	Todd Walker	.15
116	Wilton Guerrero	.15
117	Bob Abreu	.25
118	Brooks Kieschnick	.15
119	Pokey Reese	.15
120	Todd Greene	.15
121	Dmitri Young	.15
122	Raul Casanova	.15
123	Glendon Rusch	.15
124	Jason Dickson	.15
125	Jorge Posada	.15
126	*Rod Myers*	.15
127	*Bubba Trammell*	.40
128	Scott Spiezio	.15
129	*Hideki Irabu*	.40
130	Wendell Magee	.15
131	Bartolo Colon	.15
132	Chris Holt	.15
133	Calvin Maduro	.15
134	Ray Montgomery	.15
135	Shannon Stewart	.15
136	Ken Griffey Jr. (Certified Stars)	1.00
137	Vladimir Guerrero (Certified Stars)	.50
138	Roger Clemens (Certified Stars)	.75
139	Mark McGwire (Certified Stars)	1.25
140	Albert Belle (Certified Stars)	.15
141	Derek Jeter (Certified Stars)	1.50
142	Juan Gonzalez (Certified Stars)	.25
143	Greg Maddux (Certified Stars)	.60
144	Alex Rodriguez (Certified Stars)	1.25
145	Jeff Bagwell (Certified Stars)	.50
146	Cal Ripken Jr. (Certified Stars)	1.50
147	Tony Gwynn (Certified Stars)	.60
148	Frank Thomas (Certified Stars)	.50
149	Hideo Nomo (Certified Stars)	.25
150	Andruw Jones (Certified Stars)	.50

Red

	NM/M
Common Certified Red:	1.00
Certified Red Stars:	5X

(See 1997 Pinnacle Certified for checklist and base values.)

Mirror Red

	NM/M
Common Mirror Red:	3.00
Mirror Red Stars:	12X

(See 1997 Pinnacle Certified for checklist and base values.)

Mirror Blue

	NM/M
Common Mirror Blue:	4.00
Mirror Blue Stars:	15X

(See 1997 Pinnacle Certified for checklist and base values.)

Mirror Gold

	NM/M
Common Mirror Gold:	7.50
Mirror Gold Stars:	35X

(See 1997 Pinnacle Certified for checklist and base values.)

Mirror Black

	NM/M
Common Player:	100.00

(Star cards valued at 150-250X base value.)

Lasting Impression

		NM/M
Complete Set (20):		40.00
Common Player:		1.00
1	Cal Ripken Jr.	7.50
2	Ken Griffey Jr.	5.00
3	Mo Vaughn	1.00
4	Brian Jordan	1.00
5	Mark McGwire	6.00
6	Chuck Knoblauch	1.00
7	Sammy Sosa	3.00
8	Brady Anderson	1.00
9	Frank Thomas	2.00
10	Tony Gwynn	3.00
11	Roger Clemens	4.00
12	Alex Rodriguez	6.00
13	Paul Molitor	2.00
14	Kenny Lofton	1.00
15	John Smoltz	1.00
16	Roberto Alomar	1.50
17	Randy Johnson	2.00
18	Ryne Sandberg	3.00
19	Manny Ramirez	2.00
20	Mike Mussina	1.50

Team

		NM/M
Complete Set (20):		30.00
Common Player:		.50
Gold:		3X
Mirror Gold:		15X
Sample:		1X
1	Frank Thomas	1.50
2	Jeff Bagwell	1.50
3	Derek Jeter	4.00
4	Chipper Jones	2.00
5	Alex Rodriguez	3.00
6	Ken Caminiti	.50
7	Cal Ripken Jr.	4.00
8	Mo Vaughn	.50
9	Ivan Rodriguez	1.00
10	Mike Piazza	2.50
11	Juan Gonzalez	.75
12	Barry Bonds	4.00
13	Ken Griffey Jr.	2.50
14	Andruw Jones	1.50
15	Albert Belle	.50
16	Gary Sheffield	.75
17	Andy Pettitte	.65
18	Hideo Nomo	.75
19	Greg Maddux	2.00
20	John Smoltz	.50

1997 PINNACLE INSIDE

		NM/M
Complete Set (150):		15.00
Common Player:		.05
Common Club Edition:		.75
Club Edition Stars:		5X
Common Diamond Edition:		5.00
Diamond Edition Stars:		25X
Unopened Can (10):		2.00
Case Cans (48):		60.00
1	David Cone	.05
2	Sammy Sosa	1.00
3	Joe Carter	.05
4	Juan Gonzalez	.40
5	Hideo Nomo	.40
6	Moises Alou	.05
7	Marc Newfield	.05
8	Alex Rodriguez	2.00
9	Kimera Bartee	.05
10	Chuck Knoblauch	.05
11	Jason Isringhausen	.05
12	Jermaine Allensworth	.05
13	Frank Thomas	.75
14	Paul Molitor	.75
15	John Mabry	.05
16	Greg Maddux	1.00
17	Rafael Palmeiro	.65
18	Brian Jordan	.05
19	Ken Griffey Jr.	1.50
20	Brady Anderson	.05
21	Ruben Sierra	.05
22	Travis Fryman	.05
23	Cal Ripken Jr.	2.50
24	Will Clark	.05
25	Todd Hollandsworth	.05
26	Kevin Brown	.05
27	Mike Piazza	1.50
28	Craig Biggio	.05
29	Paul Wilson	.05
30	Andres Galarraga	.05
31	Chipper Jones	1.00
32	Jason Giambi	.65
33	Ernie Young	.05
34	Marty Cordova	.05
35	Albert Belle	.05
36	Roger Clemens	1.25
37	Ryne Sandberg	1.00
38	Henry Rodriguez	.05
39	Jay Buhner	.05
40	Raul Mondesi	.05
41	Jeff Fassero	.05
42	Edgar Martinez	.05
43	Trey Beamon	.05
44	Mo Vaughn	.05
45	Gary Sheffield	.40
46	Ray Durham	.05
47	Brett Butler	.05
48	Ivan Rodriguez	.65
49	Fred McGriff	.05
50	Dean Palmer	.05
51	Rickey Henderson	.75
52	Andy Pettitte	.30
53	Bobby Bonilla	.05
54	Shawn Green	.50
55	Tino Martinez	.05
56	Tony Gwynn	1.00
57	Tom Glavine	.35
58	Eric Young	.05
59	Kevin Appier	.05
60	Barry Bonds	2.50
61	Wade Boggs	1.00
62	Jason Kendall	.05
63	Jeff Bagwell	.75
64	Jeff Conine	.05
65	Greg Vaughn	.05
66	Eric Karros	.05
67	Manny Ramirez	.75
68	John Smoltz	.05
69	Terrell Wade	.05
70	John Wetteland	.05
71	Kenny Lofton	.05
72	Jim Thome	.65
73	Bill Pulsipher	.05
74	Darryl Strawberry	.05
75	Roberto Alomar	.25
76	Bobby Higginson	.05
77	James Baldwin	.05
78	Mark McGwire	2.00
79	Jose Canseco	.40
80	Mark Grudzielanek	.05
81	Ryan Klesko	.05
82	Javier Lopez	.05
83	Ken Caminiti	.05
84	Dave Nilsson	.05
85	Tim Salmon	.05
86	Cecil Fielder	.05
87	Derek Jeter	2.50
88	Garret Anderson	.05
89	Dwight Gooden	.05
90	Carlos Delgado	.50
91	Ugueth Urbina	.05
92	Chan Ho Park	.05
93	Eddie Murray	.75
94	Alex Ochoa	.05
95	Rusty Greer	.05
96	Mark Grace	.05
97	Pat Hentgen	.05
98	John Jaha	.05
99	Charles Johnson	.05
100	Jermaine Dye	.05
101	Quinton McCracken	.05
102	Troy Percival	.05
103	Shane Reynolds	.05
104	Rondell White	.05
105	Charles Nagy	.05
106	Alan Benes	.05
107	Tom Goodwin	.05
108	Ron Gant	.05
109	Dan Wilson	.05
110	Darin Erstad	.10
111	Matt Williams	.05
112	Barry Larkin	.05
113	Mariano Rivera	.15
114	Larry Walker	.05
115	Jim Edmonds	.05
116	Michael Tucker	.05
117	Todd Hundley	.05
118	Alex Fernandez	.05
119	J.T. Snow	.05
120	Ellis Burks	.05
121	Steve Finley	.05
122	Mike Mussina	.40
123	Curtis Pride	.05
124	Derek Bell	.05
125	Dante Bichette	.05
126	Terry Steinbach	.05
127	Randy Johnson	.75
128	Andruw Jones	.75
129	Vladimir Guerrero	.75
130	Ruben Rivera	.05
131	Billy Wagner	.05
132	Scott Rolen	.65
133	Rey Ordonez	.05
134	Karim Garcia	.05
135	George Arias	.05
136	Todd Greene	.05
137	Robin Jennings	.05
138	Raul Casanova	.05
139	Josh Booty	.05
140	Edgar Renteria	.05
141	Chad Mottola	.05
142	Dmitri Young	.05
143	Tony Clark	.05
144	Todd Walker	.05
145	Kevin Brown	.05
146	Nomar Garciaparra	1.00
147	Neifi Perez	.05
148	Derek Jeter, Todd Hollandsworth	.50
149	Pat Hentgen, John Smoltz	.05
150	Juan Gonzalez, Ken Caminiti	.05

Club Edition

	NM/M
Complete Club Edition Set (150):	300.00
Common Club Edition:	.75
Stars:	5X

(See 1997 Pinnacle Inside for checklist and base values.)

Diamond Edition

	NM/M
Common Diamond Edition:	5.00
Stars:	25X

(See 1997 Pinnacle Inside for checklist and base values.)

Cans

		NM/M
Complete Set (24):		10.00
Common Can:		.25
Sealed Cans:		2X
1	Ken Griffey Jr.	.75
2	Juan Gonzalez	.30
3	Frank Thomas	.40
4	Cal Ripken Jr.	1.50
5	Derek Jeter	1.50
6	Andruw Jones	.40
7	Alex Rodriguez	1.00
8	Mike Piazza	.75
9	Mo Vaughn	.25
10	Jeff Bagwell	.40
11	Ken Caminiti	.25
12	Andy Pettitte	.30
13	Barry Bonds	1.50
14	Mark McGwire	1.00
15	Ryan Klesko	.25
16	Manny Ramirez	.40
17	Ivan Rodriguez	.35
18	Chipper Jones	.50
19	Albert Belle	.25
20	Tony Gwynn	.50
21	Kenny Lofton	.25
22	Greg Maddux	.50
23	Hideo Nomo	.40
24	John Smoltz	.25

Dueling Dugouts

		NM/M
Complete Set (20):		65.00
Common Player:		1.25
1	Alex Rodriguez, Cal Ripken Jr.	10.00
2	Jeff Bagwell, Ken Caminiti	3.00
3	Barry Bonds, Albert Belle	10.00
4	Mike Piazza, Ivan Rodriguez	6.00
5	Chuck Knoblauch, Roberto Alomar	1.25
6	Ken Griffey Jr., Andruw Jones	6.00
7	Chipper Jones, Jim Thome	4.00
8	Frank Thomas, Mo Vaughn	3.00
9	Fred McGriff, Mark McGwire	7.50
10	Brian Jordan, Tony Gwynn	4.00
11	Barry Larkin, Derek Jeter	10.00
12	Kenny Lofton, Bernie Williams	1.25
13	Juan Gonzalez, Manny Ramirez	3.00
14	Will Clark, Rafael Palmeiro	2.50
15	Greg Maddux, Roger Clemens	4.50
16	John Smoltz, Andy Pettitte	1.25
17	Mariano Rivera, John Wetteland	1.25
18	Hideo Nomo, Mike Mussina	2.00
19	Todd Hollandsworth, Darin Erstad	1.25
20	Vladimir Guerrero, Karim Garcia	3.00

Fortysomething

		NM/M
Complete Set (16):		50.00
Common Player:		1.00
1	Juan Gonzalez	3.00
2	Barry Bonds	12.00
3	Ken Caminiti	1.00
4	Mark McGwire	10.00
5	Todd Hundley	1.00
6	Albert Belle	1.00
7	Ellis Burks	1.00
8	Jay Buhner	1.00
9	Brady Anderson	1.00
10	Vinny Castilla	1.00
11	Mo Vaughn	1.00
12	Ken Griffey Jr.	7.50
13	Sammy Sosa	6.50
14	Andres Galarraga	1.00
15	Gary Sheffield	2.00
16	Frank Thomas	5.00

1997 PINNACLE MINT COLLECTION

		NM/M
Complete Set (30):		25.00
Common Player:		.25
Silver Cards:		4X
Gold Cards:		6X
Die-Cuts:		50%
Wax Box (24):		25.00
1	Ken Griffey Jr.	2.00
2	Frank Thomas	1.25
3	Alex Rodriguez	2.50
4	Cal Ripken Jr.	3.00
5	Mo Vaughn	.25
6	Juan Gonzalez	.60
7	Mike Piazza	2.00
8	Albert Belle	.25
9	Chipper Jones	1.50
10	Andruw Jones	1.25
11	Greg Maddux	1.50
12	Hideo Nomo	.60
13	Jeff Bagwell	1.25
14	Manny Ramirez	1.25
15	Mark McGwire	2.50
16	Derek Jeter	3.00
17	Sammy Sosa	1.50
18	Barry Bonds	3.00
19	Chuck Knoblauch	.25
20	Dante Bichette	.25
21	Tony Gwynn	1.50
22	Ken Caminiti	.25
23	Gary Sheffield	.60
24	Tim Salmon	.25
25	Ivan Rodriguez	1.00
26	Henry Rodriguez	.25
27	Barry Larkin	.25
28	Ryan Klesko	.25
29	Brian Jordan	.25
30	Jay Buhner	.25

Coins

		NM/M
Complete Set (30):		35.00
Common Brass Coin:		.25
Nickel Coins:		2X
Gold Plated Coins:		6X
Silver Coins:		20X
24K Gold Coins: Value undermined		
1	Ken Griffey Jr.	2.50
2	Frank Thomas	1.50
3	Alex Rodriguez	3.00
4	Cal Ripken Jr.	4.00
5	Mo Vaughn	.25
6	Juan Gonzalez	.75
7	Mike Piazza	2.50
8	Albert Belle	.25
9	Chipper Jones	2.00
10	Andruw Jones	1.50
11	Greg Maddux	2.00
12	Hideo Nomo	.75
13	Jeff Bagwell	1.50
14	Manny Ramirez	1.50
15	Mark McGwire	3.00
16	Derek Jeter	4.00
17	Sammy Sosa	2.00
18	Barry Bonds	4.00
19	Chuck Knoblauch	.25
20	Dante Bichette	.25
21	Tony Gwynn	2.00
22	Ken Caminiti	.25
23	Gary Sheffield	.65
24	Tim Salmon	.25
25	Ivan Rodriguez	1.00
26	Henry Rodriguez	.25
27	Barry Larkin	.25
28	Ryan Klesko	.25
29	Brian Jordan	.25
30	Jay Buhner	.25

1997 PINNACLE X-PRESS

		NM/M
Complete Set (150):		7.50
Common Player:		.05
Men of Summer:		4X
Pack (8):		.75
Wax Box (24):		10.00

1	Larry Walker	.05
2	Andy Pettitte	.30
3	Matt Williams	.05
4	Juan Gonzalez	.40
5	Frank Thomas	.75
6	Kenny Lofton	.05
7	Ken Griffey Jr.	1.25
8	Andres Galarraga	.05
9	Greg Maddux	1.00
10	Hideo Nomo	.40
11	Cecil Fielder	.05
12	Jose Canseco	.40
13	Tony Gwynn	1.00
14	Eddie Murray	.75
15	Alex Rodriguez	1.50
16	Mike Piazza	1.25
17	Ken Hill	.05
18	Chuck Knoblauch	.05
19	Ellis Burks	.05
20	Rafael Palmeiro	.65
21	Vinny Castilla	.05
22	Rusty Greer	.05
23	Chipper Jones	1.00
24	Rey Ordonez	.05
25	Mariano Rivera	.15
26	Garret Anderson	.05
27	Edgar Martinez	.05
28	Dante Bichette	.05
29	Todd Hundley	.05
30	Barry Bonds	2.00
31	Barry Larkin	.05
32	Derek Jeter	2.00
33	Marquis Grissom	.05
34	David Justice	.05
35	Ivan Rodriguez	.65
36	Jay Buhner	.05
37	Fred McGriff	.05
38	Brady Anderson	.05
39	Tony Clark	.05
40	Eric Young	.05
41	Charles Nagy	.05
42	Mark McGwire	1.50
43	Paul O'Neill	.05
44	Tino Martinez	.05
45	Ryne Sandberg	1.00
46	Bernie Williams	.05
47	Albert Belle	.05
48	Jeff Cirillo	.05
49	Tim Salmon	.05
50	Steve Finley	.05
51	Lance Johnson	.05
52	John Smoltz	.05
53	Javier Lopez	.05
54	Roger Clemens	1.00
55	Kevin Appier	.05
56	Ken Caminiti	.05
57	Cal Ripken Jr.	2.00
58	Moises Alou	.05
59	Marty Cordova	.05
60	David Cone	.05
61	Manny Ramirez	.75
62	Ray Durham	.05
63	Jermaine Dye	.05
64	Craig Biggio	.05
65	Will Clark	.05
66	Omar Vizquel	.05
67	Bernard Gilkey	.05
68	Greg Vaughn	.05
69	Wade Boggs	1.00
70	Dave Nilsson	.05
71	Mark Grace	.05
72	Dean Palmer	.05
73	Sammy Sosa	1.00
74	Mike Mussina	.30
75	Alex Fernandez	.05
76	Henry Rodriguez	.05
77	Travis Fryman	.05
78	Jeff Bagwell	.75
79	Pat Hentgen	.05
80	Gary Sheffield	.40
81	Jim Edmonds	.05
82	Darin Erstad	.10
83	Mark Grudzielanek	.05
84	Jim Thome	.65
85	Bobby Higginson	.05
86	Al Martin	.05
87	Jason Giambi	.50
88	Mo Vaughn	.05
89	Jeff Conine	.05

90 Edgar Renteria .05
91 Andy Ashby .05
92 Ryan Klesko .05
93 John Jaha .05
94 Paul Molitor .75
95 Brian Hunter .05
96 Randy Johnson .75
97 Joey Hamilton .05
98 Billy Wagner .05
99 John Wetteland .05
100 Jeff Fassero .05
101 Rondell White .05
102 Kevin Brown .05
103 Andy Benes .05
104 Raul Mondesi .05
105 Todd Hollandsworth .05
106 Alex Ochoa .05
107 Bobby Bonilla .05
108 Brian Jordan .05
109 Tom Glavine .35
110 Ron Gant .05
111 Jason Kendall .05
112 Roberto Alomar .30
113 Troy Percival .05
114 Michael Tucker .05
115 Joe Carter .05
116 Andruw Jones .75
117 Nomar Garciaparra 1.00
118 Todd Walker .05
119 Jose Guillen .05
120 *Bubba Trammell* .20
121 Wilton Guerrero .05
122 Bob Abreu .15
123 Vladimir Guerrero .75
124 Dmitri Young .05
125 Kevin Orie .05
126 Glendon Rusch .05
127 Brooks Kieschnick .05
128 Scott Spiezio .05
129 *Brian Giles* .75
130 Jason Dickson .05
131 Damon Mashore .05
132 Wendell Magee .05
133 Matt Morris .05
134 Scott Rolen .65
135 Shannon Stewart .05
136 *Deivi Cruz* .15
137 *Hideki Irabu* .15
138 Larry Walker .05
139 Ken Griffey Jr. .65
140 Frank Thomas .40
141 Ivan Rodriguez .30
142 Randy Johnson .40
143 Mark McGwire .75
144 Tino Martinez .05
145 Tony Clark .05
146 Mike Piazza .50
147 Alex Rodriguez .75
148 Roger Clemens Checklist .50
149 Greg Maddux Checklist .45
150 Hideo Nomo Checklist .20

Men of Summer

NM/M
Complete Set (150): 50.00
Common Player: .25
(See 1997 Pinnacle X-Press for checklist and base card values.)
Stars: 3X

Far & Away

NM/M
Complete Set (18): 25.00
Common Player: .50
1 Albert Belle .50
2 Mark McGwire 4.50
3 Frank Thomas 1.75
4 Mo Vaughn .50
5 Jeff Bagwell 1.75
6 Juan Gonzalez 1.00
7 Mike Piazza 3.50
8 Andruw Jones 1.75
9 Chipper Jones 2.50
10 Gary Sheffield 1.00
11 Sammy Sosa 2.50
12 Darin Erstad .75
13 Jay Buhner .50
14 Ken Griffey Jr. 3.50
15 Ken Caminiti .50
16 Brady Anderson .50
17 Manny Ramirez 1.75
18 Alex Rodriguez 4.50

Melting Pot

NM/M
Complete Set (20): 110.00
Common Player: 1.50
Samples: 1X
1 Jose Guillen 1.50
2 Vladimir Guerrero 8.00
3 Andruw Jones 8.00
4 Larry Walker 1.50
5 Manny Ramirez 8.00
6 Ken Griffey Jr. 10.00
7 Alex Rodriguez 12.00
8 Frank Thomas 8.00
9 Juan Gonzalez 4.00
10 Ivan Rodriguez 6.00
11 Hideo Nomo 4.00
12 Rafael Palmeiro 6.00
13 Dave Nilsson 1.50
14 Nomar Garciaparra 9.00
15 Wilton Guerrero 1.50
16 Sammy Sosa 9.00
17 Edgar Renteria 1.50
18 Cal Ripken Jr. 16.00
19 Derek Jeter 16.00
20 Rey Ordonez 1.50

Metal Works

NM/M
Complete Set (20): 25.00
Common Player: .50
Silver: 3X
Gold: 6X
1 Ken Griffey Jr. 2.00
2 Frank Thomas 1.00
3 Andruw Jones 1.00
4 Alex Rodriguez 2.50
5 Derek Jeter 3.00
6 Cal Ripken Jr. 3.00
7 Mike Piazza 2.00
8 Chipper Jones 1.50
9 Juan Gonzalez .65
10 Greg Maddux 1.50
11 Tony Gwynn 1.50
12 Jeff Bagwell 1.00
13 Albert Belle .50
14 Mark McGwire 2.50
15 Nomar Garciaparra 1.50
16 Mo Vaughn .50
17 Andy Pettitte .65
18 Manny Ramirez 1.00
19 Kenny Lofton .50
20 Roger Clemens 1.75

Swing for the Fences

NM/M
Complete Set (60): 20.00
Common Player: .15
(1) Sandy Alomar Jr. .15
(2) Moises Alou .15
(3) Brady Anderson .15
(4) Jeff Bagwell 1.00
(5) Derek Bell .15
(6) Jay Bell .15
(7) Albert Belle .15
(8) Geronimo Berroa .15
(9) Dante Bichette .15
(10) Barry Bonds 2.50
(11) Bobby Bonilla .15
(12) Jay Buhner .15
(13) Ellis Burks .15
(14) Ken Caminiti .15
(15) Jose Canseco .40
(16) Joe Carter .15
(17) Vinny Castilla .15
(18) Tony Clark .15
(19) Carlos Delgado .50
(20) Jim Edmonds .15
(21) Cecil Fielder .15
(22) Andres Galarraga .15
(23) Ron Gant .15
(24) Bernard Gilkey .15
(25) Juan Gonzalez .50
(26) Ken Griffey Jr. (AL WINNER) 4.00
(27) Vladimir Guerrero 1.00
(28) Todd Hundley .15
(29) John Jaha .15
(30) Andruw Jones 1.00
(31) Chipper Jones 1.25
(32) David Justice .15
(33) Jeff Kent .15
(34) Ryan Klesko .15
(35) Barry Larkin .15
(36) Mike Lieberthal .15
(37) Javy Lopez .15
(38) Edgar Martinez .15
(39) Tino Martinez .15
(40) Fred McGriff .15
(41) Mark McGwire (AL/NL WINNER) 4.00
(42) Raul Mondesi .15
(43) Tim Naehring .15
(44) Dave Nillson .15
(45) Rafael Palmeiro .75
(46) Dean Palmer .15
(47) Mike Piazza 1.50
(48) Cal Ripken Jr. 2.50
(49) Henry Rodriguez .15
(50) Tim Salmon .15
(51) Gary Sheffield .40
(52) Sammy Sosa 1.25
(53) Terry Steinbach .15
(54) Frank Thomas 1.00
(55) Jim Thome .75
(56) Mo Vaughn .15
(57) Larry Walker (NL Winner) 1.25
(58) Rondell White .15
(59) Matt Williams .15
(60) Todd Zeile .15

Swing/ Fences Gold

NM/M
Complete Set (60): 125.00
Common Player: 1.00
Stars: 4X
Andruw Jones Autograph: 25.00
(See 1997 Pinnacle X-Press Swing for the Fences for checklist and base values.)

1998 PINNACLE

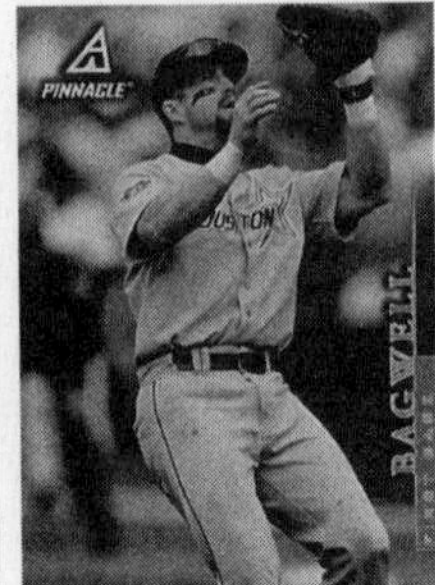

NM/M
Complete Set (200): 12.50
Common Player: .05
Pack (10): 1.00
Wax Box (18): 12.00
1 Tony Gwynn 1.00
2 Pedro Martinez .75
3 Kenny Lofton .05
4 Curt Schilling .35
5 Shawn Estes .05
6 Tom Glavine .35
7 Mike Piazza 1.50
8 Ray Lankford .05
9 Barry Larkin .05
10 Tony Womack .05
11 Jeff Blauser .05
12 Rod Beck .05
13 Larry Walker .05
14 Greg Maddux 1.00
15 Mark Grace .05
16 Ken Caminiti .05
17 Bobby Jones .05
18 Chipper Jones 1.00
19 Javier Lopez .05
20 Moises Alou .05
21 Royce Clayton .05
22 Darryl Kile .05
23 Barry Bonds 2.50
24 Steve Finley .05
25 Andres Galarraga .05
26 Denny Neagle .05
27 Todd Hundley .05
28 Jeff Bagwell .75
29 Andy Pettitte .25
30 Darin Erstad .15
31 Carlos Delgado .50
32 Matt Williams .05
33 Will Clark .05
34 Vinny Castilla .05
35 Brad Radke .05
36 John Olerud .05
37 Andruw Jones .75
38 Jason Giambi .50
39 Scott Rolen .65
40 Gary Sheffield .40
41 Jimmy Key .05
42 Kevin Appier .05
43 Wade Boggs 1.00
44 Hideo Nomo .40
45 Manny Ramirez .75
46 Wilton Guerrero .05
47 Travis Fryman .05
48 Chili Davis .05
49 Jeromy Burnitz .05
50 Craig Biggio .05
51 Tim Salmon .05
52 Jose Cruz Jr. .05
53 Sammy Sosa 1.00
54 Hideki Irabu .05
55 Chan Ho Park .05
56 Robin Ventura .05
57 Jose Guillen .05
58 Deion Sanders .05
59 Jose Canseco .40
60 Jay Buhner .05
61 Rafael Palmeiro .65
62 Vladimir Guerrero .75
63 Mark McGwire 2.00
64 Derek Jeter 2.50
65 Bobby Bonilla .05
66 Raul Mondesi .05
67 Paul Molitor .75
68 Joe Carter .05
69 Marquis Grissom .05
70 Juan Gonzalez .40
71 Kevin Orie .05
72 Rusty Greer .05
73 Henry Rodriguez .05
74 Fernando Tatis .05
75 John Valentin .05
76 Matt Morris .05
77 Ray Durham .05
78 Geronimo Berroa .05
79 Scott Brosius .05
80 Willie Greene .05
81 Rondell White .05
82 Doug Drabek .05
83 Derek Bell .05
84 Butch Huskey .05
85 Doug Jones .05
86 Jeff Kent .05
87 Jim Edmonds .05
88 Mark McLemore .05
89 Todd Zeile .05
90 Edgardo Alfonzo .05
91 Carlos Baerga .05
92 Jorge Fabregas .05
93 Alan Benes .05
94 Troy Percival .05
95 Edgar Renteria .05
96 Jeff Fassero .05
97 Reggie Sanders .05

98	Dean Palmer	.05
99	J.T. Snow	.05
100	Dave Nilsson	.05
101	Dan Wilson	.05
102	Robb Nen	.05
103	Damion Easley	.05
104	Kevin Foster	.05
105	Jose Offerman	.05
106	Steve Cooke	.05
107	Matt Stairs	.05
108	Darryl Hamilton	.05
109	Steve Karsay	.05
110	Gary DiSarcina	.05
111	Dante Bichette	.05
112	Billy Wagner	.05
113	David Segui	.05
114	Bobby Higginson	.05
115	Jeffrey Hammonds	.05
116	Kevin Brown	.05
117	Paul Sorrento	.05
118	Mark Leiter	.05
119	Charles Nagy	.05
120	Danny Patterson	.05
121	Brian McRae	.05
122	Jay Bell	.05
123	Jamie Moyer	.05
124	Carl Everett	.05
125	Greg Colbrunn	.05
126	Jason Kendall	.05
127	Luis Sojo	.05
128	Mike Lieberthal	.05
129	Reggie Jefferson	.05
130	Cal Eldred	.05
131	Orel Hershiser	.05
132	Doug Glanville	.05
133	Willie Blair	.05
134	Neifi Perez	.05
135	Sean Berry	.05
136	Chuck Finley	.05
137	Alex Gonzalez	.05
138	Dennis Eckersley	.65
139	Kenny Rogers	.05
140	Troy O'Leary	.05
141	Roger Bailey	.05
142	Yamil Benitez	.05
143	Wally Joyner	.05
144	Bobby Witt	.05
145	Pete Schourek	.05
146	Terry Steinbach	.05
147	B.J. Surhoff	.05
148	Esteban Loaiza	.05
149	Heathcliff Slocumb	.05
150	Ed Sprague	.05
151	Gregg Jefferies	.05
152	Scott Erickson	.05
153	Jaime Navarro	.05
154	David Wells	.05
155	Alex Fernandez	.05
156	Tim Belcher	.05
157	Mark Grudzielanek	.05
158	Scott Hatteberg	.05
159	Paul Konerko	.15
160	Ben Grieve	.05
161	Abraham Nunez	.05
162	Shannon Stewart	.05
163	Jaret Wright	.05
164	Derrek Lee	.50
165	Todd Dunwoody	.05
166	*Steve Woodard*	.10
167	Ryan McGuire	.05
168	Jeremi Gonzalez	.05
169	Mark Kotsay	.05
170	Brett Tomko	.05
171	Bobby Estalella	.05
172	Livan Hernandez	.05
173	Todd Helton	.75
174	Garrett Stephenson	.05
175	Pokey Reese	.05
176	Tony Saunders	.05
177	Antone Williamson	.05
178	Bartolo Colon	.05
179	Karim Garcia	.05
180	Juan Encarnacion	.05
181	Jacob Cruz	.05
182	Alex Rodriguez	2.00
183	Cal Ripken Jr., Roberto Alomar	1.00
184	Roger Clemens	1.25
185	Derek Jeter	2.00
186	Frank Thomas	.75
187	Ken Griffey Jr.	1.50
188	Mark McGwire	1.00
189	Tino Martinez	.05
190	Larry Walker	.05
191	Brady Anderson	.05
192	Jeff Bagwell	.75
193	Ken Griffey Jr.	1.50
194	Chipper Jones	1.00
195	Ray Lankford	.05
196	Jim Thome	.65
197	Nomar Garciaparra	1.00
198	Checklist	.05
199	Checklist	.05
200	Checklist	.05

9	Ken Griffey Jr.	2.00
24	Frank Thomas	1.50

Artist's Proofs

		NM/M
Complete Set (100):		375.00
Common Artist's Proof:		1.50
1	Tony Gwynn	12.50
2	Pedro Martinez	10.00
3	Kenny Lofton	1.50
4	Curt Schilling	3.00
5	Shawn Estes	1.50
6	Tom Glavine	3.00
7	Mike Piazza	16.00
8	Ray Lankford	1.50
9	Barry Larkin	1.50
10	Tony Womack	1.50
11	Jeff Blauser	1.50
12	Rod Beck	1.50
13	Larry Walker	1.50
14	Greg Maddux	12.50
15	Mark Grace	1.50
16	Ken Caminiti	1.50
17	Bobby Jones	1.50
18	Chipper Jones	12.50
19	Javier Lopez	1.50
20	Moises Alou	1.50
21	Royce Clayton	1.50
22	Darryl Kile	1.50
23	Barry Bonds	25.00
24	Steve Finley	1.50
25	Andres Galarraga	1.50
26	Denny Neagle	1.50
27	Todd Hundley	1.50
28	Jeff Bagwell	10.00
29	Andy Pettitte	2.50
30	Darin Erstad	2.00
31	Carlos Delgado	4.00
32	Matt Williams	1.50
33	Will Clark	1.50
34	Brad Radke	1.50
35	John Olerud	1.50
36	Andruw Jones	10.00
37	Scott Rolen	7.50
38	Gary Sheffield	3.00
39	Jimmy Key	1.50
40	Wade Boggs	12.50
41	Hideo Nomo	5.00
42	Manny Ramirez	10.00
43	Wilton Guerrero	1.50
44	Travis Fryman	1.50
45	Craig Biggio	1.50
46	Tim Salmon	1.50
47	Jose Cruz Jr.	1.50
48	Sammy Sosa	12.50
49	Hideki Irabu	1.50
50	Jose Guillen	1.50
51	Deion Sanders	1.50
52	Jose Canseco	4.00
53	Jay Buhner	1.50
54	Rafael Palmeiro	7.50
55	Vladimir Guerrero	10.00
56	Mark McGwire	20.00
57	Derek Jeter	25.00
58	Bobby Bonilla	1.50
59	Raul Mondesi	1.50
60	Paul Molitor	10.00
61	Joe Carter	1.50
62	Marquis Grissom	1.50
63	Juan Gonzalez	5.00
64	Dante Bichette	1.50
65	Shannon Stewart	1.50
66	Jaret Wright	1.50
67	Derrek Lee	6.00
68	Todd Dunwoody	1.50
69	Steve Woodard	1.50
70	Ryan McGuire	1.50
71	Jeremi Gonzalez	1.50
72	Mark Kotsay	1.50
73	Brett Tomko	1.50
74	Bobby Estalella	1.50
75	Livan Hernandez	1.50
76	Todd Helton	10.00
77	Garrett Stephenson	1.50
78	Pokey Reese	1.50
79	Tony Saunders	1.50
80	Antone Williamson	1.50
81	Bartolo Colon	1.50
82	Karim Garcia	1.50
83	Juan Encarnacion	1.50
84	Jacob Cruz	1.50
85	Alex Rodriguez	20.00
86	Cal Ripken Jr., Roberto Alomar	15.00
87	Roger Clemens	13.50
88	Derek Jeter	25.00
89	Frank Thomas	10.00
90	Ken Griffey Jr.	16.00
91	Mark McGwire	20.00
92	Tino Martinez	1.50
93	Larry Walker	1.50
94	Brady Anderson	1.50
95	Jeff Bagwell	10.00
96	Ken Griffey Jr.	16.00
97	Chipper Jones	12.50
98	Ray Lankford	1.50
99	Jim Thome	7.50
100	Nomar Garciaparra	12.50

Museum Collection

		NM/M
Complete Museum Set (100):		110.00
Common Museum:		.50
1	Tony Gwynn	3.00
2	Pedro Martinez	2.50
3	Kenny Lofton	.50
4	Curt Schilling	1.50
5	Shawn Estes	.50
6	Tom Glavine	1.50
7	Mike Piazza	4.00
8	Ray Lankford	.50
9	Barry Larkin	.50
10	Tony Womack	.50
11	Jeff Blauser	.50
12	Rod Beck	.50
13	Larry Walker	.50
14	Greg Maddux	3.00
15	Mark Grace	.50
16	Ken Caminiti	.50
17	Bobby Jones	.50
18	Chipper Jones	3.00
19	Javier Lopez	.50
20	Moises Alou	.50
21	Royce Clayton	.50
22	Darryl Kile	.50
23	Barry Bonds	6.00
24	Steve Finley	.50
25	Andres Galarraga	.50
26	Denny Neagle	.50
27	Todd Hundley	.50
28	Jeff Bagwell	2.50
29	Andy Pettitte	1.00
30	Darin Erstad	1.00
31	Carlos Delgado	1.50
32	Matt Williams	.50
33	Will Clark	.50
34	Brad Radke	.50
35	John Olerud	.50
36	Andruw Jones	2.50
37	Scott Rolen	2.00
38	Gary Sheffield	1.50
39	Jimmy Key	.50
40	Wade Boggs	3.00
41	Hideo Nomo	1.25
42	Manny Ramirez	2.50
43	Wilton Guerrero	.50
44	Travis Fryman	.50
45	Craig Biggio	.50
46	Tim Salmon	.50
47	Jose Cruz Jr.	.50
48	Sammy Sosa	3.00
49	Hideki Irabu	.50
50	Jose Guillen	.50
51	Deion Sanders	.50
52	Jose Canseco	1.50
53	Jay Buhner	.50
54	Rafael Palmeiro	2.00
55	Vladimir Guerrero	2.50
56	Mark McGwire	5.00
57	Derek Jeter	6.00
58	Bobby Bonilla	.50
59	Raul Mondesi	.50
60	Paul Molitor	2.50
61	Joe Carter	.50
62	Marquis Grissom	.50
63	Juan Gonzalez	1.25
64	Dante Bichette	.50
65	Shannon Stewart	.50
66	Jaret Wright	.50
67	Derrek Lee	2.00
68	Todd Dunwoody	.50
69	Steve Woodard	.50
70	Ryan McGuire	.50
71	Jeremi Gonzalez	.50
72	Mark Kotsay	.50
73	Brett Tomko	.50
74	Bobby Estalella	.50
75	Livan Hernandez	.50
76	Todd Helton	2.50
77	Garrett Stephenson	.50
78	Pokey Reese	.50
79	Tony Saunders	.50
80	Antone Williamson	.50
81	Bartolo Colon	.50
82	Karim Garcia	.50
83	Juan Encarnacion	.50
84	Jacob Cruz	.50
85	Alex Rodriguez	5.00
86	Cal Ripken Jr., Roberto Alomar	3.50
87	Roger Clemens	2.50
88	Derek Jeter	6.00
89	Frank Thomas	2.50
90	Ken Griffey Jr.	4.00
91	Mark McGwire	5.00
92	Tino Martinez	.50
93	Larry Walker	.50
94	Brady Anderson	.50
95	Jeff Bagwell	2.50
96	Ken Griffey Jr.	4.00
97	Chipper Jones	3.00
98	Ray Lankford	.50
99	Jim Thome	2.00
100	Nomar Garciaparra	3.00

Press Plates

	NM/M
Common Player:	50.00

(See 1998 Pinnacle and inserts for checklists.)

Epix

		NM/M
Complete Set (24):		45.00
Common Player:		1.00
Purples:		2X
Emeralds:		4X
1	Ken Griffey Jr. G	3.00
2	Juan Gonzalez G	1.25
3	Jeff Bagwell G	2.00
4	Ivan Rodriguez G	1.50
5	Nomar Garciaparra G	2.50
6	Ryne Sandberg G	2.50
7	Frank Thomas S	2.00
8	Derek Jeter S	5.00
9	Tony Gwynn S	2.50
10	Albert Belle S	1.00
11	Scott Rolen S	1.50
12	Barry Larkin S	1.00
13	Alex Rodriguez M	4.00
14	Cal Ripken Jr. M	5.00
15	Chipper Jones M	2.50
16	Roger Clemens M	2.75
17	Mo Vaughn M	1.00
18	Mark McGwire M	4.00
19	Mike Piazza P	3.00
20	Andruw Jones P	2.00
21	Greg Maddux P	2.50
22	Barry Bonds P	5.00
23	Paul Molitor P	2.00
24	Eddie Murray P	2.00

Hit It Here

		NM/M
Complete Set (10):		12.00
Common Player:		.50
Inserted 1:17		
Samples:		1X
1	Larry Walker	.50
2	Ken Griffey Jr.	2.00
3	Mike Piazza	2.00
4	Frank Thomas	1.50
5	Barry Bonds	3.00
6	Albert Belle	.50
7	Tino Martinez	.50
8	Mark McGwire	2.50
9	Juan Gonzalez	.75
10	Jeff Bagwell	1.00

Spellbound

		NM/M
Complete Set (50):		90.00
Common Card:		.75
Inserted 1:17		
1	Mark McGwire (M)	3.50
2	Mark McGwire (C)	3.50
3	Mark McGwire (G)	3.50
4	Mark McGwire (W)	3.50
5	Mark McGwire (I)	3.50
6	Mark McGwire (R)	3.50
7	Mark McGwire (E)	3.50
8	Roger Clemens (R)	2.50
9	Roger Clemens (O)	2.50
10	Roger Clemens (C)	2.50
11	Roger Clemens (K)	2.50
12	Roger Clemens (E)	2.50
13	Roger Clemens (T)	2.50
14	Frank Thomas (B)	1.50
15	Frank Thomas (I)	1.50
16	Frank Thomas (G)	1.50
17	Frank Thomas (H)	1.50
18	Frank Thomas (U)	1.50
19	Frank Thomas (R)	1.50
20	Frank Thomas (T)	1.50
21	Scott Rolen (R)	1.25
22	Scott Rolen (O)	1.25
23	Scott Rolen (L)	1.25
24	Scott Rolen (E)	1.25
25	Scott Rolen (N)	1.25
26	Ken Griffey Jr. (G)	3.00
27	Ken Griffey Jr. (R)	3.00
28	Ken Griffey Jr. (I)	3.00
29	Ken Griffey Jr. (F)	3.00
30	Ken Griffey Jr. (F)	3.00
31	Ken Griffey Jr. (E)	3.00
32	Ken Griffey Jr. (Y)	3.00
33	Larry Walker (W)	.75
34	Larry Walker (A)	.75
35	Larry Walker (L)	.75
36	Larry Walker (K)	.75
37	Larry Walker (E)	.75
38	Larry Walker (R)	.75
39	Nomar Garciaparra (N)	2.25
40	Nomar Garciaparra (O)	2.25
41	Nomar Garciaparra (M)	2.25
42	Nomar Garciaparra (A)	2.25
43	Nomar Garciaparra (R)	2.25
44	Cal Ripken Jr. (C)	4.50
45	Cal Ripken Jr. (A)	4.50
46	Cal Ripken Jr. (L)	4.50
47	Tony Gwynn (T)	2.25
48	Tony Gwynn (O)	2.25
49	Tony Gwynn (N)	2.25
50	Tony Gwynn (Y)	2.25

1998 PINNACLE INSIDE

		NM/M
Complete Set (150):		12.00
Common Player:		.05
Club Edition (1:7):		4X
Diamond Edition (1:67):		10X
Can (10):		1.00
Box (48):		45.00
1	Darin Erstad	.15
2	Derek Jeter	2.50
3	Alex Rodriguez	2.00
4	Bobby Higginson	.05
5	Nomar Garciaparra	1.00
6	Kenny Lofton	.05
7	Ivan Rodriguez	.65
8	Cal Ripken Jr.	2.50
9	Todd Hundley	.05
10	Chipper Jones	1.00
11	Barry Larkin	.05
12	Roberto Alomar	.15
13	Mo Vaughn	.05
14	Sammy Sosa	1.00
15	Sandy Alomar Jr.	.05
16	Albert Belle	.05
17	Scott Rolen	.65
18	Pokey Reese	.05
19	Ryan Klesko	.05
20	Andres Galarraga	.05
21	Justin Thompson	.05
22	Gary Sheffield	.40
23	David Justice	.05
24	Ken Griffey Jr.	1.50
25	Andruw Jones	.75
26	Jeff Bagwell	.75
27	Vladimir Guerrero	.75
28	Mike Piazza	1.50
29	Chuck Knoblauch	.05
30	Rondell White	.05
31	Greg Maddux	1.00
32	Andy Pettitte	.20
33	Larry Walker	.05
34	Bobby Estalella	.05
35	Frank Thomas	.75
36	Tony Womack	.05
37	Tony Gwynn	1.00
38	Barry Bonds	2.50
39	Randy Johnson	.75
40	Mark McGwire	2.00
41	Juan Gonzalez	.40
42	Tim Salmon	.05
43	John Smoltz	.05
44	Rafael Palmeiro	.65
45	Mark Grace	.05
46	Mike Cameron	.05
47	Jim Thome	.65
48	Neifi Perez	.05
49	Kevin Brown	.05
50	Craig Biggio	.05
51	Bernie Williams	.05
52	Hideo Nomo	.40
53	Bob Abreu	.15
54	Edgardo Alfonzo	.05
55	Wade Boggs	1.00
56	Jose Guillen	.05
57	Ken Caminiti	.05
58	Paul Molitor	.75
59	Shawn Estes	.05
60	Edgar Martinez	.05
61	Livan Hernandez	.05
62	Ray Lankford	.05
63	Rusty Greer	.05
64	Jim Edmonds	.05
65	Tom Glavine	.35
66	Alan Benes	.05
67	Will Clark	.05
68	Garret Anderson	.05
69	Javier Lopez	.05
70	Mike Mussina	.35
71	Kevin Orie	.05
72	Matt Williams	.05
73	Bobby Bonilla	.05
74	Ruben Rivera	.05
75	Jason Giambi	.60
76	Todd Walker	.05
77	Tino Martinez	.05
78	Matt Morris	.05
79	Fernando Tatis	.05
80	Todd Greene	.05
81	Fred McGriff	.05
82	Brady Anderson	.05
83	Mark Kotsay	.05
84	Raul Mondesi	.05
85	Moises Alou	.05
86	Roger Clemens	1.25
87	Wilton Guerrero	.05
88	Shannon Stewart	.05
89	Chan Ho Park	.05
90	Carlos Delgado	.60
91	Jose Cruz Jr.	.05
92	Shawn Green	.35
93	Robin Ventura	.05
94	Reggie Sanders	.05
95	Orel Hershiser	.05
96	Dante Bichette	.05
97	Charles Johnson	.05
98	Pedro Martinez	.75
99	Mariano Rivera	.15
100	Joe Randa	.05
101	Jeff Kent	.05
102	Jay Buhner	.05
103	Brian Jordan	.05
104	Jason Kendall	.05
105	Scott Spiezio	.05
106	Desi Relaford	.05
107	Bernard Gilkey	.05
108	Manny Ramirez	.75
109	Tony Clark	.05
110	Eric Young	.05
111	Johnny Damon	.30
112	Glendon Rusch	.05
113	Ben Grieve	.05
114	Homer Bush	.05
115	Miguel Tejada	.25
116	Lou Collier	.05
117	Derrek Lee	.60
118	Jacob Cruz	.05
119	Raul Ibanez	.05
120	Ryan McGuire	.05
121	Antone Williamson	.05
122	Abraham Nunez	.05
123	Jeff Abbott	.05
124	Brett Tomko	.05
125	Richie Sexson	.05
126	Todd Helton	.75
127	Juan Encarnacion	.05
128	Richard Hidalgo	.05
129	Paul Konerko	.10
130	Brad Fullmer	.05
131	Jeremi Gonzalez	.05
132	Jaret Wright	.05
133	Derek Jeter	1.25
134	Frank Thomas	.40
135	Nomar Garciaparra	.50
136	Kenny Lofton	.05
137	Jeff Bagwell	.40
138	Todd Hundley	.05
139	Alex Rodriguez	1.00
140	Ken Griffey Jr.	.75
141	Sammy Sosa	.50
142	Greg Maddux	.50
143	Albert Belle	.05
144	Cal Ripken Jr.	1.25
145	Mark McGwire	1.00
146	Chipper Jones	.50
147	Charles Johnson	.05
148	Ken Griffey Jr. Checklist	.75
149	Jose Cruz Jr. Checklist	.05
150	Larry Walker Checklist	.05

Behind the Numbers

		NM/M
Complete Set (20):		85.00
Common Player:		1.50
Inserted 1:23		
1	Ken Griffey Jr.	7.50
2	Cal Ripken Jr.	12.00
3	Alex Rodriguez	10.00
4	Jose Cruz Jr.	1.50
5	Mike Piazza	7.50
6	Nomar Garciaparra	5.50
7	Scott Rolen	2.50
8	Andruw Jones	4.00
9	Frank Thomas	4.00
10	Mark McGwire	10.00
11	Ivan Rodriguez	3.00
12	Greg Maddux	5.50
13	Roger Clemens	6.50
14	Derek Jeter	12.00
15	Tony Gwynn	5.50
16	Ben Grieve	1.50
17	Jeff Bagwell	4.00
18	Chipper Jones	5.50
19	Hideo Nomo	2.00
20	Sandy Alomar Jr.	1.50

Club Edition

	NM/M
Complete Set (150):	50.00
Common Player:	2.00
Stars:	4X
Inserted 1:7	

(See 1998 Pinnacle Inside for checklist and base card values.)

Diamond Edition

	NM/M
Common Card:	6.00
Stars:	10X
Inserted 1:67	

(See 1998 Pinnacle Inside for checklist and base card values.)

Cans

		NM/M
Complete Set (23):		15.00
Common Can:		.40
Gold Cans:		2X
1	Ken Griffey Jr.	1.25
2	Frank Thomas	.65
3	Alex Rodriguez	1.50
4	Andruw Jones	.65
5	Mike Piazza	1.25
6	Ben Grieve	.40
7	Hideo Nomo	.50
8	Vladimir Guerrero	.65
9	Roger Clemens	1.00
10	Tony Gwynn	.75
11	Mark McGwire	1.50
12	Cal Ripken Jr.	2.00
13	Jose Cruz Jr.	.40
14	Greg Maddux	.75
15	Chipper Jones	.75
16	Derek Jeter	2.00
17	Juan Gonzalez	.50
18	Nomar Garciaparra (AL ROY)	1.00
19	Scott Rolen (NL ROY)	.65
20	Florida Marlins World Series Winner	.40
21	Larry Walker (NL MVP)	.40
22	Tampa Bay Devil Rays	.40
23	Arizona Diamondbacks	.40

Stand Up Guys

		NM/M
Complete Set (50):		35.00
Common Card:		.25
Sample:		3X
1-A/B	Ken Griffey Jr., Cal Ripken Jr.	2.00

1-C/D	Tony Gwynn, Mike Piazza	1.25
2-A/B	Andruw Jones, Alex Rodriguez	1.50
2-C/D	Scott Rolen, Nomar Garciaparra	1.00
3-A/B	Andruw Jones, Greg Maddux	1.00
3-C/D	Javy Lopez, Chipper Jones	1.00
4-A/B	Jay Buhner, Randy Johnson	.75
4-C/D	Ken Griffey Jr., Alex Rodriguez	1.50
5-A/B	Frank Thomas, Jeff Bagwell	.75
5-C/D	Mark McGwire, Mo Vaughn	1.50
6-A/B	Nomar Garciaparra, Derek Jeter	2.00
6-C/D	Alex Rodriguez, Barry Larkin	1.50
7-A/B	Mike Piazza, Ivan Rodriguez	1.25
7-C/D	Charles Johnson, Javy Lopez	.25
8-A/B	Cal Ripken Jr., Chipper Jones	2.00
8-C/D	Ken Caminiti, Scott Rolen	.65
9-A/B	Jose Cruz Jr., Vladimir Guerrero	.75
9-C/D	Andruw Jones, Jose Guillen	.75
10-A/B	Larry Walker, Dante Bichette	.25
10-C/D	Ellis Burks, Neifi Perez	.25
11-A/B	Juan Gonzalez, Sammy Sosa	1.00
11-C/D	Vladimir Guerrero, Manny Ramirez	.75
12-A/B	Greg Maddux, Roger Clemens	1.00
12-C/D	Hideo Nomo, Randy Johnson	.75
13-A/B	Ben Grieve, Paul Konerko	.40
13-C/D	Jose Cruz Jr., Fernando Tatis	.25
14-A/B	Ryne Sandberg, Chuck Knoblauch	1.00
14-C/D	Roberto Alomar, Craig Biggio	.35
15-A/B	Cal Ripken Jr., Brady Anderson	2.00
15-C/D	Rafael Palmeiro, Roberto Alomar	.65
16-A/B	Darin Erstad, Jim Edmonds	.35
16-C/D	Tim Salmon, Garret Anderson	.25
17-A/B	Mike Piazza, Hideo Nomo	1.25
17-C/D	Raul Mondesi, Eric Karros	.25
18-A/B	Ivan Rodriguez, Juan Gonzalez	.65
18-C/D	Will Clark, Rusty Greer	.25
19-A/B	Derek Jeter, Bernie Williams	2.00
19-C/D	Tino Martinez, Andy Pettitte	.25
20-A/B	Kenny Lofton, Ken Griffey Jr.	1.25
20-C/D	Brady Anderson, Bernie Williams	.25
21-A/B	Paul Molitor, Eddie Murray	.75
21-C/D	Ryne Sandberg, Rickey Henderson	1.00
22-A/B	Tony Clark, Frank Thomas	.75
22-C/D	Jeff Bagwell, Mark McGwire	1.50
23-A/B	Manny Ramirez, Jim Thome	.75
23-C/D	David Justice, Sandy Alomar Jr.	.25
24-A/B	Barry Bonds, Albert Belle	2.00
24-C/D	Jeff Bagwell, Dante Bichette	.60
25-A/B	Ken Griffey Jr., Frank Thomas	1.25
25-C/D	Alex Rodriguez, Andruw Jones	1.50

1998 PINNACLE MINT COLLECTION

		NM/M
Complete Set (30):		10.00
Common Die-Cut:		.25
Bronze (1:1H):		2X
Silver (1:15H):		5X
Gold (1:47):		12X
Pack (3+2):		1.00
Wax Box (24):		12.00
1	Jeff Bagwell	.65
2	Albert Belle	.25
3	Barry Bonds	2.00
4	Tony Clark	.25
5	Roger Clemens	1.00
6	Juan Gonzalez	.35
7	Ken Griffey Jr.	1.25
8	Tony Gwynn	.75
9	Derek Jeter	2.00
10	Randy Johnson	.65
11	Chipper Jones	.75
12	Greg Maddux	.75
13	Tino Martinez	.25
14	Mark McGwire	1.50
15	Hideo Nomo	.35
16	Andy Pettitte	.25
17	Mike Piazza	1.25
18	Cal Ripken Jr.	2.00
19	Alex Rodriguez	1.50
20	Ivan Rodriguez	.50
21	Sammy Sosa	.75
22	Frank Thomas	.65
23	Mo Vaughn	.25
24	Larry Walker	.25
25	Jose Cruz Jr.	.25
26	Nomar Garciaparra	.75
27	Vladimir Guerrero	.65
28	Livan Hernandez	.25
29	Andruw Jones	.65
30	Scott Rolen	.50

Coins

		NM/M
Complete Set (30):		20.00
Common Brass Coin:		.25
Brass Proof (500):		5X
Nickel (1:41):		3X
Nickel Proof (250):		12X
Silver:		12X
Inserted 1:288 H, 1:960 R		
Gold Plated (1:199):		15X
Gold Proof (100):		20X
1	Jeff Bagwell	.75
2	Albert Belle	.25
3	Barry Bonds	2.00
4	Tony Clark	.25
5	Roger Clemens	1.00
6	Juan Gonzalez	.45
7	Ken Griffey Jr.	1.25
8	Tony Gwynn	1.00
9	Derek Jeter	2.00
10	Randy Johnson	.75
11	Chipper Jones	1.00
12	Greg Maddux	1.00
13	Tino Martinez	.25
14	Mark McGwire	1.50
15	Hideo Nomo	.45
16	Andy Pettitte	.35
17	Mike Piazza	1.25
18	Cal Ripken Jr.	2.00
19	Alex Rodriguez	1.50
20	Ivan Rodriguez	.65
21	Sammy Sosa	1.00
22	Frank Thomas	.75
23	Mo Vaughn	.25
24	Larry Walker	.25
25	Jose Cruz Jr.	.25
26	Nomar Garciaparra	1.00
27	Vladimir Guerrero	.75
28	Livan Hernandez	.25
29	Andruw Jones	.75
30	Scott Rolen	.65

Mint Gems

		NM/M
Complete Set (6)		20.00
Common Player:		2.00
Coins:		1X
1	Ken Griffey Jr.	6.00
2	Larry Walker	2.00
3	Roger Clemens	5.00
4	Pedro Martinez	4.00
5	Nomar Garciaparra	4.50
6	Scott Rolen	3.00

1998 PINNACLE PERFORMERS

		NM/M
Complete Set (150):		12.00
Common Player:		.05
Peak Performers (1:7):		2X
Pack (10):		1.00
Wax Box (24):		15.00
1	Ken Griffey Jr.	1.00
2	Frank Thomas	.65
3	Cal Ripken Jr.	1.50
4	Alex Rodriguez	1.25
5	Greg Maddux	.75
6	Mike Piazza	1.00
7	Chipper Jones	.75
8	Tony Gwynn	.75
9	Derek Jeter	1.50
10	Jeff Bagwell	.65
11	Juan Gonzalez	.35
12	Nomar Garciaparra	.75
13	Andruw Jones	.65
14	Hideo Nomo	.35
15	Roger Clemens	.85
16	Mark McGwire	1.25
17	Scott Rolen	.60
18	Vladimir Guerrero	.65
19	Barry Bonds	1.50
20	Darin Erstad	.15
21	Albert Belle	.05
22	Kenny Lofton	.05
23	Mo Vaughn	.05
24	Tony Clark	.05
25	Ivan Rodriguez	.60
26	Jose Cruz Jr.	.05
27	Larry Walker	.05
28	Jaret Wright	.05
29	Andy Pettitte	.25
30	Roberto Alomar	.20
31	Randy Johnson	.65
32	Manny Ramirez	.65
33	Paul Molitor	.65
34	Mike Mussina	.35
35	Jim Thome	.60
36	Tino Martinez	.05
37	Gary Sheffield	.45
38	Chuck Knoblauch	.05
39	Bernie Williams	.05
40	Tim Salmon	.05
41	Sammy Sosa	.75
42	Wade Boggs	.75
43	Will Clark	.05
44	Andres Galarraga	.05
45	Raul Mondesi	.05
46	Rickey Henderson	.65
47	Jose Canseco	.45
48	Pedro Martinez	.65
49	Jay Buhner	.05
50	Ryan Klesko	.05
51	Barry Larkin	.05
52	Charles Johnson	.05
53	Tom Glavine	.35
54	Edgar Martinez	.05
55	Fred McGriff	.05
56	Moises Alou	.05
57	Dante Bichette	.05
58	Jim Edmonds	.05
59	Mark Grace	.05
60	Chan Ho Park	.05
61	Justin Thompson	.05
62	John Smoltz	.05
63	Craig Biggio	.05
64	Ken Caminiti	.05
65	Richard Hidalgo	.05
66	Carlos Delgado	.50
67	David Justice	.05
68	J.T. Snow	.05
69	Jason Giambi	.50
70	Garret Anderson	.05
71	Rondell White	.05
72	Matt Williams	.05
73	Brady Anderson	.05
74	Eric Karros	.05
75	Javier Lopez	.05
76	Pat Hentgen	.05
77	Todd Hundley	.05
78	Ray Lankford	.05
79	Denny Neagle	.05
80	Sandy Alomar Jr.	.05
81	Jason Kendall	.05
82	Omar Vizquel	.05
83	Kevin Brown	.05
84	Kevin Appier	.05
85	Al Martin	.05
86	Rusty Greer	.05
87	Bobby Bonilla	.05
88	Shawn Estes	.05
89	Rafael Palmeiro	.60
90	Edgar Renteria	.05
91	Alan Benes	.05
92	Bobby Higginson	.05
93	Mark Grudzielanek	.05
94	Jose Guillen	.05
95	Neifi Perez	.05
96	Jeff Abbott	.05
97	Todd Walker	.05
98	Eric Young	.05
99	Brett Tomko	.05
100	Mike Cameron	.05
101	Karim Garcia	.05
102	Brian Jordan	.05
103	Jeff Suppan	.05
104	Robin Ventura	.05
105	Henry Rodriguez	.05
106	Shannon Stewart	.05
107	Kevin Orie	.05
108	Bartolo Colon	.05
109	Bob Abreu	.15

110 Vinny Castilla .05
111 Livan Hernandez .05
112 Derrek Lee .50
113 Mark Kotsay .05
114 Todd Greene .05
115 Edgardo Alfonzo .05
116 A.J. Hinch .05
117 Paul Konerko .15
118 Todd Helton .65
119 Miguel Tejada .20
120 Fernando Tatis .05
121 Ben Grieve .05
122 Travis Lee .05
123 Kerry Wood .25
124 Eli Marrero .05
125 David Ortiz .50
126 Juan Encarnacion .05
127 Brad Fullmer .05
128 Richie Sexson .05
129 Aaron Boone .05
130 Enrique Wilson .05
131 Javier Valentin .05
132 Abraham Nunez .05
133 Ricky Ledee .05
134 Carl Pavano .05
135 Bobby Estalella .05
136 Homer Bush .05
137 Brian Rose .05
138 Ken Griffey Jr. .50
139 Frank Thomas .35
140 Cal Ripken Jr. .75
141 Alex Rodriguez .65
142 Greg Maddux .40
143 Chipper Jones .40
144 Mike Piazza .50
145 Tony Gwynn .40
146 Derek Jeter .75
147 Jeff Bagwell .35
148 Hideo Nomo Checklist .20
149 Roger Clemens Checklist .45
150 Greg Maddux Checklist .35

Big Bang

NM/M
Complete Set (20): 27.50
Common Player: .50
Production 2,500 sets
Sample: 1X
1 Ken Griffey Jr. 2.50
2 Frank Thomas 1.50
3 Mike Piazza 2.50
4 Chipper Jones 2.00
5 Alex Rodriguez 3.00
6 Nomar Garciaparra 2.00
7 Jeff Bagwell 1.50
8 Cal Ripken Jr. 3.50
9 Albert Belle .50
10 Mark McGwire 3.00
11 Juan Gonzalez .75
12 Larry Walker .50
13 Tino Martinez .50
14 Jim Thome 1.00
15 Manny Ramirez 1.50
16 Barry Bonds 3.50
17 Mo Vaughn .50
18 Jose Cruz Jr. .50
19 Tony Clark .50
20 Andruw Jones 1.50

Big Bang Seasonal Outburst

NM/M
Complete Set (20): 500.00
Common Player: 10.00
#'d to player's 1997 HR total
Unnumbered: 25%
1 Ken Griffey Jr. (56) 40.00
2 Frank Thomas (35) 20.00
3 Mike Piazza (40) 40.00
4 Chipper Jones (21) 65.00
5 Alex Rodriguez (23) 75.00
6 Nomar Garciaparra (30) 40.00
7 Jeff Bagwell (43) 20.00
8 Cal Ripken Jr. (17) 80.00
9 Albert Belle (30) 10.00
10 Mark McGwire (58) 65.00
11 Juan Gonzalez (42) 12.50
12 Larry Walker (49) 10.00
13 Tino Martinez (44) 10.00
14 Jim Thome (40) 15.00
15 Manny Ramirez (26) 25.00
16 Barry Bonds (40) 75.00
17 Mo Vaughn (35) 10.00
18 Jose Cruz Jr. (26) 10.00
19 Tony Clark (32) 10.00
20 Andruw Jones (18) 25.00

Launching Pad

NM/M
Complete Set (20): 25.00
Common Player: .50
Inserted 1:9
1 Ben Grieve .50
2 Ken Griffey Jr. 2.50
3 Derek Jeter 3.50
4 Frank Thomas 1.00
5 Travis Lee .50
6 Vladimir Guerrero 1.00
7 Tony Gwynn 2.00
8 Jose Cruz Jr. .50
9 Cal Ripken Jr. 3.50
10 Chipper Jones 2.00
11 Scott Rolen .75
12 Andruw Jones 1.00
13 Ivan Rodriguez .75
14 Todd Helton 1.00
15 Nomar Garciaparra 2.00
16 Mark McGwire 3.00
17 Gary Sheffield .60
18 Bernie Williams .50
19 Alex Rodriguez 3.00
20 Mike Piazza 2.50

Power Trip

NM/M
Complete Set (10): 16.00
Common Player: 1.00
Production 10,000 sets
1 Frank Thomas 1.00
2 Alex Rodriguez 3.00
3 Nomar Garciaparra 1.50
4 Jeff Bagwell 1.00
5 Cal Ripken Jr. 4.00
6 Mike Piazza 2.00
7 Chipper Jones 1.50
8 Ken Griffey Jr. 2.00
9 Mark McGwire 3.00
10 Juan Gonzalez 1.00

Peak Performers

NM/M
Complete Set (150): 100.00
Common Player: 2.00
Stars: 6X
Inserted 1:7
(See 1998 Pinnacle Performers for checklist and base card values.)

Swing for the Fences

NM/M
Complete Set (50): 24.00
Common Player: .25
Inserted 1:1
1 Brady Anderson .25
2 Albert Belle .25

3 Jay Buhner .25
4 Jose Canseco .50
5 Tony Clark .25
6 Jose Cruz Jr. .25
7 Jim Edmonds .25
8 Cecil Fielder .25
9 Travis Fryman .25
10 Nomar Garciaparra 1.00
11 Juan Gonzalez .40
12 Ken Griffey Jr. 1.50
13 David Justice .25
14 Travis Lee .25
15 Edgar Martinez .25
16 Tino Martinez .25
17 Rafael Palmeiro .65
18 Manny Ramirez .75
19 Cal Ripken Jr. 2.50
20 Alex Rodriguez 2.00
21 Tim Salmon .25
22 Frank Thomas .75
23 Jim Thome .65
24 Mo Vaughn .25
25 Bernie Williams .25
26 Fred McGriff .25
27 Jeff Bagwell .75
28 Dante Bichette .25
29 Barry Bonds 2.50
30 Ellis Burks .25
31 Ken Caminiti .25
32 Vinny Castilla .25
33 Andres Galarraga .25
34 Vladimir Guerrero .75
35 Todd Helton .75
36 Todd Hundley .25
37 Andruw Jones .75
38 Chipper Jones 1.00
39 Eric Karros .25
40 Ryan Klesko .25
41 Ray Lankford .25
42 Mark McGwire 2.00
43 Raul Mondesi .25
44 Mike Piazza 1.50
45 Scott Rolen .65
46 Gary Sheffield .50
47 Sammy Sosa 1.00
48 Larry Walker .25
49 Matt Williams .25
50 WILDCARD .25

1998 PINNACLE PLUS

NM/M
Complete Set (200): 12.00
Common Player: .05
Pack (10): 1.00
Wax Box (20): 12.00
1 Roberto Alomar .20
2 Sandy Alomar Jr. .05
3 Brady Anderson .05
4 Albert Belle .05
5 Jeff Cirillo .05
6 Roger Clemens 1.25
7 David Cone .05
8 Nomar Garciaparra 1.00
9 Ken Griffey Jr. 1.50
10 Jason Dickson .05
11 Edgar Martinez .05
12 Tino Martinez .05
13 Randy Johnson .75
14 Mark McGwire 2.00
15 David Justice .05
16 Mike Mussina .40
17 Chuck Knoblauch .05
18 Joey Cora .05
19 Pat Hentgen .05
20 Randy Myers .05
21 Cal Ripken Jr. 2.50
22 Mariano Rivera .15
23 Jose Rosado .05
24 Frank Thomas .75
25 Alex Rodriguez 2.00
26 Justin Thompson .05
27 Ivan Rodriguez .65
28 Bernie Williams .05
29 Pedro Martinez .75
30 Tony Clark .05
31 Garret Anderson .05
32 Travis Fryman .05
33 Mike Piazza 1.50
34 Carl Pavano .05
35 *Kevin Millwood* 1.00
36 Miguel Tejada .20
37 Willie Blair .05
38 Devon White .05
39 Andres Galarraga .05
40 Barry Larkin .05
41 Al Leiter .05
42 Moises Alou .05
43 Eric Young .05
44 John Jaha .05
45 Bernard Gilkey .05
46 Freddy Garcia .05
47 Ruben Rivera .05
48 Robb Nen .05
49 Ray Lankford .05
50 Kenny Lofton .05
51 Joe Carter .05
52 Jason McDonald .05
53 Quinton McCracken .05
54 Kerry Wood .50
55 Mike Lansing .05
56 Chipper Jones 1.00
57 Barry Bonds 2.50
58 Brad Fullmer .05
59 Jeff Bagwell .75
60 Rondell White .05
61 Geronimo Berroa .05
62 *Magglio Ordonez* 1.50
63 Dwight Gooden .05
64 Brian Hunter .05
65 Todd Walker .05
66 *Frank Catalanotto* .05
67 Tony Saunders .05
68 Travis Lee .05
69 Michael Tucker .05
70 Reggie Sanders .05
71 Derrek Lee .50
72 Larry Walker .05
73 Marquis Grissom .05
74 Craig Biggio .05
75 Kevin Brown .05
76 J.T. Snow .05
77 Eric Davis .05
78 Jeff Abbott .05
79 Jermaine Dye .05
80 Otis Nixon .05
81 Curt Schilling .35
82 Enrique Wilson .05
83 Tony Gwynn 1.00
84 Orlando Cabrera .05
85 Ramon Martinez .05
86 Greg Vaughn .05
87 Alan Benes .05
88 Dennis Eckersley .65
89 Jim Thome .65
90 Juan Encarnacion .05
91 Jeff King .05
92 Shannon Stewart .05
93 Roberto Hernandez .05
94 Raul Ibanez .05
95 Darryl Kile .05
96 Charles Johnson .05
97 Rich Becker .05
98 Hal Morris .05
99 Ismael Valdes .05
100 Orel Hershiser .05
101 Mo Vaughn .05
102 Aaron Boone .05
103 Jeff Conine .05

104 Paul O'Neill .05
105 Tom Candiotti .05
106 Wilson Alvarez .05
107 Mike Stanley .05
108 Carlos Delgado .50
109 Tony Batista .05
110 Dante Bichette .05
111 Henry Rodriguez .05
112 Karim Garcia .05
113 Shane Reynolds .05
114 Ken Caminiti .05
115 Jose Silva .05
116 Juan Gonzalez .40
117 Brian Jordan .05
118 Jim Leyritz .05
119 Manny Ramirez .75
120 Fred McGriff .05
121 Brooks Kieschnick .05
122 Sean Casey .15
123 John Smoltz .05
124 Rusty Greer .05
125 Cecil Fielder .05
126 Mike Cameron .05
127 Reggie Jefferson .05
128 Bobby Higginson .05
129 Kevin Appier .05
130 Robin Ventura .05
131 Ben Grieve .05
132 Wade Boggs 1.00
133 Jose Cruz Jr. .05
134 Jeff Suppan .05
135 Vinny Castilla .05
136 Sammy Sosa 1.00
137 Mark Wohlers .05
138 Jay Bell .05
139 Brett Tomko .05
140 Gary Sheffield .40
141 Tim Salmon .05
142 Jaret Wright .05
143 Kenny Rogers .05
144 Brian Anderson .05
145 Darrin Fletcher .05
146 John Flaherty .05
147 Dmitri Young .05
148 Andruw Jones .75
149 Matt Williams .05
150 Bobby Bonilla .05
151 Mike Hampton .05
152 Al Martin .05
153 Mark Grudzielanek .05
154 Dave Nilsson .05
155 Roger Cedeno .05
156 Greg Maddux 1.00
157 Mark Kotsay .05
158 Steve Finley .05
159 Wilson Delgado .05
160 Ron Gant .05
161 Jim Edmonds .05
162 Jeff Blauser .05
163 Dave Burba .05
164 Pedro Astacio .05
165 Livan Hernandez .05
166 Neifi Perez .05
167 Ryan Klesko .05
168 Fernando Tatis .05
169 Richard Hidalgo .05
170 Carlos Perez .05
171 Bob Abreu .15
172 Francisco Cordova .05
173 Todd Helton .75
174 Doug Glanville .05
175 Brian Rose .05
176 Yamil Benitez .05
177 Darin Erstad .15
178 Scott Rolen .60
179 John Wetteland .05
180 Paul Sorrento .05
181 Walt Weiss .05
182 Vladimir Guerrero .75
183 Ken Griffey Jr. .75
184 Alex Rodriguez 1.00
185 Cal Ripken Jr. 1.25
186 Frank Thomas .40
187 Chipper Jones .50
188 Hideo Nomo .20
189 Nomar Garciaparra .60
190 Mike Piazza 1.00
191 Greg Maddux .50
192 Tony Gwynn .50
193 Mark McGwire 1.00
194 Roger Clemens .65
195 Mike Piazza .75
196 Mark McGwire 1.00
197 Chipper Jones .50
198 Larry Walker .05
199 Hideo Nomo .20
200 Barry Bonds 1.25

Artist's Proofs

NM/M
Complete Set (60): 150.00

Common Player: .75
Inserted 1:35
Golds: 10X
Production 100 sets
1 Roberto Alomar 1.50
2 Albert Belle .75
3 Roger Clemens 8.00
4 Nomar Garciaparra 7.50
5 Ken Griffey Jr. 10.00
6 Tino Martinez .75
7 Randy Johnson 6.00
8 Mark McGwire 12.50
9 David Justice .75
10 Chuck Knoblauch .75
11 Cal Ripken Jr. 15.00
12 Frank Thomas 6.00
13 Alex Rodriguez 12.50
14 Ivan Rodriguez 5.00
15 Bernie Williams .75
16 Pedro Martinez 6.00
17 Tony Clark .75
18 Mike Piazza 10.00
19 Miguel Tejada 1.00
20 Andres Galarraga .75
21 Barry Larkin .75
22 Kenny Lofton .75
23 Chipper Jones 7.50
24 Barry Bonds 15.00
25 Brad Fullmer .75
26 Jeff Bagwell 6.00
27 Todd Walker .75
28 Travis Lee .75
29 Larry Walker .75
30 Craig Biggio .75
31 Tony Gwynn 7.50
32 Jim Thome 5.00
33 Juan Encarnacion .75
34 Mo Vaughn .75
35 Karim Garcia .75
36 Ken Caminiti .75
37 Juan Gonzalez 3.00
38 Manny Ramirez 6.00
39 Fred McGriff .75
40 Rusty Greer .75
41 Bobby Higginson .75
42 Ben Grieve .75
43 Wade Boggs 7.50
44 Jose Cruz Jr. .75
45 Sammy Sosa 7.50
46 Gary Sheffield 2.00
47 Tim Salmon .75
48 Jaret Wright .75
49 Andruw Jones 6.00
50 Matt Williams .75
51 Greg Maddux 7.50
52 Jim Edmonds .75
53 Livan Hernandez .75
54 Neifi Perez .75
55 Fernando Tatis .75
56 Richard Hidalgo .75
57 Todd Helton 6.00
58 Darin Erstad 1.50
59 Scott Rolen 5.00
60 Vladimir Guerrero 6.00

A Piece of the Game

NM/M
Complete Set (10): 8.00
Common Player: .50
Inserted 1:19
1 Ken Griffey Jr. 1.00
2 Frank Thomas .65
3 Alex Rodriguez 1.50
4 Chipper Jones .75
5 Cal Ripken Jr. 2.00
6 Mike Piazza 1.00
7 Greg Maddux .75
8 Juan Gonzalez .50

9 Nomar Garciaparra .75
10 Larry Walker .50

Epix All-Star Moment

NM/M
Complete Set (12): 25.00
Common Player: 1.00
Purples: 1.5X
Emeralds: 2.5X
Inserted 1:21
13 Alex Rodriguez 3.50
14 Cal Ripken Jr. 5.00
15 Chipper Jones 2.50
16 Roger Clemens 2.75
17 Mo Vaughn 1.00
18 Mark McGwire 3.50
19 Mike Piazza 3.00
20 Andruw Jones 2.00
21 Greg Maddux 2.50
22 Barry Bonds 5.00
23 Paul Molitor 2.00
24 Hideo Nomo 1.50

Lasting Memories

NM/M
Complete Set (30): 16.00
Common Player: .25
Inserted 1:5
1 Nomar Garciaparra .75
2 Ken Griffey Jr. 1.00
3 Livan Hernandez .25
4 Hideo Nomo .40
5 Ben Grieve .25
6 Scott Rolen .50
7 Roger Clemens .85
8 Cal Ripken Jr. 2.00
9 Mo Vaughn .25
10 Frank Thomas .65
11 Mark McGwire 1.50
12 Barry Larkin .25
13 Matt Williams .25
14 Jose Cruz Jr. .25
15 Andruw Jones .65
16 Mike Piazza 1.00
17 Jeff Bagwell .65
18 Chipper Jones .75
19 Juan Gonzalez .40
20 Kenny Lofton .25
21 Greg Maddux .75
22 Ivan Rodriguez .50
23 Alex Rodriguez 1.50
24 Derek Jeter 2.00
25 Albert Belle .25
26 Barry Bonds 2.00
27 Larry Walker .25
28 Sammy Sosa .75
29 Tony Gwynn .75
30 Randy Johnson .65

Team Pinnacle

NM/M
Complete Set (15): 40.00
Common Player: 1.50
Inserted 1:71
Golds: 2X
Inserted 1:199
1 Mike Piazza, Ivan Rodriguez 4.00
2 Mark McGwire, Mo Vaughn 5.00
3 Roberto Alomar, Craig Biggio 1.50
4 Alex Rodriguez, Barry Larkin 5.00
5 Cal Ripken Jr., Chipper Jones 6.00
6 Ken Griffey Jr., Larry Walker 4.00
7 Juan Gonzalez, Tony Gwynn 3.00
8 Albert Belle, Barry Bonds 6.00
9 Kenny Lofton, Andruw Jones 2.50
10 Tino Martinez, Jeff Bagwell 2.50
11 Frank Thomas, Andres Galarraga 2.50
12 Roger Clemens, Greg Maddux 3.50
13 Pedro Martinez, Hideo Nomo 2.50
14 Nomar Garciaparra, Scott Rolen 3.50
15 Ben Grieve, Paul Konerko 1.50

Yardwork

NM/M
Complete Set (15): 12.50
Common Player: .35
Inserted 1:9
1 Mo Vaughn .35
2 Frank Thomas .75
3 Albert Belle .35
4 Nomar Garciaparra 1.00
5 Tony Clark .35
6 Tino Martinez .35
7 Ken Griffey Jr. 1.50
8 Juan Gonzalez .60
9 Sammy Sosa 1.00
10 Jose Cruz Jr. .35
11 Jeff Bagwell .75
12 Mike Piazza 1.50
13 Larry Walker .35
14 Mark McGwire 2.00
15 Barry Bonds 2.50

2001 PLAYOFF ABSOLUTE MEMORABILIA

NM/M
Complete Set (200):
Common Player: .25
Common SP (151-200): 5.00
Production 700
Pack (6): 8.00
Box (18) w/baseball: 150.00
1 Alex Rodriguez 2.50
2 Barry Bonds 3.00
3 Cal Ripken Jr. 3.00
4 Chipper Jones 1.50
5 Derek Jeter 3.00
6 Troy Glaus 1.00
7 Frank Thomas 1.00
8 Greg Maddux 1.50
9 Ivan Rodriguez .75
10 Jeff Bagwell 1.00

11	Ryan Dempster	.25
12	Todd Helton	1.00
13	Ken Griffey Jr.	2.00
14	Manny Ramirez	1.00
15	Mark McGwire	2.50
16	Mike Piazza	2.00
17	Nomar Garciaparra	2.00
18	Pedro Martinez	1.00
19	Randy Johnson	1.00
20	Rick Ankiel	.25
21	Rickey Henderson	1.00
22	Roger Clemens	1.75
23	Sammy Sosa	2.00
24	Tony Gwynn	2.00
25	Vladimir Guerrero	1.00
26	Kazuhiro Sasaki	.25
27	Roberto Alomar	.50
28	Barry Zito	.35
29	Pat Burrell	.50
30	Harold Baines	.25
31	Carlos Delgado	.65
32	J.D. Drew	.50
33	Jim Edmonds	.25
34	Darin Erstad	.50
35	Jason Giambi	.75
36	Tom Glavine	.50
37	Juan Gonzalez	1.00
38	Mark Grace	.35
39	Shawn Green	.50
40	Tim Hudson	.50
41	Andruw Jones	1.00
42	David Justice	.25
43	Jeff Kent	.25
44	Barry Larkin	.25
45	Rafael Furcal	.25
46	Mike Mussina	.50
47	Hideo Nomo	1.00
48	Rafael Palmeiro	.75
49	Adam Piatt	.25
50	Scott Rolen	.75
51	Gary Sheffield	.50
52	Bernie Williams	.35
53	Bob Abreu	.25
54	Edgardo Alfonzo	.25
55	Edgar Renteria	.25
56	Phil Nevin	.25
57	Craig Biggio	.25
58	Andres Galarraga	.25
59	Edgar Martinez	.25
60	Fred McGriff	.25
61	Magglio Ordonez	.25
62	Jim Thome	.75
63	Matt Williams	.25
64	Kerry Wood	.65
65	Moises Alou	.25
66	Brady Anderson	.25
67	Garret Anderson	.25
68	Russell Branyan	.25
69	Tony Batista	.25
70	Vernon Wells	.25
71	Carlos Beltran	.60
72	Adrian Beltre	.25
73	Kris Benson	.25
74	Lance Berkman	.25
75	Kevin Brown	.25
76	Dee Brown	.25
77	Jeromy Burnitz	.25
78	Timoniel Perez	.25
79	Sean Casey	.40
80	Luis Castillo	.25
81	Eric Chavez	.35
82	Jeff Cirillo	.25
83	Bartolo Colon	.25
84	David Cone	.25
85	Freddy Garcia	.25
86	Johnny Damon	.40
87	Ray Durham	.25
88	Jermaine Dye	.25
89	Juan Encarnacion	.25
90	Terrence Long	.25
91	Carl Everett	.25
92	Steve Finley	.25
93	Cliff Floyd	.25
94	Brad Fullmer	.25
95	Brian Giles	.25
96	Luis Gonzalez	.35
97	Rusty Greer	.25
98	Jeffrey Hammonds	.25
99	Mike Hampton	.25
100	Orlando Hernandez	.25
101	Richard Hidalgo	.25
102	Geoff Jenkins	.25
103	Jacque Jones	.25
104	Brian Jordan	.25
105	Gabe Kapler	.25
106	Eric Karros	.25
107	Jason Kendall	.25
108	Adam Kennedy	.25
109	Deion Sanders	.25
110	Ryan Klesko	.25
111	Chuck Knoblauch	.25
112	Paul Konerko	.25
113	Carlos Lee	.25
114	Kenny Lofton	.25
115	Javy Lopez	.25
116	Tino Martinez	.25
117	Ruben Mateo	.25
118	Kevin Millwood	.25
119	Jimmy Rollins	.25
120	Raul Mondesi	.25
121	Trot Nixon	.25
122	John Olerud	.25
123	Paul O'Neill	.25
124	Chan Ho Park	.25
125	Andy Pettitte	.35
126	Jorge Posada	.35
127	Mark Quinn	.25
128	Aramis Ramirez	.25
129	Mariano Rivera	.25
130	Tim Salmon	.35
131	Curt Schilling	.50
132	Richie Sexson	.25
133	John Smoltz	.25
134	J.T. Snow	.25
135	Jay Payton	.25
136	Shannon Stewart	.25
137	B.J. Surhoff	.25
138	Mike Sweeney	.25
139	Fernando Tatis	.25
140	Miguel Tejada	.35
141	Jason Varitek	.25
142	Greg Vaughn	.25
143	Mo Vaughn	.25
144	Robin Ventura	.25
145	Jose Vidro	.25
146	Omar Vizquel	.25
147	Larry Walker	.25
148	David Wells	.25
149	Rondell White	.25
150	Preston Wilson	.25
151	*Bud Smith*	5.00
152	*Cory Aldridge*	5.00
153	*Wilmy Caceres*	5.00
154	Josh Beckett	6.00
155	*Wilson Betemit*	5.00
156	*Jason Michaels*	5.00
157	*Albert Pujols*	120.00
158	*Andres Torres*	5.00
159	*Jack Wilson*	5.00
160	Alex Escobar	5.00
161	Ben Sheets	5.00
162	*Rafael Soriano*	10.00
163	*Nate Frese*	5.00
164	*Carlos Garcia*	5.00
165	*Brandon Larson*	5.00
166	*Alexis Gomez*	8.00
167	Jason Hart	5.00
168	Nick Johnson	5.00
169	*Donaldo Mendez*	5.00
170	*Christian Parker*	5.00
171	*Jackson Melian*	5.00
172	Jack Cust	5.00
173	*Adrian Hernandez*	5.00
174	Joe Crede	5.00
175	*Jose Mieses*	5.00
176	Roy Oswalt	5.00
177	Eric Munson	5.00
178	Xavier Nady	5.00
179	*Horacio Ramirez*	8.00
180	Abraham Nunez	5.00
181	Jose Ortiz	5.00
182	*Jeremy Owens*	5.00
183	*Claudio Vargas*	5.00
184	Marcus Giles	5.00
185	Aubrey Huff	5.00
186	C.C. Sabathia	5.00
187	Adam Dunn	5.00
188	*Adam Pettyjohn*	5.00
189	*Elpidio Guzman*	5.00
190	*Jay Gibbons*	10.00
191	*Wilkin Ruan*	5.00
192	*Tsuyoshi Shinjo*	8.00
193	Alfonso Soriano	8.00
194	Corey Patterson	5.00
195	*Ichiro Suzuki*	75.00
196	*Billy Sylvester*	5.00
197	*Juan Uribe*	5.00
198	*Johnny Estrada*	8.00
199	*Carlos Valderrama*	5.00
200	*Matt White*	5.00

Spectrum

Stars (1-150): No Pricing
Production 10
Rk's (151-200): 2-4X
Production 25

Ball Hoggs

NM/M

Common Player: 8.00
Production 75 unless noted

1	Vladimir Guerrero	15.00
2	Troy Glaus	10.00
3	Tony Gwynn	20.00
4	Cal Ripken/125	50.00
5	Todd Helton	15.00
6	Jacque Jones/125	8.00
7	Shawn Green/100	8.00
8	Ichiro Suzuki	85.00
9	Scott Rolen	15.00
10	Roger Clemens	30.00
11	Ken Griffey/25	50.00
14	Sammy Sosa	25.00
15	J.D. Drew	10.00
16	Barry Bonds/100	40.00
17	Pat Burrell	15.00
18	Mark McGwire/100	65.00
19	Mike Piazza	20.00
20	Magglio Ordonez/150	10.00
21	Miguel Tejada	10.00
22	Albert Pujols/100	150.00
23	Derek Jeter	40.00
24	Johnny Damon	15.00
25	Mike Sweeney	8.00
26	Ben Grieve	8.00
27	Jeff Kent	8.00
28	Andres Galarraga	8.00
29	Richie Sexson	10.00
30	Juan Encarnacion	8.00
31	Ruben Mateo	8.00
33	Manny Ramirez	15.00
35	Ivan Rodriguez	15.00
36	Darin Erstad	8.00
37	Carlos Delgado	10.00
38	Jeff Bagwell	15.00
39	Jermaine Dye	8.00
40	Jose Ortiz	8.00
41	Gary Sheffield	10.00
42	Eric Chavez	8.00
43	Mark Grace	15.00
44	Rafael Palmeiro	15.00
45	Tsuyoshi Shinjo/100	15.00
46	Terrence Long	8.00
47	Carlos Delgado/25	20.00
48	Frank Thomas	15.00
49	Chipper Jones/25	40.00
50	Jason Giambi	15.00

Ballpark Souvenirs

NM/M

Common Player: 4.00
Production 400 sets
Doubles: 1-1.5X
Production 200 sets
Triples: 1.5-2X
Production 75 sets
Home Runs: 2-4X
Production 25 sets

1	Barry Bonds	20.00
2	Cal Ripken Jr.	25.00
3	Pedro Martinez	10.00
4	Troy Glaus	6.00
5	Frank Thomas	8.00
6	Alex Rodriguez	10.00
7	Ivan Rodriguez	8.00
8	Jeff Bagwell	8.00
9	Mark McGwire	30.00
10	Todd Helton	8.00
11	Gary Sheffield	5.00
12	Manny Ramirez	8.00
13	Mike Piazza	10.00
14	Sammy Sosa	15.00
15	Preston Wilson	4.00
16	Tony Gwynn	8.00
17	Vladimir Guerrero	8.00
18	Carlos Delgado	6.00
19	Roberto Alomar	6.00
20	Todd Helton	8.00
21	Albert Pujols	50.00
22	Jason Giambi	8.00
23	Sammy Sosa	15.00
24	Ken Griffey Jr.	10.00
25	Darin Erstad	4.00
26	Mark McGwire	30.00
27	Carlos Delgado	6.00
28	Juan Gonzalez	8.00
29	Mike Sweeney	4.00
30	Alex Rodriguez	10.00
31	Roger Clemens	15.00
32	Tsuyoshi Shinjo	4.00
33	Ben Grieve	4.00
34	Jeff Kent	4.00
35	Vladimir Guerrero	8.00
36	Shawn Green	6.00
37	Rafael Palmeiro	6.00
38	Tony Gwynn	8.00
39	Scott Rolen	8.00
40	Ken Griffey Jr.	10.00
41	Albert Pujols	50.00
42	Barry Bonds	20.00
43	Mark Grace	8.00
44	Bernie Williams	6.00
45	Frank Thomas	8.00
46	Jermaine Dye	4.00
47	Mike Piazza	10.00
48	Chipper Jones	10.00
49	Richie Sexson	6.00
50	Magglio Ordonez	4.00

Boss Hoggs

NM/M

Production 25 sets

4	Cal Ripken	80.00
6	Jacque Jones	15.00
7	Shawn Green	15.00
8	Ichiro Suzuki	100.00
9	Scott Rolen	20.00
11	Ken Griffey	50.00
14	Sammy Sosa	50.00
15	J.D. Drew	15.00
16	Barry Bonds	80.00
17	Pat Burrell	20.00
18	Mark McGwire	100.00
19	Mike Piazza	75.00
20	Magglio Ordonez	20.00
21	Miguel Tejada	20.00
23	Derek Jeter	85.00
24	Johnny Damon	15.00
25	Mike Sweeney	15.00
26	Ben Grieve	15.00
27	Jeff Kent	15.00
28	Andres Galarraga	15.00
29	Richie Sexson	20.00
30	Juan Encarnacion	15.00
31	Ruben Mateo	15.00
33	Manny Ramirez	20.00
35	Ivan Rodriguez	20.00
36	Darin Erstad	15.00
37	Carlos Delgado	20.00
38	Jeff Bagwell	20.00
39	Jermaine Dye	15.00
40	Jose Ortiz	15.00
42	Eric Chavez	15.00
43	Mark Grace	30.00
44	Rafael Palmeiro	30.00
45	Tsuyoshi Shinjo	20.00
46	Terrence Long	15.00
47	Carlos Delgado	20.00
48	Frank Thomas	25.00
50	Jason Giambi	25.00

Rookie Premiere Autos

NM/M

Production 25 sets

151	Bud Smith	15.00
152	Cory Aldridge	15.00
154	Josh Beckett	40.00
155	Wilson Betemit	15.00
157	Albert Pujols	500.00
158	Andres Torres	15.00

160 Alex Escobar 15.00
161 Ben Sheets 30.00
162 Rafael Soriano 30.00
164 Carlos Garcia 15.00
165 Brandon Larson 20.00
167 Jason Hart 15.00
168 Nick Johnson 20.00
169 Donaldo Mendez 15.00
170 Christian Parker 15.00
171 Jackson Melian 15.00
173 Adrian Hernandez 15.00
174 Joe Crede 15.00
175 Jose Mieses 15.00
176 Roy Oswalt 30.00
178 Xavier Nady 20.00
179 Horacio Ramirez 20.00
180 Abraham Nunez 15.00
181 Jose Ortiz 15.00
182 Jeremy Owens 15.00
183 Claudio Vargas 15.00
184 Marcus Giles 20.00
186 C.C. Sabathia 25.00
187 Adam Dunn 50.00
188 Adam Pettyjohn 15.00
190 Jay Gibbons 25.00
191 Wilkin Ruan 15.00
193 Alfonso Soriano 85.00
194 Corey Patterson 25.00
196 Billy Sylvester 15.00
197 Juan Uribe 15.00
198 Johnny Estrada 15.00
199 Carlos Valderrama 15.00
200 Matt White 15.00

Spring Bonus Baseballs

NM/M

Common Auto. Baseball: 15.00
Inserted 1:box
Al Oliver/500 15.00
Andre Dawson/550 20.00
Barry Bonds/25 250.00
Bill Madlock/525 15.00
Bill Mazeroski/25 75.00
Billy Williams/325 20.00
Bob Feller/550 20.00
Bob Gibson/25 100.00
Bobby Doerr/300 25.00
Bobby Richardson/500 20.00
Boog Powell/500 20.00
Brian Jordan/25 40.00
Bucky Dent/500 15.00
Charles Johnson/25 40.00
Chipper Jones/25 100.00
Clete Boyer/500 20.00
Dale Murphy/25 80.00
Dave Concepcion/500 15.00
Dave Kingman/500 15.00
Don Larsen/200 40.00
Don Newcombe/500 15.00
Don Zimmer/500 15.00
Duke Snider/25 100.00
Earl Weaver/300 20.00
Enos Slaughter/525 20.00
Fergie Jenkins/1000 20.00
Frank Howard/500 20.00
Frank Robinson/25 100.00
Frank Thomas/25 85.00
Gary Carter/200 30.00
Gaylord Perry/1000 15.00
George Foster/500 15.00
George Kell/300 20.00
Goose Gossage/500 15.00
Greg Maddux/25 100.00
Hank Aaron/25 150.00
Hank Bauer/500 20.00
Harmon Killebrew/200 60.00
Henry Rodriguez/400 15.00
Herb Score/500 15.00
Hoyt Wilhelm/500 15.00
J.D. Drew/75 20.00
Javy Lopez/25 40.00
Jim Edmonds/25 50.00
Jim Palmer/500 20.00
Joe Pepitone/500 20.00
Johnny Bench/25 120.00
Johnny Podres/500 25.00
Juan Marichal/485 20.00
Kirby Puckett/25 100.00
Larry Doby/300 30.00
Lou Brock/25 75.00
Luis Tiant/500 15.00
Magglio Ordonez/200 25.00
Manny Ramirez/25 60.00
Maury Wills/500 20.00
Mike Schmidt/25 150.00
Minnie Minoso/1000 15.00
Monte Irvin/500 25.00
Moose Skowron/500 20.00
Nolan Ryan/25 200.00
Ozzie Smith/25 100.00
Phil Rizzuto/25 75.00
Ralph Kiner/100 40.00
Randy Johnson/25 100.00
Red Schoendienst/500 20.00
Reggie Jackson/25 80.00
Rickey Henderson/25 100.00
Robin Roberts/500 25.00
Roger Clemens/25 125.00
Rollie Fingers/575 20.00
Ryne Sandberg/25 100.00
Sean Casey/25 30.00
Stan Musial/25 100.00
Steve Carlton/25 75.00
Steve Garvey/1000 15.00
Todd Helton/25 50.00
Tom Glavine/25 50.00
Tom Seaver/25 75.00
Tommy John/1000 15.00
Tony Gwynn/25 75.00
Tony Perez/400 15.00
Wade Boggs/25 75.00
Warren Spahn/500 60.00
Whitey Ford/25 75.00
Willie Mays/25 150.00
Willie McCovey/25 60.00
Willie Stargell/25 75.00
Yogi Berra/25 75.00

Tools of the Trade

NM/M

Common Player: 5.00
Jerseys (1-20):
Production 300
Bats (21-40):
Production 125
Batting Glove (41-45):
Production 50
Hat (46-50):
Production 100
Autographs: No Pricing
Production 25 sets
1 Vladimir Guerrero 10.00
2 Troy Glaus 6.00
3 Tony Gwynn 10.00
4 Todd Helton 8.00
5 Scott Rolen 8.00
6 Roger Clemens 20.00
7 Pedro Martinez 10.00
8 Richie Sexson 6.00
9 Magglio Ordonez 5.00
10 Ben Grieve 5.00
11 Jeff Bagwell 8.00
12 Edgar Martinez 5.00
13 Greg Maddux 25.00
15 Frank Thomas 10.00
16 Edgardo Alfonzo 5.00
17 Cal Ripken Jr. 40.00
18 Jose Vidro 5.00
19 Andruw Jones 8.00
21 Barry Bonds 50.00
22 Juan Gonzalez 8.00
23 Andruw Jones 8.00
24 Cal Ripken Jr. 60.00
25 Greg Maddux 30.00
26 Manny Ramirez 20.00
27 Roberto Alomar 8.00
28 Shawn Green 6.00
29 Edgardo Alfonzo 5.00
30 Rafael Palmeiro 10.00
31 Hideo Nomo 100.00
32 Andres Galarraga 6.00
33 Todd Helton 15.00
34 Darin Erstad 5.00
35 Ivan Rodriguez 15.00
36 Sean Casey 6.00
37 Vladimir Guerrero 20.00
39 Troy Glaus 8.00
40 Jeff Bagwell 10.00
41 Barry Bonds 100.00
42 Cal Ripken Jr. 125.00
43 Roberto Alomar 30.00
44 Sean Casey 20.00
45 Tony Gwynn 40.00
46 Bernie Williams 25.00
47 Barry Zito 25.00
48 Greg Maddux
49 Tom Glavine 25.00
50 Troy Glaus

2002 PLAYOFF ABSOLUTE MEMORABILIA

NM/M

Complete Set (200):
Common Player: .50
Common Rk/Prospect (151-200): 3.00
Production 1,000
Pack (6): 3.00
Box + 8X10: 140.00
1 David Eckstein .50
2 Darin Erstad .75
3 Troy Glaus 1.50
4 Garret Anderson .50
5 Tim Salmon .50
6 Curt Schilling 1.00
7 Randy Johnson 1.50
8 Luis Gonzalez .50
9 Mark Grace .60
10 Tom Glavine .75
11 Greg Maddux 2.00
12 Chipper Jones 2.00
13 Gary Sheffield .75
14 John Smoltz .50
15 Andruw Jones 1.50
16 Wilson Betemit .50
17 Tony Batista .50
18 Javier Vazquez .50
19 Scott Erickson .50
20 Josh Towers .50
21 Pedro J. Martinez 1.50
22 Johnny Damon .60
23 Manny Ramirez 1.50
24 Rickey Henderson 1.50
25 Trot Nixon .50
26 Nomar Garciaparra 2.50
27 Juan Cruz .50
28 Kerry Wood 1.25
29 Fred McGriff .50
30 Moises Alou .50
31 Sammy Sosa 2.50
32 Corey Patterson .50
33 Mark Buehrle .50
34 Keith Foulke .50
35 Frank Thomas 1.50
36 Kenny Lofton .50
37 Magglio Ordonez .50
38 Barry Larkin .50
39 Ken Griffey Jr. 2.50
40 Adam Dunn .75
41 Juan Encarnacion .50
42 Sean Casey .60
43 Bartolo Colon .50
44 C.C. Sabathia .50
45 Travis Fryman .50
46 Jim Thome 1.50
47 Omar Vizquel .50
48 Ellis Burks .50
49 Russell Branyan .50
50 Mike Hampton .50
51 Todd Helton 1.50
52 Jose Ortiz .50
53 Juan Uribe .50
54 Juan Pierre .50
55 Larry Walker .50
56 Mike Rivera .50
57 Robert Fick .50
58 Bobby Higginson .50
59 Josh Beckett .50
60 Richard Hidalgo .50
61 Cliff Floyd .50
62 Mike Lowell .50
63 Roy Oswalt .50
64 Morgan Ensberg .50
65 Jeff Bagwell 1.50
66 Craig Biggio .50
67 Lance Berkman .50
68 Carlos Beltran .75
69 Mike Sweeney .50
70 Neifi Perez .50
71 Kevin Brown .50
72 Hideo Nomo 1.50
73 Paul LoDuca .50
74 Adrian Beltre .60
75 Shawn Green .75
76 Eric Karros .50
77 Brad Radke .50
78 Corey Koskie .50
79 Doug Mientkiewicz .50
80 Torii Hunter .50
81 Jacque Jones .50
82 Ben Sheets .50
83 Richie Sexson .50
84 Geoff Jenkins .50
85 Tony Armas .50
86 Michael Barrett .50
87 Jose Vidro .50
88 Vladimir Guerrero 1.50
89 Roger Clemens 2.25
90 Derek Jeter 4.00
91 Bernie Williams .60
92 Jason Giambi 1.25
93 Jorge Posada .50
94 Mike Mussina .65
95 Andy Pettitte .65
96 Nick Johnson .50
97 Alfonso Soriano 1.25
98 Shawn Estes .50
99 Al Leiter .50
100 Mike Piazza 2.50
101 Roberto Alomar .75
102 Mo Vaughn .50
103 Jeromy Burnitz .50
104 Tim Hudson .65
105 Barry Zito .50
106 Mark Mulder .50
107 Eric Chavez .65
108 Miguel Tejada .65
109 Jeremy Giambi .50
110 Jermaine Dye .50
111 Mike Lieberthal .50
112 Scott Rolen 1.25
113 Pat Burrell .75
114 Brandon Duckworth .50
115 Bobby Abreu .50
116 Jason Kendall .50
117 Aramis Ramirez .50
118 Brian Giles .50
119 Pokey Reese .50
120 Phil Nevin .50
121 Ryan Klesko .50
122 Carlos Pena .50
123 Trevor Hoffman .50
124 Barry Bonds 4.00
125 Rich Aurilia .50
126 Jeff Kent .50
127 Tsuyoshi Shinjo .50
128 Ichiro Suzuki 2.00
129 Edgar Martinez .50
130 Freddy Garcia .50
131 Bret Boone .50
132 Matt Morris .50
133 Tino Martinez .50
134 Albert Pujols 3.00
135 J.D. Drew .75
136 Jim Edmonds .50
137 Gabe Kapler .50
138 Paul Wilson .50
139 Ben Grieve .50
140 Wade Miller .50
141 Chan Ho Park .50
142 Alex Rodriguez 3.00
143 Rafael Palmeiro 1.25
144 Juan Gonzalez 1.50
145 Ivan Rodriguez 1.25
146 Carlos Delgado .75
147 Jose Cruz Jr. .50
148 Shannon Stewart .50
149 Raul Mondesi .50
150 Vernon Wells .50
151 *So Taguchi* 8.00
152 *Kazuhisa Ishii* 8.00
153 Hank Blalock 6.00
154 Sean Burroughs 3.00
155 Geronimo Gil 3.00
156 Jon Rauch 3.00
157 Fernando Rodney 3.00
158 *Miguel Asencio* 3.00
159 *Franklyn German* 3.00
160 *Luis Ugueto* 3.00
161 *Jorge Sosa* 3.00
162 *Felix Escalona* 3.00
163 Colby Lewis 3.00
164 Mark Teixeira 5.00
165 Mark Prior 10.00

166 *Francis Beltran* 3.00
167 Joe Thurston 3.00
168 *Earl Snyder* 3.00
169 *Takahito Nomura* 3.00
170 Bill Hall 3.00
171 Marlon Byrd 3.00
172 Dave Williams 3.00
173 Yorvit Torrealba 3.00
174 *Brandon Backe* 3.00
175 *Jorge de la Rosa* 3.00
176 *Brian Mallette* 3.00
177 *Rodrigo Rosario* 3.00
178 *Anderson Machado* 3.00
179 *Jorge Padilla* 3.00
180 *Allan Simpson* 3.00
181 *Doug Devore* 3.00
182 *Steve Bechler* 3.00
183 Raul Chavez 3.00
184 *Tom Shearn* 3.00
185 *Ben Howard* 3.00
186 *Chris Baker* 3.00
187 *Travis Hughes* 3.00
188 Kevin Mench 3.00
189 Drew Henson 3.00
190 *Mike Moriarty* 3.00
191 *Corey Thurman* 3.00
192 Bobby Hill 3.00
193 *Steve Kent* 3.00
194 *Satoru Komiyama* 3.00
195 Jason Lane 3.00
196 Angel Berroa 3.00
197 *Brandon Puffer* 3.00
198 *Brian Fitzgerald* 3.00
199 *Rene Reyes* 3.00
200 Hee Seop Choi 5.00

Spectrum

Stars (1-150): 3-5X
Production 100
SP's: 1-1.5X
Production 50

Absolutely Ink

NM/M

Common Autograph: 5.00
Inserted 1:27
Gold Parallel #'d to 25 not priced
Jsy Parallel #'d to Jsy # not priced
Adrian Beltre 20.00
Alex Rodriguez/50 85.00
Ben Sheets 20.00
Bernie Williams/25
Bobby Doerr 15.00
Blaine Neal 5.00
Carlos Beltran 20.00
Carlos Pena 5.00
Corey Patterson/150 15.00
Curt Schilling/15
Dave Parker 10.00
David Justice/65 25.00
Don Mattingly/75 65.00
Duaner Sanchez 5.00
Eric Chavez/100 15.00
Freddy Garcia 10.00
Gary Carter 25.00
Gary Sheffield/25
George Brett/25
Greg Maddux/25
Ivan Rodriguez/50 40.00
J.D. Drew/100 20.00
Jack Cust 5.00
Jason Michaels 5.00
Jermaine Dye/125 10.00
Jose Vidro 8.00
Josh Towers 6.00
Kerry Wood/50 40.00
Kirby Puckett/50 75.00
Luis Gonzalez/75 25.00
Luis Rivera 5.00
Manny Ramirez/50 40.00
Marcus Giles 10.00
Mark Prior/100 50.00
Mark Teixeira/100 25.00
Marlon Byrd/250 15.00
Matt Ginter 5.00
Moises Alou/150 15.00
Nate Frese 5.00
Nick Johnson 5.00
Nomar Garciaparra/15
Pablo Ozuna 5.00
Paul LoDuca/200 20.00
Richie Sexson 15.00
Roberto Alomar/100 40.00
Roy Oswalt/300 15.00
Ryan Klesko/75 15.00
Sean Casey/125 10.00
Shannon Stewart 8.00
So Taguchi 15.00
Terrence Long 8.00
Timoniel Perez 5.00
Todd Helton/25
Tony Gwynn/50 60.00
Troy Glaus/300 15.00
Vladimir Guerrero/225 40.00
Wade Miller 15.00
Wilson Betemit 5.00

Signing Bonus

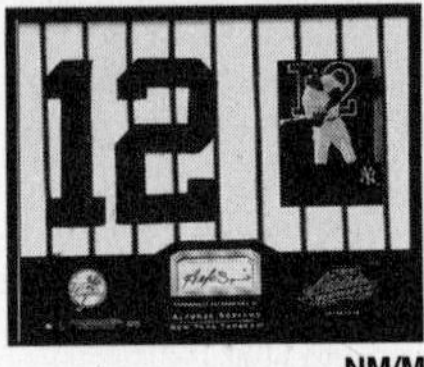

NM/M

Common Player:
Bobby Abreu/53
Grover Alexander/1
Roberto Alomar/12
Roberto Alomar/100 65.00
Moises Alou/18
Moises Alou/250 40.00
Jeff Bagwell/5
Carlos Beltran/15
Carlos Beltran/50 75.00
Adrian Beltre/29
Adrian Beltre/150 35.00
Lance Berkman/17
Angel Berroa/4
Angel Berroa/50
Angel Berroa/100 30.00
Wilson Betemit/250 30.00
Craig Biggio/7
Hank Blalock/12
Hank Blalock/50 75.00
Hank Blalock/100 50.00
George Brett/5
Lou Brock/100 60.00
Lou Brock/200 60.00
Kevin Brown/27
Kevin Brown/100
Kevin Brown/150
Mark Buehrle/56
Mark Buehrle/200 50.00
Sean Burroughs/21
Marlon Byrd/61
Steve Carlton/100 90.00
Steve Carlton/150 75.00
Sean Casey/21
Sean Casey/100
Eric Chavez/3
Eric Chavez/25
Eric Chavez/28 75.00
Roger Clemens/10
Ty Cobb/6
Eddie Collins/1
Juan Cruz/51
J.D. Drew/7
J.D. Drew/100 65.00
Brandon Duckworth/56
Brandon Duckworth/150 35.00
Adam Dunn/10
Adam Dunn/44 75.00
Jermaine Dye/100 40.00
Jermaine Dye/250 40.00
Morgan Ensberg/100 40.00
Darin Erstad/5
Darin Erstad/17
Cliff Floyd/200 40.00
Jimmie Foxx/1
Freddy Garcia/34
Freddy Garcia/125 35.00
Nomar Garciaparra/5
Troy Glaus/50 65.00
Troy Glaus/100 50.00
Tom Glavine/25
Tom Glavine/200 75.00
Luis Gonzalez/20
Luis Gonzalez/125 85.00
Hank Greenberg/1
Vladimir Guerrero/27
Vladimir Guerrero/150 150.00
Tony Gwynn/19
Richard Hidalgo/15
Richard Hidalgo/100 30.00
Richard Hidalgo/135 30.00
Richard Hidalgo/150 30.00
Rogers Hornsby/1
Tim Hudson/15
Tim Hudson/50 75.00
Tim Hudson/100 65.00
Kazuhisa Ishii/17
Reggie Jackson/44
Nick Johnson/200 40.00
Walter Johnson/4
Andruw Jones/25
Andruw Jones/75 75.00
Chipper Jones/10
Al Kaline/6
Al Kaline/250 75.00
Gabe Kapler/18
Gabe Kapler/125 35.00
Gabe Kapler/175 35.00
Ryan Klesko/30
Nap Lajoie/1
Jason Lane/100 35.00
Barry Larkin/11
Barry Larkin/50 60.00
Barry Larkin/100 50.00
Paul LoDuca/16
Paul LoDuca/50
Fred Lynn/150 40.00
Fred Lynn/250 40.00
Connie Mack/2
Greg Maddux/31
Roger Maris/3
Edgar Martinez/11
Edgar Martinez/150 55.00
Pedro J. Martinez/5
Pedro J. Martinez/45 125.00
Don Mattingly/100 175.00
Willie McCovey/190 70.00
Willie McCovey/250 60.00
Wade Miller/52
Wade Miller/150 35.00
Wade Miller/250 35.00
Paul Molitor/75 60.00
Paul Molitor/100 60.00
Paul Molitor/125 60.00
Mark Mulder/20
Mark Mulder/40
Mike Mussina/5
Jose Ortiz/125 25.00
Roy Oswalt/44
Roy Oswalt/100
Mel Ott/3
Rafael Palmeiro/25
Jim Palmer/150 40.00
Jim Palmer/250 40.00
Dave Parker/150 45.00
Corey Patterson/20
Corey Patterson/250 40.00
Carlos Pena/19
Carlos Pena/150 40.00
Carlos Pena/250 40.00
Tony Perez/24 65.00
Tony Perez/250 50.00
Juan Pierre/75
Mark Prior/22
Mark Prior/50 100.00
Mark Prior/75 80.00
Mark Prior/125 80.00
Kirby Puckett/34
Albert Pujols/5
Albert Pujols/100 180.00
Aramis Ramirez/16
Aramis Ramirez/50
Aramis Ramirez/125 40.00
Manny Ramirez/5
Manny Ramirez/24
Phil Rizzuto/10 265.00
Phil Rizzuto/250 70.00
Brooks Robinson/150 70.00
Brooks Robinson/250 60.00
Jackie Robinson/3
Alex Rodriguez/3
Alex Rodriguez/15
Ivan Rodriguez/7
Scott Rolen/17
Babe Ruth/8
Nolan Ryan/30 180.00
Nolan Ryan/34 180.00
C.C. Sabathia/10
C.C. Sabathia/15
Ryne Sandberg/23
Ryne Sandberg/50 150.00
Curt Schilling/5
Curt Schilling/10
Mike Schmidt/100 100.00
Richie Sexson/100 40.00
Ben Sheets/100 50.00
Ben Sheets/150 50.00
Gary Sheffield/11
George Sisler/3
Alfonso Soriano/12
Alfonso Soriano/100 80.00
Tris Speaker/1
Shannon Stewart/24
Shannon Stewart/100 40.00
Shannon Stewart/150 40.00
Mike Sweeney/100
So Taguchi/99 35.00
Mark Teixeira/23 60.00
Mark Teixeira/100 55.00
Miguel Tejada/4
Miguel Tejada/40
Miguel Tejada/50
Frank Thomas/10
Frank Thomas/35 120.00
Juan Uribe/4
Juan Uribe/25
Javier Vazquez/125 35.00
Jose Vidro/150 35.00
Honus Wagner/11
Bernie Williams/15
Ted Williams/1
Hack Wilson/1
Dave Winfield/25
Kerry Wood/34 100.00
Cy Young/2
Barry Zito/25
Barry Zito/50 65.00

Team Tandems

NM/M

Complete Set (40): 80.00
Common Card: 1.00
Inserted 1:12
Golds: 2-3X
Inserted 1:72
1 Troy Glaus, Darin Erstad 1.50
2 Curt Schilling, Randy Johnson 3.00
3 Chipper Jones, Andruw Jones 3.00
4 Greg Maddux, Tom Glavine 4.00
5 Nomar Garciaparra, Manny Ramirez 6.00
6 Pedro J. Martinez, Trot Nixon 3.00
7 Kerry Wood, Sammy Sosa 5.00
8 Frank Thomas, Magglio Ordonez 2.00
9 Ken Griffey Jr., Barry Larkin 5.00
10 C.C. Sabathia, Jim Thome 2.50
11 Todd Helton, Larry Walker 2.00
12 Bobby Higginson, Shane Halter 1.00
13 Cliff Floyd, Brad Penny 1.00
14 Jeff Bagwell, Craig Biggio 2.00
15 Shawn Green, Adrian Beltre 1.50
16 Ben Sheets, Richie Sexson 1.50
17 Vladimir Guerrero, Jose Vidro 3.00
18 Mike Piazza, Roberto Alomar 5.00
19 Roger Clemens, Mike Mussina 6.00
20 Derek Jeter, Jason Giambi 8.00
21 Barry Zito, Tim Hudson 1.50

22 Eric Chavez, Miguel Tejada 1.50
23 Pat Burrell, Scott Rolen 3.00
24 Brian Giles, Aramis Ramirez 1.50
25 Ryan Klesko, Phil Nevin 1.50
26 Barry Bonds, Rich Aurilia 8.00
27 Ichiro Suzuki, Kazuhiro Sasaki 5.00
28 Albert Pujols, J.D. Drew 6.00
29 Alex Rodriguez, Ivan Rodriguez 6.00
30 Carlos Delgado, Shannon Stewart 1.50
31 Mo Vaughn, Roger Cedeno 1.00
32 Carlos Beltran, Mike Sweeney 1.50
33 Edgar Martinez, Bret Boone 1.50
34 Juan Gonzalez, Rafael Palmeiro 2.00
35 Johnny Damon, Rickey Henderson 1.50
36 Sean Casey, Adam Dunn 2.00
37 Jeff Kent, Tsuyoshi Shinjo 1.50
38 Lance Berkman, Richard Hidalgo 1.50
39 So Taguchi, Tino Martinez 1.50
40 Hideo Nomo, Kazuhisa Ishii 1.50

Team Tandems G-U

NM/M
Common Card: 5.00
Inserted 1:33
Golds: 2-3X
Production 50

1 Troy Glaus, Darin Erstad 8.00
2 Curt Schilling, Randy Johnson 10.00
3 Chipper Jones, Andruw Jones 10.00
4 Greg Maddux, Tom Glavine 20.00
5 Nomar Garciaparra, Manny Ramirez 25.00
6 Pedro J. Martinez, Trot Nixon 15.00
7 Kerry Wood, Sammy Sosa 15.00
8 Frank Thomas, Magglio Ordonez 10.00
9 Ken Griffey Jr., Barry Larkin 15.00
10 C.C. Sabathia, Jim Thome 15.00
11 Todd Helton, Larry Walker 8.00
12 Bobby Higginson, Shane Halter 8.00
13 Cliff Floyd, Brad Penny 5.00
14 Jeff Bagwell, Craig Biggio 15.00
15 Shawn Green, Adrian Beltre 8.00
16 Ben Sheets, Richie Sexson 8.00
17 Vladimir Guerrero, Jose Vidro 12.00
18 Mike Piazza, Roberto Alomar 15.00
19 Roger Clemens, Mike Mussina 50.00
20 Derek Jeter, Jason Giambi 30.00
21 Barry Zito, Tim Hudson 15.00
22 Eric Chavez, Miguel Tejada 10.00
23 Pat Burrell, Scott Rolen 15.00
24 Brian Giles, Aramis Ramirez 10.00
25 Ryan Klesko, Phil Nevin 8.00
26 Barry Bonds, Rich Aurilia 15.00
27 Ichiro Suzuki, Kazuhiro Sasaki
28 Albert Pujols, J.D. Drew 15.00
29 Alex Rodriguez, Ivan Rodriguez 15.00
30 Carlos Delgado, Shannon Stewart 8.00
31 Mo Vaughn, Roger Cedeno 5.00
32 Carlos Beltran, Mike Sweeney 8.00
33 Edgar Martinez, Bret Boone 8.00
34 Juan Gonzalez, Rafael Palmeiro 12.00
35 Johnny Damon, Rickey Henderson 10.00
36 Sean Casey, Adam Dunn 15.00
37 Jeff Kent, Tsuyoshi Shinjo 10.00
38 Lance Berkman, Richard Hidalgo 8.00
39 So Taguchi, Tino Martinez 15.00
40 Hideo Nomo, Kazuhisa Ishii 35.00

Team Quads Game Used

NM/M
Numbered to 100
Prime: No Pricing
Production 25

1 Troy Glaus, Darin Erstad, Garret Anderson, Troy Percival 25.00
2 Curt Schilling, Randy Johnson, Luis Gonzalez, Mark Grace 30.00
3 Chipper Jones, Andruw Jones, Greg Maddux, Tom Glavine 40.00
4 Nomar Garciaparra, Manny Ramirez, Trot Nixon, Pedro J. Martinez 50.00
5 Kerry Wood, Sammy Sosa, Fred McGriff, Moises Alou 35.00
6 Frank Thomas, Magglio Ordonez, Mark Buehrle, Kenny Lofton 25.00
8 C.C. Sabathia, Jim Thome, Bartolo Colon, Russell Branyan 40.00
9 Todd Helton, Larry Walker, Juan Pierre, Mike Hampton 30.00
10 Jeff Bagwell, Craig Biggio, Lance Berkman, Richard Hidalgo 30.00
11 Shawn Green, Adrian Beltre, Hideo Nomo, Paul LoDuca 40.00
12 Mike Piazza, Roberto Alomar, Mo Vaughn, Roger Cedeno 40.00
13 Roger Clemens, Derek Jeter, Jason Giambi, Mike Mussina 75.00
14 Barry Zito, Tim Hudson, Eric Chavez, Miguel Tejada 20.00
15 Pat Burrell, Scott Rolen, Bobby Abreu, Marlon Byrd 35.00
16 Bernie Williams, Jorge Posada, Alfonso Soriano, Andy Pettitte 30.00
17 Barry Bonds, Rich Aurilia, Tsuyoshi Shinjo, Jeff Kent 40.00
18 Ichiro Suzuki, Kazuhiro Sasaki, Bret Boone, Edgar Martinez 50.00
19 Albert Pujols, J.D. Drew, Jim Edmonds, Tino Martinez 40.00
20 Alex Rodriguez, Ivan Rodriguez, Juan Gonzalez, Rafael Palmeiro 40.00

Tools of the Trade

NM/M
Complete Set (95): 120.00
Common Player: 1.00
Inserted 1:9
Golds: 2-3X
Inserted 1:45

1 Mike Mussina 2.00
2 Rickey Henderson 2.00
3 Raul Mondesi 1.00
4 Nomar Garciaparra 6.00
5 Randy Johnson 3.00
6 Roger Clemens 6.00
7 Shawn Green 1.00
8 Todd Helton 2.00
9 Aramis Ramirez 1.50
10 Barry Larkin 1.50
11 Byung-Hyun Kim 1.00
12 C.C. Sabathia 1.00
13 Curt Schilling 2.50
14 Darin Erstad 1.50
15 Eric Karros 1.00
16 Freddy Garcia 1.00
17 Greg Maddux 4.00
18 Jason Kendall 1.00
19 Jim Thome 3.00
20 Juan Gonzalez 2.00
21 Kazuhiro Sasaki 1.00
22 Kerry Wood 3.00
23 Luis Gonzalez 1.50
24 Mark Mulder 1.00
25 Rich Aurilia 1.00
26 Ray Durham 1.00
27 Ben Grieve 1.00
28 Bret Boone 1.00
29 Edgar Martinez 1.00
30 Ivan Rodriguez 2.00
31 Jorge Posada 2.00
32 Mike Piazza 6.00
33 Pat Burrell 1.50
34 Robin Ventura 1.00
35 Trot Nixon 1.00
36 Adrian Beltre 1.00
37 Bernie Williams 1.50
38 Bobby Abreu 1.50
39 Carlos Delgado 1.50
40 Craig Biggio 1.50
41 Garret Anderson 1.50
42 Jermaine Dye 1.00
43 Johnny Damon 1.00
44 Tim Salmon 1.00
45 Tino Martinez 1.00
46 Fred McGriff 1.50
47 Gary Sheffield 1.00
48 Adam Dunn 2.00
49 Joe Mays 1.00
50 Kenny Lofton 1.00
51 Josh Beckett 1.50
52 Bud Smith 1.00
53 Johnny Estrada 1.00
54 Charles Johnson 1.00
55 Craig Wilson 1.00
56 Terrence Long 1.00
57 Andy Pettitte 1.50
58 Brian Giles 1.50
59 Juan Pierre 1.00
60 Cliff Floyd 1.00
61 Ivan Rodriguez 2.00
62 Andruw Jones 2.00
63 Lance Berkman 1.50
64 Mark Buehrle 1.00
65 Miguel Tejada 1.50
66 Wade Miller 1.00
67 Johnny Estrada 1.00
68 Tsuyoshi Shinjo 1.00
69 Scott Rolen 2.50
70 Roberto Alomar 2.00
71 Mark Grace 2.00
72 Larry Walker 1.50
73 Jim Edmonds 1.50
74 Jeff Kent 1.50
75 Frank Thomas 2.50
76 Carlos Beltran 1.50
77 Barry Zito 1.50
78 Alex Rodriguez 8.00
79 Troy Glaus 1.50
80 Ryan Klesko 1.00
81 Tom Glavine 1.50
82 Ben Sheets 1.50
83 Manny Ramirez 2.50
84 Shannon Stewart 1.00
85 Vladimir Guerrero 4.00
86 Chipper Jones 3.00
87 Jeff Bagwell 2.50
88 Richie Sexson 1.50
89 Sean Casey 1.50
90 Tim Hudson 1.50
91 J.D. Drew 1.50
92 Ivan Rodriguez 2.00
93 Magglio Ordonez 1.50
94 John Buck 1.00
95 Paul LoDuca 1.00

Tools of Trade G-U

NM/M
Common Player: 5.00
Jerseys #'d to 300
Bats #'d to 250
Shoes #'d to 150
Shin Guard #'d to 150
Glove #'d to 125
Mask #'d to 100
Hat #'d to 50
Doubles #'d to 200
Triples #'d to 75
Quads #'d to 50

1 Mike Mussina/jsy 10.00
2 Rickey Henderson/jsy 10.00
3 Raul Mondesi/jsy 8.00
4 Nomar Garciaparra/jsy 15.00
5 Randy Johnson/jsy 10.00
6 Roger Clemens/jsy 15.00
7 Shawn Green/jsy 8.00
8 Todd Helton/jsy 8.00
9 Aramis Ramirez/jsy 8.00
10 Barry Larkin/jsy 10.00
11 Byung-Hyun Kim/jsy 5.00
12 C.C. Sabathia/jsy 5.00
13 Curt Schilling/jsy 10.00
14 Darin Erstad/jsy 5.00
15 Eric Karros/jsy 5.00
16 Freddy Garcia/jsy 5.00
17 Greg Maddux/jsy 15.00
18 Jason Kendall/jsy 5.00
19 Jim Thome/jsy 10.00
20 Juan Gonzalez/jsy 8.00
21 Kazuhiro Sasaki/jsy 5.00
22 Kerry Wood/jsy 10.00
23 Luis Gonzalez/jsy 8.00
24 Mark Mulder/jsy 8.00
25 Rich Aurilia/jsy 5.00
26 Ray Durham/jsy 5.00
27 Ben Grieve/jsy 5.00
28 Bret Boone/jsy 5.00
29 Edgar Martinez/jsy 8.00
30 Ivan Rodriguez/jsy 10.00
31 Jorge Posada/jsy 10.00
32 Mike Piazza/jsy 15.00
33 Pat Burrell/bat 8.00
34 Robin Ventura/bat 5.00
35 Trot Nixon/bat 8.00
36 Adrian Beltre/bat 5.00
37 Bernie Williams/bat 10.00
38 Bobby Abreu/bat 8.00
39 Carlos Delgado/bat 8.00
40 Craig Biggio/bat 8.00
41 Garret Anderson/bat 8.00
42 Jermaine Dye/bat 5.00
43 Johnny Damon/bat 8.00
44 Tim Salmon/bat 8.00
45 Tino Martinez/bat 10.00
46 Fred McGriff/bat 8.00
47 Gary Sheffield/bat 5.00
48 Adam Dunn/shoe 15.00
49 Joe Mays/shoe 8.00
50 Kenny Lofton/shoe 10.00
51 Josh Beckett/shoe 10.00
52 Bud Smith/shoe 5.00
53 Johnny Estrada/shin 10.00
54 Charles Johnson/shin 8.00

55 Craig Wilson/shin 15.00
56 Terrence Long/glove 8.00
57 Andy Pettitte/glove 15.00
58 Brian Giles/glove 10.00
59 Juan Pierre/glove 10.00
60 Cliff Floyd/glove 10.00
61 Ivan Rodriguez/glove 15.00
62 Andruw Jones/hat 15.00
63 Lance Berkman/hat 15.00
64 Mark Buehrle/hat 15.00
65 Miguel Tejada/hat 15.00
66 Wade Miller/hat 10.00
67 Johnny Estrada/shin 10.00
68 T. Shinjo/bat/shoe 15.00
69 S. Rolen/bat/jsy 20.00
70 R. Alomar/bat/shoe 20.00
71 M. Grace/glv/jsy 15.00
72 L. Walker/jsy/bat 10.00
73 J. Edmonds/jsy/bat 15.00
74 J. Kent/jsy/bat 10.00
75 F. Thomas/jsy/bat 15.00
76 C. Beltran/jsy/bat 10.00
77 B. Zito/shoe/jsy 15.00
78 A. Rodriguez/jsy/bat 25.00
79 T. Glaus/dualjsy 15.00
80 R. Klesko/bat/glv 10.00
81 T. Glavine/jsy/shoe 20.00
82 B. Sheets/bat/jsy 10.00
83 M. Ramirez/ shoe/glv/jsy 25.00
84 S. Stewart/hat/jsy/bat 15.00
85 V. Guerrero/glv/bat/jsy 45.00
86 C. Jones/glv/bat/jsy 40.00
87 J. Bagwell/jsy/hat/bat 40.00
88 R. Sexson/ bat/jsy/glv/shoe 40.00
89 S. Casey/ jsy/hat/shoe/bat 30.00
90 T Hudson/ shoe/hat/glv/jsy 30.00
91 JD Drew/ shoe/jsy/hat/bat 40.00
92 I Rodriguez/ jsy/mask/chst/glv 60.00
93 M Ordonez/ hat/glv/jsy/shoe 40.00
94 J Buck/ glv/chst/shin/msk 20.00
95 P LoDuca/ jsy/chst/shin/msk 30.00

2002 PLAYOFF PIECE OF THE GAME

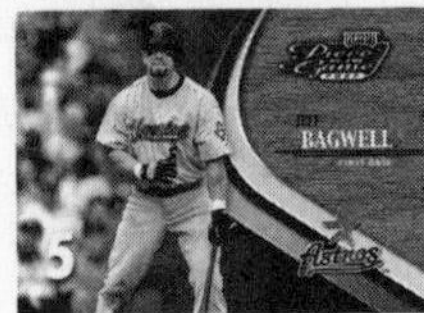

NM/M
Complete Set (100):
Common Player: .50
Common SP (51-100): 5.00
Production 500
Pack (5): 15.00
Box (6): 75.00
1 Vladimir Guerrero 1.50
2 Troy Glaus 1.50
3 Ichiro Suzuki 2.50
4 Chipper Jones 2.00
5 Roberto Alomar .75
6 Scott Rolen 1.25
7 Randy Johnson 1.50
8 Roger Clemens 2.25
9 Nomar Garciaparra 2.50
10 Greg Maddux 2.00
11 Barry Bonds 4.00
12 Derek Jeter 4.00
13 Albert Pujols 3.00
14 Kerry Wood 1.25
15 Jim Thome 1.50
16 Manny Ramirez 1.50
17 Carlos Delgado .75
18 Magglio Ordonez .50
19 Torii Hunter .50
20 Garret Anderson .50
21 Eric Chavez .60
22 Rafael Palmeiro 1.25
23 Andruw Jones 1.50
24 Cliff Floyd .50
25 Sammy Sosa 2.50
26 Mike Mussina .60
27 Jeff Bagwell 1.50
28 Miguel Tejada .60
29 Curt Schilling 1.00
30 Tom Glavine .75
31 Frank Thomas 1.50
32 Jim Edmonds .50
33 Juan Gonzalez 1.50
34 Todd Helton 1.50
35 Shawn Green .75
36 Alfonso Soriano 1.25
37 Lance Berkman .50
38 Barry Zito .60
39 Ryan Klesko .50
40 Larry Walker .50
41 Craig Biggio .50
42 Luis Gonzalez .50
43 Ivan Rodriguez 1.25
44 J.D. Drew .75
45 Roy Oswalt .50
46 Jason Giambi 1.25
47 Brian Giles .50
48 Richie Sexson .50
49 Pat Burrell .75
50 Alex Rodriguez 3.00
51 *So Taguchi* 8.00
52 *Allan Simpson* 5.00
53 *Oliver Perez* 10.00
54 *Ben Howard* 5.00
55 Kirk Saarloos 5.00
56 *Francis Beltran* 5.00
57 *Jorge Padilla* 5.00
58 *Brandon Puffer* 5.00
59 *Brian Mallette* 5.00
60 *Kyle Kane* 5.00
61 *Travis Driskill* 5.00
62 *Jeremy Lambert* 5.00
63 *Steve Kent* 5.00
64 *Julius Matos* 5.00
65 *Julio Mateo* 5.00
66 *Kazuhisa Ishii* 8.00
67 *Franklyn German* 5.00
68 *John Foster* 5.00
69 *Luis Ugueto* 5.00
70 *Shawn Sedlacek* 5.00
71 *Earl Snyder* 5.00
72 *Alex Pelaez* 5.00
73 *Victor Alvarez* 5.00
74 *Tom Shearn* 5.00
75 *Corey Thurman* 5.00
76 *Eric Junge* 5.00
77 *Hansel Izquierdo* 5.00
78 *Elio Serrano* 5.00
79 *J.J. Trujillo* 5.00
80 *Chris Snelling* 6.00
81 *Satoru Komiyama* 5.00
82 *Brandon Backe* 5.00
83 *Anderson Machado* 5.00
84 *Doug Devore* 5.00
85 *Steve Bechler* 5.00
86 *John Ennis* 5.00
87 *Rodrigo Rosario* 5.00
88 *Jorge Sosa* 5.00
89 *Ken Huckaby* 5.00
90 *Mike Moriarty* 5.00
91 *Michael Crudale* 5.00
92 *Kevin Frederick* 5.00
93 *Aaron Guiel* 5.00
94 Jose Rodriguez 5.00
95 *Andy Shibilo* 5.00
96 Deivis Santos 5.00
97 *Felix Escalona* 5.00
98 *Miguel Asencio* 5.00
99 *Takahito Nomura* 5.00
100 *Cam Esslinger* 5.00

Materials

NM/M
Common Materials (1-90): 4.00
Team Connections (91-95):
Production 500
Superstar Combos (96-100):
Production 250
Bronze Materials (1-90): 1-2X
Production 250
Bronze Team Connect. (91-95): 1.5-2X
Production 100
Bronze Combos (96-100): 2-3X
Production 50
Silver Materials (1-90): 1.5-2.5X
Production 150
Silver Tm. Connect. (91-95): 1.5-3X
Production 50
Silver Combos (96-100): No Pricing
Production 25
Gold Materials (1-90): 2-5X
Production 50
Gold Tm. Connect. (91-95): No Pricing
Production 25
Gold Combos (96-100): No Pricing
Production 10
Platinum Materials (1-90): No Pricing
Production 25
Platinum Tm Connect. (91-95): No Pricing
Production 10
Platinum Combos (96-100): No Pricing
Production 5
1 Adam Dunn/bat 8.00
2 Adrian Beltre/bat 4.00
3 Albert Pujols/base 10.00
4 Alex Rodriguez/jsy 12.00
5 Alex Rodriguez/bat 12.00
6 Andruw Jones/jsy 5.00
7 Andruw Jones/bat 5.00
8 Barry Bonds/base 15.00
9 Barry Larkin/bat 5.00
10 Juan Gonzalez/jsy 5.00
11 Bernie Williams/bat 6.00
12 Carlos Delgado/jsy 5.00
13 Chipper Jones/jsy 10.00
14 Chipper Jones/bat 10.00
15 Craig Biggio/jsy 5.00
16 Craig Biggio/bat 5.00
17 Cristian Guzman/jsy 5.00
18 Curt Schilling/jsy 6.00
19 Derek Jeter/base 15.00
20 Edgar Martinez/jsy 5.00
21 Edgardo Alfonzo/jsy 4.00
22 Ellis Burks/jsy 4.00
23 Frank Thomas/bat 6.00
24 Freddy Garcia/jsy 4.00
25 Greg Maddux/jsy 10.00
26 Harmon Killebrew/ pants 15.00
27 Hideo Nomo/jsy 12.00
28 Ichiro Suzuki/base 15.00
29 Ivan Rodriguez/jsy 8.00
30 Ivan Rodriguez/bat 8.00
31 J.D. Drew/bat 6.00
32 J.D. Drew/jsy 6.00
33 Javy Lopez/jsy 6.00
34 Jeff Bagwell/jsy 6.00
35 Jim Edmonds/jsy 6.00
36 Jim Edmonds/bat 6.00
37 John Olerud/bat 4.00
38 John Smoltz/jsy 6.00
39 Jose Cruz Jr/jsy 4.00
40 Jose Vidro/jsy 4.00
41 Juan Gonzalez/bat 6.00
42 Juan Pierre/jsy 4.00
43 Ken Griffey Jr/base 10.00
44 Kenny Lofton/bat 4.00
45 Kerry Wood/bat 8.00
46 Kevin Brown/jsy 4.00
47 Lance Berkman/jsy 6.00
48 Lance Berkman/bat 6.00
49 Larry Walker/jsy 5.00
50 Luis Gonzalez/jsy 5.00
51 Magglio Ordonez/jsy 5.00
52 Magglio Ordonez/bat 5.00
53 Manny Ramirez/jsy 8.00
54 Manny Ramirez/bat 8.00
55 Vladimir Guerrero/jsy 8.00
56 Mark Grace/bat 8.00
57 Michael Barrett/jsy 4.00
58 Miguel Tejada/jsy 8.00
59 Mike Piazza/jsy 12.00
60 Mike Piazza/bat 12.00
61 Mike Schmidt/bat 15.00
62 Mike Sweeney/jsy 4.00
63 Nolan Ryan/jsy 30.00
64 Nomar Garciaparra/jsy 15.00
65 Paul LoDuca/jsy 4.00
66 Rafael Palmeiro/jsy 8.00
67 Rafael Palmeiro/bat 8.00
68 Jose Canseco/bat 8.00
69 Raul Mondesi/jsy 4.00
70 Reggie Jackson/bat 8.00
71 Rickey Henderson/bat 8.00
72 Roberto Alomar/bat 6.00
73 Robin Ventura/jsy 4.00
74 Rod Carew/bat 10.00
75 Roger Clemens/jsy 15.00
76 Sammy Sosa/base 10.00
77 Sean Casey/jsy 5.00
78 Shannon Stewart/jsy 4.00
79 Shawn Green/jsy 6.00
80 Shawn Green/bat 6.00
81 Tim Hudson/jsy 6.00
82 Todd Helton/bat 8.00
83 Tom Glavine/jsy 6.00
84 Tony Gwynn/jsy 10.00
85 Tony Gwynn/jsy 10.00
86 Tony Gwynn/bat 10.00
87 Troy Glaus/jsy 6.00
88 Tsuyoshi Shinjo/bat 4.00
89 Vladimir Guerrero/jsy 8.00
90 Vladimir Guerrero/bat 8.00
91 Nomar Garciaparra, Pedro J. Martinez 30.00
92 Randy Johnson, Curt Schilling 15.00
93 Andruw Jones, Chipper Jones 15.00
94 Todd Helton, Larry Walker 15.00
95 Jeff Bagwell, raig Biggio 15.00
96 Alex Rodriguez 25.00
97 Greg Maddux 25.00
98 Mike Piazza 25.00
99 Lance Berkman 15.00
100 Vladimir Guerrero 20.00

2003 PLAYOFF ABSOLUTE MEMORABILIA

NM/M
Complete Set (200):
Common Player: .50
Common SP (151-200): 3.00
Production 1,500
Pack (6): 3.00
Box (18 + glass plaque): 85.00
1 Nomar Garciaparra 2.50
2 Barry Bonds 4.00
3 Greg Maddux 2.00
4 Roger Clemens 3.00
5 Derek Jeter 4.00
6 Alex Rodriguez 3.00
7 Chipper Jones 2.00
8 Sammy Sosa 2.50
9 Alfonso Soriano 1.00
10 Albert Pujols 3.00
11 Adam Dunn 1.00
12 Tom Glavine .75
13 Pedro J. Martinez 1.50
14 Jim Thome 1.00
15 Hideo Nomo 1.50
16 Roberto Alomar .75
17 Barry Zito .65
18 Troy Glaus 1.50
19 Kerry Wood 1.00
20 Magglio Ordonez .50
21 Todd Helton 1.50
22 Craig Biggio .50
23 Roy Oswalt .50
24 Torii Hunter .50
25 Miguel Tejada .65
26 Tsuyoshi Shinjo .50
27 Scott Rolen 1.00
28 Rafael Palmeiro 1.00
29 Victor Martinez .75
30 Hank Blalock .75
31 Jason Lane .50
32 Junior Spivey .50
33 Gary Sheffield .75
34 Corey Patterson .50
35 Corky Miller .50
36 Brian Tallet .50
37 Cliff Lee .50
38 Jason Jennings .50
39 Kirk Saarloos .50
40 Wade Miller .50
41 Angel Berroa .50

42 Mike Sweeney .50
43 Paul LoDuca .50
44 A.J. Pierzynski .50
45 Drew Henson .50
46 Eric Chavez .65
47 Tim Hudson .75
48 Aramis Ramirez .50
49 Jack Wilson .50
50 Ryan Klesko .50
51 Antonio Perez .50
52 Dewon Brazelton .50
53 Mark Teixeira .75
54 Eric Hinske .50
55 Freddy Sanchez .50
56 Mike Rivera .50
57 Alfredo Amezaga .50
58 Cliff Floyd .50
59 Brandon Larson .50
60 Richard Hidalgo .50
61 Cesar Izturis .50
62 Richie Sexson .50
63 Michael Cuddyer .50
64 Javier Vazquez .50
65 Brandon Claussen .50
66 Carlos Rivera .50
67 Vernon Wells .50
68 Kenny Lofton .50
69 Aubrey Huff .50
70 Adam LaRoche .50
71 Jeff Baker .50
72 Jose Castillo .50
73 Joe Borchard .50
74 Walter Young .50
75 Jose Morban .50
76 Vinnie Chulk .50
77 Christian Parker .50
78 Mike Piazza 2.50
79 Ichiro Suzuki 2.50
80 Kazuhisa Ishii .50
81 Rickey Henderson 1.50
82 Ken Griffey Jr. 2.50
83 Jason Giambi .75
84 Randy Johnson 1.50
85 Curt Schilling .75
86 Manny Ramirez 1.50
87 Barry Larkin .50
88 Jeff Bagwell 1.50
89 Vladimir Guerrero 1.50
90 Mike Mussina .65
91 Juan Gonzalez 1.50
92 Andruw Jones 1.50
93 Frank Thomas 1.50
94 Sean Casey .50
95 Josh Beckett .50
96 Lance Berkman .50
97 Shawn Green .75
98 Bernie Williams .65
99 Pat Burrell .75
100 Edgar Martinez .50
101 Ivan Rodriguez 1.00
102 Jeremy Guthrie .50
103 Alexis Rios .50
104 Nic Jackson .50
105 Jason Anderson .50
106 Travis Chapman .50
107 Mac Suzuki .50
108 Toby Hall .50
109 Mark Prior 1.50
110 So Taguchi .50
111 Marlon Byrd .50
112 Garret Anderson .50
113 Luis Gonzalez .50
114 Jay Gibbons .50
115 Mark Buehrle .50
116 Wily Mo Pena .50
117 C.C. Sabathia .50
118 Ricardo Rodriguez .50
119 Robert Fick .50
120 Rodrigo Rosario .50
121 Alexis Gomez .50
122 Carlos Beltran 1.00
123 Joe Thurston .50
124 Ben Sheets .50
125 Jose Vidro .50
126 Nick Johnson .50
127 Mark Mulder .50
128 Bobby Abreu .50
129 Brian Giles .50
130 Brian Lawrence .50
131 Jeff Kent .50
132 Chris Snelling .50
133 Kevin Mench .50
134 Carlos Delgado .75
135 Orlando Hudson .50
136 Juan Cruz .50
137 Jim Edmonds .50
138 Geronimo Gil .50
139 Joe Crede .50
140 Wilson Valdez .50
141 Runelvys Hernandez .50
142 Nick Neugebauer .50
143 Takahito Nomura .50
144 Andres Galarraga .50
145 Mark Grace .65
146 Brandon Duckworth .50
147 Oliver Perez .50
148 Xavier Nady .50
149 Rafael Soriano .50
150 Ben Kozlowski .50
151 *Prentice Redman* 3.00
152 *Craig Brazell* 5.00
153 *Nook Logan* 4.00
154 *Greg Aquino* 3.00
155 *Matt Kata* 5.00
156 *Ian Ferguson* 3.00
157 *Chien-Ming Wang* 5.00
158 *Beau Kemp* 3.00
159 *Alejandro Machado* 3.00
160 *Michael Hessman* 3.00
161 *Francisco Rosario* 4.00
162 Pedro Liriano 3.00
163 *Richard Fischer* 3.00
164 Franklin Perez 3.00
165 *Oscar Villarreal* 3.00
166 *Arnie Munoz* 3.00
167 *Tim Olson* 4.00
168 *Jose Contreras* 5.00
169 *Francisco Cruceta* 4.00
170 Jeremy Bonderman 4.00
171 Jeremy Griffiths 3.00
172 John Webb 3.00
173 *Phil Seibel* 3.00
174 *Aaron Looper* 3.00
175 *Brian Stokes* 3.00
176 *Guillermo Quiroz* 4.00
177 *Fernando Cabrera* 3.00
178 *Josh Hall* 4.00
179 *Diegomar Markwell* 3.00
180 *Andrew Brown* 3.00
181 *Doug Waechter* 4.00
182 *Felix Sanchez* 3.00
183 Gerardo Garcia 3.00
184 *Matt Bruback* 3.00
185 *Michel Hernandez* 3.00
186 *Rett Johnson* 3.00
187 *Ryan Cameron* 3.00
188 *Rob Hammock* 4.00
189 *Clint Barmes* 10.00
190 *Brandon Webb* 4.00
191 *Jon Leicester* 3.00
192 *Shane Bazzell* 4.00
193 *Joe Valentine* 3.00
194 *Josh Stewart* 4.00
195 *Pete LaForest* 3.00
196 *Shane Victorino* 4.00
197 *Terrmel Sledge* 3.00
198 *Lew Ford* 5.00
199 *Todd Wellemeyer* 4.00
200 *Hideki Matsui* 10.00

Spectrum

Stars (1-150): 3-5X
Rookies (151-200): .75-2X
Production 100 sets

Absolutely Ink

NM/M

Common Player:
Inserted 1:552
Blues: No Pricing
Production 10-25
Golds: No Pricing
Production 5-10
1 Vladimir Guerrero 50.00
6 Eric Hinske 15.00
8 Jose Vidro 8.00
16 Rodrigo Rosario 8.00
17 Brandon Claussen 20.00
18 Jermaine Dye 8.00
22 Mark Prior 75.00
24 Brian Lawrence 8.00
29 Barry Larkin 50.00
30 Drew Henson 40.00
36 Mark Teixeira 30.00
38 Roberto Alomar 30.00
39 Barry Zito 35.00

Glass Plaques

NM/M

One per box:
Roberto Alomar/bat/jsy/100 40.00
Roberto Alomar/jsy/150 30.00
Jeff Bagwell/bat/jsy/100 40.00
Jeff Bagwell/jsy/150 30.00
Ernie Banks/jsy/150 40.00
Lance Berkman/bat/jsy/100 35.00
Lance Berkman/jsy/150 25.00
Barry Bonds/ball/base/50 85.00
Barry Bonds/ball/base/100 75.00
Barry Bonds/base/200 50.00
George Brett/bat/jsy/50 125.00
George Brett/jsy/200 50.00
Pat Burrell/bat/jsy/100 35.00
Pat Burrell/jsy/150 30.00
Steve Carlton/auto/50 60.00
Steve Carlton/bat/jsy/100 40.00
Steve Carlton/jsy/150 30.00
Roger Clemens/glv/jsy/50 150.00
Roger Clemens/jsy/150 60.00
Roger Clemens/glv/jsy/50 150.00
Roger Clemens/jsy/200 60.00
Roberto Clemente/bat/jsy/150 80.00
Roberto Clemente/jsy/200 60.00
Jose Contreras/jsy/jsy/100 30.00
Jose Contreras/jsy/150 25.00
Adam Dunn/bat/jsy/100 40.00
Adam Dunn/jsy/150 30.00
Bob Feller/auto/50 65.00
Bob Feller/jsy/jsy/50 50.00
Bob Feller/jsy/100 30.00
Nomar Garciaparra/bat/jsy/100 65.00
Nomar Garciaparra/jsy/200 55.00
Jason Giambi/bat/jsy/100 50.00
Jason Giambi/jsy/150 40.00
Troy Glaus/bat/jsy/100 40.00
Troy Glaus/jsy/150 35.00
Juan Gonzalez/bat/jsy/100 40.00
Juan Gonzalez/jsy/150 30.00
Luis Gonzalez/bat/jsy/100 30.00
Luis Gonzalez/jsy/150 25.00
Mark Grace/auto/50 100.00
Mark Grace/bat/jsy/100 45.00
Mark Grace/jsy/150 35.00
Shawn Green/bat/jsy/100 30.00
Shawn Green/jsy/150 25.00
Ken Griffey Jr/ball/base/100 50.00
Ken Griffey Jr/base/200 40.00
Vladimir Guerrero/bat/jsy/100 40.00
Vladimir Guerrero/jsy/150 35.00
Tony Gwynn/bat/jsy/150 50.00
Tony Gwynn/jsy/200 40.00
Todd Helton/auto/25
Todd Helton/bat/jsy/100 40.00
Todd Helton/jsy/150 30.00
Rickey Henderson/bat/jsy/100 50.00
Rickey Henderson/jsy/200 40.00
Tim Hudson/auto/50 65.00
Tim Hudson/hat/jsy/100 30.00
Tim Hudson/jsy/150 25.00
Torii Hunter/auto/50 65.00
Torii Hunter/hat/jsy/100 40.00
Torii Hunter/jsy/150 30.00
Kazuhisa Ishii/bat/jsy/100 30.00
Kazuhisa Ishii/jsy/200 25.00
Derek Jeter/ball/base/150 60.00
Derek Jeter/base/200 50.00
Randy Johnson/bat/jsy/100 50.00
Randy Johnson/jsy/150 40.00
Andruw Jones/bat/jsy/100 35.00
Andruw Jones/jsy/150 30.00
Chipper Jones/bat/jsy/100 40.00
Chipper Jones/jsy/150 30.00
Al Kaline/bat/jsy/100 40.00
Al Kaline/jsy/150 35.00
Barry Larkin/auto/50 60.00
Barry Larkin/bat/jsy/100 40.00
Barry Larkin/jsy/150 30.00
Greg Maddux/bat/jsy/100 50.00
Greg Maddux/jsy/200 40.00
Pedro Martinez/bat/jsy/100 40.00
Pedro Martinez/jsy/150 35.00
Hideki Matsui/ball/base/50 110.00
Hideki Matsui/ball/base/150 75.00
Hideki Matsui/base/200 55.00
Don Mattingly/bat/jsy/100 65.00
Don Mattingly/jsy/200 50.00
Mark Mulder/auto/50 60.00
Mark Mulder/jsy/150 25.00
Mark Mulder/jsy/jsy/100 30.00
Stan Musial/bat/jsy/150 65.00
Stan Musial/jsy/200 60.00
Hideo Nomo/bat/jsy/50 60.00
Hideo Nomo/bat/jsy/100 40.00
Hideo Nomo/jsy/200 30.00
Magglio Ordonez/auto/50 50.00
Magglio Ordonez/bat/jsy/100 30.00
Magglio Ordonez/jsy/150 25.00
Roy Oswalt/auto/50 50.00
Roy Oswalt/b at/jsy/100 30.00
Roy Oswalt/jsy/150 25.00
Rafael Palmeiro/bat/jsy/100 40.00
Rafael Palmeiro/jsy/150 30.00
Mike Piazza/auto/15
Mike Piazza/bat/jsy/50 75.00
Mike Piazza/bat/jsy/100 50.00
Mike Piazza/jsy/200 40.00
Mark Prior/bat/jsy/100 75.00
Mark Prior/jsy/150 60.00
Albert Pujols/bat/jsy/150 75.00
Albert Pujols/jsy/150 60.00
Manny Ramirez/bat/jsy/100 40.00
Manny Ramirez/jsy/150 30.00
Cal Ripken Jr/bat/jsy/150 90.00
Cal Ripken Jr/jsy/200 70.00
Frank Robinson/auto/50 65.00
Frank Robinson/bat/jsy/100 40.00
Frank Robinson/jsy/150 30.00
Alex Rodriguez/bat/jsy/100 50.00
Alex Rodriguez/jsy/200 40.00
Nolan Ryan/jkt/jsy/150 90.00
Nolan Ryan/jsy/200 75.00
Nolan Ryan/jsy/jsy/100 100.00
Ryne Sandberg/bat/jsy/50 100.00
Ryne Sandberg/jsy/200 65.00
Curt Schilling/glv/jsy/50 50.00
Curt Schilling/jsy/150 30.00
Mike Schmidt/bat/jsy/100 70.00
Mike Schmidt/jsy/200 50.00
Ozzie Smith/bat/jsy/150 65.00
Ozzie Smith/jsy/150 50.00
Alfonso Soriano/bat/jsy/150 60.00
Alfonso Soriano/jsy/150 50.00

Sammy Sosa/ bat/jsy/150 50.00
Sammy Sosa/jsy/200 40.00
Junior Spivey/auto/50 50.00
Junior Spivey/ bat/jsy/100 30.00
Junior Spivey/jsy/150 25.00
Ichiro Suzuki/ ball/base/50 80.00
Ichiro Suzuki/ ball/base/150 60.00
Ichiro Suzuki/base/200 40.00
Mark Teixeira/ bat/jsy/100 40.00
Mark Teixeira/jsy/150 30.00
Miguel Tejada/auto/50 60.00
Miguel Tejada/ bat/jsy/100 40.00
Miguel Tejada/jsy/150 30.00
Frank Thomas/ bat/jsy/100 40.00
Frank Thomas/jsy/150 30.00
Bernie Williams/ bat/jsy/100 40.00
Bernie Williams/ jsy/150 35.00
Kerry Wood/auto/50 80.00
Kerry Wood/ bat/jsy/100 45.00
Kerry Wood/jsy/150 35.00
Barry Zito/auto/50 75.00
Barry Zito/hat/jsy/100 40.00
Barry Zito/jsy/150 30.00

Player's Collection - Jersey

NM/M
Common Player: 4.00
Production 75 sets
1 Adam Dunn 6.00
2 Adrian Beltre 4.00
3 Alex Rodriguez 15.00
4 Alfonso Soriano 12.00
5 Andruw Jones 8.00
6 Andy Pettitte 6.00
7 Barry Larkin 6.00
8 Barry Zito 6.00
9 Ben Grieve 4.00
10 Bernie Williams 8.00
11 Cal Ripken Jr. 40.00
12 Carlos Delgado 6.00
13 C.C. Sabathia 4.00
14 Chipper Jones 10.00
15 Craig Biggio 4.00
16 Curt Schilling 6.00
17 Alex Rodriguez 15.00
18 Frank Thomas 8.00
19 Freddy Garcia 4.00
20 Jay Bell 4.00
21 Roger Clemens 15.00
22 Tony Gwynn 10.00
23 Ivan Rodriguez 8.00
24 Jason Giambi 8.00
25 Jason Jennings 4.00
26 Jay Payton 4.00
27 J.D. Drew 5.00
28 Jeff Bagwell 8.00
29 Jeromy Burnitz 4.00
30 Jim Edmonds 6.00
31 Jim Thome 8.00
32 Joe Borchard 4.00
33 Joe Mays 4.00
34 John Olerud 5.00
35 David Wells 4.00
36 Juan Gonzalez 8.00
37 Kazuhiro Sasaki 4.00
38 Chan Ho Park 4.00
39 Kerry Wood 10.00
40 Kevin Brown 4.00
41 Lance Berkman 6.00
42 Larry Walker 4.00
43 Bret Boone 6.00
44 Magglio Ordonez 6.00
45 Manny Ramirez 8.00
46 Mark Mulder 6.00
47 Mark Prior 15.00
48 Matt Williams 4.00
49 Miguel Tejada 5.00
50 Mike Piazza 12.00
51 Nomar Garciaparra 15.00
52 Doug Davis 4.00
53 Paul Konerko 4.00
54 Paul LoDuca 4.00
55 Pedro J. Martinez 10.00
56 Preston Wilson 4.00
57 4.00
58 Marlon Byrd 4.00
59 Reggie Sanders 4.00
60 Richie Sexson 6.00
61 4.00
62 Rickey Henderson 8.00
63 Robert Person 4.00
64 4.00
65 Roger Clemens 15.00
66 Roy Oswalt 6.00
67 Ryan Klesko 4.00
68 Sammy Sosa 15.00
69 Shawn Green 6.00
70 Steve Finley 4.00
71 Terrence Long 4.00
72 Tim Hudson 6.00
73 Toby Hall 4.00
74 Todd Helton 8.00
75 Travis Lee 4.00
76 Troy Glaus 8.00
77 Tsuyoshi Shinjo 4.00
78 Vernon Wells 6.00
79 Vladimir Guerrero 8.00
80 Wes Helms 4.00

Player's Collection - Bat

NM/M
Common Player: 4.00
Production 75 sets
81 Alex Rodriguez 15.00
82 Alfonso Soriano 12.00
83 Barry Larkin 8.00
84 Roberto Alomar 8.00
85 Ivan Rodriguez 8.00
86 Jason Giambi 8.00
87 Jeff Bagwell 8.00
88 Juan Gonzalez 8.00
89 Larry Walker 4.00
90 Luis Gonzalez 4.00
91 Magglio Ordonez 6.00
92 Manny Ramirez 8.00
93 Marlon Byrd 4.00
94 Mike Piazza 12.00
95 Pat Burrell 8.00
96 Todd Helton 8.00
97 Rickey Henderson 8.00
98 Andruw Jones 8.00
99 Craig Biggio 4.00
100 Mark Prior 15.00

Materials Jersey Number

NM/M
Many not priced due to scarcity
2 Yogi Berra/35 40.00
3 Vladimir Guerrero/27 35.00
4 Randy Johnson/51 25.00
5 Andruw Jones/25 25.00
10 Alfonso Soriano/33 35.00
13 Rafael Palmeiro/25 20.00

Materials Season

NM/M
Common Player: 5.00
Quantity produced listed
1 Stan Musial/42 75.00
2 Yogi Berra/47 40.00
3 Vladimir Guerrero/97 15.00
4 Randy Johnson/89 20.00
5 Andruw Jones/96 10.00
6 Jeff Kent/92 5.00
8 Hideo Nomo/95 20.00
9 Ivan Rodriguez/91 10.00
10 Alfonso Soriano/101 20.00
11 Scott Rolen/96 15.00
12 Juan Gonzalez/89 15.00
13 Rafael Palmeiro/86 15.00
14 Mike Schmidt/73 60.00
15 Cal Ripken Jr./82 75.00

Spectrum Signatures

NM/M
Common Autograph: 6.00
Varying quantities produced
10 Albert Pujols/10 165.00
16 Roberto Alomar/15 100.00

17 Barry Zito/25 75.00
20 Magglio Ordonez/25 50.00
23 Roy Oswalt/25 30.00
24 Torii Hunter/25 40.00
29 Victor Martinez/100 30.00
30 Hank Blalock/50 30.00
32 Junior Spivey/50 15.00
34 Corey Patterson/50 20.00
35 Corky Miller/100 6.00
36 Brian Tallet/100 6.00
37 Cliff Lee/100 8.00
38 Jason Jennings/100 8.00
39 Kirk Saarloos/100 6.00
40 Wade Miller/50 15.00
41 Angel Berroa/100 10.00
42 Mike Sweeney/50 15.00
43 Paul LoDuca/50 20.00
44 A.J. Pierzynski/100 15.00
45 Drew Henson/50 25.00
47 Tim Hudson/50 40.00
51 Antonio Perez/25 8.00
52 Dewon Brazelton/50 15.00
53 Mark Teixeira/50 40.00
54 Eric Hinske/100 15.00
55 Freddy Sanchez/100 15.00
57 Alfredo Amezaga/100 10.00
59 Brandon Larson/100 8.00
60 Richard Hidalgo/100 10.00
62 Richie Sexson/25 30.00
63 Michael Cuddyer/100 15.00
68 Kenny Lofton/50 30.00
69 Aubrey Huff/100 15.00
70 Adam LaRoche/100 15.00
71 Jeff Baker/100 10.00
72 Jose Castillo/100 10.00
73 Joe Borchard/100 10.00
74 Walter Young/100 8.00
76 Vinnie Chulk/100 8.00
80 Kazuhisa Ishii/25 60.00
87 Barry Larkin/50 50.00
89 Vladimir Guerrero/50 50.00
92 Andruw Jones/25 60.00
95 Josh Beckett/100 25.00
100 Edgar Martinez/50 25.00
102 Jeremy Guthrie/100 15.00
103 Alexis Rios/100 20.00
104 Nic Jackson/100 8.00
105 Jason Anderson/100 8.00
106 Travis Chapman/100 8.00
107 Mac Suzuki/304 15.00
109 Mark Prior/50 75.00
111 Marlon Byrd/100 10.00
114 Jay Gibbons/100 10.00
118 Ricardo Rodriguez/100 10.00
119 Robert Fick/100 10.00
120 Rodrigo Rosario/250 8.00
121 Alexis Gomez/100 10.00
124 Ben Sheets/50 20.00
126 Nick Johnson/50 10.00
127 Mark Mulder/50 40.00
132 Chris Snelling/100 8.00
133 Kevin Mench/100 10.00
135 Orlando Hudson/50 15.00
139 Joe Crede/100 10.00
140 Wilson Valdez/25 10.00
141 Runelvys Hernandez/ 100 10.00
143 Takahito Nomura/47 15.00
147 Oliver Perez/50 15.00
148 Xavier Nady/100 12.00
150 Ben Kozlowski/100 8.00
151 Prentice Redman/250 10.00
152 Craig Brazell/250 10.00
153 Nook Logan/250 6.00
154 Greg Aquino/250 8.00
155 Matt Kata/250 15.00
156 Ian Ferguson/250 6.00
157 Chien-Ming Wang/250 20.00
158 Beau Kemp/250 6.00
159 Alejandro Machado/250 6.00
160 Michael Hessman/160 6.00
161 Francisco Rosario/250 6.00
162 Pedro Liriano/250 6.00
163 Richard Fischer/250 6.00
164 Franklin Perez/250 6.00
165 Oscar Villarreal/250 10.00
166 Arnie Munoz/250 6.00
167 Tim Olson/250 8.00
168 Jose Contreras/250 25.00
169 Francisco Cruceta/250 8.00
170 Jeremy Bonderman/ 250 15.00
171 Jeremy Griffiths/250 8.00
172 John Webb/250 6.00
173 Phil Seibel/250 6.00
174 Aaron Looper/250 6.00
175 Brian Stokes/250 6.00
176 Guillermo Quiroz/250 8.00
177 Fernando Cabrera/250 10.00
178 Josh Hall/250 10.00
179 Diegomar Markwell/250 6.00
180 Andrew Brown/250 8.00
181 Doug Waechter/250 8.00
182 Felix Sanchez/250 8.00
183 Gerardo Garcia/250 8.00
184 Matt Bruback/250 6.00
185 Michel Hernandez/250 6.00
186 Rett Johnson/250 10.00
187 Ryan Cameron/250 6.00
188 Rob Hammock/250 15.00
189 Clint Barmes/250 15.00
190 Brandon Webb/250 15.00
191 Jon Leicester/250 6.00
192 Shane Bazzell/250 10.00
193 Joe Valentine/250 8.00
194 Josh Stewart/250 15.00
195 Pete LaForest/250 8.00
196 Shane Victorino/250 8.00
197 Terrmel Sledge/250 6.00
198 Lew Ford/250 15.00
199 Todd Wellemeyer/250 10.00

Team Tandems

NM/M
Common Duo: 2.00
Inserted 1:48
Spectrums: 1-2X
Production 100 sets
1 Mark Prior, Sammy Sosa 8.00
2 Vladimir Guerrero, Jose Vidro 3.00
3 Bernie Williams, Alfonso Soriano 6.00
4 Mike Sweeney, Carlos Beltran 2.00
5 Magglio Ordonez, Paul Konerko 2.00
6 Adam Dunn, Austin Kearns 3.00
7 Randy Johnson, Curt Schilling 4.00
8 Hideo Nomo, Kazuhisa Ishii 2.00
9 Pat Burrell, Bobby Abreu 3.00
10 Todd Helton, Larry Walker 2.00

Team Tandems Material

NM/M
Common Duo:
Quantity produced listed
Spectrums: No Pricing
Production 25 or 10
1 Mark Prior, Sammy Sosa/100 35.00
2 Vladimir Guerrero, Jose Vidro/100 10.00

3 Bernie Williams, Alfonso Soriano/100 20.00
4 Mike Sweeney, Carlos Beltran/100 6.00
5 Magglio Ordonez, Paul Konerko/100 6.00
6 Adam Dunn, Austin Kearns/100 15.00
7 Randy Johnson, Curt Schilling/100 15.00
8 Hideo Nomo, Kazuhisa Ishii/40 50.00
9 Pat Burrell, Bobby Abreu/40 20.00
10 Todd Helton, Larry Walker/100 8.00

Team Trios

NM/M

Common Trio: 5.00
Inserted 1:88
Spectrums: 1-2X
Production 50 sets
1 Greg Maddux, Chipper Jones, Andruw Jones 8.00
2 Sammy Sosa, Mark Prior, Kerry Wood 8.00
3 Pedro Martinez, Nomar Garciaparra, Manny Ramirez 8.00
4 Jason Giambi, Roger Clemens, Alfonso Soriano 8.00
5 Alex Rodriguez, Rafael Palmeiro, Mark Teixeira 8.00
6 Mike Piazza, Roberto Alomar, Tsuyoshi Shinjo 6.00
7 Jeff Bagwell, Craig Biggio, Lance Berkman 5.00
8 Troy Glaus, Garret Anderson, Troy Percival 5.00
9 Miguel Tejada, Eric Chavez, Barry Zito 5.00
10 Luis Gonzalez, Randy Johnson, Curt Schilling 6.00

Team Trios Materials

NM/M

Quantity produced listed 5.00
Spectrums: No Pricing
Production 10 or 25
1 Greg Maddux, Chipper Jones, Andruw Jones/100 30.00
2 Sammy Sosa, Mark Prior, Kerry Wood/100 40.00
3 Pedro Martinez, Nomar Garciaparra, Manny Ramirez/50 50.00
4 Jason Giambi, Roger Clemens, Alfonso Soriano/100 40.00
5 Alex Rodriguez, Rafael Palmeiro, Mark Teixeira/100 25.00
6 Mike Piazza, Roberto Alomar, Tsuyoshi Shinjo/40 40.00
7 Jeff Bagwell, Craig Biggio, Lance Berkman/100 20.00
8 Troy Glaus, Garret Anderson, Troy Percival/40 25.00
9 Miguel Tejada, Eric Chavez, Barry Zito/100 20.00
10 Luis Gonzalez, Randy Johnson, Curt Schilling/100 25.00

Tools of the Trade

NM/M

Complete Set (110): 125.00
Common Player: 1.00
Inserted 1:5
1 Sammy Sosa 4.00
2 Nomar Garciaparra 5.00
3 Andruw Jones 1.50
4 Troy Glaus 1.00
5 Greg Maddux 4.00
6 Rickey Henderson 1.00
7 Alex Rodriguez 6.00
8 Manny Ramirez 1.50
9 Lance Berkman 1.00
10 Roger Clemens 5.00
11 Ivan Rodriguez 1.00
12 Kazuhisa Ishii 1.00
13 Alfonso Soriano 3.00
14 Austin Kearns 1.00
15 Mike Piazza 3.00
16 Curt Schilling 1.00
17 Jeff Bagwell 1.50
18 Todd Helton 1.50
19 Randy Johnson 2.00
20 Vladimir Guerrero 1.50
21 Kerry Wood 1.00
22 Rafael Palmeiro 1.00
23 Roy Oswalt 1.00
24 Chipper Jones 3.00
25 Pat Burrell 1.00
26 Jason Giambi 2.00
27 Pedro J. Martinez 2.00
28 Roberto Alomar 1.00
29 Shawn Green 1.00
30 Adam Dunn 1.00
31 Juan Gonzalez 1.50
32 Mark Prior 6.00
33 Hideo Nomo 1.00
34 Torii Hunter 1.00
35 Mark Teixeira 1.00
36 Craig Biggio 1.00
37 Rafael Palmeiro 1.00
38 Jeff Bagwell 1.50
39 Albert Pujols 6.00
40 Richie Sexson 1.00
41 Alex Rodriguez 6.00
42 Carlos Delgado 1.50
43 Frank Thomas 1.50
44 Sammy Sosa 4.00
45 Marlon Byrd 1.00
46 Mark Prior 6.00
47 Adrian Beltre 1.00
48 Tom Glavine 1.00
49 So Taguchi 1.00
50 Jeff Bagwell 1.50
51 Mike Sweeney 1.00
52 Luis Gonzalez 1.00
53 Chipper Jones 3.00
54 Jason Giambi 2.00
55 Miguel Tejada 1.00
56 Todd Helton 1.50
57 Andruw Jones 1.50
58 Mike Piazza 3.00
59 Manny Ramirez 1.50
60 Randy Johnson 2.00
61 Carlos Beltran 1.00
62 Victor Martinez 1.00
63 Orlando Hudson 1.00
64 Jeff Kent 1.00
65 Greg Maddux 4.00
66 Garret Anderson 1.00
67 Joe Thurston 1.00
68 Mark Teixeira 1.00
69 Kazuhisa Ishii 1.00
70 Austin Kearns 1.00
71 Pat Burrell 1.00
72 Joe Borchard 1.00
73 Josh Phelps 1.00
74 Travis Hafner 1.00
75 So Taguchi 1.00
76 Victor Martinez 1.00
77 Paul LoDuca 1.00
78 Bernie Williams 1.00
79 Josh Phelps 1.00
80 Marlon Byrd 1.00
81 Manny Ramirez 1.50
82 Jason Giambi 2.00
83 Jeff Bagwell 1.50
84 Sammy Sosa 4.00
85 Josh Phelps 1.00
86 Tim Hudson 1.00
87 Randy Johnson 2.00
88 Troy Glaus 1.00
89 Joe Thurston 1.00
90 Miguel Tejada 1.00
91 Adam Dunn 1.00
92 Magglio Ordonez 1.00
93 Mike Sweeney 1.00
94 Andruw Jones 1.50
95 Carlos Beltran 1.00
96 Joe Borchard 1.00
97 Austin Kearns 1.00
98 Richie Sexson 1.00
99 Mark Prior 6.00
100 Mark Teixeira 1.00
101 Ryan Klesko 1.00
102 Jason Jennings 1.00
103 Travis Hafner 1.00
104 Mark Buehrle 1.00
105 Eric Hinske 1.00
106 Rafael Palmeiro 1.00
107 Roy Oswalt 1.00
108 Kerry Wood 1.00
109 Brian Giles 1.00
110 Ivan Rodriguez 1.00

Tools of the Trade Materials

NM/M

Common Player: 3.00
Quantity produced listed
Spectrums: 1-2.5X
Production 10 to 50
1 Sammy Sosa/250 10.00
2 Nomar Garciaparra/250 10.00
3 Andruw Jones/250 5.00
4 Troy Glaus/250 5.00
5 Greg Maddux/250 10.00
6 Rickey Henderson/40 25.00
7 Alex Rodriguez/250 10.00
8 Manny Ramirez/250 6.00
9 Lance Berkman/250 4.00
10 Roger Clemens/250 10.00
11 Ivan Rodriguez/250 6.00
12 Kazuhisa Ishii/40 5.00
13 Alfonso Soriano/250 10.00
14 Austin Kearns/250 5.00
15 Mike Piazza/250 10.00
16 Curt Schilling/250 5.00
17 Jeff Bagwell/250 6.00
18 Todd Helton/250 6.00
19 Randy Johnson/250 6.00
20 Vladimir Guerrero/250 6.00
21 Kerry Wood/250 6.00
22 Rafael Palmeiro/250 6.00
23 Roy Oswalt/250 3.00
24 Chipper Jones/250 8.00
25 Pat Burrell/40 15.00
26 Jason Giambi/250 8.00
27 Pedro J. Martinez/250 8.00
28 Roberto Alomar/40 15.00
29 Shawn Green/250 3.00
30 Adam Dunn/250 5.00
31 Juan Gonzalez/40 15.00
32 Mark Prior/250 12.00
33 Hideo Nomo/250 8.00
34 Torii Hunter/250 5.00
35 Mark Teixeira/250 5.00
36 Craig Biggio/250 4.00
37 Rafael Palmeiro/250 5.00
38 Jeff Bagwell/250 5.00
39 Albert Pujols/200 12.00
40 Richie Sexson/250 4.00
41 Alex Rodriguez/250 10.00
42 Carlos Delgado/250 3.00
43 Frank Thomas/75 8.00
44 Sammy Sosa/250 10.00
45 Marlon Byrd/250 3.00
46 Mark Prior/250 12.00
47 Adrian Beltre/250 3.00
48 Tom Glavine/250 3.00
49 So Taguchi/250 3.00
50 Jeff Bagwell/250 5.00
51 Mike Sweeney/250 3.00
52 Luis Gonzalez/250 3.00
53 Chipper Jones/100 8.00
54 Jason Giambi/250 6.00
55 Miguel Tejada/250 4.00
56 Todd Helton/250 5.00
57 Andruw Jones/250 5.00
58 Mike Piazza/250 8.00
59 Manny Ramirez/250 6.00
60 Randy Johnson/250 6.00
61 Carlos Beltran/250 3.00
62 Victor Martinez/250 3.00
63 Orlando Hudson/250 3.00
64 Jeff Kent/250 3.00
65 Greg Maddux/250 8.00
66 Garret Anderson/150 4.00
67 Joe Thurston/250 3.00
68 Mark Teixeira/250 3.00
69 Kazuhisa Ishii/250 3.00
70 Austin Kearns/250 4.00
71 Pat Burrell/100 8.00
72 Joe Borchard/250 3.00
73 Josh Phelps/250 3.00
74 Travis Hafner/250 3.00
75 So Taguchi/125 3.00
76 Victor Martinez/125 5.00
77 Paul LoDuca/125 3.00
78 Bernie Williams/125 8.00
79 Josh Phelps/125 5.00
80 Marlon Byrd/125 5.00
81 Manny Ramirez/100 10.00
82 Jason Giambi/125 10.00
83 Jeff Bagwell/50 15.00
84 Sammy Sosa/125 20.00
85 Josh Phelps/125 3.00
86 Tim Hudson/125 5.00
87 Randy Johnson/125 10.00
88 Troy Glaus/125 8.00
89 Joe Thurston/125 4.00
90 Miguel Tejada/125 5.00
91 Adam Dunn/100 15.00
92 Magglio Ordonez/100 10.00
93 Mike Sweeney/100 10.00
94 Andruw Jones/100 15.00
95 Carlos Beltran/100 8.00
96 Joe Borchard/100 8.00
97 Austin Kearns/100 15.00
98 Richie Sexson/50 15.00
99 Mark Prior/50 75.00
100 Mark Teixeira/50 20.00
101 Ryan Klesko/50 10.00
102 Jason Jennings/50 10.00
103 Travis Hafner/50 10.00
104 Mark Buehrle/50 15.00
105 Eric Hinske/50 20.00
106 Rafael Palmeiro/50 40.00
107 Roy Oswalt/50 20.00
108 Kerry Wood/50 40.00
109 Brian Giles/50 15.00
110 Ivan Rodriguez/50 25.00

Bases Materials 1B

NM/M

Common Player: 4.00
Quantity produced listed
1 Albert Pujols/109 12.00
2 Nomar Garciaparra/112 12.00
3 Jason Giambi/100 8.00
4 Miguel Tejada/140 4.00
5 Rafael Palmeiro/58 5.00
6 Sammy Sosa/90 15.00
7 Pat Burrell/87 8.00
8 Lance Berkman/90 4.00
9 Bernie Williams/146 6.00
10 Jim Thome/73 8.00
11 Carlos Beltran/94 4.00
12 Eric Chavez/93 4.00
13 Alex Rodriguez/101 15.00
14 Magglio Ordonez/103 4.00
15 Brian Giles/68 4.00
16 Alfonso Soriano/117 10.00
17 Shawn Green/92 4.00
18 Vladimir Guerrero/128 6.00
19 Garret Anderson/107 4.00
20 Todd Helton/109 6.00
21 Barry Bonds/70 20.00
22 Jeff Kent/114 4.00
23 Torii Hunter/92 6.00
24 Ichiro Suzuki/165 25.00
25 Derek Jeter/147 25.00
26 Chipper Jones/117 8.00
27 Jeff Bagwell/100 8.00
28 Mike Piazza/76 10.00
29 Rickey Henderson/28 40.00
30 Ken Griffey Jr./36 40.00

Total Bases

NM/M

Complete Set (30): 60.00
Common Player: 1.00
Inserted 1:16
1 Albert Pujols 6.00
2 Nomar Garciaparra 6.00
3 Jason Giambi 3.00
4 Miguel Tejada 1.00
5 Rafael Palmeiro 1.50
6 Sammy Sosa 5.00
7 Pat Burrell 1.50
8 Lance Berkman 1.00
9 Bernie Williams 1.50
10 Jim Thome 2.00
11 Carlos Beltran 1.00
12 Eric Chavez 1.00
13 Alex Rodriguez 6.00
14 Magglio Ordonez 1.00

15 Brian Giles 1.00
16 Alfonso Soriano 3.00
17 Shawn Green 1.00
18 Vladimir Guerrero 2.00
19 Garret Anderson 1.00
20 Todd Helton 2.00
21 Barry Bonds 8.00
22 Jeff Kent 1.00
23 Torii Hunter 1.00
24 Ichiro Suzuki 4.00
25 Derek Jeter 8.00
26 Chipper Jones 4.00
27 Jeff Bagwell 2.00
28 Mike Piazza 4.00
29 Rickey Henderson 1.50
30 Ken Griffey Jr. 4.00

Total Bases Materials 2B

NM/M

Quantity produced listed
1 Albert Pujols/40 40.00
2 Nomar Garciaparra/56 25.00
3 Jason Giambi/34 15.00
4 Miguel Tejada/30 10.00
5 Rafael Palmeiro/34 15.00
6 Sammy Sosa/19
7 Pat Burrell/39 10.00
8 Lance Berkman/35 8.00
9 Bernie Williams/37 15.00
10 Jim Thome/19
11 Carlos Beltran/44 8.00
12 Eric Chavez/31 10.00
13 Alex Rodriguez/27 50.00
14 Magglio Ordonez/47 8.00
15 Brian Giles/37 8.00
16 Alfonso Soriano/51 25.00
17 Shawn Green/31 10.00
18 Vladimir Guerrero/37 15.00
19 Garret Anderson/56 8.00
20 Todd Helton/39 15.00
21 Barry Bonds/31 50.00
22 Jeff Kent/42 8.00
23 Torii Hunter/37 15.00
24 Ichiro Suzuki/27
25 Derek Jeter/26 50.00
26 Chipper Jones/35 25.00
27 Jeff Bagwell/33 25.00
28 Mike Piazza/23 35.00
29 Rickey Henderson/6
30 Ken Griffey Jr./8

Total Bases Materials 3B

No pricing due to scarcity

Total Bases Materials HR

NM/M

Quantity produced listed
1 Albert Pujols/34 40.00
3 Jason Giambi/41 20.00
4 Miguel Tejada/41 10.00
5 Rafael Palmeiro/43 15.00
6 Sammy Sosa/49 30.00
7 Pat Burrell/37 15.00
8 Lance Berkman/42 10.00
10 Jim Thome/52 15.00
11 Carlos Beltran/29 10.00
12 Eric Chavez/34 12.00
13 Alex Rodriguez/57 25.00
14 Magglio Ordonez/58 8.00
15 Brian Giles/38 8.00
16 Alfonso Soriano/39 30.00
17 Shawn Green/42 8.00
18 Vladimir Guerrero/39 15.00
19 Garret Anderson/29 15.00
20 Todd Helton/30 15.00
21 Barry Bonds/46 40.00
22 Jeff Kent/37 8.00
23 Torii Hunter/29 25.00
26 Chipper Jones/26 35.00
27 Jeff Bagwell/31 20.00
28 Mike Piazza/33 30.00

2003 PLAYOFF PIECE OF THE GAME

NM/M

Common Player: 4.00
Pack (1): 12.00
Box (6): 60.00
1 Adam Dunn/bat 8.00
2 Adam Dunn/jsy 8.00
3 Adrian Beltre/bat 6.00
4 Albert Pujols/jsy 15.00
5 Albert Pujols/bat 15.00
6 Alex Rodriguez/bat 10.00
7 Alex Rodriguez/ Blue jsy 10.00
8 Alex Rodriguez/ White jsy 10.00
9 Alfonso Soriano/bat 8.00
10 Alfonso Soriano/ Gray jsy 8.00
11 Alfonso Soriano/ White jsy 8.00
12 Brett Myers/jsy 4.00
13 Andruw Jones/jsy 6.00
14 Austin Kearns/jsy 6.00
15 Barry Larkin/jsy 6.00
16 Barry Zito/jsy 6.00
17 Bernie Williams/jsy 6.00
18 Brian Giles/bat 4.00
19 Zach Day/jsy 4.00
20 Carlos Beltran/bat 8.00
21 Brandon Phillips/bat 4.00
22 Carlos Lee/bat 4.00
23 Casey Fossum/jsy 4.00
24 Chipper Jones/jsy 8.00
25 Marcus Giles/jsy 4.00
26 Craig Biggio/jsy 6.00
27 Curt Schilling/jsy 8.00
28 Derek Jeter/base 15.00
29 Edgar Martinez/jsy 6.00
30 Eric Chavez/jsy 6.00
31 Eric Hinske/bat 4.00
32 Frank Thomas/190/bat 8.00
33 Aubrey Huff/jsy 4.00
34 Gary Carter/jacket 8.00
35 Greg Maddux/Gray jsy 8.00
36 Greg Maddux/White jsy 8.00
37 *Hideki Matsui/base* 15.00
38 Hideo Nomo/White jsy 8.00
39 Rod Carew/jacket 8.00
40 Ichiro Suzuki/base 10.00
41 Ivan Rodriguez/bat 8.00
42 Jason Giambi/bat 6.00
43 Jason Giambi/jsy 6.00
44 J.C. Romero/jsy 4.00
45 Jason Giambi/White jsy 6.00
46 Jeff Bagwell/jsy 6.00
47 Josh Bard/jsy 4.00
48 Jim Thome/jsy 8.00
49 Jay Gibbons/jsy 4.00
50 Jorge Posada/jsy 6.00
51 Juan Gonzalez/bat 6.00
52 Kazuhisa Ishii/bat 4.00
53 George Brett/bat 15.00
54 Kenny Lofton/bat 4.00
55 Kerry Wood/jsy 8.00
56 Kevin Brown/jsy 4.00
57 Kirk Saarloos/jsy 4.00
58 Lance Berkman/jsy 5.00
59 Larry Walker/jsy 4.00
60 Magglio Ordonez/jsy 4.00
61 Manny Ramirez/jsy 8.00
62 Mark Mulder/jsy 4.00
63 Mark Prior/jsy 10.00
64 Matt Williams/jsy 4.00
65 Miguel Tejada/jsy 6.00
66 Mike Mussina/jsy 6.00
67 Mike Piazza/bat 10.00
68 Mike Piazza/Black jsy 10.00
69 Mike Piazza/White jsy 10.00
70 Nomar Garciaparra/bat 10.00
71 Nomar Garciaparra/ Gray jsy 10.00
72 Nomar Garciaparra/ White jsy 10.00
73 Paul LoDuca/jsy 4.00
74 Pedro Martinez/jsy 8.00
75 Rafael Palmeiro/jsy 8.00
76 Randy Johnson/ Gray jsy 8.00
77 Randy Johnson/ White jsy 8.00
78 Rickey Henderson/jsy 8.00
79 Roberto Alomar/jsy 6.00
80 Rod Carew/jacket 8.00
81 Roger Clemens/ Gray jsy 15.00
82 Roger Clemens/ White jsy 15.00
83 Cal Ripken Jr./jsy 25.00
84 Roy Oswalt/jsy 4.00
85 Jeremy Bonderman/jsy 4.00
86 Ryne Sandberg/bat 15.00
87 Sammy Sosa/bat 12.00
88 Sammy Sosa/Grey jsy 15.00
89 Sammy Sosa/ White jsy 15.00
90 Scott Rolen/jsy 8.00
91 Frank Catalanotto/jsy 4.00
92 Shawn Green/jsy 5.00
93 Tim Hudson/jsy 5.00
94 Todd Helton/jsy 8.00
95 Tony Gwynn/jsy 8.00
96 Torii Hunter/jsy 6.00
97 Troy Glaus/jsy 6.00
98 Runelvys Hernandez/jsy 4.00
99 Vernon Wells/jsy 4.00
100 Vladimir Guerrero/jsy 8.00

Bronze Materials

Cards (1-100): 1-1.5X
Production 150 sets

Silver Materials

Cards (1-100): 1-2X
Production 75 sets

Gold Materials

Cards (1-100): 1.5-2.5X
Production 50 sets

Platinum Materials

No pricing due to scarcity
Production 25 sets

Autographs

NM/M

Common Player:
Varying quantities produced
Prime Autos: No Pricing
Production 4-20
12 Brett Myers 10.00
18 Brian Giles/30 30.00
19 Zach Day 8.00
21 Brandon Phillips 10.00
22 Carlos Lee 12.00
23 Casey Fossum 10.00
25 Marcus Giles 15.00
29 Edgar Martinez/100 40.00
30 Eric Chavez/75 25.00
31 Eric Hinske 10.00
33 Aubrey Huff 10.00
41 Ivan Rodriguez/50 50.00
41 Ivan Rodriguez/75 40.00
44 J.C. Romero 8.00
47 Josh Bard 8.00
49 Jay Gibbons 10.00
51 Juan Gonzalez/50 50.00
57 Kirk Saarloos 8.00
62 Mark Mulder/100 25.00
63 Mark Prior/25 100.00
64 Matt Williams 15.00
73 Paul LoDuca 15.00
84 Roy Oswalt/50 25.00
85 Jeremy Bonderman 15.00
86 Ryne Sandberg/40 100.00
90 Scott Rolen/50 40.00
91 Frank Catalanotto 8.00
96 Torii Hunter/140 20.00
98 Runelvys Hernandez 10.00
100 Vladimir Guerrero/150 40.00

Prime Materials

No Pricing
Production 25 sets

2003 PLAYOFF PORTRAITS

NM/M

Complete Set (144): 40.00
Common Player: .25
Pack (7): 4.00
Box (20): 60.00
1 Vladimir Guerrero 1.50
2 Luis Gonzalez .35
3 Andruw Jones 1.50
4 Manny Ramirez 1.50

Greg Maddux • Atlanta Braves

5 Derek Jeter 4.00
6 Eric Hinske .25
7 Curt Schilling .45
8 Adam Dunn 1.00
9 Jason Jennings .25
10 Mike Piazza 2.50
11 Jason Giambi .75
12 Jeff Bagwell 1.50
13 Rickey Henderson 1.50
14 Randy Johnson 1.50
15 Roger Clemens 3.00
16 Troy Glaus 1.50
17 Hideo Nomo 1.50
18 Joe Borchard .25
19 Torii Hunter .25
20 Lance Berkman .25
21 Todd Helton 1.50
22 Mike Mussina .40
23 Vernon Wells .25
24 Pat Burrell .50
25 Ichiro Suzuki 2.50
26 Shawn Green .50
27 Frank Thomas 1.50
28 Barry Zito .40
29 Barry Bonds 4.00
30 Ken Griffey Jr. 2.50
31 Albert Pujols 3.00
32 Roberto Alomar .50
33 Barry Larkin .25
34 Tony Gwynn 2.00
35 Chipper Jones 2.00
36 Pedro J. Martinez 1.50
37 Juan Gonzalez 1.50
38 Greg Maddux 2.00
39 Tim Hudson .35
40 Sammy Sosa 2.50
41 Victor Martinez .50
42 Mark Buehrle .25
43 Austin Kearns .25
44 Kerry Wood 1.00
45 Nomar Garciaparra 2.50
46 Alfonso Soriano 1.00
47 Mark Prior 1.50
48 Richie Sexson .25
49 Mark Teixeira .75
50 Craig Biggio .25
51 Rafael Palmeiro 1.00
52 Carlos Beltran .75
53 Bernie Williams .35
54 Eric Chavez .35
55 Paul Konerko .35
56 Nolan Ryan 4.00
57 Mark Mulder .25
58 Miguel Tejada .35
59 Roy Oswalt .25
60 Jim Edmonds .25
61 Ryan Klesko .25
62 Cal Ripken Jr. 4.00
63 Josh Beckett .25
64 Kazuhisa Ishii .25
65 Alex Rodriguez 3.00
66 Mike Sweeney .25
67 C.C. Sabathia .25
68 Jose Vidro .25
69 Magglio Ordonez .25
70 Carlos Delgado .75
71 Jorge Posada .25
72 Bobby Abreu .25
73 Brian Giles .25
74 Kirby Puckett 2.00
75 Yogi Berra 1.00
76 Ryne Sandberg 2.00
77 Tom Glavine .45
78 Jim Thome 1.00
79 Chris Snelling .25
80 Drew Henson .25
81 Junior Spivey .25
82 Mike Schmidt 3.00
83 Jeff Kent .25

84 Stan Musial 2.00
85 Garret Anderson .25
86 *Jose Contreras* 3.00
87 Ivan Rodriguez 1.00
88 *Hideki Matsui* 6.00
89 Don Mattingly 3.00
90 Angel Berroa .25
91 George Brett 3.00
92 Jermaine Dye .25
93 John Olerud .25
94 Josh Phelps .25
95 Sean Casey .35
96 Larry Walker .25
97 Jason Lane .25
98 Travis Hafner .25
99 Terrence Long .25
100 Shannon Stewart .25
101 Richard Hidalgo .25
102 Joe Thurston .25
103 Ben Sheets .25
104 Orlando Cabrera .25
105 Aramis Ramirez .25
106 So Taguchi .25
107 Frank Robinson .75
108 Phil Nevin .25
109 Dennis Tankersley .25
110 J.D. Drew .50
111 Paul LoDuca .25
112 Ozzie Smith 2.00
113 Carlos Lee .25
114 Nick Johnson .25
115 Edgar Martinez .25
116 Hank Blalock .75
117 Orlando Hudson .25
118 Corey Patterson .25
119 Steve Carlton .50
120 Wade Miller .25
121 Adrian Beltre .75
122 Scott Rolen 1.00
123 Brian Lawrence .25
124 Rich Aurilia .25
125 Tsuyoshi Shinjo .25
126 John Buck .25
127 Marlon Byrd .25
128 Michael Cuddyer .25
129 Marshall McDougall .25
130 Travis Chapman .25
131 Jose Morban .25
132 Adam LaRoche .25
133 Jose Castillo .25
134 Walter Young .25
135 Jeff Baker .25
136 Jeremy Guthrie .25
137 Pedro J. Martinez .75
138 Randy Johnson .75
139 Alex Rodriguez 1.50
140 Hideo Nomo .50
141 Roger Clemens 1.00
142 Rickey Henderson .50
143 Jason Giambi .40
144 Mike Piazza 1.00

Bronze

Bronze: 2-4X
Production 100 sets

Gold

No Pricing
Production 10 sets

Beige

Beige: 1-3X
Production 250 sets

Silver

Silver: 4-8X
Production 50 sets

Artifacts Bronze

NM/M

Common Player: 4.00
Production 100 or less
Silvers: 1-1.5X
Production 50 or less
Golds: No Pricing
Production 25 or less
Bronze Combos: 1-1.5X
Production 50 or less
Silver Combos: No Pricing
Production 25 or less
Gold Combos: No Pricing
Production 10 or less
1 Vladimir Guerrero/100 8.00
2 Luis Gonzalez/100 5.00
3 Andruw Jones/100 8.00
4 Manny Ramirez/50 10.00
5 Derek Jeter/100 20.00
6 Eric Hinske/100 4.00
7 Curt Schilling/100 8.00
8 Adam Dunn/50 10.00
9 Jason Jennings/100 4.00
10 Mike Piazza/100 12.00
11 Jason Giambi/100 6.00
12 Jeff Bagwell/50 15.00
13 Rickey Henderson/50 20.00
14 Randy Johnson/100 8.00
15 Roger Clemens/100 20.00
16 Troy Glaus/100 6.00
17 Hideo Nomo/100 20.00
18 Joe Borchard
19 Torii Hunter/100 6.00
20 Lance Berkman/100 6.00
21 Todd Helton/50 15.00
22 Mike Mussina/100 8.00
23 Vernon Wells/100 4.00
24 Pat Burrell/100 6.00
25 Ichiro Suzuki/100 25.00
26 Shawn Green/100 6.00
27 Frank Thomas/100 10.00
28 Barry Zito/100 6.00
29 Barry Bonds/100 20.00
30 Ken Griffey Jr/100 15.00
31 Albert Pujols/100 20.00
32 Roberto Alomar/50 10.00
33 Barry Larkin/50 10.00
34 Tony Gwynn/100 15.00
35 Chipper Jones/100 10.00
36 Pedro Martinez/100 10.00
37 Juan Gonzalez/50 10.00
38 Greg Maddux/100 15.00
39 Tim Hudson/100 6.00
40 Sammy Sosa/100 20.00
41 Victor Martinez/100 8.00
42 Mark Buehrle/50 6.00
43 Austin Kearns/100 6.00
44 Kerry Wood/50 15.00
45 Nomar Garciaparra/100 15.00
46 Alfonso Soriano/100 10.00
47 Mark Prior/100 15.00
48 Richie Sexson/100 6.00
49 Mark Teixeira/50 8.00
50 Craig Biggio/50 8.00
51 Rafael Palmeiro/50 10.00
52 Carlos Beltran/50 10.00
53 Bernie Williams/50 10.00
54 Eric Chavez/100 6.00
55 Paul Konerko/100 4.00
56 Nolan Ryan/100 35.00
57 Mark Mulder/100 6.00
58 Miguel Tejada/100 6.00
59 Roy Oswalt/50 8.00
60 Jim Edmonds/50 8.00
61 Ryan Klesko/50 6.00
62 Cal Ripken Jr/100 40.00
63 Josh Beckett/100 6.00
64 Kazuhisa Ishii/50 6.00
65 Alex Rodriguez/100 15.00
66 Mike Sweeney/100 4.00
67 C.C. Sabathia/100 4.00
68 Jose Vidro/100 4.00
69 Magglio Ordonez/50 6.00
70 Carlos Delgado/50 8.00
71 Jorge Posada/100 8.00
72 Bobby Abreu/100 6.00
73 Brian Giles/20
74 Kirby Puckett/50 30.00
75 Yogi Berra/50 25.00
76 Ryne Sandberg/50 40.00
77 Tom Glavine/50 8.00
78 Jim Thome/100 10.00
79 Chris Snelling/50 5.00
80 Drew Henson/50 10.00
81 Junior Spivey/50 8.00
82 Mike Schmidt/50 50.00
83 Jeff Kent/50 6.00
84 Stan Musial/100 30.00
85 Garret Anderson/50 8.00
87 Ivan Rodriguez/50 12.00
88 Hideki Matsui/100 25.00
89 Don Mattingly/100 30.00
90 Angel Berroa/100 4.00
91 George Brett/50 50.00
92 Jermaine Dye/50 4.00
93 John Olerud/100 4.00
94 Josh Phelps/50 4.00
95 Sean Casey/50 4.00
96 Larry Walker/50 8.00
97 Jason Lane/50 4.00
98 Travis Hafner/100 6.00
99 Terrence Long/50 4.00
100 Shannon Stewart/50 4.00
101 Richard Hidalgo/50 4.00
102 Joe Thurston/100 4.00
103 Ben Sheets/100 6.00
104 Orlando Cabrera/50 6.00
105 Aramis Ramirez/100 6.00
106 So Taguchi/50 5.00
107 Frank Robinson/50 12.00
109 Dennis Tankersley/100 4.00
110 J.D. Drew/100 6.00
111 Paul LoDuca/50 6.00
112 Ozzie Smith/50 40.00
113 Carlos Lee/100 4.00
114 Nick Johnson/100 4.00
115 Edgar Martinez/100 8.00
116 Hank Blalock/50 15.00
117 Orlando Hudson/100 4.00
118 Corey Patterson/100 6.00
119 Steve Carlton/50 10.00
120 Wade Miller/50 6.00
121 Adrian Beltre/50 8.00
122 Scott Rolen/50 20.00
123 Brian Lawrence/50 4.00
124 Rich Aurilia/50 4.00
125 Tsuyoshi Shinjo/50 8.00
126 John Buck/50 4.00
127 Marlon Byrd/100 4.00
128 Michael Cuddyer/50 4.00
130 Travis Chapman/100 4.00
131 Jose Morban/100 4.00
132 Adam LaRoche/100 4.00
133 Jose Castillo/100 4.00
134 Walter Young/100 4.00

Bronze Autographs

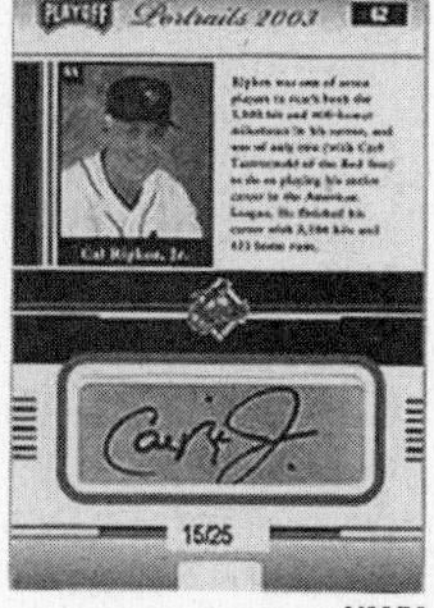

PLAYOFF
Portraits 2003
Cal Ripken, Jr.
15/25

NM/M

Common Bronze Auto.:
Production 100 or less
Silvers: 1-1.5X
Production 50 or less
No pricing for production 25 or less
Golds: No Pricing
Production 25 or less
1 Vladimir Guerrero/100 35.00
3 Andruw Jones/25 50.00
6 Eric Hinske/100 10.00
8 Adam Dunn/50 35.00
9 Jason Jennings/100 8.00
16 Troy Glaus/60 25.00
18 Joe Borchard/100 6.00
19 Torii Hunter/25 40.00
31 Albert Pujols/25 150.00
32 Roberto Alomar/100 35.00
33 Barry Larkin/95 25.00
34 Tony Gwynn/60 75.00
35 Chipper Jones/25 75.00
37 Juan Gonzalez/50 50.00
41 Victor Martinez/100 20.00
42 Mark Buehrle/100 10.00
44 Kerry Wood/40 40.00
47 Mark Prior/25 100.00
48 Richie Sexson/100 20.00
49 Mark Teixeira/25 40.00
50 Craig Biggio/25 40.00
56 Nolan Ryan/25 150.00
57 Mark Mulder/100 20.00
59 Roy Oswalt/40 25.00
61 Ryan Klesko/40 20.00
62 Cal Ripken Jr./25 150.00
67 C.C. Sabathia/50 15.00
72 Bobby Abreu/100 15.00
73 Brian Giles/50 15.00
74 Kirby Puckett/50 60.00
77 Tom Glavine/100 35.00
79 Chris Snelling/100 10.00
80 Drew Henson/25 40.00
81 Junior Spivey/100 10.00
82 Mike Schmidt/50 75.00
83 Jeff Kent/50 25.00
84 Stan Musial/50 65.00
85 Garret Anderson/25 30.00
86 Jose Contreras/50 40.00
89 Don Mattingly/50 90.00
90 Angel Berroa/100 10.00
92 Jermaine Dye/100 10.00
94 Josh Phelps/100 10.00
97 Jason Lane/100 8.00
98 Travis Hafner/100 12.00
99 Terrence Long/100 6.00
100 Shannon Stewart/100 8.00
101 Richard Hidalgo/25 20.00
102 Joe Thurston/100 8.00
103 Ben Sheets/100 15.00
105 Aramis Ramirez/40 15.00
106 So Taguchi/29 30.00
108 Phil Nevin/100 12.00
109 Dennis Tankersley/100 8.00
110 J.D. Drew/25 30.00
111 Paul LoDuca/100 15.00
113 Carlos Lee/100 10.00
114 Nick Johnson/100 10.00
115 Edgar Martinez/100 35.00
117 Orlando Hudson/100 6.00
118 Corey Patterson/100 15.00
119 Steve Carlton/25 40.00
120 Wade Miller/100 6.00
121 Adrian Beltre/25 30.00
122 Scott Rolen/100 30.00
123 Brian Lawrence/100 6.00
126 John Buck/100 6.00
127 Marlon Byrd/100 10.00
128 Michael Cuddyer/100 8.00
129 Marshall McDougall/100 6.00
130 Travis Chapman/100 6.00
131 Jose Morban/100 6.00
132 Adam LaRoche/100 12.00
133 Jose Castillo/100 6.00
134 Walter Young/100 6.00
135 Jeff Baker/100 6.00
136 Jeremy Guthrie/100 10.00

2003 PLAYOFF PRESTIGE

NM/M

Complete Set (200): 35.00
Common Player: .15
Pack (6): 2.00
Box (24): 45.00
1 Darin Erstad .25
2 David Eckstein .15
3 Garret Anderson .15
4 Jarrod Washburn .15
5 Tim Salmon .25
6 Troy Glaus .75
7 Jay Gibbons .15
8 Marty Cordova .15
9 Melvin Mora .15
10 Rodrigo Lopez .15
11 Tony Batista .15
12 Cliff Floyd .15
13 Derek Lowe .15
14 Johnny Damon .30
15 Manny Ramirez .75
16 Nomar Garciaparra 1.50
17 Pedro J. Martinez .75
18 Rickey Henderson .75
19 Shea Hillenbrand .15
20 Carlos Lee .15
21 Frank Thomas .75
22 Magglio Ordonez .15
23 Mark Buehrle .15
24 Paul Konerko .15
25 C.C. Sabathia .15
26 Danys Baez .15
27 Ellis Burks .15
28 Travis Hafner .15
29 Omar Vizquel .15
30 Bobby Higginson .15
31 Carlos Pena .15
32 Mark Redman .15
33 Robert Fick .15
34 Steve Sparks .15
35 Carlos Beltran .50
36 Joe Randa .15
37 Mike Sweeney .15
38 Paul Byrd .15
39 Raul Ibanez .15
40 Runelvys Hernandez .15
41 Brad Radke .15

42 Corey Koskie .15
43 Cristian Guzman .15
44 David Ortiz .35
45 Doug Mientkiewicz .15
46 Dustan Mohr .15
47 Jacque Jones .15
48 Torii Hunter .15
49 Alfonso Soriano .75
50 Andy Pettitte .30
51 Bernie Williams .30
52 David Wells .15
53 Derek Jeter 2.00
54 Jason Giambi .50
55 Jeff Weaver .15
56 Jorge Posada .15
57 Mike Mussina .35
58 Roger Clemens 1.25
59 Barry Zito .25
60 David Justice .15
61 Eric Chavez .30
62 Jermaine Dye .15
63 Mark Mulder .15
64 Miguel Tejada .30
65 Ray Durham .15
66 Tim Hudson .30
67 Bret Boone .15
68 Chris Snelling .15
69 Edgar Martinez .15
70 Freddy Garcia .15
71 Ichiro Suzuki 1.50
72 Jamie Moyer .15
73 John Olerud .15
74 Kazuhiro Sasaki .15
75 Aubrey Huff .15
76 Joe Kennedy .15
77 Paul Wilson .15
78 Alex Rodriguez 1.75
79 Chan Ho Park .15
80 Hank Blalock .50
81 Ivan Rodriguez .65
82 Juan Gonzalez .75
83 Kevin Mench .15
84 Rafael Palmeiro .65
85 Carlos Delgado .40
86 Eric Hinske .15
87 Jose Cruz .15
88 Josh Phelps .15
89 Roy Halladay .15
90 Shannon Stewart .15
91 Vernon Wells .15
92 Curt Schilling .40
93 Junior Spivey .15
94 Luis Gonzalez .25
95 Mark Grace .25
96 Randy Johnson .75
97 Andruw Jones .75
98 Chipper Jones 1.00
99 Gary Sheffield .40
100 Greg Maddux 1.00
101 John Smoltz .15
102 Kevin Millwood .15
103 Mike Hampton .15
104 Corey Patterson .15
105 Fred McGriff .15
106 Kerry Wood .65
107 Mark Prior .75
108 Moises Alou .15
109 Sammy Sosa 1.50
110 Adam Dunn .50
111 Austin Kearns .15
112 Barry Larkin .15
113 Ken Griffey Jr. 1.50
114 Sean Casey .30
115 Jason Jennings .15
116 Jay Payton .15
117 Larry Walker .15
118 Todd Helton .75
119 A.J. Burnett .15
120 Josh Beckett .15
121 Juan Encarnacion .15
122 Mike Lowell .15
123 Craig Biggio .15
124 Daryle Ward .15
125 Jeff Bagwell .75
126 Lance Berkman .15
127 Roy Oswalt .15
128 Adrian Beltre .35
129 Hideo Nomo .75
130 Kazuhisa Ishii .15
131 Kevin Brown .15
132 Odalis Perez .15
133 Paul LoDuca .15
134 Shawn Green .35
135 Jeff Kent .15
136 Ben Sheets .15
137 Jeffrey Hammonds .15
138 Jose Hernandez .15
139 Richie Sexson .15
140 Bartolo Colon .15
141 Brad Wilkerson .15
142 Javier Vazquez .15
143 Jose Vidro .15
144 Michael Barrett .15
145 Vladimir Guerrero .75
146 Al Leiter .15
147 Mike Piazza 1.50
148 Mo Vaughn .15
149 Pedro Astacio .15
150 Roberto Alomar .40
151 Roger Cedeno .15
152 Tom Glavine .40
153 Bobby Abreu .15
154 Jimmy Rollins .15
155 Mike Lieberthal .15
156 Pat Burrell .35
157 Vicente Padilla .15
158 Jim Thome .65
159 Aramis Ramirez .15
160 Brian Giles .15
161 Jason Kendall .15
162 Josh Fogg .15
163 Kip Wells .15
164 Mark Kotsay .15
165 Oliver Perez .15
166 Phil Nevin .15
167 Ryan Klesko .15
168 Sean Burroughs .15
169 Trevor Hoffman .15
170 Barry Bonds 2.00
171 Benito Santiago .15
172 Reggie Sanders .15
173 Rich Aurilia .15
174 Russ Ortiz .15
175 Albert Pujols 1.75
176 J.D. Drew .25
177 Jim Edmonds .15
178 Matt Morris .15
179 Tino Martinez .15
180 Scott Rolen .65
181 Joe Borchard .15
182 Freddy Sanchez .15
183 *Jose Contreras* 3.00
184 Jeff Baker .15
185 Ryan Church .15
186 Mario Ramos .15
187 Corwin Malone .15
188 Jimmy Gobble .15
189 Jon Adkins .15
190 Tim Kalita .15
191 Nelson Castro .15
192 Colin Young .15
193 Luis Martinez .15
194 Todd Donovan .15
195 Jeremy Ward .15
196 Wilson Valdez .15
197 *Hideki Matsui* 6.00
198 Mitch Wylie .15
199 Adam Walker .15
200 Clifford Bartosh .15

X-tra Points

Stars (1-180): 4-8X
Production 150
Prospects (181-200): 4-8X
Production 50

Award Winners

NM/M

Complete Set (15): 25.00
Common Player: 1.00
#'d to year of award
1 Barry Zito 1.00
2 Barry Bonds 5.00
3 Randy Johnson 1.50
4 Roger Clemens 2.50
5 Ichiro Suzuki 3.00
6 Chipper Jones 2.00
7 Ken Griffey Jr. 3.00
8 Miguel Tejada 1.00
9 Greg Maddux 2.00
10 Jeff Bagwell 1.50
11 Rickey Henderson 1.50
12 Tom Glavine 1.00
13 Albert Pujols 4.00
14 Nomar Garciaparra 3.00
15 Derek Jeter 5.00

Connections

NM/M

Complete Set (70): 90.00
Common Duo: 1.00
Inserted 1:8
Century Connections: 3-6X
Production 100 sets
1 Troy Glaus, Garret Anderson 1.50
2 Troy Glaus, Tim Salmon 1.50
3 Randy Johnson, Curt Schilling 1.50
4 Matt Williams, Luis Gonzalez 1.00
5 Greg Maddux, John Smoltz 2.00
6 Andruw Jones, Chipper Jones 2.00
7 Greg Maddux, Kevin Millwood 2.00
8 Tony Batista, Geronimo Gil 1.00
9 Pedro J. Martinez, Nomar Garciaparra 3.00
10 Manny Ramirez, Nomar Garciaparra 3.00
11 Nomar Garciaparra, Rickey Henderson 3.00
12 Trot Nixon, Manny Ramirez 1.50
13 Kerry Wood, Mark Prior 1.50
14 Sammy Sosa, Fred McGriff 3.00
15 Sammy Sosa, Corey Patterson 3.00
16 Frank Thomas, Magglio Ordonez 1.50
17 Joe Borchard, Magglio Ordonez 1.00
18 Adam Dunn, Austin Kearns 1.00
19 Barry Larkin, Ken Griffey Jr. 3.00
20 Adam Dunn, Barry Larkin 1.00
21 Adam Dunn, Ken Griffey Jr. 3.00
22 Victor Martinez, Omar Vizquel 1.00
23 C.C. Sabathia, Victor Martinez 1.00
24 Larry Walker, Todd Helton 1.00
25 Carlos Pena, Robert Fick 1.00
26 Josh Beckett, Juan Encarnacion 1.00
27 Jeff Bagwell, Craig Biggio 1.50
28 Lance Berkman, Roy Oswalt 1.00
29 Lance Berkman, Jeff Bagwell 1.50
30 Mike Sweeney, Carlos Beltran 1.00
31 Mike Sweeney, Angel Berroa 1.00
32 Kazuhisa Ishii, Shawn Green 1.00
33 Adrian Beltre, Shawn Green 1.00
34 Kazuhisa Ishii, Hideo Nomo 1.50
35 Richie Sexson, Ben Sheets 1.00
36 Jacque Jones, Torii Hunter 1.00
37 Doug Mientkiewicz, David Ortiz 1.00
38 Vladimir Guerrero, Jose Vidro 1.50
39 Derek Jeter, Jason Giambi 5.00
40 Derek Jeter, Bernie Williams 5.00
41 Roger Clemens, Mike Mussina 2.50
42 Alfonso Soriano, Jorge Posada 1.50
43 Derek Jeter, Alfonso Soriano 5.00
44 Mike Piazza, Roberto Alomar 3.00
45 Mike Piazza, Mo Vaughn 3.00
46 Eric Chavez, Miguel Tejada 1.00
47 Mark Mulder, Barry Zito 1.00
48 Tim Hudson, Barry Zito 1.00
49 Pat Burrell, Bobby Abreu 1.00
50 Jim Thome, Pat Burrell 1.00
51 Jim Thome, Marlon Byrd 1.00
52 Brian Giles, Aramis Ramirez 1.00
53 Ryan Klesko, Phil Nevin 1.00
54 Barry Bonds, Benito Santiago 5.00
55 Jeff Kent, Rich Aurilia 1.00
56 Barry Bonds, Jeff Kent 5.00
57 Ichiro Suzuki, Kazuhiro Sasaki 3.00
58 Edgar Martinez, John Olerud 1.00
59 Albert Pujols, Scott Rolen 4.00
60 Jim Edmonds, J.D. Drew 1.00
61 Albert Pujols, Jim Edmonds 4.00
62 Dewon Brazelton, Joe Kennedy 1.00
63 Alex Rodriguez, Ivan Rodriguez 4.00
64 Juan Gonzalez, Rafael Palmeiro 1.50
65 Mark Teixeira, Hank Blalock 1.00
66 Alex Rodriguez, Juan Gonzalez 4.00
67 Alex Rodriguez, Juan Gonzalez 4.00
68 Shannon Stewart, Carlos Delgado 1.00
69 Josh Phelps, Eric Hinske 1.00
70 Vernon Wells, Roy Halladay 1.00

Diamond Heritage

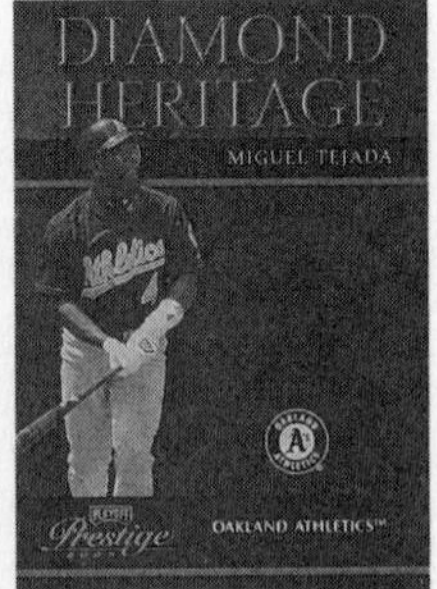

NM/M

Complete Set (30): 35.00
Common Player: 1.00
Inserted 1:21
Golds: 5-10X
Production 50 sets
1 Larry Walker 1.00
2 Troy Glaus 1.50
3 Magglio Ordonez 1.00
4 Roy Oswalt 1.00
5 Barry Zito 1.00
6 Nomar Garciaparra 3.00
7 Kerry Wood 1.25
8 Roger Clemens 2.50
9 Pedro J. Martinez 1.50
10 Mark Prior 1.50
11 Sammy Sosa 3.00

12 Randy Johnson 1.50
13 Greg Maddux 2.00
14 Manny Ramirez 1.50
15 Torii Hunter 1.00
16 Alex Rodriguez 4.00
17 Mike Piazza 3.00
18 Vladimir Guerrero 1.50
19 Ivan Rodriguez 1.25
20 Lance Berkman 1.00
21 Miguel Tejada 1.00
22 Chipper Jones 2.00
23 Todd Helton 1.50
24 Shawn Green 1.00
25 Scott Rolen 1.25
26 Adam Dunn 1.25
27 Jim Thome 1.25
28 Rafael Palmeiro 1.25
29 Eric Chavez 1.00
30 Andruw Jones 1.50

Diamond Heritage Materials

NM/M
Common Player: 5.00
Production 200 unless noted
Autographs: Not Priced
Production 15 to 25
1 Larry Walker 6.00
2 Troy Glaus 6.00
3 Magglio Ordonez 5.00
4 Roy Oswalt 5.00
5 Barry Zito 8.00
6 Nomar Garciaparra 15.00
7 Kerry Wood 8.00
8 Roger Clemens 15.00
9 Pedro J. Martinez 10.00
10 Mark Prior 10.00
11 Sammy Sosa 15.00
12 Randy Johnson 10.00
13 Greg Maddux 10.00
14 Manny Ramirez 8.00
15 Torii Hunter 10.00
16 Alex Rodriguez/ bat/100 15.00
17 Mike Piazza/bat/100 15.00
18 V. Guerrero/bat/100 10.00
19 Ivan Rodriguez/ bat/100 10.00
20 Lance Berkman/bat/100 8.00
21 Miguel Tejada/bat/100 8.00
22 Chipper Jones/bat/100 15.00
23 Todd Helton/bat/100 10.00
24 Shawn Green/bat/100 8.00
25 Scott Rolen/bat/100 15.00
26 Adam Dunn/bat/100 12.00
27 Jim Thome/bat/100 10.00
28 Rafael Palmeiro/ bat/100 10.00
29 Eric Chavez/bat/100 8.00
30 Andruw Jones/bat/100 8.00

Diamond Heritage Material Auto

No Pricing

Infield/Outfield Tandems Material

NM/M
Common Duo: 8.00
Production 100 sets
1 Troy Glaus, Garret Anderson 10.00
2 Mark Grace, Luis Gonzalez 10.00
3 Nomar Garciaparra, Manny Ramirez 20.00
4 Alfonso Soriano, Bernie Williams 15.00
5 Jeff Bagwell, Lance Berkman 15.00
6 Alex Rodriguez, Juan Gonzalez 15.00
7 Barry Larkin, Adam Dunn 15.00
8 Scott Rolen, Jim Edmonds 20.00
9 Todd Helton, Larry Walker 10.00
10 Adrian Beltre, Shawn Green 10.00
11 Jose Vidro, Vladimir Guerrero 12.00
12 Mike Sweeney, Carlos Beltran 10.00
13 Josh Phelps, Vernon Wells 8.00
14 Paul Konerko, Magglio Ordonez 10.00
15 Phil Nevin, Ryan Klesko 10.00

Inside The Numbers

NM/M
Complete Set (25): 35.00
Common Player: 1.00
Production 2,002 sets
Die-Cuts: 10-25X
#'d to jersey number
1 Roger Clemens 2.50
2 Greg Maddux 2.00
3 Miguel Tejada 1.00
4 Alex Rodriguez 4.00
5 Ichiro Suzuki 2.50
6 Sammy Sosa 3.00
7 Jim Thome 1.50
8 Derek Jeter 5.00
9 Randy Johnson 1.50
10 Barry Zito 1.00
11 Jason Giambi 1.50
12 Shawn Green 1.00
13 Curt Schilling 1.00
14 Albert Pujols 4.00
15 Vladimir Guerrero 1.50
16 Pedro J. Martinez 1.50
17 Alfonso Soriano 1.50
18 Barry Bonds 5.00
19 Magglio Ordonez 1.00
20 Chipper Jones 2.00
21 Pat Burrell 1.00
22 Luis Gonzalez 1.00
23 Jeff Bagwell 1.50
24 Garret Anderson 1.00
25 Larry Walker 1.00

League Leaders

NM/M
Complete Set (15): 25.00
Common Player: 1.00
Production 2,002 sets
1 Manny Ramirez 2.00
2 Sammy Sosa 3.00
3 Alex Rodriguez 4.00
4 Alfonso Soriano 2.00
5 Vladimir Guerrero 2.00
6 Nomar Garciaparra 3.00
7 Johnny Damon 1.00
8 Alfonso Soriano 2.00
9 Barry Bonds 5.00
10 Barry Zito 1.00
11 Pedro J. Martinez 2.00
12 John Smoltz 1.00
13 Randy Johnson 2.00
14 Lance Berkman 1.00
15 Randy Johnson 2.00

League Leaders Materials

NM/M
Common Player: 4.00
Production 250 sets
1 Manny Ramirez/jsy 8.00
2 Sammy Sosa/base 8.00
3 Alex Rodriguez/jsy 10.00
4 Alfonso Soriano/jsy 10.00
5 Vladimir Guerrero/jsy 8.00
6 Nomar Garciaparra/jsy 10.00
7 Johnny Damon/bat 4.00
8 Alfonso Soriano/jsy 10.00
9 Barry Bonds/base 12.00
10 Barry Zito/jsy 6.00
11 Pedro J. Martinez/jsy 10.00
12 John Smoltz 6.00
13 Randy Johnson/jsy 10.00
14 Lance Berkman/jsy 6.00
15 Randy Johnson/jsy 10.00

Player Collection

NM/M
Common Player: 4.00
Production 325 sets
1 Adam Dunn 8.00
2 Adrian Beltre 6.00

3 Alex Rodriguez 20.00
4 Alfonso Soriano 10.00
5 Andruw Jones 8.00
6 Andy Pettitte 6.00
7 Barry Larkin 4.00
8 Barry Zito 4.00
9 Ben Grieve 4.00
10 Bernie Williams 4.00
11 Cal Ripken Jr. 25.00
12 Carlos Delgado 5.00
13 C.C. Sabathia 4.00
14 Chipper Jones 12.00
15 Craig Biggio 4.00
16 Curt Schilling 5.00
17 Alex Rodriguez 20.00
18 Frank Thomas 8.00
19 Freddy Garcia 4.00
20 Jay Bell 4.00
21 Roger Clemens 15.00
22 Tony Gwynn 12.00
23 Ivan Rodriguez 8.00
24 Jason Giambi 8.00
25 Jason Jennings 4.00
26 Jay Payton 4.00
27 J.D. Drew 6.00
28 Jeff Bagwell 8.00
29 Jeromy Burnitz 4.00
30 Jim Edmonds 4.00
31 Jim Thome 8.00
32 Joe Borchard 4.00
33 Joe Mays 4.00
34 John Olerud 4.00
35 David Wells 4.00
36 Juan Gonzalez 8.00
37 Kazuhiro Sasaki 4.00
38 Chan Ho Park 4.00
39 Kerry Wood 8.00
40 Kevin Brown 4.00
41 Lance Berkman 4.00
42 Larry Walker 4.00
43 Bret Boone 4.00
44 Magglio Ordonez 4.00
45 Manny Ramirez 8.00
46 Mark Mulder 4.00
47 Mark Prior 10.00
48 Matt Williams 4.00
49 Miguel Tejada 4.00
50 Mike Piazza 15.00
51 Nomar Garciaparra 15.00
52 Doug Davis 4.00
53 Paul Konerko 4.00
54 Paul LoDuca 4.00
55 Pedro J. Martinez 8.00
56 Preston Wilson 4.00
57 Rafael Palmeiro 8.00
58 Marlon Byrd 4.00
59 Reggie Sanders 4.00
60 Richie Sexson 4.00
61 Rickey Henderson 10.00
62 Rickey Henderson 10.00
63 Robert Person 4.00
64 Jeff Bagwell 8.00
65 Roger Clemens 15.00
66 Roy Oswalt 4.00
67 Ryan Klesko 4.00
68 Sammy Sosa 15.00
69 Shawn Green 5.00
70 Steve Finley 4.00
71 Terrence Long 4.00
72 Tim Hudson 4.00
73 Toby Hall 4.00
74 Todd Helton 8.00
75 Travis Lee 4.00
76 Troy Glaus 8.00
77 Tsuyoshi Shinjo 4.00
78 Vernon Wells 4.00
79 Vladimir Guerrero 8.00
80 Wes Helms 4.00
81 Alex Rodriguez 20.00
82 Alfonso Soriano 10.00
83 Barry Larkin 4.00
84 Roberto Alomar 5.00
85 Ivan Rodriguez 8.00
86 Jason Giambi 6.00
87 Jeff Bagwell 8.00
88 Juan Gonzalez 8.00
89 Larry Walker 4.00
90 Luis Gonzalez 4.00
91 Magglio Ordonez 4.00
92 Manny Ramirez 8.00
93 Marlon Byrd 4.00
94 Mike Piazza 15.00
95 Pat Burrell 6.00
96 Todd Helton 8.00
97 Rickey Henderson 10.00
98 Andruw Jones 8.00
99 Craig Biggio 4.00
100 Mark Prior 10.00

Material Connections

NM/M
Common Duo: 4.00
Production 400 sets
1 Troy Glaus, Garret Anderson 8.00
2 Troy Glaus, Tim Salmon 8.00
4 Matt Williams, Luis Gonzalez 6.00
5 Greg Maddux, John Smoltz 12.00
6 Andruw Jones, Chipper Jones 12.00
7 Greg Maddux, Kevin Millwood 12.00
8 Tony Batista, Geronimo Gil 4.00
9 Pedro J. Martinez, Nomar Garciaparra 15.00
10 Manny Ramirez, Nomar Garciaparra 15.00
11 Nomar Garciaparra, Rickey Henderson 15.00
12 Trot Nixon, Manny Ramirez 10.00
13 Kerry Wood, Mark Prior 15.00
14 Sammy Sosa, Fred McGriff 10.00
15 Sammy Sosa, Corey Patterson 10.00
16 Frank Thomas, Magglio Ordonez 8.00
17 Joe Borchard, Magglio Ordonez 6.00
18 Adam Dunn, Austin Kearns 20.00
20 Adam Dunn, Barry Larkin 15.00
22 Victor Martinez, Omar Vizquel 4.00
23 C.C. Sabathia, Victor Martinez 6.00
24 Larry Walker, Todd Helton 8.00
26 Josh Beckett, Juan Encarnacion 8.00
27 Jeff Bagwell, Craig Biggio 10.00
28 Lance Berkman, Roy Oswalt 8.00
29 Lance Berkman, Jeff Bagwell 10.00
30 Mike Sweeney, Carlos Beltran 8.00
31 Mike Sweeney, Angel Berroa 4.00
32 Kazuhisa Ishii, Shawn Green 10.00
33 Adrian Beltre, Shawn Green 6.00
34 Kazuhisa Ishii, Hideo Nomo 25.00
35 Richie Sexson, Ben Sheets 8.00
36 Jacque Jones, Torii Hunter 10.00
37 Doug Mientkiewicz, David Ortiz 6.00

38 Vladimir Guerrero, Jose Vidro 10.00
39 Derek Jeter, Jason Giambi 15.00
40 Derek Jeter, Bernie Williams 15.00
41 Roger Clemens, Mike Mussina 20.00
42 Alfonso Soriano, Jorge Posada 10.00
43 Derek Jeter, Alfonso Soriano 20.00
44 Mike Piazza, Roberto Alomar 15.00
45 Mike Piazza, Mo Vaughn 10.00
46 Eric Chavez, Miguel Tejada 8.00
47 Mark Mulder, Barry Zito 10.00
48 Tim Hudson, Barry Zito 10.00
49 Pat Burrell, Bobby Abreu 8.00
50 Jim Thome, Pat Burrell 10.00
51 Jim Thome, Marlon Byrd 10.00
52 Brian Giles, Aramis Ramirez 6.00
53 Ryan Klesko, Phil Nevin 6.00
54 Barry Bonds, Benito Santiago 12.00
55 Jeff Kent, Rich Aurilia 5.00
56 Barry Bonds, Jeff Kent 12.00
57 Ichiro Suzuki, Kazuhiro Sasaki 25.00
58 Edgar Martinez, John Olerud 8.00
59 Albert Pujols, Scott Rolen 15.00
60 Jim Edmonds, J.D. Drew 8.00
61 Albert Pujols, Jim Edmonds 12.00
62 Dewon Brazelton, Joe Kennedy 8.00
63 Alex Rodriguez, Ivan Rodriguez 12.00
64 Juan Gonzalez, Rafael Palmeiro 8.00
65 Mark Teixeira, Hank Blalock 10.00
66 Alex Rodriguez, Juan Gonzalez 15.00
67 Alex Rodriguez, Juan Gonzalez 12.00
68 Shannon Stewart, Carlos Delgado 6.00
69 Josh Phelps, Eric Hinske 4.00
70 Vernon Wells, Roy Halladay 4.00

Signature Impressions

NM/M

Common Autograph:
Varying quantities produced
1 A.J. Pierzynski/50 20.00
2 Adam Dunn/25 60.00
3 Barry Zito/25 50.00
4 Bobby Abreu/20 30.00
5 Brandon Phillips/25 25.00
7 Don Mattingly/15 250.00
9 Eric Hinske/25 25.00
12 John Candelaria/50 15.00
16 Lance Berkman/25 30.00
18 Miguel Tejada/25 40.00
22 Roy Oswalt/25 30.00
27 Yogi Berra/15 100.00
28 Joe Kennedy/50 10.00
30 Lenny Dykstra/50 25.00
39 Toby Hall/50 10.00
40 Victor Martinez/25 45.00
46 Brian Giles/15 40.00
50 Jeremy Bonderman/100 15.00

Stars of MLB

NM/M

Common Player: 5.00
Production 150 sets
Patches: 4-8X
Production 25 sets
Autographs: No Pricing
Production 25
Patch Autographs: No Pricing
Production 5 to 10
1 Roger Clemens 12.00
2 Randy Johnson 8.00
3 Sammy Sosa 12.00
4 Vladimir Guerrero 8.00
5 Lance Berkman 5.00
6 Alfonso Soriano 8.00
7 Alex Rodriguez 15.00
8 Roberto Alomar 6.00
9 Miguel Tejada 5.00
10 Pedro J. Martinez 8.00
11 Greg Maddux 10.00
12 Barry Zito 5.00
13 Magglio Ordonez 5.00
14 Chipper Jones 10.00
15 Manny Ramirez 8.00
16 Troy Glaus 8.00
17 Pat Burrell 6.00
18 Roy Oswalt 5.00
19 Mike Piazza 12.00
20 Nomar Garciaparra 12.00

2004 PLAYOFF ABSOLUTE MEMORABILIA

NM/M

Complete Set (250):
Common Player (1-200): 1.50
Production 1,349
Common Non-Auto. (201-250): 2.00
Production 1,000
Common Auto. (201-250): 8.00
Production 500-700
Pack (4): 40.00
Box (6): 185.00
1 Troy Glaus 2.00
2 Garret Anderson 2.00
3 Tim Salmon 2.00
4 Bartolo Colon 1.50
5 Troy Percival 1.50
6 Nolan Ryan Angels 10.00
7 Vladimir Guerrero 4.00
8 Richie Sexson 2.00
9 Shea Hillenbrand 1.50
10 Luis Gonzalez 1.50
11 Brandon Webb 1.50
12 Randy Johnson 4.00
13 Robby Hammock 1.50
14 Edgar Gonzalez 1.50
15 Roberto Alomar 3.00
16 Andruw Jones 3.00
17 Chipper Jones 4.00
18 Dale Murphy 2.00
19 Rafael Furcal 1.50
20 J.D. Drew 2.00
21 Bubba Nelson 1.50
22 Julio Franco 1.50
23 Adam LaRoche 1.50
24 Michael Hessman 1.50
25 Warren Spahn 3.00
26 Jay Gibbons 1.50
27 Cal Ripken Jr. 10.00
28 Miguel Tejada 2.50
29 Adam Loewen 1.50
30 Rafael Palmeiro 3.00
31 Javy Lopez 2.00
32 Luis Matos 1.50
33 Jason Varitek 2.00
34 Carl Yastrzemski 3.00
35 Manny Ramirez 3.00
36 Trot Nixon 2.00
37 Curt Schilling 3.00
38 Pedro J. Martinez 4.00
39 Nomar Garciaparra 5.00
40 Luis Tiant 1.50
41 Kevin Youkilis 1.50
42 Michel Hernandez 1.50
43 Sammy Sosa 5.00
44 Greg Maddux 4.00
45 Kerry Wood 4.00
46 Mark Prior 5.00
47 Ernie Banks 4.00
48 Aramis Ramirez 2.00
49 Brendan Harris 1.50
50 Todd Wellemeyer 1.50
51 Frank Thomas 3.00
52 Magglio Ordonez 2.00
53 Carlos Lee 1.50
54 Joe Crede 1.50
55 Joe Borchard 1.50
56 Mark Buehrle 1.50
57 Sean Casey 2.00
58 Adam Dunn 2.50
59 Austin Kearns 2.00
60 Ken Griffey Jr. 5.00
61 Barry Larkin 2.00
62 Ryan Wagner 1.50
63 Jody Gerut 1.50
64 Jeremy Guthrie 1.50
65 Travis Hafner 2.00
66 Brian Tallet 1.50
67 Todd Helton 3.00
68 Preston Wilson 1.50
69 Jeff Baker 1.50
70 Clint Barmes 1.50
71 Joe Kennedy 1.50
72 Jack Morris 1.50
73 George Kell 1.50
74 Preston Larrison 1.50
75 Dmitri Young 1.50
76 Ivan Rodriguez 3.00
77 Dontrelle Willis 2.00
78 Josh Beckett 2.50
79 Miguel Cabrera 4.00
80 Mike Lowell 2.00
81 Luis Castillo 1.50
82 Juan Pierre 1.50
83 Jeff Bagwell 3.00
84 Jeff Kent 2.00
85 Craig Biggio 2.00
86 Lance Berkman 2.00
87 Andy Pettitte 2.00
88 Roy Oswalt 2.00
89 Chris Burke 1.50
90 Jason Lane 1.50
91 Roger Clemens 6.00
92 Mike Sweeney 1.50
93 Carlos Beltran 2.00
94 Angel Berroa 1.50
95 Juan Gonzalez 2.50
96 Ken Harvey 1.50
97 Byron Gettis 1.50
98 Alexis Gomez 1.50
99 Ian Ferguson 1.50
100 Duke Snider 3.00
101 Shawn Green 2.00
102 Hideo Nomo 2.00
103 Kazuhisa Ishii 1.50
104 Edwin Jackson 1.50
105 Fred McGriff 2.00
106 Hong-Chih Kou 1.50
107 *Don Sutton* 2.00
108 Rickey Henderson 2.00
109 Cesar Izturis 1.50
110 Robin Ventura 1.50
111 Paul LoDuca 1.50
112 Rickie Weeks 2.00
113 Scott Podsednik 2.00
114 Junior Spivey 1.50
115 Lyle Overbay 2.00
116 Tony Oliva 1.50
117 Jacque Jones 1.50
118 Shannon Stewart 1.50
119 Torii Hunter 2.00
120 Johan Santana 1.50
121 J.D. Durbin 1.50
122 Jason Kubel 1.50
123 Michael Cuddyer 1.50
124 Nick Johnson 1.50
125 Jose Vidro 1.50
126 Orlando Cabrera 1.50
127 Zach Day 1.50
128 Mike Piazza 5.00
129 Tom Glavine 2.00
130 Jae Weong Seo 1.50
131 Gary Carter 2.00
132 Phil Seibel 1.50
133 Edwin Almonte 1.50
134 Aaron Boone 1.50
135 Kenny Lofton 2.00
136 Don Mattingly 6.00
137 Jason Giambi 3.00
138 Alex Rodriguez Yanks 8.00
139 Jorge Posada 2.00
140 Bernie Williams 2.00
141 Hideki Matsui 5.00
142 Mike Mussina 2.00
143 Mariano Rivera 2.00
144 Gary Sheffield 2.00
145 Derek Jeter 8.00
146 Chien-Ming Wang 1.50
147 Javier Vazquez 1.50
148 Jose Contreras 1.50
149 Whitey Ford 2.00
150 Kevin Brown 2.00
151 Eric Chavez 2.00
152 Barry Zito 2.00
153 Mark Mulder 2.00
154 Tim Hudson 2.00
155 Rich Harden 1.50
156 Eric Byrnes 1.50
157 Jim Thome 4.00
158 Bobby Abreu 2.00
159 Marlon Byrd 1.50
160 Lenny Dykstra 1.50
161 Steve Carlton 2.00
162 Ryan Howard 1.50
163 Bobby Hill 1.50
164 Jose Castillo 1.50
165 Jay Payton 1.50
166 Ryan Klesko 1.50
167 Brian Giles 1.50
168 Henri Stanley 1.50
169 Jason Schmidt 2.00
170 Jerome Williams 1.50
171 J.T. Snow 1.50
172 Bret Boone 2.00
173 Edgar Martinez 2.00
174 Ichiro Suzuki 5.00
175 Jamie Moyer 1.50
176 Rich Aurilia 1.50
177 Chris Snelling 1.50
178 Scott Rolen 4.00
179 Albert Pujols 6.00
180 Jim Edmonds 2.00
181 Stan Musial 4.00
182 Dan Haren 1.50
183 Red Schoendienst 1.50
184 Aubrey Huff 1.50
185 Delmon Young 1.50
186 Rocco Baldelli 2.00
187 Dewon Brazelton 1.50
188 Mark Teixeira 2.50
189 Hank Blalock 3.00
190 Nolan Ryan Ranger 10.00
191 Alfonso Soriano 4.00
192 Michael Young 1.50
193 Vernon Wells 1.50
194 Roy Halladay 2.00
195 Carlos Delgado 2.50
196 Dustin McGowan 1.50
197 Josh Phelps 1.50
198 Alexis Rios 1.50
199 Eric Hinske 1.50
200 Josh Towers 1.50
201 *Kazuo Matsui/1000* 10.00
202 *Fernando Nieve AU/500* 8.00
203 Mike Rouse/1000 RC 3.00
204 *Dennis Sarfate AU/500* 8.00
205 *Josh Labandeira AU/500* 8.00
206 *Chris Oxspring AU/500* 8.00
207 Alfredo Simon/1000 RC 2.00
208 *Cory Sullivan AU/500* 8.00
209 *Ruddy Yan AU/500* 8.00
210 *Jason Bartlett AU/500* 8.00
211 *Akinori Otsuka/1000* 5.00
212 *Lincoln Holdzkom/1000* 2.00
213 *Justin Leone/1000* 4.00
214 *Jorge Sequea AU/500* 8.00
215 *John Gall/1000 RC* 3.00
216 *Jerome Gamble/1000 RC* 2.00
217 *Tim Bittner AU/500* 8.00
218 *Ronny Cedeno AU/500* 8.00
219 *Justin Hampson/1000 RC* 2.00
220 Ryan Wing AU/500 RC 8.00
221 *Mariano Gomez AU/500* 8.00
222 *Carlos Vasquez/1000* 2.00
223 *Casey Daigle AU/500 RC* 8.00
224 *Renyel Pinto AU/500* 8.00
225 *Chris Shelton AU/500* 30.00
226 Mike Gosling AU/700 8.00
227 *Aarom Baldiris AU/700* 8.00
228 *Ramon Ramirez AU/700* 8.00
229 *Roberto Novoa AU/500* 8.00
230 Sean Henn AU/500 10.00
231 *Jamie Brown AU/500* 8.00
232 *Nick Regilio AU/500* 8.00
233 David Crouthers AU/700 RC 8.00
234 *Greg Dobbs AU/500* 8.00
235 *Angel Chavez AU/500* 8.00
236 Willy Taveras AU/500 RC 8.00
237 *Justin Knoedler AU/500* 8.00
238 *Ian Snell AU/700* 8.00
239 *Jason Frasor AU/500* 8.00
240 *Jerry Gil AU/500 RC* 8.00
241 *Carlos Hines AU/500* 8.00
242 *Ivan Ochoa AU/500* 8.00
243 *Jose Capellan AU/700* 25.00
244 *Onil Joseph AU/700* 8.00
245 *Hector Gimenez AU/700* 8.00
246 *Shawn Hill AU/700* 8.00
247 *Freddy Guzman AU/700* 8.00
248 Graham Koonce AU/500 8.00
249 Ronald Belisario AU/500 RC 8.00
250 *Merkin Valdez AU/700* 8.00

Spectrum Gold

Stars (1-200): 2-4X
Gold Auto. (201-250): .5X
Non-Auto. (201-250): 1-2X
Production 50 sets

Spectrum Platinum

No Pricing
Production one set

Spectrum Silver

Stars (1-200): 1-2X
Gold Auto. (201-250): .25-.4X
Non-Auto. (201-250): 1X
Production 100 sets

Retail

Cards (1-200): .15X
1-200 are not serial numbered

Absolutely Ink

NM/M

Quantity Produced Listed
Spectrum: .75-1.5X
Production 1-25
No Pricing 15 or Less

1 Adam Dunn/100 25.00
2 Al Kaline/100 25.00
3 Alan Trammell/100 15.00
6 Andre Dawson Cubs/100 15.00
7 Andre Dawson Expos/100 15.00
8 Andruw Jones/50 25.00
9 Angel Berroa/50 10.00
10 Aramis Ramirez/50 25.00
11 Aubrey Huff/100 12.00
12 Austin Kearns/100 15.00
13 Barry Larkin/50 30.00
16 Bert Blyleven/100 15.00
17 Billy Williams/100 15.00
19 Bob Feller/100 20.00
20 Bob Gibson/25 35.00
21 Bobby Doerr/100 15.00
22 Brandon Webb/100 10.00
23 Brett Myers/50 15.00
24 Brooks Robinson/100 40.00
27 Carlos Beltran/100 25.00
28 Carlos Lee/100 10.00
31 Craig Biggio/50 25.00
33 Dale Murphy/100 25.00
34 Darryl Strawberry/100 15.00
35 Dave Concepcion/50 20.00
36 Dave Parker/50 15.00
38 Don Mattingly/100 60.00
39 Dontrelle Willis/100 20.00
40 Duke Snider/100 30.00
41 Dwight Gooden/100 15.00
42 Edgar Martinez/50 30.00
43 Eric Chavez/50 25.00
44 Ernie Banks/100 50.00
45 Fergie Jenkins/100 15.00
46 Frank Robinson/100 20.00
47 Frank Thomas/25 50.00
48 Fred Lynn/50 15.00
49 Fred McGriff/25 50.00
50 Garret Anderson/100 15.00
51 Gary Carter Expos/100 15.00
52 Gary Carter Mets/100 15.00
53 Gary Sheffield/50 25.00
54 Gaylord Perry/100 15.00
57 Hank Blalock/100 25.00
58 Harold Baines/50 25.00
62 Jacque Jones/100 15.00
63 Jae Weong Seo/100 15.00
64 Jamie Moyer/25 25.00
65 Jason Varitek/50 35.00
66 Jay Gibbons/50 15.00
67 Jim Edmonds/25 35.00
68 Jim Palmer/100 20.00
69 Jim Rice/50 20.00
71 Johan Santana/50 40.00
72 Jorge Posada/50 40.00
73 Josh Beckett/25 40.00
74 Juan Gonzalez/25 40.00
75 Keith Hernandez/100 15.00
76 Kirby Puckett/25 60.00
77 Luis Tiant/100 15.00
78 Maggio Ordonez/100 15.00
81 Mark Grace/25 50.00
82 Mark Mulder/100 20.00
83 Mark Prior/100 60.00
84 Mark Teixeira/100 25.00
85 Marty Marion/100 15.00
86 Mike Lowell/25 25.00
90 Nolan Ryan/25 125.00
91 Orel Hershiser/100 30.00
92 Orlando Cepeda/100 15.00
97 Phil Niekro/100 15.00
99 Ralph Kiner/100 20.00
101 Red Schoendienst/100 15.00
103 Robin Roberts/50 25.00
104 Robin Ventura/100 15.00
106 Rocco Baldelli/25 30.00
109 Sammy Sosa/21 150.00
110 Sean Casey/23 25.00
111 Shannon Stewart/50 15.00
113 Stan Musial/100 60.00
114 Steve Carlton/50 40.00
115 Steve Garvey/100 15.00
117 Tommy John/100 15.00
118 Tony Gwynn/25 60.00
119 Tony Oliva/100 15.00
120 Torii Hunter/100 15.00
121 Trot Nixon/50 30.00
122 Troy Glaus/50 20.00
123 Vernon Wells/25 20.00
124 Vladimir Guerrero/100 35.00
125 Will Clark/100 35.00

Absolutely Ink Material

NM/M

Quantity Produced Listed
Prime: .5-1X
Production 1-25
No Pricing 10 or Less

1 Adam Dunn Jsy/100 30.00
2 Al Kaline Pants/50 50.00
3 Alan Trammell Jsy/100 20.00
6 Andre Dawson Cubs Jsy/100 20.00
7 Andre Dawson Expos Jsy/100 20.00
9 Angel Berroa Jsy/100 10.00
11 Aubrey Huff Jsy/100 15.00
12 Austin Kearns Jsy/100 15.00
16 Bert Blyleven Jsy/100 15.00
17 Billy Williams Jsy/100 25.00
19 Bob Feller Jsy/100 25.00
21 Bobby Doerr Jsy/100 25.00
22 Brandon Webb Jsy/50 15.00
23 Brett Myers Jsy/100 15.00
24 Brooks Robinson Jsy/100 40.00
27 Carlos Beltran Jsy/100 40.00
28 Carlos Lee Jsy/100 15.00
33 Dale Murphy Jsy/100 30.00
34 Darryl Strawberry Jsy/100 20.00
35 Dave Concepcion Jsy/50 20.00
36 Dave Parker Jsy/100 15.00
38 Don Mattingly Jsy/50 75.00
39 Dontrelle Willis Jsy/20 25.00
41 Dwight Gooden Jsy/60 20.00
42 Edgar Martinez Jsy/100 30.00
44 Ernie Banks Jsy/50 50.00
45 Fergie Jenkins Pants/100 15.00
46 Frank Robinson Jsy/50 40.00
48 Fred Lynn Jsy/100 15.00
49 Fred McGriff Jsy/20 60.00
50 Garret Anderson Jsy/100 15.00
51 Gary Carter Expos Jsy/100 20.00
52 Gary Carter Mets Jacket/100 20.00
53 Gary Sheffield Jsy/100 20.00
54 Gaylord Perry Jsy/100 15.00
57 Hank Blalock Jsy/100 30.00
58 Harold Baines Jsy/100 20.00
63 Jae Weong Seo Jsy/100 15.00
64 Jamie Moyer Jsy/100 20.00
65 Jason Varitek Jsy/100 30.00
66 Jay Gibbons Jsy/100 15.00
67 Jim Edmonds Jsy/5
68 Jim Palmer Jsy/100 25.00
69 Jim Rice Jsy/100 20.00
70 Joe Carter Jsy/50 20.00
71 Johan Santana Jsy/100 40.00
72 Jorge Posada Jsy/15 75.00
75 Keith Hernandez Jsy/100 15.00
77 Luis Tiant Jsy/100 20.00
82 Mark Mulder Jsy/20 40.00
85 Marty Marion Jsy/100 15.00
86 Mike Lowell Jsy/60 20.00
92 Orlando Cepeda Bat/65 20.00
97 Phil Niekro Jsy/25 25.00
99 Ralph Kiner Bat/100 25.00
101 Red Schoendienst Jsy/60 20.00
103 Robin Roberts Hat/50 25.00
104 Robin Ventura Jsy/65 25.00
110 Sean Casey Jsy/75 20.00
111 Shannon Stewart Jsy/100 15.00
114 Steve Carlton Jsy/50 40.00
115 Steve Garvey Bat/100 20.00
117 Tommy John Jsy/100 15.00
119 Tony Oliva Jsy/100 20.00
120 Torii Hunter Jsy/50 20.00
121 Trot Nixon Jsy/100 30.00
124 Vladimir Guerrero Jsy/55 50.00
125 Will Clark Jsy/100 40.00

Absolutely Ink Triple

No Pricing
Production 1-10
Prime: No Pricing
Production 1-5

Fans of the Game Auto

NM/M

251 Landon Donovan 25.00
252 Jennie Finch 100.00
253 Bonnie Blair 30.00
254 Dan Jansen 40.00
255 Kerri Strug 75.00

Fans of the Game

NM/M

251 Landon Donovan 1.50
252 Jennie Finch 4.00
253 Bonnie Blair 1.50
254 Dan Jansen 2.00
255 Kerri Strug 2.00

Marks of Fame

NM/M

Production 100 Sets
Spectrum: 1-2X
Production 25 Sets

1 Nolan Ryan 15.00
2 Ernie Banks 6.00
3 Bob Feller 4.00
4 Duke Snider 5.00
5 Sammy Sosa 10.00
6 Whitey Ford 6.00
7 Steve Carlton 4.00
8 Tony Gwynn 8.00
9 Jim Bunning 4.00
10 Stan Musial 8.00
11 Cal Ripken Jr. 20.00
12 George Brett 15.00
13 Gary Carter 4.00
14 Jim Palmer 4.00
15 Gaylord Perry 4.00

Marks of Fame Signat.

NM/M

Quantity Produced Listed
Spectrum: .75-1.5X
Production 1-25
No Pricing 15 or Less

1 Nolan Ryan/50 120.00
2 Ernie Banks/50 50.00
3 Bob Feller/100 25.00
4 Duke Snider/100 25.00
5 Sammy Sosa/21 125.00
6 Whitey Ford/25 50.00
7 Steve Carlton/100 25.00
8 Tony Gwynn/25 75.00
9 Jim Bunning/100 20.00
10 Stan Musial/50 60.00
11 Cal Ripken Jr./10
12 George Brett/25 100.00
13 Gary Carter/100 15.00
14 Jim Palmer/50 25.00
15 Gaylord Perry/100 15.00

Signature Club

NM/M

Quantity Produced Listed

1 Sammy Sosa Bat/5
2 Gary Sheffield Bat/50 20.00
3 Vladimir Guerrero Bat/5
4 Will Clark Bat/50 40.00
5 Ernie Banks Bat/50 50.00

Signature Material

NM/M

Quantity Produced Listed
Prime: No Pricing
Production 5 Sets
Combo: 1X
Production 25-50
Combo Prime: No Pricing
Production 5 Sets

2 Gary Carter Jsy/50 25.00
3 Dale Murphy Jsy/50 35.00
4 Don Mattingly Jsy/25 100.00
5 Stan Musial Jsy/25 100.00

Sig. Spectrum Gold

NM/M

Quantity Produced Listed

1 Troy Glaus/15 35.00
2 Garret Anderson/100 15.00
7 Vladimir Guerrero/25 60.00
8 Richie Sexson/15 25.00
9 Shea Hillenbrand/100 10.00
11 Brandon Webb/100 10.00
15 Roberto Alomar/25 50.00
18 Dale Murphy/100 25.00
19 Rafael Furcal/100 12.00
22 Julio Franco/25 20.00
23 Adam LaRoche/100 10.00
26 Jay Gibbons/100 10.00
29 Adam Loewen/100 10.00
32 Luis Matos/50 15.00
33 Jason Varitek/25 40.00
36 Trot Nixon/100 20.00
40 Luis Tiant/50 20.00
41 Kevin Youkilis/25 40.00
45 Kerry Wood/25 50.00
46 Mark Prior/100 60.00
47 Ernie Banks/100 40.00
52 Magglio Ordonez/100 15.00
53 Carlos Lee/100 15.00
54 Joe Crede/50 10.00
59 Austin Kearns/100 15.00
61 Barry Larkin/25 40.00
62 Ryan Wagner/50 10.00
63 Jody Gerut/100 10.00
64 Jeremy Guthrie/25 15.00
65 Travis Hafner/25 25.00
68 Preston Wilson/100 10.00
69 Jeff Baker/25 15.00
73 George Kell/100 15.00
79 Miguel Cabrera/100 35.00
81 Luis Castillo/25 15.00
83 Jeff Bagwell/25 50.00
87 Andy Pettitte/25 50.00
93 Carlos Beltran/100 20.00
94 Angel Berroa/100 10.00
100 Duke Snider/100 25.00
104 Edwin Jackson/50 15.00
106 Hong-Chih Kou/25 20.00
107 Don Sutton/25 25.00
112 Rickie Weeks/24 40.00
113 Scott Podsednik/100 15.00
116 Tony Oliva/50 25.00
117 Jacque Jones/100 15.00
119 Torii Hunter/100 15.00
130 Jae Weong Seo/100 10.00
131 Gary Carter/100 15.00
136 Don Mattingly/100 50.00
139 Jorge Posada/25 50.00
144 Gary Sheffield/25 25.00
146 Chien-Ming Wang/25 25.00
153 Mark Mulder/100 25.00
155 Rich Harden/50 15.00
159 Marlon Byrd/100 10.00
160 Lenny Dykstra/100 15.00
161 Steve Carlton/50 40.00
164 Jose Castillo/50 15.00
165 Jay Payton/100 10.00
170 Jerome Williams/50 25.00
178 Scott Rolen/50 40.00
181 Stan Musial/100 60.00
182 Dan Haren/25 15.00
183 Red Schoendienst/100 15.00
184 Aubrey Huff/100 10.00
185 Delmon Young/100 20.00
187 Dewon Brazelton/25 15.00
188 Mark Teixeira/50 30.00
189 Hank Blalock/25 40.00
192 Michael Young/100 25.00
194 Roy Halladay/25 25.00
198 Alexis Rios/50 25.00
202 Fernando Nieve/100 10.00
205 Josh Labandeira/100 10.00
206 Chris Oxspring/100 15.00
208 Cory Sullivan/100 10.00
209 Ruddy Yan/100 10.00
210 Jason Bartlett/100 15.00
212 Lincoln Holdzkom/100 10.00
213 Justin Leone/100 20.00
214 Jorge Sequea/100 10.00
217 Tim Bittner/100 10.00
219 Justin Hampson/100 10.00
220 Ryan Wing/100 10.00
221 Mariano Gomez/100 10.00
222 Carlos Vasquez/100 10.00
224 Renyel Pinto/100 15.00
225 Chris Shelton/100 15.00
230 Sean Henn/100 10.00
232 Nick Regilio/100 10.00
234 Greg Dobbs/50 15.00
235 Angel Chavez/100 10.00
242 Ivan Ochoa/100 10.00
248 Graham Koonce/100 10.00

Sig. Spectrum Silver

NM/M

Quantity Produced Listed

1 Troy Glaus/34 25.00
2 Garret Anderson/100 15.00
6 Nolan Ryan Angels/25 150.00
7 Vladimir Guerrero/100 40.00

8 Richie Sexson/34 20.00
9 Shea Hillenbrand/100 10.00
11 Brandon Webb/100 10.00
13 Robby Hammock/250 10.00
14 Edgar Gonzalez/104 10.00
15 Roberto Alomar/32 50.00
16 Andruw Jones/50 20.00
18 Dale Murphy/100 25.00
19 Rafael Furcal/100 12.00
21 Bubba Nelson/250 10.00
22 Julio Franco/100 15.00
23 Adam LaRoche/100 10.00
24 Michael Hessman/250 10.00
26 Jay Gibbons/100 10.00
29 Adam Loewen/100 10.00
32 Luis Matos/100 10.00
33 Jason Varitek/50 35.00
36 Trot Nixon/100 20.00
40 Luis Tiant/100 15.00
41 Kevin Youkilis/25 40.00
42 Michel Hernandez/190 10.00
43 Sammy Sosa/21 150.00
45 Kerry Wood/50 40.00
46 Mark Prior/100 60.00
47 Ernie Banks/100 40.00
48 Aramis Ramirez/50 30.00
49 Brendan Harris/250 10.00
50 Todd Wellemeyer/250 10.00
51 Frank Thomas/50 40.00
52 Magglio Ordonez/100 20.00
53 Carlos Lee/100 15.00
54 Joe Crede/100 10.00
55 Joe Borchard/250 10.00
57 Sean Casey/50 20.00
58 Adam Dunn/100 25.00
59 Austin Kearns/100 15.00
61 Barry Larkin/50 30.00
62 Ryan Wagner/100 10.00
63 Jody Gerut/100 10.00
64 Jeremy Guthrie/50 10.00
65 Travis Hafner/50 20.00
66 Brian Tallet/250 10.00
68 Preston Wilson/100 10.00
69 Jeff Baker/50 10.00
70 Clint Barmes/250 10.00
71 Joe Kennedy/250 10.00
73 George Kell/100 15.00
74 Preston Larrison/250 10.00
77 Dontrelle Willis/100 20.00
78 Josh Beckett/25 35.00
79 Miguel Cabrera/100 35.00
80 Mike Lowell/25 25.00
81 Luis Castillo/50 10.00
83 Jeff Bagwell/50 40.00
85 Craig Biggio/50 30.00
86 Lance Berkman/25 40.00
87 Andy Pettitte/25 50.00
88 Roy Oswalt/25 25.00
89 Chris Burke/250 10.00
90 Jason Lane/231 10.00
93 Carlos Beltran/100 20.00
94 Angel Berroa/100 10.00
95 Juan Gonzalez/25 40.00
96 Ken Harvey/200 15.00
97 Byron Gettis/250 10.00
98 Alexis Gomez/250 10.00
99 Ian Ferguson/104 10.00
100 Duke Snider/100 25.00
103 Kazuhisa Ishii/25 40.00
104 Edwin Jackson/100 10.00
105 Fred McGriff/50 15.00
106 Hong-Chih Kou/50 15.00
107 Don Sutton/100 15.00
109 Cesar Izturis/101 10.00
110 Robin Ventura/25 20.00
111 Paul LoDuca/50 20.00
112 Rickie Weeks/21 40.00
113 Scott Podsednik/100 15.00
114 Junior Spivey/89 10.00
115 Lyle Overbay/89 15.00
116 Tony Oliva/72 15.00
117 Jacque Jones/100 15.00
118 Shannon Stewart/100 10.00
119 Torii Hunter/100 15.00
120 Johan Santana/50 25.00
121 J.D. Durbin/250 10.00
122 Jason Kubel/250 20.00
123 Michael Cuddyer/225 10.00
124 Nick Johnson/25 15.00
125 Jose Vidro/25 15.00
126 Orlando Cabrera/25 20.00
127 Zach Day/100 10.00
130 Jae Weong Seo/100 10.00
131 Gary Carter/100 15.00
132 Phil Seibel/177 10.00
133 Edwin Almonte/250 10.00
136 Don Mattingly/100 50.00
139 Jorge Posada/50 40.00
144 Gary Sheffield/100 15.00
146 Chien-Ming Wang/50 20.00
147 Javier Vazquez/25 40.00
148 Jose Contreras/25 35.00
149 Whitey Ford/50 40.00
151 Eric Chavez/50 25.00
153 Mark Mulder/100 25.00
154 Tim Hudson/50 25.00
155 Rich Harden/100 15.00
156 Eric Byrnes/250 10.00
159 Marlon Byrd/100 10.00
160 Lenny Dykstra/100 15.00
161 Steve Carlton/100 25.00
162 Ryan Howard/250 15.00
163 Bobby Hill/250 10.00
164 Jose Castillo/100 10.00
165 Jay Payton/100 10.00
168 Henri Stanley/112 10.00
170 Jerome Williams/100 15.00
171 J.T. Snow/89 15.00
173 Edgar Martinez/50 30.00
175 Jamie Moyer/19 25.00
176 Rich Aurilia/25 15.00
177 Chris Snelling/177 10.00
178 Scott Rolen/100 30.00
180 Jim Edmonds/50 30.00
181 Stan Musial/100 60.00
182 Dan Haren/200 10.00
183 Red Schoendienst/100 15.00
184 Aubrey Huff/100 10.00
185 Delmon Young/100 20.00
186 Rocco Baldelli/50 20.00
187 Dewon Brazelton/50 15.00
188 Mark Teixeira/100 20.00
189 Hank Blalock/50 30.00
190 Nolan Ryan Rgr/25 125.00
192 Michael Young/100 25.00
194 Roy Halladay/50 20.00
196 Dustin McGowan/250 10.00
197 Josh Phelps/25 15.00
198 Alexis Rios/100 15.00
200 Josh Towers/158 10.00
202 Fernando Nieve/250 10.00
203 Mike Rouse/100 10.00
204 Dennis Sarfate/100 10.00
205 Josh Labandeira/250 10.00
206 Chris Oxspring/250 10.00
207 Alfredo Simon/100 10.00
208 Cory Sullivan/250 10.00
209 Ruddy Yan/250 10.00
210 Jason Bartlett/250 10.00
211 Akinori Otsuka/100 50.00
212 Lincoln Holdzkom/250 10.00
213 Justin Leone/250 20.00
214 Jorge Sequea/250 10.00
215 John Gall/50 25.00
217 Tim Bittner/250 10.00
219 Justin Hampson/250 10.00
220 Ryan Wing/250 10.00
221 Mariano Gomez/250 10.00
222 Carlos Vasquez/250 10.00
223 Casey Daigle/150 10.00
224 Renyel Pinto/250 15.00
225 Chris Shelton/250 15.00
229 Roberto Novoa/225 10.00
230 Sean Henn/250 10.00
231 Jamie Brown/200 10.00
232 Nick Regilio/250 10.00
234 Greg Dobbs/250 10.00
235 Angel Chavez/250 10.00
236 Willy Taveras/225 10.00
237 Justin Knoedler/225 10.00
239 Jason Frasor/225 10.00
240 Jerry Gil/225 10.00
241 Carlos Hines/225 10.00
242 Ivan Ochoa/250 10.00
248 Graham Koonce/250 10.00
249 Ronald Belisario/225 10.00

Team Quad Material

NM/M

Production 100 Sets
Prime: No Pricing
Production 5 Sets
1 Jeff Kent, Lance Berkman, Craig Biggio, Jeff Bagwell 20.00
2 Nomar Garciaparra, Manny Ramirez, Pedro Martinez, Trot Nixon 35.00
3 Paul Konerko, Carlos Lee, Magglio Ordonez, Frank Thomas 20.00
4 John Smoltz, Chipper Jones, Andruw Jones, Rafael Furcal 20.00
5 Garret Anderson, Troy Percival, Troy Glaus, Darin Erstad 10.00
6 Steve Finley, Brandon Webb, Randy Johnson, Luis Gonzalez 20.00
7 Paul LoDuca, Hideo Nomo, Shawn Green, Kazuhisa Ishii 20.00
8 Larry Walker, Todd Helton, Jason Jennings, Preston Wilson 10.00
9 Dontrelle Willis, Brad Penny, Josh Beckett 20.00
10 Jose Reyes, Jae Weong Seo, Tom Glavine, Mike Piazza 20.00
11 Bernie Williams, Derek Jeter, Jason Giambi, Alfonso Soriano 40.00
12 Rich Harden, Tim Hudson, Barry Zito, Mark Mulder 10.00
13 Kevin Millwood, Marlon Byrd, Jim Thome, Bobby Abreu 20.00
14 Edgar Renteria, Jim Edmonds, Albert Pujols, Scott Rolen 40.00
15 Roger Clemens, Andy Pettitte, Wade Miller, Roy Oswalt 30.00

Team Tandem

NM/M

Production 250 Sets
Spectrum: 2-4X
Production 25 Sets
1 Vladimir Guerrero, Reggie Jackson 3.00
2 Dale Murphy, Chipper Jones 3.00
3 Gary Carter, Mike Piazza 4.00
4 Miguel Tejada, Cal Ripken Jr. 8.00
5 Gary Sheffield, Derek Jeter 6.00
6 Curt Schilling, Pedro J. Martinez 3.00
7 Roger Clemens, Andy Pettitte 5.00
8 Mike Sweeney, George Brett 6.00
9 Kazuhisa Ishii, Hideo Nomo 3.00
10 Austin Kearns, Adam Dunn 3.00
11 Miguel Cabrera, Dontrelle Willis 3.00
12 Don Mattingly, Derek Jeter 8.00
13 Barry Zito, Eric Chavez 2.00
14 Jim Thome, Mike Schmidt 4.00
15 Albert Pujols, Stan Musial 4.00
16 Nolan Ryan, Alex Rodriguez 8.00
17 Kerry Wood, Mark Prior 4.00
18 Rafael Palmeiro, Jay Gibbons 3.00
19 Nomar Garciaparra, Manny Ramirez 4.00
20 Ivan Rodriguez, Mike Piazza 4.00

Team Tandem Material

NM/M

Production 250 Sets
Prime: No Pricing
Production 5 Sets
1 Reggie Jackson Bat, Vladimir Guerrero Bat 10.00
2 Chipper Jones Jsy, Dale Murphy Jsy 10.00
3 Gary Carter Jsy, Mike Piazza Jsy 10.00
4 Miguel Tejada Bat, Cal Ripken Jr. Bat 25.00
5 Derek Jeter Bat, Gary Sheffield Bat 25.00
6 Curt Schilling Bat, Pedro J. Martinez Bat 10.00
7 Roger Clemens Bat, Andy Pettitte Bat 15.00
8 Mike Sweeney Jsy, George Brett Jsy 15.00
9 Kazuhisa Ishii Jsy, Hideo Nomo Jsy 10.00
10 Austin Kearns Jsy, Adam Dunn Jsy 10.00
11 Dontrelle Willis Jsy, Miguel Cabrera Jsy 10.00
12 Don Mattingly Jsy, Derek Jeter Jsy 35.00
13 Barry Zito Jsy, Eric Chavez Jsy 8.00
14 Jim Thome Jsy, Mike Schmidt Jsy 20.00
15 Albert Pujols Jsy, Stan Musial Jsy 40.00
16 Nolan Ryan Jsy, Alex Rodriguez Jsy 25.00
17 Mark Prior Jsy, Kerry Wood Jsy 20.00
18 Rafael Palmeiro Jsy, Jay Gibbons Jsy 10.00
19 Nomar Garciaparra Jsy, Manny Ramirez Jsy 15.00
20 Ivan Rodriguez Jsy, Mike Piazza Jsy 10.00

Team Trio Material

NM/M

Production 100 Sets
Prime: No Pricing
Production 5 Sets
1 Sammy Sosa, Kerry Wood, Mark Prior 35.00
2 Hank Blalock, Mark Teixeira, Alex Rodriguez 15.00
3 Vernon Wells, Roy Halladay, Carlos Delgado 8.00
4 Mike Mussina, Jorge Posada, Mariano Rivera 25.00
5 Shannon Stewart, Torii Hunter, Jacque Jones 8.00
6 Carlos Beltran, Mike Sweeney, Angel Berroa 8.00
7 Dontrelle Willis, Miguel Cabrera, Josh Beckett 15.00
8 Jeff Bagwell, Craig Biggio, Lance Berkman 10.00
9 Nomar Garciaparra, Pedro J. Martinez, Manny Ramirez 20.00
10 Shawn Green, Kazuhisa Ishii, Hideo Nomo 10.00
11 Mark Mulder, Barry Zito, Tim Hudson 8.00
12 Jim Edmonds, Scott Rolen, Albert Pujols 25.00
13 Cal Ripken Jr., Jay Gibbons, Rafael Palmeiro 40.00
14 Sammy Sosa, Mark Grace, Ryne Sandberg 35.00
15 Nolan Ryan, Roger Clemens, Randy Johnson/25 80.00

Tools of Trade Blue

NM/M

Common Player: 1.50
Production 250 Sets
Black: No Pricing
Production One Set
Blue Spectrum: 1-1.5X
Production 125 Sets
Green: 1-1.5X
Production 150 Sets
Green Spectrum: 2-3X
Production 50 Sets
Red: 1X
Production 200 Sets
Red Spectrum: 1-2X
Production 100 Sets
1 Adam Dunn H 2.50
2 Adam Dunn A 2.50
3 Alan Trammell 2.00
4 Albert Pujols H 6.00
5 Albert Pujols A 6.00
6 Alex Rodriguez M's 6.00
7 Alex Rodriguez Rgr H 6.00
8 Alex Rodriguez Rgr Alt 6.00
9 Alfonso Soriano 4.00
10 Andre Dawson 2.00
11 Andruw Jones H 2.00
12 Andruw Jones A 2.00
13 Andy Pettitte H 2.00
14 Andy Pettitte A 2.00
15 Angel Berroa 1.50
16 Aubrey Huff 1.50
17 Austin Kearns 2.00
18 Barry Zito Alt 2.00
19 Barry Zito A 2.00
20 Bernie Williams 2.00
21 Bobby Abreu 2.00
22 Brandon Webb 1.50
23 Cal Ripken Jr. H 8.00
24 Cal Ripken Jr. A 8.00
25 Cal Ripken Jr. Alt 8.00

26 Carlos Beltran 2.00
27 Carlos Delgado H 2.00
28 Carlos Delgado A 2.00
29 Carlos Lee 1.50
30 Chipper Jones H 3.00
31 Chipper Jones A 3.00
32 Craig Biggio H 2.00
33 Craig Biggio A 2.00
34 Curt Schilling D'backs 2.00
35 Curt Schilling Phils 2.00
36 Dale Murphy H 2.00
37 Dale Murphy A 2.00
38 Darryl Strawberry 1.50
39 Derek Jeter H 8.00
40 Derek Jeter A 8.00
41 Don Mattingly H 8.00
42 Don Mattingly A 8.00
43 Dontrelle Willis H 2.00
44 Dontrelle Willis A 2.00
45 Dwight Gooden 1.50
46 Edgar Martinez 1.50
47 Eric Chavez 2.00
48 Frank Thomas A 2.00
49 Frank Thomas Alt 2.00
50 Garret Anderson 2.00
51 Gary Carter 2.00
52 Gary Sheffield 2.00
53 George Brett H 6.00
54 George Brett A 6.00
55 Greg Maddux 4.00
56 Hank Blalock 2.00
57 Hideo Nomo 2.00
58 Ivan Rodriguez Marlins 2.00
59 Ivan Rodriguez Rgr 2.00
60 Jacque Jones 1.50
61 Jae Weong Seo 1.50
62 Jason Giambi Yanks 2.00
63 Jason Giambi A's 2.00
64 Javy Lopez 2.00
65 Jay Gibbons 1.50
66 Jeff Bagwell A 2.00
67 Jeff Bagwell Alt 2.00
68 Jeff Kent 1.50
69 Jim Edmonds 2.00
70 Jim Thome 3.00
71 Jorge Posada 2.00
72 Jose Canseco 2.00
73 Jose Reyes 2.00
74 Josh Beckett 2.00
75 Juan Gonzalez 2.00
76 Kazuhisa Ishii 1.50
77 Kerry Wood H 3.00
78 Kerry Wood Alt 3.00
79 Kirby Puckett 3.00
80 Lance Berkman 2.00
81 Lou Brock 2.00
82 Luis Castillo 1.50
83 Luis Gonzalez 1.50
84 Magglio Ordonez 1.50
85 Manny Ramirez Sox 2.00
86 Manny Ramirez Indians 2.00
87 Marcus Giles 1.50
88 Mark Grace 2.00
89 Mark Mulder 2.00
90 Mark Prior H 5.00
91 Mark Prior A 5.00
92 Mark Teixeira 2.00
93 Marlon Byrd 1.50
94 Miguel Cabrera 3.00
95 Miguel Tejada 2.00
96 Mike Lowell 2.00
97 Mike Mussina O's 2.00
98 Mike Mussina Yanks 2.00
99 Mike Piazza Marlins 4.00
100 Mike Piazza Dodgers 4.00
101 Mike Piazza Mets 4.00
102 Mike Schmidt H 5.00
103 Mike Schmidt A 5.00
104 Mike Sweeney 1.50
105 Nick Johnson 1.50
106 Nolan Ryan Angels 8.00
107 Nolan Ryan Astros 8.00
108 Nolan Ryan Rangers 8.00
109 Nomar Garciaparra H 5.00
110 Nomar Garciaparra A 5.00
111 Pat Burrell 2.00
112 Paul LoDuca 1.50
113 Pedro J. Martinez Sox 3.00
114 Pedro Martinez Expos 3.00
115 Preston Wilson 1.50
116 Rafael Palmeiro O's 2.00
117 Rafael Palmeiro Rgr 2.00
118 Randy Johnson D'backs 4.00
119 Randy Johnson M's 4.00
120 Richie Sexson 2.00
121 Rickey Henderson A's 2.00
122 Rickey Henderson Padres 2.00
123 Rickey Henderson M's 2.00
124 Roberto Alomar 2.00
125 Rocco Baldelli 2.00
126 Rod Carew 2.00
127 Roger Clemens Sox 6.00
128 Roger Clemens Yanks 6.00
129 Roy Halladay 2.00
130 Roy Oswalt 1.50
131 Ryne Sandberg 5.00
132 Sammy Sosa H 5.00
133 Sammy Sosa A 5.00
134 Sammy Sosa Sox 5.00
135 Scott Rolen 4.00
136 Shawn Green 2.00
137 Steve Carlton 2.00
138 Tim Hudson 2.00
139 Todd Helton H 2.00
140 Todd Helton A 2.00
141 Tom Glavine Braves 2.00
142 Tom Glavine Mets 2.00
143 Tony Gwynn A 4.00
144 Tony Gwynn Alt 4.00
145 Torii Hunter 2.00
146 Trot Nixon 2.00
147 Troy Glaus 2.00
148 Vernon Wells 2.00
149 Vladimir Guerrero 4.00
150 Will Clark 3.00

Tools of Trade Mater. Combo

NM/M

Production 25-250
Single: No Pricing
Production 1-5
Combo Price Single: 2-4X
Production 1-25
Trio: 1-3X
Production 5-100
No Pricing 15 or Less
Quad: 2-4X
Production 1-50
No Pricing 15 or Less
Five: 3-5X
Production 10-25
Six: 3-6X
Production 5-25

1 Adam Dunn H Bat-Jsy/250 6.00
2 Adam Dunn A Bat-Jsy/250 6.00
3 Alan Trammell Bat-Jsy/250 4.00
4 Albert Pujols H Bat-Jsy/250 20.00
5 Albert Pujols A Bat-Jsy/250 20.00
6 Alex Rodriguez M's Bat-Jsy/250 10.00
7 Alex Rodriguez H Bat-Jsy/250 10.00
8 Alex Rodriguez Alt Rgr Bat-Jsy/250 10.00
9 Alfonso Soriano Bat-Jsy/100 10.00
10 Andre Dawson Bat-Jsy/250 5.00
11 Andruw Jones H Bat-Jsy/100 8.00
12 Andruw Jones A Bat-Jsy/250 8.00
13 Andy Pettitte H Bat-Jsy/100 10.00
14 Andy Pettitte A Bat-Jsy/100 10.00
15 Angel Berroa Bat-Jsy/250 4.00
16 Aubrey Huff Bat-Jsy/250 4.00
17 Austin Kearns Bat-Jsy/250 6.00
18 Barry Zito Alt Bat-Jsy/250 6.00
19 Barry Zito A Bat-Jsy/250 6.00
20 Bernie Williams Bat-Jsy/250 8.00
21 Bobby Abreu Bat-Jsy/250 6.00
22 Brandon Webb Bat-Jsy/250 4.00
23 Cal Ripken Jr. H Bat-Jsy/250 30.00
24 Cal Ripken Jr. A Bat-Jsy/250 30.00
25 Cal Ripken Jr. Alt Bat-Jsy/250 30.00
26 Carlos Beltran Bat-Jsy/250 6.00
27 Carlos Delgado H Bat-Jsy/250 6.00
28 Carlos Delgado A Bat-Jsy/250 6.00
29 Carlos Lee Bat-Jsy/250 4.00
30 Chipper Jones H Bat-Jsy/250 10.00
31 Chipper Jones A Bat-Jsy/250 10.00
32 Craig Biggio H Bat-Jsy/250 6.00
33 Craig Biggio A Bat-Jsy/100 6.00
34 Curt Schilling D'backs Bat-Jsy/250 8.00
35 Curt Schilling Phils Bat-Jsy/250 8.00
36 Dale Murphy H Bat-Jsy/250 8.00
37 Dale Murphy A Bat-Jsy/100 8.00
38 Darryl Strawberry Bat-Jsy/250 4.00
39 Derek Jeter H Bat-Jsy/100 30.00
40 Derek Jeter A Bat-Jsy/100 30.00
41 Don Mattingly H Bat-Jsy/100 30.00
42 Don Mattingly A Bat-Jsy/100 30.00
43 Dontrelle Willis H Bat-Jsy/250 6.00
44 Dontrelle Willis A Bat-Jsy/250 6.00
45 Dwight Gooden Bat-Jsy/250 6.00
46 Edgar Martinez Bat-Jsy/250 6.00
47 Eric Chavez Bat-Jsy/250 6.00
48 Frank Thomas A Bat-Jsy/250 10.00
49 Frank Thomas Alt Bat-Jsy/250 10.00
50 Garret Anderson Bat-Jsy/250 6.00
51 Gary Carter Bat-Jsy/250 6.00
52 Gary Sheffield Bat-Jsy/250 6.00
53 George Brett H Bat-Jsy/250 20.00
54 George Brett A Bat-Jsy/250 20.00
55 Greg Maddux Bat-Jsy/250 10.00
56 Hank Blalock Bat-Jsy/250 8.00
57 Hideo Nomo Bat-Jsy/250 10.00
58 Ivan Rodriguez Marlins Bat-Jsy/250 8.00
59 Ivan Rodriguez Rgr Bat-Jsy/250 8.00
60 Jacque Jones Bat-Jsy/250 4.00
62 Jason Giambi Yanks Bat-Jsy/250 8.00
63 Jason Giambi A's Bat-Jsy/250 8.00
64 Javy Lopez Bat-Jsy/250 6.00
65 Jay Gibbons Bat-Jsy/250 4.00
66 Jeff Bagwell A Bat-Jsy/250 8.00
67 Jeff Bagwell Alt Bat-Jsy/250 8.00
68 Jeff Kent Bat-Jsy/250 5.00
69 Jim Edmonds B at-Jsy/250 8.00
70 Jim Thome Bat-Jsy/250 12.00
71 Jorge Posada Bat-Jsy/250 8.00
72 Jose Canseco Bat-Jsy/250 8.00
73 Jose Reyes Bat-Jsy/250 6.00
74 Josh Beckett Bat-Jsy/250 8.00
75 Juan Gonzalez Bat-Jsy/250 8.00
76 Kazuhisa Ishii Bat-Jsy/250 4.00
77 Kerry Wood H Bat-Jsy/250 10.00
78 Kerry Wood Alt Bat-Jsy/250 10.00
79 Kirby Puckett Bat-Jsy/250 10.00
80 Lance Berkman Bat-Jsy/250 6.00
81 Lou Brock Bat-Jsy/250 8.00
82 Luis Castillo Bat-Jsy/250 4.00
83 Luis Gonzalez Bat-Jsy/250 4.00
84 Magglio Ordonez Bat-Jsy/250 6.00
85 Manny Ramirez Sox Bat-Jsy/250 8.00
86 Manny Ramirez Indians Bat-Jsy/250 8.00
87 Marcus Giles Bat-Jsy/25 10.00
88 Mark Grace Bat-Jsy/250 8.00
89 Mark Mulder Bat-Jsy/250 8.00
90 Mark Prior Bat-Jsy/250 15.00
91 Mark Prior A Bat-Jsy/250 15.00
92 Mark Teixeira Bat-Jsy/250 6.00
93 Marlon Byrd Bat-Jsy/250 4.00
94 Miguel Cabrera Bat-Jsy/250 10.00
95 Miguel Tejada Bat-Jsy/250 6.00
96 Mike Lowell Bat-Jsy/250 6.00
97 Mike Mussina O's Jsy-Pants/250 8.00
98 Mike Mussina Yanks Jsy-Jsy/250 8.00
99 Mike Piazza Marlins Bat-Jsy/250 12.00
100 Mike Piazza Dodgers Bat-Jsy/250 12.00
101 Mike Piazza Mets Bat-Jsy/250 12.00
102 Mike Schmidt H Bat-Jsy/100 20.00
103 Mike Schmidt A Bat-Jsy/100 20.00
104 Mike Sweeney Bat-Jsy/250 4.00
105 Nick Johnson Bat-Jsy/250 4.00
106 Nolan Ryan Angels Jkt-Jsy/250 30.00
107 Nolan Ryan Astros Jkt-Jsy/250 30.00
108 Nolan Ryan Rgr Jsy-Pants/250 30.00
109 Nomar Garciaparra H Bat-Jsy/250 15.00
110 Nomar Garciaparra A Bat-Jsy/250 15.00
111 Pat Burrell Bat-Jsy/250 6.00
112 Paul LoDuca Bat-Jsy/250 4.00
113 Pedro J. Martinez Sox Bat-Jsy/250 10.00
114 Pedro Martinez Expos Bat-Jsy/250 10.00
115 Preston Wilson Bat-Jsy/250 4.00
116 Rafael Palmeiro O's Bat-Jsy/250 8.00
117 Rafael Palmeiro Rgr Bat-Jsy/250 8.00
118 Randy Johnson D'backs Bat-Jsy/250 10.00
119 Randy Johnson M's Bat-Jsy/250 10.00
120 Richie Sexson Bat-Jsy/250 6.00
121 Rickey Henderson A's Bat-Jsy/250 8.00
122 Rickey Henderson Padres Bat-Jsy/250 8.00
123 Rickey Henderson M's Bat-Jsy/250 8.00
124 Roberto Alomar Bat-Jsy/250 8.00
125 Rocco Baldelli Bat-Jsy/250 6.00
126 Rod Carew Bat-Jsy/250 8.00
127 Roger Clemens Sox Bat-Jsy/250 15.00
128 Roger Clemens Yanks Bat-Jsy/250 15.00
129 Roy Halladay Jsy-Jsy/250 4.00
130 Roy Oswalt Bat-Jsy/250 6.00
131 Ryne Sandberg Bat-Jsy/250 15.00
132 Sammy Sosa H Bat-Jsy/250 15.00
133 Sammy Sosa A Bat-Jsy/250 15.00

134 Sammy Sosa Sox Bat-Jsy/250 15.00
135 Scott Rolen Bat-Jsy/250 10.00
136 Shawn Green Bat-Jsy/250 6.00
137 Steve Carlton Bat-Jsy/250 6.00
138 Tim Hudson Bat-Jsy/250 6.00
139 Todd Helton H Bat-Jsy/250 8.00
140 Todd Helton A Bat-Jsy/250 8.00
141 Tom Glavine Braves Bat-Jsy/250 8.00
142 Tom Glavine Mets Bat-Jsy/250 8.00
143 Tony Gwynn A Bat-Jsy/250 12.00
144 Tony Gwynn Alt Bat-Jsy/250 12.00
145 Torii Hunter Bat-Jsy/250 6.00
146 Trot Nixon Bat-Jsy/250 8.00
147 Troy Glaus Bat-Jsy/250 6.00
148 Vernon Wells Bat-Jsy/250 4.00
149 Vladimir Guerrero Bat-Jsy/250 10.00
150 Will Clark Bat-Jsy/250 10.00

Tools of the Trade Mater. Sig. Single

NM/M

Quantity Produced Listed
Combo: 1-2X
Production 1-25
Combo Prime: No Pricing
Production 1-5
Trio: No Pricing
Production 1-10
Quad: No Pricing
Production 1-10
1 Adam Dunn H Jsy/25 50.00
2 Adam Dunn A Jsy/25 50.00
3 Alan Trammell Jsy/25 50.00
10 Andre Dawson Jsy/25 25.00
15 Angel Berroa Jsy/50 15.00
17 Austin Kearns Jsy/28 25.00
21 Bobby Abreu Jsy/25 25.00
22 Brandon Webb Jsy/25 20.00
26 Carlos Beltran Jsy/15 50.00
29 Carlos Lee Jsy/25 25.00
36 Dale Murphy H Jsy/25 40.00
37 Dale Murphy A Jsy/25 40.00
38 Darryl Strawberry Jsy/39 20.00
43 Dontrelle Willis H Jsy/25 30.00
44 Dontrelle Willis A Jsy/25 30.00
45 Dwight Gooden Jsy/16 35.00
50 Garret Anderson Jsy/16 30.00
61 Jae Weong Seo Jsy/25 20.00
71 Jorge Posada Jsy/20 60.00
74 Josh Beckett Jsy/21 40.00
82 Luis Castillo Jsy/25 20.00
89 Mark Mulder Jsy/20 40.00
93 Marlon Byrd Jsy/29 20.00
94 Miguel Cabrera Jsy/20 50.00
96 Mike Lowell Jsy/19 30.00
112 Paul LoDuca Jsy/50 25.00
115 Preston Wilson Jsy/44 20.00
125 Rocco Baldelli Jsy/25 30.00
129 Roy Halladay Jsy/32 25.00
137 Steve Carlton Jsy/25 50.00
145 Torii Hunter Jsy/25 25.00
146 Trot Nixon Jsy/25 50.00

Tools of Trade Sig. Blue Spectrum

NM/M

Quantity Produced Listed
Black: No Pricing
Production One Set
Green: No Pricing
Production 1-10
Red: .75-1.5X
Production 1-50
No Pricing 15 or Less
3 Alan Trammell/100 15.00
10 Andre Dawson/100 15.00
15 Angel Berroa/100 8.00
16 Aubrey Huff/100 10.00
17 Austin Kearns/100 15.00
22 Brandon Webb/100 8.00
26 Carlos Beltran/100 20.00
29 Carlos Lee/100 15.00
36 Dale Murphy H/50 30.00
37 Dale Murphy A/50 30.00
38 Darryl Strawberry/50 20.00
41 Don Mattingly H/50 75.00
42 Don Mattingly A/50 75.00
43 Dontrelle Willis H/25 30.00
44 Dontrelle Willis A/25 30.00
45 Dwight Gooden/50 25.00
46 Edgar Martinez/25 50.00
48 Frank Thomas A/25 50.00
49 Frank Thomas Alt/25 50.00
50 Garret Anderson/100 15.00
51 Gary Carter/100 15.00
60 Jacque Jones/50 20.00
61 Jae Weong Seo/25 25.00
65 Jay Gibbons/50 15.00
69 Jim Edmonds/25 35.00
71 Jorge Posada/25 40.00
73 Jose Reyes/25 25.00
75 Juan Gonzalez/20 40.00
77 Kerry Wood H/25 50.00
78 Kerry Wood Alt/25 50.00
81 Lou Brock/100 25.00
84 Magglio Ordonez/50 20.00
87 Marcus Giles/50 20.00
88 Mark Grace/25 40.00
89 Mark Mulder/100 20.00
90 Mark Prior H/50 75.00
91 Mark Prior A/50 75.00
92 Mark Teixeira/50 30.00
93 Marlon Byrd/50 15.00
94 Miguel Cabrera/100 35.00
102 Mike Schmidt H/25 75.00
103 Mike Schmidt A/25 75.00
106 Nolan Ryan Angels/25 125.00
107 Nolan Ryan Astros/25 125.00
108 Nolan Ryan Rangers/25 125.00
112 Paul LoDuca/50 25.00
115 Preston Wilson/100 15.00
129 Roy Halladay/25 30.00
130 Roy Oswalt/25 25.00
135 Scott Rolen/50 40.00
136 Shawn Green/1
137 Steve Carlton/50 30.00
143 Tony Gwynn A/25 60.00
144 Tony Gwynn Alt/25 60.00
145 Torii Hunter/50 25.00
146 Trot Nixon/25 30.00
149 Vladimir Guerrero/25 65.00
150 Will Clark/50 50.00

2004 PLAYOFF HONORS

NM/M

Complete Set (250):
Common Player (1-200): .15
Common SP (201-250): 3.00
Production 1,999
Common SP Auto (226-250): 8.00
Pack (6): 5.00
Box (12): 55.00
1 Bartolo Colon .15
2 Garret Anderson .40
3 Tim Salmon .25
4 Troy Glaus .25
5 Vladimir Guerrero .75
6 Brandon Webb .15
7 Brian Bruney .15
8 Luis Gonzalez .25
9 Randy Johnson .75
10 Richie Sexson .40
11 Robby Hammock .15
12 Roberto Alomar .40
13 Shea Hillenbrand .15
14 Steve Finley .15
15 Adam LaRoche .15
16 Andruw Jones .50
17 Bubba Nelson .15
18 Chipper Jones .75
19 Dale Murphy .50
20 J.D. Drew .25
21 John Smoltz .25
22 Marcus Giles .15
23 Rafael Furcal .25
24 Warren Spahn .75
25 Greg Maddux 1.00
26 Adam Loewen .15
27 Cal Ripken Jr. 3.00
28 Javy Lopez .25
29 Jay Gibbons .15
30 Luis Matos .15
31 Miguel Tejada .40
32 Rafael Palmeiro .50
33 Bobby Doerr .15
34 Curt Schilling .50
35 Edwin Almonte .15
36 Jason Varitek .25
37 Kevin Youkilis .15
38 Manny Ramirez .50
39 Nomar Garciaparra 1.00
40 Pedro J. Martinez .75
41 Trot Nixon .25
42 Andre Dawson .25
43 Aramis Ramirez .40
44 Brendan Harris .15
45 Derrek Lee .25
46 Ernie Banks .75
47 Kerry Wood .75
48 Mark Prior 1.00
49 Ryne Sandberg 1.00
50 Sammy Sosa 1.50
51 Carlos Lee .15
52 Frank Thomas .50
53 Joe Borchard .15
54 Joe Crede .15
55 Magglio Ordonez .25
56 Adam Dunn .50
57 Austin Kearns .25
58 Barry Larkin .40
59 Brandon Larson .15
60 Ken Griffey Jr. 1.00
61 Ryan Wagner .15
62 Sean Casey .25
63 Bob Feller .25
64 Brian Tallet .15
65 C.C. Sabathia .15
66 Jeremy Guthrie .15
67 Jody Gerut .15
68 Clint Barmes .15
69 Jeff Baker .15
70 Joe Kennedy .15
71 Larry Walker .25
72 Preston Wilson .15
73 Todd Helton .50
74 Alan Trammell .25
75 Dmitri Young .15
76 Ivan Rodriguez .50
77 Jeremy Bonderman .15
78 Preston Larrison .15
79 Dontrelle Willis .25
80 Josh Beckett .50
81 Juan Pierre .15
82 Luis Castillo .15
83 Miguel Cabrera .75
84 Mike Lowell .25
85 Andy Pettitte .25
86 Chris Burke .15
87 Craig Biggio .25
88 Jeff Bagwell .50
89 Jeff Kent .25
90 Lance Berkman .25
91 Morgan Ensberg .15
92 Richard Hidalgo .15
93 Roger Clemens 1.50
94 Roy Oswalt .25
95 Angel Berroa .15
96 Byron Gettis .15
97 Carlos Beltran .40
98 George Brett 2.00
99 Juan Gonzalez .50
100 Mike Sweeney .15
101 Duke Snider .50
102 Edwin Jackson .15
103 Eric Gagne .50
104 Hideo Nomo .40
105 Hong-Chih Kuo .15
106 Kazuhisa Ishii .15
107 Paul LoDuca .15
108 Robin Ventura .15
109 Shawn Green .25
110 Junior Spivey .15
111 Rickie Weeks .25
112 Scott Podsednik .25
113 J.D. Durbin .15
114 Jacque Jones .15
115 Jason Kubel .25
116 Johan Santana .15
117 Shannon Stewart .15
118 Torii Hunter .25
119 Brad Wilkerson .15
120 Jose Vidro .15
121 Nick Johnson .15
122 Orlando Cabrera .15
123 Gary Carter .25
124 Jae Weong Seo .15
125 Lenny Dykstra .15
126 Mike Piazza 1.00
127 Tom Glavine .25
128 Alex Rodriguez 1.50
129 Bernie Williams .40
130 Chien-Ming Wang .15
131 Derek Jeter 2.00
132 Don Mattingly 1.50
133 Gary Sheffield .40
134 Hideki Matsui 1.50
135 Jason Giambi .50
136 Javier Vazquez .25
137 Jorge Posada .40
138 Jose Contreras .15
139 Kevin Brown .25
140 Mariano Rivera .40
141 Mike Mussina .40
142 Whitey Ford .50
143 Barry Zito .40
144 Eric Chavez .25
145 Mark Mulder .40
146 Rich Harden .15
147 Tim Hudson .25
148 Reggie Jackson .50
149 Rickey Henderson .50
150 Brett Myers .15
151 Bobby Abreu .25
152 Jim Thome .75
153 Kevin Millwood .25
154 Marlon Byrd .15
155 Mike Schmidt 1.50
156 Ryan Howard .15
157 Jack Wilson .15
158 Jason Kendall .15
159 Brian Giles .25
160 David Wells .15
161 Jay Payton .15
162 Phil Nevin .15
163 Ryan Klesko .15
164 Sean Burroughs .15
165 A.J. Pierzynski .15
166 J.T. Snow .15
167 Jason Schmidt .50
168 Jerome Williams .15
169 Will Clark .50
170 Bret Boone .15
171 Chris Snelling .15
172 Edgar Martinez .25
173 Ichiro Suzuki 1.50
174 Randy Winn .15
175 Rich Aurilia .15
176 Shigetoshi Hasegawa .15
177 Albert Pujols .15
178 Dan Haren .15
179 Edgar Renteria .25
180 Jim Edmonds .40
181 Matt Morris .15
182 Scott Rolen .75
183 Stan Musial 1.00
184 Aubrey Huff .15
185 Chad Gaudin .15
186 Delmon Young .25
187 Fred McGriff .25
188 Rocco Baldelli .15
189 Alfonso Soriano .75
190 Hank Blalock .50
191 Mark Teixeira .40
192 Nolan Ryan 2.00
193 Alexis Rios .15
194 Carlos Delgado .40
195 Dustin McGowan .15
196 Guillermo Quiroz .15
197 Josh Phelps .15
198 Roy Halladay .25
199 Vernon Wells .15
200 Vinnie Chulk .15
201 *Jose Capellan/1999* 8.00
202 *Kazuo Matsui/1999* 10.00
203 David Crouthers/1999 3.00
204 *Akinori Otsuka/1999* 5.00
205 *Nick Regilio/1999* 3.00
206 *Justin Hampson/1999* 3.00
207 *Lincoln Holdzkom/1999* 3.00
208 *Jorge Sequea/1999* 3.00
209 *Justin Leone/1999* 5.00
210 *Renyel Pinto/1999* 3.00
211 *Mariano Gomez/1999* 3.00
212 *Onil Joseph Auto/1000* 8.00
213 *Josh Labandeira AU/1000* 10.00

214	*Cory Sullivan/1999*	3.00
215	*Carlos Vasquez Auto/675*	8.00
216	*Chris Shelton/1999*	6.00
217	*Willy Taveras/1999*	3.00
218	*John Gall/1999*	5.00
219	*Jerry Gil/1999*	3.00
220	*Jason Frasor/1999*	3.00
221	*Justin Knoedler/1999*	3.00
222	*Ronald Belisario/1999*	3.00
223	Mike Rouse/1999	3.00
224	*Dennis Sarfate/1999*	3.00
225	*Casey Daigle/1999*	3.00
226	*Shingo Takatsu Auto/800*	25.00
227	*Jason Bartlett Auto/800*	8.00
228	*Alfredo Simon Auto/1000*	8.00
229	*Chris Oxspring/1999*	3.00
230	*Fernando Nieve Auto/1000*	8.00
231	*Ruddy Yan Auto/800*	8.00
232	Ryan Wing/1999	3.00
233	*Tim Bittner Auto/1000*	8.00
234	*Ramon Ramirez Auto/1000*	8.00
235	Sean Henn Auto/1000	8.00
236	*Roberto Novoa*	8.00
237	*Jerome Gamble Auto/800*	8.00
238	*Jamie Brown Auto/800*	8.00
239	*Ian Snell Auto/800*	8.00
240	*Freddy Guzman Auto/800*	8.00
241	*Aarom Baldiris Auto/1000*	8.00
242	*Greg Dobbs/1999*	3.00
243	*Ivan Ochoa/1999*	3.00
244	*Angel Chavez Auto/800*	8.00
245	*Merkin Valdez Auto/800*	10.00
246	Mike Gosling Auto/800	8.00
247	*Carlos Hines Auto/800*	8.00
248	Graham Koonce Auto/1000	10.00
249	*William Bergolla Auto/1000*	8.00
250	*Hector Gimenez Auto/1000*	8.00

Credits Bronze

Bronze (1-200): 3-6X
Bronze (201-250): .5-1X
Production 100 sets

Credits Gold

Gold (1-200): 8-15X
Gold (201-250): No Pricing
Production 25 sets

Credits Silver

Silver (1-200): 4-8X
Silver (201-250): No Pricing
Production 50 sets

Credits Platinum

No Pricing
Production one set

Awards

NM/M

Common Player: 2.00
Quantity produced listed

1	Phil Rizzuto/1950	3.00
2	Fred Lynn/1975	2.00
3	George Brett/1980	8.00
4	Cal Ripken Jr./1983	10.00
5	Don Mattingly/1985	8.00
6	Rickey Henderson/1990	3.00
7	Stan Musial/1943	5.00
8	Marty Marion/1944	3.00
9	Ernie Banks/1958	5.00
10	Sammy Sosa/1998	6.00
11	Terry Pendleton/1991	2.00
12	Ryne Sandberg/1984	6.00
13	Andre Dawson/1987	3.00
14	George Foster/1977	2.00
15	Dave Parker/1978	2.00
16	Keith Hernandez/1979	3.00
17	Mike Schmidt/1980	6.00
18	Dale Murphy/1982	3.00
19	Whitey Ford/1961	3.00
20	Roy Halladay/2003	2.00
21	Orel Hershiser/1988	2.00
22	Bob Feller/1940	3.00
23	Dwight Gooden/1985	2.00
24	Steve Carlton/1972	3.00
25	Randy Johnson/2002	4.00

Awards Signature

NM/M

Quantity produced listed

1	Phil Rizzuto/50	25.00
2	Fred Lynn/100	15.00
7	Stan Musial/50	50.00
8	Marty Marion/50	10.00
10	Sammy Sosa/21	125.00
11	Terry Pendleton/100	10.00
13	Andre Dawson/100	15.00
14	George Foster/100	10.00
15	Dave Parker/88	15.00
16	Keith Hernandez/100	20.00
19	Whitey Ford/50	25.00
20	Roy Halladay/25	25.00
21	Orel Hershiser/25	40.00
22	Bob Feller/100	15.00
23	Dwight Gooden/100	10.00
25	Randy Johnson/5	

Champions

NM/M

Common Player: 2.00
Quantity produced listed

1	Stan Musial/1951	5.00
2	Warren Spahn/1958	3.00
3	Bob Gibson/1968	3.00
4	Mike Schmidt/1980	6.00
5	Dale Murphy/1982	4.00
6	Steve Carlton/1983	4.00
7	Will Clark/1988	4.00
8	Nolan Ryan/1990	10.00
9	Ryne Sandberg/1990	6.00
10	Roger Clemens/1990	8.00
11	George Brett/1990	8.00
12	Tony Gwynn/1997	5.00
13	Todd Helton/2000	3.00
14	Troy Glaus/2000	2.00
15	Sammy Sosa/2000	6.00
16	Pedro J. Martinez/2000	4.00
17	Mark Mulder/2001	2.00
18	Manny Ramirez/2002	3.00
19	Lance Berkman/2002	2.00
20	Alex Rodriguez Rgr/2002	6.00

Champions Jersey

NM/M

Common Jersey: 5.00
Quantity produced listed

1	Stan Musial/100	30.00
2	Warren Spahn/100	10.00
3	Bob Gibson/100	10.00
4	Mike Schmidt/100	20.00
5	Dale Murphy/82	10.00
6	Steve Carlton/100	8.00
7	Will Clark/100	10.00
8	Nolan Ryan/100	25.00
9	Ryne Sandberg/100	20.00
10	Roger Clemens/100	15.00
11	George Brett/100	25.00
12	Tony Gwynn/250	10.00
13	Todd Helton/250	8.00
14	Troy Glaus/250	5.00
15	Sammy Sosa/250	15.00
16	Pedro J. Martinez/250	8.00
17	Mark Mulder/250	5.00
18	Manny Ramirez/250	8.00
19	Lance Berkman/250	5.00
20	Alex Rodriguez/250	10.00

Champions Jersey Signature

No Pricing
Production 5 Sets

Champions Signature

NM/M

Quantity produced listed

1	Stan Musial/50	50.00
3	Bob Gibson/50	25.00
7	Will Clark/50	40.00
8	Nolan Ryan/34	100.00

Class Reunion

NM/M

Quantity produced listed

1	Eddie Murray, Gary Carter/2003	3.00
2	Carlton Fisk, Tony Perez/2000	3.00
3	Nolan Ryan, George Brett/1999	10.00
4	Rod Carew, Fergie Jenkins/1991	3.00
5	Joe Morgan, Jim Palmer/1990	3.00
6	Carl Yastrzemski, Johnny Bench/1989	5.00
7	Harmon Killebrew, Luis Aparicio/1984	3.00
8	Brooks Robinson, Juan Marichal/1983	3.00
9	Al Kaline, Duke Snider/1980	3.00
10	Roberto Clemente, Warren Spahn/1973	8.00
11	Mark Prior, Mark Teixeira/2001	4.00
12	Josh Beckett, Barry Zito/1999	3.00
13	Mark Mulder, Adam Dunn/1998	3.00
14	Vernon Wells, Lance Berkman/1997	3.00
15	Eric Chavez, Nick Johnson/1996	3.00
16	Kerry Wood, Roy Halladay/1995	4.00
17	Todd Helton, Carlos Beltran/1995	4.00
18	Derek Jeter, Jason Giambi/1992	8.00
19	Manny Ramirez, Shawn Green/1991	4.00
20	Chipper Jones, Mike Mussina/1990	4.00

Class Reunion Material

NM/M

Quantity produced listed

1	Eddie Murray Jsy, Gary Carter Jsy/100	15.00
2	Carlton Fisk Jsy, Tony Perez Bat/250	20.00
3	Nolan Ryan Jsy, George Brett Jsy/100	50.00
4	Rod Carew Jsy, Fergie Jenkins Pants/250	15.00
5	Joe Morgan Jsy, Jim Palmer Jsy/100	10.00
6	Carl Yastrzemski Jsy, Johnny Bench Jsy/250	30.00
7	Harmon Killebrew Jsy, Luis Aparicio Jsy/250	15.00
8	Brooks Robinson Jsy, Juan Marichal Jsy/100	15.00
9	Al Kaline Jsy, Duke Snider Jsy/25	35.00
10	Roger Clemens Jsy, Warren Spahn Jsy/100	80.00
11	Mark Prior Jsy, Mark Teixeira Jsy/250	15.00
12	Josh Beckett Jsy, Barry Zito Jsy/250	8.00
13	Mark Mulder Jsy, Adam Dunn Jsy/250	10.00
14	Vernon Wells Jsy, Lance Berkman Jsy/250	8.00
15	Eric Chavez Jsy, Nick Johnson Jsy/250	8.00
16	Kerry Wood Jsy, Roy Halladay Jsy/250	12.00
17	Todd Helton Jsy, Carlos Beltran Jsy/250	10.00
18	Derek Jeter Jsy, Jason Giambi Jsy/250	20.00
19	Manny Ramirez Jsy, Shawn Green Jsy/50	10.00
20	Chipper Jones Jsy, Mike Mussina Jsy/250	10.00

Fans of the Game

NM/M

251	Charlie Sheen	3.00
252	Corbin Bernsen	2.00
253	Peter Gammons	3.00
254	Jeff Garlin SP	2.00
255	Larry King	2.00

Fans of the Game Signature

NM/M

251	Charlie Sheen	100.00
252	Corbin Bernsen	25.00
253	Peter Gammons	50.00
254	Jeff Garlin SP	80.00
255	Larry King	45.00

Game Day Souvenir

NM/M

2	Bob Gibson Jsy/75	15.00
3	Frank Robinson Bat/61	10.00
4	Tony Gwynn Pants/99	20.00
5	Warren Spahn Jsy/53	20.00
6	George Brett Bat/77	25.00
7	Cal Ripken Jr. Hat/19	100.00
8	Frank Thomas Bat/93	10.00
9	Sammy Sosa Jsy/100	15.00
10	Harmon Killebrew Bat/75	15.00

Game Day Souvenir Signature

No Pricing
Production 5 Sets

Piece of the Game Bat

NM/M

1	Albert Pujols/250	15.00
2	Angel Berroa/250	4.00
3	Aubrey Huff/250	4.00
4	Barry Zito/250	6.00
5	Bobby Abreu/250	4.00
6	Carlos Beltran/250	4.00
7	Chipper Jones/250	8.00
8	Derek Jeter/250	20.00
9	Eric Chavez/150	6.00
10	Eric Hinske/50	6.00
11	Gary Sheffield/250	6.00
12	George Brett/250	15.00
13	Jay Gibbons/250	4.00
14	Jim Edmonds/250	6.00
15	Josh Beckett/250	6.00
16	Manny Ramirez/250	8.00
17	Mark Mulder/250	6.00
18	Marlon Byrd/250	4.00
19	Mike Lowell/250	4.00
20	Mike Schmidt/250	20.00
21	Nolan Ryan/250	20.00
22	Rafael Furcal/250	4.00
23	Randy Johnson/100	10.00
24	Rod Carew/250	8.00
25	Torii Hunter/250	4.00

Piece of the Game Bat Signature

No Pricing
Production 1-10

Piece of the Game Combo

NM/M

1	Albert Pujols Bat-Jsy/100	25.00
2	Angel Berroa Bat-Pants/100	6.00
3	Aubrey Huff Bat-Jsy/100	6.00
4	Barry Zito Bat-Jsy/100	8.00
5	Bobby Abreu Bat-Jsy/100	6.00
6	Carlos Beltran Bat-Jsy/100	6.00
7	Chipper Jones Bat-Jsy/100	10.00
8	Derek Jeter Bat-Jsy/100	40.00
9	Eric Chavez Bat-Jsy/50	8.00
10	Eric Hinske Bat-Jsy/25	8.00
12	George Brett Bat-Jsy/100	25.00
13	Jay Gibbons Bat-Jsy/100	6.00
14	Jim Edmonds Bat-Jsy/100	8.00
15	Josh Beckett Bat-Jsy/100	6.00
16	Manny Ramirez Bat-Jsy/100	10.00
17	Mark Mulder Bat-Jsy/25	15.00

18	Marlon Byrd Bat-Jsy/100	6.00
19	Mike Lowell Bat-Jsy/100	6.00
20	Mike Schmidt Bat-Jsy/50	50.00
21	Nolan Ryan Bat-Jsy/100	35.00
22	Rafael Furcal Bat-Jsy/100	6.00
23	Randy Johnson Bat-Jsy/100	15.00
24	Rod Carew Bat-Jsy/100	15.00
25	Torii Hunter Bat-Jsy/100	8.00

Piece of the Game Combo Signature

No Pricing
Production 1-10

Piece of the Game Jersey

NM/M

Quantity produced listed

1	Albert Pujols/250	15.00
2	Angel Berroa/250	4.00
3	Aubrey Huff/250	4.00
4	Barry Zito/250	6.00
5	Bobby Abreu/250	4.00
6	Carlos Beltran/250	4.00
7	Chipper Jones/250	8.00
8	Derek Jeter/50	40.00
9	Eric Chavez/250	5.00
10	Eric Hinske/100	4.00
12	George Brett/250	15.00
13	Jay Gibbons/250	4.00
14	Jim Edmonds/250	6.00
15	Josh Beckett/250	4.00
16	Manny Ramirez/250	6.00
17	Mark Mulder/100	6.00
18	Marlon Byrd/250	4.00
19	Mike Lowell/250	4.00
20	Mike Schmidt/50	35.00
21	Nolan Ryan/100	25.00
22	Rafael Furcal/250	4.00
23	Randy Johnson/250	8.00
24	Rod Carew/100	8.00
25	Torii Hunter/250	4.00

Piece of the Game Jersey Signature

No Pricing
Production 1-10

Prime Signature Autograph

NM/M

1	Garret Anderson/100	15.00
2	Rafael Palmeiro/50	40.00
3	Vladimir Guerrero/50	50.00
5	Dontrelle Willis/50	30.00
6	Miguel Cabrera/100	35.00
7	Shannon Stewart/100	10.00
9	Gary Sheffield/100	25.00
12	Tom Glavine/25	40.00
13	Brandon Webb/100	10.00
14	Carlos Lee/100	10.00
17	Magglio Ordonez/100	15.00
19	Andruw Jones/50	20.00
21	Sammy Sosa/50	100.00
22	Juan Gonzalez/50	25.00
23	Jeff Bagwell/25	50.00
24	Rickey Henderson/25	75.00
25	Mike Schmidt/50	60.00
26	Jim Rice/100	15.00
27	Billy Williams/100	15.00
28	Lou Brock/100	20.00
29	Robin Yount/25	75.00
30	Nolan Ryan/50	85.00
31	Darryl Strawberry/100	15.00
32	Cal Ripken Jr./25	200.00
33	Andre Dawson/100	15.00
34	Don Mattingly/50	75.00
35	Paul Molitor/25	50.00
36	Bo Jackson/50	75.00
37	Ernie Banks/50	50.00
38	Orel Hershiser/100	20.00
39	Mark Grace/50	40.00
40	Carlton Fisk/50	25.00

Prime Signature Autograph Bat

No Pricing
Production 1-10

Prime Signature Autograph Jersey

NM/M

Quantity produced listed

1	Garret Anderson/16	
2	Rafael Palmeiro/25	75.00
6	Miguel Cabrera/20	75.00
7	Shannon Stewart/23	15.00
29	Robin Yount/19	75.00
31	Darryl Strawberry/25	25.00
34	Don Mattingly/23	100.00
39	Mark Grace/17	65.00

Prime Signature Insert

NM/M

Production 2,500 Sets

1	Garret Anderson	2.00
2	Rafael Palmeiro	3.00
3	Vladimir Guerrero	3.00
4	Alex Rodriguez	5.00
5	Dontrelle Willis	2.00
6	Miguel Cabrera	3.00
7	Shannon Stewart	2.00
8	Mike Piazza	4.00
9	Gary Sheffield	2.00
10	Ivan Rodriguez	3.00
11	Randy Johnson	3.00
12	Tom Glavine	2.00
13	Brandon Webb	2.00
14	Carlos Lee	2.00
15	Hideo Nomo	2.00
16	Mike Mussina	3.00
17	Magglio Ordonez	2.00
18	Austin Kearns	2.00
19	Andruw Jones	3.00
20	Mariano Rivera	3.00
21	Sammy Sosa	4.00
22	Juan Gonzalez	3.00
23	Jeff Bagwell	3.00
24	Rickey Henderson	3.00
25	Mike Schmidt	5.00
26	Jim Rice	2.00
27	Billy Williams	2.00
28	Lou Brock	2.00
29	Robin Yount	4.00
30	Nolan Ryan	8.00
31	Darryl Strawberry	2.00
32	Cal Ripken Jr.	10.00
33	Andre Dawson	2.00
34	Don Mattingly	8.00
35	Paul Molitor	3.00
36	Bo Jackson	3.00
37	Ernie Banks	4.00
38	Orel Hershiser	2.00
39	Mark Grace	3.00
40	Carlton Fisk	3.00

Quad Material

NM/M

Quantity produced listed

1	Matt Williams, Mark Grace, Will Clark, Keith Hernandez/100	60.00
2	Jason Giambi, Jim Thome, Carlos Delgado, Rafael Palmeiro/100	20.00
3	Albert Pujols, Ernie Banks, Jeff Bagwell, Jim Thome/100	50.00
4	Paul Molitor, Joe Morgan, Ryne Sandberg, Alfonso Soriano/50	50.00
5	Cal Ripken Jr., Derek Jeter, Alex Rodriguez, Nomar Garciaparra/100	75.00
6	Ozzie Smith, Robin Yount, Alan Trammell, Dave Concepcion/50	50.00
7	George Brett, Mike Schmidt, Brooks Robinson, Wade Boggs/25	
8	Johnny Bench, Carlton Fisk, Gary Carter, Mike Piazza/100	40.00
9	Todd Helton, Brian Giles, Edgar Renteria, Scott Rolen/25	40.00
10	Carlos Delgado, Alfonso Soriano, Alex Rodriguez, Troy Glaus/100	20.00
11	Harmon Killebrew, Reggie Jackson, Mike Schmidt, Sammy Sosa/100	65.00
12	Stan Musial, Rickey Henderson, Tony Gwynn, Lou Brock/25	80.00
13	Cal Ripken Jr., George Brett, Paul Molitor, Rod Carew/100	75.00
14	Sammy Sosa, Vladimir Guerrero, Manny Ramirez, Magglio Ordonez/100	40.00
15	Andruw Jones, Jim Edmonds, Torii Hunter, Vernon Wells/100	20.00
16	Chipper Jones, Shawn Green, Andruw Jones, Lance Berkman/100	20.00
17	Tony Gwynn, Dale Murphy, Kirby Puckett, Andre Dawson/100	40.00
18	Stan Musial, Roberto Clemente, Al Kaline, Carl Yastrzemski/10	
19	Nolan Ryan, Roger Clemens, Kerry Wood, Josh Beckett/100	75.00
20	Bob Gibson, Fergie Jenkins, Tom Seaver, Jim Palmer/10	
21	Dennis Eckersley, John Smoltz, Mariano Rivera, Lee Smith/100	40.00
22	Mike Mussina, Greg Maddux, Jack Morris, Bert Blyleven/100	40.00
23	Steve Carlton, Tom Glavine, Barry Zito, Andy Pettitte/100	20.00
24	Whitey Ford, Warren Spahn, Bob Feller, Juan Marichal/25	80.00
25	Nolan Ryan, Roger Clemens, Steve Carlton, Randy Johnson/100	80.00

Rookie Year Jersey Number

NM/M

1	Gary Carter/50	10.00
2	Robin Yount/50	30.00
3	Roger Clemens/25	40.00
4	Gary Sheffield/50	8.00
5	Mike Piazza/25	30.00
6	Hideo Nomo/25	30.00
7	Alex Rodriguez/50	20.00
8	Mark Prior/25	25.00
9	Dontrelle Willis/100	10.00
10	Angel Berroa/100	8.00

Rookie Year Jersey Signature

\No Pricing
Production 1-10

Signature Bronze

NM/M

Quantity produced listed

2	Garret Anderson/100	15.00
5	Vladimir Guerrero/50	50.00
6	Brandon Webb/100	8.00
7	Brian Bruney/96	8.00
11	Robby Hammock/100	8.00
13	Shea Hillenbrand/100	10.00
15	Adam LaRoche/100	10.00
16	Andruw Jones/25	25.00
17	Bubba Nelson/100	8.00
22	Marcus Giles/100	15.00
23	Rafael Furcal/50	15.00
26	Adam Loewen/100	8.00
27	Cal Ripken Jr./25	150.00
29	Jay Gibbons/100	8.00
30	Luis Matos/100	8.00
33	Bobby Doerr/100	15.00
35	Edwin Almonte/99	8.00
36	Jason Varitek/50	30.00
37	Kevin Youkilis/100	15.00
42	Andre Dawson/100	15.00
43	Aramis Ramirez/25	25.00
44	Brendan Harris/100	8.00
45	Derrek Lee/100	20.00
46	Ernie Banks/25	60.00
47	Kerry Wood/25	50.00
48	Mark Prior/50	65.00
50	Sammy Sosa/50	125.00
51	Carlos Lee/100	10.00
52	Frank Thomas/25	50.00
53	Joe Borchard/100	8.00
54	Joe Crede/50	10.00
55	Maggio Ordonez/50	15.00
58	Barry Larkin/25	40.00
59	Brandon Larson/100	8.00
61	Ryan Wagner/100	8.00
63	Bob Feller/100	20.00
64	Brian Tallet/100	8.00
66	Jeremy Guthrie/100	8.00
67	Jody Gerut/100	10.00
68	Clint Barmes/100	8.00
69	Jeff Baker/25	20.00
72	Preston Wilson/100	15.00
74	Alan Trammell/100	15.00
78	Preston Larrison/100	8.00
79	Dontrelle Willis/25	30.00
83	Miguel Cabrera/100	40.00
85	Andy Pettitte/25	50.00
86	Chris Burke/100	8.00
88	Jeff Bagwell/25	50.00
91	Morgan Ensberg/100	10.00
96	Byron Gettis/100	8.00
97	Carlos Beltran/100	25.00
98	George Brett/25	100.00
101	Duke Snider/100	25.00
102	Edwin Jackson/100	10.00
105	Hong-Chih Kuo/100	10.00
106	Kazuhisa Ishii/25	40.00
107	Paul LoDuca/100	15.00
108	Robin Ventura/50	15.00
110	Junior Spivey/50	10.00
112	Scott Podsednik/100	15.00
113	J.D. Durbin/100	8.00
114	Jacque Jones/100	15.00
116	Johan Santana/100	20.00
117	Shannon Stewart/50	10.00
123	Gary Carter/100	15.00
125	Lenny Dykstra/100	15.00
130	Chien-Ming Wang/100	20.00
132	Don Mattingly/25	80.00
133	Gary Sheffield/50	25.00
137	Jorge Posada/50	25.00
142	Whitey Ford/50	25.00
145	Mark Mulder/100	15.00
146	Rich Harden/100	15.00
147	Tim Hudson/25	40.00
148	Reggie Jackson/25	50.00
149	Rickey Henderson/25	80.00
150	Brett Myers/100	8.00
154	Marlon Byrd/100	8.00
155	Mike Schmidt/50	60.00
156	Ryan Howard/100	15.00
161	Jay Payton/100	10.00
168	Jerome Williams/50	20.00
169	Will Clark/50	50.00
171	Chris Snelling/100	8.00
176	Shigetoshi Hasegawa/100	50.00
178	Dan Haren/100	10.00
180	Jim Edmonds/25	30.00
182	Scott Rolen/50	30.00
183	Stan Musial/50	60.00
184	Aubrey Huff/100	15.00
185	Chad Gaudin/100	8.00
186	Delmon Young/50	30.00
191	Mark Teixeira/50	25.00
192	Nolan Ryan/50	100.00
193	Alexis Rios/100	15.00
195	Dustin McGowan/100	10.00
196	Guillermo Quiroz/50	10.00
197	Josh Phelps/25	15.00
198	Roy Halladay/25	25.00
200	Vinnie Chulk/25	15.00
201	Jose Capellan/100	35.00
203	David Crouthers/100	8.00
204	Akinori Otsuka/100	35.00
205	Nick Regilio/100	8.00
206	Justin Hampson/100	8.00
207	Lincoln Holdzkom/100	8.00
208	Jorge Sequea/100	8.00
209	Justin Leone/100	15.00
210	Renyel Pinto/100	10.00
211	Mariano Gomez/100	8.00
214	Cory Sullivan/100	8.00
216	Chris Shelton/100	8.00
217	Willy Taveras/25	8.00
218	John Gall/100	15.00
222	Ronald Belisario/100	8.00
223	Mike Rouse/100	8.00
224	Dennis Sarfate/100	8.00

Signature Silver

Silver: .75-1.5X Bronze
Production 1-100
No Pricing 25 or less

Signature Gold

Gold: .75-1.5X Bronze
Production 1-50
No Pricing 25 or less

Signature Platinum

No Pricing
Production one set

Signs of Greatness

NM/M

Quantity produced listed

1	Mark Prior/25	75.00
2	Scott Podsednik/25	25.00
4	Dontrelle Willis/25	30.00
5	Rocco Baldelli/20	40.00
6	Brandon Webb/25	20.00
7	Rich Harden/25	25.00
8	Miguel Cabrera/25	50.00
9	Josh Beckett/25	40.00
10	Mark Teixeira/25	40.00

Tandem Material

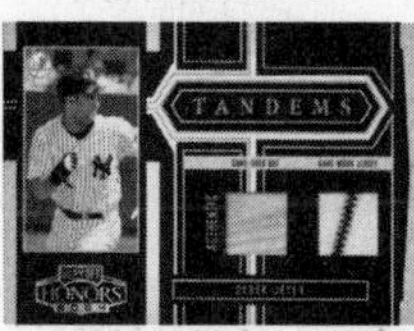

NM/M
Common Duo: 10.00
Quantity produced listed
1 Bo Jackson, Deion Sanders/100 30.00
2 Eddie Murray, Rafael Palmeiro/250 15.00
3 Alex Rodriguez, Dale Murphy/250 15.00
4 Carlton Fisk, Ivan Rodriguez/250 15.00
5 Rickey Henderson, Lou Brock/50 30.00
6 Sammy Sosa, Ernie Banks/250 25.00
7 Warren Spahn, Steve Carlton/100 15.00
8 Carl Yastrzemski, Darrell Evans/250 25.00
9 Keith Hernandez, Lenny Dykstra/250 10.00
10 Pee Wee Reese, Marty Marion/100 15.00
11 Hideo Nomo, Chipper Jones/250 15.00
12 Willie McCovey, Reggie Jackson/100 20.00
13 Mark Prior, Barry Zito/250 15.00
14 Cal Ripken Jr., Miguel Tejada Bat/100 50.00
15 Roberto Clemente, Vladimir Guerrero Bat/100 75.00
16 Gary Carter, Mike Piazza/250 15.00
17 Jim Rice, red Lynn/50 20.00
18 Willie Stargell, Keith Hernandez/250 15.00
19 Nomar Garciaparra, Mark Teixeira/100 20.00
20 Derek Jeter, Phil Rizzuto/50 50.00
21 Eric Chavez, Hank Blalock/100 10.00
22 Eric Davis, Darryl Strawberry/100 15.00
23 Rickey Henderson, Deion Sanders/100 30.00
24 Dave Parker, Austin Kearns/250 10.00
25 Luis Aparicio, Dave Concepcion/100 15.00
26 Rafael Palmeiro, Will Clark/100 25.00
27 Ryne Sandberg, Ozzie Smith/250 50.00
28 Alex Rodriguez M's, Jose Canseco/250 15.00
29 Sammy Sosa, Juan Gonzalez/250 15.00
30 Pedro J. Martinez, Juan Marichal/50 20.00
31 Stan Musial, Duke Snider/5
32 Dwight Gooden, Gary Sheffield/250 10.00
33 Lou Boudreau, Omar Vizquel/100 15.00
34 Mark Prior, Ron Santo Bat/100 40.00
35 Albert Pujols, Ken Boyer/250 25.00
36 Tom Seaver, Curt Schilling/250 15.00
37 Joe Morgan, Jeff Kent/250 10.00
38 Steve Garvey, Ozzie Smith/250 25.00
39 Mike Piazza, Ivan Rodriguez/250 15.00
40 Mike Schmidt, Jim Thome/100 25.00

2004 PLAYOFF PRESTIGE

NM/M
Complete Set (200): 35.00

Common Player: .15
Pack (6): 3.50
Box (24): 75.00
1 Bengie Molina .15
2 Garret Anderson .25
3 Jarrod Washburn .15
4 Scott Spiezio .15
5 Tim Salmon .25
6 Troy Glaus .40
7 Alex Cintron .15
8 Brandon Webb .25
9 Curt Schilling .50
10 Edgar Gonzalez PROS .50
11 Luis Gonzalez .25
12 Randy Johnson .75
13 Steve Finley .15
14 Andruw Jones .50
15 Bubba Nelson PROS .50
16 Chipper Jones 1.00
17 Gary Sheffield .40
18 Greg Maddux 1.00
19 Javy Lopez .40
20 John Smoltz .25
21 Marcus Giles .25
22 Rafael Furcal .25
23 Brian Roberts .15
24 Jason Johnson .15
25 Jay Gibbons .25
26 Luis Matos .15
27 Melvin Mora .15
28 Tony Batista .15
29 Bill Mueller .25
30 David Ortiz .40
31 Johnny Damon .25
32 Kevin Youkilis PROS 1.00
33 Manny Ramirez .50
34 Nomar Garciaparra 1.50
35 Pedro Martinez .75
36 Trot Nixon .25
37 Aramis Ramirez .25
38 Brendan Harris PROS .50
39 Carlos Zambrano .15
40 Corey Patterson .25
41 Kenny Lofton .25
42 Kerry Wood .75
43 Mark Prior 1.50
44 Sammy Sosa 1.50
45 Bartolo Colon .25
46 Carlos Lee .25
47 Esteban Loaiza .15
48 Frank Thomas .50
49 Joe Crede .15
50 Magglio Ordonez .40
51 Roberto Alomar .40
52 Adam Dunn .40
53 Austin Kearns .40
54 Josh Hall .15
55 Ken Griffey Jr. 1.00
56 Sean Casey .15
57 Micheal Nakamura .15
58 C.C. Sabathia .15
59 Casey Blake .15
60 Jody Gerut .15
61 Matt Lawton .15
62 Milton Bradley .15
63 Omar Vizquel .25
64 Jason Jennings .15
65 Jay Payton .25
66 Larry Walker .25
67 Preston Wilson .25
68 Todd Helton .50
69 Bobby Higginson .15
70 Carlos Pena .15
71 Dmitri Young .15
72 Jeremy Bonderman .15
73 Preston Larrison PROS .50
74 Derrek Lee .25
75 Dontrelle Willis .40
76 Ivan Rodriguez .50
77 Josh Beckett .50
78 Juan Pierre .15
79 Miguel Cabrera .75
80 Mike Lowell .25
81 Chris Burke PROS .15
82 Craig Biggio .25
83 Jeff Bagwell .50
84 Jeff Kent .25
85 Lance Berkman .40
86 Richard Hidalgo .25
87 Roy Oswalt .25
88 Aaron Guiel .15
89 Angel Berroa .15
90 Carlos Beltran .40
91 Jeremy Affeldt .15
92 Michael Sweeney .15
93 Runelvys Hernandez .15
94 Dave Roberts .15
95 Eric Gagne .40
96 Hideo Nomo .40
97 Kevin Brown .25
98 Paul Lo Duca .15
99 Shawn Green .40
100 Ben Sheets .25
101 Geoff Jenkins .40
102 Richie Sexson .40
103 Rickie Weeks PROS 1.00
104 Scott Podsednik .50
105 J.D. Durbin PROS .50
106 Jacque Jones .15
107 Jason Kubel PROS .50
108 Shannon Stewart .15
109 Torii Hunter .40
110 Chad Cordero PROS .50
111 Javier Vazquez .25
112 Jose Vidro .15
113 Livan Hernandez .15
114 Orlando Cabrera .25
115 Tony Armas Jr. .15
116 Vladimir Guerrero .75
117 Al Leiter .15
118 Cliff Floyd .15
119 Jae Weong So .15
120 Jose Reyes .40
121 Mike Piazza 1.00
122 Tom Glavine .25
123 Aaron Boone .15
124 Alfonso Soriano .75
125 Andy Pettitte .15
126 Derek Jeter .15
127 Hideki Matsui .15
128 Jason Giambi .15
129 Jorge Posada .50
130 Jose Contreras .25
131 Mike Mussina .50
132 Barry Zito .40
133 Eric Byrnes .15
134 Eric Chavez .40
135 Jose Guillen .15
136 Mark Mulder .40
137 Miguel Tejada .40
138 Ramon Hernandez .15
139 Rich Harden .15
140 Tim Hudson .40
141 Bobby Abreu .25
142 Brett Myers .15
143 Jim Thome .75
144 Kevin Millwood .40
145 Mike Lieberthal .15
146 Ryan Howard PROS .75
147 Craig Wilson .15
148 Jack Wilson .15
149 Jason Kendall .15
150 Kip Wells .15
151 Reggie Sanders .15
152 Albert Pujols 1.50
153 Edgar Renteria .25
154 Jim Edmonds .40
155 Matt Morris .25
156 Scott Rolen .75
157 Tino Martinez .15
158 Woody Williams .15
159 Brian Giles .25
160 *Freddy Guzman PROS RC* .50
161 Jake Peavy .15
162 Khalil Greene PROS .50
163 Phil Nevin .15
164 Ryan Klesko .25
165 Ray Durham .15
166 Jason Schmidt .25
167 Jerome Williams PROS .50
168 Jesse Foppert .15
169 Jose Cruz .15
170 Marquis Grissom .15
171 *Merkin Valdez PROS RC* 1.50
172 Rich Aurilia .15
173 Bret Boone .25
174 Freddy Garcia .15
175 Ichiro Suzuki 1.50
176 Jamie Moyer .15
177 John Olerud .25
178 Mike Cameron .15
179 Randy Winn .15
180 Aubrey Huff .25
181 Carl Crawford .25
182 Chad Gaudin PROS .50
183 Rocco Baldelli .50
184 Toby Hall .15
185 Travis Lee .15
186 Alex Rodriguez 1.50
187 Hank Blalock .40
188 John Thomson .15
189 Juan Gonzalez .50
190 Mark Teixeira .40
191 Michael Young .15
192 Rafael Palmeiro .50
193 Ramon Nivar PROS .50
194 Carlos Delgado .50
195 Dustin McGowan PROS .50
196 Frank Catalanotto .15
197 Vinnie Chulk .15
198 Orlando Hudson .15
199 Roy Halladay .40
200 Vernon Wells .25

Xtra Bases Red Autographs

No Pricing

Xtra Bases Black

Black (1-200): 4X-8X
Production 75 Sets

Xtra Bases Purple

Purple (1-200): 2X-5X
Production 150 Sets

Xtra Bases Purple Autographs

NM/M
Production 100 Sets
10 Edgar Gonzalez PROS 6.00
15 Bubba Nelson PROS 8.00
32 Kevin Youkilis PROS 15.00
38 Brendan Harris PROS 8.00
57 Micheal Nakamura 6.00
73 Preston Larrison PROS 6.00
79 Miguel Cabrera 35.00
81 Chris Burke PROS 15.00
105 J.D. Durbin PROS 10.00
107 Jason Kubel PROS 8.00
146 Ryan Howard PROS 8.00
193 Ramon Nivar PROS 8.00
195 Dustin McGowan PROS 10.00
198 Orlando Hudson 6.00

Xtra Bases Green Autographs

No Pricing

Achievements

NM/M
1 Hideo Nomo 95 ROY 1.50
2 Don Mattingly 85 MVP 6.00
3 Roger Clemens 86 CY/MVP 6.00
4 Greg Maddux 95 CY 4.00
5 Stan Musial 43 MVP 4.00
6 Roberto Clemente 66 MVP 6.00
7 Derek Jeter 96 ROY 6.00
8 Albert Pujols 01 ROY 6.00
9 Cal Ripken Jr. 91 MVP 8.00
10 George Brett 80 MVP 8.00
11 Carl Yastrzemski 67 MVP 4.00

12 Rickey Henderson 90 MVP 2.00
13 Sammy Sosa 98 MVP 5.00
14 Randy Johnson 02 CY 3.00
15 Bob Gibson 68 CY/MVP 3.00

Autographs

NM/M

Quantity produced listed
8 Brandon Webb/100 20.00
10 Edgar Gonzalez PROS/150 8.00
15 Bubba Nelson PROS/250 10.00
25 Jay Gibbons/50 20.00
32 Kevin Youkilis PROS/100 20.00
36 Trot Nixon/25 40.00
37 Aramis Ramirez/25 25.00
38 Brendan Harris PROS/400 8.00
49 Joe Crede/25 15.00
54 Josh Hall/25 15.00
57 Mike Nakamura/250 8.00
60 Jody Gerut/50 15.00
73 Preston Larrison PROS/250 8.00
75 Dontrelle Willis/25 40.00
79 Miguel Cabrera/100 30.00
81 Chris Burke PROS/250 10.00
93 Runelvys Hernandez/50 10.00
98 Paul Lo Duca/25 15.00
102 Richie Sexson/25 25.00
105 J.D. Durbin PROS/500 10.00
106 Jacque Jones/50 12.00
107 Jason Kubel PROS/400 8.00
108 Shannon Stewart/50 15.00
112 Jose Vidro/25 15.00
114 Orlando Cabrera/25 20.00
119 Jae Weong Seo/25 20.00
133 Eric Byrnes/50 15.00
136 Mark Mulder/25 20.00
139 Rich Harden/50 25.00
146 Ryan Howard PROS/400 10.00
193 Ramon Nivar PROS/100 8.00
195 Dustin McGowan PROS/100 10.00
197 Vinnie Chulk/112 8.00
198 Orlando Hudson/100 8.00

Changing Stripes

NM/M

Inserted 1:11
Foil: 1X-2X
Production 150 Sets
Holofoil: 2-3X
Production 50 Sets
1 Rickey Henderson A-s-Yanks 4.00
2 Mike Mussina O's-Yanks 2.00
3 Jim Thome Indians-Phils 3.00
4 Hideo Nomo Sox-Dodgers 1.50
5 Scott Rolen Phils-Cards 3.00
6 Jason Giambi A-s-Yanks 3.00
7 Randy Johnson Astros-D'backs 3.00
8 Shawn Green Jays-Dodgers 1.50
9 Curt Schilling Phils-D'backs 2.00
10 Alex Rodriguez M's-Rangers 5.00
11 Greg Maddux Cubs-Braves 4.00
12 Randy Johnson M's-Astros 3.00
13 Hideo Nomo Dodgers-Mets 1.50
14 Juan Rodriguez Rgr-Marlins 2.00
15 Juan Gonzalez Indians-Rangers 2.00
16 Manny Ramirez Indians-Sox 2.00
17 Mike Piazza Dodgers-Mets 4.00
18 Nolan Ryan Angels-Astros 8.00
19 Nolan Ryan Astros-Rangers 8.00
20 Pedro Martinez Expos-Sox 3.00
21 Reggie Jackson Yanks-Angels 2.00
22 Roberto Alomar Mets-Sox 1.50
23 Rod Carew Twins-Angels 2.00
24 Roger Clemens Sox-Yanks 6.00
25 Sammy Sosa Sox-Cubs 5.00

Changing Stripes Dual Jersey

NM/M

Prodcution 150 Sets
Primes: No Pricing
Production 25 Sets
1 Rickey Henderson A's-Yanks 10.00
2 Mike Mussina O's-Yanks 8.00
3 Jim Thome Indians-Phils 10.00
4 Hideo Nomo Sox-Dodgers 15.00
5 Scott Rolen Phils-Cards 10.00
6 Jason Giambi A's-Yanks 12.00
7 Randy Johnson Astros-D'backs 10.00
8 Shawn Green Jays-Dodgers 6.00
9 Curt Schilling Phils-D'backs 8.00
10 Alex Rodriguez M's-Rangers 15.00
12 Randy Johnson M's-Astros 10.00
13 Hideo Nomo Dodgers-Mets 15.00
14 Ivan Rodriguez Rgr-Marlins 10.00
15 Juan Gonzalez Indians-Rangers 8.00
16 Manny Ramirez Indians-Sox 8.00
17 Mike Piazza Dodgers-Mets 10.00
18 Nolan Ryan Angels-Astros 30.00
19 Nolan Ryan Astrs-Rangers 30.00
20 Pedro Martinez Expos-Sox 10.00
22 Roberto Alomar Mets-Sox 8.00
23 Rod Carew Twins-Angels 12.00
24 Roger Clemens Sox-Yanks 15.00
25 Sammy Sosa Sox-Cubs 15.00

Connections

NM/M

Inserted 1:9
Foil: 1.5X-2X
Production 100 Sets
Holofoil: No Pricing
Production 21 Sets
1 Derek Jeter, Alfonso Soriano 4.00
2 Greg Maddux, Chipper Jones 2.00
3 Albert Pujols, Scott Rolen 3.00
4 Randy Johnson, Curt Schilling 1.50
5 Nomar Garciaparra, Manny Ramirez 3.00
6 Alex Rodriguez, Mark Teixeira 3.00
7 Barry Zito, Tim Hudson .75
8 Sammy Sosa, Mark Prior 3.00
9 Derek Jeter, Jason Giambi 4.00
10 Roger Clemens, Mike Mussina 3.00
11 Mark Prior, Kerry Wood 3.00
12 Alex Rodriguez, Hank Blalock 3.00
13 Frank Thomas, Magglio Ordonez 1.00
14 Nomar Garciaparra, Pedro Martinez 3.00
15 Carlos Delgado, Vernon Wells 1.00
16 Miguel Tejada, Eric Chavez .75
17 Jeff Bagwell, Lance Berkman 1.00
18 Jim Thome, Bobby Abreu 1.50
19 Todd Helton, Preston Wilson 1.00
20 Vladimir Guerrero, Javier Vazquez 1.50

Connections Material

NM/M

Production 250 sets
1 Derek Jeter Bat, Alfonso Soriano Bat 20.00
2 Greg Maddux Bat, Chipper Jones Jsy 12.00
3 Albert Pujols Bat, Scott Rolen Bat 15.00
4 Randy Johnson Bat, Curt Schilling Bat 10.00
5 Nomar Garciaparra Bat, Manny Ramirez Bat 10.00
6 Alex Rodriguez Bat, Mark Teixeira Bat 10.00
7 Barry Zito Bat, Tim Hudson Bat 10.00
8 Sammy Sosa Bat, Mark Prior Bat 25.00
9 Derek Jeter Bat, Jason Giambi Bat 20.00
10 Roger Clemens Jsy, Mike Mussina Bat 15.00
11 Mark Prior Bat, Kerry Wood Bat 20.00
12 Alex Rodriguez Bat, Hank Blalock Bat 10.00
13 Frank Thomas Bat, Magglio Ordonez Bat 8.00
14 Nomar Garciaparra Bat, Pedro Martinez Bat 15.00
15 Carlos Delgado Bat, Vernon Wells Bat 8.00
16 Miguel Tejada Bat, Eric Chavez Bat 8.00
17 Jeff Bagwell Bat, Lance Berkman Bat 10.00
18 Jim Thome Jsy, Bobby Abreu Bat 10.00
19 Todd Helton Bat, Preston Wilson 8.00
20 Vladimir Guerrero Bat, Javier Vazquez Jsy 10.00

Diamond Heritage

NM/M

Inserted 1:13
1 Mike Piazza 3.00

2 Greg Maddux 2.50
3 Nomar Garciaparra 3.00
4 Chipper Jones 2.00
5 Albert Pujols 4.00
6 Derek Jeter 5.00
7 Shawn Green .75
8 Alex Rodriguez 4.00
9 Jim Thome 2.00
10 Jason Giambi 1.50
11 Sammy Sosa 3.00
12 Hank Blalock 1.00
13 Garret Anderson .75
14 Manny Ramirez 1.50
15 Scott Rolen 1.50
16 Jeff Bagwell 1.50
17 Randy Johnson 2.00
18 Ichiro Suzuki 3.00
19 Ivan Rodriguez 1.50
20 Alfonso Soriano 1.50

Diamond Heritage Material

NM/M

Inserted 1:92
1 Mike Piazza Bat 10.00
2 Greg Maddux Bat 8.00
3 Nomar Garciaparra Bat 10.00
4 Chipper Jones Jsy 8.00
5 Albert Pujols Bat 15.00
6 Derek Jeter Jsy 15.00
7 Shawn Green Bat 5.00
8 Alex Rodriguez Bat 10.00
9 Jim Thome Jsy 8.00
10 Jason Giambi Bat 8.00
11 Sammy Sosa Bat 12.00
12 Hank Blalock Bat 6.00
13 Garret Anderson Bat 5.00
14 Manny Ramirez Bat 6.00
15 Scott Rolen Bat 6.00
16 Jeff Bagwell Bat 6.00
17 Randy Johnson Bat 8.00
19 Ivan Rodriguez Bat 6.00
20 Alfonso Soriano Bat 6.00

League Leaders Double

NM/M

Production 500 sets
Foil: 1X-2X
Production 75 sets
Holofoil: No Pricing
Production 10 Sets
1 Alex Rodriguez, Jim Thome HR 5.00
2 Mark Prior, Pedro Martinez ERA 5.00
3 Roger Clemens, Kerry Wood SO 5.00
4 Nomar Garciaparra, Albert Pujols Hit 5.00
5 Derek Jeter, Albert Pujols Avg 5.00

League Leaders Double Material

NM/M

Production 100 Sets
1 Alex Rodriguez Bat, Jim Thome Bat 20.00
2 Mark Prior Jsy, Pedro Martinez Jsy 20.00
3 Roger Clemens Jsy, Kerry Wood Jsy 20.00
4 Nomar Garciaparra Bat, Albert Pujols Bat 25.00
5 Derek Jeter Jsy, Albert Pujols Bat 25.00

League Leaders Quad Material

NM/M

Production 50 sets

1	Albert Pujols, Todd Helton, Edgar Renteria, Gary Sheffield	30.00
3	Mark Prior, Curt Schilling, Hideo Nomo, Kevin Brown	40.00
4	Richie Sexson, Sammy Sosa, Albert Pujols, Jim Thome	40.00
5	Alex Rodriguez, Frank Thomas, Jason Giambi, Carlos Delgado	35.00

League Leaders Single

		NM/M
	Foil	2X-3X
	Production 100 sets	
	Holofoil:	No Pricing
	Production 25 Sets	
1	Alex Rodriguez AL HR	3.00
2	Albert Pujols NL Hit	3.00
3	Albert Pujols NL Avg	3.00
4	Nomar Garciaparra AL Hit	2.00
5	Mark Prior NL ERA	2.00
6	Pedro Martinez AL ERA	1.00
7	Kerry Wood NL SO	1.00
8	Derek Jeter AL Avg	3.00
9	Jason Giambi AL BB	1.00
10	Roger Clemens AL SO	2.00

League Leaders Single Material

		NM/M
	Production 250 sets	
1	Alex Rodriguez Bat	10.00
2	Albert Pujols Bat	15.00
3	Albert Pujols Bat	15.00
4	Nomar Garciaparra Bat	10.00
5	Mark Prior Jsy	15.00
6	Pedro Martinez Jsy	8.00
7	Kerry Wood Jsy	8.00
8	Derek Jeter Jsy	15.00
9	Jason Giambi Jsy	6.00
10	Roger Clemens Jsy	12.00

Players Collection Jersey

		NM/M
	Inserted 1:79	
	Platinum:	1X-2X
	Production 50	
1	Adam Dunn AS	5.00
2	Adam Dunn Gray	5.00
3	Adam Dunn White	5.00
4	Alex Rodriguez Ms	10.00
5	Alex Rodriguez AS	10.00
6	Alex Rodriguez Rgr Blue	10.00
7	Alex Rodriguez Rgr White	10.00
8	Andruw Jones Home	6.00
9	Andruw Jones Road	6.00
10	Austin Kearns	6.00
11	Brandon Webb	4.00
12	C.C. Sabathia	4.00
13	Cal Ripken Jr.	25.00
14	Carlos Beltran	5.00
15	Carlos Delgado	6.00
16	Carlos Lee	4.00
17	Chipper Jones Home	8.00
18	Chipper Jones Road	8.00
19	Craig Biggio	4.00
20	Curt Schilling	6.00
21	David Wells	4.00
22	Don Mattingly	15.00
23	Dontrelle Willis	6.00
24	Frank Thomas Black	8.00
25	Frank Thomas White	8.00
26	Fred McGriff	6.00
27	Garret Anderson AS	6.00
28	Gary Sheffield Braves	6.00
29	Gary Sheffield Dodgers	6.00
30	Greg Maddux Gray	10.00
31	Hank Blalock Home	6.00
32	Hank Blalock Road	6.00
33	Hee Seop Choi	4.00
34	Hideo Nomo Mets	8.00
35	Hideo Nomo Dodgers Gray	8.00
36	Hideo Nomo Dodgers White	8.00
37	Ivan Rodriguez Marlins	6.00
38	Ivan Rodriguez Rgr	6.00
39	Jason Giambi Home	6.00
40	Jim Edmonds	6.00
41	Jim Thome	8.00
42	John Olerud	4.00
43	John Smoltz	6.00
44	Josh Beckett	6.00
45	Josh Phelps	4.00
46	Juan Gonzalez Rgr	6.00
47	Juan Gonzalez Indians	6.00
48	Kazuhisa Ishii	4.00
49	Lance Berkman White	5.00
50	Larry Walker Home	5.00
51	Larry Walker Road	5.00
52	Luis Gonzalez AS	5.00
53	Magglio Ordonez Home	6.00
54	Magglio Ordonez Road	6.00
55	Manny Ramirez	6.00
56	Manny Ramirez AS	6.00
57	Mark Prior Home	12.00
58	Mark Prior Road	12.00
59	Mark Teixeira	6.00
60	Mike Mussina	6.00
61	Mike Piazza AS	8.00
62	Mike Piazza Black	8.00
63	Mike Piazza White	8.00
64	Nomar Garciaparra Gray	8.00
65	Nomar Garciaparra White	8.00
66	Pat Burrell	6.00
67	Paul Konerko	5.00
68	Paul Lo Duca	5.00
69	Pedro Martinez	8.00
70	Rafael Furcal	5.00
71	Rafael Palmeiro Blue	8.00
72	Rafael Palmeiro Gray	8.00
73	Ramon Hernandez	4.00
74	Rickey Henderson	8.00
75	Rickey Henderson Black	8.00
76	Rickey Henderson White	8.00
77	Roberto Alomar Indians	6.00
78	Roberto Alomar Mets	6.00
79	Robin Ventura AS	5.00
80	Roger Clemens Away	10.00
81	Roger Clemens Home	10.00
82	Roy Halladay	6.00
83	Sammy Sosa AS	12.00
84	Sammy Sosa Gray	12.00
85	Sammy Sosa White	12.00
86	Scott Rolen	8.00
87	Shannon Stewart	4.00
88	Shawn Green Blue	5.00
89	Shawn Green Gray	5.00
90	Shawn Green White	5.00
91	Terrence Long	4.00
92	Tim Hudson	6.00
93	Todd Helton Away	8.00
94	Todd Helton Home	8.00
95	Tom Glavine Braves	6.00
96	Tom Glavine Mets	6.00
97	Torii Hunter	6.00
98	Vernon Wells	4.00
99	Vladimir Guerrero	8.00
100	Vladimir Guerrero AS	8.00

Prestigious Pros

		NM/M
	Inserted 1:23	
1	Mark Prior	4.00
2	Derek Jeter	5.00
3	Mike Mussina	1.50
4	Nomar Garciaparra	3.00
5	Roger Clemens	4.00
6	Jason Giambi	1.50
7	Randy Johnson	2.00
8	Rafael Palmeiro	1.50
9	Barry Zito	1.00
10	Pat Burrell	1.00

Stars of MLB

		NM/M
	Foil:	1X-2X
	Production 100 sets	
	Holofoil:	No Pricing
	Prod. 25 Sets	
1	Albert Pujols	6.00
2	Derek Jeter	8.00
3	Mike Piazza	4.00
4	Greg Maddux	4.00
5	Ichiro Suzuki	5.00
6	Nomar Garciaparra	5.00
7	Ivan Rodriguez	2.00
8	Randy Johnson	3.00
9	Alex Rodriguez	6.00
10	Sammy Sosa	5.00
11	Alfonso Soriano	3.00
12	Vladimir Guerrero	3.00
13	Jason Giambi	3.00
14	Mark Prior	6.00
15	Chipper Jones	3.00

Stars of MLB Jersey

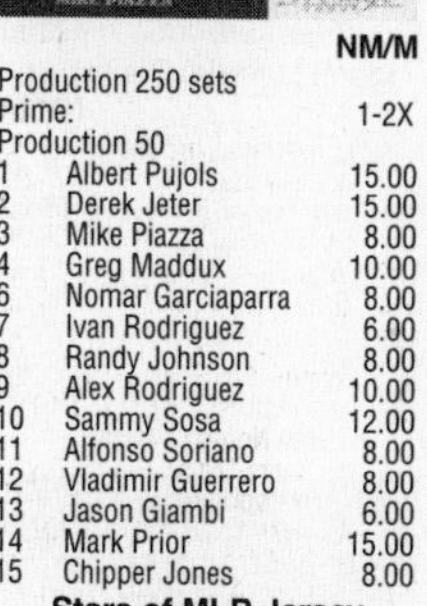

		NM/M
	Production 250 sets	
	Prime:	1-2X
	Production 50	
1	Albert Pujols	15.00
2	Derek Jeter	15.00
3	Mike Piazza	8.00
4	Greg Maddux	10.00
6	Nomar Garciaparra	8.00
7	Ivan Rodriguez	6.00
8	Randy Johnson	8.00
9	Alex Rodriguez	10.00
10	Sammy Sosa	12.00
11	Alfonso Soriano	8.00
12	Vladimir Guerrero	8.00
13	Jason Giambi	6.00
14	Mark Prior	15.00
15	Chipper Jones	8.00

Stars of MLB Jersey Autographs

		NM/M
	Quantity produced listed	
3	Mike Piazza/5	
4	Greg Maddux/15	
8	Randy Johnson/5	
9	Alex Rodriguez/25	
10	Sammy Sosa/1	
12	Vladimir Guerrero/15	
14	Mark Prior/50	100.00
15	Chipper Jones/10	

2004 PLAYOFF PRIME CUTS

		NM/M
	Complete Set (50):	150.00
	Common Player:	1.50
	Production 949 Sets	
	Box (1):	185.00
1	Roger Clemens	6.00
2	Nomar Garciaparra	6.00
3	Albert Pujols	6.00
4	Sammy Sosa	6.00
5	Greg Maddux	4.00
6	Jason Giambi	3.00
7	Hideo Nomo	1.50
8	Mike Piazza	4.00
9	Ichiro Suzuki	5.00
10	Jeff Bagwell	2.00
11	Derek Jeter	8.00
12	Manny Ramirez	2.00
13	Rickey Henderson	1.50
14	Alex Rodriguez	6.00
15	Troy Glaus	1.50
16	Mike Mussina	1.50
17	Kerry Wood	2.00
18	Kazuhisa Ishii	1.00
19	Hideki Matsui	8.00
20	Frank Thomas	2.00
21	Barry Bonds	8.00
22	Adam Dunn	1.50
23	Randy Johnson	3.00
24	Alfonso Soriano	3.00
25	Pedro J. Martinez	3.00
26	Andruw Jones	2.00
27	Mark Prior	6.00
28	Vladimir Guerrero	3.00
29	Chipper Jones	4.00
30	Todd Helton	2.00
31	Rafael Palmeiro	2.00
32	Mark Grace	2.00
33	Pedro J. Martinez	3.00
34	Randy Johnson	3.00
35	Randy Johnson	3.00
36	Roger Clemens	6.00
37	Roger Clemens	6.00
38	Alex Rodriguez	6.00
39	Greg Maddux	4.00
40	Mike Piazza	4.00
41	Mike Piazza	4.00
42	Hideo Nomo	1.50
43	Rickey Henderson	1.50
44	Rickey Henderson	1.50
45	Barry Bonds	8.00
46	Ivan Rodriguez	2.00
47	George Brett	6.00
48	Cal Ripken Jr.	8.00
49	Nolan Ryan	10.00
50	Don Mattingly	6.00

Century

		NM/M
	Cards (1-50):	1-2X
	Production 100 sets	
	Century Gold:	No Pricing
	Production 10 sets	
	Century Proof:	No Pricing
	Production one set	

Icons Material

		NM/M
	Varying quantities produced	
1	Ty Cobb/9	
2	Babe Ruth/9	
3	Lou Gehrig/9	
4	Johnny Bench/50	35.00
5	Lefty Grove/25	75.00
6	Carlton Fisk/50	25.00
7	Mel Ott/25	75.00
8	Bob Feller/25	30.00

9	Jackie Robinson/25	75.00
10	Ted Williams/50	135.00
11	Roy Campanella/50	40.00
12	Stan Musial/50	40.00
13	Yogi Berra/50	40.00
14	Babe Ruth/25	750.00
15	Roberto Clemente/50	100.00
16	Warren Spahn/50	40.00
17	Ernie Banks/50	40.00
18	Eddie Mathews/50	35.00
19	Ryne Sandberg/50	40.00
20	Rod Carew/50	25.00
21	Duke Snider/50	25.00
22	Jim Palmer/50	20.00
24	Frank Robinson/50	20.00
25	Brooks Robinson/50	25.00
26	Harmon Killebrew/50	40.00
27	Carl Yastrzemski/50	40.00
28	Reggie Jackson/50	25.00
29	Mike Schmidt/50	40.00
30	Robin Yount/50	30.00
31	George Brett/50	40.00
32	Nolan Ryan/50	40.00
33	Kirby Puckett/50	40.00
34	Cal Ripken Jr./50	60.00
35	Don Mattingly/50	35.00
36	Tony Gwynn/19	65.00
37	Deion Sanders/19	45.00
38	Dave Winfield/19	40.00
39	Eddie Murray/19	60.00
40	Tom Seaver/19	50.00
41	Willie Stargell/19	50.00
42	Wade Boggs/19	50.00
43	Ozzie Smith/19	60.00
44	Willie McCovey/19	40.00
45	Reggie Jackson/19	40.00
46	Whitey Ford/19	40.00
47	Lou Brock/19	40.00
48	Lou Boudreau/19	30.00
49	Steve Carlton/19	45.00
50	Rod Carew/19	40.00
51	Bob Gibson/19	35.00
52	Thurman Munson/19	60.00
53	Roger Maris/19	80.00
54	Nolan Ryan/50	40.00
55	Nolan Ryan/50	40.00
56	Bo Jackson/19	50.00
57	Joe Morgan/19	30.00
58	Phil Rizzuto/19	35.00
59	Gary Carter/19	40.00
60	Paul Molitor/19	50.00
61	Don Drysdale/19	50.00
62	Jim "Catfish" Hunter/19	30.00
63	Fergie Jenkins/19	30.00
64	Pee Wee Reese/19	40.00
65	Dave Winfield/19	40.00
66	Wade Boggs/19	40.00
67	Lefty Grove/19	80.00
68	Rickey Henderson/19	45.00
69	Roger Clemens/19	50.00
70	Roger Clemens/19	50.00

Icons Material Combo Prime

NM/M

Varying quantities produced

6	Carlton Fisk/25	50.00
7	Mel Ott/25	85.00
11	Roy Campanella/25	70.00
15	Roberto Clemente/25	200.00
17	Ernie Banks/25	85.00
18	Eddie Mathews/25	50.00
19	Ryne Sandberg/25	80.00
20	Rod Carew/25	50.00
24	Frank Robinson/25	40.00
25	Brooks Robinson/25	50.00
27	Carl Yastrzemski/25	80.00
28	Reggie Jackson/25	50.00
29	Mike Schmidt/25	75.00
30	Robin Yount/25	60.00
31	George Brett/25	75.00
32	Nolan Ryan/25	75.00
33	Kirby Puckett/25	60.00
34	Cal Ripken Jr./25	120.00
35	Don Mattingly/25	70.00
36	Tony Gwynn/19	80.00
37	Deion Sanders/19	60.00
38	Dave Winfield/19	50.00
39	Eddie Murray/19	70.00
41	Willie Stargell/19	60.00
42	Wade Boggs/19	60.00
43	Ozzie Smith/19	70.00
44	Willie McCovey/19	50.00
45	Reggie Jackson/19	50.00
46	Whitey Ford/19	50.00
47	Lou Brock/19	50.00
48	Lou Boudreau/19	40.00
49	Steve Carlton/19	60.00
50	Rod Carew/19	50.00
52	Thurman Munson/19	70.00
53	Roger Maris/19	110.00
54	Nolan Ryan/19	75.00
55	Nolan Ryan/19	75.00
56	Bo Jackson/19	60.00
57	Joe Morgan/19	40.00
58	Phil Rizzuto/19	45.00
59	Gary Carter/19	50.00
60	Paul Molitor/19	60.00
63	Fergie Jenkins/19	40.00
64	Pee Wee Reese/19	50.00
65	Dave Winfield/19	50.00
66	Wade Boggs/19	50.00
69	Roger Clemens/19	50.00
70	Roger Clemens/19	60.00

Icons Material Signature Prime

NM/M

Many not priced due to scarcity

6	Carlton Fisk/50	60.00
11	Roy Campanella/1 (8/05 auction)	2,020
12	Stan Musial/20	120.00
16	Warren Spahn/25	90.00
17	Ernie Banks/50	70.00
19	Ryne Sandberg/50	100.00
20	Rod Carew/50	50.00
22	Jim Palmer/50	40.00
24	Frank Robinson/50	40.00
25	Brooks Robinson/50	60.00
26	Harmon Killebrew/20	100.00
27	Carl Yastrzemski/50	90.00
28	Reggie Jackson/50	60.00
29	Mike Schmidt/20	125.00
30	Robin Yount/50	75.00
31	George Brett/50	100.00
32	Nolan Ryan/50	120.00
33	Kirby Puckett/34	70.00
34	Cal Ripken Jr./50	150.00
35	Don Mattingly/50	100.00
36	Tony Gwynn/50	70.00
37	Deion Sanders/50	50.00
38	Dave Winfield/50	45.00
39	Eddie Murray/50	75.00
42	Wade Boggs/50	60.00
43	Ozzie Smith/50	75.00
44	Willie McCovey/50	50.00
45	Reggie Jackson/50	50.00
46	Whitey Ford/50	50.00
47	Lou Brock/25	50.00
48	Lou Boudreau/50	75.00
49	Steve Carlton/50	50.00
50	Rod Carew/50	40.00
51	Bob Gibson/50	70.00
54	Nolan Ryan/50	125.00
55	Nolan Ryan/50	125.00
56	Bo Jackson/50	60.00
57	Joe Morgan/50	35.00
58	Phil Rizzuto/50	45.00
59	Gary Carter/50	50.00
60	Paul Molitor/50	55.00
63	Fergie Jenkins/50	40.00
65	Dave Winfield/50	45.00
66	Wade Boggs/50	60.00
68	Rickey Henderson/50	85.00
69	Roger Clemens/25	150.00
70	Roger Clemens/50	120.00

Icons Material Signature

NM/M

Varying quantities produced

4	Johnny Bench/18	75.00
8	Bob Feller/45	50.00
12	Stan Musial/30	100.00
13	Yogi Berra/42	65.00
21	Duke Snider/35	50.00
26	Harmon Killebrew/30	100.00
33	Kirby Puckett/16	80.00
69	Roger Clemens/25	150.00

Icons Signature

NM/M

Varying quantities produced

4	Johnny Bench/50	60.00
6	Carlton Fisk/50	40.00
8	Bob Feller/50	40.00
12	Stan Musial/50	65.00
13	Yogi Berra/50	50.00
16	Warren Spahn/25	100.00
17	Ernie Banks/50	60.00
19	Ryne Sandberg/50	70.00
21	Duke Snider/25	50.00
22	Jim Palmer/25	40.00
24	Frank Robinson/50	40.00
25	Brooks Robinson/50	50.00
26	Harmon Killebrew/25	75.00
27	Carl Yastrzemski/50	60.00
28	Reggie Jackson/50	50.00
29	Mike Schmidt/20	75.00
30	Robin Yount/25	65.00
31	George Brett/25	120.00
32	Nolan Ryan/50	110.00
33	Kirby Puckett/25	60.00
34	Cal Ripken Jr./25	200.00
35	Don Mattingly/50	85.00
36	Tony Gwynn/25	70.00
38	Dave Winfield/25	50.00
39	Eddie Murray/25	70.00
42	Wade Boggs/25	60.00
43	Ozzie Smith/25	75.00
44	Willie McCovey/25	50.00
45	Reggie Jackson/25	50.00
47	Lou Brock/25	50.00
48	Lou Boudreau/25	90.00
51	Bob Gibson/25	40.00
56	Bo Jackson/25	65.00
57	Joe Morgan/25	35.00
59	Gary Carter/25	45.00
60	Paul Molitor/25	55.00
65	Dave Winfield/25	50.00
66	Wade Boggs/25	60.00

Material Combos

NM/M

Production 25 Sets

1	Roger Clemens	60.00
2	Nomar Garciaparra	50.00
3	Albert Pujols	80.00
4	Sammy Sosa	50.00
5	Greg Maddux	50.00
6	Jason Giambi	40.00
7	Hideo Nomo	30.00
8	Mike Piazza	40.00
9	Ichiro Suzuki	70.00
10	Jeff Bagwell	40.00
11	Derek Jeter	60.00
12	Manny Ramirez	30.00
13	Rickey Henderson	40.00
14	Alex Rodriguez	70.00
15	Troy Glaus	35.00
16	Mike Mussina	40.00
17	Kerry Wood	50.00
18	Kazuhisa Ishii	35.00
19	Hideki Matsui	75.00
20	Frank Thomas	45.00
21	Barry Bonds	60.00
22	Adam Dunn	35.00
23	Randy Johnson	50.00
24	Alfonso Soriano	40.00
25	Pedro J. Martinez	45.00
26	Andruw Jones	35.00
27	Mark Prior	60.00
28	Vladimir Guerrero	45.00
29	Chipper Jones	45.00
30	Todd Helton	40.00
31	Rafael Palmeiro	45.00
32	Mark Grace	40.00
33	Pedro J. Martinez	45.00
34	Randy Johnson	50.00
35	Randy Johnson	50.00
36	Roger Clemens	60.00
38	Alex Rodriguez	70.00
40	Mike Piazza	40.00
42	Hideo Nomo	25.00
43	Rickey Henderson	40.00
44	Rickey Henderson	40.00
46	Ivan Rodriguez	35.00
47	George Brett	85.00
48	Cal Ripken Jr.	140.00
49	Nolan Ryan	75.00
50	Don Mattingly	75.00

Prime Cut Materials

NM/M

Varying quantities produced

1	Roger Clemens/150	40.00
2	Nomar Garciaparra/150	45.00
3	Albert Pujols/150	40.00
4	Sammy Sosa/150	40.00
5	Greg Maddux/150	40.00
6	Jason Giambi/125	40.00
7	Hideo Nomo/150	30.00
8	Mike Piazza/50	30.00
9	Ichiro Suzuki/25	60.00
10	Jeff Bagwell/25	35.00
11	Derek Jeter/25	50.00
12	Manny Ramirez/25	25.00
13	Rickey Henderson/50	30.00
14	Alex Rodriguez/25	60.00
15	Troy Glaus/25	30.00
17	Kerry Wood/25	40.00
18	Kazuhisa Ishii/25	30.00
19	Hideki Matsui/25	65.00
20	Frank Thomas/25	40.00
21	Barry Bonds/25	50.00
22	Adam Dunn/25	30.00
23	Randy Johnson/25	40.00
24	Alfonso Soriano/35	30.00
25	Pedro J. Martinez/25	40.00
26	Andruw Jones/25	30.00
27	Mark Prior/50	50.00
28	Vladimir Guerrero/25	40.00
29	Chipper Jones/25	40.00
30	Todd Helton/25	35.00
31	Rafael Palmeiro/25	40.00
32	Mark Grace/25	35.00
33	Pedro J. Martinez/25	40.00
34	Randy Johnson/25	40.00
35	Randy Johnson/25	40.00
36	Roger Clemens/50	45.00
38	Alex Rodriguez/25	60.00
40	Mike Piazza/50	30.00
42	Hideo Nomo/50	25.00
43	Rickey Henderson/50	30.00
44	Rickey Henderson/50	30.00
46	Ivan Rodriguez/25	30.00
47	George Brett/50	50.00
48	Cal Ripken Jr./50	65.00
49	Nolan Ryan/50	50.00
50	Don Mattingly/50	40.00

Prime Cut Material Signature

NM/M

Varying quantities produced

1	Roger Clemens/25	185.00
3	Albert Pujols/25	180.00
5	Greg Maddux/25	175.00
10	Jeff Bagwell/25	70.00
12	Manny Ramirez/25	60.00
13	Rickey Henderson/25	100.00
14	Alex Rodriguez/25	180.00
15	Troy Glaus/50	40.00
16	Mike Mussina/25	70.00
17	Kerry Wood/25	90.00
18	Kazuhisa Ishii/50	50.00
20	Frank Thomas/25	80.00
22	Adam Dunn/50	60.00
24	Alfonso Soriano/25	85.00
26	Andruw Jones/25	60.00
27	Mark Prior/50	150.00
28	Vladimir Guerrero/50	75.00
29	Chipper Jones/50	85.00
30	Todd Helton/50	60.00
31	Rafael Palmeiro/25	75.00
32	Mark Grace/50	70.00
36	Roger Clemens/25	185.00
38	Alex Rodriguez/25	180.00
44	Rickey Henderson/25	100.00
46	Ivan Rodriguez/25	60.00
47	George Brett/50	120.00
48	Cal Ripken Jr./50	200.00
49	Nolan Ryan/50	140.00
50	Don Mattingly/50	120.00

Signature

NM/M

Varying quantities produced

1	Roger Clemens/25	150.00
3	Albert Pujols/25	150.00
10	Jeff Bagwell/25	60.00
13	Rickey Henderson/25	80.00
14	Alex Rodriguez/25	150.00
15	Troy Glaus/25	35.00
16	Mike Mussina/25	60.00
17	Kerry Wood/25	80.00
18	Kazuhisa Ishii/25	40.00
20	Frank Thomas/25	70.00
22	Adam Dunn/25	50.00
24	Alfonso Soriano/25	75.00
26	Andruw Jones/25	50.00
27	Mark Prior/25	125.00
28	Vladimir Guerrero/25	60.00
29	Chipper Jones/25	75.00
31	Rafael Palmeiro/25	65.00

32 Mark Grace/25 60.00
36 Roger Clemens/25 150.00
37 Roger Clemens/25 150.00
38 Alex Rodriguez/25 150.00
43 Rickey Henderson/25 80.00
44 Rickey Henderson/25 80.00
46 Ivan Rodriguez/25 50.00
47 George Brett/25 120.00
48 Cal Ripken Jr./25 200.00
49 Nolan Ryan/25 125.00
50 Don Mattingly/25 100.00

Timeline - Material

NM/M

Varying quantities produced
4 Ted Williams/50 140.00
5 Roy Campanella/50 30.00
6 Stan Musial/50 35.00
7 Yogi Berra/50 25.00
9 Roberto Clemente/50 85.00
12 Carl Yastrzemski/50 35.00
13 Mike Schmidt/50 30.00
14 George Brett/50 30.00
15 Nolan Ryan/50 35.00
16 Stan Musial/50 35.00
17 Ted Williams/50 140.00
18 Roberto Clemente/50 90.00
19 Greg Maddux/50 25.00
21 Robin Yount/50 20.00
22 Nolan Ryan/50 35.00
23 Ted Williams/50 140.00
24 George Brett/50 30.00
25 Yogi Berra/50 25.00
26 Rod Carew/50 20.00
27 Dale Murphy/25 40.00

Timeline Dual Achieve. Material Prime

NM/M

Varying quantities produced
4 George Brett, Mike Schmidt/19 120.00
5 Cal Ripken Jr., Dale Murphy/19 120.00
6 Mike Schmidt, Roger Clemens/19 90.00
10 George Brett, Nolan Ryan/19 140.00

Timeline Dual Achieve. Material Sig.

NM/M

Varying quantities produced
4 George Brett, Mike Schmidt/24 150.00
5 Cal Ripken Jr., Dale Murphy/25 200.00
6 Mike Schmidt, Roger Clemens/24 220.00
7 Babe Ruth, Ty Cobb/1 (4/04 auction) 18,000
10 George Brett, Nolan Ryan/25 220.00

Timeline Dual Achievement Material

NM/M

Varying quantities produced
3 Stan Musial, Ted Williams/19 175.00
4 George Brett, Mike Schmidt/19 75.00
5 Cal Ripken Jr., Dale Murphy/19 90.00
6 Mike Schmidt, Roger Clemens/19 65.00
10 George Brett, Nolan Ryan/19 100.00
12 Al Kaline, Duke Snider/19 50.00

Timeline Dual Achievement Signature

NM/M

Production 24 or 25
4 George Brett, Mike Schmidt/24 160.00
5 Cal Ripken Jr., Dale Murphy/25 180.00
6 Mike Schmidt, Roger Clemens/24 220.00
10 George Brett, Nolan Ryan/25 220.00
12 Al Kaline, Duke Snider/25 100.00

Timeline Material Combo

NM/M

Varying quantities produced
10 Will Clark/19 60.00
12 Carl Yastrzemski/19 80.00
13 Mike Schmidt/19 60.00
14 George Brett/19 65.00
15 Nolan Ryan/19 100.00
19 Greg Maddux/19 50.00
21 Robin Yount/19 50.00
22 Nolan Ryan/19 100.00
24 George Brett/19 65.00
26 Rod Carew/19 40.00
27 Dale Murphy/19 50.00

Timeline Material Signature

NM/M

Varying quantities produced
6 Stan Musial/33 100.00
7 Yogi Berra/42 75.00
16 Stan Musial/38 100.00
25 Yogi Berra/42 75.00

Timeline Material Signature Prime

NM/M

Varying quantities produced
10 Will Clark/50 75.00
12 Carl Yastrzemski/50 80.00
13 Mike Schmidt/20 120.00
14 George Brett/25 100.00
15 Nolan Ryan/50 125.00
19 Greg Maddux/50 125.00
21 Robin Yount/50 75.00
22 Nolan Ryan/50 125.00

Timeline Material Prime

NM/M

Varying quantities produced
5 Roy Campanella/25 40.00
10 Will Clark/25 50.00
12 Carl Yastrzemski/25 75.00
13 Mike Schmidt/25 50.00
14 George Brett/25 50.00
15 Nolan Ryan/25 50.00
19 Greg Maddux/25 40.00
21 Robin Yount/25 40.00
22 Nolan Ryan/25 50.00
24 George Brett/25 50.00
26 Rod Carew/25 40.00
27 Dale Murphy/25 40.00

Timeline Signature

NM/M

Varying quantities produced
6 Stan Musial/50 70.00
7 Yogi Berra/50 50.00
10 Will Clark/25 100.00
12 Carl Yastrzemski/50 80.00
13 Mike Schmidt/20 85.00
14 George Brett/25 90.00
15 Nolan Ryan/50 110.00
16 Stan Musial/50 70.00
19 Greg Maddux/31 120.00
21 Robin Yount/25 75.00
22 Nolan Ryan/50 110.00
24 George Brett/25 90.00
25 Yogi Berra/50 50.00
27 Dale Murphy/25 50.00

Timeline Dual League Leader Material

NM/M

Production 9 or 19
4 Jim Palmer, Steve Carlton/19 40.00
7 Nolan Ryan, Steve Carlton/19 70.00
8 Don Mattingly, Tony Gwynn/19 70.00
9 Nolan Ryan, Roger Clemens/19 80.00

Timeline Dual League Leader Mat Prime

NM/M

Production 9 or 19
7 Nolan Ryan, Steve Carlton/19 80.00
8 Don Mattingly, Tony Gwynn/19 80.00
9 Nolan Ryan, Roger Clemens/19 100.00

Timeline Dual League Leader Mat. Sig.

NM/M

Varying quantities produced
4 Jim Palmer, Steve Carlton/50 60.00
7 Nolan Ryan, Steve Carlton/25 200.00
8 Don Mattingly, Tony Gwynn/25 150.00
9 Nolan Ryan, Roger Clemens/25 350.00

Timeline Dual League Leader Signature

NM/M

Production 25 or 50
4 Jim Palmer, Steve Carlton/50 60.00
7 Nolan Ryan, Steve Carlton/25 180.00
8 Don Mattingly, Tony Gwynn/25 140.00
9 Nolan Ryan, Roger Clemens/25 300.00

Timeline Dual League Leader Mat Combo

NM/M

Production 9 or 19
7 Nolan Ryan, Steve Carlton/19 80.00
8 Don Mattingly, Tony Gwynn/19 80.00
9 Nolan Ryan, Roger Clemens/19 100.00

2004 PLAYOFF PRIME CUTS II

NM/M

Complete Set (100):
Common (1-91): 1.50
Common (92-100): 3.00
Production 699
Wood Box (1 pack): 150.00
1 Mark Prior 3.00
2 Derek Jeter 8.00
3 Eric Chavez 1.50
4 Carlos Delgado 1.50
5 Albert Pujols 8.00
6 Miguel Cabrera 2.00
7 Ivan Rodriguez 2.00
8 Javy Lopez 1.50
9 Hank Blalock 2.00
10 Chipper Jones 3.00
11 Gary Sheffield 2.00
12 Alfonso Soriano 3.00
13 Alex Rodriguez Yanks 6.00
14 Edgar Renteria 1.50
15 Jim Edmonds 1.50
16 Garret Anderson 1.50
17 Lance Berkman 1.50
18 Brandon Webb 1.50
19 Mike Lowell 1.50
20 Mark Mulder 1.50
21 Sammy Sosa 5.00
22 Roger Clemens Astros 8.00
23 Mark Teixeira 1.50
24 Manny Ramirez 3.00
25 Rafael Palmeiro 2.00
26 Ichiro Suzuki 6.00
27 Vladimir Guerrero 3.00
28 Austin Kearns 1.50
29 Troy Glaus 1.50
30 Ken Griffey Jr. 4.00
31 Greg Maddux 4.00
32 Roy Halladay 1.50
33 Roy Oswalt 1.50
34 Kerry Wood 3.00
35 Mike Mussina Yanks 2.00
36 Michael Young 1.50
37 Juan Gonzalez 1.50
38 Curt Schilling 2.00
39 Shannon Stewart 1.50
40 Todd Helton 2.00
41 Larry Walker Cards 1.50
42 Mariano Rivera 1.50
43 Nomar Garciaparra 4.00
44 Adam Dunn 2.00
45 Pedro J. Martinez Sox 3.00
46 Bernie Williams 1.50
47 Tom Glavine 2.00
48 Torii Hunter 1.50
49 David Ortiz 3.00
50 Frank Thomas 2.00
51 Randy Johnson D'backs 3.00
52 Jason Giambi 1.50
53 Carlos Lee 1.50
54 Mike Sweeney 1.50
55 Hideki Matsui 6.00
56 Dontrelle Willis 1.50
57 Tim Hudson 1.50
58 Jose Vidro 1.50
59 Jeff Bagwell 2.00
60 Rocco Baldelli 1.50
61 Craig Biggio 1.50
62 Mike Piazza Mets 4.00
63 Magglio Ordonez 1.50
64 Hideo Nomo 1.50
65 Miguel Tejada 2.00
66 Vernon Wells 1.50
67 Barry Larkin 1.50
68 Jacque Jones 1.50
69 Scott Rolen 3.00
70 Jeff Kent 1.50
71 Steve Finley 1.50
72 Kazuo Matsui 6.00
73 Carlos Beltran 2.00
74 Shawn Green 1.50
75 Barry Zito 1.50
76 Aramis Ramirez 1.50
77 Paul LoDuca 1.50
78 Kazuhisa Ishii 1.50
79 Aubrey Huff 1.50
80 Jim Thome 3.00
81 Andy Pettitte Astros 1.50
82 Andruw Jones 1.50
83 Josh Beckett 1.50
84 Sean Casey 1.50
85 Alex Rodriguez M's 6.00
86 Roger Clemens Yanks 8.00
87 Mike Mussina O's 2.00
88 Pedro Martinez Dgr 3.00
89 Randy Johnson Astros 3.00
90 Mike Piazza Dgr 4.00
91 Andy Pettitte Yanks 1.50
92 Cal Ripken Jr. 15.00
93 Dale Murphy 3.00
94 Don Mattingly 8.00
95 Gary Carter 3.00
96 George Brett 8.00
97 Nolan Ryan 10.00
98 Ozzie Smith 8.00
99 Steve Carlton 3.00
100 Tony Gwynn 6.00

Gold

Gold (1-91): 2-4X
Gold (92-100): 1.5-2X
Production 25 sets

Silver

Silver (1-91): 1-2X
Silver (92-100): 1-1.5X
Production 50 sets

Platinum

No Pricing
Production one set

Icons

NM/M

Common Player: 4.00
Production 50 Sets
Gold: No Pricing
Production 10 Sets
Platinum: No Pricing
Production 1 Set
Silver: 1X-1.5X
Production 25 Sets
1 Dale Murphy 6.00
2 Eddie Mathews 8.00
3 Brooks Robinson 6.00
4 Cal Ripken Jr. 25.00
5 Cal Ripken Jr. 25.00
6 Eddie Murray 8.00
7 Frank Robinson 4.00
8 Jim Palmer 4.00
9 Bobby Doerr 4.00
10 Carl Yastrzemski 10.00
11 Carlton Fisk 6.00
12 Dennis Eckersley 6.00
13 Luis Aparicio 4.00
14 Luis Tiant 4.00
15 Ted Williams 12.00
16 Wade Boggs 4.00
17 Duke Snider 6.00
18 Jackie Robinson 8.00
19 Pee Wee Reese 6.00
20 Burleigh Grimes 4.00
21 Nolan Ryan 20.00
22 Reggie Jackson 6.00
23 Rod Carew 6.00
24 Rod Carew 6.00
25 Billy Williams 4.00
26 Ernie Banks 8.00
27 Mark Grace 6.00

28 Ron Santo 4.00
29 Paul Molitor 6.00
30 Bo Jackson 8.00
31 Carlton Fisk 6.00
32 Johnny Bench 8.00
33 Tom Seaver 6.00
34 Tony Perez 4.00
35 Bob Feller 4.00
36 Lou Boudreau 4.00
37 Al Kaline 8.00
38 Alan Trammell 4.00
39 Ty Cobb 8.00
40 Don Sutton 4.00
41 Nolan Ryan 20.00
42 Roger Maris 8.00
43 Bo Jackson 8.00
44 George Brett 12.00
45 George Brett 12.00
46 Maury Wills 4.00
47 Warren Spahn 6.00
48 Robin Yount 10.00
49 Harmon Killebrew 8.00
50 Kirby Puckett 8.00
51 Paul Molitor 6.00
52 Andre Dawson 4.00
53 Mel Ott 6.00
54 Mel Ott 6.00
55 Duke Snider 6.00
56 Rickey Henderson 8.00
57 Tom Seaver 6.00
58 Babe Ruth 15.00
59 Babe Ruth 15.00
60 Jim "Catfish" Hunter 4.00
61 Dave Righetti 4.00
62 Dave Winfield 4.00
63 Don Mattingly 15.00
64 Don Mattingly 15.00
65 Lou Gehrig 10.00
66 Lou Gehrig 10.00
67 Phil Niekro 4.00
68 Phil Rizzuto 6.00
69 Reggie Jackson 6.00
70 Rickey Henderson 6.00
71 Roger Maris 8.00
72 Thurman Munson 8.00
73 Thurman Munson 8.00
74 Wade Boggs 6.00
75 Whitey Ford 6.00
76 Yogi Berra 8.00
77 Lefty Grove 4.00
78 Mike Schmidt 10.00
79 Mike Schmidt 10.00
80 Steve Carlton 4.00
81 Ralph Kiner 4.00
82 Roberto Clemente 15.00
83 Roberto Clemente 15.00
84 Dave Winfield 4.00
85 Rickey Henderson 6.00
86 Steve Garvey 4.00
87 Tony Gwynn 8.00
88 Tony Gwynn 8.00
89 Gaylord Perry 4.00
90 Joe Morgan 4.00
91 Juan Marichal 4.00
92 Steve Carlton 4.00
93 Will Clark 6.00
94 Willie McCovey 4.00
95 Bob Gibson 6.00
96 Lou Brock 6.00
97 Stan Musial 10.00
98 Fergie Jenkins 4.00
99 Nolan Ryan 20.00
100 Harmon Killebrew 8.00

Icons Material Combo

NM/M

Many not priced
Prime: No Pricing
Production 1-10
4 Cal Ripken Jr. Bat-Jsy/25 75.00
5 Cal Ripken Jr. Jkt-Pants/25 75.00
6 Eddie Murray Bat-Jsy/25 30.00
7 Frank Robinson Bat-Jsy/20 20.00
10 Carl Yastrzemski Bat-Jsy/25 40.00
11 Carlton Fisk Bat-Jsy/25 25.00
15 Ted Williams Bat-Jsy/25 100.00
17 Duke Snider Jsy-Pants/25 25.00
18 Jackie Robinson Jkt-Jsy/25 80.00
21 Nolan Ryan Jkt-Jsy/25 50.00
22 Reggie Jackson Hat-Jsy/25 25.00
23 Rod Carew Bat-Jsy/25 25.00
24 Rod Carew Jkt-Jsy/25 25.00
29 Paul Molitor Jsy-Pants/25 25.00
31 Carlton Fisk Bat-Jsy/25 25.00
33 Tom Seaver Bat-Jsy/25 25.00
39 Ty Cobb Bat-Pants/25 150.00
41 Nolan Ryan Bat-Jsy/25 50.00
42 Roger Maris Jsy-Pants/25 75.00
44 George Brett Bat-Jsy/25 50.00
45 George Brett Hat-Jsy/25 50.00
47 Warren Spahn Jsy-Pants/25 30.00
48 Robin Yount Bat-Jsy/19 50.00
49 Harmon Killebrew Jsy-Jsy/25 40.00
53 Mel Ott Bat-Jsy/25 50.00
54 Mel Ott Bat-Pants/25 50.00
55 Duke Snider Jsy/Pants/25 25.00
58 Babe Ruth Bat-Jsy/25 300.00
59 Babe Ruth Bat-Pants/25 300.00
65 Lou Gehrig Bat-Jsy/25 200.00
66 Lou Gehrig Bat-Pants/25 200.00
69 Reggie Jackson Bat-Jsy/25 25.00
71 Roger Maris Bat-Pants/25 60.00
72 Thurman Munson Bat-Jsy/25 50.00
73 Thurman Munson Bat-Pants/25 50.00
75 Whitey Ford Jsy-Pants/16 40.00
76 Yogi Berra Bat-Jsy/8
78 Mike Schmidt Bat-Jsy/20 50.00
79 Mike Schmidt Hat-Jkt/20 50.00
82 Roberto Clemente Bat-Jsy/21 150.00
83 Roberto Clemente Bat-Hat/21 150.00
93 Will Clark Bat-Jsy/22 30.00
94 Willie McCovey Jsy-Jsy/25 25.00
99 Nolan Ryan Jsy-Pants/25 50.00
100 Harmon Killebrew Bat-Jsy/25 40.00

Icons Material Number

NM/M

Many not priced
1 Dale Murphy Jsy/25 20.00
3 Brooks Robinson Jsy/25 20.00
4 Cal Ripken Jr. Jsy/25 60.00
5 Cal Ripken Jr. Jkt/25 60.00
6 Eddie Murray Jsy/25 30.00
7 Frank Robinson Jsy/25 10.00
8 Jim Palmer Jsy/25 15.00
9 Bobby Doerr Jsy/25 10.00
10 Carl Yastrzemski Jsy/25 40.00
11 Carlton Fisk Jsy/25 20.00
15 Ted Williams Jsy/50 100.00
16 Wade Boggs Jsy/10
17 Duke Snider Jsy/25 20.00
18 Jackie Robinson Jkt/50 65.00
19 Pee Wee Reese Jsy/25 20.00
20 Burleigh Grimes Pants/25 50.00
21 Nolan Ryan Jsy/25 40.00
22 Reggie Jackson Jsy/25 2.00
23 Rod Carew Jsy/25 20.00
24 Rod Carew Jkt/25 20.00
25 Billy Williams Jsy/25 10.00
26 Ernie Banks Jsy/25 25.00
29 Paul Molitor Pants/25 25.00
30 Bo Jackson Jsy/1
31 Carlton Fisk Jsy/25 20.00
32 Johnny Bench Jsy/25 30.00
33 Tom Seaver Jsy/25 25.00
35 Bob Feller Jsy/25 15.00
36 Lou Boudreau Jsy/25 25.00
39 Ty Cobb Pants/50 100.00
41 Nolan Ryan Jsy/25 40.00
42 Roger Maris Jsy/25 50.00
44 George Brett Jsy/25 40.00
45 George Brett Jsy/25 40.00
47 Warren Spahn Jsy/25 25.00
48 Robin Yount Jsy/25 30.00
49 Harmon Killebrew Jsy/25 30.00
50 Kirby Puckett Jsy/25 25.00
51 Paul Molitor Jsy/25 20.00
53 Mel Ott Jsy/25 40.00
54 Mel Ott Pants/25 40.00
55 Duke Snider Jsy/25 20.00
58 Babe Ruth Jsy/25 300.00
59 Babe Ruth Pants/50 180.00
60 Jim "Catfish" Hunter Jsy/25 20.00
63 Don Mattingly Jsy/25 40.00
64 Don Mattingly Jkt/25 40.00
65 Lou Gehrig Jsy/25 150.00
66 Lou Gehrig Pants/50 100.00
68 Phil Rizzuto Pants/25 20.00
69 Reggie Jackson Jsy/25 20.00
71 Roger Maris Pants/25 40.00
72 Thurman Munson Jsy/50 35.00
73 Thurman Munson Pants/50 35.00
77 Lefty Grove Hat/25 120.00
78 Mike Schmidt Jsy/20 40.00
79 Mike Schmidt Jkt/20 40.00
82 Roberto Clemente Jsy/21 100.00
83 Roberto Clemente Hat/21 100.00
91 Juan Marichal Jsy/25 15.00
93 Will Clark Jsy/22 25.00
94 Willie McCovey Jsy/25 20.00
95 Bob Gibson Jsy/25 25.00
96 Lou Brock Jkt/20 20.00
99 Nolan Ryan Pants/25 40.00
100 Harmon Killebrew Jsy/25 35.00

Material Combo

NM/M

Many not priced due to scarcity
Prime: No Pricing
Production 1-9
1 Mark Prior Hat-Jsy/22 30.00
12 Alfonso Soriano Bat-Jsy/25 25.00
15 Jim Edmonds Bat-Jsy/15 20.00
16 Garret Anderson Bat-Jsy/16 15.00
21 Sammy Sosa Bat-Jsy/21 40.00
22 Roger Clemens Bat-Jsy/22 50.00
24 Manny Ramirez Bat-Jsy/24 25.00
25 Rafael Palmeiro Bat-Jsy/25 20.00
27 Vladimir Guerrero Bat-Jsy/27 25.00
31 Greg Maddux Bat-Jsy/31 40.00
35 Mike Mussina Bat-Jsy/35 25.00
40 Todd Helton Bat-Jsy/17 25.00
86 Roger Clemens Fld Glv-Jsy/22 50.00
92 Cal Ripken Jr. Bat-Jsy/25 75.00
93 Dale Murphy Bat-Jsy/25 20.00
94 Don Mattingly Bat-Jsy/25 50.00
95 Gary Carter Jkt-Jsy/10
96 George Brett Bat-Jsy/25 50.00
97 Nolan Ryan Bat-Jkt/25 60.00
98 Ozzie Smith Bat-Jsy/25 40.00

Material Number

NM/M

Most not priced
Prime: No Pricing
Production 1-10
86 Roger Clemens Jsy/25 40.00
92 Cal Ripken Jr. Jsy/25 60.00
93 Dale Murphy Jsy/25 20.00
94 Don Mattingly Jsy/25 40.00
96 George Brett Jsy/25 40.00
97 Nolan Ryan Jkt/25 50.00
98 Ozzie Smith Jsy/25 30.00

Icons Signature Century Gold

NM/M

Many not priced
1 Dale Murphy/25 40.00
3 Brooks Robinson/25 40.00
7 Frank Robinson/20 35.00
8 Jim Palmer/22 35.00
9 Bobby Doerr/25 30.00
17 Duke Snider/25 35.00
32 Johnny Bench/25 50.00
34 Tony Perez/24 40.00
35 Bob Feller/19 40.00
37 Al Kaline/25 50.00
43 Bo Jackson/16 75.00
49 Harmon Killebrew/25 50.00
51 Paul Molitor/25 35.00
55 Duke Snider/25 40.00
63 Don Mattingly/23 75.00
64 Don Mattingly/23 75.00
80 Steve Carlton/25 35.00
81 Ralph Kiner/25 45.00
87 Tony Gwynn/19 50.00
88 Tony Gwynn/19 50.00
92 Steve Carlton/25 35.00
95 Bob Gibson/25 40.00
96 Lou Brock/20 40.00
97 Stan Musial/25 90.00
100 Harmon Killebrew/25 50.00

Icons Sign. Century Platinum

No Pricing
Production 1 Set

Icons Sign. Century Silver

NM/M

1 Dale Murphy/25 40.00
3 Brooks Robinson/50 30.00
4 Cal Ripken Jr./25 180.00
5 Cal Ripken Jr./25 180.00
6 Eddie Murray/25 50.00
7 Frank Robinson/50 30.00
8 Jim Palmer/50 30.00
9 Bobby Doerr/25 30.00
10 Carl Yastrzemski/25 75.00
11 Carlton Fisk/27 40.00
12 Dennis Eckersley/43 30.00
13 Luis Aparicio/25 25.00
16 Wade Boggs/26 40.00
17 Duke Snider/50 30.00
21 Nolan Ryan/30 100.00
22 Reggie Jackson/25 50.00
23 Rod Carew/29 35.00
24 Rod Carew/29 35.00
25 Billy Williams/26 20.00
29 Paul Molitor/25 35.00
30 Bo Jackson/25 50.00
31 Carlton Fisk/25 40.00
32 Johnny Bench/50 30.00
33 Tom Seaver/25 40.00
34 Tony Perez/25 40.00
35 Bob Feller/25 30.00
37 Al Kaline/50 40.00
40 Don Sutton/20 20.00
41 Nolan Ryan/34 100.00
43 Bo Jackson/25 50.00
44 George Brett/25 100.00
45 George Brett/25 100.00
48 Robin Yount/19 65.00
49 Harmon Killebrew/50 40.00
51 Paul Molitor/50 30.00
55 Duke Snider/50 30.00
56 Rickey Henderson/24 60.00
57 Tom Seaver/25 40.00
62 Dave Winfield/31 35.00
63 Don Mattingly/50 60.00
64 Don Mattingly/50 60.00
67 Phil Niekro/35 20.00
68 Phil Rizzuto/25 40.00
69 Reggie Jackson/25 50.00
70 Rickey Henderson/24 60.00
75 Whitey Ford/25 50.00
76 Yogi Berra/25 50.00
78 Mike Schmidt/20 80.00
79 Mike Schmidt/20 80.00
80 Steve Carlton/32 30.00
81 Ralph Kiner/25 45.00
84 Dave Winfield/31 35.00
85 Rickey Henderson/24 60.00
87 Tony Gwynn/50 40.00
88 Tony Gwynn/50 40.00
89 Gaylord Perry/36 20.00
90 Joe Morgan/24 25.00
91 Juan Marichal/27 25.00
92 Steve Carlton/32 30.00
93 Will Clark/22 50.00
94 Willie McCovey/25 30.00
95 Bob Gibson/45 30.00
96 Lou Brock/50 30.00
97 Stan Musial/50 65.00
98 Fergie Jenkins/31 25.00
99 Nolan Ryan/34 100.00
100 Harmon Killebrew/50 40.00

Icons Sign. Material Combo

NM/M

Many not priced
Prime: No Pricing
Production 1-10

1 Dale Murphy Bat-Jsy/25 50.00
7 Frank Robinson Bat-Jsy/20 45.00
8 Jim Palmer Hat-Jsy/22 50.00
9 Bobby Doerr Bat-Jsy/25 40.00
17 Duke Snider Jsy-Pants/25 50.00
25 Billy Williams Bat-Jsy/26 30.00
29 Paul Molitor Jsy-Pants/25 50.00
34 Tony Perez Bat-Fld Glv/24 50.00
48 Robin Yount Bat-Jsy/19 100.00
49 Harmon Killebrew Jsy-Jsy/25 80.00
51 Paul Molitor Bat-Jsy/25 50.00
63 Don Mattingly Bat-Jsy/23 100.00
64 Don Mattingly Hat-Jkt/23 100.00
78 Mike Schmidt Bat-Jsy/20 100.00
79 Mike Schmidt Hat-Jkt/20 100.00
80 Steve Carlton Fld Glv-Pants/32 50.00
87 Tony Gwynn Fld Glv-Jsy/19 80.00
88 Tony Gwynn Jsy-Pants/19 80.00
92 Steve Carlton Bat-Jsy/32 50.00
93 Will Clark Bat-Jsy/22 75.00
98 Fergie Jenkins Fld Glv-Hat/31 40.00

Icons Sign. Material Number

NM/M

Many not priced
Prime: No Pricing
Production 1-10

7 Frank Robinson Jsy/20 40.00
8 Jim Palmer Jsy/22 40.00
9 Bobby Doerr Jsy/25 30.00
11 Carlton Fisk Jsy/27 40.00
12 Dennis Eckersley Jsy/43 30.00
16 Wade Boggs Jsy/26 40.00
21 Nolan Ryan Jsy/30 100.00
22 Reggie Jackson Jsy/44 50.00
25 Billy Williams Jsy/26 25.00
27 Mark Grace Jsy/17 45.00
35 Bob Feller Jsy/19 30.00
40 Don Sutton Jsy/20 25.00
41 Nolan Ryan Jsy/34 100.00
43 Bo Jackson Jsy/16 75.00
48 Robin Yount Jsy/19 65.00
62 Dave Winfield Pants/31 40.00
63 Don Mattingly Jsy/23 80.00
64 Don Mattingly Jkt/23 80.00
69 Reggie Jackson Jsy/44 50.00
78 Mike Schmidt Jsy/20 80.00
79 Mike Schmidt Jkt/20 80.00
80 Steve Carlton Pants/32 40.00
84 Dave Winfield Jsy/31 40.00
87 Tony Gwynn Jsy/19 75.00
88 Tony Gwynn Jsy/19 75.00
89 Gaylord Perry Jsy/36 20.00
91 Juan Marichal Jsy/27 25.00
92 Steve Carlton Jsy/32 40.00
93 Will Clark Jsy/22 65.00
95 Bob Gibson Jsy/45 35.00
96 Lou Brock Jkt/20 40.00
98 Fergie Jenkins Hat/31 25.00
99 Nolan Ryan Pants/34 100.00

Signature Century Gold

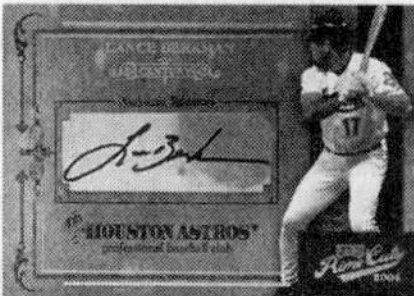

No Pricing
Production 1-17

Signature Century Platinum

No Pricing
Production 1 Set

Signature Century Silver

NM/M

Many not priced

1 Mark Prior/22 50.00
6 Miguel Cabrera/24 40.00
9 Hank Blalock/25 40.00
11 Gary Sheffield/25 40.00
15 Jim Edmonds/25 40.00
16 Garret Anderson/25 25.00
17 Lance Berkman/25 30.00
20 Mark Mulder/20 25.00
21 Sammy Sosa/21 125.00
23 Mark Teixeira/40 40.00
24 Manny Ramirez/24 75.00
25 Rafael Palmeiro/25 50.00
31 Greg Maddux/31 100.00
34 Kerry Wood/34 50.00
35 Mike Mussina/35 40.00
37 Juan Gonzalez/22 40.00
44 Adam Dunn/44 30.00
49 David Ortiz/34 50.00
50 Frank Thomas/35 40.00
61 Craig Biggio/25 35.00
63 Magglio Ordonez/30 25.00
66 Vernon Wells/25 20.00
69 Scott Rolen/27 50.00
82 Andruw Jones/25 35.00
83 Josh Beckett/21 25.00
87 Mike Mussina/35 40.00
92 Cal Ripken Jr./25 175.00
93 Dale Murphy/25 40.00
94 Don Mattingly/23 75.00
95 Gary Carter/25 25.00
97 Nolan Ryan/34 100.00
99 Steve Carlton/32 30.00
100 Tony Gwynn/25 50.00

Signature Material Combo

NM/M

Most not priced
Prime: No Pricing
Production 1-9

1 Mark Prior Hat-Jsy/22 75.00
20 Mark Mulder Jsy-Jsy/20 35.00
40 Todd Helton Bat-Jsy/17 75.00
83 Josh Beckett Bat-Jsy/21 35.00
93 Dale Murphy Bat-Jsy/25 50.00
94 Don Mattingly Bat-Jsy/25 100.00

Signature Material Number

NM/M

Most not priced
Prime: No Pricing
Production 1-9

1 Mark Prior Jsy/22 60.00
17 Lance Berkman Jsy/17 50.00
20 Mark Mulder Jsy/20 25.00
40 Todd Helton Jsy/17 60.00
57 Tim Hudson Jsy/15 35.00
83 Josh Beckett Jsy/21 25.00
94 Don Mattingly Jsy/23 100.00
97 Nolan Ryan Jkt/34 125.00
99 Steve Carlton Jsy/32 40.00
100 Tony Gwynn Jsy/19 80.00

Timeline

NM/M

Common Player: 4.00
Production 50 Sets
Century Gold: No Pricing
Production 10 Sets
Century Platinum: No Pricing
Production 1 Set
Century Silver: 1X-1.5X
Production 25 Sets

1 Al Kaline 8.00
2 Alex Rodriguez 10.00
3 Andre Dawson 4.00
4 Babe Ruth 15.00
5 Barry Zito 4.00
6 Bob Feller 4.00
7 Bob Gibson 6.00
8 Bobby Doerr 4.00
9 Brooks Robinson 6.00
10 Cal Ripken Jr. 25.00
11 Carl Hubbell 4.00
12 Carl Yastrzemski 10.00
13 Carlton Fisk 6.00
14 Jim "Catfish" Hunter 6.00
15 Chipper Jones 8.00
16 Cy Young 6.00
17 Dale Murphy 6.00
18 Dave Parker 4.00
19 Dennis Eckersley 4.00
20 Don Drysdale 6.00
21 Don Mattingly 15.00
22 Duke Snider 6.00
23 Dwight Gooden 4.00
24 Early Wynn 4.00
25 Eddie Mathews 8.00
26 Eddie Murray 6.00
27 Enos Slaughter 4.00
28 Ernie Banks 8.00
29 Fergie Jenkins 4.00
30 Frank Robinson 6.00
31 Frank Thomas 8.00
32 Frankie Frisch 4.00
33 Fred Lynn 4.00
34 Gary Carter 4.00
35 Gaylord Perry 4.00
36 George Brett 15.00
37 Greg Maddux 10.00
38 Hal Newhouser 4.00
39 Harmon Killebrew 8.00
40 Honus Wagner 6.00
41 Hoyt Wilhelm 4.00
42 Ivan Rodriguez 8.00
43 Jackie Robinson 6.00
44 Jason Giambi 4.00
45 Jeff Bagwell 6.00
46 Jim Palmer 4.00
47 Jimmie Foxx 8.00
48 Joe Morgan 4.00
49 Johnny Bench 8.00
50 Johnny Mize 4.00
51 Jose Canseco 6.00
52 Juan Gonzalez 6.00
53 Juan Marichal 4.00
54 Keith Hernandez 4.00
55 Kirby Puckett 8.00
56 Lefty Grove 4.00
57 Lou Boudreau 4.00
58 Lou Brock 6.00
59 Lou Gehrig 10.00
60 Luis Aparicio 4.00
61 Marty Marion 4.00
62 Mel Ott 6.00
63 Miguel Tejada 6.00
64 Mike Schmidt 10.00
65 Nellie Fox 6.00
66 Nolan Ryan 15.00
67 Orel Hershiser 4.00
68 Orlando Cepeda 4.00
69 Paul Molitor 6.00
70 Pedro Martinez 8.00
71 Pee Wee Reese 6.00
72 Phil Niekro 4.00
73 Phil Rizzuto 6.00
74 Ralph Kiner 4.00
75 Randy Johnson 8.00
76 Red Schoendienst 4.00
77 Reggie Jackson 6.00
78 Rickey Henderson 6.00
79 Roberto Clemente 15.00
80 Robin Yount 10.00
81 Rod Carew 6.00
82 Roger Clemens 10.00
83 Roger Maris 10.00
84 Rogers Hornsby 6.00
85 Roy Campanella 8.00
86 Ozzie Smith 10.00
87 Sammy Sosa 10.00
88 Satchel Paige 6.00
89 Stan Musial 10.00
90 Steve Carlton 4.00
91 Ted Williams 10.00
92 Thurman Munson 8.00
93 Tom Seaver 6.00
94 Ty Cobb 10.00
95 Walter Johnson 6.00
96 Warren Spahn 8.00
97 Whitey Ford 6.00
98 Willie McCovey 6.00
99 Willie Stargell 6.00
100 Yogi Berra 8.00

Timeline Material Combo

NM/M

Quantity produced listed

4 Babe Ruth Jsy-Jsy/25 350.00
7 Bob Gibson Hat-Jsy/25 35.00
10 Cal Ripken Jr. Jkt-Jsy/25 75.00
13 Carlton Fisk Bat-Jsy/27 25.00
14 Jim "Catfish" Hunter Jsy-Jsy/27 25.00
17 Dale Murphy Bat-Jsy/25 25.00
21 Don Mattingly Btg Glv-Pants/25 50.00
25 Eddie Mathews Bat-Jsy/41 40.00
26 Eddie Murray Bat-Jsy/33 40.00
36 George Brett Hat-Jsy/25 60.00
39 Harmon Killebrew Bat-Jsy/25 50.00
43 Jackie Robinson Jkt-Jsy/42 100.00
46 Jim Palmer Hat-Jsy/22 20.00
47 Jimmie Foxx Bat-Fld Glv/25 125.00
49 Johnny Bench Bat-Jsy/25 40.00
58 Lou Brock Bat-Jsy/20 25.00
59 Lou Gehrig Jsy-Pants/25 250.00
62 Mel Ott Jsy-Pants/25 50.00
64 Mike Schmidt Bat-Jsy/20 60.00
66 Nolan Ryan Jsy-Pants/25 60.00
68 Orlando Cepeda Bat-Pants/25 20.00
71 Pee Wee Reese Bat-Jsy/25 30.00
77 Reggie Jackson Jsy-Jsy/25 30.00
79 Roberto Clemente Hat-Jsy/21 150.00
80 Robin Yount Bat-Jsy/19 50.00
81 Rod Carew Bat-Jsy/29 30.00
82 Roger Clemens Jsy-Jsy/21 40.00
83 Roger Maris Jsy-Pants/25 75.00
85 Roy Campanella Bat-Pants/39 35.00
86 Ozzie Smith Bat-Jsy/21 40.00
87 Sammy Sosa Bat-Jsy/21 40.00
89 Stan Musial Bat-Jsy/6
90 Steve Carlton Hat-Jsy/32 20.00
91 Ted Williams Jsy-Jsy/25 140.00
92 Thurman Munson Jsy-Pants/10 50.00
94 Ty Cobb Bat-Pants/25 160.00
96 Warren Spahn Jsy-Jsy/21 40.00
98 Willie McCovey Bat-Jsy/25 25.00

Timeline Material Combo CY

No Pricing

Timeline Material Number

NM/M

Quantity produced listed

4 Babe Ruth Jsy/25 350.00
6 Bob Feller Pants/19 25.00
7 Bob Gibson Jsy/25 30.00
10 Cal Ripken Jr. Jsy/25 60.00
12 Carl Yastrzemski Jsy/25 40.00
13 Carlton Fisk Jsy/27 25.00
14 Jim "Catfish" Hunter Jsy/27 20.00
20 Don Drysdale Jsy/25 40.00
22 Duke Snider Pants/25 25.00
24 Early Wynn Jsy/24 15.00
25 Eddie Mathews Jsy/25 30.00
26 Eddie Murray Jsy/25 25.00
28 Ernie Banks Jsy/25 35.00
32 Frankie Frisch Jkt/25 40.00
36 George Brett Jsy/25 40.00
39 Harmon Killebrew Jsy/25 35.00
43 Jackie Robinson Jkt/42 60.00
46 Jim Palmer Jsy/22 15.00

47 Jimmie Foxx
Fld Glv/25 85.00
49 Johnny Bench Jsy/25 25.00
53 Juan Marichal Jsy/25 15.00
55 Kirby Puckett Jsy/25 30.00
58 Lou Brock Jsy/20 25.00
59 Lou Gehrig Jsy/25 180.00
62 Mel Ott Pants/25 40.00
64 Mike Schmidt Jsy/20 50.00
66 Nolan Ryan Jsy/25 50.00
68 Orlando Cepeda
Pants/25 15.00
71 Pee Wee Reese Jsy/25 25.00
74 Ralph Kiner Bat/25 25.00
77 Reggie Jackson
Jsy/25 25.00
80 Robin Yount Jsy/19 40.00
81 Rod Carew Jsy/25 25.00
82 Roger Clemens Jsy/21 30.00
83 Roger Maris Jsy/25 60.00
84 Rogers Hornsby
Bat/25 75.00
85 Roy Campanella
Pants/25 30.00
86 Ozzie Smith Jsy/25 35.00
87 Sammy Sosa Jsy/21 30.00
88 Satchel Paige Jsy/25 75.00
90 Steve Carlton Jsy/25 15.00
91 Ted Williams Jsy/25 100.00
92 Thurman Munson
Jsy/25 40.00
93 Tom Seaver Pants/25 25.00
94 Ty Cobb Pants/25 140.00
96 Warren Spahn Jsy/21 35.00
98 Willie McCovey Jsy/8 25.00

Timeline Material Position

NM/M

Quantity produced listed
4 Babe Ruth Jsy/25 350.00
6 Bob Feller Pants/19 25.00
7 Bob Gibson Jsy/25 30.00
10 Cal Ripken Jr. Jsy/25 60.00
12 Carl Yastrzemski
Jsy/25 40.00
13 Carlton Fisk Jsy/27 25.00
14 Jim "Catfish" Hunter
Jsy/27 20.00
20 Don Drysdale Jsy/25 40.00
22 Duke Snider Pants/25 25.00
24 Early Wynn Jsy/24 15.00
25 Eddie Mathews Jsy/25 30.00
26 Eddie Murray Jsy/25 25.00
28 Ernie Banks Jsy/25 35.00
32 Frankie Frisch Jkt/25 40.00
36 George Brett Jsy/25 40.00
39 Harmon Killebrew
Jsy/25 35.00
43 Jackie Robinson Jkt/42 60.00
46 Jim Palmer Jsy/22 15.00
47 Jimmie Foxx
Fld Glv/25 85.00
49 Johnny Bench Jsy/25 25.00
53 Juan Marichal Jsy/27 15.00
55 Kirby Puckett Jsy/25 30.00
58 Lou Brock Jsy/20 25.00
59 Lou Gehrig Jsy/25 180.00
62 Mel Ott Pants/25 40.00
64 Mike Schmidt Jsy/20 50.00
66 Nolan Ryan Jsy/25 50.00
68 Orlando Cepeda
Pants/25 15.00
71 Pee Wee Reese Jsy/25 25.00
74 Ralph Kiner Bat/25 25.00
77 Reggie Jackson Jsy/25 25.00
80 Robin Yount Jsy/19 40.00
81 Rod Carew Jsy/25 25.00
82 Roger Clemens Jsy/21 30.00
84 Rogers Hornsby
Bat/25 75.00
86 Ozzie Smith Jsy/25 35.00
87 Sammy Sosa Jsy/21 30.00
88 Satchel Paige CO
Jsy/25 75.00
90 Steve Carlton Jsy/25 15.00
92 Thurman Munson
Jsy/15 50.00
93 Tom Seaver Pants/25 25.00
94 Ty Cobb Pants/5
96 Warren Spahn Jsy/21 35.00
98 Willie McCovey Jsy/25 25.00

Timeline Material Quad

No Pricing
Production 1-25

Timeline Material Trio

NM/M

Most not priced
Trio HOF: No Pricing
Production 1-9
Trio MVP: No Pricing
Production 1-10
Trio Stats: No Pricing
Production 1-15
10 Cal Ripken Jr.
Jkt-Jsy-Pants/25 100.00
17 Dale Murphy
Bat-Jsy-Jsy/25 40.00
21 Don Mattingly
Bat-Jkt-Pants/25 75.00
26 Eddie Murray
Bat-Jsy-Shoe/25 85.00
80 Robin Yount
Bat-Jsy-Jsy/19 70.00
82 Roger Clemens
Bat-Jsy-Jsy/21 50.00

Timeline Sig. Material Combo

NM/M

Most not priced
7 Bob Gibson
Hat-Jsy/25 50.00
8 Bobby Doerr
Bat-Jsy/25 50.00
58 Lou Brock Bat-Jsy/20 50.00

Timeline Sign. Mat. Combo CY

NM/M

Most not priced
7 Bob Gibson Hat-Jsy/25 50.00
46 Jim Palmer Hat-Jsy/22 50.00
90 Steve Carlton
Hat-Jsy/32 50.00

Timeline Sign. Mat. Number

NM/M

Most not priced
6 Bob Feller Pants/19 40.00
7 Bob Gibson Jsy/25 50.00
8 Bobby Doerr Jsy/25 40.00
21 Don Mattingly
Pants/23 80.00
46 Jim Palmer Jsy/22 40.00
53 Juan Marichal Jsy/27 40.00
58 Lou Brock Jsy/20 50.00
66 Nolan Ryan Jsy/34 150.00
90 Steve Carlton Jsy/32 40.00

Timeline Sign. Mat. Position

NM/M

Most not priced
6 Bob Feller Pants/19 40.00
8 Bobby Doerr Jsy/25 40.00
21 Don Mattingly
Pants/23 80.00
46 Jim Palmer Jsy/22 40.00
53 Juan Marichal Jsy/27 40.00
58 Lou Brock Jsy/20 50.00
66 Nolan Ryan Jsy/34 150.00
67 Orel Hershiser Jsy/25 30.00

Timeline Sign. Mat. Prime

No Pricing
Production 1-9

Timeline Sign. Material Quad

NM/M

Most not priced
21 Don Mattingly/25 180.00

Timeline Sign. Material Trio

NM/M

No Pricing
Production 1-9
Trio HOF: No Pricing
Production 1-9
Trio MVP: No Pricing
Production 1-8
Trio Stats: No Pricing
Production 1-9

2005 PLAYOFF ABSOLUTE MEMORABILIA

NM/M

Complete Set (100):
Common Player: .50
Retail: .3X
Retail doesn't have foil front
Pack (4): 50.00
Box (4): 185.00
1 Andruw Jones .75
2 B.J. Upton .75
3 Jim Edmonds .75
4 Johan Santana 1.00
5 Jeff Bagwell .75
6 Derek Jeter 3.00
7 Eric Chavez .75
8 Albert Pujols 3.00
9 Craig Biggio .75
10 Hank Blalock .75
11 Chipper Jones 1.00
12 Jacque Jones .50
13 Alfonso Soriano 1.00
14 Carl Crawford .50
15 Ben Sheets .50
16 Garret Anderson .75
17 Luis Gonzalez .50
18 Andy Pettitte .75
19 Miguel Tejada .75
20 Carlos Delgado .75
21 Austin Kearns .50
22 Adrian Beltre .50
23 Rafael Palmeiro .75
24 Greg Maddux 2.00
25 Jason Bay .50
26 Jason Varitek .75
27 David Ortiz 1.00
28 Dontrelle Willis .75
29 Adam Dunn 1.00
30 Carlos Lee .50
31 Manny Ramirez 1.00
32 Rocco Baldelli .50
33 Jeff Kent .50
34 Jake Peavy .75
35 Vernon Wells .50
36 Ichiro Suzuki 2.00
37 C.C. Sabathia .50
38 Hideki Matsui 2.00
39 Gary Sheffield .75
40 Paul LoDuca .50
41 Vladimir Guerrero 1.00
42 Omar Vizquel .50
43 Lance Berkman .50
44 Shawn Green .50
45 Josh Beckett .50
46 Barry Zito .50
47 Roger Clemens 3.00
48 Sean Casey .50
49 Edgar Renteria .50
50 Mark Teixeira .75
51 Frank Thomas .75
52 Khalil Greene .50
53 Bobby Abreu .75
54 Rafael Furcal .50
55 Jose Vidro .50
56 Nomar Garciaparra 1.00
57 Melvin Mora .50
58 Trot Nixon .50
59 Magglio Ordonez .50
60 Michael Young .50
61 Richie Sexson .50
62 Alex Rodriguez 3.00
63 Tim Hudson .50
64 Todd Helton .75
65 Mike Lowell .50
66 Mark Mulder .50
67 Sammy Sosa 1.50
68 Mark Prior 1.00
69 Shannon Stewart .50
70 Miguel Cabrera 1.00
71 Troy Glaus .50
72 Scott Rolen 1.00
73 Ken Griffey Jr. 2.00
74 Mike Piazza 1.00
75 Roy Halladay .50
76 Larry Walker .75
77 Kerry Wood .75
78 Mike Mussina .75
79 Curt Schilling 1.00
80 Rich Harden .50
81 Victor Martinez .50
82 Roy Oswalt .50
83 Pedro Martinez 1.00
84 Tom Glavine .50
85 Randy Johnson 1.00
86 Ivan Rodriguez 1.00
87 Carlos Beltran .75
88 Torii Hunter .50
89 Hideo Nomo .50
90 Jim Thome 1.00
91 Aramis Ramirez .50
92 J.D. Drew .50
93 Javy Lopez .50
94 David Wright 2.00
95 Bobby Crosby .75
96 *Jeff Niemann* 3.00
97 *Yuniesky Betancourt* 3.00
98 *Tadahito Iguchi* 6.00
99 *Philip Humber* 3.00
100 *Justin Verlander* 3.00

Black

Black: 2X-4X
Inserted 1:18 Retail

Blue

Blue: 1X-2X
Inserted 1:3 Retail

Red

Red: 2X-3X
Inserted 1:8 Retail

Spectrum Gold

No Pricing
Production 10 sets

Spectrum Platinum

No Pricing
Production one set

Spectrum Silver

Silver: 2X-3X
Production 100 sets

Absolutely Ink Swatch Double

NM/M

Production 1-50
1 Rafael Furcal B-J/50 20.00
3 Dale Murphy B-J/50 30.00
7 Bobby Crosby J-J/50 20.00
8 Cal Ripken Jr. J-P/25 150.00
10 Vernon Wells J-J/25 20.00
11 Lyle Overbay J-J/50 15.00
13 Omar Vizquel J-J/50 25.00
16 Aramis Ramirez J-J/25 30.00
18 Travis Hafner BG-J/50 25.00
22 Juan Gonzalez B-J/25 25.00
23 Mark Teixeira FG-J/50 35.00
27 Darryl Strawberry
J-J/50 20.00
30 Magglio Ordonez
B-J/25 20.00
31 Jay Gibbons B-J/50 15.00
32 Steve Carlton FG-J/25 40.00
37 Keith Hernandez
B-J/50 20.00
38 Carlos Zambrano
J-J/50 25.00
39 Brett Myers J-J/50 15.00
41 Danny Kolb J-J/50 15.00
42 Mark Prior FG-J/25 50.00
43 Joey Gathright B-J/25 15.00
44 David Cone J-J/50 15.00
45 Carlos Lee FG-J/50 20.00
49 Garret Anderson
J-J/25 25.00
51 Dave Parker B-J/25 25.00
52 C.C. Sabathia J-J/50 20.00
53 Dennis Eckersley A's
J-P/50 20.00
55 Brandon Webb B-P/50 15.00
56 Sean Casey B-J/50 20.00
57 Johan Santana J-J/25 60.00
58 Miguel Cabrera J-J/50 40.00
59 Bert Blyleven J-J/50 15.00
60 Casey Kotchman
B-J/50 20.00
62 Milton Bradley J-J/50 15.00
63 John Kruk J-J/50 25.00
64 Michael Young B-J/50 20.00
69 Lew Ford B-J/50 15.00
70 Jody Gerut B-J/50 15.00
71 Don Sutton J-J/50 15.00
73 Austin Kearns B-J/50 15.00
77 Ryan Wagner J-J/50 15.00
78 Jermaine Dye J-J/50 15.00
80 Al Oliver B-J/50 15.00
81 Angel Berroa B-P/50 15.00
82 Edgar Renteria J-J/50 20.00
84 Roy Oswalt FG-J/25 25.00
86 Dave Righetti J-J/50 20.00
87 Aubrey Huff H-J/25 20.00
89 Jose Vidro B-J/50 15.00
90 Harold Baines J-J/50 15.00
93 Ken Harvey J-J/50 15.00
95 Jason Bay B-J/50 20.00
96 Dwight Evans B-J/50 40.00
99 Brian Roberts J-J/50 40.00

Swatch Double Spectrum

NM/M

Production 1-25
Prime: No Pricing
Production One Set
1 Rafael Furcal B-J/25 20.00
3 Dale Murphy B-J/25 40.00
7 Bobby Crosby J-J/25 25.00
10 Vernon Wells J-J/25 20.00
11 Lyle Overbay J-J/25 15.00
18 Travis Hafner BG-J/25 30.00
27 Darryl Strawberry
J-J/25 25.00
31 Jay Gibbons B-J/25 20.00
37 Keith Hernandez
B-J/25 25.00

38 Carlos Zambrano J-J/25 30.00
39 Brett Myers J-J/25 15.00
41 Danny Kolb J-J/25 15.00
45 Carlos Lee FG-J/25 20.00
55 Brandon Webb B-P/25 25.00
59 Bert Blyleven J-J/25 15.00
60 Casey Kotchman B-J/25 25.00
62 Milton Bradley J-J/25 20.00
63 John Kruk J-J/25 25.00
64 Michael Young B-J/25 25.00
69 Lew Ford B-J/25 15.00
70 Jody Gerut B-J/25 15.00
71 Don Sutton J-J/25 20.00
73 Austin Kearns B-J/25 20.00
77 Ryan Wagner J-J/25 15.00
78 Jermaine Dye J-J/25 15.00
81 Angel Berroa B-P/25 15.00
89 Jose Vidro B-J/25 15.00
90 Harold Baines J-J/25 20.00
93 Ken Harvey J-J/25 15.00
95 Jason Bay B-J/25 25.00
96 Dwight Evans B-J/25 40.00
99 Brian Roberts J-J/25 40.00

Absolutely Ink Swatch Single

NM/M

Production 5-50
1 Rafael Furcal Jsy/50 15.00
3 Dale Murphy Jsy/50 25.00
4 Duke Snider Pants/25 40.00
5 Bill Madlock Bat/50 20.00
7 Bobby Crosby Jsy/50 15.00
8 Cal Ripken Jr. Jsy/25 140.00
9 Hank Blalock Jsy/25 25.00
10 Vernon Wells Jsy/50 20.00
11 Lyle Overbay Jsy/50 15.00
13 Omar Vizquel Jsy/50 25.00
15 Ben Sheets Jsy/25 20.00
16 Aramis Ramirez Jsy/25 30.00
18 Travis Hafner Jsy/50 20.00
19 Mike Lowell Jsy/25 15.00
20 Frank Robinson Bat/50 30.00
22 Juan Gonzalez Jsy/50 25.00
27 Darryl Strawberry Jsy/50 20.00
28 Alexis Rios Bat/50 15.00
30 Magglio Ordonez Jsy/50 15.00
31 Jay Gibbons Jsy/50 15.00
32 Steve Carlton Jsy/25 35.00
34 Kerry Wood Jsy/25 35.00
36 Eric Chavez Jsy/25 25.00
37 Keith Hernandez Jsy/50 15.00
38 Carlos Zambrano Jsy/50 25.00
39 Brett Myers Jsy/50 15.00
40 Rich Harden Jsy/50 20.00
41 Danny Kolb Jsy/50 15.00
42 Mark Prior Jsy/25 50.00
43 Joey Gathright Jsy/25 15.00
44 David Cone Jsy/50 15.00
45 Carlos Lee Jsy/50 20.00
47 Jack Morris Jsy/50 20.00
48 Torii Hunter Jsy/50 20.00
49 Garret Anderson Jsy/50 25.00
51 Dave Parker Bat/50 20.00
52 C.C. Sabathia Jsy/50 15.00
53 Dennis Eckersley Jsy/50 20.00
54 Barry Larkin Jsy/25 40.00
55 Brandon Webb Pants/50 15.00
56 Sean Casey Jsy/50 20.00
57 Johan Santana Jsy/50 40.00
58 Miguel Cabrera Jsy/50 40.00
59 Bert Blyleven Jsy/50 15.00
60 Casey Kotchman Jsy/50 15.00
61 Dwight Gooden Jsy/50 20.00
62 Milton Bradley Jsy/50 15.00
63 John Kruk Jsy/50 25.00
64 Michael Young Jsy/50 20.00
66 Robin Ventura Jsy/50 20.00
67 Tim Hudson Jsy/25 30.00
68 Will Clark Bat/50 40.00
69 Lew Ford Jsy/50 15.00
70 Jody Gerut Jsy/50 15.00
71 Don Sutton Jsy/50 15.00
72 B.J. Upton Bat/25 20.00
73 Austin Kearns Jsy/50 15.00
77 Ryan Wagner Jsy/50 15.00
78 Jermaine Dye Jsy/50 15.00
80 Al Oliver Jsy/50 15.00
81 Angel Berroa Pants/50 15.00
82 Edgar Renteria Jsy/50 20.00
83 Dennis Eckersley Jsy/25 25.00
84 Roy Oswalt Jsy/50 20.00
86 Dave Righetti Jsy/50 20.00
87 Aubrey Huff Jsy/25 20.00
89 Jose Vidro Jsy/50 15.00
90 Harold Baines Jsy/50 15.00
93 Ken Harvey Jsy/50 15.00
95 Jason Bay Jsy/50 20.00
96 Dwight Evans Jsy/50 30.00
97 Luis Tiant Pants/50 15.00
98 Ron Santo Bat/50 30.00
99 Brian Roberts Jsy/50 40.00
100 Marty Marion Jsy/50 15.00

Absolutely Ink Swatch Single Spectrum

NM/M

Production 1-25
Prime: No Pricing
Production One Set
1 Rafael Furcal Jsy/25 20.00
3 Dale Murphy Jsy/25 35.00
5 Bill Madlock Bat/25 25.00
7 Bobby Crosby Jsy/25 20.00
11 Lyle Overbay Jsy/25 15.00
13 Omar Vizquel Jsy/25 25.00
18 Travis Hafner Jsy/25 25.00
23 Mark Teixeira Jsy/25 50.00
27 Darryl Strawberry Jsy/25 20.00
28 Alexis Rios Bat/25 15.00
30 Magglio Ordonez Jsy/25 15.00
31 Jay Gibbons Jsy/25 15.00
37 Keith Hernandez Jsy/25 20.00
38 Carlos Zambrano Jsy/25 30.00
39 Brett Myers Jsy/25 15.00
40 Rich Harden Jsy/25 25.00
41 Danny Kolb Jsy/25 15.00
45 Carlos Lee Jsy/25 20.00
47 Jack Morris Jsy/25 20.00
51 Dave Parker Bat/25 20.00
52 C.C. Sabathia Jsy/25 20.00
55 Brandon Webb Pants/25 25.00
56 Sean Casey Jsy/25 20.00
57 Johan Santana Jsy/25 50.00
58 Miguel Cabrera Jsy/25 50.00
59 Bert Blyleven Jsy/25 20.00
60 Casey Kotchman Jsy/25 25.00
61 Dwight Gooden Jsy/25 25.00
62 Milton Bradley Jsy/25 20.00
63 John Kruk Jsy/25 25.00
64 Michael Young Jsy/25 25.00
69 Lew Ford Jsy/25 15.00
70 Jody Gerut Jsy/25 15.00
71 Don Sutton Jsy/25 20.00
73 Austin Kearns Jsy/25 20.00
77 Ryan Wagner Jsy/25 15.00
78 Jermaine Dye Jsy/25 15.00
80 Al Oliver Jsy/25 15.00
81 Angel Berroa Pants/25 15.00
89 Jose Vidro Jsy/25 15.00
90 Harold Baines Jsy/25 20.00
92 Mark Mulder Jsy/25 25.00
93 Ken Harvey Jsy/25 15.00
95 Jason Bay Jsy/25 25.00
96 Dwight Evans Jsy/25 40.00
97 Luis Tiant Pants/25 15.00
98 Ron Santo Bat/25 30.00
99 Brian Roberts Jsy/25 40.00
100 Marty Marion Jsy/25 25.00

Absolutely Ink Swatch Triple

NM/M

Production 1-75
1 Rafael Furcal/50 20.00
3 Dale Murphy/50 30.00
8 Cal Ripken Jr./25 160.00
9 Hank Blalock/25 30.00
13 Omar Vizquel/25 30.00
16 Aramis Ramirez/25 35.00
18 Travis Hafner/50 25.00
22 Juan Gonzalez/25 30.00
23 Mark Teixeira/75 40.00
27 Darryl Strawberry/50 20.00
31 Jay Gibbons/25 20.00
37 Keith Hernandez/25 25.00
45 Carlos Lee/50 20.00
49 Garret Anderson/25 30.00
52 C.C. Sabathia/25 20.00
53 Dennis Eckersley/50 25.00
55 Brandon Webb/50 20.00
56 Sean Casey/50 25.00
58 Miguel Cabrera/25 50.00
60 Casey Kotchman/50 25.00
64 Michael Young/75 25.00
69 Lew Ford/50 15.00
70 Jody Gerut/50 15.00
73 Austin Kearns/50 20.00
77 Ryan Wagner/50 15.00
78 Jermaine Dye/50 15.00
81 Angel Berroa/50 15.00
86 Dave Righetti/50 20.00
89 Jose Vidro/50 15.00
90 Harold Baines/50 20.00
95 Jason Bay/25 25.00
96 Dwight Evans/25 40.00

Absolutely Ink Swatch Triple Spectrum

NM/M

Production 1-25
Prime: No Pricing
Production One Set
1 Rafael Furcal/25 20.00
3 Dale Murphy/25 40.00
18 Travis Hafner/25 25.00
23 Mark Teixeira/25 50.00
27 Darryl Strawberry/25 20.00
45 Carlos Lee/25 20.00
60 Casey Kotchman/25 25.00
64 Michael Young/25 30.00
69 Lew Ford/25 15.00
70 Jody Gerut/25 15.00
73 Austin Kearns/25 20.00
77 Ryan Wagner/25 15.00
78 Jermaine Dye/25 15.00
81 Angel Berroa/25 15.00
89 Jose Vidro/25 15.00
90 Harold Baines/25 20.00

Heroes

NM/M

Common Player: 1.50
Production 250 Sets
Spectrum: 1X-2X
Production 50 Sets
Reverse Spectrum: 2X-4X
Production 25 Sets
1 Billy Martin 3.00
2 Rickey Henderson 2.00
3 Alan Trammell 2.00
4 Lenny Dykstra 1.50
5 Jeff Bagwell 2.00
6 Steve Garvey 1.50
7 Jim "Catfish" Hunter 2.00
8 Cal Ripken Jr. 10.00
9 Reggie Jackson 3.00
10 Gary Sheffield 2.00
11 Edgar Martinez 1.50
12 Roberto Alomar 2.00
13 Luis Tiant 1.50
14 Jim Rice 2.00
15 Carlos Beltran 2.00
16 Hideo Nomo 2.00
17 Mark Grace 2.00
18 Joe Cronin 2.00
19 Tony Gwynn 3.00
20 Bo Jackson 3.00
21 Roger Clemens 5.00
22 Roger Clemens 5.00
23 Don Mattingly 5.00
24 Willie Mays 5.00
25 Andruw Jones 2.00
26 Andre Dawson 2.00
27 Carlton Fisk 2.00
28 Robin Yount 3.00
29 Joe Carter 1.50
30 Dale Murphy 2.00
31 Greg Maddux 3.00
32 Ichiro Suzuki 4.00
33 Jose Canseco 2.00
34 Nolan Ryan 8.00
35 Frank Thomas 2.00
36 Fred Lynn 1.50
37 Curt Schilling 2.00
38 Curt Schilling 2.00
39 Dave Parker 1.50
40 Randy Johnson 2.50
41 Randy Johnson 2.50
42 Vladimir Guerrero 2.50
43 Bernie Williams 1.50
44 Wade Boggs 2.00
45 Pedro Martinez 2.50
46 Andy Pettitte 1.50
47 Fergie Jenkins 2.00
48 Darryl Strawberry 1.50
49 Rafael Palmeiro 2.00
50 Albert Pujols 5.00

Heroes Auto Swatch Double Spec Prime

No Pricing
Production 1-15
Triple: No Pricing
Production One Set

Heroes Swatch Double

NM/M

Production 25-50
Spectrum Prime: No Pricing
Production 1-25
1 Billy Martin J-P/50 25.00
2 Rickey Henderson B-J/50 10.00
3 Alan Trammell B-J/50 10.00
4 Lenny Dykstra B-J/50 8.00
5 Jeff Bagwell B-J/50 10.00
6 Steve Garvey B-J/50 8.00
7 Jim "Catfish" Hunter J-J/25 10.00
8 Cal Ripken Jr. J-P/50 40.00
9 Reggie Jackson JK-J/50 10.00
10 Gary Sheffield FG-J/50 8.00
11 Edgar Martinez J-J/50 8.00
12 Roberto Alomar J-J/50 8.00
13 Luis Tiant H-J/25 10.00
14 Jim Rice J-P/50 8.00
15 Carlos Beltran B-J/50 8.00
16 Hideo Nomo B-J/50 10.00
17 Mark Grace FG-J/50 10.00
18 Joe Cronin J-P/50 30.00
19 Tony Gwynn B-J/50 15.00
20 Bo Jackson B-J/50 10.00
21 Roger Clemens J-J/50 25.00
22 Roger Clemens J-J/50 25.00
23 Don Mattingly B-J/50 20.00
24 Willie Mays B-J/50 50.00
25 Andruw Jones B-J/50 8.00
26 Andre Dawson J-P/50 8.00
28 Robin Yount H-J/50 15.00
29 Joe Carter B-J/50 8.00
30 Dale Murphy B-J/50 10.00
31 Greg Maddux J-J/50 15.00
33 Jose Canseco H-J/50 10.00
34 Nolan Ryan B-J/50 30.00
35 Frank Thomas J-P/50 10.00
36 Fred Lynn B-J/50 8.00
37 Curt Schilling J-J/50 10.00
38 Curt Schilling J-J/50 10.00
39 Dave Parker B-J/50 8.00
40 Randy Johnson J-J/50 10.00
41 Randy Johnson B-J/25 10.00
42 Vladimir Guerrero J-J/50 10.00
43 Bernie Williams J-J/50 8.00
44 Wade Boggs B-J/50 10.00
45 Pedro Martinez J-J/50 10.00
46 Andy Pettitte J-J/50 8.00
47 Fergie Jenkins H-J/50 8.00
48 Darryl Strawberry J-P/50 8.00
49 Rafael Palmeiro B-J/50 10.00
50 Albert Pujols J-J/50 30.00

Heroes Swatch Triple

NM/M

Production 1-50
Spectrum Prime: No Pricing
Production 1-15
1 Billy Martin/25 35.00
2 Rickey Henderson/25 15.00
3 Alan Trammell/25 10.00
4 Lenny Dykstra/25 10.00
5 Jeff Bagwell/50 10.00
6 Steve Garvey/25 10.00
8 Cal Ripken Jr./25 50.00
9 Reggie Jackson/25 15.00
10 Gary Sheffield/50 10.00
11 Edgar Martinez/25 10.00
12 Roberto Alomar/50 10.00
14 Jim Rice/25 10.00
15 Carlos Beltran/25 15.00
16 Hideo Nomo/25 20.00
17 Mark Grace/25 15.00
18 Joe Cronin/25 40.00
19 Tony Gwynn/25 25.00
20 Bo Jackson/25 20.00
21 Roger Clemens/50 25.00

22 Roger Clemens/50 25.00
23 Don Mattingly/25 30.00
25 Andruw Jones/50 10.00
26 Andre Dawson/25 10.00
28 Robin Yount/25 60.00
31 Greg Maddux/50 15.00
34 Nolan Ryan/25 40.00
35 Frank Thomas/50 15.00
36 Fred Lynn/25 10.00
37 Curt Schilling/50 15.00
38 Curt Schilling/50 15.00
39 Dave Parker/25 10.00
42 Vladimir Guerrero/50 15.00
43 Bernie Williams/25 10.00
44 Wade Boggs/25 15.00
45 Pedro Martinez/50 15.00
46 Andy Pettitte/50 10.00
47 Fergie Jenkins/25 10.00
48 Darryl Strawberry/25 10.00
49 Rafael Palmeiro/50 15.00
50 Albert Pujols/50 40.00

Marks of Fame

NM/M

Common Player: 2.00
Production 150 Sets
Spectrum: 2X-3X
Production 25 Sets
1 Bobby Doerr 2.00
2 Reggie Jackson 3.00
3 Harmon Killebrew 4.00
4 Duke Snider 3.00
5 Brooks Robinson 3.00
6 Al Kaline 4.00
7 Carlton Fisk 3.00
8 Willie Stargell 3.00
9 Enos Slaughter 2.00
10 Nolan Ryan 10.00
11 Luis Aparicio 2.00
12 Hoyt Wilhelm 2.00
13 Orlando Cepeda 2.00
14 Mike Schmidt 6.00
15 Frank Robinson 3.00
16 Whitey Ford 3.00
17 Don Sutton 2.00
18 Joe Morgan 2.00
19 Bob Feller 3.00
20 Lou Brock 3.00
21 Warren Spahn 4.00
22 Jim Palmer 2.00
23 Reggie Jackson 3.00
24 Willie Mays 8.00
25 George Brett 8.00
26 Billy Williams 2.00
27 Juan Marichal 2.00
28 Early Wynn 2.00
29 Rod Carew 3.00
30 Maury Wills 2.00
31 Fergie Jenkins 2.00
32 Steve Carlton 3.00
33 Eddie Murray 3.00
34 Kirby Puckett 3.00
35 Johnny Bench 4.00
36 Gaylord Perry 2.00
37 Gary Carter 2.00
38 Tony Perez 2.00
39 Tony Oliva 2.00
40 Luis Aparicio 2.00
41 Tom Seaver 3.00
42 Paul Molitor 3.00
43 Dennis Eckersley 2.00
44 Willie McCovey 3.00
45 Bob Gibson 3.00
46 Robin Roberts 2.00
47 Carl Yastrzemski 4.00
48 Ozzie Smith 4.00
49 Nolan Ryan 10.00
50 Stan Musial 6.00

Marks of Fame Auto. Swatch Double

NM/M

Production 1-75
Prime: No Pricing
Production 1-10
1 Bobby Doerr B-P/50 25.00
3 Harmon Killebrew B-J/50 40.00
4 Duke Snider J-P/25 40.00
5 Brooks Robinson B-J/25 40.00
7 Carlton Fisk B-JK/25 40.00
10 Nolan Ryan J-P/25 100.00
11 Luis Aparicio B-J/75 20.00
12 Hoyt Wilhelm J-J/25 25.00
13 Orlando Cepeda B-P/25 25.00
14 Mike Schmidt B-J/25 75.00
15 Frank Robinson B-S/25 50.00
16 Whitey Ford J-J/25 50.00
17 Don Sutton J-J/25 20.00
20 Lou Brock B-JK/25 50.00
22 Jim Palmer H-P/25 30.00
27 Juan Marichal J-P/25 25.00
29 Rod Carew B-J/25 40.00
31 Fergie Jenkins FG-P/25 20.00
32 Steve Carlton B-P/25 40.00
35 Johnny Bench B-J/25 50.00
36 Gaylord Perry J-J/25 20.00
37 Gary Carter B-J/25 25.00
38 Tony Perez FG-J/25 25.00
39 Tony Oliva B-J/75 20.00
41 Tom Seaver J-P/25 40.00
42 Paul Molitor B-J/25 35.00
43 Dennis Eckersley J-J/25 25.00
44 Willie McCovey J-P/25 40.00
48 Ozzie Smith H-P/25 50.00
49 Nolan Ryan JK-J/25 100.00
50 Stan Musial B-P/25 80.00

Marks of Fame Auto. Swatch Single

NM/M

Production 5-125
1 Bobby Doerr Pants/125 20.00
3 Harmon Killebrew Jsy/50 40.00
4 Duke Snider Jsy/25 40.00
5 Brooks Robinson Jsy/125 30.00
6 Al Kaline Bat/125 35.00
7 Carlton Fisk Jkt/50 40.00
10 Nolan Ryan Pants/50 80.00
11 Luis Aparicio Jsy/125 20.00
13 Orlando Cepeda Pants/50 25.00
14 Mike Schmidt Jsy/50 60.00
15 Frank Robinson Bat/125 30.00
16 Whitey Ford Jsy/50 50.00
17 Don Sutton Jsy/125 20.00
19 Bob Feller Pants/125 30.00
20 Lou Brock Jkt/125 30.00
22 Jim Palmer Pants/50 25.00
26 Billy Williams Jsy/50 25.00
27 Juan Marichal Pants/125 25.00
29 Rod Carew Jsy/50 35.00
31 Fergie Jenkins Pants/125 20.00
32 Steve Carlton Pants/125 25.00
35 Johnny Bench Pants/50 50.00
36 Gaylord Perry Jsy/125 15.00
37 Gary Carter Pants/50 20.00
38 Tony Perez Jsy/50 20.00
39 Tony Oliva Jsy/125 25.00
40 Luis Aparicio Bat/125 20.00
41 Tom Seaver Pants/50 35.00
42 Paul Molitor Pants/50 35.00
43 Dennis Eckersley Jsy/125 20.00
44 Willie McCovey Pants/50 35.00
45 Bob Gibson Hat/5
46 Robin Roberts Hat/50 35.00
48 Ozzie Smith Pants/50 50.00
49 Nolan Ryan Jkt/50 80.00
50 Stan Musial Pants/50 60.00

Marks of Fame Auto. Swatch Triple

No Pricing
Production 1-10
Prime: No Pricing
Production One Set

Marks of Fame Swatch Double

NM/M

Production 1-50
Spectrum Prime: No Pricing
Production 1-25
1 Bobby Doerr/50 10.00
2 Reggie Jackson B-P/50 10.00
3 Harmon Killebrew B-J/50 15.00
4 Duke Snider J-P/25 15.00
5 Brooks Robinson B-J/50 15.00
7 Carlton Fisk B-JK/50 10.00
8 Willie Stargell B-J/50 10.00
9 Enos Slaughter J-J/50 10.00
10 Nolan Ryan J-P/50 25.00
11 Luis Aparicio B-J/50 8.00
12 Hoyt Wilhelm J-J/50 8.00
13 Orlando Cepeda B-P/50 10.00
14 Mike Schmidt B-J/50 20.00
15 Frank Robinson B-S/50 15.00
16 Whitey Ford J-J/25 15.00
17 Don Sutton J-J/50 8.00
18 Joe Morgan B-J/50 8.00
20 Lou Brock B-JK/50 10.00
21 Warren Spahn J-P/50 12.00
22 Jim Palmer H-P/50 10.00
23 Reggie Jackson B-J/50 10.00
24 Willie Mays B-J/25 50.00
26 Billy Williams J-J/50 8.00
27 Juan Marichal J-P/50 8.00
28 Early Wynn J-J/25 10.00
29 Rod Carew B-J/50 10.00
31 Fergie Jenkins FG-P/50 8.00
32 Steve Carlton B-P/50 8.00
33 Eddie Murray B-J/50 15.00
34 Kirby Puckett B-J/50 15.00
35 Johnny Bench B-J/50 15.00
36 Gaylord Perry J-J/50 8.00
37 Gary Carter B-J/50 8.00
39 Tony Oliva B-J/50 8.00
41 Tom Seaver J-P/50 15.00
42 Paul Molitor B-J/50 15.00
43 Dennis Eckersley J-J/50 10.00
44 Willie McCovey J-P/50 10.00
47 Carl Yastrzemski B-J/50 25.00
48 Ozzie Smith H-P/50 20.00
49 Nolan Ryan JK-J/50 25.00
50 Stan Musial B-P/50 30.00

Marks of Fame Swatch Triple

NM/M

Production 1-25
Spectrum Prime: No Pricing
Production 1-15
1 Bobby Doerr/25 15.00
7 Carlton Fisk/25 15.00
8 Willie Stargell/25 15.00
10 Nolan Ryan/25 40.00
11 Luis Aparicio/25 12.00
12 Hoyt Wilhelm/25 10.00
14 Mike Schmidt/25 30.00
18 Joe Morgan/25 12.00
20 Lou Brock/25 15.00
21 Warren Spahn/25 50.00
23 Reggie Jackson/25 15.00
24 Willie Mays/25 60.00
27 Juan Marichal/25 12.00
29 Rod Carew/25 15.00
32 Steve Carlton/25 12.00
33 Eddie Murray/25 20.00
34 Kirby Puckett/25 20.00
35 Johnny Bench/25 20.00
37 Gary Carter/25 12.00
39 Tony Oliva/25 12.00
41 Tom Seaver/25 15.00
42 Paul Molitor/25 15.00
43 Dennis Eckersley/25 12.00
44 Willie McCovey/25 15.00
47 Carl Yastrzemski/25 35.00
48 Ozzie Smith/25 25.00
49 Nolan Ryan/25 40.00
50 Stan Musial/25 40.00

Team Quads

NM/M

Common Quad: 2.00
Production 150 Sets
Spectrum: 1X
Production 100 Sets
1 St. Louis Card Active 6.00
2 Cleveland Indians 2.00
3 California Angels 2.00
4 Boston Red Sox 5.00
5 New York Yanks Active 6.00
6 Atlanta Braves 3.00
7 Oakland A's 3.00
8 Anaheim Angels 3.00
9 Texas Rangers Active 2.00
10 Minnesota Twins Active 3.00
11 New York Mets 4.00
12 Houston Astros 5.00
13 San Diego Padres 4.00
14 Cincinnati Reds 2.00
15 Texas Rangers Retro 8.00
16 New York Yanks Retro 8.00
17 St. Louis Cards Retro 6.00
18 Pittsburgh Pirates 2.00
19 Chicago Cubs 4.00
20 Minnesota Twins Retro 3.00

Team Quads Swatch Double

NM/M

Production 25-75
1 St. Louis Card Active/75 25.00
3 California Angels/75 30.00
4 Boston Red Sox/75 30.00
5 New York Yanks Active/25 75.00
6 Atlanta Braves/25 60.00
7 Oakland A's/75 20.00
8 Anaheim Angels/25 40.00
9 Texas Rangers Active/75 20.00
10 Minnesota Twins Active/25 40.00
11 New York Mets/75 30.00
12 Houston Astros/25 75.00
13 San Diego Padres/75 40.00
14 Cincinnati Reds/75 20.00
15 Texas Rangers Retro/75 50.00
18 Pittsburgh Pirates/75 20.00
20 Minnesota Twins Retro/75 30.00

Team Quads Swatch Double Spectrum

NM/M

Production 1-25
Prime Black: No Pricing
Production 1-5
1 St. Louis Card Active/25 40.00
3 California Angels/25 50.00
4 Boston Red Sox/25 60.00
5 New York Yanks Active/10
6 Atlanta Braves/10
7 Oakland A's/25
8 Anaheim Angels/10
9 Texas Rangers Active/25 30.00
10 Minnesota Twins Active/10
11 New York Mets/25 50.00
12 Houston Astros/10
13 San Diego Padres/25 60.00
14 Cincinnati Reds/25 30.00
15 Texas Rangers Retro/25 70.00
16 New York Yanks Retro/5
18 Pittsburgh Pirates/25
19 Chicago Cubs/1
20 Minnesota Twins Retro/25

Team Quads Swatch Single

NM/M

Production 25-100
1 St. Louis Card Active/100 25.00
2 Cleveland Indians/100 30.00
3 California Angels/100 15.00
4 Boston Red Sox/100 20.00
5 New York Yanks Active/100 30.00
6 Atlanta Braves/100 25.00
7 Oakland A's/100 10.00
8 Anaheim Angels/100 15.00
9 Texas Rangers Active/100 10.00
10 Minnesota Twins Active/25 25.00
11 New York Mets/100 20.00
12 Houston Astros/100 30.00
13 San Diego Padres/100 25.00
14 Cincinnati Reds/100 10.00
15 Texas Rangers Retro/100 30.00
16 New York Yanks Retro/100 50.00
17 St. Louis Cards Retro/25 50.00
18 Pittsburgh Pirates/100 15.00
19 Chicago Cubs/100 25.00
20 Minnesota Twins Retro/100 20.00

Swatch Single Spectrum

NM/M

Production 10-35
Prime Black: No Pricing
Production 10 Sets
1 St. Louis Card Active/35 40.00
2 Cleveland Indians/35 50.00
3 California Angels/35 25.00
4 Boston Red Sox/35 30.00
5 New York Yanks Active/35 40.00

6 Atlanta Braves/35 40.00
7 Oakland A's/35 20.00
8 Anaheim Angels/35 25.00
9 Texas Rangers Active/35 20.00
10 Minnesota Twins Active/10
11 New York Mets/35 30.00
12 Houston Astros/35 50.00
13 San Diego Padres/35 40.00
14 Cincinnati Reds/35 20.00
15 Texas Rangers Retro/35 40.00
16 New York Yanks Retro/35 75.00
17 St. Louis Cards Retro/10
18 Pittsburgh Pirates/35 20.00
19 Chicago Cubs/35 40.00
20 Minnesota Twins Retro/35 30.00

Team Six

NM/M

Common Card: 1.50
Production 100 Sets
Spectrum: 1X-1.5X
Production 50 Sets
1 San Francisco Giants 8.00
2 Houston Astros 6.00
3 Cincinnati Reds 5.00
4 St. Louis Cardinals 8.00
5 New York Yankees 10.00
6 Chicago Cubs 6.00
7 Arizona Diamondbacks 1.50
8 Los Angeles Dodgers 6.00
9 Anaheim Angels 4.00
10 Boston Red Sox 8.00
11 Seattle Mariners 8.00
12 Chicago White Sox 4.00
13 Philadelphia Phillies 10.00
14 New York Mets 10.00
15 Atlanta Braves 4.00

Team Six Swatch Single

NM/M

Production 15-50
1 San Francisco Giants/50 80.00
2 Houston Astros/50 40.00
5 New York Yankees/50 60.00
6 Chicago Cubs/50 40.00
7 Arizona Diamondbacks/50 20.00
8 Los Angeles Dodgers/50 40.00
9 Anaheim Angeles/50 30.00
10 Boston Red Sox/50 50.00
12 Chicago White Sox/50 30.00
13 Philadelphia Phillies/50 40.00
14 New York Mets/50 40.00
15 Atlanta Braves/50 40.00

Team Six Swatch Single Spectrum

NM/M

Production 5-25
Prime Black: No Pricing
Production 5 Sets
1 San Francisco Giants/25 100.00
2 Houston Astros/25 50.00
5 New York Yankees/25 75.00
6 Chicago Cubs/25 50.00
7 Arizona Diamondbacks/25 25.00
8 Los Angeles Dodgers/25 50.00
9 Anaheim Angels/10
10 Boston Red Sox/25 65.00
12 Chicago White Sox/25 40.00
13 Philadelphia Phillies/25 50.00
14 New York Mets/25 50.00
15 Atlanta Braves/25 50.00

Team Tandems

NM/M

Common Card: 1.50
Production 250 Sets
Spectrum: .75X-1.5X
Production 150 Sets
1 Mark Prior, Kerry Wood 2.00
2 Barry Zito, Tim Hudson 1.50
3 Curt Schilling, Pedro Martinez 2.50
4 Will Clark, Matt Williams 2.00
5 Bernie Williams, Jason Giambi 2.00
6 Vernon Wells, Roy Halladay 1.50
7 Josh Beckett, A.J. Burnett 1.50
8 Dale Murphy, Phil Niekro 2.00
9 Mike Schmidt, Steve Carlton 5.00
10 Tony Oliva, Harmon Killebrew 2.00
11 Robin Yount, Paul Molitor 2.50
12 Francisco Rodriguez, Troy Percival 1.50
13 Ben Sheets, Danny Kolb 1.50
14 Andruw Jones, Rafael Furcal 1.50
15 Todd Helton, Preston Wilson 1.50
16 Wade Boggs, Fred McGriff 2.00
17 Manny Ramirez, David Ortiz 2.50
18 Miguel Cabrera, Dontrelle Willis 2.00
19 Edgar Renteria, Scott Rolen 2.00
20 Carlos Beltran, Jeff Kent 2.00
21 Eric Davis, Deion Sanders 2.00
22 Frank Thomas, Paul Konerko 2.00
23 Mike Piazza, Al Leiter 3.00
24 Sean Burroughs, Ryan Klesko 1.50
25 Ken Harvey, Mike Sweeney 1.50
26 David Sanders, Hideki Matsui 4.00
27 Steve Carlton, Mark Buehrle 2.00
28 Gaylord Perry, Randy Johnson 2.00
29 Joe Morgan, Steve Carlton 2.00
30 Vladimir Guerrero, Orlando Cabrera 2.00
31 Scott Rolen, John Kruk 2.00
32 Aaron Boone, Dmitri Young 1.50
33 Rickey Henderson, Vladimir Guerrero 2.00
34 Charles Johnson, Cliff Floyd 1.50
35 Cal Ripken Jr., Rafael Palmeiro 8.00

Team Tandems Swatch Double

NM/M

Production 1-125
Spectrum: 1X-2X
Production 1-50
No pricing 20 or less
1 Mark Prior, Kerry Wood/125 12.00
2 Barry Zito, Tim Hudson/125 8.00
3 Curt Schilling, Pedro Martinez/125 15.00
5 Bernie Williams, Jason Giambi/125 10.00
7 Josh Beckett, A.J. Burnett/125 8.00
8 Dale Murphy, Phil Niekro/125 20.00
10 Tony Oliva, Harmon Killebrew/50 30.00
11 Robin Yount, Paul Molitor/125 20.00
14 Andruw Jones, Rafael Furcal/125 8.00
15 Todd Helton, Preston Wilson/125 10.00
16 Wade Boggs, Fred McGriff/125 15.00
17 Manny Ramirez, David Ortiz/125 15.00
18 Miguel Cabrera, Dontrelle Willis/125 12.00
20 Carlos Beltran, Jeff Kent/50 12.00
21 Eric Davis, Deion Sanders/25 15.00
22 Frank Thomas, Paul Konerko/50 15.00
23 Mike Piazza, Al Leiter/125 20.00
24 Sean Burroughs, Ryan Klesko/50 10.00
26 Deion Sanders, Hideki Matsui/125 35.00
27 Steve Carlton, Mark Buehrle/50 12.00
29 Joe Morgan, Steve Carlton/25 15.00
33 Rickey Henderson, Vladimir Guerrero/50 15.00
34 Charles Johnson, Cliff Floyd/125 8.00
35 Cal Ripken Jr., Rafael Palmeiro/125 40.00

Team Tandems Swatch Single

NM/M

Production 10-125
1 Mark Prior, Kerry Wood/125 8.00
2 Barry Zito, Tim Hudson/125 5.00
3 Curt Schilling, Pedro Martinez/125 8.00
4 Will Clark, Matt Williams/125 8.00
5 Bernie Williams, Jason Giambi/125 8.00
6 Vernon Wells, Roy Halladay/125 5.00
7 Josh Beckett, A.J. Burnett/125 5.00
8 Dale Murphy, Phil Niekro/125 15.00
9 Mike Schmidt, Steve Carlton/125 15.00
10 Tony Oliva, Harmon Killebrew/50 15.00
11 Robin Yount, Paul Molitor/125 15.00
12 Felix Rodriguez, Troy Percival/25 10.00
13 Ben Sheets, Danny Kolb/125 5.00
14 Andruw Jones, Rafael Furcal/125 5.00
15 Todd Helton, Preston Wilson/125 5.00
16 Wade Boggs, Fred McGriff/50 10.00
17 Manny Ramirez, David Ortiz/125 12.00
18 Miguel Cabrera, Dontrelle Willis/125 10.00
19 Edgar Renteria, Scott Rolen/125 10.00
20 Carlos Beltran, Jeff Kent Bat/125 8.00
21 Eric Davis Bat, Deion Sanders/125 8.00
22 Frank Thomas, Paul Konerko/50 10.00
23 Mike Piazza, Al Leiter/125 12.00
24 Sean Burroughs, Ryan Klesko/125 5.00
25 Ken Harvey, Mike Sweeney/125 5.00
26 Deion Sanders, Hideki Matsui/125 25.00
27 Steve Carlton, Mark Buehrle/50 8.00
28 Gaylord Perry, Randy Johnson/125 10.00
29 Joe Morgan, Steve Carlton/25 10.00
31 Scott Rolen, John Kruk/125 10.00
32 Aaron Boone, Dmitri Young/125 5.00
33 Rickey Henderson Hat, Vladimir Guerrero/25 15.00
34 Charles Johnson, Cliff Floyd/125 5.00
35 Cal Ripken Jr., Rafael Palmeiro/125 25.00

Swatch Single Spectrum

NM/M

Production 1-75
1 Mark Prior, Kerry Wood/75 8.00
2 Barry Zito, Tim Hudson/75 5.00
3 Curt Schilling, Pedro Martinez/75 10.00
4 Will Clark, M. Williams/75 8.00
5 Bernie Williams, Jason Giambi/75 5.00
6 Vernon Wells, Roy Halladay/75 5.00
7 Josh Beckett, A.J. Burnett/75 5.00
8 Dale Murphy, Phil Niekro/75 10.00
11 Robin Yount, Paul Molitor/75 15.00
13 Ben Sheets, Danny Kolb/75 5.00
14 Andruw Jones, Rafael Furcal/75 5.00
15 Todd Helton, Preston Wilson/75 5.00
17 Manny Ramirez, David Ortiz/75 10.00
18 Miguel Cabrera, Dontrelle Willis/75 8.00
19 Edgar Renteria, Scott Rolen/75 8.00
20 Carlos Beltran, Jeff Kent Bat/75 8.00
21 Eric Davis Bat, Deion Sanders/75 8.00
23 Mike Piazza, Al Leiter/75 10.00
24 Sean Burroughs, Ryan Klesko/75 5.00
25 Ken Harvey, Mike Sweeney/75 5.00
26 Deion Sanders, Hideki Matsui/75 25.00
28 Gaylord Perry, Randy Johnson/75 8.00
31 Scott Rolen, John Kruk/75 8.00
32 Aaron Boone, D. Young/75 5.00
34 Charles Johnson, Cliff Floyd/75 5.00
35 Cal Ripken Jr., Rafael Palmeiro/75 25.00

Team Trios

NM/M

Common Card:
Production 200 Sets
Spectrum: 1X
Production 125 Sets
1 Cal Ripken Jr., Jim Palmer, Eddie Murray 10.00
2 Roger Clemens, Wade Boggs, Evans 5.00
3 Rafael Palmeiro, Miguel Tejada, Javy Lopez 2.00
4 Carl Crawford, Rocco Baldelli, B.J. Upton 1.50
5 Mark Buehrle, Magglio Ordonez, Carlos Lee 1.50
6 Victor Martinez, Travis Hafner, Jody Gerut 1.50
7 Bobby Abreu, Brett Myers, Kevin Millwood 1.50
8 Sammy Sosa, Aramis Ramirez, Carlos Zambrano 3.00
9 Bo, George Brett, Carlos Beltran 5.00
10 Hideo Nomo, Adrian Beltre, Shawn Green 2.00
11 Wilson, Wilson, Jason Bay 1.50
12 Tom Seaver, Nolan Ryan, Dwight Gooden 8.00
13 David Dellucci, Laynce Nix, Kevin Mench 1.50
14 Alan Trammell, Morris, Gibson 2.00
15 M. Will, Grace, Randy Johnson 2.00
16 Dawson, Gary Carter, Tony Perez 2.00
17 Dale Murphy, John Kruk, Lenny Dykstra 2.00
18 B. Roberts, Ian Gibb, Larry Bigbie 1.50
19 Mike Lowell, Ivan Rodriguez, Brad Penny 2.00
20 Murray, Darryl Strawberry, Oliver 2.00
21 Darryl Strawberry, Rickey Henderson, Gary Sheffield 2.00

22 Roberto Alomar, Joe Crede, Durham 2.00
23 Jason Kendall, Giles, Aramis Ramirez 1.50
24 Delmon, Aubrey Huff, Tino 2.00
25 Jeff Bagwell, Cruz, Joe Morgan 2.00
26 Snow, Rich Aurilia, Jeff Kent 1.50
27 Jenkins, Nolan Ryan, Cordero 8.00
28 Lofton, Jim Thome, Roberto Alomar 3.00
29 Atkins, Todd Helton, Jennings 2.00
30 Gary Carter, Pedro, Randy Johnson 2.50

Team Trios Swatch Double

NM/M

Production 25-100
Spectrum: .75X-1.5X
Production 5-35
No pricing production 20 or less
Prime Black: No Pricing
Production 5-10
1 Cal Ripken Jr., Jim Palmer, Murray/100 75.00
2 Roger Clemens, Wade Boggs, Evans/100 50.00
3 Rafael Palmeiro, Miguel Tejada, Javy Lopez/50 25.00
5 Mark Buehrle, Magglio Ordonez, Carlos Lee/100 15.00
6 Victor Martinez, Travis Hafner, Jody Gerut/50 20.00
9 Bo, George Brett, Carlos Beltran/100 40.00
10 Hideo Nomo, Adrian Beltre, Shawn Green/100 25.00
11 Wilson, Wilson, Jason Bay/100 15.00
12 Tom Seaver, Nolan Ryan, Dwight Gooden/100 50.00
14 Alan Trammell, Morris, Gibson/50 30.00
15 M. Will, Mark Grace, Randy Johnson/50 30.00
16 Dawson, Gary Carter, Tony Perez/100 20.00
19 Mike Lowell, Ivan Rodriguez, Brad Penny/50 25.00
20 Murray, Darryl Strawberry, Oliver/100 30.00
21 Darryl Strawberry, Rickey Henderson, Gary Sheffield/100 25.00
22 Roberto Alomar, Joe Crede, Durham/100 20.00
28 Lofton, Jim Thome, Roberto Alomar/25 40.00
29 Atkins, Todd Helton, Jennings/100 20.00
30 Gary Carter, Pedro, Randy Johnson/50 30.00

Team Trios Swatch Single

NM/M

Production 50 unless noted
1 Cal Ripken Jr., Jim Palmer, Murray 40.00
2 Roger Clemens, Wade Boggs, Evans 25.00
3 Rafael Palmeiro, Miguel Tejada, Javy Lopez 12.00
4 Carl Crawford, Rocco Baldelli, B.J. Upton 10.00
5 Mark Buehrle, Magglio Ordonez, Carlos Lee 10.00
6 Victor Martinez, Travis Hafner, Jody Gerut 10.00
7 Bobby Abreu, Brett Myers, Kevin Millwood 10.00
8 Sammy Sosa, Aramis Ramirez, Carlos Zambrano 15.00
9 Bo, George Brett, Carlos Beltran 30.00
10 Hideo Nomo, Adrian Beltre, Shawn Green 15.00
11 Wilson, Wilson, Jason Bay 10.00
12 Tom Seaver, Nolan Ryan, Dwight Gooden 35.00
13 David Dellucci, Laynce Nix, Kevin Mench 8.00
14 Alan Trammell, Morris, Gibson 15.00
15 M. Will, Grace, Randy Johnson 15.00
16 Dawson, Gary Carter, Tony Perez 10.00
17 Dale Murphy, Tomas Kurka, Lenny Dykstra 20.00
18 Roberts, Ian Gibb, Larry Bigbie 15.00
19 Mike Lowell, Ivan Rodriguez, Brad Penny 10.00
20 Murray, Darryl Strawberry, Oliver 20.00
21 Darryl Strawberry, Rickey Henderson, Gary Sheffield 15.00
22 Roberto Alomar, Joe Crede, Durham 10.00
23 Jason Kendall, Giles, Aramis Ramirez 10.00
24 Delmon, Aubrey Huff, Tino 10.00
25 Jeff Bagwell, Cruz, Joe Morgan 12.00
26 Snow, Rich Aurilia, Jeff Kent 8.00
27 Jenkins, Nolan Ryan, Cordero 25.00
28 Lofton, Jim Thome, Roberto Alomar 20.00
29 Atkins, Todd Helton, Jennings 15.00
30 Gary Carter, Pedro, Randy Johnson 15.00

Swatch Single Spectrum

NM/M

Production 10-50
Prime Black: No Pricing
Production 10 Sets
1 Cal Ripken Jr., Jim Palmer, Murray/50 40.00
2 Roger Clemens, Wade Boggs, Evans/50 30.00
4 Carl Crawford, Rocco Baldelli, B.J. Upton/50 10.00
5 Mark Buehrle, Magglio Ordonez, Carlos Lee/50 10.00
7 Bobby Abreu, Brett Myers, Kevin Millwood/50 10.00
8 Sammy Sosa, Aramis Ramirez, Carlos Zambrano/50 15.00
9 Bo, George Brett, Carlos Beltran/50 25.00
10 Hideo Nomo, Adrian Beltre, Shawn Green/50 15.00
11 Wilson, Wilson, Jason Bay/50 8.00
12 Tom Seaver, Nolan Ryan, Dwight Gooden/50 30.00
13 David Dellucci, Laynce Nix, Kevin Mench/50 10.00
14 Alan Trammell, Morris, Gibson/50 15.00
16 Dawson, Gary Carter, Tony Perez/50 10.00
17 Dale Murphy, Tomas Kurka, Lenny Dykstra/50 15.00
18 Roberts, Ian Gibb, Larry Bigbie/50 10.00
19 Mike Lowell, Ivan Rodriguez, Brad Penny/25 10.00
20 Murray, Darryl Strawberry, Oliver/50 20.00
21 Darryl Strawberry, Rickey Henderson, Gary Sheffield/50 15.00
22 Roberto Alomar, Joe Crede, Durham/50 10.00
24 Delmon, Aubrey Huff, Tino/50 10.00
25 Jeff Bagwell, Cruz, Joe Morgan/50 10.00
26 Snow, Rich Aurilia, Jeff Kent/50 8.00
27 Jenkins, Nolan Ryan, Cordero/50 25.00
28 Lofton, Jim Thome, Roberto Alomar/50 10.00
29 Atkins, Todd Helton, Jennings/50 10.00
30 Gary Carter, Pedro, Randy Johnson/50 15.00

Tools of Trade Auto Swatch Double

NM/M

Production 1-75
Prime Red: .75X-1.5X
Production 1-50
No pricing production 20 or less
Prime Black: No Pricing
Production One Set
1 Ozzie Smith B-P/25 50.00
3 Dale Murphy J-J/50 30.00
4 Paul Molitor J-P/25 40.00
20 Lou Brock B-JK/50 40.00
22 Paul LoDuca B-J/25 25.00
36 Sean Casey J-P/50 20.00
37 Juan Gonzalez J-P/25 30.00
39 Darryl Strawberry B-J/50 25.00
41 Tom Seaver J-P/25 40.00
48 Torii Hunter B-J/40 25.00
56 Brad Penny FG-J/75 10.00
57 Gary Carter J-P/25 30.00
62 Andre Dawson B-J/50 25.00
64 Adrian Beltre B-J/50 25.00
66 Juan Gonzalez B-J/25 30.00
70 Andre Dawson J-P/50 25.00
73 Cal Ripken Jr. J-P/25 160.00
88 Magglio Ordonez B-S/25 20.00
91 Gary Carter B-J/25 30.00
96 Bobby Doerr B-P/50 25.00
98 Eric Chavez B-J/25 25.00
100 Harmon Killebrew H-J/25 50.00

Tools of Trade Auto Swatch Double Reverse

NM/M

Production 1-75
20 Lou Brock B-JK/50 40.00
36 Sean Casey J-P/50 25.00
39 Darryl Strawberry B-J/75 20.00
48 Torii Hunter B-J/50 25.00
56 Brad Penny FG-J/50 12.00
62 Andre Dawson B-J/25 30.00
64 Adrian Beltre B-J/50 20.00
66 Juan Gonzalez B-J/25 30.00
70 Andre Dawson J-P/25 30.00

Tools of Trade Auto. Swatch Quad

NM/M

Production 1-25
Prime Red: No Pricing
Production 1-5
3 Dale Murphy/25 60.00
20 Lou Brock/25 80.00
23 Don Mattingly/25 120.00
36 Sean Casey/25 40.00
39 Darryl Strawberry/25 40.00
41 Tom Seaver/25 75.00
42 Mike Schmidt/25 100.00
56 Brad Penny/25 20.00
57 Gary Carter/25 40.00
73 Cal Ripken Jr./25 200.00
78 Tony Gwynn/25 75.00
88 Magglio Ordonez/25 30.00
91 Gary Carter/25 40.00
100 Harmon Killebrew/25 80.00

Tools of Trade Auto Swatch Triple

NM/M

Production 1-75
Prime Red: No Pricing
Production 1-25
Prime Black: No Pricing
Production One Set
2 Carlos Beltran/25 40.00
3 Dale Murphy/25 50.00
18 Darryl Strawberry/75 20.00
20 Lou Brock/50 40.00
36 Sean Casey/75 20.00
37 Juan Gonzalez/75 25.00
39 Darryl Strawberry/75 20.00
56 Brad Penny/25 20.00
57 Gary Carter/25 30.00
64 Adrian Beltre/25 25.00
66 Juan Gonzalez/50 25.00
70 Andre Dawson/75 25.00
73 Cal Ripken Jr./25 200.00
82 Carlos Beltran/25 40.00
91 Gary Carter/25 30.00
96 Bobby Doerr/25 30.00
100 Harmon Killebrew/25 60.00

Tools of Trade Auto Swatch Triple Revers

NM/M

Production 1-50
18 Darryl Strawberry/50 25.00
20 Lou Brock/50 50.00
36 Sean Casey/25 25.00
37 Juan Gonzalez/25 30.00
39 Darryl Strawberry/50 25.00
70 Andre Dawson/50 25.00

Tools of the Trade Red

NM/M

Common Player:
Production 250 Sets
Black: 1X-1.5X
Production 100 Sets
Blue: 1X-1.5X
Production 150 Sets
Rev. Spectrum Red: 1X-2X
Production 50 Sets
Rev. Spectrum Blue: No Pricing
Production 10 Sets
1 Ozzie Smith 5.00
2 Carlos Beltran 2.00
3 Dale Murphy 2.00
4 Paul Molitor 2.00
5 George Brett 6.00
6 Stan Musial 5.00
7 Ivan Rodriguez 2.00
8 Carl Yastrzemski 4.00
9 Reggie Jackson 2.00
10 Hideo Nomo 2.00
11 Gary Sheffield 2.00
12 Roberto Alomar 2.00
13 Pedro Martinez 3.00
14 Ernie Banks 3.00
15 Tim Hudson 1.50
16 Dwight Gooden 1.50
17 Lance Berkman 1.50
18 Darryl Strawberry 1.50
19 Larry Walker 1.50
20 Lou Brock 2.00
21 Roger Clemens 6.00
22 Paul LoDuca 1.50
23 Don Mattingly 6.00
24 Willie Mays 6.00
25 Rafael Palmeiro 2.00
26 Roy Oswalt 1.50
27 Vladimir Guerrero 3.00
28 Austin Kearns 1.50
29 Rod Carew 2.00
30 Nolan Ryan 8.00
31 Richie Sexson 2.00
32 Steve Carlton 2.00
33 Eddie Murray 3.00
34 Nolan Ryan 8.00
35 Mike Mussina 2.00
36 Sean Casey 1.50
37 Juan Gonzalez 1.50
38 Curt Schilling 2.00
39 Darryl Strawberry 1.50
40 Alfonso Soriano 3.00
41 Tom Seaver 3.00
42 Mike Schmidt 5.00
43 Todd Helton 2.00
44 Reggie Jackson 2.00
45 Shawn Green 1.50
46 Mike Mussina 2.00
47 Tom Glavine 1.50
48 Torii Hunter 1.50
49 Kerry Wood 2.00
50 Carlos Delgado 2.00
51 Randy Johnson 3.00
52 David Ortiz 3.00
53 Troy Glaus 2.00
54 Rickey Henderson 2.00
55 Craig Biggio 2.00
56 Brad Penny 1.50
57 Gary Carter 2.00
58 Andy Pettitte 1.50
59 Mark Prior 3.00
60 Kirby Puckett 3.00
61 Willie McCovey 3.00
62 Andre Dawson 2.00
63 Greg Maddux 4.00
64 Adrian Beltre 1.50
65 Andruw Jones 2.00
66 Juan Gonzalez 1.50
67 Frank Thomas 2.00
68 Victor Martinez 1.50
69 Randy Johnson 3.00
70 Andre Dawson 2.00
71 Adam Dunn 2.00
72 Carlton Fisk 2.00
73 Cal Ripken Jr. 8.00
74 Kenny Lofton 1.50

75 Barry Zito 1.50
76 Sammy Sosa 4.00
77 Deion Sanders 2.00
78 Tony Gwynn 3.00
79 Mike Piazza 4.00
80 Jeff Bagwell 2.00
81 Manny Ramirez 3.00
82 Carlos Beltran 2.00
83 Mark Grace 2.00
84 Robin Yount 4.00
85 Albert Pujols 6.00
86 Dontrelle Willis 2.00
87 Jim Thome 2.00
88 Magglio Ordonez 1.50
89 Miguel Tejada 2.00
90 Mark Teixeira 2.00
91 Gary Carter 2.00
92 Ivan Rodriguez 2.00
93 Jason Giambi 1.50
94 Rickey Henderson 2.00
95 Curt Schilling 2.00
96 Bobby Doerr 2.00
97 Chipper Jones 3.00
98 Eric Chavez 1.50
99 Johnny Bench 4.00
100 Harmon Killebrew 3.00

Tools of the Trade Swatch Double

NM/M

Production 1-150
Prime Red: No Pricing
Production 1-25
Prime Black: No Pricing
Production 1-25
1 Ozzie Smith B-P/50 15.00
2 Carlos Beltran J-S/50 8.00
3 Dale Murphy J-J/50 8.00
4 Paul Molitor J-P/150 8.00
5 George Brett B-H/25 25.00
6 Stan Musial B-P/25 30.00
7 Ivan Rodriguez J-J/150 8.00
8 Carl Yastrzemski B-J/25 30.00
9 Reggie Jackson J-J/50 10.00
10 Hideo Nomo J-P/150 10.00
11 Gary Sheffield H-J/25 8.00
12 Roberto Alomar B-J/150 8.00
13 Pedro Martinez J-P/150 8.00
15 Tim Hudson H-J/100 5.00
17 Lance Berkman B-J/150 5.00
19 Larry Walker J-J/150 5.00
20 Lou Brock B-JK/150 10.00
21 Roger Clemens B-J/150 15.00
22 Paul LoDuca B-J/50 5.00
23 Don Mattingly BG-P/50 20.00
24 Willie Mays B-P/25 50.00
25 Rafael Palmeiro B-J/150 8.00
27 Vladimir Guerrero B-J/150 8.00
29 Rod Carew JK-JK/150 8.00
30 Nolan Ryan B-JK/150 25.00
31 Richie Sexson H-J/150 8.00
32 Steve Carlton B-H/150 8.00
33 Eddie Murray B-J/150 10.00
34 Nolan Ryan B-J/150 25.00
35 Mike Mussina J-P/125 8.00
36 Sean Casey J-P/150 5.00
37 Juan Gonzalez J-P/10
38 Curt Schilling J-J/150 8.00
39 Darryl Strawberry B-J/150 5.00
40 Alfonso Soriano J-J/5
41 Tom Seaver J-P/150 10.00
42 Mike Schmidt B-J/150 15.00
43 Todd Helton B-J/150 8.00
45 Shawn Green B-J/150 5.00
46 Mike Mussina J-S/1
47 Tom Glavine B-J/150 5.00
49 Kerry Wood FG-J/150 8.00
50 Carlos Delgado B-J/100 5.00
51 R. John J-P/150 8.00
52 David Ortiz B-J/150 8.00
53 Troy Glaus J-J/150 5.00
54 Rickey Henderson B-J/150 8.00
55 Craig Biggio B-J/150 5.00
56 Brad Penny FG-J/150 5.00
57 Gary Carter J-P/150 8.00
58 Andy Pettitte J-J/150 5.00
59 Mark Prior FG-J/150 8.00
60 Kirby Puckett B-FG/100 10.00
61 Willie McCovey J-P/150 10.00
62 Andre Dawson B-J/20
63 Greg Maddux B-J/50 15.00
64 Adrian Beltre B-J/150 5.00
65 Andruw Jones B-J/150 8.00
66 Juan Gonzalez B-J/5
67 Frank Thomas J-J/150 8.00
68 Victor Martinez CP-J/150 5.00
69 R. John J-P/150 8.00
70 Andre Dawson J-P/5
71 Adam Dunn B-J/95 8.00
72 Carlton Fisk B-J/150 8.00
73 Cal Ripken Jr. J-P/150 25.00
74 Kenny Lofton B-H/150 5.00
75 Barry Zito J-J/150 5.00
76 Sammy Sosa B-J/150 10.00
77 Deion Sanders J-P/150 10.00
78 Tony Gwynn J-P/150 10.00
79 Mike Piazza J-P/150 10.00
80 Jeff Bagwell J-P/150 8.00
81 Manny Ramirez B-J/150 8.00
82 Carlos Beltran H-J/10
83 Mark Grace B-J/50 8.00
84 Robin Yount B-J/150 12.00
85 Albert Pujols B-J/150 20.00
86 Dontrelle Willis B-J/150 8.00
88 Magglio Ordonez B-S/150 5.00
89 Miguel Tejada H-J/150 8.00
90 Mark Teixeira FG-J/150 8.00
91 Gary Carter B-J/25 10.00
92 Ivan Rodriguez CP-J/150 8.00
93 Jason Giambi H-J/50 5.00
94 Rickey Henderson B-P/150 8.00
95 Curt Schilling J-J/150 8.00
96 Bobby Doerr B-P/150 8.00
97 Chipper Jones B-J/150 8.00
98 Eric Chavez B-J/1
99 Johnny Bench B-P/150 10.00
100 Harmon Killebrew H-J/50 10.00

Tools of the Trade Swatch Five

NM/M

Production 1-50
Prime Red: No Pricing
Production 1-10
Prime Black: No Pricing
Production One Set
Reverse: No Pricing
Production 1-15
4 Paul Molitor/25 35.00
7 Ivan Rodriguez/25 25.00
12 Roberto Alomar/25 20.00
13 Pedro Martinez/25 30.00
15 Tim Hudson/25 25.00
17 Lance Berkman/25 20.00
22 Paul LoDuca/50 15.00
23 Don Mattingly/25 65.00
25 Rafael Palmeiro/25 25.00
26 Roy Oswalt/25 20.00
28 Austin Kearns/25 20.00
29 Rod Carew/25 40.00
31 Richie Sexson/50 15.00
33 Eddie Murray/25 50.00
36 Sean Casey/25 20.00
42 Mike Schmidt/25 70.00
43 Todd Helton/25 25.00
52 David Ortiz/50 35.00
53 Troy Glaus/25 20.00
54 Rickey Henderson/50 25.00
55 Craig Biggio/50 25.00
56 Brad Penny/45 15.00
57 Gary Carter/40 25.00
58 Andy Pettitte/25 25.00
59 Mark Prior/25 35.00
60 Kirby Puckett/25 50.00
64 Adrian Beltre/50 20.00
65 Andruw Jones/25 20.00
67 Frank Thomas/25 25.00
68 Victor Martinez/25 20.00
73 Cal Ripken Jr./50 75.00
76 Sammy Sosa/25 35.00
78 Tony Gwynn/50 40.00
79 Mike Piazza/25 50.00
80 Jeff Bagwell/50 25.00
82 Carlos Beltran/20 25.00
84 Robin Yount/25 40.00
88 Magglio Ordonez/25 20.00
89 Miguel Tejada/50 25.00
90 Mark Teixeira/50 20.00
91 Gary Carter/25 25.00
92 Ivan Rodriguez/25 25.00
94 Rickey Henderson/50 25.00
95 Curt Schilling/50 25.00

Tools of the Trade Swatch Quad

NM/M

Production 1-100
Prime Red: No Pricing
Production 1-10
Prime Black: No Pricing
Production One Set
3 Dale Murphy/50 20.00
4 Paul Molitor/25 30.00
7 Ivan Rodriguez/50 15.00
8 Carl Yastrzemski/25 50.00
9 Reggie Jackson/100 20.00
10 Hideo Nomo/75 15.00
11 Gary Sheffield/30 15.00
12 Roberto Alomar/50 15.00
13 Pedro Martinez/50 20.00
14 Ernie Banks/25 40.00
15 Tim Hudson/50 10.00
17 Lance Berkman/65 10.00
19 Larry Walker/100 10.00
20 Lou Brock/50 20.00
21 Roger Clemens/25 40.00
22 Paul LoDuca/100 10.00
23 Don Mattingly/50 40.00
24 Willie Mays/25 80.00
25 Rafael Palmeiro/100 10.00
26 Roy Oswalt/30 15.00
27 Vladimir Guerrero/50 20.00
29 Rod Carew/75 15.00
31 Richie Sexson/100 10.00
33 Eddie Murray/100 15.00
36 Sean Casey/75 10.00
39 Darryl Strawberry/50 15.00
41 Tom Seaver/35 25.00
42 Mike Schmidt/50 40.00
43 Todd Helton/100 12.00
45 Shawn Green/100 10.00
46 Mike Mussina/25 20.00
50 Carlos Delgado/50 10.00
52 David Ortiz/90 30.00
53 Troy Glaus/50 12.00
54 Rickey Henderson/100 25.00
55 Craig Biggio/100 10.00
56 Brad Penny/25 15.00
57 Gary Carter/50 15.00
58 Andy Pettitte/50 15.00
59 Mark Prior/50 20.00
60 Kirby Puckett/50 25.00
64 Adrian Beltre/50 10.00
65 Andruw Jones/100 10.00
66 Juan Gonzalez/30 20.00
67 Frank Thomas/50 25.00
68 Victor Martinez/50 10.00
70 Andre Dawson/25 15.00
72 Carlton Fisk/25 25.00
73 Cal Ripken Jr./100 50.00
74 Kenny Lofton/100 10.00
75 Barry Zito/50 10.00
76 Sammy Sosa/100 15.00
78 Tony Gwynn/100 20.00
79 Mike Piazza/100 20.00
80 Jeff Bagwell/100 10.00
83 Mark Grace/50 20.00
85 Albert Pujols/50 60.00
86 Dontrelle Willis/50 15.00
88 Magglio Ordonez/50 10.00
89 Miguel Tejada/100 15.00
90 Mark Teixeira/100 15.00
91 Gary Carter/90 15.00
92 Ivan Rodriguez/50 15.00
93 Jason Giambi/25 15.00
94 Rickey Henderson/100 15.00
95 Curt Schilling/100 15.00
100 Harmon Killebrew/25 40.00

Tools of the Swatch Single Jumbo

NM/M

Production 1-100
Prime Red: No Pricing
Production 1-25
Reverse: 1X-2X
Production 1-50
Prime Black: No Pricing
Production One Set
1 Ozzie Smith/25 30.00
2 Carlos Beltran Jsy/50 10.00
3 Dale Murphy Jsy/25 20.00
4 Paul Molitor Jsy/25 25.00
6 Stan Musial Pants/25 50.00
7 Ivan Rodriguez Jsy/100 10.00
10 Hideo Nomo Jsy/100 15.00
11 Gary Sheffield Jsy/25 15.00
12 Roberto Alomar Jsy/100 10.00
13 Pedro Martinez Jsy/50 12.00
15 Tim Hudson Jsy/100 10.00
17 Lance Berkman Jsy/75 8.00
19 Larry Walker Jsy/100 10.00
20 Lou Brock Jkt/50 20.00
21 Roger Clemens Jsy/50 30.00
23 Don Mattingly Jsy/25 40.00
25 Rafael Palmeiro Jsy/100 10.00
27 Vladimir Guerrero Jsy/50 15.00
29 Rod Carew Jsy/50 15.00
30 Nolan Ryan Jsy/25 50.00
31 Richie Sexson Jsy/100 10.00
33 Eddie Murray Jsy/50 20.00
35 Mike Mussina Jsy/50 12.00
36 Sean Casey Jsy/100 8.00
37 Juan Gonzalez Jsy/25 15.00
38 Curt Schilling Jsy/100 15.00
39 Darryl Strawberry Jsy/50 10.00
41 Tom Seaver Jsy/50 15.00
42 Mike Schmidt Jsy/25 40.00
43 Todd Helton Jsy/50 10.00
45 Shawn Green Jsy/100 8.00
47 Tom Glavine Jsy/100 10.00
49 Kerry Wood Jsy/50 10.00
51 R. John Jsy/25 20.00
52 David Ortiz Jsy/75 15.00
53 Troy Glaus Jsy/100 10.00
54 Rickey Henderson Jsy/25 15.00
55 Craig Biggio Jsy/75 10.00
56 Brad Penny Jsy/100 8.00
57 Gary Carter Jsy/25 15.00
58 Andy Pettitte Jsy/50 10.00
59 Mark Prior Jsy/50 15.00
60 Kirby Puckett Jsy/50 20.00
61 Willie McCovey Jsy/50 15.00
63 Greg Maddux Jsy/100 20.00
65 Andruw Jones Jsy/100 10.00
68 Victor Martinez Jsy/50 8.00
70 Andre Dawson Jsy/50 10.00
72 Carlton Fisk Jsy/100 10.00
73 Cal Ripken Jr. Jsy/100 35.00
74 Kenny Lofton Hat/25 10.00
75 Barry Zito Jsy/100 8.00
76 Sammy Sosa Jsy/100 15.00
77 Deion Sanders Jsy/25 20.00
78 Tony Gwynn Jsy/100 20.00
79 Mike Piazza Jsy/100 20.00
80 Jeff Bagwell Jsy/100 10.00
83 Mark Grace Jsy/50 15.00
84 Robin Yount Jsy/50 20.00
85 Albert Pujols Jsy/100 30.00
86 Dontrelle Willis Jsy/50 10.00
89 Miguel Tejada Jsy/100 12.00
90 Mark Teixeira Jsy/25 15.00
92 Ivan Rodriguez Jsy/100 10.00
93 Jason Giambi Jsy/25 10.00
94 Rickey Henderson Jsy/25 15.00
95 Curt Schilling Jsy/50 10.00
96 Bobby Doerr Pants/25 20.00
97 Chipper Jones Jsy/25 20.00
98 Eric Chavez Jsy/100 8.00
99 Johnny Bench Jsy/25 25.00
100 Harmon Killebrew Jsy/25 40.00

Tools of the Trade Swatch Six

NM/M

Production 1-50
Reverse: No Pricing
Production 1-10
Prime Red: No Pricing
Production 1-5
Prime Black: No Pricing
Production One Set
22 Paul LoDuca/50 20.00
31 Richie Sexson/50 20.00
52 David Ortiz/50 40.00
53 Troy Glaus/50 25.00
57 Gary Carter/25 35.00
59 Mark Prior/50 30.00
73 Cal Ripken Jr./50 85.00
76 Sammy Sosa/25 40.00
78 Tony Gwynn/50 40.00
79 Mike Piazza/50 40.00
80 Jeff Bagwell/50 25.00
90 Mark Teixeira/50 25.00
92 Ivan Rodriguez/25 30.00
94 Rickey Henderson/50 30.00

Tools of the Trade Swatch Triple

NM/M

Production 1-25
Prime Red: No Pricing
Production 1-25

Prime Black: No Pricing
Production 1-15

1	Ozzie Smith/10	
2	Carlos Beltran/25	15.00
3	Dale Murphy/25	15.00
4	Paul Molitor/25	20.00
5	George Brett/25	35.00
6	Stan Musial/25	40.00
7	Ivan Rodriguez/25	10.00
9	Reggie Jackson/25	15.00
10	Hideo Nomo/25	20.00
12	Roberto Alomar/25	10.00
13	Pedro Martinez/25	15.00
15	Tim Hudson/25	10.00
17	Lance Berkman/25	10.00
19	Larry Walker/25	10.00
21	Roger Clemens/25	30.00
22	Paul LoDuca/25	10.00
23	Don Mattingly/25	30.00
25	Rafael Palmeiro/25	15.00
27	Vladimir Guerrero/25	15.00
29	Rod Carew/25	15.00
30	Nolan Ryan/25	40.00
31	Richie Sexson/25	10.00
33	Eddie Murray/25	20.00
34	Nolan Ryan/25	40.00
36	Sean Casey/25	10.00
37	Juan Gonzalez/25	10.00
38	Curt Schilling/25	15.00
42	Mike Schmidt/25	30.00
43	Todd Helton/25	12.00
45	Shawn Green/25	10.00
47	Tom Glavine/25	10.00
49	Kerry Wood/25	15.00
50	Carlos Delgado/25	10.00
51	R. John/25	15.00
52	David Ortiz/25	15.00
53	Troy Glaus/25	10.00
54	Rickey Henderson/25	15.00
55	Craig Biggio/25	12.00
56	Brad Penny/25	10.00
57	Gary Carter/25	15.00
58	Andy Pettitte/25	10.00
59	Mark Prior/25	15.00
60	Kirby Puckett/25	20.00
63	Greg Maddux/25	25.00
64	Adrian Beltre/25	10.00
65	Andruw Jones/25	12.00
67	Frank Thomas/25	15.00
68	Victor Martinez/25	10.00
70	Andre Dawson/25	12.00
72	Carlton Fisk/25	15.00
73	Cal Ripken Jr./25	40.00
74	Kenny Lofton/25	10.00
75	Barry Zito/25	10.00
76	Sammy Sosa/25	15.00
77	Deion Sanders/25	20.00
78	Tony Gwynn/25	20.00
79	Mike Piazza/25	20.00
80	Jeff Bagwell/25	15.00
81	Manny Ramirez/25	15.00
83	Mark Grace/25	15.00
84	Robin Yount/25	20.00
85	Albert Pujols/25	40.00
86	Dontrelle Willis/25	15.00
88	Magglio Ordonez/25	10.00
89	Miguel Tejada/25	15.00
90	Mark Teixeira/25	12.00
91	Gary Carter/25	15.00
92	Ivan Rodriguez/25	10.00
93	Jason Giambi/25	10.00
94	Rickey Henderson/25	15.00
95	Curt Schilling/25	15.00
96	Bobby Doerr/25	15.00
97	Chipper Jones/25	15.00
98	Eric Chavez/25	10.00
99	Johnny Bench/25	20.00
100	Harmon Killebrew/25	30.00

2005 PLAYOFF PRESTIGE

		NM/M
Complete Set (200):		35.00
Common Player:		.25
Hobby pack (8):		3.00
Hobby box (24):		65.00
1	Rafael Furcal	.25
2	Derek Jeter	2.00
3	Edgar Renteria	.40
4	Jeff Bagwell	.50
5	Nomar Garciaparra	1.25
6	Melvin Mora	.25
7	Craig Biggio	.40
8	Brad Penny	.25
9	Hank Blalock	.50
10	Vernon Wells	.25
11	Gary Sheffield	.50
12	Jeff Kent	.25
13	Carl Crawford	.25
14	Paul Konerko	.25
15	Carlos Beltran	.50
16	Garret Anderson	.40
17	Todd Helton	.50
18	Javy Lopez	.40
19	Mike Lowell	.25
20	Robb Quinlan	.25
21	Andy Pettitte	.40
22	Roger Clemens	2.00
23	Mark Teixeira	.50
24	Miguel Cabrera	.75
25	Andruw Jones	.40
26	Josh Beckett	.40
27	Scott Rolen	.75
28	J.J. Putz	.25
29	Adrian Beltre	.50
30	Magglio Ordonez	.25
31	Mike Piazza	1.00
32	Danny Graves	.25
33	Larry Walker	.40
34	Kerry Wood	.75
35	Mike Mussina	.50
36	Joe Nathan	.25
37	Chone Figgins	.25
38	Curt Schilling	.75
39	Brett Myers	.25
40	Jae Weong Seo	.25
41	Danny Kolb	.25
42	Mariano Rivera	.50
43	Francisco Cordero	.25
44	Adam Dunn	.50
45	Pedro Martinez	.75
46	Frank Thomas	.50
47	Tom Glavine	.40
48	Torii Hunter	.40
49	Ben Sheets	.40
50	Shawn Green	.25
51	Randy Johnson	.75
52	C.C. Sabathia	.25
53	Bobby Abreu	.40
54	Octavio Dotel	.25
55	Hideki Matsui	1.50
56	Mark Buehrle	.25
57	Johan Santana	.50
58	Brandon Inge	.25
59	Dewon Brazelton	.25
60	Ryan Wagner	.25
61	Kevin Brown	.25
62	Laynce Nix	.25
63	Jason Bay	.40
64	J.D. Drew	.40
65	Jacque Jones	.25
66	Jason Schmidt	.40
67	Joe Kennedy	.25
68	Miguel Tejada	.50
69	Hideo Nomo	.40
70	Michael Young	.25
71	Lyle Overbay	.25
72	Omar Vizquel	.25
73	Johnny Estrada	.25
74	Khalil Greene	.40
75	Barry Zito	.25
76	Wilson Valdez	.25
77	Nick Green	.25
78	Bucky Jacobsen	.25
79	Keith Foulke	.25
80	Sean Burroughs	.25
81	Carlos Zambrano	.40
82	Orlando Cabrera	.25
83	Shigetoshi Hasegawa	.25
84	Troy Glaus	.40
85	Mike Sweeney	.25
86	Jason Giambi	.25
87	Derrek Lee	.40
88	Carlos Delgado	.40
89	Kazuo Matsui	.25
90	Lew Ford	.25
91	Akinori Otsuka	.25
92	Bobby Crosby	.25
93	Jose Reyes	.40
94	Jose Vidro	.25
95	Shingo Takatsu	.25
96	Sean Casey	.25
97	Tim Olson	.25
98	Jeff Suppan	.25
99	Rafael Palmeiro	.50
100	Esteban Loaiza	.25
101	Brian Roberts	.25
102	Jack Wilson	.25
103	Eric Chavez	.40
104	Eric Milton	.25
105	Albert Pujols	2.00
106	Jake Peavy	.25
107	Ivan Rodriguez	.50
108	Chad Cordero	.25
109	Jody Gerut	.25
110	Chipper Jones	.75
111	Barry Larkin	.40
112	Alfonso Soriano	.75
113	Alex Rodriguez	1.50
114	Paul LoDuca	.25
115	Jim Edmonds	.40
116	Aramis Ramirez	.40
117	Lance Berkman	.40
118	Johnny Damon	.75
119	Aubrey Huff	.25
120	Mark Mulder	.40
121	Sammy Sosa	1.50
122	Mark Prior	.75
123	Shannon Stewart	.25
124	Manny Ramirez	.75
125	Jim Thome	.75
126	Doug Devore	.25
127	Vladimir Guerrero	.75
128	Ken Harvey	.25
129	Jacob Cruz	.25
130	Ken Griffey Jr.	1.00
131	Greg Maddux	1.00
132	Derek Lowe	.25
133	Craig Monroe	.25
134	David Ortiz	.75
135	Dontrelle Willis	.40
136	Tom Gordon	.25
137	David Dellucci	.25
138	Vance Wilson	.25
139	Milton Bradley	.25
140	Ichiro Suzuki	1.50
141	Victor Martinez	.40
142	Wade Miller	.25
143	Francisco Rodriguez	.25
144	Roy Oswalt	.40
145	Carlos Lee	.25
146	Kazuhisa Ishii	.25
147	Tim Hudson	.40
148	Travis Hafner	.25
149	Jermaine Dye	.25
150	Steve Finley	.25
151	*Justin Verlander*	1.50
152	Yadier Molina	.25
153	Andy Green	.25
154	Nick Swisher	.25
155	Clint Nageotte	.25
156	Grady Sizemore	.25
157	Gavin Floyd	.25
158	Josh Kroeger	.25
159	Russ Adams	.25
160	Jeff Baker	.25
161	Dioner Navarro	.25
162	Shawn Hill	.25
163	Ryan Howard	.40
164	Scott Proctor	.25
165	Jason Kubel	.25
166	Jose Lopez	.25
167	Ryan Church	.25
168	Yhency Brazoban	.25
169	Jeff Francis	.25
170	Angel Guzman	.25
171	John Van Benschoten	.25
172	Adrian Gonzalez	.25
173	Casey Kotchman	.25
174	David Wright	.75
175	B.J. Upton	.50
176	Dallas McPherson	.50
177	Rene Rivera	.25
178	Denny Bautista	.25
179	Logan Kensing	.25
180	Matt Peterson	.25
181	Jeremy Reed	.25
182	Jairo Garcia	.25
183	Val Majewski	.25
184	Victor Diaz	.25
185	David Krynzel	.25
186	Ron Cey	.25
187	Bill Madlock	.25
188	Dave Stewart	.25
189	Billy Ripken	.25
190	Gary Carter	.50
191	Darryl Strawberry	.25
192	Dave Parker	.25
193	Ron Guidry	.25
194	Gaylord Perry	.25
195	Fred Lynn	.25
196	Jack Morris	.25
197	Steve Garvey	.25
198	Andre Dawson	.50
199	Nolan Ryan	2.50
200	Paul Molitor	.75

Red Foil

Red Foil: 8-15X
Production 25 sets

Xtra Bases Black

Black: 8-15X
Production 25 sets

Xtra Bases Green

Green: 5-10X
Production 50 sets

Xtra Bases Purple

Purple: 4-8X
Production 100 sets

Xtra Bases Red

Red: 3-6X
Production 150 sets

Autographs

		NM/M
Common Autograph:		8.00
20	Robb Quinlan	8.00
28	J.J. Putz	8.00
58	Brandon Inge SP	15.00
67	Joe Kennedy	8.00
76	Wilson Valdez	8.00
77	Nick Green	8.00
78	Bucky Jacobsen	10.00
97	Tim Olson	10.00
98	Jeff Suppan SP	15.00
126	Doug Devore	8.00
129	Jacob Cruz	8.00
133	Craig Monroe	10.00
138	Vance Wilson	8.00
153	Andy Green	8.00
164	Scott Proctor	8.00

Changing Stripes

		NM/M
Complete Set (25):		25.00
Common Player:		.75
Inserted 1:8		
Foil:		2X-3X
Production 100 Sets		
Holo-Foil:		3X-6X
Production 25 Sets		
1	Ivan Rodriguez	1.00
2	Roger Clemens	4.00
3	Curt Schilling	1.50
4	Alex Rodriguez	4.00
5	Greg Maddux	2.00
6	Juan Gonzalez	.75
7	Pedro Martinez	1.50
8	Roberto Alomar	.75
9	Randy Johnson	1.50
10	Ken Griffey Jr.	2.00
11	Carlos Beltran	1.00
12	Andy Pettitte	1.00
13	Tom Glavine	.75
14	Miguel Tejada	1.50
15	Alfonso Soriano	1.50
16	Shannon Stewart	.75
17	Nomar Garciaparra	2.00
18	Jeff Kent	.75
19	David Ortiz	1.50
20	Sean Casey	.75
21	Rickey Henderson	1.00
22	Carlton Fisk	1.00
23	Phil Niekro	.75
24	Dale Murphy	1.00
25	Reggie Jackson	1.50

Changing Stripes Mat. Dual Jersey

		NM/M
Production 12-250		
1	Ivan Rodriguez/250	10.00
2	Roger Clemens/50	20.00
3	Curt Schilling/250	12.00
6	Juan Gonzalez/250	8.00
7	Pedro Martinez/100	15.00
8	Roberto Alomar/250	10.00
9	Randy Johnson/100	15.00
11	Carlos Beltran/100	15.00
12	Andy Pettitte/250	10.00
13	Tom Glavine/50	15.00
14	Miguel Tejada/250	10.00
15	Alfonso Soriano/100	10.00
16	Shannon Stewart/100	8.00
18	Jeff Kent/12	
19	David Ortiz/100	15.00
20	Sean Casey/50	10.00
21	Rickey Henderson/250	15.00
22	Carlton Fisk/250	15.00
23	Phil Niekro/250	8.00
24	Dale Murphy/250	15.00
25	Reggie Jackson/100	15.00

Connections

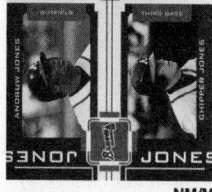

		NM/M
Complete Set (25):		40.00
Common Duo:		1.50
Inserted 1:8		
Foil:		2X-3X
Production 100 Sets		
Holo-Foil:		3X-6X
Production 25 Sets		
1	Josh Beckett, Dontrelle Willis	1.50
2	Andruw Jones, Chipper Jones	2.00
3	Kazuo Matsui, Jose Reyes	1.50
4	Bobby Abreu, Jim Thome	2.00
5	Jeff Bagwell, Lance Berkman	2.00
6	Roger Clemens, Roy Oswalt	4.00
7	Scott Rolen, Larry Walker	2.00
8	Albert Pujols, Jim Edmonds	4.00
9	Greg Maddux, Sammy Sosa	2.50
10	Mark Prior, Nomar Garciaparra	2.50
11	Barry Larkin, Sean Casey	1.50
12	Adrian Beltre, Shawn Green	1.50
13	Alex Rodriguez, Derek Jeter	6.00
14	Manny Ramirez, Jason Varitek	3.00
15	Miguel Tejada, Javy Lopez	2.00
16	B.J. Upton, Carl Crawford	1.50
17	Frank Thomas, Paul Konerko	2.00
18	Joe Mauer, Justin Morneau	2.00
19	Victor Martinez, Jody Gerut	1.50
20	Bobby Crosby, Barry Zito	1.50
21	Mark Teixeira, Hank Blalock	2.00
22	Reggie Jackson, Rod Carew	2.00
23	Rickey Henderson, Tony Gwynn	2.50
24	Tom Seaver, Johnny Bench	3.00
25	Don Mattingly, Dave Righetti	4.00

Connections Material Dual Bat

		NM/M
Production 25-250		
2	Andruw Jones, Chipper Jones/250	10.00
3	Kazuo Matsui, Jose Reyes/100	10.00
4	Bobby Abreu, Jim Thome/100	12.00
5	Jeff Bagwell, Lance Berkman/250	10.00
6	Roger Clemens, Roy Oswalt/250	15.00
10	Mark Prior, Nomar Garciaparra/100	15.00
11	Barry Larkin, Sean Casey/100	10.00
12	Shawn Green, Adrian Beltre/250	5.00
14	Jason Varitek, Manny Ramirez/100	15.00
15	Miguel Tejada, Javy Lopez/100	10.00
17	Frank Thomas, Paul Konerko/100	10.00
19	Victor Martinez, Jody Gerut/25	12.00
21	Mark Teixeira, Hank Blalock/100	10.00
22	Reggie Jackson, Rod Carew/250	10.00
23	Tony Gwynn, Rickey Henderson/250	15.00
24	Tom Seaver, Johnny Bench/250	15.00

Connections Material Dual Jersey

		NM/M
Production 10-250		
Prime:		1X-2X
Production 10-25		
No pricing 20 or less		
1	Josh Beckett, Dontrelle Willis/250	8.00
2	Andruw Jones, Chipper Jones/250	10.00
3	Kazuo Matsui, Jose Reyes/100	10.00
4	Bobby Abreu, Jim Thome/250	10.00
5	Jeff Bagwell, Lance Berkman/250	10.00
6	Roger Clemens, Roy Oswalt/250	15.00
8	Albert Pujols, Jim Edmonds/250	25.00
11	Barry Larkin, Sean Casey/50	15.00
12	Shawn Green, Adrian Beltre/250	8.00
14	Jason Varitek, Manny Ramirez/50	20.00
15	Miguel Tejada, Javy Lopez/50	12.00
17	Frank Thomas Pants, Paul Konerko/250	10.00
19	Victor Martinez, Jody Gerut/10	
20	Bobby Crosby, Barry Zito/250	10.00
21	Mark Teixeira, Hank Blalock/100	10.00
22	Reggie Jackson, Rod Carew Jkt/250	12.00
23	Rickey Henderson, Tony Gwynn/250	15.00
24	Tom Seaver, Johnny Bench Pants/100	15.00
25	Don Mattingly, Dave Righetti/250	20.00

Diamond Heritage

		NM/M
Complete Set (15):		20.00
Common Player:		.75
Inserted 1:12		
1	Pedro Martinez	1.50
2	Mark Teixeira	1.00
3	Lance Berkman	.75
4	Vladimir Guerrero	1.50
5	Albert Pujols	4.00

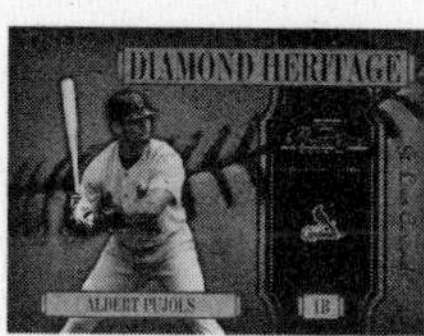

6	Roger Clemens	4.00
7	Manny Ramirez	1.50
8	Mike Piazza	2.00
9	Jim Thome	1.50
10	Mark Prior	1.50
11	Gary Sheffield	.75
12	Sammy Sosa	2.50
13	Tim Hudson	.75
14	Hideki Matsui	3.00
15	Jim Edmonds	.75

Diamond Heritage Matieral Bat

		NM/M
Production 100 Sets		
1	Pedro Martinez	10.00
2	Mark Teixeira	10.00
3	Lance Berkman	5.00
4	Vladimir Guerrero	10.00
6	Roger Clemens	15.00
7	Manny Ramirez	10.00
8	Mike Piazza	10.00
9	Jim Thome	10.00
10	Mark Prior	10.00
11	Gary Sheffield	8.00
12	Sammy Sosa	10.00
13	Tim Hudson	5.00
14	Hideki Matsui	25.00
15	Jim Edmonds	8.00

Diamond Heritage Material Jersey

		NM/M
Production 100 Sets		
1	Pedro Martinez	10.00
2	Mark Teixeira	10.00
3	Lance Berkman	5.00
4	Vladimir Guerrero	10.00
5	Albert Pujols	25.00
6	Roger Clemens	15.00
7	Manny Ramirez	10.00
8	Mike Piazza	10.00
9	Jim Thome	10.00
10	Mark Prior	10.00
11	Gary Sheffield	8.00
12	Sammy Sosa	10.00
13	Tim Hudson	5.00
14	Hideki Matsui Pants	25.00
15	Jim Edmonds	8.00

Fans of the Game

		NM/M
Inserted 1:24		
1	Tony Hawk	3.00
2	Tia Carrere	2.00
3	Mathew Modine	2.00

Fans of the Game Signature Gold

		NM/M
Production 100 Sets		
Platinum:		1X
Production 50 Sets		
1	Tony Hawk	75.00
2	Tia Carrere	85.00
3	Mathew Modine	40.00

Fans of the Game Signature Silver

		NM/M
Common Autograph:		40.00
1	Tony Hawk	75.00
2	Tia Carrere	85.00
3	Mathew Modine	40.00

League Leaders Double

		NM/M
Complete Set (5):		15.00

Inserted 1:39		
Foil:		2X-3X
Production 100 Sets		
Holo-Foil:		3X-6X
Production 25 Sets		
1	Tim Hudson, Roy Oswalt	2.00
2	Ivan Rodriguez, Todd Helton	3.00
3	Mark Teixeira, Jim Edmonds	2.00
4	Nolan Ryan, Roger Clemens	8.00
5	Sammy Sosa, Troy Glaus	3.00

League Leader Double Material Bat

		NM/M
Production 250 Sets		
1	Tim Hudson, Roy Oswalt	8.00
2	Ivan Rodriguez, Todd Helton	15.00
3	Mark Teixeira, Jim Edmonds	10.00
4	Nolan Ryan, Roger Clemens	25.00
5	Sammy Sosa, Troy Glaus	15.00

League Leaders Double Mat. Jersey

		NM/M
Production 50-250		
1	Tim Hudson, Roy Oswalt/100	10.00
2	Ivan Rodriguez, Todd Helton/50	15.00
3	Mark Teixeira, Jim Edmonds/250	15.00
4	Nolan Ryan, Roger Clemens/250	25.00
5	Sammy Sosa, Troy Glaus/250	15.00

League Leaders Quad

		NM/M
Inserted 1:39		
Foil:		1X-2X
Production 100 Sets		
Holo-Foil:		3X-5X
Production 25 Sets		
1	Wade Boggs, Paul Molitor, Alan Trammell, Kirby Puckett	4.00
2	Dale Murphy, Mike Schmidt, Gary Carter, Darryl Strawberry	6.00
3	Jose Canseco, Kirby Puckett, Will Clark, Darryl Strawberry	4.00
4	Pedro Martinez, Kevin Brown, Randy Johnson, Roger Clemens	6.00
5	Don Mattingly, Dave Parker, Eddie Murray, Dale Murphy	4.00

League Leaders Quad Material Bat

		NM/M
Production 100 Sets		
2	Dale Murphy, Mike Schmidt, Gary Carter, Darryl Strawberry	40.00
4	Pedro Martinez, Kevin Brown, Randy Johnson, Roger Clemens	50.00
5	Don Mattingly, Dave Parker, Eddie Murray, Dale Murphy	50.00

League Leaders Quad Mat. Jersey

		NM/M
Production 100 Sets		
1	Wade Boggs, Paul Molitor, Alan Trammell, Kirby Puckett	40.00

2 Dale Murphy, Mike Schmidt, Gary Carter, Darryl Strawberry 40.00
3 Jose Canseco, Kirby Puckett, Will Clark, Darryl Strawberry 40.00
4 Pedro Martinez, Kevin Brown, Randy Johnson, Roger Clemens 50.00
5 Don Mattingly, Dave Parker, Eddie Murray, Dale Murphy 50.00

League Leaders Single

NM/M
Complete Set (10): 25.00
Inserted 1:21
Foil: 2X-4X
Production 100 Sets
Holo-Foil: 4X-8X
Production 25 Sets
1 Gary Sheffield 2.00
2 Ben Sheets 2.00
3 Adrian Beltre 2.00
4 Scott Rolen 3.00
5 George Brett 4.00
6 Johan Santana 3.00
7 Manny Ramirez 3.00
8 Cal Ripken Jr. 8.00
9 Carlos Zambrano 2.00
10 Tony Gwynn 4.00

League Leader Single Material Bat

NM/M
Production 250 Sets
1 Gary Sheffield 8.00
2 Ben Sheets 5.00
3 Adrian Beltre 5.00
5 George Brett 12.00
7 Manny Ramirez 10.00
8 Cal Ripken Jr. 25.00
10 Tony Gwynn 8.00

League Leaders Single Material Jersey

NM/M
Production 25-250
1 Gary Sheffield/250 8.00
2 Ben Sheets/250 5.00
3 Adrian Beltre/50 8.00
4 Scott Rolen/250 8.00
5 George Brett/250 15.00
6 Johan Santana/25 20.00
7 Manny Ramirez/250 8.00
8 Cal Ripken Jr./250 25.00
9 Carlos Zambrano/250 5.00
10 Tony Gwynn/250 8.00

Playoff Champions Combo Wild Card

NM/M
Inserted 1:391
Division Combo: .75X-1X
League Combo: .75X-1X
World Series Combo: .75X-1X
Redemption Deadline 4-15-06
1 Andruw Jones, Johnny Estrada, Chipper Jones 10.00
2 Miguel Cabrera, Josh Beckett, Dontrelle Willis 10.00
3 Chad Cordero, Nick Johnson, Brad Wilkerson 5.00
4 Jim Thome, Bobby Abreu, Chase Utley 10.00
5 Mike Piazza, Kazuo Matsui, David Wright 10.00
6 Albert Pujols, Scott Rolen, Jim Edmonds 15.00
7 Kerry Wood, Mark Prior, Carlos Zambrano 10.00
8 Ben Sheets, Geoff Jenkins, Lyle Overbay 5.00
9 Kip Wells, Jack Wilson, Jason Bay 5.00
10 Austin Kearns, Adam Dunn, Ken Griffey Jr. 10.00
11 Roy Oswalt, Lance Berkman, Jeff Bagwell 10.00
12 Jason Jennings, Matt Holliday, Todd Helton 10.00
13 Eric Gagne, Jayson Werth, Milton Bradley 10.00
14 Alex Cintron, Brandon Webb, Luis Gonzalez 5.00
15 Jason Schmidt, Edgardo Alfonzo, Kirk Rueter 5.00
16 Khalil Greene, Jake Peavy, Trevor Hoffman 10.00
17 Manny Ramirez, Curt Schilling, David Ortiz 15.00
18 Miguel Tejada, Melvin Mora, Javy Lopez 8.00
19 Roy Halladay, Alexis Rios, Gabe Gross 5.00
20 Alex Rodriguez, Derek Jeter, Hideki Matsui 20.00
21 B.J. Upton, Scott Kazmir, Carl Crawford 10.00
22 Frank Thomas, Shingo Takatsu, Aaron Rowand 8.00
23 Victor Martinez, C.C. Sabathia, Travis Hafner 5.00
24 Torii Hunter, Johan Santana, Justin Morneau 10.00
25 Zack Greinke, Mike Sweeney, Ken Harvey 5.00
26 Ivan Rodriguez, Jeremy Bonderman, Carlos Guillen 8.00
27 Rich Harden, Bobby Crosby, Barry Zito 5.00
28 Bret Boone, Ichiro Suzuki, Jeremy Reed 12.00
29 Michael Young, Mark Teixeira, Hank Blalock 10.00
30 Vladimir Guerrero, Darin Erstad, Garret Anderson 10.00

Prestigious Pros Blue

NM/M
Common Player: 1.00
Production 900 Sets
Black: No Pricing
Production 10 Sets
Bronze: 2X-3X
Production 100 Sets
Gold: 2X-4X
Production 50 Sets
Green: 1X-2X
Production 350 Sets
Orange: 1X-1.5X
Production 500 Sets
Platinum: 3X-5X
Production 25 Sets
Purple: 1X-2X
Production 200 Sets
Red: 1X
Production 70 Sets
Silver: 2X-3X
Production 75 Sets
1 Ozzie Smith 3.00
2 Derek Jeter 6.00
3 Eric Chavez 1.00
4 Paul Molitor 2.00
5 Jeff Bagwell 1.50
6 Melvin Mora 1.00
7 Craig Biggio 1.00
8 Cal Ripken Jr. 8.00
9 Hank Blalock 1.50
10 Miguel Tejada 2.00
11 Jacque Jones 1.00
12 Alfonso Soriano 2.00
13 Omar Vizquel 1.00
14 Paul Konerko 1.00
15 Tim Hudson 1.00
16 Garret Anderson 1.00
17 Lance Berkman 1.00
18 Randy Johnson 2.00
19 Robin Yount 3.00
20 Mark Mulder 1.00
21 Sean Casey 1.00
22 Jim Palmer 1.50
23 Don Mattingly 5.00
24 Manny Ramirez 2.00
25 Rafael Palmeiro 1.50
26 Vernon Wells 1.00
27 Vladimir Guerrero 2.00
28 Ken Harvey 1.00
29 Rod Carew 1.50
30 Nolan Ryan 8.00
31 Mike Piazza 3.00
32 Steve Carlton 1.50
33 Miguel Cabrera 2.00
34 Kerry Wood 2.00
35 Mike Mussina 1.00
36 Gaylord Perry 1.00
37 Gary Sheffield 1.50
38 Curt Schilling 2.00
39 Don Sutton 1.00
40 Roger Clemens 6.00
41 Victor Martinez 1.00
42 Jason Giambi 1.00
43 Dennis Eckersley 1.00
44 Adam Dunn 1.50
45 Pedro Martinez 2.00
46 Tony Perez 1.00
47 Tom Glavine 1.00
48 Torii Hunter 1.00
49 Hideo Nomo 1.00
50 Scott Rolen 2.00
51 Ichiro Suzuki 5.00
52 C.C. Sabathia 1.00
53 George Brett 5.00
54 David Ortiz 2.00
55 Hideki Matsui 4.00
56 Nomar Garciaparra 4.00
57 Johan Santana 2.00
58 Phil Niekro 1.00
59 Dontrelle Willis 1.00
60 Magglio Ordonez 1.00
61 Livan Hernandez 1.00
62 Edgar Renteria 1.00
63 Todd Helton 1.50
64 Carlos Beltran 1.50
65 Sammy Sosa 4.00
66 Albert Pujols 6.00
67 Mike Lowell 1.00
68 Mark Prior 2.00
69 Ivan Rodriguez 1.50
70 Jake Peavy 1.00
71 Jim Thome 2.00
72 Mark Teixeira 1.50
73 Shawn Green 1.00
74 Rollie Fingers 1.00
75 Barry Zito 1.00
76 Jose Vidro 1.00
77 Ben Sheets 1.00
78 Roy Halladay 1.00
79 Frank Thomas 1.50
80 Chipper Jones 2.00
81 Jason Bay 1.00
82 Tony Gwynn 2.00
83 Shannon Stewart 1.00
84 Carl Crawford 1.00
85 Andruw Jones 1.00
86 Greg Maddux 3.00
87 Barry Larkin 1.00
88 Alex Rodriguez 5.00
89 Rickey Henderson 1.50
90 Troy Glaus 1.00
91 Roy Oswalt 1.00
92 Michael Young 1.00
93 Carlos Lee 1.00
94 Jim Edmonds 1.00
95 Fergie Jenkins 1.00
96 Paul LoDuca 1.00
97 Aubrey Huff 1.00
98 Ken Griffey Jr. 3.00
99 Carlos Delgado 1.50
100 Mike Schmidt 5.00

Prestigious Pros Material Jersey Gold

NM/M
Production 5-50
No pricing 20 or less
Platinum Patch: No Pricing
Production 5-10
1 Ozzie Smith/50 25.00
3 Eric Chavez/25 10.00
4 Paul Molitor/50 12.00
5 Jeff Bagwell/50 10.00
6 Melvin Mora/25 10.00
7 Craig Biggio/25 15.00
8 Cal Ripken Jr./50 40.00
10 Miguel Tejada/25 12.00
13 Omar Vizquel/25 15.00
14 Paul Konerko/25 8.00
15 Tim Hudson/25 10.00
17 Lance Berkman/50 8.00
18 Randy Johnson/25 20.00
19 Robin Yount/50 15.00
20 Mark Mulder/20 10.00
21 Sean Casey/25 10.00
22 Jim Palmer/50 8.00
23 Don Mattingly/50 25.00
26 Vernon Wells/25 8.00
27 Vladimir Guerrero/25 20.00
28 Ken Harvey/25 8.00
29 Rod Carew/50 10.00
30 Nolan Ryan/50 35.00
31 Mike Piazza/25 20.00
32 Steve Carlton/50 8.00
34 Kerry Wood/25 15.00
35 Mike Mussina/25 15.00
36 Gaylord Perry/50 8.00
37 Gary Sheffield/25 10.00
38 Curt Schilling/25 15.00
39 Don Sutton/50 8.00
40 Roger Clemens/25 25.00
41 Victor Martinez/25 10.00
42 Jason Giambi/25 10.00
43 Dennis Eckersley/50 10.00
45 Pedro Martinez/25 15.00
46 Tony Perez/50 8.00
49 Hideo Nomo/25 25.00
50 Scott Rolen/25 20.00
52 C.C. Sabathia/25 10.00
53 George Brett/50 25.00
55 Hideki Matsui/25 40.00
58 Phil Niekro/50 8.00
59 Dontrelle Willis/25 10.00
60 Magglio Ordonez/25 8.00
61 Livan Hernandez/25 8.00
62 Edgar Renteria/25 10.00
63 Todd Helton/25 15.00
65 Sammy Sosa/25 20.00
66 Albert Pujols/25 35.00
68 Mark Prior/25 15.00
71 Jim Thome/25 15.00
72 Mark Teixeira/25 12.00
73 Shawn Green/25 10.00
74 Rollie Fingers/50 8.00
77 Ben Sheets/25 10.00
78 Roy Halladay/25 10.00
79 Frank Thomas/25 15.00
80 Chipper Jones/25 15.00
81 Jason Bay/25 10.00
82 Tony Gwynn/50 15.00
84 Carl Crawford/25 10.00
85 Andruw Jones/25 10.00
86 Greg Maddux/25 20.00
87 Barry Larkin/25 12.00
89 Rickey Henderson/50 15.00
90 Troy Glaus/25 10.00
92 Michael Young/25 10.00
93 Carlos Lee/25 10.00
94 Jim Edmonds/25 12.00
95 Fergie Jenkins/50 10.00
97 Aubrey Huff/25 10.00
99 Carlos Delgado/25 10.00
100 Mike Schmidt/50 25.00

Stars of MLB

NM/M
Complete Set (15): 20.00
Common Player: 1.00
Inserted 1:12
Foil: 2X-4X
Production 100 Sets
Holo-Foil: 4X-8X
Production 25 Sets
1 Randy Johnson 3.00
2 Adrian Beltre 1.00
3 Eric Chavez 1.00
4 Mike Mussina 1.50
5 Todd Helton 2.00
6 Curt Schilling 2.00
7 Miguel Cabrera 3.00
8 Kerry Wood 2.50
9 David Ortiz 3.00
10 Michael Young 1.00
11 Mark Mulder 1.00
12 Victor Martinez 1.00
13 Johan Santana 2.00
14 Scott Rolen 3.00
15 Carlos Beltran 2.00

Stars of MLB Material Bat

NM/M
Production 50-100
1 Randy Johnson/100 10.00
2 Adrian Beltre/100 5.00
3 Eric Chavez/100 5.00
4 Mike Mussina/100 8.00
5 Todd Helton/100 8.00
6 Curt Schilling/100 10.00
7 Miguel Cabrera/100 8.00
8 Kerry Wood/100 10.00
9 David Ortiz/100 10.00
10 Michael Young/100 5.00
11 Mark Mulder/50 8.00
14 Scott Rolen/100 10.00
15 Carlos Beltran/100 8.00

Stars of MLB Material Jersey

NM/M
Production 100 Sets
Prime: 1X-2X
Production 25 Sets
1 Randy Johnson Pants 10.00
2 Adrian Beltre 5.00
3 Eric Chavez 5.00
4 Mike Mussina 8.00
5 Todd Helton 8.00
6 Curt Schilling 10.00
7 Miguel Cabrera 10.00
8 Kerry Wood 10.00
9 David Ortiz 12.00
10 Michael Young 5.00
11 Mark Mulder 5.00
12 Victor Martinez 5.00
13 Johan Santana 10.00
14 Scott Rolen 10.00
15 Carlos Beltran 8.00

Stars of MLB Sign. Material Bat

NM/M
Production 10-50
2 Adrian Beltre/50 25.00
3 Eric Chavez/50 20.00
8 Kerry Wood/25 50.00
9 David Ortiz/50 40.00
10 Michael Young/50 25.00
15 Carlos Beltran/25 50.00

Stars of MLB Sig. Material Jersey

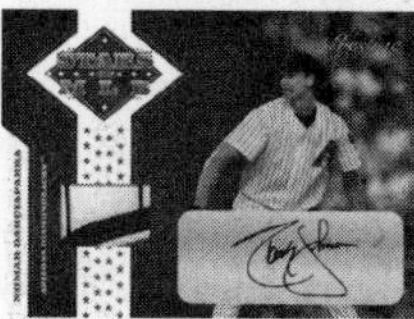

NM/M
Production 10-50
Prime: No Pricing
Production 5 Sets
2 Adrian Beltre/50 25.00
3 Eric Chavez/50 20.00
8 Kerry Wood/25 50.00
9 David Ortiz/50 40.00
10 Michael Young/50 25.00
12 Victor Martinez/50 20.00
13 Johan Santana/50 50.00
15 Carlos Beltran/25 50.00

Prestigious Pros Material Bat Silver

NM/M
Production 5-50
No pricing 20 or less
1 Ozzie Smith/50 25.00
3 Eric Chavez/25 10.00
4 Paul Molitor/50 12.00
5 Jeff Bagwell/50 10.00
7 Craig Biggio/25 15.00
8 Cal Ripken Jr./50 40.00
9 Hank Blalock/25 12.00
10 Miguel Tejada/25 12.00
14 Paul Konerko/25 8.00
15 Tim Hudson/25 10.00
16 Garret Anderson/25 10.00
17 Lance Berkman/50 8.00
18 Randy Johnson/25 20.00
19 Robin Yount/50 15.00
21 Sean Casey/25 10.00
23 Don Mattingly/50 25.00
25 Rafael Palmeiro/25 15.00
27 Vladimir Guerrero/25 20.00
28 Ken Harvey/25 8.00
29 Rod Carew/50 10.00
30 Nolan Ryan/50 35.00
31 Mike Piazza/25 20.00
32 Steve Carlton/50 8.00
34 Kerry Wood/25 15.00
35 Mike Mussina/25 15.00
37 Gary Sheffield/25 10.00
38 Curt Schilling/25 15.00
40 Roger Clemens/25 25.00
41 Victor Martinez/25 10.00
42 Jason Giambi/25 10.00
44 Adam Dunn/25 12.00
45 Pedro Martinez/25 15.00
46 Tony Perez/50 8.00
47 Tom Glavine/25 12.00
48 Torii Hunter/50 8.00
49 Hideo Nomo/25 25.00
50 Scott Rolen/25 20.00
53 George Brett/50 25.00
54 David Ortiz/50 12.00
55 Hideki Matsui/50 40.00
56 Nomar Garciaparra/25 20.00
58 Phil Niekro/50 8.00
60 Magglio Ordonez/50 8.00
62 Edgar Renteria/25 10.00
63 Todd Helton/25 15.00
64 Carlos Beltran/25 15.00
65 Sammy Sosa/50 15.00
67 Mike Lowell/25 10.00
68 Mark Prior/25 20.00
69 Ivan Rodriguez/50 10.00
71 Jim Thome/50 10.00
72 Mark Teixeira/50 10.00
73 Shawn Green/25 10.00
76 Jose Vidro/25 8.00
77 Ben Sheets/25 10.00
79 Frank Thomas/25 15.00
81 Jason Bay/25 10.00
82 Tony Gwynn/50 15.00
83 Shannon Stewart/25 8.00
85 Andruw Jones/25 10.00
87 Barry Larkin/50 10.00
89 Rickey Henderson/50 15.00
90 Troy Glaus/25 10.00
91 Roy Oswalt/25 10.00
92 Michael Young/25 10.00
93 Carlos Lee/25 10.00
94 Jim Edmonds/50 10.00
96 Paul LoDuca/25 10.00
99 Carlos Delgado/25 10.00
100 Mike Schmidt/50 25.00

Signature Xtra Bases Purple

NM/M
Production 5-50
6 Melvin Mora/25 25.00
8 Brad Penny/50 10.00
13 Carl Crawford/25 25.00
20 Robb Quinlan/50 8.00
28 J.J. Putz/50 8.00
32 Danny Graves/50 10.00
36 Joe Nathan/50 25.00
37 Chone Figgins/50 10.00
39 Brett Myers/50 10.00
41 Danny Kolb/50 15.00
43 Francisco Cordero/50 10.00
52 C.C. Sabathia/25 25.00
54 Octavio Dotel/50 15.00
56 Mark Buehrle/25 20.00
58 Brandon Inge/50 15.00
59 Dewon Brazelton/50 10.00
60 Ryan Wagner/50 8.00
62 Laynce Nix/50 15.00
63 Jason Bay/50 15.00
65 Jacque Jones/25 20.00
67 Joe Kennedy/50 8.00
71 Lyle Overbay/25 20.00
73 Johnny Estrada/50 15.00
76 Wilson Valdez/50 8.00
77 Nick Green/50 8.00
78 Bucky Jacobsen/50 10.00
79 Keith Foulke/50 35.00
81 Carlos Zambrano/25 35.00
82 Orlando Cabrera/25 20.00
90 Lew Ford/50 15.00
92 Bobby Crosby/50 20.00
97 Tim Olson/50 8.00
98 Jeff Suppan/50 10.00
100 Esteban Loaiza/50 10.00
101 Brian Roberts/50 35.00
102 Jack Wilson/50 15.00
106 Jake Peavy/25 30.00
108 Chad Cordero/50 10.00
109 Jody Gerut/25 10.00
126 Doug Devore/50 8.00
128 Ken Harvey/50 10.00
129 Jacob Cruz/50 8.00
133 Craig Monroe/50 10.00
136 Tom Gordon/50 15.00
137 David Dellucci/50 20.00
138 Vance Wilson/50 8.00
139 Milton Bradley/50 15.00
141 Victor Martinez/25 30.00
142 Wade Miller/50 15.00
145 Carlos Lee/25 20.00
148 Travis Hafner/50 15.00
149 Jermaine Dye/50 15.00
152 Yadier Molina/25 20.00
153 Andy Green/50 8.00
161 Dioner Navarro/50 12.00
162 Shawn Hill/50 8.00
164 Scott Proctor/50 10.00
165 Jason Kubel/50 15.00
168 Yhency Brazoban/50 10.00
170 Angel Guzman/50 15.00
172 Adrian Gonzalez/50 12.00
173 Casey Kotchman 15.00
187 Bill Madlock/25 20.00
189 Billy Ripken/25 10.00
190 Gary Carter/25 25.00
191 Darryl Strawberry/25 20.00
192 Dave Parker/25 25.00
195 Fred Lynn/25 20.00
196 Jack Morris/25 25.00
198 Andre Dawson/25 25.00

Signature Xtra Bases Black

No Pricing
Production 3-10

S

1988 SCORE

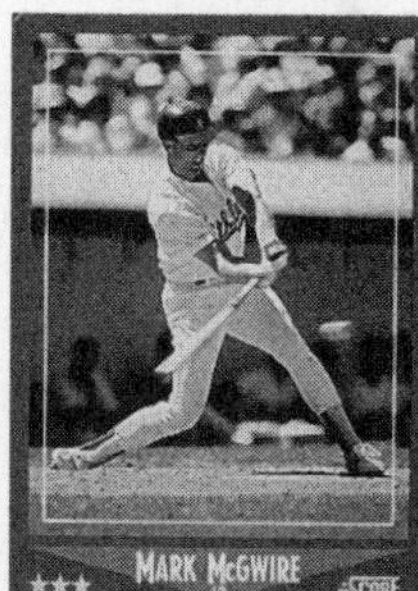

NM/M
Unopened Fact. Set (660): 9.00
Complete Set (660): 6.00
Common Player: .05
Pack: .35
Wax Box: 9.00
Rack Pack (54): .75
Rack Box (24): 12.00
1 Don Mattingly .65
2 Wade Boggs .50
3 Tim Raines .05
4 Andre Dawson .25
5 Mark McGwire .75
6 Kevin Seitzer .05
7 Wally Joyner .05
8 Jesse Barfield .05
9 Pedro Guerrero .05
10 Eric Davis .05
11 George Brett .65
12 Ozzie Smith .50
13 Rickey Henderson .40
14 Jim Rice .15
15 *Matt Nokes* .05
16 Mike Schmidt .65
17 Dave Parker .05
18 Eddie Murray .40
19 Andres Galarraga .05
20 Tony Fernandez .05
21 Kevin McReynolds .05
22 B.J. Surhoff .05
23 Pat Tabler .05
24 Kirby Puckett .50
25 Benny Santiago .05
26 Ryne Sandberg .50
27 Kelly Downs .05
28 Jose Cruz .05
29 Pete O'Brien .05
30 Mark Langston .05
31 Lee Smith .05
32 Juan Samuel .05
33 Kevin Bass .05
34 R.J. Reynolds .05
35 Steve Sax .05
36 John Kruk .05
37 Alan Trammell .05
38 Chris Bosio .05
39 Brook Jacoby .05
40 Willie McGee .05
41 Dave Magadan .05
42 Fred Lynn .05
43 Kent Hrbek .05
44 Brian Downing .05
45 Jose Canseco .30
46 Jim Presley .05
47 Mike Stanley .05
48 Tony Pena .05
49 David Cone .05
50 Rick Sutcliffe .05
51 Doug Drabek .05
52 Bill Doran .05
53 Mike Scioscia .05
54 Candy Maldonado .05
55 Dave Winfield .40
56 Lou Whitaker .05
57 Tom Henke .05
58 Ken Gerhart .05
59 Glenn Braggs .05
60 Julio Franco .05
61 Charlie Leibrandt .05
62 Gary Gaetti .05
63 Bob Boone .05
64 *Luis Polonia* .05
65 Dwight Evans .05
66 Phil Bradley .05
67 Mike Boddicker .05
68 Vince Coleman .05
69 Howard Johnson .05
70 Tim Wallach .05
71 Keith Moreland .05
72 Barry Larkin .05
73 Alan Ashby .05
74 Rick Rhoden .05
75 Darrell Evans .05
76 Dave Stieb .05
77 Dan Plesac .05
78 Will Clark .05
79 Frank White .05
80 Joe Carter .05
81 Mike Witt .05
82 Terry Steinbach .05
83 Alvin Davis .05
84 Tom Herr .05
85 Vance Law .05
86 Kal Daniels .05
87 Rick Honeycutt .05
88 Alfredo Griffin .05
89 Bret Saberhagen .05
90 Bert Blyleven .05
91 Jeff Reardon .05
92 Cory Snyder .05
93 Greg Walker .05
94 *Joe Magrane* .10
95 Rob Deer .05
96 Ray Knight .05
97 Casey Candaele .05
98 John Cerutti .05
99 Buddy Bell .05
100 Jack Clark .05
101 Eric Bell .05
102 Willie Wilson .05
103 Dave Schmidt .05
104 Dennis Eckersley .35
105 Don Sutton .35
106 Danny Tartabull .05
107 Fred McGriff .05
108 *Les Straker* .05
109 Lloyd Moseby .05
110 Roger Clemens .65
111 Glenn Hubbard .05
112 *Ken Williams* .05
113 Ruben Sierra .05
114 Stan Jefferson .05
115 Milt Thompson .05
116 Bobby Bonilla .05
117 Wayne Tolleson .05
118 Matt Williams .05
119 Chet Lemon .05
120 Dale Sveum .05
121 Dennis Boyd .05

No.	Player	Price
122	Brett Butler	.05
123	Terry Kennedy	.05
124	Jack Howell	.05
125	Curt Young	.05
126a	Dale Valle (first name incorrect)	.25
126b	Dave Valle (correct spelling)	.05
127	Curt Wilkerson	.05
128	Tim Teufel	.05
129	Ozzie Virgil	.05
130	Brian Fisher	.05
131	Lance Parrish	.05
132	Tom Browning	.05
133a	Larry Anderson (incorrect spelling)	.25
133b	Larry Andersen (correct spelling)	.05
134a	Bob Brenley (incorrect spelling)	.25
134b	Bob Brenly (correct spelling)	.05
135	Mike Marshall	.05
136	Gerald Perry	.05
137	Bobby Meacham	.05
138	Larry Herndon	.05
139	*Fred Manrique*	.05
140	Charlie Hough	.05
141	Ron Darling	.05
142	Herm Winningham	.05
143	Mike Diaz	.05
144	*Mike Jackson*	.05
145	Denny Walling	.05
146	Rob Thompson	.05
147	Franklin Stubbs	.05
148	Albert Hall	.05
149	Bobby Witt	.05
150	Lance McCullers	.05
151	Scott Bradley	.05
152	Mark McLemore	.05
153	Tim Laudner	.05
154	Greg Swindell	.05
155	Marty Barrett	.05
156	Mike Heath	.05
157	Gary Ward	.05
158a	Lee Mazilli (incorrect spelling)	.25
158b	Lee Mazzilli (correct spelling)	.05
159	Tom Foley	.05
160	Robin Yount	.40
161	Steve Bedrosian	.05
162	Bob Walk	.05
163	Nick Esasky	.05
164	*Ken Caminiti*	.15
165	Jose Uribe	.05
166	Dave Anderson	.05
167	Ed Whitson	.05
168	Ernie Whitt	.05
169	Cecil Cooper	.05
170	Mike Pagliarulo	.05
171	Pat Sheridan	.05
172	Chris Bando	.05
173	Lee Lacy	.05
174	Steve Lombardozzi	.05
175	Mike Greenwell	.05
176	Greg Minton	.05
177	Moose Haas	.05
178	Mike Kingery	.05
179	Greg Harris	.05
180	Bo Jackson	.10
181	Carmelo Martinez	.05
182	Alex Trevino	.05
183	Ron Oester	.05
184	Danny Darwin	.05
185	Mike Krukow	.05
186	Rafael Palmeiro	.40
187	Tim Burke	.05
188	Roger McDowell	.05
189	Garry Templeton	.05
190	Terry Pendleton	.05
191	Larry Parrish	.05
192	Rey Quinones	.05
193	Joaquin Andujar	.05
194	Tom Brunansky	.05
195	Donnie Moore	.05
196	Dan Pasqua	.05
197	Jim Gantner	.05
198	Mark Eichhorn	.05
199	John Grubb	.05
200	*Bill Ripken*	.05
201	*Sam Horn*	.05
202	Todd Worrell	.05
203	Terry Leach	.05
204	Garth Iorg	.05
205	Brian Dayett	.05
206	Bo Diaz	.05
207	Craig Reynolds	.05
208	Brian Holton	.05
209	Marvelle Wynne (Marvell)	.05
210	Dave Concepcion	.05
211	Mike Davis	.05
212	Devon White	.05
213	Mickey Brantley	.05
214	Greg Gagne	.05
215	Oddibe McDowell	.05
216	Jimmy Key	.05
217	Dave Bergman	.05
218	Calvin Schiraldi	.05
219	Larry Sheets	.05
220	Mike Easler	.05
221	Kurt Stillwell	.05
222	*Chuck Jackson*	.05
223	Dave Martinez	.05
224	Tim Leary	.05
225	Steve Garvey	.20
226	Greg Mathews	.05
227	Doug Sisk	.05
228	Dave Henderson	.05
229	Jimmy Dwyer	.05
230	Larry Owen	.05
231	Andre Thornton	.05
232	Mark Salas	.05
233	Tom Brookens	.05
234	Greg Brock	.05
235	Rance Mulliniks	.05
236	Bob Brower	.05
237	Joe Niekro	.05
238	Scott Bankhead	.05
239	Doug DeCinces	.05
240	Tommy John	.05
241	Rich Gedman	.05
242	Ted Power	.05
243	*Dave Meads*	.05
244	Jim Sundberg	.05
245	Ken Oberkfell	.05
246	Jimmy Jones	.05
247	Ken Landreaux	.05
248	Jose Oquendo	.05
249	*John Mitchell*	.05
250	Don Baylor	.05
251	Scott Fletcher	.05
252	Al Newman	.05
253	Carney Lansford	.05
254	Johnny Ray	.05
255	Gary Pettis	.05
256	Ken Phelps	.05
257	Rick Leach	.05
258	Tim Stoddard	.05
259	Ed Romero	.05
260	Sid Bream	.05
261a	Tom Neidenfuer (incorrect spelling)	.25
261b	Tom Niedenfuer (correct spelling)	.05
262	Rick Dempsey	.05
263	Lonnie Smith	.05
264	Bob Forsch	.05
265	Barry Bonds	1.00
266	Willie Randolph	.05
267	Mike Ramsey	.05
268	Don Slaught	.05
269	Mickey Tettleton	.05
270	Jerry Reuss	.05
271	Marc Sullivan	.05
272	Jim Morrison	.05
273	Steve Balboni	.05
274	Dick Schofield	.05
275	John Tudor	.05
276	*Gene Larkin*	.05
277	Harold Reynolds	.05
278	Jerry Browne	.05
279	Willie Upshaw	.05
280	Ted Higuera	.05
281	Terry McGriff	.05
282	Terry Puhl	.05
283	*Mark Wasinger*	.05
284	Luis Salazar	.05
285	Ted Simmons	.05
286	John Shelby	.05
287	*John Smiley*	.05
288	Curt Ford	.05
289	Steve Crawford	.05
290	Dan Quisenberry	.05
291	Alan Wiggins	.05
292	Randy Bush	.05
293	John Candelaria	.05
294	Tony Phillips	.05
295	Mike Morgan	.05
296	Bill Wegman	.05
297a	Terry Franconia (incorrect spelling)	.25
297b	Terry Francona (correct spelling)	.05
298	Mickey Hatcher	.05
299	Andres Thomas	.05
300	Bob Stanley	.05
301	*Alfredo Pedrique*	.05
302	Jim Lindeman	.05
303	Wally Backman	.05
304	Paul O'Neill	.05
305	Hubie Brooks	.05
306	Steve Buechele	.05
307	Bobby Thigpen	.05
308	George Hendrick	.05
309	John Moses	.05
310	Ron Guidry	.05
311	Bill Schroeder	.05
312	*Jose Nunez*	.05
313	Bud Black	.05
314	Joe Sambito	.05
315	Scott McGregor	.05
316	Rafael Santana	.05
317	Frank Williams	.05
318	Mike Fitzgerald	.05
319	Rick Mahler	.05
320	Jim Gott	.05
321	Mariano Duncan	.05
322	Jose Guzman	.05
323	Lee Guetterman	.05
324	Dan Gladden	.05
325	Gary Carter	.40
326	Tracy Jones	.05
327	Floyd Youmans	.05
328	Bill Dawley	.05
329	*Paul Noce*	.05
330	Angel Salazar	.05
331	Goose Gossage	.10
332	George Frazier	.05
333	Ruppert Jones	.05
334	Billy Jo Robidoux	.05
335	Mike Scott	.05
336	Randy Myers	.05
337	Bob Sebra	.05
338	Eric Show	.05
339	Mitch Williams	.05
340	Paul Molitor	.40
341	Gus Polidor	.05
342	Steve Trout	.05
343	Jerry Don Gleaton	.05
344	Bob Knepper	.05
345	Mitch Webster	.05
346	John Morris	.05
347	Andy Hawkins	.05
348	Dave Leiper	.05
349	Ernest Riles	.05
350	Dwight Gooden	.05
351	Dave Righetti	.05
352	Pat Dodson	.05
353	John Habyan	.05
354	Jim Deshaies	.05
355	Butch Wynegar	.05
356	Bryn Smith	.05
357	Matt Young	.05
358	*Tom Pagnozzi*	.05
359	Floyd Rayford	.05
360	Darryl Strawberry	.05
361	Sal Butera	.05
362	Domingo Ramos	.05
363	Chris Brown	.05
364	Jose Gonzalez	.05
365	Dave Smith	.05
366	Andy McGaffigan	.05
367	Stan Javier	.05
368	Henry Cotto	.05
369	Mike Birkbeck	.05
370	Len Dykstra	.05
371	Dave Collins	.05
372	Spike Owen	.05
373	Geno Petralli	.05
374	Ron Karkovice	.05
375	Shane Rawley	.05
376	*DeWayne Buice*	.05
377	*Bill Pecota*	.05
378	Leon Durham	.05
379	Ed Olwine	.05
380	Bruce Hurst	.05
381	Bob McClure	.05
382	Mark Thurmond	.05
383	Buddy Biancalana	.05
384	Tim Conroy	.05
385	Tony Gwynn	.50
386	Greg Gross	.05
387	*Barry Lyons*	.05
388	Mike Felder	.05
389	Pat Clements	.05
390	Ken Griffey	.05
391	Mark Davis	.05
392	Jose Rijo	.05
393	Mike Young	.05
394	Willie Fraser	.05
395	Dion James	.05
396	*Steve Shields*	.05
397	Randy St. Claire	.05
398	Danny Jackson	.05
399	Cecil Fielder	.05
400	Keith Hernandez	.05
401	Don Carman	.05
402	*Chuck Crim*	.05
403	Rob Woodward	.05
404	Junior Ortiz	.05
405	Glenn Wilson	.05
406	Ken Howell	.05
407	Jeff Kunkel	.05
408	Jeff Reed	.05
409	Chris James	.05
410	Zane Smith	.05
411	Ken Dixon	.05
412	Ricky Horton	.05
413	Frank DiPino	.05
414	*Shane Mack*	.05
415	Danny Cox	.05
416	Andy Van Slyke	.05
417	Danny Heep	.05
418	John Cangelosi	.05
419a	John Christiansen (incorrect spelling)	.25
419b	John Christensen (correct spelling)	.05
420	*Joey Cora*	.05
421	Mike LaValliere	.05
422	Kelly Gruber	.05
423	Bruce Benedict	.05
424	Len Matuszek	.05
425	Kent Tekulve	.05
426	Rafael Ramirez	.05
427	Mike Flanagan	.05
428	Mike Gallego	.05
429	Juan Castillo	.05
430	Neal Heaton	.05
431	Phil Garner	.05
432	*Mike Dunne*	.05
433	Wallace Johnson	.05
434	Jack O'Connor	.05
435	Steve Jeltz	.05
436	*Donnell Nixon*	.05
437	Jack Lazorko	.05
438	*Keith Comstock*	.05
439	Jeff Robinson	.05
440	Graig Nettles	.05
441	Mel Hall	.05
442	*Gerald Young*	.05
443	Gary Redus	.05
444	Charlie Moore	.05
445	Bill Madlock	.05
446	Mark Clear	.05
447	Greg Booker	.05
448	Rick Schu	.05
449	Ron Kittle	.05
450	Dale Murphy	.25
451	Bob Dernier	.05
452	Dale Mohorcic	.05
453	Rafael Belliard	.05
454	Charlie Puleo	.05
455	Dwayne Murphy	.05
456	Jim Eisenreich	.05
457	David Palmer	.05
458	Dave Stewart	.05
459	Pascual Perez	.05
460	Glenn Davis	.05
461	Dan Petry	.05
462	Jim Winn	.05
463	Darrell Miller	.05
464	Mike Moore	.05
465	Mike LaCoss	.05
466	Steve Farr	.05
467	Jerry Mumphrey	.05
468	Kevin Gross	.05
469	Bruce Bochy	.05
470	Orel Hershiser	.05
471	Eric King	.05
472	*Ellis Burks*	.25
473	Darren Daulton	.05
474	Mookie Wilson	.05
475	Frank Viola	.05
476	Ron Robinson	.05
477	Bob Melvin	.05
478	Jeff Musselman	.05
479	Charlie Kerfeld	.05
480	Richard Dotson	.05
481	Kevin Mitchell	.05
482	Gary Roenicke	.05
483	Tim Flannery	.05
484	Rich Yett	.05
485	Pete Incaviglia	.05
486	Rick Cerone	.05
487	Tony Armas	.05
488	Jerry Reed	.05
489	Davey Lopes	.05
490	Frank Tanana	.05
491	Mike Loynd	.05
492	Bruce Ruffin	.05
493	Chris Speier	.05
494	Tom Hume	.05
495	Jesse Orosco	.05

496 *Robby Wine, Jr.* .05
497 *Jeff Montgomery* .15
498 Jeff Dedmon .05
499 Luis Aguayo .05
500 Reggie Jackson (1968-75) .15
501 Reggie Jackson (1976) .15
502 Reggie Jackson (1977-81) .15
503 Reggie Jackson (1982-86) .15
504 Reggie Jackson (1987) .15
505 Billy Hatcher .05
506 Ed Lynch .05
507 Willie Hernandez .05
508 Jose DeLeon .05
509 Joel Youngblood .05
510 Bob Welch .05
511 Steve Ontiveros .05
512 Randy Ready .05
513 Juan Nieves .05
514 Jeff Russell .05
515 Von Hayes .05
516 Mark Gubicza .05
517 Ken Dayley .05
518 Don Aase .05
519 Rick Reuschel .05
520 *Mike Henneman* .10
521 Rick Aguilera .05
522 Jay Howell .05
523 Ed Correa .05
524 Manny Trillo .05
525 Kirk Gibson .05
526 *Wally Ritchie* .05
527 Al Nipper .05
528 Atlee Hammaker .05
529 Shawon Dunston .05
530 Jim Clancy .05
531 Tom Paciorek .05
532 Joel Skinner .05
533 Scott Garrelts .05
534 Tom O'Malley .05
535 John Franco .05
536 *Paul Kilgus* .05
537 Darrell Porter .05
538 Walt Terrell .05
539 *Bill Long* .05
540 George Bell .05
541 Jeff Sellers .05
542 *Joe Boever* .05
543 Steve Howe .05
544 Scott Sanderson .05
545 Jack Morris .05
546 *Todd Benzinger* .15
547 Steve Henderson .05
548 Eddie Milner .05
549 *Jeff Robinson* .05
550 Cal Ripken, Jr. 1.00
551 Jody Davis .05
552 Kirk McCaskill .05
553 Craig Lefferts .05
554 Darnell Coles .05
555 Phil Niekro .35
556 Mike Aldrete .05
557 Pat Perry .05
558 Juan Agosto .05
559 Rob Murphy .05
560 Dennis Rasmussen .05
561 Manny Lee .05
562 *Jeff Blauser* .10
563 Bob Ojeda .05
564 Dave Dravecky .05
565 Gene Garber .05
566 Ron Roenicke .05
567 *Tommy Hinzo* .05
568 *Eric Nolte* .05
569 Ed Hearn .05
570 *Mark Davidson* .05
571 *Jim Walewander* .05
572 Donnie Hill .05
573 Jamie Moyer .05
574 Ken Schrom .05
575 Nolan Ryan 1.00
576 Jim Acker .05
577 Jamie Quirk .05
578 *Jay Aldrich* .05
579 Claudell Washington .05
580 Jeff Leonard .05
581 Carmen Castillo .05
582 Daryl Boston .05
583 *Jeff DeWillis* .05
584 *John Marzano* .05
585 Bill Gullickson .05
586 Andy Allanson .05
587 Lee Tunnell .05
588 Gene Nelson .05
589 Dave LaPoint .05
590 Harold Baines .05
591 Bill Buckner .05

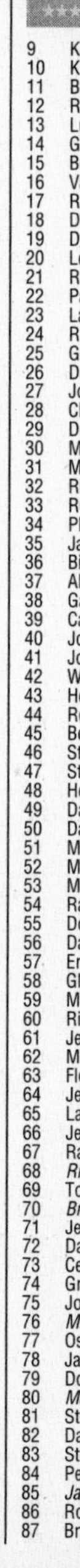

592 Carlton Fisk .40
593 Rick Manning .05
594 *Doug Jones* .10
595 Tom Candiotti .05
596 Steve Lake .05
597 *Jose Lind* .05
598 *Ross Jones* .05
599 Gary Matthews .05
600 Fernando Valenzuela .05
601 Dennis Martinez .05
602 *Les Lancaster* .05
603 Ozzie Guillen .05
604 Tony Bernazard .05
605 Chili Davis .05
606 Roy Smalley .05
607 Ivan Calderon .05
608 Jay Tibbs .05
609 Guy Hoffman .05
610 Doyle Alexander .05
611 Mike Bielecki .05
612 *Shawn Hillegas* .05
613 Keith Atherton .05
614 Eric Plunk .05
615 Sid Fernandez .05
616 Dennis Lamp .05
617 Dave Engle .05
618 Harry Spilman .05
619 Don Robinson .05
620 *John Farrell* .05
621 *Nelson Liriano* .05
622 Floyd Bannister .05
623 *Randy Milligan* .05
624 *Kevin Elster* .10
625 *Jody Reed* .05
626 *Shawn Abner* .05
627 *Kirt Manwaring* .10
628 *Pete Stanicek* .05
629 *Rob Ducey* .05
630 Steve Kiefer .05
631 *Gary Thurman* .05
632 *Darrel Akerfelds* .05
633 Dave Clark .05
634 *Roberto Kelly* .05
635 *Keith Hughes* .05
636 *John Davis* .05
637 *Mike Devereaux* .10
638 *Tom Glavine* 1.00
639 *Keith Miller* .05
640 *Chris Gwynn* .05
641 *Tim Crews* .05
642 *Mackey Sasser* .05
643 *Vicente Palacios* .05
644 Kevin Romine .05
645 *Gregg Jefferies* .25
646 *Jeff Treadway* .05
647 *Ron Gant* .25
648 Mark McGwire, Matt Nokes Rookie Sluggers .35
649 Tim Raines, Eric Davis Speed and Power .05
650 Jack Clark, Don Mattingly Game Breakers .25
651 Tony Fernandez, Cal Ripken, Jr., Alan Trammell Super Shortstops .25
652 Vince Coleman (Highlight) .05
653 Kirby Puckett (Highlight) .25
654 Benito Santiago (Highlight) .05
655 Juan Nieves (Highlight) .05
656 Steve Bedrosian (Highlight) .05
657 Mike Schmidt (Highlight) .30
658 Don Mattingly (Highlight) .30
659 Mark McGwire (Highlight) .35
660 Paul Molitor (Highlight) .20

Glossy

NM/M

Complete Set (660): 65.00
Common Player: .25
Stars: 15X
(See 1988 Score for checklist and base card values.)

Traded/Rookie

NM/M

Complete Set (110): 12.00
Common Player: .05
1 Jack Clark .05
2 Danny Jackson .05
3 Brett Butler .05
4 Kurt Stillwell .05
5 Tom Brunansky .05
6 Dennis Lamp .05
7 Jose DeLeon .05
8 Tom Herr .05

9 Keith Moreland .05
10 Kirk Gibson .05
11 Bud Black .05
12 Rafael Ramirez .05
13 Luis Salazar .05
14 Goose Gossage .05
15 Bob Welch .05
16 Vance Law .05
17 Ray Knight .05
18 Dan Quisenberry .05
19 Don Slaught .05
20 Lee Smith .25
21 Rick Cerone .05
22 Pat Tabler .05
23 Larry McWilliams .05
24 Rick Horton .05
25 Graig Nettles .05
26 Dan Petry .05
27 Jose Rijo .05
28 Chili Davis .05
29 Dickie Thon .05
30 Mackey Sasser .05
31 Mickey Tettleton .05
32 Rick Dempsey .05
33 Ron Hassey .05
34 Phil Bradley .05
35 Jay Howell .05
36 Bill Buckner .05
37 Alfredo Griffin .05
38 Gary Pettis .05
39 Calvin Schiraldi .05
40 John Candelaria .05
41 Joe Orsulak .05
42 Willie Upshaw .05
43 Herm Winningham .05
44 Ron Kittle .05
45 Bob Dernier .05
46 Steve Balboni .05
47 Steve Shields .05
48 Henry Cotto .05
49 Dave Henderson .05
50 Dave Parker .05
51 Mike Young .05
52 Mark Salas .05
53 Mike Davis .05
54 Rafael Santana .05
55 Don Baylor .05
56 Dan Pasqua .05
57 Ernest Riles .05
58 Glenn Hubbard .05
59 Mike Smithson .05
60 Richard Dotson .05
61 Jerry Reuss .05
62 Mike Jackson .05
63 Floyd Bannister .05
64 Jesse Orosco .05
65 Larry Parrish .05
66 Jeff Bittiger .05
67 Ray Hayward .05
68 *Ricky Jordan* .05
69 Tommy Gregg .05
70 *Brady Anderson* .50
71 Jeff Montgomery .05
72 Darryl Hamilton .05
73 Cecil Espy .05
74 Greg Briley .05
75 Joey Meyer .05
76 *Mike Macfarlane* .05
77 Oswald Peraza .05
78 Jack Armstrong .05
79 Don Heinkel .05
80 *Mark Grace* 1.50
81 Steve Curry .05
82 Damon Berryhill .05
83 Steve Ellsworth .05
84 Pete Smith .05
85 *Jack McDowell* .25
86 Rob Dibble .05
87 Bryan Harvey .05
88 John Dopson .05
89 Dave Gallagher .05
90 *Todd Stottlemyre* .25
91 Mike Schooler .05
92 Don Gordon .05
93 Sil Campusano .05
94 Jeff Pico .05
95 *Jay Buhner* .75
96 Nelson Santovenia .05
97 Al Leiter .05
98 Luis Alicea .05
99 Pat Borders .05
100 *Chris Sabo* .25
101 Tim Belcher .05
102 Walt Weiss .05
103 *Craig Biggio* 6.00
104 Don August .05
105 *Roberto Alomar* 4.00
106 Todd Burns .05
107 John Costello .05
108 Melido Perez .05
109 Darrin Jackson .05
110 Orestes Destrade .05

Glossy

NM/M

Complete Set (110): 60.00
Common Player: .25
Stars: 3X
(See 1988 Score Traded/Rookie for checklist and base card values.)

1989 SCORE

NM/M

Unopened Fact. Set (660): 12.00
Complete Set (660): 9.00
Common Player: .05
Pack (16): .30
Wax Box (36): 7.50
1 Jose Canseco .25
2 Andre Dawson .25
3 Mark McGwire .65
4 Benny Santiago .05
5 Rick Reuschel .05
6 Fred McGriff .05
7 Kal Daniels .05
8 Gary Gaetti .05
9 Ellis Burks .05
10 Darryl Strawberry .05
11 Julio Franco .05
12 Lloyd Moseby .05
13 *Jeff Pico* .05
14 Johnny Ray .05
15 Cal Ripken, Jr. .75
16 Dick Schofield .05
17 Mel Hall .05
18 Bill Ripken .05
19 Brook Jacoby .05
20 Kirby Puckett .50
21 Bill Doran .05
22 Pete O'Brien .05
23 Matt Nokes .05
24 Brian Fisher .05
25 Jack Clark .05
26 Gary Pettis .05
27 Dave Valle .05
28 Willie Wilson .05
29 Curt Young .05
30 Dale Murphy .20
31 Barry Larkin .05
32 Dave Stewart .05
33 Mike LaValliere .05
34 Glenn Hubbard .05
35 Ryne Sandberg .50
36 Tony Pena .05
37 Greg Walker .05
38 Von Hayes .05
39 Kevin Mitchell .05
40 Tim Raines .05

41 Keith Hernandez .05
42 Keith Moreland .05
43 Ruben Sierra .05
44 Chet Lemon .05
45 Willie Randolph .05
46 Andy Allanson .05
47 Candy Maldonado .05
48 Sid Bream .05
49 Denny Walling .05
50 Dave Winfield .40
51 Alvin Davis .05
52 Cory Snyder .05
53 Hubie Brooks .05
54 Chili Davis .05
55 Kevin Seitzer .05
56 Jose Uribe .05
57 Tony Fernandez .05
58 Tim Teufel .05
59 Oddibe McDowell .05
60 Les Lancaster .05
61 Billy Hatcher .05
62 Dan Gladden .05
63 Marty Barrett .05
64 Nick Esasky .05
65 Wally Joyner .05
66 Mike Greenwell .05
67 Ken Williams .05
68 Bob Horner .05
69 Steve Sax .05
70 Rickey Henderson .40
71 Mitch Webster .05
72 Rob Deer .05
73 Jim Presley .05
74 Albert Hall .05
75a George Brett ('At age 33 ...') 1.00
75b George Brett ('At age 35 ...') .50
76 Brian Downing .05
77 Dave Martinez .05
78 Scott Fletcher .05
79 Phil Bradley .05
80 Ozzie Smith .50
81 Larry Sheets .05
82 Mike Aldrete .05
83 Darnell Coles .05
84 Len Dykstra .05
85 Jim Rice .15
86 Jeff Treadway .05
87 Jose Lind .05
88 Willie McGee .05
89 Mickey Brantley .05
90 Tony Gwynn .50
91 R.J. Reynolds .05
92 Milt Thompson .05
93 Kevin McReynolds .05
94 Eddie Murray .40
95 Lance Parrish .05
96 Ron Kittle .05
97 Gerald Young .05
98 Ernie Whitt .05
99 Jeff Reed .05
100 Don Mattingly .60
101 Gerald Perry .05
102 Vance Law .05
103 John Shelby .05
104 Chris Sabo .05
105 Danny Tartabull .05
106 Glenn Wilson .05
107 Mark Davidson .05
108 Dave Parker .05
109 Eric Davis .05
110 Alan Trammell .05
111 Ozzie Virgil .05
112 Frank Tanana .05
113 Rafael Ramirez .05
114 Dennis Martinez .05
115 Jose DeLeon .05
116 Bob Ojeda .05
117 Doug Drabek .05
118 Andy Hawkins .05
119 Greg Maddux .50
120 Cecil Fielder (reversed negative) .05
121 Mike Scioscia .05
122 Dan Petry .05
123 Terry Kennedy .05
124 Kelly Downs .05
125 Greg Gross .05
126 Fred Lynn .05
127 Barry Bonds .75
128 Harold Baines .05
129 Doyle Alexander .05
130 Kevin Elster .05
131 Mike Heath .05
132 Teddy Higuera .05
133 Charlie Leibrandt .05
134 Tim Laudner .05
135a Ray Knight (photo reversed) .40
135b Ray Knight (correct photo) .05
136 Howard Johnson .05
137 Terry Pendleton .05
138 Andy McGaffigan .05
139 Ken Oberkfell .05
140 Butch Wynegar .05
141 Rob Murphy .05
142 *Rich Renteria* .05
143 Jose Guzman .05
144 Andres Galarraga .05
145 Rick Horton .05
146 Frank DiPino .05
147 Glenn Braggs .05
148 John Kruk .05
149 Mike Schmidt .60
150 Lee Smith .05
151 Robin Yount .40
152 Mark Eichhorn .05
153 DeWayne Buice .05
154 B.J. Surhoff .05
155 Vince Coleman .05
156 Tony Phillips .05
157 Willie Fraser .05
158 Lance McCullers .05
159 Greg Gagne .05
160 Jesse Barfield .05
161 Mark Langston .05
162 Kurt Stillwell .05
163 Dion James .05
164 Glenn Davis .05
165 Walt Weiss .05
166 Dave Concepcion .05
167 Alfredo Griffin .05
168 *Don Heinkel* .05
169 Luis Rivera .05
170 Shane Rawley .05
171 Darrell Evans .05
172 Robby Thompson .05
173 Jody Davis .05
174 Andy Van Slyke .05
175 Wade Boggs .50
176 Garry Templeton .05
177 Gary Redus .05
178 Craig Lefferts .05
179 Carney Lansford .05
180 Ron Darling .05
181 Kirk McCaskill .05
182 Tony Armas .05
183 Steve Farr .05
184 Tom Brunansky .05
185 *Bryan Harvey* .05
186 Mike Marshall .05
187 Bo Diaz .05
188 Willie Upshaw .05
189 Mike Pagliarulo .05
190 Mike Krukow .05
191 Tommy Herr .05
192 Jim Pankovits .05
193 Dwight Evans .05
194 Kelly Gruber .05
195 Bobby Bonilla .05
196 Wallace Johnson .05
197 Dave Stieb .05
198 *Pat Borders* .05
199 Rafael Palmeiro .35
200 Dwight Gooden .05
201 Pete Incaviglia .05
202 Chris James .05
203 Marvell Wynne .05
204 Pat Sheridan .05
205 Don Baylor .05
206 Paul O'Neill .05
207 Pete Smith .05
208 Mark McLemore .05
209 Henry Cotto .05
210 Kirk Gibson .05
211 Claudell Washington .05
212 Randy Bush .05
213 Joe Carter .05
214 Bill Buckner .05
215 Bert Blyleven .05
216 Brett Butler .05
217 Lee Mazzilli .05
218 Spike Owen .05
219 Bill Swift .05
220 Tim Wallach .05
221 David Cone .05
222 Don Carman .05
223 Rich Gossage .05
224 Bob Walk .05
225 Dave Righetti .05
226 Kevin Bass .05
227 Kevin Gross .05
228 Tim Burke .05
229 Rick Mahler .05
230 Lou Whitaker .05
231 *Luis Alicea* .05
232 Roberto Alomar .25
233 Bob Boone .05
234 Dickie Thon .05
235 Shawon Dunston .05
236 Pete Stanicek .05
237 Craig Biggio .05
238 Dennis Boyd .05
239 Tom Candiotti .05
240 Gary Carter .40
241 Mike Stanley .05
242 Ken Phelps .05
243 Chris Bosio .05
244 Les Straker .05
245 Dave Smith .05
246 John Candelaria .05
247 Joe Orsulak .05
248 Storm Davis .05
249 Floyd Bannister .05
250 Jack Morris .05
251 Bret Saberhagen .05
252 Tom Niedenfuer .05
253 Neal Heaton .05
254 Eric Show .05
255 Juan Samuel .05
256 Dale Sveum .05
257 Jim Gott .05
258 Scott Garrelts .05
259 Larry McWilliams .05
260 Steve Bedrosian .05
261 Jack Howell .05
262 Jay Tibbs .05
263 Jamie Moyer .05
264 Doug Sisk .05
265 Todd Worrell .05
266 John Farrell .05
267 Dave Collins .05
268 Sid Fernandez .05
269 Tom Brookens .05
270 Shane Mack .05
271 Paul Kilgus .05
272 Chuck Crim .05
273 Bob Knepper .05
274 Mike Moore .05
275 Guillermo Hernandez .05
276 Dennis Eckersley .35
277 Graig Nettles .05
278 Rich Dotson .05
279 Larry Herndon .05
280 Gene Larkin .05
281 Roger McDowell .05
282 Greg Swindell .05
283 Juan Agosto .05
284 Jeff Robinson .05
285 Mike Dunne .05
286 Greg Mathews .05
287 Kent Tekulve .05
288 Jerry Mumphrey .05
289 Jack McDowell .05
290 Frank Viola .05
291 Mark Gubicza .05
292 Dave Schmidt .05
293 Mike Henneman .05
294 Jimmy Jones .05
295 Charlie Hough .05
296 Rafael Santana .05
297 Chris Speier .05
298 Mike Witt .05
299 Pascual Perez .05
300 Nolan Ryan .75
301 Mitch Williams .05
302 Mookie Wilson .05
303 Mackey Sasser .05
304 John Cerutti .05
305 Jeff Reardon .05
306 Randy Myers .05
307 Greg Brock .05
308 Bob Welch .05
309 Jeff Robinson .05
310 Harold Reynolds .05
311 Jim Walewander .05
312 Dave Magadan .05
313 Jim Gantner .05
314 Walt Terrell .05
315 Wally Backman .05
316 Luis Salazar .05
317 Rick Rhoden .05
318 Tom Henke .05
319 Mike Macfarlane .05
320 Dan Plesac .05
321 Calvin Schiraldi .05
322 Stan Javier .05
323 Devon White .05
324 Scott Bradley .05
325 Bruce Hurst .05
326 Manny Lee .05
327 Rick Aguilera .05
328 Bruce Ruffin .05
329 Ed Whitson .05
330 Bo Jackson .10
331 Ivan Calderon .05
332 Mickey Hatcher .05
333 Barry Jones .05
334 Ron Hassey .05
335 Bill Wegman .05
336 Damon Berryhill .05
337 Steve Ontiverso .05
338 Dan Pasqua .05
339 Bill Pecota .05
340 Greg Cadaret .05
341 Scott Bankhead .05
342 Ron Guidry .10
343 Danny Heep .05
344 Bob Brower .05
345 Rich Gedman .05
346 *Nelson Santovenia* .05
347 George Bell .05
348 Ted Power .05
349 Mark Grant .05
350a Roger Clemens (778 wins) 2.00
350b Roger Clemens (78 wins) .60
351 Bill Long .05
352 Jay Bell .05
353 Steve Balboni .05
354 Bob Kipper .05
355 Steve Jeltz .05
356 Jesse Orosco .05
357 Bob Dernier .05
358 Mickey Tettleton .05
359 Duane Ward .05
360 Darrin Jackson .05
361 Rey Quinones .05
362 Mark Grace .05
363 Steve Lake .05
364 Pat Perry .05
365 Terry Steinbach .05
366 Alan Ashby .05
367 Jeff Montgomery .05
368 Steve Buechele .05
369 Chris Brown .05
370 Orel Hershiser .05
371 Todd Benzinger .05
372 Ron Gant .05
373 Paul Assenmacher .05
374 Joey Meyer .05
375 Neil Allen .05
376 Mike Davis .05
377 Jeff Parrett .05
378 Jay Howell .05
379 Rafael Belliard .05
380 Luis Polonia .05
381 Keith Atherton .05
382 Kent Hrbek .05
383 Bob Stanley .05
384 Dave LaPoint .05
385 Rance Mulliniks .05
386 Melido Perez .05
387 Doug Jones .05
388 Steve Lyons .05
389 Alejandro Pena .05
390 Frank White .05
391 Pat Tabler .05
392 Eric Plunk .05
393 Mike Maddux .05
394 Allan Anderson .05
395 Bob Brenly .05
396 Rick Cerone .05
397 Scott Terry .05
398 Mike Jackson .05
399 Bobby Thigpen .05
400 Don Sutton .35
401 Cecil Espy .05
402 Junior Ortiz .05
403 Mike Smithson .05
404 Bud Black .05
405 Tom Foley .05
406 Andres Thomas .05
407 Rick Sutcliffe .05
408 Brian Harper .05
409 John Smiley .05
410 Juan Nieves .05
411 Shawn Abner .05
412 Wes Gardner .05
413 Darren Daulton .05
414 Juan Berenguer .05
415 Charles Hudson .05
416 Rick Honeycutt .05
417 Greg Booker .05
418 Tim Belcher .05
419 Don August .05
420 Dale Mohorcic .05
421 Steve Lombardozzi .05
422 Atlee Hammaker .05
423 Jerry Don Gleaton .05
424 Scott Bailes .05
425 Bruce Sutter .40
426 Randy Ready .05
427 Jerry Reed .05
428 Bryn Smith .05

#	Player	Price
429	Tim Leary	.05
430	Mark Clear	.05
431	Terry Leach	.05
432	John Moses	.05
433	Ozzie Guillen	.05
434	Gene Nelson	.05
435	Gary Ward	.05
436	Luis Aguayo	.05
437	Fernando Valenzuela	.05
438	Jeff Russell	.05
439	Cecilio Guante	.05
440	Don Robinson	.05
441	Rick Anderson	.05
442	Tom Glavine	.35
443	Daryl Boston	.05
444	Joe Price	.05
445	Stewart Cliburn	.05
446	Manny Trillo	.05
447	Joel Skinner	.05
448	Charlie Puleo	.05
449	Carlton Fisk	.40
450	Will Clark	.05
451	Otis Nixon	.05
452	Rick Schu	.05
453	Todd Stottlemyre	.05
454	Tim Birtsas	.05
455	*Dave Gallagher*	.05
456	Barry Lyons	.05
457	Fred Manrique	.05
458	Ernest Riles	.05
459	*Doug Jennings*	.05
460	Joe Magrane	.05
461	Jamie Quirk	.05
462	*Jack Armstrong*	.05
463	Bobby Witt	.05
464	Keith Miller	.05
465	*Todd Burns*	.05
466	*John Dopson*	.05
467	Rich Yett	.05
468	Craig Reynolds	.05
469	Dave Bergman	.05
470	Rex Hudler	.05
471	Eric King	.05
472	Joaquin Andujar	.05
473	*Sil Campusano*	.05
474	Terry Mulholland	.05
475	Mike Flanagan	.05
476	Greg Harris	.05
477	Tommy John	.10
478	Dave Anderson	.05
479	Fred Toliver	.05
480	Jimmy Key	.05
481	Donell Nixon	.05
482	Mark Portugal	.05
483	Tom Pagnozzi	.05
484	Jeff Kunkel	.05
485	Frank Williams	.05
486	Jody Reed	.05
487	Roberto Kelly	.05
488	Shawn Hillegas	.05
489	Jerry Reuss	.05
490	Mark Davis	.05
491	Jeff Sellers	.05
492	Zane Smith	.05
493	Al Newman	.05
494	Mike Young	.05
495	Larry Parrish	.05
496	Herm Winningham	.05
497	Carmen Castillo	.05
498	Joe Hesketh	.05
499	Darrell Miller	.05
500	Mike LaCoss	.05
501	Charlie Lea	.05
502	Bruce Benedict	.05
503	Chuck Finley	.05
504	Brad Wellman	.05
505	Tim Crews	.05
506	Ken Gerhart	.05
507a	Brian Holton (Born: 1/25/65, Denver)	.15
507b	Brian Holton (Born: 11/29/59, McKeesport)	.05
508	Dennis Lamp	.05
509	Bobby Meacham	.05
510	Tracy Jones	.05
511	Mike Fitzgerald	.05
512	*Jeff Bittiger*	.05
513	Tim Flannery	.05
514	Ray Hayward	.05
515	Dave Leiper	.05
516	Rod Scurry	.05
517	Carmelo Martinez	.05
518	Curtis Wilkerson	.05
519	Stan Jefferson	.05
520	Dan Quisenberry	.05
521	Lloyd McClendon	.05
522	Steve Trout	.05
523	Larry Andersen	.05
524	Don Aase	.05
525	Bob Forsch	.05
526	Geno Petralli	.05
527	Angel Salazar	.05
528	*Mike Schooler*	.05
529	Jose Oquendo	.05
530	Jay Buhner	.05
531	Tom Bolton	.05
532	Al Nipper	.05
533	Dave Henderson	.05
534	*John Costello*	.05
535	Donnie Moore	.05
536	Mike Laga	.05
537	Mike Gallego	.05
538	Jim Clancy	.05
539	Joel Youngblood	.05
540	Rick Leach	.05
541	Kevin Romine	.05
542	Mark Salas	.05
543	Greg Minton	.05
544	Dave Palmer	.05
545	Dwayne Murphy	.05
546	Jim Deshaies	.05
547	Don Gordon	.05
548	Ricky Jordan	.05
549	Mike Boddicker	.05
550	Mike Scott	.05
551	Jeff Ballard	.05
552a	Jose Rijo (uniform number #24 on card back)	.15
552b	Jose Rijo (uniform number #27 on card back)	.10
553	Danny Darwin	.05
554	Tom Browning	.05
555	Danny Jackson	.05
556	Rick Dempsey	.05
557	Jeffrey Leonard	.05
558	Jeff Musselman	.05
559	Ron Robinson	.05
560	John Tudor	.05
561	Don Slaught	.05
562	Dennis Rasmussen	.05
563	Brady Anderson	.05
564	Pedro Guerrero	.05
565	Paul Molitor	.40
566	*Terry Clark*	.05
567	Terry Puhl	.05
568	Mike Campbell	.05
569	Paul Mirabella	.05
570	Jeff Hamilton	.05
571	*Oswald Peraza*	.05
572	Bob McClure	.05
573	*Jose Bautista*	.05
574	Alex Trevino	.05
575	John Franco	.05
576	*Mark Parent*	.05
577	Nelson Liriano	.05
578	Steve Shields	.05
579	Odell Jones	.05
580	Al Leiter	.05
581	Dave Stapleton	.05
582	Jose Canseco, Kirk Gibson, Orel Hershiser, Dave Stewart 1988 World Series	.10
583	Donnie Hill	.05
584	Chuck Jackson	.05
585	Rene Gonzales	.05
586	Tracy Woodson	.05
587	Jim Adduci	.05
588	Mario Soto	.05
589	Jeff Blauser	.05
590	Jim Traber	.05
591	Jon Perlman	.05
592	Mark Williamson	.05
593	Dave Meads	.05
594	Jim Eisenreich	.05
595a	*Paul Gibson* (player in background adjusting cup)	.25
595b	*Paul Gibson* (hand airbrushed away)	.05
596	Mike Birkbeck	.05
597	Terry Francona	.05
598	Paul Zuvella	.05
599	Franklin Stubbs	.05
600	Gregg Jefferies	.05
601	John Cangelosi	.05
602	Mike Sharperson	.05
603	Mike Diaz	.05
604	*Gary Varsho*	.05
605	*Terry Blocker*	.05
606	Charlie O'Brien	.05
607	Jim Eppard	.05
608	John Davis	.05
609	Ken Griffey, Sr.	.05
610	Buddy Bell	.05
611	Ted Simmons	.05
612	Matt Williams	.05
613	Danny Cox	.05
614	Al Pedrique	.05
615	Ron Oester	.05
616	John Smoltz	.05
617	Bob Melvin	.05
618	*Rob Dibble*	.10
619	Kirt Manwaring	.05
620	Felix Fermin	.05
621	*Doug Dascenzo*	.05
622	*Bill Brennan*	.05
623	*Carlos Quintana*	.05
624	*Mike Harkey*	.05
625	*Gary Sheffield*	1.25
626	*Tom Prince*	.05
627	*Steve Searcy*	.05
628	*Charlie Hayes*	.05
629	*Felix Jose*	.05
630	*Sandy Alomar*	.50
631	*Derek Lilliquist*	.05
632	Geronimo Berroa	.05
633	*Luis Medina*	.05
634	*Tom Gordon*	.10
635	*Ramon Martinez*	.25
636	*Craig Worthington*	.05
637	Edgar Martinez	.05
638	*Chad Krueter*	.05
639	*Ron Jones*	.05
640	*Van Snider*	.05
641	*Lance Blankenship*	.05
642	*Dwight Smith*	.05
643	*Cameron Drew*	.05
644	*Jerald Clark*	.05
645	*Randy Johnson*	2.00
646	*Norm Charlton*	.05
647	Todd Frohwirth	.05
648	*Luis de los Santos*	.05
649	*Tim Jones*	.05
650	*Dave West*	.05
651	*Bob Milacki*	.05
652	1988 Highlight (Wrigley Field)	.05
653	Orel Hershiser 1988 Highlight	.05
654a	Wade Boggs 1988 Highlight ('...sixth consecutive seaason...' on back)	2.00
654b	Wade Boggs 1988 Highlight ('season' corrected)	.10
655	Jose Canseco 1988 Highlight	.15
656	Doug Jones 1988 Highlight	.05
657	Rickey Henderson 1988 Highlight	.10
658	Tom Browning 1988 Highlight	.05
659	Mike Greenwell 1988 Highlight	.05
660	Joe Morgan 1988 Highlight (A.L. Win Streak)	.05

Rookie/Traded

		NM/M
Complete Set (110):		10.00
Common Player:		.05
1	Rafael Palmeiro	.35
2	Nolan Ryan	1.00
3	Jack Clark	.05
4	Dave LaPoint	.05
5	Mike Moore	.05
6	Pete O'Brien	.05
7	Jeffrey Leonard	.05
8	Rob Murphy	.05
9	Tom Herr	.05
10	Claudell Washington	.05
11	Mike Pagliarulo	.05
12	Steve Lake	.05
13	Spike Owen	.05
14	Andy Hawkins	.05
15	Todd Benzinger	.05
16	Mookie Wilson	.05
17	Bert Blyleven	.05
18	Jeff Treadway	.05
19	Bruce Hurst	.05
20	Steve Sax	.05
21	Juan Samuel	.05
22	Jesse Barfield	.05
23	Carmelo Castillo	.05
24	Terry Leach	.05
25	Mark Langston	.05
26	Eric King	.05
27	Steve Balboni	.05
28	Len Dykstra	.05
29	Keith Moreland	.05
30	Terry Kennedy	.05
31	Eddie Murray	.45
32	Mitch Williams	.05
33	Jeff Parrett	.05
34	Wally Backman	.05
35	Julio Franco	.05
36	Lance Parrish	.05
37	Nick Esasky	.05
38	Luis Polonia	.05
39	Kevin Gross	.05
40	John Dopson	.05
41	Willie Randolph	.05
42	Jim Clancy	.05
43	Tracy Jones	.05
44	Phil Bradley	.05
45	Milt Thompson	.05
46	Chris James	.05
47	Scott Fletcher	.05
48	Kal Daniels	.05
49	Steve Bedrosian	.05
50	Rickey Henderson	.45
51	Dion James	.05
52	Tim Leary	.05
53	Roger McDowell	.05
54	Mel Hall	.05
55	Dickie Thon	.05
56	Zane Smith	.05
57	Danny Heep	.05
58	Bob McClure	.05
59	Brian Holton	.05
60	Randy Ready	.05
61	Bob Melvin	.05
62	Harold Baines	.05
63	Lance McCullers	.05
64	Jody Davis	.05
65	Darrell Evans	.05
66	Joel Youngblood	.05
67	Frank Viola	.05
68	Mike Aldrete	.05
69	Greg Cadaret	.05
70	John Kruk	.05
71	Pat Sheridan	.05
72	Oddibe McDowell	.05
73	Tom Brookens	.05
74	Bob Boone	.05
75	Walt Terrell	.05
76	Joel Skinner	.05
77	Randy Johnson	1.50
78	Felix Fermin	.05
79	Rick Mahler	.05
80	Rich Dotson	.05
81	Cris Carpenter	.05
82	Bill Spiers	.05
83	Junior Felix	.05
84	Joe Girardi	.05
85	Jerome Walton	.05
86	Greg Litton	.05
87	Greg Harris	.05
88	Jim Abbott	.05
89	Kevin Brown	.05
90	*John Wetteland*	.10
91	Gary Wayne	.05
92	Rich Monteleone	.05
93	Bob Geren	.05
94	Clay Parker	.05
95	Steve Finley	.05
96	Gregg Olson	.05
97	Ken Patterson	.05
98	Ken Hill	.05
99	Scott Scudder	.05
100	*Ken Griffey, Jr.*	6.00
101	Jeff Brantley	.05
102	Donn Pall	.05
103	Carlos Martinez	.05
104	Joe Oliver	.05
105	Omar Vizquel	.25
106	*Albert Belle*	1.00
107	*Kenny Rogers*	.10
108	Mark Carreon	.05
109	Rolando Roomes	.05
110	Pete Harnisch	.05

1990 SCORE

	NM/M
Hobby Factory Set (714):	8.00
Retail Factory Set (704):	7.00

Complete Set (704):	6.00
Common Player:	.05
Plastic Pack (16):	.40
Plastic Wax Box (36):	9.00

No.	Player	Price
1	Don Mattingly	.50
2	Cal Ripken, Jr.	1.00
3	Dwight Evans	.05
4	Barry Bonds	1.00
5	Kevin McReynolds	.05
6	Ozzie Guillen	.05
7	Terry Kennedy	.05
8	Bryan Harvey	.05
9	Alan Trammell	.05
10	Cory Snyder	.05
11	Jody Reed	.05
12	Roberto Alomar	.20
13	Pedro Guerrero	.05
14	Gary Redus	.05
15	Marty Barrett	.05
16	Ricky Jordan	.05
17	Joe Magrane	.05
18	Sid Fernandez	.05
19	Rich Dotson	.05
20	Jack Clark	.05
21	Bob Walk	.05
22	Ron Karkovice	.05
23	Lenny Harris	.05
24	Phil Bradley	.05
25	Andres Galarraga	.05
26	Brian Downing	.05
27	Dave Martinez	.05
28	Eric King	.05
29	Barry Lyons	.05
30	Dave Schmidt	.05
31	Mike Boddicker	.05
32	Tom Foley	.05
33	Brady Anderson	.05
34	Jim Presley	.05
35	Lance Parrish	.05
36	Von Hayes	.05
37	Lee Smith	.05
38	Herm Winningham	.05
39	Alejandro Pena	.05
40	Mike Scott	.05
41	Joe Orsulak	.05
42	Rafael Ramirez	.05
43	Gerald Young	.05
44	Dick Schofield	.05
45	Dave Smith	.05
46	Dave Magadan	.05
47	Dennis Martinez	.05
48	Greg Minton	.05
49	Milt Thompson	.05
50	Orel Hershiser	.05
51	Bip Roberts	.05
52	Jerry Browne	.05
53	Bob Ojeda	.05
54	Fernando Valenzuela	.05
55	Matt Nokes	.05
56	Brook Jacoby	.05
57	Frank Tanana	.05
58	Scott Fletcher	.05
59	Ron Oester	.05
60	Bob Boone	.05
61	Dan Gladden	.05
62	Darnell Coles	.05
63	Gregg Olson	.05
64	Todd Burns	.05
65	Todd Benzinger	.05
66	Dale Murphy	.25
67	Mike Flanagan	.05
68	Jose Oquendo	.05
69	Cecil Espy	.05
70	Chris Sabo	.05
71	Shane Rawley	.05
72	Tom Brunansky	.05
73	Vance Law	.05
74	B.J. Surhoff	.05
75	Lou Whitaker	.05
76	Ken Caminiti	.05
77	Nelson Liriano	.05
78	Tommy Gregg	.05
79	Don Slaught	.05
80	Eddie Murray	.40
81	Joe Boever	.05
82	Charlie Leibrandt	.05
83	Jose Lind	.05
84	Tony Phillips	.05
85	Mitch Webster	.05
86	Dan Plesac	.05
87	Rick Mahler	.05
88	Steve Lyons	.05
89	Tony Fernandez	.05
90	Ryne Sandberg	.45
91	Nick Esasky	.05
92	Luis Salazar	.05
93	Pete Incaviglia	.05
94	Ivan Calderon	.05
95	Jeff Treadway	.05
96	Kurt Stillwell	.05
97	Gary Sheffield	.30
98	Jeffrey Leonard	.05
99	Andres Thomas	.05
100	Roberto Kelly	.05
101	Alvaro Espinoza	.05
102	Greg Gagne	.05
103	John Farrell	.05
104	Willie Wilson	.05
105	Glenn Braggs	.05
106	Chet Lemon	.05
107	Jamie Moyer	.05
108	Chuck Crim	.05
109	Dave Valle	.05
110	Walt Weiss	.05
111	Larry Sheets	.05
112	Don Robinson	.05
113	Danny Heep	.05
114	Carmelo Martinez	.05
115	Dave Gallagher	.05
116	Mike LaValliere	.05
117	Bob McClure	.05
118	Rene Gonzales	.05
119	Mark Parent	.05
120	Wally Joyner	.05
121	Mark Gubicza	.05
122	Tony Pena	.05
123	Carmen Castillo	.05
124	Howard Johnson	.05
125	Steve Sax	.05
126	Tim Belcher	.05
127	Tim Burke	.05
128	Al Newman	.05
129	Dennis Rasmussen	.05
130	Doug Jones	.05
131	Fred Lynn	.05
132	Jeff Hamilton	.05
133	German Gonzalez	.05
134	John Morris	.05
135	Dave Parker	.05
136	Gary Pettis	.05
137	Dennis Boyd	.05
138	Candy Maldonado	.05
139	Rick Cerone	.05
140	George Brett	.50
141	Dave Clark	.05
142	Dickie Thon	.05
143	Junior Ortiz	.05
144	Don August	.05
145	Gary Gaetti	.05
146	Kirt Manwaring	.05
147	Jeff Reed	.05
148	Jose Alvarez	.05
149	Mike Schooler	.05
150	Mark Grace	.05
151	Geronimo Berroa	.05
152	Barry Jones	.05
153	Geno Petralli	.05
154	Jim Deshaies	.05
155	Barry Larkin	.05
156	Alfredo Griffin	.05
157	Tom Henke	.05
158	Mike Jeffcoat	.05
159	Bob Welch	.05
160	Julio Franco	.05
161	Henry Cotto	.05
162	Terry Steinbach	.05
163	Damon Berryhill	.05
164	Tim Crews	.05
165	Tom Browning	.05
166	Frd Manrique	.05
167	Harold Reynolds	.05
168a	Ron Hassey (uniform #27 on back)	.05
168b	Ron Hassey (uniform #24 on back)	.50
169	Shawon Dunston	.05
170	Bobby Bonilla	.05
171	Tom Herr	.05
172	Mike Heath	.05
173	Rich Gedman	.05
174	Bill Ripken	.05
175	Pete O'Brien	.05
176a	Lloyd McClendon (uniform number 1 on back)	.50
176b	Lloyd McClendon (uniform number 10 on back)	.05
177	Brian Holton	.05
178	Jeff Blauser	.05
179	Jim Eisenreich	.05
180	Bert Blyleven	.05
181	Rob Murphy	.05
182	Bill Doran	.05
183	Curt Ford	.05
184	Mike Henneman	.05
185	Eric Davis	.05
186	Lance McCullers	.05
187	*Steve Davis*	.05
188	Bill Wegman	.05
189	Brian Harper	.05
190	Mike Moore	.05
191	Dale Mohorcic	.05
192	Tim Wallach	.05
193	Keith Hernandez	.05
194	Dave Righetti	.05
195a	Bret Saberhagen ('joke' on card back)	.10
195b	Bret Saberhagen ('joker' on card back)	.30
196	Paul Kilgus	.05
197	Bud Black	.05
198	Juan Samuel	.05
199	Kevin Seitzer	.05
200	Darryl Strawberry	.05
201	Dave Steib	.05
202	Charlie Hough	.05
203	Jack Morris	.05
204	Rance Mulliniks	.05
205	Alvin Davis	.05
206	Jack Howell	.05
207	Ken Patterson	.05
208	Terry Pendleton	.05
209	Craig Lefferts	.05
210	Kevin Brown	.05
211	Dan Petry	.05
212	Dave Leiper	.05
213	Daryl Boston	.05
214	Kevin Hickey	.05
215	Mike Krukow	.05
216	Terry Francona	.05
217	Kirk McCaskill	.05
218	Scott Bailes	.05
219	Bob Forsch	.05
220	Mike Aldrete	.05
221	Steve Buechele	.05
222	Jesse Barfield	.05
223	Juan Berenguer	.05
224	Andy McGaffigan	.05
225	Pete Smith	.05
226	Mike Witt	.05
227	Jay Howell	.05
228	Scott Bradley	.05
229	*Jerome Walton*	.05
230	Greg Swindell	.05
231	Atlee Hammaker	.05
232a	Mike Devereaux (RF)	.05
232b	Mike Devereaux (CF)	2.00
233	Ken Hill	.05
234	Craig Worthington	.05
235	Scott Terry	.05
236	Brett Butler	.05
237	Doyle Alexander	.05
238	Dave Anderson	.05
239	Bob Milacki	.05
240	Dwight Smith	.05
241	Otis Nixon	.05
242	Pat Tabler	.05
243	Derek Lilliquist	.05
244	Danny Tartabull	.05
245	Wade Boggs	.45
246	Scott Garrelts	.05
247	Spike Owen	.05
248	Norm Charlton	.05
249	Gerald Perry	.05
250	Nolan Ryan	1.00
251	Kevin Gross	.05
252	Randy Milligan	.05
253	Mike LaCoss	.05
254	Dave Bergman	.05
255	Tony Gwynn	.45
256	Felix Fermin	.05
257	Greg Harris	.05
258	*Junior Felix*	.05
259	Mark Davis	.05
260	Vince Coleman	.05
261	Paul Gibson	.05
262	Mitch Williams	.05
263	Jeff Russell	.05
264	Omar Vizquel	.05
265	Andre Dawson	.25
266	Storm Davis	.05
267	Guillermo Hernandez	.05
268	Mike Felder	.05
269	Tom Candiotti	.05
270	Bruce Hurst	.05
271	Fred McGriff	.05
272	Glenn Davis	.05
273	John Franco	.05
274	Rich Yett	.05
275	Craig Biggio	.05
276	Gene Larkin	.05
277	Rob Dibble	.05
278	Randy Bush	.05
279	Kevin Bass	.05
280a	Bo Jackson ('Watham' on back)	.15
280b	Bo Jackson ('Wathan' on back)	.50
281	Wally Backman	.05
282	Larry Andersen	.05
283	Chris Bosio	.05
284	Juan Agosto	.05
285	Ozzie Smith	.45
286	George Bell	.05
287	Rex Hudler	.05
288	Pat Borders	.05
289	Danny Jackson	.05
290	Carlton Fisk	.40
291	Tracy Jones	.05
292	Allan Anderson	.05
293	Johnny Ray	.05
294	Lee Guetterman	.05
295	Paul O'Neill	.05
296	Carney Lansford	.05
297	Tom Brookens	.05
298	Claudell Washington	.05
299	Hubie Brooks	.05
300	Will Clark	.05
301	Kenny Rogers	.05
302	Darrell Evans	.05
303	Greg Briley	.05
304	Donn Pall	.05
305	Teddy Higuera	.05
306	Dan Pasqua	.05
307	Dave Winfield	.40
308	Dennis Powell	.05
309	Jose DeLeon	.05
310	Roger Clemens	.50
311	Melido Perez	.05
312	Devon White	.05
313	Dwight Gooden	.05
314	*Carlos Martinez*	.05
315	Dennis Eckersley	.35
316	Clay Parker	.05
317	Rick Honeycutt	.05
318	Tim Laudner	.05
319	Joe Carter	.05
320	Robin Yount	.40
321	Felix Jose	.05
322	Mickey Tettleton	.05
323	Mike Gallego	.05
324	Edgar Martinez	.05
325	Dave Henderson	.05
326	Chili Davis	.05
327	Steve Balboni	.05
328	Jody Davis	.05
329	Shawn Hillegas	.05
330	Jim Abbott	.05
331	John Dopson	.05
332	Mark Williamson	.05
333	Jeff Robinson	.05
334	John Smiley	.05
335	Bobby Thigpen	.05
336	Garry Templeton	.05
337	Marvell Wynne	.05
338a	Ken Griffey, Sr. (uniform #25 on card back)	.05
338b	Ken Griffey, Sr. (uniform #30 on card back)	1.00
339	Steve Finley	.05
340	Ellis Burks	.05
341	Frank Williams	.05
342	Mike Morgan	.05
343	Kevin Mitchell	.05
344	Joel Youngblood	.05
345	Mike Greenwell	.05
346	Glenn Wilson	.05
347	John Costello	.05
348	Wes Gardner	.05
349	Jeff Ballard	.05
350	Mark Thurmond	.05
351	Randy Myers	.05
352	Shawn Abner	.05
353	Jesse Orosco	.05
354	Greg Walker	.05
355	Pete Harnisch	.05
356	Steve Farr	.05

No.	Player	Price
357	Dave LaPoint	.05
358	Willie Fraser	.05
359	Mickey Hatcher	.05
360	Rickey Henderson	.40
361	Mike Fitzgerald	.05
362	Bill Schroeder	.05
363	Mark Carreon	.05
364	Ron Jones	.05
365	Jeff Montgomery	.05
366	Bill Krueger	.05
367	John Cangelosi	.05
368	Jose Gonzalez	.05
369	*Greg Hibbard*	.05
370	John Smoltz	.05
371	*Jeff Brantley*	.05
372	Frank White	.05
373	Ed Whitson	.05
374	Willie McGee	.05
375	Jose Canseco	.30
376	Randy Ready	.05
377	Don Aase	.05
378	Tony Armas	.05
379	Steve Bedrosian	.05
380	Chuck Finley	.05
381	Kent Hrbek	.05
382	Jim Gantner	.05
383	Mel Hall	.05
384	Mike Marshall	.05
385	Mark McGwire	.75
386	Wayne Tolleson	.05
387	Brian Holton	.05
388	John Wetteland	.05
389	Darren Daulton	.05
390	Rob Deer	.05
391	John Moses	.05
392	Todd Worrell	.05
393	Chuck Cary	.05
394	Stan Javier	.05
395	Willie Randolph	.05
396	Bill Buckner	.05
397	Robby Thompson	.05
398	Mike Scioscia	.05
399	Lonnie Smith	.05
400	Kirby Puckett	.45
401	Mark Langston	.05
402	Danny Darwin	.05
403	Greg Maddux	.45
404	Lloyd Moseby	.05
405	Rafael Palmeiro	.35
406	Chad Kreuter	.05
407	Jimmy Key	.05
408	Tim Birtsas	.05
409	Tim Raines	.05
410	Dave Stewart	.05
411	*Eric Yelding*	.05
412	*Kent Anderson*	.05
413	Les Lancaster	.05
414	Rick Dempsey	.05
415	Randy Johnson	.40
416	Gary Carter	.40
417	Rolando Roomes	.05
418	Dan Schatzeder	.05
419	Bryn Smith	.05
420	Ruben Sierra	.05
421	Steve Jeltz	.05
422	Ken Oberkfell	.05
423	Sid Bream	.05
424	Jim Clancy	.05
425	Kelly Gruber	.05
426	Rick Leach	.05
427	Len Dykstra	.05
428	Jeff Pico	.05
429	John Cerutti	.05
430	David Cone	.05
431	Jeff Kunkel	.05
432	Luis Aquino	.05
433	Ernie Whitt	.05
434	Bo Diaz	.05
435	Steve Lake	.05
436	Pat Perry	.05
437	Mike Davis	.05
438	Cecilio Guante	.05
439	Duane Ward	.05
440	Andy Van Slyke	.05
441	Gene Nelson	.05
442	Luis Polonia	.05
443	Kevin Elster	.05
444	Keith Moreland	.05
445	Roger McDowell	.05
446	Ron Darling	.05
447	Ernest Riles	.05
448	Mookie Wilson	.05
449a	*Bill Spiers* (66 missing for year of birth)	.50
449b	*Bill Spiers* (1966 for birth year)	.05
450	Rick Sutcliffe	.05
451	Nelson Santovenia	.05
452	Andy Allanson	.05

No.	Player	Price
453	Bob Melvin	.05
454	Benny Santiago	.05
455	Jose Uribe	.05
456	Bill Landrum	.05
457	Bobby Witt	.05
458	Kevin Romine	.05
459	Lee Mazzilli	.05
460	Paul Molitor	.40
461	Ramon Martinez	.05
462	Frank DiPino	.05
463	Walt Terrell	.05
464	*Bob Geren*	.05
465	Rick Reuchel	.05
466	Mark Grant	.05
467	John Kruk	.05
468	Gregg Jefferies	.05
469	R.J. Reynolds	.05
470	Harold Baines	.05
471	Dennis Lamp	.05
472	Tom Gordon	.05
473	Terry Puhl	.05
474	Curtis Wilkerson	.05
475	Dan Quisenberry	.05
476	Oddibe McDowell	.05
477a	Zane Smith (Career ERA 3.93)	.50
477b	Zane Smith	.05
478	Franklin Stubbs	.05
479	Wallace Johnson	.05
480	Jay Tibbs	.05
481	Tom Glavine	.35
482	Manny Lee	.05
483	Joe Hesketh	.05
484	Mike Bielecki	.05
485	Greg Brock	.05
486	Pascual Perez	.05
487	Kirk Gibson	.05
488	Scott Sanderson	.05
489	Domingo Ramos	.05
490	Kal Daniels	.05
491a	David Wells (reversed negative on back photo)	1.50
491b	David Wells (corrected)	.05
492	Jerry Reed	.05
493	Eric Show	.05
494	Mike Pagliarulo	.05
495	Ron Robinson	.05
496	Brad Komminsk	.05
497	*Greg Litton*	.05
498	Chris James	.05
499	Luis Quinones	.05
500	Frank Viola	.05
501	Tim Teufel	.05
502	Terry Leach	.05
503	Matt Williams	.05
504	Tim Leary	.05
505	Doug Drabek	.05
506	Mariano Duncan	.05
507	Charlie Hayes	.05
508	Albert Belle	.05
509	Pat Sheridan	.05
510	Mackey Sasser	.05
511	Jose Rijo	.05
512	Mike Smithson	.05
513	Gary Ward	.05
514	Dion James	.05
515	Jim Gott	.05
516	Drew Hall	.05
517	Doug Bair	.05
518	*Scott Scudder*	.05
519	Rick Aguilera	.05
520	Rafael Belliard	.05
521	Jay Buhner	.05
522	Jeff Reardon	.05
523	Steve Rosenberg	.05
524	Randy Velarde	.05
525	Jeff Musselman	.05
526	Bill Long	.05
527	*Gary Wayne*	.05
528	*Dave Johnson*	.05
529	Ron Kittle	.05
530	Erik Hanson	.05
531	Steve Wilson	.05
532	Joey Meyer	.05
533	Curt Young	.05
534	Kelly Downs	.05
535	Joe Girardi	.05
536	Lance Blankenship	.05
537	Greg Mathews	.05
538	Donell Nixon	.05
539	Mark Knudson	.05
540	*Jeff Wetherby*	.05
541	Darrin Jackson	.05
542	Terry Mulholland	.05
543	Eric Hetzel	.05
544	*Rick Reed*	.05
545	Dennis Cook	.05
546	Mike Jackson	.05
547	Brian Fisher	.05

No.	Player	Price
548	*Gene Harris*	.05
549	Jeff King	.05
550	Dave Dravecky (Salute)	.05
551	Randy Kutcher	.05
552	Mark Portugal	.05
553	*Jim Corsi*	.05
554	Todd Stottlemyre	.05
555	Scott Bankhead	.05
556	Ken Dayley	.05
557	*Rick Wrona*	.10
558	*Sammy Sosa*	3.00
559	Keith Miller	.05
560	Ken Griffey, Jr.	.65
561a	Ryne Sandberg (Highlight, 3B on front)	2.00
561b	Ryne Sandberg (Highlight, no position)	.25
562	Billy Hatcher	.05
563	Jay Bell	.05
564	*Jack Daugherty*	.05
565	*Rich Monteleone*	.05
566	Bo Jackson (All-Star MVP)	.10
567	*Tony Fossas*	.05
568	*Roy Smith*	.05
569	*Jaime Navarro*	.05
570	Lance Johnson	.05
571	*Mike Dyer*	.05
572	*Kevin Ritz*	.05
573	Dave West	.05
574	*Gary Mielke*	.05
575	Scott Lusader	.05
576	Joe Oliver	.05
577	Sandy Alomar, Jr.	.05
578	Andy Benes	.05
579	Tim Jones	.05
580	*Randy McCament*	.05
581	Curt Schilling	.35
582	*John Orton*	.05
583a	*Milt Cuyler* (998 games)	1.00
583b	*Milt Cuyler* (98 games)	.05
584	*Eric Anthony*	.05
585	*Greg Vaughn*	.15
586	Deion Sanders	.05
587	Jose DeJesus	.05
588	*Chip Hale*	.05
589	*John Olerud*	.50
590	*Steve Olin*	.05
591	*Marquis Grissom*	.40
592	*Moises Alou*	.40
593	Mark Lemke	.05
594	*Dean Palmer*	.15
595	Robin Ventura	.05
596	Tino Martinez	.05
597	*Mike Huff*	.05
598	*Scott Hemond*	.05
599	*Wally Whitehurst*	.05
600	*Todd Zeile*	.15
601	Glenallen Hill	.05
602	Hal Morris	.05
603	Juan Bell	.05
604	*Bobby Rose*	.05
605	*Matt Merullo*	.05
606	*Kevin Maas*	.05
607	*Randy Nosek*	.05
608a	*Billy Bates* (line ine '12 triples' mentioned in second-last)	.05
608b	Billy Bates (triples not mentioned)	.75
609	*Mike Stanton*	.05
610	*Goose Gozzo*	.05
611	*Charles Nagy*	.40
612	*Scott Coolbaugh*	.05
613	*Jose Vizcaino*	.10
614	*Greg Smith*	.05
615	*Jeff Huson*	.05
616	*Mickey Weston*	.05
617	John Pawlowski	.05
618a	*Joe Skalski* (uniform #27 on card back)	.15
618b	*Joe Skalski* (uniform #67 on card back)	1.00
619	*Bernie Williams*	1.00
620	*Shawn Holman*	.05
621	*Gary Eave*	.05
622	*Darrin Fletcher*	.10
623	*Pat Combs*	.05
624	*Mike Blowers*	.05
625	Kevin Appier	.05
626	*Pat Austin*	.05
627	*Kelly Mann*	.05
628	*Matt Kinzer*	.05
629	*Chris Hammond*	.10
630	*Dean Wilkins*	.05
631	*Larry Walker*	.50
632	*Blaine Beatty*	.05
633a	Tom Barrett (uniform #29 on card back)	.05

No.	Player	Price
633b	Tom Barrett (uniform #14 on card back)	1.00
634	*Stan Belinda*	.05
635	*Tex Smith*	.05
636	*Hensley Meulens*	.10
637	*Juan Gonzalez*	1.50
638	*Lenny Webster*	.10
639	*Mark Gardner*	.05
640	*Tommy Greene*	.05
641	*Mike Hartley*	.05
642	*Phil Stephenson*	.05
643	*Kevin Mmahat*	.05
644	*Ed Whited*	.05
645	*Delino DeShields*	.15
646	Kevin Blankenship	.05
647	*Paul Sorrento*	.05
648	*Mike Roesler*	.05
649	*Jason Grimsley*	.05
650	*Dave Justice*	1.00
651	*Scott Cooper*	.05
652	Dave Eiland	.05
653	*Mike Munoz*	.05
654	*Jeff Fischer*	.05
655	*Terry Jorgenson*	.05
656	*George Canale*	.05
657	*Brian DuBois*	.05
658	Carlos Quintana	.05
659	Luis de los Santos	.05
660	Jerald Clark	.05
661	*Donald Harris*	.05
662	*Paul Coleman*	.05
663	*Frank Thomas*	2.00
664	*Brent Mayne*	.10
665	*Eddie Zosky*	.05
666	*Steve Hosey*	.05
667	*Scott Bryant*	.05
668	*Tom Goodwin*	.10
669	*Cal Eldred*	.10
670	*Earl Cunningham*	.05
671	*Alan Zinter*	.05
672	*Chuck Knoblauch*	.40
672(a)	Chuck Knoblauch	10.00
673	*Kyle Abbott*	.10
674	*Roger Salkeld*	.05
675	*Mo Vaughn*	.50
676	*Kiki Jones*	.05
677	*Tyler Houston*	.10
678	*Jeff Jackson*	.05
679	*Greg Gohr*	.05
680	*Ben McDonald*	.15
681	*Greg Blosser*	.05
682	*Willie Green*	.05
683	Wade Boggs	.25
684	Will Clark	.05
685	Tony Gwynn	.25
686	Rickey Henderson	.20
687	Bo Jackson	.15
688	Mark Langston	.05
689	Barry Larkin	.05
690	Kirby Puckett	.25
691	Ryne Sandberg	.25
692	Mike Scott	.05
693	Terry Steinbach	.05
694	Bobby Thigpen	.05
695	Mitch Williams	.05
696	Nolan Ryan	.40
697	Bo Jackson	.25
698	Rickey Henderson	.20
699	Will Clark	.05
700	World Series Games 1-2	.05
701	Lights Out: Candlestick	.15
702	World Series Game 3	.05
703	World Series Wrap-up	.05
704	Wade Boggs	.25

Traded

	NM/M
Complete Set (110):	4.00
Common Player:	.05

No.	Player	Price
1	Dave Winfield	.75
2	Kevin Bass	.05
3	Nick Esasky	.05
4	Mitch Webster	.05
5	Pascual Perez	.05
6	Gary Pettis	.05
7	Tony Pena	.05
8	Candy Maldonado	.05
9	Cecil Fielder	.05
10	Carmelo Martinez	.05
11	Mark Langston	.05
12	Dave Parker	.05
13	Don Slaught	.05
14	Tony Phillips	.05
15	John Franco	.05
16	Randy Myers	.05
17	Jeff Reardon	.05
18	Sandy Alomar, Jr.	.05
19	Joe Carter	.05
20	Fred Lynn	.05
21	Storm Davis	.05
22	Craig Lefferts	.05
23	Pete O'Brien	.05
24	Dennis Boyd	.05
25	Lloyd Moseby	.05
26	Mark Davis	.05
27	Tim Leary	.05
28	Gerald Perry	.05
29	Don Aase	.05
30	Ernie Whitt	.05
31	Dale Murphy	.35
32	Alejandro Pena	.05
33	Juan Samuel	.05
34	Hubie Brooks	.05
35	Gary Carter	.75
36	Jim Presley	.05
37	Wally Backman	.05
38	Matt Nokes	.05
39	Dan Petry	.05
40	Franklin Stubbs	.05
41	Jeff Huson	.05
42	Billy Hatcher	.05
43	Terry Leach	.05
44	Phil Bradley	.05
45	Claudell Washington	.05
46	Luis Polonia	.05
47	Daryl Boston	.05
48	Lee Smith	.05
49	Tom Brunansky	.05
50	Mike Witt	.05
51	Willie Randolph	.05
52	Stan Javier	.05
53	Brad Komminsk	.05
54	John Candelaria	.05
55	Bryn Smith	.05
56	Glenn Braggs	.05
57	Keith Hernandez	.05
58	Ken Oberkfell	.05
59	Steve Jeltz	.05
60	Chris James	.05
61	Scott Sanderson	.05
62	Bill Long	.05
63	Rick Cerone	.05
64	Scott Bailes	.05
65	Larry Sheets	.05
66	Junior Ortiz	.05
67	Francisco Cabrera	.05
68	Gary DiSarcina	.05
69	Greg Olson	.05
70	Beau Allred	.05
71	Oscar Azocar	.05
72	Kent Mercker	.05
73	John Burkett	.05
74	Carlos Baerga	.05
75	Dave Hollins	.05
76	*Todd Hundley*	.25
77	Rick Parker	.05
78	Steve Cummings	.05
79	Bill Sampen	.05
80	Jerry Kutzler	.05
81	Derek Bell	.05
82	Kevin Tapani	.05
83	*Jim Leyritz*	.25
84	*Ray Lankford*	.25
85	Wayne Edwards	.05
86	Frank Thomas	2.00
87	Tim Naehring	.05
88	Willie Blair	.05
89	*Alan Mills*	.05
90	Scott Radinsky	.05
91	Howard Farmer	.05
92	Julio Machado	.05
93	Rafael Valdez	.05
94	*Shawn Boskie*	.05
95	David Segui	.05
96	Chris Hoiles	.05
97	D.J. Dozier	.05
98	Hector Villanueva	.05
99	Eric Gunderson	.05
100	*Eric Lindros*	1.00
101	Dave Otto	.05
102	Dana Kiecker	.05
103	Tim Drummond	.05
104	Mickey Pina	.05
105	Craig Grebeck	.05
106	*Bernard Gilkey*	.25
107	Tim Layana	.05
108	Scott Chiamparino	.05
109	Steve Avery	.05
110	Terry Shumpert	.05

1991 SCORE

	NM/M
Unopened Fact. Set (900):	10.00
Complete Set (893):	6.00
Common Player:	.05
Series 1 or 2 Pack (16):	.25
Series 1 or 2 Box (36):	6.00

No.	Player	Price
1	Jose Canseco	.25
2	Ken Griffey, Jr.	.60
3	Ryne Sandberg	.50
4	Nolan Ryan	.75
5	Bo Jackson	.10
6	Bret Saberhagen	.05
7	Will Clark	.05
8	Ellis Burks	.05
9	Joe Carter	.05
10	Rickey Henderson	.40
11	Ozzie Guillen	.05
12	Wade Boggs	.50
13	Jerome Walton	.05
14	John Franco	.05
15	Ricky Jordan	.05
16	Wally Backman	.05
17	Rob Dibble	.05
18	Glenn Braggs	.05
19	Cory Snyder	.05
20	Kal Daniels	.05
21	Mark Langston	.05
22	Kevin Gross	.05
23	Don Mattingly	.55
24	Dave Righetti	.05
25	Roberto Alomar	.15
26	Robby Thompson	.05
27	Jack McDowell	.05
28	Bip Roberts	.05
29	Jay Howell	.05
30	Dave Steib	.05
31	Johnny Ray	.05
32	Steve Sax	.05
33	Terry Mulholland	.05
34	Lee Guetterman	.05
35	Tim Raines	.05
36	Scott Fletcher	.05
37	Lance Parrish	.05
38	Tony Phillips	.05
39	Todd Stottlemyre	.05
40	Alan Trammell	.05
41	Todd Burns	.05
42	Mookie Wilson	.05
43	Chris Bosio	.05
44	Jeffrey Leonard	.05
45	Doug Jones	.05
46	Mike Scott	.05
47	Andy Hawkins	.05
48	Harold Reynolds	.05
49	Paul Molitor	.40
50	John Farrell	.05
51	Danny Darwin	.05
52	Jeff Blauser	.05
53	John Tudor	.05
54	Milt Thompson	.05
55	Dave Justice	.05
56	*Greg Olson*	.05
57	*Willie Blair*	.05
58	*Rick Parker*	.05
59	Shawn Boskie	.05
60	Kevin Tapani	.05
61	Dave Hollins	.05
62	*Scott Radinsky*	.05
63	Francisco Cabrera	.05
64	*Tim Layana*	.05
65	Jim Leyritz	.05
66	Wayne Edwards	.05
67	Lee Stevens	.05
68	*Bill Sampen*	.05
69	*Craig Grebeck*	.05
70	John Burkett	.05
71	*Hector Villanueva*	.05
72	*Oscar Azocar*	.05
73	Alan Mills	.05
74	Carlos Baerga	.05
75	Charles Nagy	.05
76	Tim Drummond	.05
77	*Dana Kiecker*	.05
78	*Tom Edens*	.05
79	Kent Mercker	.05
80	Steve Avery	.05
81	Lee Smith	.05
82	Dave Martinez	.05
83	Dave Winfield	.40
84	Bill Spiers	.05
85	Dan Pasqua	.05
86	Randy Milligan	.05
87	Tracy Jones	.05
88	Greg Myers	.05
89	Keith Hernandez	.05
90	Todd Benzinger	.05
91	Mike Jackson	.05
92	Mike Stanley	.05
93	Candy Maldonado	.05
94	John Kruk	.05
95	Cal Ripken, Jr.	.75
96	Willie Fraser	.05
97	Mike Felder	.05
98	Bill Landrum	.05
99	Chuck Crim	.05
100	Chuck Finley	.05
101	Kirt Manwaring	.05
102	Jaime Navarro	.05
103	Dickie Thon	.05
104	Brian Downing	.05
105	Jim Abbott	.05
106	Tom Brookens	.05
107	Darryl Hamilton	.05
108	Bryan Harvey	.05
109	Greg Harris	.05
110	Greg Swindell	.05
111	Juan Berenguer	.05
112	Mike Heath	.05
113	Scott Bradley	.05
114	Jack Morris	.05
115	Barry Jones	.05
116	Kevin Romine	.05
117	Garry Templeton	.05
118	Scott Sanderson	.05
119	Roberto Kelly	.05
120	George Brett	.50
121	Oddibe McDowell	.05
122	Jim Acker	.05
123	Bill Swift	.05
124	Eric King	.05
125	Jay Buhner	.05
126	Matt Young	.05
127	Alvaro Espinoza	.05
128	Greg Hibbard	.05
129	Jeff Robinson	.05
130	Mike Greenwell	.05
131	Dion James	.05
132	Donn Pall	.05
133	Lloyd Moseby	.05
134	Randy Velarde	.05
135	Allan Anderson	.05
136	Mark Davis	.05
137	Eric Davis	.05
138	Phil Stephenson	.05
139	Felix Fermin	.05
140	Pedro Guerrero	.05
141	Charlie Hough	.05
142	Mike Henneman	.05
143	Jeff Montgomery	.05
144	Lenny Harris	.05
145	Bruce Hurst	.05
146	Eric Anthony	.05
147	Paul Assenmacher	.05
148	Jesse Barfield	.05
149	Carlos Quintana	.05
150	Dave Stewart	.05
151	Roy Smith	.05
152	Paul Gibson	.05
153	Mickey Hatcher	.05
154	Jim Eisenreich	.05
155	Kenny Rogers	.05
156	Dave Schmidt	.05
157	Lance Johnson	.05
158	Dave West	.05
159	Steve Balboni	.05
160	Jeff Brantley	.05
161	Craig Biggio	.05
162	Brook Jacoby	.05
163	Dan Gladden	.05
164	Jeff Reardon	.05
165	Mark Carreon	.05
166	Mel Hall	.05
167	Gary Mielke	.05
168	Cecil Fielder	.05
169	Darrin Jackson	.05
170	Rick Aguilera	.05
171	Walt Weiss	.05
172	Steve Farr	.05
173	Jody Reed	.05
174	Mike Jeffcoat	.05
175	Mark Grace	.05
176	Larry Sheets	.05
177	Bill Gullickson	.05
178	Chris Gwynn	.05
179	Melido Perez	.05
180	Sid Fernandez	.05
181	Tim Burke	.05
182	Gary Pettis	.05
183	Rob Murphy	.05
184	Craig Lefferts	.05
185	Howard Johnson	.05
186	Ken Caminiti	.05
187	Tim Belcher	.05
188	Greg Cadaret	.05
189	Matt Williams	.05
190	Dave Magadan	.05
191	Geno Petralli	.05
192	Jeff Robinson	.05
193	Jim Deshaies	.05
194	Willie Randolph	.05
195	George Bell	.05
196	Hubie Brooks	.05
197	Tom Gordon	.05
198	Mike Fitzgerald	.05
199	Mike Pagliarulo	.05
200	Kirby Puckett	.50
201	Shawon Dunston	.05
202	Dennis Boyd	.05
203	Junior Felix	.05
204	Alejandro Pena	.05
205	Pete Smith	.05
206	Tom Glavine	.35
207	Luis Salazar	.05
208	John Smoltz	.05
209	Doug Dascenzo	.05
210	Tim Wallach	.05
211	Greg Gagne	.05
212	Mark Gubicza	.05
213	Mark Parent	.05
214	Ken Oberkfell	.05
215	Gary Carter	.40
216	Rafael Palmeiro	.35
217	Tom Niedenfuer	.05
218	Dave LaPoint	.05
219	Jeff Treadway	.05
220	Mitch Williams	.05
221	Jose DeLeon	.05
222	Mike LaValliere	.05
223	Darrel Akerfelds	.05
224a	Kent Anderson ('flachy' in first line)	.05
224b	Kent Anderson ('flashy' in first line)	.05
225	Dwight Evans	.05
226	Gary Redus	.05
227	Paul O'Neill	.05
228	Marty Barrett	.05
229	Tom Browning	.05
230	Terry Pendleton	.05
231	Jack Armstrong	.05
232	Mike Boddicker	.05
233	Neal Heaton	.05
234	Marquis Grissom	.05
235	Bert Blyleven	.05
236	Curt Young	.05
237	Don Carman	.05
238	Charlie Hayes	.05
239	Mark Knudson	.05
240	Todd Zeile	.05
241	Larry Walker	.05
242	Jerald Clark	.05
243	Jeff Ballard	.05
244	Jeff King	.05
245	Tom Brunansky	.05
246	Darren Daulton	.05
247	Scott Terry	.05
248	Rob Deer	.05
249	Brady Anderson	.05
250	Len Dykstra	.05
251	Greg Harris	.05
252	Mike Hartley	.05
253	Joey Cora	.05
254	Ivan Calderon	.05
255	Ted Power	.05

No.	Player	Value
256	Sammy Sosa	.50
257	Steve Buechele	.05
258	Mike Devereaux	.05
259	Brad Komminsk	.05
260	Teddy Higuera	.05
261	Shawn Abner	.05
262	Dave Valle	.05
263	Jeff Huson	.05
264	Edgar Martinez	.05
265	Carlton Fisk	.40
266	Steve Finley	.05
267	John Wetteland	.05
268	Kevin Appier	.05
269	Steve Lyons	.05
270	Mickey Tettleton	.05
271	Luis Rivera	.05
272	Steve Jeltz	.05
273	R.J. Reynolds	.05
274	Carlos Martinez	.05
275	Dan Plesac	.05
276	Mike Morgan	.05
277	Jeff Russell	.05
278	Pete Incaviglia	.05
279	Kevin Seitzer	.05
280	Bobby Thigpen	.05
281	Stan Javier	.05
282	Henry Cotto	.05
283	Gary Wayne	.05
284	Shane Mack	.05
285	Brian Holman	.05
286	Gerald Perry	.05
287	Steve Crawford	.05
288	Nelson Liriano	.05
289	Don Aase	.05
290	Randy Johnson	.40
291	Harold Baines	.05
292	Kent Hrbek	.05
293a	Les Lancaster ('Dallas Texas')	.05
293b	Les Lancaster ('Dallas, Texas')	.05
294	Jeff Musselman	.05
295	Kurt Stillwell	.05
296	Stan Belinda	.05
297	Lou Whitaker	.05
298	Glenn Wilson	.05
299	Omar Vizquel	.05
300	Ramon Martinez	.05
301	Dwight Smith	.05
302	Tim Crews	.05
303	Lance Blankenship	.05
304	Sid Bream	.05
305	Rafael Ramirez	.05
306	Steve Wilson	.05
307	Mackey Sasser	.05
308	Franklin Stubbs	.05
309	Jack Daugherty	.05
310	Eddie Murray	.40
311	Bob Welch	.05
312	Brian Harper	.05
313	Lance McCullers	.05
314	Dave Smith	.05
315	Bobby Bonilla	.05
316	Jerry Don Gleaton	.05
317	Greg Maddux	.50
318	Keith Miller	.05
319	Mark Portugal	.05
320	Robin Ventura	.05
321	Bob Ojeda	.05
322	Mike Harkey	.05
323	Jay Bell	.05
324	Mark McGwire	.65
325	Gary Gaetti	.05
326	Jeff Pico	.05
327	Kevin McReynolds	.05
328	Frank Tanana	.05
329	Eric Yelding	.05
330	Barry Bonds	.75
331	*Brian McRae*	.05
332	*Pedro Munoz*	.05
333	*Daryl Irvine*	.05
334	Chris Hoiles	.05
335	*Thomas Howard*	.05
336	*Jeff Schulz*	.05
337	Jeff Manto	.05
338	Beau Allred	.05
339	*Mike Bordick*	.10
340	Todd Hundley	.05
341	*Jim Vatcher*	.05
342	Luis Sojo	.05
343	*Jose Offerman*	.05
344	*Pete Coachman*	.05
345	Mike Benjamin	.05
346	*Ozzie Canseco*	.05
347	Tim McIntosh	.05
348	*Phil Plantier*	.05
349	*Terry Shumpert*	.05
350	Darren Lewis	.05
351	*David Walsh*	.05
352a	*Scott Chiamparino* (Bats: Left)	.05
352b	*Scott Chiamparino* (Bats: Right)	.05
353	*Julio Valera*	.05
354	*Anthony Telford*	.05
355	Kevin Wickander	.05
356	*Tim Naehring*	.05
357	*Jim Poole*	.05
358	*Mark Whiten*	.05
359	*Terry Wells*	.05
360	*Rafael Valdez*	.05
361	*Mel Stottlemyre*	.05
362	*David Segui*	.10
363	Paul Abbott	.05
364	*Steve Howard*	.05
365	*Karl Rhodes*	.10
366	*Rafael Novoa*	.05
367	*Joe Grahe*	.05
368	*Darren Reed*	.05
369	Jeff McKnight	.05
370	Scott Leius	.05
371	*Mark Dewey*	.05
372	*Mark Lee*	.05
373	*Rosario Rodriguez*	.05
374	Chuck McElroy	.05
375	*Mike Bell*	.05
376	Mickey Morandini	.05
377	*Bill Haselman*	.05
378	*Dave Pavlas*	.05
379	Derrick May	.05
380	*Jeromy Burnitz*	.25
381	*Donald Peters*	.05
382	*Alex Fernandez*	.05
383	*Mike Mussina*	1.00
384	*Daniel Smith*	.05
385	*Lance Dickson*	.10
386	*Carl Everett*	.40
387	*Thomas Nevers*	.05
388	*Adam Hyzdu*	.05
389	*Todd Van Poppel*	.10
390	*Rondell White*	.30
391	*Marc Newfield*	.05
392	Julio Franco (AS)	.05
393	Wade Boggs (AS)	.25
394	Ozzie Guillen (AS)	.05
395	Cecil Fielder (AS)	.05
396	Ken Griffey, Jr. (AS)	.30
397	Rickey Henderson (AS)	.20
398	Jose Canseco (AS)	.15
399	Roger Clemens (AS)	.30
400	Sandy Alomar,Jr. (AS)	.05
401	Bobby Thigpen (AS)	.05
402	Bobby Bonilla	.05
403	Eric Davis	.05
404	Fred McGriff	.05
405	Glenn Davis	.05
406	Kevin Mitchell	.05
407	Rob Dibble	.05
408	Ramon Martinez	.05
409	David Cone	.05
410	Bobby Witt	.05
411	Mark Langston	.05
412	Bo Jackson	.10
413	Shawon Dunston	.05
414	Jesse Barfield	.05
415	Ken Caminiti	.05
416	Benito Santiago	.05
417	Nolan Ryan	.40
418	Bobby Thigpen (HL)	.05
419	Ramon Martinez (HL)	.05
420	Bo Jackson (HL)	.10
421	Carlton Fisk (HL)	.20
422	Jimmy Key	.05
423	Junior Noboa	.05
424	Al Newman	.05
425	Pat Borders	.05
426	Von Hayes	.05
427	Tim Teufel	.05
428	Eric Plunk	.05
429	John Moses	.05
430	Mike Witt	.05
431	Otis Nixon	.05
432	Tony Fernandez	.05
433	Rance Mulliniks	.05
434	Dan Petry	.05
435	Bob Geren	.05
436	Steve Frey	.05
437	Jamie Moyer	.05
438	Junior Ortiz	.05
439	Tom O'Malley	.05
440	Pat Combs	.05
441	Jose Canseco	.15
442	Alfredo Griffin	.05
443	Andres Galarraga	.05
444	Bryn Smith	.05
445	Andre Dawson	.25
446	Juan Samuel	.05
447	Mike Aldrete	.05
448	Ron Gant	.05
449	Fernando Valenzuela	.05
450	Vince Coleman	.05
451	Kevin Mitchell	.05
452	Spike Owen	.05
453	Mike Bielecki	.05
454	Dennis Martinez	.05
455	Brett Butler	.05
456	Ron Darling	.05
457	Dennis Rasmussen	.05
458	Ken Howell	.05
459	Steve Bedrosian	.05
460	Frank Viola	.05
461	Jose Lind	.05
462	Chris Sabo	.05
463	Dante Bichette	.05
464	Rick Mahler	.05
465	John Smiley	.05
466	Devon White	.05
467	John Orton	.05
468	Mike Stanton	.05
469	Billy Hatcher	.05
470	Wally Joyner	.05
471	Gene Larkin	.05
472	Doug Drabek	.05
473	Gary Sheffield	.30
474	David Wells	.05
475	Andy Van Slyke	.05
476	Mike Gallego	.05
477	B.J. Surhoff	.05
478	Gene Nelson	.05
479	Mariano Duncan	.05
480	Fred McGriff	.05
481	Jerry Browne	.05
482	Alvin Davis	.05
483	Bill Wegman	.05
484	Dave Parker	.05
485	Dennis Eckersley	.35
486	Erik Hanson	.05
487	Bill Ripken	.05
488	Tom Candiotti	.05
489	Mike Schooler	.05
490	Gregg Olson	.05
491	Chris James	.05
492	Pete Harnisch	.05
493	Julio Franco	.05
494	Greg Briley	.05
495	Ruben Sierra	.05
496	Steve Olin	.05
497	Mike Fetters	.05
498	Mark Williamson	.05
499	Bob Tewksbury	.05
500	Tony Gwynn	.50
501	Randy Myers	.05
502	Keith Comstock	.05
503	Craig Worthington	.05
504	Mark Eichhorn	.05
505	Barry Larkin	.05
506	Dave Johnson	.05
507	Bobby Witt	.05
508	Joe Orsulak	.05
509	Pete O'Brien	.05
510	Brad Arnsberg	.05
511	Storm Davis	.05
512	Bob Milacki	.05
513	Bill Pecota	.05
514	Glenallen Hill	.05
515	Danny Tartabull	.05
516	Mike Moore	.05
517	Ron Robinson	.05
518	Mark Gardner	.05
519	Rick Wrona	.05
520	Mike Scioscia	.05
521	Frank Wills	.05
522	Greg Brock	.05
523	Jack Clark	.05
524	Bruce Ruffin	.05
525	Robin Yount	.40
526	Tom Foley	.05
527	Pat Perry	.05
528	Greg Vaughn	.05
529	Wally Whitehurst	.05
530	Norm Charlton	.05
531	Marvell Wynne	.05
532	Jim Gantner	.05
533	Greg Litton	.05
534	Manny Lee	.05
535	Scott Bailes	.05
536	Charlie Leibrandt	.05
537	Roger McDowell	.05
538	Andy Benes	.05
539	Rick Honeycutt	.05
540	Dwight Gooden	.05
541	Scott Garrelts	.05
542	Dave Clark	.05
543	Lonnie Smith	.05
544	Rick Rueschel	.05
545	Delino DeShields	.05
546	Mike Sharperson	.05
547	Mike Kingery	.05
548	Terry Kennedy	.05
549	David Cone	.05
550	Orel Hershiser	.05
551	Matt Nokes	.05
552	Eddie Williams	.05
553	Frank DiPino	.05
554	Fred Lynn	.05
555	Alex Cole	.05
556	Terry Leach	.05
557	Chet Lemon	.05
558	Paul Mirabella	.05
559	Bill Long	.05
560	Phil Bradley	.05
561	Duane Ward	.05
562	Dave Bergman	.05
563	Eric Show	.05
564	Xavier Hernandez	.05
565	Jeff Parrett	.05
566	Chuck Cary	.05
567	Ken Hill	.05
568	Bob Welch	.05
569	John Mitchell	.05
570	Travis Fryman	.05
571	Derek Lilliquist	.05
572	Steve Lake	.05
573	*John Barfield*	.05
574	Randy Bush	.05
575	Joe Magrane	.05
576	Edgar Diaz	.05
577	Casy Candaele	.05
578	Jesse Orosco	.05
579	Tom Henke	.05
580	Rick Cerone	.05
581	Drew Hall	.05
582	Tony Castillo	.05
583	Jimmy Jones	.05
584	Rick Reed	.05
585	Joe Girardi	.05
586	*Jeff Gray*	.05
587	Luis Polonia	.05
588	Joe Klink	.05
589	Rex Hudler	.05
590	Kirk McCaskill	.05
591	Juan Agosto	.05
592	Wes Gardner	.05
593	*Rich Rodriguez*	.05
594	Mitch Webster	.05
595	Kelly Gruber	.05
596	Dale Mohorcic	.05
597	Willie McGee	.05
598	Bill Krueger	.05
599	Bob Walk	.05
600	Kevin Maas	.05
601	Danny Jackson	.05
602	Craig McMurtry	.05
603	Curtis Wilkerson	.05
604	Adam Peterson	.05
605	Sam Horn	.05
606	Tommy Gregg	.05
607	Ken Dayley	.05
608	Carmelo Castillo	.05
609	John Shelby	.05
610	Don Slaught	.05
611	Calvin Schiraldi	.05
612	Dennis Lamp	.05
613	Andres Thomas	.05
614	Jose Gonzales	.05
615	Randy Ready	.05
616	Kevin Bass	.05
617	Mike Marshall	.05
618	Daryl Boston	.05
619	Andy McGaffigan	.05
620	Joe Oliver	.05
621	Jim Gott	.05
622	Jose Oquendo	.05
623	Jose DeJesus	.05
624	Mike Brumley	.05
625	John Olerud	.05
626	Ernest Riles	.05
627	Gene Harris	.05
628	Jose Uribe	.05
629	Darnell Coles	.05
630	Carney Lansford	.05
631	Tim Leary	.05
632	Tim Hulett	.05
633	Kevin Elster	.05
634	Tony Fossas	.05
635	Francisco Oliveras	.05
636	Bob Patterson	.05
637	Gary Ward	.05
638	Rene Gonzales	.05
639	Don Robinson	.05
640	Darryl Strawberry	.05
641	Dave Anderson	.05
642	Scott Scudder	.05
643	*Reggie Harris*	.05
644	Dave Henderson	.05
645	Ben McDonald	.05

No.	Player	Price
646	Bob Kipper	.05
647	Hal Morris	.05
648	Tim Birtsas	.05
649	Steve Searcy	.05
650	Dale Murphy	.20
651	Ron Oester	.05
652	Mike LaCoss	.05
653	Ron Jones	.05
654	Kelly Downs	.05
655	Roger Clemens	.55
656	Herm Winningham	.05
657	Trevor Wilson	.05
658	Jose Rijo	.05
659	Dann Bilardello	.05
660	Gregg Jefferies	.05
661	Doug Drabek (All-Star)	.05
662	Randy Myers (AS)	.05
663	Benito Santiago (AS)	.05
664	Will Clark (AS)	.05
665	Ryne Sandberg (AS)	.25
666	Barry Larkin (AS)	.05
667	Matt Williams (AS)	.05
668	Barry Bonds (AS)	.35
669	Eric Davis	.05
670	Bobby Bonilla (AS)	.05
671	*Chipper Jones*	1.50
672	*Eric Christopherson*	.05
673	*Robbie Beckett*	.05
674	*Shane Andrews*	.15
675	*Steve Karsay*	.10
676	*Aaron Holbert*	.05
677	*Donovan Osborne*	.05
678	*Todd Ritchie*	.05
679	*Ron Walden*	.05
680	*Tim Costo*	.05
681	*Dan Wilson*	.10
682	*Kurt Miller*	.05
683	*Mike Lieberthal*	.25
684	Roger Clemens	.25
685	Dwight Gooden	.05
686	Nolan Ryan	.35
687	Frank Viola	.05
688	Erik Hanson	.05
689	Matt Williams	.05
690	Jose Canseco	.10
691	Darryl Strawberry	.05
692	Bo Jackson	.10
693	Cecil Fielder	.05
694	Sandy Alomar, Jr.	.05
695	Cory Snyder	.05
696	Eric Davis	.05
697	Ken Griffey, Jr.	.30
698	Andy Van Slyke	.05
699	Mark Langston, Mike Witt	.05
700	Randy Johnson	.20
701	Nolan Ryan	.35
702	Dave Stewart	.05
703	Fernando Valenzuela	.05
704	Andy Hawkins	.05
705	Melido Perez	.05
706	Terry Mulholland	.05
707	Dave Stieb	.05
708	*Brian Barnes*	.05
709	Bernard Gilkey	.05
710	*Steve Decker*	.05
711	*Paul Faries*	.05
712	*Paul Marak*	.05
713	*Wes Chamberlain*	.05
714	*Kevin Belcher*	.05
715	Dan Boone	.05
716	*Steve Adkins*	.05
717	*Geronimo Pena*	.05
718	*Howard Farmer*	.05
719	*Mark Leonard*	.05
720	Tom Lampkin	.05
721	*Mike Gardiner*	.05
722	*Jeff Conine*	.25
723	*Efrain Valdez*	.05
724	Chuck Malone	.05
725	*Leo Gomez*	.05
726	*Paul McClellan*	.05
727	*Mark Leiter*	.05
728	*Rich DeLucia*	.05
729	Mel Rojas	.05
730	*Hector Wagner*	.05
731	Ray Lankford	.05
732	*Turner Ward*	.05
733	*Gerald Alexander*	.05
734	*Scott Anderson*	.05
735	Tony Perezchica	.05
736	Jimmy Kremers	.05
737a	American Flag	.25
737b	American Flag	.25
738	*Mike York*	.05
739	Mike Rochford	.05
740	Scott Aldred	.05
741	*Rico Brogna*	.05
742	*Dave Burba*	.05
743	*Ray Stephens*	.05
744	*Eric Gunderson*	.05
745	*Troy Afenir*	.05
746	Jeff Shaw	.05
747	*Orlando Merced*	.10
748	*Omar Oliveras*	.05
749	Jerry Kutzler	.05
750	Mo Vaughn	.05
751	*Matt Stark*	.05
752	*Randy Hennis*	.05
753	*Andujar Cedeno*	.05
754	Kelvin Torve	.05
755	Joe Kraemer	.05
756	*Phil Clark*	.05
757	*Ed Vosberg*	.05
758	*Mike Perez*	.05
759	*Scott Lewis*	.05
760	*Steve Chitren*	.05
761	*Ray Young*	.05
762	*Andres Santana*	.05
763	*Rodney McCray*	.05
764	*Sean Berry*	.05
765	Brent Mayne	.05
766	*Mike Simms*	.05
767	*Glenn Sutko*	.05
768	Gary Disarcina	.05
769	George Brett (HL)	.25
770	Cecil Fielder (HL)	.05
771	Jim Presley	.05
772	John Dopson	.05
773	Bo Jackson (Breaker)	.10
774	Brent Knackert	.05
775	Bill Doran	.05
776	Dick Schofield	.05
777	Nelson Santovenia	.05
778	Mark Guthrie	.05
779	Mark Lemke	.05
780	Terry Steinbach	.05
781	Tom Bolton	.05
782	*Randy Tomlin*	.05
783	Jeff Kunkel	.05
784	Felix Jose	.05
785	Rick Sutcliffe	.05
786	John Cerutti	.05
787	Jose Vizcaino	.05
788	Curt Schilling	.35
789	Ed Whitson	.05
790	Tony Pena	.05
791	John Candelaria	.05
792	Carmelo Martinez	.05
793	Sandy Alomar, Jr.	.05
794	*Jim Neidlinger*	.05
795	Barry Larkin, Chris Sabo Red's October	.10
796	Paul Sorrento	.05
797	Tom Pagnozzi	.05
798	Tino Martinez	.05
799	Scott Ruskin	.05
800	Kirk Gibson	.05
801	Walt Terrell	.05
802	John Russell	.05
803	Chili Davis	.05
804	Chris Nabholz	.05
805	Juan Gonzalez	.20
806	Ron Hassey	.05
807	Todd Worrell	.05
808	Tommy Greene	.05
809	Joel Skinner	.05
810	Benito Santiago	.05
811	Pat Tabler	.05
812	*Scott Erickson*	.05
813	Moises Alou	.05
814	Dale Sveum	.05
815	Ryne Sandberg	.25
816	Rick Dempsey	.05
817	Scott Bankhead	.05
818	Jason Grimsley	.05
819	Doug Jennings	.05
820	Tom Herr	.05
821	Rob Ducey	.05
822	Luis Quinones	.05
823	Greg Minton	.05
824	Mark Grant	.05
825	Ozzie Smith	.50
826	Dave Eiland	.05
827	Danny Heep	.05
828	Hensley Meulens	.05
829	Charlie O'Brien	.05
830	Glenn Davis	.05
831	John Marzano	.05
832	Steve Ontiveros	.05
833	Ron Karkovice	.05
834	Jerry Goff	.05
835	Ken Griffey, Sr.	.05
836	Kevin Reimer	.05
837	Randy Kutcher	.05
838	Mike Blowers	.05
839	Mike Macfarlane	.05
840	Frank Thomas	.40
841	Ken Griffey Sr., Ken Griffey Jr.	.20
842	Jack Howell	.05
843	Mauro Gozzo	.05
844	Gerald Young	.05
845	Zane Smith	.05
846	Kevin Brown	.05
847	Sil Campusano	.05
848	Larry Andersen	.05
849	Cal Ripken, Jr.	.35
850	Roger Clemens	.30
851	Sandy Alomar, Jr.	.05
852	Alan Trammell	.05
853	George Brett	.25
854	Robin Yount	.25
855	Kirby Puckett	.25
856	Don Mattingly	.30
857	Rickey Henderson	.20
858	Ken Griffey, Jr.	.30
859	Ruben Sierra	.05
860	John Olerud	.05
861	Dave Justice	.05
862	Ryne Sandberg	.25
863	Eric Davis	.05
864	Darryl Strawberry	.05
865	Tim Wallach	.05
866	Dwight Gooden	.05
867	Len Dykstra	.05
868	Barry Bonds	.35
869	Todd Zeile	.05
870	Benito Santiago	.05
871	Will Clark	.05
872	Craig Biggio	.05
873	Wally Joyner	.05
874	Frank Thomas	.20
875	Rickey Henderson	.20
876	Barry Bonds	.35
877	Bob Welch	.05
878	Doug Drabek	.05
879	Sandy Alomar, Jr.	.05
880	Dave Justice	.05
881	Damon Berryhill	.05
882	Frank Viola	.05
883	Dave Stewart	.05
884	Doug Jones	.05
885	Randy Myers	.05
886	Will Clark	.05
887	Roberto Alomar	.10
888	Barry Larkin	.05
889	Wade Boggs	.25
890	Rickey Henderson	.20
891	Kirby Puckett	.25
892	Ken Griffey, Jr.	.30
893	Benito Santiago	.05

Hot Rookies

		NM/M
Complete Set (10):		2.50
Common Player:		.10
1	Dave Justice	.25
2	Kevin Maas	.10
3	Hal Morris	.10
4	Frank Thomas	1.50
5	Jeff Conine	.10
6	Sandy Alomar Jr.	.10
7	Ray Lankford	.10
8	Steve Decker	.10
9	Juan Gonzalez	.50
10	Jose Offerman	.10

Mickey Mantle

		NM/M
Complete Set (7):		35.00
Common Card:		6.00
Autographed Card:		575.00
1	The Rookie	9.00
2	Triple Crown	7.50
3	World Series	7.50
4	Going, Going, Gone	7.50
5	Speed and Grace	7.50

6	A True Yankee	7.50
7	Twilight	7.50

Traded

		NM/M
Complete Set (110):		4.00
Common Player:		.05
1	Bo Jackson	.10
2	Mike Flanagan	.05
3	Pete Incaviglia	.05
4	Jack Clark	.05
5	Hubie Brooks	.05
6	Ivan Calderon	.05
7	Glenn Davis	.05
8	Wally Backman	.05
9	Dave Smith	.05
10	Tim Raines	.05
11	Joe Carter	.05
12	Sid Bream	.05
13	George Bell	.05
14	Steve Bedrosian	.05
15	Willie Wilson	.05
16	Darryl Strawberry	.05
17	Danny Jackson	.05
18	Kirk Gibson	.05
19	Willie McGee	.05
20	Junior Felix	.05
21	Steve Farr	.05
22	Pat Tabler	.05
23	Brett Butler	.05
24	Danny Darwin	.05
25	Mickey Tettleton	.05
26	Gary Carter	.50
27	Mitch Williams	.05
28	Candy Maldonado	.05
29	Otis Nixon	.05
30	Brian Downing	.05
31	Tom Candiotti	.05
32	John Candelaria	.05
33	Rob Murphy	.05
34	Deion Sanders	.05
35	Willie Randolph	.05
36	Pete Harnisch	.05
37	Dante Bichette	.05
38	Garry Templeton	.05
39	Gary Gaetti	.05
40	John Cerutti	.05
41	Rick Cerone	.05
42	Mike Pagliarulo	.05
43	Ron Hassey	.05
44	Roberto Alomar	.20
45	Mike Boddicker	.05
46	Bud Black	.05
47	Rob Deer	.05
48	Devon White	.05
49	Luis Sojo	.05
50	Terry Pendleton	.05
51	Kevin Gross	.05
52	Mike Huff	.05

53 Dave Righetti .05
54 Matt Young .05
55 Ernest Riles .05
56 Bill Gullickson .05
57 Vince Coleman .05
58 Fred McGriff .05
59 Franklin Stubbs .05
60 Eric King .05
61 Cory Snyder .05
62 Dwight Evans .05
63 Gerald Perry .05
64 Eric Show .05
65 Shawn Hillegas .05
66 Tony Fernandez .05
67 Tim Teufel .05
68 Mitch Webster .05
69 Mike Heath .05
70 Chili Davis .05
71 Larry Andersen .05
72 Gary Varsho .05
73 Juan Berenguer .05
74 Jack Morris .05
75 Barry Jones .05
76 Rafael Belliard .05
77 Steve Buechele .05
78 Scott Sanderson .05
79 Bob Ojeda .05
80 Curt Schilling .35
81 Brian Drahman .05
82 *Ivan Rodriguez* 1.00
83 David Howard .05
84 Heath Slocumb .05
85 Mike Timlin .05
86 Darryl Kile .05
87 Pete Schourek .05
88 Bruce Walton .05
89 Al Osuna .05
90 Gary Scott .05
91 Doug Simons .05
92 Chris Jones .05
93 Chuck Knoblauch .05
94 Dana Allison .05
95 Erik Pappas .05
96 *Jeff Bagwell* 2.50
97 Kirk Dressendorfer .05
98 Freddie Benavides .05
99 *Luis Gonzalez* .50
100 Wade Taylor .05
101 Ed Sprague .05
102 Bob Scanlan .05
103 Rick Wilkins .05
104 Chris Donnels .05
105 Joe Slusarski .05
106 Mark Lewis .05
107 Pat Kelly .05
108 John Briscoe .05
109 Luis Lopez .05
110 Jeff Johnson .05

1992 SCORE

	NM/M
Unopened Fact. Set (910):	7.50
Complete Set (893):	5.00
Common Player:	.05
Wax Pack (16):	.40
Wax Box (36):	7.50

1 Ken Griffey, Jr. .65
2 Nolan Ryan 1.00
3 Will Clark .05
4 Dave Justice .05
5 Dave Henderson .05
6 Bret Saberhagen .05
7 Fred McGriff .05
8 Erik Hanson .05
9 Darryl Strawberry .05
10 Dwight Gooden .05
11 Juan Gonzalez .20
12 Mark Langston .05
13 Lonnie Smith .05
14 Jeff Montgomery .05
15 Roberto Alomar .20
16 Delino DeShields .05
17 Steve Bedrosian .05
18 Terry Pendleton .05
19 Mark Carreon .05
20 Mark McGwire .75
21 Roger Clemens .60
22 Chuck Crim .05
23 Don Mattingly .60
24 Dickie Thon .05
25 Ron Gant .05
26 Milt Cuyler .05
27 Mike Macfarlane .05
28 Dan Gladden .05
29 Melido Perez .05
30 Willie Randolph .05
31 Albert Belle .05
32 Dave Winfield .40
33 Jimmy Jones .05
34 Kevin Gross .05
35 Andres Galarraga .05
36 Mike Devereaux .05
37 Chris Bosio .05
38 Mike LaValliere .05
39 Gary Gaetti .05
40 Felix Jose .05
41 Alvaro Espinoza .05
42 Rick Aguilera .05
43 Mike Gallego .05
44 Eric Davis .05
45 George Bell .05
46 Tom Brunansky .05
47 Steve Farr .05
48 Duane Ward .05
49 David Wells .05
50 Cecil Fielder .05
51 Walt Weiss .05
52 Todd Zeile .05
53 Doug Jones .05
54 Bob Walk .05
55 Rafael Palmeiro .35
56 Rob Deer .05
57 Paul O'Neill .05
58 Jeff Reardon .05
59 Randy Ready .05
60 Scott Erickson .05
61 Paul Molitor .40
62 Jack McDowell .05
63 Jim Acker .05
64 Jay Buhner .05
65 Travis Fryman .05
66 Marquis Grissom .05
67 Mike Harkey .05
68 Luis Polonia .05
69 Ken Caminiti .05
70 Chris Sabo .05
71 Gregg Olson .05
72 Carlton Fisk .40
73 Juan Samuel .05
74 Todd Stottlemyre .05
75 Andre Dawson .25
76 Alvin Davis .05
77 Bill Doran .05
78 B.J. Surhoff .05
79 Kirk McCaskill .05
80 Dale Murphy .25
81 Jose DeLeon .05
82 Alex Fernandez .05
83 Ivan Calderon .05
84 Brent Mayne .05
85 Jody Reed .05
86 Randy Tomlin .05
87 Randy Milligan .05
88 Pascual Perez .05
89 Hensley Meulens .05
90 Joe Carter .05
91 Mike Moore .05
92 Ozzie Guillen .05
93 Shawn Hillegas .05
94 Chili Davis .05
95 Vince Coleman .05
96 Jimmy Key .05
97 Billy Ripken .05
98 Dave Smith .05
99 Tom Bolton .05
100 Barry Larkin .05
101 Kenny Rogers .05
102 Mike Boddicker .05
103 Kevin Elster .05
104 Ken Hill .05
105 Charlie Leibrandt .05
106 Pat Combs .05
107 Hubie Brooks .05
108 Julio Franco .05
109 Vicente Palacios .05
110 Kal Daniels .05
111 Bruce Hurst .05
112 Willie McGee .05
113 Ted Power .05
114 Milt Thompson .05
115 Doug Drabek .05
116 Rafael Belliard .05
117 Scott Garrelts .05
118 Terry Mulholland .05
119 Jay Howell .05
120 Danny Jackson .05
121 Scott Ruskin .05
122 Robin Ventura .05
123 Bip Roberts .05
124 Jeff Russell .05
125 Hal Morris .05
126 Teddy Higuera .05
127 Luis Sojo .05
128 Carlos Baerga .05
129 Jeff Ballard .05
130 Tom Gordon .05
131 Sid Bream .05
132 Rance Mulliniks .05
133 Andy Benes .05
134 Mickey Tettleton .05
135 Rich DeLucia .05
136 Tom Pagnozzi .05
137 Harold Baines .05
138 Danny Darwin .05
139 Kevin Bass .05
140 Chris Nabholz .05
141 Pete O'Brien .05
142 Jeff Treadway .05
143 Mickey Morandini .05
144 Eric King .05
145 Danny Tartabull .05
146 Lance Johnson .05
147 Casey Candaele .05
148 Felix Fermin .05
149 Rich Rodriguez .05
150 Dwight Evans .05
151 Joe Klink .05
152 Kevin Reimer .05
153 Orlando Merced .05
154 Mel Hall .05
155 Randy Myers .05
156 Greg Harris .05
157 Jeff Brantley .05
158 Jim Eisenreich .05
159 Luis Rivera .05
160 Cris Carpenter .05
161 Bruce Ruffin .05
162 Omar Vizquel .05
163 Gerald Alexander .05
164 Mark Guthrie .05
165 Scott Lewis .05
166 Bill Sampen .05
167 Dave Anderson .05
168 Kevin McReynolds .05
169 Jose Vizcaino .05
170 Bob Geren .05
171 Mike Morgan .05
172 Jim Gott .05
173 Mike Pagliarulo .05
174 Mike Jeffcoat .05
175 Craig Lefferts .05
176 Steve Finley .05
177 Wally Backman .05
178 Kent Mercker .05
179 John Cerutti .05
180 Jay Bell .05
181 Dale Sveum .05
182 Greg Gagne .05
183 Donnie Hill .05
184 Rex Hudler .05
185 Pat Kelly .05
186 Jeff Robinson .05
187 Jeff Gray .05
188 Jerry Willard .05
189 Carlos Quintana .05
190 Dennis Eckersley .35
191 Kelly Downs .05
192 Gregg Jefferies .05
193 Darrin Fletcher .05
194 Mike Jackson .05
195 Eddie Murray .40
196 Billy Landrum .05
197 Eric Yelding .05
198 Devon White .05
199 Larry Walker .05
200 Ryne Sandberg .50
201 Dave Magadan .05
202 Steve Chitren .05
203 Scott Fletcher .05
204 Dwayne Henry .05
205 Scott Coolbaugh .05
206 Tracy Jones .05
207 Von Hayes .05
208 Bob Melvin .05
209 Scott Scudder .05
210 Luis Gonzalez .25
211 Scott Sanderson .05
212 Chris Donnels .05
213 Heath Slocumb .05
214 Mike Timlin .05
215 Brian Harper .05
216 Juan Berenguer .05
217 Mike Henneman .05
218 Bill Spiers .05
219 Scott Terry .05
220 Frank Viola .05
221 Mark Eichhorn .05
222 Ernest Riles .05
223 Ray Lankford .05
224 Pete Harnisch .05
225 Bobby Bonilla .05
226 Mike Scioscia .05
227 Joel Skinner .05
228 Brian Holman .05
229 Gilberto Reyes .05
230 Matt Williams .05
231 Jaime Navarro .05
232 Jose Rijo .05
233 Atlee Hammaker .05
234 Tim Teufel .05
235 John Kruk .05
236 Kurt Stillwell .05
237 Dan Pasqua .05
238 Tim Crews .05
239 Dave Gallagher .05
240 Leo Gomez .05
241 Steve Avery .05
242 Bill Gullickson .05
243 Mark Portugal .05
244 Lee Guetterman .05
245 Benny Santiago .05
246 Jim Gantner .05
247 Robby Thompson .05
248 Terry Shumpert .05
249 *Mike Bell* .05
250 Harold Reynolds .05
251 Mike Felder .05
252 Bill Pecota .05
253 Bill Krueger .05
254 Alfredo Griffin .05
255 Lou Whitaker .05
256 Roy Smith .05
257 Jerald Clark .05
258 Sammy Sosa .50
259 Tim Naehring .05
260 Dave Righetti .05
261 Paul Gibson .05
262 Chris James .05
263 Larry Andersen .05
264 Storm Davis .05
265 Jose Lind .05
266 Greg Hibbard .05
267 Norm Charlton .05
268 Paul Kilgus .05
269 Greg Maddux .50
270 Ellis Burks .05
271 Frank Tanana .05
272 Gene Larkin .05
273 Ron Hassey .05
274 Jeff Robinson .05
275 Steve Howe .05
276 Daryl Boston .05
277 Mark Lee .05
278 *Jose Segura* .05
279 Lance Blankenship .05
280 Don Slaught .05
281 Russ Swan .05
282 Bob Tewksbury .05
283 Geno Petralli .05
284 Shane Mack .05
285 Bob Scanlan .05
286 Tim Leary .05
287 John Smoltz .05
288 Pat Borders .05
289 Mark Davidson .05
290 Sam Horn .05
291 Lenny Harris .05
292 Franklin Stubbs .05
293 Thomas Howard .05
294 Steve Lyons .05
295 Francisco Oliveras .05
296 Terry Leach .05
297 Barry Jones .05
298 Lance Parrish .05
299 Wally Whitehurst .05
300 Bob Welch .05
301 Charlie Hayes .05
302 Charlie Hough .05
303 Gary Redus .05
304 Scott Bradley .05
305 Jose Oquendo .05
306 Pete Incaviglia .05
307 Marvin Freeman .05
308 Gary Pettis .05
309 Joe Slusarski .05
310 Kevin Seitzer .05

No.	Player	Price
311	Jeff Reed	.05
312	Pat Tabler	.05
313	Mike Maddux	.05
314	Bob Milacki	.05
315	Eric Anthony	.05
316	Dante Bichette	.05
317	Steve Decker	.05
318	Jack Clark	.05
319	Doug Dascenzo	.05
320	Scott Leius	.05
321	Jim Lindeman	.05
322	Bryan Harvey	.05
323	Spike Owen	.05
324	Roberto Kelly	.05
325	Stan Belinda	.05
326	Joey Cora	.05
327	Jeff Innis	.05
328	Willie Wilson	.05
329	Juan Agosto	.05
330	Charles Nagy	.05
331	Scott Bailes	.05
332	Pete Schourek	.05
333	Mike Flanagan	.05
334	Omar Olivares	.05
335	Dennis Lamp	.05
336	Tommy Greene	.05
337	Randy Velarde	.05
338	Tom Lampkin	.05
339	John Russell	.05
340	Bob Kipper	.05
341	Todd Burns	.05
342	Ron Jones	.05
343	Dave Valle	.05
344	Mike Heath	.05
345	John Olerud	.05
346	Gerald Young	.05
347	Ken Patterson	.05
348	Les Lancaster	.05
349	Steve Crawford	.05
350	John Candelaria	.05
351	Mike Aldrete	.05
352	Mariano Duncan	.05
353	Julio Machado	.05
354	Ken Williams	.05
355	Walt Terrell	.05
356	Mitch Williams	.05
357	Al Newman	.05
358	Bud Black	.05
359	Joe Hesketh	.05
360	Paul Assenmacher	.05
361	Bo Jackson	.05
362	Jeff Blauser	.05
363	Mike Brumley	.05
364	Jim Deshaies	.05
365	Brady Anderson	.05
366	Chuck McElroy	.05
367	Matt Merullo	.05
368	Tim Belcher	.05
369	Luis Aquino	.05
370	Joe Oliver	.05
371	Greg Swindell	.05
372	Lee Stevens	.05
373	Mark Knudson	.05
374	Bill Wegman	.05
375	Jerry Don Gleaton	.05
376	Pedro Guerrero	.05
377	Randy Bush	.05
378	Greg Harris	.05
379	Eric Plunk	.05
380	Jose DeJesus	.05
381	Bobby Witt	.05
382	Curtis Wilkerson	.05
383	Gene Nelson	.05
384	Wes Chamberlain	.05
385	Tom Henke	.05
386	Mark Lemke	.05
387	Greg Briley	.05
388	Rafael Ramirez	.05
389	Tony Fossas	.05
390	Henry Cotto	.05
391	Tim Hulett	.05
392	Dean Palmer	.05
393	Glenn Braggs	.05
394	Mark Salas	.05
395	*Rusty Meacham*	.05
396	*Andy Ashby*	.10
397	*Jose Melendez*	.05
398	*Warren Newson*	.05
399	*Frank Castillo*	.05
400	*Chito Martinez*	.05
401	Bernie Williams	.05
402	Derek Bell	.05
403	*Javier Ortiz*	.05
404	*Tim Sherrill*	.05
405	*Rob MacDonald*	.05
406	Phil Plantier	.05
407	Troy Afenir	.05
408	*Gino Minutelli*	.05
409	*Reggie Jefferson*	.05
410	*Mike Remlinger*	.05
411	*Carlos Rodriguez*	.05
412	*Joe Redfield*	.05
413	Alonzo Powell	.05
414	*Scott Livingstone*	.05
415	*Scott Kamieniecki*	.05
416	*Tim Spehr*	.05
417	*Brian Hunter*	.05
418	*Ced Landrum*	.05
419	*Bret Barberie*	.05
420	Kevin Morton	.05
421	*Doug Henry*	.05
422	*Doug Piatt*	.05
423	*Pat Rice*	.05
424	Juan Guzman	.05
425	Nolan Ryan (No-Hit)	.50
426	Tommy Greene (No-Hit)	.05
427	Bob Milacki, Mike Flanagan, Mark Williamson, Gregg Olson (No-Hit)	.05
428	Wilson Alvarez (No-Hit)	.05
429	Otis Nixon (Highlight)	.05
430	Rickey Henderson (Highlight)	.20
431	Cecil Fielder (All-Star)	.05
432	Julio Franco (AS)	.05
433	Cal Ripken, Jr. (AS)	.50
434	Wade Boggs (AS)	.25
435	Joe Carter (AS)	.05
436	Ken Griffey, Jr. (AS)	.35
437	Ruben Sierra (AS)	.05
438	Scott Erickson (AS)	.05
439	Tom Henke (AS)	.05
440	Terry Steinbach (AS)	.05
441	Rickey Henderson (Dream Team)	.20
442	Ryne Sandberg (Dream Team)	.30
443	Otis Nixon	.05
444	Scott Radinsky	.05
445	Mark Grace	.05
446	Tony Pena	.05
447	Billy Hatcher	.05
448	Glenallen Hill	.05
449	Chris Gwynn	.05
450	Tom Glavine	.35
451	John Habyan	.05
452	Al Osuna	.05
453	Tony Phillips	.05
454	Greg Cadaret	.05
455	Rob Dibble	.05
456	Rick Honeycutt	.05
457	Jerome Walton	.05
458	Mookie Wilson	.05
459	Mark Gubicza	.05
460	Craig Biggio	.05
461	Dave Cochrane	.05
462	Keith Miller	.05
463	Alex Cole	.05
464	Pete Smith	.05
465	Brett Butler	.05
466	Jeff Huson	.05
467	Steve Lake	.05
468	Lloyd Moseby	.05
469	Tim McIntosh	.05
470	Dennis Martinez	.05
471	Greg Myers	.05
472	Mackey Sasser	.05
473	Junior Ortiz	.05
474	Greg Olson	.05
475	Steve Sax	.05
476	Ricky Jordan	.05
477	Max Venable	.05
478	Brian McRae	.05
479	Doug Simons	.05
480	Rickey Henderson	.40
481	Gary Varsho	.05
482	Carl Willis	.05
483	Rick Wilkins	.05
484	Donn Pall	.05
485	Edgar Martinez	.05
486	Tom Foley	.05
487	Mark Williamson	.05
488	Jack Armstrong	.05
489	Gary Carter	.40
490	Ruben Sierra	.05
491	Gerald Perry	.05
492	Rob Murphy	.05
493	Zane Smith	.05
494	Darryl Kile	.05
495	Kelly Gruber	.05
496	Jerry Browne	.05
497	Darryl Hamilton	.05
498	Mike Stanton	.05
499	Mark Leonard	.05
500	Jose Canseco	.30
501	Dave Martinez	.05
502	Jose Guzman	.05
503	Terry Kennedy	.05
504	Ed Sprague	.05
505	Frank Thomas	.40
506	Darren Daulton	.05
507	Kevin Tapani	.05
508	Luis Salazar	.05
509	Paul Faries	.05
510	Sandy Alomar, Jr.	.05
511	Jeff King	.05
512	Gary Thurman	.05
513	Chris Hammond	.05
514	*Pedro Munoz*	.05
515	Alan Trammell	.05
516	Geronimo Pena	.05
517	Rodney McCray	.05
518	Manny Lee	.05
519	Junior Felix	.05
520	Kirk Gibson	.05
521	Darrin Jackson	.05
522	John Burkett	.05
523	Jeff Johnson	.05
524	Jim Corsi	.05
525	Robin Yount	.40
526	Jamie Quirk	.05
527	Bob Ojeda	.05
528	Mark Lewis	.05
529	Bryn Smith	.05
530	Kent Hrbek	.05
531	Dennis Boyd	.05
532	Ron Karkovice	.05
533	Don August	.05
534	Todd Frohwirth	.05
535	Wally Joyner	.05
536	Dennis Rasmussen	.05
537	Andy Allanson	.05
538	Rich Gossage	.05
539	John Marzano	.05
540	Cal Ripken, Jr.	1.00
541	Bill Swift	.05
542	Kevin Appier	.05
543	Dave Bergman	.05
544	Bernard Gilkey	.05
545	Mike Greenwell	.05
546	Jose Uribe	.05
547	Jesse Orosco	.05
548	Bob Patterson	.05
549	Mike Stanley	.05
550	Howard Johnson	.05
551	Joe Orsulak	.05
552	Dick Schofield	.05
553	Dave Hollins	.05
554	David Segui	.05
555	Barry Bonds	1.00
556	Mo Vaughn	.05
557	Craig Wilson	.05
558	Bobby Rose	.05
559	Rod Nichols	.05
560	Len Dykstra	.05
561	Craig Grebeck	.05
562	Darren Lewis	.05
563	Todd Benzinger	.05
564	Ed Whitson	.05
565	Jesse Barfield	.05
566	Lloyd McClendon	.05
567	Dan Plesac	.05
568	Danny Cox	.05
569	Skeeter Barnes	.05
570	Bobby Thigpen	.05
571	Deion Sanders	.05
572	Chuck Knoblauch	.05
573	Matt Nokes	.05
574	Herm Winningham	.05
575	Tom Candiotti	.05
576	Jeff Bagwell	.40
577	Brook Jacoby	.05
578	Chico Walker	.05
579	Brian Downing	.05
580	Dave Stewart	.05
581	Francisco Cabrera	.05
582	Rene Gonzales	.05
583	Stan Javier	.05
584	Randy Johnson	.40
585	Chuck Finley	.05
586	Mark Gardner	.05
587	Mark Whiten	.05
588	Garry Templeton	.05
589	Gary Sheffield	.30
590	Ozzie Smith	.50
591	Candy Maldonado	.05
592	Mike Sharperson	.05
593	Carlos Martinez	.05
594	Scott Bankhead	.05
595	Tim Wallach	.05
596	Tino Martinez	.05
597	Roger McDowell	.05
598	Cory Snyder	.05
599	Andujar Cedeno	.05
600	Kirby Puckett	.50
601	Rick Parker	.05
602	Todd Hundley	.05
603	Greg Litton	.05
604	Dave Johnson	.05
605	John Franco	.05
606	Mike Fetters	.05
607	Luis Alicea	.05
608	Trevor Wilson	.05
609	Rob Ducey	.05
610	Ramon Martinez	.05
611	Dave Burba	.05
612	Dwight Smith	.05
613	Kevin Maas	.05
614	John Costello	.05
615	Glenn Davis	.05
616	Shawn Abner	.05
617	Scott Hemond	.05
618	Tom Prince	.05
619	Wally Ritchie	.05
620	Jim Abbott	.05
621	Charlie O'Brien	.05
622	Jack Daugherty	.05
623	Tommy Gregg	.05
624	Jeff Shaw	.05
625	Tony Gwynn	.50
626	Mark Leiter	.05
627	Jim Clancy	.05
628	Tim Layana	.05
629	Jeff Schaefer	.05
630	Lee Smith	.05
631	Wade Taylor	.05
632	Mike Simms	.05
633	Terry Steinbach	.05
634	Shawon Dunston	.05
635	Tim Raines	.05
636	Kirt Manwaring	.05
637	Warren Cromartie	.05
638	Luis Quinones	.05
639	Greg Vaughn	.05
640	Kevin Mitchell	.05
641	Chris Hoiles	.05
642	Tom Browning	.05
643	Mitch Webster	.05
644	Steve Olin	.05
645	Tony Fernandez	.05
646	Juan Bell	.05
647	Joe Boever	.05
648	Carney Lansford	.05
649	Mike Benjamin	.05
650	George Brett	.60
651	Tim Burke	.05
652	Jack Morris	.05
653	Orel Hershiser	.05
654	Mike Schooler	.05
655	Andy Van Slyke	.05
656	Dave Stieb	.05
657	Dave Clark	.05
658	Ben McDonald	.05
659	John Smiley	.05
660	Wade Boggs	.50
661	Eric Bullock	.05
662	Eric Show	.05
663	Lenny Webster	.05
664	Mike Huff	.05
665	Rick Sutcliffe	.05
666	Jeff Manto	.05
667	Mike Fitzgerald	.05
668	Matt Young	.05
669	Dave West	.05
670	Mike Hartley	.05
671	Curt Schilling	.35
672	Brian Bohanon	.05
673	Cecil Espy	.05
674	Joe Grahe	.05
675	Sid Fernandez	.05
676	Edwin Nunez	.05
677	Hector Villanueva	.05
678	Sean Berry	.05
679	Dave Eiland	.05
680	David Cone	.05
681	Mike Bordick	.05
682	Tony Castillo	.05
683	John Barfield	.05
684	Jeff Hamilton	.05
685	Ken Dayley	.05
686	Carmelo Martinez	.05
687	Mike Capel	.05
688	Scott Chiamparino	.05
689	Rich Gedman	.05
690	Rich Monteleone	.05
691	Alejandro Pena	.05
692	Oscar Azocar	.05
693	Jim Poole	.05
694	Mike Gardiner	.05
695	Steve Buechele	.05
696	Rudy Seanez	.05
697	Paul Abbott	.05
698	Steve Searcy	.05
699	Jose Offerman	.05
700	Ivan Rodriguez	.35
701	Joe Girardi	.05

702 Tony Perezchica .05
703 Paul McClellan .05
704 *David Howard* .05
705 Dan Petry .05
706 Jack Howell .05
707 Jose Mesa .05
708 Randy St. Claire .05
709 Kevin Brown .05
710 Ron Darling .05
711 Jason Grimsley .05
712 John Orton .05
713 Shawn Boskie .05
714 Pat Clements .05
715 Brian Barnes .05
716 *Luis Lopez* .05
717 Bob McClure .05
718 Mark Davis .05
719 Dann Billardello .05
720 Tom Edens .05
721 Willie Fraser .05
722 Curt Young .05
723 Neal Heaton .05
724 Craig Worthington .05
725 Mel Rojas .05
726 Daryl Irvine .05
727 Roger Mason .05
728 Kirk Dressendorfer .05
729 Scott Aldred .05
730 Willie Blair .05
731 Allan Anderson .05
732 Dana Kiecker .05
733 Jose Gonzalez .05
734 Brian Drahman .05
735 Brad Komminsk .05
736 *Arthur Rhodes* .10
737 *Terry Mathews* .05
738 *Jeff Fassero* .05
739 *Mike Magnante* .05
740 *Kip Gross* .05
741 *Jim Hunter* .05
742 *Jose Mota* .05
743 Joe Bitker .05
744 *Tim Mauser* .05
745 *Ramon Garcia* .05
746 *Rod Beck* .10
747 *Jim Austin* .05
748 *Keith Mitchell* .05
749 *Wayne Rosenthal* .05
750 *Bryan Hickerson* .05
751 *Bruce Egloff* .05
752 *John Wehner* .05
753 Darren Holmes .05
754 Dave Hansen .05
755 Mike Mussina .30
756 *Anthony Young* .05
757 Ron Tingley .05
758 *Ricky Bones* .05
759 *Mark Wohlers* .05
760 Wilson Alvarez .05
761 *Harvey Pulliam* .05
762 *Ryan Bowen* .05
763 Terry Bross .05
764 *Joel Johnston* .05
765 *Terry McDaniel* .05
766 *Esteban Beltre* .05
767 *Rob Maurer* .05
768 Ted Wood .05
769 *Mo Sanford* .05
770 *Jeff Carter* .05
771 *Gil Heredia* .05
772 Monty Fariss .05
773 Will Clark (AS) .05
774 Ryne Sandberg (AS) .25
775 Barry Larkin (AS) .05
776 Howard Johnson (AS) .05
777 Barry Bonds (AS) .50
778 Brett Butler (AS) .05
779 Tony Gwynn (AS) .25
780 Ramon Martinez (AS) .05
781 Lee Smith (AS) .05
782 Mike Scioscia (AS) .05
783 Dennis Martinez .05
784 Dennis Martinez .05
785 Mark Gardner .05
786 Bret Saberhagen .05
787 Kent Mercker, Mark Wohlers, Alejandro Pena .05
788 Cal Ripken (MVP) .50
789 Terry Pendleton (MVP) .05
790 Roger Clemens (CY) .35
791 Tom Glavine (CY) .05
792 Chuck Knoblauch (ROY) .05
793 Jeff Bagwell (ROY) .20
794 Cal Ripken, Jr. .50
795 David Cone .05
796 Kirby Puckett .25
797 Steve Avery .05
798 Jack Morris .05
799 *Allen Watson* .05
800 *Manny Ramirez* 2.00
801 *Cliff Floyd* .50
802 *Al Shirley* .05
803 *Brian Barber* .05
804 *Jon Farrell* .05
805 *Brent Gates* .05
806 *Scott Ruffcorn* .05
807 *Tyrone Hill* .05
808 *Benji Gil* .05
809 *Aaron Sele* .25
810 *Tyler Green* .05
811 Chris Jones .05
812 Steve Wilson .05
813 *Cliff Young* .05
814 *Don Wakamatsu* .05
815 *Mike Humphreys* .05
816 *Scott Servais* .05
817 *Rico Rossy* .05
818 *John Ramos* .05
819 Rob Mallicoat .05
820 *Milt Hill* .05
821 Carlos Carcia .05
822 Stan Royer .05
823 *Jeff Plympton* .05
824 *Braulio Castillo* .05
825 *David Haas* .05
826 *Luis Mercedes* .05
827 Eric Karros .05
828 *Shawn Hare* .05
829 Reggie Sanders .05
830 Tom Goodwin .05
831 *Dan Gakeler* .05
832 *Stacy Jones* .05
833 *Kim Batiste* .05
834 Cal Eldred .05
835 *Chris George* .05
836 *Wayne Housie* .05
837 *Mike Ignasiak* .05
838 *Josias Manzanillo* .05
839 *Jim Olander* .05
840 *Gary Cooper* .05
841 Royce Clayton .05
842 Hector Fajardo .05
843 Blaine Beatty .05
844 *Jorge Pedre* .05
845 Kenny Lofton .05
846 Scott Brosius .05
847 *Chris Cron* .05
848 Denis Boucher .05
849 Kyle Abbott .05
850 Bob Zupcic .05
851 *Rheal Cormier* .05
852 *Jim Lewis* .05
853 Anthony Telford .05
854 *Cliff Brantley* .05
855 *Kevin Campbell* .05
856 *Craig Shipley* .05
857 Chuck Carr .05
858 *Tony Eusebio* .10
859 Jim Thome .35
860 *Vinny Castilla* .30
861 Dann Howitt .05
862 *Kevin Ward* .05
863 *Steve Wapnick* .05
864 Rod Brewer .05
865 Todd Van Poppel .05
866 *Jose Hernandez* .05
867 *Amalio Carreno* .05
868 *Calvin Jones* .05
869 *Jeff Gardner* .05
870 *Jarvis Brown* .05
871 *Eddie Taubensee* .10
872 *Andy Mota* .05
873 Chris Haney .05
874 Roberto Hernandez .05
875 *Laddie Renfroe* .05
876 Scott Cooper .05
877 *Armando Reynoso* .05
878 Ty Cobb .30
879 Babe Ruth .40
880 Honus Wagner .30
881 Lou Gehrig .30
882 Satchel Paige .35
883 Will Clark .05
884 Cal Ripken, Jr. .50
885 Wade Boggs .25
886 Kirby Puckett .30
887 Tony Gwynn .30
888 Craig Biggio .05
889 Scott Erickson .05
890 Tom Glavine .10
891 Rob Dibble .05
892 Mitch Williams .05
893 Frank Thomas .25

Hot Rookies

NM/M
Complete Set (10): 4.00
Common Player: .50

1 Cal Eldred .50
2 Royce Clayton .50
3 Kenny Lofton .75
4 Todd Van Poppel .50
5 Scott Cooper .50
6 Todd Hundley .50
7 Tino Martinez .75
8 Anthony Telford .50
9 Derek Bell .50
10 Reggie Jefferson .50

Joe DiMaggio

NM/M
Complete Set (5): 25.00
Common Card: 8.00
Autographed Card: 365.00
1 Joe DiMaggio 8.00
2 Joe DiMaggio 8.00
3 Joe DiMaggio 8.00
4 Joe DiMaggio 8.00
5 Joe DiMaggio 8.00

The Franchise

NM/M
Complete Set (4): 5.00
Common Player: 1.25
Musial Autograph: 80.00
Mantle Autograph: 450.00
Yastrzemski Autograph: 80.00
Triple Autograph: 1,100
1 Stan Musial 1.50
2 Mickey Mantle 2.50
3 Carl Yastrzemski 1.25
4 Stan Musial, Mickey Mantle, Carl Yastrzemski 1.50

1992 SCORE ROOKIES

NM/M
Complete Set (40): 1.50

Common Player: .05
1 Todd Van Poppel .05
2 Kyle Abbott .05
3 Derek Bell .05
4 Jim Thome .50
5 Mark Wohlers .05
6 Todd Hundley .05
7 Arthur Rhodes .05
8 John Ramos .05
9 Chris George .05
10 Kenny Lofton .05
11 Ted Wood .05
12 Royce Clayton .05
13 Scott Cooper .05
14 Anthony Young .05
15 Joel Johnston .05
16 Andy Mota .05
17 Lenny Webster .05
18 Andy Ashby .05
19 Jose Mota .05
20 Tim McIntosh .05
21 Terry Bross .05
22 Harvey Pulliam .05
23 Hector Fajardo .05
24 Esteban Beltre .05
25 Gary DiSarcina .05
26 Mike Humphreys .05
27 Jarvis Brown .05
28 Gary Cooper .05
29 Chris Donnels .05
30 Monty Fariss .05
31 Eric Karros .05
32 Braulio Castillo .05
33 Cal Eldred .05
34 Tom Goodwin .05
35 Reggie Sanders .05
36 Scott Servais .05
37 Kim Batiste .05
38 Eric Wedge .05
39 Willie Banks .05
40 Mo Sanford .05

Rookie & Traded

NM/M
Complete Set (110): 5.00
Common Player: .05
1 Gary Sheffield .20
2 Kevin Seitzer .05
3 Danny Tartabull .05
4 Steve Sax .05
5 Bobby Bonilla .05
6 Frank Viola .05
7 Dave Winfield .60
8 Rick Sutcliffe .05
9 Jose Canseco .45
10 Greg Swindell .05
11 Eddie Murray .60
12 Randy Myers .05
13 Wally Joyner .05
14 Kenny Lofton .05

15	Jack Morris	.05
16	Charlie Hayes	.05
17	Pete Incaviglia	.05
18	Kevin Mitchell	.05
19	Kurt Stillwell	.05
20	Bret Saberhagen	.05
21	Steve Buechele	.05
22	John Smiley	.05
23	Sammy Sosa	3.00
24	George Bell	.05
25	Curt Schilling	.30
26	Dick Schofield	.05
27	David Cone	.05
28	Dan Gladden	.05
29	Kirk McCaskill	.05
30	Mike Gallego	.05
31	Kevin McReynolds	.05
32	Bill Swift	.05
33	Dave Martinez	.05
34	Storm Davis	.05
35	Willie Randolph	.05
36	Melido Perez	.05
37	Mark Carreon	.05
38	Doug Jones	.05
39	Gregg Jefferies	.05
40	Mike Jackson	.05
41	Dickie Thon	.05
42	Eric King	.05
43	Herm Winningham	.05
44	Derek Lilliquist	.05
45	Dave Anderson	.05
46	Jeff Reardon	.05
47	Scott Bankhead	.05
48	Cory Snyder	.05
49	Al Newman	.05
50	Keith Miller	.05
51	Dave Burba	.05
52	Bill Pecota	.05
53	Chuck Crim	.05
54	Mariano Duncan	.05
55	Dave Gallagher	.05
56	Chris Gwynn	.05
57	Scott Ruskin	.05
58	Jack Armstrong	.05
59	Gary Carter	.60
60	Andres Galarraga	.05
61	Ken Hill	.05
62	Eric Davis	.05
63	Ruben Sierra	.05
64	Darrin Fletcher	.05
65	Tim Belcher	.05
66	Mike Morgan	.05
67	Scott Scudder	.05
68	Tom Candiotti	.05
69	Hubie Brooks	.05
70	Kal Daniels	.05
71	Bruce Ruffin	.05
72	Billy Hatcher	.05
73	Bob Melvin	.05
74	Lee Guetterman	.05
75	Rene Gonzales	.05
76	Kevin Bass	.05
77	Tom Bolton	.05
78	John Wetteland	.05
79	Bip Roberts	.05
80	Pat Listach	.05
81	John Doherty	.05
82	Sam Militello	.05
83	Brian Jordan	.05
84	Jeff Kent	.10
85	Dave Fleming	.05
86	Jeff Tackett	.05
87	Chad Curtis	.05
88	Eric Fox	.05
89	Denny Neagle	.05
90	Donovan Osborne	.05
91	Carlos Hernandez	.05
92	Tim Wakefield	.05
93	Tim Salmon	.05
94	Dave Nilsson	.05
95	Mike Perez	.05
96	Pat Hentgen	.05
97	Frank Seminara	.05
98	Ruben Amaro Jr.	.05
99	Archi Cianfrocco	.05
100	Andy Stankiewicz	.05
101	Jim Bullinger	.05
102	Pat Mahomes	.05
103	Hipolito Pichardo	.05
104	Bret Boone	.05
105	John Vander Wal	.05
106	Vince Horsman	.05
107	James Austin	.05
108	Brian Williams	.05
109	Dan Walters	.05
110	Wil Cordero	.05

1993 SCORE

		NM/M
Complete Set (660):		15.00
Common Player:		.05
Pack (16):		.75
Wax Box (36):		17.50
1	Ken Griffey, Jr.	.65
2	Gary Sheffield	.30
3	Frank Thomas	.40
4	Ryne Sandberg	.45
5	Larry Walker	.05
6	Cal Ripken, Jr.	1.00
7	Roger Clemens	.50
8	Bobby Bonilla	.05
9	Carlos Baerga	.05
10	Darren Daulton	.05
11	Travis Fryman	.05
12	Andy Van Slyke	.05
13	Jose Canseco	.30
14	Roberto Alomar	.15
15	Tom Glavine	.30
16	Barry Larkin	.05
17	Gregg Jefferies	.05
18	Craig Biggio	.05
19	Shane Mack	.05
20	Brett Butler	.05
21	Dennis Eckersley	.35
22	Will Clark	.05
23	Don Mattingly	.50
24	Tony Gwynn	.45
25	Ivan Rodriguez	.35
26	Shawon Dunston	.05
27	Mike Mussina	.30
28	Marquis Grissom	.05
29	Charles Nagy	.05
30	Len Dykstra	.05
31	Cecil Fielder	.05
32	Jay Bell	.05
33	B.J. Surhoff	.05
34	Bob Tewksbury	.05
35	Danny Tartabull	.05
36	Terry Pendleton	.05
37	Jack Morris	.05
38	Hal Morris	.05
39	Luis Polonia	.05
40	Ken Caminiti	.05
41	Robin Ventura	.05
42	Darryl Strawberry	.05
43	Wally Joyner	.05
44	Fred McGriff	.05
45	Kevin Tapani	.05
46	Matt Williams	.05
47	Robin Yount	.40
48	Ken Hill	.05
49	Edgar Martinez	.05
50	Mark Grace	.05
51	Juan Gonzalez	.20
52	Curt Schilling	.30
53	Dwight Gooden	.05
54	Chris Hoiles	.05
55	Frank Viola	.05
56	Ray Lankford	.05
57	George Brett	.50
58	Kenny Lofton	.05
59	Nolan Ryan	1.00
60	Mickey Tettleton	.05
61	John Smoltz	.05
62	Howard Johnson	.05
63	Eric Karros	.05
64	Rick Aguilera	.05
65	Steve Finley	.05
66	Mark Langston	.05
67	Bill Swift	.05
68	John Olerud	.05
69	Kevin McReynolds	.05
70	Jack McDowell	.05
71	Rickey Henderson	.40
72	Brian Harper	.05
73	Mike Morgan	.05
74	Rafael Palmeiro	.40
75	Dennis Martinez	.05
76	Tino Martinez	.05
77	Eddie Murray	.40
78	Ellis Burks	.05
79	John Kruk	.05
80	Gregg Olson	.05
81	Bernard Gilkey	.05
82	Milt Cuyler	.05
83	Mike LaValliere	.05
84	Albert Belle	.05
85	Bip Roberts	.05
86	Melido Perez	.05
87	Otis Nixon	.05
88	Bill Spiers	.05
89	Jeff Bagwell	.40
90	Orel Hershiser	.05
91	Andy Benes	.05
92	Devon White	.05
93	Willie McGee	.05
94	Ozzie Guillen	.05
95	Ivan Calderon	.05
96	Keith Miller	.05
97	Steve Buechele	.05
98	Kent Hrbek	.05
99	Dave Hollins	.05
100	Mike Bordick	.05
101	Randy Tomlin	.05
102	Omar Vizquel	.05
103	Lee Smith	.05
104	Leo Gomez	.05
105	Jose Rijo	.05
106	Mark Whiten	.05
107	Dave Justice	.05
108	Eddie Taubensee	.05
109	Lance Johnson	.05
110	Felix Jose	.05
111	Mike Harkey	.05
112	Randy Milligan	.05
113	Anthony Young	.05
114	Rico Brogna	.05
115	Bret Saberhagen	.05
116	Sandy Alomar, Jr.	.05
117	Terry Mulholland	.05
118	Darryl Hamilton	.05
119	Todd Zeile	.05
120	Bernie Williams	.05
121	Zane Smith	.05
122	Derek Bell	.05
123	Deion Sanders	.05
124	Luis Sojo	.05
125	Joe Oliver	.05
126	Craig Grebeck	.05
127	Andujar Cedeno	.05
128	Brian McRae	.05
129	Jose Offerman	.05
130	Pedro Munoz	.05
131	Bud Black	.05
132	Mo Vaughn	.05
133	Bruce Hurst	.05
134	Dave Henderson	.05
135	Tom Pagnozzi	.05
136	Erik Hanson	.05
137	Orlando Merced	.05
138	Dean Palmer	.05
139	John Franco	.05
140	Brady Anderson	.05
141	Ricky Jordan	.05
142	Jeff Blauser	.05
143	Sammy Sosa	.45
144	Bob Walk	.05
145	Delino DeShields	.05
146	Kevin Brown	.05
147	Mark Lemke	.05
148	Chuck Knoblauch	.05
149	Chris Sabo	.05
150	Bobby Witt	.05
151	Luis Gonzalez	.05
152	Ron Karkovice	.05
153	Jeff Brantley	.05
154	Kevin Appier	.05
155	Darrin Jackson	.05
156	Kelly Gruber	.05
157	Royce Clayton	.05
158	Chuck Finley	.05
159	Jeff King	.05
160	Greg Vaughn	.05
161	Geronimo Pena	.05
162	Steve Farr	.05
163	Jose Oquendo	.05
164	Mark Lewis	.05
165	John Wetteland	.05
166	Mike Henneman	.05
167	Todd Hundley	.05
168	Wes Chamberlain	.05
169	Steve Avery	.05
170	Mike Devereaux	.05
171	Reggie Sanders	.05
172	Jay Buhner	.05
173	Eric Anthony	.05
174	John Burkett	.05
175	Tom Candiotti	.05
176	Phil Plantier	.05
177	Doug Henry	.05
178	Scott Leius	.05
179	Kirt Manwaring	.05
180	Jeff Parrett	.05
181	Don Slaught	.05
182	Scott Radinsky	.05
183	Luis Alicea	.05
184	Tom Gordon	.05
185	Rick Wilkins	.05
186	Todd Stottlemyre	.05
187	Moises Alou	.05
188	Joe Grahe	.05
189	Jeff Kent	.05
190	Bill Wegman	.05
191	Kim Batiste	.05
192	Matt Nokes	.05
193	Mark Wohlers	.05
194	Paul Sorrento	.05
195	Chris Hammond	.05
196	Scott Livingstone	.05
197	Doug Jones	.05
198	Scott Cooper	.05
199	Ramon Martinez	.05
200	Dave Valle	.05
201	Mariano Duncan	.05
202	Ben McDonald	.05
203	Darren Lewis	.05
204	Kenny Rogers	.05
205	Manuel Lee	.05
206	Scott Erickson	.05
207	Dan Gladden	.05
208	Bob Welch	.05
209	Greg Olson	.05
210	Dan Pasqua	.05
211	Tim Wallach	.05
212	Jeff Montgomery	.05
213	Derrick May	.05
214	Ed Sprague	.05
215	David Haas	.05
216	Darrin Fletcher	.05
217	Brian Jordan	.05
218	Jaime Navarro	.05
219	Randy Velarde	.05
220	Ron Gant	.05
221	Paul Quantrill	.05
222	Damion Easley	.05
223	Charlie Hough	.05
224	*Brad Brink*	.05
225	*Barry Manual*	.05
226	*Kevin Koslofski*	.05
227	*Ryan Thompson*	.05
228	*Mike Munoz*	.05
229	*Dan Wilson*	.10
230	*Peter Hoy*	.05
231	*Pedro Astacio*	.10
232	*Matt Stairs*	.10
233	*Jeff Reboulet*	.05
234	*Manny Alexander*	.05
235	*Willie Banks*	.05
236	*John Jaha*	.05
237	*Scooter Tucker*	.05
238	*Russ Springer*	.05
239	*Paul Miller*	.05
240	*Dan Peltier*	.05
241	*Ozzie Canseco*	.05
242	*Ben Rivera*	.05
243	*John Valentin*	.05
244	Henry Rodriguez	.05
245	*Derek Parks*	.05
246	*Carlos Garcia*	.10
247	*Tim Pugh*	.05
248	*Melvin Nieves*	.05
249	*Rich Amaral*	.05
250	*Willie Greene*	.05
251	*Tim Scott*	.05
252	*Dave Silvestri*	.05
253	*Rob Mallicoat*	.05
254	*Donald Harris*	.05
255	*Craig Colbert*	.05
256	Jose Guzman	.05
257	*Domingo Martinez*	.05
258	*William Suero*	.05
259	*Juan Guerrero*	.05
260	*J.T. Snow*	.45
261	Tony Pena	.05
262	*Tim Fortugno*	.05
263	*Tom Marsh*	.05
264	*Kurt Knudsen*	.05
265	*Tim Costo*	.05
266	*Steve Shifflett*	.05
267	*Billy Ashley*	.05
268	Jerry Nielsen	.05
269	*Pete Young*	.05
270	*Johnny Guzman*	.05
271	*Greg Colbrunn*	.05
272	Jeff Nelson	.05
273	*Kevin Young*	.05
274	Jeff Frye	.05

No.	Player	Price
275	*J.T. Bruett*	.05
276	*Todd Pratt*	.05
277	*Mike Butcher*	.05
278	*John Flaherty*	.05
279	*John Patterson*	.05
280	*Eric Hillman*	.05
281	*Bien Figueros*	.05
282	*Shane Reynolds*	.05
283	*Rich Rowland*	.05
284	*Steve Foster*	.05
285	*Dave Mlicki*	.05
286	Mike Piazza	.65
287	*Mike Trombley*	.05
288	*Jim Pena*	.05
289	*Bob Ayrault*	.05
290	*Henry Mercedes*	.05
291	Bob Wickman	.05
292	*Jacob Brumfield*	.05
293	*David Hulse*	.05
294	Ryan Klesko	.05
295	Doug Linton	.05
296	Steve Cooke	.05
297	Eddie Zosky	.05
298	*Gerald Williams*	.05
299	*Jonathan Hurst*	.05
300	*Larry Carter*	.05
301	*William Pennyfeather*	.05
302	*Cesar Hernandez*	.05
303	*Steve Hosey*	.05
304	*Blas Minor*	.05
305	*Jeff Grotewold*	.05
306	*Bernardo Brito*	.05
307	*Rafael Bournigal*	.05
308	*Jeff Branson*	.05
309	*Tom Quinlan*	.05
310	*Pat Gomez*	.05
311	*Sterling Hitchcock*	.10
312	Kent Bottenfield	.05
313	Alan Trammell	.05
314	*Cris Colon*	.05
315	*Paul Wagner*	.05
316	*Matt Maysey*	.05
317	Mike Stanton	.05
318	*Rick Trlicek*	.05
319	*Kevin Rogers*	.05
320	*Mark Clark*	.05
321	Pedro Martinez	.40
322	*Al Martin*	.05
323	Mike Macfarlane	.05
324	*Rey Sanchez*	.10
325	*Roger Pavlik*	.05
326	Troy Neel	.05
327	*Kerry Woodson*	.05
328	*Wayne Kirby*	.05
329	*Ken Ryan*	.05
330	*Jesse Levis*	.05
331	James Austin	.05
332	Dan Walters	.05
333	Brian Williams	.05
334	Wil Cordero	.05
335	Bret Boone	.05
336	Hipolito Pichardo	.05
337	Pat Mahomes	.05
338	Andy Stankiewicz	.05
339	Jim Bullinger	.05
340	Archi Cianfrocco	.05
341	Ruben Amaro Jr.	.05
342	Frank Seminara	.05
343	Pat Hentgen	.05
344	Dave Nilsson	.05
345	Mike Perez	.05
346	Tim Salmon	.05
347	*Tim Wakefield*	.10
348	Carlos Hernandez	.05
349	Donovan Osborne	.05
350	Denny Naegle	.05
351	Sam Militello	.05
352	Eric Fox	.05
353	John Doherty	.05
354	Chad Curtis	.05
355	Jeff Tackett	.05
356	Dave Fleming	.05
357	Pat Listach	.05
358	Kevin Wickander	.05
359	John VanderWal	.05
360	Arthur Rhodes	.05
361	Bob Scanlan	.05
362	Bob Zupcic	.05
363	Mel Rojas	.05
364	Jim Thome	.35
365	Bill Pecota	.05
366	Mark Carreon	.05
367	Mitch Williams	.05
368	Cal Eldred	.05
369	Stan Belinda	.05
370	Pat Kelly	.05
371	Pheal Cormier	.05
372	Juan Guzman	.05
373	Damon Berryhill	.05
374	Gary DiSarcina	.05
375	Norm Charlton	.05
376	Roberto Hernandez	.05
377	Scott Kamieniecki	.05
378	Rusty Meacham	.05
379	Kurt Stillwell	.05
380	Lloyd McClendon	.05
381	Mark Leonard	.05
382	Jerry Browne	.05
383	Glenn Davis	.05
384	Randy Johnson	.40
385	Mike Greenwell	.05
386	Scott Chiamparino	.05
387	George Bell	.05
388	Steve Olin	.05
389	Chuck McElroy	.05
390	Mark Gardner	.05
391	Rod Beck	.05
392	Dennis Rasmussen	.05
393	Charlie Leibrandt	.05
394	Julio Franco	.05
395	Pete Harnisch	.05
396	Sid Bream	.05
397	Milt Thompson	.05
398	Glenallen Hill	.05
399	Chico Walker	.05
400	Alex Cole	.05
401	Trevor Wilson	.05
402	Jeff Conine	.05
403	Kyle Abbott	.05
404	Tom Browning	.05
405	Jerald Clark	.05
406	Vince Horsman	.05
407	Kevin Mitchell	.05
408	Pete Smith	.05
409	Jeff Innis	.05
410	Mike Timlin	.05
411	Charlie Hayes	.05
412	Alex Fernandez	.05
413	Jeff Russell	.05
414	Jody Reed	.05
415	Mickey Morandini	.05
416	Darnell Coles	.05
417	Xavier Hernandez	.05
418	Steve Sax	.05
419	Joe Girardi	.05
420	Mike Fetters	.05
421	Danny Jackson	.05
422	Jim Gott	.05
423	Tim Belcher	.05
424	Jose Mesa	.05
425	Junior Felix	.05
426	Thomas Howard	.05
427	Julio Valera	.05
428	Dante Bichette	.05
429	Mike Sharperson	.05
430	Darryl Kile	.05
431	Lonnie Smith	.05
432	Monty Fariss	.05
433	Reggie Jefferson	.05
434	Bob McClure	.05
435	Craig Lefferts	.05
436	Duane Ward	.05
437	Shawn Abner	.05
438	Roberto Kelly	.05
439	Paul O'Neill	.05
440	Alan Mills	.05
441	Roger Mason	.05
442	Gary Pettis	.05
443	Steve Lake	.05
444	Gene Larkin	.05
445	Larry Anderson	.05
446	Doug Dascenzo	.05
447	Daryl Boston	.05
448	John Candelaria	.05
449	Storm Davis	.05
450	Tom Edens	.05
451	Mike Maddux	.05
452	Tim Naehring	.05
453	John Orton	.05
454	Joey Cora	.05
455	Chuck Crim	.05
456	Dan Plesac	.05
457	Mike Bielecki	.05
458	*Terry Jorgensen*	.05
459	John Habyan	.05
460	Pete O'Brien	.05
461	Jeff Treadway	.05
462	Frank Castillo	.05
463	Jimmy Jones	.05
464	Tommy Greene	.05
465	Tracy Woodson	.05
466	Rich Rodriguez	.05
467	Joe Hesketh	.05
468	Greg Myers	.05
469	Kirk McCaskill	.05
470	Ricky Bones	.05
471	Lenny Webster	.05
472	Francisco Cabrera	.05
473	Turner Ward	.05
474	Dwayne Henry	.05
475	Al Osuna	.05
476	Craig Wilson	.05
477	Chris Nabholz	.05
478	Rafael Belliard	.05
479	Terry Leach	.05
480	Tim Teufel	.05
481	Dennis Eckersley	.15
482	Barry Bonds	.50
483	Dennis Eckersley	.15
484	Greg Maddux	.25
485	Pat Listach (ROY)	.05
486	Eric Karros (ROY)	.05
487	*Jamie Arnold*	.05
488	B.J. Wallace	.05
489	*Derek Jeter*	6.00
490	*Jason Kendall*	.45
491	Rick Helling	.05
492	*Derek Wallace*	.05
493	*Sean Lowe*	.05
494	*Shannon Stewart*	.65
495	*Benji Grigsby*	.05
496	*Todd Steverson*	.05
497	*Dan Serafini*	.05
498	Michael Tucker	.05
499	Chris Roberts	.05
500	*Pete Janicki*	.05
501	*Jeff Schmidt*	.05
502	Edgar Martinez	.05
503	Omar Vizquel (AS)	.05
504	Ken Griffey, Jr. (AS)	.35
505	Kirby Puckett (AS)	.25
506	Joe Carter (AS)	.05
507	Ivan Rodriguez (AS)	.15
508	Jack Morris (AS)	.05
509	Dennis Eckersley (AS)	.15
510	Frank Thomas (AS)	.20
511	Roberto Alomar (AS)	.10
512	Mickey Morandini	.05
513	Dennis Eckersley	.15
514	Jeff Reardon	.05
515	Danny Tartabull	.05
516	Bip Roberts	.05
517	George Brett	.30
518	Robin Yount	.20
519	Kevin Gross	.05
520	Ed Sprague	.05
521	Dave Winfield	.20
522	Ozzie Smith (AS)	.25
523	Barry Bonds (AS)	.50
524	Andy Van Slyke (AS)	.05
525	Tony Gwynn (AS)	.25
526	Darren Daulton (AS)	.05
527	Greg Maddux (AS)	.25
528	Fred McGriff (AS)	.05
529	Lee Smith (AS)	.05
530	Ryne Sandberg (AS)	.25
531	Gary Sheffield (AS)	.10
532	Ozzie Smith	.25
533	Kirby Puckett	.25
534	Gary Sheffield	.10
535	Andy Van Slyke	.05
536	Ken Griffey, Jr.	.35
537	Ivan Rodriguez	.15
538	Charles Nagy	.05
539	Tom Glavine	.10
540	Dennis Eckersley	.15
541	Frank Thomas	.20
542	Roberto Alomar	.10
543	Sean Barry	.05
544	Mike Schooler	.05
545	Chuck Carr	.05
546	Lenny Harris	.05
547	Gary Scott	.05
548	Derek Lilliquist	.05
549	Brian Hunter	.05
550	Kirby Puckett (MOY)	.25
551	Jim Eisenreich	.05
552	Andre Dawson	.25
553	David Nied	.05
554	Spike Owen	.05
555	Greg Gagne	.05
556	Sid Fernandez	.05
557	Mark McGwire	.75
558	Bryan Harvey	.05
559	Harold Reynolds	.05
560	Barry Bonds	1.00
561	*Eric Wedge*	.05
562	Ozzie Smith	.45
563	Rick Sutcliffe	.05
564	Jeff Reardon	.05
565	*Alex Arias*	.05
566	Greg Swindell	.05
567	Brook Jacoby	.05
568	Pete Incaviglia	.05
569	*Butch Henry*	.05
570	Eric Davis	.05
571	Kevin Seitzer	.05
572	Tony Fernandez	.05
573	*Steve Reed*	.05
574	Cory Snyder	.05
575	Joe Carter	.05
576	Greg Maddux	.45
577	Bert Blyleven	.05
578	Kevin Bass	.05
579	Carlton Fisk	.40
580	Doug Drabek	.05
581	Mark Gubicza	.05
582	Bobby Thigpen	.05
583	Chili Davis	.05
584	Scott Bankhead	.05
585	Harold Baines	.05
586	*Eric Young*	.15
587	Lance Parrish	.05
588	Juan Bell	.05
589	Bob Ojeda	.05
590	Joe Orsulak	.05
591	Benito Santiago	.05
592	Wade Boggs	.45
593	Robby Thompson	.05
594	Erik Plunk	.05
595	Hensley Meulens	.05
596	Lou Whitaker	.05
597	Dale Murphy	.25
598	Paul Molitor	.40
599	Greg W. Harris	.05
600	Darren Holmes	.05
601	Dave Martinez	.05
602	Tom Henke	.05
603	Mike Benjamin	.05
604	Rene Gonzales	.05
605	Roger McDowell	.05
606	Kirby Puckett	.45
607	Randy Myers	.05
608	Ruben Sierra	.05
609	Wilson Alvarez	.05
610	Dave Segui	.05
611	Juan Samuel	.05
612	Tom Brunansky	.05
613	Willie Randolph	.05
614	Tony Phillips	.05
615	Candy Maldonado	.05
616	Chris Bosio	.05
617	Bret Barberie	.05
618	Scott Sanderson	.05
619	Ron Darling	.05
620	Dave Winfield	.40
621	Mike Felder	.05
622	Greg Hibbard	.05
623	Mike Scioscia	.05
624	John Smiley	.05
625	Alejandro Pena	.05
626	Terry Steinbach	.05
627	Freddie Benavides	.05
628	Kevin Reimer	.05
629	Braulio Castillo	.05
630	Dave Stieb	.05
631	Dave Magadan	.05
632	Scott Fletcher	.05
633	Cris Carpenter	.05
634	Kevin Maas	.05
635	Todd Worrell	.05
636	Rob Deer	.05
637	Dwight Smith	.05
638	Chito Martinez	.05
639	Jimmy Key	.05
640	Greg Harris	.05
641	Mike Moore	.05
642	Pat Borders	.05
643	Bill Gullickson	.05
644	Gary Gaetti	.05
645	David Howard	.05
646	Jim Abbott	.05
647	Willie Wilson	.05
648	David Wells	.05
649	Andres Galarraga	.05
650	Vince Coleman	.05
651	Rob Dibble	.05
652	Frank Tanana	.05
653	Steve Decker	.05
654	David Cone	.05
655	Jack Armstrong	.05
656	Dave Stewart	.05
657	Billy Hatcher	.05
658	Tim Raines	.05
659	Walt Weiss	.05
660	Jose Lind	.05

Boys of Summer

		NM/M
Complete Set (30):		12.50
Common Player:		.25
1	Billy Ashley	.25
2	Tim Salmon	.50
3	Pedro Martinez	4.00
4	Luis Mercedes	.25
5	Mike Piazza	8.00

6	Troy Neel	.25
7	Melvin Nieves	.25
8	Ryan Klesko	.25
9	Ryan Thompson	.25
10	Kevin Young	.25
11	Gerald Williams	.25
12	Willie Greene	.25
13	John Patterson	.25
14	Carlos Garcia	.25
15	Eddie Zosky	.25
16	Sean Berry	.25
17	Rico Brogna	.25
18	Larry Carter	.25
19	Bobby Ayala	.25
20	Alan Embree	.25
21	Donald Harris	.25
22	Sterling Hitchcock	.25
23	David Nied	.25
24	Henry Mercedes	.25
25	Ozzie Canseco	.25
26	David Hulse	.25
27	Al Martin	.25
28	Dan Wilson	.25
29	Paul Miller	.25
30	Rich Rowland	.25

The Franchise

		NM/M
Complete Set (28):		50.00
Common Player:		.60
1	Cal Ripken, Jr.	12.00
2	Roger Clemens	6.00
3	Mark Langston	.60
4	Frank Thomas	3.50
5	Carlos Baerga	.60
6	Cecil Fielder	.60
7	Gregg Jefferies	.60
8	Robin Yount	3.50
9	Kirby Puckett	5.00
10	Don Mattingly	6.00
11	Dennis Eckersley	3.00
12	Ken Griffey, Jr.	9.00
13	Juan Gonzalez	3.50
14	Roberto Alomar	1.50
15	Terry Pendleton	.60
16	Ryne Sandberg	5.00
17	Barry Larkin	.60
18	Jeff Bagwell	3.50
19	Brett Butler	.60
20	Larry Walker	.60
21	Bobby Bonilla	.60
22	Darren Daulton	.60
23	Andy Van Slyke	.60
24	Ray Lankford	.60
25	Gary Sheffield	1.50
26	Will Clark	.60
27	Bryan Harvey	.60
28	David Nied	.60

Dream Team

		NM/M
Complete Set (12):		5.00
Common Player:		.25
1	Ozzie Smith	1.00
2	Kirby Puckett	1.00
3	Gary Sheffield	.35
4	Andy Van Slyke	.25
5	Ken Griffey, Jr.	2.00
6	Ivan Rodriguez	.60
7	Charles Nagy	.25
8	Tom Glavine	.35
9	Dennis Eckersley	.60
10	Frank Thomas	.75
11	Roberto Alomar	.30
---	Header card	.05

1994 SCORE

		NM/M
Complete Set (660):		15.00
Common Player:		.05
Gold Rush:		2X
Pack (14):		.75
Wax Box (36):		15.00
1	Barry Bonds	1.00
2	John Olerud	.05
3	Ken Griffey, Jr.	.65
4	Jeff Bagwell	.40
5	John Burkett	.05
6	Jack McDowell	.05
7	Albert Belle	.05
8	Andres Galarraga	.05
9	Mike Mussina	.30
10	Will Clark	.05
11	Travis Fryman	.05
12	Tony Gwynn	.50
13	Robin Yount	.40
14	Dave Magadan	.05
15	Paul O'Neill	.05
16	Ray Lankford	.05
17	Damion Easley	.05
18	Andy Van Slyke	.05
19	Brian McRae	.05
20	Ryne Sandberg	.50
21	Kirby Puckett	.50
22	Dwight Gooden	.05
23	Don Mattingly	.60
24	Kevin Mitchell	.05
25	Roger Clemens	.60
26	Eric Karros	.05
27	Juan Gonzalez	.20
28	John Kruk	.05
29	Gregg Jefferies	.05
30	Tom Glavine	.30
31	Ivan Rodriguez	.35
32	Jay Bell	.05
33	Randy Johnson	.40
34	Darren Daulton	.05
35	Rickey Henderson	.40
36	Eddie Murray	.40
37	Brian Harper	.05
38	Delino DeShields	.05
39	Jose Lind	.05
40	Benito Santiago	.05
41	Frank Thomas	.40
42	Mark Grace	.05
43	Roberto Alomar	.20
44	Andy Benes	.05
45	Luis Polonia	.05
46	Brett Butler	.05
47	Terry Steinbach	.05
48	Craig Biggio	.05
49	Greg Vaughn	.05
50	Charlie Hayes	.05
51	Mickey Tettleton	.05
52	Jose Rijo	.05
53	Carlos Baerga	.05
54	Jeff Blauser	.05
55	Leo Gomez	.05
56	Bob Tewksbury	.05
57	Mo Vaughn	.05
58	Orlando Merced	.05
59	Tino Martinez	.05
60	Len Dykstra	.05
61	Jose Canseco	.25
62	Tony Fernandez	.05
63	Donovan Osborne	.05
64	Ken Hill	.05
65	Kent Hrbek	.05
66	Bryan Harvey	.05
67	Wally Joyner	.05
68	Derrick May	.05
69	Lance Johnson	.05
70	Willie McGee	.05
71	Mark Langston	.05
72	Terry Pendleton	.05
73	Joe Carter	.05
74	Barry Larkin	.05
75	Jimmy Key	.05
76	Joe Girardi	.05
77	B.J. Surhoff	.05
78	Pete Harnisch	.05
79	Lou Whitaker	.05
80	Cory Snyder	.05
81	Kenny Lofton	.05
82	Fred McGriff	.05
83	Mike Greenwell	.05
84	Mike Perez	.05
85	Cal Ripken, Jr.	1.00
86	Don Slaught	.05
87	Omar Vizquel	.05
88	Curt Schilling	.30
89	Chuck Knoblauch	.05
90	Moises Alou	.05
91	Greg Gagne	.05
92	Bret Saberhagen	.05
93	Ozzie Guillen	.05
94	Matt Williams	.05
95	Chad Curtis	.05
96	Mike Harkey	.05
97	Devon White	.05
98	Walt Weiss	.05
99	Kevin Brown	.05
100	Gary Sheffield	.25
101	Wade Boggs	.50
102	Orel Hershiser	.05
103	Tony Phillips	.05
104	Andujar Cedeno	.05
105	Bill Spiers	.05
106	Otis Nixon	.05
107	Felix Fermin	.05
108	Bip Roberts	.05
109	Dennis Eckersley	.35
110	Dante Bichette	.05
111	Ben McDonald	.05
112	Jim Poole	.05
113	John Dopson	.05
114	Rob Dibble	.05
115	Jeff Treadway	.05
116	Ricky Jordan	.05
117	Mike Henneman	.05
118	Willie Blair	.05
119	Doug Henry	.05
120	Gerald Perry	.05
121	Greg Myers	.05
122	John Franco	.05
123	Roger Mason	.05
124	Chris Hammond	.05
125	Hubie Brooks	.05
126	Kent Mercker	.05
127	Jim Abbott	.05
128	Kevin Bass	.05
129	Rick Aguilera	.05
130	Mitch Webster	.05
131	Eric Plunk	.05
132	Mark Carreon	.05
133	Dave Stewart	.05
134	Willie Wilson	.05
135	Dave Fleming	.05
136	Jeff Tackett	.05
137	Geno Petralli	.05
138	Gene Harris	.05
139	Scott Bankhead	.05
140	Trevor Wilson	.05
141	Alvaro Espinoza	.05
142	Ryan Bowen	.05
143	Mike Moore	.05
144	Bill Pecota	.05
145	Jaime Navarro	.05
146	Jack Daugherty	.05
147	Bob Wickman	.05
148	Chris Jones	.05
149	Todd Stottlemyre	.05
150	Brian Williams	.05
151	Chuck Finley	.05
152	Lenny Harris	.05
153	Alex Fernandez	.05
154	Candy Maldonado	.05
155	Jeff Montgomery	.05
156	David West	.05
157	Mark Williamson	.05
158	Milt Thompson	.05
159	Ron Darling	.05
160	Stan Belinda	.05
161	Henry Cotto	.05
162	Mel Rojas	.05
163	Doug Strange	.05
164	Rene Arocha	.05
165	Tim Hulett	.05
166	Steve Avery	.05
167	Jim Thome	.35
168	Tom Browning	.05
169	Mario Diaz	.05
170	Steve Reed	.05
171	Scott Livingstone	.05
172	Chris Donnels	.05
173	John Jaha	.05
174	Carlos Hernandez	.05
175	Dion James	.05
176	Bud Black	.05
177	Tony Castillo	.05
178	Jose Guzman	.05
179	Torey Lovullo	.05
180	John Vander Wal	.05
181	Mike LaValliere	.05
182	Sid Fernandez	.05
183	Brent Mayne	.05
184	Terry Mulholland	.05
185	Willie Banks	.05
186	Steve Cooke	.05
187	Brent Gates	.05
188	Erik Pappas	.05
189	Bill Haselman	.05
190	Fernando Valenzuela	.05
191	Gary Redus	.05
192	Danny Darwin	.05
193	Mark Portugal	.05
194	Derek Lilliquist	.05
195	Charlie O'Brien	.05
196	Matt Nokes	.05
197	Danny Sheaffer	.05
198	Bill Gullickson	.05
199	Alex Arias	.05
200	Mike Fetters	.05
201	Brian Jordan	.05
202	Joe Grahe	.05
203	Tom Candiotti	.05
204	Jeremy Stanton	.05
205	Mike Stanton	.05
206	David Howard	.05
207	Darren Holmes	.05
208	Rick Honeycutt	.05
209	Danny Jackson	.05
210	Rich Amaral	.05
211	Blas Minor	.05
212	Kenny Rogers	.05
213	Jim Leyritz	.05
214	Mike Morgan	.05
215	Dan Gladden	.05
216	Randy Velarde	.05
217	Mitch Williams	.05
218	Hipolito Pichardo	.05
219	Dave Burba	.05
220	Wilson Alvarez	.05
221	Bob Zupcic	.05
222	Francisco Cabrera	.05
223	Julio Valera	.05
224	Paul Assenmacher	.05
225	Jeff Branson	.05
226	Todd Frohwirth	.05
227	Armando Reynoso	.05
228	Rich Rowland	.05
229	Freddie Benavides	.05
230	Wayne Kirby	.05
231	Darryl Kile	.05
232	Skeeter Barnes	.05
233	Ramon Martinez	.05
234	Tom Gordon	.05
235	Dave Gallagher	.05
236	Ricky Bones	.05
237	Larry Andersen	.05
238	Pat Meares	.05
239	Zane Smith	.05
240	Tim Leary	.05
241	Phil Clark	.05
242	Danny Cox	.05
243	Mike Jackson	.05
244	Mike Gallego	.05
245	Lee Smith	.05
246	Todd Jones	.05
247	Steve Bedrosian	.05
248	Troy Neel	.05
249	Jose Bautista	.05
250	Steve Frey	.05
251	Jeff Reardon	.05
252	Stan Javier	.05
253	Mo Sanford	.05
254	Steve Sax	.05

No.	Player	Value
255	Luis Aquino	.05
256	Domingo Jean	.05
257	Scott Servais	.05
258	Brad Pennington	.05
259	Dave Hansen	.05
260	Goose Gossage	.05
261	Jeff Fassero	.05
262	Junior Ortiz	.05
263	Anthony Young	.05
264	Chris Bosio	.05
265	Ruben Amaro Jr.	.05
266	Mark Eichhorn	.05
267	Dave Clark	.05
268	Gary Thurman	.05
269	Les Lancaster	.05
270	Jamie Moyer	.05
271	Ricky Gutierrez	.05
272	Greg Harris	.05
273	Mike Benjamin	.05
274	Gene Nelson	.05
275	Damon Berryhill	.05
276	Scott Radinsky	.05
277	Mike Aldrete	.05
278	Jerry DiPoto	.05
279	Chris Haney	.05
280	Richie Lewis	.05
281	Jarvis Brown	.05
282	Juan Bell	.05
283	Joe Klink	.05
284	Graeme Lloyd	.05
285	Casey Candaele	.05
286	Bob MacDonald	.05
287	Mike Sharperson	.05
288	Gene Larkin	.05
289	Brian Barnes	.05
290	David McCarty	.05
291	Jeff Innis	.05
292	Bob Patterson	.05
293	Ben Rivera	.05
294	John Habyan	.05
295	Rich Rodriguez	.05
296	Edwin Nunez	.05
297	Rod Brewer	.05
298	Mike Timlin	.05
299	Jesse Orosco	.05
300	Gary Gaetti	.05
301	Todd Benzinger	.05
302	Jeff Nelson	.05
303	Rafael Belliard	.05
304	Matt Whiteside	.05
305	Vinny Castilla	.05
306	Matt Turner	.05
307	Eduardo Perez	.05
308	Joel Johnston	.05
309	Chris Gomez	.05
310	Pat Rapp	.05
311	Jim Tatum	.05
312	Kirk Rueter	.05
313	John Flaherty	.05
314	Tom Kramer	.05
315	Mark Whiten	.05
316	Chris Bosio	.05
317	Orioles Checklist	.05
318	Red Sox Checklist	.05
319	Angels Checklist	.05
320	White Sox Checklist	.05
321	Indians Checklist	.05
322	Tigers Checklist	.05
323	Royals Checklist	.05
324	Brewers Checklist	.05
325	Twins Checklist	.05
326	Yankees Checklist	.05
327	Athletics Checklist	.05
328	Mariners Checklist	.05
329	Rangers Checklist	.05
330	Blue Jays Checklist	.05
331	Frank Viola	.05
332	Ron Gant	.05
333	Charles Nagy	.05
334	Roberto Kelly	.05
335	Brady Anderson	.05
336	Alex Cole	.05
337	Alan Trammell	.05
338	Derek Bell	.05
339	Bernie Williams	.05
340	Jose Offerman	.05
341	Bill Wegman	.05
342	Ken Caminiti	.05
343	Pat Borders	.05
344	Kirt Manwaring	.05
345	Chili Davis	.05
346	Steve Buechele	.05
347	Robin Ventura	.05
348	Teddy Higuera	.05
349	Jerry Browne	.05
350	Scott Kamieniecki	.05
351	Kevin Tapani	.05
352	Marquis Grissom	.05
353	Jay Buhner	.05
354	Dave Hollins	.05
355	Dan Wilson	.05
356	Bob Walk	.05
357	Chris Hoiles	.05
358	Todd Zeile	.05
359	Kevin Appier	.05
360	Chris Sabo	.05
361	David Segui	.05
362	Jerald Clark	.05
363	Tony Pena	.05
364	Steve Finley	.05
365	Roger Pavlik	.05
366	John Smoltz	.05
367	Scott Fletcher	.05
368	Jody Reed	.05
369	David Wells	.05
370	Jose Vizcaino	.05
371	Pat Listach	.05
372	Orestes Destrade	.05
373	Danny Tartabull	.05
374	Greg W. Harris	.05
375	Juan Guzman	.05
376	Larry Walker	.05
377	Gary DiSarcina	.05
378	Bobby Bonilla	.05
379	Tim Raines	.05
380	Tommy Greene	.05
381	Chris Gwynn	.05
382	Jeff King	.05
383	Shane Mack	.05
384	Ozzie Smith	.50
385	*Eddie Zambrano*	.05
386	Mike Devereaux	.05
387	Erik Hanson	.05
388	Scott Cooper	.05
389	Dean Palmer	.05
390	John Wetteland	.05
391	Reggie Jefferson	.05
392	Mark Lemke	.05
393	Cecil Fielder	.05
394	Reggie Sanders	.05
395	Darryl Hamilton	.05
396	Daryl Boston	.05
397	Pat Kelly	.05
398	Joe Orsulak	.05
399	Ed Sprague	.05
400	Eric Anthony	.05
401	Scott Sanderson	.05
402	Jim Gott	.05
403	Ron Karkovice	.05
404	Phil Plantier	.05
405	David Cone	.05
406	Robby Thompson	.05
407	Dave Winfield	.40
408	Dwight Smith	.05
409	Ruben Sierra	.05
410	Jack Armstrong	.05
411	Mike Felder	.05
412	Wil Cordero	.05
413	Julio Franco	.05
414	Howard Johnson	.05
415	Mark McLemore	.05
416	Pete Incaviglia	.05
417	John Valentin	.05
418	Tim Wakefield	.05
419	Jose Mesa	.05
420	Bernard Gilkey	.05
421	Kirk Gibson	.05
422	Dave Justice	.05
423	Tom Brunansky	.05
424	John Smiley	.05
425	Kevin Maas	.05
426	Doug Drabek	.05
427	Paul Molitor	.40
428	Darryl Strawberry	.05
429	Tim Naehring	.05
430	Bill Swift	.05
431	Ellis Burks	.05
432	Greg Hibbard	.05
433	Felix Jose	.05
434	Bret Barberie	.05
435	Pedro Munoz	.05
436	Darrin Fletcher	.05
437	Bobby Witt	.05
438	Wes Chamberlain	.05
439	Mackey Sasser	.05
440	Mark Whiten	.05
441	Harold Reynolds	.05
442	Greg Olson	.05
443	Billy Hatcher	.05
444	Joe Oliver	.05
445	Sandy Alomar Jr.	.05
446	Tim Wallach	.05
447	Karl Rhodes	.05
448	Royce Clayton	.05
449	Cal Eldred	.05
450	Rick Wilkins	.05
451	Mike Stanley	.05
452	Charlie Hough	.05
453	Jack Morris	.05
454	*Jon Ratliff*	.05
455	Rene Gonzales	.05
456	Eddie Taubensee	.05
457	Roberto Hernandez	.05
458	Todd Hundley	.05
459	Mike MacFarlane	.05
460	Mickey Morandini	.05
461	Scott Erickson	.05
462	Lonnie Smith	.05
463	Dave Henderson	.05
464	Ryan Klesko	.05
465	Edgar Martinez	.05
466	Tom Pagnozzi	.05
467	Charlie Leibrandt	.05
468	*Brian Anderson*	.10
469	Harold Baines	.05
470	Tim Belcher	.05
471	Andre Dawson	.25
472	Eric Young	.05
473	Paul Sorrento	.05
474	Luis Gonzalez	.05
475	Rob Deer	.05
476	Mike Piazza	.65
477	Kevin Reimer	.05
478	Jeff Gardner	.05
479	Melido Perez	.05
480	Darren Lewis	.05
481	Duane Ward	.05
482	Rey Sanchez	.05
483	Mark Lewis	.05
484	Jeff Conine	.05
485	Joey Cora	.05
486	*Trot Nixon*	.50
487	Kevin McReynolds	.05
488	Mike Lansing	.05
489	Mike Pagliarulo	.05
490	Mariano Duncan	.05
491	Mike Bordick	.05
492	Kevin Young	.05
493	Dave Valle	.05
494	*Wayne Gomes*	.05
495	Rafael Palmeiro	.35
496	Deion Sanders	.05
497	Rick Sutcliffe	.05
498	Randy Milligan	.05
499	Carlos Quintana	.05
500	Chris Turner	.05
501	Thomas Howard	.05
502	Greg Swindell	.05
503	Chad Kreuter	.05
504	Eric Davis	.05
505	Dickie Thon	.05
506	*Matt Drews*	.05
507	Spike Owen	.05
508	Rod Beck	.05
509	Pat Hentgen	.05
510	Sammy Sosa	.50
511	J.T. Snow	.05
512	Chuck Carr	.05
513	Bo Jackson	.10
514	Dennis Martinez	.05
515	Phil Hiatt	.05
516	Jeff Kent	.05
517	*Brooks Kieschnick*	.05
518	*Kirk Presley*	.05
519	Kevin Seitzer	.05
520	Carlos Garcia	.05
521	Mike Blowers	.05
522	Luis Alicea	.05
523	David Hulse	.05
524	Greg Maddux	.50
525	Gregg Olson	.05
526	Hal Morris	.05
527	Daron Kirkreit	.05
528	David Nied	.05
529	Jeff Russell	.05
530	Kevin Gross	.05
531	John Doherty	.05
532	*Matt Brunson*	.05
533	Dave Nilsson	.05
534	Randy Myers	.05
535	Steve Farr	.05
536	*Billy Wagner*	.10
537	Darnell Coles	.05
538	Frank Tanana	.05
539	Tim Salmon	.05
540	Kim Batiste	.05
541	George Bell	.05
542	Tom Henke	.05
543	Sam Horn	.05
544	Doug Jones	.05
545	Scott Leius	.05
546	Al Martin	.05
547	Bob Welch	.05
548	*Scott Christman*	.05
549	Norm Charlton	.05
550	Mark McGwire	.75
551	Greg McMichael	.05
552	Tim Costo	.05
553	Rodney Bolton	.05
554	Pedro Martinez	.40
555	Marc Valdes	.05
556	Darrell Whitmore	.05
557	Tim Bogar	.05
558	Steve Karsay	.05
559	Danny Bautista	.05
560	Jeffrey Hammonds	.05
561	Aaron Sele	.05
562	Russ Springer	.05
563	Jason Bere	.05
564	Billy Brewer	.05
565	Sterling Hitchcock	.05
566	Bobby Munoz	.05
567	Craig Paquette	.05
568	Bret Boone	.05
569	Dan Peltier	.05
570	Jeromy Burnitz	.05
571	*John Wasdin*	.05
572	Chipper Jones	.50
573	*Jamey Wright*	.05
574	Jeff Granger	.05
575	*Jay Powell*	.05
576	Ryan Thompson	.05
577	Lou Frazier	.05
578	Paul Wagner	.05
579	Brad Ausmus	.05
580	Jack Voigt	.05
581	Kevin Rogers	.05
582	Damon Buford	.05
583	Paul Quantrill	.05
584	Marc Newfield	.05
585	*Derrek Lee*	1.00
586	Shane Reynolds	.05
587	Cliff Floyd	.05
588	Jeff Schwarz	.05
589	*Ross Powell*	.05
590	Gerald Williams	.05
591	Mike Trombley	.05
592	Ken Ryan	.05
593	John O'Donoghue	.05
594	Rod Correia	.05
595	Darrell Sherman	.05
596	Steve Scarsone	.05
597	Sherman Obando	.05
598	Kurt Abbott	.05
599	Dave Telgheder	.05
600	Rick Trlicek	.05
601	Carl Everett	.05
602	Luis Ortiz	.05
603	*Larry Luebbers*	.05
604	Kevin Roberson	.05
605	Butch Huskey	.05
606	Benji Gil	.05
607	Todd Van Poppel	.05
608	Mark Hutton	.05
609	Chip Hale	.05
610	Matt Maysey	.05
611	Scott Ruffcorn	.05
612	Hilly Hathaway	.05
613	Allen Watson	.05
614	Carlos Delgado	.30
615	Roberto Mejia	.05
616	Turk Wendell	.05
617	Tony Tarasco	.05
618	Raul Mondesi	.05
619	Kevin Stocker	.05
620	Javier Lopez	.05
621	*Keith Kessinger*	.05
622	Bob Hamelin	.05
623	John Roper	.05
624	Len Dykstra	.05
625	Joe Carter	.05
626	Jim Abbott	.05
627	Lee Smith	.05
628	Ken Griffey, Jr.	.35
629	Dave Winfield	.05
630	Darryl Kile	.05
631	Frank Thomas	.25
632	Barry Bonds	.50
633	Jack McDowell	.05
634	Greg Maddux	.25
635	Tim Salmon	.05
636	Mike Piazza	.40
637	*Brian Turang*	.05
638	Rondell White	.05
639	Nigel Wilson	.05
640	*Torii Hunter*	.75
641	Salomon Torres	.05
642	Kevin Higgins	.05
643	Eric Wedge	.05
644	Roger Salkeld	.05
645	Manny Ramirez	.40
646	Jeff McNeely	.05
647	Braves Checklist	.05
648	Cubs Checklist	.05
649	Reds Checklist	.05
650	Rockies Checklist	.05

651	Marlins Checklist	.05
652	Astros Checklist	.05
653	Dodgers Checklist	.05
654	Expos Checklist	.05
655	Mets Checklist	.05
656	Phillies Checklist	.05
657	Pirates Checklist	.05
658	Cardinals Checklist	.05
659	Padres Checklist	.05
660	Giants Checklist	.05

Gold Rush

		NM/M
Complete Set (660):		40.00
Common Player:		.15
Stars:		2X

(See 1994 Score for checklist and base card values.)

Boys of Summer

		NM/M
Complete Set (60):		25.00
Common Player:		.25
1	Jeff Conine	.25
2	Aaron Sele	.25
3	Kevin Stocker	.25
4	Pat Meares	.25
5	Jeromy Burnitz	.25
6	Mike Piazza	6.00
7	Allen Watson	.25
8	Jeffrey Hammonds	.25
9	Kevin Roberson	.25
10	Hilly Hathaway	.25
11	Kirk Reuter	.25
12	Eduardo Perez	.25
13	Ricky Gutierrez	.25
14	Domingo Jean	.25
15	David Nied	.25
16	Wayne Kirby	.25
17	Mike Lansing	.25
18	Jason Bere	.25
19	Brent Gates	.25
20	Javier Lopez	.25
21	Greg McMichael	.25
22	David Hulse	.25
23	Roberto Mejia	.25
24	Tim Salmon	.50
25	Rene Arocha	.25
26	Bret Boone	.25
27	David McCarty	.25
28	Todd Van Poppel	.25
29	Lance Painter	.25
30	Erik Pappas	.25
31	Chuck Carr	.25
32	Mark Hutton	.25
33	Jeff McNeely	.25
34	Willie Greene	.25
35	Nigel Wilson	.25
36	Rondell White	.25
37	Brian Turang	.25
38	Manny Ramirez	3.00
39	Salomon Torres	.25
40	Melvin Nieves	.25
41	Ryan Klesko	.25
42	Keith Kessinger	.25
43	Eric Wedge	.25
44	Bob Hamelin	.25
45	Carlos Delgado	2.50
46	Marc Newfield	.25
47	Raul Mondesi	.25
48	Tim Costo	.25
49	Pedro Martinez	3.00
50	Steve Karsay	.25
51	Danny Bautista	.25
52	Butch Huskey	.25
53	Kurt Abbott	.25
54	Darrell Sherman	.25
55	Damon Buford	.25
56	Ross Powell	.25
57	Darrell Whitmore	.25
58	Chipper Jones	5.00
59	Jeff Granger	.25
60	Cliff Floyd	.25

1994 SCORE CAL RIPKEN, JR.

		NM/M
Complete Set (9):		3.00
Complete Set, Gold (9):		6.00
Common Player:		.50
Common Card, Gold:		1.00
Autographed Card:		200.00
1	Double Honors	.50
1a	Double Honors (gold)	1.00
2	Perennial All-Star	.50
2a	Perennial All-Star (gold)	1.00
3	Peerless Power	.50
3a	Peerless Power (gold)	1.00
4	Fitness Fan	.50
4a	Fitness Fan (gold)	1.00
5	Prime Concerns	.50
5a	Prime Concerns (gold)	1.00
6	Home Run Club	.50
6a	Home Run Club (gold)	1.00
7	The Iron Man	.50
7a	The Iron Man (gold)	1.00
8	Heavy Hitter	.50
8a	Heavy Hitter (gold)	1.00
9	Gold Glover	.50
9a	Gold Glover (gold)	1.00

Dream Team

		NM/M
Complete Set (10):		15.00
Common Player:		1.00
1	Mike Mussina	2.00
2	Tom Glavine	2.00
3	Don Mattingly	10.00
4	Carlos Baerga	1.00
5	Barry Larkin	1.00
6	Matt Williams	1.00
7	Juan Gonzalez	4.00
8	Andy Van Slyke	1.00
9	Larry Walker	1.00
10	Mike Stanley	1.00

Gold Stars

		NM/M
Complete Set (60):		40.00
Common Player:		.25
1	Barry Bonds	6.00
2	Orlando Merced	.25
3	Mark Grace	.25
4	Darren Daulton	.25
5	Jeff Blauser	.25
6	Deion Sanders	.25
7	John Kruk	.25
8	Jeff Bagwell	2.50
9	Gregg Jefferies	.25
10	Matt Williams	.25
11	Andres Galarraga	.25
12	Jay Bell	.25
13	Mike Piazza	4.50
14	Ron Gant	.25
15	Barry Larkin	.25
16	Tom Glavine	.50
17	Len Dykstra	.25
18	Fred McGriff	.25
19	Andy Van Slyke	.25
20	Gary Sheffield	.75
21	John Burkett	.25
22	Dante Bichette	.25
23	Tony Gwynn	3.50
24	Dave Justice	.25
25	Marquis Grissom	.25
26	Bobby Bonilla	.25
27	Larry Walker	.25
28	Brett Butler	.25
29	Robby Thompson	.25
30	Jeff Conine	.25
31	Joe Carter	.25
32	Ken Griffey, Jr.	4.50
33	Juan Gonzalez	1.25
34	Rickey Henderson	2.50
35	Bo Jackson	.35
36	Cal Ripken, Jr.	6.00
37	John Olerud	.25
38	Carlos Baerga	.25
39	Jack McDowell	.25
40	Cecil Fielder	.25
41	Kenny Lofton	.25
42	Roberto Alomar	1.00
43	Randy Johnson	2.50
44	Tim Salmon	.25
45	Frank Thomas	2.50
46	Albert Belle	.25
47	Greg Vaughn	.25
48	Travis Fryman	.25
49	Don Mattingly	4.00
50	Wade Boggs	3.50
51	Mo Vaughn	.25
52	Kirby Puckett	3.50
53	Devon White	.25
54	Tony Phillips	.25
55	Brian Harper	.25
56	Chad Curtis	.25
57	Paul Molitor	2.50
58	Ivan Rodriguez	2.00
59	Rafael Palmeiro	2.00
60	Brian McRae	.25

The Cycle

		NM/M
Complete Set (20):		12.00
Common Player:		.50
1	Brett Butler	.50
2	Kenny Lofton	.50
3	Paul Molitor	2.00
4	Carlos Baerga	.50
5	Gregg Jefferies, Tony Phillips	.50
6	John Olerud	.50
7	Charlie Hayes	.50
8	Len Dykstra	.50
9	Dante Bichette	.50
10	Devon White	.50
11	Lance Johnson	.50
12	Joey Cora, Steve Finley	.50
13	Tony Fernandez	.50
14	David Hulse, Brett Butler	.50
15	Jay Bell, Brian McRae, Mickey Morandini	.50
16	Juan Gonzalez, Barry Bonds	4.00
17	Ken Griffey, Jr.	4.00
18	Frank Thomas	2.50
19	Dave Justice	.50
20	Matt Williams, Albert Belle	.50

1994 SCORE ROOKIE/TRADED

		NM/M
Complete Set (165):		5.00
Common Player:		.05
Gold Rush:		2X
Pack (10):		.40
Wax Box (36):		9.00
1	Will Clark	.05
2	Lee Smith	.05
3	Bo Jackson	.10
4	Ellis Burks	.05
5	Eddie Murray	1.00
6	Delino DeShields	.05
7	Erik Hanson	.05
8	Rafael Palmeiro	.75
9	Luis Polonia	.05
10	Omar Vizquel	.05
11	Kurt Abbott	.05
12	Vince Coleman	.05
13	Rickey Henderson	1.00
14	Terry Mulholland	.05
15	Greg Hibbard	.05
16	Walt Weiss	.05
17	Chris Sabo	.05
18	Dave Henderson	.05
19	Rick Sutcliffe	.05
20	Harold Reynolds	.05
21	Jack Morris	.05
22	Dan Wilson	.05
23	Dave Magadan	.05
24	Dennis Martinez	.05
25	Wes Chamberlain	.05
26	Otis Nixon	.05
27	Eric Anthony	.05
28	Randy Milligan	.05
29	Julio Franco	.05
30	Kevin McReynolds	.05
31	Anthony Young	.05
32	Brian Harper	.05
33	Lenny Harris	.05
34	Eddie Taubensee	.05
35	David Segui	.05
36	Stan Javier	.05
37	Felix Fermin	.05
38	Darrin Jackson	.05
39	Tony Fernandez	.05
40	Jose Vizcaino	.05
41	Willie Banks	.05
42	Brian Hunter	.05
43	Reggie Jefferson	.05
44	Junior Felix	.05
45	Jack Armstrong	.05
46	Bip Roberts	.05
47	Jerry Browne	.05
48	Marvin Freeman	.05
49	Jody Reed	.05
50	Alex Cole	.05
51	Sid Fernandez	.05
52	Pete Smith	.05
53	Xavier Hernandez	.05
54	Scott Sanderson	.05
55	Turner Ward	.05
56	Rex Hudler	.05
57	Deion Sanders	.05
58	Sid Bream	.05
59	Tony Pena	.05
60	Bret Boone	.05
61	Bobby Ayala	.05
62	Pedro Martinez	1.00
63	Howard Johnson	.05
64	Mark Portugal	.05
65	Roberto Kelly	.05
66	Spike Owen	.05
67	Jeff Treadway	.05
68	Mike Harkey	.05
69	Doug Jones	.05
70	Steve Farr	.05
71	Billy Taylor	.05
72	Manny Ramirez	1.00
73	Bob Hamelin	.05
74	Steve Karsay	.05
75	Ryan Klesko	.05
76	Cliff Floyd	.05
77	Jeffrey Hammonds	.05
78	Javier Lopez	.05
79	Roger Salkeld	.05
80	Hector Carrasco	.05
81	Gerald Williams	.05
82	Raul Mondesi	.05
83	Sterling Hitchcock	.05
84	Danny Bautista	.05
85	Chris Turner	.05
86	Shane Reynolds	.05
87	Rondell White	.05
88	Salomon Torres	.05

89	Turk Wendell	.05
90	Tony Tarasco	.05
91	Shawn Green	.65
92	Greg Colbrunn	.05
93	Eddie Zambrano	.05
94	Rich Becker	.05
95	Chris Gomez	.05
96	John Patterson	.05
97	Derek Parks	.05
98	Rich Rowland	.05
99	James Mouton	.05
100	Tim Hyers	.05
101	Jose Valentin	.05
102	Carlos Delgado	.65
103	Robert Esenhoorn	.05
104	John Hudek	.05
105	Domingo Cedeno	.05
106	Denny Hocking	.05
107	Greg Pirkl	.05
108	Mark Smith	.05
109	Paul Shuey	.05
110	Jorge Fabregas	.05
111	Rikkert Faneyte	.05
112	Rob Butler	.05
113	Darren Oliver	.05
114	Troy O'Leary	.05
115	Scott Brow	.05
116	Tony Eusebio	.05
117	Carlos Reyes	.05
118	J.R. Phillips	.05
119	Alex Diaz	.05
120	Charles Johnson	.05
121	Nate Minchey	.05
122	Scott Sanders	.05
123	Daryl Boston	.05
124	Joey Hamilton	.05
125	Brian Anderson	.05
126	Dan Miceli	.05
127	Tom Brunansky	.05
128	Dave Staton	.05
129	Mike Oquist	.05
130	John Mabry	.05
131	Norberto Martin	.05
132	Hector Fajardo	.05
133	Mark Hutton	.05
134	Fernando Vina	.05
135	Lee Tinsley	.05
136	*Chan Ho Park*	1.50
137	Paul Spoljaric	.05
138	Matias Carrillo	.05
139	Mark Kiefer	.05
140	Stan Royer	.05
141	Bryan Eversgerd	.05
143	Joe Hall	.05
144	Johnny Ruffin	.05
145	Alex Gonzalez	.05
146	Keith Lockhart	.05
147	Tom Marsh	.05
148	Tony Longmire	.05
149	Keith Mitchell	.05
150	Melvin Nieves	.05
151	Kelly Stinnett	.05
152	Miguel Jimenez	.05
153	Jeff Juden	.05
154	Matt Walbeck	.05
155	Marc Newfield	.05
156	Matt Mieske	.05
157	Marcus Moore	.05
158	*Jose Lima*	.25
159	Mike Kelly	.05
160	Jim Edmonds	.05
161	Steve Trachsel	.05
162	Greg Blosser	.05
163	Mark Acre	.05
164	AL Checklist	.05
165	NL Checklist	.05

Changing Places

		NM/M
Complete Set (10):		15.00
Common Player:		1.00
1	Will Clark	1.00
2	Rafael Palmeiro	4.00
3	Roberto Kelly	1.00
4	Bo Jackson	1.25
5	Otis Nixon	1.00
6	Rickey Henderson	5.00
7	Ellis Burks	1.00
8	Lee Smith	1.00
9	Delino DeShields	1.00
10	Deion Sanders	1.00

Rookie/Traded Super Rookies

		NM/M
Complete Set (18):		15.00
Common Player:		1.00
1	Carlos Delgado	5.00
2	Manny Ramirez	5.00
3	Ryan Klesko	1.00
4	Raul Mondesi	1.00
5	Bob Hamelin	1.00
6	Steve Karsay	1.00
7	Jeffrey Hammonds	1.00
8	Cliff Floyd	1.00
9	Kurt Abbott	1.00
10	Marc Newfield	1.00
11	Javier Lopez	1.00
12	Rich Becker	1.00
13	Greg Pirkl	1.00
14	Rondell White	1.00
15	James Mouton	1.00
16	Tony Tarasco	1.00
17	Brian Anderson	1.00
18	Jim Edmonds	1.00

1995 SCORE

		NM/M
Complete Set (605):		13.50
Common Player:		.05
Series 1 or 2 Pack (12):		.75
Series 1 or 2 Box (36):		12.50
1	Frank Thomas	.50
2	Roberto Alomar	.15
3	Cal Ripken, Jr.	1.50
4	Jose Canseco	.30
5	Matt Williams	.05
6	Esteban Beltre	.05
7	Domingo Cedeno	.05
8	John Valentin	.05
9	Glenallen Hill	.05
10	Rafael Belliard	.05
11	Randy Myers	.05
12	Mo Vaughn	.05
13	Hector Carrasco	.05
14	Chili Davis	.05
15	Dante Bichette	.05
16	Darren Jackson	.05
17	Mike Piazza	.75
18	Junior Felix	.05
19	Moises Alou	.05
20	Mark Gubicza	.05
21	Bret Saberhagen	.05
22	Len Dykstra	.05
23	Steve Howe	.05
24	Mark Dewey	.05
25	Brian Harper	.05
26	Ozzie Smith	.60
27	Scott Erickson	.05
28	Tony Gwynn	.60
29	Bob Welch	.05
30	Barry Bonds	1.50
31	Leo Gomez	.05
32	Greg Maddux	.60
33	Mike Greenwell	.05
34	Sammy Sosa	.60
35	Darnell Coles	.05
36	Tommy Greene	.05
37	Will Clark	.05
38	Steve Ontiveros	.05
39	Stan Javier	.05
40	Bip Roberts	.05
41	Paul O'Neill	.05
42	Bill Haselman	.05
43	Shane Mack	.05
44	Orlando Merced	.05
45	Kevin Seitzer	.05
46	Trevor Hoffman	.05
47	Greg Gagne	.05
48	Jeff Kent	.05
49	Tony Phillips	.05
50	Ken Hill	.05
51	Carlos Baerga	.05
52	Henry Rodriguez	.05
53	Scott Sanderson	.05
54	Jeff Conine	.05
55	Chris Turner	.05
56	Ken Caminiti	.05
57	Harold Baines	.05
58	Charlie Hayes	.05
59	Roberto Kelly	.05
60	John Olerud	.05
61	Tim Davis	.05
62	Rich Rowland	.05
63	Rey Sanchez	.05
64	Junior Ortiz	.05
65	Ricky Gutierrez	.05
66	Rex Hudler	.05
67	Johnny Ruffin	.05
68	Jay Buhner	.05
69	Tom Pagnozzi	.05
70	Julio Franco	.05
71	Eric Young	.05
72	Mike Bordick	.05
73	Don Slaught	.05
74	Goose Gossage	.05
75	Lonnie Smith	.05
76	Jimmy Key	.05
77	Dave Hollins	.05
78	Mickey Tettleton	.05
79	Luis Gonzalez	.05
80	Dave Winfield	.50
81	Ryan Thompson	.05
82	Felix Jose	.05
83	Rusty Meacham	.05
84	Darryl Hamilton	.05
85	John Wetteland	.05
86	Tom Brunansky	.05
87	Mark Lemke	.05
88	Spike Owen	.05
89	Shawon Dunston	.05
90	Wilson Alvarez	.05
91	Lee Smith	.05
92	Scott Kamieniecki	.05
93	Jacob Brumfield	.05
94	Kirk Gibson	.05
95	Joe Girardi	.05
96	Mike Macfarlane	.05
97	Greg Colbrunn	.05
98	Ricky Bones	.05
99	Delino DeShields	.05
100	Pat Meares	.05
101	Jeff Fassero	.05
102	Jim Leyritz	.05
103	Gary Redus	.05
104	Terry Steinbach	.05
105	Kevin McReynolds	.05
106	Felix Fermin	.05
107	Danny Jackson	.05
108	Chris James	.05
109	Jeff King	.05
110	Pat Hentgen	.05
111	Gerald Perry	.05
112	Tim Raines	.05
113	Eddie Williams	.05
114	Jamie Moyer	.05
115	Bud Black	.05
116	Chris Gomez	.05
117	Luis Lopez	.05
118	Roger Clemens	.65
119	Javier Lopez	.05
120	Dave Nilsson	.05
121	Karl Rhodes	.05
122	Rick Aguilera	.05
123	Tony Fernandez	.05
124	Bernie Williams	.05
125	James Mouton	.05
126	Mark Langston	.05
127	Mike Lansing	.05
128	Tino Martinez	.05
129	Joe Orsulak	.05
130	David Hulse	.05
131	Pete Incaviglia	.05
132	Mark Clark	.05
133	Tony Eusebio	.05
134	Chuck Finley	.05
135	Lou Frazier	.05
136	Craig Grebeck	.05
137	Kelly Stinnett	.05
138	Paul Shuey	.05
139	David Nied	.05
140	Billy Brewer	.05
141	Dave Weathers	.05
142	Scott Leius	.05
143	Brian Jordan	.05
144	Melido Perez	.05
145	Tony Tarasco	.05
146	Dan Wilson	.05
147	Rondell White	.05
148	Mike Henneman	.05
149	Brian Johnson	.05
150	Tom Henke	.05
151	John Patterson	.05
152	Bobby Witt	.05
153	Eddie Taubensee	.05
154	Pat Borders	.05
155	Ramon Martinez	.05
156	Mike Kingery	.05
157	Zane Smith	.05
158	Benito Santiago	.05
159	Matias Carrillo	.05
160	Scott Brosius	.05
161	Dave Clark	.05
162	Mark McLemore	.05
163	Curt Schilling	.30
164	J.T. Snow	.05
165	Rod Beck	.05
166	Scott Fletcher	.05
167	Bob Tewksbury	.05
168	Mike LaValliere	.05
169	Dave Hansen	.05
170	Pedro Martinez	.50
171	Kirk Rueter	.05
172	Jose Lind	.05
173	Luis Alicea	.05
174	Mike Moore	.05
175	Andy Ashby	.05
176	Jody Reed	.05
177	Darryl Kile	.05
178	Carl Willis	.05
179	Jeromy Burnitz	.05
180	Mike Gallego	.05
181	*W. Van Landingham*	.05
182	Sid Fernandez	.05
183	Kim Batiste	.05
184	Greg Myers	.05
185	Steve Avery	.05
186	Steve Farr	.05
187	Robb Nen	.05
188	Dan Pasqua	.05
189	Bruce Ruffin	.05
190	Jose Valentin	.05
191	Willie Banks	.05
192	Mike Aldrete	.05
193	Randy Milligan	.05
194	Steve Karsay	.05
195	Mike Stanley	.05
196	Jose Mesa	.05
197	Tom Browning	.05
198	John Vander Wal	.05
199	Kevin Brown	.05
200	Mike Oquist	.05
201	Greg Swindell	.05
202	Eddie Zambrano	.05
203	Joe Boever	.05
204	Gary Varsho	.05
205	Chris Gwynn	.05
206	David Howard	.05
207	Jerome Walton	.05
208	Danny Darwin	.05
209	Darryl Strawberry	.05
210	Todd Van Poppel	.05
211	Scott Livingstone	.05
212	Dave Fleming	.05
213	Todd Worrell	.05
214	Carlos Delgado	.40
215	Bill Pecota	.05
216	Jim Lindeman	.05
217	Rick White	.05
218	Jose Oquendo	.05
219	Tony Castillo	.05
220	Fernando Vina	.05
221	Jeff Bagwell	.50
222	Randy Johnson	.50
223	Albert Belle	.05
224	Chuck Carr	.05
225	Mark Leiter	.05
226	Hal Morris	.05
227	Robin Ventura	.05
228	Mike Munoz	.05
229	Jim Thome	.40
230	Mario Diaz	.05
231	John Doherty	.05
232	Bobby Jones	.05
233	Raul Mondesi	.05
234	Ricky Jordan	.05
235	John Jaha	.05

236	Carlos Garcia	.05
237	Kirby Puckett	.60
238	Orel Hershiser	.05
239	Don Mattingly	.65
240	Sid Bream	.05
241	Brent Gates	.05
242	Tony Longmire	.05
243	Robby Thompson	.05
244	Rick Sutcliffe	.05
245	Dean Palmer	.05
246	Marquis Grissom	.05
247	Paul Molitor	.50
248	Mark Carreon	.05
249	Jack Voight	.05
250	Greg McMichael (photo on front is Mike Stanton)	.05
251	Damon Berryhill	.05
252	Brian Dorsett	.05
253	Jim Edmonds	.05
254	Barry Larkin	.05
255	Jack McDowell	.05
256	Wally Joyner	.05
257	Eddie Murray	.50
258	Lenny Webster	.05
259	Milt Cuyler	.05
260	Todd Benzinger	.05
261	Vince Coleman	.05
262	Todd Stottlemyre	.05
263	Turner Ward	.05
264	Ray Lankford	.05
265	Matt Walbeck	.05
266	Deion Sanders	.05
267	Gerald Williams	.05
268	Jim Gott	.05
269	Jeff Frye	.05
270	Jose Rijo	.05
271	Dave Justice	.05
272	Ismael Valdes	.05
273	Ben McDonald	.05
274	Darren Lewis	.05
275	Graeme Lloyd	.05
276	Luis Ortiz	.05
277	Julian Tavarez	.05
278	Mark Dalesandro	.05
279	Brett Merriman	.05
280	Ricky Bottalico	.05
281	Robert Eenhoorn	.05
282	Rikkert Faneyte	.05
283	Mike Kelly	.05
284	Mark Smith	.05
285	Turk Wendell	.05
286	Greg Blosser	.05
287	Garey Ingram	.05
288	Jorge Fabregas	.05
289	Blaise Ilsley	.05
290	Joe Hall	.05
291	Orlando Miller	.05
292	Jose Lima	.05
293	Greg O'Halloran	.05
294	Mark Kiefer	.05
295	Jose Oliva	.05
296	Rich Becker	.05
297	Brian Hunter	.05
298	Dave Silvestri	.05
299	*Armando Benitez*	.10
300	Darren Dreifort	.05
301	John Mabry	.05
302	Greg Pirkl	.05
303	J.R. Phillips	.05
304	Shawn Green	.30
305	Roberto Petagine	.05
306	Keith Lockhart	.05
307	Jonathon Hurst	.05
308	Paul Spoljaric	.05
309	Mike Lieberthal	.05
310	Garret Anderson	.05
311	John Johnston	.05
312	Alex Rodriguez	1.50
313	Kent Mercker	.05
314	John Valentin	.05
315	Kenny Rogers	.05
316	Fred McGriff	.05
317	Atlanta Braves, Baltimore Orioles	.05
318	Chicago Cubs, Boston Red Sox	.05
319	Cincinnati Reds, California Angels	.05
320	Colorado Rockies, Chicago White Sox	.05
321	Cleveland Indians, Florida Marlins	.05
322	Houston Astros, Detroit Tigers	.05
323	Los Angels Dodgers, Kansas City Royals	.05
324	Montreal Expos, Milwaukee Brewers	.05
325	New York Mets, Minnesota Twins	.05
326	Philadelphia Phillies, New York Yankees	.05
327	Pittsburgh Pirates, Oakland Athletics	.05
328	San Diego Padres, Seattle Mariners	.05
329	San Francisco Giants, Texas Rangers	.05
330	St. Louis Cardinals, Toronto Blue Jays	.05
331	Pedro Munoz	.05
332	Ryan Klesko	.05
333a	Andre Dawson	.25
333b	Andre Dawson	.35
334	Derrick May	.05
335	Aaron Sele	.05
336	Kevin Mitchell	.05
337	Steve Traschel	.05
338	Andres Galarraga	.05
339a	Terry Pendleton	.05
339b	Terry Pendleton	.10
340	Gary Sheffield	.30
341	Travis Fryman	.05
342	Bo Jackson	.10
343	Gary Gaetti	.05
344a	Brett Butler	.05
344b	Brett Butler	.10
345	B. J. Surhoff	.05
346a	Larry Walker	.05
346b	Larry Walker	.10
347	Kevin Tapani	.05
348	Rick Wilkins	.05
349	Wade Boggs	.60
350	Mariano Duncan	.05
351	Ruben Sierra	.05
352a	Andy Van Slyke	.05
352b	Andy Van Slyke	.10
353	Reggie Jefferson	.05
354	Gregg Jefferies	.05
355	Tim Naehring	.05
356	John Roper	.05
357	Joe Carter	.05
358	Kurt Abbott	.05
359	Lenny Harris	.05
360	Lance Johnson	.05
361	Brian Anderson	.05
362	Jim Eisenreich	.05
363	Jerry Browne	.05
364	Mark Grace	.05
365	Devon White	.05
366	Reggie Sanders	.05
367	Ivan Rodriguez	.40
368	Kirt Manwaring	.05
369	Pat Kelly	.05
370	Ellis Burks	.05
371	Charles Nagy	.05
372	Kevin Bass	.05
373	Lou Whitaker	.05
374	Rene Arocha	.05
375	Derrick Parks	.05
376	Mark Whiten	.05
377	Mark McGwire	1.00
378	Doug Drabek	.05
379	Greg Vaughn	.05
380	Al Martin	.05
381	Ron Darling	.05
382	Tim Wallach	.05
383	Alan Trammell	.05
384	Randy Velarde	.05
385	Chris Sabo	.05
386	Wil Cordero	.05
387	Darrin Fletcher	.05
388	David Segui	.05
389	Steve Buechele	.05
390	Otis Nixon	.05
391	Jeff Brantley	.05
392a	Chad Curtis	.05
392b	Chad Curtis	.10
393	Cal Eldred	.05
394	Jason Bere	.05
395	Bret Barberie	.05
396	Paul Sorrento	.05
397	Steve Finley	.05
398	Cecil Fielder	.05
399	Eric Karros	.05
400	Jeff Montgomery	.05
401	Cliff Floyd	.05
402	Matt Mieske	.05
403	Brian Hunter	.05
404	Alex Cole	.05
405	Kevin Stocker	.05
406	Eric Davis	.05
407	Marvin Freeman	.05
408	Dennis Eckersley	.40
409	Todd Zeile	.05
410	Keith Mitchell	.05
411	Andy Benes	.05
412	Juan Bell	.05
413	Royce Clayton	.05
414	Ed Sprague	.05
415	Mike Mussina	.30
416	Todd Hundley	.05
417	Pat Listach	.05
418	Joe Oliver	.05
419	Rafael Palmeiro	.40
420	Tim Salmon	.05
421	Brady Anderson	.05
422	Kenny Lofton	.05
423	Craig Biggio	.05
424	Bobby Bonilla	.05
425	Kenny Rogers	.05
426	Derek Bell	.05
427a	Scott Cooper	.05
427b	Scott Cooper	.10
428	Ozzie Guillen	.05
429	Omar Vizquel	.05
430	Phil Plantier	.05
431	Chuck Knoblauch	.05
432	Darren Daulton	.05
433	Bob Hamelin	.05
434	Tom Glavine	.30
435	Walt Weiss	.05
436	Jose Vizcaino	.05
437	Ken Griffey Jr.	.75
438	Jay Bell	.05
439	Juan Gonzalez	.25
440	Jeff Blauser	.05
441	Rickey Henderson	.50
442	Bobby Ayala	.05
443a	David Cone	.05
443b	David Cone	.10
444	Pedro Martinez	.05
445	Manny Ramirez	.50
446	Mark Portugal	.05
447	Damion Easley	.05
448	Gary DiSarcina	.05
449	Roberto Hernandez	.05
450	Jeffrey Hammonds	.05
451	Jeff Treadway	.05
452a	Jim Abbott	.05
452b	Jim Abbott	.10
453	Carlos Rodriguez	.05
454	Joey Cora	.05
455	Bret Boone	.05
456	Danny Tartabull	.05
457	John Franco	.05
458	Roger Salkeld	.05
459	Fred McGriff	.05
460	Pedro Astacio	.05
461	Jon Lieber	.05
462	Luis Polonia	.05
463	Geronimo Pena	.05
464	Tom Gordon	.05
465	Brad Ausmus	.05
466	Willie McGee	.05
467	Doug Jones	.05
468	John Smoltz	.05
469	Troy Neel	.05
470	Luis Sojo	.05
471	John Smiley	.05
472	Rafael Bournigal	.05
473	Billy Taylor	.05
474	Juan Guzman	.05
475	Dave Magadan	.05
476	Mike Devereaux	.05
477	Andujar Cedeno	.05
478	Edgar Martinez	.05
479	Troy Neel	.05
480	Allen Watson	.05
481	Ron Karkovice	.05
482	Joey Hamilton	.05
483	Vinny Castilla	.05
484	Kevin Gross	.05
485	Bernard Gilkey	.05
486	John Burkett	.05
487	Matt Nokes	.05
488	Mel Rojas	.05
489	Craig Shipley	.05
490	Chip Hale	.05
491	Bill Swift	.05
492	Pat Rapp	.05
493a	Brian McRae	.05
493b	Brian McRae	.10
494	Mickey Morandini	.05
495	Tony Pena	.05
496	Danny Bautista	.05
497	Armando Reynoso	.05
498	Ken Ryan	.05
499	Billy Ripken	.05
500	Pat Mahomes	.05
501	Mark Acre	.05
502	Geronimo Berroa	.05
503	Norberto Martin	.05
504	Chad Kreuter	.05
505	Howard Johnson	.05
506	Eric Anthony	.05
507	Mark Wohlers	.05
508	Scott Sanders	.05
509	Pete Harnisch	.05
510	Wes Chamberlain	.05
511	Tom Candiotti	.05
512	Albie Lopez	.05
513	Denny Neagle	.05
514	Sean Berry	.05
515	Billy Hatcher	.05
516	Todd Jones	.05
517	Wayne Kirby	.05
518	Butch Henry	.05
519	Sandy Alomar Jr.	.05
520	Kevin Appier	.05
521	Robert Mejia	.05
522	Steve Cooke	.05
523	Terry Shumpert	.05
524	Mike Jackson	.05
525	Kent Mercker	.05
526	David Wells	.05
527	Juan Samuel	.05
528	Salomon Torres	.05
529	Duane Ward	.05
530a	Rob Dibble	.05
530b	Rob Dibble	.10
531	Mike Blowers	.05
532	Mark Eichhorn	.05
533	Alex Diaz	.05
534	Dan Miceli	.05
535	Jeff Branson	.05
536	Dave Stevens	.05
537	Charlie O'Brien	.05
538	Shane Reynolds	.05
539	Rich Amaral	.05
540	Rusty Greer	.05
541	Alex Arias	.05
542	Eric Plunk	.05
543	John Hudek	.05
544	Kirk McCaskill	.05
545	Jeff Reboulet	.05
546	Sterling Hitchcock	.05
547	Warren Newson	.05
548	Bryan Harvey	.05
549	Mike Huff	.05
550	Lance Parrish	.05
551	Ken Griffey Jr.	.65
552	Matt Williams	.05
553	Roberto Alomar	.10
554	Jeff Bagwell	.25
555	Dave Justice	.05
556	Cal Ripken Jr.	.75
557	Albert Belle	.05
558	Mike Piazza	.45
559	Kirby Puckett	.35
560	Wade Boggs	.30
561	Tony Gwynn	.35
562	Barry Bonds	.75
563	Mo Vaughn	.05
564	Don Mattingly	.40
565	Carlos Baerga	.05
566	Paul Molitor	.25
567	Raul Mondesi	.05
568	Manny Ramirez	.25
569	Alex Rodriguez	.75
570	Will Clark	.05
571	Frank Thomas	.30
572	Moises Alou	.05
573	Jeff Conine	.05
574	Joe Ausanio	.05
575	Charles Johnson	.05
576	Ernie Young	.05
577	Jeff Granger	.05
578	Robert Perez	.05
579	Melvin Nieves	.05
580	Gar Finnvold	.05
581	Duane Singleton	.05
582	Chan Ho Park	.05
583	Fausto Cruz	.05
584	Dave Staton	.05
585	Denny Hocking	.05
586	Nate Minchey	.05
587	Marc Newfield	.05
588	Jayhawk Owens	.05
589	Darren Bragg	.05
590	Kevin King	.05
591	Kurt Miller	.05
592	Aaron Small	.05
593	Troy O'Leary	.05
594	Phil Stidham	.05
595	Steve Dunn	.05
596	Cory Bailey	.05
597	Alex Gonzalez	.05
598	Jim Bowie	.05
599	Jeff Cirillo	.05
600	Mark Hutton	.05
601	Russ Davis	.05
602	Checklist #331-400	.05
603	Checklist #401-469	.05
604	Checklist #470-537	.05
605	Checklist #538-605	.05

----	"You Trade 'em" redemption card (Expired Dec. 31, 1995)	.10

Gold Rush

	NM/M
Complete Set (605):	35.00
Common Player:	.10
Gold Rush Stars:	2X

(See 1995 Score for checklist and base card values.)

Airmail

		NM/M
Complete Set (18):		8.00
Common Player:		.25
1	Bob Hamelin	.25
2	John Mabry	.25
3	Marc Newfield	.25
4	Jose Oliva	.25
5	Charles Johnson	.25
6	Russ Davis	.25
7	Ernie Young	.25
8	Billy Ashley	.25
9	Ryan Klesko	.25
10	J.R. Phillips	.25
11	Cliff Floyd	.25
12	Carlos Delgado	1.50
13	Melvin Nieves	.25
14	Raul Mondesi	.25
15	Manny Ramirez	2.00
16	Mike Kelly	.25
17	Alex Rodriguez	5.00
18	Rusty Greer	.25

Double Gold Champions

		NM/M
Complete Set (12):		25.00
Common Player:		.40
1	Frank Thomas	2.00
2	Ken Griffey Jr.	3.50
3	Barry Bonds	5.00
4	Tony Gwynn	2.50
5	Don Mattingly	3.00
6	Greg Maddux	2.50
7	Roger Clemens	3.00
8	Kenny Lofton	.40
9	Jeff Bagwell	2.00
10	Matt Williams	.40
11	Kirby Puckett	2.50
12	Cal Ripken Jr.	5.00

Draft Picks

		NM/M
Complete Set (18):		4.00
Common Player:		.50
1	McKay Christensen	.50
2	Brett Wagner	.50
3	Paul Wilson	.50
4	C.J. Nitkowski	.50
5	Josh Booty	.50
6	Antone Williamson	.50
7	Paul Konerko	1.50
8	Scott Elarton	.50
9	Jacob Shumate	.50
10	Terrence Long	.50
11	Mark Johnson	.50
12	Ben Grieve	.50
13	Doug Million	.50
14	Jayson Peterson	.50
15	Dustin Hermanson	.50
16	Matt Smith	.50
17	Kevin Witt	.50
18	Brian Buchanan	.50

Dream Team Gold

		NM/M
Complete Set (12):		12.00
Common Player:		.30

1	Frank Thomas	1.25
2	Roberto Alomar	.50
3	Cal Ripken Jr.	4.00
4	Matt Williams	.30
5	Mike Piazza	2.50
6	Albert Belle	.30
7	Ken Griffey Jr.	2.50
8	Tony Gwynn	1.50
9	Paul Molitor	1.25
10	Jimmy Key	.30
11	Greg Maddux	1.50
12	Lee Smith	.30

Hall of Gold

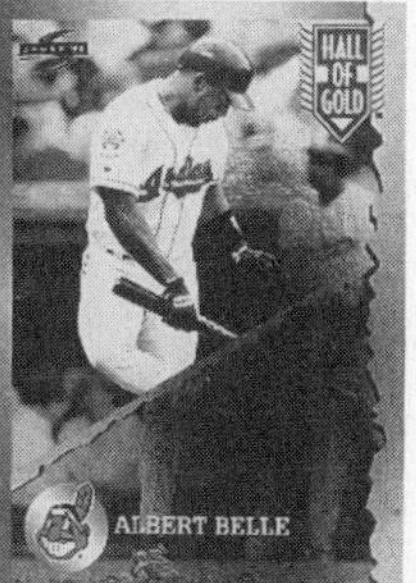

		NM/M
Complete Set (110):		25.00
Common Player:		.10
1	Ken Griffey Jr.	1.25
2	Matt Williams	.10
3	Roberto Alomar	.25
4	Jeff Bagwell	.75
5	Dave Justice	.10
6	Cal Ripken Jr.	2.00
7	Randy Johnson	.75
8	Barry Larkin	.10
9	Albert Belle	.10
10	Mike Piazza	1.25
11	Kirby Puckett	1.00
12	Moises Alou	.10
13	Jose Canseco	.45
14	Tony Gwynn	1.00
15	Roger Clemens	1.00
16	Barry Bonds	2.00
17	Mo Vaughn	.10
18	Greg Maddux	1.00
19	Dante Bichette	.10
20	Will Clark	.10
21	Len Dykstra	.10
22	Don Mattingly	1.00
23	Carlos Baerga	.10
24	Ozzie Smith	1.00
25	Paul Molitor	.75
26	Paul O'Neill	.10
27	Deion Sanders	.10
28	Jeff Conine	.10
29	John Olerud	.10
30	Jose Rijo	.10
31	Sammy Sosa	1.00
32	Robin Ventura	.10
33	Raul Mondesi	.10
34	Eddie Murray	.75
35	Marquis Grissom	.10
36	Darryl Strawberry	.10
37	Dave Nilsson	.10
38	Manny Ramirez	.75
39	Delino DeShields	.10
40	Lee Smith	.10
41	Alex Rodriguez	1.50
42	Julio Franco	.10
43	Bret Saberhagen	.10
44	Ken Hill	.10
45	Roberto Kelly	.10
46	Hal Morris	.10
47	Jimmy Key	.10
48	Terry Steinbach	.10
49	Mickey Tettleton	.10
50	Tony Phillips	.10
51	Carlos Garcia	.10
52	Jim Edmonds	.10
53	Rod Beck	.10
54	Shane Mack	.10
55	Ken Caminiti	.10
56	Frank Thomas	.75
57	Kenny Lofton	.10
58	Jack McDowell	.10
59	Jason Bere	.10
60	Joe Carter	.10
61	Gary Sheffield	.45
62	Andres Galarraga	.10
63	Gregg Jefferies	.10
64	Bobby Bonilla	.10
65	Tom Glavine	.35
66	John Smoltz	.10
67	Fred McGriff	.10
68	Craig Biggio	.10
69	Reggie Sanders	.10
70	Kevin Mitchell	.10
71a	Larry Walker (Expos)	.10
71b	Larry Walker (Rockies)	.10
72	Carlos Delgado	.50
73	Andujar Cedeno	.10
74	Ivan Rodriguez	.65
75	Ryan Klesko	.10
76a	John Kruk (Phillies)	.10
76b	John Kruk (White Sox)	.10
77a	Brian McRae (Royals)	.10
77b	Brian McRae (Cubs)	.10
78	Tim Salmon	.10
79	Travis Fryman	.10
80	Chuck Knoblauch	.10
81	Jay Bell	.10
82	Cecil Fielder	.10
83	Cliff Floyd	.10
84	Ruben Sierra	.10
85	Mike Mussina	.45
86	Mark Grace	.10
87	Dennis Eckersley	.65
88	Dennis Martinez	.10
89	Rafael Palmeiro	.65
90	Ben McDonald	.10
91	Dave Hollins	.10
92	Steve Avery	.10
93a	David Cone (Royals)	.10
93b	David Cone (Blue Jays)	.10
94	Darren Daulton	.10
95	Bret Boone	.10
96	Wade Boggs	1.00
97	Doug Drabek	.10
98	Derek Bell	.10
99	Jim Thome	.65
100	Chili Davis	.10
101	Jeffrey Hammonds	.10
102	Rickey Henderson	.75
103	Brett Butler	.10
104	Tim Wallach	.10
105	Wil Cordero	.10
106	Mark Whiten	.10
107	Bob Hamelin	.10
108	Rondell White	.10
109	Devon White	.10
110a	Tony Tarasco (Braves)	.10
110b	Tony Tarasco (Expos)	.10
----	Redemption trade card (Expired Dec. 31, 1995)	.10

Rookie Dream Team

		NM/M
Complete Set (12):		9.00
Common Player:		.50
1	J.R. Phillips	.50
2	Alex Gonzalez	.50
3	Alex Rodriguez	6.00
4	Jose Oliva	.50
5	Charles Johnson	.50
6	Shawn Green	1.50
7	Brian Hunter	.50
8	Garret Anderson	.50
9	Julian Tavarez	.50
10	Jose Lima	.50
11	Armando Benitez	.50
12	Ricky Bottalico	.50

Rookie Greatness

		NM/M
RG1	Ryan Klesko	1.00
SG1	Ryan Klesko (autographed)	7.50

Score Rules

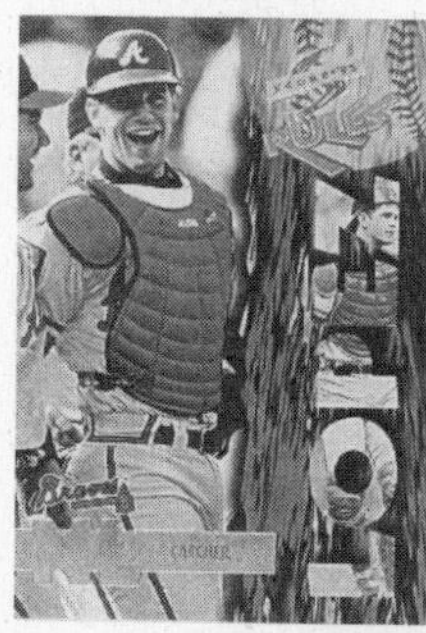

		NM/M
Complete Set (30):		30.00
Common Player:		.30
1	Ken Griffey, Jr.	3.50
2	Frank Thomas	1.50
3	Mike Piazza	3.50
4	Jeff Bagwell	1.50
5	Alex Rodriguez	4.50
6	Albert Belle	.30
7	Matt Williams	.30
8	Roberto Alomar	.45
9	Barry Bonds	5.00
10	Raul Mondesi	.30
11	Jose Canseco	.60
12	Kirby Puckett	2.50
13	Fred McGriff	.30
14	Kenny Lofton	.30
15	Greg Maddux	2.50
16	Juan Gonzalez	.75
17	Cliff Floyd	.30
18	Cal Ripken, Jr.	5.00
19	Will Clark	.30
20	Tim Salmon	.30
21	Paul O'Neill	.30
22	Jason Bere	.30
23	Tony Gwynn	2.50
24	Manny Ramirez	1.50
25	Don Mattingly	3.00
26	Dave Justice	.30
27	Javier Lopez	.30
28	Ryan Klesko	.30
29	Carlos Delgado	.90
30	Mike Mussina	.60

1996 SCORE

	NM/M
Complete Set (510):	15.00
Common Player:	.05

No.	Player	Value
	Wax Pack (10):	.45
	Wax Box (36):	10.00
1	Will Clark	.05
2	Rich Becker	.05
3	Ryan Klesko	.05
4	Jim Edmonds	.05
5	Barry Larkin	.05
6	Jim Thome	.40
7	Raul Mondesi	.05
8	Don Mattingly	.65
9	Jeff Conine	.05
10	Rickey Henderson	.50
11	Chad Curtis	.05
12	Darren Daulton	.05
13	Larry Walker	.05
14	Carlos Garcia	.05
15	Carlos Baerga	.05
16	Tony Gwynn	.60
17	Jon Nunally	.05
18	Deion Sanders	.05
19	Mark Grace	.05
20	Alex Rodriguez	1.00
21	Frank Thomas	.50
22	Brian Jordan	.05
23	J.T. Snow	.05
24	Shawn Green	.30
25	Tim Wakefield	.05
26	Curtis Goodwin	.05
27	John Smoltz	.05
28	Devon White	.05
29	Brian Hunter	.05
30	Rusty Greer	.05
31	Rafael Palmeiro	.40
32	Bernard Gilkey	.05
33	John Valentin	.05
34	Randy Johnson	.50
35	Garret Anderson	.05
36	Rikkert Faneyte	.05
37	Ray Durham	.05
38	Bip Roberts	.05
39	Jaime Navarro	.05
40	Mark Johnson	.05
41	Darren Lewis	.05
42	Tyler Green	.05
43	Bill Pulsipher	.05
44	Jason Giambi	.40
45	Kevin Ritz	.05
46	Jack McDowell	.05
47	Felipe Lira	.05
48	Rico Brogna	.05
49	Terry Pendleton	.05
50	Rondell White	.05
51	Andre Dawson	.25
52	Kirby Puckett	.60
53	Wally Joyner	.05
54	B.J. Surhoff	.05
55	Chan Ho Park	.05
56	Greg Vaughn	.05
57	Roberto Alomar	.20
58	Dave Justice	.05
59	Kevin Seitzer	.05
60	Cal Ripken Jr.	1.50
61	Ozzie Smith	.60
62	Mo Vaughn	.05
63	Ricky Bones	.05
64	Gary DiSarcina	.05
65	Matt Williams	.05
66	Wilson Alvarez	.05
67	Lenny Dykstra	.05
68	Brian McRae	.05
69	Todd Stottlemyre	.05
70	Bret Boone	.05
71	Sterling Hitchcock	.05
72	Albert Belle	.05
73	Todd Hundley	.05
74	Vinny Castilla	.05
75	Moises Alou	.05
76	Cecil Fielder	.05
77	Brad Radke	.05
78	Quilvio Veras	.05
79	Eddie Murray	.50
80	James Mouton	.05
81	Pat Listach	.05
82	Mark Gubicza	.05
83	Dave Winfield	.50
84	Fred McGriff	.05
85	Darryl Hamilton	.05
86	Jeffrey Hammonds	.05
87	Pedro Munoz	.05
88	Craig Biggio	.05
89	Cliff Floyd	.05
90	Tim Naehring	.05
91	Brett Butler	.05
92	Kevin Foster	.05
93	Patrick Kelly	.05
94	John Smiley	.05
95	Terry Steinbach	.05
96	Orel Hershiser	.05
97	Darrin Fletcher	.05
98	Walt Weiss	.05
99	John Wetteland	.05
100	Alan Trammell	.05
101	Steve Avery	.05
102	Tony Eusebio	.05
103	Sandy Alomar	.05
104	Joe Girardi	.05
105	Rick Aguilera	.05
106	Tony Tarasco	.05
107	Chris Hammond	.05
108	Mike McFarlane	.05
109	Doug Drabek	.05
110	Derek Bell	.05
111	Ed Sprague	.05
112	Todd Hollandsworth	.05
113	Otis Nixon	.05
114	Keith Lockhart	.05
115	Donovan Osborne	.05
116	Dave Magadan	.05
117	Edgar Martinez	.05
118	Chuck Carr	.05
119	J.R. Phillips	.05
120	Sean Bergman	.05
121	Andujar Cedeno	.05
122	Eric Young	.05
123	Al Martin	.05
124	Ken Hill	.05
125	Jim Eisenreich	.05
126	Benito Santiago	.05
127	Ariel Prieto	.05
128	Jim Bullinger	.05
129	Russ Davis	.05
130	Jim Abbott	.05
131	Jason Isringhausen	.05
132	Carlos Perez	.05
133	David Segui	.05
134	Troy O'Leary	.05
135	Pat Meares	.05
136	Chris Hoiles	.05
137	Ismael Valdes	.05
138	Jose Oliva	.05
139	Carlos Delgado	.35
140	Tom Goodwin	.05
141	Bob Tewksbury	.05
142	Chris Gomez	.05
143	Jose Oquendo	.05
144	Mark Lewis	.05
145	Salomon Torres	.05
146	Luis Gonzalez	.05
147	Mark Carreon	.05
148	Lance Johnson	.05
149	Melvin Nieves	.05
150	Lee Smith	.05
151	Jacob Brumfield	.05
152	Armando Benitez	.05
153	Curt Schilling	.30
154	Javier Lopez	.05
155	Frank Rodriguez	.05
156	Alex Gonzalez	.05
157	Todd Worrell	.05
158	Benji Gil	.05
159	Greg Gagne	.05
160	Tom Henke	.05
161	Randy Myers	.05
162	Joey Cora	.05
163	Scott Ruffcorn	.05
164	William VanLandingham	.05
165	Tony Phillips	.05
166	Eddie Williams	.05
167	Bobby Bonilla	.05
168	Denny Neagle	.05
169	Troy Percival	.05
170	Billy Ashley	.05
171	Andy Van Slyke	.05
172	Jose Offerman	.05
173	Mark Parent	.05
174	Edgardo Alfonzo	.05
175	Trevor Hoffman	.05
176	David Cone	.05
177	Dan Wilson	.05
178	Steve Ontiveros	.05
179	Dean Palmer	.05
180	Mike Kelly	.05
181	Jim Leyritz	.05
182	Ron Karkovice	.05
183	Kevin Brown	.05
184	*Jose Valentin*	.05
185	Jorge Fabregas	.05
186	Jose Mesa	.05
187	Brent Mayne	.05
188	Carl Everett	.05
189	Paul Sorrento	.05
190	Pete Shourek	.05
191	Scott Kamieniecki	.05
192	Roberto Hernandez	.05
193	Randy Johnson	.25
194	Greg Maddux	.35
195	Hideo Nomo	.15
196	David Cone	.05
197	Mike Mussina	.15
198	Andy Benes	.05
199	Kevin Appier	.05
200	John Smoltz	.05
201	John Wetteland	.05
202	Mark Wohlers	.05
203	Stan Belinda	.05
204	Brian Anderson	.05
205	Mike Devereaux	.05
206	Mark Wohlers	.05
207	Omar Vizquel	.05
208	Jose Rijo	.05
209	Willie Blair	.05
210	Jamie Moyer	.05
211	Craig Shipley	.05
212	Shane Reynolds	.05
213	Chad Fonville	.05
214	Jose Vizcaino	.05
215	Sid Fernandez	.05
216	Andy Ashby	.05
217	Frank Castillo	.05
218	Kevin Tapani	.05
219	Kent Mercker	.05
220	Karim Garcia	.05
221	Chris Snopek	.05
222	Tim Unroe	.05
223	Johnny Damon	.25
224	LaTroy Hawkins	.05
225	Mariano Rivera	.10
226	Jose Alberro	.05
227	Angel Martinez	.05
228	Jason Schmidt	.05
229	Tony Clark	.05
230	Kevin Jordan	.05
231	Mark Thompson	.05
232	Jim Dougherty	.05
333	Roger Cedeno	.05
234	Ugueth Urbina	.05
235	Ricky Otero	.05
236	Mark Smith	.05
237	Brian Barber	.05
238	Marc Kroon	.05
239	Joe Rosselli	.05
240	Derek Jeter	1.50
241	Michael Tucker	.05
242	*Joe Borowski*	.05
243	Joe Vitiello	.05
244	Orlando Palmeiro	.05
245	James Baldwin	.05
246	Alan Embree	.05
247	Shannon Penn	.05
248	Chris Stynes	.05
249	Oscar Munoz	.05
250	Jose Herrera	.05
251	Scott Sullivan	.05
252	Reggie Williams	.05
253	Mark Grudzielanek	.05
254	Kevin Jordan	.05
255	Terry Bradshaw	.05
256	*F.P. Santangelo*	.05
257	Doug Johns	.05
258	George Williams	.05
259	Larry Thomas	.05
260	Rudy Pemberton	.05
261	Jim Pittsley	.05
262	Les Norman	.05
263	Ruben Rivera	.05
264	*Cesar Devarez*	.05
265	Greg Zaun	.05
266	Eric Owens	.05
267	John Frascatore	.05
268	Shannon Stewart	.05
269	Checklist	.05
270	Checklist	.05
271	Checklist	.05
272	Checklist	.05
273	Checklist	.05
274	Checklist	.05
275	Checklist	.05
276	Greg Maddux	.60
277	Pedro Martinez	.50
278	Bobby Higginson	.05
279	Ray Lankford	.05
280	Shawon Dunston	.05
281	Gary Sheffield	.35
282	Ken Griffey Jr.	.75
283	Paul Molitor	.50
284	Kevin Appier	.05
285	Chuck Knoblauch	.05
286	Alex Fernandez	.05
287	Steve Finley	.05
288	Jeff Blauser	.05
289	Charles Johnson	.05
290	John Franco	.05
291	Mark Langston	.05
292	Bret Saberhagen	.05
293	John Mabry	.05
294	Ramon Martinez	.05
295	Mike Blowers	.05
296	Paul O'Neill	.05
297	Dave Nilsson	.05
298	Dante Bichette	.05
299	Marty Cordova	.05
300	Jay Bell	.05
301	Mike Mussina	.30
302	Ivan Rodriguez	.40
303	Jose Canseco	.30
304	Jeff Bagwell	.50
305	Manny Ramirez	.50
306	Dennis Martinez	.05
307	Charlie Hayes	.05
308	Joe Carter	.05
309	Travis Fryman	.05
310	Mark McGwire	1.00
311	Reggie Sanders	.05
312	Julian Tavarez	.05
313	Jeff Montgomery	.05
314	Andy Benes	.05
315	John Jaha	.05
316	Jeff Kent	.05
317	Mike Piazza	.75
318	Erik Hanson	.05
319	Kenny Rogers	.05
320	Hideo Nomo	.25
321	Gregg Jefferies	.05
322	Chipper Jones	.60
323	Jay Buhner	.05
324	Dennis Eckersley	.40
325	Kenny Lofton	.05
326	Robin Ventura	.05
327	Tom Glavine	.35
328	Tim Salmon	.05
329	Andres Galarraga	.05
330	Hal Morris	.05
331	Brady Anderson	.05
332	Chili Davis	.05
333	Roger Clemens	.65
334	Marquis Grissom	.05
335	Jeff (Mike) Greenwell	.05
336	Sammy Sosa	.60
337	Ron Gant	.05
338	Ken Caminiti	.05
339	Danny Tartabull	.05
340	Barry Bonds	1.50
341	Ben McDonald	.05
342	Ruben Sierra	.05
343	Bernie Williams	.05
344	Wil Cordero	.05
345	Wade Boggs	.60
346	Gary Gaetti	.05
347	Greg Colbrunn	.05
348	Juan Gonzalez	.25
349	Marc Newfield	.05
350	Charles Nagy	.05
351	Robby Thompson	.05
352	Roberto Petagine	.05
353	Darryl Strawberry	.05
354	Tino Martinez	.05
355	Eric Karros	.05
356	Cal Ripken Jr.	.75
357	Cecil Fielder	.05
358	Kirby Puckett	.35
359	Jim Edmonds	.05
360	Matt Williams	.05
361	Alex Rodriguez	.50
362	Barry Larkin	.05
363	Rafael Palmeiro	.20
364	David Cone	.05
365	Roberto Alomar	.10
366	Eddie Murray	.25
367	Randy Johnson	.20
368	Ryan Klesko	.05
369	Raul Mondesi	.05
370	Mo Vaughn	.05
371	Will Clark	.05
372	Carlos Baerga	.05
373	Frank Thomas	.30
374	Larry Walker	.05
375	Garret Anderson	.05
376	Edgar Martinez	.05
377	Don Mattingly	.40
378	Tony Gwynn	.35
379	Albert Belle	.05
380	Jason Isringhausen	.05
381	Ruben Rivera	.05
382	Johnny Damon	.05
383	Karim Garcia	.05
384	Derek Jeter	.75
385	David Justice	.05
386	Royce Clayton	.05
387	Mark Whiten	.05
388	Mickey Tettleton	.05
389	Steve Trachsel	.05
390	Danny Bautista	.05
391	Midre Cummings	.05
392	Scott Leius	.05
393	Manny Alexander	.05
394	Brent Gates	.05

395 Rey Sanchez .05
396 Andy Pettitte .20
397 Jeff Cirillo .05
398 Kurt Abbott .05
399 Lee Tinsley .05
400 Paul Assenmacher .05
401 Scott Erickson .05
402 Todd Zeile .05
403 Tom Pagnozzi .05
404 Ozzie Guillen .05
405 Jeff Frye .05
406 Kirt Manwaring .05
407 Chad Ogea .05
408 Harold Baines .05
409 Jason Bere .05
410 Chuck Finley .05
411 Jeff Fassero .05
412 Joey Hamilton .05
413 John Olerud .05
414 Kevin Stocker .05
415 Eric Anthony .05
416 Aaron Sele .05
417 Chris Bosio .05
418 Michael Mimbs .05
419 Orlando Miller .05
420 Stan Javier .05
421 Matt Mieske .05
422 Jason Bates .05
423 Orlando Merced .05
424 John Flaherty .05
425 Reggie Jefferson .05
426 Scott Stahoviak .05
427 John Burkett .05
428 Rod Beck .05
429 Bill Swift .05
430 Scott Cooper .05
431 Mel Rojas .05
432 Todd Van Poppel .05
433 Bobby Jones .05
434 Mike Harkey .05
435 Sean Berry .05
436 Glenallen Hill .05
437 Ryan Thompson .05
438 Luis Alicea .05
439 Esteban Loaiza .05
440 Jeff Reboulet .05
441 Vince Coleman .05
442 Ellis Burks .05
443 Allen Battle .05
444 Jimmy Key .05
445 Ricky Bottalico .05
446 Delino DeShields .05
447 Albie Lopez .05
448 Mark Petkovsek .05
449 Tim Raines .05
450 Bryan Harvey .05
451 Pat Hentgen .05
452 Tim Laker .05
453 Tom Gordon .05
454 Phil Plantier .05
455 Ernie Young .05
456 Pete Harnisch .05
457 Roberto Kelly .05
458 Mark Portugal .05
459 Mark Leiter .05
460 Tony Pena .05
461 Roger Pavlik .05
462 Jeff King .05
463 Bryan Rekar .05
464 Al Leiter .05
465 Phil Nevin .05
466 Jose Lima .05
467 Mike Stanley .05
468 David McCarty .05
469 Herb Perry .05
470 Geronimo Berroa .05
471 David Wells .05
472 Vaughn Eshelman .05
473 Greg Swindell .05
474 Steve Sparks .05
475 Luis Sojo .05
476 Derrick May .05
477 Joe Oliver .05
478 Alex Arias .05
479 Brad Ausmus .05
480 Gabe White .05
481 Pat Rapp .05
482 Damon Buford .05
483 Turk Wendell .05
484 Jeff Brantley .05
485 Curtis Leskanic .05
486 Robb Nen .05
487 Lou Whitaker .05
488 Melido Perez .05
489 Luis Polonia .05
490 Scott Brosius .05
491 Robert Perez .05
492 *Mike Sweeney* .50
493 Mark Loretta .05
494 Alex Ochoa .05
495 *Matt Lawton* .10
496 Shawn Estes .05
497 John Wasdin .05
498 Marc Kroon .05
499 Chris Snopek .05
500 Jeff Suppan .05
501 Terrell Wade .05
502 *Marvin Benard* .10
503 Chris Widger .05
504 Quinton McCracken .05
505 Bob Wolcott .05
506 C.J. Nitkowski .05
507 Aaron Ledesma .05
508 Scott Hatteberg .05
509 Jimmy Haynes .05
510 Howard Battle .05

Dugout Collection

NM/M

Complete Set (220): 60.00
Complete Series 1 (1-110): 30.00
Complete Series 2 (1-110): 30.00
Common Player: .20
Artist's Proofs: 4X

SERIES 1

1 Will Clark .20
2 Rich Becker .20
3 Ryan Klesko .20
4 Jim Edmonds .20
5 Barry Larkin .20
6 Jim Thome .65
7 Raul Mondesi .20
8 Don Mattingly 1.25
9 Jeff Conine .20
10 Rickey Henderson .75
11 Chad Curtis .20
12 Darren Daulton .20
13 Larry Walker .20
14 Carlos Baerga .20
15 Tony Gwynn 1.00
16 Jon Nunnally .20
17 Deion Sanders .20
18 Mark Grace .20
19 Alex Rodriguez 2.00
20 Frank Thomas .75
21 Brian Jordan .20
22 J.T. Snow .20
23 Shawn Green .50
24 Tim Wakefield .20
25 Curtis Goodwin .20
26 John Smoltz .20
27 Devon White .20
28 Brian Hunter .20
29 Rusty Greer .20
30 Rafael Palmeiro .65
31 Bernard Gilkey .20
32 John Valentin .20
33 Randy Johnson .75
34 Garret Anderson .20
35 Ray Durham .20
36 Bip Roberts .20
37 Tyler Green .20
38 Bill Pulsipher .20
39 Jason Giambi .50
40 Jack McDowell .20
41 Rico Brogna .20
42 Terry Pendleton .20
43 Rondell White .20
44 Andre Dawson .35
45 Kirby Puckett 1.00
46 Wally Joyner .20
47 B.J. Surhoff .20
48 Randy Velarde .20
49 Greg Vaughn .20
50 Roberto Alomar .30
51 David Justice .20
52 Cal Ripken Jr. 3.00
53 Ozzie Smith 1.00
54 Mo Vaughn .20
55 Gary DiSarcina .20
56 Matt Williams .20
57 Lenny Dykstra .20
58 Bret Boone .20
59 Albert Belle .20
60 Vinny Castilla .20
61 Moises Alou .20
62 Cecil Fielder .20
63 Brad Radke .20
64 Quilvio Veras .20
65 Eddie Murray .75
66 Dave Winfield .75
67 Fred McGriff .20
68 Craig Biggio .20
69 Cliff Floyd .20
70 Tim Naehring .20
71 John Wetteland .20
72 Alan Trammell .20
73 Steve Avery .20
74 Rick Aguilera .20
75 Derek Bell .20
76 Todd Hollandsworth .20
77 Edgar Martinez .20
78 Mark Lemke .20
79 Ariel Prieto .20
80 Russ Davis .20
81 Jim Abbott .20
82 Jason Isringhausen .20
83 Carlos Perez .20
84 David Segui .20
85 Troy O'Leary .20
86 Ismael Valdes .20
87 Carlos Delgado .50
88 Lee Smith .20
89 Javy Lopez .20
90 Frank Rodriguez .20
91 Alex Gonzalez .20
92 Benji Gil .20
93 Greg Gagne .20
94 Randy Myers .20
95 Bobby Bonilla .20
96 Billy Ashley .20
97 Andy Van Slyke .20
98 Edgardo Alfonzo .20
99 David Cone .20
100 Dean Palmer .20
101 Jose Mesa .20
102 Karim Garcia .20
103 Johnny Damon .40
104 LaTroy Hawkins .20
105 Mark Smith .20
106 Derek Jeter 3.00
107 Michael Tucker .20
108 Joe Vitiello .20
109 Ruben Rivera .20
110 Greg Zaun .20

SERIES 2

1 Greg Maddux 1.00
2 Pedro Martinez .75
3 Bobby Higginson .20
4 Ray Lankford .20
5 Shawon Dunston .20
6 Gary Sheffield .45
7 Ken Griffey Jr. 1.50
8 Paul Molitor .75
9 Kevin Appier .20
10 Chuck Knoblauch .20
11 Alex Fernandez .20
12 Steve Finley .20
13 Jeff Blauser .20
14 Charles Johnson .20
15 John Franco .20
16 Mark Langston .20
17 Bret Saberhagen .20
18 John Mabry .20
19 Ramon Martinez .20
20 Mike Blowers .20
21 Paul O'Neill .20
22 Dave Nilsson .20
23 Dante Bichette .20
24 Marty Cordova .20
25 Jay Bell .20
26 Mike Mussina .40
27 Ivan Rodriguez .65
28 Jose Canseco .50
29 Jeff Bagwell .75
30 Manny Ramirez .75
31 Dennis Martinez .20
32 Charlie Hayes .20
33 Joe Carter .20
34 Travis Fryman .20
35 Mark McGwire 2.00
36 Reggie Sanders .20
37 Julian Tavarez .20
38 Jeff Montgomery .20
39 Andy Benes .20
40 John Jaha .20
41 Jeff Kent .20
42 Mike Piazza 1.50
43 Erik Hanson .20
44 Kenny Rogers .20
45 Hideo Nomo .50
46 Gregg Jefferies .20
47 Chipper Jones 1.00
48 Jay Buhner .20
49 Dennis Eckersley .65
50 Kenny Lofton .20
51 Robin Ventura .20
52 Tom Glavine .30
53 Tim Salmon .20
54 Andres Galarraga .20
55 Hal Morris .20
56 Brady Anderson .20
57 Chili Davis .20
58 Roger Clemens 1.25
59 Marquis Grissom .20
60 Mike Greenwell .20
61 Sammy Sosa 1.00
62 Ron Gant .20
63 Ken Caminiti .20
64 Danny Tartabull .20
65 Barry Bonds 3.00
66 Ben McDonald .20
67 Ruben Sierra .20
68 Bernie Williams .20
69 Wil Cordero .20
70 Wade Boggs 1.00
71 Gary Gaetti .20
72 Greg Colbrunn .20
73 Juan Gonzalez .50
74 Marc Newfield .20
75 Charles Nagy .20
76 Robby Thompson .20
77 Roberto Petagine .20
78 Darryl Strawberry .20
79 Tino Martinez .20
80 Eric Karros .20
81 Cal Ripken Jr. 1.50
82 Cecil Fielder .20
83 Kirby Puckett .50
84 Jim Edmonds .20
85 Matt Williams .20
86 Alex Rodriguez 1.00
87 Barry Larkin .20
88 Rafael Palmeiro .40
89 David Cone .20
90 Roberto Alomar .25
91 Eddie Murray .40
92 Randy Johnson .40
93 Ryan Klesko .20
94 Raul Mondesi .20
95 Mo Vaughn .20
96 Will Clark .20
97 Carlos Baerga .20
98 Frank Thomas .45
99 Larry Walker .20
100 Garret Anderson .20
101 Edgar Martinez .20
102 Don Mattingly .60
103 Tony Gwynn .50
104 Albert Belle .20
105 Jason Isringhausen .20
106 Ruben Rivera .20
107 Johnny Damon .35
108 Karim Garcia .20
109 Derek Jeter 1.50
110 David Justice .20

Dugout Collection Artist's Proofs

NM/M

Complete Set (220): 300.00
Common Player: 1.00
Artist's Proof Stars: 4X

(See 1996 Score Dugout Collection for checklist and base card values.)

All-Stars

		NM/M
Complete Set (20):		13.50
Common Player:		.25
1	Frank Thomas	1.25
2	Albert Belle	.25
3	Ken Griffey Jr.	2.00
4	Cal Ripken Jr.	3.00
5	Mo Vaughn	.25
6	Matt Williams	.25
7	Barry Bonds	3.00
8	Dante Bichette	.25
9	Tony Gwynn	1.50
10	Greg Maddux	1.50
11	Randy Johnson	1.25
12	Hideo Nomo	.75
13	Tim Salmon	.25
14	Jeff Bagwell	1.25
15	Edgar Martinez	.25
16	Reggie Sanders	.25
17	Larry Walker	.25
18	Chipper Jones	1.50
19	Manny Ramirez	1.25
20	Eddie Murray	1.25

Big Bats

		NM/M
Complete Set (20):		12.50
Common Player:		.45
1	Cal Ripken Jr.	3.00
2	Ken Griffey Jr.	2.00
3	Frank Thomas	.75
4	Jeff Bagwell	.75
5	Mike Piazza	2.00
6	Barry Bonds	3.00
7	Matt Williams	.45
8	Raul Mondesi	.45
9	Tony Gwynn	1.25
10	Albert Belle	.45
11	Manny Ramirez	.75
12	Carlos Baerga	.45
13	Mo Vaughn	.45
14	Derek Bell	.45
15	Larry Walker	.45
16	Kenny Lofton	.45
17	Edgar Martinez	.45
18	Reggie Sanders	.45
19	Eddie Murray	.75
20	Chipper Jones	1.25

Cal Ripken Tribute

		NM/M
2131	Cal Ripken Jr. (Tribute)	4.00

Dream Team

		NM/M
Complete Set (9):		15.00
Common Player:		.75
1	Cal Ripken Jr.	4.00
2	Frank Thomas	1.50
3	Carlos Baerga	.75
4	Matt Williams	.75
5	Mike Piazza	3.00
6	Barry Bonds	4.00
7	Ken Griffey Jr.	3.00
8	Manny Ramirez	1.50
9	Greg Maddux	2.00

Diamond Aces

		NM/M
Complete Set (30):		25.00
Common Player:		.35
1	Hideo Nomo	.60
2	Brian Hunter	.35
3	Ray Durham	.35
4	Frank Thomas	1.00
5	Cal Ripken Jr.	3.50
6	Barry Bonds	3.50
7	Greg Maddux	1.25
8	Chipper Jones	1.25
9	Raul Mondesi	.35
10	Mike Piazza	2.00
11	Derek Jeter	3.50
12	Bill Pulsipher	.35
13	Larry Walker	.35
14	Ken Griffey Jr.	2.00
15	Alex Rodriguez	3.00
16	Manny Ramirez	1.00
17	Mo Vaughn	.35
18	Reggie Sanders	.35
19	Derek Bell	.35
20	Jim Edmonds	.35
21	Albert Belle	.35
22	Eddie Murray	1.00
23	Tony Gwynn	1.25
24	Jeff Bagwell	1.00
25	Carlos Baerga	.35
26	Matt Williams	.35
27	Garret Anderson	.35
28	Todd Hollandsworth	.35
29	Johnny Damon	.75
30	Tim Salmon	.35

Future Franchise

		NM/M
Complete Set (16):		20.00
Common Player:		.75
1	Jason Isringhausen	.75
2	Chipper Jones	2.50
3	Derek Jeter	5.00
4	Alex Rodriguez	4.00
5	Alex Ochoa	.75
6	Manny Ramirez	1.50
7	Johnny Damon	1.00
8	Ruben Rivera	.75
9	Karim Garcia	.75
10	Garret Anderson	.75
11	Marty Cordova	.75
12	Bill Pulsipher	.75
13	Hideo Nomo	1.00
14	Marc Newfield	.75
15	Charles Johnson	.75
16	Raul Mondesi	.75

Gold Stars

		NM/M
Complete Set (30):		20.00
Common Player:		.20
1	Ken Griffey Jr.	2.00
2	Frank Thomas	1.00
3	Reggie Sanders	.20
4	Tim Salmon	.20
5	Mike Piazza	2.00
6	Tony Gwynn	1.50
7	Gary Sheffield	.45
8	Matt Williams	.20
9	Bernie Williams	.20
10	Jason Isringhausen	.20
11	Albert Belle	.20
12	Chipper Jones	1.50
13	Edgar Martinez	.20
14	Barry Larkin	.20
15	Barry Bonds	3.00
16	Jeff Bagwell	1.00
17	Greg Maddux	1.50
18	Mo Vaughn	.20
19	Ryan Klesko	.20
20	Sammy Sosa	1.50
21	Darren Daulton	.20
22	Ivan Rodriguez	.75
23	Dante Bichette	.20
24	Hideo Nomo	.50
25	Cal Ripken Jr.	3.00
26	Rafael Palmeiro	.75
27	Larry Walker	.20
28	Carlos Baerga	.20
29	Randy Johnson	1.00
30	Manny Ramirez	1.00

Numbers Game

		NM/M
Complete Set (30):		17.50
Common Player:		.15
1	Cal Ripken Jr.	2.50
2	Frank Thomas	.75
3	Ken Griffey Jr.	1.50
4	Mike Piazza	1.50
5	Barry Bonds	2.50
6	Greg Maddux	1.00
7	Jeff Bagwell	.75
8	Derek Bell	.15
9	Tony Gwynn	1.00
10	Hideo Nomo	.50
11	Raul Mondesi	.15
12	Manny Ramirez	.75
13	Albert Belle	.15
14	Matt Williams	.15
15	Jim Edmonds	.15
16	Edgar Martinez	.15
17	Mo Vaughn	.15
18	Reggie Sanders	.15
19	Chipper Jones	1.00
20	Larry Walker	.15
21	Juan Gonzalez	.50
22	Kenny Lofton	.15
23	Don Mattingly	1.25
24	Ivan Rodriguez	.65
25	Randy Johnson	.75
26	Derek Jeter	2.50
27	J.T. Snow	.15
28	Will Clark	.15
29	Rafael Palmeiro	.65
30	Alex Rodriguez	2.00

Power Pace

		NM/M
Complete Set (18):		24.00
Common Player:		.50
1	Mark McGwire	4.00
2	Albert Belle	.50
3	Jay Buhner	.50
4	Frank Thomas	1.50
5	Matt Williams	.50
6	Gary Sheffield	.75
7	Mike Piazza	3.00
8	Larry Walker	.50
9	Mo Vaughn	.50
10	Rafael Palmeiro	1.25
11	Dante Bichette	.50
12	Ken Griffey Jr.	3.00
13	Barry Bonds	5.00
14	Manny Ramirez	1.50
15	Sammy Sosa	2.00
16	Tim Salmon	.50
17	Dave Justice	.50
18	Eric Karros	.50

Reflexions

		NM/M
Complete Set (20):		35.00
Common Player:		.45
1	Cal Ripken Jr., Chipper Jones	5.00
2	Ken Griffey Jr., Alex Rodriguez	4.50
3	Frank Thomas, Mo Vaughn	2.50
4	Kenny Lofton, Brian Hunter	.45
5	Don Mattingly, J.T. Snow	3.75
6	Manny Ramirez, Raul Mondesi	2.50
7	Tony Gwynn, Garret Anderson	3.75
8	Roberto Alomar, Carlos Baerga	.50
9	Andre Dawson, Larry Walker	.50
10	Barry Larkin, Derek Jeter	5.00
11	Barry Bonds, Reggie Sanders	5.00
12	Mike Piazza, Albert Belle	4.00
13	Wade Boggs, Edgar Martinez	3.75
14	David Cone, John Smoltz	.45
15	Will Clark, Jeff Bagwell	2.50
16	Mark McGwire, Cecil Fielder	4.50
17	Greg Maddux, Mike Mussina	3.75
18	Randy Johnson, Hideo Nomo	2.50
19	Jim Thome, Dean Palmer	2.00
20	Chuck Knoblauch, Craig Biggio	.45

Titantic Taters

		NM/M
Complete Set (18):		25.00
Common Player:		.60
1	Albert Belle	.60
2	Frank Thomas	2.00
3	Mo Vaughn	.60
4	Ken Griffey Jr.	3.00
5	Matt Williams	.60
6	Mark McGwire	3.50
7	Dante Bichette	.60
8	Tim Salmon	.60
9	Jeff Bagwell	2.00
10	Rafael Palmeiro	1.50
11	Mike Piazza	3.00
12	Cecil Fielder	.60
13	Larry Walker	.60
14	Sammy Sosa	2.50
15	Manny Ramirez	2.00
16	Gary Sheffield	.90
17	Barry Bonds	5.00
18	Jay Buhner	.60

1997 SCORE

		NM/M
Complete Set (551):		16.00
Factory Tin-Box Set (551):		17.50
Common Player:		.05
Showcase:		3X
Artist's Proofs:		10X
Premium Stocks:		3X
Wax Pack (10):		.50
Wax Box (36):		12.00
1	Jeff Bagwell	.50
2	Mickey Tettleton	.05
3	Johnny Damon	.25
4	Jeff Conine	.05
5	Bernie Williams	.05
6	Will Clark	.05
7	Ryan Klesko	.05
8	Cecil Fielder	.05

No.	Player	Price
9	Paul Wilson	.05
10	Gregg Jefferies	.05
11	Chili Davis	.05
12	Albert Belle	.05
13	Ken Hill	.05
14	Cliff Floyd	.05
15	Jaime Navarro	.05
16	Ismael Valdes	.05
17	Jeff King	.05
18	Chris Bosio	.05
19	Reggie Sanders	.05
20	Darren Daulton	.05
21	Ken Caminiti	.05
22	Mike Piazza	.75
23	Chad Mottola	.05
24	Darin Erstad	.15
25	Dante Bichette	.05
26	Frank Thomas	.50
27	Ben McDonald	.05
28	Raul Casanova	.05
29	Kevin Ritz	.05
30	Garret Anderson	.05
31	Jason Kendall	.05
32	Billy Wagner	.05
33	David Justice	.05
34	Marty Cordova	.05
35	Derek Jeter	1.50
36	Trevor Hoffman	.05
37	Geronimo Berroa	.05
38	Walt Weiss	.05
39	Kirt Manwaring	.05
40	Alex Gonzalez	.05
41	Sean Berry	.05
42	Kevin Appier	.05
43	Rusty Greer	.05
44	Pete Incaviglia	.05
45	Rafael Palmeiro	.45
46	Eddie Murray	.50
47	Moises Alou	.05
48	Mark Lewis	.05
49	Hal Morris	.05
50	Edgar Renteria	.05
51	Rickey Henderson	.50
52	Pat Listach	.05
53	John Wasdin	.05
54	James Baldwin	.05
55	Brian Jordan	.05
56	Edgar Martinez	.05
57	Wil Cordero	.05
58	Danny Tartabull	.05
59	Keith Lockhart	.05
60	Rico Brogna	.05
61	Ricky Bottalico	.05
62	Terry Pendleton	.05
63	Bret Boone	.05
64	Charlie Hayes	.05
65	Marc Newfield	.05
66	Sterling Hitchcock	.05
67	Roberto Alomar	.15
68	John Jaha	.05
69	Greg Colbrunn	.05
70	Sal Fasano	.05
71	Brooks Kieschnick	.05
72	Pedro Martinez	.50
73	Kevin Elster	.05
74	Ellis Burks	.05
75	Chuck Finley	.05
76	John Olerud	.05
77	Jay Bell	.05
78	Allen Watson	.05
79	Darryl Strawberry	.05
80	Orlando Miller	.05
81	Jose Herrera	.05
82	Andy Pettitte	.20
83	Juan Guzman	.05
84	Alan Benes	.05
85	Jack McDowell	.05
86	Ugueth Urbina	.05
87	Rocky Coppinger	.05
88	Jeff Cirillo	.05
89	Tom Glavine	.35
90	Robby Thompson	.05
91	Barry Bonds	1.50
92	Carlos Delgado	.40
93	Mo Vaughn	.05
94	Ryne Sandberg	.65
95	Alex Rodriguez	1.00
96	Brady Anderson	.05
97	Scott Brosius	.05
98	Dennis Eckersley	.45
99	Brian McRae	.05
100	Rey Ordonez	.05
101	John Valentin	.05
102	Brett Butler	.05
103	Eric Karros	.05
104	Harold Baines	.05
105	Javier Lopez	.05
106	Alan Trammell	.05
107	Jim Thome	.45
108	Frank Rodriguez	.05
109	Bernard Gilkey	.05
110	Reggie Jefferson	.05
111	Scott Stahoviak	.05
112	Steve Gibralter	.05
113	Todd Hollandsworth	.05
114	Ruben Rivera	.05
115	Dennis Martinez	.05
116	Mariano Rivera	.10
117	John Smoltz	.05
118	John Mabry	.05
119	Tom Gordon	.05
120	Alex Ochoa	.05
121	Jamey Wright	.05
122	Dave Nilsson	.05
123	Bobby Bonilla	.05
124	Al Leiter	.05
125	Rick Aguilera	.05
126	Jeff Brantley	.05
127	Kevin Brown	.05
128	George Arias	.05
129	Darren Oliver	.05
130	Bill Pulsipher	.05
131	Roberto Hernandez	.05
132	Delino DeShields	.05
133	Mark Grudzielanek	.05
134	John Wetteland	.05
135	Carlos Baerga	.05
136	Paul Sorrento	.05
137	Leo Gomez	.05
138	Andy Ashby	.05
139	Julio Franco	.05
140	Brian Hunter	.05
141	Jermaine Dye	.05
142	Tony Clark	.05
143	Ruben Sierra	.05
144	Donovan Osborne	.05
145	Mark McLemore	.05
146	Terry Steinbach	.05
147	Bob Wells	.05
148	Chan Ho Park	.05
149	Tim Salmon	.05
150	Paul O'Neill	.05
151	Cal Ripken Jr.	1.50
152	Wally Joyner	.05
153	Omar Vizquel	.05
154	Mike Mussina	.30
155	Andres Galarraga	.05
156	Ken Griffey Jr.	.75
157	Kenny Lofton	.05
158	Ray Durham	.05
159	Hideo Nomo	.25
160	Ozzie Guillen	.05
161	Roger Pavlik	.05
162	Manny Ramirez	.50
163	Mark Lemke	.05
164	Mike Stanley	.05
165	Chuck Knoblauch	.05
166	Kimera Bartee	.05
167	Wade Boggs	.65
168	Jay Buhner	.05
169	Eric Young	.05
170	Jose Canseco	.30
171	Dwight Gooden	.05
172	Fred McGriff	.05
173	Sandy Alomar Jr.	.05
174	Andy Benes	.05
175	Dean Palmer	.05
176	Larry Walker	.05
177	Charles Nagy	.05
178	David Cone	.05
179	Mark Grace	.05
180	Robin Ventura	.05
181	Roger Clemens	.70
182	Bobby Witt	.05
183	Vinny Castilla	.05
184	Gary Sheffield	.35
185	Dan Wilson	.05
186	Roger Cedeno	.05
187	Mark McGwire	1.00
188	Darren Bragg	.05
189	Quinton McCracken	.05
190	Randy Myers	.05
191	Jeromy Burnitz	.05
192	Randy Johnson	.50
193	Chipper Jones	.65
194	Greg Vaughn	.05
195	Travis Fryman	.05
196	Tim Naehring	.05
197	B.J. Surhoff	.05
198	Juan Gonzalez	.25
199	Terrell Wade	.05
200	Jeff Frye	.05
201	Joey Cora	.05
202	Raul Mondesi	.05
203	Ivan Rodriguez	.45
204	Armando Reynoso	.05
205	Jeffrey Hammonds	.05
206	Darren Dreifort	.05
207	Kevin Seitzer	.05
208	Tino Martinez	.05
209	Jim Bruske	.05
210	Jeff Suppan	.05
211	Mark Carreon	.05
212	Wilson Alvarez	.05
213	John Burkett	.05
214	Tony Phillips	.05
215	Greg Maddux	.65
216	Mark Whiten	.05
217	Curtis Pride	.05
218	Lyle Mouton	.05
219	Todd Hundley	.05
220	Greg Gagne	.05
221	Rich Amaral	.05
222	Tom Goodwin	.05
223	Chris Hoiles	.05
224	Jayhawk Owens	.05
225	Kenny Rogers	.05
226	Mike Greenwell	.05
227	Mark Wohlers	.05
228	Henry Rodriguez	.05
229	Robert Perez	.05
230	Jeff Kent	.05
231	Darryl Hamilton	.05
232	Alex Fernandez	.05
233	Ron Karkovice	.05
234	Jimmy Haynes	.05
235	Craig Biggio	.05
236	Ray Lankford	.05
237	Lance Johnson	.05
238	Matt Williams	.05
239	Chad Curtis	.05
240	Mark Thompson	.05
241	Jason Giambi	.40
242	Barry Larkin	.05
243	Paul Molitor	.50
244	Sammy Sosa	.65
245	Kevin Tapani	.05
246	Marquis Grissom	.05
247	Joe Carter	.05
248	Ramon Martinez	.05
249	Tony Gwynn	.65
250	Andy Fox	.05
251	Troy O'Leary	.05
252	Warren Newson	.05
253	Troy Percival	.05
254	Jamie Moyer	.05
255	Danny Graves	.05
256	David Wells	.05
257	Todd Zeile	.05
258	Raul Ibanez	.05
259	Tyler Houston	.05
260	LaTroy Hawkins	.05
261	Joey Hamilton	.05
262	Mike Sweeney	.05
263	Brant Brown	.05
264	Pat Hentgen	.05
265	Mark Johnson	.05
266	Robb Nen	.05
267	Justin Thompson	.05
268	Ron Gant	.05
269	Jeff D'Amico	.05
270	Shawn Estes	.05
271	Derek Bell	.05
272	Fernando Valenzuela	.05
273	Luis Castillo	.05
274	Ray Montgomery	.05
275	Ed Sprague	.05
276	F.P. Santangelo	.05
277	Todd Greene	.05
278	Butch Huskey	.05
279	Steve Finley	.05
280	Eric Davis	.05
281	Shawn Green	.30
282	Al Martin	.05
283	Michael Tucker	.05
284	Shane Reynolds	.05
285	Matt Mieske	.05
286	Jose Rosado	.05
287	Mark Langston	.05
288	Ralph Milliard	.05
289	Mike Lansing	.05
290	Scott Servais	.05
291	Royce Clayton	.05
292	Mike Grace	.05
293	James Mouton	.05
294	Charles Johnson	.05
295	Gary Gaetti	.05
296	Kevin Mitchell	.05
297	Carlos Garcia	.05
298	Desi Relaford	.05
299	Jason Thompson	.05
300	Osvaldo Fernandez	.05
301	Fernando Vina	.05
302	Jose Offerman	.05
303	Yamil Benitez	.05
304	J.T. Snow	.05
305	Rafael Bournigal	.05
306	Jason Isringhausen	.05
307	Bob Higginson	.05
308	*Nerio Rodriguez*	.05
309	*Brian Giles*	.50
310	Andruw Jones	.50
311	Billy McMillon	.05
312	Arquimedez Pozo	.05
313	Jermaine Allensworth	.05
314	Luis Andujar	.05
315	Angel Echevarria	.05
316	Karim Garcia	.05
317	Trey Beamon	.05
318	Makoto Suzuki	.05
319	Robin Jennings	.05
320	Dmitri Young	.05
321	*Damon Mashore*	.05
322	Wendell Magee	.05
323	*Dax Jones*	.05
324	Todd Walker	.05
325	Marvin Benard	.05
326	*Brian Raabe*	.05
327	Marcus Jensen	.05
328	Checklist	.05
329	Checklist	.05
330	Checklist	.05
331	Norm Charlton	.05
332	Bruce Ruffin	.05
333	John Wetteland	.05
334	Marquis Grissom	.05
335	Sterling Hitchcock	.05
336	John Olerud	.05
337	David Wells	.05
338	Chili Davis	.05
339	Mark Lewis	.05
340	Kenny Lofton	.05
341	Alex Fernandez	.05
342	Ruben Sierra	.05
343	Delino DeShields	.05
344	John Wasdin	.05
345	Dennis Martinez	.05
346	Kevin Elster	.05
347	Bobby Bonilla	.05
348	Jaime Navarro	.05
349	Chad Curtis	.05
350	Terry Steinbach	.05
351	Ariel Prieto	.05
352	Jeff Kent	.05
353	Carlos Garcia	.05
354	Mark Whiten	.05
355	Todd Zeile	.05
356	Eric Davis	.05
357	Greg Colbrunn	.05
358	Moises Alou	.05
359	Allen Watson	.05
360	Jose Canseco	.30
361	Matt Williams	.05
362	Jeff King	.05
363	Darryl Hamilton	.05
364	Mark Clark	.05
365	J.T. Snow	.05
366	Kevin Mitchell	.05
367	Orlando Miller	.05
368	Rico Brogna	.05
369	Mike James	.05
370	Brad Ausmus	.05
371	Darryl Kile	.05
372	Edgardo Alfonzo	.05
373	Julian Tavarez	.05
374	Darren Lewis	.05
375	Steve Karsay	.05
376	Lee Stevens	.05
377	Albie Lopez	.05
378	Orel Hershiser	.05
379	Lee Smith	.05
380	Rick Helling	.05
381	Carlos Perez	.05
382	Tony Tarasco	.05
383	Melvin Nieves	.05
384	Benji Gil	.05

#	Player	Price
385	Devon White	.05
386	Armando Benitez	.05
387	Bill Swift	.05
388	John Smiley	.05
389	Midre Cummings	.05
390	Tim Belcher	.05
391	Tim Raines	.05
392	Todd Worrell	.05
393	Quilvio Veras	.05
394	Matt Lawton	.05
395	Aaron Sele	.05
396	Bip Roberts	.05
397	Denny Neagle	.05
398	Tyler Green	.05
399	Hipolito Pichardo	.05
400	Scott Erickson	.05
401	Bobby Jones	.05
402	Jim Edmonds	.05
403	Chad Ogea	.05
404	Cal Eldred	.05
405	Pat Listach	.05
406	Todd Stottlemyre	.05
407	Phil Nevin	.05
408	Otis Nixon	.05
409	Billy Ashley	.05
410	Jimmy Key	.05
411	Mike Timlin	.05
412	Joe Vitiello	.05
413	Rondell White	.05
414	Jeff Fassero	.05
415	Rex Hudler	.05
416	Curt Schilling	.35
417	Rich Becker	.05
418	William VanLandingham	.05
419	Chris Snopek	.05
420	David Segui	.05
421	Eddie Murray	.50
422	Shane Andrews	.05
423	Gary DiSarcina	.05
424	Brian Hunter	.05
425	Willie Greene	.05
426	Felipe Crespo	.05
427	Jason Bates	.05
428	Albert Belle	.05
429	Rey Sanchez	.05
430	Roger Clemens	.70
431	Deion Sanders	.05
432	Ernie Young	.05
433	Jay Bell	.05
434	Jeff Blauser	.05
435	Lenny Dykstra	.05
436	Chuck Carr	.05
437	Russ Davis	.05
438	Carl Everett	.05
439	Damion Easley	.05
440	Pat Kelly	.05
441	Pat Rapp	.05
442	David Justice	.05
443	Graeme Lloyd	.05
444	Damon Buford	.05
445	Jose Valentin	.05
446	Jason Schmidt	.05
447	Dave Martinez	.05
448	Danny Tartabull	.05
449	Jose Vizcaino	.05
450	Steve Avery	.05
451	Mike Devereaux	.05
452	Jim Eisenreich	.05
453	Mark Leiter	.05
454	Roberto Kelly	.05
455	Benito Santiago	.05
456	Steve Trachsel	.05
457	Gerald Williams	.05
458	Pete Schourek	.05
459	Esteban Loaiza	.05
460	Mel Rojas	.05
461	Tim Wakefield	.05
462	Tony Fernandez	.05
463	Doug Drabek	.05
464	Joe Girardi	.05
465	Mike Bordick	.05
466	Jim Leyritz	.05
467	Erik Hanson	.05
468	Michael Tucker	.05
469	*Tony Womack*	.10
470	Doug Glanville	.05
471	Rudy Pemberton	.05
472	Keith Lockhart	.05
473	Nomar Garciaparra	.65
474	Scott Rolen	.40
475	Jason Dickson	.05
476	Glendon Rusch	.05
477	Todd Walker	.05
478	Dmitri Young	.05
479	*Rod Myers*	.05
480	Wilton Guerrero	.05
481	Jorge Posada	.05
482	Brant Brown	.05
483	*Bubba Trammell*	.10
484	Jose Guillen	.05
485	Scott Spiezio	.05
486	Bob Abreu	.10
487	Chris Holt	.05
488	*Deivi Cruz*	.15
489	Vladimir Guerrero	.50
490	Julio Santana	.05
491	Ray Montgomery	.05
492	Kevin Orie	.05
493	Todd Hundley	.05
494	Tim Salmon	.05
495	Albert Belle	.05
496	Manny Ramirez	.25
497	Rafael Palmeiro	.20
498	Juan Gonzalez	.15
499	Ken Griffey Jr.	.40
500	Andruw Jones	.25
501	Mike Piazza	.40
502	Jeff Bagwell	.25
503	Bernie Williams	.05
504	Barry Bonds	.65
505	Ken Caminiti	.05
506	Darin Erstad	.10
507	Alex Rodriguez	.50
508	Frank Thomas	.30
509	Chipper Jones	.35
510	Mo Vaughn	.05
511	Mark McGwire	.50
512	Fred McGriff	.05
513	Jay Buhner	.05
514	Jim Thome	.20
515	Gary Sheffield	.20
516	Dean Palmer	.05
517	Henry Rodriguez	.05
518	Andy Pettitte	.10
519	Mike Mussina	.10
520	Greg Maddux	.35
521	John Smoltz	.05
522	Hideo Nomo	.15
523	Troy Percival	.05
524	John Wetteland	.05
525	Roger Clemens	.40
526	Charles Nagy	.05
527	Mariano Rivera	.10
528	Tom Glavine	.15
529	Randy Johnson	.25
530	Jason Isringhausen	.05
531	Alex Fernandez	.05
532	Kevin Brown	.05
533	Chuck Knoblauch	.05
534	Rusty Greer	.05
535	Tony Gwynn	.35
536	Ryan Klesko	.05
537	Ryne Sandberg	.35
538	Barry Larkin	.05
539	Will Clark	.05
540	Kenny Lofton	.05
541	Paul Molitor	.30
542	Roberto Alomar	.10
543	Rey Ordonez	.05
544	Jason Giambi	.25
545	Derek Jeter	.75
546	Cal Ripken Jr.	.75
547	Ivan Rodriguez	.25
548	Ken Griffey Jr. Checklist	.35
549	Frank Thomas Checklist	.25
550	Mike Piazza Checklist	.40
551a	*Hideki Irabu* (SP)	.25
551b	*Hideki Irabu* (SP)	.35

Pitcher Perfect

		NM/M
Complete Set (15):		6.50
Common Player:		.15
1	Cal Ripken Jr.	2.00
2	Alex Rodriguez	1.25
3	Cal Ripken Jr., Alex Rodriguez	1.25
4	Edgar Martinez	.15
5	Ivan Rodriguez	.50
6	Mark McGwire	1.25
7	Tim Salmon	.15
8	Chili Davis	.15
9	Joe Carter	.15
10	Frank Thomas	.60
11	Will Clark	.15
12	Mo Vaughn	.15
13	Wade Boggs	.75
14	Ken Griffey Jr.	1.00
15	Randy Johnson	.60

Stellar Season

		NM/M
Complete Set (18):		15.00
Common Player:		.50
1	Juan Gonzalez	.75
2	Chuck Knoblauch	.50
3	Jeff Bagwell	1.50
4	John Smoltz	.50
5	Mark McGwire	3.00
6	Ken Griffey Jr.	2.50
7	Frank Thomas	1.50
8	Alex Rodriguez	3.00
9	Mike Piazza	2.50
10	Albert Belle	.50
11	Roberto Alomar	.60
12	Sammy Sosa	2.00
13	Mo Vaughn	.50
14	Brady Anderson	.50
15	Henry Rodriguez	.50
16	Eric Young	.50
17	Gary Sheffield	.75
18	Ryan Klesko	.50

The Franchise

		NM/M
Complete Set (9):		5.00
Common Player:		.15
Glowing:		2.5X
Samples:		2.5
1	Ken Griffey Jr.	1.00
2	John Smoltz	.15
3	Cal Ripken Jr.	2.00
4	Chipper Jones	.75
5	Mike Piazza	1.00
6	Albert Belle	.15
7	Frank Thomas	.60
8	Sammy Sosa	.75
9	Roberto Alomar	.30

Highlight Zone

		NM/M
Complete Set (18):		30.00
Common Player:		.60
1	Frank Thomas	1.50
2	Ken Griffey Jr.	3.00
3	Mo Vaughn	.60
4	Albert Belle	.60
5	Mike Piazza	3.00
6	Barry Bonds	4.50
7	Greg Maddux	2.25
8	Sammy Sosa	2.25
9	Jeff Bagwell	1.50
10	Alex Rodriguez	3.50
11	Chipper Jones	2.25
12	Brady Anderson	.60
13	Ozzie Smith	2.25
14	Edgar Martinez	.60
15	Cal Ripken Jr.	4.50
16	Ryan Klesko	.60
17	Randy Johnson	1.50
18	Eddie Murray	1.50

Titanic Taters

		NM/M
Complete Set (18):		25.00
Common Player:		.35
1	Mark McGwire	4.00
2	Mike Piazza	3.50
3	Ken Griffey Jr.	3.50
4	Juan Gonzalez	1.00
5	Frank Thomas	1.50
6	Albert Belle	.35
7	Sammy Sosa	2.50
8	Jeff Bagwell	1.50
9	Todd Hundley	.35
10	Ryan Klesko	.35
11	Brady Anderson	.35
12	Mo Vaughn	.35
13	Jay Buhner	.35
14	Chipper Jones	2.75
15	Barry Bonds	6.00
16	Gary Sheffield	.75
17	Alex Rodriguez	4.00
18	Cecil Fielder	.35

Blast Masters

		NM/M
Complete Set (18):		17.50
Common Player:		.25
1	Mo Vaughn	.25
2	Mark McGwire	2.25
3	Juan Gonzalez	.75
4	Albert Belle	.25
5	Barry Bonds	3.00
6	Ken Griffey Jr.	2.00
7	Andruw Jones	1.25
8	Chipper Jones	1.50
9	Mike Piazza	2.00
10	Jeff Bagwell	1.25
11	Dante Bichette	.25
12	Alex Rodriguez	2.25
13	Gary Sheffield	.60
14	Ken Caminiti	.25
15	Sammy Sosa	1.50
16	Vladimir Guerrero	1.25
17	Brian Jordan	.25
18	Tim Salmon	.25

Heart of the Order

		NM/M
Complete Set (36):		35.00
Complete Retail Set (1-18):		20.00
Complete Hobby Set (19-36):		15.00
Common Player:		.50
1	Ivan Rodriguez	1.00
2	Will Clark	.50
3	Juan Gonzalez	.75
4	Frank Thomas	1.25
5	Albert Belle	.50
6	Robin Ventura	.50
7	Alex Rodriguez	3.00
8	Ken Griffey Jr.	2.50
9	Jay Buhner	.50
10	Roberto Alomar	.65
11	Rafael Palmeiro	1.00
12	Cal Ripken Jr.	4.00
13	Manny Ramirez	1.25
14	Matt Williams	.50
15	Jim Thome	.50
16	Derek Jeter	4.00
17	Wade Boggs	2.00
18	Bernie Williams	.50
19	Chipper Jones	2.00
20	Andruw Jones	1.25
21	Ryan Klesko	.50
22	Wilton Guerrero	.50
23	Mike Piazza	2.50
24	Raul Mondesi	.50
25	Tony Gwynn	2.00
26	Ken Caminiti	.50
27	Greg Vaughn	.50
28	Brian Jordan	.50
29	Ron Gant	.50
30	Dmitri Young	.50
31	Darin Erstad	.50
32	Jim Edmonds	.50
33	Tim Salmon	.50

34 Chuck Knoblauch .50
35 Paul Molitor 1.25
36 Todd Walker .50

Stand & Deliver

		NM/M
Complete Set (24):		50.00
Common Player:		.50
Gold:		4X
1	Andruw Jones	3.00
2	Greg Maddux	4.00
3	Chipper Jones	4.00
4	John Smoltz	.50
5	Ken Griffey Jr.	5.00
6	Alex Rodriguez	6.00
7	Jay Buhner	.50
8	Randy Johnson	3.00
9	Derek Jeter	7.50
10	Andy Pettitte	.75
11	Bernie Williams	.50
12	Mariano Rivera	.50
13	Mike Piazza	5.00
14	Hideo Nomo	1.50
15	Raul Mondesi	.50
16	Todd Hollandsworth	.50
17	Manny Ramirez	3.00
18	Jim Thome	2.00
19	David Justice	.50
20	Matt Williams	.50
21	Juan Gonzalez	1.50
22	Jeff Bagwell	3.00
23	Cal Ripken Jr.	7.50
24	Frank Thomas	3.00

Premium Stock

	NM/M
Complete Set (330):	17.50
Common Player:	.10
Premium Stock Stars:	3X

(See 1997 Score #1-330 for checklist and base card values.)

Showcase

	NM/M
Complete Set (551):	200.00
Common Player:	.50
Showcase Stars:	3X

(See 1997 Score for checklist and base card values.)

Showcase Artist's Proofs

	NM/M
Common Player:	1.00
Showcase AP Stars:	10X

(See 1997 Score for checklist and base card values.)

1998 SCORE

		NM/M
Complete Set (270):		12.00
Common Player:		.05
Showcases:		3X
Artist's Proofs:		6X
Pack (10):		.75
Wax Box (36):		15.00
All-Star Edition Box (36/10):		10.00
Jumbo Pack (20):		1.00
Jumbo Box (24):		15.00
1	Andruw Jones	.50
2	Dan Wilson	.05
3	Hideo Nomo	.30
4	Chuck Carr	.05
5	Barry Bonds	1.50
6	Jack McDowell	.05
7	Albert Belle	.05
8	Francisco Cordova	.05
9	Greg Maddux	.65
10	Alex Rodriguez	1.00
11	Steve Avery	.05
12	Chuck McElroy	.05
13	Larry Walker	.05
14	Hideki Irabu	.05
15	Roberto Alomar	.20
16	Neifi Perez	.05
17	Jim Thome	.40
18	Rickey Henderson	.50
19	Andres Galarraga	.05
20	Jeff Fassero	.05
21	Kevin Young	.05
22	Derek Jeter	1.50
23	Andy Benes	.05
24	Mike Piazza	.75
25	Todd Stottlemyre	.05
26	Michael Tucker	.05
27	Denny Neagle	.05
28	Javier Lopez	.05
29	Aaron Sele	.05
30	Ryan Klesko	.05
31	Dennis Eckersley	.40
32	Quinton McCracken	.05
33	Brian Anderson	.05
34	Ken Griffey Jr.	.75
35	Shawn Estes	.05
36	Tim Wakefield	.05
37	Jimmy Key	.05
38	Jeff Bagwell	.50
39	Edgardo Alfonzo	.05
40	Mike Cameron	.05
41	Mark McGwire	1.00
42	Tino Martinez	.05
43	Cal Ripken Jr.	1.50
44	Curtis Goodwin	.05
45	Bobby Ayala	.05
46	Sandy Alomar Jr.	.05
47	Bobby Jones	.05
48	Omar Vizquel	.05
49	Roger Clemens	.70
50	Tony Gwynn	.65
51	Chipper Jones	.65
52	Ron Coomer	.05
53	Dmitri Young	.05
54	Brian Giles	.05
55	Steve Finley	.05
56	David Cone	.05
57	Andy Pettitte	.20
58	Wilton Guerrero	.05
59	Deion Sanders	.05
60	Carlos Delgado	.30
61	Jason Giambi	.30
62	Ozzie Guillen	.05
63	Jay Bell	.05
64	Barry Larkin	.05
65	Sammy Sosa	.65
66	Bernie Williams	.05
67	Terry Steinbach	.05
68	Scott Rolen	.40
69	Melvin Nieves	.05
70	Craig Biggio	.05
71	Todd Greene	.05
72	Greg Gagne	.05
73	Shigetosi Hasegawa	.05
74	Mark McLemore	.05
75	Darren Bragg	.05
76	Brett Butler	.05
77	Ron Gant	.05
78	Mike Difelice	.05
79	Charles Nagy	.05
80	Scott Hatteberg	.05
81	Brady Anderson	.05
82	Jay Buhner	.05
83	Todd Hollandsworth	.05
84	Geronimo Berroa	.05
85	Jeff Suppan	.05
86	Pedro Martinez	.50
87	Roger Cedeno	.05
88	Ivan Rodriguez	.40
89	Jaime Navarro	.05
90	Chris Hoiles	.05
91	Nomar Garciaparra	.65
92	Rafael Palmeiro	.40
93	Darin Erstad	.15
94	Kenny Lofton	.05
95	Mike Timlin	.05
96	Chris Clemons	.05
97	Vinny Castilla	.05
98	Charlie Hayes	.05
99	Lyle Mouton	.05
100	Jason Dickson	.05
101	Justin Thompson	.05
102	Pat Kelly	.05
103	Chan Ho Park	.05
104	Ray Lankford	.05
105	Frank Thomas	.50
106	Jermaine Allensworth	.05
107	Doug Drabek	.05
108	Todd Hundley	.05
109	Carl Everett	.05
110	Edgar Martinez	.05
111	Robin Ventura	.05
112	John Wetteland	.05
113	Mariano Rivera	.10
114	Jose Rosado	.05
115	Ken Caminiti	.05
116	Paul O'Neill	.05
117	Tim Salmon	.05
118	Eduardo Perez	.05
119	Mike Jackson	.05
120	John Smoltz	.05
121	Brant Brown	.05
122	John Mabry	.05
123	Chuck Knoblauch	.05
124	Reggie Sanders	.05
125	Ken Hill	.05
126	Mike Mussina	.25
127	Chad Curtis	.05
128	Todd Worrell	.05
129	Chris Widger	.05
130	Damon Mashore	.05
131	Kevin Brown	.05
132	Bip Roberts	.05
133	Tim Naehring	.05
134	Dave Martinez	.05
135	Jeff Blauser	.05
136	David Justice	.05
137	Dave Hollins	.05
138	Pat Hentgen	.05
139	Darren Daulton	.05
140	Ramon Martinez	.05
141	Raul Casanova	.05
142	Tom Glavine	.30
143	J.T. Snow	.05
144	Tony Graffanino	.05
145	Randy Johnson	.50
146	Orlando Merced	.05
147	Jeff Juden	.05
148	Darryl Kile	.05
149	Ray Durham	.05
150	Alex Fernandez	.05
151	Joey Cora	.05
152	Royce Clayton	.05
153	Randy Myers	.05
154	Charles Johnson	.05
155	Alan Benes	.05
156	Mike Bordick	.05
157	Heathcliff Slocumb	.05
158	Roger Bailey	.05
159	Reggie Jefferson	.05
160	Ricky Bottalico	.05
161	Scott Erickson	.05
162	Matt Williams	.05
163	Robb Nen	.05
164	Matt Stairs	.05
165	Ismael Valdes	.05
166	Lee Stevens	.05
167	Gary DiSarcina	.05
168	Brad Radke	.05
169	Mike Lansing	.05
170	Armando Benitez	.05
171	Mike James	.05
172	Russ Davis	.05
173	Lance Johnson	.05
174	Joey Hamilton	.05
175	John Valentin	.05
176	David Segui	.05
177	David Wells	.05
178	Delino DeShields	.05
179	Eric Karros	.05
180	Jim Leyritz	.05
181	Raul Mondesi	.05
182	Travis Fryman	.05
183	Todd Zeile	.05
184	Brian Jordan	.05
185	Rey Ordonez	.05
186	Jim Edmonds	.05
187	Terrell Wade	.05
188	Marquis Grissom	.05
189	Chris Snopek	.05
190	Shane Reynolds	.05
191	Jeff Frye	.05
192	Paul Sorrento	.05
193	James Baldwin	.05
194	Brian McRae	.05
195	Fred McGriff	.05
196	Troy Percival	.05
197	Rich Amaral	.05
198	Juan Guzman	.05
199	Cecil Fielder	.05
200	Willie Blair	.05
201	Chili Davis	.05
202	Gary Gaetti	.05
203	B.J. Surhoff	.05
204	Steve Cooke	.05
205	Chuck Finley	.05
206	Jeff Kent	.05
207	Ben McDonald	.05
208	Jeffrey Hammonds	.05
209	Tom Goodwin	.05
210	Billy Ashley	.05
211	Wil Cordero	.05
212	Shawon Dunston	.05
213	Tony Phillips	.05
214	Jamie Moyer	.05
215	John Jaha	.05
216	Troy O'Leary	.05
217	Brad Ausmus	.05
218	Garret Anderson	.05
219	Wilson Alvarez	.05
220	Kent Mercker	.05
221	Wade Boggs	.65
222	Mark Wohlers	.05
223	Kevin Appier	.05
224	Tony Fernandez	.05
225	Ugueth Urbina	.05
226	Gregg Jefferies	.05
227	Mo Vaughn	.05
228	Arthur Rhodes	.05
229	Jorge Fabregas	.05
230	Mark Gardner	.05
231	Shane Mack	.05
232	Jorge Posada	.05
233	Jose Cruz Jr.	.05
234	Paul Konerko	.15
235	Derrek Lee	.30
236	*Steve Woodard*	.15
237	Todd Dunwoody	.05
238	Fernando Tatis	.05
239	Jacob Cruz	.05
240	*Pokey Reese*	.25
241	Mark Kotsay	.05
242	Matt Morris	.05
243	*Antone Williamson*	.05
244	Ben Grieve	.05
245	Ryan McGuire	.05
246	*Lou Collier*	.05
247	Shannon Stewart	.05
248	*Brett Tomko*	.10
249	Bobby Estalella	.05
250	*Livan Hernandez*	.15
251	Todd Helton	.40
252	Jaret Wright	.05
253	Darryl Hamilton	.05
254	Stan Javier	.05
255	Glenallen Hill	.05
256	Mark Gardner	.05
257	Cal Ripken Jr.	.75
258	Mike Mussina	.15
259	Mike Piazza	.45
260	Sammy Sosa	.35
261	Todd Hundley	.05
262	Eric Karros	.05
263	Denny Neagle	.05
264	Jeromy Burnitz	.05
265	Greg Maddux	.35
266	Tony Clark	.05
267	Vladimir Guerrero	.25
268	Checklist	.05
269	Checklist	.05
270	Checklist	.05

Complete Players

		NM/M
Complete Set (30):		75.00
Common Player:		1.00
Inserted 1:23		
Golds:		75%
1A	Ken Griffey Jr.	3.25
1B	Ken Griffey Jr.	3.25

1C	Ken Griffey Jr.	3.25
2A	Mark McGwire	3.75
2B	Mark McGwire	3.75
2C	Mark McGwire	3.75
3A	Derek Jeter	5.00
3B	Derek Jeter	5.00
3C	Derek Jeter	5.00
4A	Cal Ripken Jr.	5.00
4B	Cal Ripken Jr.	5.00
4C	Cal Ripken Jr.	5.00
5A	Mike Piazza	3.25
5B	Mike Piazza	3.25
5C	Mike Piazza	3.25
6A	Darin Erstad	1.00
6B	Darin Erstad	1.00
6C	Darin Erstad	1.00
7A	Frank Thomas	2.00
7B	Frank Thomas	2.00
7C	Frank Thomas	2.00
8A	Andruw Jones	2.00
8B	Andruw Jones	2.00
8C	Andruw Jones	2.00
9A	Nomar Garciaparra	3.00
9B	Nomar Garciaparra	3.00
9C	Nomar Garciaparra	3.00
10A	Manny Ramirez	2.00
10B	Manny Ramirez	2.00
10C	Manny Ramirez	2.00

Epix

		NM/M
Common Card:		.50
Purple:		2X
Emeralds:		3X
1	Ken Griffey Jr. P	2.50
2	Juan Gonzalez P	.75
3	Jeff Bagwell P	1.25
4	Ivan Rodriguez P	1.00
5	Nomar Garciaparra P	2.00
6	Ryne Sandberg P	1.50
7	Frank Thomas G	1.25
8	Derek Jeter G	3.50
9	Tony Gwynn G	2.00
10	Albert Belle G	.50
11	Scott Rolen G	1.00
12	Barry Larkin G	.50
13	Alex Rodriguez S	6.00
14	Cal Ripken Jr. S	7.50
15	Chipper Jones S	4.00
16	Roger Clemens S	4.50
17	Mo Vaughn S	1.50
18	Mark McGwire S	6.00
19	Mike Piazza M	8.00
20	Andruw Jones M	4.00
21	Greg Maddux M	6.00
22	Barry Bonds M	12.00
23	Paul Molitor M	4.00
24	Eddie Murray M	4.00

All Score Team

		NM/M
Complete Set (20):		15.00
Common Player:		.25
Inserted 1:35		
1	Mike Piazza	1.50
2	Ivan Rodriguez	.65
3	Frank Thomas	.75
4	Mark McGwire	2.00
5	Ryne Sandberg	1.00
6	Roberto Alomar	.35
7	Cal Ripken Jr.	2.50
8	Barry Larkin	.25
9	Paul Molitor	.75
10	Travis Fryman	.25
11	Kirby Puckett	1.00
12	Tony Gwynn	1.00
13	Ken Griffey Jr.	1.50
14	Juan Gonzalez	.45
15	Barry Bonds	2.50
16	Andruw Jones	.75
17	Roger Clemens	1.25
18	Randy Johnson	.75
19	Greg Maddux	1.00
20	Dennis Eckersley	.65

1998 SCORE ROOKIE & TRADED

		NM/M
Complete Set (270):		10.00
Common SP (1-50):		.10
Common Player (51-270):		.05
Artist's Proofs:		4X
Inserted 1:35		
Paul Konerko Auto. (500):		15.00
Pack (10):		.65
Wax Box (36):		15.00
Jumbo Pack (20):		1.50
Jumbo Box (24):		25.00
1	Tony Clark	.10
2	Juan Gonzalez	.35
3	Frank Thomas	.60
4	Greg Maddux	.75
5	Barry Larkin	.10
6	Derek Jeter	1.50
7	Randy Johnson	.60
8	Roger Clemens	.85
9	Tony Gwynn	.75
10	Barry Bonds	1.50
11	Jim Edmonds	.10
12	Bernie Williams	.10
13	Ken Griffey Jr.	1.00
14	Tim Salmon	.10
15	Mo Vaughn	.10
16	David Justice	.10
17	Jose Cruz Jr.	.10
18	Andruw Jones	.60
19	Sammy Sosa	.75
20	Jeff Bagwell	.60
21	Scott Rolen	.50
22	Darin Erstad	.30
23	Andy Pettitte	.35
24	Mike Mussina	.40
25	Mark McGwire	1.25
26	Hideo Nomo	.35
27	Chipper Jones	.75
28	Cal Ripken Jr.	1.50
29	Chuck Knoblauch	.10
30	Alex Rodriguez	1.25
31	Jim Thome	.50
32	Mike Piazza	1.00
33	Ivan Rodriguez	.50
34	Roberto Alomar	.40
35	Nomar Garciaparra	.75
36	Albert Belle	.10
37	Vladimir Guerrero	.60
38	Raul Mondesi	.10
39	Larry Walker	.10
40	Manny Ramirez	.60
41	Tino Martinez	.10
42	Craig Biggio	.10
43	Jay Buhner	.10
44	Kenny Lofton	.10
45	Pedro Martinez	.60
46	Edgar Martinez	.10
47	Gary Sheffield	.45
48	Jose Guillen	.10
49	Ken Caminiti	.10
50	Bobby Higginson	.05
51	Alan Benes	.05
52	Shawn Green	.15
53	Ron Coomer	.05
54	Charles Nagy	.05
55	Steve Karsay	.05
56	Matt Morris	.05
57	Bobby Jones	.05
58	Jason Kendall	.05
59	Jeff Conine	.05
60	Joe Girardi	.05
61	Mark Kotsay	.05
62	Eric Karros	.05
63	Bartolo Colon	.05
64	Mariano Rivera	.10
65	Alex Gonzalez	.05
66	Scott Spiezio	.05
67	Luis Castillo	.05
68	Joey Cora	.05
69	Mark McLemore	.05
70	Reggie Jefferson	.05
71	Lance Johnson	.05
72	Damian Jackson	.05
73	Jeff D'Amico	.05
74	David Ortiz	.30
75	J.T. Snow	.05
76	Todd Hundley	.05
77	Billy Wagner	.05
78	Vinny Castilla	.05
79	Ismael Valdes	.05
80	Neifi Perez	.05
81	Derek Bell	.05
82	Ryan Klesko	.05
83	Rey Ordonez	.05
84	Carlos Garcia	.05
85	Curt Schilling	.30
86	Robin Ventura	.05
87	Pat Hentgen	.05
88	Glendon Rusch	.05
89	Hideki Irabu	.05
90	Antone Williamson	.05
91	Denny Neagle	.05
92	Kevin Orie	.05
93	Reggie Sanders	.05
94	Brady Anderson	.05
95	Andy Benes	.05
96	John Valentin	.05
97	Bobby Bonilla	.05
98	Walt Weiss	.05
99	Robin Jennings	.05
100	Marty Cordova	.05
101	Brad Ausmus	.05
102	Brian Rose	.05
103	Calvin Maduro	.05
104	Raul Casanova	.05
105	Jeff King	.05
106	Sandy Alomar	.05
107	Tim Naehring	.05
108	Mike Cameron	.05
109	Omar Vizquel	.05
110	Brad Radke	.05
111	Jeff Fassero	.05
112	Deivi Cruz	.05
113	Dave Hollins	.05
114	Dean Palmer	.05
115	Esteban Loaiza	.05
116	Brian Giles	.05
117	Steve Finley	.05
118	Jose Canseco	.30
119	Al Martin	.05
120	Eric Young	.05
121	Curtis Goodwin	.05
122	Ellis Burks	.05
123	Mike Hampton	.05
124	Lou Collier	.05
125	John Olerud	.05
126	Ramon Martinez	.05
127	Todd Dunwoody	.05
128	Jermaine Allensworth	.05
129	Eduardo Perez	.05
130	Dante Bichette	.05
131	Edgar Renteria	.05
132	Bob Abreu	.10
133	Rondell White	.05
134	Michael Coleman	.05
135	Jason Giambi	.30
136	Brant Brown	.05
137	Michael Tucker	.05
138	Dave Nilsson	.05
139	Benito Santiago	.05
140	Ray Durham	.05
141	Jeff Kent	.05
142	Matt Stairs	.05
143	Kevin Young	.05
144	Eric Davis	.05
145	John Wetteland	.05
146	Esteban Yan	.05
147	Wilton Guerrero	.05
148	Moises Alou	.05
149	Edgardo Alfonzo	.05
150	Andy Ashby	.05
151	Todd Walker	.05
152	Jermaine Dye	.05
153	Brian Hunter	.05
154	Shawn Estes	.05
155	Bernard Gilkey	.05
156	Tony Womack	.05
157	John Smoltz	.05
158	Delino DeShields	.05
159	Jacob Cruz	.05
160	Javier Valentin	.05
161	Chris Hoiles	.05
162	Garret Anderson	.05
163	Dan Wilson	.05
164	Paul O'Neill	.05
165	Matt Williams	.05
166	Travis Fryman	.05
167	Javier Lopez	.05
168	Ray Lankford	.05
169	Bobby Estalella	.05
170	Henry Rodriguez	.05
171	Quinton McCracken	.05
172	Jaret Wright	.05
173	Darryl Kile	.05
174	Wade Boggs	.65
175	Orel Hershiser	.05
176	B.J. Surhoff	.05
177	Fernando Tatis	.05
178	Carlos Delgado	.30
179	Jorge Fabregas	.05
180	Tony Saunders	.05
181	Devon White	.05
182	Dmitri Young	.05
183	Ryan McGuire	.05
184	Mark Bellhorn	.05
185	Joe Carter	.05
186	Kevin Stocker	.05
187	Mike Lansing	.05
188	Jason Dickson	.05
189	Charles Johnson	.05
190	Will Clark	.05
191	Shannon Stewart	.05
192	Johnny Damon	.20
193	Todd Greene	.05
194	Carlos Baerga	.05
195	David Cone	.05
196	Pokey Reese	.05
197	Livan Hernandez	.05
198	Tom Glavine	.25
199	Geronimo Berroa	.05
200	Darryl Hamilton	.05
201	Terry Steinbach	.05
202	Robb Nen	.05
203	Ron Gant	.05
204	Rafael Palmeiro	.40
205	Rickey Henderson	.40
206	Justin Thompson	.05
207	Jeff Suppan	.05
208	Kevin Brown	.05
209	Jimmy Key	.05
210	Brian Jordan	.05
211	Aaron Sele	.05
212	Fred McGriff	.05
213	Jay Bell	.05
214	Andres Galarraga	.05
215	Mark Grace	.05
216	Brett Tomko	.05
217	Francisco Cordova	.05
218	Rusty Greer	.05
219	Bubba Trammell	.05
220	Derrek Lee	.35
221	Brian Anderson	.05
222	Mark Grudzielanek	.05
223	Marquis Grissom	.05
224	Gary DiSarcina	.05
225	Jim Leyritz	.05
226	Jeffrey Hammonds	.05
227	Karim Garcia	.05
228	Chan Ho Park	.05
229	Brooks Kieschnick	.05
230	Trey Beamon	.05
231	Kevin Appier	.05
232	Wally Joyner	.05
233	Richie Sexson	.05
234	*Frank Catalanotto*	.15
235	Rafael Medina	.05
236	Travis Lee	.05
237	Eli Marrero	.05
238	Carl Pavano	.05

239	Enrique Wilson	.05
240	Richard Hidalgo	.05
241	Todd Helton	.40
242	Ben Grieve	.05
243	Mario Valdez	.05
244	*Magglio Ordonez*	.75
245	Juan Encarnacion	.05
246	Russell Branyan	.05
247	Sean Casey	.10
248	Abraham Nunez	.05
249	Brad Fullmer	.05
250	Paul Konerko	.20
251	Miguel Tejada	.15
252	*Mike Lowell*	.50
253	Ken Griffey Jr.	.35
254	Frank Thomas	.25
255	Alex Rodriguez	.45
256	Jose Cruz Jr.	.05
257	Jeff Bagwell	.20
258	Chipper Jones	.30
259	Mo Vaughn	.05
260	Nomar Garciaparra	.30
261	Jim Thome	.05
262	Derek Jeter	.50
263	Mike Piazza	.45
264	Tony Gwynn	.30
265	Scott Rolen	.15
266	Andruw Jones	.20
267	Cal Ripken Jr.	.50
268	Ken Griffey Jr. Checklist	.30
269	Cal Ripken Jr. Checklist	.45
270	Jose Cruz Jr. Checklist	.05

Epix All-Star Moment

		NM/M
Complete Set (12):		25.00
Common Player:		1.00
Purples:		1.5X
Emeralds:		2.5X
1	Ken Griffey Jr.	4.00
2	Juan Gonzalez	1.50
3	Jeff Bagwell	2.50
4	Ivan Rodriguez	2.00
5	Nomar Garciaparra	3.00
6	Ryne Sandberg	3.00
7	Frank Thomas	2.50
8	Derek Jeter	5.00
9	Tony Gwynn	3.00
10	Albert Belle	1.00
11	Scott Rolen	2.00
12	Barry Larkin	1.00

Complete Players

		NM/M
Complete Set (30):		65.00
Common Player:		1.00
Inserted 1:11		
Samples:		1X
1A	Ken Griffey Jr.	3.50
1B	Ken Griffey Jr.	3.50
1C	Ken Griffey Jr.	3.50
2A	Larry Walker	1.00
2B	Larry Walker	1.00
2C	Larry Walker	1.00
3A	Alex Rodriguez	4.00
3B	Alex Rodriguez	4.00
3C	Alex Rodriguez	4.00
4A	Jose Cruz Jr.	1.00
4B	Jose Cruz Jr.	1.00
4C	Jose Cruz Jr.	1.00
5A	Jeff Bagwell	2.00
5B	Jeff Bagwell	2.00
5C	Jeff Bagwell	2.00
6A	Greg Maddux	2.75
6B	Greg Maddux	2.75
6C	Greg Maddux	2.75
7A	Ivan Rodriguez	1.75
7B	Ivan Rodriguez	1.75
7C	Ivan Rodriguez	1.75
8A	Roger Clemens	3.00
8B	Roger Clemens	3.00
8C	Roger Clemens	3.00
9A	Chipper Jones	2.75
9B	Chipper Jones	2.75
9C	Chipper Jones	2.75
10A	Hideo Nomo	1.50
10B	Hideo Nomo	1.50
10C	Hideo Nomo	1.50

Star Gazing

		NM/M
Complete Set (20):		12.00
Common Player:		.25
Inserted 1:35		
1	Ken Griffey Jr.	1.00
2	Frank Thomas	.60
3	Chipper Jones	.75
4	Mark McGwire	1.25
5	Cal Ripken Jr.	1.50
6	Mike Piazza	1.00

7	Nomar Garciaparra	.75
8	Derek Jeter	1.50
9	Juan Gonzalez	.35
10	Vladimir Guerrero	.60
11	Alex Rodriguez	1.25
12	Tony Gwynn	.75
13	Andruw Jones	.60
14	Scott Rolen	.40
15	Jose Cruz Jr.	.25
16	Mo Vaughn	.25
17	Bernie Williams	.25
18	Greg Maddux	.75
19	Tony Clark	.25
20	Ben Grieve	.25

First Pitch

		NM/M
Complete Set (20):		25.00
Common Player:		.50
Inserted 1:11 All-Star Edition		
1	Ken Griffey Jr.	2.00
2	Frank Thomas	1.25
3	Alex Rodriguez	2.50
4	Cal Ripken Jr.	3.25
5	Chipper Jones	1.50
6	Juan Gonzalez	.75
7	Derek Jeter	3.25
8	Mike Piazza	2.00
9	Andruw Jones	1.25
10	Nomar Garciaparra	1.50
11	Barry Bonds	3.25
12	Jeff Bagwell	1.25
13	Scott Rolen	1.00
14	Hideo Nomo	.75
15	Roger Clemens	1.75
16	Mark McGwire	2.50
17	Greg Maddux	1.50
18	Albert Belle	.50
19	Ivan Rodriguez	1.00
20	Mo Vaughn	.50

Loaded Lineup

		NM/M
Complete Set (10):		20.00
Common Player:		.50
Inserted 1:45 All-Star Edition		
LL1	Chuck Knoblauch	.50
LL2	Tony Gwynn	2.25
LL3	Frank Thomas	1.50
LL4	Ken Griffey Jr.	3.00
LL5	Mike Piazza	3.00
LL6	Barry Bonds	4.50
LL7	Cal Ripken Jr.	4.50
LL8	Paul Molitor	1.50
LL9	Nomar Garciaparra	2.25
LL10	Greg Maddux	2.25

New Season

		NM/M
Complete Set (15):		18.00
Common Player:		.50
Inserted 1:23 All-Star Edition		
NS1	Kenny Lofton	.50
NS2	Nomar Garciaparra	2.00
NS3	Todd Helton	1.00
NS4	Miguel Tejada	.75
NS5	Jaret Wright	.50
NS6	Alex Rodriguez	3.00
NS7	Vladimir Guerrero	1.25
NS8	Ken Griffey Jr.	2.50
NS9	Ben Grieve	.50
NS10	Travis Lee	.50
NS11	Jose Cruz Jr.	.50
NS12	Paul Konerko	.75
NS13	Frank Thomas	1.25
NS14	Chipper Jones	2.00
NS15	Cal Ripken Jr.	4.00

Showcase Series

		NM/M
Complete Set (160):		10.00
Common Player:		.15
1	Tony Clark	.15
2	Juan Gonzalez	.30
3	Frank Thomas	.60
4	Greg Maddux	.75
5	Barry Larkin	.15
6	Derek Jeter	1.50
7	Randy Johnson	.60
8	Roger Clemens	.85
9	Tony Gwynn	.75
10	Barry Bonds	1.50
11	Jim Edmonds	.15
12	Bernie Williams	.15
13	Ken Griffey Jr.	1.00
14	Tim Salmon	.15
15	Mo Vaughn	.15
16	David Justice	.15
17	Jose Cruz Jr.	.15
18	Andruw Jones	.60
19	Sammy Sosa	.75
20	Jeff Bagwell	.60
21	Scott Rolen	.50
22	Darin Erstad	.25
23	Andy Pettitte	.30
24	Mike Mussina	.30
25	Mark McGwire	1.25
26	Hideo Nomo	.30
27	Chipper Jones	.75
28	Cal Ripken Jr.	1.50
29	Chuck Knoblauch	.15
30	Alex Rodriguez	1.25
31	Jim Thome	.50
32	Mike Piazza	1.00
33	Ivan Rodriguez	.50
34	Roberto Alomar	.25
35	Nomar Garciaparra	1.00
36	Albert Belle	.15
37	Vladimir Guerrero	.60
38	Raul Mondesi	.15
39	Larry Walker	.15
40	Manny Ramirez	.60
41	Tino Martinez	.15
42	Craig Biggio	.15
43	Jay Buhner	.15
44	Kenny Lofton	.15
45	Pedro Martinez	.60
46	Edgar Martinez	.15
47	Gary Sheffield	.40
48	Jose Guillen	.15
49	Ken Caminiti	.15
50	Bobby Higginson	.15
51	Alan Benes	.15
52	Shawn Green	.35
53	Matt Morris	.15
54	Jason Kendall	.15
55	Mark Kotsay	.15
56	Bartolo Colon	.15
57	Damian Jackson	.15
58	David Ortiz	.35
59	J.T. Snow	.15
60	Todd Hundley	.15
61	Neifi Perez	.15
62	Ryan Klesko	.15
63	Robin Ventura	.15
64	Pat Hentgen	.15
65	Antone Williamson	.15
66	Kevin Orie	.15
67	Brady Anderson	.15
68	Bobby Bonilla	.15
69	Brian Rose	.15
70	Sandy Alomar Jr.	.15
71	Mike Cameron	.15
72	Omar Vizquel	.15
73	Steve Finley	.15
74	Jose Canseco	.40
75	Al Martin	.15
76	Eric Young	.15
77	Ellis Burks	.15
78	Todd Dunwoody	.15
79	Dante Bichette	.15
80	Edgar Renteria	.15
81	Bobby Abreu	.15
82	Rondell White	.15
83	Michael Coleman	.15
84	Jason Giambi	.50
85	Wilton Guerrero	.15
86	Moises Alou	.15
87	Todd Walker	.15
88	Shawn Estes	.15
89	John Smoltz	.15
90	Jacob Cruz	.15
91	Javier Valentin	.15
92	Garret Anderson	.15
93	Paul O'Neill	.15
94	Matt Williams	.15
95	Travis Fryman	.15
96	Javier Lopez	.15
97	Ray Lankford	.15
98	Bobby Estalella	.15
99	Jaret Wright	.15
100	Wade Boggs	.75
101	Fernando Tatis	.15
102	Carlos Delgado	.50
103	Joe Carter	.15
104	Jason Dickson	.15
105	Charles Johnson	.15
106	Will Clark	.15
107	Shannon Stewart	.15
108	Todd Greene	.15
109	Pokey Reese	.15
110	Livan Hernandez	.15
111	Tom Glavine	.35
112	Rafael Palmeiro	.50
113	Justin Thompson	.15
114	Jeff Suppan	.15
115	Kevin Brown	.15
116	Brian Jordan	.15
117	Fred McGriff	.15
118	Andres Galarraga	.15
119	Mark Grace	.15
120	Rusty Greer	.15
121	Bubba Trammell	.15
122	Derrek Lee	.40
123	Brian Anderson	.15
124	Karim Garcia	.15
125	Chan Ho Park	.15
126	Richie Sexson	.15
127	Frank Catalanotto	.15
128	Rafael Medina	.15
129	Travis Lee	.15
130	Eli Marrero	.15
131	Carl Pavano	.15
132	Enrique Wilson	.15
133	Richard Hidalgo	.15
134	Todd Helton	.40
135	Ben Grieve	.15
136	Mario Valdez	.15

137 Magglio Ordonez .25
138 Juan Encarnacion .15
139 Russell Branyan .15
140 Sean Casey .25
141 Abraham Nunez .15
142 Brad Fullmer .15
143 Paul Konerko .25
144 Miguel Tejada .30
145 Mike Lowell .15
146 Ken Griffey Jr. (Spring Training) .50
147 Frank Thomas (Spring Training) .35
148 Alex Rodriguez (Spring Training) .65
149 Jose Cruz Jr. (Spring Training) .15
150 Jeff Bagwell (Spring Training) .35
151 Chipper Jones (Spring Training) .40
152 Mo Vaughn (Spring Training) .15
153 Nomar Garciaparra (Spring Training) .40
154 Jim Thome (Spring Training) .30
155 Derek Jeter (Spring Training) .75
156 Mike Piazza (Spring Training) .50
157 Tony Gwynn (Spring Training) .40
158 Scott Rolen (Spring Training) .25
159 Andruw Jones (Spring Training) .35
160 Cal Ripken Jr. (Spring Training) .75

Artist's Proofs

NM/M
Common Player: 1.00
AP Stars: 4X
(See 1998 Score Rookie & Traded Showcase for checklist and base card values.)

Showcase Series

NM/M
Complete Set (160): 40.00
Common Player: .25
Inserted 1:7
1 Andruw Jones .75
2 Dan Wilson .25
3 Hideo Nomo .40
4 Neifi Perez .25
5 Jim Thome .60
6 Jeff Fassero .25
7 Derek Jeter 2.00
8 Andy Benes .25
9 Michael Tucker .25
10 Ryan Klesko .25
11 Dennis Eckersley .65
12 Jimmy Key .25
13 Edgardo Alfonzo .25
14 Mike Cameron .25
15 Omar Vizquel .25
16 Ron Coomer .25
17 Dmitri Young .25
18 Brian Giles .25
19 Steve Finley .25
20 Andy Pettitte .40
21 Wilton Guerrero .25
22 Deion Sanders .25
23 Carlos Delgado .50
24 Jason Giambi .50
25 David Cone .25
26 Jay Bell .25
27 Sammy Sosa 1.00
28 Barry Larkin .25
29 Scott Rolen .60
30 Todd Greene .25
31 Bernie Williams .25
32 Brett Butler .25
33 Ron Gant .25
34 Brady Anderson .25
35 Craig Biggio .25
36 Charles Nagy .25
37 Jay Buhner .25
38 Geronimo Berroa .25
39 Jeff Suppan .25
40 Rafael Palmeiro .65
41 Darin Erstad .35
42 Mike Timlin .25
43 Vinny Castilla .25
44 Carl Everett .25
45 Robin Ventura .25
46 John Wetteland .25
47 Paul O'Neill .25
48 Tim Salmon .25
49 Mike Jackson .25
50 John Smoltz .25
51 Brant Brown .25
52 Reggie Sanders .25
53 Ken Hill .25
54 Todd Worrell .25
55 Bip Roberts .25
56 Tim Naehring .25
57 Darren Daulton .25
58 Ramon Martinez .25
59 Raul Casanova .25
60 J.T. Snow .25
61 Jeff Juden .25
62 Royce Clayton .25
63 Charles Johnson .25
64 Alan Benes .25
65 Reggie Jefferson .25
66 Ricky Bottalico .25
67 Scott Erickson .25
68 Matt Williams .25
69 Robb Nen .25
70 Matt Stairs .25
71 Ismael Valdes .25
72 Brad Radke .25
73 Armando Benitez .25
74 Russ Davis .25
75 Lance Johnson .25
76 Joey Hamilton .25
77 John Valentin .25
78 David Segui .25
79 David Wells .25
80 Eric Karros .25
81 Raul Mondesi .25
82 Travis Fryman .25
83 Todd Zeile .25
84 Brian Jordan .25
85 Rey Ordonez .25
86 Jim Edmonds .25
87 Marquis Grissom .25
88 Shane Reynolds .25
89 Paul Sorrento .25
90 Brian McRae .25
91 Fred McGriff .25
92 Troy Percival .25
93 Juan Guzman .25
94 Cecil Fielder .25
95 Chili Davis .25
96 B.J. Surhoff .25
97 Chuck Finley .25
98 Jeff Kent .25
99 Ben McDonald .25
100 Jeffrey Hammonds .25
101 Tom Goodwin .25
102 Wil Cordero .25
103 Tony Phillips .25
104 John Jaha .25
105 Garret Anderson .25
106 Wilson Alvarez .25
107 Wade Boggs 1.00
108 Mark Wohlers .25
109 Kevin Appier .25
110 Mo Vaughn .25
111 Ray Durham .25
112 Alex Fernandez .25
113 Barry Bonds 2.00
114 Albert Belle .25
115 Greg Maddux 1.00
116 Alex Rodriguez 1.50
117 Larry Walker .25
118 Roberto Alomar .35
119 Andres Galarraga .25
120 Mike Piazza 1.25
121 Denny Neagle .25
122 Javier Lopez .25
123 Ken Griffey Jr. 1.25
124 Shawn Estes .25
125 Jeff Bagwell .75
126 Mark McGwire 1.50
127 Tino Martinez .25
128 Cal Ripken Jr. 2.00
129 Sandy Alomar Jr. .25
130 Bobby Jones .25
131 Roger Clemens 1.00
132 Tony Gwynn 1.00
133 Chipper Jones 1.00
134 Orlando Merced .25
135 Todd Stottlemyre .25
136 Delino DeShields .25
137 Pedro Martinez .75
138 Ivan Rodriguez .65
139 Nomar Garciaparra 1.00
140 Kenny Lofton .25
141 Jason Dickson .25
142 Justin Thompson .25
143 Ray Lankford .25
144 Frank Thomas .75
145 Todd Hundley .25
146 Edgar Martinez .25
147 Mariano Rivera .25
148 Jose Rosado .25
149 Ken Caminiti .25
150 Chuck Knoblauch .25
151 Mike Mussina .40
152 Kevin Brown .25
153 Jeff Blauser .25
154 David Justice .25
155 Pat Hentgen .25
156 Tom Glavine .40
157 Randy Johnson .75
158 Darryl Kile .25
159 Joey Cora .25
160 Randy Myers .25

Artist's Proofs

NM/M
Complete Set (160): 125.00
Common Player: .50
Inserted 1:35
1 Andruw Jones 1.25
2 Dan Wilson .50
3 Hideo Nomo .75
4 Neifi Perez .50
5 Jim Thome 1.00
6 Jeff Fassero .50
7 Derek Jeter 4.00
8 Andy Benes .50
9 Michael Tucker .50
10 Ryan Klesko .50
11 Dennis Eckersley 1.00
12 Jimmy Key .50
13 Edgardo Alfonzo .50
14 Mike Cameron .50
15 Omar Vizquel .50
16 Ron Coomer .50
17 Dmitri Young .50
18 Brian Giles .50
19 Steve Finley .50
20 Andy Pettitte .75
21 Wilton Guerrero .50
22 Deion Sanders .50
23 Carlos Delgado .75
24 Jason Giambi .75
25 David Cone .50
26 Jay Bell .50
27 Sammy Sosa 2.00
28 Barry Larkin .50
29 Scott Rolen 1.00
30 Todd Greene .50
31 Bernie Williams .50
32 Brett Butler .50
33 Ron Gant .50
34 Brady Anderson .50
35 Craig Biggio .50
36 Charles Nagy .50
37 Jay Buhner .50
38 Geronimo Berroa .50
39 Jeff Suppan .50
40 Rafael Palmeiro 1.00
41 Darin Erstad .65
42 Mike Timlin .50
43 Vinny Castilla .50
44 Carl Everett .50
45 Robin Ventura .50
46 John Wetteland .50
47 Paul O'Neill .50
48 Tim Salmon .50
49 Mike Jackson .50
50 John Smoltz .50
51 Brant Brown .50
52 Reggie Sanders .50
53 Ken Hill .50
54 Todd Worrell .50
55 Bip Roberts .50
56 Tim Naehring .50
57 Darren Daulton .50
58 Ramon Martinez .50
59 Raul Casanova .50
60 J.T. Snow .50
61 Jeff Juden .50
62 Royce Clayton .50
63 Charles Johnson .50
64 Alan Benes .50
65 Reggie Jefferson .50
66 Ricky Bottalico .50
67 Scott Erickson .50
68 Matt Williams .50
69 Robb Nen .50
70 Matt Stairs .50
71 Ismael Valdes .50
72 Brad Radke .50
73 Armando Benitez .50
74 Russ Davis .50
75 Lance Johnson .50
76 Joey Hamilton .50
77 John Valentin .50
78 David Segui .50
79 David Wells .50
80 Eric Karros .50
81 Raul Mondesi .50
82 Travis Fryman .50
83 Todd Zeile .50
84 Brian Jordan .50
85 Rey Ordonez .50
86 Jim Edmonds .50
87 Marquis Grissom .50
88 Shane Reynolds .50
89 Paul Sorrento .50
90 Brian McRae .50
91 Fred McGriff .50
92 Troy Percival .50
93 Juan Guzman .50
94 Cecil Fielder .50
95 Chili Davis .50
96 B.J. Surhoff .50
97 Chuck Finley .50
98 Jeff Kent .50
99 Ben McDonald .50
100 Jeffrey Hammonds .50
101 Tom Goodwin .50
102 Wil Cordero .50
103 Tony Phillips .50
104 John Jaha .50
105 Garret Anderson .50
106 Wilson Alvarez .50
107 Wade Boggs 2.00
108 Mark Wohlers .50
109 Kevin Appier .50
110 Mo Vaughn .50
111 Ray Durham .50
112 Alex Fernandez .50
113 Barry Bonds 4.00
114 Albert Belle .50
115 Greg Maddux 2.00
116 Alex Rodriguez 3.00
117 Larry Walker .50
118 Roberto Alomar .60
119 Andres Galarraga .50
120 Mike Piazza 2.50
121 Denny Neagle .50
122 Javier Lopez .50
123 Ken Griffey Jr. 2.50
124 Shawn Estes .50
125 Jeff Bagwell 1.25
126 Mark McGwire 3.00
127 Tino Martinez .50
128 Cal Ripken Jr. 4.00
129 Sandy Alomar Jr. .50
130 Bobby Jones .50
131 Roger Clemens 2.25
132 Tony Gwynn 2.00
133 Chipper Jones 2.00
134 Orlando Merced .50
135 Todd Stottlemyre .50
136 Delino DeShields .50
137 Pedro Martinez 1.25

No.	Player	Price
138	Ivan Rodriguez	1.00
139	Nomar Garciaparra	2.00
140	Kenny Lofton	.50
141	Jason Dickson	.50
142	Justin Thompson	.50
143	Ray Lankford	.50
144	Frank Thomas	1.25
145	Todd Hundley	.50
146	Edgar Martinez	.50
147	Mariano Rivera	.50
148	Jose Rosado	.50
149	Ken Caminiti	.50
150	Chuck Knoblauch	.50
151	Mike Mussina	.65
152	Kevin Brown	.50
153	Jeff Blauser	.50
154	David Justice	.50
155	Pat Hentgen	.50
156	Tom Glavine	.65
157	Randy Johnson	1.25
158	Darryl Kile	.50
159	Joey Cora	.50
160	Randy Myers	.50

Reserve Collection

	NM/M
Complete Set (221):	250.00
Common Player:	1.00
Reserve Collection Stars:	8X

(See 1997 Score #331-551 for checklist and base card values.)

All Score Team Andruw Jones Autograph

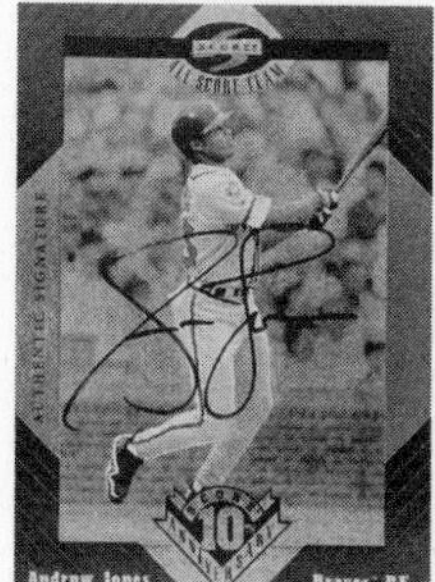

No.	Player	NM/M
16	Andruw Jones	25.00

White Border Artist's Proofs

	NM/M
Complete Set (330):	150.00
Common Player:	.50
Artist's Proof Stars:	10X

(See 1997 Score for checklist and base card values.)

Hobby Reserve

	NM/M
Complete Set (221):	35.00
Common Player:	.10
Hobby Reserve Stars:	3X

(See 1997 Score #331-551 for checklist and base card values.)

1993 SELECT

	NM/M
Complete Set (405):	13.50
Common Player:	.05
Pack (15):	.75
Wax Box (36):	22.50

No.	Player	Price
1	Barry Bonds	1.50
2	Ken Griffey, Jr.	1.00
3	Will Clark	.05
4	Kirby Puckett	.75
5	Tony Gwynn	.75
6	Frank Thomas	.65
7	Tom Glavine	.35
8	Roberto Alomar	.25
9	Andre Dawson	.25
10	Ron Darling	.05
11	Bobby Bonilla	.05
12	Danny Tartabull	.05
13	Darren Daulton	.05
14	Roger Clemens	.85
15	Ozzie Smith	.75
16	Mark McGwire	1.25
17	Terry Pendleton	.05
18	Cal Ripken, Jr.	1.50
19	Fred McGriff	.05
20	Cecil Fielder	.05
21	Darryl Strawberry	.05
22	Robin Yount	.65
23	Barry Larkin	.05
24	Don Mattingly	.85
25	Craig Biggio	.05
26	Sandy Alomar Jr.	.05
27	Larry Walker	.05
28	Junior Felix	.05
29	Eddie Murray	.65
30	Robin Ventura	.05
31	Greg Maddux	.75
32	Dave Winfield	.65
33	John Kruk	.05
34	Wally Joyner	.05
35	Andy Van Slyke	.05
36	Chuck Knoblauch	.05
37	Tom Pagnozzi	.05
38	Dennis Eckersley	.60
39	Dave Justice	.05
40	Juan Gonzalez	.35
41	Gary Sheffield	.40
42	Paul Molitor	.65
43	Delino DeShields	.05
44	Travis Fryman	.05
45	Hal Morris	.05
46	Gregg Olson	.05
47	Ken Caminiti	.05
48	Wade Boggs	.75
49	Orel Hershiser	.05
50	Albert Belle	.05
51	Bill Swift	.05
52	Mark Langston	.05
53	Joe Girardi	.05
54	Keith Miller	.05
55	Gary Carter	.65
56	Brady Anderson	.05
57	Dwight Gooden	.05
58	Julio Franco	.05
59	Len Dykstra	.05
60	Mickey Tettleton	.05
61	Randy Tomlin	.05
62	B.J. Surhoff	.05
63	Todd Zeile	.05
64	Roberto Kelly	.05
65	Rob Dibble	.05
66	Leo Gomez	.05
67	Doug Jones	.05
68	Ellis Burks	.05
69	Mike Scioscia	.05
70	Charles Nagy	.05
71	Cory Snyder	.05
72	Devon White	.05
73	Mark Grace	.05
74	Luis Polonia	.05
75	John Smiley	.05
76	Carlton Fisk	.65
77	Luis Sojo	.05
78	George Brett	.85
79	Mitch Williams	.05
80	Kent Hrbek	.05
81	Jay Bell	.05
82	Edgar Martinez	.05
83	Lee Smith	.05
84	Deion Sanders	.05
85	Bill Gullickson	.05
86	Paul O'Neill	.05
87	Kevin Seitzer	.05
88	Steve Finley	.05
89	Mel Hall	.05
90	Nolan Ryan	1.50
91	Eric Davis	.05
92	Mike Mussina	.35
93	Tony Fernandez	.05
94	Frank Viola	.05
95	Matt Williams	.05
96	Joe Carter	.05
97	Ryne Sandberg	.75
98	Jim Abbott	.05
99	Marquis Grissom	.05
100	George Bell	.05
101	Howard Johnson	.05
102	Kevin Appier	.05
103	Dale Murphy	.20
104	Shane Mack	.05
105	Jose Lind	.05
106	Rickey Henderson	.65
107	Bob Tewksbury	.05
108	Kevin Mitchell	.05
109	Steve Avery	.05
110	Candy Maldonado	.05
111	Bip Roberts	.05
112	Lou Whitaker	.05
113	Jeff Bagwell	.65
114	Dante Bichette	.05
115	Brett Butler	.05
116	Melido Perez	.05
117	Andy Benes	.05
118	Randy Johnson	.65
119	Willie McGee	.05
120	Jody Reed	.05
121	Shawon Dunston	.05
122	Carlos Baerga	.05
123	Bret Saberhagen	.05
124	John Olerud	.05
125	Ivan Calderon	.05
126	Bryan Harvey	.05
127	Terry Mulholland	.05
128	Ozzie Guillen	.05
129	Steve Buechele	.05
130	Kevin Tapani	.05
131	Felix Jose	.05
132	Terry Steinbach	.05
133	Ron Gant	.05
134	Harold Reynolds	.05
135	Chris Sabo	.05
136	Ivan Rodriguez	.60
137	Eric Anthony	.05
138	Mike Henneman	.05
139	Robby Thompson	.05
140	Scott Fletcher	.05
141	Bruce Hurst	.05
142	Kevin Maas	.05
143	Tom Candiotti	.05
144	Chris Hoiles	.05
145	Mike Morgan	.05
146	Mark Whiten	.05
147	Dennis Martinez	.05
148	Tony Pena	.05
149	Dave Magadan	.05
150	Mark Lewis	.05
151	Mariano Duncan	.05
152	Gregg Jefferies	.05
153	Doug Drabek	.05
154	Brian Harper	.05
155	Ray Lankford	.05
156	Carney Lansford	.05
157	Mike Sharperson	.05
158	Jack Morris	.05
159	Otis Nixon	.05
160	Steve Sax	.05
161	Mark Lemke	.05
162	Rafael Palmeiro	.60
163	Jose Rijo	.05
164	Omar Vizquel	.05
165	Sammy Sosa	.75
166	Milt Cuyler	.05
167	John Franco	.05
168	Darryl Hamilton	.05
169	Ken Hill	.05
170	Mike Devereaux	.05
171	Don Slaught	.05
172	Steve Farr	.05
173	Bernard Gilkey	.05
174	Mike Fetters	.05
175	Vince Coleman	.05
176	Kevin McReynolds	.05
177	John Smoltz	.05
178	Greg Gagne	.05
179	Greg Swindell	.05
180	Juan Guzman	.05
181	Kal Daniels	.05
182	Rick Sutcliffe	.05
183	Orlando Merced	.05
184	Bill Wegman	.05
185	Mark Gardner	.05
186	Rob Deer	.05
187	Dave Hollins	.05
188	Jack Clark	.05
189	Brian Hunter	.05
190	Tim Wallach	.05
191	Tim Belcher	.05
192	Walt Weiss	.05
193	Kurt Stillwell	.05
194	Charlie Hayes	.05
195	Willie Randolph	.05
196	Jack McDowell	.05
197	Jose Offerman	.05
198	Chuck Finley	.05
199	Darrin Jackson	.05
200	Kelly Gruber	.05
201	John Wetteland	.05
202	Jay Buhner	.05
203	Mike LaValliere	.05
204	Kevin Brown	.05
205	Luis Gonzalez	.05
206	Rick Aguilera	.05
207	Norm Charlton	.05
208	Mike Bordick	.05
209	Charlie Leibrandt	.05
210	Tom Brunansky	.05
211	Tom Henke	.05
212	Randy Milligan	.05
213	Ramon Martinez	.05
214	Mo Vaughn	.05
215	Randy Myers	.05
216	Greg Hibbard	.05
217	Wes Chamberlain	.05
218	Tony Phillips	.05
219	Pete Harnisch	.05
220	Mike Gallego	.05
221	Bud Black	.05
222	Greg Vaughn	.05
223	Milt Thompson	.05
224	Ben McDonald	.05
225	Billy Hatcher	.05
226	Paul Sorrento	.05
227	Mark Gubicza	.05
228	Mike Greenwell	.05
229	Curt Schilling	.35
230	Alan Trammell	.05
231	Zane Smith	.05
232	Bobby Thigpen	.05
233	Greg Olson	.05
234	Joe Orsulak	.05
235	Joe Oliver	.05
236	Tim Raines	.05
237	Juan Samuel	.05
238	Chili Davis	.05
239	Spike Owen	.05
240	Dave Stewart	.05
241	Jim Eisenreich	.05
242	Phil Plantier	.05
243	Sid Fernandez	.05
244	Dan Gladden	.05
245	Mickey Morandini	.05
246	Tino Martinez	.05
247	Kirt Manwaring	.05
248	Dean Palmer	.05
249	Tom Browning	.05
250	Brian McRae	.05
251	Scott Leius	.05
252	Bert Blyleven	.05
253	Scott Erickson	.05
254	Bob Welch	.05
255	Pat Kelly	.05
256	Felix Fermin	.05
257	Harold Baines	.05
258	Duane Ward	.05
259	Bill Spiers	.05
260	Jaime Navarro	.05
261	Scott Sanderson	.05
262	Gary Gaetti	.05
263	Bob Ojeda	.05
264	Jeff Montgomery	.05
265	Scott Bankhead	.05
266	Lance Johnson	.05
267	Rafael Belliard	.05
268	Kevin Reimer	.05
269	Benito Santiago	.05
270	Mike Moore	.05
271	Dave Fleming	.05
272	Moises Alou	.05
273	Pat Listach	.05
274	Reggie Sanders	.05
275	Kenny Lofton	.05
276	Donovan Osborne	.05
277	Rusty Meacham	.05
278	Eric Karros	.05
279	Andy Stankiewicz	.05
280	Brian Jordan	.05
281	Gary DiSarcina	.05
282	Mark Wohlers	.05
283	Dave Nilsson	.05
284	Anthony Young	.05
285	Jim Bullinger	.05
286	Derek Bell	.05
287	Brian Williams	.05
288	Julio Valera	.05
289	Dan Walters	.05
290	Chad Curtis	.05
291	Michael Tucker	.05
292	Bob Zupcic	.05
293	Todd Hundley	.05
294	Jeff Tackett	.05
295	Greg Colbrunn	.05
296	Cal Eldred	.05
297	Chris Roberts	.05

#	Player	NM/M
298	John Doherty	.05
299	Denny Neagle	.05
300	Arthur Rhodes	.05
301	Mark Clark	.05
302	Scott Cooper	.05
303	*Jamie Arnold*	.05
304	Jim Thome	.60
305	Frank Seminara	.05
306	Kurt Knudsen	.05
307	Tim Wakefield	.05
308	John Jaha	.05
309	Pat Hentgen	.05
310	B.J. Wallace	.05
311	Roberto Hernandez	.05
312	Hipolito Pichardo	.05
313	Eric Fox	.05
314	Willie Banks	.05
315	Sam Millitello	.05
316	Vince Horsman	.05
317	Carlos Hernandez	.05
318	Jeff Kent	.05
319	Mike Perez	.05
320	Scott Livingstone	.05
321	Jeff Conine	.05
322	James Austin	.05
323	John Vander Wal	.05
324	Pat Mahomes	.05
325	Pedro Astacio	.05
326	Bret Boone	.05
327	Matt Stairs	.05
328	Damion Easley	.05
329	Ben Rivera	.05
330	Reggie Jefferson	.05
331	Luis Mercedes	.05
332	Kyle Abbott	.05
333	Eddie Taubensee	.05
334	Tim McIntosh	.05
335	Phil Clark	.05
336	Wil Cordero	.05
337	Russ Springer	.05
338	Craig Colbert	.05
339	Tim Salmon	.05
340	Braulio Castillo	.05
341	Donald Harris	.05
342	Eric Young	.05
343	Bob Wickman	.05
344	John Valentin	.05
345	Dan Wilson	.05
346	Steve Hosey	.05
347	Mike Piazza	1.00
348	Willie Greene	.05
349	Tom Goodwin	.05
350	Eric Hillman	.05
351	*Steve Reed*	.05
352	*Dan Serafini*	.05
353	*Todd Steverson*	.05
354	Benji Grigsby	.05
355	*Shannon Stewart*	1.00
356	Sean Lowe	.05
357	Derek Wallace	.05
358	Rick Helling	.05
359	*Jason Kendall*	1.00
360	*Derek Jeter*	4.00
361	David Cone	.05
362	Jeff Reardon	.05
363	Bobby Witt	.05
364	Jose Canseco	.40
365	Jeff Russell	.05
366	Ruben Sierra	.05
367	Alan Mills	.05
368	Matt Nokes	.05
369	Pat Borders	.05
370	Pedro Munoz	.05
371	Danny Jackson	.05
372	Geronimo Pena	.05
373	Craig Lefferts	.05
374	Joe Grahe	.05
375	Roger McDowell	.05
376	Jimmy Key	.05
377	Steve Olin	.05
378	Glenn Davis	.05
379	Rene Gonzales	.05
380	Manuel Lee	.05
381	Ron Karkovice	.05
382	Sid Bream	.05
383	Gerald Williams	.05
384	Lenny Harris	.05
385	*J.T. Snow*	.75
386	Dave Stieb	.05
387	Kirk McCaskill	.05
388	Lance Parrish	.05
389	Craig Greback	.05
390	Rick Wilkins	.05
391	Manny Alexander	.05
392	Mike Schooler	.05
393	Bernie Williams	.05
394	Kevin Koslofski	.05
395	Willie Wilson	.05
396	Jeff Parrett	.05
397	Mike Harkey	.05
398	Frank Tanana	.05
399	Doug Henry	.05
400	Royce Clayton	.05
401	Eric Wedge	.05
402	Derrick May	.05
403	Carlos Garcia	.05
404	Henry Rodriguez	.05
405	Ryan Klesko	.05

Aces

		NM/M
Complete Set (24):		20.00
Common Player:		1.00
1	Roger Clemens	6.00
2	Tom Glavine	3.00
3	Jack McDowell	1.00
4	Greg Maddux	4.50
5	Jack Morris	1.00
6	Dennis Martinez	1.00
7	Kevin Brown	1.00
8	Dwight Gooden	1.00
9	Kevin Appier	1.00
10	Mike Morgan	1.00
11	Juan Guzman	1.00
12	Charles Nagy	1.00
13	John Smiley	1.00
14	Ken Hill	1.00
15	Bob Tewksbury	1.00
16	Doug Drabek	1.00
17	John Smoltz	1.00
18	Greg Swindell	1.00
19	Bruce Hurst	1.00
20	Mike Mussina	2.00
21	Cal Eldred	1.00
22	Melido Perez	1.00
23	Dave Fleming	1.00
24	Kevin Tapani	1.00

Rookie/Traded All-Star Rookies

		NM/M
Complete Set (10):		30.00
Common Player:		1.00
1	Jeff Conine	1.00
2	Brent Gates	1.00
3	Mike Lansing	1.00
4	Kevin Stocker	1.00
5	Mike Piazza	25.00
6	Jeffrey Hammonds	1.00
7	David Hulse	1.00
8	Tim Salmon	2.00
9	Rene Arocha	1.00
10	Greg McMichael	1.00

Rookies

		NM/M
Complete Set (21):		4.00
Common Player:		.50
1	Pat Listach	.50
2	Moises Alou	.50
3	Reggie Sanders	.50
4	Kenny Lofton	.50
5	Eric Karros	.50
6	Brian Williams	.50
7	Donovan Osborne	.50
8	Sam Militello	.50
9	Chad Curtis	.50
10	Bob Zupcic	.50
11	Tim Salmon	1.50
12	Jeff Conine	.50
13	Pedro Astacio	.50
14	Arthur Rhodes	.50
15	Cal Eldred	.50
16	Tim Wakefield	.50
17	Andy Stankiewicz	.50
18	Wil Cordero	.50
19	Todd Hundley	.50
20	Dave Fleming	.50
21	Bret Boone	1.00

Stars

		NM/M
Complete Set (24):		40.00
Common Player:		.60
1	Fred McGriff	.60
2	Ryne Sandberg	4.00
3	Ozzie Smith	4.00
4	Gary Sheffield	1.25
5	Darren Daulton	.60
6	Andy Van Slyke	.60
7	Barry Bonds	7.50
8	Tony Gwynn	4.00
9	Greg Maddux	4.00
10	Tom Glavine	1.00
11	John Franco	.60
12	Lee Smith	.60
13	Cecil Fielder	.60
14	Roberto Alomar	1.00
15	Cal Ripken, Jr.	7.50
16	Edgar Martinez	.60
17	Ivan Rodriguez	2.50
18	Kirby Puckett	4.00
19	Ken Griffey, Jr.	6.00
20	Joe Carter	.60
21	Roger Clemens	4.50
22	Dave Fleming	.60
(22)	Dave Fleming (blank-back sample card)	1.00
23	Paul Molitor	3.00
(23)	Paul Molitor (blank-back sample card)	2.75
24	Dennis Eckersley	2.50

Rookie/Traded

		NM/M
Complete Set (150):		11.00
Common Player:		.05
Pack (12):		1.25
Wax Box (24):		20.00
1	Rickey Henderson	.75
2	Rob Deer	.05
3	Tim Belcher	.05
4	Gary Sheffield	.35
5	Fred McGriff	.05
6	Mark Whiten	.05
7	Jeff Russell	.05
8	Harold Baines	.05
9	Dave Winfield	.75
10	Ellis Burks	.05
11	Andre Dawson	.25
12	Gregg Jefferies	.05
13	Jimmy Key	.05
14	Harold Reynolds	.05
15	Tom Henke	.05
16	Paul Molitor	.75
17	Wade Boggs	1.00
18	David Cone	.05
19	Tony Fernandez	.05
20	Roberto Kelly	.05
21	Paul O'Neill	.05
22	Jose Lind	.05
23	Barry Bonds	2.00
24	Dave Stewart	.05
25	Randy Myers	.05
26	Benito Santiago	.05
27	Tim Wallach	.05
28	Greg Gagne	.05
29	Kevin Mitchell	.05
30	Jim Abbott	.05
31	Lee Smith	.05
32	*Bobby Munoz*	.05
33	*Mo Sanford*	.05
34	John Roper	.05
35	*David Hulse*	.05
36	Pedro Martinez	.75
37	*Chuck Carr*	.05
38	*Armando Reynoso*	.10
39	Ryan Thompson	.05
40	*Carlos Garcia*	.05
41	Matt Whiteside	.05
42	Benji Gil	.05
43	*Rodney Bolton*	.05
44	J.T. Snow	.05
45	David McCarty	.05
46	*Paul Quantrill*	.05
47	Al Martin	.05
48	Lance Painter	.05
49	*Lou Frazier*	.05
50	Eduardo Perez	.05
51	Kevin Young	.05
52	Mike Trombley	.05
53	*Sterling Hitchcock*	.10
54	*Tim Bogar*	.05
55	*Hilly Hathaway*	.05
56	*Wayne Kirby*	.05
57	*Craig Paquette*	.05
58	Bret Boone	.05
59	*Greg McMichael*	.05
60	*Mike Lansing*	.35
61	Brent Gates	.05
62	Rene Arocha	.05
63	Ricky Gutierrez	.05
64	*Kevin Rogers*	.05
65	*Ken Ryan*	.05
66	Phil Hiatt	.05
67	*Pat Meares*	.05
68	Troy Neel	.05
69	Steve Cooke	.05
70	*Sherman Obando*	.05
71	*Blas Minor*	.05
72	*Angel Miranda*	.05
73	*Tom Kramer*	.05
74	*Chip Hale*	.05
75	*Brad Pennington*	.05
76	*Graeme Lloyd*	.05
77	*Darrell Whitmore*	.05
78	David Nied	.05
79	Todd Van Poppel	.05
80	*Chris Gomez*	.10
81	Jason Bere	.05
82	Jeffrey Hammonds	.05
83	*Brad Ausmus*	.10
84	Kevin Stocker	.05
85	Jeromy Burnitz	.05
86	Aaron Sele	.05
87	*Roberto Mejia*	.05
88	*Kirk Rueter*	.10
89	*Kevin Roberson*	.05
90	*Allen Watson*	.05
91	Charlie Leibrandt	.05
92	Eric Davis	.05
93	Jody Reed	.05
94	Danny Jackson	.05
95	Gary Gaetti	.05
96	Norm Charlton	.05
97	Doug Drabek	.05
98	Scott Fletcher	.05
99	Greg Swindell	.05
100	John Smiley	.05
101	Kevin Reimer	.05
102	Andres Galarraga	.05
103	Greg Hibbard	.05
104	Chris Hammond	.05
105	Darnell Coles	.05
106	Mike Felder	.05
107	Jose Guzman	.05
108	Chris Bosio	.05
109	Spike Owen	.05
110	Felix Jose	.05
111	Cory Snyder	.05
112	Craig Lefferts	.05
113	David Wells	.05
114	Pete Incaviglia	.05
115	Mike Pagliarulo	.05
116	Dave Magadan	.05
117	Charlie Hough	.05

No.	Player	NM/M
118	Ivan Calderon	.05
119	Manuel Lee	.05
120	Bob Patterson	.05
121	Bob Ojeda	.05
122	Scott Bankhead	.05
123	Greg Maddux	1.00
124	Chili Davis	.05
125	Milt Thompson	.05
126	Dave Martinez	.05
127	Frank Tanana	.05
128	Phil Plantier	.05
129	Juan Samuel	.05
130	Eric Young	.05
131	Joe Orsulak	.05
132	Derek Bell	.05
133	Darrin Jackson	.05
134	Tom Brunansky	.05
135	Jeff Reardon	.05
136	*Kevin Higgins*	.05
137	*Joel Johnston*	.05
138	*Rick Trlicek*	.05
139	*Richie Lewis*	.05
140	*Jeff Gardner*	.05
141	*Jack Voigt*	.05
142	*Rod Correia*	.05
143	*Billy Brewer*	.05
144	*Terry Jorgensen*	.05
145	*Rich Amaral*	.05
146	*Sean Berry*	.05
147	*Dan Peltier*	.05
148	*Paul Wagner*	.05
149	*Damon Buford*	.05
150	Wil Cordero	.05

Rookie/Traded Inserts

		NM/M
Complete Set (3):		60.00
Common Player:		6.00
1NR	Nolan Ryan	40.00
1ROY	Tim Salmon	6.00
2ROY	Mike Piazza	20.00

Stat Leaders

		NM/M
Complete Set (90):		8.00
Common Player:		.05
1	Edgar Martinez	.05
2	Kirby Puckett	.30
3	Frank Thomas	.25
4	Gary Sheffield	.15
5	Andy Van Slyke	.05
6	John Kruk	.05
7	Kirby Puckett	.30
8	Carlos Baerga	.05
9	Paul Molitor	.25
10	Andy Van Slyke, Terry Pendleton	.05
11	Ryne Sandberg	.30
12	Mark Grace	.05
13	Frank Thomas	.25
14	Don Mattingly	.35
15	Ken Griffey, Jr.	.45
16	Andy Van Slyke	.05
17	Mariano Duncan, Jerald Clark, Ray Lankford	.05
18	Marquis Grissom, Terry Pendleton	.05
19	Lance Johnson	.05
20	Mike Devereaux	.05
21	Brady Anderson	.05
22	Deion Sanders	.05
23	Steve Finley	.05
24	Andy Van Slyke	.05
25	Juan Gonzalez	.15
26	Mark McGwire	.50
27	Cecil Fielder	.05
28	Fred McGriff	.05
29	Barry Bonds	.60
30	Gary Sheffield	.15
31	Cecil Fielder	.05
32	Joe Carter	.05
33	Frank Thomas	.25
34	Darren Daulton	.05
35	Terry Pendleton	.05
36	Fred McGriff	.05
37	Tony Phillips	.05
38	Frank Thomas	.25
39	Roberto Alomar	.15
40	Barry Bonds	.60
41	Dave Hollins	.05
42	Andy Van Slyke	.05
43	Mark McGwire	.50
44	Edgar Martinez	.05
45	Frank Thomas	.25
46	Barry Bonds	.60
47	Gary Sheffield	.15
48	Fred McGriff	.05
49	Frank Thomas	.25
50	Danny Tartabull	.05
51	Roberto Alomar	.15
52	Barry Bonds	.60
53	John Kruk	.05
54	Brett Butler	.05
55	Kenny Lofton	.05
56	Pat Listach	.05
57	Brady Anderson	.05
58	Marquis Grissom	.05
59	Delino DeShields	.05
60	Steve Finley, Bip Roberts	.05
61	Jack McDowell	.05
62	Kevin Brown	.05
63	Melido Perez	.05
64	Terry Mulholland	.05
65	Curt Schilling	.20
66	John Smoltz, Doug Drabek, Greg Maddux	.05
67	Dennis Eckersley	.20
68	Rick Aguilera	.05
69	Jeff Montgomery	.05
70	Lee Smith	.05
71	Randy Myers	.05
72	John Wetteland	.05
73	Randy Johnson	.25
74	Melido Perez	.05
75	Roger Clemens	.35
76	John Smoltz	.05
77	David Cone	.05
78	Greg Maddux	.30
79	Roger Clemens	.35
80	Kevin Appier	.05
81	Mike Mussina	.15
82	Bill Swift	.05
83	Bob Tewksbury	.05
84	Greg Maddux	.30
85	Kevin Brown	.05
86	Jack McDowell	.05
87	Roger Clemens	.35
88	Tom Glavine	.10
89	Ken Hill, Bob Tewksbury	.05
90	Dennis Martinez, Mike Morgan	.05

Values quoted in this guide reflect the retail price of a card, the price a collector can expect to pay when buying a card from a dealer.

Triple Crown

		NM/M
Complete Set (3):		35.00
Common Player:		10.00
1	Mickey Mantle	22.50
2	Frank Robinson	10.00
3	Carl Yastrzemski	12.50

1994 SELECT

		NM/M
Complete Set (420):		12.50
Common Player:		.05
Pack (12):		1.25
Wax Box (24):		16.00
1	Ken Griffey, Jr.	1.50
2	Greg Maddux	1.00
3	Paul Molitor	.75
4	Mike Piazza	1.50
5	Jay Bell	.05
6	Frank Thomas	.75
7	Barry Larkin	.05
8	Paul O'Neill	.05
9	Darren Daulton	.05
10	Mike Greenwell	.05
11	Chuck Carr	.05
12	Joe Carter	.05
13	Lance Johnson	.05
14	Jeff Blauser	.05
15	Chris Hoiles	.05
16	Rick Wilkins	.05
17	Kirby Puckett	1.00
18	Larry Walker	.05
19	Randy Johnson	.75
20	Bernard Gilkey	.05
21	Devon White	.05
22	Randy Myers	.05
23	Don Mattingly	1.25
24	John Kruk	.05
25	Ozzie Guillen	.05
26	Jeff Conine	.05
27	Mike Macfarlane	.05
28	Dave Hollins	.05
29	Chuck Knoblauch	.05
30	Ozzie Smith	1.00
31	Harold Baines	.05
32	Ryne Sandberg	1.00
33	Ron Karkovice	.05
34	Terry Pendleton	.05
35	Wally Joyner	.05
36	Mike Mussina	.35
37	Felix Jose	.05
38	Derrick May	.05
39	Scott Cooper	.05
40	Jose Rijo	.05
41	Robin Ventura	.05
42	Charlie Hayes	.05
43	Jimmy Key	.05
44	Eric Karros	.05
45	Ruben Sierra	.05
46	Ryan Thompson	.05
47	Brian McRae	.05
48	Pat Hentgen	.05
49	John Valentin	.05
50	Al Martin	.05
51	Jose Lind	.05
52	Kevin Stocker	.05
53	Mike Gallego	.05
54	Dwight Gooden	.05
55	Brady Anderson	.05
56	Jeff King	.05
57	Mark McGwire	1.75
58	Sammy Sosa	1.00
59	Ryan Bowen	.05
60	Mark Lemke	.05
61	Roger Clemens	1.25
62	Brian Jordan	.05
63	Andres Galarraga	.05
64	Kevin Appier	.05
65	Don Slaught	.05
66	Mike Blowers	.05
67	Wes Chamberlain	.05
68	Troy Neel	.05
69	John Wetteland	.05
70	Joe Girardi	.05
71	Reggie Sanders	.05
72	Edgar Martinez	.05
73	Todd Hundley	.05
74	Pat Borders	.05
75	Roberto Mejia	.05
76	David Cone	.05
77	Tony Gwynn	1.00
78	Jim Abbott	.05
79	Jay Buhner	.05
80	Mark McLemore	.05
81	Wil Cordero	.05
82	Pedro Astacio	.05
83	Bob Tewksbury	.05
84	Dave Winfield	.75
85	Jeff Kent	.05
86	Todd Van Poppel	.05
87	Steve Avery	.05
88	Mike Lansing	.05
89	Len Dykstra	.05
90	Jose Guzman	.05
91	Brian Hunter	.05
92	Tim Raines	.05
93	Andre Dawson	.25
94	Joe Orsulak	.05
95	Ricky Jordan	.05
96	Billy Hatcher	.05
97	Jack McDowell	.05
98	Tom Pagnozzi	.05
99	Darryl Strawberry	.05
100	Mike Stanley	.05
101	Bret Saberhagen	.05
102	Willie Greene	.05
103	Bryan Harvey	.05
104	Tim Bogar	.05
105	Jack Voight	.05
106	Brad Ausmus	.05
107	Ramon Martinez	.05
108	Mike Perez	.05
109	Jeff Montgomery	.05
110	Danny Darwin	.05
111	Wilson Alvarez	.05
112	Kevin Mitchell	.05
113	David Nied	.05
114	Rich Amaral	.05
115	Stan Javier	.05
116	Mo Vaughn	.05
117	Ben McDonald	.05
118	Tom Gordon	.05
119	Carlos Garcia	.05
120	Phil Plantier	.05
121	Mike Morgan	.05
122	Pat Meares	.05
123	Kevin Young	.05
124	Jeff Fassero	.05
125	Gene Harris	.05
126	Bob Welch	.05
127	Walt Weiss	.05
128	Bobby Witt	.05
129	Andy Van Slyke	.05
130	Steve Cooke	.05
131	Mike Devereaux	.05
132	Joey Cora	.05
133	Bret Barberie	.05
134	Orel Hershiser	.05
135	Ed Sprague	.05
136	Shawon Dunston	.05
137	Alex Arias	.05
138	Archi Cianfrocco	.05
139	Tim Wallach	.05
140	Bernie Williams	.05
141	Karl Rhodes	.05
142	Pat Kelly	.05
143	Dave Magadan	.05
144	Kevin Tapani	.05
145	Eric Young	.05
146	Derek Bell	.05
147	Dante Bichette	.05
148	Geronimo Pena	.05
149	Joe Oliver	.05
150	Orestes Destrade	.05
151	Tim Naehring	.05
152	Ray Lankford	.05

153 Phil Clark .05
154 David McCarty .05
155 Tommy Greene .05
156 Wade Boggs 1.00
157 Kevin Gross .05
158 Hal Morris .05
159 Moises Alou .05
160 Rick Aguilera .05
161 Curt Schilling .35
162 Chip Hale .05
163 Tino Martinez .05
164 Mark Whiten .05
165 Dave Stewart .05
166 Steve Buechele .05
167 Bobby Jones .05
168 Darrin Fletcher .05
169 John Smiley .05
170 Cory Snyder .05
171 Scott Erickson .05
172 Kirk Rueter .05
173 Dave Fleming .05
174 John Smoltz .05
175 Ricky Gutierrez .05
176 Mike Bordick .05
177 *Chan Ho Park* 1.00
178 Alex Gonzalez .05
179 Steve Karsay .05
180 Jeffrey Hammonds .05
181 Manny Ramirez .75
182 Salomon Torres .05
183 Raul Mondesi .05
184 James Mouton .05
185 Cliff Floyd .05
186 Danny Bautista .05
187 *Kurt Abbott* .05
188 Javier Lopez .05
189 John Patterson .05
190 Greg Blosser .05
191 Bob Hamelin .05
192 Tony Eusebio .05
193 Carlos Delgado .50
194 Chris Gomez .05
195 Kelly Stinnett .05
196 Shane Reynolds .05
197 Ryan Klesko .05
198 Jim Edmonds .05
199 James Hurst .05
200 Dave Staton .05
201 Rondell White .05
202 Keith Mitchell .05
203 Darren Oliver .05
204 Mike Matheny .05
205 Chris Turner .05
206 Matt Mieske .05
207 N.L. team checklist .05
208 N.L. team checklist .05
209 A.L. team checklist .05
210 A.L. team checklist .05
211 Barry Bonds 2.00
212 Juan Gonzalez .40
213 Jim Eisenreich .05
214 Ivan Rodriguez .65
215 Tony Phillips .05
216 John Jaha .05
217 Lee Smith .05
218 Bip Roberts .05
219 Dave Hansen .05
220 Pat Listach .05
221 Willie McGee .05
222 Damion Easley .05
223 Dean Palmer .05
224 Mike Moore .05
225 Brian Harper .05
226 Gary DiSarcina .05
227 Delino DeShields .05
228 Otis Nixon .05
229 Roberto Alomar .30
230 Mark Grace .05
231 Kenny Lofton .05
232 Gregg Jefferies .05
233 Cecil Fielder .05
234 Jeff Bagwell .75
235 Albert Belle .05
236 Dave Justice .05
237 Tom Henke .05
238 Bobby Bonilla .05
239 John Olerud .05
240 Robby Thompson .05
241 Dave Valle .05
242 Marquis Grissom .05
243 Greg Swindell .05
244 Todd Zeile .05
245 Dennis Eckersley .65
246 Jose Offerman .05
247 Greg McMichael .05
248 Tim Belcher .05
249 Cal Ripken, Jr. 2.00
250 Tom Glavine .05
251 Luis Polonia .05
252 Bill Swift .05
253 Juan Guzman .05
254 Rickey Henderson .75
255 Terry Mulholland .05
256 Gary Sheffield .40
257 Terry Steinbach .05
258 Brett Butler .05
259 Jason Bere .05
260 Doug Strange .05
261 Kent Hrbek .05
262 Graeme Lloyd .05
263 Lou Frazier .05
264 Charles Nagy .05
265 Bret Boone .05
266 Kirk Gibson .05
267 Kevin Brown .05
269 Matt Williams .05
270 Greg Gagne .05
271 Mariano Duncan .05
272 Jeff Russell .05
273 Eric Davis .05
274 Shane Mack .05
275 Jose Vizcaino .05
276 Jose Canseco .45
277 Roberto Hernandez .05
278 Royce Clayton .05
279 Carlos Baerga .05
280 Pete Incaviglia .05
281 Brent Gates .05
282 Jeromy Burnitz .05
283 Chili Davis .05
284 Pete Harnisch .05
285 Alan Trammell .05
286 Eric Anthony .05
287 Ellis Burks .05
288 Julio Franco .05
289 Jack Morris .05
290 Erik Hanson .05
291 Chuck Finley .05
292 Reggie Jefferson .05
293 Kevin McReynolds .05
294 Greg Hibbard .05
295 Travis Fryman .05
296 Craig Biggio .05
297 Kenny Rogers .05
298 Dave Henderson .05
299 Jim Thome .50
300 Rene Arocha .05
301 Pedro Munoz .05
302 David Hulse .05
303 Greg Vaughn .05
304 Darren Lewis .05
305 Deion Sanders .05
306 Danny Tartabull .05
307 Darryl Hamilton .05
308 Andujar Cedeno .05
309 Tim Salmon .05
310 Tony Fernandez .05
311 Alex Fernandez .05
312 Roberto Kelly .05
313 Harold Reynolds .05
314 Chris Sabo .05
315 Howard Johnson .05
316 Mark Portugal .05
317 Rafael Palmeiro .65
318 Pete Smith .05
319 Will Clark .05
320 Henry Rodriguez .05
321 Omar Vizquel .05
322 David Segui .05
323 Lou Whitaker .05
324 Felix Fermin .05
325 Spike Owen .05
326 Darryl Kile .05
327 Chad Kreuter .05
328 Rod Beck .05
329 Eddie Murray .75
330 B.J. Surhoff .05
331 Mickey Tettleton .05
332 Pedro Martinez .75
333 Roger Pavlik .05
334 Eddie Taubensee .05
335 John Doherty .05
336 Jody Reed .05
337 Aaron Sele .05
338 Leo Gomez .05
339 Dave Nilsson .05
340 Rob Dibble .05
341 John Burkett .05
342 Wayne Kirby .05
343 Dan Wilson .05
344 Armando Reynoso .05
345 Chad Curtis .05
346 Dennis Martinez .05
347 Cal Eldred .05
348 Luis Gonzalez .05
349 Doug Drabek .05
350 Jim Leyritz .05
351 Mark Langston .05
352 Darrin Jackson .05
353 Sid Fernandez .05
354 Benito Santiago .05
355 Kevin Seitzer .05
356 Bo Jackson .10
357 David Wells .05
358 Paul Sorrento .05
359 Ken Caminiti .05
360 Eduardo Perez .05
361 Orlando Merced .05
362 Steve Finley .05
363 Andy Benes .05
364 Manuel Lee .05
365 Todd Benzinger .05
366 Sandy Alomar Jr. .05
367 Rex Hudler .05
368 Mike Henneman .05
369 Vince Coleman .05
370 Kirt Manwaring .05
371 Ken Hill .05
372 Glenallen Hill .05
373 Sean Berry .05
374 Geronimo Berroa .05
375 Duane Ward .05
376 Allen Watson .05
377 Marc Newfield .05
378 Dan Miceli .05
379 Denny Hocking .05
380 Mark Kiefer .05
381 Tony Tarasco .05
382 Tony Longmire .05
383 *Brian Anderson* .05
384 Fernando Vina .05
385 Hector Carrasco .05
386 Mike Kelly .05
387 Greg Colbrunn .05
388 Roger Salkeld .05
389 Steve Trachsel .05
390 Rich Becker .05
391 *Billy Taylor* .05
392 Rich Rowland .05
393 Carl Everett .05
394 Johnny Ruffin .05
395 *Keith Lockhart* .05
396 J.R. Phillips .05
397 Sterling Hitchcock .05
398 Jorge Fabregas .05
399 Jeff Granger .05
400 *Eddie Zambrano* .05
401 *Rikkert Faneyte* .05
402 Gerald Williams .05
403 Joey Hamilton .05
404 *Joe Hall* .05
405 *John Hudek* .05
406 Roberto Petagine .05
407 Charles Johnson .05
408 Mark Smith .05
409 Jeff Juden .05
410 *Carlos Pulido* .05
411 Paul Shuey .05
412 Rob Butler .05
413 Mark Acre .05
414 Greg Pirkl .05
415 Melvin Nieves .05
416 *Tim Hyers* .05
417 N.L. checklist .05
418 N.L. checklist .05
419 A.L. checklist .05
420 A.L. checklist .05

Crown Contenders

		NM/M
Complete Set (10):		12.50
Common Player:		.50
1	Len Dykstra	.50
2	Greg Maddux	1.75
3	Roger Clemens	2.00
4	Randy Johnson	1.50
5	Frank Thomas	1.50
6	Barry Bonds	3.00
7	Juan Gonzalez	1.00
8	John Olerud	.50
9	Mike Piazza	2.50
10	Ken Griffey, Jr.	2.50

MVP

		NM/M
MVP1	Paul Molitor	5.00

Rookie of the Year

		NM/M
RY1	Carlos Delgado	7.50

Rookie Surge

		NM/M
Complete Set (18):		10.00
Common Player:		.75
1	Cliff Floyd	.75
2	Bob Hamelin	.75
3	Ryan Klesko	.75
4	Carlos Delgado	3.00
5	Jeffrey Hammonds	.75
6	Rondell White	.75
7	Salomon Torres	.75
8	Steve Karsay	.75
9	Javier Lopez	.75
10	Manny Ramirez	3.00
11	Tony Tarasco	.75
12	Kurt Abbott	.75
13	Chan Ho Park	.75
14	Rich Becker	.75
15	James Mouton	.75
16	Alex Gonzalez	.75
17	Raul Mondesi	.75
18	Steve Trachsel	.75

Salute

		NM/M
Complete Set (2):		15.00
1	Cal Ripken, Jr.	12.50
2	Dave Winfield	5.00

Skills

		NM/M
Complete Set (10):		15.00
Common Player:		.75
1	Randy Johnson	3.00
2	Barry Larkin	.75
3	Len Dykstra	.75
4	Kenny Lofton	.75
5	Juan Gonzalez	1.50
6	Barry Bonds	6.00
7	Marquis Grissom	.75
8	Ivan Rodriguez	2.50
9	Larry Walker	.75
10	Travis Fryman	.75

1995 SELECT

		NM/M
Complete Set (251):		9.00
Common Player:		.05
Artist's Proofs:		10X
Pack (12):		1.50
Wax Box (24):		17.50
1	Cal Ripken Jr.	1.50
2	Robin Ventura	.05
3	Al Martin	.05
4	Jeff Frye	.05
5	Darryl Strawberry	.05
6	Chan Ho Park	.05
7	Steve Avery	.05
8	Bret Boone	.05
9	Danny Tartabull	.05
10	Dante Bichette	.05
11	Rondell White	.05
12	Dave McCarty	.05
13	Bernard Gilkey	.05
14	Mark McGwire	1.25

15 Ruben Sierra .05
16 Wade Boggs .75
17 Mike Piazza 1.00
18 Jeffrey Hammonds .05
19 Mike Mussina .35
20 Darryl Kile .05
21 Greg Maddux .75
22 Frank Thomas .65
23 Kevin Appier .05
24 Jay Bell .05
25 Kirk Gibson .05
26 Pat Hentgen .05
27 Joey Hamilton .05
28 Bernie Williams .05
29 Aaron Sele .05
30 Delino DeShields .05
31 Danny Bautista .05
32 Jim Thome .45
33 Rikkert Faneyte .05
34 Roberto Alomar .20
35 Paul Molitor .65
36 Allen Watson .05
37 Jeff Bagwell .65
38 Jay Buhner .05
39 Marquis Grissom .05
40 Jim Edmonds .05
41 Ryan Klesko .05
42 Fred McGriff .05
43 Tony Tarasco .05
44 Darren Daulton .05
45 Marc Newfield .05
46 Barry Bonds 1.50
47 Bobby Bonilla .05
48 Greg Pirkl .05
49 Steve Karsay .05
50 Bob Hamelin .05
51 Javier Lopez .05
52 Barry Larkin .05
53 Kevin Young .05
54 Sterling Hitchcock .05
55 Tom Glavine .05
56 Carlos Delgado .40
57 Darren Oliver .05
58 Cliff Floyd .05
59 Tim Salmon .05
60 Albert Belle .05
61 Salomon Torres .05
62 Gary Sheffield .35
63 Ivan Rodriguez .50
64 Charles Nagy .05
65 Eduardo Perez .05
66 Terry Steinbach .05
67 Dave Justice .05
68 Jason Bere .05
69 Dave Nilsson .05
70 Brian Anderson .05
71 Billy Ashley .05
72 Roger Clemens .85
73 Jimmy Key .05
74 Wally Joyner .05
75 Andy Benes .05
76 Ray Lankford .05
77 Jeff Kent .05
78 Moises Alou .05
79 Kirby Puckett .75
80 Joe Carter .05
81 Manny Ramirez .65
82 J.R. Phillips .05
83 Matt Mieske .05
84 John Olerud .05
85 Andres Galarraga .05
86 Juan Gonzalez .35
87 Pedro Martinez .65
88 Dean Palmer .05
89 Ken Griffey Jr. 1.00
90 Brian Jordan .05
91 Hal Morris .05
92 Lenny Dykstra .05
93 Wil Cordero .05
94 Tony Gwynn .75
95 Alex Gonzalez .05
96 Cecil Fielder .05
97 Mo Vaughn .05
98 John Valentin .05
99 Will Clark .05
100 Geronimo Pena .05
101 Don Mattingly .85
102 Charles Johnson .05
103 Raul Mondesi .05
104 Reggie Sanders .05
105 Royce Clayton .05
106 Reggie Jefferson .05
107 Craig Biggio .05
108 Jack McDowell .05
109 James Mouton .05
110 Mike Greenwell .05
111 David Cone .05
112 Matt Williams .05
113 Garret Anderson .05
114 Carlos Garcia .05
115 Alex Fernandez .05
116 Deion Sanders .05
117 Chili Davis .05
118 Mike Kelly .05
119 Jeff Conine .05
120 Kenny Lofton .05
121 Rafael Palmeiro .50
122 Chuck Knoblauch .05
123 Ozzie Smith .75
124 Carlos Baerga .05
125 Brett Butler .05
126 Sammy Sosa .75
127 Ellis Burks .05
128 Bret Saberhagen .05
129 Doug Drabek .05
130 Dennis Martinez .05
131 Paul O'Neill .05
132 Travis Fryman .05
133 Brent Gates .05
134 Rickey Henderson .65
135 Randy Johnson .65
136 Mark Langston .05
137 Greg Colbrunn .05
138 Jose Rijo .05
139 Bryan Harvey .05
140 Dennis Eckersley .50
141 Ron Gant .05
142 Carl Everett .05
143 Jeff Granger .05
144 Ben McDonald .05
145 Kurt Abbott .05
146 Jim Abbott .05
147 Jason Jacome .05
148 Rico Brogna .05
149 Cal Eldred .05
150 Rich Becker .05
151 Pete Harnisch .05
152 Roberto Petagine .05
153 Jacob Brumfield .05
154 Todd Hundley .05
155 Roger Cedeno .05
156 Harold Baines .05
157 Steve Dunn .05
158 Tim Belk .05
159 Marty Cardova .05
160 Russ Davis .05
161 Jose Malave .05
162 Brian Hunter .05
163 Andy Pettitte .20
164 Brooks Kieschnick .05
165 Midre Cummings .05
166 Frank Rodriguez .05
167 Chad Mottola .05
168 Brian Barber .05
169 Tim Unroe .05
170 Shane Andrews .05
171 Kevin Flora .05
172 Ray Durham .05
173 Chipper Jones .75
174 Butch Huskey .05
175 Ray McDavid .05
176 Jeff Cirillo .05
177 Terry Pendleton .05
178 Scott Ruffcorn .05
179 Ray Holbert .05
180 Joe Randa .05
181 Jose Oliva .05
182 Andy Van Slyke .05
183 Albie Lopez .05
184 Chad Curtis .05
185 Ozzie Guillen .05
186 Chad Ogea .05
187 Dan Wilson .05
188 Tony Fernandez .05
189 John Smoltz .05
190 Willie Greene .05
191 Darren Lewis .05
192 Orlando Miller .05
193 Kurt Miller .05
194 Andrew Lorraine .05
195 Ernie Young .05
196 Jimmy Haynes .05
197 *Raul Casanova* .05
198 Joe Vitiello .05
199 Brad Woodall .05
200 Juan Acevedo .05
201 Michael Tucker .05
202 Shawn Green .35
203 Alex Rodriguez 1.25
204 Julian Tavarez .05
205 Jose Lima .05
206 Wilson Alvarez .05
207 Rich Aude .05
208 Armando Benitez .05
209 Dwayne Hosey .05
210 Gabe White .05
211 Joey Eischen .05
212 Bill Pulsipher .05
213 Robby Thompson .05
214 Toby Borland .05
215 Rusty Greer .05
216 Fausto Cruz .05
217 Luis Ortiz .05
218 Duane Singleton .05
219 Troy Percival .05
220 Gregg Jefferies .05
221 Mark Grace .05
222 Mickey Tettleton .05
223 Phil Plantier .05
224 Larry Walker .05
225 Ken Caminiti .05
226 Dave Winfield .65
227 Brady Anderson .05
228 Kevin Brown .05
229 Andujar Cedeno .05
230 Roberto Kelly .05
231 Jose Canseco .35
231 Scott Ruffcorn .05
232 Billy Ashley .05
234 J.R. Phillips .05
235 Chipper Jones .40
236 Charles Johnson .05
237 Midre Cummings .05
238 Brian Hunter .05
239 Garret Anderson .05
240 Shawn Green .10
241 Alex Rodriguez .65
242 Frank Thomas Checklist #1 .35
243 Ken Griffey Jr. Checklist #2 .50
244 Albert Belle Checklist #3 .05
245 Cal Ripken Jr. Checklist #4 .65
246 Barry Bonds Checklist #5 .75
247 Raul Mondesi Checklist #6 .05
248 Mike Piazza Checklist #7 .65
249 Jeff Bagwell Checklist #8 .30
250 Jeff Bagwell, Frank Thomas, Ken Griffey Jr., Mike Piazza Checklist #9 .25
251 Hideo Nomo .35

Can't Miss

		NM/M
Complete Set (12):		10.00
Common Player:		.35
1	Cliff Floyd	.35
2	Ryan Klesko	.35
3	Charles Johnson	.35
4	Raul Mondesi	.35
5	Manny Ramirez	2.00
6	Billy Ashley	.35
7	Alex Gonzalez	.35
8	Carlos Delgado	.75
9	Garret Anderson	.35
10	Alex Rodriguez	5.00
11	Chipper Jones	3.00
12	Shawn Green	.75

Big Sticks

		NM/M
Complete Set (12):		40.00
Common Player:		1.50
1	Frank Thomas	4.00
2	Ken Griffey Jr.	7.50
3	Cal Ripken Jr.	10.00
4	Mike Piazza	7.50
5	Don Mattingly	6.00
6	Will Clark	1.50
7	Tony Gwynn	5.00
8	Jeff Bagwell	4.00

9	Barry Bonds	10.00
10	Paul Molitor	4.00
11	Matt Williams	1.50
12	Albert Belle	1.50

Sure Shots

		NM/M
Complete Set (10):		10.00
Common Player:		1.00
1	Ben Grieve	1.00
2	Kevin Witt	1.00
3	Mark Farris	1.00
4	Paul Konerko	3.00
5	Dustin Hermanson	1.00
6	Ramon Castro	1.00
7	McKay Christensen	1.00
8	Brian Buchanan	1.00
9	Paul Wilson	1.00
10	Terrence Long	1.00

Artist's Proofs

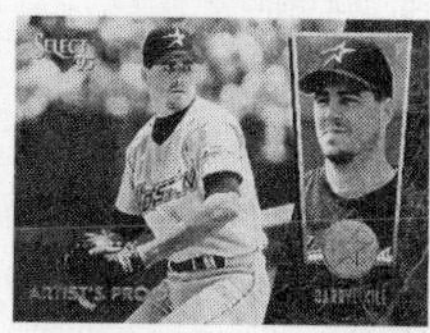

	NM/M
Complete Set (250):	100.00
Common Player:	1.00
AP Stars:	10X

(See 1995 Select for checklist and base card values.)

1995 SELECT CERTIFIED

		NM/M
Complete Set (135):		10.00
Common Player:		.05
Mirror Gold Stars:		5X
Pack (6):		2.00
Wax Box (20):		25.00
1	Barry Bonds	2.50
2	Reggie Sanders	.05
3	Terry Steinbach	.05
4	Eduardo Perez	.05
5	Frank Thomas	.75
6	Wil Cordero	.05
7	John Olerud	.05
8	Deion Sanders	.05
9	Mike Mussina	.40
10	Mo Vaughn	.05
11	Will Clark	.05
12	Chili Davis	.05
13	Jimmy Key	.05
14	Eddie Murray	.75
15	Bernard Gilkey	.05
16	David Cone	.05
17	Tim Salmon	.05
18	(Not issued, see #2131)	
19	Steve Ontiveros	.05
20	Andres Galarraga	.05
21	Don Mattingly	1.25
22	Kevin Appier	.05
23	Paul Molitor	.75
24	Edgar Martinez	.05
25	Andy Benes	.05
26	Rafael Palmeiro	.65
27	Barry Larkin	.05
28	Gary Sheffield	.25
29	Wally Joyner	.05
30	Wade Boggs	1.00
31	Rico Brogna	.05
32	Eddie Murray (Murray Tribute)	.40
33	Kirby Puckett	1.00
34	Bobby Bonilla	.05
35	Hal Morris	.05
36	Moises Alou	.05
37	Javier Lopez	.05
38	Chuck Knoblauch	.05
39	Mike Piazza	1.50
40	Travis Fryman	.05
41	Rickey Henderson	.75
42	Jim Thome	.60
43	Carlos Baerga	.05
44	Dean Palmer	.05
45	Kirk Gibson	.05
46	Bret Saberhagen	.05
47	Cecil Fielder	.05
48	Manny Ramirez	.75
49	Derek Bell	.05
50	Mark McGwire	2.00
51	Jim Edmonds	.05
52	Robin Ventura	.05
53	Ryan Klesko	.05
54	Jeff Bagwell	.75
55	Ozzie Smith	1.00
56	Albert Belle	.05
57	Darren Daulton	.05
58	Jeff Conine	.05
59	Greg Maddux	1.00
60	Lenny Dykstra	.05
61	Randy Johnson	.75
62	Fred McGriff	.05
63	Ray Lankford	.05
64	Dave Justice	.05
65	Paul O'Neill	.05
66	Tony Gwynn	1.00
67	Matt Williams	.05
68	Dante Bichette	.05
69	Craig Biggio	.05
70	Ken Griffey Jr.	1.50
71	J.T. Snow	.05
72	Cal Ripken Jr.	2.50
73	Jay Bell	.05
74	Joe Carter	.05
75	Roberto Alomar	.30
76	Benji Gil	.05
77	Ivan Rodriguez	.65
78	Raul Mondesi	.05
79	Cliff Floyd	.05
80	Eric Karros, Mike Piazza, Raul Mondesi (Dodger Dynasty)	.30
81	Royce Clayton	.05
82	Billy Ashley	.05
83	Joey Hamilton	.05
84	Sammy Sosa	1.00
85	Jason Bere	.05
86	Dennis Martinez	.05
87	Greg Vaughn	.05
88	Roger Clemens	1.25
89	Larry Walker	.05
90	Mark Grace	.05
91	Kenny Lofton	.05
92	*Carlos Perez*	.05
93	Roger Cedeno	.05
94	Scott Ruffcorn	.05
95	Jim Pittsley	.05
96	Andy Pettitte	.20
97	James Baldwin	.05
98	*Hideo Nomo*	1.50
99	Ismael Valdes	.05
100	Armando Benitez	.05
101	Jose Malave	.05
102	*Bobby Higginson*	.25
103	LaTroy Hawkins	.05
104	Russ Davis	.05
105	Shawn Green	.40
106	Joe Vitiello	.05
107	Chipper Jones	1.00
108	Shane Andrews	.05
109	Jose Oliva	.05
110	Ray Durham	.05
111	Jon Nunnally	.05
112	Alex Gonzalez	.05
113	Vaughn Eshelman	.05
114	Marty Cordova	.05
115	*Mark Grudzielanek*	.25
116	Brian Hunter	.05
117	Charles Johnson	.05
118	Alex Rodriguez	2.00
119	David Bell	.05
120	Todd Hollandsworth	.05
121	Joe Randa	.05
122	Derek Jeter	2.50
123	Frank Rodriguez	.05
124	Curtis Goodwin	.05
125	Bill Pulsipher	.05
126	John Mabry	.05
127	Julian Tavarez	.05
128	Edgardo Alfonzo	.05
129	Orlando Miller	.05
130	Juan Acevedo	.05
131	Jeff Cirillo	.05
132	Roberto Petagine	.05
133	Antonio Osuna	.05
134	Michael Tucker	.05
135	Garret Anderson	.05
2131	Cal Ripken Jr. (Consecutive Game Record)	1.00

Checklists

		NM/M
Complete Set (7):		2.00
Common Player:		.35
1	Ken Griffey Jr.	.50
2	Frank Thomas	.40
3	Cal Ripken Jr.	.65
4	Jeff Bagwell	.40
5	Mike Piazza	.50
6	Barry Bonds	.65
7	Manny Ramirez, Raul Mondesi	.40

Future

		NM/M
Complete Set (10):		10.00
Common Player:		.50
1	Chipper Jones	2.00
2	Curtis Goodwin	.50
3	Hideo Nomo	1.00
4	Shawn Green	1.00
5	Ray Durham	.50
6	Todd Hollandsworth	.50
7	Brian Hunter	.50
8	Carlos Delgado	1.00
9	Michael Tucker	.50
10	Alex Rodriguez	4.00

Gold Team

		NM/M
Complete Set (12):		40.00
Common Player:		2.00
1	Ken Griffey Jr.	7.50
2	Frank Thomas	4.00
3	Cal Ripken Jr.	10.00
4	Jeff Bagwell	4.00
5	Mike Piazza	7.50
6	Barry Bonds	10.00
7	Matt Williams	2.00
8	Don Mattingly	6.00
9	Will Clark	2.00
10	Tony Gwynn	5.00
11	Kirby Puckett	5.00
12	Jose Canseco	2.50

Potential Unlimited

		NM/M
Complete Set (20):		35.00
Common Player:		1.00
903s:		2.5X
1	Cliff Floyd	1.00
2	Manny Ramirez	4.50
3	Raul Mondesi	1.00
4	Scott Ruffcorn	1.00
5	Billy Ashley	1.00
6	Alex Gonzalez	1.00
7	Midre Cummings	1.00
8	Charles Johnson	1.00
9	Garret Anderson	1.00
10	Hideo Nomo	2.00
11	Chipper Jones	7.00
12	Curtis Goodwin	1.00
13	Frank Rodriguez	1.00
14	Shawn Green	2.00
15	Ray Durham	1.00
16	Todd Hollandsworth	1.00
17	Brian Hunter	1.00
18	Carlos Delgado	2.00
19	Michael Tucker	1.00
20	Alex Rodriguez	9.00

Mirror Gold

	NM/M
Complete Set (135):	150.00
Common Player:	1.00
Mirror Gold Stars:	5X

(See 1995 Select Certified for checklist and base card values.)

1996 SELECT

		NM/M
Complete Set (200):		9.00
Common Player:		.05
Pack (10):		1.00
Wax Box (24):		16.00
1	Wade Boggs	1.00
2	Shawn Green	.35
3	Andres Galarraga	.05
4	Bill Pulsipher	.05
5	Chuck Knoblauch	.05
6	Ken Griffey Jr.	1.25
7	Greg Maddux	1.00
8	Manny Ramirez	.75
9	Ivan Rodriguez	.65
10	Tim Salmon	.05
11	Frank Thomas	.75
12	Jeff Bagwell	.75
13	Travis Fryman	.05
14	Kenny Lofton	.05
15	Matt Williams	.05
16	Jay Bell	.05
17	Ken Caminiti	.05
18	Ray Lankford	.05
19	Cal Ripken Jr.	2.00
20	Roger Clemens	1.00
21	Carlos Baerga	.05
22	Mike Piazza	1.25
23	Gregg Jefferies	.05
24	Reggie Sanders	.05
25	Rondell White	.05
26	Sammy Sosa	1.00
27	Kevin Appier	.05
28	Kevin Seitzer	.05
29	Gary Sheffield	.40
30	Mike Mussina	.35
31	Mark McGwire	1.50
32	Barry Larkin	.05
33	Marc Newfield	.05
34	Ismael Valdes	.05
35	Marty Cordova	.05
36	Albert Belle	.05
37	Johnny Damon	.35
38	Garret Anderson	.05
39	Cecil Fielder	.05
40	John Mabry	.05
41	Chipper Jones	1.00
42	Omar Vizquel	.05
43	Jose Rijo	.05
44	Charles Johnson	.05
45	Alex Rodriguez	1.50
46	Rico Brogna	.05
47	Joe Carter	.05
48	Mo Vaughn	.05
49	Moises Alou	.05
50	Raul Mondesi	.05
51	Robin Ventura	.05
52	Jim Thome	.60
53	Dave Justice	.05
54	Jeff King	.05
55	Brian Hunter	.05
56	Juan Gonzalez	.40
57	John Olerud	.05
58	Rafael Palmeiro	.65
59	Tony Gwynn	1.00
60	Eddie Murray	.75
61	Jason Isringhausen	.05
62	Dante Bichette	.05
63	Randy Johnson	.75
64	Kirby Puckett	1.00
65	Jim Edmonds	.05
66	David Cone	.05
67	Ozzie Smith	1.00
68	Fred McGriff	.05
69	Darren Daulton	.05
70	Edgar Martinez	.05
71	J.T. Snow	.05
72	Butch Huskey	.05
73	Hideo Nomo	.40
74	Pedro Martinez	.75
75	Bobby Bonilla	.05
76	Jeff Conine	.05
77	Ryan Klesko	.05
78	Bernie Williams	.05
79	Andre Dawson	.25
80	Trevor Hoffman	.05
81	Mark Grace	.05
82	Benji Gil	.05
83	Eric Karros	.05
84	Pete Schourek	.05
85	Edgardo Alfonzo	.05
86	Jay Buhner	.05
87	Vinny Castilla	.05
88	Bret Boone	.05
89	Ray Durham	.05
90	Brian Jordan	.05
91	Jose Canseco	.40
92	Paul O'Neill	.05
93	Chili Davis	.05
94	Tom Glavine	.30
95	Julian Tavarez	.05
96	Derek Bell	.05
97	Will Clark	.05
98	Larry Walker	.05
99	Denny Neagle	.05
100	Alex Fernandez	.05
101	Barry Bonds	2.00
102	Ben McDonald	.05
103	Andy Pettitte	.25
104	Tino Martinez	.05
105	Sterling Hitchcock	.05
106	Royce Clayton	.05
107	Jim Abbott	.05
108	Rickey Henderson	.75
109	Ramon Martinez	.05
110	Paul Molitor	.75
111	Dennis Eckersley	.65
112	Alex Gonzalez	.05
113	Marquis Grissom	.05
114	Greg Vaughn	.05

115 Lance Johnson .05
116 Todd Stottlemyre .05
117 Jack McDowell .05
118 Ruben Sierra .05
119 Brady Anderson .05
120 Julio Franco .05
121 Brooks Kieshnick .05
122 Roberto Alomar .20
123 Greg Gagne .05
124 Wally Joyner .05
125 John Smoltz .05
126 John Valentin .05
127 Russ Davis .05
128 Joe Vitiello .05
129 Shawon Dunston .05
130 Frank Rodriguez .05
131 Charlie Hayes .05
132 Andy Benes .05
133 B.J. Surhoff .05
134 Dave Nilsson .05
135 Carlos Delgado .50
136 Walt Weiss .05
137 Mike Stanley .05
138 Greg Colbrunn .05
139 Mike Kelly .05
140 Ryne Sandberg 1.00
141 Lee Smith .05
142 Dennis Martinez .05
143 Bernard Gilkey .05
144 Lenny Dykstra .05
145 Danny Tartabull .05
146 Dean Palmer .05
147 Craig Biggio .05
148 Juan Acevedo .05
149 Michael Tucker .05
150 Bobby Higginson .05
151 Ken Griffey Jr. .65
152 Frank Thomas .45
153 Cal Ripken Jr. 1.00
154 Albert Belle .05
155 Mike Piazza .65
156 Barry Bonds 1.00
157 Sammy Sosa .60
158 Mo Vaughn .05
159 Greg Maddux .50
160 Jeff Bagwell .40
161 Derek Jeter 2.00
162 Paul Wilson .05
163 Chris Snopek .05
164 Jason Schmidt .05
165 Jimmy Haynes .05
166 George Arias .05
167 Steve Gibralter .05
168 Bob Wolcott .05
169 Jason Kendall .05
170 Greg Zaun .05
171 Quinton McCracken .05
172 Alan Benes .05
173 Rey Ordonez .05
174 Ugueth Urbina .05
175 *Osvaldo Fernandez* .10
176 Marc Barcelo .05
177 Sal Fasano .05
178 *Mike Grace* .05
179 Chan Ho Park .05
180 Robert Perez .05
181 Todd Hollandsworth .05
182 *Wilton Guerrero* .05
183 John Wasdin .05
184 Jim Pittsley .05
185 LaTroy Hawkins .05
186 Jay Powell .05
187 Felipe Crespo .05
188 Jermaine Dye .05
189 Bob Abreu .05
190 *Matt Luke* .05
191 Richard Hidalgo .05
192 Karim Garcia .05
193 Tavo Alvarez .05
194 *Andy Fox* .05
195 Terrell Wade .05
196 Frank Thomas (checklist) .40
197 Ken Griffey Jr. (checklist) .65
198 Greg Maddux (checklist) .50
199 Mike Piazza (checklist) .65
200 Cal Ripken Jr. (checklist) .75

Claim to Fame

NM/M
Complete Set (20): 45.00
Common Player: .75
1 Cal Ripken Jr. 7.50
2 Greg Maddux 4.50
3 Ken Griffey Jr. 6.00
4 Frank Thomas 3.50
5 Mo Vaughn .75
6 Albert Belle .75
7 Jeff Bagwell 3.50
8 Sammy Sosa 4.50
8s Sammy Sosa (overprinted 'SAMPLE') 2.50
9 Reggie Sanders .75
10 Hideo Nomo 2.00
11 Chipper Jones 4.50
12 Mike Piazza 6.00
13 Matt Williams .75
14 Tony Gwynn 4.50
15 Johnny Damon 1.50
16 Dante Bichette .75
17 Kirby Puckett 4.50
18 Barry Bonds 7.50
19 Randy Johnson 3.50
20 Eddie Murray 3.50

En Fuego

NM/M
Complete Set (25): 35.00
Common Player: .75
1 Ken Griffey Jr. 3.50
2 Frank Thomas 2.00
3 Cal Ripken Jr. 5.00
4 Greg Maddux 3.00
5 Jeff Bagwell 2.00
6 Barry Bonds 5.00
7 Mo Vaughn .75
8 Albert Belle .75
9 Sammy Sosa 3.00
10 Reggie Sanders .75
11 Mike Piazza 3.50
12 Chipper Jones 3.00
13 Tony Gwynn 3.00
14 Kirby Puckett 3.00
15 Wade Boggs 3.00
16 Dan Patrick .75
17 Gary Sheffield 1.25
18 Dante Bichette .75
19 Randy Johnson 2.00
20 Matt Williams .75
21 Alex Rodriguez 4.00
22 Tim Salmon .75
23 Johnny Damon 1.25
24 Manny Ramirez 2.00
25 Hideo Nomo 1.25

Team Nucleus

NM/M
Complete Set (28): 20.00
Common Player: .50
1 Albert Belle, Manny Ramirez, Carlos Baerga 1.00
2 Ray Lankford, Brian Jordan, Ozzie Smith 1.25
3 Jay Bell, Jeff King, Denny Neagle .50
4 Dante Bichette, Andres Galarraga, Larry Walker .50
5 Mark McGwire, Mike Bordick, Terry Steinbach 1.75
6 Bernie Williams, Wade Boggs, David Cone 1.25
7 Joe Carter, Alex Gonzalez, Shawn Green .50
8 Roger Clemens, Mo Vaughn, Jose Canseco 1.25
9 Ken Griffey Jr., Edgar Martinez, Randy Johnson 1.50
10 Gregg Jefferies, Darren Daulton, Lenny Dykstra .50
11 Mike Piazza, Raul Mondesi, Hideo Nomo 1.50
12 Greg Maddux, Chipper Jones, Ryan Klesko 1.25
13 Cecil Fielder, Travis Fryman, Phil Nevin .50
14 Ivan Rodriguez, Will Clark, Juan Gonzalez 1.00
15 Ryne Sandberg, Sammy Sosa, Mark Grace 1.50
16 Gary Sheffield, Charles Johnson, Andre Dawson .60
17 Johnny Damon, Michael Tucker, Kevin Appier .65
18 Barry Bonds, Matt Williams, Rod Beck 2.00
19 Kirby Puckett, Chuck Knoblauch, Marty Cordova 1.25
20 Cal Ripken Jr., Bobby Bonilla, Mike Mussina 2.00
21 Jason Isringhausen, Bill Pulsipher, Rico Brogna .50
22 Tony Gwynn, Ken Caminiti, Marc Newfield 1.25
23 Tim Salmon, Garret Anderson, Jim Edmonds .50
24 Moises Alou, Rondell White, Cliff Floyd .50
25 Barry Larkin, Reggie Sanders, Bret Boone .50
26 Jeff Bagwell, Craig Biggio, Derek Bell 1.00
27 Frank Thomas, Robin Ventura, Alex Fernandez 1.00
28 John Jaha, Greg Vaughn, Kevin Seitzer .50

Artist's Proofs

NM/M
Complete Set (200): 200.00
Common Player: 1.00
AP Stars: 7X
(See 1996 Select for checklist and base card values.)

1996 SELECT CERTIFIED

NM/M
Complete Set (144): 20.00
Common Player: .15
Pack (6): 2.50
Wax Box (20): 40.00
1 Frank Thomas 1.25
2 Tino Martinez .15
3 Gary Sheffield .50
4 Kenny Lofton .15
5 Joe Carter .15

6 Alex Rodriguez 2.50
7 Chipper Jones 1.50
8 Roger Clemens 1.75
9 Jay Bell .15
10 Eddie Murray 1.00
11 Will Clark .15
12 Mike Mussina .35
13 Hideo Nomo .50
14 Andres Galarraga .15
15 Marc Newfield .15
16 Jason Isringhausen .15
17 Randy Johnson 1.00
18 Chuck Knoblauch .15
19 J.T. Snow .15
20 Mark McGwire 2.50
21 Tony Gwynn 1.50
22 Albert Belle .15
23 Gregg Jefferies .15
24 Reggie Sanders .15
25 Bernie Williams .15
26 Ray Lankford .15
27 Johnny Damon .40
28 Ryne Sandberg 1.50
29 Rondell White .15
30 Mike Piazza 2.00
31 Barry Bonds 3.00
32 Greg Maddux 1.50
33 Craig Biggio .15
34 John Valentin .15
35 Ivan Rodriguez .75
36 Rico Brogna .15
37 Tim Salmon .15
38 Sterling Hitchcock .15
39 Charles Johnson .15
40 Travis Fryman .15
41 Barry Larkin .15
42 Tom Glavine .35
43 Marty Cordova .15
44 Shawn Green .40
45 Ben McDonald .15
46 Robin Ventura .15
47 Ken Griffey Jr. 2.00
48 Orlando Merced .15
49 Paul O'Neill .15
50 Ozzie Smith 1.50
51 Manny Ramirez 1.00
52 Ismael Valdes .15
53 Cal Ripken Jr. 3.00
54 Jeff Bagwell 1.00
55 Greg Vaughn .15
56 Juan Gonzalez .50
57 Raul Mondesi .15
58 Carlos Baerga .15
59 Sammy Sosa 1.50
60 Mike Kelly .15
61 Edgar Martinez .15
62 Kirby Puckett 1.50
63 Cecil Fielder .15
64 David Cone .15
65 Moises Alou .15
66 Fred McGriff .15
67 Mo Vaughn .15
68 Edgardo Alfonzo .15
69 Jim Thome .75
70 Rickey Henderson 1.00
71 Dante Bichette .15
72 Lenny Dykstra .15
73 Benji Gil .15
74 Wade Boggs 1.50
75 Jim Edmonds .15
76 Michael Tucker .15
77 Carlos Delgado .65
78 Butch Huskey .15
79 Billy Ashley .15
80 Dean Palmer .15
81 Paul Molitor 1.00
82 Ryan Klesko .15
83 Brian Hunter .15
84 Jay Buhner .15

#	Player	NM/M
85	Larry Walker	.15
86	Mike Bordick	.15
87	Matt Williams	.15
88	Jack McDowell	.15
89	Hal Morris	.15
90	Brian Jordan	.15
91	Andy Pettitte	.35
92	Melvin Nieves	.15
93	Pedro Martinez	1.00
94	Mark Grace	.15
95	Garret Anderson	.15
96	Andre Dawson	.30
97	Ray Durham	.15
98	Jose Canseco	.50
99	Roberto Alomar	.30
100	Derek Jeter	3.00
101	Alan Benes	.15
102	Karim Garcia	.15
103	*Robin Jennings*	.15
104	Bob Abreu	.15
105	Sal Fasano (Livan Hernandez' name on front)	.15
106	Steve Gibralter	.15
107	Jermaine Dye	.15
108	Jason Kendall	.15
109	*Mike Grace*	.15
110	Jason Schmidt	.15
111	Paul Wilson	.15
112	Rey Ordonez	.15
113	*Wilton Guerrero*	.15
114	Brooks Kieschnick	.15
115	George Arias	.15
116	*Osvaldo Fernandez*	.15
117	Todd Hollandsworth	.15
118	John Wasdin	.15
119	Eric Owens	.15
120	Chan Ho Park	.15
121	Mark Loretta	.15
122	Richard Hidalgo	.15
123	Jeff Suppan	.15
124	Jim Pittsley	.15
125	LaTroy Hawkins	.15
126	Chris Snopek	.15
127	Justin Thompson	.15
128	Jay Powell	.15
129	Alex Ochoa	.15
130	Felipe Crespo	.15
131	*Matt Lawton*	.15
132	Jimmy Haynes	.15
133	Terrell Wade	.15
134	Ruben Rivera	.15
135	Frank Thomas	.55
136	Ken Griffey Jr.	1.00
137	Greg Maddux	.65
138	Mike Piazza	.75
139	Cal Ripken Jr.	1.50
140	Albert Belle	.15
141	Mo Vaughn	.15
142	Chipper Jones	.65
143	Hideo Nomo	.25
144	Ryan Klesko	.15

Interleague Preview

		NM/M
Complete Set (25):		45.00
Common Card:		.75
Promos:		1X
1	Ken Griffey Jr., Hideo Nomo	3.50
2	Greg Maddux, Mo Vaughn	3.00
3	Frank Thomas, Sammy Sosa	3.00
4	Mike Piazza, Jim Edmonds	3.50
5	Ryan Klesko, Roger Clemens	3.25
6	Derek Jeter, Rey Ordonez	4.50
7	Johnny Damon, Ray Lankford	1.00
8	Manny Ramirez, Reggie Sanders	2.50
9	Barry Bonds, Jay Buhner	4.50
10	Jason Isringhausen, Wade Boggs	3.00
11	David Cone, Chipper Jones	3.00
12	Jeff Bagwell, Will Clark	2.50
13	Tony Gwynn, Randy Johnson	3.00
14	Cal Ripken Jr., Tom Glavine	4.50
15	Kirby Puckett, Alan Benes	3.00
16	Gary Sheffield, Mike Mussina	1.00
17	Raul Mondesi, Tim Salmon	.75
18	Rondell White, Carlos Delgado	1.00
19	Cecil Fielder, Ryne Sandberg	3.00
20	Kenny Lofton, Brian Hunter	.75
21	Paul Wilson, Paul O'Neill	.75
22	Ismael Valdes, Edgar Martinez	.75
23	Matt Williams, Mark McGwire	4.00
24	Albert Belle, Barry Larkin	.75
25	Brady Anderson, Marquis Grissom	.75

Select Few

		NM/M
Complete Set (18):		40.00
Common Player:		1.00
1	Sammy Sosa	3.00
2	Derek Jeter	5.00
3	Ken Griffey Jr.	3.50
4	Albert Belle	1.00
5	Cal Ripken Jr.	5.00
6	Greg Maddux	3.00
7	Frank Thomas	2.50
8	Mo Vaughn	1.00
9	Chipper Jones	3.00
10	Mike Piazza	3.50
11	Ryan Klesko	1.00
12	Hideo Nomo	1.50
13	Alan Benes	1.00
14	Manny Ramirez	2.50
15	Gary Sheffield	2.00
16	Barry Bonds	5.00
17	Matt Williams	1.00
18	Johnny Damon	2.00

Artist's Proofs

	NM/M
Complete Set (144):	200.00
Common Player:	1.00
AP Stars:	7X

(See 1996 Select Certified for checklist and base card values.)

Red, Blue

	NM/M
Common Red:	.50

Red Stars:	3X
Common Blue:	2.50
Blue Stars:	10X

(See 1996 Select Certified for checklist and base card values.)

Mirror Red, Blue, Gold

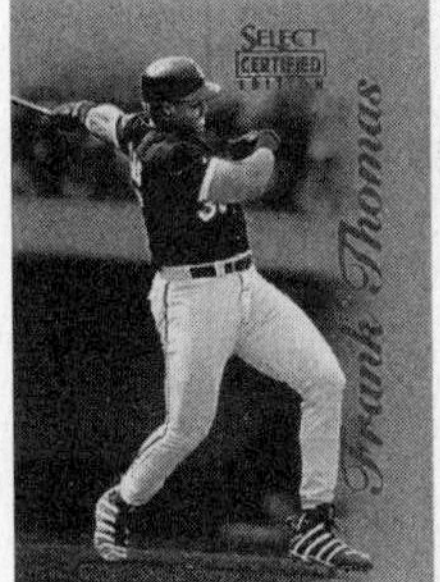

	NM/M
Common Mirror Red:	6.00
Mirror Red Stars:	20X
Common Mirror Blue:	12.00
Mirror Blue Stars:	30X
Common Mirror Gold:	20.00
Mirror Gold Stars:	100X

(See 1996 Select Certified for checklist and base card values.)

1997 SELECT

		NM/M
Complete Set (200):		30.00
Series 1 (#1-150):		20.00
High Series (#151-200):		10.00
Common High Series:		.25
Pack (6):		1.50
Wax Box (24):		25.00
1	Juan Gonzalez (B)	2.00
2	Mo Vaughn (B)	.25
3	Tony Gwynn	1.50
4	Manny Ramirez (B)	2.00
5	Jose Canseco	.50
6	David Cone	.10
7	Chan Ho Park	.10
8	Frank Thomas (B)	2.50
9	Todd Hollandsworth	.10
10	Marty Cordova	.10
11	Gary Sheffield (B)	.75
12	John Smoltz (B)	.25
13	Mark Grudzielanek	.10
14	Sammy Sosa (B)	3.00
15	Paul Molitor	1.00
16	Kevin Brown	.10
17	Albert Belle (B)	.25
18	Eric Young	.10
19	John Wetteland	.10
20	Ryan Klesko (B)	.25
21	Joe Carter	.10
22	Alex Ochoa	.10
23	Greg Maddux (B)	3.00
24	Roger Clemens (B)	3.25
25	Ivan Rodriguez (B)	1.50
26	Barry Bonds (B)	5.00
27	Kenny Lofton (B)	.25
28	Javy Lopez	.10
29	Hideo Nomo (B)	1.00
30	Rusty Greer	.10
31	Rafael Palmeiro	.75
32	Mike Piazza (B)	3.50
33	Ryne Sandberg	1.50
34	Wade Boggs	1.50
35	Jim Thome (B)	1.50
36	Ken Caminiti (B)	.25
37	Mark Grace	.10
38	Brian Jordan (B)	.25
39	Craig Biggio	.10
40	Henry Rodriguez	.10
41	Dean Palmer	.10
42	Jason Kendall	.10
43	Bill Pulsipher	.10
44	Tim Salmon (B)	.25
45	Marc Newfield	.10
46	Pat Hentgen	.10
47	Ken Griffey Jr. (B)	3.50
48	Paul Wilson	.10
49	Jay Buhner (B)	.25
50	Rickey Henderson	1.00
51	Jeff Bagwell (B)	2.00
52	Cecil Fielder	.10
53	Alex Rodriguez (B)	4.00
54	John Jaha	.10
55	Brady Anderson (B)	.25
56	Andres Galarraga	.10
57	Raul Mondesi	.10
58	Andy Pettitte	.30
59	Roberto Alomar (B)	1.00
60	Derek Jeter (B)	5.00
61	Charles Johnson	.10
62	Travis Fryman	.10
63	Chipper Jones (B)	3.00
64	Edgar Martinez	.10
65	Bobby Bonilla	.10
66	Greg Vaughn	.10
67	Bobby Higginson	.10
68	Garret Anderson	.10
69	Chuck Knoblauch (B)	.25
70	Jermaine Dye	.10
71	Cal Ripken Jr. (B)	5.00
72	Jason Giambi	.60
73	Trey Beamon	.10
74	Shawn Green	.35
75	Mark McGwire (B)	4.00
76	Carlos Delgado	.60
77	Jason Isringhausen	.10
78	Randy Johnson (B)	2.00
79	Troy Percival (B)	.25
80	Ron Gant	.10
81	Ellis Burks	.10
82	Mike Mussina (B)	1.00
83	Todd Hundley	.10
84	Jim Edmonds	.10
85	Charles Nagy	.10
86	Dante Bichette (B)	.25
87	Mariano Rivera	.20
88	Matt Williams (B)	.25
89	Rondell White	.10
90	Steve Finley	.10
91	Alex Fernandez	.10
92	Barry Larkin	.10
93	Tom Goodwin	.10
94	Will Clark	.10
95	Michael Tucker	.10
96	Derek Bell	.10
97	Larry Walker	.10
98	Alan Benes	.10
99	Tom Glavine	.35
100	Darin Erstad (B)	.35
101	Andruw Jones (B)	2.00
102	Scott Rolen	.65
103	Todd Walker (B)	.25
104	Dmitri Young	.10
105	Vladimir Guerrero (B)	2.00
106	Nomar Garciaparra	1.50
107	*Danny Patterson*	.10
108	Karim Garcia	.10
109	Todd Greene	.10
110	Ruben Rivera	.10
111	Raul Casanova	.10
112	Mike Cameron	.10
113	Bartolo Colon	.10
114	*Rod Myers*	.10

115 Todd Dunn .10
116 Torii Hunter .10
117 Jason Dickson .10
118 *Gene Kingsale* .10
119 Rafael Medina .10
120 Raul Ibanez .10
121 *Bobby Henley* .10
122 Scott Spiezio .10
123 *Bobby Smith* .10
124 J.J. Johnson .10
125 *Bubba Trammell* .50
126 Jeff Abbott .10
127 Neifi Perez .10
128 Derrek Lee .65
129 *Kevin Brown* .10
130 Mendy Lopez .10
131 Kevin Orie .10
132 Ryan Jones .10
133 Juan Encarnacion .10
134 Jose Guillen (B) .25
135 Greg Norton .10
136 Richie Sexson .10
137 Jay Payton .10
138 Bob Abreu .15
139 *Ronnie Belliard* .10
140 Wilton Guerrero (B) .25
141 Alex Rodriguez (Select Stars)(B) 2.00
142 Juan Gonzalez (Select Stars)(B) .50
143 Ken Caminiti (Select Stars)(B) .25
144 Frank Thomas (Select Stars)(B) 1.25
145 Ken Griffey Jr. (Select Stars)(B) 1.75
146 John Smoltz (Select Stars)(B) .25
147 Mike Piazza (Select Stars)(B) 1.75
148 Derek Jeter (Select Stars)(B) 3.00
149 Frank Thomas (checklist) .75
150 Ken Griffey Jr. (checklist) 1.00
151 *Jose Cruz Jr.* 1.00
152 Moises Alou .25
153 *Hideki Irabu* .50
154 Glendon Rusch .25
155 Ron Coomer .25
156 *Jeremi Gonzalez* .25
157 *Fernando Tatis* .40
158 John Olerud .25
159 Rickey Henderson 1.00
160 Shannon Stewart .25
161 Kevin Polcovich .25
162 Jose Rosado .25
163 Ray Lankford .25
164 David Justice .25
165 *Mark Kotsay* .50
166 *Deivi Cruz* .50
167 Billy Wagner .25
168 Jacob Cruz .25
169 Matt Morris .25
170 Brian Banks .25
171 Brett Tomko .25
172 Todd Helton .75
173 Eric Young .25
174 Bernie Williams .25
175 Jeff Fassero .25
176 Ryan McGuire .25
177 Darryl Kile .25
178 *Kelvim Escobar* .50
179 Dave Nilsson .25
180 Geronimo Berroa .25
181 Livan Hernandez .25
182 *Tony Womack* .50
183 Deion Sanders .25
184 Jeff Kent .25
185 Brian Hunter .25
186 Jose Malave .25
187 *Steve Woodard* .50
188 Brad Radke .25
189 Todd Dunwoody .25
190 Joey Hamilton .25
191 Denny Naegle .25
192 Bobby Jones .25
193 Tony Clark .25
194 *Jaret Wright* .50
195 Matt Stairs .25
196 Francisco Cordova .25
197 Justin Thompson .25
198 Pokey Reese .25
199 Garrett Stephenson .25
200 Carl Everett .25

Artist's Proofs

NM/M
Complete Set (150): 450.00
Common Red: 1.25
Red Stars: 5X
Common Blue: 2.50
Blue Stars: 1.5X
(See 1997 Select #1-150 for checklist and base card values.)

Registered Gold

NM/M
Complete Set (150): 300.00
Common Red Gold: .75
Common Blue Gold: 1.50
(See 1997 Select #1-150 for checklist and base card values.)
Registered Gold Stars: 2X

Autographs

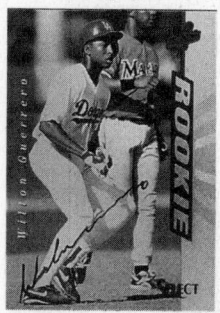

NM/M
Complete Set (4): 15.00
Common Autograph: 3.00
AU1 Wilton Guerrero 3.00
AU2 Jose Guillen 3.00
AU3 Andruw Jones 10.00
AU4 Todd Walker 3.00

Company

NM/M
Complete Set (200): 150.00
Common Player: .50
Red Stars: 3X
Blue Stars: 1.5X
High-Series Stars: 1.5X
Samples: 10X
(See 1997 Select for checklist and base card values.)

Rookie Revolution

NM/M
Complete Set (20): 21.00
Common Player: .50
1 Andruw Jones 2.50
2 Derek Jeter 6.00
3 Todd Hollandsworth .50
4 Edgar Renteria .50
5 Jason Kendall .50
6 Rey Ordonez .50
7 F.P. Santangelo .50
8 Jermaine Dye .50
9 Alex Ochoa .50
10 Vladimir Guerrero 2.50
11 Dmitri Young .50
12 Todd Walker .50
13 Scott Rolen 1.50
14 Nomar Garciaparra 3.50
15 Ruben Rivera .50
16 Darin Erstad 1.00
17 Todd Greene .50
18 Mariano Rivera 1.00
19 Trey Beamon .50
20 Karim Garcia .50

Tools of the Trade

NM/M
Complete Set (25): 25.00
Common Player: .40
Mirror Blues: 2.5X
1 Ken Griffey Jr., Andruw Jones 2.00
2 Greg Maddux, Andy Pettitte 1.50
3 Cal Ripken Jr., Chipper Jones 2.50
4 Mike Piazza, Jason Kendall 2.00
5 Albert Belle, Karim Garcia .40
6 Mo Vaughn, Dmitri Young .40
7 Juan Gonzalez, Vladimir Guerrero 1.00
8 Tony Gwynn, Jermaine Dye 1.50
9 Barry Bonds, Alex Ochoa 2.50
10 Jeff Bagwell, Jason Giambi 1.00
11 Kenny Lofton, Darin Erstad .50
12 Gary Sheffield, Manny Ramirez 1.00
13 Tim Salmon, Todd Hollandsworth .40
14 Sammy Sosa, Ruben Rivera 1.50
15 Paul Molitor, George Arias 1.00
16 Jim Thome, Todd Walker .75
17 Wade Boggs, Scott Rolen 1.50
18 Ryne Sandberg, Chuck Knoblauch 1.50
19 Mark McGwire, Frank Thomas 2.25
20 Ivan Rodriguez, Charles Johnson .75
21 Brian Jordan, Trey Beamon .40
22 Roger Clemens, Troy Percival 1.75
23 John Smoltz, Mike Mussina .65
24 Alex Rodriguez, Rey Ordonez 2.25
25 Derek Jeter, Nomar Garciaparra 2.50

1995 SKYBOX E-MOTION

NM/M
Complete Set (200): 15.00
Common Player: .05
Pack (8): 1.00
Wax Box (36): 20.00
1 Brady Anderson .05
2 Kevin Brown .05
3 Curtis Goodwin .05
4 Jeffrey Hammonds .05
5 Ben McDonald .05
6 Mike Mussina .35
7 Rafael Palmeiro .65
8 Cal Ripken Jr. 2.00
9 Jose Canseco .45
10 Roger Clemens 1.00
11 Vaughn Eshelman .05
12 Mike Greenwell .05
13 Erik Hanson .05
14 Tim Naehring .05
15 Aaron Sele .05
16 John Valentin .05
17 Mo Vaughn .05
18 Chili Davis .05
19 Gary DiSarcina .05
20 Chuck Finley .05
21 Tim Salmon .05
22 Lee Smith .05
23 J.T. Snow .05
24 Jim Abbott .05
25 Jason Bere .05
26 Ray Durham .05
27 Ozzie Guillen .05
28 Tim Raines .05
29 Frank Thomas .75
30 Robin Ventura .05
31 Carlos Baerga .05
32 Albert Belle .05
33 Orel Hershiser .05
34 Kenny Lofton .05
35 Dennis Martinez .05
36 Eddie Murray .75
37 Manny Ramirez .75
38 Julian Tavarez .05
39 Jim Thome .60
40 Dave Winfield .75
41 Chad Curtis .05
42 Cecil Fielder .05
43 Travis Fryman .05
44 Kirk Gibson .05
45 *Bob Higginson* .25
46 Alan Trammell .05
47 Lou Whitaker .05
48 Kevin Appier .05
49 Gary Gaetti .05
50 Jeff Montgomery .05
51 Jon Nunnally .05
52 Ricky Bones .05
53 Cal Eldred .05
54 Joe Oliver .05
55 Kevin Seitzer .05
56 Marty Cordova .05
57 Chuck Knoblauch .05
58 Kirby Puckett 1.00
59 Wade Boggs 1.00
60 Derek Jeter 2.00
61 Jimmy Key .05
62 Don Mattingly 1.00
63 Jack McDowell .05
64 Paul O'Neill .05
65 Andy Pettitte .30
66 Ruben Rivera .05
67 Mike Stanley .05
68 John Wetteland .05
69 Geronimo Berroa .05
70 Dennis Eckersley .65
71 Rickey Henderson .75
72 Mark McGwire 1.50
73 Steve Ontiveros .05
74 Ruben Sierra .05
75 Terry Steinbach .05
76 Jay Buhner .05
77 Ken Griffey Jr. 1.25
78 Randy Johnson .75
79 Edgar Martinez .05
80 Tino Martinez .05
81 Marc Newfield .05
82 Alex Rodriguez 1.50
83 Will Clark .05
84 Benji Gil .05
85 Juan Gonzalez .40
86 Rusty Greer .05
87 Dean Palmer .05
88 Ivan Rodriguez .65
89 Kenny Rogers .05
90 Roberto Alomar .30
91 Joe Carter .05
92 David Cone .05
93 Alex Gonzalez .05
94 Shawn Green .40
95 Pat Hentgen .05
96 Paul Molitor .75

97 John Olerud .05
98 Devon White .05
99 Steve Avery .05
100 Tom Glavine .35
101 Marquis Grissom .05
102 Chipper Jones 1.00
103 Dave Justice .05
104 Ryan Klesko .05
105 Javier Lopez .05
106 Greg Maddux 1.00
107 Fred McGriff .05
108 John Smoltz .05
109 Shawon Dunston .05
110 Mark Grace .05
111 Brian McRae .05
112 Randy Myers .05
113 Sammy Sosa 1.00
114 Steve Trachsel .05
115 Bret Boone .05
116 Ron Gant .05
117 Barry Larkin .05
118 Deion Sanders .05
119 Reggie Sanders .05
120 Pete Schourek .05
121 John Smiley .05
122 Jason Bates .05
123 Dante Bichette .05
124 Vinny Castilla .05
125 Andres Galarraga .05
126 Larry Walker .05
127 Greg Colbrunn .05
128 Jeff Conine .05
129 Andre Dawson .30
130 Chris Hammond .05
131 Charles Johnson .05
132 Gary Sheffield .45
133 Quilvio Veras .05
134 Jeff Bagwell .75
135 Derek Bell .05
136 Craig Biggio .05
137 Jim Dougherty .05
138 John Hudek .05
139 Orlando Miller .05
140 Phil Plantier .05
141 Eric Karros .05
142 Ramon Martinez .05
143 Raul Mondesi .05
144 *Hideo Nomo* 2.00
145 Mike Piazza 1.25
146 Ismael Valdes .05
147 Todd Worrell .05
148 Moises Alou .05
149 *Yamil Benitez* .05
150 Wil Cordero .05
151 Jeff Fassero .05
152 Cliff Floyd .05
153 Pedro Martinez .75
154 *Carlos Perez* .05
155 Tony Tarasco .05
156 Rondell White .05
157 Edgardo Alfonzo .05
158 Bobby Bonilla .05
159 Rico Brogna .05
160 Bobby Jones .05
161 Bill Pulsipher .05
162 Bret Saberhagen .05
163 Ricky Bottalico .05
164 Darren Daulton .05
165 Lenny Dykstra .05
166 Charlie Hayes .05
167 Dave Hollins .05
168 Gregg Jefferies .05
169 *Michael Mimbs* .05
170 Curt Schilling .35
171 Heathcliff Slocumb .05
172 Jay Bell .05
173 *Micah Franklin* .05
174 *Mark Johnson* .05
175 Jeff King .05
176 Al Martin .05
177 Dan Miceli .05
178 Denny Neagle .05
179 Bernard Gilkey .05
180 Ken Hill .05
181 Brian Jordan .05
182 Ray Lankford .05
183 Ozzie Smith 1.00
184 Andy Benes .05
185 Ken Caminiti .05
186 Steve Finley .05
187 Tony Gwynn 1.00
188 Joey Hamilton .05
189 Melvin Nieves .05
190 Scott Sanders .05
191 Rod Beck .05
192 Barry Bonds 2.00
193 Royce Clayton .05
194 Glenallen Hill .05
195 Darren Lewis .05
196 Mark Portugal .05
197 Matt Williams .05
198 Checklist .05
199 Checklist .05
200 Checklist .05

Cal Ripken Jr. Timeless

NM/M
Complete Set (15): 20.00
Common Card: 1.50
1 High School Pitcher 1.50
2 Role Model 1.50
3 Rookie of the Year 1.50
4 1st MVP Season 1.50
5 95 Consecutive Errorless Games 1.50
6 All-Star MVP 1.50
7 Conditioning 1.50
8 Shortstop HR Record 1.50
9 Literacy Work 1.50
10 2000th Consecutive Game 1.50
11 All-Star Selection 2.25
12 Record-tying Game 2.25
13 Record-breaking Game 2.25
14 2,153 and Counting 2.25
15 Birthday 2.25

Masters

NM/M
Complete Set (10): 12.00
Common Player: .50
1 Barry Bonds 2.50
2 Juan Gonzalez .65
3 Ken Griffey Jr. 2.00
4 Tony Gwynn 1.50
5 Kenny Lofton .50
6 Greg Maddux 1.50
7 Raul Mondesi .50
8 Cal Ripken Jr. 2.50
9 Frank Thomas 1.00
10 Matt Williams .50

N-Tense

NM/M
Complete Set (12): 16.00
Common Player: .50
1 Jeff Bagwell 2.00
2 Albert Belle .50
3 Barry Bonds 4.00
4 Cecil Fielder .50
5 Ron Gant .50
6 Ken Griffey Jr. 2.50
7 Mark McGwire 3.00
8 Mike Piazza 2.50
9 Manny Ramirez 2.00
10 Frank Thomas 2.00
11 Mo Vaughn .50
12 Matt Williams .50

Rookies

NM/M
Complete Set (10): 6.50
Common Player: .25
1 Edgardo Alfonzo .25
2 Jason Bates .25
3 Marty Cordova .25
4 Ray Durham .25
5 Alex Gonzalez .25
6 Shawn Green .75
7 Charles Johnson .25
8 Chipper Jones 1.50
9 Hideo Nomo 1.00
10 Alex Rodriguez 3.00

1996 SKYBOX E-MOTION XL

NM/M
Complete Set (300): 10.00
Common Player: .05
Pack (7): 1.00
Wax Box (24): 20.00
1 Roberto Alomar .15
2 Brady Anderson .05
3 Bobby Bonilla .05
4 Jeffrey Hammonds .05
5 Chris Hoiles .05
6 Mike Mussina .30
7 Randy Myers .05
8 Rafael Palmeiro .50
9 Cal Ripken Jr. 2.00
10 B.J. Surhoff .05
11 Jose Canseco .25
12 Roger Clemens 1.00
13 Wil Cordero .05
14 Mike Greenwell .05
15 Dwayne Hosey .05
16 Tim Naehring .05
17 Troy O'Leary .05
18 Mike Stanley .05
19 John Valentin .05
20 Mo Vaughn .05
21 Jim Abbott .05
22 Garret Anderson .05
23 George Arias .05
24 Chili Davis .05
25 Jim Edmonds .05
26 Chuck Finley .05
27 Todd Greene .05
28 Mark Langston .05
29 Troy Percival .05
30 Tim Salmon .05
31 Lee Smith .05
32 J.T. Snow .05
33 Harold Baines .05
34 Jason Bere .05
35 Ray Durham .05
36 Alex Fernandez .05
37 Ozzie Guillen .05
38 Darren Lewis .05
39 Lyle Mouton .05
40 Tony Phillips .05
41 Danny Tartabull .05
42 Frank Thomas .60
43 Robin Ventura .05
44 Sandy Alomar .05
45 Carlos Baerga .05
46 Albert Belle .05
47 Julio Franco .05
48 Orel Hershiser .05
49 Kenny Lofton .05
50 Dennis Martinez .05
51 Jack McDowell .05
52 Jose Mesa .05
53 Eddie Murray .60
54 Charles Nagy .05
55 Manny Ramirez .60
55p Manny Ramirez (overprinted "PROMOTIONAL SAMPLE") .60
56 Jim Thome .45
57 Omar Vizquel .05
58 Chad Curtis .05
59 Cecil Fielder .05
60 Travis Fryman .05
61 Chris Gomez .05
62 Felipe Lira .05
63 Alan Trammell .05
64 Kevin Appier .05
65 Johnny Damon .35
66 Tom Goodwin .05
67 Mark Gubicza .05
68 Jeff Montgomery .05
69 Jon Nunnally .05
70 Bip Roberts .05
71 Ricky Bones .05
72 Chuck Carr .05
73 John Jaha .05
74 Ben McDonald .05
75 Matt Mieske .05
76 Dave Nilsson .05
77 Kevin Seitzer .05
78 Greg Vaughn .05
79 Rick Aguilera .05
80 Marty Cordova .05
81 Roberto Kelly .05
82 Chuck Knoblauch .05
83 Pat Meares .05
84 Paul Molitor .60
85 Kirby Puckett .75
86 Brad Radke .05
87 Wade Boggs .75
88 David Cone .05
89 Dwight Gooden .05
90 Derek Jeter 2.00
91 Tino Martinez .05
92 Paul O'Neill .05
93 Andy Pettitte .15
94 Tim Raines .05
95 Ruben Rivera .05
96 Kenny Rogers .05
97 Ruben Sierra .05
98 John Wetteland .05
99 Bernie Williams .05
100 Allen Battle .05
101 Geronimo Berroa .05
102 Brent Gates .05
103 Doug Johns .05
104 Mark McGwire 1.50
105 Pedro Munoz .05
106 Ariel Prieto .05
107 Terry Steinbach .05
108 Todd Van Poppel .05
109 Chris Bosio .05
110 Jay Buhner .05
111 Joey Cora .05
112 Russ Davis .05
113 Ken Griffey Jr. 1.25
114 Sterling Hitchcock .05
115 Randy Johnson .60
116 Edgar Martinez .05
117 Alex Rodriguez 1.50
118 Paul Sorrento .05
119 Dan Wilson .05
120 Will Clark .05
121 Juan Gonzalez .30
122 Rusty Greer .05
123 Kevin Gross .05
124 Ken Hill .05
125 Dean Palmer .05
126 Roger Pavlik .05
127 Ivan Rodriguez .50
128 Mickey Tettleton .05
129 Joe Carter .05
130 Carlos Delgado .40
131 Alex Gonzalez .05
132 Shawn Green .25
133 Erik Hanson .05
134 Pat Hentgen .05
135 Otis Nixon .05
136 John Olerud .05
137 Ed Sprague .05
138 Steve Avery .05
139 Jermaine Dye .05
140 Tom Glavine .35
141 Marquis Grissom .05
142 Chipper Jones .75
143 David Justice .05
144 Ryan Klesko .05
145 Javier Lopez .05
146 Greg Maddux .75
147 Fred McGriff .05
148 Jason Schmidt .05
149 John Smoltz .05
150 Mark Wohlers .05
151 Jim Bullinger .05

152 Frank Castillo .05
153 Kevin Foster .05
154 Luis Gonzalez .05
155 Mark Grace .05
156 Brian McRae .05
157 Jaime Navarro .05
158 Rey Sanchez .05
159 Ryne Sandberg .75
160 Sammy Sosa .75
161 Bret Boone .05
162 Jeff Brantley .05
163 Vince Coleman .05
164 Steve Gibralter .05
165 Barry Larkin .05
166 Hal Morris .05
167 Mark Portugal .05
168 Reggie Sanders .05
169 Pete Schourek .05
170 John Smiley .05
171 Jason Bates .05
172 Dante Bichette .05
173 Ellis Burks .05
174 Vinny Castilla .05
175 Andres Galarraga .05
176 Kevin Ritz .05
177 Bill Swift .05
178 Larry Walker .05
179 Walt Weiss .05
180 Eric Young .05
181 Kurt Abbott .05
182 Kevin Brown .05
183 John Burkett .05
184 Greg Colbrunn .05
185 Jeff Conine .05
186 Chris Hammond .05
187 Charles Johnson .05
188 Terry Pendleton .05
189 Pat Rapp .05
190 Gary Sheffield .25
191 Quilvio Veras .05
192 Devon White .05
193 Jeff Bagwell .60
194 Derek Bell .05
195 Sean Berry .05
196 Craig Biggio .05
197 Doug Drabek .05
198 Tony Eusebio .05
199 Mike Hampton .05
200 Brian Hunter .05
201 Derrick May .05
202 Orlando Miller .05
203 Shane Reynolds .05
204 Mike Blowers .05
205 Tom Candiotti .05
206 Delino DeShields .05
207 Greg Gagne .05
208 Karim Garcia .05
209 Todd Hollandsworth .05
210 Eric Karros .05
211 Ramon Martinez .05
212 Raul Mondesi .05
213 Hideo Nomo .30
214 Chan Ho Park .05
215 Mike Piazza 1.25
216 Ismael Valdes .05
217 Todd Worrell .05
218 Moises Alou .05
219 Yamil Benitez .05
220 Jeff Fassero .05
221 Darrin Fletcher .05
222 Cliff Floyd .05
223 Pedro Martinez .60
224 Carlos Perez .05
225 Mel Rojas .05
226 David Segui .05
227 Rondell White .05
228 Rico Brogna .05
229 Carl Everett .05
230 John Franco .05
231 Bernard Gilkey .05
232 Todd Hundley .05
233 Jason Isringhausen .05
234 Lance Johnson .05
235 Bobby Jones .05
236 Jeff Kent .05
237 Rey Ordonez .05
238 Bill Pulsipher .05
239 Jose Vizcaino .05
240 Paul Wilson .05
241 Ricky Bottalico .05
242 Darren Daulton .05
243 Lenny Dykstra .05
244 Jim Eisenreich .05
245 Sid Fernandez .05
246 Gregg Jefferies .05
247 Mickey Morandini .05
248 Benito Santiago .05
249 Curt Schilling .35
250 Mark Whiten .05
251 Todd Zeile .05
252 Jay Bell .05
253 Carlos Garcia .05
254 Charlie Hayes .05
255 Jason Kendall .05
256 Jeff King .05
257 Al Martin .05
258 Orlando Merced .05
259 Dan Miceli .05
260 Denny Neagle .05
261 Alan Benes .05
262 Andy Benes .05
263 Royce Clayton .05
264 Dennis Eckersley .50
265 Gary Gaetti .05
266 Ron Gant .05
267 Brian Jordan .05
268 Ray Lankford .05
269 John Mabry .05
270 Tom Pagnozzi .05
271 Ozzie Smith .75
272 Todd Stottlemyre .05
273 Andy Ashby .05
274 Brad Ausmus .05
275 Ken Caminiti .05
276 Steve Finley .05
277 Tony Gwynn .75
278 Joey Hamilton .05
279 Rickey Henderson .60
280 Trevor Hoffman .05
281 Wally Joyner .05
282 Jody Reed .05
283 Bob Tewksbury .05
284 Fernando Valenzuela .05
285 Rod Beck .05
286 Barry Bonds 2.00
287 Mark Carreon .05
288 Shawon Dunston .05
289 *Osvaldo Fernandez* .10
290 Glenallen Hill .05
291 Stan Javier .05
292 Mark Leiter .05
293 Kirt Manwaring .05
294 Robby Thompson .05
295 William VanLandingham .05
296 Allen Watson .05
297 Matt Williams .05
298 Checklist .05
299 Checklist .05
300 Checklist .05

Legion of Boom

		NM/M
Complete Set (12):		27.50
Common Player:		2.00
1	Albert Belle	2.00
2	Barry Bonds	6.00
3	Juan Gonzalez	2.50
4	Ken Griffey Jr.	4.00
5	Mark McGwire	5.00
6	Mike Piazza	4.00
7	Manny Ramirez	3.00
8	Tim Salmon	2.00
9	Sammy Sosa	3.50
10	Frank Thomas	3.00
11	Mo Vaughn	2.00
12	Matt Williams	2.00

D-Fense

		NM/M
Complete Set (10):		9.00
Common Player:		.50
1	Roberto Alomar	.65
2	Barry Bonds	3.50
3	Mark Grace	.50
4	Ken Griffey Jr.	2.50
5	Kenny Lofton	.50
6	Greg Maddux	1.50
7	Raul Mondesi	.50
8	Cal Ripken Jr.	3.50
9	Ivan Rodriguez	1.00
10	Matt Williams	.50

N-Tense

		NM/M
Complete Set (10):		17.50
Common Player:		.50
1	Albert Belle	.50
2	Barry Bonds	3.50
3	Jose Canseco	1.00
4	Ken Griffey Jr.	3.00
5	Tony Gwynn	2.50
6	Randy Johnson	2.00
7	Greg Maddux	2.50
8	Cal Ripken Jr.	3.50
9	Frank Thomas	2.00
10	Matt Williams	.50

Rare Breed

		NM/M
Complete Set (10):		50.00
Common Player:		3.00
1	Garret Anderson	3.00
2	Marty Cordova	3.00
3	Brian Hunter	3.00
4	Jason Isringhausen	3.00
5	Charles Johnson	3.00
6	Chipper Jones	16.00
7	Raul Mondesi	3.00
8	Hideo Nomo	6.00
9	Manny Ramirez	12.00
10	Rondell White	3.00

1997 SKYBOX E-X2000

		NM/M
Complete Set (100):		20.00
Common Player:		.15
Pack (2):		1.25
Wax Box (24):		20.00
1	Jim Edmonds	.15
2	Darin Erstad	.25
3	Eddie Murray	1.00
4	Roberto Alomar	.25
5	Brady Anderson	.15
6	Mike Mussina	.45
7	Rafael Palmeiro	.75
8	Cal Ripken Jr.	3.00
9	Steve Avery	.15
10	Nomar Garciaparra	1.50
11	Mo Vaughn	.15
12	Albert Belle	.15
13	Mike Cameron	.15
14	Ray Durham	.15
15	Frank Thomas	1.00
16	Robin Ventura	.15
17	Manny Ramirez	1.00
18	Jim Thome	.65
19	Matt Williams	.15
20	Tony Clark	.15
21	Travis Fryman	.15
22	Bob Higginson	.15
23	Kevin Appier	.15
24	Johnny Damon	.45
25	Jermaine Dye	.15
26	Jeff Cirillo	.15
27	Ben McDonald	.15
28	Chuck Knoblauch	.15
29	Paul Molitor	1.00
30	Todd Walker	.15
31	Wade Boggs	1.50
32	Cecil Fielder	.15
33	Derek Jeter	3.00
34	Andy Pettitte	.25
35	Ruben Rivera	.15
36	Bernie Williams	.15
37	Jose Canseco	.50
38	Mark McGwire	2.50
39	Jay Buhner	.15
40	Ken Griffey Jr.	2.00
41	Randy Johnson	1.00
42	Edgar Martinez	.15
43	Alex Rodriguez	2.50
44	Dan Wilson	.15
45	Will Clark	.15
46	Juan Gonzalez	.50
47	Ivan Rodriguez	.75
48	Joe Carter	.15
49	Roger Clemens	1.75
50	Juan Guzman	.15
51	Pat Hentgen	.15
52	Tom Glavine	.35
53	Andruw Jones	1.00
54	Chipper Jones	1.50
55	Ryan Klesko	.15
56	Kenny Lofton	.15
57	Greg Maddux	1.50
58	Fred McGriff	.15
59	John Smoltz	.15
60	Mark Wohlers	.15
61	Mark Grace	.15
62	Ryne Sandberg	1.50
63	Sammy Sosa	1.50
64	Barry Larkin	.15
65	Deion Sanders	.15
66	Reggie Sanders	.15
67	Dante Bichette	.15
68	Ellis Burks	.15
69	Andres Galarraga	.15
70	Moises Alou	.15
71	Kevin Brown	.15
72	Cliff Floyd	.15
73	Edgar Renteria	.15
74	Gary Sheffield	.50
75	Bob Abreu	.15
76	Jeff Bagwell	1.00
77	Craig Biggio	.15
78	Todd Hollandsworth	.15
79	Eric Karros	.15
80	Raul Mondesi	.15
81	Hideo Nomo	.50
82	Mike Piazza	2.00
83	Vladimir Guerrero	1.00
84	Henry Rodriguez	.15
85	Todd Hundley	.15
86	Rey Ordonez	.15
87	Alex Ochoa	.15
88	Gregg Jefferies	.15
89	Scott Rolen	.65
90	Jermaine Allensworth	.15
91	Jason Kendall	.15
92	Ken Caminiti	.15
93	Tony Gwynn	1.50
94	Rickey Henderson	1.00
95	Barry Bonds	3.00
96	J.T. Snow	.15
97	Dennis Eckersley	.75
98	Ron Gant	.15
99	Brian Jordan	.15
100	Ray Lankford	.15

Essential Credentials

	NM/M
Common Player:	3.00
Essential Credentials Stars:	10X

(See 1997 SkyBox E-X2000 for checklist and base card values.)

Credentials

	NM/M
Common Player:	1.00
Credentials Stars:	6X

(See E-X2000 for checklist, base card values)

A Cut Above

	NM/M
Complete Set (10):	55.00
Common Player:	2.00

1	Frank Thomas	7.50
2	Ken Griffey Jr.	9.00
3	Alex Rodriguez	12.00
4	Albert Belle	2.00
5	Juan Gonzalez	4.00
6	Mark McGwire	10.00
7	Mo Vaughn	2.00
8	Manny Ramirez	7.50
9	Barry Bonds	12.00
10	Fred McGriff	2.00

Alex Rodriguez Jumbo

	NM/M
Alex Rodriguez	12.00

Emerald Autographs

		NM/M
Complete Set (6):		75.00
Common Player:		3.00
2	Darin Erstad	12.50
30	Todd Walker	3.00
43	Alex Rodriguez	60.00
78	Todd Hollandsworth	3.00
86	Alex Ochoa	3.00
89	Scott Rolen	16.00

Hall or Nothing

		NM/M
Complete Set (20):		55.00
Common Player:		1.00
1	Frank Thomas	2.50
2	Ken Griffey Jr.	5.00
3	Eddie Murray	2.50
4	Cal Ripken Jr.	7.00
5	Ryne Sandberg	4.00
6	Wade Boggs	4.00
7	Roger Clemens	4.50
8	Tony Gwynn	4.00
9	Alex Rodriguez	6.00
10	Mark McGwire	6.00
11	Barry Bonds	7.00
12	Greg Maddux	4.00
13	Juan Gonzalez	1.25
14	Albert Belle	1.00
15	Mike Piazza	5.00
16	Jeff Bagwell	2.50
17	Dennis Eckersley	1.50
18	Mo Vaughn	1.00
19	Roberto Alomar	1.00
20	Kenny Lofton	1.00

Star Date 2000

		NM/M
Complete Set (15):		10.00
Common Player:		.40
1	Alex Rodriguez	2.00
2	Andruw Jones	1.25
3	Andy Pettitte	.60
4	Brooks Kieschnick	.40
5	Chipper Jones	1.50
6	Darin Erstad	.60
7	Derek Jeter	2.50
8	Jason Kendall	.40
9	Jermaine Dye	.40
10	Neifi Perez	.40
11	Scott Rolen	.90
12	Todd Hollandsworth	.40
13	Todd Walker	.40
14	Tony Clark	.40
15	Vladimir Guerrero	1.25

1998 SKYBOX DUGOUT AXCESS

		NM/M
Complete Set (150):		12.00
Common Player:		.05
Inside Axcess Stars:		25X
Production 50 sets		
Pack (12):		1.00
Wax Box (36):		20.00
1	Travis Lee	.05
2	Matt Williams	.05
3	Andy Benes	.05
4	Chipper Jones	.75
5	Ryan Klesko	.05
6	Greg Maddux	.75
7	Sammy Sosa	.75
8	Henry Rodriguez	.05
9	Mark Grace	.05
10	Barry Larkin	.05
11	Bret Boone	.05
12	Reggie Sanders	.05
13	Vinny Castilla	.05
14	Larry Walker	.05
15	Darryl Kile	.05
16	Charles Johnson	.05
17	Edgar Renteria	.05
18	Gary Sheffield	.40
19	Jeff Bagwell	.65
20	Craig Biggio	.05
21	Moises Alou	.05
22	Mike Piazza	1.00
23	Hideo Nomo	.35
24	Raul Mondesi	.05
25	John Jaha	.05
26	Jeff Cirillo	.05
27	Jeromy Burnitz	.05
28	Mark Grudzielanek	.05
29	Vladimir Guerrero	.65
30	Rondell White	.05
31	Edgardo Alfonzo	.05
32	Rey Ordonez	.05
33	Bernard Gilkey	.05
34	Scott Rolen	.50
35	Curt Schilling	.35
36	Ricky Bottalico	.05
37	Tony Womack	.05
38	Al Martin	.05
39	Jason Kendall	.05
40	Ron Gant	.05
41	Mark McGwire	1.25
42	Ray Lankford	.05
43	Tony Gwynn	.75
44	Ken Caminiti	.05
45	Kevin Brown	.05
46	Barry Bonds	1.50
47	J.T. Snow	.05
48	Shawn Estes	.05
49	Jim Edmonds	.05
50	Tim Salmon	.05
51	Jason Dickson	.05
52	Cal Ripken Jr.	1.50
53	Mike Mussina	.35
54	Roberto Alomar	.20
55	Mo Vaughn	.05
56	Pedro Martinez	.65
57	Nomar Garciaparra	.75
58	Albert Belle	.05
59	Frank Thomas	.65
60	Robin Ventura	.05
61	Jim Thome	.60
62	Sandy Alomar Jr.	.05
63	Jaret Wright	.05
64	Bobby Higginson	.05
65	Tony Clark	.05
66	Justin Thompson	.05
67	Dean Palmer	.05
68	Kevin Appier	.05
69	Johnny Damon	.35
70	Paul Molitor	.65
71	Marty Cordova	.05
72	Brad Radke	.05
73	Derek Jeter	1.50
74	Bernie Williams	.05
75	Andy Pettitte	.25
76	Matt Stairs	.05
77	Ben Grieve	.05
78	Jason Giambi	.50
79	Randy Johnson	.65
80	Ken Griffey Jr.	1.00
81	Alex Rodriguez	1.25
82	Fred McGriff	.05
83	Wade Boggs	.75
84	Wilson Alvarez	.05
85	Juan Gonzalez	.35
86	Ivan Rodriguez	.50
87	Fernando Tatis	.05
88	Roger Clemens	.85
89	Jose Cruz Jr.	.05
90	Shawn Green	.30
91	Jeff Suppan	.05
92	Eli Marrero	.05
93	*Mike Lowell*	.50
94	Ben Grieve	.05
95	Cliff Politte	.05
96	*Rolando Arrojo*	.25
97	Mike Caruso	.05
98	Miguel Tejada	.15
99	Rod Myers	.05
100	Juan Encarnacion	.05
101	Enrique Wilson	.05
102	Brian Giles	.05
103	*Magglio Ordonez*	1.00
104	Brian Rose	.05
105	*Ryan Jackson*	.05
106	Mark Kotsay	.05
107	Desi Relaford	.05
108	A.J. Hinch	.05
109	Eric Milton	.05
110	Ricky Ledee	.05
111	Karim Garcia	.05
112	Derrek Lee	.60
113	Brad Fullmer	.05
114	Travis Lee	.05
115	Greg Norton	.05
116	Rich Butler	.05
117	*Masato Yoshii*	.25
118	Paul Konerko	.20
119	Richard Hidalgo	.05
120	Todd Helton	.60
121	Nomar Garciaparra	.40
122	Scott Rolen	.20
123	Cal Ripken Jr.	.75
124	Derek Jeter	.75
125	Mike Piazza	.45
126	Tony Gwynn	.40
127	Mark McGwire	.65
128	Kenny Lofton	.05
129	Greg Maddux	.40
130	Jeff Bagwell	.30
131	Randy Johnson	.30
132	Alex Rodriguez	.65
133	Mo Vaughn	.05
134	Chipper Jones	.40
135	Juan Gonzalez	.15
136	Tony Clark	.05
137	Fred McGriff	.05
138	Roger Clemens	.45
139	Ken Griffey Jr.	.65
140	Ivan Rodriguez	.25
141	Vinny Castilla	.05
142	Livan Hernandez	.05
143	Jose Cruz Jr.	.05
144	Andruw Jones	.30
145	Rafael Palmeiro	.50
146	Chuck Knoblauch	.05
147	Jay Buhner	.05
148	Andres Galarraga	.05
149	Frank Thomas	.35
150	Todd Hundley	.05

Inside Axcess

	NM/M
Common Player:	4.00
Inside Axcess Stars:	25X

(See 1998 SkyBox Dugout Axcess for checklist and base card values.)

Dishwashers

		NM/M
Complete Set (10):		7.00
Common Player:		.50
Inserted 1:8		
D1	Greg Maddux	2.00
D2	Kevin Brown	.50
D3	Pedro Martinez	1.00
D4	Randy Johnson	1.00
D5	Curt Schilling	.75
D6	John Smoltz	.50
D7	Darryl Kile	.50
D8	Roger Clemens	2.25
D9	Andy Pettitte	.60
D10	Mike Mussina	.65

Double Header

		NM/M
Complete Set (20):		2.00
Common Player:		.05
Inserted 2:1		
DH1	Jeff Bagwell	.15
DH2	Albert Belle	.05
DH3	Barry Bonds	.40
DH4	Derek Jeter	.40
DH5	Tony Clark	.05
DH6	Nomar Garciaparra	.20
DH7	Juan Gonzalez	.10
DH8	Ken Griffey Jr.	.25
DH9	Chipper Jones	.20
DH10	Kenny Lofton	.05
DH11	Mark McGwire	.30
DH12	Mo Vaughn	.05
DH13	Mike Piazza	.25
DH14	Cal Ripken Jr.	.40
DH15	Ivan Rodriguez	.10
DH16	Scott Rolen	.10
DH17	Frank Thomas	.15
DH18	Tony Gwynn	.20
DH19	Travis Lee	.05
DH20	Jose Cruz Jr.	.05

Frequent Flyers

		NM/M
Complete Set (10):		2.50
Common Player:		.25
Inserted 1:4		
FF1	Brian Hunter	.25
FF2	Kenny Lofton	.25
FF3	Chuck Knoblauch	.25
FF4	Tony Womack	.25
FF5	Marquis Grissom	.25
FF6	Craig Biggio	.25
FF7	Barry Bonds	2.00
FF8	Tom Goodwin	.25
FF9	Delino DeShields	.25
FF10	Eric Young	.25

Gronks

		NM/M
Complete Set (10):		30.00
Common Player:		1.50
Inserted 1:72		
G1	Jeff Bagwell	3.50
G2	Albert Belle	1.50
G3	Juan Gonzalez	2.00
G4	Ken Griffey Jr.	6.00
G5	Mark McGwire	7.50
G6	Mike Piazza	6.00

G7	Frank Thomas	3.50
G8	Mo Vaughn	1.50
G9	Ken Caminiti	1.50
G10	Tony Clark	1.50

Todd Helton Autograph

		NM/M
120	Todd Helton	15.00

SuperHeroes

		NM/M
Complete Set (10):		10.00
Common Player:		.50
Inserted 1:20		
SH1	Barry Bonds	3.00
SH2	Andres Galarraga	.50
SH3	Ken Griffey Jr.	1.50
SH4	Chipper Jones	1.00
SH5	Andruw Jones	.75
SH6	Hideo Nomo	.60
SH7	Cal Ripken Jr.	3.00
SH8	Alex Rodriguez	2.00
SH9	Frank Thomas	.75
SH10	Mo Vaughn	.50

1998 SKYBOX E-X2001

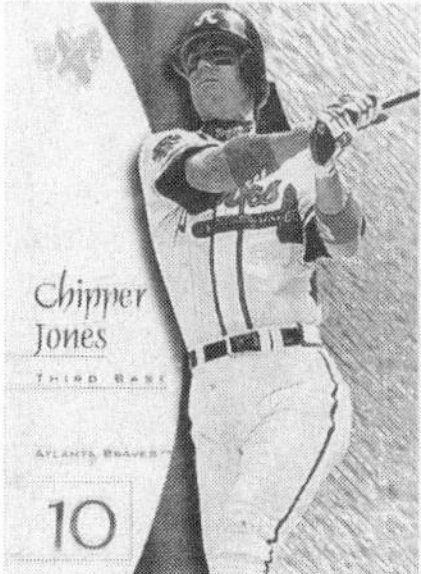

		NM/M
Complete Set (100):		25.00
Common Player:		.15
Pack (2):		1.50
Wax Box (24):		25.00
1	Alex Rodriguez	2.50
2	Barry Bonds	3.00
3	Greg Maddux	1.50
4	Roger Clemens	1.75
5	Juan Gonzalez	.50
6	Chipper Jones	1.50
7	Derek Jeter	3.00
8	Frank Thomas	1.00
9	Cal Ripken Jr.	3.00
10	Ken Griffey Jr.	2.00
11	Mark McGwire	2.50
12	Hideo Nomo	.50
13	Tony Gwynn	1.50
14	Ivan Rodriguez	.75
15	Mike Piazza	2.00
16	Roberto Alomar	.30
17	Jeff Bagwell	1.00
18	Andruw Jones	1.00
19	Albert Belle	.15
20	Mo Vaughn	.15
21	Kenny Lofton	.15
22	Gary Sheffield	.40
23	Tony Clark	.15
24	Mike Mussina	.30
25	Barry Larkin	.15
26	Moises Alou	.15
27	Brady Anderson	.15
28	Andy Pettitte	.25
29	Sammy Sosa	1.50
30	Raul Mondesi	.15
31	Andres Galarraga	.15
32	Chuck Knoblauch	.15
33	Jim Thome	.65
34	Craig Biggio	.15
35	Jay Buhner	.15
36	Rafael Palmeiro	.75
37	Curt Schilling	.35
38	Tino Martinez	.15
39	Pedro Martinez	1.00
40	Jose Canseco	.50
41	Jeff Cirillo	.15
42	Dean Palmer	.15
43	Tim Salmon	.15
44	Jason Giambi	.50
45	Bobby Higginson	.15
46	Jim Edmonds	.15
47	David Justice	.15
48	John Olerud	.15
49	Ray Lankford	.15
50	Al Martin	.15
51	Mike Lieberthal	.15
52	Henry Rodriguez	.15
53	Edgar Renteria	.15
54	Eric Karros	.15
55	Marquis Grissom	.15
56	Wilson Alvarez	.15
57	Darryl Kile	.15
58	Jeff King	.15
59	Shawn Estes	.15
60	Tony Womack	.15
61	Willie Greene	.15
62	Ken Caminiti	.15
63	Vinny Castilla	.15
64	Mark Grace	.15
65	Ryan Klesko	.15
66	Robin Ventura	.15
67	Todd Hundley	.15
68	Travis Fryman	.15
69	Edgar Martinez	.15
70	Matt Williams	.15
71	Paul Molitor	1.00
72	Kevin Brown	.15
73	Randy Johnson	1.00
74	Bernie Williams	.10
75	Manny Ramirez	1.00
76	Fred McGriff	.15
77	Tom Glavine	.35
78	Carlos Delgado	.60
79	Larry Walker	.15
80	Hideki Irabu	.15
81	Ryan McGuire	.15
82	Justin Thompson	.15
83	Kevin Orie	.15
84	Jon Nunnally	.15
85	Mark Kotsay	.15
86	Todd Walker	.15
87	Jason Dickson	.15
88	Fernando Tatis	.15
89	Karim Garcia	.15
90	Ricky Ledee	.15
91	Paul Konerko	.25
92	Jaret Wright	.15
93	Darin Erstad	.30
94	Livan Hernandez	.15
95	Nomar Garciaparra	1.50
96	Jose Cruz Jr.	.15
97	Scott Rolen	.65
98	Ben Grieve	.15
99	Vladimir Guerrero	1.00
100	Travis Lee	.15

Essential Credentials Future

		NM/M
Common Player:		5.00
1	Alex Rodriguez (100)	55.00
2	Barry Bonds (99)	60.00
3	Greg Maddux (98)	40.00
4	Roger Clemens (97)	45.00
5	Juan Gonzalez (96)	15.00
6	Chipper Jones (95)	40.00
7	Derek Jeter (94)	55.00
8	Frank Thomas (93)	35.00
9	Cal Ripken Jr. (92)	65.00
10	Ken Griffey Jr. (91)	45.00
11	Mark McGwire (90)	55.00
12	Hideo Nomo (89)	15.00
13	Tony Gwynn (88)	25.00
14	Ivan Rodriguez (87)	25.00
15	Mike Piazza (86)	40.00
16	Roberto Alomar (85)	15.00
17	Jeff Bagwell (84)	25.00
18	Andruw Jones (83)	25.00
19	Albert Belle (82)	5.00
20	Mo Vaughn (81)	5.00
21	Kenny Lofton (80)	5.00
22	Gary Sheffield (79)	12.00
23	Tony Clark (78)	5.00
24	Mike Mussina (77)	25.00
25	Barry Larkin (76)	5.00
26	Moises Alou (75)	5.00
27	Brady Anderson (74)	5.00
28	Andy Pettitte (73)	7.50
29	Sammy Sosa (72)	40.00
30	Raul Mondesi (71)	5.00
31	Andres Galarraga (70)	6.00
32	Chuck Knoblauch (69)	6.00
33	Jim Thome (68)	20.00
34	Craig Biggio (67)	6.00
35	Jay Buhner (66)	6.00
36	Rafael Palmeiro (65)	30.00
37	Curt Schilling (64)	20.00
38	Tino Martinez (63)	6.00
39	Pedro Martinez (62)	32.50
40	Jose Canseco (61)	30.00
41	Jeff Cirillo (60)	6.00
42	Dean Palmer (59)	6.00
43	Tim Salmon (58)	7.50
44	Jason Giambi (57)	25.00
45	Bobby Higginson (56)	6.00
46	Jim Edmonds (55)	6.00
47	David Justice (54)	6.00
48	John Olerud (53)	6.00
49	Ray Lankford (52)	6.00
50	Al Martin (51)	6.00
51	Mike Lieberthal (50)	6.00
52	Henry Rodriguez (49)	6.00
53	Edgar Renteria (48)	6.00
54	Eric Karros (47)	6.00
55	Marquis Grissom (46)	6.00
56	Wilson Alvarez (45)	6.00
57	Darryl Kile (44)	6.00
58	Jeff King (43)	6.00
59	Shawn Estes (42)	6.00
60	Tony Womack (41)	6.00
61	Willie Greene (40)	6.00
62	Ken Caminiti (39)	6.00
63	Vinny Castilla (38)	6.00
64	Mark Grace (37)	6.00
65	Ryan Klesko (36)	6.00
66	Robin Ventura (35)	6.00
67	Todd Hundley (34)	6.00
68	Travis Fryman (33)	6.00
69	Edgar Martinez (32)	7.50
70	Matt Williams (31)	7.50
71	Paul Molitor (30)	45.00
72	Kevin Brown (29)	7.50
73	Randy Johnson (28)	40.00
74	Bernie Williams (27)	20.00
75	Manny Ramirez (26)	45.00
76	Fred McGriff (25)	20.00
77	Tom Glavine (24)	35.00
78	Carlos Delgado (23)	35.00
79	Larry Walker (22)	9.00
80	Hideki Irabu (21)	9.00
81	Ryan McGuire (20)	9.00
82	Justin Thompson (19)	9.00
83	Kevin Orie (18)	9.00
84	Jon Nunnally (17)	9.00
85	Mark Kotsay (16)	9.00
86	Todd Walker (15)	10.00
87	Jason Dickson (14)	10.00
88	Fernando Tatis (13)	10.00
89	Karim Garcia (12)	15.00
90	Ricky Ledee (11)	10.00
91	Paul Konerko (10)	30.00
92	Jaret Wright (9)	15.00
93	Darin Erstad (8)	25.00
94	Livan Hernandez (7)	15.00
95	Nomar Garciaparra (6)	100.00
96	Jose Cruz Jr. (5)	40.00
97	Scott Rolen (4)	125.00
98	Ben Grieve (3)	100.00
99	Vladimir Guerrero (2)	350.00
100	Travis Lee (1)	200.00

Cheap Seat Treats

		NM/M
Complete Set (20):		30.00
Common Player:		1.00
Inserted 1:24		
1	Frank Thomas	2.00
2	Ken Griffey Jr.	3.00
3	Mark McGwire	4.00
4	Tino Martinez	1.00
5	Larry Walker	1.00
6	Juan Gonzalez	1.50
7	Mike Piazza	3.00
8	Jeff Bagwell	2.00
9	Tony Clark	1.00
10	Albert Belle	1.00
11	Andres Galarraga	1.00
12	Jim Thome	1.50
13	Mo Vaughn	1.00
14	Barry Bonds	5.00
15	Vladimir Guerrero	2.00
16	Scott Rolen	1.25
17	Travis Lee	1.00
18	David Justice	1.00
19	Jose Cruz Jr.	1.00
20	Andruw Jones	2.00

Destination: Cooperstown

		NM/M
Complete Set (15):		375.00
Common Player:		8.00
Inserted 1:720		
1	Alex Rodriguez	40.00
2	Frank Thomas	20.00
3	Cal Ripken Jr.	50.00
4	Roger Clemens	30.00
5	Greg Maddux	25.00
6	Chipper Jones	25.00
7	Ken Griffey Jr.	35.00
8	Mark McGwire	40.00
9	Tony Gwynn	25.00
10	Mike Piazza	35.00
11	Jeff Bagwell	20.00
12	Jose Cruz Jr.	8.00
13	Derek Jeter	50.00
14	Hideo Nomo	12.50
15	Ivan Rodriguez	15.00

Signature 2001

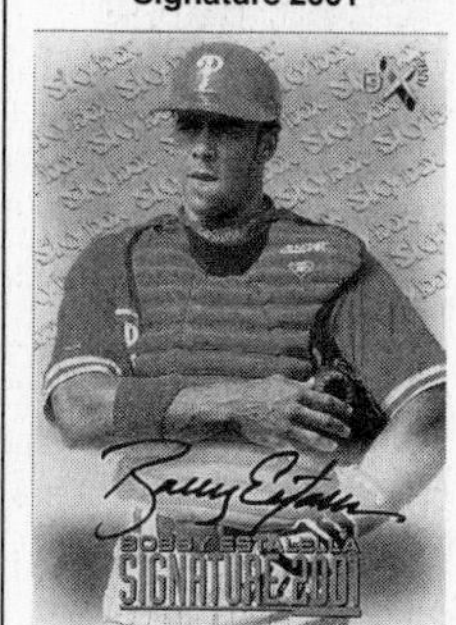

		NM/M
Complete Set (17):		100.00
Common Player:		3.00
Inserted 1:60		
1	Ricky Ledee	3.00
2	Derrick Gibson	3.00
3	Mark Kotsay	3.00
4	Kevin Millwood	10.00
5	Brad Fullmer	3.00

6	Todd Walker	4.00
7	Ben Grieve	3.00
8	Tony Clark	3.00
9	Jaret Wright	4.00
10	Randall Simon	3.00
11	Paul Konerko	4.00
12	Todd Helton	15.00
13	David Ortiz	15.00
14	Alex Gonzalez	4.00
15	Bobby Estalella	3.00
16	Alex Rodriguez	50.00
17	Mike Lowell	7.50

Star Date 2001

		NM/M
Complete Set (15):		5.00
Common Player:		.25
Inserted 1:12		
1	Travis Lee	.25
2	Jose Cruz Jr.	.25
3	Paul Konerko	1.00
4	Bobby Estalella	.25
5	Magglio Ordonez	1.00
6	Juan Encarnacion	.25
7	Richard Hidalgo	.25
8	Abraham Nunez	.25
9	Sean Casey	.50
10	Todd Helton	1.50
11	Brad Fullmer	.25
12	Ben Grieve	.25
13	Livan Hernandez	.25
14	Jaret Wright	.25
15	Todd Dunwoody	.25

Kerry Wood

		NM/M
Complete Set (2):		2.00
---	Kerry Wood (cardboard trade card)	1.00
101	Kerry Wood (plastic redemption card)	4.00

1999 SKYBOX E-X CENTURY

		NM/M
Complete Set (120):		35.00
Common Player:		.15
Common SP (91-120):		.60
Inserted 1:2		
Pack (3):		3.00
Wax Box (18):		40.00
1	Scott Rolen	.75
2	Nomar Garciaparra	1.50
3	Mike Piazza	2.00
4	Tony Gwynn	1.50
5	Sammy Sosa	1.50
6	Alex Rodriguez	2.50
7	Vladimir Guerrero	1.00
8	Chipper Jones	1.50
9	Derek Jeter	3.00
10	Kerry Wood	.50
11	Juan Gonzalez	.50
12	Frank Thomas	1.00
13	Mo Vaughn	.15
14	Greg Maddux	1.50
15	Jeff Bagwell	1.00
16	Mark McGwire	2.50
17	Ken Griffey Jr.	2.00
18	Roger Clemens	1.75
19	Cal Ripken Jr.	3.00
20	Travis Lee	.15
21	Todd Helton	.75
22	Darin Erstad	.30
23	Pedro Martinez	1.00
24	Barry Bonds	3.00
25	Andruw Jones	1.00
26	Larry Walker	.15
27	Albert Belle	.15
28	Ivan Rodriguez	.75
29	Magglio Ordonez	.25
30	Andres Galarraga	.15
31	Mike Mussina	.35
32	Randy Johnson	1.00
33	Tom Glavine	.35
34	Barry Larkin	.15
35	Jim Thome	.75
36	Gary Sheffield	.45
37	Bernie Williams	.15
38	Carlos Delgado	.60
39	Rafael Palmeiro	.75
40	Edgar Renteria	.15
41	Brad Fullmer	.15
42	David Wells	.15
43	Dante Bichette	.15
44	Jaret Wright	.15
45	Ricky Ledee	.15
46	Ray Lankford	.15
47	Mark Grace	.15
48	Jeff Cirillo	.15
49	Rondell White	.15
50	Jeromy Burnitz	.15
51	Sean Casey	.25
52	Rolando Arrojo	.15
53	Jason Giambi	.65
54	John Olerud	.15
55	Will Clark	.15
56	Raul Mondesi	.15
57	Scott Brosius	.15
58	Bartolo Colon	.15
59	Steve Finley	.15
60	Javy Lopez	.15
61	Tim Salmon	.15
62	Roberto Alomar	.30
63	Vinny Castilla	.15
64	Craig Biggio	.15
65	Jose Guillen	.15
66	Greg Vaughn	.15
67	Jose Canseco	.40
68	Shawn Green	.50
69	Curt Schilling	.35
70	Orlando Hernandez	.15
71	Jose Cruz Jr.	.15
72	Alex Gonzalez	.15
73	Tino Martinez	.15
74	Todd Hundley	.15
75	Brian Giles	.15
76	Cliff Floyd	.15
77	Paul O'Neill	.15
78	Ken Caminiti	.15
79	Ron Gant	.15
80	Juan Encarnacion	.15
81	Ben Grieve	.15
82	Brian Jordan	.15
83	Rickey Henderson	1.00
84	Tony Clark	.15
85	Shannon Stewart	.15
86	Robin Ventura	.15
87	Todd Walker	.15
88	Kevin Brown	.15
89	Moises Alou	.15
90	Manny Ramirez	1.00
91	Gabe Alvarez	.60
92	Jeremy Giambi	.60
93	Adrian Beltre	.75
94	George Lombard	.60
95	Ryan Minor	.60
96	Kevin Witt	.60
97	*Scott Hunter*	.60
98	Carlos Guillen	.60
99	Derrick Gibson	.60
100	Trot Nixon	.75
101	Troy Glaus	3.00
102	Armando Rios	.60
103	Preston Wilson	.60
104	*Pat Burrell*	3.00
105	J.D. Drew	1.50
106	Bruce Chen	.60
107	Matt Clement	.60
108	Carlos Beltran	1.50
109	Carlos Febles	.60
110	Rob Fick	.60
111	Russell Branyan	.60
112	*Roosevelt Brown*	.60
113	Corey Koskie	.60
114	Mario Encarnacion	.60
115	*Peter Tucci*	.60
116	Eric Chavez	.75
117	Gabe Kapler	.60
118	Marlon Anderson	.60
119	*A.J. Burnett*	.75
120	Ryan Bradley	.60
---	Checklist 1-96	.05
---	Checklist 97-120/Inserts	.05

Authen-Kicks

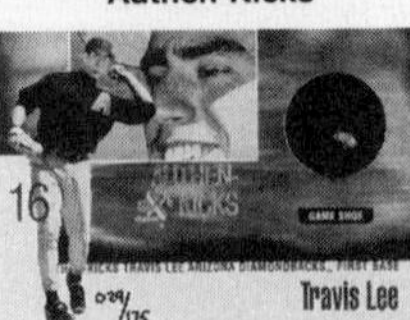

		NM/M
Complete Set (10):		125.00
Common Player:		2.50
(1)	J.D. Drew (160)	7.50
(1ab)	J.D. Drew (autographed black)(8)	75.00
(1ar)	J.D. Drew (autographed red)(8)	75.00
(2)	Travis Lee (175)	5.00
(3)	Kevin Millwood (160)	5.00
(4)	Bruce Chen (205)	2.50
(5)	Troy Glaus (205)	15.00
(6)	Todd Helton (205)	15.00
(7)	Ricky Ledee (180)	2.50
(8)	Scott Rolen (205)	15.00
(9)	Jeremy Giambi (205)	2.50

E-X Quisite

		NM/M
Complete Set (15):		17.50
Common Player:		.50
Inserted 1:18		
1	Troy Glaus	3.50
2	J.D. Drew	2.50
3	Pat Burrell	3.50
4	Russell Branyan	.50
5	Kerry Wood	2.00
6	Eric Chavez	1.00
7	Ben Grieve	.50
8	Gabe Kapler	.50
9	Adrian Beltre	1.00
10	Todd Helton	3.00
11	Roosevelt Brown	.50
12	Marlon Anderson	.50
13	Jeremy Giambi	.50
14	Magglio Ordonez	1.00
15	Travis Lee	.50

Favorites for Fenway

		NM/M
Complete Set (20):		45.00
Common Player:		1.00
Inserted 1:36		
1	Mo Vaughn	1.00
2	Nomar Garciaparra	2.25
3	Frank Thomas	2.00
4	Ken Griffey Jr.	3.00
5	Roger Clemens	2.50
6	Alex Rodriguez	4.00
7	Derek Jeter	5.00
8	Juan Gonzalez	1.50
9	Cal Ripken Jr.	5.00
10	Ivan Rodriguez	1.50
11	J.D. Drew	1.50
12	Barry Bonds	5.00
13	Tony Gwynn	2.25
14	Vladimir Guerrero	2.00
15	Chipper Jones	2.25
16	Kerry Wood	1.50
17	Mike Piazza	3.00
18	Sammy Sosa	2.25
19	Scott Rolen	1.50
20	Mark McGwire	4.00

Milestones of the Century

		NM/M
Complete Set (10):		375.00
Common Player:		10.00
Numbered to featured milestone		
1	Kerry Wood (20)	20.00
2	Mark McGwire (70)	60.00
3	Sammy Sosa (66)	40.00
4	Ken Griffey Jr. (350)	17.50
5	Roger Clemens (98)	25.00
6	Cal Ripken Jr. (17)	165.00
7	Alex Rodriguez (40)	90.00
8	Barry Bonds (400)	25.00
9	N.Y. Yankees (114)	15.00
10	Travis Lee (98)	10.00

1999 SKYBOX MOLTEN METAL

		NM/M
Complete Set (150):		35.00
Common Metalsmiths (1-100):		.15
Inserted 4:1		
Common Heavy Metal (101-130):		.25
Inserted 1:1		
Common Supernatural (131-150):		.50
Inserted 1:2		
Pack (6):		1.00
Wax Box (24):		20.00
1	Larry Walker	.15
2	Jose Canseco	.50
3	Brian Jordan	.15
4	Rafael Palmeiro	.65
5	Edgar Renteria	.15
6	Dante Bichette	.15
7	Mark Kotsay	.15
8	Denny Neagle	.15
9	Ellis Burks	.15
10	Paul O'Neill	.15
11	Miguel Tejada	.30
12	Ken Caminiti	.15
13	David Cone	.15
14	Jason Kendall	.15
15	Ruben Rivera	.15
16	Todd Walker	.15
17	Bobby Higginson	.15
18	Derrek Lee	.60
19	Rondell White	.15
20	Pedro J. Martinez	.75
21	Jeff Kent	.15
22	Randy Johnson	.75
23	Matt Williams	.15
24	Sean Casey	.25
25	Eric Davis	.15
26	Ryan Klesko	.15
27	Curt Schilling	.35
28	Geoff Jenkins	.15
29	Armand Abreu	.15
30	Vinny Castilla	.15
31	Will Clark	.15
32	Ray Durham	.15
33	Ray Lankford	.15
34	Richie Sexson	.15
35	Derrick Gibson	.15
36	Mark Grace	.15
37	Greg Vaughn	.15
38	Bartolo Colon	.15
39	Steve Finley	.15
40	Chuck Knoblauch	.15
41	Ricky Ledee	.15
42	John Smoltz	.15
43	Moises Alou	.15
44	Jim Edmonds	.15
45	Cliff Floyd	.15
46	Javy Lopez	.15
47	Jim Thome	.65
48	J.T. Snow	.15
49	Sandy Alomar Jr.	.15
50	Andy Pettitte	.25
51	Juan Encarnacion	.15
52	Travis Fryman	.15
53	Eli Marrero	.15
54	Jeff Cirillo	.15
55	Brady Anderson	.15
56	Jose Cruz Jr.	.15
57	Edgar Martinez	.15

58	Garret Anderson	.15
59	Paul Konerko	.30
60	Eric Milton	.15
61	Jason Giambi	.45
62	Tom Glavine	.35
63	Justin Thompson	.15
64	Brad Fullmer	.15
65	Marquis Grissom	.15
66	Fernando Tatis	.15
67	Carlos Beltran	.45
68	Charles Johnson	.15
69	Raul Mondesi	.15
70	Richard Hildalgo	.15
71	Barry Larkin	.15
72	David Wells	.15
73	Jay Buhner	.15
74	Matt Clement	.15
75	Eric Karros	.15
76	Carl Pavano	.15
77	Mariano Rivera	.25
78	Livan Hernandez	.15
79	A.J. Hinch	.15
80	Tino Martinez	.15
81	Rusty Greer	.15
82	Jose Guillen	.15
83	Robin Ventura	.15
84	Kevin Brown	.15
85	Chan Ho Park	.15
86	John Olerud	.15
87	Johnny Damon	.35
88	Todd Hundley	.15
89	Fred McGriff	.15
90	Wade Boggs	1.00
91	Mike Cameron	.15
92	Gary Sheffield	.50
93	Rickey Henderson	.75
94	Pat Hentgen	.15
95	Omar Vizquel	.15
96	Craig Biggio	.15
97	Mike Caruso	.15
98	Neifi Perez	.15
99	Mike Mussina	.50
100	Carlos Delgado	.45
101	Andruw Jones	1.00
102	*Pat Burrell*	3.00
103	Orlando Hernandez	.25
104	Darin Erstad	.40
105	Roberto Alomar	.35
106	Tim Salmon	.25
107	Albert Belle	.25
108	*Chad Allen*	.25
109	Travis Lee	.25
110	*Jesse Garcia*	.25
111	Tony Clark	.25
112	Ivan Rodriguez	.75
113	Troy Glaus	1.00
114	*A.J. Burnett*	1.50
115	David Justice	.25
116	Adrian Beltre	.50
117	Eric Chavez	.35
118	Kenny Lofton	.25
119	Michael Barrett	.25
120	*Jeff Weaver*	1.50
121	Manny Ramirez	1.00
122	Barry Bonds	2.00
123	Bernie Williams	.25
124	*Freddy Garcia*	1.50
125	*Scott Hunter*	.25
126	Jeremy Giambi	.25
127	*Masao Kida*	.25
128	Todd Helton	1.00
129	Mike Figga	.25
130	Mo Vaughn	.25
131	J.D. Drew	.65
132	Cal Ripken Jr.	3.00
133	Ken Griffey Jr.	1.50
134	Mark McGwire	2.00
135	Nomar Garciaparra	1.00
136	Greg Maddux	1.00
137	Mike Piazza	1.50
138	Alex Rodriguez	2.00
139	Frank Thomas	.85
140	Juan Gonzalez	.65
141	Tony Gwynn	1.00
142	Derek Jeter	3.00
143	Chipper Jones	1.00
144	Scott Rolen	.65
145	Sammy Sosa	1.00
146	Kerry Wood	.50
147	Roger Clemens	1.25
148	Jeff Bagwell	.75
149	Vladimir Guerrero	.75
150	Ben Grieve	.50

Fusion

	NM/M
Complete Set (50):	100.00
Common Heavy Metal (1-30):	1.00
Inserted 1:12	
Common Supernatural (31-50):	2.50
Inserted 1:24	
Sterling (31-50):	1.5X
Production 500 sets	
Titanium (31-50):	6X
Production 50 sets	

1	Andruw Jones	4.00
2	Pat Burrell	2.00
3	Orlando Hernandez	1.00
4	Darin Erstad	1.50
5	Roberto Alomar	1.50
6	Tim Salmon	1.00
7	Albert Belle	1.00
8	Chad Allen	1.00
9	Travis Lee	1.00
10	Jesse Garcia	1.00
11	Tony Clark	1.00
12	Ivan Rodriguez	3.00
13	Troy Glaus	3.00
14	A.J. Burnett	1.00
15	David Justice	1.00
16	Adrian Beltre	1.50
17	Eric Chavez	1.50
18	Kenny Lofton	1.00
19	Michael Barrett	1.00
20	Jeff Weaver	1.00
21	Manny Ramirez	4.00
22	Barry Bonds	10.00
23	Bernie Williams	1.00
24	Freddy Garcia	1.00
25	Scott Hunter	1.00
26	Jeremy Giambi	1.00
27	Masao Kida	1.00
28	Todd Helton	3.00
29	Mike Figga	1.00
30	Mo Vaughn	1.00
31	J.D. Drew	2.00
32	Cal Ripken Jr.	10.00
33	Ken Griffey Jr.	6.00
34	Mark McGwire	7.50
35	Nomar Garciaparra	5.00
36	Greg Maddux	5.00
37	Mike Piazza	6.00
38	Alex Rodriguez	7.50
39	Frank Thomas	4.00
40	Juan Gonzalez	1.50
41	Tony Gwynn	5.00
42	Derek Jeter	10.00
43	Chipper Jones	5.00
44	Scott Rolen	3.00
45	Sammy Sosa	5.00
46	Kerry Wood	2.00
47	Roger Clemens	5.50
48	Jeff Bagwell	4.00
49	Vladimir Guerrero	4.00
50	Ben Grieve	1.00

Oh Atlanta!

	NM/M
Complete Set (30):	30.00
Common Player:	.60
Inserted 1:1	

1	Kenny Lofton	.60
2	Kevin Millwood	.60
3	Bret Boone	.60
4	Otis Nixon	.60
5	Vinny Castilla	.60
6	Brian Jordan	.60
7	Chipper Jones	8.00
8	Dave Justice	.60
9	Micah Bowie	.60
10	Fred McGriff	.60
11	Ron Gant	.60
12	Andruw Jones	4.00
13	Kent Mercker	.60
14	Greg McMichael	.60
15	Steve Avery	.60
16	Marquis Grissom	.60
17	Jason Schmidt	.60
18	Ryan Klesko	.60
19	Charlie O'Brien	.60
20	Terry Pendleton	.60
21	Denny Neagle	.60
22	Greg Maddux	8.00
23	Tom Glavine	1.50
24	Javy Lopez	.60
25	John Rocker	.60
26	Walt Weiss	.60
27	John Smoltz	.60
28	Michael Tucker	.60
29	Odalis Perez	.60
30	Andres Galarraga	.60

Xplosion

	NM/M
Complete Set (150):	300.00
Common Player:	1.00
Stars:	3X

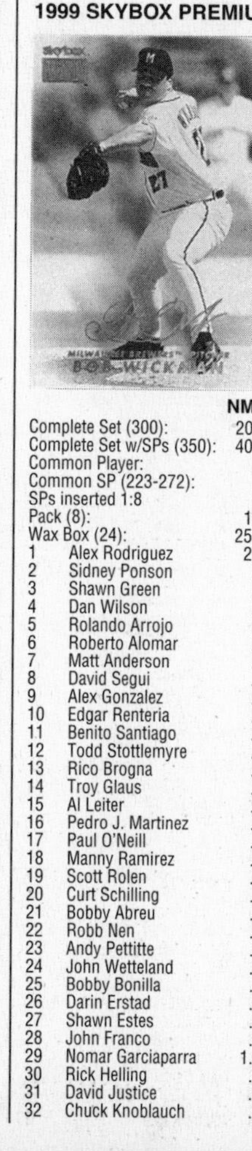

Inserted 1:2

(See 1999 SkyBox Molten Metal for checklist and base card values.)

Fusion - Sterling

	NM/M
Common Player:	1.50
Sterling Stars:	1.5X

(See 1999 Molten Metal Fusion for checklist and base card values.)

Fusion - Titanium

	NM/M
Common Player:	4.00
Titanium Stars:	6X

(See 1999 SkyBox Molten Metal Fusion for checklist and base card values.)

1999 SKYBOX PREMIUM

	NM/M
Complete Set (300):	20.00
Complete Set w/SPs (350):	40.00
Common Player:	.10
Common SP (223-272):	.60
SPs inserted 1:8	
Pack (8):	1.50
Wax Box (24):	25.00

1	Alex Rodriguez	2.00
2	Sidney Ponson	.10
3	Shawn Green	.35
4	Dan Wilson	.10
5	Rolando Arrojo	.10
6	Roberto Alomar	.30
7	Matt Anderson	.10
8	David Segui	.10
9	Alex Gonzalez	.10
10	Edgar Renteria	.10
11	Benito Santiago	.10
12	Todd Stottlemyre	.10
13	Rico Brogna	.10
14	Troy Glaus	.65
15	Al Leiter	.10
16	Pedro J. Martinez	.75
17	Paul O'Neill	.10
18	Manny Ramirez	.75
19	Scott Rolen	.65
20	Curt Schilling	.35
21	Bobby Abreu	.15
22	Robb Nen	.10
23	Andy Pettitte	.25
24	John Wetteland	.10
25	Bobby Bonilla	.10
26	Darin Erstad	.20
27	Shawn Estes	.10
28	John Franco	.10
29	Nomar Garciaparra	1.00
30	Rick Helling	.10
31	David Justice	.10
32	Chuck Knoblauch	.10

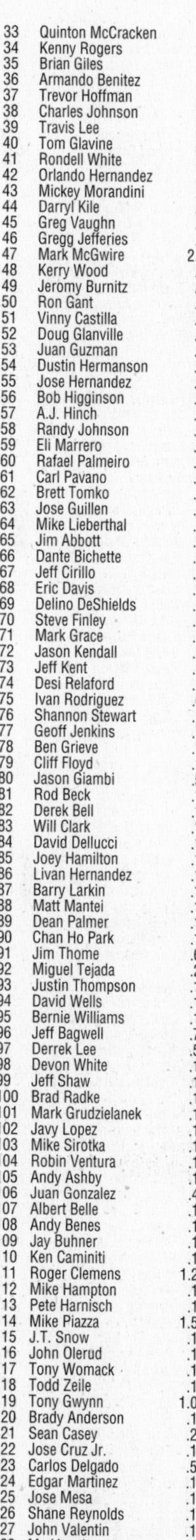

33	Quinton McCracken	.10
34	Kenny Rogers	.10
35	Brian Giles	.10
36	Armando Benitez	.10
37	Trevor Hoffman	.10
38	Charles Johnson	.10
39	Travis Lee	.10
40	Tom Glavine	.35
41	Rondell White	.10
42	Orlando Hernandez	.10
43	Mickey Morandini	.10
44	Darryl Kile	.10
45	Greg Vaughn	.10
46	Gregg Jefferies	.10
47	Mark McGwire	2.00
48	Kerry Wood	.40
49	Jeromy Burnitz	.10
50	Ron Gant	.10
51	Vinny Castilla	.10
52	Doug Glanville	.10
53	Juan Guzman	.10
54	Dustin Hermanson	.10
55	Jose Hernandez	.10
56	Bob Higginson	.10
57	A.J. Hinch	.10
58	Randy Johnson	.75
59	Eli Marrero	.10
60	Rafael Palmeiro	.65
61	Carl Pavano	.10
62	Brett Tomko	.10
63	Jose Guillen	.10
64	Mike Lieberthal	.10
65	Jim Abbott	.10
66	Dante Bichette	.10
67	Jeff Cirillo	.10
68	Eric Davis	.10
69	Delino DeShields	.10
70	Steve Finley	.10
71	Mark Grace	.10
72	Jason Kendall	.10
73	Jeff Kent	.10
74	Desi Relaford	.10
75	Ivan Rodriguez	.65
76	Shannon Stewart	.10
77	Geoff Jenkins	.10
78	Ben Grieve	.10
79	Cliff Floyd	.10
80	Jason Giambi	.50
81	Rod Beck	.10
82	Derek Bell	.10
83	Will Clark	.10
84	David Dellucci	.10
85	Joey Hamilton	.10
86	Livan Hernandez	.10
87	Barry Larkin	.10
88	Matt Mantei	.10
89	Dean Palmer	.10
90	Chan Ho Park	.10
91	Jim Thome	.65
92	Miguel Tejada	.20
93	Justin Thompson	.10
94	David Wells	.10
95	Bernie Williams	.10
96	Jeff Bagwell	.75
97	Derrek Lee	.50
98	Devon White	.10
99	Jeff Shaw	.10
100	Brad Radke	.10
101	Mark Grudzielanek	.10
102	Javy Lopez	.10
103	Mike Sirotka	.10
104	Robin Ventura	.10
105	Andy Ashby	.10
106	Juan Gonzalez	.40
107	Albert Belle	.10
108	Andy Benes	.10
109	Jay Buhner	.10
110	Ken Caminiti	.10
111	Roger Clemens	1.25
112	Mike Hampton	.10
113	Pete Harnisch	.10
114	Mike Piazza	1.50
115	J.T. Snow	.10
116	John Olerud	.10
117	Tony Womack	.10
118	Todd Zeile	.10
119	Tony Gwynn	1.00
120	Brady Anderson	.10
121	Sean Casey	.20
122	Jose Cruz Jr.	.10
123	Carlos Delgado	.50
124	Edgar Martinez	.10
125	Jose Mesa	.10
126	Shane Reynolds	.10
127	John Valentin	.10
128	Mo Vaughn	.10
129	Kevin Young	.10
130	Jay Bell	.10
131	Aaron Boone	.10

No.	Player	Price
132	John Smoltz	.10
133	Mike Stanley	.10
134	Bret Saberhagen	.10
135	Tim Salmon	.10
136	Mariano Rivera	.15
137	Ken Griffey Jr.	1.50
138	Jose Offerman	.10
139	Troy Percival	.10
140	Greg Maddux	1.00
141	Frank Thomas	.75
142	Steve Avery	.10
143	Kevin Millwood	.10
144	Sammy Sosa	1.00
145	Larry Walker	.10
146	Matt Williams	.10
147	Mike Caruso	.10
148	Todd Helton	.65
149	Andruw Jones	.75
150	Ray Lankford	.10
151	Craig Biggio	.10
152	Ugueth Urbina	.10
153	Wade Boggs	1.00
154	Derek Jeter	2.50
155	Wally Joyner	.10
156	Mike Mussina	.30
157	Gregg Olson	.10
158	Henry Rodriguez	.10
159	Reggie Sanders	.10
160	Fernando Tatis	.10
161	Dmitri Young	.10
162	Rick Aguilera	.10
163	Marty Cordova	.10
164	Johnny Damon	.30
165	Ray Durham	.10
166	Brad Fullmer	.10
167	Chipper Jones	1.00
168	Bobby Smith	.10
169	Omar Vizquel	.10
170	Todd Hundley	.10
171	David Cone	.10
172	Royce Clayton	.10
173	Ryan Klesko	.10
174	Jeff Montgomery	.10
175	Magglio Ordonez	.10
176	Billy Wagner	.10
177	Masato Yoshii	.10
178	Jason Christiansen	.10
179	Chuck Finley	.10
180	Tom Gordon	.10
181	Wilton Guerrero	.10
182	Rickey Henderson	.75
183	Sterling Hitchcock	.10
184	Kenny Lofton	.10
185	Tino Martinez	.10
186	Fred McGriff	.10
187	Matt Stairs	.10
188	Neifi Perez	.10
189	Bob Wickman	.10
190	Barry Bonds	2.50
191	Jose Canseco	.40
192	Damion Easley	.10
193	Jim Edmonds	.10
194	Juan Encarnacion	.10
195	Travis Fryman	.10
196	Tom Goodwin	.10
197	Rusty Greer	.10
198	Roberto Hernandez	.10
199	B.J. Surhoff	.10
200	Scott Brosius	.10
201	Brian Jordan	.10
202	Paul Konerko	.20
203	Ismael Valdes	.10
204	Eric Milton	.10
205	Adrian Beltre	.25
206	Tony Clark	.10
207	Bartolo Colon	.10
208	Cal Ripken Jr.	2.50
209	Moises Alou	.10
210	Wilson Alvarez	.10
211	Kevin Brown	.10
212	Orlando Cabrera	.10
213	Vladimir Guerrero	.75
214	Jose Rosado	.10
215	Raul Mondesi	.10
216	Dave Nilsson	.10
217	Carlos Perez	.10
218	Jason Schmidt	.10
219	Richie Sexson	.10
220	Gary Sheffield	.40
221	Fernando Vina	.10
222	Todd Walker	.10
223	*Scott Sauerbeck*	.10
223	*Scott Sauerbeck (sp)*	.60
224	*Pascual Matos*	.10
224	*Pascual Matos (sp)*	.60
225	*Kyle Farnsworth*	.15
225	*Kyle Farnsworth (sp)*	.60
226	*Freddy Garcia*	.75
226	*Freddy Garcia (sp)*	1.50
227	*David Lundquist*	.10
227	*David Lundquist (sp)*	.60
228	*Jolbert Cabrera*	.10
228	*Jolbert Cabrera (sp)*	.60
229	*Dan Perkins*	.10
229	*Dan Perkins (sp)*	.60
230	Warren Morris	.10
230	Warren Morris (sp)	.60
231	Carlos Febles	.10
231	Carlos Febles (sp)	.60
232	*Brett Hinchliffe*	.10
232	*Brett Hinchliffe (sp)*	.60
233	*Jason Phillips*	.10
233	*Jason Phillips (sp)*	.60
234	*Glen Barker*	.10
234	*Glen Barker (sp)*	.60
235	*Jose Macias*	.25
235	*Jose Macias (sp)*	1.00
236	*Joe Mays*	.10
236	*Joe Mays (sp)*	.60
237	*Chad Allen*	.10
237	*Chad Allen (sp)*	.60
238	*Miguel Del Toro*	.10
238	*Miguel Del Toro (sp)*	.60
239	Chris Singleton	.10
239	Chris Singleton (sp)	.60
240	*Jesse Garcia*	.10
240	*Jesse Garcia (sp)*	.60
241	Kris Benson	.10
241	Kris Benson (sp)	.60
242	*Clay Bellinger*	.10
242	*Clay Bellinger (sp)*	.60
243	Scott Williamson	.10
243	Scott Williamson (sp)	.60
244	*Masao Kida*	.10
244	*Masao Kida (sp)*	.60
245	*Guillermo Garcia*	.10
245	*Guillermo Garcia (sp)*	.60
246	*A.J. Burnett*	.25
246	*A.J. Burnett (sp)*	1.50
247	*Bo Porter*	.10
247	*Bo Porter (sp)*	.60
248	*Pat Burrell*	1.50
248	*Pat Burrell (sp)*	4.00
249	Carlos Lee	.50
249	Carlos Lee (sp)	1.50
250	*Jeff Weaver*	.50
250	*Jeff Weaver (sp)*	1.50
251	Ruben Mateo	.10
251	Ruben Mateo (sp)	.60
252	J.D. Drew	.40
252	J.D. Drew (sp)	2.00
253	Jeremy Giambi	.10
253	Jeremy Giambi (sp)	.60
254	*Gary Bennett*	.10
254	*Gary Bennett (sp)*	.60
255	*Edwards Guzman*	.10
255	*Edwards Guzman (sp)*	.60
256	Ramon Martinez	.10
256	Ramon Martinez (sp)	.60
257	*Giomar Guevara*	.10
257	*Giomar Guevara (sp)*	.60
258	*Joe McEwing*	.10
258	*Joe McEwing (sp)*	.60
259	*Tom Davey*	.10
259	*Tom Davey (sp)*	.60
260	Gabe Kapler	.10
260	Gabe Kapler (sp)	.60
261	*Ryan Rupe*	.10
261	*Ryan Rupe (sp)*	.60
262	*Kelly Dransfeldt*	.10
262	*Kelly Dransfeldt (sp)*	.60
263	Michael Barrett	.10
263	Michael Barrett (sp)	.60
264	Eric Chavez	.25
264	Eric Chavez (sp)	1.00
265	*Orber Moreno*	.10
265	*Orber Moreno (sp)*	.60
266	Marlon Anderson	.10
266	Marlon Anderson (sp)	.60
267	Carlos Beltran	.50
267	Carlos Beltran (sp)	1.50
268	Doug Mientkiewicz	.10
268	Doug Mientkiewicz (sp)	.60
269	Roy Halladay	.10
269	Roy Halladay (sp)	.60
270	Torii Hunter	.10
270	Torii Hunter (sp)	.60
271	Stan Spencer	.10
271	Stan Spencer (sp)	.60
272	Alex Gonzalez	.10
272	Alex Gonzalez (sp)	.60
273	Mark McGwire	1.00
274	Scott Rolen	.30
275	Jeff Bagwell	.40
276	Derek Jeter	1.50
277	Tony Gwynn	.50
278	Frank Thomas	.40
279	Sammy Sosa	.50
280	Nomar Garciaparra	.50
281	Cal Ripken Jr.	1.50
282	Albert Belle	.10
283	Kerry Wood	.20
284	Greg Maddux	.50
285	Barry Bonds	1.50
286	Juan Gonzalez	.25
287	Ken Griffey Jr.	.75
288	Alex Rodriguez	1.00
289	Ben Grieve	.10
290	Travis Lee	.10
291	Mo Vaughn	.10
292	Mike Piazza	.85
293	Roger Clemens	.60
294	J.D. Drew	.20
295	Randy Johnson	.40
296	Chipper Jones	.50
297	Vladimir Guerrero	.40
298	Nomar Garciaparra Checklist	.40
299	Ken Griffey Jr. Checklist	.50
300	Mark McGwire Checklist	.60

Star Rubies

Star Rubies: 50X
Production 50 sets
SP Star Rubies: 15X
Production 15 sets
(See 1999 SkyBox Premium for checklist and base card values.)

Autographics

NM/M

Common Player: 3.00
Inserted 1:68
Blue Ink: 1.5X
Production 50 sets

Player	NM/M
Roberto Alomar	10.00
Paul Bako	3.00
Michael Barrett	3.00
Kris Benson	3.00
Micah Bowie	3.00
Roosevelt Brown	3.00
A.J. Burnett	4.00
Pat Burrell	12.00
Ken Caminiti	12.00
Royce Clayton	3.00
Edgard Clemente	3.00
Bartolo Colon	3.00
J.D. Drew	12.50
Damion Easley	3.00
Derrin Ebert	3.00
Mario Encarnacion	3.00
Juan Encarnacion	3.00
Troy Glaus	10.00
Tom Glavine	12.00
Juan Gonzalez	15.00
Shawn Green	5.00
Wilton Guerrero	3.00
Jose Guillen	3.00
Tony Gwynn	20.00
Mark Harriger	3.00
Bobby Higginson	3.00
Todd Hollandsworth	3.00
Scott Hunter	3.00
Gabe Kapler	3.00
Scott Karl	3.00
Mike Kinkade	3.00
Ray Lankford	3.00
Barry Larkin	6.00
Matt Lawton	3.00
Ricky Ledee	3.00
Travis Lee	3.00
Eli Marrero	3.00
Ruben Mateo	3.00
Joe McEwing	3.00
Doug Mientkiewicz	4.00
Russ Ortiz	3.00
Jim Parque	3.00
Robert Person	3.00
Alex Rodriguez	60.00
Scott Rolen	10.00
Benj Sampson	3.00
Luis Saturria	3.00
Curt Schilling	25.00
David Segui	3.00
Fernando Tatis	3.00
Peter Tucci	3.00
Javier Vasquez	6.00
Robin Ventura	10.00

Diamond Debuts

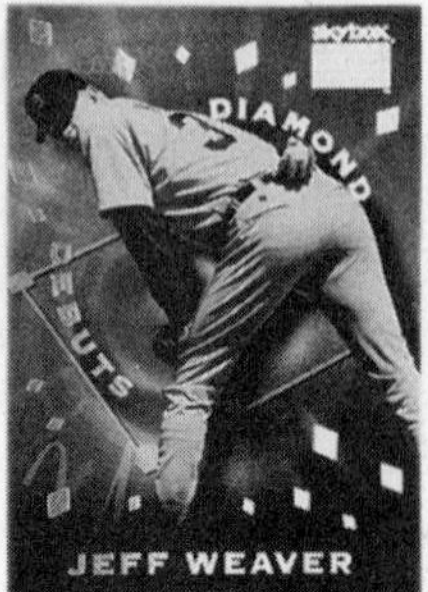

Complete Set (15): 17.50
Common Player: 2.00
Inserted 1:49

No.	Player	NM/M
1	Eric Chavez	3.00
2	Kyle Farnsworth	2.00
3	Ryan Rupe	2.00
4	Jeremy Giambi	2.00
5	Marlon Anderson	2.00
6	J.D. Drew	4.00
7	Carlos Febles	2.00
8	Joe McEwing	2.00
9	Jeff Weaver	2.00
10	Alex Gonzalez	2.00
11	Chad Allen	2.00
12	Michael Barrett	2.00
13	Gabe Kapler	2.00
14	Carlos Lee	2.00
15	Edwards Guzman	2.00

Intimidation Nation

Complete Set (15): 280.00
Common Player: 12.00
Production 99 sets

No.	Player	NM/M
1	Cal Ripken Jr.	40.00
2	Tony Gwynn	20.00
3	Nomar Garciaparra	20.00
4	Frank Thomas	15.00
5	Mike Piazza	25.00
6	Mark McGwire	30.00
7	Scott Rolen	12.00
8	Chipper Jones	20.00
9	Greg Maddux	20.00
10	Ken Griffey Jr.	25.00
11	Juan Gonzalez	12.00
12	Derek Jeter	40.00
13	J.D. Drew	12.00
14	Roger Clemens	22.50
15	Alex Rodriguez	30.00

Live Bats

Complete Set (15): 10.00
Common Player: .25
Inserted 1:7

No.	Player	NM/M
1	Juan Gonzalez	.35
2	Mark McGwire	1.50
3	Jeff Bagwell	.50
4	Frank Thomas	.50
5	Mike Piazza	1.00
6	Nomar Garciaparra	.75
7	Alex Rodriguez	1.50
8	Scott Rolen	.40
9	Travis Lee	.25
10	Tony Gwynn	.75
11	Derek Jeter	2.00
12	Ben Grieve	.25
13	Chipper Jones	.75
14	Ken Griffey Jr.	1.00
15	Cal Ripken Jr.	2.00

Soul of the Game

Complete Set (15): 15.00
Common Player: .60
Inserted 1:14

No.	Player	NM/M
1	Alex Rodriguez	2.00

2	Vladimir Guerrero	.90
3	Chipper Jones	1.25
4	Derek Jeter	2.50
5	Tony Gwynn	1.25
6	Scott Rolen	.60
7	Juan Gonzalez	.60
8	Mark McGwire	2.00
9	Ken Griffey Jr.	1.50
10	Jeff Bagwell	.90
11	Cal Ripken Jr.	2.50
12	Frank Thomas	.90
13	Mike Piazza	1.50
14	Nomar Garciaparra	1.25
15	Sammy Sosa	1.25

Show Business

		NM/M
Complete Set (15):		60.00
Common Player:		2.00
Inserted 1:70		
1	Mark McGwire	7.50
2	Tony Gwynn	5.00
3	Nomar Garciaparra	5.00
4	Juan Gonzalez	2.50
5	Roger Clemens	5.00
6	Chipper Jones	5.00
7	Cal Ripken Jr.	10.00
8	Alex Rodriguez	7.50
9	Orlando Hernandez	2.00
10	Greg Maddux	5.00
11	Mike Piazza	6.00
12	Frank Thomas	4.00
13	Ken Griffey Jr.	6.00
14	Scott Rolen	3.00
15	Derek Jeter	10.00

1999 SKYBOX THUNDER

		NM/M
Complete Set (300):		15.00
Common Player (1-240):		.05
Common Player (241-300):		.15
Raves:		15X
Production 150 sets		
SuperRaves:		45X
Production 25 sets		
Rants:		8X
Inserted 1:2 R		
Pack (8):		1.50
Wax Box (36):		25.00
1	John Smoltz	.05
2	Garret Anderson	.05
3	Matt Williams	.05
4	Daryle Ward	.05
5	Andy Ashby	.05
6	Miguel Tejada	.15
7	Dmitri Young	.05
8	Roberto Alomar	.25
9	Kevin Brown	.05
10	Eric Young	.05
11	Odalis Perez	.05
12	Preston Wilson	.05
13	Jeff Abbott	.05
14	Bret Boone	.05
15	Mendy Lopez	.05
16	B.J. Surhoff	.05
17	Steve Woodard	.05
18	Ron Coomer	.05
19	Rondell White	.05
20	Edgardo Alfonzo	.05
21	Kevin Millwood	.05
22	Jose Canseco	.45
23	Blake Stein	.05
24	Quilvio Veras	.05
25	Chuck Knoblauch	.05
26	David Segui	.05
27	Eric Davis	.05
28	Francisco Cordova	.05
29	Randy Winn	.05
30	Will Clark	.05
31	Billy Wagner	.05
32	Kevin Witt	.05
33	Jim Edmonds	.05
34	Todd Stottlemyre	.05
35	Shane Andrews	.05
36	Michael Tucker	.05
37	Sandy Alomar Jr.	.05
38	Neifi Perez	.05
39	Jaret Wright	.05
40	Devon White	.05
41	Edgar Renteria	.05
42	Shane Reynolds	.05
43	Jeff King	.05
44	Darren Dreifort	.05
45	Fernando Vina	.05
46	Marty Cordova	.05
47	Ugueth Urbina	.05
48	Bobby Bonilla	.05
49	Omar Vizquel	.05
50	Tom Gordon	.05
51	Ryan Christenson	.05
52	Aaron Boone	.05
53	Jamie Moyer	.05
54	Brian Giles	.05
55	Kevin Tapani	.05
56	Scott Brosius	.05
57	Ellis Burks	.05
58	Al Leiter	.05
59	Royce Clayton	.05
60	Chris Carpenter	.05
61	Bubba Trammell	.05
62	Tom Glavine	.35
63	Shannon Stewart	.05
64	Todd Zeile	.05
65	J.T. Snow	.05
66	Matt Clement	.05
67	Matt Stairs	.05
68	Ismael Valdes	.05
69	Todd Walker	.05
70	Jose Lima	.05
71	Mike Caruso	.05
72	Brett Tomko	.05
73	Mike Lansing	.05
74	Justin Thompson	.05
75	Damion Easley	.05
76	Derrek Lee	.50
77	Derek Bell	.05
78	Brady Anderson	.05
79	Charles Johnson	.05
80	*Rafael Roque*	.05
81	Corey Koskie	.05
82	Fernando Seguignol	.05
83	Jay Tessmer	.05
84	Jason Giambi	.50
85	Mike Lieberthal	.05
86	Jose Guillen	.05
87	Jim Leyritz	.05
88	Shawn Estes	.05
89	Ray Lankford	.05
90	Paul Sorrento	.05
91	Javy Lopez	.05
92	John Wetteland	.05
93	Sean Casey	.15
94	Chuck Finley	.05
95	Trot Nixon	.05
96	Ray Durham	.05
97	Reggie Sanders	.05
98	Bartolo Colon	.05
99	Henry Rodriguez	.05
100	Rolando Arrojo	.05
101	Geoff Jenkins	.05
102	Darryl Kile	.05
103	Mark Kotsay	.05
104	Craig Biggio	.05
105	Omar Daal	.05
106	Carlos Febles	.05
107	Eric Karros	.05
108	Matt Lawton	.05
109	Carl Pavano	.05
110	Brian McRae	.05
111	Mariano Rivera	.15
112	Jay Buhner	.05
113	Doug Glanville	.05
114	Jason Kendall	.05
115	Wally Joyner	.05
116	Jeff Kent	.05
117	Shane Monahan	.05
118	Eli Marrero	.05
119	Bobby Smith	.05
120	Shawn Green	.20
121	Kirk Rueter	.05
122	Tom Goodwin	.05
123	Andy Benes	.05
124	Ed Sprague	.05
125	Mike Mussina	.25
126	Jose Offerman	.05
127	Mickey Morandini	.05
128	Paul Konerko	.20
129	Denny Neagle	.05
130	Travis Fryman	.05
131	John Rocker	.05
132	*Rob Fick*	.05
133	Livan Hernandez	.05
134	Ken Caminiti	.05
135	Johnny Damon	.30
136	Jeff Kubenka	.05
137	Marquis Grissom	.05
138	Doug Mientkiewicz	.05
139	Dustin Hermanson	.05
140	Carl Everett	.05
141	Hideo Nomo	.40
142	Jorge Posada	.05
143	Rickey Henderson	.75
144	Robb Nen	.05
145	Ron Gant	.05
146	Aramis Ramirez	.05
147	Trevor Hoffman	.05
148	Bill Mueller	.05
149	Edgar Martinez	.05
150	Fred McGriff	.05
151	Rusty Greer	.05
152	Tom Evans	.05
153	Todd Greene	.05
154	Jay Bell	.05
155	Mike Lowell	.05
156	Orlando Cabrera	.05
157	Troy O'Leary	.05
158	Jose Hernandez	.05
159	Magglio Ordonez	.05
160	Barry Larkin	.05
161	David Justice	.05
162	Derrick Gibson	.05
163	Luis Gonzalez	.05
164	Alex Gonzalez	.05
165	Scott Elarton	.05
166	Dermal Brown	.05
167	Eric Milton	.05
168	Raul Mondesi	.05
169	Jeff Cirillo	.05
170	Benj Sampson	.05
171	John Olerud	.05
172	Andy Pettitte	.20
173	A.J. Hinch	.05
174	Rico Brogna	.05
175	Jason Schmidt	.05
176	Dean Palmer	.05
177	Matt Morris	.05
178	Quinton McCracken	.05
179	Rick Helling	.05
180	Walt Weiss	.05
181	Troy Percival	.05
182	Tony Batista	.05
183	Brian Jordan	.05
184	Jerry Hairston Jr.	.05
185	Bret Saberhagen	.05
186	Mark Grace	.05
187	Brian Simmons	.05
188	Pete Harnisch	.05
189	Kenny Lofton	.05
190	Vinny Castilla	.05
191	Bobby Higginson	.05
192	Joey Hamilton	.05
193	Cliff Floyd	.05
194	Andres Galarraga	.05
195	Chan Ho Park	.05
196	Jeromy Burnitz	.05
197	David Ortiz	.35
198	Wilton Guerrero	.05
199	Rey Ordonez	.05
200	Paul O'Neill	.05
201	Kenny Rogers	.05
202	Marlon Anderson	.05
203	Tony Womack	.05
204	Robin Ventura	.05
205	Russ Ortiz	.05
206	Mike Frank	.05
207	Fernando Tatis	.05
208	Miguel Cairo	.05
209	Ivan Rodriguez	.65
210	Carlos Delgado	.50
211	Tim Salmon	.15
212	Brian Anderson	.05
213	Ryan Klesko	.05
214	Scott Erickson	.05
215	Mike Stanley	.05
216	Brant Brown	.05
217	Rod Beck	.05
218	*Guillermo Garcia*	.05
219	David Wells	.05
220	Dante Bichette	.05
221	Armando Benitez	.05
222	Todd Dunwoody	.05
223	Kelvim Escobar	.05
224	Richard Hidalgo	.05
225	Angel Pena	.05
226	Ronnie Belliard	.05
227	Brad Radke	.05
228	Brad Fullmer	.05
229	Jay Payton	.05
230	Tino Martinez	.05
231	Scott Spiezio	.05
232	Bobby Abreu	.05
233	John Valentin	.05
234	Kevin Young	.05
235	Steve Finley	.05
236	David Cone	.05
237	Armando Rios	.05
238	Russ Davis	.05
239	Wade Boggs	1.00
240	Aaron Sele	.05
241	Jose Cruz Jr.	.15
242	George Lombard	.15
243	Todd Helton	.65
244	Andruw Jones	.75
245	Troy Glaus	.65
246	Manny Ramirez	.75
247	Ben Grieve	.15
247p	Ben Grieve ("PROMOTIONAL SAMPLE")	1.00
248	Richie Sexson	.15
249	Juan Encarnacion	.15
250	Randy Johnson	.75
251	Gary Sheffield	.45
252	Rafael Palmeiro	.65
253	Roy Halladay	.15
254	Mike Piazza	1.50
255	Tony Gwynn	1.00
256	Juan Gonzalez	.40
257	Jeremy Giambi	.15
258	Ben Davis	.15
259	Russ Branyan	.15
260	Pedro Martinez	.75
261	Frank Thomas	.75
262	Calvin Pickering	.15
263	Chipper Jones	1.00
264	Ryan Minor	.15
265	Roger Clemens	1.25
266	Sammy Sosa	1.00
267	Mo Vaughn	.15
268	Carlos Beltran	.50
269	Jim Thome	.65
270	Mark McGwire	2.00
271	Travis Lee	.15
272	Darin Erstad	.30
273	Derek Jeter	2.50
274	Greg Maddux	1.00
275	Ricky Ledee	.15
276	Alex Rodriguez	2.00
277	Vladimir Guerrero	.75
278	Greg Vaughn	.15
279	Scott Rolen	.60
280	Carlos Guillen	.15
281	Jeff Bagwell	.75
282	Bruce Chen	.15
283	Tony Clark	.15
284	Albert Belle	.05
285	Cal Ripken Jr.	2.50
286	Barry Bonds	2.50
287	Curt Schilling	.35
288	Eric Chavez	.30
289	Larry Walker	.15
290	Orlando Hernandez	.15
291	Moises Alou	.15
292	Ken Griffey Jr.	1.50
293	Kerry Wood	.50
294	Nomar Garciaparra	1.00
295	Gabe Kapler	.15
296	Bernie Williams	.05
297	Matt Anderson	.15
298	Adrian Beltre	.35
299	J.D. Drew	.40
300	Ryan Bradley	.15

Rant

	NM/M
Common Player:	.50
Rant Stars:	8X

(See 1999 SkyBox Thunder for checklist and base card values.)

Dial 1

		NM/M
Complete Set (10):		70.00
Common Player:		2.50
Inserted 1:300		
1D	Nomar Garciaparra	7.50
2D	Juan Gonzalez	3.40
3D	Ken Griffey Jr.	10.00
4D	Chipper Jones	7.50
5D	Mark McGwire	12.50
6D	Mike Piazza	10.00
7D	Manny Ramirez	6.00
8D	Alex Rodriguez	12.50
9D	Sammy Sosa	7.50
10D	Mo Vaughn	2.50

Hip-No-Tized

		NM/M
Complete Set (15):		20.00
Common Player:		1.25
Inserted 1:36		
1H	J.D. Drew	1.25
2H	Nomar Garciaparra	2.00
3H	Juan Gonzalez	1.25
4H	Ken Griffey Jr.	2.50
5H	Derek Jeter	4.00
6H	Randy Johnson	1.50
7H	Chipper Jones	2.00
8H	Mark McGwire	3.00
9H	Mike Piazza	2.50
10H	Cal Ripken Jr.	4.00
11H	Alex Rodriguez	3.00
12H	Sammy Sosa	2.00
13H	Frank Thomas	1.50
14H	Jim Thome	1.25
15H	Kerry Wood	1.25

In Depth

		NM/M
Complete Set (10):		17.50
Common Player:		1.00
Inserted 1:24		
1ID	Albert Belle	1.00
2ID	Barry Bonds	5.00
3ID	Roger Clemens	1.50
4ID	Juan Gonzalez	1.25
5ID	Ken Griffey Jr.	3.00
6ID	Mark McGwire	4.00
7ID	Mike Piazza	3.00
8ID	Sammy Sosa	2.50
9ID	Mo Vaughn	1.00
10ID	Kerry Wood	1.25

Todd Helton Autograph

		NM/M
243	Todd Helton	15.00

Turbo Charged

		NM/M
Complete Set (10):		35.00
Common Player:		2.00
Inserted 1:72		
1TC	Jose Canseco	2.50
2TC	Juan Gonzalez	2.00
3TC	Ken Griffey Jr.	5.00
4TC	Vladimir Guerrero	3.00
5TC	Mark McGwire	6.00
6TC	Mike Piazza	5.00
7TC	Manny Ramirez	3.00
8TC	Alex Rodriguez	6.00
9TC	Sammy Sosa	4.00
10TC	Mo Vaughn	2.00

Unleashed

		NM/M
Complete Set (15):		10.00
Common Player:		.50
Inserted 1:6		
1U	Carlos Beltran	1.50
2U	Adrian Beltre	1.00
3U	Eric Chavez	.75
4U	J.D. Drew	1.00
5U	Juan Encarnacion	.50
6U	Jeremy Giambi	.50
7U	Troy Glaus	2.00
8U	Ben Grieve	.50
9U	Todd Helton	2.00
10U	Orlando Hernandez	.50
11U	Gabe Kapler	.50
12U	Travis Lee	.50
13U	Calvin Pickering	.50
14U	Richie Sexson	.50
15U	Kerry Wood	1.00

www.Batterz.com

		NM/M
Complete Set (10):		12.00
Common Player:		.50
Inserted 1:18		
1WB	J.D. Drew	.60
2WB	Nomar Garciaparra	1.00
3WB	Ken Griffey Jr.	1.50
4WB	Tony Gwynn	1.00
5WB	Derek Jeter	3.00
6WB	Mark McGwire	2.00
7WB	Alex Rodriguez	2.00
8WB	Scott Rolen	.65
9WB	Sammy Sosa	1.00
10WB	Bernie Williams	.50

2000 SKYBOX

		NM/M
Complete Set (250):		25.00
Comp. Set w/SPs (300):		85.00
Common Player:		.10
Common SP (201-240):		1.00
Inserted 1:8		
Common SP (241-250):		.50
Inserted 1:12		
Pack (10):		1.50
Wax Box (24):		30.00
1	Cal Ripken Jr.	2.00
2	Ivan Rodriguez	.65
3	Chipper Jones	1.00
4	Dean Palmer	.10
5	Devon White	.10
6	Ugueth Urbina	.10
7	Doug Glanville	.10
8	Damian Jackson	.10
9	Jose Canseco	.40
10	Billy Koch	.10
11	Brady Anderson	.10
12	Vladimir Guerrero	.75
13	Dan Wilson	.10
14	Kevin Brown	.10
15	Eddie Taubensee	.10
16	Jose Lima	.10
17	Greg Maddux	1.00
18	Manny Ramirez	.75
19	Brad Fullmer	.10
20	Ron Gant	.10
21	Edgar Martinez	.10
22	Pokey Reese	.10
23	Jason Varitek	.10
24	Neifi Perez	.10
25	Shane Reynolds	.10
26	Robin Ventura	.10
27	Scott Rolen	.65
28	Trevor Hoffman	.10
29	John Valentin	.10
30	Shannon Stewart	.10
31	Troy Glaus	.75
32	Kerry Wood	.65
33	Jim Thome	.65
34	Rafael Roque	.10
35	Tino Martinez	.10
36	Jeffrey Hammonds	.10
37	Orlando Hernandez	.10
38	Kris Benson	.10
39	Fred McGriff	.10
40	Brian Jordan	.10
41	Trot Nixon	.10
42	Matt Clement	.10
43	Ray Durham	.10
44	Johnny Damon	.30
45	Todd Hollandsworth	.10
46	Edgardo Alfonzo	.10
47	Tim Hudson	.25
48	Tony Gwynn	1.00
49	Barry Bonds	2.00
50	Andruw Jones	.75
51	Pedro Martinez	.75
52	Mike Hampton	.10
53	Miguel Tejada	.25
54	Kevin Young	.10
55	J.T. Snow	.10
56	Carlos Delgado	.50
57	Bobby Howry	.10
58	Andres Galarraga	.10
59	Paul Konerko	.20
60	Mike Cameron	.10
61	Jeremy Giambi	.10
62	Todd Hundley	.10
63	Al Leiter	.10
64	Matt Stairs	.10
65	Edgar Renteria	.10
66	Jeff Kent	.10
67	John Wetteland	.10
68	Nomar Garciaparra	1.25
69	Jeff Weaver	.10
70	Matt Williams	.10
71	Kyle Farnsworth	.10
72	Brad Radke	.10
73	Eric Chavez	.25
74	J.D. Drew	.25
75	Steve Finley	.10
76	Pete Harnisch	.10
77	Chad Kreuter	.10
78	Todd Pratt	.10
79	John Jaha	.10
80	Armando Rios	.10
81	Luis Gonzalez	.25
82	Ryan Minor	.10
83	Juan Gonzalez	.75
84	Rickey Henderson	.75
85	Jason Giambi	.50
86	Shawn Estes	.10
87	Chad Curtis	.10
88	Jeff Cirillo	.10
89	Juan Encarnacion	.10
90	Tony Womack	.10
91	Mike Mussina	.35
92	Jeff Bagwell	.75
93	Rey Ordonez	.10
94	Joe McEwing	.10
95	Robb Nen	.10
96	Will Clark	.10
97	Chris Singleton	.10
98	Jason Kendall	.10
99	Ken Griffey Jr.	1.25
100	Rusty Greer	.10
101	Charles Johnson	.10
102	Carlos Lee	.10
103	Brad Ausmus	.10
104	Preston Wilson	.10
105	Ronnie Belliard	.10
106	Mike Lieberthal	.10
107	Alex Rodriguez	1.50
108	Jay Bell	.10
109	Frank Thomas	.75
110	Adrian Beltre	.30
111	Ron Coomer	.10
112	Ben Grieve	.10
113	Darryl Kile	.10
114	Erubiel Durazo	.10
115	Magglio Ordonez	.10
116	Gary Sheffield	.40
117	Joe Mays	.10
118	Fernando Tatis	.10
119	David Wells	.10
120	Tim Salmon	.20
121	Troy O'Leary	.10
122	Roberto Alomar	.40
123	Damion Easley	.10
124	Brant Brown	.10
125	Carlos Beltran	.45
126	Eric Karros	.10
127	Geoff Jenkins	.10
128	Roger Clemens	1.00
129	Warren Morris	.10
130	Eric Owens	.10
131	Jose Cruz Jr.	.10
132	Mo Vaughn	.10
133	Eric Young	.10
134	Kenny Lofton	.10
135	Marquis Grissom	.10
136	A.J. Burnett	.10
137	Bernie Williams	.25
138	Javy Lopez	.10
139	Jose Offerman	.10
140	Sean Casey	.25
141	Alex Gonzalez	.10
142	Carlos Febles	.10
143	Mike Piazza	1.25
144	Curt Schilling	.35
145	Ben Davis	.10
146	Rafael Palmeiro	.65
147	Scott Williamson	.10
148	Darin Erstad	.25
149	Joe Girardi	.10
150	Gerald Williams	.10
151	Richie Sexson	.10
152	Corey Koskie	.10
153	Paul O'Neill	.10
154	Chad Hermansen	.10
155	Randy Johnson	.75
156	Henry Rodriguez	.10
157	Bartolo Colon	.10
158	Tony Clark	.10
159	Mike Lowell	.10
160	Moises Alou	.10
161	Todd Walker	.10
162	Mariano Rivera	.20
163	Mark McGwire	1.50
164	Roberto Hernandez	.10
165	Larry Walker	.10
166	Albert Belle	.15
167	Barry Larkin	.10
168	Rolando Arrojo	.10
169	Mark Kotsay	.10
170	Ken Caminiti	.10
171	Dermal Brown	.10
172	Michael Barrett	.10
173	Jay Buhner	.10
174	Ruben Mateo	.10
175	Jim Edmonds	.10
176	Sammy Sosa	1.25

177 Omar Vizquel .10
178 Todd Helton .75
179 Kevin Barker .10
180 Derek Jeter 2.00
181 Brian Giles .10
182 Greg Vaughn .10
183 Roy Halladay .10
184 Tom Glavine .35
185 Craig Biggio .10
186 Jose Vidro .10
187 Andy Ashby .10
188 Freddy Garcia .10
189 Garret Anderson .10
190 Mark Grace .20
191 Travis Fryman .10
192 Jeromy Burnitz .10
193 Jacque Jones .10
194 David Cone .10
195 Ryan Rupe .10
196 John Smoltz .10
197 Daryle Ward .10
198 Rondell White .10
199 Bobby Abreu .10
200 Justin Thompson .10
201 Norm Hutchins .10
201 Norm Hutchins SP 1.00
202 Ramon Ortiz .10
202 Ramon Ortiz SP 1.00
203 Dan Wheeler .10
203 Dan Wheeler SP 1.00
204 Matt Riley .10
204 Matt Riley SP 1.00
205 Steve Lomasney .10
205 Steve Lomasney SP 1.00
206 Chad Meyers .10
206 Chad Meyers SP 1.00
207 *Gary Glover* .20
207 Gary Glover SP 1.00
208 Joe Crede .10
208 Joe Crede SP 1.00
209 Kip Wells .10
209 Kip Wells SP 1.00
210 Travis Dawkins .10
210 Travis Dawkins SP 1.00
211 *Denny Stark* .20
211 Denny Stark SP 1.00
212 Ben Petrick .10
212 Ben Petrick SP 1.00
213 Eric Munson .10
213 Eric Munson SP 1.00
214 Josh Beckett .25
214 Josh Beckett SP 1.50
215 Pablo Ozuna .10
215 Pablo Ozuna SP 1.00
216 Brad Penny .10
216 Brad Penny SP 1.00
217 Julio Ramirez .10
217 Julio Ramirez SP 1.00
218 Danny Peoples .10
218 Danny Peoples SP 1.00
219 *Wilfredo Rodriguez* .10
219 *Wilfredo Rodriguez SP* 1.00
220 Julio Lugo .10
220 Julio Lugo SP 1.00
221 Mark Quinn .10
221 Mark Quinn SP 1.00
222 Eric Gagne .10
222 Eric Gagne SP 1.00
223 Chad Green .10
223 Chad Green SP 1.00
224 Tony Armas Jr. .10
224 Tony Armas Jr. SP 1.00
225 Milton Bradley .10
225 Milton Bradley SP 1.00
226 Rob Bell .10
226 Rob Bell SP 1.00
227 Alfonso Soriano 1.00
227 Alfonso Soriano SP 4.00
228 Wily Pena .10
228 Wily Pena SP 1.00
229 Nick Johnson .10
229 Nick Johnson SP 1.50
230 Ed Yarnall .10
230 Ed Yarnall SP 1.00
231 Ryan Bradley .10
231 Ryan Bradley SP 1.00
232 Adam Piatt .10
232 Adam Piatt SP 1.00
233 Chad Harville .10
233 Chad Harville SP 1.00
234 Alex Sanchez .10
234 Alex Sanchez SP 1.00
235 Michael Coleman .10
235 Michael Coleman SP 1.00
236 Pat Burrell .25
236 Pat Burrell SP 1.50
237 *Wascar Serrano* .10
237 *Wascar Serrano SP* 1.00
238 Rick Ankiel .10
238 Rick Ankiel SP 1.00
239 *Mike Lamb* .10
239 *Mike Lamb SP* 1.00
240 Vernon Wells .10
240 Vernon Wells SP 1.00
241 Jorge Toca, Goefrey Tomlinson .10
241 Jorge Toca, Goefrey Tomlinson SP .50
242 *Shea Hillenbrand, Josh Phelps* 2.00
242 *Shea Hillenbrand, Josh Phelps SP* 4.00
243 Aaron Myette, Doug Davis .10
243 Aaron Myette, Doug Davis SP .50
244 Brett Laxton, Robert Ramsay .10
244 Brett Laxton, Robert Ramsay SP .50
245 B.J. Ryan, Corey Lee .10
245 B.J. Ryan, Corey Lee SP .50
246 Chris Haas, Wilton Veras .10
246 Chris Haas, Wilton Veras SP .50
247 Jimmy Anderson, Kyle Peterson .10
247 Jimmy Anderson, Kyle Peterson SP .50
248 Jason Dewey, Giuseppe Chiaramonte .10
248 Jason Dewey, Giuseppe Chiaramonte SP .50
249 Guillermo Mota, Orber Moreno .10
249 Guillermo Mota, Orber Moreno SP .50
250 *Steve Cox, Julio Zuleta* .15
250 *Steve Cox, Julio Zuleta SP* .50

Star Rubies

NM/M

Complete Set (250): 200.00
Common Player (1-200): .50
Common SP Prospect (201-250): 3.00
Stars: 6X
Star SPs: 3X
(See 2000 SkyBox for checklist and base card values.)

Star Rubies Extreme

NM/M

Common Player (1-200): 3.00
Common SP Prospect (201-250): 4.50
Stars: 25X
Star SPs: 15X
(See 2000 SkyBox for checklist and base card values.)

Autographics

NM/M

Common Player 5.00
Rick Ankiel 6.00
Michael Barrett 5.00
Josh Beckett 20.00
Rob Bell 5.00
Adrian Beltre 15.00
Peter Bergeron 5.00
Lance Berkman 15.00
Rico Brogna 5.00
Pat Burrell 20.00
Orlando Cabrera 15.00
Mike Cameron 8.00
Roger Cedeno 5.00
Eric Chavez 15.00
Bruce Chen 5.00
Johnny Damon 20.00
Ben Davis 5.00
Jason Dewey 5.00
Octavio Dotel 6.00
J.D. Drew 15.00
Erubiel Durazo 8.00
Jason Giambi 20.00
Doug Glanville 5.00
Troy Glaus 20.00
Alex Gonzalez 8.00
Shawn Green 15.00
Jason Grilli 5.00
Tony Gwynn 40.00
Mike Hampton 8.00
Tim Hudson 15.00
Norm Hutchins 5.00
John Jaha 5.00
Derek Jeter 100.00
D'Angelo Jimenez 5.00
Randy Johnson 60.00
Andruw Jones 20.00
Gabe Kapler 8.00
Jason Kendall 10.00
Adam Kennedy 8.00
Cesar King 5.00
Paul Konerko 8.00
Mark Kotsay 6.00
Carlos Lee 8.00
Mike Lieberthal 8.00
Steve Lomasney 5.00
Greg Maddux 60.00
Edgar Martinez 15.00
Aaron McNeal 5.00
Kevin Millwood 10.00
Raul Mondesi 8.00
Joe Nathan 5.00
Magglio Ordonez 15.00
Eric Owens 5.00
Rafael Palmeiro 25.00
Angel Pena 5.00
Wily Pena 15.00
Cal Ripken Jr. 85.00
Scott Rolen 20.00
Jimmy Rollins 8.00
B.J. Ryan 5.00
Tim Salmon 10.00
Chris Singleton 5.00
J.T. Snow 6.00
Mike Sweeney 8.00
Jose Vidro 8.00
Rondell White 8.00
Jaret Wright 5.00

E-Ticket

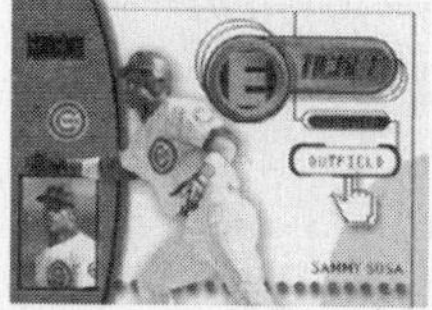

NM/M

Complete Set (14): 15.00
Common Player: .50
Inserted 1:4
Star Ruby: 4-8X
Production 100 sets
1 Alex Rodriguez 2.50
2 Derek Jeter 3.00
3 Nomar Garciaparra 1.50
4 Cal Ripken Jr. 3.00
5 Sean Casey .50
6 Mark McGwire 2.50
7 Sammy Sosa 1.50
8 Ken Griffey Jr. 2.00
9 Tony Gwynn 1.50
10 Pedro Martinez 1.00
11 Chipper Jones 1.50
12 Vladimir Guerrero 1.00
13 Roger Clemens 1.75
14 Mike Piazza 2.00

Genuine Coverage

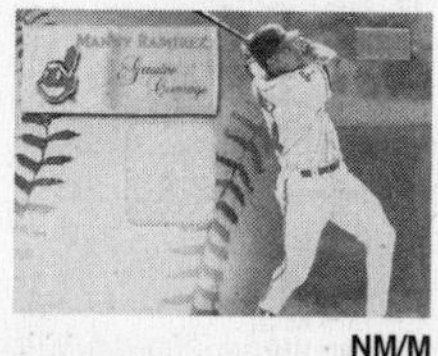

NM/M

Common Player: 8.00
Inserted 1:399
1 Troy Glaus 15.00
2 Cal Ripken Jr. 40.00
3 Alex Rodriguez 25.00
4 Mike Mussina 10.00
5 J.D. Drew 8.00
6 Robin Ventura 8.00
7 Matt Williams 8.00

Genuine Coverage HOBBY

NM/M

Common Player: 10.00
Inserted 1:144
1 Ivan Rodriguez 12.00
2 Jose Canseco 10.00
3 Frank Thomas 15.00
4 Manny Ramirez 15.00

Higher Level

NM/M

Complete Set (10): 20.00
Common Player: 1.00
Inserted 1:24
Star Ruby: 5-10X
Production 50 sets
1 Cal Ripken Jr. 4.00
2 Derek Jeter 4.00
3 Nomar Garciaparra 2.00
4 Chipper Jones 2.00
5 Mike Piazza 2.50
6 Ivan Rodriguez 1.00
7 Ken Griffey Jr. 2.50
8 Sammy Sosa 2.00
9 Alex Rodriguez 3.00
10 Mark McGwire 3.00

Preeminence

NM/M

Complete Set (10): 15.00
Common Player: .50
Inserted 1:24
Star Ruby: 5-10X
Production 50 sets
1 Pedro Martinez 1.25
2 Derek Jeter 4.00
3 Nomar Garciaparra 1.50
4 Alex Rodriguez 3.00
5 Mark McGwire 3.00
6 Sammy Sosa 1.50
7 Sean Casey .50
8 Mike Piazza 2.00
9 Chipper Jones 1.50
10 Ivan Rodriguez 1.00

SkyLines

NM/M

Complete Set (10): 10.00
Common Player: .50
Inserted 1:11
Star Ruby: 10-20X
Production 50 sets
1 Cal Ripken Jr. 2.00
2 Mark McGwire 1.50
3 Alex Rodriguez 1.50
4 Sammy Sosa .75
5 Derek Jeter 2.00
6 Mike Piazza 1.00
7 Nomar Garciaparra .75
8 Chipper Jones .75
9 Ken Griffey Jr. 1.00
10 Manny Ramirez .50

Speed Merchants

NM/M

Complete Set (10): 12.00
Common Player: .50
Inserted 1:8
Star Ruby: 3-6X
Production 100 sets

#	Player	Price
1	Derek Jeter	3.00
2	Sammy Sosa	1.25
3	Nomar Garciaparra	1.25
4	Alex Rodriguez	2.50
5	Randy Johnson	1.00
6	Ken Griffey Jr.	1.50
7	Pedro Martinez	1.00
8	Pat Burrell	.50
9	Barry Bonds	3.00
10	Mark McGwire	2.50

The Technique

		NM/M
Complete Set (15):		20.00
Common Player:		.50
Inserted 1:11		
Star Ruby:		3-6X
Production 50 sets		
1	Alex Rodriguez	3.00
2	Tony Gwynn	1.50
3	Sean Casey	.50
4	Mark McGwire	3.00
5	Sammy Sosa	1.50
6	Ken Griffey Jr.	2.00
7	Mike Piazza	2.00
8	Nomar Garciaparra	1.50
9	Derek Jeter	4.00
10	Vladimir Guerrero	1.00
11	Cal Ripken Jr.	4.00
12	Chipper Jones	1.50
13	Frank Thomas	1.00
14	Manny Ramirez	1.00
15	Jeff Bagwell	1.00

2000 SKYBOX DOMINION

		NM/M
Complete Set (300):		20.00
Common Player:		.10
Pack (10):		1.50
Wax Box (36):		30.00
1	Mark McGwire, Ken Griffey Jr.	.40
2	Mark McGwire, Manny Ramirez	.40
3	Larry Walker, Nomar Garciaparra	.25
4	Tony Womack, Brian Hunter	.10
5	Mike Hampton, Pedro Martinez	.20
6	Randy Johnson, Pedro Martinez	.20
7	Randy Johnson, Pedro Martinez	.20
8	Ugueth Urbina, Mariano Rivera	.10
9	Vinny Castilla	.10
10	Orioles host Cuban National Team	.10
11	Jose Canseco	.10
12	Fernando Tatis	.10
13	Robin Ventura	.10
14	Roger Clemens	.50
15	Jose Jimenez	.10
16	David Cone	.10
17	Mark McGwire	.65
18	Cal Ripken Jr.	.75
19	Tony Gwynn	.30
20	Wade Boggs	.25
21	Ivan Rodriguez	.20
22	Chuck Finley	.10
23	Eric Milton	.10
24	Adrian Beltre	.10
25	Brad Radke	.10
26	Derek Bell	.10
27	Garret Anderson	.10
28	Ivan Rodriguez	.40
29	Jeff Kent	.10
30	Jeremy Giambi	.10
31	John Franco	.10
32	Jose Hernandez	.10
33	Jose Offerman	.10
34	Jose Rosado	.10
35	Kevin Appier	.10
36	Kris Benson	.10
37	Mark McGwire	1.00
38	Matt Williams	.10
39	Paul O'Neill	.10
40	Rickey Henderson	.50
41	Todd Greene	.10
42	Russ Ortiz	.10
43	Sean Casey	.20
44	Tony Womack	.10
45	Troy O'Leary	.10
46	Ugueth Urbina	.10
47	Tom Glavine	.25
48	Mike Mussina	.30
49	Carlos Febles	.10
50	Jon Lieber	.10
51	Juan Gonzalez	.30
52	Matt Clement	.10
53	Moises Alou	.10
54	Ray Durham	.10
55	Robb Nen	.10
56	Tino Martinez	.10
57	Troy Glaus	.40
58	Curt Schilling	.30
59	Mike Sweeney	.10
60	Steve Finley	.10
61	Roger Cedeno	.10
62	Bobby Jones	.10
63	John Smoltz	.10
64	Darin Erstad	.20
65	Carlos Delgado	.35
66	Ray Lankford	.10
67	Todd Stottlemyre	.10
68	Andy Ashby	.10
69	Bobby Abreu	.15
70	Chuck Finley	.10
71	Damion Easley	.10
72	Dustin Hermanson	.10
73	Frank Thomas	.50
74	Kevin Brown	.10
75	Kevin Millwood	.10
76	Mark Grace	.10
77	Matt Stairs	.10
78	Mike Hampton	.10
79	Omar Vizquel	.10
80	Preston Wilson	.10
81	Robin Ventura	.10
82	Todd Helton	.40
83	Tony Clark	.10
84	Al Leiter	.10
85	Alex Fernandez	.10
86	Bernie Williams	.10
87	Edgar Martinez	.10
88	Edgar Renteria	.10
89	Fred McGriff	.10
90	Jermaine Dye	.10
91	Joe McEwing	.10
92	John Halama	.10
93	Lee Stevens	.10
94	Matt Lawton	.10
95	Mike Piazza	.75
96	Pete Harnisch	.10
97	Scott Karl	.10
98	Tony Fernandez	.10
99	Sammy Sosa	.60
100	Bobby Higginson	.10
101	Tony Gwynn	.60
102	J.D. Drew	.20
103	Roberto Hernandez	.10
104	Rondell White	.10
105	David Nilsson	.10
106	Shane Reynolds	.10
107	Jaret Wright	.10
108	Jeff Bagwell	.50
109	Jay Bell	.10
110	Kevin Tapani	.10
111	Michael Barrett	.10
112	Neifi Perez	.10
113	Pat Hentgen	.10
114	Roger Clemens	.65
115	Travis Fryman	.10
116	Aaron Sele	.10
117	Eric Davis	.10
118	Trevor Hoffman	.10
119	Chris Singleton	.10
120	Ryan Klesko	.10
121	Scott Rolen	.40
122	Jorge Posada	.10
123	Abraham Nunez	.10
124	Alex Gonzalez	.10
125	B.J. Surhoff	.10
126	Barry Bonds	1.50
127	Billy Koch	.10
128	Billy Wagner	.10
129	Brad Ausmus	.10
130	Bret Boone	.10
131	Cal Ripken Jr.	1.50
132	Chad Allen	.10
133	Chris Carpenter	.10
134	Craig Biggio	.10
135	Dante Bichette	.10
136	Dean Palmer	.10
137	Derek Jeter	1.50
138	Ellis Burks	.10
139	Freddy Garcia	.10
140	Gabe Kapler	.10
141	Greg Maddux	.60
142	Greg Vaughn	.10
143	Jason Kendall	.10
144	Jim Parque	.10
145	John Valentin	.10
146	Jose Vidro	.10
147	Ken Griffey Jr.	.75
148	Kenny Lofton	.10
149	Kenny Rogers	.10
150	Kent Bottenfield	.10
151	Chuck Knoblauch	.10
152	Larry Walker	.10
153	Manny Ramirez	.50
154	Mickey Morandini	.10
155	Mike Cameron	.10
156	Mike Lieberthal	.10
157	Mo Vaughn	.10
158	Randy Johnson	.50
159	Rey Ordonez	.10
160	Roberto Alomar	.20
161	Scott Williamson	.10
162	Shawn Estes	.10
163	Tim Wakefield	.10
164	Tony Batista	.10
165	Will Clark	.10
166	Wade Boggs	.60
167	David Cone	.10
168	Doug Glanville	.10
169	Jeff Cirillo	.10
170	John Jaha	.10
171	Mariano Rivera	.20
172	Tom Gordon	.10
173	Wally Joyner	.10
174	Alex Gonzalez	.10
175	Andruw Jones	.50
176	Barry Larkin	.10
177	Bartolo Colon	.10
178	Brian Giles	.10
179	Carlos Lee	.10
180	Darren Dreifort	.10
181	Eric Chavez	.20
182	Henry Rodriguez	.10
183	Ismael Valdes	.10
184	Jason Giambi	.40
185	John Wetteland	.10
186	Juan Encarnacion	.10
187	Luis Gonzalez	.10
188	Reggie Sanders	.10
189	Richard Hidalgo	.10
190	Ryan Rupe	.10
191	Sean Berry	.10
192	Rick Helling	.10
193	Randy Wolf	.10
194	Cliff Floyd	.10
195	Jose Lima	.10
196	Chipper Jones	.60
197	Charles Johnson	.10
198	Nomar Garciaparra	.60
199	Magglio Ordonez	.10
200	Shawn Green	.25
201	Travis Lee	.10
202	Jose Canseco	.35
203	Fernando Tatis	.10
204	Bruce Aven	.10
205	Johnny Damon	.35
206	Gary Sheffield	.25
207	Ken Caminiti	.10
208	Ben Grieve	.10
209	Sidney Ponson	.10
210	Vinny Castilla	.10
211	Alex Rodriguez	1.00
212	Chris Widger	.10
213	Carl Pavano	.10
214	J.T. Snow	.10
215	Jim Thome	.40
216	Kevin Young	.10
217	Mike Sirotka	.10
218	Rafael Palmeiro	.40
219	Rico Brogna	.10
220	Todd Walker	.10
221	Todd Zeile	.10
222	Brian Rose	.10
223	Chris Fussell	.10
224	Corey Koskie	.10
225	Rich Aurilia	.10
226	Geoff Jenkins	.10
227	Pedro Martinez	.50
228	Todd Hundley	.10
229	Brian Jordan	.10
230	Cristian Guzman	.10
231	Raul Mondesi	.10
232	Tim Hudson	.20
233	Albert Belle	.10
234	Andy Pettitte	.25
235	Brady Anderson	.10
236	Brian Bohannon	.10
237	Carlos Beltran	.35
238	Doug Mientkiewicz	.10
239	Jason Schmidt	.10
240	Jeff Zimmerman	.10
241	John Olerud	.10
242	Paul Byrd	.10
243	Vladimir Guerrero	.50
244	Warren Morris	.10
245	Eric Karros	.10
246	Jeff Weaver	.10
247	Jeromy Burnitz	.10
248	David Bell	.10
249	Rusty Greer	.10
250	Kevin Stocker	.10
251	Shea Hillenbrand	.15
252	Alfonso Soriano	.50
253	Micah Bowie	.10
254	Gary Matthews Jr.	.10
255	Lance Berkman	.10
256	Pat Burrell	.25
257	Ruben Mateo	.10
258	Kip Wells	.10
259	Wilton Veras	.10
260	Ben Davis	.10
261	Eric Munson	.10
262	Ramon Hernandez	.10
263	Tony Armas Jr.	.10
264	Erubiel Durazo	.10
265	Chad Meyers	.10
266	Rick Ankiel	.10
267	Ramon Ortiz	.10
268	Adam Kennedy	.10
269	Vernon Wells	.10
270	Chad Hermansen	.10
271	Norm Hutchins, Trent Durrington	.10
272	Gabe Molina, B.J. Ryan	.10
273	*Juan Pena, Tomokazu Ohka*	.25
274	Pat Daneker, Aaron Myette	.15
275	Jason Rakers, Russell Branyan	.10
276	Beiker Graterol, Dave Borkowski	.10
277	Mark Quinn, Dan Reichert	.10
278	Mark Redman, Jacque Jones	.15
279	Ed Yarnall, Wily Pena	.10
280	Chad Harville, Brett Laxton	.10
281	Aaron Scheffer, Gil Meche	.10
282	Jim Morris, Dan Wheeler	.10
283	Danny Kolb, Kelly Dransfeldt	.10
284	Peter Munro, Casey Blake	.10
285	Rob Ryan, Byung-Hyun Kim	.10
286	Derrin Ebert, Pascual Matos	.10
287	Richard Barker, Kyle Farnsworth	.10
288	Jason LaRue, Travis Dawkins	.10
289	Chris Sexton, Edgard Clemente	.10
290	Amaury Garcia, A.J. Burnett	.10
291	Carlos Hernandez, Daryle Ward	.10
292	Eric Gagne, Jeff Williams	.10
293	Kyle Peterson, Kevin Barker	.10
294	Fernando Seguignol, Guillermo Mota	.10
295	Melvin Mora, Octavio Dotel	.10
296	Anthony Shumaker, Cliff Politte	.10
297	Yamid Haad, Jimmy Anderson	.10
298	Rick Heiserman, Chad Hutchinson	.10
299	Mike Darr, Wiki Gonzalez	.10
300	Joe Nathan, Calvin Murray	.10

Autographics

	NM/M
Common Player:	5.00
Inserted 1:144	

1	Rick Ankiel	6.00
2	Peter Bergeron	5.00
3	Wade Boggs	25.00
4	Barry Bonds	200.00
5	Pat Burrell	20.00
6	Miguel Cairo	5.00
7	Mike Cameron	8.00
8	Ben Davis	5.00
9	Russ Davis	5.00
10	Einar Diaz	5.00
11	Scott Elarton	5.00
12	Jeremy Giambi	5.00
13	Todd Greene	5.00
14	Vladimir Guerrero	25.00
15	Tony Gwynn	30.00
16	Bobby Howry	5.00
17	Tim Hudson	15.00
18	Randy Johnson	50.00
19	Andruw Jones	20.00
20	Jacque Jones	8.00
21	Jason LaRue	5.00
22	Matt Lawton	6.00
23	Greg Maddux	50.00
24	Pedro Martinez	50.00
25	Pokey Reese	5.00
26	Alex Rodriguez	75.00
27	Ryan Rupe	5.00
28	J.T. Snow	6.00
29	Jose Vidro	6.00
30	Tony Womack	6.00
31	Ed Yarnall	5.00
32	Kevin Young	5.00

Double Play

		NM/M
Complete Set (10):		10.00
Common Player:		1.00
Inserted 1:9		
Plus:		2-4X
Inserted 1:90		
WarpTek:		10-20X
Inserted 1:900		
1	Nomar Garciaparra	1.50
2	Pedro Martinez	1.25
3	Chipper Jones	1.50
4	Mark McGwire	2.50
5	Cal Ripken Jr.	3.00
6	Roger Clemens	1.75
7	Juan Gonzalez	1.00
8	Tony Gwynn	1.50
9	Sammy Sosa	1.50
10	Mike Piazza	2.00

Eye on October

		NM/M
Complete Set (15):		25.00
Common Player:		.50
Inserted 1:24		
Plus:		2-4X
Inserted 1:240		
1	Ken Griffey Jr.	2.50
2	Mark McGwire	3.00
3	Derek Jeter	4.00
4	Juan Gonzalez	1.00
5	Chipper Jones	2.00
6	Sammy Sosa	2.00
7	Greg Maddux	2.00
8	Frank Thomas	1.50
9	Nomar Garciaparra	2.00
10	Shawn Green	1.00
11	Cal Ripken Jr.	4.00
12	Manny Ramirez	1.50
13	Scott Rolen	1.25
14	Mike Piazza	2.50
15	Alex Rodriguez	3.00

Hats Off

	NM/M
Common Player:	15.00
Inserted 1:468 H	

1	Wade Boggs	25.00
2	Barry Bonds	75.00
3	J.D. Drew	15.00
4	Shawn Green	15.00
5	Vladimir Guerrero	25.00
6	Randy Johnson	30.00
7	Andruw Jones	20.00
8	Greg Maddux	40.00
9	Pedro Martinez	25.00
10	Mike Mussina	15.00
11	Rafael Palmeiro	20.00
12	Alex Rodriguez	50.00
13	Scott Rolen	15.00
14	Tim Salmon	15.00
15	Robin Ventura	15.00

Milestones

		NM/M
Common Player:		15.00
Inserted 1:1,999		
1	Mark McGwire	60.00
2	Roger Clemens	40.00
3	Tony Gwynn	25.00
4	Wade Boggs	25.00
5	Cal Ripken Jr.	75.00
6	Jose Canseco	15.00

New Era

		NM/M
Complete Set (20):		5.00
Common Player:		.25
Inserted 1:3		
Plus:		2X to 4X
Inserted 1:30		
WarpTek:		5X to 10X
Inserted 1:300		
1	Pat Burrell	.75
2	Ruben Mateo	.25
3	Wilton Veras	.25
4	Eric Munson	.25
5	Jeff Weaver	.25
6	Tim Hudson	.50
7	Carlos Beltran	1.00
8	Chris Singleton	.25
9	Lance Berkman	.25
10	Freddy Garcia	.25
11	Erubiel Durazo	.25
12	Randy Wolf	.25
13	Shea Hillenbrand	.25
14	Kip Wells	.25
15	Alfonso Soriano	1.50
16	Rick Ankiel	.25
17	Ramon Ortiz	.25
18	Adam Kennedy	.25
19	Vernon Wells	.25
20	Chad Hermansen	.25

2004 SKYBOX AUTOGRAPHICS

		NM/M
Complete Set (100):		
Common Player:		.40
Hobby Box (4):		75.00
1	Albert Pujols	2.50
2	Richie Sexson	.75
3	Scott Rolen	1.00
4	Rafael Palmeiro	.75
5	Ichiro Suzuki	2.00
6	Craig Biggio	.50
7	Todd Helton	.75
8	Miguel Cabrera	.75
9	Ken Griffey Jr.	1.50
10	Pat Burrell	.50
11	Jose Reyes	.50
12	Hideki Matsui	2.50
13	Geoff Jenkins	.50
14	Mark Prior	2.00
15	Gary Sheffield	.50
16	Nomar Garciaparra	2.00
17	Luis Gonzalez	.50
18	Troy Glaus	.50
19	Rocco Baldelli	.75
20	Hank Blalock	.50
21	Bret Boone	.50
22	Mike Sweeney	.40
23	Dmitri Young	.40
24	Dontrelle Willis	.50
25	Austin Kearns	.50
26	Jason Kendall	.40
27	Derek Jeter	3.00
28	Miguel Tejada	.50
29	Torii Hunter	.50
30	Sammy Sosa	2.00
31	Chipper Jones	1.50
32	Pedro J. Martinez	1.00
33	Curt Schilling	.75
34	Roy Halladay	.50
35	Jim Edmonds	.50
36	Alex Rodriguez	2.50
37	Jason Schmidt	.50
38	Jeff Bagwell	.75
39	Omar Vizquel	.40
40	Ivan Rodriguez	.75
41	Magglio Ordonez	.50
42	Jim Thome	1.00
43	Mike Piazza	2.00
44	Alfonso Soriano	1.00
45	Hideo Nomo	.50
46	Kerry Wood	1.00
47	Greg Maddux	1.50
48	Tony Batista	.40
49	Randy Johnson	1.00
50	Garret Anderson	.50
51	Mark Teixeira	.50
52	Carlos Delgado	.75
53	Darin Erstad	.50
54	Shawn Green	.50
55	Josh Beckett	.75
56	Lance Berkman	.50
57	Adam Dunn	.50
58	Brian Giles	.50
59	Jason Giambi	1.00
60	Barry Zito	.50
61	Vladimir Guerrero	1.00
62	Frank Thomas	.75
63	Jay Gibbons	.40
64	Manny Ramirez	.75
65	Andruw Jones	.75
66	Rickie Weeks	5.00
67	*Chad Bentz*	4.00
68	Bobby Crosby	4.00
69	*Greg Dobbs*	5.00
70	*John Gall*	3.00
71	*Kazuo Matsui*	20.00
72	Dallas McPherson	3.00
73	Brandon Watson	3.00
74	*Jerry Gil*	3.00
75	Garrett Atkins	3.00
76	*Cory Sullivan*	3.00
77	Khalil Greene	5.00
78	*Shawn Hill*	3.00
79	Graham Koonce	3.00
80	Chien-Ming Wang	3.00
81	*Josh Labandeira*	3.00
82	Jonny Gomes	3.00
83	Edwin Jackson	3.00
84	*Alfredo Simon*	4.00
85	Delmon Young	6.00
86	*Jason Bartlett*	5.00
87	*Angel Chavez*	3.00
88	Angel Guzman	3.00
89	Ryan Howard	3.00
90	Scott Hairston	3.00
91	*Ronny Cedeno*	3.00
92	*Donald Kelly*	3.00
93	*Ivan Ochoa*	3.00
94	Edwin Encarnacion	3.00
95	Byron Gettis	3.00
96	Kevin Youkilis	4.00
97	Grady Sizemore	3.00
98	*Mariano Gomez*	3.00
99	*Hector Gimenez*	3.00
100	*Ruddy Yan*	3.00

Insignia

Cards (1-65):	3X-5X
Rookies (66-100):	1X-2X
Production 150 sets	

Royal Insignia

No Pricing
Production 25 sets

Autoclassics

	NM/M
Complete Set (15):	
Common Player:	
Johnny Bench	4.00
Wade Boggs	2.00
Steve Carlton	2.00
Albert Chandler	1.50
Ty Cobb	4.00
Carlton Fisk	1.50
George Kelly	1.50
Sal Maglie	2.00
Bill Mazeroski	1.50
Jim Palmer	2.00
Nolan Ryan	6.00
Mike Schmidt	3.00
Joe Sewell	2.00
Duke Snider	3.00
Warren Spahn	4.00

Autographics

	NM/M
Common Player:	5.00
Garrett Atkins	5.00
Rocco Baldelli/255	18.00
Josh Beckett/100	20.00
Angel Berroa/182	12.00
Hank Blalock/205	18.00
A.J. Burnett/485	10.00
Marlon Byrd/240	8.00
Edwin Encarnacion/188	5.00
Eric Gagne/225	25.00
Jonny Gomes/265	8.00
Khalil Greene/190	25.00
Rich Harden/185	10.00
Dan Haren/176	5.00
Koyie Hill/240	5.00
Shea Hillenbrand/213	10.00
Ryan Howard/170	5.00
Tim Hudson/169	8.00
Aubrey Huff/296	5.00
Torii Hunter/215	10.00
Edwin Jackson/224	10.00
Bobby Jenks/307	8.00
Austin Kearns/275	8.00
Graham Koonce/190	12.00
Barry Larkin/195	20.00
Dallas McPherson/179	8.00
Aaron Miles/140	10.00
Mark Mulder/186	15.00
Laynce Nix/185	20.00
Trot Nixon/210	15.00
Corey Patterson/220	12.00
Juan Pierre/220	8.00
Scott Podsednik/210	25.00
Albert Pujols/103	80.00
Jose Reyes/195	15.00
Juan Richardson/345	5.00
Jason Schmidt	
Gary Sheffield/210	20.00
Chris Snelling/200	5.00
Shannon Stewart/340	5.00
Cory Sullivan/170	5.00
Javier Vazquez/210	25.00

Billy Wagner/180 30.00
Ryan Wagner
Chien-Ming Wang/195 20.00
Brandon Webb/310 12.00
Rickie Weeks/187 20.00
Dontrelle Willis/225 20.00
Kerry Wood/191 30.00
Delmon Young/205 20.00

Jerseygraphics Blue

NM/M
Common Player:
Silver: 1X-2X
Production 100 sets
Gold: No Pricing
Production 25 sets
Bobby Abreu 5.00
Rocco Baldelli 5.00
Josh Beckett 10.00
Lance Berkman 5.00
Craig Biggio 5.00
Hank Blalock 8.00
Pat Burrell 8.00
Miguel Cabrera 10.00
Carlos Delgado 5.00
Adam Dunn 8.00
Jim Edmonds 5.00
Darin Erstad 5.00
Nomar Garciaparra 8.00
Jason Giambi 8.00
Jay Gibbons 8.00
Troy Glaus 8.00
Shawn Green 5.00
Vladimir Guerrero 8.00
Roy Halladay 8.00
Todd Helton 5.00
Torii Hunter 5.00
Derek Jeter 15.00
Andruw Jones 5.00
Chipper Jones 10.00
Austin Kearns 5.00
Greg Maddux 15.00
Pedro J. Martinez 10.00
Kevin Millwood 5.00
Hideo Nomo 8.00
David Ortiz 10.00
Rafael Palmeiro 5.00
Mike Piazza 10.00
Mark Prior 10.00
Albert Pujols 15.00
Manny Ramirez 5.00
Jose Reyes 5.00
Alex Rodriguez 15.00
Ivan Rodriguez 5.00
Scott Rolen 10.00
Curt Schilling 5.00
Alfonso Soriano 5.00
Sammy Sosa 15.00
Mark Teixeira 8.00
Miguel Tejada 8.00
Frank Thomas 10.00
Jim Thome 10.00
Dontrelle Willis 5.00
Kerry Wood 12.00
Barry Zito 5.00

Prospects Endorsed

NM/M
Complete Set (15): 10.00
Common Duo: .50
1 Albert Pujols, Delmon Young 3.00
2 Eric Gagne, Bobby Jenks .50
3 Barry Larkin, Kazuo Matsui 2.00
4 Andruw Jones, Jonny Gomes 1.00
5 Hideo Nomo, Chien-Ming Wang .50
6 Gary Sheffield, Cory Sullivan .75
7 Billy Wagner, Ryan Howard .30
8 Jorge Posada, Koyie Hill .75
9 Curt Schilling, Ryan Wagner .75
10 Jose Reyes, Rickie Weeks 1.25
11 Alfonso Soriano, Matt Kata 1.50
12 Barry Zito, Rich Harden .75
13 Randy Johnson, Brandon Webb 1.50
14 Alex Rodriguez, Angel Berroa 3.00
15 Dontrelle Willis, Edwin Jackson .50

2004 SKYBOX LE

NM/M
Complete Set (160):
Common Player (1-110): .25
Common SP (111-160): 4.00
Production 299 unless noted
Pack (3): 5.00
Box (18): 80.00
1 Juan Pierre .25
2 Derek Jeter 3.00
3 Brandon Webb .25
4 Jeff Bagwell .75
5 Jason Schmidt .40
6 Marlon Byrd .25
7 Garret Anderson .50
8 Miguel Cabrera .75
9 Jose Reyes .50
10 Rocco Baldelli .50
11 Tony Batista .25
12 Carlos Beltran .50
13 Nomar Garciaparra 2.00
14 Shawn Green .50
15 Albert Pujols 2.50
16 Magglio Ordonez .50
17 Kip Wells .25
18 Andruw Jones .75
19 Ryan Wagner .25
20 Alex Rodriguez 3.00
21 Vernon Wells .50
22 Todd Helton .75
23 David Ortiz .25
24 Troy Glaus .50
25 Jim Thome 1.00
26 Greg Maddux 1.50
27 Roberto Alomar .50
28 Edgardo Alfonzo .25
29 Hee Seop Choi .25
30 Ken Griffey Jr. 1.50
31 Tim Hudson .50
32 Shannon Stewart .25
33 Ichiro Suzuki 2.00
34 Luis Gonzalez .50
35 Darin Erstad .50
36 Dmitri Young .25
37 Ivan Rodriguez .75
38 Scott Podsednik .50
39 Jose Vidro .25
40 Mark Prior 2.00
41 Mike Mussina .75
42 Gary Sheffield .50
43 Manny Ramirez .75
44 C.C. Sabathia .40
45 Curt Schilling .75
46 Scott Rolen 1.00
47 Hideo Nomo .50
48 Torii Hunter .50
49 Aubrey Huff .25
50 Javy Lopez .50
51 Austin Kearns .50
52 Mike Piazza 1.50
53 Sean Burroughs .25
54 Kerry Wood .75
55 Marquis Grissom .25
56 Preston Wilson .25
57 Angel Berroa .25
58 Jason Kendall .25
59 Rafael Palmeiro .75
60 Mike Lowell .40
61 Eric Chavez .50
62 Bartolo Colon .50
63 Adam Dunn .50
64 Pedro J. Martinez 1.00
65 Lance Berkman .50
66 Bret Boone .40
67 Eric Gagne .40
68 Vladimir Guerrero 1.00
69 Jay Gibbons .25
70 Larry Walker .40
71 Orlando Cabrera .40
72 Jorge Posada .50
73 Jamie Moyer .25
74 Carl Crawford .25
75 Hank Blalock .50
76 Josh Beckett .75
77 Jody Gerut .25
78 Kevin Brown .50
79 Sammy Sosa 2.00
80 Chipper Jones 1.00
81 Tom Glavine .50
82 Barry Zito .50
83 Edgar Renteria .50
84 Esteban Loaiza .25
85 Jason Giambi 1.00
86 Miguel Tejada .50
87 Randy Johnson 1.00
88 A.J. Burnett .25
89 Richie Sexson .75
90 Reggie Sanders .25
91 Carlos Delgado .75
92 Pat Burrell .50
93 Jacque Jones .25
94 Roy Oswalt .50
95 Frank Thomas .75
96 Melvin Mora .25
97 Jeremy Bonderman .25
98 Mike Sweeney .25
99 Brian Giles .50
100 Edgar Martinez .40
101 Mark Teixeira .50
102 Sean Casey .25
103 Javier Vazquez .50
104 Hideki Matsui 2.50
105 Jim Edmonds .40
106 Roy Halladay .50
107 Craig Biggio .40
108 Geoff Jenkins .50
109 Alfonso Soriano 1.00
110 Barry Larkin .50
111 Chris Bootcheck 4.00
112 Dallas McPherson/99 6.00
113 Matt Kata/99 6.00
114 Scott Hairston 4.00
115 Bobby Crosby 8.00
116 Adam Wainright/99 6.00
117 Daniel Cabrera 4.00
118 Kevin Youkilis 8.00
119 *Ronny Cedeno* 6.00
120 *Ruddy Yan* 4.00
121 Ryan Wing 4.00
122 *William Bergolla* 5.00
123 Edwin Encarnacion 4.00
124 Jonny Gomes 4.00
125 Garrett Atkins 4.00
126 Clint Barmes 4.00
127 Wilfredo Ledezma 4.00
128 Cody Ross 6.00
129 Josh Willingham/99 6.00
130 Chin-Hui Tsao 4.00
131 *Hector Gimenez* 6.00
132 David DeJesus 4.00
133 Jimmy Gobble 4.00
134 Edwin Jackson/99 6.00
135 Koyie Hill 4.00
136 Rickie Weeks/99 8.00
137 Graham Koonce 4.00
138 Rob Bowen 6.00
139 *Shawn Hill* 4.00
140 Craig Brazell 4.00
141 Mike Hessman 4.00
142 Jorge DePaula 4.00
143 Chien-Ming Wang/99 6.00
144 Rich Harden 4.00
145 Ryan Howard/99 6.00
146 *Alfredo Simon* 4.00
147 *Ian Snell* 6.00
148 Ryan Doumit 4.00
149 Khalil Greene/99 6.00
150 *Angel Chavez* 4.00
151 Dan Haren 6.00
152 Chris Snelling 4.00
153 Aaron Miles 4.00
154 *John Gall* 8.00
155 Chris Narveson 4.00
156 Delmon Young/99 8.00
157 Chad Gaudin 4.00
158 Gerald Laird 4.00
159 Alexis Rios 8.00
160 Jason Arnold 4.00

Gold Proof

Cards (1-110): 3-5X
SP's (111-160): 1X
Production 150 sets

Artist's Proof

Cards (1-110): 3-6X
SP's (110-160): 1-1.5X
Production 50 sets

Photographer Proof

Cards (1-110): 6-12X
SP's (110-160): 2-3X
Production 25 sets

Executive Proof

No Pricing
Production one set

History of the Draft Game-Used

NM/M
Common Player: 5.00
Numbered to last 2 digits of draft yr.
Silver Proof: 1-1.5X
Production 50 sets
Gold Proof: No Pricing
Production 10 sets
Garret Anderson 6.00
Josh Beckett 10.00
Carlos Beltran 5.00
Lance Berkman 5.00
Hank Blalock 10.00
Bret Boone 8.00
A.J. Burnett 5.00
Pat Burrell 8.00
Marlon Byrd 5.00
Eric Chavez 6.00
Adam Dunn 8.00
Darin Erstad 8.00
Nomar Garciaparra 10.00
Jason Giambi 8.00
Shawn Green 5.00
Roy Halladay 6.00
Todd Helton 10.00
Tim Hudson 6.00
Aubrey Huff 8.00
Torii Hunter 8.00
Derek Jeter 15.00
Chipper Jones 10.00
Austin Kearns 8.00
Mike Lowell 5.00
Mike Mussina 10.00
Corey Patterson 6.00
Juan Pierre 5.00
Scott Podsednik 10.00
Jorge Posada 10.00
Albert Pujols 20.00
Manny Ramirez 8.00
Alex Rodriguez 10.00
Scott Rolen 10.00
Jason Schmidt 6.00
Richie Sexson 8.00
Shannon Stewart 5.00
Javier Vazquez 8.00
Vernon Wells 6.00
Kerry Wood 10.00
Barry Zito 8.00

History of the Draft Autographs

NM/M
Common Autograph: 10.00
Production 199 sets
Draft Year: 1-1.25X
#'d to last 2 digits of draft year
Silver Proof: 1-1.5X
Production 50 sets
Gold Proof: No Pricing
Production 10 sets
Hank Blalock 20.00
A.J. Burnett 10.00
Marlon Byrd 10.00
Roy Halladay 20.00
Tim Hudson 10.00
Aubrey Huff 15.00
Torii Hunter 15.00
Austin Kearns 20.00
Mike Lowell 10.00

Corey Patterson 20.00
Juan Pierre 15.00
Scott Podsednik 20.00
Albert Pujols 120.00
Scott Rolen 30.00
Shannon Stewart 10.00
Javier Vazquez 10.00
Vernon Wells 15.00

Jersey Proof

NM/M
Common Player: 5.00
Production 299 sets
Silver Proof: 1.5-2X
Production 50 sets
Gold Proof: No Pricing
Production 10 sets
1 Troy Glaus 5.00
2 Curt Schilling 6.00
3 Randy Johnson 8.00
4 Brandon Webb 5.00
5 Gary Sheffield 5.00
6 Greg Maddux 15.00
7 Chipper Jones 10.00
8 David Ortiz 10.00
9 Nomar Garciaparra 15.00
10 Pedro J. Martinez 8.00
11 Manny Ramirez 8.00
12 Kerry Wood 8.00
13 Mark Prior 15.00
14 Sammy Sosa 12.00
15 Frank Thomas 8.00
16 Austin Kearns 6.00
17 Todd Helton 8.00
18 Preston Wilson 5.00
19 Juan Pierre 5.00
20 Josh Beckett 6.00
21 Ivan Rodriguez 6.00
22 Miguel Cabrera 8.00
23 Mike Lowell 6.00
24 Lance Berkman 6.00
25 Jeff Bagwell 8.00
26 Angel Berroa 5.00
27 Hideo Nomo 10.00
28 Eric Gagne 8.00
29 Scott Podsednik 10.00
30 Richie Sexson 6.00
31 Torii Hunter 6.00
32 Mike Piazza 10.00
33 Jose Reyes 8.00
34 Tom Glavine 6.00
35 Derek Jeter 30.00
36 Jorge Posada 6.00
37 Jason Giambi 8.00
38 Alfonso Soriano 8.00
39 Eric Chavez 6.00
40 Miguel Tejada 5.00
41 Jim Thome 10.00
42 Albert Pujols 15.00
43 Scott Rolen 8.00
44 Rocco Baldelli 10.00
45 Alex Rodriguez 10.00
46 Hank Blalock 8.00
47 Mark Teixeira 6.00
48 Rafael Palmeiro 10.00
49 Carlos Delgado 6.00
50 Roy Halladay 6.00

L.E.ague L.E.aders

NM/M
Complete Set (10): 10.00
Common Player: .50
Inserted 1:18
1LL Alex Rodriguez 3.00
2LL Jim Thome 1.50
3LL Albert Pujols 3.00
4LL Pedro J. Martinez 1.50
5LL Roy Halladay .75
6LL Jason Schmidt .50
7LL Kerry Wood 1.00
8LL Juan Pierre .50
9LL Preston Wilson .50
10LL Carlos Delgado 1.00

L.E.ague L.E.eaders Game-Used

NM/M
Common Player: 6.00
Production 75 sets
Silver Proof: 1-1.5X
Production 50 sets
Gold Proof: No Pricing
Production 10 sets
Alex Rodriguez 12.00
Jim Thome 10.00
Albert Pujols 20.00
Pedro J. Martinez 10.00
Roy Halladay 8.00
Jason Schmidt 8.00
Kerry Wood 8.00
Juan Pierre 6.00
Preston Wilson 6.00
Carlos Delgado 8.00

Rare Form

NM/M
Common Player: 5.00
Inserted 1:288
1 Albert Pujols 20.00
2 Miguel Cabrera 5.00
3 Jim Thome 10.00
4 Derek Jeter 30.00
5 Nomar Garciaparra 15.00
6 Mike Piazza 15.00
7 Alex Rodriguez 20.00
8 Delmon Young 15.00
9 Chipper Jones 12.00
10 Rickie Weeks 10.00

Rare Form Autographs

NM/M
Common Autograph: 10.00
Production 299 sets
Level 2: 1-1.5X
Production 99 sets
Silver Proof: 1.5X
Production 50 sets
Gold Proof: No Pricing
Production 10 sets
Rocco Baldelli 25.00
Angel Berroa 15.00
Miguel Cabrera
Rich Harden 20.00
Edwin Jackson 20.00
Matt Kata 10.00
Dallas McPherson 15.00
Brandon Webb 15.00
Rickie Weeks 30.00
Delmon Young 30.00

Rare Form Game-Used Silver Proof

NM/M
Common Player: 8.00
Production 50 sets
Gold Proof: No Pricing
Production 10 sets
Rocco Baldelli 15.00
Miguel Cabrera 8.00
Nomar Garciaparra 15.00
Derek Jeter 30.00
Chipper Jones 12.00
Mike Piazza 25.00
Albert Pujols 25.00
Alex Rodriguez 15.00
Jim Thome 12.00

Rare Form Memorabilia Jersey Number

NM/M
Numbered to jersey number
Most not priced due to scarcity
Mike Piazza/31 30.00
Jim Thome/25 25.00

Sky's the Limit

NM/M
Complete Set (20): 20.00
Common Player: .50
Inserted 1:6
1SL Dontrelle Willis 1.00
2SL Rocco Baldelli 1.00
3SL Miguel Cabrera 1.00
4SL Mark Prior 3.00
5SL Hideki Matsui 4.00
6SL Kerry Wood 1.50
7SL Alfonso Soriano 1.50
8SL Ichiro Suzuki 2.50
9SL Brandon Webb .50
10SL Alex Rodriguez 3.00
11SL Barry Zito 1.00
12SL Hank Blalock 1.00
13SL Jose Reyes .75
14SL Torii Hunter .75
15SL Josh Beckett 1.00
16SL Manny Ramirez 1.00
17SL Andruw Jones 1.00
18SL Vladimir Guerrero 1.50
19SL Miguel Tejada .75
20SL Carlos Delgado 1.00

Sky's the Limit Game-Used

NM/M
Common Player: 5.00
Production 99 sets
Silver Proof: 1X
Production 50 sets
Gold Proof: No Pricing
Production 10 sets
Rocco Baldelli 15.00
Josh Beckett 8.00
Hank Blalock 6.00
Miguel Cabrera 8.00
Carlos Delgado 8.00
Vladimir Guerrero 8.00
Torii Hunter 8.00
Andruw Jones 6.00
Mark Prior 15.00
Manny Ramirez 8.00
Jose Reyes 6.00
Alex Rodriguez 10.00
Alfonso Soriano 8.00
Miguel Tejada 6.00
Brandon Webb 5.00
Dontrelle Willis 5.00
Kerry Wood 10.00
Barry Zito 6.00

1993 SP

NM/M
Complete Set (290): 75.00
Common Player: .10
Pack (12): 10.00
Wax Box (24): 200.00
1 Roberto Alomar .30
2 Wade Boggs 2.00
3 Joe Carter .10
4 Ken Griffey, Jr. 2.50
5 Mark Langston .10
6 John Olerud .10
7 Kirby Puckett 2.00
8 Cal Ripken, Jr. 4.00
9 Ivan Rodriguez 1.25
10 Barry Bonds 4.00
11 Darren Daulton .10
12 Marquis Grissom .10
13 Dave Justice .10
14 John Kruk .10
15 Barry Larkin .10
16 Terry Mulholland .10
17 Ryne Sandberg 2.00
18 Gary Sheffield .10
19 Chad Curtis .10
20 Chili Davis .10
21 Gary DiSarcina .10
22 Damion Easley .10
23 Chuck Finley .10
24 Luis Polonia .10
25 Tim Salmon .10
26 *J.T. Snow* 1.00
27 Russ Springer .10
28 Jeff Bagwell 1.50
29 Craig Biggio .10
30 Ken Caminiti .10
31 Andujar Cedeno .10
32 Doug Drabek .10
33 Steve Finley .10
34 Luis Gonzalez .10
35 Pete Harnisch .10
36 Darryl Kile .10
37 Mike Bordick .10
38 Dennis Eckersley 1.25
39 Brent Gates .10
40 Rickey Henderson 1.50
41 Mark McGwire 3.00
42 Craig Paquette .10
43 Ruben Sierra .10
44 Terry Steinbach .10
45 Todd Van Poppel .10
46 Pat Borders .10
47 Tony Fernandez .10
48 Juan Guzman .10
49 Pat Hentgen .10
50 Paul Molitor 1.50
51 Jack Morris .10
52 Ed Sprague .10
53 Duane Ward .10
54 Devon White .10
55 Steve Avery .10
56 Jeff Blauser .10
57 Ron Gant .10
58 Tom Glavine .40
59 Greg Maddux 2.00
60 Fred McGriff .10
61 Terry Pendleton .10
62 Deion Sanders .10
63 John Smoltz .10
64 Cal Eldred .10
65 Darryl Hamilton .10
66 John Jaha .10
67 Pat Listach .10
68 Jaime Navarro .10
69 Kevin Reimer .10
70 B.J. Surhoff .10
71 Greg Vaughn .10
72 Robin Yount 1.50
73 *Rene Arocha* .10
74 Bernard Gilkey .10
75 Gregg Jefferies .10
76 Ray Lankford .10
77 Tom Pagnozzi .10
78 Lee Smith .10
79 Ozzie Smith 2.00
80 Bob Tewksbury .10
81 Mark Whiten .10
82 Steve Buechele .10
83 Mark Grace .10
84 Jose Guzman .10
85 Derrick May .10
86 Mike Morgan .10
87 Randy Myers .10
88 *Kevin Roberson* .10
89 Sammy Sosa 2.00
90 Rick Wilkins .10
91 Brett Butler .10
92 Eric Davis .10
93 Orel Hershiser .10
94 Eric Karros .10
95 Ramon Martinez .10
96 Raul Mondesi .10

97 Jose Offerman .10
98 Mike Piazza 2.50
99 Darryl Strawberry .10
100 Moises Alou .10
101 Wil Cordero .10
102 Delino DeShields .10
103 Darrin Fletcher .10
104 Ken Hill .10
105 *Mike Lansing* .40
106 Dennis Martinez .10
107 Larry Walker .10
108 John Wetteland .10
109 Rod Beck .10
110 John Burkett .10
111 Will Clark .10
112 Royce Clayton .10
113 Darren Lewis .10
114 Willie McGee .10
115 Bill Swift .10
116 Robby Thompson .10
117 Matt Williams .10
118 Sandy Alomar Jr. .10
119 Carlos Baerga .10
120 Albert Belle .10
121 Reggie Jefferson .10
122 Kenny Lofton .10
123 Wayne Kirby .10
124 Carlos Martinez .10
125 Charles Nagy .10
126 Paul Sorrento .10
127 Rich Amaral .10
128 Jay Buhner .10
129 Norm Charlton .10
130 Dave Fleming .10
131 Erik Hanson .10
132 Randy Johnson 1.50
133 Edgar Martinez .10
134 Tino Martinez .10
135 Omar Vizquel .10
136 Bret Barberie .10
137 Chuck Carr .10
138 Jeff Conine .10
139 Orestes Destrade .10
140 Chris Hammond .10
141 Bryan Harvey .10
142 Benito Santiago .10
143 Walt Weiss .10
144 *Darrell Whitmore* .10
145 *Tim Bolger* .10
146 Bobby Bonilla .10
147 Jeromy Burnitz .10
148 Vince Coleman .10
149 Dwight Gooden .10
150 Todd Hundley .10
151 Howard Johnson .10
152 Eddie Murray 1.50
153 Bret Saberhagen .10
154 Brady Anderson .10
155 Mike Devereaux .10
156 Jeffrey Hammonds .10
157 Chris Hoiles .10
158 Ben McDonald .10
159 Mark McLemore .10
160 Mike Mussina .50
161 Gregg Olson .10
162 David Segui .10
163 Derek Bell .10
164 Andy Benes .10
165 Archi Cianfrocco .10
166 Ricky Gutierrez .10
167 Tony Gwynn 2.00
168 Gene Harris .10
169 Trevor Hoffman .10
170 *Ray McDavid* .10
171 Phil Plantier .10
172 Mariano Duncan .10
173 Len Dykstra .10
174 Tommy Greene .10
175 Dave Hollins .10
176 Pete Incaviglia .10
177 Mickey Morandini .10
178 Curt Schilling .40
179 Kevin Stocker .10
180 Mitch Williams .10
181 Stan Belinda .10
182 Jay Bell .10
183 Steve Cooke .10
184 Carlos Garcia .10
185 Jeff King .10
186 Orlando Merced .10
187 Don Slaught .10
188 Andy Van Slyke .10
189 Kevin Young .10
190 Kevin Brown .10
191 Jose Canseco .60
192 Julio Franco .10
193 Benji Gil .10
194 Juan Gonzalez .75
195 Tom Henke .10
196 Rafael Palmeiro 1.25
197 Dean Palmer .10
198 Nolan Ryan 4.00
199 Roger Clemens 2.25
200 Scott Cooper .10
201 Andre Dawson .35
202 Mike Greenwell .10
203 Carlos Quintana .10
204 Jeff Russell .10
205 Aaron Sele .10
206 Mo Vaughn .10
207 Frank Viola .10
208 Rob Dibble .10
209 Roberto Kelly .10
210 Kevin Mitchell .10
211 Hal Morris .10
212 Joe Oliver .10
213 Jose Rijo .10
214 Bip Roberts .10
215 Chris Sabo .10
216 Reggie Sanders .10
217 Dante Bichette .10
218 Jerald Clark .10
219 Alex Cole .10
220 Andres Galarraga .10
221 Joe Girardi .10
222 Charlie Hayes .10
223 *Robert Mejia* .10
224 Armando Reynoso .10
225 Eric Young .10
226 Kevin Appier .10
227 George Brett 2.25
228 David Cone .10
229 Phil Hiatt .10
230 Felix Jose .10
231 Wally Joyner .10
232 Mike Macfarlane .10
233 Brian McRae .10
234 Jeff Montgomery .10
235 Rob Deer .10
236 Cecil Fielder .10
237 Travis Fryman .10
238 Mike Henneman .10
239 Tony Phillips .10
240 Mickey Tettleton .10
241 Alan Trammell .10
242 David Wells .10
243 Lou Whitaker .10
244 Rick Aguilera .10
245 Scott Erickson .10
246 Brian Harper .10
247 Kent Hrbek .10
248 Chuck Knoblauch .10
249 Shane Mack .10
250 David McCarty .10
251 Pedro Munoz .10
252 Dave Winfield 1.50
253 Alex Fernandez .10
254 Ozzie Guillen .10
255 Bo Jackson .20
256 Lance Johnson .10
257 Ron Karkovice .10
258 Jack McDowell .10
259 Tim Raines .10
260 Frank Thomas 1.50
261 Robin Ventura .10
262 Jim Abbott .10
263 Steve Farr .10
264 Jimmy Key .10
265 Don Mattingly 2.25
266 Paul O'Neill .10
267 Mike Stanley .10
268 Danny Tartabull .10
269 Bob Wickman .10
270 Bernie Williams .10
271 Jason Bere .10
272 *Roger Cedeno* .50
273 *Johnny Damon* 12.00
274 *Russ Davis* .25
275 Carlos Delgado .75
276 Carl Everett .10
277 Cliff Floyd .10
278 Alex Gonzalez .10
279 *Derek Jeter* 60.00
280 Chipper Jones 2.00
281 Javier Lopez .10
282 *Chad Mottola* .10
283 Marc Newfield .10
284 Eduardo Perez .10
285 Manny Ramirez 1.50
286 *Todd Steverson* .10
287 Michael Tucker .10
288 Allen Watson .10
289 Rondell White .10
290 Dmitri Young .10

Platinum Power

NM/M
Complete Set (20): 27.50
Common Player: .50
1 Albert Belle .50
2 Barry Bonds 5.00
3 Joe Carter .50
4 Will Clark .50
5 Darren Daulton .50
6 Cecil Fielder .50
7 Ron Gant .50
8 Juan Gonzalez 1.00
9 Ken Griffey, Jr. 3.00
10 Dave Hollins .50
11 Dave Justice .50
12 Fred McGriff .50
13 Mark McGwire 5.00
14 Dean Palmer .50
15 Mike Piazza 3.00
16 Tim Salmon .50
17 Ryne Sandberg 2.50
18 Gary Sheffield .75
19 Frank Thomas 2.00
20 Matt Williams .50

1994 SP

NM/M
Complete Set (200): 100.00
Common Player: .10
Pack (8): 15.00
Wax Box (32): 450.00
1 *Mike Bell* .10
2 D.J. Boston .10
3 Johnny Damon .45
4 *Brad Fullmer* .75
5 Joey Hamilton .10
6 Todd Hollandsworth .10
7 Brian Hunter .10
8 *LaTroy Hawkins* .25
9 *Brooks Kieschnick* .10
10 *Derrek Lee* 25.00
11 *Trot Nixon* 3.00
12 Alex Ochoa .10
13 *Chan Ho Park* 1.50
14 *Kirk Presley* .10
15 *Alex Rodriguez* 80.00
16 *Jose Silva* .10
17 *Terrell Wade* .10
18 *Billy Wagner* 1.00
19 *Glenn Williams* .10
20 Preston Wilson .10
21 Brian Anderson .10
22 Chad Curtis .10
23 Chili Davis .10
24 Bo Jackson .25
25 Mark Langston .10
26 Tim Salmon .10
27 Jeff Bagwell 1.00
28 Craig Biggio .10
29 Ken Caminiti .10
30 Doug Drabek .10
31 John Hudek .10
32 Greg Swindell .10
33 Brent Gates .10
34 Rickey Henderson 1.00
35 Steve Karsay .10
36 Mark McGwire 2.50
37 Ruben Sierra .10
38 Terry Steinbach .10
39 Roberto Alomar .30
40 Joe Carter .10
41 Carlos Delgado .50
42 Alex Gonzalez .10
43 Juan Guzman .10
44 Paul Molitor 1.00
45 John Olerud .10
46 Devon White .10
47 Steve Avery .10
48 Jeff Blauser .10
49 Tom Glavine .35
50 Dave Justice .10
51 Roberto Kelly .10
52 Ryan Klesko .10
53 Javier Lopez .10
54 Greg Maddux 1.25
55 Fred McGriff .10
56 Ricky Bones .10
57 Cal Eldred .10
58 Brian Harper .10
59 Pat Listach .10
60 B.J. Surhoff .10
61 Greg Vaughn .10
62 Bernard Gilkey .10
63 Gregg Jefferies .10
64 Ray Lankford .10
65 Ozzie Smith 1.25
66 Bob Tewksbury .10
67 Mark Whiten .10
68 Todd Zeile .10
69 Mark Grace .10
70 Randy Myers .10
71 Ryne Sandberg 1.25
72 Sammy Sosa 1.25
73 Steve Trachsel .10
74 Rick Wilkins .10
75 Brett Butler .10
76 Delino DeShields .10
77 Orel Hershiser .10
78 Eric Karros .10
79 Raul Mondesi .10
80 Mike Piazza 2.00
81 Tim Wallach .10
82 Moises Alou .10
83 Cliff Floyd .10
84 Marquis Grissom .10
85 Pedro Martinez 1.00
86 Larry Walker .10
87 John Wetteland .10
88 Rondell White .10
89 Rod Beck .10
90 Barry Bonds 3.00
91 John Burkett .10
92 Royce Clayton .10
93 Billy Swift .10
94 Robby Thompson .10
95 Matt Williams .10
96 Carlos Baerga .10
97 Albert Belle .10
98 Kenny Lofton .10
99 Dennis Martinez .10
100 Eddie Murray 1.00
101 Manny Ramirez 1.00
102 Eric Anthony .10
103 Chris Bosio .10
104 Jay Buhner .10
105 Ken Griffey, Jr. 2.00
106 Randy Johnson 1.00
107 Edgar Martinez .10
108 Chuck Carr .10
109 Jeff Conine .10
110 Carl Everett .10
111 Chris Hammond .10
112 Bryan Harvey .10
113 Charles Johnson .10
114 Gary Sheffield .45
115 Bobby Bonilla .10
116 Dwight Gooden .10
117 Todd Hundley .10
118 Bobby Jones .10
119 Jeff Kent .10
120 Bret Saberhagen .10
121 Jeffrey Hammonds .10
122 Chris Hoiles .10
123 Ben McDonald .10
124 Mike Mussina .40
125 Rafael Palmeiro .75
126 Cal Ripken, Jr. 3.00
127 Lee Smith .10
128 Derek Bell .10
129 Andy Benes .10
130 Tony Gwynn 1.25
131 Trevor Hoffman .10
132 Phil Plantier .10
133 Bip Roberts .10
134 Darren Daulton .10
135 Len Dykstra .10
136 Dave Hollins .10
137 Danny Jackson .10
138 John Kruk .10
139 Kevin Stocker .10
140 Jay Bell .10
141 Carlos Garcia .10
142 Jeff King .10
143 Orlando Merced .10
144 Andy Van Slyke .10
145 Paul Wagner .10
146 Jose Canseco .50
147 Will Clark .10
148 Juan Gonzalez .50
149 Rick Helling .10
150 Dean Palmer .10

151 Ivan Rodriguez .75
152 Roger Clemens 1.50
153 Scott Cooper .10
154 Andre Dawson .30
155 Mike Greenwell .10
156 Aaron Sele .10
157 Mo Vaughn .10
158 Bret Boone .10
159 Barry Larkin .10
160 Kevin Mitchell .10
161 Jose Rijo .10
162 Deion Sanders .10
163 Reggie Sanders .10
164 Dante Bichette .10
165 Ellis Burks .10
166 Andres Galarraga .10
167 Charlie Hayes .10
168 David Nied .10
169 Walt Weiss .10
170 Kevin Appier .10
171 David Cone .10
172 Jeff Granger .10
173 Felix Jose .10
174 Wally Joyner .10
175 Brian McRae .10
176 Cecil Fielder .10
177 Travis Fryman .10
178 Mike Henneman .10
179 Tony Phillips .10
180 Mickey Tettleton .10
181 Alan Trammell .10
182 Rick Aguilera .10
183 Rich Becker .10
184 Scott Erickson .10
185 Chuck Knoblauch .10
186 Kirby Puckett 1.25
187 Dave Winfield 1.00
188 Wilson Alvarez .10
189 Jason Bere .10
190 Alex Fernandez .10
191 Julio Franco .10
192 Jack McDowell .10
193 Frank Thomas 1.00
194 Robin Ventura .10
195 Jim Abbott .10
196 Wade Boggs 1.25
197 Jimmy Key .10
198 Don Mattingly 1.50
199 Paul O'Neill .10
200 Danny Tartabull .10

Die-Cut

(Star cards valued at 1-2X corresponding cards in regular SP issue.)

Holoview Blue

NM/M
Complete Set (38): 85.00
Common Player: .90
1 Roberto Alomar 1.25
2 Kevin Appier .90
3 Jeff Bagwell 2.50
4 Jose Canseco 2.50
5 Roger Clemens 4.00
6 Carlos Delgado 1.50
7 Cecil Fielder .90
8 Cliff Floyd .90
9 Travis Fryman .90
10 Andres Galarraga .90
11 Juan Gonzalez 1.50
12 Ken Griffey, Jr. 5.50
13 Tony Gwynn 3.50
14 Jeffrey Hammonds .90
15 Bo Jackson 1.25
16 Michael Jordan 10.00
17 Dave Justice .90
18 Steve Karsay .90
19 Jeff Kent .90
20 Brooks Kieschnick .90
21 Ryan Klesko .90
22 John Kruk .90
23 Barry Larkin .90
24 Pat Listach .90
25 Don Mattingly 4.00
26 Mark McGwire 7.00
27 Raul Mondesi .90
28 Trot Nixon 1.50
29 Mike Piazza 5.50
30 Kirby Puckett 3.50
31 Manny Ramirez 2.50
32 Cal Ripken, Jr. 9.00
33 Alex Rodriguez 35.00
34 Tim Salmon .90
35 Gary Sheffield 1.50
36 Ozzie Smith 3.50
37 Sammy Sosa 3.50
38 Andy Van Slyke .90

Holoview Red

NM/M
Complete Set (38): 1,175
Common Player: 12.50
1 Roberto Alomar 15.00
2 Kevin Appier 12.50
3 Jeff Bagwell 30.00
4 Jose Canseco 20.00
5 Roger Clemens 45.00
6 Carlos Delgado 20.00
7 Cecil Fielder 12.50
8 Cliff Floyd 12.50
9 Travis Fryman 12.50
10 Andres Galarraga 12.50
11 Juan Gonzalez 17.50
12 Ken Griffey, Jr. 50.00
13 Tony Gwynn 40.00
14 Jeffrey Hammonds 12.50
15 Bo Jackson 15.00
16 Michael Jordan 100.00
17 Dave Justice 12.50
18 Steve Karsay 12.50
19 Jeff Kent 12.50
20 Brooks Kieschnick 12.50
21 Ryan Klesko 12.50
22 John Kruk 12.50
23 Barry Larkin 12.50
24 Pat Listach 12.50
25 Don Mattingly 45.00
26 Mark McGwire 60.00
27 Raul Mondesi 12.50
28 Trot Nixon 20.00
29 Mike Piazza 50.00
30 Kirby Puckett 40.00
31 Manny Ramirez 30.00
32 Cal Ripken, Jr. 80.00
33 Alex Rodriguez 625.00
34 Tim Salmon 12.50
35 Gary Sheffield 15.00
36 Ozzie Smith 40.00
37 Sammy Sosa 40.00
38 Andy Van Slyke 12.50

Values quoted in this guide reflect the retail price of a card, the price a collector can expect to pay when buying a card from a dealer.

Alex Rodriguez Autographed Jumbo

NM/M
15 Alex Rodriguez 125.00

1995 SP

NM/M
Complete Set (207): 12.50
Common Player: .05
Pack (8): 1.25
Wax Box (32): 25.00
1 Cal Ripken Jr. 2.00
2 Nolan Ryan 2.00
3 George Brett 1.25
4 Mike Schmidt 1.25
5 Dustin Hermanson .05
6 Antonio Osuna .05
7 *Mark Grudzielanek* .35
8 Ray Durham .05
9 Ugueth Urbina .05
10 Ruben Rivera .05
11 Curtis Goodwin .05
12 Jimmy Hurst .05
13 Jose Malave .05
14 *Hideo Nomo* 1.50
15 Juan Acevedo .05
16 Tony Clark .05
17 Jim Pittsley .05
18 *Freddy Garcia* .50
19 *Carlos Perez* .05
20 *Raul Casanova* .05
21 Quilvio Veras .05
22 Edgardo Alfonzo .05
23 Marty Cordova .05
24 C.J. Nitkowski .05
25 Wade Boggs Checklist 1-69 .30
26 Dave Winfield Checklist 70-138 .25
27 Eddie Murray Checklist 139-207 .25
28 Dave Justice .05
29 Marquis Grissom .05
30 Fred McGriff .05
31 Greg Maddux 1.00
32 Tom Glavine .35
33 Steve Avery .05
34 Chipper Jones 1.00
35 Sammy Sosa 1.00
36 Jaime Navarro .05
37 Randy Myers .05
38 Mark Grace .05
39 Todd Zeile .05
40 Brian McRae .05
41 Reggie Sanders .05
42 Ron Gant .05
43 Deion Sanders .05
44 Barry Larkin .05
45 Bret Boone .05
46 Jose Rijo .05
47 Jason Bates .05
48 Andres Galarraga .05
49 Bill Swift .05
50 Larry Walker .05
51 Vinny Castilla .05
52 Dante Bichette .05
53 Jeff Conine .05
54 John Burkett .05
55 Gary Sheffield .40
56 Andre Dawson .30
57 Terry Pendleton .05
58 Charles Johnson .05
59 Brian L. Hunter .05
60 Jeff Bagwell .75
61 Craig Biggio .05
62 Phil Nevin .05
63 Doug Drabek .05
64 Derek Bell .05
65 Raul Mondesi .05
66 Eric Karros .05
67 Roger Cedeno .05
68 Delino DeShields .05
69 Ramon Martinez .05
70 Mike Piazza 1.50
71 Billy Ashley .05
72 Jeff Fassero .05
73 Shane Andrews .05
74 Wil Cordero .05
75 Tony Tarasco .05
76 Rondell White .05
77 Pedro Martinez .75
78 Moises Alou .05
79 Rico Brogna .05
80 Bobby Bonilla .05
81 Jeff Kent .05
82 Brett Butler .05
83 Bobby Jones .05
84 Bill Pulsipher .05
85 Bret Saberhagen .05
86 Gregg Jefferies .05
87 Lenny Dykstra .05
88 Dave Hollins .05
89 Charlie Hayes .05
90 Darren Daulton .05
91 Curt Schilling .35
92 Heathcliff Slocumb .05
93 Carlos Garcia .05
94 Denny Neagle .05
95 Jay Bell .05
96 Orlando Merced .05
97 Dave Clark .05
98 Bernard Gilkey .05
99 Scott Cooper .05
100 Ozzie Smith 1.00
100 Ken Griffey Jr. (promo card) 2.00
101 Tom Henke .05
102 Ken Hill .05
103 Brian Jordan .05
104 Ray Lankford .05
105 Tony Gwynn 1.00
106 Andy Benes .05
107 Ken Caminiti .05
108 Steve Finley .05
109 Joey Hamilton .05
110 Bip Roberts .05
111 Eddie Williams .05
112 Rod Beck .05
113 Matt Williams .05
114 Glenallen Hill .05
115 Barry Bonds 2.50
116 Robby Thompson .05
117 Mark Portugal .05
118 Brady Anderson .05
119 Mike Mussina .35
120 Rafael Palmeiro .65
121 Chris Hoiles .05
122 Harold Baines .05
123 Jeffrey Hammonds .05
124 Tim Naehring .05
125 Mo Vaughn .05
126 Mike Macfarlane .05
127 Roger Clemens 1.25
128 John Valentin .05
129 Aaron Sele .05
130 Jose Canseco .50
131 J.T. Snow .05
132 Mark Langston .05
133 Chili Davis .05
134 Chuck Finley .05
135 Tim Salmon .05
136 Tony Phillips .05
137 Jason Bere .05
138 Robin Ventura .05
139 Tim Raines .05
140a Frank Thomas (5-yr. BA .326) .75

140b	Frank Thomas (5-yr. BA .303)	.75
141	Alex Fernandez	.05
142	Jim Abbott	.05
143	Wilson Alvarez	.05
144	Carlos Baerga	.05
145	Albert Belle	.05
146	Jim Thome	.65
147	Dennis Martinez	.05
148	Eddie Murray	.75
149	Dave Winfield	.75
150	Kenny Lofton	.05
151	Manny Ramirez	.75
152	Chad Curtis	.05
153	Lou Whitaker	.05
154	Alan Trammell	.05
155	Cecil Fielder	.05
156	Kirk Gibson	.05
157	Michael Tucker	.05
158	Jon Nunnally	.05
159	Wally Joyner	.05
160	Kevin Appier	.05
161	Jeff Montgomery	.05
162	Greg Gagne	.05
163	Ricky Bones	.05
164	Cal Eldred	.05
165	Greg Vaughn	.05
166	Kevin Seitzer	.05
167	Jose Valentin	.05
168	Joe Oliver	.05
169	Rick Aguilera	.05
170	Kirby Puckett	1.00
171	Scott Stahoviak	.05
172	Kevin Tapani	.05
173	Chuck Knoblauch	.05
174	Rich Becker	.05
175	Don Mattingly	1.25
176	Jack McDowell	.05
177	Jimmy Key	.05
178	Paul O'Neill	.05
179	John Wetteland	.05
180	Wade Boggs	1.00
181	Derek Jeter	2.50
182	Rickey Henderson	.75
183	Terry Steinbach	.05
184	Ruben Sierra	.05
185	Mark McGwire	2.00
186	Todd Stottlemyre	.05
187	Dennis Eckersley	.65
188	Alex Rodriguez	2.00
189	Randy Johnson	.75
190	Ken Griffey Jr.	1.50
191	Tino Martinez	.05
192	Jay Buhner	.05
193	Edgar Martinez	.05
194	Mickey Tettleton	.05
195	Juan Gonzalez	.40
196	Benji Gil	.05
197	Dean Palmer	.05
198	Ivan Rodriguez	.65
199	Kenny Rogers	.05
200	Will Clark	.05
201	Roberto Alomar	.20
202	David Cone	.05
203	Paul Molitor	.75
204	Shawn Green	.40
205	Joe Carter	.05
206	Alex Gonzalez	.05
207	Pat Hentgen	.05

SuperbaFoil

	NM/M
Complete Set (207):	30.00
Common Player:	.10
SuperbaFoil Stars:	1.5X

(See 1995 SP for checklist and base values.)

Griffey Gold Signature

		NM/M
190	Ken Griffey Jr.	65.00

Platinum Power

		NM/M
Complete Set (20):		10.00
Common Player:		.20
1	Jeff Bagwell	.75
2	Barry Bonds	2.00
3	Ron Gant	.20
4	Fred McGriff	.20
5	Raul Mondesi	.20
6	Mike Piazza	1.25
7	Larry Walker	.20
8	Matt Williams	.20
9	Albert Belle	.20
10	Cecil Fielder	.20
11	Juan Gonzalez	.40
12	Ken Griffey Jr.	1.25
13	Mark McGwire	1.50
14	Eddie Murray	.75
15	Manny Ramirez	.75
16	Cal Ripken Jr.	2.00
17	Tim Salmon	.20
18	Frank Thomas	.75
19	Jim Thome	.65
20	Mo Vaughn	.20

Special F/X

		NM/M
Complete Set (48):		110.00
Common Player:		.75
1	Jose Canseco	3.00
2	Roger Clemens	6.00
3	Mo Vaughn	.75
4	Tim Salmon	.75
5	Chuck Finley	.75
6	Robin Ventura	.75
7	Jason Bere	.75
8	Carlos Baerga	.75
9	Albert Belle	.75
10	Kenny Lofton	.75
11	Manny Ramirez	4.00
12	Jeff Montgomery	.75
13	Kirby Puckett	5.00
14	Wade Boggs	5.00
15	Don Mattingly	6.00
16	Cal Ripken Jr.	10.00
17	Ruben Sierra	.75
18	Ken Griffey Jr.	7.50
19	Randy Johnson	4.00
20	Alex Rodriguez	9.00
21	Will Clark	.75
22	Juan Gonzalez	2.00
23	Roberto Alomar	1.50
24	Joe Carter	.75
25	Alex Gonzalez	.75
26	Paul Molitor	4.00
27	Ryan Klesko	.75
28	Fred McGriff	.75
29	Greg Maddux	5.00
30	Sammy Sosa	5.00
31	Bret Boone	.75
32	Barry Larkin	.75
33	Reggie Sanders	.75
34	Dante Bichette	.75
35	Andres Galarraga	.75
36	Charles Johnson	.75
37	Gary Sheffield	3.00
38	Jeff Bagwell	4.00
39	Craig Biggio	.75
40	Eric Karros	.75
41	Billy Ashley	.75
42	Raul Mondesi	.75
43	Mike Piazza	7.50
44	Rondell White	.75
45	Bret Saberhagen	.75
46	Tony Gwynn	5.00
47	Melvin Nieves	.75
48	Matt Williams	.75

1995 SP/CHAMPIONSHIP

		NM/M
Complete Set (200):		25.00
Common Player:		.05
Wax Pack (6):		1.00
Wax Box (44):		30.00
1	*Hideo Nomo*	1.50
2	Roger Cedeno	.05
3	Curtis Goodwin	.05
4	Jon Nunnally	.05
5	Bill Pulsipher	.05
6	C.J. Nitkowski	.05
7	Dustin Hermanson	.05
8	Marty Cordova	.05
9	Ruben Rivera	.05
10	*Ariel Prieto*	.05
11	Edgardo Alfonzo	.05
12	Ray Durham	.05
13	Quilvio Veras	.05
14	Ugueth Urbina	.05
15	*Carlos Perez*	.05
16	*Glenn Dishman*	.05
17	Jeff Suppan	.05
18	Jason Bates	.05
19	Jason Isringhausen	.05
20	Derek Jeter	2.00
21	Fred McGriff	.05
22	Marquis Grissom	.05
23	Fred McGriff	.05
24	Tom Glavine	.35
25	Greg Maddux	1.00
26	Chipper Jones	1.00
27	Sammy Sosa	.50
28	Randy Myers	.05
29	Mark Grace	.05
30	Sammy Sosa	1.00
31	Todd Zeile	.05
32	Brian McRae	.05
33	Ron Gant	.05
34	Reggie Sanders	.05
35	Ron Gant	.05
36	Barry Larkin	.05
37	Bret Boone	.05
38	John Smiley	.05
39	Larry Walker	.05
40	Andres Galarraga	.05
41	Bill Swift	.05
42	Larry Walker	.05
43	Vinny Castilla	.05
44	Dante Bichette	.05
45	Jeff Conine	.05
46	Charles Johnson	.05
47	Gary Sheffield	.45
48	Andre Dawson	.25
49	Jeff Conine	.05
50	Jeff Bagwell	.40
51	Phil Nevin	.05
52	Craig Biggio	.05
53	Brian L. Hunter	.05
54	Doug Drabek	.05
55	Jeff Bagwell	.75
56	Derek Bell	.05
57	Mike Piazza	.65
58	Raul Mondesi	.05
59	Eric Karros	.05
60	Mike Piazza	1.25
61	Ramon Martinez	.05
62	Billy Ashley	.05
63	Rondell White	.05
64	Jeff Fassero	.05
65	Moises Alou	.05
66	Tony Tarasco	.05
67	Rondell White	.05
68	Pedro Martinez	.75
69	Bobby Jones	.05
70	Bobby Bonilla	.05
71	Bobby Jones	.05
72	Bret Saberhagen	.05
73	Darren Daulton	.05
74	Darren Daulton	.05
75	Gregg Jefferies	.05
76	Tyler Green	.05
77	Heathcliff Slocumb	.05
78	Lenny Dykstra	.05
79	Jay Bell	.05
80	Denny Neagle	.05
81	Orlando Merced	.05
82	Jay Bell	.05
83	Ozzie Smith	.50
84	Ken Hill	.05
85	Ozzie Smith	1.00
86	Bernard Gilkey	.05
87	Ray Lankford	.05
88	Tony Gwynn	.50
89	Ken Caminiti	.05
90	Tony Gwynn	1.00
91	Joey Hamilton	.05
92	Bip Roberts	.05
93	Deion Sanders	.05
94	Glenallen Hill	.05
95	Matt Williams	.05
96	Barry Bonds	2.00
97	Rod Beck	.05
98	Eddie Murray	.35
99	Cal Ripken Jr.	1.00
100	Roberto Alomar	.10
101	George Brett	.60
102	Joe Carter	.05
103	Will Clark	.05
104	Dennis Eckersley	.40
105	Whitey Ford	.40
106	Steve Garvey	.05
107	Kirk Gibson	.05
108	Orel Hershiser	.05
109	Reggie Jackson	.50
110	Paul Molitor	.40
111	Kirby Puckett	.50
112	Mike Schmidt	.60
113	Dave Stewart	.05
114	Alan Trammell	.05
115	Cal Ripken Jr.	1.00
116	Brady Anderson	.05
117	Mike Mussina	.30
118	Rafael Palmeiro	.65
119	Chris Hoiles	.05
120	Cal Ripken Jr.	2.00
121	Mo Vaughn	.05
122	Roger Clemens	1.25
123	Tim Naehring	.05
124	John Valentin	.05
125	Mo Vaughn	.05
126	Tim Wakefield	.05
127	Jose Canseco	.40
128	Rick Aguilera	.05
129	Chili Davis	.05
130	Lee Smith	.05
131	Jim Edmonds	.05
132	Chuck Finley	.05
133	Chili Davis	.05
134	J.T. Snow	.05
135	Tim Salmon	.05
136	Frank Thomas	.45
137	Jason Bere	.05
138	Robin Ventura	.05
139	Tim Raines	.05
140	Frank Thomas	.75
141	Alex Fernandez	.05
142	Eddie Murray	.40
143	Carlos Baerga	.05
144	Eddie Murray	.75
145	Albert Belle	.05
146	Jim Thome	.65
147	Dennis Martinez	.05
148	Dave Winfield	.75
149	Kenny Lofton	.05
150	Manny Ramirez	.75
151	Cecil Fielder	.05
152	Lou Whitaker	.05
153	Alan Trammell	.05
154	Kirk Gibson	.05
155	Cecil Fielder	.05
156	*Bobby Higginson*	.25
157	Kevin Appier	.05
158	Wally Joyner	.05
159	Jeff Montgomery	.05
160	Kevin Appier	.05
161	Gary Gaetti	.05
162	Greg Gagne	.05
163	Ricky Bones	.05
164	Greg Vaughn	.05
165	Kevin Seitzer	.05
166	Ricky Bones	.05
167	Kirby Puckett	.50
168	Pedro Munoz	.05
169	Chuck Knoblauch	.05
170	Kirby Puckett	1.00
171	Don Mattingly	.60

172	Wade Boggs	1.00
173	Paul O'Neill	.05
174	John Wetteland	.05
175	Don Mattingly	1.25
176	Jack McDowell	.05
177	Mark McGwire	.75
178	Rickey Henderson	.75
179	Terry Steinbach	.05
180	Ruben Sierra	.05
181	Mark McGwire	1.50
182	Dennis Eckersley	.05
183	Ken Griffey Jr.	.65
184	Alex Rodriguez	1.50
185	Ken Griffey Jr.	1.25
186	Randy Johnson	.75
187	Jay Buhner	.05
188	Edgar Martinez	.05
189	Will Clark	.05
190	Juan Gonzalez	.40
191	Benji Gil	.05
192	Ivan Rodriguez	.65
193	Kenny Rogers	.05
194	Will Clark	.05
195	Paul Molitor	.40
196	Roberto Alomar	.20
197	David Cone	.05
198	Paul Molitor	.75
199	Shawn Green	.30
200	Joe Carter	.05
CR1	Cal Ripken Jr.	5.00
CR1	Cal Ripken Jr. die-cut	7.50

Die-Cuts

		NM/M
	Complete Set (200):	50.00
	Common Player:	.25
	Die-Cut Stars:	1.5X

(See 1995 SP/Championship for checklist and base values.)

Classic Performances

		NM/M
	Complete Set (10):	8.00
	Common Player:	.50
	Complete Die-Cut Set (10):	16.00
	Common Die-Cuts:	1.00
CP1	Reggie Jackson	.60
CP1	Reggie Jackson	2.00
CP2	Nolan Ryan	4.00
CP2	Nolan Ryan	8.00
CP3	Kirk Gibson	.50
CP3	Kirk Gibson	1.00
CP4	Joe Carter	.50
CP4	Joe Carter	1.00
CP5	George Brett	1.25
CP5	George Brett	2.50
CP6	Roberto Alomar	.50
CP6	Roberto Alomar	1.00
CP7	Ozzie Smith	.75
CP7	Ozzie Smith	2.00
CP8	Kirby Puckett	1.25
CP8	Kirby Puckett	2.00
CP9	Bret Saberhagen	.50
CP9	Bret Saberhagen	1.00
CP10	Steve Garvey	.50
CP10	Steve Garvey	1.00

Destination: Fall Classic

		NM/M
	Complete Set (9):	18.00
	Common Player:	1.00
	Complete Die-Cut Set (9):	36.00
	Common Die-Cut:	2.00
1	Ken Griffey Jr.	3.00
1	Ken Griffey Jr. (die-cut)	6.00
2	Frank Thomas	2.00
2	Frank Thomas (die-cut)	4.00
3	Albert Belle	1.00
3	Albert Belle (die-cut)	2.00
4	Mike Piazza	3.00
4	Mike Piazza (die-cut)	6.00
5	Don Mattingly	2.75
5	Don Mattingly (die-cut)	5.50
6	Hideo Nomo	1.50
6	Hideo Nomo (die-cut)	2.00
7	Greg Maddux	2.50
7	Greg Maddux (die-cut)	5.00
8	Fred McGriff	1.00
8	Fred McGriff (die-cut)	2.00
9	Barry Bonds	5.00
9	Barry Bonds (die-cut)	8.00

Ripken Tribute Jumbo

		NM/M
CR1	Cal Ripken Jr.	12.00

1996 SP

		NM/M
	Complete Set (188):	12.50
	Common Player:	.05
	Pack (8):	1.25
	Wax Box (30):	25.00
1	Rey Ordonez	.05
2	George Arias	.05
3	*Osvaldo Fernandez*	.25
4	*Darin Erstad*	2.00
5	Paul Wilson	.05
6	Richard Hidalgo	.05
7	Bob Wolcott	.05
8	Jimmy Haynes	.05
9	Edgar Renteria	.05
10	Alan Benes	.05
11	Chris Snopek	.05
12	Billy Wagner	.05
13	*Mike Grace*	.05
14	Todd Greene	.05
15	Karim Garcia	.05
16	John Wasdin	.05
17	Jason Kendall	.05
18	Bob Abreu	.15
19	Jermaine Dye	.05
20	Jason Schmidt	.05
21	Javy Lopez	.05
22	Ryan Klesko	.05
23	Tom Glavine	.35
24	John Smoltz	.05
25	Greg Maddux	1.00
26	Chipper Jones	1.00
27	Fred McGriff	.05
28	David Justice	.05
29	Roberto Alomar	.20
30	Cal Ripken Jr.	2.00
31	Jeffrey Hammonds	.05
32	Bobby Bonilla	.05
33	Mike Mussina	.30
34	Randy Myers	.05
35	Rafael Palmeiro	.65
36	Brady Anderson	.05
37	Tim Naehring	.05
38	Jose Canseco	.40
39	Roger Clemens	1.00
40	Mo Vaughn	.05
41	*Jose Valentin*	.05
42	Kevin Mitchell	.05
43	Chili Davis	.05
44	Garret Anderson	.05
45	Tim Salmon	.05
46	Chuck Finley	.05
47	Mark Langston	.05
48	Jim Abbott	.05
49	J.T. Snow	.05
50	Jim Edmonds	.05
51	Sammy Sosa	1.00
52	Brian McRae	.05
53	Ryne Sandberg	1.00
54	Mark Grace	.05
55	Jaime Navarro	.05
56	Harold Baines	.05
57	Robin Ventura	.05
58	Tony Phillips	.05
59	Alex Fernandez	.05
60	Frank Thomas	.75
61	Ray Durham	.05
62	Bret Boone	.05
63	Barry Larkin	.05
64	Pete Schourek	.05
65	Reggie Sanders	.05
66	John Smiley	.05
67	Carlos Baerga	.05
68	Jim Thome	.65
69	Eddie Murray	.75
70	Albert Belle	.05
71	Dennis Martinez	.05
72	Jack McDowell	.05
73	Kenny Lofton	.05
74	Manny Ramirez	.75
75	Dante Bichette	.05
76	Vinny Castilla	.05
77	Andres Galarraga	.05
78	Walt Weiss	.05
79	Ellis Burks	.05
80	Larry Walker	.05
81	Cecil Fielder	.05
82	Melvin Nieves	.05
83	Travis Fryman	.05
84	Chad Curtis	.05
85	Alan Trammell	.05
86	Gary Sheffield	.45
87	Charles Johnson	.05
88	Andre Dawson	.30
89	Jeff Conine	.05
90	Greg Colbrunn	.05
91	Derek Bell	.05
92	Brian Hunter	.05
93	Doug Drabek	.05
94	Craig Biggio	.05
95	Jeff Bagwell	.75
96	Kevin Appier	.05
97	Jeff Montgomery	.05
98	Michael Tucker	.05
99	Bip Roberts	.05
100	Johnny Damon	.35
101	Eric Karros	.05
102	Raul Mondesi	.05
103	Ramon Martinez	.05
104	Ismael Valdes	.05
105	Mike Piazza	1.25
106	Hideo Nomo	.40
107	Chan Ho Park	.05
108	Ben McDonald	.05
109	Kevin Seitzer	.05
110	Greg Vaughn	.05
111	Jose Valentin	.05
112	Rick Aguilera	.05
113	Marty Cordova	.05
114	Brad Radke	.05
115	Kirby Puckett	1.00
116	Chuck Knoblauch	.05
117	Paul Molitor	.75
118	Pedro Martinez	.75
119	Mike Lansing	.05
120	Rondell White	.05
121	Moises Alou	.05
122	Mark Grudzielanek	.05
123	Jeff Fassero	.05
124	Rico Brogna	.05
125	Jason Isringhausen	.05
126	Jeff Kent	.05
127	Bernard Gilkey	.05
128	Todd Hundley	.05
129	David Cone	.05
130	Andy Pettitte	.25
131	Wade Boggs	1.00
132	Paul O'Neill	.05
133	Ruben Sierra	.05
134	John Wetteland	.05
135	Derek Jeter	2.00
136	Geronimo Pena	.05
137	Terry Steinbach	.05
138	Ariel Prieto	.05
139	Scott Brosius	.05
140	Mark McGwire	1.50
141	Lenny Dykstra	.05
142	Todd Zeile	.05
143	Benito Santiago	.05
144	Mickey Morandini	.05
145	Gregg Jefferies	.05
146	Denny Neagle	.05
147	Orlando Merced	.05
148	Charlie Hayes	.05
149	Carlos Garcia	.05
150	Jay Bell	.05
151	Ray Lankford	.05
152	Alan Benes	.05
153	Dennis Eckersley	.65
154	Gary Gaetti	.05
155	Ozzie Smith	1.00
156	Ron Gant	.05
157	Brian Jordan	.05
158	Ken Caminiti	.05
159	Rickey Henderson	.75
160	Tony Gwynn	1.00
161	Wally Joyner	.05
162	Andy Ashby	.05
163	Steve Finley	.05
164	Glenallen Hill	.05
165	Matt Williams	.05
166	Barry Bonds	2.00
167	William VanLandingham	.05
168	Rod Beck	.05
169	Randy Johnson	.75
170	Ken Griffey Jr.	1.25
170p	Ken Griffey Jr. (unmarked promo; bio on back says, ". . .against Cleveland" as opposed to ". . . against the Indians")	4.00
171	Alex Rodriguez	1.50
172	Edgar Martinez	.05
173	Jay Buhner	.05
174	Russ Davis	.05
175	Juan Gonzalez	.40
176	Mickey Tettleton	.05
177	Will Clark	.05
178	Ken Hill	.05
179	Dean Palmer	.05
180	Ivan Rodriguez	.65
181	Carlos Delgado	.50
182	Alex Gonzalez	.05
183	Shawn Green	.30
184	Erik Hanson	.05
185	Joe Carter	.05
186	Hideo Nomo Checklist	.20
187	Cal Ripken Jr. Checklist	1.00
188	Ken Griffey Jr. Checklist	.65

Baseball Heroes

		NM/M
	Complete Set (10):	65.00
	Common Player:	4.00
81	Ken Griffey Jr. Header	8.00
82	Frank Thomas	6.50
83	Albert Belle	4.00
84	Barry Bonds	12.00
85	Chipper Jones	8.00
86	Hideo Nomo	5.00
87	Mike Piazza	10.00
88	Manny Ramirez	6.50
89	Greg Maddux	8.00
90	Ken Griffey Jr.	10.00

Marquee Matchups Blue

		NM/M
	Complete Set (20):	15.00
	Common Player:	.35
1	Ken Griffey Jr.	1.50
2	Hideo Nomo	.60

3	Derek Jeter	2.00
4	Rey Ordonez	.50
5	Tim Salmon	.50
6	Mike Piazza	1.50
7	Mark McGwire	1.75
8	Barry Bonds	2.00
9	Cal Ripken Jr.	2.00
10	Greg Maddux	1.00
11	Albert Belle	.50
12	Barry Larkin	.50
13	Jeff Bagwell	.75
14	Juan Gonzalez	.60
15	Frank Thomas	.75
16	Sammy Sosa	1.00
17	Mike Mussina	.50
18	Chipper Jones	1.00
19	Roger Clemens	1.25
20	Fred McGriff	.50

Marquee Matchups Red

		NM/M
Complete Set (20):		70.00
Common Player:		1.25
1	Ken Griffey Jr.	6.00
2	Hideo Nomo	2.00
3	Derek Jeter	9.00
4	Rey Ordonez	1.25
5	Tim Salmon	1.25
6	Mike Piazza	6.00
7	Mark McGwire	7.50
8	Barry Bonds	9.00
9	Cal Ripken Jr.	9.00
10	Greg Maddux	4.50
11	Albert Belle	1.25
12	Barry Larkin	1.25
13	Jeff Bagwell	3.50
14	Juan Gonzalez	2.00
15	Frank Thomas	3.50
16	Sammy Sosa	4.50
17	Mike Mussina	1.25
18	Chipper Jones	4.50
19	Roger Clemens	5.00
20	Fred McGriff	1.25

Ripken Collection

		NM/M
Complete Set (5):		25.00
Common Card:		5.00
18	Cal Ripken Jr.	5.00
19	Cal Ripken Jr.	5.00
20	Cal Ripken Jr.	5.00
21	Cal Ripken Jr.	5.00
22	Cal Ripken Jr.	5.00

SpecialFX

		NM/M
Complete Set (48):		50.00
Common Player:		.60
1	Greg Maddux	2.50
2	Eric Karros	.60
3	Mike Piazza	3.00
4	Raul Mondesi	.60
5	Hideo Nomo	1.00
6	Jim Edmonds	.60
7	Jason Isringhausen	.60
8	Jay Buhner	.60
9	Barry Larkin	.60
10	Ken Griffey Jr.	3.00
11	Gary Sheffield	1.25
12	Craig Biggio	.60
13	Paul Wilson	.60
14	Rondell White	.60
15	Chipper Jones	2.50
16	Kirby Puckett	2.50
17	Ron Gant	.60
18	Wade Boggs	2.50
19	Fred McGriff	.60
20	Cal Ripken Jr.	5.00
21	Jason Kendall	.60
22	Johnny Damon	.90
23	Kenny Lofton	.60
24	Roberto Alomar	1.00
25	Barry Bonds	5.00
26	Dante Bichette	.60
27	Mark McGwire	4.00
28	Rafael Palmeiro	1.50
29	Juan Gonzalez	1.00
30	Albert Belle	.60
31	Randy Johnson	1.75
32	Jose Canseco	1.25
33	Sammy Sosa	2.50
34	Eddie Murray	1.75
35	Frank Thomas	1.75
36	Tom Glavine	.90
37	Matt Williams	.60
38	Roger Clemens	2.75
39	Paul Molitor	1.75
40	Tony Gwynn	2.50
41	Mo Vaughn	.60
42	Tim Salmon	.60
43	Manny Ramirez	1.75
44	Jeff Bagwell	1.75
45	Edgar Martinez	.60
46	Rey Ordonez	.60
47	Osvaldo Fernandez	.60
48	Derek Jeter	5.00

SpecialFX Red

		NM/M
Complete Set (48):		135.00
Common Player:		1.50
1	Greg Maddux	6.00
2	Eric Karros	1.50
3	Mike Piazza	8.00
4	Raul Mondesi	1.50
5	Hideo Nomo	2.25
6	Jim Edmonds	1.50
7	Jason Isringhausen	1.50
8	Jay Buhner	1.50
9	Barry Larkin	1.50
10	Ken Griffey Jr.	8.00
11	Gary Sheffield	2.50
12	Craig Biggio	1.50
13	Paul Wilson	1.50
14	Rondell White	1.50
15	Chipper Jones	6.00
16	Kirby Puckett	6.00
17	Ron Gant	1.50
18	Wade Boggs	6.00
19	Fred McGriff	1.50
20	Cal Ripken Jr.	12.50
21	Jason Kendall	1.50
22	Johnny Damon	2.50
23	Kenny Lofton	1.50
24	Roberto Alomar	2.25
25	Barry Bonds	12.50
26	Dante Bichette	1.50
27	Mark McGwire	10.00
28	Rafael Palmeiro	3.50
29	Juan Gonzalez	2.25
30	Albert Belle	1.50
31	Randy Johnson	4.50
32	Jose Canseco	2.50
33	Sammy Sosa	6.00
34	Eddie Murray	4.50
35	Frank Thomas	4.50
36	Tom Glavine	2.00
37	Matt Williams	1.50
38	Roger Clemens	7.00
39	Paul Molitor	4.50
40	Tony Gwynn	6.00
41	Mo Vaughn	1.50
42	Tim Salmon	1.50
43	Manny Ramirez	4.50
44	Jeff Bagwell	4.50
45	Edgar Martinez	1.50
46	Rey Ordonez	1.50
47	Osvaldo Fernandez	1.50
48	Derek Jeter	12.50

1996 SPX

		NM/M
Complete Set (60):		17.50
Common Player:		.15
Golds:		1.5X
Pack (1):		1.25
Wax Box (36):		25.00
1	Greg Maddux	1.50
2	Chipper Jones	1.50
3	Fred McGriff	.15
4	Tom Glavine	.50
5	Cal Ripken Jr.	3.00
6	Roberto Alomar	.50
7	Rafael Palmeiro	1.00
8	Jose Canseco	.65
9	Roger Clemens	1.75
10	Mo Vaughn	.15
11	Jim Edmonds	.15
12	Tim Salmon	.15
13	Sammy Sosa	1.50
14	Ryne Sandberg	1.50
15	Mark Grace	.15
16	Frank Thomas	1.25
17	Barry Larkin	.15
18	Kenny Lofton	.15
19	Albert Belle	.15
20	Eddie Murray	1.25
21	Manny Ramirez	1.25
22	Dante Bichette	.15
23	Larry Walker	.15
24	Vinny Castilla	.15
25	Andres Galarraga	.15
26	Cecil Fielder	.15
27	Gary Sheffield	.75
28	Craig Biggio	.15
29	Jeff Bagwell	1.25
30	Derek Bell	.15
31	Johnny Damon	.60
32	Eric Karros	.15
33	Mike Piazza	2.00
34	Raul Mondesi	.15
35	Hideo Nomo	.65
36	Kirby Puckett	1.50
37	Paul Molitor	1.25
38	Marty Cordova	.15
39	Rondell White	.15
40	Jason Isringhausen	.15
41	Paul Wilson	.15
42	Rey Ordonez	.15
43	Derek Jeter	3.00
44	Wade Boggs	1.50
45	Mark McGwire	2.50
46	Jason Kendall	.15
47	Ron Gant	.15
48	Ozzie Smith	1.50
49	Tony Gwynn	1.50
50	Ken Caminiti	.15
51	Barry Bonds	3.00
52	Matt Williams	.15
53	*Osvaldo Fernandez*	.25
54	Jay Buhner	.15
55	Ken Griffey Jr.	2.00
55p	Ken Griffey Jr. (overprinted "For Promotional Use Only")	2.00
56	Randy Johnson	1.25
57	Alex Rodriguez	2.50
58	Juan Gonzalez	.65
59	Joe Carter	.15
60	Carlos Delgado	.75

Bound for Glory

		NM/M
Complete Set (10):		18.00
Common Player:		1.00
1	Ken Griffey Jr.	3.00
2	Frank Thomas	1.50
3	Barry Bonds	4.00
4	Cal Ripken Jr.	4.00
5	Greg Maddux	2.00
6	Chipper Jones	2.00
7	Roberto Alomar	1.00
8	Manny Ramirez	1.50
9	Tony Gwynn	2.00
10	Mike Piazza	3.00

Ken Griffey Jr. Commemorative

		NM/M
KG1	Ken Griffey Jr.	2.50
KGA1	Ken Griffey Jr./ autograph	100.00

Mike Piazza Tribute

		NM/M
MP1	Mike Piazza	2.00
MP1	Mike Piazza/ autograph	125.00

1997 SP

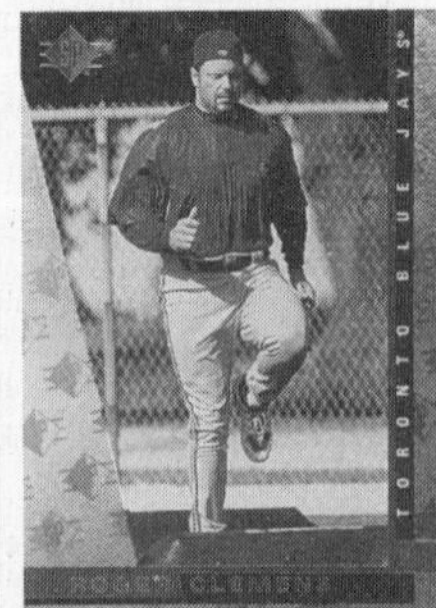

		NM/M
Complete Set (184):		12.00
Common Player:		.05
Pack (8):		2.00
Wax Box (30):		45.00
1	Andruw Jones	.75
2	Kevin Orie	.05
3	Nomar Garciaparra	1.00
4	Jose Guillen	.05
5	Todd Walker	.05
6	Derrick Gibson	.05
7	Aaron Boone	.05
8	Bartolo Colon	.05
9	Derrek Lee	.50

10	Vladimir Guerrero	.75
11	Wilton Guerrero	.05
12	Luis Castillo	.05
13	Jason Dickson	.05
14	*Bubba Trammell*	.25
15	*Jose Cruz Jr.*	.50
16	Eddie Murray	.75
17	Darin Erstad	.20
18	Garret Anderson	.05
19	Jim Edmonds	.05
20	Tim Salmon	.05
21	Chuck Finley	.05
22	John Smoltz	.05
23	Greg Maddux	1.00
24	Kenny Lofton	.05
25	Chipper Jones	1.00
26	Ryan Klesko	.05
27	Javier Lopez	.05
28	Fred McGriff	.05
29	Roberto Alomar	.20
30	Rafael Palmeiro	.65
31	Mike Mussina	.30
32	Brady Anderson	.05
33	Rocky Coppinger	.05
34	Cal Ripken Jr.	2.00
35	Mo Vaughn	.05
36	Steve Avery	.05
37	Tom Gordon	.05
38	Tim Naehring	.05
39	Troy O'Leary	.05
40	Sammy Sosa	1.00
41	Brian McRae	.05
42	Mel Rojas	.05
43	Ryne Sandberg	1.00
44	Mark Grace	.05
45	Albert Belle	.05
46	Robin Ventura	.05
47	Roberto Hernandez	.05
48	Ray Durham	.05
49	Harold Baines	.05
50	Frank Thomas	.75
51	Bret Boone	.05
52	Reggie Sanders	.05
53	Deion Sanders	.05
54	Hal Morris	.05
55	Barry Larkin	.05
56	Jim Thome	.65
57	Marquis Grissom	.05
58	David Justice	.05
59	Charles Nagy	.05
60	Manny Ramirez	.75
61	Matt Williams	.05
62	Jack McDowell	.05
63	Vinny Castilla	.05
64	Dante Bichette	.05
65	Andres Galarraga	.05
66	Ellis Burks	.05
67	Larry Walker	.05
68	Eric Young	.05
69	Brian L. Hunter	.05
70	Travis Fryman	.05
71	Tony Clark	.05
72	Bobby Higginson	.05
73	Melvin Nieves	.05
74	Jeff Conine	.05
75	Gary Sheffield	.40
76	Moises Alou	.05
77	Edgar Renteria	.05
78	Alex Fernandez	.05
79	Charles Johnson	.05
80	Bobby Bonilla	.05
81	Darryl Kile	.05
82	Derek Bell	.05
83	Shane Reynolds	.05
84	Craig Biggio	.05
85	Jeff Bagwell	.75
86	Billy Wagner	.05
87	Chili Davis	.05
88	Kevin Appier	.05
89	Jay Bell	.05
90	Johnny Damon	.35
91	Jeff King	.05
92	Hideo Nomo	.40
93	Todd Hollandsworth	.05
94	Eric Karros	.05
95	Mike Piazza	1.25
96	Ramon Martinez	.05
97	Todd Worrell	.05
98	Raul Mondesi	.05
99	Dave Nilsson	.05
100	John Jaha	.05
101	Jose Valentin	.05
102	Jeff Cirillo	.05
103	Jeff D'Amico	.05
104	Ben McDonald	.05
105	Paul Molitor	.75
106	Rich Becker	.05
107	Frank Rodriguez	.05
108	Marty Cordova	.05
109	Terry Steinbach	.05
110	Chuck Knoblauch	.05
111	Mark Grudzielanek	.05
112	Mike Lansing	.05
113	Pedro Martinez	.75
114	Henry Rodriguez	.05
115	Rondell White	.05
116	Rey Ordonez	.05
117	Carlos Baerga	.05
118	Lance Johnson	.05
119	Bernard Gilkey	.05
120	Todd Hundley	.05
121	John Franco	.05
122	Bernie Williams	.05
123	David Cone	.05
124	Cecil Fielder	.05
125	Derek Jeter	2.00
126	Tino Martinez	.05
127	Mariano Rivera	.15
128	Andy Pettitte	.15
129	Wade Boggs	1.00
130	Mark McGwire	1.50
131	Jose Canseco	.50
132	Geronimo Berroa	.05
133	Jason Giambi	.45
134	Ernie Young	.05
135	Scott Rolen	.65
136	Ricky Bottalico	.05
137	Curt Schilling	.35
138	Gregg Jefferies	.05
139	Mickey Morandini	.05
140	Jason Kendall	.05
141	Kevin Elster	.05
142	Al Martin	.05
143	Joe Randa	.05
144	Jason Schmidt	.05
145	Ray Lankford	.05
146	Brian Jordan	.05
147	Andy Benes	.05
148	Alan Benes	.05
149	Gary Gaetti	.05
150	Ron Gant	.05
151	Dennis Eckersley	.65
152	Rickey Henderson	.75
153	Joey Hamilton	.05
154	Ken Caminiti	.05
155	Tony Gwynn	1.00
156	Steve Finley	.05
157	Trevor Hoffman	.05
158	Greg Vaughn	.05
159	J.T. Snow	.05
160	Barry Bonds	2.00
161	Glenallen Hill	.05
162	William VanLandingham	.05
163	Jeff Kent	.05
164	Jay Buhner	.05
165	Ken Griffey Jr.	1.25
166	Alex Rodriguez	1.50
167	Randy Johnson	.75
168	Edgar Martinez	.05
169	Dan Wilson	.05
170	Ivan Rodriguez	.65
171	Roger Pavlik	.05
172	Will Clark	.05
173	Dean Palmer	.05
174	Rusty Greer	.05
175	Juan Gonzalez	.40
176	John Wetteland	.05
177	Joe Carter	.05
178	Ed Sprague	.05
179	Carlos Delgado	.45
180	Roger Clemens	1.00
181	Juan Guzman	.05
182	Pat Hentgen	.05
183	Ken Griffey Jr. (checklist)	.65
184	*Hideki Irabu*	.25

Buy-Back Autographed Inserts

		NM/M
Common Autograph:		7.50
	1993 SP	
4	Ken Griffey Jr. (16)	600.00
28	Jeff Bagwell (7)	100.00
167	Tony Gwynn (17)	250.00
280	Chipper Jones (34)	110.00
	1993 SP Platinum Power	
PP9	Ken Griffey Jr. (5)	800.00
	1994 SP	
6	Todd Hollandsworth (167)	7.50
15	Alex Rodriguez (94)	1,200
105	Ken Griffey Jr. (103)	125.00
114	Gary Sheffield (130)	25.00
130	Tony Gwynn (367)	25.00
	1994 SP Holoview Blue	
13	Tony Gwynn (31)	150.00
	1994 SP Holoview Red	
35	Gary Sheffield (4)	60.00
	1995 SP	
34	Chipper Jones (60)	125.00
60	Jeff Bagwell (173)	40.00
75	Gary Sheffield (221)	20.00
105	Tony Gwynn (64)	60.00
188	Alex Rodriguez (63)	200.00
190	Ken Griffey Jr. (38)	200.00
195	Jay Buhner (57)	15.00
	1996 SP	
1	Rey Ordonez (111)	7.50
18	Gary Sheffield (58)	30.00
26	Chipper Jones (102)	50.00
40	Mo Vaughn (250)	15.00
95	Jeff Bagwell (292)	20.00
160	Tony Gwynn (20)	200.00
170	Ken Griffey Jr. (312)	65.00
171	Alex Rodriguez (73)	125.00
173	Jay Buhner (79)	30.00
	1996 SP Marquee Matchups	
MM13	Jeff Bagwell (23)	65.00
MM4	Rey Ordonez (40)	15.00
	1996 SP Special F/X	
8	Jay Buhner (27)	30.00

Griffey Baseball Heroes

	NM/M
Complete Set (10):	75.00
Common Griffey Jr.:	10.00

Game Film

		NM/M
Complete Set (10):		175.00
Common Player:		12.00
1	Alex Rodriguez	22.50
2	Frank Thomas	12.00
3	Andruw Jones	12.00
4	Cal Ripken Jr.	30.00
5	Mike Piazza	17.50
6	Derek Jeter	30.00
7	Mark McGwire	22.50
8	Chipper Jones	15.00
9	Barry Bonds	30.00
10	Ken Griffey Jr.	17.50

Inside Info

		NM/M
Complete Set (25):		75.00
Common Player:		1.00
1	Ken Griffey Jr.	5.00
2	Mark McGwire	6.00
3	Kenny Lofton	1.00
4	Paul Molitor	3.00
5	Frank Thomas	3.00
6	Greg Maddux	3.50
7	Mo Vaughn	1.00
8	Cal Ripken Jr.	7.50
9	Jeff Bagwell	3.00
10	Alex Rodriguez	6.00
11	John Smoltz	1.00
12	Manny Ramirez	3.00
13	Sammy Sosa	3.50
14	Vladimir Guerrero	3.00
15	Albert Belle	1.00
16	Mike Piazza	5.00
17	Derek Jeter	7.50
18	Scott Rolen	2.00
19	Tony Gwynn	3.50
20	Barry Bonds	7.50
21	Ken Caminiti	1.00
22	Chipper Jones	3.50
23	Juan Gonzalez	1.50
24	Roger Clemens	4.00
25	Andruw Jones	3.00

Marquee Matchups

		NM/M
Complete Set (20):		20.00
Common Player:		.25
1	Ken Griffey Jr.	1.50
2	Andres Galarraga	.25
3	Barry Bonds	3.00
4	Mark McGwire	2.00
5	Mike Piazza	1.50
6	Tim Salmon	.25
7	Tony Gwynn	1.00
8	Alex Rodriguez	2.00
9	Chipper Jones	1.00
10	Derek Jeter	3.00
11	Manny Ramirez	.75
12	Jeff Bagwell	.75
13	Greg Maddux	1.00
14	Cal Ripken Jr.	3.00
15	Mo Vaughn	.25
16	Gary Sheffield	.45
17	Jim Thome	.65
18	Barry Larkin	.25
19	Frank Thomas	.75
20	Sammy Sosa	1.00

Special FX

		NM/M
Complete Set (48):		60.00
Common Player:		.60
1	Ken Griffey Jr.	3.50
2	Frank Thomas	2.00
3	Barry Bonds	5.00
4	Albert Belle	.60
5	Mike Piazza	3.50
6	Greg Maddux	2.50
7	Chipper Jones	2.50
8	Cal Ripken Jr.	5.00
9	Jeff Bagwell	2.00
10	Alex Rodriguez	4.00
11	Mark McGwire	4.00
12	Kenny Lofton	.60
13	Juan Gonzalez	1.00
14	Mo Vaughn	.60
15	John Smoltz	.60
16	Derek Jeter	5.00
17	Tony Gwynn	2.50
18	Ivan Rodriguez	1.50
19	Barry Larkin	.60
20	Sammy Sosa	2.50
21	Mike Mussina	.75
22	Gary Sheffield	1.00
23	Brady Anderson	.60
24	Roger Clemens	3.00
25	Ken Caminiti	.60

26 Roberto Alomar 1.00
27 Hideo Nomo 1.00
28 Bernie Williams .60
29 Todd Hundley .60
30 Manny Ramirez 2.00
31 Eric Karros .60
32 Tim Salmon .60
33 Jay Buhner .60
34 Andy Pettitte .60
35 Jim Thome 1.50
36 Ryne Sandberg 2.50
37 Matt Williams .60
38 Ryan Klesko .60
39 Jose Canseco 1.25
40 Paul Molitor 2.00
41 Eddie Murray 2.00
42 Darin Erstad .75
43 Todd Walker .60
44 Wade Boggs 2.50
45 Andruw Jones 2.00
46 Scott Rolen 1.50
47 Vladimir Guerrero 2.00
48 NOT ISSUED
49 Alex Rodriguez (1996 design) 4.00

SPx Force

NM/M
Complete Set (10): 60.00
Common Player: 6.00
1 Ken Griffey Jr., Jay Buhner, Andres Galarraga, Dante Bichette 7.50
2 Albert Belle, Brady Anderson, Mark McGwire, Cecil Fielder 9.00
3 Mo Vaughn, Ken Caminiti, Frank Thomas, Jeff Bagwell 6.00
4 Gary Sheffield, Sammy Sosa, Barry Bonds, Jose Canseco 12.00
5 Greg Maddux, Roger Clemens, John Smoltz, Randy Johnson 6.00
6 Alex Rodriguez, Derek Jeter, Chipper Jones, Rey Ordonez 12.00
7 Todd Hollandsworth, Mike Piazza, Raul Mondesi, Hideo Nomo 7.50
8 Juan Gonzalez, Manny Ramirez, Roberto Alomar, Ivan Rodriguez 6.00
9 Tony Gwynn, Wade Boggs, Eddie Murray, Paul Molitor 6.00
10 Andruw Jones, Vladimir Guerrero, Todd Walker, Scott Rolen 6.00

SPx Force Autographs

NM/M
Common Player: 20.00
1 Ken Griffey Jr. 125.00
2 Albert Belle 25.00
3 Mo Vaughn 20.00
4 Gary Sheffield 25.00
5 Greg Maddux 100.00
6 Alex Rodriguez 160.00
7 Todd Hollandsworth 20.00
8 Roberto Alomar 30.00
9 Tony Gwynn 75.00
10 Andruw Jones 40.00

1997 SPX

NM/M
Complete Set (50): 17.50

Common Player: .15
Steel: 1.5X
Bronze: 1.5X
Silver: 1.5X
Gold: 3X
Grand Finale: 4X
Pack (3): 2.00
Wax Box (18): 30.00
1 Eddie Murray 1.00
2 Darin Erstad .35
3 Tim Salmon .15
4 Andruw Jones 1.00
5 Chipper Jones 1.50
6 John Smoltz .15
7 Greg Maddux 1.50
8 Kenny Lofton .15
9 Roberto Alomar .30
10 Rafael Palmeiro .75
11 Brady Anderson .15
12 Cal Ripken Jr. 3.00
13 Nomar Garciaparra 1.50
14 Mo Vaughn .15
15 Ryne Sandberg 1.50
16 Sammy Sosa 1.50
17 Frank Thomas 1.00
18 Albert Belle .15
19 Barry Larkin .15
20 Deion Sanders .15
21 Manny Ramirez 1.00
22 Jim Thome .65
23 Dante Bichette .15
24 Andres Galarraga .15
25 Larry Walker .15
26 Gary Sheffield .50
27 Jeff Bagwell 1.00
28 Raul Mondesi .15
29 Hideo Nomo .50
30 Mike Piazza 2.00
31 Paul Molitor 1.00
32 Todd Walker .15
33 Vladimir Guerrero 1.00
34 Todd Hundley .15
35 Andy Pettitte .25
36 Derek Jeter 3.00
37 Jose Canseco .50
38 Mark McGwire 2.50
39 Scott Rolen .65
40 Ron Gant .15
41 Ken Caminiti .15
42 Tony Gwynn 1.50
43 Barry Bonds 3.00
44 Jay Buhner .15
45 Ken Griffey Jr. 2.00
45s Ken Griffey Jr. (overprinted SAMPLE on back) 2.00
46 Alex Rodriguez 2.50
47 *Jose Cruz Jr.* 1.00
48 Juan Gonzalez .50
49 Ivan Rodriguez .75
50 Roger Clemens 1.75

Bound for Glory

NM/M
Complete Set (20): 60.00
Common Player: 1.00
1 Andruw Jones 3.00
2 Chipper Jones 4.00
3 Greg Maddux 4.00
4 Kenny Lofton 1.00
5 Cal Ripken Jr. 7.50
6 Mo Vaughn 1.00
7 Frank Thomas 3.00
8 Albert Belle 1.00
9 Manny Ramirez 3.00
10 Gary Sheffield 1.50
11 Jeff Bagwell 3.00
12 Mike Piazza 5.00
13 Derek Jeter 7.50
14 Mark McGwire 6.00
15 Tony Gwynn 4.00
16 Ken Caminiti 1.00
17 Barry Bonds 7.50
18 Alex Rodriguez 6.00
19 Ken Griffey Jr. 5.00
20 Juan Gonzalez 1.50

Bound for Glory Supreme Signatures

NM/M
Complete Set (5): 250.00
Common Player: 25.00
1 Jeff Bagwell 35.00
2 Ken Griffey Jr. 110.00
3 Andruw Jones 25.00
4 Alex Rodriguez 140.00
5 Gary Sheffield 25.00

Cornerstones of the Game

NM/M
Complete Set (10): 150.00
Common Player: 12.00
1 Ken Griffey Jr., Barry Bonds 25.00
2 Frank Thomas, Albert Belle 12.00
3 Chipper Jones, Greg Maddux 15.00
4 Tony Gwynn, Paul Molitor 15.00
5 Andruw Jones, Vladimir Guerrero 12.00
6 Jeff Bagwell, Ryne Sandberg 15.00
7 Mike Piazza, Ivan Rodriguez 20.00
8 Cal Ripken Jr., Eddie Murray 25.00
9 Mo Vaughn, Mark McGwire 20.00
10 Alex Rodriguez, Derek Jeter 25.00

1998 SP AUTHENTIC

NM/M
Complete Set (198): 15.00
Common Player: .05
Pack (5): 2.00
Wax Box (24): 35.00
1 Travis Lee .10
2 Mike Caruso .05
3 Kerry Wood .65
4 Mark Kotsay .05
5 *Magglio Ordonez* 2.00
6 Scott Elarton .05
7 Carl Pavano .10
8 A.J. Hinch .05
9 *Rolando Arrojo* .40
10 Ben Grieve .05
11 Gabe Alvarez .05
12 *Mike Kinkade* .40
13 Bruce Chen .05
14 Juan Encarnacion .05
15 Todd Helton .75
16 Aaron Boone .05
17 Sean Casey .15
18 Ramon Hernandez .05
19 Daryle Ward .05
20 Paul Konerko .15
21 David Ortiz .50
22 Derrek Lee .50
23 Brad Fullmer .05
24 Javier Vazquez .05
25 Miguel Tejada .15
26 David Dellucci .05
27 Alex Gonzalez .05
28 Matt Clement .05
29 Eric Milton .05
30 Russell Branyan .05
31 Chuck Finley .05
32 Jim Edmonds .05
33 Darin Erstad .20
34 Jason Dickson .05
35 Tim Salmon .05
36 Cecil Fielder .05
37 Todd Greene .05
38 Andy Benes .05
39 Jay Bell .05
40 Matt Williams .05
41 Brian Anderson .05
42 Karim Garcia .05
43 Javy Lopez .05
44 Tom Glavine .35
45 Greg Maddux 1.50
46 Andruw Jones 1.00
47 Chipper Jones 1.50
48 Ryan Klesko .05
49 John Smoltz .05
50 Andres Galarraga .05
51 Rafael Palmeiro .75
52 Mike Mussina .30
53 Roberto Alomar .20
54 Joe Carter .05
55 Cal Ripken Jr. 3.00
56 Brady Anderson .05
57 Mo Vaughn .05
58 John Valentin .05
59 Dennis Eckersley .75
60 Nomar Garciaparra 1.50
61 Pedro J. Martinez 1.00
62 Jeff Blauser .05
63 Kevin Orie .05
64 Henry Rodriguez .05
65 Mark Grace .05
66 Albert Belle .05
67 Mike Cameron .05
68 Robin Ventura .05
69 Frank Thomas 1.00
70 Barry Larkin .05
71 Brett Tomko .05
72 Willie Greene .05
73 Reggie Sanders .05
74 Sandy Alomar Jr. .05
75 Kenny Lofton .05
76 Jaret Wright .05
77 David Justice .05
78 Omar Vizquel .05
79 Manny Ramirez 1.00
80 Jim Thome .75
81 Travis Fryman .05
82 Neifi Perez .05
83 Mike Lansing .05
84 Vinny Castilla .05
85 Larry Walker .05
86 Dante Bichette .05
87 Darryl Kile .05
88 Justin Thompson .05
89 Damion Easley .05
90 Tony Clark .05
91 Bobby Higginson .05
92 Brian L. Hunter .05
93 Edgar Renteria .05
94 Craig Counsell .05
95 Mike Piazza 2.00
96 Livan Hernandez .05
97 Todd Zeile .05
98 Richard Hidalgo .05
99 Moises Alou .05
100 Jeff Bagwell 1.00
101 Mike Hampton .05
102 Craig Biggio .05
103 Dean Palmer .05
104 Tim Belcher .05
105 Jeff King .05
106 Jeff Conine .05

107	Johnny Damon	.30
108	Hideo Nomo	.50
109	Raul Mondesi	.05
110	Gary Sheffield	.45
111	Ramon Martinez	.05
112	Chan Ho Park	.05
113	Eric Young	.05
114	Charles Johnson	.05
115	Eric Karros	.05
116	Bobby Bonilla	.05
117	Jeromy Burnitz	.05
118	Carl Eldred	.05
119	Jeff D'Amico	.05
120	Marquis Grissom	.05
121	Dave Nilsson	.05
122	Brad Radke	.05
123	Marty Cordova	.05
124	Ron Coomer	.05
125	Paul Molitor	1.00
126	Todd Walker	.05
127	Rondell White	.05
128	Mark Grudzielanek	.05
129	Carlos Perez	.05
130	Vladimir Guerrero	1.00
131	Dustin Hermanson	.05
132	Butch Huskey	.05
133	John Franco	.05
134	Rey Ordonez	.05
135	Todd Hundley	.05
136	Edgardo Alfonzo	.05
137	Bobby Jones	.05
138	John Olerud	.05
139	Chili Davis	.05
140	Tino Martinez	.05
141	Andy Pettitte	.15
142	Chuck Knoblauch	.05
143	Bernie Williams	.05
144	David Cone	.05
145	Derek Jeter	3.00
146	Paul O'Neill	.05
147	Rickey Henderson	1.00
148	Jason Giambi	.50
149	Kenny Rogers	.05
150	Scott Rolen	.75
151	Curt Schilling	.35
152	Ricky Bottalico	.05
153	Mike Lieberthal	.05
154	Francisco Cordova	.05
155	Jose Guillen	.05
156	Jason Schmidt	.05
157	Jason Kendall	.05
158	Kevin Young	.05
159	Delino DeShields	.05
160	Mark McGwire	2.50
161	Ray Lankford	.05
162	Brian Jordan	.05
163	Ron Gant	.05
164	Todd Stottlemyre	.05
165	Ken Caminiti	.05
166	Kevin Brown	.05
167	Trevor Hoffman	.05
168	Steve Finley	.05
169	Wally Joyner	.05
170	Tony Gwynn	1.50
171	Shawn Estes	.05
172	J.T. Snow	.05
173	Jeff Kent	.05
174	Robb Nen	.05
175	Barry Bonds	3.00
176	Randy Johnson	1.00
177	Edgar Martinez	.05
178	Jay Buhner	.05
179	Alex Rodriguez	2.50
180	Ken Griffey Jr.	2.00
181	Ken Cloude	.05
182	Wade Boggs	1.50
183	Tony Saunders	.05
184	Wilson Alvarez	.05
185	Fred McGriff	.05
186	Roberto Hernandez	.05
187	Kevin Stocker	.05
188	Fernando Tatis	.05
189	Will Clark	.05
190	Juan Gonzalez	.50
191	Rusty Greer	.05
192	Ivan Rodriguez	.75
193	Jose Canseco	.45
194	Carlos Delgado	.50
195	Roger Clemens	1.75
196	Pat Hentgen	.05
197	Randy Myers	.05
198	Ken Griffey Jr. Checklist	.85

Chirography

		NM/M
Common Card:		4.00
Inserted 1:25		
RA	Roberto Alomar	15.00
RB	Russell Branyan	4.00

SC	Sean Casey	10.00
TC	Tony Clark	4.00
RC	Roger Clemens/SP/400	80.00
JC	Jose Cruz Jr.	4.00
DE	Darin Erstad	7.50
NG	Nomar Garciaparra/SP/400	60.00
BG	Ben Grieve	4.00
KG	Ken Griffey Jr./SP/400	60.00
VG	Vladimir Guerrero	30.00
TG	Tony Gwynn/SP/850	30.00
TH	Todd Helton	15.00
LH	Livan Hernandez	6.00
CJ	Charles Johnson	6.00
AJ	Andruw Jones	17.50
CHIP	Chipper Jones/SP/800	30.00
PK	Paul Konerko	15.00
MK	Mark Kotsay	6.00
RL	Ray Lankford	6.00
TL	Travis Lee	6.00
PM	Paul Molitor/SP/800	20.00
MM	Mike Mussina	20.00
AR	Alex Rodriguez/SP/800	80.00
IR	Ivan Rodriguez	30.00
SR	Scott Rolen	20.00
GS	Gary Sheffield	15.00
MT	Miguel Tejada	20.00
JW	Jaret Wright	6.00
MV	Mo Vaughn/SP/800	12.50

Jersey Swatch

		NM/M
Complete Set (6):		130.00
Common Player:		7.50
(1)	Jay Buhner (125)	7.50
(2)	Ken Griffey Jr. (125)	50.00
(3)	Tony Gwynn (415)	10.00
(4)	Greg Maddux (125)	30.00
(5)	Alex Rodriguez (125)	60.00
(6)	Gary Sheffield (125)	12.00

Sheer Dominance

		NM/M
Complete Set (42):		32.50
Common Player:		.25
Inserted 1:3		
Gold (2,000 sets):		2X
Titanium (100 sets):		12X
SD1	Ken Griffey Jr.	1.75
SD2	Rickey Henderson	1.00
SD3	Jaret Wright	.25
SD4	Craig Biggio	.25
SD5	Travis Lee	.25
SD6	Kenny Lofton	.25
SD7	Raul Mondesi	.25
SD8	Cal Ripken Jr.	2.50
SD9	Matt Williams	.25
SD10	Mark McGwire	2.00
SD11	Alex Rodriguez	2.00
SD12	Fred McGriff	.25
SD13	Scott Rolen	.75
SD14	Paul Molitor	1.00
SD15	Nomar Garciaparra	1.50
SD16	Vladimir Guerrero	1.00
SD17	Andruw Jones	1.00
SD18	Manny Ramirez	1.00
SD19	Tony Gwynn	1.50
SD20	Barry Bonds	2.50
SD21	Ben Grieve	.25
SD22	Ivan Rodriguez	.75
SD23	Jose Cruz Jr.	.25
SD24	Pedro J. Martinez	1.00
SD25	Chipper Jones	1.50
SD26	Albert Belle	.25
SD27	Todd Helton	.75
SD28	Paul Konerko	.35
SD29	Sammy Sosa	1.50
SD30	Frank Thomas	1.00
SD31	Greg Maddux	1.50
SD32	Randy Johnson	1.00
SD33	Larry Walker	.25
SD34	Roberto Alomar	.45
SD35	Roger Clemens	1.50
SD36	Mo Vaughn	.25
SD37	Jim Thome	.75
SD38	Jeff Bagwell	1.00
SD39	Tino Martinez	.25
SD40	Mike Piazza	1.75
SD41	Derek Jeter	2.50
SD42	Juan Gonzalez	.50

Ken Griffey Jr. 300th HR Redemption

		NM/M
KG300	Ken Griffey Jr.	30.00

Sheer Dominance Gold

	NM/M
Common Player:	.50
Gold Stars:	2X

(See 1998 SP Authentic Sheer Dominance for checklist and base card values.)

Sheer Dominance Titanium

	NM/M
Common Player:	4.00
Titanium Stars:	12X

(See 1998 SP Authentic Sheer Dominance for checklist and base card values.)

Trade Cards

		NM/M
Common Card:		5.00
(1)	Roberto Alomar (autographed ball 100)	15.00
(2)	Albert Belle (autographed ball 100)	7.50
(3)	Jay Buhner (jersey card 125)	5.00
(4)	Ken Griffey Jr. (autographed glove 30)	200.00
(5)	Ken Griffey Jr. (autographed jersey 30)	200.00
(6)	Ken Griffey Jr. (jersey card 125)	25.00
(7)	Ken Griffey Jr. (standee 200)	15.00
(8)	Ken Griffey Jr. (300th HR card 1000)	5.00
(9)	Tony Gwynn (jersey card 415)	15.00
(10)	Brian Jordan (autographed ball 50)	10.00
(11)	Greg Maddux (jersey card 125)	20.00
(12)	Raul Mondesi (autographed ball 100)	5.00
(13)	Alex Rodriguez (jersey card 125)	40.00
(14)	Gary Sheffield (jersey card 125)	5.00
(15)	Robin Ventura (autographed ball 50)	10.00

1998 SPX FINITE

		NM/M
Complete Set (360):		200.00
Common Youth Movement: (#1-30, 181-210):		.50
Radiance YM (2,500):		1.5X
Spectrum YM (1,250):		2X
Common Power Explosion: (#31-50):		.50
Radiance PE (1,000):		2X
Spectrum PE (50):		25X
Common Base Card (#51-140, 241-330):		.15
Radiance Base Card (4,500):		1X
Spectrum Base Card (2,250):		2X
Common Star Focus: (#141-170):		.35
Radiance SF (3,500):		1X
Spectrum SF (1,750):		2X
Common Heroes of the Game: (#171-180):		2.50
Radiance HG (100):		15X
Common Power Passion: (#211-240):		.50
Radiance PP (3,500)		1X
Spectrum PP (1,750)		2X
Common Tradewinds: (#331-350):		.75
Radiance TW (1,000)		2X
Spectrum TW (50):		25X
Common Cornerstones/Game: (#351-360):		2.50
Radiance CG (100):		15X
Pack (3):		2.00
Wax Box:		25.00
1	Nomar Garciaparra	3.00
2	Miguel Tejada	.75
3	Mike Cameron	.50
4	Ken Cloude	.50
5	Jaret Wright	.50
6	Mark Kotsay	.50
7	Craig Counsell	.50
8	Jose Guillen	.50
9	Neifi Perez	.50
10	Jose Cruz Jr.	.50
11	Brett Tomko	.50
12	Matt Morris	.50
13	Justin Thompson	.50
14	Jeremi Gonzalez	.50
15	Scott Rolen	1.50
16	Vladimir Guerrero	2.00
17	Brad Fullmer	.50
18	Brian Giles	.50
19	Todd Dunwoody	.50
20	Ben Grieve	.50
21	Juan Encarnacion	.50
22	Aaron Boone	.50
23	Richie Sexson	.50
24	Richard Hidalgo	.50
25	Andruw Jones	2.00
26	Todd Helton	1.50
27	Paul Konerko	.75
28	Dante Powell	.50
29	Elieser Marrero	.50
30	Derek Jeter	5.00
31	Mike Piazza	3.00
32	Tony Clark	.50
33	Larry Walker	.50
34	Jim Thome	1.50
35	Juan Gonzalez	1.00
36	Jeff Bagwell	2.00
37	Jay Buhner	.50
38	Tim Salmon	.50
39	Albert Belle	.50
40	Mark McGwire	4.00
41	Sammy Sosa	2.50
42	Mo Vaughn	.50
43	Manny Ramirez	2.00
44	Tino Martinez	.50
45	Frank Thomas	2.00

46	Nomar Garciaparra	2.50
47	Alex Rodriguez	4.00
48	Chipper Jones	2.50
49	Barry Bonds	5.00
50	Ken Griffey Jr.	3.00
51	Jason Dickson	.15
52	Jim Edmonds	.15
53	Darin Erstad	.35
54	Tim Salmon	.15
55	Chipper Jones	2.00
56	Ryan Klesko	.15
57	Tom Glavine	.35
58	Denny Neagle	.15
59	John Smoltz	.15
60	Javy Lopez	.15
61	Roberto Alomar	.30
62	Rafael Palmeiro	1.25
63	Mike Mussina	.35
64	Cal Ripken Jr.	4.00
65	Mo Vaughn	.15
66	Tim Naehring	.15
67	John Valentin	.15
68	Mark Grace	.15
69	Kevin Orie	.15
70	Sammy Sosa	2.50
71	Albert Belle	.15
72	Frank Thomas	1.50
73	Robin Ventura	.15
74	David Justice	.15
75	Kenny Lofton	.15
76	Omar Vizquel	.15
77	Manny Ramirez	1.50
78	Jim Thome	.65
79	Dante Bichette	.15
80	Larry Walker	.15
81	Vinny Castilla	.15
82	Ellis Burks	.15
83	Bobby Higginson	.15
84	Brian L. Hunter	.15
85	Tony Clark	.15
86	Mike Hampton	.15
87	Jeff Bagwell	1.50
88	Craig Biggio	.15
89	Derek Bell	.15
90	Mike Piazza	3.00
91	Ramon Martinez	.15
92	Raul Mondesi	.15
93	Hideo Nomo	.75
94	Eric Karros	.15
95	Paul Molitor	1.50
96	Marty Cordova	.15
97	Brad Radke	.15
98	Mark Grudzielanek	.15
99	Carlos Perez	.15
100	Rondell White	.15
101	Todd Hundley	.15
102	Edgardo Alfonzo	.15
103	John Franco	.15
104	John Olerud	.15
105	Tino Martinez	.15
106	David Cone	.15
107	Paul O'Neill	.15
108	Andy Pettitte	.25
109	Bernie Williams	.15
110	Rickey Henderson	1.50
111	Jason Giambi	.75
112	Matt Stairs	.15
113	Gregg Jefferies	.15
114	Rico Brogna	.15
115	Curt Schilling	.35
116	Jason Schmidt	.15
117	Jose Guillen	.15
118	Kevin Young	.15
119	Ray Lankford	.15
120	Mark McGwire	3.00
121	Delino DeShields	.15
122	Ken Caminiti	.15
123	Tony Gwynn	2.00
124	Trevor Hoffman	.15
125	Barry Bonds	4.00
126	Jeff Kent	.15
127	Shawn Estes	.15
128	J.T. Snow	.15
129	Jay Buhner	.15
130	Ken Griffey Jr.	2.50
131	Dan Wilson	.15
132	Edgar Martinez	.15
133	Alex Rodriguez	3.00
134	Rusty Greer	.15
135	Juan Gonzalez	.75
136	Fernando Tatis	.15
137	Ivan Rodriguez	1.00
138	Carlos Delgado	.75
139	Pat Hentgen	.15
140	Roger Clemens	2.25
141	Chipper Jones	2.00
142	Greg Maddux	2.00
143	Rafael Palmeiro	1.25
144	Mike Mussina	.65
145	Cal Ripken Jr.	4.00
146	Nomar Garciaparra	2.00
147	Mo Vaughn	.35
148	Sammy Sosa	2.00
149	Albert Belle	.35
150	Frank Thomas	1.50
151	Jim Thome	1.25
152	Kenny Lofton	.35
153	Manny Ramirez	1.50
154	Larry Walker	.35
155	Jeff Bagwell	1.50
156	Craig Biggio	.35
157	Mike Piazza	2.50
158	Paul Molitor	1.50
159	Derek Jeter	4.00
160	Tino Martinez	.35
161	Curt Schilling	.50
162	Mark McGwire	3.00
163	Tony Gwynn	2.00
164	Barry Bonds	4.00
165	Ken Griffey Jr.	2.50
166	Randy Johnson	1.50
167	Alex Rodriguez	3.00
168	Juan Gonzalez	.75
169	Ivan Rodriguez	1.25
170	Roger Clemens	2.25
171	Greg Maddux	3.00
172	Cal Ripken Jr.	6.50
173	Frank Thomas	2.00
174	Jeff Bagwell	2.00
175	Mike Piazza	4.00
176	Mark McGwire	5.00
177	Barry Bonds	6.50
178	Ken Griffey Jr.	4.00
179	Alex Rodriguez	5.00
180	Roger Clemens	3.25
181	Mike Caruso	.50
182	David Ortiz	1.00
183	Gabe Alvarez	.50
184	Gary Matthews Jr.	.50
185	Kerry Wood	1.25
186	Carl Pavano	.50
187	Alex Gonzalez	.50
188	Masato Yoshii	.50
189	Larry Sutton	.50
190	Russell Branyan	.50
191	Bruce Chen	.50
192	Rolando Arrojo	.50
193	Ryan Christenson	.50
194	Cliff Politte	.50
195	A.J. Hinch	.50
196	Kevin Witt	.50
197	Daryle Ward	.50
198	Corey Koskie	.50
199	Mike Lowell	.50
200	Travis Lee	.50
201	*Kevin Millwood*	1.00
202	Robert Smith	.50
203	*Magglio Ordonez*	4.00
204	Eric Milton	.50
205	Geoff Jenkins	.50
206	Rich Butler	.50
207	*Mike Kinkade*	.75
208	Braden Looper	.50
209	Matt Clement	.50
210	Derrek Lee	1.50
211	Randy Johnson	1.50
212	John Smoltz	.50
213	Roger Clemens	2.25
214	Curt Schilling	.75
215	Pedro J. Martinez	1.50
216	Vinny Castilla	.50
217	Jose Cruz Jr.	.50
218	Jim Thome	1.20
219	Alex Rodriguez	3.00
220	Frank Thomas	1.50
221	Tim Salmon	.50
222	Larry Walker	.50
223	Albert Belle	.50
224	Manny Ramirez	1.50
225	Mark McGwire	3.00
226	Mo Vaughn	.50
227	Andres Galarraga	.50
228	Scott Rolen	1.25
229	Travis Lee	.50
230	Mike Piazza	2.50
231	Nomar Garciaparra	2.00
232	Andruw Jones	1.50
233	Barry Bonds	4.00
234	Jeff Bagwell	1.50
235	Juan Gonzalez	.75
236	Tino Martinez	.50
237	Vladimir Guerrero	1.50
238	Rafael Palmeiro	1.25
239	Russell Branyan	.50
240	Ken Griffey Jr.	2.50
241	Cecil Fielder	.15
242	Chuck Finley	.15
243	Jay Bell	.15
244	Andy Benes	.15
245	Matt Williams	.15
246	Brian Anderson	.15
247	David Dellucci	.15
248	Andres Galarraga	.15
249	Andruw Jones	1.50
250	Greg Maddux	2.00
251	Brady Anderson	.15
252	Joe Carter	.15
253	Eric Davis	.15
254	Pedro J. Martinez	1.50
255	Nomar Garciaparra	2.00
256	Dennis Eckersley	1.25
257	Henry Rodriguez	.15
258	Jeff Blauser	.15
259	Jaime Navarro	.15
260	Ray Durham	.15
261	Chris Stynes	.15
262	Willie Greene	.15
263	Reggie Sanders	.15
264	Bret Boone	.15
265	Barry Larkin	.15
266	Travis Fryman	.15
267	Charles Nagy	.15
268	Sandy Alomar Jr.	.15
269	Darryl Kile	.15
270	Mike Lansing	.15
271	Pedro Astacio	.15
272	Damion Easley	.15
273	Joe Randa	.15
274	Luis Gonzalez	.15
275	Mike Piazza	2.50
276	Todd Zeile	.15
277	Edgar Renteria	.15
278	Livan Hernandez	.15
279	Cliff Floyd	.15
280	Moises Alou	.15
281	Billy Wagner	.15
282	Jeff King	.15
283	Hal Morris	.15
284	Johnny Damon	.35
285	Dean Palmer	.15
286	Tim Belcher	.15
287	Eric Young	.15
288	Bobby Bonilla	.15
289	Gary Sheffield	.60
290	Chan Ho Park	.15
291	Charles Johnson	.15
292	Jeff Cirillo	.15
293	Jeromy Burnitz	.15
294	Jose Valentin	.15
295	Marquis Grissom	.15
296	Todd Walker	.15
297	Terry Steinbach	.15
298	Rick Aguilera	.15
299	Vladimir Guerrero	1.50
300	Rey Ordonez	.15
301	Butch Huskey	.15
302	Bernard Gilkey	.15
303	Mariano Rivera	.25
304	Chuck Knoblauch	.15
305	Derek Jeter	4.00
306	Ricky Bottalico	.15
307	Bob Abreu	.15
308	Scott Rolen	1.25
309	Al Martin	.15
310	Jason Kendall	.15
311	Brian Jordan	.15
312	Ron Gant	.15
313	Todd Stottlemyre	.15
314	Greg Vaughn	.15
315	J. Kevin Brown	.15
316	Wally Joyner	.15
317	Robb Nen	.15
318	Orel Hershiser	.15
319	Russ Davis	.15
320	Randy Johnson	1.50
321	Quinton McCracken	.15
322	Tony Saunders	.15
323	Wilson Alvarez	.15
324	Wade Boggs	2.00
325	Fred McGriff	.15
326	Lee Stevens	.15
327	John Wetteland	.15
328	Jose Canseco	.60
329	Randy Myers	.15
330	Jose Cruz Jr.	.15
331	Matt Williams	.50
332	Andres Galarraga	.50
333	Walt Weiss	.50
334	Joe Carter	.50
335	Pedro J. Martinez	2.00
336	Henry Rodriguez	.50
337	Travis Fryman	.50
338	Darryl Kile	.50
339	Mike Lansing	.50
340	Mike Piazza	4.00
341	Moises Alou	.50
342	Charles Johnson	.50
343	Chuck Knoblauch	.50
344	Rickey Henderson	2.00
345	J. Kevin Brown	.50
346	Orel Hershiser	.50
347	Wade Boggs	3.00
348	Fred McGriff	.50
349	Jose Canseco	1.00
350	Gary Sheffield	1.00
351	Travis Lee	2.50
352	Nomar Garciaparra	5.00
353	Frank Thomas	4.00
354	Cal Ripken Jr.	10.00
355	Mark McGwire	8.00
356	Mike Piazza	6.00
357	Alex Rodriguez	8.00
358	Barry Bonds	10.00
359	Tony Gwynn	5.00
360	Ken Griffey Jr.	6.00

1999 SP AUTHENTIC

		NM/M
Complete Set (135):		100.00
Common Player (1-90):		.10
Common Future Watch (91-120):		2.00
Production:		(2,700)
Common Season to Remember (121-135):		2.00
Production:		(2,700)
Pack (5):		3.50
Wax Box (24):		75.00
1	Mo Vaughn	.10
2	Jim Edmonds	.10
3	Darin Erstad	.25
4	Travis Lee	.10
5	Matt Williams	.10
6	Randy Johnson	1.50
7	Chipper Jones	1.75
8	Greg Maddux	1.75
9	Andruw Jones	1.50
10	Andres Galarraga	.10
11	Tom Glavine	.35
12	Cal Ripken Jr.	3.00
13	Brady Anderson	.10
14	Albert Belle	.10
15	Nomar Garciaparra	1.75
16	Donnie Sadler	.10
17	Pedro Martinez	1.50
18	Sammy Sosa	1.75
19	Kerry Wood	.60
20	Mark Grace	.10
21	Mike Caruso	.10
22	Frank Thomas	1.50
23	Paul Konerko	.20
24	Sean Casey	.20
25	Barry Larkin	.10
26	Kenny Lofton	.10
27	Manny Ramirez	1.50
28	Jim Thome	1.25
29	Bartolo Colon	.10
30	Jaret Wright	.10
31	Larry Walker	.10
32	Todd Helton	1.25
33	Tony Clark	.10
34	Dean Palmer	.10
35	Mark Kotsay	.10
36	Cliff Floyd	.10
37	Ken Caminiti	.10
38	Craig Biggio	.10
39	Jeff Bagwell	1.50
40	Moises Alou	.10
41	Johnny Damon	.35
42	Larry Sutton	.10
43	Kevin Brown	.10
44	Gary Sheffield	.40
45	Raul Mondesi	.10
46	Jeromy Burnitz	.10
47	Jeff Cirillo	.10
48	Todd Walker	.10

49	David Ortiz	.50
50	Brad Radtke	.10
51	Vladimir Guerrero	1.50
52	Rondell White	.10
53	Brad Fullmer	.10
54	Mike Piazza	2.00
55	Robin Ventura	.10
56	John Olerud	.10
57	Derek Jeter	3.00
58	Tino Martinez	.10
59	Bernie Williams	.10
60	Roger Clemens	1.75
61	Ben Grieve	.10
62	Miguel Tejada	.20
63	A.J. Hinch	.10
64	Scott Rolen	1.00
65	Curt Schilling	.35
66	Doug Glanville	.10
67	Aramis Ramirez	.10
68	Tony Womack	.10
69	Jason Kendall	.10
70	Tony Gwynn	1.75
71	Wally Joyner	.10
72	Greg Vaughn	.10
73	Barry Bonds	3.00
74	Ellis Burks	.10
75	Jeff Kent	.10
76	Ken Griffey Jr.	2.00
77	Alex Rodriguez	2.50
78	Edgar Martinez	.10
79	Mark McGwire	2.50
80	Eli Marrero	.10
81	Matt Morris	.10
82	Rolando Arrojo	.10
83	Quinton McCracken	.10
84	Jose Canseco	.50
85	Ivan Rodriguez	1.25
86	Juan Gonzalez	.75
87	Royce Clayton	.10
88	Shawn Green	.30
89	Jose Cruz Jr.	.10
90	Carlos Delgado	.60
91	Troy Glaus	6.00
92	George Lombard	2.00
93	Ryan Minor	2.00
94	Calvin Pickering	2.00
95	Jin Ho Cho	2.00
96	Russ Branyon	2.00
97	Derrick Gibson	2.00
98	Gabe Kapler	2.00
99	Matt Anderson	2.00
100	Preston Wilson	2.00
101	Alex Gonzalez	2.00
102	Carlos Beltran	6.00
103	Dee Brown	2.00
104	Jeremy Giambi	2.00
105	Angel Pena	2.00
106	Geoff Jenkins	2.00
107	Corey Koskie	2.00
108	A.J. Pierzynski	2.00
109	Michael Barrett	2.00
110	Fernando Seguignol	2.00
111	Mike Kinkade	2.00
112	Ricky Ledee	2.00
113	Mike Lowell	2.00
114	Eric Chavez	2.50
115	Matt Clement	2.00
116	Shane Monahan	2.00
117	J.D. Drew	4.00
118	Bubba Trammell	2.00
119	Kevin Witt	2.00
120	Roy Halladay	2.50
121	Mark McGwire	5.00
122	Mark McGwire, Sammy Sosa	4.00
123	Sammy Sosa	2.50
124	Ken Griffey Jr.	3.00
125	Cal Ripken Jr.	6.00
126	Juan Gonzalez	2.50
127	Kerry Wood	2.50
128	Trevor Hoffman	2.00
129	Barry Bonds	5.00
130	Alex Rodriguez	4.00
131	Ben Grieve	2.00
132	Tom Glavine	2.00
133	David Wells	2.00
134	Mike Piazza	3.00
135	Scott Brosius	2.00

Chirography

		NM/M
Common Player:		4.00
Inserted 1:24		
EC	Eric Chavez	8.00
GK	Gabe Kapler	4.00
GMj	Gary Matthews Jr.	4.00
CP	Calvin Pickering	4.00
CK	Corey Koskie	6.00
SM	Shane Monahan	4.00

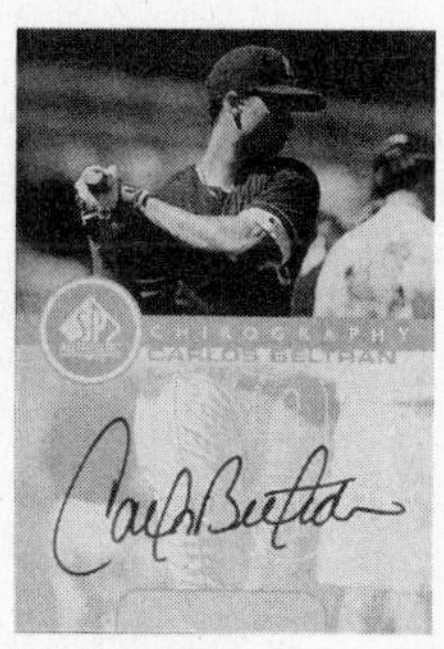

RH	Richard Hidalgo	4.00
MK	Mike Kinkade	4.00
CB	Carlos Beltran	35.00
AG	Alex Gonzalez	4.00
BC	Bruce Chen	4.00
MA	Matt Anderson	4.00
RM	Ryan Minor	4.00
RL	Ricky Ledee	4.00
RR	Ruben Rivera	4.00
BF	Brad Fullmer	4.00
RB	Russ Branyan	4.00
ML	Mike Lowell	6.00
JG	Jeremy Giambi	4.00
GL	George Lombard	4.00
KW	Kevin Witt	4.00
TW	Todd Walker	4.00
SR	Scott Rolen	20.00
KW	Kerry Wood	25.00
BG	Ben Grieve	4.00
JR	Ken Griffey Jr.	75.00
CJ	Chipper Jones	30.00
IR	Ivan Rodriguez	25.00
TGl	Troy Glaus	15.00
TL	Travis Lee	4.00
VG	Vladimir Guerrero	30.00
GV	Greg Vaughn	4.00
JT	Jim Thome	25.00
JD	J.D. Drew	15.00
TH	Todd Helton	15.00
GM	Greg Maddux	75.00
NG	Nomar Garciaparra	75.00
TG	Tony Gwynn	30.00
CR	Cal Ripken Jr.	125.00

Chirography Gold

		NM/M
Common Player:		5.00
Inserted 1:24		
EC	Eric Chavez (30)	40.00
GK	Gabe Kapler (51)	10.00
GMj	Gary Matthews Jr. (68)	5.00
CP	Calvin Pickering (6)	40.00
CK	Corey Koskie (47)	15.00
SM	Shane Monahan (12)	20.00
RH	Richard Hidalgo (15)	30.00
MK	Mike Kinkade (33)	10.00
CB	Carlos Beltran (36)	75.00
AG	Alex Gonzalez (22)	20.00
BC	Bruce Chen (48)	10.00
MA	Matt Anderson (14)	20.00
RM	Ryan Minor (10)	35.00
RL	Ricky Ledee (38)	10.00
RR	Ruben Rivera (28)	10.00
BF	Brad Fullmer (20)	10.00
RB	Russ Branyon (66)	10.00
ML	Mike Lowell (60)	15.00
JG	Jeremy Giambi (15)	20.00
GL	George Lombard (26)	10.00
KW	Kevin Witt (6)	20.00
TW	Todd Walker (12)	40.00
SR	Scott Rolen (17)	75.00
KW	Kerry Wood (34)	60.00
BG	Ben Grieve (14)	35.00
JR	Ken Griffey Jr. (24)	250.00
CJ	Chipper Jones (10)	200.00
IR	Ivan Rodriguez (7)	125.00
TGl	Troy Glaus (14)	90.00
TL	Travis Lee (16)	35.00
VG	Vladimir Guerrero (27)	75.00
GV	Greg Vaughn (23)	10.00
JT	Jim Thome (25)	40.00
JD	J.D. Drew (8)	125.00
TH	Todd Helton (17)	75.00
GM	Greg Maddux (31)	150.00
NG	Nomar Garciaparra (5)	375.00
TG	Tony Gwynn (19)	125.00
CR	Cal Ripken Jr. (8)	650.00

Epic Figures

		NM/M
Complete Set (30):		30.00
Common Player:		.50
Inserted 1:7		
E01	Mo Vaughn	.50
E02	Travis Lee	.50
E03	Andres Galarraga	.50
E04	Andruw Jones	1.00
E05	Chipper Jones	1.25
E06	Greg Maddux	1.25
E07	Cal Ripken Jr.	3.00
E08	Nomar Garciaparra	1.25
E09	Sammy Sosa	1.25
E10	Frank Thomas	1.00
E11	Kerry Wood	.60
E12	Kenny Lofton	.50
E13	Manny Ramirez	1.00
E14	Larry Walker	.50
E15	Jeff Bagwell	1.00
E16	Paul Molitor	1.00
E17	Vladimir Guerrero	1.00
E18	Derek Jeter	3.00
E19	Tino Martinez	.50
E20	Mike Piazza	1.50
E21	Ben Grieve	.50
E22	Scott Rolen	.75
E23	Mark McGwire	2.00
E24	Tony Gwynn	1.25
E25	Barry Bonds	3.00
E26	Ken Griffey Jr.	1.50
E27	Alex Rodriguez	2.00
E28	J.D. Drew	.65
E29	Juan Gonzalez	.60
E30	Kevin Brown	.50

Home Run Chronicles

		NM/M
Complete Set (70):		50.00
Common Player:		.15
Inserted 1:1		
Die-Cuts:		10X
Production 70 sets		
HR01	Mark McGwire	1.50
HR02	Sammy Sosa	1.25
HR03	Ken Griffey Jr.	1.00
HR04	Mark McGwire	1.50
HR05	Mark McGwire	1.50
HR06	Albert Belle	.15
HR07	Jose Canseco	.30
HR08	Juan Gonzalez	.45
HR09	Manny Ramirez	.65
HR10	Rafael Palmeiro	.50
HR11	Mo Vaughn	.15
HR12	Carlos Delgado	.45
HR13	Nomar Garciaparra	.75
HR14	Barry Bonds	1.50
HR15	Alex Rodriguez	1.25
HR16	Tony Clark	.15
HR17	Jim Thome	.50
HR18	Edgar Martinez	.15
HR19	Frank Thomas	.65
HR20	Greg Vaughn	.15
HR21	Vinny Castilla	.15
HR22	Andres Galarraga	.15
HR23	Moises Alou	.15
HR24	Jeromy Burnitz	.15
HR25	Vladimir Guerrero	.65
HR26	Jeff Bagwell	.65
HR27	Chipper Jones	.75
HR28	Javier Lopez	.15
HR29	Mike Piazza	1.00
HR30	Andruw Jones	.65
HR31	Henry Rodriguez	.15
HR32	Jeff Kent	.15
HR33	Ray Lankford	.15
HR34	Scott Rolen	.50
HR35	Raul Mondesi	.15
HR36	Ken Caminiti	.15
HR37	J.D. Drew	.40
HR38	Troy Glaus	.50
HR39	Gabe Kapler	.15
HR40	Alex Rodriguez	1.25
HR41	Ken Griffey Jr.	1.00
HR42	Sammy Sosa	1.25
HR43	Mark McGwire	1.50
HR44	Sammy Sosa	1.25
HR45	Mark McGwire	1.50
HR46	Vinny Castilla	.15
HR47	Sammy Sosa	1.25
HR48	Mark McGwire	1.50
HR49	Sammy Sosa	1.25
HR50	Greg Vaughn	.15
HR51	Sammy Sosa	1.25
HR52	Mark McGwire	1.50
HR53	Sammy Sosa	1.25
HR54	Mark McGwire	1.50
HR55	Sammy Sosa	1.25
HR56	Ken Griffey Jr.	1.00
HR57	Sammy Sosa	1.25
HR58	Mark McGwire	1.50
HR59	Sammy Sosa	1.25
HR60	Mark McGwire	1.50
HR61	Mark McGwire	2.50
HR62	Mark McGwire	2.50
HR63	Mark McGwire	1.50
HR64	Mark McGwire	1.50
HR65	Mark McGwire	1.50
HR66	Sammy Sosa	2.50
HR67	Mark McGwire	1.50
HR68	Mark McGwire	1.50
HR69	Mark McGwire	1.50
HR70	Mark McGwire	4.00

Reflections

		NM/M
Complete Set (30):		60.00
Common Player:		.75
Inserted 1:23		
R01	Mo Vaughn	.75
R02	Travis Lee	.75
R03	Andres Galarraga	.75
R04	Andruw Jones	2.50
R05	Chipper Jones	3.00
R06	Greg Maddux	3.00
R07	Cal Ripken Jr.	6.00
R08	Nomar Garciaparra	3.00
R09	Sammy Sosa	3.00
R10	Frank Thomas	2.50
R11	Kerry Wood	1.50
R12	Kenny Lofton	.75
R13	Manny Ramirez	2.50
R14	Larry Walker	.75
R15	Jeff Bagwell	2.50
R16	Paul Molitor	2.50
R17	Vladimir Guerrero	2.50
R18	Derek Jeter	6.00
R19	Tino Martinez	.75
R20	Mike Piazza	3.50
R21	Ben Grieve	.75
R22	Scott Rolen	2.00
R23	Mark McGwire	4.50
R24	Tony Gwynn	3.00
R25	Barry Bonds	6.00
R26	Ken Griffey Jr.	3.50
R27	Alex Rodriguez	4.50
R28	J.D. Drew	1.25
R29	Juan Gonzalez	1.25
R30	Roger Clemens	3.25

SP Authentics

		NM/M
Common Card:		10.00
(1)	K.Griffey Jr./ auto ball/75	60.00
(2)	Ken Griffey Jr./ glove/200	20.00
(3)	K. Griffey Jr./ HR Cel card/346	10.00
(4)	Ken Griffey Jr./ auto jsy/25	125.00
(5)	K. Griffey Jr/ auto mini helmet/75	80.00
(6)	Ken Griffey Jr/ SI Cover/200	15.00
(7)	K. Griffey Jr/ SI Cover Auto/75	75.00
(8)	Ken Griffey Jr/ Standee/300	10.00

(9)	Mark McGwire/ Auto 62 HR Ticket/1 (autographed 62HR ticket)(1)	
(10)	Mark McGwire/ Auto 70 HR Ticket/3	

500 Club Piece of History

		NM/M
EB	Ernie Banks	120.00
EB	Ernie Banks Auto./14	325.00

1999 SP SIGNATURE EDITION

		NM/M
Complete Set (180):		60.00
Common Player:		.15
Pack (3):		20.00
Wax Box (12):		250.00
1	Nomar Garciaparra	2.00
2	Ken Griffey Jr.	2.50
3	J.D. Drew	.50
4	Alex Rodriguez	3.00
5	Juan Gonzalez	.60
6	Mo Vaughn	.15
7	Greg Maddux	2.00
8	Chipper Jones	2.00
9	Frank Thomas	1.50
10	Vladimir Guerrero	1.50
11	Mike Piazza	2.50
12	Eric Chavez	.25
13	Tony Gwynn	2.00
14	Orlando Hernandez	.15
15	*Pat Burrell*	6.00
16	Darin Erstad	.30
17	Greg Vaughn	.15
18	Russ Branyan	.15
19	Gabe Kapler	.15
20	Craig Biggio	.15
21	Troy Glaus	1.25
22	Pedro J. Martinez	1.50
23	Carlos Beltran	.50
24	Derrek Lee	.50
25	Manny Ramirez	1.50
26	*Shea Hillenbrand*	1.00
27	Carlos Lee	.15
28	Angel Pena	.15
29	Rafael Roque	.15
30	Octavio Dotel	.15
31	Jeromy Burnitz	.15
32	Jeremy Giambi	.15
33	Andruw Jones	1.50
34	Todd Helton	1.25
35	Scott Rolen	1.25
36	Jason Kendall	.15
37	Trevor Hoffman	.15
38	Barry Bonds	4.00
39	Ivan Rodriguez	1.25
40	Roy Halladay	.15
41	Rickey Henderson	1.50
42	Ryan Minor	.15
43	Brian Jordan	.15
44	Alex Gonzalez	.15
45	Raul Mondesi	.15
46	Corey Koskie	.15
47	Paul O'Neill	.15
48	Todd Walker	.15
49	Carlos Febles	.15
50	Travis Fryman	.15
51	Albert Belle	.15
52	Travis Lee	.15
53	Bruce Chen	.15
54	Reggie Taylor	.15
55	Jerry Hairston Jr.	.15
56	Carlos Guillen	.15
57	Michael Barrett	.15
58	Jason Conti	.15
59	Joe Lawrence	.15
60	Jeff Cirillo	.15
61	Juan Melo	.15
62	Chad Hermansen	.15
63	Ruben Mateo	.15
64	Ben Davis	.15
65	Mike Caruso	.15
66	Jason Giambi	.50
67	Jose Canseco	.50
68	*Chad Hutchinson*	.15
69	Mitch Meluskey	.15
70	Adrian Beltre	.25
71	Mark Kotsay	.15
72	Juan Encarnacion	.15
73	Dermal Brown	.15
74	Kevin Witt	.15
75	Vinny Castilla	.15
76	Aramis Ramirez	.15
77	Marlon Anderson	.15
78	Mike Kinkade	.15
79	Kevin Barker	.15
80	Ron Belliard	.15
81	Chris Haas	.15
82	Bob Henley	.15
83	Fernando Seguignol	.15
84	Damon Minor	.15
85	*A.J. Burnett*	1.00
86	Calvin Pickering	.15
87	Mike Darr	.15
88	Cesar King	.15
89	Rob Bell	.15
90	Derrick Gibson	.15
91	*Ober Moreno*	.15
92	Robert Fick	.15
93	*Doug Mientkiewicz*	.75
94	A.J. Pierzynski	.15
95	Orlando Palmeiro	.15
96	Sidney Ponson	.15
97	*Ivanon Coffie*	.15
98	*Juan Pena*	1.00
99	Mark Karchner	.15
100	Carlos Castillo	.15
101	Bryan Ward	.15
102	Mario Valdez	.15
103	Billy Wagner	.15
104	Miguel Tejada	.25
105	Jose Cruz Jr.	.15
106	George Lombard	.15
107	Geoff Jenkins	.15
108	Ray Lankford	.15
109	Todd Stottlemyre	.15
110	Mike Lowell	.15
111	Matt Clement	.15
112	Scott Brosius	.15
113	Preston Wilson	.15
114	Bartolo Colon	.15
115	Rolando Arrojo	.15
116	Jose Guillen	.15
117	Ron Gant	.15
118	Ricky Ledee	.15
119	Carlos Delgado	.50
120	Abraham Nunez	.15
121	John Olerud	.15
122	Chan Ho Park	.15
123	Brad Radke	.15
124	Al Leiter	.15
125	Gary Matthews Jr.	.15
126	F.P. Santangelo	.15
127	Brad Fullmer	.15
128	Matt Anderson	.15
129	A.J. Hinch	.15
130	Sterling Hitchcock	.15
131	Edgar Martinez	.15
132	Fernando Tatis	.15
133	Bobby Smith	.15
134	Paul Konerko	.25
135	Sean Casey	.25
136	Donnie Sadler	.15
137	Denny Neagle	.15
138	Sandy Alomar	.15
139	Mariano Rivera	.25
140	Emil Brown	.15
141	J.T. Snow	.15
142	Eli Marrero	.15
143	Rusty Greer	.15
144	Johnny Damon	.35
145	Damion Easley	.15
146	Eric Milton	.15
147	Rico Brogna	.15
148	Ray Durham	.15
149	Wally Joyner	.15
150	Royce Clayton	.15
151	David Ortiz	.50
152	Wade Boggs	2.00
153	Ugueth Urbina	.15
154	Richard Hidalgo	.15
155	Bobby Abreu	.15
156	Robb Nen	.15
157	David Segui	.15
158	Sean Berry	.15
159	Kevin Tapani	.15
160	Jason Varitek	.15
161	Fernando Vina	.15
162	Jim Leyritz	.15
163	Enrique Wilson	.15
164	Jim Parque	.15
165	Doug Glanville	.15
166	Jesus Sanchez	.15
167	Nolan Ryan	4.00
168	Robin Yount	.50
169	Stan Musial	1.00
170	Tom Seaver	.50
171	Mike Schmidt	1.00
172	Willie Stargell	.50
173	Rollie Fingers	.45
174	Willie McCovey	.50
175	Harmon Killebrew	.50
176	Eddie Mathews	.50
177	Reggie Jackson	1.00
178	Frank Robinson	.50
179	Ken Griffey Sr.	.15
180	Eddie Murray	1.50

Autographs

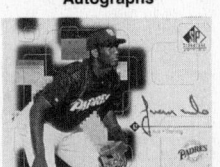

		NM/M
Common Player:		3.00
Inserted 1:1		
BA	Bobby Abreu	10.00
SA	Sandy Alomar	5.00
MA	Marlon Anderson	4.00
KB	Kevin Barker	3.00
MB	Michael Barrett	4.00
RoB	Rob Bell	3.00
AB	Albert Belle	15.00
RBe	Ron Belliard	3.00
CBe	Carlos Beltran	50.00
ABe	Adrian Beltre	25.00
BB	Barry Bonds	200.00
RB	Russ Branyan	3.00
SB	Scott Brosius/SP	30.00
DB	Dermal Brown	3.00
EB	Emil Brown	3.00
AJB	A.J. Burnett (exchange card)	3.00
AJB	A.J. Burnett (autographed)	15.00
PB	Pat Burrell	12.50
JoC	Jose Canseco	30.00
MC	Mike Caruso	3.00
SC	Sean Casey (exchange card)	3.00
SC	Sean Casey (autographed)	15.00
VC	Vinny Castilla (exchange card)	3.00
VC	Vinny Castilla (autographed)	8.00
CC	Carlos Castillo	3.00
EC	Eric Chavez	10.00
BC	Bruce Chen	3.00
JCi	Jeff Cirillo	3.00
RC	Royce Clayton	3.00
MCl	Matt Clement	6.00
IC	Ivanon Coffie	3.00
BCo	Bartolo Colon (exchange card)	3.00
BCo	Bartolo Colon (autographed)	8.00
JC	Jason Conti	3.00
JDa	Johnny Damon	25.00
BD	Ben Davis	3.00
CD	Carlos Delgado	15.00
OD	Octavio Dotel	3.00
JD	J.D. Drew	15.00
RD	Ray Durham	3.00
DEa	Damion Easley	3.00
JE	Juan Encarnacion	3.00
DE	Darin Erstad	8.00
CF	Carlos Febles	3.00
Rob	Robert Fick	3.00
Rol	Rollie Fingers	8.00
BF	Brad Fullmer	3.00
RGa	Ron Gant	8.00
NG	Nomar Garciaparra	75.00
JaG	Jason Giambi	20.00
DG	Derrick Gibson	3.00
DGl	Doug Glanville	3.00
TGl	Troy Glaus	15.00
AG	Alex Gonzalez	5.00
RGr	Rusty Greer	3.00
Jr.	Ken Griffey Jr.	80.00
1	Ken Griffey Jr. (facsimile autographed "SAMPLE")	15.00
Sr.	Ken Griffey Sr.	8.00
VG	Vladimir Guerrero	30.00
JG	Jose Guillen	8.00
TG	Tony Gwynn	35.00
CHa	Chris Haas	3.00
JHj	Jerry Hairston Jr.	4.00
RH	Roy Halladay	10.00
THe	Todd Helton	20.00
BH	Bob Henley	3.00
ED	Orlando Hernandez	40.00
CH	Chad Hermansen	3.00
ShH	Shea Hillenbrand	8.00
StH	Sterling Hitchcock	3.00
THo	Trevor Hoffman	5.00
CHu	Chad Hutchinson	3.00
RJ	Reggie Jackson/SP	40.00
GJ	Geoff Jenkins	5.00
AJ	Andruw Jones	20.00
CJ	Chipper Jones	40.00
WJ	Wally Joyner	8.00
GK	Gabe Kapler	3.00
MKa	Mark Karchner	3.00
JK	Jason Kendall	6.00
HK	Harmon Killebrew	40.00
CKi	Cesar King	3.00
MKi	Mike Kinkade	3.00
PK	Paul Konerko	10.00
CK	Corey Koskie	6.00
MK	Mark Kotsay	4.00
RL	Ray Lankford	5.00
JLa	Joe Lawrence	3.00
CL	Carlos Lee	10.00
DL	Derrek Lee	25.00
AL	Al Leiter	6.00
JLe	Jim Leyritz	6.00
GL	George Lombard	3.00
GM	Greg Maddux	80.00
Eli	Eli Marrero	3.00
EM	Edgar Martinez	20.00
PM	Pedro J. Martinez (exchange card)	5.00
PM	Pedro J. Martinez (autographed)	100.00
RMa	Ruben Mateo (exchange card)	3.00
RMa	Ruben Mateo (autographed)	8.00
EMa	Eddie Mathews	60.00
GMj	Gary Matthews Jr.	3.00
WMc	Willie McCovey	35.00
JM	Juan Melo	3.00
MMe	Mitch Meluskey	3.00
DoM	Doug Mientkiewicz	6.00
EMi	Eric Milton	3.00
DaM	Damon Minor	3.00
RM	Ryan Minor	3.00
EMu	Eddie Murray	20.00
SM	Stan Musial	50.00
RN	Robb Nen	3.00
AN	Abraham Nunez	3.00
JO	John Olerud	10.00
PO	Paul O'Neill	17.50
DO	David Ortiz	35.00
OP	Orlando Palmeiro	3.00
JP	Jim Parque	3.00
AP	Angel Pena	3.00
MP	Mike Piazza (exchange card)	6.00
MP	Mike Piazza (autographed)	175.00
CP	Calvin Pickering	3.00
AJP	A.J. Pierzynski	5.00
SP	Sidney Ponson	8.00
BR	Brad Radke	4.00
ARa	Aramis Ramirez	10.00
MR	Manny Ramirez	50.00
MRi	Mariano Rivera	25.00
FR	Frank Robinson	25.00
AR	Alex Rodriguez	120.00
PG	Ivan Rodriguez	25.00
SR	Scott Rolen (exchange card)	3.00
SR	Scott Rolen (autographed)	25.00
RR	Rafael Roque	3.00
NR	Nolan Ryan	120.00
DS	Donnie Sadler	3.00
JS	Jesus Sanchez	3.00
MS	Mike Schmidt	60.00
TSe	Tom Seaver	35.00
DSe	David Segui	3.00
FS	Fernando Seguignol	3.00
BS	Bobby Smith	3.00
JT	J.T. Snow (exchange card)	3.00

JT J.T. Snow (autographed) 6.00
POP Willie Stargell (exchange card) 3.00
POP Willie Stargell (autographed) 40.00
TSt Todd Stottlemyre 3.00
FTa Fernando Tatis 3.00
RT Reggie Taylor 3.00
MT Miguel Tejada 20.00
FT Frank Thomas 50.00
MV Mario Valdez 3.00
JV Jason Varitek 30.00
GV Greg Vaughn 3.00
MO Mo Vaughn 8.00
FV Fernando Vina 3.00
BWa Billy Wagner 10.00
TW Todd Walker 3.00
BW Bryan Ward 3.00
EW Enrique Wilson 3.00
KW Kevin Witt 3.00
RY Robin Yount 40.00

Autographs Gold

NM/M
Common Player: 12.00
Production 50 sets
MA Marlon Anderson 12.00
KB Kevin Barker 12.00
MB Michael Barrett 12.00
RoB Rob Bell 12.00
AB Albert Belle 20.00
RBe Ron Belliard 12.00
CBe Carlos Beltran 75.00
ABe Adrian Beltre 40.00
CB Craig Biggio (unsigned) 3.00
BB Barry Bonds 300.00
RB Russ Branyan 12.00
DB Dermal Brown 12.00
AJB A.J. Burnett (exchange card) 4.00
AJB A.J. Burnett (autographed edition of 20) 40.00
JB Jeromy Burnitz (unsigned) 3.00
PB Pat Burrell 40.00
JoC Jose Canseco 50.00
MC Mike Caruso 12.00
VC Vinny Castilla (exchange card) 3.00
VC Vinny Castilla (autographed) 20.00
CC Carlos Castillo 12.00
EC Eric Chavez 20.00
BC Bruce Chen 12.00
JCi Jeff Cirillo 12.00
JC Jason Conti 12.00
MD Mike Darr (unsigned) 3.00
BD Ben Davis 12.00
OD Octavio Dotel 12.00
JD J.D. Drew 30.00
JE Juan Encarnacion 12.00
DE Darin Erstad 20.00
CF Carlos Febles 12.00
TF Travis Fryman (unsigned) 3.00
BF Brad Fullmer 12.00
NG Nomar Garciaparra 100.00
JaG Jason Giambi 40.00
JeG Jeremy Giambi (unsigned) 3.00
DG Derrick Gibson 12.00
DGl Doug Glanville 12.00
TGl Troy Glaus 30.00
AG Alex Gonzalez 12.00
JG Juan Gonzalez (unsigned) 6.00
Jr. Ken Griffey Jr. 150.00
Sr. Ken Griffey Sr. 12.00
VG Vladimir Guerrero 75.00
JG Jose Guillen (unsigned) 3.00
TG Tony Gwynn 60.00
CHa Chris Haas 12.00
JHj Jerry Hairston Jr. 12.00
RH Roy Halladay 25.00
THe Todd Helton 30.00
RH Rickey Henderson (unsigned) 6.00
BH Bob Henley 12.00
ED Orlando Hernandez 25.00
CH Chad Hermansen 12.00
ShH Shea Hillenbrand 20.00
StH Sterling Hitchcock 12.00
THo Trevor Hoffman 30.00
CHu Chad Hutchinson 12.00
GJ Geoff Jenkins 12.00
AJ Andruw Jones 40.00
CJ Chipper Jones 80.00
BJ Brian Jordan (unsigned) 3.00
WJ Wally Joyner 25.00
GK Gabe Kapler 12.00
MKa Mark Karchner 12.00
JK Jason Kendall 20.00
CKi Cesar King 12.00
MKi Mike Kinkade 12.00
PK Paul Konerko 15.00
CK Corey Koskie 20.00
MK Mark Kotsay 12.00
RL Ray Lankford 12.00
JLa Joe Lawrence 12.00
CL Carlos Lee 25.00
DL Derrek Lee 50.00
TL Travis Lee (unsigned) 4.00
AL Al Leiter 12.00
JLe Jim Leyritz 12.00
GL George Lombard 12.00
GM Greg Maddux 150.00
PM Pedro Martinez (exchange card) 6.00
PM Pedro Martinez (autographed) 200.00
RMa Ruben Mateo (exchange card) 3.00
RMa Ruben Mateo (autographed) 15.00
GMj Gary Matthews Jr. 12.00
JM Juan Melo 12.00
MMe Mitch Meluskey 12.00
DoM Doug Mientkiewicz 12.00
EMi Eric Milton 12.00
DaM Damon Minor 12.00
RM Ryan Minor 12.00
PO Paul O'Neill 30.00
DO David Ortiz 75.00
OP Orlando Palmeiro 12.00
AP Angel Pena 12.00
MP Mike Piazza (exchange card) 10.00
MP Mike Piazza (autographed) 250.00
CP Calvin Pickering 12.00
ARa Aramis Ramirez 30.00
MR Manny Ramirez 80.00
AR Alex Rodriguez 185.00
PG Ivan Rodriguez 45.00
SR Scott Rolen (exchange card) 4.00
SR Scott Rolen (autographed) 75.00
RR Rafael Roque 12.00
DSe David Segui 12.00
FS Fernando Seguignol 12.00
BS Bobby Smith 12.00
RT Reggie Taylor 12.00
FT Frank Thomas 70.00
MV Mario Valdez 12.00
GV Greg Vaughn 12.00
MO Mo Vaughn 20.00
TW Todd Walker 12.00
KW Kevin Witt 12.00

Legendary Cuts

No Pricing
Production one set

500 Club Piece of History

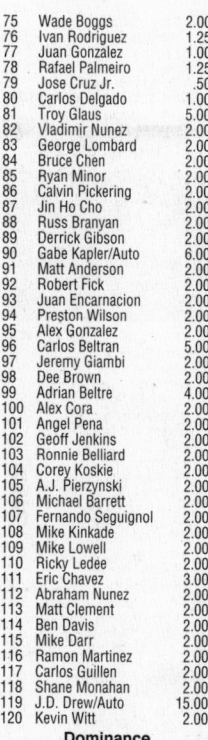

NM/M
MO Mel Ott (350) 100.00

1999 SPX

NM/M
Complete Set (120): 100.00
Common Player: .50
Common SPx Rookie (81-120): 2.00
Production 1,999 sets
Radiance (1-80): 7X

Radiance SP (81-120): 1.5X
Spectrum (1-of-1): VALUE UNDETERMINED
Pack (3): 3.00
Wax Box (18): 40.00
1 Mark McGwire #61 2.50
2 Mark McGwire #62 1.00
3 Mark McGwire #63 1.00
4 Mark McGwire #64 1.00
5 Mark McGwire #65 1.00
6 Mark McGwire #66 1.00
7 Mark McGwire #67 1.00
8 Mark McGwire #68 1.00
9 Mark McGwire #69 1.00
10 Mark McGwire #70 2.50
11 Mo Vaughn .50
12 Darin Erstad .75
13 Travis Lee .50
14 Randy Johnson 1.50
15 Matt Williams .50
16 Chipper Jones 2.00
17 Greg Maddux 2.00
18 Andruw Jones 1.50
19 Andres Galarraga .50
20 Cal Ripken Jr. 4.00
21 Albert Belle .50
22 Mike Mussina .75
23 Nomar Garciaparra 2.00
24 Pedro Martinez 1.50
25 John Valentin .50
26 Kerry Wood 1.00
27 Sammy Sosa 2.00
28 Mark Grace .50
29 Frank Thomas 1.50
30 Mike Caruso .50
31 Barry Larkin .50
32 Sean Casey .50
33 Jim Thome 1.25
34 Kenny Lofton .50
35 Manny Ramirez 1.50
36 Larry Walker .50
37 Todd Helton 1.25
38 Vinny Castilla .50
39 Tony Clark .50
40 Derrek Lee 1.00
41 Mark Kotsay .50
42 Jeff Bagwell 1.50
43 Craig Biggio .50
44 Moises Alou .50
45 Larry Sutton .50
46 Johnny Damon 1.00
47 Gary Sheffield 1.00
48 Raul Mondesi .50
49 Jeromy Burnitz .50
50 Todd Walker .50
51 David Ortiz 1.00
52 Vladimir Guerrero 1.50
53 Rondell White .50
54 Mike Piazza 2.50
55 Derek Jeter 4.00
56 Tino Martinez .50
57 David Wells .50
58 Ben Grieve .50
59 A.J. Hinch .50
60 Scott Rolen 1.25
61 Doug Glanville .50
62 Aramis Ramirez .50
63 Jose Guillen .50
64 Tony Gwynn 2.00
65 Greg Vaughn .50
66 Ruben Rivera .50
67 Barry Bonds 4.00
68 J.T. Snow .50
69 Alex Rodriguez 3.00
70 Ken Griffey Jr. 2.50
71 Jay Buhner .50
72 Mark McGwire 3.00
73 Fernando Tatis .50
74 Quinton McCracken .50
75 Wade Boggs 2.00
76 Ivan Rodriguez 1.25
77 Juan Gonzalez 1.00
78 Rafael Palmeiro 1.25
79 Jose Cruz Jr. .50
80 Carlos Delgado 1.00
81 Troy Glaus 5.00
82 Vladimir Nunez 2.00
83 George Lombard 2.00
84 Bruce Chen 2.00
85 Ryan Minor 2.00
86 Calvin Pickering 2.00
87 Jin Ho Cho 2.00
88 Russ Branyan 2.00
89 Derrick Gibson 2.00
90 Gabe Kapler/Auto 6.00
91 Matt Anderson 2.00
92 Robert Fick 2.00
93 Juan Encarnacion 2.00
94 Preston Wilson 2.00
95 Alex Gonzalez 2.00
96 Carlos Beltran 5.00
97 Jeremy Giambi 2.00
98 Dee Brown 2.00
99 Adrian Beltre 4.00
100 Alex Cora 2.00
101 Angel Pena 2.00
102 Geoff Jenkins 2.00
103 Ronnie Belliard 2.00
104 Corey Koskie 2.00
105 A.J. Pierzynski 2.00
106 Michael Barrett 2.00
107 Fernando Seguignol 2.00
108 Mike Kinkade 2.00
109 Mike Lowell 2.00
110 Ricky Ledee 2.00
111 Eric Chavez 3.00
112 Abraham Nunez 2.00
113 Matt Clement 2.00
114 Ben Davis 2.00
115 Mike Darr 2.00
116 Ramon Martinez 2.00
117 Carlos Guillen 2.00
118 Shane Monahan 2.00
119 J.D. Drew/Auto 15.00
120 Kevin Witt 2.00

Dominance

NM/M
Complete Set (20): 35.00
Common Player: 1.00
Inserted 1:17
1 Chipper Jones 2.00
2 Greg Maddux 2.00
3 Cal Ripken Jr. 4.00
4 Nomar Garciaparra 2.00
5 Mo Vaughn 1.00
6 Sammy Sosa 2.00
7 Albert Belle 1.00
8 Frank Thomas 1.50
9 Jim Thome 1.25
10 Jeff Bagwell 1.50
11 Vladimir Guerrero 1.50
12 Mike Piazza 2.50
13 Derek Jeter 4.00
14 Tony Gwynn 2.00
15 Barry Bonds 4.00
16 Ken Griffey Jr. 2.50
17 Alex Rodriguez 3.00
18 Mark McGwire 3.00
19 J.D. Drew 1.25
20 Juan Gonzalez 1.25

Power Explosion

NM/M
Complete Set (30): 15.00
Common Player: .20
Inserted 1:3
1 Troy Glaus .65
2 Mo Vaughn .20
3 Travis Lee .20
4 Chipper Jones 1.00
5 Andres Galarraga .20
6 Brady Anderson .20
7 Albert Belle .20
8 Nomar Garciaparra 1.00
9 Sammy Sosa 1.00
10 Frank Thomas .75
11 Jim Thome .65
12 Manny Ramirez .75
13 Larry Walker .20
14 Tony Clark .20
15 Jeff Bagwell .75
16 Moises Alou .20
17 Ken Caminiti .20
18 Vladimir Guerrero .75
19 Mike Piazza 1.25
20 Tino Martinez .20
21 Ben Grieve .20
22 Scott Rolen .60

23	Greg Vaughn	.20
24	Barry Bonds	2.00
25	Ken Griffey Jr.	1.25
26	Alex Rodriguez	1.50
27	Mark McGwire	1.50
28	J.D. Drew	.35
29	Juan Gonzalez	.45
30	Ivan Rodriguez	.60

Premier Stars

		NM/M
Complete Set (30):		45.00
Common Player:		1.00
Inserted 1:17		
1	Mark McGwire	3.00
2	Sammy Sosa	2.00
3	Frank Thomas	1.50
4	J.D. Drew	1.25
5	Kerry Wood	1.25
6	Moises Alou	1.00
7	Kenny Lofton	1.00
8	Jeff Bagwell	1.50
9	Tony Clark	1.00
10	Roberto Alomar	1.00
11	Cal Ripken Jr.	4.00
12	Derek Jeter	4.00
13	Mike Piazza	2.50
14	Jose Cruz Jr.	1.00
15	Chipper Jones	2.00
16	Nomar Garciaparra	2.00
17	Greg Maddux	2.00
18	Scott Rolen	1.25
19	Vladimir Guerrero	1.50
20	Albert Belle	1.00
21	Ken Griffey Jr.	2.50
22	Alex Rodriguez	3.00
23	Ben Grieve	1.00
24	Juan Gonzalez	1.25
25	Barry Bonds	4.00
26	Larry Walker	1.00
27	Tony Gwynn	2.00
28	Randy Johnson	1.50
29	Travis Lee	1.00
30	Mo Vaughn	1.00

Star Focus

		NM/M
Complete Set (30):		50.00
Common Player:		.75
Inserted 1:8		
1	Chipper Jones	2.25
2	Greg Maddux	2.25
3	Cal Ripken Jr.	4.50
4	Nomar Garciaparra	2.25
5	Mo Vaughn	.75
6	Sammy Sosa	2.25
7	Albert Belle	.75
8	Frank Thomas	1.50
9	Jim Thome	1.25
10	Kenny Lofton	.75
11	Manny Ramirez	1.50
12	Larry Walker	.75
13	Jeff Bagwell	1.50
14	Craig Biggio	.75
15	Randy Johnson	1.50
16	Vladimir Guerrero	1.50
17	Mike Piazza	3.00
18	Derek Jeter	4.50
19	Tino Martinez	.75
20	Bernie Williams	.75
21	Curt Schilling	1.00
22	Tony Gwynn	2.25
23	Barry Bonds	4.50
24	Ken Griffey Jr.	3.00
25	Alex Rodriguez	4.00
26	Mark McGwire	4.00
27	J.D. Drew	1.00
28	Juan Gonzalez	1.00
29	Ivan Rodriguez	1.25
30	Ben Grieve	.75

Winning Materials

		NM/M
Complete Set (8):		90.00
Common Player:		5.00
Inserted 1:251		
VC	Vinny Castilla	5.00
JD	J.D. Drew	7.50
JR	Ken Griffey Jr.	20.00
VG	Vladimir Guerrero	12.00
TG	Tony Gwynn	15.00
TH	Todd Helton	10.00
TL	Travis Lee	5.00
IR	Ivan Rodriguez	10.00

500 Club Piece of History

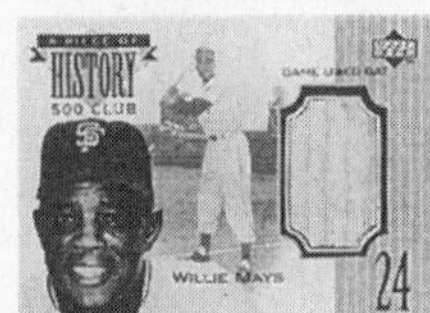

		NM/M
WM	Willie Mays (350)	275.00
WM	Willie Mays Auto./24	450.00

2000 SP AUTHENTIC

		NM/M
Complete Set (135):		150.00
Common Player:		.15
Common (91-105):		2.00
Production 2,500 sets		
Common (106-135):		2.00
Production 2,500 sets		
Pack (5):		3.00
Box (24):		60.00
1	Mo Vaughn	.15
2	Troy Glaus	1.00
3	Jason Giambi	.75
4	Tim Hudson	.30
5	Eric Chavez	.25
6	Shannon Stewart	.15
7	Raul Mondesi	.15
8	Carlos Delgado	.75
9	Jose Canseco	.45
10	Vinny Castilla	.15
11	Greg Vaughn	.15
12	Manny Ramirez	1.00
13	Roberto Alomar	.45
14	Jim Thome	.85
15	Richie Sexson	.10
16	Alex Rodriguez	2.50
17	Fred Garcia	.15
18	John Olerud	.15
19	Albert Belle	.25
20	Cal Ripken Jr.	3.00
21	Mike Mussina	.35
22	Ivan Rodriguez	.85
23	Gabe Kapler	.15
24	Rafael Palmeiro	.85
25	Nomar Garciaparra	2.00
26	Pedro Martinez	1.00
27	Carl Everett	.15
28	Carlos Beltran	.50
29	Jermaine Dye	.15
30	Juan Gonzalez	1.00
31	Dean Palmer	.15
32	Corey Koskie	.15
33	Jacque Jones	.15
34	Frank Thomas	1.00
35	Paul Konerko	.15
36	Magglio Ordonez	.15
37	Bernie Williams	.25
38	Derek Jeter	3.00
39	Roger Clemens	2.00
40	Mariano Rivera	.25
41	Jeff Bagwell	1.00
42	Craig Biggio	.15
43	Jose Lima	.15
44	Moises Alou	.15
45	Chipper Jones	1.50
46	Greg Maddux	1.50
47	Andruw Jones	1.00
48	Kevin Millwood	.15
49	Jeromy Burnitz	.15
50	Geoff Jenkins	.15
51	Mark McGwire	2.50
52	Fernando Tatis	.15
53	J.D. Drew	.25
54	Sammy Sosa	2.00
55	Kerry Wood	.85
56	Mark Grace	.25
57	Matt Williams	.15
58	Randy Johnson	1.00
59	Erubiel Durazo	.15
60	Gary Sheffield	.45
61	Kevin Brown	.15
62	Shawn Green	.60
63	Vladimir Guerrero	1.00
64	Michael Barrett	.15
65	Barry Bonds	3.00
66	Jeff Kent	.15
67	Russ Ortiz	.15
68	Preston Wilson	.15
69	Mike Lowell	.15
70	Mike Piazza	2.00
71	Mike Hampton	.15
72	Robin Ventura	.15
73	Edgardo Alfonzo	.15
74	Tony Gwynn	1.50
75	Ryan Klesko	.15
76	Trevor Hoffman	.15
77	Scott Rolen	.85
78	Bob Abreu	.15
79	Mike Lieberthal	.15
80	Curt Schilling	.50
81	Jason Kendall	.15
82	Brian Giles	.15
83	Kris Benson	.15
84	Ken Griffey Jr.	2.00
85	Sean Casey	.25
86	Pokey Reese	.15
87	Barry Larkin	.15
88	Larry Walker	.15
89	Todd Helton	1.00
90	Jeff Cirillo	.15
91	Ken Griffey Jr.	4.00
92	Mark McGwire	5.00
93	Chipper Jones	3.00
94	Derek Jeter	5.00
95	Shawn Green	2.00
96	Pedro Martinez	2.50
97	Mike Piazza	4.00
98	Alex Rodriguez	5.00
99	Jeff Bagwell	2.50
100	Cal Ripken Jr.	5.00
101	Sammy Sosa	3.00
102	Barry Bonds	5.00
103	Jose Canseco	2.00
104	Nomar Garciaparra	4.00
105	Ivan Rodriguez	2.50
106	Rick Ankiel	2.50
107	Pat Burrell	6.00
108	Vernon Wells	2.50
109	Nick Johnson	2.50
110	Kip Wells	2.50
111	Matt Riley	2.50
112	Alfonso Soriano	8.00
113	Josh Beckett	4.00
114	*Danys Baez*	6.00
115	Travis Dawkins	2.50
116	Eric Gagne	3.00
117	*Mike Lamb*	2.50
118	Eric Munson	2.50
119	*Wilfredo Rodriguez*	2.50
120	*Kazuhiro Sasaki*	4.00
121	Chad Hutchinson	2.50
122	Peter Bergeron	2.50
123	*Wascar Serrano*	2.50
124	Tony Armas Jr.	2.50
125	Ramon Ortiz	2.50
126	Adam Kennedy	2.50
127	Joe Crede	2.50
128	Roosevelt Brown	2.50
129	Mark Mulder	2.50
130	Brad Penny	2.50
131	Terrence Long	2.50
132	Ruben Mateo	2.50
133	Wily Mo Pena	2.50
134	Rafael Furcal	2.50
135	Mario Encarnacion	2.50

Limited

Cards (1-90):	4-8X
Cards (91-105):	2-3X
Cards (106-135):	1-2X
Production 100 sets	

Chirography

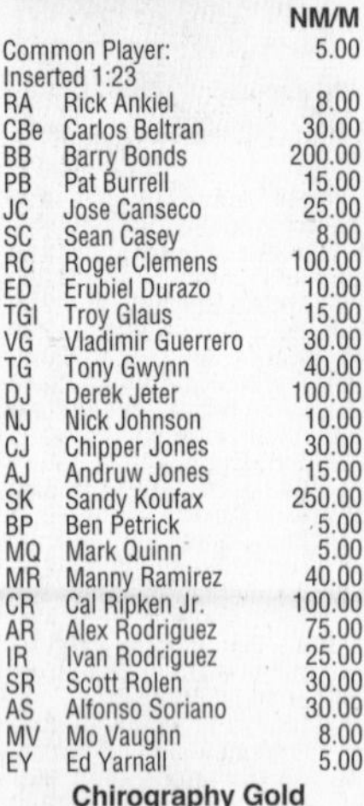

		NM/M
Common Player:		5.00
Inserted 1:23		
RA	Rick Ankiel	8.00
CBe	Carlos Beltran	30.00
BB	Barry Bonds	200.00
PB	Pat Burrell	15.00
JC	Jose Canseco	25.00
SC	Sean Casey	8.00
RC	Roger Clemens	100.00
ED	Erubiel Durazo	10.00
TGl	Troy Glaus	15.00
VG	Vladimir Guerrero	30.00
TG	Tony Gwynn	40.00
DJ	Derek Jeter	100.00
NJ	Nick Johnson	10.00
CJ	Chipper Jones	30.00
AJ	Andruw Jones	15.00
SK	Sandy Koufax	250.00
BP	Ben Petrick	5.00
MQ	Mark Quinn	5.00
MR	Manny Ramirez	40.00
CR	Cal Ripken Jr.	100.00
AR	Alex Rodriguez	75.00
IR	Ivan Rodriguez	25.00
SR	Scott Rolen	30.00
AS	Alfonso Soriano	30.00
MV	Mo Vaughn	8.00
EY	Ed Yarnall	5.00

Chirography Gold

		NM/M
Common Player:		
RA	Rick Ankiel/66 EXCH	50.00
JB	Jeff Bagwell/5 EXCH	
JOB	John Bale/49	
CBe	Carlos Beltran/15	65.00
BB	Barry Bonds/25	300.00
PB	Pat Burrell/33 EXCH	50.00
JC	Jose Canseco/33	75.00
SC	Sean Casey/21	65.00
EC	Eric Chavez/3	
RC	Roger Clemens/22	300.00
JD	J.D. Drew	
ED	Erubiel Durazo/44	25.00
RF	Rafael Furcal/1	
JG	Jason Giambi/16	
TGl	Troy Glaus/14	
VG	Vladimir Guerrero/27	100.00
WG	Wilton Guerrero/4	
TG	Tony Gwynn/19	200.00
DJ	Derek Jeter/2	
NJ	Nick Johnson/63	15.00
AJ	Andruw Jones/25 EXCH	
CJ	Chipper Jones/10 EXCH	
JK	Josh Kalinowski/62	
SK	Sandy Koufax/32	
JL	Jose Lima/42 EXCH	
KL	Kenny Lofton/7	
JMA	Joe Mays/53	
JMO	Jim Morris/63	

EM Eric Munson/17
RP Robert Person/31
BP Ben Petrick/15 40.00
MQ Mark Quinn/14
MR Manny Ramirez/24 EXCH 100.00
MRI Matt Riley/25
CR Cal Ripken Jr./8
AR Alex Rodriguez/3 EXCH
IR Ivan Rodriguez/7
SR Scott Rolen/17 EXCH
AS Alfonso Soriano/53 60.00
MV Mo Vaughn/42 25.00
VW Vernon Wells/3
EY Ed Yarnall/41 15.00

Midsummer Classics

NM/M
Complete Set (10): 10.00
Common Player: .50
Inserted 1:12
1 Cal Ripken Jr. 3.00
2 Roger Clemens 1.75
3 Jeff Bagwell .75
4 Barry Bonds 3.00
5 Jose Canseco .50
6 Frank Thomas .75
7 Mike Piazza 2.00
8 Tony Gwynn 1.50
9 Juan Gonzalez .75
10 Greg Maddux 1.50

Joe DiMaggio Game Jersey

NM/M
DiMaggio Jersey card
JD Joe DiMaggio jersey/500 120.00
JD Joe DiMaggio jersey gold/56 200.00
JD Joe DiMaggio jersey/auto/5

Premier Performers

NM/M
Complete Set (10): 10.00
Common Player: .75
Inserted 1:12
1 Mark McGwire 2.50
2 Alex Rodriguez 2.50
3 Cal Ripken Jr. 3.00
4 Nomar Garciaparra 2.00
5 Ken Griffey Jr. 2.00
6 Chipper Jones 1.50
7 Derek Jeter 3.00
8 Ivan Rodriguez .75
9 Vladimir Guerrero .75
10 Sammy Sosa 2.00

SP Buyback

NM/M
Common Player:
1 Jeff Bagwell Exch. 50.00
2 Craig Biggio '93/59 50.00
3 Craig Biggio '94/69 50.00
4 Craig Biggio '95/171 90.00
5 Craig Biggio '96/71 50.00
6 Craig Biggio '97/46 70.00
7 Craig Biggio '98/40 75.00
8 Craig Biggio '99/125 40.00
15 Barry Bonds '99/520 150.00
16 Jose Canseco '93/29 125.00
17 Jose Canseco '94/20 125.00
19 Jose Canseco '96/23 125.00
20 Jose Canseco '97/23 125.00
21 Jose Canseco '98/24 125.00
22 Jose Canseco '99/502 40.00
24 Sean Casey '99/139 25.00
25 Roger Clemens '93/68 60.00
26 Roger Clemens '94/60 60.00
27 Roger Clemens '95/68 60.00
28 Roger Clemens '96/68 60.00
30 Roger Clemens '98/25 300.00
31 Roger Clemens '99/134 60.00
32 Jason Giambi '97/34 60.00
33 Jason Giambi '98/25 90.00
34 Tom Glavine '93/99 50.00
35 Tom Glavine '94/107 40.00
36 Tom Glavine '95/97 50.00
37 Tom Glavine '96/42 75.00
38 Tom Glavine '98/40 75.00
39 Tom Glavine '99/138 40.00
40 Shawn Green '96/55 60.00
41 Shawn Green '99/530 25.00
42 Ken Griffey Jr. '96/12 275.00
47 Tony Gwynn '97/24 250.00
49 Tony Gwynn '99/129 80.00
50 Tony Gwynn '99/369 60.00
56 Derek Jeter '99/119 200.00
57 Randy Johnson '93/60 100.00
58 Randy Johnson '94/45 120.00
59 Randy Johnson '95/70 100.00
60 Randy Johnson '96/60 100.00
63 Randy Johnson '99/113 75.00
64 Andruw Jones Exch. 60.00
65 Chipper Jones Exch. 100.00
66 Kenny Lofton '94/100 25.00
67 Kenny Lofton '95/84 25.00
68 Kenny Lofton '96/34 40.00
69 Kenny Lofton '97/82 25.00
70 Kenny Lofton '98/21 60.00
71 Kenny Lofton '99/99 20.00
72 Javy Lopez '93/106 15.00
73 Javy Lopez '94/160 20.00
74 Javy Lopez '96/99 15.00
75 Javy Lopez '97/61 20.00
77 Greg Maddux '93/22 275.00
78 Greg Maddux '94/19 275.00
83 Greg Maddux '99/504 75.00
84 Paul O'Neill '93/110 25.00
85 Paul O'Neill '94/97 30.00
86 Paul O'Neill '95/142 25.00
87 Paul O'Neill '96/70 30.00
88 Paul O'Neill '98/23 75.00
89 Mario Ramirez Exch. 50.00
91 Cal Ripken Jr. '94/22 400.00
96 Cal Ripken Jr. '99/510 125.00
97 Alex Rodriguez Exch. 200.00
98 Ivan Rodriguez '93/29 100.00
100 Ivan Rodriguez '95/18 125.00
101 Ivan Rodriguez '96/22 125.00
103 Ivan Rodriguez '98/27 125.00
109 Frank Thomas '97/20 250.00
111 Frank Thomas '99/100 120.00
112 Greg Vaughn '93/79 20.00
113 Greg Vaughn '94/75 20.00
114 Greg Vaughn '95/155 15.00
115 Greg Vaughn '96/113 15.00
117 Greg Vaughn '99/527 10.00
118 Mo Vaughn '93/119 25.00
119 Mo Vaughn '94/96 30.00
120 Mo Vaughn '95/121 25.00
121 Mo Vaughn '96/114 25.00
122 Mo Vaughn '97/61 35.00
124 Mo Vaughn '99/537 15.00
125 Robin Ventura '93/59 25.00
126 Robin Ventura '94/49 30.00
127 Robin Ventura '95/125 20.00
128 Robin Ventura '96/55 25.00
129 Robin Ventura '97/44 40.00
130 Robin Ventura '98/28 50.00
131 Robin Ventura '99/370 15.00
133 Matt Williams '94/50 40.00
134 Matt Williams '95/137 40.00
135 Matt Williams '96/77 40.00
136 Matt Williams '97/54 40.00
137 Matt Williams '98/29 70.00
138 Matt Williams '99/529 15.00
139 Preston Wilson '94/249 15.00
140 Preston Wilson '99/195 15.00

SP Supremacy

NM/M
Complete Set (7): 8.00
Common Player: .75
Inserted 1:23
1 Alex Rodriguez 3.00
2 Shawn Green .75
3 Pedro Martinez 1.00
4 Chipper Jones 2.00
5 Tony Gwynn 2.00
6 Ivan Rodriguez 1.00
7 Jeff Bagwell 1.00

SP Cornerstones

NM/M
Complete Set (7): 15.00
Common Player: 2.00
Inserted 1:23
1 Ken Griffey Jr. 2.00
2 Cal Ripken Jr. 4.00
3 Mike Piazza 2.00
4 Derek Jeter 4.00
5 Mark McGwire 3.00
6 Nomar Garciaparra 2.00
7 Sammy Sosa 2.00

United Nations

NM/M
Complete Set (10): 5.00
Common Player: .50
Inserted 1:4
1 Sammy Sosa (Dominican Rep.) 1.50
2 Ken Griffey Jr. (USA) 2.00
3 Orlando Hernandez (Cuba) .50
4 Andres Galarraga (Venezuela) .50
5 Kazuhiro Sasaki (Japan) .50
6 Larry Walker (Canada) .50
7 Vinny Castilla (Mexico) .50
8 Andruw Jones (Neth. Antilles) .75
9 Ivan Rodriguez (Puerto Rico) .75
10 Chan Ho Park (So. Korea) .50

3,000 Hit Club

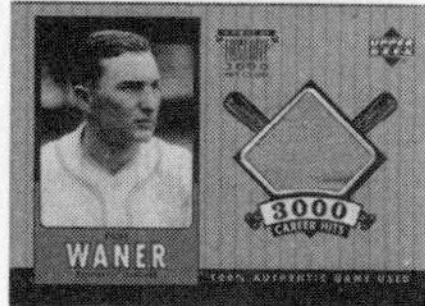

NM/M
PW Paul Waner bat/350 55.00
TS Tris Speaker bat/350 100.00
PW Paul Waner bat/auto/5
TS Tris Speaker bat/auto/5

2000 SPX

NM/M
Complete Set (120): 400.00

Common Player: .15
Common Rookie (91-120): 10.00
Pack (4): 6.00
Box (18): 80.00
1 Troy Glaus 1.00
2 Mo Vaughn .15
3 Ramon Ortiz .15
4 Jeff Bagwell 1.00
5 Moises Alou .25
6 Craig Biggio .40
7 Jose Lima .15
8 Jason Giambi .75
9 John Jaha .15
10 Matt Stairs .15
11 Chipper Jones 1.50
12 Greg Maddux 1.50
13 Andres Galarraga .15
14 Andruw Jones 1.00
15 Jeromy Burnitz .15
16 Ron Belliard .15
17 Carlos Delgado .75
18 David Wells .15
19 Tony Batista .15
20 Shannon Stewart .15
21 Sammy Sosa 2.00
22 Mark Grace .85
23 Henry Rodriguez .15
24 Mark McGwire 2.50
25 J.D. Drew .25
26 Luis Gonzalez .25
27 Randy Johnson 1.00
28 Matt Williams .15
29 Steve Finley .15
30 Shawn Green .50
31 Kevin Brown .15
32 Gary Sheffield .50
33 Jose Canseco .50
34 Greg Vaughn .15
35 Vladimir Guerrero 1.00
36 Michael Barrett .15
37 Russ Ortiz .15
38 Barry Bonds 3.00
39 Jeff Kent .15
40 Richie Sexson .40
41 Manny Ramirez 1.00
42 Jim Thome 1.00
43 Roberto Alomar .50
44 Edgar Martinez .15
45 Alex Rodriguez 2.50
46 John Olerud .15
47 Alex Gonzalez .15
48 Cliff Floyd .15
49 Mike Piazza 2.00
50 Al Leiter .15
51 Robin Ventura .15
52 Edgardo Alfonzo .15
53 Albert Belle .20
54 Cal Ripken Jr. 3.00
55 B.J. Surhoff .15
56 Tony Gwynn 1.50
57 Trevor Hoffman .15
58 Brian Giles .15
59 Jason Kendall .15
60 Kris Benson .15
61 Bob Abreu .40
62 Scott Rolen 1.00
63 Curt Schilling .75
64 Mike Lieberthal .15
65 Sean Casey .25
66 Dante Bichette .15
67 Ken Griffey Jr. 2.00
68 Pokey Reese .15
69 Mike Sweeney .15
70 Carlos Febles .15
71 Ivan Rodriguez 1.00
72 Ruben Mateo .15
73 Rafael Palmeiro 1.00
74 Larry Walker .40
75 Todd Helton 1.00

76 Nomar Garciaparra 2.00
77 Pedro Martinez 1.00
78 Troy O'Leary .15
79 Jacque Jones .15
80 Corey Koskie .15
81 Juan Gonzalez 1.00
82 Dean Palmer .15
83 Juan Encarnacion .15
84 Frank Thomas 1.00
85 Magglio Ordonez .25
86 Paul Konerko .25
87 Bernie Williams .50
88 Derek Jeter 3.00
89 Roger Clemens 2.50
90 Orlando Hernandez .15
91 Vernon Wells AU-1,000 25.00
92 Rick Ankiel AU-1,000 15.00
93 Eric Chavez AU-1,000 20.00
94 Alfonso Soriano AU-1,000 50.00
95 Eric Gagne AU-1,000 50.00
96 Rob Bell AU-1,500 10.00
97 Matt Riley AU-1,500 10.00
98 Josh Beckett AU-1,500 50.00
99 Ben Petrick AU-1,500 10.00
100 *Rob Ramsay AU-1,500* 10.00
101 Scott Williamson AU-1,500 10.00
102 Doug Davis AU-1,500 10.00
103 Eric Munson AU-1,500 12.00
104 Pat Burrell AU-500 40.00
105 Jim Morris AU-1,500 20.00
106 Gabe Kapler AU-500 15.00
107 Lance Berkman 1,500 20.00
108 Erubiel Durazo AU-1,500 15.00
109 Tim Hudson AU-1,500 50.00
110 Ben Davis AU-1,500 10.00
111 Nick Johnson AU-1,500 20.00
112 Octavio Dotel AU-1,500 10.00
113 Jerry Hairston Jr. 1,500 10.00
114 Ruben Mateo 1,500 10.00
115 Chris Singleton 1,500 10.00
116 Bruce Chen AU-1,500 10.00
117 Derrick Gibson AU-1,500 10.00
118 Carlos Beltran AU-500 140.00
119 Fred Garcia AU-500 10.00
120 Preston Wilson AU-500 15.00

Radiance

NM/M
Stars (1-90): 4-8X
Common Young Star (91-120): 10.00
Production 100 sets

Foundations

NM/M
Complete Set (10): 15.00
Common Player: .50
Inserted 1:32
1 Ken Griffey Jr. 3.00
2 Nomar Garciaparra 3.00
3 Cal Ripken Jr. 4.00
4 Chipper Jones 2.00
5 Mike Piazza 3.00
6 Derek Jeter 4.00
7 Manny Ramirez 1.00
8 Jeff Bagwell 1.00
9 Tony Gwynn 2.00
10 Larry Walker .50

Heart of the Order

NM/M
Complete Set (20): 10.00
Common Player: .40
Inserted 1:8
1 Bernie Williams .50
2 Mike Piazza 2.00
3 Ivan Rodriguez .75
4 Mark McGwire 2.50
5 Manny Ramirez 1.00
6 Ken Griffey Jr. 2.00
7 Matt Williams .40
8 Sammy Sosa 2.00
9 Mo Vaughn .40
10 Carlos Delgado .75
11 Brian Giles .40
12 Chipper Jones 1.50
13 Sean Casey .40
14 Tony Gwynn 1.50
15 Barry Bonds 3.00
16 Carlos Beltran .65
17 Scott Rolen .75
18 Juan Gonzalez 1.00
19 Larry Walker .40
20 Vladimir Guerrero 1.00

Highlight Heroes

NM/M
Complete Set (10): 10.00
Common Player: .50
Inserted 1:16
1 Pedro Martinez 1.00
2 Ivan Rodriguez .75
3 Carlos Beltran .65
4 Nomar Garciaparra 2.00
5 Ken Griffey Jr. 2.00
6 Randy Johnson 1.00
7 Chipper Jones 1.50
8 Scott Williamson .50
9 Larry Walker .50
10 Mark McGwire 2.50

Power Brokers

NM/M
Complete Set (20): 10.00
Common Player: .25
Inserted 1:8
1 Rafael Palmeiro .75
2 Carlos Delgado .65
3 Ken Griffey Jr. 2.00
4 Matt Stairs .25
5 Mike Piazza 2.00
6 Vladimir Guerrero 1.00
7 Chipper Jones 1.50
8 Mark McGwire 2.50
9 Matt Williams .25
10 Juan Gonzalez 1.00
11 Shawn Green .50
12 Sammy Sosa 2.00
13 Brian Giles .25
14 Jeff Bagwell 1.00
15 Alex Rodriguez 2.50
16 Frank Thomas 1.00
17 Larry Walker .25
18 Albert Belle .25
19 Dean Palmer .25
20 Mo Vaughn .25

SPxcitement

NM/M
Complete Set (20): 15.00
Common Player: .25
Inserted 1:4
1 Nomar Garciaparra 1.25
2 Mark McGwire 1.50
3 Derek Jeter 2.00
4 Cal Ripken Jr. 2.00
5 Barry Bonds 2.00
6 Alex Rodriguez 1.50
7 Scott Rolen .75
8 Pedro Martinez .75
9 Sean Casey .25
10 Sammy Sosa 1.25
11 Randy Johnson .75
12 Ivan Rodriguez .75
13 Frank Thomas .75
14 Greg Maddux 1.00
15 Tony Gwynn 1.00
16 Ken Griffey Jr. 1.25
17 Carlos Beltran .50
18 Mike Piazza 1.25
19 Chipper Jones 1.00
20 Craig Biggio .25

SPx Signatures

NM/M
Common Player: 10.00
Inserted 1:179
JB Jeff Bagwell 30.00
BB Barry Bonds 200.00
JC Jose Canseco 25.00
SC Sean Casey 10.00
RC Roger Clemens 125.00
KG Ken Griffey Jr. 85.00
VG Vladimir Guerrero 35.00
TG Tony Gwynn 40.00
OH Orlando Hernandez 40.00
DJ Derek Jeter 100.00
CJ Chipper Jones 40.00
MR Manny Ramirez 40.00
CR Cal Ripken Jr. 125.00
IR Ivan Rodriguez 30.00
SR Scott Rolen 30.00

Untouchable Talents

NM/M
Complete Set (10): 30.00
Common Player: 1.50
Inserted 1:96
1 Mark McGwire 8.00
2 Ken Griffey Jr. 6.00
3 Shawn Green 2.00
4 Ivan Rodriguez 2.50
5 Sammy Sosa 6.00
6 Derek Jeter 10.00
7 Sean Casey 1.50
8 Chipper Jones 4.50
9 Pedro Martinez 3.00
10 Vladimir Guerrero 3.00

3,000 Hit Club

NM/M
TC-B Ty Cobb bat/350 130.00
TC-C Ty Cobb cut sig./3
TC-BC Ty Cobb bat/cut/1

Winning Materials

NM/M
Common Bat/Jsy 6.00
AR Alex Rodriguez bat/jersey 25.00
AR Alex Rodriguez cap/jersey/100 40.00
AR Alex Rodriguez ball/jersey/50 50.00
DJ Derek Jeter bat/jersey 40.00
DJ Derek Jeter ball/jersey/50 75.00
DJ Derek Jeter bat/jersey/auto/2
BB Barry Bonds bat/jersey 30.00
BB Barry Bonds cap/jersey/100 45.00
BB Barry Bonds ball/jersey/auto/25 350.00
JB Jeff Bagwell bat/jersey 8.00
JB Jeff Bagwell cap/jersey/100 15.00
JB Jeff Bagwell ball/jersey/50 25.00
KG Ken Griffey Jr. bat/jersey 20.00
KG Ken Griffey Jr. ball/jersey/50 50.00
KG Ken Griffey Jr. jersey/bat/auto/24 225.00
TG Tony Gwynn bat/jersey 10.00
TG Tony Gwynn ball/jersey/50 40.00
TG Tony Gwynn Cap/Jersey/100 30.00
BW Bernie Williams bat/jersey 8.00
EC Eric Chavez bat/jersey 8.00
EC Eric Chavez cap/jersey/100 15.00
GM Greg Maddux bat/jersey 25.00
IR Ivan Rodriguez bat/jersey 8.00
JC Jose Canseco bat/jersey 8.00
JL Javy Lopez bat/jersey 6.00
JL Javy Lopez cap/jersey/100 8.00
MM Mark McGwire base/ball/500 50.00
MR Manny Ramirez bat/jersey 10.00
MR Manny Ramirez bat/jersey/auto./24
MW Matt Williams bat/jersey 6.00
PM Pedro Martinez cap/jersey/100 25.00
PO Paul O'Neill bat/jersey 6.00
VG Vladimir Guerrero bat/jersey 10.00
VG Vladimir Guerrero cap/jersey/100 20.00
VG Vladimir Guerrero ball/jersey/50 30.00
TG Troy Glaus bat/jersey 8.00

2001 SP AUTHENTIC

Jeff Bagwell

NM/M
Common Player: .25
Common SP (91-135): 3.00
Production 1,250
Common SP (136-180): 2.00
Production 1,250
Pack (5): 15.00
Box (24): 300.00
1 Troy Glaus .75
2 Darin Erstad .50
3 Jason Giambi .75
4 Tim Hudson .50

5 Eric Chavez .40
6 Miguel Tejada .40
7 Jose Ortiz .25
8 Carlos Delgado .75
9 Tony Batista .25
10 Raul Mondesi .25
11 Aubrey Huff .25
12 Greg Vaughn .25
13 Roberto Alomar .50
14 Juan Gonzalez 1.00
15 Jim Thome .85
16 Omar Vizquel .25
17 Edgar Martinez .25
18 Fred Garcia .25
19 Cal Ripken Jr. 3.00
20 Ivan Rodriguez .85
21 Rafael Palmeiro .85
22 Alex Rodriguez 2.50
23 Manny Ramirez 1.00
24 Pedro Martinez 1.00
25 Nomar Garciaparra 2.00
26 Mike Sweeney .25
27 Jermaine Dye .25
28 Bobby Higginson .25
29 Dean Palmer .25
30 Matt Lawton .25
31 Eric Milton .25
32 Frank Thomas 1.00
33 Magglio Ordonez .25
34 David Wells .25
35 Paul Konerko .40
36 Derek Jeter 3.00
37 Bernie Williams .50
38 Roger Clemens 2.00
39 Mike Mussina .50
40 Jorge Posada .25
41 Jeff Bagwell 1.00
42 Richard Hidalgo .25
43 Craig Biggio .25
44 Greg Maddux 1.50
45 Chipper Jones 1.50
46 Andruw Jones 1.00
47 Rafael Furcal .25
48 Tom Glavine .50
49 Jeromy Burnitz .25
50 Jeffrey Hammonds .25
51 Mark McGwire 2.00
52 Jim Edmonds .25
53 Rick Ankiel .25
54 J.D. Drew .40
55 Sammy Sosa 2.00
56 Corey Patterson .25
57 Kerry Wood .85
58 Randy Johnson 1.00
59 Luis Gonzalez .35
60 Curt Schilling .50
61 Gary Sheffield .50
62 Shawn Green .50
63 Kevin Brown .25
64 Vladimir Guerrero 1.00
65 Jose Vidro .25
66 Barry Bonds 3.00
67 Jeff Kent .25
68 Livan Hernandez .25
69 Preston Wilson .25
70 Charles Johnson .25
71 Ryan Dempster .25
72 Mike Piazza 2.00
73 Al Leiter .25
74 Edgardo Alfonzo .25
75 Robin Ventura .25
76 Tony Gwynn 1.50
77 Phil Nevin .25
78 Trevor Hoffman .25
79 Scott Rolen .85
80 Pat Burrell .50
81 Bob Abreu .25
82 Jason Kendall .25
83 Brian Giles .25
84 Kris Benson .25
85 Ken Griffey Jr. 2.00
86 Barry Larkin .25
87 Sean Casey .40
88 Todd Helton 1.00
89 Mike Hampton .25
90 Larry Walker .25
91 *Ichiro Suzuki* 200.00
92 *Wilson Betemit* 3.00
93 *Adrian Hernandez* 3.00
94 *Juan Uribe* 6.00
95 *Travis Hafner* 40.00
96 *Morgan Ensberg* 40.00
97 *Sean Douglass* 3.00
98 *Juan Diaz* 3.00
99 *Erick Almonte* 3.00
100 *Ryan Freel* 6.00
101 *Elpidio Guzman* 3.00
102 *Christian Parker* 3.00
103 *Josh Fogg* 6.00
104 *Bert Snow* 3.00
105 *Horacio Ramirez* 8.00
106 *Ricardo Rodriguez* 3.00
107 *Tyler Walker* 3.00
108 *Jose Mieses* 5.00
109 *Billy Sylvester* 3.00
110 *Martin Vargas* 3.00
111 *Andres Torres* 3.00
112 *Greg Miller* 3.00
113 *Alexis Gomez* 3.00
114 *Grant Balfour* 3.00
115 *Henry Mateo* 3.00
116 *Esix Snead* 3.00
117 *Jackson Melian* 3.00
118 *Nate Teut* 3.00
119 *Tsuyoshi Shinjo* 8.00
120 *Carlos Valderrama* 6.00
121 *Johnny Estrada* 15.00
122 *Jason Michaels* 3.00
123 *William Ortega* 3.00
124 *Jason Smith* 3.00
125 *Brian Lawrence* 3.00
126 *Albert Pujols* 375.00
127 *Wilken Ruan* 3.00
128 *Josh Towers* 8.00
129 *Kris Keller* 3.00
130 *Nick Maness* 3.00
131 *Jack Wilson* 10.00
132 *Brandon Duckworth* 8.00
133 *Mike Penney* 3.00
134 *Jay Gibbons* 10.00
135 *Cesar Crespo* 3.00
136 Ken Griffey Jr. 8.00
137 Mark McGwire 10.00
138 Derek Jeter 12.00
139 Alex Rodriguez 10.00
140 Sammy Sosa 8.00
141 Carlos Delgado 3.00
142 Cal Ripken Jr. 12.00
143 Pedro Martinez 5.00
144 Frank Thomas 5.00
145 Juan Gonzalez 5.00
146 Troy Glaus 5.00
147 Jason Giambi 3.00
148 Ivan Rodriguez 4.00
149 Chipper Jones 6.00
150 Vladimir Guerrero 5.00
151 Mike Piazza 8.00
152 Jeff Bagwell 5.00
153 Randy Johnson 5.00
154 Todd Helton 5.00
155 Gary Sheffield 3.00
156 Tony Gwynn 5.00
157 Barry Bonds 12.00
158 Nomar Garciaparra 8.00
159 Bernie Williams 2.00
160 Greg Vaughn 2.00
161 David Wells 2.00
162 Roberto Alomar 3.00
163 Jermaine Dye 2.00
164 Rafael Palmeiro 4.00
165 Andruw Jones 5.00
166 Preston Wilson 2.00
167 Edgardo Alfonzo 2.00
168 Pat Burrell 3.00
169 Jim Edmonds 2.00
170 Mike Hampton 2.00
171 Jeff Kent 2.00
172 Kevin Brown 2.00
173 Manny Ramirez 5.00
174 Magglio Ordonez 2.00
175 Roger Clemens 7.00
176 Jim Thome 4.00
177 Barry Zito 2.00
178 Brian Giles 2.00
179 Rick Ankiel 2.00
180 Corey Patterson 2.00

Limited

Stars (1-90): 8-15X
SP (91-135): 1-2X
SP (136-180): 1-3X
Production 50 sets

Buyback Autographs

NM/M

Inserted 1:144
Some not priced due to scarcity
4 Ken Griffey '93 SP/34 125.00
105 Ken Griffey '94 SP/182 80.00
190 Ken Griffey ' 95 SP/116 80.00
170 Ken Griffey '96 SP/53 100.00
84 Ken Griffey '00 SP/333 60.00
188 Alex Rodriguez '95 SP Red/117 80.00
171 Alex Rodriguez '96 SP/72 100.00

16 Alex Rodriguez '00 SP/332 60.00
260 Frank Thomas '93 SP/79 40.00
193 Frank Thomas '94 SP/165 35.00
50 Frank Thomas '97 SP/34 75.00
34 Frank Thomas '00 SP/302 25.00
34 Chipper Jones '95 SP/118 40.00
26 Chipper Jones '96 SP/72 45.00
45 Chipper Jones '00 SP/303 25.00
132 Randy Johnson '93 SP/97 60.00
106 Randy Johnson '94 SP/146 40.00
189 Randy Johnson '95 SP/121 40.00
169 Randy Johnson '96 SP/78 50.00
58 Randy Johnson '00 SP/213 40.00
41 Carlos Delgado '94 SP/279 15.00
181 Carlos Delgado '96 SP/83 20.00
8 Carlos Delgado '00 SP/174 15.00
50 Jim Edmonds '96 SP/74 20.00
167 Tony Gwynn '93 SP/101 40.00
130 Tony Gwynn '94 SP/88 40.00
105 Tony Gwynn '95 SP/179 30.00
160 Tony Gwynn '96 SP/92 40.00
74 Tony Gwynn '00 SP/95 40.00
3 Jason Giambi '00 SP/290 25.00
9 Ivan Rodriguez '93 SP/89 40.00
180 Ivan Rodriguez '96 SP/64 40.00
22 Ivan Rodriguez '00 SP/163 30.00
47 Andruw Jones '00 SP/336 20.00
10 Barry Bonds '93 SP/75 200.00
90 Barry Bonds '94 SP/103 200.00
166 Barry Bonds '96 SP/49 200.00
65 Barry Bonds '00 SP/146 200.00
18 Gary Sheffield '93 SP/83 20.00
114 Gary Sheffield '94 SP/70 20.00
86 Gary Sheffield '96 SP/69 20.00
60 Gary Sheffield '00 SP/133 15.00
89 Sammy Sosa '93 SP/73 150.00
126 Cal Ripken '94 SP/99 100.00
1 Cal Ripken '95 SP/37 150.00
20 Cal Ripken '00 SP/266 80.00
89 Todd Helton '00 SP/194 25.00
4 Tim Hudson '00 SP/291 15.00
62 Shawn Green '00 SP/340 15.00
52 Fernando Tatis '00 SP/267 8.00
57 Matt Williams '00 SP/340 10.00
72 Robin Ventura '00 SP/340 10.00
2 Troy Glaus '00 SP/340 15.00
39 Roger Clemens '00 SP/145 75.00

Chirography

NM/M

Common Player: 5.00
Inserted 1:72
EA Edgardo Alfonzo 5.00
AB Albert Belle 15.00
CB Carlos Beltran 35.00
MB Milton Bradley 12.00
PB Pat Burrell 10.00
JC Jose Canseco 30.00
CD Carlos Delgado 10.00
DD Darren Dreifort/206 5.00
JD J.D. Drew 15.00
JE Jim Edmonds 20.00
DEr Darin Erstad 10.00
DEs David Espinosa 5.00
CF Cliff Floyd 10.00
RF Rafael Furcal/222 8.00
JG Jason Giambi 15.00
TrG Troy Glaus 15.00
LG Luis Gonzalez/271 15.00
SG Shawn Green/82 25.00
KG Ken Griffey Jr/126 80.00
ToG Tony Gwynn/76 40.00
RH Rick Helling/211 5.00
ToH Todd Helton/152 30.00
TiH Tim Hudson 15.00
RJ Randy Johnson/143 50.00
AJ Andruw Jones 15.00
CJ Chipper Jones/184 40.00
DJ David Justice 8.00
MK Mark Kotsay/228 5.00
TL Travis Lee/226 5.00
AP Albert Pujols 400.00
CR Cal Ripken/109 125.00
AR Alex Rodriguez/229 90.00
DS Dane Sardinha 5.00
BS Ben Sheets 20.00
SS Sammy Sosa/76 150.00
MS Mike Sweeney 8.00
MV Mo Vaughn/103 8.00
RV Robin Ventura/92 10.00
DW David Wells 8.00
RW Rondell White 8.00
MW Matt Williams 8.00

Chirography Gold

NM/M

Common Player:
G-AB Albert Belle/88 15.00
G-CD Carlos Delgado/25 75.00
G-DD Darren Dreifort/37 25.00
G-DES David Espinosa/79 15.00
G-KG Ken Griffey Jr./30 200.00
G-RH Rick Helling/32 15.00
G-RJ Randy Johnson/51 80.00
G-DJ David Justice/28 30.00
G-DS Dane Sardinha/50 15.00
G-MS Mike Sweeney/29 30.00
G-MV Mo Vaughn/42 15.00
G-DW David Wells/33 20.00

Game Jersey

NM/M

Common Player: 5.00
Overall jersey odds 1:24
UD-JD Joe DiMaggio/243 100.00
UD-KG Ken Griffey Jr. 10.00

UD-MM Mickey Mantle/243 150.00
UD-AR Alex Rodriguez 10.00
UD-GS Gary Sheffield 5.00
UD-SS Sammy Sosa 15.00

Combo Game Jersey

NM/M

Overall jersey odds 1:24
SD Sammy Sosa, Andre Dawson 30.00
RS Alex Rodriguez, Ozzie Smith 35.00
GD Ken Griffey Jr., Joe DiMaggio/98 120.00
SW Gary Sheffield, Dave Winfield 10.00
MD Mickey Mantle, Joe DiMaggio/98 400.00
MG Mickey Mantle, Ken Griffey /98 200.00

Cooperstown Calling Game Jersey

NM/M

Common Player: 5.00
Overall jersey odds 1:24
JB Jeff Bagwell 8.00
WB Wade Boggs 8.00
GC Gary Carter 5.00
RC Roger Clemens 30.00
AD Andre Dawson 5.00
SG Steve Garvey 5.00
GG Goose Gossage 5.00
TG Tony Gwynn 10.00
RM Roger Maris/243 75.00
PM Pedro Martinez/SP 15.00
DM Don Mattingly 30.00
BM Bill Mazeroski 5.00
PM Paul Molitor 8.00
EM Eddie Murray 5.00
MP Mike Piazza/SP 25.00
KP Kirby Puckett 10.00
MR Manny Ramirez/SP 10.00
CR Cal Ripken Jr. 30.00
RS Ryne Sandberg 20.00
OS Ozzie Smith 10.00
DW Dave Winfield 5.00

Stars of Japan

NM/M

Complete Set (30): 50.00
Common Player: 1.00
One pack/hobby box
RS1 Ichiro Suzuki, Tsuyoshi Shinjo 5.00
RS2 Shigetosi Hasegawa, Hideki Irabu 1.00
RS3 Tomokazu Ohka, Mac Suzuki 1.00
RS4 Tsuyoshi Shinjo, Hideki Irabu 1.50
RS5 Ichiro Suzuki, Hideo Nomo 5.00
RS6 Tsuyoshi Shinjo, Mac Suzuki 1.50
RS7 Tsuyoshi Shinjo, Kazuhiro Sasaki 1.50
RS8 Hideo Nomo, Tomokazu Ohka 1.50
RS9 Ichiro Suzuki, Mac Suzuki 5.00
RS10 Hideo Nomo, Shigetosi Hasegawa 1.50
RS11 Hideo Nomo, Masato Yoshii 1.50
RS12 Hideo Nomo, Hideki Irabu 1.50
RS13 Shigetosi Hasegawa, Kazuhiro Sasaki 1.00
RS14 Shigetosi Hasegawa, Mac Suzuki 1.00
RS15 Tsuyoshi Shinjo, Hideo Nomo 1.50
RS16 Tsuyoshi Shinjo, Tomokazu Ohka 1.50
RS17 Ichiro Suzuki, Kazuhiro Sasaki 5.00
RS18 Masato Yoshii, Hideki Irabu 1.00
RS19 Ichiro Suzuki, Tomokazu Ohka 5.00
RS20 Hideki Irabu, Kazuhiro Sasaki 1.00
RS21 Tsuyoshi Shinjo, Masato Yoshii 1.50
RS22 Ichiro Suzuki, Shigetosi Hasegawa 5.00
RS23 Mac Suzuki, Kazuhiro Sasaki 1.00
RS24 Ichiro Suzuki, Hideki Irabu 5.00
RS25 Tomokazu Ohka, Kazuhiro Sasaki 1.00
RS26 Tsuyoshi Shinjo, Shigetosi Hasegawa 1.50
RS27 Masato Yoshii, Kazuhiro Sasaki 1.00
RS28 Hideo Nomo, Kazuhiro Sasaki 1.50
RS29 Ichiro Suzuki, Masato Yoshii 5.00
RS30 Hideo Nomo, Ichiro Suzuki 5.00

Stars of Japan Game Ball

NM/M

Common Player: 8.00
BB-SH Shigetosi Hasegawa SP/30 15.00
BB-HI Hideki Irabu 8.00
BB-KS Kazuhiro Sasaki 10.00
BB-TS Tsuyoshi Shinjo SP/50 20.00
BB-IS Ichiro Suzuki 75.00
BB-MY Masato Yoshii 10.00

Stars of Japan Game Ball Gold

NM/M

Production 25 sets
BB-SH Shigetosi Hasegawa 40.00
BB-HI Hideki Irabu 20.00
BB-KS Kazuhiro Sasaki 40.00

Stars of Japan Game Ball-Base Combos

NM/M

Inserted 1:576
HI-KS Hideki Irabu, Kazuhiro Sasaki SP/30 25.00
HN-KS Hideo Nomo, Kazuhiro Sasaki SP/50 75.00
HN-SH Hideo Nomo, Shigetosi Hasegawa 20.00
IS-KS Ichiro Suzuki, Kazuhiro Sasaki SP/30 120.00
IS-MY Ichiro Suzuki, Masato Yoshii 50.00
IS-SH Ichiro Suzuki, Shigetosi Hasegawa SP/72 75.00
IS-TS Ichiro Suzuki, Tsuyoshi Shinjo SP/40 125.00
MS-KS Mac Suzuki, Kazuhiro Sasaki SP/30 20.00
MY-KS Masato Yoshii, Kazuhiro Sasaki SP/30 25.00
SH-KS Shigetosi Hasegawa, Kazuhiro Sasaki SP/30 25.00
TO-KS Tomokazu Ohka, Kazuhiro Sasaki 20.00
TS-HI Tsuyoshi Shinjo, Hideki Irabu SP/30 25.00
TS-KS Tsuyoshi Shinjo, Kazuhiro Sasaki SP/30 25.00
TS-SH Tsuyoshi Shinjo, Shigetosi Hasegawa SP/30 25.00

Stars of Japan Game Ball-Base Combos Gold

NM/M

Common Card: 20.00
Production 25 sets
HI-KS Hideki Irabu, Kazuhiro Sasaki 25.00
HN-KS Hideo Nomo, Kazuhiro Sasaki 65.00
HN-SH Hideo Nomo, Shigetosi Hasegawa 65.00
IS-KS Ichiro Suzuki, Kazuhiro Sasaki 150.00
IS-MY Ichiro Suzuki, Masato Yoshii 150.00
IS-SH Ichiro Suzuki, Shigetosi Hasegawa 150.00
IS-TS Ichiro Suzuki, Tsuyoshi Shinjo 150.00
MS-KS Mac Suzuki, Kazuhiro Sasaki 20.00
MY-KS Masato Yoshii, Kazuhiro Sasaki 20.00
SH-KS Shigetosi Hasegawa, Kazuhiro Sasaki 20.00
TO-KS Tomokazu Ohka, Kazuhiro Sasaki 20.00
TS-HI Tsuyoshi Shinjo, Hideki Irabu 25.00
TS-KS Tsuyoshi Shinjo, Kazuhiro Sasaki 25.00
TS-SH Tsuyoshi Shinjo, Shigetosi Hasegawa 25.00

Stars of Japan Game Ball-Base Trio

NM/M

BBB-RS Kazuhiro Sasaki, Ichiro Suzuki, Hideo Nomo 175.00

Stars of Japan Game Base

NM/M

Common Player: 15.00
SH Shigetosi Hasegawa SP/33 20.00
HI Hideki Irabu SP/33 15.00
TO Tomokazu Ohka SP/33 15.00
KS Kazuhiro Sasaki SP/33 25.00
TS Tsuyoshi Shinjo SP/33 25.00
IS Ichiro Suzuki SP/23
MS Mac Suzuki SP/23 20.00
MY Masato Yoshii SP/33 20.00

Stars of Japan Game Base Gold

NM/M

Common Player: 25.00
Production 25 sets
SH Shigetosi Hasegawa 25.00
HI Hideki Irabu 25.00
TO Tomokazu Ohka 25.00
KS Kazuhiro Sasaki 30.00
TS Tsuyoshi Shinjo 35.00
IS Ichiro Suzuki
MS Mac Suzuki 25.00
MY Masato Yoshii 25.00

Stars of Japan Game Bat

NM/M

Inserted 1:12
B-HN Hideo Nomo SP/30 60.00
B-TS Tsuyoshi Shinjo SP/30 20.00
B-MY Masato Yoshii 5.00

Stars of Japan Game Bat Gold

NM/M

Common Player: 10.00
Production 25 sets
B-HN Hideo Nomo 80.00
B-TS Tsuyoshi Shinjo 30.00
B-MY Masato Yoshii 10.00

Stars of Japan Game Jersey-Bat Combos

NM/M

Common Player: 15.00
BB-HS Shigetosi Hasegawa, Tsuyoshi Shinjo 15.00
JB-NN Hideo Nomo 60.00
JB-SN Kazuhiro Sasaki, Hideo Nomo 40.00
JJ-SH Kazuhiro Sasaki, Shigetosi Hasegawa 15.00

Stars of Japan Game Bat-Jersey Combo Gold

NM/M

Production 25 sets
BB-HS Shigetosi Hasegawa, Tsuyoshi Shinjo 40.00

Stars of Japan Game Jersey

NM/M

Common Player: 5.00
Inserted 1:12
J-SH Shigetosi Hasegawa 5.00
J-HN Hideo Nomo 40.00
J-KS Kazuhiro Sasaki 8.00
J-TS Tsuyoshi Shinjo 8.00
J-IS Ichiro Suzuki SP/260 EXCH 100.00
J-MY Masato Yoshii 5.00

Stars of Japan Game Jersey Gold

NM/M

Common Player: 10.00
Production 25 sets
J-SH Shigetosi Hasegawa 10.00
J-HN Hideo Nomo 60.00
J-KS Kazuhiro Sasaki 15.00
J-TS Tsuyoshi Shinjo 15.00
J-MY Masato Yoshii 10.00

Sultan of Swatch Jersey or Pants

NM/M

Quantity produced listed
SOS1 Babe Ruth/14
SOS2 Babe Ruth/29 350.00
SOS3 Babe Ruth/94 300.00
SOS4 Babe Ruth/54 350.00
SOS5 Babe Ruth/59 350.00
SOS6 Babe Ruth/26 350.00
SOS7 Babe Ruth/27 350.00
SOS8 Babe Ruth/32 350.00
SOS9 Babe Ruth/20 350.00
SOS10 Babe Ruth/21 350.00
SOS11 Babe Ruth/23 350.00

SOS12	Babe Ruth/24	350.00
SOS13	Babe Ruth/26	350.00
SOS14	Babe Ruth/27	350.00
SOS15	Babe Ruth/28	350.00
SOS16	Babe Ruth/29	350.00
SOS17	Babe Ruth/30	350.00
SOS18	Babe Ruth/31	350.00
SOS19	Babe Ruth/33	350.00
SOS20	Babe Ruth/36	350.00
SOS21	Babe Ruth/48	350.00

2001 SP GAME BAT

		NM/M
Complete Set (90):		45.00
Common Player:		.25
Pack (4):		10.00
Box (16):		140.00
1	Troy Glaus	1.00
2	Darin Erstad	.50
3	Mo Vaughn	.25
4	Jason Giambi	.75
5	Ben Grieve	.25
6	Eric Chavez	.45
7	Carlos Delgado	.75
8	Tony Batista	.25
9	Shannon Stewart	.25
10	Jose Cruz Jr.	.25
11	Fred McGriff	.25
12	Greg Vaughn	.25
13	Roberto Alomar	.45
14	Manny Ramirez	1.00
15	Jim Thome	.85
16	Russ Branyan	.25
17	Alex Rodriguez	3.00
18	John Olerud	.25
19	Edgar Martinez	.25
20	Cal Ripken Jr.	4.00
21	Albert Belle	.35
22	Ivan Rodriguez	.85
23	Rafael Palmeiro	.85
24	Nomar Garciaparra	2.00
25	Carl Everett	.25
26	Dante Bichette	.25
27	Mike Sweeney	.25
28	Jermaine Dye	.25
29	Carlos Beltran	.75
30	Juan Gonzalez	1.00
31	Dean Palmer	.25
32	Bobby Higginson	.25
33	Matt Lawton	.25
34	Jacque Jones	.25
35	Frank Thomas	1.00
36	Magglio Ordonez	.25
37	Paul Konerko	.35
38	Carlos Lee	.25
39	Bernie Williams	.35
40	Derek Jeter	4.00
41	Paul O'Neill	.25
42	Jose Canseco	.45
43	Ken Caminiti	.25
44	Jeff Bagwell	1.00
45	Craig Biggio	.25
46	Richard Hidalgo	.25
47	Andruw Jones	1.00
48	Chipper Jones	1.50
49	Andres Galarraga	.25
50	B.J. Surhoff	.25
51	Jeromy Burnitz	.25
52	Geoff Jenkins	.25
53	Richie Sexson	.25
54	Mark McGwire	3.00
55	Jim Edmonds	.25
56	J.D. Drew	.50
57	Fernando Tatis	.25
58	Sammy Sosa	2.00
59	Mark Grace	.35
60	Eric Young	.25
61	Matt Williams	.25
62	Luis Gonzalez	.35
63	Steve Finley	.25
64	Shawn Green	.60
65	Gary Sheffield	.50
66	Eric Karros	.25
67	Vladimir Guerrero	1.00
68	Jose Vidro	.25
69	Barry Bonds	4.00
70	Jeff Kent	.25
71	Preston Wilson	.25
72	Mike Lowell	.25
73	Luis Castillo	.25
74	Mike Piazza	2.00
75	Robin Ventura	.25
76	Edgardo Alfonzo	.25
77	Tony Gwynn	1.50
78	Eric Owens	.25
79	Ryan Klesko	.25
80	Scott Rolen	.85
81	Bobby Abreu	.25
82	Pat Burrell	.75
83	Brian Giles	.25
84	Jason Kendall	.25
85	Aaron Boone	.25
86	Ken Griffey Jr.	2.00
87	Barry Larkin	.25
88	Todd Helton	1.00
89	Larry Walker	.25
90	Jeffrey Hammonds	.25

Big League Hit Parade

		NM/M
Complete Set (6):		15.00
Common Player:		1.50
Inserted 1:15		
1	Nomar Garciaparra	3.00
2	Ken Griffey Jr.	3.00
3	Sammy Sosa	3.00
4	Alex Rodriguez	4.00
5	Mark McGwire	4.00
6	Ivan Rodriguez	1.50

In the Swing

		NM/M
Complete Set (15):		25.00
Common Player:		1.00
Inserted 1:7		
1	Ken Griffey Jr.	2.50
2	Jim Edmonds	1.00
3	Carlos Delgado	1.00
4	Frank Thomas	1.50
5	Barry Bonds	4.00
6	Nomar Garciaparra	2.50
7	Gary Sheffield	1.00
8	Vladimir Guerrero	1.50
9	Alex Rodriguez	3.00
10	Todd Helton	1.50
11	Darin Erstad	1.00
12	Derek Jeter	4.00
13	Sammy Sosa	2.50
14	Mark McGwire	3.00
15	Jason Giambi	1.00

Lineup Time

		NM/M
Complete Set (11):		20.00
Common Player:		1.00
Inserted 1:8		
1	Mark McGwire	3.00
2	Roberto Alomar	1.00
3	Alex Rodriguez	3.00
4	Chipper Jones	2.00
5	Ivan Rodriguez	1.00
6	Ken Griffey Jr.	2.50
7	Sammy Sosa	2.50
8	Barry Bonds	4.00
9	Frank Thomas	1.50
10	Pedro Martinez	1.50
11	Derek Jeter	4.00

Piece of the Game

		NM/M
Common Player:		4.00
Inserted 1:1		
SP production 1,500 or fewer		
Golds:		2-5X
Production 25 sets		
EA	Edgardo Alfonzo SP	10.00
RA	Roberto Alomar	8.00
SA	Sandy Alomar	4.00
RA	Rick Ankiel	4.00
JB	Jeff Bagwell SP	15.00
TB	Tony Batista	5.00
CB	Carlos Beltran	5.00
JB	Johnny Bench SP	25.00
BB	Barry Bonds	25.00
KB	Kevin Brown SP	10.00
PB	Pat Burrell	8.00
JC	Jose Canseco	6.00
WC	Will Clark	8.00
CD	Carlos Delgado	6.00
JoD	Joe DiMaggio SP	100.00
JD	J.D. Drew	6.00
JE	Jim Edmonds	6.00
DE	Darin Erstad SP	10.00
RF	Rafael Furcal	6.00
BG	Bob Gibson SP	20.00
TGl	Tom Glavine SP	15.00
MG	Mark Grace	8.00
SG	Shawn Green	6.00
KG	Ken Griffey Jr.	15.00
TGw	Tony Gwynn	10.00
TH	Todd Helton	8.00
TH	Todd Hundley SP	10.00
RJ	Reggie Jackson SP	20.00
RJ	Randy Johnson	10.00
AJ	Andruw Jones	8.00
CJ	Chipper Jones	10.00
DJ	David Justice	5.00
KL	Kenny Lofton	4.00
GM	Greg Maddux	15.00
EM	Edgar Martinez	6.00
TM	Tino Martinez	6.00
FM	Fred McGriff SP	10.00
PN	Phil Nevin SP	10.00
JO	John Olerud	6.00
PO	Paul O'Neill	6.00
MO	Magglio Ordonez SP	10.00
MQ	Mark Quinn SP	10.00
MR	Manny Ramirez	8.00
CR	Cal Ripken Jr. SP	40.00
AR	Alex Rodriguez	10.00
IR	Ivan Rodriguez	8.00
SR	Scott Rolen	8.00
NR	Nolan Ryan SP	35.00
TS	Tim Salmon SP	10.00
GS	Gary Sheffield	5.00
SS	Sammy Sosa SP	25.00
SS	Shannon Stewart	4.00
FT	Frank Thomas	8.00
GV	Greg Vaughn	4.00
MV	Mo Vaughn	4.00
RV	Robin Ventura	4.00
BW	Bernie Williams	6.00
MW	Matt Williams	4.00
PW	Preston Wilson	4.00

Piece of the Game Autograph

		NM/M
Common Autograph:		30.00
Inserted 1:96		
BB	Barry Bonds	250.00
JC	Jose Canseco	40.00
KG	Ken Griffey Jr.	100.00
TGw	Tony Gwynn	50.00
AJ	Andruw Jones	30.00
AR	Alex Rodriguez	100.00
NR	Nolan Ryan	125.00
FT	Frank Thomas	50.00

The Lumber Yard

		NM/M
Complete Set (10):		15.00
Common Player:		.50
Inserted 1:10		
1	Jason Giambi	1.00
2	Chipper Jones	2.00
3	Carl Everett	.50
4	Alex Rodriguez	3.00
5	Frank Thomas	1.50
6	Barry Bonds	4.00
7	Jeff Bagwell	1.50
8	Sammy Sosa	2.50
9	Carlos Delgado	1.00
10	Mike Piazza	2.50

2001 SP GAME BAT - MILESTONE

		NM/M
Complete Set (96):		
Common Player:		.40
Common Rookie (91-96):		5.00
Production 500		
Pack (4):		16.00
Box (10):		140.00
1	Troy Glaus	1.00
2	Darin Erstad	.50
3	Jason Giambi	.75
4	Jermaine Dye	.40
5	Eric Chavez	.50
6	Carlos Delgado	.75
7	Raul Mondesi	.40
8	Shannon Stewart	.40
9	Greg Vaughn	.40
10	Aubrey Huff	.40
11	Juan Gonzalez	1.00
12	Roberto Alomar	.60
13	Jim Thome	.85
14	Omar Vizquel	.40
15	Mike Cameron	.40
16	Edgar Martinez	.40
17	John Olerud	.40
18	Bret Boone	.40
19	Cal Ripken Jr.	4.00
20	Tony Batista	.40
21	Alex Rodriguez	3.00
22	Ivan Rodriguez	.85
23	Rafael Palmeiro	.85
24	Manny Ramirez	1.00
25	Pedro Martinez	1.00
26	Nomar Garciaparra	2.50
27	Carl Everett	.40
28	Mike Sweeney	.40
29	Neifi Perez	.40
30	Mark Quinn	.40
31	Bobby Higginson	.40
32	Tony Clark	.40
33	Doug Mientkiewicz	.40
34	Cristian Guzman	.40
35	Joe Mays	.40
36	David Ortiz	.75
37	Frank Thomas	1.00
38	Magglio Ordonez	.40
39	Carlos Lee	.40
40	Alfonso Soriano	1.00
41	Bernie Williams	.50
42	Derek Jeter	4.00
43	Roger Clemens	2.25
44	Jeff Bagwell	1.00
45	Richard Hidalgo	.40
46	Moises Alou	.40
47	Chipper Jones	1.50
48	Greg Maddux	1.50
49	Rafael Furcal	.40
50	Andruw Jones	1.00
51	Jeromy Burnitz	.40
52	Geoff Jenkins	.40
53	Richie Sexson	.40

54 Edgar Renteria .40
55 Mark McGwire 3.00
56 Jim Edmonds .40
57 J.D. Drew .50
58 Sammy Sosa 2.50
59 Bill Mueller .40
60 Luis Gonzalez .50
61 Randy Johnson 1.00
62 Gary Sheffield .50
63 Shawn Green .65
64 Kevin Brown .40
65 Vladimir Guerrero 1.00
66 Jose Vidro .40
67 Fernando Tatis .40
68 Barry Bonds 4.00
69 Jeff Kent .40
70 Rich Aurilia .40
71 Preston Wilson .40
72 Charles Johnson .40
73 Cliff Floyd .40
74 Mike Piazza 2.50
75 Matt Lawton .40
76 Edgardo Alfonzo .40
77 Tony Gwynn 1.50
78 Phil Nevin .40
79 Scott Rolen .85
80 Pat Burrell .75
81 Bobby Abreu .40
82 Brian Giles .40
83 Jason Kendall .40
84 Aramis Ramirez .40
85 Sean Casey .50
86 Ken Griffey Jr. 2.50
87 Barry Larkin .40
88 Todd Helton 1.00
89 Mike Hampton .40
90 Larry Walker .40
91 *Ichiro Suzuki* 60.00
92 *Albert Pujols* 140.00
93 *Tsuyoshi Shinjo* 5.00
94 *Jack Wilson* 8.00
95 *Donaldo Mendez* 5.00
96 *Junior Spivey* 8.00

The Art of Hitting

NM/M

Complete Set (12): 10.00
Common Player: .50
Inserted 1:5
AH1 Tony Gwynn 1.50
AH2 Manny Ramirez 1.00
AH3 Todd Helton 1.00
AH4 Nomar Garciaparra 2.00
AH5 Vladimir Guerrero 1.00
AH6 Ichiro Suzuki 2.50
AH7 Darin Erstad .50
AH8 Alex Rodriguez 2.50
AH9 Carlos Delgado .75
AH10 Edgar Martinez .50
AH11 Luis Gonzalez .50
AH12 Barry Bonds 3.00

P.O.A. Milestone Bat

NM/M

Common Player: 5.00
Golds: 3-5X
Production 35 sets
JB Jeff Bagwell 8.00
BB Barry Bonds 20.00
RB Russell Branyan 5.00
JB Jeromy Burnitz 5.00
RC Roger Clemens 20.00
DE Darin Erstad 5.00
LG Luis Gonzalez 5.00
KG Ken Griffey Jr. 12.00
TH Todd Helton 8.00
Chj Chipper Jones 10.00
MP Mike Piazza 10.00
CR Cal Ripken Jr. 30.00
AR Alex Rodriguez 10.00
GS Gary Sheffield 5.00
SS Sammy Sosa 10.00
IS Ichiro Suzuki/203 80.00
FT Frank Thomas 8.00
JT Jim Thome 8.00

P.O.A. Int. Conn. Bat

NM/M

Common Player: 5.00
Golds: 3-5X
Production 35 sets
RA Roberto Alomar 6.00
AB Adrian Beltre 5.00
RF Rafael Furcal 5.00
JG Juan Gonzalez 6.00
AJ Andruw Jones 8.00
PM Pedro Martinez 10.00
HN Hideo Nomo/203 40.00
MO Magglio Ordonez 5.00
CP Chan Ho Park 5.00
JP Jorge Posada 10.00
AP Albert Pujols 50.00
MR Manny Ramirez 8.00
TS Tsuyoshi Shinjo 8.00
IS Ichiro Suzuki/273 80.00
MT Miguel Tejada 6.00
OV Omar Vizquel 5.00

P.O.A. BFH Bat

NM/M

Common Player: 5.00
Golds: 2-3X
Production 35 sets
BB Barry Bonds 20.00
RC Roger Clemens/203 25.00
CD Carlos Delgado 5.00
JG Jason Giambi 5.00
KG Ken Griffey Jr. 15.00
TGw Tony Gwynn 15.00
GM Greg Maddux 12.00
EM Edgar Martinez 6.00
FM Fred McGriff 6.00
RP Rafael Palmeiro 8.00
MP Mike Piazza 10.00
CR Cal Ripken Jr. 30.00
AR Alex Rodriguez 10.00
IR Ivan Rodriguez 8.00
SS Sammy Sosa 15.00

P.O.A. Autograph Bat

NM/M

Common Autograph: 15.00
Inserted 1:100
RB Russell Branyan 15.00
CD Carlos Delgado/97 25.00
JDr J.D. Drew 20.00
JDy Jermaine Dye 15.00
LG Luis Gonzalez 20.00
JK Jason Kendall 15.00
JK Jeff Kent/194 35.00
AR Alex Rodriguez/97 100.00
GS Gary Sheffield/194 40.00
IS Ichiro Suzuki/53 800.00
MT Miguel Tejada 40.00
JV Jose Vidro 15.00
PW Preston Wilson 15.00

P.O.A. Triple Bat

NM/M

Common Card: 15.00
Inserted 1:50
GRS Ken Griffey Jr., Alex Rodriguez, Sammy Sosa 40.00
JJF Chipper Jones, Andruw Jones, Rafael Furcal 15.00
RRP Alex Rodriguez, Ivan Rodriguez, Rafael Palmeiro 35.00
SGB Gary Sheffield, Shawn Green, Adrian Beltre 15.00
TVA Jim Thome, Omar Vizquel, Roberto Alomar 15.00
KGR Jason Kendall, Brian Giles, Aramis Ramirez 15.00
OJC Paul O'Neill, David Justice, Roger Clemens 35.00
CMG Roger Clemens, Greg Maddux, Tom Glavine 40.00
VSA Robin Ventura, Tsuyoshi Shinjo, Edgardo Alfonzo 15.00
OTA Magglio Ordonez, Frank Thomas, Sandy Alomar 15.00
PWS Kirby Puckett, Dave Winfield, Ozzie Smith 25.00
GRB Tony Gwynn, Cal Ripken Jr., Barry Bonds 60.00
GBM Ken Griffey Jr., Barry Bonds, Fred McGriff 35.00
SFR Alfonso Soriano, Rafael Furcal, Alex Ramirez 25.00

P.O.A. Quad Bat

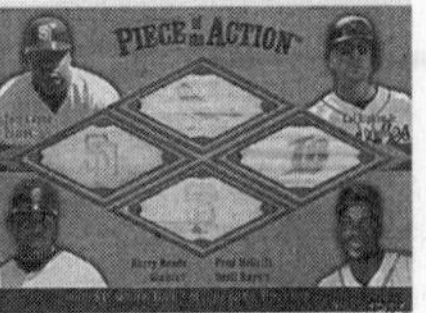

NM/M

Common Card: 15.00
Inserted 1:50
TVAL Jim Thome, Omar Vizquel, Roberto Alomar, Kenny Lofton 25.00
RRPM Alex Rodriguez, Ivan Rodriguez, Rafael Palmeiro, Ruben Mateo 50.00
OJCP Paul O'Neill, David Justice, Roger Clemens, Jorge Posada 60.00
JJFM Chipper Jones, Andruw Jones, Rafael Furcal, Greg Maddux 40.00
PWSG Kirby Puckett, Dave Winfield, Ozzie Smith, Steve Garvey 30.00
GRSB Ken Griffey Jr., Alex Rodriguez, Sammy Sosa, Barry Bonds 80.00
SGBP Gary Sheffield, Shawn Green, Adrian Beltre, Chan Ho Park 15.00
GGRR Ken Griffey Jr., Ken Griffey Jr., Alex Rodriguez, Alex Rodriguez 65.00
GRBM Tony Gwynn, Cal Ripken Jr., Barry Bonds, Fred McGriff 70.00
TDTA Frank Thomas, Jermaine Dye, Jim Thome, Roberto Alomar 25.00
GHSK Luis Gonzalez, Todd Helton, Gary Sheffield, Jeff Kent 20.00
GDBS Ken Griffey Jr., J.D. Drew, Jeromy Burnitz, Sammy Sosa 50.00
JVBW Chipper Jones, Robin Ventura, Pat Burrell, Preston Wilson 30.00
RGGM Alex Rodriguez, Troy Glaus, Jason Giambi, Edgar Martinez 40.00
ONRD Paul O'Neill, Hideo Nomo, Cal Ripken Jr., Carlos Delgado 80.00

Slugging Sensations

NM/M

Complete Set (12): 12.00
Common Player: .50
Inserted 1:5
SS1 Troy Glaus 1.00
SS2 Mark McGwire 2.50
SS3 Sammy Sosa 2.00
SS4 Juan Gonzalez 1.00
SS5 Barry Bonds 3.00
SS6 Jeff Bagwell 1.00
SS7 Jason Giambi .75
SS8 Ivan Rodriguez .85
SS9 Mike Piazza 2.00
SS10 Chipper Jones 1.50
SS11 Ken Griffey Jr. 2.00
SS12 Gary Sheffield .50

The Trophy Room

NM/M

Complete Set (6): 8.00
Common Player: 1.00
Inserted 1:10
TR1 Sammy Sosa 2.00
TR2 Jason Giambi 1.00
TR3 Todd Helton 1.00
TR4 Alex Rodriguez 2.50
TR5 Mark McGwire 2.50
TR6 Ken Griffey Jr. 2.00

2001 SP GAME-USED EDITION

NM/M

Common Player: .50
Common SP (61-90): 5.00
Production 500
Pack (3): 35.00
Box (6): 160.00
1 Garret Anderson .50
2 Troy Glaus 1.50
3 Darin Erstad .75
4 Jason Giambi 1.00
5 Tim Hudson .75
6 Johnny Damon .65
7 Carlos Delgado 1.00
8 Greg Vaughn .50
9 Juan Gonzalez 1.50
10 Roberto Alomar 1.00
11 Jim Thome 1.25
12 Edgar Martinez .50
13 Cal Ripken Jr. 5.00
14 Andres Galarraga .50
15 Alex Rodriguez 4.00
16 Rafael Palmeiro 1.25
17 Ivan Rodriguez 1.25
18 Manny Ramirez 1.50
19 Nomar Garciaparra 3.00
20 Pedro Martinez 1.50
21 Jermaine Dye .50
22 Dean Palmer .50
23 Matt Lawton .50
24 Frank Thomas 1.50

25 David Wells .50
26 Magglio Ordonez .50
27 Derek Jeter 5.00
28 Bernie Williams .50
29 Roger Clemens 2.50
30 Jeff Bagwell 1.50
31 Richard Hidalgo .50
32 Chipper Jones 2.00
33 Andruw Jones 1.50
34 Greg Maddux 2.00
35 Jeffrey Hammonds .50
36 Mark McGwire 4.00
37 Jim Edmonds .50
38 Sammy Sosa 3.00
39 Corey Patterson .50
40 Randy Johnson 1.50
41 Luis Gonzalez .50
42 Gary Sheffield .75
43 Shawn Green 1.00
44 Kevin Brown .50
45 Vladimir Guerrero 1.50
46 Barry Bonds 5.00
47 Jeff Kent .50
48 Preston Wilson .50
49 Charles Johnson .50
50 Mike Piazza 3.00
51 Edgardo Alfonzo .50
52 Tony Gwynn 2.00
53 Scott Rolen 1.25
54 Pat Burrell 1.00
55 Brian Giles .50
56 Jason Kendall .50
57 Ken Griffey Jr. 3.00
58 Mike Hampton .50
59 Todd Helton 1.50
60 Larry Walker .50
61 *Wilson Betemit* 5.00
62 *Travis Hafner* 20.00
63 *Ichiro Suzuki* 60.00
64 *Juan Diaz* 5.00
65 *Morgan Ensberg* 25.00
66 *Horacio Ramirez* 10.00
67 *Ricardo Rodriguez* 5.00
68 *Sean Douglass* 5.00
69 *Brandon Duckworth* 8.00
70 *Jackson Melian* 5.00
71 *Adrian Hernandez* 5.00
72 *Kyle Kessel* 5.00
73 *Jason Michaels* 5.00
74 *Esix Snead* 5.00
75 *Jason Smith* 5.00
76 *Tyler Walker* 5.00
77 *Juan Uribe* 8.00
78 *Adam Pettyjohn* 5.00
79 *Tsuyoshi Shinjo* 5.00
80 *Mike Penney* 5.00
81 *Josh Towers* 8.00
82 *Erick Almonte* 5.00
83 *Ryan Freel* 6.00
84 Juan Pena 5.00
85 *Albert Pujols* 220.00
86 *Henry Mateo* 5.00
87 *Greg Miller* 5.00
88 *Jose Mieses* 5.00
89 *Jack Wilson* 10.00
90 *Carlos Valderrama* 5.00

Authentic Fabric Jersey Autograph

NM/M

Production 50 sets
S-EA Edgardo Alfonzo 25.00
S-RA Rick Ankiel 15.00
S-BB Barry Bonds /50 250.00
S-JC Jose Canseco 40.00
S-CD Carlos Delgado /50 40.00
S-JDr J.D. Drew /50 40.00
S-JG Jason Giambi /50 40.00
S-TGl Troy Glaus /50 50.00
S-KG Ken Griffey Jr. 150.00
S-TH Tim Hudson /50 50.00
S-RJ Randy Johnson 100.00
S-AJ Andruw Jones 50.00
S-CJ Chipper Jones 80.00
S-CR Cal Ripken /50 200.00
S-AR Alex Rodriguez 150.00
S-IR Ivan Rodriguez 75.00
S-NR Nolan Ryan /50 200.00
S-TS Tom Seaver /50 80.00
S-SS Sammy Sosa /50 225.00
S-FTh Frank Thomas 75.00
S-DW David Wells /50 25.00

Authentic Fabric Jersey

NM/M

Common Player: 4.00
Inserted 1:1
EA Edgardo Alfonzo 4.00
RA Roberto Alomar 6.00

RA Rick Ankiel 4.00
TB Tony Batista SP 8.00
BB Barry Bonds 25.00
KB Kevin Brown 6.00
JB Jeromy Burnitz 4.00
PB Pat Burrell 8.00
JC(B) Jose Canseco BLC 8.00
JC(H) Jose Canseco Yanks 8.00
EC Eric Chavez 6.00
JCi Jeff Cirillo 4.00
RC Roger Clemens 20.00
CD Carlos Delgado SP 10.00
JDi Joe DiMaggio SP/50 180.00
JDr J.D. Drew 5.00
JDy Jermaine Dye SP 8.00
JE Jim Edmonds 6.00
DE Darin Erstad 5.00
JG Jason Giambi 8.00
BG Brian Giles SP 8.00
TGl Troy Glaus 6.00
ToG Tom Glavine 6.00
LG Luis Gonzalez 6.00
MG Mark Grace 8.00
SG Shawn Green 6.00
KG(H) Ken Griffey Reds 12.00
KG(M) Ken Griffey M's 12.00
KG(R) Ken Griffey Reds 12.00
TGw Tony Gwynn 10.00
MH Mike Hampton 4.00
THe Todd Helton 8.00
TrH Trevor Hoffman 4.00
TH Tim Hudson 6.00
AH Aubrey Huff 4.00
JI J. Isringhausen SP 8.00
CJo Charles Johnson 4.00
RJ Randy Johnson 10.00
AJ Andruw Jones 8.00
CJ Chipper Jones 10.00
JK Jason Kendall 4.00
JK Jeff Kent 5.00
BL Barry Larkin 6.00
AL Al Leiter 4.00
KL Kenny Lofton 4.00
TL Terrence Long 4.00
GM Greg Maddux 10.00
MM Mickey Mantle SP/50 250.00
RM Roger Maris SP 75.00
EM Edgar Martinez 6.00
TM Tino Martinez 5.00
FM Fred McGriff 5.00
KM Kevin Millwood 5.00
PN Phil Nevin 4.00
JO John Olerud 5.00
MO Magglio Ordonez 6.00
AP Adam Piatt 4.00
CR Cal Ripken Jr. 20.00
MR Mariano Rivera 6.00
AR(H) Alex Rodriguez Rangers 10.00
AR(M) Alex Rodriguez M's 10.00
IR Ivan Rodriguez 8.00
SR Scott Rolen 8.00
NR Nolan Ryan SP/50 50.00
TS Tom Seaver SP/50 30.00
GS Gary Sheffield 5.00
SS(H) Sammy Sosa 15.00
SS(R) Sammy Sosa 15.00
FTa Fernando Tatis 4.00
MT Miguel Tejada 6.00
FTh Frank Thomas 8.00
JT Jim Thome 8.00
GV Greg Vaughn 4.00
RV Robin Ventura 4.00
JV Jose Vidro 4.00
DW David Wells SP 8.00
MW Matt Williams 5.00
PW Preston Wilson 4.00
DY Dmitri Young 4.00
TZ Todd Zeile 4.00

2-Player Auth. Fabric Jersey

NM/M

Common Card: 25.00
Production 50 sets
R-R Alex Rodriguez, Ivan Rodriguez 50.00
M-D Mickey Mantle, Joe DiMaggio 450.00
M-M Mickey Mantle, Roger Maris 400.00
R-S Nolan Ryan, Tom Seaver 100.00
B-C Barry Bonds, Jose Canseco 70.00
S-G Gary Sheffield, Shawn Green 25.00
J-J Chipper Jones, Andruw Jones 40.00
C-W Roger Clemens, Bernie Williams 40.00
J-R Randy Johnson, Nolan Ryan 75.00
S-T Sammy Sosa, Frank Thomas 35.00
G-S Ken Griffey Jr., Sammy Sosa 50.00
G-R Ken Griffey Jr., Alex Rodriguez 50.00
S-R Sammy Sosa, Alex Rodriguez 40.00
H-G Tim Hudson, Jason Giambi 30.00

3-Player Auth. Fabric Jersey

NM/M

Production 25 sets
G-R-S Ken Griffey Jr., Alex Rodriguez, Sammy Sosa 100.00
M-J-J Greg Maddux, Chipper Jones, Andruw Jones 80.00
D-M-M Joe DiMaggio, Mickey Mantle, Roger Maris
J-B-S Andruw Jones, Barry Bonds, Sammy Sosa 120.00
J-S-M Randy Johnson, Tom Seaver, Greg Maddux 80.00
D-G-S Joe DiMaggio, Ken Griffey Jr., Sammy Sosa

2001 SP LEGENDARY CUTS

NM/M

Complete Set (90): 25.00
Common Player: .40
Pack (4): 10.00
Box (18): 150.00
1 Al Simmons .40
2 Jimmie Foxx (Height, weight and birthplace incorrect) .75
3 Mickey Cochrane .40
4 Phil Niekro .40
5 Eddie Mathews .75
6 Gary Matthews .40
7 Hank Aaron 2.50
8 Joe Adcock .40
9 Warren Spahn .75
10 George Sisler .40
11 Stan Musial 1.00
12 Dizzy Dean .40
13 Frankie Frisch .40
14 Harvey Haddix .40
15 Johnny Mize .40
16 Ken Boyer .40
17 Rogers Hornsby .75
18 Cap Anson .40
19 Andre Dawson .40
20 Billy Williams .40
21 Billy Herman .40
22 Hack Wilson .40
23 Ron Santo .40
24 Ryne Sandberg 1.00
25 Ernie Banks 1.00
26 Burleigh Grimes .40
27 Don Drysdale .75
28 Gil Hodges .40
29 Jackie Robinson 2.00
30 Tommy Lasorda .40
31 Pee Wee Reese .40
32 Roy Campanella .75
33 Tommy Davis .40
34 Branch Rickey .40
35 Leo Durocher .75
36 Walt Alston .40
37 Bill Terry .40
38 Carl Hubbell .40
39 Eddie Stanky .40
40 George Kelly .40
41 Mel Ott .75
42 Juan Marichal .40
43 Rube Marquard .40
44 Travis Jackson .40
45 Bob Feller .40
46 Earl Averill .40
47 Elmer Flick .40
48 Ken Keltner .40
49 Lou Boudreau .40
50 Early Wynn .40
51 Satchel Paige 1.50
52 Ron Hunt .40
53 Tom Seaver 1.00
54 Richie Ashburn .40
55 Mike Schmidt 1.00
56 Honus Wagner 1.00
57 Lloyd Waner .40
58 Max Carey .40
59 Paul Waner .40
60 Roberto Clemente 2.50
61 Nolan Ryan 3.00
62 Bobby Doerr .40
63 Carlton Fisk .75
64 Joe Cronin .40
65 Smokey Joe Wood .40
66 Tony Conigliaro .40
67 Edd Roush .40
68 Johnny Vander Meer .40
69 Walter Johnson .75
70 Charlie Gehringer .40
71 Al Kaline .75
72 Ty Cobb 2.00
73 Tony Oliva .40
74 Luke Appling .40
75 Minnie Minoso .40
76 Nellie Fox .40
77 Shoeless Joe Jackson 2.00
78 Babe Ruth 3.00
79 Bill Dickey .40
80 Elston Howard .40
81 Joe DiMaggio 2.50
82 Lefty Gomez .40
83 Lou Gehrig 2.50
84 Mickey Mantle 3.00
85 Reggie Jackson .75
86 Roger Maris 1.00
87 Whitey Ford .40
88 Waite Hoyt .40
89 Yogi Berra .75
90 Casey Stengel .40

Bat

NM/M

Common Player: 4.00
Inserted 1:18
HA Hank Aaron/SP 40.00

YB	Yogi Berra	10.00
WB	Wade Boggs	8.00
GB	George Brett	15.00
RCa	Roy Campanella/SP	40.00
RC	Rico Carty	4.00
RCl	Roberto Clemente	60.00
TC	Ty Cobb/SP	125.00
KC	Kiki Cuyler	8.00
TD	Tommy Davis/SP	40.00
AD	Andre Dawson	8.00
JD	Joe DiMaggio/SP	100.00
DD	Don Drysdale/SP	25.00
CF	Carlton Fisk	10.00
NF	Nellie Fox	10.00
JF	Jimmie Foxx	40.00
GH	Gil Hodges/SP	40.00
THo	Tommy Holmes (photo on front is Eddie Mathews)	8.00
RJ	Reggie Jackson	15.00
DJ	Davey Johnson	4.00
MM	Mickey Mantle/SP	120.00
RM	Roger Maris/SP	60.00
EM	Eddie Mathews	25.00
WMc	Willie McCovey	8.00
PM	Paul Molitor	15.00
MM	Manny Mota	4.00
MO	Mel Ott/SP	50.00
VP	Vada Pinson	4.00
JR	Jackie Robinson/SP	75.00
BR	Babe Ruth/SP	165.00
NR	Nolan Ryan/SP	40.00
RS	Ryne Sandberg	20.00
AS	Al Simmons/SP	25.00
BT	Bill Terry/SP	25.00
MW	Maury Wills	8.00
RY	Robin Yount	15.00

Combo Bat

No pricing due to scarcity
Production 25 sets

Debut Bat

		NM/M
Common Player:		5.00
Inserted 1:18		
JA	Joe Adcock/SP	15.00
LA	Luke Appling/SP	25.00
RA	Richie Ashburn/SP	25.00
BB	Bobby Bonds	5.00
LB	Lou Boudreau	10.00
KB	Ken Boyer/SP	10.00
BB	Bill Buckner	5.00
MC	Mickey Cochrane	30.00
TC	Tony Conigliaro/SP	15.00
JC	Joe Cronin	10.00
BD	Bobby Doerr/SP	15.00
BF	Bob Feller/SP	15.00
BF	Bill Freehan	5.00
FF	Frankie Frisch/SP	15.00
CG	Charlie Gehringer	15.00
BH	Billy Herman/SP	15.00
WH	Willie Horton	6.00
EH	Elston Howard/SP	15.00
RH	Ron Hunt	5.00
JJ	Joe Jackson	200.00
GL	Greg Luzinski	5.00
GM	Gary Matthews	5.00
MM	Minnie Minoso/SP	15.00
TO	Tony Oliva	8.00
WP	Wes Parker	5.00
BR	Bobby Richardson/SP	15.00
SS	Steve Sax	5.00
GS	George Sisler	20.00
ES	Eddie Stanky	5.00
AT	Alan Trammell	5.00
PW	Paul Waner/SP	40.00
HW	Hack Wilson/SP	40.00
SY	Steve Yeager	5.00

Game Jersey

		NM/M
Common Player:		5.00
Inserted 1:18		
YB	Yogi Berra	15.00
WB	Wade Boggs	5.00
RC	Roberto Clemente	80.00
TC	Ty Cobb	
TC	Tony Conigliaro	8.00
BD	Bill Dickey	25.00
JD	Joe DiMaggio	350.00
LD	Leo Durocher	8.00
WF	Whitey Ford	15.00
NF	Nellie Fox	8.00
JF	Jim Fregosi	5.00
GH	Gil Hodges	10.00
THo	Tommy Holmes	5.00
RJ	Reggie Jackson	15.00
TK	Ted Kluszewski	5.00
BL	Bob Lemon	5.00
VL	Vic Lombardi	5.00
MM	Mickey Mantle	275.00
JM	Juan Marichal	10.00
RM	Roger Maris	150.00
WM	Willie McCovey	10.00
JN	Joe Nuxhall	8.00
GP	Gaylord Perry	5.00
BR	Bobby Richardson	5.00
BRo	Brooks Robinson	15.00
BR	Babe Ruth	600.00
NR	Nolan Ryan	40.00
TS	Tom Seaver	100.00
CS	Casey Stengel	15.00
BT	Bobby Thomson	5.00
HW	Honus Wagner	750.00
BW	Billy Williams	6.00
MW	Maury Wills	5.00
RY	Robin Yount	15.00

Signatures

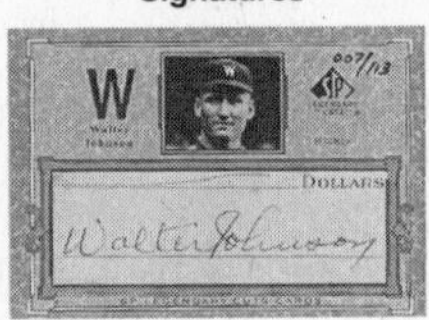

		NM/M
Inserted 1:252		
GA	Grover Cleveland Alexander/1	
WA	Walt Alston/34	175.00
CA	Cap Anson/2 (11/01 auction)	10,000
LA	Luke Appling/45	205.00
EA	Earl Averill/189	100.00
EB	E.G. Barrow/16	600.00
MC	Max Carey/73	145.00
TC	Ty Cobb/24	2,500
JC	Jocko Conlan/12	1,200
SC	Stanley Coveleski/42	315.00
JC	Joe Cronin/12	1,200
KC	Kiki Cuyler/6	4,000
DDe	Dizzy Dean/56	410.00
BD	Bill Dickey/28	275.00
JD	Joe DiMaggio/25	650.00
JD	Joe DiMaggio/50	395.00
JD	Joe DiMaggio/150	400.00
JD	Joe DiMaggio/275	285.00
DDr	Don Drysdale/12	1,500
LD	Leo Durocher/45	260.00
RF	Rick Ferrell/8	750.00
EF	Elmer Flick/22	400.00
NF	Nellie Fox/9	750.00
JF	Jimmie Foxx/16	2,500
FF	Ford Frick/21	750.00
FF	Frankie Frisch/3	3,500
LGe	Lou Gehrig/7	6,000
WG	Warren Giles/10	800.00
LGo	Lefty Gomez/85	195.00
BG	Burleigh Grimes/18	500.00
LG	Lefty Grove/34	600.00
HH	Harvey Haddix/4	3,000
BH	Bucky Harris/10	500.00
GH	Gabby Hartnett/32	380.00
BH	Billy Herman/88	140.00
GH	Gil Hodges/6	1,050
HH	Harry Hooper/14	800.00
RH	Rogers Hornsby/4	
WH	Waite Hoyt/38	245.00
CH	Carl Hubbell/30	375.00
TJ	Travis Jackson/35	225.00
JJ	Judy Johnson/9	650.00
WJ	Walter Johnson/113	510.00
CK	Charlie Keller/16	365.00
GK	George Kelly/52	140.00
KK	Ken Keltner/11	500.00
MK	Mark Koenig/30	275.00
KL	Kenesaw M. Landis/4	
BL	Bob Lemon/23	225.00
FL	Freddie Lindstrom/2	
EL	Eddie Lopat/22	275.00
TL	Ted Lyons/59	185.00
SM	Sal Maglie/19	400.00
MM	Mickey Mantle/8	5,000
HM	Heinie Manush/50	185.00
RoM	Roger Maris/73	1,675
RuM	Rube Marquard/23	375.00
JMc	Joe McCarthy/40	340.00
JM	Joe Medwick/18	750.00
BM	Bob Meusel/23	400.00
JMi	Johnny Mize/84	160.00
MO	Mel Ott/8	4,000
SP	Satchel Paige/36	900.00
RP	Roger Peckinpaugh/45	200.00
VR	Vic Raschi/26	175.00
BRi	Branch Rickey/16	1,350
JR	Jackie Robinson/147	530.00
ER	Edd Roush/83	170.00
RR	Red Ruffing/5	2,250
BRu	Babe Ruth/7	9,000
GS	George Selkirk/15	450.00
JS	Joe Sewell/55	130.00
RS	Rip Sewell/39	155.00
BS	Bob Shawkey/39	165.00
GS	George Sisler/1	
CS	Casey Stengel/10	1,500
BT	Bill Terry/184	125.00
VM	Johnny Vander Meer/65	125.00
HW	Honus Wagner/24	2,200
BW	Bucky Walters/13	400.00
LW	Lloyd Waner/217	105.00
PW	Paul Waner/4	2,250
HW	Hack Wilson/4	6,000
JW	Smokey Joe Wood/43	215.00

2001 SPX

		NM/M
Complete Set (150):		
Common Player:		.25
Common Young Star (91-120):		4.00
Production 2,000		
Common Prospect Jersey (121-135):		6.00
Common Prosp. Auto. Jersey (136-150):		10.00
Pack (4):		18.00
Box (18):		280.00
1	Darin Erstad	.50
2	Troy Glaus	1.00
3	Mo Vaughn	.25
4	Johnny Damon	.40
5	Jason Giambi	.75
6	Tim Hudson	.40
7	Miguel Tejada	.40
8	Carlos Delgado	.75
9	Raul Mondesi	.25
10	Tony Batista	.25
11	Ben Grieve	.25
12	Greg Vaughn	.25
13	Juan Gonzalez	1.00
14	Jim Thome	.85
15	Roberto Alomar	.50
16	John Olerud	.25
17	Edgar Martinez	.25
18	Albert Belle	.25
19	Cal Ripken Jr.	3.00
20	Ivan Rodriguez	.85
21	Rafael Palmeiro	.85
22	Alex Rodriguez	2.50
23	Nomar Garciaparra	2.00
24	Pedro J. Martinez	1.00
25	Manny Ramirez	1.00
26	Jermaine Dye	.25
27	Mark Quinn	.25
28	Carlos Beltran	.65
29	Tony Clark	.25
30	Bobby Higginson	.25
31	Eric Milton	.25
32	Matt Lawton	.25
33	Frank Thomas	1.00
34	Magglio Ordonez	.25
35	Ray Durham	.25
36	David Wells	.25
37	Derek Jeter	3.00
38	Bernie Williams	.40
39	Roger Clemens	1.75
40	David Justice	.25
41	Jeff Bagwell	1.00
42	Richard Hidalgo	.25
43	Moises Alou	.25
44	Chipper Jones	1.50
45	Andruw Jones	1.00
46	Greg Maddux	1.50
47	Rafael Furcal	.25
48	Jeromy Burnitz	.25
49	Geoff Jenkins	.25
50	Mark McGwire	2.50
51	Jim Edmonds	.25
52	Rick Ankiel	.25
53	Edgar Renteria	.25
54	Sammy Sosa	2.00
55	Kerry Wood	.85
56	Rondell White	.25
57	Randy Johnson	1.00
58	Steve Finley	.25
59	Matt Williams	.25
60	Luis Gonzalez	.25
61	Kevin Brown	.25
62	Gary Sheffield	.50
63	Shawn Green	.60
64	Vladimir Guerrero	1.00
65	Jose Vidro	.25
66	Barry Bonds	3.00
67	Jeff Kent	.25
68	Livan Hernandez	.25
69	Preston Wilson	.25
70	Charles Johnson	.25
71	Cliff Floyd	.25
72	Mike Piazza	2.00
73	Edgardo Alfonzo	.25
74	Jay Payton	.25
75	Robin Ventura	.25
76	Tony Gwynn	1.50
77	Phil Nevin	.25
78	Ryan Klesko	.25
79	Scott Rolen	.85
80	Pat Burrell	.50
81	Bob Abreu	.25
82	Brian Giles	.25
83	Kris Benson	.25
84	Jason Kendall	.25
85	Ken Griffey Jr.	2.00
86	Barry Larkin	.25
87	Sean Casey	.35
88	Todd Helton	1.00
89	Larry Walker	.25
90	Mike Hampton	.25
91	*Billy Sylvester*	4.00
92	*Josh Towers*	8.00
93	*Zach Day*	6.00
94	*Martin Vargas*	4.00
95	*Adam Pettyjohn*	4.00
96	*Andres Torres*	4.00
97	*Kris Keller*	4.00
98	*Blaine Neal*	4.00
99	*Kyle Kessel*	4.00
100	*Greg Miller*	4.00
101	Shawn Sonnier	4.00
102	*Alexis Gomez*	4.00

103 *Grant Balfour* 4.00
104 *Henry Mateo* 4.00
105 *Wilkin Ruan* 4.00
106 *Nick Maness* 4.00
107 *Jason Michaels* 4.00
108 *Esix Snead* 4.00
109 *William Ortega* 4.00
110 *David Elder* 4.00
111 *Jackson Melian* 4.00
112 *Nate Teut* 4.00
113 *Jason Smith* 4.00
114 *Mike Penney* 4.00
115 *Jose Mieses* 4.00
116 Juan Pena 4.00
117 *Brian Lawrence* 6.00
118 *Jeremy Owens* 4.00
119 *Carlos Valderrama* 4.00
120 *Rafael Soriano* 8.00
121 *Horacio Ramirez* 10.00
122 *Ricardo Rodriguez* 6.00
123 *Juan Diaz* 6.00
124 Donnie Bridges 6.00
125 *Tyler Walker* 6.00
126 *Erick Almonte* 6.00
127 Jesus Colome 6.00
128 *Ryan Freel* 6.00
129 *Elpidio Guzman* 6.00
130 Jack Cust 6.00
131 *Eric Hinske* 10.00
132 *Josh Fogg* 6.00
133 *Juan Uribe* 10.00
134 *Bert Snow* 6.00
135 Pedro Feliz 6.00
136 *Wilson Betemit* 15.00
137 *Sean Douglass* 10.00
138 Dernell Stenson 10.00
139 Brandon Inge 10.00
140 *Morgan Ensberg* 60.00
141 Brian Cole 10.00
142 *Adrian Hernandez* 10.00
143 *Brandon Duckworth* 10.00
144 *Jack Wilson* 15.00
145 *Travis Hafner* 50.00
146 Carlos Pena 10.00
147 Corey Patterson 15.00
148 Xavier Nady 10.00
149 Jason Hart 10.00
150 *Ichiro Suzuki* 750.00

Spectrum

Stars (1-90): 10-20X
SP's (91-120): 1-1.5X
Production 50 sets

Foundations

NM/M
Complete Set (12): 15.00
Common Player: 1.00
Inserted 1:8
F1 Mark McGwire 3.00
F2 Jeff Bagwell 1.00
F3 Alex Rodriguez 3.00
F4 Ken Griffey Jr. 2.00
F5 Andruw Jones 1.00
F6 Cal Ripken Jr. 4.00
F7 Barry Bonds 4.00
F8 Derek Jeter 4.00
F9 Frank Thomas 1.00
F10 Sammy Sosa 2.00
F11 Tony Gwynn 1.50
F12 Vladimir Guerrero 1.00

SPXcitement

NM/M
Complete Set (12): 15.00
Common Player: .75
Inserted 1:8
X1 Alex Rodriguez 3.00
X2 Jason Giambi .75
X3 Ken Griffey Jr. 2.00
X4 Sammy Sosa 2.00
X5 Frank Thomas 1.00
X6 Todd Helton 1.00
X7 Mark McGwire 3.00
X8 Mike Piazza 2.00
X9 Derek Jeter 4.00
X10 Vladimir Guerrero 1.00
X11 Carlos Delgado .75
X12 Chipper Jones 1.50

Untouchable Talents

NM/M
Complete Set (6): 10.00
Inserted 1:15
UT1 Ken Griffey Jr. 2.00
UT2 Mike Piazza 2.00
UT3 Mark McGwire 2.50
UT4 Alex Rodriguez 2.50
UT5 Sammy Sosa 2.00
UT6 Derek Jeter 3.00

Winning Materials Jersey/Bat

NM/M
Common Player: 8.00
Inserted 1:18
RA Rick Ankiel 8.00
BB1 Barry Bonds 25.00
BB2 Barry Bonds 25.00
CD Carlos Delgado 10.00
JD Joe DiMaggio 150.00
JE Jim Edmonds 8.00
KG1 Ken Griffey Jr. 15.00
KG2 Ken Griffey Jr. 15.00
RJ1 Randy Johnson 15.00
RJ2 Randy Johnson 15.00
AJ1 Andruw Jones 10.00
AJ2 Andruw Jones 10.00
CJ1 Chipper Jones 15.00
CJ2 Chipper Jones 15.00
CR Cal Ripken Jr. 40.00
AR1 Alex Rodriguez 15.00
AR2 Alex Rodriguez 15.00
IR1 Ivan Rodriguez 10.00
IR2 Ivan Rodriguez 10.00
SS Sammy Sosa 15.00
FT Frank Thomas 10.00

Winning Materials Jersey Combo

NM/M
Common Duo: 30.00
Production 50
Common Trio:
Production 25
KG-AR Ken Griffey Jr., Alex Rodriguez 65.00
KG-BB Ken Griffey Jr., Barry Bonds 80.00
KG-RJ Ken Griffey Jr., Randy Johnson 60.00
CJ-DW Chipper Jones, David Wells 30.00
BB-SS Barry Bonds, Sammy Sosa 65.00
KG-JD Ken Griffey Jr., Joe DiMaggio 180.00
KG-SS Ken Griffey Jr., Sammy Sosa 60.00
SS-CD Sammy Sosa, Carlos Delgado 30.00
SS-FT Sammy Sosa, Frank Thomas 30.00
IR-AR Ivan Rodriguez, Alex Rodriguez 40.00
AR-CR Alex Rodriguez, Cal Ripken Jr. 75.00
AJ-CJ Andruw Jones, Chipper Jones 30.00
KG-KG Ken Griffey Jr., Ken Griffey Jr. 60.00
G-R-B Ken Griffey Jr., Alex Rodriguez, Barry Bonds 125.00
S-G-C Sammy Sosa, Ken Griffey Jr., Chipper Jones 100.00
B-G-J Barry Bonds, Ken Griffey Jr., Andruw Jones 125.00
R-R-D Alex Rodriguez, Ivan Rodriguez, Carlos Delgado 75.00
D-B-S Carlos Delgado, Barry Bonds, Sammy Sosa 85.00
R-J-D Cal Ripken Jr., Chipper Jones, Carlos Delgado 125.00

Winning Materials Base/Ball

NM/M
Common Player: 10.00
Production 250 sets
B-BB Barry Bonds 50.00
B-NG Nomar Garciaparra 20.00
B-KG Ken Griffey Jr. 30.00
B-VG Vladimir Guerrero 15.00
B-DJ Derek Jeter 50.00
B-AJ Andruw Jones 10.00
B-CJ Chipper Jones 15.00
B-PM Pedro Martinez 15.00
B-MM Mark McGwire 75.00
B-MP Mike Piazza 20.00
B-AR Alex Rodriguez 20.00
B-SS Sammy Sosa 20.00
B-FT Frank Thomas 15.00

Winning Materials Base

NM/M
Common Duo: 50.00
Production 50
Trios: No Pricing
Production 25
B2-MG Mark McGwire, Ken Griffey Jr. 60.00
B2-MS Mark McGwire, Sammy Sosa 75.00
B2-MR Mark McGwire, Alex Rodriguez 60.00
B2-GJ Nomar Garciaparra, Derek Jeter 75.00
B2-TR Frank Thomas, Alex Rodriguez 50.00
B2-JG Derek Jeter, Jason Giambi 60.00
B2-PB Mike Piazza, Barry Bonds 60.00
B2-RJ Alex Rodriguez, Derek Jeter 70.00
B2-PM Mike Piazza, Mark McGwire 60.00
B2-JP Derek Jeter, Mike Piazza 60.00
B3-MGS Mark McGwire, Ken Griffey Jr., Sammy Sosa 180.00
B3-JRG Derek Jeter, Alex Rodriguez, Nomar Garciaparra 180.00
B3-PJW Mike Piazza, Derek Jeter, Bernie Williams 125.00
B3-BMS Barry Bonds, Mark McGwire, Sammy Sosa 200.00
B3-GJR Ken Griffey Jr., Derek Jeter, Alex Rodriguez 180.00

2002 SP AUTHENTIC

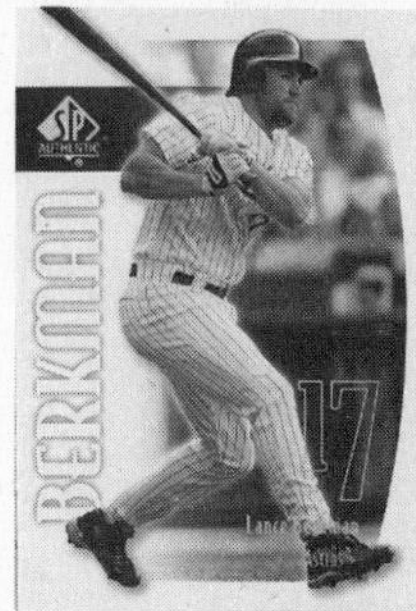

NM/M
Complete Set (170):
Common Player: .25
Common SP (91-135): 4.00
Production 1,999
Common SP Auto (136-170): 10.00
Production 999
Pack (5): 4.00
Box (24): 85.00
1 Troy Glaus .75
2 Darin Erstad .40
3 Barry Zito .40
4 Eric Chavez .40
5 Tim Hudson .40
6 Miguel Tejada .40
7 Carlos Delgado .60
8 Shannon Stewart .25
9 Ben Grieve .25
10 Jim Thome .65
11 C.C. Sabathia .25
12 Ichiro Suzuki 2.00
13 Freddy Garcia .25
14 Edgar Martinez .25
15 Bret Boone .25
16 Jeff Conine .25
17 Alex Rodriguez 2.00
18 Juan Gonzalez .75
19 Ivan Rodriguez .65
20 Rafael Palmeiro .65
21 Hank Blalock .60
22 Pedro J. Martinez .75
23 Manny Ramirez .75
24 Nomar Garciaparra 1.50
25 Carlos Beltran .60
26 Mike Sweeney .25
27 Randall Simon .25
28 Dmitri Young .25
29 Bobby Higginson .25
30 Corey Koskie .25
31 Eric Milton .25
32 Torii Hunter .25
33 Joe Mays .25
34 Frank Thomas .75
35 Mark Buehrle .25
36 Magglio Ordonez .25
37 Kenny Lofton .25
38 Roger Clemens 1.25
39 Derek Jeter 2.50
40 Jason Giambi .60
41 Bernie Williams .40
42 Alfonso Soriano .65
43 Lance Berkman .25
44 Roy Oswalt .25
45 Jeff Bagwell .75
46 Craig Biggio .25
47 Chipper Jones 1.00
48 Greg Maddux 1.00
49 Gary Sheffield .50
50 Andruw Jones .75
51 Ben Sheets .25
52 Richie Sexson .25
53 Albert Pujols 2.00
54 Matt Morris .25
55 J.D. Drew .40
56 Sammy Sosa 1.50
57 Kerry Wood .65
58 Corey Patterson .25
59 Mark Prior .75
60 Randy Johnson .75
61 Luis Gonzalez .40
62 Curt Schilling .50
63 Shawn Green .50
64 Kevin Brown .25
65 Hideo Nomo .75

66	Vladimir Guerrero	.75
67	Jose Vidro	.25
68	Barry Bonds	2.50
69	Jeff Kent	.25
70	Rich Aurilia	.25
71	Preston Wilson	.25
72	Josh Beckett	.40
73	Mike Lowell	.25
74	Roberto Alomar	.40
75	Mo Vaughn	.25
76	Jeromy Burnitz	.25
77	Mike Piazza	1.50
78	Sean Burroughs	.25
79	Phil Nevin	.25
80	Bobby Abreu	.25
81	Pat Burrell	.40
82	Scott Rolen	.65
83	Jason Kendall	.25
84	Brian Giles	.25
85	Ken Griffey Jr.	1.50
86	Adam Dunn	.50
87	Sean Casey	.40
88	Todd Helton	.75
89	Larry Walker	.25
90	Mike Hampton	.25
91	*Brandon Puffer*	4.00
92	*Tom Shearn*	4.00
93	*Chris Baker*	4.00
94	*Gustavo Chacin*	15.00
95	*Joe Orloski*	4.00
96	*Mike Smith*	4.00
97	*John Ennis*	4.00
98	*John Foster*	4.00
99	*Kevin Gryboski*	4.00
100	*Brian Mallette*	4.00
101	*Takahito Nomura*	4.00
102	*So Taguchi*	10.00
103	*Jeremy Lambert*	4.00
104	*Jason Simontacchi*	4.00
105	*Jorge Sosa*	4.00
106	*Brandon Backe*	4.00
107	*P.J. Bevis*	4.00
108	*Jeremy Ward*	4.00
109	*Doug Devore*	4.00
110	Ron Chiavacci	4.00
111	*Ron Calloway*	4.00
112	*Nelson Castro*	4.00
113	Deivis Santos	4.00
114	*Earl Snyder*	4.00
115	*Julio Mateo*	4.00
116	*J.J. Putz*	4.00
117	*Allan Simpson*	4.00
118	*Satoru Komiyama*	4.00
119	*Adam Walker*	4.00
120	*Oliver Perez*	10.00
121	*Clifford Bartosh*	4.00
122	*Todd Donovan*	4.00
123	*Elio Serrano*	4.00
124	*Peter Zamora*	4.00
125	*Mike Gonzalez*	4.00
126	*Travis Hughes*	4.00
127	*Jorge de la Rosa*	4.00
128	*Anastacio Martinez*	4.00
129	*Colin Young*	4.00
130	*Nate Field*	4.00
131	*Tim Kalita*	4.00
132	*Julius Matos*	4.00
133	*Terry Pearson*	4.00
134	*Kyle Kane*	4.00
135	*Mitch Wylie*	4.00
136	*Rodrigo Rosario*	10.00
137	*Franklyn German*	10.00
138	*Reed Johnson*	15.00
139	*Luis Martinez*	10.00
140	*Michael Crudale*	10.00
141	*Francis Beltran*	10.00
142	*Steve Kent*	10.00
143	*Felix Escalona*	10.00
144	*Jose Valverde*	15.00
145	*Victor Alvarez*	10.00
146	*Kazuhisa Ishii/249*	50.00
147	*Jorge Nunez*	10.00
148	*Eric Good*	10.00
149	*Luis Ugueto*	10.00
150	Matt Thornton	10.00
151	*Wilson Valdez*	10.00
152	*Hansel Izquierdo/249*	25.00
153	*Jaime Cerda*	10.00
154	*Mark Corey*	10.00
155	*Tyler Yates*	10.00
156	*Steve Bechler*	10.00
157	*Ben Howard/249*	25.00
158	*Anderson Machado*	15.00
159	*Jorge Padilla*	15.00
160	*Eric Junge*	10.00
161	*Adrian Burnside*	10.00
162	*Josh Hancock*	10.00
163	*Chris Booker*	10.00
164	*Cam Esslinger*	10.00
165	*Rene Reyes*	10.00
166	*Aaron Cook*	10.00
167	*Juan Brito*	10.00
168	*Miguel Ascencio*	10.00
169	*Kevin Frederick*	10.00
170	*Edwin Almonte*	10.00

Limited

Stars (1-90):	5-10X
Cards (91-135):	.5-1X
Cards (136-170):	.5-1X
Production 125 sets	
Golds (1-90):	10-20X
Golds (91-135):	.75-1.5X
Golds (136-170):	.75-1.5X
Production 50 sets	

Chirography

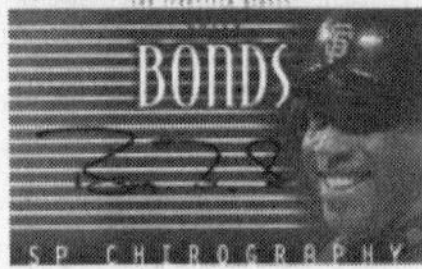

		NM/M
Common Autograph:		10.00
Inserted 1:72		
HB	Hank Blalock/282	25.00
BB	Barry Bonds/112	200.00
BBo	Bret Boone/500	15.00
MB	Milton Bradley/470	15.00
JB	John Buck/427	10.00
MB	Mark Buehrle/438	15.00
SB	Sean Burroughs/275	15.00
AD	Adam Dunn/348	30.00
DE	Darin Erstad/80	15.00
CF	Cliff Floyd/313	10.00
FG	Freddy Garcia/456	15.00
JG	Jason Giambi/244	40.00
TG	Tom Glavine/376	25.00
AG	Alex Graman/418	10.00
KG	Ken Griffey Jr/238	110.00
TG	Tony Gwynn/75	40.00
JL	Jon Lieber/462	15.00
JM	Joe Mays/469	15.00
MM	Mark McGwire/50	300.00
DM	Doug Mientkiewicz/478	15.00
AR	Alex Rodriguez/391	90.00
CS	C.C. Sabathia/442	15.00
RS	Richie Sexson/483	15.00
SS	Sammy Sosa/247	150.00
IS	Ichiro Suzuki/78	300.00
MS	Mike Sweeney/265	15.00
BZ	Barry Zito/419	20.00

Chirography Gold

		NM/M
Common Autograph:		10.00
Quantity produced listed		
HB	Hank Blalock/12	
BB	Barry Bonds/25	
MB	Milton Bradley/24	
JB	John Buck/67	
MB	Mark Buehrle/56	25.00
SB	Sean Burroughs/21	
AD	Adam Dunn/44	40.00
DE	Darin Erstad/17	
CF	Cliff Floyd/30	20.00
FG	Freddy Garcia/34	35.00
JG	Jason Giambi/25	
TG	Tom Glavine/47	50.00
AG	Alex Graman/76	15.00
KG	Ken Griffey Jr/30	200.00
JL	Jon Lieber/32	20.00
JM	Joe Mays/25	
MM	Mark McGwire/25	
DM	Doug Mientkiewicz/16	
AR	Alex Rodriguez/3	
CS	C.C. Sabathia/52	20.00
RS	Richie Sexson/11	
SS	Sammy Sosa/21	
IS	Ichiro Suzuki/51	
MS	Mike Sweeney/29	40.00
BZ	Barry Zito/75	25.00

Excellence

		NM/M
Production 25		
AE-1	Ken Griffey Jr., Sammy Sosa, Cal Ripken Jr., Jason Giambi, Mark McGwire, Ichiro Suzuki	1,500

Future USA Watch

		NM/M
Common Player:		4.00
Production 1,999 sets		
USA1	Chad Cordero	5.00
USA2	Philip Humber	10.00
USA3	Grant Johnson	5.00
USA4	Wes Littleton	5.00
USA5	Kyle Sleeth	15.00
USA6	Huston Street	15.00
USA7	Brad Sullivan	5.00
USA8	Bob Zimmermann	5.00
USA9	Abe Alvarez	5.00
USA10	Kyle Bakker	5.00
USA11	Landon Powell	8.00
USA12	Clint Sammons	5.00
USA13	Michael Aubrey	25.00
USA14	Aaron Hill	15.00
USA15	Conor Jackson	25.00
USA16	Eric Patterson	5.00
USA17	Dustin Pedroia	15.00
USA18	Rickie Weeks	50.00
USA19	Shane Costa	5.00
USA20	Mark Jurich	5.00
USA21	Sam Fuld	5.00
USA22	Carlos Quentin	20.00

Game Jerseys

		NM/M
Common Player:		5.00
Inserted 1:24		
RA	Roberto Alomar	8.00
JB	Jeff Bagwell	10.00
JB	Jeromy Burnitz/SP	5.00
RC	Roger Clemens	15.00
CD	Carlos Delgado	6.00
JE	Jim Edmonds	8.00
DE	Darin Erstad	8.00
JGi	Jason Giambi	8.00
JGo	Juan Gonzalez	8.00
SG	Shawn Green	6.00
KG	Ken Griffey Jr/95	40.00
TH	Todd Helton	8.00
KI	Kazuhisa Ishii	10.00
RJ	Randy Johnson	10.00
AJ	Andruw Jones	8.00
CJ	Chipper Jones	10.00
JK	Jason Kendall	5.00
GM	Greg Maddux	10.00
MM	Mark McGwire/SP	100.00
MO	Magglio Ordonez	8.00
AP	Andy Pettitte	10.00
MP	Mike Piazza	15.00
MR	Manny Ramirez	10.00
AR	Alex Rodriguez	15.00
IR	Ivan Rodriguez	8.00
SR	Scott Rolen	10.00
CC	C.C. Sabathia	5.00
CS	Curt Schilling	10.00
GS	Gary Sheffield	6.00
TS	Tsuyoshi Shinjo	5.00
SS	Sammy Sosa	15.00
IS	Ichiro Suzuki/SP	50.00
JT	Jim Thome	10.00
RV	Robin Ventura	5.00
OV	Omar Vizquel	5.00
BW	Bernie Williams	8.00
PW	Preston Wilson	5.00
BZ	Barry Zito	6.00

Game Jersey Gold

		NM/M
Quantity produced listed		
KG	Ken Griffey Jr./30	65.00
RJ	Randy Johnson/51	25.00
GM	Greg Maddux/31	50.00
MO	Magglio Ordonez/30	15.00
AP	Andy Pettitte/46	20.00
MP	Mike Piazza/31	50.00
CC	C.C. Sabathia/52	10.00
CS	Curt Schilling/38	30.00
IS	Ichiro Suzuki/51	85.00
BW	Bernie Williams/51	20.00
PW	Preston Wilson/44	10.00
BZ	Barry Zito/75	10.00

Prospect Signatures

		NM/M
Common Autograph:		5.00
Inserted 1:36		
JC	Jose Cueto	5.00
JDe	Jeff Deardorff	5.00
JDi	Jose Diaz	8.00
AG	Alex Graman	8.00
MG	Matt Guerrier	5.00
BH	Bill Hall	6.00
KH	Ken Huckaby	5.00
DM	Dustan Mohr	5.00
XN	Xavier Nady	8.00
MS	Marco Scutaro	5.00
ST	Steve Torrealba	6.00
DW	Danny Wright	5.00

Signed SP Big Mac

		NM/M
Quantity signed listed		
MM1	Mark McGwire/1	
MM2	Mark McGwire/25	
MM3	Mark McGwire/5	
MM4	Mark McGwire/4	
MM5	Mark McGwire/12	
MM6	Mark McGwire/70	250.00
MM7	Mark McGwire/4	
MM8	Mark McGwire/7	
MM9	Mark McGwire/5	
MM10	Mark McGwire/16	

2002 SP LEGENDARY CUTS

	NM/M
Complete Set (90):	30.00
Common Player:	.40
Pack (4):	10.00
Box (12):	100.00

1	Al Kaline	.75
2	Alvin Dark	.40
3	Andre Dawson	.75
4	Babe Ruth	3.00
5	Ernie Banks	1.00
6	Bob Lemon	.40
7	Bobby Bonds	.40
8	Carl Erskine	.40
9	Carl Hubbell	.40
10	Casey Stengel	.40
11	Charlie Gehringer	.40
12	Christy Mathewson	.60
13	Dale Murphy	.75
14	Dave Concepcion	.40
15	Dave Parker	.40
16	Dazzy Vance	.40
17	Dizzy Dean	.75
18	Don Baylor	.40
19	Don Drysdale	.75
20	Duke Snider	1.00
21	Earl Averill	.40
22	Early Wynn	.40
23	Edd Roush	.40
24	Elston Howard	.40
25	Ferguson Jenkins	.75
26	Frank Crosetti	.40
27	Frankie Frisch	.40
28	Gaylord Perry	.40
29	George Foster	.40
30	George Kell	.40
31	Gil Hodges	.75
32	Hank Greenberg	.75
33	Phil Niekro	.40
34	Harvey Haddix	.40
35	Harvey Kuenn	.40
36	Honus Wagner	1.50
37	Jackie Robinson	2.00
38	Orlando Cepeda	.40
39	Joe Adcock	.40
40	Joe Cronin	.40
41	Joe DiMaggio	2.50
42	Joe Morgan	.75
43	Johnny Mize	.40
44	Lefty Gomez	.75
45	Lefty Grove	.40
46	Jim Palmer	.75
47	Lou Boudreau	.40
48	Lou Gehrig	2.50
49	Luke Appling	.40
50	Mark McGwire	2.50
51	Mel Ott	.75
52	Mickey Cochrane	.40
53	Mickey Mantle	3.00
54	Minnie Minoso	.40
55	Brooks Robinson	.75
56	Nellie Fox	.40
57	Nolan Ryan	3.00
58	Rollie Fingers	.40
59	Pee Wee Reese	.40
60	Phil Rizzuto	.75
61	Ralph Kiner	.75
62	Ray Dandridge	.40
63	Richie Ashburn	.40
64	Robin Yount	.75
65	Rocky Colavito	.40
66	Roger Maris	2.00
67	Rogers Hornsby	.75
68	Ron Santo	.40
69	Ryne Sandberg	1.00
70	Stan Musial	1.50
71	Sam McDowell	.40
72	Satchel Paige	.75
73	Willie McCovey	.40
74	Steve Garvey	.40
75	Ted Kluszewski	.40
76	Catfish Hunter	.40
77	Terry Moore	.40
78	Thurman Munson	1.00
79	Tom Seaver	.75
80	Tommy John	.40
81	Tony Gwynn	1.00
82	Tony Kubek	.40
83	Tony Lazzeri	.40
84	Ty Cobb	1.50
85	Wade Boggs	1.00
86	Waite Hoyt	.40
87	Walter Johnson	1.00
88	Willie Stargell	.75
89	Yogi Berra	1.00
90	Zack Wheat	.40

Bat

NM/M

Common Player: 6.00
Inserted 1:8

DBa	Don Baylor	6.00
YBe	Yogi Berra/SP	20.00
BBo	Bobby Bonds	6.00
RCo	Rocky Colavito	12.00

ADa	Alvin Dark	6.00
AnD	Andre Dawson	8.00
GFo	George Foster	6.00
NFo	Nellie Fox	15.00
SGa	Steve Garvey	6.00
HGr	Hank Greenberg/SP	35.00
LGr	Lefty Grove	15.00
TGw	Tony Gwynn	12.00
EHo	Elston Howard	10.00
GKe	George Kell	8.00
RKi	Ralph Kiner	10.00
TKu	Tonk (Tony) Kubek	8.00
TLa	Tony Lazzeri	10.00
MMa	Mickey Mantle/SP	110.00
RMa	Roger Maris	50.00
MMc	Mark McGwire	60.00
JMi	Johnny Mize	12.00
TMu	Thurman Munson	25.00
DMu	Dale Murphy	10.00
DPa	Dave Parker	6.00
GPe	Gaylord Perry	8.00
PWe	Pee Wee Reese	10.00
CRi	Cal Ripken Jr.	25.00
JaR	Jackie Robinson	40.00
BRu	Babe Ruth/SP	150.00
NRy	Nolan Ryan	25.00
RSa	Ryne Sandberg	12.00
TSe	Tom Seaver/SP	15.00
DSn	Duke Snider	12.00
WSt	Willie Stargell	8.00
RYo	Robin Yount	10.00
EWy	Early Wynn	8.00

Bat Barrel

NM/M

Many not priced due to scarcity

BB-ADa	Alvin Dark/4	800.00
BB-AnD	Andre Dawson/4	750.00
BB-GFo	George Foster/5	250.00
BB-LGr	Lefty Grove/1 (8/03 auction)	10,000
BB-TGw	Tony Gwynn/11	650.00
BB-MMa	Mickey Mantle/7 (8/04 auction)	3,000
BB-MMc	Mark McGwire/4	2,000
BB-JMi	Johnny Mize/2	1,275
BB-DMu	Dale Murphy/3	600.00
BB-PWe	Pee Wee Reese/4	1,500
BB-BRu	Babe Ruth/3 (8/05 auction)	9,500
BB-NRy	Nolan Ryan/9	1,500
BB-RSa	Ryne Sandberg/3	2,250
BB-DSn	Duke Snider/2	1,500
BB-RYo	Robin Yount/8	750.00

Swatches

NM/M

Common Player: 6.00
Inserted 1:24

DBa	Don Baylor	6.00
WBo	Wade Boggs	8.00
FCr	Frank Crosetti	8.00
DDr	Don Drysdale	20.00
CEr	Carl Erskine	8.00
TGw	Tony Gwynn	10.00
FJe	Ferguson Jenkins	8.00
TJo	Tommy John	6.00
SMc	Sam McDowell	6.00
MMi	Minnie Minoso	8.00
JMo	Joe Morgan	8.00
MOt	Mel Ott	25.00
DPa	Dave Parker	6.00
CRj	Cal Ripken Jr.	25.00
RSa	Ron Santo	10.00

Jersey

NM/M

Common Player: 6.00
Inserted 1:24

DBa	Don Baylor	6.00
YBe	Yogi Berra	20.00
BBo	Bobby Bonds	6.00
FCr	Frank Crosetti	10.00
AnD	Andre Dawson	8.00
GFo	George Foster	6.00
SGa	Steve Garvey	8.00
MMa	Mickey Mantle	100.00
RMa	Roger Maris	40.00
DPa	Dave Parker	6.00
PWe	Pee Wee Reese	12.00
JRo	Jackie Robinson	45.00
NRy	Nolan Ryan	30.00
RSa	Ryne Sandberg	25.00
TSe	Tom Seaver	10.00

Signatures

NM/M

Quantity signed listed

JAd	Joe Adcock/48	145.00
LAp	Luke Appling/53	150.00
RAs	Richie Ashburn/10	550.00
EAv	Earl Averill/22	275.00
JBe	Johnny Berardino/12	450.00
LBo	Lou Boudreau/85	120.00
GBu	Guy Bush/38	125.00
GCa	George Case/36	180.00
HCh	Happy Chandler/96	95.00
SCh	Spud Chandler/17	350.00
TyC	Ty Cobb/2	5,500
MCo	Mickey Cochrane/2	5,000
JCo	Johnny Cooney/64	75.00
SCo	Stan Coveleski/85	150.00
JCr	Joe Cronin/185	120.00
BDa	Babe Dahlgren/51	180.00
RDa	Ray Dandridge/179	85.00
DDe	Dizzy Dean/4	2,000
JDi	Joe DiMaggio/103	175.00
DDo	Dick Donovan/23	200.00
TDo	Taylor Douthit/60	165.00
DDr	Don Drysdale/14	650.00
JDu	Joe Dugan/39	140.00
BFa	Bibb Falk/44	150.00
RFe	Rick Ferrell/19	225.00
NFo	Nellie Fox/1 (12/02 auction)	3,100
FoF	Ford Frick/1 (10/03 auction)	4,000
FFr	Frankie Frisch/35	
LGe	Lou Gehrig/3 (6/04 auction)	7,500
CGe	Charlie Gehringer/3	700.00
LGo	Lefty Gomez/3	750.00
BGo	Billy Goodman/53	140.00
HGr	Hank Greenberg/94	425.00
LGr	Lefty Grove/190	240.00
SHa	Stan Hack/36	200.00
HHa	Harvey Haddix/37	250.00
BHa	Buddy Hassett/56	200.00
WHo	Waite Hoyt/62	250.00
CHu	Carl Hubbell/17	475.00
LJa	Larry Jackson/37	125.00
NJa	Newton "Bucky" Jacobs/44	150.00
EJo	Earl Johnson/31	200.00
JJo	Judy Johnson/86	150.00
WJo	Walter Johnson/20	2,000
BKa	Bob Kahle/53	150.00
WKa	Willie Kamm/57	110.00
CKe	Charlie Keller/29	280.00
KKe	Ken Keltner/11	415.00
TKl	Ted Kluszewski/23	300.00
MKo	Mark Koenig/22	260.00
HKu	Harvey Kuenn/23	230.00
CLa	Cookie Lavagetto/22	200.00
BiL	Billy Lee/40	150.00
BoL	Bob Lemon/91	110.00
ELo	Ed Lopat/58	150.00
SMa	Sal Maglie/29	200.00
HMa	Hank Majeski/21	300.00
MMa	Mickey Mantle/2 (10/04 auction)	6,000
RMa	Roger Maris/1	
ChrM	Christy Mathewson/2 (5/03 auction)	2,000
RMc	Roy McMillan/18	250.00
JMi	Johnny Mize/3	2,500
JMo	Johnny Moore/22	250.00
TMo	Terry Moore/86	95.00
ChM	Chet Morgan/27	185.00
HNe	Hal Newhouser/81	135.00
GPi	George Pipgras/34	
VRa	Vic Raschi/98	110.00
PWe	Pee Wee Reese/23	450.00
PRe	Pete Reiser/73	140.00
RRe	Rip Repulski/19	275.00
LRi	Lance Richbourg/3	1,800
ORo	Oscar Roettger/9	700.00
ERo	Edd Roush/101	100.00
ERo2	Edd Roush/99	100.00
BRu	Babe Ruth/3 (6/04 auction)	12,500
BSc	Bob Scheffing/19	200.00
WSc	Willard Schmidt/10	350.00
HSc	Hal Schumacher/17	300.00
BSe	Bill Serena/16	275.00
JSe	Joe Sewell/136	125.00
LSe	Luke Sewell/2	
BSh	Bob Shawkey/10	120.00
BSh	Bill Sherdel/10	450.00
BSz	Bill Shantz/17	300.00
WSt	Willie Stargell/153	95.00
CSt	Casey Stengel/8	750.00
DVa	Dazzy Vance/5	
BVe	Bill Veeck/11	500.00
HWa	Honus Wagner/6 (2/05 auction)	5,000
BWa	Bucky Walters/31	165.00
VWe	Vic Wertz/17	300.00
ZWh	Zack Wheat/127	150.00
PWi	Pete Whisenant/13	300.00
EWy	Early Wynn/4	1,650

2002 SPX

NM/M

Common Player: .25
Common SP (91-120): 4.00
Production 1,800
Common SP Auto. (121-150): 10.00
Common Star Swatch (151-190): 5.00
Production 800
Pack (4): 4.00
Box (18): 60.00

1	Troy Glaus	.75
2	Darin Erstad	.40
3	David Justice	.25
4	Tim Hudson	.35
5	Miguel Tejada	.35
6	Barry Zito	.25
7	Carlos Delgado	.50
8	Shannon Stewart	.25
9	Greg Vaughn	.25
10	Toby Hall	.25
11	Jim Thome	.65
12	C.C. Sabathia	.25
13	Ichiro Suzuki	2.00
14	Edgar Martinez	.25
15	Freddy Garcia	.25
16	Mike Cameron	.25
17	Jeff Conine	.25
18	Tony Batista	.25
19	Alex Rodriguez	2.00
20	Rafael Palmeiro	.65
21	Ivan Rodriguez	.65
22	Carl Everett	.25
23	Pedro J. Martinez	.75
24	Manny Ramirez	.75
25	Nomar Garciaparra	1.50
26	Johnny Damon	.35
27	Mike Sweeney	.25
28	Carlos Beltran	.50
29	Dmitri Young	.25
30	Joe Mays	.25
31	Doug Mientkiewicz	.25
32	Cristian Guzman	.25
33	Corey Koskie	.25
34	Frank Thomas	.75

35 Magglio Ordonez .25
36 Mark Buehrle .25
37 Bernie Williams .35
38 Roger Clemens 1.25
39 Derek Jeter 2.50
40 Jason Giambi .50
41 Mike Mussina .45
42 Lance Berkman .25
43 Jeff Bagwell .75
44 Roy Oswalt .25
45 Greg Maddux 1.00
46 Chipper Jones 1.00
47 Andruw Jones .75
48 Gary Sheffield .40
49 Geoff Jenkins .25
50 Richie Sexson .25
51 Ben Sheets .25
52 Albert Pujols 2.00
53 J.D. Drew .40
54 Jim Edmonds .25
55 Sammy Sosa 1.50
56 Moises Alou .25
57 Kerry Wood .65
58 Jon Lieber .25
59 Fred McGriff .25
60 Randy Johnson .75
61 Luis Gonzalez .35
62 Curt Schilling .50
63 Kevin Brown .25
64 Hideo Nomo .75
65 Shawn Green .50
66 Vladimir Guerrero .75
67 Jose Vidro .25
68 Barry Bonds 2.50
69 Jeff Kent .25
70 Rich Aurilia .25
71 Cliff Floyd .25
72 Josh Beckett .35
73 Preston Wilson .25
74 Mike Piazza 1.50
75 Mo Vaughn .25
76 Jeromy Burnitz .25
77 Roberto Alomar .45
78 Phil Nevin .25
79 Ryan Klesko .25
80 Scott Rolen .65
81 Bobby Abreu .25
82 Jimmy Rollins .25
83 Brian Giles .25
84 Aramis Ramirez .25
85 Ken Griffey Jr. 1.50
86 Sean Casey .35
87 Barry Larkin .25
88 Mike Hampton .25
89 Larry Walker .25
90 Todd Helton .75
91 *Ron Calloway* 4.00
92 *Joe Orloski* 4.00
93 *Anderson Machado* 6.00
94 *Eric Good* 4.00
95 *Reed Johnson* 8.00
96 *Brendan Donnelly* 4.00
97 *Chris Baker* 4.00
98 *Wilson Valdez* 4.00
99 *Scotty Layfield* 4.00
100 *P.J. Bevis* 4.00
101 *Edwin Almonte* 4.00
102 *Francis Beltran* 4.00
103 Valentino Pasucci 4.00
104 *Nelson Castro* 4.00
105 *Michael Crudale* 4.00
106 *Colin Young* 4.00
107 *Todd Donovan* 4.00
108 *Felix Escalona* 4.00
109 *Brandon Backe* 4.00
110 *Corey Thurman* 4.00
111 *Kyle Kane* 4.00
112 *Allan Simpson* 4.00
113 *Jose Valverde* 4.00
114 *Chris Booker* 4.00
115 *Brandon Puffer* 4.00
116 *John Foster* 4.00
117 *Clifford Bartosh* 4.00
118 *Gustavo Chacin* 4.00
119 *Steve Kent* 4.00
120 *Nate Field* 4.00
121 *Victor Alvarez* 10.00
122 *Steve Bechler* 10.00
123 *Adrian Burnside* 10.00
124 Marlon Byrd 15.00
125 *Jaime Cerda* 10.00
126 Brandon Claussen 10.00
127 *Mark Corey* 10.00
128 *Doug Devore* 10.00
129 *Kazuhisa Ishii* 80.00
130 *John Ennis* 10.00
131 *Kevin Frederick* 10.00
132 *Josh Hancock* 10.00
133 *Ben Howard* 10.00
134 Orlando Hudson 10.00
135 *Hansel Izquierdo* 10.00
136 *Eric Junge* 10.00
137 Austin Kearns 20.00
138 Victor Martinez 35.00
139 *Luis Martinez* 10.00
140 *Danny Mota* 10.00
141 *Jorge Padilla* 10.00
142 *Andy Pratt* 10.00
143 *Rene Reyes* 10.00
144 *Rodrigo Rosario* 10.00
145 *Tom Shearn* 10.00
146 *So Taguchi* 30.00
147 Dennis Tankersley 15.00
148 Matt Thornton 10.00
149 *Jeremy Ward* 10.00
150 *Mitch Wylie* 10.00
151 Pedro Martinez 8.00
152 Cal Ripken Jr. 30.00
153 Roger Clemens 15.00
154 Bernie Williams 6.00
155 Jason Giambi 8.00
156 Robin Ventura 5.00
157 Carlos Delgado 5.00
158 Frank Thomas 8.00
159 Magglio Ordonez 5.00
160 Jim Thome 10.00
161 Darin Erstad 5.00
162 Tim Salmon 5.00
163 Tim Hudson 5.00
164 Barry Zito 5.00
165 Ichiro Suzuki 35.00
166 Edgar Martinez 8.00
167 Alex Rodriguez 15.00
168 Ivan Rodriguez 8.00
169 Juan Gonzalez 8.00
170 Greg Maddux 10.00
171 Chipper Jones 10.00
172 Andruw Jones 8.00
173 Tom Glavine 6.00
174 Mike Piazza 15.00
175 Roberto Alomar 8.00
176 Scott Rolen 10.00
177 Sammy Sosa 15.00
178 Moises Alou 8.00
179 Ken Griffey Jr. 15.00
180 Jeff Bagwell 8.00
181 Jim Edmonds 6.00
182 J.D. Drew 5.00
183 Brian Giles 5.00
184 Randy Johnson 10.00
185 Curt Schilling 8.00
186 Luis Gonzalez 5.00
187 Todd Helton 8.00
188 Shawn Green 5.00
189 David Wells 5.00
190 Jeff Kent 5.00

SuperStar Swatch Gold

Jersey (151-190): .75-1.5X
Production 150

SuperStar Swatch Silver

Jersey (151-190): .5-1X
Production 400

Sweet Spot Bat Barrel

No Pricing

Winning Materials Jersey Combo

NM/M
Common Card: 8.00
Inserted 1:18
AR Alex Rodriguez, Ivan Rodriguez 20.00
GC Ken Griffey Jr., Sean Casey/SP 20.00
BR Jeff Bagwell, Alex Rodriguez 15.00
WG Bernie Williams, Jason Giambi 10.00
JS Randy Johnson, Curt Schilling 15.00
MJ Greg Maddux, Chipper Jones 20.00
MC Edgar Martinez, Mike Cameron 10.00
SP Sammy Sosa, Corey Patterson 20.00
ED Jim Edmonds, J.D. Drew 10.00
PA Mike Piazza, Roberto Alomar 15.00
DH Jermaine Dye, Tim Hudson 8.00
RA Scott Rolen, Bobby Abreu 15.00
TO Frank Thomas, Magglio Ordonez 15.00
HW Mike Hampton, Larry Walker 8.00
TS Jim Thome, C.C. Sabathia 15.00
GK Shawn Green, Eric Karros 10.00
KG Jason Kendall, Brian Giles 8.00
WP David Wells, Jorge Posada 10.00
NM Hideo Nomo, Pedro Martinez/SP 20.00
RP Ivan Rodriguez, Chan Ho Park 10.00
LH Al Leiter, Mike Hampton 8.00
BA Jeromy Burnitz, Edgardo Alfonzo 8.00
DS Carlos Delgado, Shannon Stewart 10.00
BG Jeff Bagwell, Juan Gonzalez 10.00
GR Juan Gonzalez, Ivan Rodriguez 10.00
VR Omar Vizquel, Alex Rodriguez 15.00
SE Aaron Sele, Darin Erstad 8.00
JJ Chipper Jones, Andruw Jones 15.00
SH Kazuhiro Sasaki, Shigetoshi Hasegawa 8.00

Winning Materials USA Jersey Combo

NM/M
Common Card: 10.00
Production 150
AH Brent Abernathy, Orlando Hudson 8.00
BT Sean Burroughs, Mark Teixeira 25.00
GB Jason Giambi, Sean Burroughs 20.00
HD Orlando Hudson, Jeff Deardorff 10.00
GT Jason Giambi, Mark Teixeira 20.00
HOU Roy Oswalt, Adam Everett 10.00
HP Dustin Hermanson, Mark Prior 40.00
JC Jacque Jones, Michael Cuddyer 10.00
KB Austin Kearns, Sean Burroughs 15.00
KC Austin Kearns, Michael Cuddyer 15.00
MG Doug Mientkiewicz, Jason Giambi 20.00
MIN Doug Mientkiewicz, Michael Cuddyer 10.00
MO Matt Morris, Roy Oswalt 15.00
MP Matt Morris, Mark Prior 35.00
AW Matt Anderson, Jeff Weaver 10.00
MW Matt Morris, Jeff Weaver 10.00
PB Mark Prior, Dewon Brazelton 30.00
RE Brian Roberts, Adam Everett 10.00
SD Mark Kotsay, Sean Burroughs 10.00
TB Brent Abernathy, Dewon Brazelton 10.00
TP Mark Teixeira, Mark Prior 40.00
WB Jeff Weaver, Dewon Brazelton 10.00
WH Jeff Weaver, Dustin Hermanson 10.00

Winning Materials Base Combo

NM/M
Common Card: 15.00
Production 200
PE Mike Piazza, Jim Edmonds 20.00
RJ Alex Rodriguez, Derek Jeter 40.00
BG Barry Bonds, Shawn Green 20.00
IM Ichiro Suzuki, Edgar Martinez 50.00
SG Sammy Sosa, Luis Gonzalez 25.00
GR Troy Glaus, Alex Rodriguez 20.00
WJ Bernie Williams, Derek Jeter 30.00
GS Ken Griffey Jr., Sammy Sosa 30.00
PI Albert Pujols, Ichiro Suzuki 60.00
SR Kazuhiro Sasaki, Mariano Rivera 20.00

Winning Materials Base/Patch Combo

No Pricing
Production 25 sets

Winning Materials Ball/Patch Combo

No Pricing
Production 25 sets

2003 SP AUTHENTIC

NM/M
Complete Set (189):
Common Player: .25
Common Rk Archives (91-123): 1.00
Production 2,500

Common Back to '93
(124-150): 1.50
Production 1,993
Common Future Watch
(150-180): 4.00
Production 2,003
Pack (5): 3.50
Box (24): 70.00
1 Darin Erstad .40
2 Garret Anderson .40
3 Troy Glaus .40
4 Eric Chavez .40
5 Barry Zito .40
6 Miguel Tejada .50
7 Eric Hinske .25
8 Carlos Delgado .40
9 Josh Phelps .25
10 Ben Grieve .25
11 Carl Crawford .25
12 Omar Vizquel .40
13 Matt Lawton .25
14 C.C. Sabathia .25
15 Ichiro Suzuki 1.50
16 John Olerud .40
17 Freddy Garcia .25
18 Jay Gibbons .25
19 Tony Batista .25
20 Melvin Mora .25
21 Alex Rodriguez 2.00
22 Rafael Palmeiro .50
23 Hank Blalock .50
24 Nomar Garciaparra 1.50
25 Pedro J. Martinez .75
26 Johnny Damon .40
27 Mike Sweeney .25
28 Carlos Febles .25
29 Carlos Beltran .50
30 Carlos Pena .25
31 Eric Munson .25
32 Bobby Higginson .25
33 Torii Hunter .40
34 Doug Mientkiewicz .25
35 Jacque Jones .25
36 Paul Konerko .25
37 Bartolo Colon .25
38 Magglio Ordonez .40
39 Derek Jeter 2.00
40 Bernie Williams .50
41 Jason Giambi .50
42 Alfonso Soriano .75
43 Roger Clemens 1.50
44 Jeff Bagwell .50
45 Jeff Kent .40
46 Lance Berkman .40
47 Chipper Jones .75
48 Andruw Jones .50
49 Gary Sheffield .50
50 Ben Sheets .40
51 Richie Sexson .50
52 Geoff Jenkins .25
53 Jim Edmonds .40
54 Albert Pujols 1.50
55 Scott Rolen .75
56 Sammy Sosa 1.50
57 Kerry Wood .75
58 Eric Karros .25
59 Luis Gonzalez .40
60 Randy Johnson .75
61 Curt Schilling .50
62 Fred McGriff .40
63 Shawn Green .40
64 Paul LoDuca .25
65 Vladimir Guerrero .75
66 Jose Vidro .25
67 Barry Bonds 2.00
68 Rich Aurilia .25
69 Edgardo Alfonzo .25
70 Ivan Rodriguez .50
71 Mike Lowell .40
72 Derrek Lee .40
73 Tom Glavine .50
74 Mike Piazza 1.00
75 Roberto Alomar .50
76 Ryan Klesko .40
77 Phil Nevin .25
78 Mark Kotsay .25
79 Jim Thome .75
80 Pat Burrell .40
81 Bobby Abreu .40
82 Jason Kendall .40
83 Brian Giles .40
84 Aramis Ramirez .40
85 Austin Kearns .40
86 Ken Griffey Jr. 1.00
87 Adam Dunn .50
88 Larry Walker .40
89 Todd Helton .50
90 Preston Wilson .40
91 Derek Jeter 6.00
92 Johnny Damon 1.00
93 Chipper Jones 2.00
94 Manny Ramirez 2.00
95 Trot Nixon 1.00
96 Alex Rodriguez 5.00
97 Chan Ho Park 1.00
98 Brad Fullmer 1.00
99 Billy Wagner 1.00
100 Hideo Nomo 1.50
101 Freddy Garcia 1.00
102 Darin Erstad 1.00
103 Jose Cruz Jr. 1.00
104 Nomar Garciaparra 4.00
105 Magglio Ordonez 1.50
106 Kerry Wood 2.00
107 Troy Glaus 1.50
108 J.D. Drew 1.00
109 Alfonso Soriano 2.00
110 Danys Baez 1.00
111 Kazuhiro Sasaki 1.00
112 Barry Zito 1.50
113 Brent Abernathy 1.00
114 Ben Diggins 1.00
115 Ben Sheets 1.50
116 Brad Wilkerson 1.00
117 Juan Pierre 1.00
118 Jon Rauch 1.00
119 Ichiro Suzuki 4.00
120 Albert Pujols 5.00
121 Mark Prior 2.00
122 Mark Teixeira 1.50
123 Kazuhisa Ishii 1.00
124 Troy Glaus 1.50
125 Randy Johnson 3.00
126 Curt Schilling 2.00
127 Chipper Jones 3.00
128 Greg Maddux 4.00
129 Nomar Garciaparra 4.00
130 Pedro J. Martinez 3.00
131 Sammy Sosa 5.00
132 Mark Prior 3.00
133 Ken Griffey Jr. 4.00
134 Adam Dunn 2.00
135 Jeff Bagwell 2.00
136 Vladimir Guerrero 2.00
137 Mike Piazza 4.00
138 Tom Glavine 1.50
139 Derek Jeter 8.00
140 Roger Clemens 6.00
141 Jason Giambi 2.00
142 Alfonso Soriano 3.00
143 Miguel Tejada 1.50
144 Barry Zito 1.50
145 Jim Thome 2.00
146 Barry Bonds 8.00
147 Ichiro Suzuki 5.00
148 Albert Pujols 6.00
149 Alex Rodriguez 6.00
150 Carlos Delgado 1.50
151 *Richard Fischer* 4.00
152 *Brandon Webb* 10.00
153 *Rob Hammock* 6.00
154 *Matt Kata* 6.00
155 *Tim Olson* 4.00
156 *Oscar Villarreal* 4.00
157 *Michael Hessman* 4.00
158 *Daniel Cabrera* 4.00
159 *Jon Leicester* 4.00
160 *Todd Wellemeyer* 6.00
161 *Felix Sanchez* 6.00
162 *David Sanders* 4.00
163 *Josh Stewart* 4.00
164 *Arnie Munoz* 4.00
165 *Ryan Cameron* 4.00
166 *Clint Barmes* 15.00
167 *Josh Willingham* 6.00
168 .25
169 *Willie Eyre* 4.00
170 *Brent Hoard* 4.00
171 *Terrmel Sledge* 4.00
172 *Phil Seibel* 4.00
173 *Craig Brazell* 8.00
174 *Jeff Duncan* 8.00
175 .25
176 *Bernie Castro* 4.00
177 *Mike Nicolas* 4.00
178 *Rett Johnson* 6.00
179 *Bobby Madritsch* 10.00
180 *Chris Capuano* 4.00
181 *Hideki Matsui/ auto/500* 240.00
181 H. Matsui/Bronze/ auto/75 275.00
181 H. Matsui/Silver/auto/25
181 H. Matsui/Gold/auto/10
182 *Jose Contreras/ auto/500* 35.00
183 *Lew Ford/auto/500* 20.00
184 Jeremy Griffiths/ auto/500 15.00
185 *Guillermo Quiroz/ auto/500* 20.00
186 *Alejandro Machado/ auto/500* 10.00
187 *Francisco Cruceta/ auto/500* 15.00
188 *Prentice Redman/ auto/500* 15.00
189 *Shane Bazzell/ auto/500* 15.00

500 Home Run Club

NM/M

Production 25
500HR Ted Williams, Barry Bonds, Mark McGwire, Sammy Sosa, Mickey Mantle 325.00

Chirography

NM/M

Common Autograph: 10.00
Varying quantities produced
Bronze Autos: 1X
Production 100
Silver Autos: 1-1.5X
Production 50
Gold Autos: No Pricing
Production 10
GA1 Garret Anderson/245 15.00
BA Jeff Bagwell/175 50.00
JD Johnny Damon/245 15.00
AD Adam Dunn/170 30.00
JE2 Jim Edmonds/350 20.00
FL Cliff Floyd/125 12.00
FC Rafael Furcal/150 15.00
FG Freddy Garcia/345 15.00
GI Jason Giambi/250 15.00
GL Brian Giles/225 15.00
LG1 Luis Gonzalez/195 15.00
GJ Ken Griffey Jr./350 85.00
JR Ken Griffey Jr./350 85.00
TO Torii Hunter/245 15.00
KE Jason Kendall/145 10.00
MM Mark McGwire/50 275.00
MP Mark Prior/150 70.00
CR Cal Ripken Jr./250 100.00
RO Scott Rolen/345 35.00
TS Tim Salmon/350 20.00
RS Richie Sexson/245 15.00
SA Sammy Sosa/335 125.00
SO Sammy Sosa/335 125.00
IC Ichiro Suzuki/85 350.00
IS Ichiro Suzuki/75 350.00
SW Mike Sweeney/125 15.00
JT1 Jim Thome/250 35.00

Chirography Dodger Stars

NM/M

Common Autograph: 8.00
Bronze Autos: 1X
Production 100
Silver Autos: 1-1.5X
Production 50
Gold Autos: No Pricing
Production 10
BB Bill Buckner/245 10.00
CE Ron Cey/345 15.00
SG Steve Garvey/320 20.00
JN Tommy John/170 15.00
DL Davey Lopes/245 8.00
DN Don Newcombe/345 15.00
BI Bill Russell/245 15.00
DS Duke Snider/345 30.00
SU Don Sutton/245 15.00
MW Maury Wills/320 10.00
SY Steve Yeager/345 15.00

Chirography Double

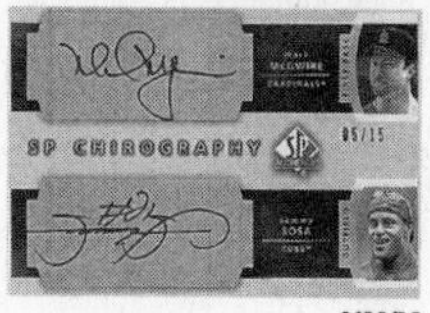

NM/M

Common Duo Auto: 40.00
FB Yogi Berra, Whitey Ford/75 150.00
FE Carlton Fisk, Dwight Evans/75 65.00
FM Carlton Fisk, Bill Mazeroski/75 40.00
GG Jason Giambi, Ken Griffey Jr. 125.00
GR Steve Garvey, Ron Cey/75 50.00
JI Ken Griffey Jr., Ichiro Suzuki 350.00
KR Tony Kubek, Bobby Richardson/75 80.00
KT Tom Seaver, Jerry Koosman/75 80.00
MG Don Mattingly, Jason Giambi/25 150.00
MS Mark McGwire, Sammy Sosa/15 725.00
SJ Sammy Sosa, Jason Giambi/25 175.00
WB Bill Buckner, Mookie Wilson/150 40.00

Chirography Flash Backs

NM/M

Common Autograph: 8.00
Bronze Autos: 1X
Production 100
Silver Autos: 1-1.5X
Production 50
Gold Autos: No Pricing
No Pricing
JE1 Jim Edmonds/350 15.00
CF1 Cliff Floyd/350 8.00
JA Jason Giambi/350 15.00
BN Brian Giles/245 15.00
LA Luis Gonzalez/200 15.00
GM Ken Griffey Jr./350 80.00
MA Mark McGwire/55 280.00
SR Sammy Sosa/245 125.00

Chirography Hall of Famers

NM/M

Common Autograph: 15.00
Bronze Autos: 1X
Production 100
Silver Autos: 1-1.5x
Production 50
Gold Autos: No Pricing
Production 10
JB1 Johnny Bench/350 40.00
GC1 Gary Carter/350 20.00
OC Orlando Cepeda/245 20.00
RF Rollie Fingers/170 15.00
CF Carlton Fisk/240 35.00
WF Whitey Ford/150 40.00
BG Bob Gibson/245 35.00
TP Tony Perez/320 20.00
RR Robin Roberts/170 30.00
NR Nolan Ryan/170 140.00
TS Tom Seaver/170 40.00
DS Duke Snider/250 30.00
DW2 Dave Winfield/350 25.00

Chirography Triple

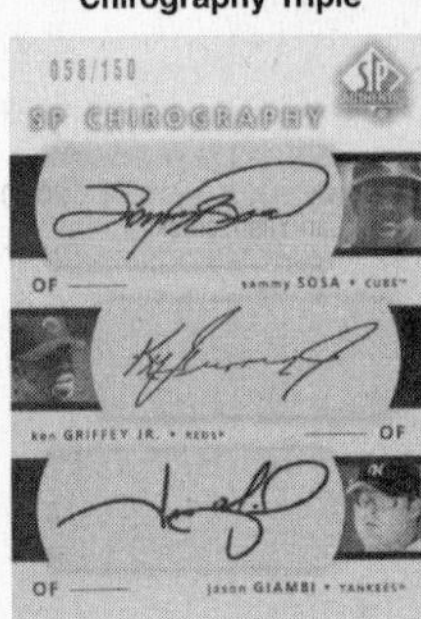

NM/M

Quantity produced listed
BKR Bobby Richardson, Yogi Berra, Tony Kubek/75 120.00
FCG Carlton Fisk, Gary Carter, Kirk Gibson/75 75.00
GIS Sammy Sosa, Ichiro Suzuki, Ken Griffey Jr./75 400.00
GLC Davey Lopes, Ron Cey, Steve Garvey/75 65.00
GRC Steve Garvey, Ron Cey, Bill Russell/75 60.00
GSG Sammy Sosa, Jason Giambi, Ken Griffey Jr./75 250.00
GSJ Ken Griffey Jr., Jason Giambi, Sammy Sosa/75 250.00
ISG Sammy Sosa, Jason Giambi, Ichiro Suzuki/75 300.00
MSG Ken Griffey Jr., Sammy Sosa, Mark McGwire/10 1,300
MSI Mark McGwire, Sammy Sosa, Ichiro Suzuki/10
SEA Tim Salmon, Garret Anderson, Darin Erstad/75 100.00
SKM Tom Seaver, Tug McGraw, Jerry Koosman/75 125.00

Chirography World Series Heroes

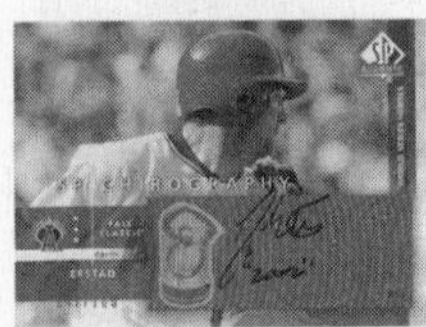

NM/M

Common Autograph: 10.00
Bronze Autos: 1X
Production 100
Silver Autos: 1-1.5X
Production 50
Gold Autos: No Pricing
Production 10
GA Garret Anderson/245 15.00
GC Gary Carter/345 20.00
DE Darin Erstad/245 15.00
CF Carlton Fisk/200 40.00
KG Kirk Gibson/145 15.00
GO Luis Gonzalez/225 15.00
GS Ken Griffey Sr/295 10.00
AJ1 Andruw Jones/350 20.00
DJ David Justice/170 20.00
JK Jerry Koosman/170 15.00
BM Bill Mazeroski/245 20.00
TM Tug McGraw/170 15.00
JP Jorge Posada/350 35.00
ER Edgar Renteria/220 15.00
CR Cal Ripken Jr./295 100.00
TI Tim Salmon/245 15.00
CS Curt Schilling/345 30.00

Chirography Yankee Stars

NM/M

Common Autograph: 8.00
Bronze Autos: 1X
Production 100
Silver Autos: 1-1.5X
Production 50
Gold Autos: No Pricing
Production 10
YB Yogi Berra/320 35.00
JB Jim Bouton/345 10.00
RC Roger Clemens/210 100.00
JG Jason Giambi/275 15.00
KS Ken Griffey Sr/350 10.00
TH Tommy Henrich/345 15.00
HK Ralph Houk/245 12.00
TJ Tommy John/245 15.00
TK Tony Kubek/345 20.00
SL Sparky Lyle/345 8.00
DM Don Mattingly/295 60.00
BR Bobby Richardson/320 20.00
ST Mel Stottlemyre/345 10.00
DW1 Dave Winfield/350 25.00

Chirography Young Stars

NM/M

Common Autograph: 6.00
Bronze Autos: 1X
Production 100
Silver Autos: 1-1.5X
Production 50
Gold Autos: No Pricing
Production 10
HB Hank Blalock/245 25.00
BO Joe Borchard/245 8.00
SB Sean Burroughs/245 15.00
MB Marlon Byrd/245 8.00
HC Hee Seop Choi/245 40.00
DI1 Ben Diggins/350 8.00
DH Drew Henson/245 25.00
EH Eric Hinske/245 10.00
OH Orlando Hudson/245 8.00
JJ Jacque Jones/245 15.00
JJ1 Jimmy Journell/350 10.00
JL Jason Lane/245 6.00
JO Joe Mays/245 6.00
MI Doug Mientkiewicz/245 15.00
MY Brett Myers/245 10.00
CP Corey Patterson/245 15.00
PE Carlos Pena/245 8.00
OP Oliver Perez/245 10.00
JP Josh Phelps/245 8.00
BP1 Brandon Phillips/350 8.00
AP A.J. Pierzynski/245 15.00
FS1 Freddy Sanchez/350 15.00
TX Mark Teixeira/245 25.00
BZ Barry Zito/350 20.00

Splendid Jerseys

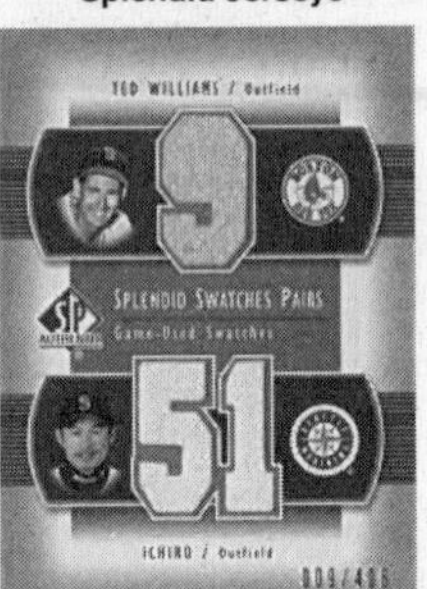

NM/M

Production 406 sets
TW Mickey Mantle, Ted Williams 180.00
SJ-TW Ted Williams 100.00
TW-IS Ted Williams, Ichiro Suzuki 100.00
TW-JG Ted Williams, Jason Giambi 60.00
TW-KG Ted Williams, Ken Griffey Jr. 75.00
TW-MM Mark McGwire, Ted Williams 110.00
TW-SS Ted Williams, Sammy Sosa 80.00
TW-NM1 Ted Williams, Nomar Garciaparra 80.00
TW-NM2 Nomar Garciaparra, Ted Williams 80.00

Splendid Signatures

NM/M

Hand Numbered to 5 or 3
GA Nomar Garciaparra/406 100.00
TW-NM3 Ted Williams, Nomar Garciaparra/3 (10/03 auction) 2,400

Simply Splendid

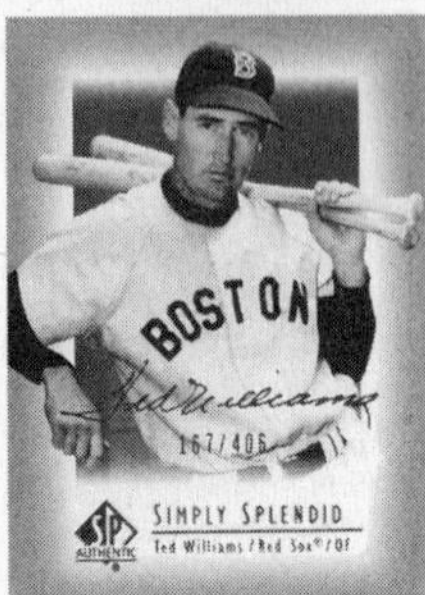

NM/M

Complete Set (30): 200.00
Common Williams: 8.00
Production 406 sets

Superstar Flashback

NM/M

Complete Set (60): 65.00
Common Player: 1.00
Production 2,003 sets
SF1 Tim Salmon 1.00
SF2 Darin Erstad 1.00
SF3 Troy Glaus 1.50
SF4 Randy Johnson 2.00
SF5 Curt Schilling 1.50
SF6 Steve Finley 1.00
SF7 Greg Maddux 3.00
SF8 Chipper Jones 3.00
SF9 Andruw Jones 1.50
SF10 Gary Sheffield 1.00
SF11 Manny Ramirez 2.00
SF12 Pedro J. Martinez 2.00
SF13 Nomar Garciaparra 4.00
SF14 Sammy Sosa 3.00
SF15 Frank Thomas 1.50
SF16 Kerry Wood 1.50
SF17 Paul Konerko 1.00
SF18 Corey Patterson 1.00
SF19 Mark Prior 2.50
SF20 Ken Griffey Jr. 3.00
SF21 Adam Dunn 1.50
SF22 Larry Walker 1.00
SF23 Preston Wilson 1.00
SF24 Todd Helton 1.50
SF25 Ivan Rodriguez 1.50
SF26 Josh Beckett 1.00
SF27 Jeff Bagwell 1.50
SF28 Jeff Kent 1.00
SF29 Lance Berkman 1.00
SF30 Carlos Beltran 1.50
SF31 Shawn Green 1.00
SF32 Richie Sexson 1.00
SF33 Vladimir Guerrero 1.50
SF34 Mike Piazza 4.00
SF35 Roberto Alomar 1.50
SF36 Roger Clemens 4.00
SF37 Derek Jeter 6.00
SF38 Jason Giambi 1.50
SF39 Bernie Williams 1.50
SF40 Nick Johnson 1.00
SF41 Alfonso Soriano 3.00
SF42 Miguel Tejada 1.00
SF43 Eric Chavez 1.00
SF44 Barry Zito 1.50
SF45 Jim Thome 1.50
SF46 Pat Burrell 1.00
SF47 Marlon Byrd 1.00
SF48 Jason Kendall 1.00
SF49 Aramis Ramirez 1.50
SF50 Brian Giles 1.00
SF51 Phil Nevin 1.00
SF52 Barry Bonds 6.00
SF53 Ichiro Suzuki 3.00
SF54 Scott Rolen 2.00
SF55 J.D. Drew 1.00
SF56 Albert Pujols 4.00
SF57 Mark Teixeira 1.50
SF58 Hank Blalock 2.00
SF59 Carlos Delgado 1.50
SF60 Roy Halladay 1.00

2003 SP LEGENDARY CUTS

NM/M

Complete Set (130):
Common Player: .25
Common SP: 3.00
Production 1,299
Pack (4): 8.00
Box (12): 85.00
1 Luis Aparicio .25
2 Al Barlick .25
3 Al Lopez .25
4 Ernie Banks 1.00
5 Alexander Cartwright .25
6 Lou Brock .50
7 Babe Ruth/SP 10.00
8 Bill Dickey .50
9 Bill Mazeroski .25
10 Bob Feller .50
11 Billy Herman .25
12 Billy Williams .25
13 Bob Gibson/SP 4.00
14 Bob Lemon .25
15 Bobby Doerr .25
16 Branch Rickey .25
17 Gary Carter .50
18 Burleigh Grimes .25
19 Cap Anson .25
20 Carl Hubbell .25
21 Carlton Fisk .50
22 Casey Stengel .25
23 Charlie Gehringer .25
24 Chief Bender .25
25 Christy Mathewson/SP 5.00
26 Cy Young 1.00
27 Dave Winfield .50
28 Dazzy Vance .25
29 Dizzy Dean/SP 4.00
30 Don Drysdale/SP 4.00
31 Duke Snider/SP 4.00
32 Earl Averill .25
33 Earle Combs .25
34 Edd Roush .25
35 Earl Weaver .25
36 Eddie Collins .25
37 Eddie Plank .25
38 Elmer Flick .25
39 Enos Slaughter .25
40 Ernie Lombardi .25
41 Ford Frick .25
42 Jim "Catfish" Hunter .25
43 Frankie Frisch .25
44 Gabby Hartnett .25
45 George Kell .25
46 Early Wynn .25
47 Ferguson Jenkins .25
48 Al Kaline 1.00
49 Harmon Killebrew 1.00
50 Hal Newhouser .25
51 Hank Greenberg/SP 5.00
52 Harry Caray .25
53 Tommy Lasorda .25
54 Honus Wagner/SP 6.00
55 Hoyt Wilhelm/SP 3.00
56 Jackie Robinson/SP 6.00
57 Jim Bottomley .25
58 Jim Bunning/SP 3.00
59 Jimmie Foxx/SP 6.00
60 Eddie Mathews 1.00
61 Joe Cronin .25
62 Joe DiMaggio/SP 8.00
63 Joe McCarthy/SP 3.00
64 Joe Morgan/SP 3.00
65 Willie McCovey .50
66 Joe Tinker .25
67 Johnny Bench/SP 6.00
68 Johnny Evers/SP 3.00
69 Johnny Mize/SP 3.00

70 Josh Gibson/SP 5.00
71 Juan Marichal .50
72 Judy Johnson .25
73 Stan Musial 1.50
74 Kiki Cuyler .25
75 Larry Doby .75
76 Nap Lajoie .25
77 Larry MacPhail .25
78 Phil Niekro .25
79 Lefty Gomez/SP 3.00
80 Lefty Grove/SP 3.00
81 Leo Durocher/SP 3.00
82 Leon Day .25
83 Gaylord Perry/SP 3.00
84 Lou Boudreau .25
85 Lou Gehrig 3.00
86 Luke Appling .25
87 Max Carey .25
88 Mel Allen/SP 3.00
89 Mel Ott/SP 5.00
90 Mickey Cochrane .50
91 Mickey Mantle 4.00
92 Brooks Robinson 1.00
93 Monte Irvin .50
94 Nellie Fox .50
95 Nolan Ryan/SP 10.00
96 Ozzie Smith/SP 6.00
97 Mike Schmidt 2.00
98 Pee Wee Reese/SP 3.00
99 Phil Rizzuto .75
100 Ralph Kiner .50
101 Ray Dandridge .25
102 Richie Ashburn .25
103 Rick Ferrell .25
104 Roberto Clemente 2.00
105 Robin Roberts .25
106 Robin Yount 1.00
107 Rogers Hornsby .25
108 Rollie Fingers .25
109 Roy Campanella .50
110 Rube Marquard .25
111 Sam Crawford .25
112 Steve Carlton .50
113 Satchel Paige/SP 5.00
114 Sparky Anderson .25
115 Stan Coveleski .25
116 Red Schoendienst .25
117 Ted Williams 3.00
118 Tom Seaver 1.00
119 Tom Yawkey .25
120 Tony Lazzeri .25
121 Tony Perez .25
122 Tris Speaker .25
123 Ty Cobb 2.00
124 Waite Hoyt/SP 3.00
125 Walter Alston .25
126 Walter Johnson .75
127 Warren Spahn 1.00
128 Whitey Ford .75
129 Willie Stargell .50
130 Yogi Berra .75

Blue

Non SP's (1-130): 2-4X
SP's: 1-2X
Production 275 sets

Green

No pricing due to scarcity
Production 25 sets

Autographs

NM/M

Common Player:
Inserted 1:196
Many not priced due to scarcity
AL Alexander Cartwright/1 (6/05 auction) 7,800
BD Bill Dickey/25
BG Burleigh Grimes/34 250.00
BI Billy Herman/30 150.00
BL Bob Lemon/34 150.00
BL1 Bob Lemon/41 150.00
CG Charlie Gehringer/17
CG1 Charlie Gehringer/20
CH Carl Hubbell/47 300.00
CH1 Carl Hubbell/63 300.00
CS Casey Stengel/3
CY Cy Young/2
DD Dizzy Dean/8
DD Don Drysdale/12
DV Dazzy Vance/2
EA Earl Averill/96 125.00
EC Earle Combs/45 150.00
EF Elmer Flick/6
EL Ernie Lombardi/1
ER Edd Roush/15
ER1 Edd Roush/14
ES Enos Slaughter/30 200.00
FF Ford Frick/10
FR Frankie Frisch/4
GH Gabby Hartnett/20
HC Harry Caray/29 225.00
HC1 Harry Caray/35 225.00
HG Hank Greenberg/30 375.00
HN Hal Newhouser TC/22
HN1 Hal Newhouser B2B/22
HW Honus Wagner/1
JB Jim Bottomley/2
JC Joe Cronin/15
JD Joe DiMaggio/50 375.00
JD1 Joe DiMaggio/28 400.00
JF Jimmie Fox/3
JJ Judy Johnson/23
JM Johnny Mize/18
JM1 Johnny Mize/12
JO Joe McCarthy/22
JR Jackie Robinson/4
LA Leon Day/6
LB Lou Boudreau/82 110.00
LB1 Lou Boudreau/49 120.00
LD Leo Durocher/20
LE Lefty Grove/9
LG Lefty Gomez/21
LM Larry MacPhail/2
LU Luke Appling/52 150.00
MA Mel Allen/2
MC Max Carey/18
MI Mickey Cochrane/3
MM Mickey Mantle/2
NF Nellie Fox/5
NL Nap Lajoie/2
RA Richie Asburn/10
RD Ray Dandridge Hands/20
RD1 Ray Dandridge MVP/20
RH Rogers Hornsby/1
RM Rube Marquard/40 200.00
RO Roy Campanella/1
SC Sam Crawford/3
SP Satchel Paige/11
ST Stan Coveleski/19
ST1 Stan Coveleski/20
TC Ty Cobb/6
TJ Travis Jackson/19
TO Tony Lazzeri/8
TS Tris Speaker/2
TW Ted Williams/7
TY Tom Yawkey/1
WA Walter Alston/30
WJ Walter Johnson/1
WS Willie Stargell/4
ZW Zack Wheat/19

Autographs Blue

NM/M

Many not priced due to scarcity
EA Earl Averill/50 125.00
HC1 Harry Caray/35 240.00
HN1 Hal Newhouser B2B/29 125.00
JD1 Joe DiMaggio/40 375.00

Combo Cuts

No Pricing
Production 1 Set

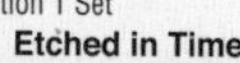

Etched in Time

NM/M

Common Player: 3.00
Production 400 sets
Etched 300: .5-1X
Production 300
Etched 175: .75-1.5X
Production 175
ME Mel Allen 3.00
RA Richie Ashburn 4.00
AB Al Barlick 3.00
LB Lou Boudreau 3.00
RO Roy Campanella 4.00
AC Alexander Cartwright 3.00
HC Harry Caray 3.00
RC Roberto Clemente 10.00
TC Ty Cobb 6.00
EC Eddie Collins 3.00
DD Dizzy Dean 3.00
JD Joe DiMaggio 8.00
DO Don Drysdale 3.00
LD Leo Durocher 3.00
JF Jimmie Foxx 5.00
LO Lou Gehrig 8.00
CG Charlie Gehringer 3.00
JG Josh Gibson 5.00
LG Lefty Gomez 3.00
HG Hank Greenberg 5.00
LE Lefty Grove 3.00
GH Gabby Hartnett 3.00
RH Rogers Hornsby 4.00
CH Carl Hubbell 3.00
TL Tony Lazzeri 3.00
EL Ernie Lombardi 3.00
MM Mickey Mantle 15.00
CM Christy Mathewson 8.00
JM Joe McCarthy 3.00
JO Johnny Mize 3.00
MO Mel Ott 4.00
SP Satchel Paige 5.00
PR Pee Wee Reese 3.00
JR Jackie Robinson 5.00
BR Babe Ruth 10.00
TS Tris Speaker 3.00
CS Casey Stengel 3.00
HW Honus Wagner 5.00
TW Ted Williams 8.00
CY Cy Young 5.00

Hall Marks Autographs

NM/M

Inserted 1:196
Many not priced due to scarcity
Greens: No Pricing
Production 10
BD1 Bobby Doerr Black/50 40.00
BM1 Bill Mazeroski Black/50 40.00
CF1 Carlton Fisk Black/50 50.00
CY1 Carl Yastrzemski Black/45 75.00
DS1 Duke Snider Black/50 40.00
GC1 Gary Carter Black/50 30.00
GK1 George Kell Black/50 20.00
JM1 Juan Marichal Black/50 35.00
JO1 Joe Morgan Black/75 30.00
LA1 Luis Aparicio Black/45 30.00
MI1 Monte Irvin Black/85 30.00
OS1 Ozzie Smith Black/45 75.00
PR1 Phil Rizzuto Black/50 40.00
RF1 Rollie Fingers Black/99 20.00
RK1 Ralph Kiner Black/50 30.00
RR1 Robin Roberts Black/55 40.00
RY1 Robin Yount Black/45 75.00
TP1 Tony Perez Black/50 30.00
WS1 Warren Spahn Black/35 70.00
YB1 Yogi Berra Black/50 60.00

Historic Lumber

NM/M

Common Player: 6.00
Inserted 1:12
BR Babe Ruth Away/150 125.00
BR1 Babe Ruth Home/150 125.00
CF Carlton Fisk R.Sox/50 15.00
CF1 Carlton Fisk W.Sox/50 15.00
CY Carl Yastrzemski w/Bat/300 20.00
CY1 Carl Yastrzemski w/Cap/350 20.00
CY2 Carl Yastrzemski w/Helmet/350 20.00
DW Dave Winfield Padres/350 10.00
DW1 Dave Winfield Yanks/350 10.00
FR Frank Robinson O's/300 10.00
FR1 Frank Robinson Reds/350 10.00
FR2 Frank Robinson Angels/350 10.00
GC Gary Carter Mets/300 6.00
GC1 Gary Carter Helmet Expos/100 6.00
GC2 Gary Carter Cap Expos/100 6.00
HK Harmon Killebrew/350 10.00
JB Johnny Bench w/Bat/350 10.00
JB1 Johnny Bench Swing/350 10.00
JM Joe Morgan Reds/350 6.00
JM1 Joe Morgan Astros/350 6.00
MM Mickey Mantle/300 100.00
NR Nolan Ryan Rgr./225 25.00
OS Ozzie Smith Cards/300 15.00
OS1 Ozzie Smith Padres/350 15.00
RS Red Schoendienst Look Right/165 6.00
RS1 Red Schoendienst Look Left/165 6.00
SC Steve Carlton/350 8.00
TP Tony Perez Swing/350 6.00
TP1 Tony Perez Portrait/350 6.00
TS Tom Seaver/100 10.00
TW Ted Williams w/3 Bats/150 75.00
TW1 Ted Williams Portrait/150 75.00
WS Willie Stargell Arms Down/150 8.00
WS1 Willie Stargell Arms Up/150 8.00
YB Yogi Berra Shout/350 10.00
YB1 Yogi Berra w/Bat/350 10.00

Historic Lumber Green

NM/M

Common Player:
BR Babe Ruth Away/75 140.00
BR1 Babe Ruth Home/75 140.00
CY Carl Yastrzemski w/Bat/125 25.00
CY1 Carl Yastrzemski w/Cap/125 25.00
CY2 Carl Yastrzemski w/Helmet/125 25.00
DW Dave Winfield Padres/125 10.00
DW1 Dave Winfield Yanks/125 10.00
FR Frank Robinson O's/125 10.00
FR1 Frank Robinson Reds/125 10.00
FR2 Frank Robinson Angels/125 10.00
GC Gary Carter Mets/125 6.00
GC1 Gary Carter Helmet Expos/125 6.00
GC2 Gary Carter Cap Expos/125 6.00
HK Harmon Killebrew/125 10.00
JB Johnny Bench w/Bat/125 10.00
JB1 Johnny Bench Swing/125 10.00
JM Joe Morgan Reds/125 6.00
JM1 Joe Morgan Astros/125 6.00
MM Mickey Mantle/75 110.00
NR Nolan Ryan Astros/50 50.00
OS Ozzie Smith Cards/125 20.00
OS1 Ozzie Smith Padres/125 20.00
RS Red Schoendienst Look Right/125 8.00
RS1 Red Schoendienst Look Left/125 8.00
SC Steve Carlton/125 10.00

TP Tony Perez Swing/125 6.00
TP1 Tony Perez Portrait/125 6.00
TS Tom Seaver/50 15.00
TW Ted Williams w/3 Bats/75 75.00
TW1 Ted Williams Portrait/75 75.00
WS Willie Stargell Arms Down/125 10.00
WS1 Willie Stargell Arms Up/125 10.00
YB Yogi Berra Shout/125 10.00
YB1 Yogi Berra w/Bat/125 10.00

Historic Swatches

NM/M

Common Player: 5.00
Inserted 1:12
Blues: .75-1.5X
Production 50 sets
Greens: .75-1X
Production 160 to 250
Purples: .75-1.5X
Production 75 to 150

BG Bob Gibson CO Jsy/350 10.00
BM Bill Mazeroski Pants/50 15.00
BW Billy Williams Jsy/190 5.00
CF Carlton Fisk Pants/350 8.00
CM Christy Mathewson Pants/300 100.00
CS Casey Stengel Jsy/275 6.00
CY Carl Yastrzemski Jsy/350 20.00
CY1 Carl Yastrzemski Pants/350 20.00
DS Duke Snider Jsy/350 10.00
DW1 Dave Winfield Twins Jsy/300 8.00
FR Frank Robinson O's Jsy/350 8.00
FR1 Frank Robinson Angels Jsy/350 8.00
GC Gary Carter Mets Jsy/350 5.00
GC1 Gary Carter Expos Jsy/350 5.00
HW Honus Wagner Pants/275 100.00
JB Johnny Bench Jsy/150 10.00
JM Joe Morgan Jsy/350 5.00
JN Juan Marichal Pants/225 5.00
JN1 Juan Marichal Jsy/48 5.00
LA Luis Aparicio Jsy/230 5.00
LB Lou Boudreau Jsy/265 5.00
MM Mickey Mantle Pants/350 100.00
NR Nolan Ryan Rgr. Pants/350 25.00
NR1 Nolan Ryan Astro Pants/350 25.00
OS Ozzie Smith Jsy/85 25.00
RF Rollie Fingers Jsy/105 5.00
RY Robin Yount Portrait Jsy/350 10.00
RY1 Robin Yount Swing Jsy/350 10.00
SA Sparky Anderson Jsy/350 5.00
SC Steve Carlton Jsy/350 10.00
SM Stan Musial Jsy/350 25.00
TC Ty Cobb Pants/350 90.00
TP Tony Perez Jsy/350 5.00
TS Tom Seaver Jsy/350 10.00
TS1 Tom Seaver Pants/350 10.00
TW Ted Williams Jsy/250 85.00
WA Walter Alston Look Left Jsy/350 5.00
WA1 Walter Alston Ahead Jsy/350 5.00
WI Willie Stargell Jsy/55 15.00
WS Warren Spahn CO Jsy/350 15.00
YB Yogi Berra Jsy/300 10.00

Historic Impressions

NM/M

Common Player: 3.00
Production 350 sets
Golds: 1X
Production 200 sets
Golds 75: 1.5-2X
Production 75
Silvers: 1X
Production 250 sets

MA Mel Allen 3.00
RA Richie Ashburn 5.00
LB Lou Boudreau 3.00
RO Roy Campanella 5.00
AC Alexander Cartwright 3.00
HC Harry Caray 4.00
RC Roberto Clemente 15.00
TY Ty Cobb 8.00
MC Mickey Cochrane 5.00
EC Eddie Collins 3.00
DD Dizzy Dean 5.00
JD Joe DiMaggio 8.00
DO Don Drysdale 3.00
LD Leo Durocher 3.00
JF Jimmie Foxx 8.00
LO Lou Gehrig 10.00
CG Charlie Gehringer 3.00
LG Lefty Gomez 3.00
HG Hank Greenberg 6.00
LE Lefty Grove 6.00
GH Gabby Hartnett 3.00
RH Rogers Hornsby 6.00
CH Carl Hubbell 6.00
TL Tony Lazzeri 3.00
MM Mickey Mantle 25.00
CM Christy Mathewson 6.00
JO Joe McCarthy 3.00
JM Johnny Mize 3.00
MO Mel Ott 6.00
SP Satchel Paige 6.00
PR Pee Wee Reese 3.00
JR Jackie Robinson 8.00
BR Babe Ruth 15.00
ES Enos Slaughter 3.00
TS Tris Speaker 5.00
CS Casey Stengel 4.00
HW Honus Wagner 8.00
HO Hoyt Wilhelm 3.00
TW Ted Williams 15.00
CY Cy Young 8.00

Presidential Cut Signatures

Production between 1-3
No Pricing

2003 SPX

NM/M

Complete Set (178):
Common Player: .25
Common SP (126-160): 4.00
Production 999
Common Jsy Auto (161-178): 10.00
Production 1,224 unless noted
Pack (4): 5.00
Box (18): 75.00

1 Darin Erstad .50
2 Garret Anderson .50
3 Tim Salmon .50
4 Troy Glaus/SP 2.00
5 Luis Gonzalez .50
6 Randy Johnson 1.50
7 Curt Schilling .75
8 Lyle Overbay .25
9 Andruw Jones/SP 2.00
10 Gary Sheffield .75
11 Rafael Furcal .40
12 Greg Maddux 2.00
13 Chipper Jones/SP 3.00
14 Tony Batista .25
15 Rodrigo Lopez .25
16 Jay Gibbons .25
17 Byung-Hyun Kim .25
18 Johnny Damon .50
19 Derek Lowe .25
20 Nomar Garciaparra/SP 4.00
21 Pedro J. Martinez 1.50
22 Manny Ramirez/SP 3.00
23 Mark Prior 2.00
24 Kerry Wood 1.00
25 Corey Patterson .50
26 Sammy Sosa/SP 5.00
27 Moises Alou .50
28 Magglio Ordonez .50
29 Frank Thomas 1.00
30 Paul Konerko .25
31 Bartolo Colon .25
32 Adam Dunn 1.00
33 Austin Kearns .50
34 Aaron Boone .25
35 Ken Griffey Jr./SP 4.00
36 Omar Vizquel .50
37 C.C. Sabathia .25
38 Jason Davis .25
39 Travis Hafner .50
40 Brandon Phillips .25
41 Larry Walker .50
42 Preston Wilson .50
43 Jay Payton .25
44 Todd Helton 1.00
45 Carlos Pena .25
46 Eric Munson .25
47 Ivan Rodriguez 1.00
48 Josh Beckett .75
49 Alex Gonzalez .25
50 Roy Oswalt .50
51 Craig Biggio .50
52 Jeff Bagwell 1.00
53 Dontrelle Willis/SP 2.00
54 Mike Sweeney .25
55 Carlos Beltran 1.00
56 Brent Mayne .25
57 Hideo Nomo .75
58 Rickey Henderson .75
59 Adrian Beltre .50
60 Miguel Cabrera/SP 3.00
61 Kazuhisa Ishii .25
62 Ben Sheets .50
63 Richie Sexson .50
64 Torii Hunter/SP 2.00
65 Jacque Jones .25
66 Joe Mays .25
67 Corey Koskie .25
68 A.J. Pierzynski .25
69 Jose Vidro .25
70 Vladimir Guerrero/SP 3.00
71 Tom Glavine .50
72 Jose Reyes/SP 2.00
73 Aaron Heilman .25
74 Mike Piazza 2.00
75 Jorge Posada .75
76 Mike Mussina .75
77 Robin Ventura .50
78 Mariano Rivera .50
79 Roger Clemens 6.00
80 Jason Giambi .75
81 Bernie Williams .75
82 Alfonso Soriano/SP 3.00
83 Derek Jeter 3.00
84 Miguel Tejada/SP 2.50
85 Eric Chavez .50
86 Tim Hudson .50
87 Barry Zito .50
88 Mark Mulder .50
89 Erubiel Durazo .25
90 Pat Burrell .50
91 Jim Thome/SP 3.00
92 Bobby Abreu .50
93 Brian Giles .50
94 Reggie Sanders/SP 2.00
95 Kenny Lofton .50
96 Ryan Klesko .50
97 Sean Burroughs .25
98 Edgardo Alfonzo .25
99 Rich Aurilia .25
100 Jose Cruz Jr. .25
101 Barry Bonds/SP 8.00
102 Mike Cameron .25
103 Kazuhiro Sasaki .25
104 Bret Boone .50
105 Ichiro Suzuki/SP 5.00
106 J.D. Drew .50
107 Jim Edmonds .50
108 Scott Rolen/SP 3.00
109 Matt Morris .25
110 Tino Martinez .25
111 Albert Pujols/SP 6.00
112 Damian Rolls .25
113 Carl Crawford .25
114 Rocco Baldelli/SP 2.00
115 Hank Blalock 1.00
116 Alex Rodriguez/SP 5.00
117 Kevin Mench .25
118 Rafael Palmeiro .75
119 Mark Teixeira .75
120 Shannon Stewart .25
121 Vernon Wells .25
122 Josh Phelps .25
123 Eric Hinske .25
124 Orlando Hudson .25
125 Carlos Delgado/SP 2.00
126 *Jason Roach* 4.00
127 Dan Haren 8.00
128 *Luis Ayala* 4.00
129 *Bo Hart* 4.00
130 *Wilfredo Ledezma* 4.00
131 *Rick Roberts* 4.00
132 *Miguel Ojeda* 4.00
133 *Aquilino Lopez* 4.00
134 *Roger Deago* 4.00
135 *Arnie Munoz* 4.00
136 *Brent Hoard* 4.00
137 *Terrmel Sledge* 4.00
138 *Ryan Cameron* 4.00
139 *Prentice Redman* 4.00
140 *Clint Barmes* 8.00
141 Jeremy Griffiths 4.00
142 *Jon Leicester* 4.00
143 *Brandon Webb* 8.00
144 *Todd Wellemeyer* 4.00
145 *Felix Sanchez* 4.00
146 *Anthony Ferrari* 4.00
147 *Ian Ferguson* 4.00
148 *Micheal Nakamura* 4.00
149 *Lew Ford* 10.00
150 *Nate Bland* 4.00
151 *Dave Matranga* 4.00
152 *Edgar Gonzalez* 4.00
153 *Carlos Mendez* 4.00
154 *Jason Gilfillan* 4.00
155 *Mike Neu* 4.00
156 *Jason Shiell* 4.00
157 *Jeff Duncan* 4.00
158 *Oscar Villarreal* 4.00
159 *Diegomar Markwell* 4.00
160 *Joe Valentine* 4.00
161 *Hideki Matsui/864* 300.00
162 *Jose Contreras/800* 30.00
163 *Willie Eyre* 10.00
164 *Matt Bruback* 10.00
165 *Rett Johnson* 15.00
166 Jeremy Griffiths 15.00
167 *Francisco Cruceta* 10.00
168 *Fernando Cabrera* 10.00
169 *Jhonny Peralta* 40.00
170 *Shane Bazzell* 10.00
171 *Bobby Madritsch* 20.00
172 *Phil Seibel* 10.00
173 *Josh Willingham* 20.00
174 *Robby Hammock* 15.00
175 *Alejandro Machado* 10.00
176 *David Sanders* 10.00
177 *Matt Kata* 15.00
178 *Heath Bell* 4.00

Spectrum

NM/M

Stars (1-125) print run 51-99: 3-6X
Stars (1-125) p/r 26-50: 6-12X
Print run 25 or less not priced
Numbered to jersey number
SP's (126-160): .75-1.5X
Production 125

Stars

NM/M

Common Player: 20.00
Quantity produced listed

LB Lance Berkman/590 25.00
PB Pat Burrell/590 25.00
NM Nomar Garciaparra/195 140.00
JG Jason Giambi/315 30.00
TG Troy Glaus/490 25.00
LG Luis Gonzalez/790 20.00
KG Ken Griffey Jr/690 80.00
VG Vladimir Guerrero/390 45.00
CJ Chipper Jones/195 50.00
MP Mark Prior/490 75.00
CS Curt Schilling/490 40.00

SPX Combos

NM/M

Common Duo: 20.00
Quantity produced listed

MJ Hideki Matsui, Derek Jeter/90 100.00

RC	Nolan Ryan, Roger Clemens/90	120.00
SJ	Curt Schilling, Randy Johnson/90	30.00
EG	Darin Erstad, Troy Glaus/90	20.00
GC	Greg Maddux, Chipper Jones/90	50.00
GS	Jason Giambi, Alfonso Soriano/90	30.00
BK	Jeff Bagwell, Jeff Kent/90	25.00
GD	Ken Griffey Jr., Adam Dunn/90	50.00
GR	Ken Griffey Jr., Sammy Sosa/90	50.00
SP	Sammy Sosa, Rafael Palmeiro/90	40.00
MG	Pedro Martinez, Nomar Garciaparra/90	40.00
RY	Nolan Ryan, Pedro Martinez/10	
RG	Alex Rodriguez, Nomar Garciaparra/90	40.00
CM	Jose Contreras, Pedro Martinez/90	40.00
FC	Carlton Fisk, Gary Carter/90	30.00
RR	Cal Ripken Jr., Scott Rolen/90	80.00
JJ	Chipper Jones, Andruw Jones/90	30.00
PM	Rafael Palmeiro, Fred McGriff/90	30.00
RT	Alex Rodriguez, Miguel Tejada/90	30.00
SB	Sammy Sosa, Barry Bonds/90	50.00
SN	Ichiro Suzuki, Hideo Nomo/90	175.00
MS	Hideki Matsui, Ichiro Suzuki/50	350.00
MW	Mickey Mantle, Ted Williams/50	300.00
CC	Jose Contreras, Roger Clemens/50	40.00
CL	Cal Ripken Jr., Lou Gehrig/90	300.00
HJ	Hideki Matsui, Jason Giambi/50	75.00
CA	Cal Ripken Jr., Alex Rodriguez/50	150.00
IA	Ichiro Suzuki, Albert Pujols/50	250.00
NI	Hideo Nomo, Kazuhisa Ishii/50	50.00
MD	Mickey Mantle, Derek Jeter/50	180.00
BT	Barry Bonds, Ted Williams/50	180.00
BM	Barry Bonds, Roger Maris/50	80.00
MC	Hideki Matsui, Jose Contreras/10	
WG	Ted Williams, Nomar Garciaparra/10	
WM	Ted Williams, Pedro Martinez/10	
HM	Hideki Matsui, Mickey Mantle/10	
RM	Babe Ruth, Hideki Matsui/10	
MB	Mickey Mantle, Barry Bonds/50	150.00
MR	Mickey Mantle, Roger Maris/10	
PS	Rafael Palmeiro, Sammy Sosa/90	40.00
RS	Nolan Ryan, Tom Seaver/90	110.00
TB	Thurman Munson, Yogi Berra/10	

Young Stars

		NM/M
	Common Player:	8.00
	Production 1,295 unless noted	
KA	Kurt Ainsworth/1,460	8.00
RB	Rocco Baldelli	20.00
JBa	Josh Bard	8.00
HB	Hank Blalock	25.00
SB	Sean Burroughs	10.00
MD	Michael Cuddyer/1,156	10.00
AD	Adam Dunn	20.00
CG	Chris George/1,260	8.00
EH	Eric Hinske	8.00
JA	Jason Jennings	8.00
NJ	Nick Johnson	8.00
JJ	Jacque Jones/1,260	12.00
AK	Austin Kearns/964	15.00
MK	Mike Kinkade	8.00
BM	Brett Myers	8.00
RO	Roy Oswalt	15.00
JP	Josh Phelps	10.00
BP	Brandon Phillips	10.00
KS	Kirk Saarloos	8.00
MT	Mark Teixeira	25.00

Winning Materials

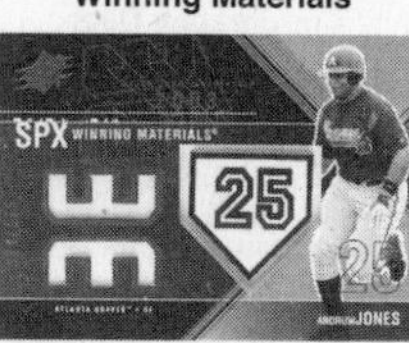

		NM/M
	Common Player:	5.00
	Version 1 Production 375	
	Golds:	1X
	Production 250	
	Version 2 Production 175	
	Golds:	1-2X
	Production 50	
RA1	Roberto Alomar	8.00
RA2	Roberto Alomar	10.00
JB1	Jeff Bagwell	6.00
JB2	Jeff Bagwell	8.00
LB1	Lance Berkman	5.00
LB2	Lance Berkman	5.00
PB1	Pat Burrell	6.00
PB2	Pat Burrell	8.00
RC1	Roger Clemens	15.00
RC2	Roger Clemens	15.00
CD1	Carlos Delgado	6.00
CD2	Carlos Delgado	8.00
RF1	Rafael Furcal	6.00
RF2	Rafael Furcal	8.00
JG1	Jason Giambi	8.00
JG2	Jason Giambi	8.00
TR1	Troy Glaus	6.00
TG2	Troy Glaus	8.00
TG1	Tom Glavine	5.00
TG2	Tom Glavine	6.00
LG1	Luis Gonzalez	5.00
LG2	Luis Gonzalez	5.00
SG1	Shawn Green	5.00
SG2	Shawn Green	5.00
KG1	Ken Griffey Jr.	12.00
KG2	Ken Griffey Jr.	15.00
VG1	Vladimir Guerrero	10.00
VG2	Vladimir Guerrero	12.00
TO1	Todd Helton	8.00
TH2	Todd Helton	10.00
TH1	Torii Hunter	8.00
RJ1	Randy Johnson	10.00
RJ2	Randy Johnson	12.00
AJ1	Andruw Jones	6.00
AJ2	Andruw Jones	8.00
CJ1	Chipper Jones	10.00
CJ2	Chipper Jones	15.00
JK1	Jeff Kent	5.00
JK2	Jeff Kent	5.00
GM1	Greg Maddux	15.00
GM2	Greg Maddux	15.00
MM2	Mickey Mantle	120.00
PM1	Pedro Martinez	10.00
PM2	Pedro Martinez	15.00
HM1	Hideki Matsui	30.00
HM2	Hideki Matsui	30.00
HN1	Hideo Nomo	15.00
HN2	Hideo Nomo	20.00
MP1	Mike Piazza	10.00
MP2	Mike Piazza	15.00
MA1	Mark Prior	15.00
MP2	Mark Prior	15.00
AP1	Albert Pujols	20.00
AP2	Albert Pujols	20.00
MR1	Manny Ramirez	10.00
MR2	Manny Ramirez	10.00
AR1	Alex Rodriguez	10.00
AR2	Alex Rodriguez	12.00
IR1	Ivan Rodriguez	8.00
IR2	Ivan Rodriguez	10.00
CS1	Curt Schilling	8.00
CS2	Curt Schilling	10.00
GS1	Gary Sheffield	6.00
GS2	Gary Sheffield	8.00
AS1	Alfonso Soriano	10.00
AS2	Alfonso Soriano	12.00
SS1	Sammy Sosa	15.00
SS2	Sammy Sosa	20.00
IS1	Ichiro Suzuki	25.00
IS2	Ichiro Suzuki	35.00
MT1	Miguel Tejada	6.00
MT2	Miguel Tejada	8.00
FT1	Frank Thomas	8.00
FT2	Frank Thomas	10.00
JT1	Jim Thome	8.00
JT2	Jim Thome	10.00
BW1	Bernie Williams	8.00
BW2	Bernie Williams	10.00
TW2	Ted Williams	80.00
TW2	Ted Williams/Gold/50	200.00
BZ1	Barry Zito	6.00
BZ2	Barry Zito	8.00

2004 SP AUTHENTIC

		NM/M
	Complete Set (191):	
	Common (1-90):	.25
	Common RC (91-132, 178-191):	4.00
	Production 999	
	Common SP (133-177):	2.00
	Production 999	
	Pack (5):	5.00
	Box (24):	100.00
1	Bret Boone	.40
2	Gary Sheffield	.50
3	Rafael Palmeiro	.75
4	Jorge Posada	.50
5	Derek Jeter	3.00
6	Garret Anderson	.50
7	Bartolo Colon	.40
8	Kevin Brown	.40
9	Shea Hillenbrand	.25
10	Ryan Klesko	.40
11	Bobby Abreu	.40
12	Scott Rolen	1.00
13	Alfonso Soriano	.75
14	Jason Giambi	1.00
15	Tom Glavine	.50
16	Hideo Nomo	.50
17	Johan Santana	.25
18	Sammy Sosa	2.00
19	Rickie Weeks	.50
20	Barry Zito	.50
21	Kerry Wood	1.00
22	Austin Kearns	.40
23	Shawn Green	.40
24	Miguel Cabrera	1.00
25	Richard Hidalgo	.25
26	Andruw Jones	.75
27	Randy Wolf	.25
28	David Ortiz	1.00
29	Roy Oswalt	.40
30	Vernon Wells	.25
31	Ben Sheets	.50
32	Mike Lowell	.50
33	Todd Helton	.75
34	Jacque Jones	.25
35	Mike Sweeney	.25
36	Hank Blalock	.50
37	Jason Schmidt	.50
38	Jeff Kent	.40
39	Josh Beckett	.75
40	Manny Ramirez	.75
41	Torii Hunter	.40
42	Brian Giles	.40
43	Javier Vazquez	.40
44	Jim Edmonds	.40
45	Dmitri Young	.25
46	Preston Wilson	.25
47	Jeff Bagwell	.75
48	Pedro J. Martinez	1.00
49	Eric Chavez	.40
50	Ken Griffey Jr.	1.50
51	Shannon Stewart	.25
52	Rafael Furcal	.40
53	Brandon Webb	.25
54	Juan Pierre	.25
55	Roger Clemens	2.00
56	Geoff Jenkins	.40
57	Lance Berkman	.50
58	Albert Pujols	2.50
59	Frank Thomas	.75
60	Edgar Martinez	.40
61	Tim Hudson	.50
62	Eric Gagne	.50
63	Richie Sexson	.50
64	Corey Patterson	.40
65	Nomar Garciaparra	2.00
66	Hideki Matsui	2.00
67	Mark Teixeira	.40
68	Troy Glaus	.50
69	Carlos Lee	.40
70	Mike Mussina	.75
71	Magglio Ordonez	.50
72	Roy Halladay	.50
73	Ichiro Suzuki	2.00
74	Randy Johnson	1.00
75	Luis Gonzalez	.40
76	Mark Prior	2.00
77	Carlos Beltran	.50
78	Ivan Rodriguez	.75
79	Alex Rodriguez	2.50
80	Dontrelle Willis	.50
81	Mike Piazza	1.50
82	Curt Schilling	.75
83	Vladimir Guerrero	1.00
84	Greg Maddux	1.50
85	Jim Thome	1.00
86	Miguel Tejada	.50
87	Carlos Delgado	.50
88	Jose Reyes	.40
89	Matt Morris	.25
90	Mark Mulder	.40
91	*Angel Chavez*	4.00
92	*Brandon Medders*	4.00
93	*Carlos Vasquez*	4.00
94	*Chris Aguila*	4.00
95	*Colby Miller*	6.00
96	David Crouthers	6.00
97	*Dennis Sarfate*	4.00
98	*Donnie Kelly*	4.00
99	*Merkin Valdez*	6.00
100	*Eddy Rodriguez*	8.00
101	*Edwin Moreno*	6.00
102	*Enemencio Pacheco*	6.00
103	*Roberto Novoa*	4.00
104	*Greg Dobbs*	4.00
105	*Hector Gimenez*	4.00
106	*Ian Snell*	4.00
107	Jake Woods	4.00
108	*Jamie Brown*	4.00
109	*Jason Frasor*	4.00
110	*Jerome Gamble*	4.00
111	*Jerry Gil*	6.00
112	*Jesse Harper*	4.00
113	*Jorge Vasquez*	4.00
114	*Jose Capellan*	8.00
115	*Josh Labandeira*	4.00
116	*Justin Hampson*	4.00
117	*Justin Huisman*	4.00
118	*Justin Leone*	8.00
119	*Lincoln Holdzkom*	4.00
120	*Lino Urdaneta*	8.00
121	Mike Gosling	6.00
122	*Mike Johnston*	4.00
123	Mike Rouse	6.00
124	*Scott Proctor*	6.00
125	*Roman Colon*	4.00
126	*Ronny Cedeno*	8.00
127	*Ryan Meaux*	4.00
128	*Scott Dohmann*	4.00
129	Sean Henn	8.00
130	*Tim Bausher*	4.00
131	*Tim Bittner*	4.00
132	*William Bergolla*	6.00
133	Rick Ferrell	2.00
134	Joe DiMaggio	6.00
135	Bob Feller	2.00
136	Ted Williams	6.00
137	Stan Musial	5.00
138	Larry Doby	2.00
139	Red Schoendienst	2.00
140	Enos Slaughter	2.00
141	Stan Musial	5.00
142	Mickey Mantle	8.00
143	Ted Williams	6.00
144	Mickey Mantle	8.00
145	Stan Musial	5.00
146	Tom Seaver	3.00

147 Willie McCovey 2.00
148 Bob Gibson 3.00
149 Frank Robinson 3.00
150 Joe Morgan 2.00
151 Billy Williams 2.00
152 Catfish Hunter 2.00
153 Joe Morgan 2.00
154 Joe Morgan 2.00
155 Mike Schmidt 5.00
156 Tommy Lasorda 2.00
157 Robin Yount 4.00
158 Nolan Ryan 8.00
159 John Franco 2.00
160 Nolan Ryan 8.00
161 Ken Griffey Jr. 4.00
162 Cal Ripken Jr. 8.00
163 Ken Griffey Jr. 4.00
164 Gary Sheffield 2.00
165 Fred McGriff 2.00
166 Hideo Nomo 2.00
167 Mike Piazza 4.00
168 Sandy Alomar Jr. 2.00
169 Roberto Alomar 2.00
170 Ted Williams 6.00
171 Pedro J. Martinez 4.00
172 Derek Jeter 6.00
173 Cal Ripken Jr. 8.00
174 Torii Hunter 2.00
175 Alfonso Soriano 3.00
176 Hank Blalock 2.00
177 Ichiro Suzuki 4.00
178 *Orlando Rodriguez* 6.00
179 *Ramon Ramirez* 10.00
180 *Kazuo Matsui* 20.00
181 *Kevin Cave* 6.00
182 *John Gall* 12.00
183 *Freddy Guzman* 4.00
184 *Chris Oxspring* 6.00
185 *Rusty Tucker* 6.00
186 *Jorge Sequea* 6.00
187 *Carlos Hines* 4.00
188 Luis Gonzalez 6.00
189 Ryan Wing 6.00
190 *Jeff Bennett* 4.00
191 Luis Gonzalez 4.00

Silver

Stars (1-90): 2-4X
Production 499
SP (91-132, 178-191): 1X
Production 249

Gold

Stars (1-90): 4-8X
Gold SP (91-132, 178-191): 2X
Production 99
Gold (133-177): 1-1.5X
Production 499

Future Watch Autograph

NM/M

Production 295 8.00
91 Angel Chavez 8.00
92 Brandon Medders 8.00
93 Carlos Vasquez 10.00
94 Chris Aguila 8.00
95 Colby Miller 15.00
96 David Crouthers 12.00
97 Dennis Sarfate 8.00
98 Donnie Kelly 10.00
99 Merkin Valdez 20.00
100 Eddy Rodriguez 15.00
101 *Edwin Moreno* 15.00
102 *Enemencio Pacheco* 10.00
103 *Roberto Novoa* 8.00
104 *Greg Dobbs* 8.00
105 *Hector Gimenez* 8.00
106 *Ian Snell* 20.00
107 Jake Woods 10.00
108 *Jamie Brown* 8.00
109 *Jason Frasor* 10.00
110 *Jerome Gamble* 8.00
111 *Jerry Gil* 10.00
112 *Jesse Harper* 8.00
113 *Jorge Vasquez* 10.00
114 *Jose Capellan* 40.00
115 *Josh Labandeira* 10.00
116 *Justin Hampson* 8.00
117 *Justin Huisman* 8.00
118 *Justin Leone* 15.00
119 *Lincoln Holdzkom* 8.00
120 *Lino Urdaneta* 12.00
121 Mike Gosling 12.00
122 *Mike Johnston* 10.00
123 Mike Rouse 10.00
124 *Scott Proctor* 25.00
125 *Roman Colon* 10.00
126 *Ronny Cedeno* 15.00
127 *Ryan Meaux* 10.00
128 *Scott Dohmann* 8.00
129 Sean Henn 15.00
130 *Tim Bausher* 10.00
131 *Tim Bittner* 8.00
132 *William Bergolla* 10.00
178 *Orlando Rodriguez* 10.00
179 *Ramon Ramirez* 20.00
180 *Kazuo Matsui*
181 *Kevin Cave* 10.00
182 *John Gall* 15.00
183 *Freddy Guzman* 10.00
184 *Chris Oxspring* 15.00
185 *Rusty Tucker* 20.00
186 *Jorge Sequea* 15.00
187 *Carlos Hines* 8.00
188 Luis Gonzalez 12.00
189 Ryan Wing 10.00
190 *Jeff Bennett* 10.00
191 Luis Gonzalez 10.00

Chirography

NM/M

Bronze: 1X
Production 65
Bronze Duo Tone: 1X
Production 60
Gold: 1-1.5X
Production 40
Gold Duo Tone: No Pricing
Production 20
Silver: 1X
Production 60
Silver Duo Tone: 1.5-2X
Production 30
Duo Tone: 1X
Production 75
AB Bobby Abreu 12.00
GA Garret Anderson 15.00
RB Rocco Baldelli 15.00
JB Josh Beckett 25.00
CB Carlos Beltran 40.00
HB Hank Blalock 30.00
BB Bret Boone 30.00
MC Miguel Cabrera 40.00
EC Eric Chavez 20.00
DE Dennis Eckersley 30.00
WE Willie Eyre 8.00
EG Eric Gagne 35.00
JG Juan Gonzalez 20.00
KG Ken Griffey Jr. 120.00
TH Travis Hafner 15.00
HY Roy Halladay 20.00
HA Robby Hammock 10.00
BH Bo Hart 8.00
HE Runelvys Hernandez 8.00
HI Bobby Hill 10.00
DJ Derek Jeter 150.00
JJ Jacque Jones 15.00
AK Austin Kearns 15.00
CL Cliff Lee 15.00
AL Al Leiter 15.00
PL Paul LoDuca 15.00
JL Javy Lopez 25.00
ML Mike Lowell 15.00
EM Edgar Martinez 25.00
RO Roy Oswalt 15.00
PA Corey Patterson 25.00
PI Mike Piazza 125.00
CP Colin Porter 10.00
JP Jorge Posada 25.00
MP Mark Prior 75.00
HR Horacio Ramirez 15.00
JR Jose Reyes 20.00
CR Cal Ripken Jr. 100.00
JS Jae Weong Seo 15.00
BS Ben Sheets 20.00
SM John Smoltz 60.00
MT Mark Teixeira 25.00
JV Javier Vazquez 25.00
CW Chien-Ming Wang 30.00
RW Rickie Weeks 25.00
BW Brandon Webb 10.00
VW Vernon Wells 15.00
JW Jerome Williams 25.00
DW Dontrelle Willis 30.00
KW Kerry Wood 40.00
DY Delmon Young 25.00
BZ Barry Zito 20.00

Chirography Dual

NM/M

Common Duo: 40.00
Production 50 sets
BC Bret Boone, Eric Chavez 50.00
BL Mike Lowell, Josh Beckett 50.00
BP Corey Patterson, Carlos Beltran 75.00
BT Hank Blalock, Mark Teixeira 50.00
EG Dennis Eckersley, Eric Gagne 75.00
HW Vernon Wells, Roy Halladay 50.00
JM Johnny Bench, Mike Piazza 200.00
KG Ken Griffey Jr., Austin Kearns 100.00
PB Yogi Berra, Jorge Posada 100.00
RR Alex Rodriguez, Cal Ripken Jr. 400.00
SG Ken Griffey Jr., Ichiro Suzuki 375.00
SM Stan Musial, Ozzie Smith 175.00
WC Miguel Cabrera, Dontrelle Willis 70.00
WJ Chien-Ming Wang, Derek Jeter 150.00
WR Nolan Ryan, Kerry Wood 225.00
WW Dontrelle Willis, Brandon Webb 50.00
YW Delmon Young, Rickie Weeks 80.00
ZC Eric Chavez, Barry Zito 50.00

Chirography Hall of Famers

NM/M

Production 40 sets
Duo Tone: No Pricing
Production 25
LA Luis Aparicio 20.00
JB Johnny Bench 60.00
YB Yogi Berra 50.00
BD Bobby Doerr 30.00
DE Dennis Eckersley 30.00
CF Carlton Fisk 30.00
BG Bob Gibson 40.00
MI Monte Irvin 20.00
AK Al Kaline 50.00
HK Harmon Killebrew 65.00
RK Ralph Kiner 25.00
PM Paul Molitor 40.00
SM Stan Musial 100.00
TP Tony Perez 30.00
KP Kirby Puckett 100.00
PR Phil Rizzuto 40.00
RR Robin Roberts 40.00
BR Brooks Robinson 40.00
NR Nolan Ryan 120.00
MS Mike Schmidt 120.00
TS Tom Seaver 40.00
OS Ozzie Smith 65.00
DS Duke Snider 30.00
CY Carl Yastrzemski 75.00
RY Robin Yount 100.00

Chirography Quad

No Pricing
Production 10 sets

Chirography Triple

NM/M

Production 25 sets
BWR Kerry Wood, Nolan Ryan, Josh Beckett 250.00
FBB Johnny Bench, Carlton Fisk, Yogi Berra 300.00
GSM Bob Gibson, Stan Musial, Ozzie Smith 220.00
JVB Derek Jeter, Yogi Berra, Javier Vazquez 250.00
PRC Jose Reyes, Miguel Cabrera, Colin Porter 100.00
RBT Hank Blalock, Mark Teixeira, Alex Rodriguez 250.00
RRR Alex Rodriguez, Cal Ripken Jr., Phil Rizzuto 400.00
SJB Rocco Baldelli, Jacque Jones, Ichiro Suzuki 275.00
WLE Chien-Ming Wang, Willie Eyre, Cliff Lee 75.00
WPB Mark Prior, Josh Beckett, Brandon Webb 250.00
YYM Robin Yount, Carl Yastrzemski, Stan Musial 300.00
ZHO Barry Zito, Roy Oswalt, Roy Halladay 200.00

USA Signature

NM/M

Production 445 sets
Reds: 1.5X
Production 50
USA-1 Ernie Young 6.00
USA-2 Chris Burke 10.00
USA-3 Jesse Crain 15.00
USA-4 Justin Duchscherer 15.00
USA-5 J.D. Durbin 12.00
USA-6 Gerald Laird 10.00
USA-7 John Grabow 8.00
USA-8 Gabe Gross 15.00
USA-9 J.J. Hardy 15.00
USA-10 Jeremy Reed 20.00
USA-11 Graham Koonce 10.00
USA-12 Mike Lamb 10.00
USA-13 Justin Leone 15.00
USA-14 Ryan Madson 12.00
USA-15 Joe Mauer 45.00
USA-16 Todd Williams 6.00
USA-17 Horacio Ramirez 15.00
USA-18 Mike Rouse 15.00
USA-19 Jason Stanford 10.00
USA-20 John Van Benschoten 10.00
USA-21 Grady Sizemore 15.00

2004 SP GAME USED PATCH

NM/M

Complete Set (119):
Common (1-60): 2.00
Common (61-90): 2.00
Quantity produced listed
Common (91-119): 6.00
Production 375
Box (1 pack): 180.00
1 Miguel Cabrera 4.00
2 Alex Rodriguez 10.00
3 Edgar Renteria 2.50
4 Juan Gonzalez 2.50
5 Mike Lowell 2.50
6 Andruw Jones 2.50
7 Eric Chavez 2.00
8 Jim Edmonds 2.00
9 Mike Piazza 5.00
10 Angel Berroa 2.00
11 Eric Gagne 3.00
12 Jody Gerut 2.00
13 Orlando Cabrera 2.00
14 Austin Kearns 2.00
15 Frank Thomas 3.00
16 Johan Santana 2.00
17 Randy Johnson 4.00
18 Preston Wilson 2.00

19 Garret Anderson 2.50
20 Jorge Posada 2.50
21 Rich Harden 2.00
22 Barry Zito 2.50
23 Gary Sheffield 2.50
24 Jose Reyes 2.00
25 Roy Halladay 2.00
26 Ben Sheets 2.00
27 Geoff Jenkins 2.00
28 Josh Beckett 3.00
29 Roy Oswalt 2.50
30 Bobby Abreu 2.50
31 Hank Blalock 2.50
32 Kerry Wood 4.00
33 Ryan Klesko 2.00
34 Rafael Furcal 2.00
35 Tom Glavine 2.50
36 Kevin Brown 2.50
37 Scott Rolen 3.00
38 Bret Boone 2.50
39 Ichiro Suzuki 6.00
40 Lance Berkman 2.00
41 Tim Hudson 2.50
42 Carlos Delgado 2.50
43 Ivan Rodriguez 3.00
44 Luis Gonzalez 2.00
45 Torii Hunter 2.00
46 Carlos Lee 2.00
47 Jacque Jones 2.00
48 Manny Ramirez 3.00
49 Troy Glaus 2.50
50 Corey Patterson 2.50
51 Jason Schmidt 2.50
52 Mark Mulder 2.00
53 Vernon Wells 2.00
54 Curt Schilling 4.00
55 Javy Lopez 2.50
56 Mark Prior 6.00
57 Dontrelle Willis 2.50
58 Derek Jeter 10.00
59 Jeff Bagwell 3.00
60 Marlon Byrd 2.00
61 Rafael Palmeiro/500 3.00
62 Kevin Millwood/165 2.00
63 Greg Maddux/273 5.00
64 Adam Dunn/400 3.00
65 Richie Sexson/469 3.00
66 Magglio Ordonez/567 2.00
67 Hideo Nomo/236 2.00
68 Albert Pujols/194 10.00
69 Rocco Baldelli/368 3.00
70 Mark Teixeira/86 4.00
71 Jason Giambi/660 3.00
72 Alfonso Soriano/230 4.00
73 Roger Clemens/300 8.00
74 Miguel Tejada/359 2.00
75 Jeff Kent/684 2.00
76 Bernie Williams/342 3.00
77 Sammy Sosa/470 8.00
78 Mike Mussina/641 3.00
79 Jim Thome/334 4.00
80 Brian Giles/506 2.00
81 Shawn Green/234 2.00
82 Mike Sweeney/340 2.00
83 John Smoltz/262 2.00
84 Carlos Beltran/319 3.00
85 Todd Helton/384 3.00
86 Nomar Garciaparra/372 8.00
87 Ken Griffey Jr./481 8.00
88 Chipper Jones/633 4.00
89 Vladimir Guerrero/226 4.00
90 Pedro Martinez/313 5.00
91 *Brandon Medders* 6.00
92 *Colby Miller* 6.00
93 David Crouthers 6.00
94 *Dennis Sarfate* 8.00
95 *Donald Kelly* 6.00
96 *Alec Zumwalt* 6.00
97 *Chris Aguila* 6.00
98 *Greg Dobbs* 6.00
99 *Ian Snell* 8.00
100 Jake Woods 6.00
101 *Jamie Brown* 6.00
102 *Jason Frasor* 6.00
103 *Jerome Gamble* 6.00
104 *Jesse Harper* 6.00
105 *Josh Labandeira* 6.00
106 *Justin Hampson* 6.00
107 *Justin Huisman* 6.00
108 *Justin Leone* 6.00
109 *Lincoln Holdzkom* 6.00
110 *Mike Bumatay* 6.00
111 Mike Gosling 6.00
112 *Mike Johnston* 6.00
113 Mike Rouse 6.00
114 *Nick Regilio* 6.00
115 *Ryan Meaux* 6.00
116 *Scott Dohmann* 6.00
117 Sean Henn 8.00
118 *Tim Bausher* 6.00
119 *Tim Bittner* 6.00

All-Star Patch Gold

NM/M
Production 50 sets
AP Albert Pujols 75.00
AR Alex Rodriguez 50.00
AS Alfonso Soriano 25.00
BZ Barry Zito 25.00
CD Carlos Delgado 20.00
CJ Chipper Jones 30.00
CS Curt Schilling 35.00
DJ Derek Jeter 85.00
EC Eric Chavez 20.00
FT Frank Thomas 30.00
GS Gary Sheffield 20.00
HE Todd Helton 25.00
HN Hideo Nomo 50.00
IS Ichiro Suzuki 80.00
JG Juan Gonzalez 20.00
JT Jim Thome 30.00
KG Ken Griffey Jr. 45.00
MP Mark Prior 65.00
SS Sammy Sosa 50.00
TH Tim Hudson 25.00
VW Vernon Wells 20.00

All-Star Patch Autograph

Production 10 Sets
No Pricing

All-Star Patch Auto-Dual

Production 10 Sets
No Pricing

All-Star Patch Number

NM/M
Quantity produced listed
AJ Andruw Jones/25 30.00
AP Andy Pettitte/46 25.00
BZ Barry Zito/50 30.00
CD Carlos Delgado/25 25.00
CS Curt Schilling/38 30.00
FT Frank Thomas/35 40.00
GM Greg Maddux/31 50.00
IS Ichiro Suzuki/50 65.00
JG Juan Gonzalez/19 35.00
JP Jorge Posada/20 30.00
JT Jim Thome/25 30.00
KG Ken Griffey Jr./30 60.00
MM Mike Mussina/35 30.00
MO Magglio Ordonez/30 25.00
PM Pedro Martinez/45 35.00
RC Roger Clemens/22 50.00
RH Roy Halladay/32 25.00
RP Rafael Palmeiro/25 30.00
SG Shawn Green/15 30.00
SR Scott Rolen/27 35.00
SS Sammy Sosa/21 80.00

Autographed 300 Win Club

Production 10 Sets
No Pricing

Autographed 500 HR Club

Production 10 Sets
No Pricing

Famous Nicknames

NM/M
Quantity produced listed
BR Brooks Robinson/23 25.00
CR Cal Ripken Jr./21 120.00
CY Carl Yastrzemski/23 70.00
DM Don Mattingly/14 50.00
DS Darryl Strawberry/17 25.00
ES Duke Snider/18 45.00
FT Frank Thomas/14 40.00
GA Sparky Anderson/27 25.00
GC Gary Carter/19 30.00
HK Harmon Killebrew/22 45.00
JF Nellie Fox/19 120.00
JG Juan Gonzalez/15 35.00
JH "Catfish" Hunter/15 35.00
KG Ken Griffey Jr./15 75.00
LB Yogi Berra/19 50.00
MM Mike Mussina/13 35.00
NR Nolan Ryan/27 60.00
OC Orlando Cepeda/17 25.00
OS Ozzie Smith/19 50.00
PN Phil Niekro/24 25.00
RC Roger Clemens/20 60.00
RI Phil Rizzuto/13 50.00
RJ Randy Johnson/16 40.00
RY Robin Yount/20 40.00
TS Tom Seaver/20 85.00
SM Stan Musial/22 85.00
SS Sammy Sosa/15 75.00
WS Willie Stargell/21 40.00

Famous Nicknames Autograph

NM/M
Production 50 sets
AD Andre Dawson 45.00
AR Alex Rodriguez 150.00
BM Bill Mazeroski 65.00
BR Brooks Robinson 60.00
DM Don Mattingly 120.00
FT Frank Thomas 70.00
HK Harmon Killebrew 70.00
HM Hideki Matsui 350.00
JB Jeff Bagwell 80.00
JG Juan Gonzalez 50.00
KG Ken Griffey Jr. 160.00
LJ Chipper Jones 80.00
MM Mike Mussina 60.00
NR Nolan Ryan 125.00
OS Ozzie Smith 90.00
PN Phil Niekro 45.00
RC Roger Clemens 150.00
RY Robin Yount 75.00
TS Tom Seaver 65.00
WI Dontrelle Willis 60.00

Hall of Fame Numbers

NM/M
Quantity produced listed
AJ Andruw Jones/25 30.00
BG Bob Gibson/45 35.00
BW Billy Williams/26 20.00
CD Carlos Delgado/25 25.00
CH Jim "Catfish" Hunter/27 40.00
CL Roger Clemens/22 50.00
CS Curt Schilling/38 25.00
DD Don Drysdale/50 35.00
DS Don Sutton/20 25.00
EG Eric Gagne/38 25.00
EM Eddie Mathews/41 50.00
FR Frank Robinson/20 25.00
FT Frank Thomas/35 40.00
GL Tom Glavine/47 25.00
GM Greg Maddux/31 45.00
GO Juan Gonzalez/35 35.00
GP Gaylord Perry/36 25.00
HE Todd Helton/17 35.00
IS Ichiro Suzuki/50 65.00
JC Jose Canseco/33 25.00
JG Jason Giambi/25 30.00
JI Jim Thome/25 30.00
JP Jim Palmer/22 35.00
KG Ken Griffey Jr./30 60.00
MA Juan Marichal/27 25.00
MP Mike Piazza/31 40.00
MR Manny Ramirez/24 30.00
MS Mike Schmidt/20 60.00
MZ Pedro Martinez/45 25.00
NR Nolan Ryan/34 70.00
OC Orlando Cepeda/30 20.00
PI Mark Prior/22 60.00
RC Roberto Clemente/21 200.00
RF Rollie Fingers/34 25.00
RH Rickey Henderson/25 40.00
RP Rafael Palmeiro/25 30.00
RY Robin Yount/19 45.00
SC Steve Carlton/32 30.00
SG Shawn Green/15 25.00
SR Scott Rolen/27 30.00
SS Sammy Sosa/21 75.00
TG Tony Gwynn/19 45.00
TH Tim Hudson/15 25.00
TS Tom Seaver/41 25.00
WB Wade Boggs/26 30.00
WS Warren Spahn/21 65.00

Hall of Fame Numbers Autograph

Production 10 Sets
No Pricing

Hall of Fame Numbers Auto. Dual

Production 10 Sets
No Pricing

Historic Cut Signatures

Production one set

Legendary Fabrics

NM/M
Production 50 unless noted 20.00
BE Johnny Bench 25.00
BG Bob Gibson 30.00
BW Billy Williams 25.00
CH "Catfish" Hunter 25.00
CR Cal Ripken Jr. 60.00
CY Carl Yastrzemski/31 45.00
EM Eddie Mathews 35.00
FR Frank Robinson 20.00
GP Gaylord Perry 20.00
HK Harmon Killebrew 40.00
JC Jose Canseco 40.00
JM Joe Morgan 20.00
JT Joe Torre 25.00
LA Luis Aparicio 25.00
LD Leo Durocher 30.00
MS Mike Schmidt 40.00
NR Nolan Ryan 50.00
OC Orlando Cepeda 20.00
OS Ozzie Smith 35.00
PO Paul O'Neill 20.00
RF Rollie Fingers 20.00
RY Robin Yount 35.00
SC Steve Carlton 25.00
TS Tom Seaver 30.00
WS Warren Spahn 40.00

Legendary Fabrics Auto. Dual

NM/M
Production 25 unless noted
AD Andre Dawson 60.00
BE Johnny Bench 75.00
BR Brooks Robinson 85.00
BW Billy Williams 65.00
CR Cal Ripken Jr. 275.00
CY Carl Yastrzemski/17 125.00
DE Dwight Evans 40.00
DM Don Mattingly 125.00
DS Don Sutton 65.00
FL Fred Lynn 70.00
FR Frank Robinson 60.00
GP Gaylord Perry 40.00
HK Harmon Killebrew 100.00
JC Jose Canseco 100.00
JM Joe Morgan 50.00
JP Jim Palmer 60.00
JT Joe Torre 70.00
KP Kirby Puckett 100.00
LA Luis Aparicio 70.00
LB Lou Brock/13 125.00
NR Nolan Ryan 200.00
OC Orlando Cepeda 45.00
OS Ozzie Smith 100.00
PM Paul Molitor 75.00
PO Paul O'Neill 70.00
RC Roger Clemens 150.00
RF Rollie Fingers 65.00
RY Robin Yount 110.00
SG Steve Garvey 60.00
ST Darryl Strawberry 65.00
TG Tony Gwynn 120.00
TS Tom Seaver 85.00
WB Wade Boggs 100.00
WI Maury Wills 45.00

Logo Threads

No Pricing
Production one set

Masters

NM/M
Quantity produced listed
AJ Andruw Jones/25 25.00
BE Josh Beckett/25 45.00
CD Carlos Delgado/25 25.00
CS Curt Schilling/38 25.00
EC Eric Chavez/3
FT Frank Thomas/35 30.00
GM Greg Maddux/31 45.00
GO Juan Gonzalez/19 30.00
HE Todd Helton/17 35.00
IS Ichiro Suzuki/50 65.00
JG Jason Giambi/25 30.00
JP Jorge Posada/20 30.00
JT Jim Thome/25 30.00
KG Ken Griffey Jr./30 60.00
MO Magglio Ordonez/30 20.00
MP Mark Prior/22 60.00
MR Manny Ramirez/24 25.00

PI Mike Piazza/31 40.00
PM Pedro Martinez/45 25.00
RC Roger Clemens/22 50.00
RH Roy Halladay/32 25.00
SG Shawn Green/15 25.00
SR Scott Rolen/27 30.00
SS Sammy Sosa/21 65.00
TH Tim Hudson/15 25.00
VW Vernon Wells/10

MVP Patch

NM/M

Production 25 sets
AR Alex Rodriguez 40.00
BR Brooks Robinson 50.00
BW Bernie Williams 35.00
CJ Chipper Jones 40.00
CR Cal Ripken Jr. 90.00
CS Curt Schilling 35.00
DJ Derek Jeter 70.00
FT Frank Thomas 40.00
GA Garret Anderson 30.00
IS Ichiro Suzuki 75.00
IV Ivan Rodriguez 40.00
JB Josh Beckett 50.00
JG Jason Giambi 30.00
KG Ken Griffey Jr. 60.00
MP Mike Piazza 50.00
MT Miguel Tejada 40.00
PM Pedro Martinez 45.00
RC Roger Clemens 60.00
RJ Randy Johnson 30.00
SS Sammy Sosa 50.00
TG Troy Glaus 25.00

Premium Patch

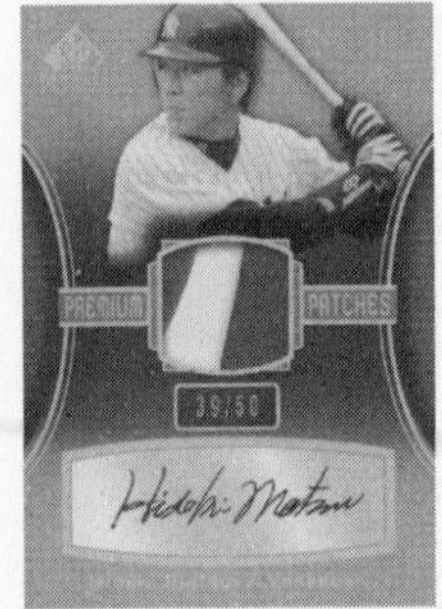

NM/M

Production 50 unless noted
AD Adam Dunn 30.00
AP Albert Pujols 50.00
AR Alex Rodriguez 50.00
AR1 Alex Rodriguez/ Yankees 65.00
AS Alfonso Soriano/34 35.00
BE Josh Beckett 30.00
BW Bernie Williams 25.00
BZ Barry Zito 25.00
CD Carlos Delgado 25.00
CJ Chipper Jones 35.00
CS Curt Schilling 25.00
DJ Derek Jeter 60.00
DW Dontrelle Willis 20.00
EC Eric Chavez 20.00
FT Frank Thomas 40.00
GM Greg Maddux 35.00
GO Juan Gonzalez 30.00
HM Hideki Matsui/17 120.00
IR Ivan Rodriguez 30.00
IS Ichiro Suzuki 65.00
JB Jeff Bagwell 30.00
JG Jason Giambi 30.00
JP Jorge Posada 30.00
JT Jim Thome 30.00
KB Kevin Brown 20.00
KG Ken Griffey Jr. 50.00
MO Magglio Ordonez 20.00
MP Mark Prior 65.00
MR Manny Ramirez 25.00
MT Miguel Tejada 20.00
PI Mike Piazza 35.00
NR Nolan Ryan 50.00
PM Pedro Martinez 30.00
RC Roger Clemens 40.00
RH Roy Halladay 20.00
RI Mariano Rivera 30.00
RJ Randy Johnson 30.00
RP Rafael Palmeiro 30.00
SG Shawn Green 20.00
SR Scott Rolen 30.00
SS Sammy Sosa 40.00
TE Mark Teixeira 20.00
TG Tom Glavine 25.00
TH Tim Hudson 25.00

Premium Patch Autograph

NM/M

Production 50 unless noted
AK Austin Kearns 45.00
AR Alex Rodriguez 150.00
BZ Barry Zito 60.00
CD Carlos Delgado 50.00
DW Dontrelle Willis 60.00
EC Eric Chavez 40.00
EG Eric Gagne 60.00
HM Hideki Matsui 350.00
IR Ivan Rodriguez 80.00
IS Ichiro Suzuki 300.00
KB Kevin Brown 45.00
KG Ken Griffey Jr. 160.00
MP Mark Prior 120.00
MT Miguel Tejada 45.00
NG Nomar Garciaparra/33 180.00
RC Roger Clemens 150.00
SG Shawn Green 50.00
TH Tim Hudson 50.00
VG Vladimir Guerrero 75.00

Significant Numbers

NM/M

Quantity produced listed
CR Cal Ripken Jr./21 120.00
CS Curt Schilling/16 40.00
CY Carl Yastrzemski/23 65.00
DS Darryl Strawberry/17 25.00
EM Eddie Mathews/17 50.00
FT Frank Thomas/14 50.00
GM Greg Maddux/18 50.00
GO Juan Gonzalez/15 40.00
GS Gary Sheffield/16 30.00
JB Jeff Bagwell/13 50.00
KG Ken Griffey Jr./15 75.00
NR Nolan Ryan/27 60.00
PO Paul O'Neill/17 25.00
RC Roger Clemens/20 50.00
RF Rollie Fingers/17 25.00
RJ Randy Johnson/16 35.00
RP Rafael Palmeiro/18 40.00
SN Duke Snider/18 50.00
SS Sammy Sosa/15 80.00
TG Tom Glavine/17 30.00
TS Tom Seaver/20 40.00

Significant Numbers Autograph

NM/M

Production 50 unless noted
AR Alex Rodriguez 150.00
BA Bobby Abreu 40.00
BG Brian Giles 40.00
BW Bernie Williams 100.00
BZ Barry Zito 60.00
CD Carlos Delgado 50.00
CJ Chipper Jones 90.00
EC Eric Chavez 40.00
EG Eric Gagne 60.00
GM Greg Maddux 110.00
HE Todd Helton 60.00
GO Juan Gonzalez 50.00
HM Hideki Matsui 350.00
KB Kevin Brown 45.00
KG Ken Griffey Jr. 160.00
LB Lou Brock/16 60.00
LG Luis Gonzalez 50.00
MM Mike Mussina 60.00
MP Mike Piazza 185.00
MS Mike Schmidt 90.00
MT Miguel Tejada 40.00
NR Nolan Ryan 140.00
PB Pat Burrell 40.00
PO Paul O'Neill 65.00
PR Mark Prior 120.00
RA Roberto Alomar 60.00
RB Rocco Baldelli 55.00
RF Rollie Fingers 40.00
RO Roy Oswalt 60.00
RP Rafael Palmeiro 70.00
RS Ryne Sandberg 90.00
SG Shawn Green 50.00
TG Tom Glavine 60.00
TH Tim Hudson 50.00
VG Vladimir Guerrero 75.00

Significant Numbers Auto. Dual

NM/M

Production 25 unless noted
AR Alex Rodriguez 200.00
BA Bobby Abreu 50.00
BG Brian Giles 50.00

BW Bernie Williams 120.00
BZ Barry Zito 80.00
CD Carlos Delgado 70.00
CJ Chipper Jones 100.00
DW Dontrelle Willis 60.00
EC Eric Chavez 65.00
EG Eric Gagne 80.00
GI Bob Gibson 100.00
GL Troy Glaus 70.00
GM Greg Maddux 125.00
HE Todd Helton 85.00
GO Juan Gonzalez 75.00
HM Hideki Matsui 500.00
KB Kevin Brown 65.00
KG Ken Griffey Jr. 200.00
KP Kirby Puckett 100.00
LB Lou Brock/14 85.00
LG Luis Gonzalez 50.00
MM Mike Mussina 80.00
MP Mike Piazza 200.00
MS Mike Schmidt 140.00
MT Miguel Tejada 50.00
NR Nolan Ryan 200.00
PB Pat Burrell 60.00
PO Paul O'Neill 80.00
RA Roberto Alomar 80.00
RF Rollie Fingers 65.00
RP Rafael Palmeiro 100.00
RS Ryne Sandberg 150.00
SG Shawn Green 60.00
TG Tom Glavine 80.00
TH Tim Hudson 75.00
VG Vladimir Guerrero 100.00
TO Tony Gwynn 120.00
TS Tom Seaver 85.00

Star Potential Patch

NM/M

Quantity produced listed
AS Alfonso Soriano/12
BW Brandon Webb/50 25.00
CP Corey Patterson/20 30.00
DW Dontrelle Willis/35 30.00
EC Eric Chavez/3
HA Roy Halladay/32 30.00
HB Hank Blalock/9
IS Ichiro Suzuki/50 65.00
HB Josh Beckett/21 40.00
JR Jose Reyes/7
LB Lance Berkman/17 30.00
MM Mark Mulder/20 35.00
MP Mark Prior/22 65.00
MT Mark Teixeira/23 25.00
RB Rocco Baldelli/5
RH Rich Harden/40 25.00
RO Roy Oswalt/44 25.00
RS Richie Sexson/11
RW Rickie Weeks/23 40.00
TE Miguel Tejada/4
TG Troy Glaus/25 40.00
TH Tim Hudson/15 30.00
VW Vernon Wells/10

Stellar Combos

NM/M

Production 25 unless noted
AD Derek Jeter, Alfonso Soriano 75.00
AJ Alex Rodriguez, Juan Gonzalez 50.00
AT Jim Thome, Bobby Abreu 40.00
BK Jeff Bagwell, Jeff Kent 30.00
BT Mark Teixeira, Hank Blalock 40.00
CA Roberto Alomar, Joe Carter 60.00
CO Roger Clemens, Roy Oswalt 60.00
CR Randy Johnson, Curt Schilling 35.00
DG Jason Giambi, Carlos Delgado 40.00
DK Austin Kearns, Adam Dunn 40.00
GH Eric Gagne, Trevor Hoffman 40.00
GT Greg Maddux, Tom Glavine 65.00
JJ Andruw Jones, Chipper Jones 50.00
KR Nolan Ryan, Jerry Koosman 85.00
LP Mike Piazza, Al Leiter 50.00
LS Fred Lynn, Ichiro Suzuki 75.00
MG Don Mattingly, Jason Giambi 80.00
MT Frank Thomas, Edgar Martinez 50.00
MY Paul Molitor, Robin Yount 70.00
NB Hideo Nomo, Kevin Brown 40.00
NY Alfonso Soriano, Jose Reyes 40.00
PC Mark Prior, Roger Clemens 80.00
PE Albert Pujols, Jim Edmonds 80.00
PM Mike Mussina, Andy Pettitte 50.00
PP Mike Piazza, Jorge Posada 60.00
PS Sammy Sosa, Rafael Palmeiro 60.00
RB Ivan Rodriguez, Josh Beckett 50.00
RJ Alex Rodriguez, Derek Jeter 100.00
RR Alex Rodriguez, Cal Ripken Jr. 180.00
RS Mike Schmidt, Brooks Robinson 75.00
SG Shawn Green, Duke Snider 40.00
SJ Randy Johnson, Gary Sheffield 40.00
SM Pedro Martinez, Curt Schilling 50.00
SR Nolan Ryan, Curt Schilling 65.00
TO Frank Thomas, Magglio Ordonez 60.00
WC Roger Clemens, David Wells 50.00
WH Larry Walker, Todd Helton 45.00
WS Sammy Sosa, Billy Williams 65.00
ZH Barry Zito, Tim Hudson 50.00
RJ Alex Rodriguez, Derek Jeter 100.00
RG Cal Ripken Jr., Lou Gehrig 350.00
SC Ty Cobb, Ichiro Suzuki 180.00

Team Threads

Production 10 unless noted
No Pricing

Triple Authentic

Production 10
No Pricing

World Series Stars

NM/M

Production 50 unless noted
AJ Andruw Jones 20.00
AP Andy Pettitte/15 40.00
AS Alfonso Soriano/15 35.00
BL Barry Larkin 25.00
BW Bernie Williams 25.00
CA Jose Canseco 30.00
CJ Chipper Jones 30.00
CS Curt Schilling 25.00
CY Carl Yastrzemski/31 50.00
DW Dontrelle Willis 20.00
GA Garret Anderson 25.00
GL Troy Glaus 40.00
GM Greg Maddux 30.00
HM Hideki Matsui/17 140.00
IR Ivan Rodriguez 30.00
JB Josh Beckett 30.00
JE Derek Jeter 50.00
JM Joe Morgan 20.00
JP Jorge Posada 30.00
JT Jim Thome 25.00
KB Kevin Brown 20.00
MM Mike Mussina/43 25.00
MP Mike Piazza 35.00
MR Mariano Rivera 30.00
MS Mike Schmidt 40.00
PM Paul Molitor 35.00
PO Paul O'Neill 20.00
RC Roger Clemens 35.00
RF Rollie Fingers 25.00
RJ Randy Johnson 30.00
TG Tom Glavine 25.00

World Series Stars Autograph

No Pricing
Production one set

300 Win Club

Production 10 Sets

3000 Hit Club

Production 10 Sets

500 HR Club

Production 10 Sets

2004 SP LEGENDARY CUTS

		NM/M
Complete Set (126):		
Common Player:		.40
Pack (4):		12.00
Box (12):		120.00
1	Al Kaline	1.00
2	Al Lopez	.40
3	Alan Trammell	.40
4	Andre Dawson	.40
5	Babe Ruth	3.00
6	Bert Campaneris	.40
7	Bill Mazeroski	.40
8	Bill Russell	.40
9	Billy Williams	.40
10	Bob Feller	.50
11	Bob Gibson	.75
12	Bob Lemon	.40
13	Bobby Doerr	.40
14	Brooks Robinson	1.00
15	Cal Ripken Jr.	3.00
16	Carl Yastrzemski	1.00
17	Carlton Fisk	.40
18	Jim "Catfish" Hunter	.40
19	Dale Murphy	.40
20	Darryl Strawberry	.40
21	Dave Concepcion	.40
22	Dave Winfield	.50
23	Dennis Eckersley	.40
24	Denny McLain	.40
25	Don Drysdale	.50
26	Don Larsen	.50
27	Don Mattingly	2.00
28	Don Sutton	.40
29	Duke Snider	1.00
30	Dusty Baker	.40
31	Dwight Gooden	.40
32	Earl Weaver	.40
33	Early Wynn	.40
34	Eddie Mathews	1.00
35	Eddie Murray	.75
36	Enos Slaughter	.40
37	Ernie Banks	1.50
38	Fergie Jenkins	.40
39	Frank Robinson	.75
40	Fred Lynn	.40
41	Gary Carter	.50
42	Gaylord Perry	.40
43	George Brett	2.00
44	George Foster	.40
45	George Kell	.40
46	Greg Luzinski	.40
47	Hal Newhouser	.40
48	Hank Greenberg	1.00
49	Harmon Killebrew	1.00
50	Honus Wagner	1.00
51	Hoyt Wilhelm	.40
52	Jackie Robinson	1.50
53	Jim Bunning	.40
54	Jim Palmer	.75
55	Jimmie Foxx	1.00
56	Joe Carter	.40
57	Joe DiMaggio	2.00
58	Joe Morgan	.40
59	Joe Torre	.40
60	Johnny Bench	1.00
61	Johnny Podres	.40
62	John Roseboro	.40
63	Johnny Sain	.40
64	Juan Marichal	.50
65	Keith Hernandez	.40
66	Kirby Puckett	.75
67	Kirk Gibson	.40
68	Will Clark	.50
69	Jim Rice	.40
70	Larry Doby	.40
71	Lou Boudreau	.40
72	Lou Brock	.50
73	Lou Gehrig	2.50
74	Lou Piniella	.40
75	Luis Aparicio	.40
76	Mark Grace	.50
77	Mel Ott	.40
78	Mickey Lolich	.40
79	Mickey Mantle	3.00
80	Mike Greenwell	.40
81	Mike Schmidt	2.00
82	Monte Irvin	.40
83	Nellie Fox	.50
84	Nolan Ryan	3.00
85	Orlando Cepeda	.40
86	Ozzie Smith	1.00
87	Paul Molitor	.75
88	Pee Wee Reese	.40
89	Phil Niekro	.40
90	Phil Rizzuto	.75
91	Ralph Kiner	.75
92	Red Rolfe	.40
93	Red Schoendienst	.40
94	Reggie Smith	.40
95	Rich "Goose" Gossage	.40
96	Richie Ashburn	.40
97	Rick Ferrell	.40
98	Elston Howard	.40
99	Roberto Clemente	2.00
100	Robin Roberts	.40
101	Robin Yount	1.00
102	Roger Maris	2.00
103	Rollie Fingers	.40
104	Ron Santo	.40
105	Roy Campanella	.75
106	Ryne Sandberg	1.50
107	Sparky Anderson	.40
108	Sparky Lyle	.40
109	Stan Musial	2.00
110	Steve Carlton	.50
111	Steve Garvey	.40
112	Ted Williams	2.50
113	Thurman Munson	1.00
114	Tom Seaver	1.00
115	Tommy Henrich	.40
116	Tommy Lasorda	.40
117	Tony Gwynn	1.00
118	Tony Perez	.40
119	Ty Cobb	1.50
120	Wade Boggs	.50
121	Warren Spahn	.75
122	Whitey Ford	.75
123	Willie McCovey	.40
124	Willie Randolph	.40
125	Willie Stargell	.50
126	Yogi Berra	.75

All-Time Autos

		NM/M
Production 50 Sets		
LA	Luis Aparicio	20.00
YB	Yogi Berra	65.00
WB	Wade Boggs	40.00
SC	Steve Carlton	20.00
GC	Gary Carter	25.00
JC	Joe Carter	20.00
OC	Orlando Cepeda	25.00
WC	Will Clark	40.00
BD	Bobby Doerr	20.00
DE	Dennis Eckersley	20.00
RF	Rollie Fingers	20.00
CF	Carlton Fisk	35.00
WF	Whitey Ford	40.00
TG	Tony Gwynn	50.00
MI	Monte Irvin	25.00
FJ	Fergie Jenkins	20.00
AK	Al Kaline	40.00
GK	George Kell	25.00
HK	Harmon Killebrew	40.00
FL	Fred Lynn	15.00
MA	Don Mattingly	60.00
BM	Bill Mazeroski	50.00
WM	Willie McCovey	40.00
MC	Denny McLain	30.00
DM	Dale Murphy	30.00
SM	Stan Musial	80.00
DN	Don Newcombe	25.00
PN	Phil Niekro	20.00
TP	Tony Perez	25.00
GP	Gaylord Perry	20.00
JP	Johnny Podres	20.00
CR	Cal Ripken Jr.	125.00
RR	Robin Roberts	30.00
NR	Nolan Ryan	125.00
SA	Ryne Sandberg	75.00
RS	Red Schoendienst	25.00
TS	Tom Seaver	50.00
DS	Don Sutton	15.00
BW	Billy Williams	20.00
MW	Maury Willis	20.00
RY	Robin Yount	75.00

Game Graphs

		NM/M
Production 25 Sets		
Gold:		No Pricing
Production 10 Sets		
LA	Luis Aparicio	25.00
EB	Ernie Banks	75.00
JB	Johnny Bench	80.00
YB	Yogi Berra	80.00
WB	Wade Boggs	50.00
GB	George Brett	100.00
LB	Lou Brock	40.00
SC	Steve Carlton	30.00
GC	Gary Carter	35.00
JC	Joe Carter	30.00
RF	Rollie Fingers	25.00
CF	Carlton Fisk	50.00
BG	Bob Gibson	40.00
TG	Tony Gwynn	65.00
AK	Al Kaline	50.00
HK	Harmon Killebrew	50.00
JM	Juan Marichal	35.00
MA	Don Mattingly	80.00
BM	Bill Mazeroski	50.00
WM	Willie McCovey	50.00
PM	Paul Molitor	40.00
MO	Joe Morgan	40.00
DM	Dale Murphy	40.00
EM	Eddie Murray	85.00
SM	Stan Musial	100.00
PN	Phil Niekro	30.00
KP	Kirby Puckett	75.00
CR	Cal Ripken Jr.	180.00
PR	Phil Rizzuto	40.00
BR	Brooks Robinson	40.00
FR	Frank Robinson	40.00
NR	Nolan Ryan	175.00
RS	Ryne Sandberg	85.00
MS	Mike Schmidt	80.00
TS	Tom Seaver	60.00
OS	Ozzie Smith	75.00
SN	Duke Snider	50.00
DS	Don Sutton	20.00
BW	Billy Williams	25.00
DW	Dave Winfield	30.00
CY	Carl Yastrzemski	85.00
RY	Robin Yount	85.00

Historic Patches

		NM/M
Production 25 Sets		
EB	Ernie Banks	50.00
GB	George Brett	60.00
DD	Don Drysdale	40.00
BG	Bob Gibson	25.00
TG	Tony Gwynn	50.00
EM	Eddie Mathews	30.00
SM	Stan Musial	60.00
CR	Cal Ripken Jr.	100.00
NR	Nolan Ryan	75.00
TS	Tom Seaver	50.00
DS	Duke Snider	30.00
CY	Carl Yastrzemski	60.00
RY	Robin Yount	50.00

Historic Quads

No Pricing
Production 10 Sets

Historic Swatches

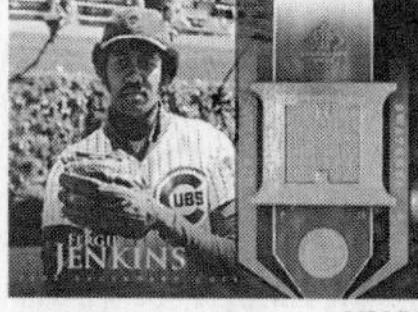

		NM/M
Common Swatch:		4.00
Golds:		2X-3X
Production 25 Sets		
AN	Sparky Anderson	4.00
JB	Johnny Bench SP	10.00
GB	George Brett	12.00
LB	Lou Brock	8.00
GC	Gary Carter	6.00
JC	Joe Carter	6.00
DC	Dave Concepcion	4.00
DD	Don Drysdale	8.00
RF	Rollie Fingers	6.00
CF	Carlton Fisk	8.00
GF	George Foster	4.00
SG	Steve Garvey	4.00
CH	Jim "Catfish" Hunter	6.00
FJ	Fergie Jenkins	8.00
HK	Harmon Killebrew	10.00
DL	Don Larsen SP	10.00
ML	Mickey Lolich	4.00
SL	Sparky Lyle	4.00
MA	Eddie Mathews	10.00
DM	Don Mattingly	15.00
PM	Paul Molitor	6.00
JM	Joe Morgan	6.00
TM	Thurman Munson	12.00
MU	Dale Murphy	8.00
EM	Eddie Murray SP	10.00
SM	Stan Musial	20.00
PN	Phil Niekro	6.00
GP	Gaylord Perry	6.00
JP	Johnny Podres	6.00
KP	Kirby Puckett	10.00
JR	Jim Rice	8.00
CR	Cal Ripken Jr.	20.00
BR	Brooks Robinson	8.00
NR	Nolan Ryan	20.00
TS	Tom Seaver	8.00
OS	Ozzie Smith	10.00
DS	Don Sutton	4.00
HW	Hoyt Wilhelm	4.00
DW	Dave Winfield	6.00
RY	Robin Yount	8.00

Historical Cuts

Quantity Produced Listed
No Pricing

Legendary Cuts

		NM/M
Quantity produced listed		
GA	Grover Alexander/2	
WA	Walter Alston/74	200.00
AN	Cap Anson/1	
LU	Luke Appling/108	150.00
RA	Richie Ashburn/31	350.00
FB	Frank Baker/3	
PB	Cool Papa Bell/47	
CB	Chief Bender/6	
BO	Jim Bottomley/2	
LB	Lou Boudreau/199	125.00
MB	"Three Finger" Mordecai Brown/2	
JA	Jack Buck/2	
JB	"Bullet" Joe Bush/1	
RC	Roy Campanella/3	
CA	Max Carey/72	
FC	Frank Chance/1	
CL	Fred Clarke/2	
RO	Roberto Clemente/9	
TC	Ty Cobb/18	
MC	Mickey Cochrane/7	
CO	Eddie Collins/6	6.00
EC	Earle Combs/27	350.00
CC	Charlie Comiskey/2	
CJ	"Colby" Jack Coombs/1	
ST	Stan Coveleski/102	150.00
SC	"Wahoo" Sam Crawford/9	
CR	Joe Cronin/84	
KC	Kiki Cuyler/4	
RD	Ray Dandridge/199	125.00
DD	Dizzy Dean/33	650.00
BD	Bill Dickey/82	250.00
JD	Joe DiMaggio/111	500.00
DO	Larry Doby/14	400.00
DR	Don Drysdale/66	450.00
DU	Joe Dugan/9	
LD	Leo Durocher/75	400.00
RF	Rick Ferrell/44	160.00
WF	Wes Ferrell/36	200.00
NF	Nellie Fox/14	
JF	Jimmie Foxx/15	
FF	Frankie Frisch/57	450.00
GE	Lou Gehrig/7	
CG	Charlie Gehringer/171	200.00
BG	A. Bartlett Giamatti/2	
LG	Lefty Gomez/98	325.00
HG	Hank Greenberg/37	500.00
BU	Burleigh Grimes/83	200.00
GR	Lefty Grove/75	375.00
GH	Gabby Hartnett/19	475.00
HH	Harry Heilmann/3	
BH	Billy Herman/134	125.00
GI	Gil Hodges/9	
RH	Rogers Hornsby/5	
EH	Elston Howard/2	

WH Waite Hoyt/106 200.00
CH Carl Hubbell/199 180.00
JH Jim "Catfish" Hunter/25 220.00
BJ "Indian" Bob Johnson/32 200.00
WJ Walter Johnson/14
SJ "Sad" Sam Jones/4
CK Chuck Klein/5
HK Harvey Kuenn/49 150.00
NL Nap Lajoie/2
LA Tony Lazzeri/5
BL Bob Lemon/199 100.00
EL Ernie Lombardi/39 450.00
TL Ted Lyons/199 150.00
MK Connie Mack/9
MM Mickey Mantle/19
HM Heinie Manush/16
RM Rabbit Maranville/5
MA Roger Maris/6
RU Rube Marquard/59 220.00
BM Billy Martin/7
EM Eddie Mathews/27
MW Christy Mathewson/1
CM Carl Mays/2
SM Stuffy McInnis/2
JM Joe Medwick/32 450.00
MI Johnny Mize/118 140.00
TM Thurman Munson/2
HN Hal Newhouser/51 140.00
KN Kid Nichols/4 2,500
MO Mel Ott/17
SP Satchel Paige/28 1,325
HP Herb Pennock/2
GP George Pipgras/46 200.00
EP Eddie Plank/1
PR Pee Wee Reese/35 350.00
AR Allie Reynolds/25
SR Sam Rice/28 500.00
JR Jackie Robinson/19
ER Edd Roush/129 125.00
RR Red Ruffing/30 500.00
BR Babe Ruth/13
JS Joe Sewell/199 140.00
AS Al Simmons/10
GS George Sisler/32 850.00
ES Enos Slaughter/147 125.00
TS Tris Speaker/4
WS Willie Stargell/39 220.00
CS Casey Stengel/38
PT Pie Traynor/6
DV Dazzy Vance/5
AV Arky Vaughan/4
HW Honus Wagner/17
BW Bobby Wallace/2
ED Ed Walsh/5
PW Paul Waner/9
WM Hoyt Wilhelm/115 100.00
TW Ted Williams/28
WI Hack Wilson/5
SW "Smokey" Joe Wood/79 400.00
EW Early Wynn/54 200.00
CY Cy Young/5

Legendary Duels

NM/M

Production 25 Sets
BG George Brett, Rich "Goose" Gossage 40.00
DW Joe DiMaggio, Ted Williams 150.00
EG Dennis Eckersley, Kirk Gibson 25.00
FM Joe Morgan, Carlton Fisk 30.00
GL Bob Gibson, Mickey Lolich 30.00
MW Mickey Mantle, Ted Williams 200.00
PL Johnny Podres, Don Larsen 30.00
RM Juan Marichal, John Roseboro 30.00
RR Pee Wee Reese, Phil Rizzuto 35.00
SM Duke Snider, Mickey Mantle 125.00
SS Ryne Sandberg, Ozzie Smith 80.00
WB Ernie Banks, Honus Wagner 125.00

Legendary Duels Patch

No Pricing
Production 15 Sets

Legendary Duos

NM/M

Production 25 Sets
DM Joe DiMaggio, Mickey Mantle 200.00
MM Mickey Mantle, Roger Maris 200.00
MY Paul Molitor, Robin Yount 30.00
PJ Jackie Robinson, Pee Wee Reese 75.00
RS Tom Seaver, Nolan Ryan 65.00
SC Roy Campanella, Duke Snider 40.00
SS Johnny Sain, Warren Spahn 40.00

Legendary Duos Patch

No Pricing
Production 15 Sets

Legendary Sigs

NM/M

Production 50 Sets
LA Luis Aparicio 20.00
EB Ernie Banks 60.00
JB Johnny Bench 60.00
WB Wade Boggs 40.00
GC Gary Carter 25.00
JC Joe Carter 20.00
WC Will Clark 40.00
BD Bobby Doerr 20.00
DE Dennis Eckersley 20.00
BF Bob Feller 30.00
RF Rollie Fingers 20.00
BG Bob Gibson 35.00
TG Tony Gwynn 50.00
MI Monte Irvin 25.00
AK Al Kaline 40.00
GK George Kell 25.00
HK Harmon Killebrew 40.00
RK Ralph Kiner 30.00
FL Fred Lynn 15.00
JM Juan Marichal 30.00
MA Don Mattingly 60.00
WM Willie McCovey 40.00
MC Denny McLain 30.00
DM Dale Murphy 30.00
EM Eddie Murray 80.00
DN Don Newcombe 25.00
PA Jim Palmer 30.00
GP Gaylord Perry 20.00
JP Johnny Podres 20.00
CR Cal Ripken Jr. 125.00
PR Phil Rizzuto 25.00
RR Robin Roberts 30.00
BR Brooks Robinson 40.00
SA Ryne Sandberg 75.00
MS Mike Schmidt 60.00
RS Red Schoendienst 25.00
OS Ozzie Smith 65.00
SN Duke Snider 40.00
DS Don Sutton 15.00
MW Maury Wills 20.00
CY Carl Yastrzemski 75.00

Legendary Swatches

NM/M

Common Swatch: 4.00
Golds: No Pricing
Production 15 Sets
EB Ernie Banks SP 15.00
JB Johnny Bench 10.00
YB Yogi Berra 12.00
WB Wade Boggs 6.00
GB George Brett 12.00
RC Roy Campanella 10.00
SC Steve Carlton 6.00
OC Orlando Cepeda 6.00
BD Bobby Doerr 8.00
DD Don Drysdale 8.00
CF Carlton Fisk 8.00
NF Nellie Fox 12.00
BG Bob Gibson 8.00
TG Tony Gwynn 10.00
EH Elston Howard 8.00
CH Jim "Catfish" Hunter 8.00
AK Al Kaline 10.00
HK Harmon Killebrew 10.00
MA Juan Marichal 8.00
EM Eddie Mathews 10.00
DM Don Mattingly 15.00
WM Willie McCovey 6.00
TM Thurman Munson 12.00
SM Stan Musial 15.00
TP Tony Perez 4.00
PO Johnny Podres 6.00
PR Pee Wee Reese 8.00
JR Jim Rice 8.00
CR Cal Ripken Jr. 20.00
RI Phil Rizzuto 10.00
FR Frank Robinson 6.00
NR Nolan Ryan 20.00
MS Mike Schmidt 15.00
TS Tom Seaver 8.00
DS Duke Snider 10.00
WS Warren Spahn 10.00
ST Willie Stargell 8.00
BW Billy Williams 4.00
DW Dave Winfield 6.00
CY Carl Yastrzemski 10.00
RY Robin Yount 8.00

Marked for the Hall

NM/M

Production 50 Sets
LA Luis Aparicio 20.00
EB Ernie Banks 60.00
JB Johnny Bench 60.00
YB Yogi Berra 65.00
GB George Brett 75.00
LB Lou Brock 30.00
SC Steve Carlton 20.00
GC Gary Carter 25.00
OC Orlando Cepeda 25.00
BD Bobby Doerr 20.00
BF Bob Feller 30.00
CF Carlton Fisk 35.00
WF Whitey Ford 40.00
BG Bob Gibson 35.00
AK Al Kaline 40.00
HK Harmon Killebrew 40.00
RK Ralph Kiner 30.00
MA Juan Marichal 30.00
BM Bill Mazeroski 50.00
WM Willie McCovey 40.00
PM Paul Molitor 40.00
JM Joe Morgan 35.00
EM Eddie Murray 80.00
SM Stan Musial 80.00
PN Phil Niekro 20.00
JP Jim Palmer 30.00
TP Tony Perez 25.00
GP Gaylord Perry 20.00
KP Kirby Puckett 60.00
PR Phil Rizzuto 25.00
RR Robin Roberts 30.00
BR Brooks Robinson 40.00
FR Frank Robinson 30.00
NR Nolan Ryan 125.00
MS Mike Schmidt 60.00
TS Tom Seaver 50.00
OS Ozzie Smith 65.00
DS Duke Snider 40.00
BW Billy Williams 20.00
DW Dave Winfield 30.00
CY Carl Yastrzemski 75.00
RY Robin Yount 75.00

Marks of Greatness

NM/M

Production 50 Sets
EB Ernie Banks 60.00
JB Johnny Bench 60.00
YB Yogi Berra 65.00
WB Wade Boggs 40.00
GB George Brett 75.00
LB Lou Brock 30.00
SC Steve Carlton 20.00
JC Joe Carter 20.00
OC Orlando Cepeda 25.00
WC Will Clark 40.00
RF Rollie Fingers 20.00
CF Carlton Fisk 35.00
WF Whitey Ford 40.00
BG Bob Gibson 35.00
TG Tony Gwynn 50.00
FJ Fergie Jenkins 20.00
AK Al Kaline 40.00
HK Harmon Killebrew 40.00
FL Fred Lynn 15.00
MA Don Mattingly 60.00
MC Denny McLain 30.00
PM Paul Molitor 40.00
JM Joe Morgan 35.00
DM Dale Murphy 30.00
SM Stan Musial 80.00
DN Don Newcombe 25.00
PN Phil Niekro 20.00
JP Jim Palmer 30.00
TP Tony Perez 25.00
KP Kirby Puckett 60.00
CR Cal Ripken Jr. 125.00
BR Brooks Robinson 40.00
FR Frank Robinson 30.00
NR Nolan Ryan 125.00
RS Ryne Sandberg 75.00
MS Mike Schmidt 60.00
TS Tom Seaver 50.00
OZ Ozzie Smith 65.00
DS Duke Snider 40.00
BW Billy Williams 20.00
DW Dave Winfield 30.00
RY Robin Yount 75.00

Significant Swatches

NM/M

Common Swatch: 4.00
Golds: 2X-3X
Production 25 Sets
SA Sparky Anderson 4.00
EB Ernie Banks SP 10.00
LB Lou Brock SP 8.00
GC Gary Carter 4.00
JC Joe Carter 4.00
OC Orlando Cepeda 6.00
DC Dave Concepcion 4.00
BD Bobby Doerr 8.00
DD Don Drysdale 8.00
RF Rollie Fingers 6.00
CF Carlton Fisk 8.00
GF George Foster 4.00
SG Steve Garvey 4.00
CH Jim "Catfish" Hunter 8.00
FJ Fergie Jenkins 4.00
SL Sparky Lyle 4.00
RM Roger Maris 30.00
ED Eddie Mathews 10.00
MA Don Mattingly 15.00
BM Bill Mazeroski 8.00
WM Willie McCovey 6.00
PM Paul Molitor 6.00
TM Thurman Munson 12.00
DM Dale Murphy 8.00
EM Eddie Murray SP 8.00
PN Phil Niekro 6.00
TP Tony Perez 4.00
GP Gaylord Perry 6.00
JP Johnny Podres 6.00
CR Cal Ripken Jr. 20.00
FR Frank Robinson 6.00
NR Nolan Ryan 20.00
MS Mike Schmidt 15.00
TS Tom Seaver 8.00
SN Duke Snider 10.00
WS Warren Spahn 10.00
ST Willie Stargell 8.00
DS Don Sutton 4.00
HW Hoyt Wilhelm 4.00
DW Dave Winfield 6.00
CY Carl Yastrzemski 10.00
RY Robin Yount 8.00

Significant Trips

No Pricing
Production 15 Sets

Significant Trips Patch

No Pricing
Production 10 Sets

Ultimate Autos

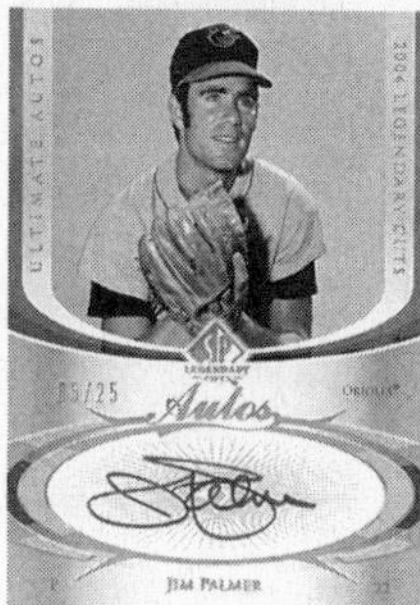

		NM/M
Production 25 Sets		
EB	Ernie Banks	75.00
JB	Johnny Bench	75.00
YB	Yogi Berra	75.00
GB	George Brett	90.00
LB	Lou Brock	35.00
SC	Steve Carlton	25.00
DE	Dennis Eckersley	25.00
BF	Bob Feller	35.00
WF	Whitey Ford	40.00
BG	Bob Gibson	40.00
MI	Monte Irvin	30.00
FJ	Fergie Jenkins	30.00
AK	Al Kaline	50.00
GK	George Kell	25.00
HK	Harmon Killebrew	50.00
RK	Ralph Kiner	40.00
MA	Juan Marichal	30.00
DM	Don Mattingly	75.00
BM	Bill Mazeroski	50.00
PM	Paul Molitor	40.00
JM	Joe Morgan	35.00
EM	Eddie Murray	80.00
SM	Stan Musial	90.00
PA	Jim Palmer	40.00
JP	Johnny Podres	25.00
KP	Kirby Puckett	70.00
PR	Phil Rizzuto	35.00
BR	Brooks Robinson	40.00
FR	Frank Robinson	40.00
NR	Nolan Ryan	150.00
SA	Ryne Sandberg	80.00
MS	Mike Schmidt	75.00
RS	Red Schoendienst	25.00
TS	Tom Seaver	50.00
OS	Ozzie Smith	65.00
SN	Duke Snider	50.00
DS	Don Sutton	20.00
MW	Maury Willis	25.00
DW	Dave Winfield	30.00
CY	Carl Yastrzemski	80.00
RY	Robin Yount	80.00

Ultimate Swatches

		NM/M
Common Swatch:		6.00
Golds:		No Pricing
Production 10 Sets		
EB	Ernie Banks	12.00
JB	Johnny Bench	10.00
YB	Yogi Berra	12.00
WB	Wade Boggs	6.00
GB	George Brett	12.00
RC	Roy Campanella	10.00
SC	Steve Carlton	6.00
JD	Joe DiMaggio SP	75.00
DD	Don Drysdale	8.00
NF	Nellie Fox	12.00
BG	Bob Gibson	8.00
HG	Hank Greenberg	20.00
TG	Tony Gwynn	10.00
CH	Jim "Catfish" Hunter	6.00
HK	Harmon Killebrew	10.00
MM	Mickey Mantle SP	
MA	Juan Marichal	8.00
RM	Roger Maris	30.00
EM	Eddie Mathews	10.00
DM	Don Mattingly	15.00
WM	Willie McCovey	6.00
TM	Thurman Munson	10.00
SM	Stan Musial	15.00
KP	Kirby Puckett	10.00
PR	Pee Wee Reese	8.00
CR	Cal Ripken Jr.	20.00
BR	Brooks Robinson	8.00
FR	Frank Robinson	6.00
JR	Jackie Robinson	40.00
NR	Nolan Ryan	20.00
MS	Mike Schmidt	15.00
TS	Tom Seaver	10.00
OS	Ozzie Smith	10.00
DS	Duke Snider SP	10.00
WS	Warren Spahn	10.00
HW	Honus Wagner SP	
BW	Billy Williams	6.00
TW	Ted Williams	75.00
DW	Dave Winfield	6.00
CY	Carl Yastrzemski	10.00
RY	Robin Yount	8.00

2004 SP PROSPECTS

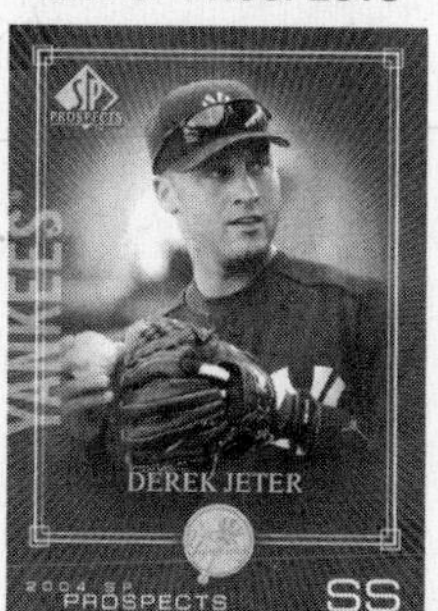

		NM/M
Complete Set (447):		
Common SP (1-90):		.50
1:pack		
Common rookie (91-290):		1.00
Common Rookie Auto (291-447):		8.00
Production 400 unless noted		
Overall Autos. 1:5		
Pack (5):		6.00
Box (24):		125.00
1	Roger Clemens	3.00
2	Melvin Mora	.50
3	Dontrelle Willis	.50
4	Jose Vidro	.50
5	Oliver Perez	.50
6	Carlos Zambrano	.50
7	Chipper Jones	1.00
8	Greg Maddux	1.50
9	Curt Schilling	1.00
10	Jose Reyes	.50
11	David Ortiz	1.00
12	Mike Piazza	2.00
13	Jason Schmidt	.50
14	Randy Johnson	1.00
15	Magglio Ordonez	.50
16	Mike Mussina	1.00
17	Jake Peavy	.50
18	Jim Edmonds	.75
19	Ken Griffey Jr.	1.50
20	Jason Giambi	.50
21	Mike Sweeney	.50
22	Carlos Lee	.50
23	Craig Wilson	.50
24	Pedro Martinez	1.00
25	Bobby Abreu	.50
26	Mike Lowell	.50
27	Miguel Cabrera	1.00
28	Hank Blalock	.75
29	Frank Thomas	.75
30	Manny Ramirez	1.00
31	Mark Mulder	.50
32	Scott Podsednik	.50
33	Albert Pujols	3.00
34	Preston Wilson	.50
35	Todd Helton	.75
36	Victor Martinez	.50
37	Kerry Wood	1.00
38	Carlos Beltran	1.00
39	Vernon Wells	.50
40	Sammy Sosa	2.00
41	Pat Burrell	.50
42	Tim Hudson	.50
43	Eric Gagne	.75
44	Jim Thome	1.00
45	Vladimir Guerrero	1.00
46	Travis Hafner	.50
47	Rickie Weeks	.50
48	Miguel Tejada	.75
49	Ivan Rodriguez	.75
50	J.D. Drew	.50
51	Ben Sheets	.50
52	Garret Anderson	.50
53	Aubrey Huff	.50
54	Nomar Garciaparra	1.50
55	Luis Gonzalez	.50
56	Lance Berkman	.50
57	Ichiro Suzuki	2.00
58	Torii Hunter	.50
59	Adam Dunn	1.00
60	Mark Teixeira	.50
61	Bret Boone	.50
62	Roy Oswalt	.50
63	Joe Mauer	.50
64	Scott Rolen	1.00
65	Hideki Matsui	2.00
66	Richie Sexson	.50
67	Jeff Kent	.50
68	Barry Zito	.50
69	C.C. Sabathia	.50
70	Carlos Delgado	.50
71	Gary Sheffield	.75
72	Shawn Green	.50
73	Jason Bay	.50
74	Andruw Jones	.50
75	Jeff Bagwell	.75
76	Rafael Palmeiro	.75
77	Alex Rodriguez	3.00
78	Adrian Beltre	.50
79	Troy Glaus	.50
80	Tom Glavine	.50
81	Paul Konerko	.50
82	Alfonso Soriano	1.00
83	Roy Halladay	.50
84	Derek Jeter	3.00
85	Josh Beckett	.50
86	Delmon Young	.50
87	Brian Giles	.50
88	Eric Chavez	.50
89	Lyle Overbay	.50
90	Mark Prior	1.00
91	*Shawn Camp*	1.00
92	Travis Smith	1.00
93	*Juan Padilla*	1.00
94	*Brad Halsey*	1.00
95	*Scott Kazmir*	4.00
96	*Sam Narron*	1.00
97	*Frank Francisco*	1.00
98	*Mike Johnston*	1.00
99	*Sam McConnell*	1.00
100	*Josh Labandeira*	1.00
101	*Kazuhito Tadano*	1.00
102	*Hector Gimenez*	1.00
103	*David Aardsma*	1.00
104	*Charles Thomas*	2.00
105	*Ian Snell*	2.00
106	*Jeff Keppinger*	1.00
107	*Michael Vento*	2.00
108	*Jerry Gil*	1.00
109	*Marty McLeary*	1.00
110	*Donnie Kelly*	1.00
111	*Roman Colon*	1.00
112	*Travis Blackley*	1.00
113	*Edwardo Sierra*	1.00
114	*Chris Shelton*	3.00
115	*Bartolome Fortunato*	1.00
116	*Brandon Medders*	1.00
117	*Merkin Valdez*	2.00
118	*Carlos Vasquez*	1.00
119	*Shingo Takatsu*	1.50
120	*Aarom Baldiris*	1.00
121	*Chris Aguila*	1.00
122	*Jimmy Serrano*	1.00
123	*Mike Gosling*	1.00
124	*Brian Dallimore*	1.00
125	*Ronald Belisario*	1.00
126	*George Sherrill*	1.00
127	*Fernando Nieve*	1.00
128	*Abe Alvarez*	1.50
129	*Jeff Bennett*	1.00
130	*Ryan Meaux*	1.00
131	*Edwin Moreno*	1.00
132	*Jesse Crain*	2.00
133	*Scott Dohmann*	1.00
134	*Ronny Cedeno*	1.00
135	*Orlando Rodriguez*	1.00
136	*Mike Wuertz*	1.00
137	*Justin Hampson*	1.00
138	*Matt Treanor*	1.00
139	*Andy Green*	1.00
140	*Yadier Molina*	2.50
141	*Joe Nelson*	1.00
142	*Justin Lehr*	1.00
143	*Ryan Wing*	1.00
144	*Kevin Cave*	1.50
145	*Evan Rust*	1.00
146	*Mike Rouse*	1.00
147	*Lance Cormier*	1.00
148	*Eduardo Villacis*	1.00
149	*Justin Knoedler*	1.00
150	*Freddy Guzman*	1.00
151	*Casey Daigle*	1.00
152	*Joey Gathright*	2.00
153	*Tim Bittner*	1.00
154	*Scott Atchison*	1.00
155	*Ivan Ochoa*	1.50
156	*Lincoln Holdzkom*	1.00
157	*Onil Joseph*	1.00
158	*Jason Bartlett*	1.00
159	*Jon Knott*	1.00
160	*Jake Woods*	1.00
161	*Jerome Gamble*	1.00
162	*Sean Henn*	1.50
163	*Kazuo Matsui*	2.00
164	*Roberto Novoa*	1.00
165	*Eddy Rodriguez*	1.00
166	*Ramon Ramirez*	1.00
167	*Enemencio Pacheco*	1.00
168	*Chad Bentz*	1.00
169	*Chris Oxspring*	1.00
170	*Justin Leone*	1.00
171	*Joe Horgan*	1.00
172	*Jose Capellan*	2.00
173	*Greg Dobbs*	1.00
174	*Jason Frasor*	1.50
175	*Shawn Hill*	1.00
176	*Carlos Hines*	1.00
177	*John Gall*	1.00
178	*Steve Andrade*	1.00
179	*Scott Proctor*	1.00
180	*Rusty Tucker*	1.00
181	*David Crouthers*	1.00
182	*Franklyn Gracesqui*	1.00
183	*Justin Germano*	1.00
184	*Alfredo Simon*	1.50
185	*Jorge Sequea*	1.00
186	*Nick Regilio*	1.00
187	*Justin Huisman*	1.00
188	*Akinori Otsuka*	1.50
189	*Luis Gonzalez*	1.00
190	*Renyel Pinto*	1.00
191	*Josh LeBlanc*	1.50
192	*Devin Ivany*	1.00
193	*Chad Blackwell*	1.50
194	*Brandon Burgess*	1.50
195	*Cory Patton*	1.50
196	*Daniel Batz*	1.50
197	*Adam Russell*	1.00
198	*Jarrett Hoffpauir*	1.50
199	*Patrick Bryant*	1.00
200	*Sean Gamble*	1.50
201	*Jermaine Brock*	1.50
202	*Benjamin Zobrist*	1.50
203	*Clay Meredith*	1.50
204	*Derek Tharpe*	1.00
205	*Brad McCann*	2.00
206	*Justin Hedrick*	1.00
207	*Clint Sammons*	2.00
208	*Richard Steik*	1.00
209	*Fernando Perez*	1.00
210	*Mark Jecmen*	1.00
211	*Benjamin Harrison*	1.00
212	*Jason Quarles*	1.00
213	*William Layman*	1.00
214	*Koley Kolberg*	1.00
215	*Randy Dicken*	1.00
216	*Barry Richmond*	1.00
217	*Timothy Murphey*	1.50
218	*John Hardy*	1.50
219	*Sebastien Boucher*	1.00
220	*Andrew Alvarado*	1.00
221	*Patrick Perry*	1.00
222	*Jarod McAuliff*	1.00
223	*Jared Gaston*	1.00
224	*William Thompson*	1.50
225	*Lucas French*	1.00
226	*Brandon Parillo*	1.00
227	*Greg Goetz*	1.00
228	*David Haehnel*	1.00
229	*James Miller*	1.00
230	*Mark Roberts*	1.00
231	*Eric Ridener*	1.00

232 *Freddy Sandoval* 1.00
234 *Carlos Medero-Stullz* 1.00
235 *Matt Shepherd* 1.00
236 *Thomas Hubbard* 1.00
238 *Kyle Bono* 1.00
239 *Craig Moldrem* 1.00
239 *Brandon Timm* 1.00
241 *Mike Carp* 2.50
242 *Joseph Muro* 1.00
243 *Derek Decarlo* 1.50
244 *Chris Niesel* 1.00
245 *Trevor Lawhorn* 1.00
246 *Joey Howell* 1.00
247 *Dustin Hahn* 1.00
248 *Jim Fasano* 2.00
249 *Hainley Statia* 1.00
250 *Brandon Conway* 1.00
251 *Christopher McConnell* 2.00
252 *Austin Shappi* 1.50
253 *Joey Metropoulos* 2.00
254 *David Nicholson* 1.50
255 *Ryan McCarthy* 2.00
256 *Michael Parisi* 1.00
257 *Andrew Macfarlane* 1.00
258 *Jeffery Dominguez* 1.50
259 *Trey Patton* 3.00
260 *Ryan Norwood* 1.50
261 *Chad Boyd* 1.00
262 *Grant Plumley* 1.00
263 *Jeffrey Katz* 2.00
264 *Cory Middleton* 1.00
265 *Andrew Moffitt* 1.00
266 *Jarrett Grube* 1.00
267 *Derek Hankins* 1.00
268 *Douglas Reinhardt* 1.00
269 *Duron Legrande* 1.00
270 *Steven Jackson* 1.00
271 *Brian Hall* 1.00
272 *Cory Wade* 1.00
273 *John Grogan* 1.00
274 *Robert Asanovich* 1.00
275 *Kevin Hart* 1.50
276 *Matt Guillory* 1.00
277 *Cliff Remole* 1.00
278 *David Trahan* 1.00
279 *Kristian Bell* 1.00
280 *Chris Westervelt* 1.00
281 *Garry Bakker* 1.00
282 *Jonny Ash* 1.00
283 *Ryan Phillips* 1.00
284 *Wes Letson* 1.00
285 *Jeff Landing* 1.00
286 *Mark Worrell* 1.00
287 *Sean Gallagher* 5.00
288 *Nick Blasi* 1.00
289 *Kevin Frandsen* 1.50
290 *Richard Mercado* 1.00
291 *Matt Bush* 50.00
292 *Mark Rogers* 25.00
293 *Homer Bailey* 40.00
294 *Chris Nelson* 75.00
295 *Thomas Diamond* 50.00
296 *Neil Walker* 30.00
297 *Bill Bray* 15.00
298 *David Purcey* 15.00
299 *Scott Elbert* 20.00
300 *Josh Fields* 35.00
301 *Chris Lambert* 10.00
302 *Trevor Plouffe* 35.00
303 *Greg Golson* 25.00
304 *Phillip Hughes* 40.00
305 *Kyle Waldrop* 30.00
306 *Richie Robnett/350* 35.00
307 *Taylor Tankersley* 25.00
308 *Blake Dewitt* 40.00
309 *Eric Hurley* 25.00
310 *James Howell* 25.00
311 *Zachary Jackson* 15.00
312 *Justin Orenduff* 20.00
313 *Tyler Lumsden* 15.00
314 *Matt Fox/600* 10.00
315 *Dan Putnam/450* 15.00
316 *Jon Poterson* 20.00
317 *Gio Gonzalez* 25.00
318 *Jay Rainville/475* 35.00
319 *Huston Street* 40.00
320 *Jeff Marquez* 15.00
321 *Eric Beattie/500* 20.00
322 *Reid Brignac/325* 50.00
323 *Yovani Gallardo* 20.00
324 *Justin Hoyman* 12.00
325 *Brandon Szymanski* 25.00
326 *Seth Smith/600* 20.00
327 *Karl Herren/600* 15.00
328 *Brian Bixler/600* 8.00
329 *Wes Whisler/600* 8.00
330 *Erick San Pedro* 10.00
331 *Billy Buckner* 15.00
332 *Jon Zeringue* 30.00
333 *Curtis Thigpen* 20.00
334 *Blake Johnson* 20.00
335 *Donny Lucy* 10.00
336 *Mike Ferris/600* 15.00
337 *Anthony Swarzak/600* 25.00
338 *Jason Jaramillo* 10.00
339 *Hunter Pence/600* 65.00
340 *Dustin Pedroia* 60.00
341 *Grant Johnson* 25.00
342 *Kurt Suzuki* 30.00
343 *Jason Vargas/600* 40.00
344 *Ray Liotta* 20.00
346 *Eric Campbell* 40.00
347 *Jeff Frazier* 15.00
348 *Gaby Hernandez* 40.00
349 *Wade Davis/600* 8.00
350 *Josh Wahpepah* 10.00
351 *Scott Lewis* 10.00
352 *Jeff Fiorentino* 25.00
353 *Steven Register/600* 10.00
354 *Michael Schlact* 15.00
355 *Eddie Prasch* 10.00
356 *Adam Lind* 25.00
357 *Ian Desmond* 50.00
358 *Josh Johnson/575* 15.00
359 *Garrett Mock/600* 8.00
360 *Danny Hill/600* 8.00
361 *Cory Dunlap/600* 25.00
362 *Grant Hansen/600* 8.00
363 *Eric Haberer* 15.00
364 *Eduardo Morlan* 20.00
365 *James Happ/600* 10.00
366 *Matt Tuiasosopo/600* 65.00
367 *Jordan Parraz* 10.00
368 *Andrew Dobies* 15.00
369 *Mark Reed* 40.00
370 *Jason Windsor* 20.00
371 *Gregory Burns/600* 20.00
372 *Christian Garcia/600* 15.00
373 *John Bowker/575* 20.00
374 *John Holt/550* 15.00
375 *Daryl Jones* 25.00
376 *Colin Mahoney* 10.00
377 *Aaron Hathaway* 15.00
378 *Matt Spring* 10.00
379 *Josh Baker* 10.00
380 *Charles Lofgren* 8.00
381 *Rafael Gonzalez* 10.00
382 *Bradley Bergesen/575* 10.00
383 *Brandon Boggs* 15.00
384 *Joseph Bauserman* 15.00
385 *Collin Balester/500* 25.00
386 *James Moore* 10.00
387 *Robert Janssen* 8.00
388 *Luis Guerra* 15.00
389 *Lucas Harrell/550* 8.00
390 *Donnie Smith/500* 10.00
391 *Mark Robinson/525* 10.00
392 *Louis Marson/550* 20.00
393 *Robert Johnson/600* 10.00
394 *Lou Santangelo/600* 8.00
395 *Tommy Hottovy* 10.00
396 *Ryan Webb* 15.00
397 *Jamar Walton* 25.00
398 *Jason Jones* 30.00
399 *Clay Timpner/600* 15.00
400 *James Parr* 30.00
401 *Sean Kazmar* 8.00
402 *Andrew Kown* 15.00
403 *Jacob McGee/600* 8.00
404 *Mike Butia/600* 15.00
405 *Paul Janish/500* 15.00
406 *Matt Macri* 25.00
407 *Mike Nickeas/500* 15.00
408 *Kyle Bloom/550* 10.00
409 *Luis Rivera/500* 10.00
410 *William Bunn/600* 15.00
411 *Enrique Barrera* 20.00
412 *Ryan Klosterman* 10.00
413 *John Raglani/515* 10.00
414 *Brandon Allen/500* 35.00
415 *Andy Baldwin/600* 8.00
416 *Mark Lowe* 15.00
417 *Mitch Einertson* 65.00
418 *Ryan Schroyer/600* 10.00
419 *Brad Davis* 10.00
420 *Jesse Hoover/500* 12.00
421 *Garrett Broshuis* 15.00
422 *Peter Pope* 15.00
423 *Brent Dlugach* 10.00
424 *Ryan Coultas* 15.00
425 *Ryan Royster* 15.00
426 *Stephen Chapman* 15.00
427 *Bryce Chamberlin* 20.00
428 *Joe Koshansky/550* 20.00
429 *William Susdorf* 8.00
430 *A.J. Johnson* 30.00
431 *Jeremy Sowers* 40.00
432 *Justin Pekarek* 20.00
433 *Brett Smith* 15.00
434 *Matt Durkin* 15.00
435 *Daniel Barone* 15.00
436 *Scott Hyde* 15.00
437 *Thomas Everidge* 15.00
444 *Mark Trumbo* 50.00
446 *Eric Patterson* 20.00
447 *Mike Rozier* 15.00

Gold

Gold (291-447): No Pricing
Production 10 sets

Platinum

No Pricing
Production one set

Draft Class

No Pricing
Production 10 sets

Draft Duos

NM/M

Common Dual Autograph: 15.00
Production 175 sets
LK Adam Lind, Ryan Klosterman 20.00
BB Bill Bray, Collin Balester 15.00
BI Bill Bray, Ian Desmond 25.00
BM William Buckner, James Moore 15.00
JH James Howell, Josh Johnson 15.00
DB Blake Dewitt, Daniel Batz 40.00
SJ Brandon Szymanski, Paul Janish 30.00
SH Brett Smith, Phillip Hughes 30.00
LS Chris Lambert, Donnie Smith 15.00
LF Chris Lambert, Mike Ferris 15.00
NS Chris Nelson, Seth Smith 50.00
NM Chris Nelson, Matt Macri 50.00
DG Cory Dunlap, Luis Guerra 30.00
BN Matt Bush, Chris Nelson 50.00
TH Curtis Thigpen, Danny Hill 15.00
PT Dan Putnam, Derek Tharpe 15.00
PJ David Purcey, Robert Janssen 15.00
DZ David Purcey, Zachary Jackson 20.00
LH Donny Lucy, Grant Hansen 15.00
PD Dustin Pedroia, Andrew Dobies 25.00
MR Eduardo Morlan, Mark Robinson 15.00
PB Eddie Prasch, Joseph Bauserman 20.00
EA Eric Beattie, Andrew Kown 20.00
EJ Eric Campbell, John Holt 30.00
EM Eric Hurley, Mike Nickeas 15.00
PI Erick San Pedro, Devin Ivany 15.00
HH Gaby Hernandez, Aaron Hathaway 20.00
SK Seth Smith, Joe Koshansky 15.00
GM Gio Gonzalez, Timothy Murphey 25.00
BH Matt Bush, Phillip Hughes 50.00
JR Grant Johnson, Mark Reed 25.00
GH Greg Golson, James Happ 20.00
GG Greg Golson, Sean Gamble 15.00
BS Homer Bailey, Brandon Szymanski 30.00
BG Homer Bailey, Rafael Gonzalez 25.00
HJ Hunter Pence, Jordan Parraz 15.00
SS Huston Street, Kurt Suzuki 50.00
SW Huston Street, Ryan Webb 40.00
HB James Howell, Chad Blackwell 25.00
JM Jason Jaramillo, Louis Marson 15.00
RS Jay Rainville, Anthony Swarzak 20.00
JP Jay Rainville, Patrick Bryant 20.00
FM Jeff Frazier, Colin Mahoney 15.00
MS Jeff Marquez, Brett Smith 20.00
MH Jeff Marquez, Jesse Hoover 25.00
SL Jeremy Sowers, Charles Lofgren 25.00
JS Jeremy Sowers, Scott Lewis 20.00
JJ Jon Poterson, Jason Jones 25.00
ZM Jon Zeringue, Garrett Mock 20.00
FH Josh Fields, Lucas Harrell 25.00
FW Josh Fields, Wes Whisler 35.00
WB Josh Wahpepah, Josh Baker 15.00
CL Justin Hoyman, Jeremy Sowers 20.00
OJ Justin Orenduff, Blake Johnson 25.00
OG Justin Orenduff, Luis Guerra 20.00
HS Karl Herren, Michael Schlact 20.00
WF Kyle Waldrop, Matt Fox 20.00
KB Kyle Waldrop, Patrick Bryant 25.00
RW Richie Robnett, Jason Windsor 25.00
SR Richie Robnett, Kurt Suzuki 35.00
RB Mark Rogers, Josh Baker 40.00
RG Mark Rogers, Yovani Gallardo 40.00
BK Matt Bush, Sean Kazmar 50.00
WE William Buckner, Enrique Barrera 15.00
WJ William Buckner, James Howell 20.00
KH Matt Durkin, Aaron Hathaway 20.00
NB Neil Walker, Brian Bixler 20.00
NK Neil Walker, Kyle Bloom 20.00
HG Phillip Hughes, Christian Garcia 25.00
HP Phillip Hughes, Jon Poterson 30.00
LA Ray Liotta, Brandon Allen 25.00
BR Reid Brignac, Ryan Royster 20.00
RP Richie Robnett, Dan Putnam 30.00
RH Richie Robnett, Huston Street 50.00
CO Steven Register, Seth Smith 25.00
TD Taylor Tankersley, Brad Davis 15.00
TV Taylor Tankersley, Jason Vargas 20.00
BT Thomas Diamond, Brandon Boggs 35.00
DH Thomas Diamond, Eric Hurley 25.00
ED Scott Elbert, Blake Dewitt 30.00
ER Scott Elbert, John Raglani 20.00
PW Trevor Plouffe, Kyle Waldrop 30.00
PR Trevor Plouffe, Mark Robinson 25.00

LR Tyler Lumsden, Adam Russell 15.00
LG Tyler Lumsden, Gio Gonzalez 25.00
JB William Buckner, Josh Johnson 20.00
BJ Matt Bush, Daryl Jones 50.00
GW Yovani Gallardo, Josh Wahpepah 15.00
JK Zachary Jackson, Ryan Klosterman 15.00
DR Blake Dewitt, John Raglani 30.00
GB Homer Bailey, Greg Goetz 30.00
WR Reid Brignac, Wade Davis 20.00
HM Jeff Marquez, Phillip Hughes 25.00
PZ Jordan Parraz, Benjamin Zobrist 20.00
RL Luis Rivera, William Layman 15.00
EC Eric Beattie, Collin Mahoney 15.00
JE Jeff Frazier, Eric Beattie 15.00
BP Matt Bush, Trevor Plouffe 50.00
CH Ryan Coultas, Aaron Hathaway 15.00
SB Jeremy Sowers, Homer Bailey 35.00
FB Jeff Fiorentino, Bradley Bergesen 25.00
CF Bryce Chamberlin, Jeff Fiorentino 20.00
RD Cory Dunlap, John Raglani 20.00
ZP Hunter Pence, Benjamin Zobrist 15.00

Draft Generations Triple Autograph

No Pricing
Production 25 sets

Draft Picks Autographs

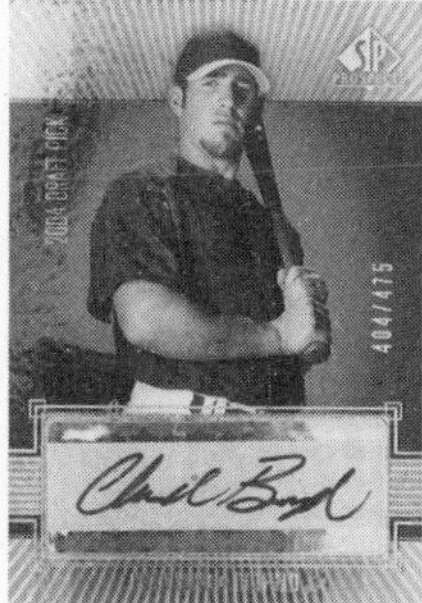

NM/M

Common Autograph: 8.00
Golds: No Pricing
Production 10 sets
Platinum: No Pricing
Production one set

AA Andrew Alvarado/400 8.00
RA Robert Asanovich/400 15.00
JA Jonny Ash/400 15.00
GB Garry Bakker/400 8.00
DB Daniel Batz/400 10.00
KB Kristian Bell/400 8.00
BL Chad Blackwell/400 10.00
NB Nick Blasi/400 8.00
BO Kyle Bono/400 10.00
SB Sebastien Boucher/325 15.00
CB Chad Boyd/475 8.00
JB Jermaine Brock/400 8.00
PB Patrick Bryant/400 10.00
BB Brandon Burgess/400 10.00
CA Mike Carp/400 50.00
BC Brandon Conway/400 8.00
DD Derek Decarlo/400 10.00
RD Randy Dicken/475 8.00
JD Jeffery Dominguez/400 15.00
JF Jim Fasano/400 15.00
KF Kevin Frandsen/400 10.00
LF Lucas French/400 15.00
SE Sean Gallagher/400 60.00
SG Sean Gamble/400 8.00
GA Jared Gaston/400 15.00
GG Greg Goetz/400 15.00
GR John Grogan/475 10.00
JG Jarrett Grube/400 8.00
MG Matt Guillory/400 10.00
DA David Haehnel/475 8.00
HA Dustin Hahn/400 8.00
BH Brian Hall/400 15.00
DH Derek Hankins/400 8.00
JO John Hardy/475 10.00
BE Benjamin Harrison/387 10.00
KH Kevin Hart/400 10.00
HE Justin Hedrick/400 8.00
JH Jarrett Hoffpauir/400 15.00
HO Joey Howell/400 15.00
TH Thomas Hubbard/400 10.00
DI Devin Ivany/550 10.00
SJ Steven Jackson/475 10.00
MJ Mark Jecmen/600 8.00
JK Jeffrey Katz/400 10.00
KK Koley Kolberg/400 10.00
LA Jeff Landing/400 8.00
TL Trevor Lawhorn/475 10.00
WL William Layman/400 8.00
JL Josh LeBlanc/400 8.00
DL Duron Legrande/400 8.00
LE Wes Letson/400 10.00
MA Andrew Macfarlane/400 8.00
MC Jarod McAuliff/400 10.00
BM Brad McCann/400 25.00
RM Ryan McCarthy/400 15.00
CH Christopher McConnell/400 30.00
ME Carlos Medero-Stullz/400 8.00
RI Richard Mercado/475 10.00
CL Clay Meredith/400 15.00
JM Joey Metropoulos/400 15.00
CM Cory Middleton/400 8.00
MI James Miller/475 8.00
AM Andrew Moffitt/400 10.00
MO Craig Molldrem/400 8.00
MU Joseph Muro/400 8.00
TM Timothy Murphey/400 10.00
DN David Nicholson/475 10.00
CN Chris Niesel/475 15.00
RN Ryan Norwood/400 30.00
BP Brandon Parillo/475 15.00
MP Michael Parisi/475 10.00
CP Cory Patton/400 10.00
TP Troy Patton/400 50.00
FP Fernando Perez/400 8.00
PP Patrick Perry/475 15.00
RP Ryan Phillips/400 15.00
GP Grant Plumley/475 10.00
JQ Jason Quarles/400 8.00
DR Douglas Reinhardt/400 8.00
CR Cliff Remole/400 10.00
BR Barry Richmond/400 10.00
ER Eric Ridener/475 10.00
MR Mark Roberts/400 8.00
AR Adam Russell/550 8.00
CS Clint Sammons/400 12.00
FS Freddy Sandoval/400 10.00
AS Austin Shappi/475 15.00
MS Matt Shepherd/400 8.00
HS Hainley Statia/400 20.00
RS Richard Steik/400 8.00
DT Derek Tharpe/400 8.00
WT William Thompson/475 10.00
BT Brandon Timm/475 15.00
TR David Trahan/400 10.00
CW Cory Wade/400 15.00
WE Chris Westervelt/400 12.00
MW Mark Worrell/400 10.00
BZ Benjamin Zobrist/600 15.00

Link to the Future Dual Autograph

NM/M

Common Dual Auto. 10.00
Production 100 sets

BD Adrian Beltre, Blake Dewitt 40.00
RF Scott Rolen, Mike Ferris 50.00
JR Andruw Jones, Richie Robnett 30.00
KB Scott Kazmir, Reid Brignac 40.00
JB Jason Kendall, Brian Bixler 20.00
SR Ben Sheets, Mark Rogers 40.00
GP Brian Giles, Dan Putnam 20.00
BG Carlos Beltran, Greg Golson 50.00
SJ Johan Santana, Jay Rainville 50.00
WT Dontrelle Willis, Taylor Tankersley 15.00
JJ Edwin Jackson, Blake Johnson 25.00
EJ Eric Chavez, Josh Fields 30.00
QT Guillermo Quiroz, Curtis Thigpen 10.00
KW Jason Kendall, Neil Walker 40.00
VM Javier Vazquez, Jeff Marquez 20.00
MP Joe Mauer, Trevor Plouffe 50.00
SW Johan Santana, Kyle Waldrop 50.00
VP Javier Vazquez, Jon Poterson 20.00
GS Ken Griffey Jr., Brandon Szymanski 75.00
WB Kerry Wood, Homer Bailey 50.00
MS Mike Mussina, Brett Smith 50.00
HS Todd Helton, Seth Smith 30.00
GZ Luis Gonzalez, Jon Zeringue 20.00
OH Magglio Ordonez, Karl Herren 20.00
MB Mark Mulder, Bill Bray 20.00
PJ Mark Prior, Grant Johnson 50.00
CF Matt Clement, Matt Fox 15.00
TN Miguel Tejada, Chris Nelson 40.00
MH Mike Mussina, Phillip Hughes 50.00
GB Nomar Garciaparra, Matt Bush 100.00
PE Odalis Perez, Scott Elbert 20.00
LS Paul LoDuca, Erick San Pedro 15.00
HW Rich Harden, Kyle Waldrop 25.00
CD Roger Clemens, Thomas Diamond 100.00
RP Alexis Rios, David Purcey 20.00
RE Roy Oswalt, Eric Hurley 20.00
RL Scott Rolen, Chris Lambert 50.00
TS Tim Hudson, Huston Street 50.00
TJ Tom Glavine, Jeremy Sowers 35.00
VD Victor Martinez, Donny Lucy 25.00
BH Angel Berroa, James Howell 10.00

Link to the Past Dual Autograph

NM/M

Common Dual Autograph
Production 50 sets

MB Bill Mazeroski, Brian Bixler 35.00
FL Carlton Fisk, Tyler Lumsden 35.00
WJ Dave Winfield, Zachary Jackson 35.00
BW Johnny Bench, Neil Walker 40.00
JD Jose Canseco, Dan Putnam 50.00
AS Billy Williams, Richie Robnett 40.00
RB Nolan Ryan, Homer Bailey 125.00
PD Gaylord Perry, Thomas Diamond 50.00
WR Wade Boggs, Reid Brignac 60.00
WB Whitey Ford, Brett Smith 30.00
WP Whitey Ford, Phillip Hughes 50.00

Link to the Future Triple Autograph

NM/M

Common Triple Auto.
Production 50 sets

BHH Hank Blalock, Eric Hurley, Benjamin Harrison 40.00
KBS Scott Kazmir, Reid Brignac, Matt Spring 75.00
SRB Ben Sheets, Mark Rogers, Josh Baker 50.00
JJB Edwin Jackson, Blake Johnson, Daniel Batz 20.00
SWM Johan Santana, Kyle Waldrop, Eduardo Morlan 60.00
VBB Jose Vidro, Bill Bray, Collin Balester 30.00
GSJ Ken Griffey Jr., Brandon Szymanski, Paul Janish 60.00
MSH Mike Mussina, Brett Smith, Jesse Hoover 50.00
OFA Magglio Ordonez, Josh Fields, Brandon Allen 25.00
PJR Mark Prior, Grant Johnson, Mark Reed 100.00
GHM Juan Gonzalez, James Howell, James Moore 40.00
HSW Rich Harden, Huston Street, Jason Windsor 50.00
GMZ Luis Gonzalez, Garrett Mock, Jon Zeringue 25.00
HRW Tim Hudson, Richie Robnett, Ryan Webb 60.00
GTR Vladimir Guerrero, Mark Trumbo, Luis Rivera 75.00

National Honors

NM/M

Common Player: 4.00
Inserted 1:12

DB Daniel Bard 8.00
TB Travis Buck 8.00
JC Jeff Clement 8.00
BC Brent Cox 8.00
TC Trevor Crowe 4.00
JD Joey Devine 4.00
AG Alex Gordon 10.00
BH Brett Hayes 4.00
LH Luke Hochevar 8.00
SK Stephen Kahn 4.00
IK Ian Kennedy 8.00
JL Jed Lowrie 4.00
JM John Mayberry Jr. 8.00
MP Mike Pelfrey 8.00
CR Cesar Ramos 8.00
MR Mark Romanczuk 4.00
RR Ricky Romero 8.00
DS Drew Stubbs 8.00
TE Taylor Teagarden 8.00
TT Troy Tulowitzki 15.00
CV Chris Valaika 4.00
RZ Ryan Zimmerman 15.00

2004 SPX

NM/M

Complete Set (202):
Common Player: .25
Common SP (111-145): 3.00
Production 1,599
Common SP (146-154): 5.00
Production 499
Common SP (155-160): 8.00

Production 299
Common Jersey Auto (161-202): 8.00
Production 799
Pack (4): 7.50
Box (18): 110.00

#	Player	Price
1	Alfonso Soriano	1.50
2	Todd Helton	1.00
3	Andruw Jones	.75
4	Eric Gagne	.75
5	Craig Wilson	.25
6	Brian Giles	.25
7	Miguel Tejada	.75
8	Kevin Brown	.50
9	Shawn Green	.50
10	Ben Sheets	.50
11	John Smoltz	.50
12	Tim Hudson	.50
13	Jason Schmidt	.50
14	Paul Konerko	.25
15	Randy Johnson	1.50
16	Roy Oswalt	.50
17	Mike Lowell	.50
18	Carlos Lee	.25
19	Sean Burroughs	.25
20	Edgar Renteria	.50
21	Michael Young	.25
22	Jose Vidro	.25
23	Scott Rolen	1.50
24	Rafael Furcal	.25
25	Tom Glavine	.75
26	Scott Podsednik	.25
27	Gary Sheffield	.75
28	Eric Chavez	.50
29	Mark Prior	1.50
30	Chipper Jones	1.50
31	Frank Thomas	1.00
32	Victor Martinez	.25
33	Jake Peavy	.25
34	Carlos Beltran	1.00
35	Roy Halladay	.25
36	Mark Teixeira	.50
37	Jacque Jones	.25
38	Mike Sweeney	.25
39	Troy Glaus	.50
40	Pat Burrell	.50
41	Ichiro Suzuki	3.00
42	Vladimir Guerrero	1.50
43	Bobby Abreu	.50
44	Jim Edmonds	.75
45	Garret Anderson	.50
46	J.D. Drew	.50
47	C.C. Sabathia	.25
48	Joe Mauer	.50
49	Phil Nevin	.25
50	Hank Blalock	1.00
51	Carlos Zambrano	.50
52	Mike Piazza	2.00
53	Manny Ramirez	1.00
54	Lance Berkman	.50
55	Delmon Young	.50
56	Nomar Garciaparra	2.00
57	Alex Rodriguez	4.00
58	Rickie Weeks	.25
59	Adrian Beltre	.75
60	Albert Pujols	4.00
61	Richie Sexson	.50
62	Maggilo Ordonez	.50
63	Derrek Lee	.50
64	Sammy Sosa	2.50
65	Jason Giambi	.50
66	Curt Schilling	1.00
67	Jorge Posada	.50
68	Rafael Palmeiro	1.00
69	Jeff Kent	.50
70	Jose Reyes	.25
71	David Ortiz	1.00
72	Aubrey Huff	.25
73	Jim Thome	1.00
74	Andy Pettitte	.50
75	Barry Zito	.50
76	Carlos Delgado	.50
77	Hideki Matsui	3.00
78	Sean Casey	.25
79	Luis Gonzalez	.25
80	Marcus Giles	.25
81	Preston Wilson	.25
82	Javy Lopez	.25
83	Mark Mulder	.50
84	Derek Jeter	4.00
85	Miguel Cabrera	1.00
86	Vernon Wells	.25
87	Roger Clemens	3.00
88	Lyle Overbay	.25
89	Bret Boone	.25
90	Melvin Mora	.25
91	Greg Maddux	2.00
92	Kerry Wood	1.50
93	Ivan Rodriguez	1.00
94	Pedro J. Martinez	1.50
95	Jeff Bagwell	1.00
96	Torii Hunter	.50
97	Ken Griffey Jr.	2.00
98	Mike Mussina	.75
99	Oliver Perez	.25
100	Josh Beckett	.75
101	Bob Gibson	4.00
102	Cal Ripken Jr.	8.00
103	Ted Williams	8.00
104	Nolan Ryan	8.00
105	Mickey Mantle	10.00
106	Ernie Banks	5.00
107	Joe DiMaggio	6.00
108	Stan Musial	5.00
109	Tom Seaver	4.00
110	Mike Schmidt	6.00
111	*Jerry Gil*	3.00
112	*Dioner Navarro*	8.00
113	*Bartolome Fortunato*	8.00
114	*Carlos Hines*	3.00
115	*Franklyn Gracesqui*	3.00
116	*Aarom Baldiris*	3.00
117	*Casey Daigle*	3.00
118	*Joey Gathright*	5.00
119	*William Bergolla*	3.00
120	*Jeff Bennett*	3.00
121	*Lincoln Holdzkom*	3.00
122	*Jorge Vasquez*	3.00
123	*Donnie Kelly*	3.00
124	*Yadier Molina*	5.00
125	Ryan Wing	5.00
126	*Justin Germano*	3.00
127	*Freddy Guzman*	3.00
128	*Onil Joseph*	5.00
129	*Roman Colon*	3.00
130	*Roberto Novoa*	3.00
131	*Renyel Pinto*	3.00
132	*Evan Rust*	3.00
133	*Orlando Rodriguez*	3.00
134	*Edwardo Sierra*	3.00
135	*Mike Rose*	10.00
136	*Phil Stockman*	5.00
137	*Greg Dobbs*	5.00
138	*Brad Halsey*	3.00
139	David Aardsma	5.00
140	*Joe Hietpas*	8.00
141	*Josh Labandeira*	3.00
142	*Mariano Gomez*	3.00
143	*Jeff Bajenaru*	8.00
144	*Travis Blackley*	5.00
145	Abe Alvarez	5.00
146	*Ramon Ramirez*	8.00
147	*Edwin Moreno*	5.00
148	*Ronny Cedeno*	5.00
149	*Hector Gimenez*	5.00
150	*Carlos Vasquez*	8.00
151	Jesse Crain	5.00
152	*Logan Kensing*	5.00
153	Sean Henn	5.00
154	*Rusty Tucker*	5.00
155	*Justin Lehr*	8.00
156	*Ian Snell*	8.00
157	*Merkin Valdez*	12.00
158	*Scott Proctor*	10.00
159	*Jose Capellan*	8.00
160	*Kazuo Matsui*	10.00
161	*Chris Oxspring*	8.00
162	*Jimmy Serrano*	10.00
163	*Jeff Keppinger*	12.00
164	*Brandon Medders*	8.00
165	*Brian Dallimore*	10.00
166	*Chad Bentz*	12.00
167	*Chris Aguila*	10.00
168	*Chris Saenz*	10.00
169	*Frank Francisco*	10.00
170	*Colby Miller*	12.00
171	David Crouthers	10.00
172	*Charles Thomas*	15.00
173	*Dennis Sarfate*	12.00
174	*Lance Cormier*	10.00
175	*Joe Horgan*	10.00
176	*Fernando Nieve*	10.00
177	Jake Woods	12.00
178	*Matt Treanor*	12.00
179	*Jerome Gamble*	15.00
180	*John Gall*	15.00
181	*Jorge Sequea*	10.00
182	*Justin Hampson*	10.00
183	*Justin Huisman*	15.00
184	*Justin Knoedler*	12.00
185	*Justin Leone*	15.00
186	*Scott Atchison*	12.00
187	*Jon Knott*	15.00
188	*Kevin Cave*	10.00
189	*Jason Frasor*	10.00
190	*George Sherrill*	12.00
191	Mike Gosling	10.00
192	*Mike Johnston*	10.00
193	Mike Rouse	10.00
194	*Nick Regilio*	10.00
195	*Ryan Meaux*	10.00
196	*Scott Dohmann*	15.00
197	*Shawn Camp*	10.00
198	*Shawn Hill*	10.00
199	*Shingo Takatsu*	25.00
200	*Tim Bausher*	10.00
201	*Tim Bittner*	10.00
202	Scott Kazmir	40.00

Spectrum

Stars (1-100): 5-10X
SP's (101-202): 2-3X
Production 25 sets

Master Player Prints

No Pricing
Production one set

Superscripts

NM/M

Common Player: 8.00
Inserted 1:18

Code	Player	Price
JB	Josh Beckett	15.00
MC	Miguel Cabrera	25.00
EC	Eric Chavez	15.00
BC	Bobby Crosby	25.00
BF	Bartolome Fortunato	10.00
NG	Nomar Garciaparra/SP	
MG	Mariano Gomez	10.00
KG	Ken Griffey Jr.	75.00
RH	Rich Harden	20.00
SH	Sean Henn	10.00
CH	Carlos Hines	8.00
LH	Lincoln Holdzkom	10.00
EJ	Edwin Jackson	15.00
DJ	Derek Jeter/SP	
DK	Donnie Kelly	8.00
LA	Josh Labandeira	8.00
JL	Justin Lehr	10.00
JM	Joe Mauer	30.00
IO	Ivan Ochoa	8.00
MP	Mark Prior	60.00
SP	Scott Proctor	10.00
AP	Albert Pujols/SP	
RR	Ramon Ramirez	12.00
JR	Jose Reyes	20.00
CR	Cal Ripken Jr./SP	
RU	Evan Rust	10.00
NR	Nolan Ryan/SP	
ES	Edwardo Sierra	10.00
AS	Alfredo Simon	10.00
IS	Ian Snell	10.00
PS	Phil Stockman	10.00
TE	Miguel Tejada	35.00
MT	Mark Teixeira	20.00
MV	Merkin Valdez	12.00
CV	Carlos Vasquez	10.00
VE	Michael Vento	10.00
BW	Brandon Webb	10.00
RW	Rickie Weeks	15.00
DW	Dontrelle Willis	25.00
DY	Delmon Young	25.00

Swatch Supremecy Signatures

NM/M

Common Player: 8.00
Production 999 unless noted
Spectrum: 1.5-3X
Production 25 sets

Code	Player	Price
GA	Garret Anderson/275	20.00
RB	Rocco Baldelli	20.00
JB	Josh Beckett	15.00
AB	Angel Berroa	15.00
HB	Hank Blalock	15.00
SB	Sean Burroughs	15.00
MC	Miguel Cabrera	25.00
EC	Eric Chavez/275	20.00
CC	Chad Cordero	10.00
BC	Bobby Crosby	25.00
AE	Adam Eaton	10.00
NG	Nomar Garciaparra/275	100.00
MG	Marcus Giles	15.00
GR	Khalil Greene	35.00
KG	Ken Griffey Jr./275	85.00
RH	Rich Harden	20.00
DJ	Derek Jeter/275	180.00
CK	Casey Kotchman	20.00
CL	Cliff Lee	10.00
DL	Derrek Lee/275	25.00
JM	Joe Mauer	30.00
RO	Roy Oswalt	15.00
LO	Lyle Overbay	15.00
CP	Corey Patterson	20.00
JP	Jake Peavy	35.00
SP	Scott Podsednik	15.00
MP	Mark Prior/275	60.00
AP	Albert Pujols/275	180.00
HR	Horacio Ramirez	10.00
JR	Jose Reyes	20.00
CR	Cal Ripken Jr./275	160.00
NR	Nolan Ryan/275	120.00
BS	Ben Sheets	20.00
MT	Mark Teixeira	20.00
BW	Brandon Webb	12.00
RW	Rickie Weeks	15.00
DW	Dontrelle Willis	25.00
JW	Jerome Williams	15.00
MY	Michael Young	10.00

Swatch Supremecy Cut Signatures

No pricing due to scarcity

Winning Materials

NM/M

Common Player: 8.00
Inserted 1:18
Spectrum: 2-3X
Production 25 sets

Code	Player	Price
JB	Jeff Bagwell	10.00
BE	Josh Beckett	10.00
HB	Hank Blalock	12.00
KB	Kevin Brown	8.00
EC	Eric Chavez	8.00
RC	Roger Clemens	20.00
CD	Carlos Delgado	8.00
JG	Jason Giambi	8.00
TG	Troy Glaus	8.00
SG	Shawn Green	8.00
VG	Vladimir Guerrero	10.00
DJ	Derek Jeter	30.00
CJ	Chipper Jones	10.00
GM	Greg Maddux	15.00
HM	Hideki Matsui	50.00
MM	Mike Mussina	8.00
RP	Rafael Palmeiro	10.00
PI	Mike Piazza	15.00
JP	Jorge Posada	10.00
MP	Mark Prior	15.00
AP	Albert Pujols	30.00
MR	Manny Ramirez	12.00
JR	Jose Reyes	10.00
SR	Scott Rolen	12.00
GS	Gary Sheffield	10.00
SS	Sammy Sosa	15.00
IS	Ichiro Suzuki	40.00
TE	Miguel Tejada	10.00
JT	Jim Thome	12.00

2005 SP COLLECTION

NM/M

Complete SPx Set (100): 25.00
Common Player: .25
Pack (5): 6.00
Box (20): 100.00

#	Player	Price
1	Aaron Harang	.25
2	Aaron Rowand	.25
3	Aaron Miles	.25
4	Adrian Gonzalez	.25
5	Alex Rios	.25
6	Angel Berroa	.25
7	B.J. Upton	.25
8	Brandon Claussen	.25
9	Andy Marte	.25
10	Brandon Webb	.25

11	Bronson Arroyo	.25
12	Casey Kotchman	.25
13	Cesar Izturis	.25
14	Chad Cordero	.25
15	Chad Tracy	.25
16	Charles Thomas	.25
17	Chase Utley	.50
18	Chone Figgins	.25
19	Chris Burke	.25
20	Cliff Lee	.25
21	Clint Barmes	.25
22	Coco Crisp	.25
23	Bill Hall	.25
24	Dallas McPherson	.25
25	Brad Halsey	.25
26	Daniel Cabrera	.25
27	Danny Haren	.25
28	David Bush	.25
29	David DeJesus	.25
30	D.J. Houlton	.25
31	Derek Jeter	3.00
32	Dewon Brazelton	.25
33	Edwin Jackson	.25
34	Brad Hawpe	.25
35	Brandon Inge	.25
36	Brett Myers	.25
37	Garrett Atkins	.25
38	Gavin Floyd	.25
39	Grady Sizemore	.25
40	Guillermo Mota	.25
41	Carlos Guillen	.25
42	Gustavo Chacin	.25
43	Huston Street	.25
44	Chris Duffy	.25
45	J.D. Closser	.25
46	J.J. Hardy	.25
47	Jason Bartlett	.25
48	Jason Dubois	.25
49	Chris Shelton	.25
50	Jason Lane	.25
51	Jayson Werth	.25
52	Jeff Baker	.25
53	Jeff Francis	.25
54	Jeremy Bonderman	.25
55	Jeremy Reed	.25
56	Jerome Williams	.25
57	Jesse Crain	.25
58	Chris Young	.25
59	Jhonny Peralta	.25
60	Joe Blanton	.25
61	Joe Crede	.25
62	Joel Pineiro	.25
63	Joey Gathright	.25
64	John Buck	.25
65	Jonny Gomes	.25
66	Jorge Cantu	.25
67	Dan Johnson	.25
68	Jose Valverde	.25
69	Ervin Santana	.25
70	Justin Morneau	.25
71	Keiichi Yabu	.25
72	Ken Griffey Jr.	2.00
73	Jason Repko	.25
74	Kevin Youkilis	.25
75	Koyie Hill	.25
76	Laynce Nix	.25
77	Luke Scott	.25
78	Juan Rivera	.25
79	Justin Duchscherer	.25
80	Mark Teahen	.25
81	Lance Niekro	.25
82	Michael Cuddyer	.25
83	Nick Swisher	.25
84	Noah Lowry	.25
85	Matt Holliday	.25
86	Reed Johnson	.25
87	Rich Harden	.25
88	Robb Quinlan	.25
89	Nick Johnson	.25
90	Ryan Howard	.50
91	Nook Logan	.25
92	Steve Schmoll	.25
93	Tadahito Iguchi	.25
94	Willy Taveras	.25
95	Wily Mo Pena	.25
96	Xavier Nady	.25
97	Yadier Molina	.25
98	Yhency Brazoban	.25
99	Ryan Freel	.25
100	Zack Greinke	.25

Complete SP Authentic Set (100): 25.00
Common Player: .25

1	A.J. Burnett	.25
2	Aaron Rowand	.25
3	Adam Dunn	.75
4	Adrian Beltre	.50
5	Adrian Gonzalez	.25
6	Akinori Otsuka	.25
7	Albert Pujols	3.00
8	Andre Dawson	.50
9	Andruw Jones	.50
10	Aramis Ramirez	.50
11	Barry Larkin	.50
12	Ben Sheets	.50
13	Bo Jackson	.50
14	Bobby Abreu	.50
15	Bobby Crosby	.50
16	Bronson Arroyo	.25
17	Cal Ripken Jr.	4.00
18	Carl Crawford	.25
19	Carlos Zambrano	.50
20	Casey Kotchman	.25
21	Cesar Izturis	.25
22	Chone Figgins	.25
23	Corey Patterson	.25
24	Craig Biggio	.50
25	Dale Murphy	.50
26	Dallas McPherson	.25
27	Danny Haren	.25
28	Darryl Strawberry	.25
29	David Ortiz	1.00
30	David Wright	1.00
31	Derek Jeter	3.00
32	Derrek Lee	.50
33	Don Mattingly	1.50
34	Dwight Gooden	.25
35	Edgar Renteria	.50
36	Eric Chavez	.50
37	Eric Gagne	.25
38	Gary Sheffield	.50
39	Gavin Floyd	.25
40	Pedro Martinez	1.00
41	Greg Maddux	2.00
42	Hank Blalock	.50
43	Huston Street	.25
44	J.D. Drew	.25
45	Jake Peavy	.50
46	Jake Westbrook	.25
47	Jason Bay	.25
48	Austin Kearns	.25
49	Jeremy Reed	.25
50	Jim Rice	.50
51	Jimmy Rollins	.25
52	Joe Blanton	.25
53	Joe Mauer	.50
54	Johan Santana	1.00
55	John Smoltz	.50
56	Johnny Estrada	.25
57	Jose Reyes	.25
58	Ken Griffey Jr.	2.00
59	Kerry Wood	.50
60	Khalil Greene	.50
61	Marcus Giles	.25
62	Melvin Mora	.25
63	Mark Grace	.50
64	Mark Mulder	.50
65	Mark Prior	1.00
66	Mark Teixeira	.50
67	Matt Clement	.25
68	Michael Young	.25
69	Miguel Cabrera	1.00
70	Miguel Tejada	.75
71	Mike Piazza	1.50
72	Mike Schmidt	2.00
73	Nolan Ryan	3.00
74	Oliver Perez	.25
75	Nick Johnson	.25
76	Paul Molitor	.75
77	Rafael Palmeiro	.50
78	Randy Johnson	1.00
79	Reggie Jackson	1.00
80	Rich Harden	.25
81	Rickie Weeks	.50
82	Robin Yount	1.00
83	Roger Clemens	3.00
84	Roy Oswalt	.25
85	Ryan Howard	.50
86	Ryne Sandberg	2.00
87	Scott Kazmir	.25
88	Scott Rolen	1.00
89	Sean Burroughs	.25
90	Sean Casey	.25
91	Shingo Takatsu	.25
92	Tim Hudson	.50
93	Tony Gwynn	1.00
94	Torii Hunter	.50
95	Travis Hafner	.25
96	Victor Martinez	.25
97	Vladimir Guerrero	1.00
98	Wade Boggs	.50
99	Will Clark	.50
100	Yadier Molina	.25

SP Authentic Chirography

No Pricing
Production 15 Sets

SP Authentic Chirography Triple

No Pricing
Production 5 Sets

SP Authentic Honors

NM/M

Common Player: 1.00
Production 299 Sets

JB	Jason Bay	1.50
AB	Adrian Beltre	1.50
WB	Wade Boggs	1.50
BO	Jeremy Bonderman	1.00
CA	Miguel Cabrera	2.00
WC	Will Clark	1.50
RC	Roger Clemens	6.00
CC	Carl Crawford	1.00
BC	Bobby Crosby	1.50
MG	Marcus Giles	1.00
DG	Dwight Gooden	1.50
GR	Khalil Greene	2.00
ZG	Zack Greinke	1.00
KG	Ken Griffey Jr.	4.00
TG	Tony Gwynn	2.00
TH	Travis Hafner	1.00
RH	Rich Harden	1.00
BJ	Bo Jackson	2.00
DJ	Derek Jeter	6.00
SK	Scott Kazmir	1.00
BL	Barry Larkin	1.50
VM	Victor Martinez	1.00
JM	Joe Mauer	1.50
MC	Dallas McPherson	1.00
PM	Paul Molitor	2.00
MO	Justin Morneau	1.00
DM	Dale Murphy	1.50
DO	David Ortiz	2.00
CP	Corey Patterson	1.00
JP	Jake Peavy	1.50
OP	Oliver Perez	1.00
AP	Albert Pujols	6.00
AR	Aramis Ramirez	1.50
RE	Jose Reyes	1.00
CR	Cal Ripken Jr.	8.00
JR	Jimmy Rollins	1.00
NR	Nolan Ryan	6.00
RS	Ryne Sandberg	4.00
JS	Johan Santana	2.00
MS	Mike Schmidt	4.00
BS	Ben Sheets	1.50
SM	John Smoltz	1.50
ST	Shingo Takatsu	1.00
MT	Mark Teixeira	1.50
TE	Miguel Tejada	2.00
BU	B.J. Upton	1.00
JW	Jake Westbrook	1.00
DW	David Wright	3.00
MY	Michael Young	1.00
CZ	Carlos Zambrano	1.50

SP Authentic Honors Jersey

NM/M

Common Player: 4.00
Production 130 Sets

JB	Jason Bay	4.00
AB	Adrian Beltre	6.00
WB	Wade Boggs	8.00
BO	Jeremy Bonderman	4.00
CA	Miguel Cabrera	8.00
WC	Will Clark	6.00
RC	Roger Clemens	10.00
CC	Carl Crawford	4.00
BC	Bobby Crosby	4.00
MG	Marcus Giles	4.00
DG	Dwight Gooden	6.00
GR	Khalil Greene	8.00
ZG	Zack Greinke	4.00
KG	Ken Griffey Jr.	15.00
TG	Tony Gwynn	8.00
TH	Travis Hafner	4.00
RH	Rich Harden	4.00
BJ	Bo Jackson	10.00
DJ	Derek Jeter	15.00
SK	Scott Kazmir	4.00
BL	Barry Larkin	6.00
VM	Victor Martinez	4.00
JM	Joe Mauer	6.00
MC	Dallas McPherson	4.00
PM	Paul Molitor	8.00
MO	Justin Morneau	4.00
DM	Dale Murphy	8.00
DO	David Ortiz	8.00
CP	Corey Patterson	4.00
JP	Jake Peavy	6.00
OP	Oliver Perez	4.00
AP	Albert Pujols	15.00
AR	Aramis Ramirez	6.00
RE	Jose Reyes	4.00
CR	Cal Ripken Jr.	20.00
JR	Jimmy Rollins	4.00
NR	Nolan Ryan	15.00
RS	Ryne Sandberg	10.00
JS	Johan Santana	8.00
MS	Mike Schmidt	8.00
BS	Ben Sheets	4.00
SM	John Smoltz	6.00
ST	Shingo Takatsu	4.00
MT	Mark Teixeira	6.00
TE	Miguel Tejada	6.00
BU	B.J. Upton	6.00
JW	Jake Westbrook	4.00
DW	David Wright	15.00
MY	Michael Young	4.00
CZ	Carlos Zambrano	6.00

SP Authentic Honors Signatures

No Pricing
Production 5 Sets

SP Authentic Materials

NM/M

Common Player:
Production 199 Sets
Gold: 1X
Production 99 Sets

1	A.J. Burnett	4.00
2	Aaron Rowand	4.00
3	Adam Dunn	6.00
4	Adrian Beltre	6.00
5	Adrian Gonzalez	4.00
6	Akinori Otsuka	4.00
7	Albert Pujols	15.00
8	Andre Dawson	6.00
9	Andruw Jones	6.00
10	Aramis Ramirez	6.00
11	Barry Larkin	6.00
12	Ben Sheets	4.00
13	Bo Jackson	8.00
14	Bobby Abreu	4.00
15	Bobby Crosby	4.00
16	Bronson Arroyo	6.00
17	Cal Ripken Jr.	20.00
18	Carl Crawford	4.00
19	Carlos Zambrano	4.00
20	Casey Kotchman	4.00
21	Cesar Izturis	4.00
22	Chone Figgins	4.00
23	Corey Patterson	4.00
24	Craig Biggio	6.00
25	Dale Murphy	6.00
26	Dallas McPherson	4.00
27	Danny Haren	4.00
28	Darryl Strawberry	4.00
29	David Ortiz	8.00
30	David Wright	10.00
31	Derek Jeter	15.00
32	Derrek Lee	8.00
33	Don Mattingly	10.00
34	Dwight Gooden	4.00
35	Edgar Renteria	6.00
36	Eric Chavez	4.00
37	Eric Gagne	6.00
38	Gary Sheffield	6.00
39	Gavin Floyd	4.00
40	Pedro Martinez	8.00
41	Greg Maddux	10.00
42	Hank Blalock	4.00
43	Huston Street	6.00
44	J.D. Drew	4.00
45	Jake Peavy	6.00
46	Jake Westbrook	4.00
47	Jason Bay	4.00
48	Austin Kearns	4.00
49	Jeremy Reed	4.00
50	Jim Rice	6.00
51	Jimmy Rollins	4.00
52	Joe Blanton	4.00
53	Joe Mauer	6.00
54	Johan Santana	6.00
55	John Smoltz	6.00
56	Johnny Estrada	4.00
57	Jose Reyes	4.00
58	Ken Griffey Jr.	12.00
59	Kerry Wood	6.00
60	Khalil Greene	6.00
61	Marcus Giles	4.00
62	Melvin Mora	4.00
63	Mark Grace	6.00
64	Mark Mulder	4.00
65	Mark Prior	8.00
66	Mark Teixeira	6.00
67	Matt Clement	4.00
68	Michael Young	4.00
69	Miguel Cabrera	6.00
70	Miguel Tejada	6.00
71	Mike Piazza	8.00
72	Mike Schmidt	8.00
73	Nolan Ryan	15.00

74 Oliver Perez 4.00
75 Nick Johnson 4.00
76 Paul Molitor 8.00
77 Rafael Palmeiro 6.00
78 Randy Johnson 8.00
79 Reggie Jackson 8.00
80 Rich Harden 6.00
81 Rickie Weeks 6.00
82 Robin Yount 8.00
83 Roger Clemens 10.00
84 Roy Oswalt 4.00
85 Ryan Howard 15.00
86 Ryne Sandberg 8.00
87 Scott Kazmir 4.00
88 Scott Rolen 6.00
89 Sean Burroughs 4.00
90 Sean Casey 4.00
91 Shingo Takatsu 4.00
92 Tim Hudson 6.00
93 Tony Gwynn 8.00
94 Torii Hunter 6.00
95 Travis Hafner 4.00
96 Victor Martinez 4.00
97 Vladimir Guerrero 8.00
98 Wade Boggs 6.00
99 Will Clark 6.00
100 Yadier Molina 4.00

SP Authentic Signature Materials

No Pricing
Production 10 Sets

SP Authentic Signatures

NM/M

Production 25-550
Gold: No Pricing
Production 10 Sets
2 Aaron Rowand 550 20.00
3 Adam Dunn 25 20.00
4 Adrian Beltre 125 15.00
5 Adrian Gonzalez 550 10.00
6 Akinori Otsuka 475 15.00
7 Albert Pujols 25
8 Andre Dawson 125 15.00
9 Andruw Jones 25
10 Aramis Ramirez 475 15.00
11 Barry Larkin 125 20.00
12 Ben Sheets 350 12.00
13 Bo Jackson 25
15 Bobby Crosby 350 10.00
16 Bronson Arroyo 550 15.00
18 Carl Crawford 475 12.00
20 Casey Kotchman 550 8.00
21 Cesar Izturis 550 8.00
22 Chone Figgins 550 10.00
23 Corey Patterson 350 10.00
24 Craig Biggio 125 30.00
25 Dale Murphy 350 20.00
26 Dallas McPherson 550 10.00
27 Danny Haren 550 10.00
28 Darryl Strawberry 125 12.00
30 David Wright 350 40.00
31 Derek Jeter 150 140.00
32 Derrek Lee 350 15.00
33 Don Mattingly 25
34 Dwight Gooden 475 15.00
36 Eric Chavez 75 12.00
38 Gary Sheffield 25
39 Gavin Floyd 550 8.00
42 Hank Blalock 25
43 Huston Street 550 25.00
45 Jake Peavy 475 15.00
46 Jake Westbrook 550 10.00
47 Jason Bay 475 12.00
48 Austin Kearns 75 10.00
49 Jeremy Reed 550 15.00
50 Jim Rice 350 15.00
52 Joe Blanton 550 10.00
53 Joe Mauer 350 20.00
55 John Smoltz 25
57 Jose Reyes 475 20.00
59 Kerry Wood 25
60 Khalil Greene 350 20.00
62 Melvin Mora 475 12.00
63 Mark Grace 25
64 Mark Mulder 350 15.00
65 Mark Prior 25
66 Mark Teixeira 125 25.00
67 Matt Clement 350 20.00
68 Michael Young 475 15.00
69 Miguel Cabrera 125 25.00
70 Miguel Tejada 25
71 Mike Piazza 25
72 Mike Schmidt 25
73 Nolan Ryan 25
74 Oliver Perez 475 15.00
75 Nick Johnson 550 10.00
76 Paul Molitor 25
77 Rafael Palmeiro 25
78 Randy Johnson 25
79 Reggie Jackson 25
80 Rich Harden 550
83 Roger Clemens 25
84 Roy Oswalt 125 20.00
85 Ryan Howard 550 30.00
86 Ryne Sandberg 25 125.00
87 Scott Kazmir 475 15.00
89 Sean Burroughs 475 10.00
91 Shingo Takatsu 550 10.00
92 Tim Hudson 25
93 Tony Gwynn 25
94 Torii Hunter 94
95 Travis Hafner 550
97 Vladimir Guerrero 25
98 Wade Boggs 25
99 Will Clark 25

SP Collection of Stars

NM/M

Common Player: 1.00
Production 299 Sets
BR Bronson Arroyo 1.00
GA Garrett Atkins 1.00
JE Jeff Baker 1.00
BA Clint Barmes 1.00
JB Jason Bartlett 1.00
JA Jason Bay 1.00
BE Adrian Beltre 1.50
BL Joe Blanton 1.00
BO Jeremy Bonderman 1.00
YB Yhency Brazoban 1.00
CB Chris Burke 1.50
AB A.J. Burnett 1.00
DB David Bush 1.00
DC Daniel Cabrera 1.00
MC Miguel Cabrera 2.00
CA Jorge Cantu 1.00
GC Gustavo Chacin 1.00
RC Roger Clemens 6.00
JD J.D. Closser 1.00
CH Chad Cordero 1.00
JC Jesse Crain 1.00
CC Carl Crawford 1.00
CO Coco Crisp 1.00
DD David DeJesus 1.00
DU Jason Dubois 1.00
CD Chris Duffy 1.00
CF Chone Figgins 1.00
GF Gavin Floyd 1.00
JF Jeff Francis 1.00
RF Ryan Freel 1.00
JG Joey Gathright 1.00
GO Jonny Gomes 1.00
AG Adrian Gonzalez 1.00
GR Khalil Greene 2.00
ZG Zack Greinke 1.00
KG Ken Griffey Jr. 4.00
CG Carlos Guillen 1.00
TR Travis Hafner 1.00
BH Bill Hall 1.00
RH Rich Harden 1.50
DH Danny Haren 1.00
MH Matt Holliday 1.00
HO Ryan Howard 2.00
BI Brandon Inge 1.00
CI Cesar Izturis 1.00
EJ Edwin Jackson 1.00
DJ Derek Jeter 6.00
NJ Nick Johnson 1.00
RJ Reed Johnson 1.00
SK Scott Kazmir 1.00
CK Casey Kotchman 1.00
JL Jason Lane 1.00
LE Brandon League 1.00
CL Cliff Lee 1.00
GM Greg Maddux 4.00
AM Andy Marte 1.00
JM Joe Mauer 1.50
DM Dallas McPherson 1.00
YM Yadier Molina 1.00
MM Melvin Mora 1.00
MO Guillermo Mota 1.00
BM Brett Myers 1.00
DO David Ortiz 2.00
CP Corey Patterson 1.00
JP Jake Peavy 1.50
WM Wily Mo Pena 1.00
OP Oliver Perez 1.00
PI Joel Pineiro 1.00
MP Mark Prior 2.00
AP Albert Pujols 6.00
RQ Robb Quinlan 1.00
RA Aramis Ramirez 1.50
JR Jeremy Reed 1.00
RE Jose Reyes 1.50
RI Alex Rios 1.00
CR Cal Ripken Jr. 8.00
RO Jimmy Rollins 1.00
AR Aaron Rowand 1.00
JS Johan Santana 2.00
MS Mike Schmidt 4.00
LS Luke Scott 1.00
CS Chris Shelton 1.00
GS Grady Sizemore 1.50
SM John Smoltz 1.50
HS Huston Street 1.00
NS Nick Swisher 1.00
ST Shingo Takatsu 1.00
WT Willy Taveras 1.00
MT Mark Teahen 1.00
TE Mark Teixeira 1.50
MI Miguel Tejada 1.50
TH Charles Thomas 1.00
CT Chad Tracy 1.00
BU B.J. Upton 1.50
WE Jayson Werth 1.00
JW Jake Westbrook 1.00
DW David Wright 3.00
KY Kevin Youkilis 1.00
MY Michael Young 1.00
CZ Carlos Zambrano 1.50

SP Collection of Stars Jersey

NM/M

Production 130 Sets
BR Bronson Arroyo 4.00
GA Garrett Atkins 4.00
JE Jeff Baker 4.00
BA Clint Barmes 6.00
JB Jason Bartlett 4.00
JA Jason Bay 4.00
BE Adrian Beltre 6.00
BL Joe Blanton 4.00
BO Jeremy Bonderman 4.00
YB Yhency Brazoban 4.00
CB Chris Burke 4.00
AB A.J. Burnett 4.00
DB David Bush 4.00
DC Daniel Cabrera 4.00
MC Miguel Cabrera 8.00
CA Jorge Cantu 4.00
GC Gustavo Chacin 4.00
RC Roger Clemens 10.00
JD J.D. Closser 4.00
CH Chad Cordero 4.00
JC Jesse Crain 4.00
CC Carl Crawford 4.00
CO Coco Crisp 4.00
DD David DeJesus 4.00
DU Jason Dubois 4.00
CD Chris Duffy 6.00
CF Chone Figgins 4.00
GF Gavin Floyd 4.00
JF Jeff Francis 4.00
RF Ryan Freel 4.00
JG Joey Gathright 4.00
GO Jonny Gomes 6.00
AG Adrian Gonzalez 6.00
GR Khalil Greene 6.00
ZG Zack Greinke 4.00
KG Ken Griffey Jr. 15.00
CG Carlos Guillen 4.00
TR Travis Hafner 4.00
BH Bill Hall 4.00
RH Rich Harden 4.00
DH Danny Haren 4.00
MH Matt Holliday 4.00
HO Ryan Howard 15.00
BI Brandon Inge 4.00
CI Cesar Izturis 4.00
EJ Edwin Jackson 4.00
DJ Derek Jeter 15.00
NJ Nick Johnson 4.00
RJ Reed Johnson 4.00
SK Scott Kazmir 4.00
CK Casey Kotchman 4.00
JL Jason Lane 4.00
LE Brandon League 4.00
CL Cliff Lee 4.00
GM Greg Maddux 10.00
AM Andy Marte 4.00
JM Joe Mauer 6.00
DM Dallas McPherson 4.00
YM Yadier Molina 4.00
MM Melvin Mora 4.00
MO Guillermo Mota 4.00
BM Brett Myers 4.00
DO David Ortiz 8.00
CP Corey Patterson 4.00
JP Jake Peavy 6.00
WM Wily Mo Pena 4.00
OP Oliver Perez 4.00
PI Joel Pineiro 4.00
MP Mark Prior 6.00
AP Albert Pujols 15.00
RQ Robb Quinlan 4.00
RA Aramis Ramirez 6.00
JR Jeremy Reed 4.00
RE Jose Reyes 4.00
RI Alex Rios 4.00
CR Cal Ripken Jr. 20.00
RO Jimmy Rollins 4.00
AR Aaron Rowand 6.00
JS Johan Santana 8.00
MS Mike Schmidt 10.00
LS Luke Scott 4.00
CS Chris Shelton 4.00
GS Grady Sizemore 6.00
SM John Smoltz 6.00
HS Huston Street 6.00
NS Nick Swisher 4.00
ST Shingo Takatsu 4.00
WT Willy Taveras 4.00
MT Mark Teahen 4.00
TE Mark Teixeira 6.00
MI Miguel Tejada 6.00
TH Charles Thomas 4.00
CT Chad Tracy 4.00
BU B.J. Upton 4.00
WE Jayson Werth 4.00
JW Jake Westbrook 4.00
DW David Wright 10.00
KY Kevin Youkilis 4.00
MY Michael Young
CZ Carlos Zambrano 6.00

SP Collection of Stars Signatures

No Pricing
Production 5 Sets

SPx Materials

NM/M

Common Player: 3.00
Production 199 Sets
Spectrum: 1X
Production 99 Sets
1 Aaron Harang 3.00
2 Aaron Rowand 5.00
3 Aaron Miles 3.00
4 Adrian Gonzalez 5.00
5 Alex Rios 3.00
6 Angel Berroa 3.00
7 B.J. Upton 5.00
8 Brandon Claussen 3.00
9 Andy Marte 3.00
10 Brandon Webb 5.00
11 Bronson Arroyo 5.00
12 Casey Kotchman 3.00
13 Cesar Izturis 3.00
14 Chad Cordero 3.00
15 Chad Tracy 3.00
16 Charles Thomas 3.00
17 Chase Utley 8.00
18 Chone Figgins 3.00
19 Chris Burke 5.00
20 Cliff Lee 3.00
21 Clint Barmes 5.00
22 Coco Crisp 3.00
23 Bill Hall 3.00
24 Dallas McPherson 3.00
25 Brad Halsey 3.00
26 Daniel Cabrera 3.00
27 Danny Haren 3.00
28 David Bush 3.00
29 David DeJesus 3.00
30 D.J. Houlton 3.00
31 Derek Jeter 20.00
32 Dewon Brazelton 3.00
33 Edwin Jackson 3.00
34 Brad Hawpe 3.00
35 Brandon Inge 3.00
36 Brett Myers 3.00
37 Garrett Atkins 3.00
38 Gavin Floyd 3.00
39 Grady Sizemore 8.00

40 Guillermo Mota 3.00
41 Carlos Guillen 3.00
42 Gustavo Chacin 3.00
43 Huston Street 5.00
44 Chris Duffy 3.00
45 J.D. Closser 3.00
46 J.J. Hardy 3.00
47 Jason Bartlett 3.00
48 Jason Dubois 3.00
49 Chris Shelton 3.00
50 Jason Lane 3.00
51 Jayson Werth 3.00
52 Jeff Baker 3.00
53 Jeff Francis 3.00
54 Jeremy Bonderman 3.00
55 Jeremy Reed 3.00
56 Jerome Williams 3.00
57 Jesse Crain 3.00
58 Chris Young 3.00
59 Jhonny Peralta 3.00
60 Joe Blanton 3.00
61 Joe Crede 3.00
62 Joel Pineiro 3.00
63 Joey Gathright 3.00
64 John Buck 3.00
65 Jonny Gomes 8.00
66 Jorge Cantu 8.00
67 Dan Johnson 3.00
68 Jose Valverde 3.00
69 Ervin Santana 3.00
70 Justin Morneau 3.00
71 Keiichi Yabu 5.00
72 Ken Griffey Jr. 15.00
73 Jason Repko 5.00
74 Kevin Youkilis 3.00
75 Koyie Hill 3.00
76 Laynce Nix 3.00
77 Luke Scott 3.00
78 Juan Rivera 3.00
79 Justin Duchscherer 3.00
80 Mark Teahen 3.00
81 Lance Niekro 3.00
82 Michael Cuddyer 3.00
83 Nick Swisher 3.00
84 Noah Lowry 3.00
85 Matt Holliday 3.00
86 Reed Johnson 3.00
87 Rich Harden 5.00
88 Robb Quinlan 3.00
89 Nick Johnson 3.00
90 Ryan Howard 20.00
91 Nook Logan 3.00
92 Steve Schmoll 3.00
93 Tadahito Iguchi 20.00
94 Willy Taveras 3.00
95 Wily Mo Pena 3.00
96 Xavier Nady 3.00
97 Yadier Molina 3.00
98 Yhency Brazoban 3.00
99 Ryan Freel 3.00
100 Zack Greinke 3.00

SPx Signatures

NM/M
Production 50-350
Spectrum: No Pricing
Production 10 Sets
Jersey Auto: No Pricing
Production 10 Sets
1 Aaron Harang 350 8.00
2 Aaron Rowand 150 20.00
4 Adrian Gonzalez 225 10.00
6 Angel Berroa 150 8.00
7 B.J. Upton 50 12.00
8 Brandon Claussen 350 8.00
9 Andy Marte 350 10.00
11 Bronson Arroyo 350 15.00
12 Casey Kotchman 225 8.00
13 Cesar Izturis 150 8.00
14 Chad Cordero 350 10.00
15 Chad Tracy 350 10.00
16 Charles Thomas 350 5.00
17 Chase Utley 50 20.00
18 Chone Figgins 150 8.00
19 Chris Burke 350 15.00
20 Cliff Lee 225 10.00
21 Clint Barmes 350 12.00
22 Coco Crisp 225 10.00
23 Bill Hall 350 8.00
24 Dallas McPherson 150 10.00
25 Brad Halsey 350 8.00
26 Daniel Cabrera 350 12.00
27 Danny Haren 225 10.00
28 David Bush 350 8.00
29 David DeJesus 225 8.00
30 D.J. Houlton 350 8.00
31 Derek Jeter 50 150.00
32 Dewon Brazelton 225 8.00
33 Edwin Jackson 150 8.00
34 Brad Hawpe 350 8.00
35 Brandon Inge 350 10.00
36 Brett Myers 150 8.00
37 Garrett Atkins 350 8.00
38 Gavin Floyd 150 8.00
39 Grady Sizemore 350 25.00
40 Guillermo Mota 225 8.00
41 Carlos Guillen 150 8.00
42 Gustavo Chacin 350 10.00
43 Huston Street 350 25.00
44 Chris Duffy 225 15.00
45 J.D. Closser 350 8.00
46 J.J. Hardy 350 10.00
47 Jason Bartlett 350 8.00
48 Jason Dubois 350 10.00
49 Chris Shelton
50 Jason Lane 350 10.00
51 Jayson Werth 350 12.00
52 Jeff Baker 350 8.00
53 Jeff Francis 150 10.00
54 Jeremy Bonderman 50 15.00
55 Jeremy Reed 150 10.00
56 Jerome Williams 50 8.00
57 Jesse Crain 350 10.00
58 Chris Young
59 Jhonny Peralta 350 15.00
60 Joe Blanton 350 10.00
61 Joe Crede 350 25.00
62 Joel Pineiro 150 12.00
63 Joey Gathright 350 8.00
64 John Buck 350 8.00
65 Jonny Gomes 350 25.00
66 Jorge Cantu 350 15.00
67 Dan Johnson 350 15.00
68 Jose Valverde 350 8.00
69 Ervin Santana 350 15.00
70 Justin Morneau 50
71 Keiichi Yabu 350 25.00
73 Jason Repko 350 25.00
74 Kevin Youkilis 225 12.00
75 Koyie Hill 350 10.00
76 Laynce Nix 150 8.00
77 Luke Scott 350 15.00
78 Juan Rivera 225 8.00
79 Justin Duchscherer 350 10.00
80 Mark Teahen 350 8.00
81 Lance Niekro 350 10.00
82 Michael Cuddyer 350 8.00
83 Nick Swisher
84 Noah Lowry 150 15.00
85 Matt Holliday 225 8.00
86 Reed Johnson 350 8.00
87 Rich Harden
88 Robb Quinlan 350 5.00
89 Nick Johnson 150 8.00
90 Ryan Howard 225 35.00
91 Nook Logan 350 8.00
92 Steve Schmoll 350 5.00
93 Tadahito Iguchi 50 250.00
95 Wily Mo Pena 150 8.00
96 Xavier Nady 150 10.00
98 Yhency Brazoban 350 8.00
100 Zack Greinke 150

SPx Superscripts Signatures

No Pricing
Production 15 Sets

SPx Superscripts Triple Signature

No Pricing
Production 5 Sets

SPx Winning Materials Dual

No Pricing
Production 20 Sets
Dual Auto: No Pricing
Production 5 Sets

SPXtreme Stats

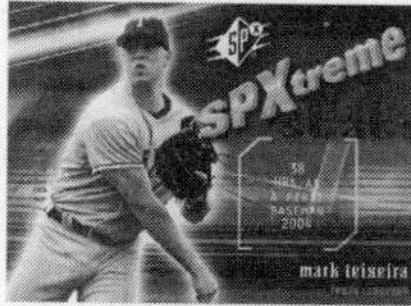

NM/M
Common Player: 1.00
Production 299 Sets
BA Bobby Abreu 1.50
AB Adrian Beltre 1.50
CB Craig Biggio 1.50
HB Hank Blalock 1.50
MC Miguel Cabrera 2.00
SC Sean Casey 1.00
EC Eric Chavez 1.00
RC Roger Clemens 6.00
CC Carl Crawford 1.00
BC Bobby Crosby 1.00
JD J.D. Drew 1.00
AD Adam Dunn 1.50
EG Eric Gagne 1.00
GR Khalil Greene 1.50
KG Ken Griffey Jr. 4.00
VG Vladimir Guerrero 2.00
TH Tim Hudson 1.50
HU Torii Hunter 1.00
DJ Derek Jeter 6.00
RJ Randy Johnson 2.00
AJ Andruw Jones 1.50
DL Derrek Lee 1.50
GM Greg Maddux 4.00
VM Victor Martinez 1.00
JM Joe Mauer 1.50
MO Melvin Mora 1.00
MM Mark Mulder 1.50
DO David Ortiz 2.00
RO Roy Oswalt 1.50
RP Rafael Palmeiro 1.50
CP Corey Patterson 1.00
JP Jake Peavy 1.50
OP Oliver Perez 1.00
PI Mike Piazza 3.00
MP Mark Prior 2.00
AP Albert Pujols 6.00
AR Aramis Ramirez 1.50
ER Edgar Renteria 1.00
JR Jose Reyes 1.00
SR Scott Rolen 2.00
SA Johan Santana 2.00
BS Ben Sheets 1.00
GS Gary Sheffield 1.50
SM John Smoltz 1.50
MT Mark Teixeira 1.50
TE Miguel Tejada 1.50
KW Kerry Wood 1.50
MY Michael Young 1.50
DW David Wright 3.00
CZ Carlos Zambrano 1.50

SPXtreme Stats Jersey

NM/M
BA Bobby Abreu 6.00
AB Adrian Beltre 6.00
CB Craig Biggio 6.00
HB Hank Blalock 4.00
MC Miguel Cabrera 8.00
SC Sean Casey 4.00
EC Eric Chavez 4.00
RC Roger Clemens 10.00
CC Carl Crawford 4.00
BC Bobby Crosby 4.00
JD J.D. Drew 4.00
AD Adam Dunn 6.00
EG Eric Gagne 4.00
GR Khalil Greene 6.00
KG Ken Griffey Jr. 15.00
VG Vladimir Guerrero 8.00
TH Tim Hudson 4.00
HU Torii Hunter 4.00
DJ Derek Jeter 15.00
RJ Randy Johnson 8.00
AJ Andruw Jones 6.00
DL Derrek Lee 6.00
GM Greg Maddux 10.00
VM Victor Martinez 4.00
JM Joe Mauer 6.00
MO Melvin Mora 4.00
MM Mark Mulder 4.00
DO David Ortiz 8.00
RO Roy Oswalt 4.00
RP Rafael Palmeiro 6.00
CP Corey Patterson 4.00
JP Jake Peavy 6.00
OP Oliver Perez 4.00
PI Mike Piazza 8.00
MP Mark Prior 6.00
AP Albert Pujols 15.00
AR Aramis Ramirez 6.00
ER Edgar Renteria 4.00
JR Jose Reyes 4.00
SR Scott Rolen 6.00
SA Johan Santana 8.00
BS Ben Sheets 4.00
GS Gary Sheffield 6.00
SM John Smoltz 6.00
MT Mark Teixeira 6.00
TE Miguel Tejada 6.00
KW Kerry Wood 6.00
DW David Wright 8.00
MY Michael Young 4.00
CZ Carlos Zambrano 6.00

SPXtreme Stats Signatures

No Pricing
Production 5 Sets

1997 SPORTS ILLUSTRATED

NM/M
Complete Set (180): 20.00
Common Player: .05
Extra Edition Stars: 8X
Pack (6): 1.25
Wax Box (24): 20.00
1 Bob Abreu .10
2 Jaime Bluma .05
3 Emil Brown .05
4 Jose Cruz, Jr. .05
5 Jason Dickson .05
6 Nomar Garciaparra 1.00
7 Todd Greene .05
8 Vladimir Guerrero .75
9 Wilton Guerrero .05
10 Jose Guillen .05
11 Hideki Irabu .05
12 Russ Johnson .05
13 Andruw Jones .75
14 Damon Mashore .05
15 Jason McDonald .05
16 Ryan McGuire .05
17 Matt Morris .05
18 Kevin Orie .05
19 Dante Powell .05
20 Pokey Reese .05
21 Joe Roa .05
22 Scott Rolen .65
23 Glendon Rusch .05
24 Scott Spiezio .05
25 Bubba Trammell .05
26 Todd Walker .05
27 Jamey Wright .05
28 Ken Griffey Jr. .75
29 Tino Martinez .05
30 Roger Clemens .65
31 Hideki Irabu .05
32 Kevin Brown .05
33 Chipper Jones, Cal Ripken Jr. .65
34 Sandy Alomar .05
35 Ken Caminiti .05
36 Randy Johnson .40
37 Andy Ashby .05
38 Jay Buhner .05
39 Joe Carter .05
40 Darren Daulton .05
41 Jeff Fassero .05
42 Andres Galarraga .05
43 Rusty Greer .05
44 Marquis Grissom .05
45 Joey Hamilton .05
46 Jimmy Key .05
47 Ryan Klesko .05
48 Eddie Murray .75
49 Charles Nagy .05
50 Dave Nilsson .05
51 Ricardo Rincon .05
52 Billy Wagner .05
53 Dan Wilson .05
54 Dmitri Young .05
55 Roberto Alomar .30
56 Sandy Alomar Jr. .05
57 Scott Brosius .05
58 Tony Clark .05
59 Carlos Delgado .45
60 Jermaine Dye .05
61 Darin Erstad .20
62 Derek Jeter 1.00
63 Jason Kendall .05
64 Hideo Nomo .20
65 Rey Ordonez .05
66 Andy Pettitte .10
67 Manny Ramirez .75
68 Edgar Renteria .05
69 Shane Reynolds .05

70	Alex Rodriguez	1.00
71	Ivan Rodriguez	.65
72	Jose Rosado	.05
73	John Smoltz	.05
74	Tom Glavine	.35
75	Greg Maddux	1.00
76	Chipper Jones	1.00
77	Kenny Lofton	.05
78	Fred McGriff	.05
79	Kevin Brown	.05
80	Alex Fernandez	.05
81	Al Leiter	.05
82	Bobby Bonilla	.05
83	Gary Sheffield	.40
84	Moises Alou	.05
85	Henry Rodriguez	.05
86	Mark Grudzielanek	.05
87	Pedro Martinez	.75
88	Todd Hundley	.05
89	Bernard Gilkey	.05
90	Bobby Jones	.05
91	Curt Schilling	.35
92	Ricky Bottalico	.05
93	Mike Lieberthal	.05
94	Sammy Sosa	1.00
95	Ryne Sandberg	1.00
96	Mark Grace	.05
97	Deion Sanders	.05
98	Reggie Sanders	.05
99	Barry Larkin	.05
100	Craig Biggio	.05
101	Jeff Bagwell	.75
102	Derek Bell	.05
103	Brian Jordan	.05
104	Ray Lankford	.05
105	Ron Gant	.05
106	Al Martin	.05
107	Kevin Elster	.05
108	Jermaine Allensworth	.05
109	Vinny Castilla	.05
110	Dante Bichette	.05
111	Larry Walker	.05
112	Mike Piazza	1.25
113	Eric Karros	.05
114	Todd Hollandsworth	.05
115	Raul Mondesi	.05
116	Hideo Nomo	.40
117	Ramon Martinez	.05
118	Ken Caminiti	.05
119	Tony Gwynn	1.00
120	Steve Finley	.05
121	Barry Bonds	2.00
122	J.T. Snow	.05
123	Rod Beck	.05
124	Cal Ripken Jr.	2.00
125	Mike Mussina	.30
126	Brady Anderson	.05
127	Bernie Williams	.05
128	Derek Jeter	2.00
129	Tino Martinez	.05
130	Andy Pettitte	.30
131	David Cone	.05
132	Mariano Rivera	.15
133	Roger Clemens	1.00
134	Pat Hentgen	.05
135	Juan Guzman	.05
136	Bob Higginson	.05
137	Tony Clark	.05
138	Travis Fryman	.05
139	Mo Vaughn	.05
140	Tim Naehring	.05
141	John Valentin	.05
142	Matt Williams	.05
143	David Justice	.05
144	Jim Thome	.65
145	Chuck Knoblauch	.05
146	Paul Molitor	.75
147	Marty Cordova	.05
148	Frank Thomas	.85
149	Albert Belle	.05
150	Robin Ventura	.05
151	John Jaha	.05
152	Jeff Cirillo	.05
153	Jose Valentin	.05
154	Jay Bell	.05
155	Jeff King	.05
156	Kevin Appier	.05
157	Ken Griffey Jr.	1.25
158	Alex Rodriguez	1.50
158p	Alex Rodriguez (overprinted "PROMOTIONAL SAMPLE")	1.50
159	Randy Johnson	.75
160	Juan Gonzalez	.40
161	Will Clark	.05
162	Dean Palmer	.05
163	Tim Salmon	.05
164	Jim Edmonds	.05
165	Jim Leyritz	.05
166	Jose Canseco	.40
167	Jason Giambi	.50
168	Mark McGwire	1.50
169	Barry Bonds	1.00
170	Alex Rodriguez	.75
171	Roger Clemens	.65
172	Ken Griffey Jr.	.65
173	Greg Maddux	.50
174	Mike Piazza	.65
175	Will Clark, Mark McGwire	1.00
176	Hideo Nomo	.20
177	Cal Ripken Jr.	1.00
178	Ken Griffey Jr., Frank Thomas	.50
179	Alex Rodriguez, Derek Jeter	1.50
180	John Wetteland	.05
---	Jose Cruz Jr. Checklist	.05

Extra Edition

	NM/M
Complete Set (180):	150.00
Common Player:	1.00
Extra Edition Stars:	8X

(See 1997 Sports Illustrated for checklist and base card values.)

Autographed Mini-Covers

	NM/M
Complete Set (6):	300.00
Common Player:	30.00
Alex Rodriguez	90.00
Cal Ripken Jr.	90.00
Kirby Puckett	45.00
Willie Mays	45.00
Frank Robinson	30.00
Hank Aaron	45.00

1997 SPORTS ILLUSTRATED BOX TOPPER

	NM/M
Alex Rodriguez	4.50

Cooperstown Collection

		NM/M
Complete Set (12):		27.50
Common Player:		2.00
1	Hank Aaron	6.00
2	Yogi Berra	3.00
3	Lou Brock	2.00
4	Rod Carew	2.00
5	Juan Marichal	2.00
6	Al Kaline	2.50
7	Joe Morgan	2.00
8	Brooks Robinson	3.00
9	Willie Stargell	2.00
10	Kirby Puckett	4.00
11	Willie Mays	6.00
12	Frank Robinson	3.00

Great Shots

		NM/M
Complete Set (25):		10.00
Common Player:		.20
(1)	Roberto Alomar	.30
(2)	Andy Ashby	.20
(3)	Albert Belle	.20
(4)	Barry Bonds	2.00
(5)	Jay Buhner	.20
(6)	Vinny Castilla, Andres Galarraga	.20
(7)	Darren Daulton	.20
(8)	Juan Gonzalez	.40
(9)	Ken Griffey Jr.	1.25
(10)	Derek Jeter	2.00
(11)	Randy Johnson	.75
(12)	Chipper Jones	1.00
(13)	Eric Karros	.20
(14)	Ryan Klesko	.20
(15)	Kenny Lofton	.20
(16)	Greg Maddux	1.00
(17)	Mark McGwire	1.50
(18)	Mike Piazza	1.25
(19)	Cal Ripken Jr.	2.00
(20)	Alex Rodriguez	1.50
(21)	Ryne Sandberg	1.00
(22)	Deion Sanders	.30
(23)	John Smoltz	.20
(24)	Frank Thomas	.75
(25)	Mo Vaughn	.20

1998 SPORTS ILLUSTRATED

		NM/M
Complete Set (201):		20.00
Common Player:		.05
Pack (6):		1.50
Wax Box (24):		25.00
1	Edgardo Alfonzo	.05
2	Roberto Alomar	.20
3	Sandy Alomar	.05
4	Moises Alou	.05
5	Brady Anderson	.05
6	Garret Anderson	.05
7	Kevin Appier	.05
8	Jeff Bagwell	.75
9	Jay Bell	.05
10	Albert Belle	.05
11	Dante Bichette	.05
12	Craig Biggio	.05
13	Barry Bonds	2.00
14	Bobby Bonilla	.05
15	Kevin Brown	.05
16	Jay Buhner	.05
17	Ellis Burks	.05
18	Mike Cameron	.05
19	Ken Caminiti	.05
20	Jose Canseco	.45
21	Joe Carter	.05
22	Vinny Castilla	.05
23	Jeff Cirillo	.05
24	Tony Clark	.05
25	Will Clark	.05
26	Roger Clemens	1.00
27	David Cone	.05
28	Jose Cruz Jr.	.05
29	Carlos Delgado	.50
30	Jason Dickson	.05
31	Dennis Eckersley	.65
32	Jim Edmonds	.05
33	Scott Erickson	.05
34	Darin Erstad	.20
35	Shawn Estes	.05
36	Jeff Fassero	.05
37	Alex Fernandez	.05
38	Chuck Finley	.05
39	Steve Finley	.05
40	Travis Fryman	.05
41	Andres Galarraga	.05
42	Ron Gant	.05
43	Nomar Garciaparra	1.00
44	Jason Giambi	.50
45	Tom Glavine	.35
46	Juan Gonzalez	.40
47	Mark Grace	.05
48	Willie Green	.05
49	Rusty Greer	.05
50	Ben Grieve	.05
51	Ken Griffey Jr.	1.25
52	Mark Grudzielanek	.05
53	Vladimir Guerrero	.75
54	Juan Guzman	.05
55	Tony Gwynn	1.00
56	Joey Hamilton	.05
57	Rickey Henderson	.75
58	Pat Hentgen	.05
59	Livan Hernandez	.05
60	Bobby Higginson	.05
61	Todd Hundley	.05
62	Hideki Irabu	.05
63	John Jaha	.05
64	Derek Jeter	2.00
65	Charles Johnson	.05
66	Randy Johnson	.75
67	Andruw Jones	.75
68	Bobby Jones	.05
69	Chipper Jones	1.00
70	Brian Jordan	.05
71	David Justice	.05
72	Eric Karros	.05
73	Jeff Kent	.05
74	Jimmy Key	.05
75	Darryl Kile	.05
76	Jeff King	.05
77	Ryan Klesko	.05
78	Chuck Knoblauch	.05
79	Ray Lankford	.05
80	Barry Larkin	.05
81	Kenny Lofton	.05
82	Greg Maddux	1.00
83	Al Martin	.05
84	Edgar Martinez	.05
85	Pedro Martinez	.75
86	Tino Martinez	.05
87	Mark McGwire	1.50
88	Paul Molitor	.75
89	Raul Mondesi	.05
90	Jamie Moyer	.05
91	Mike Mussina	.30
92	Tim Naehring	.05
93	Charles Nagy	.05
94	Denny Neagle	.05
95	Dave Nilsson	.05
96	Hideo Nomo	.40
97	Rey Ordonez	.05
98	Dean Palmer	.05
99	Rafael Palmeiro	.65
100	Andy Pettitte	.30
101	Mike Piazza	1.25
102	Brad Radke	.05
103	Manny Ramirez	.75
104	Edgar Renteria	.05
105	Cal Ripken Jr.	2.00
106	Alex Rodriguez	1.50
106p	Alex Rodriguez ("PROMOTIONAL SAMPLE")	1.50
107	Henry Rodriguez	.05
108	Ivan Rodriguez	.65
109	Scott Rolen	.65
110	Tim Salmon	.05
111	Curt Schilling	.35
112	Gary Sheffield	.45
113	John Smoltz	.05
114	J.T. Snow	.05
115	Sammy Sosa	1.00
116	Matt Stairs	.05
117	Shannon Stewart	.05
118	Frank Thomas	.75
119	Jim Thome	.65
120	Justin Thompson	.05
121	Mo Vaughn	.05
122	Robin Ventura	.05
123	Larry Walker	.05
124	Rondell White	.05
125	Bernie Williams	.05
126	Matt Williams	.05
127	Tony Womack	.05
128	Jaret Wright	.05
129	Edgar Renteria	.05
130	Kenny Lofton	.05
131	Tony Gwynn	.50
132	Mark McGwire	.75
133	Craig Biggio	.05
134	Charles Johnson	.05

135 J.T. Snow .05
136 Ken Caminiti .05
137 Vladimir Guerrero .40
138 Jim Edmonds .05
139 Randy Johnson .40
140 Darryl Kile .05
141 John Smoltz .05
142 Greg Maddux .50
143 Andy Pettitte .05
144 Ken Griffey Jr. .65
145 Mike Piazza .65
146 Todd Greene .05
147 Vinny Castilla .05
148 Derek Jeter 1.00
149 Robert Machado .05
150 Mike Gulan .05
151 Randall Simon .05
152 Michael Coleman .05
153 Brian Rose .05
154 *Scott Eyre* .05
155 *Magglio Ordonez* 1.50
156 Todd Helton .65
157 Juan Encarnacion .05
158 Mark Kotsay .05
159 Josh Booty .05
160 *Melvin Rosario* .05
161 Shane Halter .05
162 Paul Konerko .25
163 *Henry Blanco* .05
164 Antone Williamson .05
165 Brad Fullmer .05
166 Ricky Ledee .05
167 Ben Grieve .05
168 *Frank Catalanotto* .25
169 Bobby Estalella .05
170 Dennis Reyes .05
171 Kevin Polcovich .05
172 Jacob Cruz .05
173 Ken Cloude .05
174 Eli Marrero .05
175 Fernando Tatis .05
176 Tom Evans .05
177 Carl Everett, Nomar Garciaparra .35
178 Eric Davis .05
179 Roger Clemens .60
180 Brett Butler, Eddie Murray .30
181 Frank Thomas .45
182 Curt Schilling .15
183 Jeff Bagwell .40
184 Mark McGwire, Ken Griffey, Jr. .75
185 Kevin Brown .05
186 Marty Cordova, Ricardo Rincon .05
187 Charles Johnson .05
188 Hideki Irabu .05
189 Tony Gwynn .50
190 Sandy Alomar .05
191 Ken Griffey Jr. .65
192 Larry Walker .05
193 Roger Clemens .60
194 Pedro Martinez .40
195 Nomar Garciaparra .60
196 Scott Rolen .40
197 Brian Anderson .05
198 Tony Saunders .05
199 Florida Celebration .05
200 Livan Hernandez .05
201 Travis Lee 2.00

Extra Edition

NM/M
Common Player: 2.00
Extra Edition Stars: 8X
(See 1998 Sports Illustrated for checklist and base card values.)

Autographs

NM/M
Common Player: 7.50
Lou Brock (500) 40.00
Jose Cruz Jr. (250) 10.00
Rollie Fingers (500) 10.00
Ben Grieve (exchange card)(250) 3.00
Ben Grieve (signed card) 7.50
Paul Konerko (exchange card)(250) 3.00
Paul Konerko (signed card) 9.00
Brooks Robinson (250) 50.00

Covers

NM/M
Complete Set (10): 15.00
Common Player: 1.00
Inserted 1:9
1 Ken Griffey, Jr., Mike Piazza 2.00
2 Derek Jeter 3.00
3 Ken Griffey Jr. 2.50
4 Cal Ripken Jr. 3.00
5 Manny Ramirez 1.50
6 Jay Buhner 1.00
7 Matt Williams 1.00
8 Randy Johnson 1.50
9 Deion Sanders 1.00
10 Jose Canseco 1.50

Editor's Choice

NM/M
Complete Set (10): 20.00
Common Player: 1.00
Inserted 1:24
1 Ken Griffey Jr. 3.00
2 Alex Rodriguez 4.00
3 Frank Thomas 1.50
4 Mark McGwire 4.00
5 Greg Maddux 2.00
6 Derek Jeter 5.00
7 Cal Ripken Jr. 5.00
8 Nomar Garciaparra 2.50
9 Jeff Bagwell 1.50
10 Jose Cruz Jr. 1.00

Mini-Posters

NM/M
Complete Set (30): 8.00
Common Player: .10
Inserted 1:1
1 Tim Salmon .10
2 Travis Lee .10
3 John Smoltz, Greg Maddux .50
4 Cal Ripken Jr. 1.00
5 Nomar Garciaparra .50
6 Sammy Sosa .50
7 Frank Thomas .45
8 Barry Larkin .10
9 David Justice .10
10 Larry Walker .10
11 Tony Clark .10
12 Livan Hernandez .10
13 Jeff Bagwell .45
14 Kevin Appier .10
15 Mike Piazza .65
16 Fernando Vina .10
17 Chuck Knoblauch .10
18 Vladimir Guerrero .45
19 Rey Ordonez .10
20 Bernie Williams .10
21 Matt Stairs .10
22 Curt Schilling .30
23 Tony Womack .10
24 Mark McGwire .75
25 Tony Gwynn .50
26 Barry Bonds 1.00
27 Ken Griffey Jr. .65
28 Fred McGriff .10
29 Juan Gonzalez, Alex Rodriguez .50
30 Roger Clemens .60

1998 SPORTS ILLUSTRATED THEN & NOW

NM/M
Complete Set (150): 15.00
Common Player: .05
Extra Edition Stars: 6X
Production 500 sets
Pack (5): 1.00
Wax Box (24): 16.00
1 Luis Aparicio .05
2 Richie Ashburn .05
3 Ernie Banks .50
4 Yogi Berra .50
5 Lou Boudreau .05
6 Lou Brock .15
7 Jim Bunning .05
8 Rod Carew .15
9 Bob Feller .25
10 Rollie Fingers .05
11 Bob Gibson .15
12 Fergie Jenkins .05
13 Al Kaline .25
14 George Kell .05
15 Harmon Killebrew .25
16 Ralph Kiner .05
17 Tommy Lasorda .05
18 Juan Marichal .05
19 Eddie Mathews .25
20 Willie Mays 1.00
21 Willie McCovey .05
22 Joe Morgan .15
23 Gaylord Perry .05
24 Kirby Puckett 1.00
25 Pee Wee Reese .25
26 Phil Rizzuto .25
27 Robin Roberts .05
28 Brooks Robinson .35
29 Frank Robinson .35
30 Red Schoendienst .05
31 Enos Slaughter .05
32 Warren Spahn .25
33 Willie Stargell .15
34 Earl Weaver .05
35 Billy Williams .15
36 Early Wynn .05
37 Rickey Henderson .75
38 Greg Maddux 1.00
39 Mike Mussina .40
40 Cal Ripken Jr. 2.00
41 Albert Belle .05
42 Frank Thomas .75
43 Jeff Bagwell .75
44 Paul Molitor .75
45 Chuck Knoblauch .05
46 Todd Hundley .05
47 Bernie Williams .05
48 Tony Gwynn 1.00
49 Barry Bonds 2.00
50 Ken Griffey Jr. 1.25
51 Randy Johnson .75
52 Mark McGwire 1.50
53 Roger Clemens 1.00
54 Jose Cruz Jr. .05
55 Roberto Alomar .20
56 Sandy Alomar .05
57 Brady Anderson .05
58 Kevin Appier .05
59 Jeff Bagwell .75
60 Albert Belle .05
61 Dante Bichette .05
62 Craig Biggio .05
63 Barry Bonds 2.00
64 Kevin Brown .05
65 Jay Buhner .05
66 Ellis Burks .05
67 Ken Caminiti .05
68 Jose Canseco .50
69 Joe Carter .05
70 Vinny Castilla .05
71 Tony Clark .05
72 Roger Clemens 1.00
73 David Cone .05
74 Jose Cruz Jr. .05
75 Jason Dickson .05
76 Jim Edmonds .05
77 Scott Erickson .05
78 Darin Erstad .20
79 Alex Fernandez .05
80 Steve Finley .05
81 Travis Fryman .05
82 Andres Galarraga .05
83 Nomar Garciaparra 1.00
84 Tom Glavine .35
85 Juan Gonzalez .40
86 Mark Grace .05
87 Willie Greene .05
88 Ken Griffey Jr. 1.25
89 Vladimir Guerrero .75
90 Tony Gwynn 1.00
91 Livan Hernandez .05
92 Bobby Higginson .05
93 Derek Jeter 2.00
94 Charles Johnson .05
95 Randy Johnson .75
96 Andruw Jones .75
97 Chipper Jones 1.00
98 David Justice .05
99 Eric Karros .05
100 Jason Kendall .05
101 Jimmy Key .05
102 Darryl Kile .05
103 Chuck Knoblauch .05
104 Ray Lankford .05
105 Barry Larkin .05
106 Kenny Lofton .05
107 Greg Maddux 1.00
108 Al Martin .05
109 Edgar Martinez .05
110 Pedro Martinez .75
111 Ramon Martinez .05
112 Tino Martinez .05
113 Mark McGwire 1.50
114 Raul Mondesi .05
115 Matt Morris .05
116 Charles Nagy .05
117 Denny Neagle .05
118 Hideo Nomo .40
119 Dean Palmer .05
120 Andy Pettitte .25
121 Mike Piazza 1.25
122 Manny Ramirez .75
123 Edgar Renteria .05
124 Cal Ripken Jr. 2.00
125 Alex Rodriguez 1.50
126 Henry Rodriguez .05
127 Ivan Rodriguez .65
128 Scott Rolen .65
129 Tim Salmon .05
130 Curt Schilling .35
131 Gary Sheffield .45
132 John Smoltz .05
133 Sammy Sosa 1.00
134 Frank Thomas .75
135 Jim Thome .65
136 Mo Vaughn .05
137 Robin Ventura .05
138 Larry Walker .05
139 Bernie Williams .05
140 Matt Williams .05
141 Jaret Wright .05
142 Michael Coleman .05
143 Juan Encarnacion .05
144 Brad Fullmer .05
145 Ben Grieve .05
146 Todd Helton .75
147 Paul Konerko .20
148 Derrek Lee .50
149 *Magglio Ordonez* 1.50
150 Enrique Wilson .05
--- Alex Rodriguez 1.00

Values quoted in this guide reflect the retail price of a card, the price a collector can expect to pay when buying a card from a dealer.

Extra Edition

	NM/M
Common Extra Edition:	1.00
Extra Edition Stars:	6X
Production 500 sets	

(See 1998 Sports Illustrated Then & Now for checklist and base card values.)

Autographs

	NM/M
Common Autograph:	15.00
Redemption Cards:	10%
Bob Gibson (500)	15.00
Tony Gwynn (250)	35.00
Roger Clemens (250)	120.00
Scott Rolen (150)	20.00
Willie Mays (250)	90.00
Harmon Killebrew (500)	25.00

Art of the Game

		NM/M
Complete Set (8):		11.00
Common Player:		1.00
Inserted 1:9		
1	Ken Griffey Jr. It's Gone	1.50
2	Alex Rodriguez	2.00
3	Mike Piazza	1.50
4	Brooks Robinson	1.00
5	David Justice (All-Star)	1.00
6	Cal Ripken Jr.	3.00
7	The Prospect and the Prospector	1.00
8	Barry Bonds	3.00

Covers

		NM/M
Complete Set (12):		22.00
Common Player:		1.00
Inserted 1:18		
1	Lou Brock (10/16/67)	1.00
2	Kirby Puckett (4/6/92)	2.50
3	Harmon Killebrew (4/8/63 - inside)	1.00
4	Eddie Mathews (8/16/54)	1.00
5	Willie Mays (5/22/72)	2.00
6	Frank Robinson (10/6/69)	1.00
7	Cal Ripken Jr. (9/11/95)	5.00
8	Roger Clemens (5/12/86)	2.50
9	Ken Griffey Jr. (10/16/95)	3.00
10	Mark McGwire (6/1/92)	4.00
11	Tony Gwynn (7/28/97)	2.50
12	Ivan Rodriguez (8/11/97)	1.50

Great Shots!

		NM/M
Complete Set (25):		7.50
Common Player:		.10
Inserted 1:1		
1	Ken Griffey Jr.	.65
2	Frank Thomas	.45
3	Alex Rodriguez	.75
4	Andruw Jones	.45
5	Chipper Jones	.50
6	Cal Ripken Jr.	1.00
7	Mark McGwire	.75
8	Derek Jeter	1.00
9	Greg Maddux	.50
10	Jeff Bagwell	.45
11	Mike Piazza	.65
12	Scott Rolen	.35
13	Nomar Garciaparra	.50
14	Jose Cruz Jr.	.10
15	Charles Johnson	.10
16	Fergie Jenkins	.10
17	Lou Brock	.10
18	Bob Gibson	.10
19	Harmon Killebrew	.10
20	Juan Marichal	.10
21	Brooks Robinson	.10
22	Rod Carew	.10
23	Yogi Berra	.25
24	Willie Mays	.50
25	Kirby Puckett	.50

Road to Cooperstown

		NM/M
Complete Set (10):		10.00
Common Player:		.75
Inserted 1:24		
1	Barry Bonds	2.50
2	Roger Clemens	1.25
3	Ken Griffey Jr.	1.50
4	Tony Gwynn	1.00
5	Rickey Henderson	.75
6	Greg Maddux	1.00
7	Paul Molitor	.75
8	Mike Piazza	1.50
9	Cal Ripken Jr.	2.50
10	Frank Thomas	.75

1998 SPORTS ILLUSTRATED WORLD SERIES FEVER

		NM/M
Complete Set (150):		10.00
Common Player:		.05
Pack (6):		1.00
Wax Box (24):		17.50
1	Mickey Mantle	1.50
2	1957 World Series Preview	.15
3	1958 World Series Preview	.15
4	1959 World Series Preview	.15
5	1962 World Series	.10
6	Lou Brock	.10
7	Brooks Robinson	.25
8	Frank Robinson	.25
9	1974 World Series	.10
10	Reggie Jackson	.60
11	1985 World Series	.10
12	1987 World Series	.10
13	Orel Hershiser	.05
14	Rickey Henderson	.40
15	1991 World Series	.10
16	1992 World Series	.05
17	Joe Carter	.05
18	1995 World Series	.10
19	1996 World Series	.15
20	Edgar Renteria	.05
21	Bill Mazeroski	.15
22	Joe Carter	.05
23	Carlton Fisk	.40
24	Bucky Dent	.15
25	Mookie Wilson	.05
26	Enos Slaughter	.05
27	Mickey Lolich	.05
28	Bobby Richardson	.05
29	Kirk Gibson	.05
30	Edgar Renteria	.05
31	Albert Belle	.05
32	Kevin Brown	.05
33	Brian Rose	.05
34	Ron Gant	.05
35	Jeromy Burnitz	.05
36	Andres Galarraga	.05
37	Jim Edmonds	.05
38	Jose Cruz Jr.	.05
39	Mark Grudzielanek	.05
40	Shawn Estes	.05
41	Mark Grace	.05
42	Nomar Garciaparra	.50
43	Juan Gonzalez	.20
44	Tom Glavine	.25
45	Brady Anderson	.05
46	Tony Clark	.05
47	Jeff Cirillo	.05
48	Dante Bichette	.05
49	Ben Grieve	.05
50	Ken Griffey Jr.	.65
51	Edgardo Alfonzo	.05
52	Roger Clemens	.60
53	Pat Hentgen	.05
54	Todd Helton	.30
55	Andy Benes	.05
56	Tony Gwynn	.50
57	Andruw Jones	.40
58	Bobby Higginson	.05
59	Bobby Jones	.05
60	Darryl Kile	.05
61	Chan Ho Park	.05
62	Charles Johnson	.05
63	Rusty Greer	.05
64	Travis Fryman	.05
65	Derek Jeter	1.00
66	Jay Buhner	.05
67	Chuck Knoblauch	.05
68	David Justice	.05
69	Brian Hunter	.05
70	Eric Karros	.05
71	Edgar Martinez	.05
72	Chipper Jones	.50
73	Barry Larkin	.05
74	Mike Lansing	.05
75	Craig Biggio	.05
76	Al Martin	.05
77	Barry Bonds	1.00
78	Randy Johnson	.40
79	Ryan Klesko	.05
80	Mark McGwire	.75
81	Fred McGriff	.05
82	Javy Lopez	.05
83	Kenny Lofton	.05
84	Sandy Alomar Jr.	.05
85	Matt Morris	.05
86	Paul Konerko	.10
87	Ray Lankford	.05
88	Kerry Wood	.30
89	Roberto Alomar	.20
90	Greg Maddux	.50
91	Travis Lee	.05
92	Moises Alou	.05
93	Dean Palmer	.05
94	Hideo Nomo	.20
95	Ken Caminiti	.05
96	Pedro Martinez	.40
97	Raul Mondesi	.05
98	Denny Neagle	.05
99	Tino Martinez	.05
100	Mike Mussina	.20
101	Kevin Appier	.05
102	Vinny Castilla	.05
103	Jeff Bagwell	.40
104	Paul O'Neill	.05
105	Rey Ordonez	.05
106	Vladimir Guerrero	.40
107	Rafael Palmeiro	.35
108	Alex Rodriguez	.75
109	Andy Pettitte	.15
110	Carl Pavano	.05
111	Henry Rodriguez	.05
112	Gary Sheffield	.40
113	Curt Schilling	.25
114	John Smoltz	.05
115	Reggie Sanders	.05
116	Scott Rolen	.35
117	Mike Piazza	.65
118	Manny Ramirez	.40
119	Cal Ripken Jr.	1.00
120	Brad Radke	.05
121	Tim Salmon	.05
122	Brett Tomko	.05
123	Robin Ventura	.05
124	Mo Vaughn	.05
125	A.J. Hinch	.05
126	Derrek Lee	.45
127	*Orlando Hernandez*	.40
128	Aramis Ramirez	.05
129	Frank Thomas	.40
130	J.T. Snow	.05
131	*Magglio Ordonez*	1.00
132	Bobby Bonilla	.05
133	Marquis Grissom	.05
134	Jim Thome	.45
135	Justin Thompson	.05
136	Matt Williams	.05
137	Matt Stairs	.05
138	Wade Boggs	.50
139	Chuck Finley	.05
140	Jaret Wright	.05
141	Ivan Rodriguez	.35
142	Brad Fullmer	.05
143	Bernie Williams	.05
144	Jason Giambi	.30
145	Larry Walker	.05
146	Tony Womack	.05
147	Sammy Sosa	.50
148	Rondell White	.05
149	Todd Stottlemyre	.05
150	Shane Reynolds	.05

Extra Edition

	NM/M
Common EE Player:	2.00
EE Stars:	15X
Production:	98 sets
Common FE Player:	100.00
FE Stars: VALUES UNDETERMINED	
1 of 1	

(See 1998 Sports Illustrated World Series Fever for checklist and base values.)

Autumn Excellence

		NM/M
Complete Set (10):		15.00
Common Player:		.50
Inserted 1:24		
Golds:		2X
Inserted 1:240		
AE1	Willie Mays	2.50
AE2	Kirby Puckett	2.00
AE3	Babe Ruth	4.00
AE4	Reggie Jackson	1.50
AE5	Whitey Ford	.50
AE6	Lou Brock	.50
AE7	Mickey Mantle	4.00
AE8	Yogi Berra	.75
AE9	Bob Gibson	.50
AE10	Don Larsen	1.00

MVP Collection

		NM/M
Complete Set (10):		1.00
Common Player:		.10
Inserted 1:4		
1	Frank Robinson	.25
2	Brooks Robinson	.25
3	Willie Stargell	.10
4	Bret Saberhagen	.10
5	Rollie Fingers	.10
6	Orel Hershiser	.10
7	Paul Molitor	.50
8	Tom Glavine	.15
9	John Wetteland	.10
10	Livan Hernandez	.10

Reggie Jackson Picks

		NM/M
Complete Set (15):		12.50
Common Player:		.25
Inserted 1:12		
1	Paul O'Neill	.25
2	Barry Bonds	2.50
3	Ken Griffey Jr.	1.50
4	Juan Gonzalez	.40
5	Greg Maddux	1.00
6	Mike Piazza	1.50
7	Larry Walker	.25
8	Mo Vaughn	.25
9	Roger Clemens	1.25
10	John Smoltz	.25
11	Alex Rodriguez	2.00
12	Frank Thomas	.75
13	Mark McGwire	2.00
14	Jeff Bagwell	.75
15	Randy Johnson	.75

1999 SPORTS ILLUSTRATED

		NM/M
Complete Set (180):		15.00
Common Player:		.05
Wax Pack (6):		1.00
Hobby Box (24):		15.00
Retail Box (16):		10.00
1	Yankees	.25
2	Scott Brosius	.05
3	David Wells	.05
4	Sterling Hitchcock	.05
5	David Justice	.05
6	David Cone	.05
7	Greg Maddux	.50
8	Jim Leyritz	.05
9	Gary Gaetti	.05
10	Mark McGwire	.75
11	Sammy Sosa	.50
12	Larry Walker	.05
13	Tony Womack	.05
14	Tom Glavine	.10
15	Curt Schilling	.10
16	Greg Maddux	.50
17	Trevor Hoffman	.05
18	Kerry Wood	.20
19	Tom Glavine	.10
20	Sammy Sosa	.50
21	Travis Lee	.05
22	Roberto Alomar	.05
23	Roger Clemens	.60
24	Barry Bonds	1.00
25	Paul Molitor	.45
26	Todd Stottlemyre	.05
27	Chris Hoiles	.05
28	Albert Belle	.05
29	Tony Clark	.05
30	Kerry Wood	.20
31	David Wells	.05
32	Dennis Eckersley	.40
33	Mark McGwire	.75
34	Cal Ripken Jr.	1.00
35	Ken Griffey Jr.	.65
36	Alex Rodriguez	.75
37	Craig Biggio	.05
38	Sammy Sosa	.50
39	Dennis Martinez	.05
40	Curt Schilling	.10
41	Orlando Hernandez	.05
42	Troy Glaus, Ben Molina, Todd Greene	.45
43	Mitch Meluskey, Daryle Ward, Mike Grzanich	.05
44	*Eric Chavez, Mike Neill, Steve Connelly*	.10
45	Roy Halladay, Tom Evans, Kevin Witt	.05
46	George Lombard, Adam Butler, Bruce Chen	.05
47	*Ronnie Belliard, Valerio de los Santos, Rafael Roque*	.05
48	*J.D. Drew, Placido Polanco, Mark Little*	.50
49	Jason Maxwell, Jose Nieves, Jeremi Gonzalez	.05
50	*Scott McClain, Kerry Robinson, Mike Duvall*	.05
51	Ben Ford, Bryan Corey, Danny Klassen	.05
52	Angel Pena, Jeff Kubenka, Paul LoDuca	.05
53	Kirk Bullinger, Fernando Seguignol, Tim Young	.05
54	Ramon Martinez, Wilson Delgado, Armando Rios	.05
55	Russ Branyon, Jolbert Cabrera, Jason Rakers	.05
56	*Carlos Guillen, David Holdridge, Giomar Guevara*	.10
57	Alex Gonzalez, Joe Fontenot, Preston Wilson	.05
58	Mike Kinkade, Jay Payton, Masato Yoshii	.05
59	Willis Otanez, Ryan Minor, Calvin Pickering	.05
60	Ben Davis, Matt Clement, Stan Spencer	.05
61	*Marlon Anderson, Mike Welch, Gary Bennett*	.05
62	Abraham Nunez, Sean Lawrence, Aramis Ramirez	.05
63	*Jonathan Johnson, Rob Sasser, Scott Sheldon*	.05
64	Keith Glauber, Guillermo Garcia, Eddie Priest	.05
65	Brian Barkley, Jin Ho Cho, Donnie Sadler	.05
66	*Derrick Gibson, Mark Strittmatter, Edgard Clemente*	.05
67	*Jeremy Giambi, Dermal Brown, Chris Hatcher*	.05
68	Rob Fick, Gabe Kapler, Marino Santana	.10
69	Corey Koskie, A.J. Pierzynski, Benj Sampson	.05
70	Brian Simmons, Mark Johnson, Craig Wilson	.05
71	Ryan Bradley, Mike Lowell, Jay Tessmer	.05
72	Ben Grieve	.05
73	Shawn Green	.45
74	Rafael Palmeiro	.65
75	Juan Gonzalez	.40
76	Mike Piazza	1.25
77	Devon White	.05
78	Jim Thome	.65
79	Barry Larkin	.05
80	Scott Rolen	.65
81	Raul Mondesi	.05
82	Jason Giambi	.50
83	Jose Canseco	.45
84	Tony Gwynn	1.00
85	Cal Ripken Jr.	2.00
86	Andy Pettitte	.15
87	Carlos Delgado	.50
88	Jeff Cirillo	.05
89	Bret Saberhagen	.05
90	John Olerud	.05
91	Ron Coomer	.05
92	Todd Helton	.65
93	Ray Lankford	.05
94	Tim Salmon	.05
95	Fred McGriff	.05
96	Matt Stairs	.05
97	Ken Griffey Jr.	1.25
98	Chipper Jones	1.00
99	Mark Grace	.05
100	Ivan Rodriguez	.65
101	Jeromy Burnitz	.05
102	Kenny Rogers	.05
103	Kevin Millwood	.05
104	Vinny Castilla	.05
105	Jim Edmonds	.05
106	Craig Biggio	.05
107	Andres Galarraga	.05
108	Sammy Sosa	1.00
109	Juan Encarnacion	.05
110	Larry Walker	.05
111	John Smoltz	.05
112	Randy Johnson	.75
113	Bobby Higginson	.05
114	Albert Belle	.05
115	Jaret Wright	.05
116	Edgar Renteria	.05
117	Andruw Jones	.75
118	Barry Bonds	2.00
119	Rondell White	.05
120	Jamie Moyer	.05
121	Darin Erstad	.20
122	Al Leiter	.05
123	Mark McGwire	1.50
124	Mo Vaughn	.05
125	Livan Hernandez	.05
126	Jason Kendall	.05
127	Frank Thomas	.75
128	Denny Neagle	.05
129	Johnny Damon	.35
130	Derek Bell	.05
131	Jeff Kent	.05
132	Tony Womack	.05
133	Trevor Hoffman	.05
134	Gary Sheffield	.40
135	Tino Martinez	.05
136	Travis Fryman	.05
137	Rolando Arrojo	.05
138	Dante Bichette	.05
139	Nomar Garciaparra	1.00
140	Moises Alou	.05
141	Chuck Knoblauch	.05
142	Robin Ventura	.05
143	Scott Erickson	.05
144	David Cone	.05
145	Greg Vaughn	.05
146	Wade Boggs	1.00
147	Mike Mussina	.30
148	Tony Clark	.05
149	Alex Rodriguez	1.50
150	Javy Lopez	.05
151	Bartolo Colon	.05
152	Derek Jeter	2.00
153	Greg Maddux	1.00
154	Kevin Brown	.05
155	Curt Schilling	.35
156	Jeff King	.05
157	Bernie Williams	.05
158	Roberto Alomar	.20
159	Travis Lee	.05
160	Kerry Wood	.50
160p	Kerry Wood ("PROMOTIONAL SAMPLE")	1.00
161	Jeff Bagwell	.75
162	Roger Clemens	1.00
163	Matt Williams	.05
164	Chan Ho Park	.05
165	Damion Easley	.05
166	Manny Ramirez	.75
167	Quinton McCracken	.05
168	Todd Walker	.05
169	Eric Karros	.05
170	Will Clark	.05
171	Edgar Martinez	.05
172	Cliff Floyd	.05
173	Vladimir Guerrero	.75
174	Tom Glavine	.35
175	Pedro Martinez	.75
176	Chuck Finley	.05
177	Dean Palmer	.05
178	Omar Vizquel	.05
179	Checklist	.05
180	Checklist	.05

Diamond Dominators

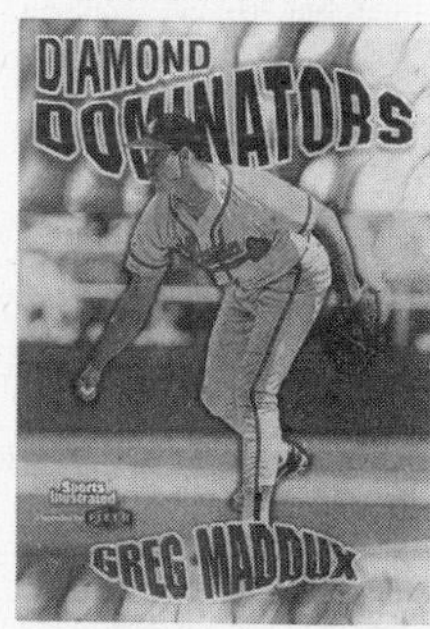

		NM/M
Complete Set (10):		30.00
Common Player:		1.50
Pitchers inserted 1:90		
Hitters inserted 1:180		
1DD	Kerry Wood	1.50
2DD	Roger Clemens	3.00
3DD	Randy Johnson	2.00
4DD	Greg Maddux	2.50
5DD	Pedro Martinez	2.00
6DD	Ken Griffey Jr.	5.00
7DD	Sammy Sosa	2.50
8DD	Nomar Garciaparra	2.50
9DD	Mark McGwire	6.00
10DD	Alex Rodriguez	6.00

Fabulous 40s

		NM/M
Complete Set (13):		9.00
Common Player:		.25
Inserted 1:20		
1FF	Mark McGwire	2.00
2FF	Sammy Sosa	1.25
3FF	Ken Griffey Jr.	1.50
4FF	Greg Vaughn	.25
5FF	Albert Belle	.25
6FF	Jose Canseco	.50
7FF	Vinny Castilla	.25
8FF	Juan Gonzalez	.50
9FF	Manny Ramirez	1.00
10FF	Andres Galarraga	.25
11FF	Rafael Palmeiro	.75
12FF	Alex Rodriguez	2.00
13FF	Mo Vaughn	.25

Fabulous 40s Extra

		NM/M
Common Player:		12.00
Numbered to amount of HRs		
1FF	Mark McGwire (70)	60.00
2FF	Sammy Sosa (66)	40.00
3FF	Ken Griffey Jr. (56)	35.00
4FF	Greg Vaughn (50)	12.00
5FF	Albert Belle (49)	12.00
6FF	Jose Canseco (46)	25.00
7FF	Vinny Castilla (46)	12.00
8FF	Juan Gonzalez (45)	20.00
9FF	Manny Ramirez (45)	30.00
10FF	Andres Galarraga (44)	12.00
11FF	Rafael Palmeiro (43)	25.00
12FF	Alex Rodriguez (42)	45.00
13FF	Mo Vaughn (40)	12.00

Headliners

		NM/M
Complete Set (25):		10.00
Common Player:		.25
Inserted 1:4		
1H	Vladimir Guerrero	.40
2H	Randy Johnson	.40
3H	Mo Vaughn	.25
4H	Chipper Jones	.50
5H	Jeff Bagwell	.40
6H	Juan Gonzalez	.30
7H	Mark McGwire	.75
8H	Cal Ripken Jr.	1.00
9H	Frank Thomas	.40
10H	Manny Ramirez	.40
11H	Ken Griffey Jr.	.65
12H	Scott Rolen	.35
13H	Alex Rodriguez	.75
14H	Barry Bonds	1.00
15H	Roger Clemens	.55
16H	Darin Erstad	.30
17H	Nomar Garciaparra	.50
18H	Mike Piazza	.65
19H	Greg Maddux	.50
20H	Ivan Rodriguez	.35

21H Derek Jeter 1.00
22H Sammy Sosa .50
23H Andruw Jones .40
24H Pedro Martinez .40
25H Kerry Wood .35

Ones To Watch

NM/M
Complete Set (15): 5.00
Common Player: .25
Inserted 1:12
10W J.D. Drew .65
20W Marlon Anderson .25
30W Roy Halladay .35
40W Ben Grieve .25
50W Todd Helton .75
60W Gabe Kapler .25
70W Troy Glaus .75
80W Ben Davis .25
90W Eric Chavez .35
100W Richie Sexson .25
110W Fernando Seguignol .25
120W Kerry Wood .50
130W Bobby Smith .25
140W Ryan Minor .25
150W Jeremy Giambi .25
J.D. Drew autograph (250) 15.00

1999 SPORTS ILLUSTRATED GREATS OF THE GAME

NM/M
Complete Set (90): 12.00
Common Player: .05
Pack (7): 15.00
Wax Box (12): 150.00
1 Jimmie Foxx .25
2 Red Schoendienst .05
3 Babe Ruth 3.00
4 Lou Gehrig 2.00
5 Mel Ott .05
6 Stan Musial .25
7 Mickey Mantle 3.00
8 Carl Yastrzemski .15
9 Enos Slaughter .05
10 Andre Dawson .05
11 Luis Aparicio .05
12 Ferguson Jenkins .05
13 Christy Mathewson .25
14 Ernie Banks .15
15 Johnny Podres .05
16 George Foster .05
17 Jerry Koosman .05
18 Curt Simmons .05
19 Bob Feller .05
20 Frank Robinson .05
21 Gary Carter .05
22 Frank Thomas .05
23 Bill Lee .05
24 Willie Mays 1.00
25 Tommie Agee .05
26 Boog Powell .05
27 Jimmy Wynn .05
28 Sparky Lyle .05
29 Bo Belinsky .05
30 Maury Wills .05
31 Bill Buckner .05
32 Steve Carlton .05
33 Harmon Killebrew .05
34 Nolan Ryan 1.00
35 Randy Jones .05
36 Robin Roberts .05
37 Al Oliver .05
38 Rico Petrocelli .05
39 Dave Parker .05
40 Eddie Mathews .05
41 Earl Weaver .05
42 Jackie Robinson 1.50
43 Lou Brock .05
44 Reggie Jackson .15
45 Bob Gibson .05
46 Jeff Burroughs .05
47 Jim Bouton .05
48 Bob Forsch .05
49 Ron Guidry .05
50 Ty Cobb 2.00
51 Roy White .05
52 Joe Rudi .05
53 Moose Skowron .05
54 Goose Gossage .05
55 Ed Kranepool .05
56 Paul Blair .05
57 Kent Hrbek .05
58 Orlando Cepeda .05
59 Buck O'Neil .05
60 Al Kaline .05
61 Vida Blue .05
62 Sam McDowell .05
63 Jesse Barfield .05
64 Dave Kingman .05
65 Ron Santo .05
66 Steve Garvey .05
67 Gaylord Perry .05
68 Darrell Evans .05
69 Rollie Fingers .05
70 Walter Johnson .25
71 Al Hrabosky .05
72 Mickey Rivers .05
73 Mike Torrez .05
74 Hank Bauer .05
75 Tug McGraw .05
76 David Clyde .05
77 Jim Lonborg .05
78 Clete Boyer .05
79 Harry Walker .05
80 Cy Young .25
81 Bud Harrelson .05
82 Paul Splittorff .05
83 Bert Campaneris .05
84 Joe Niekro .05
85 Bob Horner .05
86 Jerry Royster .05
87 Tommy John .05
88 Mark Fidrych .05
89 Dick Williams .05
90 Graig Nettles .05

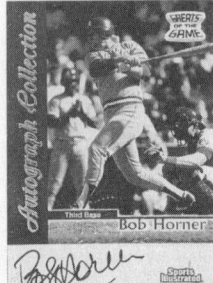

Autographs

NM/M
Common Player: 4.00
Inserted 1:1
(1) Tommie Agee 8.00
(2) Luis Aparicio 12.00
(3) Ernie Banks 25.00
(4) Jesse Barfield 6.00
(5) Hank Bauer 10.00
(6) Bo Belinsky 6.00
(7) Paul Blair 6.00
(8) Vida Blue 10.00
(9) Jim Bouton 10.00
(10) Clete Boyer 10.00
(11) Lou Brock 15.00
(12) Bill Buckner 10.00
(13) Jeff Burroughs 5.00
(14) Bert Campaneris 8.00
(15) Steve Carlton 20.00
(16) Gary Carter 10.00
(17) Orlando Cepeda 12.00
(18) David Clyde 5.00
(19) Andre Dawson 10.00
(20) Darrell Evans 8.00
(21) Bob Feller 12.00
(22) Mark Fidrych 15.00
(23) Rollie Fingers 10.00
(24) Bob Forsch 6.00
(25) George Foster 10.00
(26) Steve Garvey 10.00
(27) Bob Gibson 15.00
(28) Goose Gossage 10.00
(29) Ron Guidry 20.00
(30) Bud Harrelson 10.00
(31) Bob Horner 10.00
(32) Al Hrabosky 8.00
(33) Kent Hrbek 10.00
(34a) Reggie Jackson 150.00
(34b) Reggie Jackson ("Mr. October") 200.00
(34c) Reggie Jackson ("HoF 93") 200.00
(35) Ferguson Jenkins 10.00
(36) Tommy John 8.00
(37) Randy Jones 4.00
(38) Al Kaline 25.00
(39) Harmon Killebrew 25.00
(40) Dave Kingman 8.00
(41) Jerry Koosman 8.00
(42) Ed Kranepool 8.00
(43) Bill Lee 10.00
(44) Jim Lonborg 5.00
(45) Sparky Lyle 8.00
(46) Eddie Mathews 60.00
(47) Willie Mays 125.00
(48) Sam McDowell 8.00
(49) Tug McGraw 25.00
(50) Stan Musial 100.00
(51) Graig Nettles 10.00
(52) Joe Niekro 8.00
(53) Buck O'Neil 20.00
(54) Al Oliver 10.00
(55) Dave Parker 10.00
(56) Gaylord Perry 10.00
(57) Rico Petrocelli 12.00
(58) Johnny Podres 20.00
(59) Boog Powell 12.50
(60) Mickey Rivers 8.00
(61) Robin Roberts 20.00
(62) Frank Robinson 17.50
(63) Jerry Royster 4.00
(64) Joe Rudi 8.00
(65) Nolan Ryan 200.00
(66) Ron Santo 17.50
(67) Red Schoendienst 12.00
(68) Curt Simmons 6.00
(69) Moose Skowron 15.00
(70) Enos Slaughter 20.00
(71) Paul Splittorff 6.00
(72) Frank Thomas 8.00
(73) Mike Torrez 4.00
(74) Harry Walker 4.00
(75) Earl Weaver 10.00
(76) Roy White 9.00
(77) Dick Williams 10.00
(78) Maury Wills 10.00
(79) Jimmy Wynn 10.00
(80) Carl Yastrzemski 45.00

Cover Collection

NM/M
Complete Set (50): 25.00
Common Player: .50
Inserted 1:1
1 Johnny Podres .50
2 Mickey Mantle 5.00
3 Stan Musial .50
4 Eddie Mathews .50
5 Frank Thomas .50
6 Willie Mays 1.00
7 Red Schoendienst .50
8 Luis Aparicio .50
9 Mickey Mantle 3.00
10 Al Kaline .50
11 Maury Wills .50
12 Sam McDowell .50
13 Harry Walker .50
14 Carl Yastrzemski .50
15 Carl Yastrzemski .50
16 Lou Brock .50
17 Ron Santo .50
18 Reggie Jackson .50
19 Frank Robinson .50
20 Jerry Koosman .50
21 Bud Harrelson .50
22 Vida Blue .50
23 Ferguson Jenkins .50
24 Sparky Lyle .50
25 Steve Carlton .50
26 Bert Campaneris .50
27 Jimmy Wynn .50
28 Steve Garvey .50
29 Nolan Ryan 1.00
30 Randy Jones .50
31 Reggie Jackson .50
32 Joe Rudi .50
33 Reggie Jackson .50
34 Dave Parker .50
35 Mark Fidrych .50
36 Earl Weaver .50
37 Nolan Ryan 1.00
38 Steve Carlton .50
39 Reggie Jackson .50
40 Rollie Fingers .50
41 Gary Carter .50
42 Graig Nettles .50
43 Gaylord Perry .50
44 Kent Hrbek .50
45 Gary Carter .50
46 Steve Garvey .50
47 Steve Carlton .50
48 Nolan Ryan 1.00
49 Nolan Ryan 1.00
50 Mickey Mantle 3.00

Record Breakers

NM/M
Complete Set (10): 40.00
Common Player: 2.00
Inserted 1:12
Golds: 6X
Inserted 1:120
1 Mickey Mantle 8.00
2 Stan Musial 3.50
3 Babe Ruth 8.00
4 Christy Mathewson 2.00
5 Cy Young 2.00
6 Nolan Ryan 7.50
7 Jackie Robinson 6.00
8 Lou Gehrig 7.00
9 Ty Cobb 3.50
10 Walter Johnson 2.00

1991 STADIUM CLUB

NM/M
Complete Set (600): 20.00
Common Player: .05
Series 1 or 2 Pack (13): .60
Series 1 or 2 Box (36): 15.00
1 Dave Stewart .05
2 Wally Joyner .05
3 Shawon Dunston .05
4 Darren Daulton .05
5 Will Clark .05
6 Sammy Sosa 1.00
7 Dan Plesac .05
8 Marquis Grissom .05
9 Erik Hanson .05
10 Geno Petralli .05
11 Jose Rijo .05
12 Carlos Quintana .05
13 Junior Ortiz .05
14 Bob Walk .05
15 Mike Macfarlane .05
16 Eric Yelding .05
17 Bryn Smith .05
18 Bip Roberts .05
19 Mike Scioscia .05
20 Mark Williamson .05

No.	Player	Value
21	Don Mattingly	1.00
22	John Franco	.05
23	Chet Lemon	.05
24	Tom Henke	.05
25	Jerry Browne	.05
26	Dave Justice	.05
27	Mark Langston	.05
28	Damon Berryhill	.05
29	Kevin Bass	.05
30	Scott Fletcher	.05
31	Moises Alou	.05
32	Dave Valle	.05
33	Jody Reed	.05
34	Dave West	.05
35	Kevin McReynolds	.05
36	Pat Combs	.05
37	Eric Davis	.05
38	Bret Saberhagen	.05
39	Stan Javier	.05
40	Chuck Cary	.05
41	Tony Phillips	.05
42	Lee Smith	.05
43	Tim Teufel	.05
44	Lance Dickson	.05
45	Greg Litton	.05
46	Teddy Higuera	.05
47	Edgar Martinez	.05
48	Steve Avery	.05
49	Walt Weiss	.05
50	David Segui	.05
51	Andy Benes	.05
52	Karl Rhodes	.05
53	Neal Heaton	.05
54	Dan Gladden	.05
55	Luis Rivera	.05
56	Kevin Brown	.05
57	Frank Thomas	.75
58	Terry Mulholland	.05
59	Dick Schofield	.05
60	Ron Darling	.05
61	Sandy Alomar, Jr.	.05
62	Dave Stieb	.05
63	Alan Trammell	.05
64	Matt Nokes	.05
65	Lenny Harris	.05
66	Milt Thompson	.05
67	Storm Davis	.05
68	Joe Oliver	.05
69	Andres Galarraga	.05
70	Ozzie Guillen	.05
71	Ken Howell	.05
72	Garry Templeton	.05
73	Derrick May	.05
74	Xavier Hernandez	.05
75	Dave Parker	.05
76	Rick Aguilera	.05
77	Robby Thompson	.05
78	Pete Incaviglia	.05
79	Bob Welch	.05
80	Randy Milligan	.05
81	Chuck Finley	.05
82	Alvin Davis	.05
83	Tim Naehring	.05
84	Jay Bell	.05
85	Joe Magrane	.05
86	Howard Johnson	.05
87	Jack McDowell	.05
88	Kevin Seitzer	.05
89	Bruce Ruffin	.05
90	Fernando Valenzuela	.05
91	Terry Kennedy	.05
92	Barry Larkin	.05
93	Larry Walker	.05
94	Luis Salazar	.05
95	Gary Sheffield	.45
96	Bobby Witt	.05
97	Lonnie Smith	.05
98	Bryan Harvey	.05
99	Mookie Wilson	.05
100	Dwight Gooden	.05
101	Lou Whitaker	.05
102	Ron Karkovice	.05
103	Jesse Barfield	.05
104	Jose DeJesus	.05
105	Benito Santiago	.05
106	Brian Holman	.05
107	Rafael Ramirez	.05
108	Ellis Burks	.05
109	Mike Bielecki	.05
110	Kirby Puckett	1.00
111	Terry Shumpert	.05
112	Chuck Crim	.05
113	Todd Benzinger	.05
114	Brian Barnes	.05
115	Carlos Baerga	.05
116	Kal Daniels	.05
117	Dave Johnson	.05
118	Andy Van Slyke	.05
119	John Burkett	.05
120	Rickey Henderson	.75
121	Tim Jones	.05
122	Daryl Irvine	.05
123	Ruben Sierra	.05
124	Jim Abbott	.05
125	Daryl Boston	.05
126	Greg Maddux	1.00
127	Von Hayes	.05
128	Mike Fitzgerald	.05
129	Wayne Edwards	.05
130	Greg Briley	.05
131	Rob Dibble	.05
132	Gene Larkin	.05
133	David Wells	.05
134	Steve Balboni	.05
135	Greg Vaughn	.05
136	Mark Davis	.05
137	Dave Rohde	.05
138	Eric Show	.05
139	Bobby Bonilla	.05
140	Dana Kiecker	.05
141	Gary Pettis	.05
142	Dennis Boyd	.05
143	Mike Benjamin	.05
144	Luis Polonia	.05
145	Doug Jones	.05
146	Al Newman	.05
147	Alex Fernandez	.05
148	Bill Doran	.05
149	Kevin Elster	.05
150	Len Dykstra	.05
151	Mike Gallego	.05
152	Tim Belcher	.05
153	Jay Buhner	.05
154	Ozzie Smith	1.00
155	Jose Canseco	.50
156	Gregg Olson	.05
157	Charlie O'Brien	.05
158	Frank Tanana	.05
159	George Brett	1.00
160	Jeff Huson	.05
161	Kevin Tapani	.05
162	Jerome Walton	.05
163	Charlie Hayes	.05
164	Chris Bosio	.05
165	Chris Sabo	.05
166	Lance Parrish	.05
167	Don Robinson	.05
168	Manuel Lee	.05
169	Dennis Rasmussen	.05
170	Wade Boggs	1.00
171	Bob Geren	.05
172	Mackey Sasser	.05
173	Julio Franco	.05
174	Otis Nixon	.05
175	Bert Blyleven	.05
176	Craig Biggio	.05
177	Eddie Murray	.75
178	Randy Tomlin	.05
179	Tino Martinez	.05
180	Carlton Fisk	.75
181	Dwight Smith	.05
182	Scott Garrelts	.05
183	Jim Gantner	.05
184	Dickie Thon	.05
185	John Farrell	.05
186	Cecil Fielder	.05
187	Glenn Braggs	.05
188	Allan Anderson	.05
189	Kurt Stillwell	.05
190	Jose Oquendo	.05
191	Joe Orsulak	.05
192	Ricky Jordan	.05
193	Kelly Downs	.05
194	Delino DeShields	.05
195	Omar Vizquel	.05
196	Mark Carreon	.05
197	Mike Harkey	.05
198	Jack Howell	.05
199	Lance Johnson	.05
200	Nolan Ryan	2.00
201	John Marzano	.05
202	Doug Drabek	.05
203	Mark Lemke	.05
204	Steve Sax	.05
205	Greg Harris	.05
206	B.J. Surhoff	.05
207	Todd Burns	.05
208	Jose Gonzalez	.05
209	Mike Scott	.05
210	Dave Magadan	.05
211	Dante Bichette	.05
212	Trevor Wilson	.05
213	Hector Villanueva	.05
214	Dan Pasqua	.05
215	Greg Colbrunn	.05
216	Mike Jeffcoat	.05
217	Harold Reynolds	.05
218	Paul O'Neill	.05
219	Mark Guthrie	.05
220	Barry Bonds	2.00
221	Jimmy Key	.05
222	Billy Ripken	.05
223	Tom Pagnozzi	.05
224	Bo Jackson	.10
225	Sid Fernandez	.05
226	Mike Marshall	.05
227	John Kruk	.05
228	Mike Fetters	.05
229	Eric Anthony	.05
230	Ryne Sandberg	1.00
231	Carney Lansford	.05
232	Melido Perez	.05
233	Jose Lind	.05
234	Darryl Hamilton	.05
235	Tom Browning	.05
236	Spike Owen	.05
237	Juan Gonzalez	.40
238	Felix Fermin	.05
239	Keith Miller	.05
240	Mark Gubicza	.05
241	Kent Anderson	.05
242	Alvaro Espinoza	.05
243	Dale Murphy	.20
244	Orel Hershiser	.05
245	Paul Molitor	.75
246	Eddie Whitson	.05
247	Joe Girardi	.05
248	Kent Hrbek	.05
249	Bill Sampen	.05
250	Kevin Mitchell	.05
251	Mariano Duncan	.05
252	Scott Bradley	.05
253	Mike Greenwell	.05
254	Tom Gordon	.05
255	Todd Zeile	.05
256	Bobby Thigpen	.05
257	Gregg Jefferies	.05
258	Kenny Rogers	.05
259	Shane Mack	.05
260	Zane Smith	.05
261	Mitch Williams	.05
262	Jim DeShaies	.05
263	Dave Winfield	.75
264	Ben McDonald	.05
265	Randy Ready	.05
266	Pat Borders	.05
267	Jose Uribe	.05
268	Derek Lilliquist	.05
269	Greg Brock	.05
270	Ken Griffey, Jr.	1.25
271	Jeff Gray	.05
272	Danny Tartabull	.05
273	Dennis Martinez	.05
274	Robin Ventura	.05
275	Randy Myers	.05
276	Jack Daugherty	.05
277	Greg Gagne	.05
278	Jay Howell	.05
279	Mike LaValliere	.05
280	Rex Hudler	.05
281	Mike Simms	.05
282	Kevin Maas	.05
283	Jeff Ballard	.05
284	Dave Henderson	.05
285	Pete O'Brien	.05
286	Brook Jacoby	.05
287	Mike Henneman	.05
288	Greg Olson	.05
289	Greg Myers	.05
290	Mark Grace	.05
291	Shawn Abner	.05
292	Frank Viola	.05
293	Lee Stevens	.05
294	Jason Grimsley	.05
295	Matt Williams	.05
296	Ron Robinson	.05
297	Tom Brunansky	.05
298	Checklist	.05
299	Checklist	.05
300	Checklist	.05
301	Darryl Strawberry	.05
302	Bud Black	.05
303	Harold Baines	.05
304	Roberto Alomar	.20
305	Norm Charlton	.05
306	Gary Thurman	.05
307	Mike Felder	.05
308	Tony Gwynn	1.00
309	Roger Clemens	1.00
310	Andre Dawson	.25
311	Scott Radinsky	.05
312	Bob Melvin	.05
313	Kirk McCaskill	.05
314	Pedro Guerrero	.05
315	Walt Terrell	.05
316	Sam Horn	.05
317	*Wes Chamberlain*	.05
318	*Pedro Munoz*	.05
319	Roberto Kelly	.05
320	Mark Portugal	.05
321	Tim McIntosh	.05
322	Jesse Orosco	.05
323	Gary Green	.05
324	Greg Harris	.05
325	Hubie Brooks	.05
326	Chris Nabholz	.05
327	Terry Pendleton	.05
328	Eric King	.05
329	Chili Davis	.05
330	Anthony Telford	.05
331	Kelly Gruber	.05
332	Dennis Eckersley	.65
333	Mel Hall	.05
334	Bob Kipper	.05
335	Willie McGee	.05
336	Steve Olin	.05
337	Steve Buechele	.05
338	Scott Leius	.05
339	Hal Morris	.05
340	Jose Offerman	.05
341	Kent Mercker	.05
342	Ken Griffey	.05
343	Pete Harnisch	.05
344	Kirk Gibson	.05
345	Dave Smith	.05
346	Dave Martinez	.05
347	Atlee Hammaker	.05
348	Brian Downing	.05
349	Todd Hundley	.05
350	Candy Maldonado	.05
351	Dwight Evans	.05
352	Steve Searcy	.05
353	Gary Gaetti	.05
354	Jeff Reardon	.05
355	Travis Fryman	.05
356	Dave Righetti	.05
357	Fred McGriff	.05
358	Don Slaught	.05
359	Gene Nelson	.05
360	Billy Spiers	.05
361	Lee Guetterman	.05
362	Darren Lewis	.05
363	Duane Ward	.05
364	Lloyd Moseby	.05
365	John Smoltz	.05
366	Felix Jose	.05
367	David Cone	.05
368	Wally Backman	.05
369	Jeff Montgomery	.05
370	Rich Garces	.05
371	Billy Hatcher	.05
372	Bill Swift	.05
373	Jim Eisenreich	.05
374	Rob Ducey	.05
375	Tim Crews	.05
376	Steve Finley	.05
377	Jeff Blauser	.05
378	Willie Wilson	.05
379	Gerald Perry	.05
380	Jose Mesa	.05
381	Pat Kelly	.05
382	Matt Merullo	.05
383	Ivan Calderon	.05
384	Scott Chiamparino	.05
385	Lloyd McClendon	.05
386	Dave Bergman	.05
387	Ed Sprague	.05
388	*Jeff Bagwell*	3.00
389	Brett Butler	.05
390	Larry Andersen	.05
391	Glenn Davis	.05
392	Alex Cole (photo is Otis Nixon)	.05
393	Mike Heath	.05
394	Danny Darwin	.05
395	Steve Lake	.05
396	Tim Layana	.05
397	Terry Leach	.05
398	Bill Wegman	.05
399	Mark McGwire	1.50
400	Mike Boddicker	.05
401	Steve Howe	.05
402	Bernard Gilkey	.05
403	Thomas Howard	.05
404	Rafael Belliard	.05
405	Tom Candiotti	.05
406	Rene Gonzalez	.05
407	Chuck McElroy	.05
408	Paul Sorrento	.05
409	Randy Johnson	.75
410	Brady Anderson	.05
411	Dennis Cook	.05
412	Mickey Tettleton	.05
413	Mike Stanton	.05
414	Ken Oberkfell	.05
415	Rick Honeycutt	.05
416	Nelson Santovenia	.05
417	Bob Tewksbury	.05
418	Brent Mayne	.05
419	Steve Farr	.05
420	Phil Stephenson	.05
421	Jeff Russell	.05
422	Chris James	.05
423	Tim Leary	.05

424 Gary Carter .75
425 Glenallen Hill .05
426 Matt Young .05
427 Sid Bream .05
428 Greg Swindell .05
429 Scott Aldred .05
430 Cal Ripken, Jr. 2.00
431 Bill Landrum .05
432 Ernie Riles .05
433 Danny Jackson .05
434 Casey Candaele .05
435 Ken Hill .05
436 Jaime Navarro .05
437 Lance Blankenship .05
438 Randy Velarde .05
439 Frank DiPino .05
440 Carl Nichols .05
441 Jeff Robinson .05
442 Deion Sanders .05
443 Vincente Palacios .05
444 Devon White .05
445 John Cerutti .05
446 Tracy Jones .05
447 Jack Morris .05
448 Mitch Webster .05
449 Bob Ojeda .05
450 Oscar Azocar .05
451 Luis Aquino .05
452 Mark Whiten .05
453 Stan Belinda .05
454 Ron Gant .05
455 Jose DeLeon .05
456 Mark Salas .05
457 Junior Felix .05
458 Wally Whitehurst .05
459 *Phil Plantier* .05
460 Juan Berenguer .05
461 Franklin Stubbs .05
462 Joe Boever .05
463 Tim Wallach .05
464 Mike Moore .05
465 Albert Belle .05
466 Mike Witt .05
467 Craig Worthington .05
468 Jerald Clark .05
469 Scott Terry .05
470 Milt Cuyler .05
471 John Smiley .05
472 Charles Nagy .05
473 Alan Mills .05
474 John Russell .05
475 Bruce Hurst .05
476 Andujar Cedeno .05
477 Dave Eiland .05
478 *Brian McRae* .10
479 Mike LaCoss .05
480 Chris Gwynn .05
481 Jamie Moyer .05
482 John Olerud .05
483 Efrain Valdez .05
484 Sil Campusano .05
485 Pascual Perez .05
486 Gary Redus .05
487 Andy Hawkins .05
488 Cory Snyder .05
489 Chris Hoiles .05
490 Ron Hassey .05
491 Gary Wayne .05
492 Mark Lewis .05
493 Scott Coolbaugh .05
494 Gerald Young .05
495 Juan Samuel .05
496 Willie Fraser .05
497 Jeff Treadway .05
498 Vince Coleman .05
499 Cris Carpenter .05
500 Jack Clark .05
501 Kevin Appier .05
502 Rafael Palmeiro .65
503 Hensley Meulens .05
504 George Bell .05
505 Tony Pena .05
506 Roger McDowell .05
507 Luis Sojo .05
508 Mike Schooler .05
509 Robin Yount .75
510 Jack Armstrong .05
511 Rick Cerone .05
512 Curt Wilkerson .05
513 Joe Carter .05
514 Tim Burke .05
515 Tony Fernandez .05
516 Ramon Martinez .05
517 Tim Hulett .05
518 Terry Steinbach .05
519 Pete Smith .05
520 Ken Caminiti .05
521 Shawn Boskie .05
522 Mike Pagliarulo .05
523 Tim Raines .05
524 Alfredo Griffin .05
525 Henry Cotto .05
526 Mike Stanley .05
527 Charlie Leibrandt .05
528 Jeff King .05
529 Eric Plunk .05
530 Tom Lampkin .05
531 Steve Bedrosian .05
532 Tom Herr .05
533 Craig Lefferts .05
534 Jeff Reed .05
535 Mickey Morandini .05
536 Greg Cadaret .05
537 Ray Lankford .05
538 John Candelaria .05
539 Rob Deer .05
540 Brad Arnsberg .05
541 Mike Sharperson .05
542 Jeff Robinson .05
543 Mo Vaughn .05
544 Jeff Parrett .05
545 Willie Randolph .05
546 Herm Winningham .05
547 Jeff Innis .05
548 Chuck Knoblauch .05
549 Tommy Greene .05
550 Jeff Hamilton .05
551 Barry Jones .05
552 Ken Dayley .05
553 Rick Dempsey .05
554 Greg Smith .05
555 Mike Devereaux .05
556 Keith Comstock .05
557 Paul Faries .05
558 Tom Glavine .35
559 Craig Grebeck .05
560 Scott Erickson .05
561 Joel Skinner .05
562 Mike Morgan .05
563 Dave Gallagher .05
564 Todd Stottlemyre .05
565 Rich Rodriguez .05
566 *Craig Wilson* .05
567 Jeff Brantley .05
568 Scott Kamieniecki .05
569 Steve Decker .05
570 Juan Agosto .05
571 Tommy Gregg .05
572 Kevin Wickander .05
573 Jamie Quirk .05
574 Jerry Don Gleaton .05
575 Chris Hammond .05
576 *Luis Gonzalez* 1.00
577 Russ Swan .05
578 *Jeff Conine* .50
579 Charlie Hough .05
580 Jeff Kunkel .05
581 Darrel Akerfelds .05
582 Jeff Manto .05
583 Alejandro Pena .05
584 Mark Davidson .05
585 Bob MacDonald .05
586 Paul Assenmacher .05
587 Dan Wilson .05
588 Tom Bolton .05
589 Brian Harper .05
590 John Habyan .05
591 John Orton .05
592 Mark Gardner .05
593 Turner Ward .05
594 Bob Patterson .05
595 Edwin Nunez .05
596 Gary Scott .05
597 Scott Bankhead .05
598 Checklist .05
599 Checklist .05
600 Checklist .05

Nolan Ryan Bronze

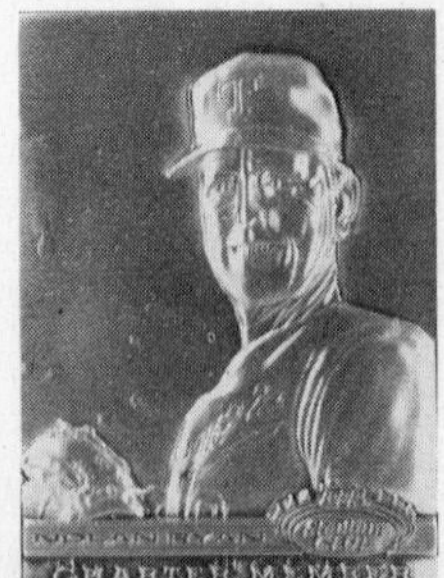

NM/M

Nolan Ryan (bronze) 15.00

1992 STADIUM CLUB

NM/M

Complete Set (900): 20.00
Common Player: .05
Series 1, 2, 3 Pack (15): .75
Series 1, 2, 3 Box (36): 15.00

1 Cal Ripken, Jr. 1.50
2 Eric Yelding .05
3 Geno Petralli .05
4 Wally Backman .05
5 Milt Cuyler .05
6 Kevin Bass .05
7 Dante Bichette .05
8 Ray Lankford .05
9 Mel Hall .05
10 Joe Carter .05
11 Juan Samuel .05
12 Jeff Montgomery .05
13 Glenn Braggs .05
14 Henry Cotto .05
15 Deion Sanders .05
16 Dick Schofield .05
17 David Cone .05
18 Chili Davis .05
19 Tom Foley .05
20 Ozzie Guillen .05
21 Luis Salazar .05
22 Terry Steinbach .05
23 Chris James .05
24 Jeff King .05
25 Carlos Quintana .05
26 Mike Maddux .05
27 Tommy Greene .05
28 Jeff Russell .05
29 Steve Finley .05
30 Mike Flanagan .05
31 Darren Lewis .05
32 Mark Lee .05
33 Willie Fraser .05
34 Mike Henneman .05
35 Kevin Maas .05
36 Dave Hansen .05
37 Erik Hanson .05
38 Bill Doran .05
39 Mike Boddicker .05
40 Vince Coleman .05
41 Devon White .05
42 Mark Gardner .05
43 Scott Lewis .05
44 Juan Berenguer .05
45 Carney Lansford .05
46 Curt Wilkerson .05
47 Shane Mack .05
48 Bip Roberts .05
49 Greg Harris .05
50 Ryne Sandberg .75
51 Mark Whiten .05
52 Jack McDowell .05
53 Jimmy Jones .05
54 Steve Lake .05
55 Bud Black .05
56 Dave Valle .05
57 Kevin Reimer .05
58 Rich Gedman .05
59 Travis Fryman .05
60 Steve Avery .05
61 Francisco de la Rosa .05
62 Scott Hemond .05
63 Hal Morris .05
64 Hensley Meulens .05
65 Frank Castillo .05
66 Gene Larkin .05
67 Jose DeLeon .05
68 Al Osuna .05
69 Dave Cochrane .05
70 Robin Ventura .05
71 John Cerutti .05
72 Kevin Gross .05
73 Ivan Calderon .05
74 Mike Macfarlane .05
75 Stan Belinda .05
76 Shawn Hillegas .05
77 Pat Borders .05
78 Jim Vatcher .05
79 Bobby Rose .05
80 Roger Clemens .85
81 Craig Worthington .05
82 Jeff Treadway .05
83 Jamie Quirk .05
84 Randy Bush .05
85 Anthony Young .05
86 Trevor Wilson .05
87 Jaime Navarro .05
88 Les Lancaster .05
89 Pat Kelly .05
90 Alvin Davis .05
91 Larry Andersen .05
92 Rob Deer .05
93 Mike Sharperson .05
94 Lance Parrish .05
95 Cecil Espy .05
96 Tim Spehr .05
97 Dave Stieb .05
98 Terry Mulholland .05
99 Dennis Boyd .05
100 Barry Larkin .05
101 Ryan Bowen .05
102 Felix Fermin .05
103 Luis Alicea .05
104 Tim Hulett .05
105 Rafael Belliard .05
106 Mike Gallego .05
107 Dave Righetti .05
108 Jeff Schaefer .05
109 Ricky Bones .05
110 Scott Erickson .05
111 Matt Nokes .05
112 Bob Scanlan .05
113 Tom Candiotti .05
114 Sean Berry .05
115 Kevin Morton .05
116 Scott Fletcher .05
117 B.J. Surhoff .05
118 Dave Magadan .05
119 Bill Gullickson .05
120 Marquis Grissom .05
121 Lenny Harris .05
122 Wally Joyner .05
123 Kevin Brown .05
124 Braulio Castillo .05
125 Eric King .05
126 Mark Portugal .05
127 Calvin Jones .05
128 Mike Heath .05
129 Todd Van Poppel .05
130 Benny Santiago .05
131 Gary Thurman .05
132 Joe Girardi .05
133 Dave Eiland .05
134 Orlando Merced .05
135 Joe Orsulak .05
136 John Burkett .05
137 Ken Dayley .05
138 Ken Hill .05
139 Walt Terrell .05
140 Mike Scioscia .05
141 Junior Felix .05
142 Ken Caminiti .05
143 Carlos Baerga .05
144 Tony Fossas .05
145 Craig Grebeck .05
146 Scott Bradley .05
147 Kent Mercker .05
148 Derrick May .05
149 Jerald Clark .05
150 George Brett .85
151 Luis Quinones .05
152 Mike Pagliarulo .05
153 Jose Guzman .05
154 Charlie O'Brien .05
155 Darren Holmes .05
156 Joe Boever .05
157 Rich Monteleone .05
158 Reggie Harris .05
159 Roberto Alomar .20
160 Robby Thompson .05
161 Chris Hoiles .05
162 Tom Pagnozzi .05
163 Omar Vizquel .05
164 John Candelaria .05
165 Terry Shumpert .05
166 Andy Mota .05
167 Scott Bailes .05
168 Jeff Blauser .05
169 Steve Olin .05

No.	Player	Price
170	Doug Drabek	.05
171	Dave Bergman	.05
172	Eddie Whitson	.05
173	Gilberto Reyes	.05
174	Mark Grace	.05
175	Paul O'Neill	.05
176	Greg Cadaret	.05
177	Mark Williamson	.05
178	Casey Candaele	.05
179	Candy Maldonado	.05
180	Lee Smith	.05
181	Harold Reynolds	.05
182	Dave Justice	.05
183	Lenny Webster	.05
184	Donn Pall	.05
185	Gerald Alexander	.05
186	Jack Clark	.05
187	Stan Javier	.05
188	Ricky Jordan	.05
189	Franklin Stubbs	.05
190	Dennis Eckersley	.60
191	Danny Tartabull	.05
192	Pete O'Brien	.05
193	Mark Lewis	.05
194	Mike Felder	.05
195	Mickey Tettleton	.05
196	Dwight Smith	.05
197	Shawn Abner	.05
198	Jim Leyritz	.05
199	Mike Devereaux	.05
200	Craig Biggio	.05
201	Kevin Elster	.05
202	Rance Mulliniks	.05
203	Tony Fernandez	.05
204	Allan Anderson	.05
205	Herm Winningham	.05
206	Tim Jones	.05
207	Ramon Martinez	.05
208	Teddy Higuera	.05
209	John Kruk	.05
210	Jim Abbott	.05
211	Dean Palmer	.05
212	Mark Davis	.05
213	Jay Buhner	.05
214	Jesse Barfield	.05
215	Kevin Mitchell	.05
216	Mike LaValliere	.05
217	Mark Wohlers	.05
218	Dave Henderson	.05
219	Dave Smith	.05
220	Albert Belle	.05
221	Spike Owen	.05
222	Jeff Gray	.05
223	Paul Gibson	.05
224	Bobby Thigpen	.05
225	Mike Mussina	.30
226	Darrin Jackson	.05
227	Luis Gonzalez	.05
228	Greg Briley	.05
229	Brent Mayne	.05
230	Paul Molitor	.65
231	Al Leiter	.05
232	Andy Van Slyke	.05
233	Ron Tingley	.05
234	Bernard Gilkey	.05
235	Kent Hrbek	.05
236	Eric Karros	.05
237	Randy Velarde	.05
238	Andy Allanson	.05
239	Willie McGee	.05
240	Juan Gonzalez	.35
241	Karl Rhodes	.05
242	Luis Mercedes	.05
243	Billy Swift	.05
244	Tommy Gregg	.05
245	David Howard	.05
246	Dave Hollins	.05
247	Kip Gross	.05
248	Walt Weiss	.05
249	Mackey Sasser	.05
250	Cecil Fielder	.05
251	Jerry Browne	.05
252	Doug Dascenzo	.05
253	Darryl Hamilton	.05
254	Dann Bilardello	.05
255	Luis Rivera	.05
256	Larry Walker	.05
257	Ron Karkovice	.05
258	Bob Tewksbury	.05
259	Jimmy Key	.05
260	Bernie Williams	.05
261	Gary Wayne	.05
262	Mike Simms	.05
263	John Orton	.05
264	Marvin Freeman	.05
265	Mike Jeffcoat	.05
266	Roger Mason	.05
267	Edgar Martinez	.05
268	Henry Rodriguez	.05
269	Sam Horn	.05
270	Brian McRae	.05
271	Kirt Manwaring	.05
272	Mike Bordick	.05
273	Chris Sabo	.05
274	Jim Olander	.05
275	Greg Harris	.05
276	Dan Gakeler	.05
277	Bill Sampen	.05
278	Joel Skinner	.05
279	Curt Schilling	.35
280	Dale Murphy	.25
281	Lee Stevens	.05
282	Lonnie Smith	.05
283	Manuel Lee	.05
284	Shawn Boskie	.05
285	Kevin Seitzer	.05
286	Stan Royer	.05
287	John Dopson	.05
288	Scott Bullett	.05
289	Ken Patterson	.05
290	Todd Hundley	.05
291	Tim Leary	.05
292	Brett Butler	.05
293	Gregg Olson	.05
294	Jeff Brantley	.05
295	Brian Holman	.05
296	Brian Harper	.05
297	Brian Bohanon	.05
298	Checklist 1-100	.05
299	Checklist 101-200	.05
300	Checklist 201-300	.05
301	Frank Thomas	.65
302	Lloyd McClendon	.05
303	Brady Anderson	.05
304	Julio Valera	.05
305	Mike Aldrete	.05
306	Joe Oliver	.05
307	Todd Stottlemyre	.05
308	Rey Sanchez	.05
309	Gary Sheffield	.35
310	Andujar Cedeno	.05
311	Kenny Rogers	.05
312	Bruce Hurst	.05
313	Mike Schooler	.05
314	Mike Benjamin	.05
315	Chuck Finley	.05
316	Mark Lemke	.05
317	Scott Livingstone	.05
318	Chris Nabholz	.05
319	Mike Humphreys	.05
320	Pedro Guerrero	.05
321	Willie Banks	.05
322	Tom Goodwin	.05
323	Hector Wagner	.05
324	Wally Ritchie	.05
325	Mo Vaughn	.05
326	Joe Klink	.05
327	Cal Eldred	.05
328	Daryl Boston	.05
329	Mike Huff	.05
330	Jeff Bagwell	.65
331	Bob Milacki	.05
332	Tom Prince	.05
333	Pat Tabler	.05
334	Ced Landrum	.05
335	Reggie Jefferson	.05
336	Mo Sanford	.05
337	Kevin Ritz	.05
338	Gerald Perry	.05
339	Jeff Hamilton	.05
340	Tim Wallach	.05
341	Jeff Huson	.05
342	Jose Melendez	.05
343	Willie Wilson	.05
344	Mike Stanton	.05
345	Joel Johnston	.05
346	Lee Guetterman	.05
347	Francisco Olivares	.05
348	Dave Burba	.05
349	Tim Crews	.05
350	Scott Leius	.05
351	Danny Cox	.05
352	Wayne Housie	.05
353	Chris Donnels	.05
354	Chris George	.05
355	Gerald Young	.05
356	Roberto Hernandez	.05
357	Neal Heaton	.05
358	Todd Frohwirth	.05
359	Jose Vizcaino	.05
360	Jim Thome	.60
361	Craig Wilson	.05
362	Dave Haas	.05
363	Billy Hatcher	.05
364	John Barfield	.05
365	Luis Aquino	.05
366	Charlie Leibrandt	.05
367	Howard Farmer	.05
368	Bryn Smith	.05
369	Mickey Morandini	.05
370	Jose Canseco (Members Choice, should have been #597)	.35
371	Jose Uribe	.05
372	Bob MacDonald	.05
373	Luis Sojo	.05
374	Craig Shipley	.05
375	Scott Bankhead	.05
376	Greg Gagne	.05
377	Scott Cooper	.05
378	Jose Offerman	.05
379	Billy Spiers	.05
380	John Smiley	.05
381	Jeff Carter	.05
382	Heathcliff Slocumb	.05
383	Jeff Tackett	.05
384	John Kiely	.05
385	John Vander Wal	.05
386	Omar Olivares	.05
387	Ruben Sierra	.05
388	Tom Gordon	.05
389	Charles Nagy	.05
390	Dave Stewart	.05
391	Pete Harnisch	.05
392	Tim Burke	.05
393	Roberto Kelly	.05
394	Freddie Benavides	.05
395	Tom Glavine	.35
396	Wes Chamberlain	.05
397	Eric Gunderson	.05
398	Dave West	.05
399	Ellis Burks	.05
400	Ken Griffey, Jr.	1.00
401	Thomas Howard	.05
402	Juan Guzman	.05
403	Mitch Webster	.05
404	Matt Merullo	.05
405	Steve Buechele	.05
406	Danny Jackson	.05
407	Felix Jose	.05
408	Doug Piatt	.05
409	Jim Eisenreich	.05
410	Bryan Harvey	.05
411	Jim Austin	.05
412	Jim Poole	.05
413	Glenallen Hill	.05
414	Gene Nelson	.05
415	Ivan Rodriguez	.60
416	Frank Tanana	.05
417	Steve Decker	.05
418	Jason Grimsley	.05
419	Tim Layana	.05
420	Don Mattingly	.85
421	Jerome Walton	.05
422	Rob Ducey	.05
423	Andy Benes	.05
424	John Marzano	.05
425	Gene Harris	.05
426	Tim Raines	.05
427	Bret Barberie	.05
428	Harvey Pulliam	.05
429	Cris Carpenter	.05
430	Howard Johnson	.05
431	Orel Hershiser	.05
432	Brian Hunter	.05
433	Kevin Tapani	.05
434	Rick Reed	.05
435	Ron Witmeyer	.05
436	Gary Gaetti	.05
437	Alex Cole	.05
438	Chito Martinez	.05
439	Greg Litton	.05
440	Julio Franco	.05
441	Mike Munoz	.05
442	Erik Pappas	.05
443	Pat Combs	.05
444	Lance Johnson	.05
445	Ed Sprague	.05
446	Mike Greenwell	.05
447	Milt Thompson	.05
448	Mike Magnante	.05
449	Chris Haney	.05
450	Robin Yount	.65
451	Rafael Ramirez	.05
452	Gino Minutelli	.05
453	Tom Lampkin	.05
454	Tony Perezchica	.05
455	Dwight Gooden	.05
456	Mark Guthrie	.05
457	Jay Howell	.05
458	Gary DiSarcina	.05
459	John Smoltz	.05
460	Will Clark	.05
461	Dave Otto	.05
462	Rob Maurer	.05
463	Dwight Evans	.05
464	Tom Brunansky	.05
465	*Shawn Hare*	.05
466	Geronimo Pena	.05
467	Alex Fernandez	.05
468	Greg Myers	.05
469	Jeff Fassero	.05
470	Len Dykstra	.05
471	Jeff Johnson	.05
472	Russ Swan	.05
473	Archie Corbin	.05
474	Chuck McElroy	.05
475	Mark McGwire	1.25
476	Wally Whitehurst	.05
477	Tim McIntosh	.05
478	Sid Bream	.05
479	Jeff Juden	.05
480	Carlton Fisk	.65
481	Jeff Plympton	.05
482	Carlos Martinez	.05
483	Jim Gott	.05
484	Bob McClure	.05
485	Tim Teufel	.05
486	Vicente Palacios	.05
487	Jeff Reed	.05
488	Tony Phillips	.05
489	Mel Rojas	.05
490	Ben McDonald	.05
491	Andres Santana	.05
492	Chris Beasley	.05
493	Mike Timlin	.05
494	Brian Downing	.05
495	Kirk Gibson	.05
496	Scott Sanderson	.05
497	Nick Esasky	.05
498	*Johnny Guzman*	.05
499	Mitch Williams	.05
500	Kirby Puckett	.75
501	Mike Harkey	.05
502	Jim Gantner	.05
503	Bruce Egloff	.05
504	Josias Manzanillo	.05
505	Delino DeShields	.05
506	Rheal Cormier	.05
507	Jay Bell	.05
508	Rich Rowland	.05
509	Scott Servais	.05
510	Terry Pendleton	.05
511	Rich DeLucia	.05
512	Warren Newson	.05
513	Paul Faries	.05
514	Kal Daniels	.05
515	Jarvis Brown	.05
516	Rafael Palmeiro	.60
517	Kelly Downs	.05
518	Steve Chitren	.05
519	Moises Alou	.05
520	Wade Boggs	.75
521	Pete Schourek	.05
522	Scott Terry	.05
523	Kevin Appier	.05
524	Gary Redus	.05
525	George Bell	.05
526	Jeff Kaiser	.05
527	Alvaro Espinoza	.05
528	Luis Polonia	.05
529	Darren Daulton	.05
530	Norm Charlton	.05
531	John Olerud	.05
532	Dan Plesac	.05
533	Billy Ripken	.05
534	Rod Nichols	.05
535	Joey Cora	.05
536	Harold Baines	.05
537	Bob Ojeda	.05
538	Mark Leonard	.05
539	Danny Darwin	.05
540	Shawon Dunston	.05
541	Pedro Munoz	.05
542	Mark Gubicza	.05
543	Kevin Baez	.05
544	Todd Zeile	.05
545	Don Slaught	.05
546	Tony Eusebio	.05
547	Alonzo Powell	.05
548	Gary Pettis	.05
549	Brian Barnes	.05
550	Lou Whitaker	.05
551	Keith Mitchell	.05
552	Oscar Azocar	.05
553	Stu Cole	.05
554	Steve Wapnick	.05
555	Derek Bell	.05
556	Luis Lopez	.05
557	Anthony Telford	.05
558	Tim Mauser	.05
559	Glenn Sutko	.05
560	Darryl Strawberry	.05
561	Tom Bolton	.05
562	Cliff Young	.05
563	Bruce Walton	.05

No.	Player	Price
564	Chico Walker	.05
565	John Franco	.05
566	Paul McClellan	.05
567	Paul Abbott	.05
568	Gary Varsho	.05
569	Carlos Maldonado	.05
570	Kelly Gruber	.05
571	Jose Oquendo	.05
572	Steve Frey	.05
573	Tino Martinez	.05
574	Bill Haselman	.05
575	Eric Anthony	.05
576	John Habyan	.05
577	Jeffrey McNeely	.05
578	Chris Bosio	.05
579	Joe Grahe	.05
580	Fred McGriff	.05
581	Rick Honeycutt	.05
582	Matt Williams	.05
583	Cliff Brantley	.05
584	Rob Dibble	.05
585	Skeeter Barnes	.05
586	Greg Hibbard	.05
587	Randy Milligan	.05
588	Checklist 301-400	.05
589	Checklist 401-500	.05
590	Checklist 501-600	.05
591	Frank Thomas	.35
592	Dave Justice	.05
593	Roger Clemens	.45
594	Steve Avery	.05
595	Cal Ripken, Jr.	.75
596	Barry Larkin	.05
597	Not issued (See #370)	.05
598	Will Clark	.05
599	Cecil Fielder	.05
600	Ryne Sandberg	.40
601	Chuck Knoblauch	.05
602	Dwight Gooden	.05
603	Ken Griffey, Jr.	.65
604	Barry Bonds	.75
605	Nolan Ryan	.75
606	Jeff Bagwell	.35
607	Robin Yount	.30
608	Bobby Bonilla	.05
609	George Brett	.50
610	Howard Johnson	.05
611	Esteban Beltre	.05
612	Mike Christopher	.05
613	Troy Afenir	.05
614	Mariano Duncan	.05
615	Doug Henry	.05
616	Doug Jones	.05
617	Alvin Davis	.05
618	Craig Lefferts	.05
619	Kevin McReynolds	.05
620	Barry Bonds	1.50
621	Turner Ward	.05
622	Joe Magrane	.05
623	Mark Parent	.05
624	Tom Browning	.05
625	John Smiley	.05
626	Steve Wilson	.05
627	Mike Gallego	.05
628	Sammy Sosa	.75
629	Rico Rossy	.05
630	Royce Clayton	.05
631	Clay Parker	.05
632	Pete Smith	.05
633	Jeff McKnight	.05
634	Jack Daugherty	.05
635	Steve Sax	.05
636	Joe Hesketh	.05
637	Vince Horsman	.05
638	Eric King	.05
639	Joe Boever	.05
640	Jack Morris	.05
641	Arthur Rhodes	.05
642	Bob Melvin	.05
643	Rick Wilkins	.05
644	Scott Scudder	.05
645	Bip Roberts	.05
646	Julio Valera	.05
647	Kevin Campbell	.05
648	Steve Searcy	.05
649	Scott Kamieniecki	.05
650	Kurt Stillwell	.05
651	Bob Welch	.05
652	Andres Galarraga	.05
653	Mike Jackson	.05
654	Bo Jackson	.10
655	Sid Fernandez	.05
656	Mike Bielecki	.05
657	Jeff Reardon	.05
658	Wayne Rosenthal	.05
659	Eric Bullock	.05
660	Eric Davis	.05
661	Randy Tomlin	.05
662	Tom Edens	.05
663	Rob Murphy	.05
664	Leo Gomez	.05
665	Greg Maddux	.75
666	Greg Vaughn	.05
667	Wade Taylor	.05
668	Brad Arnsberg	.05
669	Mike Moore	.05
670	Mark Langston	.05
671	Barry Jones	.05
672	Bill Landrum	.05
673	Greg Swindell	.05
674	Wayne Edwards	.05
675	Greg Olson	.05
676	*Bill Pulsipher*	.05
677	Bobby Witt	.05
678	Mark Carreon	.05
679	Patrick Lennon	.05
680	Ozzie Smith	.75
681	John Briscoe	.05
682	Matt Young	.05
683	Jeff Conine	.05
684	Phil Stephenson	.05
685	Ron Darling	.05
686	Bryan Hickerson	.05
687	Dale Sveum	.05
688	Kirk McCaskill	.05
689	Rich Amaral	.05
690	Danny Tartabull	.05
691	Donald Harris	.05
692	Doug Davis	.05
693	John Farrell	.05
694	Paul Gibson	.05
695	Kenny Lofton	.05
696	Mike Fetters	.05
697	Rosario Rodriguez	.05
698	Chris Jones	.05
699	Jeff Manto	.05
700	Rick Sutcliffe	.05
701	Scott Bankhead	.05
702	Donnie Hill	.05
703	Todd Worrell	.05
704	Rene Gonzales	.05
705	Rick Cerone	.05
706	Tony Pena	.05
707	Paul Sorrento	.05
708	Gary Scott	.05
709	Junior Noboa	.05
710	Wally Joyner	.05
711	Charlie Hayes	.05
712	Rich Rodriguez	.05
713	Rudy Seanez	.05
714	Jim Bullinger	.05
715	Jeff Robinson	.05
716	Jeff Branson	.05
717	Andy Ashby	.05
718	Dave Burba	.05
719	Rich Gossage	.05
720	Randy Johnson	.65
721	David Wells	.05
722	Paul Kilgus	.05
723	Dave Martinez	.05
724	Denny Neagle	.05
725	Andy Stankiewicz	.05
726	Rick Aguilera	.05
727	Junior Ortiz	.05
728	Storm Davis	.05
729	Don Robinson	.05
730	Ron Gant	.05
731	Paul Assenmacher	.05
732	Mark Gardiner	.05
733	Milt Hill	.05
734	Jeremy Hernandez	.05
735	Ken Hill	.05
736	Xavier Hernandez	.05
737	Gregg Jefferies	.05
738	Dick Schofield	.05
739	Ron Robinson	.05
740	Sandy Alomar	.05
741	Mike Stanley	.05
742	Butch Henry	.05
743	Floyd Bannister	.05
744	Brian Drahman	.05
745	Dave Winfield	.65
746	Bob Walk	.05
747	Chris James	.05
748	Don Prybylinski	.05
749	Dennis Rasmussen	.05
750	Rickey Henderson	.65
751	Chris Hammond	.05
752	Bob Kipper	.05
753	Dave Rohde	.05
754	Hubie Brooks	.05
755	Bret Saberhagen	.05
756	Jeff Robinson	.05
757	*Pat Listach*	.05
758	Bill Wegman	.05
759	John Wetteland	.05
760	Phil Plantier	.05
761	Wilson Alvarez	.05
762	Scott Aldred	.05
763	*Armando Reynoso*	.05
764	Todd Benzinger	.05
765	Kevin Mitchell	.05
766	Gary Sheffield	.35
767	Allan Anderson	.05
768	Rusty Meacham	.05
769	Rick Parker	.05
770	Nolan Ryan	1.50
771	Jeff Ballard	.05
772	Cory Snyder	.05
773	Denis Boucher	.05
774	Jose Gonzales	.05
775	Juan Guerrero	.05
776	Ed Nunez	.05
777	Scott Ruskin	.05
778	Terry Leach	.05
779	Carl Willis	.05
780	Bobby Bonilla	.05
781	Duane Ward	.05
782	Joe Slusarski	.05
783	David Segui	.05
784	Kirk Gibson	.05
785	Frank Viola	.05
786	Keith Miller	.05
787	Mike Morgan	.05
788	Kim Batiste	.05
789	Sergio Valdez	.05
790	Eddie Taubensee	.05
791	Jack Armstrong	.05
792	Scott Fletcher	.05
793	Steve Farr	.05
794	Dan Pasqua	.05
795	Eddie Murray	.65
796	John Morris	.05
797	Francisco Cabrera	.05
798	Mike Perez	.05
799	Ted Wood	.05
800	Jose Rijo	.05
801	Danny Gladden	.05
802	Arci Cianfrocco	.05
803	Monty Fariss	.05
804	Roger McDowell	.05
805	Randy Myers	.05
806	Kirk Dressendorfer	.05
807	Zane Smith	.05
808	Glenn Davis	.05
809	Torey Lovullo	.05
810	Andre Dawson	.25
811	Bill Pecota	.05
812	Ted Power	.05
813	Willie Blair	.05
814	Dave Fleming	.05
815	Chris Gwynn	.05
816	Jody Reed	.05
817	Mark Dewey	.05
818	Kyle Abbott	.05
819	Tom Henke	.05
820	Kevin Seitzer	.05
821	Al Newman	.05
822	Tim Sherrill	.05
823	Chuck Crim	.05
824	Darren Reed	.05
825	Tony Gwynn	.75
826	Steve Foster	.05
827	Steve Howe	.05
828	Brook Jacoby	.05
829	Rodney McCray	.05
830	Chuck Knoblauch	.05
831	John Wehner	.05
832	Scott Garrelts	.05
833	Alejandro Pena	.05
834	Jeff Parrett	.05
835	Juan Bell	.05
836	Lance Dickson	.05
837	Darryl Kile	.05
838	Efrain Valdez	.05
839	*Bob Zupcic*	.05
840	George Bell	.05
841	Dave Gallagher	.05
842	Tim Belcher	.05
843	Jeff Shaw	.05
844	Mike Fitzgerald	.05
845	Gary Carter	.65
846	John Russell	.05
847	*Eric Hillman*	.05
848	Mike Witt	.05
849	Curt Wilkerson	.05
850	Alan Trammell	.05
851	Rex Hudler	.05
852	*Michael Walkden*	.05
853	Kevin Ward	.05
854	Tim Naehring	.05
855	Bill Swift	.05
856	Damon Berryhill	.05
857	Mark Eichhorn	.05
858	Hector Villanueva	.05
859	Jose Lind	.05
860	Denny Martinez	.05
861	Bill Krueger	.05
862	Mike Kingery	.05
863	Jeff Innis	.05
864	Derek Lilliquist	.05
865	Reggie Sanders	.05
866	Ramon Garcia	.05
867	Bruce Ruffin	.05
868	Dickie Thon	.05
869	Melido Perez	.05
870	Ruben Amaro	.05
871	Alan Mills	.05
872	Matt Sinatro	.05
873	Eddie Zosky	.05
874	Pete Incaviglia	.05
875	Tom Candiotti	.05
876	Bob Patterson	.05
877	Neal Heaton	.05
878	*Terrel Hansen*	.05
879	Dave Eiland	.05
880	Von Hayes	.05
881	Tim Scott	.05
882	Otis Nixon	.05
883	Herm Winningham	.05
884	Dion James	.05
885	Dave Wainhouse	.05
886	Frank DiPino	.05
887	Dennis Cook	.05
888	Jose Mesa	.05
889	Mark Leiter	.05
890	Willie Randolph	.05
891	Craig Colbert	.05
892	Dwayne Henry	.05
893	Jim Lindeman	.05
894	Charlie Hough	.05
895	Gil Heredia	.05
896	Scott Chiamparino	.05
897	Lance Blankenship	.05
898	Checklist 601-700	.05
899	Checklist 701-800	.05
900	Checklist 801-900	.05

Master Photos

		NM/M
Complete Set (15):		20.00
Common Player:		.50
(1)	Wade Boggs	2.25
(2)	Barry Bonds	4.00
(3)	Jose Canseco	1.00
(4)	Will Clark	.50
(5)	Cecil Fielder	.50
(6)	Dwight Gooden	.50
(7)	Ken Griffey, Jr.	3.00
(8)	Rickey Henderson	2.00
(9)	Lance Johnson	.50
(10)	Cal Ripken, Jr.	4.00
(11)	Nolan Ryan	4.00
(12)	Deion Sanders	.50
(13)	Darryl Strawberry	.50
(14)	Danny Tartabull	.50
(15)	Frank Thomas	2.00

SkyDome

		NM/M
Unopened Factory Set (200):		15.00
Complete Set (200):		10.00
Common Player:		.05
1	*Terry Adams*	.05
2	Tommy Adams	.05
3	Rick Aguilera	.05
4	Ron Allen	.05
5	Roberto Alomar (All-Star)	.20
6	Sandy Alomar	.05
7	Greg Anthony	.05
8	James Austin	.05
9	Steve Avery	.05
10	Harold Baines	.05
11	*Brian Barber*	.05
12	Jon Barnes	.05
13	George Bell	.05

14 Doug Bennett .05
15 Sean Bergman .05
16 Craig Biggio .05
17 Bill Bliss .05
18 Wade Boggs (AS) .60
19 Bobby Bonilla (AS) .05
20 Russell Brock .05
21 Tarrik Brock .05
22 Tom Browning .05
23 Brett Butler .05
24 Ivan Calderon .05
25 Joe Carter .05
26 Joe Caruso .05
27 Dan Cholowsky .05
28 Will Clark (AS) .05
29 Roger Clemens (AS) .65
30 Shawn Curran .05
31 Chris Curtis .05
32 Chili Davis .05
33 Andre Dawson .25
34 Joe DeBerry .05
35 John Dettmer .05
36 Rob Dibble .05
37 *John Donati* .05
38 Dave Doorneweerd .05
39 Darren Dreifort .05
40 Mike Durant .05
41 Chris Durkin .05
42 Dennis Eckersley .40
43 *Brian Edmondson* .05
44 *Vaughn Eshelman* .05
45 *Shawn Estes* .50
46 *Jorge Fabregas* .10
47 Jon Farrell .05
48 Cecil Fielder (AS) .05
49 Carlton Fisk .50
50 Tim Flannelly .05
51 *Cliff Floyd* .50
52 Julio Franco .05
53 Greg Gagne .05
54 *Chris Gambs* .05
55 Ron Gant .05
56 Brent Gates .05
57 Dwayne Gerald .05
58 Jason Giambi 1.50
59 *Benji Gil* .05
60 Mark Gipner .05
61 Danny Gladden .05
62 Tom Glavine .35
63 Jimmy Gonzalez .05
64 Jeff Granger .05
65 Dan Grapenthien .05
66 Dennis Gray .05
67 *Shawn Green* 2.00
68 Tyler Green .05
69 Todd Greene .05
70 Ken Griffey, Jr. (AS) .75
71 Kelly Gruber .05
72 Ozzie Guillen .05
73 Tony Gwynn (AS) .60
74 Shane Halter .05
75 Jeffrey Hammonds .05
76 Larry Hanlon .05
77 Pete Harnisch .05
78 Mike Harrison .05
79 Bryan Harvey .05
80 Scott Hatteberg .05
81 Rick Helling .05
82 Dave Henderson .05
83 Rickey Henderson (AS) .50
84 Tyrone Hill .05
85 *Todd Hollandsworth* .10
86 Brian Holliday .05
87 Terry Horn .05
88 Jeff Hostetler .05
89 Kent Hrbek .05
90 Mark Hubbard .05
91 Charles Johnson .05
92 Howard Johnson .05
93 Todd Johnson .05
94 *Bobby Jones* .10
95 Dan Jones .05
96 Felix Jose .05
97 Dave Justice .05
98 Jimmy Key .05
99 *Marc Kroom* .05
100 John Kruk .05
101 Mark Langston .05
102 Barry Larkin .05
103 Mike LaValliere .05
104a Scott Leius (1991 N.L. All-Star - error) .05
104b Scott Leius (1991 World Series - correct) .25
105 Mark Lemke .05
106 Donnie Leshnock .05
107 Jimmy Lewis .05
108 Shawn Livesy .05
109 Ryan Long .05
110 Trevor Mallory .05
111 Denny Martinez .05
112 Justin Mashore .05
113 Jason McDonald .05
114 Jack McDowell .05
115 Tom McKinnon .05
116 Billy McKinnon .05
117 *Buck McNabb* .05
118 Jim Mecir .05
119 Dan Melendez .05
120 *Shawn Miller* .05
121 Trever Miller .05
122 Paul Molitor .50
123 Vincent Moore .05
124 Mike Morgan .05
125 Jack Morris (World Series) .05
126 Jack Morris (All-Star) .05
127 Sean Mulligan .05
128 Eddie Murray .50
129 Mike Neill .05
130 Phil Nevin .05
131 Mark O'Brien .05
132 *Alex Ochoa* .05
133 *Chad Ogea* .05
134 Greg Olson .05
135 Paul O'Neill .05
136a Jared Osentowski (1991 World Series - error) .05
136b Jared Osentowski (Draft Pick - correct) .25
137 Mike Pagliarulo .05
138 Rafael Palmeiro .40
139 Rodney Pedraza .05
140 Tony Phillips .05
141 *Scott Pisciotta* .05
142 Chris Pritchett .05
143 Jason Pruitt .05
144a Kirby Puckett (1991 N.L. All-Star - error) .60
144b Kirby Puckett (1991 World Series - correct) 3.00
145 Kirby Puckett (AS) .60
146 *Manny Ramirez* 5.00
147 Eddie Ramos .05
148 Mark Ratekin .05
149 Jeff Reardon .05
150 Sean Rees .05
151 *Calvin Reese* .50
152 *Desmond Relaford* .10
153 Eric Richardson .05
154 Cal Ripken, Jr. (AS) 1.50
155 Chris Roberts .05
156 Mike Robertson .05
157 Steve Rodriguez .05
158 Mike Rossiter .05
159 Scott Ruffcorn .05
160a Chris Sabo (1991 World Series - error) .05
160b Chris Sabo (1991 N.L. All-Star - correct) .25
161 Juan Samuel .05
162 Ryne Sandberg (AS) .60
163 Scott Sanderson .05
164 Benito Santiago .05
165 *Gene Schall* .05
166 Chad Schoenvogel .05
167 *Chris Seelbach* .05
168 *Aaron Sele* .50
169 Basil Shabazz .05
170 *Al Shirley* .05
171 Paul Shuey .05
172 Ruben Sierra .05
173 John Smiley .05
174 Lee Smith .05
175 Ozzie Smith .60
176 Tim Smith .05
177 Zane Smith .05
178 John Smoltz .05
179 Scott Stahoviak .05
180 Kennie Steenstra .05
181 Kevin Stocker .05
182 *Chris Stynes* .05
183 Danny Tartabull .05
184 Brien Taylor .05
185 Todd Taylor .05
186 Larry Thomas .05
187a *Ozzie Timmons* .05
187b David Tuttle (should be #188) .05
188 Not issued .05
189 Andy Van Slyke .05
190a Frank Viola (1991 World Series - error) .05
190b Frank Viola (1991 N.L. All-Star - correct) .25
191 Michael Walkden .05
192 Jeff Ware .05
193 *Allen Watson* .05
194 Steve Whitaker .05
195a Jerry Willard (1991 Draft Pick - error) .05
195b Jerry Willard (1991 World Series - correct) .25
196 Craig Wilson .05
197 Chris Wimmer .05
198 *Steve Wojciechowski* .05
199 Joel Wolfe .05
200 Ivan Zweig .05

1993 STADIUM CLUB

	NM/M
Complete Set (750):	25.00
Common Player:	.05
First Day:	8X
Pack (15):	.75
Wax Box (24):	9.00

1 Pat Borders .05
2 Greg Maddux .85
3 Daryl Boston .05
4 Bob Ayrault .05
5 Tony Phillips .05
6 Damion Easley .05
7 Kip Gross .05
8 Jim Thome .65
9 Tim Belcher .05
10 Gary Wayne .05
11 Sam Militello .05
12 Mike Magnante .05
13 Tim Wakefield .05
14 Tim Hulett .05
15 Rheal Cormier .05
16 Juan Guerrero .05
17 Rich Gossage .05
18 Tim Laker .05
19 Darrin Jackson .05
20 Jack Clark .05
21 Roberto Hernandez .05
22 Dean Palmer .05
23 Harold Reynolds .05
24 Dan Plesac .05
25 Brent Mayne .05
26 Pat Hentgen .05
27 Luis Sojo .05
28 Ron Gant .05
29 Paul Gibson .05
30 Bip Roberts .05
31 Mickey Tettleton .05
32 Randy Velarde .05
33 Brian McRae .05
34 Wes Chamberlain .05
35 Wayne Kirby .05
36 Rey Sanchez .05
37 Jesse Orosco .05
38 Mike Stanton .05
39 Royce Clayton .05
40 Cal Ripken, Jr. 2.50
41 John Dopson .05
42 Gene Larkin .05
43 Tim Raines .05
44 Randy Myers .05
45 Clay Parker .05
46 Mike Scioscia .05
47 Pete Incaviglia .05
48 Todd Van Poppel .05
49 Ray Lankford .05
50 Eddie Murray .75
51 Barry Bonds 2.50
52 Gary Thurman .05
53 Bob Wickman .05
54 Joey Cora .05
55 Kenny Rogers .05
56 Mike Devereaux .05
57 Kevin Seitzer .05
58 Rafael Belliard .05
59 David Wells .05
60 Mark Clark .05
61 Carlos Baerga .05
62 Scott Brosius .05
63 Jeff Grotewold .05
64 Rick Wrona .05
65 Kurt Knudsen .05
66 Lloyd McClendon .05
67 Omar Vizquel .05
68 Jose Vizcaino .05
69 Rob Ducey .05
70 Casey Candaele .05
71 Ramon Martinez .05
72 Todd Hundley .05
73 John Marzano .05
74 Derek Parks .05
75 Jack McDowell .05
76 Tim Scott .05
77 Mike Mussina .40
78 Delino DeShields .05
79 Chris Bosio .05
80 Mike Bordick .05
81 Rod Beck .05
82 Ted Power .05
83 John Kruk .05
84 Steve Shifflett .05
85 Danny Tartabull .05
86 Mike Greenwell .05
87 Jose Melendez .05
88 Craig Wilson .05
89 Melvin Nieves .05
90 Ed Sprague .05
91 Willie McGee .05
92 Joe Orsulak .05
93 Jeff King .05
94 Dan Pasqua .05
95 Brian Harper .05
96 Joe Oliver .05
97 Shane Turner .05
98 Lenny Harris .05
99 Jeff Parrett .05
100 Luis Polonia .05
101 Kent Bottenfield .05
102 Albert Belle .05
103 Mike Maddux .05
104 Randy Tomlin .05
105 Andy Stankiewicz .05
106 Rico Rossy .05
107 Joe Hesketh .05
108 Dennis Powell .05
109 Derrick May .05
110 Pete Harnisch .05
111 Kent Mercker .05
112 Scott Fletcher .05
113 Rex Hudler .05
114 Chico Walker .05
115 Rafael Palmeiro .65
116 Mark Leiter .05
117 Pedro Munoz .05
118 Jim Bullinger .05
119 Ivan Calderon .05
120 Mike Timlin .05
121 Rene Gonzales .05
122 Greg Vaughn .05
123 Mike Flanagan .05
124 Mike Hartley .05
125 Jeff Montgomery .05
126 Mike Gallego .05
127 Don Slaught .05
128 Charlie O'Brien .05
129a Jose Offerman (Home: (blank)) 2.00
129b Jose Offerman (Home: S.P. de MACORIS, D.R.) .05
130 Mark Wohlers .05
131 Eric Fox .05
132 Doug Strange .05
133 Jeff Frye .05
134 Wade Boggs .85
135 Lou Whitaker .05
136 Craig Grebeck .05
137 Rich Rodriguez .05
138 Jay Bell .05
139 Felix Fermin .05
140 Denny Martinez .05
141 Eric Anthony .05
142 Roberto Alomar .20
143 Darren Lewis .05
144 Mike Blowers .05
145 Scott Bankhead .05
146 Jeff Reboulet .05
147 Frank Viola .05
148 Bill Pecota .05
149 Carlos Hernandez .05
150 Bobby Witt .05
151 Sid Bream .05
152 Todd Zeile .05
153 Dennis Cook .05
154 Brian Bohanon .05
155 Pat Kelly .05
156 Milt Cuyler .05
157 Juan Bell .05

No.	Player	Price
158	Randy Milligan	.05
159	Mark Gardner	.05
160	Pat Tabler	.05
161	Jeff Reardon	.05
162	Ken Patterson	.05
163	Bobby Bonilla	.05
164	Tony Pena	.05
165	Greg Swindell	.05
166	Kirk McCaskill	.05
167	Doug Drabek	.05
168	Franklin Stubbs	.05
169	Ron Tingley	.05
170	Willie Banks	.05
171	Sergio Valdez	.05
172	Mark Lemke	.05
173	Robin Yount	.75
174	Storm Davis	.05
175	Dan Walters	.05
176	Steve Farr	.05
177	Curt Wilkerson	.05
178	Luis Alicea	.05
179	Russ Swan	.05
180	Mitch Williams	.05
181	Wilson Alvarez	.05
182	Carl Willis	.05
183	Craig Biggio	.05
184	Sean Berry	.05
185	Trevor Wilson	.05
186	Jeff Tackett	.05
187	Ellis Burks	.05
188	Jeff Branson	.05
189	Matt Nokes	.05
190	John Smiley	.05
191	Danny Gladden	.05
192	Mike Boddicker	.05
193	Roger Pavlik	.05
194	Paul Sorrento	.05
195	Vince Coleman	.05
196	Gary DiSarcina	.05
197	Rafael Bournigal	.05
198	Mike Schooler	.05
199	Scott Ruskin	.05
200	Frank Thomas	.75
201	Kyle Abbott	.05
202	Mike Perez	.05
203	Andre Dawson	.25
204	Bill Swift	.05
205	Alejandro Pena	.05
206	Dave Winfield	.75
207	Andujar Cedeno	.05
208	Terry Steinbach	.05
209	Chris Hammond	.05
210	Todd Burns	.05
211	Hipolito Pichardo	.05
212	John Kiely	.05
213	Tim Teufel	.05
214	Lee Guetterman	.05
215	Geronimo Pena	.05
216	Brett Butler	.05
217	Bryan Hickerson	.05
218	Rick Trlicek	.05
219	Lee Stevens	.05
220	Roger Clemens	1.25
221	Carlton Fisk	.75
222	Chili Davis	.05
223	Walt Terrell	.05
224	Jim Eisenreich	.05
225	Ricky Bones	.05
226	Henry Rodriguez	.05
227	Ken Hill	.05
228	Rick Wilkins	.05
229	Ricky Jordan	.05
230	Bernard Gilkey	.05
231	Tim Fortugno	.05
232	Geno Petralli	.05
233	Jose Rijo	.05
234	Jim Leyritz	.05
235	Kevin Campbell	.05
236	Al Osuna	.05
237	Pete Smith	.05
238	Pete Schourek	.05
239	Moises Alou	.05
240	Donn Pall	.05
241	Denny Neagle	.05
242	Dan Peltier	.05
243	Scott Scudder	.05
244	Juan Guzman	.05
245	Dave Burba	.05
246	Rick Sutcliffe	.05
247	Tony Fossas	.05
248	Mike Munoz	.05
249	Tim Salmon	.05
250	Rob Murphy	.05
251	Roger McDowell	.05
252	Lance Parrish	.05
253	Cliff Brantley	.05
254	Scott Leius	.05
255	Carlos Martinez	.05
256	Vince Horsman	.05
257	Oscar Azocar	.05
258	Craig Shipley	.05
259	Ben McDonald	.05
260	Jeff Brantley	.05
261	Damon Berryhill	.05
262	Joe Grahe	.05
263	Dave Hansen	.05
264	Rich Amaral	.05
265	*Tim Pugh*	.05
266	Dion James	.05
267	Frank Tanana	.05
268	Stan Belinda	.05
269	Jeff Kent	.05
270	Bruce Ruffin	.05
271	Xavier Hernandez	.05
272	Darrin Fletcher	.05
273	Tino Martinez	.05
274	Benny Santiago	.05
275	Scott Radinsky	.05
276	Mariano Duncan	.05
277	Kenny Lofton	.05
278	Dwight Smith	.05
279	Joe Carter	.05
280	Tim Jones	.05
281	Jeff Huson	.05
282	Phil Plantier	.05
283	Kirby Puckett	.85
284	Johnny Guzman	.05
285	Mike Morgan	.05
286	Chris Sabo	.05
287	Matt Williams	.05
288	Checklist 1-100	.05
289	Checklist 101-200	.05
290	Checklist 201-300	.05
291	Dennis Eckersley	.30
292	Eric Karros	.05
293	Pat Listach	.05
294	Andy Van Slyke	.05
295	Robin Ventura	.05
296	Tom Glavine	.05
297	Juan Gonzalez	.20
298	Travis Fryman	.05
299	Larry Walker	.05
300	Gary Sheffield	.20
301	Chuck Finley	.05
302	Luis Gonzalez	.05
303	Darryl Hamilton	.05
304	Bien Figueroa	.05
305	Ron Darling	.05
306	Jonathan Hurst	.05
307	Mike Sharperson	.05
308	Mike Christopher	.05
309	Marvin Freeman	.05
310	Jay Buhner	.05
311	Butch Henry	.05
312	Greg Harris	.05
313	Darren Daulton	.05
314	Chuck Knoblauch	.05
315	Greg Harris	.05
316	John Franco	.05
317	John Wehner	.05
318	Donald Harris	.05
319	Benny Santiago	.05
320	Larry Walker	.05
321	Randy Knorr	.05
322	*Ramon D. Martinez*	.05
323	Mike Stanley	.05
324	Bill Wegman	.05
325	Tom Candiotti	.05
326	Glenn Davis	.05
327	Chuck Crim	.05
328	Scott Livingstone	.05
329	Eddie Taubensee	.05
330	George Bell	.05
331	Edgar Martinez	.05
332	Paul Assenmacher	.05
333	Steve Hosey	.05
334	Mo Vaughn	.05
335	Bret Saberhagen	.05
336	Mike Trombley	.05
337	Mark Lewis	.05
338	Terry Pendleton	.05
339	Dave Hollins	.05
340	Jeff Conine	.05
341	Bob Tewksbury	.05
342	Billy Ashley	.05
343	Zane Smith	.05
344	John Wetteland	.05
345	Chris Hoiles	.05
346	Frank Castillo	.05
347	Bruce Hurst	.05
348	Kevin McReynolds	.05
349	Dave Henderson	.05
350	Ryan Bowen	.05
351	Sid Fernandez	.05
352	Mark Whiten	.05
353	Nolan Ryan	2.50
354	Rick Aguilera	.05
355	Mark Langston	.05
356	Jack Morris	.05
357	Rob Deer	.05
358	Dave Fleming	.05
359	Lance Johnson	.05
360	Joe Millette	.05
361	Wil Cordero	.05
362	Chito Martinez	.05
363	Scott Servais	.05
364	Bernie Williams	.05
365	Pedro Martinez	.75
366	Ryne Sandberg	.85
367	Brad Ausmus	.05
368	Scott Cooper	.05
369	Rob Dibble	.05
370	Walt Weiss	.05
371	Mark Davis	.05
372	Orlando Merced	.05
373	Mike Jackson	.05
374	Kevin Appier	.05
375	Esteban Beltre	.05
376	Joe Slusarski	.05
377	William Suero	.05
378	Pete O'Brien	.05
379	Alan Embree	.05
380	Lenny Webster	.05
381	Eric Davis	.05
382	Duane Ward	.05
383	John Habyan	.05
384	Jeff Bagwell	.75
385	Ruben Amaro	.05
386	Julio Valera	.05
387	Robin Ventura	.05
388	Archi Cianfrocco	.05
389	Skeeter Barnes	.05
390	Tim Costo	.05
391	Luis Mercedes	.05
392	Jeremy Hernandez	.05
393	Shawon Dunston	.05
394	Andy Van Slyke	.05
395	Kevin Maas	.05
396	Kevin Brown	.05
397	J.T. Bruett	.05
398	Darryl Strawberry	.05
399	Tom Pagnozzi	.05
400	Sandy Alomar	.05
401	Keith Miller	.05
402	Rich DeLucia	.05
403	Shawn Abner	.05
404	Howard Johnson	.05
405	Mike Benjamin	.05
406	*Roberto Mejia*	.05
407	Mike Butcher	.05
408	Deion Sanders	.05
409	Todd Stottlemyre	.05
410	Scott Kamieniecki	.05
411	Doug Jones	.05
412	John Burkett	.05
413	Lance Blankenship	.05
414	Jeff Parrett	.05
415	Barry Larkin	.05
416	Alan Trammell	.05
417	Mark Kiefer	.05
418	Gregg Olson	.05
419	Mark Grace	.05
420	Shane Mack	.05
421	Bob Walk	.05
422	Curt Schilling	.25
423	Erik Hanson	.05
424	George Brett	1.25
425	Reggie Jefferson	.05
426	Mark Portugal	.05
427	Ron Karkovice	.05
428	Matt Young	.05
429	Troy Neel	.05
430	Hector Fajardo	.05
431	Dave Righetti	.05
432	Pat Listach	.05
433	Jeff Innis	.05
434	Bob MacDonald	.05
435	Brian Jordan	.05
436	Jeff Blauser	.05
437	*Mike Myers*	.05
438	Frank Seminara	.05
439	Rusty Meacham	.05
440	Greg Briley	.05
441	Derek Lilliquist	.05
442	John Vander Wal	.05
443	Scott Erickson	.05
444	Bob Scanlan	.05
445	Todd Frohwirth	.05
446	Tom Goodwin	.05
447	William Pennyfeather	.05
448	Travis Fryman	.05
449	Mickey Morandini	.05
450	Greg Olson	.05
451	Trevor Hoffman	.05
452	Dave Magadan	.05
453	Shawn Jeter	.05
454	Andres Galarraga	.05
455	Ted Wood	.05
456	Freddie Benavides	.05
457	Junior Felix	.05
458	Alex Cole	.05
459	John Orton	.05
460	Eddie Zosky	.05
461	Dennis Eckersley	.65
462	Lee Smith	.05
463	John Smoltz	.05
464	Ken Caminiti	.05
465	Melido Perez	.05
466	Tom Marsh	.05
467	Jeff Nelson	.05
468	Jesse Levis	.05
469	Chris Nabholz	.05
470	Mike Mcfarlane	.05
471	Reggie Sanders	.05
472	Chuck McElroy	.05
473	Kevin Gross	.05
474	*Matt Whiteside*	.05
475	Cal Eldred	.05
476	Dave Gallagher	.05
477	Len Dykstra	.05
478	Mark McGwire	2.00
479	David Segui	.05
480	Mike Henneman	.05
481	Bret Barberie	.05
482	Steve Sax	.05
483	Dave Valle	.05
484	Danny Darwin	.05
485	Devon White	.05
486	Eric Plunk	.05
487	Jim Gott	.05
488	Scooter Tucker	.05
489	Omar Oliveres	.05
490	Greg Myers	.05
491	Brian Hunter	.05
492	Kevin Tapani	.05
493	Rich Monteleone	.05
494	Steve Buechele	.05
495	Bo Jackson	.10
496	Mike LaValliere	.05
497	Mark Leonard	.05
498	Daryl Boston	.05
499	Jose Canseco	.45
500	Brian Barnes	.05
501	Randy Johnson	.75
502	Tim McIntosh	.05
503	Cecil Fielder	.05
504	Derek Bell	.05
505	Kevin Koslofski	.05
506	Darren Holmes	.05
507	Brady Anderson	.05
508	John Valentin	.05
509	Jerry Browne	.05
510	Fred McGriff	.05
511	Pedro Astacio	.05
512	Gary Gaetti	.05
513	*John Burke*	.05
514	Dwight Gooden	.05
515	Thomas Howard	.05
516	*Darrell Whitmore*	.05
517	Ozzie Guillen	.05
518	Darryl Kile	.05
519	Rich Rowland	.05
520	Carlos Delgado	.50
521	Doug Henry	.05
522	Greg Colbrunn	.05
523	Tom Gordon	.05
524	Ivan Rodriguez	.65
525	Kent Hrbek	.05
526	Eric Young	.05
527	Rod Brewer	.05
528	Eric Karros	.05
529	Marquis Grissom	.05
530	Rico Brogna	.05
531	Sammy Sosa	1.00
532	Bret Boone	.05
533	Luis Rivera	.05
534	Hal Morris	.05
535	Monty Fariss	.05
536	Leo Gomez	.05
537	Wally Joyner	.05
538	Tony Gwynn	.85
539	Mike Williams	.05
540	Juan Gonzalez	.40
541	Ryan Klesko	.05
542	Ryan Thompson	.05
543	Chad Curtis	.05
544	Orel Hershiser	.05
545	Carlos Garcia	.05
546	Bob Welch	.05
547	Vinny Castilla	.05
548	Ozzie Smith	.85
549	Luis Salazar	.05
550	Mark Guthrie	.05
551	Charles Nagy	.05
552	Alex Fernandez	.05
553	Mel Rojas	.05

554 Orestes Destrade .05
555 Mark Gubicza .05
556 Steve Finley .05
557 Don Mattingly 1.25
558 Rickey Henderson .75
559 Tommy Greene .05
560 Arthur Rhodes .05
561 Alfredo Griffin .05
562 Will Clark .05
563 Bob Zupcic .05
564 Chuck Carr .05
565 Henry Cotto .05
566 Billy Spiers .05
567 Jack Armstrong .05
568 Kurt Stillwell .05
569 David McCarty .05
570 Joe Vitiello .05
571 Gerald Williams .05
572 Dale Murphy .25
573 Scott Aldred .05
574 Bill Gullickson .05
575 Bobby Thigpen .05
576 Glenallen Hill .05
577 Dwayne Henry .05
578 Calvin Jones .05
579 Al Martin .05
580 Ruben Sierra .05
581 Andy Benes .05
582 Anthony Young .05
583 Shawn Boskie .05
584 *Scott Pose* .05
585 Mike Piazza 1.50
586 Donovan Osborne .05
587 James Austin .05
588 Checklist 301-400 .05
589 Checklist 401-500 .05
590 Checklist 501-600 .05
591 Ken Griffey, Jr. (Members Choice) .75
592 Ivan Rodriguez (Members Choice) .40
593 Carlos Baerga (Members Choice) .05
594 Fred McGriff (Members Choice) .05
595 Mark McGwire (Members Choice) 1.00
596 Roberto Alomar (Members Choice) .10
597 Kirby Puckett (Members Choice) .45
598 Marquis Grissom (Members Choice) .05
599 John Smoltz (Members Choice) .05
600 Ryne Sandberg (Members Choice) .45
601 Wade Boggs .85
602 Jeff Reardon .05
603 Billy Ripken .05
604 Bryan Harvey .05
605 Carlos Quintana .05
606 Greg Hibbard .05
607 Ellis Burks .05
608 Greg Swindell .05
609 Dave Winfield .75
610 Charlie Hough .05
611 Chili Davis .05
612 Jody Reed .05
613 Mark Williamson .05
614 Phil Plantier .05
615 Jim Abbott .05
616 Dante Bichette .05
617 Mark Eichhorn .05
618 Gary Sheffield .45
619 *Richie Lewis* .05
620 Joe Girardi .05
621 Jaime Navarro .05
622 Willie Wilson .05
623 Scott Fletcher .05
624 Bud Black .05
625 Tom Brunansky .05
626 Steve Avery .05
627 Paul Molitor .75
628 Gregg Jefferies .05
629 Dave Stewart .05
630 Javier Lopez .05
631 Greg Gagne .05
632 Bobby Kelly .05
633 Mike Fetters .05
634 Ozzie Canseco .05
635 Jeff Russell .05
636 Pete Incaviglia .05
637 Tom Henke .05
638 Chipper Jones 1.00
639 Jimmy Key .05
640 Dave Martinez .05
641 Dave Stieb .05
642 Milt Thompson .05
643 Alan Mills .05
644 Tony Fernandez .05
645 Randy Bush .05
646 Joe Magrane .05
647 Ivan Calderon .05
648 Jose Guzman .05
649 John Olerud .05
650 Tom Glavine .25
651 Julio Franco .05
652 Armando Reynoso .05
653 Felix Jose .05
654 Ben Rivera .05
655 Andre Dawson .25
656 Mike Harkey .05
657 Kevin Seitzer .05
658 Lonnie Smith .05
659 Norm Charlton .05
660 Dave Justice .05
661 Fernando Valenzuela .05
662 Dan Wilson .05
663 Mark Gardner .05
664 Doug Dascenzo .05
665 Greg Maddux .85
666 Harold Baines .05
667 Randy Myers .05
668 Harold Reynolds .05
669 Candy Maldonado .05
670 Al Leiter .05
671 Jerald Clark .05
672 Doug Drabek .05
673 Kirk Gibson .05
674 *Steve Reed* .05
675 Mike Felder .05
676 Ricky Gutierrez .05
677 Spike Owen .05
678 Otis Nixon .05
679 Scott Sanderson .05
680 Mark Carreon .05
681 Troy Percival .05
682 Kevin Stocker .05
683 *Jim Converse* .05
684 Barry Bonds 2.50
685 Greg Gohr .05
686 Tim Wallach .05
687 Matt Mieske .05
688 Robby Thompson .05
689 Brien Taylor .05
690 Kirt Manwaring .05
691 *Mike Lansing* .25
692 Steve Decker .05
693 Mike Moore .05
694 Kevin Mitchell .05
695 Phil Hiatt .05
696 *Tony Tarasco* .05
697 Benji Gil .05
698 Jeff Juden .05
699 Kevin Reimer .05
700 Andy Ashby .05
701 John Jaha .05
702 *Tim Bogar* .05
703 David Cone .05
704 Willie Greene .05
705 *David Hulse* .05
706 Cris Carpenter .05
707 Ken Griffey, Jr. 1.50
708 Steve Bedrosian .05
709 Dave Nilsson .05
710 Paul Wagner .05
711 B.J. Surhoff .05
712 *Rene Arocha* .05
713 Manny Lee .05
714 Brian Williams .05
715 *Sherman Obando* .05
716 Terry Mulholland .05
717 Paul O'Neill .05
718 David Nied .05
719 *J.T. Snow* .50
720 Nigel Wilson .05
721 Mike Bielecki .05
722 Kevin Young .05
723 Charlie Leibrandt .05
724 Frank Bolick .05
725 *Jon Shave* .05
726 Steve Cooke .05
727 *Domingo Martinez* .05
728 Todd Worrell .05
729 Jose Lind .05
730 *Jim Tatum* .05
731 Mike Hampton .05
732 Mike Draper .05
733 Henry Mercedes .05
734 *John Johnstone* .05
735 Mitch Webster .05
736 Russ Springer .05
737 Rob Natal .05
738 Steve Howe .05
739 *Darrell Sherman* .05
740 Pat Mahomes .05
741 Alex Arias .05
742 Damon Buford .05
743 Charlie Hayes .05
744 Guillermo Velasquez .05
745 Checklist 601-750 .05
746 Frank Thomas .40
747 Barry Bonds 1.50
748 Roger Clemens .50
749 Joe Carter .05
750 Greg Maddux .45

1st Day Production

NM/M
Common Player: 1.00
1st Day Stars: 8X
(See 1993 Stadium Club for checklist and base card values.)

Master Photos

NM/M
Complete Set (30): 15.00
Common Player: .20
Series 1
(1) Carlos Baerga .20
(2) Delino DeShields .20
(3) Brian McRae .20
(4) Sam Militello .20
(5) Joe Oliver .20
(6) Kirby Puckett 1.50
(7) Cal Ripken Jr. 4.00
(8) Bip Roberts .20
(9) Mike Scioscia .20
(10) Rick Sutcliffe .20
(11) Danny Tartabull .20
(12) Tim Wakefield .20
Series 2
(13) George Brett 3.00
(14) Jose Canseco .50
(15) Will Clark .20
(16) Travis Fryman .20
(17) Dwight Gooden .20
(18) Mark Grace .30
(19) Rickey Henderson 1.00
(20) Mark McGwire 2.50
(21) Nolan Ryan 4.00
(22) Ruben Sierra .20
(23) Darryl Strawberry .20
(24) Larry Walker .20
Series 3
(25) Barry Bonds 5.00
(26) Ken Griffey, Jr. 2.50
(27) Greg Maddux 2.00
(28) David Nied .20
(29) J.T. Snow .20
(30) Brien Taylor .20
Redemption Card: 3X

Series 1 Inserts

NM/M
Complete Set (4): 3.00
Common Player: .25
1 Robin Yount (3,000 hits) 1.00
2 George Brett (3,000 hits) 2.00
3 David Nied (#1 pick) .25
4 Nigel Wilson (#1 pick) .25

Series 2 Inserts

NM/M
Complete Set (4): 5.00
Common Card: 1.50
1 Will Clark, Mark McGwire Pacific Terrific 2.00
2 Dwight Gooden, Don Mattingly Broadway Stars 1.50
3 Ryne Sandberg, Frank Thomas Second City Sluggers 1.50
4 Ken Griffey, Jr., Darryl Strawberry Pacific Terrific 1.50

Series 3 Inserts

NM/M
Complete Set (2): .50
Common Player: .25
1 David Nied .25
2 Charlie Hough .25

Special

NM/M
Unopened Set (200): 40.00
Complete Set (200): 30.00
Common Player: .05
1 Dave Winfield .75
2 Juan Guzman .05
3 Tony Gwynn .85
4 Chris Roberts .05
5 Benny Santiago .05
6 Sherard Clinkscales .05
7 *Jonathan Nunnally* .05
8 Chuck Knoblauch .05
9 *Bob Wolcott* .05
10 Steve Rodriguez .05
11 *Mark Williams* .05
12 *Danny Clyburn* .05
13 Darren Dreifort .05
14 Andy Van Slyke .05
15 Wade Boggs .85
16 Scott Patton .05
17 Gary Sheffield .45
18 Ron Villone .05
19 Roberto Alomar .20
20 Marc Valdes .05
21 Daron Kirkreit .05
22 Jeff Granger .05
23 Levon Largusa .05
24 Jimmy Key .05
25 Kevin Pearson .05
26 Michael Moore .05
27 *Preston Wilson* 1.00
28 Kirby Puckett .85
29 *Tim Crabtree* .05
30 Bip Roberts .05
31 Kelly Gruber .05
32 Tony Fernandez .05
33 Jason Angel .05
34 Calvin Murray .05
35 Chad McConnell .05
36 Jason Moler .05
37 Mark Lemke .05
38 Tom Knauss .05
39 Larry Mitchell .05
40 Doug Mirabelli .05
41 Everett Stull II .05
42 Chris Wimmer .05
43 *Dan Serafini* .05
44 Ryne Sandberg .85
45 Steve Lyons .05
46 Ryan Freeburg .05
47 Ruben Sierra .05
48 David Mysel .05
49 Joe Hamilton .05
50 Steve Rodriguez .05
51 Tim Wakefield .05
52 Scott Gentile .05
53 Doug Jones .05
54 Willie Brown .05
55 *Chad Mottola* .05
56 Ken Griffey, Jr. 1.50
57 *Jon Lieber* .50
58 Denny Martinez .05
59 Joe Petcka .05
60 Benji Simonton .05
61 Brett Backlund .05
62 Damon Berryhill .05
63 Juan Guzman .05
64 Doug Hecker .05
65 Jamie Arnold .05
66 Bob Tewksbury .05
67 Tim Leger .05
68 Todd Etler .05
69 Lloyd McClendon .05
70 Kurt Ehmann .05
71 Rick Magdaleno .05
72 Tom Pagnozzi .05
73 Jeffrey Hammonds .05
74 Joe Carter .05

75	Chris Holt	.05
76	Charles Johnson	.05
77	Bob Walk	.05
78	Fred McGriff	.05
79	Tom Evans	.05
80	Scott Klingenbeck	.05
81	Chad McConnell	.05
82	Chris Eddy	.05
83	Phil Nevin	.05
84	John Kruk	.05
85	Tony Sheffield	.05
86	John Smoltz	.05
87	Trevor Humphry	.05
88	Charles Nagy	.05
89	Sean Runyan	.05
90	Mike Gulan	.05
91	Darren Daulton	.05
92	Otis Nixon	.05
93	Nomar Garciaparra	8.00
94	Larry Walker	.05
95	Hut Smith	.05
96	Rick Helling	.05
97	Roger Clemens	1.00
98	Ron Gant	.05
99	Kenny Felder	.05
100	Steve Murphy	.05
101	Mike Smith	.05
102	Terry Pendleton	.05
103	Tim Davis	.05
104	Jeff Patzke	.05
105	Craig Wilson	.05
106	Tom Glavine	.35
107	Mark Langston	.05
108	Mark Thompson	.05
109	*Eric Owens*	.05
110	Keith Johnson	.05
111	Robin Ventura	.05
112	Ed Sprague	.05
113	*Jeff Schmidt*	.05
114	Don Wengert	.05
115	Craig Biggio	.05
116	Kenny Carlyle	.05
117	*Derek Jeter*	20.00
118	Manuel Lee	.05
119	Jeff Haas	.05
120	Roger Bailey	.05
121	Sean Lowe	.05
122	Rick Aguilera	.05
123	Sandy Alomar	.05
124	Derek Wallace	.05
125	B.J. Wallace	.05
126	Greg Maddux	.85
127	Tim Moore	.05
128	Lee Smith	.05
129	Todd Steverson	.05
130	Chris Widger	.05
131	Paul Molitor	.75
132	Chris Smith	.05
133	*Chris Gomez*	.05
134	Jimmy Baron	.05
135	John Smoltz	.05
136	Pat Borders	.05
137	Donnie Leshnock	.05
138	Gus Gandarillos	.05
139	Will Clark	.05
140	*Ryan Luzinski*	.05
141	Cal Ripken, Jr.	2.50
142	B.J. Wallace	.05
143	*Trey Beamon*	.05
144	Norm Charlton	.05
145	Mike Mussina	.30
146	Billy Owens	.05
147	Ozzie Smith	.85
148	*Jason Kendall*	1.00
149	*Mike Matthews*	.05
150	David Spykstra	.05
151	Benji Grigsby	.05
152	Sean Smith	.05
153	Mark McGwire	2.00
154	David Cone	.05
155	*Shon Walker*	.05
156	Jason Giambi	.50
157	Jack McDowell	.05
158	Paxton Briley	.05
159	Edgar Martinez	.05
160	Brian Sackinsky	.05
161	Barry Bonds	2.50
162	Roberto Kelly	.05
163	Jeff Alkire	.05
164	Mike Sharperson	.05
165	Jamie Taylor	.05
166	John Saffer	.05
167	Jerry Browne	.05
168	Travis Fryman	.05
169	Brady Anderson	.05
170	Chris Roberts	.05
171	Lloyd Peever	.05
172	Francisco Cabrera	.05
173	Ramiro Martinez	.05
174	Jeff Alkire	.05
175	Ivan Rodriguez	.65
176	Kevin Brown	.05
177	Chad Roper	.05
178	Rod Henderson	.05
179	Dennis Eckersley	.65
180	*Shannon Stewart*	1.00
181	DeShawn Warren	.05
182	Lonnie Smith	.05
183	Willie Adams	.05
184	Jeff Montgomery	.05
185	Damon Hollins	.05
186	Byron Matthews	.05
187	Harold Baines	.05
188	Rick Greene	.05
189	Carlos Baerga	.05
190	Brandon Cromer	.05
191	Roberto Alomar	.20
192	Rich Ireland	.05
193	Steve Montgomery	.05
194	Brant Brown	.05
195	Ritchie Moody	.05
196	Michael Tucker	.05
197	*Jason Varitek*	6.00
198	David Manning	.05
199	Marquis Riley	.05
200	Jason Giambi	.60

1994 STADIUM CLUB

	NM/M
Complete Set (720):	20.00
Common Player:	.05
1st Day:	8X
Golden Rainbow:	2X
Series 1, 2, 3 Pack (12):	1.00
Series 1, 2, 3 Wax Box (24):	15.00

1	Robin Yount	.65
2	Rick Wilkins	.05
3	Steve Scarsone	.05
4	Gary Sheffield	.40
5	George Brett	1.00
6	Al Martin	.05
7	Joe Oliver	.05
8	Stan Belinda	.05
9	Denny Hocking	.05
10	Roberto Alomar	.20
11	Luis Polonia	.05
12	Scott Hemond	.05
13	Joey Reed	.05
14	Mel Rojas	.05
15	Junior Ortiz	.05
16	Harold Baines	.05
17	Brad Pennington	.05
18	Jay Bell	.05
19	Tom Henke	.05
20	Jeff Branson	.05
21	Roberto Mejia	.05
22	Pedro Munoz	.05
23	Matt Nokes	.05
24	Jack McDowell	.05
25	Cecil Fielder	.05
26	Tony Fossas	.05
27	Jim Eisenreich	.05
28	Anthony Young	.05
29	Chuck Carr	.05
30	Jeff Treadway	.05
31	Chris Nabholz	.05
32	Tom Candiotti	.05
33	Mike Maddux	.05
34	Nolan Ryan	2.00
35	Luis Gonzalez	.05
36	Tim Salmon	.05
37	Mark Whiten	.05
38	Roger McDowell	.05
39	Royce Clayton	.05
40	Troy Neel	.05
41	Mike Harkey	.05
42	Darrin Fletcher	.05
43	Wayne Kirby	.05
44	Rich Amaral	.05
45	Robb Nen	.05
46	Tim Teufel	.05
47	Steve Cooke	.05
48	Jeff McNeely	.05
49	Jeff Montgomery	.05
50	Skeeter Barnes	.05
51	Scott Stahoviak	.05
52	Pat Kelly	.05
53	Brady Anderson	.05
54	Mariano Duncan	.05
55	Brian Bohanon	.05
56	Jerry Spradlin	.05
57	Ron Karkovice	.05
58	Jeff Gardner	.05
59	Bobby Bonilla	.05
60	Tino Martinez	.05
61	Todd Benzinger	.05
62	*Steve Trachsel*	.25
63	Brian Jordan	.05
64	Steve Bedrosian	.05
65	Brent Gates	.05
66	Shawn Green	.35
67	Sean Berry	.05
68	Joe Klink	.05
69	Fernando Valenzuela	.05
70	Andy Tomberlin	.05
71	Tony Pena	.05
72	Eric Young	.05
73	Chris Gomez	.05
74	Paul O'Neill	.05
75	Ricky Gutierrez	.05
76	Brad Holman	.05
77	Lance Painter	.05
78	Mike Butcher	.05
79	Sid Bream	.05
80	Sammy Sosa	.75
81	Felix Fermin	.05
82	Todd Hundley	.05
83	Kevin Higgins	.05
84	Todd Pratt	.05
85	Ken Griffey, Jr.	1.25
86	John O'Donoghue	.05
87	Rick Renteria	.05
88	John Burkett	.05
89	Jose Vizcaino	.05
90	Kevin Seitzer	.05
91	Bobby Witt	.05
92	Chris Turner	.05
93	Omar Vizquel	.05
94	Dave Justice	.05
95	David Segui	.05
96	Dave Hollins	.05
97	Doug Strange	.05
98	Jerald Clark	.05
99	Mike Moore	.05
100	Joey Cora	.05
101	Scott Kamieniecki	.05
102	Andy Benes	.05
103	Chris Bosio	.05
104	Rey Sanchez	.05
105	John Jaha	.05
106	Otis Nixon	.05
107	Rickey Henderson	.65
108	Jeff Bagwell	.65
109	Gregg Jefferies	.05
110	Roberto Alomar, Paul Molitor, John Olerud Topps Trios	.25
111	Ron Gant, David Justice, Fred McGriff Topps Trios	.05
112	Juan Gonzalez, Rafael Palmeiro, Dean Palmer Topps Trios	.25
113	Greg Swindell	.05
114	Bill Hasleman	.05
115	Phil Plantier	.05
116	Ivan Rodriguez	.60
117	Kevin Tapani	.05
118	Mike LaValliere	.05
119	Tim Costo	.05
120	Mickey Morandini	.05
121	Brett Butler	.05
122	Tom Pagnozzi	.05
123	Ron Gant	.05
124	Damion Easley	.05
125	Dennis Eckersley	.60
126	Matt Mieske	.05
127	Cliff Floyd	.05
128	*Julian Tavarez*	.05
129	Arthur Rhodes	.05
130	Dave West	.05
131	Tim Naehring	.05
132	Freddie Benavides	.05
133	Paul Assenmacher	.05
134	David McCarty	.05
135	Jose Lind	.05
136	Reggie Sanders	.05
137	Don Slaught	.05
138	Andujar Cedeno	.05
139	Rob Deer	.05
140	Mike Piazza	1.25
141	Moises Alou	.05
142	Tom Foley	.05
143	Benny Santiago	.05
144	Sandy Alomar	.05
145	Carlos Hernandez	.05
146	Luis Alicea	.05
147	Tom Lampkin	.05
148	Ryan Klesko	.05
149	Juan Guzman	.05
150	Scott Servais	.05
151	Tony Gwynn	.75
152	Tim Wakefield	.05
153	David Nied	.05
154	Chris Haney	.05
155	Danny Bautista	.05
156	Randy Velarde	.05
157	Darrin Jackson	.05
158	*J.R. Phillips*	.05
159	Greg Gagne	.05
160	Luis Aquino	.05
161	John Vander Wal	.05
162	Randy Myers	.05
163	Ted Power	.05
164	Scott Brosius	.05
165	Len Dykstra	.05
166	Jacob Brumfield	.05
167	Bo Jackson	.10
168	Eddie Taubensee	.05
169	Carlos Baerga	.05
170	Tim Bogar	.05
171	Jose Canseco	.50
172	Greg Blosser	.05
173	Chili Davis	.05
174	Randy Knorr	.05
175	Mike Perez	.05
176	Henry Rodriguez	.05
177	*Brian Turang*	.05
178	Roger Pavlik	.05
179	Aaron Sele	.05
180	Fred McGriff, Gary Sheffield Tale of 2 Players	.05
181	J.T. Snow, Tim Salmon Tale of 2 Players	.05
182	Roberto Hernandez	.05
183	Jeff Reboulet	.05
184	John Doherty	.05
185	Danny Sheaffer	.05
186	Bip Roberts	.05
187	Denny Martinez	.05
188	Darryl Hamilton	.05
189	Eduardo Perez	.05
190	Pete Harnisch	.05
191	Rick Gossage	.05
192	Mickey Tettleton	.05
193	Lenny Webster	.05
194	Lance Johnson	.05
195	Don Mattingly	1.00
196	Gregg Olson	.05
197	Mark Gubicza	.05
198	Scott Fletcher	.05
199	Jon Shave	.05
200	Tim Mauser	.05
201	Jeromy Burnitz	.05
202	Rob Dibble	.05
203	Will Clark	.05
204	Steve Buechele	.05
205	Brian Williams	.05
206	Carlos Garcia	.05
207	Mark Clark	.05
208	Rafael Palmeiro	.60
209	Eric Davis	.05
210	Pat Meares	.05
211	Chuck Finley	.05
212	Jason Bere	.05
213	Gary DiSarcina	.05
214	Tony Fernandez	.05
215	B.J. Surhoff	.05
216	Lee Guetterman	.05
217	Tim Wallach	.05
218	Kirt Manwaring	.05
219	Albert Belle	.05
220	Dwight Gooden	.05
221	Archi Cianfrocco	.05
222	Terry Mulholland	.05
223	Hipolito Pichardo	.05
224	Kent Hrbek	.05
225	Criag Grebeck	.05
226	Todd Jones	.05
227	Mike Bordick	.05
228	John Olerud	.05
229	Jeff Blauser	.05
230	Alex Arias	.05
231	Bernard Gilkey	.05
232	Denny Neagle	.05
233	*Pedro Borbon*	.05
234	Dick Schofield	.05

No.	Card	Value
235	Matias Carrillo	.05
236	Juan Bell	.05
237	Mike Hampton	.05
238	Barry Bonds	2.00
239	Cris Carpenter	.05
240	Eric Karros	.05
241	Greg McMichael	.05
242	Pat Hentgen	.05
243	Tim Pugh	.05
244	Vinny Castilla	.05
245	Charlie Hough	.05
246	Bobby Munoz	.05
247	Kevin Baez	.05
248	Todd Frohwirth	.05
249	Charlie Hayes	.05
250	Mike Macfarlane	.05
251	Danny Darwin	.05
252	Ben Rivera	.05
253	Dave Henderson	.05
254	Steve Avery	.05
255	Tim Belcher	.05
256	Dan Plesac	.05
257	Jim Thome	.60
258	Albert Belle	.05
259	Barry Bonds	1.00
260	Ron Gant	.05
261	Juan Gonzalez	.20
262	Ken Griffey, Jr.	.65
263	Dave Justice	.05
264	Fred McGriff	.05
265	Rafael Palmeiro	.20
266	Mike Piazza	.65
267	Frank Thomas	.35
268	Matt Williams	.05
269a	Checklist 1-135	.05
269b	Checklist 271-408	.05
270a	Checklist 136-270	.05
270b	Checklist 409-540	.05
271	Mike Stanley	.05
272	Tony Tarasco	.05
273	Teddy Higuera	.05
274	Ryan Thompson	.05
275	Rick Aguilera	.05
276	Ramon Martinez	.05
277	Orlando Merced	.05
278	Guillermo Velasquez	.05
279	Mark Hutton	.05
280	Larry Walker	.05
281	Kevin Gross	.05
282	Jose Offerman	.05
283	Jim Leyritz	.05
284	Jamie Moyer	.05
285	Frank Thomas	.65
286	Derek Bell	.05
287	Derrick May	.05
288	Dave Winfield	.65
289	Curt Schilling	.35
290	Carlos Quintana	.05
291	Bob Natal	.05
292	David Cone	.05
293	Al Osuna	.05
294	Bob Hamelin	.05
295	Chad Curtis	.05
296	Danny Jackson	.05
297	Bob Welch	.05
298	Felix Jose	.05
299	Jay Buhner	.05
300	Joe Carter	.05
301	Kenny Lofton	.05
302	*Kirk Rueter*	.15
303	Kim Batiste	.05
304	Mike Morgan	.05
305	Pat Borders	.05
306	Rene Arocha	.05
307	Ruben Sierra	.05
308	Steve Finley	.05
309	Travis Fryman	.05
310	Zane Smith	.05
311	Willie Wilson	.05
312	Trevor Hoffman	.05
313	Terry Pendleton	.05
314	Salomon Torres	.05
315	Robin Ventura	.05
316	Randy Tomlin	.05
317	Dave Stewart	.05
318	Mike Benjamin	.05
319	Matt Turner	.05
320	Manny Ramirez	.65
321	Kevin Young	.05
322	Ken Caminiti	.05
323	Joe Girardi	.05
324	Jeff McKnight	.05
325	Gene Harris	.05
326	Devon White	.05
327	Darryl Kile	.05
328	Craig Paquette	.05
329	Cal Eldred	.05
330	Bill Swift	.05
331	Alan Trammell	.05
332	Armando Reynoso	.05
333	Brent Mayne	.05
334	Chris Donnels	.05
335	Darryl Strawberry	.05
336	Dean Palmer	.05
337	Frank Castillo	.05
338	Jeff King	.05
339	John Franco	.05
340	Kevin Appier	.05
341	Lance Blankenship	.05
342	Mark McLemore	.05
343	Pedro Astacio	.05
344	Rich Batchelor	.05
345	Ryan Bowen	.05
346	Terry Steinbach	.05
347	Troy O'Leary	.05
348	Willie Blair	.05
349	Wade Boggs	.75
350	Tim Raines	.05
351	Scott Livingstone	.05
352	Rod Carreia	.05
353	Ray Lankford	.05
354	Pat Listach	.05
355	Milt Thompson	.05
356	Miguel Jimenez	.05
357	Marc Newfield	.05
358	Mark McGwire	1.50
359	Kirby Puckett	.75
360	Kent Mercker	.05
361	John Kruk	.05
362	Jeff Kent	.05
363	Hal Morris	.05
364	Edgar Martinez	.05
365	Dave Magadan	.05
366	Dante Bichette	.05
367	Chris Hammond	.05
368	Bret Saberhagen	.05
369	Billy Ripken	.05
370	Bill Gullickson	.05
371	Andre Dawson	.35
372	Bobby Kelly	.05
373	Cal Ripken, Jr.	2.00
374	Craig Biggio	.05
375	Dan Pasqua	.05
376	Dave Nilsson	.05
377	Duane Ward	.05
378	Greg Vaughn	.05
379	Jeff Fassero	.05
380	Jerry Dipoto	.05
381	John Patterson	.05
382	Kevin Brown	.05
383	Kevin Roberson	.05
384	Joe Orsulak	.05
385	Hilly Hathaway	.05
386	Mike Greenwell	.05
387	Orestes Destrade	.05
388	Mike Gallego	.05
389	Ozzie Guillen	.05
390	Raul Mondesi	.05
391	Scott Lydy	.05
392	Tom Urbani	.05
393	Wil Cordero	.05
394	Tony Longmire	.05
395	Todd Zeile	.05
396	Scott Cooper	.05
397	Ryne Sandberg	.75
398	Ricky Bones	.05
399	Phil Clark	.05
400	Orel Hershiser	.05
401	Mike Henneman	.05
402	Mark Lemke	.05
403	Mark Grace	.05
404	Ken Ryan	.05
405	John Smoltz	.05
406	Jeff Conine	.05
407	Greg Harris	.05
408	Doug Drabek	.05
409	Dave Fleming	.05
410	Danny Tartabull	.05
411	Chad Kreuter	.05
412	Brad Ausmus	.05
413	Ben McDonald	.05
414	Barry Larkin	.05
415	Bret Barberie	.05
416	Chuck Knoblauch	.05
417	Ozzie Smith	.75
418	Ed Sprague	.05
419	Matt Williams	.05
420	Jeremy Hernandez	.05
421	Jose Bautista	.05
422	Kevin Mitchell	.05
423	Manuel Lee	.05
424	Mike Devereaux	.05
425	Omar Olivares	.05
426	Rafael Belliard	.05
427	Richie Lewis	.05
428	Ron Darling	.05
429	Shane Mack	.05
430	Tim Hulett	.05
431	Wally Joyner	.05
432	Wes Chamberlain	.05
433	Tom Browning	.05
434	Scott Radinsky	.05
435	Rondell White	.05
436	Rod Beck	.05
437	Rheal Cormier	.05
438	Randy Johnson	.65
439	Pete Schourek	.05
440	Mo Vaughn	.05
441	Mike Timlin	.05
442	Mark Langston	.05
443	Lou Whitaker	.05
444	Kevin Stocker	.05
445	Ken Hill	.05
446	John Wetteland	.05
447	J.T. Snow	.05
448	Erik Pappas	.05
449	David Hulse	.05
450	Darren Daulton	.05
451	Chris Hoiles	.05
452	Bryan Harvey	.05
453	Darren Lewis	.05
454	Andres Galarraga	.05
455	Joe Hesketh	.05
456	Jose Valentin	.05
457	Dan Peltier	.05
458	Joe Boever	.05
459	Kevin Rogers	.05
460	Craig Shipley	.05
461	Alvaro Espinoza	.05
462	Wilson Alvarez	.05
463	Cory Snyder	.05
464	Candy Maldonado	.05
465	Blas Minor	.05
466	Rod Bolton	.05
467	Kenny Rogers	.05
468	Greg Myers	.05
469	Jimmy Key	.05
470	Tony Castillo	.05
471	Mike Stanton	.05
472	Deion Sanders	.05
473	Tito Navarro	.05
474	Mike Gardiner	.05
475	Steve Reed	.05
476	John Roper	.05
477	Mike Trombley	.05
478	Charles Nagy	.05
479	Larry Casian	.05
480	Eric Hillman	.05
481	Bill Wertz	.05
482	Jeff Schwarz	.05
483	John Valentin	.05
484	Carl Willis	.05
485	Gary Gaetti	.05
486	Bill Pecota	.05
487	John Smiley	.05
488	Mike Mussina	.35
489	*Mike Ignasiak*	.05
490	Billy Brewer	.05
491	Jack Voigt	.05
492	Mike Munoz	.05
493	Lee Tinsley	.05
494	Bob Wickman	.05
495	Roger Salkeld	.05
496	Thomas Howard	.05
497	Mark Davis	.05
498	Dave Clark	.05
499	Turk Wendell	.05
500	Rafael Bournigal	.05
501	Chip Hale	.05
502	Matt Whiteside	.05
503	Brian Koelling	.05
504	Jeff Reed	.05
505	Paul Wagner	.05
506	Torey Lovullo	.05
507	Curtis Leskanic	.05
508	Derek Lilliquist	.05
509	Joe Magrane	.05
510	Mackey Sasser	.05
511	Lloyd McClendon	.05
512	*Jayhawk Owens*	.05
513	*Woody Williams*	.05
514	Gary Redus	.05
515	Tim Spehr	.05
516	Jim Abbott	.05
517	Lou Frazier	.05
518	Erik Plantenberg	.05
519	Tim Worrell	.05
520	Brian McRae	.05
521	*Chan Ho Park*	1.00
522	Mark Wohlers	.05
523	Geronimo Pena	.05
524	Andy Ashby	.05
525	Tim Raines, Andre Dawson Tale of 2 Players	.05
526	Paul Molitor, Dave Winfield Tale of 2 Players	.40
527	Joe Carter	.05
528	Frank Thomas	.35
529	Ken Griffey, Jr.	.65
530	Dave Justice	.05
531	Gregg Jefferies	.05
532	Barry Bonds	1.00
533	John Kruk	.05
534	Roger Clemens	.50
535	Cecil Fielder	.05
536	Ruben Sierra	.05
537	Tony Gwynn	.40
538	Tom Glavine	.10
539	Not issued, see #269	
540	Not issued, see #270	
541	Ozzie Smith	.40
542	Eddie Murray	.30
543a	Lee Smith	.05
543b	Lonnie Smith	.05
544	Greg Maddux	.75
545	Denis Boucher	.05
546	Mark Gardner	.05
547	Bo Jackson	.10
548	Eric Anthony	.05
549	Delino DeShields	.05
550	Turner Ward	.05
551	Scott Sanderson	.05
552	Hector Carrasco	.05
553	Tony Phillips	.05
554	Melido Perez	.05
555	Mike Felder	.05
556	Jack Morris	.05
557	Rafael Palmeiro	.60
558	Shane Reynolds	.05
559	Pete Incaviglia	.05
560	Greg Harris	.05
561	Matt Walbeck	.05
562	Todd Van Poppel	.05
563	Todd Stottlemyre	.05
564	Ricky Bones	.05
565	Mike Jackson	.05
566	Kevin McReynolds	.05
567	Melvin Nieves	.05
568	Juan Gonzalez	.35
569	Frank Viola	.05
570	Vince Coleman	.05
571	*Brian Anderson*	.25
572	Omar Vizquel	.05
573	Bernie Williams	.05
574	Tom Glavine	.35
575	Mitch Williams	.05
576	Shawon Dunston	.05
577	Mike Lansing	.05
578	Greg Pirkl	.05
579	Sid Fernandez	.05
580	Doug Jones	.05
581	Walt Weiss	.05
582	Tim Belcher	.05
583	Alex Fernandez	.05
584	Alex Cole	.05
585	Greg Cadaret	.05
586	Bob Tewksbury	.05
587	Dave Hansen	.05
588	*Kurt Abbott*	.25
589	*Rick White*	.05
590	Kevin Bass	.05
591	Geronimo Berroa	.05
592	Jaime Navarro	.05
593	Steve Farr	.05
594	Jack Armstrong	.05
595	Steve Howe	.05
596	Jose Rijo	.05
597	Otis Nixon	.05
598	Robby Thompson	.05
599	Kelly Stinnett	.05
600	Carlos Delgado	.50
601	*Brian Johnson*	.05
602	Gregg Olson	.05
603	Jim Edmonds	.05
604	Mike Blowers	.05
605	Lee Smith	.05
606	Pat Rapp	.05
607	Mike Magnante	.05
608	Karl Rhodes	.05
609	Jeff Juden	.05
610	Rusty Meacham	.05
611	Pedro Martinez	.65
612	Todd Worrell	.05
613	Stan Javier	.05
614	Mike Hampton	.05
615	Jose Guzman	.05
616	Xavier Hernandez	.05
617	David Wells	.05
618	John Habyan	.05
619	Chris Nabholz	.05
620	Bobby Jones	.05
621	Chris James	.05
622	Ellis Burks	.05
623	Erik Hanson	.05
624	Pat Meares	.05
625	Harold Reynolds	.05

626	Bob Hamelin	.05
627	Manny Ramirez	.30
628	Ryan Klesko	.05
629	Carlos Delgado	.30
630	Javier Lopez	.05
631	Steve Karsay	.05
632	Rick Helling	.05
633	Steve Trachsel	.05
634	Hector Carrasco	.05
635	Andy Stankiewicz	.05
636	Paul Sorrento	.05
637	Scott Erickson	.05
638	Chipper Jones	.75
639	Luis Polonia	.05
640	Howard Johnson	.05
641	John Dopson	.05
642	Jody Reed	.05
643	Not issued, see #543	
644	Mark Portugal	.05
645	Paul Molitor	.65
646	Paul Assenmacher	.05
647	Hubie Brooks	.05
648	Gary Wayne	.05
649	Sean Berry	.05
650	Roger Clemens	1.00
651	Brian Hunter	.05
652	Wally Whitehurst	.05
653	Allen Watson	.05
654	Rickey Henderson	.65
655	Sid Bream	.05
656	Dan Wilson	.05
657	Ricky Jordan	.05
658	Sterling Hitchcock	.05
659	Darrin Jackson	.05
660	Junior Felix	.05
661	Tom Brunansky	.05
662	Jose Vizcaino	.05
663	Mark Leiter	.05
664	Gil Heredia	.05
665	Fred McGriff	.05
666	Will Clark	.05
667	Al Leiter	.05
668	James Mouton	.05
669	Billy Bean	.05
670	Scott Leius	.05
671	Bret Boone	.05
672	Darren Holmes	.05
673	Dave Weathers	.05
674	Eddie Murray	.65
675	Felix Fermin	.05
676	Chris Sabo	.05
677	Billy Spiers	.05
678	Aaron Sele	.05
679	Juan Samuel	.05
680	Julio Franco	.05
681	Heathcliff Slocumb	.05
682	Denny Martinez	.05
683	Jerry Browne	.05
684	*Pedro A. Martinez*	.05
685	Rex Hudler	.05
686	Willie McGee	.05
687	Andy Van Slyke	.05
688	Pat Mahomes	.05
689	Dave Henderson	.05
690	Tony Eusebio	.05
691	Rick Sutcliffe	.05
692	Willie Banks	.05
693	Alan Mills	.05
694	Jeff Treadway	.05
695	Alex Gonzalez	.05
696	David Segui	.05
697	Rick Helling	.05
698	Bip Roberts	.05
699	*Jeff Cirillo*	.25
700	Terry Mulholland	.05
701	Marvin Freeman	.05
702	Jason Bere	.05
703	Javier Lopez	.05
704	Greg Hibbard	.05
705	Tommy Greene	.05
706	Marquis Grissom	.05
707	Brian Harper	.05
708	Steve Karsay	.05
709	Jeff Brantley	.05
710	Jeff Russell	.05
711	Bryan Hickerson	.05
712	*Jim Pittsley*	.05
713	Bobby Ayala	.05
714	John Smoltz	.05
715	Jose Rijo	.05
716	Greg Maddux	.40
717	Matt Williams	.05
718	Frank Thomas	.35
719	Ryne Sandberg	.40
720	Checklist	.05

1st Day Issue

	NM/M
Common Player:	1.00
Stars:	8X

(See 1994 Stadium Club for checklist and base card values.)

Dugout Dirt

		NM/M
Complete Set (12):		5.00
Common Player:		.25
1	Mike Piazza (Catch of the Day)	1.00
2	Dave Winfield (The Road to 3,000)	.65
3	John Kruk (From Coal Mine to Gold Mine)	.25
4	Cal Ripken, Jr. (On Track)	2.00
5	Jack McDowell (Chin Music)	.25
6	Barry Bonds (The Bonds Market)	2.00
7	Ken Griffey, Jr. (Gold Gloves/All-Star)	1.00
8	Tim Salmon (The Salmon Run)	.25
9	Frank Thomas (Big Hurt)	.65
10	Jeff Kent (Super Kent)	.25
11	Randy Johnson (High Heat)	.65
12	Darren Daulton (Daulton's Gym)	.25

Finest

		NM/M
Complete Set (10):		11.00
Common Player:		.50
1	Jeff Bagwell	1.25
2	Albert Belle	.50
3	Barry Bonds	3.00
4	Juan Gonzalez	.75
5	Ken Griffey, Jr.	2.00
6	Marquis Grissom	.50
7	David Justice	.50
8	Mike Piazza	2.00
9	Tim Salmon	.50
10	Frank Thomas	1.50

Finest Jumbo

		NM/M
Complete Set (10):		30.00
Common Player:		2.00
1	Jeff Bagwell	4.00
2	Albert Belle	2.00
3	Barry Bonds	6.50
4	Juan Gonzalez	3.00
5	Ken Griffey, Jr.	5.00
6	Marquis Grissom	2.00
7	David Justice	2.00
8	Mike Piazza	5.00
9	Tim Salmon	2.00
10	Frank Thomas	4.00

Golden Rainbow

	NM/M
Complete Set (720):	60.00
Common Player:	.25
Stars:	2X

(See 1994 Stadium Club for checklist and base card values.)

Super Teams

		NM/M
Complete Set (28):		25.00
Common Team:		.70
Expired Jan. 31, 1996		
1	Atlanta Braves	5.00
2	Chicago Cubs	.70
3	Cincinnati Reds	1.25
4	Colorado Rockies	1.00
5	Florida Marlins	.70
6	Houston Astros	1.00
7	Los Angeles Dodgers	1.75
8	Montreal Expos	1.00
9	New York Mets	.70
10	Philadelphia Phillies	.70
11	Pittsburgh Pirates	.70
12	St. Louis Cardinals	.70
13	San Diego Padres	.70
14	San Francisco Giants	1.25
15	Baltimore Orioles	1.25
16	Boston Red Sox	1.00
17	California Angels	.70
18	Chicago White Sox	1.50
19	Cleveland Indians	2.00
20	Detroit Tigers	.70
21	Kansas City Royals	1.00
22	Milwaukee Brewers	.70
23	Minnesota Twins	1.00
24	New York Yankees	1.50
25	Oakland Athletics	1.00
26	Seattle Mariners	2.00
27	Texas Rangers	1.00
28	Toronto Blue Jays	1.00

1995 STADIUM CLUB

		NM/M
Complete Set (630):		25.00
Common Player:		.05
Series 1 or 2 Pack (14):		1.25
Series 1 or 2 Wax Box (24):		20.00
Series 3 Pack (13):		1.25
Series 3 Wax Box (24):		20.00
1	Cal Ripken Jr.	2.50
2	Bo Jackson	.10
3	Bryan Harvey	.05
4	Curt Schilling	.35
5	Bruce Ruffin	.05
6	Travis Fryman	.05
7	Jim Abbott	.05
8	David McCarty	.05
9	Gary Gaetti	.05
10	Roger Clemens	1.25
11	Carlos Garcia	.05
12	Lee Smith	.05
13	Bobby Ayala	.05
14	Charles Nagy	.05
15	Lou Frazier	.05
16	Rene Arocha	.05
17	Carlos Delgado	.50
18	Steve Finley	.05
19	Ryan Klesko	.05
20	Cal Eldred	.05
21	Rey Sanchez	.05
22	Ken Hill	.05
23	Benny Santiago	.05
24	Julian Tavarez	.05
25	Jose Vizcaino	.05
26	Andy Benes	.05
27	Mariano Duncan	.05
28	Checklist A	.05
29	Shawon Dunston	.05
30	Rafael Palmeiro	.65
31	Dean Palmer	.05
32	Andres Galarraga	.05
33	Joey Cora	.05
34	Mickey Tettleton	.05
35	Barry Larkin	.05
36	Carlos Baerga	.05
37	Orel Hershiser	.05
38	Jody Reed	.05
39	Paul Molitor	.75
40	Jim Edmonds	.05
41	Bob Tewksbury	.05
42	John Patterson	.05
43	Ray McDavid	.05
44	Zane Smith	.05
45	Bret Saberhagen	.05
46	Greg Maddux	1.00
47	Frank Thomas	.75
48	Carlos Baerga	.05
49	Billy Spiers	.05
50	Stan Javier	.05
51	Rex Hudler	.05
52	Denny Hocking	.05
53	Todd Worrell	.05
54	Mark Clark	.05
55	Hipilito Pichardo	.05
56	Bob Wickman	.05
57	Raul Mondesi	.05
58	Steve Cooke	.05
59	Rod Beck	.05
60	Tim Davis	.05
61	Jeff Kent	.05
62	John Valentin	.05
63	Alex Arias	.05
64	Steve Reed	.05
65	Ozzie Smith	1.00
66	Terry Pendleton	.05
67	Kenny Rogers	.05
68	Vince Coleman	.05
69	Tom Pagnozzi	.05
70	Roberto Alomar	.20
71	Darrin Jackson	.05
72	Dennis Eckersley	.65
73	Jay Buhner	.05
74	Darren Lewis	.05
75	Dave Weathers	.05
76	Matt Walbeck	.05
77	Brad Ausmus	.05
78	Danny Bautista	.05
79	Bob Hamelin	.05
80	Steve Traschel	.05
81	Ken Ryan	.05
82	Chris Turner	.05
83	David Segui	.05
84	Ben McDonald	.05
85	Wade Boggs	1.00
86	John Vander Wal	.05
87	Sandy Alomar	.05
88	Ron Karkovice	.05
89	Doug Jones	.05
90	Gary Sheffield	.40
91	Ken Caminiti	.05
92	Chris Bosio	.05
93	Kevin Tapani	.05
94	Walt Weiss	.05
95	Erik Hanson	.05
96	Ruben Sierra	.05
97	Nomar Garciaparra	1.00
98	Terrence Long	.05
99	Jacob Shumate	.05
100	Paul Wilson	.05
101	Kevin Witt	.05
102	Paul Konerko	.15
103	Ben Grieve	.05
104	*Mark Johnson*	.05
105	*Cade Gaspar*	.05
106	Mark Farris	.05
107	Dustin Hermanson	.05
108	*Scott Elarton*	.15
109	Doug Million	.05
110	Matt Smith	.05
111	*Brian Buchanan*	.05
112	*Jayson Peterson*	.05
113	Bret Wagner	.05
114	C.J. Nitkowski	.05
115	*Ramon Castro*	.05
116	Rafael Bournigal	.05
117	Jeff Fassero	.05
118	Bobby Bonilla	.05
119	Ricky Gutierrez	.05
120	Roger Pavlik	.05
121	Mike Greenwell	.05
122	Deion Sanders	.05
123	Charlie Hayes	.05
124	Paul O'Neill	.05
125	Jay Bell	.05
126	Royce Clayton	.05
127	Willie Banks	.05

No.	Player	Price
128	Mark Wohlers	.05
129	Todd Jones	.05
130	Todd Stottlemyre	.05
131	Will Clark	.05
132	Wilson Alvarez	.05
133	Chili Davis	.05
134	Dave Burba	.05
135	Chris Hoiles	.05
136	Jeff Blauser	.05
137	Jeff Reboulet	.05
138	Bret Saberhagen	.05
139	Kirk Rueter	.05
140	Dave Nilsson	.05
141	Pat Borders	.05
142	Ron Darling	.05
143	Derek Bell	.05
144	Dave Hollins	.05
145	Juan Gonzalez	.40
146	Andre Dawson	.25
147	Jim Thome	.65
148	Larry Walker	.05
149	Mike Piazza	1.50
150	Mike Perez	.05
151	Steve Avery	.05
152	Dan Wilson	.05
153	Andy Van Slyke	.05
154	Junior Felix	.05
155	Jack McDowell	.05
156	Danny Tartabull	.05
157	Willie Blair	.05
158	William Van Landingham	.05
159	Robb Nen	.05
160	Lee Tinsley	.05
161	Ismael Valdes	.05
162	Juan Guzman	.05
163	Scott Servais	.05
164	Cliff Floyd	.05
165	Allen Watson	.05
166	Eddie Taubensee	.05
167	Scott Hemond	.05
168	Jeff Tackett	.05
169	Chad Curtis	.05
170	Rico Brogna	.05
171	Luis Polonia	.05
172	Checklist B	.05
173	Lance Johnson	.05
174	Sammy Sosa	1.00
175	Mike MacFarlane	.05
176	Darryl Hamilton	.05
177	Rick Aguilera	.05
178	Dave West	.05
179	Mike Gallego	.05
180	Marc Newfield	.05
181	Steve Buechele	.05
182	David Wells	.05
183	Tom Glavine	.35
184	Joe Girardi	.05
185	Craig Biggio	.05
186	Eddie Murray	.75
187	Kevin Gross	.05
188	Sid Fernandez	.05
189	John Franco	.05
190	Bernard Gilkey	.05
191	Matt Williams	.05
192	Darrin Fletcher	.05
193	Jeff Conine	.05
194	Ed Sprague	.05
195	Eduardo Perez	.05
196	Scott Livingstone	.05
197	Ivan Rodriguez	.65
198	Orlando Merced	.05
199	Ricky Bones	.05
200	Javier Lopez	.05
201	Miguel Jimenez	.05
202	Terry McGriff	.05
203	Mike Lieberthal	.05
204	David Cone	.05
205	Todd Hundley	.05
206	Ozzie Guillen	.05
207	Alex Cole	.05
208	Tony Phillips	.05
209	Jim Eisenreich	.05
210	Greg Vaughn	.05
211	Barry Larkin	.05
212	Don Mattingly	1.00
213	Mark Grace	.05
214	Jose Canseco	.50
215	Joe Carter	.05
216	David Cone	.05
217	Sandy Alomar	.05
218	Al Martin	.05
219	Roberto Kelly	.05
220	Paul Sorrento	.05
221	Tony Fernandez	.05
222	Stan Belinda	.05
223	Mike Stanley	.05
224	Doug Drabek	.05
225	Todd Van Poppel	.05
226	Matt Mieske	.05
227	Tino Martinez	.05
228	Andy Ashby	.05
229	Midre Cummings	.05
230	Jeff Frye	.05
231	Hal Morris	.05
232	Jose Lind	.05
233	Shawn Green	.30
234	Rafael Belliard	.05
235	Randy Myers	.05
236	Frank Thomas	.45
237	Darren Daulton	.05
238	Sammy Sosa	.65
239	Cal Ripken Jr.	1.00
240	Jeff Bagwell	.40
241	Ken Griffey Jr.	1.50
242	Brett Butler	.05
243	Derrick May	.05
244	Pat Listach	.05
245	Mike Bordick	.05
246	Mark Langston	.05
247	Randy Velarde	.05
248	Julio Franco	.05
249	Chuck Knoblauch	.05
250	Bill Gullickson	.05
251	Dave Henderson	.05
252	Bret Boone	.05
253	Al Martin	.05
254	Armando Benitez	.05
255	Wil Cordero	.05
256	Al Leiter	.05
257	Luis Gonzalez	.05
258	Charlie O'Brien	.05
259	Tim Wallach	.05
260	Scott Sanders	.05
261	Tom Henke	.05
262	Otis Nixon	.05
263	Darren Daulton	.05
264	Manny Ramirez	.75
265	Bret Barberie	.05
266	Mel Rojas	.05
267	John Burkett	.05
268	Brady Anderson	.05
269	John Roper	.05
270	Shane Reynolds	.05
271	Barry Bonds	2.50
272	Alex Fernandez	.05
273	Brian McRae	.05
274	Todd Zeile	.05
275	Greg Swindell	.05
276	Johnny Ruffin	.05
277	Troy Neel	.05
278	Eric Karros	.05
279	John Hudek	.05
280	Thomas Howard	.05
281	Joe Carter	.05
282	Mike Devereaux	.05
283	Butch Henry	.05
284	Reggie Jefferson	.05
285	Mark Lemke	.05
286	Jeff Montgomery	.05
287	Ryan Thompson	.05
288	Paul Shuey	.05
289	Mark McGwire	2.00
290	Bernie Williams	.05
291	Mickey Morandini	.05
292	Scott Leius	.05
293	David Hulse	.05
294	Greg Gagne	.05
295	Moises Alou	.05
296	Geronimo Berroa	.05
297	Eddie Zambrano	.05
298	Alan Trammell	.05
299	Don Slaught	.05
300	Jose Rijo	.05
301	Joe Ausanio	.05
302	Tim Raines	.05
303	Melido Perez	.05
304	Kent Mercker	.05
305	James Mouton	.05
306	Luis Lopez	.05
307	Mike Kingery	.05
308	Willie Greene	.05
309	Cecil Fielder	.05
310	Scott Kamieniecki	.05
311	Mike Greenwell	.05
312	Bobby Bonilla	.05
313	Andres Galarraga	.05
314	Cal Ripken Jr.	1.25
315	Matt Williams	.05
316	Tom Pagnozzi	.05
317	Len Dykstra	.05
318	Frank Thomas	.40
319	Kirby Puckett	.50
320	Mike Piazza	1.00
321	Jason Jacome	.05
322	Brian Hunter	.05
323	Brent Gates	.05
324	Jim Converse	.05
325	Damion Easley	.05
326	Dante Bichette	.05
327	Kurt Abbott	.05
328	Scott Cooper	.05
329	Mike Henneman	.05
330	Orlando Miller	.05
331	John Kruk	.05
332	Jose Oliva	.05
333	Reggie Sanders	.05
334	Omar Vizquel	.05
335	Devon White	.05
336	Mike Morgan	.05
337	J.R. Phillips	.05
338	Gary DiSarcina	.05
339	Joey Hamilton	.05
340	Randy Johnson	.75
341	Jim Leyritz	.05
342	Bobby Jones	.05
343	Jaime Navarro	.05
344	Bip Roberts	.05
345	Steve Karsay	.05
346	Kevin Stocker	.05
347	Jose Canseco	.50
348	Bill Wegman	.05
349	Rondell White	.05
350	Mo Vaughn	.05
351	Joe Orsulak	.05
352	Pat Meares	.05
353	Albie Lopez	.05
354	Edgar Martinez	.05
355	Brian Jordan	.05
356	Tommy Greene	.05
357	Chuck Carr	.05
358	Pedro Astacio	.05
359	Russ Davis	.05
360	Chris Hammond	.05
361	Gregg Jefferies	.05
362	Shane Mack	.05
363	Fred McGriff	.05
364	Pat Rapp	.05
365	Bill Swift	.05
366	Checklist	.05
367	Robin Ventura	.05
368	Bobby Witt	.05
369	Karl Rhodes	.05
370	Eddie Williams	.05
371	John Jaha	.05
372	Steve Howe	.05
373	Leo Gomez	.05
374	Hector Fajardo	.05
375	Jeff Bagwell	.75
376	Mark Acre	.05
377	Wayne Kirby	.05
378	Mark Portugal	.05
379	Jesus Tavarez	.05
380	Jim Lindeman	.05
381	Don Mattingly	1.25
382	Trevor Hoffman	.05
383	Chris Gomez	.05
384	Garret Anderson	.05
385	Bobby Munoz	.05
386	Jon Lieber	.05
387	Rick Helling	.05
388	Marvin Freeman	.05
389	Juan Castillo	.05
390	Jeff Cirillo	.05
391	Sean Berry	.05
392	Hector Carrasco	.05
393	Mark Grace	.05
394	Pat Kelly	.05
395	Tim Naehring	.05
396	Greg Pirkl	.05
397	John Smoltz	.05
398	Robby Thompson	.05
399	Rick White	.05
400	Frank Thomas	.75
401	Jeff Conine	.05
402	Jose Valentin	.05
403	Carlos Baerga	.05
404	Rick Aguilera	.05
405	Wilson Alvarez	.05
406	Juan Gonzalez	.20
407	Barry Larkin	.05
408	Ken Hill	.05
409	Chuck Carr	.05
410	Tim Raines	.05
411	Bryan Eversgerd	.05
412	Phil Plantier	.05
413	Josias Manzanillo	.05
414	Roberto Kelly	.05
415	Rickey Henderson	.75
416	John Smiley	.05
417	Kevin Brown	.05
418	Jimmy Key	.05
419	Wally Joyner	.05
420	Roberto Hernandez	.05
421	Felix Fermin	.05
422	Checklist	.05
423	Greg Vaughn	.05
424	Ray Lankford	.05
425	Greg Maddux	1.00
426	Mike Mussina	.30
427	Geronimo Pena	.05
428	David Nied	.05
429	Scott Erickson	.05
430	Kevin Mitchell	.05
431	Mike Lansing	.05
432	Brian Anderson	.05
433	Jeff King	.05
434	Ramon Martinez	.05
435	Kevin Seitzer	.05
436	Salomon Torres	.05
437	Brian Hunter	.05
438	Melvin Nieves	.05
439	Mike Kelly	.05
440	Marquis Grissom	.05
441	Chuck Finley	.05
442	Len Dykstra	.05
443	Ellis Burks	.05
444	Harold Baines	.05
445	Kevin Appier	.05
446	Dave Justice	.05
447	Darryl Kile	.05
448	John Olerud	.05
449	Greg McMichael	.05
450	Kirby Puckett	1.00
451	Jose Valentin	.05
452	Rick Wilkins	.05
453	Arthur Rhodes	.05
454	Pat Hentgen	.05
455	Tom Gordon	.05
456	Tom Candiotti	.05
457	Jason Bere	.05
458	Wes Chamberlain	.05
459	Greg Colbrunn	.05
460	John Doherty	.05
461	Kevin Foster	.05
462	Mark Whiten	.05
463	Terry Steinbach	.05
464	Aaron Sele	.05
465	Kirt Manwaring	.05
466	Darren Hall	.05
467	Delino DeShields	.05
468	Andujar Cedeno	.05
469	Billy Ashley	.05
470	Kenny Lofton	.05
471	Pedro Munoz	.05
472	John Wetteland	.05
473	Tim Salmon	.05
474	Denny Neagle	.05
475	Tony Gwynn	1.00
476	Vinny Castilla	.05
477	Steve Dreyer	.05
478	Jeff Shaw	.05
479	Chad Ogea	.05
480	Scott Ruffcorn	.05
481	Lou Whitaker	.05
482	J.T. Snow	.05
483	Rich Rowland	.05
484	Dennis Martinez	.05
485	Pedro Martinez	.75
486	Rusty Greer	.05
487	Dave Fleming	.05
488	John Dettmer	.05
489	Albert Belle	.05
490	Ravelo Manzanillo	.05
491	Henry Rodriguez	.05
492	Andrew Lorraine	.05
493	Dwayne Hosey	.05
494	Mike Blowers	.05
495	Turner Ward	.05
496	Fred McGriff	.05
497	Sammy Sosa	.50
498	Barry Larkin	.05
499	Andres Galarraga	.05
500	Gary Sheffield	.15
501	Jeff Bagwell	.40
502	Mike Piazza	1.00
503	Moises Alou	.05
504	Bobby Bonilla	.05
505	Darren Daulton	.05
506	Jeff King	.05
507	Ray Lankford	.05
508	Tony Gwynn	.50
509	Barry Bonds	1.25
510	Cal Ripken Jr.	1.25
511	Mo Vaughn	.05
512	Tim Salmon	.05
513	Frank Thomas	.45
514	Albert Belle	.05
515	Cecil Fielder	.05
516	Kevin Appier	.05
517	Greg Vaughn	.05
518	Kirby Puckett	.50
519	Paul O'Neill	.05
520	Ruben Sierra	.05
521	Ken Griffey Jr.	.75
522	Will Clark	.05
523	Joe Carter	.05

524	Antonio Osuna	.05
525	Glenallen Hill	.05
526	Alex Gonzalez	.05
527	Dave Stewart	.05
528	Ron Gant	.05
529	Jason Bates	.05
530	Mike Macfarlane	.05
531	Esteban Loaiza	.05
532	Joe Randa	.05
533	Dave Winfield	.75
534	Danny Darwin	.05
535	Pete Harnisch	.05
536	Joey Cora	.05
537	Jaime Navarro	.05
538	Marty Cordova	.05
539	Andujar Cedeno	.05
540	Mickey Tettleton	.05
541	Andy Van Slyke	.05
542	*Carlos Perez*	.05
543	Chipper Jones	1.00
544	Tony Fernandez	.05
545	Tom Henke	.05
546	Pat Borders	.05
547	Chad Curtis	.05
548	Ray Durham	.05
549	Joe Oliver	.05
550	Jose Mesa	.05
551	Steve Finley	.05
552	Otis Nixon	.05
553	Jacob Brumfield	.05
554	Bill Swift	.05
555	Quilvio Veras	.05
556	*Hideo Nomo*	1.50
557	Joe Vitiello	.05
558	Mike Perez	.05
559	Charlie Hayes	.05
560	*Brad Radke*	.25
561	Darren Bragg	.05
562	Orel Hershiser	.05
563	Edgardo Alfonzo	.05
564	Doug Jones	.05
565	Andy Pettitte	.25
566	Benito Santiago	.05
567	John Burkett	.05
568	Brad Clontz	.05
569	Jim Abbott	.05
570	Joe Rosselli	.05
571	*Mark Grudzielanek*	.25
572	Dustin Hermanson	.05
573	Benji Gil	.05
574	Mark Whiten	.05
575	Mike Ignasiak	.05
576	Kevin Ritz	.05
577	Paul Quantrill	.05
578	Andre Dawson	.25
579	Jerald Clark	.05
580	Frank Rodriguez	.05
581	Mark Kiefer	.05
582	Trevor Wilson	.05
583	*Gary Wilson*	.05
584	Andy Stankiewicz	.05
585	Felipe Lira	.05
586	*Mike Mimbs*	.05
587	Jon Nunnally	.05
588	*Tomas Perez*	.05
589	Checklist	.05
590	Todd Hollandsworth	.05
591	Roberto Petagine	.05
592	Mariano Rivera	.15
593	Mark McLemore	.05
594	Bobby Witt	.05
595	Jose Offerman	.05
596	Jason Christiansen	.05
597	Jeff Manto	.05
598	Jim Dougherty	.05
599	Juan Acevedo	.05
600	Troy O'Leary	.05
601	Ron Villone	.05
602	Tripp Cromer	.05
603	Steve Scarsone	.05
604	Lance Parrish	.05
605	Ozzie Timmons	.05
606	Ray Holbert	.05
607	Tony Phillips	.05
608	Phil Plantier	.05
609	Shane Andrews	.05
610	Heathcliff Slocumb	.05
611	*Bobby Higginson*	.25
612	Bob Tewksbury	.05
613	Terry Pendleton	.05
614	Scott Cooper	.05
615	John Wetteland	.05
616	Ken Hill	.05
617	Marquis Grissom	.05
618	Larry Walker	.05
619	Derek Bell	.05
620	David Cone	.05
621	Ken Caminiti	.05
622	Jack McDowell	.05
623	Vaughn Eshelman	.05
624	Brian McRae	.05
625	Gregg Jefferies	.05
626	Kevin Brown	.05
627	Lee Smith	.05
628	Tony Tarasco	.05
629	Brett Butler	.05
630	Jose Canseco	.35

1st Day Issue

	NM/M
Common Player:	.50
Stars:	7X

(See 1995 Stadium Club #1-270 for checklist and base card values.)

Clear Cut

		NM/M
Complete Set (28):		20.00
Common Player:		.65
1	Mike Piazza	3.00
2	Ruben Sierra	.65
3	Tony Gwynn	2.50
4	Frank Thomas	2.00
5	Fred McGriff	.65
6	Rafael Palmeiro	1.50
7	Bobby Bonilla	.65
8	Chili Davis	.65
9	Hal Morris	.65
10	Jose Canseco	1.00
11	Jay Bell	.65
12	Kirby Puckett	2.50
13	Gary Sheffield	1.00
14	Bob Hamelin	.65
15	Jeff Bagwell	2.00
16	Albert Belle	.65
17	Sammy Sosa	2.50
18	Ken Griffey Jr.	3.00
19	Todd Zeile	.65
20	Mo Vaughn	.65
21	Moises Alou	.65
22	Paul O'Neill	.65
23	Andres Galarraga	.65
24	Greg Vaughn	.65
25	Len Dykstra	.65
26	Joe Carter	.65
27	Barry Bonds	4.50
28	Cecil Fielder	.65

Crunch Time

		NM/M
Complete Set (20):		15.00
Common Player:		1.00
1	Jeff Bagwell	2.50
2	Kirby Puckett	3.00
3	Frank Thomas	2.50
4	Albert Belle	1.00
5	Julio Franco	1.00
6	Jose Canseco	1.50
7	Paul Molitor	2.50
8	Joe Carter	1.00
9	Ken Griffey Jr.	4.00
10	Larry Walker	1.00
11	Dante Bichette	1.00
12	Carlos Baerga	1.00
13	Fred McGriff	1.00
14	Ruben Sierra	1.00
15	Will Clark	1.00
16	Moises Alou	1.00
17	Rafael Palmeiro	2.00
18	Travis Fryman	1.00
19	Barry Bonds	5.00
20	Cal Ripken Jr.	5.00

Crystal Ball

		NM/M
Complete Set (15):		15.00
Common Player:		.75
1	Chipper Jones	5.00
2	Dustin Hermanson	.75
3	Ray Durham	.75
4	Phil Nevin	.75
5	Billy Ashley	.75
6	Shawn Green	2.50
7	Jason Bates	.75
8	Benji Gil	.75
9	Marty Cordova	.75
10	Quilvio Veras	.75
11	Mark Grudzielanek	.75
12	Ruben Rivera	.75
13	Bill Pulsipher	.75
14	Derek Jeter	7.50
15	LaTroy Hawkins	.75

Power Zone

		NM/M
Complete Set (12):		9.00
Common Player:		.50
1	Jeff Bagwell	1.00
2	Albert Belle	.50
3	Barry Bonds	3.00
4	Joe Carter	.50
5	Cecil Fielder	.50
6	Andres Galarraga	.50
7	Ken Griffey Jr.	2.00
8	Paul Molitor	1.00
9	Fred McGriff	.50
10	Rafael Palmeiro	.75
11	Frank Thomas	1.00
12	Matt Williams	.50

Ring Leaders

		NM/M
Complete Set (40):		70.00
Common Player:		.75
1	Jeff Bagwell	3.00
2	Mark McGwire	7.50
3	Ozzie Smith	4.00
4	Paul Molitor	3.00
5	Darryl Strawberry	.75
6	Eddie Murray	3.00
7	Tony Gwynn	4.00
8	Jose Canseco	2.00
9	Howard Johnson	.75
10	Andre Dawson	1.25
11	Matt Williams	.75
12	Tim Raines	.75
13	Fred McGriff	.75
14	Ken Griffey Jr.	6.00
15	Gary Sheffield	2.00
16	Dennis Eckersley	2.50
17	Kevin Mitchell	.75
18	Will Clark	.75
19	Darren Daulton	.75
20	Paul O'Neill	.75
21	Julio Franco	.75
22	Albert Belle	.75
23	Juan Gonzalez	1.50
24	Kirby Puckett	4.00
25	Joe Carter	.75
26	Frank Thomas	3.00
27	Cal Ripken Jr.	9.00
28	John Olerud	.75
29	Ruben Sierra	.75
30	Barry Bonds	9.00
31	Cecil Fielder	.75
32	Roger Clemens	5.00
33	Don Mattingly	5.00
34	Terry Pendleton	.75
35	Rickey Henderson	3.00
36	Dave Winfield	3.00
37	Edgar Martinez	.75
38	Wade Boggs	4.00
39	Willie McGee	.75
40	Andres Galarraga	.75

Super Skills

		NM/M
Complete Set (20):		30.00

Common Player:		.75
1	Roberto Alomar	1.00
2	Barry Bonds	10.00
3	Jay Buhner	.75
4	Chuck Carr	.75
5	Don Mattingly	5.00
6	Raul Mondesi	.75
7	Tim Salmon	.75
8	Deion Sanders	.75
9	Devon White	.75
10	Mark Whiten	.75
11	Ken Griffey Jr.	7.50
12	Marquis Grissom	.75
13	Paul O'Neill	.75
14	Kenny Lofton	.75
15	Larry Walker	.75
16	Scott Cooper	.75
17	Barry Larkin	.75
18	Matt Williams	.75
19	John Wetteland	.75
20	Randy Johnson	2.50

Virtual Reality

		NM/M
Complete Set (270):		35.00
Common Player:		.10
1	Cal Ripken Jr.	2.50
2	Travis Fryman	.10
3	Jim Abbott	.10
4	Gary Gaetti	.10
5	Roger Clemens	1.25
6	Carlos Garcia	.10
7	Lee Smith	.10
8	Bobby Ayala	.10
9	Charles Nagy	.10
10	Rene Arocha	.10
11	Carlos Delgado	.50
12	Steve Finley	.10
13	Ryan Klesko	.10
14	Cal Eldred	.10
15	Rey Sanchez	.10
16	Ken Hill	.10
17	Jose Vizcaino	.10
18	Andy Benes	.10
19	Shawon Dunston	.10
20	Rafael Palmeiro	.65
21	Dean Palmer	.10
22	Joey Cora	.10
23	Mickey Tettleton	.10
24	Barry Larkin	.10
25	Carlos Baerga	.10
26	Orel Hershiser	.10
27	Jody Reed	.10
28	Paul Molitor	.75
29	Jim Edmonds	.10
30	Bob Tewksbury	.10
31	Ray McDavid	.10
32	Stan Javier	.10
33	Todd Worrell	.10
34	Bob Wickman	.10
35	Raul Mondesi	.10
36	Rod Beck	.10
37	Jeff Kent	.10
38	John Valentin	.10
39	Ozzie Smith	1.00
40	Terry Pendleton	.10
41	Kenny Rogers	.10
42	Vince Coleman	.10
43	Roberto Alomar	.20
44	Darrin Jackson	.10
45	Dennis Eckersley	.65
46	Jay Buhner	.10
47	Dave Weathers	.10
48	Danny Bautista	.10
49	Bob Hamelin	.10
50	Steve Trachsel	.10
51	Ben McDonald	.10
52	Wade Boggs	1.00
53	Sandy Alomar	.10
54	Ron Karkovice	.10
55	Doug Jones	.10
56	Gary Sheffield	.40
57	Ken Caminiti	.10
58	Kevin Tapani	.10
59	Ruben Sierra	.10
60	Bobby Bonilla	.10
61	Deion Sanders	.10
62	Charlie Hayes	.10
63	Paul O'Neill	.10

#	Player	Value
64	Jay Bell	.10
65	Todd Jones	.10
66	Todd Stottlemyre	.10
67	Will Clark	.10
68	Wilson Alvarez	.10
69	Chili Davis	.10
70	Chris Hoiles	.10
71	Bret Saberhagen	.10
72	Dave Nilsson	.10
73	Derek Bell	.10
74	Juan Gonzalez	.40
75	Andre Dawson	.30
76	Jim Thome	.65
77	Larry Walker	.10
78	Mike Piazza	1.50
79	Dan Wilson	.10
80	Junior Felix	.10
81	Jack McDowell	.10
82	Danny Tartabull	.10
83	William Van Landingham	.10
84	Robb Nen	.10
85	Ismael Valdes	.10
86	Juan Guzman	.10
87	Cliff Floyd	.10
88	Rico Brogna	.10
89	Luis Polonia	.10
90	Lance Johnson	.10
91	Sammy Sosa	1.00
92	Dave West	.10
93	Tom Glavine	.35
94	Joe Girardi	.10
95	Craig Biggio	.10
96	Eddie Murray	.75
97	Kevin Gross	.10
98	John Franco	.10
99	Matt Williams	.10
100	Darrin Fletcher	.10
101	Jeff Conine	.10
102	Ed Sprague	.10
103	Ivan Rodriguez	.65
104	Orlando Merced	.10
105	Ricky Bones	.10
106	David Cone	.10
107	Todd Hundley	.10
108	Alex Cole	.10
109	Tony Phillips	.10
110	Jim Eisenreich	.10
111	Paul Sorrento	.10
112	Mike Stanley	.10
113	Doug Drabek	.10
114	Matt Mieske	.10
115	Tino Martinez	.10
116	Midre Cummings	.10
117	Hal Morris	.10
118	Shawn Green	.40
119	Randy Myers	.10
120	Ken Griffey Jr.	1.50
121	Brett Butler	.10
122	Julio Franco	.10
123	Chuck Knoblauch	.10
124	Bret Boone	.10
125	Wil Cordero	.10
126	Luis Gonzalez	.10
127	Tim Wallach	.10
128	Scott Sanders	.10
129	Tom Henke	.10
130	Otis Nixon	.10
131	Darren Daulton	.10
132	Manny Ramirez	.75
133	Bret Barberie	.10
134	Brady Anderson	.10
135	Shane Reynolds	.10
136	Barry Bonds	2.50
137	Alex Fernandez	.10
138	Brian McRae	.10
139	Todd Zeile	.10
140	Greg Swindell	.10
141	Troy Neel	.10
142	Eric Karros	.10
143	John Hudek	.10
144	Joe Carter	.10
145	Mike Devereaux	.10
146	Butch Henry	.10
147	Mark Lemke	.10
148	Jeff Montgomery	.10
149	Ryan Thompson	.10
150	Bernie Williams	.10
151	Scott Leius	.10
152	Greg Gagne	.10
153	Moises Alou	.10
154	Geronimo Berroa	.10
155	Alan Trammell	.10
156	Don Slaught	.10
157	Jose Rijo	.10
158	Tim Raines	.10
159	Melido Perez	.10
160	Kent Mercker	.10
161	James Mouton	.10
162	Luis Lopez	.10
163	Mike Kingery	.10
164	Cecil Fielder	.10
165	Scott Kamieniecki	.10
166	Brent Gates	.10
167	Jason Jacome	.10
168	Dante Bichette	.10
169	Kurt Abbott	.10
170	Mike Henneman	.10
171	John Kruk	.10
172	Jose Oliva	.10
173	Reggie Sanders	.10
174	Omar Vizquel	.10
175	Devon White	.10
176	Mark McGwire	2.00
177	Gary DiSarcina	.10
178	Joey Hamilton	.10
179	Randy Johnson	.75
180	Jim Leyritz	.10
181	Bobby Jones	.10
182	Bip Roberts	.10
183	Jose Canseco	.40
184	Mo Vaughn	.10
185	Edgar Martinez	.10
186	Tommy Greene	.10
187	Chuck Carr	.10
188	Pedro Astacio	.10
189	Shane Mack	.10
190	Fred McGriff	.10
191	Pat Rapp	.10
192	Bill Swift	.10
193	Robin Ventura	.10
194	Bobby Witt	.10
195	Steve Howe	.10
196	Leo Gomez	.10
197	Hector Fajardo	.10
198	Jeff Bagwell	.75
199	Rondell White	.10
200	Don Mattingly	1.25
201	Trevor Hoffman	.10
202	Chris Gomez	.10
203	Bobby Munoz	.10
204	Marvin Freeman	.10
205	Sean Berry	.10
206	Mark Grace	.10
207	Pat Kelly	.10
208	Eddie Williams	.10
209	Frank Thomas	.75
210	Bryan Eversgerd	.10
211	Phil Plantier	.10
212	Roberto Kelly	.10
213	Rickey Henderson	.75
214	John Smiley	.10
215	Kevin Brown	.10
216	Jimmy Key	.10
217	Wally Joyner	.10
218	Roberto Hernandez	.10
219	Felix Fermin	.10
220	Greg Vaughn	.10
221	Ray Lankford	.10
222	Greg Maddux	1.00
223	Mike Mussina	.30
224	David Nied	.10
225	Scott Erickson	.10
226	Kevin Mitchell	.10
227	Brian Anderson	.10
228	Jeff King	.10
229	Ramon Martinez	.10
230	Kevin Seitzer	.10
231	Marquis Grissom	.10
232	Chuck Finley	.10
233	Len Dykstra	.10
234	Ellis Burks	.10
235	Harold Baines	.10
236	Kevin Appier	.10
237	Dave Justice	.10
238	Darryl Kile	.10
239	John Olerud	.10
240	Greg McMichael	.10
241	Kirby Puckett	1.00
242	Jose Valentin	.10
243	Rick Wilkins	.10
244	Pat Hentgen	.10
245	Tom Gordon	.10
246	Tom Candiotti	.10
247	Jason Bere	.10
248	Wes Chamberlain	.10
249	Jeff Cirillo	.10
250	Kevin Foster	.10
251	Mark Whiten	.10
252	Terry Steinbach	.10
253	Aaron Sele	.10
254	Kirt Manwaring	.10
255	Delino DeShields	.10
256	Andujar Cedeno	.10
257	Kenny Lofton	.10
258	John Wetteland	.10
259	Tim Salmon	.10
260	Denny Neagle	.10
261	Tony Gwynn	1.00
262	Lou Whitaker	.10
263	J.T. Snow	.10
264	Dennis Martinez	.10
265	Pedro Martinez	.75
266	Rusty Greer	.10
267	Dave Fleming	.10
268	John Dettmer	.10
269	Albert Belle	.10
270	Henry Rodriguez	.10

VR Extremist

		NM/M
Complete Set (10):		25.00
Common Player:		1.50
1	Barry Bonds	7.50
2	Ken Griffey Jr.	6.00
3	Jeff Bagwell	3.50
4	Albert Belle	1.50
5	Frank Thomas	3.50
6	Tony Gwynn	4.50
7	Kenny Lofton	1.50
8	Deion Sanders	1.50
9	Ken Hill	1.50
10	Jimmy Key	1.50

World Series Winners

	NM/M
Complete Set (585):	40.00
Common Player:	.25
Stars:	3X

(See 1995 Stadium Club for checklist and base card values.)

1996 STADIUM CLUB

		NM/M
Complete Set (450):		25.00
Common Player:		.05
Series 1 or 2 Pack (10):		1.00
Series 1 or 2 Wax Box (24):		20.00
1	Hideo Nomo	.40
2	Paul Molitor	.75
3	Garret Anderson	.05
4	Jose Mesa	.05
5	Vinny Castilla	.05
6	Mike Mussina	.30
7	Ray Durham	.05
8	Jack McDowell	.05
9	Juan Gonzalez	.40
10	Chipper Jones	1.00
11	Deion Sanders	.05
12	Rondell White	.05
13	Tom Henke	.05
14	Derek Bell	.05
15	Randy Myers	.05
16	Randy Johnson	.75
17	Len Dykstra	.05
18	Bill Pulsipher	.05
19	Greg Colbrunn	.05
20	David Wells	.05
21	Chad Curtis	.05
22	Roberto Hernandez	.05
23	Kirby Puckett	1.00
24	Joe Vitiello	.05
25	Roger Clemens	1.25
26	Al Martin	.05
27	Chad Ogea	.05
28	David Segui	.05
29	Joey Hamilton	.05
30	Dan Wilson	.05
31	Chad Fonville	.05
32	Bernard Gilkey	.05
33	Kevin Seitzer	.05
34	Shawn Green	.35
35	Rick Aguilera	.05
36	Gary DiSarcina	.05
37	Jaime Navarro	.05
38	Doug Jones	.05
39	Brent Gates	.05
40	Dean Palmer	.05
41	Pat Rapp	.05
42	Tony Clark	.05
43	Bill Swift	.05
44	Randy Velarde	.05
45	Matt Williams	.05
46	John Mabry	.05
47	Mike Fetters	.05
48	Orlando Miller	.05
49	Tom Glavine	.35
50	Delino DeShields	.05
51	Scott Erickson	.05
52	Andy Van Slyke	.05
53	Jim Bullinger	.05
54	Lyle Mouton	.05
55	Bret Saberhagen	.05
56	Benito Santiago	.05
57	Dan Miceli	.05
58	Carl Everett	.05
59	Rod Beck	.05
60	Phil Nevin	.05
61	Jason Giambi	.50
62	Paul Menhart	.05
63	Eric Karros	.05
64	Allen Watson	.05
65	Jeff Cirillo	.05
66	Lee Smith	.05
67	Sean Berry	.05
68	Luis Sojo	.05
69	Jeff Montgomery	.05
70	Todd Hundley	.05
71	John Burkett	.05
72	Mark Gubicza	.05
73	Don Mattingly	1.25
74	Jeff Brantley	.05
75	Matt Walbeck	.05
76	Steve Parris	.05
77	Ken Caminiti	.05
78	Kirt Manwaring	.05
79	Greg Vaughn	.05
80	Pedro Martinez	.75
81	Benji Gil	.05
82	Heathcliff Slocumb	.05
83	Joe Girardi	.05
84	Sean Bergman	.05
85	Matt Karchner	.05
86	Butch Huskey	.05
87	Mike Morgan	.05
88	Todd Worrell	.05
89	Mike Bordick	.05
90	Bip Roberts	.05
91	Mike Hampton	.05
92	Troy O'Leary	.05
93	Wally Joyner	.05
94	Dave Stevens	.05
95	Cecil Fielder	.05
96	Wade Boggs	1.00
97	Hal Morris	.05
98	Mickey Tettleton	.05

99 Jeff Kent .05
100 Denny Martinez .05
101 Luis Gonzalez .05
102 John Jaha .05
103 Javy Lopez .05
104 Mark McGwire 2.00
105 Ken Griffey Jr. 1.50
106 Darren Daulton .05
107 Bryan Rekar .05
108 Mike Macfarlane .05
109 Gary Gaetti .05
110 Shane Reynolds .05
111 Pat Meares .05
112 Jason Schmidt .05
113 Otis Nixon .05
114 John Franco .05
115 Marc Newfield .05
116 Andy Benes .05
117 Ozzie Guillen .05
118 Brian Jordan .05
119 Terry Pendleton .05
120 Chuck Finley .05
121 Scott Stahoviak .05
122 Sid Fernandez .05
123 Derek Jeter 3.00
124 John Smiley .05
125 David Bell .05
126 Brett Butler .05
127 Doug Drabek .05
128 J.T. Snow .05
129 Joe Carter .05
130 Dennis Eckersley .65
131 Marty Cordova .05
132 Greg Maddux 1.00
133 Tom Goodwin .05
134 Andy Ashby .05
135 Paul Sorrento .05
136 Ricky Bones .05
137 Shawon Dunston .05
138 Moises Alou .05
139 Mickey Morandini .05
140 Ramon Martinez .05
141 Royce Clayton .05
142 Brad Ausmus .05
143 Kenny Rogers .05
144 Tim Naehring .05
145 Chris Gomez .05
146 Bobby Bonilla .05
147 Wilson Alvarez .05
148 Johnny Damon .35
149 Pat Hentgen .05
150 Andres Galarraga .05
151 David Cone .05
152 Lance Johnson .05
153 Carlos Garcia .05
154 Doug Johns .05
155 Midre Cummings .05
156 Steve Sparks .05
157 *Sandy Martinez* .05
158 William Van Landingham .05
159 Dave Justice .05
160 Mark Grace .05
161 Robb Nen .05
162 Mike Greenwell .05
163 Brad Radke .05
164 Edgardo Alfonzo .05
165 Mark Leiter .05
166 Walt Weiss .05
167 Mel Rojas .05
168 Bret Boone .05
169 Ricky Bottalico .05
170 Bobby Higginson .05
171 Trevor Hoffman .05
172 Jay Bell .05
173 Gabe White .05
174 Curtis Goodwin .05
175 Tyler Green .05
176 Roberto Alomar .20
177 Sterling Hitchcock .05
178 Ryan Klesko .05
179 *Donne Wall* .05
180 Brian McRae .05
181 Will Clark .05
182 Frank Thomas .60
183 Jeff Bagwell .60
184 Mo Vaughn .05
185 Tino Martinez .05
186 Craig Biggio .05
187 Chuck Knoblauch .05
188 Carlos Baerga .05
189 Quilvio Veras .05
190 Luis Alicea .05
191 Jim Thome .40
192 Mike Blowers .05
193 Robin Ventura .05
194 Jeff King .05
195 Tony Phillips .05
196 John Valentin .05
197 Barry Larkin .05
198 Cal Ripken Jr. 2.00
199 Omar Vizquel .05
200 Kurt Abbott .05
201 Albert Belle .05
202 Barry Bonds 2.00
203 Ron Gant .05
204 Dante Bichette .05
205 Jeff Conine .05
206 Jim Edmonds .05
207 Stan Javier .05
208 Kenny Lofton .05
209 Ray Lankford .05
210 Bernie Williams .05
211 Jay Buhner .05
212 Paul O'Neill .05
213 Tim Salmon .05
214 Reggie Sanders .05
215 Manny Ramirez .60
216 Mike Piazza 1.50
217 Mike Stanley .05
218 Tony Eusebio .05
219 Chris Hoiles .05
220 Ron Karkovice .05
221 Edgar Martinez .05
222 Chili Davis .05
223 Jose Canseco .35
224 Eddie Murray .60
225 Geronimo Berroa .05
226 Chipper Jones .75
227 Garret Anderson .05
228 Marty Cordova .05
229 Jon Nunnally .05
230 Brian Hunter .05
231 Shawn Green .20
232 Ray Durham .05
233 Alex Gonzalez .05
234 Bobby Higginson .05
235 Randy Johnson .60
236 Al Leiter .05
237 Tom Glavine .10
238 Kenny Rogers .05
239 Mike Hampton .05
240 David Wells .05
241 Jim Abbott .05
242 Denny Neagle .05
243 Wilson Alvarez .05
244 John Smiley .05
245 Greg Maddux .75
246 Andy Ashby .05
247 Hideo Nomo .30
248 Pat Rapp .05
249 Tim Wakefield .05
250 John Smoltz .05
251 Joey Hamilton .05
252 Frank Castillo .05
253 Denny Martinez .05
254 Jaime Navarro .05
255 Karim Garcia .05
256 Bob Abreu .05
257 Butch Huskey .05
258 Ruben Rivera .05
259 Johnny Damon .20
260 Derek Jeter 2.00
261 Dennis Eckersley .50
262 Jose Mesa .05
263 Tom Henke .05
264 Rick Aguilera .05
265 Randy Myers .05
266 John Franco .05
267 Jeff Brantley .05
268 John Wetteland .05
269 Mark Wohlers .05
270 Rod Beck .05
271 Barry Larkin .05
272 Paul O'Neill .05
273 Bobby Jones .05
274 Will Clark .05
275 Steve Avery .05
276 Jim Edmonds .05
277 John Olerud .05
278 Carlos Perez .05
279 Chris Hoiles .05
280 Jeff Conine .05
281 Jim Eisenreich .05
282 Jason Jacome .05
283 Ray Lankford .05
284 John Wasdin .05
285 Frank Thomas .75
286 Jason Isringhausen .05
287 Glenallen Hill .05
288 Esteban Loaiza .05
289 Bernie Williams .05
290 Curtis Leskanic .05
291 Scott Cooper .05
292 Curt Schilling .35
293 Eddie Murray .75
294 Rick Krivda .05
295 Domingo Cedeno .05
296 Jeff Fassero .05
297 Albert Belle .05
298 Craig Biggio .05
299 Fernando Vina .05
300 Edgar Martinez .05
301 Tony Gwynn 1.00
302 Felipe Lira .05
303 Mo Vaughn .05
304 Alex Fernandez .05
305 Keith Lockhart .05
306 Roger Pavlik .05
307 Lee Tinsley .05
308 Omar Vizquel .05
309 Scott Servais .05
310 Danny Tartabull .05
311 Chili Davis .05
312 Cal Eldred .05
313 Roger Cedeno .05
314 Chris Hammond .05
315 Rusty Greer .05
316 Brady Anderson .05
317 Ron Villone .05
318 Mark Carreon .05
319 Larry Walker .05
320 Pete Harnisch .05
321 Robin Ventura .05
322 Tim Belcher .05
323 Tony Tarasco .05
324 Juan Guzman .05
325 Kenny Lofton .05
326 Kevin Foster .05
327 Wil Cordero .05
328 Troy Percival .05
329 Turk Wendell .05
330 Thomas Howard .05
331 Carlos Baerga .05
332 B.J. Surhoff .05
333 Jay Buhner .05
334 Andujar Cedeno .05
335 Jeff King .05
336 Dante Bichette .05
337 Alan Trammell .05
338 Scott Leius .05
339 Chris Snopek .05
340 Roger Bailey .05
341 Jacob Brumfield .05
342 Jose Canseco .50
343 Rafael Palmeiro .65
344 Quilvio Veras .05
345 Darrin Fletcher .05
346 Carlos Delgado .50
347 Tony Eusebio .05
348 Ismael Valdes .05
349 Terry Steinbach .05
350 Orel Hershiser .05
351 Kurt Abbott .05
352 Jody Reed .05
353 David Howard .05
354 Ruben Sierra .05
355 John Ericks .05
356 Buck Showalter .05
357 Jim Thome .65
358 Geronimo Berroa .05
359 Robby Thompson .05
360 Jose Vizcaino .05
361 Jeff Frye .05
362 Kevin Appier .05
363 Pat Kelly .05
364 Ron Gant .05
365 Luis Alicea .05
366 Armando Benitez .05
367 Rico Brogna .05
368 Manny Ramirez .75
369 Mike Lansing .05
370 Sammy Sosa 1.00
371 Don Wengert .05
372 Dave Nilsson .05
373 Sandy Alomar .05
374 Joey Cora .05
375 Larry Thomas .05
376 John Valentin .05
377 Kevin Ritz .05
378 Steve Finley .05
379 Frank Rodriguez .05
380 Ivan Rodriguez .65
381 Alex Ochoa .05
382 Mark Lemke .05
383 Scott Brosius .05
384 James Mouton .05
385 Mark Langston .05
386 Ed Sprague .05
387 Joe Oliver .05
388 Steve Ontiveros .05
389 Rey Sanchez .05
390 Mike Henneman .05
391 *Jose Valentin* .05
392 Tom Candiotti .05
393 Damon Buford .05
394 Erik Hanson .05
395 Mark Smith .05
396 Pete Schourek .05
397 John Flaherty .05
398 Dave Martinez .05
399 Tommy Greene .05
400 Gary Sheffield .45
401 Glenn Dishman .05
402 Barry Bonds 3.00
403 Tom Pagnozzi .05
404 Todd Stottlemyre .05
405 Tim Salmon .05
406 John Hudek .05
407 Fred McGriff .05
408 Orlando Merced .05
409 Brian Barber .05
410 Ryan Thompson .05
411 Mariano Rivera .10
412 Eric Young .05
413 Chris Bosio .05
414 Chuck Knoblauch .05
415 Jamie Moyer .05
416 Chan Ho Park .05
417 Mark Portugal .05
418 Tim Raines .05
419 Antonio Osuna .05
420 Todd Zeile .05
421 Steve Wojciechowski .05
422 Marquis Grissom .05
423 Norm Charlton .05
424 Cal Ripken Jr. 3.00
425 Gregg Jefferies .05
426 Mike Stanton .05
427 Tony Fernandez .05
428 Jose Rijo .05
429 Jeff Bagwell .75
430 Raul Mondesi .05
431 Travis Fryman .05
432 Ron Karkovice .05
433 Alan Benes .05
434 Tony Phillips .05
435 Reggie Sanders .05
436 Andy Pettitte .25
437 *Matt Lawton* .25
438 Jeff Blauser .05
439 Michael Tucker .05
440 Mark Loretta .05
441 Charlie Hayes .05
442 Mike Piazza 1.50
443 Shane Andrews .05
444 Jeff Suppan .05
445 Steve Rodriguez .05
446 Mike Matheny .05
447 Trenidad Hubbard .05
448 Denny Hocking .05
449 Mark Grudzielanek .05
450 Joe Randa .05

Bash & Burn

		NM/M
Complete Set (10):		10.00
Common Player:		.75
1	Sammy Sosa	3.50
2	Barry Bonds	6.00
3	Reggie Sanders	.75
4	Craig Biggio	.75
5	Raul Mondesi	.75
6	Ron Gant	.75
7	Ray Lankford	.75
8	Glenallen Hill	.75
9	Chad Curtis	.75
10	John Valentin	.75

Mega Heroes

		NM/M
Complete Set (10):		10.00
Common Player:		1.00
1	Frank Thomas	1.50
2	Ken Griffey Jr.	3.00
3	Hideo Nomo	1.25
4	Ozzie Smith	1.75
5	Will Clark	1.00

#	Player	NM/M
6	Jack McDowell	1.00
7	Andres Galarraga	1.00
8	Roger Clemens	2.00
9	Deion Sanders	1.00
10	Mo Vaughn	1.00

Metalists

		NM/M
Complete Set (8):		12.00
Common Player:		1.00
1	Jeff Bagwell	1.25
2	Barry Bonds	3.50
3	Jose Canseco	1.00
4	Roger Clemens	2.50
5	Dennis Eckersley	1.00
6	Greg Maddux	2.00
7	Cal Ripken Jr.	3.50
8	Frank Thomas	1.25

Mickey Mantle Retrospective

		NM/M
Complete Set (19):		35.00
Common Series 1:		4.00
Common Series 2:		2.00
1	Mickey Mantle (1950, minor league)	4.00
2	Mickey Mantle (1951)	4.00
3	Mickey Mantle (1951)	4.00
4	Mickey Mantle (1953)	4.00
5	Mickey Mantle (1954) (w/ Yogi Berra)	4.00
6	Mickey Mantle (1956)	4.00
7	Mickey Mantle (1957)	4.00
8	Mickey Mantle (1958) (w/ Casey Stengel)	4.00
9	Mickey Mantle (1959)	4.00
10	Mickey Mantle (1960) (w/ Elston Howard)	2.00
11	Mickey Mantle (1961)	2.00
12	Mickey Mantle (1961) (w/ Roger Maris)	4.00
13	Mickey Mantle (1962)	2.00
14	Mickey Mantle (1963)	2.00
15	Mickey Mantle (1964)	2.00
16	Mickey Mantle	2.00
17	Mickey Mantle (1968)	2.00
18	Mickey Mantle (1969)	2.00
19	Mickey Mantle (In Memoriam)	3.50

Mickey Mantle "Cereal Box" Set

	NM/M
Unopened Set:	30.00
Common Player:	.10

(See 1996 Stadium Club for checklist and values.)

Midsummer Matchups

		NM/M
Complete Set (10):		20.00
Common Player:		1.00
1	Hideo Nomo, Randy Johnson	2.00
2	Mike Piazza, Ivan Rodriguez	4.00
3	Fred McGriff, Frank Thomas	2.00
4	Craig Biggio, Carlos Baerga	1.00
5	Vinny Castilla, Wade Boggs	2.50
6	Barry Larkin, Cal Ripken Jr.	5.00
7	Barry Bonds, Albert Belle	5.00
8	Len Dykstra, Kenny Lofton	1.00
9	Tony Gwynn, Kirby Puckett	3.00
10	Ron Gant, Edgar Martinez	1.00

Power Packed

		NM/M
Complete Set (15):		15.00
Common Player:		1.00
1	Albert Belle	1.00
2	Mark McGwire	4.00
3	Jose Canseco	1.75
4	Mike Piazza	3.00
5	Ron Gant	1.00
6	Ken Griffey Jr.	3.00
7	Mo Vaughn	1.00
8	Cecil Fielder	1.00
9	Tim Salmon	1.00
10	Frank Thomas	2.50
11	Juan Gonzalez	1.50
12	Andres Galarraga	1.00
13	Fred McGriff	1.00
14	Jay Buhner	1.00
15	Dante Bichette	1.00

Power Streak

		NM/M
Complete Set (15):		20.00
Common Player:		1.00
1	Randy Johnson	2.00
2	Hideo Nomo	1.25
3	Albert Belle	1.00
4	Dante Bichette	1.00
5	Jay Buhner	1.00
6	Frank Thomas	2.00
7	Mark McGwire	4.00
8	Rafael Palmeiro	1.50
9	Mo Vaughn	1.00
10	Sammy Sosa	3.00
11	Larry Walker	1.00
12	Gary Gaetti	1.00
13	Tim Salmon	1.00
14	Barry Bonds	5.00
15	Jim Edmonds	1.00

Prime Cuts

		NM/M
Complete Set (8):		20.00
Common Player:		1.50
1	Albert Belle	1.50
2	Barry Bonds	6.00
3	Ken Griffey Jr.	4.00
4	Tony Gwynn	3.00
5	Edgar Martinez	1.50
6	Rafael Palmeiro	2.00
7	Mike Piazza	4.00
8	Frank Thomas	2.50

TSC Awards

		NM/M
Complete Set (10):		15.00
Common Player:		.50
1	Cal Ripken Jr.	5.00
2	Albert Belle	.60
3	Tom Glavine	1.00
4	Jeff Conine	.50
5	Ken Griffey Jr.	4.00
6	Hideo Nomo	1.25
7	Greg Maddux	3.00
8	Chipper Jones	3.00
9	Randy Johnson	2.00
10	Jose Mesa	.50

1997 STADIUM CLUB

		NM/M
Complete Set (390):		35.00
Common Player:		.05
Series 1 or 2 Pack (9):		1.50
Series 1 or 2 Wax Box (24):		27.50
1	Chipper Jones	1.50
2	Gary Sheffield	.50
3	Kenny Lofton	.05
4	Brian Jordan	.05
5	Mark McGwire	2.50
6	Charles Nagy	.05
7	Tim Salmon	.05
8	Cal Ripken Jr.	3.00
9	Jeff Conine	.05
10	Paul Molitor	1.00
11	Mariano Rivera	.15
12	Pedro Martinez	1.00
13	Jeff Bagwell	1.00
14	Bobby Bonilla	.05
15	Barry Bonds	3.00
16	Ryan Klesko	.05
17	Barry Larkin	.05
18	Jim Thome	.65
19	Jay Buhner	.05
20	Juan Gonzalez	.50
21	Mike Mussina	.30
22	Kevin Appier	.05
23	Eric Karros	.05
24	Steve Finley	.05
25	Ed Sprague	.05
26	Bernard Gilkey	.05
27	Tony Phillips	.05
28	Henry Rodriguez	.05
29	John Smoltz	.05
30	Dante Bichette	.05
31	Mike Piazza	2.00
32	Paul O'Neill	.05
33	Billy Wagner	.05
34	Reggie Sanders	.05
35	John Jaha	.05
36	Eddie Murray	1.00
37	Eric Young	.05
38	Roberto Hernandez	.05
39	Pat Hentgen	.05
40	Sammy Sosa	1.50
41	Todd Hundley	.05
42	Mo Vaughn	.05
43	Robin Ventura	.05
44	Mark Grudzielanek	.05
45	Shane Reynolds	.05
46	Andy Pettitte	.25
47	Fred McGriff	.05
48	Rey Ordonez	.05
49	Will Clark	.05
50	Ken Griffey Jr.	2.00
51	Todd Worrell	.05
52	Rusty Greer	.05
53	Mark Grace	.05
54	Tom Glavine	.35
55	Derek Jeter	3.00
56	Rafael Palmeiro	.75
57	Bernie Williams	.05
58	Marty Cordova	.05
59	Andres Galarraga	.05
60	Ken Caminiti	.05
61	Garret Anderson	.05
62	Denny Martinez	.05
63	Mike Greenwell	.05
64	David Segui	.05
65	Julio Franco	.05
66	Rickey Henderson	1.00
67	Ozzie Guillen	.05
68	Pete Harnisch	.05
69	Chan Ho Park	.05
70	Harold Baines	.05
71	Mark Clark	.05
72	Steve Avery	.05
73	Brian Hunter	.05
74	Pedro Astacio	.05
75	Jack McDowell	.05
76	Gregg Jefferies	.05
77	Jason Kendall	.05
78	Todd Walker	.05
79	B.J. Surhoff	.05
80	Moises Alou	.05
81	Fernando Vina	.05
82	Darryl Strawberry	.05
83	Jose Rosado	.05
84	Chris Gomez	.05
85	Chili Davis	.05
86	Alan Benes	.05
87	Todd Hollandsworth	.05
88	Jose Vizcaino	.05
89	Edgardo Alfonzo	.05
90	Ruben Rivera	.05
91	Donovan Osborne	.05
92	Doug Glanville	.05
93	Gary DiSarcina	.05
94	Brooks Kieschnick	.05
95	Bobby Jones	.05
96	Raul Casanova	.05
97	Jermaine Allensworth	.05
98	Kenny Rogers	.05
99	Mark McLemore	.05
100	Jeff Fassero	.05
101	Sandy Alomar	.05
102	Chuck Finley	.05
103	Eric Owens	.05
104	Billy McMillon	.05
105	Dwight Gooden	.05
106	Sterling Hitchcock	.05
107	Doug Drabek	.05
108	Paul Wilson	.05
109	Chris Snopek	.05
110	Al Leiter	.05
111	Bob Tewksbury	.05
112	Todd Greene	.05
113	Jose Valentin	.05
114	Delino DeShields	.05
115	Mike Bordick	.05
116	Pat Meares	.05
117	Mariano Duncan	.05
118	Steve Trachsel	.05
119	Luis Castillo	.05
120	Andy Benes	.05
121	Donne Wall	.05
122	Alex Gonzalez	.05
123	Dan Wilson	.05
124	Omar Vizquel	.05
125	Devon White	.05
126	Darryl Hamilton	.05
127	Orlando Merced	.05
128	Royce Clayton	.05
129	William VanLandingham	.05
130	Terry Steinbach	.05
131	Jeff Blauser	.05
132	Jeff Cirillo	.05
133	Roger Pavlik	.05
134	Danny Tartabull	.05
135	Jeff Montgomery	.05
136	Bobby Higginson	.05
137	Mike Grace	.05
138	Kevin Elster	.05
139	*Brian Giles*	1.00
140	Rod Beck	.05
141	Ismael Valdes	.05
142	Scott Brosius	.05
143	Mike Fetters	.05
144	Gary Gaetti	.05
145	Mike Lansing	.05
146	Glenallen Hill	.05
147	Shawn Green	.35
148	Mel Rojas	.05
149	Joey Cora	.05
150	John Smiley	.05
151	Marvin Benard	.05
152	Curt Schilling	.35
153	Dave Nilsson	.05
154	Edgar Renteria	.05
155	Joey Hamilton	.05
156	Carlos Garcia	.05
157	Nomar Garciaparra	2.00
158	Kevin Ritz	.05
159	Keith Lockhart	.05
160	Justin Thompson	.05

161	Terry Adams	.05
162	Jamey Wright	.05
163	Otis Nixon	.05
164	Michael Tucker	.05
165	Mike Stanley	.05
166	Ben McDonald	.05
167	John Mabry	.05
168	Troy O'Leary	.05
169	Mel Nieves	.05
170	Bret Boone	.05
171	Mike Timlin	.05
172	Scott Rolen	.75
173	Reggie Jefferson	.05
174	Neifi Perez	.05
175	Brian McRae	.05
176	Tom Goodwin	.05
177	Aaron Sele	.05
178	Benny Santiago	.05
179	Frank Rodriguez	.05
180	Eric Davis	.05
181	Andruw Jones	.75
182	Todd Walker	.15
183	Wes Helms	.15
184	*Nelson Figueroa*	.15
185	Vladimir Guerrero	.75
186	Billy McMillon	.15
187	Todd Helton	.65
188	Nomar Garciaparra	2.00
189	Katsuhiro Maeda	.15
190	Russell Branyan	.15
191	Glendon Rusch	.15
192	Bartolo Colon	.15
193	Scott Rolen	.50
194	Angel Echevarria	.15
195	Bob Abreu	.20
196	Greg Maddux	1.50
197	Joe Carter	.05
198	Alex Ochoa	.05
199	Ellis Burks	.05
200	Ivan Rodriguez	.75
201	Marquis Grissom	.05
202	Trevor Hoffman	.05
203	Matt Williams	.05
204	Carlos Delgado	.50
205	Ramon Martinez	.05
206	Chuck Knoblauch	.05
207	Juan Guzman	.05
208	Derek Bell	.05
209	Roger Clemens	1.75
210	Vladimir Guerrero	1.00
211	Cecil Fielder	.05
212	Hideo Nomo	.50
213	Frank Thomas	1.00
214	Greg Vaughn	.05
215	Javy Lopez	.05
216	Raul Mondesi	.05
217	Wade Boggs	1.50
218	Carlos Baerga	.05
219	Tony Gwynn	1.50
220	Tino Martinez	.05
221	Vinny Castilla	.05
222	Lance Johnson	.05
223	David Justice	.05
224	Rondell White	.05
225	Dean Palmer	.05
226	Jim Edmonds	.05
227	Albert Belle	.05
228	Alex Fernandez	.05
229	Ryne Sandberg	1.50
230	Jose Mesa	.05
231	David Cone	.05
232	Troy Percival	.05
233	Edgar Martinez	.05
234	Jose Canseco	.50
235	Kevin Brown	.05
236	Ray Lankford	.05
237	Karim Garcia	.05
238	J.T. Snow	.05
239	Dennis Eckersley	.75
240	Roberto Alomar	.35
241	John Valentin	.05
242	Ron Gant	.05
243	Geronimo Berroa	.05
244	Manny Ramirez	1.00
245	Travis Fryman	.05
246	Denny Neagle	.05
247	Randy Johnson	1.00
248	Darin Erstad	.15
249	Mark Wohlers	.05
250	Ken Hill	.05
251	Larry Walker	.05
252	Craig Biggio	.05
253	Brady Anderson	.05
254	John Wetteland	.05
255	Andruw Jones	1.00
256	Turk Wendell	.05
257	Jason Isringhausen	.05
258	Jaime Navarro	.05
259	Sean Berry	.05
260	Albie Lopez	.05
261	Jay Bell	.05
262	Bobby Witt	.05
263	Tony Clark	.05
264	Tim Wakefield	.05
265	Brad Radke	.05
266	Tim Belcher	.05
267	Mark Lewis	.05
268	Roger Cedeno	.05
269	Tim Naehring	.05
270	Kevin Tapani	.05
271	Joe Randa	.05
272	Randy Myers	.05
273	Dave Burba	.05
274a	Mike Sweeney	.05
274b	Tom Pagnozzi (should be #374)	.05
275	Danny Graves	.05
276	Chad Mottola	.05
277	Ruben Sierra	.05
278	Norm Charlton	.05
279	Scott Servais	.05
280	Jacob Cruz	.05
281	Mike Macfarlane	.05
282	Rich Becker	.05
283	Shannon Stewart	.05
284	Gerald Williams	.05
285	Jody Reed	.05
286	Jeff D'Amico	.05
287	Walt Weiss	.05
288	Jim Leyritz	.05
289	Francisco Cordova	.05
290	F.P. Santangelo	.05
291	Scott Erickson	.05
292	Hal Morris	.05
293	Ray Durham	.05
294	Andy Ashby	.05
295	Darryl Kile	.05
296	Jose Paniagua	.05
297	Mickey Tettleton	.05
298	Joe Girardi	.05
299	Rocky Coppinger	.05
300	Bob Abreu	.05
301	John Olerud	.05
302	Paul Shuey	.05
303	Jeff Brantley	.05
304	Bob Wells	.05
305	Kevin Seitzer	.05
306	Shawon Dunston	.05
307	Jose Herrera	.05
308	Butch Huskey	.05
309	Jose Offerman	.05
310	Rick Aguilera	.05
311	Greg Gagne	.05
312	John Burkett	.05
313	Mark Thompson	.05
314	Alvaro Espinoza	.05
315	Todd Stottlemyre	.05
316	Al Martin	.05
317	James Baldwin	.05
318	Cal Eldred	.05
319	Sid Fernandez	.05
320	Mickey Morandini	.05
321	Robb Nen	.05
322	Mark Lemke	.05
323	Pete Schourek	.05
324	Marcus Jensen	.05
325	Rich Aurilia	.05
326	Jeff King	.05
327	Scott Stahoviak	.05
328	Ricky Otero	.05
329	Antonio Osuna	.05
330	Chris Hoiles	.05
331	Luis Gonzalez	.05
332	Wil Cordero	.05
333	Johnny Damon	.35
334	Mark Langston	.05
335	Orlando Miller	.05
336	Jason Giambi	.50
337	Damian Jackson	.05
338	David Wells	.05
339	Bip Roberts	.05
340	Matt Ruebel	.05
341	Tom Candiotti	.05
342	Wally Joyner	.05
343	Jimmy Key	.05
344	Tony Batista	.05
345	Paul Sorrento	.05
346	Ron Karkovice	.05
347	Wilson Alvarez	.05
348	John Flaherty	.05
349	Rey Sanchez	.05
350	John Vander Wal	.05
351a	Jermaine Dye	.05
351b	Brant Brown (should be #361)	.05
352	Mike Hampton	.05
353	Greg Colbrunn	.05
354	Heathcliff Slocumb	.05
355	Ricky Bottalico	.05
356	Marty Janzen	.05
357	Orel Hershiser	.05
358	Rex Hudler	.05
359	Amaury Telemaco	.05
360	Darrin Fletcher	.05
361	Not issued - see #351	.05
362	Russ Davis	.05
363	Allen Watson	.05
364	Mike Lieberthal	.05
365	Dave Stevens	.05
366	Jay Powell	.05
367	Tony Fossas	.05
368	Bob Wolcott	.05
369	Mark Loretta	.05
370	Shawn Estes	.05
371	Sandy Martinez	.05
372	Wendell Magee Jr.	.05
373	John Franco	.05
374	Not issued - see #274	.05
375	Willie Adams	.05
376	Chipper Jones	2.00
377	Mo Vaughn	.15
378	Frank Thomas	1.50
379	Albert Belle	.15
380	Andres Galarraga	.15
381	Gary Sheffield	.85
382	Jeff Bagwell	1.50
383	Mike Piazza	3.00
384	Mark McGwire	3.00
385	Ken Griffey Jr.	2.50
386	Barry Bonds	3.50
387	Juan Gonzalez	.40
388	Brady Anderson	.15
389	Ken Caminiti	.15
390	Jay Buhner	.15

Co-Signers

		NM/M
Complete Set (10):		200.00
Common Card:		5.00
CO1	Andy Pettitte, Derek Jeter	100.00
CO2	Paul Wilson, Todd Hundley	5.00
CO3	Jermaine Dye, Mark Wohlers	6.00
CO4	Scott Rolen, Gregg Jefferies	15.00
CO5	Todd Hollandsworth, Jason Kendall	8.00
CO6	Alan Benes, Robin Ventura	8.00
CO7	Eric Karros, Raul Mondesi	15.00
CO8	Rey Ordonez, Nomar Garciaparra	45.00
CO9	Rondell White, Marty Cordova	6.00
CO10	Tony Gwynn, Karim Garcia	30.00

Firebrand

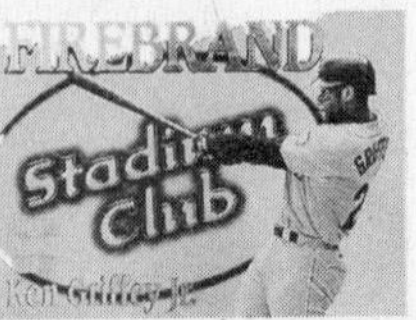

		NM/M
Complete Set (12):		25.00
Common Player:		1.00
1	Jeff Bagwell	2.50
2	Albert Belle	1.00
3	Barry Bonds	6.50
4	Andres Galarraga	1.00
5	Ken Griffey Jr.	4.50
6	Brady Anderson	1.00
7	Mark McGwire	5.50
8	Chipper Jones	3.50
9	Frank Thomas	2.50
10	Mike Piazza	4.50
11	Mo Vaughn	1.00
12	Juan Gonzalez	1.50

1997 STADIUM CLUB FIREBRAND REDEMPTION

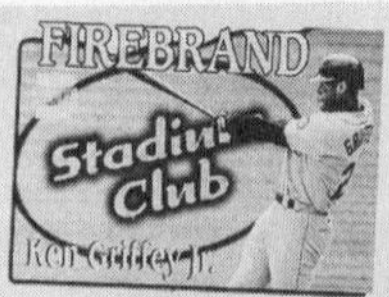

		NM/M
Complete Set (12):		15.00
Common Player:		.60
F1	Jeff Bagwell	1.25
F2	Albert Belle	.60
F3	Barry Bonds	4.00
F4	Andres Galarraga	.60
F5	Ken Griffey Jr.	2.50
F6	Brady Anderson	.60
F7	Mark McGwire	3.25
F8	Chipper Jones	2.00
F9	Frank Thomas	1.25
F10	Mike Piazza	2.50
F11	Mo Vaughn	.60
F12	Juan Gonzalez	.85

Instavision

		NM/M
Complete Set (22):		10.00
Common Player:		.35
I1	Eddie Murray	.75
I2	Paul Molitor	.75
I3	Todd Hundley	.35
I4	Roger Clemens	1.50
I5	Barry Bonds	3.00
I6	Mark McGwire	2.00
I7	Brady Anderson	.35
I8	Barry Larkin	.35
I9	Ken Caminiti	.35
I10	Hideo Nomo	.45
I11	Bernie Williams	.35
I12	Juan Gonzalez	.45
I13	Andy Pettitte	.45
I14	Albert Belle	.35
I15	John Smoltz	.35
I16	Brian Jordan	.35
I17	Derek Jeter	3.00
I18	Ken Caminiti	.35
I19	John Wetteland	.35
I20	Brady Anderson	.35
I21	Andruw Jones	.75
I22	Jim Leyritz	.35

Millennium

		NM/M
Complete Set (40):		12.50
Common Player:		.25
1	Derek Jeter	5.00
2	Mark Grudzielanek	.25
3	Jacob Cruz	.25
4	Ray Durham	.25
5	Tony Clark	.25
6	Chipper Jones	2.50
7	Luis Castillo	.25
8	Carlos Delgado	.50
9	Brant Brown	.25
10	Jason Kendall	.25
11	Alan Benes	.25
12	Rey Ordonez	.25
13	Justin Thompson	.25
14	Jermaine Allensworth	.25
15	Brian Hunter	.25
16	Marty Cordova	.25
17	Edgar Renteria	.25

18	Karim Garcia	.25
19	Todd Greene	.25
20	Paul Wilson	.25
21	Andruw Jones	1.50
22	Todd Walker	.25
23	Alex Ochoa	.25
24	Bartolo Colon	.25
25	Wendell Magee Jr.	.25
26	Jose Rosado	.25
27	Katsuhiro Maeda	.25
28	Bob Abreu	.25
29	Brooks Kieschnick	.25
30	Derrick Gibson	.25
31	Mike Sweeney	.25
32	Jeff D'Amico	.25
33	Chad Mottola	.25
34	Chris Snopek	.25
35	Jaime Bluma	.25
36	Vladimir Guerrero	1.50
37	Nomar Garciaparra	2.50
38	Scott Rolen	1.25
39	Dmitri Young	.25
40	Neifi Perez	.25

Patent Leather

		NM/M
Complete Set (13):		25.00
Common Player:		1.00
1	Ivan Rodriguez	3.00
2	Ken Caminiti	1.00
3	Barry Bonds	6.00
4	Ken Griffey Jr.	5.00
5	Greg Maddux	4.00
6	Craig Biggio	1.00
7	Andres Galarraga	1.00
8	Kenny Lofton	1.00
9	Barry Larkin	1.00
10	Mark Grace	1.00
11	Rey Ordonez	1.00
12	Roberto Alomar	1.25
13	Derek Jeter	6.00

Pure Gold

		NM/M
Complete Set (20):		60.00
Common Player:		1.25
1	Brady Anderson	1.25
2	Albert Belle	1.25
3	Dante Bichette	1.25
4	Barry Bonds	12.00
5	Jay Buhner	1.25
6	Tony Gwynn	6.00
7	Chipper Jones	6.00
8	Mark McGwire	9.00
9	Gary Sheffield	2.25
10	Frank Thomas	4.50
11	Juan Gonzalez	2.50
12	Ken Caminiti	1.25
13	Kenny Lofton	1.25
14	Jeff Bagwell	4.50
15	Ken Griffey Jr.	7.50
16	Cal Ripken Jr.	12.00
17	Mo Vaughn	1.25
18	Mike Piazza	7.50
19	Derek Jeter	12.00
20	Andres Galarraga	1.25

TSC Matrix

		NM/M
Complete Set (120):		70.00
Common Player:		.50
1	Chipper Jones	2.50
2	Gary Sheffield	1.00
3	Kenny Lofton	.50
4	Brian Jordan	.50
5	Mark McGwire	4.25
6	Charles Nagy	.50
7	Tim Salmon	.50
8	Cal Ripken Jr.	5.00
9	Jeff Conine	.50
10	Paul Molitor	1.75
11	Mariano Rivera	.65
12	Pedro Martinez	1.75
13	Jeff Bagwell	1.75
14	Bobby Bonilla	.50
15	Barry Bonds	5.00
16	Ryan Klesko	.50
17	Barry Larkin	.50
18	Jim Thome	1.50
19	Jay Buhner	.50
20	Juan Gonzalez	1.00
21	Mike Mussina	.75
22	Kevin Appier	.50
23	Eric Karros	.50
24	Steve Finley	.50
25	Ed Sprague	.50
26	Bernard Gilkey	.50
27	Tony Phillips	.50
28	Henry Rodriguez	.50
29	John Smoltz	.50
30	Dante Bichette	.50
31	Mike Piazza	3.25
32	Paul O'Neill	.50
33	Billy Wagner	.50
34	Reggie Sanders	.50
35	John Jaha	.50
36	Eddie Murray	1.75
37	Eric Young	.50
38	Roberto Hernandez	.50
39	Pat Hentgen	.50
40	Sammy Sosa	2.50
41	Todd Hundley	.50
42	Mo Vaughn	.50
43	Robin Ventura	.50
44	Mark Grudzielanek	.50
45	Shane Reynolds	.50
46	Andy Pettitte	.65
47	Fred McGriff	.50
48	Rey Ordonez	.50
49	Will Clark	.50
50	Ken Griffey Jr.	3.25
51	Todd Worrell	.50
52	Rusty Greer	.50
53	Mark Grace	.50
54	Tom Glavine	.75
55	Derek Jeter	5.00
56	Rafael Palmeiro	1.50
57	Bernie Williams	.50
58	Marty Cordova	.50
59	Andres Galarraga	.50
60	Ken Caminiti	.50
196	Greg Maddux	2.50
197	Joe Carter	.50
198	Alex Ochoa	.50
199	Ellis Burks	.50
200	Ivan Rodriguez	1.50
201	Marquis Grissom	.50
202	Trevor Hoffman	.50
203	Matt Williams	.50
204	Carlos Delgado	1.25
205	Ramon Martinez	.50
206	Chuck Knoblauch	.50
207	Juan Guzman	.50
208	Derek Bell	.50
209	Roger Clemens	3.00
210	Vladimir Guerrero	1.75
211	Cecil Fielder	.50
212	Hideo Nomo	1.00
213	Frank Thomas	1.75
214	Greg Vaughn	.50
215	Javy Lopez	.50
216	Raul Mondesi	.50
217	Wade Boggs	2.50
218	Carlos Baerga	.50
219	Tony Gwynn	2.50
220	Tino Martinez	.50
221	Vinny Castilla	.50
222	Lance Johnson	.50
223	David Justice	.50
224	Rondell White	.50
225	Dean Palmer	.50
226	Jim Edmonds	.50
227	Albert Belle	.50
228	Alex Fernandez	.50
229	Ryne Sandberg	2.50
230	Jose Mesa	.50
231	David Cone	.50
232	Troy Percival	.50
233	Edgar Martinez	.50
234	Jose Canseco	1.25
235	Kevin Brown	.50
236	Ray Lankford	.50
237	Karim Garcia	.50
238	J.T. Snow	.50
239	Dennis Eckersley	1.50
240	Roberto Alomar	.75
241	John Valentin	.50
242	Ron Gant	.50
243	Geronimo Berroa	.50
244	Manny Ramirez	1.75
245	Travis Fryman	.50
246	Denny Neagle	.50
247	Randy Johnson	1.75
248	Darin Erstad	.65
249	Mark Wohlers	.50
250	Ken Hill	.50
251	Larry Walker	.50
252	Craig Biggio	.50
253	Brady Anderson	.50
254	John Wetteland	.50
255	Andruw Jones	1.75

1998 STADIUM CLUB

		NM/M
Complete Set (400):		30.00
Common Player:		.05
Hobby Pack (10):		1.50
Retail Pack (7):		1.50
Home Team Adv. Pack (16):		4.00
Hobby Box (24):		30.00
1	Chipper Jones	1.00
2	Frank Thomas	.75
3	Vladimir Guerrero	.75
4	Ellis Burks	.05
5	John Franco	.05
6	Paul Molitor	.75
7	Rusty Greer	.05
8	Todd Hundley	.05
9	Brett Tomko	.05
10	Eric Karros	.05
11	Mike Cameron	.05
12	Jim Edmonds	.05
13	Bernie Williams	.05
14	Denny Neagle	.05
15	Jason Dickson	.05
16	Sammy Sosa	1.00
17	Brian Jordan	.05
18	Jose Vidro	.05
19	Scott Spiezio	.05
20	Jay Buhner	.05
21	Jim Thome	.65
22	Sandy Alomar	.05
23	Devon White	.05
24	Roberto Alomar	.20
25	John Flaherty	.05
26	John Wetteland	.05
27	Willie Greene	.05
28	Gregg Jefferies	.05
29	Johnny Damon	.35
30	Barry Larkin	.05
31	Chuck Knoblauch	.05
32	Mo Vaughn	.05
33	Tony Clark	.05
34	Marty Cordova	.05
35	Vinny Castilla	.05
36	Jeff King	.05
37	Reggie Jefferson	.05
38	Mariano Rivera	.15
39	Jermaine Allensworth	.05
40	Livan Hernandez	.05
41	Heathcliff Slocumb	.05
42	Jacob Cruz	.05
43	Barry Bonds	2.50
44	Dave Magadan	.05
45	Chan Ho Park	.05
46	Jeremi Gonzalez	.05
47	Jeff Cirillo	.05
48	Delino DeShields	.05
49	Craig Biggio	.05
50	Benito Santiago	.05
51	Mark Clark	.05
52	Fernando Vina	.05
53	F.P. Santangelo	.05
54	*Pep Harris*	.05
55	Edgar Renteria	.05
56	Jeff Bagwell	.75
57	Jimmy Key	.05
58	Bartolo Colon	.05
59	Curt Schilling	.35
60	Steve Finley	.05
61	Andy Ashby	.05
62	John Burkett	.05
63	Orel Hershiser	.05
64	Pokey Reese	.05
65	Scott Servais	.05
66	Todd Jones	.05
67	Javy Lopez	.05
68	Robin Ventura	.05
69	Miguel Tejada	.15
70	Raul Casanova	.05
71	Reggie Sanders	.05
72	Edgardo Alfonzo	.05
73	Dean Palmer	.05
74	Todd Stottlemyre	.05
75	David Wells	.05
76	Troy Percival	.05
77	Albert Belle	.05
78	Pat Hentgen	.05
79	Brian Hunter	.05
80	Richard Hidalgo	.05
81	Darren Oliver	.05
82	Mark Wohlers	.05
83	Cal Ripken Jr.	2.50
84	Hideo Nomo	.40
85	Derrek Lee	.50
86	Stan Javier	.05
87	Rey Ordonez	.05
88	Randy Johnson	.75
89	Jeff Kent	.05
90	Brian McRae	.05
91	Manny Ramirez	.75
92	Trevor Hoffman	.05
93	Doug Glanville	.05
94	Todd Walker	.05
95	Andy Benes	.05
96	Jason Schmidt	.05
97	Mike Matheny	.05
98	Tim Naehring	.05
99	Jeff Blauser	.05
100	Jose Rosado	.05
101	Roger Clemens	1.25
102	Pedro Astacio	.05
103	Mark Bellhorn	.05
104	Paul O'Neill	.05
105	Darin Erstad	.15
106	Mike Lieberthal	.05
107	Wilson Alvarez	.05
108	Mike Mussina	.30
109	George Williams	.05
110	Cliff Floyd	.05
111	Shawn Estes	.05
112	Mark Grudzielanek	.05
113	Tony Gwynn	1.00
114	Alan Benes	.05
115	Terry Steinbach	.05
116	Greg Maddux	1.00
117	Andy Pettitte	.25
118	Dave Nilsson	.05
119	Deivi Cruz	.05
120	Carlos Delgado	.50
121	Scott Hatteberg	.05
122	John Olerud	.05
123	Moises Alou	.05
124	Garret Anderson	.05
125	Royce Clayton	.05
126	Dante Powell	.05
127	Tom Glavine	.35
128	Gary DiSarcina	.05
129	Terry Adams	.05
130	Raul Mondesi	.05
131	Dan Wilson	.05
132	Al Martin	.05
133	Mickey Morandini	.05
134	Rafael Palmeiro	.65
135	Juan Encarnacion	.05
136	Jim Pittsley	.05
137	*Magglio Ordonez*	1.00

No.	Player	NM/M
138	Will Clark	.05
139	Todd Helton	.65
140	Kelvim Escobar	.05
141	Esteban Loaiza	.05
142	John Jaha	.05
143	Jeff Fassero	.05
144	Harold Baines	.05
145	Butch Huskey	.05
146	Pat Meares	.05
147	Brian Giles	.05
148	Ramiro Mendoza	.05
149	John Smoltz	.05
150	Felix Martinez	.05
151	Jose Valentin	.05
152	Brad Rigby	.05
153	Ed Sprague	.05
154	Mike Hampton	.05
155	Mike Lansing	.05
156	Ray Lankford	.05
157	Bobby Bonilla	.05
158	Bill Mueller	.05
159	Jeffrey Hammonds	.05
160	Charles Nagy	.05
161	Rich Loiselle	.05
162	Al Leiter	.05
163	Larry Walker	.05
164	Chris Hoiles	.05
165	Jeff Montgomery	.05
166	Francisco Cordova	.05
167	James Baldwin	.05
168	Mark McLemore	.05
169	Kevin Appier	.05
170	Jamey Wright	.05
171	Nomar Garciaparra	1.00
172	Matt Franco	.05
173	Armando Benitez	.05
174	Jeromy Burnitz	.05
175	Ismael Valdes	.05
176	Lance Johnson	.05
177	Paul Sorrento	.05
178	Rondell White	.05
179	Kevin Elster	.05
180	Jason Giambi	.50
181	Carlos Baerga	.05
182	Russ Davis	.05
183	Ryan McGuire	.05
184	Eric Young	.05
185	Ron Gant	.05
186	Manny Alexander	.05
187	Scott Karl	.05
188	Brady Anderson	.05
189	Randall Simon	.05
190	Tim Belcher	.05
191	Jaret Wright	.05
192	Dante Bichette	.05
193	John Valentin	.05
194	Darren Bragg	.05
195	Mike Sweeney	.05
196	Craig Counsell	.05
197	Jaime Navarro	.05
198	Todd Dunn	.05
199	Ken Griffey Jr.	1.50
200	Juan Gonzalez	.40
201	Billy Wagner	.05
202	Tino Martinez	.05
203	Mark McGwire	2.00
204	Jeff D'Amico	.05
205	Rico Brogna	.05
206	Todd Hollandsworth	.05
207	Chad Curtis	.05
208	Tom Goodwin	.05
209	Neifi Perez	.05
210	Derek Bell	.05
211	Quilvio Veras	.05
212	Greg Vaughn	.05
213	Roberto Hernandez	.05
214	Arthur Rhodes	.05
215	Cal Eldred	.05
216	Bill Taylor	.05
217	Todd Greene	.05
218	Mario Valdez	.05
219	Ricky Bottalico	.05
220	Frank Rodriguez	.05
221	Rich Becker	.05
222	Roberto Duran	.05
223	Ivan Rodriguez	.65
224	Mike Jackson	.05
225	Deion Sanders	.05
226	Tony Womack	.05
227	Mark Kotsay	.05
228	Steve Trachsel	.05
229	Ryan Klesko	.05
230	Ken Cloude	.05
231	Luis Gonzalez	.05
232	Gary Gaetti	.05
233	Michael Tucker	.05
234	Shawn Green	.35
235	Ariel Prieto	.05
236	Kirt Manwaring	.05
237	Omar Vizquel	.05
238	Matt Beech	.05
239	Justin Thompson	.05
240	Bret Boone	.05
241	Derek Jeter	2.50
242	Ken Caminiti	.05
243	Jay Bell	.05
244	Kevin Tapani	.05
245	Jason Kendall	.05
246	Jose Guillen	.05
247	Mike Bordick	.05
248	Dustin Hermanson	.05
249	Darrin Fletcher	.05
250	Dave Hollins	.05
251	Ramon Martinez	.05
252	Hideki Irabu	.05
253	Mark Grace	.05
254	Jason Isringhausen	.05
255	Jose Cruz Jr.	.05
256	Brian Johnson	.05
257	Brad Ausmus	.05
258	Andruw Jones	.75
259	Doug Jones	.05
260	Jeff Shaw	.05
261	Chuck Finley	.05
262	Gary Sheffield	.45
263	David Segui	.05
264	John Smiley	.05
265	Tim Salmon	.05
266	J.T. Snow Jr.	.05
267	Alex Fernandez	.05
268	Matt Stairs	.05
269	B.J. Surhoff	.05
270	Keith Foulke	.05
271	Edgar Martinez	.05
272	Shannon Stewart	.05
273	Eduardo Perez	.05
274	Wally Joyner	.05
275	Kevin Young	.05
276	Eli Marrero	.05
277	Brad Radke	.05
278	Jamie Moyer	.05
279	Joe Girardi	.05
280	Troy O'Leary	.05
281	Aaron Sele	.05
282	Jose Offerman	.05
283	Scott Erickson	.05
284	Sean Berry	.05
285	Shigetosi Hasegawa	.05
286	Felix Heredia	.05
287	Willie McGee	.05
288	Alex Rodriguez	2.00
289	Ugueth Urbina	.05
290	Jon Lieber	.05
291	Fernando Tatis	.05
292	Chris Stynes	.05
293	Bernard Gilkey	.05
294	Joey Hamilton	.05
295	Matt Karchner	.05
296	Paul Wilson	.05
297	Mel Nieves	.05
298	*Kevin Millwood*	.75
299	Quinton McCracken	.05
300	Jerry DiPoto	.05
301	Jermaine Dye	.05
302	Travis Lee	.05
303	Ron Coomer	.05
304	Matt Williams	.05
305	Bobby Higginson	.05
306	Jorge Fabregas	.05
307	Hal Morris	.05
308	Jay Bell	.05
309	Joe Randa	.05
310	Andy Benes	.05
311	Sterling Hitchcock	.05
312	Jeff Suppan	.05
313	Shane Reynolds	.05
314	Willie Blair	.05
315	Scott Rolen	.65
316	Wilson Alvarez	.05
317	David Justice	.05
318	Fred McGriff	.05
319	Bobby Jones	.05
320	Wade Boggs	1.00
321	Tim Wakefield	.05
322	Tony Saunders	.05
323	David Cone	.05
324	Roberto Hernandez	.05
325	Jose Canseco	.45
326	Kevin Stocker	.05
327	Gerald Williams	.05
328	Quinton McCracken	.05
329	Mark Gardner	.05
330	Ben Grieve	.05
331	Kevin Brown	.05
332	*Mike Lowell*	1.00
333	Jed Hansen	.05
334	Abraham Nunez	.05
335	John Thomson	.05
336	Derrek Lee	.05
337	Mike Piazza	1.50
338	Brad Fullmer	.05
339	Ray Durham	.05
340	Kerry Wood	.50
341	*Kevin Polcovich*	.05
342	Russ Johnson	.05
343	Darryl Hamilton	.05
344	David Ortiz	.45
345	Kevin Orie	.05
346	Sean Casey	.25
347	Juan Guzman	.05
348	Ruben Rivera	.05
349	Rick Aguilera	.05
350	Bobby Estalella	.05
351	Bobby Witt	.05
352	Paul Konerko	.25
353	Matt Morris	.05
354	Carl Pavano	.05
355	Todd Zeile	.05
356	Kevin Brown	.05
357	Alex Gonzalez	.05
358	Chuck Knoblauch	.05
359	Joey Cora	.05
360	Mike Lansing	.05
361	Adrian Beltre	.45
362	Dennis Eckersley	.65
363	A.J. Hinch	.05
364	Kenny Lofton	.05
365	Alex Gonzalez	.05
366	Henry Rodriguez	.05
367	*Mike Stoner*	.05
368	Darryl Kile	.05
369	Carl Pavano	.05
370	Walt Weiss	.05
371	Kris Benson	.05
372	Cecil Fielder	.05
373	Dermal Brown	.05
374	Rod Beck	.05
375	Eric Milton	.05
376	Travis Fryman	.05
377	Preston Wilson	.10
378	Chili Davis	.05
379	Travis Lee	.10
380	Jim Leyritz	.05
381	Vernon Wells	.05
382	Joe Carter	.05
383	J.J. Davis	.05
384	Marquis Grissom	.05
385	*Mike Cuddyer*	.50
386	Rickey Henderson	.75
387	*Chris Enochs*	.10
388	Andres Galarraga	.05
389	Jason Dellaero	.05
390	Robb Nen	.05
391	Mark Mangum	.05
392	Jeff Blauser	.05
393	Adam Kennedy	.05
394	Bob Abreu	.05
395	*Jack Cust*	.25
396	Jose Vizcaino	.05
397	Jon Garland	.05
398	Pedro Martinez	.75
399	Aaron Akin	.05
400	Jeff Conine	.05

One of a Kind

	NM/M
Common Player:	2.00
Stars:	12X

Production 150 sets
(See 1998 Stadium Club for checklist and base card values.)

First Day Issue

	NM/M
Common Player:	2.00
Stars:	10X

Production 200 sets
(See 1998 Stadium Club for checklist and base card values.)

Printing Plates

	NM/M
Common Player:	25.00

(See 1998 Stadium Club for checklist.)

Bowman Preview

		NM/M
Complete Set (10):		10.00
Common Player:		.25
Inserted 1:12		
BP1	Nomar Garciaparra	1.00
BP2	Scott Rolen	.65
BP3	Ken Griffey Jr.	1.50
BP4	Frank Thomas	.75
BP5	Larry Walker	.25
BP6	Mike Piazza	1.50
BP7	Chipper Jones	1.00
BP8	Tino Martinez	.25
BP9	Mark McGwire	2.00
BP10	Barry Bonds	2.50

Bowman Prospect Preview

		NM/M
Complete Set (10):		3.00
Common Player:		.25
Inserted 1:12		
BP1	Ben Grieve	.25
BP2	Brad Fullmer	.25
BP3	Ryan Anderson	.25
BP4	Mark Kotsay	.25
BP5	Bobby Estalella	.25
BP6	Juan Encarnacion	.25
BP7	Todd Helton	2.00
BP8	Mike Lowell	.25
BP9	A.J. Hinch	.25
BP10	Richard Hidalgo	.25

Co-Signers

		NM/M
Common Card:		10.00
Group A 1:4,372		
Group B 1:1,457		
Group C 1:121		
CS1	Nomar Garciaparra, Scott Rolen (A)	120.00
CS2	Nomar Garciaparra, Derek Jeter (B)	250.00
CS3	Nomar Garciaparra, Eric Karros (C)	60.00
CS4	Scott Rolen, Derek Jeter (C)	100.00
CS5	Scott Rolen, Eric Karros (B)	40.00
CS6	Derek Jeter, Eric Karros (A)	150.00
CS7	Travis Lee, Jose Cruz Jr. (B)	15.00
CS8	Travis Lee, Mark Kotsay (C)	10.00
CS9	Travis Lee, Paul Konerko (A)	25.00
CS10	Jose Cruz Jr., Mark Kotsay (A)	25.00
CS11	Jose Cruz Jr., Paul Konerko (C)	12.00
CS12	Mark Kotsay, Paul Konerko (B)	20.00
CS13	Tony Gwynn, Larry Walker (A)	120.00
CS14	Tony Gwynn, Mark Grudzielanek (C)	30.00
CS15	Tony Gwynn, Andres Galarraga (B)	60.00

CS16	Larry Walker, Mark Grudzielanek (B)	40.00
CS17	Larry Walker, Andres Galarraga (C)	30.00
CS18	Mark Grudzielanek, Andres Galarraga (A)	25.00
CS19	Sandy Alomar, Roberto Alomar (A)	75.00
CS20	Sandy Alomar, Andy Pettitte (C)	20.00
CS21	Sandy Alomar, Tino Martinez (B)	40.00
CS22	Roberto Alomar, Andy Pettitte (B)	50.00
CS23	Roberto Alomar, Tino Martinez (C)	25.00
CS24	Andy Pettitte, Tino Martinez (A)	75.00
CS25	Tony Clark, Todd Hundley (A)	25.00
CS26	Tony Clark, Tim Salmon (B)	30.00
CS27	Tony Clark, Robin Ventura (C)	10.00
CS28	Todd Hundley, Tim Salmon (C)	15.00
CS29	Todd Hundley, Robin Ventura (B)	12.00
CS30	Tim Salmon, Robin Ventura (A)	50.00
CS31	Roger Clemens, Randy Johnson (B)	175.00
CS32	Roger Clemens, Jaret Wright (A)	140.00
CS33	Roger Clemens, Matt Morris (C)	100.00
CS34	Randy Johnson, Jaret Wright (C)	50.00
CS35	Randy Johnson, Matt Morris (A)	85.00
CS36	Jaret Wright, Matt Morris (B)	20.00

In the Wings

		NM/M
Complete Set (15):		6.00
Common Player:		.50
Inserted 1:36		
W1	Juan Encarnacion	.50
W2	Brad Fullmer	.50
W3	Ben Grieve	.50
W4	Todd Helton	3.00
W5	Richard Hidalgo	.50
W6	Russ Johnson	.50
W7	Paul Konerko	.75
W8	Mark Kotsay	.50
W9	Derrek Lee	1.00
W10	Travis Lee	.50
W11	Eli Marrero	.50
W12	David Ortiz	.75
W13	Randall Simon	.50
W14	Shannon Stewart	.50
W15	Fernando Tatis	.50

Never Compromise

		NM/M
Complete Set (20):		10.00
Common Player:		.15
Inserted 1:12		
NC1	Cal Ripken Jr.	2.00
NC2	Ivan Rodriguez	.50
NC3	Ken Griffey Jr.	1.00
NC4	Frank Thomas	.60
NC5	Tony Gwynn	.75
NC6	Mike Piazza	1.00
NC7	Randy Johnson	.60
NC8	Greg Maddux	.75
NC9	Roger Clemens	.85
NC10	Derek Jeter	2.00
NC11	Chipper Jones	.75
NC12	Barry Bonds	2.00
NC13	Larry Walker	.15
NC14	Jeff Bagwell	.60
NC15	Barry Larkin	.15
NC16	Ken Caminiti	.15
NC17	Mark McGwire	1.50
NC18	Manny Ramirez	.60
NC19	Tim Salmon	.15
NC20	Paul Molitor	.60

Playing with Passion

		NM/M
Complete Set (10):		10.00
Common Player:		.35
Inserted 1:12		
P1	Bernie Williams	.35
P2	Jim Edmonds	.35
P3	Chipper Jones	1.00
P4	Cal Ripken Jr.	3.00
P5	Craig Biggio	.35
P6	Juan Gonzalez	.45
P7	Alex Rodriguez	2.25
P8	Tino Martinez	.35
P9	Mike Piazza	1.50
P10	Ken Griffey Jr.	1.50

Royal Court

		NM/M
Complete Set (15):		15.00
Common Player:		.50
Inserted 1:36		
RC1	Ken Griffey Jr.	2.00
RC2	Frank Thomas	1.25
RC3	Mike Piazza	2.00
RC4	Chipper Jones	1.50
RC5	Mark McGwire	2.50
RC6	Cal Ripken Jr.	3.00
RC7	Jeff Bagwell	1.25
RC8	Barry Bonds	3.00
RC9	Juan Gonzalez	.85
RC10	Alex Rodriguez	2.50
RC11	Travis Lee	.50
RC12	Paul Konerko	.75
RC13	Todd Helton	1.00
RC14	Ben Grieve	.50
RC15	Mark Kotsay	.50

Screen Plays Sound Chips

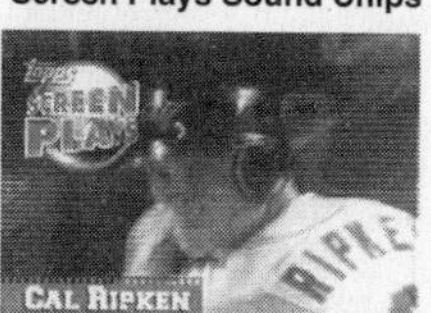

		NM/M
SC1	Cal Ripken Jr.	5.00

Triumvirate

		NM/M
Complete Set (54):		70.00
Complete Series 1 (24):		30.00
Complete Series 2 (30):		40.00
Common Player:		.50
Luminous 1:48		
Luminescents 1:192:		1.5X
Illuminators 1:384:		2.5X
T1a	Chipper Jones	2.50
T1b	Andruw Jones	2.00
T1c	Kenny Lofton	.50
T2a	Derek Jeter	5.00
T2b	Bernie Williams	.50
T2c	Tino Martinez	.50
T3a	Jay Buhner	.50
T3b	Edgar Martinez	.50
T3c	Ken Griffey Jr.	3.00
T4a	Albert Belle	.50
T4b	Robin Ventura	.50
T4c	Frank Thomas	2.00
T5a	Brady Anderson	.50
T5b	Cal Ripken Jr.	5.00
T5c	Rafael Palmeiro	1.50
T6a	Mike Piazza	3.00
T6b	Raul Mondesi	.50
T6c	Eric Karros	.50
T7a	Vinny Castilla	.50
T7b	Andres Galarraga	.50
T7c	Larry Walker	.50
T8a	Jim Thome	1.50
T8b	Manny Ramirez	2.00
T8c	David Justice	.50
T9a	Mike Mussina	.75
T9b	Greg Maddux	2.50
T9c	Randy Johnson	2.00
T10a	Mike Piazza	3.00
T10b	Sandy Alomar	.50
T10c	Ivan Rodriguez	1.50
T11a	Mark McGwire	4.00
T11b	Tino Martinez	.50
T11c	Frank Thomas	2.00
T12a	Roberto Alomar	.75
T12b	Chuck Knoblauch	.50
T12c	Craig Biggio	.50
T13a	Cal Ripken Jr.	5.00
T13b	Chipper Jones	2.50
T13c	Ken Caminiti	.50
T14a	Derek Jeter	5.00
T14b	Nomar Garciaparra	2.50
T14c	Alex Rodriguez	4.00
T15a	Barry Bonds	5.00
T15b	David Justice	.50
T15c	Albert Belle	.50
T16a	Bernie Williams	.50
T16b	Ken Griffey Jr.	3.00
T16c	Ray Lankford	.50
T17a	Tim Salmon	.50
T17b	Larry Walker	.50
T17c	Tony Gwynn	2.50
T18a	Paul Molitor	2.00
T18b	Edgar Martinez	.50
T18c	Juan Gonzalez	1.00

1999 STADIUM CLUB

		NM/M
Complete Set (355):		40.00
Complete Series 1 (170):		20.00
Complete Series 2 (185):		20.00
Common Player:		.05
Common SP (141-160; 336-355):		.50
Inserted 1:3		
Pack (6):		1.25
Wax Box (24):		25.00
1	Alex Rodriguez	2.00
2	Chipper Jones	1.50
3	Rusty Greer	.05
4	Jim Edmonds	.05
5	Ron Gant	.05
6	Kevin Polcovich	.05
7	Darryl Strawberry	.05
8	Bill Mueller	.05
9	Vinny Castilla	.05
10	Wade Boggs	1.50
11	Jose Lima	.05
12	Darren Dreifort	.05
13	Jay Bell	.05
14	Ben Grieve	.05
15	Shawn Green	.35
16	Andres Galarraga	.05
17	Bartolo Colon	.05
18	Francisco Cordova	.05
19	Paul O'Neill	.05
20	Trevor Hoffman	.05
21	Darren Oliver	.05
22	John Franco	.05
23	Eli Marrero	.05
24	Roberto Hernandez	.05
25	Craig Biggio	.05
26	Brad Fullmer	.05
27	Scott Erickson	.05
28	Tom Gordon	.05
29	Brian Hunter	.05
30	Raul Mondesi	.05
31	Rick Reed	.05
32	Jose Canseco	.50
33	Robb Nen	.05
34	Turner Ward	.05
35	Bret Boone	.05
36	Jose Offerman	.05
37	Matt Lawton	.05
38	David Wells	.05
39	Bob Abreu	.10
40	Jeromy Burnitz	.05
41	Deivi Cruz	.05
42	Mike Cameron	.05
43	Rico Brogna	.05
44	Dmitri Young	.05
45	Chuck Knoblauch	.05
46	Johnny Damon	.35
47	Brian Meadows	.05
48	Jeremi Gonzalez	.05
49	Gary DiSarcina	.05
50	Frank Thomas	1.00
51	F.P. Santangelo	.05
52	Tom Candiotti	.05
53	Shane Reynolds	.05
54	Rod Beck	.05
55	Rey Ordonez	.05
56	Todd Helton	.75
57	Mickey Morandini	.05
58	Jorge Posada	.05
59	Mike Mussina	.30
60	Bobby Bonilla	.05
61	David Segui	.05
62	Brian McRae	.05
63	Fred McGriff	.05
64	Brett Tomko	.05
65	Derek Jeter	2.50
66	Sammy Sosa	1.50
67	Kenny Rogers	.05
68	Dave Nilsson	.05
69	Eric Young	.05
70	Mark McGwire	2.00
71	Kenny Lofton	.05
72	Tom Glavine	.35
73	Joey Hamilton	.05
74	John Valentin	.05
75	Mariano Rivera	.15
76	Ray Durham	.05
77	Tony Clark	.05
78	Livan Hernandez	.05
79	Rickey Henderson	1.00
80	Vladimir Guerrero	1.00
81	J.T. Snow Jr.	.05
82	Juan Guzman	.05
83	Darryl Hamilton	.05
84	Matt Anderson	.05
85	Travis Lee	.05
86	Joe Randa	.05
87	Dave Dellucci	.05
88	Moises Alou	.05
89	Alex Gonzalez	.05
90	Tony Womack	.05
91	Neifi Perez	.05
92	Travis Fryman	.05
93	Masato Yoshii	.05
94	Woody Williams	.05
95	Ray Lankford	.05
96	Roger Clemens	1.50
97	Dustin Hermanson	.05
98	Joe Carter	.05
99	Jason Schmidt	.05
100	Greg Maddux	1.50
101	Kevin Tapani	.05
102	Charles Johnson	.05
103	Derrek Lee	.50
104	Pete Harnisch	.05
105	Dante Bichette	.05
106	Scott Brosius	.05
107	Mike Caruso	.05
108	Eddie Taubensee	.05
109	Jeff Fassero	.05
110	Marquis Grissom	.05
111	Jose Hernandez	.05
112	Chan Ho Park	.05
113	Wally Joyner	.05
114	Bobby Estalella	.05
115	Pedro Martinez	1.00
116	Shawn Estes	.05
117	Walt Weiss	.05
118	John Mabry	.05
119	Brian Johnson	.05
120	Jim Thome	.65
121	Bill Spiers	.05
122	John Olerud	.05
123	Jeff King	.05
124	Tim Belcher	.05
125	John Wetteland	.05
126	Tony Gwynn	1.50
127	Brady Anderson	.05
128	Randy Winn	.05
129	Devon White	.05
130	Eric Karros	.05
131	Kevin Millwood	.05
132	Andy Benes	.05
133	Andy Ashby	.05
134	Ron Comer	.05
135	Juan Gonzalez	.50
136	Randy Johnson	1.00
137	Aaron Sele	.05
138	Edgardo Alfonzo	.05
139	B.J. Surhoff	.05
140	Jose Vizcaino	.05
141	*Chad Moeller*	.75

142	*Mike Zwicka*	.50
143	Angel Pena	.50
144	*Nick Johnson*	2.00
145	*Giuseppe Chiaramonte*	.50
146	*Kit Pellow*	.50
147	*Clayton Andrews*	.50
148	*Jerry Hairston Jr.*	.75
149	*Jason Tyner*	.50
150	*Chip Ambres*	.50
151	*Pat Burrell*	2.00
152	*Josh McKinley*	.75
153	*Choo Freeman*	.75
154	*Rick Elder*	.50
155	*Eric Valent*	.75
156	*Jeff Winchester*	.50
157	*Mike Nannini*	.50
158	*Mamon Tucker*	.50
159	*Nate Bump*	.50
160	*Andy Brown*	.50
161	Troy Glaus	1.00
162	Adrian Beltre	.45
163	Mitch Meluskey	.05
164	Alex Gonzalez	.05
165	George Lombard	.05
166	Eric Chavez	.25
167	Ruben Mateo	.05
168	Calvin Pickering	.05
169	Gabe Kapler	.05
170	Bruce Chen	.05
171	Darin Erstad	.15
172	Sandy Alomar	.05
173	Miguel Cairo	.05
174	Jason Kendall	.05
175	Cal Ripken Jr.	2.50
176	Darryl Kile	.05
177	David Cone	.05
178	Mike Sweeney	.05
179	Royce Clayton	.05
180	Curt Schilling	.25
181	Barry Larkin	.05
182	Eric Milton	.05
183	Ellis Burks	.05
184	A.J. Hinch	.05
185	Garret Anderson	.05
186	Sean Bergman	.05
187	Shannon Stewart	.05
188	Bernard Gilkey	.05
189	Jeff Blauser	.05
190	Andruw Jones	1.00
191	Omar Daal	.05
192	Jeff Kent	.05
193	Mark Kotsay	.05
194	Dave Burba	.05
195	Bobby Higginson	.05
196	Hideki Irabu	.05
197	Jamie Moyer	.05
198	Doug Glanville	.05
199	Quinton McCracken	.05
200	Ken Griffey Jr.	1.75
201	Mike Lieberthal	.05
202	Carl Everett	.05
203	Omar Vizquel	.05
204	Mike Lansing	.05
205	Manny Ramirez	1.00
206	Ryan Klesko	.05
207	Jeff Montgomery	.05
208	Chad Curtis	.05
209	Rick Helling	.05
210	Justin Thompson	.05
211	Tom Goodwin	.05
212	Todd Dunwoody	.05
213	Kevin Young	.05
214	Tony Saunders	.05
215	Gary Sheffield	.45
216	Jaret Wright	.05
217	Quilvio Veras	.05
218	Marty Cordova	.05
219	Tino Martinez	.05
220	Scott Rolen	.75
221	Fernando Tatis	.05
222	Damion Easley	.05
223	Aramis Ramirez	.05
224	Brad Radke	.05
225	Nomar Garciaparra	1.50
226	Maggio Ordonez	.05
227	Andy Pettitte	.20
228	David Ortiz	.45
229	Todd Jones	.05
230	Larry Walker	.05
231	Tim Wakefield	.05
232	Jose Guillen	.05
233	Gregg Olson	.05
234	Ricky Gutierrez	.05
235	Todd Walker	.05
236	Abraham Nunez	.05
237	Sean Casey	.15
238	Greg Norton	.05
239	Bret Saberhagen	.05
240	Bernie Williams	.05
241	Tim Salmon	.05
242	Jason Giambi	.50
243	Fernando Vina	.05
244	Darrin Fletcher	.05
245	Greg Vaughn	.05
246	Dennis Reyes	.05
247	Hideo Nomo	.50
248	Reggie Sanders	.05
249	Mike Hampton	.05
250	Kerry Wood	.50
251	Ismael Valdes	.05
252	Pat Hentgen	.05
253	Scott Spiezio	.05
254	Chuck Finley	.05
255	Troy Glaus	.75
256	Bobby Jones	.05
257	Wayne Gomes	.05
258	Rondell White	.05
259	Todd Zeile	.05
260	Matt Williams	.05
261	Henry Rodriguez	.05
262	Matt Stairs	.05
263	Jose Valentin	.05
264	David Justice	.05
265	Javy Lopez	.05
266	Matt Morris	.05
267	Steve Trachsel	.05
268	Edgar Martinez	.05
269	Al Martin	.05
270	Ivan Rodriguez	.75
271	Carlos Delgado	.50
272	Mark Grace	.05
273	Ugueth Urbina	.05
274	Jay Buhner	.05
275	Mike Piazza	1.75
276	Rick Aguilera	.05
277	Javier Valentin	.05
278	Brian Anderson	.05
279	Cliff Floyd	.05
280	Barry Bonds	2.50
281	Troy O'Leary	.05
282	Seth Greisinger	.05
283	Mark Grudzielanek	.05
284	Jose Cruz Jr.	.05
285	Jeff Bagwell	1.00
286	John Smoltz	.05
287	Jeff Cirillo	.05
288	Richie Sexson	.05
289	Charles Nagy	.05
290	Pedro Martinez	1.00
291	Juan Encarnacion	.05
292	Phil Nevin	.05
293	Terry Steinbach	.05
294	Miguel Tejada	.15
295	Dan Wilson	.05
296	Chris Peters	.05
297	Brian Moehler	.05
298	Jason Christiansen	.05
299	Kelly Stinnett	.05
300	Dwight Gooden	.05
301	Randy Velarde	.05
302	Kirt Manwaring	.05
303	Jeff Abbott	.05
304	Dave Hollins	.05
305	Kerry Ligtenberg	.05
306	Aaron Boone	.05
307	Carlos Hernandez	.05
308	Mike DiFelice	.05
309	Brian Meadows	.05
310	Tim Bogar	.05
311	Greg Vaughn	.05
312	Brant Brown	.05
313	Steve Finley	.05
314	Bret Boone	.05
315	Albert Belle	.05
316	Robin Ventura	.05
317	Eric Davis	.05
318	Todd Hundley	.05
319	Jose Offerman	.05
320	Kevin Brown	.05
321	Denny Neagle	.05
322	Brian Jordan	.05
323	Brian Giles	.05
324	Bobby Bonilla	.05
325	Roberto Alomar	.20
326	Ken Caminiti	.05
327	Todd Stottlemyre	.05
328	Randy Johnson	1.00
329	Luis Gonzalez	.05
330	Rafael Palmeiro	.75
331	Devon White	.05
332	Will Clark	.05
333	Dean Palmer	.05
334	Gregg Jefferies	.05
335	Mo Vaughn	.05
336	*Brad Lidge*	2.00
337	*Chris George*	.75
338	*Austin Kearns*	1.50
339	*Matt Belisle*	.75
340	*Nate Cornejo*	.75
341	*Matt Holliday*	.75
342	*J.M. Gold*	.50
343	*Matt Roney*	.50
344	*Seth Etherton*	.75
345	*Adam Everett*	.75
346	Marlon Anderson	.50
347	Ron Belliard	.50
348	Fernando Seguignol	.50
349	Michael Barrett	.50
350	Dernell Stenson	.50
351	Ryan Anderson	.50
352	Ramon Hernandez	.50
353	Jeremy Giambi	.50
354	Ricky Ledee	.50
355	Carlos Lee	1.00

One of a Kind

	NM/M
Common Player:	2.00
Stars:	8X
SP Stars:	4X

(See 1999 Stadium Club for checklist and base card values.)

First Day Issue

	NM/M
Common Player:	2.00
Stars:	8X
SP Stars:	4X

(See 1999 Stadium Club for checklist and base card values.)

Printing Plates

	NM/M
Common Player:	25.00

(See 1999 Stadium Club for checklist.)

Autographs

		NM/M
Common Player:		10.00
Inserted 1:1,107		
1	Alex Rodriguez	75.00
2	Chipper Jones	30.00
3	Barry Bonds	175.00
4	Tino Martinez	25.00
5	Ben Grieve	10.00
6	Juan Gonzalez	17.50
7	Vladimir Guerrero	30.00
8	Albert Belle	17.50
9	Kerry Wood	25.00
10	Todd Helton	17.50

Co-Signers

		NM/M
Common Group A:		90.00
Inserted 1:18,085		
Common Group B:		20.00
Inserted 1:9043		
Common Group C:		9.00
Inserted 1:3014		
Common Group D:		6.00
Inserted 1:254		
CS1	Ben Grieve, Richie Sexson (D)	15.00
CS2	Todd Helton, Troy Glaus (D)	50.00
CS3	Alex Rodriguez, Scott Rolen (D)	85.00
CS4	Derek Jeter, Chipper Jones (D)	150.00
CS5	Cliff Floyd, Eli Marrero (D)	6.00
CS6	Jay Buhner, Kevin Young (D)	8.00
CS7	Ben Grieve, Troy Glaus (C)	40.00
CS8	Todd Helton, Richie Sexson (C)	40.00
CS9	Alex Rodriguez, Chipper Jones (C)	125.00
CS10	Derek Jeter, Scott Rolen (C)	125.00
CS11	Cliff Floyd, Kevin Young (C)	10.00
CS12	Jay Buhner, Eli Marrero (B)	10.00
CS13	Ben Grieve, Todd Helton (B)	50.00
CS14	Richie Sexson, Troy Glaus (B)	40.00
CS15	Alex Rodriguez, Derek Jeter (B)	350.00
CS16	Chipper Jones, Scott Rolen (B)	150.00
CS17	Cliff Floyd, Jay Buhner (B)	15.00
CS18	Eli Marrero, Kevin Young (B)	20.00
CS19	Ben Grieve, Todd Helton, Richie Sexson, Troy Glaus (A)	180.00
CS20	Alex Rodriguez, Derek Jeter, Chipper Jones, Scott Rolen (A)	2,500
CS21	Cliff Floyd, Jay Buhner, Eli Marrero, Kevin Young (A)	100.00
CS22	Edgardo Alfonzo, Jose Guillen (D)	15.00
CS23	Mike Lowell, Ricardo Rincon (D)	10.00
CS24	Juan Gonzalez, Vinny Castilla (D)	20.00
CS25	Moises Alou, Roger Clemens (D)	60.00
CS26	Scott Spezio, Tony Womack (D)	10.00
CS27	Fernando Vina, Quilvio Veras (D)	10.00
CS28	Edgardo Alfonzo, Ricardo Rincon (C)	10.00
CS29	Jose Guillen, Mike Lowell (C)	10.00
CS30	Juan Gonzalez, Moises Alou (C)	25.00
CS31	Roger Clemens, Vinny Castilla (C)	85.00
CS32	Scott Spezio, Fernando Vina (C)	10.00
CS33	Tony Womack, Quilvio Veras (B)	20.00
CS34	Edgardo Alfonzo, Mike Lowell (B)	30.00
CS35	Jose Guillen, Ricardo Rincon (B)	30.00
CS36	Juan Gonzalez, Roger Clemens (B)	135.00
CS37	Moises Alou, Vinny Castilla (B)	30.00
CS38	Scott Spezio, Quilvio Veras (B)	20.00
CS39	Tony Womack, Fernando Vina (B)	20.00
CS40	Edgardo Alfonzo, Jose Guillen, Mike Lowell, Ricardo Rincon (A)	90.00
CS41	Juan Gonzalez, Moises Alou, Roger Clemens, Vinny Castilla (A)	900.00
CS42	Scott Spezio, Tony Womack, Fernando Vina, Quilvio Veras (A)	90.00

Chrome

		NM/M
Complete Set (40):		45.00
Common Player:		.50
Inserted 1:24		
Refractors:		2X
Inserted 1:96		
1	Nomar Garciaparra	2.00
2	Kerry Wood	1.00
3	Jeff Bagwell	1.50
4	Ivan Rodriguez	1.25
5	Albert Belle	.50
6	Gary Sheffield	1.00
7	Andruw Jones	1.50
8	Kevin Brown	.50

9	David Cone	.50
10	Darin Erstad	.75
11	Manny Ramirez	1.50
12	Larry Walker	.50
13	Mike Piazza	2.50
14	Cal Ripken Jr.	4.00
15	Pedro Martinez	1.50
16	Greg Vaughn	.50
17	Barry Bonds	4.00
18	Mo Vaughn	.50
19	Bernie Williams	.50
20	Ken Griffey Jr.	2.50
21	Alex Rodriguez	3.00
22	Chipper Jones	2.00
23	Ben Grieve	.50
24	Frank Thomas	1.50
25	Derek Jeter	4.00
26	Sammy Sosa	2.00
27	Mark McGwire	3.00
28	Vladimir Guerrero	1.50
29	Greg Maddux	2.00
30	Juan Gonzalez	.75
31	Troy Glaus	1.25
32	Adrian Beltre	1.25
33	Mitch Meluskey	.50
34	Alex Gonzalez	.50
35	George Lombard	.50
36	Eric Chavez	.75
37	Ruben Mateo	.50
38	Calvin Pickering	.50
39	Gabe Kapler	.50
40	Bruce Chen	.50

Never Compromise

		NM/M
Complete Set (20):		10.00
Common Player:		.25
Inserted 1:12		
NC1	Mark McGwire	1.00
NC2	Sammy Sosa	.65
NC3	Ken Griffey Jr.	.75
NC4	Greg Maddux	.65
NC5	Barry Bonds	1.50
NC6	Alex Rodriguez	1.00
NC7	Darin Erstad	.35
NC8	Roger Clemens	.65
NC9	Nomar Garciaparra	.65
NC10	Derek Jeter	1.50
NC11	Cal Ripken Jr.	1.50
NC12	Mike Piazza	.75
NC13	Greg Vaughn	.25
NC14	Andres Galarraga	.25
NC15	Vinny Castilla	.25
NC16	Jeff Bagwell	.50
NC17	Chipper Jones	.65
NC18	Eric Chavez	.35
NC19	Orlando Hernandez	.25
NC20	Troy Glaus	.40

Photography

		NM/M
Complete Set (10):		200.00
Common Player:		20.00
1	Alex Rodriguez	20.00
65	Derek Jeter	20.00
66	Sammy Sosa	20.00
135	Juan Gonzalez	20.00
NC1	Mark McGwire	20.00
NC3	Ken Griffey Jr.	20.00
SCA5	Ben Grieve	20.00
SCC1	Nomar Garciaparra	20.00
SCC2	Kerry Wood	20.00
SCC13	Mike Piazza	20.00

Triumvirate

		NM/M
Complete Set (48):		75.00
Common Player:		.50
Inserted 1:36		
Luminescents:		1.5X

Inserted 1:144		
Illuminators:		2.5X
Inserted 1:288		
T1A	Greg Vaughn	.50
T1B	Ken Caminiti	.50
T1C	Tony Gwynn	2.50
T2A	Andruw Jones	2.00
T2B	Chipper Jones	2.50
T2C	Andres Galarraga	.50
T3A	Jay Buhner	.50
T3B	Ken Griffey Jr.	3.00
T3C	Alex Rodriguez	4.00
T4A	Derek Jeter	6.00
T4B	Tino Martinez	.50
T4C	Bernie Williams	.50
T5A	Brian Jordan	.50
T5B	Ray Lankford	.50
T5C	Mark McGwire	4.00
T6A	Jeff Bagwell	2.00
T6B	Craig Biggio	.50
T6C	Randy Johnson	2.00
T7A	Nomar Garciaparra	2.50
T7B	Pedro Martinez	2.00
T7C	Mo Vaughn	.50
T8A	Mark Grace	.50
T8B	Sammy Sosa	2.50
T8C	Kerry Wood	1.00
T9A	Alex Rodriguez	4.00
T9B	Nomar Garciaparra	2.50
T9C	Derek Jeter	6.00
T10A	Todd Helton	1.50
T10B	Travis Lee	.50
T10C	Pat Burrell	1.50
T11A	Greg Maddux	2.50
T11B	Kerry Wood	1.00
T11C	Tom Glavine	.75
T12A	Chipper Jones	2.50
T12B	Vinny Castilla	.50
T12C	Scott Rolen	1.50
T13A	Juan Gonzalez	1.00
T13B	Ken Griffey Jr.	3.00
T13C	Ben Grieve	.50
T14A	Sammy Sosa	3.00
T14B	Vladimir Guerrero	2.00
T14C	Barry Bonds	6.00
T15A	Frank Thomas	2.00
T15B	Jim Thome	1.50
T15C	Tino Martinez	.50
T16A	Mark McGwire	4.00
T16B	Andres Galarraga	.50
T16C	Jeff Bagwell	2.00

2000 STADIUM CLUB

		NM/M
Complete Set (250):		80.00
Common Player:		.15
Common SP (201-250):		2.00
Inserted 1:5		
Pack (6):		1.50
Wax Box (24):		30.00
1	Nomar Garciaparra	1.25
2	Brian Jordan	.15
3	Mark Grace	.25
4	Jeromy Burnitz	.15
5	Shane Reynolds	.15
6	Alex Gonzalez	.15
7	Jose Offerman	.15
8	Orlando Hernandez	.15
9	Mike Caruso	.15
10	Tony Clark	.15
11	Sean Casey	.25
12	Johnny Damon	.25
13	Dante Bichette	.15
14	Kevin Young	.15
15	Juan Gonzalez	.75
16	Chipper Jones	1.00
17	Quilvio Veras	.15
18	Trevor Hoffman	.15
19	Roger Cedeno	.15
20	Ellis Burks	.15
21	Richie Sexson	.15
22	Gary Sheffield	.40
23	Delino DeShields	.15
24	Wade Boggs	1.00
25	Ray Lankford	.15
26	Kevin Appier	.15
27	Roy Halladay	.15
28	Harold Baines	.15
29	Todd Zeile	.15
30	Barry Larkin	.15
31	Ron Coomer	.15
32	Jorge Posada	.15
33	Magglio Ordonez	.15
34	Brian Giles	.15
35	Jeff Kent	.15
36	Henry Rodriguez	.15
37	Fred McGriff	.15
38	Shawn Green	.50
39	Derek Bell	.15
40	Ben Grieve	.15
41	Dave Nilsson	.15
42	Mo Vaughn	.15
43	Rondell White	.15
44	Doug Glanville	.15
45	Paul O'Neill	.15
46	Carlos Lee	.15
47	Vinny Castilla	.15
48	Mike Sweeney	.15
49	Rico Brogna	.15
50	Alex Rodriguez	1.50
51	Luis Castillo	.15
52	Kevin Brown	.15
53	Jose Vidro	.15
54	John Smoltz	.15
55	Garret Anderson	.15
56	Matt Stairs	.15
57	Omar Vizquel	.15
58	Tom Goodwin	.15
59	Scott Brosius	.15
60	Robin Ventura	.15
61	B.J. Surhoff	.15
62	Andy Ashby	.15
63	Chris Widger	.15
64	Tim Hudson	.40
65	Javy Lopez	.15
66	Tim Salmon	.25
67	Warren Morris	.15
68	John Wetteland	.15
69	Gabe Kapler	.15
70	Bernie Williams	.30
71	Rickey Henderson	.75
72	Andruw Jones	.75
73	Eric Young	.15
74	Bob Abreu	.15
75	David Cone	.15
76	Rusty Greer	.15
77	Ron Belliard	.15
78	Troy Glaus	.75
79	Mike Hampton	.15
80	Miguel Tejada	.30
81	Jeff Cirillo	.15
82	Todd Hundley	.15
83	Roberto Alomar	.40
84	Charles Johnson	.15
85	Rafael Palmeiro	.65
86	Doug Mientkiewicz	.15
87	Mariano Rivera	.25
88	Neifi Perez	.15
89	Jermaine Dye	.15
90	Ivan Rodriguez	.65
91	Jay Buhner	.15
92	Pokey Reese	.15
93	John Olerud	.15
94	Brady Anderson	.15
95	Manny Ramirez	.75
96	Keith Osik	.15
97	Mickey Morandini	.15
98	Matt Williams	.15
99	Eric Karros	.15
100	Ken Griffey Jr.	1.25
101	Bret Boone	.15
102	Ryan Klesko	.15
103	Craig Biggio	.15
104	John Jaha	.15
105	Vladimir Guerrero	.75
106	Devon White	.15
107	Tony Womack	.15
108	Marvin Benard	.15
109	Kenny Lofton	.15
110	Preston Wilson	.15
111	Al Leiter	.15
112	Reggie Sanders	.15
113	Scott Williamson	.15
114	Deivi Cruz	.15
115	Carlos Beltran	.50
116	Ray Durham	.15
117	Ricky Ledee	.15
118	Torii Hunter	.15
119	John Valentin	.15
120	Scott Rolen	.65
121	Jason Kendall	.15
122	Dave Martinez	.15
123	Jim Thome	.65
124	David Bell	.15
125	Jose Canseco	.45
126	Jose Lima	.15
127	Carl Everett	.15
128	Kevin Millwood	.15
129	Bill Spiers	.15
130	Omar Daal	.15
131	Miguel Cairo	.15
132	Mark Grudzielanek	.15
133	David Justice	.15
134	Russ Ortiz	.15
135	Mike Piazza	1.25
136	Brian Meadows	.15
137	Tony Gwynn	1.00
138	Cal Ripken Jr.	2.00
139	Kris Benson	.15
140	Larry Walker	.15
141	Cristian Guzman	.15
142	Tino Martinez	.25
143	Chris Singleton	.15
144	Lee Stevens	.15
145	Rey Ordonez	.15
146	Russ Davis	.15
147	J.T. Snow Jr.	.15
148	Luis Gonzalez	.25
149	Marquis Grissom	.15
150	Greg Maddux	1.00
151	Fernando Tatis	.15
152	Jason Giambi	.50
153	Carlos Delgado	.50
154	Joe McEwing	.15
155	Raul Mondesi	.15
156	Rich Aurilia	.15
157	Alex Fernandez	.15
158	Albert Belle	.25
159	Pat Meares	.15
160	Mike Lieberthal	.15
161	Mike Cameron	.15
162	Juan Encarnacion	.15
163	Chuck Knoblauch	.15
164	Pedro Martinez	.75
165	Randy Johnson	.75
166	Shannon Stewart	.15
167	Jeff Bagwell	.75
168	Edgar Renteria	.15
169	Barry Bonds	2.00
170	Steve Finley	.15
171	Brian Hunter	.15
172	Tom Glavine	.35
173	Mark Kotsay	.15
174	Tony Fernandez	.15
175	Sammy Sosa	1.25
176	Geoff Jenkins	.15
177	Adrian Beltre	.15
178	Jay Bell	.15
179	Mike Bordick	.15
180	Ed Sprague	.15
181	Dave Roberts	.15
182	Greg Vaughn	.15
183	Brian Daubach	.15
184	Damion Easley	.15
185	Carlos Febles	.15
186	Kevin Tapani	.15
187	Frank Thomas	.75
188	Roger Clemens	1.00
189	Mike Benjamin	.15
190	Curt Schilling	.40
191	Edgardo Alfonzo	.15
192	Mike Mussina	.40
193	Todd Helton	.75
194	Todd Jones	.15
195	Dean Palmer	.15
196	John Flaherty	.15
197	Derek Jeter	2.00

198 Todd Walker .15
199 Brad Ausmus .15
200 Mark McGwire 1.50
201 Erubiel Durazo 2.00
202 Nick Johnson 2.50
203 Ruben Mateo 2.00
204 Lance Berkman 2.50
205 Pat Burrell 3.00
206 Pablo Ozuna 2.00
207 Roosevelt Brown 2.00
208 Alfonso Soriano 4.00
209 A.J. Burnett 2.00
210 Rafael Furcal 2.00
211 Scott Morgan 2.00
212 Adam Piatt 2.00
213 Dee Brown 2.00
214 Corey Patterson 2.50
215 Mickey Lopez 2.00
216 Rob Ryan 2.00
217 Sean Burroughs 2.00
218 Jack Cust 2.00
219 John Patterson 2.00
220 Kit Pellow 2.00
221 Chad Hermansen 2.00
222 Daryle Ward 2.00
223 Jayson Werth 2.00
224 Jason Standridge 2.00
225 Mark Mulder 2.50
226 Peter Bergeron 2.00
227 Willi Mo Pena 2.00
228 Aramis Ramirez 2.00
229 *John Sneed* 2.00
230 Wilton Veras 2.00
231 Josh Hamilton 2.00
232 Eric Munson 2.00
233 *Bobby Bradley* 2.00
234 *Larry Bigbie* 2.00
235 *B.J. Garbe* 2.00
236 *Brett Myers* 6.00
237 *Jason Stumm* 2.00
238 *Corey Myers* 2.00
239 *Ryan Christianson* 2.00
240 David Walling 2.00
241 Josh Girdley 2.00
242 Omar Ortiz 2.00
243 Jason Jennings 2.00
244 *Kyle Snyder* 2.00
245 Jay Gehrke 2.00
246 *Mike Paradis* 2.00
247 *Chance Caple* 2.00
248 *Ben Christiansen* 2.00
249 *Brad Baker* 2.00
250 *Rick Asadoorian* 2.00
--- Nomar Garciaparra Checklist .25

One of a Kind

Stars: 5-10X
Short-prints: 2-3X
Production 150 sets H
(See 2000 Stadium Club for checklist and base card values.)

First Day Issue

Stars: 5X-10X
Short-prints: 2X-3X
Production 150 sets R
(See 2000 Stadium Club for checklist and base card values.)

Printing Plates

NM/M
Common Player: 60.00
(See 2000 Stadium Club for checklist.)

Bats of Brilliance

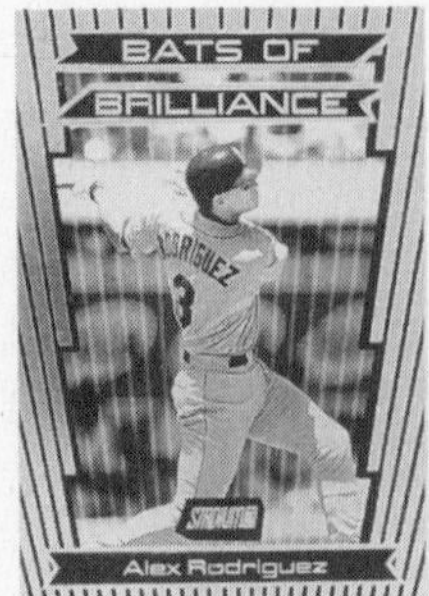

NM/M
Complete Set (10): 10.00
Common Player: .50
Inserted 1:12
1 Mark McGwire 2.50
2 Sammy Sosa 1.50
3 Jose Canseco .50
4 Jeff Bagwell .75
5 Ken Griffey Jr. 1.50
6 Nomar Garciaparra 1.50
7 Mike Piazza 1.50
8 Alex Rodriguez 2.50
9 Vladimir Guerrero .75
10 Chipper Jones 1.50

Capture The Action

NM/M
Complete Set (20): 20.00
Common Player: .50
Inserted 1:12
Game View Stars: 3X-6X
Production 100 sets H
1 Josh Hamilton .50
2 Pat Burrell .75
3 Erubiel Durazo .50
4 Alfonso Soriano 1.00
5 A.J. Burnett .50
6 Alex Rodriguez 3.00
7 Sean Casey .50
8 Derek Jeter 4.00
9 Vladimir Guerrero 1.00
10 Nomar Garciaparra 2.00
11 Mike Piazza 2.00
12 Ken Griffey Jr. 2.00
13 Sammy Sosa 2.00
14 Juan Gonzalez 1.00
15 Mark McGwire 3.00
16 Ivan Rodriguez .75
17 Barry Bonds 4.00
18 Wade Boggs 1.50
19 Tony Gwynn 1.50
20 Cal Ripken Jr. 4.00

Co-Signers

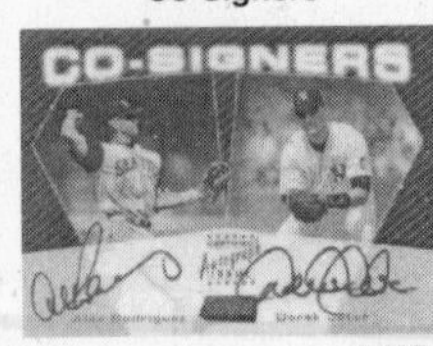

NM/M
Common Card: 15.00
Group A 1:10,184
Group B 1:5,092
Group C 1:508
1 Alex Rodriguez, Derek Jeter 400.00
2 Derek Jeter, Omar Vizquel 150.00
3 Alex Rodriguez, Rey Ordonez 100.00
4 Derek Jeter, Rey Ordonez 150.00
5 Omar Vizquel, Alex Rodriguez 100.00
6 Rey Ordonez, Omar Vizquel 15.00
7 Wade Boggs, Robin Ventura 30.00
8 Randy Johnson, Mike Mussina 90.00
9 Pat Burrell, Magglio Ordonez 40.00
10 Chad Hermansen, Pat Burrell 20.00
11 Magglio Ordonez, Chad Hermansen 20.00
12 Josh Hamilton, Corey Myers 15.00
13 B.J. Garbe, Josh Hamilton 15.00
14 Corey Myers, B.J. Garbe 15.00
15 Tino Martinez, Fred McGriff 60.00

Lone Star Signatures

NM/M
Common Player: 8.00
Group 1 1:1,979
Group 2 1:2,374
Group 3 1:1,979
Group 4 1:424
1 Derek Jeter 100.00
2 Alex Rodriguez 100.00
3 Wade Boggs 25.00
4 Robin Ventura 15.00
5 Randy Johnson 60.00
6 Mike Mussina 25.00

7 Tino Martinez 35.00
8 Fred McGriff 25.00
9 Omar Vizquel 15.00
10 Rey Ordonez 8.00
11 Pat Burrell 15.00
12 Chad Hermansen 8.00
13 Magglio Ordonez 10.00
14 Josh Hamilton 8.00
15 Corey Myers 8.00
16 B.J. Garbe 8.00

Onyx Extreme

NM/M
Complete Set (10): 10.00
Common Player: .40
Inserted 1:12
Die-cuts: 2-3X
Inserted 1:60
1 Ken Griffey Jr. 1.50
2 Derek Jeter 3.00
3 Vladimir Guerrero 1.00
4 Nomar Garciaparra 1.50
5 Barry Bonds 3.00
6 Alex Rodriguez 2.50
7 Sammy Sosa 1.50
8 Ivan Rodriguez .75
9 Larry Walker .40
10 Andruw Jones 1.00

Scenes

NM/M
Complete Set (9): 10.00
Common Player: .50
Inserted 1:box
1 Mark McGwire 2.50
2 Alex Rodriguez 2.50
3 Cal Ripken Jr. 3.00
4 Sammy Sosa 2.00
5 Derek Jeter 3.00
6 Ken Griffey Jr. 2.00
7 Raul Mondesi .50
8 Chipper Jones 1.50
9 Nomar Garciaparra 2.00

Souvenirs

NM/M
Complete Set (3): 35.00
Common Player: 8.00
Inserted 2:339
1 Wade Boggs 20.00
2 Randy Johnson 20.00
3 Robin Ventura 8.00

3 X 3

NM/M
Complete Set (30): 40.00
Common Player: .75
Inserted 1:18
Luminescent: 2X
Inserted 1:72
Illuminator: 3X-4X
Inserted 1:144
1A Randy Johnson 1.50
1B Pedro Martinez 1.50
1C Greg Maddux 2.00
2A Mike Piazza 3.00
2B Ivan Rodriguez 1.25
2C Mike Lieberthal .75
3A Mark McGwire 4.50
3B Jeff Bagwell 1.50
3C Sean Casey .75
4A Craig Biggio .75
4B Roberto Alomar 1.00
4C Jay Bell .75
5A Chipper Jones 2.00
5B Matt Williams .75
5C Robin Ventura .75
6A Alex Rodriguez 4.50
6B Derek Jeter 6.00
6C Nomar Garciaparra 3.00
7A Barry Bonds 6.00
7B Luis Gonzalez 1.00
7C Dante Bichette .75
8A Ken Griffey Jr. 3.00
8B Bernie Williams 1.00
8C Andruw Jones 1.50
9A Manny Ramirez 1.50
9B Sammy Sosa 3.00
9C Juan Gonzalez 1.50
10A Jose Canseco 1.00
10B Frank Thomas 1.50
10C Rafael Palmeiro 1.00

2000 STADIUM CLUB CHROME

NM/M
Complete Set (250): 40.00
Common Player: .15
Pack (11): 1.50
Wax Box (36): 40.00
1 Nomar Garciaparra 1.50
2 Brian Jordan .15
3 Mark Grace .25
4 Jeromy Burnitz .15
5 Shane Reynolds .15
6 Alex Gonzalez .15
7 Jose Offerman .15
8 Orlando Hernandez .15
9 Mike Caruso .15
10 Tony Clark .15
11 Sean Casey .25
12 Johnny Damon .25
13 Dante Bichette .15
14 Kevin Young .15
15 Juan Gonzalez .75
16 Chipper Jones 1.00
17 Quilvio Veras .15
18 Trevor Hoffman .15
19 Roger Cedeno .15
20 Ellis Burks .15
21 Richie Sexson .15
22 Gary Sheffield .45
23 Delino DeShields .15
24 Wade Boggs 1.00
25 Ray Lankford .15
26 Kevin Appier .15
27 Roy Halladay .15
28 Harold Baines .15
29 Todd Zeile .15
30 Barry Larkin .15
31 Ron Coomer .15
32 Jorge Posada .15
33 Magglio Ordonez .15
34 Brian Giles .15
35 Jeff Kent .15
36 Henry Rodriguez .15
37 Fred McGriff .15
38 Shawn Green .50
39 Derek Bell .15
40 Ben Grieve .15
41 Dave Nilsson .15
42 Mo Vaughn .15
43 Rondell White .15
44 Doug Glanville .15
45 Paul O'Neill .15
46 Carlos Lee .15
47 Vinny Castilla .15
48 Mike Sweeney .15
49 Rico Brogna .15
50 Alex Rodriguez 2.50

51	Luis Castillo	.15
52	Kevin Brown	.15
53	Jose Vidro	.15
54	John Smoltz	.15
55	Garret Anderson	.15
56	Matt Stairs	.15
57	Omar Vizquel	.15
58	Tom Goodwin	.15
59	Scott Brosius	.15
60	Robin Ventura	.15
61	B.J. Surhoff	.15
62	Andy Ashby	.15
63	Chris Widger	.15
64	Tim Hudson	.40
65	Javy Lopez	.15
66	Tim Salmon	.25
67	Warren Morris	.15
68	John Wetteland	.15
69	Gabe Kapler	.15
70	Bernie Williams	.25
71	Rickey Henderson	.75
72	Andruw Jones	.75
73	Eric Young	.15
74	Bobby Abreu	.15
75	David Cone	.15
76	Rusty Greer	.15
77	Ron Belliard	.15
78	Troy Glaus	.75
79	Mike Hampton	.15
80	Miguel Tejada	.30
81	Jeff Cirillo	.15
82	Todd Hundley	.15
83	Roberto Alomar	.35
84	Charles Johnson	.15
85	Rafael Palmeiro	.65
86	Doug Mientkiewicz	.15
87	Mariano Rivera	.25
88	Neifi Perez	.15
89	Jermaine Dye	.15
90	Ivan Rodriguez	.65
91	Jay Buhner	.15
92	Pokey Reese	.15
93	John Olerud	.15
94	Brady Anderson	.15
95	Manny Ramirez	.75
96	Keith Osik	.15
97	Mickey Morandini	.15
98	Matt Williams	.15
99	Eric Karros	.15
100	Ken Griffey Jr.	1.50
101	Bret Boone	.15
102	Ryan Klesko	.15
103	Craig Biggio	.15
104	John Jaha	.15
105	Vladimir Guerrero	.75
106	Devon White	.15
107	Tony Womack	.15
108	Marvin Benard	.15
109	Kenny Lofton	.15
110	Preston Wilson	.15
111	Al Leiter	.15
112	Reggie Sanders	.15
113	Scott Williamson	.15
114	Deivi Cruz	.15
115	Carlos Beltran	.50
116	Ray Durham	.15
117	Ricky Ledee	.15
118	Torii Hunter	.15
119	John Valentin	.15
120	Scott Rolen	.65
121	Jason Kendall	.15
122	Dave Martinez	.15
123	Jim Thome	.65
124	David Bell	.15
125	Jose Canseco	.50
126	Jose Lima	.15
127	Carl Everett	.15
128	Kevin Millwood	.15
129	Bill Spiers	.15
130	Omar Daal	.15
131	Miguel Cairo	.15
132	Mark Grudzielanek	.15
133	David Justice	.15
134	Russ Ortiz	.15
135	Mike Piazza	1.50
136	Brian Meadows	.15
137	Tony Gwynn	1.00
138	Cal Ripken Jr.	3.00
139	Kris Benson	.15
140	Larry Walker	.15
141	Cristian Guzman	.15
142	Tino Martinez	.15
143	Chris Singleton	.15
144	Lee Stevens	.15
145	Rey Ordonez	.15
146	Russ Davis	.15
147	J.T. Snow Jr.	.15
148	Luis Gonzalez	.25
149	Marquis Grissom	.15
150	Greg Maddux	1.00
151	Fernando Tatis	.15
152	Jason Giambi	.50
153	Carlos Delgado	.50
154	Joe McEwing	.15
155	Raul Mondesi	.15
156	Rich Aurilia	.15
157	Alex Fernandez	.15
158	Albert Belle	.25
159	Pat Meares	.15
160	Mike Lieberthal	.15
161	Mike Cameron	.15
162	Juan Encarnacion	.15
163	Chuck Knoblauch	.15
164	Pedro Martinez	.75
165	Randy Johnson	.75
166	Shannon Stewart	.15
167	Jeff Bagwell	.75
168	Edgar Renteria	.15
169	Barry Bonds	3.00
170	Steve Finley	.15
171	Brian Hunter	.15
172	Tom Glavine	.40
173	Mark Kotsay	.15
174	Tony Fernandez	.15
175	Sammy Sosa	1.50
176	Geoff Jenkins	.15
177	Adrian Beltre	.45
178	Jay Bell	.15
179	Mike Bordick	.15
180	Ed Sprague	.15
181	Dave Roberts	.15
182	Greg Vaughn	.15
183	Brian Daubach	.15
184	Damion Easley	.15
185	Carlos Febles	.15
186	Kevin Tapani	.15
187	Frank Thomas	.75
188	Roger Clemens	1.25
189	Mike Benjamin	.15
190	Curt Schilling	.40
191	Edgardo Alfonzo	.15
192	Mike Mussina	.45
193	Todd Helton	.75
194	Todd Jones	.15
195	Dean Palmer	.15
196	John Flaherty	.15
197	Derek Jeter	3.00
198	Todd Walker	.15
199	Brad Ausmus	.15
200	Mark McGwire	2.50
201	Erubiel Durazo	.15
202	Nick Johnson	.15
203	Ruben Mateo	.15
204	Lance Berkman	.15
205	Pat Burrell	.65
206	Pablo Ozuna	.15
207	Roosevelt Brown	.15
208	Alfonso Soriano	1.00
209	A.J. Burnett	.15
210	Rafael Furcal	.15
211	Scott Morgan	.15
212	Adam Piatt	.15
213	Dee Brown	.15
214	Corey Patterson	.15
215	Mickey Lopez	.15
216	Rob Ryan	.15
217	Sean Burroughs	.15
218	Jack Cust	.15
219	John Patterson	.15
220	Kit Pellow	.15
221	Chad Hermansen	.15
222	Daryle Ward	.15
223	Jayson Werth	.15
224	Jason Standridge	.15
225	Mark Mulder	.15
226	Peter Bergeron	.15
227	Willi Mo Pena	.15
228	Aramis Ramirez	.15
229	John Sneed	.15
230	Wilton Veras	.15
231	Josh Hamilton	.15
232	Eric Munson	.15
233	*Bobby Bradley*	1.00
234	*Larry Bigbie*	1.00
235	*B.J. Garbe*	1.00
236	*Brett Myers*	4.00
237	*Jason Stumm*	1.00
238	*Corey Myers*	1.00
239	*Ryan Christianson*	1.00
240	David Walling	.15
241	Josh Girdley	.15
242	Omar Ortiz	.15
243	Jason Jennings	.15
244	Kyle Snyder	.15
245	Jay Gehrke	.15
246	Mike Paradis	.15
247	*Chance Caple*	1.00
248	*Ben Christensen*	1.00
249	*Brad Baker*	1.00
250	*Rick Asadoorian*	1.00

Refractor

Stars:	2-4X
Rookies:	1-2X
Inserted 1:12	

First Day Issue

Stars:	4-8X
Rookies:	1-3X
Production 100 sets	
Refractor:	25-40X
Rookies:	5-10X
Production 25 sets	

Capture The Action

		NM/M
Complete Set (20):		40.00
Common Player:		1.00
Inserted 1:18		
Refractors:		2-3X
Inserted 1:90		
1	Josh Hamilton	1.00
2	Pat Burrell	1.50
3	Erubiel Durazo	1.00
4	Alfonso Soriano	1.50
5	A.J. Burnett	1.00
6	Alex Rodriguez	5.00
7	Sean Casey	1.00
8	Derek Jeter	6.00
9	Vladimir Guerrero	1.50
10	Nomar Garciaparra	3.00
11	Mike Piazza	3.00
12	Ken Griffey Jr.	3.00
13	Sammy Sosa	3.00
14	Juan Gonzalez	1.50
15	Mark McGwire	5.00
16	Ivan Rodriguez	1.50
17	Barry Bonds	6.00
18	Wade Boggs	2.00
19	Tony Gwynn	2.00
20	Cal Ripken Jr.	6.00

Clear Shots

		NM/M
Complete Set (10):		10.00
Common Player:		.50
Inserted 1:24		
Refractor:		2-3X
Inserted 1:120		
1	Derek Jeter	4.00
2	Bernie Williams	.50
3	Roger Clemens	2.50
4	Chipper Jones	2.00
5	Greg Maddux	2.00
6	Andruw Jones	1.00
7	Juan Gonzalez	1.00
8	Manny Ramirez	1.00
9	Ken Griffey Jr.	3.00
10	Josh Hamilton	.50

Eyes of the Game

		NM/M
Complete Set (10):		10.00
Common Player:		.50
Inserted 1:16		
Refractors:		2-3X
Inserted 1:80		
1	Randy Johnson	1.00
2	Mike Piazza	1.50
3	Nomar Garciaparra	1.50
4	Mark McGwire	2.50
5	Alex Rodriguez	2.50
6	Derek Jeter	3.00
7	Tony Gwynn	1.00
8	Sammy Sosa	1.50
9	Larry Walker	.50
10	Ken Griffey Jr.	1.50

True Colors

		NM/M
Complete Set (10):		15.00
Common Player:		1.00
Inserted 1:32		
Refractors:		2-3X
Inserted 1:160		
1	Sammy Sosa	2.00
2	Nomar Garciaparra	2.00
3	Alex Rodriguez	3.00
4	Derek Jeter	4.00
5	Mark McGwire	3.00
6	Chipper Jones	1.50
7	Mike Piazza	2.00
8	Ken Griffey Jr.	2.00
9	Manny Ramirez	1.00
10	Vladimir Guerrero	1.00

Visionaries

		NM/M
Complete Set (20):		17.50
Common Player:		1.00
Inserted 1:18		
Refractors:		2X
Inserted 1:90		
1	Alfonso Soriano	3.00
2	Josh Hamilton	1.00
3	A.J. Burnett	1.50
4	Pat Burrell	2.50
5	Ruben Salazar	1.00
6	Aaron Rowand	1.00
7	Adam Piatt	1.00
8	Nick Johnson	1.00
9	Rafael Furcal	1.00
10	Jack Cust	1.00
11	Corey Patterson	1.00
12	Sean Burroughs	1.50
13	Pablo Ozuna	1.00
14	Dee Brown	1.00
15	John Patterson	1.00
16	Willi Mo Pena	1.00
17	Mark Mulder	1.00
18	Eric Munson	1.00
19	Alex Escobar	1.00
20	Rob Ryan	1.00

2001 STADIUM CLUB

		NM/M
Complete Set (200):		65.00
Common Player:		.15
Common SP:		1.50
Inserted 1:6		
Pack (7):		2.00
Box (24):		35.00
1	Nomar Garciaparra	1.25
2	Chipper Jones	1.00
3	Jeff Bagwell	.75
4	Chad Kreuter	.15
5	Randy Johnson	.75
6	Mike Hampton	.15
7	Barry Larkin	.15
8	Bernie Williams	.30

No.	Player	Price
9	Chris Singleton	.15
10	Larry Walker	.15
11	Brad Ausmus	.15
12	Ron Coomer	.15
13	Edgardo Alfonzo	.15
14	Delino DeShields	.15
15	Tony Gwynn	1.00
16	Andruw Jones	.75
17	Raul Mondesi	.15
18	Troy Glaus	.75
19	Ben Grieve	.15
20	Sammy Sosa	1.25
21	Fernando Vina	.15
22	Jeromy Burnitz	.15
23	Jay Bell	.15
24	Pete Harnisch	.15
25	Barry Bonds	2.00
26	Eric Karros	.15
27	Alex Gonzalez	.15
28	Mike Lieberthal	.15
29	Juan Encarnacion	.15
30	Derek Jeter	2.00
31	Bruce Aven	.15
32	Eric Milton	.15
33	Aaron Boone	.15
34	Roberto Alomar	.40
35	John Olerud	.15
36	Orlando Cabrera	.15
37	Shawn Green	.45
38	Roger Cedeno	.15
39	Garret Anderson	.15
40	Jim Thome	.65
41	Gabe Kapler	.15
42	Mo Vaughn	.15
43	Sean Casey	.25
44	Preston Wilson	.15
45	Javy Lopez	.15
46	Ryan Klesko	.15
47	Ray Durham	.15
48	Dean Palmer	.15
49	Jorge Posada	.15
50	Alex Rodriguez	1.50
51	Tom Glavine	.40
52	Ray Lankford	.15
53	Jose Canseco	.40
54	Tim Salmon	.25
55	Cal Ripken Jr.	2.00
56	Bob Abreu	.15
57	Robin Ventura	.15
58	Damion Easley	.15
59	Paul O'Neill	.15
60	Ivan Rodriguez	.65
61	Carl Everett	.15
62	Doug Glanville	.15
63	Jeff Kent	.15
64	Jay Buhner	.15
65	Cliff Floyd	.15
66	Rick Ankiel	.15
67	Mark Grace	.25
68	Brian Jordan	.15
69	Craig Biggio	.15
70	Carlos Delgado	.50
71	Brad Radke	.15
72	Greg Maddux	1.00
73	Al Leiter	.15
74	Pokey Reese	.15
75	Todd Helton	.75
76	Mariano Rivera	.25
77	Shane Spencer	.15
78	Jason Kendall	.15
79	Chuck Knoblauch	.15
80	Scott Rolen	.65
81	Jose Offerman	.15
82	J.T. Snow Jr.	.15
83	Pat Meares	.15
84	Quilvio Veras	.15
85	Edgar Renteria	.15
86	Luis Matos	.15
87	Adrian Beltre	.15
88	Luis Gonzalez	.25
89	Rickey Henderson	.75
90	Brian Giles	.15
91	Carlos Febles	.15
92	Tino Martinez	.15
93	Magglio Ordonez	.15
94	Rafael Furcal	.15
95	Mike Mussina	.30
96	Gary Sheffield	.40
97	Kenny Lofton	.15
98	Fred McGriff	.15
99	Ken Caminiti	.15
100	Mark McGwire	1.50
101	Tom Goodwin	.15
102	Mark Grudzielanek	.15
103	Derek Bell	.15
104	Mike Lowell	.15
105	Jeff Cirillo	.15
106	Orlando Hernandez	.15
107	Jose Valentin	.15
108	Warren Morris	.15
109	Mike Williams	.15
110	Greg Zaun	.15
111	Jose Vidro	.15
112	Omar Vizquel	.15
113	Vinny Castilla	.15
114	Gregg Jefferies	.15
115	Kevin Brown	.15
116	Shannon Stewart	.15
117	Marquis Grissom	.15
118	Manny Ramirez	.75
119	Albert Belle	.15
120	Bret Boone	.15
121	Johnny Damon	.25
122	Juan Gonzalez	.75
123	David Justice	.15
124	Jeffrey Hammonds	.15
125	Ken Griffey Jr.	1.25
126	Mike Sweeney	.15
127	Tony Clark	.15
128	Todd Zeile	.15
129	Mark Johnson	.15
130	Matt Williams	.15
131	Geoff Jenkins	.15
132	Jason Giambi	.50
133	Steve Finley	.15
134	Derrek Lee	.15
135	Royce Clayton	.15
136	Joe Randa	.15
137	Rafael Palmeiro	.65
138	Kevin Young	.15
139	Curt Schilling	.40
140	Vladimir Guerrero	.75
141	Greg Vaughn	.15
142	Jermaine Dye	.15
143	Roger Clemens	1.00
144	Denny Hocking	.15
145	Frank Thomas	.75
146	Carlos Beltran	.50
147	Eric Young	.15
148	Pat Burrell	.50
149	Pedro Martinez	.75
150	Mike Piazza	1.25
151	Adrian Gonzalez	.50
152	Adam Johnson	.15
153	*Luis Montanez*	1.50
154	Mike Stodolka	.15
155	Phil Dumatrait	.15
156	Sean Burnett	1.50
157	*Dominic Rich*	1.50
158	Adam Wainwright	.50
159	Scott Thorman	.15
160	Scott Heard	.25
161	*Chad Petty*	1.50
162	Matt Wheatland	2.00
163	Brad Digby	.15
164	Rocco Baldelli	1.00
165	Grady Sizemore	.15
166	*Brian Sellier*	1.50
167	*Rick Brosseau*	1.50
168	*Shawn Fagan*	1.50
169	Sean Smith	1.50
170	*Chris Bass*	1.50
171	Corey Patterson	.25
172	Sean Burroughs	.25
173	Ben Petrick	.15
174	Mike Glendenning	.15
175	Barry Zito	.50
176	Milton Bradley	.15
177	Bobby Bradley	.15
178	Jason Hart	.15
179	Ryan Anderson	.15
180	Ben Sheets	.25
181	Adam Everett	.15
182	Alfonso Soriano	.75
183	Josh Hamilton	.25
184	Eric Munson	.15
185	Chin-Feng Chen	.25
186	*Tim Christman*	1.50
187	J.R. House	2.00
188	*Brandon Parker*	1.50
189	*Sean Fesh*	1.50
190	*Joel Pieniero*	2.00
191	*Oscar Ramirez*	1.50
192	*Alex Santos*	1.50
193	*Eddy Reyes*	1.50
194	*Mike Jacobs*	1.50
195	*Erick Almonte*	2.00
196	*Brandon Claussen*	6.00
197	*Kris Keller*	1.50
198	*Wilson Betemit*	1.50
199	*Andy Phillips*	1.50
200	*Adam Pettyjohn*	1.50
---	Derek Jeter (Checklist)	.25

Beam Team

NM/M

Complete Set (30): 100.00
Common Player: 1.50
Production 500 sets

No.	Player	Price
1	Sammy Sosa	6.00
2	Mark McGwire	8.00
3	Vladimir Guerrero	3.00
4	Chipper Jones	4.50
5	Manny Ramirez	3.00
6	Derek Jeter	10.00
7	Alex Rodriguez	8.00
8	Cal Ripken Jr.	10.00
9	Ken Griffey Jr.	6.00
10	Greg Maddux	4.50
11	Barry Bonds	10.00
12	Pedro Martinez	3.00
13	Nomar Garciaparra	6.00
14	Randy Johnson	3.00
15	Frank Thomas	3.00
16	Ivan Rodriguez	2.50
17	Jeff Bagwell	3.00
18	Mike Piazza	6.00
19	Todd Helton	3.00
20	Shawn Green	2.00
21	Juan Gonzalez	3.00
22	Larry Walker	1.50
23	Tony Gwynn	4.50
24	Pat Burrell	2.00
25	Rafael Furcal	1.50
26	Corey Patterson	1.50
27	Chin-Feng Chen	1.50
28	Sean Burroughs	1.50
29	Ryan Anderson	1.50
30	Josh Hamilton	1.50

Capture The Action

NM/M

Complete Set (15): 15.00
Common Player: 1.00
Inserted 1:8

No.	Player	Price
1	Cal Ripken Jr.	3.00
2	Alex Rodriguez	2.50
3	Mike Piazza	2.00
4	Mark McGwire	2.50
5	Greg Maddux	1.50
6	Derek Jeter	3.00
7	Chipper Jones	1.50
8	Pedro Martinez	1.00
9	Ken Griffey Jr.	2.00
10	Nomar Garciaparra	2.00
11	Randy Johnson	1.00
12	Sammy Sosa	2.00
13	Vladimir Guerrero	1.00
14	Barry Bonds	3.00
15	Ivan Rodriguez	1.00

Capture The Action Game View

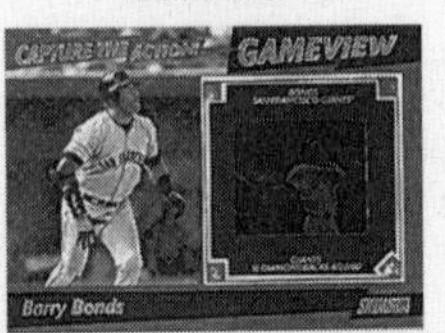

NM/M

Common Player: 10.00
Production 100 sets

No.	Player	Price
1	Cal Ripken Jr.	30.00
2	Alex Rodriguez	25.00
3	Mike Piazza	20.00
4	Mark McGwire	25.00
5	Greg Maddux	15.00
6	Derek Jeter	30.00
7	Chipper Jones	15.00
8	Pedro Martinez	10.00
9	Ken Griffey Jr.	20.00
10	Nomar Garciaparra	20.00
11	Randy Johnson	10.00
12	Sammy Sosa	20.00
13	Vladimir Guerrero	10.00
14	Barry Bonds	30.00
15	Ivan Rodriguez	10.00

Diamond Pearls

NM/M

Complete Set (20): 20.00
Common Player: .65
Inserted 1:8

No.	Player	Price
1	Ken Griffey Jr.	2.00
2	Alex Rodriguez	2.50
3	Derek Jeter	3.00
4	Chipper Jones	1.50
5	Nomar Garciaparra	2.00
6	Vladimir Guerrero	1.00
7	Jeff Bagwell	1.00
8	Cal Ripken Jr.	3.00
9	Sammy Sosa	2.00
10	Mark McGwire	2.50
11	Frank Thomas	1.00
12	Pedro Martinez	1.00
13	Manny Ramirez	1.00
14	Randy Johnson	1.00
15	Barry Bonds	3.00
16	Ivan Rodriguez	.75
17	Greg Maddux	1.50
18	Mike Piazza	2.00
19	Todd Helton	1.00
20	Shawn Green	.65

Co-Signers

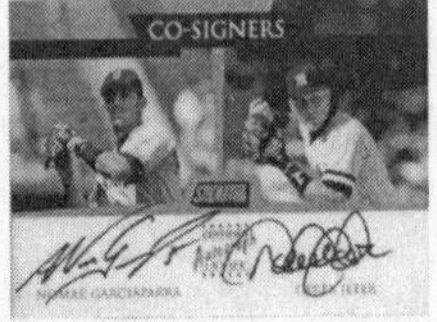

NM/M

Common Duo: 15.00
Inserted 1:1,117

No.	Players	Price
1	Nomar Garciaparra, Derek Jeter	400.00
2	Roberto Alomar, Edgardo Alfonzo	50.00
3	Rick Ankiel, Kevin Millwood	15.00
4	Chipper Jones, Troy Glaus	65.00
5	Magglio Ordonez, Bobby Abreu	20.00
6	Adam Piatt, Sean Burroughs	20.00
7	Corey Patterson, Nick Johnson	40.00
8	Adrian Gonzalez, Rocco Baldelli	40.00
9	Adam Johnson, Mike Stodolka	15.00

Game-Used Cards

NM/M

Common Player: 5.00
Inserted 1:285

No.	Player	Price
12	Sammy Sosa	20.00
13	Vladimir Guerrero	10.00
14	Barry Bonds	30.00
15	Ivan Rodriguez	10.00

1	Chin-Feng Chen	20.00
2	Bobby Bradley	5.00
3	Tomokazu Ohka	5.00
4	Kurt Ainsworth	5.00
5	Craig Anderson	5.00
6	Josh Hamilton	5.00
7	Felipe Lopez	5.00
8	Ryan Anderson	5.00
9	Alex Escobar	5.00
10	Ben Sheets	8.00
11	Ntema Ndungidi	5.00
12	Eric Munson	5.00
13	Aaron Myette	5.00
14	Jack Cust	5.00
15	Julio Zuleta	5.00
16	Corey Patterson	10.00
17	Carlos Pena	5.00
18	Marcus Giles	5.00
19	Travis Wilson	5.00
20	Barry Zito	8.00

Lone Star Signatures

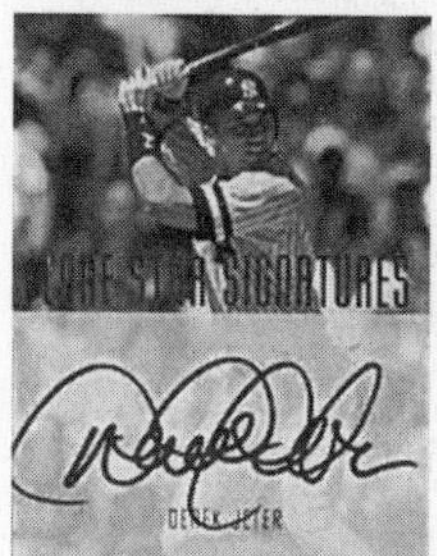

		NM/M
Common Player:		6.00
Inserted 1:196		
1	Nomar Garciaparra	100.00
2	Derek Jeter	120.00
3	Edgardo Alfonzo	20.00
4	Roberto Alomar	40.00
5	Magglio Ordonez	20.00
6	Bobby Abreu	40.00
7	Chipper Jones	40.00
8	Troy Glaus	30.00
9	Nick Johnson	15.00
10	Adam Piatt	6.00
11	Sean Burroughs	8.00
12	Corey Patterson	15.00
13	Rick Ankiel	6.00
14	Kevin Millwood	10.00
15	Adrian Gonzalez	6.00
16	Adam Johnson	6.00
17	Rocco Baldelli	25.00
18	Mike Stodolka	6.00

King of the Hill

		NM/M
Complete Set (5):		30.00
Common Player:		3.00
Inserted 1:21		
1	Pedro Martinez	10.00
2	Randy Johnson	10.00
3	Greg Maddux	15.00
4	Rick Ankiel	3.00
5	Kevin Brown	3.00

Play at the Plate

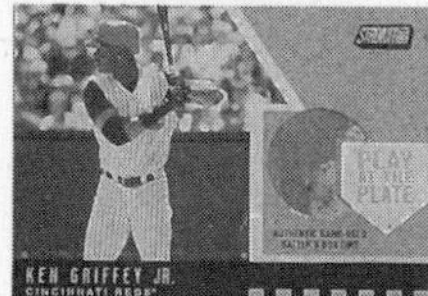

		NM/M
Common Player:		10.00
Inserted 1:11		
1	Mark McGwire	20.00
2	Sammy Sosa	15.00
3	Vladimir Guerrero	8.00
4	Ken Griffey Jr.	15.00
5	Mike Piazza	15.00
6	Chipper Jones	10.00
7	Barry Bonds	25.00
8	Alex Rodriguez	20.00
9	Jeff Bagwell	8.00
10	Nomar Garciaparra	15.00

Souvenirs

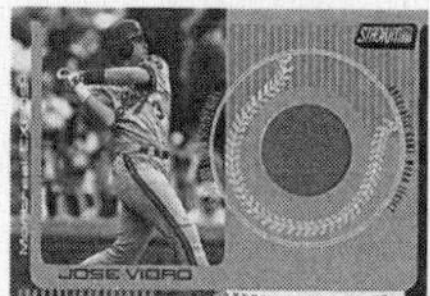

		NM/M
Common Player:		4.00
1	Scott Rolen bat	8.00
2	Larry Walker bat	5.00
3	Rafael Furcal bat	5.00
4	Darin Erstad bat	5.00
5	Mike Sweeney jersey	4.00
6	Matt Lawton jersey	4.00
7	Jose Vidro jersey	4.00
8	Pat Burrell jersey	6.00

2002 STADIUM CLUB RELIC EDITION

		NM/M
Complete Set (125):		
Common Player:		.15
Common SP (101-125):		5.00
Production 2,999		
Pack (6):		1.50
Box (24):		30.00
1	Pedro Martinez	.75
2	Derek Jeter	2.00
3	Chipper Jones	1.00
4	Roberto Alomar	.40
5	Albert Pujols	1.50
6	Bret Boone	.15
7	Alex Rodriguez	1.50
8	Jose Cruz	.15
9	Mike Hampton	.15
10	Vladimir Guerrero	.75
11	Jim Edmonds	.25
12	Luis Gonzalez	.25
13	Jeff Kent	.15
14	Mike Piazza	1.25
15	Ben Sheets	.15
16	Tsuyoshi Shinjo	.15
17	Pat Burrell	.40
18	Jermaine Dye	.15
19	Rafael Furcal	.15
20	Randy Johnson	.75
21	Carlos Delgado	.50
22	Roger Clemens	1.00
23	Eric Chavez	.25
24	Nomar Garciaparra	1.25
25	Ivan Rodriguez	.65
26	Juan Gonzalez	.75
27	Reggie Sanders	.15
28	Jeff Bagwell	.75
29	Kazuhiro Sasaki	.15
30	Larry Walker	.15
31	Ben Grieve	.15
32	David Justice	.15
33	David Wells	.15
34	Kevin Brown	.15
35	Miguel Tejada	.25
36	Jorge Posada	.15
37	Javy Lopez	.15
38	Cliff Floyd	.15
39	Carlos Lee	.15
40	Manny Ramirez	.75
41	Jim Thome	.65
42	Pokey Reese	.15
43	Scott Rolen	.65
44	Richie Sexson	.15
45	Dean Palmer	.15
46	Rafael Palmeiro	.65
47	Alfonso Soriano	.75
48	Craig Biggio	.15
49	Troy Glaus	.75
50	Andruw Jones	.75
51	Ichiro Suzuki	1.50
52	Kenny Lofton	.15
53	Hideo Nomo	.75
54	Magglio Ordonez	.15
55	Brad Penny	.15
56	Omar Vizquel	.15
57	Mike Sweeney	.15
58	Gary Sheffield	.25
59	Ken Griffey Jr.	1.25
60	Curt Schilling	.40
61	Bobby Higginson	.15
62	Terrence Long	.15
63	Moises Alou	.15
64	Sandy Alomar	.15
65	Cristian Guzman	.15
66	Sammy Sosa	1.25
67	Jose Vidro	.15
68	Edgar Martinez	.15
69	Jason Giambi	.50
70	Mark McGwire	1.50
71	Barry Bonds	2.00
72	Greg Vaughn	.15
73	Phil Nevin	.15
74	Jason Kendall	.15
75	Greg Maddux	1.00
76	Jeromy Burnitz	.15
77	Mike Mussina	.40
78	Johnny Damon	.25
79	Shawn Green	.40
80	Jimmy Rollins	.15
81	Edgardo Alfonzo	.15
82	Barry Larkin	.15
83	Raul Mondesi	.15
84	Preston Wilson	.15
85	Mike Lieberthal	.15
86	J.D. Drew	.40
87	Ryan Klesko	.15
88	David Segui	.15
89	Derek Bell	.15
90	Bernie Williams	.40
91	Doug Mientkiewicz	.15
92	Rich Aurilia	.15
93	Ellis Burks	.15
94	Placido Polanco	.15
95	Darin Erstad	.25
96	Brian Giles	.15
97	Geoff Jenkins	.15
98	Kerry Wood	.65
99	Mariano Rivera	.40
100	Todd Helton	.75
101	Adam Dunn	15.00
102	Grant Balfour	5.00
103	Jae Weong Seo	5.00
104	Hank Blalock	10.00
105	Chris George	5.00
106	Jack Cust	5.00
107	Juan Cruz	5.00
108	Adrian Gonzalez	5.00
109	Nick Johnson	5.00
110	*Jeff Devanon*	5.00
111	Juan Diaz	10.00
112	Brandon Duckworth	5.00
113	Jason Lane	5.00
114	Seung Jun Song	5.00
115	Morgan Ensberg	5.00
116	*Marlyn Tisdale*	5.00
117	*Jason Botts*	5.00
118	*Henry Pichardo*	5.00
119	*John Rodriguez*	5.00
120	*Mike Peeples*	5.00
121	*Rob Bowen*	5.00
122	Jeremy Affeldt	5.00
123	*Jorge Buret*	5.00
124	*Manny Ravelo*	10.00
125	*Eudy Lajara*	5.00

All-Star Relics

		NM/M
Common Player:		5.00
RA	Roberto Alomar	7.50
MA	Moises Alou	5.00
BB	Barry Bonds	40.00
BRB	Bret Boone	5.00
MC	Mike Cameron	5.00
SC	Sean Casey	7.50
CF	Cliff Floyd	5.00
BG	Brian Giles	5.00
JG	Juan Gonzalez	12.00
LG3	Luis Gonzalez	5.00
CG	Cristian Guzman	5.00
TG	Tony Gwynn	15.00
MH	Mike Hampton	5.00
TH	Todd Helton	12.00
RJ	Randy Johnson	12.00
CJ	Chipper Jones	15.00
JK	Jeff Kent	5.00
RK	Ryan Klesko	5.00
EM	Edgar Martinez	5.00
ERM	Eric Milton	5.00
JO	John Olerud	5.00
MO	Magglio Ordonez	5.00
MP	Mike Piazza	20.00
JP	Jorge Posada	5.00
AP	Albert Pujols	30.00
MR	Manny Ramirez	12.00
CR	Cal Ripken Jr.	
IR	Ivan Rodriguez	10.00
KS	Kazuhiro Sasaki	5.00
MS	Mike Sweeney	5.00
LW	Larry Walker	5.00

Barry Bonds Auto. Ball

	NM/M
Inserted as a redemption	
Barry Bonds	250.00

Chasing 500-500

		NM/M
Common Player:		
BB1	Barry Bonds dual	40.00
BB2	Barry Bonds jsy/600	30.00
BB3	Barry Bonds mult/200	75.00

Passport to the Majors

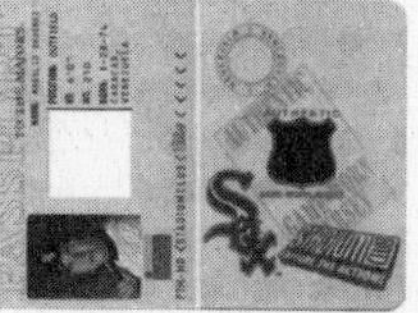

		NM/M
Common Player:		5.00
Jsy 1:84		
Bat 1:795		
BA	Bobby Abreu/400	6.00
EA	Edgardo Alfonzo	5.00
RA	Roberto Alomar	6.00
WB	Wilson Betemit/325	5.00
BC	Bartolo Colon	5.00
RF	Rafael Furcal	5.00
AG	Andres Galarraga	5.00
JG	Juan Gonzalez	8.00
SH	Shigetoshi Hasegawa	5.00
AJ	Andruw Jones	8.00
CL	Carlos Lee	5.00
JL	Javy Lopez	5.00
PM	Pedro Martinez	10.00
RM	Raul Mondesi	5.00
MO	Magglio Ordonez	5.00
RP	Rafael Palmeiro	8.00
CP	Chan Ho Park	5.00
AP	Albert Pujols/450	40.00
MR	Manny Ramirez	10.00
IR	Ivan Rodriguez	10.00
KS	Kazuhiro Sasaki	5.00
TS	Tsuyoshi Shinjo/400	6.00
AS	Alfonso Soriano/400	10.00
MT	Miguel Tejada/375	6.00
LW	Larry Walker	5.00

Reel Time

		NM/M
Complete Set (20):		25.00
Common Player:		.50
Inserted 1:8		
RT1	Luis Gonzalez	.50
RT2	Derek Jeter	4.00
RT3	Ken Griffey Jr.	2.50
RT4	Alex Rodriguez	3.00
RT5	Barry Bonds	4.00
RT6	Ichiro Suzuki	2.50
RT7	Carlos Delgado	1.00
RT8	Manny Ramirez	1.50
RT9	Mike Piazza	2.50
RT10	Mark McGwire	3.00
RT11	Todd Helton	1.50
RT12	Vladimir Guerrero	1.50
RT13	Jim Thome	1.50
RT14	Rich Aurilia	.50
RT15	Bret Boone	.50
RT16	Roberto Alomar	.75
RT17	Jason Giambi	1.00
RT18	Chipper Jones	2.00
RT19	Albert Pujols	3.00
RT20	Sammy Sosa	2.50

Stadium Shots

		NM/M
Complete Set (10):		15.00
Common Player:		1.50
Inserted 1:12		
SS1	Sammy Sosa	2.00

SS2 Manny Ramirez 1.50
SS3 Jason Giambi 1.00
SS4 Mike Piazza 2.00
SS5 Barry Bonds 4.00
SS6 Ken Griffey Jr. 2.00
SS7 Juan Gonzalez 1.50
SS8 Jeff Bagwell 1.50
SS9 Jim Thome 1.00
SS10 Mark McGwire 3.00

Stadium Slices Handle

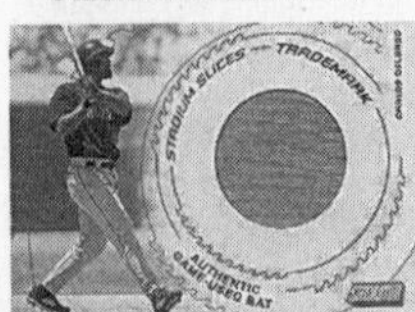

		NM/M
Common Player:		15.00
BB	Barry Bonds	50.00
LG	Luis Gonzalez	15.00
AP	Albert Pujols	50.00
IR	Ivan Rodriguez	20.00
BW	Bernie Williams	15.00

Stadium Slices Barrel

		NM/M
Common Player:		15.00
BB	Barry Bonds	75.00
LG	Luis Gonzalez	15.00
AP	Albert Pujols	75.00
IR	Ivan Rodriguez	35.00
BW	Bernie Williams	25.00

Stadium Slices Trademar

		NM/M
Common Player:		15.00
BB	Barry Bonds	60.00
LG	Luis Gonzalez	15.00
AP	Albert Pujols	60.00
IR	Ivan Rodriguez	20.00
BW	Bernie Williams	15.00

World Champions Relics

		NM/M
Common Player:		4.00
Jersey 1:106		
Bat 1:94		
Pants 1:795		
Spikes 1:38,400		
RA	Roberto Alomar	15.00
MA	Moises Alou	8.00
DB	Don Baylor	8.00
JB	Johnny Bench	20.00
BB	Bert Blyleven	8.00
WB	Wade Boggs	15.00
BRB	Bob Boone	4.00
GB	George Brett	50.00
SB	Scott Brosius	10.00
AB	Al Bumbry	4.00
JC1	Jose Canseco	15.00
JC2	Jose Canseco	15.00
GC1	Gary Carter	15.00
GC2	Gary Carter	15.00
JC	Joe Carter	10.00
RC	Ron Cey	10.00
CC	Chris Chambliss	8.00
DC	Dave Concepcion	8.00
ED	Eric Davis	10.00
BD	Bucky Dent	8.00
GF	George Foster	8.00
PG	Phil Garner	4.00
KG1	Kirk Gibson	10.00
KG2	Kirk Gibson	10.00
TG	Tom Glavine	15.00
KG	Ken Griffey Sr.	10.00
RH	Rickey Henderson/50	80.00
GH	George Hendrick	6.00
KH	Keith Hernandez	15.00
WH	Willie Hernandez	8.00
OH	Orel Hershiser	10.00
RJ	Reggie Jackson	15.00
CWJ	Chipper Jones	15.00
DJ	David Justice	8.00
CK	Chuck Knoblauch	4.00
AL	Al Leiter	8.00
DL	Davey Lopes	8.00
JL	Javy Lopez	8.00
GL	Greg Luzinski	6.00
GM	Greg Maddux	30.00
BM	Bill Madlock	8.00
TLM	Tino Martinez	15.00
HM	Hal McCrae	8.00
FM	Fred McGriff	10.00
PM	Paul Molitor	15.00
TM	Thurman Munson	50.00
EM1	Eddie Murray	15.00
EM2	Eddie Murray	15.00
JO	John Olerud	6.00
PO	Paul O'Neill	15.00
DP	Dave Parker	10.00
TP	Tony Perez	10.00
LVP	Lou Pinella	8.00
JP	Jorge Posada	10.00
KP	Kirby Puckett	20.00
WR	Willie Randolph	10.00
MJS	Mike Schmidt	50.00
MS	Mike Scoscia	10.00
OS	Ozzie Smith	30.00
JS	John Smoltz	10.00
ES	Ed Sprague	4.00
WS	Willie Stargell	15.00
AT	Alan Trammell	10.00
LW	Lou Whitaker	10.00
BW	Bernie Williams	15.00
MW	Mookie Wilson	10.00
DW	Dave Winfield	10.00
FV	Fernando Valenzuela	8.00
JV	Jose Vizcaino	4.00

2003 STADIUM CLUB

		NM/M
Complete Set (125):		30.00
Common Player:		.15
Hobby pack (6):		1.50
Hobby box (24):		30.00
1	Rafael Furcal	.15
2	Randy Winn	.15
3	Eric Chavez	.25
4	Fernando Vina	.15
5	Pat Burrell	.25
6	Derek Jeter	2.00
7	Ivan Rodriguez	.65
8	Eric Hinske	.15
9	Roberto Alomar	.40
10	Tony Batista	.15
11	Jacque Jones	.15
12	Alfonso Soriano	.75
13	Omar Vizquel	.15
14	Paul Konerko	.25
15	Shawn Green	.45
16	Garret Anderson	.15
17	Darin Erstad	.25
18	Johnny Damon	.25
19	Juan Gonzalez	.75
20	Luis Gonzalez	.25
21	Sean Burroughs	.15
22	Mark Prior	.75
23	Javier Vazquez	.15
24	Shannon Stewart	.15
25	Jay Gibbons	.15
26	A.J. Pierzynski	.15
27	Vladimir Guerrero	.75
28	Austin Kearns	.25
29	Shea Hillenbrand	.15
30	Magglio Ordonez	.15
31	Mike Cameron	.15
32	Tim Salmon	.25
33	Brian Jordan	.15
34	Moises Alou	.15
35	Rich Aurilia	.15
36	Nick Johnson	.15
37	Junior Spivey	.15
38	Curt Schilling	.40
39	Jose Vidro	.15
40	Orlando Cabrera	.15
41	Jeff Bagwell	.75
42	Mo Vaughn	.15
43	Luis Castillo	.15
44	Vicente Padilla	.15
45	Pedro J. Martinez	.75
46	John Olerud	.15
47	Tom Glavine	.40
48	Torii Hunter	.15
49	J.D. Drew	.25
50	Alex Rodriguez	1.50
51	Randy Johnson	.75
52	Richie Sexson	.15
53	Jimmy Rollins	.15
54	Cristian Guzman	.15
55	Tim Hudson	.25
56	Mark Buehrle	.15
57	Paul LoDuca	.15
58	Aramis Ramirez	.25
59	Todd Helton	.75
60	Lance Berkman	.15
61	Josh Beckett	.25
62	Bret Boone	.15
63	Miguel Tejada	.35
64	Nomar Garciaparra	1.25
65	Albert Pujols	1.50
66	Chipper Jones	1.00
67	Scott Rolen	.65
68	Kerry Wood	.65
69	Jorge Posada	.15
70	Ichiro Suzuki	1.50
71	Jeff Kent	.15
72	David Eckstein	.15
73	Phil Nevin	.15
74	Brian Giles	.15
75	Barry Zito	.25
76	Andruw Jones	.75
77	Jim Thome	.65
78	Robert Fick	.15
79	Rafael Palmeiro	.65
80	Barry Bonds	2.00
81	Gary Sheffield	.40
82	Jim Edmonds	.25
83	Kazuhisa Ishii	.15
84	Jose Hernandez	.15
85	Jason Giambi	.40
86	Mark Mulder	.15
87	Roger Clemens	1.00
88	Troy Glaus	.75
89	Carlos Delgado	.50
90	Mike Sweeney	.15
91	Ken Griffey Jr.	1.25
92	Manny Ramirez	.75
93	Ryan Klesko	.15
94	Larry Walker	.15
95	Adam Dunn	.65
96	Raul Ibanez	.15
97	Preston Wilson	.15
98	Roy Oswalt	.15
99	Sammy Sosa	1.25
100	Mike Piazza	1.25
101	Jose Reyes	.25
102	Ed Rogers	.15
103	Hank Blalock	.75
104	Mark Teixeira	.65
105	Orlando Hudson	.15
106	Drew Henson	.25
107	Joe Mauer	.75
108	Carl Crawford	.15
109	Marlon Byrd	.15
110	Jason Stokes	.15
111	Miguel Cabrera	.50
112	Wilson Betemit	.15
113	Jerome Williams	.15
114	Walter Young	.15
115	*Juan Camacho*	.15
116	*Chris Duncan*	.50
117	*Franklin Gutierrez*	3.00
118	Adam LaRoche	.50
119	*Manuel Ramirez*	.50
120	*Il Kim*	.50
121	*Wayne Lydon*	.50
122	*Daryl Clark*	.50
123	Sean Pierce	.15
124	*Andy Marte*	3.00
125	*Matthew Peterson*	.75

Photographer's Proof

Stars (1-100): 4-8X
Cards (101-125): 2-4X
Production 299 sets

Royal Gold

Stars: 1-3X
Inserted 1:1

Beam Team

		NM/M
Complete Set (20):		50.00
Common Player:		1.00
Inserted 1:12		
BT1	Larry Walker	1.00
BT2	Miguel Tejada	1.50
BT3	Ichiro Suzuki	5.00
BT4	Sammy Sosa	5.00
BT5	Ivan Rodriguez	2.50
BT6	Alex Rodriguez	6.00
BT7	Mike Piazza	5.00
BT8	Jeff Kent	1.00
BT9	Chipper Jones	4.00
BT10	Derek Jeter	8.00
BT11	Todd Helton	3.00
BT12	Vladimir Guerrero	3.00
BT13	Shawn Green	1.50
BT14	Brian Giles	1.00
BT15	Jason Giambi	2.00
BT16	Nomar Garciaparra	5.00
BT17	Adam Dunn	2.00
BT18	Carlos Delgado	1.50
BT19	Barry Bonds	8.00
BT20	Lance Berkman	1.00

Born In The USA

		NM/M
Common Player:		5.00
Jerseys inserted 1:52		
Bats inserted 1:76		
RA	Rich Aurilia/jsy	5.00
JB	Jeff Bagwell/jsy	12.00
CB	Craig Biggio/jsy	8.00
BB	Bret Boone/jsy	5.00
AB	A.J. Burnett/jsy	5.00
JNB	Jeromy Burnitz/bat	6.00
PB	Pat Burrell/bat	10.00
SB	Sean Burroughs/bat	6.00
EC	Eric Chavez/jsy	6.00
TC	Tony Clark/bat	5.00
JD	Johnny Damon/bat	8.00
JDD	J.D. Drew/bat	6.00
AD	Adam Dunn/bat	12.00
JE	Jim Edmonds/jsy	8.00
CF	Cliff Floyd/bat	5.00
BF	Brad Fullmer/bat	5.00
NG	Nomar Garciaparra/bat	20.00
LG	Luis Gonzalez/bat	6.00
MG	Mark Grace/jsy	12.00
SG	Shawn Green/bat	6.00
TJH	Toby Hall	5.00
JH	Josh Hamilton/bat	5.00
TH	Todd Helton/bat	8.00
RH	Rickey Henderson/bat	15.00
RJ	Randy Johnson/bat	12.00
CJ	Chipper Jones/jsy	12.00
RK	Ryan Klesko/bat	5.00
PK	Paul Konerko/bat	8.00
BL	Barry Larkin/jsy	10.00
TRL	Travis Lee/bat	5.00
TL	Terrence Long/jsy	5.00
GM	Greg Maddux/jsy	15.00
TM	Tino Martinez/bat	10.00
WM	Willie Mays/bat	40.00
EM	Eric Milton/jsy	6.00
JO	John Olerud/jsy	6.00
CP	Corey Patterson/bat	8.00
MP	Mike Piazza/jsy	15.00
AR	Alex Rodriguez/bat	15.00
SR	Scott Rolen/bat	15.00
RS	Richie Sexson/bat	6.00
GS	Gary Sheffield/bat	8.00
JS	John Smoltz/jsy	6.00
FT	Frank Thomas/bat	8.00
JT	Jim Thome/jsy	15.00
MV	Mo Vaughn/bat	6.00
RV	Robin Ventura/bat	8.00
MW	Matt Williams/bat	8.00
PW	Preston Wilson/jsy	5.00
KW	Kerry Wood/bat	10.00

Clubhouse Exclusive

		NM/M
Jersey inserted 1:488		
Jersey & Bat 1:2,073		
Jersey, Bat & Spikes 1:2,750		
CE1	Albert Pujols/jsy	15.00
CE2	Albert Pujols/bat/jsy	35.00
CE3	Albert Pujols/ jsy/bat/spike	100.00

Co-Signers

		NM/M
HTA Exclusive		
MI	Masanori Murakami, Kazuhisa Ishii	180.00
AM	Hank Aaron, Willie Mays	400.00

License To Drive

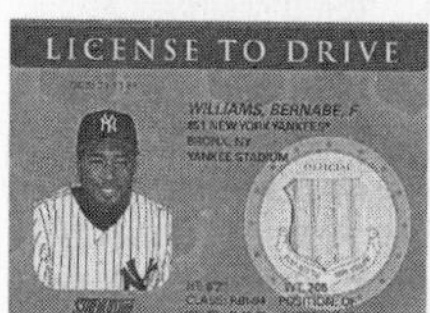

		NM/M
Common Player:		5.00
Inserted 1:98		
RA	Roberto Alomar	8.00
MA	Moises Alou	6.00
AB	Adrian Beltre	8.00
LB	Lance Berkman	6.00
EC	Eric Chavez	6.00
AD	Adam Dunn	8.00
NG	Nomar Garciaparra	15.00
JG	Juan Gonzalez	8.00
LG	Luis Gonzalez	6.00
SG	Shawn Green	8.00
TH	Todd Helton	10.00
AJ	Andruw Jones	10.00
CJ	Chipper Jones	12.00
TM	Tino Martinez	6.00
RP	Rafael Palmeiro	8.00
MP	Mike Piazza	15.00
AP	Albert Pujols	25.00
ANR	Aramis Ramirez	6.00
AR	Alex Rodriguez	20.00
IR	Ivan Rodriguez	8.00
SR	Scott Rolen	10.00
GS	Gary Sheffield	8.00
FT	Frank Thomas	10.00
LW	Larry Walker	6.00
BW	Bernie Williams	6.00

MLB Match-Ups

		NM/M
Inserted 1:485		
BB	Bret Boone	15.00
TH	Todd Helton	15.00
AJ	Andruw Jones	12.00
GM	Greg Maddux	30.00
AP	Albert Pujols	30.00

Stadium Shots

		NM/M
Complete Set (10):		25.00
Common Player:		1.00
Inserted 1:24		
SS1	Lance Berkman	1.00
SS2	Barry Bonds	6.00
SS3	Jason Giambi	2.50
SS4	Shawn Green	1.50
SS5	Vladimir Guerrero	3.00
SS6	Paul Konerko	1.00
SS7	Mike Piazza	4.50
SS8	Alex Rodriguez	6.00
SS9	Sammy Sosa	4.50
SS10	Jim Thome	2.00

Stadium Slices Handle

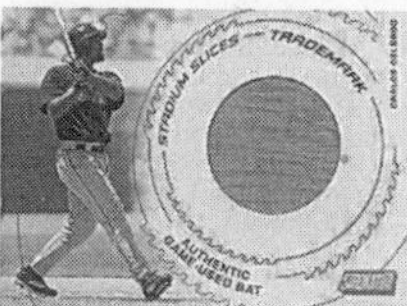

		NM/M
Common Player:		5.00
Inserted 1:237		
Trademarks:		1-1.5X
Inserted 1:415		
Barrels:		1.5-2X
Inserted 1:550		
RA	Roberto Alomar	15.00
CD	Carlos Delgado	8.00
NG	Nomar Garciaparra	20.00
TH	Todd Helton	10.00
AJ	Andruw Jones	8.00
RP	Rafael Palmeiro	10.00
MP	Mike Piazza	15.00
AP	Albert Pujols	20.00
AR	Alex Rodriguez	15.00
GS	Gary Sheffield	10.00

World Stage

		NM/M
Common Player:		5.00
Jerseys inserted 1:118		
Bats inserted 1:809		
AB	Adrian Beltre/jsy	6.00
KI	Kazuhisa Ishii/jsy	5.00
BK	Byung-Hyun Kim/jsy	5.00
HN	Hideo Nomo/bat	20.00
AP	Albert Pujols/jsy	15.00
IR	Ivan Rodriguez/jsy	8.00
KS	Kazuhiro Sasaki/jsy	5.00
TS	Tsuyoshi Shinjo/bat	5.00
AS	Alfonso Soriano/bat	15.00
MT	Miguel Tejada/jsy	8.00

1991 STUDIO PREVIEW

		NM/M
Complete Set (18):		5.00
Common Player:		.50
1	Juan Bell	.50
2	Roger Clemens	3.00
3	Dave Parker	.50
4	Tim Raines	.50
5	Kevin Seitzer	.50
6	Teddy Higuera	.50
7	Bernie Williams	.50
8	Harold Baines	.50
9	Gary Pettis	.50
10	Dave Justice	.50
11	Eric Davis	.50
12	Andujar Cedeno	.50
13	Tom Foley	.50
14	Dwight Gooden	.50
15	Doug Drabek	.50
16	Steve Decker	.50
17	Joe Torre	.75
18	Header card	.10

1991 STUDIO

		NM/M
Complete Set (264):		7.50
Common Player:		.05
Foil Pack (10):		.50
Foil Box (48):		12.50
1	Glenn Davis	.05
2	Dwight Evans	.05
3	Leo Gomez	.05
4	Chris Hoiles	.05
5	Sam Horn	.05
6	Ben McDonald	.05
7	Randy Milligan	.05
8	Gregg Olson	.05
9	Cal Ripken, Jr.	1.00
10	David Segui	.05
11	Wade Boggs	.40
12	Ellis Burks	.05
13	Jack Clark	.05
14	Roger Clemens	.45
15	Mike Greenwell	.05
16	Tim Naehring	.05
17	Tony Pena	.05
18	*Phil Plantier*	.05
19	Jeff Reardon	.05
20	Mo Vaughn	.05
21	Jimmy Reese	.05
22	Jim Abbott	.05
23	Bert Blyleven	.05
24	Chuck Finley	.05
25	Gary Gaetti	.05
26	Wally Joyner	.05
27	Mark Langston	.05
28	Kirk McCaskill	.05
29	Lance Parrish	.05
30	Dave Winfield	.30
31	Alex Fernandez	.05
32	Carlton Fisk	.30
33	Scott Fletcher	.05
34	Greg Hibbard	.05
35	Charlie Hough	.05
36	Jack McDowell	.05
37	Tim Raines	.05
38	Sammy Sosa	.40
39	Bobby Thigpen	.05
40	Frank Thomas	.30
41	Sandy Alomar	.05
42	John Farrell	.05
43	Glenallen Hill	.05
44	Brook Jacoby	.05
45	Chris James	.05
46	Doug Jones	.05
47	Eric King	.05
48	Mark Lewis	.05
49	Greg Swindell	.05
50	Mark Whiten	.05
51	Milt Cuyler	.05
52	Rob Deer	.05
53	Cecil Fielder	.05
54	Travis Fryman	.05
55	Bill Gullickson	.05
56	Lloyd Moseby	.05
57	Frank Tanana	.05
58	Mickey Tettleton	.05
59	Alan Trammell	.05
60	Lou Whitaker	.05
61	Mike Boddicker	.05
62	George Brett	.45
63	Jeff Conine	.05
64	Warren Cromartie	.05
65	Storm Davis	.05
66	Kirk Gibson	.05
67	Mark Gubicza	.05
68	*Brian McRae*	.05
69	Bret Saberhagen	.05
70	Kurt Stillwell	.05
71	Tim McIntosh	.05
72	Candy Maldonado	.05
73	Paul Molitor	.30
74	Willie Randolph	.05
75	Ron Robinson	.05
76	Gary Sheffield	.20
77	Franklin Stubbs	.05
78	B.J. Surhoff	.05
79	Greg Vaughn	.05
80	Robin Yount	.30
81	Rick Aguilera	.05
82	Steve Bedrosian	.05
83	Scott Erickson	.05
84	Greg Gagne	.05
85	Dan Gladden	.05
86	Brian Harper	.05
87	Kent Hrbek	.05
88	Shane Mack	.05
89	Jack Morris	.05
90	Kirby Puckett	.40
91	Jesse Barfield	.05
92	Steve Farr	.05
93	Steve Howe	.05
94	Roberto Kelly	.05
95	Tim Leary	.05
96	Kevin Maas	.05
97	Don Mattingly	.45
98	Hensley Meulens	.05
99	Scott Sanderson	.05
100	Steve Sax	.05
101	Jose Canseco	.20
102	Dennis Eckersley	.25
103	Dave Henderson	.05
104	Rickey Henderson	.30
105	Rick Honeycutt	.05
106	Mark McGwire	.75
107	Dave Stewart	.05
108	Eric Show	.05
109	*Todd Van Poppel*	.05
110	Bob Welch	.05
111	Alvin Davis	.05
112	Ken Griffey, Jr.	.50
113	Ken Griffey, Sr.	.05
114	Erik Hanson	.05
115	Brian Holman	.05
116	Randy Johnson	.30
117	Edgar Martinez	.05
118	Tino Martinez	.05
119	Harold Reynolds	.05
120	David Valle	.05
121	Kevin Belcher	.05
122	Scott Chiamparino	.05
123	Julio Franco	.05
124	Juan Gonzalez	.20
125	Rich Gossage	.05
126	Jeff Kunkel	.05
127	Rafael Palmeiro	.25
128	Nolan Ryan	1.00
129	Ruben Sierra	.05
130	Bobby Witt	.05
131	Roberto Alomar	.10
132	Tom Candiotti	.05
133	Joe Carter	.05
134	Ken Dayley	.05
135	Kelly Gruber	.05
136	John Olerud	.05
137	Dave Stieb	.05
138	Turner Ward	.05
139	Devon White	.05
140	Mookie Wilson	.05
141	Steve Avery	.05
142	Sid Bream	.05
143	Nick Esasky	.05
144	Ron Gant	.05
145	Tom Glavine	.20
146	Dave Justice	.05
147	Kelly Mann	.05
148	Terry Pendleton	.05
149	John Smoltz	.05
150	Jeff Treadway	.05
151	George Bell	.05
152	Shawn Boskie	.05
153	Andre Dawson	.20
154	Lance Dickson	.05
155	Shawon Dunston	.05
156	Joe Girardi	.05
157	Mark Grace	.05

#	Player	Price
158	Ryne Sandberg	.40
159	Gary Scott	.05
160	Dave Smith	.05
161	Tom Browning	.05
162	Eric Davis	.05
163	Rob Dibble	.05
164	Mariano Duncan	.05
165	Chris Hammond	.05
166	Billy Hatcher	.05
167	Barry Larkin	.05
168	Hal Morris	.05
169	Paul O'Neill	.05
170	Chris Sabo	.05
171	Eric Anthony	.05
172	*Jeff Bagwell*	1.50
173	Craig Biggio	.05
174	Ken Caminitti	.05
175	Jim Deshaies	.05
176	Steve Finley	.05
177	Pete Harnisch	.05
178	Darryl Kile	.05
179	Curt Schilling	.20
180	Mike Scott	.05
181	Brett Butler	.05
182	Gary Carter	.30
183	Orel Hershiser	.05
184	Ramon Martinez	.05
185	Eddie Murray	.30
186	Jose Offerman	.05
187	Bob Ojeda	.05
188	Juan Samuel	.05
189	Mike Scioscia	.05
190	Darryl Strawberry	.05
191	Moises Alou	.05
192	Brian Barnes	.05
193	Oil Can Boyd	.05
194	Ivan Calderon	.05
195	Delino DeShields	.05
196	Mike Fitzgerald	.05
197	Andres Galarraga	.05
198	Marquis Grissom	.05
199	Bill Sampen	.05
200	Tim Wallach	.05
201	Daryl Boston	.05
202	Vince Coleman	.05
203	John Franco	.05
204	Dwight Gooden	.05
205	Tom Herr	.05
206	Gregg Jefferies	.05
207	Howard Johnson	.05
208	Dave Magadan	.05
209	Kevin McReynolds	.05
210	Frank Viola	.05
211	Wes Chamberlain	.05
212	Darren Daulton	.05
213	Len Dykstra	.05
214	Charlie Hayes	.05
215	Ricky Jordan	.05
216	Steve Lake	.05
217	Roger McDowell	.05
218	Mickey Morandini	.05
219	Terry Mulholland	.05
220	Dale Murphy	.15
221	Jay Bell	.05
222	Barry Bonds	1.00
223	Bobby Bonilla	.05
224	Doug Drabek	.05
225	Bill Landrum	.05
226	Mike LaValliere	.05
227	Jose Lind	.05
228	Don Slaught	.05
229	John Smiley	.05
230	Andy Van Slyke	.05
231	Bernard Gilkey	.05
232	Pedro Guerrero	.05
233	Rex Hudler	.05
234	Ray Lankford	.05
235	Joe Magrane	.05
236	Jose Oquendo	.05
237	Lee Smith	.05
238	Ozzie Smith	.40
239	Milt Thompson	.05
240	Todd Zeile	.05
241	Larry Andersen	.05
242	Andy Benes	.05
243	Paul Faries	.05
244	Tony Fernandez	.05
245	Tony Gwynn	.40
246	Atlee Hammaker	.05
247	Fred McGriff	.05
248	Bip Roberts	.05
249	Benito Santiago	.05
250	Ed Whitson	.05
251	Dave Anderson	.05
252	Mike Benjamin	.05
253	John Burkett	.05
254	Will Clark	.05
255	Scott Garrelts	.05
256	Willie McGee	.05
257	Kevin Mitchell	.05
258	Dave Righetti	.05
259	Matt Williams	.05
260	Bud Black, Steve Decker (Black & Decker)	.10
261	Checklist	.03
262	Checklist	.03
263	Checklist	.03
---	Header card	.03

1992 STUDIO PREVIEW

		NM/M
	Complete Set (22):	75.00
	Common Player:	1.50
1	Ruben Sierra	1.50
2	Kirby Puckett	6.00
3	Ryne Sandberg	6.00
4	John Kruk	1.50
5	Cal Ripken, Jr.	12.00
6	Robin Yount	4.50
7	Dwight Gooden	1.50
8	David Justice	1.50
9	Don Mattingly	7.50
10	Wally Joyner	1.50
11	Will Clark	1.50
12	Rob Dibble	1.50
13	Roberto Alomar	2.50
14	Wade Boggs	6.00
15	Barry Bonds	12.00
16	Jeff Bagwell	4.50
17	Mark McGwire	9.00
18	Frank Thomas	6.00
19	Brett Butler	1.50
20	Ozzie Smith	6.00
21	Jim Abbott	1.50
22	Tony Gwynn	6.00

1992 STUDIO

		NM/M
	Complete Set (264):	8.00
	Common Player:	.05
	Pack (10):	.65
	Wax Box (48):	15.00
1	Steve Avery	.05
2	Sid Bream	.05
3	Ron Gant	.05
4	Tom Glavine	.25
5	Dave Justice	.05
6	Mark Lemke	.05
7	Greg Olson	.05
8	Terry Pendleton	.05
9	Deion Sanders	.05
10	John Smoltz	.05
11	Doug Dascenzo	.05
12	Andre Dawson	.25
13	Joe Girardi	.05
14	Mark Grace	.05
15	Greg Maddux	.50
16	Chuck McElroy	.05
17	Mike Morgan	.05
18	Ryne Sandberg	.50
19	Gary Scott	.05
20	Sammy Sosa	.50
21	Norm Charlton	.05
22	Rob Dibble	.05
23	Barry Larkin	.05
24	Hal Morris	.05
25	Paul O'Neill	.05
26	Jose Rijo	.05
27	Bip Roberts	.05
28	Chris Sabo	.05
29	Reggie Sanders	.05
30	Greg Swindell	.05
31	Jeff Bagwell	.45
32	Craig Biggio	.05
33	Ken Caminiti	.05
34	Andujar Cedeno	.05
35	Steve Finley	.05
36	Pete Harnisch	.05
37	Butch Henry	.05
38	Doug Jones	.05
39	Darryl Kile	.05
40	Eddie Taubensee	.05
41	Brett Butler	.05
42	Tom Candiotti	.05
43	Eric Davis	.05
44	Orel Hershiser	.05
45	Eric Karros	.05
46	Ramon Martinez	.05
47	Jose Offerman	.05
48	Mike Scioscia	.05
49	Mike Sharperson	.05
50	Darryl Strawberry	.05
51	Bret Barbarie	.05
52	Ivan Calderon	.05
53	Gary Carter	.45
54	Delino DeShields	.05
55	Marquis Grissom	.05
56	Ken Hill	.05
57	Dennis Martinez	.05
58	Spike Owen	.05
59	Larry Walker	.05
60	Tim Wallach	.05
61	Bobby Bonilla	.05
62	Tim Burke	.05
63	Vince Coleman	.05
64	John Franco	.05
65	Dwight Gooden	.05
66	Todd Hundley	.05
67	Howard Johnson	.05
68	Eddie Murray	.45
69	Bret Saberhagen	.05
70	Anthony Young	.05
71	Kim Batiste	.05
72	Wes Chamberlain	.05
73	Darren Daulton	.05
74	Mariano Duncan	.05
75	Len Dykstra	.05
76	John Kruk	.05
77	Mickey Morandini	.05
78	Terry Mulholland	.05
79	Dale Murphy	.20
80	Mitch Williams	.05
81	Jay Bell	.05
82	Barry Bonds	1.00
83	Steve Buechele	.05
84	Doug Drabek	.05
85	Mike LaValliere	.05
86	Jose Lind	.05
87	Denny Neagle	.05
88	Randy Tomlin	.05
89	Andy Van Slyke	.05
90	Gary Varsho	.05
91	Pedro Guerrero	.05
92	Rex Hudler	.05
93	Brian Jordan	.05
94	Felix Jose	.05
95	Donovan Osborne	.05
96	Tom Pagnozzi	.05
97	Lee Smith	.05
98	Ozzie Smith	.50
99	Todd Worrell	.05
100	Todd Zeile	.05
101	Andy Benes	.05
102	Jerald Clark	.05
103	Tony Fernandez	.05
104	Tony Gwynn	.50
105	Greg Harris	.05
106	Fred McGriff	.05
107	Benito Santiago	.05
108	Gary Sheffield	.30
109	Kurt Stillwell	.05
110	Tim Teufel	.05
111	Kevin Bass	.05
112	Jeff Brantley	.05
113	John Burkett	.05
114	Will Clark	.05
115	Royce Clayton	.05
116	Mike Jackson	.05
117	Darren Lewis	.05
118	Bill Swift	.05
119	Robby Thompson	.05
120	Matt Williams	.05
121	Brady Anderson	.05
122	Glenn Davis	.05
123	Mike Devereaux	.05
124	Chris Hoiles	.05
125	Sam Horn	.05
126	Ben McDonald	.05
127	Mike Mussina	.25
128	Gregg Olson	.05
129	Cal Ripken, Jr.	1.00
130	Rick Sutcliffe	.05
131	Wade Boggs	.50
132	Roger Clemens	.60
133	Greg Harris	.05
134	Tim Naehring	.05
135	Tony Pena	.05
136	Phil Plantier	.05
137	Jeff Reardon	.05
138	Jody Reed	.05
139	Mo Vaughn	.05
140	Frank Viola	.05
141	Jim Abbott	.05
142	Hubie Brooks	.05
143	*Chad Curtis*	.05
144	Gary DiSarcina	.05
145	Chuck Finley	.05
146	Bryan Harvey	.05
147	Von Hayes	.05
148	Mark Langston	.05
149	Lance Parrish	.05
150	Lee Stevens	.05
151	George Bell	.05
152	Alex Fernandez	.05
153	Greg Hibbard	.05
154	Lance Johnson	.05
155	Kirk McCaskill	.05
156	Tim Raines	.05
157	Steve Sax	.05
158	Bobby Thigpen	.05
159	Frank Thomas	.45
160	Robin Ventura	.05
161	Sandy Alomar, Jr.	.05
162	Jack Armstrong	.05
163	Carlos Baerga	.05
164	Albert Belle	.05
165	Alex Cole	.05
166	Glenallen Hill	.05
167	Mark Lewis	.05
168	Kenny Lofton	.05
169	Paul Sorrento	.05
170	Mark Whiten	.05
171	Milt Cuyler (color photo is Lou Whitaker)	.05
172	Rob Deer	.05
173	Cecil Fielder	.05
174	Travis Fryman	.05
175	Mike Henneman	.05
176	Tony Phillips	.05
177	Frank Tanana	.05
178	Mickey Tettleton	.05
179	Alan Trammell	.05
180	Lou Whitaker	.05
181	George Brett	.60
182	Tom Gordon	.05
183	Mark Gubicza	.05
184	Gregg Jefferies	.05
185	Wally Joyner	.05
186	Brent Mayne	.05
187	Brian McRae	.05
188	Kevin McReynolds	.05
189	Keith Miller	.05
190	Jeff Montgomery	.05
191	Dante Bichette	.05
192	Ricky Bones	.05
193	Scott Fletcher	.05
194	Paul Molitor	.45
195	Jaime Navarro	.05
196	Franklin Stubbs	.05
197	B.J. Surhoff	.05
198	Greg Vaughn	.05
199	Bill Wegman	.05
200	Robin Yount	.45
201	Rick Aguilera	.05
202	Scott Erickson	.05
203	Greg Gagne	.05
204	Brian Harper	.05
205	Kent Hrbek	.05
206	Scott Leius	.05
207	Shane Mack	.05
208	Pat Mahomes	.05
209	Kirby Puckett	.50
210	John Smiley	.05
211	Mike Gallego	.05
212	Charlie Hayes	.05
213	Pat Kelly	.05

214	Roberto Kelly	.05
215	Kevin Maas	.05
216	Don Mattingly	.60
217	Matt Nokes	.05
218	Melido Perez	.05
219	Scott Sanderson	.05
220	Danny Tartabull	.05
221	Harold Baines	.05
222	Jose Canseco	.30
223	Dennis Eckersley	.35
224	Dave Henderson	.05
225	Carney Lansford	.05
226	Mark McGwire	.75
227	Mike Moore	.05
228	Randy Ready	.05
229	Terry Steinbach	.05
230	Dave Stewart	.05
231	Jay Buhner	.05
232	Ken Griffey, Jr.	.65
233	Erik Hanson	.05
234	Randy Johnson	.45
235	Edgar Martinez	.05
236	Tino Martinez	.05
237	Kevin Mitchell	.05
238	Pete O'Brien	.05
239	Harold Reynolds	.05
240	David Valle	.05
241	Julio Franco	.05
242	Juan Gonzalez	.25
243	Jose Guzman	.05
244	Rafael Palmeiro	.35
245	Dean Palmer	.05
246	Ivan Rodriguez	.35
247	Jeff Russell	.05
248	Nolan Ryan	1.00
249	Ruben Sierra	.05
250	Dickie Thon	.05
251	Roberto Alomar	.20
252	Derek Bell	.05
253	Pat Borders	.05
254	Joe Carter	.05
255	Kelly Gruber	.05
256	Juan Guzman	.05
257	Jack Morris	.05
258	John Olerud	.05
259	Devon White	.05
260	Dave Winfield	.45
261	Checklist	.05
262	Checklist	.05
263	Checklist	.05
264	History card	.05

Heritage

		NM/M
Complete Set (14):		6.00
Common Player:		.50
1	Ryne Sandberg	1.00
2	Carlton Fisk	.75
3	Wade Boggs	1.00
4	Jose Canseco	.65
5	Don Mattingly	1.25
6	Darryl Strawberry	.50
7	Cal Ripken, Jr.	1.50
8	Will Clark	.50
9	Andre Dawson	.50
10	Andy Van Slyke	.50
11	Paul Molitor	.75
12	Jeff Bagwell	.75
13	Darren Daulton	.50
14	Kirby Puckett	1.00

1993 STUDIO

		NM/M
Complete Set (220):		15.00
Common Player:		.05
Pack (12):		.75
Wax Box (36):		12.50
1	Dennis Eckersley	.35
2	Chad Curtis	.05
3	Eric Anthony	.05
4	Roberto Alomar	.20
5	Steve Avery	.05
6	Cal Eldred	.05
7	Bernard Gilkey	.05
8	Steve Buechele	.05
9	Brett Butler	.05
10	Terry Mulholland	.05
11	Moises Alou	.05
12	Barry Bonds	1.00
13	Sandy Alomar Jr.	.05
14	Chris Bosio	.05
15	Scott Sanderson	.05
16	Bobby Bonilla	.05
17	Brady Anderson	.05
18	Derek Bell	.05
19	Wes Chamberlain	.05
20	Jay Bell	.05
21	Kevin Brown	.05
22	Roger Clemens	.60
23	Roberto Kelly	.05
24	Dante Bichette	.05
25	George Brett	.60
26	Rob Deer	.05
27	Brian Harper	.05
28	George Bell	.05
29	Jim Abbott	.05
30	Dave Henderson	.05
31	Wade Boggs	.50
32	Chili Davis	.05
33	Ellis Burks	.05
34	Jeff Bagwell	.40
35	Kent Hrbek	.05
36	Pat Borders	.05
37	Cecil Fielder	.05
38	Sid Bream	.05
39	Greg Gagne	.05
40	Darryl Hamilton	.05
41	Jerald Clark	.05
42	Mark Grace	.05
43	Barry Larkin	.05
44	John Burkett	.05
45	Scott Cooper	.05
46	*Mike Lansing*	.25
47	Jose Canseco	.30
48	Will Clark	.05
49	Carlos Garcia	.05
50	Carlos Baerga	.05
51	Darren Daulton	.05
52	Jay Buhner	.05
53	Andy Benes	.05
54	Jeff Conine	.05
55	Mike Devereaux	.05
56	Vince Coleman	.05
57	Terry Steinbach	.05
58	*J.T. Snow*	.40
59	Greg Swindell	.05
60	Devon White	.05
61	John Smoltz	.05
62	Todd Zeile	.05
63	Rick Wilkins	.05
64	Tim Wallach	.05
65	John Wetteland	.05
66	Matt Williams	.05
67	Paul Sorrento	.05
68	David Valle	.05
69	Walt Weiss	.05
70	John Franco	.05
71	Nolan Ryan	1.00
72	Frank Viola	.05
73	Chris Sabo	.05
74	David Nied	.05
75	Kevin McReynolds	.05
76	Lou Whitaker	.05
77	Dave Winfield	.40
78	Robin Ventura	.05
79	Spike Owen	.05
80	Cal Ripken, Jr.	1.00
81	Dan Walter	.05
82	Mitch Williams	.05
83	Tim Wakefield	.05
84	Rickey Henderson	.40
85	Gary DiSarcina	.05
86	Craig Biggio	.05
87	Joe Carter	.05
88	Ron Gant	.05
89	John Jaha	.05
90	Gregg Jefferies	.05
91	Jose Guzman	.05
92	Eric Karros	.05
93	Wil Cordero	.05
94	Royce Clayton	.05
95	Albert Belle	.05
96	Ken Griffey, Jr.	.65
97	Orestes Destrade	.05
98	Tony Fernandez	.05
99	Leo Gomez	.05
100	Tony Gwynn	.50
101	Len Dykstra	.05
102	Jeff King	.05
103	Julio Franco	.05
104	Andre Dawson	.25
105	Randy Milligan	.05
106	Alex Cole	.05
107	Phil Hiatt	.05
108	Travis Fryman	.05
109	Chuck Knoblauch	.05
110	Bo Jackson	.10
111	Pat Kelly	.05
112	Bret Saberhagen	.05
113	Ruben Sierra	.05
114	Tim Salmon	.05
115	Doug Jones	.05
116	Ed Sprague	.05
117	Terry Pendleton	.05
118	Robin Yount	.40
119	Mark Whiten	.05
120	Checklist	.05
121	Sammy Sosa	.50
122	Darryl Strawberry	.05
123	Larry Walker	.05
124	Robby Thompson	.05
125	Carlos Martinez	.05
126	Edgar Martinez	.05
127	Benito Santiago	.05
128	Howard Johnson	.05
129	Harold Reynolds	.05
130	Craig Shipley	.05
131	Curt Schilling	.30
132	Andy Van Slyke	.05
133	Ivan Rodriguez	.35
134	Mo Vaughn	.05
135	Bip Roberts	.05
136	Charlie Hayes	.05
137	Brian McRae	.05
138	Mickey Tettleton	.05
139	Frank Thomas	.40
140	Paul O'Neill	.05
141	Mark McGwire	.75
142	Damion Easley	.05
143	Ken Caminiti	.05
144	Juan Guzman	.05
145	Tom Glavine	.25
146	Pat Listach	.05
147	Lee Smith	.05
148	Derrick May	.05
149	Ramon Martinez	.05
150	Delino DeShields	.05
151	Kirt Manwaring	.05
152	Reggie Jefferson	.05
153	Randy Johnson	.40
154	Dave Magadan	.05
155	Dwight Gooden	.05
156	Chris Hoiles	.05
157	Fred McGriff	.05
158	Dave Hollins	.05
159	Al Martin	.05
160	Juan Gonzalez	.20
161	Mike Greenwell	.05
162	Kevin Mitchell	.05
163	Andres Galarraga	.05
164	Wally Joyner	.05
165	Kirk Gibson	.05
166	Pedro Munoz	.05
167	Ozzie Guillen	.05
168	Jimmy Key	.05
169	Kevin Seitzer	.05
170	Luis Polonia	.05
171	Luis Gonzalez	.05
172	Paul Molitor	.40
173	Dave Justice	.05
174	B.J. Surhoff	.05
175	Ray Lankford	.05
176	Ryne Sandberg	.50
177	Jody Reed	.05
178	Marquis Grissom	.05
179	Willie McGee	.05
180	Kenny Lofton	.05
181	Junior Felix	.05
182	Jose Offerman	.05
183	John Kruk	.05
184	Orlando Merced	.05
185	Rafael Palmeiro	.35
186	Billy Hatcher	.05
187	Joe Oliver	.05
188	Joe Girardi	.05
189	Jose Lind	.05
190	Harold Baines	.05
191	Mike Pagliarulo	.05
192	Lance Johnson	.05
193	Don Mattingly	.60
194	Doug Drabek	.05
195	John Olerud	.05
196	Greg Maddux	.50
197	Greg Vaughn	.05
198	Tom Pagnozzi	.05
199	Willie Wilson	.05
200	Jack McDowell	.05
201	Mike Piazza	.65
202	Mike Mussina	.30
203	Charles Nagy	.05
204	Tino Martinez	.05
205	Charlie Hough	.05
206	Todd Hundley	.05
207	Gary Sheffield	.30
208	Mickey Morandini	.05
209	Don Slaught	.05
210	Dean Palmer	.05
211	Jose Rijo	.05
212	Vinny Castilla	.05
213	Tony Phillips	.05
214	Kirby Puckett	.50
215	Tim Raines	.05
216	Otis Nixon	.05
217	Ozzie Smith	.50
218	Jose Vizcaino	.05
220	Checklist	.05

Heritage

		NM/M
Complete Set (12):		12.00
Common Player:		.50
1	George Brett	2.00
2	Juan Gonzalez	.75
3	Roger Clemens	2.00
4	Mark McGwire	4.00
5	Mark Grace	.50
6	Ozzie Smith	1.50
7	Barry Larkin	.50
8	Frank Thomas	1.00
9	Carlos Baerga	.50
10	Eric Karros	.50
11	J.T. Snow	.50
12	John Kruk	.50

Silhouettes

		NM/M
Complete Set (10):		7.00
Common Player:		.15
1	Frank Thomas	.65
2	Barry Bonds	3.00
3	Jeff Bagwell	.65
4	Juan Gonzalez	.40
5	Travis Fryman	.15
6	J.T. Snow	.15
7	John Kruk	.15
8	Jeff Blauser	.15
9	Mike Piazza	2.00
10	Nolan Ryan	3.00

Superstars on Canvas

		NM/M
Complete Set (10):		8.00
Common Player:		.25
1	Ken Griffey, Jr.	1.50
2	Jose Canseco	.60
3	Mark McGwire	2.00
4	Mike Mussina	.50

5	Joe Carter	.25
6	Frank Thomas	1.00
7	Darren Daulton	.25
8	Mark Grace	.25
9	Andres Galarraga	.25
10	Barry Bonds	2.50

Frank Thomas

		NM/M
Complete Set (5):		5.00
Common Card:		1.00
1	Childhood	1.00
2	Baseball Memories	1.00
3	Importance of Family	1.00
4	Performance	1.00
5	On Being a Role Model	1.00

1994 STUDIO

		NM/M
Complete Set (220):		7.50
Common Player:		.05
Pack (12):		.45
Wax Box (36):		10.00
1	Dennis Eckersley	.45
2	Brent Gates	.05
3	Rickey Henderson	.55
4	Mark McGwire	1.00
5	Troy Neel	.05
6	Ruben Sierra	.05
7	Terry Steinbach	.05
8	Chad Curtis	.05
9	Chili Davis	.05
10	Gary DiSarcina	.05
11	Damion Easley	.05
12	Bo Jackson	.10
13	Mark Langston	.05
14	Eduardo Perez	.05
15	Tim Salmon	.05
16	Jeff Bagwell	.55
17	Craig Biggio	.05
18	Ken Caminiti	.05
19	Andujar Cedeno	.05
20	Doug Drabek	.05
21	Steve Finley	.05
22	Luis Gonzalez	.05
23	Darryl Kile	.05
24	Roberto Alomar	.20
25	Pat Borders	.05
26	Joe Carter	.05
27	Carlos Delgado	.40
28	Pat Hentgen	.05
29	Paul Molitor	.55
30	John Olerud	.05
31	Ed Sprague	.05
32	Devon White	.05
33	Steve Avery	.05
34	Tom Glavine	.25
35	David Justice	.05
36	Roberto Kelly	.05
37	Ryan Klesko	.05
38	Javier Lopez	.05
39	Greg Maddux	.60
40	Fred McGriff	.05
41	Terry Pendleton	.05
42	Ricky Bones	.05
43	Darryl Hamilton	.05
44	Brian Harper	.05
45	John Jaha	.05
46	Dave Nilsson	.05
47	Kevin Seitzer	.05
48	Greg Vaughn	.05
49	Turner Ward	.05
50	Bernard Gilkey	.05
51	Gregg Jefferies	.05
52	Ray Lankford	.05
53	Tom Pagnozzi	.05
54	Ozzie Smith	.60
55	Bob Tewksbury	.05
56	Mark Whiten	.05
57	Todd Zeile	.05
58	Steve Buechele	.05
59	Shawon Dunston	.05
60	Mark Grace	.05
61	Derrick May	.05
62	Tuffy Rhodes	.05
63	Ryne Sandberg	.60
64	Sammy Sosa	.60
65	Rick Wilkins	.05
66	Brett Butler	.05
67	Delino DeShields	.05
68	Orel Hershiser	.05
69	Eric Karros	.05
70	Raul Mondesi	.05
71	Jose Offerman	.05
72	Mike Piazza	.75
73	Tim Wallach	.05
74	Moises Alou	.05
75	Sean Berry	.05
76	Wil Cordero	.05
77	Cliff Floyd	.05
78	Marquis Grissom	.05
79	Ken Hill	.05
80	Larry Walker	.05
81	John Wetteland	.05
82	Rod Beck	.05
83	Barry Bonds	1.50
84	Royce Clayton	.05
85	Darren Lewis	.05
86	Willie McGee	.05
87	Bill Swift	.05
88	Robby Thompson	.05
89	Matt Williams	.05
90	Sandy Alomar Jr.	.05
91	Carlos Baerga	.05
92	Albert Belle	.05
93	Kenny Lofton	.05
94	Eddie Murray	.55
95	Manny Ramirez	.55
96	Paul Sorrento	.05
97	Jim Thome	.45
98	Rich Amaral	.05
99	Eric Anthony	.05
100	Jay Buhner	.05
101	Ken Griffey, Jr.	.75
102	Randy Johnson	.55
103	Edgar Martinez	.05
104	Tino Martinez	.05
105	*Kurt Abbott*	.05
106	Bret Barberie	.05
107	Chuck Carr	.05
108	Jeff Conine	.05
109	Chris Hammond	.05
110	Bryan Harvey	.05
111	Benito Santiago	.05
112	Gary Sheffield	.30
113	Bobby Bonilla	.05
114	Dwight Gooden	.05
115	Todd Hundley	.05
116	Bobby Jones	.05
117	Jeff Kent	.05
118	Kevin McReynolds	.05
119	Bret Saberhagen	.05
120	Ryan Thompson	.05
121	Harold Baines	.05
122	Mike Devereaux	.05
123	Jeffrey Hammonds	.05
124	Ben McDonald	.05
125	Mike Mussina	.25
126	Rafael Palmeiro	.45
127	Cal Ripken, Jr.	1.50
128	Lee Smith	.05
129	Brad Ausmus	.05
130	Derek Bell	.05
131	Andy Benes	.05
132	Tony Gwynn	.60
133	Trevor Hoffman	.05
134	Scott Livingstone	.05
135	Phil Plantier	.05
136	Darren Daulton	.05
137	Mariano Duncan	.05
138	Len Dykstra	.05
139	Dave Hollins	.05
140	Pete Incaviglia	.05
141	Danny Jackson	.05
142	John Kruk	.05
143	Kevin Stocker	.05
144	Jay Bell	.05
145	Carlos Garcia	.05
146	Jeff King	.05
147	Al Martin	.05
148	Orlando Merced	.05
149	Don Slaught	.05
150	Andy Van Slyke	.05
151	Kevin Brown	.05
152	Jose Canseco	.40
153	Will Clark	.05
154	Juan Gonzalez	.30
155	David Hulse	.05
156	Dean Palmer	.05
157	Ivan Rodriguez	.45
158	Kenny Rogers	.05
159	Roger Clemens	.65
160	Scott Cooper	.05
161	Andre Dawson	.25
162	Mike Greenwell	.05
163	Otis Nixon	.05
164	Aaron Sele	.05
165	John Valentin	.05
166	Mo Vaughn	.05
167	Bret Boone	.05
168	Barry Larkin	.05
169	Kevin Mitchell	.05
170	Hal Morris	.05
171	Jose Rijo	.05
172	Deion Sanders	.05
173	Reggie Sanders	.05
174	John Smiley	.05
175	Dante Bichette	.05
176	Ellis Burks	.05
177	Andres Galarraga	.05
178	Joe Girardi	.05
179	Charlie Hayes	.05
180	Roberto Mejia	.05
181	Walt Weiss	.05
182	David Cone	.05
183	Gary Gaetti	.05
184	Greg Gagne	.05
185	Felix Jose	.05
186	Wally Joyner	.05
187	Mike Macfarlane	.05
188	Brian McRae	.05
189	Eric Davis	.05
190	Cecil Fielder	.05
191	Travis Fryman	.05
192	Tony Phillips	.05
193	Mickey Tettleton	.05
194	Alan Trammell	.05
195	Lou Whitaker	.05
196	Kent Hrbek	.05
197	Chuck Knoblauch	.05
198	Shane Mack	.05
199	Pat Meares	.05
200	Kirby Puckett	.60
201	Matt Walbeck	.05
202	Dave Winfield	.55
203	Wilson Alvarez	.05
204	Alex Fernandez	.05
205	Julio Franco	.05
206	Ozzie Guillen	.05
207	Jack McDowell	.05
208	Tim Raines	.05
209	Frank Thomas	.55
210	Robin Ventura	.05
211	Jim Abbott	.05
212	Wade Boggs	.60
213	Pat Kelly	.05
214	Jimmy Key	.05
215	Don Mattingly	.65
216	Paul O'Neill	.05
217	Mike Stanley	.05
218	Danny Tartabull	.05
219	Checklist	.05
220	Checklist	.05

Gold Stars

		NM/M
Complete Set (10):		80.00
Common Player:		4.50
1	Tony Gwynn	9.00
2	Barry Bonds	16.00
3	Frank Thomas	7.50
4	Ken Griffey, Jr.	12.50
5	Joe Carter	4.50
6	Mike Piazza	12.50
7	Cal Ripken, Jr.	16.00
8	Greg Maddux	9.00
9	Juan Gonzalez	5.00
10	Don Mattingly	10.00

Silver Stars

		NM/M
Complete Set (10):		35.00
Common Player:		1.50
1	Tony Gwynn	3.50
2	Barry Bonds	7.50
3	Frank Thomas	2.50
4	Ken Griffey, Jr.	4.50
5	Joe Carter	1.50
6	Mike Piazza	4.50
7	Cal Ripken, Jr.	7.50
8	Greg Maddux	3.50
9	Juan Gonzalez	2.00
10	Don Mattingly	4.00

Editor's Choice

		NM/M
Complete Set (8):		12.00
Common Player:		.50
1	Barry Bonds	3.00
2	Frank Thomas	1.50
3	Ken Griffey, Jr.	2.50
4	Andres Galarraga	.50
5	Juan Gonzalez	.75
6	Tim Salmon	.50
7	Paul O'Neill	.50
8	Mike Piazza	2.50

Heritage

		NM/M
Complete Set (8):		9.00
Common Player:		.50
1	Barry Bonds	4.00
2	Frank Thomas	1.50
3	Joe Carter	.50
4	Don Mattingly	3.00
5	Ryne Sandberg	2.00
6	Javier Lopez	.50
7	Gregg Jefferies	.50
8	Mike Mussina	.65

1995 STUDIO

		NM/M
Complete Set (200):		25.00
Common Player:		.05
Pack (5):		1.00
Wax Box (36):		20.00
1	Frank Thomas	.75
2	Jeff Bagwell	.75
3	Don Mattingly	1.25
4	Mike Piazza	1.50
5	Ken Griffey Jr.	1.50
6	Greg Maddux	1.00
7	Barry Bonds	2.50
8	Cal Ripken Jr.	2.50
9	Jose Canseco	.40
10	Paul Molitor	.75
11	Kenny Lofton	.05
12	Will Clark	.05
13	Tim Salmon	.05
14	Joe Carter	.05
15	Albert Belle	.05
`6	Roger Clemens	1.25
17	Roberto Alomar	.30
18	Alex Rodriguez	2.00
19	Raul Mondesi	.05
20	Deion Sanders	.05
21	Juan Gonzalez	.40

#	Player	Price
22	Kirby Puckett	1.00
23	Fred McGriff	.05
24	Matt Williams	.05
25	Tony Gwynn	1.00
26	Cliff Floyd	.05
27	Travis Fryman	.05
28	Shawn Green	.30
29	Mike Mussina	.35
30	Bob Hamelin	.05
31	Dave Justice	.05
32	Manny Ramirez	.75
33	David Cone	.05
34	Marquis Grissom	.05
35	Moises Alou	.05
36	Carlos Baerga	.05
37	Barry Larkin	.05
38	Robin Ventura	.05
39	Mo Vaughn	.05
40	Jeffrey Hammonds	.05
41	Ozzie Smith	1.00
42	Andres Galarraga	.05
43	Carlos Delgado	.50
44	Lenny Dykstra	.05
45	Cecil Fielder	.05
46	Wade Boggs	1.00
47	Gregg Jefferies	.05
48	Randy Johnson	.75
49	Rafael Palmeiro	.65
50	Craig Biggio	.05
51	Steve Avery	.05
52	Ricky Bottalico	.05
53	Chris Gomez	.05
54	Carlos Garcia	.05
55	Brian Anderson	.05
56	Wilson Alvarez	.05
57	Roberto Kelly	.05
58	Larry Walker	.05
59	Dean Palmer	.05
60	Rick Aguilera	.05
61	Javy Lopez	.05
62	Shawon Dunston	.05
63	William Van Landingham	.05
64	Jeff Kent	.05
65	David McCarty	.05
66	Armando Benitez	.05
67	Brett Butler	.05
68	Bernard Gilkey	.05
69	Joey Hamilton	.05
70	Chad Curtis	.05
71	Dante Bichette	.05
72	Chuck Carr	.05
73	Pedro Martinez	.75
74	Ramon Martinez	.05
75	Rondell White	.05
76	Alex Fernandez	.05
77	Dennis Martinez	.05
78	Sammy Sosa	1.00
79	Bernie Williams	.05
80	Lou Whitaker	.05
81	Kurt Abbott	.05
82	Tino Martinez	.05
83	Willie Greene	.05
84	Garret Anderson	.05
85	Jose Rijo	.05
86	Jeff Montgomery	.05
87	Mark Langston	.05
88	Reggie Sanders	.05
89	Rusty Greer	.05
90	Delino DeShields	.05
91	Jason Bere	.05
92	Lee Smith	.05
93	Devon White	.05
94	John Wetteland	.05
95	Luis Gonzalez	.05
96	Greg Vaughn	.05
97	Lance Johnson	.05
98	Alan Trammell	.05
99	Bret Saberhagen	.05
100	Jack McDowell	.05
101	Trevor Hoffman	.05
102	Dave Nilsson	.05
103	Bryan Harvey	.05
104	Chuck Knoblauch	.05
105	Bobby Bonilla	.05
106	Hal Morris	.05
107	Mark Whiten	.05
108	Phil Plantier	.05
109	Ryan Klesko	.05
110	Greg Gagne	.05
111	Ruben Sierra	.05
112	J.R. Phillips	.05
113	Terry Steinbach	.05
114	Jay Buhner	.05
115	Ken Caminiti	.05
116	Gary DiSarcina	.05
117	Ivan Rodriguez	.65
118	Bip Roberts	.05
119	Jay Bell	.05
120	Ken Hill	.05
121	Mike Greenwell	.05
122	Rick Wilkins	.05
123	Rickey Henderson	.75
124	Dave Hollins	.05
125	Terry Pendleton	.05
126	Rich Becker	.05
127	Billy Ashley	.05
128	Derek Bell	.05
129	Dennis Eckersley	.65
130	Andujar Cedeno	.05
131	John Jaha	.05
132	Chuck Finley	.05
133	Steve Finley	.05
134	Danny Tartabull	.05
135	Jeff Conine	.05
136	Jon Lieber	.05
137	Jim Abbott	.05
138	Steve Traschel	.05
139	Bret Boone	.05
140	Charles Johnson	.05
141	Mark McGwire	2.00
142	Eddie Murray	.75
143	Doug Drabek	.05
144	Steve Cooke	.05
145	Kevin Seitzer	.05
146	Rod Beck	.05
147	Eric Karros	.05
148	Tim Raines	.05
149	Joe Girardi	.05
150	Aaron Sele	.05
151	Robby Thompson	.05
152	Chan Ho Park	.05
153	Ellis Burks	.05
154	Brian McRae	.05
155	Jimmy Key	.05
156	Rico Brogna	.05
157	Ozzie Guillen	.05
158	Chili Davis	.05
159	Darren Daulton	.05
160	Chipper Jones	1.00
161	Walt Weiss	.05
162	Paul O'Neill	.05
163	Al Martin	.05
164	John Valentin	.05
165	Tim Wallach	.05
166	Scott Erickson	.05
167	Ryan Thompson	.05
168	Todd Zeile	.05
169	Scott Cooper	.05
170	Matt Mieske	.05
171	Allen Watson	.05
172	Brian Hunter	.05
173	Kevin Stocker	.05
174	Cal Eldred	.05
175	Tony Phillips	.05
176	Ben McDonald	.05
177	Mark Grace	.05
178	Midre Cummings	.05
179	Orlando Merçed	.05
180	Jeff King	.05
181	Gary Sheffield	.40
182	Tom Glavine	.35
183	Edgar Martinez	.05
184	Steve Karsay	.05
185	Pat Listach	.05
186	Wil Cordero	.05
187	Brady Anderson	.05
188	Bobby Jones	.05
189	Andy Benes	.05
190	Ray Lankford	.05
191	John Doherty	.05
192	Wally Joyner	.05
193	Jim Thome	.65
194	Royce Clayton	.05
195	John Olerud	.05
196	Steve Buechele	.05
197	Harold Baines	.05
198	Geronimo Berroa	.05
199	Checklist	.05
200	Checklist	.05

Gold

		NM/M
Complete Set (50):		25.00
Common Player:		.15
1	Frank Thomas	1.00
2	Jeff Bagwell	1.00
3	Don Mattingly	1.75
4	Mike Piazza	2.00
5	Ken Griffey Jr.	2.00
6	Greg Maddux	1.50
7	Barry Bonds	3.00
8	Cal Ripken Jr.	3.00
9	Jose Canseco	.50
10	Paul Molitor	1.00
11	Kenny Lofton	.15
12	Will Clark	.15
13	Tim Salmon	.15
14	Joe Carter	.15
15	Albert Belle	.15
16	Roger Clemens	1.75
17	Roberto Alomar	.35
18	Alex Rodriguez	2.50
19	Raul Mondesi	.15
20	Deion Sanders	.15
21	Juan Gonzalez	.50
22	Kirby Puckett	1.50
23	Fred McGriff	.15
24	Matt Williams	.15
25	Tony Gwynn	1.50
26	Cliff Floyd	.15
27	Travis Fryman	.15
28	Shawn Green	.40
29	Mike Mussina	.35
30	Bob Hamelin	.15
31	Dave Justice	.15
32	Manny Ramirez	1.00
33	David Cone	.15
34	Marquis Grissom	.15
35	Moises Alou	.15
36	Carlos Baerga	.15
37	Barry Larkin	.15
38	Robin Ventura	.15
39	Mo Vaughn	.15
40	Jeffrey Hammonds	.15
41	Ozzie Smith	1.50
42	Andres Galarraga	.15
43	Carlos Delgado	.50
44	Lenny Dykstra	.15
45	Cecil Fielder	.15
46	Wade Boggs	1.50
47	Gregg Jefferies	.15
48	Randy Johnson	1.00
49	Rafael Palmeiro	.75
50	Craig Biggio	.15

Platinum

		NM/M
Complete Set (25):		25.00
Common Player:		.50
1	Frank Thomas	2.00
2	Jeff Bagwell	2.00
3	Don Mattingly	3.25
4	Mike Piazza	3.50
5	Ken Griffey Jr.	3.50
6	Greg Maddux	3.00
7	Barry Bonds	5.00
8	Cal Ripken Jr.	5.00
9	Jose Canseco	1.00
10	Paul Molitor	2.00
11	Kenny Lofton	.50
12	Will Clark	.50
13	Tim Salmon	.50
14	Joe Carter	.50
15	Albert Belle	.50
16	Roger Clemens	3.25
17	Roberto Alomar	.75
18	Alex Rodriguez	4.00
19	Raul Mondesi	.50
20	Deion Sanders	.50
21	Juan Gonzalez	1.00
22	Kirby Puckett	3.00
23	Fred McGriff	.50
24	Matt Williams	.50
25	Tony Gwynn	3.00

1996 STUDIO

		NM/M
Complete Set (150):		9.00
Common Player:		.05
Pack (7):		1.25
Wax Box (24):		20.00
1	Cal Ripken Jr.	1.50
2	Alex Gonzalez	.05
3	Roger Cedeno	.05
4	Todd Hollandsworth	.05
5	Gregg Jefferies	.05
6	Ryne Sandberg	.65
7	Eric Karros	.05
8	Jeff Conine	.05
9	Rafael Palmeiro	.45
10	Bip Roberts	.05
11	Roger Clemens	.70
12	Tom Glavine	.30
13	Jason Giambi	.40
14	Rey Ordonez	.05
15	Chan Ho Park	.05
16	Vinny Castilla	.05
17	Butch Huskey	.05
18	Greg Maddux	.65
19	Bernard Gilkey	.05
20	Marquis Grissom	.05
21	Chuck Knoblauch	.05
22	Ozzie Smith	.65
23	Garret Anderson	.05
24	J.T. Snow	.05
25	John Valentin	.05
26	Barry Larkin	.05
27	Bobby Bonilla	.05
28	Todd Zeile	.05
29	Roberto Alomar	.20
30	Ramon Martinez	.05
31	Jeff King	.05
32	Dennis Eckersley	.45
33	Derek Jeter	1.50
34	Edgar Martinez	.05
35	Geronimo Berroa	.05
36	Hal Morris	.05
37	Troy Percival	.05
38	Jason Isringhausen	.05
39	Greg Vaughn	.05
40	Robin Ventura	.05
41	Craig Biggio	.05
42	Will Clark	.05
43	Sammy Sosa	.65
44	Bernie Williams	.05
45	Kenny Lofton	.05
46	Wade Boggs	.65
47	Javy Lopez	.05
48	Reggie Sanders	.05
49	Jeff Bagwell	.55
50	Fred McGriff	.05
51	Charles Johnson	.05
52	Darren Daulton	.05
53	Jose Canseco	.40
54	Cecil Fielder	.05
55	Hideo Nomo	.30
56	Tim Salmon	.05
57	Carlos Delgado	.40
58	David Cone	.05
59	Tim Raines	.05
60	Lyle Mouton	.05
61	Wally Joyner	.05
62	Bret Boone	.05
63	Raul Mondesi	.05
64	Gary Sheffield	.35
65	Alex Rodriguez	1.00
66	Russ Davis	.05
67	Checklist	.05
68	Marty Cordova	.05
69	Ruben Sierra	.05
70	Jose Mesa	.05
71	Matt Williams	.05
72	Chipper Jones	.65
73	Randy Johnson	.55
74	Kirby Puckett	.65
75	Jim Edmonds	.05
76	Barry Bonds	1.50
77	David Segui	.05
78	Larry Walker	.05
79	Jason Kendall	.05
80	Mike Piazza	.75
81	Brian Hunter	.05
82	Julio Franco	.05
83	Jay Bell	.05
84	Kevin Seitzer	.05
85	John Smoltz	.05

86	Joe Carter	.05
87	Ray Durham	.05
88	Carlos Baerga	.05
89	Ron Gant	.05
90	Orlando Merced	.05
91	Lee Smith	.05
92	Pedro Martinez	.55
93	Frank Thomas	.55
94	Al Martin	.05
95	Chad Curtis	.05
96	Eddie Murray	.55
97	Rusty Greer	.05
98	Jay Buhner	.05
99	Rico Brogna	.05
100	Todd Hundley	.05
101	Moises Alou	.05
102	Chili Davis	.05
103	Ismael Valdes	.05
104	Mo Vaughn	.05
105	Juan Gonzalez	.30
106	Mark Grudzielanek	.05
107	Derek Bell	.05
108	Shawn Green	.30
109	David Justice	.05
110	Paul O'Neill	.05
111	Kevin Appier	.05
112	Ray Lankford	.05
113	Travis Fryman	.05
114	Manny Ramirez	.55
115	Brooks Kieschnick	.05
116	Ken Griffey Jr.	.75
117	Jeffrey Hammonds	.05
118	Mark McGwire	1.00
119	Denny Neagle	.05
120	Quilvio Veras	.05
121	Alan Benes	.05
122	Rondell White	.05
123	*Osvaldo Fernandez*	.20
124	Andres Galarraga	.05
125	Johnny Damon	.35
126	Lenny Dykstra	.05
127	Jason Schmidt	.05
128	Mike Mussina	.30
129	Ken Caminiti	.05
130	Michael Tucker	.05
131	LaTroy Hawkins	.05
132	Checklist	.05
133	Delino DeShields	.05
134	Dave Nilsson	.05
135	Jack McDowell	.05
136	Joey Hamilton	.05
137	Dante Bichette	.05
138	Paul Molitor	.55
139	Ivan Rodriguez	.45
140	Mark Grace	.05
141	Paul Wilson	.05
142	Orel Hershiser	.05
143	Albert Belle	.05
144	Tino Martinez	.05
145	Tony Gwynn	.65
146	George Arias	.05
147	Brian Jordan	.05
148	Brian McRae	.05
149	Rickey Henderson	.55
150	Ryan Klesko	.05

1996 STUDIO PRESS PROOFS

	NM/M
Common Player, Bronze:	.50
Bronze Stars:	3X
Common Player, Gold:	1.00
Gold Stars:	7X
Common Player, Silver:	4.00
Silver Stars:	25X

(See 1996 Studio for checklist, base card values)

Hit Parade

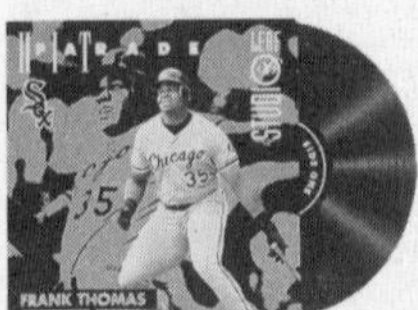

		NM/M
Complete Set (10):		10.00
Common Player:		.75
1	Tony Gwynn	1.50
2	Ken Griffey Jr.	2.00
3	Frank Thomas	1.00
4	Jeff Bagwell	1.00
5	Kirby Puckett	1.50
6	Mike Piazza	2.00
7	Barry Bonds	2.50
8	Albert Belle	.75
9	Tim Salmon	.75
10	Mo Vaughn	.75

Masterstrokes

		NM/M
Complete Set (8):		30.00
Common Player:		4.00
Samples:		75%
1	Tony Gwynn	6.00
2	Mike Piazza	8.00
3	Jeff Bagwell	4.00
4	Manny Ramirez	4.00
5	Cal Ripken Jr.	12.00
6	Frank Thomas	4.00
7	Ken Griffey Jr.	8.00
8	Greg Maddux	6.00

Stained Glass Stars

		NM/M
Complete Set (12):		24.00
Common Player:		1.00
1	Cal Ripken Jr.	5.00
2	Ken Griffey Jr.	3.50
3	Frank Thomas	2.00
4	Greg Maddux	2.50
5	Chipper Jones	2.50
6	Mike Piazza	3.50
7	Albert Belle	1.00
8	Jeff Bagwell	2.00
9	Hideo Nomo	1.50
10	Barry Bonds	5.00
11	Manny Ramirez	2.00
12	Kenny Lofton	1.00

1997 STUDIO

		NM/M
Complete Set (165):		17.50
Common Player:		.05
Silver Press Proofs:		4X
Gold Press Proofs:		8X
Pack (5):		3.00
Wax Box (18):		40.00
1	Frank Thomas	.65
2	Gary Sheffield	.45
3	Jason Isringhausen	.05
4	Ron Gant	.05
5	Andy Pettitte	.25
6	Todd Hollandsworth	.05
7	Troy Percival	.05
8	Mark McGwire	1.50
9	Barry Larkin	.05
10	Ken Caminiti	.05
11	Paul Molitor	.65
12	Travis Fryman	.05
13	Kevin Brown	.05
14	Robin Ventura	.05
15	Andres Galarraga	.05
16	Ken Griffey Jr.	1.00
17	Roger Clemens	.85
18	Alan Benes	.05
19	David Justice	.05
20	Damon Buford	.05
21	Mike Piazza	1.00
22	Ray Durham	.05
23	Billy Wagner	.05
24	Dean Palmer	.05
25	David Cone	.05
26	Ruben Sierra	.05
27	Henry Rodriguez	.05
28	Ray Lankford	.05
29	Jamey Wright	.05
30	Brady Anderson	.05
31	Tino Martinez	.05
32	Manny Ramirez	.65
33	Jeff Conine	.05
34	Dante Bichette	.05
35	Jose Canseco	.50
36	Mo Vaughn	.05
37	Sammy Sosa	.75
38	Mark Grudzielanek	.05
39	Mike Mussina	.35
40	Bill Pulsipher	.05
41	Ryne Sandberg	.75
42	Rickey Henderson	.65
43	Alex Rodriguez	1.50
44	Eddie Murray	.65
45	Ernie Young	.05
46	Joey Hamilton	.05
47	Wade Boggs	.75
48	Rusty Greer	.05
49	Carlos Delgado	.50
50	Ellis Burks	.05
51	Cal Ripken Jr.	2.00
52	Alex Fernandez	.05
53	Wally Joyner	.05
54	James Baldwin	.05
55	Juan Gonzalez	.35
56	John Smoltz	.05
57	Omar Vizquel	.05
58	Shane Reynolds	.05
59	Barry Bonds	2.00
60	Jason Kendall	.05
61	Marty Cordova	.05
62	Charles Johnson	.05
63	John Jaha	.05
64	Chan Ho Park	.05
65	Jermaine Allensworth	.05
66	Mark Grace	.05
67	Tim Salmon	.05
68	Edgar Martinez	.05
69	Marquis Grissom	.05
70	Craig Biggio	.05
71	Bobby Higginson	.05
72	Kevin Seitzer	.05
73	Hideo Nomo	.35
74	Dennis Eckersley	.60
75	Bobby Bonilla	.05
76	Dwight Gooden	.05
77	Jeff Cirillo	.05
78	Brian McRae	.05
79	Chipper Jones	.75
80	Jeff Fassero	.05
81	Fred McGriff	.05
82	Garret Anderson	.05
83	Eric Karros	.05
84	Derek Bell	.05
85	Kenny Lofton	.05
86	John Mabry	.05
87	Pat Hentgen	.05
88	Greg Maddux	.75
89	Jason Giambi	.45
90	Al Martin	.05
91	Derek Jeter	2.00
92	Rey Ordonez	.05
93	Will Clark	.05
94	Kevin Appier	.05
95	Roberto Alomar	.30
96	Joe Carter	.05
97	Bernie Williams	.05
98	Albert Belle	.05
99	Greg Vaughn	.05
100	Tony Clark	.05
101	Matt Williams	.05
102	Jeff Bagwell	.65
103	Reggie Sanders	.05
104	Mariano Rivera	.15
105	Larry Walker	.05
106	Shawn Green	.30
107	Alex Ochoa	.05
108	Ivan Rodriguez	.60
109	Eric Young	.05
110	Javier Lopez	.05
111	Brian Hunter	.05
112	Raul Mondesi	.05
113	Randy Johnson	.65
114	Tony Phillips	.05
115	Carlos Garcia	.05
116	Moises Alou	.05
117	Paul O'Neill	.05
118	Jim Thome	.60
119	Jermaine Dye	.05
120	Wilson Alvarez	.05
121	Rondell White	.05
122	Michael Tucker	.05
123	Mike Lansing	.05
124	Tony Gwynn	.75
125	Ryan Klesko	.05
126	Jim Edmonds	.05
127	Chuck Knoblauch	.05
128	Rafael Palmeiro	.60
129	Jay Buhner	.05
130	Tom Glavine	.35
131	Julio Franco	.05
132	Cecil Fielder	.05
133	Paul Wilson	.05
134	Deion Sanders	.05
135	Alex Gonzalez	.05
136	Charles Nagy	.05
137	Andy Ashby	.05
138	Edgar Renteria	.05
139	Pedro Martinez	.65
140	Brian Jordan	.05
141	Todd Hundley	.05
142	Marc Newfield	.05
143	Darryl Strawberry	.05
144	Dan Wilson	.05
145	*Brian Giles*	.50
146	Bartolo Colon	.05
147	Shannon Stewart	.05
148	Scott Spiezio	.05
149	Andruw Jones	.65
150	Karim Garcia	.05
151	Vladimir Guerrero	.65
152	George Arias	.05
153	Brooks Kieschnick	.05
154	Todd Walker	.05
155	Scott Rolen	.60
156	Todd Greene	.05
157	Dmitri Young	.05
158	Ruben Rivera	.05
159	Trey Beamon	.05
160	Nomar Garciaparra	.75
161	Bob Abreu	.05
162	Darin Erstad	.15
163	Ken Griffey Jr. (checklist)	.50
164	Frank Thomas (checklist)	.35
165	Alex Rodriguez (checklist)	.75

1997 STUDIO PRESS PROOFS

	NM/M
Common Player, Silver:	.50
Silver Stars:	4X
Common Player, Gold:	1.00
Gold Stars:	8X

(See 1997 Studio for checklist and base card values.)

Hard Hats

		NM/M
Complete Set (24):		50.00
Common Player:		1.50
1	Ivan Rodriguez	3.00
2	Albert Belle	1.50

3	Ken Griffey Jr.	6.00
4	Chuck Knoblauch	1.50
5	Frank Thomas	4.00
6	Cal Ripken Jr.	8.00
7	Todd Walker	1.50
8	Alex Rodriguez	7.00
9	Jim Thome	3.00
10	Mike Piazza	6.00
11	Barry Larkin	1.50
12	Chipper Jones	5.00
13	Derek Jeter	8.00
14	Jermaine Dye	1.50
15	Jason Giambi	2.00
16	Tim Salmon	1.50
17	Brady Anderson	1.50
18	Rondell White	1.50
19	Bernie Williams	1.50
20	Juan Gonzalez	2.00
21	Karim Garcia	1.50
22	Scott Rolen	3.00
23	Darin Erstad	2.00
24	Brian Jordan	1.50

Master Strokes

		NM/M
Complete Set (24):		120.00
Common Player:		2.00
1	Derek Jeter	12.00
2	Jeff Bagwell	4.50
3	Ken Griffey Jr.	8.00
4	Barry Bonds	12.00
5	Frank Thomas	4.50
6	Andy Pettitte	2.25
7	Mo Vaughn	2.00
8	Alex Rodriguez	10.00
9	Andruw Jones	4.50
10	Kenny Lofton	2.00
11	Cal Ripken Jr.	12.00
12	Greg Maddux	6.00
13	Manny Ramirez	4.50
14	Mike Piazza	8.00
14p	Mike Piazza (promo)	3.50
15	Vladimir Guerrero	4.50
16	Albert Belle	2.00
17	Chipper Jones	6.00
18	Hideo Nomo	2.50
19	Sammy Sosa	6.00
20	Tony Gwynn	6.00
21	Gary Sheffield	2.50
22	Mark McGwire	10.00
23	Juan Gonzalez	2.50
24	Paul Molitor	4.50

Master Strokes 8x10

		NM/M
Complete Set (24):		45.00
Common Player:		.75
1	Derek Jeter	5.00
2	Jeff Bagwell	2.00
3	Ken Griffey Jr.	3.00
4	Barry Bonds	5.00
5	Frank Thomas	2.00
6	Andy Pettitte	1.00
7	Mo Vaughn	.75
8	Alex Rodriguez	4.00
9	Andruw Jones	2.00
10	Kenny Lofton	.75
11	Cal Ripken Jr.	5.00
12	Greg Maddux	2.50
13	Manny Ramirez	2.00
14	Mike Piazza	3.00
15	Vladimir Guerrero	2.00
16	Albert Belle	.75
17	Chipper Jones	2.50
18	Hideo Nomo	1.50
19	Sammy Sosa	2.50
20	Tony Gwynn	2.50
21	Gary Sheffield	1.50
22	Mark McGwire	4.00
23	Juan Gonzalez	1.50
24	Paul Molitor	2.00

Portraits

		NM/M
Complete Set (24):		10.00
Common Player:		.25
1	Ken Griffey Jr.	1.00
1s	Frank Thomas (overprinted "SAMPLE")	.75
2	Frank Thomas	.65
3	Alex Rodriguez	1.50
4	Andruw Jones	.65
5	Cal Ripken Jr.	2.00
6	Greg Maddux	.75
7	Mike Piazza	1.00
8	Chipper Jones	.75
9	Albert Belle	.25
10	Derek Jeter	2.00
11	Juan Gonzalez	.45
12	Todd Walker	.25
12a	Todd Walker (autographed edition of 1,250)	10.00
13	Mark McGwire	1.50
14	Barry Bonds	2.00
15	Jeff Bagwell	.65
16	Manny Ramirez	.65
17	Kenny Lofton	.25
18	Mo Vaughn	.25
19	Hideo Nomo	.45
20	Tony Gwynn	.75
21	Vladimir Guerrero	.65
21a	Vladimir Guerrero (autographed edition of 500)	30.00
22	Gary Sheffield	.45
23	Ryne Sandberg	.75
24	Scott Rolen	.50
24a	Scott Rolen (autographed edition of 1,000)	12.00

1998 STUDIO

		NM/M
Complete Set (220):		25.00
Common Player:		.05
Pack (7 cards+8x10):		2.00
Wax Box (18):		20.00
1	Tony Clark	.05
2	Jose Cruz Jr.	.05
3	Ivan Rodriguez	.65
4	Mo Vaughn	.05
5	Kenny Lofton	.05
6	Will Clark	.05
7	Barry Larkin	.05
8	Jay Bell	.05
9	Kevin Young	.05
10	Francisco Cordova	.05
11	Justin Thompson	.05
12	Paul Molitor	.75
13	Jeff Bagwell	.75
14	Jose Canseco	.45
15	Scott Rolen	.65
16	Wilton Guerrero	.05
17	Shannon Stewart	.05
18	Hideki Irabu	.05
19	Michael Tucker	.05
20	Joe Carter	.05
21	Gabe Alvarez	.05
22	Ricky Ledee	.05
23	Karim Garcia	.05
24	Eli Marrero	.05
25	Scott Elarton	.05
26	Mario Valdez	.05
27	Ben Grieve	.05
28	Paul Konerko	.15
29	*Esteban Yan*	.05
30	Esteban Loaiza	.05
31	Delino DeShields	.05
32	Bernie Williams	.05
33	Joe Randa	.05
34	Randy Johnson	.75
35	Brett Tomko	.05
36	*Todd Erdos*	.05
37	Bobby Higginson	.05
38	Jason Kendall	.05
39	Ray Lankford	.05
40	Mark Grace	.05
41	Andy Pettitte	.25
42	Alex Rodriguez	2.00
43	Hideo Nomo	.45
44	Sammy Sosa	1.00
45	J.T. Snow	.05
46	Jason Varitek	.05
47	Vinny Castilla	.05
48	Neifi Perez	.05
49	Todd Walker	.05
50	Mike Cameron	.05
51	Jeffrey Hammonds	.05
52	Deivi Cruz	.05
53	Brian Hunter	.05
54	Al Martin	.05
55	Ron Coomer	.05
56	Chan Ho Park	.05
57	Pedro Martinez	.75
58	Darin Erstad	.15
59	Albert Belle	.05
60	Nomar Garciaparra	1.00
61	Tony Gwynn	1.00
62	Mike Piazza	1.50
63	Todd Helton	.65
64	David Ortiz	.45
65	Todd Dunwoody	.05
66	Orlando Cabrera	.05
67	Ken Cloude	.05
68	Andy Benes	.05
69	Mariano Rivera	.15
70	Cecil Fielder	.05
71	Brian Jordan	.05
72	Darryl Kile	.05
73	Reggie Jefferson	.05
74	Shawn Estes	.05
75	Bobby Bonilla	.05
76	Denny Neagle	.05
77	Robin Ventura	.05
78	Omar Vizquel	.05
79	Craig Biggio	.05
80	Moises Alou	.05
81	Garret Anderson	.05
82	Eric Karros	.05
83	Dante Bichette	.05
84	Charles Johnson	.05
85	Rusty Greer	.05
86	Travis Fryman	.05
87	Fernando Tatis	.05
88	Wilson Alvarez	.05
89	Carl Pavano	.05
90	Brian Rose	.05
91	Geoff Jenkins	.05
92	*Magglio Ordonez*	1.50
93	David Segui	.05
94	David Cone	.05
95	John Smoltz	.05
96	Jim Thome	.65
97	Gary Sheffield	.45
98	Barry Bonds	2.50
99	Andres Galarraga	.05
100	Brad Fullmer	.05
101	Bobby Estalella	.05
102	Enrique Wilson	.05
103	*Frank Catalanotto*	.25
104	*Mike Lowell*	1.00
105	Kevin Orie	.05
106	Matt Morris	.05
107	Pokey Reese	.05
108	Shawn Green	.35
109	Tony Womack	.05
110	Ken Caminiti	.05
111	Roberto Alomar	.20
112	Ken Griffey Jr.	1.50
113	Cal Ripken Jr.	2.50
114	Lou Collier	.05
115	Larry Walker	.05
116	Fred McGriff	.05
117	Jim Edmonds	.05
118	Edgar Martinez	.05
119	Matt Williams	.05
120	Ismael Valdes	.05
121	Bartolo Colon	.05
122	Jeff Cirillo	.05
123	*Steve Woodard*	.25
124	*Kevin Millwood*	1.00
125	Derrick Gibson	.05
126	Jacob Cruz	.05
127	Russell Branyan	.05
128	Sean Casey	.15
129	Derrek Lee	.50
130	Paul O'Neill	.05
131	Brad Radke	.05
132	Kevin Appier	.05
133	John Olerud	.05
134	Alan Benes	.05
135	Todd Greene	.05
136	*Carlos Mendoza*	.05
137	Wade Boggs	1.00
138	Jose Guillen	.05
139	Tino Martinez	.05
140	Aaron Boone	.05
141	Abraham Nunez	.05
142	Preston Wilson	.05
143	Randall Simon	.05
144	Dennis Reyes	.05
145	Mark Kotsay	.05
146	Richard Hidalgo	.05
147	Travis Lee	.05
148	*Hanley Frias*	.05
149	Ruben Rivera	.05
150	Rafael Medina	.05
151	Dave Nilsson	.05
152	Curt Schilling	.35
153	Brady Anderson	.05
154	Carlos Delgado	.50
155	Jason Giambi	.45
156	Pat Hentgen	.05
157	Tom Glavine	.35
158	Ryan Klesko	.05
159	Chipper Jones	1.00
160	Juan Gonzalez	.45
161	Mark McGwire	2.00
162	Vladimir Guerrero	.75
163	Derek Jeter	2.50
164	Manny Ramirez	.75
165	Mike Mussina	.30
166	Rafael Palmeiro	.65
167	Henry Rodriguez	.05
168	Jeff Suppan	.05
169	Eric Milton	.05
170	Scott Spiezio	.05
171	Wilson Delgado	.05
172	Bubba Trammell	.05
173	Ellis Burks	.05
174	Jason Dickson	.05
175	Butch Huskey	.05
176	Edgardo Alfonzo	.05
177	Eric Young	.05
178	Marquis Grissom	.05
179	Lance Johnson	.05
180	Kevin Brown	.05
181	Sandy Alomar Jr.	.05
182	Todd Hundley	.05
183	Rondell White	.05
184	Javier Lopez	.05
185	Damian Jackson	.05
186	Raul Mondesi	.05
187	Rickey Henderson	.75
188	David Justice	.05
189	Jay Buhner	.05
190	Jaret Wright	.05
191	Miguel Tejada	.25
192	Ron Wright	.05
193	Livan Hernandez	.05
194	A.J. Hinch	.05
195	Richie Sexson	.05
196	Bob Abreu	.05
197	Luis Castillo	.05
198	Michael Coleman	.05
199	Greg Maddux	1.00
200	Frank Thomas	.75
201	Andruw Jones	.75
202	Roger Clemens	1.25
203	Tim Salmon	.05
204	Chuck Knoblauch	.05
205	Wes Helms	.05
206	Juan Encarnacion	.05
207	Russ Davis	.05
208	John Valentin	.05
209	Tony Saunders	.05
210	Mike Sweeney	.05
211	Steve Finley	.05
212	*David Dellucci*	.25
213	Edgar Renteria	.05

214	Jeremi Gonzalez	.05
215	Jeff Bagwell Checklist	.40
216	Mike Piazza Checklist	1.00
217	Greg Maddux Checklist	.50
218	Cal Ripken Jr. Checklist	1.25
219	Frank Thomas Checklist	.45
220	Ken Griffey Jr. Checklist	.75

Silver Proofs

NM/M

Common Player: 1.00
Silver Stars: 3X
(See 1998 Studio for checklist, base cardvalues.)

Gold Proofs

NM/M

Common Player: 3.00
Stars: 6X
(See 1998 Studio for checklist and base card values.)

Autographs

		NM/M
1	Travis Lee (500)	20.00
2	Todd Helton (1000)	20.00
3	Ben Grieve (1000)	10.00

Freeze Frame

NM/M

Complete Set (30): 75.00
Common Player: 1.25
Production 4,500 sets
Die-Cuts: 1.5X
Production 500 sets

1	Ken Griffey Jr.	5.00
2	Derek Jeter	7.50
3	Ben Grieve	1.25
4	Cal Ripken Jr.	7.50
5	Alex Rodriguez	6.00
6	Greg Maddux	4.00
7	David Justice	1.25
8	Mike Piazza	5.00
9	Chipper Jones	4.00
10	Randy Johnson	3.00
11	Jeff Bagwell	3.00
12	Nomar Garciaparra	4.00
13	Andruw Jones	3.00
14	Frank Thomas	3.00
15	Scott Rolen	2.50
16	Barry Bonds	7.50
17	Kenny Lofton	1.25
18	Ivan Rodriguez	2.50
19	Chuck Knoblauch	1.25
20	Jose Cruz Jr.	1.25
21	Bernie Williams	1.25
22	Tony Gwynn	4.00
23	Juan Gonzalez	2.00
24	Gary Sheffield	2.25
25	Roger Clemens	4.50
26	Travis Lee	1.25
27	Brad Fullmer	1.25
28	Tim Salmon	1.25
29	Raul Mondesi	1.25
30	Roberto Alomar	2.00

Hit Parade

NM/M

Complete Set (20): 30.00
Common Player: 1.00
Production 5,000 sets

1	Tony Gwynn	2.50
2	Larry Walker	1.00
3	Mike Piazza	3.00
4	Frank Thomas	2.00
5	Manny Ramirez	2.00
6	Ken Griffey Jr.	3.00
7	Todd Helton	1.50
8	Vladimir Guerrero	2.00
9	Albert Belle	1.00
10	Jeff Bagwell	2.00
11	Juan Gonzalez	1.25
12	Jim Thome	1.50
13	Scott Rolen	1.50
14	Tino Martinez	1.00
15	Mark McGwire	4.00
16	Barry Bonds	5.00
17	Tony Clark	1.00
18	Mo Vaughn	1.00
19	Darin Erstad	1.25
20	Paul Konerko	1.25

Masterstrokes

NM/M

Complete Set (20): 95.00
Common Player: 2.00
Production 1,000 sets
Samples: 3X

1	Travis Lee	2.00
2	Kenny Lofton	2.00
3	Mo Vaughn	2.00
4	Ivan Rodriguez	3.50
5	Roger Clemens	6.50
6	Mark McGwire	10.00
7	Hideo Nomo	2.50
8	Andruw Jones	4.50
9	Nomar Garciaparra	6.00
10	Juan Gonzalez	2.50
11	Jeff Bagwell	4.50
12	Derek Jeter	12.50
13	Tony Gwynn	6.00
14	Chipper Jones	6.00
15	Mike Piazza	7.50
16	Greg Maddux	6.00
17	Alex Rodriguez	10.00
18	Cal Ripken Jr.	12.50
19	Frank Thomas	4.50
20	Ken Griffey Jr.	7.50

Sony MLB 99

NM/M

Complete Set (20): 8.00
Common Player: .15

1	Cal Ripken Jr.	1.50
2	Nomar Garciaparra	.75
3	Barry Bonds	1.50
4	Mike Mussina	.35
5	Pedro Martinez	.60
6	Derek Jeter	1.50
7	Andruw Jones	.60
8	Kenny Lofton	.15
9	Gary Sheffield	.45
10	Raul Mondesi	.15
11	Jeff Bagwell	.60
12	Tim Salmon	.15
13	Tom Glavine	.35
14	Ben Grieve	.15
15	Matt Williams	.15
16	Juan Gonzalez	.35
17	Mark McGwire	1.00
18	Bernie Williams	.15
19	Andres Galarraga	.15
20	Jose Cruz Jr.	.15

8x10 Portraits

NM/M

Complete Set (36): 65.00
Common Player: .50
Inserted 1:1

1	Travis Lee	.50
2	Todd Helton	1.50
3	Ben Grieve	.50
4	Paul Konerko	.65
5	Jeff Bagwell	2.00
6	Derek Jeter	7.00
7	Ivan Rodriguez	1.50
8	Cal Ripken Jr.	7.00
9	Mike Piazza	4.00
10	Chipper Jones	3.00
11	Frank Thomas	2.00
12	Tony Gwynn	3.00
13	Nomar Garciaparra	3.00
14	Juan Gonzalez	1.00
15	Greg Maddux	3.00
16	Hideo Nomo	1.00
17	Scott Rolen	1.50
18	Barry Bonds	7.00
19	Ken Griffey Jr.	4.00
20	Alex Rodriguez	5.00
21	Roger Clemens	3.50
22	Mark McGwire	5.00
23	Jose Cruz Jr.	.50
24	Andruw Jones	2.00
25	Tino Martinez	.50
26	Mo Vaughn	.50
27	Vladimir Guerrero	2.00
28	Tony Clark	.50
29	Andy Pettitte	.65
30	Jaret Wright	.50
31	Paul Molitor	2.00
32	Darin Erstad	.65
33	Larry Walker	.50
34	Chuck Knoblauch	.50
35	Barry Larkin	.50
36	Kenny Lofton	.50

1995 SUMMIT

NM/M

Complete Set (200): 10.00
Common Player: .05
Pack (7): 1.00
Wax Box (24): 12.50

1	Ken Griffey Jr.	1.00
2	Alex Fernandez	.05
3	Fred McGriff	.05
4	Ben McDonald	.05
5	Rafael Palmeiro	.60
6	Tony Gwynn	.75
7	Jim Thome	.60
8	Ken Hill	.05
9	Barry Bonds	2.00
10	Barry Larkin	.05
11	Albert Belle	.05
12	Billy Ashley	.05
13	Matt Williams	.05
14	Andy Benes	.05
15	Midre Cummings	.05
16	J.R. Phillips	.05
17	Edgar Martinez	.05
18	Manny Ramirez	.65
19	Jose Canseco	.40
20	Chili Davis	.05
21	Don Mattingly	.85
22	Bernie Williams	.05
23	Tom Glavine	.35
24	Robin Ventura	.05
25	Jeff Conine	.05
26	Mark Grace	.05
27	Mark McGwire	1.50
28	Carlos Delgado	.45
29	Greg Colbrunn	.05
30	Greg Maddux	.75
31	Craig Biggio	.05
32	Kirby Puckett	.75
33	Derek Bell	.05
34	Lenny Dykstra	.05
35	Tim Salmon	.05
36	Deion Sanders	.05
37	Moises Alou	.05
38	Ray Lankford	.05
39	Willie Greene	.05
40	Ozzie Smith	.75
41	Roger Clemens	.85
42	Andres Galarraga	.05
43	Gary Sheffield	.35
44	Sammy Sosa	.75
45	Larry Walker	.05
46	Kevin Appier	.05
47	Raul Mondesi	.05
48	Kenny Lofton	.05
49	Darryl Hamilton	.05
50	Roberto Alomar	.20
51	Hal Morris	.05
52	Cliff Floyd	.05
53	Brent Gates	.05
54	Rickey Henderson	.65
55	John Olerud	.05
56	Gregg Jefferies	.05
57	Cecil Fielder	.05
58	Paul Molitor	.65
59	Bret Boone	.05
60	Greg Vaughn	.05
61	Wally Joyner	.05
62	Jeffrey Hammonds	.05
63	James Mouton	.05
64	Omar Vizquel	.05
65	Wade Boggs	.75
66	Terry Steinbach	.05
67	Wil Cordero	.05
68	Joey Hamilton	.05
69	Rico Brogna	.05
70	Darren Daulton	.05
71	Chuck Knoblauch	.05
72	Bob Hamelin	.05
73	Carl Everett	.05
74	Joe Carter	.05
75	Dave Winfield	.65
76	Bobby Bonilla	.05
77	Paul O'Neill	.05
78	Javier Lopez	.05
79	Cal Ripken Jr.	2.00
80	David Cone	.05
81	Bernard Gilkey	.05
82	Ivan Rodriguez	.60
83	Dean Palmer	.05
84	Jason Bere	.05
85	Will Clark	.05
86	Scott Cooper	.05
87	Royce Clayton	.05
88	Mike Piazza	1.00
89	Ryan Klesko	.05
90	Juan Gonzalez	.35
91	Travis Fryman	.05
92	Frank Thomas	.65
93	Eduardo Perez	.05
94	Mo Vaughn	.05
95	Jay Bell	.05
96	Jeff Bagwell	.65
97	Randy Johnson	.65
98	Jimmy Key	.05
99	Dennis Eckersley	.60
100	Carlos Baerga	.05
101	Eddie Murray	.65
102	Mike Mussina	.30
103	Brian Anderson	.05
104	Jeff Cirillo	.05
105	Dante Bichette	.05
106	Bret Saberhagen	.05
107	Jeff Kent	.05
108	Ruben Sierra	.05
109	Kirk Gibson	.05
110	Reggie Sanders	.05
111	Dave Justice	.05
112	Benji Gil	.05
113	Vaughn Eshelman	.05
114	*Carlos Perez*	.05
115	Chipper Jones	.75
116	Shane Andrews	.05
117	Orlando Miller	.05
118	Scott Ruffcorn	.05
119	Jose Oliva	.05
120	Joe Vitiello	.05
121	Jon Nunnally	.05
122	Garret Anderson	.05
123	Curtis Goodwin	.05
124	*Mark Grudzielanek*	.25
125	Alex Gonzalez	.05
126	David Bell	.05
127	Dustin Hermanson	.05
128	Dave Nilsson	.05
129	Wilson Heredia	.05
130	Charles Johnson	.05
131	Frank Rodriguez	.05
132	Alex Ochoa	.05
133	Alex Rodriguez	1.50
134	*Bobby Higginson*	.25
135	Edgardo Alfonzo	.05
136	Armando Benitez	.05
137	Rich Aude	.05
138	Tim Naehring	.05
139	Joe Randa	.05
140	Quilvio Veras	.05
141	*Hideo Nomo*	1.00
142	Ray Holbert	.05
143	Michael Tucker	.05
144	Chad Mottola	.05
145	John Valentin	.05

146	James Baldwin	.05
147	Esteban Loaiza	.05
148	Marty Cordova	.05
149	*Juan Acevedo*	.05
150	*Tim Unroe*	.05
151	Brad Clontz	.05
152	Steve Rodriguez	.05
153	Rudy Pemberton	.05
154	Ozzie Timmons	.05
155	Ricky Otero	.05
156	Allen Battle	.05
157	Joe Roselli	.05
158	Roberto Petagine	.05
159	Todd Hollandsworth	.05
160	Shannon Penn	.05
161	Antonio Osuna	.05
162	Russ Davis	.05
163	Jason Giambi	.40
164	Terry Bradshaw	.05
165	Ray Durham	.05
166	Todd Steverson	.05
167	Tim Belk	.05
168	Andy Pettitte	.25
169	Roger Cedeno	.05
170	Jose Parra	.05
171	Scott Sullivan	.05
172	LaTroy Hawkins	.05
173	Jeff McCurry	.05
174	Ken Griffey Jr. (Bat Speed)	.50
175	Frank Thomas (Bat Speed)	.30
176	Cal Ripken Jr. (Bat Speed)	1.00
177	Jeff Bagwell (Bat Speed)	.30
178	Mike Piazza (Bat Speed)	.50
179	Barry Bonds (Bat Speed)	1.00
180	Matt Williams (Bat Speed)	.05
181	Don Mattingly (Bat Speed)	.45
182	Will Clark (Bat Speed)	.05
183	Tony Gwynn (Bat Speed)	.40
184	Kirby Puckett (Bat Speed)	.40
185	Jose Canseco (Bat Speed)	.25
186	Paul Molitor (Bat Speed)	.30
187	Albert Belle (Bat Speed)	.05
188	Joe Carter (Bat Speed)	.05
189	Greg Maddux (Special Delivery)	.40
190	Roger Clemens (Special Delivery)	.45
191	David Cone (Special Delivery)	.05
192	Mike Mussina (Special Delivery)	.15
193	Randy Johnson (Special Delivery)	.30
194	Frank Thomas Checklist	.30
195	Ken Griffey Jr. Checklist	.50
196	Cal Ripken Jr. Checklist	.75
197	Jeff Bagwell Checklist	.30
198	Mike Piazza Checklist	.50
199	Barry Bonds Checklist	.75
200	Mo Vaughn, Matt Williams Checklist	.05

Nth Degree

		NM/M
Complete Set (200):		50.00
Common Player:		.25
Stars:		2X

(See 1995 Summit for checklist, base cardvalues.)

Big Bang

		NM/M
Complete Set (20):		45.00
Common Player:		1.00
1	Ken Griffey Jr.	6.00
2	Frank Thomas	3.25
3	Cal Ripken Jr.	8.00
4	Jeff Bagwell	3.25
5	Mike Piazza	6.00
6	Barry Bonds	8.00
7	Matt Williams	1.00
8	Don Mattingly	4.50
9	Will Clark	1.00
10	Tony Gwynn	4.00
11	Kirby Puckett	4.00
12	Jose Canseco	2.00
13	Paul Molitor	3.25
14	Albert Belle	1.00
15	Joe Carter	1.00
16	Rafael Palmeiro	3.00
17	Fred McGriff	1.00
18	Dave Justice	1.00
19	Tim Salmon	1.00
20	Mo Vaughn	1.00

New Age

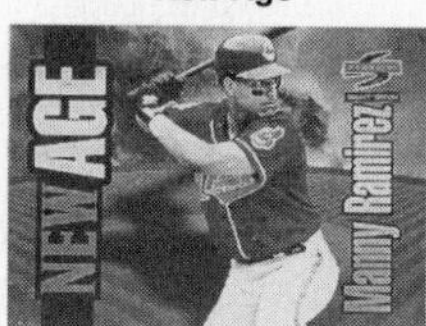

		NM/M
Complete Set (15):		10.00
Common Player:		.25
1	Cliff Floyd	.25
2	Manny Ramirez	2.00
3	Raul Mondesi	.25
4	Alex Rodriguez	5.00
5	Billy Ashley	.25
6	Alex Gonzalez	.25
7	Michael Tucker	.25
8	Charles Johnson	.25
9	Carlos Delgado	1.00
10	Benji Gil	.25
11	Chipper Jones	3.00
12	Todd Hollandsworth	.25
13	Frank Rodriguez	.25
14	Shawn Green	.60
15	Ray Durham	.25

21 Club

		NM/M
Complete Set (9):		4.00
Common Player:		.50
1	Bob Abreu	.65
2	Pokey Reese	.50
3	Edgardo Alfonzo	.50
4	Jim Pittsley	.50
5	Ruben Rivera	.50
6	Chan Ho Park	.50
7	Julian Tavarez	.50
8	Ismael Valdes	.50
9	Dmitri Young	.50

1996 SUMMIT

		NM/M
Complete Set (200):		10.00
Common Player:		.05
Pack (7):		1.25
Wax Box (18):		15.00
1	Mike Piazza	1.25
2	Matt Williams	.05
3	Tino Martinez	.05
4	Reggie Sanders	.05
5	Ray Durham	.05
6	Brad Radke	.05
7	Jeff Bagwell	.65
8	Ron Gant	.05
9	Lance Johnson	.05
10	Kevin Seitzer	.05
11	Dante Bichette	.05
12	Ivan Rodriguez	.60
13	Jim Abbott	.05
14	Greg Colbrunn	.05
15	Rondell White	.05
16	Shawn Green	.40
17	Gregg Jefferies	.05
18	Omar Vizquel	.05
19	Cal Ripken Jr.	2.00
20	Mark McGwire	1.50
21	Wally Joyner	.05
22	Chili Davis	.05
23	Jose Canseco	.40
24	Royce Clayton	.05
25	Jay Bell	.05
26	Travis Fryman	.05
27	Jeff King	.05
28	Todd Hundley	.05
29	Joe Vitiello	.05
30	Russ Davis	.05
31	Mo Vaughn	.05
32	Raul Mondesi	.05
33	Ray Lankford	.05
34	Mike Stanley	.05
35	B.J. Surhoff	.05
36	Greg Vaughn	.05
37	Todd Stottlemyre	.05
38	Carlos Delgado	.50
39	Kenny Lofton	.05
40	Hideo Nomo	.35
41	Sterling Hitchcock	.05
42	Pete Schourek	.05
43	Edgardo Alfonzo	.05
44	Ken Hill	.05
45	Ken Caminiti	.05
46	Bobby Higginson	.05
47	Michael Tucker	.05
48	David Cone	.05
49	Cecil Fielder	.05
50	Brian Hunter	.05
51	Charles Johnson	.05
52	Bobby Bonilla	.05
53	Eddie Murray	.65
54	Kenny Rogers	.05
55	Jim Edmonds	.05
56	Trevor Hoffman	.05
57	Kevin Mitchell	.05
58	Ruben Sierra	.05
59	Benji Gil	.05
60	Juan Gonzalez	.35
61	Larry Walker	.05
62	Jack McDowell	.05
63	Shawon Dunston	.05
64	Andy Benes	.05
65	Jay Buhner	.05
66	Rickey Henderson	.65
67	Alex Gonzalez	.05
68	Mike Kelly	.05
69	Fred McGriff	.05
70	Ryne Sandberg	.75
71	Ernie Young	.05
72	Kevin Appier	.05
73	Moises Alou	.05
74	John Jaha	.05
75	J.T. Snow	.05
76	Jim Thome	.60
77	Kirby Puckett	.75
78	Hal Morris	.05
79	Robin Ventura	.05
80	Ben McDonald	.05
81	Tim Salmon	.05
82	Albert Belle	.05
83	Marquis Grissom	.05
84	Alex Rodriguez	1.50
85	Manny Ramirez	.65
86	Ken Griffey Jr.	1.25
87	Sammy Sosa	.75
88	Frank Thomas	.65
89	Lee Smith	.05
90	Marty Cordova	.05
91	Greg Maddux	.75
92	Lenny Dykstra	.05
93	Butch Huskey	.05
94	Garret Anderson	.05
95	Mike Bordick	.05
96	Dave Justice	.05
97	Chad Curtis	.05
98	Carlos Baerga	.05
99	Jason Isringhausen	.05
100	Gary Sheffield	.35
101	Roger Clemens	1.00
102	Ozzie Smith	.75
103	Ramon Martinez	.05
104	Paul O'Neill	.05
105	Will Clark	.05
106	Tom Glavine	.35
107	Barry Bonds	2.00
108	Barry Larkin	.05
109	Derek Bell	.05
110	Randy Johnson	.65
111	Jeff Conine	.05
112	John Mabry	.05
113	Julian Tavarez	.05
114	Gary DiSarcina	.05
115	Andres Galarraga	.05
116	Marc Newfield	.05
117	Frank Rodriguez	.05
118	Brady Anderson	.05
119	Mike Mussina	.30
120	Orlando Merced	.05
121	Melvin Nieves	.05
122	Brian Jordan	.05
123	Rafael Palmeiro	.60
124	Johnny Damon	.35
125	Wil Cordero	.05
126	Chipper Jones	.75
127	Eric Karros	.05
128	Darren Daulton	.05
129	Vinny Castilla	.05
130	Joe Carter	.05
131	Bernie Williams	.05
132	Bernard Gilkey	.05
133	Bret Boone	.05
134	Tony Gwynn	.75
135	Dave Nilsson	.05
136	Ryan Klesko	.05
137	Paul Molitor	.65
138	John Olerud	.05
139	Craig Biggio	.05
140	John Valentin	.05
141	Chuck Knoblauch	.05
142	Edgar Martinez	.05
143	Rico Brogna	.05
144	Dean Palmer	.05
145	Mark Grace	.05
146	Roberto Alomar	.20
147	Alex Fernandez	.05
148	Andre Dawson	.25
149	Wade Boggs	.75
150	Mark Lewis	.05
151	Gary Gaetti	.05
152	Paul Wilson, Roger Clemens	.45
153	Rey Ordonez, Ozzie Smith	.35
154	Derek Jeter, Cal Ripken Jr.	1.00
155	Alan Benes, Andy Benes	.05
156	Jason Kendall, Mike Piazza	.75
157	Ryan Klesko, Frank Thomas	.30
158	Johnny Damon, Ken Griffey Jr.	.65
159	Karim Garcia, Sammy Sosa	.40
160	Raul Mondesi, Tim Salmon	.05
161	Chipper Jones, Matt Williams	.40
162	Rey Ordonez	.05
163	Bob Wolcott	.05
164	Brooks Kieschnick	.05
165	Steve Gibralter	.05
166	Bob Abreu	.05
167	Greg Zaun	.05
168	Tavo Alvarez	.05
169	Sal Fasano	.05
170	George Arias	.05
171	Derek Jeter	2.00
172	*Livan Hernandez*	.25
173	Alan Benes	.05
174	George Williams	.05
175	John Wasdin	.05
176	Chan Ho Park	.05
177	Paul Wilson	.05
178	Jeff Suppan	.05
179	Quinton McCracken	.05
180	*Wilton Guerrero*	.05
181	Eric Owens	.05
182	Felipe Crespo	.05
183	LaTroy Hawkins	.05
184	Jason Schmidt	.05
185	Terrell Wade	.05
186	*Mike Grace*	.05
187	Chris Snopek	.05
188	Jason Kendall	.05
189	Todd Hollandsworth	.05
190	Jim Pittsley	.05
191	Jermaine Dye	.05
192	*Mike Busby*	.05
193	Richard Hidalgo	.05
194	Tyler Houston	.05
195	Jimmy Haynes	.05
196	Karim Garcia	.05
197	Ken Griffey Jr.	.50
198	Frank Thomas	.30
199	Greg Maddux	.40
200	Cal Ripken Jr.	1.00

Artist's Proof

		NM/M
Complete Set (200):		100.00
Common Player:		1.00
Stars:		8X

(See 1996 Summit for checklist, base cardvalues.)

1996 SUMMIT FOIL

NM/M
Complete Set (200): 30.00
Common Player: .25
Stars: 3X
(See 1996 Summit for checklist and base card values.)

Above & Beyond

NM/M
Complete Set (200): 50.00
Common Player: .25
Stars: 3X
(See 1996 Summit for checklist, base card values.)

Ballparks

NM/M
Complete Set (18): 45.00
Common Player: 1.00
1 Cal Ripken Jr. 7.50
2 Albert Belle 1.00
3 Dante Bichette 1.00
4 Mo Vaughn 1.00
5 Ken Griffey Jr. 6.00
6 Derek Jeter 7.50
7 Juan Gonzalez 1.50
8 Greg Maddux 4.00
9 Frank Thomas 3.00
10 Ryne Sandberg 4.00
11 Mike Piazza 6.00
12 Johnny Damon 1.50
13 Barry Bonds 7.50
14 Jeff Bagwell 3.00
15 Paul Wilson 1.00
16 Tim Salmon 1.00
17 Kirby Puckett 4.00
18 Tony Gwynn 4.00

Big Bang

NM/M
Complete Set (16): 60.00
Common Player: 1.50
1 Frank Thomas 4.00
2 Ken Griffey Jr. 7.50
3 Albert Belle 1.50
4 Mo Vaughn 1.50
5 Barry Bonds 12.00
6 Cal Ripken Jr. 12.00
7 Jeff Bagwell 4.00
8 Mike Piazza 7.50
9 Ryan Klesko 1.50
10 Manny Ramirez 4.00
11 Tim Salmon 1.50
12 Dante Bichette 1.50
13 Sammy Sosa 6.00
14 Raul Mondesi 1.50
15 Chipper Jones 6.00
16 Garret Anderson 1.50

Hitters, Inc.

NM/M
Complete Set (16): 40.00
Common Player: 1.25
1 Tony Gwynn 4.00
2 Mo Vaughn 1.25
3 Tim Salmon 1.25
4 Ken Griffey Jr. 5.00

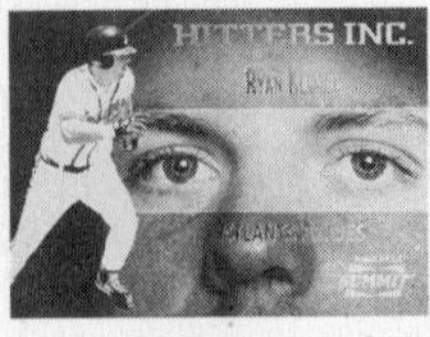

5 Sammy Sosa 4.00
6 Frank Thomas 3.00
7 Wade Boggs 4.00
8 Albert Belle 1.25
9 Cal Ripken Jr. 8.00
10 Manny Ramirez 3.00
11 Ryan Klesko 1.25
11p Ryan Klesko (overprinted "SAMPLE") 1.25
12 Dante Bichette 1.25
13 Mike Piazza 5.00
14 Chipper Jones 4.00
15 Ryne Sandberg 4.00
16 Matt Williams 1.25

Positions

NM/M
Complete Set (9): 100.00
Common Card: 6.00
1 Jeff Bagwell, Mo Vaughn, Frank Thomas (First Base) 10.00
2 Roberto Alomar, Craig Biggio, Chuck Knoblauch (Second Base) 6.00
3 Matt Williams, Jim Thome, Chipper Jones (Third Base) 12.50
4 Barry Larkin, Cal Ripken Jr., Alex Rodriguez (Short Stop) 20.00
5 Mike Piazza, Ivan Rodriguez, Charles Johnson (Catcher) 15.00
6 Hideo Nomo, Greg Maddux, Randy Johnson (Pitcher) 12.50
7 Barry Bonds, Albert Belle, Ryan Klesko (Left Field) 20.00
8 Johnny Damon, Jim Edmonds, Ken Griffey Jr. (Center Field) 15.00
9 Manny Ramirez, Gary Sheffield, Sammy Sosa (Right Field) 12.50

T

1981 TOPPS

NM/M
Complete Set (726): 37.00
Common Player: .08
Wax Pack (15):
Wax Box (36):
Cello Pack (28):
Cello Box (24):
Rack Pack (48):
Rack Box (24):
Vending Box (500):
1 George Brett, Bill Buckner Batting Leaders .60
2 Reggie Jackson, Ben Oglivie, Mike Schmidt Home Run Leaders .60
3 Cecil Cooper, Mike Schmidt RBI Leaders .20
4 Rickey Henderson, Ron LeFlore Stolen Base Leaders .40
5 Steve Carlton, Steve Stone Victory Leaders .11
6 Len Barker, Steve Carlton Strikeout Leaders .11
7 Rudy May, Don Sutton ERA Leaders .08
8 Rollie Fingers, Tom Hume, Dan Quisenberry Leading Firemen .08
9 Pete LaCock (DP) .08
10 Mike Flanagan .08
11 Jim Wohlford (DP) .08
12 Mark Clear .08
13 *Joe Charboneau* .40
14 *John Tudor* .15
15 Larry Parrish .08
16 Ron Davis .08
17 Cliff Johnson .08
18 Glenn Adams .08
19 Jim Clancy .08
20 Jeff Burroughs .08
21 Ron Oester .08
22 Danny Darwin .08
23 Alex Trevino .08
24 Don Stanhouse .08
25 Sixto Lezcano .08
26 U.L. Washington .08
27 Champ Summers (DP) .08
28 Enrique Romo .08
29 Gene Tenace .08
30 Jack Clark .08
31 Checklist 1-121 (DP) .08
32 Ken Oberkfell .08
33 Rick Honeycutt .08
34 Aurelio Rodriguez .08
35 Mitchell Page .08
36 Ed Farmer .08
37 Gary Roenicke .08
38 Win Remmerswaal .08
39 Tom Veryzer .08
40 Tug McGraw .08
41 Bob Babcock, John Butcher, Jerry Don Gleaton Rangers Future Stars .08
42 Jerry White (DP) .08
43 Jose Morales .08
44 Larry McWilliams .08
45 Enos Cabell .08
46 Rick Bosetti .08
47 Ken Brett .08
48 Dave Skaggs .08
49 Bob Shirley .08
50 Dave Lopes .08
51 Bill Robinson (DP) .08
52 Hector Cruz .08
53 Kevin Saucier .08
54 Ivan DeJesus .08
55 Mike Norris .08
56 Buck Martinez .08
57 Dave Roberts .08
58 Joel Youngblood .08
59 Dan Petry .08
60 Willie Randolph .08
61 Butch Wynegar .08
62 Joe Pettini .08
63 Steve Renko (DP) .08
64 Brian Asselstine .08
65 Scott McGregor .08
66 Manny Castillo, Tim Ireland, Mike Jones Royals Future Stars .08
67 Ken Kravec .08
68 Matt Alexander (DP) .08
69 Ed Halicki .08
70 Al Oliver (DP) .08
71 Hal Dues .08
72 Barry Evans (DP) .08
73 Doug Bair .08
74 Mike Hargrove .08
75 Reggie Smith .08
76 Mario Mendoza .08
77 Mike Barlow .08
78 Steve Dillard .08
79 Bruce Robbins .08
80 Rusty Staub .11
81 Dave Stapleton .08
82 Danny Heep, Alan Knicely, Bobby Sprowl Astros Future Stars (DP) .08
83 Mike Proly .08
84 Johnnie LeMaster .08
85 Mike Caldwell .08
86 Wayne Gross .08
87 Rick Camp .08
88 Joe Lefebvre .08
89 Darrell Jackson .08
90 Bake McBride .08
91 Tim Stoddard (DP) .08
92 Mike Easler .08
93 Ed Glynn (DP) .08
94 Harry Spilman (DP) .08
95 Jim Sundberg .08
96 Dave Beard, Ernie Camacho, Pat Dempsey A's Future Stars .08
97 Chris Speier .08
98 Clint Hurdle .08
99 Eric Wilkins .08
100 Rod Carew 1.50
101 Benny Ayala .08
102 Dave Tobik .08
103 Jerry Martin .08
104 Terry Forster .08
105 Jose Cruz .08
106 Don Money .08
107 Rich Wortham .08
108 Bruce Benedict .08
109 Mike Scott .08
110 Carl Yastrzemski 1.50
111 Greg Minton .08
112 Rusty Kuntz, Fran Mullins, Leo Sutherland White Sox Future Stars .08
113 Mike Phillips .08
114 Tom Underwood .08
115 Roy Smalley .08
116 Joe Simpson .08
117 Pete Falcone .08
118 Kurt Bevacqua .08
119 Tippy Martinez .08
120 Larry Bowa .08
121 Larry Harlow .08
122 John Denny .08
123 Al Cowens .08
124 Jerry Garvin .08
125 Andre Dawson 1.25
126 *Charlie Leibrandt* .30
127 Rudy Law .08
128 Gary Allenson (DP) .08
129 Art Howe .08
130 Larry Gura .08
131 *Keith Moreland* .15
132 Tommy Boggs .08
133 Jeff Cox .08
134 Steve Mura .08
135 Gorman Thomas .08
136 Doug Capilla .08
137 Hosken Powell .08
138 *Rich Dotson* (DP) .15
139 Oscar Gamble .08
140 Bob Forsch .08
141 Miguel Dilone .08
142 Jackson Todd .08
143 Dan Meyer .08
144 Allen Ripley .08
145 Mickey Rivers .08
146 Bobby Castillo .08
147 Dale Berra .08
148 Randy Niemann .08
149 Joe Nolan .08
150 Mark Fidrych .11
151 Claudell Washington (DP) .08
152 John Urrea .08
153 Tom Poquette .08
154 Rick Langford .08
155 Chris Chambliss .08
156 Bob McClure .08
157 John Wathan .08
158 Fergie Jenkins .70
159 Brian Doyle .08
160 Garry Maddox .08
161 Dan Graham .08
162 Doug Corbett .08
163 Billy Almon .08
164 *Lamarr Hoyt (LaMarr)* .11
165 Tony Scott .08
166 Floyd Bannister .08
167 Terry Whitfield .08
168 Don Robinson (DP) .08
169 John Mayberry .08
170 Ross Grimsley .08
171 Gene Richards .08
172 Gary Woods .08
173 Bump Wills .08
174 Doug Rau .08
175 Dave Collins .08
176 Mike Krukow .08
177 Rick Peters .08
178 Jim Essian (DP) .08
179 Rudy May .08
180 Pete Rose 3.75
181 Elias Sosa .08

182 Bob Grich .08
183 Dick Davis (DP) .08
184 Jim Dwyer .08
185 Dennis Leonard .08
186 Wayne Nordhagen .08
187 Mike Parrott .08
188 Doug DeCinces .08
189 Craig Swan .08
190 Cesar Cedeno .08
191 Rick Sutcliffe .08
192 *Terry Harper, Ed Miller, Rafael Ramirez* Braves Future Stars .08
193 Pete Vuckovich .08
194 *Rod Scurry* .08
195 Rich Murray .08
196 Duffy Dyer .08
197 Jim Kern .08
198 Jerry Dybzinski .08
199 Chuck Rainey .08
200 George Foster .08
201 Johnny Bench (Record Breaker) .35
202 Steve Carlton (Record Breaker) .20
203 Bill Gullickson (Record Breaker) .08
204 Ron LeFlore, Rodney Scott (Record Breaker) .08
205 Pete Rose (Record Breaker) 1.25
206 Mike Schmidt (Record Breaker) .70
207 Ozzie Smith (Record Breaker) .70
208 Willie Wilson (Record Breaker) .08
209 Dickie Thon (DP) .08
210 Jim Palmer 1.25
211 Derrel Thomas .08
212 Steve Nicosia .08
213 *Al Holland* .08
214 Ralph Botting, Jim Dorsey, John Harris Angels Future Stars .08
215 Larry Hisle .08
216 John Henry Johnson .08
217 Rich Hebner .08
218 Paul Splittorff .08
219 Ken Landreaux .08
220 Tom Seaver 1.50
221 Bob Davis .08
222 Jorge Orta .08
223 Roy Lee Jackson .08
224 Pat Zachry .08
225 Ruppert Jones .08
226 Manny Sanguillen (DP) .08
227 Fred Martinez .08
228 Tom Paciorek .08
229 Rollie Fingers .70
230 George Hendrick .08
231 Joe Beckwith .08
232 Mickey Klutts .08
233 Skip Lockwood .08
234 Lou Whitaker .08
235 Scott Sanderson .08
236 Mike Ivie .08
237 Charlie Moore .08
238 Willie Hernandez .08
239 Rick Miller (DP) .08
240 Nolan Ryan 3.75
241 Checklist 122-242 (DP) .08
242 Chet Lemon .08
243 Sal Butera .08
244 Tito Landrum, Al Olmsted, Andy Rincon Cardinals Future Stars .08
245 Ed Figueroa .08
246 Ed Ott (DP) .08
247 Glenn Hubbard (DP) .08
248 Joey McLaughlin .08
249 Larry Cox .08
250 Ron Guidry .11
251 Tom Brookens .08
252 Victor Cruz .08
253 Dave Bergman .08
254 Ozzie Smith 2.25
255 Mark Littell .08
256 Bombo Rivera .08
257 Rennie Stennett .08
258 *Joe Price* .08
259 *Juan Berenguer, Hubie Brooks, Mookie Wilson* Mets Future Stars .60
260 Ron Cey .08
261 Rickey Henderson 3.50
262 Sammy Stewart .08
263 Brian Downing .08
264 Jim Norris .08
265 John Candelaria .08
266 Tom Herr .08
267 Stan Bahnsen .08
268 Jerry Royster .08
269 Ken Forsch .08
270 Greg Luzinski .08
271 Bill Castro .08
272 Bruce Kimm .08
273 Stan Papi .08
274 Craig Chamberlain .08
275 Dwight Evans .08
276 Dan Spillner .08
277 Alfredo Griffin .08
278 Rick Sofield .08
279 Bob Knepper .08
280 Ken Griffey .08
281 Fred Stanley .08
282 Rick Anderson, Greg Biercevicz, Rodney Craig Mariners Future Stars .08
283 Billy Sample .08
284 Brian Kingman .08
285 Jerry Turner .08
286 Dave Frost .08
287 Lenn Sakata .08
288 Bob Clark .08
289 Mickey Hatcher .08
290 Bob Boone (DP) .08
291 Aurelio Lopez .08
292 Mike Squires .08
293 *Charlie Lea* .11
294 Mike Tyson (DP) .08
295 Hal McRae .08
296 Bill Nahorodny (DP) .08
297 Bob Bailor .08
298 Buddy Solomon .08
299 Elliott Maddox .08
300 Paul Molitor 1.50
301 Matt Keough .08
302 *Jack Perconte, Mike Scioscia, Fernando Valenzuela* Dodgers Future Stars 1.50
303 Johnny Oates .08
304 John Castino .08
305 Ken Clay .08
306 Juan Beniquez (DP) .08
307 Gene Garber .08
308 Rick Manning .08
309 *Luis Salazar* .08
310 Vida Blue (DP) .08
311 Freddie Patek .08
312 Rick Rhoden .08
313 Luis Pujols .08
314 Rich Dauer .08
315 *Kirk Gibson* 2.25
316 Craig Minetto .08
317 Lonnie Smith .08
318 Steve Yeager .08
319 Rowland Office .08
320 Tom Burgmeier .08
321 *Leon Durham* .11
322 Neil Allen .08
323 Jim Morrison (DP) .08
324 Mike Willis .08
325 Ray Knight .08
326 Biff Pocoroba .08
327 Moose Haas .08
328 Dave Engle, Greg Johnston, Gary Ward Twins Future Stars .11
329 Joaquin Andujar .08
330 Frank White .08
331 Dennis Lamp .08
332 Lee Lacy (DP) .08
333 Sid Monge .08
334 Dane Iorg .08
335 Rick Cerone .08
336 Eddie Whitson .08
337 Lynn Jones .08
338 Checklist 243-363 .08
339 John Ellis .08
340 Bruce Kison .08
341 Dwayne Murphy .08
342 Eric Rasmussen (DP) .08
343 Frank Taveras .08
344 Byron McLaughlin .08
345 Warren Cromartie .08
346 Larry Christenson (DP) .08
347 *Harold Baines* 3.00
348 Bob Sykes .08
349 Glenn Hoffman .08
350 J.R. Richard .08
351 Otto Velez .08
352 Dick Tidrow (DP) .08
353 Terry Kennedy .08
354 Mario Soto .08
355 Bob Horner .08
356 George Stablein, Craig Stimac, Tom Tellmann Padres Future Stars .08
357 Jim Slaton .08
358 Mark Wagner .08
359 Tom Hausman .08
360 Willie Wilson .08
361 Joe Strain .08
362 Bo Diaz .08
363 Geoff Zahn .08
364 *Mike Davis* .08
365 Graig Nettles (DP) .11
366 Mike Ramsey .08
367 Denny Martinez .08
368 Leon Roberts .08
369 Frank Tanana .08
370 Dave Winfield 1.50
371 Charlie Hough .08
372 Jay Johnstone .08
373 Pat Underwood .08
374 Tom Hutton .08
375 Dave Concepcion .08
376 Ron Reed .08
377 Jerry Morales .08
378 Dave Rader .08
379 Lary Sorensen .08
380 Willie Stargell 1.50
381 Carlos Lezcano, Steve Macko, Randy Martz Cubs Future Stars .08
382 *Paul Mirabella* .08
383 Eric Soderholm (DP) .08
384 Mike Sadek .08
385 Joe Sambito .08
386 Dave Edwards .08
387 Phil Niekro .70
388 Andre Thornton .08
389 Marty Pattin .08
390 Cesar Geronimo .08
391 Dave Lemanczyk (DP) .08
392 Lance Parrish .08
393 Broderick Perkins .08
394 Woodie Fryman .08
395 Scot Thompson .08
396 Bill Campbell .08
397 Julio Cruz .08
398 Ross Baumgarten .08
399 *Mike Boddicker, Mark Corey, Floyd Rayford* Orioles Future Stars .15
400 Reggie Jackson 2.25
401 A.L. Championships (Royals Sweep Yankees) .40
402 N.L. Championships (Phillies Squeak Past Astros) .20
403 World Series (Phillies Beat Royals In 6) .20
404 World Series Summary (Phillies Win First World Series) .20
405 Nino Espinosa .08
406 Dickie Noles .08
407 Ernie Whitt .08
408 Fernando Arroyo .08
409 Larry Herndon .08
410 Bert Campaneris .08
411 Terry Puhl .08
412 *Britt Burns* .08
413 Tony Bernazard .08
414 John Pacella (DP) .08
415 Ben Oglivie .08
416 Gary Alexander .08
417 Dan Schatzeder .08
418 Bobby Brown .08
419 Tom Hume .08
420 Keith Hernandez .08
421 Bob Stanley .08
422 Dan Ford .08
423 Shane Rawley .08
424 Tim Lollar, Bruce Robinson, Dennis Werth Yankees Future Stars .08
425 Al Bumbry .08
426 Warren Brusstar .08
427 John D'Acquisto .08
428 John Stearns .08
429 Mick Kelleher .08
430 Jim Bibby .08
431 Dave Roberts .08
432 Len Barker .08
433 Rance Mulliniks .08
434 Roger Erickson .08
435 Jim Spencer .08
436 Gary Lucas .08
437 Mike Heath (DP) .08
438 John Montefusco .08
439 Denny Walling .08
440 Jerry Reuss .08
441 Ken Reitz .08
442 Ron Pruitt .08
443 Jim Beattie (DP) .08
444 Garth Iorg .08
445 Ellis Valentine .08
446 Checklist 364-484 .08
447 Junior Kennedy (DP) .08
448 Tim Corcoran .08
449 Paul Mitchell .08
450 Dave Kingman (DP) .08
451 Chris Bando, Tom Brennan, Sandy Wihtol Indians Future Stars .08
452 Renie Martin .08
453 Rob Wilfong (DP) .08
454 Andy Hassler .08
455 Rick Burleson .08
456 *Jeff Reardon* 1.25
457 Mike Lum .08
458 Randy Jones .08
459 Greg Gross .08
460 Rich Gossage .08
461 Dave McKay .08
462 Jack Brohamer .08
463 Milt May .08
464 Adrian Devine .08
465 Bill Russell .08
466 Bob Molinaro .08
467 Dave Stieb .08
468 Johnny Wockenfuss .08
469 Jeff Leonard .08
470 Manny Trillo .08
471 Mike Vail .08
472 Dyar Miller (DP) .08
473 Jose Cardenal .08
474 Mike LaCoss .08
475 Buddy Bell .08
476 Jerry Koosman .08
477 Luis Gomez .08
478 Juan Eichelberger .08
479 *Bobby Pate, Tim Raines, Roberto Ramos* Expos Future Stars 2.25
480 Carlton Fisk 1.50
481 Bob Lacey (DP) .08
482 Jim Gantner .08
483 Mike Griffin .08
484 Max Venable (DP) .08
485 Garry Templeton .08
486 Marc Hill .08
487 Dewey Robinson .08
488 *Damaso Garcia* .08
489 John Littlefield (photo actually Mark Riggins) .08
490 Eddie Murray 1.50
491 Gordy Pladson .08
492 Barry Foote .08
493 Dan Quisenberry .08
494 *Bob Walk* .15
495 Dusty Baker .11
496 Paul Dade .08
497 Fred Norman .08
498 Pat Putnam .08
499 Frank Pastore .08
500 Jim Rice .20
501 Tim Foli (DP) .08
502 Chris Bourjos, Al Hargesheimer, Mike Rowland Giants Future Stars .08
503 Steve McCatty .08
504 Dale Murphy .60
505 Jason Thompson .08
506 Phil Huffman .08
507 Jamie Quirk .08
508 Rob Dressler .08
509 Pete Mackanin .08
510 Lee Mazzilli .08
511 Wayne Garland .08
512 Gary Thomasson .08
513 Frank LaCorte .08
514 George Riley .08
515 Robin Yount 1.50
516 Doug Bird .08
517 Richie Zisk .08
518 Grant Jackson .08
519 John Tamargo (DP) .08
520 Steve Stone .08
521 Sam Mejias .08
522 Mike Colbern .08
523 John Fulgham .08
524 Willie Aikens .08
525 Mike Torrez .08
526 Marty Bystrom, Jay Loviglio, Jim Wright Phillies Future Stars .08
527 Danny Goodwin .08
528 Gary Matthews .08
529 Dave LaRoche .08
530 Steve Garvey .60

531	John Curtis	.08
532	Bill Stein	.08
533	Jesus Figueroa	.08
534	*Dave Smith*	.08
535	Omar Moreno	.08
536	Bob Owchinko (DP)	.08
537	Ron Hodges	.08
538	Tom Griffin	.08
539	Rodney Scott	.08
540	Mike Schmidt (DP)	2.25
541	Steve Swisher	.08
542	Larry Bradford (DP)	.08
543	Terry Crowley	.08
544	Rich Gale	.08
545	Johnny Grubb	.08
546	Paul Moskau	.08
547	Mario Guerrero	.08
548	Dave Goltz	.08
549	Jerry Remy	.08
550	Tommy John	.15
551	*Vance Law, Tony Pena, Pascual Perez* Pirates Future Stars	.60
552	Steve Trout	.08
553	Tim Blackwell	.08
554	Bert Blyleven	.08
555	Cecil Cooper	.08
556	Jerry Mumphrey	.08
557	Chris Knapp	.08
558	Barry Bonnell	.08
559	Willie Montanez	.08
560	Joe Morgan	1.50
561	Dennis Littlejohn	.08
562	Checklist 485-605	.08
563	Jim Kaat	.11
564	Ron Hassey (DP)	.08
565	Burt Hooton	.08
566	Del Unser	.08
567	Mark Bomback	.08
568	Dave Revering	.08
569	Al Williams (DP)	.08
570	Ken Singleton	.08
571	Todd Cruz	.08
572	Jack Morris	.08
573	Phil Garner	.08
574	Bill Caudill	.08
575	Tony Perez	.70
576	Reggie Cleveland	.08
577	*Luis Leal, Brian Milner, Ken Schrom* Blue Jays Future Stars	.08
578	*Bill Gullickson*	.15
579	Tim Flannery	.08
580	Don Baylor	.11
581	Roy Howell	.08
582	Gaylord Perry	.70
583	Larry Milbourne	.08
584	Randy Lerch	.08
585	Amos Otis	.08
586	Silvio Martinez	.08
587	Jeff Newman	.08
588	Gary Lavelle	.08
589	Lamar Johnson	.08
590	Bruce Sutter	.70
591	John Lowenstein	.08
592	Steve Comer	.08
593	Steve Kemp	.08
594	Preston Hanna (DP)	.08
595	Butch Hobson	.08
596	Jerry Augustine	.08
597	Rafael Landestoy	.08
598	George Vukovich (DP)	.08
599	Dennis Kinney	.08
600	Johnny Bench	1.50
601	Don Aase	.08
602	Bobby Murcer	.08
603	John Verhoeven	.08
604	Rob Picciolo	.08
605	Don Sutton	.70
606	Bruce Berenyi, Geoff Combe, Paul Householder Reds Future Stars (DP)	.08
607	Dave Palmer	.08
608	Greg Pryor	.08
609	Lynn McGlothen	.08
610	Darrell Porter	.08
611	Rick Matula (DP)	.08
612	Duane Kuiper	.08
613	Jim Anderson	.08
614	Dave Rozema	.08
615	Rick Dempsey	.08
616	Rick Wise	.08
617	Craig Reynolds	.08
618	John Milner	.08
619	Steve Henderson	.08
620	Dennis Eckersley	.70
621	Tom Donohue	.08
622	Randy Moffitt	.08
623	Sal Bando	.08
624	Bob Welch	.08
625	Bill Buckner	.08
626	Dave Steffen, Jerry Ujdur, Roger Weaver Tigers Future Stars	.08
627	Luis Tiant	.08
628	Vic Correll	.08
629	Tony Armas	.08
630	Steve Carlton	1.50
631	Ron Jackson	.08
632	Alan Bannister	.08
633	Bill Lee	.08
634	Doug Flynn	.08
635	Bobby Bonds	.08
636	Al Hrabosky	.08
637	Jerry Narron	.08
638	Checklist 606	.08
639	Carney Lansford	.08
640	Dave Parker	.08
641	Mark Belanger	.08
642	Vern Ruhle	.08
643	*Lloyd Moseby*	.15
644	Ramon Aviles (DP)	.08
645	Rick Reuschel	.08
646	Marvis Foley	.08
647	Dick Drago	.08
648	Darrell Evans	.08
649	Manny Sarmiento	.08
650	Bucky Dent	.08
651	Pedro Guerrero	.08
652	John Montague	.08
653	Bill Fahey	.08
654	Ray Burris	.08
655	Dan Driessen	.08
656	Jon Matlack	.08
657	Mike Cubbage (DP)	.08
658	Milt Wilcox	.08
659	John Flinn, Ed Romero, Ned Yost Brewers Future Stars	.08
660	Gary Carter	1.50
661	Earl Weaver Orioles Team	.20
662	Ralph Houk Red Sox Team	.15
663	Jim Fregosi Angels Team	.08
664	Tony LaRussa White Sox Team	.20
665	Dave Garcia Indians Team	.08
666	Sparky Anderson Tigers Team	.20
667	Jim Frey Royals Team	.08
668	Bob Rodgers Brewers Team	.08
669	John Goryl Twins Team	.08
670	Gene Michael Yankees Team	.11
671	Billy Martin A's Team	.20
672	Maury Wills Mariners Team	.15
673	Don Zimmer Rangers Team	.15
674	Bobby Mattick Blue Jays Team	.08
675	Bobby Cox Braves Team	.20
676	Joe Amalfitano Cubs Team	.08
677	John McNamara Reds Team	.08
678	Bill Virdon Astros Team	.08
679	Tom Lasorda Dodgers Team	.20
680	Dick Williams Expos Team	.15
681	Joe Torre Mets Team	.20
682	Dallas Green Phillies Team	.11
683	Chuck Tanner Pirates Team	.08
684	Whitey Herzog Cardinals Team	.11
685	Frank Howard Padres Team	.15
686	Dave Bristol Giants Team	.08
687	Jeff Jones	.08
688	Kiko Garcia	.08
689	*Bruce Hurst, Keith MacWhorter, Reid Nichols* Red Sox Future Stars	.25
690	Bob Watson	.08
691	Dick Ruthven	.08
692	Lenny Randle	.08
693	*Steve Howe*	.15
694	Bud Harrelson (DP)	.08
695	Kent Tekulve	.08
696	Alan Ashby	.08
697	Rick Waits	.08
698	Mike Jorgensen	.08
699	Glenn Abbott	.08
700	George Brett	2.75
701	Joe Rudi	.08
702	George Medich	.08
703	Alvis Woods	.08
704	Bill Travers (DP)	.08
705	Ted Simmons	.08
706	Dave Ford	.08
707	Dave Cash	.08
708	Doyle Alexander	.08
709	Alan Trammell (DP)	.08
710	Ron LeFlore (DP)	.08
711	Joe Ferguson	.08
712	Bill Bonham	.08
713	Bill North	.08
714	Pete Redfern	.08
715	Bill Madlock	.08
716	Glenn Borgmann	.08
717	Jim Barr (DP)	.08
718	Larry Biittner	.08
719	Sparky Lyle	.08
720	Fred Lynn	.08
721	Toby Harrah	.08
722	Joe Niekro	.08
723	Bruce Bochte	.08
724	Lou Piniella	.11
725	Steve Rogers	.08
726	Rick Monday	.08

Traded

		NM/M
Complete Set (132):		
Common Player:		
727	Danny Ainge	1.50
728	Doyle Alexander	.11
729	Gary Alexander	.11
730	Billy Almon	.11
731	Joaquin Andujar	.11
732	Bob Bailor	.11
733	Juan Beniquez	.11
734	Dave Bergman	.11
735	Tony Bernazard	.11
736	Larry Biittner	.11
737	Doug Bird	.11
738	Bert Blyleven	.20
739	Mark Bomback	.11
740	Bobby Bonds	.11
741	Rick Bosetti	.11
742	Hubie Brooks	.11
743	Rick Burleson	.11
744	Ray Burris	.11
745	Jeff Burroughs	.11
746	Enos Cabell	.11
747	Ken Clay	.11
748	Mark Clear	.11
749	Larry Cox	.11
750	Hector Cruz	.11
751	Victor Cruz	.11
752	Mike Cubbage	.11
753	Dick Davis	.11
754	Brian Doyle	.11
755	Dick Drago	.11
756	Leon Durham	.11
757	Jim Dwyer	.11
758	Dave Edwards	.11
759	Jim Essian	.11
760	Bill Fahey	.11
761	Rollie Fingers	.70
762	Carlton Fisk	1.50
763	Barry Foote	.11
764	Ken Forsch	.11
765	Kiko Garcia	.11
766	Cesar Geronimo	.11
767	Gary Gray	.11
768	Mickey Hatcher	.11
769	Steve Henderson	.11
770	Marc Hill	.11
771	Butch Hobson	.11
772	Rick Honeycutt	.11
773	Roy Howell	.11
774	Mike Ivie	.11
775	Roy Lee Jackson	.11
776	Cliff Johnson	.11
777	Randy Jones	.11
778	Ruppert Jones	.11
779	Mick Kelleher	.11
780	Terry Kennedy	.11
781	Dave Kingman	.11
782	Bob Knepper	.11
783	Ken Kravec	.11
784	Bob Lacey	.11
785	Dennis Lamp	.11
786	Rafael Landestoy	.11
787	Ken Landreaux	.11
788	Carney Lansford	.11
789	Dave LaRoche	.11
790	Joe Lefebvre	.11
791	Ron LeFlore	.11
792	Randy Lerch	.11
793	Sixto Lezcano	.11
794	John Littlefield	.11
795	Mike Lum	.11
796	Greg Luzinski	.11
797	Fred Lynn	.11
798	Jerry Martin	.11
799	Buck Martinez	.11
800	Gary Matthews	.11
801	Mario Mendoza	.11
802	Larry Milbourne	.11
803	Rick Miller	.11
804	John Montefusco	.11
805	Jerry Morales	.11
806	Jose Morales	.11
807	Joe Morgan	1.50
808	Jerry Mumphrey	.11
809	*Gene Nelson*	.11
810	Ed Ott	.11
811	Bob Owchinko	.11
812	Gaylord Perry	.70
813	Mike Phillips	.11
814	Darrell Porter	.11
815	Mike Proly	.11
816	Tim Raines	2.25
817	Lenny Randle	.11
818	Doug Rau	.11
819	Jeff Reardon	.11
820	Ken Reitz	.11
821	Steve Renko	.11
822	Rick Reuschel	.11
823	Dave Revering	.11
824	Dave Roberts	.11
825	Leon Roberts	.11
826	Joe Rudi	.11
827	Kevin Saucier	.11
828	Tony Scott	.11
829	Bob Shirley	.11
830	Ted Simmons	.11
831	Lary Sorensen	.11
832	Jim Spencer	.11
833	Harry Spilman	.11
834	Fred Stanley	.11
835	Rusty Staub	.20
836	Bill Stein	.11
837	Joe Strain	.11
838	Bruce Sutter	.70
839	Don Sutton	.70
840	Steve Swisher	.11
841	Frank Tanana	.11
842	Gene Tenace	.11
843	Jason Thompson	.11
844	Dickie Thon	.11
845	Bill Travers	.11
846	Tom Underwood	.11
847	John Urrea	.11
848	Mike Vail	.11
849	Ellis Valentine	.11
850	Fernando Valenzuela	1.50
851	Pete Vuckovich	.11
852	Mark Wagner	.11
853	Bob Walk	.11
854	Claudell Washington	.11
855	Dave Winfield	3.00
856	Geoff Zahn	.11
857	Richie Zisk	.11
858	Checklist 727-858	.04

1982 TOPPS

		NM/M
Unopened Fact. Set (792):		180.00
Complete Set (792):		60.00
Common Player:		.10
Wax Pack (15):		5.00
Wax Box (36):		130.00
Cello Pack (28):		6.00
Cello Box (24):		130.00
Rack Pack (51):		8.00
Rack Box (24):		210.00
Vending Box (500):		60.00
1	Steve Carlton	.25

2 Ron Davis .10
3 Tim Raines .10
4 Pete Rose .75
5 Nolan Ryan 3.00
6 Fernando Valenzuela .10
7 Scott Sanderson .10
8 Rich Dauer .10
9 Ron Guidry .15
10 Ron Guidry (In Action) .10
11 Gary Alexander .10
12 Moose Haas .10
13 Lamar Johnson .10
14 Steve Howe .10
15 Ellis Valentine .10
16 Steve Comer .10
17 Darrell Evans .10
18 Fernando Arroyo .10
19 Ernie Whitt .10
20 Garry Maddox .10
21 *Bob Bonner, Cal Ripken, Jr., Jeff Schneider* Orioles Future Stars 50.00
22 Jim Beattie .10
23 Willie Hernandez .10
24 Dave Frost .10
25 Jerry Remy .10
26 Jorge Orta .10
27 Tom Herr .10
28 John Urrea .10
29 Dwayne Murphy .10
30 Tom Seaver 1.50
31 Tom Seaver (In Action) 1.00
32 Gene Garber .10
33 Jerry Morales .10
34 Joe Sambito .10
35 Willie Aikens .10
36 George Medich, Al Oliver Rangers Batting/Pitching Leaders .10
37 Dan Graham .10
38 Charlie Lea .10
39 Lou Whitaker .10
40 Dave Parker .10
41 Dave Parker (In Action) .10
42 Rick Sofield .10
43 Mike Cubbage .10
44 Britt Burns .10
45 Rick Cerone .10
46 Jerry Augustine .10
47 Jeff Leonard .10
48 Bobby Castillo .10
49 Alvis Woods .10
50 Buddy Bell .10
51 *Jay Howell, Carlos Lezcano, Ty Waller* Chicago Cubs Future Stars .40
52 Larry Andersen .10
53 Greg Gross .10
54 Ron Hassey .10
55 Rick Burleson .10
56 Mark Littell .10
57 Craig Reynolds .10
58 John D'Acquisto .10
59 *Rich Gedman* .10
60 Tony Armas .10
61 Tommy Boggs .10
62 Mike Tyson .10
63 Mario Soto .10
64 Lynn Jones .10
65 Terry Kennedy .10
66 Art Howe, Nolan Ryan Astros Batting/Pitching Leaders .75
67 Rich Gale .10
68 Roy Howell .10
69 Al Williams .10
70 Tim Raines .50
71 Roy Lee Jackson .10
72 Rick Auerbach .10
73 Buddy Solomon .10
74 Bob Clark .10
75 Tommy John .20
76 Greg Pryor .10
77 Miguel Dilone .10
78 George Medich .10
79 Bob Bailor .10
80 Jim Palmer 1.00
81 Jim Palmer (In Action) .30
82 Bob Welch .10
83 *Steve Balboni, Andy McGaffigan, Andre Robertson* Yankees Future Stars .15
84 Rennie Stennett .10
85 Lynn McGlothen .10
86 Dane Iorg .10
87 Matt Keough .10
88 Biff Pocoroba .10
89 Steve Henderson .10
90 Nolan Ryan 4.00
91 Carney Lansford .10
92 Brad Havens .10
93 Larry Hisle .10
94 Andy Hassler .10
95 Ozzie Smith 2.00
96 George Brett, Larry Gura Royals Batting/Pitching Leaders .35
97 Paul Moskau .10
98 Terry Bulling .10
99 Barry Bonnell .10
100 Mike Schmidt 3.00
101 Mike Schmidt (In Action) 1.50
102 Dan Briggs .10
103 Bob Lacey .10
104 Rance Mulliniks .10
105 Kirk Gibson .10
106 Enrique Romo .10
107 Wayne Krenchicki .10
108 Bob Sykes .10
109 Dave Revering .10
110 Carlton Fisk 1.50
111 Carlton Fisk (In Action) .65
112 Billy Sample .10
113 Steve McCatty .10
114 Ken Landreaux .10
115 Gaylord Perry 1.00
116 Jim Wohlford .10
117 Rawly Eastwick .10
118 *Terry Francona, Brad Mills, Bryn Smith* Expos Future Stars .20
119 Joe Pittman .10
120 Gary Lucas .10
121 Ed Lynch .10
122 Jamie Easterly .10
123 Danny Goodwin .10
124 Reid Nichols .10
125 Danny Ainge 1.00
126 Rick Mahler, Claudell Washington Braves Batting/Pitching Leaders .10
127 Lonnie Smith .10
128 Frank Pastore .10
129 Checklist 1-132 .10
130 Julio Cruz .10
131 Stan Bahnsen .10
132 Lee May .10
133 Pat Underwood .10
134 Dan Ford .10
135 Andy Rincon .10
136 Lenn Sakata .10
137 George Cappuzzello .10
138 Tony Pena .10
139 Jeff Jones .10
140 Ron LeFlore .10
141 *Chris Bando, Tom Brennan, Von Hayes* Indians Future Stars .20
142 Dave LaRoche .10
143 Mookie Wilson .10
144 Fred Breining .10
145 Bob Horner .10
146 Mike Griffin .10
147 Denny Walling .10
148 Mickey Klutts .10
149 Pat Putnam .10
150 Ted Simmons .10
151 Dave Edwards .10
152 Ramon Aviles .10
153 Roger Erickson .10
154 Dennis Werth .10
155 Otto Velez .10
156 Rickey Henderson, Steve McCatty A's Batting/Pitching Leaders .10
157 Steve Crawford .10
158 Brian Downing .10
159 Larry Biittner .10
160 Luis Tiant .10
161 Carney Lansford, Bill Madlock Batting Leaders .10
162 Tony Armas, Dwight Evans, Bobby Grich, Eddie Murray, Mike Schmidt Home Run Leaders .25
163 Eddie Murray, Mike Schmidt RBI Leaders .40
164 Rickey Henderson, Tim Raines Stolen Base Leaders .35
165 Denny Martinez, Steve McCatty, Jack Morris, Tom Seaver, Pete Vuckovich Victory Leaders .10
166 Len Barker, Fernando Valenzuela Strikeout Leaders .10
167 Steve McCatty, Nolan Ryan ERA Leaders 1.50
168 Rollie Fingers, Bruce Sutter Leading Relievers .15
169 Charlie Leibrandt .10
170 Jim Bibby .10
171 *Bob Brenly, Chili Davis, Bob Tufts* Giants Future Stars 2.00
172 Bill Gullickson .10
173 Jamie Quirk .10
174 Dave Ford .10
175 Jerry Mumphrey .10
176 Dewey Robinson .10
177 John Ellis .10
178 Dyar Miller .10
179 Steve Garvey .75
180 Steve Garvey (In Action) .30
181 Silvio Martinez .10
182 Larry Herndon .10
183 Mike Proly .10
184 Mick Kelleher .10
185 Phil Niekro 1.00
186 Bob Forsch, Keith Hernandez Cardinals Batting/Pitching Leaders .10
187 Jeff Newman .10
188 Randy Martz .10
189 Glenn Hoffman .10
190 J.R. Richard .05
191 *Tim Wallach* 2.00
192 Broderick Perkins .10
193 Darrell Jackson .10
194 Mike Vail .10
195 Paul Molitor 1.50
196 Willie Upshaw .10
197 Shane Rawley .10
198 Chris Speier .10
199 Don Aase .10
200 George Brett 3.00
201 George Brett (In Action) 2.00
202 Rick Manning .10
203 Jesse Barfield, Brian Milner, Boomer Wells Blue Jays Future Stars .50
204 Gary Roenicke .10
205 Neil Allen .10
206 Tony Bernazard .10
207 Rod Scurry .10
208 Bobby Murcer .10
209 Gary Lavelle .10
210 Keith Hernandez .10
211 Dan Petry .10
212 Mario Mendoza .10
213 *Dave Stewart* 4.00
214 Brian Asselstine .10
215 Mike Krukow .10
216 Dennis Lamp, Chet Lemon White Sox Batting/Pitching Leaders .10
217 Bo McLaughlin .10
218 Dave Roberts .10
219 John Curtis .10
220 Manny Trillo .10
221 Jim Slaton .10
222 Butch Wynegar .10
223 Lloyd Moseby .10
224 Bruce Bochte .10
225 Mike Torrez .10
226 Checklist 133-264 .10
227 Ray Burris .10
228 Sam Mejias .10
229 Geoff Zahn .10
230 Willie Wilson .10
231 *Mark Davis, Bob Dernier, Ozzie Virgil* Phillies Future Stars .20
232 Terry Crowley .10
233 Duane Kuiper .10
234 Ron Hodges .10
235 Mike Easler .10
236 John Martin .10
237 Rusty Kuntz .10
238 Kevin Saucier .10
239 Jon Matlack .10
240 Bucky Dent .10
241 Bucky Dent (In Action) .10
242 Milt May .10
243 Bob Owchinko .10
244 Rufino Linares .10
245 Ken Reitz .10
246 Hubie Brooks, Mike Scott Mets Batting/Pitching Leaders .10
247 Pedro Guerrero .10
248 Frank LaCorte .10
249 Tim Flannery .10
250 Tug McGraw .10
251 Fred Lynn .10
252 Fred Lynn (In Action) .10
253 Chuck Baker .10
254 *George Bell* 1.00
255 Tony Perez 1.00
256 Tony Perez (In Action) .10
257 Larry Harlow .10
258 Bo Diaz .10
259 Rodney Scott .10
260 Bruce Sutter 1.00
261 Howard Bailey, Marty Castillo, Dave Rucker Tigers Future Stars .10
262 Doug Bair .10
263 Victor Cruz .10
264 Dan Quisenberry .10
265 Al Bumbry .10
266 Rick Leach .10
267 Kurt Bevacqua .10
268 Rickey Keeton .10
269 Jim Essian .10
270 Rusty Staub .15
271 Larry Bradford .10
272 Bump Wills .10
273 Doug Bird .10
274 *Bob Ojeda* .50
275 Bob Watson .10
276 Rod Carew, Ken Forsch Angels Batting/Pitching Leaders .25
277 Terry Puhl .10
278 John Littlefield .10
279 Bill Russell .10
280 Ben Oglivie .10
281 John Verhoeven .10
282 Ken Macha .10
283 Brian Allard .10
284 Bob Grich .10
285 Sparky Lyle .10
286 Bill Fahey .10
287 Alan Bannister .10
288 Garry Templeton .10
289 Bob Stanley .10
290 Ken Singleton .10
291 *Vance Law, Bob Long, Johnny Ray* Pirates Future Stars .15
292 Dave Palmer .10
293 Rob Picciolo .10
294 Mike LaCoss .10
295 Jason Thompson .10
296 Bob Walk .10
297 Clint Hurdle .10
298 Danny Darwin .10
299 Steve Trout .10
300 Reggie Jackson 2.00
301 Reggie Jackson (In Action) 1.50
302 Doug Flynn .10
303 Bill Caudill .10
304 Johnnie LeMaster .10
305 Don Sutton 1.00
306 Don Sutton (In Action) .20
307 Randy Bass .10
308 Charlie Moore .10
309 Pete Redfern .10
310 Mike Hargrove .10
311 Dusty Baker, Burt Hooton Dodgers Batting/Pitching Leaders .10
312 Lenny Randle .10
313 John Harris .10
314 Buck Martinez .10
315 Burt Hooton .10
316 Steve Braun .10
317 Dick Ruthven .10
318 Mike Heath .10
319 Dave Rozema .10
320 Chris Chambliss .10
321 Chris Chambliss (In Action) .10

No.	Card	Value
322	Garry Hancock	.10
323	Bill Lee	.10
324	Steve Dillard	.10
325	Jose Cruz	.10
326	Pete Falcone	.10
327	Joe Nolan	.10
328	Ed Farmer	.10
329	U.L. Washington	.10
330	Rick Wise	.10
331	Benny Ayala	.10
332	Don Robinson	.10
333	Frank DiPino, Marshall Edwards, Chuck Porter Brewers Future Stars	.10
334	Aurelio Rodriguez	.10
335	Jim Sundberg	.10
336	Glenn Abbott, Tom Paciorek Mariners Batting/Pitching Leaders	.10
337	Pete Rose (All-Star)	1.50
338	Dave Lopes (All-Star)	.10
339	Mike Schmidt (All-Star)	1.00
340	Dave Concepcion (All-Star)	.10
341	Andre Dawson (All-Star)	.25
342a	George Foster (All-Star no autograph)	2.00
342b	George Foster (All-Star autograph on front)	.10
343	Dave Parker (All-Star)	.10
344	Gary Carter (All-Star)	.60
345	Fernando Valenzuela (All-Star)	.10
346	Tom Seaver (All-Star)	.75
347	Bruce Sutter (All-Star)	.50
348	Derrel Thomas	.10
349	George Frazier	.10
350	Thad Bosley	.10
351	Scott Brown, Geoff Combe, Paul Householder Reds Future Stars	.10
352	Dick Davis	.10
353	Jack O'Connor	.10
354	Roberto Ramos	.10
355	Dwight Evans	.10
356	Denny Lewallyn	.10
357	Butch Hobson	.10
358	Mike Parrott	.10
359	Jim Dwyer	.10
360	Len Barker	.10
361	Rafael Landestoy	.10
362	Jim Wright	.10
363	Bob Molinaro	.10
364	Doyle Alexander	.10
365	Bill Madlock	.10
366	Juan Eichelberger, Luis Salazar Padres Batting/ Pitching Leaders	.10
367	Jim Kaat	.10
368	Alex Trevino	.10
369	Champ Summers	.10
370	Mike Norris	.10
371	Jerry Don Gleaton	.10
372	Luis Gomez	.10
373	*Gene Nelson*	.10
374	Tim Blackwell	.10
375	Dusty Baker	.15
376	Chris Welsh	.10
377	Kiko Garcia	.10
378	Mike Caldwell	.10
379	Rob Wilfong	.10
380	Dave Stieb	.10
381	Bruce Hurst, Dave Schmidt, Julio Valdez Red Sox Future Stars	.25
382	Joe Simpson	.10
383a	Pascual Perez (no position on front)	20.00
383b	Pascual Perez ("Pitcher" on front)	.10
384	Keith Moreland	.10
385	Ken Forsch	.10
386	Jerry White	.10
387	Tom Veryzer	.10
388	Joe Rudi	.10
389	George Vukovich	.10
390	Eddie Murray	1.50
391	Dave Tobik	.10
392	Rick Bosetti	.10
393	Al Hrabosky	.10
394	Checklist 265-396	.10
395	Omar Moreno	.10
396	Fernando Arroyo, John Castino Twins Batting/ Pitching Leaders	.10
397	Ken Brett	.10
398	Mike Squires	.10
399	Pat Zachry	.10
400	Johnny Bench	1.50
401	Johnny Bench (In Action)	.45
402	Bill Stein	.10
403	Jim Tracy	.10
404	Dickie Thon	.10
405	Rick Reuschel	.10
406	Al Holland	.10
407	Danny Boone	.10
408	Ed Romero	.10
409	Don Cooper	.10
410	Ron Cey	.10
411	Ron Cey (In Action)	.10
412	Luis Leal	.10
413	Dan Meyer	.10
414	Elias Sosa	.10
415	Don Baylor	.15
416	Marty Bystrom	.10
417	Pat Kelly	.10
418	*John Butcher, Bobby Johnson, Dave Schmidt* Rangers Future Stars	.10
419	Steve Stone	.10
420	George Hendrick	.10
421	Mark Clear	.10
422	Cliff Johnson	.10
423	Stan Papi	.10
424	Bruce Benedict	.10
425	John Candelaria	.10
426	Eddie Murray, Sammy Stewart Orioles Batting/Pitching Leaders	.25
427	Ron Oester	.10
428	Lamarr Hoyt (LaMarr)	.10
429	John Wathan	.10
430	Vida Blue	.10
431	Vida Blue (In Action)	.10
432	Mike Scott	.10
433	Alan Ashby	.10
434	Joe Lefebvre	.10
435	Robin Yount	1.50
436	Joe Strain	.10
437	Juan Berenguer	.10
438	Pete Mackanin	.10
439	*Dave Righetti*	.75
440	Jeff Burroughs	.10
441	Danny Heep, Billy Smith, Bobby Sprowl Astros Future Stars	.10
442	Bruce Kison	.10
443	Mark Wagner	.10
444	Terry Forster	.10
445	Larry Parrish	.10
446	Wayne Garland	.10
447	Darrell Porter	.10
448	Darrell Porter (In Action)	.10
449	*Luis Aguayo*	.10
450	Jack Morris	.10
451	Ed Miller	.10
452	*Lee Smith*	4.00
453	Art Howe	.10
454	Rick Langford	.10
455	Tom Burgmeier	.10
456	Bill Buckner, Randy Martz Cubs Batting & Pitching Ldrs.	.10
457	Tim Stoddard	.10
458	Willie Montanez	.10
459	Bruce Berenyi	.10
460	Jack Clark	.10
461	Rich Dotson	.10
462	Dave Chalk	.10
463	Jim Kern	.10
464	Juan Bonilla	.10
465	Lee Mazzilli	.10
466	Randy Lerch	.10
467	Mickey Hatcher	.10
468	Floyd Bannister	.10
469	Ed Ott	.10
470	John Mayberry	.10
471	Atlee Hammaker, Mike Jones, Darryl Motley Royals Future Stars	.15
472	Oscar Gamble	.10
473	Mike Stanton	.10
474	Ken Oberkfell	.10
475	Alan Trammell	.10
476	Brian Kingman	.10
477	Steve Yeager	.10
478	Ray Searage	.10
479	Rowland Office	.10
480	Steve Carlton	1.50
481	Steve Carlton (In Action)	.40
482	Glenn Hubbard	.10
483	Gary Woods	.10
484	Ivan DeJesus	.10
485	Kent Tekulve	.10
486	Tommy John, Jerry Mumphrey Yankees Batting & Pitching Ldrs.	.10
487	Bob McClure	.10
488	Ron Jackson	.10
489	Rick Dempsey	.10
490	Dennis Eckersley	1.00
491	Checklist 397-528	.10
492	Joe Price	.10
493	Chet Lemon	.10
494	Hubie Brooks	.10
495	Dennis Leonard	.10
496	Johnny Grubb	.10
497	Jim Anderson	.10
498	Dave Bergman	.10
499	Paul Mirabella	.10
500	Rod Carew	1.50
501	Rod Carew (In Action)	.40
502	Steve Bedrosian, Brett Butler, Larry Owen Braves Future Stars	2.00
503	Julio Gonzalez	.10
504	Rick Peters	.10
505	Graig Nettles	.10
506	Graig Nettles (In Action)	.10
507	Terry Harper	.10
508	*Jody Davis*	.15
509	Harry Spilman	.10
510	Fernando Valenzuela	.10
511	Ruppert Jones	.10
512	Jerry Dybzinski	.10
513	Rick Rhoden	.10
514	Joe Ferguson	.10
515	Larry Bowa	.10
516	Larry Bowa (In Action)	.10
517	Mark Brouhard	.10
518	Garth Iorg	.10
519	Glenn Adams	.10
520	Mike Flanagan	.10
521	Billy Almon	.10
522	Chuck Rainey	.10
523	Gary Gray	.10
524	Tom Hausman	.10
525	Ray Knight	.10
526	Warren Cromartie, Bill Gullickson Expos Batting & Pitching Ldrs.	.10
527	John Henry Johnson	.10
528	Matt Alexander	.10
529	Allen Ripley	.10
530	Dickie Noles	.10
531	Rich Bordi, Mark Budaska, Kelvin Moore A's Future Stars	.10
532	Toby Harrah	.10
533	Joaquin Andujar	.10
534	Dave McKay	.10
535	Lance Parrish	.10
536	Rafael Ramirez	.10
537	Doug Capilla	.10
538	Lou Piniella	.10
539	Vern Ruhle	.10
540	Andre Dawson	.75
541	Barry Evans	.10
542	Ned Yost	.10
543	Bill Robinson	.10
544	Larry Christenson	.10
545	Reggie Smith	.10
546	Reggie Smith (In Action)	.10
547	Rod Carew (All-Star)	.25
548	Willie Randolph (All-Star)	.10
549	George Brett (All-Star)	1.50
550	Bucky Dent (All-Star)	.10
551	Reggie Jackson (All-Star)	.75
552	Ken Singleton (All-Star)	.10
553	Dave Winfield (All-Star)	.60
554	Carlton Fisk (All-Star)	.25
555	Scott McGregor (All-Star)	.10
556	Jack Morris (All-Star)	.10
557	Rich Gossage (All-Star)	.10
558	John Tudor	.10
559	Bert Blyleven, Mike Hargrove Indians Batting & Pitching Ldrs.	.10
560	Doug Corbett	.10
561	Glenn Brummer, Luis DeLeon, Gene Roof Cardinals Future Stars	.10
562	Mike O'Berry	.10
563	Ross Baumgarten	.10
564	Doug DeCinces	.10
565	Jackson Todd	.10
566	Mike Jorgensen	.10
567	Bob Babcock	.10
568	Joe Pettini	.10
569	Willie Randolph	.10
570	Willie Randolph (In Action)	.10
571	Glenn Abbott	.10
572	Juan Beniquez	.10
573	Rick Waits	.10
574	Mike Ramsey	.10
575	Al Cowens	.10
576	Vida Blue, Milt May Giants Batting & Pitching Ldrs.	.10
577	Rick Monday	.10
578	Shooty Babitt	.10
579	*Rick Mahler*	.10
580	Bobby Bonds	.10
581	Ron Reed	.10
582	Luis Pujols	.10
583	Tippy Martinez	.10
584	Hosken Powell	.10
585	Rollie Fingers	1.00
586	Rollie Fingers (In Action)	.15
587	Tim Lollar	.10
588	Dale Berra	.10
589	Dave Stapleton	.10
590	Al Oliver	.10
591	Al Oliver (In Action)	.10
592	Craig Swan	.10
593	Billy Smith	.10
594	Renie Martin	.10
595	Dave Collins	.10
596	Damaso Garcia	.10
597	Wayne Nordhagen	.10
598	Bob Galasso	.10
599	Jay Loviglio, Reggie Patterson, Leo Sutherland White Sox Future Stars	.10
600	Dave Winfield	1.50
601	Sid Monge	.10
602	Freddie Patek	.10
603	Rich Hebner	.10
604	Orlando Sanchez	.10
605	Steve Rogers	.10
606	John Mayberry, Dave Stieb Blue Jays Batting & Pitching Ldrs.	.10
607	Leon Durham	.10
608	Jerry Royster	.10
609	Rick Sutcliffe	.10
610	Rickey Henderson	1.50
611	Joe Niekro	.10
612	Gary Ward	.10
613	Jim Gantner	.10
614	Juan Eichelberger	.10
615	Bob Boone	.10
616	Bob Boone (In Action)	.10
617	Scott McGregor	.10
618	Tim Foli	.10
619	Bill Campbell	.10
620	Ken Griffey	.10
621	Ken Griffey (In Action)	.10
622	Dennis Lamp	.10
623	*Ron Gardenhire, Terry Leach, Tim Leary* Mets Future Stars	.20
624	Fergie Jenkins	1.00
625	Hal McRae	.10
626	Randy Jones	.10
627	Enos Cabell	.10
628	Bill Travers	.10
629	Johnny Wockenfuss	.10
630	Joe Charboneau	.10
631	Gene Tenace	.10
632	Bryan Clark	.10
633	Mitchell Page	.10
634	Checklist 529-660	.10
635	Ron Davis	.10
636	Steve Carlton, Pete Rose Phillies Batting & Pitching Ldrs.	.50
637	Rick Camp	.10
638	John Milner	.10
639	Ken Kravec	.10
640	Cesar Cedeno	.10
641	Steve Mura	.10
642	Mike Scioscia	.10
643	Pete Vuckovich	.10
644	John Castino	.10
645	Frank White	.10
646	Frank White (In Action)	.10
647	Warren Brusstar	.10
648	Jose Morales	.10
649	Ken Clay	.10
650	Carl Yastrzemski	1.50
651	Carl Yastrzemski (In Action)	.65
652	Steve Nicosia	.10
653	*Tom Brunansky, Luis Sanchez, Daryl Sconiers* Angels Future Stars	.40
654	Jim Morrison	.10
655	Joel Youngblood	.10
656	Eddie Whitson	.10
657	Tom Poquette	.10
658	Tito Landrum	.10
659	Fred Martinez	.10
660	Dave Concepcion	.10

#	Player	Price
661	Dave Concepcion (In Action)	.10
662	Luis Salazar	.10
663	Hector Cruz	.10
664	Dan Spillner	.10
665	Jim Clancy	.10
666	Steve Kemp, Dan Petry Tigers Batting & Pitching Ldrs.	.10
667	Jeff Reardon	.15
668	Dale Murphy	.75
669	Larry Milbourne	.10
670	Steve Kemp	.10
671	Mike Davis	.10
672	Bob Knepper	.10
673	Keith Drumright	.10
674	Dave Goltz	.10
675	Cecil Cooper	.10
676	Sal Butera	.10
677	Alfredo Griffin	.10
678	Tom Paciorek	.10
679	Sammy Stewart	.10
680	Gary Matthews	.10
681	*Mike Marshall, Ron Roenicke, Steve Sax* Dodgers Future Stars	.75
682	Jesse Jefferson	.10
683	Phil Garner	.10
684	Harold Baines	.05
685	Bert Blyleven	.10
686	Gary Allenson	.10
687	Greg Minton	.10
688	Leon Roberts	.10
689	Lary Sorensen	.10
690	Dave Kingman	.10
691	Dan Schatzeder	.10
692	Wayne Gross	.10
693	Cesar Geronimo	.10
694	Dave Wehrmeister	.10
695	Warren Cromartie	.10
696	Bill Madlock, Buddy Solomon Pirates Batting & Pitching Ldrs.	.10
697	John Montefusco	.10
698	Tony Scott	.10
699	Dick Tidrow	.10
700	George Foster	.10
701	George Foster (In Action)	.10
702	Steve Renko	.10
703	Cecil Cooper, Pete Vuckovich Brewers Batting & Pitching Ldrs.	.10
704	Mickey Rivers	.10
705	Mickey Rivers (In Action)	.10
706	Barry Foote	.10
707	Mark Bomback	.10
708	Gene Richards	.10
709	Don Money	.10
710	Jerry Reuss	.10
711	*Dave Edler, Dave Henderson, Reggie Walton* Mariners Future Stars	.25
712	Denny Martinez	.10
713	Del Unser	.10
714	Jerry Koosman	.10
715	Willie Stargell	1.50
716	Willie Stargell (In Action)	.30
717	Rick Miller	.10
718	Charlie Hough	.10
719	Jerry Narron	.10
720	Greg Luzinski	.10
721	Greg Luzinski (In Action)	.10
722	Jerry Martin	.10
723	Junior Kennedy	.10
724	Dave Rosello	.10
725	Amos Otis	.10
726	Amos Otis (In Action)	.10
727	Sixto Lezcano	.10
728	Aurelio Lopez	.10
729	Jim Spencer	.10
730	Gary Carter	1.50
731	Mike Armstrong, Doug Gwosdz, Fred Kuhaulua Padres Future Stars	.10
732	Mike Lum	.10
733	Larry McWilliams	.10
734	Mike Ivie	.10
735	Rudy May	.10
736	Jerry Turner	.10
737	Reggie Cleveland	.10
738	Dave Engle	.10
739	Joey McLaughlin	.10
740	Dave Lopes	.10
741	Dave Lopes (In Action)	.10
742	Dick Drago	.10
743	John Stearns	.10
744	*Mike Witt*	.25
745	Bake McBride	.10
746	Andre Thornton	.10
747	John Lowenstein	.10
748	Marc Hill	.10
749	Bob Shirley	.10
750	Jim Rice	.20
751	Rick Honeycutt	.10
752	Lee Lacy	.10
753	Tom Brookens	.10
754	Joe Morgan	1.50
755	Joe Morgan (In Action)	.25
756	Ken Griffey, Tom Seaver Reds Batting & Pitching Ldrs.	.25
757	Tom Underwood	.10
758	Claudell Washington	.10
759	Paul Splittorff	.10
760	Bill Buckner	.10
761	Dave Smith	.10
762	Mike Phillips	.10
763	Tom Hume	.10
764	Steve Swisher	.10
765	Gorman Thomas	.10
766	*Lenny Faedo, Kent Hrbek, Tim Laudner* Twins Future Stars	2.00
767	Roy Smalley	.10
768	Jerry Garvin	.10
769	Richie Zisk	.10
770	Rich Gossage	.10
771	Rich Gossage (In Action)	.10
772	Bert Campaneris	.10
773	John Denny	.10
774	Jay Johnstone	.10
775	Bob Forsch	.10
776	Mark Belanger	.10
777	Tom Griffin	.10
778	Kevin Hickey	.10
779	Grant Jackson	.10
780	Pete Rose	3.50
781	Pete Rose (In Action)	2.00
782	Frank Taveras	.10
783	*Greg Harris*	.10
784	Milt Wilcox	.10
785	Dan Driessen	.10
786	Carney Lansford, Mike Torrez Red Sox Batting & Pitching Ldrs.	.10
787	Fred Stanley	.10
788	Woodie Fryman	.10
789	Checklist 661-792	.10
790	Larry Gura	.10
791	Bobby Brown	.10
792	Frank Tanana	.10

Traded

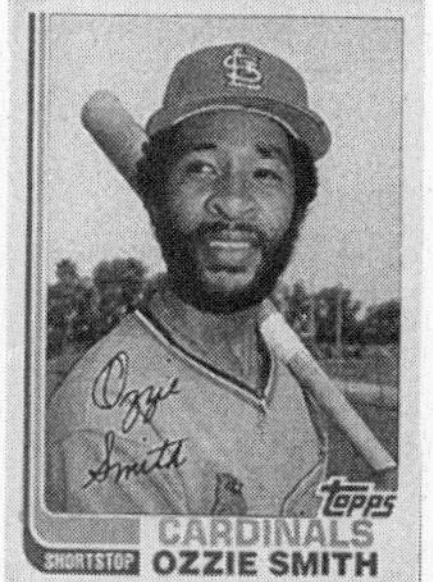

		NM/M
Complete Set (132):		125.00
Common Player:		.10
1T	Doyle Alexander	.10
2T	Jesse Barfield	.10
3T	Ross Baumgarten	.10
4T	Steve Bedrosian	.10
5T	Mark Belanger	.10
6T	Kurt Bevacqua	.10
7T	Tim Blackwell	.10
8T	Vida Blue	.10
9T	Bob Boone	.30
10T	Larry Bowa	.10
11T	Dan Briggs	.10
12T	Bobby Brown	.10
13T	Tom Brunansky	.10
14T	Jeff Burroughs	.10
15T	Enos Cabell	.10
16T	Bill Campbell	.10
17T	Bobby Castillo	.10
18T	Bill Caudill	.10
19T	Cesar Cedeno	.10
20T	Dave Collins	.10
21T	Doug Corbett	.10
22T	Al Cowens	.10
23T	Chili Davis	.50
24T	Dick Davis	.10
25T	Ron Davis	.10
26T	Doug DeCinces	.10
27T	Ivan DeJesus	.10
28T	Bob Dernier	.10
29T	Bo Diaz	.10
30T	Roger Erickson	.10
31T	Jim Essian	.10
32T	Ed Farmer	.10
33T	Doug Flynn	.10
34T	Tim Foli	.10
35T	Dan Ford	.10
36T	George Foster	.10
37T	Dave Frost	.10
38T	Rich Gale	.10
39T	Ron Gardenhire	.10
40T	Ken Griffey	.10
41T	Greg Harris	.10
42T	Von Hayes	.10
43T	Larry Herndon	.10
44T	Kent Hrbek	2.00
45T	Mike Ivie	.10
46T	Grant Jackson	.10
47T	Reggie Jackson	5.00
48T	Ron Jackson	.10
49T	Fergie Jenkins	2.00
50T	Lamar Johnson	.10
51T	Randy Johnson	.10
52T	Jay Johnstone	.10
53T	Mick Kelleher	.10
54T	Steve Kemp	.10
55T	Junior Kennedy	.10
56T	Jim Kern	.10
57T	Ray Knight	.10
58T	Wayne Krenchicki	.10
59T	Mike Krukow	.10
60T	Duane Kuiper	.10
61T	Mike LaCoss	.10
62T	Chet Lemon	.10
63T	Sixto Lezcano	.10
64T	Dave Lopes	.10
65T	Jerry Martin	.10
66T	Renie Martin	.10
67T	John Mayberry	.10
68T	Lee Mazzilli	.10
69T	Bake McBride	.10
70T	Dan Meyer	.10
71T	Larry Milbourne	.10
72T	Eddie Milner	.10
73T	Sid Monge	.10
74T	John Montefusco	.10
75T	Jose Morales	.10
76T	Keith Moreland	.10
77T	Jim Morrison	.10
78T	Rance Mulliniks	.10
79T	Steve Mura	.10
80T	Gene Nelson	.10
81T	Joe Nolan	.10
82T	Dickie Noles	.10
83T	Al Oliver	.10
84T	Jorge Orta	.10
85T	Tom Paciorek	.10
86T	Larry Parrish	.10
87T	Jack Perconte	.10
88T	Gaylord Perry	2.00
89T	Rob Picciolo	.10
90T	Joe Pittman	.10
91T	Hosken Powell	.10
92T	Mike Proly	.10
93T	Greg Pryor	.10
94T	Charlie Puleo	.10
95T	Shane Rawley	.10
96T	Johnny Ray	.10
97T	Dave Revering	.10
98T	Cal Ripken, Jr.	110.00
99T	Allen Ripley	.10
100T	Bill Robinson	.10
101T	Aurelio Rodriguez	.10
102T	Joe Rudi	.10
103T	Steve Sax	.50
104T	Dan Schatzeder	.10
105T	Bob Shirley	.10
106T	Eric Show	.10
107T	Roy Smalley	.10
108T	Lonnie Smith	.10
109T	Ozzie Smith	20.00
110T	Reggie Smith	.10
111T	Lary Sorensen	.10
112T	Elias Sosa	.10
113T	Mike Stanton	.10
114T	Steve Stroughter	.10
115T	Champ Summers	.10
116T	Rick Sutcliffe	.10
117T	Frank Tanana	.10
118T	Frank Taveras	.10
119T	Garry Templeton	.10
120T	Alex Trevino	.10
121T	Jerry Turner	.10
122T	Ed Vande Berg	.10
123T	Tom Veryzer	.10
124T	Ron Washington	.10
125T	Bob Watson	.10
126T	Dennis Werth	.10
127T	Eddie Whitson	.10
128T	Rob Wilfong	.10
129T	Bump Wills	.10
130T	Gary Woods	.10
131T	Butch Wynegar	.10
132T	Checklist 1-132	.10

1983 TOPPS

		NM/M
Complete Set (792):		75.00
Common Player:		.05
Wax Pack (15):		3.00
Wax Box (36):		110.00
Crimp-End Test Pack (15):		4.00
Crimp-end Test Box (36):		110.00
Cello Pack (28):		5.00
Cello Box (24):		125.00
Rack Pack (51):		9.00
Rack Box (24):		200.00
Vending Box (500):		70.00
1	Tony Armas	.05
2	Rickey Henderson	.75
3	Greg Minton	.05
4	Lance Parrish	.05
5	Manny Trillo	.05
6	John Wathan	.05
7	Gene Richards	.05
8	Steve Balboni	.05
9	Joey McLaughlin	.05
10	Gorman Thomas	.05
11	Billy Gardner	.05
12	Paul Mirabella	.05
13	Larry Herndon	.05
14	Frank LaCorte	.05
15	Ron Cey	.05
16	George Vukovich	.05
17	Kent Tekulve	.05
18	Kent Tekulve (Super Veteran)	.05
19	Oscar Gamble	.05
20	Carlton Fisk	2.00
21	Eddie Murray, Jim Palmer Orioles Batting & Pitching Ldrs.	.25
22	Randy Martz	.05
23	Mike Heath	.05
24	Steve Mura	.05
25	Hal McRae	.05
26	Jerry Royster	.05
27	Doug Corbett	.05
28	Bruce Bochte	.05
29	Randy Jones	.05
30	Jim Rice	.15
31	Bill Gullickson	.05
32	Dave Bergman	.05
33	Jack O'Connor	.05
34	Paul Householder	.05
35	Rollie Fingers	.75
36	Rollie Fingers (Super Veteran)	.15
37	Darrell Johnson	.05
38	Tim Flannery	.05
39	Terry Puhl	.05
40	Fernando Valenzuela	.05
41	Jerry Turner	.05
42	Dale Murray	.05
43	Bob Dernier	.05
44	Don Robinson	.05
45	John Mayberry	.05
46	Richard Dotson	.05
47	Dave McKay	.05
48	Lary Sorensen	.05
49	*Willie McGee*	1.50
50	Bob Horner	.05

No.	Card	Value
51	Leon Durham, Fergie Jenkins Cubs Batting & Pitching Ldrs.	.05
52	*Onix Concepcion*	.05
53	Mike Witt	.05
54	Jim Maler	.05
55	Mookie Wilson	.05
56	Chuck Rainey	.05
57	Tim Blackwell	.05
58	Al Holland	.05
59	Benny Ayala	.05
60	Johnny Bench	2.00
61	Johnny Bench (Super Veteran)	.75
62	Bob McClure	.05
63	Rick Monday	.05
64	Bill Stein	.05
65	Jack Morris	.05
66	Bob Lillis	.05
67	Sal Butera	.05
68	*Eric Show*	.15
69	Lee Lacy	.05
70	Steve Carlton	2.00
71	Steve Carlton (Super Veteran)	.30
72	Tom Paciorek	.05
73	Allen Ripley	.05
74	Julio Gonzalez	.05
75	Amos Otis	.05
76	Rick Mahler	.05
77	Hosken Powell	.05
78	Bill Caudill	.05
79	Mick Kelleher	.05
80	George Foster	.05
81	Jerry Mumphrey, Dave Righetti Yankees Batting & Pitching Ldrs.	.05
82	Bruce Hurst	.05
83	*Ryne Sandberg*	15.00
84	Milt May	.05
85	Ken Singleton	.05
86	Tom Hume	.05
87	Joe Rudi	.05
88	Jim Gantner	.05
89	Leon Roberts	.05
90	Jerry Reuss	.05
91	Larry Milbourne	.05
92	Mike LaCoss	.05
93	John Castino	.05
94	Dave Edwards	.05
95	Alan Trammell	.05
96	Dick Howser	.05
97	Ross Baumgarten	.05
98	Vance Law	.05
99	Dickie Noles	.05
100	Pete Rose	4.00
101	Pete Rose (Super Veteran)	2.00
102	Dave Beard	.05
103	Darrell Porter	.05
104	Bob Walk	.05
105	Don Baylor	.15
106	Gene Nelson	.05
107	Mike Jorgensen	.05
108	Glenn Hoffman	.05
109	Luis Leal	.05
110	Ken Griffey	.05
111	Al Oliver, Steve Rogers Expos Batting & Pitching Ldrs.	.05
112	Bob Shirley	.05
113	Ron Roenicke	.05
114	Jim Slaton	.05
115	Chili Davis	.05
116	Dave Schmidt	.05
117	Alan Knicely	.05
118	Chris Welsh	.05
119	Tom Brookens	.05
120	Len Barker	.05
121	Mickey Hatcher	.05
122	Jimmy Smith	.05
123	George Frazier	.05
124	Marc Hill	.05
125	Leon Durham	.05
126	Joe Torre	.25
127	Preston Hanna	.05
128	Mike Ramsey	.05
129	Checklist 1-132	.05
130	Dave Stieb	.05
131	Ed Ott	.05
132	Todd Cruz	.05
133	Jim Barr	.05
134	Hubie Brooks	.05
135	Dwight Evans	.05
136	Willie Aikens	.05
137	Woodie Fryman	.05
138	Rick Dempsey	.05
139	Bruce Berenyi	.05
140	Willie Randolph	.05
141	Toby Harrah, Rick Sutcliffe Indians Batting & Pitching Ldrs.	.05
142	Mike Caldwell	.05
143	Joe Pettini	.05
144	Mark Wagner	.05
145	Don Sutton	.75
146	Don Sutton (Super Veteran)	.20
147	Rick Leach	.05
148	Dave Roberts	.05
149	Johnny Ray	.05
150	Bruce Sutter	.75
151	Bruce Sutter (Super Veteran)	.50
152	Jay Johnstone	.05
153	Jerry Koosman	.05
154	Johnnie LeMaster	.05
155	Dan Quisenberry	.05
156	Billy Martin	.15
157	Steve Bedrosian	.05
158	Rob Wilfong	.05
159	Mike Stanton	.05
160	Dave Kingman	.05
161	Dave Kingman (Super Veteran)	.05
162	Mark Clear	.05
163	Cal Ripken, Jr.	6.00
164	Dave Palmer	.05
165	Dan Driessen	.05
166	John Pacella	.05
167	Mark Brouhard	.05
168	Juan Eichelberger	.05
169	Doug Flynn	.05
170	Steve Howe	.05
171	Bill Laskey, Joe Morgan Giants Batting & Pitching Ldrs.	.05
172	Vern Ruhle	.05
173	Jim Morrison	.05
174	Jerry Ujdur	.05
175	Bo Diaz	.05
176	Dave Righetti	.05
177	Harold Baines	.05
178	Luis Tiant	.05
179	Luis Tiant (Super Veteran)	.05
180	Rickey Henderson	2.00
181	Terry Felton	.05
182	Mike Fischlin	.05
183	*Ed Vande Berg*	.05
184	Bob Clark	.05
185	Tim Lollar	.05
186	Whitey Herzog	.05
187	Terry Leach	.05
188	Rick Miller	.05
189	Dan Schatzeder	.05
190	Cecil Cooper	.05
191	Joe Price	.05
192	Floyd Rayford	.05
193	Harry Spilman	.05
194	Cesar Geronimo	.05
195	Bob Stoddard	.05
196	Bill Fahey	.05
197	*Jim Eisenreich*	.50
198	Kiko Garcia	.05
199	Marty Bystrom	.05
200	Rod Carew	2.00
201	Rod Carew (Super Veteran)	.35
202	Damaso Garcia, Dave Stieb Blue Jays Batting & Pitching Ldrs.	.05
203	Mike Morgan	.05
204	Junior Kennedy	.05
205	Dave Parker	.05
206	Ken Oberkfell	.05
207	Rick Camp	.05
208	Dan Meyer	.05
209	*Mike Moore*	.15
210	Jack Clark	.05
211	John Denny	.05
212	John Stearns	.05
213	Tom Burgmeier	.05
214	Jerry White	.05
215	Mario Soto	.05
216	Tony LaRussa	.05
217	Tim Stoddard	.05
218	Roy Howell	.05
219	Mike Armstrong	.05
220	Dusty Baker	.05
221	Joe Niekro	.05
222	Damaso Garcia	.05
223	John Montefusco	.05
224	Mickey Rivers	.05
225	Enos Cabell	.05
226	Enrique Romo	.05
227	Chris Bando	.05
228	Joaquin Andujar	.05
229	Steve Carlton, Bo Diaz Phillies Batting/ Pitching Leaders	.15
230	Fergie Jenkins	.75
231	Fergie Jenkins (Super Veteran)	.20
232	Tom Brunansky	.05
233	Wayne Gross	.05
234	Larry Andersen	.05
235	Claudell Washington	.05
236	Steve Renko	.05
237	Dan Norman	.05
238	*Bud Black*	.25
239	Dave Stapleton	.05
240	Rich Gossage	.05
241	Rich Gossage (Super Veteran)	.05
242	Joe Nolan	.05
243	Duane Walker	.05
244	Dwight Bernard	.05
245	Steve Sax	.05
246	George Bamberger	.05
247	Dave Smith	.05
248	Bake McBride	.05
249	Checklist 133-264	.05
250	Bill Buckner	.05
251	*Alan Wiggins*	.05
252	Luis Aguayo	.05
253	Larry McWilliams	.05
254	Rick Cerone	.05
255	Gene Garber	.05
256	Gene Garber (Super Veteran)	.05
257	Jesse Barfield	.05
258	Manny Castillo	.05
259	Jeff Jones	.05
260	Steve Kemp	.05
261	Larry Herndon, Dan Petry Tigers Batting & Pitching Ldrs.	.05
262	Ron Jackson	.05
263	Renie Martin	.05
264	Jamie Quirk	.05
265	Joel Youngblood	.05
266	Paul Boris	.05
267	Terry Francona	.05
268	*Storm Davis*	.05
269	Ron Oester	.05
270	Dennis Eckersley	.75
271	Ed Romero	.05
272	Frank Tanana	.05
273	Mark Belanger	.05
274	Terry Kennedy	.05
275	Ray Knight	.05
276	Gene Mauch	.05
277	Rance Mulliniks	.05
278	Kevin Hickey	.05
279	Greg Gross	.05
280	Bert Blyleven	.05
281	Andre Robertson	.05
282	Reggie Smith	.05
283	Reggie Smith (Super Veteran)	.05
284	Jeff Lahti	.05
285	Lance Parrish	.05
286	Rick Langford	.05
287	Bobby Brown	.05
288	*Joe Cowley*	.05
289	Jerry Dybzinski	.05
290	Jeff Reardon	.05
291	John Candelaria, Bill Madlock Pirates Batting & Pitching Ldrs.	.05
292	Craig Swan	.05
293	Glenn Gulliver	.05
294	Dave Engle	.05
295	Jerry Remy	.05
296	Greg Harris	.05
297	Ned Yost	.05
298	Floyd Chiffer	.05
299	George Wright	.05
300	Mike Schmidt	3.00
301	Mike Schmidt (Super Veteran)	1.50
302	Ernie Whitt	.05
303	Miguel Dilone	.05
304	Dave Rucker	.05
305	Larry Bowa	.05
306	Tom Lasorda	.25
307	Lou Piniella	.05
308	Jesus Vega	.05
309	Jeff Leonard	.05
310	Greg Luzinski	.05
311	Glenn Brummer	.05
312	Brian Kingman	.05
313	Gary Gray	.05
314	Ken Dayley	.05
315	Rick Burleson	.05
316	Paul Splittorff	.05
317	Gary Rajsich	.05
318	John Tudor	.05
319	Lenn Sakata	.05
320	Steve Rogers	.05
321	Pete Vuckovich, Robin Yount Brewers Batting & Pitching Ldrs.	.10
322	Dave Van Gorder	.05
323	Luis DeLeon	.05
324	Mike Marshall	.05
325	Von Hayes	.05
326	Garth Iorg	.05
327	Bobby Castillo	.05
328	Craig Reynolds	.05
329	Randy Niemann	.05
330	Buddy Bell	.05
331	Mike Krukow	.05
332	*Glenn Wilson*	.05
333	Dave LaRoche	.05
334	Dave LaRoche (Super Veteran)	.05
335	Steve Henderson	.05
336	Rene Lachemann	.05
337	Tito Landrum	.05
338	Bob Owchinko	.05
339	Terry Harper	.05
340	Larry Gura	.05
341	Doug DeCinces	.05
342	Atlee Hammaker	.05
343	Bob Bailor	.05
344	Roger LaFrancois	.05
345	Jim Clancy	.05
346	Joe Pittman	.05
347	Sammy Stewart	.05
348	Alan Bannister	.05
349	Checklist 265-396	.05
350	Robin Yount	2.00
351	Cesar Cedeno, Mario Soto Reds Batting & Pitching Ldrs.	.05
352	Mike Scioscia	.05
353	Steve Comer	.05
354	Randy S. Johnson	.05
355	Jim Bibby	.05
356	Gary Woods	.05
357	*Len Matuszek*	.05
358	Jerry Garvin	.05
359	Dave Collins	.05
360	Nolan Ryan	5.00
361	Nolan Ryan (Super Veteran)	4.00
362	Bill Almon	.05
363	*John Stuper*	.05
364	Brett Butler	.05
365	Dave Lopes	.05
366	Dick Williams	.05
367	Bud Anderson	.05
368	Richie Zisk	.05
369	Jesse Orosco	.05
370	Gary Carter	2.00
371	Mike Richardt	.05
372	Terry Crowley	.05
373	Kevin Saucier	.05
374	Wayne Krenchicki	.05
375	Pete Vuckovich	.05
376	Ken Landreaux	.05
377	Lee May	.05
378	Lee May (Super Veteran)	.05
379	Guy Sularz	.05
380	Ron Davis	.05
381	Jim Rice, Bob Stanley Red Sox Batting & Pitching Ldrs.	.05
382	Bob Knepper	.05
383	Ozzie Virgil	.05
384	*Dave Dravecky*	.50
385	Mike Easler	.05
386	Rod Carew	.35
387	Bob Grich	.05
388	George Brett	1.50
389	Robin Yount	.60
390	Reggie Jackson	1.00
391	Rickey Henderson	.50
392	Fred Lynn	.05
393	Carlton Fisk	.35
394	Pete Vuckovich	.05
395	Larry Gura	.05
396	Dan Quisenberry	.05
397	Pete Rose	2.00
398	Manny Trillo	.05
399	Mike Schmidt	1.50
400	Dave Concepcion	.05
401	Dale Murphy	.20
402	Andre Dawson	.35
403	Tim Raines	.05
404	Gary Carter	.35
405	Steve Rogers	.05
406	Steve Carlton	.30
407	Bruce Sutter	.25

408 Rudy May .05
409 Marvis Foley .05
410 Phil Niekro .75
411 Phil Niekro (Super Veteran) .25
412 Buddy Bell, Charlie Hough Rangers Batting & Pitching Ldrs. .05
413 Matt Keough .05
414 Julio Cruz .05
415 Bob Forsch .05
416 Joe Ferguson .05
417 Tom Hausman .05
418 Greg Pryor .05
419 Steve Crawford .05
420 Al Oliver .05
421 Al Oliver (Super Veteran) .05
422 George Cappuzzello .05
423 *Tom Lawless* .05
424 Jerry Augustine .05
425 Pedro Guerrero .05
426 Earl Weaver .25
427 Roy Lee Jackson .05
428 Champ Summers .05
429 Eddie Whitson .05
430 Kirk Gibson .05
431 *Gary Gaetti* .75
432 Porfirio Altamirano .05
433 Dale Berra .05
434 Dennis Lamp .05
435 Tony Armas .05
436 Bill Campbell .05
437 Rick Sweet .05
438 *Dave LaPoint* .05
439 Rafael Ramirez .05
440 Ron Guidry .20
441 Ray Knight, Joe Niekro Astros Batting & Pitching Ldrs. .05
442 Brian Downing .05
443 Don Hood .05
444 Wally Backman .05
445 Mike Flanagan .05
446 Reid Nichols .05
447 Bryn Smith .05
448 Darrell Evans .05
449 *Eddie Milner* .05
450 Ted Simmons .05
451 Ted Simmons (Super Veteran) .05
452 Lloyd Moseby .05
453 Lamar Johnson .05
454 Bob Welch .05
455 Sixto Lezcano .05
456 Lee Elia .05
457 Milt Wilcox .05
458 Ron Washington .05
459 Ed Farmer .05
460 Roy Smalley .05
461 Steve Trout .05
462 Steve Nicosia .05
463 Gaylord Perry .75
464 Gaylord Perry (Super Veteran) .20
465 Lonnie Smith .05
466 Tom Underwood .05
467 Rufino Linares .05
468 Dave Goltz .05
469 Ron Gardenhire .05
470 Greg Minton .05
471 Vida Blue, Willie Wilson Royals Batting & Pitching Ldrs. .05
472 Gary Allenson .05
473 John Lowenstein .05
474 Ray Burris .05
475 Cesar Cedeno .05
476 Rob Picciolo .05
477 Tom Niedenfuer .05
478 Phil Garner .05
479 Charlie Hough .05
480 Toby Harrah .05
481 Scot Thompson .05
482 *Tony Gwynn* 25.00
483 Lynn Jones .05
484 Dick Ruthven .05
485 Omar Moreno .05
486 Clyde King .05
487 Jerry Hairston Sr. .05
488 Alfredo Griffin .05
489 Tom Herr .05
490 Jim Palmer 1.50
491 Jim Palmer (Super Veteran) .20
492 Paul Serna .05
493 Steve McCatty .05
494 Bob Brenly .05
495 Warren Cromartie .05
496 Tom Veryzer .05
497 Rick Sutcliffe .05
498 *Wade Boggs* 15.00
499 Jeff Little .05
500 Reggie Jackson 2.00
501 Reggie Jackson (Super Veteran) .75
502 Dale Murphy, Phil Niekro Braves Batting & Pitching Ldrs. .20
503 Moose Haas .05
504 Don Werner .05
505 Garry Templeton .05
506 *Jim Gott* .25
507 Tony Scott .05
508 Tom Filer .05
509 Lou Whitaker .05
510 Tug McGraw .05
511 Tug McGraw (Super Veteran) .05
512 Doyle Alexander .05
513 Fred Stanley .05
514 Rudy Law .05
515 Gene Tenace .05
516 Bill Virdon .05
517 Gary Ward .05
518 Bill Laskey .05
519 Terry Bulling .05
520 Fred Lynn .05
521 Bruce Benedict .05
522 Pat Zachry .05
523 Carney Lansford .05
524 Tom Brennan .05
525 Frank White .05
526 Checklist 397-528 .05
527 Larry Biittner .05
528 Jamie Easterly .05
529 Tim Laudner .05
530 Eddie Murray 2.00
531 Rickey Henderson, Rick Langford Athletics Batting & Pitching Ldrs. .15
532 Dave Stewart .05
533 Luis Salazar .05
534 John Butcher .05
535 Manny Trillo .05
536 Johnny Wockenfuss .05
537 Rod Scurry .05
538 Danny Heep .05
539 Roger Erickson .05
540 Ozzie Smith 2.00
541 Britt Burns .05
542 Jody Davis .05
543 Alan Fowlkes .05
544 Larry Whisenton .05
545 Floyd Bannister .05
546 Dave Garcia .05
547 Geoff Zahn .05
548 Brian Giles .05
549 *Charlie Puleo* .05
550 Carl Yastrzemski 2.00
551 Carl Yastrzemski (Super Veteran) .50
552 Tim Wallach .05
553 Denny Martinez .05
554 Mike Vail .05
555 Steve Yeager .05
556 Willie Upshaw .05
557 Rick Honeycutt .05
558 Dickie Thon .05
559 Pete Redfern .05
560 Ron LeFlore .05
561 Joaquin Andujar, Lonnie Smith Cardinals Batting & Pitching Ldrs. .05
562 Dave Rozema .05
563 Juan Bonilla .05
564 Sid Monge .05
565 Bucky Dent .05
566 Manny Sarmiento .05
567 Joe Simpson .05
568 Willie Hernandez .05
569 Jack Perconte .05
570 Vida Blue .05
571 Mickey Klutts .05
572 Bob Watson .05
573 Andy Hassler .05
574 Glenn Adams .05
575 Neil Allen .05
576 Frank Robinson .25
577 Luis Aponte .05
578 David Green .05
579 Rich Dauer .05
580 Tom Seaver 2.00
581 Tom Seaver (Super Veteran) .50
582 Marshall Edwards .05
583 Terry Forster .05
584 Dave Hostetler .05
585 Jose Cruz .05
586 *Frank Viola* 1.50
587 Ivan DeJesus .05
588 Pat Underwood .05
589 Alvis Woods .05
590 Tony Pena .05
591 LaMarr Hoyt, Greg Luzinski White Sox Batting & Pitching Ldrs. .05
592 Shane Rawley .05
593 Broderick Perkins .05
594 Eric Rasmussen .05
595 Tim Raines .05
596 Randy S. Johnson .05
597 Mike Proly .05
598 Dwayne Murphy .05
599 Don Aase .05
600 George Brett 3.00
601 Ed Lynch .05
602 Rich Gedman .05
603 Joe Morgan 2.00
604 Joe Morgan (Super Veteran) .35
605 Gary Roenicke .05
606 Bobby Cox .05
607 Charlie Leibrandt .05
608 Don Money .05
609 Danny Darwin .05
610 Steve Garvey .50
611 Bert Roberge .05
612 Steve Swisher .05
613 Mike Ivie .05
614 Ed Glynn .05
615 Garry Maddox .05
616 Bill Nahorodny .05
617 Butch Wynegar .05
618 LaMarr Hoyt .05
619 Keith Moreland .05
620 Mike Norris .05
621 Craig Swan, Mookie Wilson Mets Batting & Pitching Ldrs. .05
622 Dave Edler .05
623 Luis Sanchez .05
624 Glenn Hubbard .05
625 Ken Forsch .05
626 Jerry Martin .05
627 Doug Bair .05
628 Julio Valdez .05
629 Charlie Lea .05
630 Paul Molitor 2.00
631 Tippy Martinez .05
632 Alex Trevino .05
633 Vicente Romo .05
634 Max Venable .05
635 Graig Nettles .05
636 Graig Nettles (Super Veteran) .05
637 Pat Corrales .05
638 Dan Petry .05
639 Art Howe .05
640 Andre Thornton .05
641 Billy Sample .05
642 Checklist 529-660 .05
643 Bump Wills .05
644 Joe Lefebvre .05
645 Bill Madlock .05
646 Jim Essian .05
647 Bobby Mitchell .05
648 Jeff Burroughs .05
649 Tommy Boggs .05
650 George Hendrick .05
651 Rod Carew, Mike Witt Angels Batting & Pitching Ldrs. .05
652 Butch Hobson .05
653 Ellis Valentine .05
654 Bob Ojeda .05
655 Al Bumbry .05
656 Dave Frost .05
657 Mike Gates .05
658 Frank Pastore .05
659 Charlie Moore .05
660 Mike Hargrove .05
661 Bill Russell .05
662 Joe Sambito .05
663 Tom O'Malley .05
664 Bob Molinaro .05
665 Jim Sundberg .05
666 Sparky Anderson .25
667 Dick Davis .05
668 Larry Christenson .05
669 Mike Squires .05
670 Jerry Mumphrey .05
671 Lenny Faedo .05
672 Jim Kaat .10
673 Jim Kaat (Super Veteran) .05
674 Kurt Bevacqua .05
675 Jim Beattie .05
676 Biff Pocoroba .05
677 Dave Revering .05
678 Juan Beniquez .05
679 Mike Scott .05
680 Andre Dawson .60
681 Pedro Guerrero, Fernando Valenzuela Dodgers Batting & Pitching Ldrs. .05
682 Bob Stanley .05
683 Dan Ford .05
684 Rafael Landestoy .05
685 Lee Mazzilli .05
686 Randy Lerch .05
687 U.L. Washington .05
688 Jim Wohlford .05
689 Ron Hassey .05
690 Kent Hrbek .05
691 Dave Tobik .05
692 Denny Walling .05
693 Sparky Lyle .05
694 Sparky Lyle (Super Veteran) .05
695 Ruppert Jones .05
696 Chuck Tanner .05
697 Barry Foote .05
698 Tony Bernazard .05
699 Lee Smith .05
700 Keith Hernandez .05
701 Al Oliver, Willie Wilson Batting Leaders .05
702 Reggie Jackson, Dave Kingman, Gorman Thomas Home Run Leaders .15
703 Hal McRae, Dale Murphy, Al Oliver Runs Batted In Leaders .05
704 Rickey Henderson, Tim Raines Stolen Base Leaders .10
705 Steve Carlton, LaMarr Hoyt Victory Leaders .05
706 Floyd Bannister, Steve Carlton Strikeout Leaders .05
707 Steve Rogers, Rick Sutcliffe Earned Run Average Leaders .05
708 Dan Quisenberry, Bruce Sutter Leading Firemen .10
709 Jimmy Sexton .05
710 Willie Wilson .05
711 Jim Beattie, Bruce Bochte Mariners Batting & Pitching Ldrs. .05
712 Bruce Kison .05
713 Ron Hodges .05
714 Wayne Nordhagen .05
715 Tony Perez 1.50
716 Tony Perez (Super Veteran) .05
717 Scott Sanderson .05
718 Jim Dwyer .05
719 Rich Gale .05
720 Dave Concepcion .05
721 John Martin .05
722 Jorge Orta .05
723 Randy Moffitt .05
724 Johnny Grubb .05
725 Dan Spillner .05
726 Harvey Kuenn .05
727 Chet Lemon .05
728 Ron Reed .05
729 Jerry Morales .05
730 Jason Thompson .05
731 Al Williams .05
732 Dave Henderson .05
733 Buck Martinez .05
734 Steve Braun .05
735 Tommy John .20
736 Tommy John (Super Veteran) .05
737 Mitchell Page .05
738 Tim Foli .05
739 Rick Ownbey .05
740 Rusty Staub .05
741 Rusty Staub (Super Veteran) .05
742 Terry Kennedy, Tim Lollar Padres Batting & Pitching Ldrs. .05
743 Mike Torrez .05
744 Brad Mills .05
745 Scott McGregor .05
746 John Wathan .05
747 Fred Breining .05
748 Derrel Thomas .05
749 Jon Matlack .05
750 Ben Oglivie .05
751 Brad Havens .05

752	Luis Pujols	.05
753	Elias Sosa	.05
754	Bill Robinson	.05
755	John Candelaria	.05
756	Russ Nixon	.05
757	Rick Manning	.05
758	Aurelio Rodriguez	.05
759	Doug Bird	.05
760	Dale Murphy	.60
761	Gary Lucas	.05
762	Cliff Johnson	.05
763	Al Cowens	.05
764	Pete Falcone	.05
765	Bob Boone	.05
766	Barry Bonnell	.05
767	Duane Kuiper	.05
768	Chris Speier	.05
769	Checklist 661-792	.05
770	Dave Winfield	2.00
771	Bobby Castillo, Kent Hrbek Twins Batting & Pitching Ldrs.	.05
772	Jim Kern	.05
773	Larry Hisle	.05
774	Alan Ashby	.05
775	Burt Hooton	.05
776	Larry Parrish	.05
777	John Curtis	.05
778	Rich Hebner	.05
779	Rick Waits	.05
780	Gary Matthews	.05
781	Rick Rhoden	.05
782	Bobby Murcer	.05
783	Bobby Murcer (Super Veteran)	.05
784	Jeff Newman	.05
785	Dennis Leonard	.05
786	Ralph Houk	.05
787	Dick Tidrow	.05
788	Dane Iorg	.05
789	Bryan Clark	.05
790	Bob Grich	.05
791	Gary Lavelle	.05
792	Chris Chambliss	.05

Traded

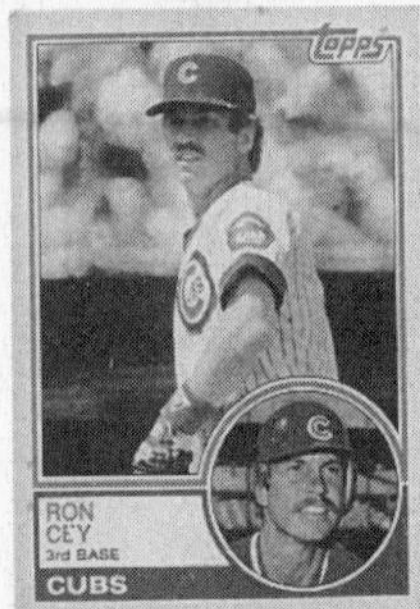

		NM/M
Complete Set (132):		22.50
Common Player:		.05
1T	Neil Allen	.05
2T	Bill Almon	.05
3T	Joe Altobelli	.05
4T	Tony Armas	.05
5T	Doug Bair	.05
6T	Steve Baker	.05
7T	Floyd Bannister	.05
8T	Don Baylor	.25
9T	Tony Bernazard	.05
10T	Larry Biittner	.05
11T	Dann Bilardello	.05
12T	Doug Bird	.05
13T	Steve Boros	.05
14T	Greg Brock	.05
15T	Mike Brown	.05
16T	Tom Burgmeier	.05
17T	Randy Bush	.05
18T	Bert Campaneris	.05
19T	Ron Cey	.05
20T	Chris Codiroli	.05
21T	Dave Collins	.05
22T	Terry Crowley	.05
23T	Julio Cruz	.05
24T	Mike Davis	.05
25T	Frank DiPino	.05
26T	Bill Doran	.05
27T	Jerry Dybzinski	.05
28T	Jamie Easterly	.05
29T	Juan Eichelberger	.05
30T	Jim Essian	.05
31T	Pete Falcone	.05
32T	Mike Ferraro	.05
33T	Terry Forster	.05
34T	*Julio Franco*	3.00
35T	Rich Gale	.05
36T	Kiko Garcia	.05
37T	Steve Garvey	1.00
38T	Johnny Grubb	.05
39T	Mel Hall	.05
40T	Von Hayes	.05
41T	Danny Heep	.05
42T	Steve Henderson	.05
43T	Keith Hernandez	.15
44T	Leo Hernandez	.05
45T	Willie Hernandez	.05
46T	Al Holland	.05
47T	Frank Howard	.05
48T	Bobby Johnson	.05
49T	Cliff Johnson	.05
50T	Odell Jones	.05
51T	Mike Jorgensen	.05
52T	Bob Kearney	.05
53T	Steve Kemp	.05
54T	Matt Keough	.05
55T	Ron Kittle	.05
56T	Mickey Klutts	.05
57T	Alan Knicely	.05
58T	Mike Krukow	.05
59T	Rafael Landestoy	.05
60T	Carney Lansford	.05
61T	Joe Lefebvre	.05
62T	Bryan Little	.05
63T	Aurelio Lopez	.05
64T	Mike Madden	.05
65T	Rick Manning	.05
66T	Billy Martin	.25
67T	Lee Mazzilli	.05
68T	Andy McGaffigan	.05
69T	Craig McMurtry	.05
70T	John McNamara	.05
71T	Orlando Mercado	.05
72T	Larry Milbourne	.05
73T	Randy Moffitt	.05
74T	Sid Monge	.05
75T	Jose Morales	.05
76T	Omar Moreno	.05
77T	Joe Morgan	4.00
78T	Mike Morgan	.05
79T	Dale Murray	.05
80T	Jeff Newman	.05
81T	Pete O'Brien	.05
82T	Jorge Orta	.05
83T	Alejandro Pena	.05
84T	Pascual Perez	.05
85T	Tony Perez	1.00
86T	Broderick Perkins	.05
87T	*Tony Phillips*	.15
88T	Charlie Puleo	.05
89T	Pat Putnam	.05
90T	Jamie Quirk	.05
91T	Doug Rader	.05
92T	Chuck Rainey	.05
93T	Bobby Ramos	.05
94T	Gary Redus	.05
95T	Steve Renko	.05
96T	Leon Roberts	.05
97T	Aurelio Rodriguez	.05
98T	Dick Ruthven	.05
99T	Daryl Sconiers	.05
100T	Mike Scott	.05
101T	Tom Seaver	6.00
102T	John Shelby	.05
103T	Bob Shirley	.05
104T	Joe Simpson	.05
105T	Doug Sisk	.05
106T	Mike Smithson	.05
107T	Elias Sosa	.05
108T	*Darryl Strawberry*	7.50
109T	Tom Tellmann	.05
110T	Gene Tenace	.05
111T	Gorman Thomas	.05
112T	Dick Tidrow	.05
113T	Dave Tobik	.05
114T	Wayne Tolleson	.05
115T	Mike Torrez	.05
116T	Manny Trillo	.05
117T	Steve Trout	.05
118T	Lee Tunnell	.05
119T	Mike Vail	.05
120T	Ellis Valentine	.05
121T	Tom Veryzer	.05
122T	George Vukovich	.05
123T	Rick Waits	.05
124T	Greg Walker	.05
125T	Chris Welsh	.05
126T	Len Whitehouse	.05
127T	Eddie Whitson	.05
128T	Jim Wohlford	.05
129T	Matt Young	.05
130T	Joel Youngblood	.05
131T	Pat Zachry	.05
132T	Checklist 1-132	.05

1984 TOPPS

		NM/M
Complete Set (792):		40.00
Common Player:		.05
Wax Pack (15):		1.75
Wax Box (36):		40.00
Cello Pack (28):		2.50
Cello Box (24):		45.00
Rack Pack (54+1):		3.00
Rack Box (24):		40.00
Vending Box (500):		20.00
1	Steve Carlton	.25
2	Rickey Henderson	.25
3	Dan Quisenberry	.05
4	Steve Carlton, Gaylord Perry, Nolan Ryan	.50
5	Bob Forsch, Dave Righetti, Mike Warren	.05
6	Johnny Bench, Gaylord Perry, Carl Yastrzemski	.25
7	Gary Lucas	.05
8	*Don Mattingly*	12.00
9	Jim Gott	.05
10	Robin Yount	1.00
11	Kent Hrbek, Ken Schrom Twins Batting & Pitching Leaders	.05
12	Billy Sample	.05
13	Scott Holman	.05
14	Tom Brookens	.05
15	Burt Hooton	.05
16	Omar Moreno	.05
17	John Denny	.05
18	Dale Berra	.05
19	*Ray Fontenot*	.05
20	Greg Luzinski	.05
21	Joe Altobelli	.05
22	Bryan Clark	.05
23	Keith Moreland	.05
24	John Martin	.05
25	Glenn Hubbard	.05
26	Bud Black	.05
27	Daryl Sconiers	.05
28	Frank Viola	.05
29	Danny Heep	.05
30	Wade Boggs	3.00
31	Andy McGaffigan	.05
32	Bobby Ramos	.05
33	Tom Burgmeier	.05
34	Eddie Milner	.05
35	Don Sutton	.65
36	Denny Walling	.05
37	Buddy Bell, Rick Honeycutt Rangers Batting & Pitching Leaders	.05
38	Luis DeLeon	.05
39	Garth Iorg	.05
40	Dusty Baker	.05
41	Tony Bernazard	.05
42	Johnny Grubb	.05
43	Ron Reed	.05
44	Jim Morrison	.05
45	Jerry Mumphrey	.05
46	Ray Smith	.05
47	Rudy Law	.05
48	Julio Franco	.05
49	John Stuper	.05
50	Chris Chambliss	.05
51	Jim Frey	.05
52	Paul Splittorff	.05
53	Juan Beniquez	.05
54	Jesse Orosco	.05
55	Dave Concepcion	.05
56	Gary Allenson	.05
57	Dan Schatzeder	.05
58	Max Venable	.05
59	Sammy Stewart	.05
60	Paul Molitor	1.00
61	*Chris Codiroli*	.05
62	Dave Hostetler	.05
63	Ed Vande Berg	.05
64	Mike Scioscia	.05
65	Kirk Gibson	.05
66	Jose Cruz, Nolan Ryan Astros Batting & Pitching Leaders	.25
67	Gary Ward	.05
68	Luis Salazar	.05
69	Rod Scurry	.05
70	Gary Matthews	.05
71	Leo Hernandez	.05
72	Mike Squires	.05
73	Jody Davis	.05
74	Jerry Martin	.05
75	Bob Forsch	.05
76	Alfredo Griffin	.05
77	Brett Butler	.05
78	Mike Torrez	.05
79	Rob Wilfong	.05
80	Steve Rogers	.05
81	Billy Martin	.15
82	Doug Bird	.05
83	Richie Zisk	.05
84	Lenny Faedo	.05
85	Atlee Hammaker	.05
86	*John Shelby*	.05
87	Frank Pastore	.05
88	Rob Picciolo	.05
89	*Mike Smithson*	.05
90	Pedro Guerrero	.05
91	Dan Spillner	.05
92	Lloyd Moseby	.05
93	Bob Knepper	.05
94	Mario Ramirez	.05
95	Aurelio Lopez	.05
96	Larry Gura, Hal McRae Royals Batting & Pitching Leaders	.05
97	LaMarr Hoyt	.05
98	Steve Nicosia	.05
99	*Craig Lefferts*	.25
100	Reggie Jackson	1.50
101	Porfirio Altamirano	.05
102	Ken Oberkfell	.05
103	Dwayne Murphy	.05
104	Ken Dayley	.05
105	Tony Armas	.05
106	Tim Stoddard	.05
107	Ned Yost	.05
108	Randy Moffitt	.05
109	Brad Wellman	.05
110	Ron Guidry	.05
111	Bill Virdon	.05
112	Tom Niedenfuer	.05
113	Kelly Paris	.05
114	Checklist 1-132	.05
115	Andre Thornton	.05
116	George Bjorkman	.05
117	Tom Veryzer	.05
118	Charlie Hough	.05
119	Johnny Wockenfuss	.05
120	Keith Hernandez	.05
121	*Pat Sheridan*	.05
122	Cecilio Guante	.05
123	Butch Wynegar	.05
124	Damaso Garcia	.05
125	Britt Burns	.05
126	Craig McMurtry, Dale Murphy Braves Batting & Pitching Leaders	.05
127	Mike Madden	.05
128	Rick Manning	.05
129	Bill Laskey	.05
130	Ozzie Smith	2.00
131	Wade Boggs, Bill Madlock Batting Leaders	.25
132	Jim Rice, Mike Schmidt Home Run Leaders	.25
133	Cecil Cooper, Dale Murphy, Jim Rice RBI Leaders	.10
134	Rickey Henderson, Tim Raines Stolen Base Leaders	.25
135	John Denny, LaMarr Hoyt Victory Leaders	.05
136	Steve Carlton, Jack Morris Strikeout Leaders	.05
137	Atlee Hammaker, Rick Honeycutt Earned Run Average Leaders	.05
138	Al Holland, Dan Quisenberry Leading Firemen	.05
139	Bert Campaneris	.05

140 Storm Davis .05
141 Pat Corrales .05
142 Rich Gale .05
143 Jose Morales .05
144 *Brian Harper* .20
145 Gary Lavelle .05
146 Ed Romero .05
147 Dan Petry .05
148 Joe Lefebvre .05
149 Jon Matlack .05
150 Dale Murphy .50
151 Steve Trout .05
152 Glenn Brummer .05
153 Dick Tidrow .05
154 Dave Henderson .05
155 Frank White .05
156 Tim Conroy, Rickey Henderson Athletics Batting & Pitching Leaders .15
157 Gary Gaetti .05
158 John Curtis .05
159 Darryl Cias .05
160 Mario Soto .05
161 *Junior Ortiz* .05
162 Bob Ojeda .05
163 Lorenzo Gray .05
164 Scott Sanderson .05
165 Ken Singleton .05
166 Jamie Nelson .05
167 Marshall Edwards .05
168 Juan Bonilla .05
169 Larry Parrish .05
170 Jerry Reuss .05
171 Frank Robinson .25
172 Frank DiPino .05
173 *Marvell Wynne* .05
174 Juan Berenguer .05
175 Graig Nettles .05
176 Lee Smith .05
177 Jerry Hairston Sr. .05
178 Bill Krueger .05
179 Buck Martinez .05
180 Manny Trillo .05
181 Roy Thomas .05
182 Darryl Strawberry .25
183 Al Williams .05
184 Mike O'Berry .05
185 Sixto Lezcano .05
186 Lonnie Smith, John Stuper Cardinals Batting & Pitching Leaders .05
187 Luis Aponte .05
188 Bryan Little .05
189 *Tim Conroy* .05
190 Ben Oglivie .05
191 Mike Boddicker .05
192 *Nick Esasky* .05
193 Darrell Brown .05
194 Domingo Ramos .05
195 Jack Morris .05
196 Don Slaught .05
197 Garry Hancock .05
198 *Bill Doran* .05
199 Willie Hernandez .05
200 Andre Dawson .60
201 Bruce Kison .05
202 Bobby Cox .05
203 Matt Keough .05
204 *Bobby Meacham* .05
205 Greg Minton .05
206 *Andy Van Slyke* .75
207 Donnie Moore .05
208 *Jose Oquendo* .05
209 Manny Sarmiento .05
210 Joe Morgan 1.00
211 Rick Sweet .05
212 Broderick Perkins .05
213 Bruce Hurst .05
214 Paul Householder .05
215 Tippy Martinez .05
216 Richard Dotson, Carlton Fisk White Sox Batting & Pitching Leaders .05
217 Alan Ashby .05
218 Rick Waits .05
219 Joe Simpson .05
220 Fernando Valenzuela .05
221 Cliff Johnson .05
222 Rick Honeycutt .05
223 Wayne Krenchicki .05
224 Sid Monge .05
225 Lee Mazzilli .05
226 Juan Eichelberger .05
227 Steve Braun .05
228 John Rabb .05
229 Paul Owens .05
230 Rickey Henderson 1.00
231 Gary Woods .05
232 Tim Wallach .05
233 Checklist 133-264 .05
234 Rafael Ramirez .05
235 *Matt Young* .05
236 Ellis Valentine .05
237 John Castino .05
238 Reid Nichols .05
239 Jay Howell .05
240 Eddie Murray 1.00
241 Billy Almon .05
242 Alex Trevino .05
243 Pete Ladd .05
244 Candy Maldonado .05
245 Rick Sutcliffe .05
246 Tom Seaver, Mookie Wilson Mets Batting & Pitching Leaders .25
247 Onix Concepcion .05
248 *Bill Dawley* .05
249 Jay Johnstone .05
250 Bill Madlock .05
251 Tony Gwynn 4.00
252 Larry Christenson .05
253 Jim Wohlford .05
254 Shane Rawley .05
255 Bruce Benedict .05
256 Dave Geisel .05
257 Julio Cruz .05
258 Luis Sanchez .05
259 Sparky Anderson .15
260 Scott McGregor .05
261 Bobby Brown .05
262 *Tom Candiotti* .25
263 Jack Fimple .05
264 Doug Frobel .05
265 *Donnie Hill* .05
266 Steve Lubratich .05
267 *Carmelo Martinez* .05
268 Jack O'Connor .05
269 Aurelio Rodriguez .05
270 *Jeff Russell* .05
271 Moose Haas .05
272 Rick Dempsey .05
273 Charlie Puleo .05
274 Rick Monday .05
275 Len Matuszek .05
276 Rod Carew, Geoff Zahn Angels Batting & Pitching Leaders .10
277 Eddie Whitson .05
278 Jorge Bell .05
279 Ivan DeJesus .05
280 Floyd Bannister .05
281 Larry Milbourne .05
282 Jim Barr .05
283 Larry Biittner .05
284 Howard Bailey .05
285 Darrell Porter .05
286 Lary Sorensen .05
287 Warren Cromartie .05
288 Jim Beattie .05
289 Randy S. Johnson .05
290 Dave Dravecky .05
291 Chuck Tanner .05
292 Tony Scott .05
293 Ed Lynch .05
294 U.L. Washington .05
295 Mike Flanagan .05
296 Jeff Newman .05
297 Bruce Berenyi .05
298 Jim Gantner .05
299 John Butcher .05
300 Pete Rose 5.00
301 Frank LaCorte .05
302 Barry Bonnell .05
303 Marty Castillo .05
304 Warren Brusstar .05
305 Roy Smalley .05
306 Pedro Guerrero, Bob Welch Dodgers Batting & Pitching Leaders .05
307 Bobby Mitchell .05
308 Ron Hassey .05
309 Tony Phillips .05
310 Willie McGee .05
311 Jerry Koosman .05
312 Jorge Orta .05
313 Mike Jorgensen .05
314 Orlando Mercado .05
315 Bob Grich .05
316 Mark Bradley .05
317 Greg Pryor .05
318 Bill Gullickson .05
319 Al Bumbry .05
320 Bob Stanley .05
321 Harvey Kuenn .05
322 Ken Schrom .05
323 Alan Knicely .05
324 *Alejandro Pena* .05
325 Darrell Evans .05
326 Bob Kearney .05
327 Ruppert Jones .05
328 Vern Ruhle .05
329 Pat Tabler .05
330 John Candelaria .05
331 Bucky Dent .05
332 *Kevin Gross* .05
333 Larry Herndon .05
334 Chuck Rainey .05
335 Don Baylor .15
336 Pat Putnam, Matt Young Mariners Batting & Pitching Leaders .05
337 Kevin Hagen .05
338 Mike Warren .05
339 Roy Lee Jackson .05
340 Hal McRae .05
341 Dave Tobik .05
342 Tim Foli .05
343 Mark Davis .05
344 Rick Miller .05
345 Kent Hrbek .05
346 Kurt Bevacqua .05
347 Allan Ramirez .05
348 Toby Harrah .05
349 Bob L. Gibson .05
350 George Foster .05
351 Russ Nixon .05
352 Dave Stewart .05
353 Jim Anderson .05
354 Jeff Burroughs .05
355 Jason Thompson .05
356 Glenn Abbott .05
357 Ron Cey .05
358 Bob Dernier .05
359 *Jim Acker* .05
360 Willie Randolph .05
361 Dave Smith .05
362 David Green .05
363 Tim Laudner .05
364 Scott Fletcher .05
365 Steve Bedrosian .05
366 Dave Dravecky, Terry Kennedy Padres Batting & Pitching Leaders .05
367 Jamie Easterly .05
368 Hubie Brooks .05
369 Steve McCatty .05
370 Tim Raines .05
371 Dave Gumpert .05
372 Gary Roenicke .05
373 Bill Scherrer .05
374 Don Money .05
375 Dennis Leonard .05
376 *Dave Anderson* .05
377 Danny Darwin .05
378 Bob Brenly .05
379 Checklist 265-396 .05
380 Steve Garvey .45
381 Ralph Houk .05
382 Chris Nyman .05
383 Terry Puhl .05
384 *Lee Tunnell* .05
385 Tony Perez 1.00
386 George Hendrick .05
387 Johnny Ray .05
388 Mike Schmidt .75
389 Ozzie Smith .50
390 Tim Raines .05
391 Dale Murphy .20
392 Andre Dawson .25
393 Gary Carter .30
394 Steve Rogers .05
395 Steve Carlton .25
396 Jesse Orosco .05
397 Eddie Murray .40
398 Lou Whitaker .05
399 George Brett .75
400 Cal Ripken, Jr. 4.00
401 Jim Rice .05
402 Dave Winfield .30
403 Lloyd Moseby .05
404 Ted Simmons .05
405 LaMarr Hoyt .05
406 Ron Guidry .05
407 Dan Quisenberry .05
408 Lou Piniella .05
409 *Juan Agosto* .05
410 Claudell Washington .05
411 Houston Jimenez .05
412 Doug Rader .05
413 *Spike Owen* .05
414 Mitchell Page .05
415 Tommy John .15
416 Dane Iorg .05
417 Mike Armstrong .05
418 Ron Hodges .05
419 John Henry Johnson .05
420 Cecil Cooper .05
421 Charlie Lea .05
422 Jose Cruz .05
423 Mike Morgan .05
424 Dann Bilardello .05
425 Steve Howe .05
426 Mike Boddicker, Cal Ripken, Jr. Orioles Batting & Pitching Leaders .50
427 Rick Leach .05
428 Fred Breining .05
429 *Randy Bush* .05
430 Rusty Staub .05
431 Chris Bando .05
432 *Charlie Hudson* .05
433 Rich Hebner .05
434 Harold Baines .05
435 Neil Allen .05
436 Rick Peters .05
437 Mike Proly .05
438 Biff Pocoroba .05
439 Bob Stoddard .05
440 Steve Kemp .05
441 Bob Lillis .05
442 Byron McLaughlin .05
443 Benny Ayala .05
444 Steve Renko .05
445 Jerry Remy .05
446 Luis Pujols .05
447 Tom Brunansky .05
448 Ben Hayes .05
449 Joe Pettini .05
450 Gary Carter 1.00
451 Bob Jones .05
452 Chuck Porter .05
453 Willie Upshaw .05
454 Joe Beckwith .05
455 Terry Kennedy .05
456 Fergie Jenkins, Keith Moreland Cubs Batting & Pitching Leaders .05
457 Dave Rozema .05
458 Kiko Garcia .05
459 Kevin Hickey .05
460 Dave Winfield 1.00
461 Jim Maler .05
462 Lee Lacy .05
463 Dave Engle .05
464 Jeff Jones .05
465 Mookie Wilson .05
466 Gene Garber .05
467 Mike Ramsey .05
468 Geoff Zahn .05
469 Tom O'Malley .05
470 Nolan Ryan 6.00
471 Dick Howser .05
472 Mike Brown .05
473 Jim Dwyer .05
474 Greg Bargar .05
475 *Gary Redus* .05
476 Tom Tellmann .05
477 Rafael Landestoy .05
478 Alan Bannister .05
479 Frank Tanana .05
480 Ron Kittle .05
481 *Mark Thurmond* .05
482 Enos Cabell .05
483 Fergie Jenkins .65
484 Ozzie Virgil .05
485 Rick Rhoden .05
486 Don Baylor, Ron Guidry Yankees Batting & Pitching Leaders .05
487 Ricky Adams .05
488 Jesse Barfield .05
489 Dave Von Ohlen .05
490 Cal Ripken, Jr. 6.00
491 Bobby Castillo .05
492 Tucker Ashford .05
493 Mike Norris .05
494 Chili Davis .05
495 Rollie Fingers .65
496 Terry Francona .05
497 Bud Anderson .05
498 Rich Gedman .05
499 Mike Witt .05
500 George Brett 2.00
501 Steve Henderson .05
502 Joe Torre .05
503 Elias Sosa .05
504 Mickey Rivers .05
505 Pete Vuckovich .05
506 Ernie Whitt .05
507 Mike LaCoss .05
508 Mel Hall .05
509 Brad Havens .05
510 Alan Trammell .05
511 Marty Bystrom .05

512 Oscar Gamble .05
513 Dave Beard .05
514 Floyd Rayford .05
515 Gorman Thomas .05
516 Charlie Lea, Al Oliver Expos Batting & Pitching Leaders .05
517 John Moses .05
518 *Greg Walker* .05
519 Ron Davis .05
520 Bob Boone .05
521 Pete Falcone .05
522 Dave Bergman .05
523 Glenn Hoffman .05
524 Carlos Diaz .05
525 Willie Wilson .05
526 Ron Oester .05
527 Checklist 397-528 .05
528 Mark Brouhard .05
529 *Keith Atherton* .05
530 Dan Ford .05
531 Steve Boros .05
532 Eric Show .05
533 Ken Landreaux .05
534 Pete O'Brien .05
535 Bo Diaz .05
536 Doug Bair .05
537 Johnny Ray .05
538 Kevin Bass .05
539 George Frazier .05
540 George Hendrick .05
541 Dennis Lamp .05
542 Duane Kuiper .05
543 *Craig McMurtry* .05
544 Cesar Geronimo .05
545 Bill Buckner .05
546 Mike Hargrove, Lary Sorensen Indians Batting & Pitching Leaders .05
547 Mike Moore .05
548 Ron Jackson .05
549 *Walt Terrell* .05
550 Jim Rice .15
551 Scott Ullger .05
552 Ray Burris .05
553 Joe Nolan .05
554 Ted Power .05
555 Greg Brock .05
556 Joey McLaughlin .05
557 Wayne Tolleson .05
558 Mike Davis .05
559 Mike Scott .05
560 Carlton Fisk 1.00
561 Whitey Herzog .05
562 Manny Castillo .05
563 Glenn Wilson .05
564 Al Holland .05
565 Leon Durham .05
566 Jim Bibby .05
567 Mike Heath .05
568 Pete Filson .05
569 Bake McBride .05
570 Dan Quisenberry .05
571 Bruce Bochy .05
572 Jerry Royster .05
573 Dave Kingman .05
574 Brian Downing .05
575 Jim Clancy .05
576 Atlee Hammaker, Jeff Leonard Giants Batting & Pitching Leaders .05
577 Mark Clear .05
578 Lenn Sakata .05
579 Bob James .05
580 Lonnie Smith .05
581 *Jose DeLeon* .05
582 Bob McClure .05
583 Derrel Thomas .05
584 Dave Schmidt .05
585 Dan Driessen .05
586 Joe Niekro .05
587 Von Hayes .05
588 Milt Wilcox .05
589 Mike Easler .05
590 Dave Stieb .05
591 Tony LaRussa .05
592 Andre Robertson .05
593 Jeff Lahti .05
594 Gene Richards .05
595 Jeff Reardon .05
596 Ryne Sandberg 3.00
597 Rick Camp .05
598 Rusty Kuntz .05
599 *Doug Sisk* .05
600 Rod Carew 1.00
601 John Tudor .05
602 John Wathan .05
603 Renie Martin .05
604 John Lowenstein .05
605 Mike Caldwell .05
606 Lloyd Moseby, Dave Stieb Blue Jays Batting & Pitching Leaders .05
607 Tom Hume .05
608 Bobby Johnson .05
609 Dan Meyer .05
610 Steve Sax .05
611 Chet Lemon .05
612 Harry Spilman .05
613 Greg Gross .05
614 Len Barker .05
615 Garry Templeton .05
616 Don Robinson .05
617 Rick Cerone .05
618 Dickie Noles .05
619 Jerry Dybzinski .05
620 Al Oliver .05
621 Frank Howard .05
622 Al Cowens .05
623 Ron Washington .05
624 Terry Harper .05
625 Larry Gura .05
626 Bob Clark .05
627 Dave LaPoint .05
628 Ed Jurak .05
629 Rick Langford .05
630 Ted Simmons .05
631 Denny Martinez .05
632 Tom Foley .05
633 Mike Krukow .05
634 Mike Marshall .05
635 Dave Righetti .05
636 Pat Putnam .05
637 John Denny, Gary Matthews Phillies Batting & Pitching Leaders .05
638 George Vukovich .05
639 Rick Lysander .05
640 Lance Parrish .05
641 Mike Richardt .05
642 Tom Underwood .05
643 Mike Brown .05
644 Tim Lollar .05
645 Tony Pena .05
646 Checklist 529-660 .05
647 Ron Roenicke .05
648 Len Whitehouse .05
649 Tom Herr .05
650 Phil Niekro .65
651 John McNamara .05
652 Rudy May .05
653 Dave Stapleton .05
654 Bob Bailor .05
655 Amos Otis .05
656 Bryn Smith .05
657 Thad Bosley .05
658 Jerry Augustine .05
659 Duane Walker .05
660 Ray Knight .05
661 Steve Yeager .05
662 Tom Brennan .05
663 Johnnie LeMaster .05
664 Dave Stegman .05
665 Buddy Bell .05
666 Jack Morris, Lou Whitaker Tigers Batting & Pitching Leaders .05
667 Vance Law .05
668 Larry McWilliams .05
669 Dave Lopes .05
670 Rich Gossage .05
671 Jamie Quirk .05
672 Ricky Nelson .05
673 Mike Walters .05
674 Tim Flannery .05
675 Pascual Perez .05
676 Brian Giles .05
677 Doyle Alexander .05
678 Chris Speier .05
679 Art Howe .05
680 Fred Lynn .05
681 Tom Lasorda .15
682 Dan Morogiello .05
683 *Marty Barrett* .05
684 Bob Shirley .05
685 Willie Aikens .05
686 Joe Price .05
687 Roy Howell .05
688 George Wright .05
689 Mike Fischlin .05
690 Jack Clark .05
691 *Steve Lake* .05
692 Dickie Thon .05
693 Alan Wiggins .05
694 Mike Stanton .05
695 Lou Whitaker .05
696 Bill Madlock, Rick Rhoden Pirates Batting & Pitching Leaders .05
697 Dale Murray .05
698 Marc Hill .05
699 Dave Rucker .05
700 Mike Schmidt 2.00
701 Bill Madlock, Dave Parker, Pete Rose NL Active Career Batting Leaders .25
702 Tony Perez, Pete Rose, Rusty Staub NL Active Career Hit Leaders .25
703 Dave Kingman, Tony Perez, Mike Schmidt NL Active Career Home Run Leaders .15
704 Al Oliver, Tony Perez, Rusty Staub NL Active Career RBI Leaders .05
705 Larry Bowa, Cesar Cedeno, Joe Morgan NL Active Career Stolen Bases Leaders .05
706 Steve Carlton, Fergie Jenkins, Tom Seaver NL Active Career Victory Leaders .05
707 Steve Carlton, Nolan Ryan, Tom Seaver NL Active Career Strikeout Leaders .35
708 Steve Carlton, Steve Rogers, Tom Seaver NL Active Career ERA Leaders .05
709 Gene Garber, Tug McGraw, Bruce Sutter NL Active Career Save Leaders .10
710 George Brett, Rod Carew, Cecil Cooper AL Active Career Batting Leaders .25
711 Bert Campaneris, Rod Carew, Reggie Jackson AL Active Career Hit Leaders .15
712 Reggie Jackson, Greg Luzinski, Graig Nettles AL Active Career Home Run Leaders .15
713 Reggie Jackson, Graig Nettles, Ted Simmons AL Active Career RBI Leaders .15
714 Bert Campaneris, Dave Lopes, Omar Moreno AL Active Career Stolen Bases Leaders .05
715 Tommy John, Jim Palmer, Don Sutton AL Active Career Victory Leaders .05
716 Bert Blyleven, Jerry Koosman, Don Sutton AL Active Strikeout Leaders .05
717 Rollie Fingers, Ron Guidry, Jim Palmer AL Active Career ERA Leaders .05
718 Rollie Fingers, Rich Gossage, Dan Quisenberry AL Active Career Save Leaders .05
719 Andy Hassler .05
720 Dwight Evans .05
721 Del Crandall .05
722 Bob Welch .05
723 Rich Dauer .05
724 Eric Rasmussen .05
725 Cesar Cedeno .05
726 Moose Haas, Ted Simmons Brewers Batting & Pitching Leaders .05
727 Joel Youngblood .05
728 Tug McGraw .05
729 Gene Tenace .05
730 Bruce Sutter .75
731 Lynn Jones .05
732 Terry Crowley .05
733 Dave Collins .05
734 Odell Jones .05
735 Rick Burleson .05
736 Dick Ruthven .05
737 Jim Essian .05
738 *Bill Schroeder* .05
739 Bob Watson .05
740 Tom Seaver 1.00
741 Wayne Gross .05
742 Dick Williams .05
743 Don Hood .05
744 Jamie Allen .05
745 Dennis Eckersley .65
746 Mickey Hatcher .05
747 Pat Zachry .05
748 Jeff Leonard .05
749 Doug Flynn .05
750a Jim Palmer 1.00
750b Jim Palmer (missing 1980-82 losses on back) 3.00
750c Jim Palmer (missing 1979-83 losses on back) 4.00
751 Charlie Moore .05
752 Phil Garner .05
753 Doug Gwosdz .05
754 Kent Tekulve .05
755 Garry Maddox .05
756 Ron Oester, Mario Soto Reds Batting & Pitching Leaders .05
757 Larry Bowa .05
758 Bill Stein .05
759 Richard Dotson .05
760 Bob Horner .05
761 John Montefusco .05
762 Rance Mulliniks .05
763 Craig Swan .05
764 Mike Hargrove .05
765 Ken Forsch .05
766 Mike Vail .05
767 Carney Lansford .05
768 Champ Summers .05
769 Bill Caudill .05
770 Ken Griffey .05
771 Billy Gardner .05
772 Jim Slaton .05
773 Todd Cruz .05
774 Tom Gorman .05
775 Dave Parker .05
776 Craig Reynolds .05
777 Tom Paciorek .05
778 *Andy Hawkins* .05
779 Jim Sundberg .05
780 Steve Carlton 1.00
781 Checklist 661-792 .05
782 Steve Balboni .05
783 Luis Leal .05
784 Leon Roberts .05
785 Joaquin Andujar .05
786 Wade Boggs, Bob Ojeda Red Sox Batting & Pitching Leaders .25
787 Bill Campbell .05
788 Milt May .05
789 Bert Blyleven .05
790 Doug DeCinces .05
791 Terry Forster .05
792 Bill Russell .05

Tiffany

	NM/M
Unopened Set (792):	175.00
Complete Set (792):	95.00
Common Player:	.15
Stars:	6X
8 Don Mattingly	80.00

(See 1984 Topps for checklist and base card values.)

Traded

	NM/M
Complete Set (132):	16.00
Common Player:	.05
1T Willie Aikens	.05
2T Luis Aponte	.05
3T Mike Armstrong	.05
4T Bob Bailor	.05
5T Dusty Baker	.15
6T Steve Balboni	.05
7T Alan Bannister	.05
8T Dave Beard	.05
9T Joe Beckwith	.05
10T Bruce Berenyi	.05
11T Dave Bergman	.05
12T Tony Bernazard	.05
13T Yogi Berra	.25
14T Barry Bonnell	.05

15T	Phil Bradley	.05
16T	Fred Breining	.05
17T	Bill Buckner	.05
18T	Ray Burris	.05
19T	John Butcher	.05
20T	Brett Butler	.05
21T	Enos Cabell	.05
22T	Bill Campbell	.05
23T	Bill Caudill	.05
24T	Bob Clark	.05
25T	Bryan Clark	.05
26T	Jaime Cocanower	.05
27T	*Ron Darling*	.50
28T	*Alvin Davis*	.05
29T	Ken Dayley	.05
30T	Jeff Dedmon	.05
31T	Bob Dernier	.05
32T	Carlos Diaz	.05
33T	Mike Easler	.05
34T	Dennis Eckersley	1.50
35T	Jim Essian	.05
36T	Darrell Evans	.05
37T	Mike Fitzgerald	.05
38T	Tim Foli	.05
39T	George Frazier	.05
40T	Rich Gale	.05
41T	Barbaro Garbey	.05
42T	*Dwight Gooden*	3.00
43T	Rich Gossage	.05
44T	Wayne Gross	.05
45T	*Mark Gubicza*	.25
46T	Jackie Gutierrez	.05
47T	Mel Hall	.05
48T	Toby Harrah	.05
49T	Ron Hassey	.05
50T	Rich Hebner	.05
51T	Willie Hernandez	.05
52T	Ricky Horton	.05
53T	Art Howe	.05
54T	Dane Iorg	.05
55T	Brook Jacoby	.05
56T	Mike Jeffcoat	.05
57T	Dave Johnson	.05
58T	Lynn Jones	.05
59T	Ruppert Jones	.05
60T	Mike Jorgensen	.05
61T	Bob Kearney	.05
62T	*Jimmy Key*	.50
63T	Dave Kingman	.05
64T	Jerry Koosman	.05
65T	Wayne Krenchicki	.05
66T	Rusty Kuntz	.05
67T	Rene Lachemann	.05
68T	Frank LaCorte	.05
69T	Dennis Lamp	.05
70T	*Mark Langston*	.50
71T	Rick Leach	.05
72T	Craig Lefferts	.05
73T	Gary Lucas	.05
74T	Jerry Martin	.05
75T	Carmelo Martinez	.05
76T	Mike Mason	.05
77T	Gary Matthews	.05
78T	Andy McGaffigan	.05
79T	Larry Milbourne	.05
80T	Sid Monge	.05
81T	Jackie Moore	.05
82T	Joe Morgan	2.00
83T	Graig Nettles	.05
84T	Phil Niekro	1.00
85T	Ken Oberkfell	.05
86T	Mike O'Berry	.05
87T	Al Oliver	.05
88T	Jorge Orta	.05
89T	Amos Otis	.05
90T	Dave Parker	.05
91T	Tony Perez	1.00
92T	Gerald Perry	.05
93T	Gary Pettis	.05
94T	Rob Picciolo	.05
95T	Vern Rapp	.05
96T	Floyd Rayford	.05
97T	Randy Ready	.05
98T	Ron Reed	.05
99T	Gene Richards	.05
100T	*Jose Rijo*	.25
101T	Jeff Robinson	.05
102T	Ron Romanick	.05
103T	Pete Rose	7.50
104T	*Bret Saberhagen*	3.00
105T	Juan Samuel	.05
106T	Scott Sanderson	.05
107T	Dick Schofield	.05
108T	Tom Seaver	3.00
109T	Jim Slaton	.05
110T	Mike Smithson	.05
111T	Lary Sorensen	.05
112T	Tim Stoddard	.05
113T	Champ Summers	.05
114T	Jim Sundberg	.05
115T	Rick Sutcliffe	.05
116T	Craig Swan	.05
117T	Tim Teufel	.05
118T	Derrel Thomas	.05
119T	Gorman Thomas	.05
120T	Alex Trevino	.05
121T	Manny Trillo	.05
122T	John Tudor	.05
123T	Tom Underwood	.05
124T	Mike Vail	.05
125T	Tom Waddell	.05
126T	Gary Ward	.05
127T	Curt Wilkerson	.05
128T	Frank Williams	.05
129T	Glenn Wilson	.05
130T	Johnny Wockenfuss	.05
131T	Ned Yost	.05
132T	Checklist 1-132	.05

Tiffany

	NM/M
Complete Set (132):	35.00
Common Player:	.25
Stars:	2X

(See 1984 Topps Traded for checklist and base card values.)

1985 TOPPS

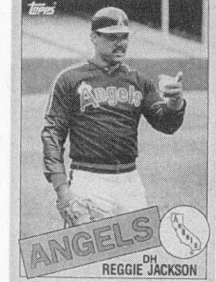

	NM/M
Unopened Fact. Set (792):	150.00
Complete Set (792):	80.00
Common Player:	.05
Wax Pack (15):	4.50
Wax Box (36):	130.00
Cello Pack (28):	6.00
Cello Box (24):	160.00
Rack Pack (51+1):	9.00
Rack Box (24):	190.00
Vending Box (500):	65.00

1	Carlton Fisk	.25
2	Steve Garvey	.05
3	Dwight Gooden	.05
4	Cliff Johnson	.05
5	Joe Morgan	.10
6	Pete Rose	.50
7	Nolan Ryan	1.50
8	Juan Samuel	.05
9	Bruce Sutter	.10
10	Don Sutton	.05
11	Ralph Houk	.05
12	Dave Lopes	.05
13	Tim Lollar	.05
14	Chris Bando	.05
15	Jerry Koosman	.05
16	Bobby Meacham	.05
17	Mike Scott	.05
18	Mickey Hatcher	.05
19	George Frazier	.05
20	Chet Lemon	.05
21	Lee Tunnell	.05
22	Duane Kuiper	.05
23	Bret Saberhagen	.05
24	Jesse Barfield	.05
25	Steve Bedrosian	.05
26	Roy Smalley	.05
27	Bruce Berenyi	.05
28	Dann Bilardello	.05
29	Odell Jones	.05
30	Cal Ripken, Jr.	4.00
31	Terry Whitfield	.05
32	Chuck Porter	.05
33	Tito Landrum	.05
34	Ed Nunez	.05
35	Graig Nettles	.05
36	Fred Breining	.05
37	Reid Nichols	.05
38	Jackie Moore	.05
39	Johnny Wockenfuss	.05
40	Phil Niekro	.60
41	Mike Fischlin	.05
42	Luis Sanchez	.05
43	Andre David	.05
44	Dickie Thon	.05
45	Greg Minton	.05
46	Gary Woods	.05
47	Dave Rozema	.05
48	Tony Fernandez	.05
49	Butch Davis	.05
50	John Candelaria	.05
51	Bob Watson	.05
52	Jerry Dybzinski	.05
53	Tom Gorman	.05
54	Cesar Cedeno	.05
55	Frank Tanana	.05
56	Jim Dwyer	.05
57	Pat Zachry	.05
58	Orlando Mercado	.05
59	Rick Waits	.05
60	George Hendrick	.05
61	Curt Kaufman	.05
62	Mike Ramsey	.05
63	Steve McCatty	.05
64	*Mark Bailey*	.05
65	Bill Buckner	.05
66	Dick Williams	.05
67	*Rafael Santana*	.05
68	Von Hayes	.05
69	*Jim Winn*	.05
70	Don Baylor	.10
71	Tim Laudner	.05
72	Rick Sutcliffe	.05
73	Rusty Kuntz	.05
74	Mike Krukow	.05
75	Willie Upshaw	.05
76	Alan Bannister	.05
77	Joe Beckwith	.05
78	Scott Fletcher	.05
79	Rick Mahler	.05
80	Keith Hernandez	.05
81	Lenn Sakata	.05
82	Joe Price	.05
83	Charlie Moore	.05
84	Spike Owen	.05
85	Mike Marshall	.05
86	Don Aase	.05
87	David Green	.05
88	Bryn Smith	.05
89	Jackie Gutierrez	.05
90	Rich Gossage	.05
91	Jeff Burroughs	.05
92	Paul Owens	.05
93	*Don Schulze*	.05
94	Toby Harrah	.05
95	Jose Cruz	.05
96	Johnny Ray	.05
97	Pete Filson	.05
98	Steve Lake	.05
99	Milt Wilcox	.05
100	George Brett	2.00
101	Jim Acker	.05
102	Tommy Dunbar	.05
103	Randy Lerch	.05
104	Mike Fitzgerald	.05
105	Ron Kittle	.05
106	Pascual Perez	.05
107	Tom Foley	.05
108	Darnell Coles	.05
109	Gary Roenicke	.05
110	Alejandro Pena	.05
111	Doug DeCinces	.05
112	Tom Tellmann	.05
113	Tom Herr	.05
114	Bob James	.05
115	Rickey Henderson	.75
116	Dennis Boyd	.05
117	Greg Gross	.05
118	Eric Show	.05
119	Pat Corrales	.05
120	Steve Kemp	.05
121	Checklist 1-132	.05
122	Tom Brunansky	.05
123	Dave Smith	.05
124	Rich Hebner	.05
125	Kent Tekulve	.05
126	Ruppert Jones	.05
127	Mark Gubicza	.05
128	Ernie Whitt	.05
129	Gene Garber	.05
130	Al Oliver	.05
131	Buddy Bell, Gus Bell Father - Son	.05
132	Dale Berra, Yogi Berra Father - Son	.10
133	Bob Boone, Ray Boone Father - Son	.05
134	Terry Francona, Tito Francona Father - Son	.05
135	Bob Kennedy, Terry Kennedy Father - Son	.05
136	Bill Kunkel, Jeff Kunkel Father - Son	.05
137	Vance Law, Vern Law Father - Son	.05
138	Dick Schofield, Dick Schofield, Jr. Father - Son	.05
139	Bob Skinner, Joel Skinner Father - Son	.05
140	Roy Smalley, Jr., Roy Smalley III Father - Son	.05
141	Dave Stenhouse, Mike Stenhouse Father - Son	.05
142	Dizzy Trout, Steve Trout Father - Son	.05
143	Ozzie Virgil, Ozzie Virgil Father - Son	.05
144	Ron Gardenhire	.05
145	Alvin Davis	.05
146	Gary Redus	.05
147	Bill Swaggerty	.05
148	Steve Yeager	.05
149	Dickie Noles	.05
150	Jim Rice	.15
151	Moose Haas	.05
152	Steve Braun	.05
153	Frank LaCorte	.05
154	Argenis Salazar	.05
155	Yogi Berra	.10
156	Craig Reynolds	.05
157	Tug McGraw	.05
158	Pat Tabler	.05
159	Carlos Diaz	.05
160	Lance Parrish	.05
161	Ken Schrom	.05
162	*Benny Distefano*	.05
163	Dennis Eckersley	.60
164	Jorge Orta	.05
165	Dusty Baker	.05
166	Keith Atherton	.05
167	Rufino Linares	.05
168	Garth Iorg	.05
169	Dan Spillner	.05
170	George Foster	.05
171	Bill Stein	.05
172	Jack Perconte	.05
173	Mike Young	.05
174	Rick Honeycutt	.05
175	Dave Parker	.05
176	Bill Schroeder	.05
177	Dave Von Ohlen	.05
178	Miguel Dilone	.05
179	Tommy John	.10
180	Dave Winfield	.75
181	Roger Clemens	35.00
182	Tim Flannery	.05
183	Larry McWilliams	.05
184	Carmen Castillo	.05
185	Al Holland	.05
186	Bob Lillis	.05
187	Mike Walters	.05
188	Greg Pryor	.05
189	Warren Brusstar	.05
190	Rusty Staub	.05
191	Steve Nicosia	.05
192	Howard Johnson	.05
193	Jimmy Key	.05
194	Dave Stegman	.05
195	Glenn Hubbard	.05
196	Pete O'Brien	.05
197	Mike Warren	.05
198	Eddie Milner	.05
199	Denny Martinez	.05
200	Reggie Jackson	1.50
201	Burt Hooton	.05
202	Gorman Thomas	.05
203	Bob McClure	.05
204	Art Howe	.05
205	Steve Rogers	.05
206	Phil Garner	.05
207	Mark Clear	.05
208	Champ Summers	.05
209	Bill Campbell	.05
210	Gary Matthews	.05
211	Clay Christiansen	.05
212	George Vukovich	.05
213	Billy Gardner	.05
214	John Tudor	.05
215	Bob Brenly	.05
216	Jerry Don Gleaton	.05
217	Leon Roberts	.05
218	Doyle Alexander	.05
219	Gerald Perry	.05
220	Fred Lynn	.05
221	Ron Reed	.05

No.	Player	Price
222	Hubie Brooks	.05
223	Tom Hume	.05
224	Al Cowens	.05
225	Mike Boddicker	.05
226	Juan Beniquez	.05
227	Danny Darwin	.05
228	Dion James	.05
229	Dave LaPoint	.05
230	Gary Carter	.75
231	Dwayne Murphy	.05
232	Dave Beard	.05
233	Ed Jurak	.05
234	Jerry Narron	.05
235	Garry Maddox	.05
236	Mark Thurmond	.05
237	Julio Franco	.05
238	Jose Rijo	.05
239	Tim Teufel	.05
240	Dave Stieb	.05
241	Jim Frey	.05
242	Greg Harris	.05
243	Barbaro Garbey	.05
244	Mike Jones	.05
245	Chili Davis	.05
246	Mike Norris	.05
247	Wayne Tolleson	.05
248	Terry Forster	.05
249	Harold Baines	.05
250	Jesse Orosco	.05
251	Brad Gulden	.05
252	Dan Ford	.05
253	*Sid Bream*	.10
254	Pete Vuckovich	.05
255	Lonnie Smith	.05
256	Mike Stanton	.05
257	Brian Little (Bryan)	.05
258	Mike Brown	.05
259	Gary Allenson	.05
260	Dave Righetti	.05
261	Checklist 133-264	.05
262	*Greg Booker*	.05
263	Mel Hall	.05
264	Joe Sambito	.05
265	Juan Samuel	.05
266	Frank Viola	.05
267	*Henry Cotto*	.05
268	Chuck Tanner	.05
269	*Doug Baker*	.05
270	Dan Quisenberry	.05
271	Tim Foli (#1 Draft Pick)	.05
272	Jeff Burroughs (#1 Draft Pick)	.05
273	Bill Almon (#1 Draft Pick)	.05
274	Floyd Bannister (#1 Draft Pick)	.05
275	Harold Baines (#1 Draft Pick)	.10
276	Bob Horner (#1 Draft Pick)	.10
277	Al Chambers (#1 Draft Pick)	.05
278	Darryl Strawberry (#1 Draft Pick)	.30
279	Mike Moore (#1 Draft Pick)	.05
280	*Shawon Dunston* (#1 Draft Pick)	.40
281	*Tim Belcher* (#1 Draft Pick)	.30
282	*Shawn Abner* (#1 Draft Pick)	.05
283	Fran Mullins	.05
284	Marty Bystrom	.05
285	Dan Driessen	.05
286	Rudy Law	.05
287	Walt Terrell	.05
288	*Jeff Kunkel*	.05
289	Tom Underwood	.05
290	Cecil Cooper	.05
291	Bob Welch	.05
292	Brad Komminsk	.05
293	*Curt Young*	.05
294	*Tom Nieto*	.05
295	Joe Niekro	.05
296	Ricky Nelson	.05
297	Gary Lucas	.05
298	Marty Barrett	.05
299	Andy Hawkins	.05
300	Rod Carew	.75
301	John Montefusco	.05
302	Tim Corcoran	.05
303	*Mike Jeffcoat*	.05
304	Gary Gaetti	.05
305	Dale Berra	.05
306	Rick Reuschel	.05
307	Sparky Anderson	.10
308	John Wathan	.05
309	Mike Witt	.05
310	Manny Trillo	.05
311	Jim Gott	.05
312	Marc Hill	.05
313	Dave Schmidt	.05
314	Ron Oester	.05
315	Doug Sisk	.05
316	John Lowenstein	.05
317	*Jack Lazorko*	.05
318	Ted Simmons	.05
319	Jeff Jones	.05
320	Dale Murphy	.35
321	*Ricky Horton*	.05
322	Dave Stapleton	.05
323	Andy McGaffigan	.05
324	Bruce Bochy	.05
325	John Denny	.05
326	Kevin Bass	.05
327	Brook Jacoby	.05
328	Bob Shirley	.05
329	Ron Washington	.05
330	Leon Durham	.05
331	Bill Laskey	.05
332	Brian Harper	.05
333	Willie Hernandez	.05
334	Dick Howser	.05
335	Bruce Benedict	.05
336	Rance Mulliniks	.05
337	Billy Sample	.05
338	Britt Burns	.05
339	Danny Heep	.05
340	Robin Yount	.75
341	Floyd Rayford	.05
342	Ted Power	.05
343	Bill Russell	.05
344	Dave Henderson	.05
345	Charlie Lea	.05
346	*Terry Pendleton*	.75
347	Rick Langford	.05
348	Bob Boone	.05
349	Domingo Ramos	.05
350	Wade Boggs	1.00
351	Juan Agosto	.05
352	Joe Morgan	.75
353	Julio Solano	.05
354	Andre Robertson	.05
355	Bert Blyleven	.05
356	Dave Meier	.05
357	Rich Bordi	.05
358	Tony Pena	.05
359	Pat Sheridan	.05
360	Steve Carlton	.75
361	Alfredo Griffin	.05
362	Craig McMurtry	.05
363	Ron Hodges	.05
364	Richard Dotson	.05
365	Danny Ozark	.05
366	Todd Cruz	.05
367	Keefe Cato	.05
368	Dave Bergman	.05
369	*R.J. Reynolds*	.05
370	Bruce Sutter	.65
371	Mickey Rivers	.05
372	Roy Howell	.05
373	Mike Moore	.05
374	Brian Downing	.05
375	Jeff Reardon	.05
376	Jeff Newman	.05
377	Checklist 265-396	.05
378	Alan Wiggins	.05
379	Charles Hudson	.05
380	Ken Griffey	.05
381	Roy Smith	.05
382	Denny Walling	.05
383	Rick Lysander	.05
384	Jody Davis	.05
385	Jose DeLeon	.05
386	*Dan Gladden*	.30
387	*Buddy Biancalana*	.05
388	Bert Roberge	.05
389	Rod Dedeaux	.05
390	Sid Akins	.05
391	Flavio Alfaro	.05
392	Don August	.05
393	*Scott Bankhead*	.10
394	Bob Caffrey	.05
395	Mike Dunne	.05
396	Gary Green	.05
397	John Hoover	.05
398	*Shane Mack*	.10
399	John Marzano	.05
400	Oddibe McDowell	.05
401	*Mark McGwire*	40.00
402	Pat Pacillo	.05
403	*Cory Snyder*	.30
404	*Billy Swift*	.40
405	Tom Veryzer	.05
406	Len Whitehouse	.05
407	Bobby Ramos	.05
408	Sid Monge	.05
409	Brad Wellman	.05
410	Bob Horner	.05
411	Bobby Cox	.05
412	Bud Black	.05
413	Vance Law	.05
414	Gary Ward	.05
415	Ron Darling	.05
416	Wayne Gross	.05
417	*John Franco*	.45
418	Ken Landreaux	.05
419	Mike Caldwell	.05
420	Andre Dawson	.50
421	Dave Rucker	.05
422	Carney Lansford	.05
423	Barry Bonnell	.05
424	*Al Nipper*	.05
425	Mike Hargrove	.05
426	Verne Ruhle	.05
427	Mario Ramirez	.05
428	Larry Andersen	.05
429	Rick Cerone	.05
430	Ron Davis	.05
431	U.L. Washington	.05
432	Thad Bosley	.05
433	Jim Morrison	.05
434	Gene Richards	.05
435	Dan Petry	.05
436	Willie Aikens	.05
437	Al Jones	.05
438	Joe Torre	.10
439	Junior Ortiz	.05
440	Fernando Valenzuela	.05
441	Duane Walker	.05
442	Ken Forsch	.05
443	George Wright	.05
444	Tony Phillips	.05
445	Tippy Martinez	.05
446	Jim Sundberg	.05
447	Jeff Lahti	.05
448	Derrel Thomas	.05
449	*Phil Bradley*	.10
450	Steve Garvey	.25
451	Bruce Hurst	.05
452	John Castino	.05
453	Tom Waddell	.05
454	Glenn Wilson	.05
455	Bob Knepper	.05
456	Tim Foli	.05
457	Cecilio Guante	.05
458	Randy S. Johnson	.05
459	Charlie Leibrandt	.05
460	Ryne Sandberg	1.00
461	Marty Castillo	.05
462	Gary Lavelle	.05
463	Dave Collins	.05
464	*Mike Mason*	.05
465	Bob Grich	.05
466	Tony LaRussa	.10
467	Ed Lynch	.05
468	Wayne Krenchicki	.05
469	Sammy Stewart	.05
470	Steve Sax	.05
471	Pete Ladd	.05
472	Jim Essian	.05
473	Tim Wallach	.05
474	Kurt Kepshire	.05
475	Andre Thornton	.05
476	*Jeff Stone*	.05
477	Bob Ojeda	.05
478	Kurt Bevacqua	.05
479	Mike Madden	.05
480	Lou Whitaker	.05
481	Dale Murray	.05
482	Harry Spilman	.05
483	Mike Smithson	.05
484	Larry Bowa	.05
485	Matt Young	.05
486	Steve Balboni	.05
487	*Frank Williams*	.05
488	Joel Skinner	.05
489	Bryan Clark	.05
490	Jason Thompson	.05
491	Rick Camp	.05
492	Dave Johnson	.05
493	*Orel Hershiser*	1.50
494	Rich Dauer	.05
495	Mario Soto	.05
496	Donnie Scott	.05
497	Gary Pettis	.05
498	Ed Romero	.05
499	Danny Cox	.05
500	Mike Schmidt	2.00
501	Dan Schatzeder	.05
502	Rick Miller	.05
503	Tim Conroy	.05
504	Jerry Willard	.05
505	Jim Beattie	.05
506	*Franklin Stubbs*	.05
507	Ray Fontenot	.05
508	John Shelby	.05
509	Milt May	.05
510	Kent Hrbek	.05
511	Lee Smith	.05
512	Tom Brookens	.05
513	Lynn Jones	.05
514	Jeff Cornell	.05
515	Dave Concepcion	.05
516	Roy Lee Jackson	.05
517	Jerry Martin	.05
518	Chris Chambliss	.05
519	Doug Rader	.05
520	LaMarr Hoyt	.05
521	Rick Dempsey	.05
522	Paul Molitor	.75
523	Candy Maldonado	.05
524	Rob Wilfong	.05
525	Darrell Porter	.05
526	Dave Palmer	.05
527	Checklist 397-528	.05
528	Bill Krueger	.05
529	Rich Gedman	.05
530	Dave Dravecky	.05
531	Joe Lefebvre	.05
532	Frank DiPino	.05
533	Tony Bernazard	.05
534	Brian Dayett	.05
535	Pat Putnam	.05
536	Kirby Puckett	6.00
537	Don Robinson	.05
538	Keith Moreland	.05
539	Aurelio Lopez	.05
540	Claudell Washington	.05
541	Mark Davis	.05
542	Don Slaught	.05
543	Mike Squires	.05
544	Bruce Kison	.05
545	Lloyd Moseby	.05
546	Brent Gaff	.05
547	Pete Rose	1.50
548	Larry Parrish	.05
549	Mike Scioscia	.05
550	Scott McGregor	.05
551	Andy Van Slyke	.05
552	Chris Codiroli	.05
553	Bob Clark	.05
554	Doug Flynn	.05
555	Bob Stanley	.05
556	Sixto Lezcano	.05
557	Len Barker	.05
558	Carmelo Martinez	.05
559	Jay Howell	.05
560	Bill Madlock	.05
561	Darryl Motley	.05
562	Houston Jimenez	.05
563	Dick Ruthven	.05
564	Alan Ashby	.05
565	Kirk Gibson	.05
566	Ed Vande Berg	.05
567	Joel Youngblood	.05
568	Cliff Johnson	.05
569	Ken Oberkfell	.05
570	Darryl Strawberry	.10
571	Charlie Hough	.05
572	Tom Paciorek	.05
573	*Jay Tibbs*	.05
574	Joe Altobelli	.05
575	Pedro Guerrero	.05
576	Jaime Cocanower	.05
577	Chris Speier	.05
578	Terry Francona	.05
579	*Ron Romanick*	.05
580	Dwight Evans	.05
581	Mark Wagner	.05
582	Ken Phelps	.05
583	Bobby Brown	.05
584	Kevin Gross	.05
585	Butch Wynegar	.05
586	Bill Scherrer	.05
587	Doug Frobel	.05
588	Bobby Castillo	.05
589	Bob Dernier	.05
590	Ray Knight	.05
591	Larry Herndon	.05
592	*Jeff Robinson*	.05
593	Rick Leach	.05
594	Curt Wilkerson	.05
595	Larry Gura	.05
596	Jerry Hairston Sr.	.05
597	Brad Lesley	.05
598	Jose Oquendo	.05
599	Storm Davis	.05
600	Pete Rose	3.00
601	Tom Lasorda	.10
602	*Jeff Dedmon*	.05
603	Rick Manning	.05
604	Daryl Sconiers	.05
605	Ozzie Smith	1.00
606	Rich Gale	.05
607	Bill Almon	.05

608	Craig Lefferts	.05
609	Broderick Perkins	.05
610	Jack Morris	.05
611	Ozzie Virgil	.05
612	Mike Armstrong	.05
613	Terry Puhl	.05
614	Al Williams	.05
615	Marvell Wynne	.05
616	Scott Sanderson	.05
617	Willie Wilson	.05
618	Pete Falcone	.05
619	Jeff Leonard	.05
620	Dwight Gooden	.50
621	Marvis Foley	.05
622	Luis Leal	.05
623	Greg Walker	.05
624	Benny Ayala	.05
625	Mark Langston	.05
626	German Rivera	.05
627	*Eric Davis*	.45
628	Rene Lachemann	.05
629	Dick Schofield	.05
630	Tim Raines	.05
631	Bob Forsch	.05
632	Bruce Bochte	.05
633	Glenn Hoffman	.05
634	Bill Dawley	.05
635	Terry Kennedy	.05
636	Shane Rawley	.05
637	Brett Butler	.05
638	*Mike Pagliarulo*	.10
639	Ed Hodge	.05
640	Steve Henderson	.05
641	Rod Scurry	.05
642	Dave Owen	.05
643	Johnny Grubb	.05
644	Mark Huismann	.05
645	Damaso Garcia	.05
646	Scot Thompson	.05
647	Rafael Ramirez	.05
648	Bob Jones	.05
649	Sid Fernandez	.05
650	Greg Luzinski	.05
651	Jeff Russell	.05
652	Joe Nolan	.05
653	Mark Brouhard	.05
654	Dave Anderson	.05
655	Joaquin Andujar	.05
656	Chuck Cottier	.05
657	Jim Slaton	.05
658	Mike Stenhouse	.05
659	Checklist 529-660	.05
660	Tony Gwynn	1.00
661	Steve Crawford	.05
662	Mike Heath	.05
663	Luis Aguayo	.05
664	*Steve Farr*	.05
665	Don Mattingly	2.00
666	Mike LaCoss	.05
667	Dave Engle	.05
668	Steve Trout	.05
669	Lee Lacy	.05
670	Tom Seaver	.75
671	Dane Iorg	.05
672	Juan Berenguer	.05
673	Buck Martinez	.05
674	Atlee Hammaker	.05
675	Tony Perez	.75
676	*Albert Hall*	.05
677	Wally Backman	.05
678	Joey McLaughlin	.05
679	Bob Kearney	.05
680	Jerry Reuss	.05
681	Ben Oglivie	.05
682	Doug Corbett	.05
683	Whitey Herzog	.05
684	Bill Doran	.05
685	Bill Caudill	.05
686	Mike Easler	.05
687	Bill Gullickson	.05
688	Len Matuszek	.05
689	Luis DeLeon	.05
690	Alan Trammell	.05
691	Dennis Rasmussen	.05
692	Randy Bush	.05
693	Tim Stoddard	.05
694	Joe Carter	.05
695	Rick Rhoden	.05
696	John Rabb	.05
697	Onix Concepcion	.05
698	Jorge Bell	.05
699	Donnie Moore	.05
700	Eddie Murray	.75
701	Eddie Murray	.40
702	Damaso Garcia	.05
703	George Brett	.50
704	Cal Ripken, Jr.	1.50
705	Dave Winfield	.40
706	Rickey Henderson	.35
707	Tony Armas	.05
708	Lance Parrish	.05
709	Mike Boddicker	.05
710	Frank Viola	.05
711	Dan Quisenberry	.05
712	Keith Hernandez	.05
713	Ryne Sandberg	.40
714	Mike Schmidt	.75
715	Ozzie Smith	.50
716	Dale Murphy	.15
717	Tony Gwynn	.75
718	Jeff Leonard	.05
719	Gary Carter	.35
720	Rick Sutcliffe	.05
721	Bob Knepper	.05
722	Bruce Sutter	.30
723	Dave Stewart	.05
724	Oscar Gamble	.05
725	Floyd Bannister	.05
726	Al Bumbry	.05
727	Frank Pastore	.05
728	Bob Bailor	.05
729	Don Sutton	.60
730	Dave Kingman	.05
731	Neil Allen	.05
732	John McNamara	.05
733	Tony Scott	.05
734	John Henry Johnson	.05
735	Garry Templeton	.05
736	Jerry Mumphrey	.05
737	Bo Diaz	.05
738	Omar Moreno	.05
739	Ernie Camacho	.05
740	Jack Clark	.05
741	John Butcher	.05
742	Ron Hassey	.05
743	Frank White	.05
744	Doug Bair	.05
745	Buddy Bell	.05
746	Jim Clancy	.05
747	Alex Trevino	.05
748	Lee Mazzilli	.05
749	Julio Cruz	.05
750	Rollie Fingers	.60
751	Kelvin Chapman	.05
752	Bob Owchinko	.05
753	Greg Brock	.05
754	Larry Milbourne	.05
755	Ken Singleton	.05
756	Rob Picciolo	.05
757	Willie McGee	.05
758	Ray Burris	.05
759	Jim Fanning	.05
760	Nolan Ryan	4.00
761	Jerry Remy	.05
762	Eddie Whitson	.05
763	Kiko Garcia	.05
764	Jamie Easterly	.05
765	Willie Randolph	.05
766	Paul Mirabella	.05
767	Darrell Brown	.05
768	Ron Cey	.05
769	Joe Cowley	.05
770	Carlton Fisk	.75
771	Geoff Zahn	.05
772	Johnnie LeMaster	.05
773	Hal McRae	.05
774	Dennis Lamp	.05
775	Mookie Wilson	.05
776	Jerry Royster	.05
777	Ned Yost	.05
778	Mike Davis	.05
779	Nick Esasky	.05
780	Mike Flanagan	.05
781	Jim Gantner	.05
782	Tom Niedenfuer	.05
783	Mike Jorgensen	.05
784	Checklist 661-792	.05
785	Tony Armas	.05
786	Enos Cabell	.05
787	Jim Wohlford	.05
788	Steve Comer	.05
789	Luis Salazar	.05
790	Ron Guidry	.10
791	Ivan DeJesus	.05
792	Darrell Evans	.05

Tiffany

	NM/M
Complete Unopened Set (792):	500.00
Complete Set, Opened (792):	325.00
Common Player:	.25
Stars:	4X
181 Roger Clemens	100.00
401 Mark McGwire	90.00

(See 1985 Topps for checklist and base card values.)

Traded

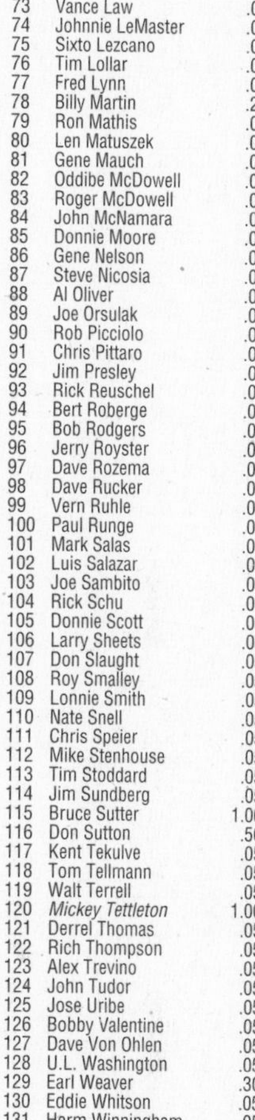

	NM/M
Complete Set (132):	10.00
Common Player:	.05
Wax Test Pack (8):	10.00
Wax Test Wax Box (36):	150.00

1	Don Aase	.05
2	Bill Almon	.05
3	Benny Ayala	.05
4	Dusty Baker	.25
5	George Bamberger	.05
6	Dale Berra	.05
7	Rich Bordi	.05
8	Daryl Boston	.05
9	Hubie Brooks	.05
10	Chris Brown	.05
11	Tom Browning	.05
12	Al Bumbry	.05
13	Ray Burris	.05
14	Jeff Burroughs	.05
15	Bill Campbell	.05
16	Don Carman	.05
17	Gary Carter	1.50
18	Bobby Castillo	.05
19	Bill Caudill	.05
20	Rick Cerone	.05
21	Bryan Clark	.05
22	Jack Clark	.05
23	Pat Clements	.05
24	*Vince Coleman*	.50
25	Dave Collins	.05
26	Danny Darwin	.05
27	Jim Davenport	.05
28	Jerry Davis	.05
29	Brian Dayett	.05
30	Ivan DeJesus	.05
31	Ken Dixon	.05
32	Mariano Duncan	.05
33	John Felske	.05
34	Mike Fitzgerald	.05
35	Ray Fontenot	.05
36	Greg Gagne	.05
37	Oscar Gamble	.05
38	Scott Garrelts	.05
39	Bob L. Gibson	.05
40	Jim Gott	.05
41	David Green	.05
42	Alfredo Griffin	.05
43	*Ozzie Guillen*	3.00
44	Eddie Haas	.05
45	Terry Harper	.05
46	Toby Harrah	.05
47	Greg Harris	.05
48	Ron Hassey	.05
49	Rickey Henderson	2.50
50	Steve Henderson	.05
51	George Hendrick	.05
52	Joe Hesketh	.05
53	Teddy Higuera	.05
54	Donnie Hill	.05
55	Al Holland	.05
56	Burt Hooton	.05
57	Jay Howell	.05
58	Ken Howell	.05
59	LaMarr Hoyt	.05
60	Tim Hulett	.05
61	Bob James	.05
62	Steve Jeltz	.05
63	Cliff Johnson	.05
64	Howard Johnson	.05
65	Ruppert Jones	.05
66	Steve Kemp	.05
67	Bruce Kison	.05
68	Alan Knicely	.05
69	Mike LaCoss	.05
70	Lee Lacy	.05
71	Dave LaPoint	.05
72	Gary Lavelle	.05
73	Vance Law	.05
74	Johnnie LeMaster	.05
75	Sixto Lezcano	.05
76	Tim Lollar	.05
77	Fred Lynn	.05
78	Billy Martin	.25
79	Ron Mathis	.05
80	Len Matuszek	.05
81	Gene Mauch	.05
82	Oddibe McDowell	.05
83	Roger McDowell	.05
84	John McNamara	.05
85	Donnie Moore	.05
86	Gene Nelson	.05
87	Steve Nicosia	.05
88	Al Oliver	.05
89	Joe Orsulak	.05
90	Rob Picciolo	.05
91	Chris Pittaro	.05
92	Jim Presley	.05
93	Rick Reuschel	.05
94	Bert Roberge	.05
95	Bob Rodgers	.05
96	Jerry Royster	.05
97	Dave Rozema	.05
98	Dave Rucker	.05
99	Vern Ruhle	.05
100	Paul Runge	.05
101	Mark Salas	.05
102	Luis Salazar	.05
103	Joe Sambito	.05
104	Rick Schu	.05
105	Donnie Scott	.05
106	Larry Sheets	.05
107	Don Slaught	.05
108	Roy Smalley	.05
109	Lonnie Smith	.05
110	Nate Snell	.05
111	Chris Speier	.05
112	Mike Stenhouse	.05
113	Tim Stoddard	.05
114	Jim Sundberg	.05
115	Bruce Sutter	1.00
116	Don Sutton	.50
117	Kent Tekulve	.05
118	Tom Tellmann	.05
119	Walt Terrell	.05
120	*Mickey Tettleton*	1.00
121	Derrel Thomas	.05
122	Rich Thompson	.05
123	Alex Trevino	.05
124	John Tudor	.05
125	Jose Uribe	.05
126	Bobby Valentine	.05
127	Dave Von Ohlen	.05
128	U.L. Washington	.05
129	Earl Weaver	.30
130	Eddie Whitson	.05
131	Herm Winningham	.05
132	Checklist 1-132	.05

Tiffany

	NM/M
Complete Set (132):	35.00
Common Player:	.25
Stars:	4X

(See 1985 Topps Traded for checklist and base card values.)

1986 TOPPS

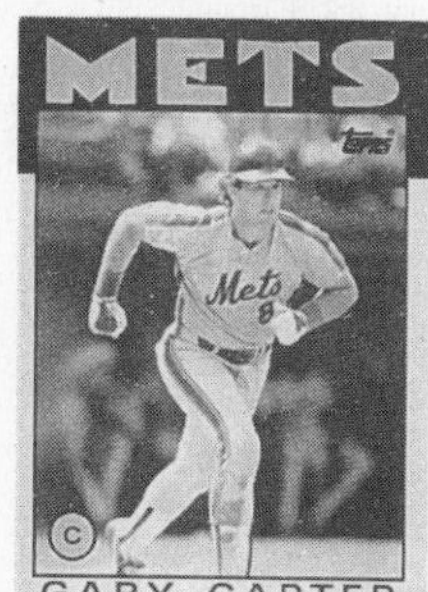

	NM/M
Unopened Factory Set, Retail (792):	60.00
Unopened Factory Set, Hobby (792):	30.00
Complete Set (792):	25.00
Common Player:	.05
Wax Pack (15):	.65
Wax Box (36):	16.00

#	Player	Value
	Cello Pack (28):	1.00
	Cello Box (24):	16.00
	Rack Pack (51):	1.25
	Rack Box (24):	18.00
	Vending Box (500):	9.00
1	Pete Rose	1.50
2	Pete Rose	.50
3	Pete Rose	.50
4	Pete Rose	.50
5	Pete Rose	.50
6	Pete Rose	.50
7	Pete Rose	.50
8	Dwayne Murphy	.05
9	Roy Smith	.05
10	Tony Gwynn	.75
11	Bob Ojeda	.05
12	*Jose Uribe*	.05
13	Bob Kearney	.05
14	Julio Cruz	.05
15	Eddie Whitson	.05
16	Rick Schu	.05
17	Mike Stenhouse	.05
18	Brent Gaff	.05
19	Rich Hebner	.05
20	Lou Whitaker	.05
21	George Bamberger	.05
22	Duane Walker	.05
23	*Manny Lee*	.05
24	Len Barker	.05
25	Willie Wilson	.05
26	Frank DiPino	.05
27	Ray Knight	.05
28	Eric Davis	.05
29	Tony Phillips	.05
30	Eddie Murray	.50
31	Jamie Easterly	.05
32	Steve Yeager	.05
33	Jeff Lahti	.05
34	Ken Phelps	.05
35	Jeff Reardon	.05
36	Lance Parrish Tigers Leaders	.05
37	Mark Thurmond	.05
38	Glenn Hoffman	.05
39	Dave Rucker	.05
40	Ken Griffey	.05
41	Brad Wellman	.05
42	Geoff Zahn	.05
43	Dave Engle	.05
44	*Lance McCullers*	.05
45	Damaso Garcia	.05
46	Billy Hatcher	.05
47	Juan Berenguer	.05
48	Bill Almon	.05
49	Rick Manning	.05
50	Dan Quisenberry	.05
51	Not issued, see #57	
52	Chris Welsh	.05
53	*Len Dykstra*	.50
54	John Franco	.05
55	Fred Lynn	.05
56	Tom Niedenfuer	.05
57a	Bill Doran	.05
57b	Bobby Wine (supposed to be #51)	.05
58	Bill Krueger	.05
59	Andre Thornton	.05
60	Dwight Evans	.05
61	Karl Best	.05
62	Bob Boone	.05
63	Ron Roenicke	.05
64	Floyd Bannister	.05
65	Dan Driessen	.05
66	Bob Forsch Cardinals Leaders	.05
67	Carmelo Martinez	.05
68	Ed Lynch	.05
69	Luis Aguayo	.05
70	Dave Winfield	.50
71	Ken Schrom	.05
72	Shawon Dunston	.05
73	Randy O'Neal	.05
74	Rance Mulliniks	.05
75	Jose DeLeon	.05
76	Dion James	.05
77	Charlie Leibrandt	.05
78	Bruce Benedict	.05
79	Dave Schmidt	.05
80	Darryl Strawberry	.05
81	Gene Mauch	.05
82	Tippy Martinez	.05
83	Phil Garner	.05
84	Curt Young	.05
85	Tony Perez	.40
86	Tom Waddell	.05
87	Candy Maldonado	.05
88	Tom Nieto	.05
89	Randy St. Claire	.05
90	Garry Templeton	.05
91	Steve Crawford	.05
92	Al Cowens	.05
93	Scot Thompson	.05
94	Rich Bordi	.05
95	Ozzie Virgil	.05
96	Jim Clancy Blue Jay Leaders	.05
97	Gary Gaetti	.05
98	Dick Ruthven	.05
99	Buddy Biancalana	.05
100	Nolan Ryan	2.00
101	Dave Bergman	.05
102	*Joe Orsulak*	.15
103	Luis Salazar	.05
104	Sid Fernandez	.05
105	Gary Ward	.05
106	Ray Burris	.05
107	Rafael Ramirez	.05
108	Ted Power	.05
109	Len Matuszek	.05
110	Scott McGregor	.05
111	Roger Craig	.05
112	Bill Campbell	.05
113	U.L. Washington	.05
114	Mike Brown	.05
115	Jay Howell	.05
116	Brook Jacoby	.05
117	Bruce Kison	.05
118	Jerry Royster	.05
119	Barry Bonnell	.05
120	Steve Carlton	.50
121	Nelson Simmons	.05
122	Pete Filson	.05
123	Greg Walker	.05
124	Luis Sanchez	.05
125	Dave Lopes	.05
126	Mookie Wilson Mets Leaders	.05
127	*Jack Howell*	.05
128	John Wathan	.05
129	Jeff Dedmon	.05
130	Alan Trammell	.05
131	Checklist 1-132	.05
132	Razor Shines	.05
133	Andy McGaffigan	.05
134	Carney Lansford	.05
135	Joe Niekro	.05
136	Mike Hargrove	.05
137	Charlie Moore	.05
138	Mark Davis	.05
139	Daryl Boston	.05
140	John Candelaria	.05
141a	Chuck Cottier	.05
141b	Bob Rodgers (supposed to be #171)	.05
142	Bob Jones	.05
143	Dave Van Gorder	.05
144	Doug Sisk	.05
145	Pedro Guerrero	.05
146	Jack Perconte	.05
147	Larry Sheets	.05
148	Mike Heath	.05
149	Brett Butler	.05
150	Joaquin Andujar	.05
151	Dave Stapleton	.05
152	Mike Morgan	.05
153	Ricky Adams	.05
154	Bert Roberge	.05
155	Bob Grich	.05
156	Richard Dotson White Sox Leaders	.05
157	Ron Hassey	.05
158	Derrel Thomas	.05
159	Orel Hershiser	.05
160	Chet Lemon	.05
161	Lee Tunnell	.05
162	Greg Gagne	.05
163	Pete Ladd	.05
164	Steve Balboni	.05
165	Mike Davis	.05
166	Dickie Thon	.05
167	Zane Smith	.05
168	Jeff Burroughs	.05
169	George Wright	.05
170	Gary Carter	.50
171	Not issued, see #141	
172	Jerry Reed	.05
173	Wayne Gross	.05
174	Brian Snyder	.05
175	Steve Sax	.05
176	Jay Tibbs	.05
177	Joel Youngblood	.05
178	Ivan DeJesus	.05
179	*Stu Cliburn*	.05
180	Don Mattingly	1.00
181	Al Nipper	.05
182	Bobby Brown	.05
183	Larry Andersen	.05
184	Tim Laudner	.05
185	Rollie Fingers	.40
186	Jose Cruz Astros Leaders	.05
187	Scott Fletcher	.05
188	Bob Dernier	.05
189	Mike Mason	.05
190	George Hendrick	.05
191	Wally Backman	.05
192	Milt Wilcox	.05
193	Daryl Sconiers	.05
194	Craig McMurtry	.05
195	Dave Concepcion	.05
196	Doyle Alexander	.05
197	Enos Cabell	.05
198	Ken Dixon	.05
199	Dick Howser	.05
200	Mike Schmidt	1.00
201	Vince Coleman	.05
202	Dwight Gooden	.05
203	Keith Hernandez	.05
204	Phil Niekro	.05
205	Tony Perez	.05
206	Pete Rose	.25
207	Fernando Valenzuela	.05
208	Ramon Romero	.05
209	Randy Ready	.05
210	Calvin Schiraldi	.05
211	Ed Wojna	.05
212	Chris Speier	.05
213	Bob Shirley	.05
214	Randy Bush	.05
215	Frank White	.05
216	Dwayne Murphy A's Leaders	.05
217	Bill Scherrer	.05
218	Randy Hunt	.05
219	Dennis Lamp	.05
220	Bob Horner	.05
221	Dave Henderson	.05
222	Craig Gerber	.05
223	Atlee Hammaker	.05
224	Cesar Cedeno	.05
225	Ron Darling	.05
226	Lee Lacy	.05
227	Al Jones	.05
228	Tom Lawless	.05
229	Bill Gullickson	.05
230	Terry Kennedy	.05
231	Jim Frey	.05
232	Rick Rhoden	.05
233	Steve Lyons	.05
234	Doug Corbett	.05
235	Butch Wynegar	.05
236	Frank Eufemia	.05
237	Ted Simmons	.05
238	Larry Parrish	.05
239	Joel Skinner	.05
240	Tommy John	.10
241	Tony Fernandez	.05
242	Rich Thompson	.05
243	Johnny Grubb	.05
244	Craig Lefferts	.05
245	Jim Sundberg	.05
246	Steve Carlton Phillies Leaders	.10
247	Terry Harper	.05
248	Spike Owen	.05
249	Rob Deer	.05
250	Dwight Gooden	.05
251	Rich Dauer	.05
252	Bobby Castillo	.05
253	Dann Bilardello	.05
254	*Ozzie Guillen*	.30
255	Tony Armas	.05
256	Kurt Kepshire	.05
257	Doug DeCinces	.05
258	*Tim Burke*	.05
259	Dan Pasqua	.05
260	Tony Pena	.05
261	Bobby Valentine	.05
262	Mario Ramirez	.05
263	Checklist 133-264	.05
264	Darren Daulton	.05
265	Ron Davis	.05
266	Keith Moreland	.05
267	Paul Molitor	.50
268	Mike Scott	.05
269	Dane Iorg	.05
270	Jack Morris	.05
271	Dave Collins	.05
272	Tim Tolman	.05
273	Jerry Willard	.05
274	Ron Gardenhire	.05
275	Charlie Hough	.05
276	Willie Randolph Yankees Leaders	.05
277	Jaime Cocanower	.05
278	Sixto Lezcano	.05
279	Al Pardo	.05
280	Tim Raines	.05
281	Steve Mura	.05
282	Jerry Mumphrey	.05
283	Mike Fischlin	.05
284	Brian Dayett	.05
285	Buddy Bell	.05
286	Luis DeLeon	.05
287	*John Christensen*	.05
288	Don Aase	.05
289	Johnnie LeMaster	.05
290	Carlton Fisk	.50
291	Tom Lasorda	.10
292	Chuck Porter	.05
293	Chris Chambliss	.05
294	Danny Cox	.05
295	Kirk Gibson	.05
296	Geno Petralli	.05
297	Tim Lollar	.05
298	Craig Reynolds	.05
299	Bryn Smith	.05
300	George Brett	1.00
301	Dennis Rasmussen	.05
302	Greg Gross	.05
303	Curt Wardle	.05
304	*Mike Gallego*	.10
305	Phil Bradley	.05
306	Terry Kennedy Padres Leaders	.05
307	Dave Sax	.05
308	Ray Fontenot	.05
309	John Shelby	.05
310	Greg Minton	.05
311	Dick Schofield	.05
312	Tom Filer	.05
313	Joe DeSa	.05
314	Frank Pastore	.05
315	Mookie Wilson	.05
316	Sammy Khalifa	.05
317	Ed Romero	.05
318	Terry Whitfield	.05
319	Rick Camp	.05
320	Jim Rice	.15
321	Earl Weaver	.10
322	Bob Forsch	.05
323	Jerry Davis	.05
324	Dan Schatzeder	.05
325	Juan Beniquez	.05
326	Kent Tekulve	.05
327	Mike Pagliarulo	.05
328	Pete O'Brien	.05
329	Kirby Puckett	.75
330	Rick Sutcliffe	.05
331	Alan Ashby	.05
332	Darryl Motley	.05
333	Tom Henke	.05
334	Ken Oberkfell	.05
335	Don Sutton	.40
336	Andre Thornton Indians Leaders	.05
337	Darnell Coles	.05
338	Jorge Bell	.05
339	Bruce Berenyi	.05
340	Cal Ripken, Jr.	2.00
341	Frank Williams	.05
342	Gary Redus	.05
343	Carlos Diaz	.05
344	Jim Wohlford	.05
345	Donnie Moore	.05
346	Bryan Little	.05
347	*Teddy Higuera*	.10
348	Cliff Johnson	.05
349	Mark Clear	.05
350	Jack Clark	.05
351	Chuck Tanner	.05
352	Harry Spilman	.05
353	Keith Atherton	.05
354	Tony Bernazard	.05
355	Lee Smith	.05
356	Mickey Hatcher	.05
357	Ed Vande Berg	.05
358	Rick Dempsey	.05
359	Mike LaCoss	.05
360	Lloyd Moseby	.05
361	Shane Rawley	.05
362	Tom Paciorek	.05
363	Terry Forster	.05
364	Reid Nichols	.05
365	Mike Flanagan	.05
366	Dave Concepcion Reds Leaders	.05
367	Aurelio Lopez	.05
368	Greg Brock	.05
369	Al Holland	.05
370	*Vince Coleman*	.35
371	Bill Stein	.05
372	Ben Oglivie	.05
373	*Urbano Lugo*	.05
374	Terry Francona	.05
375	Rich Gedman	.05
376	Bill Dawley	.05

377 Joe Carter .05
378 Bruce Bochte .05
379 Bobby Meacham .05
380 LaMarr Hoyt .05
381 Ray Miller .05
382 *Ivan Calderon* .05
383 *Chris Brown* .05
384 Steve Trout .05
385 Cecil Cooper .05
386 *Cecil Fielder* .75
387 Steve Kemp .05
388 Dickie Noles .05
389 Glenn Davis .05
390 Tom Seaver .60
391 Julio Franco .05
392 John Russell .05
393 Chris Pittaro .05
394 Checklist 265-396 .05
395 Scott Garrelts .05
396 Dwight Evans Red Sox Leaders .05
397 *Steve Buechele* .10
398 *Earnie Riles* .05
399 Bill Swift .05
400 Rod Carew .50
401 Fernando Valenzuela .05
402 Tom Seaver .25
403 Willie Mays .35
404 Frank Robinson .10
405 Roger Maris .30
406 Scott Sanderson .05
407 Sal Butera .05
408 Dave Smith .05
409 *Paul Runge* .05
410 Dave Kingman .05
411 Sparky Anderson .10
412 Jim Clancy .05
413 Tim Flannery .05
414 Tom Gorman .05
415 Hal McRae .05
416 Denny Martinez .05
417 R.J. Reynolds .05
418 Alan Knicely .05
419 Frank Wills .05
420 Von Hayes .05
421 Dave Palmer .05
422 Mike Jorgensen .05
423 Dan Spillner .05
424 Rick Miller .05
425 Larry McWilliams .05
426 Charlie Moore Brewers Leaders .05
427 Joe Cowley .05
428 Max Venable .05
429 Greg Booker .05
430 Kent Hrbek .05
431 George Frazier .05
432 Mark Bailey .05
433 Chris Codiroli .05
434 Curt Wilkerson .05
435 Bill Caudill .05
436 Doug Flynn .05
437 Rick Mahler .05
438 Clint Hurdle .05
439 Rick Honeycutt .05
440 Alvin Davis .05
441 Whitey Herzog .05
442 Ron Robinson .05
443 Bill Buckner .05
444 Alex Trevino .05
445 Bert Blyleven .05
446 Lenn Sakata .05
447 Jerry Don Gleaton .05
448 *Herm Winningham* .05
449 Rod Scurry .05
450 Graig Nettles .05
451 Mark Brown .05
452 Bob Clark .05
453 Steve Jeltz .05
454 Burt Hooton .05
455 Willie Randolph .05
456 Dale Murphy Braves Leaders .10
457 Mickey Tettleton .05
458 Kevin Bass .05
459 Luis Leal .05
460 Leon Durham .05
461 Walt Terrell .05
462 Domingo Ramos .05
463 Jim Gott .05
464 Ruppert Jones .05
465 Jesse Orosco .05
466 Tom Foley .05
467 Bob James .05
468 Mike Scioscia .05
469 Storm Davis .05
470 Bill Madlock .05
471 Bobby Cox .05
472 Joe Hesketh .05
473 Mark Brouhard .05
474 John Tudor .05
475 Juan Samuel .05
476 Ron Mathis .05
477 Mike Easler .05
478 Andy Hawkins .05
479 *Bob Melvin* .05
480 *Oddibe McDowell* .05
481 Scott Bradley .05
482 Rick Lysander .05
483 George Vukovich .05
484 Donnie Hill .05
485 Gary Matthews .05
486 Bob Grich Angels Leaders .05
487 Bret Saberhagen .05
488 Lou Thornton .05
489 Jim Winn .05
490 Jeff Leonard .05
491 Pascual Perez .05
492 Kelvin Chapman .05
493 Gene Nelson .05
494 Gary Roenicke .05
495 Mark Langston .05
496 Jay Johnstone .05
497 John Stuper .05
498 Tito Landrum .05
499 Bob L. Gibson .05
500 Rickey Henderson .50
501 Dave Johnson .05
502 Glen Cook .05
503 Mike Fitzgerald .05
504 Denny Walling .05
505 Jerry Koosman .05
506 Bill Russell .05
507 *Steve Ontiveros* .05
508 Alan Wiggins .05
509 Ernie Camacho .05
510 Wade Boggs .75
511 Ed Nunez .05
512 Thad Bosley .05
513 Ron Washington .05
514 Mike Jones .05
515 Darrell Evans .05
516 Greg Minton Giants Leaders .05
517 *Milt Thompson* .05
518 Buck Martinez .05
519 Danny Darwin .05
520 Keith Hernandez .05
521 Nate Snell .05
522 Bob Bailor .05
523 Joe Price .05
524 Darrell Miller .05
525 Marvell Wynne .05
526 Charlie Lea .05
527 Checklist 397-528 .05
528 Terry Pendleton .05
529 Marc Sullivan .05
530 Rich Gossage .05
531 Tony LaRussa .05
532 *Don Carman* .05
533 Billy Sample .05
534 Jeff Calhoun .05
535 Toby Harrah .05
536 Jose Rijo .05
537 Mark Salas .05
538 Dennis Eckersley .40
539 Glenn Hubbard .05
540 Dan Petry .05
541 Jorge Orta .05
542 Don Schulze .05
543 Jerry Narron .05
544 Eddie Milner .05
545 Jimmy Key .05
546 Dave Henderson Mariners Leaders .05
547 Roger McDowell .05
548 Mike Young .05
549 Bob Welch .05
550 Tom Herr .05
551 Dave LaPoint .05
552 Marc Hill .05
553 Jim Morrison .05
554 Paul Householder .05
555 Hubie Brooks .05
556 John Denny .05
557 Gerald Perry .05
558 Tim Stoddard .05
559 Tommy Dunbar .05
560 Dave Righetti .05
561 Bob Lillis .05
562 Joe Beckwith .05
563 Alejandro Sanchez .05
564 Warren Brusstar .05
565 Tom Brunansky .05
566 Alfredo Griffin .05
567 Jeff Barkley .05
568 Donnie Scott .05
569 Jim Acker .05
570 Rusty Staub .10
571 Mike Jeffcoat .05
572 Paul Zuvella .05
573 Tom Hume .05
574 Ron Kittle .05
575 Mike Boddicker .05
576 Andre Dawson Expos Leaders .05
577 Jerry Reuss .05
578 Lee Mazzilli .05
579 Jim Slaton .05
580 Willie McGee .05
581 Bruce Hurst .05
582 Jim Gantner .05
583 Al Bumbry .05
584 *Brian Fisher* .05
585 Garry Maddox .05
586 Greg Harris .05
587 Rafael Santana .05
588 Steve Lake .05
589 Sid Bream .05
590 Bob Knepper .05
591 Jackie Moore .05
592 Frank Tanana .05
593 Jesse Barfield .05
594 Chris Bando .05
595 Dave Parker .05
596 Onix Concepcion .05
597 Sammy Stewart .05
598 Jim Presley .05
599 *Rick Aguilera* .25
600 Dale Murphy .25
601 Gary Lucas .05
602 Mariano Duncan .05
603 Bill Laskey .05
604 Gary Pettis .05
605 Dennis Boyd .05
606 Hal McRae Royals Leaders .05
607 Ken Dayley .05
608 Bruce Bochy .05
609 Barbaro Garbey .05
610 Ron Guidry .05
611 Gary Woods .05
612 Richard Dotson .05
613 Roy Smalley .05
614 Rick Waits .05
615 Johnny Ray .05
616 Glenn Brummer .05
617 Lonnie Smith .05
618 Jim Pankovits .05
619 Danny Heep .05
620 Bruce Sutter .40
621 John Felske .05
622 Gary Lavelle .05
623 Floyd Rayford .05
624 Steve McCatty .05
625 Bob Brenly .05
626 Roy Thomas .05
627 Ron Oester .05
628 *Kirk McCaskill* .15
629 *Mitch Webster* .05
630 Fernando Valenzuela .05
631 Steve Braun .05
632 Dave Von Ohlen .05
633 Jackie Gutierrez .05
634 Roy Lee Jackson .05
635 Jason Thompson .05
636 Lee Smith Cubs Leaders .05
637 Rudy Law .05
638 John Butcher .05
639 Bo Diaz .05
640 Jose Cruz .05
641 Wayne Tolleson .05
642 Ray Searage .05
643 Tom Brookens .05
644 Mark Gubicza .05
645 Dusty Baker .05
646 Mike Moore .05
647 Mel Hall .05
648 Steve Bedrosian .05
649 Ronn Reynolds .05
650 Dave Stieb .05
651 Billy Martin .10
652 Tom Browning .05
653 Jim Dwyer .05
654 Ken Howell .05
655 Manny Trillo .05
656 Brian Harper .05
657 Juan Agosto .05
658 Rob Wilfong .05
659 Checklist 529-660 .05
660 Steve Garvey .20
661 Roger Clemens 3.00
661 Roger Clemens (blue streak upper-right) 7.50
662 Bill Schroeder .05
663 Neil Allen .05
664 Tim Corcoran .05
665 Alejandro Pena .05
666 Charlie Hough Rangers Leaders .05
667 Tim Teufel .05
668 Cecilio Guante .05
669 Ron Cey .05
670 Willie Hernandez .05
671 Lynn Jones .05
672 Rob Picciolo .05
673 Ernie Whitt .05
674 Pat Tabler .05
675 Claudell Washington .05
676 Matt Young .05
677 Nick Esasky .05
678 Dan Gladden .05
679 Britt Burns .05
680 George Foster .05
681 Dick Williams .05
682 Junior Ortiz .05
683 Andy Van Slyke .05
684 Bob McClure .05
685 Tim Wallach .05
686 Jeff Stone .05
687 Mike Trujillo .05
688 Larry Herndon .05
689 Dave Stewart .05
690 Ryne Sandberg .75
691 Mike Madden .05
692 Dale Berra .05
693 Tom Tellmann .05
694 Garth Iorg .05
695 Mike Smithson .05
696 Bill Russell Dodgers Leaders .05
697 Bud Black .05
698 Brad Komminsk .05
699 Pat Corrales .05
700 Reggie Jackson .75
701 Keith Hernandez .05
702 Tom Herr .05
703 Tim Wallach .05
704 Ozzie Smith .35
705 Dale Murphy .10
706 Pedro Guerrero .05
707 Willie McGee .05
708 Gary Carter .25
709 Dwight Gooden .05
710 John Tudor .05
711 Jeff Reardon .05
712 Don Mattingly .50
713 Damasco Garcia .05
714 George Brett .45
715 Cal Ripken, Jr. 1.00
716 Rickey Henderson .25
717 Dave Winfield .25
718 George Bell .05
719 Carlton Fisk .20
720 Bret Saberhagen .05
721 Ron Guidry .05
722 Dan Quisenberry .05
723 Marty Bystrom .05
724 Tim Hulett .05
725 Mario Soto .05
726 Rick Dempsey Orioles Leaders .05
727 David Green .05
728 Mike Marshall .05
729 Jim Beattie .05
730 Ozzie Smith .75
731 Don Robinson .05
732 *Floyd Youmans* .05
733 Ron Romanick .05
734 Marty Barrett .05
735 Dave Dravecky .05
736 Glenn Wilson .05
737 Pete Vuckovich .05
738 Andre Robertson .05
739 Dave Rozema .05
740 Lance Parrish .05
741 Pete Rose 1.00
742 Frank Viola .05
743 Pat Sheridan .05
744 Lary Sorensen .05
745 Willie Upshaw .05
746 Denny Gonzalez .05
747 Rick Cerone .05
748 Steve Henderson .05
749 Ed Jurak .05
750 Gorman Thomas .05
751 Howard Johnson .05
752 Mike Krukow .05
753 Dan Ford .05
754 *Pat Clements* .05
755 Harold Baines .05
756 Rick Rhoden Pirates Leaders .05
757 Darrell Porter .05
758 Dave Anderson .05

759	Moose Haas	.05
760	Andre Dawson	.30
761	Don Slaught	.05
762	Eric Show	.05
763	Terry Puhl	.05
764	Kevin Gross	.05
765	Don Baylor	.05
766	Rick Langford	.05
767	Jody Davis	.05
768	Vern Ruhle	.05
769	*Harold Reynolds*	.25
770	Vida Blue	.05
771	John McNamara	.05
772	Brian Downing	.05
773	Greg Pryor	.05
774	Terry Leach	.05
775	Al Oliver	.05
776	Gene Garber	.05
777	Wayne Krenchicki	.05
778	Jerry Hairston Sr.	.05
779	Rick Reuschel	.05
780	Robin Yount	.50
781	Joe Nolan	.05
782	Ken Landreaux	.05
783	Ricky Horton	.05
784	Alan Bannister	.05
785	Bob Stanley	.05
786	Mickey Hatcher Twins Leaders	.05
787	Vance Law	.05
788	Marty Castillo	.05
789	Kurt Bevacqua	.05
790	Phil Niekro	.40
791	Checklist 661-792	.05
792	Charles Hudson	.05

Tiffany

	NM/M
Unopened Set (792):	100.00
Complete Set (792):	45.00
Common Player:	.25

(Star cards valued at 4X corresponding cards in regular 1986 Topps issue)

Traded

	NM/M
Unopened Set (132):	45.00
Complete Set (132):	40.00
Common Player:	.05

1T	Andy Allanson	.05
2T	Neil Allen	.05
3T	Joaquin Andujar	.05
4T	Paul Assenmacher	.05
5T	Scott Bailes	.05
6T	Don Baylor	.15
7T	Steve Bedrosian	.05
8T	Juan Beniquez	.05
9T	Juan Berenguer	.05
10T	Mike Bielecki	.05
11T	*Barry Bonds*	35.00
12T	*Bobby Bonilla*	.50
13T	Juan Bonilla	.05
14T	Rich Bordi	.05
15T	Steve Boros	.05
16T	Rick Burleson	.05
17T	Bill Campbell	.05
18T	Tom Candiotti	.05
19T	John Cangelosi	.05
20T	*Jose Canseco*	4.00
21T	Carmen Castillo	.05
22T	Rick Cerone	.05
23T	John Cerutti	.05
24T	*Will Clark*	1.50
25T	Mark Clear	.05
26T	Darnell Coles	.05
27T	Dave Collins	.05
28T	Tim Conroy	.05
29T	Joe Cowley	.05
30T	Joel Davis	.05
31T	Rob Deer	.05
32T	John Denny	.05
33T	Mike Easler	.05
34T	Mark Eichhorn	.05
35T	Steve Farr	.05
36T	Scott Fletcher	.05
37T	Terry Forster	.05
38T	Terry Francona	.05
39T	Jim Fregosi	.05
40T	Andres Galarraga	.35
41T	Ken Griffey	.05
42T	Bill Gullickson	.05
43T	Jose Guzman	.05
44T	Moose Haas	.05
45T	Billy Hatcher	.05
46T	Mike Heath	.05
47T	Tom Hume	.05
48T	*Pete Incaviglia*	.20
49T	Dane Iorg	.05
50T	*Bo Jackson*	1.50
51T	*Wally Joyner*	.40
52T	Charlie Kerfeld	.05
53T	Eric King	.05
54T	Bob Kipper	.05
55T	Wayne Krenchicki	.05
56T	*John Kruk*	.35
57T	Mike LaCoss	.05
58T	Pete Ladd	.05
59T	Mike Laga	.05
60T	Hal Lanier	.05
61T	Dave LaPoint	.05
62T	Rudy Law	.05
63T	Rick Leach	.05
64T	Tim Leary	.05
65T	Dennis Leonard	.05
66T	Jim Leyland	.05
67T	Steve Lyons	.05
68T	Mickey Mahler	.05
69T	Candy Maldonado	.05
70T	Roger Mason	.05
71T	Bob McClure	.05
72T	Andy McGaffigan	.05
73T	Gene Michael	.05
74T	*Kevin Mitchell*	.25
75T	Omar Moreno	.05
76T	Jerry Mumphrey	.05
77T	Phil Niekro	.25
78T	Randy Niemann	.05
79T	Juan Nieves	.05
80T	Otis Nixon	.05
81T	Bob Ojeda	.05
82T	Jose Oquendo	.05
83T	Tom Paciorek	.05
84T	Dave Palmer	.05
85T	Frank Pastore	.05
86T	Lou Piniella	.05
87T	Dan Plesac	.05
88T	Darrell Porter	.05
89T	Rey Quinones	.05
90T	Gary Redus	.05
91T	Bip Roberts	.05
92T	Billy Jo Robidoux	.05
93T	Jeff Robinson	.05
94T	Gary Roenicke	.05
95T	Ed Romero	.05
96T	Argenis Salazar	.05
97T	Joe Sambito	.05
98T	Billy Sample	.05
99T	Dave Schmidt	.05
100T	Ken Schrom	.05
101T	Tom Seaver	.50
102T	Ted Simmons	.05
103T	Sammy Stewart	.05
104T	Kurt Stillwell	.05
105T	Franklin Stubbs	.05
106T	Dale Sveum	.05
107T	Chuck Tanner	.05
108T	Danny Tartabull	.05
109T	Tim Teufel	.05
110T	Bob Tewksbury	.05
111T	Andres Thomas	.05
112T	Milt Thompson	.05
113T	Robby Thompson	.05
114T	Jay Tibbs	.05
115T	Wayne Tolleson	.05
116T	Alex Trevino	.05
117T	Manny Trillo	.05
118T	Ed Vande Berg	.05
119T	Ozzie Virgil	.05
120T	Bob Walk	.05
121T	Gene Walter	.05
122T	Claudell Washington	.05
123T	Bill Wegman	.05
124T	Dick Williams	.05
125T	Mitch Williams	.05
126T	Bobby Witt	.05
127T	Todd Worrell	.05
128T	George Wright	.05
129T	Ricky Wright	.05
130T	Steve Yeager	.05
131T	Paul Zuvella	.05
132T	Checklist	.05

Tiffany

	NM/M
Unopened Set (132):	750.00
Complete Set (132):	500.00
Common Player:	.25
11T Barry Bonds	475.00

(Star cards valued at 4X corresponding cards in regular Topps Traded)

1987 TOPPS

	NM/M
Unopened Factory Set, Retail (792):	30.00
Unopened Factory Set, Hobby (792):	25.00
Complete Set (792):	20.00
Uncut Sheet Set (6):	45.00
Common Player:	.05
Wax Pack (15):	.65
Wax Box (36):	16.00
Cello Pack (31):	1.00
Cello Box (24):	17.50
Rack Pack (49):	1.50
Rack Box (24):	25.00
Vending Box (500):	12.00

1	Roger Clemens	.45
2	Jim Deshaies	.05
3	Dwight Evans	.05
4	Dave Lopes	.05
5	Dave Righetti	.05
6	Ruben Sierra	.05
7	Todd Worrell	.05
8	Terry Pendleton	.05
9	Jay Tibbs	.05
10	Cecil Cooper	.05
11	Jack Aker, Chris Bando, Phil Niekro Indians Leaders	.05
12	*Jeff Sellers*	.05
13	Nick Esasky	.05
14	Dave Stewart	.05
15	Claudell Washington	.05
16	Pat Clements	.05
17	Pete O'Brien	.05
18	Dick Howser	.05
19	Matt Young	.05
20	Gary Carter	.40
21	Mark Davis	.05
22	Doug DeCinces	.05
23	Lee Smith	.05
24	Tony Walker	.05
25	Bert Blyleven	.05
26	Greg Brock	.05
27	Joe Cowley	.05
28	Rick Dempsey	.05
29	Jimmy Key	.05
30	Tim Raines	.05
31	Glenn Hubbard, Rafael Ramirez Braves Leaders	.05
32	Tim Leary	.05
33	Andy Van Slyke	.05
34	Jose Rijo	.05
35	Sid Bream	.05
36	*Eric King*	.05
37	Marvell Wynne	.05
38	Dennis Leonard	.05
39	Marty Barrett	.05
40	Dave Righetti	.05
41	Bo Diaz	.05
42	Gary Redus	.05
43	Gene Michael	.05
44	Greg Harris	.05
45	Jim Presley	.05
46	Danny Gladden	.05
47	Dennis Powell	.05
48	Wally Backman	.05
49	Terry Harper	.05
50	Dave Smith	.05
51	Mel Hall	.05
52	Keith Atherton	.05
53	Ruppert Jones	.05
54	Bill Dawley	.05
55	Tim Wallach	.05
56	Jamie Cocanower, Paul Molitor, Charlie Moore, Herm Starrette Brewers Leaders	.10
57	*Scott Nielsen*	.05
58	Thad Bosley	.05
59	Ken Dayley	.05
60	Tony Pena	.05
61	*Bobby Thigpen*	.05
62	Bobby Meacham	.05
63	Fred Toliver	.05
64	Harry Spilman	.05
65	Tom Browning	.05
66	Marc Sullivan	.05
67	Bill Swift	.05
68	Tony LaRussa	.05
69	Lonnie Smith	.05
70	Charlie Hough	.05
71	*Mike Aldrete*	.05
72	Walt Terrell	.05
73	Dave Anderson	.05
74	Dan Pasqua	.05
75	Ron Darling	.05
76	Rafael Ramirez	.05
77	Bryan Oelkers	.05
78	Tom Foley	.05
79	Juan Nieves	.05
80	*Wally Joyner*	.35
81	Andy Hawkins, Terry Kennedy Padres Leaders	.05
82	*Rob Murphy*	.05
83	Mike Davis	.05
84	Steve Lake	.05
85	Kevin Bass	.05
86	Nate Snell	.05
87	Mark Salas	.05
88	Ed Wojna	.05
89	Ozzie Guillen	.05
90	Dave Stieb	.05
91	Harold Reynolds	.05
92a	Urbano Lugo (no trademark on front)	.10
92b	Urbano Lugo (trademark on front)	.05
93	Jim Leyland	.05
94	Calvin Schiraldi	.05
95	Oddibe McDowell	.05
96	Frank Williams	.05
97	Glenn Wilson	.05
98	Bill Scherrer	.05
99	Darryl Motley	.05
100	Steve Garvey	.15
101	*Carl Willis*	.05
102	Paul Zuvella	.05
103	Rick Aguilera	.05
104	Billy Sample	.05
105	Floyd Youmans	.05
106	George Bell, Willie Upshaw Blue Jays Leaders	.05
107	John Butcher	.05
108	Jim Gantner (photo reversed)	.05
109	R.J. Reynolds	.05
110	John Tudor	.05
111	Alfredo Griffin	.05
112	Alan Ashby	.05
113	Neil Allen	.05
114	Billy Beane	.05
115	Donnie Moore	.05
116	*Mike Stanley*	.05
117	Jim Beattie	.05
118	Bobby Valentine	.05
119	Ron Robinson	.05
120	Eddie Murray	.40
121	*Kevin Romine*	.05
122	Jim Clancy	.05
123	John Kruk	.05
124	Ray Fontenot	.05
125	Bob Brenly	.05
126	*Mike Loynd*	.05
127	Vance Law	.05
128	Checklist 1-132	.05
129	Rick Cerone	.05
130	Dwight Gooden	.05
131	Sid Bream, Tony Pena Pirates Leaders	.05
132	*Paul Assenmacher*	.05

No.	Player	Price
133	Jose Oquendo	.05
134	*Rich Yett*	.05
135	Mike Easler	.05
136	Ron Romanick	.05
137	Jerry Willard	.05
138	Roy Lee Jackson	.05
139	*Devon White*	.40
140	Bret Saberhagen	.05
141	Herm Winningham	.05
142	Rick Sutcliffe	.05
143	Steve Boros	.05
144	Mike Scioscia	.05
145	Charlie Kerfeld	.05
146	*Tracy Jones*	.05
147	Randy Niemann	.05
148	Dave Collins	.05
149	Ray Searage	.05
150	Wade Boggs	.45
151	Mike LaCoss	.05
152	Toby Harrah	.05
153	*Duane Ward*	.05
154	Tom O'Malley	.05
155	Eddie Whitson	.05
156	Bob Kearney, Phil Regan, Matt Young Mariners Leaders	.05
157	Danny Darwin	.05
158	Tim Teufel	.05
159	Ed Olwine	.05
160	Julio Franco	.05
161	Steve Ontiveros	.05
162	*Mike LaValliere*	.10
163	Kevin Gross	.05
164	Sammy Khalifa	.05
165	Jeff Reardon	.05
166	Bob Boone	.05
167	*Jim Deshaies*	.10
168	Lou Piniella	.05
169	Ron Washington	.05
170	Bo Jackson (Future Stars)	.35
171	*Chuck Cary*	.05
172	Ron Oester	.05
173	Alex Trevino	.05
174	Henry Cotto	.05
175	Bob Stanley	.05
176	Steve Buechele	.05
177	Keith Moreland	.05
178	Cecil Fielder	.05
179	Bill Wegman	.05
180	Chris Brown	.05
181	Mike LaValliere, Ozzie Smith, Ray Soff Cardinals Leaders	.10
182	Lee Lacy	.05
183	Andy Hawkins	.05
184	Bobby Bonilla	.05
185	Roger McDowell	.05
186	Bruce Benedict	.05
187	Mark Huismann	.05
188	Tony Phillips	.05
189	Joe Hesketh	.05
190	Jim Sundberg	.05
191	Charles Hudson	.05
192	Cory Snyder	.05
193	Roger Craig	.05
194	Kirk McCaskill	.05
195	Mike Pagliarulo	.05
196	Randy O'Neal	.05
197	Mark Bailey	.05
198	Lee Mazzilli	.05
199	Mariano Duncan	.05
200	Pete Rose	.75
201	*John Cangelosi*	.05
202	Ricky Wright	.05
203	*Mike Kingery*	.05
204	Sammy Stewart	.05
205	Graig Nettles	.05
206	Tim Laudner, Frank Viola Twins Leaders	.05
207	George Frazier	.05
208	John Shelby	.05
209	Rick Schu	.05
210	Lloyd Moseby	.05
211	John Morris	.05
212	Mike Fitzgerald	.05
213	*Randy Myers*	.20
214	Omar Moreno	.05
215	Mark Langston	.05
216	*B.J. Surhoff* (Future Stars)	.20
217	Chris Codiroli	.05
218	Sparky Anderson	.10
219	Cecilio Guante	.05
220	Joe Carter	.05
221	Vern Ruhle	.05
222	Denny Walling	.05
223	Charlie Leibrandt	.05
224	Wayne Tolleson	.05
225	Mike Smithson	.05
226	Max Venable	.05
227	*Jamie Moyer*	.05
228	Curt Wilkerson	.05
229	*Mike Birkbeck*	.05
230	Don Baylor	.05
231	Bob Brenly, Mike Krukow Giants Leaders	.05
232	*Reggie Williams*	.05
233	*Russ Morman*	.05
234	Pat Sheridan	.05
235	Alvin Davis	.05
236	Tommy John	.10
237	Jim Morrison	.05
238	Bill Krueger	.05
239	Juan Espino	.05
240	Steve Balboni	.05
241	Danny Heep	.05
242	Rick Mahler	.05
243	Whitey Herzog	.05
244	Dickie Noles	.05
245	Willie Upshaw	.05
246	Jim Dwyer	.05
247	Jeff Reed	.05
248	Gene Walter	.05
249	Jim Pankovits	.05
250	Teddy Higuera	.05
251	Rob Wilfong	.05
252	Denny Martinez	.05
253	Eddie Milner	.05
254	*Bob Tewksbury*	.20
255	Juan Samuel	.05
256	George Brett, Frank White Royals Leaders	.15
257	Bob Forsch	.05
258	Steve Yeager	.05
259	*Mike Greenwell*	.25
260	Vida Blue	.05
261	Ruben Sierra	.05
262	Jim Winn	.05
263	Stan Javier	.05
264	Checklist 133-264	.05
265	Darrell Evans	.05
266	*Jeff Hamilton*	.05
267	Howard Johnson	.05
268	Pat Corrales	.05
269	Cliff Speck	.05
270	Jody Davis	.05
271	Mike Brown	.05
272	Andres Galarraga	.05
273	Gene Nelson	.05
274	*Jeff Hearron*	.05
275	LaMarr Hoyt	.05
276	Jackie Gutierrez	.05
277	Juan Agosto	.05
278	Gary Pettis	.05
279	*Dan Plesac*	.05
280	Jeffrey Leonard	.05
281	Bo Diaz, Bill Gullickson, Pete Rose Reds Leaders	.10
282	Jeff Calhoun	.05
283	*Doug Drabek*	.25
284	John Moses	.05
285	Dennis Boyd	.05
286	Mike Woodard	.05
287	Dave Von Ohlen	.05
288	Tito Landrum	.05
289	Bob Kipper	.05
290	Leon Durham	.05
291	Mitch Williams	.05
292	Franklin Stubbs	.05
293	Bob Rodgers	.05
294	Steve Jeltz	.05
295	Len Dykstra	.05
296	*Andres Thomas*	.05
297	Don Schulze	.05
298	Larry Herndon	.05
299	Joel Davis	.05
300	Reggie Jackson	.50
301	*Luis Aquino*	.05
302	Bill Schroeder	.05
303	Juan Berenguer	.05
304	Phil Garner	.05
305	John Franco	.05
306	Rich Gedman, John McNamara, Tom Seaver Red Sox Leaders	.10
307	*Lee Guetterman*	.05
308	Don Slaught	.05
309	Mike Young	.05
310	Frank Viola	.05
311	Rickey Henderson	.10
312	Reggie Jackson	.10
313	Roberto Clemente	.50
314	Carl Yastrzemski	.10
315	Maury Wills	.05
316	Brian Fisher	.05
317	Clint Hurdle	.05
318	Jim Fregosi	.05
319	*Greg Swindell*	.10
320	Barry Bonds	10.00
321	Mike Laga	.05
322	Chris Bando	.05
323	*Al Newman*	.05
324	Dave Palmer	.05
325	Garry Templeton	.05
326	Mark Gubicza	.05
327	*Dale Sveum*	.05
328	Bob Welch	.05
329	Ron Roenicke	.05
330	Mike Scott	.05
331	Gary Carter, Keith Hernandez, Dave Johnson, Darryl Strawberry Mets Leaders	.10
332	Joe Price	.05
333	Ken Phelps	.05
334	*Ed Correa*	.05
335	Candy Maldonado	.05
336	*Allan Anderson*	.05
337	Darrell Miller	.05
338	Tim Conroy	.05
339	Donnie Hill	.05
340	Roger Clemens	.65
341	Mike Brown	.05
342	Bob James	.05
343	Hal Lanier	.05
344a	Joe Niekro (copyright outside yellow on back)	.25
344b	Joe Niekro (copyright inside yellow on back)	.05
345	Andre Dawson	.25
346	Shawon Dunston	.05
347	Mickey Brantley	.05
348	Carmelo Martinez	.05
349	Storm Davis	.05
350	Keith Hernandez	.05
351	Gene Garber	.05
352	Mike Felder	.05
353	Ernie Camacho	.05
354	Jamie Quirk	.05
355	Don Carman	.05
356	Ed Brinkman, Julio Cruz White Sox Leaders	.05
357	*Steve Fireovid*	.05
358	Sal Butera	.05
359	Doug Corbett	.05
360	Pedro Guerrero	.05
361	Mark Thurmond	.05
362	*Luis Quinones*	.05
363	Jose Guzman	.05
364	Randy Bush	.05
365	Rick Rhoden	.05
366	Mark McGwire	3.00
367	Jeff Lahti	.05
368	John McNamara	.05
369	Brian Dayett	.05
370	Fred Lynn	.05
371	*Mark Eichhorn*	.05
372	Jerry Mumphrey	.05
373	Jeff Dedmon	.05
374	Glenn Hoffman	.05
375	Ron Guidry	.10
376	Scott Bradley	.05
377	John Henry Johnson	.05
378	Rafael Santana	.05
379	John Russell	.05
380	Rich Gossage	.05
381	Mike Fitzgerald, Bob Rodgers Expos Leaders	.05
382	Rudy Law	.05
383	Ron Davis	.05
384	Johnny Grubb	.05
385	Orel Hershiser	.05
386	Dickie Thon	.05
387	*T.R. Bryden*	.05
388	Geno Petralli	.05
389	Jeff Robinson	.05
390	Gary Matthews	.05
391	Jay Howell	.05
392	Checklist 265-396	.05
393	Pete Rose	.60
394	Mike Bielecki	.05
395	Damaso Garcia	.05
396	Tim Lollar	.05
397	Greg Walker	.05
398	Brad Havens	.05
399	Curt Ford	.05
400	George Brett	.50
401	Billy Jo Robidoux	.05
402	Mike Trujillo	.05
403	Jerry Royster	.05
404	Doug Sisk	.05
405	Brook Jacoby	.05
406	Rickey Henderson, Don Mattingly Yankees Leaders	.25
407	Jim Acker	.05
408	John Mizerock	.05
409	Milt Thompson	.05
410	Fernando Valenzuela	.05
411	Darnell Coles	.05
412	Eric Davis	.05
413	Moose Haas	.05
414	Joe Orsulak	.05
415	*Bobby Witt*	.05
416	Tom Nieto	.05
417	Pat Perry	.05
418	Dick Williams	.05
419	*Mark Portugal*	.10
420	Will Clark	.40
421	Jose DeLeon	.05
422	Jack Howell	.05
423	Jaime Cocanower	.05
424	Chris Speier	.05
425	Tom Seaver	.40
426	Floyd Rayford	.05
427	Ed Nunez	.05
428	Bruce Bochy	.05
429	*Tim Pyznarski* (Future Stars)	.05
430	Mike Schmidt	.50
431	Tom Niedenfuer, Ron Perranoski, Alex Trevino Dodgers Leaders	.05
432	Jim Slaton	.05
433	*Ed Hearn*	.05
434	Mike Fischlin	.05
435	Bruce Sutter	.35
436	*Andy Allanson*	.05
437	Ted Power	.05
438	*Kelly Downs*	.05
439	Karl Best	.05
440	Willie McGee	.05
441	*Dave Leiper*	.05
442	Mitch Webster	.05
443	John Felske	.05
444	Jeff Russell	.05
445	Dave Lopes	.05
446	*Chuck Finley*	.25
447	Bill Almon	.05
448	*Chris Bosio*	.10
449	*Pat Dodson* (Future Stars)	.05
450	Kirby Puckett	.45
451	Joe Sambito	.05
452	Dave Henderson	.05
453	*Scott Terry*	.05
454	Luis Salazar	.05
455	Mike Boddicker	.05
456	Carney Lansford, Tony LaRussa, Mickey Tettleton, Dave Von Ohlen A's Leaders	.05
457	Len Matuszek	.05
458	Kelly Gruber	.05
459	Dennis Eckersley	.35
460	Darryl Strawberry	.05
461	Craig McMurtry	.05
462	Scott Fletcher	.05
463	Tom Candiotti	.05
464	Butch Wynegar	.05
465	Todd Worrell	.05
466	Kal Daniels	.05
467	Randy St. Claire	.05
468	George Bamberger	.05
469	*Mike Diaz*	.05
470	Dave Dravecky	.05
471	Ronn Reynolds	.05
472	Bill Doran	.05
473	Steve Farr	.05
474	Jerry Narron	.05
475	Scott Garrelts	.05
476	Danny Tartabull	.05
477	Ken Howell	.05
478	Tim Laudner	.05
479	*Bob Sebra*	.05
480	Jim Rice	.15
481	Von Hayes, Juan Samuel, Glenn Wilson Phillies Leaders	.05
482	Daryl Boston	.05
483	Dwight Lowry	.05
484	Jim Traber	.05
485	Tony Fernandez	.05
486	Otis Nixon	.05
487	Dave Gumpert	.05
488	Ray Knight	.05
489	Bill Gullickson	.05
490	Dale Murphy	.20
491	*Ron Karkovice*	.05
492	Mike Heath	.05
493	Tom Lasorda	.10
494	*Barry Jones*	.05
495	Gorman Thomas	.05
496	Bruce Bochte	.05
497	*Dale Mohorcic*	.05

498 Bob Kearney .05
499 *Bruce Ruffin* .05
500 Don Mattingly .65
501 Craig Lefferts .05
502 Dick Schofield .05
503 Larry Andersen .05
504 Mickey Hatcher .05
505 Bryn Smith .05
506 Rich Bordi, Rick Dempsey, Earl Weaver Orioles Leaders .05
507 Dave Stapleton .05
508 *Scott Bankhead* .05
509 Enos Cabell .05
510 Tom Henke .05
511 Steve Lyons .05
512 *Dave Magadan* (Future Stars) .20
513 Carmen Castillo .05
514 Orlando Mercado .05
515 Willie Hernandez .05
516 Ted Simmons .05
517 Mario Soto .05
518 Gene Mauch .05
519 Curt Young .05
520 Jack Clark .05
521 Rick Reuschel .05
522 Checklist 397-528 .05
523 Earnie Riles .05
524 Bob Shirley .05
525 Phil Bradley .05
526 Roger Mason .05
527 Jim Wohlford .05
528 Ken Dixon .05
529 *Alvaro Espinoza* .05
530 Tony Gwynn .45
531 Yogi Berra, Hal Lanier, Denis Menke, Gene Tenace Astros Leaders .05
532 Jeff Stone .05
533 Argenis Salazar .05
534 Scott Sanderson .05
535 Tony Armas .05
536 *Terry Mulholland* .15
537 Rance Mulliniks .05
538 Tom Niedenfuer .05
539 Reid Nichols .05
540 Terry Kennedy .05
541 *Rafael Belliard* .05
542 Ricky Horton .05
543 Dave Johnson .05
544 Zane Smith .05
545 Buddy Bell .05
546 Mike Morgan .05
547 Rob Deer .05
548 *Bill Mooneyham* .05
549 Bob Melvin .05
550 Pete Incaviglia .05
551 Frank Wills .05
552 Larry Sheets .05
553 *Mike Maddux* .05
554 Buddy Biancalana .05
555 Dennis Rasmussen .05
556 Bob Boone, Marcel Lachemann, Mike Witt Angels Leaders .05
557 *John Cerutti* .05
558 Greg Gagne .05
559 Lance McCullers .05
560 Glenn Davis .05
561 *Rey Quinones* .05
562 *Bryan Clutterbuck* .05
563 John Stefero .05
564 Larry McWilliams .05
565 Dusty Baker .05
566 Tim Hulett .05
567 *Greg Mathews* .05
568 Earl Weaver .10
569 Wade Rowdon .05
570 Sid Fernandez .05
571 Ozzie Virgil .05
572 Pete Ladd .05
573 Hal McRae .05
574 Manny Lee .05
575 Pat Tabler .05
576 Frank Pastore .05
577 Dann Bilardello .05
578 Billy Hatcher .05
579 Rick Burleson .05
580 Mike Krukow .05
581 Ron Cey, Steve Trout Cubs Leaders .05
582 Bruce Berenyi .05
583 Junior Ortiz .05
584 Ron Kittle .05
585 *Scott Bailes* .05
586 Ben Oglivie .05
587 Eric Plunk .05
588 Wallace Johnson .05
589 Steve Crawford .05
590 Vince Coleman .05
591 Spike Owen .05
592 Chris Welsh .05
593 Chuck Tanner .05
594 Rick Anderson .05
595 Keith Hernandez .05
596 Steve Sax .05
597 Mike Schmidt .35
598 Ozzie Smith .30
599 Tony Gwynn .30
600 Dave Parker .05
601 Darryl Strawberry .05
602 Gary Carter .25
603a Dwight Gooden .25
603b Dwight Gooden .05
604 Fernando Valenzuela .05
605 Todd Worrell .05
606a Don Mattingly .75
606b Don Mattingly .35
607 Tony Bernazard .05
608 Wade Boggs .30
609 Cal Ripken, Jr. .45
610 Jim Rice .05
611 Kirby Puckett .30
612 George Bell .05
613 Lance Parrish .05
614 Roger Clemens .35
615 Teddy Higuera .05
616 Dave Righetti .05
617 Al Nipper .05
618 Tom Kelly .05
619 Jerry Reed .05
620 Jose Canseco .60
621 Danny Cox .05
622 *Glenn Braggs* .05
623 *Kurt Stillwell* .05
624 Tim Burke .05
625 Mookie Wilson .05
626 Joel Skinner .05
627 Ken Oberkfell .05
628 Bob Walk .05
629 Larry Parrish .05
630 John Candelaria .05
631 Sparky Anderson, Mike Heath, Willie Hernandez Tigers Leaders .05
632 Rob Woodward .05
633 Jose Uribe .05
634 *Rafael Palmeiro* 2.00
635 Ken Schrom .05
636 Darren Daulton .05
637 *Bip Roberts* .10
638 Rich Bordi .05
639 Gerald Perry .05
640 Mark Clear .05
641 Domingo Ramos .05
642 Al Pulido .05
643 Ron Shepherd .05
644 John Denny .05
645 Dwight Evans .05
646 Mike Mason .05
647 Tom Lawless .05
648 *Barry Larkin* .60
649 Mickey Tettleton .05
650 Hubie Brooks .05
651 Benny Distefano .05
652 Terry Forster .05
653 Kevin Mitchell .05
654 Checklist 529-660 .05
655 Jesse Barfield .05
656 Bobby Valentine, Rickey Wright Rangers Leaders .05
657 Tom Waddell .05
658 *Robby Thompson* .05
659 Aurelio Lopez .05
660 Bob Horner .05
661 Lou Whitaker .05
662 Frank DiPino .05
663 Cliff Johnson .05
664 Mike Marshall .05
665 Rod Scurry .05
666 Von Hayes .05
667 Ron Hassey .05
668 Juan Bonilla .05
669 Bud Black .05
670 Jose Cruz .05
671a Ray Soff (no "D*" before copyright line) .20
671b Ray Soff ("D*" before copyright line) .05
672 Chili Davis .05
673 Don Sutton .35
674 Bill Campbell .05
675 Ed Romero .05
676 Charlie Moore .05
677 Bob Grich .05
678 Carney Lansford .05
679 Kent Hrbek .05
680 Ryne Sandberg .45
681 George Bell .05
682 Jerry Reuss .05
683 Gary Roenicke .05
684 Kent Tekulve .05
685 Jerry Hairston Sr. .05
686 Doyle Alexander .05
687 Alan Trammell .05
688 Juan Beniquez .05
689 Darrell Porter .05
690 Dane Iorg .05
691 Dave Parker .05
692 Frank White .05
693 Terry Puhl .05
694 Phil Niekro .35
695 Chico Walker .05
696 Gary Lucas .05
697 Ed Lynch .05
698 Ernie Whitt .05
699 Ken Landreaux .05
700 Dave Bergman .05
701 Willie Randolph .05
702 Greg Gross .05
703 Dave Schmidt .05
704 Jesse Orosco .05
705 Bruce Hurst .05
706 Rick Manning .05
707 Bob McClure .05
708 Scott McGregor .05
709 Dave Kingman .05
710 Gary Gaetti .05
711 Ken Griffey .05
712 Don Robinson .05
713 Tom Brookens .05
714 Dan Quisenberry .05
715 Bob Dernier .05
716 Rick Leach .05
717 Ed Vande Berg .05
718 Steve Carlton .40
719 Tom Hume .05
720 Richard Dotson .05
721 Tom Herr .05
722 Bob Knepper .05
723 Brett Butler .05
724 Greg Minton .05
725 George Hendrick .05
726 Frank Tanana .05
727 Mike Moore .05
728 Tippy Martinez .05
729 Tom Paciorek .05
730 Eric Show .05
731 Dave Concepcion .05
732 Manny Trillo .05
733 Bill Caudill .05
734 Bill Madlock .05
735 Rickey Henderson .40
736 Steve Bedrosian .05
737 Floyd Bannister .05
738 Jorge Orta .05
739 Chet Lemon .05
740 Rich Gedman .05
741 Paul Molitor .40
742 Andy McGaffigan .05
743 Dwayne Murphy .05
744 Roy Smalley .05
745 Glenn Hubbard .05
746 Bob Ojeda .05
747 Johnny Ray .05
748 Mike Flanagan .05
749 Ozzie Smith .45
750 Steve Trout .05
751 Garth Iorg .05
752 Dan Petry .05
753 Rick Honeycutt .05
754 Dave LaPoint .05
755 Luis Aguayo .05
756 Carlton Fisk .40
757 Nolan Ryan .75
758 Tony Bernazard .05
759 Joel Youngblood .05
760 Mike Witt .05
761 Greg Pryor .05
762 Gary Ward .05
763 Tim Flannery .05
764 Bill Buckner .05
765 Kirk Gibson .05
766 Don Aase .05
767 Ron Cey .05
768 Dennis Lamp .05
769 Steve Sax .05
770 Dave Winfield .40
771 Shane Rawley .05
772 Harold Baines .05
773 Robin Yount .40
774 Wayne Krenchicki .05
775 Joaquin Andujar .05
776 Tom Brunansky .05
777 Chris Chambliss .05
778 Jack Morris .05
779 Craig Reynolds .05
780 Andre Thornton .05
781 Atlee Hammaker .05
782 Brian Downing .05
783 Willie Wilson .05
784 Cal Ripken, Jr. .75
785 Terry Francona .05
786 Jimy Williams .05
787 Alejandro Pena .05
788 Tim Stoddard .05
789 Dan Schatzeder .05
790 Julio Cruz .05
791 Lance Parrish .05
792 Checklist 661-792 .05

Tiffany

NM/M

Unopened Set (792): 100.00
Complete Set (792): 60.00
Common Player: .15
320 Barry Bonds 45.00
(Star cards valued at 4X corresponding cards in regular 1987 Topps)

Traded

NM/M

Complete Set (132): 4.00
Common Player: .05
1 Bill Almon .05
2 Scott Bankhead .05
3 Eric Bell .05
4 Juan Beniquez .05
5 Juan Berenguer .05
6 Greg Booker .05
7 Thad Bosley .05
8 Larry Bowa .05
9 Greg Brock .05
10 Bob Brower .05
11 Jerry Browne .05
12 Ralph Bryant .05
13 DeWayne Buice .05
14 *Ellis Burks* .50
15 Ivan Calderon .05
16 Jeff Calhoun .05
17 Casey Candaele .05
18 John Cangelosi .05
19 Steve Carlton .25
20 Juan Castillo .05
21 Rick Cerone .05
22 Ron Cey .05
23 John Christensen .05
24 Dave Cone .15
25 Chuck Crim .05
26 Storm Davis .05
27 Andre Dawson .25
28 Rick Dempsey .05
29 Doug Drabek .05
30 Mike Dunne .05
31 Dennis Eckersley .25
32 Lee Elia .05
33 Brian Fisher .05
34 Terry Francona .05
35 Willie Fraser .05
36 Billy Gardner .05
37 Ken Gerhart .05
38 Danny Gladden .05
39 Jim Gott .05
40 Cecilio Guante .05
41 Albert Hall .05
42 Terry Harper .05
43 Mickey Hatcher .05
44 Brad Havens .05
45 Neal Heaton .05
46 *Mike Henneman* .20
47 Donnie Hill .05
48 Guy Hoffman .05
49 Brian Holton .05
50 Charles Hudson .05

51	Danny Jackson	.05
52	Reggie Jackson	.40
53	Chris James	.05
54	Dion James	.05
55	Stan Jefferson	.05
56	Joe Johnson	.05
57	Terry Kennedy	.05
58	Mike Kingery	.05
59	Ray Knight	.05
60	Gene Larkin	.05
61	Mike LaValliere	.05
62	Jack Lazorko	.05
63	Terry Leach	.05
64	Tim Leary	.05
65	Jim Lindeman	.05
66	Steve Lombardozzi	.05
67	Bill Long	.05
68	Barry Lyons	.05
69	*Shane Mack*	.05
70	*Greg Maddux*	3.00
71	Bill Madlock	.05
72	Joe Magrane	.05
73	Dave Martinez	.05
74	Fred McGriff	.25
75	Mark McLemore	.05
76	Kevin McReynolds	.05
77	Dave Meads	.05
78	Eddie Milner	.05
79	Greg Minton	.05
80	John Mitchell	.05
81	Kevin Mitchell	.05
82	Charlie Moore	.05
83	Jeff Musselman	.05
84	Gene Nelson	.05
85	Graig Nettles	.05
86	Al Newman	.05
87	Reid Nichols	.05
88	Tom Niedenfuer	.05
89	Joe Niekro	.05
90	Tom Nieto	.05
91	*Matt Nokes*	.10
92	Dickie Noles	.05
93	Pat Pacillo	.05
94	Lance Parrish	.05
95	Tony Pena	.05
96	Luis Polonia	.05
97	Randy Ready	.05
98	Jeff Reardon	.05
99	Gary Redus	.05
100	Jeff Reed	.05
101	Rick Rhoden	.05
102	Cal Ripken, Sr.	.05
103	Wally Ritchie	.05
104	Jeff Robinson	.05
105	Gary Roenicke	.05
106	Jerry Royster	.05
107	Mark Salas	.05
108	Luis Salazar	.05
109	Benny Santiago	.15
110	Dave Schmidt	.05
111	Kevin Seitzer	.05
112	John Shelby	.05
113	Steve Shields	.05
114	*John Smiley*	.20
115	Chris Speier	.05
116	Mike Stanley	.05
117	Terry Steinbach	.15
118	Les Straker	.05
119	Jim Sundberg	.05
120	Danny Tartabull	.05
121	Tom Trebelhorn	.05
122	Dave Valle	.05
123	Ed Vande Berg	.05
124	Andy Van Slyke	.05
125	Gary Ward	.05
126	Alan Wiggins	.05
127	Bill Wilkinson	.05
128	Frank Williams	.05
129	*Matt Williams*	.75
130	Jim Winn	.05
131	Matt Young	.05
132	Checklist 1T-132T	.05

Traded Tiffany

	NM/M
Complete Set (132):	30.00
Common Player:	.15

(Star cards valued at 2X corresponding cards in regular Topps Traded)

1988 TOPPS

	NM/M
Unopened Factory Set, Retail (792):	17.50
Unopened Factory Set, Hobby (792):	16.00
Complete Set (792):	12.50
Common Player:	.05
Wax Pack (15):	.40

Wax Box (36):	15.00
Cello Pack (28):	.70
Cello Box (24):	13.50
Rack Pack (43):	.75
Rack Box (24):	15.00
Vending Box (500):	7.50

1	Vince Coleman	.05
2	Don Mattingly	.25
3a	Mark McGwire	1.00
3b	Mark McGwire	.40
4a	Eddie Murray	.25
4b	Eddie Murray	.20
5	Joe Niekro, Phil Niekro	.05
6	Nolan Ryan	.40
7	Benito Santiago	.05
8	Kevin Elster (Future Stars)	.05
9	Andy Hawkins	.05
10	Ryne Sandberg	.50
11	Mike Young	.05
12	Bill Schroeder	.05
13	Andres Thomas	.05
14	Sparky Anderson	.10
15	Chili Davis	.05
16	Kirk McCaskill	.05
17	Ron Oester	.05
18a	*Al Leiter* (actually Steve George Future Stars, no "NY" on shirt, photo)	.40
18b	*Al Leiter* (photo Future Stars, "NY" on shirt, correct)	.20
19	*Mark Davidson*	.05
20	Kevin Gross	.05
21	Wade Boggs, Spike Owen Red Sox Leaders	.10
22	Greg Swindell	.05
23	Ken Landreaux	.05
24	Jim Deshaies	.05
25	Andres Galarraga	.05
26	Mitch Williams	.05
27	R.J. Reynolds	.05
28	*Jose Nunez*	.05
29	Argenis Salazar	.05
30	Sid Fernandez	.05
31	Bruce Bochy	.05
32	Mike Morgan	.05
33	Rob Deer	.05
34	Ricky Horton	.05
35	Harold Baines	.05
36	Jamie Moyer	.05
37	Ed Romero	.05
38	Jeff Calhoun	.05
39	Gerald Perry	.05
40	Orel Hershiser	.05
41	Bob Melvin	.05
42	*Bill Landrum*	.05
43	Dick Schofield	.05
44	Lou Piniella	.05
45	Kent Hrbek	.05
46	Darnell Coles	.05
47	Joaquin Andujar	.05
48	Alan Ashby	.05
49	Dave Clark	.05
50	Hubie Brooks	.05
51	Eddie Murray, Cal Ripken, Jr. Orioles Leaders	.25
52	Don Robinson	.05
53	Curt Wilkerson	.05
54	Jim Clancy	.05
55	Phil Bradley	.05
56	Ed Hearn	.05
57	*Tim Crews*	.05
58	Dave Magadan	.05
59	Danny Cox	.05
60	Rickey Henderson	.40
61	*Mark Knudson*	.05
62	Jeff Hamilton	.05
63	Jimmy Jones	.05
64	*Ken Caminiti*	.25
65	Leon Durham	.05
66	Shane Rawley	.05
67	Ken Oberkfell	.05
68	Dave Dravecky	.05
69	*Mike Hart*	.05
70	Roger Clemens	.60
71	Gary Pettis	.05
72	Dennis Eckersley	.30
73	Randy Bush	.05
74	Tom Lasorda	.05
75	Joe Carter	.05
76	Denny Martinez	.05
77	Tom O'Malley	.05
78	Dan Petry	.05
79	Ernie Whitt	.05
80	Mark Langston	.05
81	John Franco, Ron Robinson Reds Leaders	.05
82	*Darrel Akerfelds*	.05
83	Jose Oquendo	.05
84	Cecilio Guante	.05
85	Howard Johnson	.05
86	Ron Karkovice	.05
87	Mike Mason	.05
88	Earnie Riles	.05
89	*Gary Thurman*	.05
90	Dale Murphy	.20
91	*Joey Cora*	.10
92	Len Matuszek	.05
93	Bob Sebra	.05
94	*Chuck Jackson*	.05
95	Lance Parrish	.05
96	*Todd Benzinger*	.05
97	Scott Garrelts	.05
98	*Rene Gonzales*	.05
99	Chuck Finley	.05
100	Jack Clark	.05
101	Allan Anderson	.05
102	Barry Larkin	.05
103	Curt Young	.05
104	Dick Williams	.05
105	Jesse Orosco	.05
106	*Jim Walewander*	.05
107	Scott Bailes	.05
108	Steve Lyons	.05
109	Joel Skinner	.05
110	Teddy Higuera	.05
111	Hubie Brooks, Vance Law Expos Leaders	.05
112	*Les Lancaster*	.05
113	Kelly Gruber	.05
114	Jeff Russell	.05
115	Johnny Ray	.05
116	Jerry Don Gleaton	.05
117	*James Steels*	.05
118	Bob Welch	.05
119	*Robbie Wine*	.05
120	Kirby Puckett	.50
121	Checklist 1-132	.05
122	Tony Bernazard	.05
123	Tom Candiotti	.05
124	Ray Knight	.05
125	Bruce Hurst	.05
126	Steve Jeltz	.05
127	Jim Gott	.05
128	Johnny Grubb	.05
129	Greg Minton	.05
130	Buddy Bell	.05
131	Don Schulze	.05
132	Donnie Hill	.05
133	Greg Mathews	.05
134	Chuck Tanner	.05
135	Dennis Rasmussen	.05
136	Brian Dayett	.05
137	Chris Bosio	.05
138	Mitch Webster	.05
139	Jerry Browne	.05
140	Jesse Barfield	.05
141	George Brett, Bret Saberhagen Royals Leaders	.20
142	Andy Van Slyke	.05
143	Mickey Tettleton	.05
144	*Don Gordon*	.05
145	Bill Madlock	.05
146	*Donell Nixon*	.05
147	Bill Buckner	.05
148	Carmelo Martinez	.05
149	Ken Howell	.05
150	Eric Davis	.05
151	Bob Knepper	.05
152	*Jody Reed*	.10
153	John Habyan	.05
154	Jeff Stone	.05
155	Bruce Sutter	.30
156	Gary Matthews	.05
157	Atlee Hammaker	.05
158	Tim Hulett	.05
159	*Brad Arnsberg*	.05
160	Willie McGee	.05
161	Bryn Smith	.05
162	Mark McLemore	.05
163	Dale Mohorcic	.05
164	Dave Johnson	.05
165	Robin Yount	.40
166	*Rick Rodriguez*	.05
167	Rance Mulliniks	.05
168	Barry Jones	.05
169	*Ross Jones*	.05
170	Rich Gossage	.05
171	Shawon Dunston, Manny Trillo Cubs Leaders	.05
172	*Lloyd McClendon*	.05
173	Eric Plunk	.05
174	Phil Garner	.05
175	Kevin Bass	.05
176	Jeff Reed	.05
177	Frank Tanana	.05
178	Dwayne Henry	.05
179	Charlie Puleo	.05
180	Terry Kennedy	.05
181	Dave Cone	.05
182	Ken Phelps	.05
183	Tom Lawless	.05
184	Ivan Calderon	.05
185	Rick Rhoden	.05
186	Rafael Palmeiro	.35
187	Steve Kiefer	.05
188	John Russell	.05
189	*Wes Gardner*	.05
190	Candy Maldonado	.05
191	John Cerutti	.05
192	Devon White	.05
193	Brian Fisher	.05
194	Tom Kelly	.05
195	Dan Quisenberry	.05
196	Dave Engle	.05
197	Lance McCullers	.05
198	Franklin Stubbs	.05
199	*Dave Meads*	.05
200	Wade Boggs	.50
201	Steve Buechele, Pete Incaviglia, Pete O'Brien, Bobby Valentine Rangers Leaders	.05
202	Glenn Hoffman	.05
203	Fred Toliver	.05
204	Paul O'Neill	.05
205	*Nelson Liriano*	.05
206	Domingo Ramos	.05
207	*John Mitchell*	.05
208	Steve Lake	.05
209	Richard Dotson	.05
210	Willie Randolph	.05
211	Frank DiPino	.05
212	Greg Brock	.05
213	Albert Hall	.05
214	Dave Schmidt	.05
215	Von Hayes	.05
216	Jerry Reuss	.05
217	Harry Spilman	.05
218	Dan Schatzeder	.05
219	Mike Stanley	.05
220	Tom Henke	.05
221	Rafael Belliard	.05
222	Steve Farr	.05
223	Stan Jefferson	.05
224	Tom Trebelhorn	.05
225	Mike Scioscia	.05
226	Dave Lopes	.05
227	Ed Correa	.05
228	Wallace Johnson	.05
229	Jeff Musselman	.05
230	Pat Tabler	.05
231	Barry Bonds, Bobby Bonilla Pirates Leaders	.50
232	Bob James	.05
233	Rafael Santana	.05
234	Ken Dayley	.05
235	Gary Ward	.05
236	Ted Power	.05
237	Mike Heath	.05
238	*Luis Polonia*	.10
239	Roy Smalley	.05
240	Lee Smith	.05
241	Damaso Garcia	.05
242	Tom Niedenfuer	.05
243	Mark Ryal	.05
244	Jeff Robinson	.05
245	Rich Gedman	.05
246	*Mike Campbell* (Future Stars)	.05
247	Thad Bosley	.05
248	Storm Davis	.05
249	Mike Marshall	.05
250	Nolan Ryan	.75

251 Tom Foley .05
252 Bob Brower .05
253 Checklist 133-264 .05
254 Lee Elia .05
255 Mookie Wilson .05
256 Ken Schrom .05
257 Jerry Royster .05
258 Ed Nunez .05
259 Ron Kittle .05
260 Vince Coleman .05
261 Will Clark, Candy Maldonado, Kevin Mitchell, Robby Thompson, Jose Uribe Giants Leaders .05
262 Drew Hall .05
263 Glenn Braggs .05
264 *Les Straker* .05
265 Bo Diaz .05
266 Paul Assenmacher .05
267 *Billy Bean* .05
268 Bruce Ruffin .05
269 Ellis Burks .05
270 Mike Witt .05
271 Ken Gerhart .05
272 Steve Ontiveros .05
273 Garth Iorg .05
274 Junior Ortiz .05
275 Kevin Seitzer .05
276 Luis Salazar .05
277 Alejandro Pena .05
278 Jose Cruz .05
279 Randy St. Claire .05
280 Pete Incaviglia .05
281 Jerry Hairston Sr. .05
282 Pat Perry .05
283 Phil Lombardi .05
284 Larry Bowa .05
285 Jim Presley .05
286 *Chuck Crim* .05
287 Manny Trillo .05
288 *Pat Pacillo* .05
289 Dave Bergman .05
290 Tony Fernandez .05
291 Kevin Bass, Billy Hatcher Astros Leaders .05
292 Carney Lansford .05
293 *Doug Jones* .05
294 *Al Pedrique* .05
295 Bert Blyleven .05
296 Floyd Rayford .05
297 Zane Smith .05
298 Milt Thompson .05
299 Steve Crawford .05
300 Don Mattingly .60
301 Bud Black .05
302 Jose Uribe .05
303 Eric Show .05
304 George Hendrick .05
305 Steve Sax .05
306 Billy Hatcher .05
307 Mike Trujillo .05
308 Lee Mazzilli .05
309 *Bill Long* .05
310 Tom Herr .05
311 Scott Sanderson .05
312 Joey Meyer (Future Stars) .05
313 Bob McClure .05
314 Jimy Williams .05
315 Dave Parker .05
316 Jose Rijo .05
317 Tom Nieto .05
318 Mel Hall .05
319 Mike Loynd .05
320 Alan Trammell .05
321 Harold Baines, Carlton Fisk White Sox Leaders .05
322 *Vicente Palacios* .05
323 Rick Leach .05
324 Danny Jackson .05
325 Glenn Hubbard .05
326 Al Nipper .05
327 Larry Sheets .05
328 *Greg Cadaret* .05
329 Chris Speier .05
330 Eddie Whitson .05
331 Brian Downing .05
332 Jerry Reed .05
333 Wally Backman .05
334 Dave LaPoint .05
335 Claudell Washington .05
336 Ed Lynch .05
337 Jim Gantner .05
338 Brian Holton .05
339 Kurt Stillwell .05
340 Jack Morris .05
341 Carmen Castillo .05
342 Larry Andersen .05
343 Greg Gagne .05
344 Tony LaRussa .05
345 Scott Fletcher .05
346 Vance Law .05
347 Joe Johnson .05
348 Jim Eisenreich .05
349 Bob Walk .05
350 Will Clark .05
351 Tony Pena, Red Schoendienst Cardinals Leaders .05
352 *Billy Ripken* .05
353 Ed Olwine .05
354 Marc Sullivan .05
355 Roger McDowell .05
356 Luis Aguayo .05
357 Floyd Bannister .05
358 Rey Quinones .05
359 Tim Stoddard .05
360 Tony Gwynn .50
361 Greg Maddux .50
362 Juan Castillo .05
363 Willie Fraser .05
364 Nick Esasky .05
365 Floyd Youmans .05
366 Chet Lemon .05
367 Tim Leary .05
368 *Gerald Young* .05
369 Greg Harris .05
370 Jose Canseco .25
371 Joe Hesketh .05
372 Matt Williams .05
373 Checklist 265-396 .05
374 Doc Edwards .05
375 Tom Brunansky .05
376 *Bill Wilkinson* .05
377 *Sam Horn* .05
378 *Todd Frohwirth* .05
379 Rafael Ramirez .05
380 *Joe Magrane* .05
381 Jack Howell, Wally Joyner Angels Leaders .05
382 *Keith Miller* .05
383 Eric Bell .05
384 Neil Allen .05
385 Carlton Fisk .40
386 Don Mattingly (All-Star) .30
387 Willie Randolph (All-Star) .05
388 Wade Boggs (All-Star) .20
389 Alan Trammell (All-Star) .05
390 George Bell (All-Star) .05
391 Kirby Puckett (All-Star) .25
392 Dave Winfield (All-Star) .20
393 Matt Nokes (All-Star) .05
394 Roger Clemens (All-Star) .35
395 Jimmy Key (All-Star) .05
396 Tom Henke (All-Star) .05
397 Jack Clark (All-Star) .05
398 Juan Samuel (All-Star) .05
399 Tim Wallach (All-Star) .05
400 Ozzie Smith (All-Star) .25
401 Andre Dawson (All-Star) .15
402 Tony Gwynn (All-Star) .25
403 Tim Raines (All-Star) .05
404 Benny Santiago (All-Star) .05
405 Dwight Gooden (All-Star) .05
406 Shane Rawley (All-Star) .05
407 Steve Bedrosian (All-Star) .05
408 Dion James .05
409 Joel McKeon .05
410 Tony Pena .05
411 Wayne Tolleson .05
412 Randy Myers .05
413 John Christensen .05
414 John McNamara .05
415 Don Carman .05
416 Keith Moreland .05
417 *Mark Ciardi* .05
418 Joel Youngblood .05
419 Scott McGregor .05
420 Wally Joyner .05
421 Ed Vande Berg .05
422 Dave Concepcion .05
423 John Smiley .05
424 Dwayne Murphy .05
425 Jeff Reardon .05
426 Randy Ready .05
427 *Paul Kilgus* .05
428 John Shelby .05
429 Kirk Gibson, Alan Trammell Tigers Leaders .05
430 Glenn Davis .05
431 Casey Candaele .05
432 Mike Moore .05
433 *Bill Pecota* .05
434 Rick Aguilera .05
435 Mike Pagliarulo .05
436 Mike Bielecki .05
437 *Fred Manrique* .05
438 *Rob Ducey* .05
439 Dave Martinez .05
440 Steve Bedrosian .05
441 Rick Manning .05
442 *Tom Bolton* .05
443 Ken Griffey .05
444 Cal Ripken, Sr. .05
445 Mike Krukow .05
446 Doug DeCinces .05
447 *Jeff Montgomery* .20
448 Mike Davis .05
449 *Jeff Robinson* .05
450 Barry Bonds .75
451 Keith Atherton .05
452 Willie Wilson .05
453 Dennis Powell .05
454 Marvell Wynne .05
455 *Shawn Hillegas* .05
456 Dave Anderson .05
457 Terry Leach .05
458 Ron Hassey .05
459 Willie Randolph, Dave Winfield Yankees Leaders .05
460 Ozzie Smith .50
461 Danny Darwin .05
462 Don Slaught .05
463 Fred McGriff .05
464 Jay Tibbs .05
465 Paul Molitor .40
466 Jerry Mumphrey .05
467 Don Aase .05
468 Darren Daulton .05
469 Jeff Dedmon .05
470 Dwight Evans .05
471 Donnie Moore .05
472 Robby Thompson .05
473 Joe Niekro .05
474 Tom Brookens .05
475 Pete Rose .65
476 Dave Stewart .05
477 Jamie Quirk .05
478 Sid Bream .05
479 Brett Butler .05
480 Dwight Gooden .05
481 Mariano Duncan .05
482 Mark Davis .05
483 *Rod Booker* .05
484 Pat Clements .05
485 Harold Reynolds .05
486 *Pat Keedy* .05
487 Jim Pankovits .05
488 Andy McGaffigan .05
489 Pedro Guerrero, Fernando Valenzuela Dodgers Leaders .05
490 Larry Parrish .05
491 B.J. Surhoff .05
492 Doyle Alexander .05
493 Mike Greenwell .05
494 *Wally Ritchie* .05
495 Eddie Murray .40
496 Guy Hoffman .05
497 Kevin Mitchell .05
498 Bob Boone .05
499 Eric King .05
500 Andre Dawson .25
501 Tim Birtsas .05
502 Danny Gladden .05
503 *Junior Noboa* .05
504 Bob Rodgers .05
505 Willie Upshaw .05
506 John Cangelosi .05
507 Mark Gubicza .05
508 Tim Teufel .05
509 Bill Dawley .05
510 Dave Winfield .40
511 Joel Davis .05
512 Alex Trevino .05
513 Tim Flannery .05
514 Pat Sheridan .05
515 Juan Nieves .05
516 Jim Sundberg .05
517 Ron Robinson .05
518 Greg Gross .05
519 Phil Bradley, Harold Reynolds Mariners Leaders .05
520 Dave Smith .05
521 Jim Dwyer .05
522 *Bob Patterson* .05
523 Gary Roenicke .05
524 Gary Lucas .05
525 Marty Barrett .05
526 Juan Berenguer .05
527 Steve Henderson .05
528a Checklist 397-528 (#455 is Steve Carlton) .05
528b Checklist 397-528 (#455 is Shawn Hillegas) .05
529 Tim Burke .05
530 Gary Carter .40
531 Rich Yett .05
532 Mike Kingery .05
533 *John Farrell* .05
534 John Wathan .05
535 Ron Guidry .05
536 John Morris .05
537 Steve Buechele .05
538 Bill Wegman .05
539 Mike LaValliere .05
540 Bret Saberhagen .05
541 Juan Beniquez .05
542 *Paul Noce* .05
543 Kent Tekulve .05
544 Jim Traber .05
545 Don Baylor .05
546 John Candelaria .05
547 *Felix Fermin* .05
548 Shane Mack .05
549 Ken Griffey, Dion James, Dale Murphy, Gerald Perry Braves Leaders .05
550 Pedro Guerrero .05
551 Terry Steinbach .05
552 Mark Thurmond .05
553 Tracy Jones .05
554 Mike Smithson .05
555 Brook Jacoby .05
556 *Stan Clarke* .05
557 Craig Reynolds .05
558 Bob Ojeda .05
559 *Ken Williams* .05
560 Tim Wallach .05
561 Rick Cerone .05
562 Jim Lindeman .05
563 Jose Guzman .05
564 Frank Lucchesi .05
565 Lloyd Moseby .05
566 *Charlie O'Brien* .05
567 Mike Diaz .05
568 Chris Brown .05
569 Charlie Leibrandt .05
570 Jeffrey Leonard .05
571 *Mark Williamson* .05
572 Chris James .05
573 Bob Stanley .05
574 Graig Nettles .05
575 Don Sutton .30
576 *Tommy Hinzo* .05
577 Tom Browning .05
578 Gary Gaetti .05
579 Gary Carter, Kevin McReynolds Mets Leaders .05
580 Mark McGwire .65
581 Tito Landrum .05
582 Mike Henneman .05
583 Dave Valle .05
584 Steve Trout .05
585 Ozzie Guillen .05
586 Bob Forsch .05
587 Terry Puhl .05
588 *Jeff Parrett* .05
589 Geno Petralli .05
590 George Bell .05
591 Doug Drabek .05
592 Dale Sveum .05
593 Bob Tewksbury .05
594 Bobby Valentine .05
595 Frank White .05
596 John Kruk .05
597 Gene Garber .05
598 Lee Lacy .05
599 Calvin Schiraldi .05
600 Mike Schmidt .60
601 Jack Lazorko .05
602 Mike Aldrete .05
603 Rob Murphy .05
604 Chris Bando .05
605 Kirk Gibson .05
606 Moose Haas .05
607 Mickey Hatcher .05
608 Charlie Kerfeld .05
609 Gary Gaetti, Kent Hrbek Twins Leaders .05
610 Keith Hernandez .05
611 Tommy John .05
612 Curt Ford .05
613 Bobby Thigpen .05
614 Herm Winningham .05
615 Jody Davis .05
616 *Jay Aldrich* .05
617 Oddibe McDowell .05
618 Cecil Fielder .05
619 *Mike Dunne* .05
620 Cory Snyder .05
621 Gene Nelson .05
622 Kal Daniels .05

623 Mike Flanagan .05
624 Jim Leyland .05
625 Frank Viola .05
626 Glenn Wilson .05
627 *Joe Boever* .05
628 Dave Henderson .05
629 Kelly Downs .05
630 Darrell Evans .05
631 Jack Howell .05
632 *Steve Shields* .05
633 *Barry Lyons* .05
634 Jose DeLeon .05
635 Terry Pendleton .05
636 Charles Hudson .05
637 *Jay Bell* .25
638 Steve Balboni .05
639 Glenn Braggs, Tony Muser Brewers Leaders .05
640 Garry Templeton .05
641 Rick Honeycutt .05
642 Bob Dernier .05
643 *Rocky Childress* .05
644 Terry McGriff .05
645 Matt Nokes .05
646 Checklist 529-660 .05
647 Pascual Perez .05
648 Al Newman .05
649 *DeWayne Buice* .05
650 Cal Ripken, Jr. .75
651 *Mike Jackson* .05
652 Bruce Benedict .05
653 Jeff Sellers .05
654 Roger Craig .05
655 Len Dykstra .05
656 Lee Guetterman .05
657 Gary Redus .05
658 Tim Conroy .05
659 Bobby Meacham .05
660 Rick Reuschel .05
661 Nolan Ryan (Turn Back the Clock) .35
662 Jim Rice (Turn Back the Clock) .05
663 Ron Blomberg (Turn Back the Clock) .05
664 Bob Gibson (Turn Back the Clock) .10
665 Stan Musial (Turn Back the Clock) .20
666 Mario Soto .05
667 Luis Quinones .05
668 Walt Terrell .05
669 Lance Parrish, Mike Ryan Phillies Leaders .05
670 Dan Plesac .05
671 Tim Laudner .05
672 *John Davis* .05
673 Tony Phillips .05
674 Mike Fitzgerald .05
675 Jim Rice .20
676 Ken Dixon .05
677 Eddie Milner .05
678 Jim Acker .05
679 Darrell Miller .05
680 Charlie Hough .05
681 Bobby Bonilla .05
682 Jimmy Key .05
683 Julio Franco .05
684 Hal Lanier .05
685 Ron Darling .05
686 Terry Francona .05
687 Mickey Brantley .05
688 Jim Winn .05
689 *Tom Pagnozzi* .05
690 Jay Howell .05
691 Dan Pasqua .05
692 Mike Birkbeck .05
693 Benny Santiago .05
694 *Eric Nolte* .05
695 Shawon Dunston .05
696 Duane Ward .05
697 Steve Lombardozzi .05
698 Brad Havens .05
699 Tony Gwynn, Benny Santiago Padres Leaders .15
700 George Brett .60
701 Sammy Stewart .05
702 Mike Gallego .05
703 Bob Brenly .05
704 Dennis Boyd .05
705 Juan Samuel .05
706 Rick Mahler .05
707 Fred Lynn .05
708 Gus Polidor .05
709 George Frazier .05
710 Darryl Strawberry .05
711 Bill Gullickson .05
712 John Moses .05
713 Willie Hernandez .05
714 Jim Fregosi .05
715 Todd Worrell .05
716 Lenn Sakata .05
717 Jay Baller .05
718 Mike Felder .05
719 Denny Walling .05
720 Tim Raines .05
721 Pete O'Brien .05
722 Manny Lee .05
723 Bob Kipper .05
724 Danny Tartabull .05
725 Mike Boddicker .05
726 Alfredo Griffin .05
727 Greg Booker .05
728 Andy Allanson .05
729 George Bell, Fred McGriff Blue Jays Leaders .05
730 John Franco .05
731 Rick Schu .05
732 Dave Palmer .05
733 Spike Owen .05
734 Craig Lefferts .05
735 Kevin McReynolds .05
736 Matt Young .05
737 Butch Wynegar .05
738 Scott Bankhead .05
739 Daryl Boston .05
740 Rick Sutcliffe .05
741 Mike Easler .05
742 Mark Clear .05
743 Larry Herndon .05
744 Whitey Herzog .05
745 Bill Doran .05
746 *Gene Larkin* .05
747 Bobby Witt .05
748 Reid Nichols .05
749 Mark Eichhorn .05
750 Bo Jackson .10
751 Jim Morrison .05
752 Mark Grant .05
753 Danny Heep .05
754 Mike LaCoss .05
755 Ozzie Virgil .05
756 Mike Maddux .05
757 *John Marzano* .05
758 *Eddie Williams* .05
759 Jose Canseco, Mark McGwire A's Leaders .35
760 Mike Scott .05
761 Tony Armas .05
762 Scott Bradley .05
763 Doug Sisk .05
764 Greg Walker .05
765 Neal Heaton .05
766 Henry Cotto .05
767 *Jose Lind* (Future Stars) .10
768 Dickie Noles .05
769 Cecil Cooper .05
770 Lou Whitaker .05
771 Ruben Sierra .05
772 Sal Butera .05
773 Frank Williams .05
774 Gene Mauch .05
775 Dave Stieb .05
776 Checklist 661-792 .05
777 Lonnie Smith .05
778a *Keith Comstock* (white team letters) .40
778b *Keith Comstock* (blue team letters, white name) .10
778c *Keith Comstock* (blue team letters, yellow name) 2.00
779 *Tom Glavine* .75
780 Fernando Valenzuela .05
781 *Keith Hughes* .05
782 *Jeff Ballard* .05
783 Ron Roenicke .05
784 Joe Sambito .05
785 Alvin Davis .05
786 Joe Price .05
787 Bill Almon .05
788 Ray Searage .05
789 Joe Carter, Cory Snyder Indians Leaders .05
790 Dave Righetti .05
791 Ted Simmons .05
792 John Tudor .05

Traded

NM/M

Complete Set (132): 5.00
Common Player: .05
1 *Jim Abbott* (USA) .25
2 Juan Agosto .05
3 Luis Alicea .05
4 *Roberto Alomar* 1.50
5 *Brady Anderson* .25
6 Jack Armstrong .05
7 Don August .05
8 Floyd Bannister .05

9 Bret Barberie (USA) .05
10 Jose Bautista .05
11 Don Baylor .05
12 Tim Belcher .05
13 Buddy Bell .05
14 *Andy Benes* (USA) .25
15 Damon Berryhill .05
16 Bud Black .05
17 Pat Borders .05
18 Phil Bradley .05
19 Jeff Branson (USA) .05
20 Tom Brunansky .05
21 *Jay Buhner* .75
22 Brett Butler .05
23 Jim Campanis (USA) .05
24 Sil Campusano .05
25 John Candelaria .05
26 Jose Cecena .05
27 Rick Cerone .05
28 Jack Clark .05
29 Kevin Coffman .05
30 Pat Combs (USA) .05
31 Henry Cotto .05
32 Chili Davis .05
33 Mike Davis .05
34 Jose DeLeon .05
35 Richard Dotson .05
36 Cecil Espy .05
37 Tom Filer .05
38 Mike Fiore (USA) .05
39 *Ron Gant* .25
40 Kirk Gibson .05
41 Rich Gossage .05
42 *Mark Grace* 1.00
43 Alfredo Griffin .05
44 Ty Griffin (USA) .05
45 Bryan Harvey .05
46 Ron Hassey .05
47 Ray Hayward .05
48 Dave Henderson .05
49 Tom Herr .05
50 Bob Horner .05
51 Ricky Horton .05
52 Jay Howell .05
53 Glenn Hubbard .05
54 Jeff Innis .05
55 Danny Jackson .05
56 Darrin Jackson .05
57 Roberto Kelly .05
58 Ron Kittle .05
59 Ray Knight .05
60 Vance Law .05
61 Jeffrey Leonard .05
62 *Mike Macfarlane* .05
63 Scotti Madison .05
64 Kirt Manwaring .05
65 Mark Marquess (USA) .05
66 *Tino Martinez* (USA) .75
67 Billy Masse (USA) .05
68 *Jack McDowell* .25
69 Jack McKeon .05
70 Larry McWilliams .05
71 Mickey Morandini (USA) .05
72 Keith Moreland .05
73 Mike Morgan .05
74 Charles Nagy (USA) .10
75 Al Nipper .05
76 Russ Nixon .05
77 Jesse Orosco .05
78 Joe Orsulak .05
79 Dave Palmer .05
80 Mark Parent .05
81 Dave Parker .05
82 Dan Pasqua .05
83 Melido Perez .05
84 Steve Peters .05
85 Dan Petry .05
86 Gary Pettis .05
87 Jeff Pico .05
88 Jim Poole (USA) .05
89 Ted Power .05
90 Rafael Ramirez .05
91 Dennis Rasmussen .05
92 Jose Rijo .05
93 Earnie Riles .05
94 Luis Rivera .05
95 Doug Robbins (USA) .05
96 Frank Robinson .15
97 Cookie Rojas .05
98 *Chris Sabo* .10
99 Mark Salas .05
100 Luis Salazar .05
101 Rafael Santana .05
102 Nelson Santovenia .05
103 Mackey Sasser .05
104 Calvin Schiraldi .05
105 Mike Schooler .05
106 Scott Servais (USA) .05
107 Dave Silvestri (USA) .05
108 Don Slaught .05
109 Joe Slusarski (USA) .05
110 Lee Smith .05
111 Pete Smith .05
112 Jim Snyder .05
113 Ed Sprague (USA) .05
114 Pete Stanicek .05
115 Kurt Stillwell .05
116 Todd Stottlemyre .05
117 Bill Swift .05
118 Pat Tabler .05
119 Scott Terry .05
120 Mickey Tettleton .05
121 Dickie Thon .05
122 Jeff Treadway .05
123 Willie Upshaw .05
124 *Robin Ventura* .25
125 Ron Washington .05
126 Walt Weiss .05
127 Bob Welch .05
128 David Wells .25
129 Glenn Wilson .05
130 Ted Wood (USA) .05
131 Don Zimmer .05
132 Checklist 1T-132T .05

Traded Tiffany

NM/M

Complete Set (132): 25.00
Common Player: .15
(Star cards valued at 3X corresponding cards in regular Topps Traded issue)

1989 TOPPS

NM/M

Unopened Factory Set, Retail (792): 17.50
Unopened Factory Set, Hobby (792): 15.00
Complete Set (792): 11.00
Common Player: .05
Wax Pack (15): .75
Wax Box (36): 11.00
Cello Pack (29): 1.00
Cello Box (24): 16.00
Rack Pack (43): .75
Rack Box (24): 12.50
Vending Box (500): 6.00
1 George Bell .05
2 Wade Boggs .25
3 Gary Carter .20
4 Andre Dawson .10
5 Orel Hershiser .05
6 Doug Jones .05
7 Kevin McReynolds .05
8 *Dave Eiland* .05
9 Tim Teufel .05
10 Andre Dawson .25

No.	Player	Price
11	Bruce Sutter	.35
12	Dale Sveum	.05
13	Doug Sisk	.05
14	Tom Kelly	.05
15	Robby Thompson	.05
16	Ron Robinson	.05
17	Brian Downing	.05
18	Rick Rhoden	.05
19	Greg Gagne	.05
20	Steve Bedrosian	.05
21	Greg Walker White Sox Leaders	.05
22	Tim Crews	.05
23	Mike Fitzgerald	.05
24	Larry Andersen	.05
25	Frank White	.05
26	Dale Mohorcic	.05
27	*Orestes Destrade*	.05
28	Mike Moore	.05
29	Kelly Gruber	.05
30	Dwight Gooden	.05
31	Terry Francona	.05
32	Dennis Rasmussen	.05
33	B.J. Surhoff	.05
34	Ken Williams	.05
35	John Tudor	.05
36	Mitch Webster	.05
37	Bob Stanley	.05
38	Paul Runge	.05
39	Mike Maddux	.05
40	Steve Sax	.05
41	Terry Mulholland	.05
42	Jim Eppard	.05
43	Guillermo Hernandez	.05
44	Jim Snyder	.05
45	Kal Daniels	.05
46	Mark Portugal	.05
47	Carney Lansford	.05
48	Tim Burke	.05
49	Craig Biggio	.05
50	George Bell	.05
51	Mark McLemore Angels Leaders	.05
52	Bob Brenly	.05
53	Ruben Sierra	.05
54	Steve Trout	.05
55	Julio Franco	.05
56	Pat Tabler	.05
57	Alejandro Pena	.05
58	Lee Mazzilli	.05
59	Mark Davis	.05
60	Tom Brunansky	.05
61	Neil Allen	.05
62	Alfredo Griffin	.05
63	Mark Clear	.05
64	Alex Trevino	.05
65	Rick Reuschel	.05
66	Manny Trillo	.05
67	Dave Palmer	.05
68	Darrell Miller	.05
69	Jeff Ballard	.05
70	Mark McGwire	.65
71	Mike Boddicker	.05
72	John Moses	.05
73	Pascual Perez	.05
74	Nick Leyva	.05
75	Tom Henke	.05
76	*Terry Blocker*	.05
77	Doyle Alexander	.05
78	Jim Sundberg	.05
79	Scott Bankhead	.05
80	Cory Snyder	.05
81	Tim Raines Expos Leaders	.05
82	Dave Leiper	.05
83	Jeff Blauser	.05
84	*Bill Bene* (#1 Draft Pick)	.05
85	Kevin McReynolds	.05
86	Al Nipper	.05
87	Larry Owen	.05
88	*Darryl Hamilton*	.05
89	Dave LaPoint	.05
90	Vince Coleman	.05
91	Floyd Youmans	.05
92	Jeff Kunkel	.05
93	Ken Howell	.05
94	Chris Speier	.05
95	Gerald Young	.05
96	Rick Cerone	.05
97	Greg Mathews	.05
98	Larry Sheets	.05
99	*Sherman Corbett*	.05
100	Mike Schmidt	.50
101	Les Straker	.05
102	Mike Gallego	.05
103	Tim Birtsas	.05
104	Dallas Green	.05
105	Ron Darling	.05
106	Willie Upshaw	.05
107	Jose DeLeon	.05
108	Fred Manrique	.05
109	*Hipolito Pena*	.05
110	Paul Molitor	.40
111	Eric Davis Reds Leaders	.05
112	Jim Presley	.05
113	Lloyd Moseby	.05
114	Bob Kipper	.05
115	Jody Davis	.05
116	Jeff Montgomery	.05
117	Dave Anderson	.05
118	Checklist 1-132	.05
119	Terry Puhl	.05
120	Frank Viola	.05
121	Garry Templeton	.05
122	Lance Johnson	.05
123	Spike Owen	.05
124	Jim Traber	.05
125	Mike Krukow	.05
126	Sid Bream	.05
127	Walt Terrell	.05
128	Milt Thompson	.05
129	*Terry Clark*	.05
130	Gerald Perry	.05
131	Dave Otto	.05
132	Curt Ford	.05
133	Bill Long	.05
134	Don Zimmer	.05
135	Jose Rijo	.05
136	Joey Meyer	.05
137	Geno Petralli	.05
138	Wallace Johnson	.05
139	Mike Flanagan	.05
140	Shawon Dunston	.05
141	Brook Jacoby Indians Leaders	.05
142	Mike Diaz	.05
143	Mike Campbell	.05
144	Jay Bell	.05
145	Dave Stewart	.05
146	Gary Pettis	.05
147	DeWayne Buice	.05
148	Bill Pecota	.05
149	*Doug Dascenzo*	.05
150	Fernando Valenzuela	.05
151	Terry McGriff	.05
152	Mark Thurmond	.05
153	Jim Pankovits	.05
154	Don Carman	.05
155	Marty Barrett	.05
156	*Dave Gallagher*	.05
157	Tom Glavine	.25
158	Mike Aldrete	.05
159	Pat Clements	.05
160	Jeffrey Leonard	.05
161	*Gregg Olson* (#1 Draft Pick)	.05
162	John Davis	.05
163	Bob Forsch	.05
164	Hal Lanier	.05
165	Mike Dunne	.05
166	*Doug Jennings*	.05
167	*Steve Searcy* (Future Star)	.05
168	Willie Wilson	.05
169	Mike Jackson	.05
170	Tony Fernandez	.05
171	Andres Thomas Braves Leaders	.05
172	Frank Williams	.05
173	Mel Hall	.05
174	*Todd Burns*	.05
175	John Shelby	.05
176	Jeff Parrett	.05
177	*Monty Fariss* (#1 Draft Pick)	.05
178	Mark Grant	.05
179	Ozzie Virgil	.05
180	Mike Scott	.05
181	*Craig Worthington*	.05
182	Bob McClure	.05
183	Oddibe McDowell	.05
184	*John Costello*	.05
185	Claudell Washington	.05
186	Pat Perry	.05
187	Darren Daulton	.05
188	Dennis Lamp	.05
189	Kevin Mitchell	.05
190	Mike Witt	.05
191	*Sil Campusano*	.05
192	Paul Mirabella	.05
193	Sparky Anderson	.10
194	*Greg Harris*	.05
195	Ozzie Guillen	.05
196	Denny Walling	.05
197	Neal Heaton	.05
198	Danny Heep	.05
199	*Mike Schooler*	.05
200	George Brett	.50
201	Kelly Gruber Blue Jays Leaders	.05
202	*Brad Moore*	.05
203	Rob Ducey	.05
204	Brad Havens	.05
205	Dwight Evans	.05
206	Roberto Alomar	.35
207	Terry Leach	.05
208	Tom Pagnozzi	.05
209	*Jeff Bittiger*	.05
210	Dale Murphy	.15
211	Mike Pagliarulo	.05
212	Scott Sanderson	.05
213	Rene Gonzales	.05
214	Charlie O'Brien	.05
215	Kevin Gross	.05
216	Jack Howell	.05
217	Joe Price	.05
218	Mike LaValliere	.05
219	Jim Clancy	.05
220	Gary Gaetti	.05
221	Cecil Espy	.05
222	*Mark Lewis* (#1 Draft Pick)	.05
223	Jay Buhner	.05
224	Tony LaRussa	.05
225	*Ramon Martinez*	.25
226	Bill Doran	.05
227	John Farrell	.05
228	*Nelson Santovenia*	.05
229	Jimmy Key	.05
230	Ozzie Smith	.45
231	Roberto Alomar Padres Leaders	.05
232	Ricky Horton	.05
233	Gregg Jefferies (Future Star)	.20
234	Tom Browning	.05
235	John Kruk	.05
236	Charles Hudson	.05
237	Glenn Hubbard	.05
238	Eric King	.05
239	Tim Laudner	.05
240	Greg Maddux	.45
241	Brett Butler	.05
242	Ed Vande Berg	.05
243	Bob Boone	.05
244	Jim Acker	.05
245	Jim Rice	.15
246	Rey Quinones	.05
247	Shawn Hillegas	.05
248	Tony Phillips	.05
249	Tim Leary	.05
250	Cal Ripken, Jr.	.75
251	*John Dopson*	.05
252	Billy Hatcher	.05
253	*Jose Alvarez*	.05
254	Tom LaSorda	.05
255	Ron Guidry	.10
256	Benny Santiago	.05
257	Rick Aguilera	.05
258	Checklist 133-264	.05
259	Larry McWilliams	.05
260	Dave Winfield	.40
261	Tom Brunansky Cardinals Leaders	.05
262	*Jeff Pico*	.05
263	Mike Felder	.05
264	*Rob Dibble*	.10
265	Kent Hrbek	.05
266	Luis Aquino	.05
267	Jeff Robinson	.05
268	Keith Miller	.05
269	Tom Bolton	.05
270	Wally Joyner	.05
271	Jay Tibbs	.05
272	Ron Hassey	.05
273	Jose Lind	.05
274	Mark Eichhorn	.05
275	Danny Tartabull	.05
276	Paul Kilgus	.05
277	Mike Davis	.05
278	Andy McGaffigan	.05
279	Scott Bradley	.05
280	Bob Knepper	.05
281	Gary Redus	.05
282	*Cris Carpenter*	.05
283	Andy Allanson	.05
284	Jim Leyland	.05
285	John Candelaria	.05
286	Darrin Jackson	.05
287	Juan Nieves	.05
288	Pat Sheridan	.05
289	Ernie Whitt	.05
290	John Franco	.05
291	Darryl Strawberry Mets Leaders	.05
292	*Jim Corsi*	.05
293	Glenn Wilson	.05
294	Juan Berenguer	.05
295	Scott Fletcher	.05
296	Ron Gant	.05
297	*Oswald Peraza*	.05
298	Chris James	.05
299	*Steve Ellsworth*	.05
300	Darryl Strawberry	.05
301	Charlie Leibrandt	.05
302	Gary Ward	.05
303	Felix Fermin	.05
304	Joel Youngblood	.05
305	Dave Smith	.05
306	Tracy Woodson	.05
307	Lance McCullers	.05
308	Ron Karkovice	.05
309	Mario Diaz	.05
310	Rafael Palmeiro	.35
311	Chris Bosio	.05
312	Tom Lawless	.05
313	Denny Martinez	.05
314	Bobby Valentine	.05
315	Greg Swindell	.05
316	Walt Weiss	.05
317	*Jack Armstrong*	.05
318	Gene Larkin	.05
319	Greg Booker	.05
320	Lou Whitaker	.05
321	Jody Reed Red Sox Leaders	.05
322	John Smiley	.05
323	Gary Thurman	.05
324	*Bob Milacki*	.05
325	Jesse Barfield	.05
326	Dennis Boyd	.05
327	*Mark Lemke*	.05
328	Rick Honeycutt	.05
329	Bob Melvin	.05
330	Eric Davis	.05
331	Curt Wilkerson	.05
332	Tony Armas	.05
333	Bob Ojeda	.05
334	Steve Lyons	.05
335	Dave Righetti	.05
336	Steve Balboni	.05
337	Calvin Schiraldi	.05
338	Jim Adduci	.05
339	Scott Bailes	.05
340	Kirk Gibson	.05
341	Jim Deshaies	.05
342	Tom Brookens	.05
343	*Gary Sheffield* (Future Star)	1.50
344	Tom Trebelhorn	.05
345	Charlie Hough	.05
346	Rex Hudler	.05
347	John Cerutti	.05
348	Ed Hearn	.05
349	*Ron Jones*	.05
350	Andy Van Slyke	.05
351	Bob Melvin Giants Leaders	.05
352	Rick Schu	.05
353	Marvell Wynne	.05
354	Larry Parrish	.05
355	Mark Langston	.05
356	Kevin Elster	.05
357	Jerry Reuss	.05
358	*Ricky Jordan*	.05
359	Tommy John	.10
360	Ryne Sandberg	.45
361	Kelly Downs	.05
362	Jack Lazorko	.05
363	Rich Yett	.05
364	Rob Deer	.05
365	Mike Henneman	.05
366	Herm Winningham	.05
367	*Johnny Paredes*	.05
368	Brian Holton	.05
369	Ken Caminiti	.05
370	Dennis Eckersley	.35
371	Manny Lee	.05
372	Craig Lefferts	.05
373	Tracy Jones	.05
374	John Wathan	.05
375	Terry Pendleton	.05
376	Steve Lombardozzi	.05
377	Mike Smithson	.05
378	Checklist 265-396	.05
379	Tim Flannery	.05
380	Rickey Henderson	.40
381	Larry Sheets Orioles Leaders	.05
382	John Smoltz	.50
383	Howard Johnson	.05
384	Mark Salas	.05
385	Von Hayes	.05
386	Andres Galarraga	.05
387	Ryne Sandberg	.20
388	Bobby Bonilla	.05

No.	Card	Price
389	Ozzie Smith	.25
390	Darryl Strawberry	.05
391	Andre Dawson	.05
392	Andy Van Slyke	.05
393	Gary Carter	.05
394	Orel Hershiser	.05
395	Danny Jackson	.05
396	Kirk Gibson	.05
397	Don Mattingly	.30
398	Julio Franco	.05
399	Wade Boggs	.20
400	Alan Trammell	.05
401	Jose Canseco	.15
402	Mike Greenwell	.05
403	Kirby Puckett	.25
404	Bob Boone	.05
405	Roger Clemens	.30
406	Frank Viola	.05
407	Dave Winfield	.20
408	Greg Walker	.05
409	Ken Dayley	.05
410	Jack Clark	.05
411	Mitch Williams	.05
412	Barry Lyons	.05
413	Mike Kingery	.05
414	Jim Fregosi	.05
415	Rich Gossage	.05
416	Fred Lynn	.05
417	Mike LaCoss	.05
418	Bob Dernier	.05
419	Tom Filer	.05
420	Joe Carter	.05
421	Kirk McCaskill	.05
422	Bo Diaz	.05
423	Brian Fisher	.05
424	Luis Polonia	.05
425	Jay Howell	.05
426	Danny Gladden	.05
427	Eric Show	.05
428	Craig Reynolds	.05
429	Greg Gagne Twins Leaders	.05
430	Mark Gubicza	.05
431	Luis Rivera	.05
432	*Chad Kreuter*	.10
433	Albert Hall	.05
434	*Ken Patterson*	.05
435	Len Dykstra	.05
436	Bobby Meacham	.05
437	Andy Benes (#1 Draft Pick)	.05
438	Greg Gross	.05
439	Frank DiPino	.05
440	Bobby Bonilla	.05
441	Jerry Reed	.05
442	Jose Oquendo	.05
443	*Rod Nichols*	.05
444	Moose Stubing	.05
445	Matt Nokes	.05
446	Rob Murphy	.05
447	Donell Nixon	.05
448	Eric Plunk	.05
449	Carmelo Martinez	.05
450	Roger Clemens	.50
451	Mark Davidson	.05
452	*Israel Sanchez*	.05
453	Tom Prince	.05
454	Paul Assenmacher	.05
455	Johnny Ray	.05
456	Tim Belcher	.05
457	Mackey Sasser	.05
458	*Donn Pall*	.05
459	Dave Valle Mariners Leaders	.05
460	Dave Stieb	.05
461	Buddy Bell	.05
462	Jose Guzman	.05
463	Steve Lake	.05
464	Bryn Smith	.05
465	Mark Grace	.05
466	Chuck Crim	.05
467	Jim Walewander	.05
468	Henry Cotto	.05
469	*Jose Bautista*	.05
470	Lance Parrish	.05
471	*Steve Curry*	.05
472	Brian Harper	.05
473	Don Robinson	.05
474	Bob Rodgers	.05
475	Dave Parker	.05
476	Jon Perlman	.05
477	Dick Schofield	.05
478	Doug Drabek	.05
479	Mike Macfarlane	.05
480	Keith Hernandez	.05
481	Chris Brown	.05
482	*Steve Peters*	.05
483	Mickey Hatcher	.05
484	Steve Shields	.05
485	Hubie Brooks	.05
486	Jack McDowell	.05
487	Scott Lusader	.05
488	Kevin Coffman	.05
489	Mike Schmidt Phillies Leaders	.15
490	Chris Sabo	.05
491	Mike Birkbeck	.05
492	Alan Ashby	.05
493	Todd Benzinger	.05
494	Shane Rawley	.05
495	Candy Maldonado	.05
496	Dwayne Henry	.05
497	Pete Stanicek	.05
498	Dave Valle	.05
499	*Don Heinkel*	.05
500	Jose Canseco	.35
501	Vance Law	.05
502	Duane Ward	.05
503	Al Newman	.05
504	Bob Walk	.05
505	Pete Rose	.65
506	Kirt Manwaring	.05
507	Steve Farr	.05
508	Wally Backman	.05
509	Bud Black	.05
510	Bob Horner	.05
511	Richard Dotson	.05
512	Donnie Hill	.05
513	Jesse Orosco	.05
514	Chet Lemon	.05
515	Barry Larkin	.05
516	Eddie Whitson	.05
517	Greg Brock	.05
518	Bruce Ruffin	.05
519	Willie Randolph Yankees Leaders	.05
520	Rick Sutcliffe	.05
521	Mickey Tettleton	.05
522	*Randy Kramer*	.05
523	Andres Thomas	.05
524	Checklist 397-528	.05
525	Chili Davis	.05
526	Wes Gardner	.05
527	Dave Henderson	.05
528	*Luis Medina*	.05
529	Tom Foley	.05
530	Nolan Ryan	.75
531	Dave Hengel	.05
532	Jerry Browne	.05
533	Andy Hawkins	.05
534	Doc Edwards	.05
535	Todd Worrell	.05
536	Joel Skinner	.05
537	Pete Smith	.05
538	Juan Castillo	.05
539	Barry Jones	.05
540	Bo Jackson	.10
541	Cecil Fielder	.05
542	Todd Frohwirth	.05
543	Damon Berryhill	.05
544	Jeff Sellers	.05
545	Mookie Wilson	.05
546	Mark Williamson	.05
547	Mark McLemore	.05
548	Bobby Witt	.05
549	Jamie Moyer Cubs Leaders	.05
550	Orel Hershiser	.05
551	Randy Ready	.05
552	Greg Cadaret	.05
553	Luis Salazar	.05
554	Nick Esasky	.05
555	Bert Blyleven	.05
556	Bruce Fields	.05
557	*Keith Miller*	.05
558	Dan Pasqua	.05
559	Juan Agosto	.05
560	Tim Raines	.05
561	Luis Aguayo	.05
562	Danny Cox	.05
563	Bill Schroeder	.05
564	Russ Nixon	.05
565	Jeff Russell	.05
566	Al Pedrique	.05
567	David Wells	.05
568	Mickey Brantley	.05
569	*German Jimenez*	.05
570	Tony Gwynn	.45
571	Billy Ripken	.05
572	Atlee Hammaker	.05
573	Jim Abbott (#1 Draft Pick)	.10
574	Dave Clark	.05
575	Juan Samuel	.05
576	Greg Minton	.05
577	Randy Bush	.05
578	John Morris	.05
579	Glenn Davis Astros Leaders	.05
580	Harold Reynolds	.05
581	Gene Nelson	.05
582	Mike Marshall	.05
583	*Paul Gibson*	.05
584	Randy Velarde	.05
585	Harold Baines	.05
586	Joe Boever	.05
587	Mike Stanley	.05
588	*Luis Alicea*	.05
589	Dave Meads	.05
590	Andres Galarraga	.05
591	Jeff Musselman	.05
592	John Cangelosi	.05
593	Drew Hall	.05
594	Jimy Williams	.05
595	Teddy Higuera	.05
596	Kurt Stillwell	.05
597	*Terry Taylor*	.05
598	Ken Gerhart	.05
599	Tom Candiotti	.05
600	Wade Boggs	.45
601	Dave Dravecky	.05
602	Devon White	.05
603	Frank Tanana	.05
604	Paul O'Neill	.05
605a	Bob Welch (missing Complete Major League Pitching Record line)	3.00
605b	Bob Welch (contains Complete Major League Pitching Record line)	.05
606	Rick Dempsey	.05
607	*Willie Ansley*	.05
608	Phil Bradley	.05
609	Frank Tanana Tigers Leaders	.05
610	Randy Myers	.05
611	Don Slaught	.05
612	Dan Quisenberry	.05
613	*Gary Varsho*	.05
614	Joe Hesketh	.05
615	Robin Yount	.40
616	*Steve Rosenberg*	.05
617	*Mark Parent*	.05
618	Rance Mulliniks	.05
619	Checklist 529-660	.05
620	Barry Bonds	.75
621	Rick Mahler	.05
622	Stan Javier	.05
623	Fred Toliver	.05
624	Jack McKeon	.05
625	Eddie Murray	.40
626	Jeff Reed	.05
627	Greg Harris	.05
628	Matt Williams	.05
629	Pete O'Brien	.05
630	Mike Greenwell	.05
631	Dave Bergman	.05
632	*Bryan Harvey*	.10
633	Daryl Boston	.05
634	Marvin Freeman	.05
635	Willie Randolph	.05
636	Bill Wilkinson	.05
637	Carmen Castillo	.05
638	Floyd Bannister	.05
639	Walt Weiss Athletics Leaders	.05
640	Willie McGee	.05
641	Curt Young	.05
642	Argenis Salazar	.05
643	*Louie Meadows*	.05
644	Lloyd McClendon	.05
645	Jack Morris	.05
646	Kevin Bass	.05
647	*Randy Johnson*	3.00
648	*Sandy Alomar* (Future Star)	.25
649	Stewart Cliburn	.05
650	Kirby Puckett	.45
651	Tom Niedenfuer	.05
652	Rich Gedman	.05
653	*Tommy Barrett*	.05
654	Whitey Herzog	.05
655	Dave Magadan	.05
656	Ivan Calderon	.05
657	Joe Magrane	.05
658	R.J. Reynolds	.05
659	Al Leiter	.05
660	Will Clark	.05
661	Dwight Gooden	.05
662	Lou Brock	.05
663	Hank Aaron	.15
664	Gil Hodges	.05
665a	Tony Oliva	12.50
665b	Tony Oliva	.05
666	Randy St. Claire	.05
667	Dwayne Murphy	.05
668	Mike Bielecki	.05
669	Orel Hershiser Dodgers Leaders	.05
670	Kevin Seitzer	.05
671	Jim Gantner	.05
672	Allan Anderson	.05
673	Don Baylor	.05
674	Otis Nixon	.05
675	Bruce Hurst	.05
676	Ernie Riles	.05
677	Dave Schmidt	.05
678	Dion James	.05
679	Willie Fraser	.05
680	Gary Carter	.40
681	Jeff Robinson	.05
682	Rick Leach	.05
683	*Jose Cecena*	.05
684	Dave Johnson	.05
685	Jeff Treadway	.05
686	Scott Terry	.05
687	Alvin Davis	.05
688	Zane Smith	.05
689a	Stan Jefferson (pink triangle at bottom-left photo)	.05
689b	Stan Jefferson (pink/purple triangle)	.05
689c	Stan Jefferson (purple triangle)	.05
690	Doug Jones	.05
691	Roberto Kelly	.05
692	Steve Ontiveros	.05
693	*Pat Borders*	.05
694	Les Lancaster	.05
695	Carlton Fisk	.40
696	Don August	.05
697	Franklin Stubbs	.05
698	Keith Atherton	.05
699	Al Pedrique Pirates Leaders	.05
700	Don Mattingly	.50
701	Storm Davis	.05
702	Jamie Quirk	.05
703	Scott Garrelts	.05
704	*Carlos Quintana*	.05
705	Terry Kennedy	.05
706	Pete Incaviglia	.05
707	Steve Jeltz	.05
708	Chuck Finley	.05
709	Tom Herr	.05
710	Dave Cone	.05
711	*Candy Sierra*	.05
712	Bill Swift	.05
713	*Ty Griffin* (#1 Draft Pick)	.05
714	Joe M. Morgan	.05
715	Tony Pena	.05
716	Wayne Tolleson	.05
717	Jamie Moyer	.05
718	Glenn Braggs	.05
719	Danny Darwin	.05
720	Tim Wallach	.05
721	*Ron Tingley*	.05
722	Todd Stottlemyre	.05
723	Rafael Belliard	.05
724	Jerry Don Gleaton	.05
725	Terry Steinbach	.05
726	Dickie Thon	.05
727	Joe Orsulak	.05
728	Charlie Puleo	.05
729	Steve Buechele Rangers Leaders	.05
730	Danny Jackson	.05
731	Mike Young	.05
732	Steve Buechele	.05
733	*Randy Bockus*	.05
734	Jody Reed	.05
735	Roger McDowell	.05
736	Jeff Hamilton	.05
737	*Norm Charlton*	.05
738	Darnell Coles	.05
739	Brook Jacoby	.05
740	Dan Plesac	.05
741	Ken Phelps	.05
742	*Mike Harkey* (Future Star)	.05
743	Mike Heath	.05
744	Roger Craig	.05
745	Fred McGriff	.05
746	*German Gonzalez*	.05
747	Wil Tejada	.05
748	Jimmy Jones	.05
749	Rafael Ramirez	.05
750	Bret Saberhagen	.05
751	Ken Oberkfell	.05
752	Jim Gott	.05
753	Jose Uribe	.05
754	Bob Brower	.05
755	Mike Scioscia	.05
756	*Scott Medvin*	.05
757	Brady Anderson	.05
758	Gene Walter	.05
759	Rob Deer Brewers Leaders	.05

760 Lee Smith .05
761 *Dante Bichette* .25
762 Bobby Thigpen .05
763 Dave Martinez .05
764 Robin Ventura (#1 Draft Pick) .25
765 Glenn Davis .05
766 Cecilio Guante .05
767 *Mike Capel* .05
768 Bill Wegman .05
769 Junior Ortiz .05
770 Alan Trammell .05
771 Ron Kittle .05
772 Ron Oester .05
773 Keith Moreland .05
774 Frank Robinson .15
775 Jeff Reardon .05
776 Nelson Liriano .05
777 Ted Power .05
778 Bruce Benedict .05
779 Craig McMurtry .05
780 Pedro Guerrero .05
781 *Greg Briley* .05
782 Checklist 661-792 .05
783 *Trevor Wilson* .05
784 *Steve Avery* (#1 Draft Pick) .15
785 Ellis Burks .05
786 Melido Perez .05
787 *Dave West* .05
788 Mike Morgan .05
789 Bo Jackson Royals Leaders .05
790 Sid Fernandez .05
791 Jim Lindeman .05
792 Rafael Santana .05

Tiffany

NM/M
Unopened Set (792): 75.00
Complete Set (792): 40.00
Common Player: .10
(Star cards valued at 3X corresponding cards in regular 1989 Topps issue)

Traded

NM/M
Unopened Set, Retail (132): 12.50
Unopened Set, Hobby (132): 10.00
Complete Set (132): 7.50
Common Player: .05
1T Don Aase .05
2T Jim Abbott .05
3T Kent Anderson .05
4T Keith Atherton .05
5T Wally Backman .05
6T Steve Balboni .05
7T Jesse Barfield .05
8T Steve Bedrosian .05
9T Todd Benzinger .05
10T Geronimo Berroa .05
11T Bert Blyleven .05
12T Bob Boone .05
13T Phil Bradley .05
14T *Jeff Brantley* .05
15T Kevin Brown .05
16T Jerry Browne .05
17T Chuck Cary .05
18T Carmen Castillo .05
19T Jim Clancy .05
20T Jack Clark .05
21T Bryan Clutterbuck .05
22T Jody Davis .05
23T Mike Devereaux .05
24T Frank DiPino .05
25T Benny Distefano .05
26T John Dopson .05
27T Len Dykstra .05
28T Jim Eisenreich .05
29T Nick Esasky .05
30T Alvaro Espinoza .05
31T Darrell Evans .05
32T Junior Felix .05
33T Felix Fermin .05
34T Julio Franco .05
35T Terry Francona .05
36T Cito Gaston .05
37T Bob Geren (photo actually Mike Fennell) .05
38T *Tom Gordon* .10
39T Tommy Gregg .05
40T Ken Griffey .05
41T *Ken Griffey, Jr.* 6.00
42T Kevin Gross .05
43T Lee Guetterman .05
44T Mel Hall .05
45T Erik Hanson .05
46T Gene Harris .05
47T Andy Hawkins .05
48T Rickey Henderson .40
49T Tom Herr .05
50T *Ken Hill* .05
51T Brian Holman .05
52T Brian Holton .05
53T Art Howe .05
54T Ken Howell .05
55T Bruce Hurst .05
56T Chris James .05
57T Randy Johnson 1.50
58T Jimmy Jones .05
59T Terry Kennedy .05
60T Paul Kilgus .05
61T Eric King .05
62T Ron Kittle .05
63T John Kruk .05
64T Randy Kutcher .05
65T Steve Lake .05
66T Mark Langston .05
67T Dave LaPoint .05
68T Rick Leach .05
69T Terry Leach .05
70T Jim Levebvre .05
71T Al Leiter .05
72T Jeffrey Leonard .05
73T Derek Lilliquist .05
74T Rick Mahler .05
75T Tom McCarthy .05
76T Lloyd McClendon .05
77T Lance McCullers .05
78T Oddibe McDowell .05
79T Roger McDowell .05
80T Larry McWilliams .05
81T Randy Milligan .05
82T Mike Moore .05
83T Keith Moreland .05
84T Mike Morgan .05
85T Jamie Moyer .05
86T Rob Murphy .05
87T Eddie Murray .40
88T Pete O'Brien .05
89T Gregg Olson .05
90T Steve Ontiveros .05
91T Jesse Orosco .05
92T Spike Owen .05
93T Rafael Palmeiro .35
94T Clay Parker .05
95T Jeff Parrett .05
96T Lance Parrish .05
97T Dennis Powell .05
98T Rey Quinones .05
99T Doug Rader .05
100T Willie Randolph .05
101T Shane Rawley .05
102T Randy Ready .05
103T Bip Roberts .05
104T *Kenny Rogers* .10
105T Ed Romero .05
106T Nolan Ryan 1.00
107T Luis Salazar .05
108T Juan Samuel .05
109T Alex Sanchez .05
110T *Deion Sanders* .50
111T Steve Sax .05
112T Rick Schu .05
113T Dwight Smith .05
114T Lonnie Smith .05
115T Billy Spiers .05
116T Kent Tekulve .05
117T Walt Terrell .05
118T Milt Thompson .05
119T Dickie Thon .05
120T Jeff Torborg .05
121T Jeff Treadway .05
122T *Omar Vizquel* .50
123T Jerome Walton .05
124T Gary Ward .05
125T Claudell Washington .05
126T Curt Wilkerson .05
127T Eddie Williams .05
128T Frank Williams .05
129T Ken Williams .05
130T Mitch Williams .05
131T Steve Wilson .05
--- Topps Magazine subscription offer card .05

Traded Tiffany

NM/M
Unopened Set (132): 85.00
Complete Set (132): 50.00
Common Player: .10
(Star cards valued at 3X corresponding cards in regular Topps Traded issue)

1990 TOPPS

NM/M
Unopened Factory Set, Retail (792): 25.00
Unopened Factory Set, Hobby (792): 20.00
Complete Set (792): 15.00
Common Player: .05
Wax Pack (16): .60
Wax Box (36): 12.00
Cello Pack (31): 1.00
Cello Box (24): 15.00
Rack Pack (45): 1.00
Rack Box (24): 16.00
Vending Box (500): 7.50
1 Nolan Ryan .75
2 Nolan Ryan (Mets) .35
3 Nolan Ryan (Angels) .25
4 Nolan Ryan (Astros) .25
5 Nolan Ryan (Rangers) .25
6 Vince Coleman .05
7 Rickey Henderson .20
8 Cal Ripken, Jr. .40
9 Eric Plunk .05
10 Barry Larkin .05
11 Paul Gibson .05
12 Joe Girardi .05
13 Mark Williamson .05
14 *Mike Fetters* .05
15 Teddy Higuera .05
16 *Kent Anderson* .05
17 Kelly Downs .05
18 Carlos Quintana .05
19 Al Newman .05
20 Mark Gubicza .05
21 Jeff Torborg .05
22 Bruce Ruffin .05
23 Randy Velarde .05
24 Joe Hesketh .05
25 Willie Randolph .05
26 Don Slaught .05
27 Rick Leach .05
28 Duane Ward .05
29 John Cangelosi .05
30 David Cone .05
31 Henry Cotto .05
32 John Farrell .05
33 Greg Walker .05
34 *Tony Fossas* .05
35 Benito Santiago .05
36 John Costello .05
37 Domingo Ramos .05
38 Wes Gardner .05
39 Curt Ford .05
40 Jay Howell .05
41 Matt Williams .05
42 Jeff Robinson .05
43 Dante Bichette .05
44 *Roger Salkeld* .10
45 Dave Parker .05
46 Rob Dibble .05
47 Brian Harper .05
48 Zane Smith .05
49 Tom Lawless .05
50 Glenn Davis .05
51 Doug Rader .05
52 *Jack Daugherty* .05
53 Mike LaCoss .05
54 Joel Skinner .05
55 Darrell Evans .05
56 Franklin Stubbs .05
57 Greg Vaughn .05
58 Keith Miller .05
59 Ted Power .05
60 George Brett .50
61 Deion Sanders .10
62 Ramon Martinez .05
63 Mike Pagliarulo .05
64 Danny Darwin .05
65 Devon White .05
66 *Greg Litton* .05
67 Scott Sanderson .05
68 Dave Henderson .05
69 Todd Frohwirth .05
70 Mike Greenwell .05
71 Allan Anderson .05
72 *Jeff Huson* .05
73 Bob Milacki .05
74 *Jeff Jackson* .05
75 Doug Jones .05
76 Dave Valle .05
77 Dave Bergman .05
78 Mike Flanagan .05
79 Ron Kittle .05
80 Jeff Russell .05
81 Bob Rodgers .05
82 Scott Terry .05
83 Hensley Meulens .05
84 Ray Searage .05
85 Juan Samuel .05
86 Paul Kilgus .05
87 *Rick Luecken* .05
88 Glenn Braggs .05
89 *Clint Zavaras* .05
90 Jack Clark .05
91 *Steve Frey* .05
92 Mike Stanley .05
93 Shawn Hillegas .05
94 Herm Winningham .05
95 Todd Worrell .05
96 Jody Reed .05
97 Curt Schilling .25
98 Jose Gonzalez .05
99 *Rich Monteleone* .05
100 Will Clark .05
101 Shane Rawley .05
102 Stan Javier .05
103 Marvin Freeman .05
104 Bob Knepper .05
105 Randy Myers .05
106 Charlie O'Brien .05
107 Fred Lynn .05
108 Rod Nichols .05
109 Roberto Kelly .05
110 Tommy Helms .05
111 Ed Whited .05
112 Glenn Wilson .05
113 Manny Lee .05
114 Mike Bielecki .05
115 Tony Pena .05
116 Floyd Bannister .05
117 Mike Sharperson .05
118 Erik Hanson .05
119 Billy Hatcher .05
120 John Franco .05
121 Robin Ventura .05
122 Shawn Abner .05
123 Rich Gedman .05
124 Dave Dravecky .05
125 Kent Hrbek .05
126 Randy Kramer .05
127 Mike Devereaux .05
128 Checklist 1-132 .05
129 Ron Jones .05
130 Bert Blyleven .05
131 Matt Nokes .05
132 Lance Blankenship .05
133 Ricky Horton .05
134 *Earl Cunningham* .05
135 Dave Magadan .05
136 Kevin Brown .05
137 *Marty Pevey* .05
138 Al Leiter .05
139 Greg Brock .05
140 Andre Dawson .25
141 John Hart .05
142 *Jeff Wetherby* .05
143 Rafael Belliard .05
144 Bud Black .05
145 Terry Steinbach .05

146 *Rob Richie* .05
147 Chuck Finley .05
148 Edgar Martinez .05
149 Steve Farr .05
150 Kirk Gibson .05
151 Rick Mahler .05
152 Lonnie Smith .05
153 Randy Milligan .05
154 Mike Maddux .05
155 Ellis Burks .05
156 Ken Patterson .05
157 Craig Biggio .05
158 Craig Lefferts .05
159 Mike Felder .05
160 Dave Righetti .05
161 Harold Reynolds .05
162 *Todd Zeile* .20
163 Phil Bradley .05
164 *Jeff Juden* .05
165 Walt Weiss .05
166 Bobby Witt .05
167 Kevin Appier .05
168 Jose Lind .05
169 Richard Dotson .05
170 George Bell .05
171 Russ Nixon .05
172 Tom Lampkin .05
173 Tim Belcher .05
174 Jeff Kunkel .05
175 Mike Moore .05
176 Luis Quinones .05
177 Mike Henneman .05
178 Chris James .05
179 Brian Holton .05
180 Rock Raines .05
181 Juan Agosto .05
182 Mookie Wilson .05
183 Steve Lake .05
184 Danny Cox .05
185 Ruben Sierra .05
186 Dave LaPoint .05
187 *Rick Wrona* .05
188 Mike Smithson .05
189 Dick Schofield .05
190 Rick Reuschel .05
191 Pat Borders .05
192 Don August .05
193 Andy Benes .05
194 Glenallen Hill .05
195 Tim Burke .05
196 Gerald Young .05
197 Doug Drabek .05
198 Mike Marshall .05
199 *Sergio Valdez* .05
200 Don Mattingly .50
201 Cito Gaston .05
202 Mike Macfarlane .05
203 *Mike Roesler* .05
204 Bob Dernier .05
205 Mark Davis .05
206 Nick Esasky .05
207 Bob Ojeda .05
208 Brook Jacoby .05
209 Greg Mathews .05
210 Ryne Sandberg .45
211 John Cerutti .05
212 Joe Orsulak .05
213 Scott Bankhead .05
214 Terry Francona .05
215 Kirk McCaskill .05
216 Ricky Jordan .05
217 Don Robinson .05
218 Wally Backman .05
219 Donn Pall .05
220 Barry Bonds .75
221 *Gary Mielke* .05
222 Kurt Stillwell .05
223 Tommy Gregg .05
224 *Delino DeShields* .15
225 Jim Deshaies .05
226 Mickey Hatcher .05
227 *Kevin Tapani* .15
228 Dave Martinez .05
229 David Wells .05
230 Keith Hernandez .05
231 Jack McKeon .05
232 Darnell Coles .05
233 Ken Hill .05
234 Mariano Duncan .05
235 Jeff Reardon .05
236 Hal Morris .05
237 *Kevin Ritz* .05
238 Felix Jose .05
239 Eric Show .05
240 Mark Grace .05
241 Mike Krukow .05
242 Fred Manrique .05
243 Barry Jones .05
244 Bill Schroeder .05
245 Roger Clemens .50
246 Jim Eisenreich .05
247 Jerry Reed .05
248 Dave Anderson .05
249 *Mike Smith* .05
250 Jose Canseco .25
251 Jeff Blauser .05
252 Otis Nixon .05
253 Mark Portugal .05
254 Francisco Cabrera .05
255 Bobby Thigpen .05
256 Marvell Wynne .05
257 Jose DeLeon .05
258 Barry Lyons .05
259 Lance McCullers .05
260 Eric Davis .05
261 Whitey Herzog .05
262 Checklist 133-264 .05
263 *Mel Stottlemyre, Jr.* .10
264 Bryan Clutterbuck .05
265 Pete O'Brien .05
266 German Gonzalez .05
267 Mark Davidson .05
268 Rob Murphy .05
269 Dickie Thon .05
270 Dave Stewart .05
271 Chet Lemon .05
272 Bryan Harvey .05
273 Bobby Bonilla .05
274 *Goose Gozzo* .05
275 Mickey Tettleton .05
276 Gary Thurman .05
277 Lenny Harris .05
278 Pascual Perez .05
279 Steve Buechele .05
280 Lou Whitaker .05
281 Kevin Bass .05
282 Derek Lilliquist .05
283 Albert Belle .15
284 *Mark Gardner* .05
285 Willie McGee .05
286 Lee Guetterman .05
287 Vance Law .05
288 Greg Briley .05
289 Norm Charlton .05
290 Robin Yount .35
291 Dave Johnson .05
292 Jim Gott .05
293 Mike Gallego .05
294 Craig McMurtry .05
295 Fred McGriff .05
296 Jeff Ballard .05
297 Tom Herr .05
298 Danny Gladden .05
299 Adam Peterson .05
300 Bo Jackson .10
301 Don Aase .05
302 *Marcus Lawton* .05
303 Rick Cerone .05
304 Marty Clary .05
305 Eddie Murray .35
306 Tom Niedenfuer .05
307 Bip Roberts .05
308 Jose Guzman .05
309 *Eric Yelding* .05
310 Steve Bedrosian .05
311 Dwight Smith .05
312 Dan Quisenberry .05
313 Gus Polidor .05
314 *Donald Harris* .05
315 Bruce Hurst .05
316 Carney Lansford .05
317 *Mark Guthrie* .05
318 Wallace Johnson .05
319 Dion James .05
320 Dave Steib .05
321 Joe M. Morgan .05
322 Junior Ortiz .05
323 Willie Wilson .05
324 Pete Harnisch .05
325 Robby Thompson .05
326 *Tom McCarthy* .05
327 Ken Williams .05
328 Curt Young .05
329 Oddibe McDowell .05
330 Ron Darling .05
331 *Juan Gonzalez* 1.50
332 Paul O'Neill .05
333 Bill Wegman .05
334 Johnny Ray .05
335 Andy Hawkins .05
336 Ken Griffey, Jr. .75
337 Lloyd McClendon .05
338 Dennis Lamp .05
339 Dave Clark .05
340 Fernando Valenzuela .05
341 Tom Foley .05
342 Alex Trevino .05
343 Frank Tanana .05
344 *George Canale* .05
345 Harold Baines .05
346 Jim Presley .05
347 *Junior Felix* .05
348 *Gary Wayne* .05
349 *Steve Finley* .15
350 Bret Saberhagen .05
351 Roger Craig .05
352 Bryn Smith .05
353 Sandy Alomar .05
354 *Stan Belinda* .05
355 Marty Barrett .05
356 Randy Ready .05
357 Dave West .05
358 Andres Thomas .05
359 Jimmy Jones .05
360 Paul Molitor .35
361 *Randy McCament* .05
362 Damon Berryhill .05
363 Dan Petry .05
364 Rolando Roomes .05
365 Ozzie Guillen .05
366 Mike Heath .05
367 Mike Morgan .05
368 Bill Doran .05
369 Todd Burns .05
370 Tim Wallach .05
371 Jimmy Key .05
372 Terry Kennedy .05
373 Alvin Davis .05
374 *Steve Cummings* .05
375 Dwight Evans .05
376 Checklist 265-396 .05
377 *Mickey Weston* .05
378 Luis Salazar .05
379 Steve Rosenberg .05
380 Dave Winfield .35
381 Frank Robinson .10
382 Jeff Musselman .05
383 John Morris .05
384 *Pat Combs* .05
385 Fred McGriff .05
386 Julio Franco .05
387 Wade Boggs .20
388 Cal Ripken, Jr. .40
389 Robin Yount .20
390 Ruben Sierra .05
391 Kirby Puckett .25
392 Carlton Fisk .20
393 Bret Saberhagen .05
394 Jeff Ballard .05
395 Jeff Russell .05
396 A. Bartlett Giamatti .20
397 Will Clark .05
398 Ryne Sandberg .20
399 Howard Johnson .05
400 Ozzie Smith .20
401 Kevin Mitchell .05
402 Eric Davis .05
403 Tony Gwynn .25
404 Craig Biggio .05
405 Mike Scott .05
406 Joe Magrane .05
407 Mark Davis .05
408 Trevor Wilson .05
409 Tom Brunansky .05
410 Joe Boever .05
411 Ken Phelps .05
412 Jamie Moyer .05
413 *Brian DuBois* .05
414a *Frank Thomas No Name* (#1 Draft Pick, no name on front) 450.00
414b *Frank Thomas* (#1 Draft Pick, name on front) 2.00
415 Shawon Dunston .05
416 *Dave Johnson* .05
417 Jim Gantner .05
418 Tom Browning .05
419 *Beau Allred* .05
420 Carlton Fisk .35
421 Greg Minton .05
422 Pat Sheridan .05
423 Fred Toliver .05
424 Jerry Reuss .05
425 Bill Landrum .05
426 Jeff Hamilton .05
427 Carmem Castillo .05
428 *Steve Davis* .05
429 Tom Kelly .05
430 Pete Incaviglia .05
431 Randy Johnson .35
432 Damaso Garcia .05
433 *Steve Olin* .05
434 Mark Carreon .05
435 Kevin Seitzer .05
436 Mel Hall .05
437 Les Lancaster .05
438 Greg Myers .05
439 Jeff Parrett .05
440 Alan Trammell .05
441 Bob Kipper .05
442 Jerry Browne .05
443 Cris Carpenter .05
444 *Kyle Abbott* (FDP) .10
445 Danny Jackson .05
446 Dan Pasqua .05
447 Atlee Hammaker .05
448 Greg Gagne .05
449 Dennis Rasmussen .05
450 Rickey Henderson .35
451 Mark Lemke .05
452 Luis de los Santos .05
453 Jody Davis .05
454a Jeff King (no white on back) 15.00
454b Jeff King (correct use of white) .05
455 Jeffrey Leonard .05
456 Chris Gwynn .05
457 Gregg Jefferies .05
458 Bob McClure .05
459 Jim Lefebvre .05
460 Mike Scott .05
461 *Carlos Martinez* .05
462 Denny Walling .05
463 Drew Hall .05
464 *Jerome Walton* .05
465 Kevin Gross .05
466 Rance Mulliniks .05
467 Juan Nieves .05
468 Billy Ripken .05
469 John Kruk .05
470 Frank Viola .05
471 Mike Brumley .05
472 Jose Uribe .05
473 Joe Price .05
474 Rich Thompson .05
475 Bob Welch .05
476 Brad Komminsk .05
477 Willie Fraser .05
478 Mike LaValliere .05
479 Frank White .05
480 Sid Fernandez .05
481 Garry Templeton .05
482 *Steve Carter* .05
483 Alejandro Pena .05
484 Mike Fitzgerald .05
485 John Candelaria .05
486 Jeff Treadway .05
487 Steve Searcy .05
488 Ken Oberkfell .05
489 Nick Leyva .05
490 Dan Plesac .05
491 *Dave Cochrane* .05
492 Ron Oester .05
493 *Jason Grimsley* .05
494 Terry Puhl .05
495 Lee Smith .05
496 Cecil Espy .05
497 Dave Schmidt .05
498 Rick Schu .05
499 Bill Long .05
500 Kevin Mitchell .05
501 Matt Young .05
502 Mitch Webster .05
503 Randy St. Claire .05
504 Tom O'Malley .05
505 Kelly Gruber .05
506 Tom Glavine .25
507 Gary Redus .05
508 Terry Leach .05
509 Tom Pagnozzi .05
510 Dwight Gooden .05
511 Clay Parker .05
512 Gary Pettis .05
513 Mark Eichhorn .05
514 Andy Allanson .05
515 Len Dykstra .05
516 Tim Leary .05
517 Roberto Alomar .15
518 Bill Krueger .05
519 Bucky Dent .05
520 Mitch Williams .05
521 Craig Worthington .05
522 Mike Dunne .05
523 Jay Bell .05
524 Daryl Boston .05
525 Wally Joyner .05
526 Checklist 397-528 .05
527 Ron Hassey .05
528 *Kevin Wickander* .05
529 Greg Harris .05
530 Mark Langston .05
531 Ken Caminiti .05
532 Cecilio Guante .05
533 Tim Jones .05
534 Louie Meadows .05

535 John Smoltz .05
536 *Bob Geren* .05
537 Mark Grant .05
538 *Billy Spiers* .05
539 Neal Heaton .05
540 Danny Tartabull .05
541 Pat Perry .05
542 Darren Daulton .05
543 Nelson Liriano .05
544 Dennis Boyd .05
545 Kevin McReynolds .05
546 Kevin Hickey .05
547 Jack Howell .05
548 Pat Clements .05
549 Don Zimmer .05
550 Julio Franco .05
551 Tim Crews .05
552 *Mike Smith* .05
553 *Scott Scudder* .05
554 Jay Buhner .05
555 Jack Morris .05
556 Gene Larkin .05
557 *Jeff Innis* .05
558 Rafael Ramirez .05
559 Andy McGaffigan .05
560 Steve Sax .05
561 Ken Dayley .05
562 Chad Kreuter .05
563 Alex Sanchez .05
564 *Tyler Houston* (#1 Draft Pick) .10
565 Scott Fletcher .05
566 Mark Knudson .05
567 Ron Gant .05
568 John Smiley .05
569 Ivan Calderon .05
570 Cal Ripken, Jr. .75
571 Brett Butler .05
572 Greg Harris .05
573 Danny Heep .05
574 Bill Swift .05
575 Lance Parrish .05
576 *Mike Dyer* .05
577 Charlie Hayes .05
578 Joe Magrane .05
579 Art Howe .05
580 Joe Carter .05
581 Ken Griffey .05
582 Rick Honeycutt .05
583 Bruce Benedict .05
584 *Phil Stephenson* .05
585 Kal Daniels .05
586 Ed Nunez .05
587 Lance Johnson .05
588 Rick Rhoden .05
589 Mike Aldrete .05
590 Ozzie Smith .45
591 Todd Stottlemyre .05
592 R.J. Reynolds .05
593 Scott Bradley .05
594 *Luis Sojo* .05
595 Greg Swindell .05
596 Jose DeJesus .05
597 Chris Bosio .05
598 Brady Anderson .05
599 Frank Williams .05
600 Darryl Strawberry .05
601 Luis Rivera .05
602 Scott Garrelts .05
603 Tony Armas .05
604 Ron Robinson .05
605 Mike Scioscia .05
606 Storm Davis .05
607 Steve Jeltz .05
608 *Eric Anthony* .10
609 Sparky Anderson .10
610 Pedro Guerrero .05
611 Walt Terrell .05
612 Dave Gallagher .05
613 Jeff Pico .05
614 Nelson Santovenia .05
615 Rob Deer .05
616 Brian Holman .05
617 Geronimo Berroa .05
618 Eddie Whitson .05
619 Rob Ducey .05
620 *Tony Castillo* .05
621 Melido Perez .05
622 Sid Bream .05
623 Jim Corsi .05
624 Darrin Jackson .05
625 Roger McDowell .05
626 Bob Melvin .05
627 Jose Rijo .05
628 Candy Maldonado .05
629 Eric Hetzel .05
630 Gary Gaetti .05
631 *John Wetteland* .15
632 Scott Lusader .05
633 Dennis Cook .05
634 Luis Polonia .05
635 Brian Downing .05
636 Jesse Orosco .05
637 Craig Reynolds .05
638 Jeff Montgomery .05
639 Tony LaRussa .05
640 Rick Sutcliffe .05
641 *Doug Strange* .05
642 Jack Armstrong .05
643 Alfredo Griffin .05
644 Paul Assenmacher .05
645 Jose Oquendo .05
646 Checklist 529-660 .05
647 Rex Hudler .05
648 Jim Clancy .05
649 *Dan Murphy* .05
650 Mike Witt .05
651 Rafael Santana .05
652 Mike Boddicker .05
653 John Moses .05
654 *Paul Coleman* (#1 Draft Pick) .05
655 Gregg Olson .05
656 Mackey Sasser .05
657 Terry Mulholland .05
658 Donell Nixon .05
659 Greg Cadaret .05
660 Vince Coleman .05
661 Dick Howser .05
662 Mike Schmidt .10
663 Fred Lynn .05
664 Johnny Bench .05
665 Sandy Koufax .15
666 Brian Fisher .05
667 Curt Wilkerson .05
668 *Joe Oliver* .05
669 Tom Lasorda .05
670 Dennis Eckersley .30
671 Bob Boone .05
672 Roy Smith .05
673 Joey Meyer .05
674 Spike Owen .05
675 Jim Abbott .05
676 Randy Kutcher .05
677 Jay Tibbs .05
678 Kirt Manwaring .05
679 Gary Ward .05
680 Howard Johnson .05
681 Mike Schooler .05
682 Dann Bilardello .05
683 Kenny Rogers .05
684 *Julio Machado* .05
685 Tony Fernandez .05
686 Carmelo Martinez .05
687 Tim Birtsas .05
688 Milt Thompson .05
689 Rich Yett .05
690 Mark McGwire .65
691 Chuck Cary .05
692 *Sammy Sosa* 4.00
693 Calvin Schiraldi .05
694 *Mike Stanton* .05
695 Tom Henke .05
696 B.J. Surhoff .05
697 Mike Davis .05
698 Omar Vizquel .05
699 Jim Leyland .05
700 Kirby Puckett .45
701 *Bernie Williams* 1.00
702 Tony Phillips .05
703 Jeff Brantley .05
704 *Chip Hale* .05
705 Claudell Washington .05
706 Geno Petralli .05
707 Luis Aquino .05
708 Larry Sheets .05
709 Juan Berneguer .05
710 Von Hayes .05
711 Rick Aguilera .05
712 Todd Benzinger .05
713 *Tim Drummond* .05
714 *Marquis Grissom* .25
715 Greg Maddux .45
716 Steve Balboni .05
717 Ron Kakovice .05
718 Gary Sheffield .30
719 *Wally Whitehurst* .05
720 Andres Galarraga .05
721 Lee Mazzilli .05
722 Felix Fermin .05
723 Jeff Robinson .05
724 Juan Bell .05
725 Terry Pendleton .05
726 Gene Nelson .05
727 Pat Tabler .05
728 Jim Acker .05
729 Bobby Valentine .05
730 Tony Gwynn .45
731 Don Carman .05
732 Ernie Riles .05
733 John Dopson .05
734 Kevin Elster .05
735 Charlie Hough .05
736 Rick Dempsey .05
737 Chris Sabo .05
738 *Gene Harris* .05
739 Dale Sveum .05
740 Jesse Barfield .05
741 Steve Wilson .05
742 Ernie Whitt .05
743 Tom Candiotti .05
744 *Kelly Mann* .05
745 Hubie Brooks .05
746 Dave Smith .05
747 Randy Bush .05
748 Doyle Alexander .05
749 Mark Parent .05
750 Dale Murphy .15
751 Steve Lyons .05
752 Tom Gordon .05
753 Chris Speier .05
754 Bob Walk .05
755 Rafael Palmeiro .30
756 Ken Howell .05
757 *Larry Walker* .75
758 Mark Thurmond .05
759 Tom Trebelhorn .05
760 Wade Boggs .45
761 Mike Jackson .05
762 Doug Dascenzo .05
763 Denny Martinez .05
764 Tim Teufel .05
765 Chili Davis .05
766 Brian Meyer .05
767 Tracy Jones .05
768 Chuck Crim .05
769 *Greg Hibbard* .05
770 Cory Snyder .05
771 Pete Smith .05
772 Jeff Reed .05
773 Dave Leiper .05
774 *Ben McDonald* .20
775 Andy Van Slyke .05
776 Charlie Leibrandt .05
777 Tim Laudner .05
778 Mike Jeffcoat .05
779 Lloyd Moseby .05
780 Orel Hershiser .05
781 Mario Diaz .05
782 Jose Alvarez .05
783 Checklist 661-792 .05
784 Scott Bailes .05
785 Jim Rice .15
786 Eric King .05
787 Rene Gonzales .05
788 Frank DiPino .05
789 John Wathan .05
790 Gary Carter .35
791 Alvaro Espinoza .05
792 Gerald Perry .05

Tiffany

	NM/M
Unopened Set (792):	115.00
Complete Set (792):	90.00
Common Player:	.10

(Star cards valued at 5X corresponding cards in regular Topps issue)

Traded

	NM/M
Complete Set, Retail (132):	6.00
Complete Set, Hobby (132):	4.00
Common Player:	.05
Wax Pack (7):	.75
Wax Box (36):	9.00

1 Darrel Akerfelds .05
2 Sandy Alomar, Jr. .05
3 Brad Arnsberg .05
4 Steve Avery .05
5 Wally Backman .05
6 *Carlos Baerga* .10
7 Kevin Bass .05
8 Willie Blair .05
9 Mike Blowers .05
10 Shawn Boskie .05
11 Daryl Boston .05
12 Dennis Boyd .05
13 Glenn Braggs .05
14 Hubie Brooks .05
15 Tom Brunansky .05
16 John Burkett .05
17 Casey Candaele .05
18 John Candelaria .05
19 Gary Carter .75
20 Joe Carter .05
21 Rick Cerone .05
22 Scott Coolbaugh .05
23 Bobby Cox .05
24 Mark Davis .05
25 Storm Davis .05
26 Edgar Diaz .05
27 Wayne Edwards .05
28 Mark Eichhorn .05
29 Scott Erickson .05
30 Nick Esasky .05
31 Cecil Fielder .05
32 John Franco .05
33 *Travis Fryman* .25
34 Bill Gullickson .05
35 Darryl Hamilton .05
36 Mike Harkey .05
37 Bud Harrelson .05
38 Billy Hatcher .05
39 Keith Hernandez .05
40 Joe Hesketh .05
41 Dave Hollins .05
42 Sam Horn .05
43 Steve Howard .05
44 *Todd Hundley* .15
45 Jeff Huson .05
46 Chris James .05
47 Stan Javier .05
48 *Dave Justice* .75
49 Jeff Kaiser .05
50 Dana Kiecker .05
51 Joe Klink .05
52 Brent Knackert .05
53 Brad Komminsk .05
54 Mark Langston .05
55 Tim Layana .05
56 Rick Leach .05
57 Terry Leach .05
58 Tim Leary .05
59 Craig Lefferts .05
60 Charlie Leibrandt .05
61 Jim Leyritz .05
62 Fred Lynn .05
63 Kevin Maas .05
64 Shane Mack .05
65 Candy Maldonado .05
66 Fred Manrique .05
67 Mike Marshall .05
68 Carmelo Martinez .05
69 John Marzano .05
70 Ben McDonald .05
71 Jack McDowell .05
72 John McNamara .05
73 Orlando Mercado .05
74 Stump Merrill .05
75 Alan Mills .05
76 Hal Morris .05
77 Lloyd Moseby .05
78 Randy Myers .05
79 Tim Naehring .05
80 Junior Noboa .05
81 Matt Nokes .05
82 Pete O'Brien .05
83 *John Olerud* .75
84 Greg Olson .05
85 Junior Ortiz .05
86 Dave Parker .05
87 Rick Parker .05
88 Bob Patterson .05
89 Alejandro Pena .05
90 Tony Pena .05
91 Pascual Perez .05
92 Gerald Perry .05
93 Dan Petry .05
94 Gary Pettis .05
95 Tony Phillips .05
96 Lou Pinella .05
97 Luis Polonia .05
98 Jim Presley .05
99 Scott Radinsky .05
100 Willie Randolph .05

101 Jeff Reardon .05
102 Greg Riddoch .05
103 Jeff Robinson .05
104 Ron Robinson .05
105 Kevin Romine .05
106 Scott Ruskin .05
107 John Russell .05
108 Bill Sampen .05
109 Juan Samuel .05
110 Scott Sanderson .05
111 Jack Savage .05
112 Dave Schmidt .05
113 Red Schoendienst .10
114 Terry Shumpert .05
115 Matt Sinatro .05
116 Don Slaught .05
117 Bryn Smith .05
118 Lee Smith .05
119 Paul Sorrento .05
120 Franklin Stubbs .05
121 Russ Swan .05
122 Bob Tewksbury .05
123 Wayne Tolleson .05
124 John Tudor .05
125 Randy Veres .05
126 Hector Villanueva .05
127 Mitch Webster .05
128 Ernie Whitt .05
129 Frank Wills .05
130 Dave Winfield .75
131 Matt Young .05
132 Checklist .05

Traded Tiffany

NM/M
Complete Set (132): 25.00
Common Player: .15
(Star cards valued at 4X corresponding cards in regular Topps Traded issue)

1991 TOPPS

NM/M
Unopened Factory Set, Retail (792): 30.00
Unopened Factory Set, Hobby (792): 25.00
Complete Set (792): 20.00
Common Player: .05
Wax Pack (15): .50
Wax Box (36): 12.50
Cello Pack (34): 1.00
Cello Box (24): 15.00
Rack Pack (45): 1.00
Rack Box (24): 15.00
Vending Box (500): 7.50
1 Nolan Ryan .75
2 George Brett .25
3 Carlton Fisk .20
4 Kevin Maas .05
5 Cal Ripken, Jr. .40
6 Nolan Ryan .40
7 Ryne Sandberg .30
8 Bobby Thigpen .05
9 Darrin Fletcher .05
10 Gregg Olson .05
11 Roberto Kelly .05
12 Paul Assenmacher .05
13 Mariano Duncan .05
14 Dennis Lamp .05
15 Von Hayes .05
16 Mike Heath .05
17 Jeff Brantley .05
18 Nelson Liriano .05
19 Jeff Robinson .05
20 Pedro Guerrero .05
21 Joe M. Morgan .05
22 Storm Davis .05
23 Jim Gantner .05
24 Dave Martinez .05
25 Tim Belcher .05
26 Luis Sojo .05
27 Bobby Witt .05
28 Alvaro Espinoza .05
29 Bob Walk .05
30 Gregg Jefferies .05
31 *Colby Ward* .05
32 *Mike Simms* .05
33 Barry Jones .05
34 Atlee Hammaker .05
35 Greg Maddux .50
36 Donnie Hill .05
37 Tom Bolton .05
38 Scott Bradley .05
39 *Jim Neidlinger* .05
40 Kevin Mitchell .05
41 Ken Dayley .05
42a *Chris Hoiles* (white inner photo frame) .20
42b *Chris Hoiles* (gray inner photo frame) .10
43 Roger McDowell .05
44 Mike Felder .05
45 Chris Sabo .05
46 Tim Drummond .05
47 Brook Jacoby .05
48 Dennis Boyd .05
49a Pat Borders (40 stolen bases in Kinston 1986) .20
49b Pat Borders (0 stolen bases in Kinston 1986) .10
50 Bob Welch .05
51 Art Howe .05
52 *Francisco Oliveras* .05
53 Mike Sharperson .05
54 Gary Mielke .05
55 Jeffrey Leonard .05
56 Jeff Parrett .05
57 Jack Howell .05
58 Mel Stottlemyre .05
59 Eric Yelding .05
60 Frank Viola .05
61 Stan Javier .05
62 Lee Guetterman .05
63 Milt Thompson .05
64 Tom Herr .05
65 Bruce Hurst .05
66 Terry Kennedy .05
67 Rick Honeycutt .05
68 Gary Sheffield .25
69 Steve Wilson .05
70 Ellis Burks .05
71 Jim Acker .05
72 Junior Ortiz .05
73 Craig Worthington .05
74 *Shane Andrews* (#1 Draft Pick) .10
75 Jack Morris .05
76 Jerry Browne .05
77 Drew Hall .05
78 Geno Petralli .05
79 Frank Thomas .35
80a Fernando Valenzuela (no diamond after 104 ER in 1990) .25
80b Fernando Valenzuela (diamond after 104 ER in 1990) .05
81 Cito Gaston .05
82 Tom Glavine .20
83 Daryl Boston .05
84 Bob McClure .05
85 Jesse Barfield .05
86 Les Lancaster .05
87 Tracy Jones .05
88 Bob Tewksbury .05
89 Darren Daulton .05
90 Danny Tartabull .05
91 *Greg Colbrunn* (Future Star) .05
92 Danny Jackson .05
93 Ivan Calderon .05
94 John Dopson .05
95 Paul Molitor .35
96 Trevor Wilson .05
97a Brady Anderson (3H, 2RBI in Sept. scoreboard) .25
97b Brady Anderson (14H, 3 RBI in Sept. scoreboard) .05
98 Sergio Valdez .05
99 Chris Gwynn .05
100a Don Mattingly (10 hits 1990) .50
100b Don Mattingly (101 hits in 1990) .50
101 Rob Ducey .05
102 Gene Larkin .05
103 *Tim Costo* (#1 Draft Pick) .05
104 Don Robinson .05
105 Kevin McReynolds .05
106 Ed Nunez .05
107 Luis Polonia .05
108 Matt Young .05
109 Greg Riddoch .05
110 Tom Henke .05
111 Andres Thomas .05
112 Frank DiPino .05
113 *Carl Everett* (#1 Draft Pick) .50
114 *Lance Dickson* (Future Star) .05
115 Hubie Brooks .05
116 Mark Davis .05
117 Dion James .05
118 *Tom Edens* .05
119 Carl Nichols .05
120 Joe Carter .05
121 Eric King .05
122 Paul O'Neill .05
123 Greg Harris .05
124 Randy Bush .05
125 Steve Bedrosian .05
126 *Bernard Gilkey* .10
127 Joe Price .05
128 Travis Fryman .05
129 Mark Eichhorn .05
130 Ozzie Smith .50
131a Checklist 1 (Phil Bradley #727) .05
131b Checklist 1 (Phil Bradley #717) .05
132 Jamie Quirk .05
133 Greg Briley .05
134 Kevin Elster .05
135 Jerome Walton .05
136 Dave Schmidt .05
137 Randy Ready .05
138 Jamie Moyer .05
139 Jeff Treadway .05
140 Fred McGriff .05
141 Nick Leyva .05
142 Curtis Wilkerson .05
143 John Smiley .05
144 Dave Henderson .05
145 Lou Whitaker .05
146 Dan Plesac .05
147 Carlos Baerga .05
148 Rey Palacios .05
149 *Al Osuna* .05
150 Cal Ripken, Jr. .75
151 Tom Browning .05
152 Mickey Hatcher .05
153 Bryan Harvey .05
154 Jay Buhner .05
155a Dwight Evans (diamond after 162 G 1982) .10
155b Dwight Evans (no diamond after 162 G 1982) .05
156 Carlos Martinez .05
157 John Smoltz .05
158 Jose Uribe .05
159 Joe Boever .05
160 Vince Coleman .05
161 Tim Leary .05
162 *Ozzie Canseco* .10
163 Dave Johnson .05
164 Edgar Diaz .05
165 Sandy Alomar .05
166 Harold Baines .05
167a *Randy Tomlin* ("Harriburg" 1989-90) .10
167b *Randy Tomlin* ("Harrisburg" 1989-90) .05
168 John Olerud .05
169 Luis Aquino .05
170 Carlton Fisk .35
171 Tony LaRussa .05
172 Pete Incaviglia .05
173 Jason Grimsley .05
174 Ken Caminiti .05
175 Jack Armstrong .05
176 John Orton .05
177 *Reggie Harris* .05
178 Dave Valle .05
179 Pete Harnisch .05
180 Tony Gwynn .50
181 Duane Ward .05
182 Junior Noboa .05
183 Clay Parker .05
184 Gary Green .05
185 Joe Magrane .05
186 Rod Booker .05
187 Greg Cadaret .05
188 Damon Berryhill .05
189 *Daryl Irvine* .05
190 Matt Williams .05
191 *Willie Blair* .05
192 Rob Deer .05
193 Felix Fermin .05
194 Xavier Hernandez .05
195 Wally Joyner .05
196 *Jim Vatcher* .05
197 *Chris Nabholz* .05
198 R.J. Reynolds .05
199 Mike Hartley .05
200 Darryl Strawberry .05
201 Tom Kelly .05
202 *Jim Leyritz* .20
203 Gene Harris .05
204 Herm Winningham .05
205 *Mike Perez* .05
206 Carlos Quintana .05
207 Gary Wayne .05
208 Willie Wilson .05
209 Ken Howell .05
210 Lance Parrish .05
211 *Brian Barnes* (Future Star) .05
212 Steve Finley .05
213 Frank Wills .05
214 Joe Girardi .05
215 Dave Smith .05
216 Greg Gagne .05
217 Chris Bosio .05
218 *Rick Parker* .05
219 Jack McDowell .05
220 Tim Wallach .05
221 Don Slaught .05
222 *Brian McRae* .10
223 Allan Anderson .05
224 Juan Gonzalez .20
225 Randy Johnson .35
226 Alfredo Griffin .05
227 Steve Avery .05
228 Rex Hudler .05
229 Rance Mulliniks .05
230 Sid Fernandez .05
231 Doug Rader .05
232 Jose DeJesus .05
233 Al Leiter .05
234 *Scott Erickson* .10
235 Dave Parker .05
236a Frank Tanana (no diamond after 269 SO 1975) .10
236b Frank Tanana (diamond after 269 SO 1975) .05
237 Rick Cerone .05
238 Mike Dunne .05
239 *Darren Lewis* .05
240 Mike Scott .05
241 Dave Clark .05
242 Mike LaCoss .05
243 Lance Johnson .05
244 Mike Jeffcoat .05
245 Kal Daniels .05
246 Kevin Wickander .05
247 Jody Reed .05
248 Tom Gordon .05
249 Bob Melvin .05
250 Dennis Eckersley .30
251 Mark Lemke .05
252 *Mel Rojas* .05
253 Garry Templeton .05
254 *Shawn Boskie* .05
255 Brian Downing .05
256 Greg Hibbard .05
257 Tom O'Malley .05
258 Chris Hammond .05
259 Hensley Meulens .05
260 Harold Reynolds .05
261 Bud Harrelson .05
262 Tim Jones .05
263 Checklist 2 .05
264 *Dave Hollins* .05
265 Mark Gubicza .05
266 Carmen Castillo .05
267 Mark Knudson .05
268 Tom Brookens .05
269 Joe Hesketh .05
270a Mark McGwire (1987 SLG .618) .75
270b Mark McGwire (1987 SLG 618) .75
271 *Omar Olivares* .05
272 Jeff King .05
273 Johnny Ray .05
274 Ken Williams .05
275 Alan Trammell .05
276 Bill Swift .05
277 Scott Coolbaugh .05
278 *Alex Fernandez* .10
279a Jose Gonzalez (photo of Billy Bean, left-handed batter) .75
279b Jose Gonzalez (correct photo, right-handed batter) .05
280 Bret Saberhagen .05

281	Larry Sheets	.05
282	Don Carman	.05
283	Marquis Grissom	.05
284	Bill Spiers	.05
285	Jim Abbott	.05
286	Ken Oberkfell	.05
287	Mark Grant	.05
288	Derrick May	.05
289	Tim Birtsas	.05
290	Steve Sax	.05
291	John Wathan	.05
292	Bud Black	.05
293	Jay Bell	.05
294	Mike Moore	.05
295	Rafael Palmeiro	.30
296	Mark Williamson	.05
297	Manny Lee	.05
298	Omar Vizquel	.05
299	*Scott Radinsky*	.05
300	Kirby Puckett	.50
301	Steve Farr	.05
302	Tim Teufel	.05
303	Mike Boddicker	.05
304	Kevin Reimer	.05
305	Mike Scioscia	.05
306a	Lonnie Smith (136 G 1990)	.10
306b	Lonnie Smith (135 G 1990)	.05
307	Andy Benes	.05
308	Tom Pagnozzi	.05
309	Norm Charlton	.05
310	Gary Carter	.35
311	Jeff Pico	.05
312	Charlie Hayes	.05
313	Ron Robinson	.05
314	Gary Pettis	.05
315	Roberto Alomar	.15
316	Gene Nelson	.05
317	Mike Fitzgerald	.05
318	Rick Aguilera	.05
319	Jeff McKnight	.05
320	Tony Fernandez	.05
321	Bob Rodgers	.05
322	*Terry Shumpert*	.05
323	Cory Snyder	.05
324a	Ron Kittle ("6 Home Runs" in career summary)	.10
324b	Ron Kittle ("7 Home Runs" in career summary)	.05
325	Brett Butler	.05
326	Ken Patterson	.05
327	Ron Hassey	.05
328	Walt Terrell	.05
329	Dave Justice	.05
330	Dwight Gooden	.05
331	Eric Anthony	.05
332	Kenny Rogers	.05
333	*Chipper Jones* (#1 Draft Pick)	2.00
334	Todd Benzinger	.05
335	Mitch Williams	.05
336	Matt Nokes	.05
337a	Keith Comstock (Mariners logo)	.05
337b	Keith Comstock (Cubs logo)	1.50
338	Luis Rivera	.05
339	Larry Walker	.05
340	Ramon Martinez	.05
341	John Moses	.05
342	*Mickey Morandini*	.10
343	Jose Oquendo	.05
344	Jeff Russell	.05
345	Len Dykstra	.05
346	Jesse Orosco	.05
347	Greg Vaughn	.05
348	Todd Stottlemyre	.05
349	Dave Gallagher	.05
350	Glenn Davis	.05
351	Joe Torre	.05
352	Frank White	.05
353	Tony Castillo	.05
354	Sid Bream	.05
355	Chili Davis	.05
356	Mike Marshall	.05
357	Jack Savage	.05
358	Mark Parent	.05
359	Chuck Cary	.05
360	Tim Raines	.05
361	Scott Garrelts	.05
362	*Hector Villanueva*	.05
363	Rick Mahler	.05
364	Dan Pasqua	.05
365	Mike Schooler	.05
366a	Checklist 3 (Carl Nichols #19)	.05
366b	Checklist 3 (Carl Nichols #119)	.05
367	*Dave Walsh*	.05
368	Felix Jose	.05
369	Steve Searcy	.05
370	Kelly Gruber	.05
371	Jeff Montgomery	.05
372	Spike Owen	.05
373	Darrin Jackson	.05
374	*Larry Casian*	.05
375	Tony Pena	.05
376	Mike Harkey	.05
377	Rene Gonzales	.05
378a	*Wilson Alvarez* (no 1989 Port Charlotte stats)	.50
378b	*Wilson Alvarez* (1989 Port Charlotte stats)	.20
379	Randy Velarde	.05
380	Willie McGee	.05
381	Jim Leyland	.05
382	Mackey Sasser	.05
383	Pete Smith	.05
384	Gerald Perry	.05
385	Mickey Tettleton	.05
386	Cecil Fielder	.05
387	Julio Franco	.05
388	Kelly Gruber	.05
389	Alan Trammell	.05
390	Jose Canseco	.15
391	Rickey Henderson	.20
392	Ken Griffey, Jr.	.35
393	Carlton Fisk	.20
394	Bob Welch	.05
395	Chuck Finley	.05
396	Bobby Thigpen	.05
397	Eddie Murray	.20
398	Ryne Sandberg	.30
399	Matt Williams	.05
400	Barry Larkin	.05
401	Barry Bonds	.40
402	Darryl Strawberry	.05
403	Bobby Bonilla	.05
404	Mike Scoscia	.05
405	Doug Drabek	.05
406	Frank Viola	.05
407	John Franco	.05
408	Ernie Riles	.05
409	Mike Stanley	.05
410	Dave Righetti	.05
411	Lance Blankenship	.05
412	Dave Bergman	.05
413	Terry Mulholland	.05
414	Sammy Sosa	.60
415	Rick Sutcliffe	.05
416	Randy Milligan	.05
417	Bill Krueger	.05
418	Nick Esasky	.05
419	Jeff Reed	.05
420	Bobby Thigpen	.05
421	Alex Cole	.05
422	Rick Rueschel	.05
423	Rafael Ramirez	.05
424	Calvin Schiraldi	.05
425	Andy Van Slyke	.05
426	*Joe Grahe*	.05
427	Rick Dempsey	.05
428	*John Barfield*	.05
429	Stump Merrill	.05
430	Gary Gaetti	.05
431	Paul Gibson	.05
432	Delino DeShields	.05
433	Pat Tabler	.05
434	Julio Machado	.05
435	Kevin Maas	.05
436	Scott Bankhead	.05
437	Doug Dascenzo	.05
438	Vicente Palacios	.05
439	Dickie Thon	.05
440	George Bell	.05
441	Zane Smith	.05
442	Charlie O'Brien	.05
443	Jeff Innis	.05
444	Glenn Braggs	.05
445	Greg Swindell	.05
446	*Craig Grebeck*	.05
447	John Burkett	.05
448	Craig Lefferts	.05
449	Juan Berenguer	.05
450	Wade Boggs	.50
451	Neal Heaton	.05
452	Bill Schroeder	.05
453	Lenny Harris	.05
454a	Kevin Appier (no 1990 Omaha stats)	.15
454b	Kevin Appier (1990 Omaha stats)	.05
455	Walt Weiss	.05
456	Charlie Leibrandt	.05
457	Todd Hundley	.05
458	Brian Holman	.05
459	Tom Trebelhorn	.05
460	Dave Steib	.05
461a	Robin Ventura (gray inner photo frame at left)	.15
461b	Robin Ventura (red inner photo frame at left)	.05
462	Steve Frey	.05
463	Dwight Smith	.05
464	Steve Buechele	.05
465	Ken Griffey	.05
466	Charles Nagy	.05
467	Dennis Cook	.05
468	Tim Hulett	.05
469	Chet Lemon	.05
470	Howard Johnson	.05
471	*Mike Lieberthal* (#1 Draft Pick)	.50
472	Kirt Manwaring	.05
473	Curt Young	.05
474	*Phil Plantier*	.10
475	Teddy Higuera	.05
476	Glenn Wilson	.05
477	Mike Fetters	.05
478	Kurt Stillwell	.05
479	Bob Patterson	.05
480	Dave Magadan	.05
481	Eddie Whitson	.05
482	Tino Martinez	.05
483	Mike Aldrete	.05
484	Dave LaPoint	.05
485	Terry Pendleton	.05
486	Tommy Greene	.05
487	Rafael Belliard	.05
488	Jeff Manto	.05
489	Bobby Valentine	.05
490	Kirk Gibson	.05
491	*Kurt Miller*	.05
492	Ernie Whitt	.05
493	Jose Rijo	.05
494	Chris James	.05
495	Charlie Hough	.05
496	Marty Barrett	.05
497	Ben McDonald	.05
498	Mark Salas	.05
499	Melido Perez	.05
500	Will Clark	.05
501	Mike Bielecki	.05
502	Carney Lansford	.05
503	Roy Smith	.05
504	*Julio Valera*	.05
505	Chuck Finley	.05
506	Darnell Coles	.05
507	Steve Jeltz	.05
508	*Mike York*	.05
509	Glenallen Hill	.05
510	John Franco	.05
511	Steve Balboni	.05
512	Jose Mesa	.05
513	Jerald Clark	.05
514	Mike Stanton	.05
515	Alvin Davis	.05
516	*Karl Rhodes*	.05
517	Joe Oliver	.05
518	Cris Carpenter	.05
519	Sparky Anderson	.10
520	Mark Grace	.05
521	Joe Orsulak	.05
522	Stan Belinda	.05
523	*Rodney McCray*	.05
524	Darrel Akerfelds	.05
525	Willie Randolph	.05
526a	Moises Alou (37 R 1990 Pirates)	.20
526b	Moises Alou (0 R 1990 Pirates)	.15
527a	Checklist 4 (Kevin McReynolds #719)	.05
527b	Checklist 4 (Kevin McReynolds #105)	.05
528	Denny Martinez	.05
529	*Mark Newfield*	.05
530	Roger Clemens	.60
531	*Dave Rhode*	.05
532	Kirk McCaskill	.05
533	Oddibe McDowell	.05
534	Mike Jackson	.05
535	Ruben Sierra	.05
536	Mike Witt	.05
537	Jose Lind	.05
538	Bip Roberts	.05
539	Scott Terry	.05
540	George Brett	.60
541	Domingo Ramos	.05
542	Rob Murphy	.05
543	Junior Felix	.05
544	Alejandro Pena	.05
545	Dale Murphy	.15
546	Jeff Ballard	.05
547	Mike Pagliarulo	.05
548	Jaime Navarro	.05
549	John McNamara	.05
550	Eric Davis	.05
551	Bob Kipper	.05
552	Jeff Hamilton	.05
553	*Joe Klink*	.05
554	Brian Harper	.05
555	*Turner Ward*	.05
556	Gary Ward	.05
557	Wally Whitehurst	.05
558	Otis Nixon	.05
559	Adam Peterson	.05
560	Greg Smith	.05
561	Tim McIntosh (Future Star)	.05
562	Jeff Kunkel	.05
563	*Brent Knackert*	.05
564	Dante Bichette	.05
565	Craig Biggio	.05
566	*Craig Wilson*	.05
567	Dwayne Henry	.05
568	Ron Karkovice	.05
569	Curt Schilling	.05
570	Barry Bonds	.75
571	Pat Combs	.05
572	Dave Anderson	.05
573	*Rich Rodriguez*	.05
574	John Marzano	.05
575	Robin Yount	.35
576	Jeff Kaiser	.05
577	Bill Doran	.05
578	Dave West	.05
579	Roger Craig	.05
580	Dave Stewart	.05
581	Luis Quinones	.05
582	Marty Clary	.05
583	Tony Phillips	.05
584	Kevin Brown	.05
585	Pete O'Brien	.05
586	Fred Lynn	.05
587	Jose Offerman (Future Star)	.05
588a	Mark Whiten (hand inside left border)	.05
588b	Mark Whiten (hand over left border)	.20
589	*Scott Ruskin*	.05
590	Eddie Murray	.35
591	Ken Hill	.05
592	B.J. Surhoff	.05
593a	*Mike Walker* (No 1990 Canton-Akron stats)	.15
593b	*Mike Walker* (1990 Canton-Akron stats)	.05
594	*Rich Garces* (Future Star)	.05
595	Bill Landrum	.05
596	*Ronnie Walden* (#1 Draft Pick)	.05
597	Jerry Don Gleaton	.05
598	Sam Horn	.05
599a	Greg Myers (no 1990 Syracuse stats)	.10
599b	Greg Myers (1990 Syracuse stats)	.05
600	Bo Jackson	.10
601	Bob Ojeda	.05
602	Casey Candaele	.05
603a	*Wes Chamberlain* (photo of Louie Meadows, no bat)	.75
603b	*Wes Chamberlain* (correct photo, holding bat)	.05
604	Billy Hatcher	.05
605	Jeff Reardon	.05
606	Jim Gott	.05
607	Edgar Martinez	.05
608	Todd Burns	.05
609	Jeff Torborg	.05
610	Andres Galarraga	.05
611	Dave Eiland	.05
612	Steve Lyons	.05
613	Eric Show	.05
614	Luis Salazar	.05
615	Bert Blyleven	.05
616	Todd Zeile	.05
617	Bill Wegman	.05
618	Sil Campusano	.05
619	David Wells	.05
620	Ozzie Guillen	.05
621	Ted Power	.05
622	Jack Daugherty	.05
623	Jeff Blauser	.05
624	Tom Candiotti	.05
625	Terry Steinbach	.05
626	Gerald Young	.05
627	*Tim Layana*	.05
628	Greg Litton	.05
629	Wes Gardner	.05
630	Dave Winfield	.35
631	Mike Morgan	.05
632	Lloyd Moseby	.05

#	Player	Value
633	Kevin Tapani	.05
634	Henry Cotto	.05
635	Andy Hawkins	.05
636	Geronimo Pena	.05
637	Bruce Ruffin	.05
638	Mike Macfarlane	.05
639	Frank Robinson	.05
640	Andre Dawson	.20
641	Mike Henneman	.05
642	Hal Morris	.05
643	Jim Presley	.05
644	Chuck Crim	.05
645	Juan Samuel	.05
646	*Andujar Cedeno*	.05
647	Mark Portugal	.05
648	Lee Stevens	.05
649	*Bill Sampen*	.05
650	Jack Clark	.05
651	*Alan Mills*	.05
652	Kevin Romine	.05
653	*Anthony Telford*	.05
654	Paul Sorrento	.05
655	Erik Hanson	.05
656a	Checklist 5 (Vincente Palacios #348)	.05
656b	Checklist 5 (Palacios #433)	.05
656c	Checklist 5 (Palacios #438)	.05
657	Mike Kingery	.05
658	*Scott Aldred*	.05
659	*Oscar Azocar*	.05
660	Lee Smith	.05
661	Steve Lake	.05
662	Rob Dibble	.05
663	Greg Brock	.05
664	John Farrell	.05
665	Mike LaValliere	.05
666	Danny Darwin	.05
667	Kent Anderson	.05
668	Bill Long	.05
669	Lou Pinella	.05
670	Rickey Henderson	.35
671	Andy McGaffigan	.05
672	Shane Mack	.05
673	*Greg Olson*	.05
674a	Kevin Gross (no diamond after 89 BB 1988)	.10
674b	Kevin Gross (diamond after 89 BB 1988)	.05
675	Tom Brunansky	.05
676	*Scott Chiamparino*	.05
677	Billy Ripken	.05
678	Mark Davidson	.05
679	Bill Bathe	.05
680	David Cone	.05
681	*Jeff Schaefer*	.05
682	*Ray Lankford*	.15
683	Derek Lilliquist	.05
684	Milt Cuyler	.05
685	Doug Drabek	.05
686	Mike Gallego	.05
687a	John Cerutti (4.46 ERA 1990)	.05
687b	John Cerutti (4.76 ERA 1990)	.05
688	*Rosario Rodriguez*	.05
689	John Kruk	.05
690	Orel Hershiser	.05
691	Mike Blowers	.05
692a	*Efrain Valdez* (no text below stats)	.15
692b	*Efrain Valdez* (two lines of text below stats)	.05
693	Francisco Cabrera	.05
694	Randy Veres	.05
695	Kevin Seitzer	.05
696	Steve Olin	.05
697	Shawn Abner	.05
698	Mark Guthrie	.05
699	Jim Lefebvre	.05
700	Jose Canseco	.25
701	Pascual Perez	.05
702	*Tim Naehring*	.05
703	Juan Agosto	.05
704	Devon White	.05
705	Robby Thompson	.05
706a	Brad Arnsberg (68.2 IP Rangers 1990)	.05
706b	Brad Arnsberg (62.2 IP Rangers 1990)	.05
707	Jim Eisenreich	.05
708	John Mitchell	.05
709	Matt Sinatro	.05
710	Kent Hrbek	.05
711	Jose DeLeon	.05
712	Ricky Jordan	.05
713	Scott Scudder	.05
714	Marvell Wynne	.05
715	Tim Burke	.05
716	Bob Geren	.05
717	Phil Bradley	.05
718	Steve Crawford	.05
719	Keith Miller	.05
720	Cecil Fielder	.05
721	*Mark Lee*	.05
722	Wally Backman	.05
723	Candy Maldonado	.05
724	*David Segui*	.10
725	Ron Gant	.05
726	Phil Stephenson	.05
727	Mookie Wilson	.05
728	Scott Sanderson	.05
729	Don Zimmer	.05
730	Barry Larkin	.05
731	*Jeff Gray*	.05
732	Franklin Stubbs	.05
733	Kelly Downs	.05
734	John Russell	.05
735	Ron Darling	.05
736	Dick Schofield	.05
737	Tim Crews	.05
738	Mel Hall	.05
739	*Russ Swan*	.05
740	Ryne Sandberg	.50
741	Jimmy Key	.05
742	Tommy Gregg	.05
743	Bryn Smith	.05
744	Nelson Santovenia	.05
745	Doug Jones	.05
746	John Shelby	.05
747	Tony Fossas	.05
748	Al Newman	.05
749	Greg Harris	.05
750	Bobby Bonilla	.05
751	*Wayne Edwards*	.05
752	Kevin Bass	.05
753	*Paul Marak*	.05
754	Bill Pecota	.05
755	Mark Langston	.05
756	Jeff Huson	.05
757	Mark Gardner	.05
758	Mike Devereaux	.05
759	Bobby Cox	.05
760	Benny Santiago	.05
761	Larry Andersen	.05
762	Mitch Webster	.05
763	*Dana Kiecker*	.05
764	Mark Carreon	.05
765	Shawon Dunston	.05
766	Jeff Robinson	.05
767	*Dan Wilson*	.10
768	Donn Pall	.05
769	*Tim Sherrill*	.05
770	Jay Howell	.05
771	Gary Redus	.05
772	Kent Mercker	.05
773	Tom Foley	.05
774	Dennis Rasmussen	.05
775	Julio Franco	.05
776	Brent Mayne	.05
777	John Candelaria	.05
778	Danny Gladden	.05
779	Carmelo Martinez	.05
780a	Randy Myers (Career losses 15)	.10
780b	Randy Myers (Career losses 19)	.05
781	Darryl Hamilton	.05
782	Jim Deshaies	.05
783	Joel Skinner	.05
784	Willie Fraser	.05
785	Scott Fletcher	.05
786	Eric Plunk	.05
787	Checklist 6	.05
788	Bob Milacki	.05
789	Tom Lasorda	.05
790	Ken Griffey, Jr.	.60
791	Mike Benjamin	.05
792	Mike Greenwell	.05

Tiffany

	NM/M
Unopened Set (792):	135.00
Complete Set (792):	85.00
Common Player:	.10

(Star cards valued at 3X corresponding regular issue Topps cards)

Traded

	NM/M
Unopened Retail or Hobby Set (132):	8.00
Complete Set (132):	7.50
Common Player:	.05
Wax Pack (7):	.65
Wax Box (36):	15.00

#	Player	Value
1	Juan Agosto	.05
2	Roberto Alomar	.15
3	Wally Backman	.05
4	*Jeff Bagwell*	3.00
5	Skeeter Barnes	.05
6	Steve Bedrosian	.05
7	Derek Bell	.05
8	George Bell	.05
9	Rafael Belliard	.05
10	Dante Bichette	.05
11	Bud Black	.05
12	Mike Boddicker	.05
13	Sid Bream	.05
14	Hubie Brooks	.05
15	Brett Butler	.05
16	Ivan Calderon	.05
17	John Candelaria	.05
18	Tom Candiotti	.05
19	Gary Carter	.50
20	Joe Carter	.05
21	Rick Cerone	.05
22	Jack Clark	.05
23	Vince Coleman	.05
24	Scott Coolbaugh	.05
25	Danny Cox	.05
26	Danny Darwin	.05
27	Chili Davis	.05
28	Glenn Davis	.05
29	Steve Decker	.05
30	Rob Deer	.05
31	Rich DeLucia	.05
32	*John Dettmer* (USA)	.05
33	Brian Downing	.05
34	*Darren Dreifort* (USA)	.25
35	Kirk Dressendorfer	.05
36	Jim Essian	.05
37	Dwight Evans	.05
38	Steve Farr	.05
39	Jeff Fassero	.05
40	Junior Felix	.05
41	Tony Fernandez	.05
42	Steve Finley	.05
43	Jim Fregosi	.05
44	Gary Gaetti	.05
45	*Jason Giambi* (USA)	4.00
46	Kirk Gibson	.05
47	Leo Gomez	.05
48	*Luis Gonzalez*	1.00
49	*Jeff Granger* (USA)	.10
50	*Todd Greene* (USA)	.15
51	*Jeffrey Hammonds* (USA)	.15
52	Mike Hargrove	.05
53	Pete Harnisch	.05
54	*Rick Helling* (USA)	.10
55	Glenallen Hill	.05
56	Charlie Hough	.05
57	Pete Incaviglia	.05
58	Bo Jackson	.10
59	Danny Jackson	.05
60	Reggie Jefferson	.05
61	*Charles Johnson* (USA)	.15
62	Jeff Johnson	.05
63	*Todd Johnson* (USA)	.05
64	Barry Jones	.05
65	Chris Jones	.05
66	Scott Kamieniecki	.05
67	*Pat Kelly*	.05
68	Darryl Kile	.05
69	Chuck Knoblauch	.05
70	Bill Krueger	.05
71	Scott Leius	.05
72	*Donnie Leshnock* (USA)	.05
73	Mark Lewis	.05
74	Candy Maldonado	.05
75	*Jason McDonald* (USA)	.05
76	Willie McGee	.05
77	Fred McGriff	.05
78	*Billy McMillon* (USA)	.05
79	Hal McRae	.05
80	*Dan Melendez* (USA)	.05
81	Orlando Merced	.05
82	Jack Morris	.05
83	*Phil Nevin* (USA)	.50
84	Otis Nixon	.05
85	Johnny Oates	.05
86	Bob Ojeda	.05
87	Mike Pagliarulo	.05
88	Dean Palmer	.05
89	Dave Parker	.05
90	Terry Pendleton	.05
91	*Tony Phillips* (USA)	.10
92	Doug Piatt	.05
93	Ron Polk (U.S.A.)	.05
94	Tim Raines	.05
95	Willie Randolph	.05
96	Dave Righetti	.05
97	Ernie Riles	.05
98	*Chris Roberts* (USA)	.05
99	Jeff Robinson (Angels)	.05
100	Jeff Robinson (Orioles)	.05
101	*Ivan Rodriguez*	2.00
102	*Steve Rodriguez* (USA)	.05
103	Tom Runnells	.05
104	Scott Sanderson	.05
105	Bob Scanlan	.05
106	*Pete Schourek*	.10
107	Gary Scott	.05
108	*Paul Shuey* (USA)	.10
109	*Doug Simons*	.05
110	Dave Smith	.05
111	Cory Snyder	.05
112	Luis Sojo	.05
113	*Kennie Steenstra* (USA)	.05
114	Darryl Strawberry	.05
115	Franklin Stubbs	.05
116	*Todd Taylor* (USA)	.05
117	Wade Taylor	.05
118	Garry Templeton	.05
119	Mickey Tettleton	.05
120	Tim Teufel	.05
121	Mike Timlin	.05
122	*David Tuttle* (USA)	.05
123	Mo Vaughn	.25
124	*Jeff Ware* (USA)	.05
125	Devon White	.05
126	Mark Whiten	.05
127	Mitch Williams	.05
128	*Craig Wilson* (USA)	.05
129	Willie Wilson	.05
130	*Chris Wimmer* (USA)	.05
131	*Ivan Zweig* (USA)	.05
132	Checklist	.05

Traded Tiffany

	NM/M
Unopened Set (132):	165.00
Complete Set (132):	90.00
Common Player:	.25
Stars and Rookies:	4X

(See 1991 Topps Traded for checklist and base card values.)

1992 TOPPS 1991 MAJOR LEAGUE DEBUT

	NM/M
Complete Set (194):	12.50
Common Player:	.05

#	Player	Value
1	Kyle Abbott	.05
2	Dana Allison	.05
3	Rich Amaral	.05
4	Ruben Amaro	.05
5	Andy Ashby	.05
6	Jim Austin	.05
7	Jeff Bagwell	4.00
8	Jeff Banister	.05
9	Willie Banks	.05
10	Bret Barberie	.05
11	Kim Batiste	.05
12	Chris Beasley	.05

13	Rod Beck	.05
14	Derek Bell	.05
15	Esteban Beltre	.05
16	Freddie Benavides	.05
17	Rickey Bones	.05
18	Denis Boucher	.05
19	Ryan Bowen	.05
20	Cliff Brantley	.05
21	John Briscoe	.05
22	Scott Brosius	.05
23	Terry Bross	.05
24	Jarvis Brown	.05
25	Scott Bullett	.05
26	Kevin Campbell	.05
27	Amalio Carreno	.05
28	Matias Carrillo	.05
29	Jeff Carter	.05
30	Vinny Castilla	.05
31	Braulio Castillo	.05
32	Frank Castillo	.05
33	Darrin Chapin	.05
34	Mike Christopher	.05
35	Mark Clark	.05
36	Royce Clayton	.05
37	Stu Cole	.05
38	Gary Cooper	.05
39	Archie Corbin	.05
40	Rheal Cormier	.05
41	Chris Cron	.05
42	Mike Dalton	.05
43	Mark Davis	.05
44	Francisco de la Rosa	.05
45	Chris Donnels	.05
46	Brian Drahman	.05
47	Tom Drees	.05
48	Kirk Dressendorfer	.05
49	Bruce Egloff	.05
50	Cal Eldred	.05
51	Jose Escobar	.05
52	Tony Eusebio	.05
53	Hector Fajardo	.05
54	Monty Farriss	.05
55	Jeff Fassero	.05
56	Dave Fleming	.05
57	Kevin Flora	.05
58	Steve Foster	.05
59	Dan Gakeler	.05
60	Ramon Garcia	.05
61	Chris Gardner	.05
62	Jeff Gardner	.05
63	Chris George	.05
64	Ray Giannelli	.05
65	Tom Goodwin	.05
66	Mark Grater	.05
67	Johnny Guzman	.05
68	Juan Guzman	.05
69	Dave Haas	.05
70	Chris Haney	.05
71	Shawn Hare	.05
72	Donald Harris	.05
73	Doug Henry	.05
74	Pat Hentgen	.05
75	Gil Heredia	.05
76	Jeremy Hernandez	.05
77	Jose Hernandez	.05
78	Roberto Hernandez	.05
79	Bryan Hickerson	.05
80	Milt Hill	.05
81	Vince Horsman	.05
82	Wayne Housie	.05
83	Chris Howard	.05
84	David Howard	.05
85	Mike Humphreys	.05
86	Brian Hunter	.05
87	Jim Hunter	.05
88	Mike Ignasiak	.05
89	Reggie Jefferson	.05
90	Jeff Johnson	.05
91	Joel Johnson	.05
92	Calvin Jones	.05
93	Chris Jones	.05
94	Stacy Jones	.05
95	Jeff Juden	.05
96	Scott Kamieniecki	.05
97	Eric Karros	.05
98	Pat Kelly	.05
99	John Kiely	.05
100	Darryl Kile	.05
101	Wayne Kirby	.05
102	Garland Kiser	.05
103	Chuck Knoblauch	.05
104	Randy Knorr	.05
105	Tom Kramer	.05
106	Ced Landrum	.05
107	Patrick Lennon	.05
108	Jim Lewis	.05
109	Mark Lewis	.05
110	Doug Lindsey	.05
111	Scott Livingstone	.05
112	Kenny Lofton	.10
113	Ever Magallanes	.05
114	Mike Magnante	.05
115	Barry Manuel	.05
116	Josias Manzanillo	.05
117	Chito Martinez	.05
118	Terry Mathews	.05
119	Rob Mauer	.05
120	Tim Mauser	.05
121	Terry McDaniel	.05
122	Rusty Meacham	.05
123	Luis Mercedes	.05
124	Paul Miller	.05
125	Keith Mitchell	.05
126	Bobby Moore	.05
127	Kevin Morton	.05
128	Andy Mota	.05
129	Jose Mota	.05
130	Mike Mussina	2.00
131	Jeff Mutis	.05
132	Denny Neagle	.05
133	Warren Newson	.05
134	Jim Olander	.05
135	Erik Pappas	.05
136	Jorge Pedre	.05
137	Yorkis Perez	.05
138	Mark Petkovsek	.05
139	Doug Piatt	.05
140	Jeff Plympton	.05
141	Harvey Pulliam	.05
142	John Ramos	.05
143	Mike Remlinger	.05
144	Laddie Renfroe	.05
145	Armando Reynoso	.05
146	Arthur Rhodes	.05
147	Pat Rice	.05
148	Nikco Riesgo	.05
149	Carlos Rodriguez	.05
150	Ivan Rodriguez	3.00
151	Wayne Rosenthal	.05
152	Rico Rossy	.05
153	Stan Royer	.05
154	Rey Sanchez	.05
155	Reggie Sanders	.05
156	Mo Sanford	.05
157	Bob Scanlan	.05
158	Pete Schourek	.05
159	Gary Scott	.05
160	Tim Scott	.05
161	Tony Scruggs	.05
162	Scott Servais	.05
163	Doug Simons	.05
164	Heathcliff Slocumb	.05
165	Joe Slusarski	.05
166	Tim Spehr	.05
167	Ed Sprague	.05
168	Jeff Tackett	.05
169	Eddie Taubensee	.05
170	Wade Taylor	.05
171	Jim Thome	2.50
172	Mike Timlin	.05
173	Jose Tolentino	.05
174	John Vander Wal	.05
175	Todd Van Poppel	.05
176	Mo Vaughn	.50
177	Dave Wainhouse	.05
178	Don Wakamatsu	.05
179	Bruce Walton	.05
180	Kevin Ward	.05
181	Dave Weathers	.05
182	Eric Wedge	.05
183	John Wehner	.05
184	Rick Wilkins	.05
185	Bernie Williams	.50
186	Brian Williams	.05
187	Ron Witmeyer	.05
188	Mark Wohlers	.05
189	Ted Wood	.05
190	Anthony Young	.05
191	Eddie Zosky	.05
192	Bob Zupcic	.05
193	Checklist	.05
194	Checklist	.05

1992 TOPPS

	NM/M
Unopened Fact. Set (802):	30.00
Complete Set (792):	20.00
Common Player:	.05
Golds:	4X
Wax Pack (14):	.50
Wax Box (36):	12.50
Cello Pack (34):	1.00
Cello Box (24):	16.00
Vending Box (500):	6.00

1	Nolan Ryan	.75
2	Rickey Henderson	.20
3	Jeff Reardon	.05
4	Nolan Ryan	.40
5	Dave Winfield	.20
6	*Brien Taylor*	.05
7	*Jim Olander*	.05
8	*Bryan Hickerson*	.05
9	John Farrell	.05
10	Wade Boggs	.45
11	Jack McDowell	.05
12	Luis Gonzalez	.05
13	Mike Scioscia	.05
14	Wes Chamberlain	.05
15	Denny Martinez	.05
16	Jeff Montgomery	.05
17	Randy Milligan	.05
18	Greg Cadaret	.05
19	Jamie Quirk	.05
20	Bip Roberts	.05
21	Buck Rodgers	.05
22	Bill Wegman	.05
23	Chuck Knoblauch	.05
24	Randy Myers	.05
25	Ron Gant	.05
26	Mike Bielecki	.05
27	Juan Gonzalez	.20
28	Mike Schooler	.05
29	Mickey Tettleton	.05
30	John Kruk	.05
31	Bryn Smith	.05
32	Chris Nabholz	.05
33	Carlos Baerga	.05
34	Jeff Juden	.05
35	Dave Righetti	.05
36	*Scott Ruffcorn*	.05
37	Luis Polonia	.05
38	Tom Candiotti	.05
39	Greg Olson	.05
40	Cal Ripken, Jr.	.75
41	Craig Lefferts	.05
42	Mike Macfarlane	.05
43	Jose Lind	.05
44	Rick Aguilera	.05
45	Gary Carter	.35
46	Steve Farr	.05
47	Rex Hudler	.05
48	Scott Scudder	.05
49	Damon Berryhill	.05
50	Ken Griffey, Jr.	.55
51	Tom Runnells	.05
52	Juan Bell	.05
53	Tommy Gregg	.05
54	David Wells	.05
55	Rafael Palmeiro	.30
56	Charlie O'Brien	.05
57	Donn Pall	.05
58	*Brad Ausmus, Jim Campanis, Dave Nilsson, Doug Robbins* Top Prospects-Catchers	.15
59	Mo Vaughn	.05
60	Tony Fernandez	.05
61	Paul O'Neill	.05
62	Gene Nelson	.05
63	Randy Ready	.05
64	Bob Kipper	.05
65	Willie McGee	.05
66	*Scott Stahoviak*	.05
67	Luis Salazar	.05
68	Marvin Freeman	.05
69	Kenny Lofton	.05
70	Gary Gaetti	.05
71	Erik Hanson	.05
72	Eddie Zosky	.05
73	Brian Barnes	.05
74	Scott Leius	.05
75	Bret Saberhagen	.05
76	Mike Gallego	.05
77	Jack Armstrong	.05
78	Ivan Rodriguez	.35
79	Jesse Orosco	.05
80	Dave Justice	.05
81	*Ced Landrum*	.05
82	*Doug Simons*	.05
83	Tommy Greene	.05
84	Leo Gomez	.05
85	Jose DeLeon	.05
86	Steve Finley	.05
87	*Bob MacDonald*	.05
88	Darrin Jackson	.05
89	Neal Heaton	.05
90	Robin Yount	.35
91	Jeff Reed	.05
92	Lenny Harris	.05
93	Reggie Jefferson	.05
94	Sammy Sosa	.45
95	Scott Bailes	.05
96	*Tom McKinnon*	.05
97	Luis Rivera	.05
98	Mike Harkey	.05
99	Jeff Treadway	.05
100	Jose Canseco	.25
101	Omar Vizquel	.05
102	*Scott Kamieniecki*	.05
103	Ricky Jordan	.05
104	Jeff Ballard	.05
105	Felix Jose	.05
106	Mike Boddicker	.05
107	Dan Pasqua	.05
108	*Mike Timlin*	.10
109	Roger Craig	.05
110	Ryne Sandberg	.45
111	Mark Carreon	.05
112	Oscar Azocar	.05
113	Mike Greenwell	.05
114	Mark Portugal	.05
115	Terry Pendleton	.05
116	Willie Randolph	.05
117	Scott Terry	.05
118	Chili Davis	.05
119	Mark Gardner	.05
120	Alan Trammell	.05
121	Derek Bell	.05
122	Gary Varsho	.05
123	Bob Ojeda	.05
124	*Shawn Livsey*	.05
125	Chris Hoiles	.05
126	Rico Brogna, John Jaha, Ryan Klesko, Dave Staton Top Prospects-1st Baseman	.05
127	Carlos Quintana	.05
128	Kurt Stillwell	.05
129	Melido Perez	.05
130	Alvin Davis	.05
131	Checklist 1	.05
132	Eric Show	.05
133	Rance Mulliniks	.05
134	Darryl Kile	.05
135	Von Hayes	.05
136	Bill Doran	.05
137	Jeff Robinson	.05
138	Monty Fariss	.05
139	Jeff Innis	.05
140	Mark Grace	.05
141	Jim Leyland	.05
142	Todd Van Poppel	.05
143	Paul Gibson	.05
144	Bill Swift	.05
145	Danny Tartabull	.05
146	Al Newman	.05
147	Cris Carpenter	.05
148	*Anthony Young*	.05
149	*Brian Bohanon*	.05
150	Roger Clemens	.50
151	Jeff Hamilton	.05
152	Charlie Leibrandt	.05
153	Ron Karkovice	.05
154	Hensley Meulens	.05
155	Scott Bankhead	.05
156	*Manny Ramirez*	3.00
157	Keith Miller	.05
158	Todd Frohwirth	.05
159	Darrin Fletcher	.05
160	Bobby Bonilla	.05
161	Casey Candaele	.05
162	Paul Faries	.05
163	Dana Kiecker	.05
164	Shane Mack	.05
165	Mark Langston	.05
166	Geronimo Pena	.05
167	Andy Allanson	.05
168	Dwight Smith	.05
169	Chuck Crim	.05
170	Alex Cole	.05
171	Bill Plummer	.05
172	Juan Berenguer	.05
173	Brian Downing	.05
174	Steve Frey	.05
175	Orel Hershiser	.05
176	*Ramon Garcia*	.05
177	Danny Gladden	.05

178 Jim Acker .05
179 *Cesar Bernhardt, Bobby DeJardin, Armando Moreno, Andy Stankiewicz* Top Prospects-2nd Baseman .05
180 Kevin Mitchell .05
181 Hector Villanueva .05
182 Jeff Reardon .05
183 Brent Mayne .05
184 Jimmy Jones .05
185 Benny Santiago .05
186 *Cliff Floyd* .50
187 Ernie Riles .05
188 Jose Guzman .05
189 Junior Felix .05
190 Glenn Davis .05
191 Charlie Hough .05
192 *Dave Fleming* .05
193 Omar Oliveras .05
194 Eric Karros .05
195 David Cone .05
196 *Frank Castillo* .05
197 Glenn Braggs .05
198 Scott Aldred .05
199 Jeff Blauser .05
200 Len Dykstra .05
201 Buck Showalter .05
202 Rick Honeycutt .05
203 Greg Myers .05
204 Trevor Wilson .05
205 Jay Howell .05
206 Luis Sojo .05
207 Jack Clark .05
208 Julio Machado .05
209 Lloyd McClendon .05
210 Ozzie Guillen .05
211 *Jeremy Hernandez* .05
212 Randy Velarde .05
213 Les Lancaster .05
214 *Andy Mota* .05
215 Rich Gossage .05
216 *Brent Gates* .05
217 Brian Harper .05
218 Mike Flanagan .05
219 Jerry Browne .05
220 Jose Rijo .05
221 Skeeter Barnes .05
222 Jaime Navarro .05
223 Mel Hall .05
224 *Brett Barberie* .05
225 Roberto Alomar .15
226 Pete Smith .05
227 Daryl Boston .05
228 Eddie Whitson .05
229 Shawn Boskie .05
230 Dick Schofield .05
231 *Brian Drahman* .05
232 John Smiley .05
233 Mitch Webster .05
234 Terry Steinbach .05
235 Jack Morris .05
236 Bill Pecota .05
237 *Jose Hernandez* .05
238 Greg Litton .05
239 Brian Holman .05
240 Andres Galarraga .05
241 Gerald Young .05
242 Mike Mussina .30
243 Alvaro Espinoza .05
244 Darren Daulton .05
245 John Smoltz .05
246 *Jason Pruitt* .05
247 Chuck Finley .05
248 Jim Gantner .05
249 Tony Fossas .05
250 Ken Griffey .05
251 Kevin Elster .05
252 Dennis Rasmussen .05
253 Terry Kennedy .05
254 *Ryan Bowen* .05
255 Robin Ventura .05
256 Mike Aldrete .05
257 Jeff Russell .05
258 Jim Lindeman .05
259 Ron Darling .05
260 Devon White .05
261 Tom Lasorda .05
262 Terry Lee .05
263 Bob Patterson .05
264 Checklist 2 .05
265 Teddy Higuera .05
266 Roberto Kelly .05
267 Steve Bedrosian .05
268 Brady Anderson .05
269 *Ruben Amaro* .05
270 Tony Gwynn .45
271 Tracy Jones .05
272 Jerry Don Gleaton .05
273 Craig Grebeck .05
274 *Bob Scanlan* .05
275 Todd Zeile .05
276 *Shawn Green* 1.50
277 Scott Chiamparino .05
278 Darryl Hamilton .05
279 Jim Clancy .05
280 Carlos Martinez .05
281 Kevin Appier .05
282 *John Wehner* .05
283 Reggie Sanders .05
284 Gene Larkin .05
285 Bob Welch .05
286 Gilberto Reyes .05
287 Pete Schourek .05
288 Andujar Cedeno .05
289 Mike Morgan .05
290 Bo Jackson .10
291 Phil Garner .05
292 Ray Lankford .05
293 Mike Henneman .05
294 Dave Valle .05
295 Alonzo Powell .05
296 Tom Brunansky .05
297 Kevin Brown .05
298 Kelly Gruber .05
299 Charles Nagy .05
300 Don Mattingly .50
301 Kirk McCaskill .05
302 Joey Cora .05
303 Dan Plesac .05
304 Joe Oliver .05
305 Tom Glavine .25
306 *Al Shirley* .05
307 Bruce Ruffin .05
308 *Craig Shipley* .05
309 Dave Martinez .05
310 Jose Mesa .05
311 Henry Cotto .05
312 Mike LaValliere .05
313 Kevin Tapani .05
314 Jeff Huson .05
315 Juan Samuel .05
316 Curt Schilling .25
317 Mike Bordick .05
318 Steve Howe .05
319 Tony Phillips .05
320 George Bell .05
321 Lou Pinella .05
322 Tim Burke .05
323 Milt Thompson .05
324 Danny Darwin .05
325 Joe Orsulak .05
326 Eric King .05
327 Jay Buhner .05
328 *Joel Johnston* .05
329 Franklin Stubbs .05
330 Will Clark .05
331 Steve Lake .05
332 *Chris Jones* .05
333 Pat Tabler .05
334 Kevin Gross .05
335 Dave Henderson .05
336 *Greg Anthony* .05
337 Alejandro Pena .05
338 Shawn Abner .05
339 Tom Browning .05
340 Otis Nixon .05
341 Bob Geren .05
342 *Tim Spehr* .05
343 *Jon Vander Wal* .20
344 Jack Daugherty .05
345 Zane Smith .05
346 *Rheal Cormier* .05
347 Kent Hrbek .05
348 *Rick Wilkins* .10
349 Steve Lyons .05
350 Gregg Olson .05
351 Greg Riddoch .05
352 Ed Nunez .05
353 *Braulio Castillo* .05
354 Dave Bergman .05
355 *Warren Newson* .05
356 Luis Quinones .05
357 Mike Witt .05
358 *Ted Wood* .05
359 Mike Moore .05
360 Lance Parrish .05
361 Barry Jones .05
362 *Javier Ortiz* .05
363 John Candelaria .05
364 Glenallen Hill .05
365 Duane Ward .05
366 Checklist 3 .05
367 Rafael Belliard .05
368 Bill Krueger .05
369 *Steve Whitaker* .05
370 Shawon Dunston .05
371 Dante Bichette .05
372 *Kip Gross* .05
373 Don Robinson .05
374 Bernie Williams .05
375 Bert Blyleven .05
376 *Chris Donnels* .05
377 *Bob Zupcic* .05
378 Joel Skinner .05
379 Steve Chitren .05
380 Barry Bonds .75
381 Sparky Anderson .10
382 Sid Fernandez .05
383 Dave Hollins .05
384 Mark Lee .05
385 Tim Wallach .05
386 Will Clark .05
387 Ryne Sandberg .20
388 Howard Johnson .05
389 Barry Larkin .05
390 Barry Bonds .40
391 Ron Gant .05
392 Bobby Bonilla .05
393 Craig Biggio .05
394 Denny Martinez .05
395 Tom Glavine .05
396 Lee Smith .05
397 Cecil Fielder .05
398 Julio Franco .05
399 Wade Boggs .20
400 Cal Ripken, Jr. .40
401 Jose Canseco .15
402 Joe Carter .05
403 Ruben Sierra .05
404 Matt Nokes .05
405 Roger Clemens .25
406 Jim Abbott .05
407 Bryan Harvey .05
408 Bob Milacki .05
409 Geno Petralli .05
410 Dave Stewart .05
411 Mike Jackson .05
412 Luis Aquino .05
413 Tim Teufel .05
414 Jeff Ware .05
415 Jim Deshaies .05
416 Ellis Burks .05
417 Allan Anderson .05
418 Alfredo Griffin .05
419 Wally Whitehurst .05
420 Sandy Alomar .05
421 Juan Agosto .05
422 Sam Horn .05
423 *Jeff Fassero* .05
424 *Paul McClellan* .05
425 Cecil Fielder .05
426 Tim Raines .05
427 *Eddie Taubensee* .05
428 Dennis Boyd .05
429 Tony LaRussa .05
430 Steve Sax .05
431 Tom Gordon .05
432 Billy Hatcher .05
433 Cal Eldred .05
434 Wally Backman .05
435 Mark Eichhorn .05
436 Mookie Wilson .05
437 *Scott Servais* .10
438 Mike Maddux .05
439 *Chico Walker* .05
440 Doug Drabek .05
441 Rob Deer .05
442 Dave West .05
443 Spike Owen .05
444 *Tyrone Hill* .05
445 Matt Williams .05
446 Mark Lewis .05
447 David Segui .05
448 Tom Pagnozzi .05
449 *Jeff Johnson* .05
450 Mark McGwire .65
451 Tom Henke .05
452 Wilson Alvarez .05
453 Gary Redus .05
454 Darren Holmes .05
455 Pete O'Brien .05
456 Pat Combs .05
457 Hubie Brooks .05
458 Frank Tanana .05
459 Tom Kelly .05
460 Andre Dawson .25
461 Doug Jones .05
462 Rich Rodriguez .05
463 *Mike Simms* .05
464 Mike Jeffcoat .05
465 Barry Larkin .05
466 Stan Belinda .05
467 Lonnie Smith .05
468 Greg Harris .05
469 Jim Eisenreich .05
470 Pedro Guerrero .05
471 Jose DeJesus .05
472 *Rich Rowland* .05
473 *Frank Bolick, Craig Paquette, Tom Redington, Paul Russo* Top Prospects-3rd Baseman .05
474 *Mike Rossiter* .05
475 Robby Thompson .05
476 Randy Bush .05
477 Greg Hibbard .05
478 Dale Sveum .05
479 *Chito Martinez* .05
480 Scott Sanderson .05
481 Tino Martinez .05
482 Jimmy Key .05
483 Terry Shumpert .05
484 Mike Hartley .05
485 Chris Sabo .05
486 Bob Walk .05
487 John Cerutti .05
488 Scott Cooper .05
489 Bobby Cox .05
490 Julio Franco .05
491 Jeff Brantley .05
492 Mike Devereaux .05
493 Jose Offerman .05
494 Gary Thurman .05
495 Carney Lansford .05
496 Joe Grahe .05
497 *Andy Ashby* .10
498 Gerald Perry .05
499 Dave Otto .05
500 Vince Coleman .05
501 *Rob Mallicoat* .05
502 Greg Briley .05
503 Pascual Perez .05
504 *Aaron Sele* .25
505 Bobby Thigpen .05
506 Todd Benzinger .05
507 Candy Maldonado .05
508 Bill Gullickson .05
509 Doug Dascenzo .05
510 Frank Viola .05
511 Kenny Rogers .05
512 Mike Heath .05
513 Kevin Bass .05
514 *Kim Batiste* .05
515 Delino DeShields .05
516 *Ed Sprague* .05
517 Jim Gott .05
518 *Jose Melendez* .05
519 Hal McRae .05
520 Jeff Bagwell .35
521 Joe Hesketh .05
522 Milt Cuyler .05
523 Shawn Hillegas .05
524 Don Slaught .05
525 Randy Johnson .35
526 *Doug Piatt* .05
527 Checklist 4 .05
528 *Steve Foster* .05
529 Joe Girardi .05
530 Jim Abbott .05
531 Larry Walker .05
532 Mike Huff .05
533 Mackey Sasser .05
534 *Benji Gil* .05
535 Dave Stieb .05
536 Willie Wilson .05
537 *Mark Leiter* .05
538 Jose Uribe .05
539 Thomas Howard .05
540 Ben McDonald .05
541 *Jose Tolentino* .05
542 *Keith Mitchell* .05
543 Jerome Walton .05
544 *Cliff Brantley* .05
545 Andy Van Slyke .05
546 Paul Sorrento .05
547 Herm Winningham .05
548 Mark Guthrie .05
549 Joe Torre .05
550 Darryl Strawberry .05
551 Manny Alexander, Alex Arias, Wil Cordero, Chipper Jones Top Prospects-Shortstops .25
552 Dave Gallagher .05
553 Edgar Martinez .05
554 Donald Harris .05
555 Frank Thomas .35
556 Storm Davis .05
557 Dickie Thon .05
558 Scott Garrelts .05
559 Steve Olin .05
560 Rickey Henderson .35
561 Jose Vizcaino .05
562 *Wade Taylor* .05
563 Pat Borders .05

564 *Jimmy Gonzalez* .05
565 Lee Smith .05
566 Bill Sampen .05
567 Dean Palmer .05
568 Bryan Harvey .05
569 Tony Pena .05
570 Lou Whitaker .05
571 Randy Tomlin .05
572 Greg Vaughn .05
573 Kelly Downs .05
574 Steve Avery .05
575 Kirby Puckett .45
576 *Heathcliff Slocumb* .05
577 Kevin Seitzer .05
578 Lee Guetterman .05
579 Johnny Oates .05
580 Greg Maddux .45
581 Stan Javier .05
582 Vicente Palacios .05
583 Mel Rojas .05
584 *Wayne Rosenthal* .05
585 Lenny Webster .05
586 Rod Nichols .05
587 Mickey Morandini .05
588 Russ Swan .05
589 Mariano Duncan .05
590 Howard Johnson .05
591 Jacob Brumfield, Jeromy Burnitz, Alan Cockrell, D.J. Dozier Top Prospects-Outfielders .25
592 *Denny Neagle* .10
593 Steve Decker .05
594 *Brian Barber* .05
595 Bruce Hurst .05
596 Kent Mercker .05
597 *Mike Magnante* .05
598 Jody Reed .05
599 Steve Searcy .05
600 Paul Molitor .35
601 Dave Smith .05
602 Mike Fetters .05
603 *Luis Mercedes* .05
604 Chris Gwynn .05
605 Scott Erickson .05
606 Brook Jacoby .05
607 Todd Stottlemyre .05
608 Scott Bradley .05
609 Mike Hargrove .05
610 Eric Davis .05
611 *Brian Hunter* .05
612 Pat Kelly .05
613 Pedro Munoz .05
614 Al Osuna .05
615 Matt Merullo .05
616 Larry Andersen .05
617 Junior Ortiz .05
618 *Cesar Hernandez, Steve Hosey, Dan Peltier, Jeff McNeely* Top Prospects-Outfielders .10
619 Danny Jackson .05
620 George Brett .50
621 *Dan Gakeler* .05
622 Steve Buechele .05
623 Bob Tewksbury .05
624 *Shawn Estes* .25
625 Kevin McReynolds .05
626 *Chris Haney* .05
627 Mike Sharperson .05
628 Mark Williamson .05
629 Wally Joyner .05
630 Carlton Fisk .35
631 *Armando Reynoso* .05
632 Felix Fermin .05
633 Mitch Williams .05
634 Manuel Lee .05
635 Harold Baines .05
636 Greg Harris .05
637 Orlando Merced .05
638 Chris Bosio .05
639 *Wayne Housie* .05
640 Xavier Hernandez .05
641 *David Howard* .05
642 Tim Crews .05
643 Rick Cerone .05
644 Terry Leach .05
645 Deion Sanders .10
646 Craig Wilson .05
647 Marquis Grissom .05
648 Scott Fletcher .05
649 Norm Charlton .05
650 Jesse Barfield .05
651 *Joe Slusarski* .05
652 Bobby Rose .05
653 Dennis Lamp .05
654 *Allen Watson* .05
655 Brett Butler .05
656 *Rudy Pemberton, Henry Rodriguez, Lee Tinsley, Gerald Williams* Top Prospects-Outfielders .10
657 Dave Johnson .05
658 Checklist 5 .05
659 Brian McRae .05
660 Fred McGriff .05
661 Bill Landrum .05
662 Juan Guzman .05
663 Greg Gagne .05
664 Ken Hill .05
665 *Dave Haas* .05
666 Tom Foley .05
667 *Roberto Hernandez* .10
668 Dwayne Henry .05
669 Jim Fregosi .05
670 Harold Reynolds .05
671 Mark Whiten .05
672 Eric Plunk .05
673 Todd Hundley .05
674 *Mo Sanford* .05
675 Bobby Witt .05
676 *Pat Mahomes, Sam Militello, Roger Salkeld, Turk Wendell* Top Prospects-Pitchers .15
677 John Marzano .05
678 Joe Klink .05
679 Pete Incaviglia .05
680 Dale Murphy .15
681 Rene Gonzales .05
682 Andy Benes .05
683 Jim Poole .05
684 *Trever Miller* .10
685 *Scott Livingstone* .05
686 Rich DeLucia .05
687 *Harvey Pulliam* .05
688 Tim Belcher .05
689 Mark Lemke .05
690 John Franco .05
691 Walt Weiss .05
692 Scott Ruskin .05
693 Jeff King .05
694 Mike Gardiner .05
695 Gary Sheffield .30
696 Joe Boever .05
697 Mike Felder .05
698 John Habyan .05
699 Cito Gaston .05
700 Ruben Sierra .05
701 Scott Radinsky .05
702 Lee Stevens .05
703 *Mark Wohlers* .05
704 Curt Young .05
705 Dwight Evans .05
706 Rob Murphy .05
707 Gregg Jefferies .05
708 Tom Bolton .05
709 Chris James .05
710 Kevin Maas .05
711 *Ricky Bones* .05
712 Curt Wilkerson .05
713 Roger McDowell .05
714 *Calvin Reese* .10
715 Craig Biggio .05
716 *Kirk Dressendorfer* .05
717 Ken Dayley .05
718 B.J. Surhoff .05
719 Terry Mulholland .05
720 Kirk Gibson .05
721 Mike Pagliarulo .05
722 Walt Terrell .05
723 Jose Oquendo .05
724 Kevin Morton .05
725 Dwight Gooden .05
726 Kirt Manwaring .05
727 Chuck McElroy .05
728 Dave Burba .05
729 Art Howe .05
730 Ramon Martinez .05
731 Donnie Hill .05
732 Nelson Santovenia .05
733 Bob Melvin .05
734 *Scott Hatteberg* .10
735 Greg Swindell .05
736 Lance Johnson .05
737 Kevin Reimer .05
738 Dennis Eckersley .35
739 Rob Ducey .05
740 Ken Caminiti .05
741 Mark Gubicza .05
742 Billy Spiers .05
743 Darren Lewis .05
744 Chris Hammond .05
745 Dave Magadan .05
746 Bernard Gilkey .05
747 Willie Banks .05
748 Matt Nokes .05
749 Jerald Clark .05
750 Travis Fryman .05
751 Steve Wilson .05
752 Billy Ripken .05
753 Paul Assenmacher .05
754 Charlie Hayes .05
755 Alex Fernandez .05
756 Gary Pettis .05
757 Rob Dibble .05
758 Tim Naehring .05
759 Jeff Torborg .05
760 Ozzie Smith .45
761 Mike Fitzgerald .05
762 John Burkett .05
763 Kyle Abbott .05
764 *Tyler Green* .05
765 Pete Harnisch .05
766 Mark Davis .05
767 Kal Daniels .05
768 Jim Thome .35
769 Jack Howell .05
770 Sid Bream .05
771 *Arthur Rhodes* .10
772 Garry Templeton .05
773 Hal Morris .05
774 Bud Black .05
775 Ivan Calderon .05
776 *Doug Henry* .05
777 John Olerud .05
778 Tim Leary .05
779 Jay Bell .05
780 Eddie Murray .35
781 Paul Abbott .05
782 Phil Plantier .05
783 Joe Magrane .05
784 Ken Patterson .05
785 Albert Belle .05
786 Royce Clayton .05
787 Checklist 6 .05
788 Mike Stanton .05
789 Bobby Valentine .05
790 Joe Carter .05
791 Danny Cox .05
792 Dave Winfield .35

Gold

NM/M

Unopened Fact. Set (793): 75.00
Complete Set (792): 35.00
Common Player: .20
(Star cards valued at 4X corresponding cards in regular-issue 1992 Topps)
86 Steve Finley (incorrect name, Mark Davidson, on gold strip) .20
131 Terry Mathews .20
264 Rod Beck 1.00
288 Andujar Cedeno (incorrect team, Yankees, listed on gold strip) .60
366 Tony Perezchica .20
465 Barry Larkin (incorrect team, Astros, listed on gold strip) 2.50
527 Terry McDaniel .20
532 Mike Huff (incorrect team, Red Sox, listed on gold strip) .20
658 John Ramos .20
787 Brian Williams .20
793 Brien Taylor (autographed edition of 12,000; factory sets only) 7.50

Traded

NM/M

Complete Set (132): 50.00
Common Player: .05
Golds: 2-4X
1 *Willie Adams* (USA) .05
2 Jeff Alkire (USA) .05
3 Felipe Alou .05
4 Moises Alou .10
5 Ruben Amaro .05
6 Jack Armstrong .05
7 Scott Bankhead .05
8 Tim Belcher .05
9 George Bell .05
10 Freddie Benavides .05
11 Todd Benzinger .05
12 Joe Boever .05
13 Ricky Bones .05
14 Bobby Bonilla .05
15 Hubie Brooks .05
16 Jerry Browne .05
17 Jim Bullinger .05
18 Dave Burba .05
19 Kevin Campbell .05
20 Tom Candiotti .05
21 Mark Carreon .05
22 Gary Carter .75
23 Archi Cianfrocco .05
24 Phil Clark .05
25 *Chad Curtis* .50
26 Eric Davis .05
27 Tim Davis (USA) .05
28 Gary DiSarcina .05
29 Darren Dreifort (USA) .05
30 Mariano Duncan .05
31 Mike Fitzgerald .05
32 John Flaherty .05
33 Darrin Fletcher .05
34 Scott Fletcher .05
35 Ron Fraser (USA) .05
36 Andres Galarraga .05
37 Dave Gallagher .05
38 Mike Gallego .05
39 *Nomar Garciaparra* (USA) 30.00
40 Jason Giambi (USA) 1.00
41 Danny Gladden .05
42 Rene Gonzales .05
43 Jeff Granger (USA) .05
44 Rick Greene (USA) .05
45 Jeffrey Hammonds (USA) .05
46 Charlie Hayes .05
47 Von Hayes .05
48 Rick Helling (USA) .05
49 Butch Henry .05
50 Carlos Hernandez .05
51 Ken Hill .05
52 Butch Hobson .05
53 Vince Horsman .05
54 Pete Incaviglia .05
55 Gregg Jefferies .05
56 Charles Johnson (USA) .05
57 Doug Jones .05
58 *Brian Jordan* 2.00
59 Wally Joyner .05
60 *Daron Kirkreit* (USA) .20
61 Bill Krueger .05
62 Gene Lamont .05
63 Jim Lefebvre .05
64 *Danny Leon* .05
65 Pat Listach .05
66 Kenny Lofton .05
67 Dave Martinez .05
68 Derrick May .05
69 Kirk McCaskill .05
70 *Chad McConnell* (USA) .05
71 Kevin McReynolds .05
72 Rusty Meacham .05
73 Keith Miller .05
74 Kevin Mitchell .05
75 *Jason Moler* (USA) .05
76 Mike Morgan .05
77 Jack Morris .05

78	*Calvin Murray* (USA)	.05
79	Eddie Murray	.75
80	Randy Myers	.05
81	Denny Neagle	.05
82	Phil Nevin (USA)	.10
83	Dave Nilsson	.05
84	Junior Ortiz	.05
85	Donovan Osborne	.05
86	Bill Pecota	.05
87	Melido Perez	.05
88	Mike Perez	.05
89	Hipolito Pena	.05
90	Willie Randolph	.05
91	Darren Reed	.05
92	Bip Roberts	.05
93	Chris Roberts (USA)	.05
94	Steve Rodriguez (USA)	.05
95	Bruce Ruffin	.05
96	Scott Ruskin	.05
97	Bret Saberhagen	.05
98	Rey Sanchez	.05
99	Steve Sax	.05
100	Curt Schilling	.25
101	Dick Schofield	.05
102	Gary Scott	.05
103	Kevin Seitzer	.05
104	Frank Seminara	.05
105	Gary Sheffield	.35
106	John Smiley	.05
107	Cory Snyder	.05
108	Paul Sorrento	.05
109	Sammy Sosa	1.50
110	*Matt Stairs*	.25
111	Andy Stankiewicz	.05
112	Kurt Stillwell	.05
113	Rick Sutcliffe	.05
114	Bill Swift	.05
115	Jeff Tackett	.05
116	Danny Tartabull	.05
117	Eddie Taubensee	.05
118	Dickie Thon	.05
119	*Michael Tucker* (USA)	.25
120	Scooter Tucker	.05
121	*Marc Valdes* (USA)	.05
122	Julio Valera	.05
123	*Jason Varitek* (USA)	15.00
124	*Ron Villone* (USA)	.05
125	Frank Viola	.05
126	*B.J. Wallace* (USA)	.05
127	Dan Walters	.05
128	Craig Wilson (USA)	.05
129	Chris Wimmer (USA)	.05
130	Dave Winfield	.75
131	Herm Winningham	.05
132	Checklist	.05

Traded Gold

	NM/M
Complete Unopened Set (132):	75.00
Complete Set (132):	65.00
Common Player:	.25
Stars/Rookies:	4X

(See 1992 Topps Traded for checklist and base card values.)

1993 TOPPS

	NM/M
Unopened Fact. Set (847):	40.00
Complete Set (825):	30.00
Common Player:	.05
Golds:	3X
Series 1 Wax Pack (15):	.75
Series 1 Wax Box (36):	20.00
Series 2 Wax Pack (15):	.50
Series 2 Wax Box (36):	15.00

1	Robin Yount	.50
2	Barry Bonds	1.00
3	Ryne Sandberg	.60

4	Roger Clemens	.65
5	Tony Gwynn	.60
6	*Jeff Tackett*	.05
7	Pete Incaviglia	.05
8	Mark Wohlers	.05
9	Kent Hrbek	.05
10	Will Clark	.05
11	Eric Karros	.05
12	Lee Smith	.05
13	Esteban Beltre	.05
14	Greg Briley	.05
15	Marquis Grissom	.05
16	Dan Plesac	.05
17	Dave Hollins	.05
18	Terry Steinbach	.05
19	Ed Nunez	.05
20	Tim Salmon	.05
21	Luis Salazar	.05
22	Jim Eisenreich	.05
23	Todd Stottlemyre	.05
24	Tim Naehring	.05
25	John Franco	.05
26	Skeeter Barnes	.05
27	*Carlos Garcia*	.05
28	Joe Orsulak	.05
29	Dwayne Henry	.05
30	Fred McGriff	.05
31	Derek Lilliquist	.05
32	Don Mattingly	.65
33	B.J. Wallace	.05
34	Juan Gonzalez	.25
35	John Smoltz	.05
36	Scott Servais	.05
37	Lenny Webster	.05
38	Chris James	.05
39	Roger McDowell	.05
40	Ozzie Smith	.60
41	Alex Fernandez	.05
42	Spike Owen	.05
43	Ruben Amaro	.05
44	Kevin Seitzer	.05
45	Dave Fleming	.05
46	*Eric Fox*	.05
47	Bob Scanlan	.05
48	Bert Blyleven	.05
49	Brian McRae	.05
50	Roberto Alomar	.20
51	Mo Vaughn	.05
52	Bobby Bonilla	.05
53	Frank Tanana	.05
54	Mike LaValliere	.05
55	Mark McLemore	.05
56	*Chad Mottola*	.10
57	Norm Charlton	.05
58	Jose Melendez	.05
59	Carlos Martinez	.05
60	Roberto Kelly	.05
61	Gene Larkin	.05
62	Rafael Belliard	.05
63	Al Osuna	.05
64	Scott Chiamparino	.05
65	Brett Butler	.05
66	John Burkett	.05
67	Felix Jose	.05
68	Omar Vizquel	.05
69	John Vander Wal	.05
70	Roberto Hernandez	.05
71	Ricky Bones	.05
72	*Jeff Grotewold*	.05
73	Mike Moore	.05
74	Steve Buechele	.05
75	Juan Guzman	.05
76	Kevin Appier	.05
77	Junior Felix	.05
78	Greg Harris	.05
79	Dick Schofield	.05
80	Cecil Fielder	.05
81	Lloyd McClendon	.05
82	David Segui	.05

83	Reggie Sanders	.05
84	Kurt Stillwell	.05
85	Sandy Alomar	.05
86	John Habyan	.05
87	Kevin Reimer	.05
88	Mike Stanton	.05
89	Eric Anthony	.05
90	Scott Erickson	.05
91	Craig Colbert	.05
92	Tom Pagnozzi	.05
93	*Pedro Astacio*	.10
94	Lance Johnson	.05
95	Larry Walker	.05
96	Russ Swan	.05
97	Scott Fletcher	.05
98	*Derek Jeter*	8.00
99	*Mike Williams*	.05
100	Mark McGwire	.85
101	*Jim Bullinger*	.05
102	Brian Hunter	.05
103	Jody Reed	.05
104	*Mike Butcher*	.05
105	Gregg Jefferies	.05
106	Howard Johnson	.05
107	*John Kiely*	.05
108	Jose Lind	.05
109	Sam Horn	.05
110	Barry Larkin	.05
111	Bruce Hurst	.05
112	Brian Barnes	.05
113	Thomas Howard	.05
114	Mel Hall	.05
115	Robby Thompson	.05
116	Mark Lemke	.05
117	Eddie Taubensee	.05
118	David Hulse	.05
119	Pedro Munoz	.05
120	Ramon Martinez	.05
121	Todd Worrell	.05
122	Joey Cora	.05
123	Moises Alou	.05
124	Franklin Stubbs	.05
125	Pete O'Brien	.05
126	*Bob Ayrault*	.05
127	Carney Lansford	.05
128	Kal Daniels	.05
129	Joe Grahe	.05
130	Jeff Montgomery	.05
131	Dave Winfield	.50
132	*Preston Wilson*	.75
133	Steve Wilson	.05
134	Lee Guetterman	.05
135	Mickey Tettleton	.05
136	Jeff King	.05
137	Alan Mills	.05
138	Joe Oliver	.05
139	Gary Gaetti	.05
140	Gary Sheffield	.30
141	Dennis Cook	.05
142	Charlie Hayes	.05
143	Jeff Huson	.05
144	Kent Mercker	.05
145	*Eric Young*	.10
146	Scott Leius	.05
147	Bryan Hickerson	.05
148	Steve Finley	.05
149	Rheal Cormier	.05
150	Frank Thomas	.50
151	*Archi Cianfrocco*	.05
152	Rich DeLucia	.05
153	Greg Vaughn	.05
154	Wes Chamberlain	.05
155	Dennis Eckersley	.40
156	Sammy Sosa	.60
157	Gary DiSarcina	.05
158	*Kevin Koslofski*	.05
159	*Doug Linton*	.05
160	Lou Whitaker	.05
161	Chad McDonnell	.05
162	Joe Hesketh	.05
163	*Tim Wakefield*	.10
164	Leo Gomez	.05
165	Jose Rijo	.05
166	*Tim Scott*	.05
167	Steve Olin	.05
168	Kevin Maas	.05
169	Kenny Rogers	.05
170	Dave Justice	.05
171	Doug Jones	.05
172	*Jeff Reboulet*	.05
173	Andres Galarraga	.05
174	Randy Velarde	.05
175	Kirk McCaskill	.05
176	Darren Lewis	.05
177	Lenny Harris	.05
178	Jeff Fassero	.05
179	Ken Griffey, Jr.	.75
180	Darren Daulton	.05
181	John Jaha	.05

182	Ron Darling	.05
183	Greg Maddux	.60
184	*Damion Easley*	.10
185	Jack Morris	.05
186	Mike Magnante	.05
187	John Dopson	.05
188	Sid Fernandez	.05
189	Tony Phillips	.05
190	Doug Drabek	.05
191	*Sean Lowe*	.05
192	Bob Milacki	.05
193	*Steve Foster*	.05
194	Jerald Clark	.05
195	Pete Harnisch	.05
196	Pat Kelly	.05
197	Jeff Frye	.05
198	Alejandro Pena	.05
199	Junior Ortiz	.05
200	Kirby Puckett	.60
201	Jose Uribe	.05
202	Mike Scioscia	.05
203	Bernard Gilkey	.05
204	Dan Pasqua	.05
205	Gary Carter	.50
206	Henry Cotto	.05
207	Paul Molitor	.50
208	Mike Hartley	.05
209	Jeff Parrett	.05
210	Mark Langston	.05
211	Doug Dascenzo	.05
212	Rick Reed	.05
213	Candy Maldonado	.05
214	Danny Darwin	.05
215	*Pat Howell*	.05
216	Mark Leiter	.05
217	Kevin Mitchell	.05
218	Ben McDonald	.05
219	Bip Roberts	.05
220	Benny Santiago	.05
221	Carlos Baerga	.05
222	Bernie Williams	.05
223	*Roger Pavlik*	.05
224	Sid Bream	.05
225	Matt Williams	.05
226	Willie Banks	.05
227	Jeff Bagwell	.50
228	Tom Goodwin	.05
229	Mike Perez	.05
230	Carlton Fisk	.50
231	John Wetteland	.05
232	Tino Martinez	.05
233	*Rick Greene*	.05
234	Tim McIntosh	.05
235	Mitch Williams	.05
236	*Kevin Campbell*	.05
237	Jose Vizcaino	.05
238	Chris Donnels	.05
239	Mike Boddicker	.05
240	John Olerud	.05
241	Mike Gardiner	.05
242	Charlie O'Brien	.05
243	Rob Deer	.05
244	Denny Neagle	.05
245	Chris Sabo	.05
246	Gregg Olson	.05
247	Frank Seminara	.05
248	Scott Scudder	.05
249	Tim Burke	.05
250	Chuck Knoblauch	.05
251	Mike Bielecki	.05
252	Xavier Hernandez	.05
253	Jose Guzman	.05
254	Cory Snyder	.05
255	Orel Hershiser	.05
256	Wil Cordero	.05
257	Luis Alicea	.05
258	Mike Schooler	.05
259	Craig Grebeck	.05
260	Duane Ward	.05
261	Bill Wegman	.05
262	Mickey Morandini	.05
263	*Vince Horsman*	.05
264	Paul Sorrento	.05
265	Andre Dawson	.25
266	Rene Gonzales	.05
267	Keith Miller	.05
268	Derek Bell	.05
269	*Todd Steverson*	.05
270	Frank Viola	.05
271	Wally Whitehurst	.05
272	*Kurt Knudsen*	.05
273	*Dan Walters*	.05
274	Rick Sutcliffe	.05
275	Andy Van Slyke	.05
276	Paul O'Neill	.05
277	Mark Whiten	.05
278	Chris Nabholz	.05
279	Todd Burns	.05
280	Tom Glavine	.25

281 *Butch Henry* .05
282 Shane Mack .05
283 Mike Jackson .05
284 Henry Rodriguez .05
285 Bob Tewksbury .05
286 Ron Karkovice .05
287 Mike Gallego .05
288 Dave Cochrane .05
289 Jesse Orosco .05
290 Dave Stewart .05
291 Tommy Greene .05
292 Rey Sanchez .05
293 Rob Ducey .05
294 Brent Mayne .05
295 Dave Stieb .05
296 Luis Rivera .05
297 Jeff Innis .05
298 Scott Livingstone .05
299 Bob Patterson .05
300 Cal Ripken, Jr. 1.00
301 Cesar Hernandez .05
302 Randy Myers .05
303 Brook Jacoby .05
304 Melido Perez .05
305 Rafael Palmeiro .40
306 Damon Berryhill .05
307 *Dan Serafini* .05
308 Darryl Kile .05
309 *J.T. Bruett* .05
310 Dave Righetti .05
311 Jay Howell .05
312 Geronimo Pena .05
313 Greg Hibbard .05
314 Mark Gardner .05
315 Edgar Martinez .05
316 Dave Nilsson .05
317 Kyle Abbott .05
318 Willie Wilson .05
319 Paul Assenmacher .05
320 *Tim Fortugno* .05
321 Rusty Meacham .05
322 Pat Borders .05
323 Mike Greenwell .05
324 Willie Randolph .05
325 Bill Gullickson .05
326 Gary Varsho .05
327 Tim Hulett .05
328 Scott Ruskin .05
329 Mike Maddux .05
330 Danny Tartabull .05
331 Kenny Lofton .05
332 Geno Petralli .05
333 Otis Nixon .05
334 *Jason Kendall* .50
335 Mark Portugal .05
336 Mike Pagliarulo .05
337 Kirt Manwaring .05
338 Bob Ojeda .05
339 *Mark Clark* .05
340 John Kruk .05
341 Mel Rojas .05
342 Erik Hanson .05
343 Doug Henry .05
344 Jack McDowell .05
345 Harold Baines .05
346 Chuck McElroy .05
347 Luis Sojo .05
348 Andy Stankiewicz .05
349 *Hipolito Pichardo* .05
350 Joe Carter .05
351 Ellis Burks .05
352 Pete Schourek .05
353 *Buddy Groom* .05
354 Jay Bell .05
355 Brady Anderson .05
356 Freddie Benavides .05
357 Phil Stephenson .05
358 Kevin Wickander .05
359 Mike Stanley .05
360 Ivan Rodriguez .40
361 Scott Bankhead .05
362 Luis Gonzalez .05
363 John Smiley .05
364 Trevor Wilson .05
365 Tom Candiotti .05
366 Craig Wilson .05
367 Steve Sax .05
368 Delino Deshields .05
369 Jaime Navarro .05
370 Dave Valle .05
371 Mariano Duncan .05
372 Rod Nichols .05
373 Mike Morgan .05
374 Julio Valera .05
375 Wally Joyner .05
376 Tom Henke .05
377 Herm Winningham .05
378 Orlando Merced .05
379 Mike Munoz .05
380 Todd Hundley .05
381 Mike Flanagan .05
382 Tim Belcher .05
383 Jerry Browne .05
384 Mike Benjamin .05
385 Jim Leyritz .05
386 Ray Lankford .05
387 Devon White .05
388 Jeremy Hernandez .05
389 Brian Harper .05
390 Wade Boggs .60
391 Derrick May .05
392 Travis Fryman .05
393 Ron Gant .05
394 Checklist 1-132 .05
395 Checklist 133-264 .05
396 Checklist 265-396 .05
397 George Brett .65
398 Bobby Witt .05
399 Daryl Boston .05
400 Bo Jackson .10
401 Fred McGriff, Frank Thomas .20
402 Ryne Sandberg, Carlos Baerga .30
403 Gary Sheffield, Edgar Martinez .05
404 Barry Larkin, Travis Fryman .05
405 Andy Van Slyke, Ken Griffey, Jr. .40
406 Larry Walker, Kirby Puckett .20
407 Barry Bonds, Joe Carter .50
408 Darren Daulton, Brian Harper .05
409 Greg Maddux, Roger Clemens .25
410 Tom Glavine, Dave Fleming .05
411 Lee Smith, Dennis Eckersley .15
412 Jamie McAndrew .05
413 Pete Smith .05
414 Juan Guerrero .05
415 Todd Frohwirth .05
416 Randy Tomlin .05
417 B.J. Surhoff .05
418 Jim Gott .05
419 Mark Thompson .05
420 Kevin Tapani .05
421 Curt Schilling .25
422 *J.T. Snow* .40
423 Ryan Klesko, Ivan Cruz, Bubba Smith, Larry Sutton Top Prospects 1B .05
424 John Valentin .05
425 Joe Girardi .05
426 *Nigel Wilson* .05
427 Bob MacDonald .05
428 Todd Zeile .05
429 Milt Cuyler .05
430 Eddie Murray .50
431 Rich Amaral .05
432 Pete Young .05
433 Roger Bailey, Tom Schmidt Rockies Future Stars .05
434 Jack Armstrong .05
435 Willie McGee .05
436 Greg Harris .05
437 Chris Hammond .05
438 *Ritchie Moody* .05
439 Bryan Harvey .05
440 Ruben Sierra .05
441 Don Lemon, Todd Pridy Marlins Future Stars .05
442 Kevin McReynolds .05
443 Terry Leach .05
444 David Nied .05
445 Dale Murphy .15
446 Luis Mercedes .05
447 *Keith Shepherd* .05
448 Ken Caminiti .05
449 James Austin .05
450 Darryl Strawberry .05
451 *Ramon Caraballo, Jon Shave, Brent Gates, Quinton McCracken* Top Prospects 2B .10
452 Bob Wickman .05
453 Victor Cole .05
454 *John Johnstone* .05
455 Chili Davis .05
456 Scott Taylor .05
457 Tracy Woodson .05
458 David Wells .05
459 *Derek Wallace* .05
460 Randy Johnson .50
461 *Steve Reed* .05
462 Felix Fermin .05
463 Scott Aldred .05
464 Greg Colbrunn .05
465 Tony Fernandez .05
466 Mike Felder .05
467 Lee Stevens .05
468 Matt Whiteside .05
469 Dave Hansen .05
470 Rob Dibble .05
471 Dave Gallagher .05
472 Chris Gwynn .05
473 Dave Henderson .05
474 Ozzie Guillen .05
475 Jeff Reardon .05
476 Mark Voisard, Will Scalzitti Rockies Future Stars .05
477 Jimmy Jones .05
478 Greg Cadaret .05
479 Todd Pratt .05
480 Pat Listach .05
481 *Ryan Luzinski* .05
482 Darren Reed .05
483 *Brian Griffiths* .05
484 John Wehner .05
485 Glenn Davis .05
486 *Eric Wedge* .05
487 Jesse Hollins .05
488 Manuel Lee .05
489 *Scott Fredrickson* .05
490 Omar Olivares .05
491 Shawn Hare .05
492 Tom Lampkin .05
493 Jeff Nelson .05
494 Kevin Young, Adell Davenport, Eduardo Perez, Lou Lucca Top Prospects 3B .05
495 Ken Hill .05
496 Reggie Jefferson .05
497 Matt Petersen, Willie Brown Marlins Future Stars .05
498 Bud Black .05
499 Chuck Crim .05
500 Jose Canseco .30
501 Johnny Oates, Bobby Cox Major League Managers .05
502 Butch Hobson, Jim Lefebvre Major League Managers .05
503 Buck Rodgers, Tony Perez Major League Managers .05
504 Gene Lamont, Don Baylor Major League Managers .05
505 Mike Hargrove, Rene Lachemann Major League Managers .05
506 Sparky Anderson, Art Howe Major League Managers .10
507 Hal McRae, Tommy Lasorda Major League Managers .05
508 Phil Garner, Felipe Alou Major League Manager .05
509 Tom Kelly, Jeff Torborg Major League Managers .05
510 Buck Showalter, Jim Fregosi Major League Managers .05
511 Tony LaRussa, Jim Leyland Major League Managers .10
512 Lou Piniella, Joe Torre Major League Managers .10
513 Toby Harrah, Jim Riggleman Major League Managers .05
514 Cito Gaston, Dusty Baker Major League Managers .05
515 Greg Swindell .05
516 Alex Arias .05
517 Bill Pecota .05
518 *Benji Grigsby* .05
519 David Howard .05
520 Charlie Hough .05
521 Kevin Flora .05
522 Shane Reynolds .05
523 *Doug Bochtler* .05
524 Chris Hoiles .05
525 Scott Sanderson .05
526 Mike Sharperson .05
527 Mike Fetters .05
528 Paul Quantrill .05
529 Dave Silvestri, Chipper Jones, Benji Gil, Jeff Patzke Top Propsects SS .25
530 Sterling Hitchcock .05
531 Joe Millette .05
532 Tom Brunansky .05
533 Frank Castillo .05
534 Randy Knorr .05
535 Jose Oquendo .05
536 Dave Haas .05
537 Jason Hutchins, Ryan Turner Rockies Future Stars .05
538 Jimmy Baron .05
539 Kerry Woodson .05
540 Ivan Calderon .05
541 Denis Boucher .05
542 Royce Clayton .05
543 Reggie Williams .05
544 Steve Decker .05
545 Dean Palmer .05
546 Hal Morris .05
547 *Ryan Thompson* .05
548 Lance Blankenship .05
549 Hensley Meulens .05
550 Scott Radinsky .05
551 *Eric Young* .10
552 Jeff Blauser .05
553 Andujar Cedeno .05
554 Arthur Rhodes .05
555 Terry Mulholland .05
556 Darryl Hamilton .05
557 Pedro Martinez .50
558 Ryan Whitman, Mark Skeels Marlins Future Stars .05
559 *Jamie Arnold* .05
560 Zane Smith .05
561 Matt Nokes .05
562 Bob Zupcic .05
563 Shawn Boskie .05
564 Mike Timlin .05
565 Jerald Clark .05
566 Rod Brewer .05
567 Mark Carreon .05
568 Andy Benes .05
569 Shawn Barton .05
570 Tim Wallach .05
571 Dave Mlicki .05
572 Trevor Hoffman .05
573 John Patterson .05
574 DeShawn Warren .05
575 Monty Fariss .05
576 Darrell Sherman, Damon Buford, Cliff Floyd, Michael Moore Top Prospects OF .05
577 Tim Costo .05
578 Dave Magadan .05
579 Neil Garret, Jason Bates Rockies Future Stars .05
580 Walt Weiss .05
581 Chris Haney .05
582 Shawn Abner .05
583 Marvin Freeman .05
584 Casey Candaele .05
585 Ricky Jordan .05
586 Jeff Tabaka .05
587 Manny Alexander .05
588 Mike Trombley .05
589 Carlos Hernandez .05
590 Cal Eldred .05
591 Alex Cole .05
592 Phil Plantier .05
593 Brett Merriman .05
594 Jerry Nielsen .05
595 Shawon Dunston .05
596 Jimmy Key .05
597 Gerald Perry .05
598 Rico Brogna .05
599 Clemente Nunez, Dan Robinson Marlins Future Stars .05
600 Bret Saberhagen .05
601 Craig Shipley .05
602 Henry Mercedes .05
603 Jim Thome .40
604 Rod Beck .05
605 Chuck Finley .05
606 J. Owens .05
607 Dan Smith .05
608 Bill Doran .05
609 Lance Parrish .05
610 Denny Martinez .05
611 Tom Gordon .05
612 Byron Mathews .05
613 Joel Adamson .05
614 Brian Williams .05
615 Steve Avery .05
616 Matt Mieske, Tracy Sanders, Midre Cummings, Ryan Freeburg Top Prospects OF .05
617 Craig Lefferts .05
618 Tony Pena .05
619 Billy Spiers .05
620 Todd Benzinger .05
621 Mike Kotarski, Greg Boyd Rockies Future Stars .05
622 Ben Rivera .05
623 Al Martin .05
624 Sam Militello .05
625 Rick Aguilera .05

626 Danny Gladden .05
627 Andres Berumen .05
628 Kelly Gruber .05
629 Cris Carpenter .05
630 Mark Grace .05
631 Jeff Brantley .05
632 Chris Widger .05
633 Rodolf Razjigaev, Evgenyi Puchkov, Ilya Bogatyrev Russian Angels .10
634 Mo Sanford .05
635 Albert Belle .05
636 Tim Teufel .05
637 Greg Myers .05
638 Brian Bohanon .05
639 Mike Bordick .05
640 Dwight Gooden .05
641 Pat Leahy, Gavin Baugh Marlins Future Stars .05
642 Milt Hill .05
643 Luis Aquino .05
644 Dante Bichette .05
645 Bobby Thigpen .05
646 Rich Scheid .05
647 Brian Sackinsky .05
648 Ryan Hawblitzel .05
649 Tom Marsh .05
650 Terry Pendleton .05
651 *Rafael Bournigal* .05
652 Dave West .05
653 Steve Hosey .05
654 Gerald Williams .05
655 Scott Cooper .05
656 Gary Scott .05
657 Mike Harkey .05
658 Jeromy Burnitz, Melvin Nieves, Rich Becker, Shon Walker Top Prospects OF .05
659 Ed Sprague .05
660 Alan Trammell .05
661 Garvin Alston, Mike Case Rockies Future Stars .05
662 Donovan Osborne .05
663 Jeff Gardner .05
664 Calvin Jones .05
665 Darrin Fletcher .05
666 Glenallen Hill .05
667 Jim Rosenbohm .05
668 Scott Lewis .05
669 Kip Yaughn .05
670 Julio Franco .05
671 Dave Martinez .05
672 Kevin Bass .05
673 Todd Van Poppel .05
674 Mark Gubicza .05
675 Tim Raines .05
676 Rudy Seanez .05
677 Charlie Leibrandt .05
678 Randy Milligan .05
679 Kim Batiste .05
680 Craig Biggio .05
681 Darren Holmes .05
682 John Candelaria .05
683 Jerry Stafford, Eddie Christian Marlins Future Stars .05
684 Pat Mahomes .05
685 Bob Walk .05
686 Russ Springer .05
687 Tony Sheffield .05
688 Dwight Smith .05
689 Eddie Zosky .05
690 Bien Figueroa .05
691 Jim Tatum .05
692 Chad Kreuter .05
693 Rich Rodriguez .05
694 Shane Turner .05
695 Kent Bottenfield .05
696 Jose Mesa .05
697 *Darrell Whitmore* .05
698 Ted Wood .05
699 Chad Curtis .05
700 Nolan Ryan 1.00
701 Mike Piazza, Carlos Delgado, Brook Fordyce, Donnie Leshnock Top Prospects C .85
702 *Tim Pugh* .05
703 Jeff Kent .05
704 Jon Goodrich, Danny Figueroa Rockies Future Stars .05
705 Bob Welch .05
706 Sherard Clinkscales .05
707 Donn Pall .05
708 Greg Olson .05
709 Jeff Juden .05
710 Mike Mussina .30
711 Scott Champarino .05
712 Stan Javier .05
713 John Doherty .05
714 Kevin Gross .05
715 Greg Gagne .05
716 Steve Cooke .05
717 Steve Farr .05
718 Jay Buhner .05
719 Butch Henry .05
720 David Cone .05
721 Rick Wilkins .05
722 Chuck Carr .05
723 *Kenny Felder* .05
724 Guillermo Velasquez .05
725 Billy Hatcher .05
726 Mike Veneziale, Ken Kendrena Marlins Future Stars .05
727 Jonathan Hurst .05
728 Steve Frey .05
729 Mark Leonard .05
730 Charles Nagy .05
731 Donald Harris .05
732 Travis Buckley .05
733 Tom Browning .05
734 Anthony Young .05
735 Steve Shifflett .05
736 Jeff Russell .05
737 Wilson Alvarez .05
738 Lance Painter .05
739 Dave Weathers .05
740 Len Dykstra .05
741 Mike Devereaux .05
742 Rene Arocha, Alan Embree, Tim Crabtree, Brien Taylor Top Prospects SP .05
743 Dave Landaker .05
744 Chris George .05
745 Eric Davis .05
746 Mark Strittmatter, LaMarr Rogers Rockies Future Stars .05
747 Carl Willis .05
748 Stan Belinda .05
749 Scott Kamieniecki .05
750 Rickey Henderson .50
751 Eric Hillman .05
752 Pat Hentgen .05
753 Jim Corsi .05
754 Brian Jordan .05
755 Bill Swift .05
756 Mike Henneman .05
757 Harold Reynolds .05
758 Sean Berry .05
759 Charlie Hayes .05
760 Luis Polonia .05
761 Darrin Jackson .05
762 Mark Lewis .05
763 Rob Maurer .05
764 Willie Greene .05
765 Vince Coleman .05
766 Todd Revenig .05
767 Rich Ireland .05
768 Mike MacFarlane .05
769 Francisco Cabrera .05
770 Robin Ventura .05
771 Kevin Ritz .05
772 Chito Martinez .05
773 Cliff Brantley .05
774 Curtis Leskanic .05
775 Chris Bosio .05
776 Jose Offerman .05
777 Mark Guthrie .05
778 Don Slaught .05
779 Rich Monteleone .05
780 Jim Abbott .05
781 Jack Clark .05
782 Rafael Mendoza, Dan Roman Marlins Future Stars .05
783 Heathcliff Slocumb .05
784 Jeff Branson .05
785 Kevin Brown .05
786 Mike Christopher, Ken Ryan, Aaron Taylor, Gus Gandarillas Top Prospects RP .05
787 Mike Matthews .05
788 Mackey Sasser .05
789 Jeff Conine .05
790 George Bell .05
791 Pat Rapp .05
792 Joe Boever .05
793 Jim Poole .05
794 Andy Ashby .05
795 Deion Sanders .10
796 Scott Brosius .05
797 Brad Pennington .05
798 Greg Blosser .05
799 *Jim Edmonds* 1.00
800 Shawn Jeter .05
801 Jesse Levis .05
802 Phil Clark .05
803 Ed Pierce .05
804 *Jose Valentin* .05
805 Terry Jorgensen .05
806 Mark Hutton .05
807 Troy Neel .05
808 Bret Boone .05
809 Chris Colon .05
810 *Domingo Martinez* .05
811 Javier Lopez .05
812 Matt Walbeck .05
813 Dan Wilson .05
814 Scooter Tucker .05
815 *Billy Ashley* .05
816 *Tim Laker* .05
817 Bobby Jones .05
818 Brad Brink .05
819 William Pennyfeather .05
820 Stan Royer .05
821 Doug Brocail .05
822 Kevin Rogers .05
823 Checklist 397-528 .05
824 Checklist 541-691 .05
825 Checklist 692-825 .05

Gold

NM/M
Complete Set (825): 40.00
Common Player: .15
(Star cards valued at 3X corresponding cards in regular 1993 Topps issue)
394 Bernardo Brito .25
395 Jim McNamara .25
396 Rich Sauveur .25
823 Keith Brown .25
824 Russ McGinnis .25
825 Mike Walker .25

Black Gold

NM/M
Complete Set (44): 7.50
Common Player: .10
Winner A (1-11): 1.00
Winner B (12-22): 1.00
Winner C (23-33): 1.00
Winner D (34-44): 1.00
Winner AB (1-22): 3.00
Winner CD (23-44): 3.00
Winner ABCD (1-44): 5.00
1 Barry Bonds 1.50
2 Will Clark .10
3 Darren Daulton .10
4 Andre Dawson .25
5 Delino DeShields .10
6 Tom Glavine .20
7 Marquis Grissom .10
8 Tony Gwynn .75
9 Eric Karros .10
10 Ray Lankford .10
11 Barry Larkin .10
12 Greg Maddux .75
13 Fred McGriff .10
14 Joe Oliver .10
15 Terry Pendleton .10
16 Bip Roberts .10
17 Ryne Sandberg .75
18 Gary Sheffield .40
19 Lee Smith .10
20 Ozzie Smith .75
21 Andy Van Slyke .10
22 Larry Walker .10
23 Roberto Alomar .20
24 Brady Anderson .10
25 Carlos Baerga .10
26 Joe Carter .10
27 Roger Clemens .85
28 Mike Devereaux .10
29 Dennis Eckersley .60
30 Cecil Fielder .10
31 Travis Fryman .10
32 Juan Gonzalez .35
33 Ken Griffey Jr. 1.00
34 Brian Harper .10
35 Pat Listach .10
36 Kenny Lofton .10
37 Edgar Martinez .10
38 Jack McDowell .10
39 Mark McGwire 1.00
40 Kirby Puckett .75
41 Mickey Tettleton .10
42 Frank Thomas .65
43 Robin Ventura .10
44 Dave Winfield .65

Traded

NM/M
Complete Set (132): 25.00
Common Player: .05
1 Barry Bonds 2.00
2 Rich Renteria .05
3 Aaron Sele .05
4 *Carlton Loewer* (USA) .10
5 Erik Pappas .05
6 *Greg McMichael* .05
7 Freddie Benavides .05
8 Kirk Gibson .05
9 Tony Fernandez .05
10 *Jay Gainer* (USA) .05
11 Orestes Destrade .05
12 *A.J. Hinch* (USA) .40
13 Bobby Munoz .05
14 Tom Henke .05
15 Rob Butler .05
16 Gary Wayne .05
17 David McCarty .05
18 Walt Weiss .05
19 *Todd Helton* (USA) 20.00
20 Mark Whiten .05
21 Ricky Gutierrez .05
22 *Dustin Hermanson* (USA) .40
23 *Sherman Obando* .05
24 Mike Piazza 2.00
25 Jeff Russell .05
26 Jason Bere .05
27 *Jack Voight* .05
28 Chris Bosio .05
29 Phil Hiatt .05
30 *Matt Beaumont* (USA) .05
31 Andres Galarraga .05
32 Greg Swindell .05
33 Vinny Castilla .05
34 *Pat Clougherty* (USA) .05
35 Greg Briley .05
36 Dallas Green, Davey Johnson .05
37 Tyler Green .05
38 Craig Paquette .05
39 Danny Sheaffer .05
40 Jim Converse .05
41 Terry Harvey .05
42 Phil Plantier .05
43 *Doug Saunders* .05
44 Benny Santiago .05
45 *Dante Powell* (USA) .10
46 Jeff Parrett .05
47 Wade Boggs .85
48 Paul Molitor .75
49 Turk Wendell .05
50 David Wells .05
51 Gary Sheffield .35
52 Kevin Young .05
53 Nelson Liriano .05
54 Greg Maddux .85
55 Derek Bell .05

56	*Matt Turner*	.05
57	*Charlie Nelson* (USA)	.05
58	Mike Hampton	.05
59	*Troy O'Leary*	.10
60	Benji Gil	.05
61	*Mitch Lyden*	.05
62	J.T. Snow	.05
63	Damon Buford	.05
64	Gene Harris	.05
65	Randy Myers	.05
66	Felix Jose	.05
67	*Todd Dunn* (USA)	.05
68	Jimmy Key	.05
69	Pedro Castellano	.05
70	*Mark Merila* (USA)	.05
71	Rich Rodriguez	.05
72	Matt Mieske	.05
73	Pete Incaviglia	.05
74	Carl Everett	.05
75	Jim Abbott	.05
76	Luis Aquino	.05
77	*Rene Arocha*	.05
78	*Jon Shave*	.05
79	*Todd Walker* (USA)	1.00
80	Jack Armstrong	.05
81	Jeff Richardson	.05
82	Blas Minor	.05
83	Dave Winfield	.75
84	Paul O'Neill	.05
85	*Steve Reich* (USA)	.10
86	Chris Hammond	.05
87	*Hilly Hathaway*	.05
88	Fred McGriff	.05
89	*Dave Telgheder*	.05
90	*Richie Lewis*	.05
91	Brent Gates	.05
92	Andre Dawson	.15
93	*Andy Barkett* (USA)	.05
94	Doug Drabek	.05
95	Joe Klink	.05
96	Willie Blair	.05
97	*Danny Graves* (USA)	.05
98	Pat Meares	.05
99	Mike Lansing	.05
100	*Marcos Armas*	.05
101	*Darren Grass* (USA)	.05
102	Chris Jones	.05
103	*Ken Ryan*	.05
104	Ellis Burks	.05
105	Bobby Kelly	.05
106	Dave Magadan	.05
107	*Paul Wilson* (USA)	.25
108	Rob Natal	.05
109	Paul Wagner	.05
110	Jeromy Burnitz	.05
111	Monty Fariss	.05
112	Kevin Mitchell	.05
113	*Scott Pose*	.05
114	Dave Stewart	.05
115	*Russ Johnson* (USA)	.10
116	Armando Reynoso	.05
117	Geronimo Berroa	.05
118	*Woody Williams*	.15
119	*Tim Bogar*	.05
120	*Bob Scafa* (USA)	.05
121	Henry Cotto	.05
122	Gregg Jefferies	.05
123	Norm Charlton	.05
124	*Bret Wagner* (USA)	.05
125	David Cone	.05
126	Daryl Boston	.05
127	Tim Wallach	.05
128	*Mike Martin* (USA)	.05
129	*John Cummings*	.05
130	Ryan Bowen	.05
131	*John Powell* (USA)	.05
132	Checklist	.05

1994 TOPPS

		NM/M
Unopened Retail Set (818):		60.00
Unopened Hobby Set (808)		50.00
Complete Set (792):		35.00
Common Player:		.05
Series 1 or 2 Pack (12):		.50
Series 1 or 2 Wax Box (36):		15.00
1	Mike Piazza (All-Star Rookie)	.85
2	Bernie Williams	.05
3	Kevin Rogers	.05
4	Paul Carey (Future Star)	.05
5	Ozzie Guillen	.05
6	Derrick May	.05
7	Jose Mesa	.05
8	Todd Hundley	.05
9	Chris Haney	.05
10	John Olerud	.05
11	Andujar Cedeno	.05
12	John Smiley	.05
13	Phil Plantier	.05
14	Willie Banks	.05
15	Jay Bell	.05
16	Doug Henry	.05
17	Lance Blankenship	.05
18	Greg Harris	.05
19	Scott Livingstone	.05
20	Bryan Harvey	.05
21	Wil Cordero (All-Star Rookie)	.05
22	Roger Pavlik	.05
23	Mark Lemke	.05
24	Jeff Nelson	.05
25	Todd Zeile	.05
26	Billy Hatcher	.05
27	Joe Magrane	.05
28	Tony Longmire (Future Star)	.05
29	Omar Daal	.05
30	Kirt Manwaring	.05
31	Melido Perez	.05
32	Tim Hulett	.05
33	Jeff Schwarz	.05
34	Nolan Ryan	1.00
35	Jose Guzman	.05
36	Felix Fermin	.05
37	Jeff Innis	.05
38	Brent Mayne	.05
39	*Huck Flener*	.05
40	Jeff Bagwell	.50
41	Kevin Wickander	.05
42	Ricky Gutierrez	.05
43	Pat Mahomes	.05
44	Jeff King	.05
45	Cal Eldred	.05
46	Craig Paquette	.05
47	Richie Lewis	.05
48	Tony Phillips	.05
49	Armando Reynoso	.05
50	Moises Alou	.05
51	Manuel Lee	.05
52	Otis Nixon	.05
53	Billy Ashley (Future Star)	.05
54	Mark Whiten	.05
55	Jeff Russell	.05
56	Chad Curtis	.05
57	Kevin Stocker	.05
58	Mike Jackson	.05
59	Matt Nokes	.05
60	Chris Bosio	.05
61	Damon Buford	.05
62	Tim Belcher	.05
63	Glenallen Hill	.05
64	Bill Wertz	.05
65	Eddie Murray	.50
66	Tom Gordon	.05
67	Alex Gonzalez (Future Star)	.05
68	Eddie Taubensee	.05
69	Jacob Brumfield	.05
70	Andy Benes	.05
71	Rich Becker (Future Star)	.05
72	Steve Cooke (All-Star Rookie)	.05
73	Billy Spiers	.05
74	Scott Brosius	.05
75	Alan Trammell	.05
76	Luis Aquino	.05
77	Jerald Clark	.05
78	Mel Rojas	.05
79	Billy Masse, Stanton Cameron, Tim Clark, Craig McClure OF Prospects	.05
80	Jose Canseco	.30
81	Greg McMichael (All-Star Rookie)	.05
82	Brian Turang	.05
83	Tom Urban	.05
84	Garret Anderson (Future Star)	.05
85	Tony Pena	.05
86	Ricky Jordan	.05
87	Jim Gott	.05
88	Pat Kelly	.05
89	Bud Black	.05
90	Robin Ventura	.05
91	Rick Sutcliffe	.05
92	Jose Bautista	.05
93	Bob Ojeda	.05
94	Phil Hiatt	.05
95	Tim Pugh	.05
96	Randy Knorr	.05
97	Todd Jones (Future Star)	.05
98	Ryan Thompson	.05
99	Tim Mauser	.05
100	Kirby Puckett	.60
101	Mark Dewey	.05
102	B.J. Surhoff	.05
103	Sterling Hitchcock	.05
104	Alex Arias	.05
105	David Wells	.05
106	Daryl Boston	.05
107	Mike Stanton	.05
108	Gary Redus	.05
109a	Delino DeShields (red "Expos, 2B")	2.00
109b	Delino DeShields (yellow "Expos, 2B")	.05
110	Lee Smith	.05
111	Greg Litton	.05
112	Frank Rodriguez (Future Star)	.05
113	Russ Springer	.05
114	Mitch Williams	.05
115	Eric Karros	.05
116	Jeff Brantley	.05
117	Jack Voight	.05
118	Jason Bere	.05
119	Kevin Roberson	.05
120	Jimmy Key	.05
121	Reggie Jefferson	.05
122	Jeromy Burnitz	.05
123	Billy Brewer (Future Star)	.05
124	Willie Canate	.05
125	Greg Swindell	.05
126	Hal Morris	.05
127	Brad Ausmus	.05
128	George Tsamis	.05
129	Denny Neagle	.05
130	Pat Listach	.05
131	Steve Karsay	.05
132	Bret Barberie	.05
133	Mark Leiter	.05
134	Greg Colbrunn	.05
135	David Nied	.05
136	Dean Palmer	.05
137	Steve Avery	.05
138	Bill Haselman	.05
139	Tripp Cromer (Future Star)	.05
140	Frank Viola	.05
141	Rene Gonzales	.05
142	Curt Schilling	.25
143	Tim Wallach	.05
144	Bobby Munoz	.05
145	Brady Anderson	.05
146	Rod Beck	.05
147	Mike LaValliere	.05
148	Greg Hibbard	.05
149	Kenny Lofton	.05
150	Dwight Gooden	.05
151	Greg Gagne	.05
152	Ray McDavid (Future Star)	.05
153	Chris Donnels	.05
154	Dan Wilson	.05
155	Todd Stottlemyre	.05
156	David McCarty	.05
157	Paul Wagner	.05
158	Orlando Miller, Brandon Wilson, Derek Jeter, Mike Neal SS Prospects	1.00
159	Mike Fetters	.05
160	Scott Lydy	.05
161	Darrell Whitmore	.05
162	Bob MacDonald	.05
163	Vinny Castilla	.05
164	Denis Boucher	.05
165	Ivan Rodriguez	.40
166	Ron Gant	.05
167	Tim Davis	.05
168	Steve Dixon	.05
169	Scott Fletcher	.05
170	Terry Mulholland	.05
171	Greg Myers	.05
172	Brett Butler	.05
173	Bob Wickman	.05
174	Dave Martinez	.05
175	Fernando Valenzuela	.05
176	Craig Grebeck	.05
177	Shawn Boskie	.05
178	Albie Lopez	.05
179	Butch Huskey (Future Star)	.05
180	George Brett	.65
181	Juan Guzman	.05
182	Eric Anthony	.05
183	Rob Dibble	.05
184	Craig Shipley	.05
185	Kevin Tapani	.05
186	Marcus Moore	.05
187	Graeme Lloyd	.05
188	Mike Bordick	.05
189	Chris Hammond	.05
190	Cecil Fielder	.05
191	Curtis Leskanic	.05
192	Lou Frazier	.05
193	Steve Dreyer	.05
194	Javier Lopez (Future Star)	.05
195	Edgar Martinez	.05
196	Allen Watson	.05
197	John Flaherty	.05
198	Kurt Stillwell	.05
199	Danny Jackson	.05
200	Cal Ripken, Jr.	1.00
201	Mike Bell	.05
202	*Alan Benes*	.10
203	Matt Farner	.05
204	*Jeff Granger*	.05
205	*Brooks Kieschnick*	.05
206	Jeremy Lee	.05
207	*Charles Peterson*	.05
208	Andy Rice	.05
209	*Billy Wagner*	.25
210	Kelly Wunsch	.05
211	Tom Candiotti	.05
212	Domingo Jean	.05
213	John Burkett	.05
214	George Bell	.05
215	Dan Plesac	.05
216	Manny Ramirez	.60
217	Mike Maddux	.05
218	Kevin McReynolds	.05
219	Pat Borders	.05
220	Doug Drabek	.05
221	Larry Luebbers	.05
222	Trevor Hoffman	.05
223	Pat Meares	.05
224	Danny Miceli	.05
225	Greg Vaughn	.05
226	Scott Hemond	.05
227	Pat Rapp	.05
228	Kirk Gibson	.05
229	Lance Painter	.05
230	Larry Walker	.05
231	Benji Gil	.05
232	Mark Wohlers	.05
233	Rich Amaral	.05
234	Erik Pappas	.05
235	Scott Cooper	.05
236	Mike Butcher	.05
237	Curtis Pride, Shawn Green, Mark Sweeney, Eddie Davis OF Prospects	.35
238	Kim Batiste	.05
239	Paul Assenmacher	.05
240	Will Clark	.05
241	Jose Offerman	.05
242	Todd Frohwirth	.05
243	Tim Raines	.05
244	Rick Wilkins	.05
245	Bret Saberhagen	.05
246	Thomas Howard	.05
247	Stan Belinda	.05
248	Rickey Henderson	.50
249	Brian Williams	.05
250	Barry Larkin	.05
251	Jose Valentin	.05
252	Lenny Webster	.05
253	Blas Minor	.05
254	Tim Teufel	.05
255	Bobby Witt	.05
256	Walt Weiss	.05
257	Chad Kreuter	.05
258	Roberto Mejia	.05
259	Cliff Floyd (Future Star)	.05
260	Julio Franco	.05
261	Rafael Belliard	.05
262	Marc Newfield	.05
263	Gerald Perry	.05
264	Ken Ryan	.05
265	Chili Davis	.05
266	Dave West	.05
267	Royce Clayton	.05
268	Pedro Martinez	.50

269 Mark Hutton .05
270 Frank Thomas .50
271 Brad Pennington .05
272 Mike Harkey .05
273 Sandy Alomar .05
274 Dave Gallagher .05
275 Wally Joyner .05
276 Ricky Trlicek .05
277 Al Osuna .05
278 Calvin Reese .05
279 Kevin Higgins .05
280 Rick Aguilera .05
281 Orlando Merced .05
282 Mike Mohler .05
283 John Jaha .05
284 Robb Nen .05
285 Travis Fryman .05
286 Mark Thompson .05
287 Mike Lansing .05
288 Craig Lefferts .05
289 Damon Berryhill .05
290 Randy Johnson .50
291 Jeff Reed .05
292 Danny Darwin .05
293 J.T. Snow .05
294 Tyler Green .05
295 Chris Hoiles .05
296 Roger McDowell .05
297 Spike Owen .05
298 Salomon Torres .05
299 Wilson Alvarez .05
300 Ryne Sandberg .60
301 Derek Lilliquist .05
302 Howard Johnson .05
303 Greg Cadaret .05
304 Pat Hentgen .05
305 Craig Biggio .05
306 Scott Service .05
307 Melvin Nieves .05
308 Mike Trombley .05
309 Carlos Garcia .05
310 Robin Yount .50
311 Marcos Armas .05
312 Rich Rodriguez .05
313 Justin Thompson .05
314 Danny Sheaffer .05
315 Ken Hill .05
316 *Chad Ogea, Duff Brumley, Terrell Wade, Chris Michalak* P Propsects .10
317 Cris Carpenter .05
318 Jeff Blauser .05
319 Ted Power .05
320 Ozzie Smith .60
321 John Dopson .05
322 Chris Turner .05
323 Pete Incaviglia .05
324 Alan Mills .05
325 Jody Reed .05
326 Rich Monteleone .05
327 Mark Carreon .05
328 Donn Pall .05
329 Matt Walbeck .05
330 Charles Nagy .05
331 Jeff McKnight .05
332 Jose Lind .05
333 Mike Timlin .05
334 Doug Jones .05
335 Kevin Mitchell .05
336 Luis Lopez .05
337 Shane Mack .05
338 Randy Tomlin .05
339 Matt Mieske .05
340 Mark McGwire .85
341 Nigel Wilson .05
342 Danny Gladden .05
343 Mo Sanford .05
344 Sean Berry .05
345 Kevin Brown .05
346 Greg Olson .05
347 Dave Magadan .05
348 Rene Arocha .05
349 Carlos Quintana .05
350 Jim Abbott .05
351 Gary DiSarcina .05
352 Ben Rivera .05
353 Carlos Hernandez .05
354 Darren Lewis .05
355 Harold Reynolds .05
356 Scott Ruffcorn .05
357 Mark Gubicza .05
358 Paul Sorrento .05
359 Anthony Young .05
360 Mark Grace .05
361 Rob Butler .05
362 Kevin Bass .05
363 Eric Helfand .05
364 Derek Bell .05
365 Scott Erickson .05
366 Al Martin .05
367 Ricky Bones .05
368 Jeff Branson .05
369 *Luis Ortiz, David Bell, Jason Giambi, George Arias* 3B Prospects .30
370a Benny Santiago .05
370b Mark McLemore (originally checklisted as #379) .05
371 John Doherty .05
372 Joe Girardi .05
373 Tim Scott .05
374 Marvin Freeman .05
375 Deion Sanders .10
376 Roger Salkeld .05
377 Bernard Gilkey .05
378 Tony Fossas .05
379 (Not issued, see #370)
380 Darren Daulton .05
381 Chuck Finley .05
382 Mitch Webster .05
383 Gerald Williams .05
384 Frank Thomas, Fred McGriff .30
385 Roberto Alomar, Robby Thompson .05
386 Wade Boggs, Matt Williams .35
387 Cal Ripken, Jr., Jeff Blauser .50
388 Ken Griffey, Jr., Len Dykstra .40
389 Juan Gonzalez, Dave Justice .10
390 Albert Belle, Barry Bonds .45
391 Mike Stanley, Mike Piazza .45
392 Jack McDowell, Greg Maddux .35
393 Jimmy Key, Tom Glavine .05
394 Jeff Montgomery, Randy Myers .05
395 Checklist 1 .05
396 Checklist 2 .05
397 Tim Salmon .10
398 Todd Benzinger .05
399 Frank Castillo .05
400 Ken Griffey, Jr. .75
401 John Kruk .05
402 Dave Telgheder .05
403 Gary Gaetti .05
404 Jim Edmonds .05
405 Don Slaught .05
406 Jose Oquendo .05
407 Bruce Ruffin .05
408 Phil Clark .05
409 Joe Klink .05
410 Lou Whitaker .05
411 Kevin Seitzer .05
412 Darrin Fletcher .05
413 Kenny Rogers .05
414 Bill Pecota .05
415 Dave Fleming .05
416 Luis Alicea .05
417 Paul Quantrill .05
418 Damion Easley .05
419 Wes Chamberlain .05
420 Harold Baines .05
421 Scott Radinsky .05
422 Rey Sanchez .05
423 Junior Ortiz .05
424 Jeff Kent .05
425 Brian McRae .05
426 Ed Sprague .05
427 Tom Edens .05
428 Willie Greene .05
429 Bryan Hickerson .05
430 Dave Winfield .50
431 Pedro Astacio .05
432 Mike Gallego .05
433 Dave Burba .05
434 Bob Walk .05
435 Darryl Hamilton .05
436 Vince Horsman .05
437 Bob Natal .05
438 Mike Henneman .05
439 Willie Blair .05
440 Denny Martinez .05
441 Dan Peltier .05
442 Tony Tarasco .05
443 John Cummings .05
444 Geronimo Pena .05
445 Aaron Sele .05
446 Stan Javier .05
447 Mike Williams .05
448 Greg Pirkl, Roberto Petagine, D.J. Boston, Shawn Wooten 1B Prospects .05
449 Jim Poole .05
450 Carlos Baerga .05
451 Bob Scanlan .05
452 Lance Johnson .05
453 Eric Hillman .05
454 Keith Miller .05
455 Dave Stewart .05
456 Pete Harnisch .05
457 Roberto Kelly .05
458 Tim Worrell .05
459 Pedro Munoz .05
460 Orel Hershiser .05
461 Randy Velarde .05
462 Trevor Wilson .05
463 Jerry Goff .05
464 Bill Wegman .05
465 Dennis Eckersley .40
466 Jeff Conine .05
467 Joe Boever .05
468 Dante Bichette .05
469 Jeff Shaw .05
470 Rafael Palmeiro .40
471 *Phil Leftwich* .05
472 Jay Buhner .05
473 Bob Tewksbury .05
474 Tim Naehring .05
475 Tom Glavine .25
476 Dave Hollins .05
477 Arthur Rhodes .05
478 Joey Cora .05
479 Mike Morgan .05
480 Albert Belle .05
481 John Franco .05
482 Hipolito Pichardo .05
483 Duane Ward .05
484 Luis Gonzalez .05
485 Joe Oliver .05
486 Wally Whitehurst .05
487 Mike Benjamin .05
488 Eric Davis .05
489 Scott Kamieniecki .05
490 Kent Hrbek .05
491 *John Hope* .05
492 Jesse Orosco .05
493 Troy Neel .05
494 Ryan Bowen .05
495 Mickey Tettleton .05
496 Chris Jones .05
497 John Wetteland .05
498 David Hulse .05
499 Greg Maddux .60
500 Bo Jackson .10
501 Donovan Osborne .05
502 Mike Greenwell .05
503 Steve Frey .05
504 Jim Eisenreich .05
505 Robby Thompson .05
506 Leo Gomez .05
507 Dave Staton .05
508 Wayne Kirby .05
509 Tim Bogar .05
510 David Cone .05
511 Devon White .05
512 Xavier Hernandez .05
513 Tim Costo .05
514 Gene Harris .05
515 Jack McDowell .05
516 Kevin Gross .05
517 Scott Leius .05
518 Lloyd McClendon .05
519 *Alex Diaz* .05
520 Wade Boggs .60
521 Bob Welch .05
522 Henry Cotto .05
523 Mike Moore .05
524 Tim Laker .05
525 Andres Galarraga .05
526 Jamie Moyer .05
527 Norberto Martin, Ruben Santana, Jason Hardtke, Chris Sexton 2B Prospects .05
528 Sid Bream .05
529 Erik Hanson .05
530 Ray Lankford .05
531 Rob Deer .05
532 Rod Correia .05
533 Roger Mason .05
534 Mike Devereaux .05
535 Jeff Montgomery .05
536 Dwight Smith .05
537 Jeremy Hernandez .05
538 Ellis Burks .05
539 Bobby Jones .05
540 Paul Molitor .50
541 Jeff Juden .05
542 Chris Sabo .05
543 Larry Casian .05
544 Jeff Gardner .05
545 Ramon Martinez .05
546 Paul O'Neill .05
547 Steve Hosey .05
548 Dave Nilsson .05
549 Ron Darling .05
550 Matt Williams .05
551 Jack Armstrong .05
552 Bill Krueger .05
553 Freddie Benavides .05
554 Jeff Fassero .05
555 Chuck Knoblauch .05
556 Guillermo Velasquez .05
557 Joel Johnston .05
558 Tom Lampkin .05
559 Todd Van Poppel .05
560 Gary Sheffield .30
561 Skeeter Barnes .05
562 Darren Holmes .05
563 John Vander Wal .05
564 Mike Ignasiak .05
565 Fred McGriff .05
566 Luis Polonia .05
567 Mike Perez .05
568 John Valentin .05
569 Mike Felder .05
570 Tommy Greene .05
571 David Segui .05
572 Roberto Hernandez .05
573 Steve Wilson .05
574 Willie McGee .05
575 Randy Myers .05
576 Darrin Jackson .05
577 Eric Plunk .05
578 Mike MacFarlane .05
579 Doug Brocail .05
580 Steve Finley .05
581 John Roper .05
582 Danny Cox .05
583 Chip Hale .05
584 Scott Bullett .05
585 Kevin Reimer .05
586 Brent Gates .05
587 Matt Turner .05
588 Rich Rowland .05
589 Kent Bottenfield .05
590 Marquis Grissom .05
591 Doug Strange .05
592 Jay Howell .05
593 Omar Vizquel .05
594 Rheal Cormier .05
595 Andre Dawson .25
596 Hilly Hathaway .05
597 Todd Pratt .05
598 Mike Mussina .30
599 Alex Fernandez .05
600 Don Mattingly .65
601 Frank Thomas .25
602 Ryne Sandberg .30
603 Wade Boggs .30
604 Cal Ripken, Jr. .50
605 Barry Bonds .50
606 Ken Griffey, Jr. .40
607 Kirby Puckett .35
608 Darren Daulton .05
609 Paul Molitor .25
610 Terry Steinbach .05
611 Todd Worrell .05
612 Jim Thome .40
613 Chuck McElroy .05
614 John Habyan .05
615 Sid Fernandez .05
616 *Eddie Zambrano, Glenn Murray, Chad Mottola, Jermaine Allensworth* OF Prospects .05
617 Steve Bedrosian .05
618 Rob Ducey .05
619 Tom Browning .05
620 Tony Gwynn .60
621 Carl Willis .05
622 Kevin Young .05
623 Rafael Novoa .05
624 Jerry Browne .05
625 Charlie Hough .05
626 Chris Gomez .05
627 Steve Reed .05
628 Kirk Rueter .05
629 Matt Whiteside .05
630 Dave Justice .05
631 Brad Holman .05
632 Brian Jordan .05
633 Scott Bankhead .05
634 Torey Lovullo .05
635 Len Dykstra .05
636 Ben McDonald .05
637 Steve Howe .05
638 Jose Vizcaino .05
639 Bill Swift .05
640 Darryl Strawberry .05
641 Steve Farr .05
642 Tom Kramer .05

643 Joe Orsulak .05
644 Tom Henke .05
645 Joe Carter .05
646 Ken Caminiti .05
647 Reggie Sanders .05
648 Andy Ashby .05
649 Derek Parks .05
650 Andy Van Slyke .05
651 Juan Bell .05
652 Roger Smithberg .05
653 Chuck Carr .05
654 Bill Gullickson .05
655 Charlie Hayes .05
656 Chris Nabholz .05
657 Karl Rhodes .05
658 Pete Smith .05
659 Bret Boone .05
660 Gregg Jefferies .05
661 Bob Zupcic .05
662 Steve Sax .05
663 Mariano Duncan .05
664 Jeff Tackett .05
665 Mark Langston .05
666 Steve Buechele .05
667 Candy Maldonado .05
668 Woody Williams .05
669 Tim Wakefield .05
670 Danny Tartabull .05
671 Charlie O'Brien .05
672 Felix Jose .05
673 Bobby Ayala .05
674 Scott Servais .05
675 Roberto Alomar .15
676 Pedro Martinez .05
677 Eddie Guardado .05
678 Mark Lewis .05
679 Jaime Navarro .05
680 Ruben Sierra .05
681 Rick Renteria .05
682 Storm Davis .05
683 Cory Snyder .05
684 Ron Karkovice .05
685 Juan Gonzalez .25
686 Chris Howard, Carlos Delgado, Jason Kendall, Paul Bako C Prospects .40
687 John Smoltz .05
688 Brian Dorsett .05
689 Omar Olivares .05
690 Mo Vaughn .05
691 Joe Grahe .05
692 Mickey Morandini .05
693 Tino Martinez .05
694 Brian Barnes .05
695 Mike Stanley .05
696 Mark Clark .05
697 Dave Hansen .05
698 Willie Wilson .05
699 Pete Schourek .05
700 Barry Bonds 1.00
701 Kevin Appier .05
702 Tony Fernandez .05
703 Darryl Kile .05
704 Archi Cianfrocco .05
705 Jose Rijo .05
706 Brian Harper .05
707 Zane Smith .05
708 Dave Henderson .05
709 Angel Miranda .05
710 Orestes Destrade .05
711 Greg Gohr .05
712 Eric Young .05
713 Todd Williams, Ron Watson, Kirk Bullinger, Mike Welch P Prospects .05
714 Tim Spehr .05
715 Hank Aaron (20th Anniversary #715) .50
716 Nate Minchey .05
717 Mike Blowers .05
718 Kent Mercker .05
719 Tom Pagnozzi .05
720 Roger Clemens .65
721 Eduardo Perez .05
722 Milt Thompson .05
723 Gregg Olson .05
724 Kirk McCaskill .05
725 Sammy Sosa .60
726 Alvaro Espinoza .05
727 Henry Rodriguez .05
728 Jim Leyritz .05
729 Steve Scarsone .05
730 Bobby Bonilla .05
731 Chris Gwynn .05
732 Al Leiter .05
733 Bip Roberts .05
734 Mark Portugal .05
735 Terry Pendleton .05
736 Dave Valle .05
737 Paul Kilgus .05
738 Greg Harris .05
739 *Jon Ratliff* .05
740 *Kirk Presley* .05
741 *Josue Estrada* .05
742 *Wayne Gomes* .10
743 *Pat Watkins* .05
744 *Jamey Wright* .05
745 *Jay Powell* .05
746 *Ryan McGuire* .05
747 *Marc Barcelo* .05
748 *Sloan Smith* .05
749 *John Wasdin* .05
750 Marc Valdes .05
751 *Dan Ehler* .05
752 *Andre King* .05
753 *Greg Keagle* .05
754 *Jason Myers* .05
755 *Dax Winslett* .05
756 *Casey Whitten* .05
757 *Tony Fuduric* .05
758 *Greg Norton* .05
759 *Jeff D'Amico* .05
760 *Ryan Hancock* .05
761 *David Cooper* .05
762 *Kevin Orie* .05
763 John O'Donoghue, Mike Oquist .05
764 Cory Bailey, Scott Hatteberg .05
765 Mark Holzemer, Paul Swingle .05
766 James Baldwin, Rod Bolton .05
767 *Jerry DiPoto, Julian Tavarez* .10
768 Danny Bautista, Sean Bergman .05
769 Bob Hamelin, Joe Vitiello .05
770 Mark Kiefer, Troy O'Leary .05
771 Denny Hocking, Oscar Munoz .05
772 Russ Davis, Brien Taylor .05
773 Kurt Abbott, Miguel Jimenez .05
774 Kevin King, Eric Plantenberg .05
775 Jon Shave, Desi Wilson .05
776 Domingo Cedeno, Paul Spoljaric .05
777 Chipper Jones, Ryan Klesko .60
778 Steve Trachsel, Turk Wendell .05
779 Johnny Ruffin, Jerry Spradlin .05
780 Jason Bates, John Burke .05
781 Carl Everett, Dave Weathers .05
782 Gary Mota, James Mouton .05
783 Raul Mondesi, Ben Van Ryn .05
784 Gabe White, Rondell White .05
785 Brook Fordyce, Bill Pulsipher .05
786 Kevin Foster, Gene Schall .05
787 Rich Aude, Midre Cummings .05
788 Brian Barber, Richard Batchelor .05
789 Brian Johnson, Scott Sanders .05
790 Rikkert Faneyte, J.R. Phillips .05
791 Checklist 3 .05
792 Checklist 4 .05

Gold

NM/M
Complete Set (792): 50.00
Common Player: .15
(Star cards valued at 2X corresponding cards in regular Topps issue)

Black Gold

NM/M
Complete Set (44): 10.00
Complete Series 1 (22): 6.00
Complete Series 2 (22): 4.00
Common Player: .10
1 Roberto Alomar .20
2 Carlos Baerga .10
3 Albert Belle .10
4 Joe Carter .10
5 Cecil Fielder .10
6 Travis Fryman .10
7 Juan Gonzalez .25
8 Ken Griffey, Jr. .75
9 Chris Hoiles .10
10 Randy Johnson .45
11 Kenny Lofton .10
12 Jack McDowell .10
13 Paul Molitor .45
14 Jeff Montgomery .10
15 John Olerud .10
16 Rafael Palmeiro .45
17 Kirby Puckett .60
18 Cal Ripken, Jr. 1.50
19 Tim Salmon .10
20 Mike Stanley .10
21 Frank Thomas .50
22 Robin Ventura .10
23 Jeff Bagwell .45
24 Jay Bell .10
25 Craig Biggio .10
26 Jeff Blauser .10
27 Barry Bonds 1.50
28 Darren Daulton .10
29 Len Dykstra .10
30 Andres Galarraga .10
31 Ron Gant .10
32 Tom Glavine .10
33 Mark Grace .10
34 Marquis Grissom .10
35 Gregg Jefferies .10
36 Dave Justice .10
37 John Kruk .10
38 Greg Maddux .60
39 Fred McGriff .10
40 Randy Myers .10
41 Mike Piazza 1.00
42 Sammy Sosa .60
43 Robby Thompson .10
44 Matt Williams .10
--- Winner A .50
--- Winner B .50
--- Winner C .50
--- Winner D .50
--- Winner A/B .60
--- Winner C/D .60
--- Winner A/B/C/D .75

Traded

NM/M
Complete Set (140): 30.00
Common Player: .05
1 Paul Wilson .05
2 Bill Taylor .05
3 Dan Wilson .05
4 Mark Smith .05
5 Toby Borland .05
6 Dave Clark .05
7 Denny Martinez .05
8 Dave Gallagher .05
9 Josias Manzanillo .05
10 Brian Anderson .05
11 Damon Berryhill .05
12 Alex Cole .05
13 Jacob Shumate .05
14 Oddibe McDowell .05
15 Willie Banks .05
16 Jerry Browne .05
17 Donnie Elliott .05
18 Ellis Burks .05
19 Chuck McElroy .05
20 Luis Polonia .05
21 Brian Harper .05
22 Mark Portugal .05
23 Dave Henderson .05
24 Mark Acre .05
25 Julio Franco .05
26 Darren Hall .05
27 Eric Anthony .05
28 Sid Fernandez .05
29 *Rusty Greer* .25
30 Riccardo Ingram .05
31 Gabe White .05
32 Tim Belcher .05
33 *Terrence Long* 1.00
34 *Mark Dalesandro* .05
35 Mike Kelly .05
36 Jack Morris .05
37 Jeff Brantley .05
38 *Larry Barnes* .05
39 Brian Hunter .05
40 Otis Nixon .05
41 Bret Wagner .05
42 Pedro Martinez, Delino DeShields Anatomy of a Trade .25
43 Heathcliff Slocumb .05
44 *Ben Grieve* .35
45 John Hudek .05
46 Shawon Dunston .05
47 Greg Colbrunn .05
48 Joey Hamilton .05
49 Marvin Freeman .05
50 Terry Mulholland .05
51 Keith Mitchell .05
52 Dwight Smith .05
53 Shawn Boskie .05
54 *Kevin Witt* .05
55 Ron Gant .05
56 Trenidad Hubbard, Jason Schmidt, Larry Sutton, Stephen Larkin 1994 Prospects 10.00
57 Jody Reed .05
58 Rick Helling .05
59 John Powell .05
60 Eddie Murray .60
61 Joe Hall .05
62 Jorge Fabregas .05
63 Mike Mordecai .05
64 Ed Vosberg .05
65 Rickey Henderson .60
66 Tim Grieve .05
67 Jon Lieber .05
68 Chris Howard .05
69 Matt Walbeck .05
70 Chan Ho Park .15
71 Bryan Eversgerd .05
72 John Dettmer .05
73 Erik Hanson .05
74 Mike Thurman (Draft pick) .05
75 Bobby Ayala .05
76 Rafael Palmeiro .50
77 Bret Boone .05
78 Paul Shuey .05
79 Kevin Foster .05
80 Dave Magadan .05
81 Bip Roberts .05
82 Howard Johnson .05
83 Xavier Hernandez .05
84 Ross Powell .05
85 *Doug Million* .05
86 Geronimo Berroa .05
87 *Mark Farris* .05
88 Butch Henry .05
89 Junior Felix .05
90 Bo Jackson .10
91 Hector Carrasco .05
92 Charlie O'Brien .05
93 Omar Vizquel .05
94 David Segui .05
95 Dustin Hermanson .05
96 Gar Finnvold .05
97 Dave Stevens .05
98 Corey Pointer .05
99 Felix Fermin .05
100 Lee Smith .05
101 Reid Ryan .15
102 Bobby Munoz .05
103 Deion Sanders, Roberto Kelly Anatomy of a Trade .05
104 Turner Ward .05
105 William Van Landingham .05
106 Vince Coleman .05
107 Stan Javier .05
108 Darrin Jackson .05
109 C.J. Nitkowski .05
110 Anthony Young .05
111 Kurt Miller .05
112 *Paul Konerko* 15.00
113 Walt Weiss .05
114 Daryl Boston .05
115 Will Clark .05
116 *Matt Smith* .05
117 Mark Leiter .05
118 Gregg Olson .05
119 Tony Pena .05
120 Jose Vizcaino .05

121 Rick White .05
122 Rich Rowland .05
123 Jeff Reboulet .05
124 Greg Hibbard .05
125 Chris Sabo .05
126 Doug Jones .05
127 Tony Fernandez .05
128 Carlos Reyes .05
129 Kevin Brown .05
130 Ryne Sandberg Commemorative 1.00
131 Ryne Sandberg Commemorative 1.00
132 Checklist 1-132 .05

Traded Finest Inserts

	NM/M
Complete Set (8):	6.00
Common Player:	.25
1 Greg Maddux	1.50
2 Mike Piazza	2.00
3 Matt Williams	.25
4 Raul Mondesi	.25
5 Ken Griffey Jr.	2.00
6 Kenny Lofton	.25
7 Frank Thomas	1.25
8 Manny Ramirez	1.00

1995 TOPPS

	NM/M
Unopened Hobby Set (677):	100.00
Unopened Retail Set (684):	75.00
Unopened Retail Set (677):	85.00
Complete Set (660):	45.00
Common Player:	.05
Series 1 or 2 Pack (15):	1.25
Series 1 or 2 Wax Box (36):	25.00

1 Frank Thomas .75
2 Mickey Morandini .05
3a Babe Ruth (100th Birthday, no gold "Topps" logo) 2.00
3b Babe Ruth (100th Birthday, gold "Topps" logo) 2.00
4 Scott Cooper .05
5 David Cone .05
6 Jacob Shumate .05
7 Trevor Hoffman .05
8 Shane Mack .05
9 Delino DeShields .05
10 Matt Williams .05
11 Sammy Sosa 1.00
12 Gary DiSarcina .05
13 Kenny Rogers .05
14 Jose Vizcaino .05
15 Lou Whitaker .05
16 Ron Darling .05
17 Dave Nilsson .05
18 Chris Hammond .05
19 Sid Bream .05
20 Denny Martinez .05
21 Orlando Merced .05
22 John Wetteland .05
23 Mike Devereaux .05
24 Rene Arocha .05
25 Jay Buhner .05
26 Darren Holmes .05
27 Hal Morris .05
28 *Brian Buchanan* .10
29 Keith Miller .05
30 Paul Molitor .75
31 Dave West .05
32 Tony Tarasco .05
33 Scott Sanders .05
34 Eddie Zambrano .05
35 Ricky Bones .05
36 John Valentin .05
37 Kevin Tapani .05
38 Tim Wallach .05
39 Darren Lewis .05
40 Travis Fryman .05
41 Mark Leiter .05
42 Jose Bautista .05
43 Pete Smith .05
44 Bret Barberie .05
45 Dennis Eckersley .65
46 Ken Hill .05
47 Chad Ogea .05
48 Pete Harnisch .05
49 James Baldwin .05
50 Mike Mussina .45
51 Al Martin .05
52 Mark Thompson .05
53 Matt Smith .05
54 Joey Hamilton .05
55 Edgar Martinez .05
56 John Smiley .05
57 Rey Sanchez .05
58 Mike Timlin .05
59 Ricky Bottalico .05
60 Jim Abbott .05
61 Mike Kelly .05
62 Brian Jordan .05
63 Ken Ryan .05
64 Matt Mieske .05
65 Rick Aguilera .05
66 Ismael Valdes .05
67 Royce Clayton .05
68 Junior Felix .05
69 Harold Reynolds .05
70 Juan Gonzalez .35
71 Kelly Stinnett .05
72 Carlos Reyes .05
73 Dave Weathers .05
74 Mel Rojas .05
75 Doug Drabek .05
76 Charles Nagy .05
77 Tim Raines .05
78 Midre Cummings .05
79 *Gene Schall, Scott Talanoa, Harold Williams, Ray Brown* 1B Prospects .05
80 Rafael Palmeiro .65
81 Charlie Hayes .05
82 Ray Lankford .05
83 Tim Davis .05
84 *C.J. Nitkowski* .05
85 Andy Ashby .05
86 Gerald Williams .05
87 Terry Shumpert .05
88 Heathcliff Slocumb .05
89 Domingo Cedeno .05
90 Mark Grace .05
91 *Brad Woodall* .10
92 Gar Finnvold .05
93 Jaime Navarro .05
94 Carlos Hernandez .05
95 Mark Langston .05
96 Chuck Carr .05
97 Mike Gardiner .05
98 David McCarty .05
99 Cris Carpenter .05
100 Barry Bonds 2.00
101 David Segui .05
102 Scott Brosius .05
103 Mariano Duncan .05
104 Kenny Lofton .05
105 Ken Caminiti .05
106 Darrin Jackson .05
107 Jim Poole .05
108 Wil Cordero .05
109 Danny Miceli .05
110 Walt Weiss .05
111 Tom Pagnozzi .05
112 Terrence Long .05
113 Bret Boone .05
114 Daryl Boston .05
115 Wally Joyner .05
116 Rob Butler .05
117 Rafael Belliard .05
118 Luis Lopez .05
119 Tony Fossas .05
120 Len Dykstra .05
121 Mike Morgan .05
122 Denny Hocking .05
123 Kevin Gross .05
124 Todd Benzinger .05
125 John Doherty .05
126 Eduardo Perez .05
127 Dan Smith .05
128 Joe Orsulak .05
129 Brent Gates .05
130 Jeff Conine .05
131 Doug Henry .05
132 Paul Sorrento .05
133 Mike Hampton .05
134 Tim Spehr .05
135 Julio Franco .05
136 Mike Dyer .05
137 Chris Sabo .05
138 Rheal Cormier .05
139 Paul Konerko .25
140 Dante Bichette .05
141 Chuck McElroy .05
142 Mike Stanley .05
143 Bob Hamelin .05
144 Tommy Greene .05
145 John Smoltz .05
146 Ed Sprague .05
147 Ray McDavid .05
148 Otis Nixon .05
149 Turk Wendell .05
150 Chris James .05
151 Derek Parks .05
152 Jose Offerman .05
153 Tony Clark .05
154 Chad Curtis .05
155 Mark Portugal .05
156 Bill Pulsipher .05
157 Troy Neel .05
158 Dave Winfield .75
159 Bill Wegman .05
160 Benny Santiago .05
161 Jose Mesa .05
162 Luis Gonzalez .05
163 Alex Fernandez .05
164 Freddie Benavides .05
165 Ben McDonald .05
166 Blas Minor .05
167 Bret Wagner .05
168 Mac Suzuki .05
169 Roberto Mejia .05
170 Wade Boggs 1.00
171 Calvin Reese .05
172 Hipolito Pichardo .05
173 Kim Batiste .05
174 Darren Hall .05
175 Tom Glavine .25
176 Phil Plantier .05
177 Chris Howard .05
178 Karl Rhodes .05
179 LaTroy Hawkins .05
180 Raul Mondesi .05
181 Jeff Reed .05
182 Milt Cuyler .05
183 Jim Edmonds .05
184 Hector Fajardo .05
185 Jeff Kent .05
186 Wilson Alvarez .05
187 Geronimo Berroa .05
188 Billy Spiers .05
189 Derek Lilliquist .05
190 Craig Biggio .05
191 Roberto Hernandez .05
192 Bob Natal .05
193 Bobby Ayala .05
194 *Travis Miller* .10
195 Bob Tewksbury .05
196 Rondell White .05
197 Steve Cooke .05
198 Jeff Branson .05
199 Derek Jeter 2.00
200 Tim Salmon .05
201 Steve Frey .05
202 Kent Mercker .05
203 Randy Johnson .75
204 Todd Worrell .05
205 Mo Vaughn .05
206 Howard Johnson .05
207 John Wasdin .05
208 Eddie Williams .05
209 Tim Belcher .05
210 Jeff Montgomery .05
211 Kirt Manwaring .05
212 Ben Grieve .05
213 Pat Hentgen .05
214 Shawon Dunston .05
215 Mike Greenwell .05
216 Alex Diaz .05
217 Pat Mahomes .05
218 Dave Hanson .05
219 Kevin Rogers .05
220 Cecil Fielder .05
221 Andrew Lorraine .05
222 Jack Armstrong .05
223 Todd Hundley .05
224 Mark Acre .05
225 Darrell Whitmore .05
226 Randy Milligan .05
227 Wayne Kirby .05
228 Darryl Kile .05
229 Bob Zupcic .05
230 Jay Bell .05
231 Dustin Hermanson .05
232 Harold Baines .05
233 Alan Benes .05
234 Felix Fermin .05
235 Ellis Burks .05
236 Jeff Brantley .05
237 *Brian Hunter, Jose Malave, Shane Pullen, Karim Garcia* OF Prospects .40
238 Matt Nokes .05
239 Ben Rivera .05
240 Joe Carter .05
241 Jeff Granger .05
242 Terry Pendleton .05
243 Melvin Nieves .05
244 Frank Rodriguez .05
245 Darryl Hamilton .05
246 Brooks Kieschnick .05
247 Todd Hollandsworth .05
248 Joe Rosselli .05
249 Bill Gullickson .05
250 Chuck Knoblauch .05
251 Kurt Miller .05
252 Bobby Jones .05
253 Lance Blankenship .05
254 Matt Whiteside .05
255 Darrin Fletcher .05
256 Eric Plunk .05
257 Shane Reynolds .05
258 Norberto Martin .05
259 Mike Thurman .05
260 Andy Van Slyke .05
261 Dwight Smith .05
262 Allen Watson .05
263 Dan Wilson .05
264 Brent Mayne .05
265 Bip Roberts .05
266 Sterling Hitchcock .05
267 Alex Gonzalez .05
268 Greg Harris .05
269 Ricky Jordan .05
270 Johnny Ruffin .05
271 Mike Stanton .05
272 Rich Rowland .05
273 Steve Trachsel .05
274 Pedro Munoz .05
275 Ramon Martinez .05
276 Dave Henderson .05
277 Chris Gomez .05
278 Joe Grahe .05
279 Rusty Greer .05
280 John Franco .05
281 Mike Bordick .05
282 Jeff D'Amico .05
283 Dave Magadan .05
284 Tony Pena .05
285 Greg Swindell .05
286 Doug Million .05
287 Gabe White .05
288 Trey Beamon .05
289 Arthur Rhodes .05
290 Juan Guzman .05
291 Jose Oquendo .05
292 Willie Blair .05
293 Eddie Taubensee .05
294 Steve Howe .05
295 Greg Maddux 1.00
296 Mike MacFarlane .05
297 Curt Schilling .25
298 Phil Clark .05
299 Woody Williams .05
300 Jose Canseco .40
301 Aaron Sele .05
302 Carl Willis .05
303 Steve Buechele .05
304 Dave Burba .05
305 Orel Hershiser .05
306 Damion Easley .05
307 Mike Henneman .05
308 Josias Manzanillo .05
309 Kevin Seitzer .05
310 Ruben Sierra .05
311 Bryan Harvey .05
312 Jim Thome .45

313 *Ramon Castro* .05
314 Lance Johnson .05
315 Marquis Grissom .05
316 *Terrell Wade, Juan Acevedo, Matt Arrandale, Eddie Priest* SP Prospects .05
317 Paul Wagner .05
318 Jamie Moyer .05
319 Todd Zeile .05
320 Chris Bosio .05
321 Steve Reed .05
322 Erik Hanson .05
323 Luis Polonia .05
324 Ryan Klesko .05
325 Kevin Appier .05
326 Jim Eisenreich .05
327 Randy Knorr .05
328 Craig Shipley .05
329 Tim Naehring .05
330 Randy Myers .05
331 Alex Cole .05
332 Jim Gott .05
333 Mike Jackson .05
334 John Flaherty .05
335 Chili Davis .05
336 Benji Gil .05
337a Jason Jacome (No Diamond Vision logo on back photo) .25
337b Jason Jacome (Diamond Vision logo on back photo) .05
338 Stan Javier .05
339 Mike Fetters .05
340 Rick Renteria .05
341 Kevin Witt .05
342 Scott Servais .05
343 Craig Grebeck .05
344 Kirk Rueter .05
345 Don Slaught .05
346 *Armando Benitez* (Star Track) .15
347 Ozzie Smith 1.00
348 Mike Blowers .05
349 Armando Reynoso .05
350 Barry Larkin .05
351 Mike Williams .05
352 Scott Kamieniecki .05
353 Gary Gaetti .05
354 Todd Stottlemyre .05
355 Fred McGriff .05
356 Tim Mauser .05
357 Chris Gwynn .05
358 Frank Castillo .05
359 Jeff Reboulet .05
360 Roger Clemens 1.00
361 Mark Carreon .05
362 Chad Kreuter .05
363 Mark Farris .05
364 Bob Welch .05
365 Dean Palmer .05
366 Jeromy Burnitz .05
367 B.J. Surhoff .05
368 Mike Butcher .05
369 Brad Clontz, Steve Phoenix, Scott Gentile, Bucky Buckles RP Prospects .05
370 Eddie Murray .75
371 Orlando Miller .05
372 Ron Karkovice .05
373 Richie Lewis .05
374 Lenny Webster .05
375 Jeff Tackett .05
376 Tom Urbani .05
377 Tino Martinez .05
378 Mark Dewey .05
379 Charlie O'Brien .05
380 Terry Mulholland .05
381 Thomas Howard .05
382 Chris Haney .05
383 Billy Hatcher .05
384 Jeff Bagwell, Frank Thomas .45
385 Bret Boone, Carlos Baerga .05
386 Matt Williams, Wade Boggs .30
387 Wil Cordero, Cal Ripken Jr. 1.00
388 Barry Bonds, Ken Griffey Jr. 1.00
389 Tony Gwynn, Albert Belle .50
390 Dante Bichette, Kirby Puckett .50
391 Mike Piazza, Mike Stanley .75
392 Greg Maddux, David Cone .50
393 Danny Jackson, Jimmy Key .05
394 John Franco, Lee Smith .05
395 Checklist 1-198 .05
396 Checklist 199-396 .05
397 Ken Griffey Jr. 1.25
398 *Rick Heiserman* .05
399 Don Mattingly 1.00
400 Henry Rodriguez .05
401 Lenny Harris .05
402 Ryan Thompson .05
403 Darren Oliver .05
404 Omar Vizquel .05
405 Jeff Bagwell .75
406 *Doug Webb* .05
407 Todd Van Poppel .05
408 Leo Gomez .05
409 Mark Whiten .05
410 Pedro Martinez .05
411 Reggie Sanders .05
412 Kevin Foster .05
413 Danny Tartabull .05
414 Jeff Blauser .05
415 Mike Magnante .05
416 Tom Candiotti .05
417 Rod Beck .05
418 Jody Reed .05
419 Vince Coleman .05
420 Danny Jackson .05
421 *Ryan Nye* .05
422 Larry Walker .05
423 Russ Johnson .05
424 Pat Borders .05
425 Lee Smith .05
426 Paul O'Neill .05
427 Devon White .05
428 Jim Bullinger .05
429 Greg Hansell, Brian Sackinsky, Carey Paige, Rob Welch SP Prospects .05
430 Steve Avery .05
431 Tony Gwynn 1.00
432 Pat Meares .05
433 Bill Swift .05
434 David Wells .05
435 John Briscoe .05
436 Roger Pavlik .05
437 *Jayson Peterson* .05
438 Roberto Alomar .15
439 Billy Brewer .05
440 Gary Sheffield .40
441 Lou Frazier .05
442 Terry Steinbach .05
443 *Jay Payton* .25
444 Jason Bere .05
445 Denny Neagle .05
446 Andres Galarraga .05
447 Hector Carrasco .05
448 Bill Risley .05
449 Andy Benes .05
450 Jim Leyritz .05
451 Jose Oliva .05
452 Greg Vaughn .05
453 Rich Monteleone .05
454 Tony Eusebio .05
455 Chuck Finley .05
456 Kevin Brown .05
457 Joe Boever .05
458 Bobby Munoz .05
459 Bret Saberhagen .05
460 Kurt Abbott .05
461 Bobby Witt .05
462 Cliff Floyd .05
463 Mark Clark .05
464 Andujar Cedeno .05
465 Marvin Freeman .05
466 Mike Piazza 1.25
467 Willie Greene .05
468 Pat Kelly .05
469 Carlos Delgado .40
470 Willie Banks .05
471 Matt Walbeck .05
472 Mark McGwire 1.50
473 McKay Christensen .05
474 Alan Trammell .05
475 Tom Gordon .05
476 Greg Colbrunn .05
477 Darren Daulton .05
478 Albie Lopez .05
479 Robin Ventura .05
480 Eddie Perez, Jason Kendall, Einar Diaz, Bret Hemphill C Prospects .20
481 Bryan Eversgerd .05
482 Dave Fleming .05
483 Scott Livingstone .05
484 Pete Schourek .05
485 Bernie Williams .05
486 Mark Lemke .05
487 Eric Karros .05
488 Scott Ruffcorn .05
489 Billy Ashley .05
490 Rico Brogna .05
491 John Burkett .05
492 *Cade Gaspar* .05
493 Jorge Fabregas .05
494 Greg Gagne .05
495 Doug Jones .05
496 Troy O'Leary .05
497 Pat Rapp .05
498 Butch Henry .05
499 John Olerud .05
500 John Hudek .05
501 Jeff King .05
502 Bobby Bonilla .05
503 Albert Belle .05
504 Rick Wilkins .05
505 John Jaha .05
506 Nigel Wilson .05
507 Sid Fernandez .05
508 Deion Sanders .05
509 Gil Heredia .05
510 *Scott Elarton* .10
511 Melido Perez .05
512 Greg McMichael .05
513 Rusty Meacham .05
514 Shawn Green .35
515 Carlos Garcia .05
516 Dave Stevens .05
517 Eric Young .05
518 Omar Daal .05
519 Kirk Gibson .05
520 Spike Owen .05
521 *Jacob Cruz* .05
522 Sandy Alomar .05
523 Steve Bedrosian .05
524 Ricky Gutierrez .05
525 Dave Veres .05
526 Gregg Jefferies .05
527 Jose Valentin .05
528 Robb Nen .05
529 Jose Rijo .05
530 Sean Berry .05
531 Mike Gallego .05
532 Roberto Kelly .05
533 Kevin Stocker .05
534 Kirby Puckett 1.00
535 Chipper Jones 1.00
536 Russ Davis .05
537 Jon Lieber .05
538 *Trey Moore* .05
539 Joe Girardi .05
540 Quilvio Veras, Arquimedez Pozo, Miguel Cairo, Jason Camilli 2B Prospects .05
541 Tony Phillips .05
542 Brian Anderson .05
543 Ivan Rodriguez .65
544 Jeff Cirillo .05
545 Joey Cora .05
546 Chris Hoiles .05
547 Bernard Gilkey .05
548 Mike Lansing .05
549 Jimmy Key .05
550 Mark Wohlers .05
551 *Chris Clemons* .05
552 Vinny Castilla .05
553 Mark Guthrie .05
554 Mike Lieberthal .05
555 *Tommy Davis* .05
556 Robby Thompson .05
557 Danny Bautista .05
558 Will Clark .05
559 Rickey Henderson .75
560 Todd Jones .05
561 Jack McDowell .05
562 Carlos Rodriguez .05
563 Mark Eichhorn .05
564 Jeff Nelson .05
565 Eric Anthony .05
566 Randy Velarde .05
567 Javy Lopez .05
568 Kevin Mitchell .05
569 Steve Karsay .05
570 *Brian Meadows* .10
571 Rey Ordonez, Mike Metcalfe, Ray Holbert, Kevin Orie SS Propects .40
572 John Kruk .05
573 Scott Leius .05
574 John Patterson .05
575 Kevin Brown .05
576 Mike Moore .05
577 Manny Ramirez .75
578 Jose Lind .05
579 Derrick May .05
580 Cal Eldred .05
581 *David Bell, Joel Chelmis, Lino Diaz, Aaron Boone* 3B Prospects .15
582 J.T. Snow .05
583 Luis Sojo .05
584 Moises Alou .05
585 Dave Clark .05
586 Dave Hollins .05
587 Nomar Garciaparra 2.00
588 Cal Ripken Jr. 2.00
589 Pedro Astacio .05
590 J.R. Phillips .05
591 Jeff Frye .05
592 Bo Jackson .10
593 Steve Ontiveros .05
594 David Nied .05
595 Brad Ausmus .05
596 Carlos Baerga .05
597 James Mouton .05
598 Ozzie Guillen .05
599 *Ozzie Timmons, Curtis Goodwin, Johnny Damon, Jeff Abbott* OF Prospects .25
600 Yorkis Perez .05
601 Rich Rodriguez .05
602 Mark McLemore .05
603 Jeff Fassero .05
604 John Roper .05
605 *Mark Johnson* .10
606 Wes Chamberlain .05
607 Felix Jose .05
608 Tony Longmire .05
609 Duane Ward .05
610 Brett Butler .05
611 William Van Landingham .05
612 Mickey Tettleton .05
613 Brady Anderson .05
614 Reggie Jefferson .05
615 Mike Kingery .05
616 Derek Bell .05
617 Scott Erickson .05
618 Bob Wickman .05
619 Phil Leftwich .05
620 Dave Justice .05
621 Paul Wilson .05
622 Pedro Martinez .75
623 Terry Mathews .05
624 Brian McRae .05
625 Bruce Ruffin .05
626 Steve Finley .05
627 Ron Gant .05
628 Rafael Bournigal .05
629 Darryl Strawberry .05
630 Luis Alicea .05
631 Mark Smith, Scott Klingenbeck .05
632 Cory Bailey, Scott Hatteberg .05
633 Todd Greene, Troy Percival .05
634 Rod Bolton, Olmedo Saenz .05
635 Herb Perry, Steve Kline .05
636 Sean Bergman, Shannon Penn .05
637 Joe Vitiello, Joe Randa .05
638 Jose Mercedes, Duane Singleton .05
639 Marty Cordova, Marc Barcelo .10
640 Ruben Rivera, Andy Pettitte .10
641 Willie Adams, Scott Spiezio .05
642 Eddie Diaz, Desi Relaford .05
643 Jon Shave, Terrell Lowery .05
644 Paul Spoljaric, Angel Martinez .05
645 Damon Hollins, Tony Graffanino .05
646 Darron Cox, Doug Glanville .05
647 Tim Belk, Pat Watkins .05
648 Rod Pedraza, Phil Schneider .05
649 Marc Valdes, Vic Darensbourg .05
650 Rick Huisman, Roberto Petagine .05
651 Ron Coomer, Roger Cedeno .05
652 Carlos Perez, Shane Andrews .10
653 Jason Isringhausen, Chris Roberts .05
654 Kevin Jordan, Wayne Gomes .05
655 Esteban Loaiza, Steve Pegues .05
656 John Frascatore, Terry Bradshaw .05

657 Bryce Florie, Andres Berumen .05
658 Keith Williams, Dan Carlson .05
659 Checklist .05
660 Checklist .05

League Leaders

NM/M
Complete Set (50): 20.00
Common Player: .15
1 Albert Belle .15
2 Kevin Mitchell .15
3 Wade Boggs 1.50
4 Tony Gwynn 1.50
5 Moises Alou .15
6 Andres Galarraga .15
7 Matt Williams .15
8 Barry Bonds 4.00
9 Frank Thomas .75
10 Jose Canseco .50
11 Jeff Bagwell .75
12 Kirby Puckett 1.50
13 Julio Franco .15
14 Albert Belle .15
15 Fred McGriff .15
16 Kenny Lofton .15
17 Otis Nixon .15
18 Brady Anderson .15
19 Deion Sanders .15
20 Chuck Carr .15
21 Pat Hentgen .15
22 Andy Benes .15
23 Roger Clemens 1.75
24 Greg Maddux 1.50
25 Pedro Martinez .75
26 Paul O'Neill .15
27 Jeff Bagwell .75
28 Frank Thomas .75
29 Hal Morris .15
30 Kenny Lofton .15
31 Ken Griffey Jr. 2.00
32 Jeff Bagwell .75
33 Albert Belle .15
34 Fred McGriff .15
35 Cecil Fielder .15
36 Matt Williams .15
37 Joe Carter .15
38 Dante Bichette .15
39 Frank Thomas .75
40 Mike Piazza 2.00
41 Craig Biggio .15
42 Vince Coleman .15
43 Marquis Grissom .15
44 Chuck Knoblauch .15
45 Darren Lewis .15
46 Randy Johnson .75
47 Jose Rijo .15
48 Chuck Finley .15
49 Bret Saberhagen .15
50 Kevin Appier .15

Cyberstats

NM/M
Complete Set (396): 25.00
Common Player: .10
1 Frank Thomas .75
2 Mickey Morandini .10
3 Todd Worrell .10
4 David Cone .10
5 Trevor Hoffman .10
6 Shane Mack .10
7 Delino DeShields .10
8 Matt Williams .10
9 Sammy Sosa 1.00
10 Gary DiSarcina .10
11 Kenny Rogers .10
12 Jose Vizcaino .10
13 Lou Whitaker .10
14 Ron Darling .10
15 Dave Nilsson .10
16 Dennis Martinez .10
17 Orlando Merced .10
18 John Wetteland .10
19 Mike Devereaux .10
20 Rene Arocha .10
21 Jay Buhner .10
22 Hal Morris .10
23 Paul Molitor .75
24 Dave West .10
25 Scott Sanders .10
26 Eddie Zambrano .10
27 Ricky Bones .10
28 John Valentin .10
29 Kevin Tapani .10
30 Tim Wallach .10
31 Darren Lewis .10
32 Travis Fryman .10
33 Bret Barberie .10
34 Dennis Eckersley .65
35 Ken Hill .10
36 Pete Harnisch .10
37 Mike Mussina .50
38 Dave Winfield .75
39 Joey Hamilton .10
40 Edgar Martinez .10
41 John Smiley .10
42 Jim Abbott .10
43 Mike Kelly .10
44 Brian Jordan .10
45 Ken Ryan .10
46 Matt Mieske .10
47 Rick Aguilera .10
48 Ismael Valdes .10
49 Royce Clayton .10
50 Juan Gonzalez .35
51 Mel Rojas .10
52 Doug Drabek .10
53 Charles Nagy .10
54 Tim Raines .10
55 Midre Cummings .10
56 Rafael Palmeiro .65
57 Charlie Hayes .10
58 Ray Lankford .10
59 Tim Davis .10
60 Andy Ashby .10
61 Mark Grace .10
62 Mark Langston .10
63 Chuck Carr .10
64 Barry Bonds 2.00
65 David Segui .10
66 Mariano Duncan .10
67 Kenny Lofton .10
68 Ken Caminiti .10
69 Darrin Jackson .10
70 Wil Cordero .10
71 Walt Weiss .10
72 Tom Pagnozzi .10
73 Bret Boone .10
74 Wally Joyner .10
75 Luis Lopez .10
76 Len Dykstra .10
77 Pedro Munoz .10
78 Kevin Gross .10
79 Eduardo Perez .10
80 Brent Gates .10
81 Jeff Conine .10
82 Paul Sorrento .10
83 Julio Franco .10
84 Chris Sabo .10
85 Dante Bichette .10
86 Mike Stanley .10
87 Bob Hamelin .10
88 Tommy Greene .10
89 Jeff Brantley .10
90 Ed Sprague .10
91 Otis Nixon .10
92 Chad Curtis .10
93 Chuck McElroy .10
94 Troy Neel .10
95 Benito Santiago .10
96 Jose Mesa .10
97 Luis Gonzalez .10
98 Alex Fernandez .10
99 Ben McDonald .10
100 Wade Boggs 1.00
101 Tom Glavine .35
102 Phil Plantier .10
103 Raul Mondesi .10
104 Jim Edmonds .10
105 Jeff Kent .10
106 Wilson Alvarez .10
107 Geronimo Berroa .10
108 Craig Biggio .10
109 Roberto Hernandez .10
110 Bobby Ayala .10
111 Bob Tewksbury .10
112 Rondell White .10
113 Steve Cooke .10
114 Tim Salmon .10
115 Kent Mercker .10
116 Randy Johnson .75
117 Mo Vaughn .10
118 Eddie Williams .10
119 Jeff Montgomery .10
120 Kirt Manwaring .10
121 Pat Hentgen .10
122 Shawon Dunston .10
123 Tim Belcher .10
124 Cecil Fielder .10
125 Todd Hundley .10
126 Mark Acre .10
127 Darrell Whitmore .10
128 Darryl Kile .10
129 Jay Bell .10
130 Harold Baines .10
131 Felix Fermin .10
132 Ellis Burks .10
133 Joe Carter .10
134 Terry Pendleton .10
135 Junior Felix .10
136 Bill Gullickson .10
137 Melvin Nieves .10
138 Chuck Knoblauch .10
139 Bobby Jones .10
140 Darrin Fletcher .10
141 Andy Van Slyke .10
142 Allen Watson .10
143 Dan Wilson .10
144 Bip Roberts .10
145 Sterling Hitchcock .10
146 Johnny Ruffin .10
147 Steve Trachsel .10
148 Ramon Martinez .10
149 Dave Henderson .10
150 Chris Gomez .10
151 Rusty Greer .10
152 John Franco .10
153 Mike Bordick .10
154 Dave Magadan .10
155 Greg Swindell .10
156 Arthur Rhodes .10
157 Juan Guzman .10
158 Greg Maddux 1.00
159 Mike Macfarlane .10
160 Curt Schilling .35
161 Jose Canseco .40
162 Aaron Sele .10
163 Steve Buechele .10
164 Orel Hershiser .10
165 Mike Henneman .10
166 Kevin Seitzer .10
167 Ruben Sierra .10
168 Alex Cole .10
169 Jim Thome .65
170 Lance Johnson .10
171 Marquis Grissom .10
172 Jamie Moyer .10
173 Todd Zeile .10
174 Chris Bosio .10
175 Steve Howe .10
176 Luis Polonia .10
177 Ryan Klesko .10
178 Kevin Appier .10
179 Tim Naehring .10
180 Randy Myers .10
181 Mike Jackson .10
182 Chili Davis .10
183 Jason Jacome .10
184 Stan Javier .10
185 Scott Servais .10
186 Kirk Rueter .10
187 Don Slaught .10
188 Ozzie Smith 1.00
189 Barry Larkin .10
190 Gary Gaetti .10
191 Fred McGriff .10
192 Roger Clemens 1.00
193 Dean Palmer .10
194 Jeromy Burnitz .10
195 Scott Kamieniecki .10
196 Eddie Murray .75
197 Ron Karkovice .10
198 Tino Martinez .10
199 Ken Griffey Jr. 1.25
200 Don Mattingly 1.00
201 Henry Rodriguez .10
202 Lenny Harris .10
203 Ryan Thompson .10
204 Darren Oliver .10
205 Omar Vizquel .10
206 Jeff Bagwell .75
207 Todd Van Poppel .10
208 Leo Gomez .10
209 Mark Whiten .10
210 Pedro Martinez .10
211 Reggie Sanders .10
212 Kevin Foster .10
213 Danny Tartabull .10
214 Jeff Blauser .10
215 Mike Magnante .10
216 Tom Candiotti .10
217 Rod Beck .10
218 Jody Reed .10
219 Vince Coleman .10
220 Danny Jackson .10
221 Larry Walker .10
222 Pat Borders .10
223 Lee Smith .10
224 Paul O'Neill .10
225 Devon White .10
226 Jim Bullinger .10
227 Steve Avery .10
228 Tony Gwynn 1.00
229 Pat Meares .10
230 Bill Swift .10
231 David Wells .10
232 John Briscoe .10
233 Roger Pavlik .10
234 Roberto Alomar .30
235 Billy Brewer .10
236 Gary Sheffield .40
237 Lou Frazier .10
238 Terry Steinbach .10
239 Omar Daal .10
240 Jason Bere .10
241 Denny Neagle .10
242 Danny Bautista .10
243 Hector Carrasco .10
244 Bill Risley .10
245 Andy Benes .10
246 Jim Leyritz .10
247 Jose Oliva .10
248 Greg Vaughn .10
249 Rich Monteleone .10
250 Tony Eusebio .10
251 Chuck Finley .10
252 Joe Boever .10
253 Bobby Munoz .10
254 Bret Saberhagen .10
255 Kurt Abbott .10
256 Bobby Witt .10
257 Cliff Floyd .10
258 Mark Clark .10
259 Andujar Cedeno .10
260 Marvin Freeman .10
261 Mike Piazza 1.25
262 Pat Kelly .10
263 Carlos Delgado .45
264 Willie Banks .10
265 Matt Walbeck .10
266 Mark McGwire 1.50
267 Alan Trammell .10
268 Tom Gordon .10
269 Greg Colbrunn .10
270 Darren Daulton .10
271 Albie Lopez .10
272 Robin Ventura .10
273 Bryan Eversgerd .10
274 Dave Fleming .10
275 Scott Livingstone .10
276 Pete Schourek .10
277 Bernie Williams .10
278 Mark Lemke .10
279 Eric Karros .10
280 Billy Ashley .10
281 Rico Brogna .10
282 John Burkett .10
283 Jorge Fabregas .10
284 Greg Gagne .10
285 Doug Jones .10
286 Troy O'Leary .10
287 Pat Rapp .10
288 Butch Henry .10
289 John Olerud .10
290 John Hudek .10
291 Jeff King .10
292 Bobby Bonilla .10
293 Albert Belle .10
294 Rick Wilkins .10
295 John Jaha .10
296 Sid Fernandez .10
297 Deion Sanders .10
298 Gil Heredia .10
299 Melido Perez .10
300 Greg McMichael .10
301 Rusty Meacham .10
302 Shawn Green .35
303 Carlos Garcia .10
304 Dave Stevens .10
305 Eric Young .10
306 Kirk Gibson .10
307 Spike Owen .10
308 Sandy Alomar .10
309 Ricky Gutierrez .10
310 Dave Veres .10

311	Gregg Jefferies	.10
312	Jose Valentin	.10
313	Robb Nen	.10
314	Jose Rijo	.10
315	Sean Berry	.10
316	Mike Gallego	.10
317	Roberto Kelly	.10
318	Kevin Stocker	.10
319	Kirby Puckett	1.00
320	Jon Lieber	.10
321	Joe Girardi	.10
322	Tony Phillips	.10
323	Brian Anderson	.10
324	Ivan Rodriguez	.65
325	Jeff Cirillo	.10
326	Joey Cora	.10
327	Chris Hoiles	.10
328	Bernard Gilkey	.10
329	Mike Lansing	.10
330	Jimmy Key	.10
331	Vinny Castilla	.10
332	Mark Guthrie	.10
333	Mike Lieberthal	.10
334	Will Clark	.10
335	Rickey Henderson	.75
336	Todd Jones	.10
337	Jack McDowell	.10
338	Carlos Rodriguez	.10
339	Mark Eichhorn	.10
340	Jeff Nelson	.10
341	Eric Anthony	.10
342	Randy Velarde	.10
343	Javier Lopez	.10
344	Kevin Mitchell	.10
345	Steve Bedrosian	.10
346	John Kruk	.10
347	Scott Leius	.10
348	John Patterson	.10
349	Kevin Brown	.10
350	Mike Moore	.10
351	Manny Ramirez	.75
352	Jose Lind	.10
353	Derrick May	.10
354	Cal Eldred	.10
355	J.T. Snow	.10
356	Luis Sojo	.10
357	Moises Alou	.10
358	Dave Clark	.10
359	Dave Hollins	.10
360	Cal Ripken Jr.	2.00
361	Pedro Astacio	.10
362	Tony Longmire	.10
363	Jeff Frye	.10
364	Bo Jackson	.20
365	Steve Ontiveros	.10
366	David Nied	.10
367	Brad Ausmus	.10
368	Carlos Baerga	.10
369	James Mouton	.10
370	Ozzie Guillen	.10
371	Yorkis Perez	.10
372	Rich Rodriguez	.10
373	Mark McLemore	.10
374	Jeff Fassero	.10
375	John Roper	.10
376	Wes Chamberlain	.10
377	Felix Jose	.10
378	Brett Butler	.10
379	William Van Landingham	.10
380	Mickey Tettleton	.10
381	Brady Anderson	.10
382	Reggie Jefferson	.10
383	Mike Kingery	.10
384	Derek Bell	.10
385	Scott Erickson	.10
386	Bob Wickman	.10
387	Phil Leftwich	.10
388	Dave Justice	.10
389	Pedro Martinez	.75
390	Terry Mathews	.10
391	Brian McRae	.10
392	Bruce Ruffin	.10
393	Steve Finley	.10
394	Rafael Bournigal	.10
395	Darryl Strawberry	.10
396	Luis Alicea	.10

1995 TOPPS TOTAL BASES FINEST

		NM/M
Complete Set (15):		12.00
Common Player:		.50
1	Jeff Bagwell	1.25
2	Albert Belle	.50
3	Ken Griffey Jr.	2.00
4	Frank Thomas	1.25
5	Matt Williams	.50
6	Dante Bichette	.50
7	Barry Bonds	2.50

8	Moises Alou	.50
9	Andres Galarraga	.50
10	Kenny Lofton	.50
11	Rafael Palmeiro	1.00
12	Tony Gwynn	1.50
13	Kirby Puckett	1.50
14	Jose Canseco	.75
15	Jeff Conine	.50

Traded and Rookies

		NM/M
Complete Set (165):		40.00
Common Player:		.05
Pack (11):		3.00
Wax Box (36):		90.00
1	Frank Thomas	.50
2	Ken Griffey Jr.	.65
3	Barry Bonds	1.00
4	Albert Belle	.05
5	Cal Ripken Jr.	1.00
6	Mike Piazza	.75
7	Tony Gwynn	.60
8	Jeff Bagwell	.45
9	Mo Vaughn	.05
10	Matt Williams	.05
11	Ray Durham	.05
12	*Juan LeBron (photo Carlos Beltran)*	5.00
13	Shawn Green	.50
14	Kevin Gross	.05
15	Jon Nunnally	.05
16	*Brian Maxcy*	.05
17	Mark Kiefer	.05
18	*Carlos Beltran* (photo actually Juan Beltran)	20.00
19	*Mike Mimbs*	.05
20	Larry Walker	.05
21	Chad Curtis	.05
22	Jeff Barry	.05
23	Joe Oliver	.05
24	*Tomas Perez*	.05
25	*Michael Barrett*	.40
26	Brian McRae	.05
27	Derek Bell	.05
28	Ray Durham	.05
29	Todd Williams	.05
30	*Ryan Jaroncyk*	.05
31	Todd Steverson	.05
32	Mike Devereaux	.05
33	Rheal Cormier	.05
34	Benny Santiago	.05
35	*Bobby Higginson*	.50
36	Jack McDowell	.05
37	Mike Macfarlane	.05
38	*Tony McKnight*	.05
39	Brian Hunter	.05
40	*Hideo Nomo*	2.00
41	Brett Butler	.05
42	Donovan Osborne	.05
43	Scott Karl	.05
44	Tony Phillips	.05
45	Marty Cordova	.20
46	Dave Mlicki	.05
47	*Bronson Arroyo*	4.00
48	John Burkett	.05
49	*J.D. Smart*	.05
50	Mickey Tettleton	.05
51	Todd Stottlemyre	.05
52	Mike Perez	.05
53	Terry Mulholland	.05
54	Edgardo Alfonzo	.05
55	Zane Smith	.05
56	Jacob Brumfield	.05
57	Andujar Cedeno	.05
58	Jose Parra	.05
59	Manny Alexander	.05
60	Tony Tarasco	.05
61	Orel Hershiser	.05
62	Tim Scott	.05
63	*Felix Rodriguez*	.05
64	Ken Hill	.05
65	Marquis Grissom	.05
66	Lee Smith	.05
67	Jason Bates	.05
68	Felipe Lira	.05
69	*Alex Hernandez*	.10
70	Tony Fernandez	.05
71	Scott Radinsky	.05
72	Jose Canseco	.50
73	*Mark Grudzielanek*	.50
74	*Ben Davis*	.25
75	Jim Abbott	.05
76	Roger Bailey	.05
77	Gregg Jefferies	.05
78	Erik Hanson	.05
79	*Brad Radke*	1.50
80	Jaime Navarro	.05
81	John Wetteland	.05
82	*Chad Fonville*	.10
83	John Mabry	.05
84	Glenallen Hill	.05
85	Ken Caminiti	.05
86	Tom Goodwin	.05
87	Darren Bragg	.05
88	*Pat Ahearne, Gary Rath, Larry Wimberly, Robbie Bell* 1995 Prospects (Pitchers)	.10
89	Jeff Russell	.05
90	Dave Gallagher	.05
91	Steve Finley	.05
92	Vaughn Eshelman	.05
93	Kevin Jarvis	.05
94	Mark Gubicza	.05
95	Tim Wakefield	.05
96	Bob Tewksbury	.05
97	*Sid Roberson*	.05
98	Tom Henke	.05
99	Michael Tucker	.05
100	Jason Bates	.05
101	Otis Nixon	.05
102	Mark Whiten	.05
103	Dilson Torres	.05
104	*Melvin Bunch*	.05
105	Terry Pendleton	.05
106	*Corey Jenkins*	.05
107	*Glenn Dishman, Rob Grable* On Deck	.05
108	*Reggie Taylor*	.05
109	Curtis Goodwin	.05
110	David Cone	.05
111	Antonio Osuna	.05
112	Paul Shuey	.05
113	Doug Jones	.05
114	Mark McLemore	.05
115	Kevin Ritz	.05
116	John Kruk	.05
117	Trevor Wilson	.05
118	Jerald Clark	.05
119	Julian Tavarez	.05
120	Tim Pugh	.05
121	Todd Zeile	.05
122	*Mark Sweeney, George Arias, Richie Sexson, Brian Schneider* 1995 Prospects (Fielders)	4.00
123	Bobby Witt	.05
124	Hideo Nomo	1.00
125	Joey Cora	.05
126	*Jim Scharrer*	.05
127	Paul Quantrill	.05
128	Chipper Jones	.75
129	*Kenny James*	.05
130	Lyle Mouton, Mariano Rivera On Deck	.15
131	Tyler Green	.05
132	Brad Clontz	.05
133	Jon Nunnally	.05
134	Dave Magadan	.05
135	Al Leiter	.05
136	Bret Barberie	.05
137	Bill Swift	.05
138	Scott Cooper	.05
139	Roberto Kelly	.05
140	Charlie Hayes	.05
141	Pete Harnisch	.05
142	Rich Amaral	.05
143	Rudy Seanez	.05
144	Pat Listach	.05
145	Quilvio Veras	.05
146	*Jose Olmeda*	.05
147	Roberto Petagine	.05
148	Kevin Brown	.05
149	Phil Plantier	.05
150	*Carlos Perez*	.05
151	Pat Borders	.05
152	Tyler Green	.05
153	Stan Belinda	.05
154	Dave Stewart	.05
155	Andre Dawson	.25
156	Frank Thomas, Fred McGriff	.30
157	Carlos Baerga, Craig Biggio	.05
158	Wade Boggs, Matt Williams	.35
159	Cal Ripken Jr., Ozzie Smith	.75
160	Ken Griffey Jr., Tony Gwynn	.40
161	Albert Belle, Barry Bonds	.75
162	Kirby Puckett, Len Dykstra	.35
163	Ivan Rodriguez, Mike Piazza	.40
164	Randy Johnson, Hideo Nomo	.25
165	Checklist	.05

Traded and Rookies Power Boosters

		NM/M
Complete Set (10):		20.00
Common Player:		.75
1	Frank Thomas	1.50
2	Ken Griffey Jr.	3.00
3	Barry Bonds	5.00
4	Albert Belle	.75
5	Cal Ripken Jr.	5.00
6	Mike Piazza	3.00
7	Tony Gwynn	2.50
8	Jeff Bagwell	1.50
9	Mo Vaughn	.75
10	Matt Williams	.75

1995 TOPPS EMBOSSED

		NM/M
Complete Set (140):		7.50
Common Player:		.10
Wax Pack (6+1):		1.50
Wax Box (24):		22.50
1	Kenny Lofton	.10
2	Gary Sheffield	.35
3	Hal Morris	.10
4	Cliff Floyd	.10
5	Pat Hentgen	.10
6	Tony Gwynn	.75
7	Jose Valentin	.10
8	Jason Bere	.10
9	Jeff Kent	.10
10	John Valentin	.10
11	Brian Anderson	.10
12	Deion Sanders	.10
13	Ryan Thompson	.10
14	Ruben Sierra	.10
15	Jay Bell	.10
16	Chuck Carr	.10
17	Brent Gates	.10
18	Bret Boone	.10
19	Paul Molitor	.60
20	Chili Davis	.10
21	Ryan Klesko	.10
22	Will Clark	.10
23	Greg Vaughn	.10
24	Moises Alou	.10
25	Ray Lankford	.10
26	Jose Rijo	.10
27	Bobby Jones	.10
28	Rick Wilkins	.10
29	Cal Eldred	.10
30	Juan Gonzalez	.30
31	Royce Clayton	.10
32	Bryan Harvey	.10
33	Dave Nilsson	.10
34	Chris Hoiles	.10
35	David Nied	.10
36	Javy Lopez	.10
37	Tim Wallach	.10
38	Bobby Bonilla	.10
39	Danny Tartabull	.10
40	Andy Benes	.10
41	Dean Palmer	.10
42	Chris Gomez	.10
43	Kevin Appier	.10
44	Brady Anderson	.10
45	Alex Fernandez	.10
46	Roberto Kelly	.10
47	Dave Hollins	.10
48	Chuck Finley	.10
49	Wade Boggs	.75
50	Travis Fryman	.10
51	Ken Griffey Jr.	1.00
52	John Olerud	.10
53	Delino DeShields	.10
54	Ivan Rodriguez	.50
55	Tommy Greene	.10
56	Tom Pagnozzi	.10
57	Bip Roberts	.10
58	Luis Gonzalez	.10
59	Rey Sanchez	.10
60	Ken Ryan	.10
61	Darren Daulton	.10
62	Rick Aguilera	.10
63	Wally Joyner	.10
64	Mike Greenwell	.10
65	Jay Buhner	.10
66	Craig Biggio	.10
67	Charles Nagy	.10
68	Devon White	.10
69	Randy Johnson	.60
70	Shawon Dunston	.10
71	Kirby Puckett	.75
72	Paul O'Neill	.10
73	Tino Martinez	.10
74	Carlos Garcia	.10
75	Ozzie Smith	.75
76	Cecil Fielder	.10
77	Mike Stanley	.10
78	Lance Johnson	.10
79	Tony Phillips	.10
80	Bobby Munoz	.10
81	Kevin Tapani	.10
82	William Van Landingham	.10
83	Dante Bichette	.10
84	Tom Candiotti	.10
85	Wil Cordero	.10
86	Jeff Conine	.10
87	Joey Hamilton	.10
88	Mark Whiten	.10
89	Jeff Montgomery	.10
90	Andres Galarraga	.10
91	Roberto Alomar	.20
92	Orlando Merced	.10
93	Mike Mussina	.35
94	Pedro Martinez	.60
95	Carlos Baerga	.10
96	Steve Trachsel	.10
97	Lou Whitaker	.10
98	David Cone	.10
99	Chuck Knoblauch	.10
100	Frank Thomas	.60
101	Dave Justice	.10
102	Raul Mondesi	.10
103	Rickey Henderson	.60
104	Doug Drabek	.10
105	Sandy Alomar	.10
106	Roger Clemens	.85
107	Mark McGwire	1.20
108	Tim Salmon	.10
109	Greg Maddux	.75
110	Mike Piazza	1.00
111	Tom Glavine	.30
112	Walt Weiss	.10
113	Cal Ripken Jr.	1.50
114	Eddie Murray	.60
115	Don Mattingly	.85
116	Ozzie Guillen	.10
117	Bob Hamelin	.10
118	Jeff Bagwell	.60
119	Eric Karros	.10
120	Barry Bonds	1.50
121	Mickey Tettleton	.10
122	Mark Langston	.10
123	Robin Ventura	.10
124	Bret Saberhagen	.10
125	Albert Belle	.10
126	Rafael Palmeiro	.50
127	Fred McGriff	.10
128	Jimmy Key	.10
129	Barry Larkin	.10
130	Tim Raines	.10
131	Len Dykstra	.10
132	Todd Zeile	.10
133	Joe Carter	.10
134	Matt Williams	.10
135	Terry Steinbach	.10
136	Manny Ramirez	.60
137	John Wetteland	.10
138	Rod Beck	.10
139	Mo Vaughn	.10
140	Darren Lewis	.10

1995 TOPPS EMBOSSED GOLDEN IDOLS

	NM/M
Complete Set (140):	25.00
Common Player:	.25

(Star cards valued at 2X corresponding regular Embossed cards)

1996 TOPPS

		NM/M
Unopened Hobby Set (449):		40.00
Unopened Retail Set (450):		40.00
Unopened Cereal Box Set (444):		35.00
Complete Set (440):		25.00
Common Player:		.05
Wax Pack (12):		1.50
Wax Box (36):		35.00
Cello Pack (17):		2.50
Cello Box (24):		40.00
Vending Box (500):		12.50
1	Tony Gwynn	.50
2	Mike Piazza	.75
3	Greg Maddux	.50
4	Jeff Bagwell	.40
5	Larry Walker	.05
6	Barry Larkin	.05
7	Mickey Mantle	4.00
8	Tom Glavine	.05
9	Craig Biggio	.05
10	Barry Bonds	1.00
11	Heathcliff Slocumb	.05
12	Matt Williams	.05
13	Todd Helton	.75
14	Mark Redman	.05
15	Michael Barrett	.05
16	Ben Davis	.05
17	Juan LeBron	.05
18	Tony McKnight	.05
19	Ryan Jaroncyk	.05
20	Corey Jenkins	.05
21	Jim Scharrer	.05
22	*Mark Bellhorn*	.10
23	*Jarrod Washburn*	.50
24	*Geoff Jenkins*	1.00
25	*Sean Casey*	3.00
26	*Brett Tomko*	.10
27	Tony Fernandez	.05
28	Rich Becker	.05
29	Andujar Cedeno	.05
30	Paul Molitor	.75
31	Brent Gates	.05
32	Glenallen Hill	.05
33	Mike MacFarlane	.05
34	Manny Alexander	.05
35	Todd Zeile	.05
36	Joe Girardi	.05
37	Tony Tarasco	.05
38	Tim Belcher	.05
39	Tom Goodwin	.05
40	Orel Hershiser	.05
41	Tripp Cromer	.05
42	Sean Bergman	.05
43	Troy Percival	.05
44	Kevin Stocker	.05
45	Albert Belle	.05
46	Tony Eusebio	.05
47	Sid Roberson	.05
48	Todd Hollandsworth	.05
49	Mark Wohlers	.05
50	Kirby Puckett	1.00
51	Darren Holmes	.05
52	Ron Karkovice	.05
53	Al Martin	.05
54	Pat Rapp	.05
55	Mark Grace	.05
56	Greg Gagne	.05
57	Stan Javier	.05
58	Scott Sanders	.05
59	J.T. Snow	.05
60	David Justice	.05
61	Royce Clayton	.05
62	Kevin Foster	.05
63	Tim Naehring	.05
64	Orlando Miller	.05
65	Mike Mussina	.35
66	Jim Eisenreich	.05
67	Felix Fermin	.05
68	Bernie Williams	.05
69	Robb Nen	.05
70	Ron Gant	.05
71	Felipe Lira	.05
72	Jacob Brumfield	.05
73	John Mabry	.05
74	Mark Carreon	.05
75	Carlos Baerga	.05
76	Jim Dougherty	.05
77	Ryan Thompson	.05
78	Scott Leius	.05
79	Roger Pavlik	.05
80	Gary Sheffield	.45
81	Julian Tavarez	.05
82	Andy Ashby	.05
83	Mark Lemke	.05
84	Omar Vizquel	.05
85	Darren Daulton	.05
86	Mike Lansing	.05
87	Rusty Greer	.05
88	Dave Stevens	.05
89	Jose Offerman	.05
90	Tom Henke	.05
91	Troy O'Leary	.05
92	Michael Tucker	.05
93	Marvin Freeman	.05
94	Alex Diaz	.05
95	John Wetteland	.05
96	Cal Ripken Jr.	1.00
97	Mike Mimbs	.05
98	Bobby Higginson	.05
99	Edgardo Alfonzo	.05
100	Frank Thomas	.75
101	Steve Gibralter, Bob Abreu	.05
102	Brian Givens, T.J. Mathews	.05
103	Chris Pritchett, Trenidad Hubbard	.05
104	Eric Owens, Butch Huskey	.05
105	Doug Drabek	.05
106	Tomas Perez	.05
107	Mark Leiter	.05
108	Joe Oliver	.05
109	Tony Castillo	.05
110	Checklist	.05
111	Kevin Seitzer	.05
112	Pete Schourek	.05
113	Sean Berry	.05
114	Todd Stottlemyre	.05
115	Joe Carter	.05
116	Jeff King	.05
117	Dan Wilson	.05
118	Kurt Abbott	.05
119	Lyle Mouton	.05
120	Jose Rijo	.05
121	Curtis Goodwin	.05
122	*Jose Valentin*	.05
123	Ellis Burks	.05
124	David Cone	.05
125	Eddie Murray	.75
126	Brian Jordan	.05
127	Darrin Fletcher	.05
128	Curt Schilling	.25
129	Ozzie Guillen	.05
130	Kenny Rogers	.05
131	Tom Pagnozzi	.05
132	Garret Anderson	.05
133	Bobby Jones	.05
134	Chris Gomez	.05
135	Mike Stanley	.05
136	Hideo Nomo	.35
137	Jon Nunnally	.05
138	Tim Wakefield	.05
139	Steve Finley	.05
140	Ivan Rodriguez	.65
141	Quilvio Veras	.05
142	Mike Fetters	.05
143	Mike Greenwell	.05
144	Bill Pulsipher	.05
145	Mark McGwire	1.50
146	Frank Castillo	.05
147	Greg Vaughn	.05
148	Pat Hentgen	.05
149	Walt Weiss	.05
150	Randy Johnson	.75
151	David Segui	.05
152	Benji Gil	.05
153	Tom Candiotti	.05
154	Geronimo Berroa	.05
155	John Franco	.05
156	Jay Bell	.05
157	Mark Gubicza	.05
158	Hal Morris	.05
159	Wilson Alvarez	.05
160	Derek Bell	.05
161	Ricky Bottalico	.05
162	Bret Boone	.05
163	Brad Radke	.05
164	John Valentin	.05
165	Steve Avery	.05
166	Mark McLemore	.05
167	Danny Jackson	.05
168	Tino Martinez	.05
169	Shane Reynolds	.05
170	Terry Pendleton	.05
171	Jim Edmonds	.05
172	Esteban Loaiza	.05
173	Ray Durham	.05
174	Carlos Perez	.05
175	Raul Mondesi	.05
176	Steve Ontiveros	.05
177	Chipper Jones	1.00
178	Otis Nixon	.05
179	John Burkett	.05
180	Gregg Jefferies	.05
181	Denny Martinez	.05
182	Ken Caminiti	.05
183	Doug Jones	.05
184	Brian McRae	.05
185	Don Mattingly	1.00
186	Mel Rojas	.05
187	Marty Cordova	.05
188	Vinny Castilla	.05
189	John Smoltz	.05
190	Travis Fryman	.05
191	Chris Hoiles	.05
192	Chuck Finley	.05
193	Ryan Klesko	.05
194	Alex Fernandez	.05
195	Dante Bichette	.05
196	Eric Karros	.05
197	Roger Clemens	1.00
198	Randy Myers	.05
199	Tony Phillips	.05
200	Cal Ripken Jr.	2.00
201	Rod Beck	.05
202	Chad Curtis	.05
203	Jack McDowell	.05
204	Gary Gaetti	.05

#	Player	Price
205	Ken Griffey Jr.	1.25
206	Ramon Martinez	.05
207	Jeff Kent	.05
208	Brad Ausmus	.05
209	Devon White	.05
210	Jason Giambi	.45
211	Nomar Garciaparra	1.00
212	Billy Wagner	.05
213	Todd Greene	.05
214	Paul Wilson	.05
215	Johnny Damon	.25
216	Alan Benes	.05
217	Karim Garcia	.10
218	Dustin Hermanson	.05
219	Derek Jeter	2.00
220	Checklist	.05
221	Kirby Puckett	.50
222	Cal Ripken Jr.	1.00
223	Albert Belle	.05
224	Randy Johnson	.40
225	Wade Boggs	.50
226	Carlos Baerga	.05
227	Ivan Rodriguez	.30
228	Mike Mussina	.25
229	Frank Thomas	.40
230	Ken Griffey Jr.	.75
231	Jose Mesa	.05
232	*Matt Morris*	1.00
233	*Craig Wilson*	.50
234	*Alvie Shepherd*	.05
235	*Randy Winn*	.05
236	*David Yocum*	.05
237	*Jason Brester*	.05
238	*Shane Monahan*	.05
239	*Brian McNichol*	.05
240	Reggie Taylor	.05
241	Garrett Long	.05
242	*Jonathan Johnson*	.05
243	*Jeff Liefer*	.05
244	*Brian Powell*	.05
245	Brian Buchanan	.05
246	Mike Piazza	1.25
247	Edgar Martinez	.05
248	Chuck Knoblauch	.05
249	Andres Galarraga	.05
250	Tony Gwynn	1.00
251	Lee Smith	.05
252	Sammy Sosa	1.00
253	Jim Thome	.45
254	Frank Rodriguez	.05
255	Charlie Hayes	.05
256	Bernard Gilkey	.05
257	John Smiley	.05
258	Brady Anderson	.05
259	Rico Brogna	.05
260	Kirt Manwaring	.05
261	Len Dykstra	.05
262	Tom Glavine	.25
263	Vince Coleman	.05
264	John Olerud	.05
265	Orlando Merced	.05
266	Kent Mercker	.05
267	Terry Steinbach	.05
268	Brian Hunter	.05
269	Jeff Fassero	.05
270	Jay Buhner	.05
271	Jeff Brantley	.05
272	Tim Raines	.05
273	Jimmy Key	.05
274	Mo Vaughn	.05
275	Andre Dawson	.25
276	Jose Mesa	.05
277	Brett Butler	.05
278	Luis Gonzalez	.05
279	Steve Sparks	.05
280	Chili Davis	.05
281	Carl Everett	.05
282	Jeff Cirillo	.05
283	Thomas Howard	.05
284	Paul O'Neill	.05
285	Pat Meares	.05
286	Mickey Tettleton	.05
287	Rey Sanchez	.05
288	Bip Roberts	.05
289	Roberto Alomar	.15
290	Ruben Sierra	.05
291	John Flaherty	.05
292	Bret Saberhagen	.05
293	Barry Larkin	.05
294	Sandy Alomar	.05
295	Ed Sprague	.05
296	Gary DiSarcina	.05
297	Marquis Grissom	.05
298	John Frascatore	.05
299	Will Clark	.05
300	Barry Bonds	2.00
301	Ozzie Smith	1.00
302	Dave Nilsson	.05
303	Pedro Martinez	.75
304	Joey Cora	.05
305	Rick Aguilera	.05
306	Craig Biggio	.05
307	Jose Vizcaino	.05
308	Jeff Montgomery	.05
309	Moises Alou	.05
310	Robin Ventura	.05
311	David Wells	.05
312	Delino DeShields	.05
313	Trevor Hoffman	.05
314	Andy Benes	.05
315	Deion Sanders	.05
316	Jim Bullinger	.05
317	John Jaha	.05
318	Greg Maddux	1.00
319	Tim Salmon	.05
320	Ben McDonald	.05
321	*Sandy Martinez*	.05
322	Dan Miceli	.05
323	Wade Boggs	1.00
324	Ismael Valdes	.05
325	Juan Gonzalez	.35
326	Charles Nagy	.05
327	Ray Lankford	.05
328	Mark Portugal	.05
329	Bobby Bonilla	.05
330	Reggie Sanders	.05
331	Jamie Brewington	.05
332	Aaron Sele	.05
333	Pete Harnisch	.05
334	Cliff Floyd	.05
335	Cal Eldred	.05
336	Jason Bates	.05
337	Tony Clark	.05
338	Jose Herrera	.05
339	Alex Ochoa	.05
340	Mark Loretta	.05
341	*Donne Wall*	.05
342	Jason Kendall	.05
343	Shannon Stewart	.05
344	Brooks Kieschnick	.05
345	Chris Snopek	.05
346	Ruben Rivera	.05
347	Jeff Suppan	.05
348	Phil Nevin	.05
349	John Wasdin	.05
350	Jay Payton	.05
351	Tim Crabtree	.05
352	Rick Krivda	.05
353	Bob Wolcott	.05
354	Jimmy Haynes	.05
355	Herb Perry	.05
356	Ryne Sandberg	1.00
357	Harold Baines	.05
358	Chad Ogea	.05
359	Lee Tinsley	.05
360	Matt Williams	.05
361	Randy Velarde	.05
362	Jose Canseco	.40
363	Larry Walker	.05
364	Kevin Appier	.05
365	Darryl Hamilton	.05
366	Jose Lima	.05
367	Javy Lopez	.05
368	Dennis Eckersley	.65
369	Jason Isringhausen	.05
370	Mickey Morandini	.05
371	Scott Cooper	.05
372	Jim Abbott	.05
373	Paul Sorrento	.05
374	Chris Hammond	.05
375	Lance Johnson	.05
376	Kevin Brown	.05
377	Luis Alicea	.05
378	Andy Pettitte	.25
379	Dean Palmer	.05
380	Jeff Bagwell	.75
381	Jaime Navarro	.05
382	Rondell White	.05
383	Erik Hanson	.05
384	Pedro Munoz	.05
385	Heathcliff Slocumb	.05
386	Wally Joyner	.05
387	Bob Tewksbury	.05
388	David Bell	.05
389	Fred McGriff	.05
390	Mike Henneman	.05
391	Robby Thompson	.05
392	Norm Charlton	.05
393	Cecil Fielder	.05
394	Benito Santiago	.05
395	Rafael Palmeiro	.65
396	Ricky Bones	.05
397	Rickey Henderson	.75
398	C.J. Nitkowski	.05
399	Shawon Dunston	.05
400	Manny Ramirez	.75
401	Bill Swift	.05
402	Chad Fonville	.05
403	Joey Hamilton	.05
404	Alex Gonzalez	.05
405	Roberto Hernandez	.05
406	Jeff Blauser	.05
407	LaTroy Hawkins	.05
408	Greg Colbrunn	.05
409	Todd Hundley	.05
410	Glenn Dishman	.05
411	Joe Vitiello	.05
412	Todd Worrell	.05
413	Wil Cordero	.05
414	Ken Hill	.05
415	Carlos Garcia	.05
416	Bryan Rekar	.05
417	Shawn Green	.40
418	Tyler Green	.05
419	Mike Blowers	.05
420	Kenny Lofton	.05
421	Denny Neagle	.05
422	Jeff Conine	.05
423	Mark Langston	.05
424	*Steve Cox, Jesse Ibarra, Derrek Lee, Ron Wright*	.10
425	*Jim Bonnici, Billy Owens, Richie Sexson, Daryle Ward*	.10
426	*Kevin Jordan, Bobby Morris, Desi Relaford, Adam Riggs*	.10
427	Tim Harkrider, Rey Ordonez, Neifi Perez, Enrique Wilson	.05
428	*Bartolo Colon, Doug Million, Rafael Orellano, Ray Ricken*	.05
429	Jeff D'Amico, Marty Janzen, Gary Rath, Clint Sodowsky	.05
430	Matt Drews, Rich Hunter, Matt Ruebel, Bret Wagner	.05
431	Jaime Bluma, Dave Coggin, Steve Montgomery, Brandon Reed	.05
432	Mike Figga, Raul Ibanez, Paul Konerko, Julio Mosquera	.25
433	Brian Barber, Marc Kroon, Marc Valdes, Don Wengert	.05
434	George Arias, Chris Haas, Scott Rolen, Scott Spiezio	.50
435	Brian Banks, Vladimir Guerrero, Andruw Jones, Billy McMillon	.50
436	*Roger Cedeno, Derrick Gibson, Ben Grieve, Shane Spencer*	.50
437	Anton French, Demond Smith, Darond Stovall, Keith Williams	.05
438	Michael Coleman, Jacob Cruz, Richard Hidalgo, Charles Peterson	.10
439	Trey Beamon, Yamil Benitez, Jermaine Dye, Angel Echevarria	.05
440	Checklist	.05

Classic Confrontations

		NM/M
Complete Set (15):		3.50
Common Player:		.06
1	Ken Griffey Jr.	.65
2	Cal Ripken Jr.	1.00
3	Edgar Martinez	.05
4	Kirby Puckett	.45
5	Frank Thomas	.35
6	Barry Bonds	1.00
7	Reggie Sanders	.05
8	Andres Galarraga	.05
9	Tony Gwynn	.45
10	Mike Piazza	.65
11	Randy Johnson	.35
12	Mike Mussina	.25
13	Roger Clemens	.50
14	Tom Glavine	.25
15	Greg Maddux	.45

League Leaders Finest Bronze

		NM/M
Complete Set (6):		75.00
Common Player:		10.00
(1)	Mo Vaughn	10.00
(2)	Barry Larkin	10.00
(3)	Randy Johnson	15.00
(4)	Greg Maddux	30.00
(5)	Marty Cordova	10.00
(6)	Hideo Nomo	15.00

Masters of the Game

		NM/M
Complete Set (20):		20.00
Common Player:		.35
1	Dennis Eckersley	.75
2	Denny Martinez	.35
3	Eddie Murray	1.00
4	Paul Molitor	1.00
5	Ozzie Smith	1.50
6	Rickey Henderson	1.00
7	Tim Raines	.35
8	Lee Smith	.35
9	Cal Ripken Jr.	4.00
10	Chili Davis	.35
11	Wade Boggs	1.50
12	Tony Gwynn	1.50
13	Don Mattingly	2.00
14	Bret Saberhagen	.35
15	Kirby Puckett	1.50
16	Joe Carter	.35
17	Roger Clemens	2.00
18	Barry Bonds	4.00
19	Greg Maddux	1.50
20	Frank Thomas	1.00

Mickey Mantle Reprints

		NM/M
Complete Set (19):		55.00
Common Mantle:		2.50
Common SP Mantle (15-19):		3.00
1	1951 Bowman #253	6.00
2	1952 Topps #311	10.00
3	1953 Topps #82	4.50
4	1954 Bowman #65	2.50
5	1955 Bowman #202	2.50
6	1956 Topps #135	2.50
7	1957 Topps #95	2.50
8	1958 Topps #150	2.50
9	1959 Topps #10	2.50
10	1960 Topps #350	2.50
11	1961 Topps #300	2.50
12	1962 Topps #200	2.50
13	1963 Topps #200	2.50
14	1964 Topps #50	2.50
15	1965 Topps #350	3.00
16	1966 Topps #50	3.00
17	1967 Topps #150	3.00
18	1968 Topps #280	3.00
19	1969 Topps #500	3.00

Mickey Mantle Case Inserts

		NM/M
Complete Set (19):		375.00
Common Mantle:		20.00
Common SP Mantle (15-19):		25.00
1	1951 Bowman #253	45.00
2	1952 Topps #311	55.00
3	1953 Topps #82	40.00
4	1954 Bowman #65	20.00
5	1955 Bowman #202	20.00
6	1956 Topps #135	20.00
7	1957 Topps #95	20.00
8	1958 Topps #150	20.00
9	1959 Topps #10	20.00
10	1960 Topps #350	20.00
11	1961 Topps #300	20.00
12	1962 Topps #200	20.00
13	1963 Topps #200	20.00

14	1964 Topps #50	20.00
15	1965 Topps #350	25.00
16	1966 Topps #50	25.00
17	1967 Topps #150	25.00
18	1968 Topps #280	25.00
19	1969 Topps #500	25.00

Mickey Mantle Finest Reprints

		NM/M
Complete Set (19):		75.00
Common Card (1-14):		5.00
Common Shortprint (15-19):		7.50
Refractors:		2X
Inserted 1:144		
1	1951 Bowman #253	10.00
2	1952 Topps #311	15.00
3	1953 Topps #82	6.00
4	1954 Bowman #65	5.00
5	1955 Bowman #202	5.00
6	1956 Topps #135	5.00
7	1957 Topps #95	5.00
8	1958 Topps #150	5.00
9	1959 Topps #10	5.00
10	1960 Topps #350	5.00
11	1961 Topps #300	5.00
12	1962 Topps #200	5.00
13	1963 Topps #200	5.00
14	1964 Topps #50	5.00
15	1965 Topps #350	7.50
16	1966 Topps #50	7.50
17	1967 Topps #150	7.50
18	1968 Topps #280	7.50
19	1969 Topps #500	7.50

Mickey Mantle Commemorative Card Sheet

	NM/M
Framed Sheet:	80.00
Mickey Mantle	

Mickey Mantle Commemorative Last Day

		NM/M
7	Mickey Mantle	5.00

Mystery Finest

		NM/M
Complete Set (21)		25.00
Common Player:		.50
Refractors:		1.5X
M1	Hideo Nomo	1.00
M2	Greg Maddux	2.00
M3	Randy Johnson	1.50
M4	Chipper Jones	2.00
M5	Marty Cordova	.50
M6	Garret Anderson	.50
M7	Cal Ripken Jr.	4.00
M8	Kirby Puckett	2.00
M9	Tony Gwynn	2.00
M10	Manny Ramirez	1.50
M11	Jim Edmonds	.50
M12	Mike Piazza	2.50
M13	Barry Bonds	4.00
M14	Raul Mondesi	.50
M15	Sammy Sosa	2.00
M16	Ken Griffey Jr.	2.50
M17	Albert Belle	.50
M18	Dante Bichette	.50
M19	Mo Vaughn	.50
M20	Jeff Bagwell	1.50
M21	Frank Thomas	1.50

Power Boosters

		NM/M
Complete Set (26):		30.00
Common Player:		1.00
1	Tony Gwynn	2.00
2	Mike Piazza	3.00
3	Greg Maddux	2.00
4	Jeff Bagwell	1.50
5	Larry Walker	1.00
6	Barry Larkin	1.00
8	Tom Glavine	1.25
9	Craig Biggio	1.00
10	Barry Bonds	4.00
11	Heathcliff Slocumb	1.00
12	Matt Williams	1.00
13	Todd Helton	4.00
14	Mark Redman	1.00
15	Michael Barrett	1.00
16	Ben Davis	1.00
17	Juan LeBron	1.00
18	Tony McKnight	1.00
19	Ryan Jaroncyk	1.00
20	Corey Jenkins	1.00
21	Jim Scharrer	1.00
22	Mark Bellhorn	1.00
23	Jarrod Washburn	1.00
24	Geoff Jenkins	1.00
25	Sean Casey	2.00
26	Brett Tomko	1.00

Profiles-AL

		NM/M
Complete Set (20):		8.00
Common Player:		.25
1	Roberto Alomar	.30
2	Carlos Baerga	.25
3	Albert Belle	.25
4	Cecil Fielder	.25
5	Ken Griffey Jr.	1.00
6	Randy Johnson	.60
7	Paul O'Neill	.25
8	Cal Ripken Jr.	1.50
9	Frank Thomas	.60
10	Mo Vaughn	.25
11	Jay Buhner	.25
12	Marty Cordova	.25
13	Jim Edmonds	.25
14	Juan Gonzalez	.35
15	Kenny Lofton	.25
16	Edgar Martinez	.25
17	Don Mattingly	.75
18	Mark McGwire	1.25
19	Rafael Palmeiro	.50
20	Tim Salmon	.25

Profiles-NL

		NM/M
Complete Set (20):		7.00
Common Player:		.25
1	Jeff Bagwell	.60
2	Derek Bell	.25
3	Barry Bonds	1.50
4	Greg Maddux	.75
5	Fred McGriff	.25
6	Raul Mondesi	.25
7	Mike Piazza	1.00
8	Reggie Sanders	.25
9	Sammy Sosa	.75
10	Larry Walker	.25
11	Dante Bichette	.25
12	Andres Galarraga	.25
13	Ron Gant	.25
14	Tom Glavine	.35
15	Chipper Jones	.75
16	David Justice	.25
17	Barry Larkin	.25
18	Hideo Nomo	.40
19	Gary Sheffield	.40
20	Matt Williams	.25

1996 TOPPS ROAD WARRIORS

		NM/M
Complete Set (20):		9.00
Common Player:		.25
1	Derek Bell	.25
2	Albert Belle	.25
3	Craig Biggio	.25
4	Barry Bonds	2.50
5	Jay Buhner	.25
6	Jim Edmonds	.25
7	Gary Gaetti	.25
8	Ron Gant	.25
9	Edgar Martinez	.25
10	Tino Martinez	.25
11	Mark McGwire	1.50
12	Mike Piazza	1.25
13	Manny Ramirez	1.00
14	Tim Salmon	.25
15	Reggie Sanders	.25
16	Frank Thomas	1.00
17	John Valentin	.25
18	Mo Vaughn	.25
19	Robin Ventura	.25
20	Matt Williams	.25

Wrecking Crew

		NM/M
Complete Set (15):		20.00
Common Player:		.50
1	Jeff Bagwell	1.50
2	Albert Belle	.50
3	Barry Bonds	5.00
4	Jose Canseco	.75
5	Joe Carter	.50
6	Cecil Fielder	.50
7	Ron Gant	.50
8	Juan Gonzalez	.75
9	Ken Griffey Jr.	3.00
10	Fred McGriff	.50
11	Mark McGwire	4.00
12	Mike Piazza	3.00
13	Frank Thomas	1.50
14	Mo Vaughn	.50
15	Matt Williams	.50

5-Star Mystery Finest

		NM/M
Complete Set (5):		12.50
Common Player:		2.00
Refractors:		2X
M22	Hideo Nomo	2.00
M23	Cal Ripken Jr.	5.00
M24	Mike Piazza	3.00
M25	Ken Griffey Jr.	3.00
M26	Frank Thomas	2.50

1996 TOPPS CHROME

		NM/M
Complete Set (165):		40.00
Common Player:		.10
Refractors:		3X
Pack (4):		2.00
Wax Box (24):		30.00
1	Tony Gwynn	1.00
2	Mike Piazza	1.25
3	Greg Maddux	1.00
4	Jeff Bagwell	.75
5	Larry Walker	.10
6	Barry Larkin	.10
7	Mickey Mantle	9.00
8	Tom Glavine	.10
9	Craig Biggio	.10
10	Barry Bonds	2.00
11	Heathcliff Slocumb	.10
12	Matt Williams	.10
13	Todd Helton	2.00
14	Paul Molitor	1.50
15	Glenallen Hill	.10
16	Troy Percival	.10
17	Albert Belle	.10
18	Mark Wohlers	.10
19	Kirby Puckett	2.00
20	Mark Grace	.10
21	J.T. Snow	.10
22	David Justice	.10
23	Mike Mussina	.75
24	Bernie Williams	.10
25	Ron Gant	.10
26	Carlos Baerga	.10
27	Gary Sheffield	.65
28	Cal Ripken Jr.	2.00
29	Frank Thomas	1.50
30	Kevin Seitzer	.10
31	Joe Carter	.10
32	Jeff King	.10
33	David Cone	.10
34	Eddie Murray	1.50
35	Brian Jordan	.10
36	Garret Anderson	.10
37	Hideo Nomo	.75
38	Steve Finley	.10
39	Ivan Rodriguez	1.25
40	Quilvio Veras	.10
41	Mark McGwire	3.00
42	Greg Vaughn	.10
43	Randy Johnson	1.50
44	David Segui	.10
45	Derek Bell	.10
46	John Valentin	.10
47	Steve Avery	.10
48	Tino Martinez	.10
49	Shane Reynolds	.10
50	Jim Edmonds	.10
51	Raul Mondesi	.10
52	Chipper Jones	2.00
53	Gregg Jefferies	.10
54	Ken Caminiti	.10
55	Brian McRae	.10
56	Don Mattingly	2.25
57	Marty Cordova	.10
58	Vinny Castilla	.10
59	John Smoltz	.10
60	Travis Fryman	.10
61	Ryan Klesko	.10
62	Alex Fernandez	.10
63	Dante Bichette	.10
64	Eric Karros	.10
65	Roger Clemens	2.25
66	Randy Myers	.10
67	Cal Ripken Jr.	4.00
68	Rod Beck	.10
69	Jack McDowell	.10
70	Ken Griffey Jr.	2.50
71	Ramon Martinez	.10
72	Jason Giambi	.75
73	Nomar Garciaparra	2.00
74	Billy Wagner	.10
75	Todd Greene	.10
76	Paul Wilson	.10
77	Johnny Damon	.35
78	Alan Benes	.10
79	Karim Garcia	.25
80	Derek Jeter	4.00
81	Kirby Puckett	1.00
82	Cal Ripken Jr.	2.00
83	Albert Belle	.10
84	Randy Johnson	.40
85	Wade Boggs	1.00
86	Carlos Baerga	.10
87	Ivan Rodriguez	.35
88	Mike Mussina	.30
89	Frank Thomas	.75
90	Ken Griffey Jr.	1.25
91	Jose Mesa	.10
92	*Matt Morris*	1.00
93	Mike Piazza	2.50
94	Edgar Martinez	.10
95	Chuck Knoblauch	.10
96	Andres Galarraga	.10
97	Tony Gwynn	2.00
98	Lee Smith	.10
99	Sammy Sosa	2.00
100	Jim Thome	1.25

101	Bernard Gilkey	.10
102	Brady Anderson	.10
103	Rico Brogna	.10
104	Lenny Dykstra	.10
105	Tom Glavine	.35
106	John Olerud	.10
107	Terry Steinbach	.10
108	Brian Hunter	.10
109	Jay Buhner	.10
110	Mo Vaughn	.10
111	Jose Mesa	.10
112	Brett Butler	.10
113	Chili Davis	.10
114	Paul O'Neill	.10
115	Roberto Alomar	.35
116	Barry Larkin	.10
117	Marquis Grissom	.10
118	Will Clark	.10
119	Barry Bonds	4.00
120	Ozzie Smith	2.00
121	Pedro Martinez	1.50
122	Craig Biggio	.10
123	Moises Alou	.10
124	Robin Ventura	.10
125	Greg Maddux	2.00
126	Tim Salmon	.10
127	Wade Boggs	2.00
128	Ismael Valdes	.10
129	Juan Gonzalez	.75
130	Ray Lankford	.10
131	Bobby Bonilla	.10
132	Reggie Sanders	.10
133	Alex Ochoa	.10
134	Mark Loretta	.10
135	Jason Kendall	.10
136	Brooks Kieschnick	.10
137	Chris Snopek	.10
138	Ruben Rivera	.10
139	Jeff Suppan	.10
140	John Wasdin	.10
141	Jay Payton	.10
142	Rick Krivda	.10
143	Jimmy Haynes	.10
144	Ryne Sandberg	2.00
145	Matt Williams	.10
146	Jose Canseco	.65
147	Larry Walker	.10
148	Kevin Appier	.10
149	Javy Lopez	.10
150	Dennis Eckersley	1.25
151	Jason Isringhausen	.10
152	Dean Palmer	.10
153	Jeff Bagwell	1.50
154	Rondell White	.10
155	Wally Joyner	.10
156	Fred McGriff	.10
157	Cecil Fielder	.10
158	Rafael Palmeiro	1.25
159	Rickey Henderson	1.50
160	Shawon Dunston	.10
161	Manny Ramirez	1.50
162	Alex Gonzalez	.10
163	Shawn Green	.45
164	Kenny Lofton	.10
165	Jeff Conine	.10

Masters of the Game

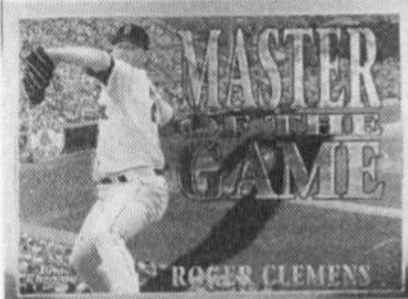

		NM/M
Complete Set (20):		35.00
Common Player:		1.00
Refractors:		1.5X
1	Dennis Eckersley	2.00
2	Denny Martinez	1.00
3	Eddie Murray	2.50
4	Paul Molitor	2.50
5	Ozzie Smith	3.50
6	Rickey Henderson	2.50
7	Tim Raines	1.00
8	Lee Smith	1.00
9	Cal Ripken Jr.	6.00
10	Chili Davis	1.00
11	Wade Boggs	3.50
12	Tony Gwynn	3.50
13	Don Mattingly	4.00
14	Bret Saberhagen	1.00
15	Kirby Puckett	3.50
16	Joe Carter	1.00
17	Roger Clemens	4.00
18	Barry Bonds	6.00
19	Greg Maddux	3.50
20	Frank Thomas	2.50

Wrecking Crew

		NM/M
Complete Set (15):		25.00
Common Player:		1.00
Refractors:		1.5X
1	Jeff Bagwell	2.50
2	Albert Belle	1.00
3	Barry Bonds	5.00
4	Jose Canseco	1.50
5	Joe Carter	1.00
6	Cecil Fielder	1.00
7	Ron Gant	1.00
8	Juan Gonzalez	1.25
9	Ken Griffey Jr.	3.50
10	Fred McGriff	1.00
11	Mark McGwire	4.00
12	Mike Piazza	4.00
13	Frank Thomas	2.50
14	Mo Vaughn	1.00
15	Matt Williams	1.00

1996 TOPPS GALLERY

		NM/M
Complete Set (180):		20.00
Common Player:		.10
Private Issue:		8X
Pack (8):		1.50
Wax Box (24):		27.50
1	Tom Glavine	.35
2	Carlos Baerga	.10
3	Dante Bichette	.10
4	Mark Langston	.10
5	Ray Lankford	.10
6	Moises Alou	.10
7	Marquis Grissom	.10
8	Ramon Martinez	.10
8p	Ramon Martinez (unmarked promo, "Pitcher" spelled out under photo on back)	2.50
9	Steve Finley	.10
10	Todd Hundley	.10
11	Brady Anderson	.10
12	John Valentin	.10
13	Heathcliff Slocumb	.10
14	Ruben Sierra	.10
15	Jeff Conine	.10
16	Jay Buhner	.10
16p	Jay Buhner (unmarked promo; height, weight and "Bats" on same line)	2.50
17	Sammy Sosa	1.00
18	Doug Drabek	.10
19	Jose Mesa	.10
20	Jeff King	.10
21	Mickey Tettleton	.10
22	Jeff Montgomery	.10
23	Alex Fernandez	.10
24	Greg Vaughn	.10
25	Chuck Finley	.10
26	Terry Steinbach	.10
27	Rod Beck	.10
28	Jack McDowell	.10
29	Mark Wohlers	.10
30	Lenny Dykstra	.10
31	Bernie Williams	.10
32	Travis Fryman	.10
33	Jose Canseco	.45
34	Ken Caminiti	.10
35	Devon White	.10
36	Bobby Bonilla	.10
37	Paul Sorrento	.10
38	Ryne Sandberg	1.00
39	Derek Bell	.10
40	Bobby Jones	.10
41	J.T. Snow	.10
42	Denny Neagle	.10
43	Tim Wakefield	.10
44	Andres Galarraga	.10
45	David Segui	.10
46	Lee Smith	.10
47	Mel Rojas	.10
48	John Franco	.10
49	Pete Schourek	.10
50	John Wetteland	.10
51	Paul Molitor	.75
52	Ivan Rodriguez	.65
53	Chris Hoiles	.10
54	Mike Greenwell	.10
55	Orel Hershiser	.10
56	Brian McRae	.10
57	Geronimo Berroa	.10
58	Craig Biggio	.10
59	David Justice	.10
59p	David Justice (unmarked promo; height,weight and "Bats"on same line)	2.50
60	Lance Johnson	.10
61	Andy Ashby	.10
62	Randy Myers	.10
63	Gregg Jefferies	.10
64	Kevin Appier	.10
65	Rick Aguilera	.10
66	Shane Reynolds	.10
67	John Smoltz	.10
68	Ron Gant	.10
69	Eric Karros	.10
70	Jim Thome	.65
71	Terry Pendleton	.10
72	Kenny Rogers	.10
73	Robin Ventura	.10
74	Dave Nilsson	.10
75	Brian Jordan	.10
76	Glenallen Hill	.10
77	Greg Colbrunn	.10
78	Roberto Alomar	.25
79	Rickey Henderson	.75
80	Carlos Garcia	.10
81	Dean Palmer	.10
82	Mike Stanley	.10
83	Hal Morris	.10
84	Wade Boggs	1.00
85	Chad Curtis	.10
86	Roberto Hernandez	.10
87	John Olerud	.10
88	Frank Castillo	.10
89	Rafael Palmeiro	.65
90	Trevor Hoffman	.10
91	Marty Cordova	.10
92	Hideo Nomo	.35
93	Johnny Damon	.30
94	Bill Pulsipher	.10
95	Garret Anderson	.10
96	Ray Durham	.10
97	Ricky Bottalico	.10
98	Carlos Perez	.10
99	Troy Percival	.10
100	Chipper Jones	1.00
101	Esteban Loaiza	.10
102	John Mabry	.10
103	Jon Nunnally	.10
104	Andy Pettitte	.35
105	Lyle Mouton	.10
106	Jason Isringhausen	.10
107	Brian Hunter	.10
108	Quilvio Veras	.10
109	Jim Edmonds	.10
110	Ryan Klesko	.10
111	Pedro Martinez	.75
112	Joey Hamilton	.10
113	Vinny Castilla	.10
114	Alex Gonzalez	.10
115	Raul Mondesi	.10
116	Rondell White	.10
117	Dan Miceli	.10
118	Tom Goodwin	.10
119	Bret Boone	.10
120	Shawn Green	.35
121	Jeff Cirillo	.10
122	Rico Brogna	.10
123	Chris Gomez	.10
124	Ismael Valdes	.10
125	Javy Lopez	.10
126	Manny Ramirez	.75
127	Paul Wilson	.10
128	Billy Wagner	.10
129	Eric Owens	.10
130	Todd Greene	.10
131	Karim Garcia	.10
132	Jimmy Haynes	.10
133	Michael Tucker	.10
134	John Wasdin	.10
135	Brooks Kieschnick	.10
136	Alex Ochoa	.10
137	Ariel Prieto	.10
138	Tony Clark	.10
139	Mark Loretta	.10
140	Rey Ordonez	.10
141	Chris Snopek	.10
142	Roger Cedeno	.10
143	Derek Jeter	2.00
144	Jeff Suppan	.10
145	Greg Maddux	1.00
146	Ken Griffey Jr.	1.25
147	Tony Gwynn	1.00
148	Darren Daulton	.10
149	Will Clark	.10
150	Mo Vaughn	.10
151	Reggie Sanders	.10
152	Kirby Puckett	1.00
153	Paul O'Neill	.10
154	Tim Salmon	.10
155	Mark McGwire	1.50
156	Barry Bonds	2.00
157	Albert Belle	.10
158	Edgar Martinez	.10
159	Mike Mussina	.35
160	Cecil Fielder	.10
161	Kenny Lofton	.10
162	Randy Johnson	.75
163	Juan Gonzalez	.35
164	Jeff Bagwell	.75
165	Joe Carter	.10
166	Mike Piazza	1.25
167	Eddie Murray	.75
168	Cal Ripken Jr.	2.00
169	Barry Larkin	.10
170	Chuck Knoblauch	.10
171	Chili Davis	.10
172	Fred McGriff	.10
173	Matt Williams	.10
174	Roger Clemens	1.00
175	Frank Thomas	.75
176	Dennis Eckersley	.10
177	Gary Sheffield	.40
178	David Cone	.10
179	Larry Walker	.10
180	Mark Grace	.10

Players Private Issue

	NM/M
Complete Set (180):	200.00
Common Player:	1.00
Stars:	8X

(See 1996 Topps Gallery for checklist and base card values.)

Expressionists

		NM/M
Complete Set (20):		20.00
Common Player:		.35
1	Mike Piazza	3.00
2	J.T. Snow	.35
3	Ken Griffey Jr.	3.00
4	Kirby Puckett	2.00
5	Carlos Baerga	.35
6	Chipper Jones	2.00
7	Hideo Nomo	.75
8	Mark McGwire	4.00
9	Gary Sheffield	.75
10	Randy Johnson	1.25
11	Ray Lankford	.35
12	Sammy Sosa	2.00
13	Denny Martinez	.35
14	Jose Canseco	.75
15	Tony Gwynn	2.00
16	Edgar Martinez	.35
17	Reggie Sanders	.35
18	Andres Galarraga	.35
19	Albert Belle	.35
20	Barry Larkin	.35

Masterpiece

		NM/M
MP1	Mickey Mantle	6.00

Photo Gallery

		NM/M
Complete Set (15):		20.00
Common Player:		.75
1	Eddie Murray	2.00
2	Randy Johnson	2.00
3	Cal Ripken Jr.	5.00
4	Bret Boone	.75
5	Frank Thomas	2.00
6	Jeff Conine	.75
7	Johnny Damon	.85
8	Roger Clemens	3.00
9	Albert Belle	.75
10	Ken Griffey Jr.	4.00
11	Kirby Puckett	2.50
12	David Justice	.75
13	Bobby Bonilla	.75
14	Larry Walker, Andres Galarraga, Vinny Castilla, Dante Bichette	1.00
15	Mark Wohlers, Javier Lopez	.75

1996 TOPPS LASER

		NM/M
Complete Set (128):		27.50
Common Player:		.10
Series 1 or 2 Pack (4):		1.50
Series 1 or 2 Wax Box (24):		22.50
1	Moises Alou	.10
2	Derek Bell	.10
3	Joe Carter	.10
4	Jeff Conine	.10
5	Darren Daulton	.10
6	Jim Edmonds	.10
7	Ron Gant	.10
8	Juan Gonzalez	.50
9	Brian Jordan	.10
10	Ryan Klesko	.10
11	Paul Molitor	1.00
12	Tony Phillips	.10
13	Manny Ramirez	1.00
14	Sammy Sosa	1.50
15	Devon White	.10
16	Bernie Williams	.10
17	Garret Anderson	.10
18	Jay Bell	.10
19	Craig Biggio	.10
20	Bobby Bonilla	.10
21	Ken Caminiti	.10
22	Shawon Dunston	.10
23	Mark Grace	.10
23p	Mark Grace (unmarked promo, plain, rather than brushed, gold foil)	2.00
24	Gregg Jefferies	.10
25	Jeff King	.10
26	Javy Lopez	.10
27	Edgar Martinez	.10
28	Dean Palmer	.10
29	J.T. Snow	.10
30	Mike Stanley	.10
30p	Mike Stanley (unmarked promo; plain, rather than brushed, gold foil)	1.00
31	Terry Steinbach	.10
32	Robin Ventura	.10
33	Roberto Alomar	.20
34	Jeff Bagwell	1.00
35	Dante Bichette	.10
36	Wade Boggs	1.50
37	Barry Bonds	3.00
38	Jose Canseco	.50
39	Vinny Castilla	.10
40	Will Clark	.10
41	Marty Cordova	.10
42	Ken Griffey Jr.	2.00
43	Tony Gwynn	1.50
44	Rickey Henderson	1.00
45	Chipper Jones	1.50
46	Mark McGwire	2.50
47	Brian McRae	.10
48	Ryne Sandberg	1.50
49	Andy Ashby	.10
50	Alan Benes	.10
51	Andy Benes	.10
52	Roger Clemens	1.75
53	Doug Drabek	.10
54	Dennis Eckersley	.75
55	Tom Glavine	.35
56	Randy Johnson	1.00
57	Mark Langston	.10
58	Denny Martinez	.10
59	Jack McDowell	.10
60	Hideo Nomo	.50
61	Shane Reynolds	.10
62	John Smoltz	.10
63	Paul Wilson	.10
64	Mark Wohlers	.10
65	Shawn Green	.35
66	Marquis Grissom	.10
67	Dave Hollins	.10
68	Todd Hundley	.10
69	David Justice	.10
70	Eric Karros	.10
71	Ray Lankford	.10
72	Fred McGriff	.10
73	Hal Morris	.10
74	Eddie Murray	1.00
75	Paul O'Neill	.10
76	Rey Ordonez	.10
77	Reggie Sanders	.10
78	Gary Sheffield	.45
79	Jim Thome	.75
80	Rondell White	.10
81	Travis Fryman	.10
82	Derek Jeter	3.00
83	Chuck Knoblauch	.10
84	Barry Larkin	.10
85	Tino Martinez	.10
86	Raul Mondesi	.10
87	John Olerud	.10
88	Rafael Palmeiro	.75
89	Mike Piazza	2.00
90	Cal Ripken Jr.	3.00
91	Ivan Rodriguez	.75
92	Frank Thomas	1.00
93	John Valentin	.10
94	Mo Vaughn	.10
95	Quilvio Veras	.10
96	Matt Williams	.10
97	Brady Anderson	.10
98	Carlos Baerga	.10
99	Albert Belle	.10
100	Jay Buhner	.10
101	Johnny Damon	.35
102	Chili Davis	.10
103	Ray Durham	.10
104	Lenny Dykstra	.10
105	Cecil Fielder	.10
106	Andres Galarraga	.10
107	Brian Hunter	.10
108	Kenny Lofton	.10
109	Kirby Puckett	1.50
110	Tim Salmon	.10
111	Greg Vaughn	.10
112	Larry Walker	.10
113	Rick Aguilera	.10
114	Kevin Appier	.10
115	Kevin Brown	.10
116	David Cone	.10
117	Alex Fernandez	.10
118	Chuck Finley	.10
119	Joey Hamilton	.10
120	Jason Isringhausen	.10
121	Greg Maddux	1.50
122	Pedro Martinez	1.00
123	Jose Mesa	.10
124	Jeff Montgomery	.10
125	Mike Mussina	.50
126	Randy Myers	.10
127	Kenny Rogers	.10
128	Ismael Valdes	.10

Bright Spots

		NM/M
Complete Set (16):		17.50
Common Player:		.50
1	Brian Hunter	.50
2	Derek Jeter	4.50
3	Jason Kendall	.50
4	Brooks Kieschnick	.50
5	Rey Ordonez	.50
6	Jason Schmidt	.50
7	Chris Snopek	.50
8	Bob Wolcott	.50
9	Alan Benes	.50
10	Marty Cordova	.50
11	Jimmy Haynes	.50
12	Todd Hollandsworth	.50
13	Derek Jeter	4.50
14	Chipper Jones	3.00
15	Hideo Nomo	1.00
16	Paul Wilson	.50

Power Cuts

		NM/M
Complete Set (16):		20.00
Common Player:		.75
1	Albert Belle	.75
2	Jay Buhner	.75
3	Fred McGriff	.75
4	Mike Piazza	3.00
5	Tim Salmon	.75
6	Frank Thomas	2.00
7	Mo Vaughn	.75
8	Matt Williams	.75
9	Jeff Bagwell	2.00
10	Barry Bonds	5.00
11	Jose Canseco	1.00
12	Cecil Fielder	.75
13	Juan Gonzalez	1.00
14	Ken Griffey Jr.	3.00
15	Sammy Sosa	2.50
16	Larry Walker	.75

Stadium Stars

		NM/M
Complete Set (16):		45.00
Common Player:		1.50
1	Carlos Baerga	1.50
2	Barry Bonds	10.00
3	Andres Galarraga	1.50
4	Ken Griffey Jr.	7.50
5	Barry Larkin	1.50
6	Raul Mondesi	1.50
7	Kirby Puckett	5.00
8	Cal Ripken Jr.	10.00
9	Will Clark	1.50
10	Roger Clemens	6.00
11	Tony Gwynn	5.00
12	Randy Johnson	4.00
13	Kenny Lofton	1.50
14	Edgar Martinez	1.50
15	Ryne Sandberg	5.00
16	Frank Thomas	4.00

1997 TOPPS

		NM/M
Unopened Fact. Set (504):		110.00
Unopened Fact. Set (503):		145.00
Complete Set (495):		65.00
Common Player:		.05
Ser. 1 or 2 Pack (11):		1.00
Ser. 1 or 2 Wax Box (36):		20.00
Ser. 1 or 2 Vending Box (500):		12.00
1	Barry Bonds	2.00
2	Tom Pagnozzi	.05
3	Terrell Wade	.05
4	Jose Valentin	.05
5	Mark Clark	.05
6	Brady Anderson	.05
7	Not issued	
8	Wade Boggs	1.00
9	Scott Stahoviak	.05
10	Andres Galarraga	.05
11	Steve Avery	.05
12	Rusty Greer	.05
13	Derek Jeter	2.00
14	Ricky Bottalico	.05
15	Andy Ashby	.05
16	Paul Shuey	.05
17	F.P. Santangelo	.05
18	Royce Clayton	.05
19	Mike Mohler	.05
20	Mike Piazza	1.50
21	Jaime Navarro	.05
22	Billy Wagner	.05
23	Mike Timlin	.05
24	Garret Anderson	.05
25	Ben McDonald	.05
26	Mel Rojas	.05
27	John Burkett	.05
28	Jeff King	.05
29	Reggie Jefferson	.05
30	Kevin Appier	.05
31	Felipe Lira	.05
32	Kevin Tapani	.05
33	Mark Portugal	.05
34	Carlos Garcia	.05
35	Joey Cora	.05
36	David Segui	.05
37	Mark Grace	.05
38	Erik Hanson	.05
39	Jeff D'Amico	.05
40	Jay Buhner	.05
41	B.J. Surhoff	.05
42	Jackie Robinson	1.50
43	Roger Pavlik	.05
44	Hal Morris	.05
45	Mariano Duncan	.05
46	Harold Baines	.05
47	Jorge Fabregas	.05
48	Jose Herrera	.05
49	Jeff Cirillo	.05
50	Tom Glavine	.25
51	Pedro Astacio	.05
52	Mark Gardner	.05
53	Arthur Rhodes	.05
54	Troy O'Leary	.05
55	Bip Roberts	.05
56	Mike Lieberthal	.05
57	Shane Andrews	.05
58	Scott Karl	.05
59	Gary DiSarcina	.05
60	Andy Pettitte	.25
61a	Kevin Elster	.05
61b	Mike Fetters (should be #84)	.05
62	Mark McGwire	1.75
63	Dan Wilson	.05
64	Mickey Morandini	.05
65	Chuck Knoblauch	.05
66	Tim Wakefield	.05
67	Raul Mondesi	.05
68	Todd Jones	.05
69	Albert Belle	.05
70	Trevor Hoffman	.05

71 Eric Young .05
72 Robert Perez .05
73 Butch Huskey .05
74 Brian McRae .05
75 Jim Edmonds .05
76 Mike Henneman .05
77 Frank Rodriguez .05
78 Danny Tartabull .05
79 Robby Nen .05
80 Reggie Sanders .05
81 Ron Karkovice .05
82 Benny Santiago .05
83 Mike Lansing .05
84 Not issued - see #61b
85 Craig Biggio .05
86 Mike Bordick .05
87 Ray Lankford .05
88 Charles Nagy .05
89 Paul Wilson .05
90 John Wetteland .05
91 Tom Candiotti .05
92 Carlos Delgado .45
93 Derek Bell .05
94 Mark Lemke .05
95 Edgar Martinez .05
96 Rickey Henderson .75
97 Greg Myers .05
98 Jim Leyritz .05
99 Mark Johnson .05
100 Dwight Gooden .05
101 Al Leiter .05
102a John Mabry (last line on back ends "... Mabry") .05
102b John Mabry (last line on back ends "...walked.") .05
103 Alex Ochoa .05
104 Mike Piazza .75
105 Jim Thome .65
106 Ricky Otero .05
107 Jamey Wright .05
108 Frank Thomas .75
109 Jody Reed .05
110 Orel Hershiser .05
111 Terry Steinbach .05
112 Mark Loretta .05
113 Turk Wendell .05
114 Marvin Benard .05
115 Kevin Brown .05
116 Robert Person .05
117 Joey Hamilton .05
118 Francisco Cordova .05
119 John Smiley .05
120 Travis Fryman .05
121 Jimmy Key .05
122 Tom Goodwin .05
123 Mike Greenwell .05
124 Juan Gonzalez .35
125 Pete Harnisch .05
126 Roger Cedeno .05
127 Ron Gant .05
128 Mark Langston .05
129 Tim Crabtree .05
130 Greg Maddux 1.00
131 William VanLandingham .05
132 Wally Joyner .05
133 Randy Myers .05
134 John Valentin .05
135 Bret Boone .05
136 Bruce Ruffin .05
137 Chris Snopek .05
138 Paul Molitor .75
139 Mark McLemore .05
140 Rafael Palmeiro .65
141 Herb Perry .05
142 Luis Gonzalez .05
143 Doug Drabek .05
144 Ken Ryan .05
145 Todd Hundley .05
146 Ellis Burks .05
147 Ozzie Guillen .05
148 Rich Becker .05
149 Sterling Hitchcock .05
150 Bernie Williams .05
151 Mike Stanley .05
152 Roberto Alomar .25
153 Jose Mesa .05
154 Steve Trachsel .05
155 Alex Gonzalez .05
156 Troy Percival .05
157 John Smoltz .05
158 Pedro Martinez .75
159 Jeff Conine .05
160 Bernard Gilkey .05
161 Jim Eisenreich .05
162 Mickey Tettleton .05
163 Justin Thompson .05
164 Jose Offerman .05
165 Tony Phillips .05
166 Ismael Valdes .05
167 Ryne Sandberg 1.00
168 Matt Mieske .05
169 Geronimo Berroa .05
170 Otis Nixon .05
171 John Mabry .05
172 Shawon Dunston .05
173 Omar Vizquel .05
174 Chris Holles .05
175 Doc Gooden .05
176 Wilson Alvarez .05
177 Todd Hollandsworth .05
178 Roger Salkeld .05
179 Rey Sanchez .05
180 Rey Ordonez .05
181 Denny Martinez .05
182 Ramon Martinez .05
183 Dave Nilsson .05
184 Marquis Grissom .05
185 Randy Velarde .05
186 Ron Coomer .05
187 Tino Martinez .05
188 Jeff Brantley .05
189 Steve Finley .05
190 Andy Benes .05
191 Terry Adams .05
192 Mike Blowers .05
193 Russ Davis .05
194 Darryl Hamilton .05
195 Jason Kendall .05
196 Johnny Damon .25
197 Dave Martinez .05
198 Mike Macfarlane .05
199 Norm Charlton .05
200 Doug Million, Damian Moss, Bobby Rodgers .05
201 Geoff Jenkins, Raul Ibanez, Mike Cameron .05
202 Sean Casey, Jim Bonnici, Dmitri Young .15
203 Jed Hansen, Homer Bush, Felipe Crespo .05
204 Kevin Orie, Gabe Alvarez, Aaron Boone .05
205 Ben Davis, Kevin Brown, Bobby Estalella .05
206 Billy McMillon, Bubba Trammell, Dante Powell .25
207 Jarrod Washburn, Marc Wilkins, Glendon Rusch .05
208 Brian Hunter .05
209 Jason Giambi .45
210 Henry Rodriguez .05
211 Edgar Renteria .05
212 Edgardo Alfonzo .05
213 Fernando Vina .05
214 Shawn Green .40
215 Ray Durham .05
216 Joe Randa .05
217 Armando Reynoso .05
218 Eric Davis .05
219 Bob Tewksbury .05
220 Jacob Cruz .05
221 Glenallen Hill .05
222 Gary Gaetti .05
223 Donne Wall .05
224 Brad Clontz .05
225 Marty Janzen .05
226 Todd Worrell .05
227 John Franco .05
228 David Wells .05
229 Gregg Jefferies .05
230 Tim Naehring .05
231 Thomas Howard .05
232 Roberto Hernandez .05
233 Kevin Ritz .05
234 Julian Tavarez .05
235 Ken Hill .05
236 Greg Gagne .05
237 Bobby Chouinard .05
238 Joe Carter .05
239 Jermaine Dye .05
240 Antonio Osuna .05
241 Julio Franco .05
242 Mike Grace .05
243 Aaron Sele .05
244 David Justice .05
245 Sandy Alomar .05
246 Jose Canseco .45
247 Paul O'Neill .05
248 Sean Berry .05
249 *Nick Bierbrodt, Kevin Sweeney* .05
250 *Larry Rodriguez, Vladimir Nunez* .10
251 Ron Hartman, David Hayman .05
252 Alex Sanchez, Matt Quatraro .05
253 *Ronni Seberino, Pablo Ortega* .05
254 Rex Hudler .05
255 Orlando Miller .05
256 Mariano Rivera .10
257 Brad Radke .05
258 Bobby Higginson .05
259 Jay Bell .05
260 Mark Grudzielanek .05
261 Lance Johnson .05
262 Ken Caminiti .05
263 J.T. Snow .05
264 Gary Sheffield .45
265 Darrin Fletcher .05
266 Eric Owens .05
267 Luis Castillo .05
268 Scott Rolen .65
269 Todd Noel, John Oliver .05
270 *Robert Stratton, Corey Lee* .05
271 *Gil Meche, Matt Halloran* .50
272 Eric Milton, Dermal Brown .25
273 *Josh Garrett, Chris Reitsma* .10
274 *A.J. Zapp, Jason Marquis* .50
275 Checklist .05
276a Checklist .05
276b Chipper Jones (should be #277) 1.00
277 Not issued
278 Orlando Merced .05
279 Ariel Prieto .05
280 Al Leiter .05
281 Pat Meares .05
282 Darryl Strawberry .05
283 Jamie Moyer .05
284 Scott Servais .05
285 Delino DeShields .05
286 Danny Graves .05
287 Gerald Williams .05
288 Todd Greene .05
289 Rico Brogna .05
290 Derrick Gibson .05
291 Joe Girardi .05
292 Darren Lewis .05
293 Nomar Garciaparra 1.00
294 Greg Colbrunn .05
295 Jeff Bagwell .75
296 Brent Gates .05
297 Jose Vizcaino .05
298 Alex Ochoa .05
299 Sid Fernandez .05
300 Ken Griffey Jr. 1.50
301 Chris Gomez .05
302 Wendell Magee .05
303 Darren Oliver .05
304 Mel Nieves .05
305 Sammy Sosa 1.00
306 George Arias .05
307 Jack McDowell .05
308 Stan Javier .05
309 Kimera Bartee .05
310 James Baldwin .05
311 Rocky Coppinger .05
312 Keith Lockhart .05
313 C.J. Nitkowski .05
314 Allen Watson .05
315 Darryl Kile .05
316 Amaury Telemaco .05
317 Jason Isringhausen .05
318 Manny Ramirez .75
319 Terry Pendleton .05
320 Tim Salmon .05
321 Eric Karros .05
322 Mark Whiten .05
323 Rick Krivda .05
324 Brett Butler .05
325 Randy Johnson .75
326 Eddie Taubensee .05
327 Mark Leiter .05
328 Kevin Gross .05
329 Ernie Young .05
330 Pat Hentgen .05
331 Rondell White .05
332 Bobby Witt .05
333 Eddie Murray .75
334 Tim Raines .05
335 Jeff Fassero .05
336 Chuck Finley .05
337 Willie Adams .05
338 Chan Ho Park .05
339 Jay Powell .05
340 Ivan Rodriguez .65
341 Jermaine Allensworth .05
342 Jay Payton .05
343 T.J. Mathews .05
344 Tony Batista .05
345 Ed Sprague .05
346 Jeff Kent .05
347 Scott Erickson .05
348 Jeff Suppan .05
349 Pete Schourek .05
350 Kenny Lofton .05
351 Alan Benes .05
352 Fred McGriff .05
353 Charlie O'Brien .05
354 Darren Bragg .05
355 Alex Fernandez .05
356 Al Martin .05
357 Bob Wells .05
358 Chad Mottola .05
359 Devon White .05
360 David Cone .05
361 Bobby Jones .05
362 Scott Sanders .05
363 Karim Garcia .15
364 Kirt Manwaring .05
365 Chili Davis .05
366 Mike Hampton .05
367 Chad Ogea .05
368 Curt Schilling .25
369 Phil Nevin .05
370 Roger Clemens 1.25
371 Willie Greene .05
372 Kenny Rogers .05
373 Jose Rijo .05
374 Bobby Bonilla .05
375 Mike Mussina .35
376 Curtis Pride .05
377 Todd Walker .05
378 Jason Bere .05
379 Heathcliff Slocumb .05
380 Dante Bichette .05
381 Carlos Baerga .05
382 Livan Hernandez .05
383 Jason Schmidt .05
384 Kevin Stocker .05
385 Matt Williams .05
386 Bartolo Colon .05
387 Will Clark .05
388 Dennis Eckersley .65
389 Brooks Kieschnick .05
390 Ryan Klesko .05
391 Mark Carreon .05
392 Tim Worrell .05
393 Dean Palmer .05
394 Wil Cordero .05
395 Javy Lopez .05
396 Rich Aurilia .05
397 Greg Vaughn .05
398 Vinny Castilla .05
399 Jeff Montgomery .05
400 Cal Ripken Jr. 2.00
401 Walt Weiss .05
402 Brad Ausmus .05
403 Ruben Rivera .05
404 Mark Wohlers .05
405 Rick Aguilera .05
406 Tony Clark .05
407 Lyle Mouton .05
408 Bill Pulsipher .05
409 Jose Rosado .05
410 Tony Gwynn 1.00
411 Cecil Fielder .05
412 John Flaherty .05
413 Lenny Dykstra .05
414 Ugueth Urbina .05
415 Brian Jordan .05
416 Bob Abreu .05
417 Craig Paquette .05
418 Sandy Martinez .05
419 Jeff Blauser .05
420 Barry Larkin .05
421 Kevin Seitzer .05
422 Tim Belcher .05
423 Paul Sorrento .05
424 Cal Eldred .05
425 Robin Ventura .05
426 John Olerud .05
427 Bob Wolcott .05
428 Matt Lawton .05
429 Rod Beck .05
430 Shane Reynolds .05
431 Mike James .05
432 Steve Wojciechowski .05
433 Vladimir Guerrero .75
434 Dustin Hermanson .05
435 Marty Cordova .05
436 Marc Newfield .05
437 Todd Stottlemyre .05
438 Jeffrey Hammonds .05
439 Dave Stevens .05
440 Hideo Nomo .35
441 Mark Thompson .05
442 Mark Lewis .05

443 Quinton McCracken .05
444 Cliff Floyd .05
445 Denny Neagle .05
446 John Jaha .05
447 Mike Sweeney .05
448 John Wasdin .05
449 Chad Curtis .05
450 Mo Vaughn .05
451 Donovan Osborne .05
452 Ruben Sierra .05
453 Michael Tucker .05
454 Kurt Abbott .05
455 Andruw Jones .75
456 Shannon Stewart .05
457 Scott Brosius .05
458 Juan Guzman .05
459 Ron Villone .05
460 Moises Alou .05
461 Larry Walker .05
462 Eddie Murray .40
463 Paul Molitor .40
464 Hideo Nomo .20
465 Barry Bonds 1.00
466 Todd Hundley .05
467 Rheal Cormier .05
468 *Jason Conti* .05
469 *Rod Barajas* .05
470 *Jared Sandberg, Cedric Bowers* .05
471 *Paul Wilders, Chie Gunner* .05
472 *Mike Decelle, Marcus McCain* .05
473 Todd Zeile .05
474 Neifi Perez .05
475 Jeromy Burnitz .05
476 Trey Beamon .05
477 *John Patterson, Braden Looper* .15
478 *Danny Peoples, Jake Westbrook* .25
479 Eric Chavez, Adam Eaton .75
480 Joe Lawrence, Pete Tucci .05
481 *Kris Benson, Billy Koch* .25
482 John Nicholson, Andy Prater .05
483 Mark Kotsay, Mark Johnson .25
484 Armando Benitez .05
485 Mike Matheny .05
486 Jeff Reed .05
487 Mark Bellhorn, Russ Johnson, Enrique Wilson .05
488 *Ben Grieve, Richard Hidalgo, Scott Morgan* .05
489 Paul Konerko, Derrek Lee, Ron Wright .50
490 Wes Helms, Bill Mueller, Brad Seitzer .50
491 Jeff Abbott, Shane Monahan, Edgard Velazquez .05
492 Jimmy Anderson, Ron Blazier, Gerald Witasick Jr. .05
493 Darin Blood, Heath Murray, Carl Pavano .05
494 Mark Redman, Mike Villano, Nelson Figueroa .05
495 Checklist .05
496 Checklist .05

Awesome Impact

NM/M
Complete Set (20): 20.00
Common Player: .40
1 Jaime Bluma .40
2 Tony Clark .40
3 Jermaine Dye .40
4 Nomar Garciaparra 4.50
5 Vladimir Guerrero 3.00
6 Todd Hollandsworth .40
7 Derek Jeter 6.00
8 Andruw Jones 3.00
9 Chipper Jones 4.50
10 Jason Kendall .40
11 Brooks Kieschnick .40
12 Alex Ochoa .40
13 Rey Ordonez .40
14 Neifi Perez .40
15 Edgar Renteria .40
16 Mariano Rivera .50
17 Ruben Rivera .40
18 Scott Rolen 2.25
19 Billy Wagner .40
20 Todd Walker .40

Derek Jeter Autograph

NM/M
Derek Jeter 85.00

HOBBY MASTERS

NM/M
Complete Set (20): 30.00
Common Player: .75
1 Ken Griffey Jr. 3.00
2 Cal Ripken Jr. 4.50
3 Greg Maddux 2.25
4 Albert Belle .75
5 Tony Gwynn 2.25
6 Jeff Bagwell 1.50
7 Randy Johnson 1.50
8 Raul Mondesi .75
9 Juan Gonzalez 1.00
10 Kenny Lofton .75
11 Frank Thomas 1.50
12 Mike Piazza 3.00
13 Chipper Jones 2.25
14 Brady Anderson .75
15 Ken Caminiti .75
16 Barry Bonds 4.50
17 Mo Vaughn .75
18 Derek Jeter 4.50
19 Sammy Sosa 2.25
20 Andres Galarraga .75

Inter-League Match Ups

NM/M
Complete Set (14): 16.00
Common Card: .50
Refractors: 1.5X
1 Mark McGwire, Barry Bonds 3.00
2 Tim Salmon, Mike Piazza 2.00
3 Ken Griffey Jr., Dante Bichette 2.00
4 Juan Gonzalez, Tony Gwynn 1.50
5 Frank Thomas, Sammy Sosa 1.50
6 Albert Belle, Barry Larkin .50
7 Johnny Damon, Brian Jordan .75
8 Paul Molitor, Jeff King 1.00
9 John Jaha, Jeff Bagwell 1.00
10 Bernie Williams, Todd Hundley .50
11 Joe Carter, Henry Rodriguez .50
12 Cal Ripken Jr., Gregg Jefferies 3.00
13 Mo Vaughn, Chipper Jones 1.50
14 Travis Fryman, Gary Sheffield .75

Mickey Mantle Reprints

NM/M
Complete Set (16): 40.00
Common Card: 3.00
21 1953 Bowman #44 3.00
22 1953 Bowman #59 5.00
23 1957 Topps #407 3.00
24 1958 Topps #418 3.00
25 1958 Topps #487 3.00
26 1959 Topps #461 3.00
27 1959 Topps #564 3.00
28 1960 Topps #160 3.00
29 1960 Topps #563 3.00
30 1961 Topps #406 3.00
31 1961 Topps #475 3.00
32 1961 Topps #578 3.00
33 1962 Topps #18 3.00
34 1962 Topps #318 3.00
35 1962 Topps #471 3.00
36 1964 Topps #331 3.00

Mickey Mantle Finest

NM/M
Complete Set (16): 70.00
Common Card: 5.00
Refractor: 2.5X
Inserted 1:216
21 1953 Bowman #44 5.00
22 1953 Bowman #59 7.50
23 1957 Topps #407 5.00
24 1958 Topps #418 5.00
25 1958 Topps #487 5.00
26 1959 Topps #461 5.00
27 1959 Topps #564 5.00
28 1960 Topps #160 5.00
29 1960 Topps #563 5.00
30 1961 Topps #406 5.00
31 1961 Topps #475 5.00
32 1961 Topps #578 5.00
33 1962 Topps #18 5.00
34 1962 Topps #318 5.00
35 1962 Topps #471 5.00
36 1964 Topps #331 5.00

1997 TOPPS MICKEY MANTLE CASE INSERTS

NM/M
Complete Set (16): 160.00
Common Card: 12.50
21 1953 Bowman #44 12.50
22 1953 Bowman #59 18.00
23 1957 Topps #407 12.50
24 1958 Topps #418 12.50
25 1958 Topps #487 12.50
26 1959 Topps #461 12.50
27 1959 Topps #564 12.50
28 1960 Topps #160 12.50
29 1960 Topps #563 12.50
30 1961 Topps #406 12.50

WORLD SERIES BATTING FOES
MICKEY MANTLE - HANK AARON

31 1961 Topps #475 12.50
32 1961 Topps #578 12.50
33 1962 Topps #18 12.50
34 1962 Topps #318 12.50
35 1962 Topps #471 12.50
36 1964 Topps #331 12.50

Season's Best

NM/M
Complete Set (25): 12.00
Common Player: .25
1 Tony Gwynn 1.50
2 Frank Thomas 1.25
3 Ellis Burks .25
4 Paul Molitor 1.25
5 Chuck Knoblauch .25
6 Mark McGwire 3.00
7 Brady Anderson .25
8 Ken Griffey Jr. 2.00
9 Albert Belle .25
10 Andres Galarraga .25
11 Andres Galarraga .25
12 Albert Belle .25
13 Juan Gonzalez .75
14 Mo Vaughn .25
15 Rafael Palmeiro 1.00
16 John Smoltz .25
17 Andy Pettitte .50
18 Pat Hentgen .25
19 Mike Mussina .50
20 Andy Benes .25
21 Kenny Lofton .25
22 Tom Goodwin .25
23 Otis Nixon .25
24 Eric Young .25
25 Lance Johnson .25

Sweet Strokes

NM/M
Complete Set (15): 15.00
Common Player: .35
1 Roberto Alomar .50
2 Jeff Bagwell 1.25
3 Albert Belle .35
4 Barry Bonds 3.00
5 Mark Grace .35
6 Ken Griffey Jr. 2.00
7 Tony Gwynn 1.50
8 Chipper Jones 1.50
9 Edgar Martinez .35
10 Mark McGwire 2.50
11 Rafael Palmeiro 1.00
12 Mike Piazza 2.00
13 Gary Sheffield .75
14 Frank Thomas 1.25
15 Mo Vaughn .35

Team Timber

NM/M
Complete Set (16): 24.00
Common Player: .50
1 Ken Griffey Jr. 3.00
2 Ken Caminiti .50
3 Bernie Williams .50
4 Jeff Bagwell 1.50
5 Frank Thomas 1.50
6 Andres Galarraga .50
7 Barry Bonds 5.00
8 Rafael Palmeiro 1.25

9	Brady Anderson	.50
10	Juan Gonzalez	.75
11	Mo Vaughn	.50
12	Mark McGwire	4.00
13	Gary Sheffield	.90
14	Albert Belle	.50
15	Chipper Jones	2.50
16	Mike Piazza	3.00

Willie Mays Reprints

		NM/M
Complete Set (27):		35.00
Common Card:		2.00
Autographed Card:		90.00
1	1951 Bowman #305	4.00
2	1952 Topps #261	2.00
3	1953 Topps #244	2.00
4	1954 Bowman #89	2.00
5	1954 Topps #90	2.00
6	1955 Bowman #184	2.00
7	1955 Topps #194	2.00
8	1956 Topps #130	2.00
9	1957 Topps #10	2.00
10	1958 Topps #5	2.00
11	1959 Topps #50	2.00
12	1960 Topps #200	2.00
13	1960 Topps #564	2.00
14	1961 Topps #150	2.00
15	1961 Topps #579	2.00
16	1962 Topps #300	2.00
17	1963 Topps #300	2.00
18	1964 Topps #150	2.00
19	1965 Topps #250	2.00
20	1966 Topps #1	2.00
21	1967 Topps #200	2.00
22	1968 Topps #50	2.00
23	1969 Topps #190	2.00
24	1970 Topps #600	2.00
25	1971 Topps #600	2.00
26	1972 Topps #49	2.00
27	1973 Topps #305	2.00

Willie Mays Finest

		NM/M
Complete Set (27):		50.00
Common Card:		3.00
Refractor:		2X
Inserted 1:180		
1	1951 Bowman #305	4.00
2	1952 Topps #261	3.00
3	1953 Topps #244	3.00
4	1954 Bowman #89	3.00
5	1954 Topps #90	3.00
6	1955 Bowman #184	3.00
7	1955 Topps #194	3.00
8	1956 Topps #130	3.00
9	1957 Topps #10	3.00
10	1958 Topps #5	3.00
11	1959 Topps #50	3.00
12	1960 Topps #200	3.00
13	1960 Topps #564	3.00
14	1961 Topps #150	3.00
15	1961 Topps #579	3.00
16	1962 Topps #300	3.00
17	1963 Topps #300	3.00
18	1964 Topps #150	3.00
19	1965 Topps #250	3.00
20	1966 Topps #1	3.00
21	1967 Topps #200	3.00
22	1968 Topps #50	3.00
23	1969 Topps #190	3.00
24	1970 Topps #600	3.00
25	1971 Topps #600	3.00
26	1972 Topps #49	3.00
27	1973 Topps #305	3.00

Willie Mays Reprint Autographs

		NM/M
Common Card:		90.00
1	1951 Bowman #305	125.00
2	1952 Topps #261	90.00
3	1953 Topps #244	90.00
6	1955 Bowman #184	90.00
7	1955 Topps #194	90.00
9	1957 Topps #10	90.00
10	1958 Topps #5	90.00
12	1960 Topps #200	90.00
13	1960 Topps #564	90.00
14	1961 Topps #150	90.00
15	1961 Topps #579	90.00
17	1963 Topps #300	90.00
18	1964 Topps #150	90.00
19	1965 Topps #250	90.00
20	1966 Topps #1	90.00
23	1969 Topps #190	90.00
24	1970 Topps #600	90.00
26	1972 Topps #49	90.00
27	1973 Topps #305	90.00

1997 TOPPS CHROME

		NM/M
Complete Set (165):		35.00
Common Player:		.10
Refractors:		2X
Pack (4):		1.50
Wax Box (24):		25.00
1	Barry Bonds	3.00
2	Jose Valentin	.10
3	Brady Anderson	.10
4	Wade Boggs	1.50
5	Andres Galarraga	.10
6	Rusty Greer	.10
7	Derek Jeter	3.00
8	Ricky Bottalico	.10
9	Mike Piazza	2.00
10	Garret Anderson	.10
11	Jeff King	.10
12	Kevin Appier	.10
13	Mark Grace	.10
14	Jeff D'Amico	.10
15	Jay Buhner	.10
16	Hal Morris	.10
17	Harold Baines	.10
18	Jeff Cirillo	.10
19	Tom Glavine	.35
20	Andy Pettitte	.35
21	Mark McGwire	2.50
22	Chuck Knoblauch	.10
23	Raul Mondesi	.10
24	Albert Belle	.10
25	Trevor Hoffman	.10
26	Eric Young	.10
27	Brian McRae	.10
28	Jim Edmonds	.10
29	Robb Nen	.10
30	Reggie Sanders	.10
31	Mike Lansing	.10
32	Craig Biggio	.10
33	Ray Lankford	.10
34	Charles Nagy	.10
35	Paul Wilson	.10
36	John Wetteland	.10
37	Derek Bell	.10
38	Edgar Martinez	.10
39	Rickey Henderson	1.00
40	Jim Thome	.75
41	Frank Thomas	1.00
42	Jackie Robinson (Tribute)	2.00
43	Terry Steinbach	.10
44	Kevin Brown	.10
45	Joey Hamilton	.10
46	Travis Fryman	.10
47	Juan Gonzalez	.50
48	Ron Gant	.10
49	Greg Maddux	1.50
50	Wally Joyner	.10
51	John Valentin	.10
42	Bret Boone	.10
53	Paul Molitor	1.00
54	Rafael Palmeiro	.75
55	Todd Hundley	.10
56	Ellis Burks	.10
57	Bernie Williams	.10
58	Roberto Alomar	.25
59	Jose Mesa	.10
60	Troy Percival	.10
61	John Smoltz	.10
62	Jeff Conine	.10
63	Bernard Gilkey	.10
64	Mickey Tettleton	.10
65	Justin Thompson	.10
66	Tony Phillips	.10
67	Ryne Sandberg	1.50
68	Geronimo Berroa	.10
69	Todd Hollandsworth	.10
70	Rey Ordonez	.10
71	Marquis Grissom	.10
72	Tino Martinez	.10
73	Steve Finley	.10
74	Andy Benes	.10
75	Jason Kendall	.10
76	Johnny Damon	.35
77	Jason Giambi	.50
78	Henry Rodriguez	.10
79	Edgar Renteria	.10
80	Ray Durham	.10
81	Gregg Jefferies	.10
82	Roberto Hernandez	.10
83	Joe Carter	.10
84	Jermaine Dye	.10
85	Julio Franco	.10
86	David Justice	.10
87	Jose Canseco	.50
88	Paul O'Neill	.10
89	Mariano Rivera	.15
90	Bobby Higginson	.10
91	Mark Grudzielanek	.10
92	Lance Johnson	.10
93	Ken Caminiti	.10
94	Gary Sheffield	.50
95	Luis Castillo	.10
96	Scott Rolen	.75
97	Chipper Jones	1.50
98	Darryl Strawberry	.10
99	Nomar Garciaparra	1.50
100	Jeff Bagwell	1.00
101	Ken Griffey Jr.	2.00
102	Sammy Sosa	1.50
103	Jack McDowell	.10
104	James Baldwin	.10
105	Rocky Coppinger	.10
106	Manny Ramirez	1.00
107	Tim Salmon	.10
108	Eric Karros	.10
109	Brett Butler	.10
110	Randy Johnson	1.00
111	Pat Hentgen	.10
112	Rondell White	.10
113	Eddie Murray	1.00
114	Ivan Rodriguez	.75
115	Jermaine Allensworth	.10
116	Ed Sprague	.10
117	Kenny Lofton	.10
118	Alan Benes	.10
119	Fred McGriff	.10
120	Alex Fernandez	.10
121	Al Martin	.10
122	Devon White	.10
123	David Cone	.10
124	Karim Garcia	.25
125	Chili Davis	.10
126	Roger Clemens	1.75
127	Bobby Bonilla	.10
128	Mike Mussina	.50
129	Todd Walker	.10
130	Dante Bichette	.10
131	Carlos Baerga	.10
132	Matt Williams	.10
133	Will Clark	.10
134	Dennis Eckersley	.75
135	Ryan Klesko	.10
136	Dean Palmer	.10
137	Javy Lopez	.10
138	Greg Vaughn	.10
139	Vinny Castilla	.10
140	Cal Ripken Jr.	3.00
141	Ruben Rivera	.10
142	Mark Wohlers	.10
143	Tony Clark	.10
144	Jose Rosado	.10
145	Tony Gwynn	1.50
146	Cecil Fielder	.10
147	Brian Jordan	.10
148	Bob Abreu	.10
149	Barry Larkin	.10
150	Robin Ventura	.10
151	John Olerud	.10
152	Rod Beck	.10
153	Vladimir Guerrero	1.00
154	Marty Cordova	.10
155	Todd Stottlemyre	.10
156	Hideo Nomo	.50
157	Denny Neagle	.10
158	John Jaha	.10
159	Mo Vaughn	.10
160	Andruw Jones	1.00
161	Moises Alou	.10
162	Larry Walker	.10
163	Eddie Murray (Season Highlights)	.75
164	Paul Molitor (Season Highlights)	.75
165	Checklist	.10

All-Stars

		NM/M
Complete Set (22):		25.00
Common Player:		.75
Refractors:		1.5X
1	Ivan Rodriguez	1.50
2	Todd Hundley	.75
3	Frank Thomas	2.00
4	Andres Galarraga	.75
5	Chuck Knoblauch	.75
6	Eric Young	.75
7	Jim Thome	1.50
8	Chipper Jones	3.00
9	Cal Ripken Jr.	6.00
10	Barry Larkin	.75
11	Albert Belle	.75
12	Barry Bonds	6.00
13	Ken Griffey Jr.	4.00
14	Ellis Burks	.75
15	Juan Gonzalez	1.00
16	Gary Sheffield	1.25
17	Andy Pettitte	1.00
18	Tom Glavine	1.00
19	Pat Hentgen	.75
20	John Smoltz	.75
21	Roberto Hernandez	.75
22	Mark Wohlers	.75

Diamond Duos

		NM/M
Complete Set (10):		17.50
Common Player:		.50
Refractors:		1.5X
1	Chipper Jones, Andruw Jones	2.00
2	Derek Jeter, Bernie Williams	4.00
3	Ken Griffey Jr., Jay Buhner	2.50
4	Kenny Lofton, Manny Ramirez	1.50

5	Jeff Bagwell, Craig Biggio	1.50
6	Juan Gonzalez, Ivan Rodriguez	1.25
7	Cal Ripken Jr., Brady Anderson	4.00
8	Mike Piazza, Hideo Nomo	2.50
9	Andres Galarraga, Dante Bichette	.50
10	Frank Thomas, Albert Belle	1.50

Jumbos

		NM/M
Complete Set (6):		10.00
Common Player:		.75
9	Mike Piazza	2.00
94	Gary Sheffield	.75
97	Chipper Jones	1.50
101	Ken Griffey Jr.	2.00
102	Sammy Sosa	1.50
140	Cal Ripken Jr.	3.00

Season's Best

		NM/M
Complete Set (25):		17.50
Common Player:		.50
Refractors:		1.5X
1	Tony Gwynn	2.00
2	Frank Thomas	1.50
3	Ellis Burks	.50
4	Paul Molitor	1.50
5	Chuck Knoblauch	.50
6	Mark McGwire	4.00
7	Brady Anderson	.50
8	Ken Griffey Jr.	3.00
9	Albert Belle	.50
10	Andres Galarraga	.50
11	Andres Galarraga	.50
12	Albert Belle	.50
13	Juan Gonzalez	.75
14	Mo Vaughn	.50
15	Rafael Palmeiro	1.25
16	John Smoltz	.50
17	Andy Pettitte	.75
18	Pat Hentgen	.50
19	Mike Mussina	.75
20	Andy Benes	.50
21	Kenny Lofton	.50
22	Tom Goodwin	.50
23	Otis Nixon	.50
24	Eric Young	.50
25	Lance Johnson	.50

1997 TOPPS GALLERY

		NM/M
Complete Set (180):		20.00
Common Player:		.10
Pack (8):		1.50
Wax Box (24):		25.00
1	Paul Molitor	.75
2	Devon White	.10
3	Andres Galarraga	.10
4	Cal Ripken Jr.	3.00
5	Tony Gwynn	1.50
6	Mike Stanley	.10
7	Orel Hershiser	.10
8	Jose Canseco	.50
9	Chili Davis	.10
10	Harold Baines	.10
11	Rickey Henderson	.75
12	Darryl Strawberry	.10
13	Todd Worrell	.10
14	Cecil Fielder	.10
15	Gary Gaetti	.10
16	Bobby Bonilla	.10
17	Will Clark	.10
18	Kevin Brown	.10
19	Tom Glavine	.35
20	Wade Boggs	1.50
21	Edgar Martinez	.10
22	Lance Johnson	.10
23	Gregg Jefferies	.10
24	Bip Roberts	.10
25	Tony Phillips	.10
26	Greg Maddux	1.50
27	Mickey Tettleton	.10
28	Terry Steinbach	.10
29	Ryne Sandberg	1.50
30	Wally Joyner	.10
31	Joe Carter	.10
32	Ellis Burks	.10
33	Fred McGriff	.10
34	Barry Larkin	.10
35	John Franco	.10
36	Rafael Palmeiro	.65
37	Mark McGwire	2.50
38	Ken Caminiti	.10
39	David Cone	.10
40	Julio Franco	.10
41	Roger Clemens	1.75
42	Barry Bonds	3.00
43	Dennis Eckersley	.65
44	Eddie Murray	.75
45	Paul O'Neill	.10
46	Craig Biggio	.10
47	Roberto Alomar	.20
48	Mark Grace	.10
49	Matt Williams	.10
50	Jay Buhner	.10
51	John Smoltz	.10
52	Randy Johnson	.75
53	Ramon Martinez	.10
54	Curt Schilling	.35
55	Gary Sheffield	.50
56	Jack McDowell	.10
57	Brady Anderson	.10
58	Dante Bichette	.10
59	Ron Gant	.10
60	Alex Fernandez	.10
61	Moises Alou	.10
62	Travis Fryman	.10
63	Dean Palmer	.10
64	Todd Hundley	.10
65	Jeff Brantley	.10
66	Bernard Gilkey	.10
67	Geronimo Berroa	.10
68	John Wetteland	.10
69	Robin Ventura	.10
70	Ray Lankford	.10
71	Kevin Appier	.10
72	Larry Walker	.10
73	Juan Gonzalez	.40
74	Jeff King	.10
75	Greg Vaughn	.10
76	Steve Finley	.10
77	Brian McRae	.10
78	Paul Sorrento	.10
79	Ken Griffey Jr.	2.00
80	Omar Vizquel	.10
81	Jose Mesa	.10
82	Albert Belle	.10
83	Glenallen Hill	.10
84	Sammy Sosa	1.50
85	Andy Benes	.10
86	David Justice	.10
87	Marquis Grissom	.10
88	John Olerud	.10
89	Tino Martinez	.10
90	Frank Thomas	.75
91	Raul Mondesi	.10
92	Steve Trachsel	.10
93	Jim Edmonds	.10
94	Rusty Greer	.10
95	Joey Hamilton	.10
96	Ismael Valdes	.10
97	Dave Nilsson	.10
98	John Jaha	.10
99	Alex Gonzalez	.10
100	Javy Lopez	.10
101	Ryan Klesko	.10
102	Tim Salmon	.10
103	Bernie Williams	.10
104	Roberto Hernandez	.10
105	Chuck Knoblauch	.10
106	Mike Lansing	.10
107	Vinny Castilla	.10
108	Reggie Sanders	.10
109	Mo Vaughn	.10
110	Rondell White	.10
111	Ivan Rodriguez	.65
112	Mike Mussina	.40
113	Carlos Baerga	.10
114	Jeff Conine	.10
115	Jim Thome	.65
116	Manny Ramirez	.75
117	Kenny Lofton	.10
118	Wilson Alvarez	.10
119	Eric Karros	.10
120	Robb Nen	.10
121	Mark Wohlers	.10
122	Ed Sprague	.10
123	Pat Hentgen	.10
124	Juan Guzman	.10
125	Derek Bell	.10
126	Jeff Bagwell	.75
127	Eric Young	.10
128	John Valentin	.10
129	Al Martin (photo actually Javy Lopez)	.10
130	Trevor Hoffman	.10
131	Henry Rodriguez	.10
132	Pedro Martinez	.75
133	Mike Piazza	2.00
134	Brian Jordan	.10
135	Jose Valentin	.10
136	Jeff Cirillo	.10
137	Chipper Jones	1.50
138	Ricky Bottalico	.10
139	Hideo Nomo	.40
140	Troy Percival	.10
141	Rey Ordonez	.10
142	Edgar Renteria	.10
143	Luis Castillo	.10
144	Vladimir Guerrero	.75
145	Jeff D'Amico	.10
146	Andruw Jones	.75
147	Darin Erstad	.25
148	Bob Abreu	.10
149	Carlos Delgado	.45
150	Jamey Wright	.10
151	Nomar Garciaparra	1.50
152	Jason Kendall	.10
153	Jermaine Allensworth	.10
154	Scott Rolen	.65
155	Rocky Coppinger	.10
156	Paul Wilson	.10
157	Garret Anderson	.10
158	Mariano Rivera	.15
159	Ruben Rivera	.10
160	Andy Pettitte	.35
161	Derek Jeter	3.00
162	Neifi Perez	.10
163	Ray Durham	.10
164	James Baldwin	.10
165	Marty Cordova	.10
166	Tony Clark	.10
167	Michael Tucker	.10
168	Mike Sweeney	.10
169	Johnny Damon	.25
170	Jermaine Dye	.10
171	Alex Ochoa	.10
172	Jason Isringhausen	.10
173	Mark Grudzielanek	.10
174	Jose Rosado	.10
175	Todd Hollandsworth	.10
176	Alan Benes	.10
177	Jason Giambi	.45
178	Billy Wagner	.10
179	Justin Thompson	.10
180	Todd Walker	.10

Gallery Players Private Issue

	NM/M
Common Player:	1.00
Stars:	5X

(See 1997 Topps/Gallery for checklist and base card values.)

Gallery of Heroes

		NM/M
Complete Set (10):		30.00
Common Player:		1.50
1	Derek Jeter	6.00
2	Chipper Jones	3.00
3	Frank Thomas	2.50
4	Ken Griffey Jr.	4.00
5	Cal Ripken Jr.	6.00
6	Mark McGwire	5.00
7	Mike Piazza	4.00
8	Jeff Bagwell	2.50
9	Tony Gwynn	3.00
10	Mo Vaughn	1.50

Peter Max

		NM/M
Complete Set (10):		60.00
Common Player:		2.00
Peter Max Autographed:		100.00
1	Derek Jeter	10.00
2	Albert Belle	3.00
3	Ken Caminiti	3.00
4	Chipper Jones	6.00
5	Ken Griffey Jr.	7.50
6	Frank Thomas	5.00
7	Cal Ripken Jr.	10.00
8	Mark McGwire	9.00
9	Barry Bonds	10.00
10	Mike Piazza	7.50

Photo Gallery

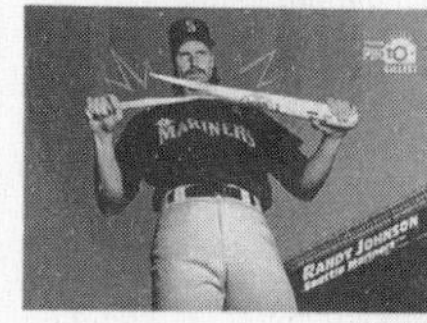

		NM/M
Complete Set (16):		15.00
Common Player:		.50
1	World Series	.50
2	Paul Molitor	1.00
3	Eddie Murray	1.00
4	Ken Griffey Jr.	2.50
5	Chipper Jones	1.50
6	Derek Jeter	3.50
7	Frank Thomas	1.00
8	Mark McGwire	3.00
9	Kenny Lofton	.50
10	Gary Sheffield	.65
11	Mike Piazza	2.50
12	Vinny Castilla	.50
13	Andres Galarraga	.50
14	Andy Pettitte	.50
15	Robin Ventura	.50
16	Barry Larkin	.50

1997 TOPPS STARS

		NM/M
Complete Set (125):		30.00
Common Player:		.10
Pack (7):		3.00
Wax Box (24):		65.00
1	Larry Walker	.10
2	Tino Martinez	.10
3	Cal Ripken Jr.	3.00
4	Ken Griffey Jr.	2.00
5	Chipper Jones	1.50
6	David Justice	.10
7	Mike Piazza	2.00
8	Jeff Bagwell	1.00
9	Ron Gant	.10
10	Sammy Sosa	2.00
11	Tony Gwynn	1.50
12	Carlos Baerga	.10
13	Frank Thomas	1.00
14	Moises Alou	.10
15	Barry Larkin	.10
16	Ivan Rodriguez	.75
17	Greg Maddux	1.50
18	Jim Edmonds	.10
19	Jose Canseco	.50

20 Rafael Palmeiro .75
21 Paul Molitor 1.00
22 Kevin Appier .10
23 Raul Mondesi .10
24 Lance Johnson .10
25 Edgar Martinez .10
26 Andres Galarraga .10
27 Mo Vaughn .10
28 Ken Caminiti .10
29 Cecil Fielder .10
30 Harold Baines .10
31 Roberto Alomar .25
32 Shawn Estes .10
33 Tom Glavine .35
34 Dennis Eckersley .75
35 Manny Ramirez 1.00
36 John Olerud .10
37 Juan Gonzalez .50
38 Chuck Knoblauch .10
39 Albert Belle .10
40 Vinny Castilla .10
41 John Smoltz .10
42 Barry Bonds 3.00
43 Randy Johnson 1.00
44 Brady Anderson .10
45 Jeff Blauser .10
46 Craig Biggio .10
47 Jeff Conine .10
48 Marquis Grissom .10
49 Mark Grace .10
50 Roger Clemens 1.75
51 Mark McGwire 2.50
52 Fred McGriff .10
53 Gary Sheffield .50
54 Bobby Jones .10
55 Eric Young .10
56 Robin Ventura .10
57 Wade Boggs 1.50
58 Joe Carter .10
59 Ryne Sandberg 1.50
60 Matt Williams .10
61 Todd Hundley .10
62 Dante Bichette .10
63 Chili Davis .10
64 Kenny Lofton .10
65 Jay Buhner .10
66 Will Clark .10
67 Travis Fryman .10
68 Pat Hentgen .10
69 Ellis Burks .10
70 Mike Mussina .40
71 Hideo Nomo .50
72 Sandy Alomar .10
73 Bobby Bonilla .10
74 Rickey Henderson 1.00
75 David Cone .10
76 Terry Steinbach .10
77 Pedro Martinez 1.00
78 Jim Thome .75
79 Rod Beck .10
80 Randy Myers .10
81 Charles Nagy .10
82 Mark Wohlers .10
83 Paul O'Neill .10
84 Curt Schilling .35
85 Joey Cora .10
86 John Franco .10
87 Kevin Brown .10
88 Benito Santiago .10
89 Ray Lankford .10
90 Bernie Williams .10
91 Jason Dickson .10
92 Jeff Cirillo .10
93 Nomar Garciaparra 2.00
94 Mariano Rivera .15
95 Javy Lopez .10
96 *Tony Womack* .25
97 Jose Rosado .10
98 Denny Neagle .10
99 Darryl Kile .10
100 Justin Thompson .10
101 Juan Encarnacion .10
102 Brad Fullmer .10
103 *Kris Benson* .75
104 Todd Helton 1.00
105 Paul Konerko .10
106 *Travis Lee* 1.00
107 Todd Greene .10
108 *Mark Kotsay* .50
109 Carl Pavano .10
110 *Kerry Wood* 4.50
111 *Jason Romano* .10
112 *Geoff Goetz* .10
113 *Scott Hodges* .10
114 *Aaron Akin* .10
115 *Vernon Wells* 2.00
116 *Chris Stowe* .10
117 *Brett Caradonna* .10
118 *Adam Kennedy* 1.00
119 *Jayson Werth* .10
120 *Glenn Davis* .10
121 *Troy Cameron* .10
122 *J.J. Davis* .10
123 *Jason Dellaero* .10
124 *Jason Standridge* .10
125 *Lance Berkman* 2.00

Always Mint

NM/M
Complete Set (125): 250.00
Common Player: .50
Stars/Rookies: 8X
(See 1997 Topps Stars for checklist and base card values.)

All-Star Memories

NM/M
Complete Set (10): 20.00
Common Player: 1.00
1 Cal Ripken Jr. 6.00
2 Jeff Conine 1.00
3 Mike Piazza 4.00
4 Randy Johnson 2.00
5 Ken Griffey Jr. 4.00
6 Fred McGriff 1.00
7 Moises Alou 1.00
8 Hideo Nomo 1.25
9 Larry Walker 1.00
10 Sandy Alomar 1.00

Autographed Rookie Reprints

NM/M
Common Player: 15.00
(1) Luis Aparicio 20.00
(3) Jim Bunning 30.00
(4) Bob Feller 35.00
(5) Rollie Fingers 15.00
(6) Monte Irvin 15.00
(7) Al Kaline 30.00
(8) Ralph Kiner 25.00
(9) Eddie Mathews 75.00
(10) Hal Newhouser 40.00
(11) Gaylord Perry 15.00
(12) Robin Roberts 30.00
(13) Brooks Robinson 40.00
(14) Enos Slaughter 30.00
(15) Earl Weaver 20.00

Future All-Stars

NM/M
Complete Set (15): 17.50
Common Player: .75
1 Derek Jeter 4.00
2 Andruw Jones 2.50
3 Vladimir Guerrero 3.00
4 Scott Rolen 2.50
5 Jose Guillen .75
6 Jose Cruz, Jr. .75
7 Darin Erstad 2.50
8 Tony Clark .75
9 Scott Spiezio .75
10 Kevin Orie .75
11 Calvin Reese .75
12 Billy Wagner .75
13 Matt Morris .75
14 Jeremi Gonzalez .75
15 Hideki Irabu .75

Rookie Reprints

NM/M
Complete Set (15): 25.00
Common Player: 2.00
(1) Luis Aparicio 2.00
(2) Richie Ashburn 2.00
(3) Jim Bunning 2.00
(4) Bob Feller 2.00
(5) Rollie Fingers 2.00
(6) Monte Irvin 2.00

(7) Al Kaline 3.00
(8) Ralph Kiner 2.00
(9) Eddie Mathews 3.00
(10) Hal Newhouser 2.00
(11) Gaylord Perry 2.00
(12) Robin Roberts 2.00
(13) Brooks Robinson 3.00
(14) Enos Slaughter 2.00
(15) Earl Weaver 2.00

1997 ALL-STARS

NM/M
Complete Set (20): 60.00
Common Player: 1.50
1 Greg Maddux 6.00
2 Randy Johnson 4.50
3 Tino Martinez 1.50
4 Jeff Bagwell 4.50
5 Ivan Rodriguez 3.50
6 Mike Piazza 7.50
7 Cal Ripken Jr. 12.00
8 Ken Caminiti 1.50
9 Tony Gwynn 6.00
10 Edgar Martinez 1.50
11 Craig Biggio 1.50
12 Roberto Alomar 2.00
13 Larry Walker 1.50
14 Brady Anderson 1.50
15 Barry Bonds 12.00
16 Ken Griffey Jr. 7.50
17 Ray Lankford 1.50
18 Paul O'Neill 1.50
19 Jeff Blauser 1.50
20 Sandy Alomar 1.50

1998 TOPPS

NM/M
Unopened Fact. Set (511): 85.00
Complete Set (503): 40.00
Common Player: .05
Series 1 or 2 Pack (11): 1.00
Series 1 or 2 Wax Box (36): 25.00
1 Tony Gwynn 1.00
2 Larry Walker .05
3 Billy Wagner .05
4 Denny Neagle .05
5 Vladimir Guerrero .75
6 Kevin Brown .05
7 NOT ISSUED
8 Mariano Rivera .10
9 Tony Clark .05
10 Deion Sanders .05
11 Francisco Cordova .05
12 Matt Williams .05
13 Carlos Baerga .05
14 Mo Vaughn .05
15 Bobby Witt .05
16 Matt Stairs .05
17 Chan Ho Park .05
18 Mike Bordick .05
19 Michael Tucker .05
20 Frank Thomas .75
21 Roberto Clemente 1.50
22 Dmitri Young .05
23 Steve Trachsel .05
24 Jeff Kent .05
25 Scott Rolen .50
26 John Thomson .05
27 Joe Vitiello .05
28 Eddie Guardado .05
29 Charlie Hayes .05
30 Juan Gonzalez .40
31 Garret Anderson .05
32 John Jaha .05
33 Omar Vizquel .05
34 Brian Hunter .05
35 Jeff Bagwell .75
36 Mark Lemke .05
37 Doug Glanville .05
38 Dan Wilson .05
39 Steve Cooke .05
40 Chili Davis .05
41 Mike Cameron .05
42 F.P. Santangelo .05
43 Brad Ausmus .05
44 Gary DiSarcina .05
45 Pat Hentgen .05
46 Wilton Guerrero .05
47 Devon White .05
48 Danny Patterson .05
49 Pat Meares .05
50 Rafael Palmeiro .65
51 Mark Gardner .05
52 Jeff Blauser .05
53 Dave Hollins .05
54 Carlos Garcia .05
55 Ben McDonald .05
56 John Mabry .05
57 Trevor Hoffman .05
58 Tony Fernandez .05
59 Rich Loiselle .05
60 Mark Leiter .05
61 Pat Kelly .05
62 John Flaherty .05
63 Roger Bailey .05
64 Tom Gordon .05
65 Ryan Klesko .05
66 Darryl Hamilton .05
67 Jim Eisenreich .05
68 Butch Huskey .05
69 Mark Grudzielanek .05
70 Marquis Grissom .05
71 Mark McLemore .05
72 Gary Gaetti .05
73 Greg Gagne .05
74 Lyle Mouton .05
75 Jim Edmonds .05
76 Shawn Green .25
77 Greg Vaughn .05
78 Terry Adams .05
79 *Kevin Polcovich* .05
80 Troy O'Leary .05
81 Jeff Shaw .05
82 Rich Becker .05
83 David Wells .05
84 Steve Karsay .05
85 Charles Nagy .05
86 B.J. Surhoff .05
87 Jamey Wright .05
88 James Baldwin .05
89 Edgardo Alfonzo .05
90 Jay Buhner .05
91 Brady Anderson .05
92 Scott Servais .05
93 Edgar Renteria .05
94 Mike Lieberthal .05
95 Rick Aguilera .05
96 Walt Weiss .05
97 Deivi Cruz .05
98 Kurt Abbott .05
99 Henry Rodriguez .05
100 Mike Piazza 1.25
101 Bill Taylor .05
102 Todd Zeile .05
103 Rey Ordonez .05
104 Willie Greene .05
105 Tony Womack .05
106 Mike Sweeney .05
107 Jeffrey Hammonds .05
108 Kevin Orie .05
109 Alex Gonzalez .05
110 Jose Canseco .50
111 Paul Sorrento .05
112 Joey Hamilton .05
113 Brad Radke .05
114 Steve Avery .05
115 Esteban Loaiza .05
116 Stan Javier .05

No.	Player	Value
117	Chris Gomez	.05
118	Royce Clayton	.05
119	Orlando Merced	.05
120	Kevin Appier	.05
121	Mel Nieves	.05
122	Joe Girardi	.05
123	Rico Brogna	.05
124	Kent Mercker	.05
125	Manny Ramirez	.75
126	Jeromy Burnitz	.05
127	Kevin Foster	.05
128	Matt Morris	.05
129	Jason Dickson	.05
130	Tom Glavine	.25
131	Wally Joyner	.05
132	Rick Reed	.05
133	Todd Jones	.05
134	Dave Martinez	.05
135	Sandy Alomar	.05
136	Mike Lansing	.05
137	Sean Berry	.05
138	Doug Jones	.05
139	Todd Stottlemyre	.05
140	Jay Bell	.05
141	Jaime Navarro	.05
142	Chris Hoiles	.05
143	Joey Cora	.05
144	Scott Spiezio	.05
145	Joe Carter	.05
146	Jose Guillen	.05
147	Damion Easley	.05
148	Lee Stevens	.05
149	Alex Fernandez	.05
150	Randy Johnson	.75
151	J.T. Snow	.05
152	Chuck Finley	.05
153	Bernard Gilkey	.05
154	David Segui	.05
155	Dante Bichette	.05
156	Kevin Stocker	.05
157	Carl Everett	.05
158	Jose Valentin	.05
159	Pokey Reese	.05
160	Derek Jeter	2.00
161	Roger Pavlik	.05
162	Mark Wohlers	.05
163	Ricky Bottalico	.05
164	Ozzie Guillen	.05
165	Mike Mussina	.50
166	Gary Sheffield	.50
167	Hideo Nomo	.40
168	Mark Grace	.05
169	Aaron Sele	.05
170	Darryl Kile	.05
171	Shawn Estes	.05
172	Vinny Castilla	.05
173	Ron Coomer	.05
174	Jose Rosado	.05
175	Kenny Lofton	.05
176	Jason Giambi	.50
177	Hal Morris	.05
178	Darren Bragg	.05
179	Orel Hershiser	.05
180	Ray Lankford	.05
181	Hideki Irabu	.05
182	Kevin Young	.05
183	Javy Lopez	.05
184	Jeff Montgomery	.05
185	Mike Holtz	.05
186	George Williams	.05
187	Cal Eldred	.05
188	Tom Candiotti	.05
189	Glenallen Hill	.05
190	Brian Giles	.05
191	Dave Mlicki	.05
192	Garrett Stephenson	.05
193	Jeff Frye	.05
194	Joe Oliver	.05
195	Bob Hamelin	.05
196	Luis Sojo	.05
197	LaTroy Hawkins	.05
198	Kevin Elster	.05
199	Jeff Reed	.05
200	Dennis Eckersley	.65
201	Bill Mueller	.05
202	Russ Davis	.05
203	Armando Benitez	.05
204	Quilvio Veras	.05
205	Tim Naehring	.05
206	Quinton McCracken	.05
207	Raul Casanova	.05
208	Matt Lawton	.05
209	Luis Alicea	.05
210	Luis Gonzalez	.05
211	Allen Watson	.05
212	Gerald Williams	.05
213	David Bell	.05
214	Todd Hollandsworth	.05
215	Wade Boggs	1.00
216	Jose Mesa	.05
217	Jamie Moyer	.05
218	Darren Daulton	.05
219	Mickey Morandini	.05
220	Rusty Greer	.05
221	Jim Bullinger	.05
222	Jose Offerman	.05
223	Matt Karchner	.05
224	Woody Williams	.05
225	Mark Loretta	.05
226	Mike Hampton	.05
227	Willie Adams	.05
228	Scott Hatteberg	.05
229	Rich Amaral	.05
230	Terry Steinbach	.05
231	Glendon Rusch	.05
232	Bret Boone	.05
233	Robert Person	.05
234	Jose Hernandez	.05
235	Doug Drabek	.05
236	Jason McDonald	.05
237	Chris Widger	.05
238	*Tom Martin*	.05
239	Dave Burba	.05
240	Pete Rose II	.05
241	Bobby Ayala	.05
242	Tim Wakefield	.05
243	Dennis Springer	.05
244	Tim Belcher	.05
245	Jon Garland, Geoff Goetz	.05
246	Glenn Davis, Lance Berkman	.05
247	Vernon Wells, Aaron Akin	.10
248	Adam Kennedy, Jason Romano	.10
249	Jason Dellaero, Troy Cameron	.05
250	*Alex Sanchez, Jared Sandberg*	.10
251	Pablo Ortega, Jim Manias	.05
252	*Jason Conti, Mike Stoner*	.10
253	John Patterson, Larry Rodriguez	.05
254	Adrian Beltre, Ryan Minor, Aaron Boone	.15
255	Ben Grieve, Brian Buchanan, Dermal Brown	.05
256	Carl Pavano, Kerry Wood, Gil Meche	.15
257	David Ortiz, Daryle Ward, Richie Sexson	.50
258	Randy Winn, Juan Encarnacion, Andrew Vessel	.10
259	Kris Benson, Travis Smith, Courtney Duncan	.05
260	*Chad Hermansen, Brent Butler, Warren Morris*	.10
261	Ben Davis, Elieser Marrero, Ramon Hernandez	.05
262	Eric Chavez, Russell Branyan, Russ Johnson	.20
263	*Todd Dunwoody, John Barnes, Ryan Jackson*	.10
264	*Matt Clement, Roy Halladay, Brian Fuentes*	.05
265	Randy Johnson	.15
266	Kevin Brown	.05
267	Ricardo Rincon, Francisco Cordova	.05
268	Nomar Garciaparra	.50
269	Tino Martinez	.05
270	Chuck Knoblauch	.05
271	Pedro Martinez	.40
272	Denny Neagle	.05
273	Juan Gonzalez	.20
274	Andres Galarraga	.05
275	Checklist	.05
276	Checklist	.05
277	Moises Alou	.05
278	Sandy Alomar	.05
279	Gary Sheffield	.05
280	Matt Williams	.05
281	Livan Hernandez	.05
282	Chad Ogea	.05
283	Marlins Win	.05
284	Tino Martinez	.05
285	Roberto Alomar	.20
286	Jeff King	.05
287	Brian Jordan	.05
288	Darin Erstad	.15
289	Ken Caminiti	.05
290	Jim Thome	.60
291	Paul Molitor	.75
292	Ivan Rodriguez	.65
293	Bernie Williams	.05
294	Todd Hundley	.05
295	Andres Galarraga	.05
296	Greg Maddux	1.00
297	Edgar Martinez	.05
298	Ron Gant	.05
299	Derek Bell	.05
300	Roger Clemens	1.00
301	Rondell White	.05
302	Barry Larkin	.05
303	Robin Ventura	.05
304	Jason Kendall	.05
305	Chipper Jones	1.00
306	John Franco	.05
307	Sammy Sosa	1.00
308	Troy Percival	.05
309	Chuck Knoblauch	.05
310	Ellis Burks	.05
311	Al Martin	.05
312	Tim Salmon	.05
313	Moises Alou	.05
314	Lance Johnson	.05
315	Justin Thompson	.05
316	Will Clark	.05
317	Barry Bonds	2.00
318	Craig Biggio	.05
319	John Smoltz	.05
320	Cal Ripken Jr.	2.00
321	Ken Griffey Jr.	1.25
322	Paul O'Neill	.05
323	Todd Helton	.65
324	John Olerud	.05
325	Mark McGwire	1.50
326	Jose Cruz Jr.	.05
327	Jeff Cirillo	.05
328	Dean Palmer	.05
329	John Wetteland	.05
330	Steve Finley	.05
331	Albert Belle	.05
332	Curt Schilling	.25
333	Raul Mondesi	.05
334	Andruw Jones	.75
335	Nomar Garciaparra	1.00
336	David Justice	.05
337	Andy Pettitte	.25
338	Pedro Martinez	.75
339	Travis Miller	.05
340	Chris Stynes	.05
341	Gregg Jefferies	.05
342	Jeff Fassero	.05
343	Craig Counsell	.05
344	Wilson Alvarez	.05
345	Bip Roberts	.05
346	Kelvim Escobar	.05
347	Mark Bellhorn	.05
348	*Cory Lidle*	.05
349	Fred McGriff	.05
350	Chuck Carr	.05
351	Bob Abreu	.05
352	Juan Guzman	.05
353	Fernando Vina	.05
354	Andy Benes	.05
355	Dave Nilsson	.05
356	Bobby Bonilla	.05
357	Ismael Valdes	.05
358	Carlos Perez	.05
359	Kirk Rueter	.05
360	Bartolo Colon	.05
361	Mel Rojas	.05
362	Johnny Damon	.25
363	Geronimo Berroa	.05
364	Reggie Sanders	.05
365	Jermaine Allensworth	.05
366	Orlando Cabrera	.05
367	Jorge Fabregas	.05
368	Scott Stahoviak	.05
369	Ken Cloude	.05
370	Donovan Osborne	.05
371	Roger Cedeno	.05
372	Neifi Perez	.05
373	Chris Holt	.05
374	Cecil Fielder	.05
375	Marty Cordova	.05
376	Tom Goodwin	.05
377	Jeff Suppan	.05
378	Jeff Brantley	.05
379	Mark Langston	.05
380	Shane Reynolds	.05
381	Mike Fetters	.05
382	Todd Greene	.05
383	Ray Durham	.05
384	Carlos Delgado	.30
385	Jeff D'Amico	.05
386	Brian McRae	.05
387	Alan Benes	.05
388	Heathcliff Slocumb	.05
389	Eric Young	.05
390	Travis Fryman	.05
391	David Cone	.05
392	Otis Nixon	.05
393	Jeremi Gonzalez	.05
394	Jeff Juden	.05
395	Jose Vizcaino	.05
396	Ugueth Urbina	.05
397	Ramon Martinez	.05
398	Robb Nen	.05
399	Harold Baines	.05
400	Delino DeShields	.05
401	John Burkett	.05
402	Sterling Hitchcock	.05
403	Mark Clark	.05
404	Terrell Wade	.05
405	Scott Brosius	.05
406	Chad Curtis	.05
407	Brian Johnson	.05
408	Roberto Kelly	.05
409	*Dave Dellucci*	.15
410	Michael Tucker	.05
411	Mark Kotsay	.05
412	Mark Lewis	.05
413	Ryan McGuire	.05
414	Shawon Dunston	.05
415	Brad Rigby	.05
416	Scott Erickson	.05
417	Bobby Jones	.05
418	Darren Oliver	.05
419	John Smiley	.05
420	T.J. Mathews	.05
421	Dustin Hermanson	.05
422	Mike Timlin	.05
423	Willie Blair	.05
424	Manny Alexander	.05
425	Bob Tewksbury	.05
426	Pete Schourek	.05
427	Reggie Jefferson	.05
428	Ed Sprague	.05
429	Jeff Conine	.05
430	Roberto Hernandez	.05
431	Tom Pagnozzi	.05
432	Jaret Wright	.05
433	Livan Hernandez	.05
434	Andy Ashby	.05
435	Todd Dunn	.05
436	Bobby Higginson	.05
437	Rod Beck	.05
438	Jim Leyritz	.05
439	Matt Williams	.05
440	Brett Tomko	.05
441	Joe Randa	.05
442	Chris Carpenter	.05
443	Dennis Reyes	.05
444	Al Leiter	.05
445	Jason Schmidt	.05
446	Ken Hill	.05
447	Shannon Stewart	.05
448	Enrique Wilson	.05
449	Fernando Tatis	.05
450	Jimmy Key	.05
451	Darrin Fletcher	.05
452	John Valentin	.05
453	Kevin Tapani	.05
454	Eric Karros	.05
455	Jay Bell	.05
456	Walt Weiss	.05
457	Devon White	.05
458	Carl Pavano	.05
459	Mike Lansing	.05
460	John Flaherty	.05
461	Richard Hidalgo	.05
462	Quinton McCracken	.05
463	Karim Garcia	.15
464	Miguel Cairo	.05
465	Edwin Diaz	.05
466	Bobby Smith	.05
467	Yamil Benitez	.05
468	*Rich Butler*	.05
469	*Ben Ford*	.05
470	Bubba Trammell	.05
471	Brent Brede	.05
472	Brooks Kieschnick	.05
473	Carlos Castillo	.05
474	Brad Radke	.05
475	Roger Clemens	.50
476	Curt Schilling	.05
477	John Olerud	.05
478	Mark McGwire	.75
479	Mike Piazza, Ken Griffey Jr.	.75
480	Jeff Bagwell, Frank Thomas	.50
481	Chipper Jones, Nomar Garciaparra	.65
482	Larry Walker, Juan Gonzalez	.30
483	Gary Sheffield, Tino Martinez	.05
484	Derrick Gibson, Michael Coleman, Norm Hutchins	.05
485	Braden Looper, Cliff Politte, Brian Rose	.05

486	Eric Milton, Jason Marquis, Corey Lee	.05
487	*A.J. Hinch, Mark Osborne, Robert Fick*	.10
488	Aramis Ramirez, Alex Gonzalez, Sean Casey	.15
489	*Donnie Bridges, Tim Drew*	.10
490	*Ntema Ndungidi, Darnell McDonald*	.10
491	Ryan Anderson, Mark Mangum	.25
492	*J.J. Davis, Troy Glaus*	2.00
493	*Jayson Werth, Dan Reichert*	.10
494	*John Curtice, Mike Cuddyer*	.25
495	Jack Cust, Jason Standridge	.15
496	Brian Anderson	.05
497	Tony Saunders	.05
498	*Vladimir Nunez, Jhensy Sandoval*	.10
499	Brad Penny, Nick Bierbrodt	.05
500	*Dustin Carr, Luis Cruz*	.05
501	*Marcus McCain, Cedrick Bowers*	.05
502	Checklist	.05
503	Checklist	.05
504	Alex Rodriguez	1.50

Minted in Cooperstown

	NM/M
Common Card:	.50
Stars/Rookies:	6X

(See 1998 Topps for checklist and base card values.)

Baby Boomers

		NM/M
Complete Set (15):		15.00
Common Player:		.75
Inserted 1:36 retail		
1	Derek Jeter	6.00
2	Scott Rolen	1.00
3	Nomar Garciaparra	3.50
4	Jose Cruz Jr.	.75
5	Darin Erstad	.85
6	Todd Helton	1.50
7	Tony Clark	.75
8	Jose Guillen	.75
9	Andruw Jones	1.00
10	Vladimir Guerrero	1.50
11	Mark Kotsay	.75
12	Todd Greene	.75
13	Andy Pettitte	.85
14	Justin Thompson	.75
15	Alan Benes	.75

Clout 9

		NM/M
Complete Set (9):		17.50
Common Player:		1.00
Inserted 1:72		
1	Edgar Martinez	1.00
2	Mike Piazza	5.00
3	Frank Thomas	2.00
4	Craig Biggio	1.00
5	Vinny Castilla	1.00
6	Jeff Blauser	1.00
7	Barry Bonds	7.50
8	Ken Griffey Jr.	5.00
9	Larry Walker	1.00

Etch-A-Sketch

		NM/M
Complete Set (9):		20.00
Common Player:		1.00
Inserted 1:36		
1	Albert Belle	1.00
2	Barry Bonds	6.00
3	Ken Griffey Jr.	4.00
4	Greg Maddux	3.00
5	Hideo Nomo	1.50
6	Mike Piazza	4.00
7	Cal Ripken Jr.	6.00
8	Frank Thomas	2.00
9	Mo Vaughn	1.00

Flashback

		NM/M
Complete Set (10):		22.50
Common Player:		1.00
Inserted 1:72		
1	Barry Bonds	7.50
2	Ken Griffey Jr.	5.00
3	Paul Molitor	2.00
4	Randy Johnson	2.00
5	Cal Ripken Jr.	7.50
6	Tony Gwynn	3.00
7	Kenny Lofton	1.00
8	Gary Sheffield	1.50
9	Deion Sanders	1.00
10	Brady Anderson	1.00

Focal Point

		NM/M
Complete Set (15):		25.00
Common Player:		.75
Inserted 1:36		
1	Juan Gonzalez	.85
2	Nomar Garciaparra	2.50
3	Jose Cruz Jr.	.75
4	Cal Ripken Jr.	5.00
5	Ken Griffey Jr.	3.50
6	Ivan Rodriguez	1.00
7	Larry Walker	.75
8	Barry Bonds	5.00
9	Roger Clemens	3.00
10	Frank Thomas	1.50
11	Chuck Knoblauch	.75
12	Mike Piazza	3.50
13	Greg Maddux	2.50
14	Vladimir Guerrero	1.50
15	Andruw Jones	1.50

Hallbound

		NM/M
Complete Set (15):		45.00
Common Player:		1.50
1	Paul Molitor	2.50
2	Tony Gwynn	3.50
3	Wade Boggs	3.50
4	Roger Clemens	4.00
5	Dennis Eckersley	2.00
6	Cal Ripken Jr.	7.50
7	Greg Maddux	3.50
8	Rickey Henderson	2.50
9	Ken Griffey Jr.	5.00
10	Frank Thomas	2.50
11	Mark McGwire	6.00
12	Barry Bonds	7.50
13	Mike Piazza	5.00
14	Juan Gonzalez	1.50
15	Randy Johnson	2.50

Inter-League Mystery Finest

		NM/M
Complete Set (20):		35.00
Common Player:		.75
Inserted 1:36		
Refractors:		1.5X
Inserted 1:144		
1	Chipper Jones	3.00
2	Cal Ripken Jr.	6.50
3	Greg Maddux	3.00
4	Rafael Palmeiro	1.50
5	Todd Hundley	.75
6	Derek Jeter	6.50
7	John Olerud	.75
8	Tino Martinez	.75
9	Larry Walker	.75
10	Ken Griffey Jr.	4.00
11	Andres Galarraga	.75
12	Randy Johnson	2.00
13	Mike Piazza	4.00
14	Jim Edmonds	.75
15	Eric Karros	.75
16	Tim Salmon	.75
17	Sammy Sosa	3.00
18	Frank Thomas	2.00
19	Mark Grace	.75
20	Albert Belle	.75

Milestones

		NM/M
Complete Set (10):		17.50
Common Player:		.75
MS1	Barry Bonds	5.00
MS2	Roger Clemens	2.50
MS3	Dennis Eckersley	1.00
MS4	Juan Gonzalez	.75
MS5	Ken Griffey Jr.	3.00
MS6	Tony Gwynn	2.00
MS7	Greg Maddux	2.00
MS8	Mark McGwire	4.00
MS9	Cal Ripken Jr.	5.00
MS10	Frank Thomas	1.25

Mystery Finest

		NM/M
Complete Set (20):		25.00
Common Player:		.50
Inserted 1:36		
Borderless 1:72:		1.5X
Bordered Refractors 1:108:		1.5X
Borderless Refractors 1:288:		2X
1	Nomar Garciaparra	1.50
2	Chipper Jones	1.50
3	Scott Rolen	.75
4	Albert Belle	.50
5	Mo Vaughn	.50
6	Jose Cruz Jr.	.50
7	Mark McGwire	3.00
8	Derek Jeter	3.50
9	Tony Gwynn	1.50
10	Frank Thomas	1.00
11	Tino Martinez	.50
12	Greg Maddux	1.50
13	Juan Gonzalez	.75
14	Larry Walker	.50
15	Mike Piazza	2.50
16	Cal Ripken Jr.	3.50
17	Jeff Bagwell	1.00
18	Andruw Jones	1.00
19	Barry Bonds	3.50
20	Ken Griffey Jr.	2.50

Roberto Clemente Finest

		NM/M
Complete Set (19):		60.00
Common Card:		3.50
Inserted 1:72		
Refractors:		2X
Inserted 1:288		
1	1955	6.00
2	1956	3.50
3	1957	3.50
4	1958	3.50
5	1959	3.50
6	1960	3.50
7	1961	3.50
8	1962	3.50
9	1963	3.50
10	1964	3.50
11	1965	3.50
12	1966	3.50
13	1967	3.50
14	1968	3.50
15	1969	3.50
16	1970	3.50
17	1971	3.50
18	1972	3.50
19	1973	3.50

Roberto Clemente Reprints

		NM/M
Complete Set (19):		50.00
Common Card:		2.50
Inserted 1:18		
1	1955	4.00
2	1956	2.50
3	1957	2.50
4	1958	2.50
5	1959	2.50
6	1960	2.50
7	1961	2.50
8	1962	2.50
9	1963	2.50
10	1964	2.50
11	1965	2.50
12	1966	2.50
13	1967	2.50
14	1968	2.50
15	1969	2.50
16	1970	2.50
17	1971	2.50
18	1972	2.50
19	1973	2.50

Roberto Clemente Tribute

		NM/M
Complete Set (5):		3.00
Common Clemente:		.75
Inserted 1:12		
1	Roberto Clemente	.75
2	Roberto Clemente	.75
3	Roberto Clemente	.75
4	Roberto Clemente	.75
5	Roberto Clemente	.75

Rookie Class

		NM/M
Complete Set (10):		4.00
Common Player:		.25
Inserted 1:12		
1	Travis Lee	.50
2	Richard Hidalgo	.25
3	Todd Helton	2.00
4	Paul Konerko	.75
5	Mark Kotsay	.25
6	Derrek Lee	1.50
7	Eli Marrero	.25
8	Fernando Tatis	.25
9	Juan Encarnacion	.25
10	Ben Grieve	.25

1998 TOPPS CHROME

		NM/M
	Complete Set (502):	100.00
	Common Player:	.10
	Foil Pack (4):	1.50
	Foil Box (24):	25.00
1	Tony Gwynn	2.00
2	Larry Walker	.10
3	Billy Wagner	.10
4	Denny Neagle	.10
5	Vladimir Guerrero	1.50
6	Kevin Brown	.10
7	Not Issued	
8	Mariano Rivera	.10
9	Tony Clark	.10
10	Deion Sanders	.10
11	Francisco Cordova	.10
12	Matt Williams	.10
13	Carlos Baerga	.10
14	Mo Vaughn	.10
15	Bobby Witt	.10
16	Matt Stairs	.10
17	Chan Ho Park	.10
18	Mike Bordick	.10
19	Michael Tucker	.10
20	Frank Thomas	1.50
21	Roberto Clemente (Tribute)	2.50
22	Dmitri Young	.10
23	Steve Trachsel	.10
24	Jeff Kent	.10
25	Scott Rolen	.75
26	John Thomson	.10
27	Joe Vitiello	.10
28	Eddie Guardado	.10
29	Charlie Hayes	.10
30	Juan Gonzalez	.75
31	Garret Anderson	.10
32	John Jaha	.10
33	Omar Vizquel	.10
34	Brian Hunter	.10
35	Jeff Bagwell	1.50
36	Mark Lemke	.10
37	Doug Glanville	.10
38	Dan Wilson	.10
39	Steve Cooke	.10
40	Chili Davis	.10
41	Mike Cameron	.10
42	F.P. Santangelo	.10
43	Brad Ausmus	.10
44	Gary DiSarcina	.10
45	Pat Hentgen	.10
46	Wilton Guerrero	.10
47	Devon White	.10
48	Danny Patterson	.10
49	Pat Meares	.10
50	Rafael Palmeiro	1.00
51	Mark Gardner	.10
52	Jeff Blauser	.10
53	Dave Hollins	.10
54	Carlos Garcia	.10
55	Ben McDonald	.10
56	John Mabry	.10
57	Trevor Hoffman	.10
58	Tony Fernandez	.10
59	Rich Loiselle	.10
60	Mark Leiter	.10
61	Pat Kelly	.10
62	John Flaherty	.10
63	Roger Bailey	.10
64	Tom Gordon	.10
65	Ryan Klesko	.10
66	Darryl Hamilton	.10
67	Jim Eisenreich	.10
68	Butch Huskey	.10
69	Mark Grudzielanek	.10
70	Marquis Grissom	.10
71	Mark McLemore	.10
72	Gary Gaetti	.10
73	Greg Gagne	.10
74	Lyle Mouton	.10
75	Jim Edmonds	.10
76	Shawn Green	.35
77	Terry Vaughn	.10
78	Terry Adams	.10
79	*Kevin Polcovich*	.10
80	Troy O'Leary	.10
81	Jeff Shaw	.10
82	Rich Becker	.10
83	David Wells	.10
84	Steve Karsay	.10
85	Charles Nagy	.10
86	B.J. Surhoff	.10
87	Jamey Wright	.10
88	James Baldwin	.10
89	Edgardo Alfonzo	.10
90	Jay Buhner	.10
91	Brady Anderson	.10
92	Scott Servais	.10
93	Edgar Renteria	.10
94	Mike Lieberthal	.10
95	Rick Aguilera	.10
96	Walt Weiss	.10
97	Deivi Cruz	.10
98	Kurt Abbott	.10
99	Henry Rodriguez	.10
100	Mike Piazza	2.25
101	Bill Taylor	.10
102	Todd Zeile	.10
103	Rey Ordonez	.10
104	Willie Greene	.10
105	Tony Womack	.10
106	Mike Sweeney	.10
107	Jeffrey Hammonds	.10
108	Kevin Orie	.10
109	Alex Gonzalez	.10
110	Jose Canseco	.60
111	Paul Sorrento	.10
112	Joey Hamilton	.10
113	Brad Radke	.10
114	Steve Avery	.10
115	Esteban Loaiza	.10
116	Stan Javier	.10
117	Chris Gomez	.10
118	Royce Clayton	.10
119	Orlando Merced	.10
120	Kevin Appier	.10
121	Mel Nieves	.10
122	Joe Girardi	.10
123	Rico Brogna	.10
124	Kent Mercker	.10
125	Manny Ramirez	1.50
126	Jeromy Burnitz	.10
127	Kevin Foster	.10
128	Matt Morris	.10
129	Jason Dickson	.10
130	Tom Glavine	.35
131	Wally Joyner	.10
132	Rick Reed	.10
133	Todd Jones	.10
134	Dave Martinez	.10
135	Sandy Alomar	.10
136	Mike Lansing	.10
137	Sean Berry	.10
138	Doug Jones	.10
139	Todd Stottlemyre	.10
140	Jay Bell	.10
141	Jaime Navarro	.10
142	Chris Hoiles	.10
143	Joey Cora	.10
144	Scott Spiezio	.10
145	Joe Carter	.10
146	Jose Guillen	.10
147	Damion Easley	.10
148	Lee Stevens	.10
149	Alex Fernandez	.10
150	Randy Johnson	1.50
151	J.T. Snow	.10
152	Chuck Finley	.10
153	Bernard Gilkey	.10
154	David Segui	.10
155	Dante Bichette	.10
156	Kevin Stocker	.10
157	Carl Everett	.10
158	Jose Valentin	.10
159	Pokey Reese	.10
160	Derek Jeter	3.00
161	Roger Pavlik	.10
162	Mark Wohlers	.10
163	Ricky Bottalico	.10
164	Ozzie Guillen	.10
165	Mike Mussina	.60
166	Gary Sheffield	.50
167	Hideo Nomo	.75
168	Mark Grace	.10
169	Aaron Sele	.10
170	Darryl Kile	.10
171	Shawn Estes	.10
172	Vinny Castilla	.10
173	Ron Coomer	.10
174	Jose Rosado	.10
175	Kenny Lofton	.10
176	Jason Giambi	.65
177	Hal Morris	.10
178	Darren Bragg	.10
179	Orel Hershiser	.10
180	Ray Lankford	.10
181	Hideki Irabu	.10
182	Kevin Young	.10
183	Javy Lopez	.10
184	Jeff Montgomery	.10
185	Mike Holtz	.10
186	George Williams	.10
187	Cal Eldred	.10
188	Tom Candiotti	.10
189	Glenallen Hill	.10
190	Brian Giles	.10
191	Dave Mlicki	.10
192	Garrett Stephenson	.10
193	Jeff Frye	.10
194	Joe Oliver	.10
195	Bob Hamelin	.10
196	Luis Sojo	.10
197	LaTroy Hawkins	.10
198	Kevin Elster	.10
199	Jeff Reed	.10
200	Dennis Eckersley	1.00
201	Bill Mueller	.10
202	Russ Davis	.10
203	Armando Benitez	.10
204	Quilvio Veras	.10
205	Tim Naehring	.10
206	Quinton McCracken	.10
207	Raul Casanova	.10
208	Matt Lawton	.10
209	Luis Alicea	.10
210	Luis Gonzalez	.10
211	Allen Watson	.10
212	Gerald Williams	.10
213	David Bell	.10
214	Todd Hollandsworth	.10
215	Wade Boggs	2.00
216	Jose Mesa	.10
217	Jamie Moyer	.10
218	Darren Daulton	.10
219	Mickey Morandini	.10
220	Rusty Greer	.10
221	Jim Bullinger	.10
222	Jose Offerman	.10
223	Matt Karchner	.10
224	Woody Williams	.10
225	Mark Loretta	.10
226	Mike Hampton	.10
227	Willie Adams	.10
228	Scott Hatteberg	.10
229	Rich Amaral	.10
230	Terry Steinbach	.10
231	Glendon Rusch	.10
232	Bret Boone	.10
233	Robert Person	.10
234	Jose Hernandez	.10
235	Doug Drabek	.10
236	Jason McDonald	.10
237	Chris Widger	.10
238	*Tom Martin*	.10
239	Dave Burba	.10
240	Pete Rose	.10
241	Bobby Ayala	.10
242	Tim Wakefield	.10
243	Dennis Springer	.10
244	Tim Belcher	.10
245	Jon Garland, Geoff Goetz	.10
246	Glenn Davis, Lance Berkman	.25
247	Vernon Wells, Aaron Akin	.15
248	Adam Kennedy, Jason Romano	.25
249	Jason Dellaero, Troy Cameron	.10
250	*Alex Sanchez, Jared Sandberg*	.25
251	*Pablo Ortega, James Manias*	.10
252	*Jason Conti, Mike Stoner*	.10
253	John Patterson, Larry Rodriguez	.10
254	Adrian Beltre, Ryan Minor, Aaron Boone	.25
255	Ben Grieve, Brian Buchanan, Dermal Brown	.10
256	Carl Pavano, Kerry Wood, Gil Meche	.75
257	David Ortiz, Daryle Ward, Richie Sexson	.65
258	Randy Winn, Juan Encarnacion, Andrew Vessel	.10
259	Kris Benson, Travis Smith, Courtney Duncan	.15
260	*Chad Hermansen, Brent Butler, Warren Morris*	.15
261	Ben Davis, Elieser Marrero, Ramon Hernandez	.10
262	Eric Chavez, Russell Branyan, Russ Johnson	.25
263	*Todd Dunwoody, John Barnes, Ryan Jackson*	.15
264	Matt Clement, Roy Halladay, Brian Fuentes	.20
265	Randy Johnson	.50
266	Kevin Brown	.10
267	Francisco Cordova, Ricardo Rincon	.10
268	Nomar Garciaparra	.75
269	Tino Martinez	.10
270	Chuck Knoblauch	.10
271	Pedro Martinez	.40
272	Denny Neagle	.10
273	Juan Gonzalez	.20
274	Andres Galarraga	.10
275	Checklist	.10
276	Checklist	.10
277	Moises Alou	.10
278	Sandy Alomar	.10
279	Gary Sheffield	.10
280	Matt Williams	.10
281	Livan Hernandez	.10
282	Chad Ogea	.10
283	Marlins Win	.10
284	Tino Martinez	.10
285	Roberto Alomar	.35
286	Jeff King	.10
287	Brian Jordan	.10
288	Darin Erstad	.30
289	Ken Caminiti	.10
290	Jim Thome	.90
291	Paul Molitor	1.50
292	Ivan Rodriguez	1.00
293	Bernie Williams	.10
294	Todd Hundley	.10
295	Andres Galarraga	.10
296	Greg Maddux	2.00
297	Edgar Martinez	.10
298	Ron Gant	.10
299	Derek Bell	.10
300	Roger Clemens	2.00
301	Rondell White	.10
302	Barry Larkin	.10
303	Robin Ventura	.10
304	Jason Kendall	.10
305	Chipper Jones	2.00
306	John Franco	.10
307	Sammy Sosa	2.00
308	Troy Percival	.10
309	Chuck Knoblauch	.10
310	Ellis Burks	.10
311	Al Martin	.10
312	Tim Salmon	.10
313	Moises Alou	.10
314	Lance Johnson	.10
315	Justin Thompson	.10
316	Will Clark	.10
317	Barry Bonds	3.00
318	Craig Biggio	.10
319	John Smoltz	.10
320	Cal Ripken Jr.	3.00
321	Ken Griffey Jr.	2.25
322	Paul O'Neill	.10
323	Todd Helton	1.50
324	John Olerud	.10
325	Mark McGwire	2.50
326	Jose Cruz Jr.	.10
327	Jeff Cirillo	.10
328	Dean Palmer	.10
329	John Wetteland	.10
330	Steve Finley	.10
331	Albert Belle	.10
332	Curt Schilling	.35
333	Raul Mondesi	.10
334	Andruw Jones	1.50
335	Nomar Garciaparra	2.00
336	David Justice	.10
337	Andy Pettitte	.30
338	Pedro Martinez	1.50
339	Travis Miller	.10
340	Chris Stynes	.10
341	Gregg Jefferies	.10
342	Jeff Fassero	.10
343	Craig Counsell	.10
344	Wilson Alvarez	.10
345	Bip Roberts	.10

346 Kelvim Escobar .10
347 Mark Bellhorn .10
348 Cory Lidle .10
349 Fred McGriff .10
350 Chuck Carr .10
351 Bob Abreu .10
352 Juan Guzman .10
353 Fernando Vina .10
354 Andy Benes .10
355 Dave Nilsson .10
356 Bobby Bonilla .10
357 Ismael Valdes .10
358 Carlos Perez .10
359 Kirk Rueter .10
360 Bartolo Colon .10
361 Mel Rojas .10
362 Johnny Damon .35
363 Geronimo Berroa .10
364 Reggie Sanders .10
365 Jermaine Allensworth .10
366 Orlando Cabrera .10
367 Jorge Fabregas .10
368 Scott Stahoviak .10
369 Ken Cloude .10
370 Donovan Osborne .10
371 Roger Cedeno .10
372 Neifi Perez .10
373 Chris Holt .10
374 Cecil Fielder .10
375 Marty Cordova .10
376 Tom Goodwin .10
377 Jeff Suppan .10
378 Jeff Brantley .10
379 Mark Langston .10
380 Shane Reynolds .10
381 Mike Fetters .10
382 Todd Greene .10
383 Ray Durham .10
384 Carlos Delgado .35
385 Jeff D'Amico .10
386 Brian McRae .10
387 Alan Benes .10
388 Heathcliff Slocumb .10
389 Eric Young .10
390 Travis Fryman .10
391 David Cone .10
392 Otis Nixon .10
393 Jeremi Gonzalez .10
394 Jeff Juden .10
395 Jose Vizcaino .10
396 Ugueth Urbina .10
397 Ramon Martinez .10
398 Robb Nen .10
399 Harold Baines .10
400 Delino DeShields .10
401 John Burkett .10
402 Sterling Hitchcock .10
403 Mark Clark .10
404 Terrell Wade .10
405 Scott Brosius .10
406 Chad Curtis .10
407 Brian Johnson .10
408 Roberto Kelly .10
409 *Dave Dellucci* .25
410 Michael Tucker .10
411 Mark Kotsay .10
412 Mark Lewis .10
413 Ryan McGuire .10
414 Shawon Dunston .10
415 Brad Rigby .10
416 Scott Erickson .10
417 Bobby Jones .10
418 Darren Oliver .10
419 John Smiley .10
420 T.J. Mathews .10
421 Dustin Hermanson .10
422 Mike Timlin .10
423 Willie Blair .10
424 Manny Alexander .10
425 Bob Tewksbury .10
426 Pete Schourek .10
427 Reggie Jefferson .10
428 Ed Sprague .10
429 Jeff Conine .10
430 Roberto Hernandez .10
431 Tom Pagnozzi .10
432 Jaret Wright .10
433 Livan Hernandez .10
434 Andy Ashby .10
435 Todd Dunn .10
436 Bobby Higginson .10
437 Rod Beck .10
438 Jim Leyritz .10
439 Matt Williams .10
440 Brett Tomko .10
441 Joe Randa .10
442 Chris Carpenter .10
443 Dennis Reyes .10
444 Al Leiter .10
445 Jason Schmidt .10
446 Ken Hill .10
447 Shannon Stewart .10
448 Enrique Wilson .10
449 Fernando Tatis .10
450 Jimmy Key .10
451 Darrin Fletcher .10
452 John Valentin .10
453 Kevin Tapani .10
454 Eric Karros .10
455 Jay Bell .10
456 Walt Weiss .10
457 Devon White .10
458 Carl Pavano .10
459 Mike Lansing .10
460 John Flaherty .10
461 Richard Hidalgo .10
462 Quinton McCracken .10
463 Karim Garcia .20
464 Miguel Cairo .10
465 Edwin Diaz .10
466 Bobby Smith .10
467 Yamil Benitez .10
468 *Rich Butler* .10
469 *Ben Ford* .10
470 Bubba Trammell .10
471 Brent Brede .10
472 Brooks Kieschnick .10
473 Carlos Castillo .10
474 Brad Radke .10
475 Roger Clemens 1.00
476 Curt Schilling .15
477 John Olerud .10
478 Mark McGwire 1.25
479 Mike Piazza, Ken Griffey Jr. 1.25
480 Jeff Bagwell, Frank Thomas 1.00
481 Chipper Jones, Nomar Garciaparra 1.00
482 Larry Walker, Juan Gonzalez .20
483 Gary Sheffield, Tino Martinez .10
484 Derrick Gibson, Michael Coleman, Norm Hutchins .10
485 Braden Looper, Cliff Politte, Brian Rose .15
486 Eric Milton, Jason Marquis, Corey Lee .25
487 *A.J. Hinch, Mark Osborne, Robert Fick* .25
488 Aramis Ramirez, Alex Gonzalez, Sean Casey .25
489 *Donnie Bridges, Tim Drew* .20
490 *Ntema Ndungidi, Darnell McDonald* .10
491 Ryan Anderson, Mark Mangum .50
492 *J.J. Davis, Troy Glaus* 3.00
493 Jayson Werth, Dan Reichert .10
494 *John Curtice, Mike Cuddyer* .50
495 Jack Cust, Jason Standridge .50
496 Brian Anderson .10
497 Tony Saunders .10
498 *Vladimir Nunez, Jhensy Sandoval* .10
499 Brad Penny, Nick Bierbrodt .10
500 *Dustin Carr, Luis Cruz* .10
501 *Marcus McCain, Cedrick Bowers* .10
502 Checklist .10
503 Checklist .10
504 Alex Rodriguez 2.50

Refractors

NM/M
Common Player: .50
Stars/Rookies: 5X
(See 1998 Topps Chrome for checklist and base card values.)

Baby Boomers

NM/M
Complete Set (15): 16.00
Common Player: .75
Inserted 1:24
Refractors: 1.5X
Inserted 1:72
1 Derek Jeter 6.00
2 Scott Rolen .90
3 Nomar Garciaparra 3.50
4 Jose Cruz Jr. .75
5 Darin Erstad .90
6 Todd Helton 1.50
7 Tony Clark .75
8 Jose Guillen .75
9 Andruw Jones 1.50
10 Vladimir Guerrero 1.50
11 Mark Kotsay .75
12 Todd Greene .75
13 Andy Pettitte .90
14 Justin Thompson .75
15 Alan Benes .75

Clout 9

NM/M
Complete Set (9): 15.00
Common Player: .75
Inserted 1:24
Refractors: 1.5X
Inserted 1:72
1 Edgar Martinez .75
2 Mike Piazza 3.50
3 Frank Thomas 1.50
4 Craig Biggio .75
5 Vinny Castilla .75
6 Jeff Blauser .75
7 Barry Bonds 6.00
8 Ken Griffey Jr. 3.50
9 Larry Walker .75

Flashback

NM/M
Complete Set (10): 16.00
Common Player: .75
Inserted 1:24
Refractors: 1.5X
Inserted 1:72
1 Barry Bonds 6.00
2 Ken Griffey Jr. 3.50
3 Paul Molitor 1.50
4 Randy Johnson 1.50
5 Cal Ripken Jr. 6.00
6 Tony Gwynn 2.50
7 Kenny Lofton .75
8 Gary Sheffield .85
9 Deion Sanders .75
10 Brady Anderson .75

Hallbound

NM/M
Complete Set (15): 35.00
Common Player: 1.50
Inserted 1:24
Refractors: 1.5X
Inserted 1:72
1 Paul Molitor 2.00
2 Tony Gwynn 2.50
3 Wade Boggs 2.50
4 Roger Clemens 3.00
5 Dennis Eckersley 1.50
6 Cal Ripken Jr. 6.00
7 Greg Maddux 2.50
8 Rickey Henderson 2.00
9 Ken Griffey Jr. 3.50
10 Frank Thomas 2.00
11 Mark McGwire 4.50
12 Barry Bonds 6.00
13 Mike Piazza 3.50
14 Juan Gonzalez 1.50
15 Randy Johnson 2.00

Milestones

NM/M
Complete Set (10): 25.00
Common Player: 1.00
Inserted 1:24
Refractors: 1.5X
Inserted 1:72
1 Barry Bonds 6.00
2 Roger Clemens 3.00
3 Dennis Eckersley 1.00
4 Juan Gonzalez 1.00
5 Ken Griffey Jr. 3.50
6 Tony Gwynn 2.50
7 Greg Maddux 2.50
8 Mark McGwire 4.50
9 Cal Ripken Jr. 6.00
10 Frank Thomas 1.50

Rookie Class

NM/M
Complete Set (10): 10.00
Common Player: .75
Inserted 1:12
Refractors: 1.5X
Inserted 1:24
1 Travis Lee 1.00
2 Richard Hidalgo .75
3 Todd Helton 4.50
4 Paul Konerko 1.50
5 Mark Kotsay .75
6 Derrek Lee 3.00
7 Eli Marrero .75
8 Fernando Tatis .75
9 Juan Encarnacion .75
10 Ben Grieve .75

1998 TOPPS GALLERY

NM/M
Complete Set (150): 15.00
Common Player: .10
Pack (6): 1.50
Wax Box (24): 25.00
1 Andruw Jones 1.00
2 Fred McGriff .10
3 Wade Boggs 1.50
4 Pedro Martinez 1.00
5 Matt Williams .10
6 Wilson Alvarez .10
7 Henry Rodriguez .10
8 Jay Bell .10
9 Marquis Grissom .10
10 Darryl Kile .10
11 Chuck Knoblauch .10
12 Kenny Lofton .10
13 Quinton McCracken .10
14 Andres Galarraga .10
15 Brian Jordan .10
16 Mike Lansing .10
17 Travis Fryman .10
18 Tony Saunders .10
19 Moises Alou .10
20 Travis Lee .10
21 Garret Anderson .10
22 Ken Caminiti .10
23 Pedro Astacio .10
24 Ellis Burks .10
25 Albert Belle .10
26 Alan Benes .10
27 Jay Buhner .10
28 Derek Bell .10
29 Jeromy Burnitz .10

30 Kevin Appier .10
31 Jeff Cirillo .10
32 Bernard Gilkey .10
33 David Cone .10
34 Jason Dickson .10
35 Jose Cruz Jr. .10
36 Marty Cordova .10
37 Ray Durham .10
38 Jaret Wright .10
39 Billy Wagner .10
40 Roger Clemens 1.75
41 Juan Gonzalez .50
42 Jeremi Gonzalez .10
43 Mark Grudzielanek .10
44 Tom Glavine .35
45 Barry Larkin .10
46 Lance Johnson .10
47 Bobby Higginson .10
48 Mike Mussina .50
49 Al Martin .10
50 Mark McGwire 2.50
51 Todd Hundley .10
52 Ray Lankford .10
53 Jason Kendall .10
54 Javy Lopez .10
55 Ben Grieve .10
56 Randy Johnson 1.00
57 Jeff King .10
58 Mark Grace .10
59 Rusty Greer .10
60 Greg Maddux 1.50
61 Jeff Kent .10
62 Rey Ordonez .10
63 Hideo Nomo .50
64 Charles Nagy .10
65 Rondell White .10
66 Todd Helton .75
67 Jim Thome .75
68 Denny Neagle .10
69 Ivan Rodriguez .75
70 Vladimir Guerrero 1.00
71 Jorge Posada .10
72 J.T. Snow Jr. .10
73 Reggie Sanders .10
74 Scott Rolen .75
75 Robin Ventura .10
76 Mariano Rivera .15
77 Cal Ripken Jr. 3.00
78 Justin Thompson .10
79 Mike Piazza 2.00
80 Kevin Brown .10
81 Sandy Alomar .10
82 Craig Biggio .10
83 Vinny Castilla .10
84 Eric Young .10
85 Bernie Williams .10
86 Brady Anderson .10
87 Bobby Bonilla .10
88 Tony Clark .10
89 Dan Wilson .10
90 John Wetteland .10
91 Barry Bonds 3.00
92 Chan Ho Park .10
93 Carlos Delgado .35
94 David Justice .10
95 Chipper Jones 1.50
96 Shawn Estes .10
97 Jason Giambi .60
98 Ron Gant .10
99 John Olerud .10
100 Frank Thomas 1.00
101 Jose Guillen .10
102 Brad Radke .10
103 Troy Percival .10
104 John Smoltz .10
105 Edgardo Alfonzo .10
106 Dante Bichette .10
107 Larry Walker .10
108 John Valentin .10
109 Roberto Alomar .30
110 Mike Cameron .10
111 Eric Davis .10
112 Johnny Damon .35
113 Darin Erstad .30
114 Omar Vizquel .10
115 Derek Jeter 3.00
116 Tony Womack .10
117 Edgar Renteria .10
118 Raul Mondesi .10
119 Tony Gwynn 1.50
120 Ken Griffey Jr. 2.00
121 Jim Edmonds .10
122 Brian Hunter .10
123 Neifi Perez .10
124 Dean Palmer .10
125 Alex Rodriguez 2.50
126 Tim Salmon .10
127 Curt Schilling .35
128 Kevin Orie .10
129 Andy Pettitte .30
130 Gary Sheffield .50
131 Jose Rosado .10
132 Manny Ramirez 1.00
133 Rafael Palmeiro .75
134 Sammy Sosa 1.50
135 Jeff Bagwell 1.00
136 Delino DeShields .10
137 Ryan Klesko .10
138 Mo Vaughn .10
139 Steve Finley .10
140 Nomar Garciaparra 1.50
141 Paul Molitor 1.00
142 Pat Hentgen .10
143 Eric Karros .10
144 Bobby Jones .10
145 Tino Martinez .10
146 Matt Morris .10
147 Livan Hernandez .10
148 Edgar Martinez .10
149 Paul O'Neill .10
150 Checklist .10

Player's Private Issue

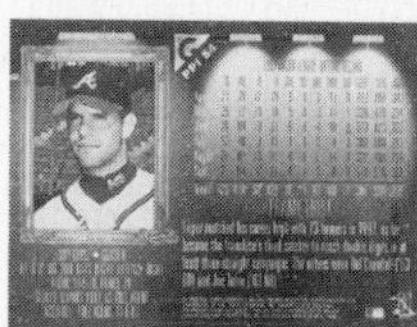

NM/M
Common Player: 1.00
Stars/Rookies: 4
Production 250 sets
(See 1998 Topps Gallery for checklist and base card values.)

Printing Plates

NM/M
Common Player, Front: 50.00
Common Player, Back: 35.00
(See 1998 Topps Gallery for checklist.)

Awards Gallery

NM/M
Complete Set (10): 18.00
Common Player: 1.00
Inserted 1:24
1 Ken Griffey Jr. 4.00
2 Larry Walker 1.00
3 Roger Clemens 2.50
4 Pedro Martinez 1.50
5 Nomar Garciaparra 2.00
6 Scott Rolen 1.00
7 Frank Thomas 1.50
8 Tony Gwynn 2.00
9 Mark McGwire 5.00
10 Livan Hernandez 1.00

Gallery Proofs

NM/M
Common Player: 1.50
Stars/Rookies: 4X
Production 125 sets
(See 1998 Topps Gallery for checklist and base card values.)

Gallery of Heroes

NM/M
Complete Set (15): 80.00
Common Player: 1.25
Inserted 1:24
Jumbo Version (1:24): 75%
1 Ken Griffey Jr. 8.00
2 Derek Jeter 15.00
3 Barry Bonds 15.00
4 Alex Rodriguez 12.00
5 Frank Thomas 4.00
6 Nomar Garciaparra 6.00
7 Mark McGwire 12.00
8 Mike Piazza 8.00
9 Cal Ripken Jr. 15.00
10 Jose Cruz Jr. 1.25

11 Jeff Bagwell 4.00
12 Chipper Jones 6.00
13 Juan Gonzalez 2.00
14 Hideo Nomo 2.00
15 Greg Maddux 6.00

Photo Gallery

NM/M
Complete Set (10): 25.00
Common Player: 1.00
Inserted 1:24
1 Alex Rodriguez 3.00
2 Frank Thomas 2.00
3 Derek Jeter 4.00
4 Cal Ripken Jr. 4.00
5 Ken Griffey Jr. 2.50
6 Mike Piazza 2.50
7 Nomar Garciaparra 2.25
8 Tim Salmon 1.00
9 Jeff Bagwell 2.00
10 Barry Bonds 4.00

1998 TOPPS GOLD LABEL CLASS 1

(Fielding, Follow-thru)

NM/M
Complete Set (100): 12.00
Gold Label Common Player: .10
Black Label Common Player: .35
Black Label Stars/RCs: 4X
Red Label Common Player: 1.50
Red Label Stars/RCs: 12X
Pack (5): 2.00
Wax Box (24): 50.00
1 Kevin Brown .10
2 Greg Maddux 1.25
3 Albert Belle .10
4 Andres Galarraga .10
5 Craig Biggio .10
6 Matt Williams .10
7 Derek Jeter 3.00
8 Randy Johnson 1.00
9 Jay Bell .10
10 Jim Thome .75
11 Roberto Alomar .30
12 Tom Glavine .35
13 Reggie Sanders .10
14 Tony Gwynn 1.25
15 Mark McGwire 2.00
16 Jeromy Burnitz .10
17 Andruw Jones 1.00
18 Jay Buhner .10
19 Robin Ventura .10
20 Jeff Bagwell 1.00
21 Roger Clemens 1.25
22 *Masato Yoshii* .25
23 Travis Fryman .10
24 Rafael Palmeiro .75
25 Alex Rodriguez 2.00
26 Sandy Alomar .10
27 Chipper Jones 1.25
28 Rusty Greer .10
29 Cal Ripken Jr. 3.00
30 Tony Clark .10
31 Derek Bell .10
32 Fred McGriff .10
33 Paul O'Neill .10
34 Moises Alou .10
35 Henry Rodriguez .10
36 Steve Finley .10
37 Marquis Grissom .10
38 Jason Giambi .60
39 Javy Lopez .10
40 Damion Easley .10
41 Mariano Rivera .15
42 Mo Vaughn .10
43 Mike Mussina .40
44 Jason Kendall .10
45 Pedro Martinez 1.00
46 Frank Thomas 1.00
47 Jim Edmonds .10
48 Hideki Irabu .10
49 Eric Karros .10
50 Juan Gonzalez .50
51 Ellis Burks .10
52 Dean Palmer .10
53 Scott Rolen .60
54 Raul Mondesi .10
55 Quinton McCraken .10
56 John Olerud .10
57 Ken Caminiti .10
58 Brian Jordan .10
59 Wade Boggs 1.25
60 Mike Piazza 1.50
61 Darin Erstad .30
62 Curt Schilling .35
63 David Justice .10
64 Kenny Lofton .10
65 Barry Bonds 3.00
66 Ray Lankford .10
67 Brian Hunter .10
68 Chuck Knoblauch .10
69 Vinny Castilla .10
70 Vladimir Guerrero 1.00
71 Tim Salmon .10
72 Larry Walker .10
73 Paul Molitor 1.00
74 Barry Larkin .10
75 Edgar Martinez .10
76 Bernie Williams .10
77 Dante Bichette .10
78 Nomar Garciaparra 1.25
79 Ben Grieve .10
80 Ivan Rodriguez .75
81 Todd Helton .75
82 Ryan Klesko .10
83 Sammy Sosa 1.25
84 Travis Lee .10
85 Jose Cruz .10
86 Mark Kotsay .10
87 Richard Hidalgo .10
88 Rondell White .10
89 Greg Vaughn .10
90 Gary Sheffield .50
91 Paul Konerko .25
92 Mark Grace .10
93 *Kevin Millwood* 1.00
94 Manny Ramirez 1.00
95 Tino Martinez .10
96 Brad Fullmer .10
97 Todd Walker .10
98 Carlos Delgado .45
99 Kerry Wood .60
100 Ken Griffey Jr. 1.50

Class 2

NM/M
Complete Set (100): 50.00
Gold Label Common Player: .35
Gold Label Stars/RCs: 2X
Black Label Common Player: 1.00
Black Label Stars/RCs: 4X
Red Label Common Player: 4.00
Red Label Stars/RCs: 25X

(See 1998 Topps Gold Label Class 1 for checklist and base card values.)

Class 3

Complete Set (100):	120.00
Common Player:	.75
Gold Label Stars/RCs:	2.5X
Black Label Common Player:	2.00
Black Label Stars/RCs 6X	
Red Label Common Player:	6.00
Red Label Stars/RCs:	35X

(See 1998 Topps Gold Label Class 1 for checklist and base card values.)

Home Run Race

Complete Set (4):	7.50
Common Player:	2.00
Black Label:	2X
Red Label:	4X
HR1 Roger Maris	3.00
HR2 Mark McGwire	3.00
HR3 Ken Griffey Jr.	2.50
HR4 Sammy Sosa	2.00

1998 TOPPS OPENING DAY

		NM/M
Complete Set (165):		10.00
Common Player:		.05
Wax Pack (7):		.65
Wax Box (22):		10.00
1	Tony Gwynn	.65
2	Larry Walker	.05
3	Billy Wagner	.05
4	Denny Neagle	.05
5	Vladimir Guerrero	.50
6	Kevin Brown	.05
7	Mariano Rivera	.15
8	Tony Clark	.05
9	Deion Sanders	.05
10	Matt Williams	.05
11	Carlos Baerga	.05
12	Mo Vaughn	.05
13	Chan Ho Park	.05
14	Frank Thomas	.50
15	John Jaha	.05
16	Steve Trachsel	.05
17	Jeff Kent	.05
18	Scott Rolen	.40
19	Juan Gonzalez	.25
20	Garret Anderson	.05
21	Roberto Clemente	1.00
22	Omar Vizquel	.05
23	Brian Hunter	.05
24	Jeff Bagwell	.50
25	Chili Davis	.05
26	Mike Cameron	.05
27	Pat Hentgen	.05
28	Wilton Guerrero	.05
29	Devon White	.05
30	Rafael Palmeiro	.40
31	Jeff Blauser	.05
32	Dave Hollins	.05
33	Trevor Hoffman	.05
34	Ryan Klesko	.05
35	Butch Huskey	.05
36	Mark Grudzielanek	.05
37	Marquis Grissom	.05
38	Jim Edmonds	.05
39	Greg Vaughn	.05
40	David Wells	.05
41	Charles Nagy	.05
42	B.J. Surhoff	.05
43	Edgardo Alfonzo	.05
44	Jay Buhner	.05
45	Brady Anderson	.05
46	Edgar Renteria	.05
47	Rick Aguilera	.05
48	Henry Rodriguez	.05
49	Mike Piazza	.75
50	Todd Zeile	.05
51	Rey Ordonez	.05
52	Tony Womack	.05
53	Mike Sweeney	.05
54	Jeffrey Hammonds	.05
55	Kevin Orie	.05
56	Alex Gonzalez	.05
57	Jose Canseco	.35
58	Joey Hamilton	.05
59	Brad Radke	.05
60	Kevin Appier	.05
61	Manny Ramirez	.50
62	Jeromy Burnitz	.05
63	Matt Morris	.05
64	Jason Dickson	.05
65	Tom Glavine	.25
66	Wally Joyner	.05
67	Todd Jones	.05
68	Sandy Alomar	.05
69	Mike Lansing	.05
70	Todd Stottlemyre	.05
71	Jay Bell	.05
72	Joey Cora	.05
73	Scott Spiezio	.05
74	Joe Carter	.05
75	Jose Guillen	.05
76	Damion Easley	.05
77	Alex Fernandez	.05
78	Randy Johnson	.50
79	J.T. Snow	.05
80	Bernard Gilkey	.05
81	David Segui	.05
82	Dante Bichette	.05
83	Derek Jeter	1.50
84	Mark Wohlers	.05
85	Ricky Bottalico	.05
86	Mike Mussina	.35
87	Gary Sheffield	.35
88	Hideo Nomo	.25
89	Mark Grace	.05
90	Darryl Kile	.05
91	Shawn Estes	.05
92	Vinny Castilla	.05
93	Jose Rosado	.05
94	Kenny Lofton	.05
95	Jason Giambi	.35
96	Ray Lankford	.05
97	Hideki Irabu	.05
98	Javy Lopez	.05
99	Jeff Montgomery	.05
100	Dennis Eckersley	.40
101	Armando Benitez	.05
102	Tim Naehring	.05
103	Luis Gonzalez	.05
104	Todd Hollandsworth	.05
105	Wade Boggs	.65
106	Mickey Morandini	.05
107	Rusty Greer	.05
108	Terry Steinbach	.05
109	Pete Rose II	.05
110	Checklist	.05
111	Tino Martinez	.05
112	Roberto Alomar	.20
113	Jeff King	.05
114	Brian Jordan	.05
115	Darin Erstad	.25
116	Ken Caminiti	.05
117	Jim Thome	.60
118	Paul Molitor	.50
119	Ivan Rodriguez	.40
120	Bernie Williams	.05
121	Todd Hundley	.05
122	Andres Galarraga	.05
123	Greg Maddux	.65
124	Edgar Martinez	.05
125	Ron Gant	.05
126	Derek Bell	.05
127	Roger Clemens	.70
128	Rondell White	.05
129	Barry Larkin	.05
130	Robin Ventura	.05
131	Jason Kendall	.05
132	Chipper Jones	.65
133	John Franco	.05
134	Sammy Sosa	.65
135	Chuck Knoblauch	.05
136	Ellis Burks	.05
137	Al Martin	.05
138	Tim Salmon	.05
139	Moises Alou	.05
140	Lance Johnson	.05
141	Justin Thompson	.05
142	Will Clark	.05
143	Barry Bonds	1.50
144	Craig Biggio	.05
145	John Smoltz	.05
146	Cal Ripken Jr.	1.50
147	Ken Griffey Jr.	.75
148	Paul O'Neill	.05
149	Todd Helton	.40
150	John Olerud	.05
151	Mark McGwire	1.00
152	Jose Cruz Jr.	.05
153	Jeff Cirillo	.05
154	Dean Palmer	.05
155	John Wetteland	.05
156	Eric Karros	.05
157	Steve Finley	.05
158	Albert Belle	.05
159	Curt Schilling	.25
160	Raul Mondesi	.05
161	Andruw Jones	.50
162	Nomar Garciaparra	.65
163	David Justice	.05
164	Andy Pettitte	.20
165	Pedro Martinez	.50

1998 TOPPS STARS

		NM/M
Complete Set, Red or Bronze (150):		24.00
Common Player, Red or Bronze:		.10
Production 9,799 sets each		
Pack (6):		1.25
Wax Box (24):		25.00
1	Greg Maddux	1.50
2	Darryl Kile	.10
3	Rod Beck	.10
4	Ellis Burks	.10
5	Gary Sheffield	.40
6	David Ortiz	.10
7	Marquis Grissom	.10
8	Tony Womack	.10
9	Mike Mussina	.60
10	Bernie Williams	.10
11	Andy Benes	.10
12	Rusty Greer	.10
13	Carlos Delgado	.35
14	Jim Edmonds	.10
15	Raul Mondesi	.10
16	Andres Galarraga	.10
17	Wade Boggs	1.50
18	Paul O'Neill	.10
19	Edgar Renteria	.10
20	Tony Clark	.10
21	Vladimir Guerrero	1.00
22	Moises Alou	.10
23	Bernard Gilkey	.10
24	Lance Johnson	.10
25	Ben Grieve	.10
26	Sandy Alomar	.10
27	Ray Durham	.10
28	Shawn Estes	.10
29	David Segui	.10
30	Javy Lopez	.10
31	Steve Finley	.10
32	Rey Ordonez	.10
33	Derek Jeter	3.00
34	Henry Rodriguez	.10
35	Mo Vaughn	.10
36	Richard Hidalgo	.10
37	Omar Vizquel	.10
38	Johnny Damon	.35
39	Brian Hunter	.10
40	Matt Williams	.10
41	Chuck Finley	.10
42	Jeromy Burnitz	.10
43	Livan Hernandez	.10
44	Delino DeShields	.10
45	Charles Nagy	.10
46	Scott Rolen	.75
47	Neifi Perez	.10
48	John Wetteland	.10
49	Eric Milton	.10
50	Mike Piazza	2.00
51	Cal Ripken Jr.	3.00
52	Mariano Rivera	.25
53	Butch Huskey	.10
54	Quinton McCracken	.10
55	Jose Cruz Jr.	.10
56	Brian Jordan	.10
57	Hideo Nomo	.50
58	Masato Yoshii	.10
59	Cliff Floyd	.10
60	Jose Guillen	.10
61	Jeff Shaw	.10
62	Edgar Martinez	.10
63	Rondell White	.10
64	Hal Morris	.10
65	Barry Larkin	.10
66	Eric Young	.10
67	Ray Lankford	.10
68	Derek Bell	.10
69	Charles Johnson	.10
70	Robin Ventura	.10
71	Chuck Knoblauch	.10
72	Kevin Brown	.10
73	Jose Valentin	.10
74	Jay Buhner	.10
75	Tony Gwynn	1.50
76	Andy Pettitte	.30
77	Edgardo Alfonzo	.10
78	Kerry Wood	.40
79	Darin Erstad	.30
80	Paul Konerko	.15
81	Jason Kendall	.10
82	Tino Martinez	.10
83	Brad Radke	.10
84	Jeff King	.10
85	Travis Lee	.10
86	Jeff Kent	.10
87	Trevor Hoffman	.10
88	David Cone	.10
89	Jose Canseco	.40
90	Juan Gonzalez	.50
91	Todd Hundley	.10
92	John Valentin	.10
93	Sammy Sosa	1.50
94	Jason Giambi	.40
95	Chipper Jones	1.50
96	Jeff Blauser	.10
97	Brad Fullmer	.10
98	Derrek Lee	.60
99	Denny Neagle	.10
100	Ken Griffey Jr.	2.00
101	David Justice	.10
102	Tim Salmon	.10
103	J.T. Snow	.10
104	Fred McGriff	.10
105	Brady Anderson	.10
106	Larry Walker	.10
107	Jeff Cirillo	.10
108	Andruw Jones	1.00
109	Manny Ramirez	1.00
110	Justin Thompson	.10
111	Vinny Castilla	.10
112	Chan Ho Park	.10
113	Mark Grudzielanek	.10
114	Mark Grace	.10
115	Ken Caminiti	.10
116	Ryan Klesko	.10
117	Rafael Palmeiro	.75
118	Pat Hentgen	.10
119	Eric Karros	.10
120	Randy Johnson	1.00
121	Roberto Alomar	.25
122	John Olerud	.10
123	Paul Molitor	1.00
124	Dean Palmer	.10
125	Nomar Garciaparra	1.50
126	Curt Schilling	.30
127	Jay Bell	.10
128	Craig Biggio	.10
129	Marty Cordova	.10

130	Ivan Rodriguez	.75
131	Todd Helton	.75
132	Jim Thome	.65
133	Albert Belle	.10
134	Mike Lansing	.10
135	Mark McGwire	2.50
136	Roger Clemens	1.75
137	Tom Glavine	.30
138	Ron Gant	.10
139	Alex Rodriguez	2.50
140	Jeff Bagwell	1.00
141	John Smoltz	.10
142	Kenny Lofton	.10
143	Dante Bichette	.10
144	Pedro Martinez	1.00
145	Barry Bonds	3.00
146	Travis Fryman	.10
147	Bobby Jones	.10
148	Bobby Higginson	.10
149	Reggie Sanders	.10
150	Frank Thomas	1.00

Silver

	NM/M
Common Silver:	.50
Silver Stars:	1.5X

Production 4,399 sets
(See 1998 Topps Stars for checklist and base card values.)

Gold

	NM/M
Common Gold:	1.00
Gold Stars:	2X

Production 2,299 sets
(See 1998 Topps Stars for checklist and base card values.)

Gold Rainbow

	NM/M
Common Gold Rainbow:	4.00
Gold Rainbow Stars:	8X

Production 99 sets
(See 1998 Topps Stars for checklist and base card values.)

Galaxy

		NM/M
Complete Set (10):		150.00
Common Player:		7.50
Production 100 sets		
Silvers:		1.5X
Production 75 sets		
Golds:		2X
Production 50 sets		
Gold Rainbows:		
VALUES UNDETERMINED		
Production 5 sets		
G1	Barry Bonds	40.00
G2	Jeff Bagwell	15.00
G3	Nomar Garciaparra	20.00
G4	Chipper Jones	20.00
G5	Ken Griffey Jr.	25.00
G6	Sammy Sosa	20.00
G7	Larry Walker	7.50
G8	Alex Rodriguez	35.00
G9	Craig Biggio	7.50
G10	Raul Mondesi	7.50

Luminaries

		NM/M
Complete Set (15):		140.00
Common Player:		4.00
Production 100 sets		
Silver (75 sets):		1.5X
Gold (50 sets):		1.5X
Gold Rainbow (5 sets):		
VALUES UNDETERMINED		
L1	Ken Griffey Jr.	15.00
L2	Mark McGwire	20.00
L3	Juan Gonzalez	5.00
L4	Tony Gwynn	12.50
L5	Frank Thomas	10.00
L6	Mike Piazza	15.00
L7	Chuck Knoblauch	4.00
L8	Kenny Lofton	4.00
L9	Barry Bonds	25.00
L10	Matt Williams	4.00
L11	Raul Mondesi	4.00
L12	Ivan Rodriguez	7.50
L13	Alex Rodriguez	20.00
L14	Nomar Garciaparra	12.50
L15	Ken Caminiti	4.00

Rookie Reprints

		NM/M
Complete Set (5):		7.00
Common Player:		1.50
1968	Johnny Bench	1.50
1953	Whitey Ford	1.50
1965	Joe Morgan	1.50
1973	Mike Schmidt	2.50
1960	Carl Yastrzemski	2.00

Rookie Reprints Autographs

		NM/M
Complete Set (5):		175.00
Common Player:		25.00
1968	Johnny Bench	75.00
1953	Whitey Ford	35.00
1965	Joe Morgan	25.00
1973	Mike Schmidt	90.00
1960	Carl Yastrzemski	75.00

Supernovas

		NM/M
Complete Set (10):		35.00
Common Player:		2.00
Production 100 sets		
Silver:		1.5X
Production 75 sets		
Gold:		1.5X
Production 50 sets		
Gold Rainbow:		
VALUES UNDETERMINED		
Production 5 sets		
S1	Ben Grieve	2.00
S2	Travis Lee	2.00
S3	Todd Helton	10.00
S4	Adrian Beltre	2.50
S5	Derrek Lee	6.00
S6	David Ortiz	6.00
S7	Brad Fullmer	2.00
S8	Mark Kotsay	2.00
S9	Paul Konerko	2.50
S10	Kerry Wood	6.00

1998 TOPPS STARS 'N STEEL

		NM/M
Complete Set (44):		40.00
Common Player:		.25
Golds:		2X
Holographics:		7X
Pack (3):		3.50
Wax Box (12):		30.00
1	Roberto Alomar	.50

2	Jeff Bagwell	1.25
3	Albert Belle	.25
4	Dante Bichette	.25
5	Barry Bonds	4.00
6	Jay Buhner	.25
7	Ken Caminiti	.25
8	Vinny Castilla	.25
9	Roger Clemens	2.25
10	Jose Cruz Jr.	.25
11	Andres Galarraga	.25
12	Nomar Garciaparra	2.00
13	Juan Gonzalez	.65
14	Mark Grace	.25
15	Ken Griffey Jr.	2.50
16	Tony Gwynn	2.00
17	Todd Hundley	.25
18	Derek Jeter	4.00
19	Randy Johnson	1.25
20	Andruw Jones	1.25
21	Chipper Jones	2.00
22	David Justice	.25
23	Ray Lankford	.25
24	Barry Larkin	.25
25	Kenny Lofton	.25
26	Greg Maddux	2.00
27	Edgar Martinez	.25
28	Tino Martinez	.25
29	Mark McGwire	3.00
30	Paul Molitor	1.25
31	Rafael Palmeiro	1.00
32	Mike Piazza	2.50
33	Manny Ramirez	1.25
34	Cal Ripken Jr.	4.00
35	Ivan Rodriguez	1.00
36	Scott Rolen	.75
37	Tim Salmon	.25
38	Gary Sheffield	.50
39	Sammy Sosa	2.00
40	Frank Thomas	1.25
41	Jim Thome	1.00
42	Mo Vaughn	.25
43	Larry Walker	.25
44	Bernie Williams	.25

1998 TOPPS TEK

		NM/M
Complete Set (90):		75.00
Common Player:		.25
Pack (4):		4.00
Wax Box (20):		80.00
1	Ben Grieve	.25
2	Kerry Wood	1.50
3	Barry Bonds	8.00
4	John Olerud	.25
5	Ivan Rodriguez	2.00
6	Frank Thomas	2.50
7	Bernie Williams	.25
8	Dante Bichette	.25
9	Alex Rodriguez	6.00
10	Tom Glavine	.50
11	Eric Karros	.25
12	Craig Biggio	.25
13	Mark McGwire	6.00
14	Derek Jeter	8.00
15	Nomar Garciaparra	4.00
16	Brady Anderson	.25
17	Vladimir Guerrero	2.50
18	David Justice	.25
19	Chipper Jones	4.00
20	Jim Edmonds	.25
21	Roger Clemens	4.50
22	Mark Kotsay	.25
23	Tony Gwynn	4.00
24	Todd Walker	.25
25	Tino Martinez	.25
26	Andruw Jones	2.50
27	Sandy Alomar	.25
28	Sammy Sosa	4.00
29	Gary Sheffield	1.50
30	Ken Griffey Jr.	5.00
31	Aramis Ramirez	.25
32	Curt Schilling	.50
33	Robin Ventura	.25
34	Larry Walker	.25
35	Darin Erstad	1.25
36	Todd Dunwoody	.25
37	Paul O'Neill	.25
38	Vinny Castilla	.25
39	Randy Johnson	2.50
40	Rafael Palmeiro	2.00
41	Pedro Martinez	2.50
42	Derek Bell	.25
43	Carlos Delgado	.50
44	Matt Williams	.25
45	Kenny Lofton	.25
46	Edgar Renteria	.25
47	Albert Belle	.25
48	Jeromy Burnitz	.25
49	Adrian Beltre	.40
50	Greg Maddux	4.00
51	Cal Ripken Jr.	8.00
52	Jason Kendall	.25
53	Ellis Burks	.25
54	Paul Molitor	2.50
55	Moises Alou	.25
56	Raul Mondesi	.25
57	Barry Larkin	.25
58	Tony Clark	.25
59	Travis Lee	.25
60	Juan Gonzalez	1.25
61	*Troy Glaus*	3.00
62	Jose Cruz Jr.	.25
63	Paul Konerko	.40
64	Edgar Martinez	.25
65	Javy Lopez	.25
66	Manny Ramirez	2.50
67	Roberto Alomar	.75
68	Ken Caminiti	.25
69	Todd Helton	1.50
70	Chuck Knoblauch	.25
71	Kevin Brown	.25
72	Tim Salmon	.25
73	*Orlando Hernandez*	1.00
74	Jeff Bagwell	2.50
75	Brian Jordan	.25
76	Derrek Lee	1.50
77	Brad Fullmer	.25
78	Mark Grace	.25
79	Jeff King	.25
80	Mike Mussina	1.50
81	Jay Buhner	.25
82	Quinton McCracken	.25
83	A.J. Hinch	.25
84	Richard Hidalgo	.25
85	Andres Galarraga	.25
86	Mike Piazza	5.00
87	Mo Vaughn	.25
88	Scott Rolen	1.50
89	Jim Thome	2.00
90	Ray Lankford	.25

Diffraction

	NM/M
Complete Set (90):	400.00
Common Player:	4.00
Stars/RCs:	4X

(See 1998 Topps TEK for checklist and base card values.)

1999 TOPPS

	NM/M
Unop. Hobby Set (462):	40.00
Unop. Retail Set (463):	50.00
Complete Set (462):	35.00
Common Player:	.05
MVP Stars/Rookies:	20X
Ser. 1 or 2 Hobby Pack (11):	1.25
Ser. 1 or 2 Hobby Box (36):	40.00
Ser. 1 or 2 Retail Pack (8):	1.00

Ser. 1 or 2 Retail Box (22): 20.00
Ser. 1 or 2 Jumbo Pack (40): 3.50
Ser. 1 or 2 Jumbo Box (12): 30.00
1 Roger Clemens 1.00
2 Andres Galarraga .05
3 Scott Brosius .05
4 John Flaherty .05
5 Jim Leyritz .05
6 Ray Durham .05
7 NOT ISSUED
8 Joe Vizcaino .05
9 Will Clark .05
10 David Wells .05
11 Jose Guillen .05
12 Scott Hatteberg .05
13 Edgardo Alfonzo .05
14 Mike Bordick .05
15 Manny Ramirez .75
16 Greg Maddux 1.00
17 David Segui .05
18 Darryl Strawberry .05
19 Brad Radke .05
20 Kerry Wood .40
21 Matt Anderson .05
22 Derrek Lee .60
23 Mickey Morandini .05
24 Paul Konerko .15
25 Travis Lee .15
26 Ken Hill .05
27 Kenny Rogers .05
28 Paul Sorrento .05
29 Quilvio Veras .05
30 Todd Walker .05
31 Ryan Jackson .05
32 John Olerud .05
33 Doug Glanville .05
34 Nolan Ryan 2.00
35 Ray Lankford .05
36 Mark Loretta .05
37 Jason Dickson .05
38 Sean Bergman .05
39 Quinton McCracken .05
40 Bartolo Colon .05
41 Brady Anderson .05
42 Chris Stynes .05
43 Jorge Posada .05
44 Justin Thompson .05
45 Johnny Damon .30
46 Armando Benitez .05
47 Brant Brown .05
48 Charlie Hayes .05
49 Darren Dreifort .05
50 Juan Gonzalez .40
51 Chuck Knoblauch .05
52 Todd Helton .75
53 Rick Reed .05
54 Chris Gomez .05
55 Gary Sheffield .45
56 Rod Beck .05
57 Rey Sanchez .05
58 Garret Anderson .05
59 Jimmy Haynes .05
60 Steve Woodard .05
61 Rondell White .05
62 Vladimir Guerrero .75
63 Eric Karros .05
64 Russ Davis .05
65 Mo Vaughn .05
66 Sammy Sosa 1.00
67 Troy Percival .05
68 Kenny Lofton .05
69 Bill Taylor .05
70 Mark McGwire 1.50
71 Roger Cedeno .05
72 Javy Lopez .05
73 Damion Easley .05
74 Andy Pettitte .25
75 Tony Gwynn 1.00
76 Ricardo Rincon .05
77 F.P. Santangelo .05
78 Jay Bell .05
79 Scott Servais .05
80 Jose Canseco .40
81 Roberto Hernandez .05
82 Todd Dunwoody .05
83 John Wetteland .05
84 Mike Caruso .05
85 Derek Jeter 2.00
86 Aaron Sele .05
87 Jose Lima .05
88 Ryan Christenson .05
89 Jeff Cirillo .05
90 Jose Hernandez .05
91 Mark Kotsay .05
92 Darren Bragg .05
93 Albert Belle .05
94 Matt Lawton .05
95 Pedro Martinez .75
96 Greg Vaughn .05
97 Neifi Perez .05
98 Gerald Williams .05
99 Derek Bell .05
100 Ken Griffey Jr. 1.25
101 David Cone .05
102 Brian Johnson .05
103 Dean Palmer .05
104 Javier Valentin .05
105 Trevor Hoffman .05
106 Butch Huskey .05
107 Dave Martinez .05
108 Billy Wagner .05
109 Shawn Green .30
110 Ben Grieve .05
111 Tom Goodwin .05
112 Jaret Wright .05
113 Aramis Ramirez .05
114 Dmitri Young .05
115 Hideki Irabu .05
116 Roberto Kelly .05
117 Jeff Fassero .05
118 Mark Clark .05
119 Jason McDonald .05
120 Matt Williams .05
121 Dave Burba .05
122 Bret Saberhagen .05
123 Deivi Cruz .05
124 Chad Curtis .05
125 Scott Rolen .65
126 Lee Stevens .05
127 J.T. Snow Jr. .05
128 Rusty Greer .05
129 Brian Meadows .05
130 Jim Edmonds .05
131 Ron Gant .05
132 A.J. Hinch .05
133 Shannon Stewart .05
134 Brad Fullmer .05
135 Cal Eldred .05
136 Matt Walbeck .05
137 Carl Everett .05
138 Walt Weiss .05
139 Fred McGriff .05
140 Darin Erstad .25
141 Dave Nilsson .05
142 Eric Young .05
143 Dan Wilson .05
144 Jeff Reed .05
145 Brett Tomko .05
146 Terry Steinbach .05
147 Seth Greisinger .05
148 Pat Meares .05
149 Livan Hernandez .05
150 Jeff Bagwell .75
151 Bob Wickman .05
152 Omar Vizquel .05
153 Eric Davis .05
154 Larry Sutton .05
155 Magglio Ordonez .40
156 Eric Milton .05
157 Darren Lewis .05
158 Rick Aguilera .05
159 Mike Lieberthal .05
160 Robb Nen .05
161 Brian Giles .05
162 Jeff Brantley .05
163 Gary DiSarcina .05
164 John Valentin .05
165 David Dellucci .05
166 Chan Ho Park .05
167 Masato Yoshii .05
168 Jason Schmidt .05
169 LaTroy Hawkins .05
170 Bret Boone .05
171 Jerry DiPoto .05
172 Mariano Rivera .10
173 Mike Cameron .05
174 Scott Erickson .05
175 Charles Johnson .05
176 Bobby Jones .05
177 Francisco Cordova .05
178 Todd Jones .05
179 Jeff Montgomery .05
180 Mike Mussina .40
181 Bob Abreu .05
182 Ismael Valdes .05
183 Andy Fox .05
184 Woody Williams .05
185 Denny Neagle .05
186 Jose Valentin .05
187 Darrin Fletcher .05
188 Gabe Alvarez .05
189 Eddie Taubensee .05
190 Edgar Martinez .05
191 Jason Kendall .05
192 Darryl Kile .05
193 Jeff King .05
194 Rey Ordonez .05
195 Andruw Jones .75
196 Tony Fernandez .05
197 Jamey Wright .05
198 B.J. Surhoff .05
199 Vinny Castilla .05
200 David Wells .05
201 Mark McGwire .75
202 Sammy Sosa .50
203 Roger Clemens .50
204 Kerry Wood .15
205 Lance Berkman, Mike Frank, Gabe Kapler .15
206 Alex Escobar, Ricky Ledee, Mike Stoner .25
207 Peter Bergeron, Jeremy Giambi, George Lombard .30
208 Michael Barrett, Ben Davis, Robert Fick .05
209 Pat Cline, Ramon Hernandez, Jayson Werth .05
210 Bruce Chen, Chris Enochs, Ryan Anderson .05
211 Mike Lincoln, Octavio Dotel, Brad Penny .05
212 Chuck Abbott, Brent Butler, Danny Klassen .05
213 *Chris Jones, Jeff Urban* (Draft Pick) .05
214 *Arturo McDowell, Tony Torcato* .25
215 *Josh McKinley, Jason Tyner* .25
216 *Matt Burch, Seth Etherton* .25
217 *Mamon Tucker, Rick Elder* .10
218 *J.M. Gold, Ryan Mills* .10
219 *Adam Brown, Choo Freeman* .25
220 M. McGwire Home Run Record #1 20.00
220 M. McGwire HR Record #2-60 6.00
220 M. McGwire HR Record #61-62 10.00
220 M. McGwire HR Record #63-69 15.00
220 Mark McGwire HR Record #70 40.00
221 Larry Walker .05
222 Bernie Williams .05
223 Mark McGwire .75
224 Ken Griffey Jr. .65
225 Sammy Sosa .50
226 Juan Gonzalez .20
227 Dante Bichette .05
228 Alex Rodriguez .75
229 Sammy Sosa .50
230 Derek Jeter 1.00
231 Greg Maddux .50
232 Roger Clemens .50
233 Ricky Ledee .05
234 Chuck Knoblauch .05
235 Bernie Williams .05
236 Tino Martinez .05
237 Orlando Hernandez .05
238 Scott Brosius .05
239 Andy Pettitte .05
240 Mariano Rivera .05
241 Checklist .05
242 Checklist .05
243 Tom Glavine .25
244 Andy Benes .05
245 Sandy Alomar .05
246 Wilton Guerrero .05
247 Alex Gonzalez .05
248 Roberto Alomar .30
249 Ruben Rivera .05
250 Eric Chavez .15
251 Ellis Burks .05
252 Richie Sexson .05
253 Steve Finley .05
254 Dwight Gooden .05
255 Dustin Hermanson .05
256 Kirk Rueter .05
257 Steve Trachsel .05
258 Gregg Jefferies .05
259 Matt Stairs .05
260 Shane Reynolds .05
261 Gregg Olson .05
262 Kevin Tapani .05
263 Matt Morris .05
264 Carl Pavano .05
265 Nomar Garciaparra 1.00
266 Kevin Young .05
267 Rick Helling .05
268 Mark Leiter .05
269 Brian McRae .05
270 Cal Ripken Jr. 2.00
271 Jeff Abbott .05
272 Tony Batista .05
273 Bill Simas .05
274 Brian Hunter .05
275 John Franco .05
276 Devon White .05
277 Rickey Henderson .75
278 Chuck Finley .05
279 Mike Blowers .05
280 Mark Grace .05
281 Randy Winn .05
282 Bobby Bonilla .05
283 David Justice .05
284 Shane Monahan .05
285 Kevin Brown .05
286 Todd Zeile .05
287 Al Martin .05
288 Troy O'Leary .05
289 Darryl Hamilton .05
290 Tino Martinez .05
291 David Ortiz .45
292 Tony Clark .05
293 Ryan Minor .05
294 Reggie Sanders .05
295 Wally Joyner .05
296 Cliff Floyd .05
297 Shawn Estes .05
298 Pat Hentgen .05
299 Scott Elarton .05
300 Alex Rodriguez 1.50
301 Ozzie Guillen .05
302 Manny Martinez .05
303 Ryan McGuire .05
304 Brad Ausmus .05
305 Alex Gonzalez .05
306 Brian Jordan .05
307 John Jaha .05
308 Mark Grudzielanek .05
309 Juan Guzman .05
310 Tony Womack .05
311 Dennis Reyes .05
312 Marty Cordova .05
313 Ramiro Mendoza .05
314 Robin Ventura .05
315 Rafael Palmeiro .60
316 Ramon Martinez .05
317 John Mabry .05
318 Dave Hollins .05
319 Tom Candiotti .05
320 Al Leiter .05
321 Rico Brogna .05
322 Jimmy Key .05
323 Bernard Gilkey .05
324 Jason Giambi .45
325 Craig Biggio .05
326 Troy Glaus .65
327 Delino DeShields .05
328 Fernando Vina .05
329 John Smoltz .05
330 Jeff Kent .05
331 Roy Halladay .05
332 Andy Ashby .05
333 Tim Wakefield .05
334 Tim Belcher .05
335 Bernie Williams .05
336 Desi Relaford .05
337 John Burkett .05
338 Mike Hampton .05
339 Royce Clayton .05
340 Mike Piazza 1.25
341 Jeremi Gonzalez .05
342 Mike Lansing .05
343 Jamie Moyer .05
344 Ron Coomer .05
345 Barry Larkin .05
346 Fernando Tatis .05
347 Chili Davis .05
348 Bobby Higginson .05
349 Hal Morris .05

350 Larry Walker .05
351 Carlos Guillen .05
352 Miguel Tejada .05
353 Travis Fryman .05
354 Jarrod Washburn .05
355 Chipper Jones 1.00
356 Todd Stottlemyre .05
357 Henry Rodriguez .05
358 Eli Marrero .05
359 Alan Benes .05
360 Tim Salmon .05
361 Luis Gonzalez .05
362 Scott Spiezio .05
363 Chris Carpenter .05
364 Bobby Howry .05
365 Raul Mondesi .05
366 Ugueth Urbina .05
367 Tom Evans .05
368 *Kerry Ligtenberg* .15
369 Adrian Beltre .15
370 Ryan Klesko .05
371 Wilson Alvarez .05
372 John Thomson .05
373 Tony Saunders .05
374 Mike Stanley .05
375 Ken Caminiti .05
376 Jay Buhner .05
377 Bill Mueller .05
378 Jeff Blauser .05
379 Edgar Renteria .05
380 Jim Thome .60
381 Joey Hamilton .05
382 Calvin Pickering .05
383 Marquis Grissom .05
384 Omar Daal .05
385 Curt Schilling .25
386 Jose Cruz Jr. .05
387 Chris Widger .05
388 Pete Harnisch .05
389 Charles Nagy .05
390 Tom Gordon .05
391 Bobby Smith .05
392 Derrick Gibson .05
393 Jeff Conine .05
394 Carlos Perez .05
395 Barry Bonds 2.00
396 Mark McLemore .05
397 Juan Encarnacion .05
398 Wade Boggs 1.00
399 Ivan Rodriguez .65
400 Moises Alou .05
401 Jeromy Burnitz .05
402 Sean Casey .10
403 Jose Offerman .05
404 Joe Fontenot .05
405 Kevin Millwood .05
406 Lance Johnson .05
407 Richard Hidalgo .05
408 Mike Jackson .05
409 Brian Anderson .05
410 Jeff Shaw .05
411 Preston Wilson .05
412 Todd Hundley .05
413 Jim Parque .05
414 Justin Baughman .05
415 Dante Bichette .05
416 Paul O'Neill .05
417 Miguel Cairo .05
418 Randy Johnson .75
419 Jesus Sanchez .05
420 Carlos Delgado .30
421 Ricky Ledee .05
422 Orlando Hernandez .05
423 Frank Thomas .75
424 Pokey Reese .05
425 *Carlos Lee, Mike Lowell, Kit Pellow* .25
426 Michael Cuddyer, Mark DeRosa, Jerry Hairston Jr. .05
427 Marlon Anderson, Ron Belliard, Orlando Cabrera .10
428 Micah Bowie, Phil Norton, Randy Wolf .10
429 Jack Cressend, Jason Rakers, John Rocker .10
430 *Ruben Mateo, Scott Morgan, Mike Zywica* .10
431 Jason LaRue, Matt LeCroy, Mitch Meluskey .10
432 Gabe Kapler, Armando Rios, Fernando Seguignol .05
433 Adam Kennedy, Mickey Lopez, Jackie Rexrode .10
434 Jose Fernandez, Jeff Liefer, Chris Truby .10
435 Corey Koskie, Doug Mientkiewicz, Damon Minor .10
436 Roosevelt Brown, Dernell Stenson, Vernon Wells .10
437 A.J. Burnett, John Nicholson, Billy Koch .25
438 *Matt Belisle, Matt Roney* .10
439 *Austin Kearns, Chris George* 2.50
440 *Nate Bump, Nate Cornejo* .40
441 *Brad Lidge, Mike Nannini* .25
442 *Matt Holiday, Jeff Winchester* .25
443 *Adam Everett, Chip Ambres* .25
444 *Pat Burrell, Eric Valent* 1.50
445 Roger Clemens .50
446 Kerry Wood .15
447 Curt Schilling .05
448 Randy Johnson .40
449 Pedro Martinez .40
450 Jeff Bagwell, Andres Galarraga, Mark McGwire .50
451 John Olerud, Jim Thome, Tino Martinez .30
452 Alex Rodriguez, Nomar Garciaparra, Derek Jeter .60
453 Vinny Castilla, Chipper Jones, Scott Rolen .40
454 Sammy Sosa, Ken Griffey Jr., Juan Gonzalez .50
455 Barry Bonds, Manny Ramirez, Larry Walker .60
456 Frank Thomas, Tim Salmon, David Justice .30
457 Travis Lee, Todd Helton, Ben Grieve .30
458 Vladimir Guerrero, Greg Vaughn, Bernie Williams .25
459 Mike Piazza, Ivan Rodriguez, Jason Kendall .50
460 Roger Clemens, Kerry Wood, Greg Maddux .45
461 Sammy Sosa Home Run Parade #1 10.00
461 Sammy Sosa HR Parade #2-60 4.00
461 Sammy Sosa HR Parade #61-62 10.00
461 Sammy Sosa HR Parade #63-65 6.00
461 Sammy Sosa HR Parade #66 20.00
462 Checklist .05
463 Checklist .05

1999 TOPPS MVP PROMOTION

NM/M

Common Player: 3.00
Stars/Rookies: 20X
(See 1999 Topps for checklist and base card values.)

Autographs

NM/M

Common Player: 8.00
Series 1 Inserted 1:532 H
Series 2 Inserted 1:501 H

A1 Roger Clemens 100.00
A2 Chipper Jones 40.00
A3 Scott Rolen 25.00
A4 Alex Rodriguez 100.00

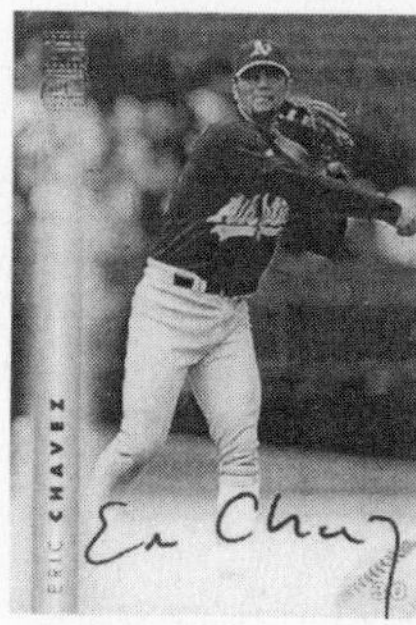

A5 Andres Galarraga 8.00
A6 Rondell White 8.00
A7 Ben Grieve 8.00
A8 Troy Glaus 20.00
A9 Moises Alou 15.00
A10 Barry Bonds 200.00
A11 Vladimir Guerrero 35.00
A12 Andruw Jones 20.00
A13 Darin Erstad 12.00
A14 Shawn Green 16.00
A15 Eric Chavez 20.00
A16 Pat Burrell 25.00

All-Matrix

NM/M

Complete Set (30): 45.00
Common Player: .75
Inserted 1:18

AM1 Mark McGwire 6.00
AM2 Sammy Sosa 3.50
AM3 Ken Griffey Jr. 4.50
AM4 Greg Vaughn .75
AM5 Albert Belle .75
AM6 Vinny Castilla .75
AM7 Jose Canseco 1.25
AM8 Juan Gonzalez 1.25
AM9 Manny Ramirez 2.50
AM10 Andres Galarraga .75
AM11 Rafael Palmeiro 2.00
AM12 Alex Rodriguez 6.00
AM13 Mo Vaughn .75
AM14 Eric Chavez 1.25
AM15 Gabe Kapler .75
AM16 Calvin Pickering .75
AM17 Ruben Mateo .75
AM18 Roy Halladay 1.25
AM19 Jeremy Giambi .75
AM20 Alex Gonzalez .75
AM21 Ron Belliard .75
AM22 Marlon Anderson .75
AM23 Carlos Lee .75
AM24 Kerry Wood 1.25
AM25 Roger Clemens 3.50
AM26 Curt Schilling 1.25
AM27 Kevin Brown .75
AM28 Randy Johnson 2.50
AM29 Pedro Martinez 2.50
AM30 Orlando Hernandez .75

All-Topps Mystery Finest

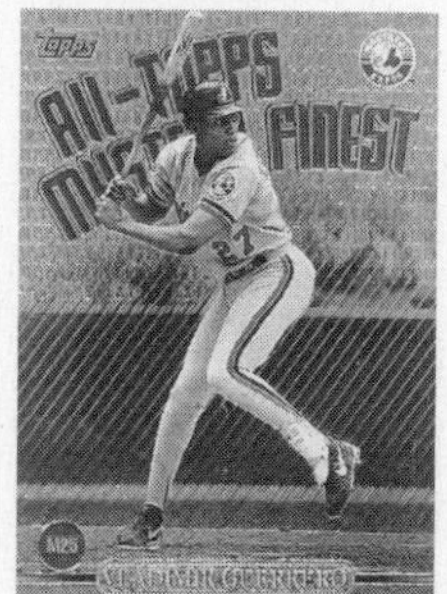

NM/M

Complete Set (33): 100.00
Common Player: 1.00
Inserted 1:36
Refractors: 1.5X
Inserted 1:144

M1 Jeff Bagwell 4.25
M2 Andres Galarraga 1.00
M3 Mark McGwire 9.00
M4 John Olerud 1.00
M5 Jim Thome 2.50
M6 Tino Martinez 1.00
M7 Alex Rodriguez 9.00
M8 Nomar Garciaparra 5.00
M9 Derek Jeter 12.50
M10 Vinny Castilla 1.00
M11 Chipper Jones 5.00
M12 Scott Rolen 3.00
M13 Sammy Sosa 5.00
M14 Ken Griffey Jr. 7.50
M15 Juan Gonzalez 2.00
M16 Barry Bonds 12.50
M17 Manny Ramirez 4.50
M18 Larry Walker 1.00
M19 Frank Thomas 4.50
M20 Tim Salmon 1.00
M21 David Justice 1.00
M22 Travis Lee 1.50
M23 Todd Helton 4.50
M24 Ben Grieve 1.00
M25 Vladimir Guerrero 4.50
M26 Greg Vaughn 1.00
M27 Bernie Williams 1.00
M28 Mike Piazza 7.50
M29 Ivan Rodriguez 3.50
M30 Jason Kendall 1.00
M31 Roger Clemens 6.00
M32 Kerry Wood 2.00
M33 Greg Maddux 5.00

Hall of Fame

NM/M

Complete Set (10): 8.00
Common Player: .50
Inserted 1:12 H

HOF1 Mike Schmidt 1.50
HOF2 Brooks Robinson .75
HOF3 Stan Musial 1.50
HOF4 Willie McCovey .50
HOF5 Eddie Mathews .75
HOF6 Reggie Jackson 1.50
HOF7 Ernie Banks 1.00
HOF8 Whitey Ford .75
HOF9 Bob Feller .50
HOF10 Yogi Berra 1.00

Lords of the Diamond

NM/M

Complete Set (15): 13.00
Common Player: .25
Inserted 1:18

LD1 Ken Griffey Jr. 1.25
LD2 Chipper Jones 1.00
LD3 Sammy Sosa 1.00
LD4 Frank Thomas .75
LD5 Mark McGwire 1.50
LD6 Jeff Bagwell .75
LD7 Alex Rodriguez 1.50
LD8 Juan Gonzalez .40
LD9 Barry Bonds 2.00
LD10 Nomar Garciaparra 1.00
LD11 Darin Erstad .35
LD12 Tony Gwynn 1.00
LD13 Andres Galarraga .25
LD14 Mike Piazza 1.25
LD15 Greg Maddux 1.00

New Breed

NM/M

Complete Set (15): 9.00
Common Player: .25
Inserted 1:18

NB1 Darin Erstad .50
NB2 Brad Fullmer .25
NB3 Kerry Wood .50
NB4 Nomar Garciaparra 1.50
NB5 Travis Lee .35
NB6 Scott Rolen .75

NB7	Todd Helton	.75
NB8	Vladimir Guerrero	1.00
NB9	Derek Jeter	3.00
NB10	Alex Rodriguez	2.00
NB11	Ben Grieve	.25
NB12	Andruw Jones	1.00
NB13	Paul Konerko	.40
NB14	Aramis Ramirez	.25
NB15	Adrian Beltre	.35

Nolan Ryan Reprints

		NM/M
Complete Set (27):		40.00
Common Ryan:		3.00
Inserted 1:18		
Nolan Ryan Autograph:		150.00
1	Nolan Ryan (1968)	7.50
2	Nolan Ryan (1969)	4.50
3	Nolan Ryan (1970)	3.00
4	Nolan Ryan (1971)	3.00
5	Nolan Ryan (1972)	3.00
6	Nolan Ryan (1973)	3.00
7	Nolan Ryan (1974)	3.00
8	Nolan Ryan (1975)	3.00
9	Nolan Ryan (1976)	3.00
10	Nolan Ryan (1977)	3.00
11	Nolan Ryan (1978)	3.00
12	Nolan Ryan (1979)	3.00
13	Nolan Ryan (1980)	3.00
14	Nolan Ryan (1981)	3.00
15	Nolan Ryan (1982)	3.00
16	Nolan Ryan (1983)	3.00
17	Nolan Ryan (1984)	3.00
18	Nolan Ryan (1985)	3.00
19	Nolan Ryan (1986)	3.00
20	Nolan Ryan (1987)	3.00
21	Nolan Ryan (1988)	3.00
22	Nolan Ryan (1989)	3.00
23	Nolan Ryan (1990)	3.00
24	Nolan Ryan (1991)	3.00
25	Nolan Ryan (1992)	3.00
26	Nolan Ryan (1993)	3.00
27	Nolan Ryan (1994)	3.00

Nolan Ryan Finest Reprints

		NM/M
Complete Set (27):		125.00
Common Card:		5.00
Inserted 1:72		
Refractors:		2X
Inserted 1:288		
1	1968	12.50
2	1969	7.50
3	1970	5.00
4	1971	5.00
5	1972	5.00
6	1973	5.00
7	1974	5.00
8	1975	5.00
9	1976	5.00
10	1977	5.00
11	1978	5.00
12	1979	5.00
13	1980	5.00
14	1981	5.00
15	1982	5.00
16	1983	5.00
17	1984	5.00
18	1985	5.00
19	1986	5.00
20	1987	5.00
21	1988	5.00
22	1989	5.00
23	1990	5.00
24	1991	5.00
25	1992	5.00
26	1992	5.00
27	1992	5.00

Nolan Ryan Reprint Autographs

		NM/M
Common Card:		150.00
1	Nolan Ryan (1968)	200.00
2	Nolan Ryan (1969)	150.00
3	Nolan Ryan (1970)	150.00
4	Nolan Ryan (1971)	150.00
5	Nolan Ryan (1972)	150.00
6	Nolan Ryan (1973)	150.00
7	Nolan Ryan (1974)	150.00
8	Nolan Ryan (1975)	150.00
9	Nolan Ryan (1976)	150.00
10	Nolan Ryan (1977)	150.00
11	Nolan Ryan (1978)	150.00
12	Nolan Ryan (1979)	150.00
13	Nolan Ryan (1980)	150.00
14	Nolan Ryan (1981)	150.00
15	Nolan Ryan (1982)	150.00
16	Nolan Ryan (1983)	150.00
17	Nolan Ryan (1984)	150.00
18	Nolan Ryan (1985)	150.00
19	Nolan Ryan (1986)	150.00
20	Nolan Ryan (1987)	150.00
21	Nolan Ryan (1988)	150.00
22	Nolan Ryan (1989)	150.00
23	Nolan Ryan (1990)	150.00
24	Nolan Ryan (1991)	150.00
25	Nolan Ryan (1992)	150.00
26	Nolan Ryan (1993)	150.00
27	Nolan Ryan (1994)	150.00

Picture Perfect

		NM/M
Complete Set (10):		5.00
Common Player:		.25
Inserted 1:8		
P1	Ken Griffey Jr.	.75
P2	Kerry Wood	.30
P3	Pedro Martinez	.45
P4	Mark McGwire	.90
P5	Greg Maddux	.60
P6	Sammy Sosa	.60
P7	Greg Vaughn	.25
P8	Juan Gonzalez	.30
P9	Jeff Bagwell	.45
P10	Derek Jeter	1.50

Power Brokers

		NM/M
Complete Set (20):		20.00
Common Player:		.25
Inserted 1:36		
Refractors:		1.5X
Inserted 1:144		
PB1	Mark McGwire	3.00
PB2	Andres Galarraga	.25
PB3	Ken Griffey Jr.	2.00
PB4	Sammy Sosa	1.50
PB5	Juan Gonzalez	.50
PB6	Alex Rodriguez	3.00
PB7	Frank Thomas	1.00
PB8	Jeff Bagwell	1.00
PB9	Vinny Castilla	.25
PB10	Mike Piazza	2.00
PB11	Greg Vaughn	.25
PB12	Barry Bonds	4.00
PB13	Mo Vaughn	.25
PB14	Jim Thome	.65
PB15	Larry Walker	.25
PB16	Chipper Jones	1.50
PB17	Nomar Garciaparra	1.50
PB18	Manny Ramirez	1.00
PB19	Roger Clemens	1.75
PB20	Kerry Wood	.65

Record Numbers

		NM/M
Complete Set (10):		7.50
Common Player:		.35
Inserted 1:8		
RN1	Mark McGwire	1.50
RN2	Mike Piazza	1.00
RN3	Curt Schilling	.35
RN4	Ken Griffey Jr.	1.00
RN5	Sammy Sosa	.65
RN6	Nomar Garciaparra	.65
RN7	Kerry Wood	.40
RN8	Roger Clemens	.75
RN9	Cal Ripken Jr.	2.00
RN10	Mark McGwire	1.50

1999 TOPPS TRADED AND ROOKIES

		NM/M
Unopened Set (122):		30.00
Complete Set, No Autograph (121):		10.00
Common Player:		.10
1	Seth Etherton	.10
2	*Mark Harriger*	.10
3	*Matt Wise*	.25
4	*Carlos Hernandez*	.15
5	*Julio Lugo*	.25
6	Mike Nannini	.10
7	*Justin Bowles*	.10
8	*Mark Mulder*	1.00
9	*Roberto Vaz*	.10
10	*Felipe Lopez*	.50
11	Matt Belisle	.10
12	Micah Bowie	.10
13	*Ruben Quevedo*	.10
14	*Jose Garcia*	.10
15	*David Kelton*	.25
16	Phillip Norton	.10
17	*Corey Patterson*	1.50
18	*Ron Walker*	.10
19	*Paul Hoover*	.10
20	*Ryan Rupe*	.15
21	*J.D. Closser*	.10
22	*Rob Ryan*	.10
23	*Steve Colyer*	.10
24	*Bubba Crosby*	.50
25	*Luke Prokopec*	.10
26	*Matt Blank*	.10
27	Josh McKinley	.10
28	Nate Bump	.10
29	*Giuseppe Chiaramonte*	.10
30	Arturo McDowell	.10
31	Tony Torcato	.10
32	Dave Roberts	.10
33	*C.C. Sabathia*	.75
34	*Sean Spencer*	.10
35	Chip Ambres	.10
36	A.J. Burnett	.15
37	*Mo Bruce*	.10
38	Jason Tyner	.10
39	Mamon Tucker	.10
40	*Sean Burroughs*	1.00
41	*Kevin Eberwein*	.10
42	*Junior Herndon*	.10
43	*Bryan Wolff*	.10
44	Pat Burrell	.50
45	Eric Valent	.10
46	*Carlos Pena*	.50
47	Mike Zywica	.10
48	Adam Everett	.10
49	*Juan Pena*	.50
50	*Adam Dunn*	3.00
51	Austin Kearns	.75
52	*Jacobo Sequea*	.10
53	Choo Freeman	.10
54	Jeff Winchester	.10
55	Matt Burch	.10
56	Chris George	.10
57	*Scott Mullen*	.10
58	Kit Pellow	.10
59	*Mark Quinn*	.15
60	Nate Cornejo	.10
61	*Ryan Mills*	.25
62	*Kevin Beirne*	.10
63	*Kip Wells*	.50
64	*Juan Rivera*	.25
65	*Alfonso Soriano*	4.00
66	*Josh Hamilton*	.25
67	*Josh Girdley*	.10
68	*Kyle Snyder*	.15
69	*Mike Paradis*	.10
70	*Jason Jennings*	.25
71	*David Walling*	.10
72	*Omar Ortiz*	.10
73	*Jay Gehrke*	.10
74	*Casey Burns*	.10
75	*Carl Crawford*	.75
76	Reggie Sanders	.10
77	Will Clark	.10
78	David Wells	.10
79	Paul Konerko	.20
80	Armando Benitez	.10
81	Brant Brown	.10
82	Mo Vaughn	.10
83	Jose Canseco	.30
84	Albert Belle	.10
85	Dean Palmer	.10
86	Greg Vaughn	.10
87	Mark Clark	.10
88	Pat Meares	.10
89	Eric Davis	.10
90	Brian Giles	.10
91	Jeff Brantley	.10
92	Bret Boone	.10
93	Ron Gant	.10
94	Mike Cameron	.10
95	Charles Johnson	.10
96	Denny Neagle	.10
97	Brian Hunter	.10
98	Jose Hernandez	.10
99	Rick Aguilera	.10
100	Tony Batista	.10
101	Roger Cedeno	.10
102	Creighton Gubanich	.10
103	Tim Belcher	.10
104	Bruce Aven	.10
105	*Brian Daubach*	.30
106	Ed Sprague	.10
107	Michael Tucker	.10
108	Homer Bush	.10
109	Armando Reynoso	.10
110	Brook Fordyce	.10
111	Matt Mantei	.10
112	Jose Guillen	.10
113	Kenny Rogers	.10
114	Livan Hernandez	.10
115	Butch Huskey	.10
116	David Segui	.10
117	Darryl Hamilton	.10
118	Jim Leyritz	.10
119	Randy Velarde	.10
120	Bill Taylor	.10
121	Kevin Appier	.10

Autographs

		NM/M
Common Player:		3.00
Inserted 1:set		
1	Seth Etherton	3.00
2	Mark Harriger	3.00
3	Matt Wise	5.00
4	Carlos Hernandez	5.00
5	Julio Lugo	5.00
6	Mike Nannini	3.00
7	Justin Bowles	3.00
8	Mark Mulder	50.00
9	Roberto Vaz	3.00
10	Felipe Lopez	30.00
11	Matt Belisle	3.00
12	Micah Bowie	3.00

13	Ruben Quevedo	5.00
14	Jose Garcia	5.00
15	David Kelton	10.00
16	Phillip Norton	5.00
17	Corey Patterson	35.00
18	Ron Walker	3.00
19	Paul Hoover	3.00
20	Ryan Rupe	4.00
21	J.D. Closser	8.00
22	Rob Ryan	3.00
23	Steve Colyer	5.00
24	Bubba Crosby	15.00
25	Luke Prokopec	3.00
26	Matt Blank	3.00
27	Josh McKinley	5.00
28	Nate Bump	5.00
29	Giuseppe Chiaramonte	3.00
30	Arturo McDowell	3.00
31	Tony Torcato	5.00
32	Dave Roberts	10.00
33	C.C. Sabathia	25.00
34	Sean Spencer	3.00
35	Chip Ambres	3.00
36	A.J. Burnett	25.00
37	Mo Bruce	3.00
38	Jason Tyner	3.00
39	Mamon Tucker	3.00
40	Sean Burroughs	15.00
41	Kevin Eberwein	3.00
42	Junior Herndon	3.00
43	Bryan Wolff	3.00
44	Pat Burrell	50.00
45	Eric Valent	8.00
46	Carlos Pena	10.00
47	Mike Zywica	3.00
48	Adam Everett	15.00
49	Juan Pena	5.00
50	Adam Dunn	100.00
51	Austin Kearns	30.00
52	Jacobo Sequea	3.00
53	Choo Freeman	8.00
54	Jeff Winchester	3.00
55	Matt Burch	3.00
56	Chris George	4.00
57	Scott Mullen	3.00
58	Kit Pellow	3.00
59	Mark Quinn	3.00
60	Nate Cornejo	8.00
61	Ryan Mills	3.00
62	Kevin Beirne	4.00
63	Kip Wells	8.00
64	Juan Rivera	10.00
65	Alfonso Soriano	125.00
66	Josh Hamilton	10.00
67	Josh Girdley	3.00
68	Kyle Snyder	5.00
69	Mike Paradis	3.00
70	Jason Jennings	10.00
71	David Walling	3.00
72	Omar Ortiz	3.00
73	Jay Gehrke	5.00
74	Casey Burns	3.00
75	Carl Crawford	30.00

1999 TOPPS CHROME

	NM/M
Complete Set (461):	75.00
Common Player:	.15
Refractors:	4X
Inserted 1:12	
Ser. 1 or 2 Pack (4):	1.50
Ser. 1 or 2 Box (24):	30.00

1	Roger Clemens	1.75
2	Andres Galarraga	.15
3	Scott Brosius	.15
4	John Flaherty	.15
5	Jim Leyritz	.15
6	Ray Durham	.15
7	NOT ISSUED	
8	Joe Vizcaino	.15
9	Will Clark	.15
10	David Wells	.15
11	Jose Guillen	.15
12	Scott Hatteberg	.15
13	Edgardo Alfonzo	.15
14	Mike Bordick	.15
15	Manny Ramirez	1.00
16	Greg Maddux	1.50
17	David Segui	.15
18	Darryl Strawberry	.15
19	Brad Radke	.15
20	Kerry Wood	.40
21	Matt Anderson	.15
22	Derrek Lee	.60
23	Mickey Morandini	.15
24	Paul Konerko	.30
25	Travis Lee	.15
26	Ken Hill	.15
27	Kenny Rogers	.15
28	Paul Sorrento	.15
29	Quilvio Veras	.15
30	Todd Walker	.15
31	Ryan Jackson	.15
32	John Olerud	.15
33	Doug Glanville	.15
34	Nolan Ryan	3.00
35	Ray Lankford	.15
36	Mark Loretta	.15
37	Jason Dickson	.15
38	Sean Bergman	.15
39	Quinton McCracken	.15
40	Bartolo Colon	.15
41	Brady Anderson	.15
42	Chris Stynes	.15
43	Jorge Posada	.15
44	Justin Thompson	.15
45	Johnny Damon	.40
46	Armando Benitez	.15
47	Brant Brown	.15
48	Charlie Hayes	.15
49	Darren Dreifort	.15
50	Juan Gonzalez	.50
51	Chuck Knoblauch	.15
52	Todd Helton	1.00
53	Rick Reed	.15
54	Chris Gomez	.15
55	Gary Sheffield	.50
56	Rod Beck	.15
57	Rey Sanchez	.15
58	Garret Anderson	.15
59	Jimmy Haynes	.15
60	Steve Woodard	.15
61	Rondell White	.15
62	Vladimir Guerrero	1.00
63	Eric Karros	.15
64	Russ Davis	.15
65	Mo Vaughn	.15
66	Sammy Sosa	1.50
67	Troy Percival	.15
68	Kenny Lofton	.15
69	Bill Taylor	.15
70	Mark McGwire	2.50
71	Roger Cedeno	.15
72	Javy Lopez	.15
73	Damion Easley	.15
74	Andy Pettitte	.35
75	Tony Gwynn	1.50
76	Ricardo Rincon	.15
77	F.P. Santangelo	.15
78	Jay Bell	.15
79	Scott Servais	.15
80	Jose Canseco	.50
81	Roberto Hernandez	.15
82	Todd Dunwoody	.15
83	John Wetteland	.15
84	Mike Caruso	.15
85	Derek Jeter	3.00
86	Aaron Sele	.15
87	Jose Lima	.15
88	Ryan Christenson	.15
89	Jeff Cirillo	.15
90	Jose Hernandez	.15
91	Mark Kotsay	.15
92	Darren Bragg	.15
93	Albert Belle	.15
94	Matt Lawton	.15
95	Pedro Martinez	1.00
96	Greg Vaughn	.15
97	Neifi Perez	.15
98	Gerald Williams	.15
99	Derek Bell	.15
100	Ken Griffey Jr.	2.00
101	David Cone	.15
102	Brian Johnson	.15
103	Dean Palmer	.15
104	Javier Valentin	.15
105	Trevor Hoffman	.15
106	Butch Huskey	.15
107	Dave Martinez	.15
108	Billy Wagner	.15
109	Shawn Green	.35
110	Ben Grieve	.15
111	Tom Goodwin	.15
112	Jaret Wright	.15
113	Aramis Ramirez	.15
114	Dmitri Young	.15
115	Hideki Irabu	.15
116	Roberto Kelly	.15
117	Jeff Fassero	.15
118	Mark Clark	.15
119	Jason McDonald	.15
120	Matt Williams	.15
121	Dave Burba	.15
122	Bret Saberhagen	.15
123	Deivi Cruz	.15
124	Chad Curtis	.15
125	Scott Rolen	.75
126	Lee Stevens	.15
127	J.T. Snow Jr.	.15
128	Rusty Greer	.15
129	Brian Meadows	.15
130	Jim Edmonds	.15
131	Ron Gant	.15
132	A.J. Hinch	.15
133	Shannon Stewart	.15
134	Brad Fullmer	.15
135	Cal Eldred	.15
136	Matt Walbeck	.15
137	Carl Everett	.15
138	Walt Weiss	.15
139	Fred McGriff	.15
140	Darin Erstad	.40
141	Dave Nilsson	.15
142	Eric Young	.15
143	Dan Wilson	.15
144	Jeff Reed	.15
145	Brett Tomko	.15
146	Terry Steinbach	.15
147	Seth Greisinger	.15
148	Pat Meares	.15
149	Livan Hernandez	.15
150	Jeff Bagwell	1.00
151	Bob Wickman	.15
152	Omar Vizquel	.15
153	Eric Davis	.15
154	Larry Sutton	.15
155	Magglio Ordonez	.45
156	Eric Milton	.15
157	Darren Lewis	.15
158	Rick Aguilera	.15
159	Mike Lieberthal	.15
160	Robb Nen	.15
161	Brian Giles	.15
162	Jeff Brantley	.15
163	Gary DiSarcina	.15
164	John Valentin	.15
165	David Dellucci	.15
166	Chan Ho Park	.15
167	Masato Yoshii	.15
168	Jason Schmidt	.15
169	LaTroy Hawkins	.15
170	Bret Boone	.15
171	Jerry DiPoto	.15
172	Mariano Rivera	.25
173	Mike Cameron	.15
174	Scott Erickson	.15
175	Charles Johnson	.15
176	Bobby Jones	.15
177	Francisco Cordova	.15
178	Todd Jones	.15
179	Jeff Montgomery	.15
180	Mike Mussina	.50
181	Bob Abreu	.15
182	Ismael Valdes	.15
183	Andy Fox	.15
184	Woody Williams	.15
185	Denny Neagle	.15
186	Jose Valentin	.15
187	Darrin Fletcher	.15
188	Gabe Alvarez	.15
189	Eddie Taubensee	.15
190	Edgar Martinez	.15
191	Jason Kendall	.15
192	Darryl Kile	.15
193	Jeff King	.15
194	Rey Ordonez	.15
195	Andruw Jones	1.00
196	Tony Fernandez	.15
197	Jamey Wright	.15
198	B.J. Surhoff	.15
199	Vinny Castilla	.15
200	David Wells	.15
201	Mark McGwire	1.25
202	Sammy Sosa	.75
203	Roger Clemens	.85
204	Kerry Wood	.20
205	Lance Berkman, Mike Frank, Gabe Kapler	.15
206	Alex Escobar, Ricky Ledee, Mike Stoner	.50
207	Peter Bergeron, Jeremy Giambi, George Lombard	.50
208	Michael Barrett, Ben Davis, Robert Fick	.15
209	Pat Cline, Ramon Hernandez, Jayson Werth	.20
210	Bruce Chen, Chris Enochs, Ryan Anderson	.15
211	Mike Lincoln, Octavio Dotel, Brad Penny	.15
212	Chuck Abbott, Brent Butler, Danny Klassen	.15
213	*Chris Jones, Jeff Urban*	.15
214	*Arturo McDowell, Tony Torcato*	.25
215	*Josh McKinley, Jason Tyner*	.30
216	*Matt Burch, Seth Etherton*	.15
217	*Mamon Tucker, Rick Elder*	.20
218	*J.M. Gold, Ryan Mills*	.15
219	*Adam Brown, Choo Freeman*	.20
220	Mark McGwire HR #1	15.00
220	Mark McGwire HR #2-60	10.00
220	McGwire HR #61-62	15.00
220	McGwire HR #63-69	12.50
220	McGwire HR #70	40.00
221	Larry Walker	.15
222	Bernie Williams	.15
223	Mark McGwire	1.25
224	Ken Griffey Jr.	1.00
225	Sammy Sosa	.75
226	Juan Gonzalez	.35
227	Dante Bichette	.15
228	Alex Rodriguez	1.25
229	Sammy Sosa	.75
230	Derek Jeter	1.50
231	Greg Maddux	.75
232	Roger Clemens	.75
233	Ricky Ledee	.15
234	Chuck Knoblauch	.15
235	Bernie Williams	.15
236	Tino Martinez	.15
237	Orlando Hernandez	.15
238	Scott Brosius	.15
239	Andy Pettitte	.15
240	Mariano Rivera	.15
241	Checklist	.15
242	Checklist	.15
243	Tom Glavine	.35
244	Andy Benes	.15
245	Sandy Alomar	.15
246	Wilton Guerrero	.15
247	Alex Gonzalez	.15
248	Roberto Alomar	.30
249	Ruben Rivera	.15
250	Eric Chavez	.15
251	Ellis Burks	.15
252	Richie Sexson	.15
253	Steve Finley	.15
254	Dwight Gooden	.15
255	Dustin Hermanson	.15
256	Kirk Rueter	.15
257	Steve Trachsel	.15
258	Gregg Jefferies	.15
259	Matt Stairs	.15
260	Shane Reynolds	.15
261	Gregg Olson	.15
262	Kevin Tapani	.15
263	Matt Morris	.15
264	Carl Pavano	.15

265 Nomar Garciaparra 1.50
266 Kevin Young .15
267 Rick Helling .15
268 Matt Franco .15
269 Brian McRae .15
270 Cal Ripken Jr. 3.00
271 Jeff Abbott .15
272 Tony Batista .15
273 Bill Simas .15
274 Brian Hunter .15
275 John Franco .15
276 Devon White .15
277 Rickey Henderson 1.00
278 Chuck Finley .15
279 Mike Blowers .15
280 Mark Grace .15
281 Randy Winn .15
282 Bobby Bonilla .15
283 David Justice .15
284 Shane Monahan .15
285 Kevin Brown .15
286 Todd Zeile .15
287 Al Martin .15
288 Troy O'Leary .15
289 Darryl Hamilton .15
290 Tino Martinez .15
291 David Ortiz .50
292 Tony Clark .15
293 Ryan Minor .15
294 Reggie Sanders .15
295 Wally Joyner .15
296 Cliff Floyd .15
297 Shawn Estes .15
298 Pat Hentgen .15
299 Scott Elarton .15
300 Alex Rodriguez 2.50
301 Ozzie Guillen .15
302 Hideo Martinez .15
303 Ryan McGuire .15
304 Brad Ausmus .15
305 Alex Gonzalez .15
306 Brian Jordan .15
307 John Jaha .15
308 Mark Grudzielanek .15
309 Juan Guzman .15
310 Tony Womack .15
311 Dennis Reyes .15
312 Marty Cordova .15
313 Ramiro Mendoza .15
314 Robin Ventura .15
315 Rafael Palmeiro .65
316 Ramon Martinez .15
317 Pedro Astacio .15
318 Dave Hollins .15
319 Tom Candiotti .15
320 Al Leiter .15
321 Rico Brogna .15
322 Reggie Jefferson .15
323 Bernard Gilkey .15
324 Jason Giambi .40
325 Craig Biggio .15
326 Troy Glaus .75
327 Delino DeShields .15
328 Fernando Vina .15
329 John Smoltz .15
330 Jeff Kent .15
331 Roy Halladay .15
332 Andy Ashby .15
333 Tim Wakefield .15
334 Roger Clemens 1.75
335 Bernie Williams .15
336 Desi Relaford .15
337 John Burkett .15
338 Mike Hampton .15
339 Royce Clayton .15
340 Mike Piazza 2.00
341 Jeremi Gonzalez .15
342 Mike Lansing .15
343 Jamie Moyer .15
344 Ron Coomer .15
345 Barry Larkin .15
346 Fernando Tatis .15
347 Chili Davis .15
348 Bobby Higginson .15
349 Hal Morris .15
350 Larry Walker .15
351 Carlos Guillen .15
352 Miguel Tejada .30
353 Travis Fryman .15
354 Jarrod Washburn .15
355 Chipper Jones 1.50
356 Todd Stottlemyre .15
357 Henry Rodriguez .15
358 Eli Marrero .15
359 Alan Benes .15
360 Tim Salmon .15
361 Luis Gonzalez .15
362 Scott Spiezio .15
363 Chris Carpenter .15
364 Bobby Howry .15
365 Raul Mondesi .15
366 Ugueth Urbina .15
367 Tom Evans .15
368 *Kerry Ligtenberg* .40
369 Adrian Beltre .35
370 Ryan Klesko .15
371 Wilson Alvarez .15
372 John Thomson .15
373 Tony Saunders .15
374 Mike Stanley .15
375 Ken Caminiti .15
376 Jay Buhner .15
377 Bill Mueller .15
378 Jeff Blauser .15
379 Edgar Renteria .15
380 Jim Thome .60
381 Joey Hamilton .15
382 Calvin Pickering .15
383 Marquis Grissom .15
384 Omar Daal .15
385 Curt Schilling .35
386 Jose Cruz Jr. .15
387 Chris Widger .15
388 Pete Harnisch .15
389 Charles Nagy .15
390 Tom Gordon .15
391 Bobby Smith .15
392 Derrick Gibson .15
393 Jeff Conine .15
394 Carlos Perez .15
395 Barry Bonds 3.00
396 Mark McLemore .15
397 Juan Encarnacion .15
398 Wade Boggs 1.50
399 Ivan Rodriguez .75
400 Moises Alou .15
401 Jeromy Burnitz .15
402 Sean Casey .25
403 Jose Offerman .15
404 Joe Fontenot .15
405 Kevin Millwood .15
406 Lance Johnson .15
407 Richard Hidalgo .15
408 Mike Jackson .15
409 Brian Anderson .15
410 Jeff Shaw .15
411 Preston Wilson .15
412 Todd Hundley .15
413 Jim Parque .15
414 Justin Baughman .15
415 Dante Bichette .15
416 Paul O'Neill .15
417 Miguel Cairo .15
418 Randy Johnson 1.00
419 Jesus Sanchez .15
420 Carlos Delgado .35
421 Ricky Ledee .15
422 Orlando Hernandez .15
423 Frank Thomas 1.00
424 Pokey Reese .15
425 *Carlos Lee, Mike Lowell, Kit Pellow* .30
426 *Michael Cuddyer, Mark DeRosa, Jerry Hairston Jr.* .60
427 Marlon Anderson, Ron Belliard, Orlando Cabrera .45
428 Micah Bowie, Phil Norton, Randy Wolf .35
429 Jack Cressend, Jason Rakers, John Rocker .25
430 *Ruben Mateo, Scott Morgan, Mike Zywica* .25
431 *Jason LaRue, Matt LeCroy, Mitch Meluskey* .25
432 Gabe Kapler, Armando Rios, Fernando Seguignol .25
433 Adam Kennedy, Mickey Lopez, Jackie Rexrodet .25
434 Jose Fernandez, Jeff Liefer, Chris Truby .25
435 Corey Koskie, Doug Mientkiewicz, Damon Minor .60
436 Roosevelt Brown, Dernell Stenson, Vernon Wells .25
437 A.J. Burnett, John Nicholson, Billy Koch .75
438 *Matt Belisle, Matt Roney* .30
439 *Austin Kearns, Chris George* 3.00
440 *Nate Bump, Nate Cornejo* .40
441 *Brad Lidge, Mike Nannini* .60
442 *Matt Holliday, Jeff Winchester* .40
443 *Adam Everett, Chip Ambres* .30
444 *Pat Burrell, Eric Valent* 3.00
445 Roger Clemens .85
446 Kerry Wood .20
447 Curt Schilling .15
448 Randy Johnson .50
449 Pedro Martinez .50
450 Jeff Bagwell, Andres Galarraga, Mark McGwire 1.25
451 John Olerud, Jim Thome, Tino Martinez .40
452 Alex Rodriguez, Nomar Garciaparra, Derek Jeter 1.50
453 Vinny Castilla, Chipper Jones, Scott Rolen .75
454 Sammy Sosa, Ken Griffey Jr., Juan Gonzalez 1.00
455 Barry Bonds, Manny Ramirez, Larry Walker 1.50
456 Frank Thomas, Tim Salmon, David Justice) .60
457 Travis Lee, Todd Helton, Ben Grieve .50
458 Vladimir Guerrero, Greg Vaughn, Bernie Williams .50
459 Mike Piazza, Ivan Rodriguez, Jason Kendall 1.00
460 Roger Clemens, Kerry Wood, Greg Maddux 1.00
461 Sammy Sosa #1 (Home Run Parade) 10.00
461 Sammy Sosa HR #2-60 6.00
461 S. Sosa HR #61-62 10.00
461 S. Sosa HR #63-65 7.50
461 S. Sosa HR #66 20.00

All-Etch

NM/M

Complete Set (30): 15.00
Common Player: .35
Inserted 1:6
Refractors: 1.5X
Inserted 1:24

1 Mark McGwire 3.00
2 Sammy Sosa 1.50
3 Ken Griffey Jr. 2.00
4 Greg Vaughn .25
5 Albert Belle .25
6 Vinny Castilla .25
7 Jose Canseco .50
8 Juan Gonzalez .50
9 Manny Ramirez 1.00
10 Andres Galarraga .25
11 Rafael Palmeiro .75
12 Alex Rodriguez 3.00
13 Mo Vaughn .25
14 Eric Chavez .40
15 Gabe Kapler .25
16 Calvin Pickering .25
17 Ruben Mateo .25
18 Roy Halladay .40
19 Jeremy Giambi .25
20 Alex Gonzalez .25
21 Ron Belliard .25
22 Marlon Anderson .25
23 Carlos Lee .25
24 Kerry Wood .50
25 Roger Clemens 1.50
26 Curt Schilling .50
27 Kevin Brown .25
28 Randy Johnson 1.00
29 Pedro Martinez 1.00
30 Orlando Hernandez .25

Early Road to the Hall

NM/M

Complete Set (10): 12.00
Common Player: .50
Inserted 1:12
Refractors (#d to 100): 6X

ER1 Nomar Garciaparra 1.50
ER2 Derek Jeter 3.00
ER3 Alex Rodriguez 2.50
ER4 Juan Gonzalez .50
ER5 Ken Griffey Jr. 2.00
ER6 Chipper Jones 1.50
ER7 Vladimir Guerrero 1.00
ER8 Jeff Bagwell 1.00
ER9 Ivan Rodriguez .75
ER10 Frank Thomas 1.00

Fortune 15

NM/M

Complete Set (15): 17.50
Common Player: .50
Inserted 1:12
Refractors (# to 100): 4X

1 Alex Rodriguez 2.25
2 Nomar Garciaparra 1.25
3 Derek Jeter 3.00
4 Troy Glaus .75
5 Ken Griffey Jr. 1.50
6 Vladimir Guerrero 1.00
7 Kerry Wood .65
8 Eric Chavez .65
9 Greg Maddux 1.25
10 Mike Piazza 1.50
11 Sammy Sosa 1.25
12 Mark McGwire 2.25
13 Ben Grieve .50
14 Chipper Jones 1.25
15 Manny Ramirez 1.00

Lords of the Diamond

NM/M

Complete Set (15): 20.00
Common Player: .40
Inserted 1:8
Refractors: 2X
Inserted 1:24

LD1 Ken Griffey Jr. 2.00
LD2 Chipper Jones 1.50
LD3 Sammy Sosa 1.50
LD4 Frank Thomas 1.25
LD5 Mark McGwire 2.50
LD6 Jeff Bagwell 1.25
LD7 Alex Rodriguez 2.25
LD8 Juan Gonzalez .65
LD9 Barry Bonds 3.00
LD10 Nomar Garciaparra 1.50
LD11 Darin Erstad .50
LD12 Tony Gwynn 1.50
LD13 Andres Galarraga .40
LD14 Mike Piazza 2.00
LD15 Greg Maddux 1.50

New Breed

		NM/M
Complete Set (15):		30.00
Common Player:		.50
Inserted 1:24		
Refractors:		1.5X
Inserted 1:72		
NB1	Darin Erstad	.75
NB2	Brad Fullmer	.50
NB3	Kerry Wood	.75
NB4	Nomar Garciaparra	5.00
NB5	Travis Lee	.65
NB6	Scott Rolen	2.00
NB7	Todd Helton	3.00
NB8	Vladimir Guerrero	3.00
NB9	Derek Jeter	7.50
NB10	Alex Rodriguez	6.00
NB11	Ben Grieve	.50
NB12	Andruw Jones	3.00
NB13	Paul Konerko	.75
NB14	Aramis Ramirez	.50
NB15	Adrian Beltre	.75

Record Numbers

		NM/M
Complete Set (10):		20.00
Common Player:		.50
Inserted 1:36		
Refractors:		1.5X
Inserted 1:144		
1	Mark McGwire	3.00
2	Craig Biggio	.50
3	Barry Bonds	4.00
4	Ken Griffey Jr.	2.50
5	Sammy Sosa	2.00
6	Alex Rodriguez	3.00
7	Kerry Wood	1.00
8	Roger Clemens	2.00
9	Cal Ripken Jr.	4.00
10	Mark McGwire	3.00

1999 TOPPS CHROME TRADED AND ROOKIES

		NM/M
Complete Set (121):		60.00
Common Player:		.15
1	Seth Etherton	.15
2	*Mark Harriger*	.25
3	*Matt Wise*	.50
4	*Carlos Hernandez*	.50
5	*Julio Lugo*	.75
6	Mike Nannini	.15
7	*Justin Bowles*	.25
8	*Mark Mulder*	5.00
9	*Roberto Vaz*	.15
10	*Felipe Lopez*	2.50
11	Matt Belisle	.15
12	Micah Bowie	.15
13	*Ruben Quevedo*	.25
14	*Jose Garcia*	.15
15	*David Kelton*	1.00
16	Phillip Norton	.15
17	*Corey Patterson*	2.00
18	*Ron Walker*	.15
19	*Paul Hoover*	.15
20	*Ryan Rupe*	.25
21	*J.D. Closser*	.15
22	*Rob Ryan*	.15
23	*Steve Colyer*	.15
24	*Bubba Crosby*	1.00
25	*Luke Prokopec*	.15
26	*Matt Blank*	.15
27	Josh McKinley	.15
28	Nate Bump	.15
29	*Giuseppe Chiaramonte*	.15
30	Arturo McDowell	.15
31	Tony Torcato	.15
32	Dave Roberts	.15
33	*C.C. Sabathia*	1.50
34	*Sean Spencer*	.15
35	Chip Ambres	.15
36	A.J. Burnett	.50
37	*Mo Bruce*	.15
38	Jason Tyner	.15
39	Mamon Tucker	.15
40	*Sean Burroughs*	1.00
41	*Kevin Eberwein*	.15
42	*Junior Herndon*	.25
43	*Bryan Wolff*	.15
44	Pat Burrell	1.00
45	Eric Valent	.15
46	*Carlos Pena*	1.00
47	Mike Zywica	.15
48	Adam Everett	.15
49	*Juan Pena*	.75
50	*Adam Dunn*	10.00
51	Austin Kearns	2.00
52	*Jacobo Sequea*	.15
53	Choo Freeman	.50
54	Jeff Winchester	.15
55	Matt Burch	.15
56	Chris George	.25
57	*Scott Mullen*	.15
58	Kit Pellow	.15
59	*Mark Quinn*	.75
60	Nate Cornejo	.15
61	*Ryan Mills*	.15
62	*Kevin Beirne*	.15
63	*Kip Wells*	.75
64	*Juan Rivera*	1.00
65	*Alfonso Soriano*	10.00
66	*Josh Hamilton*	.50
67	*Josh Girdley*	.15
68	*Kyle Snyder*	.25
69	*Mike Paradis*	.25
70	*Jason Jennings*	.25
71	*David Walling*	.25
72	*Omar Ortiz*	.15
73	*Jay Gehrke*	.15
74	*Casey Burns*	.15
75	*Carl Crawford*	3.00
76	Reggie Sanders	.15
77	Will Clark	.15
78	David Wells	.15
79	Paul Konerko	.30
80	Armando Benitez	.15
81	Brant Brown	.15
82	Mo Vaughn	.15
83	Jose Canseco	.75
84	Albert Belle	.15
85	Dean Palmer	.15
86	Greg Vaughn	.15
87	Mark Clark	.15
88	Pat Meares	.15
89	Eric Davis	.15
90	Brian Giles	.15
91	Jeff Brantley	.15
92	Bret Boone	.15
93	Ron Gant	.15
94	Mike Cameron	.15
95	Charles Johnson	.15
96	Denny Neagle	.15
97	Brian Hunter	.15
98	Jose Hernandez	.15
99	Rick Aguilera	.15
100	Tony Batista	.15
101	Roger Cedeno	.15
102	Creighton Gubanich	.15
103	Tim Belcher	.15
104	Bruce Aven	.15
105	*Brian Daubach*	.75
106	Ed Sprague	.15
107	Michael Tucker	.15
108	Homer Bush	.15
109	Armando Reynoso	.15
110	Brook Fordyce	.15
111	Matt Mantei	.15
112	Jose Guillen	.15
113	Kenny Rogers	.15
114	Livan Hernandez	.15
115	Butch Huskey	.15
116	David Segui	.15
117	Darryl Hamilton	.15
118	Jim Leyritz	.15
119	Randy Velarde	.15
120	Bill Taylor	.15
121	Kevin Appier	.15

1999 TOPPS GALLERY

		NM/M
Complete Set (150):		60.00
Common Player (1-100):		.10
Common Player (101-150):		.25
Pack (6):		3.00
Wax Box (24):		45.00
1	Mark McGwire	1.50
2	Jim Thome	.35
3	Bernie Williams	.10
4	Larry Walker	.10
5	Juan Gonzalez	.30
6	Ken Griffey Jr.	1.00
7	Raul Mondesi	.10
8	Sammy Sosa	.75
9	Greg Maddux	.75
10	Jeff Bagwell	.60
11	Vladimir Guerrero	.60
12	Scott Rolen	.50
13	Nomar Garciaparra	.75
14	Mike Piazza	1.00
15	Travis Lee	.15
16	Carlos Delgado	.35
17	Darin Erstad	.25
18	David Justice	.10
19	Cal Ripken Jr.	2.00
20	Derek Jeter	2.00
21	Tony Clark	.10
22	Barry Larkin	.10
23	Greg Vaughn	.10
24	Jeff Kent	.10
25	Wade Boggs	.75
26	Andres Galarraga	.10
27	Ken Caminiti	.10
28	Jason Kendall	.10
29	Todd Helton	.60
30	Chuck Knoblauch	.10
31	Roger Clemens	.85
32	Jeromy Burnitz	.10
33	Javy Lopez	.10
34	Roberto Alomar	.25
35	Eric Karros	.10
36	Ben Grieve	.10
37	Eric Davis	.10
38	Rondell White	.10
39	Dmitri Young	.10
40	Ivan Rodriguez	.50
41	Paul O'Neill	.10
42	Jeff Cirillo	.10
43	Kerry Wood	.30
44	Albert Belle	.10
45	Frank Thomas	.60
46	Manny Ramirez	.60
47	Tom Glavine	.25
48	Mo Vaughn	.10
49	Jose Cruz Jr.	.10
50	Sandy Alomar	.10
51	Edgar Martinez	.10
52	John Olerud	.10
53	Todd Walker	.10
54	Tim Salmon	.10
55	Derek Bell	.10
56	Matt Williams	.10
57	Alex Rodriguez	1.50
58	Rusty Greer	.10
59	Vinny Castilla	.10
60	Jason Giambi	.30
61	Mark Grace	.10
62	Jose Canseco	.40
63	Gary Sheffield	.40
64	Brad Fullmer	.10
65	Trevor Hoffman	.10
66	Mark Kotsay	.10
67	Mike Mussina	.25
68	Johnny Damon	.30
69	Tino Martinez	.10
70	Curt Schilling	.25
71	Jay Buhner	.10
72	Kenny Lofton	.10
73	Randy Johnson	.60
74	Kevin Brown	.10
75	Brian Jordan	.10
76	Craig Biggio	.10
77	Barry Bonds	2.00
78	Tony Gwynn	.75
79	Jim Edmonds	.10
80	Shawn Green	.35
81	Todd Hundley	.10
82	Cliff Floyd	.10
83	Jose Guillen	.10
84	Dante Bichette	.10
85	Moises Alou	.10
86	Chipper Jones	.75
87	Ray Lankford	.10
88	Fred McGriff	.10
89	Rod Beck	.10
90	Dean Palmer	.10
91	Pedro Martinez	.60
92	Andruw Jones	.60
93	Robin Ventura	.10
94	Ugueth Urbina	.10
95	Orlando Hernandez	.10
96	Sean Casey	.15
97	Denny Neagle	.10
98	Troy Glaus	.60
99	John Smoltz	.10
100	Al Leiter	.10
101	Ken Griffey Jr.	1.50
102	Frank Thomas	.75
103	Mark McGwire	2.00
104	Sammy Sosa	1.00
105	Chipper Jones	1.00
106	Alex Rodriguez	2.00
107	Nomar Garciaparra	1.00
108	Juan Gonzalez	.40
109	Derek Jeter	3.00
110	Mike Piazza	1.50
111	Barry Bonds	3.00
112	Tony Gwynn	1.00
113	Cal Ripken Jr.	3.00
114	Greg Maddux	1.00
115	Roger Clemens	1.25
116	Brad Fullmer	.25
117	Kerry Wood	.50
118	Ben Grieve	.25
119	Todd Helton	.65
120	Kevin Millwood	.25
121	Sean Casey	.35
122	Vladimir Guerrero	.75
123	Travis Lee	.25
124	Troy Glaus	.65
125	Bartolo Colon	.25
126	Andruw Jones	.75
127	Scott Rolen	.60
128	*Alfonso Soriano*	3.00
129	*Nick Johnson*	1.00
130	*Matt Belisle*	.25
131	*Jorge Toca*	.25
132	*Masao Kida*	.25
133	*Carlos Pena*	1.00
134	Adrian Beltre	.40
135	Eric Chavez	.40
136	Carlos Beltran	.65
137	Alex Gonzalez	.25
138	Ryan Anderson	.25
139	Ruben Mateo	.25
140	Bruce Chen	.25
141	*Pat Burrell*	3.00
142	Michael Barrett	.25
143	Carlos Lee	.25
144	*Mark Mulder*	1.00
145	*Choo Freeman*	.50
146	Gabe Kapler	.25
147	Juan Encarnacion	.25
148	Jeremy Giambi	.25
149	*Jason Tyner*	.35
150	George Lombard	.25

Player's Private Issue

	NM/M
Common Player:	1.00
Stars:	5X
SPs:	3X
Production 250 sets	

(See 1999 Topps Gallery for checklist andbase card values.)

Press Plates

		NM/M
Common Player:		25.00

(See 1999 Topps Gallery for checklist.)

Awards Gallery

		NM/M
Complete Set (10):		12.50
Common Player:		.50
Inserted 1:12		
AG1	Kerry Wood	.75
AG2	Ben Grieve	.50
AG3	Roger Clemens	2.50
AG4	Tom Glavine	.75
AG5	Juan Gonzalez	.75
AG6	Sammy Sosa	3.00
AG7	Ken Griffey Jr.	3.00
AG8	Mark McGwire	4.00
AG9	Bernie Williams	.50
AG10	Larry Walker	.50

Autograph Cards

		NM/M
Complete Set (3):		20.00
Common Player:		6.00
Inserted 1:209		
GA1	Troy Glaus	12.00
GA2	Adrian Beltre	16.00
GA3	Eric Chavez	8.00

Exhibitions

		NM/M
Complete Set (20):		75.00
Common Player:		2.00
Inserted 1:48		
E1	Sammy Sosa	4.50
E2	Mark McGwire	7.50
E3	Greg Maddux	4.50
E4	Roger Clemens	5.00
E5	Ben Grieve	2.00
E6	Kerry Wood	2.25
E7	Ken Griffey Jr.	6.00
E8	Tony Gwynn	4.50
E9	Cal Ripken Jr.	10.00
E10	Frank Thomas	4.00
E11	Jeff Bagwell	4.00
E12	Derek Jeter	10.00
E13	Alex Rodriguez	7.50
E14	Nomar Garciaparra	4.50
E15	Manny Ramirez	4.00
E16	Vladimir Guerrero	4.00
E17	Darin Erstad	2.25
E18	Scott Rolen	3.00
E19	Mike Piazza	6.00
E20	Andres Galarraga	2.00

Gallery of Heroes

		NM/M
Complete Set (10):		30.00
Common Player:		.75
Inserted 1:24		
GH1	Mark McGwire	6.00
GH2	Sammy Sosa	3.50
GH3	Ken Griffey Jr.	4.50
GH4	Mike Piazza	4.50
GH5	Derek Jeter	7.50
GH6	Nomar Garciaparra	4.50
GH7	Kerry Wood	1.50
GH8	Ben Grieve	.75
GH9	Chipper Jones	3.50
GH10	Alex Rodriguez	6.00

Heritage

		NM/M
Complete Set (20):		100.00
Common Player:		2.50
Inserted 1:12		
Heritage Proofs:		1.5X
Inserted 1:48		
TH1	Hank Aaron	10.00
TH2	Ben Grieve	2.50
TH3	Nomar Garciaparra	7.50
TH4	Roger Clemens	8.50
TH5	Travis Lee	2.50
TH6	Tony Gwynn	7.50
TH7	Alex Rodriguez	12.50
TH8	Ken Griffey Jr.	10.00
TH9	Derek Jeter	15.00
TH10	Sammy Sosa	7.50
TH11	Scott Rolen	2.50
TH12	Chipper Jones	7.50
TH13	Cal Ripken Jr.	15.00
TH14	Kerry Wood	3.00
TH15	Barry Bonds	15.00
TH16	Juan Gonzalez	3.00
TH17	Mike Piazza	10.00
TH18	Greg Maddux	7.50
TH19	Frank Thomas	6.00
TH20	Mark McGwire	12.50

Heritage Lithographs

		NM/M
Complete Set (8):		480.00
Single Player:		60.00
(1)	Roger Clemens	60.00
(2)	Nomar Garciaparra	60.00
(3)	Ken Griffey Jr.	60.00
(4)	Derek Jeter	60.00
(5)	Mark McGwire	60.00
(6)	Mike Piazza	60.00
(7)	Cal Ripken Jr.	60.00
(8)	Sammy Sosa	60.00

1999 TOPPS GOLD LABEL CLASS 1

		NM/M
Complete Set (100):		30.00
Common Gold Label:		.10
Common Black Label:		.50
Black Label Stars:		3X
Common Red Label:		2.00
Red Label Stars:		12X
Pack (5):		3.00
Wax Box (24):		50.00
1	Mike Piazza	2.00
2	Andres Galarraga	.10
3	Mark Grace	.10
4	Tony Clark	.10
5	Jim Thome	.60
6	Tony Gwynn	1.50
7	*Kelly Dransfeldt*	.15
8	Eric Chavez	.25
9	Brian Jordan	.10
10	Todd Hundley	.10
11	Rondell White	.10
12	Dmitri Young	.10
13	Jeff Kent	.10
14	Derek Bell	.10
15	Todd Helton	.75
16	Chipper Jones	1.50
17	Albert Belle	.10
18	Barry Larkin	.10
19	Dante Bichette	.10
20	Gary Sheffield	.50
21	Cliff Floyd	.10
22	Derek Jeter	3.00
23	Jason Giambi	.50
24	Ray Lankford	.10
25	Alex Rodriguez	2.50
26	Ruben Mateo	.10
27	Wade Boggs	1.50
28	Carlos Delgado	.45
29	Tim Salmon	.10
30	*Alfonso Soriano*	3.00
31	Javy Lopez	.10
32	Jason Kendall	.10
33	*Nick Johnson*	1.00
34	*A.J. Burnett*	1.00
35	Troy Glaus	.75
36	*Pat Burrell*	3.00
37	Jeff Cirillo	.10
38	David Justice	.10
39	Ivan Rodriguez	.75
40	Bernie Williams	.10
41	Jay Buhner	.10
42	Mo Vaughn	.10
43	Randy Johnson	1.00
44	Pedro Martinez	1.00
45	Larry Walker	.10
46	Todd Walker	.10
47	Roberto Alomar	.25
48	Kevin Brown	.10
49	Mike Mussina	.40
50	Tom Glavine	.25
51	Curt Schilling	.25
52	Ken Caminiti	.10
53	Brad Fullmer	.10
54	*Bobby Seay*	.10
55	Orlando Hernandez	.10
56	Sean Casey	.10
57	Al Leiter	.10
58	Sandy Alomar	.10
59	Mark Kotsay	.10
60	Matt Williams	.10
61	Raul Mondesi	.10
62	*Joe Crede*	5.00
63	Jim Edmonds	.10
64	Jose Cruz Jr.	.10
65	Juan Gonzalez	.50
66	Sammy Sosa	1.50
67	Cal Ripken Jr.	3.00
68	Vinny Castilla	.10
69	Craig Biggio	.10
70	Mark McGwire	2.50
71	Greg Vaughn	.10
72	Greg Maddux	1.50
73	Paul O'Neill	.10
74	Scott Rolen	.65
75	Ben Grieve	.10
76	Vladimir Guerrero	1.00
77	John Olerud	.10
78	Eric Karros	.10
79	Jeromy Burnitz	.10
80	Jeff Bagwell	1.00
81	Kenny Lofton	.10
82	Manny Ramirez	1.00
83	Andruw Jones	1.00
84	Travis Lee	.15
85	Darin Erstad	.25
86	Nomar Garciaparra	1.50
87	Frank Thomas	1.00
88	Moises Alou	.10
89	Tino Martinez	.10
90	*Carlos Pena*	1.00
91	Shawn Green	.40
92	Rusty Greer	.10
93	*Matt Belisle*	.25
94	Adrian Beltre	.25
95	Roger Clemens	1.75
96	John Smoltz	.10
97	*Mark Mulder*	1.00
98	Kerry Wood	.50
99	Barry Bonds	3.00
100	Ken Griffey Jr.	2.00

Class 2

	NM/M
Complete Set (100):	75.00
Common Gold Label:	.25
Gold Label Stars:	1.5
Common Black Label:	2.00
Black Label Stars:	4X
Common Red Label:	6.00
Red Label Stars:	15X

(See 1999 Topps Gold Label Class 1 for checklist and base card values.)

Class 3

Complete Set (100):	125.00
Common Gold Label:	.50
Gold Label Stars:	2
Common Black Label:	3.00
Black Label Stars:	6X
Common Red Label:	12.00
Red Label Stars:	35X

(See 1999 Topps Gold Label Class 1 for checklist and base card values.)

One

	NM/M
Common Player, Base Set:	50.00
Common Player, Race to Aaron:	150.00

(Star/rookie card values cannot be determined due to scarcity.)

Race to Aaron

		NM/M
Complete Set (10):		20.00
Common Player:		1.00
Blacks:		2X
Reds:		12X
1	Mark McGwire	4.50
2	Ken Griffey Jr.	3.00
3	Alex Rodriguez	4.50
4	Vladimir Guerrero	1.50
5	Albert Belle	1.00
6	Nomar Garciaparra	2.50
7	Ken Griffey Jr.	3.00
8	Alex Rodriguez	4.50
9	Juan Gonzalez	1.00
10	Barry Bonds	7.50

1999 TOPPS STARS

	NM/M
Complete Set (180):	20.00

Common Player: .05
Pack (6): 1.50
Wax Box (24): 25.00
1 Ken Griffey Jr. .75
2 Chipper Jones .50
3 Mike Piazza .75
4 Nomar Garciaparra .50
5 Derek Jeter 1.50
6 Frank Thomas .40
7 Ben Grieve .05
8 Mark McGwire 1.00
9 Sammy Sosa .50
10 Alex Rodriguez 1.00
11 Troy Glaus .35
12 Eric Chavez .25
13 Kerry Wood .30
14 Barry Bonds 1.50
15 Vladimir Guerrero .40
16 Albert Belle .05
17 Juan Gonzalez .20
18 Roger Clemens .60
19 Ruben Mateo .05
20 Cal Ripken Jr. 1.50
21 Darin Erstad .25
22 Jeff Bagwell .40
23 Roy Halladay .10
24 Todd Helton .35
25 Michael Barrett .05
26 Manny Ramirez .40
27 Fernando Seguignol .05
28 *Pat Burrell* 2.00
29 Andruw Jones .40
30 Randy Johnson .40
31 Jose Canseco .30
32 Brad Fullmer .05
33 *Alex Escobar* .10
34 *Alfonso Soriano* 2.00
35 Larry Walker .05
36 Matt Clement .05
37 Mo Vaughn .05
38 Bruce Chen .05
39 Travis Lee .20
40 Adrian Beltre .10
41 Alex Gonzalez .05
42 *Jason Tyner* .10
43 George Lombard .05
44 Scott Rolen .25
45 *Mark Mulder* .50
46 Gabe Kapler .05
47 *Choo Freeman* .10
48 Tony Gwynn .50
49 *A.J. Burnett* .25
50 *Matt Belisle* .10
51 Greg Maddux .50
52 John Smoltz .05
53 Mark Grace .05
54 Wade Boggs .50
55 Bernie Williams .05
56 Pedro Martinez .40
57 Barry Larkin .05
58 Orlando Hernandez .05
59 Jason Kendall .05
60 Mark Kotsay .05
61 Jim Thome .35
62 Gary Sheffield .30
63 Preston Wilson .05
64 Rafael Palmeiro .35
65 David Wells .05
66 Shawn Green .30
67 Tom Glavine .25
68 Jeromy Burnitz .05
69 Kevin Brown .05
70 Rondell White .05
71 Roberto Alomar .25
72 Cliff Floyd .05
73 Craig Biggio .05
74 Greg Vaughn .05
75 Ivan Rodriguez .35
76 Vinny Castilla .05
77 Todd Walker .05
78 Paul Konerko .15
79 *Andy Brown* .05
80 Todd Hundley .05
81 Dmitri Young .05
82 Tony Clark .05
83 *Nick Johnson* .50
84 Mike Caruso .05
85 David Ortiz .35
86 Matt Williams .05
87 Raul Mondesi .05
88 Kenny Lofton .05
89 Miguel Tejada .10
90 Dante Bichette .05
91 Jorge Posada .05
92 Carlos Beltran .25
93 Carlos Delgado .30
94 Javy Lopez .05
95 Aramis Ramirez .05
96 Neifi Perez .05
97 Marlon Anderson .05
98 David Cone .05
99 Moises Alou .05
100 John Olerud .05
101 Tim Salmon .05
102 Jason Giambi .30
103 Sandy Alomar .05
104 Curt Schilling .25
105 Andres Galarraga .05
106 Rusty Greer .05
107 *Bobby Seay* .05
108 Eric Young .05
109 Brian Jordan .05
110 Eric Davis .05
111 Will Clark .05
112 Andy Ashby .05
113 Edgardo Alfonzo .05
114 Paul O'Neill .05
115 Denny Neagle .05
116 Eric Karros .05
117 Ken Caminiti .05
118 Garret Anderson .05
119 Todd Stottlemyre .05
120 David Justice .05
121 Francisco Cordova .05
122 Robin Ventura .05
123 Mike Mussina .25
124 Hideki Irabu .05
125 Justin Thompson .05
126 Mariano Rivera .15
127 Delino DeShields .05
128 Steve Finley .05
129 Jose Cruz Jr. .05
130 Ray Lankford .05
131 Jim Edmonds .05
132 Charles Johnson .05
133 Al Leiter .05
134 Jose Offerman .05
135 Eric Milton .05
136 Dean Palmer .05
137 Johnny Damon .25
138 Andy Pettitte .20
139 Ray Durham .05
140 Ugueth Urbina .05
141 Marquis Grissom .05
142 Ryan Klesko .05
143 Brady Anderson .05
144 Bobby Higginson .05
145 Chuck Knoblauch .05
146 Rickey Henderson .40
147 Kevin Millwood .05
148 Fred McGriff .05
149 Damion Easley .05
150 Tino Martinez .05
151 Greg Maddux .30
152 Scott Rolen .20
153 Pat Burrell .75
154 Roger Clemens .35
155 Albert Belle .05
156 Troy Glaus .25
157 Cal Ripken Jr. .75
158 Alfonso Soriano .75
159 Manny Ramirez .25
160 Eric Chavez .10
161 Kerry Wood .20
162 Tony Gwynn .30
163 Barry Bonds .75
164 Ruben Mateo .05
165 Todd Helton .20
166 Darin Erstad .05
167 Jeff Bagwell .25
168 Juan Gonzalez .15
169 Mo Vaughn .05
170 Vladimir Guerrero .25
171 Nomar Garciaparra .35
172 Derek Jeter .75
173 Alex Rodriguez .50
174 Ben Grieve .05
175 Mike Piazza .40
176 Chipper Jones .35
177 Frank Thomas .25
178 Ken Griffey Jr. .40
179 Sammy Sosa .35
180 Mark McGwire .50

One-Star

NM/M
Complete Set (100): 25.00
Common Player: .10
Foils (249 each): 2X
1 Ken Griffey Jr. 1.25
2 Chipper Jones 1.00
3 Mike Piazza 1.25
4 Nomar Garciaparra 1.00
5 Derek Jeter 2.00
6 Frank Thomas .75
7 Ben Grieve .10
8 Mark McGwire 1.50
9 Sammy Sosa 1.00
10 Alex Rodriguez 1.50
11 Troy Glaus .65
12 Eric Chavez .25
13 Kerry Wood .35
14 Barry Bonds 2.00
15 Vladimir Guerrero .75
16 Albert Belle .10
17 Juan Gonzalez .40
18 Roger Clemens 1.00
19 Ruben Mateo .10
20 Cal Ripken Jr. 2.00
21 Darin Erstad .30
22 Jeff Bagwell .75
23 Roy Halladay .20
24 Todd Helton .65
25 Michael Barrett .10
26 Manny Ramirez .75
27 Fernando Seguignol .10
28 Pat Burrell 1.00
29 Andruw Jones .75
30 Randy Johnson .75
31 Jose Canseco .40
32 Brad Fullmer .10
33 Alex Escobar .10
34 Alfonso Soriano 1.00
35 Larry Walker .10
36 Matt Clement .25
37 Mo Vaughn .10
38 Bruce Chen .10
39 Travis Lee .15
40 Adrian Beltre .20
41 Alex Gonzalez .10
42 Jason Tyner .10
43 George Lombard .10
44 Scott Rolen .50
45 Mark Mulder .50
46 Gabe Kapler .10
47 Choo Freeman .10
48 Tony Gwynn 1.00
49 A.J. Burnett .15
50 Matt Belisle .10
51 Greg Maddux 1.00
52 John Smoltz .10
53 Mark Grace .10
54 Wade Boggs 1.00
55 Bernie Williams .10
56 Pedro Martinez .75
57 Barry Larkin .10
58 Orlando Hernandez .10
59 Jason Kendall .10
60 Mark Kotsay .10
61 Jim Thome .45
62 Gary Sheffield .40
63 Preston Wilson .10
64 Rafael Palmeiro .60
65 David Wells .10
66 Shawn Green .30
67 Tom Glavine .30
68 Jeromy Burnitz .10
69 Kevin Brown .10
70 Rondell White .10
71 Roberto Alomar .25
72 Cliff Floyd .10
73 Craig Biggio .10
74 Greg Vaughn .10
75 Ivan Rodriguez .60
76 Vinny Castilla .10
77 Todd Walker .10
78 Paul Konerko .20
79 Andy Brown .10
80 Todd Hundley .10
81 Dmitri Young .10
82 Tony Clark .10
83 Nick Johnson .50
84 Mike Caruso .10
85 David Ortiz .40
86 Matt Williams .10
87 Raul Mondesi .10
88 Kenny Lofton .10
89 Miguel Tejada .20
90 Dante Bichette .10
91 Jorge Posada .10
92 Carlos Beltran .20
93 Carlos Delgado .25
94 Javy Lopez .10
95 Aramis Ramirez .10
96 Neifi Perez .10
97 Marlon Anderson .10
98 David Cone .10
99 Moises Alou .10
100 John Olerud .10

Two-Star

NM/M
Complete Set (50): 50.00
Common Player: .25
Foils: 3X
1 Ken Griffey Jr. 2.00
2 Chipper Jones 1.50
3 Mike Piazza 2.00
4 Nomar Garciaparra 1.50
5 Derek Jeter 3.00
6 Frank Thomas 1.00
7 Ben Grieve .25
8 Mark McGwire 2.50
9 Sammy Sosa 1.50
10 Alex Rodriguez 2.50
11 Troy Glaus .75
12 Eric Chavez .30
13 Kerry Wood .40
14 Barry Bonds 3.00
15 Vladimir Guerrero 1.00
16 Albert Belle .25
17 Juan Gonzalez .50
18 Roger Clemens 1.75
19 Ruben Mateo .25
20 Cal Ripken Jr. 3.00
21 Darin Erstad .75
22 Jeff Bagwell 1.00
23 Roy Halladay .40
24 Todd Helton .75
25 Michael Barrett .25
26 Manny Ramirez 1.00
27 Fernando Seguignol .25
28 Pat Burrell 1.50
29 Andruw Jones 1.00
30 Randy Johnson 1.00
31 Jose Canseco .50
32 Brad Fullmer .25
33 Alex Escobar .25
34 Alfonso Soriano 1.50
35 Larry Walker .25
36 Matt Clement .30
37 Mo Vaughn .25
38 Bruce Chen .25
39 Travis Lee .30
40 Adrian Beltre .30
41 Alex Gonzalez .25
42 Jason Tyner .25
43 George Lombard .25
44 Scott Rolen .65
45 Mark Mulder .45
46 Gabe Kapler .25
47 Choo Freeman .25
48 Tony Gwynn 1.50
49 A.J. Burnett .30
50 Matt Belisle .25

Three-Star

NM/M
Complete Set (20): 30.00
Common Player: .50
Foils: 4X
1 Ken Griffey Jr. 2.50
2 Chipper Jones 2.00
3 Mike Piazza 2.50
4 Nomar Garciaparra 2.00
5 Derek Jeter 4.00
6 Frank Thomas 1.50
7 Ben Grieve .50

8	Mark McGwire	3.00
9	Sammy Sosa	2.00
10	Alex Rodriguez	3.00
11	Troy Glaus	1.25
12	Eric Chavez	.60
13	Kerry Wood	.75
14	Barry Bonds	4.00
15	Vladimir Guerrero	1.50
16	Albert Belle	.50
17	Juan Gonzalez	.75
18	Roger Clemens	2.25
19	Ruben Mateo	.50
20	Cal Ripken Jr.	4.00

Four-Star

		NM/M
Complete Set (10):		30.00
Common Player:		1.00
Foils:		2X
1	Ken Griffey Jr.	4.00
2	Chipper Jones	3.00
3	Mike Piazza	4.00
4	Nomar Garciaparra	3.00
5	Derek Jeter	6.00
6	Frank Thomas	2.50
7	Ben Grieve	1.00
8	Mark McGwire	5.00
9	Sammy Sosa	3.00
10	Alex Rodriguez	5.00

Foil

	NM/M
Complete Base Set (180):	90.00
Common Foil Player:	.15
Foil Stars:	3X

(See 1999 Topps Stars for checklist and base card values.)

Bright Futures

		NM/M
Complete Set (10):		20.00
Common Player:		1.50
Production 1,999 sets		
Foil (30 each):		8X
1	Troy Glaus	3.00
2	Eric Chavez	2.00
3	Adrian Beltre	2.00
4	Michael Barrett	1.50
5	Fernando Seguignol	1.50
6	Alex Gonzalez	1.50
7	Matt Clement	1.50
8	Pat Burrell	6.00
9	Ruben Mateo	1.50
10	Alfonso Soriano	6.00

Galaxy

		NM/M
Complete Set (10):		25.00
Common Player:		1.00
Production 1,999 sets		
Foil (30 each):		8X
1	Mark McGwire	5.00
2	Roger Clemens	3.00
3	Nomar Garciaparra	4.00
4	Alex Rodriguez	5.00
5	Kerry Wood	1.50
6	Ben Grieve	1.00
7	Derek Jeter	6.00
8	Vladimir Guerrero	2.50
9	Ken Griffey Jr.	4.00
10	Sammy Sosa	3.00

Rookie Reprints

		NM/M
Complete Set (5):		10.00
Common Player:		2.00
Production 2,500 sets		
1	Frank Robinson	2.00
2	Ernie Banks	3.00
3	Yogi Berra	3.00
4	Bob Gibson	2.00
5	Tom Seaver	3.00

Rookie Reprints Autographs

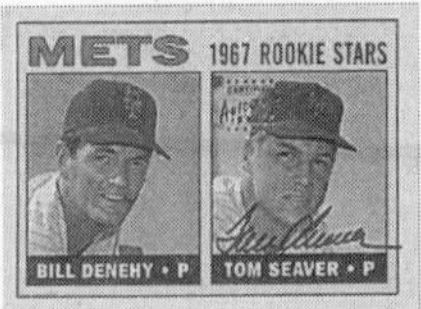

		NM/M
Complete Set (5):		150.00
Common Player:		20.00
Inserted 1:406		
Banks inserted 1:812		
1	Frank Robinson	25.00
2	Ernie Banks	70.00
3	Yogi Berra	35.00
4	Bob Gibson	20.00
5	Tom Seaver	65.00

1999 TOPPS STARS 'N STEEL

		NM/M
Complete Set (44):		65.00
Common Player:		.50
Gold:		4X
Inserted 1:12		
Holographic Dome:		6X
Inserted 1:24		
Pack (3):		4.00
Wax Box (12):		40.00
1	Kerry Wood	1.00
2	Ben Grieve	.50
3	Chipper Jones	3.00
4	Alex Rodriguez	5.00
5	Mo Vaughn	.50
6	Bernie Williams	.50
7	Juan Gonzalez	1.00
8	Vinny Castilla	.50
9	Tony Gwynn	3.00
10	Manny Ramirez	2.00
11	Raul Mondesi	.50
12	Roger Clemens	3.50
13	Darin Erstad	.75
14	Barry Bonds	6.00
15	Cal Ripken Jr.	6.00
16	Barry Larkin	.50
17	Scott Rolen	1.00
18	Albert Belle	.50
19	Craig Biggio	.50
20	Tony Clark	.50
21	Mark McGwire	5.00
22	Andres Galarraga	.50
23	Kenny Lofton	.50
24	Pedro Martinez	2.00
25	Paul O'Neill	.50
26	Ken Griffey Jr.	4.00
27	Travis Lee	75.00
28	Tim Salmon	.50
29	Frank Thomas	2.00
30	Larry Walker	.50
31	Moises Alou	.50
32	Vladimir Guerrero	2.00
33	Ivan Rodriguez	1.50
34	Derek Jeter	6.00
35	Greg Vaughn	.50
36	Gary Sheffield	1.00
37	Carlos Delgado	1.00
38	Greg Maddux	3.00
39	Sammy Sosa	3.00
40	Mike Piazza	4.00
41	Nomar Garciaparra	3.00
42	Dante Bichette	.50
43	Jeff Bagwell	2.00
44	Jim Thome	1.50

1999 TOPPS TEK

		NM/M
Complete Set (45):		30.00
Common Player:		.25
Pack (4):		3.00
Wax Box (20):		45.00
1	Ben Grieve	.25
2	Andres Galarraga	.25
3	Travis Lee	.35
4	Larry Walker	.25
5	Ken Griffey Jr.	2.50
6	Sammy Sosa	2.00
7	Mark McGwire	3.00
8	Roberto Alomar	.40
9	Wade Boggs	2.00
10	Troy Glaus	.75
11	Craig Biggio	.25
12	Kerry Wood	.50
13	Vladimir Guerrero	1.00
14	Albert Belle	.25
15	Mike Piazza	2.50
16	Chipper Jones	2.00
17	Randy Johnson	1.00
18	Adrian Beltre	.45
19	Barry Bonds	4.00
20	Jim Thome	.65
21	Greg Vaughn	.25
22	Scott Rolen	.65
23	Ivan Rodriguez	.75
24	Derek Jeter	4.00
25	Cal Ripken Jr.	4.00
26	Mark Grace	.25
27	Bernie Williams	.25
28	Darin Erstad	.75
29	Eric Chavez	.35
30	Tom Glavine	.50
31	Jeff Bagwell	1.00
32	Manny Ramirez	1.00
33	Tino Martinez	.25
34	Todd Helton	.75
35	Jason Kendall	.25
36	*Pat Burrell*	2.50
37	Tony Gwynn	2.00
38	Nomar Garciaparra	2.00
39	Frank Thomas	1.00
40	Orlando Hernandez	.25
41	Juan Gonzalez	.50
42	Alex Rodriguez	3.00
43	Greg Maddux	2.00
44	Mo Vaughn	.25
45	Roger Clemens	2.25

Gold

	NM/M
Common Gold:	2.00
Gold Stars:	10X

(See 1999 Topps TEK for checklist, base card values.)

Fantastek Phenoms

		NM/M
Complete Set (10):		15.00
Common Player:		.75
Inserted 1:18		
F1	Eric Chavez	1.50
F2	Troy Glaus	4.00
F3	Pat Burrell	4.00
F4	Alex Gonzalez	.75
F5	Carlos Lee	1.00
F6	Ruben Mateo	.75
F7	Carlos Beltran	2.00
F8	Adrian Beltre	1.50
F9	Bruce Chen	.75
F10	Ryan Anderson	.75

Teknicians

		NM/M
Complete Set (10):		24.00
Common Player:		1.00
Inserted 1:18		
T1	Ken Griffey Jr.	3.00
T2	Mark McGwire	4.00
T3	Kerry Wood	1.00
T4	Ben Grieve	1.00
T5	Sammy Sosa	2.50
T6	Derek Jeter	6.00
T7	Alex Rodriguez	4.00
T8	Roger Clemens	2.50
T9	Nomar Garciaparra	2.50
T10	Vladimir Guerrero	1.50

2000 TOPPS

	NM/M
Complete Set (478):	50.00

Complete Series I set (239):	25.00
Complete Series II set (239):	25.00
Common Player:	.10
MVP Stars:	20X to 40X
Yng Stars & RCs:	10X to 20X
Production 100 sets	
5 Versions for 236-240, 475-479	
Pack (11):	1.00
Wax Box (36):	30.00

No.	Player	Value
1	Mark McGwire	1.00
2	Tony Gwynn	.75
3	Wade Boggs	.75
4	Cal Ripken Jr.	1.50
5	Matt Williams	.10
6	Jay Buhner	.10
7	Not Issued	
8	Jeff Conine	.10
9	Todd Greene	.10
10	Mike Lieberthal	.10
11	Steve Avery	.10
12	Bret Saberhagen	.10
13	Magglio Ordonez	.20
14	Brad Radke	.10
15	Derek Jeter	1.50
16	Javy Lopez	.10
17	Russ David	.10
18	Armando Benitez	.10
19	B.J. Surhoff	.10
20	Darryl Kile	.10
21	Mark Lewis	.10
22	Mike Williams	.10
23	Mark McLemore	.10
24	Sterling Hitchcock	.10
25	Darin Erstad	.20
26	Ricky Gutierrez	.10
27	John Jaha	.10
28	Homer Bush	.10
29	Darrin Fletcher	.10
30	Mark Grace	.10
31	Fred McGriff	.10
32	Omar Daal	.10
33	Eric Karros	.10
34	Orlando Cabrera	.15
35	J.T. Snow Jr.	.10
36	Luis Castillo	.10
37	Rey Ordonez	.10
38	Bob Abreu	.20
39	Warren Morris	.10
40	Juan Gonzalez	.20
41	Mike Lansing	.10
42	Chili Davis	.10
43	Dean Palmer	.10
44	Hank Aaron	1.00
45	Jeff Bagwell	.60
46	Jose Valentin	.10
47	Shannon Stewart	.10
48	Kent Bottenfield	.10
49	Jeff Shaw	.10
50	Sammy Sosa	.75
51	Randy Johnson	.60
52	Benny Agbayani	.10
53	Dante Bichette	.10
54	Pete Harnisch	.10
55	Frank Thomas	.60
56	Jorge Posada	.10
57	Todd Walker	.10
58	Juan Encarnacion	.15
59	Mike Sweeney	.10
60	Pedro Martinez	.60
61	Lee Stevens	.10
62	Brian Giles	.10
63	Chad Ogea	.10
64	Ivan Rodriguez	.50
65	Roger Cedeno	.10
66	David Justice	.10
67	Steve Trachsel	.10
68	Eli Marrero	.10
69	Dave Nilsson	.10
70	Ken Caminiti	.10
71	Tim Raines	.10
72	Brian Jordan	.10
73	Jeff Blauser	.10
74	Bernard Gilkey	.10
75	John Flaherty	.10
76	Brent Mayne	.10
77	Jose Vidro	.10
78	Jeff Fassero	.10
79	Bruce Aven	.10
80	John Olerud	.10
81	Pokey Reese	.10
82	Woody Williams	.10
83	Ed Sprague	.10
84	Joe Girardi	.10
85	Barry Larkin	.10
86	Mike Caruso	.10
87	Bobby Higginson	.10
88	Roberto Kelly	.10
89	Edgar Martinez	.10
90	Mark Kotsay	.10
91	Paul Sorrento	.10
92	Eric Young	.10
93	Carlos Delgado	.40
94	Troy Glaus	.50
95	Ben Grieve	.10
96	Jose Lima	.10
97	Garret Anderson	.10
98	Luis Gonzalez	.10
99	Carl Pavano	.10
100	Alex Rodriguez	1.25
101	Preston Wilson	.10
102	Ron Gant	.10
103	Harold Baines	.10
104	Rickey Henderson	.60
105	Gary Sheffield	.40
106	Mickey Morandini	.10
107	Jim Edmonds	.10
108	Kris Benson	.10
109	Adrian Beltre	.20
110	Alex Fernandez	.10
111	Dan Wilson	.10
112	Mark Clark	.10
113	Greg Vaughn	.10
114	Neifi Perez	.10
115	Paul O'Neill	.10
116	Jermaine Dye	.10
117	Todd Jones	.10
118	Terry Steinbach	.10
119	Greg Norton	.10
120	Curt Schilling	.25
121	Todd Zeile	.10
122	Edgardo Alfonzo	.10
123	Ryan McGuire	.10
124	Stan Javier	.10
125	John Smoltz	.10
126	Bob Wickman	.10
127	Richard Hidalgo	.10
128	Chuck Finley	.10
129	Billy Wagner	.10
130	Todd Hundley	.10
131	Dwight Gooden	.10
132	Russ Ortiz	.10
133	Mike Lowell	.10
134	Reggie Sanders	.10
135	John Valentin	.10
136	Brad Ausmus	.10
137	Chad Kreuter	.10
138	David Cone	.10
139	Brook Fordyce	.10
140	Roberto Alomar	.25
141	Charles Nagy	.10
142	Brian Hunter	.10
143	Mike Mussina	.30
144	Robin Ventura	.10
145	Kevin Brown	.10
146	Pat Hentgen	.10
147	Ryan Klesko	.10
148	Derek Bell	.10
149	Andy Sheets	.10
150	Larry Walker	.10
151	Scott Williamson	.10
152	Jose Offerman	.10
153	Doug Mientkiewicz	.10
154	*John Snyder*	.10
155	Sandy Alomar	.10
156	Joe Nathan	.10
157	Lance Johnson	.10
158	Odalis Perez	.10
159	Hideo Nomo	.25
160	Steve Finley	.10
161	Dave Martinez	.10
162	Matt Walbeck	.10
163	Bill Spiers	.10
164	Fernando Tatis	.10
165	Kenny Lofton	.10
166	Paul Byrd	.10
167	Aaron Sele	.10
168	Eddie Taubensee	.10
169	Reggie Jefferson	.10
170	Roger Clemens	.85
171	Francisco Cordova	.10
172	Mike Bordick	.10
173	Wally Joyner	.10
174	Marvin Benard	.10
175	Jason Kendall	.10
176	Mike Stanley	.10
177	Chad Allen	.10
178	Carlos Beltran	.25
179	Deivi Cruz	.10
180	Chipper Jones	.75
181	Vladimir Guerrero	.60
182	Dave Burba	.10
183	Tom Goodwin	.10
184	Brian Daubach	.10
185	Jay Bell	.10
186	Roy Halladay	.25
187	Miguel Tejada	.25
188	Armando Rios	.10
189	Fernando Vina	.10
190	Eric Davis	.10
191	Henry Rodriguez	.10
192	Joe McEwing	.10
193	Jeff Kent	.10
194	Mike Jackson	.10
195	Mike Morgan	.10
196	Jeff Montgomery	.10
197	Jeff Zimmerman	.10
198	Tony Fernandez	.10
199	Jason Giambi	.40
200	Jose Canseco	.40
201	Alex Gonzalez	.10
202	Jack Cust, Mike Colangelo, Dee Brown	.10
203	Felipe Lopez, Alfonso Soriano, Pablo Ozuna	.75
204	Erubiel Durazo, Pat Burrell, Nick Johnson	.25
205	John Sneed, Kip Wells, Matt Blank	.10
206	Josh Kalinowski, Michael Tejera, Chris Mears	.10
207	Roosevelt Brown, Corey Patterson, Lance Berkman	.25
208	Kit Pellow, Kevin Barker, Russ Branyan	.10
209	*B.J. Garbe, Larry Bigbie*	1.00
210	*Eric Munson, Bobby Bradley*	.25
211	Josh Girdley, Kyle Snyder	.10
212	Chance Caple, Jason Jennings	.25
213	*Ryan Christiansen, Brett Myers*	1.50
214	*Jason Stumm, Rob Purvis*	.25
215	David Walling, Mike Paradis	.10
216	Omar Ortiz, Jay Gehrke	.10
217	David Cone	.10
218	Jose Jimenez	.10
219	Chris Singleton	.10
220	Fernando Tatis	.10
221	Todd Helton	.20
222	Kevin Millwood	.15
223	Todd Pratt	.10
224	Orlando Hernandez	.20
225	Post-Season Highlights	.10
226	Post-Season Highlights	.10
227	Bernie Williams	.25
228	Mariano Rivera	.20
229	Tony Gwynn	.50
230	Wade Boggs	.25
231	Tim Raines	.10
232	Mark McGwire	2.00
233	Rickey Henderson	.25
234	Rickey Henderson	.25
235	Roger Clemens	1.50
236	Mark McGwire	2.00
237	Hank Aaron	2.00
238	Cal Ripken Jr.	3.00
239	Wade Boggs	.75
240	Tony Gwynn	1.00
241	Tom Glavine	.25
242	David Wells	.10
243	Kevin Appier	.10
244	Troy Percival	.10
245	Ray Lankford	.10
246	Marquis Grissom	.10
247	Randy Winn	.10
248	Miguel Batista	.10
249	Darren Dreifort	.10
250	Barry Bonds	1.50
251	Harold Baines	.10
252	Cliff Floyd	.10
253	Freddy Garcia	.10
254	Kenny Rogers	.10
255	Ben Davis	.10
256	Charles Johnson	.10
257	John Burkett	.10
258	Desi Relaford	.10
259	Al Martin	.10
260	Andy Pettitte	.20
261	Carlos Lee	.10
262	Matt Lawton	.10
263	Andy Fox	.10
264	Chan Ho Park	.10
265	Billy Koch	.10
266	Dave Roberts	.10
267	Carl Everett	.10
268	Orel Hershiser	.10
269	Trot Nixon	.10
270	Rusty Greer	.10
271	Will Clark	.10
272	Quilvio Veras	.10
273	Rico Brogna	.10
274	Devon White	.10
275	Tim Hudson	.25
276	Mike Hampton	.10
277	Miguel Cairo	.10
278	Darren Oliver	.10
279	Jeff Cirillo	.10
280	Al Leiter	.10
281	Brant Brown	.10
282	Carlos Febles	.10
283	Pedro Astacio	.10
284	Juan Guzman	.10
285	Orlando Hernandez	.20
286	Paul Konerko	.15
287	Tony Clark	.10
288	Aaron Boone	.10
289	Ismael Valdes	.10
290	Moises Alou	.10
291	Kevin Tapani	.10
292	John Franco	.10
293	Todd Zeile	.10
294	Jason Schmidt	.15
295	Johnny Damon	.25
296	Scott Brosius	.10
297	Travis Fryman	.10
298	Jose Vizcaino	.10
299	Eric Chavez	.20
300	Mike Piazza	1.00
301	Matt Clement	.10
302	Cristian Guzman	.10
303	Darryl Strawberry	.10
304	Jeff Abbott	.10
305	Brett Tomko	.10
306	Mike Lansing	.10
307	Eric Owens	.10
308	Livan Hernandez	.10
309	Rondell White	.10
310	Todd Stottlemyre	.10
311	Chris Carpenter	.10
312	Ken Hill	.10
313	Mark Loretta	.10
314	John Rocker	.10
315	Richie Sexson	.25
316	Ruben Mateo	.10
317	Joe Randa	.10
318	Mike Sirotka	.10
319	Jose Rosado	.10
320	Matt Mantei	.10
321	Kevin Millwood	.10
322	Gary DiSarcina	.10
323	Dustin Hermanson	.10
324	Mike Stanton	.10
325	Kirk Rueter	.10
326	Damian Miller	.10
327	Doug Glanville	.10
328	Scott Rolen	.50
329	Ray Durham	.10
330	Butch Huskey	.10
331	Mariano Rivera	.20
332	Darren Lewis	.10
333	Ramiro Mendoza	.10
334	Mark Grudzielanek	.10
335	Mike Cameron	.10
336	Kelvim Escobar	.10
337	Bret Boone	.10
338	Mo Vaughn	.10
339	Craig Biggio	.10
340	Michael Barrett	.10
341	Marlon Anderson	.10
342	Bobby Jones	.10
343	John Halama	.10
344	Todd Ritchie	.10
345	Chuck Knoblauch	.10
346	Rick Reed	.10
347	Kelly Stinnett	.10
348	Tim Salmon	.10
349	A.J. Hinch	.10
350	Jose Cruz Jr.	.10
351	Roberto Hernandez	.10
352	Edgar Renteria	.10

353 Jose Hernandez .10
354 Brad Fullmer .10
355 Trevor Hoffman .10
356 Troy O'Leary .10
357 Justin Thompson .10
358 Kevin Young .10
359 Hideki Irabu .10
360 Jim Thome .50
361 Todd Dunwoody .10
362 Octavio Dotel .10
363 Omar Vizquel .10
364 Raul Mondesi .10
365 Shane Reynolds .10
366 Bartolo Colon .10
367 Chris Widger .10
368 Gabe Kapler .10
369 Bill Simas .10
370 Tino Martinez .10
371 John Thomson .10
372 Delino DeShields .10
373 Carlos Perez .10
374 Eddie Perez .10
375 Jeromy Burnitz .10
376 Jimmy Haynes .10
377 Travis Lee .10
378 Darryl Hamilton .10
379 Jamie Moyer .10
380 Alex Gonzalez .10
381 John Wetteland .10
382 Vinny Castilla .10
383 Jeff Suppan .10
384 Chad Curtis .10
385 Robb Nen .10
386 Wilson Alvarez .10
387 Andres Galarraga .10
388 Mike Remlinger .10
389 Geoff Jenkins .10
390 Matt Stairs .10
391 Bill Mueller .10
392 Mike Lowell .10
393 Andy Ashby .10
394 Ruben Rivera .10
395 Todd Helton .50
396 Bernie Williams .10
397 Royce Clayton .10
398 Manny Ramirez .60
399 Kerry Wood .25
400 Ken Griffey Jr. .75
401 Enrique Wilson .10
402 Joey Hamilton .10
403 Shawn Estes .10
404 Ugueth Urbina .10
405 Albert Belle .10
406 Rick Helling .10
407 Steve Parris .10
408 Eric Milton .10
409 Dave Mlicki .10
410 Shawn Green .25
411 Jaret Wright .10
412 Tony Womack .10
413 Vernon Wells .15
414 Ron Belliard .10
415 Ellis Burks .10
416 Scott Erickson .10
417 Rafael Palmeiro .35
418 Damion Easley .10
419 Jamey Wright .10
420 Corey Koskie .10
421 Bobby Howry .10
422 Ricky Ledee .10
423 Dmitri Young .10
424 Sidney Ponson .10
425 Greg Maddux .75
426 Jose Guillen .10
427 Jon Lieber .10
428 Andy Benes .10
429 Randy Velarde .10
430 Sean Casey .20
431 Torii Hunter .20
432 Ryan Rupe .10
433 David Segui .10
434 Rich Aurilia .10
435 Nomar Garciaparra .75
436 Denny Neagle .10
437 Ron Coomer .10
438 Chris Singleton .10
439 Tony Batista .10
440 Andruw Jones .60
441 Adam Piatt, Aubrey Huff, Sean Burroughs .20
442 Rafael Furcal, Jason Dallero, Travis Dawkins .20
443 *Wilton Veras, Joe Crede, Mike Lamb* .10
444 Julio Zuleta, Dernell Stenson, Jorge Toca .20
445 *Tim Raines Jr., Gary Mathews Jr., Garry Maddox Jr.* .20
446 Matt Riley, Mark Mulder, C.C. Sabathia .10
447 Scott Downs, Chris George, Matt Belisle .10
448 Doug Mirabelli, Ben Petrick, Jayson Werth .10
449 *Josh Hamilton, Corey Myers* .25
450 Ben Christensen, Brett Myers .20
451 *Barry Zito, Ben Sheets* 2.00
452 *Ty Howington, Kurt Ainsworth* .25
453 *Rick Asadoorian, Vince Faison* .10
454 *Keith Reed, Jeff Heaverlo* .20
455 Mike MacDougal, Jay Gehrke .25
456 Mark McGwire .75
457 Cal Ripken Jr. 1.00
458 Wade Boggs .25
459 Tony Gwynn .50
460 Jesse Orosco .10
461 Nomar Garciaparra, Larry Walker .50
462 Mark McGwire, Ken Griffey Jr. .50
463 Mark McGwire, Manny Ramirez .50
464 Randy Johnson, Pedro Martinez .25
465 Randy Johnson, Pedro Martinez .25
466 Luis Gonzalez, Derek Jeter .50
467 Manny Ramirez, Larry Walker .25
468 Tony Gwynn .75
469 Mark McGwire 2.00
470 Frank Thomas .50
471 Harold Baines .10
472 Roger Clemens .75
473 John Franco .10
474 John Franco .10
475 Ken Griffey Jr. 1.50
476 Barry Bonds 2.00
477 Sammy Sosa 1.25
478 Derek Jeter 2.50
479 Alex Rodriguez 2.00

Limited Edition

NM/M

Complete Factory Set (619): 100.00
Common Player: .50
Stars/Rookies: 1-2X
Inserts: 1X
(See 2000 Topps and inserts for checklists and base card values.)

All-Topps Team

NM/M

Complete Set (20): 15.00
Common Player: .25
Inserted 1:12
"Limited Edition" 4,000 Sets: 1X
1 Greg Maddux 1.50
2 Mike Piazza 1.50
3 Mark McGwire 2.50
4 Craig Biggio .40
5 Chipper Jones 1.50
6 Barry Larkin .40
7 Barry Bonds 2.50
8 Andruw Jones .75
9 Sammy Sosa 1.50
10 Larry Walker .40
11 Pedro Martinez 1.00
12 Ivan Rodriguez .50
13 Rafael Palmeiro .50
14 Roberto Alomar .50
15 Cal Ripken Jr. 3.00
16 Derek Jeter 3.00
17 Albert Belle .25
18 Ken Griffey Jr. 1.50
19 Manny Ramirez .75
20 Jose Canseco .50

All-Star Rookie Team

NM/M

Complete Set (10): 10.00
Common Player: .25
Inserted 1:36
"Limited Edition" 4,000 Sets: 1X
1 Mark McGwire 3.00
2 Chuck Knoblauch .25
3 Chipper Jones 2.00
4 Cal Ripken Jr. 4.00
5 Manny Ramirez 1.00
6 Jose Canseco .75
7 Ken Griffey Jr. 2.00
8 Mike Piazza 2.00
9 Dwight Gooden .25
10 Billy Wagner .25

Autographs

NM/M

Common Player: 8.00
Group A 1:7,589
Group B 1:4,553
Group C 1:518
Group D 1:911
Group E 1:1,138
1 Alex Rodriguez (A) 100.00
2 Tony Gwynn (A) 50.00
3 Vinny Castilla (B) 15.00
4 Sean Casey (B) 15.00
5 Shawn Green (C) 25.00
6 Rey Ordonez (C) 8.00
7 Matt Lawton (C) 15.00
8 Tony Womack (C) 8.00
9 Gabe Kapler (D) 10.00
10 Pat Burrell (D) 20.00
11 Preston Wilson (D) 15.00
12 Troy Glaus (D) 30.00
13 Carlos Beltran (D) 40.00
14 Josh Girdley (E) 8.00
15 B.J. Garbe (E) 8.00
16 Derek Jeter (A) 125.00
17 Cal Ripken Jr. (A) 150.00
18 Ivan Rodriguez (B) 40.00
19 Rafael Palmeiro (B) 40.00
20 Vladimir Guerrero (E) 45.00
21 Raul Mondesi (C) 15.00
22 Scott Rolen (C) 40.00
23 Billy Wagner (C) 10.00
24 Fernando Tatis (C) 8.00
25 Ruben Mateo (D) 8.00
26 Carlos Febles (D) 8.00
27 Mike Sweeney (E) 10.00
28 Alex Gonzalez (D) 10.00
29 Miguel Tejada (D) 40.00
30 Josh Hamilton (E) 8.00

Century Best

NM/M

Common Player: 2.00
Ser. 1 1:869 H
Ser. 2 1:362
CB1 Tony Gwynn (339) 8.00
CB2 Wade Boggs (578) 4.00
CB3 Lance Johnson (117) 2.00
CB4 Mark McGwire (522) 20.00
CB5 Rickey Henderson (1,334) 4.00
CB6 Rickey Henderson (2,103) 4.00
CB7 Roger Clemens (247) 12.00
CB8 Tony Gwynn (3,067) 6.00
CB9 Mark McGwire (587) 20.00
CB10 Frank Thomas (440) 6.00
CB11 Harold Baines (1,583) 2.00
CB12 Roger Clemens (3,316) 8.00
CB13 John Franco (264) 2.00
CB14 John Franco (416) 2.00

Combos

NM/M

Complete Set (10): 15.00
Common Card: 1.00
Inserted 1:18
"Limited Edition" 4,000 Sets: 1X
1 Roberto Alomar, Manny Ramirez, Kenny Lofton, Jim Thome 1.00
2 Tom Glavine, Greg Maddux, John Smoltz 1.50
3 Derek Jeter, Bernie Williams, Tino Martinez 3.00
4 Ivan Rodriguez, Mike Piazza 1.50
5 Nomar Garciaparra, Alex Rodriguez, Derek Jeter 3.00
6 Sammy Sosa, Mark McGwire 3.00
7 Pedro Martinez, Randy Johnson 1.00
8 Barry Bonds, Ken Griffey Jr. 2.50
9 Chipper Jones, Ivan Rodriguez 1.50
10 Cal Ripken Jr., Tony Gwynn, Wade Boggs 3.00

Hands of Gold

NM/M

Complete Set (7): 5.00
Common Player: .25
Inserted 1:18
"Limited Edition" 4,000 Sets: 1X
1 Barry Bonds 2.50
2 Ivan Rodriguez .75
3 Ken Griffey Jr. 1.50
4 Roberto Alomar .75
5 Tony Gwynn 1.00
6 Omar Vizquel .25
7 Greg Maddux 1.50

Hank Aaron Reprints

NM/M

Complete Set (23): 40.00
Common Aaron: 2.00
Inserted 1:18
Autographed: 260.00
"Limited Edition" 4,000 Sets: 1X
1 Hank Aaron - 1954 6.00
2 Hank Aaron - 1955 2.00
3 Hank Aaron - 1956 2.00

4	Hank Aaron - 1957	2.00
5	Hank Aaron - 1958	2.00
6	Hank Aaron - 1959	2.00
7	Hank Aaron - 1960	2.00
8	Hank Aaron - 1961	2.00
9	Hank Aaron - 1962	2.00
10	Hank Aaron - 1963	2.00
11	Hank Aaron - 1964	2.00
12	Hank Aaron - 1965	2.00
13	Hank Aaron - 1966	2.00
14	Hank Aaron - 1967	2.00
15	Hank Aaron - 1968	2.00
16	Hank Aaron - 1969	2.00
17	Hank Aaron - 1970	2.00
18	Hank Aaron - 1971	2.00
19	Hank Aaron - 1972	2.00
20	Hank Aaron - 1973	2.00
21	Hank Aaron - 1974	2.00
22	Hank Aaron - 1975	2.00
23	Hank Aaron - 1976	2.00

Hank Aaron Chrome Reprints

		NM/M
Complete Set (23):		90.00
Common Aaron:		5.00
Inserted 1:72		
Refractors:		2x to 3x
Inserted 1:288		
1	Hank Aaron - 1954	10.00
2	Hank Aaron - 1955	5.00
3	Hank Aaron - 1956	5.00
4	Hank Aaron - 1957	5.00
5	Hank Aaron - 1958	5.00
6	Hank Aaron - 1959	5.00
7	Hank Aaron - 1960	5.00
8	Hank Aaron - 1961	5.00
9	Hank Aaron - 1962	5.00
10	Hank Aaron - 1963	5.00
11	Hank Aaron - 1964	5.00
12	Hank Aaron - 1965	5.00
13	Hank Aaron - 1966	5.00
14	Hank Aaron - 1967	5.00
15	Hank Aaron - 1968	5.00
16	Hank Aaron - 1969	5.00
17	Hank Aaron - 1970	5.00
18	Hank Aaron - 1971	5.00
19	Hank Aaron - 1972	5.00
20	Hank Aaron - 1973	5.00
21	Hank Aaron - 1974	5.00
22	Hank Aaron - 1975	5.00
23	Hank Aaron - 1976	5.00

Mark McGwire 1985 Rookie Reprint

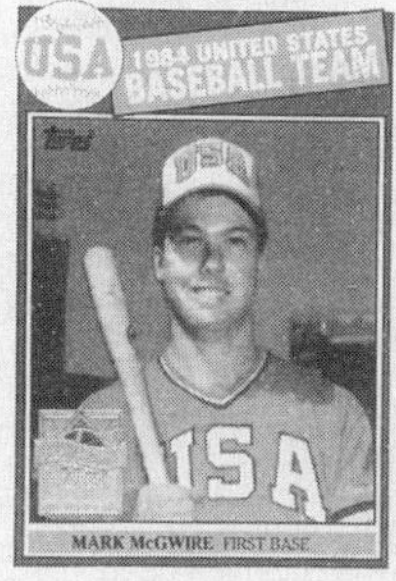

	NM/M
Complete Set (1):	6.00
Mark McGwire	6.00

Own the Game

		NM/M
Complete Set (30):		15.00
Common Player:		.15
Inserted 1:12		
"Limited Edition" 4,000 Sets:		1X
1	Derek Jeter	2.00
2	B.J. Surhoff	.15
3	Luis Gonzalez	.25
4	Manny Ramirez	.50
5	Rafael Palmeiro	.40
6	Mark McGwire	1.50
7	Mark McGwire	1.50
8	Sammy Sosa	1.00
9	Ken Griffey Jr.	1.00
10	Larry Walker	.25
11	Nomar Garciaparra	1.50
12	Derek Jeter	2.00
13	Larry Walker	.25
14	Mark McGwire	1.50
15	Manny Ramirez	.50
16	Pedro Martinez	.75
17	Randy Johnson	.75
18	Kevin Millwood	.25
19	Pedro Martinez	.75
20	Randy Johnson	.75
21	Kevin Brown	.25
22	Chipper Jones	1.00
23	Ivan Rodriguez	.50
24	Mariano Rivera	.25
25	Scott Williamson	.15
26	Carlos Beltran	.25
27	Randy Johnson	.75
28	Pedro Martinez	.75
29	Sammy Sosa	1.00
30	Manny Ramirez	.50

Perennial All-Stars

		NM/M
Complete Set (10):		10.00
Common Player:		.50
Inserted 1:18		
"Limited Edition" 4,000 Sets:		1X
1	Ken Griffey Jr.	1.00
2	Derek Jeter	2.00
3	Sammy Sosa	1.00
4	Cal Ripken Jr.	2.00
5	Mike Piazza	1.00
6	Nomar Garciaparra	1.50
7	Jeff Bagwell	.50
8	Barry Bonds	1.50
9	Alex Rodriguez	1.50
10	Mark McGwire	1.50

Power Players

		NM/M
Complete Set (20):		10.00
Common Player:		.25
Inserted 1:8		
"Limited Edition" 4,000 Sets:		1X
1	Juan Gonzalez	.50
2	Ken Griffey Jr.	1.00
3	Mark McGwire	1.50
4	Nomar Garciaparra	1.50
5	Barry Bonds	1.50
6	Mo Vaughn	.25
7	Larry Walker	.25
8	Alex Rodriguez	1.50
9	Jose Canseco	.25
10	Jeff Bagwell	.50
11	Manny Ramirez	.50
12	Albert Belle	.25
13	Frank Thomas	.50
14	Mike Piazza	1.00
15	Chipper Jones	1.00
16	Sammy Sosa	1.00
17	Vladimir Guerrero	.50
18	Scott Rolen	.50
19	Raul Mondesi	.25
20	Derek Jeter	2.00

Stadium Relics

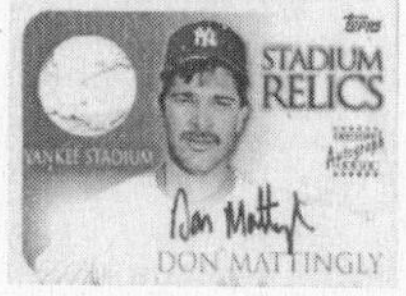

		NM/M
Common Player:		40.00
Inserted 1:165 HTA		
1	Don Mattingly	150.00
2	Carl Yastrzemski	100.00
3	Ernie Banks	75.00
4	Johnny Bench	75.00
5	Willie Mays	150.00
6	Mike Schmidt	100.00
7	Lou Brock	50.00
8	Al Kaline	75.00
9	Paul Molitor	60.00
10	Eddie Matthews	75.00

21st Century Topps

		NM/M
Complete Set (10):		5.00
Common Player:		.25
Inserted 1:18		
"Limited Edition" 4000 Sets:		1X
1	Ben Grieve	.25
2	Alex Gonzalez	.25
3	Derek Jeter	2.00
4	Sean Casey	.25
5	Nomar Garciaparra	1.50
6	Alex Rodriguez	1.50
7	Scott Rolen	.50
8	Andruw Jones	.50
9	Vladimir Guerrero	.50
10	Todd Helton	.50

2000 TOPPS TRADED AND ROOKIES

		NM/M
Complete Set (135):		25.00
Common Player:		.10
Unopened Set (136):		40.00
1	*Mike MacDougal*	.10
2	*Andy Tracy*	.20
3	*Brandon Phillips*	.50
4	*Brandon Inge*	.75
5	*Robbie Morrison*	.25
6	*Josh Pressley*	.10
7	*Todd Moser*	.25
8	*Rob Purvis*	.25
9	*Chance Caple*	.10
10	Ben Sheets	.75
11	*Russ Jacobson*	.10
12	*Brian Cole*	.10
13	*Brad Baker*	.25
14	*Alex Cintron*	.40
15	*Lyle Overbay*	1.00
16	*Mike Edwards*	.10
17	*Sean McGowan*	.25
18	*Jose Molina*	.25
19	*Marcos Castillo*	.10
20	*Josue Espada*	.10
21	*Alex Gordon*	.10
22	*Rob Pugmire*	.10
23	*Jason Stumm*	.25
24	*Ty Howington*	.40
25	Brett Myers	.50
26	*Maicer Izturis*	.10
27	*John McDonald*	.10
28	*Wilfredo Rodriguez*	.40
29	*Carlos Zambrano*	3.00
30	*Alejandro Diaz*	.20
31	*Geraldo Guzman*	.20
32	*J.R. House*	.50
33	*Elvin Nina*	.10
34	*Juan Pierre*	.50
35	*Ben Johnson*	.20
36	*Jeff Bailey*	.20
37	*Miguel Olivo*	.10
38	*Francisco Rodriguez*	2.00
39	*Tony Pena Jr.*	.25
40	*Miguel Cabrera*	15.00
41	*Asdrubal Oropeza*	.10
42	*Junior Zamora*	.10
43	*Jovanny Cedeno*	.40
44	*John Sneed*	.10
45	*Josh Kalinowski*	.10
46	*Mike Young*	3.00
47	*Rico Washington*	.10
48	*Chad Durbin*	.40
49	*Junior Brignac*	.25
50	*Carlos Hernandez*	.40
51	*Cesar Izturis*	.60
52	*Oscar Salazar*	.25
53	*Pat Strange*	.30
54	Rick Asadoorian	.15
55	*Keith Reed*	.25
56	*Leo Estrella*	.10
57	*Wascar Serrano*	.10
58	*Richard Gomez*	.25
59	*Ramon Santiago*	.40
60	*Jovanny Sosa*	.25
61	*Aaron Rowand*	.50
62	*Junior Guerrero*	.25
63	*Luis Terrero*	.25
64	*Brian Sanches*	.10
65	*Scott Sobkowiak*	.25
66	*Gary Majewski*	.10
67	Barry Zito	1.00
68	*Ryan Christianson*	.40
69	*Cristian Guerrero*	.40
70	*Tomas de la Rosa*	.10
71	*Andrew Beinbrink*	.25
72	*Ryan Knox*	.10
73	*Alex Graman*	.25
74	*Juan Guzman*	.10
75	*Ruben Salazar*	.40
76	*Luis Matos*	1.00
77	*Tony Mota*	.10
78	*Doug Davis*	.50
79	*Ben Christensen*	.25
80	Mike Lamb	.10
81	*Adrian Gonzalez*	1.00
82	*Mike Stodolka*	.25
83	*Adam Johnson*	.25
84	*Matt Wheatland*	.25
85	*Corey Smith*	.50
86	*Rocco Baldelli*	1.50
87	*Keith Bucktrot*	.25
88	*Adam Wainwright*	.50
89	*Scott Thorman*	.50
90	*Tripper Johnson*	.50
91	Jim Edmonds	.25
92	Masato Yoshii	.10
93	Adam Kennedy	.10
94	Darryl Kile	.10
95	Mark McLemore	.10
96	Ricky Gutierrez	.10
97	Juan Gonzalez	.40
98	Melvin Mora	.10
99	Dante Bichette	.10
100	Lee Stevens	.10
101	Roger Cedeno	.10
102	John Olerud	.25
103	Eric Young	.10
104	Mickey Morandini	.10
105	Travis Lee	.10
106	Greg Vaughn	.10
107	Todd Zeile	.10
108	Chuck Finley	.10
109	Ismael Valdes	.10
110	Ron Henika	.10
111	Pat Hentgen	.10
112	Ryan Klesko	.10
113	Derek Bell	.10
114	Hideo Nomo	.40
115	Aaron Sele	.10
116	Fernando Vina	.10
117	Wally Joyner	.10
118	Brian Hunter	.10
119	Joe Girardi	.10
120	Omar Daal	.10
121	Brook Fordyce	.10
122	Jose Valentin	.10
123	Curt Schilling	.40
124	B.J. Surhoff	.10
125	Henry Rodriguez	.10
126	Mike Bordick	.10
127	David Justice	.25
128	Charles Johnson	.10

129 Will Clark .25
130 Dwight Gooden .10
131 David Segui .10
132 Denny Neagle .10
133 Andy Ashby .10
134 Bruce Chen .10
135 Jason Bere .10

Autographs

	NM/M
Common Player:	4.00
Inserted 1:set	

1 Mike MacDougal 8.00
2 Andy Tracy 4.00
3 Brandon Phillips 10.00
4 Brandon Inge 20.00
5 Robbie Morrison 4.00
6 Josh Pressley 4.00
7 Todd Moser 4.00
8 Rob Purvis 4.00
9 Chance Caple 4.00
10 Ben Sheets 50.00
11 Russ Jacobson 4.00
12 Brian Cole 4.00
13 Brad Baker 4.00
14 Alex Cintron 10.00
15 Lyle Overbay 20.00
16 Mike Edwards 4.00
17 Sean McGowan 4.00
18 Jose Molina 4.00
19 Marcos Castillo 4.00
20 Josue Espada 4.00
21 Alex Gordon 4.00
22 Rob Pugmire 4.00
23 Jason Stumm 4.00
24 Ty Howington 10.00
25 Brett Myers 40.00
26 Maicer Izturis 4.00
27 John McDonald 4.00
28 Wilfredo Rodriguez 4.00
29 Carlos Zambrano 100.00
30 Alejandro Diaz 4.00
31 Geraldo Guzman 4.00
32 J.R. House 8.00
33 Elvin Nina 4.00
34 Juan Pierre 25.00
35 Ben Johnson 4.00
36 Jeff Bailey 4.00
37 Miguel Olivo 10.00
38 Francisco Rodriguez 50.00
39 Tony Pena Jr. 4.00
40 Miguel Cabrera 550.00
41 Asdrubal Oropeza 4.00
42 Junior Zamora 4.00
43 Jovanny Cedeno 4.00
44 John Sneed 4.00
45 Josh Kalinowski 4.00
46 Mike Young 75.00
47 Rico Washington 4.00
48 Chad Durbin 4.00
49 Junior Brignac 4.00
50 Carlos Hernandez 8.00
51 Cesar Izturis 20.00
52 Oscar Salazar 4.00
53 Pat Strange 4.00
54 Rick Asadoorian 4.00
55 Keith Reed 4.00
56 Leo Estrella 4.00
57 Wascar Serrano 4.00
58 Richard Gomez 4.00
59 Ramon Santiago 4.00
60 Jovanny Sosa 4.00
61 Aaron Rowand 35.00
62 Junior Guerrero 4.00
63 Luis Terrero 15.00
64 Brian Sanches 4.00
65 Scott Sobkowiak 4.00
66 Gary Majewski 8.00
67 Barry Zito 40.00
68 Ryan Christianson 8.00
69 Cristian Guerrero 8.00
70 Tomas de la Rosa 4.00
71 Andrew Beinbrink 4.00
72 Ryan Knox 4.00
73 Alex Graman 4.00
74 Juan Guzman 4.00
75 Ruben Salazar 4.00
76 Luis Matos 15.00
77 Tony Mota 4.00
78 Doug Davis 20.00
79 Ben Christensen 4.00
80 Mike Lamb 10.00

2000 TOPPS CHROME

	NM/M
Complete Set (478):	100.00
Complete Series I Set (239):	50.00
Complete Series II Set (239):	50.00
Common Player:	.25
Pack (4):	1.50
Wax Box (24):	30.00

1 Mark McGwire 3.00
2 Tony Gwynn 1.50
3 Wade Boggs .75
4 Cal Ripken Jr. 4.00
5 Matt Williams .40
6 Jay Buhner .40
7 Not Issued
8 Jeff Conine .25
9 Todd Greene .25
10 Mike Lieberthal .25
11 Steve Avery .25
12 Bret Saberhagen .25
13 Magglio Ordonez .50
14 Brad Radke .25
15 Derek Jeter 4.00
16 Javy Lopez .50
17 Russ David .25
18 Armando Benitez .25
19 B.J. Surhoff .25
20 Darryl Kile .25
21 Mark Lewis .25
22 Mike Williams .25
23 Mark McLemore .25
24 Sterling Hitchcock .25
25 Darin Erstad .50
26 Ricky Gutierrez .25
27 John Jaha .25
28 Homer Bush .25
29 Darrin Fletcher .25
30 Mark Grace .75
31 Fred McGriff .50
32 Omar Daal .25
33 Eric Karros .40
34 Orlando Cabrera .40
35 J.T. Snow Jr. .25
36 Luis Castillo .25
37 Rey Ordonez .25
38 Bob Abreu .40
39 Warren Morris .25
40 Juan Gonzalez 1.00
41 Mike Lansing .25
42 Chili Davis .25
43 Dean Palmer .25
44 Hank Aaron 3.00
45 Jeff Bagwell 1.00
46 Jose Valentin .25
47 Shannon Stewart .25
48 Kent Bottenfield .25
49 Jeff Shaw .25
50 Sammy Sosa 2.00
51 Randy Johnson 1.50
52 Benny Agbayani .25
53 Dante Bichette .25
54 Pete Harnisch .25
55 Frank Thomas 1.00
56 Jorge Posada .75
57 Todd Walker .25
58 Juan Encarnacion .40
59 Mike Sweeney .25
60 Pedro Martinez 1.50
61 Lee Stevens .25
62 Brian Giles .50
63 Chad Ogea .25
64 Ivan Rodriguez 1.00
65 Roger Cedeno .25
66 David Justice .50
67 Steve Trachsel .25
68 Eli Marrero .25
69 Dave Nilsson .25
70 Ken Caminiti .25
71 Tim Raines .25
72 Brian Jordan .25
73 Jeff Blauser .25
74 Bernard Gilkey .25
75 John Flaherty .25
76 Brent Mayne .25
77 Jose Vidro .25
78 Jeff Fassero .25
79 Bruce Aven .25
80 John Olerud .50
81 Juan Guzman .25
82 Woody Williams .25
83 Ed Sprague .25
84 Joe Girardi .25
85 Barry Larkin .50
86 Mike Caruso .25
87 Bobby Higginson .25
88 Roberto Kelly .25
89 Edgar Martinez .40
90 Mark Kotsay .25
91 Paul Sorrento .25
92 Eric Young .25
93 Carlos Delgado 1.00
94 Troy Glaus 1.00
95 Ben Grieve .25
96 Jose Lima .25
97 Garret Anderson .50
98 Luis Gonzalez .50
99 Carl Pavano .25
100 Alex Rodriguez 3.00
101 Preston Wilson .40
102 Ron Gant .40
103 Harold Baines .25
104 Rickey Henderson .50
105 Gary Sheffield .75
106 Mickey Morandini .25
107 Jim Edmonds .50
108 Kris Benson .25
109 Adrian Beltre .25
110 Alex Fernandez .25
111 Dan Wilson .25
112 Mark Clark .25
113 Greg Vaughn .25
114 Neifi Perez .25
115 Paul O'Neill .50
116 Jermaine Dye .25
117 Todd Jones .25
118 Terry Steinbach .25
119 Greg Norton .25
120 Curt Schilling .75
121 Todd Zeile .25
122 Edgardo Alfonzo .25
123 Ryan McGuire .25
124 Stan Javier .25
125 John Smoltz .40
126 Bob Wickman .25
127 Richard Hidalgo .25
128 Chuck Finley .25
129 Billy Wagner .25
130 Todd Hundley .25
131 Dwight Gooden .40
132 Russ Ortiz .25
133 Mike Lowell .25
134 Reggie Sanders .25
135 John Valentin .25
136 Brad Ausmus .25
137 Chad Kreuter .25
138 David Cone .40
139 Brook Fordyce .25
140 Roberto Alomar .75
141 Charles Nagy .25
142 Brian Hunter .25
143 Mike Mussina .75
144 Robin Ventura .40
145 Kevin Brown .40
146 Pat Hentgen .25
147 Ryan Klesko .40
148 Derek Bell .25
149 Andy Sheets .25
150 Larry Walker .50
151 Scott Williamson .25
152 Jose Offerman .25
153 Doug Mientkiewicz .25
154 *John Snyder* .40
155 Sandy Alomar .25
156 Joe Nathan .25
157 Lance Johnson .25
158 Odalis Perez .25
159 Hideo Nomo .75
160 Steve Finley .25
161 Dave Martinez .25
162 Matt Walbeck .25
163 Bill Spiers .25
164 Fernando Tatis .25
165 Kenny Lofton .40
166 Paul Byrd .25
167 Aaron Sele .25
168 Eddie Taubensee .25
169 Reggie Jefferson .25
170 Roger Clemens 2.50
171 Francisco Cordova .25
172 Mike Bordick .25
173 Wally Joyner .25
174 Marvin Benard .25
175 Jason Kendall .40
176 Mike Stanley .25
177 Chad Allen .25
178 Carlos Beltran .50
179 Deivi Cruz .25
180 Chipper Jones 2.00
181 Vladimir Guerrero 1.50
182 Dave Burba .25
183 Tom Goodwin .25
184 Brian Daubach .25
185 Jay Bell .25
186 Roy Halladay .50
187 Miguel Tejada .50
188 Armando Rios .25
189 Fernando Vina .25
190 Eric Davis .40
191 Henry Rodriguez .25
192 Joe McEwing .25
193 Jeff Kent .50
194 Mike Jackson .25
195 Mike Morgan .25
196 Jeff Montgomery .25
197 Jeff Zimmerman .25
198 Tony Fernandez .25
199 Jason Giambi 1.00
200 Jose Canseco .75
201 Alex Gonzalez .25
202 Jack Cust, Mike Colangelo, Dee Brown .50
203 Felipe Lopez, Alfonso Soriano, Pablo Ozuna 3.00
204 Erubiel Durazo, Pat Burrell, Nick Johnson .75
205 John Sneed, Kip Wells, Matt Blank .50
206 Josh Kalinowski, Michael Tejera, Chris Mears .50
207 Roosevelt Brown, Corey Patterson, Lance Berkman .50
208 Kit Pellow, Kevin Barker, Russ Branyan .40
209 *B.J. Garbe, Larry Bigbie* 3.00
210 *Eric Munson, Bobby Bradley* .75
211 Josh Girdley, Kyle Snyder .50
212 Chance Caple, Jason Jennings .50
213 *Ryan Christiansen, Brett Myers* 6.00
214 *Jason Stumm, Rob Purvis* .75
215 David Walling, Mike Paradis .40
216 Omar Ortiz, Jay Gehrke .40
217 David Cone .40
218 Jose Jimenez .25
219 Chris Singleton .25
220 Fernando Tatis .25
221 Todd Helton 1.00
222 Kevin Millwood .50
223 Todd Pratt .25
224 Orlando Hernandez .25
225 Post-Season Highlights .25
226 Post-Season Highlights .25
227 Bernie Williams .75
228 Mariano Rivera .50
229 Tony Gwynn 1.50
230 Wade Boggs .50
231 Tim Raines .25
232 Mark McGwire 3.00
233 Rickey Henderson .75
234 Rickey Henderson .75
235 Roger Clemens 2.00
236 Mark McGwire 5.00
237 Hank Aaron 5.00
238 Cal Ripken Jr. 6.00
239 Wade Boggs 1.00
240 Tony Gwynn 3.00

Series 1 checklist (1-201) .05
Series 1 checklist (202-240, inserts) .05
241 Tom Glavine .50
242 David Wells .25
243 Kevin Appier .25
244 Troy Percival .25
245 Ray Lankford .25
246 Marquis Grissom .25
247 Randy Winn .25
248 Miguel Batista .25
249 Darren Dreifort .25
250 Barry Bonds 3.00
251 Harold Baines .25
252 Cliff Floyd .25
253 Freddy Garcia .40
254 Kenny Rogers .25
255 Ben Davis .25
256 Charles Johnson .25
257 John Burkett .25
258 Desi Relaford .25
259 Al Martin .25
260 Andy Pettitte .50
261 Carlos Lee .25
262 Matt Lawton .25
263 Andy Fox .25
264 Chan Ho Park .25
265 Billy Koch .25
266 Dave Roberts .25
267 Carl Everett .25
268 Orel Hershiser .25
269 Trot Nixon .25
270 Rusty Greer .25
271 Will Clark .75
272 Quilvio Veras .25
273 Rico Brogna .25
274 Devon White .25
275 Tim Hudson .50
276 Mike Hampton .25
277 Miguel Cairo .25
278 Darren Oliver .25
279 Jeff Cirillo .25
280 Al Leiter .25
281 Brant Brown .25
282 Carlos Febles .25
283 Pedro Astacio .25
284 Juan Guzman .25
285 Orlando Hernandez .25
286 Paul Konerko .25
287 Tony Clark .25
288 Aaron Boone .50
289 Ismael Valdes .25
290 Moises Alou .50
291 Kevin Tapani .25
292 John Franco .25
293 Todd Zeile .25
294 Jason Schmidt .25
295 Johnny Damon .40
296 Scott Brosius .25
297 Travis Fryman .40
298 Jose Vizcaino .25
299 Eric Chavez .50
300 Mike Piazza 2.00
301 Matt Clement .25
302 Cristian Guzman .25
303 Darryl Strawberry .40
304 Jeff Abbott .25
305 Brett Tomko .25
306 Mike Lansing .25
307 Eric Owens .25
308 Livan Hernandez .25
309 Rondell White .40
310 Todd Stottlemyre .25
311 Chris Carpenter .25
312 Ken Hill .25
313 Mark Loretta .25
314 John Rocker .25
315 Richie Sexson .75
316 Ruben Mateo .25
317 Ramon Martinez .25
318 Mike Sirotka .25
319 Jose Rosado .25
320 Matt Mantei .25
321 Kevin Millwood .50
322 Gary DiSarcina .25
323 Dustin Hermanson .25
324 Mike Stanton .25
325 Kirk Rueter .25
326 Damian Miller .25
327 Doug Glanville .25
328 Scott Rolen 1.00
329 Ray Durham .25
330 Butch Huskey .25
331 Mariano Rivera .50
332 Darren Lewis .25
333 Ramiro Mendoza .25
334 Mark Grudzielanek .25
335 Mike Cameron .25
336 Kelvim Escobar .25
337 Bret Boone .40
338 Mo Vaughn .40
339 Craig Biggio .40
340 Michael Barrett .25
341 Marlon Anderson .25
342 Bobby Jones .25
343 John Halama .25
344 Todd Ritchie .25
345 Chuck Knoblauch .25
346 Rick Reed .25
347 Kelly Stinnett .25
348 Tim Salmon .50
349 A.J. Hinch .25
350 Jose Cruz Jr. .25
351 Roberto Hernandez .25
352 Edgar Renteria .25
353 Jose Hernandez .25
354 Brad Fullmer .25
355 Trevor Hoffman .25
356 Troy O'Leary .25
357 Justin Thompson .25
358 Kevin Young .25
359 Hideki Irabu .25
360 Jim Thome 1.00
361 Todd Dunwoody .25
362 Octavio Dotel .25
363 Omar Vizquel .40
364 Raul Mondesi .40
365 Shane Reynolds .25
366 Bartolo Colon .25
367 Chris Widger .25
368 Gabe Kapler .25
369 Bill Simas .25
370 Tino Martinez .50
371 John Thomson .25
372 Delino DeShields .25
373 Carlos Perez .25
374 Eddie Perez .25
375 Jeromy Burnitz .25
376 Jimmy Haynes .25
377 Travis Lee .25
378 Darryl Hamilton .25
379 Jamie Moyer .25
380 Alex Gonzalez .25
381 John Wetteland .25
382 Vinny Castilla .40
383 Jeff Suppan .25
384 Chad Curtis .25
385 Robb Nen .25
386 Wilson Alvarez .25
387 Andres Galarraga .50
388 Mike Remlinger .25
389 Geoff Jenkins .40
390 Matt Stairs .25
391 Bill Mueller .25
392 Mike Lowell .25
393 Andy Ashby .25
394 Ruben Rivera .25
395 Todd Helton 1.00
396 Bernie Williams .75
397 Royce Clayton .25
398 Manny Ramirez 1.00
399 Kerry Wood .75
400 Ken Griffey Jr. 2.00
401 Enrique Wilson .25
402 Joey Hamilton .25
403 Shawn Estes .25
404 Ugueth Urbina .25
405 Albert Belle .30
406 Rick Helling .25
407 Steve Parris .25
408 Eric Milton .25
409 Dave Mlicki .25
410 Shawn Green .50
411 Jaret Wright .25
412 Tony Womack .25
413 Vernon Wells .50
414 Ron Belliard .25
415 Ellis Burks .25
416 Scott Erickson .25
417 Rafael Palmeiro .75
418 Damion Easley .25
419 Jamey Wright .25
420 Corey Koskie .25
421 Bobby Howry .25
422 Ricky Ledee .25
423 Dmitri Young .25
424 Sidney Ponson .25
425 Greg Maddux 2.00
426 Jose Guillen .25
427 Jon Lieber .25
428 Andy Benes .25
429 Randy Velarde .25
430 Sean Casey .40
431 Torii Hunter .50
432 Ryan Rupe .25
433 David Segui .25
434 Rich Aurilia .25
435 Nomar Garciaparra 3.00
436 Denny Neagle .25
437 Ron Coomer .25
438 Chris Singleton .25
439 Tony Batista .25
440 Andruw Jones 1.00
441 Adam Piatt, Aubrey Huff, Sean Burroughs .50
442 Rafael Furcal, Jason Dallero, Travis Dawkins .50
443 *Wilton Veras, Joe Crede, Mike Lamb* .25
444 Julio Zuleta, Dernell Stenson, Jorge Toca .25
445 *Tim Raines Jr., Gary Mathews Jr., Garry Maddox Jr.* .50
446 Matt Riley, Mark Mulder, C.C. Sabathia .25
447 Scott Downs, Chris George, Matt Belisle .50
448 Doug Mirabelli, Ben Petrick, Jayson Werth .25
449 *Josh Hamilton, Corey Myers* .50
450 Ben Christensen, Brett Myers .50
451 *Barry Zito, Ben Sheets* 10.00
452 *Ty Howington, Kurt Ainsworth* 2.00
453 *Rick Asadoorian, Vince Faison* .50
454 *Keith Reed, Jeff Heaverlo* .50
455 Mike MacDougal, Jay Gehrke 1.50
456 Mark McGwire 3.00
457 Cal Ripken Jr. 4.00
458 Wade Boggs .75
459 Tony Gwynn 1.50
460 Jesse Orosco .25
461 Nomar Garciaparra, Larry Walker 1.50
462 Mark McGwire, Ken Griffey Jr. 1.50
463 Mark McGwire, Manny Ramirez 1.50
464 Randy Johnson, Pedro Martinez 1.00
465 Randy Johnson, Pedro Martinez 1.00
466 Luis Gonzalez, Derek Jeter 2.00
467 Manny Ramirez, Larry Walker .75
468 Tony Gwynn 1.50
469 Mark McGwire 3.00
470 Frank Thomas .75
471 Harold Baines .25
472 Roger Clemens 1.50
473 John Franco .25
474 John Franco .25
475 Ken Griffey Jr. 3.00
476 Barry Bonds 5.00
477 Sammy Sosa 4.00
478 Derek Jeter 6.00
479 Alex Rodriguez 5.00

Refractors

Stars: 3-5X
Young Stars/RCs: 1-2X
Inserted 1:12
(See 2000 Topps Chrome for checklist and base card values.)

Allegiance

NM/M
Complete Set (20): 30.00
Common Player: .75
Inserted 1:16
Refractors: 5X
Inserted 1:424

1 Derek Jeter 6.00
2 Ivan Rodriguez 1.00
3 Alex Rodriguez 5.00
4 Cal Ripken Jr. 6.00
5 Mark Grace 1.00
6 Tony Gwynn 2.00
7 Juan Gonzalez 1.50
8 Frank Thomas 1.50
9 Manny Ramirez 1.50
10 Barry Larkin .75
11 Bernie Williams 1.50
12 Raul Mondesi .75
13 Vladimir Guerrero 1.50
14 Craig Biggio .75
15 Nomar Garciaparra 4.00
16 Andruw Jones 1.50
17 Jim Thome 1.50
18 Scott Rolen 1.50
19 Chipper Jones 3.00
20 Ken Griffey Jr. 3.00

All-Topps Team

NM/M
Complete Set (20): 40.00
Complete Series I Set (10): 20.00
Complete Series II Set (10): 20.00
Common Player: .50
Inserted 1:32
Refractors: 2-3X
Inserted 1:160

1 Greg Maddux 3.00
2 Mike Piazza 3.00
3 Mark McGwire 5.00
4 Craig Biggio 1.00
5 Chipper Jones 3.00
6 Barry Larkin 1.00
7 Barry Bonds 5.00
8 Andruw Jones 1.50
9 Sammy Sosa 3.00
10 Larry Walker 1.00
11 Pedro Martinez 2.00
12 Ivan Rodriguez 1.00
13 Rafael Palmeiro 1.00
14 Roberto Alomar 1.00
15 Cal Ripken Jr. 6.00
16 Derek Jeter 6.00
17 Albert Belle .50
18 Ken Griffey Jr. 3.00
19 Manny Ramirez 1.50
20 Jose Canseco 1.00

All-Star Rookie Team

NM/M
Complete Set (10): 10.00
Common Player: .50
Inserted 1:16
Refractors: 2-3X
Inserted 1:80

1 Mark McGwire 3.00
2 Chuck Knoblauch .50
3 Chipper Jones 2.00
4 Cal Ripken Jr. 4.00
5 Manny Ramirez 1.00
6 Jose Canseco .75
7 Ken Griffey Jr. 2.00
8 Mike Piazza 2.00
9 Dwight Gooden .50
10 Billy Wagner .50

Combos

NM/M
Complete Set (10): 20.00
Common Player: 1.00
Inserted 1:16
Refractors: 2-3X
Inserted 1:80

1 Roberto Alomar, Manny Ramirez, Kenny Lofton, Jim Thome 1.00

2 Tom Glavine, Greg Maddux, John Smoltz 2.00
3 Derek Jeter, Bernie Williams, Tino Martinez 4.00
4 Ivan Rodriguez, Mike Piazza 2.00
5 Nomar Garciaparra, Alex Rodriguez, Derek Jeter 4.00
6 Sammy Sosa, Mark McGwire 4.00
7 Pedro Martinez, Randy Johnson 1.50
8 Barry Bonds, Ken Griffey Jr. 3.00
9 Chipper Jones, Ivan Rodriguez 2.00
10 Cal Ripken Jr., Tony Gwynn, Wade Boggs 4.00

Kings

NM/M

Complete Set (10): 25.00
Common Player: 1.50
Inserted 1:32
1 Mark McGwire 5.00
2 Sammy Sosa 3.00
3 Ken Griffey Jr. 3.00
4 Mike Piazza 3.00
5 Alex Rodriguez 5.00
6 Manny Ramirez 1.50
7 Barry Bonds 6.00
8 Nomar Garciaparra 4.00
9 Chipper Jones 3.00
10 Vladimir Guerrero 1.50

Mark McGwire 1985 Rookie Reprint

NM/M

Inserted 1:32
Refractor: 50.00
Production 70 cards
Mark McGwire 5.00

Millennium Stars

NM/M

Complete Set (10): 10.00
Common Player: .50
Inserted 1:32
Refractors: 2-3X
Inserted 1:160
1 Nomar Garciaparra 4.00
2 Vladimir Guerrero 1.50
3 Sean Casey .75
4 Richie Sexson 1.00
5 Todd Helton 1.50
6 Carlos Beltran .75
7 Kevin Millwood .75
8 Ruben Mateo .50
9 Pat Burrell 1.00
10 Alfonso Soriano 2.00

Own the Game

NM/M

Complete Set (30): 30.00
Common Player: .25
Inserted 1:12
Refractors: 2-3X
Inserted 1:55
1 Derek Jeter 4.00
2 B.J. Surhoff .25
3 Luis Gonzalez .50
4 Manny Ramirez 1.00
5 Rafael Palmeiro 1.00
6 Mark McGwire 3.00
7 Mark McGwire 3.00
8 Sammy Sosa 2.00
9 Ken Griffey Jr. 2.00
10 Larry Walker .50
11 Nomar Garciaparra 3.00
12 Derek Jeter 4.00
13 Larry Walker .50
14 Mark McGwire 3.00
15 Manny Ramirez 1.00
16 Pedro Martinez 1.50
17 Randy Johnson 1.50
18 Kevin Millwood .50
19 Pedro Martinez 1.50
20 Randy Johnson 1.50
21 Kevin Brown .50
22 Chipper Jones 2.00
23 Ivan Rodriguez 1.00
24 Mariano Rivera .50
25 Scott Williamson .25
26 Carlos Beltran .50
27 Randy Johnson 1.50
28 Pedro Martinez 1.50
29 Sammy Sosa 2.00
30 Manny Ramirez 1.00

Power Players

NM/M

Complete Set (20): 25.00
Common Player: .25
Inserted 1:8
Refractors: 2-3X
Inserted 1:40
1 Juan Gonzalez 1.00
2 Ken Griffey Jr. 2.00
3 Mark McGwire 3.00
4 Nomar Garciaparra 3.00
5 Barry Bonds 3.00
6 Mo Vaughn .40
7 Larry Walker .50
8 Alex Rodriguez 3.00
9 Jose Canseco .75
10 Jeff Bagwell 1.00
11 Manny Ramirez 1.00
12 Albert Belle .25
13 Frank Thomas 1.00
14 Mike Piazza 2.00
15 Chipper Jones 2.00
16 Sammy Sosa 2.00
17 Vladimir Guerrero 1.00
18 Scott Rolen 1.00
19 Raul Mondesi .40
20 Derek Jeter 4.00

21st Century Topps

NM/M

Complete Set (10): 10.00
Common Player: .25
Inserted 1:16
Refractors: 2-3X
Inserted 1:80
1 Ben Grieve .25
2 Alex Gonzalez .25
3 Derek Jeter 4.00
4 Sean Casey .50
5 Nomar Garciaparra 3.00
6 Alex Rodriguez 3.00
7 Scott Rolen 1.00
8 Andruw Jones 1.00
9 Vladimir Guerrero 1.00
10 Todd Helton 1.00

2000 TOPPS CHROME TRADED AND ROOKIES

NM/M

Complete Set (135): 70.00
Common Player: .25
1 *Mike MacDougal* 1.00
2 *Andy Tracy* .50
3 *Brandon Phillips* 1.50
4 *Brandon Inge* 1.00
5 *Robbie Morrison* .50
6 *Josh Pressley* .50
7 *Todd Moser* .50
8 *Rob Purvis* .50
9 *Chance Caple* .50
10 Ben Sheets 2.00
11 *Russ Jacobson* .50
12 *Brian Cole* .50
13 *Brad Baker* .50
14 *Alex Cintron* 1.00
15 *Lyle Overbay* 2.00
16 *Mike Edwards* .50
17 *Sean McGowan* .50
18 *Jose Molina* .50
19 *Marcos Castillo* .50
20 *Josue Espada* .50
21 *Alex Gordon* .50
22 *Rob Pugmire* .50
23 *Jason Stumm* .50
24 *Ty Howington* 1.00
25 Brett Myers 1.00
26 *Maicer Izturis* .50
27 *John McDonald* .50
28 *Wilfredo Rodriguez* .50
29 *Carlos Zambrano* 6.00
30 *Alejandro Diaz* .50
31 *Geraldo Guzman* .50
32 *J.R. House* 1.00
33 *Elvin Nina* .50
34 *Juan Pierre* 2.00
35 *Ben Johnson* .50
36 *Jeff Bailey* .50
37 *Miguel Olivo* .50
38 *Francisco Rodriguez* 4.00
39 *Tony Pena Jr.* .50
40 *Miguel Cabrera* 50.00
41 *Asdrubal Oropeza* .50
42 *Junior Zamora* .50
43 *Jovanny Cedeno* .50
44 *John Sneed* .50
45 *Josh Kalinowski* .50
46 *Mike Young* 8.00
47 *Rico Washington* .50
48 *Chad Durbin* .50
49 *Junior Brignac* .50
50 *Carlos Hernandez* .50
51 *Cesar Izturis* 1.00
52 *Oscar Salazar* .50
53 *Pat Strange* .50
54 Rick Asadoorian .50
55 *Keith Reed* .50
56 *Leo Estrella* .50
57 *Wascar Serrano* .50
58 *Richard Gomez* .50
59 *Ramon Santiago* .50
60 *Jovanny Sosa* .50
61 *Aaron Rowand* 3.00
62 *Junior Guerrero* .50
63 *Luis Terrero* 1.50
64 *Brian Sanches* .50
65 *Scott Sobkowiak* .50
66 *Gary Majewski* .50
67 Barry Zito 2.00
68 *Ryan Christianson* .50
69 *Cristian Guerrero* .50
70 *Tomas de la Rosa* .50
71 *Andrew Beinbrink* .50
72 *Ryan Knox* .50
73 *Alex Graman* .50
74 *Juan Guzman* .50
75 *Ruben Salazar* .50
76 *Luis Matos* 2.00
77 *Tony Mota* .50
78 *Doug Davis* .50
79 *Ben Christensen* .50
80 Mike Lamb .50
81 *Adrian Gonzalez* 2.00
82 *Mike Stodolka* .50
83 *Adam Johnson* 1.00
84 *Matt Wheatland* .50
85 *Corey Smith* 1.00
86 *Rocco Baldelli* 4.00
87 *Keith Bucktrot* .50
88 *Adam Wainwright* 2.00
89 *Scott Thorman* .75
90 *Tripper Johnson* 1.50
91 Jim Edmonds .50
92 Masato Yoshii .25
93 Adam Kennedy .25
94 Darryl Kile .25
95 Mark McLemore .25
96 Ricky Gutierrez .25
97 Juan Gonzalez 1.00
98 Melvin Mora .25
99 Dante Bichette .25
100 Lee Stevens .25
101 Roger Cedeno .25
102 John Olerud .40
103 Eric Young .25
104 Mickey Morandini .25
105 Travis Lee .25
106 Greg Vaughn .25
107 Todd Zeile .25
108 Chuck Finley .25
109 Ismael Valdes .25
110 Ron Henika .25
111 Pat Hentgen .25
112 Ryan Klesko .40
113 Derek Bell .25
114 Hideo Nomo 1.00
115 Aaron Sele .25
116 Fernando Vina .25
117 Wally Joyner .25
118 Brian Hunter .25
119 Joe Girardi .25
120 Omar Daal .25
121 Brook Fordyce .25
122 Jose Valentin .25
123 Curt Schilling .50
124 B.J. Surhoff .25
125 Henry Rodriguez .25
126 Mike Bordick .25
127 David Justice .50
128 Charles Johnson .25
129 Will Clark .75
130 Dwight Gooden .25
131 David Segui .25
132 Denny Neagle .25
133 Andy Ashby .25
134 Bruce Chen .25
135 Jason Bere .25

2000 TOPPS GALLERY

NM/M

Complete Set (150): 40.00
Common Player: .15
Common (101-150): .50
Inserted 1:1
Pack (6): 2.00
Wax Box (24): 40.00
1 Nomar Garciaparra 1.50
2 Kevin Millwood .25
3 Jay Bell .15
4 Rusty Greer .15
5 Bernie Williams .50
6 Barry Larkin .25
7 Carlos Beltran .25
8 Damion Easley .15
9 Magglio Ordonez .25
10 Matt Williams .20
11 Shannon Stewart .15
12 Ray Lankford .15
13 Vinny Castilla .20
14 Miguel Tejada .25
15 Craig Biggio .25
16 Chipper Jones 1.00
17 Albert Belle .20
18 Doug Glanville .15
19 Brian Giles .25
20 Shawn Green .25
21 J.T. Snow Jr. .15
22 Luis Gonzalez .25
23 Carlos Delgado .50
24 J.D. Drew .25

25 Ivan Rodriguez .50
26 Tino Martinez .25
27 Erubiel Durazo .20
28 Scott Rolen .50
29 Gary Sheffield .40
30 Manny Ramirez .50
31 Luis Castillo .15
32 Fernando Tatis .15
33 Darin Erstad .25
34 Tim Hudson .25
35 Sammy Sosa 1.00
36 Jason Kendall .25
37 Todd Walker .15
38 Orlando Hernandez .25
39 Pokey Reese .15
40 Mike Piazza 1.00
41 B.J. Surhoff .15
42 Tony Gwynn .75
43 Kevin Brown .25
44 Preston Wilson .25
45 Kenny Lofton .25
46 Rondell White .20
47 Frank Thomas .50
48 Neifi Perez .15
49 Edgardo Alfonzo .15
50 Ken Griffey Jr. 1.00
51 Barry Bonds 1.50
52 Brian Jordan .15
53 Raul Mondesi .25
54 Troy Glaus .50
55 Curt Schilling .40
56 Mike Mussina .50
57 Brian Daubach .15
58 Roger Clemens 1.00
59 Carlos Febles .15
60 Todd Helton .50
61 Mark Grace .40
62 Randy Johnson .75
63 Jeff Bagwell .50
64 Tom Glavine .25
65 Adrian Beltre .20
66 Rafael Palmeiro .50
67 Paul O'Neill .25
68 Robin Ventura .25
69 Ray Durham .15
70 Mark McGwire 1.50
71 Greg Vaughn .15
72 Javy Lopez .25
73 Jeromy Burnitz .15
74 Mike Lieberthal .15
75 Cal Ripken Jr. 2.00
76 Juan Gonzalez .50
77 Sean Casey .25
78 Jermaine Dye .15
79 John Olerud .25
80 Jose Canseco .40
81 Eric Karros .20
82 Roberto Alomar .40
83 Ben Grieve .15
84 Greg Maddux 1.00
85 Pedro Martinez .75
86 Tony Clark .15
87 Richie Sexson .25
88 Cliff Floyd .15
89 Eric Chavez .25
90 Andruw Jones .50
91 Vladimir Guerrero .50
92 Alex Gonzalez .15
93 Jim Thome .50
94 Bob Abreu .25
95 Derek Jeter 2.00
96 Larry Walker .25
97 John Smoltz .25
98 Mo Vaughn .20
99 Jason Giambi .50
100 Alex Rodriguez 1.50
101 Mark McGwire 2.50
102 Sammy Sosa 1.50
103 Alex Rodriguez 2.50
104 Derek Jeter 3.00
105 Greg Maddux 1.50
106 Jeff Bagwell .75
107 Nomar Garciaparra 2.00
108 Mike Piazza 1.50
109 Pedro Martinez 1.00
110 Chipper Jones 1.50
111 Randy Johnson 1.00
112 Barry Bonds 2.50
113 Ken Griffey Jr. 1.50
114 Manny Ramirez .75
115 Ivan Rodriguez .75
116 Juan Gonzalez .75
117 Vladimir Guerrero .75
118 Tony Gwynn 1.00
119 Larry Walker .50
120 Cal Ripken Jr. 3.00
121 Josh Hamilton .50
122 Corey Patterson .50
123 Pat Burrell .50
124 Nick Johnson .50
125 Adam Piatt .50
126 Rick Ankiel .50
127 A.J. Burnett .50
128 Ben Petrick .50
129 Rafael Furcal .75
130 Alfonso Soriano 2.00
131 Dee Brown .50
132 Ruben Mateo .50
133 Pablo Ozuna .50
134 Sean Burroughs .75
135 Mark Mulder .75
136 Jason Jennings .50
137 Eric Munson .50
138 Vernon Wells .75
139 *Brett Myers* 3.00
140 *Ben Christensen* .50
141 *Bobby Bradley* .50
142 *Ruben Salazar* .50
143 *Ryan Christianson* .50
144 *Corey Myers* .50
145 *Aaron Rowand* 1.00
146 *Julio Zuleta* .50
147 *Kurt Ainsworth* 1.00
148 *Scott Downs* .50
149 *Larry Bigbie* 1.50
150 *Chance Caple* .50

Press Plates

NM/M
Common Player: 50.00
(See 2000 Topps Gallery for checklist.)

Players Private Issue

Stars (1-100): 4-8X
SPs (101-150): 2-4X
Production 250 sets

Lithos

NM/M
Complete Set (8): 675.00
Common Player: 80.00
(1) Shawn Green (1954 Topps Style) 80.00
(2) Ken Griffey Jr. (1954 Topps Style) 80.00
(3) Chipper Jones (1954 Topps Style) 80.00
(4) Pedro Martinez (1954 Topps Style) 80.00
(5) Alex Rodriguez (1954 Topps Style) 80.00
(6) Ivan Rodriguez (1954 Topps Style) 80.00
(7) Nomar Garciaparra, Alex Rodriguez, Derek Jeter Three of a Kind 100.00
(8) Paul O'Neill, Derek Jeter, Bernie Williams, Tino Martinez Torre's Terrors 100.00

Autographs

NM/M
Common Player: 5.00
Inserted 1:153
RA Rick Ankiel 5.00
RM Ruben Mateo 5.00
CP Corey Patterson 20.00
BP Ben Petrick 5.00
VW Vernon Wells 15.00

Gallery Exhibits

NM/M
Complete Set (30): 50.00
Common Player: .50
Inserted 1:18
1 Mark McGwire 5.00
2 Jeff Bagwell 1.50
3 Mike Piazza 3.00
4 Alex Rodriguez 5.00
5 Nomar Garciaparra 4.00
6 Ivan Rodriguez 1.50
7 Chipper Jones 3.00
8 Cal Ripken Jr. 6.00
9 Tony Gwynn 2.00
10 Jose Canseco 1.00
11 Albert Belle .50
12 Greg Maddux 3.00
13 Barry Bonds 5.00
14 Ken Griffey Jr. 3.00
15 Juan Gonzalez 1.50
16 Rickey Henderson 1.00
17 Craig Biggio .75
18 Vladimir Guerrero 1.50
19 Rey Ordonez .50
20 Roberto Alomar 1.00
21 Derek Jeter 6.00
22 Manny Ramirez 1.50
23 Shawn Green 1.00
24 Sammy Sosa 3.00
25 Larry Walker 1.00
26 Pedro Martinez 2.00
27 Randy Johnson 2.00
28 Pat Burrell 1.00
29 Josh Hamilton .50
30 Corey Patterson 1.00

Gallery of Heroes

NM/M
Complete Set (10): 20.00
Common Player: 1.00
Inserted 1:24
1 Alex Rodriguez 3.00
2 Chipper Jones 2.00
3 Pedro Martinez 1.50
4 Sammy Sosa 2.00
5 Mark McGwire 3.00
6 Nomar Garciaparra 3.00
7 Vladimir Guerrero 1.00
8 Ken Griffey Jr. 2.00
9 Mike Piazza 2.00
10 Derek Jeter 4.00

Proof Positive

NM/M
Complete Set (10): 40.00
Common Player: 3.00
Inserted 1:48
1 Ken Griffey Jr., Ruben Mateo 4.00
2 Derek Jeter, Alfonso Soriano 6.00
3 Mark McGwire, Pat Burrell 6.00
4 Pedro Martinez, A.J. Burnett 3.00
5 Alex Rodriguez, Rafael Furcal 6.00
6 Sammy Sosa, Corey Patterson 4.00
7 Randy Johnson, Rick Ankiel 3.00
8 Chipper Jones, Adam Piatt 4.00
9 Nomar Garciaparra, Pablo Ozuna 6.00
10 Mike Piazza, Eric Munson 4.00

Topps Heritage

NM/M
Complete Set (20): 100.00
Common Player: 2.00
Inserted 1:12
Proofs: 1-2X
Inserted 1:27
1 Mark McGwire 12.00
2 Sammy Sosa 8.00
3 Greg Maddux 8.00
4 Mike Piazza 8.00
5 Ivan Rodriguez 4.00
6 Manny Ramirez 4.00
7 Jeff Bagwell 4.00
8 Sean Casey 2.00
9 Orlando Hernandez 2.00
10 Randy Johnson 5.00
11 Pedro Martinez 5.00
12 Vladimir Guerrero 4.00

13 Shawn Green 2.50
14 Ken Griffey Jr. 8.00
15 Alex Rodriguez 12.00
16 Nomar Garciaparra 10.00
17 Derek Jeter 15.00
18 Tony Gwynn 5.00
19 Chipper Jones 8.00
20 Cal Ripken Jr. 15.00

2000 TOPPS GOLD LABEL CLASS 1

NM/M
Complete Set (100): 25.00
Common Player: .25
Gold parallel: 4-8X
Production 100 sets
Pack (3): 2.00
Wax Box (24): 30.00
1 Sammy Sosa 1.50
2 Greg Maddux 1.50
3 Dee Brown .25
4 Rondell White .40
5 Fernando Tatis .25
6 Troy Glaus .75
7 Nick Johnson .40
8 Albert Belle .30
9 Scott Rolen .75
10 Rafael Palmeiro .50
11 Tony Gwynn 1.00
12 Kevin Brown .40
13 Roberto Alomar .50
14 John Olerud .40
15 Rick Ankiel .25
16 Chipper Jones 1.50
17 Craig Biggio .40
18 Mark Mulder .40
19 Carlos Delgado .75
20 Alex Gonzalez .25
21 Gabe Kapler .25
22 Derek Jeter 3.00
23 Carlos Beltran .40
24 Todd Helton .75
25 Mark McGwire 2.50
26 Ben Grieve .25
27 Rafael Furcal .40
28 Vernon Wells .40
29 Greg Vaughn .25
30 Vladimir Guerrero .75
31 Mike Piazza 1.50
32 Roger Clemens 2.00
33 Barry Larkin .40
34 Pedro Martinez 1.00
35 Matt Williams .30
36 Mo Vaughn .30
37 Tim Hudson .40
38 Andruw Jones .75
39 Vinny Castilla .25

40 Frank Thomas .75
41 Pokey Reese .25
42 Corey Patterson .40
43 Jeromy Burnitz .25
44 Preston Wilson .40
45 Juan Gonzalez .75
46 Brian Giles .40
47 Todd Walker .25
48 Magglio Ordonez .40
49 Alfonso Soriano 1.00
50 Ken Griffey Jr. 1.50
51 Michael Barrett .25
52 Shawn Green .50
53 Erubiel Durazo .40
54 Adam Piatt .25
55 Pat Burrell .50
56 Mike Mussina .50
57 Bernie Williams .75
58 Sean Casey .40
59 Randy Johnson 1.00
60 Jeff Bagwell .75
61 Eric Chavez .50
62 Josh Hamilton .25
63 A.J. Burnett .25
64 Jim Thome .75
65 Raul Mondesi .40
66 Jason Kendall .40
67 Mike Lieberthal .25
68 Robin Ventura .40
69 Ivan Rodriguez .50
70 Larry Walker .40
71 Eric Munson .25
72 Brian Jordan .25
73 Edgardo Alfonzo .25
74 Curt Schilling .50
75 Nomar Garciaparra 2.00
76 Mark Grace .50
77 Shannon Stewart .25
78 J.D. Drew .40
79 Jack Cust .25
80 Cal Ripken Jr. 3.00
81 Bob Abreu .40
82 Ruben Mateo .25
83 Orlando Hernandez .25
84 Kris Benson .25
85 Barry Bonds 2.50
86 Manny Ramirez .75
87 Jose Canseco .50
88 Sean Burroughs .25
89 Kevin Millwood .40
90 Alex Rodriguez 2.50
91 *Brett Myers* 3.00
92 *Rick Asadoorian* .40
93 *Ben Christensen* .40
94 *Bobby Bradley* .50
95 *Corey Myers* .50
96 *Brad Baisley* .50
97 *Aaron McNeal* .50
98 *Aaron Rowand* .75
99 *Scott Downs* .40
100 *Michael Tejera* .40

Class 2

NM/M

Same prices as Class 1
Gold Parallel: 4-8X
Same prices as Class 1
Gold parallel: 4-8X
Production 100 sets
Complete Set Bullion (10): 125.00
Common Player: 4.00
Inserted 1:53
1 Jim Thome, Manny Ramirez, Roberto Alomar 6.00
2 Derek Jeter, Orlando Hernandez, Bernie Williams 15.00
3 Chipper Jones, Andruw Jones, Greg Maddux 12.00
4 Alex Rodriguez, Jay Buhner, John Olerud 20.00
5 Nomar Garciaparra, Pedro Martinez, Brian Daubach 15.00
6 Mark McGwire, J.D. Drew, Rick Ankiel 20.00
7 Sammy Sosa, Mark Grace, Kerry Wood 15.00
8 Ken Griffey Jr., Sean Casey, Barry Larkin 20.00
9 Mike Piazza, Edgardo Alfonzo, Robin Ventura 15.00
10 Randy Johnson, Matt Williams, Erubiel Durazo 6.00

End of the Rainbow

NM/M

Complete Set (15): 8.00
Common Player: .50
Inserted 1:11
1 Pat Burrell 1.50
2 Corey Patterson 1.00
3 Josh Hamilton .50
4 Eric Munson .50
5 Sean Burroughs .75
6 Jack Cust .50
7 Rafael Furcal .75
8 Ruben Salazar .50
9 Brett Myers 1.00
10 Wes Anderson .50
11 Nick Johnson 1.00
12 Scott Downs .50
13 Choo Freeman .50
14 Brad Baisley .50
15 A.J. Burnett .75

Prospector's Dream

NM/M

Complete Set (10): 15.00
Common Player: .50
Inserted 1:26
1 Mark McGwire 3.00
2 Alex Rodriguez 3.00
3 Nomar Garciaparra 3.00
4 Pat Burrell .75
5 Todd Helton 1.00
6 Derek Jeter 4.00
7 Adam Piatt .50
8 Chipper Jones 2.00
9 Shawn Green .75
10 Josh Hamilton .50

The Treasury

NM/M

Complete Set (25): 40.00
Common Player: .50
Inserted 1:21
1 Ken Griffey Jr. 3.00
2 Derek Jeter 6.00
3 Chipper Jones 3.00
4 Manny Ramirez 1.50
5 Nomar Garciaparra 4.00
6 Sammy Sosa 3.00
7 Cal Ripken Jr. 6.00
8 Alex Rodriguez 5.00
9 Mike Piazza 3.00
10 Pedro Martinez 2.00
11 Vladimir Guerrero 1.50
12 Jeff Bagwell 1.50
13 Shawn Green 1.00
14 Greg Maddux 3.00
15 Mark McGwire 5.00
16 Josh Hamilton .50
17 Corey Patterson 1.00
18 Dee Brown .50
19 Rafael Furcal .75
20 Pat Burrell 1.00
21 Alfonso Soriano 3.00
22 Adam Piatt .50
23 A.J. Burnett .75
24 Mark Mulder .75
25 Ruben Mateo .50

2000 TOPPS HD

NM/M

Complete Set (100): 30.00
Common Player: .25
Platinums: 4-8X
Production 99 sets
Pack (4): 1.50
Wax Box (20): 30.00
1 Derek Jeter 3.00
2 Andruw Jones .75
3 Ben Grieve .25
4 Carlos Beltran .40
5 Randy Johnson 1.00
6 Javy Lopez .40
7 Gary Sheffield .50
8 John Olerud .40
9 Vinny Castilla .25
10 Barry Larkin .40
11 Tony Clark .25
12 Roberto Alomar .50
13 Brian Jordan .25
14 Wade Boggs .50
15 Carlos Febles .25
16 Alfonso Soriano 1.50
17 A.J. Burnett .25
18 Matt Williams .25
19 Alex Gonzalez .25
20 Larry Walker .40
21 Jeff Bagwell .75
22 Al Leiter .25
23 Ken Griffey Jr. 1.50
24 Ruben Mateo .25
25 Mark Grace .50
26 Carlos Delgado .75
27 Vladimir Guerrero .75
28 Kenny Lofton .40
29 Rusty Greer .25
30 Pedro Martinez 1.00
31 Todd Helton .75
32 Ray Lankford .25
33 Jose Canseco .50
34 Raul Mondesi .40
35 Mo Vaughn .40
36 Eric Chavez .40
37 Manny Ramirez .75
38 Jason Kendall .40
39 Mike Mussina .50
40 Dante Bichette .25
41 Troy Glaus .75
42 Rickey Henderson .50
43 Pablo Ozuna .25
44 Michael Barrett .25
45 Tony Gwynn 1.00
46 John Smoltz .40
47 Rafael Palmeiro .50
48 Curt Schilling .50
49 Todd Walker .25
50 Greg Vaughn .25
51 Orlando Hernandez .25
52 Jim Thome .75
53 Pat Burrell .50
54 Tim Salmon .40
55 Tom Glavine .40
56 Travis Lee .25
57 Gabe Kapler .25
58 Greg Maddux 1.50
59 Scott Rolen .75
60 Cal Ripken Jr. 3.00
61 Preston Wilson .40
62 Ivan Rodriguez .50
63 Johnny Damon .40
64 Bernie Williams .50
65 Barry Bonds 2.50
66 Sammy Sosa 1.50
67 Robin Ventura .40
68 Tony Fernandez .25
69 Jay Bell .25
70 Mark McGwire 2.50
71 Jeromy Burnitz .25
72 Chipper Jones 1.50
73 Josh Hamilton .25
74 Darin Erstad .40
75 Alex Rodriguez 2.50
76 Sean Casey .40
77 Tino Martinez .40
78 Juan Gonzalez .75
79 Cliff Floyd .25
80 Craig Biggio .40
81 Shawn Green .50
82 Adrian Beltre .25
83 Mike Piazza 1.50
84 Nomar Garciaparra 2.00
85 Kevin Brown .40
86 Roger Clemens 2.00
87 Frank Thomas .75
88 Albert Belle .25
89 Erubiel Durazo .25
90 David Walling .25
91 *John Sneed* .50
92 *Larry Bigbie* 1.50
93 *B.J. Garbe* .50
94 *Bobby Bradley* .75
95 *Ryan Christiansen* .50
96 *Jay Gerhke* .50
97 *Jason Stumm* .50
98 *Brett Myers* 4.00
99 *Chance Caple* .50
100 *Corey Myers* .75

Autographs

NM/M

Jeter 1:859
Ripken 1:4,386
1 Derek Jeter 150.00
2 Cal Ripken Jr. 250.00

Ballpark Figures

NM/M

Complete Set (10): 15.00
Common Player: .50
Inserted 1:11
1 Mark McGwire 3.00
2 Ken Griffey Jr. 2.00
3 Nomar Garciaparra 3.00
4 Derek Jeter 4.00
5 Sammy Sosa 2.00
6 Mike Piazza 2.00
7 Juan Gonzalez 1.00
8 Larry Walker .75
9 Ben Grieve .50
10 Barry Bonds 3.00

Clearly Refined

NM/M

Complete Set (10): 8.00
Common Player: .50
Inserted 1:20
1 Alfonso Soriano 3.00
2 Ruben Mateo .50
3 Josh Hamilton .75
4 Chad Hermansen .50
5 Ryan Anderson .50
6 Nick Johnson 1.00
7 Octavio Dotel .50
8 Peter Bergeron .50
9 Adam Piatt .50
10 Pat Burrell 2.00

Image

NM/M

Complete Set (10): 30.00

Common Player:		1.00
Inserted 1:44		
1	Sammy Sosa	3.00
2	Mark McGwire	5.00
3	Derek Jeter	6.00
4	Albert Belle	1.00
5	Vladimir Guerrero	1.50
6	Ken Griffey Jr.	3.00
7	Mike Piazza	3.00
8	Alex Rodriguez	5.00
9	Barry Bonds	5.00
10	Nomar Garciaparra	4.00

On The Cutting Edge

		NM/M
Complete Set (10):		15.00
Common Player:		.50
Inserted 1:22		
1	Andruw Jones	1.00
2	Nomar Garciaparra	3.00
3	Barry Bonds	3.00
4	Larry Walker	.50
5	Vladimir Guerrero	1.00
6	Jeff Bagwell	1.00
7	Derek Jeter	4.00
8	Sammy Sosa	2.00
9	Alex Rodriguez	3.00
10	Ken Griffey Jr.	2.00

2000 TOPPS OPENING DAY

		NM/M
Complete Set (165):		30.00
Common Player:		.15
Pack (8):		1.00
Wax Box (36):		25.00
1	Mark McGwire	2.00
2	Tony Gwynn	1.00
3	Wade Boggs	.40
4	Cal Ripken Jr.	2.50
5	Matt Williams	.20
6	Jay Buhner	.15
7	Mike Lieberthal	.15
8	Magglio Ordonez	.25
9	Derek Jeter	2.00
10	Javy Lopez	.25
11	Armando Benitez	.15
12	Darin Erstad	.25
13	Mark Grace	.25
14	Eric Karros	.15
15	J.T. Snow Jr.	.15
16	Luis Castillo	.15
17	Rey Ordonez	.15
18	Bob Abreu	.25
19	Warren Morris	.15
20	Juan Gonzalez	.75
21	Dean Palmer	.15
22	Hank Aaron	2.00
23	Jeff Bagwell	.75
24	Sammy Sosa	1.50
25	Randy Johnson	.75
26	Dante Bichette	.15
27	Frank Thomas	.75
28	Pedro Martinez	.75
29	Brian Giles	.20
30	Ivan Rodriguez	.50
31	Roger Cedeno	.15
32	David Justice	.25
33	Ken Caminiti	.15
34	Brian Jordan	.15
35	John Olerud	.25
36	Pokey Reese	.15
37	Barry Larkin	.25
38	Edgar Martinez	.15
39	Carlos Delgado	.50
40	Troy Glaus	.40
41	Ben Grieve	.15
42	Jose Lima	.15
43	Luis Gonzalez	.15
44	Alex Rodriguez	2.00
45	Preston Wilson	.20
46	Rickey Henderson	.40
47	Gary Sheffield	.25
48	Jim Edmonds	.25
49	Greg Vaughn	.15
50	Neifi Perez	.15
51	Paul O'Neill	.25
52	Jermaine Dye	.15
53	Curt Schilling	.25
54	Edgardo Alfonzo	.15
55	John Smoltz	.20
56	Chuck Finley	.15
57	Billy Wagner	.15
58	David Cone	.25
59	Roberto Alomar	.50
60	Charles Nagy	.15
61	Mike Mussina	.50
62	Robin Ventura	.25
63	Kevin Brown	.15
64	Pat Hentgen	.15
65	Ryan Klesko	.15
66	Derek Bell	.15
67	Larry Walker	.25
68	Scott Williamson	.15
69	Jose Offerman	.15
70	Doug Mientkiewicz	.15
71	John Snyder	.15
72	Sandy Alomar	.15
73	Joe Nathan	.15
74	Steve Finley	.15
75	Dave Martinez	.15
76	Fernando Tatis	.15
77	Kenny Lofton	.20
78	Paul Byrd	.15
79	Aaron Sele	.15
80	Roger Clemens	1.50
81	Francisco Cordova	.15
82	Wally Joyner	.15
83	Jason Kendall	.25
84	Carlos Beltran	.15
85	Chipper Jones	1.50
86	Vladimir Guerrero	.75
87	Tom Goodwin	.15
88	Brian Daubach	.15
89	Jay Bell	.15
90	Roy Halladay	.25
91	Miguel Tejada	.40
92	Eric Davis	.15
93	Henry Rodriguez	.15
94	Joe McEwing	.15
95	Jeff Kent	.25
96	Jeff Zimmerman	.15
97	Tony Fernandez	.15
98	Jason Giambi	.75
99	Jose Canseco	.40
100	Alex Gonzalez	.15
101	Erubiel Durazo, Pat Burrell, Nick Johnson	.40
102	Corey Patterson, Roosevelt Brown, Lance Berkman	.25
103	*Eric Munson, Bobby Bradley*	.25
104	*Josh Hamilton, Corey Myers*	.25
105	Mark McGwire	2.00
106	Hank Aaron	2.00
107	Cal Ripken Jr.	2.50
108	Wade Boggs	.40
109	Tony Gwynn	1.00
(110)	Hank Aaron	2.00
111	Tom Glavine	.40
112	Mo Vaughn	.20
113	Tino Martinez	.25
114	Craig Biggio	.25
115	Tim Hudson	.25
116	John Wetteland	.15
117	Ellis Burks	.15
118	David Wells	.15
119	Rico Brogna	.15
120	Greg Maddux	1.50
121	Jeromy Burnitz	.15
122	Raul Mondesi	.25
123	Rondell White	.25
124	Barry Bonds	2.00
125	Orlando Hernandez	.25
126	Bartolo Colon	.15
127	Tim Salmon	.25
128	Kevin Young	.15
129	Troy O'Leary	.15
130	Jim Thome	.50
131	Ray Durham	.15
132	Tony Clark	.15
133	Mariano Rivera	.25
134	Omar Vizquel	.15
135	Ken Griffey Jr.	1.50
136	Shawn Green	.40
137	Cliff Floyd	.15
138	Al Leiter	.15
139	Mike Hampton	.15
140	Mike Piazza	1.50
141	Andy Pettitte	.25
142	Albert Belle	.20
143	Scott Rolen	.75
144	Rusty Greer	.15
145	Kevin Millwood	.25
146	Ivan Rodriguez	.75
147	Nomar Garciaparra	1.50
148	Denny Neagle	.15
149	Manny Ramirez	.75
150	Vinny Castilla	.15
151	Andruw Jones	.50
152	Johnny Damon	.15
153	Eric Milton	.15
154	Todd Helton	.50
155	Rafael Palmeiro	.50
156	Damion Easley	.15
157	Carlos Febles	.15
158	Paul Konerko	.25
159	Bernie Williams	.50
160	Ken Griffey Jr.	1.50
161	Barry Bonds	2.00
162	Sammy Sosa	2.00
163	Derek Jeter	2.00
164	Alex Rodriguez	2.00
165	Checklist	.15

Autographs

		NM/M
Common Player:		25.00
1	Edgardo Alfonzo	25.00
2	Wade Boggs	60.00
3	Robin Ventura	25.00
4	Josh Hamilton	25.00
5	Vernon Wells	30.00

2000 TOPPS STARS

		NM/M
Complete Set (200):		35.00
Common Player:		.10
Pack (6):		2.00
Box (24):		40.00
1	Vladimir Guerrero	.75
2	Eric Karros	.10
3	Omar Vizquel	.20
4	Ken Griffey Jr.	1.50
5	Preston Wilson	.20
6	Albert Belle	.20
7	Ryan Klesko	.10
8	Bob Abreu	.20
9	Warren Morris	.10
10	Rafael Palmeiro	.40
11	Nomar Garciaparra	2.00
12	Dante Bichette	.10
13	Jeff Cirillo	.10
14	Carlos Beltran	.10
15	Tony Clark	.10
16	Ray Durham	.10
17	Mark McGwire	2.00
18	Jim Thome	.50
19	Todd Walker	.10
20	Richie Sexson	.40
21	Adrian Beltre	.10
22	Jay Bell	.10
23	Craig Biggio	.25
24	Ben Grieve	.15
25	Greg Maddux	1.50
26	Fernando Tatis	.10
27	Jeromy Burnitz	.10
28	Vinny Castilla	.10
29	Mark Grace	.25
30	Derek Jeter	2.00
31	Larry Walker	.25
32	Ivan Rodriguez	.50
33	Curt Schilling	.40
34	*Mike Lamb*	.25
35	Kevin Brown	.20
36	Andruw Jones	.40
37	*Chris Mears*	.10
38	Bartolo Colon	.10
39	Edgardo Alfonzo	.15
40	Brady Anderson	.20
41	Andres Galarraga	.25
42	Scott Rolen	.50
43	Manny Ramirez	.75
44	Carlos Delgado	.50
45	David Cone	.10
46	Carl Everett	.10
47	Chipper Jones	1.50
48	Barry Bonds	2.00
49	Dean Palmer	.10
50	Frank Thomas	.75
51	Paul O'Neill	.25
52	Mo Vaughn	.20
53	Todd Helton	.75
54	Jason Giambi	1.00
55	Brian Jordan	.10
56	Luis Gonzalez	.25
57	Alex Rodriguez	2.00
58	J.D. Drew	.10
59	Javy Lopez	.20
60	Tony Gwynn	1.00
61	Jason Kendall	.20
62	Pedro Martinez	.75
63	Matt Williams	.20
64	Gary Sheffield	.40
65	Roberto Alomar	.50
66	*Lyle Overbay*	1.00
67	Jeff Bagwell	.75
68	Tim Hudson	.40
69	Sammy Sosa	1.50
70	*Keith Reed*	.10
71	Robin Ventura	.20
72	Cal Ripken Jr.	2.50
73	Alex Gonzalez	.10
74	*Aaron McNeal*	.10
75	Mike Lieberthal	.10
76	Brian Giles	.25
77	Kevin Millwood	.10
78	Troy O'Leary	.10
79	Raul Mondesi	.20
80	John Olerud	.20
81	David Justice	.25
82	Erubiel Durazo	.10
83	Shawn Green	.40
84	Tino Martinez	.20
85	Greg Vaughn	.15
86	Tom Glavine	.25
87	Jose Canseco	.40
88	Kenny Lofton	.25
89	Brian Daubach	.10
90	Mike Piazza	1.50
91	Randy Johnson	.75
92	Pokey Reese	.10
93	Troy Glaus	.50
94	Kerry Wood	.25

95	Sean Casey	.20
96	Magglio Ordonez	.40
97	Bernie Williams	.50
98	Juan Gonzalez	.75
99	Barry Larkin	.25
100	Orlando Hernandez	.20
101	Roger Clemens	1.50
102	Bob Gibson	.40
103	Gary Carter	.10
104	Willie Stargell	.10
105	Joe Morgan	.40
106	Brooks Robinson	.50
107	Ozzie Smith	.50
108	Carl Yastrzemski	.25
109	Al Kaline	.40
110	Frank Robinson	.50
111	Lance Berkman	.10
112	Adam Piatt	.20
113	Vernon Wells	.25
114	Rafael Furcal	.25
115	Rick Ankiel	.20
116	Corey Patterson	.25
117	Josh Hamilton	.25
118	Jack Cust	.20
119	Josh Girdley	.10
120	Pablo Ozuna	.10
121	Sean Burroughs	.25
122	Pat Burrell	.25
123	Chad Hermansen	.10
124	Ruben Mateo	.10
125	Ben Petrick	.10
126	Dee Brown	.10
127	Eric Munson	.10
128	Ruben Salazar	.10
129	Kip Wells	.10
130	Alfonso Soriano	1.00
131	Mark Mulder	.25
132	Roosevelt Brown	.10
133	Nick Johnson	.40
134	Kyle Snyder	.10
135	David Walling	.10
136	*Geraldo Guzman*	.25
137	*John Sneed*	.25
138	*Ben Christensen*	.40
139	*Corey Myers*	.25
140	*Jose Ortiz*	3.00
141	*Ryan Christianson*	.25
142	*Brett Myers*	3.00
143	*Bobby Bradley*	.25
144	*Rick Asadoorian*	.25
145	*Julio Zuleta*	.40
146	*Ty Howington*	1.00
147	*Josh Kalinowski*	.40
148	*B.J. Garbe*	.50
149	*Scott Downs*	.40
150	*Dan Wright*	.25
151	Jeff Bagwell	.40
152	Vladimir Guerrero	.50
153	Mike Piazza	1.00
154	Juan Gonzalez	.40
155	Ivan Rodriguez	.40
156	Manny Ramirez	.40
157	Sammy Sosa	1.00
158	Chipper Jones	.75
159	Shawn Green	.20
160	Ken Griffey Jr.	.75
161	Cal Ripken Jr.	1.25
162	Nomar Garciaparra	1.00
163	Derek Jeter	1.00
164	Barry Bonds	1.00
165	Greg Maddux	.75
166	Mark McGwire	1.00
167	Roberto Alomar	.25
168	Alex Rodriguez	1.25
169	Randy Johnson	.40
170	Tony Gwynn	.50
171	Pedro Martinez	.40
172	Bob Gibson	.25
173	Gary Carter	.10
174	Willie Stargell	.25
175	Joe Morgan	.25
176	Brooks Robinson	.40
177	Ozzie Smith	.50
178	Carl Yastrzemski	.20
179	Al Kaline	.25
180	Frank Robinson	.40
181	Adam Piatt	.20
182	Alfonso Soriano	.75
183	Corey Patterson	.25
184	Vernon Wells	.40
185	Pat Burrell	.20
186	Mark Mulder	.10
187	Eric Munson	.10
188	Rafael Furcal	.15
189	Rick Ankiel	.20
190	Ruben Mateo	.10
191	Sean Burroughs	.20
192	Josh Hamilton	.20
193	Brett Myers	1.00
194	Ben Christensen	.20
195	Ty Howington	.25
196	Rick Asadoorian	.20
197	Josh Kalinowski	.20
198	Corey Myers	.25
199	Ryan Christianson	.25
200	John Sneed	.25

Blue

Stars (1-150): 3-5X
Production 299 sets
Stars (151-180): 4-8X
Rookies (181-200): 2-4X
Production 99 sets

Autographs

NM/M

Common Player: 10.00
Group A 1:382
Group B 1:1,636

RA	Rick Ankiel A	10.00
GC	Gary Carter B	60.00
RF	Rafael Furcal A	15.00
BG	Bob Gibson A	25.00
DJ	Derek Jeter A	90.00
AK	Al Kaline B	50.00
KM	Kevin Millwood A	15.00
JM	Joe Morgan B	40.00
BR	Brooks Robinson B	40.00
FR	Frank Robinson B	20.00
OS	Ozzie Smith B	35.00
WS	Willie Stargell B	50.00
CY	Carl Yastrzemski B	65.00

All-Star Authority

NM/M

Complete Set (14): 25.00
Common Player: 1.00
Inserted 1:13

1	Mark McGwire	3.00
2	Sammy Sosa	2.00
3	Ken Griffey Jr.	2.00
4	Cal Ripken Jr.	4.00
5	Tony Gwynn	1.50
6	Barry Bonds	4.00
7	Mike Piazza	2.00
8	Pedro Martinez	1.50
9	Chipper Jones	2.00
10	Manny Ramirez	1.00
11	Alex Rodriguez	3.00
12	Derek Jeter	4.00
13	Nomar Garciaparra	3.00
14	Roberto Alomar	1.00

Game Gear Jersey

NM/M

Common Player: 10.00
Inserted 1:382

1	Kevin Millwood	10.00
2	Brad Penny	10.00
3	J.D. Drew	15.00

Game Gear Bats

NM/M

Common Player: 10.00
Group A 1:2,289
Group B 1:1,153
Group C 1:409

1	Rafael Furcal C	10.00
2	Sean Burroughs B	10.00
3	Corey Patterson B	10.00
4	Chipper Jones B	40.00
5	Vernon Wells C	15.00
6	Alfonso Soriano B	25.00
7	Eric Munson C	10.00
8	Ben Petrick B	10.00
9	Dee Brown A	10.00
10	Lance Berkman C	15.00

Progression

NM/M

Complete Set (9): 15.00
Common Player: 1.00
Inserted 1:13

1	Bob Gibson, Pedro Martinez, Rick Ankiel	1.50
2	Gary Carter, Mike Piazza, Ben Petrick	2.00
3	Willie Stargell, Mark McGwire, Pat Burrell	3.00
4	Joe Morgan, Roberto Alomar, Ruben Salazar	1.00
5	Brooks Robinson, Chipper Jones, Sean Burroughs	2.00
6	Ozzie Smith, Derek Jeter, Rafael Furcal	3.00
7	Carl Yastrzemski, Barry Bonds, Josh Hamilton	3.00
8	Al Kaline, Ken Griffey Jr., Ruben Mateo	2.00
9	Frank Robinson, Manny Ramirez, Corey Patterson	1.50

Walk of Fame

NM/M

Complete Set (15): 15.00
Common Player: .75
Inserted 1:8

1	Cal Ripken Jr.	3.00
2	Ken Griffey Jr.	1.50
3	Mark McGwire	2.00
4	Sammy Sosa	1.50
5	Alex Rodriguez	2.00
6	Derek Jeter	2.50
7	Nomar Garciaparra	2.00
8	Chipper Jones	1.50
9	Manny Ramirez	1.00
10	Mike Piazza	1.50
11	Vladimir Guerrero	1.00
12	Barry Bonds	3.00
13	Tony Gwynn	1.00
14	Roberto Alomar	.75
15	Pedro Martinez	1.00

2000 TOPPS SUBWAY SERIES

NM/M

Complete Fact. Set (101): 70.00
Complete Set (100): 20.00
Common Player: .20

1	Mike Piazza	3.00
2	Jay Payton	.20
3	Edgardo Alfonzo	.40
4	Todd Pratt	.20
5	Todd Zeile	.20
6	Mike Bordick	.20
7	Robin Ventura	.40
8	Benny Agbayani	.20
9	Timo Perez	.50
10	Kurt Abbott	.20
11	Matt Franco	.20
12	Bubba Trammell	.20
13	Darryl Hamilton	.20
14	Lenny Harris	.20
15	Joe McEwing	.20
16	Mike Hampton	.40
17	Al Leiter	.40
18	Rick Reed	.20
19	Bobby Jones	.20
20	Glendon Rusch	.20
21	Armando Benitez	.20
22	John Franco	.20
23	Rick White	.20
24	Dennis Cook	.20
25	Turk Wendell	.20
26	Bobby Valentine	.20
27	Derek Jeter	4.00
28	Chuck Knoblauch	.40
29	Tino Martinez	.30
30	Jorge Posada	.40
31	Luis Sojo	.20
32	Scott Brosius	.20
33	Chris Turner	.20
34	Bernie Williams	.75
35	David Justice	.75
36	Paul O'Neill	.40
37	Glenallen Hill	.20
38	Jose Vizcaino	.20
39	Luis Polonia	.20
40	Clay Bellinger	.20
41	Orlando Hernandez	.40
42	Roger Clemens	1.50
43	Andy Pettitte	.50
44	Denny Neagle	.20
45	Dwight Gooden	.30
46	David Cone	.20
47	Mariano Rivera	.50
48	Jeff Nelson	.20
49	Mike Stanton	.20
50	Jason Grimsley	.20
51	Jose Canseco	.75
52	Joe Torre	.50
53	Edgardo Alfonzo	.40
54	Darryl Hamilton	.20
55	John Franco	.20
56	Benny Agbayani	.20
57	Bobby Jones	.20
58	New York Mets	.20
59	Bobby Valentine	.20
60	Mike Piazza	3.00
61	Armando Benitez	.20
62	Mike Piazza	3.00
63	Mike Piazza	3.00
64	Todd Zeile	.20
65	Timo Perez	.50
66	Timo Perez	.50
67	Mike Hampton	.40
68	Andy Pettitte	.50
69	Tino Martinez	.30
70	Joe Torre	.50
71	New York Yankees	.40
72	Orlando Hernandez	.40
73	Bernie Williams	.75
74	Andy Pettitte	.50
75	Mariano Rivera	.50
76	New York Yankees	.40
77	Roger Clemens	1.50
78	Derek Jeter	4.00
79	David Justice	.75
80	Mariano Rivera	.50
81	Tino Martinez	.30
82	New York Yankees	.40
83	Jorge Posada	.40
84	Chuck Knoblauch	.40
85	Jose Vizcaino	.20
86	Roger Clemens	1.50
87	Mike Piazza	3.00
88	Clay Bellinger	.20
89	Robin Ventura	.40
90	Benny Agbayani	.20
91	Orlando Hernandez	.40
92	Derek Jeter	4.00
93	Mike Piazza	3.00
94	Mariano Rivera	.50
95	Derek Jeter	3.00
96	Luis Sojo	.20
97	New York Yankees	.40
98	Mike Hampton	.40
99	David Justice	.75
100	Derek Jeter	4.00

Fan Fare

		NM/M
Common Player:		25.00
Inserted 1:set		
1	Timo Perez	35.00
2	Edgardo Alfonzo	40.00
3	Mike Piazza	120.00
4	Robin Ventura	35.00
5	Todd Zeile	25.00
6	Benny Agbayani	25.00
7	Jay Payton	25.00
8	Mike Bordick	25.00
9	Matt Franco	25.00
10	Mike Hampton	40.00
11	Al Leiter	40.00
12	Rick Reed	25.00
13	Bobby Jones	25.00
14	Glendon Rusch	25.00
15	Darryl Hamilton	25.00
16	Turk Wendell	25.00
17	John Franco	25.00
18	Armando Benitez	25.00
19	Chuck Knoblauch	35.00
20	Derek Jeter	200.00
21	David Justice	40.00
22	Bernie Williams	50.00
23	Jorge Posada	40.00
24	Paul O'Neill	50.00
25	Tino Martinez	35.00
26	Luis Sojo	25.00
27	Scott Brosius	25.00
28	Jose Canseco	50.00
29	Orlando Hernandez	35.00
30	Roger Clemens	100.00
31	Andy Pettitte	40.00
32	Denny Neagle	25.00
33	David Cone	25.00
34	Jeff Nelson	25.00
35	Mike Stanton	25.00
36	Mariano Rivera	60.00

2000 TOPPS TEK

		NM/M
Complete Set (45):		25.00
Common Player:		.40
Common Rookie (41-45):		.75
2,000 serial numbered rookies		
Pack (4):		2.00
Box (20):		30.00
1	Mike Piazza	1.50
2	Chipper Jones	1.50
3	Juan Gonzalez	.75
4	Ivan Rodriguez	.50
5	Cal Ripken Jr.	3.00
6	A.J. Burnett	.40
7	Jim Thome	.75
8	Mo Vaughn	.40
9	Andruw Jones	.75
10	Mark McGwire	2.00
11	Jose Canseco	.50
12	Shawn Green	.50
13	Barry Bonds	3.00
14	Bernie Williams	.50
15	Manny Ramirez	.75
16	Greg Maddux	1.50
17	Carlos Beltran	.40
18	Pedro Martinez	1.00
19	Jeff Bagwell	.75
20	Sammy Sosa	2.00
21	J.D. Drew	.40
22	Randy Johnson	1.00
23	Larry Walker	.40
24	Frank Thomas	.75
25	Orlando Hernandez	.40
26	Scott Rolen	.75
27	Tony Gwynn	1.00
28	Rick Ankiel	.40
29	Roberto Alomar	.75
30	Ken Griffey Jr.	1.50
31	Vladimir Guerrero	1.00
32	Derek Jeter	3.00
33	Nomar Garciaparra	2.00
34	Alex Rodriguez	2.50
35	Sean Casey	.40
36	Adam Piatt	.40
37	Corey Patterson	.40
38	Josh Hamilton	.40
39	Pat Burrell	.50
40	Eric Munson	.40
41	*Ruben Salazar*	.75
42	*John Sneed*	.75
43	*Josh Girdley*	.75
44	*Brett Myers*	4.00
45	*Rick Asadoorian*	.75

Color

Patterns 16-20:	1-2X
Inserted 1:10	

Gold

Stars:	8-15X
Rookies:	4-8X
Production 10 sets	

ArchiTEKs

		NM/M
Complete Set (18):		20.00
Common Player:		.50
Inserted 1:5		
1	Nomar Garciaparra	2.00
2	Derek Jeter	3.00
3	Chipper Jones	1.50
4	Vladimir Guerrero	1.00
5	Mark McGwire	2.50
6	Ken Griffey Jr.	1.50
7	Mike Piazza	1.50
8	Jeff Bagwell	1.00
9	Larry Walker	.50
10	Manny Ramirez	1.00
11	Alex Rodriguez	2.00
12	Sammy Sosa	2.00
13	Shawn Green	.50
14	Juan Gonzalez	.75
15	Barry Bonds	3.00
16	Pedro Martinez	1.00
17	Cal Ripken Jr.	3.00
18	Ivan Rodriguez	.75

DramaTEK Performers

		NM/M
Complete Set (9):		15.00
Common Player:		1.00
Inserted 1:10		
1	Mark McGwire	3.00
2	Sammy Sosa	2.50
3	Ken Griffey Jr.	2.00
4	Nomar Garciaparra	3.00
5	Chipper Jones	2.00
6	Mike Piazza	2.00
7	Alex Rodriguez	3.00
8	Derek Jeter	3.00
9	Vladimir Guerrero	1.50

TEKtonics

		NM/M
Complete Set (9):		35.00
Common Player:		4.00
Inserted 1:30		
1	Derek Jeter	6.00
2	Mark McGwire	6.00
3	Ken Griffey Jr.	4.00
4	Mike Piazza	4.00
5	Alex Rodriguez	6.00
6	Chipper Jones	4.00
7	Nomar Garciaparra	6.00
8	Sammy Sosa	5.00
9	Cal Ripken Jr.	8.00

2001 TOPPS

		NM/M
Complete Set (790):		70.00
Complete Ser. 1 Set (405):		30.00
Complete Ser. 2 Set (385):		40.00
Common Player:		.10
Complete Factory Set, Blue (795):		75.00
Complete Factory Set, Gold (795):		75.00
Ser. 1 Pack (10):		1.50
Ser. 1 Box (36):		45.00
Ser. 2 Pack (10):		1.50
Ser. 2 Box (36):		45.00
1	Cal Ripken Jr.	1.50
2	Chipper Jones	1.00
3	Roger Cedeno	.10
4	Garret Anderson	.10
5	Robin Ventura	.20
6	Daryle Ward	.10
7	Not Issued	.10
8	Ron Gant	.20
9	Phil Nevin	.10
10	Jermaine Dye	.10
11	Chris Singleton	.10
12	Mike Stanton	.10
13	Brian Hunter	.10
14	Mike Redmond	.10
15	Jim Thome	.25
16	Brian Jordan	.10
17	Joe Girardi	.10
18	Steve Woodard	.10
19	Dustin Hermanson	.10
20	Shawn Green	.30
21	Todd Stottlemyre	.10
22	Dan Wilson	.10
23	Todd Pratt	.10
24	Derek Lowe	.10
25	Juan Gonzalez	.40
26	Clay Bellinger	.10
27	Jeff Fassero	.10
28	Pat Meares	.10
29	Eddie Taubensee	.10
30	Paul O'Neill	.25
31	Jeffrey Hammonds	.10
32	Pokey Reese	.10
33	Mike Mussina	.30
34	Rico Brogna	.10
35	Jay Buhner	.10
36	Steve Cox	.10
37	Quilvio Veras	.10
38	Marquis Grissom	.10
39	Shigetoshi Hasegawa	.10
40	Shane Reynolds	.10
41	Adam Piatt	.10
42	Luis Polonia	.10
43	Brook Fordyce	.10
44	Preston Wilson	.10
45	Ellis Burks	.10
46	Armando Rios	.10
47	Chuck Finley	.10
48	Dan Plesac	.10
49	Shannon Stewart	.10
50	Mark McGwire	1.00
51	Mark Loretta	.10
52	Gerald Williams	.10
53	Eric Young	.10
54	Peter Bergeron	.10
55	Dave Hansen	.10
56	Arthur Rhodes	.10
57	Bobby Jones	.10
58	Matt Clement	.10
59	Mike Benjamin	.10
60	Pedro Martinez	.50
61	Jose Canseco	.40
62	Matt Anderson	.10
63	Torii Hunter	.10
64	Carlos Lee	.10
65	David Cone	.10
66	Ray Sanchez	.10
67	Eric Chavez	.20
68	Rick Helling	.10
69	Manny Alexander	.10
70	John Franco	.10
71	Mike Bordick	.10
72	Andres Galarraga	.25
73	Jose Cruz Jr.	.10
74	Mike Matheny	.10
75	Randy Johnson	.50
76	Richie Sexson	.10
77	Vladimir Nunez	.10
78	Harold Baines	.10
79	Aaron Boone	.10
80	Darin Erstad	.40
81	Alex Gonzalez	.10
82	Gil Heredia	.10
83	Shane Andrews	.10
84	Todd Hundley	.10
85	Bill Mueller	.10
86	Mark McLemore	.10
87	Scott Spiezio	.10
88	Kevin McGlinchy	.10
89	Bubba Trammell	.10
90	Manny Ramirez	.50
91	Mike Lamb	.10
92	Scott Karl	.10
93	Brian Buchanan	.10
94	Chris Turner	.10
95	Mike Sweeney	.10
96	John Wetteland	.10
97	Rob Bell	.10
98	Pat Rapp	.10
99	John Burkett	.10
100	Derek Jeter	1.50
101	J.D. Drew	.25
102	Jose Offerman	.10
103	Rick Reed	.10
104	Will Clark	.30
105	Rickey Henderson	.25
106	Dave Berg	.10
107	Kirk Rueter	.10
108	Lee Stevens	.10
109	Jay Bell	.10
110	Fred McGriff	.20
111	Julio Zuleta	.10
112	Brian Anderson	.10
113	Orlando Cabrera	.10
114	Alex Fernandez	.10
115	Derek Bell	.10
116	Eric Owens	.10
117	Brian Bohannon	.10
118	Dennys Reyes	.10
119	Mike Stanley	.10
120	Jorge Posada	.20
121	Rich Becker	.10
122	Paul Konerko	.10
123	Mike Remlinger	.10
124	Travis Lee	.10
125	Ken Caminiti	.10

No.	Player	Price
126	Kevin Barker	.10
127	Paul Quantrill	.10
128	Ozzie Guillen	.10
129	Kevin Tapani	.10
130	Mark Johnson	.10
131	Randy Wolf	.10
132	Michael Tucker	.10
133	Darren Lewis	.10
134	Joe Randa	.10
135	Jeff Cirillo	.10
136	David Ortiz	.10
137	Herb Perry	.10
138	Jeff Nelson	.10
139	Chris Stynes	.10
140	Johnny Damon	.10
141	Desi Relaford	.10
142	Jason Schmidt	.10
143	Charles Johnson	.10
144	Pat Burrell	.40
145	Gary Sheffield	.25
146	Tom Glavine	.25
147	Jason Isringhausen	.10
148	Chris Carpenter	.10
149	Jeff Suppan	.10
150	Ivan Rodriguez	.50
151	Luis Sojo	.10
152	Ron Villone	.10
153	Mike Sirotka	.10
154	Chuck Knoblauch	.20
155	Jason Kendall	.10
156	Dennis Cook	.10
157	Bobby Estalella	.10
158	Jose Guillen	.10
159	Thomas Howard	.10
160	Carlos Delgado	.50
161	Benji Gil	.10
162	Tim Bogar	.10
163	Kevin Elster	.10
164	Scott Downs	.10
165	Andy Benes	.10
166	Adrian Beltre	.10
167	David Bell	.10
168	Turk Wendell	.10
169	Pete Harnisch	.10
170	Roger Clemens	.75
171	Scott Williamson	.10
172	Kevin Jordan	.10
173	Brad Penny	.10
174	John Flaherty	.10
175	Troy Glaus	.50
176	Kevin Appier	.10
177	Walt Weiss	.10
178	Tyler Houston	.10
179	Michael Barrett	.10
180	Mike Hampton	.10
181	Francisco Cordova	.10
182	Mike Jackson	.10
183	David Segui	.10
184	Carlos Febles	.10
185	Roy Halladay	.10
186	Seth Etherton	.10
187	Charlie Hayes	.10
188	Fernando Tatis	.10
189	Steve Trachsel	.10
190	Livan Hernandez	.10
191	Joe Oliver	.10
192	Stan Javier	.10
193	B.J. Surhoff	.10
194	Rob Ducey	.10
195	Barry Larkin	.25
196	Danny Patterson	.10
197	Bobby Howry	.10
198	Dmitri Young	.10
199	Brian Hunter	.10
200	Alex Rodriguez	1.00
201	Hideo Nomo	.25
202	Luis Alicea	.10
203	Warren Morris	.10
204	Antonio Alfonseca	.10
205	Edgardo Alfonzo	.20
206	Mark Grudzielanek	.10
207	Fernando Vina	.10
208	Willie Greene	.10
209	Homer Bush	.10
210	Jason Giambi	.30
211	Mike Morgan	.10
212	Steve Karsay	.10
213	Matt Lawton	.10
214	Wendell Magee Jr.	.10
215	Rusty Greer	.10
216	Keith Lockhart	.10
217	Billy Koch	.10
218	Todd Hollandsworth	.10
219	Raul Ibanez	.10
220	Tony Gwynn	.75
221	Carl Everett	.20
222	Hector Carrasco	.10
223	Jose Valentin	.10
224	Deivi Cruz	.10
225	Bret Boone	.10
226	Kurt Abbott	.10
227	Melvin Mora	.10
228	Danny Graves	.10
229	Jose Jimenez	.10
230	James Baldwin	.10
231	C.J. Nitkowski	.10
232	Jeff Zimmerman	.10
233	Mike Lowell	.10
234	Hideki Irabu	.10
235	Greg Vaughn	.20
236	Omar Daal	.10
237	Darren Dreifort	.10
238	Gil Meche	.10
239	Damian Jackson	.10
240	Frank Thomas	.75
241	Travis Miller	.10
242	Jeff Frye	.10
243	Dave Magadan	.10
244	Luis Castillo	.10
245	Bartolo Colon	.10
246	Steve Kline	.10
247	Shawon Dunston	.10
248	Rick Aguilera	.10
249	Omar Olivares	.10
250	Craig Biggio	.20
251	Scott Schoeneweis	.10
252	Dave Veres	.10
253	Ramon Martinez	.10
254	Jose Vidro	.10
255	Todd Helton	.50
256	Greg Norton	.10
257	Jacque Jones	.10
258	Jason Grimsley	.10
259	Dan Reichert	.10
260	Robb Nen	.10
261	Mark Clark	.10
262	Scott Hatteberg	.10
263	Doug Brocail	.10
264	Mark Johnson	.10
265	Eric Davis	.20
266	Terry Shumpert	.10
267	Kevin Millar	.10
268	Ismael Valdes	.10
269	Richard Hidalgo	.20
270	Randy Velarde	.10
271	Bengie Molina	.10
272	Tony Womack	.10
273	Enrique Wilson	.10
274	Jeff Brantley	.10
275	Rick Ankiel	.25
276	Terry Mulholland	.10
277	Ron Belliard	.10
278	Terrence Long	.10
279	Alberto Castillo	.10
280	Royce Clayton	.10
281	Joe McEwing	.10
282	Jason McDonald	.10
283	Ricky Bottalico	.10
284	Keith Foulke	.10
285	Brad Radke	.10
286	Gabe Kapler	.10
287	Pedro Astacio	.10
288	Armando Reynoso	.10
289	Darryl Kile	.10
290	Reggie Sanders	.10
291	Esteban Yan	.10
292	Joe Nathan	.10
293	Jay Payton	.10
294	Francisco Cordero	.10
295	Gregg Jefferies	.10
296	LaTroy Hawkins	.10
297	Jeff Tam	.10
298	Jacob Cruz	.10
299	Chris Holt	.10
300	Vladimir Guerrero	.75
301	Marvin Benard	.10
302	Matt Franco	.10
303	Mike Williams	.10
304	Sean Bergman	.10
305	Juan Encarnacion	.10
306	Russ Davis	.10
307	Hanley Frias	.10
308	Ramon Hernandez	.10
309	Matt Walbeck	.10
310	Bill Spiers	.10
311	Bob Wickman	.10
312	Sandy Alomar	.10
313	Eddie Guardado	.10
314	Shane Halter	.10
315	Geoff Jenkins	.20
316	Gerald Witasick	.10
317	Damian Miller	.10
318	Darrin Fletcher	.10
319	Rafael Furcal	.25
320	Mark Grace	.25
321	Mark Mulder	.10
322	Joe Torre	.10
323	Bobby Cox	.10
324	Mike Scioscia	.10
325	Mike Hargrove	.10
326	Jimy Williams	.10
327	Jerry Manuel	.10
328	Buck Showalter	.10
329	Charlie Manuel	.10
330	Don Baylor	.10
331	Phil Garner)	.10
332	Jack McKeon	.10
333	Tony Muser	.10
334	Buddy Bell	.10
335	Tom Kelly	.10
336	John Boles	.10
337	Art Howe	.10
338	Larry Dierker	.10
339	Lou Pinella	.10
340	Davey Johnson	.10
341	Larry Rothschild	.10
342	Davey Lopes	.10
343	Johnny Oates	.10
344	Felipe Alou	.10
345	Jim Fregosi	.10
346	Bobby Valentine	.10
347	Terry Francona	.10
348	Gene Lamont	.10
349	Tony LaRussa	.10
350	Bruce Bochy	.10
351	Dusty Baker	.10
352	Adrian Gonzalez, Adam Johnson	.75
353	Matt Wheatland, Brian Digby	.40
354	Tripper Johnson, Scott Thorman	.40
355	Phil Dumatrait, Adam Wainwright	.40
356	*Scott Heard, David Parrish*	.40
357	*Rocco Baldelli, Mark Folsom*	.40
358	Dominic Rich, Aaron Herr	.40
359	Mike Stodolka, Sean Burnett	.25
360	Derek Thompson, Corey Smith	.40
361	*Danny Borrell, Jason Bourgeois*	.40
362	Chin-Feng Chen, Corey Patterson, Josh Hamilton	.25
363	Ryan Anderson, Barry Zito, C.C. Sabathia	.50
364	Scott Sobkowiak, David Walling, Ben Sheets	.50
365	Ty Howington, Josh Kalinowski, Josh Girdley	.10
366	Hee Seop Choi, Aaron McNeal, Jason Hart	1.50
367	Bobby Bradley, Kurt Ainsworth, Chin-Hui Tsao	.40
368	*Mike Glendenning, Kenny Kelly, Juan Silvestri*	.25
369	J.R. House, Ramon Castro, Ben Davis	.25
370	Chance Caple, Rafael Soriano, Pasqual Coco	.50
371	Travis Hafner, Eric Munson, Bucky Jacobsen	.75
372	Jason Conti, Chris Wakeland, Brian Cole	.20
373	Scott Seabol, Aubrey Huff, Joe Crede	.40
374	Adam Everett, Jose Ortiz, Keith Ginter	.25
375	Carlos Hernandez, Geraldo Guzman, Adam Eaton	.25
376	Bobby Kielty, Milton Bradley, Juan Rivera	.25
377	Mark McGwire	.75
378	Don Larsen	.20
379	Bobby Thomson	.10
380	Bill Mazeroski	.20
381	Reggie Jackson	.40
382	Kirk Gibson	.10
383	Roger Maris	.40
384	Cal Ripken Jr.	.75
385	Hank Aaron	.75
386	Joe Carter	.10
387	Cal Ripken Jr.	.75
388	Randy Johnson	.30
389	Ken Griffey Jr.	.50
390	Troy Glaus	.30
391	Kazuhiro Sasaki	.40
392	Sammy Sosa, Troy Glaus	.50
393	Todd Helton, Edgar Martinez	.25
394	Nomar Garciaparra, Todd Helton	.50
395	Barry Bonds, Jason Giambi	.40
396	Todd Helton, Manny Ramirez	.25
397	Todd Helton, Darin Erstad	.25
398	Kevin Brown, Pedro Martinez	.25
399	Randy Johnson, Pedro Martinez	.25
400	Will Clark	.20
401	NY Mets Divisional Highlight	.10
402	NY Yankees Divisional Highlight	.10
403	Seattle Mariners Divisional Highlight	.10
404	Mike Hampton	.10
405	NY Yankees ALCS Highlight	.75
406	World Series Highlight	1.00
407	Jeff Bagwell	.50
408	Brant Brown	.10
409	Brad Fullmer	.10
410	Dean Palmer	.10
411	Greg Zaun	.10
412	Jose Vizcaino	.10
413	Jeff Abbott	.10
414	Travis Fryman	.15
415	Mike Cameron	.10
416	Matt Mantei	.10
417	Alan Benes	.10
418	Mickey Morandini	.10
419	Troy Percival	.10
420	Eddie Perez	.10
421	Vernon Wells	.10
422	Ricky Gutierrez	.10
423	Carlos Hernandez	.10
424	Chan Ho Park	.15
425	Armando Benitez	.10
426	Sidney Ponson	.10
427	Adrian Brown	.10
428	Ruben Mateo	.20
429	Alex Ochoa	.10
430	Jose Rosado	.10
431	Masato Yoshii	.10
432	Corey Koskie	.10
433	Andy Pettitte	.20
434	Brian Daubach	.10
435	Sterling Hitchcock	.10
436	Timo Perez	.10
437	Shawn Estes	.10
438	Tony Armas Jr.	.10
439	Danny Bautista	.10
440	Randy Winn	.10
441	Wilson Alvarez	.10
442	Rondell White	.15
443	Jeromy Burnitz	.10
444	Kelvim Escobar	.10
445	Paul Bako	.10
446	Javier Vazquez	.10
447	Eric Gagne	.10
448	Kenny Lofton	.20
449	Mark Kotsay	.10
450	Jamie Moyer	.10
451	Delino DeShields	.10
452	Rey Ordonez	.10
453	Russ Ortiz	.10
454	Dave Burba	.10
455	Eric Karros	.15
456	Felix Martinez	.10
457	Tony Batista	.10
458	Bobby Higginson	.10
459	Jeff D'Amico	.10
460	Shane Spencer	.10
461	Brent Mayne	.10
462	Glendon Rusch	.10
463	Chris Gomez	.10
464	Jeff Shaw	.10
465	Damon Buford	.10
466	Mike DiFelice	.10
467	Jimmy Haynes	.10
468	Billy Wagner	.10
469	A.J. Hinch	.10
470	Gary DiSarcina	.10
471	Tom Lampkin	.10
472	Adam Eaton	.10
473	Brian Giles	.15
474	John Thomson	.10
475	Cal Eldred	.10
476	Ramiro Mendoza	.10
477	Scott Sullivan	.10
478	Scott Rolen	.25
479	Todd Ritchie	.10
480	Pablo Ozuna	.10
481	Carl Pavano	.10

482 Matt Morris .10
483 Matt Stairs .10
484 Tim Belcher .10
485 Lance Berkman .15
486 Brian Meadows .10
487 Bobby Abreu .10
488 John Vander Wal .10
489 Donnie Sadler .10
490 Damion Easley .10
491 David Justice .25
492 Ray Durham .10
493 Todd Zeile .10
494 Desi Relaford .10
495 Cliff Floyd .10
496 Scott Downs .10
497 Barry Bonds 1.00
498 Jeff D'Amico .10
499 Octavio Dotel .10
500 Kent Mercker .10
501 Craig Grebeck .10
502 Roberto Hernandez .10
503 Matt Williams .15
504 Bruce Aven .10
505 Brett Tomko .10
506 Kris Benson .10
507 Neifi Perez .10
508 Alfonso Soriano .50
509 Keith Osik .10
510 Matt Franco .10
511 Steve Finley .10
512 Olmedo Saenz .10
513 Esteban Loaiza .10
514 Adam Kennedy .10
515 Scott Elarton .10
516 Moises Alou .15
517 Bryan Rekar .10
518 Darryl Hamilton .10
519 Osvaldo Fernandez .10
520 Kip Wells .10
521 Bernie Williams .40
522 Mike Darr .10
523 Marlon Anderson .10
524 Derrek Lee .10
525 Ugueth Urbina .10
526 Vinny Castilla .10
527 David Wells .10
528 Jason Marquis .10
529 Orlando Palmeiro .10
530 Carlos Perez .10
531 J.T. Snow Jr. .10
532 Al Leiter .15
533 Jimmy Anderson .10
534 Brett Laxton .10
535 Butch Huskey .10
536 Orlando Hernandez .20
537 Magglio Ordonez .15
538 Willie Blair .10
539 Kevin Sefcik .10
540 Chad Curtis .10
541 John Halama .10
542 Andy Fox .10
543 Juan Guzman .10
544 Frank Menechino .10
545 Raul Mondesi .15
546 Tim Salmon .15
547 Ryan Rupe .10
548 Jeff Reed .10
549 Mike Mordecai .10
550 Jeff Kent .15
551 Wiki Gonzalez .10
552 Kenny Rogers .10
553 Kevin Young .10
554 Brian Johnson .10
555 Tom Goodwin .10
556 Tony Clark .10
557 Mac Suzuki .10
558 Brian Moehler .10
559 Jim Parque .10
560 Mariano Rivera .20
561 Trot Nixon .10
562 Mike Mussina .30
563 Nelson Figueroa .10
564 Alex Gonzalez .10
565 Benny Agbayani .10
566 Ed Sprague .10
567 Scott Erickson .10
568 Abraham Nunez .10
569 Jerry DiPoto .10
570 Sean Casey .10
571 Wilton Veras .10
572 Joe Mays .10
573 Bill Simas .10
574 Doug Glanville .10
575 Scott Sauerbeck .10
576 Ben Davis .10
577 Jesus Sanchez .10
578 Ricardo Rincon .10
579 John Olerud .15
580 Curt Schilling .15
581 Alex Cora .10
582 Pat Hentgen .10
583 Javy Lopez .15
584 Ben Grieve .15
585 Frank Castillo .10
586 Kevin Stocker .10
587 Mark Sweeney .10
588 Ray Lankford .10
589 Turner Ward .10
590 Felipe Crespo .10
591 Omar Vizquel .15
592 Mike Lieberthal .10
593 Ken Griffey Jr. 1.00
594 Troy O'Leary .10
595 Dave Mlicki (Front photo actually Brian Moehler.) .10
596 Manny Ramirez .50
597 Mike Lansing .10
598 Rich Aurilia .10
599 Russ Branyan .10
600 Russ Johnson .10
601 Gregg Colbrunn .10
602 Andruw Jones .40
603 Henry Blanco .10
604 Jarrod Washburn .10
605 Tony Eusebio .10
606 Aaron Sele .10
607 Charles Nagy .10
608 Ryan Klesko .10
609 Dante Bichette .10
610 Bill Haselman .10
611 Jerry Spradlin .10
612 Alex Rodriguez 1.00
613 Jose Silva .10
614 Darren Oliver .10
615 Pat Mahomes .10
616 Roberto Alomar .40
617 Edgar Renteria .10
618 Jon Lieber .10
619 John Rocker .10
620 Miguel Tejada .15
621 Mo Vaughn .15
622 Jose Lima .10
623 Kerry Wood .15
624 Mike Timlin .10
625 Wil Cordero .10
626 Albert Belle .15
627 Bobby Jones .10
628 Doug Mirabelli .10
629 Jason Tyner .10
630 Andy Ashby .10
631 Jose Hernandez .10
632 Devon White .10
633 Ruben Rivera .10
634 Steve Parris .10
635 David McCarty .10
636 Jose Canseco .25
637 Todd Walker .10
638 Stan Spencer .10
639 Wayne Gomes .10
640 Freddy Garcia .10
641 Jeremy Giambi .10
642 Luis Lopez .10
643 John Smoltz .10
644 Kelly Stinnett .10
645 Kevin Brown .10
646 Wilton Guerrero .10
647 Al Martin .10
648 Woody Williams .10
649 Brian Rose .10
650 Rafael Palmeiro .30
651 Pete Schourek .10
652 Kevin Jarvis .10
653 Mark Redman .10
654 Ricky Ledee .10
655 Larry Walker .20
656 Paul Byrd .10
657 Jason Bere .10
658 Rick White .10
659 Calvin Murray .10
660 Greg Maddux 1.00
661 Ron Gant .10
662 Eli Marrero .10
663 Graeme Lloyd .10
664 Trevor Hoffman .10
665 Nomar Garciaparra 1.00
666 Glenallen Hill .10
667 Matt LeCroy .10
668 Justin Thompson .10
669 Brady Anderson .10
670 Miguel Batista .10
671 Erubiel Durazo .10
672 Kevin Millwood .10
673 Mitch Meluskey .10
674 Luis Gonzalez .15
675 Edgar Martinez .10
676 Robert Person .10
677 Benito Santiago .10
678 Todd Jones .10
679 Tino Martinez .15
680 Carlos Beltran .10
681 Gabe White .10
682 Bret Saberhagen .10
683 Jeff Conine .10
684 Jaret Wright .10
685 Bernard Gilkey .10
686 Garrett Stephenson .10
687 Jamey Wright .10
688 Sammy Sosa 1.00
689 John Jaha .10
690 Ramon Martinez .10
691 Robert Fick .10
692 Eric Milton .10
693 Denny Neagle .10
694 Ron Coomer .10
695 John Valentin .10
696 Placido Polanco .10
697 Tim Hudson .15
698 Marty Cordova .10
699 Chad Kreuter .10
700 Frank Catalanotto .10
701 Tim Wakefield .10
702 Jim Edmonds .15
703 Michael Tucker .10
704 Cristian Guzman .10
705 Joey Hamilton .10
706 Mike Piazza 1.00
707 Dave Martinez .10
708 Mike Hampton .15
709 Bobby Bonilla .10
710 Juan Pierre .10
711 John Parrish .10
712 Kory DeHaan .10
713 Brian Tollberg .10
714 Chris Truby .10
715 Emil Brown .10
716 Ryan Dempster .10
717 Rich Garces .10
718 Mike Myers .10
719 Luis Ordaz .10
720 Kazuhiro Sasaki .10
721 Mark Quinn .10
722 Ramon Ortiz .10
723 Kerry Ligtenberg .10
724 Rolando Arrojo .10
725 *Tsuyoshi Shinjo* 1.00
726 *Ichiro Suzuki* 15.00
727 Roy Oswalt, Pat Strange, Jon Rauch .25
728 *Phil Wilson, Jake Peavy, Darwin Cubillan* .75
729 Steve Smyth, Mike Bynum, Nathan Haynes .40
730 Michael Cuddyer, Joe Lawrence, Choo Freeman .10
731 Carlos Pena, Larry Barnes, Dewayne Wise .10
732 Gookie Dawkins, Erick Almonte, Felipe Lopez .40
733 Alex Escobar, Eric Valent, Brad Wilkerson .10
734 *Toby Hall, Rod Barajas, Jeff Goldbach* .10
735 Jason Romano, Marcus Giles, Pablo Ozuna .10
736 Dee Brown, Jack Cust, Vernon Wells .10
737 *David Espinosa, Luis Montanez* .40
738 *John Lackey, Justin Wayne* .50
739 *Josh Axelson, Carmen Cali* .50
740 *Shaun Boyd, Chris Morris* .50
741 *Tommy Arko, Dan Moylan* .50
742 Luis Cotto, Luis Escobar .40
743 *Brandon Mims, Blake Williams* .40
744 Chris Russ, Bryan Edwards .40
745 Joe Torres, Ben Diggins .10
746 *Mark Dalesandro, Edwin Encarnacion* .50
747 *Brian Bass, Odannis Ayala* .40
748 *Jason Kaanoi, Michael Mathews* .10
749 *Stuart McFarland, Adam Sterrett* .40
750 David Krynzel, Grady Sizemore .50
751 Keith Bucktrot, Dane Sardinha .10
752 Anaheim Angels .10
753 Arizona Diamondbacks .10
754 Atlanta Braves .10
755 Baltimore Orioles .10
756 Boston Red Sox .10
757 Chicago Cubs .10
758 Chicago White Sox .10
759 Cincinnati Reds .10
760 Cleveland Indians .10
761 Colorado Rockies .10
762 Detroit Tigers .10
763 Florida Marlins .10
764 Houston Astros .10
765 Kansas City Royals .10
766 Los Angeles Dodgers .10
767 Milwaukee Brewers .10
768 Minnesota Twins .10
769 Montreal Expos .10
770 New York Mets .10
771 New York Yankees .75
772 Oakland Athletics .10
773 Philadelphia Phillies .10
774 Pittsburgh Pirates .10
775 San Diego Padres .10
776 San Francisco Giants .10
777 Seattle Mariners .10
778 St. Louis Cardinals .10
779 Tampa Bay Devil Rays .10
780 Texas Rangers .10
781 Toronto Blue Jays .10
782 Bucky Dent .10
783 Jackie Robinson 1.00
784 Roberto Clemente 1.00
785 Nolan Ryan 1.50
786 Kerry Wood .10
787 Rickey Henderson .20
788 Lou Brock .25
789 David Wells .10
790 Andruw Jones .25
791 Carlton Fisk .10

Gold

Stars: 8-15X
Prospects and RCs: 3-6X
Inserted 1:17

Autographs

NM/M

Common Player:
Group A 1:22,866
Group B 1:3,054
Group C 1:1,431
Group D 1:18,339
Group E 1:13,737
Group F 1:11,015
Group G 1:625
HA Hank Aaron 250.00
DA Dick Allen 25.00
RA Rick Ankiel 10.00
RB Rocco Baldelli 30.00
EB Ernie Banks 100.00
YB Yogi Berra 80.00
LB Lou Brock 50.00
PB Pat Burrell 15.00
RC Rod Carew 50.00
MC Mike Cuellar 15.00
WF Whitey Ford 40.00
RF Rafael Furcal 25.00
BG Bob Gibson 40.00
AG Adrian Gonzalez 15.00
SH Scott Heard 15.00
WH Willie Hernandez 10.00
KH Ken Holtzman
AJ Adam Johnson 10.00
CJ Chipper Jones 80.00
SK Sandy Koufax 500.00
ML Mike Lamb 10.00
VL Vernon Law 15.00
JM Jason Marquis 10.00
GM Gary Matthews

WM	Willie Mays	250.00
BO	Ben Oglivie	
MO	Magglio Ordonez	20.00
AP	Andy Pafko	30.00
BR	Brooks Robinson	80.00
JR	Joe Rudi	15.00
MS	Mike Schmidt	100.00
MS	Mike Stodolka	15.00
RS	Ron Swoboda	30.00
KT	Kent Tekulve	
GT	Garry Templeton	30.00
JV	Jose Vidro	20.00
MW	Matt Wheatland	20.00
TW	Ted Williams	
TZ	Todd Zeile	20.00

Autographs Series 2

		NM/M
Common Player:		10.00
DA	Denny Abreu	10.00
TA	Tony Alvarez	10.00
RB	Rocco Baldelli	30.00
GB	George Bell	10.00
JB	Johnny Bench	60.00
BB	Barry Bonds	250.00
MB	Milton Bradley	15.00
GHB	George Brett	175.00
KB	Keith Bucktrot	
MAB	Mike Bynum	10.00
EB	Eric Byrnes	10.00
JC	Jorge Cantu	10.00
CC	Chris Clapinski	10.00
WD	Willie Davis	40.00
JDD	J.D. Drew	30.00
TDLR	Tomas de la Rosa	10.00
PD	Phil Dumatrait	
CD	Chad Durbin	10.00
CE	Carl Erskine	25.00
BE	Brian Esposito	15.00
WF	Whitey Ford	40.00
EF	Eddy Furniss	15.00
BG	Bob Gibson	40.00
MG	Mike Glendenning	15.00
AG	Adrian Gonzalez	15.00
NG	Nick Green	10.00
KG	Kevin Gregg	10.00
DG	Dick Groat	25.00
GG	Geraldo Guzman	10.00
YH	Yamid Haad	10.00
TH	Todd Helton	40.00
AH	Aaron Herr	15.00
KH	Ken Holtzman	20.00
RJ	Reggie Jackson	100.00
NJ	Neil Jenkins	15.00
AJ	Adam Johnson	10.00
TJ	Tripper Johnson	15.00
BK	Bobby Kielty	10.00
JL	John Lackey	10.00
YL	Yovanny Lara	
ML	Matt Lawton	15.00
CL	Colby Lewis	10.00
MFL	Mike Lockwood	10.00
GM	Gary Matthews	20.00
PM	Phil Merrell	
LM	Luis Montanez	15.00
EM	Eric Munson	15.00
SM	Stan Musial	150.00
BO	Ben Oglivie	15.00
AO	Augie Ojeda	10.00
ER	Erasmo Ramirez	15.00
CR	Chris Richard	15.00
JR	Juan Rincon	10.00
LR	Luis Rivas	20.00
SR	Scott Rolen	35.00
NR	Nolan Ryan	200.00
JS	Juan Salas	10.00
TS	Tom Seaver	150.00
CS	Carlos Silva	10.00
GS	Grady Sizemore	20.00
CCS	Corey Smith	10.00
MS	Mike Stodolka	10.00
MS	Mike Sweeney	15.00
KT	Kent Tekulve	20.00
DT	Derek Thompson	10.00
ST	Scott Thorman	10.00
BT	Brian Tollberg	15.00
YT	Yorvit Torrealba	
JW	Justin Wayne	20.00
MW	Michael Wenner	15.00
MJW	Matt Wheatland	15.00
WW	Wilbur Wood	20.00
CY	Carl Yastrzemski	75.00

A Look Ahead

		NM/M
Complete Set (10):		15.00
Common Player:		.50
Inserted 1:25		
1	Vladimir Guerrero	1.50
2	Derek Jeter	4.00
3	Todd Helton	1.00
4	Alex Rodriguez	3.00
5	Ken Griffey Jr.	2.00
6	Nomar Garciaparra	3.00
7	Chipper Jones	2.00
8	Ivan Rodriguez	1.00
9	Pedro Martinez	1.50
10	Rick Ankiel	.50

A Tradition Continued

		NM/M
Complete Set (30):		50.00
Common Player:		.50
Inserted 1:17		
1	Chipper Jones	3.00
2	Cal Ripken Jr.	6.00
3	Mike Piazza	3.00
4	Ken Griffey Jr.	3.00
5	Randy Johnson	1.50
6	Derek Jeter	5.00
7	Scott Rolen	1.50
8	Nomar Garciaparra	4.00
9	Roberto Alomar	1.00
10	Greg Maddux	3.00
11	Ivan Rodriguez	1.50
12	Jeff Bagwell	1.50
13	Ivan Rodriguez	1.50
14	Pedro Martinez	2.00
15	Sammy Sosa	4.00
16	Jim Edmonds	1.00
17	Mo Vaughn	.50
18	Barry Bonds	5.00
19	Larry Walker	.75
20	Mark McGwire	4.00
21	Vladimir Guerrero	2.00
22	Andruw Jones	1.50
23	Todd Helton	1.50
24	Kevin Brown	.75
25	Tony Gwynn	2.00
26	Manny Ramirez	1.50
27	Roger Clemens	4.00
28	Frank Thomas	1.50
29	Shawn Green	.75
30	Jim Thome	1.50

Base Hit

		NM/M
Complete Set (28):		450.00
Common Player:		25.00
BH1	Mike Scioscia	35.00
BH2	Larry Dierker	25.00
BH3	Art Howe	25.00
BH4	Jim Fregosi	25.00
BH5	Bobby Cox	35.00
BH6	Davey Lopes	25.00
BH7	Tony LaRussa	30.00
BH8	Don Baylor	35.00
BH9	Larry Rothschild	25.00
BH10	Buck Showalter	30.00
BH11	Davey Johnson	30.00
BH12	Felipe Alou	30.00
BH13	Charlie Manuel	25.00
BH14	Lou Piniella	30.00
BH15	John Boles	25.00
BH16	Bobby Valentine	30.00
BH17	Mike Hargrove	25.00
BH18	Bruce Bochy	25.00
BH19	Terry Francona	25.00
BH20	Gene Lamont	25.00
BH21	Johnny Oates	25.00
BH22	Jimy Williams	25.00
BH23	Jack McKeon	25.00
BH24	Buddy Bell	25.00
BH25	Tony Muser	25.00
BH26	Phil Garner	25.00
BH27	Tom Kelly	25.00
BH28	Jerry Manuel	25.00

Before There Was Topps

		NM/M
Complete Set (10):		20.00
Common Player:		1.50
Inserted 1:25		
BT1	Lou Gehrig	4.00
BT2	Babe Ruth	5.00
BT3	Cy Young	2.00
BT4	Walter Johnson	2.00
BT5	Ty Cobb	4.00
BT6	Tris Speaker	1.50
BT7	Honus Wagner	2.00
BT8	Christy Mathewson	1.50
BT9	Grover Alexander	1.50
BT0	Joe DiMaggio	4.00

Combos

		NM/M
Complete Set (20):		25.00
Common Player:		1.50
Inserted 1:12		
1	Yogi Berra, Whitey Ford, Reggie Jackson, Don Mattingly, Derek Jeter	3.00
2	Brooks Robinson, Cal Ripken Jr.	3.00
3	Barry Bonds, Willie Mays	3.00
4	Bob Gibson, Pedro Martinez	1.50
5	Ivan Rodriguez, Johnny Bench	2.00
6	Ernie Banks, A lex Rodriguez	2.50
7	Joe Morgan, Ken Griffey Jr., Barry Larkin, Johnny Bench	2.50
8	Vladimir Guerrero, Roberto Clemente	2.50
9	Ted Williams, Carl Yastrzemski, Nomar Garciaparra	3.00
10	Joe Torre, Casey Stengel	1.50
11	Kevin Brown, Sandy Koufax, Don Drysdale	3.00
12	Mark McGwire, Sammy Sosa, Roger Maris, Babe Ruth	3.00
13	Ted Williams, Carl Yastrzemski, Nomar Garciaparra	3.00
14	Greg Maddux, Roger Clemens, Cy Young	2.00
15	Tony Gwynn, Ted Williams	3.00
16	Cal Ripken Jr., Lou Gehrig	4.00
17	Sandy Koufax, Randy Johnson, Warren Spahn, Steve Carlton	3.00
18	Mike Piazza, Josh Gibson	2.00
19	Barry Bonds, Willie Mays	3.00
20	Jackie Robinson, Larry Doby	2.50

Golden Anniversary

		NM/M
Complete Set (50):		60.00
Common Player:		.50
Inserted 1:10		
1	Hank Aaron	3.00
2	Ernie Banks	1.50
3	Mike Schmidt	3.00
4	Willie Mays	4.00
5	Johnny Bench	1.50
6	Tom Seaver	1.00
7	Frank Robinson	1.00
8	Sandy Koufax	3.00
9	Bob Gibson	1.00
10	Ted Williams	4.00
11	Cal Ripken Jr.	5.00
12	Tony Gwynn	1.50
13	Mark McGwire	3.00

14	Ken Griffey Jr.	2.00
15	Greg Maddux	2.00
16	Roger Clemens	3.00
17	Barry Bonds	4.00
18	Rickey Henderson	.75
19	Mike Piazza	2.00
20	Jose Canseco	1.00
21	Derek Jeter	4.00
22	Nomar Garciaparra	3.00
23	Alex Rodriguez	3.00
24	Sammy Sosa	2.50
25	Ivan Rodriguez	1.00
26	Vladimir Guerrero	1.50
27	Chipper Jones	2.00
28	Jeff Bagwell	1.00
29	Pedro Martinez	1.50
30	Randy Johnson	1.50
31	Pat Burrell	1.00
32	Josh Hamilton	.50
33	Nick Johnson	.50
34	Corey Patterson	.50
35	Eric Munson	.50
36	Sean Burroughs	.50
37	Alfonso Soriano	1.50
38	Chin-Feng Chen	.50
39	Barry Zito	.75
40	Adrian Gonzalez	.50
41	Mark McGwire	3.00
42	Nomar Garciaparra	3.00
43	Todd Helton	1.00
44	Matt Williams	.50
45	Troy Glaus	.75
46	Geoff Jenkins	.50
47	Frank Thomas	1.00
48	Mo Vaughn	.50
49	Barry Larkin	.75
50	J.D. Drew	.50

Hit Parade

		NM/M
Complete Set (6):		
Common Player:		25.00
1:2,600 Retail		
HP1	Reggie Jackson	40.00
HP2	Dave Winfield	25.00
HP3	Eddie Murray	25.00
HP4	Rickey Henderson	25.00
HP5	Robin Yount	25.00
HP6	Carl Yastrzemski	65.00

King of Kings

		NM/M
Common card:		25.00
Inserted 1:2,056		
1	Hank Aaron	50.00
2	Nolan Ryan	50.00
3	Rickey Henderson	30.00
4	Mark McGwire	100.00
5	Bob Gibson	25.00
6	Nolan Ryan	50.00

King of Kings Golden Edition

		NM/M
Production 50 cards		
KKGE	Hank Aaron, Nolan Ryan, Rickey Henderson	250.00
KKLE2	Mark McGwire, Bob Gibson, Nolan Ryan	300.00

Noteworthy

		NM/M
Complete Set (50):		40.00
Common Player:		.50
Inserted 1:8		
TN1	Mark McGwire	2.00
TN2	Derek Jeter	2.50
TN3	Sammy Sosa	2.00
TN4	Todd Helton	1.00
TN5	Alex Rodriguez	2.00
TN6	Chipper Jones	1.50
TN7	Barry Bonds	3.00
TN8	Ken Griffey Jr.	1.50
TN9	Nomar Garciaparra	2.00
TN10	Frank Thomas	1.00
TN11	Randy Johnson	1.00
TN12	Cal Ripken Jr.	3.00
TN13	Mike Piazza	1.50
TN14	Ivan Rodriguez	1.00
TN15	Jeff Bagwell	1.00
TN16	Vladimir Guerrero	1.00
TN17	Greg Maddux	1.50
TN18	Tony Gwynn	1.00
TN19	Larry Walker	.50
TN20	Juan Gonzalez	.75
TN21	Scott Rolen	1.00
TN22	Jason Giambi	1.00
TN23	Jeff Kent	.50
TN24	Pat Burrell	.75
TN25	Pedro Martinez	1.00
TN26	Willie Mays	2.00
TN27	Whitey Ford	.75
TN28	Jackie Robinson	2.00
TN29	Ted Williams	2.50
TN30	Babe Ruth	3.00
TN31	Warren Spahn	1.00
TN32	Nolan Ryan	3.00
TN33	Yogi Berra	1.00
TN34	Mike Schmidt	2.00
TN35	Steve Carlton	.75
TN36	Brooks Robinson	1.00
TN37	Bob Gibson	1.00
TN38	Reggie Jackson	1.00
TN39	Johnny Bench	1.50
TN40	Ernie Banks	1.00
TN41	Eddie Mathews	.50
TN42	Don Mattingly	2.50
TN43	Duke Snider	.75
TN44	Hank Aaron	2.00
TN45	Roberto Clemente	2.00
TN46	Harmon Killebrew	1.00
TN47	Frank Robinson	1.00
TN48	Stan Musial	2.00
TN49	Lou Brock	.50
TN50	Joe Morgan	.50

Through the Years

		NM/M
Complete Set (50):		100.00
Common Player:		1.50
Inserted 1:8		
1	Yogi Berra	2.00
2	Roy Campanella	2.00
3	Willie Mays	5.00
4	Andy Pafko	1.50
5	Jackie Robinson	4.00
6	Stan Musial	4.00
7	Duke Snider	2.00
8	Warren Spahn	2.50
9	Ted Williams	6.00
10	Eddie Matthews	2.00
11	Willie McCovey	1.50
12	Frank Robinson	2.00
13	Ernie Banks	3.00
14	Hank Aaron	5.00
15	Sandy Koufax	4.00
16	Bob Gibson	2.00
17	Harmon Killebrew	2.00
18	Whitey Ford	2.00
19	Roberto Clemente	5.00
20	Juan Marichal	1.50
21	Johnny Bench	3.00
22	Willie Stargell	1.50
23	Joe Morgan	1.50
24	Carl Yastrzemski	2.00
25	Reggie Jackson	2.00
26	Tom Seaver	2.00
27	Steve Carlton	1.50
28	Jim Palmer	1.50
29	Rod Carew	1.50
30	George Brett	5.00
31	Roger Clemens	4.00
32	Don Mattingly	5.00
33	Ryne Sandberg	3.00
34	Mike Schmidt	4.00
35	Cal Ripken Jr.	6.00
36	Tony Gwynn	2.00
37	Ozzie Smith	3.00
38	Wade Boggs	1.50
39	Nolan Ryan	6.00
40	Robin Yount	2.00
41	Mark McGwire	5.00
42	Ken Griffey Jr.	4.00
43	Sammy Sosa	4.00
44	Alex Rodriguez	4.00
45	Barry Bonds	6.00
46	Mike Piazza	3.00
47	Chipper Jones	3.00
48	Greg Maddux	3.00
49	Nomar Garciaparra	4.00
50	Derek Jeter	5.00

Two of a Kind

		NM/M
Inserted 1:30,167		
TK	Bo Jackson, Deion Sanders	75.00

The Shot Heard Round The World Autograph

	NM/M
B. Thomson/R. Branca	
Ralph Branca, Bobby Thomson	40.00

What Could've Been

		NM/M
Complete Set (10):		15.00
Common Player:		1.00
Inserted 1:25		
WCB1	Josh Gibson	3.00
WCB2	Leroy "Satchel" Paige	3.00
WCB3	Walter "Buck" Leonard	2.00
WCB4	James "Cool Papa" Bell	2.00
WCB5	Andrew "Rube" Foster	2.00
WCB6	Martin Dihigo	1.00
WCB7	William "Judy" Johnson	1.50
WCB8	Mule Suttles	1.00
WCB9	Ray Dandridge	1.00
WCB10	John Henry "Pop" Lloyd	2.00

2001 TOPPS & TOPPS CHROME TRADED & ROOKIES

		NM/M
Complete Topps Set (265):		50.00
Common Player:		.10
Chrome cards:		2-3X
Pack (10):		8.00
Box (24):		175.00
T1	Sandy Alomar Jr.	.10
T2	Kevin Appier	.10
T3	Brad Ausmus	.10
T4	Derek Bell	.10
T5	Bret Boone	.20
T6	Rico Brogna	.10
T7	Ellis Burks	.10
T8	Ken Caminiti	.10
T9	Roger Cedeno	.10
T10	Royce Clayton	.10
T11	Enrique Wilson	.10
T12	Rheal Cormier	.10
T13	Eric Davis	.10
T14	Shawon Duston	.10
T15	Andres Galarraga	.20
T16	Tom Gordon	.10
T17	Mark Grace	.50
T18	Jeffrey Hammonds	.10
T19	Dustin Hermanson	.10
T20	Quinton McCracken	.10
T21	Todd Hundley	.10
T22	Charles Johnson	.10
T23	Marquis Grissom	.10
T24	Jose Mesa	.10
T25	Terry Mulholland	.10
T26	John Rocker	.10
T27	Jeff Frye	.10
T28	Reggie Sanders	.10
T29	David Segui	.10
T30	Mike Sirotka	.10
T31	Fernando Tatis	.10
T32	Steve Trachsel	.10
T33	Ismael Valdes	.10
T34	Randy Velarde	.10
T35	Brian Boehringer	.10
T36	Mike Bordick	.10
T37	Ken Bottenfield	.10
T38	Pat Rapp	.10
T39	Jeff Nelson	.10
T40	Ricky Bottalico	.10
T41	Deion Sanders	.20
T42	Hideo Nomo	.50
T43	Bill Mueller	.10
T44	Roberto Kelly	.10
T45	Chris Holt	.10
T46	Mike Jackson	.10
T47	Devon White	.10
T48	Gerald Williams	.10
T49	Eddie Taubensee	.10
T50	Brian Hunter	.10
T51	Nelson Cruz	.10
T52	Jeff Fassero	.10
T53	Bubba Trammell	.10
T54	Bo Porter	.10
T55	Greg Norton	.10
T56	Benito Santiago	.10
T57	Ruben Rivera	.10
T58	Dee Brown	.10
T59	Jose Canseco	.40
T60	Chris Michalak	.10
T61	Tim Worrell	.10
T62	Matt Clement	.10
T63	Bill Pulsipher	.10
T64	Troy Brohawn	.10
T65	Mark Kotsay	.10
T66	Jose Lima	.10
T67	Shea Hillenbrand	.10
T68	Ted Lilly	.10
T69	Jermaine Dye	.10

T70	Jerry Hairston Jr.	.10
T71	John Mabry	.10
T72	Kurt Abbott	.10
T73	Eric Owens	.10
T74	Jeff Brantley	.10
T75	Vinny Castilla	.10
T76	Ron Villone	.10
T77	Ricky Henderson	.40
T78	Jason Grimsley	.10
T79	*Christian Parker*	.10
T80	Donnie Wall	.10
T81	Alex Arias	.10
T82	Willis Roberts	.10
T83	Ryan Minor	.10
T84	Jason LaRue	.10
T85	Ruben Sierra	.10
T86	Johnny Damon	.10
T87	Juan Gonzalez	.60
T88	Mac Suzuki	.10
T89	Tony Batista	.10
T90	Jay Witasick	.10
T91	Brent Abernathy	.10
T92	Paul LoDuca	.10
T93	Wes Helms	.10
T94	Milton Bradley	.10
T95	Matt LeCroy	.10
T96	A.J. Hinch	.10
T97	*Bud Smith*	.10
T98	Adam Dunn	.75
T99	Albert Pujols, Ichiro Suzuki	15.00
T100	Carlton Fisk	.25
T101	Tim Raines	.10
T102	Juan Marichal	.10
T103	Dave Winfield	.25
T104	Reggie Jackson	.50
T105	Cal Ripken Jr.	2.50
T106	Ozzie Smith	.50
T107	Tom Seaver	.50
T108	Lou Piniella	.10
T109	Dwight Gooden	.10
T110	Bret Saberhagen	.10
T111	Gary Carter	.10
T112	Jack Clark	.10
T113	Rickey Henderson	.50
T114	Barry Bonds	1.00
T115	Bobby Bonilla	.10
T116	Jose Canseco	.40
T117	Will Clark	.25
T118	Andres Galarraga	.10
T119	Bo Jackson	.10
T120	Wally Joyner	.10
T121	Ellis Burks	.10
T122	David Cone	.10
T123	Greg Maddux	.50
T124	Willie Randolph	.10
T125	Dennis Eckersley	.25
T126	Matt Williams	.20
T127	Joe Morgan	.10
T128	Fred McGriff	.10
T129	Roberto Alomar	.25
T130	Lee Smith	.10
T131	David Wells	.10
T132	Ken Griffey Jr.	1.50
T133	Deion Sanders	.10
T134	Nolan Ryan	2.00
T135	David Justice	.25
T136	Joe Carter	.10
T137	Jack Morris	.10
T138	Mike Piazza	1.50
T139	Barry Bonds	1.00
T140	Terrence Long	.10
T141	Ben Grieve	.10
T142	Richie Sexson	.10
T143	Sean Burroughs	.10
T144	Alfonso Soriano	.50
T145	Bob Boone	.10
T146	Larry Bowa	.10
T147	Bob Brenly	.10
T148	Buck Martinez	.10
T149	Lloyd McClendon	.10
T150	Jim Tracy	.10
T151	*Jared Abruzzo*	.50
T152	Kurt Ainsworth	.10
T153	Willie Bloomquist	.10
T154	Ben Broussard	.10
T155	Bobby Bradley	.10
T156	Mike Bynum	.10
T157	Ken Harvey	.10
T158	Ryan Christianson	.10
T159	Ryan Kohlmeier	.10
T160	Joe Crede	.10
T161	Jack Cust	.10
T162	Ben Diggins	.10
T163	Phil Dumatrait	.10
T164	Alex Escobar	.10
T165	Miguel Olivo	.10
T166	Chris George	.10
T167	Marcus Giles	.10
T168	Keith Ginter	.10
T169	Josh Girdley	.10
T170	Tony Alvarez	.10
T171	Scott Seabol	.10
T172	Josh Hamilton	.25
T173	Jason Hart	.10
T174	Israel Alcantara	.10
T175	Jake Peavy	5.00
T176	*Stubby Clapp*	.40
T177	D'Angelo Jimenez	.10
T178	Nick Johnson	.10
T179	Ben Johnson	.10
T180	Larry Bigbie	.10
T181	Allen Levrault	.10
T182	Felipe Lopez	.10
T183	Sean Burnett	.10
T184	Nick Neugebauer	.10
T185	Austin Kearns	.10
T186	Corey Patterson	.25
T187	Carlos Pena	.10
T188	*Ricardo Rodriguez*	.50
T189	Juan Rivera	.10
T190	Grant Roberts	.10
T191	*Adam Pettyjohn*	.10
T192	Jared Sandberg	.10
T193	Xavier Nady	.20
T194	Dane Sardinha	.10
T195	Shawn Sonnier	.10
T196	Rafael Soriano	.50
T197	*Brian Specht*	.25
T198	Aaron Myette	.10
T199	*Juan Uribe*	.40
T200	Jayson Werth	.10
T201	Brad Wilkerson	.10
T202	Horacio Estrada	.10
T203	Joel Pineiro	.10
T204	Matt LeCroy	.10
T205	Michael Coleman	.10
T206	Ben Sheets	.25
T207	Eric Byrnes	.10
T208	Sean Burroughs	.10
T209	Ken Harvey	.10
T210	Travis Hafner	.75
T211	Erick Almonte	.10
T212	*Jason Belcher*	.50
T213	*Wilson Betemit*	.50
T214	*Hank Blalock*	5.00
T215	Danny Borrell	.10
T216	*John Buck*	.50
T217	*Freddie Bynum*	.50
T218	*Noel Devarez*	.25
T219	*Juan Diaz*	.25
T220	*Felix Diaz*	.25
T221	*Josh Fogg*	.50
T222	*Matt Ford*	.25
T223	Scott Heard	.10
T224	*Ben Hendrickson*	.25
T225	*Cody Ross*	.50
T226	*Adrian Hernandez*	.40
T227	*Alfredo Amezaga*	.50
T228	*Bob Keppel*	.25
T229	*Ryan Madson*	.50
T230	*Octavio Martinez*	.25
T231	Hee Seop Choi	1.00
T232	Thomas Mitchell	.10
T233	Luis Montanez	.10
T234	*Andy Morales*	.40
T235	*Justin Morneau*	3.00
T236	*Greg "Toe" Nash*	.50
T237	*Valentino Pasucci*	.10
T238	*Roy Smith*	.40
T239	*Antonio Perez*	.40
T240	*Chad Petty*	.50
T241	Steve Smyth	.10
T242	*Jose Reyes*	3.00
T243	*Eric Reynolds*	.40
T244	Dominic Rich	.10
T245	*Jason Richardson*	.25
T246	*Ed Rogers*	.40
T247	*Albert Pujols*	40.00
T248	*Esix Snead*	.25
T249	*Luis Torres*	.25
T250	*Matt White*	.40
T251	Blake Williams	.10
T252	Chris Russ	.10
T253	*Joe Kennedy*	.25
T254	*Jeff Randazzo*	.25
T255	*Beau Hale*	.40
256	*Brad Hennessey*	.25
257	*Jake Gautreau*	.10
258	*Jeff Mathis*	1.50
259	*Aaron Heilman*	.50
260	*Bronson Sardinha*	.75
261	*Irvin Guzman*	5.00
262	*Gabe Gross*	1.00
263	*J.D. Martin*	.40
264	*Chris Smith*	.25
265	*Kenny Baugh*	.40
266	*Ichiro Suzuki (chrome)*	25.00

Dual Traded Relics

NM/M

Common Player:		5.00
TTR-DB	Derek Bell	5.00
TTR-MG	Mark Grace	10.00
TTR-BG	Ben Grieve	5.00
TTR-DH	Dustin Hermanson	5.00
TTR-MR	Manny Ramirez	15.00

Hall of Fame Relics

NM/M

Complete Set (1):		
PW	Kirby Puckett, Dave Winfield	40.00

Dual Relic

NM/M

Inserted 1:4,693		
RG	Cal Ripken, Tony Gwynn	85.00

Relics

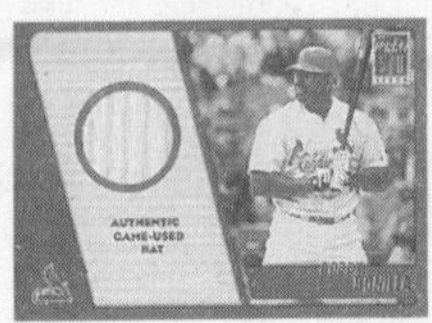

NM/M

Common Player:		5.00
Inserted 1:91		
AP	Albert Pujols	50.00
TS	Tsuyoshi Shinjo	8.00
AB	Angel Berroa	8.00
BO	Bill Ortega	5.00
HC	Humberto Cota	5.00
JL	Jason Lane	5.00
JS	Jamal Strong	5.00
JV	Jose Valverde	5.00
JY	Jason Young	5.00
NC	Nate Cornejo	5.00
NN	Nick Neugebauer	5.00
PF	Pedro Feliz	5.00
RS	Richard Stahl	5.00
SB	Sean Burroughs	6.00
SS	Jae Weong Seo	5.00
WB	Wilson Betemit	5.00
WR	Wilken Ruan	5.00

Autographs

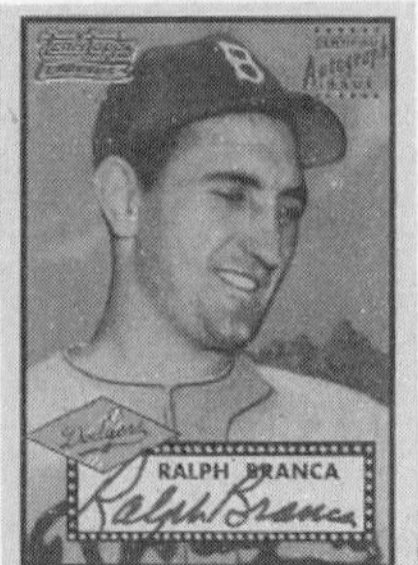

NM/M

Common Player:		
TT51	Ralph Branca	15.00
TT6F	Whitey Ford	
TTF47	Frank Howard	25.00
TTF50	Mickey Lolich	15.00
TTF1	Willie Mays	
TT37	Tug McGraw	15.00
TT35F	Joe Pepitone	
TT48F	Bobby Richardson	20.00
TT36F	Enos Slaughter	25.00
TT13	Warren Spahn	40.00
TT43	Bobby Thomson	20.00

Who Would Have Thought

NM/M

Complete Set (20):		15.00
Common Player:		.75
Inserted 1:8		
WWH1	Nolan Ryan	4.00
WWH2	Ozzie Smith	1.50
WWH3	Tom Seaver	1.50
WWH4	Steve Carlton	.75
WWH5	Reggie Jackson	1.50
WWH6	Frank Robinson	1.00
WWH7	Keith Hernandez	.75
WWH8	Andre Dawson	.75
WWH9	Lou Brock	.75
WWH10	Dennis Eckersley	.75
WWH11	Dave Winfield	1.00
WWH12	Rod Carew	1.00
WWH13	Willie Randolph	.75
WWH14	Doc Gooden	.75
WWH15	Carlton Fisk	1.00
WWH16	Dale Murphy	.75
WWH17	Paul Molitor	1.00
WWH18	Gary Carter	.75
WWH19	Wade Boggs	1.00
WWH20	Willie Mays	3.00

Relics

NM/M

Common Player:		4.00
Inserted 1:29		
SA	Sandy Alomar Jr.	4.00
DB	Derek Bell	4.00
BB	Bobby Bonilla	4.00
BB	Bret Boone	8.00
RB	Rico Brogna	4.00
KC	Ken Caminiti	4.00
JC	Jose Canseco	8.00
ROC	Roger Cedeno	4.00
RSC	Royce Clayton	4.00
JD	Johnny Damon	5.00
ED	Eric Davis	5.00
JD	Jermaine Dye	4.00
AG	Andres Galarraga	4.00
RG	Ron Gant	4.00
JG	Juan Gonzalez	8.00
MG	Mark Grace	8.00
MG	Marquis Grissom	4.00
JH	Jeffrey Hammonds	4.00
MH	Mike Hampton	4.00
DH	Dustin Hermanson	4.00
TH	Todd Hundley	4.00
CJ	Charles Johnson	4.00
FM	Fred McGriff	5.00
BM	Bill Mueller	4.00
DN	Denny Neagle	4.00
HR	Hideo Nomo	30.00
NP	Neifi Perez	4.00
TR	Tim Raines	5.00
RS	Ruben Sierra	4.00
MS	Matt Stairs	4.00
KS	Kelly Stinnett	4.00
FT	Fernando Tatis	4.00
DW	David Wells	4.00
GW	Gerald Williams	4.00
EW	Enrique Wilson	4.00

Autographs

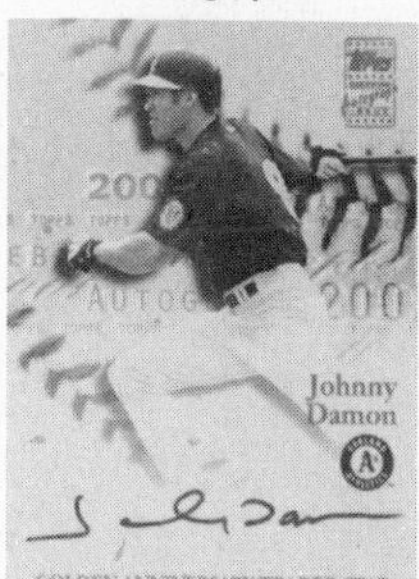

		NM/M
Common Autograph:		15.00
TTA-JD	Johnny Damon	20.00
TTA-MM	Mike Mussina	25.00

2001 TOPPS AMERICAN PIE

		NM/M
Complete Set (150):		30.00
Common Player:		.20
Pack (5):		3.00
Box (24):		60.00
1	Al Kaline	.40
2	Al Oliver	.20
3	Andre Dawson	.20
4	Bert Blyleven	.20
5	Bill Buckner	.20
6	Bill Mazeroski	.20
7	Bob Gibson	.50
8	Bill Freeman	.20
9	Bobby Grich	.20
10	Bobby Murcer	.20
11	Bobby Richardson	.20
12	Boog Powell	.20
13	Brooks Robinson	.50
14	Carl Yastrzemski	.75
15	Carlton Fisk	.40
16	Clete Boyer	.20
17	Curt Flood	.20
18	Dale Murphy	.30
19	Tony Conigliaro	.20
20	Dave Parker	.20
21	Dave Winfield	.50
22	Dick Allen	.20
23	Dick Groat	.20
24	Don Drysdale	.50
25	Don Sutton	.20
26	Dwight Evans	.20
27	Eddie Mathews	.75
28	Elston Howard	.20
29	Frank Howard	.20
30	Frank Robinson	.50
31	Fred Lynn	.20
32	Gary Carter	.20
33	Gaylord Perry	.20
34	Norm Cash	.20
35	George Brett	1.50
36	George Foster	.20
37	Goose Gossage	.20
38	Graig Nettles	.20
39	Greg Luzinski	.20
41	Harmon Killebrew	.75
42	Jack Clark	.20
43	Jack Morris	.20
44	Jim Wynn	.20
45	Jim Kaat	.20
46	Jim Palmer	.20
47	Joe Pepitone	.20
48	Joe Rudi	.20
49	Johnny Bench	1.00
50	Juan Marichal	.40
51	Keith Hernandez	.20
52	Bucky Dent	.20
53	Lou Brock	.40
54	Ron Cey	.20
55	Luis Aparicio	.20
56	Luis Tiant	.20
57	Mark Fidrych	.20
58	Maury Wills	.20
59	Mickey Lolich	.20
60	Mickey Rivers	.20
61	Mike Schmidt	1.00
62	Moose Skowron	.20
63	Nolan Ryan	3.00
64	Orlando Cepeda	.20
65	Ozzie Smith	.75
66	Phil Niekro	.20
67	Reggie Jackson	.75
68	Reggie Smith	.20
69	Rico Carty	.20
70	Roberto Clemente	2.00
71	Robin Yount	.75
72	Roger Maris	1.50
73	Rollie Fingers	.20
74	Ron Guidry	.20
75	Ron Santo	.20
76	Ron Swoboda	.20
77	Sal Bando	.20
78	Sam McDowell	.20
79	Steve Carlton	.40
80	Thurman Munson	1.00
81	Tim McCarver	.20
82	Tom Seaver	.75
83	Mike Cuellar	.20
84	Tony Kubek	.20
85	Tommy John	.20
86	Tony Perez	.20
87	Tug McGraw	.20
88	Vida Blue	.20
89	Warren Spahn	.75
90	Whitey Ford	.50
91	Willie Mays	2.00
92	Willie McCovey	.20
93	Willie Stargell	.50
94	Yogi Berra	1.00
95	Stan Musial	1.00
96	Jim Piersall	.20
97	Duke Snider	.50
98	Bruce Sutter	.30
99	Dave Concepcion	.20
100	Darrell Evans	.20
101	Dennis Eckersley	.40
102	Hoyt Wilhelm	.20
103	Minnie Minoso	.20
104	Don Newcombe	.20
105	Richie Ashburn	.20
106	Alan Trammell	.20
107	Jim "Catfish" Hunter	.20
108	Lou Whitaker	.20
109	Johnny Podres	.20
110	Denny Martinez	.20
111	Willie Horton	.20
112	Dean Chance	.20
113	Fergie Jenkins	.20
114	Cecil Cooper	.20
115	Rick Reuschel	.20
116	Space Race	.20
117	Man On The Moon	.50
118	Woodstock	.50
119	Peace Movement/Flower Power	.20
120	N.Y. Worlds Fair	.20
121	Vietnam War	.20
122	Vietnam Cease Fire	.20
123	Kennedy Elected President	.50
124	Kennedy Assassination	.20
125	Malcom X	.20
126	Nixon Elected President	.20
127	Watergate	.20
128	Nixon Resigns	.20
129	Cuban Missile Crisis	.20
130	Astrodome	.20
131	Secretariat	.20
132	Lyndon Johnson Signs Civil Rights Bill	.20
133	Atomic Bomb Test Ban Treaty	.20
134	Bi Centennial	.20
135	String Bikini	.20
136	Birth Control Pill	.20
137	Studio 54	.20
138	Motown	.20
139	Microsoft Started	.20
140	Internet Developed	.20
141	John F. Kennedy	1.50
142	Marilyn Monroe	1.50
143	Elvis Presley	1.50
144	Jimi Hendrix	1.00
145	Arthur Ashe	.20
146	Richard Nixon	.20
147	James Dean	.20
148	Janis Joplin	.50
149	Frank Sinatra	1.00
150	Malcom X	.50

Decade Leaders

		NM/M
Complete Set (10):		15.00
Common Player:		1.00
Inserted 1:12		
DL1	Willie Stargell	1.50
DL2	Harmon Killebrew	1.50
DL3	Johnny Bench	2.00
DL4	Hank Aaron	3.00
DL5	Rod Carew	1.00
DL6	Roberto Clemente	3.00
DL7	Nolan Ryan	4.00
DL8	Bob Gibson	1.50
DL9	Jim Palmer	1.00
DL10	Juan Marichal	1.00

Entertainment Stars

		NM/M
Production 500 sets		
1	Lou Ferrigno (Incredible Hulk)	50.00
2	Adam West (Batman)	60.00
3	Danny Bonaduce (Partridge Family)	30.00

Legends Autographs

		NM/M
Common Player:		10.00
Inserted 1:211		
TT1R	Willie Mays	100.00
TT14R	Johnny Bench	60.00
TT48R	Bobby Richardson	20.00
TT8R	Carl Yastrzemski	50.00
TT13R	Warren Spahn	25.00
TT15R	Reggie Jackson	50.00
TT18R	Bob Gibson	20.00
TT25R	Luis Tiant	10.00
TT29R	Moose Skowron	10.00
TT31R	Clete Boyer	10.00
TT33R	Vida Blue	15.00
TT35R	Joe Pepitone	10.00
TT37R	Tug McGraw	15.00
TT47R	Frank Howard	10.00
TT49R	Tony Kubek	40.00
TT50R	Mickey Lolich	10.00

Profiles In Courage

		NM/M
Complete Set (20):		25.00
Common Player:		1.00
Inserted 1:8		
PIC1	Roger Maris	2.00
PIC2	Lou Brock	1.00
PIC3	Brooks Robinson	1.50
PIC4	Carl Yastrzemski	1.50
PIC5	Mike Schmidt	2.50
PIC6	Hank Aaron	3.00
PIC7	Tom Seaver	1.50
PIC8	Willie Mays	3.00
PIC9	Graig Nettles	1.00
PIC10	Frank Robinson	1.50
PIC11	Rollie Fingers	1.00
PIC12	Tony Perez	1.00
PIC13	George Brett	3.00
PIC14	Robin Yount	1.50
PIC15	Nolan Ryan	4.00
PIC16	Warren Spahn	1.50
PIC17	Johnny Bench	2.00
PIC18	Vida Blue	1.00
PIC19	Roberto Clemente	3.00
PIC20	Thurman Munson	2.00

Piece of American Pie Relics

		NM/M
Common Card:		10.00
Inserted 1:29		
PAPM1	Frank Sinatra	60.00
PAPM2	JFK/Berlin Wall	10.00
PAPM3	Elvis Presley	90.00
PAPM4	Janis Joplin	50.00
PAPM5	Jimi Hendrix	

Rookie Reprint Relics

		NM/M
Common Player:		10.00
Inserted 1:116		
JB	Johnny Bench	20.00
GB	George Brett	40.00
SC	Steve Carlton	15.00
GC	Gary Carter	10.00
AD	Andre Dawson	10.00
DE	Dennis Eckersley	10.00
MF	Mark Fidrych	10.00
BG	Bobby Grich	10.00
RJ	Reggie Jackson	15.00
JK	Jim Kaat	10.00
TMC	Tim McCarver	10.00
TM	Thurman Munson	35.00
BM	Bobby Murcer	10.00
AO	Al Oliver	10.00
BP	Boog Powell	10.00
OS	Ozzie Smith	20.00
DS	Don Sutton	10.00
DW	Dave Winfield	10.00
RY	Robin Yount	20.00

Timeless Classics Relics

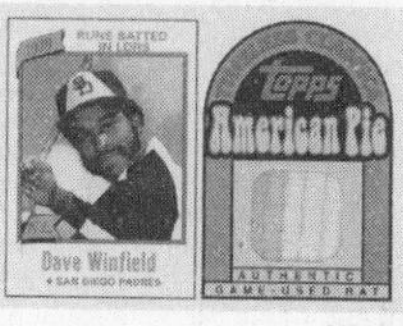

		NM/M
Common Player:		8.00
Inserted 1:80		
	Sam McDowell	8.00
	Frank Howard	8.00
	Dick Groat	8.00
	Roger Maris	50.00
	Orlando Cepeda	10.00
	Willie Mays	40.00
	Carl Yastrzemski	30.00
	Roberto Clemente	60.00
	Harmon Killebrew	20.00
	Brooks Robinson	20.00
	Tony Conigliaro	15.00
	Frank Robinson	15.00
	Hank Aaron	40.00
	Willie McCovey	15.00
	Rico Carty	8.00
	Johnny Bench	20.00
	Willie Stargell	15.00
	Steve Carlton	15.00

Player	NM/M
Norm Cash	8.00
Reggie Jackson	15.00
Mike Schmidt	30.00
Mickey Rivers	8.00
Tom Seaver	20.00
George Brett	40.00
George Foster	8.00
Graig Nettles	8.00
Nolan Ryan	40.00
Dave Parker	10.00
Dick Allen	8.00
Fred Lynn	8.00
Keith Hernandez	8.00
Dave Winfield	15.00

Woodstock Relics

		NM/M
Common Player:		8.00
Inserted 1:138		
GB	George Brett	40.00
BB	Bill Buckner	8.00
OC	Orlando Cepeda	10.00
DE	Dwight Evans	8.00
CF	Carlton Fisk	15.00
BF	Bill Freehan	8.00
DG	Dick Groat	8.00
RJ	Reggie Jackson	15.00
TK	Ted Kluszewski	8.00
FL	Fred Lynn	8.00
WM	Willie Mays	45.00
SM	Stan Musial	40.00
TP	Tony Perez	8.00
JP	Jimmy Piersall	8.00
BR	Brooks Robinson	15.00
FR	Frank Robinson	15.00
JR	Joe Rudi	8.00
DS	Duke Snider	15.00
WS	Willie Stargell	15.00
MW	Maury Wills	8.00
DW	Dave Winfield	8.00
WS	Woodstock	15.00
JW	Jim Wynn	8.00
CY	Carl Yastrzemski	30.00
RY	Robin Yount	20.00

2001 TOPPS ARCHIVES

		NM/M
Complete Set (450):		150.00
Complete Series 1 (225):		75.00
Complete Series 2 (225):		75.00
Common Player:		.40
Pack (8):		4.50
Box (20):		80.00
1	Johnny Antonelli	.40
2	Yogi Berra	2.50
3	Dom DiMaggio	.40
4	Carl Erskine	.40
5	Joe Garagiola	.50
6	Monte Irvin	.40
7	Vernon Law	.40
8	Eddie Mathews	2.00
9	Willie Mays	5.00
10	Gil McDougald	.40
11	Andy Pafko	.40
12	Phil Rizzuto	.75
13	Preacher Roe	.40
14	Hank Sauer	.50
15	Bobby Shantz	.40
16	Enos Slaughter	.50
17	Warren Spahn	2.00
18	Mickey Vernon	.40
19	Early Wynn	.40
20	Whitey Ford	1.00
21	Johnny Podres	.40
22	Ernie Banks	2.00
23	Moose Skowron	.40
24	Harmon Killebrew	2.00
25	Ted Williams	6.00
26	Jimmy Piersall	.40
27	Frank Thomas	.40
28	Bill Mazeroski	.50
29	Bobby Richardson	.40
30	Frank Robinson	1.50
31	Stan Musial	3.00
32	Johnny Callison	.40
33	Bob Gibson	2.00
34	Frank Howard	.50
35	Willie McCovey	.40
36	Carl Yastrzemski	2.00
37	Jim Maloney	.40
38	Ron Santo	.40
39	Lou Brock	.75
40	Tim McCarver	.50
41	Joe Pepitone	.40
42	Boog Powell	.50
43	Bill Freehan	.40
44	Dick Allen	.40
45	Willie Horton	.40
46	Mickey Lolich	.40
47	Wilbur Wood	.40
48	Bert Campaneris	.40
49	Rod Carew	1.50
50	Tug McGraw	.40
51	Tony Perez	.75
52	Luis Tiant	.40
53	Bobby Murcer	.40
54	Don Sutton	.75
55	Ken Holtzman	.40
56	Reggie Smith	.40
57	Hal McRae	.40
58	Roy White	.40
59	Reggie Jackson	3.00
60	Graig Nettles	.40
61	Joe Rudi	.40
62	Vida Blue	.50
63	Darrell Evans	.40
64	David Concepcion	.40
65	Bobby Grich	.40
66	Greg Luzinski	.40
67	Cecil Cooper	.40
68	George Hendrick	.40
69	Dwight Evans	.40
70	Gary Matthews	.40
71	Mike Schmidt	3.00
72	Dave Parker	.40
73	Dave Winfield	1.00
74	Gary Carter	.40
75	Dennis Eckersley	.75
76	Kent Tekulve	.40
77	Andre Dawson	.75
78	Denny Martinez	.40
79	Bruce Sutter	.75
80	Jack Morris	.40
81	Ozzie Smith	1.50
82	Lee Smith	.40
83	Don Mattingly	4.00
84	Joe Carter	.40
85	Kirby Puckett	3.00
86	Joe Adcock	.40
87	Gus Bell	.40
88	Roy Campanella	2.00
89	Jackie Jensen	.40
90	Johnny Mize	.75
91	Allie Reynolds	.40
92	Al Rosen	.40
93	Hal Newhouser	.40
94	Harvey Kuenn	.40
95	Nellie Fox	.75
96	Elston Howard	.40
97	Sal Maglie	.40
98	Roger Maris	3.00
99	Norm Cash	.40
100	Thurman Munson	2.50
101	Roy Campanella	1.50
102	Joe Garagiola	.75
103	Dom DiMaggio	.40
104	Johnny Mize	.50
105	Allie Reynolds	.40
106	Preacher Roe	.40
107	Hal Newhouser	.40
108	Monte Irvin	.40
109	Carl Erskine	.40
110	Enos Slaughter	.40
111	Gil McDougald	.40
112	Andy Pafko	.40
113	Sal Maglie	.40
114	Johnny Antonelli	.40
115	Phil Rizzuto	.50
116	Yogi Berra	1.50
117	Early Wynn	.40
118	Mickey Vernon	.40
119	Gus Bell	.40
120	Ted Williams	4.00
121	Frank Thomas	.40
122	Bobby Richardson	.40
123	Whitey Ford	1.00
124	Vernon Law	.40
125	Jimmy Piersall	.40
126	Moose Skowron	.40
127	Joe Adcock	.40
128	Johnny Podres	.40
129	Ernie Banks	1.50
130	Jim Maloney	.40
131	Johnny Callison	.40
132	Eddie Mathews	1.50
133	Joe Pepitone	.40
134	Warren Spahn	1.50
135	Bill Mazeroski	.40
136	Norm Cash	.40
137	Bob Gibson	1.00
138	Harmon Killebrew	1.50
139	Frank Robinson	1.00
140	Ron Santo	.40
141	Hank Sauer	.40
142	Bobby Shantz	.40
143	Nellie Fox	.50
144	Elston Howard	.40
145	Jackie Jensen	.40
146	Al Rosen	.40
147	Dick Allen	.40
148	Bill Freehan	.40
149	Boog Powell	.40
150	Lou Brock	.75
151	Rod Carew	.75
152	Wilbur Wood	.40
153	Thurman Munson	1.50
154	Ken Holtzman	.40
155	Willie Horton	.40
156	Mickey Lolich	.40
157	Tim McCarver	.40
158	Willie McCovey	.40
159	Roy White	.40
160	Bobby Murcer	.40
161	Joe Rudi	.40
162	Reggie Smith	.40
163	Luis Tiant	.40
164	Bert Campaneris	.40
165	Frank Howard	.40
166	Harvey Kuenn	.50
167	Greg Luzinski	.40
168	Tug McGraw	.40
169	Willie Mays	3.00
170	Roger Maris	2.00
171	Vida Blue	.40
172	Bobby Grich	.40
173	Reggie Jackson	2.00
174	Hal McRae	.40
175	Carl Yastrzemski	1.00
176	David Concepcion	.40
177	Cecil Cooper	.40
178	George Hendrick	.40
179	Gary Matthews	.40
180	Stan Musial	2.00
181	Graig Nettles	.40
182	Don Sutton	.50
183	Kent Tekulve	.40
184	Bruce Sutter	.75
185	Darrell Evans	.40
186	Mike Schmidt	2.00
187	Dave Parker	.40
188	Dwight Evans	.40
189	Gary Carter	.40
190	Jack Morris	.40
191	Tony Perez	.50
192	Dave Winfield	.75
193	Andre Dawson	.50
194	Lee Smith	.40
195	Ozzie Smith	1.00
196	Denny Martinez	.40
197	Don Mattingly	2.50
198	Joe Carter	.40
199	Dennis Eckersley	.75
200	Kirby Puckett	2.00
201	Walter Alston	.40
202	Casey Stengel	.75
203	Sparky Anderson	.40
204	Tommy Lasorda	.75
205	Whitey Herzog	.40
206	Harmon Killebrew, Frank Howard, Reggie Jackson	.40
207	Hank Aaron, Early Wynn, Ron Santo, Willie McCovey	2.50
208	Frank Robinson, Harmon Killebrew, Boog Powell	1.50
209	Tony Oliva, Frank Robinson, Frank Howard	.75
210	Hank Aaron, Willie McCovey, Willie Mays, Orlando Cepeda	2.50
211	Hank Aaron, Frank Robinson, Willie Mays, Ernie Banks	2.50
212	Carl Yastrzemski, Harmon Killebrew, Frank Howard	1.50
213	Ernie Banks	1.50
214	Hank Aaron	2.50
215	Willie Mays	2.50
216	Al Kaline	.75
217	Stan Musial	2.00
218	Duke Snider	.75
219	Frank Robinson, Hank Bauer, Frank Robinson	.50
220	Willie Mays, Stan Musial	1.50
221	Whitey Ford	.75
222	Jerry Koosman	.40
223	Bob Gibson	.75
224	Gil Hodges	.40
225	Reggie Jackson	1.50
226	Hank Bauer	.40
227	Ralph Branca	.40
228	Joe Garagiola	.75
229	Bob Feller	2.00
230	Dick Groat	.40
231	George Kell	.40
232	Bob Boone	.40
233	Minnie Minoso	.40
234	Billy Pierce	.40
235	Robin Roberts	.50
236	Johnny Sain	.40
237	Red Schoendienst	.40
238	Curt Simmons	.40
239	Duke Snider	2.00
240	Bobby Thomson	.40
241	Hoyt Wilhelm	.40
242	Elroy Face	.40
243	Ralph Kiner	.75
244	Hank Aaron	4.00
245	Al Kaline	2.00
246	Don Larsen	1.50
247	Tug McGraw	.40
248	Don Newcombe	.75
249	Herb Score	.40
250	Clete Boyer	.40
251	Lindy McDaniel	.40
252	Brooks Robinson	2.50
253	Orlando Cepeda	.60
254	Larry Bowa	.40
255	Mike Cuellar	.40
256	Jim Perry	.40
257	Dave Parker	.40
258	Maury Wills	.40
259	Willie Davis	.40
260	Juan Marichal	.60
261	Jim Bouton	.40
262	Dean Chance	.40
263	Sam McDowell	.40
264	Whitey Ford	3.00
265	Bob Uecker	2.00
266	Willie Stargell	2.00
267	Rico Carty	.40
268	Tommy John	.40
269	Phil Niekro	.60
270	Paul Blair	.40
271	Steve Carlton	3.00
272	Jim Lonborg	.40
273	Tony Perez	.60
274	Ron Swoboda	.40
275	Fergie Jenkins	.75
276	Jim Palmer	1.50
277	Sal Bando	.40
278	Tom Seaver	4.00
279	Johnny Bench	4.00
280	Nolan Ryan	6.00
281	Rollie Fingers	.50
282	Sparky Lyle	.40
283	Al Oliver	.40
284	Bob Watson	.40
285	Bill Buckner	.40
286	Bert Blyleven	.40
287	George Foster	.40
288	Al Hrabosky	.40
289	Cecil Cooper	.40
290	Carlton Fisk	1.00
291	Mickey Rivers	.40
292	Goose Gossage	.40
293	Rick Reuschel	.40
294	Bucky Dent	.40
295	Frank Tanana	.40
296	George Brett	4.00
297	Keith Hernandez	.40
298	Fred Lynn	.40
299	Robin Yount	3.00
300	Ron Guidry	.40
301	Jack Clark	.40
302	Mark Fidrych	.40
303	Dale Murphy	1.50
304	Willie Hernandez	.40
305	Lou Whitaker	.40
306	Kirk Gibson	.75
307	Wade Boggs	3.00
308	Ryne Sandberg	4.00
309	Orel Hershiser	.40
310	Jimmy Key	.40

311 Richie Ashburn .40
312 Smokey Burgess .40
313 Gil Hodges 1.50
314 Ted Kluszewski .40
315 Pee Wee Reese 1.00
316 Jackie Robinson 4.00
317 Harvey Haddix .40
318 Satchel Paige 3.00
319 Roberto Clemente 5.00
320 Carl Furillo .40
321 Don Drysdale 2.00
322 Curt Flood .40
323 Bob Allison .40
324 Tony Conigliaro .40
325 Dan Quisenberry .40
326 Ralph Branca .40
327 Bob Feller 1.00
328 Satchel Paige 3.00
329 George Kell .40
330 Pee Wee Reese 1.00
331 Bobby Thomson .40
332 Carl Furillo .40
333 Hank Bauer .40
334 Herb Score .40
335 Richie Ashburn .40
336 Billy Pierce .40
337 Duke Snider 2.00
338 Harvey Haddix .40
339 Robin Roberts .40
340 Dick Groat .40
341 Curt Simmons .40
342 Bob Uecker 1.00
343 Smokey Burgess .40
344 Jim Bouton .40
345 Elroy Face .40
346 Don Drysdale 1.00
347 Bob Allison .40
348 Clete Boyer .40
349 Dean Chance .40
350 Tony Conigliaro .40
351 Curt Flood .40
352 Hoyt Wilhelm .40
353 Ron Swoboda .40
354 Roberto Clemente 3.00
355 Tug McGraw .40
356 Orlando Cepeda .40
357 Joe Garagiola .40
358 Juan Marichal .50
359 Sam McDowell .40
360 Johnny Sain .40
361 Ted Kluszewski .40
362 Al Kaline 2.00
363 Lindy McDaniel .40
364 Don Newcombe .40
365 Jim Perry .40
366 Hank Aaron 4.00
367 Don Larsen 1.00
368 Mike Cuellar .40
369 Willie Davis .40
370 Ralph Kiner .50
371 Minnie Minoso .40
372 Larry Bowa .40
373 Brooks Robinson 1.00
374 Bob Boone .40
375 Jim Lonborg .40
376 Paul Blair .40
377 Rico Carty .40
378 Sal Bando .40
379 Mark Fidrych .40
380 Al Hrabosky .40
381 Willie Stargell 1.00
382 Johnny Bench 2.50
383 Dave Parker .40
384 Sparky Lyle .40
385 Fergie Jenkins .50
386 Jim Palmer 1.00
387 Whitey Ford 2.00
388 Tony Perez .40
389 Mickey Rivers .40
390 Bob Watson .40
391 Rollie Fingers .40
392 George Foster .40
393 Al Oliver .40
394 Tom Seaver 3.00
395 Maury Wills .40
396 Steve Carlton 1.00
397 Cecil Cooper .40
398 Bill Buckner .40
399 Phil Niekro .40
400 Red Schoendienst .40
401 Ron Guidry .40
402 Willie Hernandez .40
403 Tommy John .40
404 Gil Hodges .40
405 Bucky Dent .40
406 Keith Hernandez .40
407 Dan Quisenberry .40
408 Fred Lynn .40
409 Rick Reuschel .40
410 Jackie Robinson 3.00
411 Goose Gossage .40
412 Bert Blyleven .40
413 Jack Clark .40
414 Carlton Fisk .50
415 Dale Murphy .75
416 Frank Tanana .40
417 George Brett 3.00
418 Robin Yount 2.50
419 Kirk Gibson .50
420 Lou Whitaker .40
421 Ryne Sandberg 2.50
422 Jimmy Key .40
423 Nolan Ryan 5.00
424 Wade Boggs .75
425 Orel Hershiser .40
426 Billy Martin .40
427 Ralph Houk .40
428 Chuck Tanner .40
429 Earl Weaver .40
430 Leo Durocher .40
431 Tony Conigliaro, Norm Cash, Willie Horton .40
432 Ernie Banks, Hank Aaron, Eddie Mathews, Clete Boyer 1.50
433 Norm Cash, Frank Howard, Al Kaline, Jimmy Piersall .40
434 Goose Gossage, Rollie Fingers .40
435 Nolan Ryan, Tom Seaver .40
436 Reggie Jackson, Willie Stargell .75
437 Johnny Bench, Dick Allen .75
438 Roger Maris 3.00
439 Carl Yastrzemski 2.00
440 Nolan Ryan 4.00
441 Cincinnati Reds .75
442 Tony Perez .40
443 Steve Carlton .75
444 Wade Boggs .75
445 Andre Dawson .40
446 Whitey Ford 1.50
447 Hank Aaron 4.00
448 Bob Gibson .75
449 Roberto Clemente 4.00
450 Orioles/Jackie Robinson 1.50

Autographs

NM/M
Common Player: 10.00
Inserted 1:box
TAA1 Johnny Antonelli 15.00
TAA2 Hank Bauer 20.00
TAA3 Yogi Berra/50 275.00
TAA4 Ralph Branca 20.00
TAA5 Dom DiMaggio 30.00
TAA6 Joe Garagiola 30.00
TAA7 Carl Erskine 25.00
TAA8 Bob Feller 25.00
TAA10 Dick Groat 20.00
TAA11 Monte Irvin 20.00
TAA12 George Kell 20.00
TAA13 Vernon Law 10.00
TAA14 Bob Boone 10.00
TAA16 Willie Mays/50 375.00
TAA17 Gil McDougald 20.00
TAA18 Minnie Minoso 20.00
TAA19 Andy Pafko 20.00
TAA20 Billy Pierce 10.00
TAA21 Phil Rizzuto/200 80.00
TAA22 Robin Roberts 40.00
TAA23 Preacher Roe 20.00
TAA24 Johnny Sain 15.00
TAA25 Hank Sauer 15.00
TAA26 Red Schoendienst 15.00
TAA27 Bobby Shantz 10.00
TAA28 Curt Simmons 10.00
TAA29 Enos Slaughter 25.00
TAA30 Duke Snider 80.00
TAA31 Warren Spahn 80.00
TAA32 Bobby Thomson 20.00
TAA33 Mickey Vernon 15.00
TAA34 Hoyt Wilhelm 30.00
TAA35 Jim Wynn 10.00
TAA36 Elroy Face 10.00
TAA37 Gaylord Perry 25.00
TAA38 Ralph Kiner 50.00
TAA39 Johnny Podres 10.00
TAA40 Hank Aaron/50 375.00
TAA41 Ernie Banks/50 300.00
TAA42 Al Kaline 125.00
TAA43 Moose Skowron 15.00
TAA44 Don Larsen 160.00
TAA45 Harmon Killebrew 120.00
TAA46 Tug McGraw 30.00
TAA48 Don Newcombe 15.00
TAA49 Jimmy Piersall 10.00
TAA50 Herb Score 10.00
TAA51 Frank Thomas 10.00
TAA52 Clete Boyer 15.00
TAA53 Bill Mazeroski 40.00
TAA54 Lindy McDaniel 10.00
TAA55 Bobby Richardson 15.00
TAA56 Brooks Robinson/SP 180.00
TAA57 Frank Robinson 80.00
TAA58 Orlando Cepeda 40.00
TAA59 Stan Musial/50 250.00
TAA60 Larry Bowa 15.00
TAA61 Johnny Callison 10.00
TAA62 Mike Cuellar 15.00
TAA63 Bob Gibson/SP/50 125.00
TAA64 Jim Perry 10.00
TAA65 Frank Howard 15.00
TAA66 David Palmer 15.00
TAA67 Willie McCovey 60.00
TAA68 Maury Wills 15.00
TAA69 Carl Yastrzemski 180.00
TAA70 Willie Davis 10.00
TAA71 Jim Maloney 10.00
TAA73 Ron Santo 25.00
TAA74 Jim Bouton 25.00
TAA75 Lou Brock/50 125.00
TAA76 Dean Chance 10.00
TAA77 Tim McCarver/200 50.00
TAA78 Sam McDowell 15.00
TAA79 Joe Pepitone 15.00
TAA80 Whitey Ford 60.00
TAA81 Boog Powell 15.00
TAA82 Bob Uecker 25.00
TAA83 Bill Freehan 10.00
TAA85 Dick Allen 25.00
TAA86 Rico Carty 10.00
TAA87 Willie Horton 10.00
TAA88 Tommy John 15.00
TAA89 Mickey Lolich 10.00
TAA90 Phil Niekro 25.00
TAA91 Wilbur Wood 10.00
TAA92 Paul Blair 10.00
TAA93 Bert Campaneris 10.00
TAA94 Steve Carlton 40.00
TAA96 Jim Lonborg 10.00
TAA97 Luis Aparicio 40.00
TAA98 Tony Perez 40.00
TAA99 Joe Morgan/200 60.00
TAA100 Ron Swoboda 20.00
TAA101 Luis Tiant 15.00
TAA102 Fergie Jenkins 20.00
TAA103 Bobby Murcer 15.00
TAA104 Jim Palmer 50.00
TAA105 Don Sutton/200 40.00
TAA106 Sal Bando 10.00
TAA107 Ken Holtzman 40.00
TAA108 Tom Seaver/50 180.00
TAA110 Johnny Bench 220.00
TAA111 Hal McRae 10.00
TAA112 Nolan Ryan 300.00
TAA113 Roy White 10.00
TAA114 Rollie Fingers 20.00
TAA115 Reggie Jackson/50 175.00
TAA116 Sparky Lyle 15.00
TAA117 Graig Nettles 15.00
TAA118 Al Oliver 10.00
TAA119 Joe Rudi 15.00
TAA120 Bob Watson 10.00
TAA121 Vida Blue 10.00
TAA122 Bill Buckner 10.00
TAA123 Darrell Evans 10.00
TAA124 Bert Blyleven 15.00
TAA125 David Concepcion 15.00
TAA126 George Foster 10.00
TAA127 Bobby Grich 10.00
TAA128 Al Hrabosky 10.00
TAA129 Greg Luzinski 15.00
TAA130 Cecil Cooper 10.00
TAA131 Ron Cey 10.00
TAA132 Carlton Fisk 75.00
TAA133 George Hendrick 10.00
TAA134 Mickey Rivers 10.00
TAA135 Dwight Evans 15.00
TAA136 Goose Gossage 10.00
TAA137 Gary Matthews 10.00
TAA138 Rick Reuschel 10.00
TAA139 Mike Schmidt 300.00
TAA140 Bucky Dent 15.00
TAA141 Jim Kaat 25.00
TAA142 Frank Tanana 10.00
TAA143 Dave Winfield/200 75.00
TAA144 George Brett 275.00
TAA145 Gary Carter/200 60.00
TAA146 Keith Hernandez 25.00
TAA147 Fred Lynn 15.00
TAA148 Robin Yount SP/200 150.00
TAA149 Dennis Eckersley/SP/200 60.00
TAA150 Ron Guidry 15.00
TAA151 Kent Tekulve 15.00
TAA152 Jack Clark 10.00
TAA153 Andre Dawson SP/200 50.00
TAA154 Mark Fidrych 15.00
TAA155 Denny Martinez SP/200 35.00
TAA156 Dale Murphy 50.00
TAA157 Bruce Sutter 35.00
TAA158 Willie Hernandez 10.00
TAA160 Lou Whitaker 15.00
TAA162 Kirk Gibson 20.00
TAA163 Lee Smith 10.00
TAA164 Wade Boggs 80.00
TAA165 Ryne Sandberg SP/200 150.00
TAA166 Don Mattingly 100.00
TAA167 Joe Carter SP/200 25.00
TAA168 Orel Hershiser 25.00
TAA169 Kirby Puckett 75.00
TAA170 Jimmy Key 30.00

Game-Used Bat

NM/M
Common Player: 15.00
1 Johnny Bench 30.00
2 George Brett 50.00
3 Fred Lynn 15.00
4 Reggie Jackson 25.00
5 Mike Schmidt 50.00
6 Willie Stargell 20.00

Game-Used Bat Autograph

NM/M
Common Player: 120.00
Production 25 sets
1 Johnny Bench 150.00
2 George Brett 200.00
3 Fred Lynn 75.00
4 Reggie Jackson

5	Mike Schmidt	
6	Willie Stargell	

Topps Final Autoproof

		NM/M
Common Player:		30.00
	Carlton Fisk	60.00
	Wade Boggs	40.00
	Willie Mays	120.00
	Willie McCovey	30.00
	Jim Palmer	30.00
	Robin Roberts	30.00
	Duke Snider	40.00
	Warren Spahn	40.00
	Hoyt Wilhelm	30.00
	Carl Yastrzemski	80.00

2001 TOPPS ARCHIVES RESERVE

		NM/M
Complete Set (100):		90.00
Common Player:		.75
Hobby Pack (5):		10.00
Hobby Box (10 + auto. ball):		150.00
1	Joe Adcock	.75
2	Brooks Robinson	3.00
3	Luis Aparicio	.75
4	Richie Ashburn	.75
5	Hank Bauer	.75
6	Johnny Bench	4.00
7	Wade Boggs	2.00
8	Moose Skowron	.75
9	George Brett	5.00
10	Lou Brock	2.00
11	Roy Campanella	4.00
12	Willie Hernandez	.75
13	Steve Carlton	2.00
14	Gary Carter	.75
15	Hoyt Wilhelm	.75
16	Orlando Cepeda	.75
17	Roberto Clemente	8.00
18	Dale Murphy	1.50
19	Dave Concepcion	.75
20	Dom DiMaggio	.75
21	Larry Doby	.75
22	Don Drysdale	4.00
23	Dennis Eckersley	.75
24	Bob Feller	2.00
25	Rollie Fingers	.75
26	Carlton Fisk	2.00
27	Nellie Fox	1.50
28	Mickey Rivers	.75
29	Tommy John	.75
30	Johnny Sain	.75
31	Keith Hernandez	.75
32	Gil Hodges	.75
33	Elston Howard	3.00
34	Frank Howard	.75
35	Bob Gibson	5.00
36	Fergie Jenkins	.75
37	Jackie Jensen	.75
38	Al Kaline	3.00
39	Harmon Killebrew	5.00
40	Ralph Kiner	.75
41	Dick Groat	.75
42	Don Larsen	.75
43	Ralph Branca	.75
44	Mickey Lolich	.75
45	Juan Marichal	3.00
46	Roger Maris	6.00
47	Bobby Thomson	.75
48	Eddie Mathews	4.00
49	Don Mattingly	8.00
50	Willie McCovey	2.00
51	Gil McDougald	.75
52	Tug McGraw	.75
53	Billy Pierce	.75
54	Minnie Minoso	.75
55	Johnny Mize	2.00
56	Elroy Face	.75
57	Joe Morgan	1.50
58	Thurman Munson	5.00
59	Stan Musial	5.00
60	Phil Niekro	.75
61	Paul Blair	.75
62	Andy Pafko	.75
63	Satchel Paige	5.00
64	Tony Perez	.75
65	Sal Bando	.75
66	Jimmy Piersall	.75
67	Kirby Puckett	5.00
68	Phil Rizzuto	3.00
69	Robin Roberts	.75
70	Jackie Robinson	8.00
71	Ryne Sandberg	3.00
72	Mike Schmidt	4.00
73	Red Schoendienst	.75
74	Herb Score	.75
75	Enos Slaughter	.75
76	Ozzie Smith	3.00
77	Warren Spahn	2.00
78	Don Sutton	.75
79	Luis Tiant	.75
80	Ted Kluszewski	.75
81	Whitey Ford	3.00
82	Maury Wills	.75
83	Dave Winfield	2.00
84	Early Wynn	.75
85	Carl Yastrzemski	3.00
86	Robin Yount	4.00
87	Bob Allison	.75
88	Clete Boyer	.75
89	Reggie Jackson	3.00
90	Yogi Berra	5.00
91	Willie Mays	8.00
92	Jim Palmer	.75
93	Pee Wee Reese	2.00
94	Frank Robinson	2.00
95	Boog Powell	.75
96	Willie Stargell	3.00
97	Nolan Ryan	10.00
98	Tom Seaver	4.00
99	Duke Snider	3.00
100	Bill Mazeroski	.75

Autographs

		NM/M
Common Autograph:		10.00
Inserted 1:10		
1	Willie Mays	160.00
2	Whitey Ford	60.00
3	Nolan Ryan	175.00
4	Carl Yastrzemski	90.00
5	Frank Robinson	40.00
6	Tom Seaver	80.00
7	Warren Spahn	75.00
8	Johnny Bench	100.00
9	Reggie Jackson	80.00
10	Bob Gibson	40.00
11	Bob Feller	20.00
12	Gil McDougald	15.00
13	Luis Tiant	10.00
14	Minnie Minoso	10.00
16	Herb Score	10.00
17	Moose Skowron	15.00
18	Maury Wills	10.00
19	Clete Boyer	15.00
21	Don Larsen	20.00
23	Tug McGraw	20.00
25	Robin Roberts	20.00
26	Frank Howard	20.00
27	Mickey Lolich	10.00
29	Tommy John	10.00
32	Dick Groat	15.00
33	Elroy Face	10.00
34	Paul Blair	10.00

Bat Relics

		NM/M
Common Player:		8.00
Overall Relic Odds 1:10		
21	Al Kaline	20.00
22	Carl Yastrzemski	25.00
23	Carlton Fisk	15.00
24	Dale Murphy	15.00
25	Dave Winfield	10.00
26	Dick Groat	8.00
27	Dom DiMaggio	15.00
28	Don Mattingly	40.00
29	Gary Carter	8.00
30	George Kell	15.00
31	Harmon Killebrew	20.00
32	Jackie Jensen	15.00
33	Jackie Robinson	75.00
34	Jimmy Piersall	8.00
35	Joe Adcock	8.00
36	Joe Carter	8.00
37	Johnny Mize	10.00
38	Kirk Gibson	8.00
39	Mickey Vernon	8.00
40	Mike Schmidt	40.00
41	Ryne Sandberg	40.00
42	Ozzie Smith	20.00
43	Ted Kluszewski	10.00
44	Wade Boggs	10.00
45	Willie Mays	60.00
46	Duke Snider	15.00
47	Harvey Kuenn	8.00
48	Robin Yount	20.00
49	Red Schoendienst	8.00
50	Elston Howard	10.00
51	Bob Allison	8.00

Jersey Relics

		NM/M
Common Player:		8.00
Overall Relic Odds 1:10		
1	Brooks Robinson	15.00
2	Tony Conigliaro	15.00
3	Frank Howard	8.00
4	Don Sutton	10.00
5	Ferguson Jenkins	8.00
6	Frank Robinson	15.00
7	Don Mattingly	40.00
8	Willie Stargell	15.00
9	Moose Skowron	15.00
10	Fred Lynn	8.00
11	George Brett	40.00
12	Nolan Ryan	50.00
13	Orlando Cepeda	10.00
14	Reggie Jackson	15.00
15	Steve Carlton	15.00
16	Tom Seaver	20.00
17	Thurman Munson	25.00
18	Yogi Berra	20.00
19	Willie McCovey	10.00
20	Robin Yount	20.00

Autographed Baseball

		NM/M
Common Autograph:		15.00
Inserted 1:box		
1	Johnny Bench/100	80.00
2	Paul Blair/1,000	15.00
3	Clete Boyer/1,000	15.00
4	Ralph Branca/400	25.00
5	Elroy Face/1,000	15.00
6	Bob Feller/1,000	25.00
7	Whitey Ford/100	60.00
8	Bob Gibson/1,000	30.00
9	Dick Groat/1,000	15.00
10	Frank Howard/1,000	15.00
11	Reggie Jackson/100	75.00
12	Don Larsen/100	30.00
13	Mickey Lolich/500	15.00
14	Willie Mays/100	150.00
15	Gil McDougald/500	20.00
16	Tug McGraw/1,000	15.00
17	Minnie Minoso/1,000	15.00
18	Andy Pafko/500	25.00
19	Joe Pepitone/1,000	15.00
20	Robin Roberts/1,000	25.00
21	Frank Robinson/100	50.00
22	Nolan Ryan/100	150.00
23	Herb Score/500	20.00
24	Tom Seaver/100	80.00
25	Moose Skowron/1,000	15.00
26	Warren Spahn/100	50.00
27	Bobby Thomson/400	20.00
28	Luis Tiant/500	20.00
29	Carl Yastrzemski/100	100.00
30	Maury Wills/1,000	20.00

2001 TOPPS CHROME

		NM/M
Complete Set (660):		225.00
Complete Series 1 (330):		100.00
Complete Series 2 (330):		125.00
Common Player:		.25
Series 1 Pack (4):		2.50
Series 1 Box (24):		45.00
Series 2 Pack (4):		6.00
Series 2 Box (24):		120.00
1	Cal Ripken Jr.	4.00
2	Chipper Jones	2.00
3	Roger Cedeno	.25
4	Garret Anderson	.50
5	Robin Ventura	.40
6	Daryle Ward	.25
7	Not Issued (Retired)	.25
8	Phil Nevin	.25
9	Jermaine Dye	.25
10	Chris Singleton	.25
11	Mike Redmond	.25
12	Jim Thome	1.00
13	Brian Jordan	.25
14	Dustin Hermanson	.25
15	Shawn Green	.50
16	Todd Stottlemyre	.25
17	Dan Wilson	.25
18	Derek Lowe	.25
19	Juan Gonzalez	1.00
20	Pat Meares	.25
21	Paul O'Neill	.50
22	Jeffrey Hammonds	.25
23	Pokey Reese	.25
24	Mike Mussina	.75
25	Rico Brogna	.25
26	Jay Buhner	.25
27	Steve Cox	.25
28	Quilvio Veras	.25
29	Marquis Grissom	.25
30	Shigetoshi Hasegawa	.25
31	Shane Reynolds	.25
32	Adam Piatt	.25
33	Preston Wilson	.25
34	Ellis Burks	.25
35	Armando Rios	.25
36	Chuck Finley	.25
37	Shannon Stewart	.25
38	Mark McGwire	3.00
39	Gerald Williams	.25
40	Eric Young	.25
41	Peter Bergeron	.25
42	Arthur Rhodes	.25
43	Bobby Jones	.25
44	Matt Clement	.25
45	Pedro Martinez	1.50
46	Jose Canseco	.75

47 Matt Anderson .25
48 Torii Hunter .50
49 Carlos Lee .25
50 Eric Chavez .50
51 Rick Helling .25
52 John Franco .25
53 Mike Bordick .25
54 Andres Galarraga .40
55 Jose Cruz Jr. .25
56 Mike Matheny .25
57 Randy Johnson 1.50
58 Richie Sexson .75
59 Vladimir Nunez .25
60 Aaron Boone .25
61 Darin Erstad .50
62 Alex Gonzalez .25
63 Gil Heredia .25
64 Shane Andrews .25
65 Todd Hundley .25
66 Bill Mueller .25
67 Mark McLemore .25
68 Scott Spiezio .25
69 Kevin McGlinchy .25
70 Manny Ramirez 1.00
71 Mike Lamb .25
72 Brian Buchanan .25
73 Mike Sweeney .25
74 John Wetteland .25
75 Rob Bell .25
76 John Burkett .25
77 Derek Jeter 3.00
78 J.D. Drew .50
79 Jose Offerman .25
80 Rick Reed .25
81 Will Clark .75
82 Rickey Henderson .75
83 Kirk Rueter .25
84 Lee Stevens .25
85 Jay Bell .25
86 Fred McGriff .50
87 Julio Zuleta .25
88 Brian Anderson .25
89 Orlando Cabrera .25
90 Alex Fernandez .25
91 Derek Bell .25
92 Eric Owens .25
93 Dennys Reyes .25
94 Mike Stanley .25
95 Jorge Posada .75
96 Paul Konerko .25
97 Mike Remlinger .25
98 Travis Lee .25
99 Ken Caminiti .25
100 Kevin Barker .25
101 Ozzie Guillen .25
102 Randy Wolf .25
103 Michael Tucker .25
104 Darren Lewis .25
105 Joe Randa .25
106 Jeff Cirillo .25
107 David Ortiz .25
108 Herb Perry .25
109 Jeff Nelson .25
110 Chris Stynes .25
111 Johnny Damon .50
112 Jason Schmidt .25
113 Charles Johnson .25
114 Pat Burrell .75
115 Gary Sheffield .75
116 Tom Glavine .75
117 Jason Isringhausen .25
118 Chris Carpenter .25
119 Jeff Suppan .25
120 Ivan Rodriguez 1.00
121 Luis Sojo .25
122 Ron Villone .25
123 Mike Sirotka .25
124 Chuck Knoblauch .25
125 Jason Kendall .50
126 Bobby Estalella .25
127 Jose Guillen .25
128 Carlos Delgado 1.00
129 Benji Gil .25
130 Einar Diaz .25
131 Andy Benes .25
132 Adrian Beltre .50
133 Roger Clemens 3.00
134 Scott Williamson .25
135 Brad Penny .25
136 Troy Glaus .75
137 Kevin Appier .25
138 Walt Weiss .25
139 Michael Barrett .25
140 Mike Hampton .25
141 Francisco Cordova .25
142 David Segui .25
143 Carlos Febles .25
144 Roy Halladay .50
145 Seth Etherton .25
146 Fernando Tatis .25
147 Livan Hernandez .25
148 B.J. Surhoff .25
149 Barry Larkin .75
150 Bobby Howry .25
151 Dmitri Young .25
152 Brian Hunter .25
153 Alex Rodriguez 3.00
154 Hideo Nomo .75
155 Warren Morris .25
156 Antonio Alfonseca .25
157 Edgardo Alfonzo .25
158 Mark Grudzielanek .25
159 Fernando Vina .25
160 Homer Bush .25
161 Jason Giambi 1.00
162 Steve Karsay .25
163 Matt Lawton .25
164 Rusty Greer .25
165 Billy Koch .25
166 Todd Hollandsworth .25
167 Raul Ibanez .25
168 Tony Gwynn 1.50
169 Carl Everett .25
170 Hector Carrasco .25
171 Jose Valentin .25
172 Deivi Cruz .25
173 Bret Boone .50
174 Melvin Mora .25
175 Danny Graves .25
176 Jose Jimenez .25
177 James Baldwin .25
178 C.J. Nitkowski .25
179 Jeff Zimmerman .25
180 Mike Lowell .50
181 Hideki Irabu .25
182 Greg Vaughn .25
183 Omar Daal .25
184 Darren Dreifort .25
185 Gil Meche .25
186 Damian Jackson .25
187 Frank Thomas 1.50
188 Luis Castillo .25
189 Bartolo Colon .50
190 Craig Biggio .50
191 Scott Schoeneweis .25
192 Dave Veres .25
193 Ramon Martinez .25
194 Jose Vidro .25
195 Todd Helton 1.00
196 Greg Norton .25
197 Jacque Jones .25
198 Jason Grimsley .25
199 Dan Reichert .25
200 Robb Nen .25
201 Scott Hatteberg .25
202 Terry Shumpert .25
203 Kevin Millar .25
204 Ismael Valdes .25
205 Richard Hidalgo .25
206 Randy Velarde .25
207 Bengie Molina .25
208 Tony Womack .25
209 Enrique Wilson .25
210 Jeff Brantley .25
211 Rick Ankiel .25
212 Terry Mulholland .25
213 Ron Belliard .25
214 Terrence Long .25
215 Alberto Castillo .25
216 Royce Clayton .25
217 Joe McEwing .25
218 Jason McDonald .25
219 Ricky Bottalico .25
220 Keith Foulke .25
221 Brad Radke .25
222 Gabe Kapler .25
223 Pedro Astacio .25
224 Armando Reynoso .25
225 Darryl Kile .25
226 Reggie Sanders .25
227 Esteban Yan .25
228 Joe Nathan .25
229 Jay Payton .25
230 Francisco Cordero .25
231 Gregg Jefferies .25
232 LaTroy Hawkins .25
233 Jacob Cruz .25
234 Chris Holt .25
235 Vladimir Guerrero 1.50
236 Marvin Benard .25
237 Alex Ramirez .25
238 Mike Williams .25
239 Sean Bergman .25
240 Juan Encarnacion .25
241 Russ Davis .25
242 Ramon Hernandez .25
243 Sandy Alomar .25
244 Eddie Guardado .25
245 Shane Halter .25
246 Geoff Jenkins .50
247 Brian Meadows .25
248 Damian Miller .25
249 Darrin Fletcher .25
250 Rafael Furcal .50
251 Mark Grace .75
252 Mark Mulder .50
253 Joe Torre .75
254 Bobby Cox .25
255 Mike Scioscia .25
256 Mike Hargrove .25
257 Jimy Williams .25
258 Jerry Manuel .25
259 Charlie Manuel .25
260 Don Baylor .25
261 Phil Garner .25
262 Tony Muser .25
263 Buddy Bell .25
264 Tom Kelly .25
265 John Boles .25
266 Art Howe .25
267 Larry Dierker .25
268 Lou Pinella .25
269 Larry Rothschild .25
270 Davey Lopes .25
271 Johnny Oates .25
272 Felipe Alou .25
273 Bobby Valentine .25
274 Tony LaRussa .25
275 Bruce Bochy .25
276 Dusty Baker .25
277 Adrian Gonzalez, Adam Johnson .75
278 Matt Wheatland, Brian Digby .75
279 Tripper Johnson, Scott Thorman .75
280 Phil Dumatrait, Adam Wainwright .75
281 *Scott Heard, David Parrish* .75
282 *Rocco Baldelli, Mark Folsom* 4.00
283 Dominic Rich, Aaron Herr .75
284 Mike Stodolka, Sean Burnett .75
285 Derek Thompson, Corey Smith .75
286 *Danny Borrell, Jason Bourgeois* .75
287 Chin-Feng Chen, Corey Patterson, Josh Hamilton .75
288 Ryan Anderson, Barry Zito, C.C. Sabathia .75
289 Scott Sobkowiak, David Walling, Ben Sheets .75
290 Ty Howington, Josh Kalinowski, Josh Girdley .50
291 Hee Seop Choi, Aaron McNeal, Jason Hart 4.00
292 Bobby Bradley, Kurt Ainsworth, Chin-Hui Tsao .75
293 Mike Glendenning, Kenny Kelly, Juan Silvestri .50
294 J.R. House, Ramon Castro, Ben Davis .50
295 Chance Caple, Rafael Soriano, Pascual Coco 3.00
296 Travis Hafner, Eric Munson, Bucky Jacobsen 3.00
297 Jason Conti, Chris Wakeland, Brian Cole .75
298 Scott Seabol, Aubrey Huff, Joe Crede .50
299 Adam Everett, Jose Ortiz, Keith Ginter .50
300 Carlos Hernandez, Geraldo Guzman, Adam Eaton .75
301 Bobby Kielty, Milton Bradley, Juan Rivera .50
302 Mark McGwire 2.00
303 Don Larsen .75
304 Bobby Thomson .25
305 Bill Mazeroski .25
306 Reggie Jackson 1.00
307 Kirk Gibson .25
308 Roger Maris 1.50
309 Cal Ripken Jr. 3.00
310 Hank Aaron 3.00
311 Joe Carter .25
312 Cal Ripken Jr. 3.00
313 Randy Johnson 1.00
314 Ken Griffey Jr. 2.00
315 Troy Glaus .75
316 Kazuhiro Sasaki .25
317 Sammy Sosa, Troy Glaus 1.00
318 Todd Helton, Edgar Martinez .50
319 Todd Helton, Nomar Garciaparra 1.50
320 Barry Bonds, Jason Giambi 1.50
321 Todd Helton, Manny Ramirez .50
322 Todd Helton, Darin Erstad .50
323 Kevin Brown, Pedro Martinez .75
324 Randy Johnson, Pedro Martinez .75
325 Will Clark .40
326 New York Mets .25
327 New York Yankees 1.00
328 Seattle Mariners .25
329 Mike Hampton .25
330 New York Yankees 1.00
331 World Series 1.50
332 Jeff Bagwell 1.00
333 Andy Pettitte .75
334 Tony Armas Jr. .25
335 Jeromy Burnitz .25
336 Javier Vazquez .25
337 Eric Karros .25
338 Brian Giles .50
339 Scott Rolen 1.00
340 David Justice .50
341 Ray Durham .25
342 Todd Zeile .25
343 Cliff Floyd .25
344 Barry Bonds 4.00
345 Matt Williams .50
346 Steve Finley .25
347 Scott Elarton .25
348 Bernie Williams .75
349 David Wells .25
350 J.T. Snow .25
351 Al Leiter .40
352 Magglio Ordonez .50
353 Raul Mondesi .25
354 Tim Salmon .50
355 Jeff Kent .40
356 Mariano Rivera .50
357 John Olerud .50
358 Javy Lopez .50
359 Ben Grieve .25
360 Ray Lankford .25
361 Ken Griffey Jr. 2.00
362 Rich Aurilia .25
363 Andruw Jones 1.00
364 Ryan Klesko .50
365 Roberto Alomar .75
366 Miguel Tejada .50
367 Mo Vaughn .25
368 Albert Belle .25
369 Jose Canseco .75
370 Kevin Brown .50
371 Rafael Palmeiro .75
372 Mark Redman .25
373 Larry Walker .50
374 Greg Maddux 2.00
375 Nomar Garciaparra 2.50
376 Kevin Millwood .50
377 Edgar Martinez .50
378 Sammy Sosa 2.50
379 Tim Hudson .50
380 Jim Edmonds .50
381 Mike Piazza 2.00
382 Brant Brown .25
383 Brad Fullmer .25
384 Alan Benes .25
385 Mickey Morandini .25
386 Troy Percival .25
387 Eddie Perez .25
388 Vernon Wells .50
389 Ricky Gutierrez .25
390 Rondell White .25
391 Kevin Escobar .25
392 Tony Batista .25
393 Jimmy Haynes .25
394 Billy Wagner .50
395 A.J. Hinch .25
396 Matt Morris .25
397 Lance Berkman .75
398 Jeff D'Amico .25
399 Octavio Dotel .25
400 Olmedo Saenz .25
401 Esteban Loaiza .25
402 Adam Kennedy .25
403 Moises Alou .50
404 Orlando Palmeiro .25
405 Kevin Young .25
406 Tom Goodwin .25
407 Mac Suzuki .25
408 Pat Hentgen .25
409 Kevin Stocker .25
410 Mark Sweeney .25
411 Tony Eusebio .25
412 Edgar Renteria .25

413 John Rocker .25
414 Jose Lima .25
415 Kerry Wood .75
416 Mike Timlin .25
417 Jose Hernandez .25
418 Jeremy Giambi .25
419 Luis Lopez .25
420 Mitch Meluskey .25
421 Garrett Stephenson .25
422 Jamey Wright .25
423 John Jaha .25
424 Placido Polanco .25
425 Marty Cordova .25
426 Joey Hamilton .25
427 Travis Fryman .25
428 Mike Cameron .25
429 Matt Mantei .25
430 Chan Ho Park .25
431 Shawn Estes .25
432 Danny Bautista .25
433 Wilson Alvarez .25
434 Kenny Lofton .40
435 Russ Ortiz .25
436 Dave Burba .25
437 Felix Martinez .25
438 Jeff Shaw .25
439 Mike Difelice .25
440 Roberto Hernandez .25
441 Bryan Rekar .25
442 Ugueth Urbina .25
443 Vinny Castilla .25
444 Carlos Perez .25
445 Juan Guzman .25
446 Ryan Rupe .25
447 Mike Mordecai .25
448 Ricardo Rincon .25
449 Curt Schilling .75
450 Alex Cora .25
451 Turner Ward .25
452 Omar Vizquel .40
453 Russ Branyan .25
454 Russ Johnson .25
455 Gregg Colbrunn .25
456 Charles Nagy .25
457 Wil Cordero .25
458 Jason Tyner .25
459 Devon White .25
460 Kelly Stinnett .25
461 Wilton Guerrero .25
462 Jason Bere .25
463 Calvin Murray .25
464 Miguel Batista .25
465 Erubiel Durazo .25
466 Luis Gonzalez .50
467 Jaret Wright .25
468 Chad Kreuter .25
469 Armando Benitez .25
470 Sidney Ponson .25
471 Adrian Brown .25
472 Sterling Hitchcock .25
473 Timoniel Perez .25
474 Jamie Moyer .25
475 Delino DeShields .25
476 Glendon Rusch .25
477 Chris Gomez .25
478 Adam Eaton .25
479 Pablo Ozuna .25
480 Bob Abreu .50
481 Kris Benson .25
482 Keith Osik .25
483 Darryl Hamilton .25
484 Marlon Anderson .25
485 Jimmy Anderson .25
486 John Halama .25
487 Nelson Figueroa .25
488 Alex Gonzalez .25
489 Benny Agbayani .25
490 Ed Sprague .25
491 Scott Erickson .25
492 Doug Glanville .25
493 Jesus Sanchez .25
494 Mike Lieberthal .25
495 Aaron Sele .25
496 Pat Mahomes .25
497 Ruben Rivera .25
498 Wayne Gomes .25
499 Freddy Garcia .25
500 Al Martin .25
501 Woody Williams .25
502 Paul Byrd .25
503 Rick White .25
504 Trevor Hoffman .25
505 Brady Anderson .25
506 Robert Person .25
507 Jeff Conine .25
508 Chris Truby .25
509 Emil Brown .25
510 Ryan Dempster .25
511 Ruben Mateo .25
512 Alex Ochoa .25
513 Jose Rosado .25
514 Masato Yoshii .25
515 Brian Daubach .25
516 Jeff D'Amico .25
517 Brent Mayne .25
518 John Thomson .25
519 Todd Ritchie .25
520 John Vander Wal .25
521 Neifi Perez .25
522 Chad Curtis .25
523 Kenny Rogers .25
524 Trot Nixon .25
525 Sean Casey .25
526 Wilton Veras .25
527 Troy O'Leary .25
528 Dante Bichette .25
529 Jose Silva .25
530 Darren Oliver .25
531 Steve Parris .25
532 David McCarty .25
533 Todd Walker .25
534 Brian Rose .25
535 Pete Schourek .25
536 Ricky Ledee .25
537 Justin Thompson .25
538 Benito Santiago .25
539 Carlos Beltran .40
540 Gabe White .25
541 Bret Saberhagen .25
542 Ramon Martinez .25
543 John Valentin .25
544 Frank Catalanotto .25
545 Tim Wakefield .25
546 Michael Tucker .25
547 Juan Pierre .25
548 Rich Garces .25
549 Luis Ordaz .25
550 Jerry Spradlin .25
551 Corey Koskie .25
552 Cal Eldred .25
553 Alfonso Soriano 1.50
554 Kip Wells .25
555 Orlando Hernandez .40
556 Bill Simas .25
557 Jim Parque .25
558 Joe Mays .25
559 Tim Belcher .25
560 Shane Spencer .25
561 Glenallen Hill .25
562 Matt LeCroy .25
563 Tino Martinez .25
564 Eric Milton .25
565 Ron Coomer .25
566 Cristian Guzman .25
567 Kazuhiro Sasaki .25
568 Mark Quinn .25
569 Eric Gagne .25
570 Kerry Ligtenberg .25
571 Rolando Arrojo .25
572 Jon Lieber .25
573 Jose Vizcaino .25
574 Jeff Abbott .25
575 Carlos Hernandez .25
576 Scott Sullivan .25
577 Matt Stairs .25
578 Tom Lampkin .25
579 Donnie Sadler .25
580 Desi Relaford .25
581 Scott Downs .25
582 Mike Mussina .75
583 Ramon Ortiz .25
584 Mike Myers .25
585 Frank Castillo .25
586 Manny Ramirez 1.00
587 Alex Rodriguez 3.00
588 Andy Ashby .25
589 Felipe Crespo .25
590 Bobby Bonilla .25
591 Denny Neagle .25
592 Dave Martinez .25
593 Mike Hampton .25
594 Gary DiSarcina .25
595 *Tsuyoshi Shinjo* 2.00
596 *Albert Pujols* 65.00
597 Roy Oswalt, Pat Strange, Jon Rauch .75
598 *Phil Wilson, Jake Peavy, Darwin Cubillan* 10.00
599 Nathan Haynes, Steve Smyth, Mike Bynum .75
600 Joe Lawrence, Choo Freeman, Michael Cuddyer .50
601 Larry Barnes, Dewayne Wise, Carlos Pena .25
602 *Felipe Lopez, Gookie Dawkins, Erick Almonte* 1.00
603 Brad Wilkerson, Alex Escobar, Eric Valent .25
604 Jeff Goldbach, Toby Hall, Rod Barajas (Prospects) .25
605 Marcus Giles, Pablo Ozuna, Jason Romano .25
606 Vernon Wells, Jack Cust, Dee Brown .25
607 Luis Montanez, David Espinosa 1.00
608 *John Lackey, Justin Wayne* 1.50
609 *Josh Axelson, Carmen Cali* 1.00
610 *Shaun Boyd, Chris Morris* 1.00
611 *Dan Moylan, Tommy Arko* 1.00
612 Luis Cotto, Luis Escobar 1.00
613 *Blake Williams, Brandon Mims* 1.00
614 Chris Russ, Bryan Edwards 1.00
615 Joe Torres, Ben Diggins .25
616 *Mark Dalesandro, Edwin Encarnacion* 2.00
617 *Brian Bass, Odannis Ayala* 1.00
618 *Jason Kaanoi, Michael Mathews* .50
619 *Stuart McFarland, Adam Sterrett* 1.00
620 David Krynzel, Grady Sizemore 1.00
621 Keith Bucktrot, Dane Sardinha .25
622 Anaheim Angels .25
623 Arizona Diamondbacks .25
624 Atlanta Braves .25
625 Baltimore Orioles .25
626 Boston Red Sox .25
627 Chicago Cubs .25
628 Chicago White Sox .25
629 Cincinnati Reds .25
630 Cleveland Indians .25
631 Colorado Rockies .25
632 Detroit Tigers .25
633 Florida Marlins .25
634 Houston Astros .25
635 Kansas City Royals .25
636 Los Angeles Dodgers .25
637 Milwaukee Brewers .25
638 Minnesota Twins .25
639 Montreal Expos .25
640 New York Mets .25
641 New York Yankees 1.50
642 Oakland Athletics .25
643 Philadelphia Phillies .25
644 Pittsburgh Pirates .25
645 San Diego Padres .25
646 San Francisco Giants .25
647 Seattle Mariners .25
648 St. Louis Cardinals .25
649 Tampa Bay Devil Rays .25
650 Texas Rangers .25
651 Toronto Blue Jays .25
652 Bucky Dent .25
653 Jackie Robinson 1.50
654 Roberto Clemente 1.50
655 Nolan Ryan 2.50
656 Kerry Wood .75
657 Rickey Henderson .75
658 Lou Brock .50
659 David Wells .25
660 Andruw Jones .75
661 Carlton Fisk .25

Retrofractors

Stars: 3-5X
Inserted 1:12

Combos

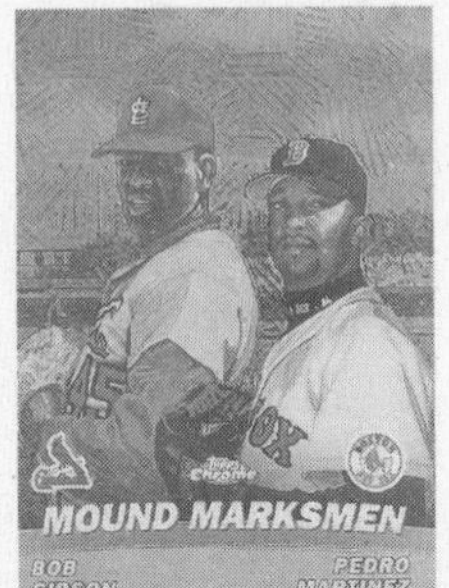

NM/M
Complete Set (20): 80.00
Common Card: 2.00
Inserted 1:12
Refractors: 2-4X
Inserted 1:120
1 Derek Jeter, Yogi Berra, Whitey Ford, Don Mattingly, Reggie Jackson 6.00
2 Chipper Jones, Mike Schmidt 6.00
3 Brooks Robinson, Cal Ripken Jr. 8.00
4 Bob Gibson, Pedro Martinez 3.00
5 Ivan Rodriguez, Johnny Bench 4.00
6 Ernie Banks, Alex Rodriguez 6.00
7 Joe Morgan, Ken Griffey Jr., Barry Larkin 5.00
8 Vladimir Guerrero, Roberto Clemente 6.00
9 Ken Griffey Jr., Hank Aaron 6.00
10 Casey Stengel, Joe Torre 2.00
TC11 Kevin Brown, Sandy Koufax, Don Drysdale 5.00
TC12 Mark McGwire, Sammy Sosa, Roger Marris, Babe Ruth 8.00
TC13 Ted Williams, Carl Yastrzemski, Nomar Garciaparra 8.00
TC14 Greg Maddux, Roger Clemens, Cy Young 5.00
TC15 Tony Gwynn, Ted Williams 6.00
TC16 Cal Ripken Jr., Lou Gehrig 10.00
TC17 Sandy Koufax, Randy Johnson, Warren Spahn, S teve Carlton 4.00
TC18 Mike Piazza, Josh Gibson 5.00
TC19 Barry Bonds, Willie Mays 8.00
TC20 Jackie Robinson, Larry Doby 5.00

Golden Anniversary

NM/M
Complete Set (50): 120.00
Common Player: 1.00
Inserted 1:10
Refractors: 2-4X
Inserted 1:100
1 Hank Aaron 6.00
2 Ernie Banks 3.00
3 Mike Schmidt 5.00
4 Willie Mays 6.00
5 Johnny Bench 4.00
6 Tom Seaver 3.00
7 Frank Robinson 2.00
8 Sandy Koufax 5.00
9 Bob Gibson 3.00
10 Ted Williams 8.00
11 Cal Ripken Jr. 8.00
12 Tony Gwynn 3.00
13 Mark McGwire 6.00
14 Ken Griffey Jr. 4.00
15 Greg Maddux 4.00
16 Roger Clemens 6.00
17 Barry Bonds 8.00
18 Rickey Henderson 1.50
19 Mike Piazza 4.00
20 Jose Canseco 2.00

21 Derek Jeter 6.00
22 Nomar Garciaparra 5.00
23 Alex Rodriguez 5.00
24 Sammy Sosa 5.00
25 Ivan Rodriguez 2.00
26 Vladimir Guerrero 3.00
27 Chipper Jones 4.00
28 Jeff Bagwell 2.00
29 Pedro Martinez 3.00
30 Randy Johnson 3.00
31 Pat Burrell 1.50
32 Josh Hamilton 1.00
33 Ryan Anderson 1.00
34 Corey Patterson 1.50
35 Eric Munson 1.00
36 Sean Burroughs 1.00
37 C.C. Sabathia 1.00
38 Chin-Feng Chen 1.00
39 Barry Zito 1.50
40 Adrian Gonzalez 1.00
41 Mark McGwire 6.00
42 Nomar Garciaparra 5.00
43 Todd Helton 2.00
44 Matt Williams 1.00
45 Troy Glaus 1.50
46 Geoff Jenkins 1.00
47 Frank Thomas 2.00
48 Mo Vaughn 1.00
49 Barry Larkin 1.50
50 J.D. Drew 1.00

King of Kings

NM/M
Common Player: 40.00
Inserted 1:5,175 H
Inserted 1:5,209 R
KKR1 Hank Aaron 80.00
KKR2 Nolan Ryan 120.00
KKR3 Rickey Henderson 40.00
KKR5 Bob Gibson 40.00
KKR6 Nolan Ryan 120.00

Past To Present

NM/M
Complete Set (10): 20.00
Common Player: 1.50
Inserted 1:18
Refractors: 1.5-3X
Inserted 1:180
1 Phil Rizzuto, Derek Jeter 6.00
2 Warren Spahn, Greg Maddux 4.00
3 Yogi Berra, Jorge Posada 3.00
4 Willie Mays, Barry Bonds 6.00
5 Red Schoendienst, Fernando Vina 1.50
6 Duke Snider, Shawn Green 2.00
7 Bob Feller, Bartolo Colon 1.50
8 Johnny Mize, Tino Martinez 1.50
9 Larry Doby, Manny Ramirez 2.00
10 Eddie Mathews, Chipper Jones 3.00

Through The Years

NM/M
Complete Set (50): 200.00
Common Player: 2.00
Inserted 1:10
Refractors: 2-4X
Inserted 1:100
1 Yogi Berra 4.00
2 Roy Campanella 4.00

3 Willie Mays 8.00
4 Andy Pafko 2.00
5 Jackie Robinson 8.00
6 Stan Musial 5.00
7 Duke Snider 4.00
8 Warren Spahn 4.00
9 Ted Williams 10.00
10 Eddie Matthews 4.00
11 Willie McCovey 2.00
12 Frank Robinson 3.00
13 Ernie Banks 5.00
14 Hank Aaron 8.00
15 Sandy Koufax 6.00
16 Bob Gibson 4.00
17 Harmon Killebrew 3.00
18 Whitey Ford 3.00
19 Roberto Clemente 8.00
20 Juan Marichal 2.00
21 Johnny Bench 5.00
22 Willie Stargell 3.00
23 Joe Morgan 2.00
24 Carl Yastrzemski 5.00
25 Reggie Jackson 4.00
26 Tom Seaver 4.00
27 Steve Carlton 3.00
28 Jim Palmer 2.00
29 Rod Carew 3.00
30 George Brett 8.00
31 Roger Clemens 8.00
32 Don Mattingly 8.00
33 Ryne Sandberg 6.00
34 Mike Schmidt 8.00
35 Cal Ripken Jr. 10.00
36 Tony Gwynn 4.00
37 Ozzie Smith 5.00
38 Wade Boggs 3.00
39 Nolan Ryan 10.00
40 Robin Yount 4.00
41 Mark McGwire 8.00
42 Ken Griffey Jr. 5.00
43 Sammy Sosa 6.00
44 Alex Rodriguez 6.00
45 Barry Bonds 8.00
46 Mike Piazza 5.00
47 Chipper Jones 5.00
48 Greg Maddux 5.00
49 Nomar Garciaparra 6.00
50 Derek Jeter 8.00

Topps Originals

NM/M
Common Player: 15.00
Inserted 1:1,783 H
Inserted 1:1,788 R
Refractors 10 sets produced
1 Roberto Clemente 180.00
2 Carl Yastrzemski 60.00
3 Mike Schmidt 75.00
4 Wade Boggs 20.00
5 Chipper Jones 40.00
6 Willie Mays
7 Lou Brock 20.00
8 Dave Parker 15.00
9 Barry Bonds 80.00
10 Alex Rodriguez 50.00

What Could've Been

NM/M
Complete Set (10): 25.00
Common Player: 2.00
Inserted 1:30
Refractors: 2-4X
Inserted 1:300
WCB1 Josh Gibson 6.00
WCB2 Satchel Paige 6.00
WCB3 Buck Leonard 3.00
WCB4 James "Cool Pap Bell 4.00
WCB5 Andrew "Rube" Foster 3.00
WCB6 Martin Dihigo 2.00
WCB7 William "Judy" Johnson 3.00
WCB8 Mule Suttles 2.00
WCB9 Ray Dandridge 2.00
WCB10 John Henry Lloyd 2.00

Before There Was Topps

NM/M
Complete Set (10): 40.00
Common Player: 3.00
Inserted 1:20
Refractors: 2-4X
Inserted 1:200
BT1 Lou Gehrig 8.00
BT2 Babe Ruth 10.00
BT3 Cy Young 5.00
BT4 Walter Johnson 3.00
BT5 Ty Cobb 8.00
BT6 Rogers Hornsby 3.00
BT7 Honus Wagner 4.00
BT8 Christy Mathewson 3.00
BT9 Grover Alexander 3.00
BT10 Joe DiMaggio 8.00

2001 TOPPS FUSION

NM/M
Complete Set (250): 150.00
Common Player: .25
Pack (5): 2.50
Box (24): 50.00
1 Albert Belle .25
2 Albert Belle .25
3 Albert Belle .25
4 Nick Bierbrodt .25
5 Alex Rodriguez 2.50
6 Alex Rodriguez 2.50
7 Alex Rodriguez 2.50
8 Alex Rodriguez 2.50

9 Eric Munson .25
10 Barry Bonds 3.00
11 Andruw Jones .75
12 Antonio Alfonseca .25
13 Andres Galarraga .40
14 Joe Crede .25
15 Barry Larkin .40
16 Barry Bonds 3.00
17 Barry Bonds 3.00
18 Andruw Jones .75
19 C.C. Sabathia .25
20 Bobby Higginson .25
21 Barry Larkin .40
22 Ben Grieve .25
23 Barry Bonds 3.00
24 Corey Patterson .25
25 Carlos Delgado .75
26 Bernie Williams .50
27 Brian Giles .40
28 Barry Larkin .40
29 Gookie Dawkins .25
30 Chipper Jones 1.50
31 Brian Giles .40
32 Carlos Delgado .75
33 Ben Grieve .25
34 Geoff Goetz .25
35 Cristian Guzman .25
36 Cal Ripken Jr. 3.00
37 Chipper Jones 1.50
38 Bernie Williams .50
39 Pablo Ozuna .25
40 Dante Bichette .25
41 Carlos Delgado .75
42 Craig Biggio .25
43 Cal Ripken Jr. 3.00
44 Tim Redding .25
45 Darin Erstad .50
46 Chipper Jones 1.50
47 Darin Erstad .50
48 Carlos Delgado .75
49 Josh Hamilton .25
50 Derek Jeter 3.00
51 Darin Erstad .50
52 Dean Palmer .25
53 Chipper Jones 1.50
54 Chin-Feng Chen .25
55 Edgar Martinez .25
56 Derek Jeter 3.00
57 Derek Jeter 3.00
58 Craig Biggio .25
59 Keith Ginter .25
60 Edgardo Alfonzo .25
61 Edgar Martinez .25
62 Edgardo Alfonzo .25
63 David Justice .50
64 Roy Oswalt .25
65 Eric Karros .25
66 Edgardo Alfonzo .25
67 Frank Thomas 1.00
68 Dean Palmer .25
69 Alfonso Soriano 1.00
70 Fernando Vina .25
71 Frank Thomas 1.00
72 Garret Anderson .40
73 Derek Jeter 3.00
74 Bobby Bradley .25
75 Frank Thomas 1.00
76 Gary Sheffield .50
77 Geoff Jenkins .25
78 Edgar Martinez .25
79 Nick Johnson .25
80 Fred McGriff .40
81 Geoff Jenkins .25
82 Greg Maddux 1.50
83 Edgardo Alfonzo .25
84 *Hee Seop Choi* 3.00
85 Garret Anderson .50
86 Greg Maddux 1.50
87 Ivan Rodriguez .75

88 Eric Karros .25
89 Scott Seabol .25
90 Ivan Rodriguez .75
91 Ivan Rodriguez .75
92 J.D. Drew .25
93 Frank Thomas 1.00
94 Ryan Anderson .25
95 Jason Giambi .75
96 Jason Giambi .75
97 Jason Kendall .25
98 Gary Sheffield .50
99 Milton Bradley .25
100 Jason Kendall .25
101 Jason Kendall .25
102 Jeff Bagwell .75
103 Greg Maddux 1.50
104 Sean Burroughs .25
105 Jay Bell .25
106 Jeff Bagwell .75
107 Jeffrey Hammonds .25
108 Ivan Rodriguez .75
109 Ben Petrick .25
110 Jeff Bagwell .75
111 Jeff Cirillo .25
112 Jermaine Dye .25
113 J.T. Snow Jr. .25
114 Ben Davis .25
115 Jeff Cirillo .25
116 Jeff Kent .25
117 Jeromy Burnitz .25
118 Jay Bell .25
119 Jason Hart .25
120 Jeff Kent .25
121 Jermaine Dye .25
122 John Olerud .25
123 Jeff Bagwell .75
124 *Jeff Segar* .50
125 Jeromy Burnitz .25
126 Jeromy Burnitz .25
127 Johnny Damon .25
128 Jim Edmonds .40
129 *Tim Christman* .50
130 Jim Thome .75
131 Jim Edmonds .40
132 Jorge Posada .50
133 Jim Thome .75
134 *Danny Borrell* .50
135 Johnny Damon .25
136 Jim Thome .75
137 Jose Vidro .25
138 Ken Griffey Jr. 1.50
139 Sean Burnett .25
140 Larry Walker .40
141 Jose Vidro .25
142 Ken Griffey Jr. 1.50
143 Larry Walker .40
144 *Robert Keppell* 1.00
145 Luis Castillo .25
146 Ken Griffey Jr. 1.50
147 Kevin Brown .40
148 Manny Ramirez .75
149 *David Parrish* .25
150 Manny Ramirez .75
151 Kevin Brown .40
152 Luis Castillo .25
153 Mark Grace .50
154 *Mike Jacobs* .50
155 Mark Grace .50
156 Larry Walker .40
157 Magglio Ordonez .40
158 Mark McGwire 2.00
159 Adam Johnson .25
160 Mark McGwire 2.00
161 Magglio Ordonez .50
162 Mark McGwire 2.00
163 Matt Williams .40
164 *Oscar Ramirez* .50
165 Mike Piazza 1.50
166 Manny Ramirez .75
167 Mike Piazza 1.50
168 Mike Mussina .50
169 *Odannis Ayala* .25
170 Mike Sweeney .25
171 Mark McGwire 2.00
172 Nomar Garciaparra 2.50
173 Mike Piazza 1.50
174 J.R. House .25
175 Neifi Perez .25
176 Mike Piazza 1.50
177 Pedro Martinez 1.00
178 Mo Vaughn .25
179 *Shawn Fagan* .50
180 Nomar Garciaparra 2.50
181 Mo Vaughn .25
182 Rafael Palmeiro .50
183 Nomar Garciaparra 2.50
184 *Chris Bass* .75
185 Raul Mondesi .25
186 Nomar Garciaparra 2.50
187 Randy Johnson 1.00
188 Omar Vizquel .25
189 *Erick Almonte* 1.00
190 Ray Durham .25
191 Pedro Martinez 1.00
192 Robb Nen .25
193 Pedro Martinez 1.00
194 *Luis Montanez* 1.00
195 Ray Lankford .25
196 Rafael Palmeiro .50
197 Roberto Alomar .75
198 Rafael Palmeiro .50
199 *Chad Petty* .50
200 Richard Hidalgo .25
201 Randy Johnson 1.00
202 Robin Ventura .25
203 Randy Johnson 1.00
204 Derek Thompson .25
205 Sammy Sosa 2.00
206 Roberto Alomar .75
207 Sammy Sosa 2.00
208 Raul Mondesi .25
209 Scott Heard .25
210 Scott Rolen .75
211 Sammy Sosa 2.00
212 Scott Rolen .75
213 Roberto Alomar .75
214 *Dominic Rich* .50
215 Sean Casey .25
216 Scott Rolen .75
217 Sean Casey .25
218 Robin Ventura .25
219 *William Smith* .50
220 Tim Salmon .40
221 Sean Casey .25
222 Shannon Stewart .25
223 Sammy Sosa 2.00
224 *Joel Pieniero* .50
225 Tino Martinez .25
226 Shawn Green .40
227 Shawn Green .40
228 Scott Rolen .50
229 *Greg Morrison* .50
230 Tony Gwynn 1.00
231 Todd Helton .75
232 Steve Finley .25
233 Scott Williamson .25
234 Talmadge Nunnari .25
235 Tony Womack .25
236 Tony Batista .25
237 Tim Salmon .40
238 Shawn Green .40
239 *Carlos Villalobos* .50
240 Troy Glaus .50
241 Troy Glaus .50
242 Todd Helton .75
243 Tim Salmon .40
244 *Marco Scutaro* .50
245 Troy O'Leary .25
246 Vladimir Guerrero 1.00
247 Vladimir Guerrero 1.00
248 Vladimir Guerrero 1.00
249 Horacio Estrada .25
250 Vladimir Guerrero 1.00

Autographs

NM/M
Common Player: 5.00
Inserted 1:23
1 Rafael Furcal 10.00
2 Mike Lamb 5.00
3 Jason Marquis 5.00
4 Milton Bradley 5.00
5 Barry Zito 20.00
6 Derrek Lee 20.00
7 Corey Patterson 10.00
8 Josh Hamilton 5.00
9 Sean Burroughs 8.00
10 Jason Hart 5.00
11 Luis Montanez 5.00
12 Robert Keppell 5.00
13 Blake Williams 10.00
14 Phil Wilson 5.00
15 Jake Peavy 40.00
16 Alex Rodriguez 70.00
17 Ivan Rodriguez 20.00
18 Don Larsen 20.00
19 Todd Helton 20.00
20 Carlos Delgado 15.00
21 Geoff Jenkins 10.00
22 Willie Stargell 30.00
23 Frank Robinson 30.00
24 Warren Spahn 40.00
25 Harmon Killebrew 30.00
26 Chipper Jones 30.00
27 Chipper Jones 30.00
28 Chipper Jones 30.00
29 Chipper Jones 30.00
30 Chipper Jones 30.00
31 Rocco Baldelli 25.00
32 Keith Ginter 5.00
33 J.R. House 8.00
34 Alex Cabrera 5.00
35 Tony Alvarez 5.00
36 Pablo Ozuna 5.00
37 Juan Salas 5.00

Double Feature

NM/M
Common Duo: 10.00
1 Ivan Rodriguez, Rickey Henderson 40.00
2 John Smoltz, Tom Glavine 15.00
3 Willie Stargell, Frank Thomas 20.00
4 Carlos Delgado, Todd Helton 15.00
5 Adrian Gonzalez, Pat Burrell 15.00
6 Jose Vidro, Roberto Alomar 15.00
7 Chipper Jones, Robin Ventura 20.00
8 J.D. Drew, Matt Lawton 10.00
9 Josh Hamilton, Chin-Feng Chen 25.00
10 Rafael Furcal, Miguel Tejada 15.00
11 Josh Beckett, Ryan Anderson 15.00

Feature

NM/M
Common Player: 4.00
Inserted 1:51
1 Ivan Rodriguez 8.00
2 Rickey Henderson 15.00
3 John Smoltz 5.00
4 Tom Glavine 8.00
5 Willie Stargell 8.00
6 Frank Thomas 8.00
7 Carlos Delgado 8.00
8 Todd Helton 8.00
9 Adrian Gonzalez 5.00
10 Pat Burrell 8.00
11 Jose Vidro 4.00
12 Roberto Alomar 8.00
13 Chipper Jones 10.00
14 Robin Ventura 5.00
15 J.D. Drew 5.00
16 Matt Lawton 4.00
17 Josh Hamilton 4.00
18 Chin-Feng Chen 25.00
19 Rafael Furcal 8.00
20 Miguel Tejada 8.00
21 Josh Beckett 8.00
22 Ryan Anderson 4.00

2001 TOPPS GALLERY

NM/M
Complete Set (152): 75.00
Common Player: .15
Common Rookie: 1.50
Inserted 1:3.5
Common Prospect: .50
Inserted 1:2.5
Common Retired: 1.00
Inserted 1:5
Pack (6): 4.00
Box (24): 75.00
set price includes one Suzuki rookie
1 Darin Erstad .40
2 Chipper Jones 1.50
3 Nomar Garciaparra 2.50
4 Fernando Vina .15
5 Bartolo Colon .25
6 Bobby Higginson .15
7 Antonio Alfonseca .15
8 Mike Sweeney .15
9 Kevin Brown .25
10 Jose Vidro .15
11 Derek Jeter 3.00
12 Jason Giambi .75
13 Pat Burrell .50
14 Jeff Kent .25
15 Alex Rodriguez 2.50
16 Rafael Palmeiro .50
17 Garret Anderson .40
18 Brad Fullmer .15
19 Doug Glanville .15
20 Mark Quinn .15
21 Mo Vaughn .25
22 Andruw Jones .75
23 Pedro Martinez 1.00
24 Ken Griffey Jr. 1.50
25 Roberto Alomar .75
26 Dean Palmer .15
27 Jeff Bagwell .75
28 Jermaine Dye .15
29 Chan Ho Park .15
30 Vladimir Guerrero 1.00
31 Bernie Williams .50
32 Ben Grieve .15
33 Jason Kendall .15
34 Barry Bonds 3.00
35 Jim Edmonds .40
36 Ivan Rodriguez .75
37 Javy Lopez .25
38 J.T. Snow .15
39 Erubiel Durazo .15
40 Terrence Long .15
41 Tim Salmon .25
42 Greg Maddux 1.50
43 Sammy Sosa 2.00
44 Sean Casey .25
45 Jeff Cirillo .15
46 Juan Gonzalez .75
47 Richard Hidalgo .25
48 Shawn Green .25
49 Jeromy Burnitz .15
50 Willie Mays 15.00
51 David Justice .25
52 Tim Hudson .40
53 Brian Giles .25
54 Robb Nen .15
55 Fernando Tatis .15
56 Tony Batista .15
57 Pokey Reese .15
58 Ray Durham .15
59 Greg Vaughn .15
60 Kazuhiro Sasaki .15
61 Troy Glaus .50
62 Rafael Furcal .40
63 Magglio Ordonez .40
64 Jim Thome .75
65 Todd Helton .75

66	Preston Wilson	.15
67	Moises Alou	.25
68	Gary Sheffield	.40
69	Geoff Jenkins	.25
70	Mike Piazza	1.50
71	Jorge Posada	.50
72	Bobby Abreu	.25
73	Phil Nevin	.15
74	John Olerud	.25
75	Mark McGwire	2.00
76	Jose Cruz Jr.	.15
77	David Segui	.15
78	Neifi Perez	.15
79	Omar Vizquel	.25
80	Rick Ankiel	.15
81	Randy Johnson	1.00
82	Albert Belle	.15
83	Frank Thomas	.75
84	Manny Ramirez	.75
85	Larry Walker	.25
86	Luis Castillo	.15
87	Johnny Damon	.25
88	Adrian Beltre	.25
89	Cristian Guzman	.15
90	Jay Payton	.15
91	Miguel Tejada	.40
92	Scott Rolen	.75
93	Ryan Klesko	.40
94	Edgar Martinez	.25
95	Fred McGriff	.25
96	Carlos Delgado	.75
97	Barry Zito	.50
98	Mike Lieberthal	.15
99	Trevor Hoffman	.15
100	Gabe Kapler	.15
101	Edgardo Alfonzo	.15
102	Corey Patterson	.50
103	Alfonso Soriano	1.00
104	Keith Ginter	.50
105	Keith Reed	.50
106	Nick Johnson	.50
107	Carlos Pena	.50
108	Vernon Wells	.50
109	Roy Oswalt	.75
110	Alex Escobar	.50
111	Adam Everett	.50
112	Jimmy Rollins	.50
113	Marcus Giles	.50
114	Jack Cust	.50
115	Chin-Feng Chen	1.00
116	Pablo Ozuna	.50
117	Ben Sheets	.50
118	Adrian Gonzalez	.50
119	Ben Davis	.50
120	Eric Valent	.50
121	Scott Heard	.50
122	*David Parrish*	1.50
123	Sean Burnett	.50
124	Derek Thompson	.50
125	*Tim Christman*	1.50
126	*Mike Jacobs*	1.00
127	*Luis Montanez*	1.50
128	*Chris Bass*	1.50
129	*William Smith*	1.50
130	*Justin Wayne*	2.00
131	*Shawn Fagan*	1.50
132	*Chad Petty*	1.50
133	J.R. House	.50
134	Joel Pineiro	.50
135	*Albert Pujols*	60.00
136	*Carmen Cali*	1.50
137	*Steve Smyth*	1.50
138	John Lackey	.50
139	*Bob Keppel*	1.50
140	*Dominic Rich*	1.50
141	Josh Hamilton	.50
142	Nolan Ryan	5.00
143	Tom Seaver	1.50
144	Reggie Jackson	1.50
145	Johnny Bench	1.50
146	Warren Spahn	1.50
147	Brooks Robinson	1.50
148	Carl Yastrzemski	1.00
149	Al Kaline	1.00
150	Bob Feller	1.00
151a	*Ichiro Suzuki english*	25.00
151b	*Ichiro Suzuki japanese*	25.00

Press Plates

	NM/M
Common Player:	50.00

(See 2001 Topps Gallery for checklist.)

Autographs

		NM/M
Common Autograph:		15.00
Inserted 1:232		
GA-RA	Rick Ankiel	15.00
GA-BB	Barry Bonds	150.00

GA-PB	Pat Burrell	20.00
GA-AG	Adrian Gonzalez	15.00
GA-AR	Alex Rodriguez	100.00
GA-IR	Ivan Rodriguez	50.00

Heritage

		NM/M
Complete Set (10):		30.00
Common Player:		2.00
Inserted 1:12		
GH1	Todd Helton	3.00
GH2	Greg Maddux	4.00
GH3	Pedro Martinez	3.00
GH4	Orlando Cepeda	2.00
GH5	Willie McCovey	2.00
GH6	Ken Griffey Jr.	4.00
GH7	Alex Rodriguez	6.00
GH8	Derek Jeter	8.00
GH9	Mark McGwire	6.00
GH10	Vladimir Guerrero	3.00

Heritage Relic

		NM/M
Common Player:		10.00
Inserted 1:133		
	Orlando Cepeda	10.00
	Greg Maddux	25.00
	Pedro Martinez	20.00
	Willie McCovey	10.00

Heritage Autographed Relic

		NM/M
Production 25 sets		
	Orlando Cepeda	75.00
	Willie McCovey	100.00

Originals Relics

		NM/M
Common Player:		8.00
Inserted 1:133		

GR-RA	Roberto Alomar	10.00
GR-JD	Jermaine Dye	8.00
GR-DE	Darin Erstad	8.00
GR-JG	Jason Giambi	10.00
GR-AG	Adrian Gonzalez	8.00
GR-SG	Shawn Green	10.00
GR-AJ	Andruw Jones	10.00
GR-JK	Jason Kendall	8.00
GR-JFK	Jeff Kent	8.00
GR-RP	Rafael Palmeiro	10.00
GR-PR	Pokey Reese	8.00
GR-SS	Sammy Sosa	20.00
GR-RV	Robin Ventura	8.00
GR-BW	Bernie Williams	10.00
GR-PW	Preston Wilson	8.00

Star Gallery

		NM/M
Complete Set (10):		15.00
Common Player:		1.00
Inserted 1:8		
SG1	Vladimir Guerrero	1.00
SG2	Alex Rodriguez	2.50
SG3	Derek Jeter	3.00
SG4	Nomar Garciaparra	2.50
SG5	Ken Griffey Jr.	1.50
SG6	Mark McGwire	2.00
SG7	Chipper Jones	1.50
SG8	Sammy Sosa	2.00
SG9	Barry Bonds	3.00
SG10	Mike Piazza	1.50

Team Topps Legends Autographs

		NM/M
Common Autograph:		10.00
Inserted 1:286		
TT23R	Gil McDougald	10.00
TT27F	Andy Pafko	20.00
TT10R	Frank Robinson	20.00
TT28F	Herb Score	10.00
TT25R	Luis Tiant	10.00

2001 TOPPS GOLD LABEL

		NM/M
Complete Set (115):		80.00
Common Player:		.25
Common Rookie:		4.00
Production 999		
Golds:		2-3X
Production 999		
Gold Rookies:		2-3X
Production 99		
Pack (5):		3.00
Box (24):		50.00
1	Adrian Beltre	.40
2	*Danny Borrell*	4.00
3	Albert Belle	.25
4	Alex Cabrera	.25
5	Alex Rodriguez	2.50
6	Andruw Jones	.75
7	Antonio Alfonseca	.25
8	Barry Bonds	3.00
9	Barry Larkin	.50
10	Ben Grieve	.25
11	Ben Molina	.25
12	Bernie Williams	.50
13	Bobby Abreu	.40
14	Bobby Higginson	.25
15	Brad Fullmer	.25
16	Brian Giles	.40
17	Cal Ripken Jr.	3.00
18	Carlos Delgado	.75
19	*Chad Petty*	4.00
20	Charles Johnson	.25
21	Chipper Jones	1.50
22	Cristian Guzman	.25
23	Darin Erstad	.40
24	David Justice	.40
25	David Segui	.25
26	Derek Jeter	2.50
27	Edgar Martinez	.40
28	Edgardo Alfonzo	.25
29	Fernando Tatis	.25
30	Eric Karros	.25
31	Eric Munson	.25
32	Eric Young	.25
33	Frank Thomas	.75
34	Fernando Vina	.25
35	Garret Anderson	.50
36	Gary Sheffield	.50
37	Geoff Jenkins	.40
38	Greg Maddux	1.50
39	Ivan Rodriguez	.75
40	J.D. Drew	.40
41	J.R. House	.25
42	J.T. Snow Jr.	.25
43	Jason Giambi	.75
44	Jason Kendall	.40
45	Jay Payton	.25
46	Jeff Bagwell	.75
47	Jeff Cirillo	.25
48	Jeff Kent	.40
49	Chan Ho Park	.25
50	Jermaine Dye	.25
51	Jeromy Burnitz	.25
52	Jim Edmonds	.50
53	Jim Thome	.75
54	John Olerud	.50
55	Johnny Damon	.40
56	Jorge Posada	.50
57	Jose Cruz Jr.	.25
58	Jose Vidro	.25
59	Josh Hamilton	.25
60	Juan Gonzalez	.75
61	*Steve Smyth*	4.00
62	*Justin Wayne*	8.00
63	Kazuhiro Sasaki	.25
64	Ken Griffey Jr.	1.50
65	Kevin Brown	.40
66	Kevin Young	.25
67	Larry Walker	.40
68	Luis Castillo	.25
69	Steve Finley	.25
70	Magglio Ordonez	.50
71	Manny Ramirez	.75
72	Mark McGwire	2.50
73	Mark Quinn	.25
74	Miguel Tejada	.50
75	Mike Piazza	1.50
76	Mike Sweeney	.25
77	Mo Vaughn	.25
78	Moises Alou	.40
79	Nomar Garciaparra	2.00
80	Pat Burrell	.50
81	Paul Konerko	.25
82	Pedro Martinez	1.00
83	Phil Nevin	.25
84	Preston Wilson	.25
85	Rafael Furcal	.25
86	Todd Zeile	.25
87	Randy Johnson	1.00
88	Travis Lee	.25
89	Carl Everett	.25
90	Quilvio Veras	.25
91	Rick Ankiel	.25

92	*Rick Brosseau*	4.00
93	*Robert Keppell*	4.00
94	Roberto Alomar	.50
95	Ryan Klesko	.40
96	Sammy Sosa	2.00
97	Scott Heard	4.00
98	Scott Rolen	.75
99	Sean Casey	.50
100	Shawn Green	.40
101	Terrence Long	.25
102	Tim Salmon	.40
103	Todd Helton	.75
104	Tom Glavine	.50
105	Tony Batista	.25
106	*Travis Baptist*	4.00
107	Troy Glaus	.50
108	*Victor Hall*	4.00
109	Vladimir Guerrero	1.00
110	Tim Hudson	.40
111	*Brian Roberts*	4.00
112	*Virgil Chevalier*	4.00
113	*Fernando Rodney*	4.00
114	*Paul Phillips*	4.00
115	*Cesar Bolivar*	4.00

Class 2

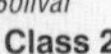

Stars:	1-2X
Inserted 1:4	
Rookies:	1-1.5X
Production 699	
Golds:	2-3X
Production 699	
Gold Rookies:	2-3X
Production 69	

(See 2001 Topps Gold Label for checklist and base card values.)

Class 3

Stars:	2-3X
Inserted 1:12	
Rookies:	1-2X
Production 299	
Golds:	3-5X
Production 299	
Gold Rookies:	2-4X
Production 29	

(See 2001 Topps Gold Label for checklist and base card values.)

Masterpiece

	NM/M
Common Player:	50.00

(See 2001 Topps Gold Label for checklist.)

Gold Fixtures

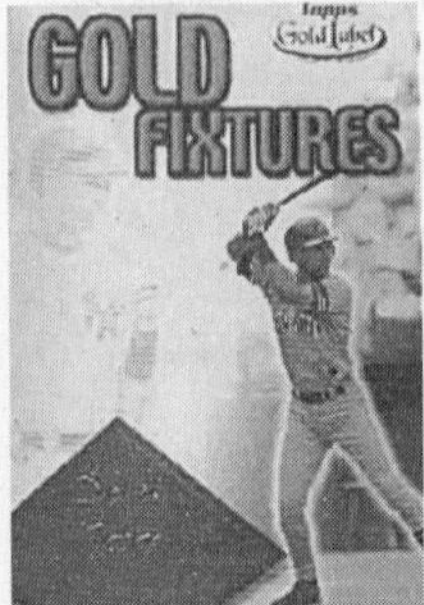

	NM/M
Complete Set (10):	150.00
Common Player:	8.00
Inserted 1:374	

1	Alex Rodriguez	20.00
2	Mark McGwire	20.00
3	Derek Jeter	25.00
4	Nomar Garciaparra	20.00
5	Chipper Jones	15.00
6	Sammy Sosa	20.00
7	Ken Griffey Jr.	15.00
8	Carlos Delgado	8.00
9	Frank Thomas	10.00
10	Barry Bonds	25.00

MLB Awards Ceremony

	NM/M
Common Player:	4.00
Inserted 1:24	

SA	Sandy Alomar bat	4.00
JB	Jeff Bagwell bat	8.00
AB	Albert Belle bat	4.00
CB	Carlos Beltran bat	4.00
DB	Dante Bichette	4.00
BB	Barry Bonds jersey	25.00
BB	Barry Bonds bat	25.00
SB	Scott Brosius bat	5.00
JC	Jose Canseco jersey	6.00
JC	Jose Canseco bat	6.00
WC	Will Clark bat	6.00
RC	Roger Clemens jersey	20.00
MC	Marty Cordova bat	4.00
RF	Rafael Furcal bat	6.00
AG	Andres Galarraga bat	4.00
NG	Nomar Garciaparra jsy	20.00
NG	Nomar Garciaparra bat	20.00
JG	Jason Giambi bat	8.00
TG	Troy Glaus bat	8.00
TG	Tom Glavine jsy	6.00
JG	Juan Gonzalez jsy	8.00
JG	Juan Gonzalez bat	8.00
DG	Dwight Gooden jsy	4.00
BG	Ben Grieve jsy	4.00
KG	Ken Griffey Jr. jsy	15.00
KG	Ken Griffey Jr. bat	15.00
TG	Tony Gwynn bat	10.00
TH	Todd Helton bat	8.00
RH	Rickey Henderson jsy	15.00
TH	Todd Hollandsworth bat	4.00
DJ	Derek Jeter bat	25.00
RJ	Randy Johnson jsy	10.00
CJ	Chipper Jones jsy	10.00
DJ	David Justice jsy	5.00
JK	Jeff Kent bat	4.00
CK	Chuck Knoblauch bat	4.00
BL	Barry Larkin bat	8.00
GM	Greg Maddux jsy	15.00
EM	Edgar Martinez bat	6.00
PM	Pedro Martinez jsy	10.00
FM	Fred McGriff bat	5.00
MM	Mark McGwire bat	60.00
MM	Mark McGwire jsy	60.00
RM	Raul Mondesi bat	4.00
HN	Hideo Nomo jsy	25.00
JO	John Olerud bat	4.00
PO	Paul O'Neill bat	5.00
MP	Mike Piazza bat	12.00
CR	Cal Ripken Jr. jsy	35.00
AR	Alex Rodriguez bat	15.00
IR	Ivan Rodriguez jsy	8.00
SR	Scott Rolen jsy	8.00
TS	Tim Salmon jsy	4.00
KS	Kazuhiro Sasaki jsy	5.00
GS	Gary Sheffield bat	6.00
JS	John Smoltz jsy	4.00
SS	Sammy Sosa bat	15.00
SS	Sammy Sosa jsy	15.00
DS	Darryl Strawberry jsy	4.00
DS	Darryl Strawberry bat	4.00
FT	Frank Thomas bat	8.00
FT	Frank Thomas jsy	8.00
MV	Mo Vaughn jsy	4.00
MV	Mo Vaughn bat	4.00
LW	Larry Walker bat	5.00
LW	Larry Walker jsy	5.00
JW	John Wetteland jsy	4.00
BW	Bernie Williams bat	8.00
MW	Matt Williams bat	5.00

2001 TOPPS HERITAGE

	NM/M
Complete Set (407):	300.00

Complete Master Set (487):	375.00
Common Player:	.50
Common SP (311-407):	2.50
Inserted 1:2	
Pack (8):	10.00
Box (24):	200.00

1	Kris Benson	.50
2	Brian Jordan	.50
3	Fernando Vina	.50
4	Mike Sweeney	.50
5	Rafael Palmeiro	2.00
6	Paul O'Neill	1.00
7	Todd Helton	2.50
8	Ramiro Mendoza	.50
9	Kevin Millwood	1.00
10	Chuck Knoblauch	.75
11	Derek Jeter	10.00
12	Alex Rodriguez	8.00
13	Geoff Jenkins	.75
14	David Justice	1.00
15	David Cone	.50
16	Andres Galarraga	1.00
17	Garret Anderson	1.00
18	Roger Cedeno	.50
19	Randy Velarde	.50
20	Carlos Delgado	2.00
21	Quilvio Veras	.50
22	Jose Vidro	.50
23	Corey Patterson	.75
24	Jorge Posada	1.00
25	Eddie Perez	.50
26	Jack Cust	.50
27	Sean Burroughs	.75
28	Randy Wolf	.50
29	Mike Lamb	.50
30	Rafael Furcal	.75
31	Barry Bonds	8.00
32	Tim Hudson	.75
33	Tom Glavine	1.50
34	Javy Lopez	.75
35	Aubrey Huff	.50
36	Wally Joyner	.50
37	Magglio Ordonez	1.00
38	Matt Lawton	.50
39	Mariano Rivera	1.00
40	Andy Ashby	.50
41	Mark Buehrle	3.00
42	Esteban Loaiza	.50
43	Mark Redman	.50
44	Mark Quinn	.50
45	Tino Martinez	.75
46	Joe Mays	.50
47	Walt Weiss	.50
48	Roger Clemens	6.00
49	Greg Maddux	5.00
50	Richard Hidalgo	.75
51	Orlando Hernandez	.75
52	Chipper Jones	5.00
53	Ben Grieve	.50
54	Jimmy Haynes	.50
55	Ken Caminiti	.50
56	Tim Salmon	1.00
57	Andy Pettitte	1.00
58	Darin Erstad	1.00
59	Marquis Grissom	.50
60	Raul Mondesi	.75
61	Bengie Molina	.50
62	Miguel Tejada	1.00
63	Jose Cruz Jr.	.50
64	Billy Koch	.50
65	Troy Glaus	2.00
66	Cliff Floyd	.50
67	Tony Batista	.50
68	Jeff Bagwell	2.50
69	Billy Wagner	.50
70	Eric Chavez	.75
71	Troy Percival	.50
72	Andruw Jones	2.50
73	Shane Reynolds	.50
74	Barry Zito	2.50
75	Roy Halladay	1.00
76	David Wells	.50
77	Jason Giambi	1.50
78	Scott Elarton	.50
79	Moises Alou	.75
80	Adam Piatt	.75
81	Wilton Veras	.50
82	Darryl Kile	.50
83	Johnny Damon	.50
84	Tony Armas Jr.	.50
85	Ellis Burks	.50
86	Jamey Wright	.50
87	Jose Vizcaino	.50
88	Bartolo Colon	.50
89	*Carmen Cali*	.50
90	Kevin Brown	.75
91	Josh Hamilton	.50
92	Jay Buhner	.50
93	*Scott Pratt*	.50
94	Alex Cora	.50
95	*Luis Montanez*	1.00
96	Dmitri Young	.50
97	J.T. Snow Jr.	.50
98	Damion Easley	.50
99	Greg Norton	.50
100	Matt Wheatland	.50
101	Chin-Feng Chen	.50
102	Tony Womack	.50
103	Adam Kennedy	.50
104	J.D. Drew	.50
105	Carlos Febles	.50
106	Jim Thome	1.00
107	Danny Graves	.50
108	Dave Mlicki	.50
109	Ron Coomer	.50
110	James Baldwin	.50
111	*Shaun Boyd*	.75
112	Brian Bohannon	.50
113	Jacque Jones	.50
114	Alfonso Soriano	1.50
115	Tony Clark	.50
116	Terrence Long	.50
117	Todd Hundley	.50
118	Kazuhiro Sasaki	.50
119	*Brian Sellier*	.50
120	John Olerud	.75
121	Javier Vazquez	.50
122	Sean Burnett	.50
123	Matt LeCroy	.50
124	Erubiel Durazo	.50
125	Juan Encarnacion	.50
126	Pablo Ozuna	.50
127	Russ Ortiz	.50
128	David Segui	.50
129	Mark McGwire	3.00
130	Mark Grace	1.00
131	Fred McGriff	.75
132	Carl Pavano	.50
133	Derek Thompson	.50
134	Shawn Green	.75
135	B.J. Surhoff	.50
136	Michael Tucker	.50
137	Jason Isringhausen	.50
138	Eric Milton	.50
139	Mike Stodolka	.50
140	Milton Bradley	.50
141	Curt Schilling	.75
142	Sandy Alomar	.50
143	Brent Mayne	.50
144	Todd Jones	.50
145	Charles Johnson	.50
146	Dean Palmer	.50
147	Masato Yoshii	.50
148	Edgar Renteria	.50
149	Joe Randa	.50
150	Adam Johnson	.50
151	Greg Vaughn	.50
152	Adrian Beltre	.75
153	Glenallen Hill	.50
154	*David Parrish*	.75
155	Neifi Perez	.50
156	Pete Harnisch	.50
157	Paul Konerko	.50
158	Dennys Reyes	.50
159	Jose Lima	.50
160	Eddie Taubensee	.50
161	Miguel Cairo	.50
162	Jeff Kent	.75
163	Dustin Hermanson	.50
164	Alex Gonzalez	.50
165	Hideo Nomo	.75
166	Sammy Sosa	2.00
167	C.J. Nitkowski	.50
168	Cal Eldred	.50
169	Jeff Abbott	.50
170	Jim Edmonds	.75
171	Mark Mulder	.75
172	*Dominic Rich*	.50

173	Ray Lankford	.50
174	*Danny Borrell*	.75
175	Rick Aguilera	.50
176	Shannon Stewart	.50
177	Steve Finley	.50
178	Jim Parque	.50
179	Kevin Appier	.50
180	Adrian Gonzalez	.75
181	Tom Goodwin	.50
182	Kevin Tapani	.50
183	Fernando Tatis	.50
184	Mark Grudzielanek	.50
185	Ryan Anderson	.50
186	Jeffrey Hammonds	.50
187	Corey Koskie	.50
188	Brad Fullmer	.50
189	Rey Sanchez	.50
190	Michael Barrett	.50
191	Rickey Henderson	1.00
192	Jermaine Dye	.50
193	Scott Brosius	.50
194	Matt Anderson	.50
195	Brian Buchanan	.50
196	Derrek Lee	.50
197	Larry Walker	.75
198	David Krynzel	.50
199	Vinny Castilla	.50
200	Ken Griffey Jr.	2.00
201	Matt Stairs	.50
202	Ty Howington	.50
203	Andy Benes	.50
204	Luis Gonzalez	.75
205	Brian Moehler	.50
206	Harold Baines	.50
207	Pedro Astacio	.50
208	Cristian Guzman	.50
209	Kip Wells	.50
210	Frank Thomas	1.00
211	Jose Rosado	.50
212	Vernon Wells	.50
213	Bobby Higginson	.50
214	Juan Gonzalez	1.00
215	Omar Vizquel	.75
216	Bernie Williams	1.00
217	Aaron Sele	.50
218	Shawn Estes	.50
219	Roberto Alomar	1.00
220	Rick Ankiel	.50
221	Josh Kalinowski	.50
222	David Bell	.50
223	Keith Foulke	.50
224	Craig Biggio	.75
225	*Shawn Fagan*	.50
226	Scott Williamson	.50
227	Ron Belliard	.50
228	Chris Singleton	.50
229	Alex Serrano	.50
230	Deivi Cruz	.50
231	Eric Munson	.50
232	Luis Castillo	.50
233	Edgar Martinez	.75
234	Jeff Shaw	.50
235	Jeromy Burnitz	.50
236	Richie Sexson	.75
237	Will Clark	1.00
238	Ron Villone	.50
239	Kerry Wood	1.00
240	Rich Aurilia	.50
241	Mo Vaughn	.50
242	Travis Fryman	.75
243	Manny Ramirez	1.00
244	Chris Stynes	.50
245	Ray Durham	.50
246	*Juan Uribe*	.50
247	Juan Guzman	.50
248	Lee Stevens	.50
249	Devon White	.50
250	*Kyle Lohse*	1.50
251	Bryan Wolff	.50
252	*Rick Brousseau*	.50
253	Eric Young	.50
254	Freddy Garcia	.50
255	Jay Bell	.50
256	Steve Cox	.50
257	Torii Hunter	.75
258	Jose Canseco	.75
259	Brad Ausmus	.50
260	Jeff Cirillo	.50
261	Brad Penny	.50
262	Antonio Alfonseca	.50
263	Russ Branyan	.50
264	Scott Heard	.50
265	John Lackey	.50
266	*Justin Wayne*	1.00
267	Brad Radke	.50
268	Todd Stottlemyre	.50
269	Mark Loretta	.50
270	Matt Williams	.50
271	Kenny Lofton	.50
272	Jeff D'Amico	.50
273	Jamie Moyer	.50
274	Darren Dreifort	.50
275	Denny Neagle	.50
276	Orlando Cabrera	.50
277	Chuck Finley	.50
278	Miguel Batista	.50
279	Carlos Beltran	.50
280	Eric Karros	.50
281	Mark Kotsay	.50
282	Ryan Dempster	.50
283	Barry Larkin	.75
284	Jeff Suppan	.50
285	Gary Sheffield	.75
286	Jose Valentin	.50
287	Robb Nen	.50
288	Chan Ho Park	.50
289	John Halama	.50
290	*Steve Smyth*	.50
291	Gerald Williams	.50
292	Preston Wilson	.50
293	*Victor Hall*	.75
294	Ben Sheets	.50
295	Eric Davis	.50
296	Kirk Rueter	.50
297	*Chad Petty*	.75
298	Kevin Millar	.50
299	Marvin Benard	.50
300	Vladimir Guerrero	1.00
301	Livan Hernandez	.50
302	*Travis Baptist*	.75
303	Bill Mueller	.50
304	Mike Cameron	.50
305	Randy Johnson	1.50
306	*Alan Mahaffey*	.50
307	Timo Perez (no facsimile autograph)	.50
308	Pokey Reese	.50
309	Ryan Rupe	.50
310	Carlos Lee	.50
311	Doug Glanville	2.50
312	Jay Payton	2.50
313	Troy O'Leary	2.50
314	Francisco Cordero	2.50
315	Rusty Greer	2.50
316	Cal Ripken Jr.	25.00
317	Ricky Ledee	2.50
318	Brian Daubach	2.50
319	Robin Ventura	3.00
320	Todd Zeile	3.00
321	Francisco Cordova	2.50
322	Henry Rodriguez	2.50
323	Pat Meares	2.50
324	Glendon Rusch	2.50
325	Keith Osik	2.50
326	*Robert Keppell*	4.00
327	Bobby Jones	2.50
328	Alex Ramirez	2.50
329	Robert Person	2.50
330	Ruben Mateo	2.50
331	Rob Bell	2.50
332	Carl Everett	2.50
333	Jason Schmidt	3.00
334	Scott Rolen	5.00
335	Jimmy Anderson	2.50
336	Bret Boone	3.00
337	Delino DeShields	2.50
338	Trevor Hoffman	2.50
339	Bob Abreu	3.00
340	Mike Williams	2.50
341	Mike Hampton	3.00
342	John Wetteland	2.50
343	Scott Erickson	2.50
344	Enrique Wilson	2.50
345	Tim Wakefield	2.50
346	Mike Lowell	2.50
347	Todd Pratt	2.50
348	Brook Fordyce	2.50
349	Benny Agbayani	2.50
350	Gabe Kapler	3.00
351	Sean Casey	3.00
352	Darren Oliver	2.50
353	Todd Ritchie	2.50
354	Kenny Rogers	2.50
355	Jason Kendall	3.00
356	John Vander Wal	2.50
357	Ramon Martinez	2.50
358	Edgardo Alfonzo	2.50
359	Phil Nevin	2.50
360	Albert Belle	2.50
361	Ruben Rivera	2.50
362	Pedro Martinez	10.00
363	Derek Lowe	2.50
364	Pat Burrell	5.00
365	Mike Mussina	5.00
366	Brady Anderson	2.50
367	Darren Lewis	2.50
368	Sidney Ponson	2.50
369	Adam Eaton	2.50
370	Eric Owens	2.50
371	Aaron Boone	2.50
372	Matt Clement	2.50
373	Derek Bell	2.50
374	Trot Nixon	2.50
375	Travis Lee	2.50
376	Mike Benjamin	2.50
377	Jeff Zimmerman	2.50
378	Mike Lieberthal	2.50
379	Rick Reed	2.50
380	Nomar Garciaparra	15.00
381	Omar Daal	2.50
382	Ryan Klesko	3.00
383	Rey Ordonez	2.50
384	Kevin Young	2.50
385	Rick Helling	2.50
386	Brian Giles	4.00
387	Tony Gwynn	8.00
388	Ed Sprague	2.50
389	J.R. House	2.50
390	Scott Hatteberg	2.50
391	John Valentin	2.50
392	Melvin Mora	2.50
393	Royce Clayton	2.50
394	Jeff Fassero	2.50
395	Manny Alexander	2.50
396	John Franco	2.50
397	Luis Alicea	2.50
398	Ivan Rodriguez	5.00
399	Kevin Jordan	2.50
400	Jose Offerman	2.50
401	Jeff Conine	2.50
402	Seth Etherton	2.50
403	Mike Bordick	2.50
404	Al Leiter	3.00
405	Mike Piazza	10.00
406	Armando Benitez	2.50
407	Warren Morris	2.50

Chrome

		NM/M
Common Player:		3.00
Production 552 sets		
1	Cal Ripken Jr.	40.00
2	Jim Thome	10.00
3	Derek Jeter	40.00
4	Andres Galarraga	4.00
5	Carlos Delgado	8.00
6	Roberto Alomar	8.00
7	Tom Glavine	8.00
8	Gary Sheffield	5.00
9	Mo Vaughn	3.00
10	Preston Wilson	3.00
11	Mike Mussina	8.00
12	Greg Maddux	30.00
13	Ivan Rodriguez	10.00
14	Al Leiter	3.00
15	Seth Etherton	3.00
16	Edgardo Alfonzo	3.00
17	Richie Sexson	3.00
18	Andruw Jones	10.00
19	Bartolo Colon	3.00
20	Darin Erstad	5.00
21	Kevin Brown	4.00
22	Mike Sweeney	3.00
23	Mike Piazza	30.00
24	Rafael Palmeiro	10.00
25	Terrence Long	3.00
26	Kazuhiro Sasaki	3.00
27	John Olerud	5.00
28	Mark McGwire	30.00
29	Fred McGriff	5.00
30	Todd Helton	10.00
31	Curt Schilling	5.00
32	Alex Rodriguez	30.00
33	Jeff Kent	4.00
34	Pat Burrell	8.00
35	Jim Edmonds	6.00
36	Mark Mulder	3.00
37	Troy Glaus	8.00
38	Jay Payton	3.00
39	Jermaine Dye	3.00
40	Larry Walker	5.00
41	Ken Griffey Jr.	30.00
42	Jeff Bagwell	10.00
43	Rick Ankiel	3.00
44	Mark Redman	3.00
45	Edgar Martinez	3.00
46	Mike Hampton	4.00
47	Manny Ramirez	10.00
48	Ray Durham	3.00
49	Rafael Furcal	3.00
50	Sean Casey	4.00
51	Jose Canseco	10.00
52	Barry Bonds	40.00
53	Tim Hudson	5.00
54	Barry Zito	10.00
55	Chuck Finley	3.00
56	Magglio Ordonez	4.00
57	David Wells	3.00
58	Jason Giambi	8.00
59	Tony Gwynn	15.00
60	Vladimir Guerrero	15.00
61	Randy Johnson	15.00
62	Bernie Williams	8.00
63	Craig Biggio	5.00
64	Jason Kendall	3.00
65	Pedro Martinez	15.00
66	Mark Quinn	3.00
67	Frank Thomas	15.00
68	Nomar Garciaparra	30.00
69	Brian Giles	5.00
70	Shawn Green	5.00
71	Roger Clemens	25.00
72	Sammy Sosa	30.00
73	Juan Gonzalez	10.00
74	Orlando Hernandez	4.00
75	Chipper Jones	20.00
76	Josh Hamilton	3.00
77	Adam Johnson	3.00
78	Shaun Boyd	3.00
79	Alfonso Soriano	15.00
80	Derek Thompson	3.00
81	Adrian Gonzalez	3.00
82	Ryan Anderson	3.00
83	Corey Patterson	5.00
84	J.R. House	3.00
85	Sean Burroughs	3.00
86	Scott Heard	3.00
87	John Lackey	3.00
88	Ben Sheets	4.00
89	Wilson Betemit	3.00
90	Robert Keppell	3.00
91	Luis Montanez	3.00
92	Sean Burnett	3.00
93	Justin Wayne	5.00
94	Eric Munson	3.00
95	Steve Smyth	3.00
96	Rick Brousseau	3.00
97	Carmen Cali	3.00
98	Brian Sellier	3.00
99	David Parrish	3.00
100	Danny Borrell	3.00
101	Chad Petty	3.00
102	Dominic Rich	3.00
103	Shawn Fagan	3.00
104	Alex Serrano	3.00
105	Juan Uribe	3.00
106	Travis Baptist	3.00
107	Alan Mahaffey	3.00
108	Kyle Lohse	4.00
109	Victor Hall	3.00
110	Scott Pratt	3.00

Classic Renditions

		NM/M
Complete Set (10):		15.00
Common Player:		1.00
Inserted 1:5		
1	Mark McGwire	2.50
2	Nomar Garciaparra	2.00
3	Barry Bonds	3.00
4	Sammy Sosa	2.00
5	Chipper Jones	1.50
6	Pat Burrell	1.00
7	Frank Thomas	1.00
8	Manny Ramirez	1.00
9	Derek Jeter	3.00
10	Ken Griffey Jr.	2.00

Clubhouse Collection Game-used

		NM/M
Common Player:		25.00
MM	Minnie Monoso	25.00
RS	Red Schoendienst	30.00
DS	Duke Snider	40.00
EM	Eddie Mathews	40.00

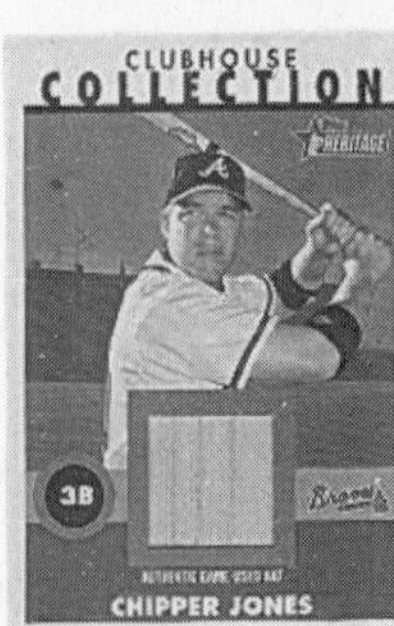

CJ	Chipper Jones	40.00
RA	Richie Ashburn	30.00
FT	Frank Thomas	40.00
FV	Fernando Vina	25.00
SG	Shawn Green	30.00
WM	Willie Mays	150.00
BB	Barry Bonds	80.00
SR	Scott Rolen	40.00

Clubhouse Collection Autographs

		NM/M
Common Player:		
MM	Minnie Monoso/25	120.00
RS	Red Schoendienst/25	150.00
DS	Duke Snider	

Clubhouse Collection Dual Game-used

		NM/M
Common Card:		75.00
Production 52 sets		
MMFT	Minnie Monoso, Frank Thomas	100.00
RSFV	Red Schoendienst, Fernando Vina	75.00
DSSG	Duke Snider, Shawn Green	150.00
RAPB	Richie Ashburn, Scott Rolen	100.00
EMCJ	Eddie Mathews, Chipper Jones	125.00
WMBB	Willie Mays, Barry Bonds	300.00
1:20,000 packs; numbered to 25 each		
CRA-BB	Barry Bonds	650.00
CRA-CJ	Chipper Jones	350.00
CRA-NG	Nomar Garciaparra	450.00

Grandstand Glory

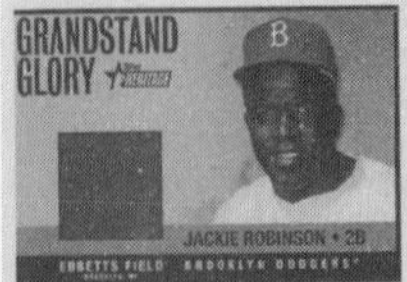

		NM/M
Common Player:		20.00
Inserted 1:211		
PR	Phil Rizzuto	30.00
YB	Yogi Berra	30.00
RA	Richie Ashburn	20.00
RR	Robin Roberts	20.00
WM	Willie Mays	60.00
NF	Nellie Fox	20.00
JR	Jackie Robinson	50.00

New Age Performers

		NM/M
Complete Set (15):		20.00
Common Player:		1.00
Inserted 1:8		
1	Mike Piazza	1.50
2	Sammy Sosa	2.00
3	Alex Rodriguez	2.50
4	Barry Bonds	3.00
5	Ken Griffey Jr.	1.50
6	Chipper Jones	1.50
7	Randy Johnson	1.00
8	Derek Jeter	3.00
9	Nomar Garciaparra	2.00
10	Mark McGwire	2.50
11	Jeff Bagwell	1.00
12	Pedro Martinez	1.00
13	Todd Helton	1.00
14	Vladimir Guerrero	1.00
15	Greg Maddux	2.00

Real One Autographs

		NM/M
Common Player:		20.00
Current MLB Players		
200 Blue-inked produced		
52 Red-inked produced		
Prices listed for Blue sigs		
RH	Richard Hidalgo	40.00
TL	Terrence Long	30.00
CD	Carlos Delgado	50.00
CJ	Chipper Jones	100.00
TG	Tom Glavine	75.00
GJ	Geoff Jenkins	40.00
JM	Joe Mays	25.00
FV	Fernando Vina	25.00
CP	Corey Patterson	40.00
JV	Jose Vidro	25.00
BB	Barry Bonds	300.00
AR	Alex Rodriguez	160.00
AH	Aubrey Huff	25.00
SPB	Sean Burroughs	25.00
RW	Randy Wolf	30.00
KB	Kris Benson	25.00
ML	Mike Lamb	20.00
TH	Todd Helton	60.00
MQ	Mark Quinn	20.00
MS	Mike Sweeney	25.00
ML	Matt Lawton	35.00
MO	Magglio Ordonez	40.00
MB	Mark Buehrle	25.00
MR	Mark Redman	20.00
CF	Cliff Floyd	25.00
NG	Nomar Garciaparra	125.00
1952 MLB Players		
MV	Mickey Vernon	25.00
HB	Hank Bauer	80.00
DD	Dom DiMaggio	90.00
LD	Larry Doby	80.00
JG	Joe Garagiola	60.00
DG	Dick Groat	40.00
MI	Monte Irvin	50.00
VL	Vernon Law	25.00
EM	Eddie Matthews	200.00
WM	Willie Mays	200.00
GM	Gil McDougald	40.00
MM	Minnie Monoso	80.00
AP	Andy Pafko	50.00
PFR	Phil Rizzuto	100.00
PR	Preacher Roe	100.00
JS	Johnny Sain	60.00
HS	Hank Sauer	40.00
RS	Red Schoendienst	40.00
BS	Bobby Shantz	30.00
CS	Curt Simmons	30.00
ES	Enos Slaughter	75.00
DS	Duke Snider	150.00
WS	Warren Spahn	100.00
BT	Bobby Thomson	75.00
HW	Hoyt Wilhelm	75.00
RR	Robin Roberts	75.00

Time Capsule

		NM/M
Common Player:		20.00

Inserted 1:369		
WM	Willie Mays	75.00
TW	Ted Williams	85.00
DN	Don Newcombe	20.00
WF	Whitey Ford	30.00
WMTW	Ted Williams, Willie Mays/52	200.00

Then and Now

		NM/M
Complete Set (10):		15.00
Common Player:		1.50
Inserted 1:8		
1	Yogi Berra, Mike Piazza	1.50
2	Duke Snider, Sammy Sosa	2.00
3	Willie Mays, Ken Griffey Jr.	2.00
4	Phil Rizzuto, Derek Jeter	3.00
5	Pee Wee Reese, Nomar Garciaparra	2.00
6	Jackie Robinson, Alex Rodriguez	2.50
7	Johnny Mize, Mark McGwire	2.50
8	Bob Feller, Pedro Martinez	1.50
9	Robin Roberts, Greg Maddux	2.00
10	Warren Spahn, Randy Johnson	1.50

2001 TOPPS HD

		NM/M
Complete Set (120):		50.00
Common Player:		.25
Common (101-120):		1.00
Inserted 1:6		
Pack (4):		2.50
Box (20):		40.00
1	Derek Jeter	3.00
2	Magglio Ordonez	.50
3	Eric Munson	.25
4	Jermaine Dye	.25
5	Larry Walker	.40
6	Pokey Reese	.25
7	Pedro Martinez	1.00
8	Rafael Palmeiro	.75
9	Jason Kendall	.40
10	Mike Lieberthal	.25
11	Ryan Klesko	.40
12	Cal Ripken Jr.	3.00
13	Mike Piazza	1.50
14	*Adam Sterrett*	.75
15	John Olerud	.40
16	Manny Ramirez	.75
17	*Chad Petty*	.75
18	Vladimir Guerrero	1.00
19	Kevin Brown	.40
20	*Luis Cotto*	.50
21	Josh Hamilton	.25
22	Mark Grace	.50
23	Mark McGwire	2.50
24	Jeromy Burnitz	.25
25	Andruw Jones	.75
26	Raul Mondesi	.40
27	*Stuart McFarland*	.50
28	Craig Biggio	.40
29	Troy Glaus	.50
30	Carlos Delgado	.75
31	Rafael Furcal	.40
32	J.D. Drew	.25
33	Corey Patterson	.40
34	Gary Sheffield	.50
35	Jeff Kent	.40
36	Alex Rodriguez	2.50
37	Edgardo Alfonzo	.25
38	*Jeff Segar*	.50
39	Bobby Abreu	.40
40	Brian Giles	.40
41	*Jason Smith*	.40
42	Mo Vaughn	.25
43	Pat Burrell	.50
44	Barry Larkin	.50
45	Carlos Beltran	.50
46	*Eric Mosley*	.50
47	Alfonso Soriano	1.00
48	Tim Salmon	.40
49	Jason Giambi	.75
50	Greg Maddux	1.50
51	Randy Johnson	1.00
52	Jose Vidro	.25
53	Edgar Martinez	.40
54	Albert Belle	.25
55	Ivan Rodriguez	.75
56	Sean Casey	.25
57	Jorge Posada	.50
58	Preston Wilson	.25
59	Paul Konerko	.25
60	Todd Helton	.75
61	*Dominic Rich*	.50
62	Tony Gwynn	1.00
63	Bernie Williams	.75
64	*Anthony Brewer*	.50
65	Shawn Green	.50
66	Jeff Bagwell	.75
67	Jose Cruz Jr.	.25
68	Darin Erstad	.40
69	Jim Edmonds	.50
70	Frank Thomas	.75
71	Ryan Anderson	.25
72	Scott Rolen	.75
73	Jeff Cirillo	.25
74	*Chris Bass*	.50
75	*William Smith*	.50
76	Trot Nixon	.25
77	Bobby Bradley	.25
78	*Odannis Ayala*	.50
79	Jim Thome	.75
80	Sammy Sosa	2.00
81	Geoff Jenkins	.40
82	Ben Grieve	.25
83	Andres Galarraga	.40
84	Rick Ankiel	.25
85	Barry Bonds	3.00
86	Alex Gonzalez	.25
87	Sean Burroughs	.25
88	Nomar Garciaparra	2.00
89	Ken Griffey Jr.	1.50
90	Tim Hudson	.50
91	Chipper Jones	1.50
92	Matt Williams	.40
93	Roberto Alomar	.75
94	Adrian Gonzalez	.40
95	Juan Gonzalez	.75
96	*Brian Bass*	.50
97	*Rick Brosseau*	.50
98	Mariano Rivera	.40
99	James Baldwin	.25
100	Dean Palmer	.25
101	Pedro Martinez	2.00
102	Randy Johnson	2.00
103	Greg Maddux	3.00
104	Sammy Sosa	4.00
105	Mark McGwire	5.00
106	Ivan Rodriguez	1.50

107	Mike Piazza	3.00
108	Chipper Jones	3.00
109	Vladimir Guerrero	2.00
110	Alex Rodriguez	5.00
111	Ken Griffey Jr.	3.00
112	Cal Ripken Jr.	6.00
113	Derek Jeter	6.00
114	Barry Bonds	6.00
115	Nomar Garciaparra	4.00
116	Jeff Bagwell	1.50
117	Todd Helton	1.50
118	Darin Erstad	1.00
119	Shawn Green	1.00
120	Roberto Alomar	1.00

Platinum

Stars (1-100): 4-8X
Stars (101-120): 2-4X
Production 199 sets

Autographed Cards

		NM/M
Common Player:		10.00
Inserted 1:431		
1	Todd Helton	25.00
2	Rick Ankiel	10.00
3	Mark Quinn	10.00
4	Adrian Gonzalez	10.00

Game Defined

		NM/M
Complete Set (10):		25.00
Common Player:		1.50
Inserted 1:24		
Platinum:		1.5-2X
Inserted 1:72		
1	Ken Griffey Jr.	3.00
2	Derek Jeter	5.00
3	Sammy Sosa	3.00
4	Mark McGwire	4.00
5	Todd Helton	1.50
6	Mike Piazza	3.00
7	Chipper Jones	2.50
8	Vladimir Guerrero	1.50
9	Alex Rodriguez	4.00
10	Nomar Garciaparra	3.00

Game-Worn Jersey

		NM/M
Common Card:		5.00
Inserted 1:108		
Cards 5-8 are redemptions		
1	Grant Roberts	5.00
2	Vernon Wells	10.00
3	Travis Dawkins	5.00
4	Ramon Ortiz	5.00
5	Steve Finley	5.00
6	Ramon Hernandez	5.00
7	Jay Payton	8.00
8	Jeromy Burnitz	5.00

Images of Excellence

		NM/M
Complete Set (10):		15.00
Common Player:		1.00
Inserted 1:8		
Platinum:		1.5-2X
Inserted 1:24		
1	Willie Mays	2.50
2	Reggie Jackson	1.00
3	Ernie Banks	1.50
4	Hank Aaron	2.50
5	Ted Williams	2.50
6	Mike Schmidt	2.00
7	Tom Seaver	1.00
8	Johnny Bench	1.50
9	George Brett	2.50
10	Nolan Ryan	3.00

20-20

		NM/M
Complete Set (10):		15.00
Common Player:		.50
Inserted 1:12		
Platinum:		1.5-2X
Inserted 1:36		
1	Barry Bonds	4.00
2	Chipper Jones	2.00
3	Ken Griffey Jr.	2.00
4	Alex Rodriguez	3.00
5	Ivan Rodriguez	1.00
6	Sammy Sosa	2.50
7	Roberto Alomar	.75
8	Larry Walker	.50
9	Shawn Green	.75
10	Jeff Bagwell	1.00

2001 TOPPS OPENING DAY

		NM/M
Complete Set (165):		35.00
Common Player:		.15
Pack (7):		1.00
Box (24):		20.00
1	Cal Ripken Jr.	2.50
2	Chipper Jones	1.50
3	Garret Anderson	.40
4	Robin Ventura	.20
5	Jermaine Dye	.15
6	Jim Thome	.75
7	Brian Jordan	.15
8	Shawn Green	.40
9	Juan Gonzalez	.75
10	Paul O'Neill	.25
11	Pokey Reese	.15
12	Mike Mussina	.40
13	Jay Buhner	.15
14	Shane Reynolds	.15
15	Adam Piatt	.15
16	Preston Wilson	.15
17	Ellis Burks	.15
18	Chuck Finley	.15
19	Shannon Stewart	.15
20	Mark McGwire	2.00
21	Mark Loretta	.15
22	Bobby Jones	.15
23	Matt Clement	.15
24	Pedro J. Martinez	1.00
25	Carlos Lee	.15
26	John Franco	.15
27	Andres Galarraga	.25
28	Jose Cruz Jr.	.15
29	Randy Johnson	.75
30	Richie Sexson	.40
31	Darin Erstad	.30
32	Manny Ramirez	.75
33	Mike Sweeney	.15
34	John Wetteland	.15
35	Derek Jeter	2.50
36	J.D. Drew	.15
37	Rick Reed	.15
38	Jay Bell	.15
39	Fred McGriff	.25
40	Orlando Cabrera	.15
41	Eric Owens	.15
42	Jorge Posada	.40
43	Jeff Cirillo	.15
44	Johnny Damon	.25
45	Charles Johnson	.15
46	Pat Burrell	.40
47	Gary Sheffield	.40
48	Tom Glavine	.30
49	Ivan Rodriguez	.75
50	Chuck Knoblauch	.15
51	Jason Kendall	.15
52	Carlos Delgado	.60
53	Roger Clemens	1.50
54	Brad Penny	.15
55	Troy Glaus	.75
56	Mike Hampton	.15
57	Carlos Febles	.15
58	Seth Etherton	.15
59	Fernando Tatis	.15
60	Livan Hernandez	.15
61	Barry Larkin	.30
62	Alex Rodriguez	2.00
63	Warren Morris	.15
64	Antonio Alfonseca	.15
65	Edgardo Alfonzo	.15
66	Fernando Vina	.15
67	Jason Giambi	.75
68	Matt Lawton	.15
69	Rusty Greer	.15
70	Tony Gwynn	1.00
71	Carl Everett	.15
72	Bret Boone	.25
73	James Baldwin	.15
74	Greg Vaughn	.15
75	Darren Dreifort	.15
76	Frank Thomas	1.00
77	Luis Castillo	.15
78	Bartolo Colon	.25
79	Craig Biggio	.25
80	Jose Vidro	.15
81	Todd Helton	.75
82	Jacque Jones	.15
83	Robb Nen	.15
84	Richard Hidalgo	.15
85	Tony Womack	.15
86	Rick Ankiel	.15
87	Terrence Long	.15
88	Brad Radke	.15
89	Gabe Kapler	.15
90	Pedro Astacio	.15
91	Darryl Kile	.15
92	Jay Payton	.15
93	Vladimir Guerrero	1.00
94	Juan Encarnacion	.15
95	Ramon Hernandez	.15
96	Sandy Alomar	.15
97	Geoff Jenkins	.25
98	Rafael Furcal	.25
99	Mark Grace	.25
100	Mark Mulder	.25
101	Jim Edmonds	.40
102	Tim Salmon	.25
103	Jeff Bagwell	.75
104	Jose Canseco	.40
105	Ben Grieve	.15
106	Ryan Klesko	.25
107	Javy Lopez	.25
108	Greg Maddux	1.50
109	Andruw Jones	.50
110	Jeromy Burnitz	.15
111	Ray Lankford	.15
112	Sammy Sosa	1.50
113	Raul Mondesi	.25
114	Mike Piazza	1.50
115	Todd Zeile	.15
116	Eric Karros	.15
117	Barry Bonds	2.50
118	J.T. Snow	.15
119	Jeff Kent	.15
120	David Justice	.25
121	Matt Williams	.25
122	Brian Giles	.25
123	Edgar Martinez	.15
124	Ken Griffey Jr.	1.50
125	Al Leiter	.25
126	Kevin Brown	.25
127	John Olerud	.25
128	Roberto Alomar	.50
129	Rafael Palmeiro	.40
130	Steve Finley	.15
131	Tim Hudson	.40
132	Scott Rolen	.75
133	Nomar Garciaparra	1.50
134	Mo Vaughn	.15
135	Larry Walker	.30
136	Albert Belle	.15
137	Ray Durham	.15
138	Andy Pettitte	.40
139	Mariano Rivera	.25
140	Bernie Williams	.50
141	David Wells	.15
142	Magglio Ordonez	.40
143	Kevin Millwood	.15
144	Cliff Floyd	.15
145	Rich Aurilia	.15
146	Eric Chavez	.15
147	Scott Elarton	.15
148	Tony Armas Jr.	.15
149	Mark Redman	.15
150	Javier Vazquez	.15
151	Adrian Gonzalez, Adam Johnson	.50
152	Mike Stodolka, Sean Burnett	.15
153	David Walling, Ben Sheets	.50
154	Chin-Feng Chen, Corey Patterson, Josh Hamilton	.25
155	Mark McGwire	1.00
156	Bobby Thomson	.15
157	Bill Mazeroski	.15
158	Cal Ripken Jr.	1.00
159	Hank Aaron	1.00
160	Bucky Dent	.15
161	Jackie Robinson	1.00
162	Roberto Clemente	1.00
163	Nolan Ryan	1.00
164	Kerry Wood	.25
165	Checklist	.15

Autographs

		NM/M
Common Autograph:		20.00
TH	Todd Helton	40.00
CJ	Chipper Jones	100.00
MO	Magglio Ordonez	25.00
CP	Corey Patterson	20.00

2001 TOPPS RESERVE

		NM/M
Complete Set (151):		
Common Player:		.40
Common SP (101-150):		4.00
Production 1,500		
Sealed Hobby Box (10):		150.00
1	Darin Erstad	.50
2	Moises Alou	.50
3	Tony Batista	.40
4	Andruw Jones	.75
5	Edgar Renteria	.40
6	Eric Young	.40
7	Steve Finley	.40
8	Adrian Beltre	.40
9	Vladimir Guerrero	1.00
10	Barry Bonds	3.00
11	Juan Gonzalez	.75
12	Jay Buhner	.40
13	Luis Castillo	.40
14	Cal Ripken Jr.	3.00
15	Bob Abreu	.40
16	Ivan Rodriguez	.75
17	Nomar Garciaparra	2.00
18	Todd Helton	.75

19 Bobby Higginson .40
20 Jorge Posada .50
21 Tim Salmon .50
22 Jason Giambi .75
23 Jose Cruz Jr. .40
24 Chipper Jones 1.50
25 Jim Edmonds .50
26 Gerald Williams .40
27 Randy Johnson 1.00
28 Gary Sheffield .50
29 Jeff Kent .40
30 Jim Thome .75
31 John Olerud .50
32 Cliff Floyd .40
33 Mike Lowell .40
34 Phil Nevin .40
35 Scott Rolen .75
36 Alex Rodriguez 2.50
37 Ken Griffey Jr. 2.00
38 Neifi Perez .40
39 Christian Guzman .40
40 Mariano Rivera .40
41 Troy Glaus .75
42 Johnny Damon .40
43 Rafael Furcal .40
44 Jeromy Burnitz .40
45 Mark McGwire 2.00
46 Fred McGriff .40
47 Matt Williams .40
48 Kevin Brown .40
49 J.T. Snow .40
50 Kenny Lofton .40
51 Al Martin .40
52 Antonio Alfonseca .40
53 Edgardo Alfonzo .40
54 Ryan Klesko .40
55 Pat Burrell .50
56 Rafael Palmeiro .75
57 Sean Casey .40
58 Jeff Cirillo .40
59 Ray Durham .40
60 Derek Jeter 3.00
61 Jeff Bagwell .75
62 Carlos Delgado .75
63 Tom Glavine .50
64 Richie Sexson .50
65 J.D. Drew .40
66 Ben Grieve .40
67 Mark Grace .50
68 Shawn Green .40
69 Robb Nen .40
70 Omar Vizquel .40
71 Edgar Martinez .40
72 Preston Wilson .40
73 Mike Piazza 1.50
74 Tony Gwynn 1.00
75 Jason Kendall .40
76 Manny Ramirez .75
77 Pokey Reese .40
78 Mike Sweeney .40
79 Magglio Ordonez .50
80 Bernie Williams .75
81 Richard Hidalgo .40
82 Brad Fullmer .40
83 Greg Maddux 2.00
84 Geoff Jenkins .40
85 Sammy Sosa 2.00
86 Luis Gonzalez .50
87 Eric Karros .40
88 Jose Vidro .40
89 Rich Aurilia .40
90 Roberto Alomar .75
91 Mike Cameron .40
92 Mike Mussina .60
93 Albert Belle .40
94 Mike Lieberthal .40
95 Brian Giles .40
96 Pedro Martinez 1.00
97 Barry Larkin .50
98 Jermaine Dye .40
99 Frank Thomas .75
100 David Justice .50
101 *Gary Johnson* 4.00
102 *Matt Ford* 4.00
103 *Albert Pujols* 100.00
104 Brad Cresse 4.00
105 *Valentino Pascucci* 4.00
106 *Bob Keppel* 4.00
107 *Luis Torres* 4.00
108 *Tony Blanco* 6.00
109 *Ronnie Corona* 4.00
110 *Phil Wilson* 4.00
111 *John Buck* 4.00
112 *Jim Journell* 4.00
113 *Victor Hall* 4.00
114 *Jeff Andra* 4.00
115 *Greg Nash* 4.00
116 *Travis Hafner* 12.00
117 *Casey Fossum* 4.00
118 Miguel Olivo 4.00
119 *Elpidio Guzman* 4.00
120 *Jason Belcher* 4.00
121 *Esix Snead* 4.00
122 *Joe Thurston* 4.00
123 *Rafael Soriano* 6.00
124 *Ed Rogers* 4.00
125 *Omar Beltre* 4.00
126 *Brett Gray* 4.00
127 *Deivi Mendez* 4.00
128 *Freddie Bynum* 4.00
129 David Kryznel 4.00
130 *Blake Williams* 4.00
131 *Reggie Abercrombie* 4.00
132 *Miguel Villilo* 4.00
133 *Ryan Madson* 8.00
134 *Matt Thompson* 4.00
135 *Mark Burnett* 4.00
136 *Andy Beal* 4.00
137 *Ryan Ludwick* 6.00
138 *Roberto Miniel* 4.00
139 *Steve Smyth* 4.00
140 *Ben Washburn* 4.00
141 *Marvin Seale* 4.00
142 *Reggie Griggs* 4.00
143 *Seung Song* 4.00
144 *Chad Petty* 4.00
145 *Noel Devarez* 4.00
146 *Matt Butler* 4.00
147 *Brett Evert* 4.00
148 Cesar Izturis 4.00
149 *Troy Farnsworth* 4.00
150 *Brian Schmitt* 4.00
151 *Ichiro Suzuki* 50.00

Rookie Autographed Baseballs

NM/M

Common Player: 10.00
Inserted 1:box w/holder

Reggie Abercrombie 10.00
Jeff Andra 10.00
Andy Beal 10.00
Jason Belcher 10.00
Omar Beltre 10.00
Tony Blanco 15.00
John Buck 15.00
Mark Burnett 10.00
Freddie Bynum 10.00
Ronnie Corona 10.00
Noel Devarez 10.00
Matt Ford 10.00
Casey Fossum 15.00
Brett Gray 10.00
Reggie Griggs 10.00
Elpidio Guzman 10.00
Travis Hafner 40.00
Victor Hall 10.00
Gary Johnson 10.00
Jim Journell 10.00
Bob Keppel 15.00
David Kryznel 15.00
Ryan Ludwick 15.00
Ryan Madson 15.00
Deivi Mendez 10.00
Roberto Miniel 10.00
Greg Nash 10.00
Miguel Olivo
Valentino Pascucci
Chad Petty 10.00
Albert Pujols 400.00
Ed Rogers 10.00
Marvin Seale 10.00
Steve Smyth 10.00
Esix Snead 10.00
Seung Song 10.00
Rafael Soriano 15.00
Matt Thompson 10.00
Joe Thurston 10.00
Luis Torres 10.00
Miguel Villilo 10.00
Ben Washburn 10.00
Blake Williams
Phil Wilson

Rookie Graded Autograph

NM/M

Common Rookie: 10.00
Inserted 1:box
Prices for PSA 8
PSA 9s: 1.5X

Reggie Abercrombie 10.00
Jeff Andra 10.00
Andy Beal 10.00
Jason Belcher 10.00
Omar Beltre 10.00
Tony Blanco 10.00
John Buck 10.00
Mark Burnett 10.00
Freddie Bynum 10.00
Ronnie Corona 10.00
Noel Devarez 10.00
Matt Ford 10.00
Casey Fossum 15.00
Brett Gray 10.00
Reggie Griggs 10.00
Elpidio Guzman 10.00
Travis Hafner 25.00
Victor Hall 10.00
Gary Johnson 10.00
Jim Journell 10.00
Bob Keppel
David Kryznel 10.00
Ryan Ludwick 20.00
Ryan Madson 10.00
Deivi Mendez 10.00
Roberto Miniel 10.00
Greg Nash 10.00
Miguel Olivo 10.00
Valentino Pascucci 10.00
Chad Petty 10.00
Albert Pujols 250.00
Ed Rogers 10.00
Marvin Seale 10.00
Steve Smyth 10.00
Esix Snead 10.00
Seung Song 10.00
Rafael Soriano 15.00
Matt Thompson 10.00
Joe Thurston 15.00
Luis Torres 10.00
Miguel Villilo 10.00
Ben Washburn 10.00
Blake Williams 10.00
Phil Wilson 10.00

Game-Worn Uniform

NM/M

Common Player: 4.00
Inserted 1:box

RA Roberto Alomar 8.00
BB Barry Bonds 25.00
CD Carlos Delgado 8.00
JE Jim Edmonds 6.00
NG Nomar Garciaparra 15.00
JG Juan Gonzalez 8.00
SG Shawn Green 5.00
VG Vladimir Guerrero 8.00
TG Tony Gwynn 10.00
TH Todd Helton 8.00
RJ Randy Johnson 8.00
CJ Chipper Jones 10.00
DJ David Justice 4.00
GM Greg Maddux 15.00
PM Pedro Martinez 8.00
RP Rafael Palmeiro 8.00
AR Alex Rodriguez 15.00
IR Ivan Rodriguez 8.00
SR Scott Rolen 8.00
FT Frank Thomas 8.00

Game-Used Bat

NM/M

Common Player: 4.00
Inserted 1:box

JB Jeff Bagwell 8.00
BB Barry Bonds 25.00
CD Carlos Delgado 6.00
JE Jim Edmonds 6.00
DE Darin Erstad 4.00
RF Rafael Furcal 4.00
NG Nomar Garciaparra 20.00
VG Vladimir Guerrero 10.00
TG Tony Gwynn 10.00
CJ Chipper Jones 10.00
MP Mike Piazza 15.00
AR Alex Rodriguez 15.00
IR Ivan Rodriguez 8.00
BW Bernie Williams 8.00

2001 TOPPS STARS

NM/M

Complete Set (200): 40.00
Common Player: .15
Pack (6): 4.00
Box (24): 80.00

1 Darin Erstad .25
2 Luis Gonzalez .25
3 Rafael Furcal .25
4 Dante Bichette .15
5 Sammy Sosa 1.25
6 Ken Griffey Jr. 1.00
7 Jim Thome .50
8 Bobby Higginson .15
9 Cliff Floyd .15
10 Lance Berkman .25
11 Eric Karros .15
12 Jeromy Burnitz .15
13 Jose Vidro .15
14 Benny Agbayani .15
15 Jorge Posada .40
16 Ramon Hernandez .15
17 Jason Kendall .25
18 Jeff Kent .25
19 John Olerud .25
20 Al Martin .15
21 Gerald Williams .15
22 Gabe Kapler .15
23 Carlos Delgado .50
24 Mariano Rivera .25
25 Javy Lopez .25
26 Paul Konerko .15
27 Daryle Ward .15
28 Mike Lieberthal .15
29 Tom Goodwin .15
30 Garret Anderson .40
31 Steve Finley .15

32	Brian Jordan	.15
33	Nomar Garciaparra	1.50
34	Ray Durham	.15
35	Sean Casey	.25
36	Kenny Lofton	.25
37	Dean Palmer	.15
38	Jeff Bagwell	.50
39	Mike Sweeney	.15
40	Adrian Beltre	.25
41	Richie Sexson	.40
42	Vladimir Guerrero	.75
43	Derek Jeter	2.00
44	Miguel Tejada	.25
45	Doug Glanville	.15
46	Brian Giles	.25
47	Marvin Benard	.15
48	Edgar Martinez	.25
49	Edgar Renteria	.15
50	Fred McGriff	.25
51	Ivan Rodriguez	.50
52	Brad Fullmer	.15
53	Antonio Alfonseca	.15
54	Tom Glavine	.40
55	Warren Morris	.15
56	Johnny Damon	.25
57	Dmitri Young	.15
58	Mo Vaughn	.15
59	Randy Johnson	.75
60	Greg Maddux	1.00
61	Carl Everett	.15
62	Magglio Ordonez	.25
63	Pokey Reese	.15
64	Todd Helton	.50
65	Preston Wilson	.15
66	Richard Hidalgo	.15
67	Jermaine Dye	.15
68	Gary Sheffield	.40
69	Geoff Jenkins	.25
70	Edgardo Alfonzo	.15
71	Paul O'Neill	.25
72	Terrence Long	.15
73	Bob Abreu	.25
74	Kevin Young	.15
75	J.T. Snow	.15
76	Alex Rodriguez	1.50
77	Jim Edmonds	.25
78	Mark McGwire	1.50
79	Tony Batista	.15
80	Darrin Fletcher	.15
81	Robb Nen	.15
82	Jose Offerman	.15
83	Travis Fryman	.25
84	Joe Randa	.15
85	Omar Vizquel	.25
86	Tim Salmon	.25
87	Andruw Jones	.50
88	Albert Belle	.15
89	Manny Ramirez	.50
90	Frank Thomas	.50
91	Barry Larkin	.40
92	Neifi Perez	.15
93	Luis Castillo	.15
94	Moises Alou	.25
95	Mark Quinn	.15
96	Kevin Brown	.25
97	Cristian Guzman	.15
98	Mike Piazza	1.00
99	Bernie Williams	.40
100	Jason Giambi	.50
101	Scott Rolen	.75
102	Phil Nevin	.15
103	Rich Aurilia	.15
104	Mike Cameron	.15
105	Fernando Vina	.15
106	Greg Vaughn	.15
107	Jose Cruz	.15
108	Raul Mondesi	.15
109	Ben Molina	.15
110	Pedro Martinez	.75
111	Todd Hollandsworth	.15
112	Jacque Jones	.15
113	Rickey Henderson	.25
114	Troy Glaus	.40
115	Chipper Jones	1.00
116	Delino DeShields	.15
117	Eric Young	.15
118	Jose Valentin	.15
119	Roberto Alomar	.40
120	Jeff Cirillo	.15
121	Mike Lowell	.15
122	Julio Lugo	.15
123	Shawn Green	.25
124	Marquis Grissom	.15
125	Matt Lawton	.15
126	Jay Payton	.15
127	David Justice	.25
128	Eric Chavez	.25
129	Pat Burrell	.50
130	Ryan Klesko	.25
131	Barry Bonds	2.00
132	Jay Buhner	.15
133	J.D. Drew	.25
134	Rafael Palmeiro	.50
135	Shannon Stewart	.15
136	Juan Gonzalez	.50
137	Tony Womack	.15
138	Carlos Lee	.15
139	Derrek Lee	.15
140	Ben Grieve	.15
141	Ron Belliard	.15
142	Stan Musial	1.50
143	Ernie Banks	1.00
144	Jim Palmer	.50
145	Tony Perez	.25
146	Duke Snider	.50
147	Rod Carew	.40
148	Warren Spahn	.75
149	Yogi Berra	.75
150	Juan Marichal	.25
151	Eric Munson	.15
152	Carlos Pena	.15
153	Joe Crede	.15
154	Ryan Anderson	.15
155	Milton Bradley	.15
156	Sean Burroughs	.15
157	Corey Patterson	.25
158	C.C. Sabathia	.15
159	Ben Petrick	.15
160	Aubrey Huff	.15
161	Gookie Dawkins	.15
162	Ben Sheets	.25
163	Pablo Ozuna	.15
164	Eric Valent	.15
165	Rod Barajas	.15
166	Chin-Feng Chen	.40
167	Josh Hamilton	.25
168	Keith Ginter	.15
169	Vernon Wells	.25
170	Dernell Stenson	.15
171	Alfonso Soriano	.75
172	Jason Marquis	.15
173	Nick Johnson	.15
174	Adam Everett	.15
175	Jimmy Rollins	.15
176	Ben Diggins	.15
177	John Lackey	.15
178	Scott Heard	.15
179	*Brian Hitchcox*	.50
180	*Odannis Ayala*	.50
181	*Scott Pratt*	.50
182	*Greg Runser*	.50
183	*Chris Russ*	.50
184	Derek Thompson	.50
185	*Jason Jones*	.50
186	*Dominic Rich*	.50
187	*Chad Petty*	.50
188	*Steve Smyth*	.50
189	*Bryan Hebson*	.50
190	*Danny Borrell*	.50
191	*Bob Keppel*	.50
192	*Justin Wayne*	1.00
193	*Reggie Abercrombie*	.75
194	*Travis Baptist*	.50
195	*Shawn Fagan*	.50
196	*Jose Reyes*	4.00
197	*Chris Bass*	.50
198	*Albert Pujols*	50.00
199	*Luis Cotto*	.50
200	*Jake Peavy*	4.00

Gold

Stars: 2-5X
Production 499 sets

Onyx

Stars: 6-12X
Rookies: 4-6X
Production 99 sets

Autographs

		NM/M
Common Player:		15.00
Inserted 1:353		
EB	Ernie Banks	50.00
YB	Yogi Berra	40.00
RC	Rod Carew	30.00
CD	Carlos Delgado	15.00
TH	Todd Helton	30.00
JM	Juan Marichal	30.00
EM	Eric Munson	10.00
SM	Stan Musial	80.00
JP	Jim Palmer	25.00
TP	Tony Perez	25.00
IR	Ivan Rodriguez	30.00
DS	Duke Snider	35.00
WS	Warren Spahn	40.00

Game Gear Bats

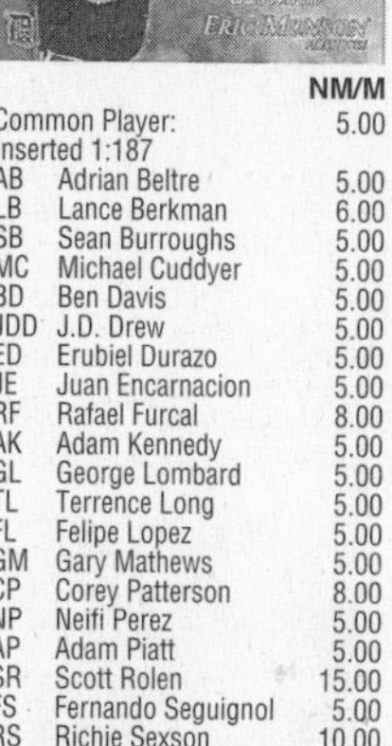

		NM/M
Common Player:		5.00
Inserted 1:187		
AB	Adrian Beltre	5.00
LB	Lance Berkman	6.00
SB	Sean Burroughs	5.00
MC	Michael Cuddyer	5.00
BD	Ben Davis	5.00
JDD	J.D. Drew	5.00
ED	Erubiel Durazo	5.00
JE	Juan Encarnacion	5.00
RF	Rafael Furcal	8.00
AK	Adam Kennedy	5.00
GL	George Lombard	5.00
TL	Terrence Long	5.00
FL	Felipe Lopez	5.00
GM	Gary Mathews	5.00
CP	Corey Patterson	8.00
NP	Neifi Perez	5.00
AP	Adam Piatt	5.00
SR	Scott Rolen	15.00
FS	Fernando Seguignol	5.00
RS	Richie Sexson	10.00

Game Gear Jerseys

		NM/M
Common Player:		4.00
Inserted 1:61		
EA	Edgardo Alfonzo	4.00
RA	Roberto Alomar	8.00
BB	Barry Bonds	25.00
LC	Luis Castillo	4.00
TG	Tony Gwynn	10.00
TH	Todd Helton	8.00
AJ	Andruw Jones	8.00
CJ	Chipper Jones	10.00
EM	Edgar Martinez	8.00
MO	Magglio Ordonez	5.00
MP	Mike Piazza	15.00
SS	Sammy Sosa	25.00
SHS	Shannon Stewart	4.00
FT	Frank Thomas	8.00
JV	Jose Vidro	4.00

Game Gear Jerseys Autographs

Inserted 1:19,288
No pricing due to scarcity
BB Barry Bonds
TH Todd Helton

Elimination

Stars: 5-10X
Production 100 sets
Redemp. deadline 10/19/01

Player Choice Awards Relics

		NM/M
Common Player:		10.00
Inserted 1:1,530		
1	Carlos Delgado	15.00
2	Eric Davis	10.00
3	Carlos Delgado	15.00
4	Pedro Martinez	25.00
5	Terrence Long	10.00
6	Frank Thomas	20.00
7	Todd Helton	15.00
8	Randy Johnson	25.00
9	Rafael Furcal	15.00
10	Andres Galarraga	10.00

Progression

		NM/M
Complete Set (9):		10.00
Common Player:		1.00
Inserted 1:8		
P1	Ernie Banks, Alex Rodriguez, Felipe Lopez	3.00
P2	Yogi Berra, Ivan Rodriguez, Ramon Hernandez	2.00
P3	Tony Perez, Carlos Delgado, Eric Munson	1.00
P4	Rod Carew, Roberto Alomar, Jose Ortiz	1.00
P5	Stan Musial, Darin Erstad, Alex Escobar	2.00
P6	Jim Palmer, Kevin Brown, Kurt Ainsworth	1.00
P7	Duke Snider, Jim Edmonds, Vernon Wells	1.00
P8	Warren Spahn, Randy Johnson, Ryan Anderson	1.50
P9	Juan Marichal, Bartolo Colon, Bobby Bradley	1.00

Players Choice Award Nominees

	NM/M
Complete Set (10):	15.00
Common Player:	1.50

Inserted 1:12
1 Barry Bonds, Carlos Delgado, Todd Helton 4.00
2 Gary Sheffield, Eric Davis, Turk Wendell 1.50
3 Alex Rodriguez, Carlos Delgado, Frank Thomas 3.00
4 David Wells, Pedro Martinez, Andy Pettitte 2.00
5 Mark Quinn, Terrence Long, Kazuhiro Sasaki 1.50
6 Jay Buhner, Frank Thomas, Bobby Higginson 1.50
7 Barry Bonds, Todd Helton, Jeff Kent 4.00
8 Tom Glavine, Randy Johnson, Greg Maddux 2.50
9 Rick Ankiel, Rafael Furcal, Jay Payton 1.50
10 Moises Alou, Andres Galarraga, Jeff D'Amico 1.50

2001 TOPPS TRIBUTE

NM/M
Complete Set (90): 300.00
Common Player: 2.00
Pack (3): 75.00
Box (6): 425.00
1 Pee Wee Reese 2.00
2 Babe Ruth 15.00
3 Ralph Kiner 2.00
4 Brooks Robinson 5.00
5 Don Sutton 2.00
6 Carl Yastrzemski 8.00
7 Roger Maris 10.00
8 Andre Dawson 2.00
9 Luis Aparicio 2.00
10 Wade Boggs 4.00
11 Johnny Bench 8.00
12 Ernie Banks 6.00
13 Thurman Munson 5.00
14 Harmon Killebrew 5.00
15 Ted Kluszewski 2.00
16 Bob Feller 3.00
17 Mike Schmidt 10.00
18 Warren Spahn 4.00
19 Jim Palmer 3.00
20 Don Mattingly 12.00
21 Willie Mays 10.00
22 Gil Hodges 2.00
23 Juan Marichal 2.00
24 Robin Yount 6.00
25 Nolan Ryan 12.00
26 Dave Winfield 3.00
27 Hank Greenberg 2.00
28 Honus Wagner 8.00
29 Nolan Ryan 12.00
30 Phil Niekro 2.00
31 Robin Roberts 2.00
32 Casey Stengel 3.00
33 Willie McCovey 2.00
34 Roy Campanella 4.00
35 Rollie Fingers 2.00
36 Tom Seaver 5.00
37 Jackie Robinson 10.00
38 Hank Aaron 10.00
39 Bob Gibson 4.00
40 Carlton Fisk 4.00
41 Hank Aaron 10.00
42 George Brett 10.00
43 Orlando Cepeda 2.00
44 Red Schoendienst 2.00
45 Don Drysdale 4.00
46 Mel Ott 4.00
47 Casey Stengel 3.00
48 Al Kaline 4.00
49 Reggie Jackson 5.00
50 Tony Perez 2.00
51 Ozzie Smith 6.00
52 Billy Martin 4.00
53 Bill Dickey 2.00
54 Catfish Hunter 2.00
55 Duke Snider 4.00
56 Dale Murphy 2.00
57 Bobby Doerr 2.00
58 Earl Averill 2.00
59 Carlton Fisk 4.00
60 Tom Lasorda 2.00
61 Lou Gehrig 12.00
62 Enos Slaughter 2.00
63 Jim Bunning 2.00
64 Rollie Fingers 2.00
65 Frank Robinson 4.00
66 Earl Weaver 2.00
67 Eddie Mathews 5.00
68 Kirby Puckett 5.00
69 Phil Rizzuto 4.00
70 Lou Brock 4.00
71 Walt Alston 2.00
72 Bill Pierce 2.00
73 Joe Morgan 2.00
74 Roberto Clemente 12.00
75 Whitey Ford 4.00
76 Richie Ashburn 2.00
77 Elston Howard 2.00
78 Gary Carter 2.00
79 Carl Hubbell 2.00
80 Yogi Berra 6.00
81 Ken Boyer 2.00
82 Nolan Ryan 12.00
83 Bill Mazeroski 2.00
84 Dizzy Dean 4.00
85 Nellie Fox 2.00
86 Stan Musial 10.00
87 Steve Carlton 4.00
88 Willie Stargell 4.00
89 Hal Newhouser 2.00
90 Frank Robinson 4.00

Casey Stengel Dual Relic

NM/M
Inserted 1:860
CS Casey Stengel 100.00

Franchise Figures

NM/M
Inserted 1:34
AL Walt Alston, Tommy Lasorda 50.00
AFF Luis Aparicio, Nellie Fox, Carlton Fisk 125.00
BPKR Johnny Bench, Tony Perez, Ted Kluszewski, Frank Robinson, Joe Morgan 150.00
CD Gary Carter, Andre Dawson 40.00
HDB Bill Dickey, Elston Howard, Yogi Berra 150.00
FY Carlton Fisk, Carl Yastrzemski 150.00
HSS Gil Hodges, Casey Stengel, Tom Seaver 150.00
JM Reggie Jackson, Billy Martin 125.00
KG Al Kaline, Hank Greenberg 150.00
MMC Willie Mays, Willie McCovey, Orlando Cepeda 200.00
MCS Bill Mazeroski, Roberto Clemente, Willie Stargell 185.00
MM Thurman Munson, Don Mattingly 200.00
MMA Dale Murphy, Ed Mathews, Hank Aaron 185.00
PK Kirby Puckett, Harmon Killebrew 100.00
RSC Pee Wee Reese, Duke Snider, Roy Campanella 160.00
RR Brooks Robinson, Frank Robinson 75.00
RG Babe Ruth, Lou Gehrig 500.00
SAC Mike Schmidt, Richie Ashburn, Steve Carlton 125.00
SBSM Ozzie Smith, Lou Brock, Red Schoendienst, Stan Musial 125.00

Frank Robinson Dual Relic

NM/M
Inserted 1:860
FR-RO Frank Robinson 90.00

Game-Used Bat Relics

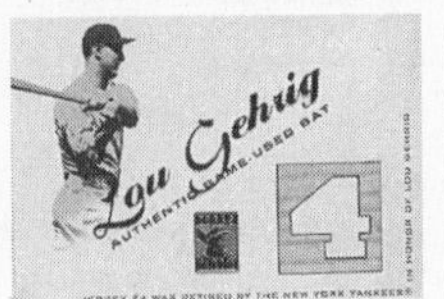

NM/M
Common Player: 20.00
Inserted 1:2
HA Hank Aaron 50.00
LA Luis Aparicio 20.00
RA Richie Ashburn 25.00
KB Ken Boyer 20.00
GB George Brett 40.00
LB Lou Brock 20.00
RC Roy Campanella 30.00
RCL Roberto Clemente 80.00
CF Carlton Fisk 25.00
LG Lou Gehrig 160.00
HG Hank Greenberg 50.00
GH Gil Hodges 25.00
RJ Reggie Jackson 30.00
AK Al Kaline 30.00
HK Harmon Killebrew 30.00
RM Roger Maris 50.00
BM Billy Martin 20.00
DM Don Mattingly 50.00
WM Willie McCovey 25.00
TM Thurman Munson 35.00
PWR Pee Wee Reese 20.00
BRO Brooks Robinson 30.00
FRR Frank Robinson 30.00
JR Jackie Robinson
BR Babe Ruth 200.00
OS Ozzie Smith 35.00
CS Casey Stengel 20.00
HW Honus Wagner 200.00
CY Carl Yastrzemski 40.00

Game-Worn Patch And Number Relics

NM/M
Common Player: 60.00
Inserted 1:61
WA Walt Alston 60.00
JB Johnny Bench 180.00
YB Yogi Berra 150.00
WB Wade Boggs 80.00
GB George Brett
LB Lou Brock 60.00
BD Bill Dickey 150.00
BDO Bobby Doerr 100.00
HK Harmon Killebrew 250.00
TL Tom Lasorda 80.00
JM Juan Marichal 75.00
EM Eddie Mathews 150.00
DM Don Mattingly
JP Jim Palmer
KB Kirby Puckett 250.00
NR Nolan Ryan 300.00
MS Mike Schmidt 250.00
RS Red Schoendienst 80.00
DW Dave Winfield 80.00
CY Carl Yastrzemski 200.00
RY Robin Yount 100.00

Nolan Ryan Tri-Relic

NM/M
Randomly inserted
NR Nolan Ryan 475.00

Retired Game-Worn Relics

NM/M
Common Player: 20.00
Inserted 1:2
WA Walt Alston 20.00
EB Ernie Banks 30.00
EBA Ernie Banks 30.00
JB Johnny Bench 30.00
YB Yogi Berra 30.00
WB Wade Boggs 20.00
GB George Brett 50.00
LB Lou Brock 25.00
SC Steve Carlton 25.00
DD Dizzy Dean 40.00
BD Bill Dickey 20.00
BDO Bobby Doerr 25.00
NF Nellie Fox 20.00
HK Harmon Killebrew 30.00
TL Tom Lasorda 20.00
JMG Juan Marichal 30.00
EM Eddie Mathews 30.00
DM Don Mattingly 50.00
WMF Willie Mays 75.00
WMW Willie Mays 75.00
SM Stan Musial 75.00
JP Jim Palmer 20.00
KP Kirby Puckett 30.00
FR Frank Robinson 25.00
NRA Nolan Ryan 80.00
NRH Nolan Ryan 80.00
NRR Nolan Ryan 80.00
MSB Mike Schmidt 50.00
MSW Mike Schmidt 50.00
RS Red Schoendienst 20.00
WST Willie Stargell 20.00
CS Casey Stengel 20.00
DW Dave Winfield 20.00
CY Carl Yastrzemski/white 40.00
CYA Carl Yastrzemski/gray 40.00
RY Robin Yount 30.00

2002 TOPPS

		NM/M
	Complete Set (718):	70.00
	Complete Factory Set (723):	80.00
	Complete Series 1 (365):	35.00
	Complete Series 2 (354):	35.00
	Common Player:	.10
	Pack (10):	1.50
	Box (36):	40.00
1	Pedro Martinez	.50
2	Mike Stanton	.10
3	Brad Penny	.10
4	Mike Matheny	.10
5	Johnny Damon	.20
6	Bret Boone	.20
7	not issued (retired)	.10
8	Chris Truby	.10
9	B.J. Surhoff	.10
10	Mike Hampton	.10
11	Juan Pierre	.10
12	Mark Buehrle	.10
13	Bob Abreu	.20
14	David Cone	.10
15	Aaron Sele	.10
16	Fernando Tatis	.10
17	Bobby Jones	.10
18	Rick Helling	.10
19	Dmitri Young	.10
20	Mike Mussina	.40
21	Mike Sweeney	.10
22	Cristian Guzman	.10
23	Ryan Kohlmeier	.10
24	Adam Kennedy	.10
25	Larry Walker	.25
26	Eric Davis	.10
27	Jason Tyner	.10
28	Eric Young	.10
29	Jason Marquis	.10
30	Luis Gonzalez	.20
31	Kevin Tapani	.10
32	Orlando Cabrera	.10
33	Marty Cordova	.10
34	Brad Ausmus	.10
35	Livan Hernandez	.10
36	Alex Gonzalez	.10
37	Edgar Renteria	.20
38	Bengie Molina	.10
39	Frank Menechino	.10
40	Rafael Palmeiro	.40
41	Brad Fullmer	.10
42	Julio Zuleta	.10
43	Darren Dreifort	.10
44	Trot Nixon	.10
45	Trevor Hoffman	.10
46	Vladimir Nunez	.10
47	Mark Kotsay	.10
48	Kenny Rogers	.10
49	Ben Petrick	.10
50	Jeff Bagwell	.40
51	Juan Encarnacion	.10
52	Ramiro Mendoza	.10
53	Brian Meadows	.10
54	Chad Curtis	.10
55	Aramis Ramirez	.25
56	Mark McLemore	.10
57	Dante Bichette	.10
58	Scott Schoeneweis	.10
59	Jose Cruz Jr.	.10
60	Roger Clemens	1.00
61	Jose Guillen	.10
62	Darren Oliver	.10
63	Chris Reitsma	.10
64	Jeff Abbott	.10
65	Robin Ventura	.10
66	Denny Neagle	.10
67	Al Martin	.10
68	Benito Santiago	.10
69	Roy Oswalt	.20
70	Juan Gonzalez	.40
71	Garret Anderson	.25
72	Bobby Bonilla	.10
73	Danny Bautista	.10
74	J.T. Snow Jr.	.10
75	Derek Jeter	1.50
76	John Olerud	.20
77	Kevin Appier	.10
78	Phil Nevin	.20
79	Sean Casey	.20
80	Troy Glaus	.40
81	Joe Randa	.10
82	Jose Valentin	.10
83	Ricky Bottalico	.10
84	Todd Zeile	.10
85	Barry Larkin	.25
86	Bob Wickman	.10
87	Jeff Shaw	.10
88	Greg Vaughn	.10
89	Fernando Vina	.10
90	Mark Mulder	.25
91	Paul Bako	.10
92	Aaron Boone	.10
93	Esteban Loaiza	.10
94	Richie Sexson	.40
95	Alfonso Soriano	.50
96	Tony Womack	.10
97	Paul Shuey	.10
98	Melvin Mora	.10
99	Tony Gwynn	.50
100	Vladimir Guerrero	.50
101	Keith Osik	.10
102	Randy Velarde	.10
103	Scott Williamson	.10
104	Daryle Ward	.10
105	Doug Mientkiewicz	.10
106	Stan Javier	.10
107	Russ Ortiz	.10
108	Wade Miller	.10
109	Luke Prokopec	.10
110	Andruw Jones	.40
111	Ron Coomer	.10
112	Dan Wilson	.10
113	Luis Castillo	.10
114	Derek Bell	.10
115	Gary Sheffield	.20
116	Ruben Rivera	.10
117	Paul O'Neill	.20
118	Craig Paquette	.10
119	Chris Michalak	.10
120	Brad Radke	.10
121	Jorge Fabregas	.10
122	Randy Winn	.10
123	Tom Goodwin	.10
124	Jaret Wright	.10
125	Manny Ramirez	.40
126	Al Leiter	.20
127	Ben Davis	.10
128	Frank Catalanotto	.10
129	Jose Cabrera	.10
130	Magglio Ordonez	.20
131	Jose Macias	.10
132	Ted Lilly	.10
133	Chris Holt	.10
134	Eric Milton	.10
135	Shannon Stewart	.10
136	Omar Olivares	.10
137	David Segui	.10
138	Jeff Nelson	.10
139	Matt Williams	.25
140	Ellis Burks	.10
141	Jason Bere	.10
142	Jimmy Haynes	.10
143	Ramon Hernandez	.10
144	Craig Counsell (Front photo actually Greg Colbrunn)	.10
145	John Smoltz	.10
146	Homer Bush	.10
147	Quilvio Veras	.10
148	Esteban Yan	.10
149	Ramon Ortiz	.10
150	Carlos Delgado	.30
151	Lee Stevens	.10
152	Wil Cordero	.10
153	Mike Bordick	.10
154	John Flaherty	.10
155	Omar Daal	.10
156	Todd Ritchie	.10
157	Carl Everett	.10
158	Scott Sullivan	.10
159	Deivi Cruz	.10
160a	Albert Pujols (back photo is Placido Polanco) (in cap)	1.00
160b	Albert Pujols (back photo corrected)(no cap)	1.00
161	Royce Clayton	.10
162	Jeff Suppan	.10
163	C.C. Sabathia	.10
164	Jimmy Rollins	.10
165	Rickey Henderson	.25
166	Rey Ordonez	.10
167	Shawn Estes	.10
168	Reggie Sanders	.10
169	Jon Lieber	.10
170	Armando Benitez	.10
171	Mike Remlinger	.10
172	Billy Wagner	.10
173	Troy Percival	.10
174	Devon White	.10
175	Ivan Rodriguez	.40
176	Dustin Hermanson	.10
177	Brian Anderson	.10
178	Graeme Lloyd	.10
179	Russ Branyan	.10
180	Bobby Higginson	.10
181	Alex Gonzalez	.10
182	John Franco	.10
183	Sidney Ponson	.10
184	Jose Mesa	.10
185	Todd Hollandsworth	.10
186	Kevin Young	.10
187	Tim Wakefield	.10
188	Craig Biggio	.20
189	Jason Isringhausen	.10
190	Mark Quinn	.10
191	Glendon Rusch	.10
192	Damian Miller	.10
193	Sandy Alomar	.10
194	Scott Brosius	.10
195	Dave Martinez	.10
196	Danny Graves	.10
197	Shea Hillenbrand	.10
198	Jimmy Anderson	.10
199	Travis Lee	.10
200	Randy Johnson	.50
201	Carlos Beltran	.25
202	Jerry Hairston Jr.	.10
203	Jesus Sanchez	.10
204	Eddie Taubensee	.10
205	David Wells	.10
206	Russ Davis	.10
207	Michael Barrett	.10
208	Marquis Grissom	.10
209	Byung-Hyun Kim	.10
210	Hideo Nomo	.25
211	Ryan Rupe	.10
212	Ricky Gutierrez	.10
213	Darryl Kile	.10
214	Rico Brogna	.10
215	Terrence Long	.10
216	Mike Jackson	.10
217	Jamey Wright	.10
218	Adrian Beltre	.20
219	Benny Agbayani	.10
220	Chuck Knoblauch	.10
221	Randy Wolf	.10
222	Andy Ashby	.10
223	Corey Koskie	.10
224	Roger Cedeno	.10
225	Ichiro Suzuki	1.00
226	Keith Foulke	.10
227	Ryan Minor	.10
228	Shawon Dunston	.10
229	Alex Cora	.10
230	Jeromy Burnitz	.10
231	Mark Grace	.25
232	Aubrey Huff	.10
233	Jeffrey Hammonds	.10
234	Olmedo Saenz	.10
235	Brian Jordan	.10
236	Jeremy Giambi	.10
237	Joe Girardi	.10
238	Eric Gagne	.25
239	Masato Yoshii	.10
240	Greg Maddux	.75
241	Bryan Rekar	.10
242	Ray Durham	.10
243	Torii Hunter	.20
244	Derrek Lee	.20
245	Jim Edmonds	.25
246	Einar Diaz	.10
247	Brian Bohanon	.10
248	Ron Belliard	.10
249	Mike Lowell	.20
250	Sammy Sosa	1.00
251	Richard Hidalgo	.10
252	Bartolo Colon	.10
253	Jorge Posada	.25
254	LaTroy Hawkins	.10
255	Paul LoDuca	.10
256	Carlos Febles	.10
257	Nelson Cruz	.10
258	Edgardo Alfonzo	.10
259	Joey Hamilton	.10
260	Cliff Floyd	.10
261	Wes Helms	.10
262	Jay Bell	.10
263	Mike Cameron	.10
264	Paul Konerko	.10
265	Jeff Kent	.20
266	Robert Fick	.10
267	Allen Levrault	.10
268	Placido Polanco	.10
269	Marlon Anderson	.10
270	Mariano Rivera	.20
271	Chan Ho Park	.10
272	Jose Vizcaino	.10
273	Jeff D'Amico	.10
274	Mark Gardner	.10
275	Travis Fryman	.10
276	Darren Lewis	.10
277	Bruce Bochy	.10
278	Jerry Manuel	.10
279	Bob Brenly	.10
280	Don Baylor	.10
281	Davey Lopes	.10
282	Jerry Narron	.10
283	Tony Muser	.10
284	Hal McRae	.10
285	Bobby Cox	.10
286	Larry Dierker	.10
287	Phil Garner	.10
288	Jimy Williams	.10
289	Bobby Valentine	.10
290	Dusty Baker	.10
291	Lloyd McLendon	.10
292	Mike Scioscia	.10
293	Buck Martinez	.10
294	Larry Bowa	.10
295	Tony LaRussa	.10
296	Jeff Torborg	.10
297	Tom Kelly	.10
298	Mike Hargrove	.10
299	Art Howe	.10
300	Lou Pinella	.10
301	Charlie Manuel	.10
302	Buddy Bell	.10
303	Tony Perez	.10
304	Bob Boone	.10
305	Joe Torre	.25
306	Jim Tracy	.10
307	Jason Lane	.10
308	Chris George	.10
309	Hank Blalock	.25
310	Joe Borchard	.10
311	Marlon Byrd	.10
312	*Raymond Cabrera*	.25
313	*Freddy Sanchez*	.40
314	*Scott Wiggins*	.40
315	*Jason Maule*	.30
316	*Dionys Cesar*	.40
317	Boof Bonser	.10
318	*Juan Tolentino*	.40
319	*Earl Snyder*	.25
320	*Travis Wade*	.25
321	*Napoleon Calzado*	.40
322	*Eric Glaser*	.40
323	*Craig Kuzmic*	.40
324	*Nic Jackson*	.50
325	Mike Rivera	.10
326	*Jason Bay*	.75
327	Chris Smith	.10
328	Jake Gautreau	.10
329	Gabe Gross	.10
330	Kenny Baugh	.10
331	J.D. Martin	.10
332	Barry Bonds	1.00
333	Rickey Henderson	.25
334	Bud Smith	.10
335	Rickey Henderson	.25
336	Barry Bonds	1.00
337	Ichiro Suzuki, Jason Giambi, Roberto Alomar	.50
338	Alex Rodriguez, Ichiro Suzuki, Bret Boone	.50
339	Alex Rodriguez, Jim Thome, Rafael Palmeiro	.40
340	Bret Boone, Juan Gonzalez, Alex Rodriguez	.40
341	Freddy Garcia, Mike Mussina, Joe Mays	.15
342	Hideo Nomo, Mike Mussina, Roger Clemens	.40
343	Larry Walker, Todd Helton, Moises Alou	.25
344	Sammy Sosa, Todd Helton, Barry Bonds	.40
345	Barry Bonds, Sammy Sosa, Luis Gonzalez	.40
346	Sammy Sosa, Todd Helton, Luis Gonzalez	.40
347	Curt Schilling, Randy Johnson, John Burkett	.20
348	Randy Johnson, Curt Schilling, Chan Ho Park	.20
349	Seattle Mariners	.25
350	Oakland A's	.10
351	New York Yankees	.50
352	Cleveland Indians	.10
353	Arizona Diamondbacks	.10
354	Atlanta Braves	.10
355	St. Louis Cardinals	.10
356	Houston Astros	.10
357	D'backs vs. Rockies	.10
358	Mets vs. Pirates	.10
359	Braves vs. Phillies	.10
360	D'backs vs. Phillies	.10
361	Yankees vs. White Sox	.10
362	Cubs vs. Reds	.10
363	Angels vs. Mariners	.10
364	Astros vs. Giants	.10
365	Barry Bonds Race to 70 #1	10.00
365	Barry Bonds HR #2-69	8.00
365	Barry Bonds HR #70	15.00
365	Barry Bonds HR #71	10.00

No.	Player	Price
365	Barry Bonds HR #72	10.00
365	Barry Bonds HR #73	50.00
366	Pat Meares	.10
367	Mike Lieberthal	.10
368	Scott Erickson	.10
369	Ron Gant	.10
370	Moises Alou	.25
371	Chad Kreuter	.10
372	Willis Roberts	.10
373	Toby Hall	.10
374	Miguel Batista	.10
375	John Burkett	.10
376	Cory Lidle	.10
377	Nick Neugebauer	.10
378	Jay Payton	.10
379	Steve Karsay	.10
380	Eric Chavez	.20
381	Kelly Stinnett	.10
382	Jarrod Washburn	.10
383	C.J. Nitkowski	.10
384	Jeff Conine	.10
385	Fred McGriff	.10
386	Marvin Benard	.10
387	Dave Burba	.10
388	Dennis Cook	.10
389	Rick Reed	.10
390	Tom Glavine	.25
391	Rondell White	.15
392	Matt Morris	.20
393	Pat Rapp	.10
394	Robert Person	.10
395	Omar Vizquel	.15
396	Jeff Cirillo	.10
397	Dave Mlicki	.10
398	Jose Ortiz	.10
399	Ryan Dempster	.10
400	Curt Schilling	.25
401	Peter Bergeron	.10
402	Kyle Lohse	.10
403	Craig Wilson	.10
404	David Justice	.20
405	Darin Erstad	.20
406	Jose Mercedes	.10
407	Carl Pavano	.10
408	Albie Lopez	.10
409	Alex Ochoa	.10
410	Chipper Jones	.50
411	Tyler Houston	.10
412	Dean Palmer	.10
413	Damian Jackson	.10
414	Josh Towers	.10
415	Rafael Furcal	.20
416	Ken Caminiti	.10
417	Herb Perry	.10
418	Mike Sirotka	.10
419	Mark Wohlers	.10
420	Nomar Garciaparra	1.00
421	Felipe Lopez	.10
422	Joe McEwing	.10
423	Jacque Jones	.10
424	Julio Franco	.10
425	Frank Thomas	.40
426	*So Taguchi*	.50
427	*Kazuhisa Ishii*	1.00
428	D'Angelo Jimenez	.10
429	Chris Stynes	.10
430	Kerry Wood	.50
431	Chris Singleton	.10
432	Erubiel Durazo	.10
433	Matt Lawton	.10
434	Bill Mueller	.10
435	Jose Canseco	.25
436	Ben Grieve	.10
437	Terry Mulholland	.10
438	David Bell	.10
439	A.J. Pierzynski	.10
440	Adam Dunn	.40
441	Jon Garland	.10
442	Jeff Fassero	.10
443	Julio Lugo	.10
444	Carlos Guillen	.10
445	Orlando Hernandez	.20
446	Mark Loretta	.10
447	Scott Spiezio	.10
448	Kevin Millwood	.20
449	Jamie Moyer	.10
450	Todd Helton	.40
451	Todd Walker	.10
452	Jose Lima	.10
453	Brook Fordyce	.10
454	Aaron Rowand	.10
455	Barry Zito	.20
456	Eric Owens	.10
457	Charles Nagy	.10
458	Raul Ibanez	.10
459	Joe Mays	.10
460	Jim Thome	.50
461	Adam Eaton	.10
462	Felix Martinez	.10
463	Vernon Wells	.10
464	Donnie Sadler	.10
465	Tony Clark	.10
466	Jose Hernandez	.10
467	Ramon Martinez	.10
468	Rusty Greer	.10
469	Rod Barajas	.10
470	Lance Berkman	.25
471	Brady Anderson	.10
472	Pedro Astacio	.10
473	Shane Halter	.10
474	Bret Prinz	.10
475	Edgar Martinez	.20
476	Steve Trachsel	.10
477	Gary Matthews Jr.	.10
478	Ismael Valdes	.10
479	Juan Uribe	.10
480	Shawn Green	.20
481	Kirk Rueter	.10
482	Damion Easley	.10
483	Chris Carpenter	.10
484	Kris Benson	.10
485	Antonio Alfonseca	.10
486	Kyle Farnsworth	.10
487	Brandon Lyon	.10
488	Hideki Irabu	.10
489	David Ortiz	.25
490	Mike Piazza	1.00
491	Derek Lowe	.10
492	Chris Gomez	.10
493	Mark Johnson	.10
494	John Rocker	.10
495	Eric Karros	.10
496	Bill Haselman	.10
497	Dave Veres	.10
498	Gil Heredia	.10
499	Tomokazu Ohka	.10
500	Barry Bonds	1.50
501	David Dellucci	.10
502	Ed Sprague	.10
503	Tom Gordon	.10
504	Javier Vazquez	.10
505	Ben Sheets	.25
506	Wilton Guerrero	.10
507	John Halama	.10
508	Mark Redman	.10
509	Jack Wilson	.10
510	Bernie Williams	.40
511	Miguel Cairo	.10
512	Denny Hocking	.10
513	Tony Batista	.10
514	Mark Grudzielanek	.10
515	Jose Vidro	.10
516	Sterling Hitchcock	.10
517	Billy Koch	.10
518	Matt Clement	.10
519	Bruce Chen	.10
520	Roberto Alomar	.40
521	Orlando Palmeiro	.10
522	Steve Finley	.10
523	Danny Patterson	.10
524	Terry Adams	.10
525	Tino Martinez	.10
526	Tony Armas Jr.	.10
527	Geoff Jenkins	.20
528	Chris Michalak	.10
529	Corey Patterson	.20
530	Brian Giles	.20
531	Jose Jimenez	.10
532	Joe Kennedy	.10
533	Armando Rios	.10
534	Osvaldo Fernandez	.10
535	Ruben Sierra	.10
536	Octavio Dotel	.10
537	Luis Sojo	.10
538	Brent Butler	.10
539	Pablo Ozuna	.10
540	Freddy Garcia	.10
541	Chad Durbin	.10
542	Orlando Merced	.10
543	Michael Tucker	.10
544	Roberto Hernandez	.10
545	Pat Burrell	.25
546	A.J. Burnett	.10
547	Bubba Trammell	.10
548	Scott Elarton	.10
549	Mike Darr	.10
550	Ken Griffey Jr.	1.00
551	Ugueth Urbina	.10
552	Todd Jones	.10
553	Delino DeShields	.10
554	Adam Piatt	.10
555	Jason Kendall	.10
556	Hector Ortiz	.10
557	Turk Wendell	.10
558	Rob Bell	.10
559	Sun-Woo Kim	.10
560	Raul Mondesi	.10
561	Brent Abernathy	.10
562	Seth Etherton	.10
563	Shawn Wooten	.10
564	Jay Buhner	.10
565	Andres Galarraga	.10
566	Shane Reynolds	.10
567	Rod Beck	.10
568	Dee Brown	.10
569	Pedro Feliz	.10
570	Ryan Klesko	.10
571	John Vander Wal	.10
572	Nick Bierbrodt	.10
573	Joe Nathan	.10
574	James Baldwin	.10
575	J.D. Drew	.20
576	Greg Colbrunn	.10
577	Doug Glanville	.10
578	Rey Sanchez	.10
579	Todd Van Poppel	.10
580	Rich Aurilia	.10
581	Chuck Finley	.10
582	Abraham Nunez	.10
583	Kenny Lofton	.20
584	Brian Daubach	.10
585	Miguel Tejada	.25
586	Nate Cornejo	.10
587	Kazuhiro Sasaki	.10
588	Chris Richard	.10
589	Armando Reynoso	.10
590	Tim Hudson	.20
591	Neifi Perez	.10
592	Steve Cox	.10
593	Henry Blanco	.10
594	Ricky Ledee	.10
595	Tim Salmon	.20
596	Luis Rivas	.10
597	Jeff Zimmerman	.10
598	Matt Stairs	.10
599	Preston Wilson	.10
600	Mark McGwire	1.50
601	Timo Perez	.10
602	Matt Anderson	.10
603	Todd Hundley	.10
604	Rick Ankiel	.10
605	Tsuyoshi Shinjo	.10
606	Woody Williams	.10
607	Jason LaRue	.10
608	Carlos Lee	.10
609	Russ Johnson	.10
610	Scott Rolen	.50
611	Brent Mayne	.10
612	Darrin Fletcher	.10
613	Ray Lankford	.10
614	Troy O'Leary	.10
615	Javier Lopez	.20
616	Randy Velarde	.10
617	Vinny Castilla	.10
618	Milton Bradley	.10
619	Ruben Mateo	.10
620	Jason Giambi	.40
621	Andy Benes	.10
622	Tony Eusebio	.10
623	Andy Pettitte	.20
624	Jose Offerman	.10
625	Mo Vaughn	.20
626	Steve Sparks	.10
627	Mike Matthews	.10
628	Robb Nen	.10
629	Kip Wells	.10
630	Kevin Brown	.20
631	Arthur Rhodes	.10
632	Gabe Kapler	.10
633	Jermaine Dye	.10
634	Josh Beckett	.25
635	Pokey Reese	.10
636	Benji Gil	.10
637	Marcus Giles	.10
638	Julian Tavarez	.10
639	Jason Schmidt	.25
640	Alex Rodriguez	1.25
641	Anaheim Angels	.10
642	Arizona Diamondbacks	.10
643	Atlanta Braves	.10
644	Baltimore Orioles	.10
645	Boston Red Sox	.10
646	Chicago Cubs	.10
647	Chicago White Sox	.10
648	Cincinnati Reds	.10
649	Cleveland Indians	.10
650	Colorado Rockies	.10
651	Detroit Tigers	.10
652	Florida Marlins	.10
653	Houston Astros	.10
654	Kansas City Royals	.10
655	Los Angeles Dodgers	.10
656	Milwaukee Brewers	.10
657	Minnesota Twins	.10
658	Montreal Expos	.10
659	New York Mets	.10
660	New York Yankees	.10
661	Oakland Athletics	.10
662	Philadelphia Phillies	.10
663	Pittsburgh Pirates	.10
664	San Diego Padres	.10
665	San Francisco Giants	.10
666	Seattle Mariners	.10
667	St. Louis Cardinals	.10
668	Tampa Bay Devil Rays	.10
669	Texas Rangers	.10
670	Toronto Blue Jays	.10
671	Juan Cruz	.25
672	*Kevin Cash*	.50
673	*Jimmy Gobble*	.75
674	*Mike Hill*	.40
675	*Taylor Buchholz*	.40
676	Bill Hall	.10
677	*Brett Roneberg*	.40
678	*Royce Huffman*	.40
679	*Chris Tritle*	.40
680	*Nate Espy*	.40
681	*Nick Alvarez*	.50
682	*Jason Botts*	.40
683	*Ryan Gripp*	.40
684	*Dan Phillips*	.50
685	*Pablo Arias*	.50
686	*John Rodriguez*	.40
687	*Rich Harden*	3.00
688	*Neal Frendling*	.50
689	*Rich Thompson*	.40
690	*Greg Montalbano*	.40
691	*Leonard Dinardo*	.40
692	*Ryan Raburn*	.40
693	Josh Barfield	1.00
694	*David Bacani*	.40
695	*Dan Johnson*	.50
696	Mike Mussina	.25
697	Ivan Rodriguez	.25
698	Doug Mientkiewicz	.10
699	Roberto Alomar	.25
700	Eric Chavez	.15
701	Omar Vizquel	.10
702	Mike Cameron	.10
703	Torii Hunter	.10
704	Ichiro Suzuki	.50
705	Greg Maddux	.50
706	Brad Ausmus	.10
707	Todd Helton	.25
708	Fernando Vina	.10
709	Scott Rolen	.40
710	Orlando Cabrera	.10
711	Andruw Jones	.15
712	Jim Edmonds	.10
713	Larry Walker	.15
714	Roger Clemens	.50
715	Randy Johnson	.25
716	Ichiro Suzuki	.50
717	Barry Bonds	.75
718	Ichiro Suzuki	.50
719	Albert Pujols	.50

Limited

	NM/M
Complete Set (790):	165.00
Includes all 73 B. Bonds #365 HR cards	

Autographs

		NM/M
Common Player:		10.00
TA1	Carlos Delgado	40.00
TA2	Ivan Rodriguez	50.00
TA3	Miguel Tejada	30.00
TA4	Geoff Jenkins	10.00
TA5	Johnny Damon	40.00
TA6	Tim Hudson	25.00
TA7	Terrence Long	10.00
TA8	Gabe Kapler	10.00
TA9	Magglio Ordonez	20.00
TA10	Barry Bonds	250.00
TA11	Pat Burrell	20.00
TA12	Mike Mussina	40.00
TA13	Eric Valent	5.00
TA14	Xavier Nady	8.00
TA15	Cristian Guerrero	5.00
TA16	Ben Sheets	15.00
TA17	Corey Patterson	15.00
TA18	Carlos Pena	5.00
TA19	Alex Rodriguez	80.00
Series 2		
TA-AB	Adrian Beltre	25.00
TA-JD	Jermaine Dye	15.00
TA-AE	Alex Escobar	8.00
TA-CF	Cliff Floyd	15.00
TA-RF	Rafael Furcal	20.00
TA-BG	Brian Giles	20.00
TA-KG	Keith Ginter	8.00
TA-TG	Troy Glaus	40.00
TA-BGR	Ben Grieve	20.00
TA-CG	Cristian Guzman	15.00
TA-JH	Josh Hamilton	8.00

TA-NJ	Nick Johnson	5.00
TA-RK	Ryan Klesko	20.00
TA-JO	Jose Ortiz	10.00
TA-RO	Roy Oswalt	15.00
TA-RP	Rafael Palmeiro	50.00
TA-AR	Alex Rodriguez	80.00
TA-JR	Jimmy Rollins	20.00
TA-RS	Richie Sexson	25.00
TA-MS	Mike Sweeney	20.00
TA-JW	Justin Wayne	10.00
TA-BW	Brad Wilkerson	10.00

All-World Team

NM/M

Complete Set (25): 25.00
Common Player: .50
Inserted 1:12

AW-1	Ichiro Suzuki	3.00
AW-2	Barry Bonds	4.00
AW-3	Pedro Martinez	1.50
AW-4	Juan Gonzalez	1.00
AW-5	Larry Walker	.50
AW-6	Sammy Sosa	3.00
AW-7	Mariano Rivera	.75
AW-8	Vladimir Guerrero	1.50
AW-9	Alex Rodriguez	3.00
AW-10	Albert Pujols	3.00
AW-11	Luis Gonzalez	.50
AW-12	Ken Griffey Jr.	2.50
AW-13	Kazuhiro Sasaki	.50
AW-14	Bob Abreu	.50
AW-15	Todd Helton	1.00
AW-16	Nomar Garciaparra	2.50
AW-17	Miguel Tejada	.75
AW-18	Roger Clemens	3.00
AW-19	Mike Piazza	2.50
AW-20	Carlos Delgado	1.00
AW-21	Derek Jeter	4.00
AW-22	Hideo Nomo	.75
AW-23	Randy Johnson	1.50
AW-24	Ivan Rodriguez	1.00
AW-25	Chan Ho Park	.50

East Meets West

NM/M

Complete Set (8): 6.00
Common Player: 1.00
Inserted 1:24

EW-HN	Hideo Nomo, Masanori Murakami	2.00
EW-HI	Hideki Irabu, Masanori Murakami	1.00
EW-SH	Shigetoshi Hasegawa, Masanori Murakami	1.00
EW-MY	Masato Yoshii, Masanori Murakami	1.00
EW-TS	Tsuyoshi Shinjo, Masanori Murakami	1.00
EW-KS	Kazuhiro Sasaki, Masanori Murakami	1.00
EW-MS	Mac Suzuki, Masanori Murakami	1.00
EW-TO	Tomo Ohka, Masanori Murakami	1.00

Aces

NM/M

Common Player: 10.00
Inserted 1:1,180

MH	Mike Hampton	10.00
RJ	Randy Johnson	20.00
GM	Greg Maddux	30.00
PM	Pedro Martinez	20.00
MM	Mark Mulder	10.00

Battery Mates Relic

NM/M

Inserted 1:4,401

ML	Greg Maddux, Javy Lopez	30.00
LP	Al Leiter, Mike Piazza	30.00

Draft Picks

NM/M

Complete Set (10): 40.00
1-5 in Green Factory sets
6-10 in Holiday Factory sets

1	Scott Moore	6.00
2	Val Majewski	6.00
3	Brian Slocum	4.00
4	Chris Gruler	6.00
5	Mark Schramek	6.00
6	Joe Saunders	4.00
7	Jeff Francis	8.00
8	Royce Ring	6.00
9	Greg Miller	8.00
10	Brandon Weeden	4.00

Dueces Are Wild

NM/M

Common Card: 15.00
Inserted 1:1,962

JG	Randy Johnson, Luis Gonzalez	30.00
BK	Barry Bonds, Jeff Kent	40.00
TA	Jim Thome, Roberto Alomar	30.00
WH	Larry Walker, Todd Helton	25.00
BG	Bret Boone, Freddy Garcia	15.00

East Meets West Relics

NM/M

Common Player: 15.00
Inserted 1:3,419

HN	Hideo Nomo	40.00
KS	Kazuhiro Sasaki	15.00
TS	Tsuyoshi Shinjo	15.00

Ebbets Field Seat Relics

NM/M

Inserted 1:9,116

JB	Joe Black	100.00
RC	Roy Campanella	250.00
BC	Billy Cox	100.00
CF	Carl Furillo	100.00
GH	Gil Hodges	250.00
AP	Andy Pafko	100.00
PWR	Pee Wee Reese	250.00
JR	Jackie Robinson	250.00
DS	Duke Snider	200.00

Ebbets Field/Yankee Stadium Seat Dual Relic

Complete Set (1):
EFYS-SB Duke Snider, Yogi Berra

Hall of Fame Vintage BuyBacks AutoProofs

NM/M

Common Autograph: 15.00

BR16	Brooks Robinson 82 KM/200	50.00
EW10	Earl Weaver 87/100	15.00
FJ33	Fergie Jenkins 84/100	15.00
GP26	Gaylord Perry 82/100	15.00
GP29	Gaylord Perry 83/100	15.00
GP30	Gaylord Perry 83 SV/200	15.00
OC1	Orlando Cepeda 82 KM/200	15.00
RF15	Rollie Fingers 81/300	15.00
RF16	Rollie Fingers 81 LL/100	15.00
RF18	Rollie Fingers 82/100	15.00
RF19	Rollie Fingers 82 IA/200	15.00
RF21	Rollie Fingers 82 KM/300	15.00
RF22	Rollie Fingers 83/200	15.00
RF24	Rollie Fingers 84/200	15.00
RF27	Rollie Fingers 85/300	15.00
RF28	Rollie Fingers 86/100	15.00
SC5	Steve Carlton 84 LL/100	25.00
SC6	Steve Carlton 85/200	25.00
SC8	Steve Carlton 87/200	25.00

Heart of the Order Relic

NM/M

Inserted 1:4,247

KBA	Jeff Kent, Barry Bonds, Rich Aurilia	75.00
TGA	Jim Thome, Juan Gonzalez, Roberto Alomar	50.00
ARB	Bob Abreu, Scott Rolen, Pat Burrell	50.00
OWM	Paul O'Neill, Bernie Williams, Tino Martinez	50.00

Hit and Run Relic

NM/M

Inserted 1:4,241

JD	Johnny Damon	10.00
DE	Darin Erstad	10.00
RF	Rafael Furcal	10.00

Hobby Masters

NM/M

Complete Set (20): 40.00
Common Player: 1.00
Inserted 1:25

1	Mark McGwire	5.00
2	Derek Jeter	5.00
3	Chipper Jones	2.00
4	Roger Clemens	4.00
5	Vladimir Guerrero	2.00
6	Ichiro Suzuki	3.00
7	Todd Helton	1.50
8	Alex Rodriguez	4.00
9	Albert Pujols	4.00
10	Sammy Sosa	3.00
11	Ken Griffey Jr.	3.00
12	Randy Johnson	2.00
13	Nomar Garciaparra	3.00
14	Ivan Rodriguez	1.50
15	Manny Ramirez	1.50
16	Barry Bonds	5.00
17	Mike Piazza	3.00
18	Pedro Martinez	1.50
19	Jeff Bagwell	1.50
20	Luis Gonzalez	1.00

Jack of All Trades

NM/M

Inserted 1:1,350

RO	Roberto Alomar/bat	20.00
BB	Barry Bonds/jsy	35.00
AJ	Andruw Jones/jsy	10.00
IR	Ivan Rodriguez/jsy	15.00
BW	Bernie Williams/jsy	15.00

Kings of the Clubhouse

NM/M

Common Player: 10.00
Inserted 1:1,449 Ser. 2

TG	Tom Glavine/jsy	15.00
TH	Todd Helton/jsy	15.00
RJ	Randy Johnson/jsy	20.00
EM	Edgar Martinez/jsy	10.00
PO	Paul O'Neill/bat	20.00

Like Father Like Son Relic

NM/M

Common Duo:
Inserted 1:1,304 Retail

AL	Roberto Alomar, Sandy Alomar, Sandy Alomar Jr.	40.00
BE	Dale Berra, Yogi Berra	50.00
BON	Bobby Bonds, Barry Bonds	80.00
BOO	Bob Boone, Bret Boone, Aaron Boone	40.00
CR	Jose Cruz, Jose Cruz Jr.	40.00

Own The Game

NM/M

Complete Set (30): 25.00
Common Player: .50
Inserted 1:12

OG1	Moises Alou	.75
OG2	Roberto Alomar	.75
OG3	Luis Gonzalez	.50
OG4	Bret Boone	.75
OG5	Barry Bonds	4.00
OG6	Jim Thome	1.50
OG7	Jimmy Rollins	.50
OG8	Cristian Guzman	.50
OG9	Lance Berkman	.75
OG10	Mike Sweeney	.50
OG11	Rich Aurilia	.50
OG12	Ichiro Suzuki	2.50
OG13	Luis Gonzalez	.50
OG14	Ichiro Suzuki	2.50
OG15	Jimmy Rollins	.50
OG16	Roger Cedeno	.50
OG17	Barry Bonds	4.00
OG18	Jim Thome	1.50
OG19	Curt Schilling	1.00
OG20	Roger Clemens	3.00
OG21	Curt Schilling	1.00
OG22	Brad Radke	.50
OG23	Greg Maddux	2.00
OG24	Mark Mulder	.75
OG25	Jeff Shaw	.50
OG26	Mariano Rivera	.75
OG27	Randy Johnson	1.50
OG28	Pedro Martinez	1.50
OG29	John Burkett	.50
OG30	Tim Hudson	.75

Prime Cuts Pine Tar Series

NM/M

Common Player: 15.00
Inserted 1:4,420

BB	Barry Bonds	60.00
LG	Luis Gonzalez	20.00
TG	Tony Gwynn	40.00
TH	Todd Helton	25.00
AP	Albert Pujols	40.00

Series 2
Inserted 1:1,043
Trademark Series: 1.5-2X
Inserted 1:2,087 Ser. 2
Prime Cuts Barrel: 2-4X
Inserted 1:7,824 Ser. 2

WB	Wilson Betemit	15.00
SB	Sean Burroughs	15.00
JC	Joe Crede	20.00
AD	Adam Dunn	30.00
AE	Alex Escobar	15.00
MG	Marcus Giles	15.00
AG	Alexis Gomez	15.00
TH	Toby Hall	15.00
JH	Josh Hamilton	15.00
NJ	Nick Johnson	15.00
XN	Xavier Nady	15.00
CP	Corey Patterson	20.00
CPE	Carlos Pena	15.00
AR	Aaron Rowand	25.00
RS	Ruben Salazar	15.00

Ring Masters

NM/M

Complete Set (10): 15.00
Common Player: .50
Inserted 1:25

1	Derek Jeter	4.00
2	Mark McGwire	4.00
3	Mariano Rivera	1.00
4	Gary Sheffield	.75
5	Al Leiter	.50
6	Chipper Jones	1.50
7	Roger Clemens	3.00
8	Greg Maddux	2.00
9	Roberto Alomar	1.00
10	Paul O'Neill	.50

Turn Two Relic

NM/M

Inserted 1:4,401

TW	Alan Trammell, Lou Whitaker	40.00
VA	Omar Vizquel, Roberto Alomar	40.00

Three of a Kind

NM/M

Common Card:
Inserted 1:2,039

SPA	Tsuyoshi Shinjo, Mike Piazza, Edgardo Alfonzo	50.00
LOC	Carlos Lee, Magglio Ordonez, Jose Canseco	50.00
FBJ	Rafael Furcal, Wilson Betemit, Andruw Jones	40.00
PSW	Jorge Posada, Alfonso Soriano, Bernie Williams	50.00
BDB	A.J. Burnett, Ryan Dempster, Josh Beckett	40.00

Yankee Stadium Seat Relics

NM/M

Inserted 1:579

HB	Hank Bauer	100.00
YB	Yogi Berra	250.00
JC	Joe Collins	100.00
BM	Billy Martin	250.00
GM	Gil McDougald	100.00
JM	Johnny Mize	100.00
AR	Allie Reynolds	100.00
PR	Phil Rizzuto	250.00
GW	Gene Woodling	100.00

1952 PLAYER AUTOGRAPHS

NM/M

Inserted 1:7,524

HBA	Hank Bauer	75.00
YBA	Yogi Berra	100.00
RHA	Ralph Houk	
PRA	Preacher Roe	70.00
JSA	Johnny Sain	

1952 WORLD SERIES TRIBUTE

		NM/M
Complete Set (19):		50.00
Common Player:		3.00
Inserted 1:25		
1	Roy Campanella	4.00
2	Duke Snider	4.00
3	Carl Erskine	3.00
4	Andy Pafko	3.00
5	Johnny Mize	3.00
6	Billy Martin	4.00
7	Phil Rizzuto	4.00
8	Gil McDougal	3.00
9	Allie Reynolds	3.00
10	Jackie Robinson	4.00
Series 2		
11	Preacher Roe	3.00
12	Gil Hodges	3.00
13	Billy Cox	3.00
14	Yogi Berra	4.00
15	Gene Woodling	3.00
16	Jerry Sain	3.00
17	Ralph Houk	3.00
18	Joe Collins	3.00
19	Hank Bauer	3.00

1952 REPRINT AUTOGRAPHS

		NM/M
Common Autograph:		25.00
Inserted 1:10,268		
JBA	Joe Black	90.00
CEA	Carl Erskine	50.00
GMA	Gil McDougal	40.00
APA	Andy Pafko	60.00
PRA	Phil Rizzuto	80.00
DSA	Duke Snider	100.00

1952 WORLD SERIES HIGHLIGHTS

		NM/M
Complete Set (7):		10.00
Common Player:		2.00
Inserted 1:25		
52WS-1	Dodgers' Game 1 Starting Line Up	3.00
52WS-2	Dodgers Celebrate Game 3 Win!	2.00
52WS-3	Carl Erskine Wins Game 5	2.00
Series 2		
52WS-2	Game 2	2.00
52WS-4	Game 4	2.00
52WS-6	Game 6	2.00
52WS-7	Game 7	2.00

2 BAGGER RELIC

		NM/M
Inserted 1:3,733		
TG	Tony Gwynn	30.00
TH	Todd Helton	20.00
SR	Scott Rolen	20.00

2002 TOPPS TRADED & ROOKIES

		NM/M
Complete Set (275):		125.00
Common Player:		.15
Common SP (1-110):		.50
Chrome cards:		2-4X
2:pack		
Pack (10):		3.00
Box (24):		60.00
T1	Jeff Weaver	.50
T2	Jay Powell	.50
T3	Alex Gonzalez	.50
T4	Jason Isringhausen	.50
T5	Darren Oliver	.50
T6	Hector Ortiz	.50
T7	Chuck Knoblauch	.50
T8	Brian L. Hunter	.50
T9	Dustan Mohr	.50
T10	Eric Hinske	.50
T11	Roger Cedeno	.50
T12	Eddie Perez	.50
T13	Jeromy Burnitz	.50
T14	Bartolo Colon	.50
T15	Rick Helling	.50
T16	Dan Plesac	.50
T17	Scott Strickland	.50
T18	Antonio Alfonseca	.50
T19	Ricky Gutierrez	.50
T20	John Valentin	.50
T21	Raul Mondesi	.50
T22	Ben Davis	.50
T23	Nelson Figueroa	.50
T24	Earl Snyder	.50
T25	Robin Ventura	.50
T26	Jimmy Haynes	.50
T27	Kenny Kelly	.50
T28	Morgan Ensberg	.50
T29	Reggie Sanders	.50
T30	Shigetoshi Hasegawa	.50
T31	Allen Levrault	.50
T32	Russell Branyan	.50
T33	Jose Guillen	.50
T34	Jose Paniagua	.50
T35	Kent Mercker	.50
T36	Jesse Orosco	.50
T37	Gregg Zaun	.50
T38	Reggie Taylor	.50
T39	Andres Galarraga	.50
T40	Chris Truby	.50
T41	Bruce Chen	.50
T42	Darren Lewis	.50
T43	Ryan Kohlmeier	.50
T44	John McDonald	.50
T45	Omar Daal	.50
T46	Matt Clement	.50
T47	Glendon Rusch	.50
T48	Chan Ho Park	.50
T49	Benny Agbayani	.50
T50	Juan Gonzalez	1.50
T51	Carlos Baerga	.50
T52	Tim Raines	.50
T53	Kevin Appier	.50
T54	Marty Cordoua	.50
T55	Jeff D'Amico	.50
T56	Dmitri Young	.50
T57	Roosevelt Brown	.50
T58	Dustin Hermanson	.50
T59	Jose Rijo	.50
T60	Todd Ritchie	.50
T61	Lee Stevens	.50
T62	Shane Heams	.50
T63	Eric Young	.50
T64	Chuck Finley	.50
T65	Dicky Gonzalez	.50
T66	Jose Macias	.50
T67	Gabe Kapler	.50
T68	Sandy Alomar Jr.	.50
T69	Henry Blanco	.50
T70	Julian Tavarez	.50
T71	Paul Bako	.50
T72	Dave Burba	.50
T73	Brian Jordan	.50
T74	Rickey Henderson	1.00
T75	Kevin Mench	.50
T76	Hideo Nomo	1.00
T77	Mark Sweeney	.50
T78	Brad Fullmer	.50
T79	Carl Everett	.50
T80	Boomer Wells	.50
T81	Aaron Sele	.50
T82	Todd Hollandsworth	.50
T83	Vicente Padilla	.50
T84	Chris Latham	.50
T85	Corky Miller	.50
T86	Josh Fogg	.50
T87	Calvin Murray	.50
T88	Craig Paquette	.50
T89	Jay Payton	.50
T90	Carlos Pena	.50
T91	Juan Encarnacion	.50
T92	Rey Sanchez	.50
T93	Ryan Dempster	.50
T94	Mario Encarnacion	.50
T95	Jorge Julio	.50
T96	John Mabry	.50
T97	Todd Zeile	.50
T98	Johnny Damon	.50
T99	Deivi Cruz	.50
T100	Gary Sheffield	1.00
T101	Ted Lilly	.50
T102	Todd Van Poppel	.50
T103	Shawn Estes	.50
T104	Cesar Izturis	.50
T105	Ron Coomer	.50
T106	Grady Little	.50
T107	Jimy Williams	.50
T108	Tony Pena	.50
T109	Frank Robinson	.50
T110	Ron Gardenhire	.50
T111	Dennis Tankersley	.15
T112	*Alejandro Cadena*	.25
T113	*Justin Reid*	.25
T114	*Nate Field*	.25
T115	*Rene Reyes*	.25
T116	*Nelson Castro*	.25
T117	Miguel Olivo	.15
T118	David Espinosa	.15
T119	*Chris Bootcheck*	.40
T120	*Rob Henkel*	.25
T121	*Steve Bechler*	.25
T122	*Mark Outlaw*	.25
T123	*Henry Pichardo*	.25
T124	*Michael Floyd*	.25
T125	*Richard Lane*	.25
T126	*Peter Zamora*	.25
T127	Javier Colina	.15
T128	*Greg Sain*	.25
T129	Ronnie Merrill	.25
T130	Gavin Floyd	1.50
T131	*Josh Bonifay*	.25
T132	*Tommy Marx*	.25
T133	*Gary Cates Jr.*	.25
T134	Neal Cotts	.50
T135	Angel Berroa	.25
T136	*Elio Serrano*	.25
T137	*J.J. Putz*	.25
T138	*Ruben Gotay*	.25
T139	*Eddie Rogers*	.25
T140	Wily Mo Pena	.25
T141	*Tyler Yates*	.25
T142	*Colin Young*	.25
T143	Chance Caple	.15
T144	*Ben Howard*	.25
T145	*Ryan Bukvich*	.25
T146	*Clifford Bartosh*	.25
T147	Brandon Claussen	.25
T148	Cristian Guerrero	.15
T149	Derrick Lewis	.15
T150	*Eric Miller*	.25
T151	*Justin Huber*	.75
T152	Adrian Gonzalez	.15
T153	*Brian West*	.25
T154	*Chris Baker*	.25
T155	Drew Henson	.15
T156	Scott Hairston	.75
T157	*Jason Simontacchi*	.75
T158	Jason Arnold	.40
T159	Brandon Phillips	.15
T160	*Adam Roller*	.25
T161	*Scotty Layfield*	.25
T162	*Freddie Money*	.25
T163	*Noochie Varner*	.50
T164	*Terrance Hill*	.25
T165	*Jeremy Hill*	.25
T166	*Carlos Cabrera*	.25
T167	*Jose Morban*	.25
T168	*Kevin Frederick*	.25
T169	Mark Teixeira	.40
T170	Brian Rogers	.15
T171	*Anastacio Martinez*	.25
T172	*Bobby Jenks*	.75
T173	*David Gil*	.25
T174	Andres Torres	.15
T175	*James Barrett*	.25
T176	Jimmy Journell	.15
T177	*Brett Kay*	.25
T178	*Jason Young*	.25
T179	*Mark Hamilton*	.25
T180	*Jose Bautista*	.50
T181	*Blake McGinley*	.25
T182	*Ryan Mottl*	.25
T183	*Jeff Austin*	.25
T184	Xavier Nady	.15
T185	*Kyle Kane*	.25
T186	Travis Foley	.15
T187	*Nathan Kaup*	.25
T188	*Eric Cyr*	.25
T189	*Josh Cisneros*	.25
T190	*Brad Nelson*	.75
T191	*Clint Weibl*	.25
T192	*Ron Calloway*	.25
T193	Jung Bong	.15
T194	*Rolando Viera*	.25
T195	*Jason Bulger*	.25
T196	*Chone Figgins*	.75
T197	*Jimmy Alvarez*	.25
T198	*Joel Crump*	.25
T199	*Ryan Doumit*	1.50
T200	*Demetrius Heath*	.25
T201	*John Ennis*	.25
T202	*Doug Sessions*	.25
T203	*Clinton Hosford*	.25
T204	*Chris Narveson*	.25
T205	*Ross Peeples*	.25
T206	*Alexander Requena*	.25
T207	*Matt Erickson*	.25
T208	*Brian Forystek*	.25
T209	Dewon Brazelton	.15
T210	Nathan Haynes	.15
T211	Jack Cust	.15
T212	Jesse Foppert	.75
T213	*Jesus Cota*	.25
T214	Juan Gonzalez	.15
T215	*Tim Kalita*	.25
T216	*Manny Delcarmen*	2.00
T217	Jim Kavourias	.15
T218	*C.J. Wilson*	.25
T219	*Edwin Yan*	.25
T220	Andy Van Hekken	.15
T221	Michael Cuddyer	.15
T222	*Jeff Verplancke*	.25
T223	*Mike Wilson*	.25
T224	Corwin Malone	.15
T225	*Chris Snelling*	.50
T226	*Joe Rogers*	.25
T227	Jason Bay	.50
T228	*Ezequiel Astacio*	.25
T229	*Joey Hammond*	.25
T230	*Chris Duffy*	.25
T231	Mark Prior	1.00
T232	*Hansel Izquierdo*	.25
T233	*Franklyn German*	.25
T234	Alexis Gomez	.15
T235	*Jorge Padilla*	.25
T236	*Ryan Snare*	.25
T237	Deivis Santos	.15
T238	*Taggert Bozied*	1.00
T239	*Mike Peeples*	.25
T240	*Ronald Acuna*	.25
T241	Koyie Hill	.15
T242	*Garrett Guzman*	.25
T243	*Ryan Church*	1.00
T244	*Tony Fontana*	.25
T245	*Keto Anderson*	.25
T246	*Brad Bouras*	.25
T247	*Jason Dubois*	1.00
T248	*Angel Guzman*	2.00
T249	*Joel Hanrahan*	.50
T250	*Joe Jiannetti*	.25
T251	*Sean Pierce*	.25
T252	*Jake Mauer*	.25
T253	*Marshall McDougall*	.50
T254	*Edwin Almonte*	.25
T255	*Shawn Riggans*	.25
T256	Steven Shell	.15
T257	*Kevin Hooper*	.40
T258	*Michael Frick*	.25
T259	*Travis Chapman*	.40

T260 *Tim Hummel* .25
T261 *Adam Morrissey* .25
T262 *Dontrelle Willis* 5.00
T263 *Justin Sherrod* .25
T264 *Gerald Smiley* .25
T265 *Tony Miller* .25
T266 Nolan Ryan 1.50
T267 Reggie Jackson .50
T268 Steve Garvey .15
T269 Wade Boggs .25
T270 Sammy Sosa 1.00
T271 Curt Schilling .25
T272 Mark Grace .25
T273 Jason Giambi .50
T274 Ken Griffey Jr. .75
T275 Roberto Alomar .40

Gold

Gold Stars: 2-4X
Production 2,002 sets
Chrome Refractors: 3-5X
Inserted 1:12

Farewell Relics

NM/M
Randomly inserted
JC Jose Canseco 10.00

Hall of Fame Relics

NM/M
Randomly inserted
HOF-OSOzzie Smith 25.00

Tools of the Trade Relics

NM/M
Common Player: 5.00
Bat Relics 1:34
Jersey Relics 1:426
RAB Roberto Alomar/bat 8.00
MA Moises Alou/bat 8.00
DB David Bell/bat 5.00
JBU Jeromy Burnitz/bat 5.00
JC Jose Canseco/bat 10.00
VC Vinny Castilla/bat 5.00
JCI Jeff Cirillo/bat 5.00
TC Tony Clark/bat 5.00
JDB Johnny Damon/bat 6.00
CE Carl Everett/bat 5.00
BF Brad Fullmer/bat 5.00
AG Andres Galarraga/bat 6.00
JG Juan Gonzalez/jsy 8.00
RHB Rickey Henderson/bat 10.00
BJ Brian Jordan/bat 5.00
DJ David Justice/bat 5.00
CK Chuck Knoblauch/bat 5.00
MLB Matt Lawton/bat 5.00
KL Kenny Lofton/bat 5.00
TM Tino Martinez/bat 6.00
CP Carlos Pena/bat 8.00
JP Josh Phelps/jsy 6.00
TR Tim Raines/bat 5.00
RS Reggie Sanders/bat 5.00
GS Gary Sheffield/bat 5.00
TS Tsuyoshi Shinjo/bat 5.00
RSI Ruben Sierra/bat 5.00
MT Michael Tucker/bat 5.00
JV John Vander Wal
MV Mo Vaughn/jsy 6.00
MVB Mo Vaughn/bat 6.00
RV Robin Ventura/bat 6.00
RW Rondell White/bat 5.00
EY Eric Young/bat 5.00

Tools of the Trade Dual Relics

NM/M
Common Card: 8.00
Inserted 1:539
MA Moises Alou 10.00
HN Hideo Nomo 35.00
CP Chan Ho Park 8.00

Legends Autographs

NM/M
Common Autograph: 10.00
Inserted 1:1,097
Johnny Bench 40.00
Vida Blue 10.00
Clete Boyer 12.00
Whitey Ford 30.00
Bob Gibson 25.00
Joe Pepitone 10.00
Bobby Richardson 10.00
Bill "Moose" Skowron 10.00
Enos Slaughter 18.00
Carl Yastrzemski 60.00

Signature Moves Autographs

NM/M
Common Autograph: 8.00
Inserted 1:91
RA Roberto Alomar 30.00
MA Moises Alou 15.00
TBL Tony Blanco 8.00
BB Boof Bonser 8.00
AC Antoine Cameron 10.00
BC Brandon Claussen 15.00
MC Matt Cooper 8.00
JD Johnny Damon 30.00
JDA Jeff DaVanon 8.00
VD Victor Diaz 12.00
RH Ryan Hannaman 8.00
KI Kazuhisa Ishii 40.00
FJ Forrest Johnson 8.00
TL Todd Linden 15.00
CM Corwin Malone 8.00
JM Jake Mauer 8.00
AM Andy Morales 8.00
RM Ramon Moreta 8.00
JMO Justin Morneau 15.00
JP Juan Pena 8.00
JS Juan Silvestre 8.00
CS Chris Smith 8.00
DT Dennis Tankersley 8.00
MT Marcus Thames 8.00
CU Chase Utley 15.00
JW Justin Wayne 8.00

2002 TOPPS AMERICAN PIE SPIRIT OF AMERICA

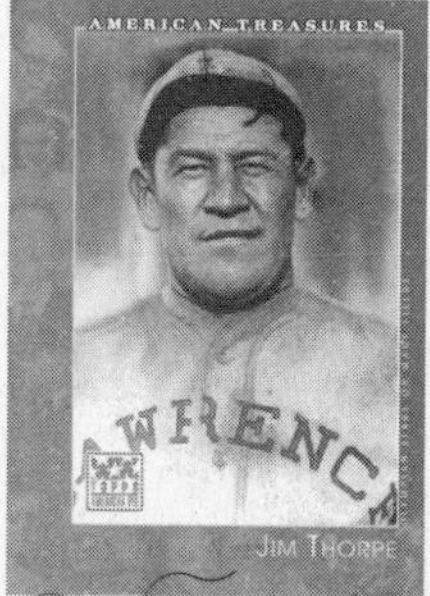

NM/M
Complete Set (150): 30.00
Common Player: .25
Pack (7): 5.00
Box (24): 100.00
1 Warren Spahn .75
2 Reggie Jackson .75
3 Bill Mazeroski .25
4 Carl Yastrzemski .75
5 Whitey Ford .75
6 Ralph Houk .25
7 Rod Carew .50
8 Kirk Gibson .25
9 Bobby Thomson .25
10 Don Newcombe .25
11 Gaylord Perry .25
12 Bruce Sutter .40
13 Bob Gibson .50
14 Brooks Robinson 1.00
15 Steve Carlton .50
16 Robin Yount 1.00
17 Ernie Banks .75
18 Lou Brock .25
19 Al Kaline .75
20 Carlton Fisk .75
21 Frank Robinson .75
22 Bobby Bonds .25
23 Andre Dawson .25
24 Rich "Goose" Gossage .25
25 Fred Lynn .25
26 Keith Hernandez .25
27 Rollie Fingers .25
28 Juan Marichal .25
29 Maury Wills .25
30 Dave Winfield .50
31 Frank Howard .25
32 Tony Gwynn 1.00
33 Jim Palmer .50
34 Mike Schmidt 1.50
35 Bo Jackson .75
36 Ferguson Jenkins .25
37 Bobby Richardson .25
38 Harmon Killebrew .75
39 Monte Irvin .25
40 Jim Abbott .50
41 Wade Boggs .75
42 Jackie Robinson 2.00
43 Ralph Branca .25
44 Minnie Minoso .25
45 Tug McGraw .25
46 Willie Mays 2.00
47 Nolan Ryan 3.00
48 Duke Snider 1.00
49 Tom Seaver 1.00
50 Casey Stengel .50
51 D-Day .75
52 Gulf War .25
53 Vietnam War .25
54 Korean War .25
55 Secret Service .25
56 Crayons .25
57 Hoover Dam .25
58 Penicillin .25
59 Polio Vaccine .25
60 Empire State Building .25
61 Television .25
62 Free Speech .25
63 Voyager Mission .25
64 Space Shuttle .25
65 Ellis Island .25
66 Statue of Liberty .25
67 Battle of the Bulge .25
68 Battle of Midway .25
69 Iwo Jima .25
70 Panama Canal .25
71 Spirit of St. Louis/Lindbergh .25
72 Civil Rights/We Shall Overcome .25
73 Space Race .25
74 Alaska Pipeline .25
75 Teddy Bear .25
76 Sea Biscuit .25
77 Bazooka Joe .25
78 Mt. Rushmore .25
79 Yellowstone Park .25
80 Niagara Falls .25
81 Grand Canyon .25
82 Hoola Hoop .25
83 George Patton .50
84 Audie Murphy .25
85 Amelia Earhart .25
86 Glen Miller .25
87 Rick Monday .25
88 Buzz Aldrin .25
89 Rosa Parks .25
90 Edward R. Murrow .25
91 Susan B. Anthony .25
92 Bobby Kennedy .25
93 Gloria Steinem .25
94 Hank Greenberg .75
95 Jimmy Doolittle .25
96 Thurgood Marshall .25
97 Ernest Hemingway .75
98 Henry Ford .25
99 Wright Brothers .25
100 Thomas Edison .75
101 Albert Einstein .75
102 Will Rogers .25
103 George Gershwin .25
104 Irving Berlin .25
105 Frank Lloyd Wright .25
106 Howard Hughes .25
107 George M. Cohan .25
108 Jack Kerouac .25
109 Harry Houdini .25
110 Helen Keller .25
111 John McCain .25
112 Andrew Carnegie .25
113 Sandra Day O'Connor .25
114 Brooklyn Bridge .25
115 Douglas MacArthur .25
116 Elvis Presley 1.00
117 George Burns .25
118 Judy Garland .50
119 Buddy Holly .25
120 Don McLean .25
121 Marilyn Monroe 1.00
122 Humphrey Bogart .50
123 Gary Cooper .25
124 The Andrews Sisters .25
125 Jim Thorpe 1.00
126 Joe Louis .75
127 Jesse Owens .50
128 Kate Smith .25
129 W.C. Fields .25
130 Bette Davis .25
131 Jayne Mansfield .25
132 Teddy Roosevelt .50
133 Franklin D. Roosevelt .75
134 Harry Truman .25
135 Dwight Eisenhower .50
136 George H.W. Bush .50
137 George W. Bush .50
138 John F. Kennedy 1.00
139 Lyndon B. Johnson .25
140 William Taft .25
141 Horace Harding .25
142 Woodrow Wilson .25
143 Richard Nixon .25
144 Bill Clinton .25
145 Jimmy Carter .25
146 Herbert Hoover .25
147 Gerald Ford .25
148 Ronald Reagan .25
149 Calvin Coolidge .25
150 William McKinley .25

Pie

NM/M
Common Card: 25.00
Inserted 1:119
HB Humphrey Bogart 120.00
GB George Burns 60.00
GC Gary Cooper 60.00
JD Judy Garland 80.00
MM Marilyn Monroe 350.00
EP Elvis Presley/shirt 125.00
EP2 Elvis Presley/coat 125.00
RR Ronald Reagan/Berlin Wall 25.00
JM Jayne Mansfield 80.00
BD Bette Davis 75.00

American Sluggers

NM/M
Complete Set (25): 25.00
Common Player: .50
Inserted 1:1

Each card issued in blue, gold, silver and red; no value differential

AD Andre Dawson .50
AK Al Kaline 1.00
BR Brooks Robinson 1.00
CC Cecil Cooper .50

CF Carlton Fisk 1.00
CY Carl Yastrzemski 2.00
DS Duke Snider 1.00
DW Dave Winfield 1.00
EM Eddie Mathews 1.00
FH Frank Howard .50
FL Fred Lynn .50
FR Frank Robinson 1.00
GB George Brett 3.00
GF George Foster .50
HK Harmon Killebrew 1.00
JC Jack Clark .50
JCC Joe Carter .50
KG Kirk Gibson .50
MI Monte Irvin .50
MS Mike Schmidt 3.00
RC Rod Carew 1.00
RJ Reggie Jackson 2.50
RS Ryne Sandberg 2.00
TK Ted Kluszewski 1.00
WM Willie Mays 4.00

Relics

NM/M
Common Player: 10.00
Inserted 1:32
GHWB George H.W. Bush 10.00
GWB George W. Bush 30.00
BC Bill Clinton 40.00
CC Calvin Coolidge 10.00
DE Dwight Eisenhower 20.00
GF Gerald Ford 20.00
WH Warren Harding 10.00
HH Herbert Hoover 10.00
LBJ Lyndon B. Johnson 15.00
JFK John F. Kennedy 35.00
RN Richard Nixon 30.00
RR Ronald Reagan 40.00
FDR Franklin D. Roosevelt 15.00
WT William Taft 10.00
HT Harry Truman 20.00
WW Woodrow Wilson 10.00
Common Player: 8.00
Inserted 1:11
JA Jim Abbott 15.00
DA Dick Allen 8.00
JB Johnny Bench 20.00
WB Wade Boggs 10.00
BB Bill Buckner 8.00
JC Jack Clark 8.00
AD Andre Dawson 10.00
KT Jim Kaat 10.00
EM Eddie Mathews 15.00
DM Don Mattingly 40.00
WM Willie Mays 40.00
MM Minnie Minoso 15.00
RM Rick Monday 10.00
JM Joe Morgan 10.00
TM Thurman Munson 30.00
AL Al Oliver 8.00
DP Dave Parker 10.00
GP Gaylord Perry 10.00
FR Frank Robinson 15.00
JR Joe Rudi 10.00
NR Nolan Ryan 40.00
TS Tom Seaver 20.00
WS Willie Stargell 15.00
DS Darryl Strawberry 15.00
DW Dave Winfield 12.00
CY Carl Yastrzemski 20.00

2002 TOPPS ARCHIVES

NM/M
Complete Set (200): 70.00
Common Player: .40
Pack (8): 3.00
Box (20): 50.00
1 Willie Mays 3.00
2 Dale Murphy .40
3 Dave Winfield .75
4 Roger Maris 2.00
5 Ron Cey .40
6 Lee Smith .40
7 Len Dykstra .40
8 Ray Fosse .40
9 Warren Spahn 1.00
10 Herb Score .40
11 Jim Wynn .40
12 Sam McDowell .40
13 Fred Lynn .40
14 Yogi Berra 1.50
15 Ron Santo .40
16 Alvin Dark .40
17 Bill Buckner .40
18 Rollie Fingers .60
19 Tony Gwynn 1.50
20 Red Schoendienst .40
21 Gaylord Perry .40
22 Jose Cruz .40
23 Dennis Martinez .40
24 Dave McNally .40
25 Norm Cash .40
26 Ted Kluszewski .40
27 Rick Reuschel .40
28 Bruce Sutter .75
29 Don Larsen .40
30 Claudell Washington .40
31 Luis Aparicio .40
32 Clete Boyer .40
33 Rich "Goose" Gossage .40
34 Ray Knight .40
35 Roy Campanella 1.50
36 Tug McGraw .40
37 Bob Lemon .40
38 Willie Stargell 1.00
39 Roberto Clemente 3.00
40 Jim Fregosi .40
41 Reggie Smith .40
42 Dave Parker .40
43 Darrell Evans .40
44 Ryne Sandberg 2.00
45 Manny Mota .40
46 Dennis Eckersley .60
47 Nellie Fox .40
48 Gil Hodges .40
49 Reggie Jackson 1.50
50 Bobby Shantz .40
51 Cecil Cooper .40
52 Jim Kaat .40
53 George Hendrick .40
54 Johnny Podres .40
55 Bob Gibson 1.00
56 Vern Law .40
57 Joe Adcock .40
58 Jack Clark .40
59 Bill Mazeroski .40
60 Carl Yastrzemski 1.50
61 Bobby Murcer .40
62 Davey Johnson .40
63 Jim Palmer .75
64 Roy Face .40
65 Dean Chance .40
66 Bill "Moose" Skowron .40
67 Dwight Evans .40
68 Kirk Gibson .40
69 Sal Bando .40
70 Mike Schmidt 2.00
71 Bo Jackson .75
72 Chris Chambliss .40
73 Fergie Jenkins .75
74 Brooks Robinson 1.50
75 Bobby Richardson .40
76 Duke Snider 1.50
77 Allie Reynolds .40
78 Harmon Killebrew 1.50
79 Steve Carlton 1.00
80 Bert Blyleven .40
81 Phil Niekro .40
82 Lew Burdette .40
83 Hoyt Wilhelm .40
84 Curt Flood .40
85 Guillermo Hernandez .40
86 Robin Yount 1.50
87 Robin Roberts .40
88 Whitey Ford 1.00
89 Tony Oliva .75
90 Don Newcombe .40
91 Al Oliver .40
92 Mike Cuellar .40
93 Mike Scott .40
94 Dick Allen .40
95 Jimmy Piersall .40
96 Bill Freehan .40
97 Willie Horton .40
98 Bob Friend .40
99 Ken Holtzman .40
100 Rico Carty .40
101 Gil McDougald .40
102 Lee May .40
103 Joe Pepitone .40
104 Gene Tenace .40
105 Gary Carter .40
106 Tim McCarver .40
107 Ernie Banks 1.50
108 George Foster .40
109 Lou Brock 1.00
110 Dick Groat .40
111 Graig Nettles .40
112 Boog Powell .40
113 Joe Carter .40
114 Juan Marichal .75
115 Larry Doby .40
116 Fernando Valenzuela .40
117 Luis Tiant .40
118 Early Wynn .40
119 Bill Madlock .40
120 Eddie Mathews 1.50
121 George Brett 3.00
122 Al Kaline 1.50
123 Frank Howard .40
124 Mickey Lolich .40
125 Kirby Puckett 3.00
126 Bob Cerv .40
127 Will Clark 1.00
128 Vida Blue .40
129 Kevin Mitchell .40
130 Bucky Dent .40
131 Tom Seaver 2.00
132 Jerry Koosman .40
133 Orlando Cepeda .40
134 Nolan Ryan 4.00
135 Tony Kubek .40
136 Don Drysdale 1.00
137 Paul Blair .40
138 Elston Howard .40
139 Joe Rudi .40
140 Tommie Agee .40
141 Richie Ashburn .40
142 Jim Bunning .40
143 Hank Sauer .40
144 Greg Luzinski .40
145 Ron Guidry .40
146 Rod Carew 1.00
147 Andre Dawson .75
148 Keith Hernandez .40
149 Carlton Fisk 1.00
150 Cleon Jones .40
151 Don Mattingly 3.00
152 Vada Pinson .40
153 Ozzie Smith 1.50
154 Dave Concepcion .40
155 Al Rosen .40
156 Tommy John .40
157 Bob Ojeda .40
158 Frank Robinson 1.50
159 Darryl Strawberry .40
160 Bobby Bonds .40
161 Bert Campaneris .40
162 Jim "Catfish" Hunter .40
163 Bud Harrelson .40
164 Dwight Gooden .40
165 Wade Boggs 1.00
166 Joe Morgan 1.00
167 Ron Swoboda .40
168 Hank Aaron 4.00
169 Steve Garvey .40
170 Mickey Rivers .40
171 Johnny Bench 3.00
172 Ralph Terry .40
173 Billy Pierce .40
174 Thurman Munson 2.50
175 Don Sutton .40
176 Sparky Anderson .40
177 Gil Hodges .40
178 Davey Johnson .40
179 Frank Robinson 1.50
180 Red Schoendienst .40
181 Roger Maris 2.00
182 Willie Mays 3.00
183 Luis Aparicio .40
184 Nellie Fox .40
185 Ernie Banks 1.50
186 Orlando Cepeda .75
187 Whitey Ford 1.00
188 Bob Gibson 1.00
189 Bill Mazeroski .40
190 Hank Aaron 3.00
191 Elston Howard, Harmon Killebrew, Carl Yastrzemski League Leaders .75
192 Orlando Cepeda, Jackie Robinson, Willie Mays League Leaders 2.00
193 Hank Aaron, Roberto Clemente, Dick Allen League Leaders 2.00
194 Tom Seaver, Phil Niekro, Fergie Jenkins, Juan Marichal League Leaders 1.00
195 Jim Palmer, Jim Hunter, Dennis Eckersley League Leaders .65
196 Hank Aaron 3.00
197 Brooks Robinson 1.50
198 Tom Seaver 1.50
199 Jim Palmer .75
200 Lou Brock 1.00

Autographs

NM/M
Common Autograph: 10.00
Inserted 1:22
HA Hank Aaron 250.00
DA Dick Allen 25.00
SB Sal Bando 20.00
EB Ernie Banks 125.00
BB Bobby Bonds 25.00
GB George Brett 250.00
JBU Jim Bunning 40.00
LB Lew Burdette 20.00
BC Bert Campaneris 10.00
GC Gary Carter 50.00
RCE Ron Cey 15.00
CC Chris Chambliss 15.00
JCR Jose Cruz 15.00
AD Alvin Dark 25.00
BD Bucky Dent 20.00
LD Len Dykstra 20.00
DEV Darrell Evans 15.00
GF George Foster 15.00
JF Jim Fregosi 10.00
SG Steve Garvey 15.00
DG Dwight Gooden 25.00
DGR Dick Groat 15.00
BH Bud Harrelson 15.00
WH Willie Hernandez 10.00
KH Keith Hernandez 40.00
BJ Bo Jackson 80.00
FJ Fergie Jenkins 20.00
TJ Tommy John 15.00
JK Jim Kaat 20.00
AK Al Kaline 125.00
HK Harmon Killebrew 110.00
JKO Jerry Koosman 65.00
GL Greg Luzinski 20.00
FL Fred Lynn 20.00
DM Dave McNally 20.00
KM Kevin Mitchell 20.00
DN Don Newcombe 15.00
TO Tony Oliva 30.00
JP Jim Palmer 50.00
DP Dave Parker 20.00
GP Gaylord Perry 20.00
BP Billy Pierce 10.00
JPI Jimmy Piersall 15.00
JPO Johnny Podres 15.00
BPO Boog Powell 25.00
KP Kirby Puckett 150.00
MR Mickey Rivers 10.00
BRO Brooks Robinson 80.00
JR Joe Rudi 15.00
RS Ron Santo 30.00
MS Mike Schmidt 150.00
LS Lee Smith 20.00
RSM Reggie Smith 15.00

DS Duke Snider
BS Bruce Sutter 35.00
RT Ralph Terry 25.00
HW Hoyt Wilhelm 20.00
DW Dave Winfield 85.00
RY Robin Yount 100.00

AutoProofs

NM/M

Quantity produced listed
1 Gary Carter/80 40.00
2 Jose Cruz/95 25.00
3 Steve Garvey/5
4 Bo Jackson/300 50.00
5 Kevin Mitchell/65 25.00
6 Kirby Puckett/65 75.00
7 Mike Schmidt/147 90.00
8 Ozzie Smith/105 75.00
9 Darryl Strawberry/181 40.00
10 Dave Winfield/16
11 Robin Yount/39 100.00

Game-Used Bat

NM/M

Common Player:
Group A 1:106
Group B 1:282
JB Johnny Bench 20.00
GB George Brett 40.00
GC Gary Carter 10.00
JC Joe Carter 10.00
NC Norm Cash 10.00
AD Andre Dawson 8.00
DE Dwight Evans 8.00
BF Bill Freehan 8.00
WH Willie Horton 10.00
RJ Reggie Jackson 15.00
DM Don Mattingly 50.00
RM Roger Maris 50.00
JM Joe Morgan 10.00
DP Dave Parker 10.00
BR Brooks Robinson 20.00
RS Ron Santo 20.00
WS Willie Stargell 15.00
CY Carl Yastrzemski 40.00
RY Robin Yount 20.00

Game-Worn Uniform

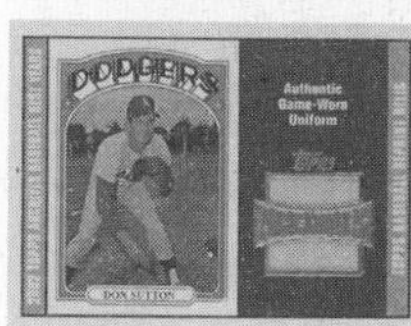

NM/M

Common Player: 8.00
Inserted 1:28
SA Sparky Anderson 10.00
WB Wade Boggs 15.00
BB Bobby Bonds 8.00
GB George Brett 30.00
OC Orlando Cepeda 10.00
WC Will Clark 20.00
DC Dave Concepcion 8.00
DE Dennis Eckersley 10.00
SG Steve Garvey 10.00
FL Fred Lynn 8.00
DM Dale Murphy 20.00
PN Phil Niekro 10.00
GP Gaylord Perry 10.00
KP Kirby Puckett 20.00
FR Frank Robinson 15.00
NR Nolan Ryan 40.00
RS Ryne Sandberg 30.00
OS Ozzie Smith 20.00
DS Don Sutton 10.00
DW Dave Winfield 10.00

Stadium Seat

NM/M

Common Player: 8.00
RA Richie Ashburn 15.00
SA Sparky Anderson 10.00
EB Ernie Banks 25.00
YB Yogi Berra 20.00
JB Jim Bunning 10.00
RC Rod Carew 20.00
JC Joe Carter 10.00
NF Nellie Fox 15.00
RG Ron Guidry 10.00
TK Ted Kluszewski 15.00
BL Bob Lemon 10.00
ML Mickey Lolich 10.00
EM Eddie Mathews 20.00
SM Sam McDowell 8.00
JP Jim Palmer 10.00
DP Dave Parker 10.00
HS Herb Score 10.00
DS Duke Snider 20.00
WS Warren Spahn 15.00

2002 TOPPS ARCHIVES RESERVE

NM/M

Complete Set (100): 100.00
Common Player: .75
Box (10 packs + Auto. Baseball): 125.00
1 Lee Smith .75
2 Gaylord Perry .75
3 Al Oliver .75
4 Rich "Goose" Gossage .75
5 Bill Madlock .75
6 Rod Carew 1.50
7 Fred Lynn .75
8 Frank Robinson 2.00
9 Al Kaline 2.50
10 Len Dykstra .75
11 Carlton Fisk 1.50
12 Nellie Fox 1.00
13 Reggie Jackson 3.00
14 Bob Gibson 2.00
15 Bill Buckner .75
16 Harmon Killebrew 2.00
17 Gary Carter 1.50
18 Dave Winfield 1.50
19 Ozzie Smith 2.50
20 Dwight Evans .75
21 Dave Concepcion .75
22 Joe Morgan 1.00
23 Clete Boyer .75
24 Will Clark 1.50
25 Lee May .75
26 Kevin Mitchell .75
27 Roger Maris 3.00
28 Mickey Lolich .75
29 Luis Aparicio .75
30 George Foster .75
31 Don Mattingly 6.00
32 Fernando Valenzuela .75
33 Bobby Bonds .75
34 Jim Palmer 1.50
35 Dennis Eckersley 1.00
36 Kirby Puckett 3.00
37 Jose Cruz .75
38 Richie Ashburn .75
39 Whitey Ford 2.00
40 Robin Roberts .75
41 Don Newcombe .75
42 Roy Campanella 2.50
43 Dennis Martinez .75
44 Larry Doby 1.00
45 Steve Garvey .75
46 Thurman Munson 3.00
47 Dale Murphy 1.50
48 Bill "Moose" Skowron .75
49 Tom Seaver 3.00
50 Orlando Cepeda .75
51 Graig Nettles .75
52 Willie Stargell 1.50
53 Yogi Berra 2.50
54 Steve Carlton 1.50
55 Don Sutton .75
56 Brooks Robinson 1.50
57 Vida Blue .75
58 Rollie Fingers 1.00
59 Jim Bunning .75
60 Nolan Ryan 8.00
61 Hank Aaron 6.00
62 Fergie Jenkins .75
63 Andre Dawson 1.00
64 Ernie Banks 2.50
65 Early Wynn .75
66 Duke Snider 1.50
67 Red Schoendienst .75
68 Don Drysdale 1.00
69 Jim "Catfish" Hunter 1.00
70 George Brett 6.00
71 Elston Howard 1.00
72 Wade Boggs 1.50
73 Keith Hernandez .75
74 Billy Pierce .75
75 Ted Kluszewski .75
76 Carl Yastrzemski 4.00
77 Bert Blyleven .75
78 Tony Oliva .75
79 Joe Carter .75
80 Johnny Bench 3.00
81 Tony Gwynn 3.00
82 Mike Schmidt 4.00
83 Phil Niekro .75
84 Juan Marichal .75
85 Eddie Mathews 2.50
86 Boog Powell .75
87 Dwight Gooden .75
88 Darryl Strawberry .75
89 Roberto Clemente 6.00
90 Ryne Sandberg 5.00
91 Jack Clark .75
92 Willie Mays 6.00
93 Ron Guidry .75
94 Kirk Gibson .75
95 Lou Brock 1.00
96 Robin Yount 2.50
97 Bill Mazeroski .75
98 Dave Parker .75
99 Hoyt Wilhelm .75
100 Warren Spahn 1.50

Autographed Baseballs

NM/M

Common Auto. Ball: 15.00
Inserted 1:box
Luis Aparicio/1,600 25.00
Ernie Banks/50 75.00
Yogi Berra/100 85.00
Lou Brock/400 40.00
Jim Bunning/500 35.00
Gary Carter/500 40.00
Rich Gossage/500 20.00
Fergie Jenkins/1,000 20.00
Al Kaline/250 75.00
Harmon Killebrew/250 60.00
Willie Mays/50
Joe Morgan/250 40.00
Graig Nettles/1,600 15.00
Jim Palmer/400 25.00
Gaylord Perry/500 15.00
Brooks Robinson/500 40.00
Mike Schmidt/250 125.00
Duke Snider/100 65.00
Dave Winfield/1650 30.00
Robin Yount/250 90.00

Best Years Autographs

NM/M

Common Autograph: 12.00
Inserted 1:15 Hobby
LA Luis Aparicio 15.00
EB Ernie Banks 70.00
YB Yogi Berra 60.00
LB Lou Brock 25.00
GC Gary Carter 20.00
FJ Fergie Jenkins 12.00
AK Al Kaline 40.00
HK Harmon Killebrew 40.00
WM Willie Mays 120.00
JM Joe Morgan 25.00
GN Graig Nettles 12.00
GP Gaylord Perry 15.00
BR Brooks Robinson 25.00
MS Mike Schmidt 125.00
LS Lee Smith 12.00
DS Duke Snider 60.00
RY Robin Yount 80.00

Best Years Game-Worn Uni.

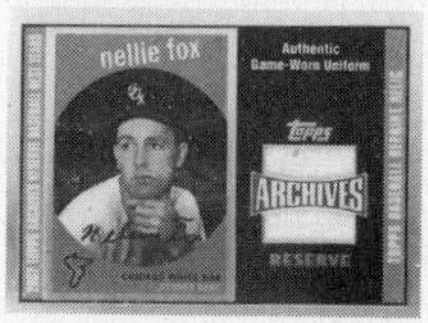

NM/M

Common Player: 10.00
Inserted 1:7 Hobby
EB Ernie Banks 25.00
JBU Johnny Bench 15.00
WBJ Wade Boggs 10.00
GCJ Gary Carter 12.00
WC Will Clark 15.00
NF Nellie Fox 15.00
TG Tony Gwynn 15.00
JM Juan Marichal 12.00
WM Willie Mays 35.00
KPJ Kirby Puckett 15.00
BR Brooks Robinson 12.00
NR Nolan Ryan 30.00
RSJ Red Schoendienst 10.00
WS Willie Stargell 15.00
RYU Robin Yount 12.00

Best Years Game-Used Bat

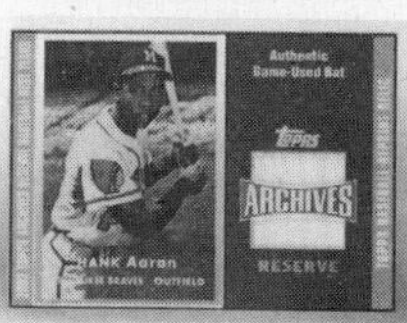

NM/M

Common Player: 10.00
Inserted 1:22
HAB Hank Aaron 40.00
GBB George Brett 25.00
OC Orlando Cepeda 10.00
CF Carlton Fisk 10.00
RM Roger Maris 70.00
EMB Eddie Mathews 20.00
DMB Don Mattingly 30.00
TM Thurman Munson 30.00
DW Dave Winfield 10.00
CYB Carl Yastrzemski 25.00

Team Topps Legends Autographs

NM/M

Common Player:
Rich "Goose" Gossage 10.00
Graig Nettles 10.00
Jim Palmer 15.00
Gaylord Perry 15.00

2002 TOPPS CHROME

NM/M

Complete Set (685): 200.00
Common Player: .25
Pack (4): 2.00
Box (24): 40.00
1 Pedro Martinez 1.25
2 Mike Stanton .25
3 Brad Penny .25
4 Mike Matheny .25
5 Johnny Damon .40
6 Bret Boone .40
7 Retired # not issued .25
8 Chris Truby .25
9 B.J. Surhoff .25
10 Mike Hampton .40

No.	Player	Value
11	Juan Pierre	.25
12	Mark Buehrle	.25
13	Bob Abreu	.50
14	David Cone	.25
15	Aaron Sele	.25
16	Fernando Tatis	.25
17	Bobby Jones	.25
18	Rick Helling	.25
19	Dmitri Young	.25
20	Mike Mussina	1.00
21	Mike Sweeney	.25
22	Cristian Guzman	.25
23	Ryan Kohlmeier	.25
24	Adam Kennedy	.25
25	Larry Walker	.50
26	Eric Davis	.40
27	Jason Tyner	.25
28	Eric Young	.25
29	Jason Marquis	.25
30	Luis Gonzalez	.50
31	Kevin Tapani	.25
32	Orlando Cabrera	.25
33	Marty Cordova	.25
34	Brad Ausmus	.25
35	Livan Hernandez	.25
36	Alex Gonzalez	.25
37	Edgar Renteria	.50
38	Bengie Molina	.25
39	Frank Menechino	.25
40	Rafael Palmeiro	1.00
41	Brad Fullmer	.25
42	Julio Zuleta	.25
43	Darren Dreifort	.25
44	Trot Nixon	.50
45	Trevor Hoffman	.25
46	Vladimir Nunez	.25
47	Mark Kotsay	.25
48	Kenny Rogers	.25
49	Ben Petrick	.25
50	Jeff Bagwell	1.00
51	Juan Encarnacion	.25
52	Ramiro Mendoza	.25
53	Brian Meadows	.25
54	Chad Curtis	.25
55	Aramis Ramirez	.50
56	Mark McLemore	.25
57	Dante Bichette	.25
58	Scott Schoeneweis	.25
59	Jose Cruz	.25
60	Roger Clemens	3.00
61	Jose Guillen	.25
62	Darren Oliver	.25
63	Chris Reitsma	.25
64	Jeff Abbott	.25
65	Robin Ventura	.25
66	Denny Neagle	.25
67	Al Martin	.25
68	Benito Santiago	.25
69	Roy Oswalt	.50
70	Juan Gonzalez	1.00
71	Garret Anderson	.75
72	Bobby Bonilla	.25
73	Danny Bautista	.25
74	J.T. Snow	.25
75	Derek Jeter	4.00
76	John Olerud	.50
77	Kevin Appier	.25
78	Phil Nevin	.25
79	Sean Casey	.50
80	Troy Glaus	.75
81	Joe Randa	.25
82	Jose Valentin	.25
83	Ricky Bottalico	.25
84	Todd Zeile	.25
85	Barry Larkin	.75
86	Bob Wickman	.25
87	Jeff Shaw	.25
88	Greg Vaughn	.25
89	Fernando Vina	.25
90	Mark Mulder	.50
91	Paul Bako	.25
92	Aaron Boone	.25
93	Esteban Loaiza	.25
94	Richie Sexson	.75
95	Alfonso Soriano	1.00
96	Tony Womack	.25
97	Paul Shuey	.25
98	Melvin Mora	.25
99	Tony Gwynn	1.50
100	Vladimir Guerrero	1.50
101	Keith Osik	.25
102	Randy Velarde	.25
103	Scott Williamson	.25
104	Daryle Ward	.25
105	Doug Mientkiewicz	.25
106	Stan Javier	.25
107	Russ Ortiz	.25
108	Wade Miller	.25
109	Luke Prokopec	.25
110	Andruw Jones	1.00
111	Ron Coomer	.25
112	Dan Wilson	.25
113	Luis Castillo	.25
114	Derek Bell	.25
115	Gary Sheffield	.75
116	Ruben Rivera	.25
117	Paul O'Neill	.50
118	Craig Paquette	.25
119	Kelvim Escobar	.25
120	Brad Radke	.25
121	Jorge Fabregas	.25
122	Randy Winn	.25
123	Tom Goodwin	.25
124	Jaret Wright	.25
125	Bonds-Race to 73	40.00
126	Al Leiter	.50
127	Ben Davis	.25
128	Frank Catalanotto	.25
129	Jose Cabrera	.25
130	Magglio Ordonez	.50
131	Jose Macias	.25
132	Ted Lilly	.25
133	Chris Holt	.25
134	Eric Milton	.25
135	Shannon Stewart	.25
136	Omar Olivares	.25
137	David Segui	.25
138	Jeff Nelson	.25
139	Matt Williams	.25
140	Ellis Burks	.25
141	Jason Bere	.25
142	Jimmy Haynes	.25
143	Ramon Hernandez	.25
144	Craig Counsell	.25
145	John Smoltz	.50
146	Homer Bush	.25
147	Quilvio Veras	.25
148	Esteban Yan	.25
149	Ramon Ortiz	.25
150	Carlos Delgado	.75
151	Lee Stevens	.25
152	Wil Cordero	.25
153	Mike Bordick	.25
154	John Flaherty	.25
155	Omar Daal	.25
156	Todd Ritchie	.25
157	Carl Everett	.25
158	Scott Sullivan	.25
159	Deivi Cruz	.25
160	Albert Pujols	3.00
161	Royce Clayton	.25
162	Jeff Suppan	.25
163	C.C. Sabathia	.25
164	Jimmy Rollins	.25
165	Rickey Henderson	.50
166	Rey Ordonez	.25
167	Shawn Estes	.25
168	Reggie Sanders	.25
169	Jon Lieber	.25
170	Armando Benitez	.25
171	Mike Remlinger	.25
172	Billy Wagner	.25
173	Troy Percival	.25
174	Devon White	.25
175	Ivan Rodriguez	1.00
176	Dustin Hermanson	.25
177	Brian Anderson	.25
178	Graeme Lloyd	.25
179	Russell Branyan	.25
180	Bobby Higginson	.25
181	Alex Gonzalez	.25
182	John Franco	.25
183	Sidney Ponson	.25
184	Jose Mesa	.25
185	Todd Hollandsworth	.25
186	Kevin Young	.25
187	Tim Wakefield	.25
188	Craig Biggio	.50
189	Jason Isringhausen	.25
190	Mark Quinn	.25
191	Glendon Rusch	.25
192	Damian Miller	.25
193	Sandy Alomar	.25
194	Scott Brosius	.25
195	Dave Martinez	.25
196	Danny Graves	.25
197	Shea Hillenbrand	.25
198	Jimmy Anderson	.25
199	Travis Lee	.25
200	Randy Johnson	1.50
201	Carlos Beltran	.50
202	Jerry Hairston Jr.	.25
203	Jesus Sanchez	.25
204	Eddie Taubensee	.25
205	David Wells	.25
206	Russ Davis	.25
207	Michael Barrett	.25
208	Marquis Grissom	.25
209	Byung-Hyun Kim	.25
210	Hideo Nomo	.75
211	Ryan Rupe	.25
212	Ricky Gutierrez	.25
213	Darryl Kile	.25
214	Rico Brogna	.25
215	Terrence Long	.25
216	Mike Jackson	.25
217	Jamey Wright	.25
218	Adrian Beltre	.50
219	Benny Agbayani	.25
220	Chuck Knoblauch	.25
221	Randy Wolf	.25
222	Andy Ashby	.25
223	Corey Koskie	.25
224	Roger Cedeno	.25
225	Ichiro Suzuki	3.00
226	Keith Foulke	.25
227	Ryan Minor	.25
228	Shawon Dunston	.25
229	Alex Cora	.25
230	Jeromy Burnitz	.25
231	Mark Grace	.75
232	Aubrey Huff	.25
233	Jeffrey Hammonds	.25
234	Olmedo Saenz	.25
235	Brian Jordan	.25
236	Jeremy Giambi	.25
237	Joe Girardi	.25
238	Eric Gagne	.50
239	Masato Yoshii	.25
240	Greg Maddux	2.00
241	Bryan Rekar	.25
242	Ray Durham	.25
243	Torii Hunter	.50
244	Derrek Lee	.50
245	Jim Edmonds	.75
246	Einar Diaz	.25
247	Brian Bohanon	.25
248	Ron Belliard	.25
249	Mike Lowell	.50
250	Sammy Sosa	2.50
251	Richard Hidalgo	.40
252	Bartolo Colon	.25
253	Jorge Posada	.50
254	LaTroy Hawkins	.25
255	Paul LoDuca	.25
256	Carlos Febles	.25
257	Nelson Cruz	.25
258	Edgardo Alfonzo	.25
259	Joey Hamilton	.25
260	Cliff Floyd	.25
261	Wes Helms	.25
262	Jay Bell	.25
263	Mike Cameron	.25
264	Paul Konerko	.25
265	Jeff Kent	.50
266	Robert Fick	.25
267	Allen Levrault	.25
268	Placido Polanco	.25
269	Marlon Anderson	.25
270	Mariano Rivera	.50
271	Chan Ho Park	.25
272	Jose Vizcaino	.25
273	Jeff D'Amico	.25
274	Mark Gardner	.25
275	Travis Fryman	.25
276	Darren Lewis	.25
277	Bruce Bochy	.25
278	Jerry Manuel	.25
279	Bob Brenly	.25
280	Don Baylor	.25
281	Davey Lopes	.25
282	Jerry Narron	.25
283	Tony Muser	.25
284	Hal McRae	.25
285	Bobby Cox	.25
286	Larry Dierker	.25
287	Phil Garner	.25
288	Jimy Williams	.25
289	Bobby Valentine	.25
290	Dusty Baker	.25
291	Lloyd McLendon	.25
292	Mike Scioscia	.25
293	Buck Martinez	.25
294	Larry Bowa	.25
295	Tony LaRussa	.25
296	Jeff Torborg	.25
297	Tom Kelly	.25
298	Mike Hargrove	.25
299	Art Howe	.25
300	Lou Piniella	.25
301	Charlie Manuel	.25
302	Buddy Bell	.25
303	Tony Perez	.25
304	Bob Boone	.25
305	Joe Torre	.25
306	Jim Tracy	.25
307	Jason Lane	1.00
308	Chris George	.25
309	Hank Blalock	2.00
310	Joe Borchard	.25
311	Marlon Byrd	.50
312	*Raymond Cabrera*	1.00
313	*Freddy Sanchez*	1.50
314	*Scott Wiggins*	1.00
315	*Jason Maule*	1.00
316	*Dionys Cesar*	1.50
317	Boof Bonser	.25
318	*Juan Tolentino*	1.50
319	*Earl Snyder*	1.50
320	*Travis Wade*	1.50
321	*Napoleon Calzado*	1.50
322	*Eric Glaser*	1.50
323	*Craig Kuzmic*	1.50
324	*Nic Jackson*	1.50
325	Mike Rivera	.25
326	*Jason Bay*	5.00
327	Chris Smith	.25
328	Jake Gautreau	.25
329	Gabe Gross	.25
330	Kenny Baugh	.25
331	J.D. Martin	.25
366	Pat Meares	.25
367	Mike Lieberthal	.25
368	Scott Erickson	.25
369	Ron Gant	.25
370	Moises Alou	.50
371	Chad Kreuter	.25
372	Willis Roberts	.25
373	Toby Hall	.25
374	Miguel Batista	.25
375	John Burkett	.25
376	Cory Lidle	.25
377	Nick Neugebauer	.25
378	Jay Payton	.25
379	Steve Karsay	.25
380	Eric Chavez	.50
381	Kelly Stinnett	.25
382	Jarrod Washburn	.25
383	C.J. Nitkowski	.25
384	Jeff Conine	.25
385	Fred McGriff	.50
386	Marvin Benard	.25
387	Dave Burba	.25
388	Dennis Cook	.25
389	Rick Reed	.25
390	Tom Glavine	.75
391	Rondell White	.25
392	Matt Morris	.50
393	Pat Rapp	.25
394	Robert Person	.25
395	Omar Vizquel	.40
396	Jeff Cirillo	.25
397	Dave Mlicki	.25
398	Jose Ortiz	.25
399	Ryan Dempster	.25
400	Curt Schilling	.75
401	Peter Bergeron	.25
402	Kyle Lohse	.25
403	Craig Wilson	.25
404	David Justice	.75
405	Darin Erstad	.50
406	Jose Mercedes	.25
407	Carl Pavano	.25
408	Albie Lopez	.25
409	Alex Ochoa	.25
410	Chipper Jones	1.50
411	Tyler Houston	.25
412	Dean Palmer	.25
413	Damian Jackson	.25
414	Josh Towers	.25
415	Rafael Furcal	.50
416	Mike Morgan	.25
417	Herb Perry	.25
418	Mike Sirotka	.25
419	Mark Wohlers	.25
420	Nomar Garciaparra	2.50

421	Felipe Lopez	.25
422	Joe McEwing	.25
423	Jacque Jones	.25
424	Julio Franco	.25
425	Frank Thomas	1.00
426	Kent Bottenfield	.25
427	Mac Suzuki	.25
428	D'Angelo Jimenez	.25
429	Chris Stynes	.25
430	Kerry Wood	1.50
431	Chris Singleton	.25
432	Erubiel Durazo	.25
433	Matt Lawton	.25
434	Bill Mueller	.25
435	Jose Canseco	.50
436	Ben Grieve	.25
437	Terry Mulholland	.25
438	David Bell	.25
439	A.J. Pierzynski	.25
440	Adam Dunn	1.00
441	Jon Garland	.25
442	Jeff Fassero	.25
443	Julio Lugo	.25
444	Carlos Guillen	.25
445	Orlando Hernandez	.25
446	Mark Loretta	.25
447	Scott Spiezio	.25
448	Kevin Millwood	.50
449	Jamie Moyer	.25
450	Todd Helton	1.00
451	Todd Walker	.25
452	Jose Lima	.25
453	Brook Fordyce	.25
454	Aaron Rowand	.25
455	Barry Zito	.50
456	Eric Owens	.25
457	Charles Nagy	.25
458	Raul Ibanez	.25
459	Joe Mays	.25
460	Jim Thome	1.50
461	Adam Eaton	.25
462	Felix Martinez	.25
463	Vernon Wells	.25
464	Donnie Sadler	.25
465	Tony Clark	.25
466	Jose Hernandez	.25
467	Ramon Martinez	.25
468	Rusty Greer	.25
469	Rod Barajas	.25
470	Lance Berkman	.75
471	Brady Anderson	.25
472	Pedro Astacio	.25
473	Shane Halter	.25
474	Bret Prinz	.25
475	Edgar Martinez	.50
476	Steve Trachsel	.25
477	Gary Matthews Jr.	.25
478	Ismael Valdes	.25
479	Juan Uribe	.25
480	Shawn Green	.75
481	Kirk Rueter	.25
482	Damion Easley	.25
483	Chris Carpenter	.25
484	Kris Benson	.25
485	Antonio Alfonseca	.25
486	Kyle Farnsworth	.25
487	Brandon Lyon	.25
488	Hideki Irabu	.25
489	David Ortiz	.50
490	Mike Piazza	2.50
491	Derek Lowe	.25
492	Chris Gomez	.25
493	Mark Johnson	.25
494	John Rocker	.25
495	Eric Karros	.25
496	Bill Haselman	.25
497	Dave Veres	.25
498	Gil Heredia	.25
499	Tomokazu Ohka	.25
500	Barry Bonds	4.00
501	David Dellucci	.25
502	Ed Sprague	.25
503	Tom Gordon	.25
504	Javier Vazquez	.25
505	Ben Sheets	.75
506	Wilton Guerrero	.25
507	John Halama	.25
508	Mark Redman	.25
509	Jack Wilson	.25
510	Bernie Williams	.75
511	Miguel Cairo	.25
512	Denny Hocking	.25
513	Tony Batista	.25
514	Mark Grudzielanek	.25
515	Jose Vidro	.25
516	Sterling Hitchcock	.25
517	Billy Koch	.25
518	Matt Clement	.25
519	Bruce Chen	.25
520	Roberto Alomar	1.00
521	Orlando Palmeiro	.25
522	Steve Finley	.25
523	Danny Patterson	.25
524	Terry Adams	.25
525	Tino Martinez	.25
526	Tony Armas Jr.	.25
527	Geoff Jenkins	.50
528	Chris Michalak	.25
529	Corey Patterson	.50
530	Brian Giles	.50
531	Jose Jimenez	.25
532	Joe Kennedy	.25
533	Armando Rios	.25
534	Osvaldo Fernandez	.25
535	Ruben Sierra	.25
536	Octavio Dotel	.25
537	Luis Sojo	.25
538	Brent Butler	.25
539	Pablo Ozuna	.25
540	Freddy Garcia	.25
541	Chad Durbin	.25
542	Orlando Merced	.25
543	Michael Tucker	.25
544	Roberto Hernandez	.25
545	Pat Burrell	.50
546	A.J. Burnett	.25
547	Bubba Trammell	.25
548	Scott Elarton	.25
549	Mike Darr	.25
550	Ken Griffey Jr.	2.00
551	Ugueth Urbina	.25
552	Todd Jones	.25
553	Delino DeShields	.25
554	Adam Piatt	.25
555	Jason Kendall	.25
556	Hector Ortiz	.25
557	Turk Wendell	.25
558	Rob Bell	.25
559	Sun-Woo Kim	.25
560	Raul Mondesi	.50
561	Brent Abernathy	.25
562	Seth Etherton	.25
563	Shawn Wooten	.25
564	Jay Buhner	.25
565	Andres Galarraga	.50
566	Shane Reynolds	.25
567	Rod Beck	.25
568	Dee Brown	.25
569	Pedro Feliz	.25
570	Ryan Klesko	.25
571	John Vander Wal	.25
572	Nick Bierbrodt	.25
573	Joe Nathan	.25
574	James Baldwin	.25
575	J.D. Drew	.75
576	Greg Colbrunn	.25
577	Doug Glanville	.25
578	Rey Sanchez	.25
579	Todd Van Poppel	.25
580	Rich Aurilia	.25
581	Chuck Finley	.25
582	Abraham Nunez	.25
583	Kenny Lofton	.50
584	Brian Daubach	.25
585	Miguel Tejada	.75
586	Nate Cornejo	.25
587	Kazuhiro Sasaki	.50
588	Chris Richard	.25
589	Armando Reynoso	.25
590	Tim Hudson	.75
591	Neifi Perez	.25
592	Steve Cox	.25
593	Henry Blanco	.25
594	Ricky Ledee	.25
595	Tim Salmon	.50
596	Luis Rivas	.25
597	Jeff Zimmerman	.25
598	Matt Stairs	.25
599	Preston Wilson	.25
600	Mark McGwire	4.00
601	Timo Perez	.25
602	Matt Anderson	.25
603	Todd Hundley	.25
604	Rick Ankiel	.25
605	Tsuyoshi Shinjo	.25
606	Woody Williams	.25
607	Jason LaRue	.25
608	Carlos Lee	.25
609	Russ Johnson	.25
610	Scott Rolen	1.50
611	Brent Mayne	.25
612	Darrin Fletcher	.25
613	Ray Lankford	.25
614	Troy O'Leary	.25
615	Javier Lopez	.50
616	Randy Velarde	.25
617	Vinny Castilla	.25
618	Milton Bradley	.25
619	Ruben Mateo	.25
620	Jason Giambi	1.00
621	Andy Benes	.25
622	Tony Eusebio	.25
623	Andy Pettitte	.75
624	Jose Offerman	.25
625	Mo Vaughn	.50
626	Steve Sparks	.25
627	Mike Matthews	.25
628	Robb Nen	.25
629	Kip Wells	.25
630	Kevin Brown	.50
631	Arthur Rhodes	.25
632	Gabe Kapler	.25
633	Jermaine Dye	.25
634	Josh Beckett	.75
635	Pokey Reese	.25
636	Benji Gil	.25
637	Marcus Giles	.25
638	Julian Tavarez	.25
639	Jason Schmidt	.50
640	Alex Rodriguez	3.00
641	Anaheim Angels	.25
642	Arizona Diamondbacks	.25
643	Atlanta Braves	.25
644	Baltimore Orioles	.25
645	Boston Red Sox	.25
646	Chicago Cubs	.25
647	Chicago White Sox	.25
648	Cincinnati Reds	.25
649	Cleveland Indians	.25
650	Colorado Rockies	.25
651	Detroit Tigers	.25
652	Florida Marlins	.25
653	Houston Astros	.25
654	Kansas City Royals	.25
655	Los Angeles Dodgers	.25
656	Milwaukee Brewers	.25
657	Minnesota Twins	.25
658	Montreal Expos	.25
659	New York Mets	.25
660	New York Yankees	1.00
661	Oakland Athletics	.25
662	Philadelphia Phillies	.25
663	Pittsburgh Pirates	.25
664	San Diego Padres	.25
665	San Francisco Giants	.25
666	Seattle Mariners	.25
667	St. Louis Cardinals	.25
668	Tampa Bay Devil Rays	.25
669	Texas Rangers	.25
670	Toronto Blue Jays	.25
671	Juan Cruz	.25
672	*Kevin Cash*	1.00
673	*Jimmy Gobble*	3.00
674	*Mike Hill*	.75
675	*Taylor Buchholz*	.75
676	Bill Hall	.75
677	*Brett Roneberg*	.75
678	*Royce Huffman*	.75
679	*Chris Tritle*	1.00
680	*Nate Espy*	.50
681	*Nick Alvarez*	1.00
682	*Jason Botts*	1.50
683	*Ryan Gripp*	.75
684	*Dan Phillips*	.50
685	*Pablo Arias*	.75
686	*John Rodriguez*	.75
687	*Rich Harden*	10.00
688	*Neal Frendling*	1.00
689	*Rich Thompson*	.50
690	*Greg Montalbano*	1.00
691	*Leonard Dinardo*	.75
692	*Ryan Raburn*	.50
693	Josh Barfield	5.00
694	*David Bacani*	.75
695	*Dan Johnson*	2.00
696	Mike Mussina	.50
697	Ivan Rodriguez	.50
698	Doug Mientkiewicz	.25
699	Roberto Alomar	.50
700	Eric Chavez	.25
701	Omar Vizquel	.25
702	Mike Cameron	.25
703	Torii Hunter	.25
704	Ichiro Suzuki	1.50
705	Greg Maddux	1.00
706	Brad Ausmus	.25
707	Todd Helton	.75
708	Fernando Vina	.25
709	Scott Rolen	.75
710	Orlando Cabrera	.25
711	Andruw Jones	.50
712	Jim Edmonds	.25
713	Larry Walker	.25
714	Roger Clemens	1.50
715	Randy Johnson	.75
716	Ichiro Suzuki	1.50
717	Barry Bonds	2.00
718	Ichiro Suzuki	
719	Albert Pujols	

Black Refracto

Stars:
Production 50 sets

Gold Refractor

Stars: 2-4X
Inserted 1:4

Aces

		NM/M
Common Player:		10.00
KB	Kevin Brown	10.00
TH	Tim Hudson	10.00
AL	Al Leiter	10.00
CS	Curt Schilling	15.00
BZ	Barry Zito	10.00

Batterymates

		NM/M
Inserted 1:349		
GL	Tom Glavine, Javy Lopez	20.00
HP	Mike Hampton, Ben Petrick	10.00

Deuces Are Wild

		NM/M
Common Card:		
Inserted 1:428		
CA	Andruw Jones, Chipper Jones	40.00
BT	Bernie Williams, Tino Martinez	25.00
RC	Ryan Dempster, Cliff Floyd	10.00

Jack of All Trades

		NM/M
Common Player:		10.00
CJ	Chipper Jones	20.00
MO	Magglio Ordonez	10.00
AR	Alex Rodriguez	25.00

Kings of the Clubhouse

		NM/M
Common Player:		15.00
JB	Jeff Bagwell	15.00
TG	Tony Gwynn	20.00
AR	Alex Rodriguez	25.00

Like Father, Like Son Relics

		NM/M
Inserted 1:790		
WI	Preston Wilson, Mookie Wilson	10.00

Three of a Kind

		NM/M
Common Card		
AIR	Alex Rodriguez, Ivan Rodriguez, Rafael Palmeiro	50.00
BEJ	Bret Boone, Edgar Martinez, John Olerud	25.00
JCL	Jeff Bagwell, Craig Biggio, Lance Berkman	40.00

Top of the Order

		NM/M
Common Player:		8.00
Inserted 1:106		
BA	Benny Agbayani/jsy	8.00
PB	Peter Bergeron/jsy	8.00
CB	Craig Biggio/jsy	15.00
JD	Johnny Damon/bat	10.00
RF	Rafael Furcal/bat	10.00
RH	Rickey Henderson/bat	20.00
JK	Jason Kendall/bat	10.00

ɔblauch/bat 8.00
CYca/bat 10.00
Pton/jsy 10.00
Ye/bat 10.00
Stewart/jsy 10.00

ER REPRINTS

NM/M
ɔet (19): 50.00
Card: 3.00
:8
rs: 2X
1:24
Roy Campanella 4.00
Duke Snider 4.00
3 Carl Erskine 3.00
-4 Andy Pafko 3.00
-5 Johnny Mize 3.00
R-6 Billy Martin 4.00
2R-7 Phil Rizzuto 4.00
2R-8 Gil McDougald 3.00
52R-9 Allie Reynolds 3.00
52R-10 Jackie Robinson 5.00
52R-11 Preacher Roe 3.00
52R-12 Gil Hodges 3.00
52R-13 Billy Cox 3.00
52R-14 Yogi Berra 4.00
52R-15 Gene Woodling 3.00
52R-16 Johnny Sain 3.00
52R-17 Ralph Houk 3.00
52R-18 Joe Collins 3.00
52R-19 Hank Bauer 3.00

2002 TOPPS GALLERY

NM/M
Complete Set (200): 60.00
Common Player: .25
Common (151-200): .75
Inserted 1:1
Pack (6): 1.50
Box (24): 30.00
1 Jason Giambi .50
2 Mark Grace .40
3 Bret Boone .40
4 Antonio Alfonseca .25
5 Kevin Brown .40
6 Cristian Guzman .25
7 Magglio Ordonez .40
8 Luis Gonzalez .40
9 Jorge Posada .40
10 Roberto Alomar .50
11 Mike Sweeney .25
12 Jeff Kent .40
13 Matt Morris .40
14 Alfonso Soriano .75
15 Adam Dunn .50
16 Neifi Perez .25
17 Todd Walker .25
18 J.D. Drew .40
19 Eric Chavez .40
20 Alex Rodriguez 1.50
21 Ray Lankford .25
22 Roger Cedeno .25
23 Chipper Jones .75
24 Jose Canseco .50
25 Mike Piazza 1.50
26 Freddy Garcia .25
27 Todd Helton .50
28 Tino Martinez .40
29 Kazuhiro Sasaki .25
30 Curt Schilling .50
31 Mark Buehrle .25
32 John Olerud .40
33 Brad Radke .25
34 Steve Sparks .25
35 Jason Tyner .25
36 Jeff Shaw .25
37 Mariano Rivera .40
38 Russ Ortiz .25
39 Richard Hidalgo .25
40 Barry Bonds 2.00
41 John Burkett .25
42 Tim Hudson .40
43 Mike Hampton .25
44 Orlando Cabrera .25
45 Barry Zito .40
46 C.C. Sabathia .25
47 Chan Ho Park .25
48 Tom Glavine .50
49 Aramis Ramirez .40
50 Lance Berkman .40
51 Al Leiter .25
52 Phil Nevin .25
53 Javier Vazquez .25
54 Troy Glaus .40
55 Tsuyoshi Shinjo .25
56 Albert Pujols 1.50
57 John Smoltz .40
58 Derek Jeter 2.00
59 Robb Nen .25
60 Jason Kendall .25
61 Eric Gagne .50
62 Vladimir Guerrero .75
63 Corey Patterson .40
64 Rickey Henderson .50
65 Jack Wilson .25
66 Jason LaRue .25
67 Sammy Sosa 1.50
68 Ken Griffey Jr. 1.00
69 Randy Johnson .75
70 Nomar Garciaparra 1.50
71 Ivan Rodriguez .50
72 J.T. Snow .25
73 Darryl Kile .25
74 Andruw Jones .50
75 Brian Giles .40
76 Pedro Martinez .75
77 Jeff Bagwell .50
78 Rafael Palmeiro .50
79 Ryan Dempster .25
80 Jeff Cirillo .25
81 Geoff Jenkins .40
82 Brandon Duckworth .25
83 Roger Clemens 1.50
84 Fred McGriff .40
85 Hideo Nomo .50
86 Larry Walker .40
87 Sean Casey .40
88 Trevor Hoffman .25
89 Robert Fick .25
90 Armando Benitez .25
91 Jeromy Burnitz .25
92 Bernie Williams .50
93 Carlos Delgado .50
94 Troy Percival .25
95 Nate Cornejo .25
96 Derrek Lee .40
97 Jose Ortiz .25
98 Brian Jordan .25
99 Jose Cruz .25
100 Ichiro Suzuki 1.50
101 Jose Mesa .25
102 Tim Salmon .40
103 Bud Smith .25
104 Paul LoDuca .25
105 Juan Pierre .25
106 Ben Grieve .25
107 Russell Branyan .25
108 Bobby Abreu .40
109 Moises Alou .40
110 Richie Sexson .50
111 Jerry Hairston Jr. .25
112 Marlon Anderson .25
113 Juan Gonzalez .50
114 Craig Biggio .40
115 Carlos Beltran .50
116 Eric Milton .25
117 Cliff Floyd .25
118 Rich Aurilia .25
119 Adrian Beltre .40
120 Jason Bere .25
121 Darin Erstad .40
122 Ben Sheets .40
123 Johnny Damon .40
124 Jimmy Rollins .25
125 Shawn Green .40
126 Greg Maddux 1.00
127 Mark Mulder .40
128 Bartolo Colon .25
129 Shannon Stewart .25
130 Ramon Ortiz .25
131 Kerry Wood .75
132 Ryan Klesko .25
133 Preston Wilson .25
134 Roy Oswalt .40
135 Rafael Furcal .25
136 Eric Karros .25
137 Nick Neugebauer .25
138 Doug Mientkiewicz .25
139 Paul Konerko .40
140 Bobby Higginson .25
141 Garret Anderson .40
142 Wes Helms .25
143 Brent Abernathy .25
144 Scott Rolen .75
145 Dmitri Young .25
146 Jim Thome .75
147 Raul Mondesi .25
148 Pat Burrell .40
149 Gary Sheffield .40
150 Miguel Tejada .40
151 Brandon Inge .75
152 Carlos Pena .75
153 Jason Lane .75
154 Nathan Haynes .75
155 Hank Blalock 1.50
156 Juan Cruz .75
157 Morgan Ensberg .75
158 Sean Burroughs .75
159 Ed Rogers .75
160 Nick Johnson .75
161 Orlando Hudson .75
162 *Anastacio Martinez* .75
163 Jeremy Affeldt .75
164 Brandon Claussen .75
165 Deivis Santos .75
166 Mike Rivera .75
167 Carlos Silva .75
168 Valentino Pascucci .75
169 Xavier Nady .75
170 David Espinosa .75
171 *Dan Phillips* .75
172 *Tony Fontana* .75
173 Juan Silvestre .75
174 *Henry Pichardo* .75
175 *Pablo Arias* .75
176 *Brett Roneberg* .75
177 *Chad Qualls* .75
178 *Greg Sain* .75
179 *Rene Reyes* .75
180 *So Taguchi* 2.00
181 *Dan Johnson* 2.50
182 *Justin Backsmeyer* .75
183 Juan Gonzalez .75
184 *Jason Ellison* .75
185 *Kazuhisa Ishii* 3.00
186 *Joe Mauer* 6.00
187 *James Shanks* .75
188 *Kevin Cash* .75
189 *J.J. Trujillo* .75
190 *Jorge Padilla* 1.00
191 Nolan Ryan 4.00
192 George Brett 3.00
193 Ryne Sandberg 2.00
194 Robin Yount 1.50
195 Tom Seaver 1.00
196 Mike Schmidt 2.00
197 Frank Robinson 1.00
198 Harmon Killebrew 1.00
199 Kirby Puckett 2.00
200 Don Mattingly 4.00

Press Plates

NM/M
Common Player: 50.00
(See 2002 Topps Gallery for checklist.)

Autographs

NM/M
Common Player: 8.00
Inserted 1:192
LB Lance Berkman 30.00
BBO Bret Boone 20.00
JD J.D. Drew 25.00
LG Luis Gonzalez 20.00
SG Shawn Green 25.00
JL Jason Lane 8.00
MO Magglio Ordonez 20.00
JP Jorge Posada 40.00
JS Juan Silvestre 8.00

Heritage

NM/M
Complete Set (25): 100.00
Common Player: 2.00
Inserted 1:12
GH-RA Roberto Alomar 4.00
GH-BBO Bret Boone 2.00
GH-RC Roger Clemens 8.00
GH-JG Jason Giambi 3.00
GH-LG Luis Gonzalez 2.00
GH-SG Shawn Green 3.00
GH-KG Ken Griffey Jr. 6.00
GH-TG Tony Gwynn 4.00
GH-RJ Reggie Jackson 4.00
GH-CJ Chipper Jones 4.00
GH-AK Al Kaline 4.00
GH-GM Greg Maddux 5.00
GH-PM Pedro Martinez 4.00
GH-MM Mark McGwire 10.00
GH-SM Stan Musial 5.00
GH-MP Mike Piazza 6.00
GH-BR Brooks Robinson 4.00
GH-AR Alex Rodriguez 8.00
GH-NR Nolan Ryan 10.00
GH-MS Mike Schmidt 6.00
GH-TS Tom Seaver 4.00
GH-TSH Tsuyoshi Shinjo 2.00
GH-SS Sammy Sosa 8.00
GH-CY Carl Yastrzemski 5.00
GH-RY Robin Yount 5.00

Heritage Relics

NM/M
Common Player: 8.00
Inserted 1:85
BBO Bret Boone 8.00
LG Luis Gonzalez 8.00
TG Tony Gwynn 15.00
CJ Chipper Jones 10.00
GM Greg Maddux 15.00
PM Pedro Martinez 15.00
MP Mike Piazza 15.00
AR Alex Rodriguez 15.00
TS Tsuyoshi Shinjo 8.00

Heritage Autographs

NM/M
Inserted 1:240
BBO Bret Boone 20.00
LG Luis Gonzalez 25.00
SG Shawn Green 25.00

Originals Relics

NM/M
Common Player: 8.00
Inserted 1:169
BBO Bret Boone 8.00
JC Jose Canseco 10.00
CD Carlos Delgado 8.00
JG Juan Gonzalez 10.00
LG Luis Gonzalez 8.00
TG Tony Gwynn 15.00
TH Todd Helton 12.00
AJ Andruw Jones 8.00
CJ Chipper Jones 10.00

TM Tino Martinez 10.00
MP Mike Piazza 20.00
AP Albert Pujols 35.00
AR Alex Rodriguez 15.00
AS Alfonso Soriano 10.00
BW Bernie Williams 10.00

Team Topps Legends Autographs

NM/M

Inserted 1:1,019
Luis Aparicio 15.00
Jim Bunning 20.00
Fergie Jenkins 15.00
Carl Yastrzemski 65.00

2002 TOPPS GOLD LABEL

NM/M

Complete Set (200): 60.00
Common Player: .25
Pack (4): 3.00
Box (18): 40.00
1 Alex Rodriguez 1.50
2 Derek Jeter 2.00
3 Luis Gonzalez .40
4 Troy Glaus .40
5 Albert Pujols 1.50
6 Lance Berkman .40
7 J.D. Drew .40
8 Chipper Jones .75
9 Miguel Tejada .40
10 Randy Johnson .75
11 Mike Cameron .25
12 Brian Giles .40
13 Roger Cedeno .25
14 Kerry Wood .75
15 Ken Griffey Jr. 1.00
16 Carlos Lee .25
17 Todd Helton .50
18 Gary Sheffield .40
19 Richie Sexson .40
20 Vladimir Guerrero .75
21 Bobby Higginson .25
22 Roger Clemens 1.50
23 Barry Zito .40
24 Juan Pierre .25
25 Pedro Martinez .75
26 Sean Casey .40
27 David Segui .25
28 Jose Garcia .25
29 Curt Schilling .50
30 Bernie Williams .40
31 Ben Grieve .25
32 Hideo Nomo .40
33 Aramis Ramirez .40
34 Cristian Guzman .25
35 Rich Aurilia .25
36 Greg Maddux 1.00
37 Eric Chavez .40
38 Shawn Green .40
39 Luis Rivas .25
40 Magglio Ordonez .40
41 Jose Vidro .25
42 Mariano Rivera .40
43 *Chris Tritle* .50
44 C.C. Sabathia .25
45 Larry Walker .40
46 Raul Mondesi .25
47 Kevin Brown .40
48 Jeff Bagwell .50
49 *Earl Snyder* .50
50 Jason Giambi .50
51 Ichiro Suzuki 1.50
52 Andruw Jones .50
53 Ivan Rodriguez .50
54 Jim Edmonds .40
55 Preston Wilson .25
56 Greg Vaughn .25
57 Jon Lieber .25
58 *Justin Sherrod* .50
59 Marcus Giles .25
60 Roberto Alomar .40
61 Pat Burrell .40
62 Doug Mientkiewicz .25
63 Mark Mulder .40
64 Mike Hampton .25
65 Adam Dunn .50
66 Moises Alou .40
67 Jose Cruz Jr. .25
68 Derek Bell .25
69 Sammy Sosa 1.50
70 Joe Mays .25
71 Phil Nevin .25
72 Edgardo Alfonzo .25
73 Barry Bonds 2.00
74 Edgar Martinez .40
75 Juan Encarnacion .25
76 Jason Tyner .25
77 Edgar Renteria .40
78 Bret Boone .40
79 Scott Rolen .75
80 Nomar Garciaparra 1.50
81 Frank Thomas .50
82 Roy Oswalt .40
83 Tsuyoshi Shinjo .25
84 Ben Sheets .40
85 Hank Blalock .40
86 Carlos Delgado .50
87 Tim Hudson .40
88 Alfonso Soriano .75
89 *Michael Hill* .50
90 Jim Thome .75
91 Craig Biggio .40
92 Ryan Klesko .25
93 Geoff Jenkins .40
94 Matt Morris .40
95 Jorge Posada .40
96 Cliff Floyd .40
97 Jimmy Rollins .25
98 Mike Sweeney .25
99 Frank Catalanotto .25
100 Mike Piazza 1.25
101 Mark Quinn .25
102 Torii Hunter .40
103 Lee Stevens .25
104 Byung-Hyug Kim .25
105 *Freddy Sanchez* .50
106 David Cone .25
107 Jerry Hairston Jr. .25
108 Kyle Farnsworth .25
109 Rafael Furcal .25
110 Bartolo Colon .25
111 Juan Rivera .25
112 Kevin Young .25
113 *Chris Narveson* 1.00
114 Richard Hidalgo .25
115 Andy Pettitte .40
116 Darin Erstad .40
117 Corey Koskie .25
118 Rickey Henderson .50
119 Derrek Lee .40
120 Sean Burroughs .25
121 Paul Konerko .25
122 *Ross Peeples* .50
123 Terrence Long .25
124 John Smoltz .40
125 Brandon Duckworth .25
126 Luis Maza .25
127 Morgan Ensberg .25
128 Eric Valent .25
129 Shannon Stewart .25
130 D'Angelo Jimenez .25
131 Jeff Cirillo .25
132 Jack Cust .25
133 Dmitri Young .25
134 Darryl Kile .25
135 Reggie Sanders .25
136 Marlon Byrd .25
137 *Napoleon Calzado* .50
138 Javy Lopez .40
139 Orlando Cabrera .25
140 Mike Mussina .40
141 Josh Beckett .40
142 Kazuhiro Sasaki .25
143 Jermaine Dye .25
144 Carlos Beltran .40
145 Trevor Hoffman .25
146 *Kazuhisa Ishii* 2.00
147 Alex Gonzalez .25
148 Marty Cordova .25
149 *Kevin Deaton* .50
150 Toby Hall .25
151 Rafael Palmeiro .50
152 John Olerud .40
153 David Eckstein .25
154 Doug Glanville .25
155 Johnny Damon .40
156 Javier Vazquez .25
157 *Jason Bay* 2.00
158 Robb Nen .25
159 Rafael Soriano .25
160 Placido Polanco .25
161 Garret Anderson .40
162 Aaron Boone .25
163 Mike Lieberthal .25
164 *Joe Mauer* 6.00
165 Matt Lawton .25
166 *Juan Tolentino* .50
167 Alex Gonzalez .25
168 Steve Finley .25
169 Troy Percival .25
170 Bud Smith .25
171 Freddie Garcia .25
172 Ray Lankford .25
173 Tim Redding .25
174 Ryan Dempster .25
175 Travis Lee .25
176 Jeff Kent .40
177 Ramon Hernandez .25
178 Carl Everett .25
179 Tom Glavine .40
180 Juan Gonzalez .50
181 Nick Johnson .25
182 Mike Lowell .40
183 Al Leiter .25
184 *Jason Maule* .50
185 Wilson Betemit .25
186 Tino Martinez .25
187 Jason Standridge .25
188 *Mike Peeples* .50
189 Jason Kendall .40
190 Fred McGriff .40
191 *John Rodriguez* .50
192 *Brett Roneberg* .50
193 *Marlyn Tisdale* .50
194 J.T. Snow .25
195 *Craig Kuzmic* .75
196 Cory Lidle .25
197 Alex Cintron .25
198 Fernando Vina .25
199 Austin Kearns .50
200 Paul LoDuca .25

Class One Gold

Stars: 2-4X
Production 500 sets

Class Two Platinum

Stars: 4-8X
Production 250 sets

Class Three Titanium

Stars: 6-10X
Production 100 sets

Platinum Memorabilia

Platinum: .75-1.5X
Titanium Memorabilia: 1-2X

All-Star MVP Winners

NM/M

Common Player: 8.00
RA Roberto Alomar 10.00
SA Sandy Alomar 8.00
BLB Bobby Bonds 8.00
DC Dave Concepcion 8.00
SG2 Steve Garvey 10.00
KG Ken Griffey Sr. 8.00
BM1 Bill Madlock 8.00
FM Fred McGriff 10.00
DP3 Dave Parker 8.00
TP Tony Perez 10.00
MP Mike Piazza 15.00
KP2 Kirby Puckett 15.00
TR Tim Raines 8.00

Batting Average

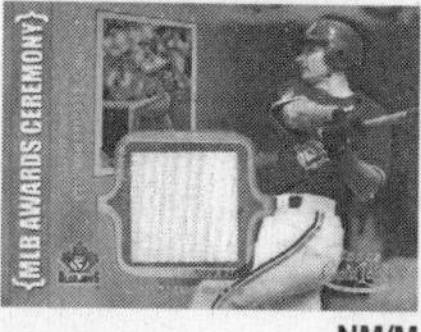

NM/M

Common Player: 8.00
WB Wade Boggs 15.00
BB Bill Buckner 8.00
RC2 Rod Carew 15.00
RAC Rico Carty 8.00
NC Norm Cash 15.00
TG1 Tony Gwynn 15.00
TG2 Tony Gwynn 15.00
BM2 Bill Madlock 8.00
DP4 Dave Parker 8.00
KP3 Kirby Puckett 15.00
LW Larry Walker 8.00
CY2 Carl Yastrzemski 30.00

Cy Young Winners

NM/M

Common Player: 8.00
RWC Roger Clemens 15.00
DE Dennis Eckersley 8.00
RJ Randy Johnson 12.00
BS Bret Saberhagen 8.00
JS John Smoltz 8.00

Home Run Champions

NM/M

Common Player: 8.00
BB2 Barry Bonds 20.00
GF George Foster 8.00
TK2 Ted Kluszewski 15.00
KM2 Kevin Mitchell 8.00
DM2 Dale Murphy 40.00
AR Alex Rodriguez 15.00
DS1 Darryl Strawberry 10.00

League Championship MVP Winners

NM/M

Common Player: 8.00
GB2 George Brett 40.00
WC Will Clark 15.00
CC Craig Counsell 8.00
RH Rickey Henderson 15.00
JL Javier Lopez 8.00
AEP Andy Pettitte 12.00
KP1 Kirby Puckett 15.00
FW Frank White 8.00
BFW Bernie Williams 10.00

MVP Winners

NM/M

Common Player: 8.00
EB Ernie Banks 20.00
DB Don Baylor 8.00
YB Yogi Berra 15.00
BB1 Barry Bonds 20.00
GB1 George Brett 40.00
SG1 Steve Garvey 8.00
KHG Kirk Gibson 8.00
KH Keith Hernandez 10.00
RJ1 Reggie Jackson 15.00
DM Don Mattingly 40.00
KM1 Kevin Mitchell 8.00
JM Joe Morgan 8.00
DM1 Dale Murphy 40.00
DP1 Dave Parker 8.00
BR Brooks Robinson 15.00
FR Frank Robinson 12.00
RS Ryne Sandberg 40.00
HS Hank Sauer 8.00
WS Willie Stargell 15.00
JT Joe Torre 10.00
MW Maury Wills 8.00
CY1 Carl Yastrzemski 30.00
RY Robin Yount 20.00

MLB Moments in Time

NM/M

Common Player: 8.00
BLB Barry Bonds 20.00
BB1 Bret Boone 8.00
BB2 Bret Boone 8.00
CD Carlos Delgado 8.00
TG Tony Gwynn 15.00
TH Toby Hall 8.00
CL Carlos Lee 8.00
JL Javy Lopez 8.00
MO Magglio Ordonez 10.00
RP1 Rafael Palmeiro 10.00
RP2 Rafael Palmeiro 10.00
AR Alex Rodriguez 15.00

Rookie of the Year Winners

NM/M

Common Player: 8.00
DA Dick Allen 15.00
AB Al Bumbry 8.00
RC1 Rod Carew 15.00
CF Carlton Fisk 15.00
MH Mike Hargrove 8.00
DJ Dave Justice 10.00

EM2	Eddie Murray	12.00
LP	Lou Piniella	10.00
AP	Albert Pujols	20.00
DS2	Darryl Strawberry	15.00
FV	Fernando Valenzuela	8.00
BW	Billy Williams	10.00

RBI Leaders

		NM/M
Common Player:		8.00
BRB	Bret Boone	8.00
BRB2	Bret Boone	8.00
GC	Gary Carter	8.00
GL	Greg Luzinski	8.00
EM1	Eddie Murray	12.00
AO	Al Oliver	8.00
DP2	Dave Parker	8.00
DW	Dave Winfield	12.00

World Series MVP Winners

		NM/M
Common Player:		8.00
JB	Johnny Bench	15.00
RCC	Ron Cey	8.00
RJ2	Reggie Jackson	15.00
PM	Paul Molitor	15.00
MR	Mariano Rivera	10.00

2002 TOPPS HERITAGE

		NM/M
Complete Set (440):		200.00
Common Player:		.25
Common (364-446):		3.00
Inserted 1:2		
Pack (8):		4.00
Box (24):		90.00
1	Ichiro Suzuki SP	10.00
2	Darin Erstad	.50
3	Rod Beck	.25
4	Doug Mientkiewicz	.25
5	Mike Sweeney	.25
6	Roger Clemens	2.50
7	Jason Tyner	.25
8	Alex Gonzalez	.25
9	Eric Young	.25
10	Randy Johnson	1.50
10	Randy Johnson SP	6.00
11	Aaron Sele	.25
12	Tony Clark	.25
13	C.C. Sabathia	.25
14	Melvin Mora	.25
15	Tim Hudson	.50
16	Ben Petrick	.25
17	Tom Glavine	.75
18	Jason Lane	.25
19	Larry Walker	.50
20	Mark Mulder	.50
21	Steve Finley	.25
22	Bengie Molina	.25
23	Rob Bell	.25
24	Nathan Haynes	.25
25	Rafael Furcal	.50
25	Rafael Furcal SP	3.00
26	Mike Mussina	1.00
27	Paul LoDuca	.25
28	Torii Hunter	.50
29	Carlos Lee	.25
30	Jimmy Rollins	.25
31	Arthur Rhodes	.25
32	Ivan Rodriguez	1.00
33	Wes Helms	.25
34	Cliff Floyd	.25
35	Julian Tavarez	.25
36	Mark McGwire	4.00
37	Chipper Jones SP	6.00
38	Denny Neagle	.25
39	Odalis Perez	.25
40	Antonio Alfonseca	.25
41	Edgar Renteria	.50
42	Troy Glaus	.75
43	Scott Brosius	.25
44	Abraham Nunez	.25
45	Jamey Wright	.25
46	Bobby Bonilla	.25
47	Ismael Valdes	.25
48	Chris Reitsma	.25
49	Neifi Perez	.25
50	Juan Cruz	.25
51	Kevin Brown	.50
52	Ben Grieve	.25
53	Alex Rodriguez SP	10.00
54	Charles Nagy	.25
55	Reggie Sanders	.25
56	Nelson Figueroa	.25
57	Felipe Lopez	.25
58	Bill Ortega	.25
59	Mac Suzuki	.25
60	Johnny Estrada	.25
61	Bob Wickman	.25
62	Doug Glanville	.25
63	Jeff Cirillo	.50
63	Jeff Cirillo SP	3.00
64	Corey Patterson	.50
65	Aaron Myette	.25
66	Magglio Ordonez	.50
67	Ellis Burks	.25
68	Miguel Tejada	.50
69	John Olerud	.50
69	John Olerud SP	4.00
70	Greg Vaughn	.25
71	Andy Pettitte	.75
72	Mike Matheny	.25
73	Brandon Duckworth	.25
74	Scott Schoeneweis	.25
75	Mike Lowell	.50
76	Einar Diaz	.25
77	Tino Martinez	.50
78	Matt Williams	.50
79	*Jason Young*	1.00
80	Nate Cornejo	.25
81	Andres Galarraga	.40
82	Bernie Williams SP	6.00
83	Ryan Klesko	.25
84	Dan Wilson	.25
85	*Henry Pichardo*	.50
86	Ray Durham	.25
87	Omar Daal	.25
88	Derrek Lee	.50
89	Al Leiter	.50
90	Darrin Fletcher	.25
91	Josh Beckett	.75
92	Johnny Damon	.50
92	Johnny Damon SP	5.00
93	Abraham Nunez	.25
94	Ricky Ledee	.25
95	Richie Sexson	.75
96	Adam Kennedy	.25
97	Raul Mondesi	.25
98	John Burkett	.25
99	Ben Sheets	.50
99	Ben Sheets SP	4.00
100	Preston Wilson	.25
100	Preston Wilson SP	3.00
101	Boof Bonser	.25
102	Shigetoshi Hasegawa	.25
103	Carlos Febles	.25
104	Jorge Posada SP	5.00
105	Michael Tucker	.25
106	Roberto Hernandez	.25
107	*John Rodriguez*	.75
108	Danny Graves	.25
109	Rich Aurilia	.25
110	Jon Lieber	.25
111	*Tim Hummel*	.50
112	J.T. Snow	.25
113	Kris Benson	.25
114	Derek Jeter	4.00
115	John Franco	.25
116	Matt Stairs	.25
117	Ben Davis	.25
118	Darryl Kile	.25
119	*Mike Peeples*	.50
120	Kevin Tapani	.25
121	Armando Benitez	.25
122	Damian Miller	.25
123	Jose Jimenez	.25
124	Pedro Astacio	.25
125	*Marlyn Tisdale*	.50
126	Deivi Cruz	.25
127	Paul O'Neill	.75
128	Jermaine Dye	.25
129	Marcus Giles	.25
130	Mark Loretta	.25
131	Garret Anderson	.50
132	Todd Ritchie	.25
133	Joe Crede	.25
134	Kevin Millwood	.50
135	Shane Reynolds	.25
136	Mark Grace	.75
137	Shannon Stewart	.25
138	Nick Neugebauer	.25
139	*Nic Jackson*	.75
140	Robb Nen	.25
141	Dmitri Young	.25
142	Kevin Appier	.25
143	Jack Cust	.25
144	Andres Torres	.25
145	Frank Thomas	1.00
146	Jason Kendall	.25
147	Greg Maddux	2.00
148	David Justice	.50
149	Hideo Nomo	.75
150	Bret Boone	.50
151	Wade Miller	.25
152	Jeff Kent	.50
153	Scott Williamson	.25
154	Julio Lugo	.25
155	Bobby Higginson	.25
156	Geoff Jenkins	.50
157	Darren Dreifort	.25
158	*Freddy Sanchez*	.75
159	Bud Smith	.25
160	Phil Nevin	.25
161	Cesar Izturis	.25
162	Sean Casey	.50
163	Jose Ortiz	.25
164	Brent Abernathy	.25
165	Kevin Young	.25
166	Daryle Ward	.25
167	Trevor Hoffman	.25
168	Rondell White	.25
169	Kip Wells	.25
170	John Vander Wal	.25
171	Jose Lima	.25
172	Wilton Guerrero	.25
173	Aaron Dean	.25
174	Rick Helling	.25
175	Juan Pierre	.25
176	Jay Bell	.25
177	Craig House	.25
178	David Bell	.25
179	Pat Burrell	.50
180	Eric Gagne	.75
181	Adam Pettyjohn	.25
182	Ugueth Urbina	.25
183	Peter Bergeron	.25
184	Adrian Gonzalez	.25
184	Adrian Gonzalez SP	4.00
185	Damion Easley	.25
186	Gookie Dawkins	.25
187	Matt Lawton	.25
188	Frank Catalanotto	.25
189	David Wells	.25
190	Roger Cedeno	.25
191	Brian Giles	.50
192	Julio Zuleta	.25
193	Timo Perez	.25
194	Billy Wagner	.25
195	Craig Counsell	.25
196	Bart Miadich	.25
197	Gary Sheffield	.75
198	Richard Hidalgo	.50
199	Juan Uribe	.25
200	Curt Schilling	1.00
201	Javy Lopez	.50
202	Jimmy Haynes	.25
203	Jim Edmonds	.75
204	Pokey Reese	.25
204	Pokey Reese SP	3.00
205	Matt Clement	.25
206	Dean Palmer	.25
207	Nick Johnson	.25
208	*Nate Espy*	.75
209	Pedro Feliz	.25
210	Aaron Rowand	.25
211	Masato Yoshii	.25
212	Jose Cruz	.25
213	Paul Byrd	.25
214	*Mark Phillips*	1.00
215	Benny Agbayani	.25
216	Frank Menechino	.25
217	John Flaherty	.25
218	Brian Boehringer	.25
219	Todd Hollandsworth	.25
220	Sammy Sosa SP	8.00
221	Steve Sparks	.25
222	Homer Bush	.25
223	Mike Hampton	.50
224	Bobby Abreu	.50
225	Barry Larkin	.75
226	Ryan Rupe	.25
227	Bubba Trammell	.25
228	Todd Zeile	.25
229	Jeff Shaw	.25
230	Alex Ochoa	.25
231	Orlando Cabrera	.25
232	Jeremy Giambi	.25
233	Tomo Ohka	.25
234	Luis Castillo	.25
235	Chris Holt	.25
236	Shawn Green	.50
237	Sidney Ponson	.25
238	Lee Stevens	.25
239	Hank Blalock	.50
240	Randy Winn	.25
241	Pedro Martinez	1.50
242	Vinny Castillo	.25
243	Steve Karsay	.25
244	Barry Bonds SP	15.00
245	Jason Bere	.25
246	Scott Rolen	1.50
246	Scott Rolen SP	6.00
247	Ryan Kohlmeier	.25
248	Kerry Wood	1.50
249	Aramis Ramirez	.50
250	Lance Berkman	.75
251	Omar Vizquel	.50
252	Juan Encarnacion	.25
254	David Segui	.25
255	Brian Anderson	.25
256	Jay Payton	.25
257	Mark Grudzielanek	.25
258	Jimmy Anderson	.25
259	Eric Valent	.25
260	Chad Durbin	.25
262	Alex Gonzalez	.25
263	Scott Dunn	.25
264	Scott Elarton	.25
265	Tom Gordon	.25
266	Moises Alou	.50
269	Mark Buehrle	.25
270	Jerry Hairston Jr.	.25
272	Luke Prokopec	.25
273	Graeme Lloyd	.25
274	Bret Prinz	.25
276	Chris Carpenter	.25
277	Ryan Minor	.25
278	Jeff D'Amico	.25
279	Raul Ibanez	.25
280	Joe Mays	.25
281	Livan Hernandez	.25
282	Robin Ventura	.40
283	Gabe Kapler	.40
284	Tony Batista	.25
285	Ramon Hernandez	.25
286	Craig Paquette	.25
287	Mark Kotsay	.25
288	Mike Lieberthal	.25
289	Joe Borchard	.25
290	Cristian Guzman	.25
291	Craig Biggio	.50
292	Joaquin Benoit	.25
293	Ken Caminiti	.25
294	Sean Burroughs	.25
295	Eric Karros	.50
296	Eric Chavez	.50
297	LaTroy Hawkins	.25
298	Alfonso Soriano	1.00
299	John Smoltz	.50
300	Adam Dunn	1.00
301	Ryan Dempster	.25
302	Travis Hafner	.50
303	Russell Branyan	.25
304	Dustin Hermanson	.25
305	Jim Thome	1.50
306	Carlos Beltran	.75
307	*Jason Botts*	.75
308	David Cone	.25
309	Ivanon Coffie	.25
310	Brian Jordan	.25
311	Todd Walker	.25
312	Jeromy Burnitz	.25
313	Tony Armas	.25
314	Jeff Conine	.25
315	Todd Jones	.25
316	Roy Oswalt	.50
317	Aubrey Huff	.25
318	Josh Fogg	.25
319	Jose Vidro	.25
320	Jace Brewer	.25
321	Mike Redmond	.25
322	*Noochie Varner*	1.00
323	Russ Ortiz	.25
324	Edgardo Alfonzo	.25
325	Ruben Sierra	.25
326	Calvin Murray	.25

327 Marlon Anderson .25
328 Albie Lopez .25
329 Chris Gomez .25
330 Fernando Tatis .25
331 Stubby Clapp .25
332 Rickey Henderson .75
333 Brad Radke .25
334 Brent Mayne .25
335 Cory Lidle .25
336 Edgar Martinez .50
337 Aaron Boone .25
338 Jay Witasick .25
339 Benito Santiago .25
340 Jose Mercedes .25
341 Fernando Vina .25
342 A.J. Pierzynski .25
343 Jeff Bagwell 1.00
344 Brian Bohanon .25
345 Adrian Beltre .50
346 Troy Percival .25
347 *Napoleon Calzado* .75
348 Ruben Rivera .25
349 Rafael Soriano .25
350 Damian Jackson .25
351 Joe Randa .25
352 Chan Ho Park .25
353 Dante Bichette .25
354 Bartolo Colon .25
355 *Jason Bay* 1.50
356 Shea Hillenbrand .25
357 Matt Morris .50
358 Brad Penny .25
359 Mark Quinn .25
360 Marquis Grissom .25
361 Henry Blanco .25
362 Billy Koch .25
363 Mike Cameron .25
364 Albert Pujols 10.00
365 Paul Konerko 3.00
366 Eric Milton 3.00
367 Nick Bierbrodt 3.00
368 Rafael Palmeiro 5.00
369 *Jorge Padilla* 4.00
370 Jason Giambi 4.00
371 Mike Piazza 10.00
372 Alex Cora 3.00
373 Todd Helton 6.00
374 Juan Gonzalez 6.00
375 Mariano Rivera 4.00
376 Jason LaRue 3.00
377 Tony Gwynn 6.00
378 Wilson Betemit 3.00
379 *J.J. Trujillo* 3.00
380 Brad Ausmus 3.00
381 Chris George 3.00
382 Jose Canseco 5.00
383 Ramon Ortiz 3.00
384 John Rocker 3.00
385 Rey Ordonez 3.00
386 Ken Griffey Jr. 10.00
387 Juan Pena 3.00
388 Michael Barrett 3.00
389 J.D. Drew 4.00
390 Corey Koskie 3.00
391 Vernon Wells 3.00
392 *Juan Tolentino* 3.00
393 Luis Gonzalez 4.00
394 Terrance Long 3.00
395 Travis Lee 3.00
396 *Earl Snyder* 3.00
397 Nomar Garciaparra 10.00
398 Jason Schmidt 4.00
399 David Espinosa 3.00
400 Steve Green 3.00
401 Jack Wilson 3.00
402 *Chris Tritle* 3.00
403 Angel Berroa 3.00
404 Josh Towers 3.00
405 Andruw Jones 4.00
406 Brent Butler 3.00
407 *Craig Kuzmic* 3.00
408 Derek Bell 3.00
409 *Eric Glaser* 3.00
410 Joel Pineiro 3.00
411 Alexis Gomez 3.00
412 Mike Rivera 3.00
413 Shawn Estes 3.00
414 Milton Bradley 3.00
415 Carl Everett 3.00
416 Kazuhiro Sasaki 3.00
417 *Tony Fontana* 3.00
418 Josh Pearce 3.00
419 Gary Matthews Jr. 3.00
420 *Raymond Cabrera* 3.00
421 Joe Kennedy 3.00
422 *Jason Maule* 3.00
423 Casey Fossum 3.00
424 Christian Parker 3.00
425 *Laynce Nix* 15.00
426 Byung-Hyun Kim 3.00
427 Freddy Garcia 3.00
428 Herbert Perry 3.00
429 Jason Marquis 3.00
430 Sandy Alomar Jr. 3.00
431 Roberto Alomar 5.00
432 Tsuyoshi Shinjo 3.00
433 Tim Wakefield 3.00
434 Robert Fick 3.00
435 Vladimir Guerrero 6.00
436 Jose Mesa 3.00
437 Scott Spiezio 3.00
438 Jose Hernandez 3.00
439 Jose Acevedo 3.00
440 *Brian West* 3.00
441 Barry Zito 4.00
442 Luis Maza 3.00
443 Marlon Byrd 4.00
444 A.J. Burnett 3.00
445 Dee Brown 3.00
446 Carlos Delgado 5.00

Chrome

Stars (1-100): 6-10X
RC's: 3-6X
Production 553 sets

Classic Renditions

NM/M
Complete Set (10): 10.00
Common Player: .50
Inserted 1:12
CR-1 Kerry Wood 2.00
CR-2 Brian Giles 1.00
CR-3 Roger Cedeno .50
CR-4 Jason Giambi 1.50
CR-5 Albert Pujols 4.00
CR-6 Mark Buehrle .50
CR-7 Cristian Guzman .50
CR-8 Jimmy Rollins .50
CR-9 Jim Thome 2.00
CR-10 Shawn Green 1.00

Classic Renditions Autographs

Production 25 sets
BG Brian Giles
CG Cristian Guzman
JR Jimmy Rollins

Clubhouse Collection

NM/M
Common Player: 15.00
Jersey 1:332
Bat 1:498
RA Rich Aurilia/bat 15.00
YB Yogi Berra/jsy 40.00
BB Barry Bonds/bat 60.00
AD Alvin Dark/bat 25.00
NG Nomar Garciaparra/bat 50.00
GK George Kell/jsy 25.00
GM Greg Maddux/jsy 30.00
EM Eddie Mathews/jsy 35.00
WM Willie Mays/bat 75.00
CP Corey Patterson/bat 20.00
JP Jorge Posada/bat 25.00
HS Hank Sauer/bat 20.00

Clubhouse Collection Auto. Relics

No Pricing
Production 25 sets
CCA-YB Yogi Berra
CCA-AD Alvin Dark
CCA-GK George Kell
CCA-WM Willie Mays

Clubhouse Collection Dual Relics

NM/M
Production 53 sets
SM Eddie Mathews, Greg Maddux 150.00
BP Yogi Berra, Jorge Posada 125.00
SP Hank Sauer, Corey Patterson 75.00
KR George Kell, Nomar Garciaparra 100.00
DA Alvin Dark, Rich Aurilia 100.00
MB Willie Mays, Barry Bonds 200.00

Grandstand Glory Stadium Seat

NM/M
Common Player: 10.00
Inserted 1:133
RC Roy Campanella 25.00
BF Bob Feller 20.00
WF Whitey Ford 20.00
TK Ted Kluszewski 20.00
BM Billy Martin 25.00
HN Hal Newhouser 15.00
SP Satchel Paige 40.00
BP Billy Pierce 15.00
HS Hank Sauer 10.00
BS Bobby Shantz 15.00
WS Warren Spahn 20.00
EW Early Wynn 15.00

New Age Performers

NM/M
Complete Set (15): 30.00
Common Player: 1.00
Inserted 1:15
NA-1 Luis Gonzalez 1.00
NA-2 Mark McGwire 5.00
NA-3 Barry Bonds 5.00
NA-4 Ken Griffey Jr. 3.00
NA-5 Ichiro Suzuki 3.00
NA-6 Sammy Sosa 3.00
NA-7 Andruw Jones 1.00
NA-8 Derek Jeter 5.00
NA-9 Todd Helton 1.50
NA-10 Alex Rodriguez 4.00
NA-11 Jason Giambi 1.50
NA-12 Bret Boone 1.00
NA-13 Roberto Alomar 1.00
NA-14 Albert Pujols 4.00
NA-15 Vladimir Guerrero 1.50

Real One Autographs

NM/M
Common Autograph: 20.00
Inserted 1:180
Red Ink: .75-1.5X
Production 53
YB Yogi Berra 100.00
JB Joe Black 50.00
RB Ray Boone 60.00
AC Andy Carey 40.00
RCL Roger Clemens 125.00
AD Alvin Dark 60.00
DD Dom DiMaggio 80.00
JE Jim Edmonds 50.00
RF Roy Face 60.00
BF Bob Feller 60.00
WF Whitey Ford 80.00
CG Brian Giles 25.00
CG Cristian Guzman 20.00
MI Monte Irvin 60.00
GK George Kell 60.00
WM Willie Mays 200.00
GM Gil McDougald 75.00
OM Orestes Minoso 60.00
JP John Podres 60.00
PR Phil Rizzuto 80.00
ARO Alex Rodriguez 140.00
PRO Preacher Roe 60.00
AR Al Rosen 75.00
HS Hank Sauer
ASC Al Schoendienst 50.00
BS Bobby Shantz 50.00
ES Enos Slaughter 80.00
WS Warren Spahn 100.00
HW Hoyt Wilhelm 60.00

Team Topps Legends Autographs

NM/M
Inserted 1:613
Vida Blue 20.00
Frank Howard 30.00
Mickey Lolich 25.00
Frank Robinson 40.00
Bobby Thomson 30.00

Then and Now

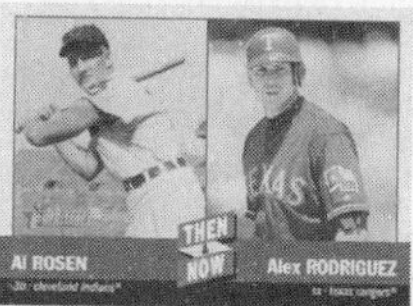

NM/M
Complete Set (10): 15.00
Common Player: 1.00
Inserted 1:15
TN-1 Ed Mathews, Barry Bonds 4.00
TN-2 Al Rosen, Alex Rodriguez 4.00
TN-3 Carl Furillo, Larry Walker 1.00
TN-4 Mickey Vernon, Ichiro Suzuki 3.00
TN-5 Roy Campanella, Sammy Sosa 3.00
TN-6 Al Rosen, Bret Boone 1.00
TN-7 Warren Spahn, Randy Johnson 2.00
TN-8 Ed Lopat, Freddy Garcia 1.00
TN-9 Robin Roberts, Randy Johnson 2.00
TN-10 Billy Pierce, Hideo Nomo 1.50

2002 TOPPS OPENING DAY

NM/M
Complete Set (165): 40.00
Common Player: .10
Pack (7): 1.00
Box (36): 30.00
1 Roy Oswalt .25
2 Derek Jeter 2.00
3 Dmitri Young .10
4 Ramon Hernandez .10
5 Albert Pujols 1.50
6 Sean Casey .25
7 Joe Randa .10
8 Craig Counsell .10
9 John Olerud .25
10 Troy Glaus .40
11 Adam Kennedy .10
12 Carlos Delgado .40
13 Bobby Abreu .20
14 J.T. Snow Jr. .10
15 Ivan Rodriguez .50
16 Mike Lowell .25
17 Juan Pierre .10

18	Magglio Ordonez	.30
19	Greg Maddux	1.00
20	Jorge Posada	.25
21	Johnny Damon	.20
22	Mike Hampton	.10
23	Paul LoDuca	.10
24	Terrence Long	.10
25	Jeff Bagwell	.50
26	Shannon Stewart	.10
27	Brad Radke	.10
28	Brian Jordan	.10
29	Lee Stevens	.10
30	Cliff Floyd	.10
31	Roger Clemens	1.00
32	Mike Matheny	.10
33	Alfonso Soriano	.50
34	Randy Johnson	.75
35	Mike Sweeney	.10
36	Jose Cruz Jr.	.20
37	Fernando Tatis	.10
38	Eric Young	.10
39	Ruben Rivera	.10
40	Mike Mussina	.50
41	Alex Gonzalez	.10
42	Edgardo Alfonzo	.10
43	Torii Hunter	.25
44	Richie Sexson	.25
45	Bret Boone	.20
46	John Smoltz	.20
47	Bengie Molina	.10
48	Trot Nixon	.10
49	Mike Cameron	.10
50	Mariano Rivera	.20
51	Ichiro Suzuki	1.50
52	Cristian Guzman	.10
53	Andruw Jones	.40
54	Jerry Hairston Jr.	.10
55	Brad Fullmer	.10
56	Luis Gonzalez	.25
57	Placido Polanco	.10
58	Jason Tyner	.10
59	Dan Wilson	.10
60	Jim Edmonds	.25
61	Larry Walker	.25
62	Edgar Renteria	.25
63	Orlando Cabrera	.10
64	Sammy Sosa	1.50
65	Derrek Lee	.20
66	C.C. Sabathia	.10
67	Aaron Boone	.10
68	Royce Clayton	.10
69	Darryl Kile	.10
70	Vladimir Guerrero	.75
71	Bud Smith	.10
72	Adrian Beltre	.20
73	Barry Bonds	15.00
74	Ben Petrick	.10
75	Derek Bell	.10
76	Jeff Kent	.20
77	Ricky Gutierrez	.10
78	Rafael Palmeiro	.50
79	Doug Mientkiewicz	.10
80	Fernando Vina	.10
81	Mark Mulder	.20
82	Carlos Beltran	.25
83	Juan Encarnacion	.10
84	Jimmy Rollins	.10
85	Pedro J. Martinez	.50
86	Aramis Ramirez	.25
87	Reggie Sanders	.10
88	Gary Sheffield	.25
89	Bartolo Colon	.10
90	Jose Macias	.10
91	Bobby Higginson	.10
92	Craig Biggio	.20
93	Al Leiter	.20
94	Juan Gonzalez	.50
95	Jose Valentin	.10
96	Jon Lieber	.10
97	Alex Gonzalez	.10
98	Jose Mesa	.10
99	Sandy Alomar	.10
100	Barry Bonds	2.00
101	Todd Walker	.10
102	Kevin Young	.10
103	Ken Griffey Jr.	1.00
104	Mark McGwire	2.00
105	Jason Giambi	.50
106	Todd Helton	.50
107	Mike Piazza	1.00
108	Nomar Garciaparra	1.50
109	Bernie Williams	.40
110	Shawn Wooten	.10
111	Eric Chavez	.20
112	Curt Schilling	.40
113	Roberto Alomar	.50
114	Chipper Jones	.75
115	Edgar Martinez	.20
116	Shawn Green	.20
117	Ben Grieve	.10
118	Jermaine Dye	.10
119	Steve Finley	.10
120	Adam Dunn	.25
121	Preston Wilson	.10
122	Lance Berkman	.20
123	Ben Sheets	.25
124	Ryan Klesko	.10
125	Brian Giles	.25
126	Marcus Giles	.10
127	Craig Wilson	.10
128	Miguel Tejada	.25
129	Andres Galarraga	.20
130	Alex Rodriguez	1.50
131	David Justice	.25
132	Barry Zito	.25
133	Scott Rolen	.75
134	Brent Abernathy	.10
135	Raul Mondesi	.20
136	Josh Towers	.10
137	Rafael Furcal	.10
138	Gabe Kapler	.10
139	Fred McGriff	.25
140	Jeff Conine	.10
141	Mike Lieberthal	.10
142	Frank Thomas	.50
143	Jason Kendall	.10
144	Toby Hall	.10
145	Pat Burrell	.30
146	J.D. Drew	.25
147	Javier Lopez	.25
148	Carlos Lee	.10
149	Doug Glanville	.10
150	Ruben Sierra	.10
151	Julio Franco	.10
152	Tim Hudson	.20
153	Rich Aurilia	.10
154	Geoff Jenkins	.10
155	Tsuyoshi Shinjo	.10
156	Moises Alou	.20
157	Jim Thome	.75
158	Steve Cox	.10
159	Kevin Brown	.20
160	Barry Bonds	.50
161	Rickey Henderson	.20
162	Bud Smith	.10
163	Rickey Henderson	.20
164	Barry Bonds	.50
165	Checklist	.10

Autographs

		NM/M
Common Auto.:		10.00
GJ	Geoff Jenkins	15.00
NJ	Nick Johnson	10.00
BS	Ben Sheets	25.00

2002 TOPPS PRISTINE

		NM/M
Complete Set (210):		
Common Player:		.75
Common Uncommon RC:		3.00
Production 1,999		
Common Rare RC:		5.00
Production 799		
Pack (8):		30.00
Box (5):		125.00
1	Alex Rodriguez	5.00
2	Carlos Delgado	1.50
3	Jimmy Rollins	.75
4	Jason Kendall	.75
5	John Olerud	1.00
6	Albert Pujols	5.00
7	Curt Schilling	2.00
8	Gary Sheffield	1.00
9	Johnny Damon	1.00
10	Ichiro Suzuki	4.00
11	Pat Burrell	1.00
12	Garret Anderson	1.00
13	Andruw Jones	1.50
14	Kerry Wood	2.00
15	Kenny Lofton	1.00
16	Adam Dunn	1.50
17	Juan Pierre	.75
18	Josh Beckett	1.00
19	Roy Oswalt	1.00
20	Derek Jeter	6.00
21	Jose Vidro	.75
22	Richie Sexson	1.50
23	Mike Sweeney	.75
24	Jeff Kent	1.00
25	Jason Giambi	1.50
26	Bret Boone	1.00
27	J.D. Drew	1.00
28	Shannon Stewart	.75
29	Miguel Tejada	1.00
30	Barry Bonds	6.00
31	Randy Johnson	2.00
32	Pedro J. Martinez	2.00
33	Magglio Ordonez	1.00
34	Todd Helton	1.50
35	Craig Biggio	1.00
36	Shawn Green	1.00
37	Vladimir Guerrero	2.00
38	Mo Vaughn	1.00
39	Alfonso Soriano	2.00
40	Barry Zito	1.00
41	Aramis Ramirez	1.00
42	Ryan Klesko	1.00
43	Ruben Sierra	.75
44	Tino Martinez	.75
45	Toby Hall	.75
46	Ivan Rodriguez	1.50
47	Raul Mondesi	.75
48	Carlos Pena	.75
49	Darin Erstad	1.00
50	Sammy Sosa	4.00
51	Bartolo Colon	1.00
52	Robert Fick	.75
53	Cliff Floyd	.75
54	Brian Jordan	.75
55	Torii Hunter	1.00
56	Roberto Alomar	1.00
57	Roger Clemens	4.00
58	Mark Mulder	1.00
59	Brian Giles	1.00
60	Mike Piazza	4.00
61	Rich Aurilia	.75
62	Freddy Garcia	.75
63	Jim Edmonds	1.50
64	Eric Hinske	.75
65	Jeremy Giambi	.75
66	Javier Vazquez	.75
67	Cristian Guzman	.75
68	Paul LoDuca	.75
69	Bobby Abreu	1.00
70	Nomar Garciaparra	4.00
71	Troy Glaus	1.00
72	Chipper Jones	2.00
73	Scott Rolen	2.00
74	Lance Berkman	1.00
75	C.C. Sabathia	.75
76	Bernie Williams	1.00
77	Rafael Palmeiro	1.50
78	Phil Nevin	.75
79	Kazuhiro Sasaki	.75
80	Eric Chavez	1.00
81	Jorge Posada	1.00
82	Edgardo Alfonzo	.75
83	Geoff Jenkins	1.00
84	Preston Wilson	.75
85	Jim Thome	2.00
86	Frank Thomas	1.50
87	Jeff Bagwell	1.50
88	Greg Maddux	3.00
89	Mark Prior	3.00
90	Larry Walker	1.00
91	Luis Gonzalez	1.00
92	Tim Hudson	1.00
93	Tsuyoshi Shinjo	.75
94	Juan Gonzalez	1.50
95	Shea Hillenbrand	.75
96	Paul Konerko	.75
97	Tom Glavine	1.50
98	Marty Cordova	.75
99	Moises Alou	1.00
100	Ken Griffey Jr.	4.00
101	Hank Blalock	1.50
102	Matt Morris	1.00
103	Robb Nen	.75
104	Mike Cameron	.75
105	Mark Buehrle	.75
106	Sean Burroughs	.75
107	Orlando Cabrera	.75
108	Jeromy Burnitz	.75
109	Juan Uribe	.75
110	Eric Milton	.75
111	Carlos Lee	.75
112	Jose Mesa	.75
113	Morgan Ensberg	.75
114	Mike Rivera	.75
115	Juan Cruz	.75
116	Mike Lieberthal	.75
117	Armando Benitez	.75
118	Vinny Castilla	.75
119	Russ Ortiz	.75
120	Mike Lowell	1.00
121	Corey Patterson	1.00
122	Mike Mussina	1.50
123	Rafael Furcal	.75
124	Mark Grace	1.50
125	Ben Sheets	1.00
126	John Smoltz	1.00
127	Fred McGriff	1.00
128	Nick Johnson	.75
129	J.T. Snow	.75
130	Jeff Cirillo	.75
131	Trevor Hoffman	.75
132	Kevin Brown	1.00
133	Mariano Rivera	1.50
134	Marlon Anderson	.75
135	Al Leiter	.75
136	Doug Mientkiewicz	.75
137	Eric Karros	.75
138	Bobby Higginson	.75
139	Sean Casey	1.00
140	Troy Percival	.75
141	Willie Mays	5.00
142	Carl Yastrzemski	3.00
143	Stan Musial	4.00
144	Harmon Killebrew	3.00
145	Mike Schmidt	5.00
146	Duke Snider	2.00
147	Brooks Robinson	3.00
148	Frank Robinson	2.00
149	Nolan Ryan	8.00
150	Reggie Jackson	3.00
151	*Joe Mauer C*	8.00
152	*Joe Mauer U*	15.00
153	*Joe Mauer R*	25.00
154	Colt Griffin C	3.00
155	Colt Griffin U	5.00
156	Colt Griffin R	8.00
157	*Jason Simontacchi C*	2.00
158	*Jason Simontacchi U*	3.00
159	*Jason Simontacchi R*	5.00
160	Casey Kotchman C	5.00
161	Casey Kotchman U	10.00
162	Casey Kotchman R	20.00
163	*Greg Sain C*	1.50
164	*Greg Sain U*	3.00
165	*Greg Sain R*	5.00
166	David Wright C	10.00
167	David Wright U	20.00
168	David Wright R	30.00
169	Scott Hairston C	4.00
170	Scott Hairston U	6.00
171	Scott Hairston R	10.00
172	*Rolando Viera C*	1.50
173	*Rolando Viera U*	3.00
174	*Rolando Viera R*	5.00
175	Tyrell Godwin C	1.50
176	Tyrell Godwin U	3.00
177	Tyrell Godwin R	5.00
178	*Jesus Cota C*	1.50
179	*Jesus Cota U*	3.00
180	*Jesus Cota R*	5.00
181	*Dan Johnson C*	6.00
182	*Dan Johnson U*	12.00
183	*Dan Johnson R*	20.00
184	Mario Ramos C	1.50
185	Mario Ramos U	3.00
186	Mario Ramos R	5.00
187	*Jason Dubois C*	4.00
188	*Jason Dubois U*	6.00
189	*Jason Dubois R*	10.00
190	*Jonny Gomes C*	5.00
191	*Jonny Gomes U*	10.00
192	*Jonny Gomes R*	15.00
193	*Chris Snelling C*	2.00
194	*Chris Snelling U*	4.00
195	*Chris Snelling R*	6.00
196	*Hansel Izquierdo C*	2.00
197	*Hansel Izquierdo U*	4.00
198	*Hansel Izquierdo R*	6.00
199	*So Taguchi C*	3.00
200	*So Taguchi U*	5.00
201	*So Taguchi R*	8.00
202	*Kazuhisa Ishii C*	3.00
203	*Kazuhisa Ishii U*	5.00
204	*Kazuhisa Ishii R*	8.00
205	*Jorge Padilla C*	1.50
206	*Jorge Padilla U*	3.00
207	*Jorge Padilla R*	5.00
208	*Earl Snyder C*	2.00
209	*Earl Snyder U*	4.00
210	*Earl Snyder R*	6.00

Refractors

Stars (1-150): 2-4X
Production 149
Common Rookies: .75-1.5X
Production 1,999
Uncommon Rookies: 1-2X
Production 799
Rare Rookies: 2-3X
Production 149
Gold Refractors (1-150): 3-5X
Gold Common RC's: 4-8X
Gold Uncommon RC's: 2-4X
Gold Rare RC's: 1-2X
Production 70 sets
All Refractors are Uncirculated

Fall Memories

NM/M
Common Player: 5.00
Varying quantities produced
JB Johnny Bench 15.00
BB Barry Bonds 30.00
GB George Brett 25.00
TG Tom Glavine 8.00
LG Luis Gonzalez 5.00
MG Mark Grace 12.00
SG Shawn Green 6.00
TH Todd Helton 8.00
RJ Reggie Jackson 15.00
AJ Andruw Jones 8.00
CP Chipper Jones 10.00
TM Tino Martinez 8.00
WM Willie Mays 40.00
EM Eddie Murray 15.00
JP Jorge Posada 8.00
KP Kirby Puckett 15.00
CS Curt Schilling 8.00
GS Gary Sheffield 5.00
AS Alfonso Soriano 10.00
BW Bernie Williams 8.00

In The Gap

NM/M
Common Player: 5.00
Varying quantities produced
RA Roberto Alomar 10.00
LB Lance Berkman 8.00
WBE Wilson Betemit 5.00
WB Wade Boggs 8.00
BBO Barry Bonds 25.00
BB Bret Boone 6.00
EC Eric Chavez 8.00
CD Carlos Delgado 6.00
AD Adam Dunn 10.00
JE Jim Edmonds 6.00
DE Darin Erstad 5.00
NG Nomar Garciaparra 15.00
TG Tony Gwynn 15.00
TH Todd Helton 8.00
RH Rickey Henderson 10.00
AJ Andruw Jones 10.00
JK Jeff Kent 5.00
RK Ryan Klesko 8.00
PL Paul LoDuca 10.00
RP Rafael Palmeiro 10.00
MP Mike Piazza 15.00
AP Albert Pujols 15.00
ARA Aramis Ramirez 8.00
AR Alex Rodriguez 15.00
IR Ivan Rodriguez 8.00
TS Tsuyoshi Shinjo 5.00
AS Alfonso Soriano 10.00
LW Larry Walker 5.00
BW Bernie Williams 15.00
PW Preston Wilson 5.00

Patches

No Pricing
Production 25 sets

Personal Endorsements

NM/M
Common Autograph: 8.00
Inserted 1:box
RA Roberto Alomar 30.00
KB Kenny Baugh 8.00
LB Lance Berkman 30.00
BB Barry Bonds 220.00
DB Dewon Brazelton 15.00
JD Johnny Damon 30.00
GF Gavin Floyd 25.00
CG Cristian Guzman 10.00
IG Irvin Guzman 10.00
OH Orlando Hudson 10.00
KI Kazuhisa Ishii 30.00
CK Casey Kotchman 20.00
JL Jason Lane 8.00
CW Corwin Malone 8.00
NN Nick Neugebauer 8.00
AP Albert Pujols 125.00
JR Jimmy Rollins 15.00
BS Ben Sheets 20.00
JS Juan Silvestre 8.00
ST So Taguchi 15.00
MT Marcus Thames 8.00

Popular Demand

NM/M
Common Player: 5.00
Varying quantities produced
RA Roberto Alomar 10.00
JB Jeff Bagwell 10.00
WB Wade Boggs 8.00
BBO Barry Bonds 25.00
BB Bret Boone 5.00
CD Carlos Delgado 5.00
AD Adam Dunn 8.00
NG Nomar Garciaparra 15.00
SG Shawn Green 5.00
TG Tony Gwynn 12.00
TH Todd Helton 8.00
CJ Chipper Jones 12.00
DM Don Mattingly 35.00
MP Mike Piazza 15.00
AP Albert Pujols 20.00
AR Alex Rodriguez 15.00
IR Ivan Rodriguez 8.00
CS Curt Schilling 8.00
FT Frank Thomas 10.00
LW Larry Walker 5.00

Portions

NM/M
Common Player: 5.00
Varying quantities produced
RA Roberto Alomar 10.00
JB Jeff Bagwell 10.00
LB Lance Berkman 10.00
CB Craig Biggio 8.00
BBO Barry Bonds 20.00
BB Bret Boone 5.00
CD Carlos Delgado 5.00
RD Ryan Dempster 5.00
AD Adam Dunn 8.00
CF Cliff Floyd 5.00
RF Rafael Furcal 5.00
NG Nomar Garciaparra 15.00
CG Cristian Guzman 5.00
TH Todd Helton 8.00
NJ Nick Johnson 5.00
LD Paul LoDuca 5.00
GM Greg Maddux 10.00
EM Edgar Martinez 10.00
MM Mike Mussina 10.00
MO Magglio Ordonez 5.00
RP Rafael Palmeiro 8.00
MP Mike Piazza 15.00
JP Jorge Posada 8.00
AP Albert Pujols 15.00
AR Alex Rodriguez 15.00
IR Ivan Rodriguez 8.00
NR Nolan Ryan 30.00
KS Kazuhiro Sasaki 5.00

2002 TOPPS RESERVE

NM/M
Complete Set (150): 120.00
Common Player: .25
Common (136-150): 4.00
Production 999
Silver parallel (1-135): 4-8X
Silver (136-150): .75-1.5X
Production 150
Box (10 packs & 1 auto. helmet): 100.00
1 Alex Rodriguez 2.50
2 Tsuyoshi Shinjo .25
3 Craig Biggio .40
4 Troy Glaus .50
5 Mike Rivera .25
6 Curt Schilling .75
7 Garret Anderson .50
8 Ben Sheets .50
9 Todd Helton .75
10 Paul Konerko .50
11 Sammy Sosa 2.00
12 Bud Smith .25
13 Jeff Bagwell .75
14 Albert Pujols 2.00
15 Jose Vidro .25
16 Carlos Delgado .50
17 Torii Hunter .50
18 Jerry Hairston Jr. .25
19 Troy Percival .25
20 Vladimir Guerrero 1.00
21 Geoff Jenkins .40
22 Carlos Pena .25
23 Juan Gonzalez .75
24 Raul Mondesi .25
25 Jimmy Rollins .25
26 Mariano Rivera .50
27 Jorge Posada .50
28 Magglio Ordonez .50
29 Roberto Alomar .50
30 Randy Johnson 1.00
31 Xavier Nady .25
32 Terrence Long .25
33 Chipper Jones 1.00
34 Rich Aurilia .25
35 Aramis Ramirez .50
36 Jim Thome 1.00
37 Bret Boone .50
38 Angel Berroa .25
39 Jeff Conine .25
40 Cliff Floyd .25
41 Pedro J. Martinez 1.00
42 J.D. Drew .50
43 Kazuhiro Sasaki .25
44 Jon Rauch .25
45 Orlando Hudson .25
46 Scott Rolen 1.00
47 Rafael Furcal .25
48 Brad Penny .25
49 Miguel Tejada .50
50 Orlando Cabrera .25
51 Bobby Abreu .50
52 Darin Erstad .50
53 Edgar Martinez .40
54 Ben Grieve .25
55 Shawn Green .50
56 Ivan Rodriguez .75
57 Josh Beckett .50
58 Ray Durham .25
59 Jason Hart .25
60 Nathan Haynes .25
61 Jason Giambi .75
62 Eric Chavez .50
63 Matt Morris .40
64 Lance Berkman .50
65 Jeff Kent .40
66 Andruw Jones .50
67 Brian Giles .50
68 Morgan Ensberg .25
69 Pat Burrell .50
70 Ken Griffey Jr. 2.00
71 Carlos Beltran .50
72 Ichiro Suzuki 2.00
73 Larry Walker .50
74 *J.J. Putz* .50
75 Mike Piazza 2.00
76 Rafael Palmeiro .75
77 Mark Prior 2.00
78 Toby Hall .25
79 Pokey Reese .25
80 Mike Mussina .50
81 Omar Vizquel .25
82 Shannon Stewart .25
83 Jeromy Burnitz .25
84 Bernie Williams .50
85 C.C. Sabathia .25
86 Mike Hampton .25
87 Kevin Brown .50
88 Juan Cruz .25
89 Jeff Weaver .25
90 Jason Lane .25
91 Adam Dunn .75
92 Jose Cruz Jr. .25
93 Marlon Anderson .25
94 Jeff Cirillo .25
95 Mark Buehrle .25
96 Austin Kearns .50
97 Tim Hudson .50
98 Brian Jordan .25
99 Phil Nevin .25
100 Barry Bonds 3.00
101 Derek Jeter 3.00
102 Javier Vazquez .25
103 Jason Kendall .40
104 Jim Edmonds .50
105 Kenny Kelly .25
106 Juan Pena .25
107 Mark Grace .50
108 Roger Clemens 2.00
109 Barry Zito .50
110 Greg Vaughn .25
111 Greg Maddux 1.50
112 Richie Sexson .50
113 Jermaine Dye .25
114 Kerry Wood 1.00
115 Matt Lawton .25
116 Sean Casey .50
117 Gary Sheffield .50
118 Preston Wilson .25
119 Cristian Guzman .25
120 Mike Sweeney .25
121 Neifi Perez .25
122 Paul LoDuca .25
123 Luis Gonzalez .50
124 Ryan Klesko .25
125 Alfonso Soriano 1.00
126 Bobby Higginson .25
127 Juan Pierre .25
128 Moises Alou .50
129 Roy Oswalt .50
130 Nomar Garciaparra 2.00
131 Fred McGriff .40
132 Edgardo Alfonzo .25
133 Johnny Damon .40
134 Dewon Brazelton .25
135 Mark Mulder .50
136 *So Taguchi* 8.00
137 Mario Ramos 4.00
138 *Dan Johnson* 20.00
139 *Hansel Izquierdo* 5.00
140 *Kazuhisa Ishii* 10.00
141 Jon Switzer 4.00
142 *Chris Tritle* 6.00
143 *Chris Snelling* 8.00
144 *Chone Figgins* 8.00
145 *Dan Phillips* 4.00
146 *John Rodriguez* 4.00
147 Colt Griffin 8.00
148 *Jonny Gomes* 12.00
149 Josh Barfield 10.00
150 *Joe Mauer* 30.00

Silver

Stars (1-135): 4-8X
SP's (136-150): .75-1.5X

Autographed Mini-Helmets

NM/M
Common Helmet: 20.00
1:box
Gold Ink Autographs: No Pricing
Production 25
Roberto Alomar 45.00

Moises Alou 25.00
Lance Berkman 35.00
Bret Boone 25.00
Eric Chavez 30.00
Adam Dunn 40.00
Cliff Floyd 20.00
Troy Glaus 40.00
Luis Gonzalez 30.00
Todd Helton 50.00
Magglio Ordonez 25.00
Rafael Palmeiro 40.00
Albert Pujols 100.00
Alex Rodriguez 100.00
Scott Rolen 35.00
Jimmy Rollins 20.00
Alfonso Soriano 50.00
Barry Zito 30.00

Game-Used Bat

NM/M

Common Player: 5.00
Inserted 1:12
RA Roberto Alomar 10.00
JB Jeff Bagwell 10.00
BB Barry Bonds 20.00
CD Carlos Delgado 8.00
JG Juan Gonzalez 8.00
LG Luis Gonzalez 5.00
TG Tony Gwynn 12.00
RH Rickey Henderson 10.00
CJ Chipper Jones 10.00
AJ Andruw Jones 8.00
TM Tino Martinez 8.00
RP Rafael Palmeiro 8.00
MB Mike Piazza 15.00
AP Albert Pujols 15.00
AR Alex Rodriguez 12.00
IR Ivan Rodriguez 8.00
TS Tsuyoshi Shinjo 5.00
AS Alfonso Soriano 10.00
FT Frank Thomas 8.00
BW Bernie Williams 8.00

Game-Worn Uniform

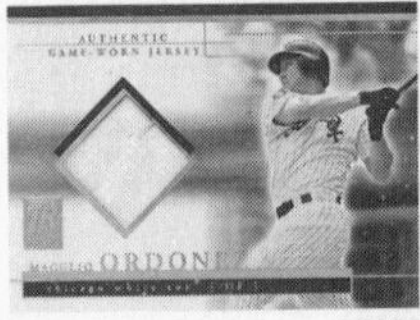

NM/M

Common Player: 5.00
Inserted 1:5
BB Barry Bonds 20.00
BBO Bret Boone 5.00
DE Darin Erstad 5.00
NG Nomar Garciaparra 15.00
LG Luis Gonzalez 5.00
TG Tony Gwynn 10.00
TH Todd Helton 8.00
RJ Randy Johnson 10.00
AJ Andruw Jones 6.00
CJ Chipper Jones 10.00
GM Greg Maddux 12.00
PM Pedro Martinez 10.00
MM Mark Mulder 5.00
MO Magglio Ordonez 5.00
RP Rafael Palmeiro 8.00
MP Mike Piazza 12.00
AP Albert Pujols 15.00
AR Alex Rodriguez 12.00
IR Ivan Rodriguez 8.00
SR Scott Rolen 10.00
KS Kazuhiro Sasaki 5.00
CS Curt Schilling 8.00
FT Frank Thomas 8.00
KW Kerry Wood 10.00

Game-Worn Patch

No Pricing
Production 25 sets

Game-Used Baseball

NM/M

Inserted 1:1,761
AR Alex Rodriguez
I Ichiro Suzuki 65.00

2002 TOPPS SUPER TEAMS

NM/M

Complete Set: 40.00
Common Player: .25
Pack (7): 3.50
Box (20): 60.00
1 Leo Durocher .25
2 Whitey Lockman .25
3 Alvin Dark .25
4 Monte Irvin .50
5 Willie Mays 2.50
6 Wes Westrum .25
7 Johnny Antonelli .25
8 Sal Maglie .25
9 Dusty Rhodes .25
10 Davey Williams .25
11 Hoyt Wilhelm .25
12 Don Mueller .25
13 Dusty Rhodes .25
14 Willie Mays, Monte Irvin, Dusty Rhodes .75
15 Walt Alston .25
16 Gil Hodges .75
17 Jim Gilliam .25
18 Pee Wee Reese .50
19 Jackie Robinson 2.00
20 Duke Snider 1.00
21 Carl Furillo .25
22 Roy Campanella 1.00
23 Don Newcombe .25
24 Don Hoak .25
25 Johnny Podres .25
26 Clem Labine .25
27 Johnny Podres .25
28 Pee Wee Reese, Jackie Robinson, Duke Snider 1.00
29 Fred Haney .25
30 Joe Adcock .25
31 Frank Torre .25
32 Red Schoendienst .25
33 Johnny Logan .25
34 Eddie Mathews 1.00
35 Hank Aaron 3.00
36 Andy Pafko .25
37 Wes Covington .25
38 Lew Burdette .25
39 Warren Spahn 1.00
40 Del Crandall .25
41 Lew Burdette .25
42 Warren Spahn, Eddie Mathews, Hank Aaron 1.50
43 Danny Murtaugh .25
44 Dick Stuart .25
45 Bill Mazeroski .25
46 Dick Groat .25
47 Don Hoak .25
48 Gino Cimoli .25
49 Bill Virdon .25
50 Roberto Clemente 2.50
51 Smokey Burgess .25
52 Bob Friend .25
53 Vernon Law .25
55 Roy Face .25
56 Bill Mazeroski .25
57 Roberto Clemente, Bill Mazeroski, Dick Groat 1.00
58 Ralph Houk .25
59 Bill "Moose" Skowron .50
60 Bobby Richardson .25
61 Tony Kubek .25
62 Clete Boyer .25
63 Yogi Berra 1.50
64 Bob Cerv .25
65 Roger Maris 1.50
66 Elston Howard .25
67 Whitey Ford 1.00
68 Ralph Terry .25
69 Johnny Blanchard .25
70 Whitey Ford 1.00
71 Yogi Berra, Roger Maris, Elston Howard, Bill "Moose" Skowron 1.00
72 Red Schoendienst .25
73 Orlando Cepeda .40
74 Julian Javier .25
75 Dal Maxvill .25
76 Mike Shannon .25
77 Lou Brock .75
78 Roger Maris 1.50
79 Curt Flood .25
80 Tim McCarver .25
81 Steve Carlton .75
82 Bob Gibson 1.00
83 Nelson Briles .25
84 Bobby Tolan .25
85 Bob Gibson 1.00
86 Bob Gibson, Steve Carlton, Orlando Cepeda, Lou Brock .50
87 Gil Hodges .25
88 Ed Kranepool .25
89 Buddy Harrelson .25
90 Wayne Garrett .25
91 Cleon Jones .25
92 Tommie Agee .25
93 Ron Swoboda .25
94 Al Weis .25
95 Jerry Grote .25
96 Tom Seaver 1.00
97 Jerry Koosman .25
98 Tug McGraw .25
99 Nolan Ryan 3.00
100 Donn Clendenon .25
101 Tom Seaver, Jerry Koosman, Tug McGraw, Nolan Ryan 1.00
102 Earl Weaver .25
103 Boog Powell .25
104 Davey Johnson .25
105 Mark Belanger .25
106 Brooks Robinson 1.00
107 Don Buford .25
108 Paul Blair .25
109 Frank Robinson 1.00
110 Dick Hall .25
111 Jim Palmer .75
112 Mike Cuellar .25
113 Dave McNally .25
114 Andy Etchebarren .25
115 Brooks Robinson 1.00
116 Dick Hall, Jim Palmer, Mike Cuellar, Dave McNally .40
117 Alvin Dark .25
118 Gene Tenace .25
119 Dick Green .25
120 Bert Campaneris .25
121 Sal Bando .25
122 Reggie Jackson 1.00
123 Joe Rudi .25
124 Claudell Washington .25
125 Ray Fosse .25
126 Vida Blue .40
127 Rollie Fingers .25
128 Jim "Catfish" Hunter .50
129 Ken Holtzman .25
130 Rollie Fingers .25
131 Jim "Catfish" Hunter, Sal Bando, Reggie Jackson, Rollie Fingers .50
132 Davey Johnson .25
133 Keith Hernandez .25
134 Wally Backman .25
135 Rafael Santana .25
136 Ray Knight .25
137 Len Dykstra .25
138 Darryl Strawberry .25
139 Kevin Mitchell .25
140 Dwight Gooden .25
141 Bob Ojeda .25
142 Sid Fernandez .25
143 Ron Darling .25
144 Gary Carter .25
145 Ray Knight .25
146 Darryl Strawberry, Dwight Gooden, Keith Hernandez .25

Retrofractor

Cards (1-146): 2-4X
#'d to year team won World Series

Autographs

NM/M

Common Autograph: 10.00
Inserted 1:19
YB Yogi Berra 40.00
VB Vida Blue 15.00
CB Clete Boyer 15.00
SC Steve Carlton 25.00
MI Monte Irvin 15.00
RJ Reggie Jackson 40.00
TK Tony Kubek 30.00
TM Tug McGraw 15.00
AP Andy Pafko 15.00
JP Jim Palmer 25.00
JPO Johnny Podres 15.00
BR Bobby Richardson 15.00
BRO Brooks Robinson 30.00
NR Nolan Ryan 150.00
TS Tom Seaver 40.00
MS Bill "Moose" Skowron 20.00
WS Warren Spahn 25.00
HW Hoyt Wilhelm 15.00

A View To A Thrill Auto. Relics

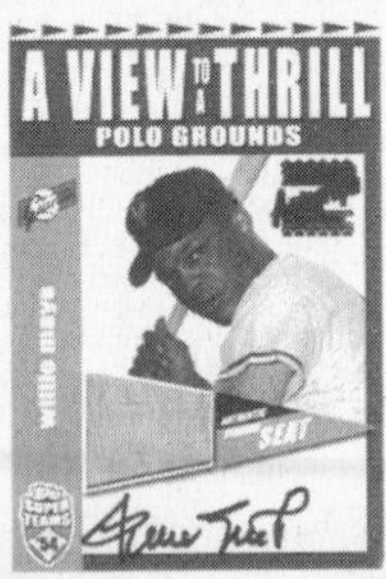

NM/M

Produced listed
WFA Whitey Ford/61 100.00
BGA Bob Gibson/67 60.00
WMA Willie Mays/54 150.00
DSA Duke Snider/55 80.00
WSA Warren Spahn/57 60.00

A View To a Thrill Seat Relics

NM/M

Common Player: 10.00
Inserted 1:30
HA Hank Aaron 20.00
YB Yogi Berra 15.00
LB Lew Burdette 10.00
RC Roberto Clemente 50.00
WF Whitey Ford 15.00
BG Bob Gibson 15.00
RMB Roger Maris/Cardinals 20.00
RMY Roger Maris/Yankees 40.00
EM Eddie Mathews 15.00
WM Willie Mays 30.00
BM Bill Mazeroski 10.00
JP Jim Palmer 10.00
BP Boog Powell 10.00
BR Brooks Robinson 15.00
FR Frank Robinson 15.00
RS Red Schoendienst 10.00
DS Duke Snider 15.00
WS Warren Spahn 15.00

Classic Combos

NM/M

Common Card: 40.00
Inserted 1:865
AJ Tommie Agee, Cleon Jones 40.00
JR Reggie Jackson, Joe Rudi 40.00
RR Brooks Robinson, Frank Robinson 50.00
SK Tom Seaver, Jerry Koosman 50.00

SRBK "Moose" Skowron, Bobby Richardson, Clete Boyer, Tony Kubek 80.00

Relics

		NM/M
Common Player:		10.00
TA	Tommie Agee/bat	20.00
SBB	Sal Bando/bat	10.00
SBJ	Sal Bando/jsy	10.00
MB	Mark Belanger/bat	10.00
PB	Paul Blair/bat	10.00
CB	Clete Boyer/bat	10.00
LB	Lew Burdette/jsy	15.00
SB	Smokey Burgess/bat	10.00
BC	Bert Campaneris/jsy	15.00
GC	Gary Carter/jacket	20.00
GCB	Gary Carter/bat	15.00
GCJ	Gary Carter/jsy	15.00
OC	Orlando Cepeda/bat	15.00
BCE	Bob Cerv/bat	10.00
GCI	Gino Cimoli/bat	10.00
DC	Del Crandel/bat	10.00
MC	Mike Cuellar/jsy	10.00
RD	Ron Darling/jsy	10.00
LD	Len Dykstra/bat	15.00
RF	Ray Fosse/bat	10.00
BF	Bob Friend/jsy	10.00
WG	Wayne Garrett/bat	10.00
DG	Dwight Gooden/jsy	15.00
DH	Don Hoak/bat	10.00
RH	Ralph Houk/jsy	10.00
RJ	Reggie Jackson/bat	35.00
DJ	Davey Johnson/bat	10.00
CJ	Cleon Jones/bat	20.00
RK	Ray Knight/bat	10.00
JK	Jerry Koosman/jsy	10.00
EK	Ed Kranepool/jsy	15.00
TK	Tony Kubek/bat	25.00
TM	Tug McGraw/jsy	15.00
DM	Dave McNally/jsy	10.00
KM	Kevin Mitchell/bat	10.00
AP	Andy Pafko/bat	10.00
BR	Bobby Richardson/bat	25.00
BRO	Brooks Robinson/bat	25.00
FR	Frank Robinson/bat	20.00
JR	Joe Rudi/bat	10.00
NR	Nolan Ryan/bat	75.00
RS	Red Schoendienst/bat	10.00
TS	Tom Seaver/bat	20.00
MS	"Moose" Skowron/bat	20.00
DS	Darryl Strawberry/bat	20.00
CW	Claudell Washington/bat	10.00

Super Teammates Autographs

		NM/M
Production 50 sets		
BGA	Lou Brock, Bob Gibson	100.00
FBA	Whitey Ford, Yogi Berra	150.00
MIA	Willie Mays, Monte Irvin	180.00
RRA	Brooks Robinson, Frank Robinson	100.00
SRBKA	Bill "Moose" Skowron, Bobby Richardson, Clete Boyer, Tony Kubek	200.00

2002 TOPPS TEN

	NM/M
Complete Set (200):	40.00
Common Player:	.15
Pack (7):	2.00
Box (24):	40.00

1	Ichiro Suzuki	1.00
2	Rich Aurilia	.15
3	Bret Boone	.25
4	Juan Pierre	.15
5	Shannon Stewart	.15
6	Alex Rodriguez	1.00
7	Luis Gonzalez	.25
8	Todd Helton	.50
9	Garret Anderson	.25
10	Albert Pujols	1.00
11	Lance Berkman	.25
12	Todd Helton	.50
13	Jeff Kent	.15
14	Bob Abreu	.25
15	Jason Giambi	.40
16	Albert Pujols	1.00
17	Mike Sweeney	.15
18	Vladimir Guerrero	.50
19	Cliff Floyd	.15
20	Shannon Stewart	.15
21	Cristian Guzman	.15
22	Roberto Alomar	.40
23	Carlos Beltran	.25
24	Jimmy Rollins	.15
25	Roger Cedeno	.15
26	Juan Pierre	.15
27	Juan Uribe	.15
28	Luis Castillo	.15
29	Ray Durham	.15
30	Mark McLemore	.15
31	Barry Bonds	1.50
32	Sammy Sosa	1.00
33	Luis Gonzalez	.25
34	Alex Rodriguez	1.00
35	Shawn Green	.25
36	Todd Helton	.50
37	Jim Thome	.50
38	Rafael Palmeiro	.40
39	Richie Sexson	.25
40	Phil Nevin	.15
41	Troy Glaus	.40
42	Sammy Sosa	1.00
43	Todd Helton	.50
44	Luis Gonzalez	.25
45	Bret Boone	.25
46	Juan Gonzalez	.40
47	Barry Bonds	1.50
48	Alex Rodriguez	1.00
49	Jeff Bagwell	.50
50	Albert Pujols	1.00
51	Phil Nevin	.15
52	Ichiro Suzuki	1.00
53	Larry Walker	.25
54	Jason Giambi	.40
55	Roberto Alomar	.40
56	Todd Helton	.50
57	Moises Alou	.25
58	Lance Berkman	.25
59	Bret Boone	.25
60	Frank Catalanotto	.15
61	Chipper Jones	.50
62	Barry Bonds	1.50
63	Sammy Sosa	1.00
64	Luis Gonzalez	.25
65	Todd Helton	.50
66	Larry Walker	.25
67	Jason Giambi	.40
68	Jim Thome	.50
69	Alex Rodriguez	1.00
70	Lance Berkman	.25
71	Albert Pujols	1.00
72	Ichiro Suzuki	1.00
73	Roger Cedeno	.15
74	Juan Pierre	.15
75	Jimmy Rollins	.15
76	Alfonso Soriano	.50
77	Mark McLemore	.15
78	Chuck Knoblauch	.15
79	Vladimir Guerrero	.50
80	Bob Abreu	.25
81	Mike Cameron	.15
82	Sammy Sosa	1.00
83	Alex Rodriguez	1.00
84	Todd Helton	.50
85	Barry Bonds	1.50
86	Luis Gonzalez	.25
87	Ichiro Suzuki	1.00
88	Jeff Bagwell	.50
89	Cliff Floyd	.15
90	Shawn Green	.25
91	Craig Biggio	.15
92	Juan Pierre	.15
93	Fernando Vina	.15
94	Paul LoDuca	.15
95	Mark Grace	.25
96	Eric Young	.15
97	Placido Polanco	.15
98	Jason Kendall	.15
99	Ichiro Suzuki	1.00
100	Orlando Cabrera	.15
101	Rey Sanchez	.15
102	Ichiro Suzuki	1.00
103	Edgar Martinez	.25
104	Bret Boone	.25
105	Barry Bonds	1.50
106	Ivan Rodriguez	.40
107	Mike Piazza	1.00
108	Sammy Sosa	1.00
109	John Olerud	.25
110	Roberto Alomar	.40
111	Roberto Alomar	.40
112	Mark McGwire	1.50
113	Barry Larkin	.25
114	Ken Griffey Jr.	1.00
115	Rickey Henderson	.25
116	Barry Bonds	1.50
117	Ivan Rodriguez	.40
118	Mike Piazza	1.00
119	Roger Clemens	1.00
120	Randy Johnson	.50
121	Albert Pujols	1.00
122	Ichiro Suzuki	1.00
123	Roy Oswalt	.25
124	C.C. Sabathia	.15
125	Jimmy Rollins	.15
126	Alfonso Soriano	.50
127	David Eckstein	.15
128	Adam Dunn	.50
129	Bud Smith	.15
130	Tsuyoshi Shinjo	.15
131	Matt Morris	.15
132	Curt Schilling	.25
133	Randy Johnson	.50
134	Mark Mulder	.25
135	Roger Clemens	1.00
136	Jon Lieber	.15
137	Jamie Moyer	.15
138	Freddy Garcia	.15
139	Tim Hudson	.25
140	C.C. Sabathia	.15
141	Randy Johnson	.50
142	Curt Schilling	.25
143	John Burkett	.15
144	Freddy Garcia	.15
145	Greg Maddux	.75
146	Darryl Kile	.15
147	Mike Mussina	.40
148	Joe Mays	.15
149	Matt Morris	.25
150	Russ Ortiz	.15
151	Randy Johnson	.50
152	Curt Schilling	.25
153	Hideo Nomo	.15
154	Chan Ho Park	.15
155	Kerry Wood	.50
156	Mike Mussina	.40
157	Roger Clemens	1.00
158	Javier Vazquez	.15
159	Barry Zito	.25
160	Bartolo Colon	.15
161	Mariano Rivera	.25
162	Robb Nen	.15
163	Kazuhiro Sasaki	.15
164	Armando Benitez	.15
165	Trevor Hoffman	.15
166	Jeff Shaw	.15
167	Keith Foulke	.15
168	Jose Mesa	.15
169	Troy Percival	.15
170	Billy Wagner	.15
171	Pat Burrell	.25
172	Raul Mondesi	.15
173	Gary Sheffield	.25
174	Carlos Beltran	.25
175	Vladimir Guerrero	.50
176	Torii Hunter	.25
177	Jeromy Burnitz	.15
178	Tim Salmon	.15
179	Jim Edmonds	.25
180	Tsuyoshi Shinjo	.15
181	Greg Maddux	.75
182	Roberto Alomar	.40
183	Ken Griffey Jr.	1.00
184	Ivan Rodriguez	.40
185	Omar Vizquel	.15
186	Barry Bonds	1.50
187	Devon White	.15
188	J.T. Snow	.15
189	Larry Walker	.25
190	Robin Ventura	.15
191	*Mark Phillips*	3.00
192	*Clint Nageotte*	2.00
193	*Mauricio Lara*	.75
194	*Nic Jackson*	.75
195	*Chris Tritle*	.75
196	*Ryan Gripp*	.75
197	*Greg Montalbano*	.75
198	*Noochie Varner*	.75
199	*Nick Alvarez*	.75
200	*Craig Kuzmic*	.75

Autographs

		NM/M
Common Autograph:		10.00
Inserted 1:67		
BB	Barry Bonds	200.00
BBO	Bret Boone	20.00
RCL	Roger Clemens	100.00
JE	Jim Edmonds	25.00
CF	Cliff Floyd	10.00
LG	Luis Gonzalez	15.00
CG	Cristian Guzman	10.00
RO	Roy Oswalt	15.00
JR	Jimmy Rollins	10.00
BZ	Barry Zito	20.00

Die-Cut

Stars (1-200):	2-4X
Inserted 1:4	

Relics

		NM/M
Common Player:		8.00
Bat Relic 1:27		
Jersey Relic 1:26		
BA	Bob Abreu/bat	12.00
RA	Roberto Alomar/bat	15.00
MA	Moises Alou/bat	8.00
GA	Garret Anderson/bat	10.00
JBA	Jeff Bagwell/jsy	15.00
CB	Carlos Beltran/bat	10.00
AB	Armando Benitez/jsy	8.00
LB	Lance Berkman/bat	15.00
CBI	Craig Biggio/jsy	15.00
BB	Barry Bonds/jsy	25.00
BBO	Bret Boone/bat	10.00
JBU	John Burkett/jsy	8.00
JB	Jeromy Burnitz/jsy	8.00
MC	Mike Cameron/bat	10.00
LC	Luis Castillo/bat	8.00
RC	Roger Cedeno/bat	8.00
BC	Bartolo Colon/jsy	8.00
RD	Ray Durham/bat	8.00
JE	Jim Edmonds/bat	15.00
CF	Cliff Floyd/bat	8.00
FG	Freddy Garcia/jsy	8.00
JGO	Juan Gonzalez/bat	10.00
LG	Luis Gonzalez/bat	10.00
MG	Mark Grace/bat	20.00
SG	Shawn Green/bat	10.00
CG	Cristian Guzman/bat	10.00
TH	Todd Helton/bat	15.00
THO	Trevor Hoffman/jsy	10.00
THU	Torii Hunter/bat	15.00
RJ	Randy Johnson/jsy	20.00
CJ	Chipper Jones/bat	20.00
JK	Jason Kendall/jsy	10.00
JKE	Jeff Kent/jsy	10.00
CK	Chuck Knoblauch/bat	10.00
PL	Paul LoDuca/bat	10.00
GM	Greg Maddux/jsy	20.00
EM	Edgar Martinez/jsy	10.00
MM	Mark McLemore/bat	8.00
PM	Raul Mondesi/bat	8.00
PN	Phil Nevin/bat	8.00
JO	John Olerud/jsy	10.00
RP	Rafael Palmeiro/jsy	12.00
CP	Chan Ho Park/jsy	8.00
MP	Mike Piazza/jsy	20.00
JP	Juan Pierre/jsy	10.00
PP	Placido Polanco/bat	10.00
AP	Albert Pujols/bat	25.00
AR	Alex Rodriguez/jsy	15.00
TS	Tim Salmon/bat	10.00
CS	Curt Schilling/jsy	15.00
RS	Richie Sexson/bat	10.00
GS	Gary Sheffield/jsy	10.00
TSH	Tsuyoshi Shinjo/bat	10.00
JS	J.T. Snow/bat	8.00
AS	Alfonso Soriano/bat	15.00
SS	Shannon Stewart/bat	8.00
MS	Mike Sweeney/bat	15.00
JT	Jim Thome/bat	20.00
RV	Robin Ventura/bat	8.00
FV	Fernando Vina/bat	10.00
OV	Omar Vizquel/bat	10.00
BW	Billy Wagner/jsy	10.00
LW	Larry Walker/bat	10.00

DW	Devon White/bat	8.00
BZ	Barry Zito/jsy	10.00

Team Topps Legends Autographs

	NM/M
Carl Yastrzemski	65.00

2002 TOPPS TOTAL

	NM/M
Complete Set (990):	125.00
Common Player:	.10
Pack (10):	1.00
Box (36):	30.00

No.	Player	NM/M
1	*Joe Mauer*	3.00
2	Derek Jeter	2.00
3	Shawn Green	.25
4	Vladimir Guerrero	.50
5	Mike Piazza	1.50
6	Brandon Duckworth	.10
7	Aramis Ramirez	.10
8	Josh Barfield	.50
9	Troy Glaus	.40
10	Sammy Sosa	1.00
11	Rod Barajas	.10
12	Tsuyoshi Shinjo	.25
13	Larry Bigbie	.10
14	Tino Martinez	.10
15	Craig Biggio	.25
16	*Anastacio Martinez*	.40
17	John McDonald	.10
18	*Kyle Kane*	.30
19	Aubrey Huff	.10
20	Juan Cruz	.10
21	Doug Creek	.10
22	Luther Hackman	.10
23	Rafael Furcal	.10
24	Andres Torres	.10
25	Jason Giambi	.50
26	Jose Paniagua	.10
27	Jose Offerman	.10
28	Alex Arias	.10
29	J.M. Gold	.10
30	Jeff Bagwell	.50
31	*Brent Cookson*	.20
32	Kelly Wunsch	.10
33	Larry Walker	.25
34	Luis Gonzalez	.25
35	John Franco	.10
36	Roy Oswalt	.25
37	Tom Glavine	.25
38	C.C. Sabathia	.10
39	Jay Gibbons	.10
40	Wilson Betemit	.10
41	Tony Armas	.10
42	Mo Vaughn	.10
43	*Gerard Oakes*	.40
44	Dmitri Young	.10
45	Tim Salmon	.10
46	Barry Zito	.10
47	Adrian Gonzalez	.10
48	Joe Davenport	.10
49	Adrian Hernandez	.10
50	Randy Johnson	.50
51	Benito Baez	.10
52	Adam Pettyjohn	.10
53	Alex Escobar	.10
54	*Stevenson Agosto*	.25
55	Omar Daal	.10
56	Mike Buddie	.10
57	Dave Williams	.10
58	Marquis Grissom	.10
59	Pat Burrell	.25
60	Mark Prior	2.00
61	Mike Bynum	.10
62	*Mike Hill*	.25
63	*Brandon Backe*	.25
64	Dan Wilson	.10
65	Nick Johnson	.10
66	Jason Grimsley	.10
67	Russ Johnson	.10
68	Todd Walker	.10
69	Kyle Farnsworth	.10
70	Ben Broussard	.10
71	*Garrett Guzman*	.50
72	Terry Mulholland	.10
73	Tyler Houston	.10
74	Jace Brewer	.10
75	*Chris Baker*	.25
76	Frank Catalanotto	.10
77	Mike Redmond	.10
78	Matt Wise	.10
79	Fernando Vina	.10
80	Kevin Brown	.10
81	Grant Balfour	.10
82	*Clint Nageotte*	.75
83	Jeff Tam	.10
84	Steve Trachsel	.10
85	Tomokazu Ohka	.10
86	Keith McDonald	.10
87	Jose Ortiz	.10
88	Rusty Greer	.10
89	Jeff Suppan	.10
90	Moises Alou	.10
91	Juan Encarnacion	.10
92	*Tyler Yates*	.40
93	Scott Strickland	.10
94	Brent Butler	.10
95	Jon Rauch	.10
96	*Brian Mallette*	.25
97	Joe Randa	.10
98	Cesar Crespo	.10
99	Felix Rodriguez	.10
100	Chipper Jones	.75
101	Victor Martinez	.10
102	Danny Graves	.10
103	*Brandon Berger*	.10
104	Carlos Garcia	.10
105	Alfonso Soriano	.75
106	*Allan Simpson*	.25
107	Brad Thomas	.10
108	Devon White	.10
109	Scott Chiasson	.10
110	Cliff Floyd	.10
111	Scott Williamson	.10
112	Julio Zuleta	.10
113	Terry Adams	.10
114	Zach Day	.10
115	Ben Grieve	.10
116	Mark Ellis	.10
117	*Bobby Jenks*	.75
118	LaTroy Hawkins	.10
119	Tim Raines Jr.	.10
120	Juan Uribe	.10
121	Bob Scanlan	.10
122	*Brad Nelson*	1.50
123	Adam Johnson	.10
124	Raul Casanova	.10
125	Jeff D'Amico	.10
126	*Aaron Cook*	.50
127	Alan Benes	.10
128	Mark Little	.10
129	Randy Wolf	.10
130	Phil Nevin	.10
131	Guillermo Mota	.10
132	Nick Neugebauer	.10
133	Pedro Borbon	.10
134	Doug Mientkiewicz	.10
135	Edgardo Alfonzo	.10
136	Dustan Mohr	.10
137	Dan Reichert	.10
138	Dewon Brazelton	.10
139	Orlando Cabrera	.10
140	Todd Hollandsworth	.10
141	Darren Dreifort	.10
142	Jose Valentin	.10
143	Josh Kalinowski	.10
144	Randy Keisler	.10
145	Bret Boone	.10
146	Roosevelt Brown	.10
147	Brent Abernathy	.10
148	Jorge Julio	.10
149	Alex Gonzalez	.10
150	Juan Pierre	.10
151	Roger Cedeno	.10
152	Javier Vazquez	.10
153	Armando Benitez	.10
154	Dave Burba	.10
155	Brad Penny	.10
156	Ryan Jensen	.10
157	Jeromy Burnitz	.10
158	*Matt Childers*	.40
159	Wilmy Caceres	.10
160	Roger Clemens	.10
161	Michael Tejera	.10
162	Jason Christiansen	.10
163	Pokey Reese	.10
164	Ivanon Coffie	.10
165	Joaquin Benoit	.10
166	Mike Matheny	.10
167	Eric Cammack	.10
168	Alex Graman	.10
169	Brook Fordyce	.10
170	Mike Lieberthal	.10
171	Giovanni Carrara	.10
172	Antonio Perez	.10
173	Fernando Tatis	.10
174	*Jason Bay*	1.00
175	*Jason Botts*	.50
176	Danys Baez	.10
177	Shea Hillenbrand	.10
178	Jack Cust	.10
179	Clay Bellinger	.10
180	Roberto Alomar	.10
181	Graeme Lloyd	.10
182	*Clint Weibl*	.40
183	Royce Clayton	.10
184	Ben Davis	.10
185	Brian Adams	.25
186	Jack Wilson	.10
187	David Coggin	.10
188	Derrick Turnbow	.10
189	Vladimir Nunez	.10
190	Mariano Rivera	.10
191	Wilson Guzman	.10
192	Michael Barrett	.10
193	Corey Patterson	.10
194	Luis Sojo	.10
195	Scott Elarton	.10
196	Charles Thomas	.25
197	Ricky Bottalico	.10
198	Wilfredo Rodriguez	.10
199	Ricardo Rincon	.10
200	John Smoltz	.10
201	Travis Miller	.10
202	Ben Weber	.10
203	T.J. Tucker	.10
204	Terry Shumpert	.10
205	Bernie Williams	.10
206	Russ Ortiz	.10
207	Nate Rolison	.10
208	Jose Cruz Jr.	.10
209	Bill Ortega	.10
210	Carl Everett	.10
211	Luis Lopez	.10
212	*Brian Wolfe*	.25
213	Doug Davis	.10
214	Troy Mattes	.10
215	Al Leiter	.10
216	Joe Mays	.10
217	Bobby Smith	.10
218	*J.J. Trujillo*	.25
219	Hideo Nomo	.25
220	Jimmy Rollins	.10
221	Bobby Seay	.10
222	Mike Thurman	.10
223	Bartolo Colon	.10
224	Jesus Sanchez	.10
225	Ray Durham	.10
226	Juan Diaz	.10
227	Lee Stevens	.10
228	*Ben Howard*	.75
229	James Moulton	.10
230	Paul Quantrill	.10
231	Randy Knorr	.10
232	Abraham Nunez	.10
233	Mike Fetters	.10
234	Mario Encarnacion	.10
235	Jeremy Fikac	.10
236	Travis Lee	.10
237	Bob File	.10
238	Pete Harnisch	.10
239	*Randy Galvez*	.25
240	Geoff Goetz	.10
241	Gary Glover	.10
242	Troy Percival	.10
243	*Lenny Dinardo*	.40
244	*Jonny Gomes*	1.00
245	*Jesus Medrano*	.25
246	Rey Ordonez	.10
247	Juan Gonzalez	.50
248	Jose Guillen	.10
249	*Franklin German*	.25
250	Mike Mussina	.40
251	Ugueth Urbina	.10
252	Melvin Mora	.10
253	Gerald Williams	.10
254	Jared Sandberg	.10
255	Darrin Fletcher	.10
256	A.J. Pierzynski	.10
257	Lenny Harris	.10
258	Blaine Neal	.10
259	Denny Neagle	.10
260	Jason Hart	.10
261	Henry Mateo	.10
262	Rheal Cormier	.10
263	Luis Terrero	.10
264	Shigetoshi Hasegawa	.10
265	Bill Haselman	.10
266	Scott Hatteberg	.10
267	Adam Hyzdu	.10
268	Mike Williams	.10
269	Marlon Anderson	.10
270	Bruce Chen	.10
271	Eli Marrero	.10
272	Jimmy Haynes	.10
273	Bronson Arroyo	.10
274	Kevin Jordan	.10
275	Rick Helling	.10
276	Mark Loretta	.10
277	Dustin Hermanson	.10
278	Pablo Ozuna	.10
279	*Syketo Anderson*	.25
280	Jermaine Dye	.10
281	Will Smith	.10
282	Brian Daubach	.10
283	Eric Hinske	.10
284	*Joe Jiannetti*	.40
285	Chan Ho Park	.10
286	*Curtis Legendre*	.25
287	Jeff Reboulet	.10
288	Scott Rolen	.50
289	Chris Richard	.10
290	Eric Chavez	.25
291	Scot Shields	.10
292	Donnie Sadler	.10
293	Dave Veres	.10
294	Craig Counsell	.10
295	Armando Reynoso	.10
296	Kyle Lohse	.10
297	Arthur Rhodes	.10
298	Sidney Ponson	.10
299	Trevor Hoffman	.10
300	Kerry Wood	.25
301	Danny Bautista	.10
302	Scott Sauerbeck	.10
303	Johnny Estrada	.10
304	Mike Timlin	.10
305	Orlando Hernandez	.25
306	Tony Clark	.10
307	Tomas Perez	.10
308	Marcus Giles	.10
309	Mike Bordick	.10
310	Jorge Posada	.25
311	Jason Conti	.10
312	Kevin Millar	.10
313	Paul Shuey	.10
314	*Jake Mauer*	.75
315	Luke Hudson	.10
316	Angel Berroa	.10
317	*Fred Bastardo*	.25
318	Shawn Estes	.10
319	Andy Ashby	.10
320	Ryan Klesko	.10
321	Kevin Appier	.10
322	Juan Pena	.10
323	Alex Herrera	.10
324	Robb Nen	.10
325	Orlando Hudson	.10
326	Lyle Overbay	.10
327	Ben Sheets	.25
328	Mike DiFelice	.10
329	*Pablo Arias*	.25
330	Mike Sweeney	.10
331	Rick Ankiel	.10
332	Tomas De La Rosa	.25
333	*Kazuhisa Ishii*	1.00
334	Jose Reyes	.10
335	Jeremy Giambi	.10
336	Jose Mesa	.10
337	*Ralph Roberts*	.25
338	Jose Nunez	.10
339	Curt Schilling	.40
340	Sean Casey	.20
341	Bob Wells	.10
342	Carlos Beltran	.10
343	Alexis Gomez	.10
344	Brandon Claussen	.25
345	Buddy Groom	.10
346	*Mark Phillips*	.50
347	Francisco Cordova	.10
348	Joe Oliver	.10
349	Danny Patterson	.10
350	Joel Pineiro	.10
351	J.R. House	.10
352	Benny Agbayani	.10
353	Jose Vidro	.10
354	*Reed Johnson*	.10
355	Mike Lowell	.10
356	Scott Schoeneweis	.10
357	Brian Jordan	.10
358	Steve Finley	.10
359	Randy Choate	.10
360	Jose Lima	.10
361	Miguel Olivo	.10
362	Kenny Rogers	.10

No.	Player	Value
363	David Justice	.20
364	Brandon Knight	.10
365	Joe Kennedy	.10
366	Eric Valent	.10
367	Nelson Cruz	.10
368	Brian Giles	.25
369	Charles Gibson Jr.	.10
370	Juan Pena	.10
371	Mark Redman	.10
372	Billy Koch	.10
373	Ted Lilly	.10
374	Craig Paquette	.10
375	Kevin Jarvis	.10
376	Scott Erickson	.10
377	Josh Paul	.10
378	Darwin Cubillan	.10
379	Nelson Figueroa	.10
380	Darin Erstad	.20
381	*Jeremy Hill*	.25
382	Elvin Nina	.10
383	*Boomer Wells*	.25
384	*Jay Caligiuri*	.40
385	Freddy Garcia	.10
386	Damian Miller	.10
387	Bobby Higginson	.10
388	*Alejandro Giron*	.25
389	Ivan Rodriguez	.40
390	Ed Rogers	.10
391	Andy Benes	.10
392	Matt Blank	.10
393	Ryan Vogelsong	.10
394	*Kelly Ramos*	.25
395	Eric Karros	.10
396	Bobby Jones	.10
397	Omar Vizquel	.25
398	Matt Perisho	.10
399	Delino DeShields	.10
400	Carlos Hernandez	.10
401	Derrek Lee	.10
402	Kirk Rueter	.10
403	David Wright	1.50
404	Paul LoDuca	.10
405	Brian Schneider	.10
406	Milton Bradley	.10
407	Daryle Ward	.10
408	Cody Ransom	.10
409	Fernando Rodney	.10
410	*John Suomi*	.20
411	Joe Girardi	.10
412	*Demetrius Heath*	.25
413	*John Foster*	.25
414	Doug Glanville	.10
415	Ryan Kohlmeier	.10
416	Mike Matthews	.10
417	Craig Wilson	.10
418	Jay Witasick	.10
419	Jay Payton	.10
420	Andruw Jones	.40
421	Benji Gil	.10
422	Jeff Liefer	.10
423	Kevin Young	.10
424	Richie Sexson	.25
425	Cory Lidle	.10
426	Shane Halter	.10
427	Jesse Foppert	.40
428	Jose Molina	.10
429	*Nick Alvarez*	.40
430	Brian L. Hunter	.10
431	*Clifford Bartosh*	.25
432	Junior Spivey	.10
433	*Eric Good*	.25
434	Chin-Feng Chen	.10
435	T.J. Mathews	.10
436	Rich Rodriguez	.10
437	Bobby Abreu	.20
438	Joe McEwing	.10
439	Michael Tucker	.10
440	Preston Wilson	.10
441	Mike MacDougal	.10
442	Shannon Stewart	.10
443	Bob Howry	.10
444	Mike Benjamin	.10
445	Erik Hiljus	.10
446	*Ryan Gripp*	.25
447	Jose Vizcaino	.10
448	Shawn Wooten	.10
449	*Steve Kent*	.25
450	Ramiro Mendoza	.10
451	Jake Westbrook	.10
452	Joe Lawrence	.10
453	Jae Weong Seo	.10
454	*Ryan Fry*	.20
455	Darren Lewis	.10
456	Brad Wilkerson	.10
457	*Gustavo Chacin*	.25
458	Adrian Brown	.10
459	Mike Cameron	.10
460	Bud Smith	.10
461	Derrick Lewis	.10
462	Derek Lowe	.10
463	Matt Williams	.10
464	Jason Jennings	.10
465	Albie Lopez	.10
466	Felipe Lopez	.10
467	Luke Allen	.10
468	Brian Anderson	.10
469	Matt Riley	.10
470	Ryan Dempster	.10
471	Matt Ginter	.10
472	David Ortiz	.10
473	Cole Barthel	.10
474	Damian Jackson	.10
475	Andy Van Hekken	.10
476	Doug Brocail	.10
477	Denny Hocking	.10
478	Sean Douglass	.10
479	Eric Owens	.10
480	Ryan Ludwick	.10
481	Todd Pratt	.10
482	Aaron Sele	.10
483	Edgar Renteria	.10
484	*Raymond Cabrera*	.25
485	Brandon Lyon	.10
486	Chase Utley	.10
487	Robert Fick	.10
488	Wilfredo Cordero	.10
489	Octavio Dotel	.10
490	Paul Abbott	.10
491	Jason Kendall	.10
492	Jarrod Washburn	.10
493	Dane Sardinha	.10
494	Jung Bong	.10
495	J.D. Drew	.10
496	Jason Schmidt	.10
497	Mike Magnante	.10
498	*Jorge Padilla*	.50
499	Eric Gagne	.10
500	Todd Helton	.50
501	Jeff Weaver	.10
502	Alex Sanchez	.10
503	Ken Griffey Jr.	.10
504	Abraham Nunez	.10
505	Reggie Sanders	.10
506	Casey Kotchman	2.00
507	Jim Mann	.10
508	Matt LeCroy	.10
509	Frank Castillo	.10
510	Geoff Jenkins	.20
511	*Jayson Durocher*	.20
512	Ellis Burks	.10
513	Aaron Fultz	.10
514	Hiram Bocachica	.10
515	*Nate Espy*	.10
516	Placido Polanco	.10
517	Kerry Ligtenberg	.10
518	Doug Nickle	.10
519	Ramon Ortiz	.10
520	Greg Swindell	.10
521	J.J. Davis	.10
522	Sandy Alomar	.10
523	Chris Carpenter	.10
524	Vance Wilson	.10
525	Nomar Garciaparra	1.00
526	Jim Mecir	.10
527	*Taylor Buchholz*	.25
528	Brent Mayne	.10
529	*John Rodriguez*	.25
530	David Segui	.10
531	Nate Cornejo	.10
532	Gil Heredia	.10
533	Esteban Loaiza	.10
534	Pat Mahomes	.10
535	Matt Morris	.20
536	Todd Stottlemyre	.10
537	Brian Lesher	.10
538	Arturo McDowell	.10
539	Felix Diaz	.10
540	Mark Mulder	.10
541	*Kevin Frederick*	.25
542	Andy Fox	.10
543	*Dionys Cesar*	.10
544	Justin Miller	.10
545	Keith Osik	.10
546	Shane Reynolds	.10
547	Mike Myers	.10
548	*Raul Chavez*	.25
549	Joe Nathan	.10
550	Ryan Anderson	.10
551	Jason Marquis	.10
552	Marty Cordova	.10
553	Kevin Tapani	.10
554	Jimmy Anderson	.10
555	Pedro Martinez	.50
556	Rocky Biddle	.10
557	Alex Ochoa	.10
558	D'Angelo Jimenez	.10
559	Wilkin Ruan	.10
560	Terrence Long	.10
561	Mark Lukasiewicz	.10
562	Jose Santiago	.10
563	Brad Fullmer	.10
564	Corky Miller	.10
565	Matt White	.10
566	Mark Grace	.30
567	Raul Ibanez	.10
568	Josh Towers	.10
569	Juan Gonzalez	.40
570	Brian Buchanan	.10
571	Ken Harvey	.10
572	Jeffrey Hammonds	.10
573	Wade Miller	.10
574	Elpidio Guzman	.10
575	Kevin Olsen	.10
576	Austin Kearns	.40
577	*Tim Kalita*	.40
578	David Dellucci	.10
579	Alex Gonzalez	.10
580	*Joe Orloski*	.20
581	Gary Matthews Jr.	.10
582	Ryan Mills	.10
583	Erick Almonte	.10
584	Jeremy Affeldt	.10
585	*Chris Tritle*	1.00
586	Michael Cuddyer	.10
587	Kris Foster	.10
588	Russell Branyan	.10
589	Darren Oliver	.10
590	*Freddie Money*	.25
591	Carlos Lee	.10
592	Tim Wakefield	.10
593	Bubba Trammell	.10
594	*John Koronka*	.20
595	Geoff Blum	.10
596	Darryl Kile	.10
597	Neifi Perez	.10
598	Torii Hunter	.10
599	Luis Castillo	.10
600	Mark Buehrle	.10
601	Jeff Zimmerman	.10
602	Mike DeJean	.10
603	Julio Lugo	.10
604	Chad Hermansen	.10
605	Keith Foulke	.10
606	Lance Davis	.10
607	*Jeff Austin*	.25
608	Brandon Inge	.10
609	Orlando Merced	.10
610	Johnny Damon	.10
611	Doug Henry	.10
612	Adam Kennedy	.10
613	Wiki Gonzalez	.10
614	*Brian West*	.25
615	Andy Pettitte	.25
616	*Chone Figgins*	.25
617	Matt Lawton	.10
618	Paul Rigdon	.10
619	Keith Lockhart	.10
620	Tim Redding	.10
621	John Parrish	.10
622	Chad Hutchinson	.10
623	Todd Greene	.10
624	David Eckstein	.10
625	*Greg Montalbano*	1.00
626	Joe Beimel	.10
627	Adrian Beltre	.20
628	Charles Nagy	.10
629	Cristian Guzman	.10
630	Toby Hall	.10
631	Jose Hernandez	.10
632	Jose Macias	.10
633	Jaret Wright	.10
634	Steve Parris	.10
635	Gene Kingsdale	.10
636	Tim Worrell	.10
637	Billy Martin	.10
638	Jovanny Cedeno	.10
639	Curt Leskanic	.10
640	Tim Hudson	.20
641	Juan Castro	.10
642	Rafael Soriano	.10
643	Juan Rincon	.10
644	Mark DeRosa	.10
645	Carlos Pena	.10
646	Robin Ventura	.20
647	Odalis Perez	.10
648	Damion Easley	.10
649	Benito Santiago	.10
650	Alex Rodriguez	1.50
651	Aaron Rowand	.10
652	Alex Cora	.10
653	Bobby Kielty	.10
654	Jose Rodriguez	.10
655	Herbert Perry	.10
656	Jeff Urban	.10
657	Paul Bako	.10
658	Shane Spencer	.10
659	Pat Hentgen	.10
660	Jeff Kent	.20
661	Mark McLemore	.10
662	Chuck Knoblauch	.10
663	Blake Stein	.10
664	*Brett Roneberg*	.25
665	Josh Phelps	.10
666	Byung-Hyun Kim	.10
667	Dave Martinez	.10
668	Mike Maroth	.10
669	Shawn Chacon	.10
670	Billy Wagner	.10
671	Luis Alicea	.10
672	Sterling Hitchcock	.10
673	Adam Piatt	.10
674	Ryan Franklin	.10
675	Luke Prokopec	.10
676	Alfredo Amezega	.10
677	Gookie Dawkins	.10
678	Eric Byrnes	.10
679	Barry Larkin	.25
680	Albert Pujols	1.00
681	Edwards Guzman	.10
682	Jason Bere	.10
683	Adam Everett	.10
684	Greg Colbrunn	.10
685	*Brandon Puffer*	.40
686	Mark Kotsay	.10
687	Willie Bloomquist	.10
688	Hank Blalock	.25
689	Travis Hafner	.10
690	Lance Berkman	.40
691	Joe Crede	.10
692	Chuck Finley	.10
693	John Grabow	.10
694	Randy Winn	.10
695	Mike James	.10
696	Kris Benson	.10
697	Bret Prinz	.10
698	Jeff Williams	.10
699	Eric Munson	.10
700	Mike Hampton	.10
701	Ramon E. Martinez	.10
702	*Hansel Izquierdo*	.25
703	Nathan Haynes	.10
704	Eddie Taubensee	.10
705	Esteban German	.10
706	Ross Gload	.10
707	*Matthew Merricks*	.20
708	*Chris Piersoll*	.25
709	Seth Greisinger	.10
710	Ichiro Suzuki	1.00
711	Cesar Izturis	.10
712	Brad Cresse	.10
713	Carl Pavano	.10
714	Steve Sparks	.10
715	Dennis Tankersley	.10
716	Kelvim Escobar	.10
717	Jason LaRue	.10
718	Corey Koskie	.10
719	Vinny Castilla	.10
720	Tim Drew	.10
721	Chin-Hui Tsao	.10
722	Paul Byrd	.10
723	Alex Cintron	.10
724	Orlando Palmeiro	.10
725	Ramon Hernandez	.10
726	Mark Johnson	.10
727	B.J. Ryan	.10
728	Wendell Magee	.10
729	Michael Coleman	.10
730	Mario Ramos	.50
731	Mike Stanton	.10
732	Dee Brown	.10
733	Brad Ausmus	.10
734	*Napoleon Calzado*	.25
735	Woody Williams	.10
736	Paxton Crawford	.10
737	Jason Karnuth	.10
738	Michael Restovich	.10
739	Ramon Castro	.10
740	Magglio Ordonez	.25
741	Tom Gordon	.10
742	Mark Grudzielanek	.10
743	Jamie Moyer	.10
744	*Marlyn Tisdale*	.20
745	Steve Kline	.10
746	Adam Eaton	.10
747	*Eric Glaser*	.25
748	Sean DePaula	.10
749	Greg Norton	.10
750	Steve Reed	.10
751	Ricardo Aramboles	.10
752	Matt Mantei	.10
753	Gene Stechschulte	.10
754	Chuck McElroy	.10
755	Barry Bonds	1.50
756	Matt Anderson	.10
757	Yorvit Torrealba	.10
758	Jason Standridge	.10

759 Desi Relaford .10
760 Jolbert Cabrera .10
761 Chris George .10
762 Erubiel Durazo .10
763 Paul Konerko .25
764 Tike Redman .10
765 *Chad Ricketts* .20
766 Roberto Hernandez .10
767 Mark Lewis .10
768 Livan Hernandez .10
769 *Carlos Brackley* .25
770 Kazuhiro Sasaki .10
771 Bill Hall .10
772 *Nelson Castro* .25
773 Eric Milton .10
774 Tom Davey .10
775 Todd Ritchie .10
776 Seth Etherton .10
777 Chris Singleton .10
778 *Robert Averette* .20
779 Robert Person .10
780 Fred McGriff .25
781 Richard Hidalgo .10
782 Kris Wilson .10
783 John Rocker .10
784 Justin Kaye .10
785 Glendon Rusch .10
786 Greg Vaughn .10
787 Mike Lamb .10
788 Greg Myers .10
789 *Nate Field* .25
790 Jim Edmonds .25
791 Olmedo Saenz .10
792 Jason Johnson .10
793 Mike Lincoln .10
794 Todd Coffey .10
795 Jesus Sanchez .10
796 Aaron Myette .10
797 Tony Womack .10
798 Chad Kreuter .10
799 Brady Clark .10
800 Adam Dunn .50
801 Jacque Jones .10
802 Kevin Millwood .10
803 Mike Rivera .10
804 Jim Thome .40
805 Jeff Conine .10
806 Elmer Dessens .10
807 Randy Velarde .10
808 Carlos Delgado .30
809 Steve Karsay .10
810 Casey Fossum .10
811 J.C. Romero .10
812 Chris Truby .10
813 Tony Graffanino .10
814 Wascar Serrano .10
815 Delvin James .10
816 Pedro Feliz .10
817 Damian Rolls .10
818 Scott Linebrink .10
819 Rafael Palmeiro .40
820 Javy Lopez .10
821 Larry Barnes .10
822 Brian Lawrence .10
823 *Scotty Layfield* .25
824 Jeff Cirillo .10
825 Willis Roberts .10
826 *Rich Harden* 4.00
827 *Chris Snelling* 1.00
828 Gary Sheffield .25
829 Jeff Heaverlo .10
830 Matt Clement .10
831 Rich Garces .10
832 Rondell White .10
833 *Henry Pichardo* .25
834 Aaron Boone .10
835 Ruben Sierra .10
836 Deivis Santos .10
837 Tony Batista .10
838 Rob Bell .10
839 Frank Thomas .50
840 Jose Silva .10
841 *Dan Johnson* .50
842 Steve Cox .10
843 Jose Acevedo .10
844 Jay Bell .10
845 Mike Sirotka .10
846 Garret Anderson .10
847 *James Shanks* .25
848 Trot Nixon .10
849 Keith Ginter .10
850 Tim Spooneybarger .10
851 Matt Stairs .10
852 Chris Stynes .10
853 Marvin Bernard .10
854 Raul Mondesi .20
855 Jeremy Owens .10
856 Jon Garland .10
857 Mitch Meluskey .10
858 Chad Durbin .10
859 John Burkett .10
860 Jon Switzer .10
861 Peter Bergeron .10
862 Jesus Colome .10
863 Todd Hundley .10
864 Ben Petrick .10
865 *So Taguchi* .75
866 Ryan Drese .10
867 Mike Trombley .10
868 Rick Reed .10
869 Mark Teixeira .20
870 *Corey Thurman* .10
871 Brian Roberts .10
872 Mike Timlin .10
873 Chris Reitsma .10
874 Jeff Fassero .10
875 Carlos Valderrama .10
876 John Lackey .10
877 Travis Fryman .10
878 Ismael Valdes .10
879 Rick White .10
880 Edgar Martinez .10
881 Dean Palmer .10
882 *Matt Allegra* .20
883 *Greg Sain* .25
884 Carlos Silva .10
885 *Jose Valverde* .25
886 Dernell Stenson .10
887 Todd Van Poppel .10
888 Wes Anderson .10
889 Bill Mueller .10
890 Morgan Ensberg .10
891 Marcus Thames .10
892 *Adam Walker* .10
893 John Halama .10
894 Frank Menechino .10
895 Greg Maddux 1.00
896 Gary Bennett .10
897 *Mauricio Lara* .25
898 Mike Young .10
899 Travis Phelps .10
900 Rich Aurilia .10
901 Henry Blanco .10
902 Carlos Febles .10
903 Scott MacRae .10
904 Lou Merloni .10
905 Dicky Gonzalez .10
906 Jeff DaVanon .10
907 A.J. Burnett .10
908 Einar Diaz .10
909 Julio Franco .10
910 John Olerud .25
911 *Mark Hamilton* .25
912 David Riske .10
913 Jason Tyner .10
914 Britt Reames .10
915 Vernon Wells .10
916 Eddie Perez .10
917 *Edwin Almonte* .25
918 Enrique Wilson .10
919 Chris Gomez .10
920 Jayson Werth .10
921 Jeff Nelson .10
922 *Freddy Sanchez* .75
923 John Vander Wal .10
924 *Chad Qualls* .25
925 Gabe White .10
926 Chad Harville .10
927 Ricky Gutierrez .10
928 Carlos Guillen .10
929 B.J. Surhoff .10
930 Chris Woodard .10
931 Ricardo Rodriguez .10
932 *Jimmy Gobble* 1.00
933 Jon Lieber .10
934 *Craig Kuzmic* .25
935 Eric Young .10
936 Greg Zaun .10
937 Miguel Batista .10
938 Danny Wright .10
939 Todd Zeile .10
940 Chad Zerbe .10
941 *Jason Young* .50
942 Ronnie Belliard .10
943 *John Ennis* .10
944 John Flaherty .10
945 Jerry Hairston Jr. .10
946 Al Levine .10
947 Antonio Alfonseca .10
948 Brian Moehler .10
949 Calvin Murray .10
950 Nick Bierbrodt .10
951 Sun-Woo Kim .10
952 *Noochie Varner* .50
953 Luis Rivas .10
954 Donnie Bridges .10
955 Ramon Vazquez .10
956 Luis Garcia .10
957 Mark Quinn .10
958 Armando Rios .10
959 Chad Fox .10
960 Hee Seop Choi .10
961 Turk Wendell .10
962 *Adam Roller* .20
963 Grant Roberts .10
964 Ben Molina .10
965 Juan Rivera .10
966 Matt Kinney .10
967 Rod Beck .10
968 Xavier Nady .10
969 Masato Yoshii .10
970 Miguel Tejada .25
971 Danny Kolb .10
972 Mike Remlinger .10
973 Ray Lankford .10
974 Ryan Minor .10
975 J.T. Snow .10
976 Brad Radke .10
977 Jason Lane .10
978 Jamey Wright .10
979 Tom Goodwin .10
980 Erik Bedard .10
981 Gabe Kapler .10
982 Brian Reith .10
983 *Nic Jackson* .50
984 Kurt Ainsworth .10
985 Jason Isringhausen .10
986 Willie Harris .10
987 David Cone .10
988 Bob Wickman .10
989 Wes Helms .10
990 Josh Beckett .25

Award Winners

NM/M
Complete Set (30): 25.00
Common Player: .75
Inserted 1:6
AW1 Ichiro Suzuki 2.00
AW2 Albert Pujols 2.00
AW3 Barry Bonds 3.00
AW4 Ichiro Suzuki 2.00
AW5 Randy Johnson 1.00
AW6 Roger Clemens 2.00
AW7 Jason Giambi .75
AW8 Bret Boone .50
AW9 Troy Glaus .75
AW10 Alex Rodriguez 2.50
AW11 Juan Gonzalez .75
AW12 Ichiro Suzuki 2.00
AW13 Jorge Posada .75
AW14 Edgar Martinez .50
AW15 Todd Helton .75
AW16 Jeff Kent .50
AW17 Albert Pujols 2.00
AW18 Rich Aurilia .50
AW19 Barry Bonds 3.00
AW20 Luis Gonzalez .50
AW21 Sammy Sosa 2.00
AW22 Mike Piazza 2.00
AW23 Mike Hampton .50
AW24 Ruben Sierra .50
AW25 Matt Morris .50
AW26 Curt Schilling .75
AW27 Alex Rodriguez 2.50
AW28 Barry Bonds 3.00
AW29 Jim Thome 1.00
AW30 Barry Bonds 3.00

Total Production

NM/M
Complete Set (10): 15.00
Common Player: .75
Inserted 1:12
TP1 Alex Rodriguez 3.00
TP2 Barry Bonds 3.00
TP3 Ichiro Suzuki 2.00
TP4 Edgar Martinez .75
TP5 Jason Giambi 1.00
TP6 Todd Helton 1.00
TP7 Nomar Garciaparra 2.50
TP8 Vladimir Guerrero 1.00
TP9 Sammy Sosa 2.00
TP10 Chipper Jones 2.00

Total Topps

NM/M
Complete Set (50): 35.00
Common Player: .50
Inserted 1:3
TT1 Roberto Alomar .75
TT2 Moises Alou .50
TT3 Jeff Bagwell 1.00
TT4 Lance Berkman .75
TT5 Barry Bonds 2.00
TT6 Bret Boone .50
TT7 Kevin Brown .50
TT8 Eric Chavez .50
TT9 Roger Clemens 1.50
TT10 Carlos Delgado .50
TT11 Cliff Floyd .50
TT12 Nomar Garciaparra 2.50
TT13 Jason Giambi 1.00
TT14 Brian Giles .75
TT15 Troy Glaus .75
TT16 Tom Glavine .50
TT17 Luis Gonzalez .50
TT18 Juan Gonzalez .75
TT19 Shawn Green .50
TT20 Ken Griffey Jr. 2.50
TT21 Vladimir Guerrero 1.00
TT22 Jorge Posada .50
TT23 Todd Helton .75
TT24 Tim Hudson .50
TT25 Derek Jeter 4.00
TT26 Randy Johnson 1.00
TT27 Andruw Jones .75
TT28 Chipper Jones 2.00
TT29 Jeff Kent .50
TT30 Greg Maddux 2.00
TT31 Edgar Martinez .50
TT32 Pedro Martinez 1.00
TT33 Magglio Ordonez .50
TT34 Rafael Palmeiro .50
TT35 Mike Piazza 3.00
TT36 Albert Pujols 2.00
TT37 Aramis Ramirez .50
TT38 Mariano Rivera .50
TT39 Alex Rodriguez 3.00
TT40 Ivan Rodriguez .75
TT41 Curt Schilling .75
TT42 Gary Sheffield .50
TT43 Sammy Sosa 2.00
TT44 Ichiro Suzuki 4.00
TT45 Miguel Tejada .50
TT46 Frank Thomas 1.00
TT47 Jim Thome .75
TT48 Larry Walker .50
TT49 Bernie Williams .50
TT50 Kerry Wood .50

2002 TOPPS TRIBUTE

NM/M
Complete Set (90): 120.00
Common Player: 1.50
Pack (5): 35.00
Box (6): 150.00
1 Hank Aaron 6.00
2 Rogers Hornsby 2.50
3 Bobby Thomson 1.50
4 Eddie Collins 1.50
5 Joe Carter 1.50
6 Jim Palmer 1.50
7 Willie Mays 6.00
8 Willie Stargell 2.50
9 Vida Blue 1.50

10	Whitey Ford	3.00
11	Bob Gibson	3.00
12	Nellie Fox	2.00
13	Napoleon Lajoie	2.00
14	Frankie Frisch	1.50
15	Nolan Ryan	10.00
16	Brooks Robinson	2.50
17	Kirby Puckett	5.00
18	Fergie Jenkins	1.50
19	Edd Roush	1.50
20	Honus Wagner	6.00
21	Richie Ashburn	1.50
22	Bob Feller	1.50
23	Joe Morgan	1.50
24	Orlando Cepeda	1.50
25	Steve Garvey	1.50
26	Hank Greenberg	1.50
27	Stan Musial	5.00
28	Sam Crawford	1.50
29	Jim Rice	1.50
30	Hack Wilson	2.50
31	Lou Brock	1.50
32	Mickey Vernon	1.50
33	Chuck Klein	1.50
34	Joe Jackson	6.00
35	Duke Snider	3.00
36	Ryne Sandberg	5.00
37	Johnny Bench	5.00
38	Sam Rice	1.50
39	Lou Gehrig	8.00
40	Robin Yount	3.00
41	Don Sutton	1.50
42	Jim Bottomley	1.50
43	Billy Herman	1.50
44	Zach Wheat	1.50
45	Juan Marichal	1.50
46	Bert Blyleven	1.50
47	Jackie Robinson	6.00
48	Gil Hodges	1.50
49	Mike Schmidt	6.00
50	Dale Murphy	1.50
51	Phil Rizzuto	1.50
52	Ty Cobb	6.00
53	Andre Dawson	1.50
54	Fred Lindstrom	1.50
55	Roy Campanella	3.00
56	Don Larsen	2.00
57	Harry Heilmann	1.50
58	Jim "Catfish" Hunter	1.50
59	Frank Robinson	2.00
60	Bill Mazeroski	1.50
61	Roger Maris	6.00
62	Dave Winfield	2.50
63	Warren Spahn	2.50
64	Babe Ruth	10.00
65	Ernie Banks	4.00
66	Wade Boggs	2.00
67	Carl Yastrzemski	3.00
68	Ron Santo	1.50
69	Dennis Martinez	1.50
70	Yogi Berra	4.00
71	Paul Waner	1.50
72	George Brett	6.00
73	Eddie Mathews	3.00
74	Bill Dickey	1.50
75	Carlton Fisk	2.00
76	Thurman Munson	5.00
77	Reggie Jackson	4.00
78	Phil Niekro	1.50
79	Luis Aparicio	1.50
80	Steve Carlton	1.50
81	Tris Speaker	1.50
82	Johnny Mize	1.50
83	Tom Seaver	4.00
84	Heinie Manush	1.50
85	Tommy John	1.50
86	Joe Cronin	1.50
87	Don Mattingly	8.00
88	Kirk Gibson	1.50
89	Bo Jackson	3.00
90	Mel Ott	1.50

First Impressions

Cards #'d 51-86: 3-5X
Cards #'d 26-50: 4-8X
#'d to last two digits of Rk year
Lasting Impressions
Cards #'d 51-96: 3-5X
Cards #'d 26-50: 4-8X
#'d to last two digits of final season
Production under 25 not priced

Matching Marks Dual

		NM/M
Common Card:		10.00
Inserted 1:11		
SBA	Ron Santo, Ernie Banks	25.00
YK	Carl Yastrzemski, Chuck Klein	65.00
WY	Dave Winfield, Carl Yastrzemski	25.00
WYO	Dave Winfield, Robin Yount	20.00
SM	Duke Snider, Willie Mays	85.00
RJ	Frank Robinson, Reggie Jackson	50.00
BMA	George Brett, Don Mattingly	90.00
GH	Steve Garvey, Gil Hodges	20.00
AR	Hank Aaron, Babe Ruth	300.00
GA	Hank Greenberg, Richie Ashburn	80.00
PJ	Jim Palmer, Tommy John	20.00
NS	Phil Niekro, Tom Seaver	15.00
SR	Willie Stargell, Jim Rice	15.00
BF	Johnny Bench, Carlton Fisk	50.00
RS	Nolan Ryan, Tom Seaver	125.00
JS	Fergie Jenkins, Tom Seaver	35.00
YP	Robin Yount, Kirby Puckett	60.00
SB	Tris Speaker, George Brett	100.00
BM	Vida Blue, Dennis Martinez	10.00
BB	Wade Boggs, George Brett	40.00
MA	Willie Mays, Hank Aaron	200.00
BS	Bert Blyleven, Don Sutton	15.00

Marks of Excellence

		NM/M
Inserted 1:61		
LB	Lou Brock	50.00
SC	Steve Carlton	50.00
DL	Don Larsen	50.00
SM	Stan Musial	100.00
MS	Mike Schmidt	85.00
WS	Warren Spahn	65.00

Marks of Excellence Relics

		NM/M
Inserted 1:61		
FJ	Fergie Jenkins	40.00
DM	Don Mattingly	120.00
JP	Jim Palmer	40.00
BR	Brooks Robinson	75.00
DS	Duke Snider	60.00
RY	Robin Yount	70.00

Memorable Materials

		NM/M
Common Player:		10.00
Season parallel:		1.5-3X
#'d to last two digits yr event occurred		
Jsy Number para.#'d 40-75:		1.5-3X
Under 40 not priced		
Numbered to jersey #		
HA	Hank Aaron	40.00

GB	George Brett	35.00
RC	Roy Campanella	30.00
JC	Joe Carter	10.00
CF	Carlton Fisk	20.00
LG	Lou Gehrig	
KG	Kirk Gibson	15.00
BJ	Bo Jackson	25.00
RJ	Reggie Jackson	20.00
CK	Chuck Klein	25.00
RM	Roger Maris	75.00
DM	Don Mattingly	40.00
BM	Bill Mazeroski	15.00
JM	Joe Morgan	15.00
TM	Thurman Munson	50.00
KP	Kirby Puckett	30.00
PR	Phil Rizzuto	25.00
JR	Jackie Robinson	50.00
NR	Nolan Ryan	50.00
BT	Bobby Thomson	15.00
HW	Hack Wilson	40.00
CY	Carl Yastrzemski	30.00

Milestone Materials

		NM/M
Common Player:		10.00
Inserted 1:4		
Season parallel #'d 51-95:		1.5-3X
#'d to last two digits milestone season		
Jersey Number par.#'d 51-95:		1.5-3X
Numbered to Jersey Number		
Under 50 not priced yet		
LA	Luis Aparicio	15.00
EB	Ernie Banks	30.00
JB	Johnny Bench	20.00
YB	Yogi Berra	25.00
WB	Wade Boggs	15.00
JBO	Jim Bottomley	20.00
OC	Orlando Cepeda	15.00
TC	Ty Cobb	150.00
EC	Eddie Collins	30.00
SC	Sam Crawford	25.00
JC	Joe Cronin	20.00
AD	Andre Dawson	15.00
BD	Bill Dickey	15.00
BF	Bob Feller	15.00
WF	Whitey Ford	25.00
NF	Nellie Fox	30.00
FF	Frankie Frisch	25.00
LG	Lou Gehrig	150.00
BG	Bob Gibson	15.00
HG	Hank Greenberg	
HH	Harry Heilmann	20.00
BH	Billy Herman	10.00
RH	Rogers Hornsby	50.00
CH	Jim "Catfish" Hunter	12.00
JJ	Joe Jackson	
RJ	Reggie Jackson	20.00
NL	Napoleon Lajoie	60.00
FL	Fred Lindstrom	15.00
HM	Heinie Manush	20.00
JMA	Juan Marichal	15.00
EM	Eddie Mathews	20.00
WH	Willie Mays	45.00
JM	Johnny Mize	15.00
DM	Dale Murphy	20.00
MO	Mel Ott	40.00
JP	Jim Palmer	15.00
SR	Sam Rice	20.00
BRO	Brooks Robinson	20.00
FR	Frank Robinson	20.00
ER	Edd Roush	25.00
BR	Babe Ruth	160.00
NR	Nolan Ryan	50.00
RS	Ryne Sandberg	30.00
TS	Tom Seaver	15.00
DS	Duke Snider	20.00
TSP	Tris Speaker	65.00
WS	Willie Stargell	15.00
MV	Mickey Vernon	15.00
HW	Honus Wagner	140.00
PW	Paul Waner	30.00
ZW	Zach Wheat	40.00
RY	Robin Yount	25.00

Pasttime Patches

		NM/M
Inserted 1:92		
JB	Johnny Bench	125.00
WB	Wade Boggs	90.00
GB	George Brett	200.00
BD	Bill Dickey	100.00
JM	Juan Marichal	
EM	Eddie Mathews	125.00
DM	Don Mattingly	160.00
JP	Jim Palmer	75.00
KP	Kirby Puckett	125.00
NRA	Nolan Ryan	200.00
NRR	Nolan Ryan	200.00
DW	Dave Winfield	100.00
CY	Carl Yastrzemski	180.00
RY	Robin Yount	100.00

"The Catch" Dual

		NM/M
Inserted 1:1,023		
MW	Willie Mays, Vic Wertz	250.00
MW	Willie Mays, Vic Wertz/54	300.00

Signature Cuts

		NM/M
Reported production 2 each		
Inserted 1:9936		
SC-BR	Babe Ruth	
SC-JR	Jackie Robinson	
SC-LG	Lou Gehrig	
SC-TC	Ty Cobb (4/04 auction)	4,725

2002 TOPPS206

		NM/M
Complete Set (456):		150.00
Common Player:		.20
Common (141-155,271-285):		1.00
Inserted 1:2		
Series I Pack (8):		6.00
Series I Box (20):		100.00
Series II Pack (8):		4.00
Series II Box (20):		60.00
Series III Pack (8):		6.00
Series III Box (20):		100.00
1	Vladimir Guerrero	.75
2	Sammy Sosa	1.50
3	Garret Anderson	.40
4	Rafael Palmeiro	.50
5	Juan Gonzalez	.50
6	John Smoltz	.40
7	Mark Mulder	.40
8	Jon Lieber	.20
9	Greg Maddux	1.00
10	Moises Alou	.40
11	Joe Randa	.20
12	Bobby Abreu	.40
13	Ryan Kohlmeier	.20
14	Kerry Wood	.75

No.	Player	Price
15	Craig Biggio	.40
16	Curt Schilling	.50
17	Brian Jordan	.20
18	Edgardo Alfonzo	.20
19	Darren Dreifort	.20
20	Todd Helton	.50
21	Ramon Ortiz	.20
22	Ichiro Suzuki	1.50
23	Jimmy Rollins	.20
24	Darin Erstad	.40
25	Shawn Green	.40
26	Tino Martinez	.30
27	Bret Boone	.40
28	Alfonso Soriano	.75
29	Chan Ho Park	.40
30	Roger Clemens	1.50
31	Cliff Floyd	.20
32	Johnny Damon	.40
33	Frank Thomas	.50
34	Barry Bonds	2.00
35	Luis Gonzalez	.40
36	Carlos Lee	.20
37	Roberto Alomar	.50
38	Carlos Delgado	.50
39	Nomar Garciaparra	1.50
40	Jason Kendall	.40
41	Scott Rolen	.75
42	Tom Glavine	.40
43	Ryan Klesko	.20
44	Brian Giles	.40
45	Bud Smith	.20
46	Charles Nagy	.20
47	Tony Gwynn	.75
48	C.C. Sabathia	.20
49	Manny Ramirez	.75
50	Jerry Hairston Jr.	.20
51	Jeromy Burnitz	.20
52	David Justice	.40
53	Bartolo Colon	.20
54	Andres Galarraga	.30
55	Jeff Weaver	.20
56	Terrance Long	.20
57	Tsuyoshi Shinjo	.20
58	Barry Zito	.40
59	Mariano Rivera	.40
60	John Olerud	.20
61	Randy Johnson	.75
62	Kenny Lofton	.40
63	Jermaine Dye	.20
64	Troy Glaus	.50
65	Larry Walker	.40
66	Hideo Nomo	.40
67	Mike Mussina	.50
68	Paul LoDuca	.20
69	Magglio Ordonez	.40
70	Paul O'Neill	.40
71	Sean Casey	.40
72	Lance Berkman	.40
73	Adam Dunn	.50
74	Aramis Ramirez	.40
75	Rafael Furcal	.40
76	Gary Sheffield	.40
77	Todd Hollandsworth	.20
78	Chipper Jones	1.00
79	Bernie Williams	.50
80	Richard Hidalgo	.25
81	Eric Chavez	.40
82	Mike Piazza	1.50
83	J.D. Drew	.40
84	Ken Griffey Jr.	1.00
85	Joe Kennedy	.20
86	Joel Pineiro	.20
87	Josh Towers	.20
88	Andruw Jones	.50
89	Carlos Beltran	.40
90	Mike Cameron	.20
91	Albert Pujols	1.50
92	Alex Rodriguez	1.50
93	Omar Vizquel	.30
94	Juan Encarnacion	.20
95	Jeff Bagwell	.50
96	Jose Canseco	.40
97	Ben Sheets	.40
98	Mark Grace	.40
99	Mike Sweeney	.20
100	Mark McGwire	2.00
101	Ivan Rodriguez	.75
102	Rich Aurilia	.20
103	Cristian Guzman	.20
104	Roy Oswalt	.40
105	Tim Hudson	.40
106	Brent Abernathy	.20
107	Mike Hampton	.20
108	Miguel Tejada	.40
109	Bobby Higginson	.20
110	Edgar Martinez	.40
111	Jorge Posada	.40
112	Jason Giambi	.50
113	Pedro Astacio	.20
114	Kazuhiro Sasaki	.20
115	Preston Wilson	.20
116	Jason Bere	.20
117	Mark Quinn	.20
118	Pokey Reese	.20
119	Derek Jeter	2.00
120	Shannon Stewart	.20
121	Jeff Kent	.40
122	Jeremy Giambi	.20
123	Pat Burrell	.40
124	Jim Edmonds	.40
125	Mark Buehrle	.20
126	Kevin Brown	.40
127	Raul Mondesi	.20
128	Pedro Martinez	.75
129	Jim Thome	.75
130	Russ Ortiz	.20
131	Brandon Duckworth	.20
132	*Ryan Jamison*	.50
133	Brandon Inge	.20
134	Felipe Lopez	.20
135	Jason Lane	.20
136	*Forrest Johnson*	.50
137	Greg Nash	.20
138	Covelli Crisp	.20
139	Nick Neugebauer	.20
140	Dustan Mohr	.20
141	*Freddy Sanchez*	1.00
142	*Justin Backsmeyer*	1.00
143	Jorge Julio	1.00
144	*Ryan Mottl*	1.00
145	*Chris Tritle*	1.00
146	*Noochie Varner*	1.00
147	Brian Rogers	1.00
148	*Michael Hill*	1.00
149	Luis Pineda	1.00
150	*Rich Thompson*	1.00
151	Bill Hall	1.00
152	*Jose Dominguez*	1.50
153	*Justin Woodrow*	1.00
154	*Nic Jackson*	1.00
155	*Layce Nix*	4.00
156	Hank Aaron	3.00
157	Ernie Banks	1.50
158	Johnny Bench	1.50
159	George Brett	4.00
160	Carlton Fisk	.50
161	Bob Gibson	.75
162	Reggie Jackson	1.00
163	Don Mattingly	4.00
164	Kirby Puckett	1.50
165	Frank Robinson	1.00
166	Nolan Ryan	5.00
167	Tom Seaver	1.00
168	Mike Schmidt	2.00
169	Dave Winfield	.50
170	Carl Yastrzemski	1.00
171	Frank Chance	.75
172	Ty Cobb	3.00
173	Sam Crawford	1.00
174	Johnny Evers	.75
175	John McGraw	1.00
176	Eddie Plank	.50
177	Tris Speaker	1.00
178	Joe Tinker	.50
179	Honus Wagner	5.00
180	Cy Young	2.50
181	Javier Vazquez	.20
182	Mark Mulder	.40
183	Roger Clemens	1.50
184	*Kazuhisa Ishii*	1.50
185	Roberto Alomar	.50
186	Lance Berkman	.40
187	Adam Dunn	.50
188	Aramis Ramirez	.40
189	Chuck Knoblauch	.20
190	Nomar Garciaparra	1.50
191	Brad Penny	.20
192	Gary Sheffield	.40
193	Alfonso Soriano	.75
194	Andruw Jones	.50
195	Randy Johnson	.75
196	Corey Patterson	.40
197	Milton Bradley	.20
198	Johnny Damon	.40
199	Paul LoDuca	.20
200	Albert Pujols	1.50
201	Scott Rolen	.75
202	J.D. Drew	.40
203	Vladimir Guerrero	.75
204	Jason Giambi	.50
205	Moises Alou	.40
206	Magglio Ordonez	.40
207	Carlos Febles	.20
208	*So Taguchi*	.75
209	Rafael Palmeiro	.50
210	*Boomer Wells*	.50
211	Orlando Cabrera	.20
212	Sammy Sosa	1.50
213	Armando Benitez	.20
214	Wes Helms	.20
215	Mariano Rivera	.40
216	Jimmy Rollins	.20
217	Matt Lawton	.20
218	Shawn Green	.40
219	Bernie Williams	.50
220	Bret Boone	.40
221	Alex Rodriguez	2.00
222	Roger Cedeno	.20
223	Marty Cordova	.20
224	Fred McGriff	.40
225	Chipper Jones	.75
226	Kerry Wood	.75
227	Larry Walker	.40
228	Robin Ventura	.40
229	Robert Fick	.20
230	Tino Martinez	.40
231	Ben Petrick	.20
232	Neifi Perez	.20
233	Pedro Martinez	.75
234	Brian Jordan	.20
235	Freddy Garcia	.20
236	Derek Jeter	2.00
237	Ben Grieve	.20
238	Barry Bonds	2.00
239	Luis Gonzalez	.40
240	Shane Halter	.20
241	Brian Giles	.40
242	Bud Smith	.20
243	Richie Sexson	.40
244	Barry Zito	.40
245	Eric Milton	.20
246	Ivan Rodriguez	.50
247	Toby Hall	.20
248	Mike Piazza	1.50
249	Ruben Sierra	.20
250	Tsuyoshi Shinjo	.20
251	Jermaine Dye	.20
252	Roy Oswalt	.40
253	Todd Helton	.50
254	Adrian Beltre	.40
255	Doug Mientkiewicz	.20
256	Ichiro Suzuki	1.50
257	C.C. Sabathia	.20
258	Paul Konerko	.20
259	Ken Griffey Jr.	1.00
260	Jeromy Burnitz	.20
261	Hank Blalock	.50
262	Mark Prior	1.50
263	Josh Beckett	.50
264	Carlos Pena	.20
265	Sean Burroughs	.20
266	Austin Kearns	.40
267	Chin-Hui Tsao	.20
268	Dewon Brazelton	.20
269	J.D. Martin	.20
270	Marlon Byrd	.20
271	*Joe Mauer*	6.00
272	*Jason Botts*	1.00
273	*Mauricio Lara*	1.00
274	*Jonny Gomes*	2.00
275	Gavin Floyd	1.50
276	*Alexander Requena*	1.00
277	*Jimmy Gobble*	1.00
278	*Chris Duffy*	1.00
279	Colt Griffin	1.00
280	*Ryan Church*	1.50
281	Beltran Perez	1.00
282	*Clint Nageotte*	1.50
283	*Justin Schuda*	1.00
284	Scott Hairston	1.50
285	Mario Ramos	1.00
286	Tom Seaver	2.00
287	Hank Aaron	3.00
288	Mike Schmidt	3.00
289	Robin Yount	1.50
290	Joe Morgan	1.00
291	Frank Robinson	1.00
292	Reggie Jackson	2.00
293	Nolan Ryan	4.00
294	Dave Winfield	1.00
295	Willie Mays	3.00
296	Brooks Robinson	1.50
297	Mark McGwire	3.00
298	Honus Wagner	3.00
299	Sherry Magee	1.00
300	Frank Chance	1.00
301	Larry Doyle	1.00
302	John McGraw	2.00
303	Jimmy Collins	1.00
304	Buck Herzog	1.00
305	Sam Crawford	1.00
306	Cy Young	2.50
307	Honus Wagner	3.00
308	Alex Rodriguez	2.00
308	Alex Rodriguez/ SP Blue Jsy	4.00
309	Vernon Wells	.20
310	Barry Bonds	2.00
310	Barry Bonds/ SP Cream Jsy	6.00
311	Vicente Padilla	.20
312	Alfonso Soriano	.75
312	A.Soriano/ SP No wristband	1.50
313	Mike Piazza	1.50
314	Jacque Jones	.20
315	Shawn Green/SP	1.50
316	Paul Byrd	.20
317	Lance Berkman	.40
318	Larry Walker	.40
319	Ken Griffey Jr./SP	3.00
320	Shea Hillenbrand	.20
321	Jay Gibbons	.20
322	Andruw Jones	.50
323	Luis Gonzalez/SP	1.50
324	Garret Anderson	.40
325	Roy Halladay	.40
326	Randy Winn	.20
327	Matt Morris	.40
328	Robb Nen	.20
329	Trevor Hoffman	.20
330	Kip Wells	.20
331	Orlando Hernandez	.30
332	Rey Ordonez	.20
333	Torii Hunter	.40
334	Geoff Jenkins	.40
335	Eric Karros	.20
336	Mike Lowell	.40
337	Nick Johnson	.20
338	Randall Simon	.20
339	Ellis Burks	.20
340	Sammy Sosa	1.50
340	Sammy Sosa/ SP Blue Jsy	4.00
341	Pedro J. Martinez	.75
342	Junior Spivey	.20
343	Vinny Castilla	.20
344	Randy Johnson/SP	2.00
345	Chipper Jones/SP	1.50
346	Orlando Hudson	.20
347	Albert Pujols/SP	5.00
348	Rondell White	.20
349	Vladimir Guerrero	.75
350	Mark Prior	1.00
350	Mark Prior/ SP Red background	3.00
351	Eric Gagne	.50
352	Todd Zeile	.20
353	Manny Ramirez/SP	2.00
354	Kevin Millwood	.40
355	Troy Percival	.20
356	Jason Giambi	.50
356	Jason Giambi/ SP White Jsy	1.50
357	Bartolo Colon	.20
358	Jeremy Giambi	.20
359	Jose Cruz Jr.	.20
360	Ichiro Suzuki	1.50
360	Ichiro/SP Blue warm-up	3.00
361	Eddie Guardado	.20
362	Ivan Rodriguez	.50
363	Carl Crawford	.20
364	*Jason Simontacchi*	.50
365	Kenny Lofton	.40
366	Raul Mondesi	.20
367	A.J. Pierzynski	.20
368	Ugueth Urbina	.20
369	Rodrigo Lopez	.20
370	Nomar Garciaparra	1.50
370	N. Garciaparra/SP 1 bat	3.00
371	Craig Counsell	.20
372	Barry Larkin	.40
373	Carlos Pena	.20
374	Luis Castillo	.20
375	Raul Ibanez	.20
376	Kazuhisa Ishii/SP	1.50
377	Derek Lowe	.20
378	Curt Schilling	.50
379	Jim Thome	.75
380	Derek Jeter	2.00
380	D. Jeter/ SP Blue background	5.00
381	Pat Burrell	.50
382	Jamie Moyer	.20
383	Eric Hinske	.20
384	Scott Rolen	.75
385	Miguel Tejada/SP	1.50
386	Andy Pettitte	.40
387	Mike Lieberthal	.20
388	Al Leiter	.40
389	Todd Helton/SP	2.00
390	Adam Dunn	.50
390	Adam Dunn/SP with bat	2.00
391	Cliff Floyd	.20
392	Tim Salmon	.40
393	Joe Torre	.50

394 Bobby Cox .20
395 Tony LaRussa .20
396 Art Howe .20
397 Bob Brenly .20
398 Ron Gardenhire .20
399 Mike Cuddyer .20
400 Joe Mauer 2.50
401 Mark Teixeira .50
402 Hee Seop Choi .20
403 Angel Berroa .20
404 Jesse Foppert .50
405 Bobby Crosby .50
406 Jose Reyes .40
407 Casey Kotchman 1.00
408 Aaron Heilman .20
409 Adrian Gonzalez .20
410 *Delwyn Young* .75
411 Brett Myers .20
412 *Justin Huber* 1.00
413 Drew Henson .20
414 *Taggert Bozied* 1.00
415 *Dontrelle Willis* 6.00
416 Rocco Baldelli .50
417 *Jason Stokes* 2.50
418 Brandon Phillips .20
419 *Jake Blalock/SP* 2.00
420 *Micah Schilling/SP* 1.00
421 *Denard Span/SP* 1.00
422 *James Loney/SP* 3.00
423 *Wes Bankston/SP* 1.50
424 *Jeremy Hermida/SP* 2.50
425 *Curtis Granderson/SP* 1.00
426 *Jason Pridie/SP* 1.00
427 *Larry Broadway/SP* 1.00
428 *Khalil Greene/SP* 5.00
429 *Joey Votto/SP* 1.00
430 *B.J. Upton/SP* 8.00
431 *Sergio Santos/SP* 2.00
432 *Brian Dopirak/SP* 2.00
433 Ozzie Smith/SP 2.00
434 Wade Boggs/SP 1.00
435 Yogi Berra/SP 3.00
436 Al Kaline/SP 2.00
437 Robin Roberts/SP 1.00
438 Roberto Clemente/SP 8.00
439 Gary Carter/SP 1.00
440 Fergie Jenkins/SP 1.00
441 Orlando Cepeda/SP 1.00
442 Rod Carew/SP 1.50
443 Harmon Killebrew/SP 2.50
444 Duke Snider/SP 2.00
445 Stan Musial/SP 5.00
446 Hank Greenberg/SP 1.00
447 Lou Brock/SP 1.00
448 Jim Palmer .50
449 John McGraw .75
450 Mordecai Brown .50
451 Christy Mathewson 1.00
452 Sam Crawford .50
453 Bill O'Hara .50
454 Joe Tinker .50
455 Napoleon Lajoie .75
456 Honus Wagner 3.00

T206 mini parallel

Polar Bear: 2-3X
Tolstoi Black: 2-5X
Average 4:box
Tolstoi Red: 4-8X
Average 2:box
Cycle: 6-12X
Average 1:box
Series 2
Polar Bear: 2-3X
Piedmont Black: 3-5X
Piedmond Red: 4-8X
Carolina Brights: 6-12X
Series 3
Polar Bear: 2-3X
Sweet Caporal Red: 3-5X
Sweet Caporal Blue or Black: 4-6X
Uzit: 6-12X
Bazooka Backs: No Pricing
Production 30
Drum Backs: No Pricing
Production 20
Lenox variations: No Pricing
Production 10
American Beauty variation: No Pricing
Production 5

Autographs

NM/M
Common Player: 8.00
Inserted 1:41
BB Barry Bonds 200.00
RC Roger Clemens 150.00
JE Jim Edmonds 30.00
BG Brian Giles 15.00
CG Cristian Guzman 15.00
BI Brandon Inge 10.00
RJ Ryan Jamison 8.00
FJ Forrest Johnson 8.00
JJ Jorge Julio 10.00
FL Felipe Lopez 15.00
GN Greg Nash 8.00
MO Magglio Ordonez 20.00
AR Alex Rodriguez 100.00
JR Jimmy Rollins 15.00
BZ Barry Zito 20.00

Autographs Series 2

NM/M
Common Player: 8.00
Inserted 1:55
MA Moises Alou 30.00
LB Lance Berkman 35.00
HB Hank Blalock 30.00
DB Dewon Brazelton 8.00
MB Marlon Byrd 10.00
EC Eric Chavez 30.00
JD Johnny Damon 25.00
GF Gavin Floyd 20.00
LG Luis Gonzalez 20.00
KI Kazuhisa Ishii 40.00
JDM J.D. Martin 8.00
JM Joe Mauer 50.00
MP Mark Prior 50.00
AP Albert Pujols 140.00
SR Scott Rolen 40.00
RS Richie Sexson 15.00
BS Ben Sheets 20.00
BSM Bud Smith 10.00
ST So Taguchi 25.00
CT Chris Tritle 10.00

Autographs Series 3

NM/M
Common Autograph: 8.00
MB Milton Bradley 10.00
JC Jose Cruz Jr. 15.00
DE David Eckstein 8.00
DH Drew Henson 15.00
ML Mike Lamb 8.00
AS Alfonso Soriano
MT Marcus Thames 8.00
JV Jose Vidro 10.00

Relics

NM/M
Common Player: 5.00
Overall Relics 1:11
RA Roberto Alomar/jsy 10.00
JB Jeff Bagwell/jsy 10.00
CB Craig Biggio/jsy 8.00
BB Barry Bonds/jsy 25.00
BBO Bret Boone/jsy 8.00
MC Mike Cameron/jsy 5.00
JC Jose Canseco/bat 10.00
CD Carlos Delgado/jsy 8.00
JED Jim Edmonds/jsy 10.00
CF Cliff Floyd/jsy 5.00
JGI Jason Giambi/jsy 8.00
JG Jeremy Giambi/jsy 5.00
TG Tom Glavine/jsy 8.00
SG Shawn Green/jsy 8.00
TGW Tony Gwynn/jsy 15.00
TH Todd Helton/jsy 10.00
RJ Randy Johnson/jsy 15.00
AJ Andruw Jones/jsy 8.00
CJ Chipper Jones/jsy 10.00
CL Carlos Lee/jsy 5.00
KL Kenny Lofton/jsy 5.00
GM Greg Maddux/jsy 15.00
EM Edgar Martinez/jsy 10.00
TM Tino Martinez/jsy 10.00
JO John Olerud/jsy 5.00
PO Paul O'Neill/jsy 8.00
MO Magglio Ordonez/jsy 6.00
CP Chan Ho Park/bat 5.00
MP Mike Piazza/jsy 15.00
AP Albert Pujols/bat 25.00
IR Ivan Rodriguez/jsy 10.00
AS Alfonso Soriano/bat 10.00
SS Shannon Stewart/bat 8.00
FT Frank Thomas/jsy 10.00
JT Jim Thome/jsy 20.00
LW Larry Walker/jsy 5.00
JW Jeff Weaver/jsy 5.00
BW Bernie Williams/jsy 8.00
BZ Barry Zito/jsy 8.00

Relics Series 2

NM/M
Common Player: 5.00
Jerseys 1:18
Bats 1:40
RA Roberto Alomar/bat 10.00
JB Jeff Bagwell/jsy 8.00
BB Barry Bonds/jsy 20.00
BBO Bret Boone/jsy 6.00
KB Kevin Brown/jsy 6.00
AB A.J. Burnett/jsy 5.00
SB Sean Burroughs/bat 8.00
EC Eric Chavez/bat 8.00
TC Ty Cobb/bat 400.00
JC Jimmy Collins/bat 45.00
SCR Sam Crawford/bat 50.00
JD Johnny Damon/bat 12.00
RD Ryan Dempster/jsy 5.00
BD Brandon Duckworth/jsy 5.00
AD Adam Dunn/bat 10.00
DE Darin Erstad/jsy 5.00
JEV Johnny Evers/bat 50.00
CF Cliff Floyd/jsy 5.00
TGL Tom Glavine/jsy 8.00
JG Juan Gonzalez/bat 10.00
MG Mark Grace/bat 10.00
SG Shawn Green/jsy 6.00
CG Cristian Guzman/jsy 5.00
TG Tony Gwynn/jsy 15.00
TH Toby Hall/jsy 5.00
JH Josh Hamilton/bat 5.00
THE Todd Helton/jsy 8.00
RH Rickey Henderson/bat 15.00
BH Buck Herzog/bat 30.00
JJ Jason Jennings/jsy 5.00
RJ Randy Johnson/jsy 10.00
AJ Andruw Jones/jsy 8.00
CJO Chipper Jones/jsy 10.00
JK Jeff Kent/jsy 5.00
BL Barry Larkin/jsy 8.00
TL Travis Lee/bat 5.00
GM Greg Maddux/jsy 12.00
EM Edgar Martinez/jsy 8.00
TM Tino Martinez/bat 10.00
JM Joe Mays/jsy 5.00
JMC John McGraw/bat 60.00
FM Fred McGriff/bat 8.00
JO John Olerud/jsy 5.00
RP Rafael Palmeiro/jsy 8.00
BP Brad Penny/jsy 5.00
MP Mike Piazza/jsy 15.00
AP Albert Pujols/jsy 15.00
ARA Aramis Ramirez/bat 10.00
AR Alex Rodriguez/bat 20.00
IR Ivan Rodriguez/jsy 8.00
CS Curt Schilling/bat 15.00
GS Gary Sheffield/bat 8.00
TS Tsuyoshi Shinjo/bat 5.00
AS Alfonso Soriano/bat 10.00
MT Miguel Tejada/bat 8.00
FT Frank Thomas/jsy 8.00
JTH Jim Thome/bat 15.00
JT Joe Tinker/bat 40.00
MV Mo Vaughn/bat 8.00
RV Robin Ventura/bat 5.00
HWA Honus Wagner/bat 400.00
LW Larry Walker/jsy 5.00
BW Bernie Williams/jsy 8.00
MW Matt Williams/jsy 5.00
PW Preston Wilson/jsy 5.00

Relics Series 3

NM/M
Common Player: 5.00
RA Roberto Alomar/bat 8.00
JB Jeff Bagwell/bat 8.00
WB Wilson Betemit/bat 5.00
PB Pat Burrell/bat 10.00
EC Eric Chavez/jsy 8.00
AD Adam Dunn/bat 10.00
JE Jim Edmonds/jsy 8.00
NG Nomar Garciaparra/bat 20.00
LG Luis Gonzalez/jsy 5.00
TG Tony Gwynn/jsy 10.00
TH Todd Helton/jsy 8.00
RH Rickey Henderson/bat 15.00
NJ Nick Johnson/bat 5.00
RJ Randy Johnson/jsy 10.00
AJ Andruw Jones/jsy 8.00
CJ Chipper Jones/jsy 10.00
PM Pedro Martinez/jsy 12.00
DM Doug Mientkiewicz/jsy 6.00
RP Rafael Palmeiro/jsy 8.00
CP Corey Patterson/bat 6.00
MP Mike Piazza/jsy 15.00
AP Albert Pujols/bat 20.00
AR Alex Rodriguez/bat 15.00
IR Ivan Rodriguez/bat 8.00
SR Scott Rolen/bat 10.00
CS Curt Schilling/bat 8.00
GS Gary Sheffield/bat 8.00
TS Tsuyoshi Shinjo/bat 5.00
AS Alfonso Soriano/bat 10.00
MTE Miguel Tejada/jsy 8.00
FT Frank Thomas/jsy 8.00
JT Jim Thome/jsy 10.00
MV Mo Vaughn/jsy 5.00
HW Honus Wagner/bat/25
BW Bernie Williams/jsy 8.00
BZ Barry Zito/jsy 6.00

Reprint Relics

NM/M
Common Player: 75.00
SC Sam Crawford 90.00
JE Johnny Evers 90.00
JM John McGraw 75.00
TS Tris Speaker 140.00
HW Honus Wagner 400.00

Team 206

NM/M
Complete Set (20): 10.00
Common Player: .25
Inserted 1:pack
1 Barry Bonds 2.00
2 Ivan Rodriguez .50
3 Luis Gonzalez .25
4 Jason Giambi .50
5 Pedro Martinez .75
6 Larry Walker .25
7 Bobby Abreu .40
8 Derek Jeter 2.00
9 Bret Boone .40
10 Mike Piazza 1.00
11 Alex Rodriguez 1.50
12 Roger Clemens 1.50
13 Albert Pujols 1.50
14 Randy Johnson .75
15 Sammy Sosa 1.50
16 Cristian Guzman .25
17 Shawn Green .40
18 Curt Schilling .50
19 Ichiro Suzuki 1.00
20 Chipper Jones .75

Team 206 Series 2

NM/M
Complete Set (25): 10.00
Common Player: .25
Inserted 1:1
1 Alex Rodriguez 1.50
2 Sammy Sosa 1.50
3 Jason Giambi .50
4 Nomar Garciaparra 1.25
5 Ichiro Suzuki 1.00
6 Chipper Jones .75
7 Derek Jeter 2.00
8 Barry Bonds 2.00
9 Mike Piazza 1.50
10 Randy Johnson .75
11 Shawn Green .25
12 Todd Helton .50
13 Luis Gonzalez .25
14 Albert Pujols 1.50
15 Curt Schilling .50
16 Scott Rolen .75

17 Ivan Rodriguez .50
18 Roberto Alomar .50
19 Cristian Guzman .25
20 Bret Boone .25
21 Barry Zito .40
22 Larry Walker .25
23 Eric Chavez .25
24 Roger Clemens 1.50
25 Pedro Martinez .75

Team 206 Series 3

NM/M

Complete Set (30): 10.00
Common Player: .25
Inserted 1:1
1 Ichiro Suzuki 1.00
2 Kazuhisa Ishii .25
3 Alex Rodriguez 1.50
4 Mark Prior 1.00
5 Derek Jeter 2.00
6 Sammy Sosa 1.50
7 Nomar Garciaparra 1.25
8 Mike Piazza 1.00
9 Jason Giambi .50
10 Vladimir Guerrero .75
11 Curt Schilling .50
12 Jim Thome .75
13 Adam Dunn .50
14 Albert Pujols 1.50
15 Pat Burrell .50
16 Chipper Jones .75
17 Randy Johnson .75
18 Todd Helton .50
19 Luis Gonzalez .25
20 Alfonso Soriano .75
21 Shawn Green .40
22 Pedro J. Martinez .75
23 Lance Berkman .40
24 Ivan Rodriguez .50
25 Larry Walker .25
26 Andruw Jones .40
27 Ken Griffey Jr. 1.00
28 Eric Hinske .25
29 Mike Sweeney .25
30 Miguel Tejada .50

Team Topps Legends Autographs

NM/M

Inserted 1:7,093
Vida Blue
Lou Brock
Rich "Goose" Gossage
Fergie Jenkins
Al Kaline
Don Larsen
Vern Law
Jim Palmer
Nolan Ryan 400.00
Moose Skowron

Team Topps Legends Autographs Series 2

NM/M

Inserted 1:260
Ralph Branca 25.00
Andy Pafko 20.00
Joe Pepitone 10.00
Herb Score
Tom Seaver 60.00
Warren Spahn 25.00
Bobby Thomson
Luis Tiant 10.00

2003 Topps

NM/M

Complete Set (720): 70.00
Sealed Factory Set (725): 70.00
Complete Series 1 Set (366): 35.00
Complete Series 2 Set (355): 35.00
Common Player: .10
Series 1 & 2 Pack (10): 1.50
Series 1 & 2 Box (36): 35.00
Series 2 Jumbo Box: 45.00
White Topps "throw-back" logo
Series 1 (1:8852):
VALUE UNDETERMINED
Series 2 (1:4487):
VALUE UNDETERMINED
1a Alex Rodriguez (red Topps) 1.00
1b Alex Rodriguez (white Topps)
2 Dan Wilson .10
3 Jimmy Rollins .10
4 Jermaine Dye .10
5 Steve Karsay .10
6 Timoniel Perez .10
7 Not Issued
8 Jose Vidro .10
9 Eddie Guardado .10
10a Mark Prior (red Topps) .50
10b Mark Prior (white Topps)
11a Curt Schilling (red Topps) .40
11b Curt Schilling (white Topps)
12 Dennis Cook .10
13 Andruw Jones .40
14 David Segui .10
15 Trot Nixon .10
16 Antonio Alfonseca .10
17 Magglio Ordonez .20
18 Jason LaRue .10
19 Danys Baez .10
20a Todd Helton (red Topps) .40
20b Todd Helton (white Topps)
21 Denny Neagle .10
22 Dave Mlicki .10
23 Roberto Hernandez .10
24 Odalis Perez .10
25 Nick Neugebauer .10
26 David Ortiz .10
27 Andres Galarraga .15
28 Edgardo Alfonzo .10
29 Chad Bradford .10
30a Jason Giambi (red Topps) .40
30b Jason Giambi (white Topps)
31 Brian Giles .25
32 Deivi Cruz .10
33 Robb Nen .10
34 Jeff Nelson .10
35 Edgar Renteria .10
36 Aubrey Huff .10
37 Brandon Duckworth .10
38 Juan Gonzalez .40
39 Sidney Ponson .10
40 Eric Hinske .10
41 Kevin Appier .10
42 Danny Bautista .10
43 Javier Lopez .10
44 Jeff Conine .10
45 Carlos Baerga .10
46 Ugueth Urbina .10
47 Mark Buehrle .10
48 Aaron Boone .10
49 Chuck Finley .10
50a Sammy Sosa (red Topps) 1.00
50b Sammy Sosa (white Topps)
51 Jose Jimenez .10
52 Chris Truby .10
53 Luis Castillo .10
54 Orlando Merced .10
55 Brian Jordan .10
56 Eric Young .10
57 Bobby Kielty .10
58 Luis Rivas .10
59 Brad Wilkerson .10
60 Roberto Alomar .40
61a Roger Clemens (red Topps) 1.00
61b Roger Clemens (white Topps)
62 Scott Hatteberg .10
63 Andy Ashby .10
64 Mike Williams .10
65 Ron Gant .10
66 Benito Santiago .10
67 Bret Boone .10
68 Matt Morris .10
69 Troy Glaus .40
70 Austin Kearns .25
71 Jim Thome .40
72 Rickey Henderson .40
73a Luis Gonzalez (red Topps) .20
73b Luis Gonzalez (white Topps)
74 Brad Fullmer .10
75 Benny Agbayani .10
76 Randy Wolf .10
77a Miguel Tejada (red Topps) .25
77b Miguel Tejada (white Topps)
78 Jimmy Anderson .10
79 Ramon Martinez .10
80a Ivan Rodriguez (red Topps) .40
80b Ivan Rodriguez (white Topps)
81 John Flaherty .10
82 Shannon Stewart .10
83 Orlando Palmeiro .10
84 Rafael Furcal .10
85 Kenny Rogers .10
86 Bud Smith .10
87 Mo Vaughn .15
88 Jose Cruz Jr. .10
89 Mike Matheny .10
90a Alfonso Soriano (red Topps) .50
90b Alfonso Soriano (white Topps)
91 Orlando Cabrera .10
92 Jeffrey Hammonds .10
93 Hideo Nomo .25
94 Carlos Febles .10
95 Billy Wagner .10
96 Alex Gonzalez .10
97 Todd Zeile .10
98 Omar Vizquel .20
99 Jose Rijo .10
100a Ichiro Suzuki (red Topps) 1.00
100b Ichiro Suzuki (white Topps)
101 Steve Cox .10
102 Hideki Irabu .10
103 Roy Halladay .10
104 David Eckstein .10
105 Greg Maddux .75
106 Chris Richard .10
107 Travis Driskill .10
108 Fred McGriff .15
109 Frank Thomas .50
110 Shawn Green .20
111 Ruben Quevedo .10
112 Jacque Jones .10
113 Tomokazu Ohka .10
114 Joe McEwing .10
115 Ramiro Mendoza .10
116 Mark Mulder .20
117 Mike Lieberthal .10
118 Jack Wilson .10
119 Randall Simon .10
120 Bernie Williams .40
121 Marvin Benard .10
122 Jamie Moyer .10
123 Andy Benes .10
124 Tino Martinez .10
125 Esteban Yan .10
126 Gabe Kapler .10
127 Jason Isringhausen .10
128 Chris Carpenter .10
129 Mike Cameron .10
130a Gary Sheffield (red Topps) .25
130b Gary Sheffield (white Topps)
131 Geronimo Gil .10
132 Brian Daubach .10
133 Corey Patterson .10
134 Aaron Rowand .10
135 Chris Reitsma .10
136 Bob Wickman .10
137 Paul Shuey .10
138 Jason Jennings .10
139 Brandon Inge .10
140 Larry Walker .20
141 Ramon Santiago .10
142 Hansel Izquierdo .10
143 Jose Vizcaino .10
144 Mark Quinn .10
145 Michael Tucker .10
146 Darren Dreifort .10
147 Mark Loretta .10
148 Corey Koskie .10
149 Tony Armas Jr. .10
150a Kazuhisa Ishii (red Topps) .10
150b Kazuhisa Ishii (white Topps)
151 Al Leiter .10
152 Steve Trachsel .10
153 Mike Stanton .10
154 David Justice .15
155 Marlon Anderson .10
156 Jason Kendall .10
157 Brian Lawrence .10
158 J.T. Snow Jr. .10
159 Edgar Martinez .10
160a Pat Burrell (red Topps) .25
160b Pat Burrell (white Topps)
161 Kerry Robinson .10
162 Greg Vaughn .10
163 Carl Everett .10
164 Vernon Wells .10
165 Jose Mesa .10
166 Troy Percival .10
167 Erubiel Durazo .10
168 Jason Marquis .10
169 Jerry Hairston Jr. .10
170a Vladimir Guerrero (red Topps) .50
170b Vladimir Guerrero (white Topps)
171 Byung-Hyun Kim .10
172 Marcus Giles .10
173 Johnny Damon .10
174 Jon Lieber .10
175 Ray Durham .10
176 Sean Casey .10
177a Adam Dunn (red Topps) .40
177b Adam Dunn (white Topps)
178 Juan Pierre .10
179 Damion Easley .10
180a Barry Zito (red Topps) .25
180b Barry Zito (white Topps)
181 Abraham Nunez .10
182 Pokey Reese .10
183 Jeff Kent .20
184 Russ Ortiz .10
185 Ruben Sierra .10
186 Brent Abernathy .10
187 Ismael Valdes .10
188 Darrin Fletcher .10
189 Craig Counsell .10
190 Boomer Wells .10
191 Ramon Hernandez .10
192 Adam Kennedy .10
193 Tony Womack .10
194 Wes Helms .10
195 Tony Batista .10
196 Rolando Arrojo .10
197 Matt Clement .10
198 Sandy Alomar .10
199 Scott Sullivan .10
200a Albert Pujols (red Topps) 1.00
200b Albert Pujols (white Topps)
201 Kirk Rueter .10
202 Phil Nevin .10
203 Kip Wells .10
204 Ron Coomer .10
205 Jeromy Burnitz .10
206 Kyle Lohse .10
207 Paul Bako .10
208 Paul LoDuca .10
209 Carlos Beltran .10
210 Roy Oswalt .25
211 Mike Lowell .10
212 Robert Fick .10
213 Todd Jones .10
214 C.C. Sabathia .10
215 Danny Graves .10
216 Todd Hundley .10
217 Tim Wakefield .10
218 Dustin Hermanson .10
219 Kevin Millwood .10
220 Jorge Posada .25
221 Bobby Jones .10
222 Carlos Guillen .10
223 Fernando Vina .10
224 Ryan Rupe .10
225 Kelvim Escobar .10
226 Ramon Ortiz .10
227 Junior Spivey .10
228 Juan Cruz .10
229 Melvin Mora .10
230a Lance Berkman (red Topps) .25
230b Lance Berkman (white Topps)
231 Brent Butler .10
232 Matt Anderson .10
233 Derrek Lee .10
234 Matt Lawton .10
235 Chuck Knoblauch .10
236 Eric Gagne .10
237 Alex Sanchez .10
238 Denny Hocking .10
239 Rick Reed .10
240 Rey Ordonez .10
241 Orlando Hernandez .10
242 Robert Person .10
243 Sean Burroughs .10
244 Jeff Cirillo .10
245 Mike Lamb .10
246 Jose Valentin .10
247 Ellis Burks .10
248 Shawn Chacon .10
249 Josh Beckett .10
250a Nomar Garciaparra (red Topps) 1.00

250b Nomar Garciaparra (white Topps)
251 Craig Biggio .20
252 Joe Randa .10
253 Mark Grudzielanek .10
254 Glendon Rusch .10
255 Michael Barrett .10
256 Tyler Houston .10
257 Ryan Dempster .10
258 Wade Miller .10
259 Adrian Beltre .20
260 Vicente Padilla .10
261 Kazuhiro Sasaki .10
262 Mike Scioscia .10
263 Bobby Cox .10
264 Mike Hargrove .10
265 Grady Little .10
266 Alex Gonzalez .10
267 Jerry Manuel .10
268 Bob Boone .10
269 Joel Skinner .10
270 Clint Hurdle .10
271 Luis Pujols .10
272 Bob Brenly .10
273 Jeff Torborg .10
274 Jimy Williams .10
275 Tony Pena .10
276 Jim Tracy .10
277 Jerry Royster .10
278 Ron Gardenhire .10
279 Frank Robinson .10
280 Bobby Valentine .10
281 Joe Torre .10
282 Art Howe .10
283 Larry Bowa .10
284 Lloyd McClendon .10
285 Bruce Bochy .10
286 Dusty Baker .10
287 Lou Pinella .10
288 Tony LaRussa .10
289 Hal McRae .10
290 Jerry Narron .10
291 Carlos Tosca .10
292 *Chris Duncan* .10
293 *Franklin Gutierrez* 1.00
294 Adam LaRoche .10
295 *Manuel Ramirez* .10
296 *Il Kim* .10
297 *Wayne Lydon* .20
298 *Daryl Clark* .25
299 Sean Pierce .10
300a *Andy Marte* (red Topps) 1.00
200b *Andy Marte* (white Topps)
301 *Matt Peterson* .25
302 *Gonzalo Lopez* .25
303 *Bernie Castro* .10
304 Cliff Lee .10
305 *Jason Perry* .50
306 *Jaime Bubela* .10
307 Alexis Rios .10
308 *Brendan Harris* .25
309 Ramon Martinez .25
310 *Terry Tiffee* .40
311 *Kevin Youkilis* 1.00
312 *Ruddy Lugo* .20
313 C.J. Wilson .10
314 *Mike McNutt* .10
315 *Jeff Clark* .10
316 *Mark Malaska* .10
317 *Doug Waechter* .25
318 *Derell McCall* .10
319 Scott Tyler .10
320 *Craig Brazell* .40
321a Walter Young (red Topps) .10
321b Walter Young (white Topps)
322a Marlon Byrd, Jorge Padilla (red Topps) .10
322b Marlon Byrd, Jorge Padilla (white Topps)
323 Chris Snelling, Shin-Soo Choo .10
324a Hank Blalock, Mark Teixeira (red Topps) .10
324b Hank Blalock, Mark Teixeira (white Topps)
325 Josh Hamilton, Carl Crawford .10
326 Orlando Hudson, Josh Phelps .10
327 Jack Cust, Rene Reyes .10
328 Angel Berroa, Alexis Gomez .10
329 Michael Cuddyer, Michael Restovich .10
330 Juan Rivera, Marcus Thames .10
331 Brandon Puffer, Jung Bong .10
332 Mike Cameron .10
333 Shawn Green .25
334 Team Shot .10
335 Jason Giambi .25
336 Derek Lowe .10
337 Manny Ramirez, Mike Sweeney, Bernie Williams .25
338 Alfonso Soriano, Alex Rodriguez, Derek Jeter .50
339 Alex Rodriguez, Jim Thome, Rafael Palmeiro .40
340 Magglio Ordonez, Alex Rodriguez, Miguel Tejada .40
341 Pedro Martinez, Derek Lowe, Barry Zito .25
342 Pedro Martinez, Roger Clemens, Mike Mussina .25
343 Larry Walker, Vladimir Guerrero, Todd Helton .25
344 Sammy Sosa, Albert Pujols, Shawn Green .40
345 Sammy Sosa, Lance Berkman, Shawn Green .40
346 Lance Berkman, Albert Pujols, Pat Burrell .25
347 Randy Johnson, Greg Maddux, Tom Glavine .25
348 Randy Johnson, Curt Schilling, Kerry Wood .25
349 AL Divison Series .20
350 AL & NL Divison Series .20
351 AL & NL Divison Series .20
352 NL Divison Series .20
353 AL Championship Series .20
354 Postseason Highlight .20
355 NL Championship Series .10
356 Jason Giambi .25
357 Alfonso Soriano .50
358 Alex Rodriguez .75
359 Eric Chavez .10
360 Torii Hunter .10
361 Bernie Williams .20
362 Garret Anderson .10
363 Jorge Posada .20
364 Derek Lowe .10
365 Barry Zito .20
366 Manny Ramirez .25
367 Mike Scioscia .10
368a Francisco Rodriguez (red Topps) .10
368b Francisco Rodriguez (white Topps)
369 Andres Galarraga .10
370a Chipper Jones (red Topps) .50
370b Chipper Jones (white Topps)
371 Chris Singleton .10
372 Cliff Floyd .10
373 Bobby Hill .10
374 Antonio Osuna .10
375 Barry Larkin .25
376 Charles Nagy .10
377 Denny Stark .10
378 Dean Palmer .10
379 Eric Owens .10
380a Randy Johnson (red Topps) .50
380b Randy Johnson (white Topps)
381 Jeff Suppan .10
382 Eric Karros .10
383 Luis Vizcaino .10
384 Johan Santana .10
385 Javier Vazquez .10
386 John Thomson .10
387a Nick Johnson (red Topps) .10
387b Nick Johnson (white Topps)
388 Mark Ellis .10
389 Doug Glanville .10
390a Ken Griffey Jr. (red Topps) .75
390b Ken Griffey Jr. (white Topps)
391 Bubba Trammell .10
392 Livan Hernandez .10
393 Desi Relaford .10
394 Eli Marrero .10
395 Jared Sandberg .10
396a Barry Bonds (red Topps) 1.50
396b Barry Bonds (white Topps)
397 Esteban Loaiza .10
398 Aaron Sele .10
399 Geoff Blum .10
400a Derek Jeter (red Topps) 1.50
400b Derek Jeter (white Topps)
401 Eric Byrnes .10
402 Mike Timlin .10
403 Mark Kotsay .10
404 Rich Aurilia .10
405 Joel Pineiro .10
406 Chuck Finley .10
407 Bengie Molina .10
408 Steve Finley .10
409 Julio Franco .10
410 Marty Cordova .10
411 Shea Hillenbrand .10
412 Mark Bellhorn .10
413 Jon Garland .10
414 Reggie Taylor .10
415 Milton Bradley .10
416 Carlos Pena .10
417 Andy Fox .10
418 Brad Ausmus .10
419 Brent Mayne .10
420 Paul Quantrill .10
421a Carlos Delgado (red Topps) .20
421b Carlos Delgado (white Topps)
422 Kevin Mench .10
423 Joe Kennedy .10
424 Mike Crudale .10
425 Mark McLemore .10
426 Bill Mueller .10
427 Robert Mackowiak .10
428 Ricky Ledee .10
429 Ted Lilly .10
430 Sterling Hitchcock .10
431 Scott Strickland .10
432 Damion Easley .10
433a Torii Hunter (red Topps) .25
433b Torii Hunter (white Topps)
434 Brad Radke .10
435 Geoff Jenkins .10
436 Paul Byrd .10
437 Morgan Ensberg .10
438 Mike Maroth .10
439 Mike Hampton .10
440 Adam Hyzdu .10
441 Vance Wilson .10
442 Todd Ritchie .10
443 Flash Gordon .10
444 John Burkett .10
445 Rodrigo Lopez .10
446 Tim Spooneybarger .10
447 Quinton McCracken .10
448 Tim Salmon .20
449 Jarrod Washburn .10
450a Pedro Martinez (red Topps) .50
450b Pedro Martinez (white Topps)
451 Dustan Mohr .10
452 Julio Lugo .10
453 Scott Stewart .10
454 Armando Benitez .10
455 Raul Mondesi .20
456 Robin Ventura .20
457 Bobby Abreu .20
458 Josh Fogg .10
459 Ryan Klesko .20
460 Tsuyoshi Shinjo .10
461a Jim Edmonds (red Topps) .25
461b Jim Edmonds (white Topps)
462 Cliff Politte .10
463 Chan Ho Park .10
464 John Mabry .10
465 Woody Williams .10
466 Jason Michaels .10
467 Scott Schoeneweis .10
468 Brian Anderson .10
469 Brett Tomko .10
470 Scott Erickson .10
471 Tony Clark .10
472 Danny Wright .10
473 Jason Schmidt .10
474 Scott Williamson .10
475 Einar Diaz .10
476 Jay Payton .10
477 Juan Acevedo .10
478 Ben Grieve .10
479 Raul Ibanez .10
480 Richie Sexson .25
481 Rick Reed .10
482 Pedro Astacio .10
483 Adam Piatt .10
484 Bud Smith .10
485 Tomas Perez .10
486 Adam Eaton .10
487 Rafael Palmeiro .25
488 Jason Tyner .10
489a Scott Rolen (red Topps) .50
489b Scott Rolen (white Topps)
490 Randy Winn .10
491 Ryan Jensen .10
492 Trevor Hoffman .10
493 Craig Wilson .10
494 Jeremy Giambi .10
495 Daryle Ward .10
496 Shane Spencer .10
497 Andy Pettitte .25
498 John Franco .10
499 Masato Yoshii .10
500a Mike Piazza (red Topps) 1.00
500b Mike Piazza (white Topps)
501 Cristian Guzman .10
502 Jose Hernandez .10
503 Octavio Dotel .10
504 Brad Penny .10
505 Jose Ortiz .10
506 Ryan Dempster .10
507 Joe Crede .10
508 Chad Hermansen .10
509 Gary Matthews Jr. .10
510 Matt Franco .10
511 Ben Weber .10
512 Dave Berg .10
513 Michael Young .10
514 Frank Catalanotto .10
515a Darin Erstad (red Topps) .25
515b Darin Erstad (white Topps)
516 Matt Williams .10
517 B.J. Surhoff .10
518 Kerry Ligtenberg .10
519 Mike Bordick .10
520 Arthur Rhodes .10
521 Joe Girardi .10
522 D'Angelo Jimenez .10
523 Paul Konerko .10
524 Jose Macias .10
525 Joe Mays .10
526 Marquis Grissom .10
527 Neifi Perez .10
528 Preston Wilson .10
529 Jeff Weaver .10
530a Eric Chavez (red Topps) .25
530b Eric Chavez (white Topps)
531 Placido Polanco .10
532 Ray Lankford .10
533 James Baldwin .10
534 Toby Hall .10
535 Brendan Donnelly .10
536 Benji Gil .10
537 Damian Moss .10
538 Jorge Julio .10
539 Matt Clement .10
540 Brian Moehler .10
541 Lee Stevens .10
542 Jimmy Haynes .10
543 Kevin Millar .10
544 Dave Roberts .10
545 J.C. Romero .10
546 Bartolo Colon .10
547 Roger Cedeno .10
548 Mariano Rivera .20
549 Billy Koch .10
550a Manny Ramirez (red Topps) .50
550b Manny Ramirez (white topps)
551 Travis Lee .10
552 Oliver Perez .10
553 Tim Worrell .10
554 Rafael Soriano .10
555 Damian Miller .10
556 John Smoltz .10
557 Willis Roberts .10
558a Tim Hudson (red Topps) .25
558b Tim Hudson (white Topps)
559 Moises Alou .20
560 Gary Glover .10
561 Corky Miller .10
562 Ben Broussard .10
563 Gabe Kapler .10
564 Chris Woodward .10
565 Paul Wilson .10
566 Todd Hollandsworth .10
567 So Taguchi .10
568 John Olerud .20
569 Reggie Sanders .10
570 Jake Peavy .10
571 Kris Benson .10
572 Todd Pratt .10
573 Ray Durham .10
574 Boomer Wells .10
575 Chris Widger .10
576 Shawn Wooten .10
577 Tom Glavine .25
578 Antonio Alfonseca .10
579 Keith Foulke .10
580 Shawn Estes .10

581 Travis Fryman .10
582 Dmitri Young .10
583 A.J. Burnett .10
584 Richard Hidalgo .10
585a Mike Sweeney (red Topps) .10
585b Mike Sweeney (white Topps)
586 Alex Cora .10
587 Matt Stairs .10
588 Doug Mientkiewicz .10
589 Fernando Tatis .10
590 David Weathers .10
591 Cory Lidle .10
592 Dan Plesac .10
593a Jeff Bagwell (red Topps) .50
593b Jeff Bagwell (white Topps)
594 Steve Sparks .10
595 Sandy Alomar Jr. .10
596 John Lackey .10
597 Rick Helling .10
598 Mark DeRosa .10
599 Carlos Lee .10
600a Garret Anderson (red Topps) .20
600b Garret Anderson (white Topps)
601 Vinny Castilla .10
602 Ryan Drese .10
603 LaTroy Hawkins .10
604 David Bell .10
605 Freddy Garcia .10
606 Miguel Cairo .10
607 Scott Spiezio .10
608 Mike Remlinger .10
609 Tony Graffanino .10
610 Russell Branyan .10
611 Chris Magruder .10
612 *Jose Contreras* .75
613 Carl Pavano .10
614 Kevin Brown .10
615 Tyler Houston .10
616 A.J. Pierzynski .10
617 Tony Fiore .10
618 Peter Bergeron .10
619 Rondell White .10
620 Brett Myers .10
621 Kevin Young .10
622 Kenny Lofton .10
623 Ben Davis .10
624 J.D. Drew .10
625 Chris Gomez .10
626 Karim Garcia .10
627 Ricky Gutierrez .10
628 Mark Redman .10
629 Juan Encarnacion .10
630 Anaheim Angels .25
631 Arizona Diamondbacks .10
632 Atlanta Braves .25
633 Baltimore Orioles .10
634 Boston Red Sox .25
635 Chicago Cubs .10
636 Chicago White Sox .10
637 Cincinnati Reds .10
638 Cleveland Indians .10
639 Colorado Rockies .10
640 Detroit Tigers .10
641 Florida Marlins .10
642 Houston Astros .10
643 Kansas City Royals .10
644 Los Angeles Dodgers .10
645 Milwaukee Brewers .10
646 Minnesota Twins .10
647 Montreal Expos .10
648 New York Mets .10
649 New York Yankees .50
650 Oakland Athletics .10
651 Philadelphia Phillies .10
652 Pittsburgh Pirates .10
653 San Diego Padres .10
654 San Francisco Giants .10
655 Seattle Mariners .10
656 St. Louis Cardinals .10
657 Tampa Bay Devil Rays .10
658 Texas Rangers .10
659 Toronto Blue Jays .10
660 *Bryan Bullington* 1.00
661 Jeremy Guthrie .10
662 Joey Gomes .25
663 *Evel Bastida-Martinez* .40
664 *Brian Wright* .10
665 B.J. Upton .10
666 Jeff Francis .10
667 Drew Meyer .10
668 Jeremy Hermida .10
669 Khalil Greene .75
670 Darrell Rasner .10
671 Cole Hamels .10
672 James Loney .10
673 Sergio Santos .10
674 Jason Pridie .10
675 Brandon Phillips, Victor Martinez .10
676 Hee Seop Choi, Nic Jackson .10
677 Dontrelle Willis, Jason Stokes .10
678 Chad Tracy, Lyle Overbay .10
679 Joe Borchard, Corwin Malone .10
680 Joe Mauer, Justin Morneau .10
681 Drew Henson, Brandon Claussen .10
682 Chase Utley, Gavin Floyd .10
683 Taggert Bozied, Xavier Nady .25
684 Aaron Heilman, Jose Reyes .10
685 Kenny Rogers .10
686 Bengie Molina .10
687 John Olerud .10
688 Bret Boone .10
689 Eric Chavez .15
690 Alex Rodriguez .75
691 Darin Erstad .15
692 Ichiro Suzuki .50
693 Torii Hunter .15
694 Greg Maddux .50
695 Brad Ausmus .10
696 Todd Helton .20
697 Fernando Vina .10
698 Scott Rolen .25
699 Edgar Renteria .10
700 Andruw Jones .20
701 Larry Walker .10
702 Jim Edmonds .10
703 Barry Zito .10
704 Randy Johnson .40
705 Miguel Tejada .15
706 Barry Bonds .75
707 Eric Hinske .10
708 Jason Jennings .10
709 Todd Helton .20
710 Jeff Kent .10
711 Edgar Renteria .10
712 Scott Rolen .25
713 Barry Bonds .75
714 Sammy Sosa .50
715 Vladimir Guerrero .40
716 Mike Piazza .75
717 Curt Schilling .20
718 Randy Johnson .40
719 Bobby Cox .10
720 World Series Card .10
721 World Series Card .10

Blue Backs

NM/M

Complete Set (40): 50.00
Common Player: .75
Inserted 1:12

BB1 Albert Pujols 2.00
BB2 Barry Bonds 5.00
BB3 Ichiro Suzuki 3.00
BB4 Sammy Sosa 2.50
BB5 Kazuhisa Ishii .75
BB6 Alex Rodriguez 4.00
BB7 Derek Jeter 5.00
BB8 Vladimir Guerrero 2.00
BB9 Ken Griffey Jr. 2.50
BB10 Jason Giambi 2.50
BB11 Todd Helton 1.00
BB12 Mike Piazza 3.00
BB13 Nomar Garciaparra 3.00
BB14 Chipper Jones 2.50
BB15 Ivan Rodriguez 1.00
BB16 Luis Gonzalez .75
BB17 Pat Burrell 1.00
BB18 Mark Prior 1.50
BB19 Adam Dunn 1.50
BB20 Jeff Bagwell 1.50
BB21 Austin Kearns 1.00
BB22 Alfonso Soriano 2.00
BB23 Jim Thome 1.50
BB24 Bernie Williams 1.00
BB25 Pedro J. Martinez 2.00
BB26 Lance Berkman 1.00
BB27 Randy Johnson 2.00
BB28 Rafael Palmeiro 1.00
BB29 Richie Sexson .75
BB30 Troy Glaus 1.50
BB31 Shawn Green .75
BB32 Larry Walker .75
BB33 Eric Hinske .75
BB34 Andruw Jones 1.50
BB35 Carlos Delgado 1.00
BB36 Curt Schilling 1.50
BB37 Greg Maddux 2.50
BB38 Jimmy Rollins .75
BB39 Eric Chavez 1.00
BB40 Scott Rolen 1.00

Gold

Stars: 3-6X
Production 2003 sets

Black

Stars: 10-20X
Production 52 sets

All-Stars

NM/M

Complete Set (20): 20.00
Common Player: .50
Inserted 1:15

TAS1 Alfonso Soriano 1.50
TAS2 Barry Bonds 4.00
TAS3 Ichiro Suzuki 2.00
TAS4 Alex Rodriguez 3.00
TAS5 Miguel Tejada .75
TAS6 Nomar Garciaparra 2.50
TAS7 Jason Giambi 2.00
TAS8 Manny Ramirez 1.00
TAS9 Derek Jeter 4.00
TAS10 Garret Anderson .50
TAS11 Barry Zito .50
TAS12 Sammy Sosa 2.00
TAS13 Adam Dunn 1.00
TAS14 Vladimir Guerrero 1.50
TAS15 Mike Piazza 2.50
TAS16 Shawn Green .50
TAS17 Luis Gonzalez .50
TAS18 Todd Helton .75
TAS19 Torii Hunter .75
TAS20 Curt Schilling .75

Autographs

NM/M

Common Autograph: 8.00
HB Hank Blalock 20.00
MB Mark Buehrle 20.00
EC Eric Chavez 25.00
DE Darin Erstad 15.00
OH Orlando Hudson 8.00
AJ Andruw Jones
AK Austin Kearns 15.00
JL Jason Lane 10.00
PL Paul LoDuca 12.00
JDM J.D. Martin 8.00
JM Joe Mauer 20.00
EM Eric Milton 10.00
NN Nick Neugebauer 10.00
MP Mark Prior 50.00
SR Scott Rolen 50.00
BS Ben Sheets 15.00
AS Alfonso Soriano
MTE Mark Teixeira 20.00
MT Miguel Tejada
MTH Marcus Thames 8.00

Autographs Series 2

NM/M

Common Autograph: 8.00
JB Josh Beckett 30.00
LB Lance Berkman 40.00
CE Clint Everts 8.00
CF Cliff Floyd 20.00
BH Brad Hawpe 8.00
EH Eric Hinske 10.00
TH Torii Hunter 20.00
AK Austin Kearns 15.00
PK Paul Konerko 20.00
PL Paul LoDuca 15.00
MO Magglio Ordonez 20.00
JPH Josh Phelps 10.00
AP Albert Pujols 120.00
MT Miguel Tejada 30.00
BU B.J. Upton 25.00
JV Jose Vidro 10.00
DW Dontrelle Willis 25.00
BZ Barry Zito 30.00

Draft Picks

NM/M

Complete Set (10): 30.00
1-5 issued in retail sets
6-10 issued in holiday sets

1 Brandon Wood 10.00
2 Ryan Wagner 5.00
3 Sean Rodriguez 3.00
4 Chris Lubanski 5.00
5 Chad Billingsley 3.00
6 Javi Herrera 3.00
7 Brian McFall 3.00
8 Nicholas Markakis 5.00
9 Adam Miller 3.00
10 Daric Barton 5.00

Flashback

NM/M

Complete Set (14): 50.00
Common Player: 2.00
HTA exclusive

GB George Brett 6.00
LD Lenny Dykstra 3.00
HK Harmon Killebrew 6.00
BM Bill Madlock 2.00
EM Eddie Mathews 4.00
DM Dale Murphy 5.00
JP Jim Palmer 3.00
MP Mike Piazza 6.00
RR Robin Roberts 3.00
AR Al Rosen 4.00
NR Nolan Ryan 10.00
TS Tom Seaver 5.00
WS Warren Spahn 4.00
CY Carl Yastrzemski 6.00

Futures Game

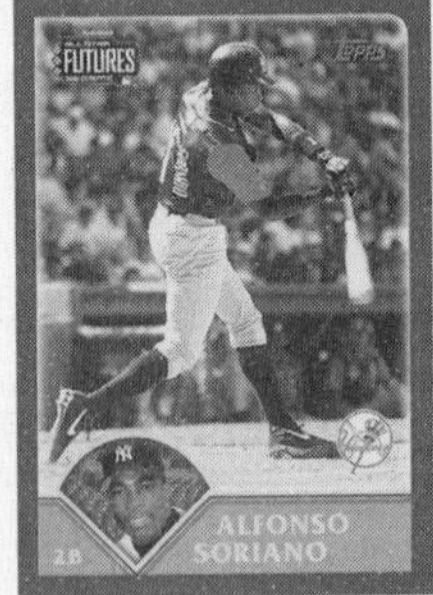

NM/M

Complete Set (6): 5.00
Common Player: .50

1 Alfonso Soriano 2.00
2 Pat Burrell 1.00
3 Adam Dunn 1.00
4 Barry Zito .75
5 Mark Buehrle .50
6 Rafael Furcal .75

Hit Parade

NM/M

Complete Set (30): 30.00
Common Player: .50
Inserted 1:15

HP1 Barry Bonds 4.00
HP2 Sammy Sosa 2.50
HP3 Rafael Palmeiro 1.00
HP4 Fred McGriff .75
HP5 Ken Griffey Jr. 2.50

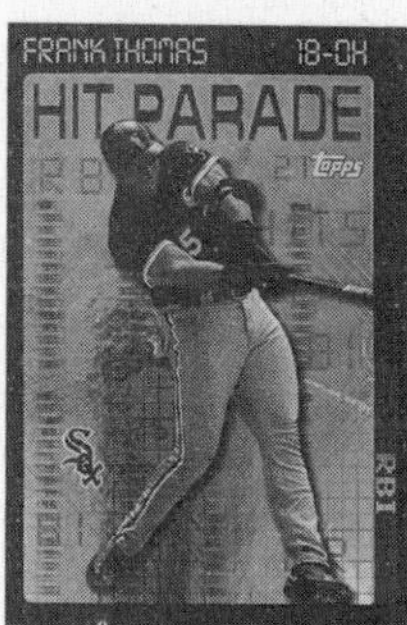

HP6 Juan Gonzalez 1.00
HP7 Andres Galarraga .50
HP8 Jeff Bagwell 1.50
HP9 Frank Thomas 1.50
HP10 Matt Williams .50
HP11 Barry Bonds 4.00
HP12 Rafael Palmeiro 1.00
HP13 Fred McGriff .75
HP14 Andres Galarraga .50
HP15 Ken Griffey Jr. 2.50
HP16 Sammy Sosa 2.50
HP17 Jeff Bagwell 1.50
HP18 Juan Gonzalez 1.00
HP19 Frank Thomas 1.50
HP20 Matt Williams .50
HP21 Rickey Henderson 1.00
HP22 Rafael Palmeiro 1.00
HP23 Roberto Alomar 1.00
HP24 Barry Bonds 4.00
HP25 Mark Grace 1.00
HP26 Fred McGriff .75
HP27 Julio Franco .50
HP28 Craig Biggio .50
HP29 Andres Galarraga .50
HP30 Barry Larkin .50

Hobby Masters

NM/M
Complete Set (20): 40.00
Common Player: 1.00
Inserted 1:18
HM1 Ichiro Suzuki 4.00
HM2 Kazuhisa Ishii 1.00
HM3 Derek Jeter 6.00
HM4 Barry Bonds 5.00
HM5 Sammy Sosa 3.00
HM6 Alex Rodriguez 5.00
HM7 Mike Piazza 4.00
HM8 Chipper Jones 3.00
HM9 Vladimir Guerrero 2.00
HM10 Nomar Garciaparra 4.00
HM11 Todd Helton 1.00
HM12 Jason Giambi 3.00
HM13 Ken Griffey Jr. 3.00
HM14 Albert Pujols 2.00
HM15 Ivan Rodriguez 1.00
HM16 Mark Prior 1.00
HM17 Adam Dunn 1.50
HM18 Randy Johnson 2.00
HM19 Pedro J. Martinez 2.00
HM20 Alfonso Soriano 3.00

Nolan Ryan No-Hitters

NM/M
Complete Set (7): 45.00
Common Ryan (1-7): 8.00
RB-NR1 Nolan Ryan 8.00
RB-NR2 Nolan Ryan 8.00
RB-NR3 Nolan Ryan 8.00
RB-NR4 Nolan Ryan 8.00
RB-NR5 Nolan Ryan 8.00
RB-NR6 Nolan Ryan 8.00
RB-NR7 Nolan Ryan 8.00

Nolan Ryan Record Breakers Autographs

NM/M
Inserted 1:1,894
HTA Exclusive
NR Nolan Ryan 200.00
NRA Nolan Ryan 200.00
NRR Nolan Ryan 200.00

Own The Game

NM/M
Complete Set (30): 30.00
Common Player: .50
Inserted 1:12
OG1 Ichiro Suzuki 3.00
OG2 Barry Bonds 4.00
OG3 Todd Helton .75
OG4 Larry Walker .75
OG5 Mike Sweeney .50
OG6 Sammy Sosa 2.50
OG7 Lance Berkman .75
OG8 Alex Rodriguez 4.00
OG9 Jim Thome 1.25
OG10 Shawn Green .75
OG11 Troy Glaus 1.00
OG12 Richie Sexson .50
OG13 Paul Konerko .50
OG14 Jason Giambi 2.50
OG15 Chipper Jones 2.50
OG16 Torii Hunter .50
OG17 Albert Pujols 1.50
OG18 Jose Vidro .50
OG19 Alfonso Soriano 2.00
OG20 Luis Castillo .50
OG21 Mike Lowell .50
OG22 Garret Anderson .50
OG23 Jimmy Rollins .50
OG24 Curt Schilling 1.00
OG25 Kazuhisa Ishii .50
OG26 Randy Johnson 1.50
OG27 Tom Glavine .75
OG28 Roger Clemens 2.50
OG29 Pedro J. Martinez 1.50
OG30 Derek Lowe .50

Prime Cuts Autograph

NM/M
Production 50 sets
EC Eric Chavez 100.00
LB Lance Berkman 120.00
DE Darin Erstad
AJ Andruw Jones 100.00
CJ Chipper Jones 150.00
MO Magglio Ordonez 100.00
RP Rafael Palmeiro
AP Albert Pujols
SR Scott Rolen
MT Miguel Tejada 120.00

Prime Cuts Pine Tar Series

NM/M
Pine Tar Series
Production 200 sets
Trademark Series: 1-1.5X
Production 100 sets
Prime Cuts Series: 1.5-2X
Production 50 sets
RA Roberto Alomar 20.00
LB Lance Berkman 15.00
EC Eric Chavez 20.00
AD Adam Dunn 25.00
DE Darin Erstad 15.00
NG Nomar Garciaparra 40.00
JG Juan Gonzalez 15.00
TH Todd Helton 25.00
AJ Andruw Jones 20.00
CJ Chipper Jones 30.00
RP Rafael Palmeiro 20.00
MP Mike Piazza 30.00
AP Albert Pujols 40.00
AR Alex Rodriguez 25.00
IR Ivan Rodriguez 25.00
SR Scott Rolen 25.00
AS Alfonso Soriano 25.00
MT Miguel Tejada 15.00
FT Frank Thomas 30.00
MV Mo Vaughn 10.00
BW Bernie Williams 25.00
Pine Tar Series:
Production 200
RA Roberto Alomar 20.00
LB Lance Berkman 15.00
HB Hank Blalock 25.00
BBO Barry Bonds 40.00
EC Eric Chavez 15.00
CD Carlos Delgado 10.00
AD Adam Dunn 25.00
NG Nomar Garciaparra 30.00
LG Luis Gonzalez 8.00
TG Tony Gwynn 20.00
RH Rickey Henderson 25.00
RJ Randy Johnson 25.00
EM Edgar Martinez 20.00
TM Tino Martinez 15.00
MO Magglio Ordonez 10.00
RP Rafael Palmeiro 15.00
JP Jorge Posada 15.00
AP Albert Pujols 40.00
MP Mark Prior 25.00
AR Alex Rodriguez 25.00
AS Alfonso Soriano 20.00

Record Breakers

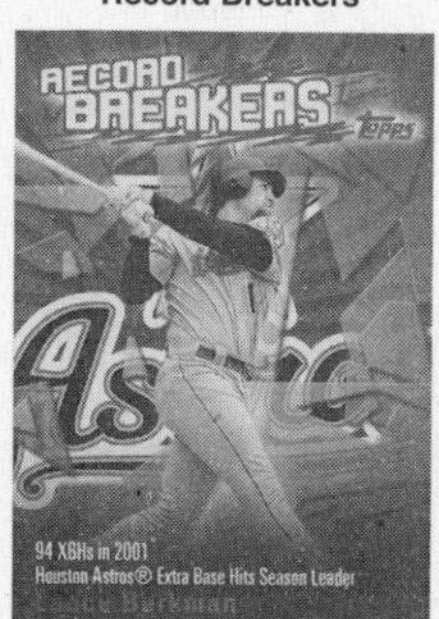

RECORD BREAKERS
94 XBHs in 2001
Houston Astros® Extra Base Hits Season Leader

NM/M
Complete Set (50): 40.00
Common Player: .50
Inserted 1:6
JB Jeff Bagwell 1.50
LBE Lance Berkman 1.00
BB Barry Bonds 5.00
GB George Brett 2.50
LB Lou Brock .50
RCA Rod Carew .50
LC Luis Castillo .50
RC Roger Clemens 2.50
CD Carlos Delgado .50
CF Cliff Floyd .50
GF George Foster .50
AG Andres Galarraga .50
JG Jason Giambi 2.50
BG Bob Gibson 1.00
TG Troy Glaus 1.00
JGO Juan Gonzalez 1.00
LGO Luis Gonzalez .50
SG Shawn Green .75
HG Hank Greenberg .50
KG Ken Griffey Jr. 3.00
VG Vladimir Guerrero 1.50
RG Ron Guidry .50
TH Todd Helton 1.00
RH Rickey Henderson .75
FJ Fergie Jenkins .50
RJ Randy Johnson 1.50
CJ Chipper Jones 3.00
HK Harmon Killebrew 1.00
CK Chuck Klein .50
JM Juan Marichal .50
PM Pedro J. Martinez 1.50
EM Eddie Mathews 1.00
DM Don Mattingly 4.00
FM Fred McGriff .50
JO John Olerud .50
RP Rafael Palmeiro 1.00
MP Mike Piazza 3.00
FR Frank Robinson 1.00
AR Alex Rodriguez 4.00
NR Nolan Ryan 6.00
MSC Mike Schmidt 3.00
CS Curt Schilling 1.00
TS Tom Seaver 1.00
RS Richie Sexson .50
GS Gary Sheffield .50
SS Sammy Sosa 3.00
MS Mike Sweeney .50
HW Hack Wilson .50
PW Preston Wilson .50
RY Robin Yount 1.00

Record Breakers Series 2

NM/M
Complete Set (50): 40.00
Common Player: .50
Inserted 1:6
RA Roberto Alomar 1.00
GA Garret Anderson .75
LA Luis Aparicio .50
JB Jeff Bagwell 1.50
LB Lance Berkman 1.00
CB Craig Biggio .75
WB Wade Boggs .75
BB Barry Bonds 5.00
GB George Brett 2.50
LBR Lou Brock .75
JD Johnny Damon .50
CD Carlos Delgado .50
LD Lenny Dykstra .50
DE Darin Erstad .50
BF Bob Feller .75
GF George Foster .50
NG Nomar Garciaparra 3.00
LG Luis Gonzalez .50
DG Dwight Gooden .50
SG Shawn Green .75
KG Ken Griffey Jr. 2.50
VG Vladimir Guerrero 1.50
TG Tony Gwynn 1.50
TH Todd Helton 1.00
RH Rickey Henderson 1.00
RJ Randy Johnson 1.50
JK Jeff Kent .50
TK Ted Kluszewski .50
GM Greg Maddux 2.50
JM Juan Marichal .50
EM Edgar Martinez .50
WM Willie Mays 4.00
JME Jose Mesa .50
PM Paul Molitor 1.00
JP Jim Palmer .75
TR Tim Raines .50
MR Manny Ramirez 1.50
JR Jim Rice .50
FR Frank Robinson 1.00
AR Alex Rodriguez 4.00
TS Tom Seaver 2.00
RS Richie Sexson .75
JS John Smoltz .50
SS Sammy Sosa 2.50
WS Willie Stargell 1.00
IS Ichiro Suzuki 2.50
FT Frank Thomas 1.50
JT Jim Thome 1.50
LW Larry Walker .50
RY Robin Yount 2.00

Record Breakers Autographs

NM/M
Common Autograph:
CF Cliff Floyd 20.00
LG Luis Gonzalez 30.00
FJ Fergie Jenkins 25.00
CJ Chipper Jones 75.00
HK Harmon Killebrew 60.00
RP Rafael Palmeiro 60.00
MS Mike Schmidt 100.00
RS Richie Sexson 30.00
MSW Mike Sweeney 30.00
RY Robin Yount 75.00

Record Breakers Autographs Series 2

NM/M
Common Autograph: 25.00
Inserted 1:2,218
LA Luis Aparicio 40.00
LB Lance Berkman 40.00
LBR Lou Brock 40.00
GF George Foster 25.00
JM Juan Marichal 40.00
DM Don Mattingly 125.00
WM Willie Mays 150.00

Record Breakers Relics

		NM/M
Common Player:		6.00
JB	Jeff Bagwell/jsy	8.00
LB	Lance Berkman/bat	10.00
GB	George Brett/bat	25.00
LC	Luis Castillo/bat	6.00
CD	Carlos Delgado/jsy	8.00
LGO	Luis Gonzalez/jsy	6.00
SG	Shawn Green/jsy	8.00
HG	Hank Greenberg/bat	30.00
TH	Todd Helton/jsy	10.00
RH	Rickey Henderson/bat	15.00
CJ	Chipper Jones/jsy	12.00
PM	Pedro Martinez/jsy	10.00
DM	Don Mattingly/bat	35.00
MP	Mike Piazza/bat	15.00
FR	Frank Robinson/bat	12.00
AR	Alex Rodriguez/jsy	15.00
NR	Nolan Ryan/jsy	35.00
MS	Mike Sweeney/bat	8.00
HW	Hack Wilson/bat	50.00
RY	Robin Yount/jsy	15.00

Record Breaker Relics Series 2

		NM/M
Common Player:		5.00
WB	Wade Boggs/bat	10.00
GB	George Brett/bat	25.00
CD	Carlos Delgado/jsy	6.00
DE	Darin Erstad/jsy	8.00
LG	Luis Gonzalez/jsy	5.00
TH	Todd Helton/jsy	8.00
RH	Rogers Hornsby/bat	35.00
TK	Ted Kluszewski/bat	15.00
EM	Edgar Martinez/bat	12.00
JR	Jim Rice/jsy	8.00
FR	Frank Robinson/bat	12.00
AR	Alex Rodriguez/jsy	15.00
NRA	Nolan Ryan/jsy	30.00
RS	Richie Sexson/jsy	8.00
FT	Frank Thomas/bat	10.00
RY	Robin Yount	12.00

Red Backs

		NM/M
Complete Set (40):		50.00
Common Player:		.50
Inserted 1:12		
TRB1	Nomar Garciaparra	3.00
TRB2	Ichiro Suzuki	2.50
TRB3	Alex Rodriguez	4.00
TRB4	Sammy Sosa	2.50
TRB5	Barry Bonds	5.00
TRB6	Vladimir Guerrero	1.50
TRB7	Derek Jeter	5.00
TRB8	Miguel Tejada	1.00
TRB9	Alfonso Soriano	2.00
TRB10	Manny Ramirez	1.50
TRB11	Adam Dunn	1.50
TRB12	Jason Giambi	2.50
TRB13	Mike Piazza	3.00
TRB14	Scott Rolen	1.50
TRB15	Shawn Green	.75
TRB16	Randy Johnson	1.50
TRB17	Todd Helton	1.00
TRB18	Garret Anderson	.50
TRB19	Curt Schilling	1.00
TRB20	Albert Pujols	2.00
TRB21	Chipper Jones	2.50
TRB22	Luis Gonzalez	.50
TRB23	Mark Prior	1.50
TRB24	Jim Thome	1.50
TRB25	Ivan Rodriguez	1.00
TRB26	Torii Hunter	1.00
TRB27	Lance Berkman	1.00
TRB28	Troy Glaus	1.50
TRB29	Andruw Jones	1.00
TRB30	Barry Zito	.75
TRB31	Jeff Bagwell	1.50
TRB32	Magglio Ordonez	.75
TRB33	Pat Burrell	1.50
TRB34	Mike Sweeney	.50
TRB35	Rafael Palmeiro	1.00
TRB36	Larry Walker	.50
TRB37	Carlos Delgado	.50
TRB38	Brian Giles	.50
TRB39	Pedro J. Martinez	1.50
TRB40	Greg Maddux	2.50

Stadium Seat Relics

		NM/M
Common Player:		15.00
Inserted 1:37 Series 2 HTA		
JB	Johnny Bench	30.00
DC	Dave Concepcion	20.00
AD	Adam Dunn	20.00
KG	Ken Griffey Jr.	25.00
AK	Austin Kearns	20.00
BL	Barry Larkin	25.00
JM	Joe Morgan	15.00
PO	Paul O'Neill	15.00
TP	Tony Perez	20.00
TS	Tom Seaver	25.00

Team Topps Legends Autographs

	NM/M
Common Player:	
Vida Blue	20.00
Bob Feller	25.00
Willie Mays	125.00
Gil McDougald	12.00
Robin Roberts	25.00
Bobby Thomson	20.00
Luis Tiant	8.00
Carl Yastrzemski	50.00

Turn Back The Clock Autographs

		NM/M
Common Player:		
LD	Lenny Dykstra	15.00
BM	Bill Madlock	10.00
DM	Dale Murphy	40.00
JP	Jim Palmer	20.00
AR	Al Rosen	

2003 TOPPS TRADED & ROOKIES

		NM/M
Complete Set (275):		50.00
Common Player:		.15
Pack (8 + 2 Chrome):		2.00
Box (24):		40.00
Chrome cards:		2-4X
T1	Juan Pierre	.15
T2	Mark Grudzielanek	.15
T3	Tanyon Sturtze	.15
T4	Greg Vaughn	.15
T5	Greg Myers	.15
T6	Randall Simon	.15
T7	Todd Hundley	.15
T8	Marlon Anderson	.15
T9	Jeff Reboulet	.15
T10	Alex Sanchez	.15
T11	Mike Rivera	.15
T12	Todd Walker	.15
T13	Ray King	.15
T14	Shawn Estes	.15
T15	Gary Mathews Jr.	.15
T16	Jaret Wright	.15
T17	Edgardo Alfonzo	.15
T18	Omar Daal	.15
T19	Ryan Rupe	.15
T20	Tony Clark	.15
T21	Damon Minor	.15
T22	Mike Stanton	.15
T23	Ramon Martinez	.15
T24	Armando Rios	.15
T25	Johnny Estrada	.15
T26	Joe Girardi	.15
T27	Ivan Rodriguez	.75
T28	Robert Fick	.15
T29	Rick White	.15
T30	Robert Person	.15
T31	Alan Benes	.15
T32	Chris Carpenter	.15
T33	Chris Widger	.15
T34	Travis Hafner	.15
T35	Mike Venafro	.15
T36	Jon Lieber	.15
T37	Orlando Hernandez	.15
T38	Aaron Myette	.15
T39	Paul Bako	.15
T40	Erubiel Durazo	.15
T41	Mark Guthrie	.15
T42	Steve Avery	.15
T43	Damian Jackson	.15
T44	Rey Ordonez	.15
T45	John Flaherty	.15
T46	Byung-Hyun Kim	.15
T47	Tom Goodwin	.15
T48	Elmer Dessens	.15
T49	Al Martin	.15
T50	Gene Kingsale	.15
T51	Lenny Harris	.15
T52	David Ortiz	.15
T53	John Rocker	.15
T54	Mike DiFelice	.15
T55	Nick Bierbrodt	.15
T56	Todd Zeile	.15
T57	Roberto Hernandez	.15
T58	Albie Lopez	.15
T59	Roberto Alomar	.50
T60	Russ Ortiz	.15
T61	Brian Daubach	.15
T62	Carl Everett	.15
T63	Jeromy Burnitz	.15
T64	Mark Bellhorn	.15
T65	Ruben Sierra	.15
T66	Mike Fetters	.15
T67	Armando Benitez	.15
T68	Deivi Cruz	.15
T69	Jose Cruz Jr.	.15
T70	Jeremy Fikac	.15
T71	Jeff Kent	.25
T72	Andres Galarraga	.25
T73	Rickey Henderson	.50
T74	Royce Clayton	.15
T75	Troy O'Leary	.15
T76	Ron Coomer	.15
T77	Greg Colbrunn	.15
T78	Wes Helms	.15
T79	Kevin Millwood	.25
T80	Damion Easley	.15
T81	Bobby Kielty	.15
T82	Keith Osik	.15
T83	Ramiro Mendoza	.15
T84	Shea Hillenbrand	.15
T85	Shannon Stewart	.15
T86	Eddie Perez	.15
T87	Ugueth Urbina	.15
T88	Orlando Palmeiro	.15
T89	Graeme Lloyd	.15
T90	John Vander Wal	.15
T91	Gary Bennett	.15
T92	Shane Reynolds	.15
T93	Steve Parris	.15
T94	Julio Lugo	.15
T95	John Halama	.15
T96	Carlos Baerga	.15
T97	Jim Parque	.15
T98	Mike Williams	.15
T99	Fred McGriff	.15
T100	Kenny Rogers	.15
T101	Matt Herges	.15
T102	Jay Bell	.15
T103	Esteban Yan	.15
T104	Eric Owens	.15
T105	Aaron Fultz	.15
T106	Rey Sanchez	.15
T107	Jim Thome	1.00
T108	Aaron Boone	.25
T109	Raul Mondesi	.25
T110	Kenny Lofton	.25
T111	Jose Guillen	.15
T112	Aramis Ramirez	.25
T113	Sidney Ponson	.15
T114	Scott Williamson	.15
T115	Robin Ventura	.25
T116	Dusty Baker	.15
T117	Felipe Alou	.15
T118	Buck Showalter	.15
T119	Jack McKeon	.15
T120	Art Howe	.15
T121	Bobby Crosby	.40
T122	Adrian Gonzalez	.15
T123	Kevin Cash	.15
T124	Shin-Soo Choo	.15
T125	Chin-Feng Chen	.25
T126	Miguel Cabrera	.75
T127	Jason Young	.15
T128	Alex Herrera	.15
T129	Jason Dubois	.15
T130	Jeff Mathis	.15
T131	Casey Kotchman	.25
T132	Ed Rogers	.15
T133	Wilson Betemit	.15
T134	Jim Kavourias	.15
T135	Taylor Buchholz	.15
T136	Adam LaRoche	.15
T137	Dallas McPherson	.50
T138	Jesus Cota	.15
T139	Clint Nageotte	.15
T140	Boof Bonser	.15
T141	Walter Young	.15
T142	Joe Crede	.15
T143	Denny Bautista	.15
T144	Victor Diaz	.15
T145	Chris Narveson	.15
T146	Gabe Gross	.15
T147	Jimmy Journell	.15
T148	Rafael Soriano	.15
T149	Jerome Williams	.15
T150	Aaron Cook	.15
T151	Anastacio Martinez	.15
T152	Scott Hairston	.15
T153	John Buck	.15
T154	Ryan Ludwick	.15
T155	Chris Bootcheck	.15
T156	John Rheinecker	.15
T157	Jason Lane	.15
T158	Shelley Duncan	.15
T159	Adam Wainwright	.15
T160	Jason Arnold	.15
T161	Jonny Gomes	.15
T162	James Loney	.15
T163	Mike Fontenot	.15
T164	Khalil Greene	1.00
T165	Sean Burnett	.15
T166	David Martinez	.15
T167	*Felix Pie*	3.00
T168	*Joe Valentine*	.50
T169	*Brandon Webb*	.75
T170	*Matt Diaz*	.25
T171	*Lew Ford*	.75
T172	Jeremy Griffiths	.25
T173	*Matt Hensley*	.50
T174	*Charlie Manning*	.25
T175	*Elizardo Ramirez*	.75
T176	*Greg Aquino*	.25
T177	*Felix Sanchez*	.50
T178	*Kelly Shoppach*	.75
T179	*Bubba Nelson*	.50

T180	*Mike O'Keefe*	.25
T181	*Hanley Ramirez*	3.00
T182	*Todd Wellemeyer*	.75
T183	*Dustin Moseley*	.25
T184	*Eric Crozier*	.50
T185	*Ryan Shealy*	.50
T186	Jeremy Bonderman	.75
T187	*Thomari Story-Harden*	.40
T188	*Dusty Brown*	.50
T189	*Rob Hammock*	.40
T190	*Jorge Piedra*	.25
T191	*Chris De La Cruz*	.25
T192	*Eli Whiteside*	.25
T193	*Jason Kubel*	1.50
T194	*Jon Schuerholz*	.25
T195	*Stephen Randolph*	.25
T196	Andy Sisco	1.00
T197	Sean Smith	.15
T198	*Jon-Mark Sprowl*	.75
T199	*Matt Kata*	.40
T200	*Robinson Cano*	.50
T201	*Nook Logan*	.25
T202	*Ben Francisco*	.50
T203	*Arnie Munoz*	.25
T204	Eric Chavez	.15
T205	*Eric Riggs*	.25
T206	*Beau Kemp*	.25
T207	*Travis Wong*	.50
T208	*Dustin Yount*	.50
T209	Brian McCann	.75
T210	*Wilton Reynolds*	.25
T211	*Matt Bruback*	.50
T212	*Andrew Brown*	.50
T213	*Edgar Gonzalez*	.25
T214	*Eider Torres*	.25
T215	*Aquilino Lopez*	.25
T216	*Bobby Basham*	.50
T217	*Tim Olson*	.50
T218	*Nathan Panther*	.50
T219	*Bryan Grace*	.25
T220	*Dusty Gomon*	.25
T221	*Wilfredo Ledezma*	.25
T222	*Josh Willingham*	.50
T223	*David Cash*	.25
T224	*Oscar Villarreal*	.25
T225	*Jeff Duncan*	.50
T226	*Kade Johnson*	.25
T227	*Luke Steidlmayer*	.25
T228	*Brandon Watson*	.50
T229	Jose Morales	.15
T230	*Mike Gallo*	.25
T231	*Tyler Adamczyk*	.50
T232	Adam Stern	.15
T233	*Brennan King*	.25
T234	Dan Haren	.75
T235	*Michel Hernandez*	.25
T236	Ben Fritz	.15
T237	*Clay Hensley*	.25
T238	*Tyler Johnson*	.25
T239	*Pete LaForest*	.25
T240	*Tyler Martin*	.25
T241	*J.D. Durbin*	.50
T242	*Shane Victorino*	.25
T243	*Rajai Davis*	.50
T244	*Ismael Castro*	.25
T245	*Chien-Ming Wang*	2.00
T246	*Travis Ishikawa*	.40
T247	*Corey Shafer*	.50
T248	*Gary Schneidmiller*	.25
T249	*David Pember*	.25
T250	*Keith Stamler*	.25
T251	*Tyson Graham*	.25
T252	*Ryan Cameron*	.25
T253	Eric Eckenstahler	.15
T254	*Matthew Peterson*	.25
T255	*Dustin McGowan*	.50
T256	*Prentice Redman*	.40
T257	*Haj Turay*	.25
T258	*Carlos Guzman*	.40
T259	*Matt DeMarco*	.25
T260	*Derek Michaelis*	.25
T261	*Brian Burgamy*	.25
T262	*Jay Sitzman*	.25
T263	*Chris Fallon*	.25
T264	*Mike Adams*	.25
T265	*Clint Barmes*	.75
T266	*Eric Reed*	.50
T267	*Willie Eyre*	.25
T268	*Carlos Duran*	.40
T269	*Nick Trzesniak*	.25
T270	*Ferdin Tejeda*	.50
T271	Michael Garciaparra	.25
T272	*Michael Hinckley*	.75
T273	*Branden Florence*	.25
T274	*Trent Oeltjen*	.40
T275	*Mike Neu*	.25

Gold

Stars: 5-10X
Rookies: 1-2.5X
Production 2003 sets

Chrome Refractor

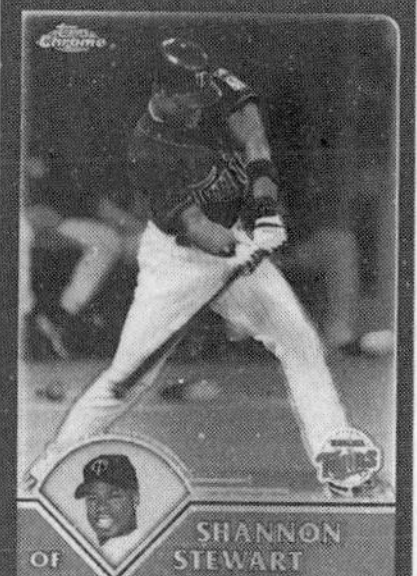

Stars: 4-8X
Rookies: 2-4X
Inserted 1:12

Future Phenoms

		NM/M
Common Player:		4.00
RB	Rocco Baldelli	6.00
WB	Wilson Betemit	4.00
HB	Hank Blalock	8.00
WPB	Willie Bloomquist	15.00
MB	Marlon Byrd	4.00
CC	Chin-Feng Chen	20.00
CDC	Carl Crawford	4.00
TH	Travis Hafner	4.00
TAH	Trey Hodges	4.00
JM	Justin Morneau	8.00
BP	Brandon Phillips	4.00
MR	Michael Restovich	8.00
CS	Chris Snelling	4.00
MT	Mark Teixeira	8.00
JT	Joe Thurston	4.00

Hall of Fame

		NM/M
Common Player:		8.00
GC	Gary Carter	8.00
EM	Eddie Murray	15.00

Hall of Fame Dual

		NM/M
Complete Set (1):		
CM	Gary Carter, Eddie Murray	25.00

Signature Moves

		NM/M
Common Player:		8.00
EA	Erick Almonte	8.00
DB	David Bell	10.00
JB	Joe Borchard	8.00
BC	Bartolo Colon	12.00
JC	Jose Cruz Jr.	8.00
JJC	Jack Cust	10.00
RF	Robert Fick	8.00
CF	Cliff Floyd	15.00
JF	Jesse Foppert	10.00
JG	Joey Gomes	8.00
KG	Khalil Greene	40.00
JL	James Loney	10.00
VM	Victor Martinez	20.00
FP	Felix Pie	50.00
ER	Elizardo Ramirez	12.00
JR	Jose Reyes	20.00
JS	Jason Stokes	15.00
MT	Mark Teixeira	25.00
BU	B.J. Upton	25.00
WY	Walter Young	10.00

Tools of the Trade

		NM/M
Common Player:		4.00
EA	Edgardo Alfonzo	4.00
DB	David Bell	4.00
JC	Jose Cruz Jr.	4.00
ED	Erubiel Durazo	4.00
RD	Ray Durham	4.00
RF	Robert Fick	4.00
CF	Cliff Floyd	4.00
AG	Andres Galarraga	5.00
JG	Jeremy Giambi	4.00
TG	Tom Glavine	6.00
EK	Eric Karros	5.00
JK	Jeff Kent	5.00
KL	Kenny Lofton	10.00
FL	Felipe Lopez	6.00
FM	Fred McGriff	5.00
KM	Kevin Millar	5.00
RO	Rey Ordonez	4.00
JP	Juan Pierre	5.00
SH	Tsuyoshi Shinjo	4.00
SS	Shane Spencer	4.00
JT	Jim Thome	15.00
BT	Bubba Trammell	4.00
RW	Rondell White	4.00
PW	Preston Wilson	4.00
TZ	Todd Zeile	6.00

Tools of the Trade Dual

		NM/M
Common Player:		10.00
KM	Kevin Millwood	10.00
IR	Ivan Rodriguez	15.00
JT	Jim Thome	15.00

2003 TOPPS ALL-TIME FAN FAVORITES

		NM/M
Complete Set (150):		30.00
Common Player:		.25
Pack (6):		4.00
Box (24):		75.00
1	Willie Mays	3.00
2	Whitey Ford	1.00
3	Stan Musial	2.50
4	Paul Blair	.25
5	Harold Reynolds	.25
6	Bob Friend	.25
7	Rod Carew	.75
8	Kirk Gibson	.25
9	Graig Nettles	.25
10	Ozzie Smith	1.00
11	Tony Perez	.25
12	Tim Wallach	.25
13	Bert Campaneris	.25
14	Cory Snyder	.25
15	Dave Parker	.25
16	Darrell Evans	.25
17	Joe Pepitone	.25
18	Don Sutton	.25
19	Dale Murphy	1.00
20	George Brett	2.50
21	Carlton Fisk	.50
22	Bob Watson	.25
23	Wally Joyner	.25
24	Paul Molitor	1.00
25	Keith Hernandez	.25
26	Jerry Koosman	.25
27	George Bell	.25
28	Boog Powell	.25
29	Bruce Sutter	.75
30	Ernie Banks	1.50
31	Steve Lyons	.25
32	Earl Weaver	.25
33	Dave Stieb	.25
34	Alan Trammell	.25
35	Bret Saberhagen	.25
36	J.R. Richard	.25
37	Mickey Rivers	.25
38	Juan Marichal	.75
39	Gaylord Perry	.25
40	Don Mattingly	3.00
41	Bobby Grich	.25
42	Steve Sax	.25
43	Sparky Anderson	.25
44	Luis Aparicio	.25
45	Fergie Jenkins	.50
46	Jim Palmer	.75
47	Howard Johnson	.25
48	Dwight Evans	.25
49	Bill Buckner	.25
50	Cal Ripken Jr.	4.00
51	Jose Cruz	.25
52	Tony Oliva	.25
53	Bobby Richardson	.25
54	Luis Tiant	.25
55	Warren Spahn	1.00
56	Phil Rizzuto	1.00
57	Eric Davis	.25
58	Vida Blue	.25
59	Steve Balboni	.25
60	Mike Schmidt	2.50
61	Ken Griffey Sr.	.25
62	Jim Abbott	.25
63	Whitey Herzog	.25
64	Rich "Goose" Gossage	.25
65	Tony Armas	.25
66	Bill "Moose" Skowron	.25
67	Don Newcombe	.25
68	Bill Madlock	.25
69	Lance Parrish	.25
70	Reggie Jackson	1.50
71	Willie Wilson	.25
72	Terry Pendleton	.25
73	Jimmy Piersall	.25
74	George Foster	.25
75	Bob Horner	.25
76	Chris Sabo	.25
77	Fred Lynn	.25
78	Jim Rice	.25
79	Maury Wills	.25
80	Yogi Berra	1.50
81	Johnny Sain	.25
82	Tom Lasorda	.50
83	Bill Mazeroski	.25
84	John Kruk	.25
85	Bob Feller	.75
86	Frank Robinson	.75
87	Red Schoendienst	.25
88	Gary Carter	.50
89	Andre Dawson	.50
90	Tim McCarver	.25
91	Robin Yount	1.00
92	Phil Niekro	.25
93	Joe Morgan	.25
94	Darren Daulton	.25
95	Bobby Thomson	.25
96	Alvin Davis	.25
97	Robin Roberts	.25
98	Kirby Puckett	1.50
99	Jack Clark	.25
100	Hank Aaron	3.00
101	Orlando Cepeda	.50
102	Vern Law	.25
103	Cecil Cooper	.25
104	Don Larsen	.50
105	Mario Mendoza	.25
106	Tony Gwynn	1.50
107	Ernie Harwell	.25
108a	Monte Irvin (no facsimile autograph)	.75
108b	Monte Irvin (w/ facsimile autograph)	1.50
109	Tommy John	.25
110	Rollie Fingers	.75
111	Johnny Podres	.25
112	Jeff Reardon	.25
113	Buddy Bell	.25
114	Dwight Gooden	.50
115	Garry Templeton	.25
116	Johnny Bench	2.00
117	Joe Rudi	.25
118	Ron Guidry	.50
119	Vince Coleman	.25
120	Al Kaline	2.00
121	Carl Yastrzemski	1.50
122	Hank Bauer	.25
123	Mark Fidrych	.25
124	Paul O'Neill	.50
125	Ron Cey	.25
126	Willie McGee	.25
127	Harmon Killebrew	1.50
128	Dave Concepcion	.25
129	Harold Baines	.25
130	Lou Brock	.50
131	Lee Smith	.25

132 Willie McCovey .75
133 Steve Garvey .25
134 Kent Tekulve .25
135 Tom Seaver 1.50
136 Bo Jackson 1.00
137 Walt Weiss .25
138 Brook Jacoby .25
139 Dennis Eckersley .50
140 Duke Snider 1.00
141 Lenny Dykstra .25
142 Greg Luzinski .25
143 Jim Bunning .25
144 Jose Canseco .75
145 Ron Santo .25
146 Bert Blyleven .25
147 Wade Boggs .75
148 Brooks Robinson 1.00
149 Ray Knight .25
150 Nolan Ryan 4.00

Refractors

Cards (1-150): 3-6X
Production 299 sets

Autographs

NM/M

Common Autograph: 8.00
SP's production 50
HA Hank Aaron/SP 250.00
JA Jim Abbott 10.00
SA Sparky Anderson/SP 30.00
LA Luis Aparicio 10.00
TA Tony Armas 10.00
HBA Harold Baines 15.00
SB Steve Balboni 8.00
EB Ernie Banks/SP 120.00
HB Hank Bauer/SP 35.00
BBE Buddy Bell 15.00
GB George Bell 10.00
JBE Johnny Bench/SP 100.00
YB Yogi Berra/SP 100.00
BBI Buddy Biancalana 8.00
PB Paul Blair 10.00
VB Vida Blue 15.00
BB Bert Blyleven 15.00
WB Wade Boggs/SP 75.00
GBR George Brett/SP 250.00
LB Lou Brock/SP 60.00
BBU Bill Buckner 10.00
JB Jim Bunning/SP 75.00
BC Bert Campaneris 10.00
JOS Jose Canseco/SP 60.00
RCA Rod Carew/SP 75.00
GC Gary Carter/SP 40.00
JCA Joe Carter/SP 35.00
OC Orlando Cepeda/SP 60.00
RCE Ron Cey 10.00
JC Jack Clark 15.00
VC Vince Coleman 10.00
DC Dave Concepcion/SP 35.00
CC Cecil Cooper 10.00
JCR Jose Cruz 10.00
RDA Ron Darling 10.00
DD Darren Daulton 15.00
AD Alvin Davis 8.00
ED Eric Davis 15.00
ADA Andre Dawson/SP 50.00
DDE Doug DeCinces 15.00
RD Rob Dibble 15.00
LDU Leon Durham 10.00
LD Lenny Dykstra 10.00
DEC Dennis Eckersley/SP 60.00
DE Darrell Evans 10.00
DEV Dwight Evans/SP 40.00
BF Bob Feller 15.00
MF Mark Fidrych 10.00
RF Rollie Fingers/SP 40.00
CF Carlton Fisk/SP 60.00
WF Whitey Ford/SP 100.00
GF George Foster 10.00
BFR Bob Friend 10.00
SG Steve Garvey 20.00
KGI Kirk Gibson/SP 75.00
DG Dwight Gooden/SP 30.00
RG Rich "Goose" Gossage/SP 30.00
BGR Bobby Grich 10.00
KG Ken Griffey Sr/SP 30.00
RGU Ron Guidry 15.00
TG Tony Gwynn/SP 100.00
EH Ernie Harwell 40.00
KH Keith Hernandez/SP 60.00
WHE Willie Hernandez 10.00
TH Tom Herr 10.00
WH Whitey Herzog 20.00
BH Bob Horner 8.00
MI Monte Irvin/SP 40.00
BJ Bo Jackson/SP 100.00
RJ Reggie Jackson/SP 100.00
BJA Brook Jacoby 8.00
FJ Fergie Jenkins 15.00
TJ Tommy John 15.00
HJ Howard Johnson 10.00
WJ Wally Joyner 10.00
AK Al Kaline/SP 75.00
HK Harmon Killebrew/SP 80.00
RK Ralph Kiner/SP 65.00
RKI Ron Kittle 10.00
RY Ray Knight 10.00
JK Jerry Koosman 20.00
JKR John Kruk/SP 60.00
CL Carney Lansford 15.00
DL Don Larsen 15.00
TL Tom Lasorda/SP 40.00
VL Vern Law 15.00
BL Bill Lee 10.00
CLE Chet Lemon 10.00
GL Greg Luzinski 15.00
FL Fred Lynn/SP 25.00
SL Steve Lyons 15.00
BMA Bill Madlock 10.00
JMA Juan Marichal/SP 75.00
DON Don Mattingly/SP 100.00
WM Willie Mays/SP 150.00
BMZ Bill Mazeroski/SP 50.00
TM Tim McCarver/SP 40.00
WMC Willie McCovey/SP 60.00
MCG Willie McGee/SP 60.00
TMC Tug McGraw 20.00
MM Mario Mendoza 10.00
KM Kevin Mitchell 10.00
PM Paul Molitor/SP 60.00
JMO John Montefusco 10.00
JM Joe Morgan/SP 30.00
DM Dale Murphy/SP 60.00
SM Stan Musial/SP 120.00
GN Graig Nettles 15.00
DN Don Newcombe/SP 40.00
PN Phil Niekro/SP 40.00
AO Al Oliver 10.00
PO Paul O'Neill/SP 75.00
MP Mike Pagliarulo 10.00
JP Jim Palmer/SP 60.00
DP Dave Parker/SP 40.00
LP Lance Parrish 10.00
TP Terry Pendleton 15.00
JPE Joe Pepitone 10.00
TPE Tony Perez/SP 65.00
GP Gaylord Perry 25.00
BP Boog Powell 15.00
KP Kirby Puckett/SP 65.00
JRE Jeff Reardon 10.00
HR Harold Reynolds/SP 40.00
JRI Jim Rice/SP 45.00
JR J.R. Richard 10.00
CR Cal Ripken Jr./SP 225.00
MR Mickey Rivers 10.00
PR Phil Rizzuto/SP 75.00
RR Robin Roberts 25.00
BRO Brooks Robinson/SP 100.00
FR Frank Robinson/SP 75.00
JRU Joe Rudi 10.00
NR Nolan Ryan/SP 200.00
BSA Bret Saberhagen/SP 40.00
CS Chris Sabo 8.00
RSA Ron Santo 25.00
SS Steve Sax 8.00
MS Mike Schmidt/SP 150.00
RS Red Schoendienst 15.00
TSE Tom Seaver/SP 100.00
KS Kevin Seitzer 10.00
BS Bill "Moose" Skowron 15.00
LS Lee Smith 10.00
OS Ozzie Smith/SP 100.00
DSN Duke Snider/SP 60.00
CN Cory Snyder 15.00
WS Warren Spahn 40.00
CSP Chris Speier 10.00
DS Dave Stieb 15.00
BSU Bruce Sutter 35.00
DSU Don Sutton/SP 40.00
KT Kent Tekulve 10.00
GT Garry Templeton 10.00
BT Bobby Thomson/SP 25.00
LT Luis Tiant/SP 40.00
AT Alan Trammell 20.00
TW Tim Wallach 10.00
BW Bob Watson 10.00
EW Earl Weaver 10.00
WW Walt Weiss 8.00
MW Maury Wills 10.00
WWI Willie Wilson/SP 25.00
CY Carl Yastrzemski/SP 150.00
SY Steve Yeager 10.00
RYO Robin Yount/SP 100.00

Best Seat Relics

NM/M

Common Card: 20.00
BS1 Jim Palmer, Frank Robinson, Brooks Robinson 25.00
BS2 Wally Joyner, Rod Carew, Bobby Grich 20.00
BS3 Phil Garner, Willie Stargell, Dave Parker, Kent Tekulve 20.00
BS4 Rollie Fingers, Robin Yount, Paul Molitor 25.00
BS5 Phil Niekro, Dale Murphy, Bob Horner 20.00

Relics

NM/M

Common Player: 8.00
HBA Harold Baines/bat 12.00
GBR George Brett/jsy 25.00
JOS Jose Canseco/bat 12.00
RCA Rod Carew/bat 10.00
GC Gary Carter/bat 10.00
NC Norm Cash/jsy 25.00
VC Vince Coleman/bat 8.00
JCR Jose Cruz/bat 6.00
RDA Ron Darling/jsy 8.00
ADA Andre Dawson/bat 8.00
LD Lenny Dykstra/bat 8.00
DEC Dennis Eckersley/jsy 10.00
CF Curt Flood/bat 10.00
GF George Foster/bat 8.00
BFR Bob Friend/jsy 6.00
SG Steve Garvey/bat 6.00
KGI Kirk Gibson/bat 8.00
KH Keith Hernandez/bat 12.00
WHE Willie Hernandez/bat 8.00
BH Bob Horner/bat 6.00
BJ Bo Jackson/bat 20.00
WJ Wally Joyner/bat 8.00
GL Greg Luzinski/bat 6.00
FL Fred Lynn/bat 10.00
DON Don Mattingly/bat 30.00
MCG Willie McGee/bat 15.00
TMC Tug McGraw/jsy 10.00
KM Kevin Mitchell/bat 6.00
JM Joe Morgan/bat 10.00
DM Dale Murphy/bat 15.00
PO Paul O'Neill/bat 8.00
DP Dave Parker/bat 6.00
LP Lance Parrish/bat 12.00
KP Kirby Puckett/bat 15.00
HR Harold Reynolds/bat 6.00
JRI Jim Rice/bat 8.00
BR Bobby Richardson/bat 15.00
JRU Joe Rudi/bat 6.00
CS Chris Sabo/bat 8.00
MS Mike Schmidt/bat 25.00
WS Willie Stargell/bat 12.00
AT Alan Trammell/bat 15.00
MW Maury Wills/bat 6.00

Team Topps Leg. Auto.

NM/M

Common Autograph: 10.00
Ernie Banks
Paul Blair 10.00
Lou Brock 30.00
Jim Bunning 15.00
Gary Carter 30.00
Rich "Goose" Gossage 15.00
Al Kaline 50.00
Willie Mays 120.00
Joe Morgan 30.00
Stan Musial 75.00
Graig Nettles 15.00
Johnny Sain 15.00
Mike Schmidt 75.00
Robin Yount

2003 TOPPS BAZOOKA

NM/M

Complete Set (280): 40.00
Common Player: .15
Pack (8): 2.00
Box (24): 40.00
Card #7 has 31 variations
1 Luis Castillo .15
2 Randy Winn .15
3 Orlando Hudson .15
4 Fernando Vina .15
5 Pat Burrell .25
6 Brad Wilkerson .15
7 Bazooka Joe .25
8 Javy Lopez .25
9 Juan Pierre .15
10 Hideo Nomo .40
11 Barry Larkin .25
12 Alfonso Soriano .75
13 Rodrigo Lopez .15
14 Mark Ellis .15
15 Tim Salmon .25
16 Garret Anderson .25
17 Aaron Boone .15
18 Jason Kendall .15
19 Hee Seop Choi .15
20 Jorge Posada .40
21 Sammy Sosa 1.50
22 Mark Prior .75
23 Mark Teixeira .50
24 Manny Ramirez .50
25 Jim Thome .75
26 A.J. Pierzynski .15
27 Scott Rolen .75
28 Austin Kearns .25
29 Bret Boone .15
30 Ken Griffey Jr. 1.00
31 Greg Maddux 1.00
32 Derek Lowe .15
33 David Wells .15
34 A.J. Burnett .15
35 Randall Simon .15
36 Nick Johnson .15
37 Junior Spivey .15
38 Eric Gagne .40
39 Darin Erstad .25
40 Marty Cordova .15
41 Brett Myers .15
42 Mo Vaughn .15
43 Randy Wolf .15
44 Vicente Padilla .15
45 Elmer Dessens .15
46 Jason Simontacchi .15
47 John Mabry .15
48 Torii Hunter .25
49 Lyle Overbay .15
50 Kirk Saarloos .15
51 Bernie Williams .50
52 Wade Miller .15
53 Bobby Abreu .25
54 Wilson Betemit .15
55 Edwin Almonte .15
56 Jarrod Washburn .15
57 Drew Henson .25
58 Tony Batista .15
59 Juan Rivera .15
60 Larry Walker .25
61 Brandon Phillips .15
62 Franklyn German .15
63 Victor Martinez .25
64 Moises Alou .25

No.	Player	NM/M
65	Nomar Garciaparra	1.00
66	Willie Harris	.15
67	Sean Casey	.25
68	Omar Vizquel	.25
69	Robert Fick	.15
70	Curt Schilling	.50
71	Adam Kennedy	.15
72	Scott Hairston	.15
73	Jimmy Journell	.15
74	Rafael Furcal	.25
75	Barry Zito	.25
76	Ed Rogers	.15
77	Cliff Floyd	.15
78	Matt Clement	.15
79	Mike Lowell	.25
80	Randy Johnson	.75
81	Craig Biggio	.25
82	Carlos Beltran	.50
83	Paul LoDuca	.15
84	Jose Vidro	.15
85	Gary Sheffield	.40
86	Jacque Jones	.15
87	Corey Hart	.15
88	Roberto Alomar	.40
89	Robin Ventura	.25
90	Pedro Martinez	.75
91	Scott Hatteberg	.15
92	Marlon Byrd	.15
93	Pokey Reese	.15
94	Sean Burroughs	.15
95	Magglio Ordonez	.25
96	Tsuyoshi Shinjo	.15
97	John Olerud	.15
98	Edgar Renteria	.25
99	Ben Grieve	.15
100	Mariano Rivera	.25
101	Ivan Rodriguez	.50
102	Josh Phelps	.15
103	*Nobuaki Yoshida*	.40
104	Roy Halladay	.15
105	Mark Buehrle	.15
106	Chan Ho Park	.15
107	Joe Kennedy	.15
108	Shin-Soo Choo	.15
109	Ryan Jensen	.15
110	Todd Helton	.50
111	*Chris Duncan*	.40
112	Taggert Bozied	.15
113	Sean Burnett	.15
114	Mike Lieberthal	.15
115	Josh Beckett	.40
116	Andy Pettitte	.40
117	Jose Reyes	.15
118	Bartolo Colon	.15
119	Justin Morneau	.15
120	Lance Berkman	.25
121	*Mike Wodnicki*	.40
122	*Craig Brazell*	.50
123	Troy Glaus	.40
124	John Smoltz	.25
125	Mike Sweeney	.15
126	Jay Gibbons	.15
127	Kerry Wood	.75
128	Ellis Burks	.15
129	Carlos Pena	.15
130	Shawn Green	.25
131	Jason Stokes	.15
132	Raul Ibanez	.15
133	Francisco Rodriguez	.15
134	Adrian Beltre	.25
135	Richie Sexson	.40
136	Paul Byrd	.15
137	Bobby Kielty	.15
138	Dewon Brazelton	.15
139	Jeremy Griffiths	.15
140	Vladimir Guerrero	.75
141	Jake Peavy	.15
142	*Bryan Bullington*	1.00
143	Orlando Cabrera	.15
144	Scott Erickson	.15
145	Doug Mientkiewicz	.15
146	Derrek Lee	.25
147	*Daryl Clark*	.40
148	Trevor Hoffman	.15
149	Gabe Gross	.15
150	Roger Clemens	1.50
151	Khalil Greene	1.00
152	*Cory Doyne*	.40
153	*Brandon Roberson*	.40
154	Josh Fogg	.15
155	Eric Chavez	.25
156	Kris Benson	.15
157	Billy Koch	.15
158	Jermaine Dye	.15
159	*Kip Bouknight*	.40
160	Brian Giles	.25
161	Justin Huber	.15
162	Mike Restovich	.15
163	*Brandon Webb*	.50
164	Odalis Perez	.15
165	Phil Nevin	.15
166	Dontrelle Willis	.25
167	Aaron Heilman	.15
168	*Dustin Moseley*	.50
169	*Rylan Reed*	.40
170	Miguel Tejada	.40
171	Nic Jackson	.15
172	*Anthony Webster*	.40
173	Jorge Julio	.15
174	Kevin Millwood	.25
175	Brian Jordan	.15
176	*Terry Tiffee*	.40
177	Dallas McPherson	.15
178	Freddy Garcia	.15
179	Jamie Moyer	.15
180	Rafael Palmeiro	.50
181	*Mike O'Keefe*	.40
182	*Kevin Youkilis*	1.00
183	Kip Wells	.15
184	Joe Mauer	.25
185	Edgar Martinez	.25
186	*Jaime Bubela*	.40
187	Jose Hernandez	.15
188	Josh Hamilton	.15
189	*Matt Diaz*	.40
190	Chipper Jones	.75
191	Kevin Mench	.15
192	Joey Gomes	.15
193	Shannon Stewart	.15
194	Damian Miller	.15
195	Mike Piazza	1.00
196	Damian Moss	.15
197	Mike Fontenot	.15
198	Shea Hillenbrand	.15
199	*Evel Bastida-Martinez*	.40
200	Jason Giambi	.40
201	*Aron Weston*	.40
202	Frank Thomas	.50
203	Carlos Lee	.15
204	C.C. Sabathia	.15
205	Jim Edmonds	.40
206	*Jemel Spearman*	.40
207	Jason Jennings	.15
208	Jeremy Bonderman	.15
209	Preston Wilson	.15
210	Eric Hinske	.15
211	Will Smith	.15
212	*Matthew Hagen*	.40
213	Joe Randa	.15
214	James Loney	.15
215	Carlos Delgado	.25
216	*Kris Kroski*	.50
217	Cristian Guzman	.15
218	Tomokazu Ohka	.15
219	Al Leiter	.15
220	Adam Dunn	.50
221	Raul Mondesi	.25
222	*Donald Hood*	.40
223	Mark Mulder	.25
224	Mike Williams	.15
225	Ryan Klesko	.25
226	Rich Aurilia	.15
227	Chris Snelling	.15
228	*Gary Schneidmiller*	.40
229	Ichiro Suzuki	1.50
230	Luis Gonzalez	.25
231	Rocco Baldelli	.15
232	*Callix Crabbe*	.40
233	Adrian Gonzalez	.15
234	Corey Koskie	.15
235	Tom Glavine	.40
236	*Kevin Beavers*	.40
237	Frank Catalanotto	.15
238	Kevin Cash	.15
239	*Nick Trzesniak*	.50
240	Paul Konerko	.25
241	Jose Cruz Jr.	.15
242	Hank Blalock	.50
243	J.D. Drew	.25
244	Kazuhiro Sasaki	.15
245	Jeff Bagwell	.50
246	Jason Schmidt	.25
247	Xavier Nady	.15
248	Aramis Ramirez	.40
249	Jimmy Rollins	.15
250	Alex Rodriguez	1.50
251	Terrence Long	.15
252	Derek Jeter	2.00
253	Edgardo Alfonzo	.15
254	Toby Hall	.15
255	Kazuhisa Ishii	.15
256	Brad Nelson	.15
257	Kevin Brown	.25
258	Roy Oswalt	.25
259	Mike Cameron	.15
260	Juan Gonzalez	.40
261	Dmitri Young	.15
262	Jose Jimenez	.15
263	Wily Mo Pena	.25
264	Joe Borchard	.15
265	Mike Mussina	.50
266	Fred McGriff	.25
267	Johnny Damon	.25
268	Joel Pineiro	.15
269	Andruw Jones	.50
270	Tim Hudson	.25
271	Chad Tracy	.15
272	Brad Fullmer	.15
273	Boof Bonser	.15
274	Clint Nageotte	.15
275	Jeff Kent	.25
276	Tino Martinez	.25
277	Matt Morris	.15
278	Jonny Gomes	.15
279	Benito Santiago	.15
280	Albert Pujols	1.50

Silver

Stars: 1-3X
Inserted 1:1

Mini

Stars: 1-3X
Inserted 1:1

Comics

	NM/M
Complete Set (12):	4.00
Common Player:	.25
Inserted 1:4	
Roger Clemens	.40
Nomar Garciaparra	.60
Jason Giambi	.40
Derek Jeter	.75
Randy Johnson	.30
Chipper Jones	.40
Mike Piazza	.50
Albert Pujols	.30
Alex Rodriguez	.60
Alfonso Soriano	.40
Sammy Sosa	.40
Ichiro Suzuki	.50

Blasts

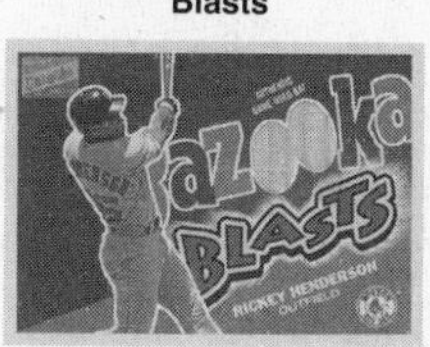

		NM/M
Common Player:		4.00
Refractors:		3-4X
Production 25 sets		
RA	Roberto Alomar	6.00
LB	Lance Berkman	6.00
WB	Wilson Betemit	4.00
JD	Johnny Damon	6.00
CD	Carlos Delgado	5.00
JDD	J.D. Drew	8.00
DE	Darin Erstad	4.00
AG	Andres Galarraga	4.00
LG	Luis Gonzalez	4.00
MG	Mark Grace	
SG	Shawn Green	6.00
TG	Tony Gwynn	8.00
RH	Rickey Henderson	10.00
DH	Drew Henson	4.00
NJ	Nick Johnson	4.00
CJ	Chipper Jones	10.00
RK	Ryan Klesko	4.00
BL	Barry Larkin	
PL	Paul LoDuca	4.00
EM	Edgar Martinez	8.00
TM	Tino Martinez	8.00
RM	Raul Mondesi	4.00
RP	Rafael Palmeiro	6.00
MP	Mike Piazza	12.00
JP	Jorge Posada	8.00
ANR	Aramis Ramirez	6.00
MR	Manny Ramirez	8.00
AR	Alex Rodriguez	12.00
IR	Ivan Rodriguez	8.00
GS	Gary Sheffield	6.00
TS	Tsuyoshi Shinjo	4.00
AS	Alfonso Soriano	10.00
MS	Mike Sweeney	4.00
RV	Robin Ventura	4.00
BW	Bernie Williams	10.00

Piece of Americana

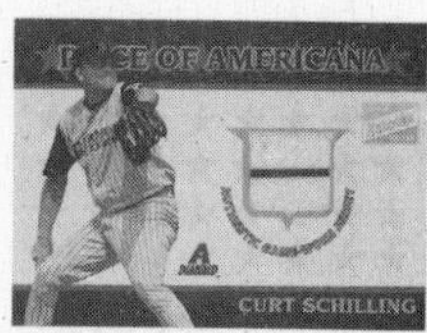

		NM/M
Common Player:		5.00
Refractors:		3-4X
Production 25 sets		
JB	Jeff Bagwell	10.00
CB	Craig Biggio	5.00
BB	Bret Boone	5.00
DB	Dewon Brazelton	5.00
CD	Carlos Delgado	5.00
AD	Adam Dunn	10.00
JE	Jim Edmonds	6.00
RF	Rafael Furcal	5.00
NG	Nomar Garciaparra	15.00
SG	Shawn Green	6.00
CG	Cristian Guzman	5.00
TG	Tony Gwynn	10.00
THA	Toby Hall	5.00
TH	Todd Helton	6.00
AH	Aubrey Huff	5.00
AJ	Andruw Jones	5.00
CJ	Chipper Jones	10.00
JK	Jeff Kent	5.00
AL	Al Leiter	5.00
PL	Paul LoDuca	6.00
MM	Mike Mussina	8.00
MO	Magglio Ordonez	6.00
RP	Rafael Palmeiro	6.00
MP	Mike Piazza	12.00
PA	Albert Pujols	10.00
IR	Ivan Rodriguez	5.00
CS	Curt Schilling	8.00
FT	Frank Thomas	6.00
LW	Larry Walker	5.00
PW	Preston Wilson	5.00

Stand-Ups

		NM/M
Complete Set (25):		20.00
Common Player:		.40
Inserted 1:8		
1	Albert Pujols	2.50
2	Alfonso Soriano	1.00
3	Ichiro Suzuki	2.00
4	Sammy Sosa	2.00
5	Randy Johnson	1.00
6	Torii Hunter	.50
7	Vladimir Guerrero	1.00
8	Nomar Garciaparra	2.00
9	Alex Rodriguez	3.00
10	Troy Glaus	.50
11	Greg Maddux	1.50
12	Derek Jeter	3.00
13	Lance Berkman	.40
14	Larry Walker	.40
15	Adam Dunn	.50
16	Shawn Green	.50
17	Curt Schilling	.75
18	Todd Helton	.75
19	Pedro Martinez	1.00
20	Pat Burrell	.50
21	Miguel Tejada	.50
22	Manny Ramirez	1.00
23	Mike Piazza	1.50
24	Chipper Jones	1.00
25	Jason Giambi	1.00

2003 TOPPS CHROME

	NM/M
Complete Set (440):	160.00
Common Player:	.25
Series 1 & 2 Hobby Pack (4):	2.50

No.	Player	Price
	Hobby Box (24):	50.00
1	Alex Rodriguez	4.00
2	Eddie Guardado	.25
3	Curt Schilling	1.50
4	Andruw Jones	1.00
5	Magglio Ordonez	.75
6	Todd Helton	1.00
7	Odalis Perez	.25
8	Edgardo Alfonzo	.25
9	Eric Hinske	.25
10	Danny Bautista	.25
11	Sammy Sosa	2.50
12	Roberto Alomar	1.00
13	Roger Clemens	3.00
14	Austin Kearns	1.00
15	Luis Gonzalez	.50
16	Mo Vaughn	.50
17	Alfonso Soriano	1.50
18	Orlando Cabrera	.25
19	Hideo Nomo	.75
20	Omar Vizquel	.25
21	Greg Maddux	2.50
22	Fred McGriff	.50
23	Frank Thomas	1.25
24	Shawn Green	.75
25	Jacque Jones	.25
26	Bernie Williams	1.00
27	Corey Patterson	.75
28	Cesar Izturis	.25
29	Larry Walker	.75
30	Darren Dreifort	.25
31	Al Leiter	.25
32	Jason Marquis	.25
33	Sean Casey	.25
34	Craig Counsell	.25
35	Albert Pujols	3.00
36	Kyle Lohse	.25
37	Paul LoDuca	.25
38	Roy Oswalt	.50
39	Danny Graves	.25
40	Kevin Millwood	.25
41	Lance Berkman	1.00
42	Denny Hocking	.25
43	Jose Valentin	.25
44	Josh Beckett	.75
45	Nomar Garciaparra	3.00
46	Craig Biggio	.50
47	Omar Daal	.25
48	Jimmy Rollins	.25
49	Jermaine Dye	.25
50	Edgar Renteria	.50
51	Brandon Duckworth	.25
52	Luis Castillo	.25
53	Andy Ashby	.25
54	Mike Williams	.25
55	Benito Santiago	.25
56	Bret Boone	.25
57	Randy Wolf	.25
58	Ivan Rodriguez	1.50
59	Shannon Stewart	.25
60	Jose Cruz Jr.	.25
61	Billy Wagner	.25
62	Alex Gonzalez	.25
63	Ichiro Suzuki	3.00
64	Joe McEwing	.25
65	Mark Mulder	.50
66	Mike Cameron	.25
67	Corey Koskie	.25
68	Marlon Anderson	.25
69	Jason Kendall	.25
70	J.T. Snow Jr.	.25
71	Edgar Martinez	.50
72	Vernon Wells	.25
73	Vladimir Guerrero	2.00
74	Adam Dunn	1.50
75	Barry Zito	.50
76	Jeff Kent	.50
77	Russ Ortiz	.25
78	Phil Nevin	.25
79	Carlos Beltran	1.00
80	Mike Lowell	.50
81	Bob Wickman	.25
82	Junior Spivey	.25
83	Melvin Mora	.25
84	Derrek Lee	.50
85	Chuck Knoblauch	.25
86	Eric Gagne	.75
87	Orlando Hernandez	.50
88	Robert Person	.25
89	Elmer Dessens	.25
90	Wade Miller	.25
91	Adrian Beltre	.50
92	Kazuhiro Sasaki	.25
93	Timoniel Perez	.25
94	Jose Vidro	.25
95	Geronimo Gil	.25
96	Trot Nixon	.25
97	Denny Neagle	.25
98	Roberto Hernandez	.25
99	David Ortiz	1.50
100	Robb Nen	.25
101	Sidney Ponson	.25
102	Kevin Appier	.25
103	Javier Lopez	.50
104	Jeff Conine	.25
105	Mark Buehrle	.25
106	Jason Simontacchi	.25
107	Jose Jimenez	.25
108	Brian Jordan	.25
109	Brad Wilkerson	.25
110	Scott Hatteberg	.25
111	Matt Morris	.50
112	Miguel Tejada	.75
113	Rafael Furcal	.50
114	Steve Cox	.25
115	Roy Halladay	.25
116	David Eckstein	.25
117	Tomokazu Ohka	.25
118	Jack Wilson	.25
119	Randall Simon	.25
120	Jamie Moyer	.25
121	Andy Benes	.25
122	Tino Martinez	.50
123	Esteban Yan	.25
124	Jason Isringhausen	.25
125	Chris Carpenter	.25
126	Aaron Rowand	.25
127	Brandon Inge	.25
128	Jose Vizcaino	.25
129	Jose Mesa	.25
130	Troy Percival	.25
131	Jon Lieber	.25
132	Brian Giles	.50
133	Aaron Boone	.25
134	Bobby Higginson	.25
135	Luis Rivas	.25
136	Troy Glaus	1.00
137	Jim Thome	1.50
138	Ramon Martinez	.25
139	Jay Gibbons	.25
140	Mike Lieberthal	.25
141	Juan Uribe	.25
142	Gary Sheffield	.75
143	Ramon Santiago	.25
144	Ben Sheets	.50
145	Tony Armas Jr.	.25
146	Kazuhisa Ishii	.25
147	Erubiel Durazo	.25
148	Jerry Hairston Jr.	.25
149	Byung-Hyun Kim	.25
150	Marcus Giles	.25
151	Johnny Damon	.75
152	Terrence Long	.25
153	Juan Pierre	.25
154	Aramis Ramirez	.75
155	Brent Abernathy	.25
156	Ismael Valdes	.25
157	Mike Mussina	1.00
158	Ramon Hernandez	.25
159	Adam Kennedy	.25
160	Tony Womack	.25
161	Tony Batista	.25
162	Kip Wells	.25
163	Jeromy Burnitz	.25
164	Todd Hundley	.25
165	Tim Wakefield	.25
166	Derek Lowe	.25
167	Jorge Posada	.75
168	Ramon Ortiz	.25
169	Brent Butler	.25
170	Shane Halter	.25
171	Matt Lawton	.25
172	Alex Sanchez	.25
173	Eric Milton	.25
174	Vicente Padilla	.25
175	Steve Karsay	.25
176	Mark Prior	1.50
177	Kerry Wood	1.50
178	Jason LaRue	.25
179	Danys Baez	.25
180	Nick Neugebauer	.25
181	Andres Galarraga	.25
182	Jason Giambi	1.00
183	Aubrey Huff	.25
184	Juan Gonzalez	1.00
185	Ugueth Urbina	.25
186	Rickey Henderson	.75
187	Brad Fullmer	.25
188	Todd Zeile	.25
189	Jason Jennings	.25
190	Vladimir Nunez	.25
191	David Justice	.50
192	Brian Lawrence	.25
193	Pat Burrell	.50
194	Pokey Reese	.25
195	Robert Fick	.25
196	C.C. Sabathia	.25
197	Fernando Vina	.25
198	Sean Burroughs	.25
199	Ellis Burks	.25
200	Joe Randa	.25
201	*Chris Duncan*	1.00
202	*Franklin Gutierrez*	1.00
203	Adam LaRoche	.25
204	*Manuel Ramirez*	1.00
205	*Il Kim*	1.00
206	*Daryl Clark*	1.00
207	Sean Pierce	.25
208	*Andy Marte*	5.00
209	*Bernie Castro*	1.00
210	*Jason Perry*	1.00
211	*Jaime Bubela*	1.00
212	Alexis Rios	.25
213	*Brendan Harris*	2.00
214	*Ramon A. Martinez*	.25
215	*Terry Tiffee*	1.00
216	*Kevin Youkilis*	4.00
217	*Derell McCall*	1.00
218	Scott Tyler	1.00
219	*Craig Brazell*	2.50
220	Walter Young	1.00
221	Francisco Rodriguez	.40
222	Chipper Jones	2.00
223	Chris Singleton	.25
224	Cliff Floyd	.25
225	Bobby Hill	.25
226	Antonio Osuna	.25
227	Barry Larkin	.50
228	Dean Palmer	.25
229	Eric Owens	.25
230	Randy Johnson	1.50
231	Jeff Suppan	.25
232	Eric Karros	.25
233	Johan Santana	.25
234	Javier Vazquez	.25
235	John Thomson	.25
236	Nick Johnson	.25
237	Mark Ellis	.25
238	Doug Glanville	.25
239	Ken Griffey Jr.	2.50
240	Bubba Trammell	.25
241	Livan Hernandez	.25
242	Desi Relaford	.25
243	Eli Marrero	.25
244	Jared Sandberg	.25
245	Barry Bonds	4.00
246	Aaron Sele	.25
247	Derek Jeter	5.00
248	Eric Byrnes	.25
249	Rich Aurilia	.25
250	Joel Pineiro	.25
251	Chuck Finley	.25
252	Bengie Molina	.25
253	Steve Finley	.25
254	Marty Cordova	.25
255	Shea Hillenbrand	.25
256	Milton Bradley	.25
257	Carlos Pena	.25
258	Brad Ausmus	.25
259	Carlos Delgado	.75
260	Kevin Mench	.25
261	Joe Kennedy	.25
262	Mark McLemore	.25
263	Bill Mueller	.25
264	Ricky Ledee	.25
265	Ted Lilly	.25
266	Sterling Hitchcock	.25
267	Scott Strickland	.25
268	Damion Easley	.25
269	Torii Hunter	.50
270	Brad Radke	.25
271	Geoff Jenkins	.25
272	Paul Byrd	.25
273	Morgan Ensberg	.25
274	Mike Hampton	.25
275	Flash Gordon	.25
276	John Burkett	.25
277	Rodrigo Lopez	.25
278	Tim Spooneybarger	.25
279	Quinton McCracken	.25
280	Tim Salmon	.50
281	Jarrod Washburn	.25
282	Pedro J. Martinez	1.50
283	Julio Lugo	.25
284	Armando Benitez	.25
285	Raul Mondesi	.50
286	Robin Ventura	.25
287	Bobby Abreu	.50
288	Josh Fogg	.25
289	Ryan Klesko	.50
290	Tsuyoshi Shinjo	.25
291	Jim Edmonds	.75
292	Chan Ho Park	.25
293	John Mabry	.25
294	Woody Williams	.25
295	Scott Schoeneweis	.25
296	Brian Anderson	.25
297	Brett Tomko	.25
298	Scott Erickson	.25
299	Tony Clark	.25
300	Danny Wright	.25
301	Jason Schmidt	.75
302	Scott Williamson	.25
303	Einar Diaz	.25
304	Jay Payton	.25
305	Juan Acevedo	.25
306	Ben Grieve	.25
307	Raul Ibanez	.25
308	Richie Sexson	.75
309	Rick Reed	.25
310	Pedro Astacio	.25
311	Bud Smith	.25
312	Tomas Perez	.25
313	Adam Eaton	.25
314	Rafael Palmeiro	1.50
315	Jason Tyner	.25
316	Scott Rolen	2.00
317	Randy Winn	.25
318	Ryan Jensen	.25
319	Trevor Hoffman	.25
320	Craig Wilson	.25
321	Jeremy Giambi	.25
322	Andy Pettitte	.50
323	John Franco	.25
324	Felipe Lopez	.25
325	Mike Piazza	3.00
326	Cristian Guzman	.25
327	Jose Hernandez	.25
328	Octavio Dotel	.25
329	Brad Penny	.25
330	Charles Johnson	.25
331	Ryan Dempster	.25
332	Joe Crede	.25
333	Chad Hermansen	.25
334	Gary Matthews Jr.	.25
335	Frank Catalanotto	.25
336	Darin Erstad	.50
337	Matt Williams	.25
338	B.J. Surhoff	.25
339	Kerry Ligtenberg	.25
340	Mike Bordick	.25
341	Joe Girardi	.25
342	D'Angelo Jimenez	.25
343	Paul Konerko	.25
344	Joe Mays	.25
345	Marquis Grissom	.25
346	Neifi Perez	.25
347	Preston Wilson	.25
348	Jeff Weaver	.25
349	Eric Chavez	.50
350	Placido Polanco	.25
351	Ray Lankford	.25
352	James Baldwin	.25
353	Toby Hall	.25
354	Benji Gil	.25
355	Damian Moss	.25
356	Jorge Julio	.25
357	Matt Clement	.25
358	Lee Stevens	.25
359	Dave Roberts	.25
360	J.C. Romero	.25
361	Bartolo Colon	.25
362	Roger Cedeno	.25
363	Mariano Rivera	.50
364	Billy Koch	.25
365	Manny Ramirez	1.50
366	Travis Lee	.25
367	Oliver Perez	.25
368	Rafael Soriano	.25
369	Damian Miller	.25
370	John Smoltz	.50
371	Willis Roberts	.25
372	Tim Hudson	.50
373	Moises Alou	.50
374	Corky Miller	.25
375	Ben Broussard	.25

376 Gabe Kapler .25
377 Chris Woodward .25
378 Todd Hollandsworth .25
379 So Taguchi .25
380 John Olerud .50
381 Reggie Sanders .25
382 Jake Peavy .25
383 Kris Benson .25
384 Ray Durham .25
385 Boomer Wells .25
386 Tom Glavine .75
387 Antonio Alfonseca .25
388 Keith Foulke .25
389 Shawn Estes .25
390 Mark Grace .50
391 Dmitri Young .25
392 A.J. Burnett .25
393 Richard Hidalgo .25
394 Mike Sweeney .25
395 Doug Mientkiewicz .25
396 Cory Lidle .25
397 Jeff Bagwell 1.50
398 Steve Sparks .25
399 Sandy Alomar Jr. .25
400 John Lackey .25
401 Rick Helling .25
402 Carlos Lee .25
403 Garret Anderson .50
404 Vinny Castilla .25
405 David Bell .25
406 Freddy Garcia .25
407 Scott Spiezio .25
408 Russell Branyan .25
409 *Jose Contreras* 3.00
410 Kevin Brown .50
411 Tyler Houston .25
412 A.J. Pierzynski .25
413 Peter Bergeron .25
414 Brett Myers .25
415 Kenny Lofton .25
416 Ben Davis .25
417 J.D. Drew .50
418 Ricky Gutierrez .25
419 Mark Redman .25
420 Juan Encarnacion .25
421 *Bryan Bullington* 4.00
422 Jeremy Guthrie .25
423 Joey Gomes .25
424 *Evel Bastida-Martinez* 1.50
425 *Brian Wright* 1.00
426 B.J. Upton .25
427 Jeff Francis .25
428 Jeremy Hermida .25
429 Khalil Greene 3.00
430 Darrell Rasner .25
431 Brandon Phillips, Victor Martinez .75
432 Hee Seop Choi, Nic Jackson .75
433 Dontrelle Willis, Jason Stokes 1.00
434 Chad Tracy, Lyle Overbay .25
435 Joe Borchard, Corwin Malone .25
436 Joe Mauer, Justin Morneau 1.00
437 Drew Henson, Brandon Claussen .50
438 Chase Utley, Gavin Floyd .25
439 Taggert Bozied, Xavier Nady .25
440 Aaron Heilman, Jose Reyes 1.50

Refractors

Stars: 1-2X
Production 699 sets
Gold Refractors: 1.5-3X
Production 449 sets
Black Refractors: 3-5X
Production 199 sets

Uncirculated X-Fractors

Stars: 5-10X
Inserted 1:hobby box
Production 50 sets

Blue Backs Relics

NM/M
Common Player: 6.00
Bat Relics inserted 1:236
RA Roberto Alomar/bat 10.00
JBA Jeff Bagwell/jsy 10.00
JB Josh Beckett/jsy 10.00
LB Lance Berkman/bat 8.00
EC Eric Chavez/jsy 6.00
AD Adam Dunn/jsy 15.00
NG Nomar Garciaparra/jsy 15.00
SG Shawn Green/jsy 6.00
NJ Nick Johnson/bat 8.00
PK Paul Konerko/jsy 8.00
MO Magglio Ordonez/jsy 8.00
MP Mike Piazza/jsy 15.00
AP Albert Pujols/jsy 15.00
AR Alex Rodriguez/bat 15.00
JR Jimmy Rollins/jsy 6.00
TS Tsuyoshi Shinjo/bat 8.00
AS Alfonso Soriano/bat 10.00
FT Frank Thomas/jsy 8.00
BW Bernie Williams/bat 10.00
KW Kerry Wood/jsy 8.00

Red Backs Relics

NM/M
Common Player: 5.00
Inserted 1:49
RA Roberto Alomar 8.00
GA Garret Anderson 8.00
JB Jeff Bagwell 8.00
PB Pat Burrell 5.00
AD Adam Dunn 8.00
NG Nomar Garciaparra 12.00
TH Todd Helton 8.00
TKH Torii Hunter 8.00
RJ Randy Johnson 8.00
AJ Andruw Jones 8.00
CJ Chipper Jones 10.00
PM Pedro J. Martinez 10.00
MP Mike Piazza 10.00
AP Albert Pujols 15.00
MR Manny Ramirez 8.00
AR Alex Rodriguez 10.00
SR Scott Rolen 10.00
CS Curt Schilling 8.00
AS Alfonso Soriano 10.00
MS Mike Sweeney 5.00

Record Breakers Relics

NM/M
Common Player: 5.00
Bat Relics 1:364
JB Jeff Bagwell 10.00
CB Craig Biggio 5.00
LB Lou Brock 15.00
CD Carlos Delgado 5.00
CF Cliff Floyd 5.00
JG Juan Gonzalez 8.00
LG Luis Gonzalez 5.00
TH Todd Helton 8.00
RH Rickey Henderson 15.00
RJ Randy Johnson 10.00
HK Harmon Killebrew 15.00
JM Joe Morgan 8.00
SM Stan Musial 25.00
MP Mike Piazza 15.00
AR Alex Rodriguez 15.00
MS Mike Schmidt 25.00
FT Frank Thomas 8.00
KS Kazuhiro Sasaki 5.00
LW Larry Walker 5.00
RY Robin Yount 15.00

Record Breakers Relics Series 2

NM/M
Common Player: 5.00
JB Jeff Bagwell 8.00
BB Barry Bonds 20.00
BB2 Barry Bonds 20.00
BB3 Barry Bonds 20.00
JC Jose Canseco 10.00
RC Rod Carew 8.00
RC2 Rod Carew 8.00
DLE Dennis Eckersley 8.00
DE Darin Erstad 5.00
LG Luis Gonzalez 5.00
RH Rickey Henderson 15.00
RJ Randy Johnson 8.00
DM Don Mattingly 30.00
PM Paul Molitor 15.00
MR Manny Ramirez 15.00
HR Harold Reynolds 5.00
AR Alex Rodriguez 15.00
TS Tom Seaver 20.00
JS John Smoltz 8.00
SS Sammy Sosa 15.00

2003 TOPPS GALLERY

NM/M
Complete Set (200): 60.00
Common Player: .25
SP's inserted 1:20
Pack (5): 2.50
Box (20): 45.00
1 Jason Giambi .50
1 Jason Giambi/ SP/Drk Blue Jsy 2.00
2 Miguel Tejada .50
3 Mike Lieberthal .25
4 Jason Kendall .40
5 Robb Nen .25
6 Freddy Garcia .25
7 Scott Rolen .75
8 David Wells .25
9 Rafael Palmeiro .75
10 Garret Anderson .50
11 Curt Schilling .75
12 Greg Maddux 1.00
13 Rodrigo Lopez .25
14 Nomar Garciaparra 1.50
14 N.Garciaparra/ SP/Navy elbow pad 4.00
15 Kerry Wood .75
16 Frank Thomas .75
17 Ken Griffey Jr. 1.00
18 Jim Thome .75
19 Todd Helton .75
20 Lance Berkman .50
21 Robert Fick .25
22 Kevin Brown .40
23 Richie Sexson .50
24 Eddie Guardado .25
25 Vladimir Guerrero 1.00
26 Mike Piazza 1.50
27 Bernie Williams .50
28 Eric Chavez .40
29 Jimmy Rollins .25
30 Ichiro Suzuki 1.50
30 Ichiro Suzuki/SP/ black long shirt 3.00
31 J.D. Drew .25
32 Nick Johnson .25
33 Shannon Stewart .25
34 Tim Salmon .40
35 Andruw Jones .75
36 Jay Gibbons .25
37 Johnny Damon .50
38 Fred McGriff .40
39 Carlos Lee .25
40 Adam Dunn .75
40 Adam Dunn/ SP/red sleeves & helmet 1.50
41 Jason Jennings .25
42 Mike Lowell .40
43 Mike Sweeney .25
44 Shawn Green .50
45 Doug Mientkiewicz .25
46 Bartolo Colon .40
47 Edgardo Alfonzo .25
48 Roger Clemens 2.00
49 Randy Wolf .25
50 Alex Rodriguez 2.00
50 Alex Rodriguez/ SP/red undershirt 4.00
51 Vernon Wells .40
52 Kenny Lofton .40
53 Mariano Rivera .40
54 Brian Jordan .25
55 Roberto Alomar .50
56 Carlos Pena .25
57 Moises Alou .40
58 John Smoltz .40
59 Adam Kennedy .25
60 Randy Johnson 1.00
61 Mark Buehrle .25
62 C.C. Sabathia .25
63 Craig Biggio .40
64 Eric Karros .25
65 Jose Vidro .25
66 Tim Hudson .40
67 Trevor Hoffman .25
68 Bret Boone .25
69 Carl Crawford .25
70 Derek Jeter 2.50
71 Troy Percival .25
72 Gary Sheffield .50
73 Rickey Henderson .50
74 Paul Konerko .25
75 Larry Walker .40
76 Pat Burrell .50
77 Brian Giles .40
78 Jeff Kent .40
79 Kazuhiro Sasaki .25
80 Chipper Jones 1.00
81 Darin Erstad .40
82 Sean Casey .40
83 Luis Gonzalez .40
84 Roy Oswalt .40
85 Dustan Mohr .25
86 Al Leiter .25
87 Mike Mussina .50
88 Vicente Padilla .25
89 Rich Aurilia .25
90 Albert Pujols 2.00
91 John Olerud .40
92 Ivan Rodriguez .75
93 Eric Hinske .25
94 Phil Nevin .25
95 Barry Zito .50
96 Armando Benitez .25
97 Torii Hunter .50
98 Paul LoDuca .25
99 Preston Wilson .40
100 Sammy Sosa 1.50
100 Sammy Sosa/ SP/No shin guard 4.00
101 Jarrod Washburn .25
102 Steve Finley .25
103 Cliff Floyd .25
104 Mark Prior 1.00
105 Austin Kearns .50
106 Jeff Bagwell .75
107 A.J. Pierzynski .25
108 Pedro J. Martinez 1.00
109 Orlando Cabrera .25
110 Raul Mondesi .25
111 Russ Ortiz .25
112 Ruben Sierra .25
113 Tino Martinez .25
114 Manny Ramirez .75
115 Troy Glaus .50
116 Magglio Ordonez .50
117 Omar Vizquel .40
118 Carlos Beltran .40
119 Jose Hernandez .25
120 Javier Vazquez .25
121 Jorge Posada .50
122 Aramis Ramirez .25
123 Jason Schmidt .40
124 Jamie Moyer .25
125 Jim Edmonds .50
126 Aubrey Huff .25
127 Carlos Delgado .50
128 Junior Spivey .25
129 Tom Glavine .50
130 Marty Cordova .25
131 Derek Lowe .25
132 Ellis Burks .25
133 Barry Bonds 2.50
134 Josh Beckett .25
135 Raul Ibanez .25
136 Kazuhisa Ishii .25
137 Geoff Jenkins .25
138 Eric Milton .25
139 Mo Vaughn .25
140 Mark Mulder .40
141 Bobby Abreu .40
142 Ryan Klesko .40
143 Tsuyoshi Shinjo .25
144 Jose Mesa .25
145 Shea Hillenbrand .25
146 Edgar Renteria .25
147 Juan Gonzalez .50
148 Edgar Martinez .25
149 Matt Morris .25
150 Alfonso Soriano 1.00
150 Alfonso Soriano/ SP/No elbow pad 2.50

151	*Bryan Bullington*	2.50
151	*Bryan Bullington/ SP/red background*	6.00
152	*Andy Marte*	3.00
152	*Andy Marte/ SP/No necklace*	4.00
153	*Brendan Harris*	1.00
154	*Juan Camacho*	1.00
155	Byron Gettis	1.00
156	*Daryl Clark*	1.00
157	*J.D. Durbin*	1.50
158	*Craig Brazell*	1.50
158	*Craig Brazell/ SP/black jersey*	3.00
159	*Jason Kubel*	4.00
160	*Brandon Roberson*	1.00
161	*Jose Contreras*	2.00
162	*Hanley Ramirez*	3.00
163	*Jaime Bubela*	1.00
164	*Chris Duncan*	1.50
165	*Tyler Johnson*	1.00
166	Adam LaRoche	.25
167	Walter Young	.25
168	Ryan Kibler	.25
169	*Tommy Whiteman*	.25
170	Trey Hodges	.25
171	Francisco Rodriguez	.25
172	Jason Arnold	.25
173	Brett Myers	.25
174	Rocco Baldelli	.50
175	Adrian Gonzalez	.25
176	Dontrelle Willis	1.00
177	Kris Honel	.25
178	Marlon Byrd	.25
179	Aaron Heilman	.25
180	Casey Kotchman	.25
181	Miguel Cabrera	.25
182	Hee Seop Choi	.50
183	Drew Henson	.25
184	Jose Reyes	.50
185	Michael Cuddyer	.25
186	Brandon Phillips	.25
187	Victor Martinez	.25
188	Joe Mauer	.25
189	Hank Blalock	.75
190	Mark Teixeira	.25
191	Willie Mays	2.00
192	George Brett	2.00
193	Tony Gwynn	1.00
194	Carl Yastrzemski	1.00
195	Nolan Ryan	3.00
196	Reggie Jackson	.75
197	Mike Schmidt	1.50
198	Cal Ripken Jr.	3.00
199	Don Mattingly	2.00
200	Tom Seaver	.75

Rainbow Refractors

Stars (1-200): 2-3X
Inserted 1:1
Rookies (151-165): 1X
Inserted 1:1

Currency Collection

		NM/M
	Common Player:	4.00
	Inserted 1:box	
BA	Bobby Abreu	6.00
HC	Hee Seop Choi	6.00
BC	Bartolo Colon	4.00
LG	Luis Gonzalez	4.00
VG	Vladimir Guerrero	12.00
KI	Kazuhisa Ishii	4.00
AJ	Andruw Jones	8.00
RL	Rodrigo Lopez	6.00
PM	Pedro J. Martinez	10.00
RM	Raul Mondesi	4.00
MO	Magglio Ordonez	8.00
VP	Vicente Padilla	6.00
RP	Rafael Palmeiro	6.00
AP	Albert Pujols	20.00
MR	Manny Ramirez	8.00
ER	Edgar Renteria	6.00
JR	Jose Reyes	8.00
MRI	Mariano Rivera	10.00
FR	Francisco Rodriguez	4.00
KS	Kazuhiro Sasaki	4.00
AS	Alfonso Soriano	8.00
SS	Sammy Sosa	15.00
IS	Ichiro Suzuki	15.00
OV	Omar Vizquel	10.00
LW	Larry Walker	5.00

Heritage

		NM/M
	Complete Set (25):	75.00
	Common Player:	1.50
	Inserted 1:10	
WB	Wade Boggs	1.50
GB	George Brett	8.00
JC	Jose Canseco	1.50
RC	Roger Clemens	6.00
AD	Adam Dunn	2.00
NG	Nomar Garciaparra	5.00
TG	Tom Glavine	1.50
SG	Shawn Green	1.50
TGW	Tony Gwynn	3.00
RH	Rickey Henderson	2.00
DJ	Derek Jeter	8.00
RJ	Randy Johnson	3.00
HK	Harmon Killebrew	4.00
KR	Jerry Koosman, Nolan Ryan	10.00
WM	Willie Mays	8.00
HN	Hideo Nomo	2.00
KP	Kirby Puckett	3.00
IR	Ivan Rodriguez	2.00
DS	Duke Snider	2.00
AS	Alfonso Soriano	3.00
IS	Ichiro Suzuki	5.00
MT	Miguel Tejada	1.50
JT	Jim Thome	2.00
BW	Bernie Williams	2.00
CY	Carl Yastrzemski	3.00

Heritage Relics

		NM/M
	Common Player:	5.00
WB	Wade Boggs	5.00
GB	George Brett	20.00
JC	Jose Canseco	8.00
RC	Roger Clemens	15.00
SG	Shawn Green	5.00
TG	Tony Gwynn	10.00
RH	Rickey Henderson	10.00
HK	Harmon Killebrew	25.00
HN	Hideo Nomo	15.00
KP	Kirby Puckett	15.00

Heritage Autographed Relics

		NM/M
	Inserted 1:3,260	
WB	Wade Boggs	70.00
GB	George Brett/25	
TG	Tony Gwynn	
KP	Kirby Puckett/25	80.00

Originals Relics

		NM/M
	Common Player:	5.00
RA	Roberto Alomar	6.00
MA	Moises Alou	5.00
LB	Lance Berkman	5.00
BB	Bret Boone	5.00
AD	Adam Dunn	6.00
NG	Nomar Garciaparra	12.00
LG	Luis Gonzalez	5.00
SG	Shawn Green	5.00
TG	Tony Gwynn	8.00
TH	Todd Helton	8.00
RH	Rickey Henderson	8.00
DH	Drew Henson	5.00
THU	Torii Hunter	8.00
AJ	Andruw Jones	6.00
CJ	Chipper Jones	8.00
JM	Joe Mauer	8.00
MO	Magglio Ordonez	5.00
RP	Rafael Palmeiro	8.00
MP	Mike Piazza	10.00
AP	Albert Pujols	15.00
MR	Manny Ramirez	8.00
AR	Alex Rodriguez	10.00
IR	Ivan Rodriguez	8.00
GS	Gary Sheffield	6.00
AS	Alfonso Soriano	8.00
MT	Miguel Tejada	5.00
FT	Frank Thomas	8.00
JT	Jim Thome	8.00
BW	Bernie Williams	6.00
CY	Carl Yastrzemski	20.00

2003 TOPPS GALLERY HOF EDITION

		NM/M
	Complete Set (74):	35.00
	Common Player:	.40
	SP variations:	2-4X
	Inserted 1:1	
	Pack (5):	4.00
	Box (20):	70.00
1	Willie Mays	2.00
1	Willie Mays/ SP/Gold Background	
2	Al Kaline	1.50
2	Al Kaline/No orange & white	
3	Hank Aaron	2.00
3	Hank Aaron/blue hat/red bill	
4	Carl Yastrzemski	1.00
4	Carl Yastrzemski/Red letters	
5	Luis Aparicio	.40
5	Luis Aparicio/black bat	
6	Sam Crawford	.40
6	Sam Crawford/Navy uni.	
7	Tom Lasorda	.40
7	Tom Lasorda/ Red background	
8	John McGraw	.40
8	John McGraw/NY on jsy	
9	Edd Roush	.40
9	Edd Roush/Red "C" on hat	
10	Reggie Jackson	1.00
10	Reggie Jackson/ Red background	
11	Jim "Catfish" Hunter	.40
11	Catfish Hunter/White jsy	
12	Roberto Clemente	2.00
12	Roberto Clemente/ Yellow uni.	
13	Ralph Kiner	.40
13	Eddie Collins/Navy uni.	
14	Frankie Frisch	.40
14	Frankie Frisch/ Blue background	
15	Nolan Ryan	4.00
15	Nolan Ryan/red sleeves	
16	Brooks Robinson	1.00
16	Brooks Robinson/ Green background	
17	Phil Niekro	.40
17	Phil Niekro/ Blue hat w/red bill	
18	Joe Cronin	.40
18	Joe Cronin/White sleeves	
19	Joe Tinker	.40
19	Joe Tinker/Blue hat	
20	Johnny Bench	1.50
20	Johnny Bench/ Night background	
21	Harry Heilmann	.40
21	Harry Heilmann/ Night background	
22	Ernie Harwell	.40
22	Ernie Harwell/ Green background	
23	Warren Spahn	1.00
23	Warren Spahn/No Patch	
24	George Kelly	.40
24	George Kelly/Red Bill on hat	
25	Phil Rizzuto	1.00
25	Phil Rizzuto/ Green background	
26	Robin Roberts	.40
26	Robin Roberts/ Night background	
27	Ozzie Smith	1.00
27	Ozzie Smith/Black Bat	
28	Jim Palmer	.40
28	Jim Palmer/Black Hat	
29	Duke Snider	1.00
29	Duke Snider/USA Flag Patch	
30	Bob Feller	.40
30	Bob Feller/Gray uni.	
31	Buck Leonard	.40
31	Buck Leonard/Red background	
32	Kirby Puckett	1.00
32	Kirby Puckett/Black Bat	
33	Monte Irvin	.40
33	Monte Irvin/Gray Jsy	
34	Chuck Klein	.40
34	Chuck Klein/Red Socks	
35	Willie Stargell	.75
35	Willie Stargell/White uni.	
36	Juan Marichal	.40
36	Juan Marichal/ Gold background	
37	Lou Brock	.40
37	Lou Brock/Night background	
38	Bucky Harris	.40
38	Bucky Harris/Red "W"	
39	Bobby Doerr	.40
39	Bobby Doerr/Red background	
40	Lee MacPhail	.40
40	Lee MacPhail/Blue background	
41	Heinie Manush	.40
41	Heinie Manush/Navy sleeve	
42	George Brett	1.50
42	George Brett/No Patch	
43	Harmon Killebrew	1.50
43	Harmon Killebrew/White uni.	
44	Whitey Ford	1.00
44	Whitey Ford/Night background	
45	Eddie Mathews	1.50
45	Eddie Mathews/ Night background	
46	Gaylord Perry	.40
46	Gaylord Perry/ Green background	
47	Red Schoendienst	.40
47	Red Schoendienst/ No red uni. stripes	
48	Earl Weaver	.40
48	Earl Weaver/Night background	
49	Joe Morgan	.40
49	Joe Morgan/Night background	
50	Mike Schmidt	2.00

50	Mike Schmidt/White uni.	
51	Willie McCovey	.40
51	Willie McCovey/Black bat	
52	Stan Musial	2.00
52	Stan Musial/ Night background	
53	Don Sutton	.40
53	Don Sutton/Gray background	
54	Hank Greenberg	.40
54	Hank Greenberg/ No player background	
55	Robin Yount	1.00
55	Robin Yount/ No people background	
56	Tom Seaver	1.00
56	Tom Seaver/Black glove	
57	Tony Perez	.40
57	Tony Perez/Gray uni.	
58	George Sisler	.40
58	George Sisler/ No ad background	
59	Jim Bottomley	.40
59	Jim Bottomley/Red hat	
60	Yogi Berra	1.50
60	Yogi Berra/ Navy chest protector	
61	Fred Lindstrom	.40
61	Fred Lindstrom/Red bill	
62	Napoleon Lajoie	.40
62	Napoleon Lajoie/Navy uni.	
63	Frank Robinson	1.00
63	Frank Robinson/White uni.	
64	Carlton Fisk	.40
64	Carlton Fisk/Red letters	
65	Orlando Cepeda	.40
65	Orlando Cepeda/Sunset sky	
66	Fergie Jenkins	.40
66	Fergie Jenkins/Black glove	
67	Ernie Banks	1.50
67	Ernie Banks/Night background	
68	Bill Mazeroski	.40
68	Bill Mazeroski/White sleeves	
69	Jim Bunning	.40
69	Jim Bunning/White uni.	
70	Rollie Fingers	.40
70	Rollie Fingers/ Night background	
71	Jimmie Foxx	1.50
71	Jimmie Foxx/White sleeves	
72	Rod Carew	.40
72	Rod Carew/Blue batting gloves	
73	Sparky Anderson	.40
73	Sparky Anderson/ Yellow background	
74	George Kell	.40
74	George Kell/White "D" on hat	

Refractors

Cards (1-74):	2-4X
Inserted 1:1	
SP Refractors:	4-8X
Inserted 1:box	

Currency Connection

		NM/M
Common Player:		12.00
1:box		
EB	Ernie Banks	20.00
OC	Orlando Cepeda	15.00
TC	Ty Cobb	40.00
BF	Bob Feller	25.00
LG	Lou Gehrig	35.00
HG	Hank Greenberg	20.00
WM	Willie Mays	20.00
WMA	Willie Mays	20.00
WMC	Willie McCovey	12.00
SM	Stan Musial	30.00
JR	Jackie Robinson	25.00
BR	Babe Ruth	60.00

Accent Mark Autograph

		NM/M
Common Player:		
Refractors:		1-2X
Production 25 sets		
YB	Yogi Berra	65.00
BD	Bobby Doerr	40.00
LM	Lee MacPhail	40.00
RR	Robin Roberts	40.00
RS	Red Schoendienst	30.00
WS	Warren Spahn	30.00

ARTifact Relics

		NM/M
Common Player:		6.00
Refractors:		1.5-3X
Production 25 sets		
HA	Hank Aaron/bat	25.00
SA	Sparky Anderson/jsy	8.00
LA	Luis Aparicio/bat	15.00
EB	Ernie Banks/jsy	30.00
JBE	Johnny Bench/bat	12.00
JB	Jim Bottomley/bat	15.00
GB	George Brett/jsy	25.00
LB	Lou Brock/bat	
RCA	Rod Carew/jsy	10.00
OC	Orlando Cepeda/bat	8.00
TC	Ty Cobb/bat	80.00
EC	Eddie Collins/bat	12.00
SC	Sam Crawford/bat	20.00
BD	Bobby Doerr/jsy	15.00
CF	Carlton Fisk/bat	8.00
JF	Jimmie Foxx/bat	
FF	Frankie Frisch/bat	15.00
LG	Lou Gehrig/bat	125.00
HG	Hank Greenberg/bat	25.00
BH	Bucky Harris/bat	12.00
HH	Harry Heilmann/bat	20.00
RJ	Reggie Jackson/bat	10.00
AK	Al Kaline/bat	15.00
GK	George Kelly/bat	20.00
HK	Harmon Killebrew/jsy	25.00
CK	Chuck Klein/bat	15.00
TLA	Tom Lasorda/jsy	15.00
HM	Heinie Manush/bat	15.00
EM	Eddie Mathews/jsy	30.00
WM	Willie Mays/jsy	45.00
WMC	Willie McCovey/bat	8.00
JM	Joe Morgan/bat	8.00
SM	Stan Musial/bat	20.00
PN	Phil Niekro/jsy	6.00
JP	Jim Palmer/jsy	20.00
TP	Tony Perez/bat	8.00
GP	Gaylord Perry/jsy	8.00
KP	Kirby Puckett/bat	12.00
BRO	Brooks Robinson/bat	20.00
FR	Frank Robinson/bat	10.00
JR	Jackie Robinson/bat	35.00
ER	Edd Roush/bat	20.00
BR	Babe Ruth/bat	140.00
NR	Nolan Ryan/bat	40.00
MS	Mike Schmidt/jsy	25.00
RSC	Red Schoendienst/jsy	
TS	Tom Seaver/bat	25.00
GS	George Sisler/bat	12.00
OS	Ozzie Smith/bat	15.00
DS	Duke Snider/bat	12.00
WS	Willie Stargell/jsy	10.00
DSU	Don Sutton/bat	8.00
JT	Joe Tinker/bat	20.00
HW	Honus Wagner/bat	140.00
PW	Paul Waner/bat	20.00
HWI	Hoyt Wilhelm/jsy	8.00
CY	Carl Yastrzemski/bat	20.00
RY	Robin Yount/bat	10.00

ARTifact Auto. Relics

		NM/M
Common Player:		30.00
Refractors:		1-1.5X
Production 25 sets		
OC	Orlando Cepeda	30.00
BD	Bobby Doerr	45.00
AK	Al Kaline	75.00
HK	Harmon Killebrew	75.00
JM	Joe Morgan	40.00
JP	Jim Palmer	50.00
BRO	Brooks Robinson	60.00
MS	Mike Schmidt	225.00
RS	Red Schoendienst	30.00
DS	Duke Snider	50.00
RY	Robin Yount	125.00

Patch Relics

		NM/M
Common Player:		40.00
Production 25 sets		
GB	George Brett	125.00
CH	Jim "Catfish" Hunter	40.00
FJ	Fergie Jenkins	40.00
HK	Harmon Killebrew	80.00
TL	Tom Lasorda	40.00
EM	Eddie Matthews	80.00
WM	Willie McCovey	40.00
JP	Jim Palmer	40.00
NR	Nolan Ryan	125.00
MS	Mike Schmidt	125.00
OS	Ozzie Smith	75.00
DS	Don Sutton	
CY	Carl Yastrzemski	80.00
RY	Robin Yount	85.00

Team Topps Legends Autos

	NM/M
Common Player:	
Vern Law	20.00
Al Kaline	
Johnny Sain	30.00

2003 TOPPS HERITAGE

		NM/M
Complete Set (430):		350.00
Common Player:		.40
Common High # SP (364-430):		4.00
Pack (8):		4.00
Box (24):		90.00
1	Alex Rodriguez	3.00
1	Alex Rodriguez/ black SP	10.00
2	Jose Cruz Jr.	.40
3	Ichiro Suzuki/SP	10.00
4	Rich Aurilia	.40
5	Trevor Hoffman	.40
6	Brian Giles	.75
6	Brian Giles/old logo SP	5.00
7	Albert Pujols	2.00
7	Albert Pujols/black SP	10.00
8	Vicente Padilla	.40
9	Bobby Crosby	.40
10	Derek Jeter	4.00
10	Derek Jeter/ old logo SP	15.00
11	Pat Burrell	.50
11	Pat Burrell/old logo SP	5.00
12	Armando Benitez	.40
13	Javier Vazquez	.40
14	Justin Morneau	.40
15	Doug Mientkiewicz	.40
16	Kevin Brown	.40
17	Alexis Gomez	.40
18	Lance Berkman	.50
18	Lance Berkman/ black SP	5.00
19	Adrian Gonzalez	.40
20	Todd Helton	.75
20	Todd Helton/black SP	6.00
21	Carlos Pena	.40
22	Matt Lawton	.40
23	Elmer Dessens	.40
24	Hee Seop Choi	.40
25	*Chris Duncan/SP*	5.00
26	Ugueth Urbina	.40
27	Rodrigo Lopez	.40
27	Rodrigo Lopez/ old logo SP	4.00
28	Damian Moss	.40
29	Steve Finley	.40
30	Sammy Sosa	2.00
30	Sammy Sosa/ old logo SP	10.00
31	Kevin Cash	.40
32	Kenny Rogers	.40
33	Ben Grieve	.40
34	Jason Simontacchi	.40
35	Shin-Soo Choo	.40
36	Freddy Garcia	.40
37	Jesse Foppert	.40
38	Tony LaRussa	.40
39	Mark Kotsay	.40
40	Barry Zito	.75
41	Josh Fogg	.40
42	Marlon Byrd	.40
43	Marcus Thames	.40
44	Al Leiter	.50
45	Michael Barrett	.40
46	Jake Peavy	.40
47	Dustan Mohr	.40
48	Alex Sanchez	.40
49	Chin-Feng Chen	.40
50	Kazuhisa Ishii	.40
50	Kazuhisa Ishii/black SP	5.00
51	Carlos Beltran	.75
52	*Franklin Gutierrez*	2.00
53	Miguel Cabrera	.75
54	Roger Clemens	2.50
55	Juan Cruz	.40
56	Jason Young	.40
57	Alex Herrera	.40
58	Aaron Boone	.40
59	Mark Buehrle	.40
60	Larry Walker	.75
61	Morgan Ensberg	.40
62	Barry Larkin	.75
63	Joe Borchard	.40
64	Jason Dubois	.40
65	Juan Acevedo	.40
66	Jay Gibbons	.40
67	Vinny Castilla	.40
68	Jeff Mathis	.40
69	Curt Schilling	1.00
70	Garret Anderson	.50
71	Josh Phelps	.40
72	Chan Ho Park	.40
73	Edgar Renteria	.50
74	Kazuhiro Sasaki	.40
75	Lloyd McClendon	.40
76	Jon Lieber	.40
77	Rolando Viera	.40
78	Jeff Conine	.40
79	Kevin Millwood	.40
80	Randy Johnson	1.50
80	Randy Johnson/ black SP	8.00
81	Troy Percival	.40
82	Cliff Floyd	.40
83	Tony Graffanino	.40
84	Austin Kearns	.50
85	*Manuel Ramirez/SP*	5.00
86	Jim Tracy	.40
87	Rondell White	.40
88	Trot Nixon	.40
89	Carlos Lee	.40
90	Mike Lowell	.50
91	Raul Ibanez	.40
92	Ricardo Rodriguez	.40
93	Ben Sheets	.50
94	*Jason Perry/SP*	4.00

95 Mark Teixeira .75
96 Brad Fullmer .40
97 Casey Kotchman .40
98 Craig Counsell .40
99 Jason Marquis .40
100 Nomar Garciaparra 2.00
100 Nomar Garciaparra/old logo SP 10.00
101 Ed Rogers .40
102 Wilson Betemit .40
103 *Wayne Lydon* 1.00
104 Jack Cust .40
105 Derrek Lee .50
106 Jim Kavourias .40
107 Joe Randa .40
108 Taylor Buchholz .40
109 Gabe Kapler .40
110 Preston Wilson .40
111 Craig Biggio .50
112 Paul LoDuca .40
113 Eddie Guardado .40
114 Andres Galarraga .40
115 Edgardo Alfonzo .40
116 Robin Ventura .40
117 Jeremy Giambi .40
118 Ray Durham .40
119 Mariano Rivera .50
120 Jimmy Rollins .40
121 Dennis Tankersley .40
122 Jason Schmidt .50
123 Bret Boone .40
124 Josh Hamilton .40
125 Scott Rolen .75
126 Steve Cox .40
127 Larry Bowa .40
128 Adam LaRoche/SP 5.00
129 Ryan Klesko .40
130 Tim Hudson .50
131 Brandon Claussen .40
132 *Craig Brazell/SP* 6.00
133 Grady Little .40
134 Jarrod Washburn .40
135 Lyle Overbay .40
136 John Burkett .40
137 *Daryl Clark* .75
138 Kirk Rueter .40
139 Joe Mauer, Jake Mauer .75
139 Joe Mauer, Jake Mauer/black SP 4.00
140 Troy Glaus .50
141 Trey Hodges/SP 4.00
142 Dallas McPherson .40
143 Art Howe .40
144 Jesus Cota .40
145 J.R. House .40
146 Reggie Sanders .40
147 Clint Nageotte .40
148 Jim Edmonds .50
149 Carl Crawford .40
150 Mike Piazza 2.00
150 Mike Piazza/black SP 10.00
151 Seung Jun Song .40
152 Roberto Hernandez .40
153 Marquis Grissom .40
154 Billy Wagner .40
155 Josh Beckett .40
156 Randall Simon .40
156 Randall Simon/old logo SP 4.00
157 Ben Broussard .40
158 Russell Branyan .40
159 Frank Thomas 1.00
160 Alex Escobar .40
161 Mark Bellhorn .40
162 Melvin Mora .40
163 Andruw Jones .75
164 Danny Bautista .40
165 Ramon Ortiz .40
166 Wily Mo Pena .50
167 Jose Jimenez .40
168 Mark Redman .40
169 Angel Berroa .40
170 *Andy Marte/SP* 10.00
171 Juan Gonzalez .75
172 Fernando Vina .40
173 Joel Pineiro .40
174 Boof Bonser .40
175 *Bernie Castro/SP* 4.00
176 Bobby Cox .40
177 Jeff Kent .50
178 Oliver Perez .40
179 Chase Utley .40
180 Mark Mulder .50
181 Bobby Abreu .50
182 Ramiro Mendoza .40
183 Aaron Heilman .40
184 A.J. Pierzynski .40
185 Eric Gagne .75
186 Kirk Saarloos .40
187 Ron Gardenhire .40
188 Dmitri Young .40
189 Todd Zeile .40
190 Jim Thome 1.00
190 Jim Thome/old logo SP 8.00
191 Cliff Lee .40
192 Matt Morris .40
193 Robert Fick .40
194 C.C. Sabathia .40
195 Alexis Rios .40
196 D'Angelo Jimenez .40
197 Edgar Martinez .50
198 Robb Nen .40
199 Taggert Bozied .40
200 Vladimir Guerrero/SP 8.00
201 Walter Young/SP 4.00
202 *Brendan Harris* .75
203 Mike Hargrove .40
204 Vernon Wells .40
205 Hank Blalock .75
206 Mike Cameron .40
207 Tony Batista .40
208 Matt Williams .40
209 Tony Womack .40
210 *Ramon A. Martinez* .40
211 Aaron Sele .40
212 Mark Grace .75
213 Joe Crede .40
214 Ryan Dempster .40
215 Omar Vizquel .40
216 Juan Pierre .40
217 Denny Bautista .40
218 Chuck Knoblauch .40
219 Eric Karros .40
220 Victor Diaz .40
221 Jacque Jones .40
222 Jose Vidro .40
223 Joe McEwing .40
224 Nick Johnson .40
225 Eric Chavez .50
226 Jose Mesa .40
227 Aramis Ramirez .50
228 John Lackey .40
229 David Bell .40
230 John Olerud .50
231 Tino Martinez .40
232 Randy Winn .40
233 Todd Hollandsworth .40
234 *Ruddy Lugo* .75
235 Carlos Delgado .75
236 Chris Narveson .40
237 Tim Salmon .75
238 Orlando Palmeiro .40
239 *Jeff Clark/SP* 4.00
240 Byung-Hyun Kim .40
241 Mike Remlinger .40
242 Johnny Damon .50
243 Corey Patterson .50
244 Paul Konerko .50
245 Danny Graves .40
246 Ellis Burks .40
247 Gavin Floyd .40
248 *Jaime Bubela* .75
249 Sean Burroughs .40
250 Alex Rodriguez/SP 10.00
251 Gabe Gross .40
252 Rafael Palmeiro .75
253 Dewon Brazelton .40
254 Jimmy Journell .40
255 Rafael Soriano .40
256 Jerome Williams .40
257 Xavier Nady .40
258 Mike Williams .40
259 Randy Wolf .40
260 Miguel Tejada .75
260 Miguel Tejada/black SP 5.00
261 Juan Rivera .40
262 Rey Ordonez .40
263 Bartolo Colon .40
264 Eric Milton .40
265 Jeffrey Hammonds .40
266 Odalis Perez .40
267 Mike Sweeney .40
268 Richard Hidalgo .40
269 Alex Gonzalez .40
270 Aaron Cook .40
271 Earl Snyder .40
272 Todd Walker .40
273 Aaron Rowand .40
274 Matt Clement .40
275 Anastacio Martinez .40
276 Mike Bordick .40
277 John Smoltz .50
278 Scott Hairston .40
279 David Eckstein .40
280 Shannon Stewart .40
281 Carl Everett .40
282 Aubrey Huff .40
283 Mike Mussina .75
284 Ruben Sierra .40
285 Russ Ortiz .40
286 Brian Lawrence .40
287 Kip Wells .40
288 Placido Polanco .40
289 Ted Lilly .40
290 Andy Pettitte .50
291 John Buck .40
292 Orlando Cabrera .40
293 Cristian Guzman .40
294 Ruben Quevedo .40
295 Cesar Izturis .40
296 Ryan Ludwick .40
297 Roy Oswalt .50
298 Jason Stokes .40
299 Mike Hampton .40
300 Pedro Martinez 1.50
301 Nic Jackson .40
302 Magglio Ordonez .50
302 Magglio Ordonez/old logo SP 5.00
303 Manny Ramirez 1.00
304 Jorge Julio .40
305 Javy Lopez .50
306 Roy Halladay .40
307 Kevin Mench .40
308 Jason Isringhausen .40
309 Carlos Guillen .40
310 Tsuyoshi Shinjo .40
311 Phil Nevin .40
312 Pokey Reese .40
313 Jorge Padilla .40
314 Jermaine Dye .40
315 Boomer Wells .40
316 Mo Vaughn .40
317 Bernie Williams .75
318 Michael Restovich .40
319 Jose Hernandez .40
320 Richie Sexson .60
321 Daryle Ward .40
322 Luis Castillo .40
323 Rene Reyes .40
324 Victor Martinez .40
325 Adam Dunn 1.00
325 Adam Dunn/old logo SP 8.00
326 Corwin Malone .40
327 Kerry Wood 1.00
328 Rickey Henderson .75
329 Marty Cordova .40
330 Greg Maddux 2.00
331 Miguel Batista .40
332 Chris Bootcheck .40
333 Carlos Baerga .40
334 Antonio Alfonseca .40
335 Shane Halter .40
336 Juan Encarnacion .40
337 Flash Gordon .40
338 Hideo Nomo .75
339 Torii Hunter .75
340 Alfonso Soriano 1.00
340 Alfonso Soriano/black SP 6.00
341 Roberto Alomar .75
342 David Justice .50
343 Mike Lieberthal .40
344 Jeff Weaver .40
345 Timoniel Perez .40
346 Travis Lee .40
347 Sean Casey .40
348 Willie Harris .40
349 Derek Lowe .40
350 Tom Glavine .75
351 Eric Hinske .40
352 Rocco Baldelli .40
353 J.D. Drew .60
354 Jamie Moyer .40
355 Todd Linden .40
356 Benito Santiago .40
357 Brad Baker .40
358 Alex Gonzalez .40
359 Brandon Duckworth .40
360 John Rheinecker .40
361 Orlando Hernandez .40
362 Pedro Astacio .40
363 Brad Wilkerson .40
364 David Ortiz 6.00
365 Geoff Jenkins 4.00
366 Brian Jordan 4.00
367 Paul Byrd 4.00
368 Jason Lane 4.00
369 Jeff Bagwell 6.00
370 Bobby Higginson 4.00
371 Juan Uribe 4.00
372 Lee Stevens 4.00
373 Jimmy Haynes 4.00
374 Jose Valentin 4.00
375 Ken Griffey Jr. 10.00
376 Shea Hillenbrand 4.00
377 Gary Matthews Jr. 4.00
378 Gary Sheffield 5.00
379 Rick Helling 4.00
380 Junior Spivey 4.00
381 Francisco Rodriguez 4.00
382 Chipper Jones 6.00
383 Orlando Hudson 4.00
384 Ivan Rodriguez 6.00
385 Chris Snelling 4.00
386 Kenny Lofton 4.00
387 Eric Cyr 4.00
388 Jason Kendall 4.00
389 Marlon Anderson 4.00
390 Billy Koch 4.00
391 Shelly Duncan 4.00
392 Jose Reyes 4.00
393 Fernando Tatis 4.00
394 Michael Cuddyer 4.00
395 Mark Prior 6.00
396 Dontrelle Willis 4.00
397 Jay Payton 4.00
398 Brandon Phillips 4.00
399 *Dustin Moseley* 4.00
400 Jason Giambi 4.00
401 John Mabry 4.00
402 Ron Gant 4.00
403 J.T. Snow 4.00
404 Jeff Cirillo 4.00
405 Darin Erstad 4.00
406 Luis Gonzalez 4.00
407 Marcus Giles 4.00
408 Brian Daubach 4.00
409 Moises Alou 4.00
410 Raul Mondesi 4.00
411 Adrian Beltre 6.00
412 A.J. Burnett 4.00
413 Jason Jennings 4.00
414 Edwin Almonte 4.00
415 Fred McGriff 5.00
416 Tim Raines Jr. 4.00
417 Rafael Furcal 4.00
418 Erubiel Durazo 4.00
419 Drew Henson 4.00
420 Kevin Appier 4.00
421 Chad Tracy 4.00
422 Adam Wainwright 4.00
423 Choo Freeman 4.00
424 Sandy Alomar Jr. 4.00
425 Corey Koskie 4.00
426 Jeromy Burnitz 4.00
427 Jorge Posada 6.00
428 Jason Arnold 4.00
429 Brett Myers 4.00
430 Shawn Green 5.00

Chrome

NM/M

Common Player: 1.00
Production 1,954 sets
Refractors: 1.5-2X
Production 554 sets

THC1 Alex Rodriguez 8.00
THC2 Ichiro Suzuki 8.00
THC3 Brian Giles 1.50
THC4 Albert Pujols 4.00
THC5 Derek Jeter 10.00
THC6 Pat Burrell 3.00
THC7 Lance Berkman 2.00
THC8 Todd Helton 2.00
THC9 Chris Duncan 1.00
THC10 Rodrigo Lopez 1.00
THC11 Sammy Sosa 5.00
THC12 Barry Zito 2.00
THC13 Marlon Byrd 1.00
THC14 Al Leiter 1.00
THC15 Kazuhisa Ishii 1.50
THC16 Franklin Gutierrez 1.00
THC17 Roger Clemens 5.00
THC18 Mark Buehrle 1.00
THC19 Larry Walker 1.50
THC20 Curt Schilling 2.50
THC21 Garret Anderson 1.50
THC22 Randy Johnson 3.00
THC23 Cliff Floyd 1.00
THC24 Austin Kearns 2.00
THC25 Manuel Ramirez 1.00
THC26 Raul Ibanez 1.00
THC27 Jason Perry 1.00
THC28 Mark Teixeira 2.00
THC29 Nomar Garciaparra 6.00
THC30 Wayne Lydon 1.00
THC31 Preston Wilson 1.00
THC32 Paul LoDuca 1.00
THC33 Edgardo Alfonzo 1.00
THC34 Jeremy Giambi 1.00
THC35 Mariano Rivera 1.50
THC36 Jimmy Rollins 1.00
THC37 Bret Boone 1.00
THC38 Scott Rolen 2.00
THC39 Adam LaRoche 1.00
THC40 Tim Hudson 1.50

THC41 Craig Brazell 1.00
THC42 Daryl Clark 1.00
THC43 Joe Mauer, Jake Mauer 2.00
THC44 Troy Glaus 2.50
THC45 Sean Pierce 1.00
THC46 Carl Crawford 1.00
THC47 Mike Piazza 6.00
THC48 Josh Beckett 1.00
THC49 Randall Simon 1.00
THC50 Frank Thomas 2.50
THC51 Andruw Jones 2.00
THC52 Andy Marte 1.00
THC53 Bernie Castro 1.00
THC54 Jim Thome 3.00
THC55 Alexis Rios 1.00
THC56 Vladimir Guerrero 4.00
THC57 Walter Young 1.00
THC58 Hank Blalock 1.50
THC59 Ramon A. Martinez 1.00
THC60 Jacque Jones 1.00
THC61 Nick Johnson 1.00
THC62 Ruddy Lugo 1.00
THC63 Carlos Delgado 1.50
THC64 Jeff Clark 1.00
THC65 Johnny Damon 1.00
THC66 Jaime Bubela 1.00
THC67 Alex Rodriguez 8.00
THC68 Rafael Palmeiro 2.00
THC69 Miguel Tejada 2.00
THC70 Bartolo Colon 1.00
THC71 Mike Sweeney 1.00
THC72 John Smoltz 1.00
THC73 Shannon Stewart 1.00
THC74 Mike Mussina 2.00
THC75 Roy Oswalt 1.50
THC76 Pedro Martinez 4.00
THC77 Magglio Ordonez 2.00
THC78 Manny Ramirez 3.00
THC79 Boomer Wells 1.00
THC80 Richie Sexson 1.50
THC81 Adam Dunn 2.50
THC82 Greg Maddux 5.00
THC83 Alfonso Soriano 5.00
THC84 Roberto Alomar 2.00
THC85 Derek Lowe 1.00
THC86 Tom Glavine 2.00
THC87 Jeff Bagwell 2.50
THC88 Ken Griffey Jr. 6.00
THC89 Shea Hillenbrand 1.00
THC90 Gary Sheffield 1.50
THC91 Chipper Jones 5.00
THC92 Orlando Hudson 1.00
THC93 Jose Cruz Jr. 1.00
THC94 Mark Prior 2.50
THC95 Jason Giambi 5.00
THC96 Luis Gonzalez 1.50
THC97 Drew Henson 1.50
THC98 Cristian Guzman 1.00
THC99 Shawn Green 1.50
THC100 Jose Vidro 1.00

Clubhouse Collection Relics

NM/M
Common Player: 10.00
EB Ernie Banks 25.00
AD Adam Dunn 15.00
JG Jim Gilliam 12.00
SG Shawn Green 10.00
CJ Chipper Jones 15.00
AK Al Kaline 25.00
EM Eddie Mathews 20.00
WM Willie Mays 40.00
AP Albert Pujols 15.00
AR Alex Rodriguez 15.00
DS Duke Snider 25.00
KW Kerry Wood 10.00

Clubhouse Collection Autographed

Production 25 sets No Pricing

Clubhouse Collection Dual Relics

NM/M
Production 54 sets
SG Duke Snider, Shawn Green 80.00
BW Ernie Banks, Kerry Wood 80.00
MJ Eddie Mathews, Chipper Jones 100.00

Flashbacks

NM/M
Complete Set (10): 12.00
Common Player: .75
Inserted 1:12
F1 Willie Mays 3.00
F2 Yogi Berra 2.00
F3 Ted Kluszewski .75
F4 Stan Musial 3.00
F5 Hank Aaron 3.00
F6 Duke Snider 1.50
F7 Richie Ashburn .75
F8 Robin Roberts .75
F9 Mickey Vernon .75
F10 Don Larsen .75

Flashbacks Autographs

NM/M
Production 25:
WM Willie Mays

Grandstand Glory

NM/M
Common Player: 10.00
RA Richie Ashburn 15.00
EB Ernie Banks 20.00
YB Yogi Berra 20.00
DG Dick Groat 12.00
AK Al Kaline 15.00
TK Ted Kluszewski 12.00
EM Eddie Mathews 12.00
WM Willie Mays 35.00
AP Andy Pafko 10.00
PR Phil Rizzuto 15.00
HS Hank Sauer 10.00
DS Duke Snider 15.00
WS Warren Spahn 15.00

New Age Performers

NM/M
Complete Set (15): 20.00
Common Player: .75
Inserted 1:15
NA1 Mike Piazza 3.00
NA2 Ichiro Suzuki 3.00
NA3 Derek Jeter 4.00
NA4 Alex Rodriguez 3.00
NA5 Sammy Sosa 2.00
NA6 Jason Giambi 2.00
NA7 Vladimir Guerrero 1.50
NA8 Albert Pujols 1.50
NA9 Todd Helton .75
NA10 Nomar Garciaparra 2.50
NA11 Randy Johnson 1.50
NA12 Jim Thome 1.00
NA13 Andruw Jones .75
NA14 Miguel Tejada .75
NA15 Alfonso Soriano 1.50

Real One Special Edition Autographs

NM/M
Production 54 sets
RO-MB Matt Batts 50.00
RO-HB Hank Bauer 75.00
RO-MBL Mike Blyzka 40.00
RO-RF Roy Face 60.00
RO-WF Whitey Ford 120.00
RO-DG Dick Groat 60.00
RO-MI Monte Irvin 80.00
RO-LJ Larry Jansen 35.00
RO-CK Charlie Kress 60.00
RO-TL Tom Lasorda 65.00
RO-VL Vern Law 40.00
RO-DL Don Lenhardt 75.00
RO-EM Eddie Mayo 45.00
RO-MM Mickey Micelotta 40.00
RO-RM Ray Murray 45.00
RO-PP Paul Penson 40.00
RO-JPO Johnny Podres 70.00
RO-JP Joe Presko 50.00
RO-PR Phil Rizzuto 75.00
RO-PRO Preacher Roe 80.00
RO-BR Bob Ross 40.00
RO-JS Johnny Sain 65.00
RO-MS Mike Sandlock 50.00
RO-CS Carl Scheib 35.00
RO-BSH Bobby Shantz 60.00
RO-BS Bill "Moose" Skowron 80.00
RO-BT Bob Talbot 50.00
RO-BWE Bill Werle 60.00
RO-LW Leroy Wheat 50.00
RO-JW Jim Willis 60.00

Team Legends Autographs

NM/M
Common Autograph: 35.00
Luis Aparicio 35.00
Jim Bunning 35.00
Al Kaline 70.00
Don Larsen 40.00
Duke Snider 70.00

Then and Now

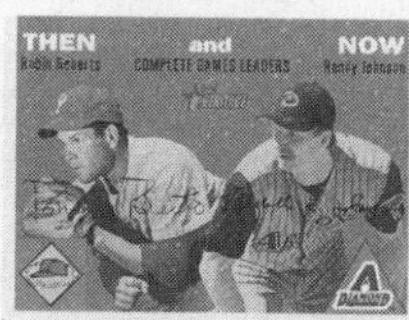

NM/M
Complete Set (10): 12.00
Common Card: .75
Inserted 1:15
TN1 Ted Kluszewski, Alex Rodriguez 3.00
TN2 Ted Kluszewski, Alex Rodriguez 3.00
TN3 Robin Roberts, Randy Johnson 1.00
TN4 Don Mueller, Alfonso Soriano 1.50
TN5 Stan Musial, Garret Anderson 2.00
TN6 Minnie Minoso, Johnny Damon .75
TN7 Robin Roberts, Randy Johnson 1.00
TN8 Duke Snider, Alex Rodriguez 3.00
TN9 Robin Roberts, Randy Johnson 1.00
TN10 Johnny Antonelli, Pedro Martinez 1.00

2003 TOPPS PRISTINE

NM/M
Complete Set (190):

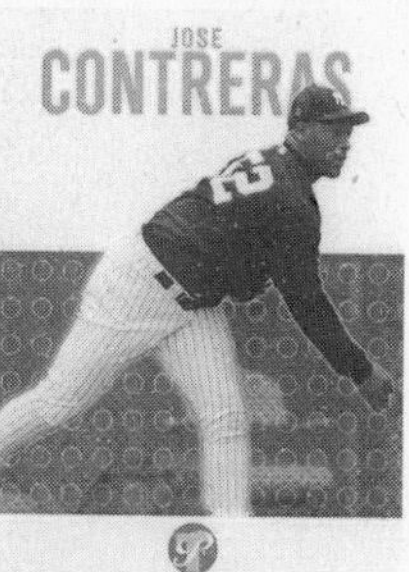

Common Player: 1.00
Common Rookie: 1.00
Common Uncommon RC: 2.50
Production 1,499
Common Rare RC: 5.00
Production 499
Pack (8): 25.00
Box (5): 110.00
1 Pedro J. Martinez 3.00
2 Derek Jeter 6.00
3 Alex Rodriguez 6.00
4 Miguel Tejada 1.00
5 Nomar Garciaparra 4.00
6 Austin Kearns 1.50
7 Jose Vidro 1.00
8 Bret Boone 1.00
9 Scott Rolen 2.00
10 Mike Sweeney 1.00
11 Jason Schmidt 1.00
12 Alfonso Soriano 2.50
13 Tim Hudson 1.50
14 A.J. Pierzynski 1.00
15 Lance Berkman 1.50
16 Frank Thomas 2.00
17 Gary Sheffield 1.50
18 Jarrod Washburn 1.00
19 Hideo Nomo 1.50
20 Barry Zito 1.50
21 Kevin Millwood 1.50
22 Matt Morris 1.00
23 Carl Crawford 1.00
24 Carlos Delgado 1.50
25 Mike Piazza 4.00
26 Brad Radke 1.00
27 Richie Sexson 1.50
28 Kevin Brown 1.50
29 Carlos Beltran 2.00
30 Curt Schilling 1.50
31 Chipper Jones 3.00
32 Paul Konerko 1.00
33 Larry Walker 1.50
34 Jeff Bagwell 2.00
35 Jason Giambi 1.50
36 Mark Mulder 1.50
37 Vicente Padilla 1.00
38 Kris Benson 1.00
39 Bernie Williams 1.50
40 Jim Thome 2.00
41 Roger Clemens 5.00
42 Roberto Alomar 1.50
43 Torii Hunter 1.50
44 Bobby Abreu 1.00
45 Jeff Kent 1.00
46 Roy Oswalt 1.00
47 Bartolo Colon 1.00
48 Greg Maddux 4.00
49 Tom Glavine 1.50
50 Sammy Sosa 5.00
51 Ichiro Suzuki 4.00
52 Mark Prior 4.00
53 Manny Ramirez 2.00
54 Andruw Jones 1.50
55 Randy Johnson 3.00
56 Garret Anderson 1.50
57 Roy Halladay 1.00
58 Rafael Palmeiro 2.00
59 Rocco Baldelli 1.50
60 Albert Pujols 5.00
61 Edgar Renteria 1.00
62 John Olerud 1.00
63 Rich Aurilia 1.00
64 Ryan Klesko 1.00
65 Brian Giles 1.50
66 Eric Chavez 1.50
67 Jorge Posada 1.50
68 Cliff Floyd 1.00
69 Vladimir Guerrero 2.00
70 Cristian Guzman 1.00
71 Raul Ibanez 1.00

72 Paul LoDuca 1.00
73 A.J. Burnett 1.00
74 Ken Griffey Jr. 4.00
75 Mark Buehrle 1.00
76 Moises Alou 1.50
77 Adam Dunn 2.00
78 Tony Batista 1.00
79 Troy Glaus 1.50
80 Luis Gonzalez 1.00
81 Shea Hillenbrand 1.00
82 Kerry Wood 2.00
83 Magglio Ordonez 1.00
84 Omar Vizquel 1.00
85 Bobby Higginson 1.00
86 Mike Lowell 1.00
87 Runelvys Hernandez 1.00
88 Shawn Green 1.50
89 Erubiel Durazo 1.00
90 Pat Burrell 1.50
91 Todd Helton 2.00
92 Jim Edmonds 1.50
93 Aubrey Huff 1.00
94 Eric Hinske 1.00
95 Barry Bonds 6.00
96 Willie Mays 5.00
97 Bo Jackson 2.00
98 Carl Yastrzemski 2.00
99 Don Mattingly 5.00
100 Gary Carter 1.50
101 *Jose Contreras/C* 2.00
102 *Jose Contreras/U* 4.00
103 *Jose Contreras/R* 8.00
104 Dan Haren/C 1.50
105 Dan Haren/U 4.00
106 Dan Haren/R 8.00
107 *Michel Hernandez/C* 1.00
108 *Michel Hernandez/U* 2.50
109 *Michel Hernandez/R* 5.00
110 *Bobby Basham/C* 1.00
111 *Bobby Basham/U* 2.50
112 *Bobby Basham/R* 5.00
113 *Bryan Bullington/C* 2.00
114 *Bryan Bullington/U* 5.00
115 *Bryan Bullington/R* 8.00
116 *Bernie Castro/C* 1.00
117 *Bernie Castro/U* 2.50
118 *Bernie Castro/R* 5.00
119 *Chien-Ming Wang/C* 3.00
120 *Chien-Ming Wang/U* 6.00
121 *Chien-Ming Wang/R* 10.00
122 *Eric Crozier/C* 1.00
123 *Eric Crozier/U* 2.50
124 *Eric Crozier/R* 5.00
125 Michael Garciaparra/C 1.00
126 Michael Garciaparra/U 2.50
127 Michael Garciaparra/R 5.00
128 Joey Gomes/C 1.00
129 Joey Gomes/U 2.50
130 Joey Gomes/R 5.00
131 *Wilfredo Ledezma/C* 1.00
132 *Wilfredo Ledezma/U* 2.50
133 *Wilfredo Ledezma/R* 5.00
134 *Branden Florence/C* 1.00
135 *Branden Florence/U* 2.50
136 *Branden Florence/R* 5.00
137 Jeremy Bonderman/C 3.00
138 Jeremy Bonderman/U 8.00
139 Jeremy Bonderman/R 12.00
140 *Travis Ishikawa/C* 1.00
141 *Travis Ishikawa/U* 2.50
142 *Travis Ishikawa/R* 5.00
143 *Ben Francisco/C* 1.00
144 *Ben Francisco/U* 2.50
145 *Ben Francisco/R* 5.00
146 *Jason Kubel/C* 3.00
147 *Jason Kubel/U* 6.00
148 *Jason Kubel/R* 10.00
149 *Tyler Martin/C* 1.00
150 *Tyler Martin/U* 2.50
151 *Tyler Martin/R* 5.00
152 Jason Perry/C 1.50
153 Jason Perry/U 3.00
154 Jason Perry/R 5.00
155 *Ryan Shealy/C* 1.50
156 *Ryan Shealy/U* 4.00
157 *Ryan Shealy/R* 6.00
158 *Hanley Ramirez/C* 5.00
159 *Hanley Ramirez/U* 10.00
160 *Hanley Ramirez/R* 15.00
161 *Rajai Davis/C* 1.00
162 *Rajai Davis/U* 2.50
163 *Rajai Davis/R* 5.00
164 *Gary Schneidmiller/C* 1.00
165 *Gary Schneidmiller/U* 2.50
166 *Gary Schneidmiller/R* 6.00
167 *Haj Turay/C* 1.00
168 *Haj Turay/U* 2.50
169 *Haj Turay/R* 5.00
170 *Kevin Youkilis/C* 3.00
171 *Kevin Youkilis/U* 6.00
172 *Kevin Youkilis/R* 12.00
173 *Shane Bazzell/C* 1.00
174 *Shane Bazzell/U* 2.50
175 *Shane Bazzell/R* 5.00
176 *Elizardo Ramirez/C* 2.00
177 *Elizardo Ramirez/U* 4.00
178 *Elizardo Ramirez/R* 8.00
179 *Robinson Cano/C* 5.00
180 *Robinson Cano/U* 10.00
181 *Robinson Cano/R* 20.00
182 *Nook Logan/C* 1.00
183 *Nook Logan/U* 2.50
184 *Nook Logan/R* 5.00
185 *Dustin McGowan/C* 1.00
186 *Dustin McGowan/U* 3.00
187 *Dustin McGowan/R* 5.00
188 Ryan Howard/C 8.00
189 Ryan Howard/U 15.00
190 Ryan Howard/R 30.00

Refractors

Veterans (1-100): 4-6X
Production 99
Common RC's: .75-1.5X
Production 1,599
Uncommon RC's: 1-2X
Production 499
Rare RC's: 1.5-3X
Production 99
Veteran Gold Refrac.(1-100): 4-8X
Rookie Golds (101-190): 2-4X
Production 69 sets

Plates

No pricing due to Scarcity
Four plates per player

Mini

NM/M
Common Player: 1.00
RB Rocco Baldelli 1.50
BWB Bobby Basham 1.00
JB Jeremy Bonderman 1.50
BB Barry Bonds 6.00
BPB Bryan Bullington 3.00
RJC Robinson Cano 1.00
BC Bernie Castro 1.00
EC Eric Chavez 1.00
RC Roger Clemens 5.00
JC Jose Contreras 2.00
ELC Eric Crozier 1.00
RD Rajai Davis 1.00
NG Nomar Garciaparra 5.00
JG Jason Giambi 2.00
BG Brian Giles 1.50
VG Vladimir Guerrero 3.00
DH Dan Haren 2.00
MH .Michel Hernandez 1.00
RH Ryan Howard 3.00
DJ Derek Jeter 6.00
AK Austin Kearns 2.00
JK Jeff Kent 1.50
JJK Jason Kubel 4.00
WL Wilfredo Ledezma 1.00
NL Nook Logan 1.00
TM Tyler Martin 1.00
DM Dustin McGowan 1.00
MO Magglio Ordonez 1.00
MJP Mike Piazza 4.00
MP Mark Prior 6.00
ER Elizardo Ramirez 1.00
AR Alex Rodriguez 6.00
RS Ryan Shealy 1.50
AS Alfonso Soriano 3.00
SS Sammy Sosa 4.00
IS Ichiro Suzuki 3.00
MT Miguel Tejada 1.50
JT Jim Thome 2.00
CW Chien-Ming Wang 5.00
KY Kevin Youkilis 6.00

Mini Autograph

NM/M
Production 100
RC Roger Clemens 125.00

Bomb Squad

NM/M
Common Player: 4.00
Refractors: No Pricing
Production 25 sets
MO1 Moises Alou 4.00
MO2 Moises Alou 4.00
GA1 Garret Anderson 5.00
GA2 Garret Anderson 5.00
JRB Jeff Bagwell 6.00
JB Johnny Bench 10.00
LB1 Lance Berkman 5.00
LB2 Lance Berkman 5.00
HB Hank Blalock 5.00
BB Barry Bonds 15.00
GB1 George Brett 12.00
GB2 George Brett 12.00
GC Gary Carter 5.00
EC1 Eric Chavez 4.00
EC2 Eric Chavez 4.00
CC Carl Crawford 4.00
AD Adam Dunn 6.00
DE1 Darin Erstad 4.00
DE2 Darin Erstad 4.00
CF Cliff Floyd 4.00
NG1 Nomar Garciaparra 10.00
NG2 Nomar Garciaparra 10.00
JG Jason Giambi 6.00
TG1 Troy Glaus 5.00
TG2 Troy Glaus 5.00
JAG Juan Gonzalez 6.00
LG Luis Gonzalez 4.00
SG Shawn Green 5.00
VG1 Vladimir Guerrero 8.00
VG2 Vladimir Guerrero 8.00
TH Todd Helton 6.00
RH Rickey Henderson 10.00
AJ Andruw Jones 6.00
CJ Chipper Jones 8.00
JK Jeff Kent 4.00
MO Maggio Ordonez 4.00
RP Rafael Palmeiro 6.00
MP Mike Piazza 10.00
AP1 Albert Pujols 15.00
AP2 Albert Pujols 15.00
MR Manny Ramirez 6.00
AR1 Alex Rodriguez 10.00
AR2 Alex Rodriguez 10.00
TS Tim Salmon 4.00
MS1 Mike Schmidt 12.00
MS2 Mike Schmidt 12.00
GS Gary Sheffield 5.00
AS Alfonso Soriano 8.00
SS1 Sammy Sosa 10.00
SS2 Sammy Sosa 10.00
MT Miguel Tejada 4.00
FT Frank Thomas 6.00
JT Jim Thome 10.00

Borders

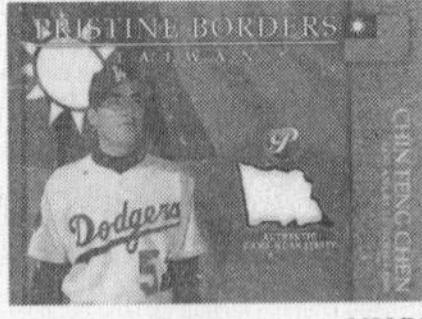

NM/M
Common Player: 4.00
Inserted 1:9
Refractors: No Pricing
Production 25 sets
CC Chin-Feng Chen 40.00
VG Vladimir Guerrero 8.00
CG Cristian Guzman 4.00
KI Kazuhisa Ishii 4.00
AJ Andruw Jones 6.00
PM Pedro J. Martinez 8.00
MO Magglio Ordonez 4.00
AP Albert Pujols 15.00
MR Manny Ramirez 6.00
IR Ivan Rodriguez 6.00
TS Tsuyoshi Shinjo 4.00
AS Alfonso Soriano 8.00
SS Sammy Sosa 10.00
MT Miguel Tejada 4.00
BW Bernie Williams 6.00

Corners

NM/M
Common Duo: 6.00
Inserted 1:12
Refractors: No Pricing
Production 25 sets
CD Eric Chavez, Erubiel Durazo 6.00
VG Robin Ventura, Jason Giambi 10.00
WG Matt Williams, Mark Grace 8.00
RM Scott Rolen, Tino Martinez 10.00
BM Adrian Beltre, Fred McGriff 6.00
GS Troy Glaus, Scott Spiezio 8.00
KM Corey Koskie, Doug Mientkiewicz 6.00
BT David Bell, Jim Thome 10.00
BK Sean Burroughs, Ryan Klesko 6.00
AS Edgardo Alfonzo, J.T. Snow 6.00
TP Mark Teixeira, Rafael Palmeiro 10.00

Double Bonds

NM/M
Common Duo: 25.00
Refractors: No Pricing
Production 25
BJ Barry Bonds, Randy Johnson 50.00
BT Miguel Tejada, Barry Bonds 25.00
BM Willie Mays, Barry Bonds 75.00
BR Alex Rodriguez, Barry Bonds 35.00

Solo Bonds

NM/M
Common Bonds: 20.00
Refractors: No Pricing
Production 25
GG Barry Bonds 20.00
HR Barry Bonds 20.00
BB Barry Bonds 20.00
MVP Barry Bonds 20.00

Factor

NM/M
Common Player: 4.00
Inserted 1:9
Refractors: No Pricing
Production 25 sets
LB Lance Berkman 4.00
AD Adam Dunn 6.00
DE Darin Erstad 4.00
NG Nomar Garciaparra 10.00
JG Jason Giambi 6.00
TG Troy Glaus 5.00
VG Vladimir Guerrero 8.00
TH Todd Helton 6.00
TKH Torii Hunter 5.00
MO Magglio Ordonez 4.00
MP Mike Piazza 10.00
MR Manny Ramirez 6.00
AR Alex Rodriguez 10.00
AS Alfonso Soriano 8.00
SS Sammy Sosa 10.00

Personal Endorsements

NM/M
Common Autograph: 6.00
Golds: No Pricing
Production 25 sets

AB Andrew Brown 6.00
RYC Ryan Church 10.00
DE David Eckstein 10.00
LF Lew Ford 10.00
JG Jay Gibbons 10.00
RJH Rich Harden 25.00
KH Ken Harvey 6.00
PK Paul Konerko 20.00
ML Mike Lowell 10.00
VM Victor Martinez 20.00
BM Brett Myers 10.00
JP Josh Phelps 8.00
SR Scott Rolen 25.00
FS Felix Sanchez 6.00
KS Kelly Shoppach 15.00
MS Mike Sweeney 10.00
FV Fernando Vina 6.00

Primary Elements

NM/M

Many not priced due to scarcity
Production 50 sets
Refractors: No Pricing
Production 10
BRB Bret Boone 15.00
NG Nomar Garciaparra 35.00
LG Luis Gonzalez 10.00
SG Shawn Green 10.00
TH Todd Helton 20.00
TKH Torii Hunter 20.00
KI Kazuhisa Ishii 10.00
AJ Andruw Jones 15.00
CJ Chipper Jones 20.00
PM Pedro J. Martinez 20.00
MO Magglio Ordonez 10.00
RP Rafael Palmeiro 15.00
MP Mike Piazza 25.00
AR Alex Rodriguez 50.00
MT Miguel Tejada 15.00
BZ Barry Zito 15.00

2003 TOPPS RETIRED SIGNATURE EDITION

NM/M

Complete Set (110): 100.00
Common Player: .50
Pack (5): 30.00
Box (5): 120.00
1 Willie Mays 4.00
2 Tony Perez 1.00
3 Tom Seaver 2.00
4 Johnny Bench 4.00
5 Rod Carew 1.50
6 Red Schoendienst .50
7 Phil Rizzuto 1.00
8 Ozzie Smith 2.50
9 Maury Wills .50
10 Hank Aaron 4.00
11 Jim Palmer 1.00
12 Jose Cruz .50
13 Dave Parker .50
14 Don Sutton .75
15 Brooks Robinson 2.00
16 Bo Jackson 1.50
17 Andre Dawson .75
18 Fergie Jenkins .75
19 George Foster .50
20 George Brett 5.00
21 Jerry Koosman .50
22 John Kruk .50
23 Kent Tekulve .50
24 Lee Smith .50
25 Nolan Ryan 6.00
26 Paul O'Neill .50
27 Rich "Goose" Gossage .50
28 Ron Santo .50
29 Tom Lasorda .75
30 Tony Gwynn 2.00
31 Vida Blue .50
32 Whitey Herzog .50
33 Willie McGee .50
34 Bill Mazeroski .50
35 Al Kaline 3.00
36 Bobby Richardson .50
37 Carlton Fisk 1.00
38 Darrell Evans .50
39 Dave Concepcion .50
40 Cal Ripken Jr. 5.00
41 Dwight Evans .50
42 Earl Weaver .50
43 Fred Lynn .50
44 Greg Luzinski .50
45 Duke Snider 1.50
46 Hank Bauer .50
47 Jim Rice .50
48 Johnny Sain .50
49 Lenny Dykstra .50
50 Mike Schmidt 4.00
51 Orlando Cepeda 1.00
52 Ralph Kiner .75
53 Robin Roberts .50
54 Ron Guidry .50
55 Steve Garvey .50
56 Tony Oliva .75
57 Whitey Ford 1.00
58 Willie McCovey 1.00
59 Phil Niekro .50
60 Stan Musial 3.00
61 Rollie Fingers 1.00
62 Robin Yount 2.00
63 Alan Trammell 1.00
64 Bill Buckner .50
65 Bob Feller 1.00
66 Bruce Sutter .75
67 Dale Murphy 1.00
68 Dennis Eckersley 1.00
69 Don Newcombe .50
70 Don Mattingly 5.00
71 Dwight Gooden .50
72 Frank Robinson 1.50
73 Gary Carter .50
74 Graig Nettles .50
75 Harmon Killebrew 2.00
76 Jim Bunning .50
77 Joe Morgan 1.00
78 Joe Rudi .50
79 Jose Canseco 1.00
80 Ernie Banks 3.00
81 Luis Aparicio .50
82 Luis Tiant .50
83 Mark Fidrych .50
84 Kirk Gibson .50
85 Lou Brock 1.00
86 Juan Marichal 1.00
87 Monte Irvin 1.00
88 Paul Molitor 1.00
89 Tommy John .50
90 Warren Spahn 1.50
91 Wade Boggs 1.00
92 Reggie Jackson 2.00
93 Kirby Puckett 3.00
94 Boog Powell .50
95 Carl Yastrzemski 2.00
96 Bobby Thomson .50
97 Bill "Moose" Skowron .50
98 Bill Madlock .50
99 Sparky Anderson .50
100 Yogi Berra 2.00
101 Bobby Doerr .50
102 Gaylord Perry .50
103 George Kell .50
104 Harold Reynolds .50
105 Joe Carter .50
106 Johnny Podres .50
107 Ron Cey .50
108 Tim McCarver .50
109 Tug McGraw .50
110 Don Larsen 1.00

Black

Cards (1-110): 2-4X
Production 99 sets

Autographs

NM/M

Common Autograph: 10.00
Inserted 1:1
Refractors: 1-2.5X
Production 25 sets
HA Hank Aaron/30 300.00
JA Jim Abbott 20.00
SA Sparky Anderson 20.00
LA Luis Aparicio 12.00
HB Harold Baines 10.00
EB Ernie Banks/24 175.00
HBA Hank Bauer 20.00
JBE Johnny Bench 65.00
YB Yogi Berra/25 150.00
VB Vida Blue 15.00
BB Bert Blyleven 10.00
WB Wade Boggs/77 125.00
GB George Brett/25 180.00
LB Lou Brock/76 120.00
BBU Bill Buckner 10.00
JB Jim Bunning/76 100.00
JCA Jose Canseco 40.00
RCA Rod Carew 60.00
GC Gary Carter/77 100.00
JC Joe Carter 25.00
OC Orlando Cepeda/75 180.00
RCE Ron Cey 10.00
DC Dave Concepcion
JCR Jose Cruz 10.00
AD Andre Dawson 20.00
BD Bobby Doerr 20.00
LD Lenny Dykstra 20.00
DEC Dennis Eckersley 65.00
DE Darrell Evans 10.00
DEV Dwight Evans/78 80.00
BF Bob Feller 20.00
MF Mark Fidrych 20.00
RF Rollie Fingers 25.00
CF Carlton Fisk 65.00
WF Whitey Ford 65.00
GF George Foster 10.00
SG Steve Garvey 15.00
KG Kirk Gibson 40.00
DG Dwight Gooden 30.00
RG Rich "Goose" Gossage 15.00
BGR Bobby Grich 15.00
KGR Ken Griffey Sr. 25.00
RGU Ron Guidry 35.00
TG Tony Gwynn/25 165.00
WH Whitey Herzog 15.00
BH Bob Horner 10.00
MI Monte Irvin 60.00
BJ Bo Jackson 75.00
RJ Reggie Jackson 100.00
FJ Fergie Jenkins 20.00
TJ Tommy John 25.00
AK Al Kaline 75.00
GK George Kell 30.00
HK Harmon Killebrew/76 150.00
RK Ralph Kiner 125.00
JK Jerry Koosman 25.00
JKR John Kruk 35.00
DL Don Larsen 15.00
TL Tom Lasorda/76 100.00
GL Greg Luzinski 15.00
FL Fred Lynn 20.00
BM Bill Madlock 10.00
JMA Juan Marichal 35.00
DON Don Mattingly/81 175.00
WM Willie Mays/25
BMA Bill Mazeroski 15.00
TM Tim McCarver 25.00
WMC Willie McCovey 50.00
WMG Willie McGee 25.00
TMC Tug McGraw 50.00
PM Paul Molitor 75.00
JM Joe Morgan 35.00
DM Dale Murphy 40.00
SM Stan Musial/28 185.00
PN Phil Niekro 15.00
GN Graig Nettles 10.00
DN Don Newcombe 15.00
TO Tony Oliva 25.00
PO Paul O'Neill 50.00
JP Jim Palmer 50.00
DP Dave Parker 20.00
LP Lance Parrish 10.00
TP Terry Pendleton 10.00
TP Tony Perez 40.00
GP Gaylord Perry 10.00
JPI Jimmy Piersall 10.00
JPO Johnny Podres 10.00
BP Boog Powell 10.00
KP Kirby Puckett/75
HR Harold Reynolds 20.00
JR Jim Rice 30.00
BR Bobby Richardson 15.00
CR Cal Ripken Jr./25 340.00
PR Phil Rizzuto/70 140.00
RR Robin Roberts 25.00
BRO Brooks Robinson/75 140.00
FR Frank Robinson 60.00
JRU Joe Rudi 10.00
NR Nolan Ryan/77 200.00
BSA Bret Saberhagen 25.00
JS Johnny Sain
RSA Ron Santo 20.00
MS Mike Schmidt/83 200.00
RS Red Schoendienst/83 100.00
TS Tom Seaver 65.00
BS Bill "Moose" Skowron 10.00
LS Lee Smith 15.00
OS Ozzie Smith 65.00
DSN Duke Snider/75 100.00
WS Warren Spahn 50.00
DS Dave Stieb 15.00
BSU Bruce Sutter 35.00
DSU Don Sutton 20.00
KT Kent Tekulve 20.00
BT Bobby Thomson 10.00
LT Luis Tiant 10.00
AT Alan Trammell 20.00
BW Bob Watson 10.00
EW Earl Weaver 12.00
MW Maury Wills 10.00
CY Carl Yastrzemski 80.00
RY Robin Yount/25 150.00

2003 TOPPS TOTAL

NM/M

Complete Set (990): 125.00
Common Player: .10
Pack (10): 1.00
Box (36): 25.00
1 Brent Abernathy .10
2 Bobby Hill .10
3 Victor Martinez .10
4 Chip Ambres .10
5 Matt Anderson .10
6 Ricardo Aramboles .10
7 Carlos Pena .10
8 Aaron Guiel .10
9 Luke Allen .10
10 Francisco Rodriguez .20
11 Jason Marquis .10
12 Edwin Almonte .10
13 Grant Balfour .10
14 Adam Piatt .10
15 Andy Phillips .10
16 Adrian Beltre .10
17 Brandon Backe .10
18 Dave Berg .10
19 Brett Myers .10
20 Brian Meadows .10
21 Chin-Feng Chen .25
22 Blake Williams .10
23 Josh Bard .10
24 Josh Beckett .10
25 *Kip Bouknight* .20
26 Matt Childers .10
27 Adam Everett .10
28 Mike Bordick .10
29 Antonio Alfonseca .10
30 Doug Creek .10
31 J.D. Drew .20
32 Milton Bradley .10
33 Boomer Wells .10
34 Vance Wilson .10
35 Jeff Fassero .10
36 Sandy Alomar .10
37 Ryan Vogelsong .10
38 Roger Clemens 1.25
39 Juan Gonzalez .40

No.	Player	Value
40	Dustin Hermanson	.10
41	Andy Ashby	.10
42	Adam Hyzdu	.10
43	Ben Broussard	.10
44	Ryan Klesko	.10
45	Chris Buglovsky	.10
46	Bud Smith	.10
47	Aaron Boone	.10
48	Cliff Floyd	.10
49	Alex Cora	.10
50	Curt Schilling	.40
51	Michael Cuddyer	.10
52	Mike Venafro	.10
53	Carlos Gullien	.10
54	Angel Berroa	.10
55	Eli Marrero	.10
56	A.J. Burnett	.10
57	Oliver Perez	.10
58	Matt Morris	.25
59	Valerio De Los Santos	.10
60	Austin Kearns	.50
61	Darren Dreifort	.10
62	Jason Standridge	.10
63	Carlos Silva	.10
64	Moises Alou	.20
65	Jason Anderson	.10
66	Russell Branyan	.10
67	B.J. Ryan	.10
68	Cory Aldridge	.10
69	Ellis Burks	.10
70	Troy Glaus	.50
71	Kelly Wunsch	.10
72	Brad Wilkerson	.10
73	Jayson Durocher	.10
74	Tony Fiore	.10
75	Brian Giles	.25
76	Billy Wagner	.10
77	Neifi Perez	.10
78	Jose Valverde	.10
79	Brent Butler	.10
80	Mario Ramos	.10
81	Kerry Robinson	.10
82	Brent Mayne	.10
83	Sean Casey	.10
84	Danys Baez	.10
85	Chase Utley	.10
86	Jared Sandberg	.10
87	Terrence Long	.10
88	Kevin Walker	.10
89	Royce Clayton	.10
90	Shea Hillenbrand	.10
91	Brad Lidge	.10
92	Shawn Chacon	.10
93	Kevin Frederick	.10
94	Chris Snelling	.10
95	Omar Vizquel	.20
96	Joe Borchard	.10
97	Matt Belisle	.10
98	Steve Smyth	.10
99	Raul Mondesi	.20
100	Chipper Jones	1.00
101	Victor Alvarez	.10
102	J.M. Gold	.10
103	Willis Roberts	.10
104	Eddie Guardado	.10
105	Brad Voyles	.10
106	Bronson Arroyo	.10
107	Juan Castro	.10
108	Dan Pleasac	.10
109	Ramon Castro	.10
110	Tim Salmon	.25
111	Damion Easley	.10
112	J.D. Closser	.10
113	Mark Buehrle	.10
114	Steve Karsay	.10
115	Cristian Guerrero	.10
116	Brad Ausmus	.10
117	Cristian Guzman	.10
118	Dan Wilson	.10
119	Jake Westbrook	.10
120	Manny Ramirez	.50
121	Jason Giambi	.75
122	Bob Wickman	.10
123	Aaron Cook	.10
124	Alfredo Amezaga	.10
125	Corey Thurman	.10
126	Brandon Puffer	.10
127	Hee Seop Choi	.25
128	Javier Vazquez	.10
129	Carlos Valderrama	.10
130	Jerome Williams	.10
131	Wilson Betemit	.10
132	Bruce Chen	.10
133	Esteban Yan	.10
134	Brandon Berger	.10
135	Bill Hall	.10
136	LaTroy Hawkins	.10
137	Nate Cornejo	.10
138	Jim Mecir	.10
139	Joe Crede	.10
140	Andres Galarraga	.10
141	Dave Williams	.10
142	Joey Eischen	.10
143	Mike Timlin	.10
144	Jose Cruz Jr.	.10
145	Wes Helms	.10
146	Brian Roberts	.10
147	Bret Prinz	.10
148	Brian Hunter	.10
149	Chad Hermansen	.10
150	Andruw Jones	.40
151	Kurt Ainsworth	.10
152	Clifford Bartosh	.10
153	Kyle Lohse	.10
154	Brian Jordan	.10
155	Coco Crisp	.10
156	Tomas Perez	.10
157	Keith Foulke	.10
158	Chris Carpenter	.10
159	Mike Remlinger	.10
160	Dewon Brazelton	.10
161	Brook Fordyce	.10
162	Rusty Greer	.10
163	Scott Downs	.10
164	Jason Dubois	.10
165	David Coggin	.10
166	Jose Hernandez	.10
167	Carlos Hernandez	.10
168	Matt Williams	.10
169	Rheal Cormier	.10
170	Duaner Sanchez	.10
171	Craig Counsell	.10
172	Edgar Martinez	.20
173	Zack Greinke	.10
174	Pedro Feliz	.10
175	Randy Choate	.10
176	Jon Garland	.10
177	Keith Ginter	.10
178	Carlos Febles	.10
179	*Gregor Blanco*	.10
180	Jack Cust	.10
181	Koyie Hill	.10
182	Ricky Gutierrez	.10
183	Ben Grieve	.10
184	Livan Hernandez	.10
185	Jason Isringhausen	.10
186	Gookie Dawkins	.10
187	Roberto Alomar	.40
188	Eric Junge	.10
189	Carlos Beltran	.10
190	Denny Hocking	.10
191	Jason Schmidt	.10
192	Cory Lidle	.10
193	Robert Mackowiak	.10
194	Charlton Jimerson	.10
195	Darin Erstad	.25
196	Jason Davis	.10
197	Luis Castillo	.10
198	Juan Encarnacion	.10
199	Jeffrey Hammonds	.10
200	Nomar Garciaparra	1.50
201	Ryan Christianson	.10
202	Willie Banks	.10
203	Damian Moss	.10
204	Chris Richard	.10
205	Todd Hundley	.10
206	Paul Bako	.10
207	Adam Kennedy	.10
208	Scott Hatteberg	.10
209	Andy Pratt	.10
210	Ken Griffey Jr.	1.00
211	Chris George	.10
212	Lance Niekro	.10
213	Greg Colbrunn	.10
214	Herbert Perry	.10
215	Cody Ransom	.10
216	Craig Biggio	.25
217	Miguel Batista	.10
218	Alex Escobar	.10
219	Willie Harris	.10
220	Scott Strickland	.10
221	Felix Rodriguez	.10
222	Torii Hunter	.25
223	Tyler Houston	.10
224	Darrell May	.10
225	Benito Santiago	.10
226	Ryan Dempster	.10
227	Andy Fox	.10
228	Jung Bong	.10
229	Jose Macias	.10
230	Shannon Stewart	.10
231	Buddy Groom	.10
232	Eric Valent	.10
233	Scott Schoeneweis	.10
234	Corey Hart	.10
235	Brett Tomko	.10
236	*Shane Bazzell*	.20
237	Tim Hummel	.10
238	Al Reyes	.10
239	Daryle Ward	.10
240	Ismael Valdes	.10
241	Brian Fuentes	.10
242	Cesar Izturis	.10
243	Mark Bellhorn	.10
244	Geoff Jenkins	.10
245	Derek Jeter	2.00
246	Anderson Machado	.10
247	Dave Roberts	.10
248	Jaime Cerda	.10
249	Woody Williams	.10
250	Vernon Wells	.20
251	Jon Lieber	.10
252	Franklyn German	.10
253	David Segui	.10
254	Freddy Garcia	.10
255	James Baldwin	.10
256	Tony Alvarez	.10
257	Walter Young	.10
258	Alex Herrera	.10
259	Robert Fick	.10
260	Rob Bell	.10
261	Ross Gload	.10
262	Dee Brown	.10
263	Mike Bacsik	.10
264	Corey Patterson	.10
265	Marvin Bernard	.10
266	Eddie Rogers	.10
267	Elio Serrano	.10
268	D'Angelo Jimenez	.10
269	Adam Johnson	.10
270	Gregg Zaun	.10
271	Nick Johnson	.10
272	Geoff Goetz	.10
273	Ryan Drese	.10
274	Eric DuBose	.10
275	Barry Zito	.25
276	Mike Crudale	.10
277	Paul Byrd	.10
278	Eric Gagne	.10
279	Aramis Ramirez	.10
280	Ray Durham	.10
281	Tony Graffanino	.10
282	Jeremy Guthrie	.10
283	Erik Bedard	.10
284	Vince Faison	.10
285	Bobby Kielty	.10
286	Francis Beltran	.10
287	Alexis Gomez	.10
288	Vladimir Guerrero	.75
289	Kevin Appier	.10
290	Gil Meche	.10
291	Marquis Grissom	.10
292	John Burkett	.10
293	Vinny Castilla	.10
294	Tyler Walker	.10
295	Shane Halter	.10
296	Geronimo Gil	.10
297	Eric Hinske	.10
298	Adam Dunn	.50
299	Mike Kinkade	.10
300	Mark Prior	.50
301	Corey Koskie	.10
302	David Dellucci	.10
303	Todd Helton	.40
304	Greg Miller	.10
305	Delvin James	.10
306	Humberto Cota	.10
307	Aaron Harang	.10
308	Jeremy Hill	.10
309	Billy Koch	.10
310	Brandon Claussen	.10
311	Matt Ginter	.10
312	Jason Lane	.10
313	Ben Weber	.10
314	Alan Benes	.10
315	Oscar Herinquez	.10
316	Danny Graves	.10
317	Jason Johnson	.10
318	Jason Grimsley	.10
319	Steve Kline	.10
320	Johnny Damon	.10
321	Jay Gibbons	.10
322	J.J. Putz	.10
323	*Stephen Randolph*	.10
324	Bobby Higginson	.10
325	Kazuhisa Ishii	.10
326	Carlos Lee	.10
327	J.R. House	.10
328	Mark Loretta	.10
329	Mike Matheny	.10
330	Ben Diggins	.10
331	Seth Etherton	.10
332	*Eli Whiteside*	.20
333	Juan Rivera	.10
334	Jeff Conine	.10
335	John McDonald	.10
336	Erik Hiljus	.10
337	David Eckstein	.10
338	Jeff Bagwell	.50
339	Matt Holliday	.10
340	Jeff Liefer	.10
341	Greg Myers	.10
342	Scott Sauerbeck	.10
343	Omar Infante	.10
344	Ryan Langerhans	.10
345	Abraham Nunez	.10
346	Mike MacDougal	.10
347	Travis Phelps	.10
348	Dan Reichert	.10
349	Alex Rodriguez	1.50
350	Bobby Seay	.10
351	Ichiro Suzuki	1.00
352	Brandon Inge	.10
353	Jack Wilson	.10
354	John Ennis	.10
355	Jamal Strong	.10
356	Jason Jennings	.10
357	Jeff Kent	.20
358	Scott Chiasson	.10
359	Jeremy Griffiths	.10
360	Paul Konerko	.10
361	Jeff Austin	.10
362	Todd Van Poppel	.10
363	Sun-Woo Kim	.10
364	Jerry Hairston	.10
365	Tony Torcato	.10
366	Arthur Rhodes	.10
367	Jose Jimenez	.10
368	Matt LeCroy	.10
369	Curtis Lesanic	.10
370	Ramon Vasquez	.10
371	Joe Randa	.10
372	John Franco	.10
373	Charles Johnson	.10
374	Craig Wilson	.10
375	Michael Young	.10
376	Mark Ellis	.10
377	Joe Mauer	.10
378	Checklist	.10
379	Jason Kendall	.10
380	Checklist	.10
381	Alex Gonzalez	.10
382	Flash Gordon	.10
383	John Buck	.10
384	Shigetoshi Hasegawa	.10
385	Scott Stewart	.10
386	Luke Hudson	.10
387	Todd Jones	.10
388	Fred McGriff	.25
389	Mike Sweeney	.10
390	Marlon Anderson	.10
391	Terry Adams	.10
392	Mark DeRosa	.10
393	Doug Mientkiewicz	.10
394	Miguel Cairo	.10
395	Jamie Moyer	.10
396	Josh Towers	.10
397	Matt Clement	.10
398	Bengie Molina	.10
399	Marcus Thames	.10
400	Nick Bierbrodt	.10
401	Tim Kalita	.10
402	Corwin Malone	.10
403	Jesse Orosco	.10
404	Brandon Phillips	.10
405	Eric Cyr	.10
406	Jason Michaels	.10
407	Julio Lugo	.10
408	Gabe Kapler	.10
409	Mark Mulder	.25
410	Adam Eaton	.10
411	Ken Harvey	.10
412	Jolbert Cabrera	.10
413	Eric Milton	.10
414	*Josh Hall*	.20
415	Bob File	.10
416	Brett Evert	.10
417	Ron Chiavacci	.10
418	Jorge De La Rosa	.10
419	Quinton McCracken	.10
420	Luther Hackman	.10
421	Gary Knotts	.10
422	Kevin Brown	.20
423	Jeff Cirillo	.10
424	Damaso Marte	.10
425	Chan Ho Park	.10
426	Nathan Haynes	.10
427	Matt Lawton	.10
428	Mike Stanton	.10
429	Bernie Williams	.40
430	Kevin Jarvis	.10
431	Joe McEwing	.10
432	Mark Kotsay	.10
433	Juan Cruz	.10
434	Russ Ortiz	.10
435	Jeff Nelson	.10

No.	Player	Value
436	Alan Embree	.10
437	Miguel Tejada	.25
438	Kirk Saarloos	.10
439	Cliff Lee	.10
440	Ryan Ludwick	.10
441	Derrek Lee	.10
442	Bobby Abreu	.20
443	Dustan Mohr	.10
444	*Nook Logan*	.25
445	Seth McClung	.10
446	Miguel Olivo	.10
447	Henry Blanco	.10
448	Seung Jun Song	.10
449	Kris Wilson	.10
450	Xavier Nady	.10
451	Corky Miller	.10
452	Jim Thome	.50
453	George Lombard	.10
454	Rey Ordonez	.10
455	Deivis Santos	.10
456	Mike Myers	.10
457	Edgar Renteria	.10
458	Braden Looper	.10
459	Guillermo Mota	.10
460	Scott Rolen	.50
461	Lance Berkman	.10
462	Jeff Heaverlo	.10
463	Ramon Hernandez	.10
464	Jason Simontacchi	.10
465	So Taguchi	.10
466	Dave Veres	.10
467	Shane Loux	.10
468	Rodrigo Lopez	.10
469	Bubba Trammell	.10
470	Scott Sullivan	.10
471	Mike Mussina	.40
472	Ramon Ortiz	.10
473	Lyle Overbay	.10
474	Mike Lowell	.10
475	Greg Vaughn	.10
476	Larry Bigbie	.10
477	Rey Sanchez	.10
478	Magglio Ordonez	.25
479	Rondell White	.10
480	Jay Witasick	.10
481	Jimmy Rollins	.10
482	Mike Maroth	.10
483	Mark Quinn	.10
484	Nick Neugebauer	.10
485	Victor Zambrano	.10
486	Travis Lee	.10
487	Bobby Bradley	.10
488	Marcus Giles	.10
489	Steve Trachsel	.10
490	Derek Lowe	.10
491	Hideo Nomo	.25
492	Brad Hawpe	.10
493	Jesus Medrano	.10
494	Rick Ankiel	.10
495	Pasqual Coco	.10
496	Michael Barrett	.10
497	Joe Beimel	.10
498	Marty Cordova	.10
499	Aaron Sele	.10
500	Sammy Sosa	1.00
501	Ivan Rodriguez	.40
502	Keith Osik	.10
503	Hank Blalock	.25
504	Craig Monroe	.10
505	Junior Spivey	.10
506	Edgardo Alfonzo	.10
507	Alex Graman	.10
508	J.J. Davis	.10
509	Roger Cedeno	.10
510	Joe Roa	.10
511	Wily Mo Pena	.10
512	Eric Munson	.10
513	*Arnie Munoz*	.10
514	Miguel Asencio	.10
515	Andy Pettitte	.25
516	Jim Edmonds	.25
517	Jeff DaVanon	.10
518	Aaron Myette	.10
519	C.C. Sabathia	.10
520	Gerardo Garcia	.10
521	Brian Schneider	.10
522	Wes Obermueller	.10
523	John Mabry	.10
524	Casey Fossum	.10
525	Toby Hall	.10
526	Denny Neagle	.10
527	Willie Bloomquist	.10
528	A.J. Pierzynski	.10
529	Bartolo Colon	.10
530	Chad Harville	.10
531	Blaine Neal	.10
532	Luis Terrero Jr.	.10
533	Reggie Taylor	.10
534	Melvin Mora	.10
535	Tino Martinez	.10
536	Peter Bergeron	.10
537	Jorge Padilla	.10
538	*Oscar Villarreal*	.20
539	David Weathers	.10
540	Mike Lamb	.10
541	Greg Norton	.10
542	Michael Tucker	.10
543	Ben Kozlowski	.10
544	Alex Sanchez	.10
545	Trey Lunsford	.10
546	Abraham Nunez	.10
547	Mike Lincoln	.10
548	Orlando Hernandez	.10
549	Kevin Mench	.10
550	Garret Anderson	.25
551	Kyle Farnsworth	.10
552	Kevin Olsen	.10
553	Joel Pineiro	.10
554	Jorge Julio	.10
555	Jose Mesa	.10
556	Jorge Posada	.40
557	Jose Ortiz	.10
558	Mike Tonis	.10
559	Gabe White	.10
560	Rafael Furcal	.10
561	Matt Franco	.10
562	Trey Hodges	.10
563	Esteban German	.10
564	Josh Fogg	.10
565	Fernando Tatis	.10
566	Alex Cintron	.10
567	Grant Roberts	.10
568	Gene Stechschulte	.10
569	Rafael Palmeiro	.25
570	Mike Hampton	.10
571	Ben Davis	.10
572	Dean Palmer	.10
573	Jerrod Riggan	.10
574	Nate Frese	.10
575	Josh Phelps	.10
576	Freddie Bynum	.10
577	Morgan Ensberg	.10
578	Juan Rincon	.10
579	Kazuhiro Sasaki	.10
580	Yorvit Torrealba	.10
581	Tim Wakefield	.10
582	Sterling Hitchcock	.10
583	Craig Paquette	.10
584	Kevin Millwood	.25
585	Damian Rolls	.10
586	Brad Baisley	.10
587	Kyle Snyder	.10
588	Paul Quantrill	.10
589	Trot Nixon	.10
590	J.T. Snow	.10
591	Kevin Young	.10
592	Tomokazu Ohka	.10
593	Brian Boehringer	.10
594	Danny Patterson	.10
595	Jeff Tam	.10
596	Anastacio Martinez	.10
597	Rod Barajas	.10
598	Octavio Dotel	.10
599	Jason Tyner	.10
600	Gary Sheffield	.40
601	Ruben Quevedo	.10
602	Jay Payton	.10
603	Mo Vaughn	.10
604	Pat Burrell	.40
605	Fernando Vina	.10
606	Wes Anderson	.10
607	Alex Gonzalez	.10
608	Ted Lilly	.10
609	Nick Punto	.10
610	Ryan Madson	.10
611	Odalis Perez	.10
612	Chris Woodward	.10
613	John Olerud	.25
614	Brad Cresse	.10
615	Chad Zerbe	.10
616	Brad Penny	.10
617	Barry Larkin	.40
618	Brandon Duckworth	.10
619	Brad Radke	.10
620	Giovanni Carrara	.10
621	Juan Pierre	.10
622	Rick Reed	.10
623	Omar Daal	.10
624	Jose Hernandez	.10
625	Greg Maddux	1.00
626	Henry Mateo	.10
627	Kip Wells	.10
628	Kevin Cash	.10
629	Mark Redman	.10
630	Luis Gonzalez	.25
631	Jason Conti	.10
632	Ricardo Rincon	.10
633	Mike Bynum	.10
634	Mike Redmond	.10
635	Chance Capel	.10
636	Chris Widger	.10
637	Michael Restovich	.10
638	Mark Grudzielanek	.10
639	Brandon Larson	.10
640	Luis De Los Santos	.10
641	Javy Lopez	.20
642	Rene Reyes	.10
643	Orlando Merced	.10
644	Jason Phillips	.10
645	Luis Ugueto	.10
646	Ron Calloway	.10
647	Josh Paul	.10
648	Todd Greene	.10
649	Joe Giradi	.10
650	Todd Ritchie	.10
651	Lou Merloni	.10
652	Shawn Wooten	.10
653	David Riske	.10
654	Luis Rivas	.10
655	Roy Halladay	.10
656	Travis Driskill	.10
657	Ricky Ledee	.10
658	Tony Perez	.10
659	Fernando Rodney	.10
660	Trevor Hoffman	.10
661	Pat Hentgen	.10
662	Bret Boone	.10
663	Ryan Jensen	.10
664	Ricardo Rodriguez	.10
665	Jeremy Lambert	.10
666	Troy Percival	.10
667	Jon Rauch	.10
668	Mariano Rivera	.25
669	Jason LaRue	.10
670	J.C. Romero	.10
671	Cody Ross	.10
672	Eric Byrnes	.10
673	Paul LoDuca	.10
674	Brad Fullmer	.10
675	Cliff Politte	.10
676	Justin Miller	.10
677	Nic Jackson	.10
678	Kris Benson	.10
679	Carl Sadler	.10
680	Joe Nathan	.10
681	Julio Santana	.10
682	Wade Miller	.10
683	Josh Pearce	.10
684	Tony Armas	.10
685	Al Leiter	.10
686	Raul Ibanez	.10
687	Danny Bautista	.10
688	Travis Hafner	.10
689	*Rylan Reed*	.20
690	Pedro J. Martinez	.75
691	Ramon Santiago	.10
692	Felipe Lopez	.10
693	David Ross	.10
694	Chone Figgins	.10
695	Antonio Osuna	.10
696	Jay Powell	.10
697	Roy Smith	.10
698	Alexis Rios	.10
699	Tanyon Sturtze	.10
700	Turk Wendell	.10
701	Richard Hidalgo	.10
702	Joe Mays	.10
703	Jorge Sosa	.10
704	Eric Karros	.10
705	Steve Finley	.10
706	Sean Smith	.10
707	Jeremy Giambi	.10
708	Scott Hodges	.10
709	Vicente Padilla	.10
710	Bert Snow	.10
711	Aaron Rowand	.10
712	Dennis Tankersley	.10
713	Rick Bauer	.10
714	*Tim Olson*	.25
715	Jeff Urban	.10
716	Steve Sparks	.10
717	Glendon Rusch	.10
718	Ricky Stone	.10
719	Benji Gil	.10
720	Pete Walker	.10
721	Tim Worrell	.10
722	Michael Tejera	.10
723	David Kelton	.10
724	Britt Reames	.10
725	John Stephens	.10
726	Mark McLemore	.10
727	Jeff Zimmerman	.10
728	Checklist	.10
729	Andres Torres	.10
730	Checklist	.10
731	Johan Santana	.10
732	Dane Sardinha	.10
733	Rodrigo Rosario	.10
734	Frank Thomas	.50
735	Tom Glavine	.25
736	Doug Mirabelli	.10
737	Juan Uribe	.10
738	Ryan Anderson	.10
739	Sean Burroughs	.10
740	Eric Chavez	.25
741	Enrique Wilson	.10
742	Elmer Dessens	.10
743	Marlon Byrd	.10
744	Brendan Donnelly	.10
745	Gary Bennett	.10
746	Roy Oswalt	.25
747	Andy Van Hekken	.10
748	Jesus Colome	.10
749	Erick Almonte	.10
750	Frank Catalanotto	.10
751	Matt Herges	.10
752	Carlos Delgado	.40
753	Ryan Franklin	.10
754	Wilken Ruan	.10
755	Kelvim Escobar	.10
756	Tim Drew	.10
757	Jarrod Washburn	.10
758	Runelvys Hernandez	.10
759	Cory Vance	.10
760	Doug Glanville	.10
761	Ryan Rupe	.10
762	Jermaine Dye	.10
763	Mike Cameron	.10
764	Scott Erickson	.10
765	Richie Sexson	.25
766	Jose Vidro	.10
767	Brian West	.10
768	Shawn Estes	.10
769	Brian Tallet	.10
770	Larry Walker	.25
771	Josh Hamilton	.10
772	Orlando Hudson	.10
773	Justin Morneau	.10
774	Ryan Bukvich	.10
775	Mike Gonzalez	.10
776	Tsuyoshi Shinjo	.10
777	Matt Mantei	.10
778	Jimmy Journell	.10
779	Brian Lawrence	.10
780	Mike Lieberthal	.10
781	Scott Mullen	.10
782	Zach Day	.10
783	John Thomson	.10
784	Ben Sheets	.10
785	Damon Minor	.10
786	Jose Valentin	.10
787	Armando Benitez	.10
788	Jamie Walker	.10
789	Preston Wilson	.10
790	Josh Wilson	.10
791	Phil Nevin	.10
792	Roberto Hernandez	.10
793	Mike Williams	.10
794	Jake Peavy	.10
795	Paul Shuey	.10
796	Chad Bradford	.10
797	Bobby Jenks	.10
798	Sean Douglass	.10
799	Damian Miller	.10
800	Mark Wohlers	.10
801	Ty Wigginton	.10
802	Alfonso Soriano	1.00
803	Randy Johnson	.75
804	Placido Polanco	.10
805	Drew Henson	.10
806	Tony Womack	.10
807	Pokey Reese	.10
808	Albert Pujols	.75
809	Shane Reynolds	.10
810	Mike Rivera	.10
811	John Lackey	.10
812	*Brian Wright*	.20
813	Eric Good	.10
814	Dernell Stenson	.10
815	Kirk Rueter	.10
816	Todd Zeile	.10
817	Brad Thomas	.10
818	Shawn Sedlacek	.10
819	Garrett Stephenson	.10
820	Mark Teixeira	.25
821	Tim Hudson	.25
822	Mike Koplove	.10
823	Chris Reitsma	.10
824	Rafael Soriano	.10
825	Ugueth Urbina	.10
826	Matt White	.10
827	Colin Young	.10
828	Pat Strange	.10
829	Juan Pena	.10
830	Joe Thurston	.10
831	Shawn Green	.25

832 Pedro Astacio .10
833 Danny Wright .10
834 *Weston O'Brien* .20
835 Luis Lopez .10
836 Randall Simon .10
837 Jaret Wright .10
838 Jayson Werth .10
839 Endy Chavez .10
840 Checklist .10
841 Chad Paronto .10
842 Randy Winn .10
843 Sidney Ponson .10
844 Robin Ventura .10
845 Rich Aurilia .10
846 Joaquin Benoit .10
847 Barry Bonds 2.00
848 Carl Crawford .10
849 Jeromy Burnitz .10
850 Orlando Cabrera .10
851 Luis Vizcaino .10
852 Randy Wolf .10
853 Benny Agbayani .10
854 Jeremy Affeldt .10
855 Einar Diaz .10
856 Carl Everett .10
857 Wiki Gonzalez .10
858 Steve Belcher .10
859 Travis Harper .10
860 Mike Piazza 1.25
861 Will Ohman .10
862 Eric Young .10
863 Jason Grabowski .10
864 *Rett Johnson* .20
865 Aubrey Huff .10
866 John Smoltz .10
867 Mickey Callaway .10
868 Joe Kennedy .10
869 Tim Redding .10
870 Colby Lewis .10
871 Salomon Torres .10
872 Marco Scutaro .10
873 Tony Batista .10
874 Dmitri Young .10
875 Scott Williamson .10
876 Scott Spezio .10
877 John Webb .10
878 Jose Acevedo .10
879 Kevin Orie .10
880 Jacque Jones .10
881 *Ben Francisco* .25
882 *Bobby Basham* .25
883 *Corey Shafer* .20
884 *J.D. Durbin* .20
885 *Chien-Ming Wang* 1.00
886 Adam Stern .10
887 *Wayne Lydon* .20
888 *Derell McCall* .20
889 *Jon Nelson* .20
890 *Willie Eyre* .20
891 *Ramon A. Martinez* .20
892 *Adrian Myers* .20
893 *Jamie Athas* .20
894 *Ismael Castro* .20
895 David Martinez .10
896 *Terry Tiffee* .20
897 *Nathan Panther* .25
898 *Kyle Roat* .20
899 *Kason Gabbard* .20
900 *Hanley Ramirez* 1.50
901 *Bryan Grace* .15
902 *B.J. Barns* .50
903 *Greg Bruso* .15
904 *Mike Neu* .15
905 *Dustin Yount* .50
906 *Shane Victorino* .20
907 *Brian Burgamy* .20
908 *Beau Kemp* .20
909 *Eny Cabreja* .20
910 *Dexter Cooper* .20
911 *Chris Colton* .20
912 *David Cash* .20
913 *Bernie Castro* .20
914 *Luis Hodge* .20
915 *Jeff Clark* .20
916 *Jason Kubel* .50
917 *T.J. Bohn* .20
918 *Luke Steidlmayer* .20
919 Natthew Petterson .10
920 Darrell Rasner .10
921 Scott Tyler .10
922 *Gary Schneidmiller* .20
923 Kerry Wood .40
924 *Ryan Cameron* .20
925 Wilfredo Rodriguez .10
926 *Rajai Davis* .20
927 *Evel Bastida-Martinez* .20
928 *Chris Duncan* .20
929 *David Pember* .20
930 *Branden Florence* .20
931 Eric Eckenstahler .10
932 *Hong-Chih Kuo* .10
933 *Il Kim* .20
934 Michael Garciaparra .50
935 *Tommy Whiteman* .10
936 *Gary Harris* .20
937 Derry Hammond .10
938 Joey Gomes .10
939 *Donald Hood* .20
940 *Clay Hensley* .50
941 *David Pahucki* .20
942 *Wilton Reynolds* .20
943 *Michael Hinckley* .20
944 *Josh Willingham* .20
945 *Pete LaForest* .20
946 Pete Smart .10
947 Jay Stizman .10
948 *Mark Malaska* .20
949 *Mike Gallo* .20
950 *Tyler Martin* .20
951 Shane Victorino .10
952 Ryan Howard 1.00
953 *Daryl Clark* .20
954 Dayton Buller .10
955 Carlos Zambrano .10
956 Chris Booker .10
957 *Brandon Watson* .20
958 *Matt DeMarco* .20
959 *Doug Waechter* .75
960 *Callix Crabbe* .20
961 *Jairo Garcia* .20
962 *Jason Perry* .20
963 *Eric Riggs* .20
964 *Travis Ishikawa* .40
965 *Jorge Piedra* .20
966 *Manuel Ramirez* .20
967 *Tyler Johnson* .20
968 *Jaime Bubela* .20
969 *Haj Turay* .20
970 *Tyson Graham* .20
971 *David DeJesus* .20
972 *Franklin Gutierrez* .20
973 *Craig Brazell* 1.00
974 *Keith Stamler* .20
975 *Jemel Spearman* .20
976 *Kade Johnson* .10
977 *Nick Trzesniak* .20
978 *Bill Simon* .20
979 *Matthew Hagen* .20
980 *Kris Kroski* .20
981 *Prentice Redman* .50
982 *Kevin Randel* .20
983 Thomari Stori-Harden .10
984 *Brian Shackelford* .20
985 *Mike Adams* .20
986 Brian McCann .10
987 *Mike McNutt* .20
988 *Aron Weston* .20
989 *Dustin Moseley* .20
990 *Bryan Bullington* 1.50

Silver

Stars (1-990): 1-2X
Inserted 1:1

Award Winners

NM/M
Complete Set (30): 20.00
Common Player: .50
Inserted 1:12
AW1 Barry Zito .75
AW2 Randy Johnson 1.50
AW3 Miguel Tejada .75
AW4 Barry Bonds 3.00
AW5 Sammy Sosa 2.00
AW6 Barry Bonds 3.00
AW7 Mike Piazza 2.50
AW8 Todd Helton .75
AW9 Jeff Kent .50
AW10 Edgar Renteria .50
AW11 Scott Rolen .75
AW12 Vladimir Guerrero 1.00
AW13 Mike Hampton .50
AW14 Jason Giambi 1.50
AW15 Alfonso Soriano 1.50
AW16 Alex Rodriguez 3.00
AW17 Eric Chavez .50
AW18 Jorge Posada .50
AW19 Bernie Williams .75
AW20 Magglio Ordonez .50
AW21 Garret Anderson .50
AW22 Manny Ramirez 1.00
AW23 Jason Jennings .50
AW24 Eric Hinske .50
AW25 Billy Koch .50
AW26 John Smoltz .50
AW27 Alex Rodriguez 3.00
AW28 Barry Bonds 3.00
AW29 Tony LaRussa .50
AW30 Mike Scioscia .50

Total Production

NM/M
Complete Set (10): 10.00
Common Player: .40
Inserted 1:18
TP1 Barry Bonds 2.50
TP2 Manny Ramirez .75
TP3 Albert Pujols 1.00
TP4 Jason Giambi 1.00
TP5 Magglio Ordonez .40
TP6 Mike Piazza 1.50
TP7 Todd Helton .75
TP8 Miguel Tejada .50
TP9 Sammy Sosa 1.50
TP10 Alex Rodriguez 2.50

Total Signatures

NM/M
Common Autograph:
Inserted 1:176
MB Marlon Byrd 10.00
EM Eli Marrero 8.00
BP Brandon Phillips 10.00
MT Marcus Thames 8.00
TT Tony Torcato 8.00

Total Topps

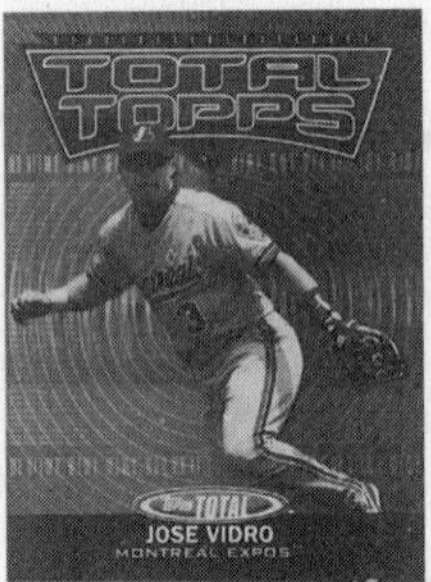

NM/M
Complete Set (50): 25.00
Common Player: .25
Inserted 1:7
TT1 Ichiro Suzuki 1.50
TT2 Alex Rodriguez 2.50
TT3 Barry Bonds 2.50
TT4 Jason Giambi 1.00
TT5 Troy Glaus .75
TT6 Greg Maddux 1.50
TT7 Albert Pujols 1.00
TT8 Randy Johnson 1.00
TT9 Chipper Jones 1.50
TT10 Magglio Ordonez .25
TT11 Jim Thome .75
TT12 Jeff Kent .40
TT13 Curt Schilling .50
TT14 Alfonso Soriano 1.00
TT15 Rafael Palmeiro .50
TT16 Carlos Delgado .50
TT17 Torii Hunter .50
TT18 Pat Burrell .50
TT19 Adam Dunn .75
TT20 Roberto Alomar .50
TT21 Eric Chavez .40
TT22 Derek Jeter 3.00
TT23 Nomar Garciaparra 2.00
TT24 Lance Berkman .40
TT25 Jim Edmonds .40
TT26 Todd Helton .75
TT27 Sammy Sosa 1.50
TT28 Phil Nevin .25
TT29 Andruw Jones .40
TT30 Barry Zito .50
TT31 Richie Sexson .40
TT32 Ken Griffey Jr. 1.50
TT33 Gary Sheffield .40
TT34 Shawn Green .40
TT35 Mike Sweeney .25
TT36 Mike Lowell .25
TT37 Larry Walker .40
TT38 Manny Ramirez .75
TT39 Miguel Tejada .40
TT40 Mike Piazza 2.00
TT41 Scott Rolen .75
TT42 Brian Giles .40
TT43 Garret Anderson .40
TT44 Vladimir Guerrero .75
TT45 Bartolo Colon .25
TT46 Jorge Posada .40
TT47 Ivan Rodriguez .50
TT48 Ryan Klesko .25
TT49 Jose Vidro .25
TT50 Pedro J. Martinez .75

2003 TOPPS TRIBUTE

NM/M
Complete Set (110): 300.00
Common Player: 1.00
Common Auto. (101-110): 10.00
Pack (5): 40.00
Box (6): 180.00
1 Jim Thome 2.50
2 Edgardo Alfonzo 1.00
3 Edgar Martinez 1.50
4 Scott Rolen 2.50
5 Eric Hinske 1.00
6 Mark Mulder 1.50
7 Jason Giambi 3.00
8 Bernie Williams 2.00
9 Cliff Floyd 1.00
10 Ichiro Suzuki 5.00
11 Pat Burrell 2.00
12 Garret Anderson 1.50
13 Gary Sheffield 1.50
14 Johnny Damon 1.50
15 Kerry Wood 2.00
16 Bartolo Colon 1.00
17 Adam Dunn 2.00
18 Omar Vizquel 1.50
19 Todd Helton 2.50
20 Nomar Garciaparra 6.00
21 A.J. Burnett 1.00
22 Craig Biggio 1.50
23 Carlos Beltran 1.50
24 Kazuhisa Ishii 1.00
25 Vladimir Guerrero 2.50
26 Roberto Alomar 2.00
27 Roger Clemens 6.00
28 Tim Hudson 2.00
29 Brian Giles 1.50
30 Barry Bonds 8.00
31 Jim Edmonds 1.50
32 Rafael Palmeiro 2.00
33 Francisco Rodriguez 1.00
34 Andruw Jones 2.00
35 Shea Hillenbrand 1.00
36 Moises Alou 1.50
37 Luis Gonzalez 1.50
38 Darin Erstad 1.50
39 John Smoltz 1.50
40 Derek Jeter 8.00
41 Aubrey Huff 1.00
42 Eric Chavez 1.50
43 Doug Mientkiewicz 1.00
44 Lance Berkman 1.50
45 Josh Beckett 1.00
46 Austin Kearns 2.00
47 Frank Thomas 2.50
48 Pedro J. Martinez 3.00
49 Tim Salmon 1.50

50 Alex Rodriguez 8.00
51 Ryan Klesko 1.50
52 Tom Glavine 1.50
53 Shawn Green 1.50
54 Jeff Kent 1.50
55 Carlos Pena 1.00
56 Paul Konerko 1.00
57 Troy Glaus 2.00
58 Manny Ramirez 2.50
59 Jason Jennings 1.00
60 Randy Johnson 3.00
61 Ivan Rodriguez 2.00
62 Roy Oswalt 1.50
63 Kevin Brown 1.50
64 Jose Vidro 1.00
65 Jorge Posada 1.50
66 Mike Piazza 5.00
67 Bret Boone 1.50
68 Carlos Delgado 2.50
69 Jimmy Rollins 1.00
70 Alfonso Soriano 4.00
71 Greg Maddux 5.00
72 Mark Prior 4.00
73 Jeff Bagwell 2.50
74 Richie Sexson 2.00
75 Sammy Sosa 5.00
76 Curt Schilling 2.00
77 Mike Sweeney 1.00
78 Torii Hunter 1.50
79 Larry Walker 1.50
80 Miguel Tejada 1.50
81 Rich Aurilia 1.00
82 Bobby Abreu 1.50
83 Phil Nevin 1.00
84 Rodrigo Lopez 1.00
85 Chipper Jones 5.00
86 Ken Griffey Jr. 5.00
87 Mike Lowell 1.00
88 Magglio Ordonez 1.50
89 Barry Zito 2.00
90 Albert Pujols 6.00
91 *Corey Shafer* 2.00
92 Dan Haren 5.00
93 Jeremy Bonderman 6.00
94 *Branden Florence* 2.00
95 *Evel Bastida-Martinez* 2.00
96 *Brian Wright* 2.00
97 *Elizardo Ramirez* 2.00
98 Michael Garciaparra 4.00
99 *Clay Hensley* 2.00
100 *Bobby Basham* 2.00
101 *Jose Contreras* 20.00
102 *Bryan Bullington* 25.00
103 Joey Gomes 10.00
104 *Craig Brazell* 15.00
105 *Andy Marte* 50.00
106 *Hanley Ramirez* 50.00
107 *Ryan Shealy* 15.00
108 *Daryl Clark* 10.00
109 *Tyler Johnson* 15.00
110 *Ben Francisco* 10.00

Red Proof

Stars (1-100): 2-4X
Production 225
Autos (101-110): 1-2.5X
Production 50

Gold Proof

Cards (1-100): No Pricing
Production 25
Autos (101-110) are 1 of 1

Double Bonds

NM/M
Premiere Proof: 1.5X
Production 50
BT-DB Barry Bonds 40.00

Solo Bonds

NM/M
Premiere Proof: 1.5X
Production 50
SB Barry Bonds 25.00

Triple Bonds

NM/M
Premiere Proof: 1.5X
Production 50
TB Barry Bonds 60.00

Matching Marks Dual Relics

NM/M
Common Duo: 10.00
Premiere Proofs: 1.5X
Production 50
PH Rafael Palmeiro, Rickey Henderson 15.00
GR Nomar Garciaparra, Alex Rodriguez 25.00
AP Roberto Alomar, Rafael Palmeiro 15.00
MP Fred McGriff, Rafael Palmeiro 10.00
HR Rickey Henderson, Manny Ramirez 15.00
RP Manny Ramirez, Mike Piazza 20.00
BG Jeff Bagwell, Juan Gonzalez 10.00
BP Barry Bonds, Rafael Palmeiro 35.00
SB Sammy Sosa, Jeff Bagwell 20.00
SG Alfonso Soriano, Vladimir Guerrero 15.00
PS Rafael Palmeiro, Sammy Sosa 20.00
MG Fred McGriff, Juan Gonzalez 10.00
PA Rafael Palmeiro, Roberto Alomar 15.00

Modern Marks Autographs

NM/M
Common Autograph: 10.00
Premiere Proofs: 1.5X
Production 50
LB Lance Berkman 20.00
RC Roger Clemens 120.00
CF Cliff Floyd 10.00
EH Eric Hinske 10.00
TH Torii Hunter 15.00
PK Paul Konerko 15.00
PL Paul LoDuca 15.00
MO Magglio Ordonez 20.00
JP Josh Phelps

Milestone Materials

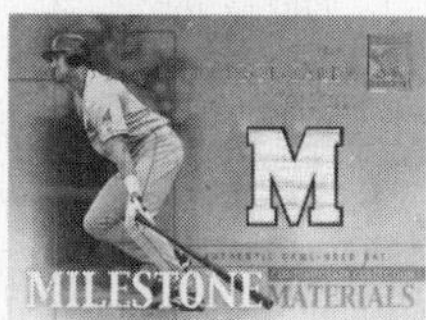

NM/M
Common Player: 8.00
Premiere Proofs: 1.5X
Production 50
RA Roberto Alomar 10.00
JB1 Jeff Bagwell 10.00
JB2 Jeff Bagwell 10.00
BB1 Barry Bonds 25.00
BB2 Barry Bonds 25.00
BB3 Barry Bonds 25.00
BB4 Barry Bonds 25.00
BB5 Barry Bonds 25.00
NG Nomar Garciaparra 20.00
JG1 Juan Gonzalez 10.00
JG2 Juan Gonzalez 10.00
VG Vladimir Guerrero 10.00
TH Todd Helton 10.00
RH1 Rickey Henderson 10.00
RH2 Rickey Henderson 10.00
RH3 Rickey Henderson 10.00
RH4 Rickey Henderson 10.00
RH5 Rickey Henderson 10.00
CJ Chipper Jones 12.00
FM1 Fred McGriff 8.00
FM2 Fred McGriff 8.00
FM3 Fred McGriff 8.00
RP1 Rafael Palmeiro 10.00
RP2 Rafael Palmeiro 10.00
RP3 Rafael Palmeiro 10.00
RP4 Rafael Palmeiro 10.00
MP1 Mike Piazza 15.00
MP2 Mike Piazza 15.00
MR1 Manny Ramirez 10.00
MR2 Manny Ramirez 10.00
AR Alex Rodriguez 15.00
SS1 Sammy Sosa 15.00
SS2 Sammy Sosa 15.00
SS3 Sammy Sosa 15.00
FT Frank Thomas 12.00

Memorable Materials

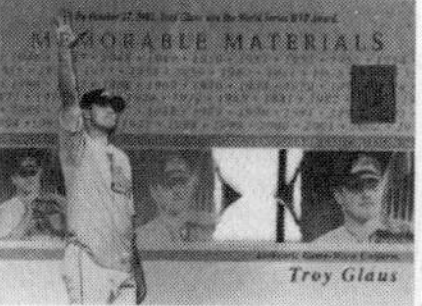

NM/M
Common Player: 8.00
Premiere Proofs: 1.5X
Production 50
BB Barry Bonds 30.00
JG Jason Giambi 8.00
JG2 Jason Giambi 8.00
TG Troy Glaus 8.00
LG Luis Gonzalez 8.00
SG Shawn Green 8.00
VG Vladimir Guerrero 10.00
RH Rickey Henderson 10.00
TH Torii Hunter 8.00
AJ Andruw Jones 8.00
GM Greg Maddux 15.00
AP Albert Pujols 20.00
CR Cal Ripken Jr. 45.00
AR Alex Rodriguez 15.00
AS Alfonso Soriano 10.00
SS Sammy Sosa 15.00
SS2 Sammy Sosa 15.00
MT Miguel Tejada 8.00
KW Kerry Wood 15.00

Perennial All-Stars Relics

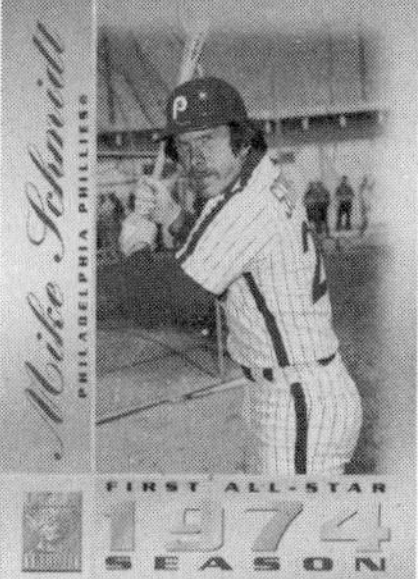

NM/M
Common Player: 8.00
Premiere Proofs: 1.5X
Production 50
RA Roberto Alomar 10.00
CB Craig Biggio 8.00
BB Barry Bonds 25.00
RC Roger Clemens 20.00
RH Rickey Henderson 15.00
CJ Chipper Jones 10.00
GM Greg Maddux 15.00
EM Edgar Martinez 15.00
EM Pedro J. Martinez 15.00
MM Mike Mussina 10.00
MP Mike Piazza 20.00
MR Manny Ramirez 10.00
AR Alex Rodriguez 15.00
IR Ivan Rodriguez 8.00
BS Benito Santiago 8.00
CS Curt Schilling 8.00
GS Gary Sheffield 8.00
JS John Smoltz 8.00
SS Sammy Sosa 20.00
FT Frank Thomas 10.00
LW Larry Walker 8.00
BW Bernie Williams 10.00

Performance Tribute Doubles

NM/M
Common Duo: 10.00
Premiere Proofs: 1.5X
Production 50
ZJ Barry Zito, Randy Johnson 15.00
SA Alfonso Soriano, Roberto Alomar 15.00
RR Cal Ripken Jr., Alex Rodriguez 60.00
RT Alex Rodriguez, Miguel Tejada 15.00
GG Luis Gonzalez, Troy Glaus 10.00
PW Albert Pujols, Kerry Wood 25.00
RG Alex Rodriguez, Nomar Garciaparra 30.00
BJ Barry Bonds, Chipper Jones 25.00
SG Sammy Sosa, Juan Gonzalez 15.00
PS Mike Piazza, Benito Santiago 15.00
PR Mike Piazza, Ivan Rodriguez 15.00
MM Pedro J. Martinez, Greg Maddux 15.00
CM Roger Clemens, Greg Maddux 35.00
JP Chipper Jones, Mike Piazza 20.00

Team Tribute Doubles

NM/M
Common Duo: 10.00
Premiere Proofs: 1.5X
Production 50
MS Greg Maddux, John Smoltz 35.00
IN Kazuhisa Ishii, Hideo Nomo 25.00
WH Larry Walker, Todd Helton 10.00
BB Craig Biggio, Jeff Bagwell 15.00
RP Alex Rodriguez, Rafael Palmeiro 15.00
GR Nomar Garciaparra, Manny Ramirez 20.00

Team Tribute Triples

NM/M
Common Trio: 15.00
Premiere Proofs: 1.5X
Production 50
JSJ Andruw Jones, Gary Sheffield, Chipper Jones 30.00
GRM Nomar Garciaparra, Manny Ramirez, Pedro J. Martinez 40.00
ASP Moises Alou, Sammy Sosa, Corey Patterson 30.00
TOK Frank Thomas, Magglio Ordonez, Paul Konerko 20.00
BBB Craig Biggio, Lance Berkman, Jeff Bagwell 20.00
MHM Joe Mauer, Torii Hunter, Doug Mientkiewicz 25.00
SGV Alfonso Soriano, Jason Giambi, Robin Ventura 25.00
CTM Eric Chavez, Miguel Tejada, Mark Mulder 15.00
HZM Tim Hudson, Barry Zito, Mark Mulder 25.00
TBB Jim Thome, Marlon Byrd, Pat Burrell 25.00
MOB Edgar Martinez, John Olerud, Bret Boone 20.00
PER Albert Pujols, Jim Edmonds, Scott Rolen 40.00
RGP Alex Rodriguez, Juan Gonzalez, Rafael Palmeiro 25.00
RBT Alex Rodriguez, Hank Blalock, Mark Teixeira 25.00

600 HR Club Relic

NM/M
Premiere Proofs: 1.5X
Production 50

Gold: No Pricing
Production one set
HA-600 Hank Aaron 35.00
BB-600 Barry Bonds 30.00
WM-600 Willie Mays 45.00
BR-600 Babe Ruth 125.00

600 HR Club Quad Relic

NM/M
Premiere Proof: 1X
Production 25
BA-600 Hank Aaron, Babe Ruth, Willie Mays, Barry Bonds 625.00

600 HR Club Double Relic

NM/M
Premiere Proofs: 1.5X
Production 50
BA-600 Barry Bonds, Hank Aaron 80.00
BA-600 Barry Bonds, Willie Mays 80.00
BA-600 Barry Bonds, Babe Ruth 200.00

40/40 Club

NM/M
Premiere Proof: 1.5X
Production 50
CBR Jose Canseco, Barry Bonds, Alex Rodriguez 85.00

Tribute to the Stars

NM/M
Common Player: 10.00
Premiere Proofs: 1.5X
Production 50
RA Roberto Alomar 15.00
GA Garret Anderson 15.00
LB Lance Berkman 10.00
BB Barry Bonds 50.00
PB Pat Burrell 15.00
EC Eric Chavez 15.00
AD Adam Dunn 15.00
NG Nomar Garciaparra 40.00
TG Troy Glaus 15.00
VG Vladimir Guerrero 15.00
TH Todd Helton 15.00
RH Rickey Henderson 15.00
THU Torii Hunter 10.00
AJ Andruw Jones 10.00
CJ Chipper Jones 15.00
GM Greg Maddux 20.00
RP Rafael Palmeiro 10.00
MP Mike Piazza 20.00
AP Albert Pujols 40.00
AR Alex Rodriguez 30.00
AS Alfonso Soriano 15.00
SS Sammy Sosa 25.00
FT Frank Thomas 15.00
JT Jim Thome 15.00
LW Larry Walker 10.00

Tribute to the Stars Patchworks

NM/M
Common Player: 25.00
Production 50 sets
JB Jeff Bagwell 35.00
BB Barry Bonds 80.00
NG Nomar Garciaparra 50.00
LG Luis Gonzalez 25.00
SG Shawn Green 25.00
TH Todd Helton 35.00
THU Torii Hunter 25.00
RJ Randy Johnson 40.00
CJ Chipper Jones 35.00
GM Greg Maddux 50.00
PM Pedro J. Martinez 40.00
RP Rafael Palmeiro 30.00
AP Albert Pujols 80.00
MR Manny Ramirez 35.00
AR Alex Rodriguez 50.00
AR2 Alex Rodriguez 50.00
CS Curt Schilling 25.00
SS Sammy Sosa 40.00
FT Frank Thomas 35.00
KW Kerry Wood 30.00

Performance Tribute Triples

NM/M
Common Trio: 20.00
Premiere Proofs: 1.5X
Production 50
SMP Sammy Sosa, Rafael Palmeiro, Fred McGriff 25.00
CMJ Roger Clemens, Greg Maddux, Randy Johnson 30.00
RHP Manny Ramirez, Mike Piazza, Rickey Henderson 30.00
STB Sammy Sosa, Frank Thomas, Jeff Bagwell 20.00
BMP Barry Bonds, Fred McGriff, Rafael Palmeiro 30.00

2003 TOPPS TRIBUTE ALL-STAR EDITION

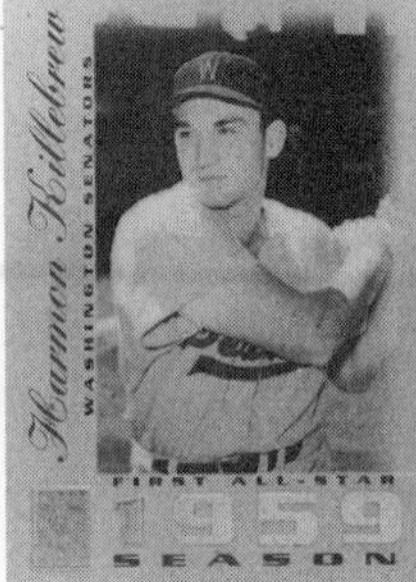

NM/M
Complete Set (50): 50.00
Common Player: 1.00
Pack (5): 40.00
Box (6): 200.00
1 Willie Mays 8.00
2 Don Mattingly 8.00
3 Hoyt Wilhelm 1.00
4 Hank Aaron 8.00
5 Hank Greenberg 1.00
6 Johnny Bench 5.00
7 Duke Snider 3.00
8 Carl Yastrzemski 3.00
9 Jim Palmer 1.00
10 Roberto Clemente 8.00
11 Mike Schmidt 8.00
12 Joe Cronin 1.00
13 Lou Brock 1.00
14 Orlando Cepeda 1.00
15 Bill Mazeroski 1.00
16 Whitey Ford 3.00
17 Rod Carew 1.00
18 Joe Morgan 1.00
19 Luis Aparicio 1.00
20 Nolan Ryan 10.00
21 Bobby Doerr 1.00
22 Dale Murphy 2.00
23 Bob Feller 1.00
24 Paul Molitor 2.00
25 Tom Seaver 3.00
26 Ozzie Smith 3.00
27 Stan Musial 6.00
28 Willie McCovey 1.00
29 Gary Carter 1.00
30 Reggie Jackson 3.00
31 Gaylord Perry 1.00
32 George Brett 8.00
33 Rocky Colavito 1.00
34 Wade Boggs 2.00
35 Cal Ripken Jr. 8.00
36 Carlton Fisk 1.00
37 Al Kaline 3.00
38 Kirby Puckett 4.00
39 Phil Rizzuto 2.00
40 Willie Stargell 1.00
41 Harmon Killebrew 3.00
42 Red Schoendienst 1.00
43 Tony Gwynn 3.00
44 Ralph Kiner 1.00
45 Yogi Berra 4.00
46 Jim "Catfish" Hunter 1.00
47 Frank Robinson 2.00
48 Ernie Banks 4.00
49 Warren Spahn 2.00
50 Brooks Robinson 3.00

1st Class Cuts

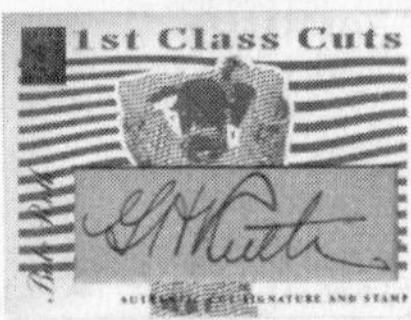

NM/M
Production 1 Set
FC-TC Ty Cobb (3/03 auction) 7,600
FC-DD Dizzy Dean
FC-LG Lou Gehrig
FC-JR Jackie Robinson (3/03 auction) 3,500
FC-BR Babe Ruth (6/04 auction) 7,300
FC-TS Tris Speaker
FC-HW Honus Wagner

Premier Proof

Cards (1-50): 4-8X
Numbered to last two digits of 1st All-Star Year

All-Star Signing

NM/M
Common Autograph: 40.00
Premier Proofs: 1.5-2X
Production 25 sets
LB Lou Brock 50.00
GC Gary Carter 40.00
OC Orlando Cepeda 40.00
AD Andre Dawson 40.00
TG Tony Gwynn 80.00
AK Al Kaline 75.00
DMA Don Mattingly 125.00
DM Dale Murphy 75.00
JP Jim Palmer 40.00
MS Mike Schmidt 100.00
DSN Duke Snider 45.00

Memorable Match-up Relic

NM/M
Common Card: 50.00
Production 150 sets
Premier Proofs: 1.5-2X
Production 25 sets
YB Carl Yastrzemski, Johnny Bench 70.00
BS George Brett, Mike Schmidt 120.00
MJ Willie Mays, Reggie Jackson 65.00
BF Johnny Bench, Carlton Fisk 50.00
CM Gary Carter, Don Mattingly 85.00
KA Harmon Killebrew, Hank Aaron 125.00
BG Wade Boggs, Tony Gwynn 60.00
PG Kirby Puckett, Tony Gwynn 60.00
YBR Carl Yastrzemski, Lou Brock 60.00

Perennial Patch Relics

NM/M
Common Player: 40.00
Production 30 sets
WB Wade Boggs 75.00
GB George Brett 220.00
GC Gary Carter 40.00
TG Tony Gwynn 125.00
HK Harmon Killebrew 90.00
WM Willie McCovey 40.00
JM Joe Morgan 40.00
DMU Dale Murphy 120.00
CR Cal Ripken Jr. 225.00
NR Nolan Ryan/Rangers 200.00
NRA Nolan Ryan/Astros 200.00
MS Mike Schmidt 200.00
OS Ozzie Smith 120.00
WS Willie Stargell 75.00
CY Carl Yastrzemski 190.00

Tribute Relics

NM/M
Common Player: 10.00
Inserted 1:1
HA Hank Aaron 35.00
LA Luis Aparicio 10.00
EB Ernie Banks 20.00
JBE Johnny Bench 20.00
YB Yogi Berra 40.00
WB Wade Boggs 15.00
GB George Brett 20.00
LB Lou Brock/bat 30.00
LBU Lou Brock/Jersey 15.00
RCA Roy Campanella 20.00
ROD Rod Carew 15.00
GC Gary Carter 10.00
OC Orlando Cepeda 12.00
RC Roberto Clemente 60.00
TC Ty Cobb 100.00
JCR Joe Cronin 15.00
AD Andre Dawson 10.00
DD Dizzy Dean 40.00
BD Bobby Doerr 10.00
BF Bob Feller 15.00
CF Carlton Fisk 15.00
WF Whitey Ford 30.00
JF Jimmie Foxx 40.00
LG Lou Gehrig 125.00
HG Hank Greenberg 40.00
TG Tony Gwynn 20.00
RH Rogers Hornsby 40.00
CH Jim "Catfish" Hunter 20.00
RJ Reggie Jackson 15.00
AK Al Kaline 25.00
HK Harmon Killebrew 20.00
NL Napoleon Lajoie 60.00
EM Eddie Mathews 15.00
DMA Don Mattingly 30.00
WM Willie Mays 40.00
BM Bill Mazeroski 20.00
WMC Willie McCovey 18.00
JMI Johnny Mize 30.00
PM Paul Molitor 15.00
JMO Joe Morgan 10.00
TM Thurman Munson 30.00
DM Dale Murphy 50.00
SM Stan Musial 30.00
DN Don Newcombe 10.00
MO Mel Ott 30.00
JP Jim Palmer 10.00
KP Kirby Puckett 20.00
CRB Cal Ripken Jr. 40.00
PR Phil Rizzuto 15.00
BRO Brooks Robinson 15.00
FR Frank Robinson 10.00
JR Jackie Robinson 40.00
BR Babe Ruth 140.00
NR Nolan Ryan/Rangers 40.00
NRA Nolan Ryan/Astros 40.00
MS Mike Schmidt 20.00
RS Red Schoendienst 15.00
TSE Tom Seaver 25.00
OS Ozzie Smith 15.00
DSN Duke Snider 20.00
TS Tris Speaker 75.00
WST Willie Stargell 20.00
HW Honus Wagner 125.00
WHI Hoyt Wilhelm 10.00
CY Carl Yastrzemski 30.00

2003 TOPPS TRIBUTE WORLD SERIES

		NM/M
Complete Set (150):		150.00
Common Player:		1.00
Pack (5):		50.00
Box (6):		260.00
1	Willie Mays	8.00
2	Gary Carter	1.50
3	Yogi Berra	4.00
4	Dennis Eckersley	1.50
5	Willie McCovey	1.50
6	Willie Stargell	2.00
7	Mike Schmidt	8.00
8	Robin Yount	4.00
9	Bucky Harris	1.00
10	Carl Yastrzemski	4.00
11	Lenny Dykstra	1.00
12	Boog Powell	1.00
13	Bill Lee	1.00
14	Lou Brock	1.50
15	Bob Friend	1.00
16	Hank Greenberg	1.50
17	Maury Wills	1.00
18	Tommy Lasorda	1.00
19	Bill "Moose" Skowron	1.00
20	Frank Robinson	2.00
21	Rollie Fingers	1.00
22	Doug DeCinces	1.00
23	Eric Davis	1.00
24	Johnny Podres	1.00
25	Darrell Evans	1.00
26	Ron Cey	1.00
27	Ray Knight	1.00
28	Don Larsen	1.00
29	Harold Baines	1.00
30	Brooks Robinson	4.00
31	Wade Boggs	2.00
32	Joe Morgan	1.00
33	Kirk Gibson	1.00
34	Tommy John	1.00
35	Monte Irvin	2.00
36	Rich "Goose" Gossage	1.00
37	Tug McGraw	1.00
38	Walt Weiss	1.00
39	Bill Madlock	1.00
40	Juan Marichal	2.00
41	Willie McGee	1.00
42	Joe Cronin	1.00
43	Paul Blair	1.00
44	Norm Cash	1.00
45	Ken Griffey Sr.	1.00
46	Bret Saberhagen	1.00
47	Don Sutton	1.00
48	Kirby Puckett	4.00
49	Keith Hernandez	1.00
50	George Brett	8.00
51	Bobby Richardson	1.00
52	Jose Canseco	2.00
53	Greg Luzinski	1.00
54	Bill Mazeroski	1.00
55	Red Schoendienst	1.00
56	Graig Nettles	1.00
57	Jerry Koosman	1.00
58	Tony Perez	1.00
59	Jim Rice	1.00
60	Duke Snider	4.00
61	David Justice	1.00
62	Johnny Sain	1.00
63	Chuck Klein	1.00
64	Sparky Anderson	1.00
65	Alan Trammell	2.00
66	Willie Wilson	1.00
67	Hoyt Wilhelm	1.00
68	Joe Pepitone	1.00
69	Darren Daulton	1.00
70	Tom Seaver	4.00
71	Jim "Catfish" Hunter	1.00
72	Tim McCarver	1.00
73	Dave Parker	1.00
74	Earl Weaver	1.00
75	Ted Kluszewski	1.00
76	John Kruk	1.00
77	Dwight Evans	1.00
78	Ron Darling	1.00
79	Tony Oliva	1.00
80	Johnny Bench	5.00
81	Sam Crawford	1.00
82	Steve Yeager	1.00
83	Paul Molitor	2.00
84	Bert Campaneris	1.00
85	Mickey Rivers	1.00
86	Vince Coleman	1.00
87	Kent Tekulve	1.00
88	Dwight Gooden	1.00
89	Whitey Herzog	1.00
90	Whitey Ford	4.00
91	Warren Spahn	3.00
92	Fred Lynn	1.00
93	Joe Tinker	1.00
94	Bill Buckner	1.00
95	Bob Feller	2.00
96	Hank Bauer	1.00
97	Joe Rudi	1.00
98	Steve Sax	1.00
99	Bruce Sutter	1.50
100	Nolan Ryan	10.00
101	Bobby Thomson	1.00
102	Bob Watson	1.00
103	Vida Blue	1.00
104	Robin Roberts	1.00
105	Orlando Cepeda	2.00
106	Jim Bottomley	1.00
107	Heinie Manush	1.00
108	Jim Gilliam	1.00
109	Dave Concepcion	1.00
110	Al Kaline	5.00
111	Howard Johnson	1.00
112	Phil Rizzuto	2.00
113	Steve Garvey	1.00
114	George Foster	1.00
115	Carlton Fisk	2.00
116	Don Newcombe	1.00
117	Lance Parrish	1.00
118	Reggie Jackson	4.00
119	Luis Aparicio	1.00
120	Jim Palmer	1.50
121	Ron Guidry	1.00
122	Frankie Frisch	1.00
123	Chet Lemon	1.00
124	Cecil Cooper	1.00
125	Harmon Killebrew	4.00
126	Luis Tiant	1.00
127	John McGraw	1.00
128	Paul O'Neill	1.00
129	Jack Clark	1.00
130	Stan Musial	6.00
131	Mike Schmidt	4.00
132	Kirby Puckett	2.00
133	Carlton Fisk	1.50
134	Bill Mazeroski	1.00
135	Johnny Podres	1.00
136	Robin Yount	1.50
137	David Justice	1.00
138	Bobby Thomson	1.00
139	Joe Carter	1.00
140	Reggie Jackson	1.50
141	Kirk Gibson	1.00
142	Whitey Ford	1.50
143	Don Larsen	1.00
144	Duke Snider	1.50
145	Carl Yastrzemski	1.50
146	Johnny Bench	2.00
147	Lou Brock	1.00
148	Ted Kluszewski	1.00
149	Jim Palmer	1.00
150	Willie Mays	5.00

Gold

Golds (1-150): 4-8X
Production 100 sets

Cut Signature Relic

No pricing due to scarcity
Production one set

Fan Fare Relic

		NM/M
Common Player:		10.00
Inserted 1:box		
HB	Hank Bauer	10.00
YB	Yogi Berra	20.00
WF	Whitey Ford	15.00
DJ	David Justice	10.00
DL	Don Larsen	15.00
BM	Billy Martin	15.00
DN	Don Newcombe	10.00
PO	Paul O'Neill	15.00

JP	Johnny Podres	15.00
PR	Phil Rizzuto	15.00
MS	Bill "Moose" Skowron	10.00
DS	Duke Snider	15.00

Pastime Patches Relics

No pricing due to scarcity
Production 15 sets

Memorab. Match-Up Relic

		NM/M
Common Player:		
Varying quantities produced		
WC	Honus Wagner, Ty Cobb/9	
CR	Eddie Collins, Edd Roush/19	
GF	Hank Greenberg, Frankie Frisch/34	90.00
GK	Hank Greenberg, Chuck Klein/35	90.00
PR	Phil Rizzuto, Willie Mays/51	150.00
FS	Whitey Ford, Duke Snider/53	75.00
AS	Luis Aparicio, Duke Snider/59	35.00
MF	Bill Mazeroski, Whitey Ford/60	50.00
KB	Al Kaline, Lou Brock/68	75.00
RS	Frank Robinson, Tom Seaver/69	40.00
RBE	Brooks Robinson, Johnny Bench/70	55.00
AM	Sparky Anderson, Billy Martin/76	25.00
SP	Willie Stargell, Jim Palmer/79	40.00
SB	Mike Schmidt, George Brett/80	80.00
SY	Ozzie Smith, Robin Yount/82	50.00
SRI	Mike Schmidt, Cal Ripken Jr./83	120.00
TG	Alan Trammell, Tony Gwynn/84	50.00
WB	Mookie Wilson, Bill Buckner/86	40.00
EG	Dennis Eckersley, Kirk Gibson/88	35.00

Relic

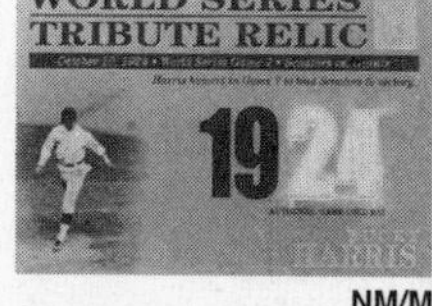

		NM/M
Common Player:		10.00
Production 425 unless noted		
Golds:		No Pricing
Production 25		
HA	Hank Aaron/50	60.00
HB	Hank Bauer/50	30.00
JBE	Johnny Bench	25.00
YB	Yogi Berra	20.00
WB	Wade Boggs	15.00
JB	Jim Bottomley/50	30.00
GB	George Brett	25.00
LB	Lou Brock	10.00
JC	Jose Canseco	15.00
NC	Norm Cash/50	25.00
OC	Orlando Cepeda/50	30.00
RC	Roberto Clemente/50	120.00
TC	Ty Cobb	120.00
SC	Sam Crawford/50	50.00
CF	Carlton Fisk	40.00
JF	Jimmie Foxx/50	80.00
FF	Frankie Frisch	15.00
LG	Lou Gehrig/50	185.00
HG	Hank Greenberg/50	60.00
TG	Tony Gwynn	20.00
BH	Bucky Harris	10.00
RH	Rogers Hornsby	35.00
CH	Jim "Catfish" Hunter	15.00
RJ	Reggie Jackson	15.00
HK	Harmon Killebrew	25.00
CK	Chuck Klein	10.00
TK	Ted Kluszewski	15.00
HM	Heinie Manush/50	35.00
JM	Juan Marichal	10.00
RM	Roger Maris/50	75.00
BMA	Billy Martin	15.00
WM	Willie Mays	50.00
BM	Bill Mazeroski	15.00
WMC	Willie McCovey	10.00
TM	Thurman Munson	30.00
SM	Stan Musial	30.00
KP	Kirby Puckett	20.00
CR	Cal Ripken Jr.	35.00
FR	Frank Robinson	15.00
JR	Jackie Robinson	40.00
ER	Edd Roush/50	40.00
BR	Babe Ruth	140.00
MS	Mike Schmidt	25.00
RS	Red Schoendienst	10.00
TS	Tom Seaver	15.00
OS	Ozzie Smith	20.00
TSP	Tris Speaker/50	90.00
WS	Willie Stargell/50	30.00
BT	Bobby Thomson	15.00
JT	Joe Tinker	30.00
HW	Honus Wagner/50	150.00
CY	Carl Yastrzemski	30.00
RY	Robin Yount	20.00

Autographed Relic

		NM/M
Inserted 1:55		
Golds:		No Pricing
Production 25 sets		
LB	Lou Brock	40.00
JC	Jose Canseco	40.00
CF	Carlton Fisk	120.00
HK	Harmon Killebrew	75.00
WM	Willie Mays	275.00
BM	Bill Mazeroski	60.00
MS	Mike Schmidt	100.00
BT	Bobby Thomson	40.00

Series Signatures

		NM/M
Common Autograph:		25.00
Golds:		No Pricing
Production 25		
SA	Sparky Anderson	25.00
JC	Joe Carter	25.00
WF	Whitey Ford	60.00
SG	Steve Garvey	25.00
KG	Kirk Gibson	30.00
DJ	David Justice	40.00
AK	Al Kaline	50.00
DN	Don Newcombe	40.00
JP	Jim Palmer	30.00
BR	Brooks Robinson	75.00
MS	Bill "Moose" Skowron	25.00
AT	Alan Trammell	25.00
EW	Earl Weaver	25.00
MW	Maury Willis	25.00
MWI	Mookie Wilson	30.00

Team Tribute Relic

	NM/M
Common Card:	15.00

Production 275 unless noted
YLK Carl Yastrzemski, Fred Lynn, Carlton Fisk 50.00
OSD Paul O'Neill, Chris Sabo, Eric Davis 25.00
FPG George Foster, Tony Perez, Ken Griffey Jr. 25.00
CPM Dave Concepcion, Tony Perez, Joe Morgan 50.00
KCA Al Kaline, Norm Cash 40.00
TA Alan Trammell, Sparky Anderson 15.00
GT Kirk Gibson, Alan Trammell 25.00
SB Bret Saberhagen, George Brett 40.00
CYG Ron Cey, Steve Yeager, Steve Garvey 30.00
YM Robin Yount, Paul Molitor 35.00
SRK Tom Seaver, Nolan Ryan, Jerry Koosman 50.00
HCD Keith Hernandez, Gary Carter, Lenny Dykstra 30.00
GB Lou Gehrig, Babe Ruth/25 500.00
SR Bill "Moose" Skowron, Bobby Richardson
FB Whitey Ford, Yogi Berra/25
EC Dennis Eckersley, Jose Canseco 25.00
HJ Jim "Catfish" Hunter, Reggie Jackson 30.00
SPM Willie Stargell, Dave Parker, Bill Madlock 30.00
CM Orlando Cepeda, Juan Marichal 30.00
MM Willie Mays, Willie McCovey 50.00
SMC Ozzie Smith, Willie McGee, Vince Coleman 40.00

World Series Tribute Singles

NM/M
Common Player: 8.00
Premiere Proofs: 1.5X
Production 50
TG Troy Glaus 8.00
MR Mariano Rivera 10.00

World Series Tribute Doubles

NM/M
Common Duo: 10.00
Premiere Proofs: 1.5X
Production 50
PP Jorge Posada, Andy Pettitte 15.00
WO Bernie Williams, Paul O'Neill 15.00
LP John Lackey, Troy Percival 10.00
SJ Curt Schilling, Randy Johnson 15.00
BG Barry Bonds, Troy Glaus 35.00
WG Bernie Williams, Luis Gonzalez 10.00
PC Mike Piazza, Roger Clemens 35.00

World Series Tribute Triples

NM/M
Common Trio: 15.00
Premiere Proofs: 1.5X
Production 50
LGP John Lackey, Troy Glaus, Troy Percival 15.00
EGS Darin Erstad, Troy Glaus, Tim Salmon 15.00

2003 TOPPS 205

NM/M
Complete Set (335): 150.00
Common Player: .20
SP's inserted 1:5
25 variations in base set and minis
Mini-Cards(316-335):Exclusive Mini Cards
Price for minis (316-335) are Polar Bear
Series 1 or 2 Pack (8): 4.00
Series 1 or 2 Box (20): 65.00
1 Barry Bonds 2.50
1 Barry Bonds/variation 3.00
2 Bret Boone .40
3 Albert Pujols 2.00
3 Albert Pujols/variation 2.00
4 Carl Crawford .20
5 Bartolo Colon .20
6 Cliff Floyd .20
7 John Olerud .40
8 Jason Giambi .50
8 Jason Giambi/variation .75
9 Edgardo Alfonzo .20
10 Ivan Rodriguez .50
11 Jim Edmonds .50
12 Mike Piazza 1.50
12 Mike Piazza/variation 2.00
13 Greg Maddux 1.50
14 Jose Vidro .20
15 Vladimir Guerrero .75
15 Vladimir Guerrero/variation 1.00
16 Bernie Williams .50
17 Roger Clemens 2.00
18 Miguel Tejada .50
18 Miguel Tejada/variation .75
19 Carlos Delgado .50
20 Alfonso Soriano .75
20 Alfonso Soriano/variation .75
21 Bobby Cox .20
22 Mike Scioscia .20
23 John Smoltz .40
24 Luis Gonzalez .40
25 Shawn Green .40
26 Raul Ibanez .20
27 Andruw Jones .50
28 Josh Beckett .40
29 Derek Lowe .20
30 Todd Helton .75
31 Barry Larkin .40
32 Jason Jennings .20
33 Darin Erstad .40
34 Magglio Ordonez .40
35 Mike Sweeney .20
36 Kazuhisa Ishii .20
37 Ron Gardenhire .20
38 Tim Hudson .40
39 Tim Salmon .50
40 Pat Burrell .40
40 Pat Burrell/variation .50
41 Manny Ramirez .75
42 Nick Johnson .20
43 Tom Glavine .40
44 Mark Mulder .40
45 Brian Jordan .20
46 Rafael Palmeiro .50
47 Vernon Wells .40
48 Bob Brenly .20
49 C.C. Sabathia .20
50 Alex Rodriguez 2.50
50 Alex Rodriguez/variation 2.50
51 Sammy Sosa 1.50
51 Sammy Sosa/variation 2.00
52 Paul Konerko .20
53 Craig Biggio .40
54 Moises Alou .40
55 Johnny Damon .50
56 Torii Hunter .40
57 Omar Vizquel .40
58 Orlando Hernandez .20
59 Barry Zito .40
60 Lance Berkman .50
61 Carlos Beltran .50
62 Edgar Renteria .40
63 Ben Sheets .40
64 Doug Mientkiewicz .20
65 Troy Glaus .50
66 Preston Wilson .20
67 Kerry Wood .75
68 Frank Thomas .75
69 Jimmy Rollins .20
70 Brian Giles .40
71 Bobby Higginson .20
72 Larry Walker .40
73 Randy Johnson 1.00
74 Tony LaRussa .20
75 Derek Jeter 3.00
75 Derek Jeter/variation 3.00
76 Bobby Abreu .40
77 Adam Dunn .75
77 Adam Dunn/variation .75
78 Ryan Klesko .20
79 Francisco Rodriguez .20
80 Scott Rolen .75
81 Roberto Alomar .50
82 Joe Torre .50
83 Jim Thome .75
84 Kevin Millwood .40
85 J.T. Snow .20
86 Trevor Hoffman .20
87 Jay Gibbons .20
88 Mark Prior 1.00
88 Mark Prior/variation 1.50
89 Rich Aurilia .20
90 Chipper Jones 1.00
91 Richie Sexson .50
92 Gary Sheffield .50
93 Pedro J. Martinez 1.00
94 Rodrigo Lopez .20
95 Al Leiter .20
96 Jorge Posada .50
97 Luis Castillo .20
98 Aubrey Huff .20
99 A.J. Pierzynski .20
100 Ichiro Suzuki 2.00
100 Ichiro Suzuki/variation 2.00
101 Eric Chavez .40
102 Brett Myers .20
103 Jason Kendall .40
104 Jeff Kent .40
105 Eric Hinske .20
106 Jacque Jones .20
107 Phil Nevin .20
108 Roy Oswalt .40
109 Curt Schilling .75
110 Nomar Garciaparra 2.00
110 Nomar Garciaparra/variation 2.00
111 Garret Anderson .40
112 Eric Gagne .40
113 Javier Vazquez .40
114 Jeff Bagwell .75
115 Mike Lowell .40
116 Carlos Pena .20
117 Ken Griffey Jr. 1.50
118 Tony Batista .20
119 Edgar Martinez .20
120 Austin Kearns .50
121 Jason Stokes .20
122 Jose Reyes .40
123 Rocco Baldelli .40
124 Joe Borchard .20
125 Joe Mauer .50
126 Gavin Floyd .20
127 Mark Teixeira .50
128 Jeremy Guthrie .20
129 B.J. Upton .40
130 Khalil Greene 2.00
131 *Hanley Ramirez* 3.00
132 *Andy Marte* 3.00
133 *J.D. Durbin* 1.00
134 *Jason Kubel* 2.00
135 *Craig Brazell* .75
136 *Bryan Bullington* 1.00
137 *Jose Contreras* 1.00
138 *Brian Burgamy* .75
139 *Evel Bastida-Martinez* .50
140 Joey Gomes 1.00
141 *Ismael Castro* .75
142 *Travis Wong* .75
143 Michael Garciaparra .50
144 *Arnaldo Munoz* .50
145 Louis Sockalexis 2.00
146 Dick Hoblitzell 1.00
147 George "Peaches" Graham .50
148 Hal Chase .50
149 John McGraw 1.00
150 Bobby Wallace .50
151 Dave Shean .20
152 Dick Hoblitzell SP 3.00
153 Hal Chase .20
154 George Wiltse .20
155 George Brett 2.00
156 Willie Mays 3.00
157 Honus Wagner SP 4.00
158 Nolan Ryan 3.00
159 Reggie Jackson 1.00
160 Mike Schmidt 1.50
161 Josh Barfield .20
162 Grady Sizemore .20
163 Justin Morneau .20
164 Laynce Nix .20
165 Zack Greinke .20
166 Victor Martinez .50
167 Jeff Mathis .20
168 Casey Kotchman .20
169 Gabe Gross .20
170 *Edwin Jackson* 1.50
171 *Delmon Young SP* 10.00
172 Eric Duncan SP 2.00
173 Brian Snyder SP 1.50
174 *Chris Lubanski SP* 4.00
175 *Ryan Harvey SP* 5.00
176 *Nicholas Markakis SP* 3.00
177 *Chad Billingsley SP* 3.00
178 Elizardo Ramirez .50
179 Ben Francisco .50
180 Franklin Gutierrez SP 4.00
181 Aaron Hill SP 2.00
182 Kevin Correia .50
183 Kelly Shoppach .50
184 *Felix Pie SP* 5.00
185 *Adam Loewen SP* 5.00
186 Danny Garcia .50
187 *Rickie Weeks SP* 8.00
188 Robby Hammock SP 2.00
189 *Ryan Wagner SP* 2.00
190 Matt Kata SP 1.50
191 *Bo Hart SP* 2.00
192 *Brandon Webb SP* 2.00
193 Bengie Molina .20
194 Junior Spivey .20
195 Gary Sheffield .50
196 Jason Johnson .20
197 David Ortiz .75
198 Roberto Alomar .50
199 Wily Mo Pena .20
200 Sammy Sosa 2.00
201 Jay Payton .20
202 Dmitri Young .20
203 Derek Lee .40
204 Jeff Bagwell .75
204 Jeff Bagwell/variation .75
205 Runelvys Hernandez .20
206 Kevin Brown .40
207 Wes Helms .20
208 Eddie Guardado .20
209 Orlando Cabrera .20
210 Alfonso Soriano .75
211 Ty Wigginton .20
212 Rich Harden .40
212 Rich Harden/variation .50
213 Mike Lieberthal .20
214 Brian Giles .40
215 Jason Schmidt .40
216 Jamie Moyer .20
217 Matt Morris .20
218 Victor Zambrano .20
219 Roy Halladay .50
220 Mike Hampton .20
221 Kevin Millar .20
222 Hideo Nomo .50
223 Milton Bradley .20
224 Jose Guillen .20
225 Derek Jeter 3.00
226 Rondell White .20
227 Hank Blalock .50
227 Hank Blalock/variation .50
228 Shigetoshi Hasegawa .20
229 Mike Mussina .50
230 Cristian Guzman .20
231 Todd Helton .75
231 Todd Helton/variation .75
232 Kenny Lofton .40
233 Carl Everett .20
234 Shea Hillenbrand .20
235 Brad Fullmer .20
236 Bernie Williams .50
237 Vicente Padilla .20
238 Tim Worrell .20
239 Juan Gonzalez .40
240 Ichiro Suzuki 2.00
241 Aaron Boone .20
242 Shannon Stewart .20
243 Barry Zito .40
243 Barry Zito/variation .40
244 Reggie Sanders .20
245 Scott Podsednik .40
246 Miguel Cabrera .75
247 Angel Berroa .20
248 Carlos Zambrano .40
249 Marlon Byrd .20

250	Mark Prior	1.00
251	Esteban Loaiza	.20
252	David Eckstein	.20
253	Alex Cintron	.20
254	Melvin Mora	.20
255	Russ Ortiz	.20
256	Carlos Lee	.20
257	Tino Martinez	.20
258	Randy Wolf	.20
259	Jason Phillips	.20
260	Vladimir Guerrero	1.00
261	Brad Wilkerson	.20
262	Ivan Rodriguez	.75
263	Matt Lawton	.20
264	Adam Dunn	.50
265	Joe Borowski	.20
266	Jody Gerut	.20
267	Alex Rodriguez	2.50
268	Brendan Donnelly	.20
269	Randy Johnson	1.00
269	Randy Johnson/ variation	1.00
270	Nomar Garciaparra	2.50
271	Javy Lopez	.50
272	Travis Hafner	.20
273	Juan Pierre	.20
274	Morgan Ensberg	.20
275	Albert Pujols	2.00
276	Jason LaRue	.20
277	Paul LoDuca	.20
278	Andy Pettitte	.50
279	Mike Piazza	1.50
280	Jim Thome	1.00
280	Jim Thome/variation	1.00
281	Marquis Grissom	.20
282	Woody Williams	.20
283	Curt Schilling	.75
283	Curt Schilling/variation	.75
284	Chipper Jones	1.00
284	Chipper Jones/variation	1.00
285	Deivi Cruz	.20
286	Johnny Damon	.50
287	Chin-Hui Tsao	.20
288	Alex Gonzalez	.20
289	Billy Wagner	.40
290	Jason Giambi	.50
291	Keith Foulke	.20
292	Jerome Williams	.20
293	Livan Hernandez	.20
294	Aaron Guiel	.20
295	Randall Simon	.20
296	Byung-Hyun Kim	.20
297	Jorge Julio	.20
298	Miguel Batista	.20
299	Rafael Furcal	.40
300	Dontrelle Willis SP	1.00
300	Dontrelle Willis/variation	1.00
301	Alex Sanchez	.20
302	Shawn Chacon	.20
303	Matt Clement	.20
304	Luis Matos	.20
305	Steve Finley	.20
306	Marcus Giles	.40
307	Boomer Wells	.20
308	Jeromy Burnitz	.20
309	Mike MacDougal	.20
310	Mariano Rivera	.40
311	Adrian Beltre	.40
312	Mark Loretta	.20
313	Ugueth Urbina	.20
314	Bill Mueller	.20
315	Johan Santana	.50
316	Willie Mays	2.00
317	Delmon Young	4.00
318	Rickie Weeks	4.00
319	Ryan Wagner	.50
320	Brandon Webb	.50
321	Chris Lubanski	1.00
322	Ryan Harvey	3.00
323	Nicholas Markakis	1.00
324	Chad Billingsley	.75
325	Aaron Hill	.40
326	Brian Snyder	.40
327	Eric Duncan	.40
328	Sammy Sosa	1.50
329	Alfonso Soriano	1.00
330	Ichiro Suzuki	2.00
331	Alex Rodriguez	2.00
332	Nomar Garciaparra	2.00
333	Albert Pujols	2.00
334	Jim Thome	1.00
335	Dontrelle Willis	.50

Mini Parallel

	NM/M
Polar Bear:	1-2X
Sovereign:	1-2X
Sovereign Green:	2-3X
American Beauty:	1-2X
Amer. Beauty Purple:	3-5X
Cycle:	1-2X
Cycle Purple:	3-5X
Drum:	2-4X
Honest:	1-2X
Honest Purple:	3-5X
Piedmont:	1-2X
Piedmont Purple:	3-5X
Sweet Caporal:	1-2X
Sweet Caporal Purple:	3-5X
Bazooka:	No Pricing
Production 5 sets	
Brooklyn:	1.5-4X
Brooklyn: Varies for common, rare & Unc.	

T-205 Relics

		NM/M
Common Player:		4.00
RA	Roberto Alomar/bat	6.00
GA	Garret Anderson/jsy	5.00
JB	Jeff Bagwell/jsy	6.00
LB	Lance Berkman/bat	8.00
BB	Barry Bonds	25.00
AB	A.J. Burnett/jsy	4.00
LC	Luis Castillo/jsy	4.00
EC	Eric Chavez/bat	5.00
JD	Johnny Damon/bat	6.00
AD	Adam Dunn/bat	8.00
RF	Rafael Furcal/bat	6.00
EG	Eric Gagne/jsy	8.00
NG	Nomar Garciaparra/jsy	15.00
BG	Brian Giles/bat	5.00
LG	Luis Gonzalez/jsy	4.00
TH	Todd Helton/jsy	10.00
KI	Kazuhisa Ishii/jsy	6.00
JJ	Jason Jennings/jsy	4.00
NJ	Nick Johnson/bat	4.00
RJ	Randy Johnson/jsy	8.00
JK	Jeff Kent/bat	4.00
AL	Al Leiter/jsy	4.00
KL	Kenny Lofton/bat	4.00
DL	Derek Lowe/jsy	4.00
GM	Greg Maddux/jsy	15.00
PM	Pedro Martinez/jsy	10.00
MO	Magglio Ordonez/jsy	4.00
RO	Roy Oswalt/jsy	4.00
RP	Rafael Palmeiro/jsy	6.00
TP	Troy Percival/jsy	4.00
MP	Mike Piazza/bat	10.00
AP	Albert Pujols/jsy	20.00
MR	Manny Ramirez/bat	8.00
AR	Alex Rodriguez/jsy	10.00
SR	Scott Rolen/bat	15.00
CS	Curt Schilling/jsy	6.00
JS	John Smoltz/jsy	8.00
AS	Alfonso Soriano/jsy	10.00
MS	Mike Sweeney/bat	4.00
JT	Jim Thome/bat	12.00
MV	Mo Vaughn/jsy	4.00
BW	Bernie Williams/bat	10.00
BZ	Barry Zito/jsy	4.00
Series 2		
RA	Roberto Alomar	6.00
JB	Jeff Bagwell	8.00
RBB	Rocco Baldelli/bat	8.00
RB	Rocco Baldelli/jersey	8.00
CB	Craig Biggio	4.00
HB	Hank Blalock	6.00
WB	Wade Boggs	15.00
BB	Bret Boone	10.00
GB	George Brett	25.00
KB	Kevin Brown	4.00
SB	Sean Burroughs	4.00
MC	Mike Cameron	4.00
JC	Jose Canseco	8.00
GC	Gary Carter	8.00
RC	Roger Clemens	15.00
CD	Carlos Delgado	6.00
BD	Brandon Duckworth	4.00
JE	Jim Edmonds	6.00
DE	Darin Erstad	4.00
RF	Rafael Furcal	4.00
NG	Nomar Garciaparra	10.00
JG	Jason Giambi	6.00
JGI	Jeremy Giambi	4.00
BG	Brian Giles	4.00
TG	Troy Glaus	6.00
JGO	Juan Gonzalez	6.00
LG	Luis Gonzalez	4.00
MG	Mark Grace	10.00
MGR	Marquis Grissom	4.00
VG	Vladimir Guerrero	8.00
CG	Cristian Guzman	4.00
RH	Rickey Henderson	8.00
RJ	Randy Johnson	8.00
AJ	Andruw Jones	6.00
CJB	Chipper Jones	8.00
KL	Kenny Lofton	4.00
GM	Greg Maddux	10.00
EM	Edgar Martinez	4.00
PM	Pedro J. Martinez	8.00
TM	Tino Martinez	6.00
FM	Fred McGriff	6.00
MM	Mark Mulder	4.00
EMU	Eddie Murray	25.00
JO	John Olerud	4.00
PO	Paul O'Neill	4.00
RP	Rafael Palmeiro	8.00
CP	Corey Patterson	10.00
BP	Brad Penny	4.00
MP	Mike Piazza	10.00
JP	Jorge Posada	15.00
APB	Albert Pujols/bat	20.00
AP	Albert Pujols/jersey	20.00
ARA	Aramis Ramirez	6.00
FR	Frank Robinson	15.00
AR	Alex Rodriguez	10.00
IR	Ivan Rodriguez	8.00
SR	Scott Rolen	8.00
NR	Nolan Ryan	40.00
CS	Curt Schilling	6.00
MS	Mike Schmidt	25.00
GS	Gary Sheffield	6.00
TS	Tsuyoshi Shinjo	4.00
AS	Alfonso Soriano	8.00
SS	Sammy Sosa	15.00
SST	Shannon Stewart	4.00
MT	Mark Teixeira	6.00
MTE	Miguel Tejada	6.00
FT	Frank Thomas	8.00
RV	Robin Ventura	4.00
LW	Larry Walker	4.00
VW	Vernon Wells	8.00
BW	Bernie Williams	6.00
DW	Dontrelle Willis	8.00

T-205 Autographs

		NM/M
Common Autograph:		12.00
LB	Lance Berkman	25.00
MB	Marlon Byrd	10.00
CF	Cliff Floyd	15.00
TH	Torii Hunter	15.00
PL	Paul LoDuca	15.00
MO	Magglio Ordonez	20.00
JR	Jose Reyes	20.00
SR	Scott Rolen	40.00
MS	Mike Sweeney	20.00
Series 2		
HA	Hank Aaron/50	280.00
LC	Luis Castillo	10.00
ED	Eric Duncan	20.00
RH	Rich Harden	25.00
FP	Felix Pie	20.00
RWA	Ryan Wagner	15.00
JW	Jerome Williams	20.00
DW	Dontrelle Willis	25.00

Team Topps Legends Autographs

	NM/M
Stan Musial	65.00
Jim Palmer	20.00
Gaylord Perry	10.00
Robin Yount	75.00

Triple Folder

		NM/M
Complete Set (100):		60.00
Common Card:		.25
Inserted 1:1		
Series 1 Brooklyn Variation:		4-8X
Inserted 1:72		
Series 2 Brooklyn Variation:		2-4X
Inserted 1:29		
TF1	Barry Bonds, Jason LaRue	1.50
TF2	Alfonso Soriano, Derek Jeter	1.50
TF3	Alex Rodriguez, Miguel Tejada	1.50
TF4	Nomar Garciaparra, Derek Jeter	2.00
TF5	Omar Vizquel, Alex Rodriguez	1.50
TF6	Paul Konerko, Omar Vizquel	.25
TF7	Paul Konerko, Magglio Ordonez	.25
TF8	Doug Mientkiewicz, Darin Erstad	.25
TF9	Jason Kendall, Jimmy Rollins	.25
TF10	Shawn Green, Roberto Alomar	.25
TF11	Derek Jeter, Roberto Alomar	1.50
TF12	Bobby Abreu, Luis Castillo	.25
TF13	Randy Johnson, Curt Schilling	.75
TF14	Mike Piazza, Kerry Wood	1.00
TF15	Roger Clemens, Jorge Posada	1.00
TF16	Ichiro Suzuki, Ryan Klesko	1.00
TF17	Alfonso Soriano, Chipper Jones	1.00
TF18	Barry Bonds, Nick Johnson	1.50
TF19	Chipper Jones, Andruw Jones	.75
TF20	Bobby Abreu, Paul Konerko	.25
TF21	Rafael Palmeiro, Alex Rodriguez	1.50
TF22	Eric Hinske, Carlos Delgado	.25
TF23	Nomar Garciaparra, Jay Gibbons	1.00
TF24	Mike Piazza, Luis Gonzalez	1.00
TF25	J.T. Snow, Vladimir Guerrero	.50
TF26	Jason Giambi, Bernie Williams	.75
TF27	Miguel Tejada, Richie Sexson	.25
TF28	Doug Mientkiewicz, Jimmy Rollins	.25
TF29	Eric Chavez, Derek Jeter	2.00
TF30	Alfonso Soriano, Bret Boone	1.00
TF31	Chipper Jones, Mike Piazza	1.00
TF32	Ichiro Suzuki, Bret Boone	1.00
TF33	Bobby Abreu, Mike Piazza	1.00
TF34	Jimmy Rollins, Pat Burrell	.25
TF35	Ichiro Suzuki, Miguel Tejada	1.00

TF36 Jason LaRue, Barry Bonds 1.50
TF37 Derek Jeter, Alfonso Soriano 1.50
TF38 Miguel Tejada, Alex Rodriguez 1.50
TF39 Derek Jeter, Nomar Garciaparra 2.00
TF40 Alex Rodriguez, Omar Vizquel 1.50
TF41 Curt Schilling, Randy Johnson .75
TF42 Jorge Posada, Roger Clemens 1.50
TF43 Ryan Klesko, Ichiro Suzuki 1.00
TF44 Nick Johnson, Barry Bonds 1.50
TF45 Alex Rodriguez, Rafael Palmeiro 1.50
TF46 Vladimir Guerrero, J.T. Snow .50
TF47 Derek Jeter, Eric Chavez 2.00
TF48 Bret Boone, Ichiro Suzuki 1.00
TF49 Mike Piazza, Bobby Abreu 1.00
TF50 Miguel Tejada, Ichiro Suzuki 1.00
TF51 Juan Pierre, Jim Thome .50
TF52 Kevin Millwood, Jim Thome .50
TF53 Hank Blalock, Jorge Posada .40
TF54 Deivi Cruz, Hank Blalock .25
TF55 Rafael Furcal, Ty Wigginton .25
TF56 Jim Thome, Nomar Garciaparra 1.50
TF57 Craig Biggio, Jason Giambi .75
TF58 Aaron Boone, Jason Giambi .75
TF59 Jason Giambi, Bernie Williams .75
TF60 Cristian Guzman, Jody Gerut .25
TF61 Todd Helton, Jose Reyes .50
TF62 Derek Jeter, Hank Blalock 2.00
TF63 Mike Piazza, Jimmy Rollins 1.00
TF64 Bernie Williams, Derek Jeter 2.00
TF65 Andruw Jones, Rafael Furcal .50
TF66 Mike Piazza, Andruw Jones 1.00
TF67 Mike Piazza, Cliff Floyd 1.00
TF68 Jason Kendall, Albert Pujols 1.50
TF69 Nomar Garciaparra, Manny Ramirez 1.50
TF70 Jorge Posada, Alex Rodriguez 1.50
TF71 Derek Jeter, Alex Rodriguez 2.00
TF72 Mike Sweeney, Alex Rodriguez 1.50
TF73 Marquis Grissom, Ivan Rodriguez .50
TF74 Jason Phillips, Gary Sheffield .40
TF75 Chipper Jones, Gary Sheffield 1.00
TF76 Junior Spivey, Gary Sheffield .40
TF77 Al Leiter, Ichiro Suzuki 1.00
TF78 Jose Vidro, Jim Thome .75
TF79 Jimmy Rollins, Paul LoDuca .25
TF80 Alex Rodriguez, Rafael Palmeiro 1.50
TF81 Albert Pujols, Jim Edmonds 1.50
TF82 Eric Chavez, Mike Sweeney .25
TF83 Cristian Guzman, Jimmy Rollins .25
TF84 Alfonso Soriano, Bernie Williams .50
TF85 Ichiro Suzuki, Derek Jeter 2.00
TF86 Jimmy Rollins, Derek Lee .25
TF87 Shawn Green, Paul LoDuca .25
TF88 Carlos Delgado, Jorge Posada .50
TF89 Dmitri Young, C.C. Sabathia .25
TF90 Dontrelle Willis, Shawn Chacon .25
TF91 Edgar Martinez, Alex Rodriguez 1.50
TF92 Edgar Martinez, Carlos Delgado .50
TF93 Edgar Martinez, Esteban Loaiza .25
TF94 Roy Halladay, C.C. Sabathia .25
TF95 Ichiro Suzuki, Albert Pujols 1.50
TF96 Ichiro Suzuki, Shigetoshi Hasegawa 1.00
TF97 Geoff Jenkins, Aaron Boone .25
TF98 Nomar Garciaparra, Alfonso Soriano 1.50
TF99 Jorge Posada, Alfonso Soriano .75
TF100 Vernon Wells, Garret Anderson .25

Triple Folder Autographs

NM/M

Inserted 1:355
RH Rich Harden 40.00
RW Ryan Wagner 40.00
JW Jerome Williams 35.00
DW Dontrelle Willis 40.00

2004 TOPPS

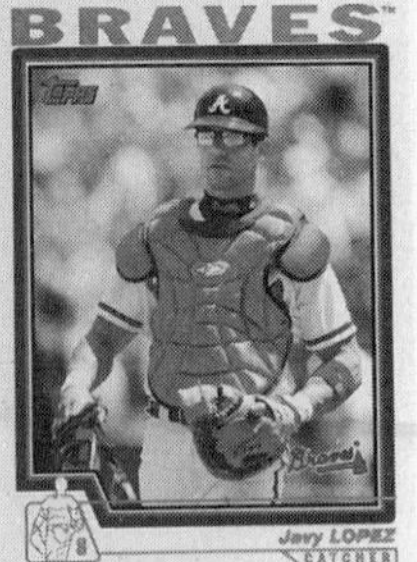

NM/M

Complete Set (732): 60.00
Complete Factory Set (732): 70.00
Common Player: .15
Pack (10): 2.00
Box (36): 55.00
Jumbo Box (12): 65.00
1 Jim Thome .40
2 Aramis Ramirez .25
3 Mark Kotsay .15
4 Edgardo Alfonzo .15
5 Ben Davis .15
6 Mike Matheny .15
8 Marlon Anderson .15
9 Chan Ho Park .15
10 Ichiro Suzuki .75
11 Kevin Millwood .25
12 Bengie Molina .15
13 Tom Glavine .25
14 Junior Spivey .15
15 Marcus Giles .15
16 David Segui .15
17 Kevin Millar .15
18 Corey Patterson .15
19 Aaron Rowand .15
20 Derek Jeter 1.00
21 Jason LaRue .15
22 Chris Hammond .15
23 Jay Payton .15
24 Bobby Higginson .15
25 Lance Berkman .25
26 Juan Pierre .15
27 Brent Mayne .15
28 Fred McGriff .25
29 Richie Sexson .25
30 Tim Hudson .25
31 Mike Piazza .50
32 Brad Radke .15
33 Jeff Weaver .15
34 Ramon Hernandez .15
35 David Bell .15
36 Craig Wilson .15
37 Jake Peavy .15
38 Tim Worrell .15
39 Gil Meche .15
40 Albert Pujols 1.00
41 Michael Young .15
42 Josh Phelps .15
43 Brendan Donnelly .15
44 Steve Finley .15
45 John Smoltz .15
46 Jay Gibbons .15
47 Trot Nixon .15
48 Carl Pavano .15
49 Frank Thomas .40
50 Mark Prior 1.00
51 Danny Graves .15
52 Milton Bradley .15
53 Jose Jimenez .15
54 Shane Halter .15
55 Mike Lowell .15
56 Geoff Blum .15
57 Michael Tucker .15
58 Paul LoDuca .15
59 Vicente Padilla .15
60 Jacque Jones .15
61 Fernando Tatis .15
62 Ty Wigginton .15
63 Pedro Astacio .15
64 Andy Pettitte .25
65 Terrence Long .15
66 Cliff Floyd .15
67 Mariano Rivera .25
68 Mike Williams .15
69 Marlon Byrd .15
70 Mark Mulder .25
71 Damian Moss .15
72 Carlos Guillen .15
73 Fernando Vina .15
74 Lance Carter .15
75 Hank Blalock .25
76 Jimmy Rollins .15
77 Kevin Appier .15
78 Javy Lopez .25
79 Jerry Hairston Jr. .15
80 Andruw Jones .40
81 Rodrigo Lopez .15
82 Johnny Damon .25
83 Hee Seop Choi .15
84 Miguel Olivo .15
85 Scott Sullivan .15
86 Matt Lawton .15
87 Juan Uribe .15
88 Steve Sparks .15
89 Tim Spooneybarger .15
90 Jose Vidro .15
91 Luis Rivas .15
92 Hideo Nomo .25
93 Javier Vazquez .15
94 Al Leiter .15
95 Darren Dreifort .15
96 Mike DeJean .15
97 Zach Day .15
98 Jorge Posada .25
99 John Halama .15
100 Alex Rodriguez 1.00
101 Orlando Palmeiro .15
102 Dave Berg .15
103 Brad Fullmer .15
104 Mike Hampton .15
105 Willis Roberts .15
106 Ramiro Mendoza .15
107 Juan Cruz .15
108 Esteban Loaiza .15
109 Aaron Boone .15
110 Todd Helton .40
111 Braden Looper .15
112 Octavio Dotel .15
113 Mike MacDougal .15
114 Cesar Izturis .15
115 Johan Santana .15
116 Jose Contreras .25
117 Placido Polanco .15
118 Kenny Lofton .25
119 Adam Eaton .15
120 Vernon Wells .25
121 Ben Grieve .15
122 Randy Winn .15
123 Ismael Valdes .15
124 Eric Owens .15
125 Curt Schilling .25
126 Russ Ortiz .15
127 Mark Buehrle .15
128 Danys Baez .15
129 Dmitri Young .15
130 Kazuhisa Ishii .15
131 A.J. Pierzynski .15
132 Michael Barrett .15
133 Joe McEwing .15
134 Robin Ventura .15
135 Tom Wilson .15
136 Carlos Zambrano .15
137 Brett Tomko .15
138 Jeff Nelson .15
139 Jarrod Washburn .15
140 Greg Maddux .75
141 Craig Counsell .15
142 Reggie Taylor .15
143 Omar Vizquel .25
144 Alex Gonzalez .15
145 Billy Wagner .15
146 Brian Jordan .15
147 Wes Helms .15
148 Kyle Lohse .15
149 Timoniel Perez .15
150 Jason Giambi .50
151 Erubiel Durazo .15
152 Mike Lieberthal .15
153 Jason Kendall .15
154 Xavier Nady .15
155 Kirk Rueter .15
156 Mike Cameron .15
157 Miguel Cairo .15
158 Woody Williams .15
159 Toby Hall .15
160 Bernie Williams .40
161 Darin Erstad .25
162 Matt Mantei .15
163 Geronimo Gil .15
164 Bill Mueller .15
165 Damian Miller .15
166 Tony Graffanino .15
167 Sean Casey .15
168 Brandon Phillips .15
169 Mike Remlinger .15
170 Adam Dunn .25
171 Carlos Lee .15
172 Juan Encarnacion .15
173 Angel Berroa .15
174 Desi Relaford .15
175 Paul Quantrill .15
176 Ben Sheets .15
177 Eddie Guardado .15
178 Rocky Biddle .15
179 Mike Stanton .15
180 Eric Chavez .25
181 Jason Michaels .15
182 Terry Adams .15
183 Kip Wells .15
184 Brian Lawrence .15
185 Bret Boone .25
186 Tino Martinez .25
187 Aubrey Huff .15
188 Kevin Mench .15
189 Tim Salmon .25
190 Carlos Delgado .40
191 John Lackey .15
192 Oscar Villarreal .15
193 Sidney Ponson .15
194 Derek Lowe .15
195 Mark Grudzielanek .15
196 Flash Gordon .15
197 Matt Clement .15
198 Scott Williamson .15
199 Brandon Inge .15
200 Nomar Garciaparra 1.00
201 Antonio Osuna .15
202 Jose Mesa .15
203 Randall Simon .15
204 Jack Wilson .15
205 Ray Durham .15
206 Freddy Garcia .15
207 J.D. Drew .15
208 Einar Diaz .15
209 Roy Halladay .25
210 David Eckstein .15
211 Jason Marquis .15
212 Jorge Julio .15
213 Tim Wakefield .15
214 Moises Alou .25
215 Bartolo Colon .25
216 Jimmy Haynes .15
217 Preston Wilson .15
218 Luis Castillo .15
219 Richard Hidalgo .15
220 Manny Ramirez .40
221 Mike Mussina .40
222 Randy Wolf .15
223 Kris Benson .15
224 Ryan Klesko .25
225 Rich Aurilia .15
226 Kelvim Escobar .15
227 Francisco Cordero .15
228 Kazuhiro Sasaki .15
229 Danny Bautista .15
230 Rafael Furcal .15
231 Travis Driskill .15
232 Kyle Farnsworth .15
233 Jose Valentin .15
234 Felipe Lopez .15
235 C.C. Sabathia .15

236 Brad Penny .15
237 Brad Ausmus .15
238 Raul Ibanez .15
239 Adrian Beltre .15
240 Rocco Baldelli .25
241 Orlando Hudson .15
242 Dave Roberts .15
243 Doug Mientkiewicz .15
244 Brad Wilkerson .15
245 Scott Strickland .15
246 Sterling Hitchcock .15
247 Chad Bradford .15
248 Gary Bennett .15
249 Jose Cruz Jr. .15
250 Jeff Kent .25
251 Josh Beckett .25
252 Ramon Ortiz .15
253 Miguel Batista .15
254 Jung Bong .15
255 Deivi Cruz .15
256 Alex Gonzalez .15
257 Shawn Chacon .15
258 Runelvys Hernandez .15
259 Joe Mays .15
260 Eric Gagne .15
261 Dustan Mohr .15
262 Tomokazu Ohka .15
263 Eric Byrnes .15
264 Frank Catalanotto .15
265 Cristian Guzman .15
266 Orlando Cabrera .15
267 Mike Scioscia .15
268 Bob Brenly .15
269 Bobby Cox .15
270 Mike Hargrove .15
271 Grady Little .15
272 Dusty Baker .15
273 Jerry Manuel .15
274 Bob Boone .15
275 Eric Wedge .15
276 Clint Hurdle .15
277 Alan Trammell .15
278 Jack McKeon .15
279 Jimy Williams .15
280 Tony Pena .15
281 Jim Tracy .15
282 Ned Yost .15
283 Ron Gardenhire .15
284 Frank Robinson .25
285 Art Howe .15
286 Joe Torre .25
287 Ken Macha .15
288 Larry Bowa .15
289 Lloyd McClendon .15
290 Bruce Bochy .15
291 Felipe Alou .15
292 Bob Melvin .15
293 Tony LaRussa .15
294 Lou Piniella .15
295 Buck Showalter .15
296 Carlos Tosca .15
297 *Anthony Acevedo* .25
298 *Anthony Lerew* .75
299 *Blake Hawksworth* .50
300 *Brayan Pena* .50
301 *Casey Myers* .50
302 *Craig Ansman* .50
303 David Murphy .40
304 David Crouthers .15
305 *Dioner Navarro* .40
306 Donald Levinski .15
307 *Jesse Roman* .40
308 *Sung Ki Jung* .25
309 *Jon Knott* .40
310 *Josh Labandeira* .25
311 *Kenny Perez* .25
312 *Khalid Ballouli* .25
313 *Kyle Davies* .40
314 *Marcus McBeth* .40
315 *Matt Creighton* .40
316 *Chris O'Riordan* .50
317 Mike Gosling .15
318 *Nic Ungs* .40
319 *Omar Falcon* .40
320 *Rodney Choy Foo* .40
321 *Tim Frend* .50
322 *Todd Self* .50
323 *Tydus Meadows* .40
324 *Yadier Molina* .50
325 *Zachary Duke* 2.00
326 *Zach Miner* .40
327 Bernie Castro, Khalil Greene .15
328 Ryan Madson, Elizardo Ramirez .15
329 Rich Harden, Bobby Crosby .15
330 Zack Greinke, Jimmy Gobble .15
331 Bobby Jenks, Casey Kotchman .15
332 Sammy Sosa .50
333 Kevin Millwood .25
334 Rafael Palmeiro .25
335 Roger Clemens .75
336 Eric Gagne .15
337 Bill Mueller, Manny Ramirez, Derek Jeter .50
338 Vernon Wells, Ichiro Suzuki, Michael Young .40
339 Alex Rodriguez, Frank Thomas, Carlos Delgado .50
340 Carlos Delgado, Alex Rodriguez, Bret Boone .50
341 Pedro Martinez, Tim Hudson, Esteban Loaiza .25
342 Esteban Loaiza, Pedro Martinez, Roy Halladay .25
343 Albert Pujols, Todd Helton, Edgar Renteria .50
344 Albert Pujols, Todd Helton, Juan Pierre .50
345 Jim Thome, Richie Sexson, Javy Lopez .25
346 Preston Wilson, Gary Sheffield, Jim Thome .25
347 Jason Schmidt, Kevin Brown, Mark Prior .50
348 Kerry Wood, Mark Prior, Javier Vazquez .50
349 AL Division Series .15
350 NL Division Series .15
351 NL Championship Series .15
352 AL Championship Series .25
353 AL & NL Division Series .15
354 AL Championship Series .15
355 World Series Highlights .25
356 Carlos Delgado .25
357 Bret Boone .15
358 Alex Rodriguez .50
359 Bill Mueller .15
360 Vernon Wells .15
361 Garret Anderson .15
362 Magglio Ordonez .15
363 Jorge Posada .15
364 Roy Halladay .15
365 Andy Pettitte .15
366 Frank Thomas .25
367 Jody Gerut .15
368 Sammy Sosa .75
369 Joe Crede .15
370 Gary Sheffield .25
371 Coco Crisp .15
372 Torii Hunter .25
373 Derrek Lee .15
374 Adam Everett .15
375 Miguel Tejada .25
376 Jeremy Affeldt .15
377 Robin Ventura .15
378 Scott Podsednik .40
379 Matthew LeCroy .15
380 Vladimir Guerrero .40
381 Tony Clark .15
382 Jeff Nelson .15
383 Chris Singleton .15
384 Bobby Abreu .25
385 Josh Fogg .15
386 Trevor Hoffman .15
387 Jesse Foppert .15
388 Edgar Martinez .25
389 Edgar Renteria .25
390 Chipper Jones .50
391 Eric Munson .15
392 Dewon Brazelton .15
393 John Thomson .15
394 Chris Woodward .15
395 Aaron Sele .15
396 Elmer Dessens .15
397 Johnny Estrada .15
398 Damian Moss .15
399 Gabe Kapler .15
400 Dontrelle Willis .40
401 Troy Glaus .25
402 Raul Mondesi .20
403 Shane Reynolds .15
404 Kurt Ainsworth .15
405 Pedro J. Martinez .50
406 Eric Karros .15
407 Billy Koch .15
408 Scott Schoeneweis .15
409 Paul Wilson .15
410 Mike Sweeney .15
411 Jason Bay .15
412 Mark Redman .15
413 Jason Jennings .15
414 Rondell White .25
415 Todd Hundley .15
416 Shannon Stewart .15
417 Jae Weong Seo .15
418 Livan Hernandez .15
419 Mark Ellis .15
420 Pat Burrell .25
421 Mark Loretta .15
422 Robb Nen .15
423 Joel Pineiro .15
424 Jason Simontacchi .15
425 Sterling Hitchcock .15
426 Rey Ordonez .15
427 Greg Myers .15
428 Shane Spencer .15
429 Carlos Baerga .15
430 Garret Anderson .25
431 Horacio Ramirez .15
432 Brian Roberts .15
433 Damian Jackson .15
434 Doug Glanville .15
435 Brian Daubach .15
436 Alex Escobar .15
437 Alex Sanchez .15
438 Jeff Bagwell .40
439 Darrell May .15
440 Shawn Green .25
441 Geoff Jenkins .25
442 Endy Chavez .15
443 Nick Johnson .15
444 Jose Guillen .15
445 Tomas Perez .15
446 Phil Nevin .15
447 Jason Schmidt .25
448 Julio Mateo .15
449 So Taguchi .15
450 Randy Johnson .40
451 Paul Byrd .15
452 Chone Figgins .15
453 Larry Bigbie .15
454 Scott Williamson .15
455 Ramon Martinez .15
456 Roberto Alomar .25
457 Ryan Dempster .15
458 Ryan Ludwick .15
459 Ramon Santiago .15
460 Jeff Conine .15
461 Brad Lidge .15
462 Ken Harvey .15
463 Guillermo Mota .15
464 Rick Reed .15
465 Joey Eischen .15
466 Wade Miller .15
467 Steve Karsay .15
468 Chase Utley .15
469 Matt Stairs .15
470 Yorvit Torrealba .15
471 Joe Kennedy .15
472 Reed Johnson .15
473 Victor Zambrano .15
474 Jeff DaVanon .15
475 Luis Gonzalez .25
476 Rod Barajas .15
477 Ray King .15
478 Jack Cust .15
479 Omar Daal .15
480 Todd Walker .15
481 Shawn Estes .15
482 Chris Reitsma .15
483 Jake Westbrook .15
484 Jeremy Bonderman .15
485 A.J. Burnett .15
486 Roy Oswalt .25
487 Kevin Brown .25
488 Eric Milton .15
489 Claudio Vargas .15
490 Roger Cedeno .15
491 Boomer Wells .15
492 Scott Hatteberg .15
493 Ricky Ledee .15
494 Eric Young .15
495 Armando Benitez .15
496 Dan Haren .15
497 Carl Crawford .15
498 Laynce Nix .15
499 Eric Hinske .15
500 Ivan Rodriguez .40
501 Scot Shields .15
502 Brandon Webb .15
503 Mark DeRosa .15
504 Jhonny Peralta .15
505 Adam Kennedy .15
506 Tony Batista .15
507 Jeff Suppan .15
508 Kenny Lofton .25
509 Scott Sullivan .15
510 Ken Griffey Jr. .60
511 Billy Traber .15
512 Larry Walker .25
513 Mike Maroth .15
514 Todd Hollandsworth .15
515 Kirk Saarloos .15
516 Carlos Beltran .25
517 Andy Ashby .15
518 Jose Macias .15
519 Karim Garcia .15
520 Jose Reyes .15
521 Brandon Duckworth .15
522 Brian Giles .25
523 J.T. Snow Jr. .15
524 Jamie Moyer .15
525 Jason Isringhausen .15
526 Julio Lugo .15
527 Mark Teixeira .25
528 Cory Lidle .15
529 Lyle Overbay .15
530 Troy Percival .15
531 Robby Hammock .15
532 Robert Fick .15
533 Jason Johnson .15
534 Brandon Lyon .15
535 Antonio Alfonseca .15
536 Tom Goodwin .15
537 Paul Konerko .15
538 D'Angelo Jimenez .15
539 Ben Broussard .15
540 Magglio Ordonez .25
541 Ellis Burks .15
542 Carlos Pena .15
543 Chad Fox .15
544 Jeriome Robertson .15
545 Travis Hafner .15
546 Joe Randa .15
547 Wil Cordero .15
548 Brady Clark .15
549 Ruben Sierra .15
550 Barry Zito .25
551 Brett Myers .15
552 Oliver Perez .15
553 Trey Hodges .15
554 Benito Santiago .15
555 David Ross .15
556 Ramon Vazquez .15
557 Joe Nathan .15
558 Dan Wilson .15
559 Garrett Stephenson .15
560 Jim Edmonds .25
561 Shawn Wooten .15
562 Matt Kata .15
563 Vinny Castilla .15
564 Marty Cordova .15
565 Aramis Ramirez .15
566 Carl Everett .15
567 Ryan Freel .15
568 Jason Davis .15
569 Mark Bellhorn .15
570 Craig Monroe .15
571 Ugueth Urbina .15
572 Tim Redding .15
573 Kevin Appier .15
574 Jeromy Burnitz .15
575 Miguel Cabrera .40
576 Orlando Hernandez .15
577 Casey Blake .15
578 Aaron Boone .15
579 Jermaine Dye .15
580 Jerome Williams .15
581 John Olerud .15
582 Scott Rolen .40
583 Bobby Kielty .15
584 Travis Lee .15
585 Jeff Cirillo .15
586 Scott Spiezio .15
587 Stephen Randolph .15
588 Melvin Mora .15
589 Mike Timlin .15
590 Kerry Wood .50
591 Tony Womack .15
592 Jody Gerut .15
593 Franklyn German .15
594 Morgan Ensberg .15
595 Odalis Perez .15
596 Michael Cuddyer .15
597 Jon Lieber .15
598 Mike Williams .15
599 Jose Hernandez .15
600 Alfonso Soriano .50
601 Marquis Grissom .15
602 Matt Morris .25
603 Damian Rolls .15
604 Juan Gonzalez .25
605 Aquilino Lopez .15
606 Jose Valverde .15
607 Scott Sauerbeck .15
608 Joe Borowski .15
609 Josh Bard .15
610 Austin Kearns .25

611 Chin-Hui Tsao .15
612 Wilfredo Ledezma .15
613 Aaron Guiel .15
614 LaTroy Hawkins .15
615 Tony Armas Jr. .15
616 Steve Trachsel .15
617 Ted Lilly .15
618 Todd Pratt .15
619 Sean Burroughs .15
620 Rafael Palmeiro .40
621 Jeremi Gonzalez .15
622 Quinton McCracken .15
623 David Ortiz .25
624 Randall Simon .15
625 Wily Mo Pena .15
626 Nate Cornejo .15
627 Brian Anderson .15
628 Corey Koskie .15
629 Keith Foulke .15
630 Rheal Cormier .15
631 Sidney Ponson .15
632 Gary Matthews Jr. .15
633 Herbert Perry .15
634 Shea Hillenbrand .15
635 Craig Biggio .25
636 Barry Larkin .25
637 Orlando Merced .15
638 Anaheim Angels .15
639 Arizona Diamondbacks .15
640 Atlanta Braves .15
641 Baltimore Orioles .15
642 Boston Red Sox .25
643 Chicago Cubs .40
644 Chicago White Sox .15
645 Cincinnati Reds .15
646 Cleveland Indians .15
647 Colorado Rockies .15
648 Detroit Tigers .15
649 Florida Marlins .15
650 Houston Astros .15
651 Kansas City Royals .15
652 Los Angeles Dodgers .15
653 Milwaukee Brewers .15
654 Minnesota Twins .15
655 Montreal Expos .15
656 New York Mets .15
657 New York Yankees .50
658 Oakland Athletics .15
659 Philadelphia Phillies .15
660 Pittsburgh Pirates .15
661 San Diego Padres .15
662 San Francisco Giants .15
663 Seattle Mariners .15
664 St. Louis Cardinals .15
665 Tampa Bay Devil Rays .15
666 Texas Rangers .15
667 Toronto Blue Jays .15
668 Kyle Sleeth .15
669 Bradley Sullivan .15
670 Carlos Quentin .15
671 Conor Jackson .15
672 Jeffrey Allison .15
673 Matthew Moses .25
674 Tim Stauffer .15
675 *Estee Harris* .25
676 David Aardsma .15
677 Omar Quintanilla .25
678 Aaron Hill .15
679 Tony Richie .15
680 Lastings Milledge .15
681 Brad Snyder .15
682 Jason Hirsh .15
683 *Logan Kensing* .40
684 Chris Lubanski .15
685 Ryan Harvey .15
686 Ryan Wagner .15
687 Rickie Weeks .50
688 Jeremy Guthrie, Grady Sizemore .15
689 Edwin Jackson, Greg Miller .15
690 Neal Cotts, Jeremy Reed .15
691 Nicholas Markakis, Adam Loewen .15
692 Delmon Young, B.J. Upton .75
693 Nomar Garciaparra, Alfonso Soriano .50
694 Ichiro Suzuki, Albert Pujols .50
695 Jim Thome, Mike Schmidt .40
696 Mike Mussina .25
697 Bengie Molina .15
698 John Olerud .15
699 Bret Boone .25
700 Eric Chavez .25
701 Alex Rodriguez .75
702 Mike Cameron .15
703 Ichiro Suzuki .75
704 Torii Hunter .25
705 Mike Hampton .15
706 Mike Matheny .15
707 Derrek Lee .15
708 Luis Castillo .15
709 Scott Rolen .40
710 Edgar Renteria .25
711 Andruw Jones .25
712 Jose Cruz Jr. .15
713 Jim Edmonds .25
714 Roy Halladay .25
715 Eric Gagne .25
716 Alex Rodriguez .75
717 Angel Berroa .15
718 Dontrelle Willis .25
719 Todd Helton .25
720 Marcus Giles .15
721 Edgar Renteria .25
722 Scott Rolen .40
723 Albert Pujols .75
724 Gary Sheffield .25
725 Javy Lopez .25
726 Eric Gagne .25
727 Randy Wolf .15
728 Bobby Cox .15
729 Scott Podsednik .40
730 World Series Game 4 .15
731 World Series Game 5 .15
732 World Series Game 6 .15
733 World Series MVP .25

Black

Black (1-733): 15-30X
Production 53 sets

Gold

Stars (1-733): 5-10X
Production 2,004 sets

1st Edition

NM/M
Stars: 3-5X
HTA Exclusive
1st Edition Pack (10): 3.00
1st Edition Box (20): 55.00

All-Stars

NM/M
Complete Set (20): 20.00
Common Player: .50
Inserted 1:16
TAS1 Jason Giambi 1.50
TAS2 Ichiro Suzuki 2.50
TAS3 Alex Rodriguez 3.00
TAS4 Albert Pujols 3.00
TAS5 Alfonso Soriano 1.50
TAS6 Nomar Garciaparra 2.50
TAS7 Andruw Jones 1.00
TAS8 Carlos Delgado .75
TAS9 Gary Sheffield .75
TAS10 Jorge Posada .75
TAS11 Magglio Ordonez .75
TAS12 Kerry Wood 1.50
TAS13 Garret Anderson .75
TAS14 Bret Boone .50
TAS15 Hank Blalock .75
TAS16 Mike Lowell .50
TAS17 Todd Helton 1.00
TAS18 Vernon Wells .50
TAS19 Roger Clemens 3.00
TAS20 Scott Rolen 1.50

All-Star Stitches

NM/M
Common Player: 5.00
Inserted 1:137
GA Garret Anderson 6.00
HB Hank Blalock 6.00
AB Aaron Boone 5.00
BD Brendan Donnelly 5.00
CE Carl Everett 5.00
KF Keith Foulke 5.00
RF Rafael Furcal 8.00
EGA Eric Gagne 8.00
NG Nomar Garciaparra 15.00
TG Troy Glaus 8.00
EG Eddie Guardado 5.00
SH Shigetoshi Hasegawa 5.00
TH Todd Helton 8.00
RH Ramon Hernandez 5.00
AJ Andruw Jones 8.00
EL Esteban Loaiza 5.00
PL Paul LoDuca 5.00
JL Javy Lopez 8.00
ML Mike Lowell 5.00
EM Edgar Martinez 8.00
MMO Melvin Mora 5.00
JM Jamie Moyer 5.00
MM Mark Mulder 6.00
RO Russ Ortiz 6.00
JP Jorge Posada 8.00
ER Edgar Renteria 5.00
AR Alex Rodriguez 15.00
SR Scott Rolen 10.00
JS Jason Schmidt 6.00
JV Jose Vidro 5.00
BW Billy Wagner 5.00
VW Vernon Wells 6.00
RWH Rondell White 5.00
WW Woody Williams 6.00
PW Preston Wilson 5.00
RW Randy Wolf 5.00
KW Kerry Wood 8.00

All-Star Patch Relics

No Pricing
Inserted 1:7,698

American Treasures Presidential Signatures

No Pricing
Production 1 set

American Treasures Cut Signatures

No Pricing
Inserted 1:658,152

Autographs

NM/M
Common Player:
JB Josh Beckett 50.00
HB Hank Blalock 20.00
CF Cliff Floyd 8.00
JG Jay Gibbons 15.00
KG Khalil Greene 10.00
EH Eric Hinske 10.00
TH Torii Hunter 25.00
AK Austin Kearns 25.00
PK Paul Konerko 15.00
PL Paul LoDuca 10.00
ML Mike Lowell 8.00
VM Victor Martinez 20.00
MO Magglio Ordonez 15.00
JP Josh Phelps 8.00
MP Mark Prior 60.00
ER Elizardo Ramirez 8.00
BS Benito Santiago 15.00
MS Mike Sweeney 20.00
MT Mark Teixeira 25.00
BU B.J. Upton 20.00
JV Jose Vidro 8.00
Series 2
GA Garret Anderson 35.00
LB Lance Berkman 35.00
AB Aaron Boone 35.00
BB Bobby Brownlie 30.00
MC Miguel Cabrera 40.00
ZG Zack Greinke 20.00
AH Aubrey Huff 20.00
DM Dustin McGowan 15.00
SP Scott Podsednik 25.00
JP Jorge Posada 40.00
IR Ivan Rodriguez 45.00
SR Scott Rolen 30.00
DW Dontrelle Willis 30.00

Derby Digs

NM/M
Common Player: 8.00
Inserted 1:585
GA Garret Anderson 8.00
BB Bret Boone 8.00
CD Carlos Delgado 8.00
JE Jim Edmonds 8.00
JG Jason Giambi 15.00
AP Albert Pujols 25.00
RS Richie Sexson 8.00

Fall Classic Covers

NM/M
Complete Set (99): 125.00
Common Card: 2.00
Inserted 1:12

Hobby Masters

NM/M
Complete Set (20): 40.00
Common Player: .75
Inserted 1:12
HM1 Albert Pujols 3.00
HM2 Mark Prior 4.00
HM3 Alex Rodriguez 4.00
HM4 Nomar Garciaparra 3.00
HM5 Barry Bonds 4.00
HM6 Sammy Sosa 3.00
HM7 Alfonso Soriano 2.00
HM8 Ichiro Suzuki 2.50
HM9 Derek Jeter 4.00
HM10 Jim Thome 1.50
HM11 Jason Giambi 1.50
HM12 Mike Piazza 2.50
HM13 Barry Zito 1.00
HM14 Randy Johnson 2.00
HM15 Adam Dunn 1.00
HM16 Vladimir Guerrero 2.00
HM17 Gary Sheffield .75
HM18 Carlos Delgado 1.00
HM19 Chipper Jones 2.50
HM20 Dontrelle Willis 1.00

Hit Parade

NM/M
Complete Set (30): 20.00
Common Player: .50
Inserted 1:7
HP1 Sammy Sosa 3.00

HP2	Rafael Palmeiro	1.00
HP3	Fred McGriff	.50
HP4	Ken Griffey Jr.	2.00
HP5	Juan Gonzalez	1.00
HP6	Frank Thomas	1.00
HP7	Andres Galarraga	.50
HP8	Jim Thome	1.50
HP9	Jeff Bagwell	1.00
HP10	Mike Piazza	2.00
HP11	Rafael Palmeiro	1.00
HP12	Sammy Sosa	3.00
HP13	Fred McGriff	.50
HP14	Andres Galarraga	.50
HP15	Juan Gonzalez	1.00
HP16	Frank Thomas	1.00
HP17	Jeff Bagwell	1.00
HP18	Ken Griffey Jr.	2.00
HP19	Ruben Sierra	.50
HP20	Ellis Burks	.50
HP21	Rafael Palmeiro	1.00
HP22	Roberto Alomar	.75
HP23	Julio Franco	.50
HP24	Andres Galarraga	.50
HP25	Fred McGriff	.50
HP26	Craig Biggio	.75
HP27	Barry Larkin	.75
HP28	Edgar Martinez	.50
HP29	Ellis Burks	.50
HP30	Sammy Sosa	3.00

Own the Game

		NM/M
Complete Set (30):		25.00
Common Player:		.50
Inserted 1:18		
OG1	Jim Thome	1.50
OG2	Albert Pujols	3.00
OG3	Alex Rodriguez	3.00
OG4	Barry Bonds	4.00
OG5	Ichiro Suzuki	2.00
OG6	Derek Jeter	3.00
OG7	Nomar Garciaparra	3.00
OG8	Alfonso Soriano	1.50
OG9	Gary Sheffield	.75
OG10	Jason Giambi	1.00
OG11	Todd Helton	1.00
OG12	Garret Anderson	.50
OG13	Carlos Delgado	1.00
OG14	Manny Ramirez	1.00
OG15	Richie Sexson	.75
OG16	Vernon Wells	.50
OG17	Preston Wilson	.50
OG18	Frank Thomas	1.00
OG19	Shawn Green	.75
OG20	Rafael Furcal	.50
OG21	Juan Pierre	.50
OG22	Javy Lopez	.50
OG23	Edgar Renteria	.50
OG24	Mark Prior	3.00
OG25	Pedro J. Martinez	1.50
OG26	Kerry Wood	1.00
OG27	Curt Schilling	.75
OG28	Roy Halladay	.50
OG29	Eric Gagne	.50
OG30	Brandon Webb	.50

Presidential Pastime

		NM/M
Complete Set (42):		100.00
Common President:		3.00
Inserted 1:6		
PP1	George Washington	8.00
PP2	John Adams	4.00
PP3	Thomas Jefferson	4.00
PP4	James Madison	4.00
PP5	James Monroe	4.00
PP6	John Quincy Adams	4.00
PP7	Andrew Jackson	3.00
PP8	Martin Van Buren	3.00
PP9	William H. Harrison	3.00
PP10	John Tyler	4.00
PP11	James K. Polk	4.00
PP12	Zachary Taylor	3.00
PP13	Millard Fillmore	3.00
PP14	Franklin Pierce	3.00
PP15	James Buchanan	3.00
PP16	Abraham Lincoln	6.00
PP17	Andrew Johnson	3.00
PP18	Ulysses S. Grant	5.00
PP19	Rutherford B. Hayes	3.00
PP20	James Garfield	3.00
PP21	Chester A. Arthur	3.00
PP22	Grover Cleveland	3.00
PP23	Benjamin Harrison	3.00
PP24	William McKinley	3.00
PP25	Theodore Roosevelt	4.00
PP26	William H. Taft	4.00
PP27	Woodrow Wilson	4.00
PP28	Warren Harding	4.00
PP29	Calvin Coolidge	4.00
PP30	Herbert Hoover	3.00
PP31	Franklin D. Roosevelt	4.00
PP32	Harry S. Truman	4.00
PP33	Dwight D. Eisenhower	4.00
PP34	John F. Kennedy	6.00
PP35	Lyndon B. Johnson	3.00
PP36	Richard Nixon	4.00
PP37	Gerald Ford	3.00
PP38	Jimmy Carter	3.00
PP39	Ronald Reagan	3.00
PP40	George H.W. Bush	3.00
PP41	Bill Clinton	4.00
PP42	George W. Bush	3.00

Presidential First Pitch Relics

		NM/M
Common Player:		15.00
Inserted 1:592		
GHB	George H.W. Bush	25.00
GB	George W. Bush	25.00
BC	Bill Clinton	40.00
CC	Calvin Coolidge	15.00
DE	Dwight D. Eisenhower	15.00
GF	Gerald Ford	30.00
WH	Warren Harding	30.00
HH	Herbert Hoover	30.00
LJ	Lyndon B. Johnson	20.00
JK	John F. Kennedy	50.00
RN	Richard Nixon	30.00
RR	Ronald Reagan	30.00
FR	Franklin D. Roosevelt	40.00
WT	William H. Taft	25.00
HT	Harry S. Truman	30.00
WW	Woodrow Wilson	25.00

Series Seats Relics

		NM/M
Common Player:		10.00
Inserted 1:316		
LA	Luis Aparicio	15.00
BF	Bob Feller	12.00
RJ	Reggie Jackson	20.00
AK	Al Kaline	20.00
HK	Harmon Killebrew	25.00
WM	Willie Mays	25.00
BM	Bill Mazeroski	20.00
PM	Paul Molitor	20.00
JP	Jim Palmer	15.00
LP	Lou Piniella	10.00
BP	Boog Powell	10.00
BR	Brooks Robinson	15.00
FR	Frank Robinson	15.00
WS	Warren Spahn	15.00
RY	Robin Yount	20.00

Series Stitches Relics

		NM/M
Common Player:		10.00
JBE	Josh Beckett	10.00
JB	Johnny Bench	25.00
GB	George Brett	30.00
JCA	Jose Canseco	15.00
GC	Gary Carter	12.00
JC	Joe Carter	10.00
RC	Roger Clemens	20.00
LD	Lenny Dykstra	15.00
SG	Steve Garvey	15.00
KG	Kirk Gibson	10.00
DG	Dwight Gooden	15.00
RJA	Reggie Jackson	20.00
RJ	Randy Johnson	10.00
CJ	Chipper Jones	15.00
DJ	David Justice	15.00
HK	Harmon Killebrew	30.00
WM	Willie Mays	50.00
PO	Paul O'Neill	20.00
KP	Kirby Puckett	25.00
FR	Frank Robinson	20.00
MS	Mike Schmidt	30.00
TS	Tom Seaver	25.00
AS	Alfonso Soriano	15.00
RY	Robin Yount	20.00

Team Topps Legends Autographs

		NM/M
Inserted 1:766		
SG	Steve Garvey	15.00
BP	Boog Powell	10.00

World Series Highlights

		NM/M
Complete Set (30):		35.00
Common Player:		1.00
Inserted 1:18		
LB	Lou Brock	1.00
CF	Carlton Fisk	1.50
KG	Kirk Gibson	1.00
RJ	Reggie Jackson	2.00
DL	Don Larsen	1.00
MM	Willie Mays	4.00
BM	Bill Mazeroski	1.00
SM	Stan Musial	3.00
JP	Jim Palmer	1.00
KP	Kirby Puckett	2.00
BR	Brooks Robinson	2.00
MS	Mike Schmidt	4.00
TS	Tom Seaver	2.00
CY	Carl Yastrzemski	2.00
RY	Robin Yount	2.00
Series 2		
DB	Dusty Baker	1.00
JB	Johnny Bench	2.50
JCA	Jose Canseco	1.50
JC	Joe Carter	1.00
WF	Whitey Ford	2.00
LG	Luis Gonzalez	1.00
AJ	Andruw Jones	1.50
DJ	David Justice	1.00
AK	Al Kaline	2.00
WM	Willie McCovey	1.00
JP	Johnny Podres	1.00
FR	Frank Robinson	1.50
OS	Ozzie Smith	2.00
DS	Duke Snider	1.50
BT	Bobby Thomson	1.00

World Series Highlights Autographs

		NM/M
Common Player:		
LB	Lou Brock	30.00
CF	Carlton Fisk	50.00
KG	Kirk Gibson	30.00
DL	Don Larsen	25.00
WM	Willie Mays	
BM	Bill Mazeroski	30.00
JP	Jim Palmer	25.00
BR	Brooks Robinson	40.00
MS	Mike Schmidt	65.00
TS	Tom Seaver	
RY	Robin Yount	50.00
Series 2		
DB	Dusty Baker	20.00
JB	Johnny Bench	50.00
WF	Whitey Ford	35.00
RJ	Reggie Jackson	40.00
DJ	David Justice	30.00
AK	Al Kaline	40.00
SM	Stan Musial	75.00
JP	Johnny Podres	15.00
DS	Duke Snider	35.00
BT	Bobby Thomson	20.00

2004 TOPPS TRADED & ROOKIES

		NM/M
Complete Set (220):		50.00
Common Player:		.10
Chrome cards:		2-4X
Pack (10):		3.00
Box (24):		65.00
T1	Pokey Reese	.10
T2	Tony Womack	.10
T3	Michael Barrett	.10
T4	Juan Uribe	.10
T5	J.D. Drew	.25
T6	Marlon Anderson	.10
T7	Carlos Guillen	.10
T8	Royce Clayton	.10
T9	Fernando Vina	.10
T10	Milton Bradley	.10
T11	Eddie Perez	.10
T12	Ben Grieve	.10
T13	Brian Jordan	.10
T14	Tony Graffanino	.10
T15	Billy Wagner	.10
T16	Terrence Long	.10
T17	Casey Fossum	.10
T18	Denny Hocking	.10
T19	Reggie Sanders	.10
T20	Javy Lopez	.25
T21	Jay Payton	.10
T22	Cliff Politte	.10
T23	Eddie Guardado	.10
T24	Andy Pettitte	.50
T25	Richie Sexson	.40
T26	Ronnie Belliard	.10
T27	Michael Tucker	.10
T28	Brad Fullmer	.10
T29	Orlando Palmeiro	.10
T30	Bartolo Colon	.25
T31	Larry Walker	.40
T32	Mark Kotsay	.10
T33	Jason Marquis	.10
T34	Dustan Mohr	.10
T35	Javier Vazquez	.25
T36	Nomar Garciaparra	1.50
T37	Tino Martinez	.25
T38	Hee Seop Choi	.10
T39	Damian Miller	.10
T40	Jose Lima	.10
T41	Todd Zeile	.10
T42	Raul Ibanez	.10
T43	Danys Baez	.10

T44 Tony Clark .10
T45 Greg Maddux 1.00
T46 Craig Counsell .10
T47 Orlando Cabrera .25
T48 Jose Cruz Jr. .10
T49 Kris Benson .10
T50 Alex Rodriguez 2.00
T51 Steve Finley .10
T52 Ramon Hernandez .10
T53 Esteban Loaiza .10
T54 Ugueth Urbina .10
T55 Jeff Weaver .10
T56 Flash Gordon .10
T57 Jose Contreras .10
T58 Paul LoDuca .10
T59 Junior Spivey .10
T60 Curt Schilling 1.00
T61 Brad Penny .10
T62 Braden Looper .10
T63 Miguel Cairo .10
T64 Juan Encarnacion .10
T65 Miguel Batista .10
T66 Terry Francona .10
T67 Lee Mazzilli .10
T68 Al Pedrique .10
T69 Ozzie Guillen .10
T70 Phil Garner .10
T71 *Matt Bush* 2.50
T72 *Homer Bailey* 1.50
T73 *Greg Golson* 2.00
T74 *Kyle Waldrop* 1.50
T75 *Richie Robnett* 1.00
T76 *Jay Rainville* 2.00
T77 *Bill Bray* .50
T78 *Phillip Hughes* 1.00
T79 *Scott Elbert* .75
T80 *Josh Fields* 1.50
T81 *Justin Orenduff* 1.00
T82 *Dan Putnam* .50
T83 *Chris Nelson* 2.50
T84 *Blake DeWitt* 2.00
T85 *J.P. Howell* 1.00
T86 *Huston Street* 2.00
T87 *Kurt Suzuki* 1.50
T88 *Erick San Pedro* .50
T89 *Matt Tuiasosopo* 4.00
T90 *Matt Macri* 1.00
T91 Chad Tracy .10
T92 Scott Hairston .10
T93 Jonny Gomes .10
T94 Chin-Feng Chen .10
T95 Chien-Ming Wang .10
T96 Dustin McGowan .10
T97 Chris Burke .10
T98 Denny Bautista .10
T99 Preston Larrison .10
T100 Kevin Youkilis .10
T101 John Maine .10
T102 Guillermo Quiroz .10
T103 David Krynzel .10
T104 David Kelton .10
T105 Edwin Encarnacion .10
T106 Chad Gaudin .10
T107 Sergio Mitre .10
T108 Laynce Nix .10
T109 David Parrish .10
T110 Brandon Claussen .10
T111 *Frank Francisco* .25
T112 *Brian Dallimore* .25
T113 *Jim Crowell* .25
T114 *Andres Blanco* .75
T115 *Eduardo Villacis* .50
T116 *Kazuhito Tadano* .50
T117 *Aarom Baldiris* .25
T118 *Justin Germano* .25
T119 *Joey Gathright* 1.00
T120 *Franklyn Gracesqui* .25
T121 *Chin-Lung Hu* .50
T122 *Scott Olsen* .75
T123 Tyler Davidson .25
T124 *Fausto Carmona* .50
T125 *Tim Hutting* .25
T126 *Ryan Meaux* .25
T127 *Jon Connolly* .75
T128 *Hector Made* .50
T129 *Jamie Brown* .25
T130 *Paul McAnulty* .50
T131 *Chris Saenz* .25
T132 *Marland Williams* .25
T133 *Mike Huggins* .25
T134 Jesse Crain .50
T135 *Chad Bentz* .50
T136 *Kazuo Matsui* 1.00
T137 *Paul Maholm* .50
T138 *Brock Jacobsen* .25
T139 *Casey Daigle* .25
T140 *Nyjer Morgan* .25
T141 *Tom Mastny* .50
T142 *Kody Kirkland* .50
T143 *Jose Capellan* 1.00
T144 *Felix Hernandez* 15.00
T145 *Shawn Hill* .25
T146 *Danny Gonzalez* .25
T147 *Scott Dohmann* .25
T148 *Tommy Murphy* .50
T149 *Akinori Otsuka* .50
T150 *Miguel Perez* .50
T151 Mike Rouse .25
T152 *Ramon Ramirez* .50
T153 *Luke Hughes* .25
T154 *Howard Kendrick* 4.00
T155 Ryan Budde .25
T156 *Charlie Zink* .25
T157 *Warner Madrigal* .50
T158 *Jason Szuminski* .25
T159 *Chad Chop* .25
T160 *Shingo Takatsu* .25
T161 *Matt Lemanczyk* .25
T162 *Wardell Starling* .50
T163 *Nick Gorneault* .25
T164 *Scott Proctor* .25
T165 *Brooks Conrad* .50
T166 *Hector Gimenez* .50
T167 *Kevin Howard* .50
T168 *Vince Perkins* .50
T169 *Brock Peterson* .25
T170 *Chris Shelton* 3.00
T171 *Erick Aybar* 1.00
T172 *Paul Bacot* .25
T173 *Matt Capps* .25
T174 Kory Casto .25
T175 *Juan Cedeno* .25
T176 *Vito Chiaravalloti* .50
T177 *Alec Zumwalt* .25
T178 *J.J. Furmaniak* .25
T179 *Lee Gwaltney* .50
T180 *Donald Kelly* .25
T181 *Benji DeQuin* .25
T182 *Brant Colamarino* .50
T183 *Juan Gutierrez* .50
T184 *Carl Loadenthal* .50
T185 Ricky Nolasco .50
T186 *Jeff Salazar* .75
T187 *Rob Tejeda* .25
T188 *Alex Romero* .25
T189 *Yoann Torrealba* .25
T190 *Carlos Sosa* .25
T191 *Tim Bittner* .50
T192 *Chris Aguila* .25
T193 *Jason Frasor* .25
T194 *Reid Gorecki* .50
T195 *Dustin Nippert* .50
T196 *Javier Guzman* .25
T197 *Harvey Garcia* .50
T198 *Ivan Ochoa* .25
T199 *Dave Wallace* .25
T200 *Joel Zumaya* 1.50
T201 *Casey Kopitzke* .25
T202 *Lincoln Holdzkom* .25
T203 *Chad Santos* .25
T204 *Brian Pilkington* .25
T205 *Terry Jones* .25
T206 *Jerome Gamble* .25
T207 *Brad Eldred* 3.00
T208 *David Pauley* .25
T209 *Kevin Davidson* .25
T210 *Damaso Espino* .25
T211 *Tom Farmer* .50
T212 *Michael Mooney* .25
T213 *James Tomlin* .25
T214 *Greg Thissen* .25
T215 *Calvin Hayes* .25
T216 *Fernando Cortez* .25
T217 *Sergio Silva* .25
T218 *Jon DeVries* .25
T219 *Don Sutton* 1.50
T220 *Leo Nunez* .25

Gold

Stars: 5-10X
Rookies: 2-3X
Production 2,004 sets

Printing Plates

No pricing due to scarcity

Chrome Refractor

Stars: 4-8X
Rookies: 2-4X
Inserted 1:12

Blue Refractor

No Pricing
Production one set

X-Fractor

No Pricing
Production 20 sets

Dual Transactions Relic

NM/M
Common Player:
Inserted 1:562
RP Rafael Palmeiro 15.00
AR Alex Rodriguez 35.00
CS Curt Schilling 20.00

Future Phenoms

NM/M
Common Player: 5.00
KC Kevin Cash 5.00
BC Bobby Crosby 20.00
ED Eric Duncan 5.00
AG Adrian Gonzalez 5.00
NG Nick Green 8.00
JH J.J. Hardy 5.00
EJ Edwin Jackson 8.00
MM Mark Malaska 5.00
VM Victor Martinez 8.00
KM Kazuo Matsui 12.00
LM Lastings Milledge 5.00
JM Justin Morneau 12.00
DN Dioner Navarro 8.00
RN Ramon Nivar 5.00
BU B.J. Upton 12.00
JW Jayson Werth 10.00
DY Delmon Young 10.00

Hall of Fame Relic

NM/M
Common Player:
DE Dennis Eckersley 10.00
PM Paul Molitor 15.00

Hall of Fame Dual Relic

NM/M
Inserted 1:3,388
ME Paul Molitor, Dennis Eckersley 40.00

Signature Cuts

No Pricing
RM Roger Maris
CH Jim "Catfish" Hunter
JM Johnny Mize
BR Babe Ruth
WS Warren Spahn

Signature Moves

NM/M
Common Autograph: 10.00
MB Milton Bradley 15.00
MK Mark Kotsay 10.00
EM Eli Marrero 10.00
MN Mike Neu 10.00
AR Alex Rodriguez 160.00
RS Richie Sexson
JV Javier Vazquez 20.00
FV Fernando Vina 10.00
AW Adam Wainwright 20.00

Transactions Relics

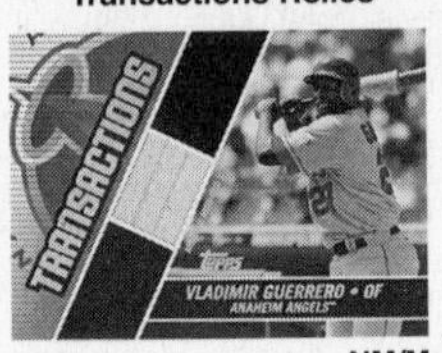

NM/M
Common Player: 5.00
Inserted 1:106
RA Roberto Alomar 8.00
JB Jeromy Burnitz 5.00
HC Hee Seop Choi 5.00
RC Roger Clemens 15.00
CE Carl Everett 5.00
JG Juan Gonzalez 8.00
VG Vladimir Guerrero 12.00
BJ Brian Jordan 5.00
KL Kenny Lofton 5.00
JL Javy Lopez 8.00
RP Rafael Palmeiro 8.00
AP Andy Pettitte 8.00
AR Alex Rodriguez 25.00
IR Ivan Rodriguez 12.00
RS Reggie Sanders 8.00
RLS Richie Sexson 8.00
GS Gary Sheffield 10.00
MT Miguel Tejada 8.00
RW Rondell White 5.00

2004 TOPPS ALL-TIME FAN FAVORITES

NM/M
Complete Set (150): 35.00
Common Player: .25
Pack (6): 4.00
Box (24): 80.00

1 Willie Mays 2.50
2 Bob Gibson .75
3 Dave Steib .25
4 Tim McCarver .25
5 Reggie Jackson .75
6 John Candelaria .25
7 Lenny Dykstra .25
8 Tony Oliva .50
9 Frank Viola .25
10 Don Mattingly 2.50
11 Garry Maddox .25
12 Randy Jones .25
13 Joe Carter .25
14 Orlando Cepeda .50
15 Bob Sheppard .25
16 Bobby Grich .25
17 George Scott .25
18 Mickey Rivers .25
19 Ron Santo .25
20 Mike Schmidt 2.00
21 Luis Aparicio .25
22 Cesar Geronimo .25
23 Jack Morris .25
24 Jeffrey Loria .25
25 George Brett 2.00
26 Paul O'Neill .25
27 Reggie Smith .25
28 Robin Yount 1.00
29 Andre Dawson .50
30 Whitey Ford .75
31 Ralph Kiner .50
32 Will Clark .50
33 Keith Hernandez .25
34 Tony Fernandez .25
35 Willie McGee .25
36 Harmon Killebrew .75
37 Dave Kingman .25
38 Kirk Gibson .25
39 Terry Steinbach .25
40 Frank Robinson .75
41 Chet Lemon .25
42 Mike Cuellar .25
43 Darrell Evans .25
44 Don Kessinger .25
45 Dave Concepcion .25
46 Sparky Anderson .25
47 Bret Saberhagen .25
48 Brett Butler .25
49 Kent Hrbek .25
50 Hank Aaron 2.50
51 Rudolph Giuliani .25
52 Clete Boyer .25
53 Mookie Wilson .25
54 Dave Stewart .25
55 Gary Matthews .25
56 Roy Face .25
57 Vida Blue .25
58 Jimmy Key .25
59 Al Hrabosky .25
60 Al Kaline .75
61 Mike Scott .25
62 Jack McDowell .25
63 Reggie Jackson .75
64 Earl Weaver .25
65 Ernie Harwell .25
66 David Justice .25
67 Wilbur Wood .25
68 Mike Boddicker .25
69 Don Zimmer .25
70 Jim Palmer .50
71 Doug DeCinces .25
72 Ryne Sandberg 1.00
73 Don Newcombe .25
74 Denny Martinez .25
75 Carl Yastrzemski 1.50
76 Bake McBride .25
77 Andy Van Slyke .25
78 Bruce Sutter .50
79 Bobby Valentine .25

80 Johnny Bench 1.50
81 Orel Hershiser .25
82 Danny Tartabull .25
83 Lou Whitaker .25
84 Alan Trammell .50
85 Sam McDowell .25
86 Ray Knight .25
87 Fernando Valenzuela .25
88 Ben Oglivie .25
89 Billy Beane .25
90 Yogi Berra 1.00
91 Jose Canseco .50
92 Bobby Bonilla .25
93 Darren Daulton .25
94 Harold Reynolds .25
95 Lou Brock .50
96 Pete Incaviglia .25
97 Eric Gregg .25
98 Devon White .25
99 Kelly Gruber .25
100 Nolan Ryan 3.00
101 Carlton Fisk .50
102 George Foster .25
103 Dennis Eckersley .25
104 Rick Sutcliffe .25
105 Cal Ripken Jr. 3.00
106 Norm Cash .25
107 Charlie Hough .25
108 Paul Molitor .75
109 Maury Wills .25
110 Tom Seaver 1.00
111 Brooks Robinson 1.00
112 Jim Rice .25
113 Dwight Gooden .25
114 Harold Baines .25
115 Tim Raines .25
116 Roy Smalley .25
117 Richie Allen .25
118 Ron Swoboda .25
119 Ron Guidry .25
120 Duke Snider .75
121 Ferguson Jenkins .50
122 Mark Fidrych .25
123 Buddy Bell .25
124 Bo Jackson .50
125 Stan Musial 1.50
126 Jesse Barfield .25
127 Tony Gwynn 1.00
128 Phil Garner .25
129 Dale Murphy .75
130 Wade Boggs .50
131 Sid Fernandez .25
132 Monte Irvin .25
133 Peter Ueberroth .25
134 Gary Gaetti .25
135 Gorman Thomas .25
136 Davey Lopes .25
137 Sy Berger .25
138 Buck O'Neil .25
139 Herb Score .25
140 Rod Carew .75
141 Joe Buck .25
142 Willie Horton .25
143 Hal McRae .25
144 Rollie Fingers .25
145 Tom Brunansky .25
146 Fay Vincent .25
147 Gary Carter .50
148 Bobby Richardson .25
149 Steve Garvey .25
150 Don Larsen .50

Refractor

Cards (1-150): 3-6X
Production 299 sets

Autographs

NM/M
Common Autograph: 10.00
Inserted 2:box
SP's noted
HA Hank Aaron/50 350.00
RA Richie Allen 15.00
SA Sparky Anderson/100 20.00
LA Luis Aparicio/100 40.00
HB Harold Baines/100 20.00
JB Jesse Barfield 10.00
BB Billy Beane/100 25.00
BBE Buddy Bell 20.00
JBE Johnny Bench/100 150.00
SB Sy Berger 50.00
YB Yogi Berra/100 90.00
VB Vida Blue 15.00
MB Mike Boddicker 15.00
WB Wade Boggs/50 100.00
BMB Bobby Bonilla 20.00
GB George Brett/50 100.00
LB Lou Brock/100 60.00
TB Tom Brunansky 25.00
JB Joe Buck/100 30.00
JCA Jose Canseco/100 65.00
RC Rod Carew/100 60.00
GC Gary Carter/50 60.00
JC Joe Carter/100 45.00
OC Orlando Cepeda/100 65.00
DC Dave Concepcion/100 40.00
DD Darren Daulton 15.00
AD Andre Dawson/100 40.00
LD Lenny Dykstra/100 20.00
DEC Dennis Eckersley/100 40.00
DE Darrell Evans 10.00
SF Sid Fernandez/100 40.00
TF Tony Fernandez 15.00
MF Mark Fidrych/100 40.00
RF Rollie Fingers/100 40.00
CF Carlton Fisk/50
WF Whitey Ford/100 100.00
GF George Foster 10.00
SG Steve Garvey/100 30.00
CG Cesar Geronimo/100 65.00
BG Bob Gibson/100 90.00
KG Kirk Gibson/50
DG Dwight Gooden/50 60.00
EG Eric Gregg 15.00
BGR Bobby Grich 10.00
RG Ron Guidry/100 50.00
TG Tony Gwynn/50 100.00
EH Ernie Harwell 25.00
KH Keith Hernandez/50 25.00
OH Orel Hershiser 30.00
WH Willie Horton 10.00
CH Charlie Hough 15.00
AH Al Hrabosky 15.00
PI Pete Incaviglia 20.00
MI Monte Irvin/100 25.00
BJ Bo Jackson/50 100.00
RJ2 Reggie Jackson 80.00
FJ Ferguson Jenkins 15.00
RJO Randy Jones 10.00
DJ David Justice 25.00
AK Al Kaline/50 100.00
DKE Don Kessinger 15.00
JK Jimmy Key/100 45.00
HK Harmon Killebrew/100 85.00
RK Ralph Kiner 40.00
DK Dave Kingman 40.00
RKN Ray Knight/100 40.00
DLA Don Larsen 15.00
CL Chet Lemon 15.00
DL Davey Lopes 10.00
GM Gary Mathews 10.00
DON Don Mattingly/50 125.00
WM Willie Mays/50 225.00
TM Tim McCarver 40.00
JM Jack McDowell 15.00
SM Sam McDowell/100 15.00
WMC Willie McGee/100 50.00
PM Paul Molitor/50 85.00
JMO Jack Morris 10.00
DM Dale Murphy/50 75.00
SM Stan Musial/100 100.00
BO Buck O'Neil 30.00
PO Paul O'Neill/50 60.00
BO Ben Oglivie 15.00
TO Tony Oliva 30.00
JP Jim Palmer/50 100.00
TR Tim Raines 25.00
HR Harold Reynolds/100 30.00
JR Jim Rice/100 40.00
BR Bobby Richardson 15.00
CR Cal Ripken Jr./50 200.00
MR Mickey Rivers 10.00
BRO Brooks Robinson/50 100.00
FR Frank Robinson/100 80.00
NR Nolan Ryan 175.00
BS Bret Saberhagen/100 45.00
RYN Ryne Sandberg/100 100.00
RS Ron Santo 30.00
MS Mike Schmidt/50 120.00
GS George Scott 15.00
MSC Mike Scott 10.00
TSE Tom Seaver/50 100.00
BS Bob Sheppard/10
DSN Duke Snider/100 75.00
DS Dave Stewart 10.00
DST Dave Stieb 25.00
RSU Rick Sutcliffe/100 40.00
BSU Bruce Sutter 35.00
RSW Ron Swoboda 15.00
AT Alan Trammell/100 60.00
PU Peter Ueberroth/100 60.00
BV Bobby Valentine/100 50.00
AV Andy Van Slyke/100 65.00
FVI Fay Vincent/100 50.00
EW Earl Weaver 15.00
MW Maury Wills 15.00
MWI Mookie Wilson 10.00
WW Wilbur Wood 15.00
CY Carl Yastrzemski/50 100.00
RY Robin Yount/50 100.00
DZ Don Zimmer 30.00

Best Seat In The Hous

NM/M
Common Card: 15.00
BS1 Tom Seaver, Johnny Bench, George Foster 15.00
BS2 Frank Robinson, Jim Palmer, Brooks Robinson 15.00
BS3 Dave Parker, Bill Madlock, Bill Mazeroski 15.00
BS4 Kent Hrbek, Rod Carew, Harmon Killebrew 30.00

Relics

NM/M
Common Player: 5.00
WB Wade Boggs 10.00
GB George Brett 15.00
LB Lou Brock 10.00
JC Jose Canseco/jsy 8.00
JCB Jose Canseco/bat 8.00
GC Gary Carter 8.00
DE Dennis Eckersley 5.00
CF Carlton Fisk 10.00
GF George Foster 5.00
KG Kirk Gibson 5.00
KH Keith Hernandez 8.00
RJ Reggie Jackson 10.00
DJ David Justice 5.00
HK Harmon Killebrew 20.00
WM Willie Mays 30.00
JM Joe Morgan 5.00
GN Graig Nettles 8.00
JP Jim Palmer 8.00
DP Dave Parker 5.00
KP Kirby Puckett 10.00
HR Harold Reynolds 5.00
JR Jim Rice 5.00
BR Brooks Robinson 12.00
FRB Frank Robinson/bat 8.00
FR Frank Robinson/jsy 8.00
NR Nolan Ryan 25.00
BS Bret Saberhagen 5.00
MS Mike Schmidt 15.00
DS Darryl Strawberry 8.00
EW Earl Weaver 8.00
MW Maury Wills 5.00
CY Carl Yastrzemski 20.00

2004 TOPPS BAZOOKA

NM/M
Complete Set (300): 40.00
Common Player: .15
Variations (30): same price
Pack (8): 2.00
Box (24): 40.00
1 Bobby Abreu .25
2 Jesse Foppert .15
3 Shea Hillenbrand .15
4 Jose Lima .15
5 Manny Ramirez .50
6 Denny Neagle .15
7 Frank Thomas .50
8 A.J. Burnett .15
9 Carl Everett .15
10 Scott Podsednik .25
11 Travis Lee .15
12 Mike Mussina .40
13 Runelvys Hernandez .15
14 Shannon Stewart .15
15 Miguel Cabrera .40
16 Edgardo Alfonzo .15
17 Victor Zambrano .15
18 Rafael Furcal .25
19 Eric Hinske .15
20 Paul LoDuca .15
21 Phil Nevin .15
22 Aramis Ramirez .15
23 Jim Thome .75
24 Jeromy Burnitz .15
25 Mark Prior 1.50
26 Ramon Hernandez .15
27 Cliff Lee .15
28 Greg Myers .15
29 Robert Fick .15
30 Mike Sweeney .15
31 Carlos Zambrano .15
32 Roberto Alomar .40
33 Orlando Cabrera .25
34 Orlando Hudson .15
35 Nomar Garciaparra 1.50
36 Esteban Loaiza .15
37 Laynce Nix .15
38 Joe Randa .15
39 Juan Uribe .15
40 Pat Burrell .40
41 Steve Finley .15
42 Livan Hernandez .15
43 Al Leiter .15
44 Brett Myers .15
45 Jody Gerut .15
46 Mark Teixeira .40
47 Barry Zito .40
48 Moises Alou .25
49 Mike Cameron .15
50 Albert Pujols 1.50
51 Tim Hudson .25
52 Kenny Lofton .25
53 Trot Nixon .15
54 Tim Redding .15
55 Marlon Byrd .15
56 Javier Vazquez .25
57 Sean Burroughs .15
58 Cliff Floyd .15
59 Juan Rivera .15
60 Mike Lieberthal .15
61 Xavier Nady .15
62 Brad Radke .15
63 Miguel Tejada .40
64 Ichiro Suzuki 1.00
65 Garret Anderson .25
66 Sean Casey .15
67 Jason Giambi .75
68 Aubrey Huff .15
69 Javy Lopez .25

70	Hideo Nomo	.25
71	Mark Redman	.15
72	Jose Vidro	.15
73	Rich Aurilia	.15
74	Luis Castillo	.15
75	Jay Gibbons	.15
76	Torii Hunter	.25
77	Derek Lowe	.15
78	Wes Obermueller	.15
79	Edgar Renteria	.15
80	Jeff Bagwell	.50
81	Fernando Vina	.15
82	Frank Catalanotto	.15
83	Marcus Giles	.15
84	Raul Ibanez	.15
85	Mike Lowell	.25
86	Tomokazu Ohka	.15
87	Jose Reyes	.25
88	Omar Vizquel	.25
89	Shawn Chacon	.15
90	Rocco Baldelli	.25
91	Brian Giles	.25
92	Kazuhisa Ishii	.15
93	Greg Maddux	1.00
94	John Olerud	.25
95	Eric Chavez	.25
96	Doug Waechter	.15
97	Tony Batista	.15
98	Jeriome Robertson	.15
99	Troy Glaus	.25
100	Eric Gagne	.25
101	Pedro J. Martinez	.75
102	Magglio Ordonez	.25
103	Alex Rodriguez	2.00
104	Jason Bay	.15
105	Larry Walker	.25
106	Matt Clement	.15
107	Tom Glavine	.25
108	Geoff Jenkins	.25
109	Victor Martinez	.15
110	David Ortiz	.15
111	Ivan Rodriguez	.40
112	Jarrod Washburn	.15
113	Josh Beckett	.25
114	Bartolo Colon	.25
115	Juan Gonzalez	.40
116	Derek Jeter	2.00
117	Edgar Martinez	.25
118	Ramon Ortiz	.15
119	Scott Rolen	.75
120	Brandon Webb	.15
121	Carlos Beltran	.25
122	Jose Contreras	.25
123	Luis Gonzalez	.25
124	Jason Johnson	.15
125	Luis Matos	.15
126	Russ Ortiz	.15
127	Damian Rolls	.15
128	Boomer Wells	.15
129	Adrian Beltre	.15
130	Shawn Green	.25
131	Nate Cornejo	.15
132	Nick Johnson	.15
133	Joe Mays	.15
134	Roy Oswalt	.25
135	C.C. Sabathia	.15
136	Vernon Wells	.25
137	Kris Benson	.15
138	Carl Crawford	.15
139	Ken Griffey Jr.	1.00
140	Randy Johnson	.75
141	Fred McGriff	.25
142	Vicente Padilla	.15
143	Tim Salmon	.25
144	Kip Wells	.15
145	Lance Berkman	.25
146	Jose Cruz Jr.	.15
147	Marquis Grissom	.15
148	Jacque Jones	.15
149	Gil Meche	.15
150	Vladimir Guerrero	.75
151	Reggie Sanders	.15
152	Ty Wigginton	.15
153	Angel Berroa	.15
154	Johnny Damon	.25
155	Rafael Palmeiro	.50
156	Chipper Jones	.75
157	Kevin Millar	.15
158	Corey Patterson	.25
159	Johan Santana	.15
160	Bernie Williams	.40
161	Craig Biggio	.25
162	Carlos Delgado	.50
163	Aaron Guiel	.15
164	Wade Miller	.15
165	Andruw Jones	.50
166	Jay Payton	.15
167	Benito Santiago	.15
168	Woody Williams	.15
169	Casey Blake	.15
170	Adam Dunn	.40
171	Jose Guillen	.15
172	Brian Jordan	.15
173	Kevin Millwood	.25
174	Carlos Pena	.15
175	Curt Schilling	.50
176	Jerome Williams	.15
177	Hank Blalock	.25
178	Erubiel Durazo	.15
179	Cristian Guzman	.15
180	Austin Kearns	.40
181	Raul Mondesi	.15
182	Andy Pettitte	.25
183	Jason Schmidt	.25
184	Jeremy Bonderman	.15
185	Dontrelle Willis	.25
186	Ray Durham	.15
187	Jerry Hairston Jr.	.15
188	Jason Kendall	.15
189	Melvin Mora	.15
190	Jeff Kent	.25
191	Jae Weong Seo	.15
192	Jack Wilson	.15
193	Cesar Izturis	.15
194	Jermaine Dye	.15
195	Roy Halladay	.25
196	Jason Phillips	.15
197	Matt Morris	.25
198	Mike Piazza	1.00
199	Richie Sexson	.40
200	Alfonso Soriano	.75
201	Mark Mulder	.25
202	David Eckstein	.15
203	Mike Hampton	.15
204	Ryan Klesko	.25
205	Damian Moss	.15
206	Juan Pierre	.15
207	Ben Sheets	.25
208	Randy Winn	.15
209	Bret Boone	.25
210	Jim Edmonds	.25
211	Rich Harden	.15
212	Paul Konerko	.15
213	Jamie Moyer	.15
214	A.J. Pierzynski	.15
215	Gary Sheffield	.25
216	Randy Wolf	.15
217	Kevin Brown	.25
218	Morgan Ensberg	.15
219	Bo Hart	.15
220	Bill Mueller	.15
221	Corey Koskie	.15
222	Joel Pineiro	.15
223	Preston Wilson	.15
224	Aaron Boone	.15
225	Kerry Wood	.50
226	Darin Erstad	.25
227	Wes Helms	.15
228	Brian Lawrence	.15
229	Mark Buehrle	.15
230	Sammy Sosa	1.25
231	Sidney Ponson	.15
232	Dmitri Young	.15
233	Ellis Burks	.15
234	Kelvim Escobar	.15
235	Todd Helton	.50
236	Matt Lawton	.15
237	Eric Munson	.15
238	Jorge Posada	.50
239	Junior Spivey	.15
240	Michael Young	.15
241	Ramon Nivar	.15
242	Edwin Jackson	.15
243	Felix Pie	.15
244	Ryan Wagner	.15
245	Grady Sizemore	.15
246	Bobby Jenks	.15
247	Chad Billingsley	.15
248	Casey Kotchman	.15
249	Bobby Crosby	.15
250	Khalil Greene	.15
251	Danny Garcia	.15
252	Nicholas Markakis	.15
253	Bernie Castro	.15
254	Aaron Hill	.15
255	Josh Barfield	.15
256	Ryan Wagner	.15
257	Ryan Harvey	.15
258	Jimmy Gobble	.15
259	Ryan Madson	.15
260	Zack Greinke	.15
261	Rene Reyes	.15
262	Eric Duncan	.15
263	Chris Lubanski	.15
264	Jeff Mathis	.15
265	Rickie Weeks	.25
266	Justin Morneau	.15
267	Brian Snyder	.15
268	Neal Cotts	.15
269	Joe Borchard	.15
270	Larry Bigbie	.15
271	*Marcus McBeth*	.40
272	*Tydus Meadows*	.40
273	*Zach Miner*	.40
274	*Anthony Lerew*	.40
275	*Yadier Molina*	.40
276	*Jon Knott*	.40
277	Matthew Moses	.40
278	*Sung Jung*	.40
279	Mike Gosling	.15
280	David Murphy	.15
281	*Tim Frend*	.40
282	*Casey Myers*	.40
283	*Brayan Pena*	.40
284	*Omar Falcon*	.40
285	*Blake Hawksworth*	.40
286	*Jesse Roman*	.40
287	*Kyle Davies*	.40
288	*Matt Creighton*	.40
289	*Rodney Choy Foo*	.40
290	Kyle Sleeth	.15
291	Carlos Quentin	.15
292	*Khalid Ballouli*	.40
293	Tim Stauffer	.15
294	*Craig Ansman*	.40
295	*Dioner Navarro*	.40
296	*Josh Labandeira*	.40
297	Jeff Allison	.15
298	*Anthony Acevedo*	.40
299	Brad Sullivan	.15
300	Conor Jackson	.15

Mini

Stars (1-300): 1-2X
Inserted 1:1

Red

Cards (1-300): 1-2X
Inserted 1:1

Adventures

		NM/M
Common Player:		4.00
EA	Edgardo Alfonzo	4.00
JB	Jeff Bagwell	8.00
LB	Lance Berkman	6.00
CB	Craig Biggio	4.00
KB	Kevin Brown	4.00
PB	Pat Burrell	6.00
MB	Marlon Byrd	4.00
SC	Sean Casey	4.00
LC	Luis Castillo	4.00
EC	Eric Chavez	5.00
AD1	Adam Dunn	6.00
AD2	Adam Dunn	6.00
CE	Carl Everett	4.00
CF	Cliff Floyd	4.00
NG	Nomar Garciaparra	10.00
JG	Jason Giambi	8.00
JDG	Jeremy Giambi	4.00
TEG	Troy Glaus	5.00
TG	Tom Glavine	5.00
LG	Luis Gonzalez	4.00
SG	Shawn Green	5.00
BG	Ben Grieve	4.00
VG	Vladimir Guerrero	8.00
CG	Cristian Guzman	4.00
TH	Toby Hall	4.00
TAH1	Tim Hudson	4.00
TAH2	Tim Hudson	4.00
GJ	Geoff Jenkins	4.00
RJ	Randy Johnson	8.00
AJ	Andruw Jones	6.00
CJ	Chipper Jones	8.00
JK	Jason Kendall	4.00
PK	Paul Konerko	4.00
PL	Paul LoDuca	4.00
ML	Mike Lowell	4.00
GM	Greg Maddux	8.00
KM	Kevin Millwood	6.00
MM	Mark Mulder	5.00
MCM	Mike Mussina	6.00
HN	Hideo Nomo	8.00
JO	John Olerud	4.00
RP1	Rafael Palmeiro	6.00
RP2	Rafael Palmeiro	6.00
BP	Brad Penny	4.00
MP1	Mike Piazza	10.00
MP2	Mike Piazza	10.00
AP	Albert Pujols	15.00
MR	Manny Ramirez	6.00
AR1	Alex Rodriguez	10.00
AR2	Alex Rodriguez	10.00
TJS	Tim Salmon	5.00
CS	Curt Schilling	8.00
AS	Alfonso Soriano	6.00
MT	Miguel Tejada	6.00
JT	Jim Thome	8.00
LW	Larry Walker	4.00
JW	Jarrod Washburn	4.00
BW	Bernie Williams	6.00
DW	Dontrelle Willis	6.00
PW	Preston Wilson	4.00
KW	Kerry Wood	6.00
BZ	Barry Zito	6.00

Blasts

		NM/M
Common Player:		4.00
RA	Roberto Alomar	6.00
MA	Moises Alou	4.00
RSA	Rich Aurilia	4.00
JB	Jeff Bagwell	8.00
RB	Rocco Baldelli	8.00
TB	Tony Batista	4.00
CIB	Carlos Beltran	4.00
LB	Lance Berkman	5.00
CB	Craig Biggio	4.00
HB	Hank Blalock	6.00
BB	Bret Boone	5.00
JNB	Jeromy Burnitz	4.00
SB	Sean Burroughs	4.00
CC	Carl Crawford	4.00
AD	Adam Dunn	6.00
CE	Carl Everett	4.00
BF	Brad Fullmer	4.00
RF	Rafael Furcal	5.00
AJG	Andres Galarraga	4.00
NG	Nomar Garciaparra	12.00
JG	Jason Giambi	8.00
TG	Troy Glaus	5.00
AG	Adrian Gonzalez	4.00
JAG	Juan Gonzalez	6.00
LG	Luis Gonzalez	4.00
SG	Shawn Green	6.00
MG	Marquis Grissom	4.00
VG	Vladimir Guerrero	8.00
CG	Cristian Guzman	4.00
NH	Nathan Haynes	4.00
TKH	Todd Helton	6.00
AH	Aubrey Huff	4.00
TH	Torii Hunter	5.00
CJ	Chipper Jones	8.00
PK	Paul Konerko	4.00
ML	Matt Lawton	4.00
CL	Carlos Lee	4.00
PL	Paul LoDuca	4.00
EM	Edgar Martinez	4.00
TM	Tino Martinez	6.00
FM	Fred McGriff	5.00
DM	Doug Mientkiewicz	4.00
JO	John Olerud	4.00
MO	Magglio Ordonez	4.00
RP	Rafael Palmeiro	8.00
CP	Corey Patterson	4.00
MP	Mike Piazza	10.00
JP	Jorge Posada	6.00
AP	Albert Pujols	15.00
ANR	Aramis Ramirez	4.00
MR	Manny Ramirez	6.00
JR	Juan Rivera	4.00
AR	Alex Rodriguez	10.00
IR	Ivan Rodriguez	6.00
SR	Scott Rolen	8.00
TJS	Tim Salmon	6.00
GS	Gary Sheffield	6.00
RS	Ruben Sierra	4.00

AS Alfonso Soriano 8.00
SS Shannon Stewart 4.00
ST So Taguchi 5.00
MCT Mark Teixeira 5.00
MT Miguel Tejada 5.00
FT Frank Thomas 8.00
MAT Michael Tucker 4.00
MV Mo Vaughn 4.00
OV Omar Vizquel 4.00
LW Larry Walker 5.00
VW Vernon Wells 5.00
RW Rondell White 4.00
BW Bernie Williams 6.00

Comics

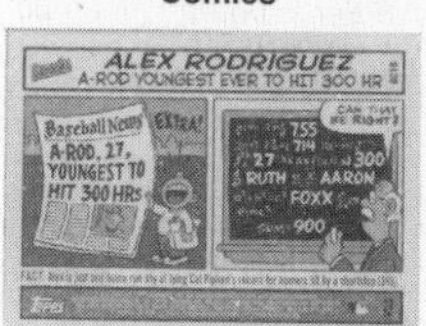

NM/M
Complete Set (24): 6.00
Common Player: .25
Inserted 1:4
BC1 Garret Anderson .25
BC2 Jeff Bagwell .50
BC3 Hank Blalock .25
BC4 Roy Halladay .25
BC5 Dontrelle Willis .25
BC6 Roger Clemens .75
BC7 Carlos Delgado .40
BC8 Rafael Furcal .25
BC9 Eric Gagne .25
BC10 Nomar Garciaparra .75
BC11 Derek Jeter .75
BC12 Esteban Loaiza .25
BC13 Kevin Millwood .25
BC14 Bill Mueller .25
BC15 Rafael Palmeiro .40
BC16 Albert Pujols .75
BC17 Jose Reyes .25
BC18 Alex Rodriguez .75
BC19 Alfonso Soriano .40
BC20 Sammy Sosa .50
BC21 Ichiro Suzuki .50
BC22 Frank Thomas .40
BC23 Brad Wilkerson .25
BC24 Houston Astros .25

One-Liners

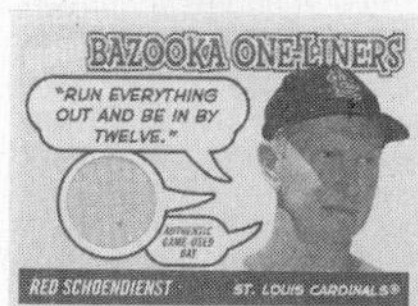

NM/M
Common Player: 5.00
DA Dick Allen 8.00
JB Johnny Bench 10.00
BB Bert Blyleven 5.00
WB1 Wade Boggs 6.00
WB2 Wade Boggs 6.00
GB George Brett 20.00
BC Bert Campaneris 5.00
RC Rod Carew 8.00
GC Gary Carter 5.00
JCA Joe Carter 5.00
OC Orlando Cepeda 5.00
RD Ron Darling 5.00
AD Andre Dawson 8.00
DE Dennis Eckersley 10.00
KG1 Kirk Gibson 5.00
KG2 Kirk Gibson 5.00
DW Dwight Gooden 5.00
KH Keith Hernandez 5.00
RJ Reggie Jackson 10.00
DJ1 David Justice 8.00
DJ2 David Justice 8.00
HK Harmon Killebrew 20.00
JK Jerry Koosman 5.00
BM Bill Madlock 5.00
WM Willie Mays 30.00
WMC Willie McGee 8.00
TM Tug McGraw 8.00
JM Joe Morgan 8.00
DM Dale Murphy 15.00
EM Eddie Murray 10.00
PN Phil Niekro 5.00
DP Dave Parker 5.00
GP Gaylord Perry 5.00
KP1 Kirby Puckett 10.00
KP2 Kirby Puckett 10.00
FR Frank Robinson 10.00
NR Nolan Ryan 15.00
BS Bret Saberhagen 5.00
RSA Ron Santo 10.00
MS Mike Schmidt 15.00
RS Red Schoendienst 5.00
TS Tom Seaver 8.00
WS Willie Stargell 8.00
CY Carl Yastrzemski 15.00
RY Robin Yount 10.00

Stand-Ups

NM/M
Complete Set (25): 20.00
Common Player: .50
Inserted 1:8
1 Jose Reyes .50
2 Jim Thome 1.00
3 Roy Halladay .50
4 Jason Giambi 1.00
5 Dontrelle Willis .50
6 Mike Piazza 1.50
7 Chipper Jones 1.00
8 Mark Prior 2.00
9 Todd Helton .75
10 Miguel Cabrera .75
11 Derek Jeter 3.00
12 Nomar Garciaparra 2.00
13 Alex Rodriguez 3.00
14 Miguel Tejada .50
15 Carlos Delgado .75
16 Pedro J. Martinez 1.00
17 Sammy Sosa 2.00
18 Ichiro Suzuki 1.50
19 Vladimir Guerrero 1.00
20 Alfonso Soriano 1.00
21 Eric Chavez .50
22 Albert Pujols 2.50
23 Ivan Rodriguez .75
24 Vernon Wells .50
25 Eric Gagne .50

Tattoos

NM/M
Complete Set (55): 8.00
Common Player: .15
Inserted 1:4
JB Jeff Bagwell .25
BAZ Bazooka Logo .15
LB Lance Berkman .15
CB Craig Biggio .15
KB Kevin Brown .15
PB Pat Burrell .15
MB Marlon Byrd .15
SC Sean Casey .15
LC Luis Castillo .15
EC Eric Chavez .15
AD Adam Dunn .15
CF Cliff Floyd .15
NG Nomar Garciaparra .75
JG Jason Giambi .40
TFG Troy Glaus .25
TG Tom Glavine .25
LG Luis Gonzalez .15
SG Shawn Green .15
VG Vladimir Guerrero .40
CG Cristian Guzman .15
TH Toby Hall .15
TAH Tim Hudson .15
GJ Geoff Jenkins .15
RJ Randy Johnson .40
AJ Andruw Jones .25
CJ Chipper Jones .40
JK Jason Kendall .15
PK Paul Konerko .15
PL Paul LoDuca .15
ML Mike Lowell .15
GM Greg Maddux .50
KM Kevin Millwood .15
MM Mark Mulder .15
MCM Mike Mussina .25
HN Hideo Nomo .15
JO John Olerud .15
RP Rafael Palmeiro .25
BP Brad Penny .15
MP Mike Piazza .50
AP Albert Pujols 1.00
MR Manny Ramirez .25
AR Alex Rodriguez 1.00
TJS Tim Salmon .25
CS Curt Schilling .25
AS Alfonso Soriano .40
MT Miguel Tejada .25
JT Jim Thome .40
TOP Topps Logo .15
LW Larry Walker .15
JW Jarrod Washburn .15
BW Bernie Williams .25
DW Dontrelle Willis .15
PW Preston Wilson .15
KW Kerry Wood .25
BZ Barry Zito .25

2004 TOPPS CHROME

NM/M
Complete Set (466):
Common Player: .25
Common Rookie Auto
(221-246): 10.00
Inserted 1:21
Series 1 Pack (4): 3.50
Series 1 Box (20): 50.00
Series 2 Pack (4): 3.50
Series 2 Box (20): 50.00
1 Jim Thome 1.00
2 Reggie Sanders .25
3 Mark Kotsay .25
4 Edgardo Alfonzo .25
5 Tim Wakefield .25
6 Moises Alou .50
7 Jorge Julio .25
8 Bartolo Colon .50
9 Chan Ho Park .25
10 Ichiro Suzuki 2.00
11 Kevin Millwood .50
12 Preston Wilson .40
13 Tom Glavine .75
14 Junior Spivey .25
15 Marcus Giles .40
16 David Segui .25
17 Kevin Millar .25
18 Corey Patterson .40
19 Aaron Rowand .25
20 Derek Jeter 4.00
21 Luis Castillo .25
22 Manny Ramirez 1.00
23 Jay Payton .25
24 Bobby Higginson .25
25 Lance Berkman .75
26 Juan Pierre .25
27 Mike Mussina 1.00
28 Fred McGriff .50
29 Richie Sexson .75
30 Tim Hudson .50
31 Mike Piazza 2.00
32 Brad Radke .25
33 Jeff Weaver .25
34 Ramon Hernandez .25
35 David Bell .25
36 Randy Wolf .25
37 Jake Peavy .25
38 Tim Worrell .25
39 Gil Meche .25
40 Albert Pujols 3.00
41 Michael Young .25
42 Josh Phelps .25
43 Brendan Donnelly .25
44 Steve Finley .25
45 John Smoltz .50
46 Jay Gibbons .25
47 Trot Nixon .25
48 Carl Pavano .25
49 Frank Thomas 1.00
50 Mark Prior 2.50
51 Danny Graves .25
52 Milton Bradley .25
53 Kris Benson .25
54 Ryan Klesko .50
55 Mike Lowell .25
56 Geoff Blum .25
57 Michael Tucker .25
58 Paul LoDuca .25
59 Vicente Padilla .25
60 Jacque Jones .25
61 Fernando Tatis .25
62 Ty Wigginton .25
63 Rich Aurilia .25
64 Andy Pettitte .75
65 Terrence Long .25
66 Cliff Floyd .25
67 Mariano Rivera .50
68 Kelvim Escobar .25
69 Marlon Byrd .25
70 Mark Mulder .50
71 Francisco Cordero .25
72 Carlos Guillen .25
73 Fernando Vina .25
74 Lance Carter .25
75 Hank Blalock .75
76 Jimmy Rollins .25
77 Francisco Rodriguez .25
78 Javy Lopez .50
79 Jerry Hairston Jr. .25
80 Andruw Jones .75
81 Rodrigo Lopez .25
82 Johnny Damon .50
83 Hee Seop Choi .25
84 Kazuhiro Sasaki .25
85 Danny Bautista .25
86 Matt Lawton .25
87 Juan Uribe .25
88 Rafael Furcal .50
89 Kyle Farnsworth .25
90 Jose Vidro .25
91 Luis Rivas .25
92 Hideo Nomo .75
93 Javier Vazquez .50
94 Al Leiter .40
95 Jose Valentin .25
96 Alex Cintron .25
97 Zach Day .25
98 Jorge Posada .75
99 C.C. Sabathia .25
100 Alex Rodriguez 3.00
101 Brad Penny .25
102 Brad Ausmus .25
103 Raul Ibanez .25
104 Mike Hampton .25
105 Adrian Beltre .50
106 Ramiro Mendoza .25
107 Rocco Baldelli .75
108 Esteban Loaiza .25
109 Russell Branyan .25
110 Todd Helton 1.00
111 Braden Looper .25
112 Octavio Dotel .25
113 Mike MacDougal .25
114 Cesar Izturis .25
115 Johan Santana .25
116 Jose Contreras .50
117 Placido Polanco .25
118 Jason Phillips .25
119 Orlando Hudson .25
120 Vernon Wells .40
121 Ben Grieve .25
122 Dave Roberts .25
123 Ismael Valdes .25
124 Eric Owens .25
125 Curt Schilling .75
126 Russ Ortiz .25
127 Mark Buehrle .25
128 Doug Mientkiewicz .25
129 Dmitri Young .25
130 Kazuhisa Ishii .25
131 A.J. Pierzynski .25
132 Brad Wilkerson .25
133 Joe McEwing .25
134 Alex Cora .25
135 Jose Cruz Jr. .25
136 Carlos Zambrano .25
137 Jeff Kent .40
138 Shigetoshi Hasegawa .25
139 Jarrod Washburn .25
140 Greg Maddux 2.00

141 Josh Beckett .75
142 Miguel Batista .25
143 Omar Vizquel .40
144 Alex Gonzalez .25
145 Billy Wagner .25
146 Brian Jordan .25
147 Wes Helms .25
148 Deivi Cruz .25
149 Alex Gonzalez .25
150 Jason Giambi 1.00
151 Erubiel Durazo .25
152 Mike Lieberthal .25
153 Jason Kendall .25
154 Xavier Nady .25
155 Kirk Rueter .25
156 Mike Cameron .25
157 Miguel Cairo .25
158 Woody Williams .25
159 Toby Hall .25
160 Bernie Williams .75
161 Darin Erstad .50
162 Matt Mantei .25
163 Shawn Chacon .25
164 Bill Mueller .25
165 Damian Miller .25
166 Tony Graffanino .25
167 Sean Casey .25
168 Brandon Phillips .25
169 Runelvys Hernandez .25
170 Adam Dunn .75
171 Carlos Lee .25
172 Juan Encarnacion .25
173 Angel Berroa .25
174 Desi Relaford .25
175 Joe Mays .25
176 Ben Sheets .40
177 Eddie Guardado .25
178 Rocky Biddle .25
179 Eric Gagne .50
180 Eric Chavez .50
181 Jason Michaels .25
182 Dustan Mohr .25
183 Kip Wells .25
184 Brian Lawrence .25
185 Bret Boone .50
186 Tino Martinez .40
187 Aubrey Huff .25
188 Kevin Mench .25
189 Tim Salmon .50
190 Carlos Delgado 1.00
191 John Lackey .25
192 Eric Byrnes .25
193 Luis Matos .25
194 Derek Lowe .50
195 Mark Grudzielanek .25
196 Flash Gordon .25
197 Matt Clement .25
198 Byung-Hyun Kim .25
199 Brandon Inge .25
200 Nomar Garciaparra 3.00
201 Frank Catalanotto .25
202 Cristian Guzman .25
203 Bo Hart .25
204 Jack Wilson .25
205 Ray Durham .25
206 Freddy Garcia .25
207 J.D. Drew .25
208 Orlando Cabrera .25
209 Roy Halladay .50
210 David Eckstein .25
211 *Omar Falcon* 2.00
212 *Todd Self* 2.00
213 David Murphy 3.00
214 *Dioner Navarro* 6.00
215 *Marcus McBeth* 3.00
216 *Chris O'Riordan* 3.00
217 *Rodney Choy Foo* 2.00
218 *Tim Frend* 3.00
219 *Yadier Molina* 6.00
220 *Zachary Duke* 8.00
221 *Anthony Lerew/auto* 20.00
222 *Blake Hawksworth/auto.* 15.00
223 *Brayan Pena/auto.* 10.00
224 *Craig Ansman/auto.* 15.00
225 *Jon Knott/auto.* 15.00
226 *Josh Labandeira/auto.* 10.00
227 *Khalid Ballouli/auto.* 12.00
228 *Kyle Davies/auto.* 25.00
229 *Matt Creighton/auto.* 15.00
230 Mike Gosling/auto. 15.00
231 *Nic Ungs/auto.* 15.00
232 *Zach Miner/auto.* 15.00
233 Donald Levinski/auto. 15.00
234 Bradley Sullivan 15.00
235 Carlos Quentin 30.00
236 Conor Jackson 50.00
237 *Estee Harris* 20.00
238 Jeffrey Allison 20.00
239 Kyle Sleeth 20.00
240 Matthew Moses 15.00
241 Tim Stauffer 20.00
242 Brad Snyder 15.00
243 Jason Hirsh 15.00
244 Lastings Milledge 30.00
245 *Logan Kensing* 15.00
246 Kory Casto 10.00
247 David Aardsma 1.50
248 Omar Quintanilla 2.00
249 *Ervin Santana* 3.00
250 *Merkin Valdez* 2.00
251 *Vito Chiaravalloti* 3.00
252 *Travis Blackley* 3.00
253 *Chris Shelton* 6.00
254 *Rudy Guillen* 3.00
255 *Bobby Brownlie* 4.00
256 *Paul Maholm* 5.00
257 Roger Clemens 3.00
258 Laynce Nix .50
259 Eric Hinske .25
260 Ivan Rodriguez 1.00
261 Brandon Webb .25
262 Jhonny Peralta .25
263 Adam Kennedy .25
264 Tony Batista .25
265 Jeff Suppan .25
266 Kenny Lofton .50
267 Scott Sullivan .25
268 Ken Griffey Jr. 2.00
269 Billy Traber .25
270 Larry Walker .50
271 Todd Hollandsworth .25
272 Carlos Beltran 1.00
273 Carl Crawford .25
274 Karim Garcia .25
275 Jose Reyes .50
276 Brandon Duckworth .25
277 Brian Giles .50
278 J.T. Snow Jr. .25
279 Jamie Moyer .25
280 Julio Lugo .25
281 Mark Teixeira .50
282 Cory Lidle .25
283 Lyle Overbay .50
284 Troy Percival .25
285 Robby Hammock .25
286 Jason Johnson .25
287 Brandon Lyon .25
288 Antonio Alfonseca .25
289 Tom Goodwin .25
290 Paul Konerko .25
291 D'Angelo Jimenez .25
292 Ben Broussard .25
293 Magglio Ordonez .75
294 Carlos Pena .25
295 Chad Fox .25
296 Jeriome Robertson .25
297 Travis Hafner .50
298 Joe Randa .25
299 Brady Clark .25
300 Barry Zito .75
301 Ruben Sierra .25
302 Brett Myers .25
303 Oliver Perez .25
304 Benito Santiago .25
305 David Ross .25
306 Joe Nathan .25
307 Jim Edmonds .50
308 Matt Kata .25
309 Vinny Castilla .25
310 Marty Cordova .25
311 Aramis Ramirez .25
312 Carl Everett .25
313 Ryan Freel .25
314 Mark Bellhorn .25
315 Ugueth Urbina .25
316 Tim Redding .25
317 Jeromy Burnitz .25
318 Miguel Cabrera 1.00
319 Orlando Hernandez .25
320 Casey Blake .25
321 Aaron Boone .25
322 Jermaine Dye .25
323 Jerome Williams .25
324 John Olerud .50
325 Scott Rolen 1.50
326 Bobby Kielty .25
327 Travis Lee .25
328 Jeff Cirillo .25
329 Scott Spiezio .25
330 Melvin Mora .25
331 Mike Timlin .25
332 Kerry Wood 1.50
333 Tony Womack .25
334 Jody Gerut .25
335 Morgan Ensberg .25
336 Odalis Perez .25
337 Michael Cuddyer .25
338 Jose Hernandez .25
339 LaTroy Hawkins .25
340 Marquis Grissom .25
341 Matt Morris .50
342 Juan Gonzalez .75
343 Jose Valverde .25
344 Joe Borowski .25
345 Josh Bard .25
346 Austin Kearns .50
347 Chin-Hui Tsao .25
348 Wilfredo Ledezma .25
349 Aaron Guiel .25
350 Alfonso Soriano 1.50
351 Ted Lilly .25
352 Sean Burroughs .25
353 Rafael Palmeiro 1.00
354 Quinton McCracken .25
355 David Ortiz 1.00
356 Randall Simon .25
357 Wily Mo Pena .25
358 Brian Anderson .25
359 Corey Koskie .25
360 Keith Foulke .25
361 Sidney Ponson .25
362 Gary Matthews Jr. .25
363 Herbert Perry .25
364 Shea Hillenbrand .25
365 Craig Biggio .50
366 Barry Larkin .50
367 Orlando Merced .25
368 Sammy Sosa 2.50
369 Joe Crede .25
370 Gary Sheffield .75
371 Coco Crisp .25
372 Torii Hunter .50
373 Derrek Lee .50
374 Adam Everett .25
375 Miguel Tejada .75
376 Jeremy Affeldt .25
377 Robin Ventura .25
378 Scott Podsednik .75
379 Matthew LeCroy .25
380 Vladimir Guerrero 1.50
381 Steve Karsay .25
382 Jeff Nelson .25
383 Chase Utley .25
384 Bobby Abreu .50
385 Josh Fogg .25
386 Trevor Hoffman .25
387 Matt Stairs .25
388 Edgar Martinez .50
389 Edgar Renteria .50
390 Chipper Jones 1.50
391 Eric Munson .25
392 Dewon Brazelton .25
393 John Thomson .25
394 Chris Woodward .25
395 Joe Kennedy .25
396 Reed Johnson .25
397 Johnny Estrada .25
398 Damian Moss .25
399 Victor Zambrano .25
400 Dontrelle Willis .50
401 Troy Glaus .75
402 Raul Mondesi .50
403 Jeff DaVanon .25
404 Kurt Ainsworth .25
405 Pedro J. Martinez 1.50
406 Eric Karros .25
407 Billy Koch .25
408 Luis Gonzalez .50
409 Jack Cust .25
410 Mike Sweeney .25
411 Jason Bay .25
412 Mark Redman .25
413 Jason Jennings .25
414 Rondell White .50
415 Todd Hundley .25
416 Shannon Stewart .25
417 Jae Weong Seo .25
418 Livan Hernandez .25
419 Mark Ellis .25
420 Pat Burrell .50
421 Mark Loretta .25
422 Robb Nen .25
423 Joel Pineiro .25
424 Todd Walker .25
425 Jeremy Bonderman .25
426 A.J. Burnett .25
427 Greg Myers .25
428 Roy Oswalt .50
429 Carlos Baerga .25
430 Garret Anderson .75
431 Horacio Ramirez .25
432 Brian Roberts .25
433 Kevin Brown .50
434 Eric Milton .25
435 Brian Daubach .25
436 Alex Escobar .25
437 Alex Sanchez .25
438 Jeff Bagwell 1.00
439 Claudio Vargas .25
440 Shawn Green .50
441 Geoff Jenkins .50
442 Boomer Wells .25
443 Nick Johnson .25
444 Jose Guillen .25
445 Scott Hatteberg .25
446 Phil Nevin .25
447 Jason Schmidt .50
448 Ricky Ledee .25
449 So Taguchi .25
450 Randy Johnson .25
451 Eric Young .25
452 Chone Figgins .25
453 Larry Bigbie .25
454 Scott Williamson .25
455 Ramon Martinez .25
456 Roberto Alomar .75
457 Ryan Dempster .25
458 Ryan Ludwick .25
459 Ramon Santiago .25
460 Jeff Conine .25
461 Brad Lidge .25
462 Ken Harvey .25
463 Guillermo Mota .25
464 Rick Reed .25
465 Armando Benitez .25
466 Wade Miller .25

Refractors

Cards (1-220, 247-466): 1-2X
Inserted 1:4
Rookie Auto (221-246): 1.5-2X
Production 100
Gold Refractor (1-220): 1-2X
Inserted 1:5
Rookie Gold Refractor (221-246) 2-3X
Production 50
Black Refractor (1-220): 2-4X
Inserted 1:10
Rookie Black Refractor: No Pricing
Production 25

Fashionably Great

NM/M

Common Player: 5.00
Inserted 1:box
JB Jeff Bagwell 10.00
CB Craig Biggio 5.00
HB Hank Blalock 8.00
JBO Joe Borchard 5.00
KB Kevin Brown 5.00
EC Eric Chavez 6.00
CD Carlos Delgado 6.00
AD Adam Dunn 6.00
FG Freddy Garcia 5.00
CF Cliff Floyd 5.00
NG Nomar Garciaparra 10.00
TH Trevor Hoffman 5.00
TH Tim Hudson 6.00
AJ Andruw Jones 6.00
CJ Chipper Jones 8.00
DL Derek Lowe 6.00
PM Pedro J. Martinez 8.00
FM Fred McGriff 8.00
MM Mark Mulder 6.00
BM Brett Myers 5.00
JO John Olerud 6.00
RP Rafael Palmeiro 8.00
WP Wily Mo Pena 5.00
MP Mike Piazza 10.00
AP Albert Pujols 15.00
MR Manny Ramirez 8.00
JR Juan Rivera 5.00
AR Alex Rodriguez 12.00
IR Ivan Rodriguez 8.00
CS Curt Schilling 6.00
JS John Smoltz 6.00
SS Sammy Sosa 12.00
MS Mike Sweeney 5.00
FT Frank Thomas 10.00
JV Jose Vidro 5.00
BW Billy Wagner 6.00
VW Vernon Wells 5.00

Handle With Care

No pricing due to scarcity
Production 5 sets

HCR-JB	Johnny Bench
HCR-LB	Lance Berkman
HCR-WB	Wade Boggs
HCR-GB	George Brett
HCR-LBR	Lou Brock
HCR-CF	Carlton Fisk
HCR-NG	Nomar Garciaparra
HCR-JG	Jason Giambi
HCR-LG	Luis Gonzalez
HCR-TH	Torii Hunter
HCR-RJ	Reggie Jackson
HCR-AK	Al Kaline
HCR-HK	Harmon Killebrew
HCR-WM	Willie Mays
HCR-PM	Paul Molitor
HCR-AP	Albert Pujols
HCR-BR	Brooks Robinson
HCR-FR	Frank Robinson
HCR-AR	Alex Rodriguez
HCR-AS	Alfonso Soriano
HCR-WS	Willie Stargell
HCR-MT	Miguel Tejada
HCR-JT	Jim Thome
HCR-CY	Carl Yastrzemski
HCR-RY	Robin Yount

Presidential Pastime

		NM/M
Common President:		3.00
X-fractors:		3-5X
Inserted 1:400		
PP1	George Washington	10.00
PP2	John Adams	3.00
PP3	Thomas Jefferson	6.00
PP4	James Madison	4.00
PP5	James Monroe	4.00
PP6	John Quincy Adams	4.00
PP7	Andrew Jackson	3.00
PP8	Martin Van Buren	3.00
PP9	William H. Harrison	3.00
PP10	John Tyler	3.00
PP11	James K. Polk	3.00
PP12	Zachary Taylor	3.00
PP13	Millard Fillmore	3.00
PP14	Franklin Pierce	3.00
PP15	James Buchanan	3.00
PP16	Abraham Lincoln	8.00
PP17	Andrew Johnson	3.00
PP18	Ulysses S. Grant	5.00
PP19	Rutherford B. Hayes	3.00
PP20	James Garfield	3.00
PP21	Chester A. Arthur	3.00
PP22	Grover Cleveland	3.00
PP23	Benjamin Harrison	3.00
PP24	William McKinley	3.00
PP25	Theodore Roosevelt	5.00
PP26	William H. Taft	3.00
PP27	Woodrow Wilson	3.00
PP28	Warren Harding	3.00
PP29	Calvin Coolidge	3.00
PP30	Herbert Hoover	3.00
PP31	Franklin D. Roosevelt	5.00
PP32	Harry S. Truman	3.00
PP33	Dwight D. Eisenhower	3.00
PP34	John F. Kennedy	8.00
PP35	Lyndon B. Johnson	3.00
PP36	Richard Nixon	4.00
PP37	Gerald Ford	3.00
PP38	Jimmy Carter	3.00
PP39	Ronald Reagan	3.00
PP40	George H.W. Bush	3.00
PP41	Bill Clinton	4.00
PP42	George W. Bush	3.00

Presidential First Pitch Relics

		NM/M
Common President:		10.00
Inserted 1:15		
GHB	George H.W. Bush	20.00
GB	George W. Bush	25.00
BC	Bill Clinton	20.00
CC	Calvin Coolidge	20.00
DE	Dwight D. Eisenhower	20.00
GF	Gerald Ford	30.00
WH	Warren Harding	15.00
HH	Herbert Hoover	25.00
LJ	Lyndon B. Johnson	30.00
JK	John F. Kennedy	
RN	Richard Nixon	25.00
RR	Ronald Reagan	30.00
FR	Franklin D. Roosevelt	20.00
WT	William H. Taft	25.00
HT	Harry S. Truman	25.00
WW	Woodrow Wilson	10.00

Town Heroes

		NM/M
Common Player:		5.00
LB	Lance Berkman	5.00
EC	Eric Chavez	5.00
NG	Nomar Garciaparra	12.00
JG	Jason Giambi	8.00
RH	Rich Harden	5.00
TH	Tim Hudson	5.00
CJ	Chipper Jones	8.00
MM	Mark Mulder	5.00
HN	Hideo Nomo	8.00
RP	Rafael Palmeiro	8.00
MP	Mark Prior	12.00
AP	Albert Pujols	15.00
MR	Manny Ramirez	8.00
JR	Jose Reyes	5.00
AR	Alex Rodriguez	10.00
SS	Sammy Sosa	15.00
SST	Shannon Stewart	5.00
MT	Miguel Tejada	5.00
FT	Frank Thomas	8.00
KW	Kerry Wood	10.00
BZ	Barry Zito	6.00

2004 TOPPS CLUBHOUSE COLLECTION RELICS

		NM/M
Common Player:		4.00
2 Relics per pack		
Pack (2):		18.00
Box (10):		140.00
HA	Hank Aaron/113	50.00
BA	Bobby Abreu	6.00
RA	Roberto Alomar	6.00
EA	Edgardo Alfonzo/286	4.00
TA	Tony Armas Jr.	4.00
JB	Jeff Bagwell	8.00
RB	Rocco Baldelli	6.00
TB	Tony Batista	4.00
HB	Hank Bauer	10.00
JPB	Josh Beckett/195	6.00
JBE	Johnny Bench	10.00
AB	Armando Benitez	4.00
LB	Lance Berkman	6.00
YB	Yogi Berra	10.00
HBL	Hank Blalock	6.00
WB	Wade Boggs/250	6.00
BB	Bret Boone	4.00
GB	George Brett	12.00
KB	Kevin Brown	6.00
JBU	Jeromy Burnitz	4.00
PB	Pat Burrell	6.00
MB	Marlon Byrd	4.00
MC	Miguel Cabrera	8.00
GC	Gary Carter/221	8.00
JCA	Joe Carter/259	6.00
RLC	Roger Cedeno	4.00
OC	Orlando Cepeda	8.00
RCE	Ron Cey	6.00
EC	Eric Chavez	6.00
CFC	Chin-Feng Chen	8.00
JC	Jeff Cirillo	4.00
WC	Will Clark	8.00
RC	Roberto Clemente	75.00
DC	Dave Concepcion	8.00
CCR	Carl Crawford	4.00
CD	Carlos Delgado/200	6.00
AD	Adam Dunn	8.00
DE	Dennis Eckersley	10.00
CE	Carl Everett	4.00
SF	Steve Finley	4.00
CFL	Cliff Floyd	4.00
WF	Whitey Ford/296	15.00
BF	Brad Fullmer/200	4.00
JF	Jonathan Fulton	6.00
RF	Rafael Furcal	4.00
EG	Eric Gagne	8.00
NG	Nomar Garciaparra	12.00
JG	Jason Giambi	8.00
TGL	Troy Glaus	6.00
TG	Tom Glavine	8.00
AG	Adrian Gonzalez	4.00
LG	Luis Gonzalez	4.00
JGO	Juan Gonzalez	8.00
MG	Mark Grace	8.00
SG	Shawn Green	6.00
KG	Ken Griffey Jr./200	15.00
MDG	Marquis Grissom	4.00
VG	Vladimir Guerrero	8.00
CG	Cristian Guzman	4.00
TGW	Tony Gwynn	10.00
MH	Mickey Hall	4.00
EH	Estee Harris/206	4.00
THE	Todd Helton	8.00
RHE	Rickey Henderson	10.00
RH	Ramon Hernandez	4.00
OH	Orel Hershiser	8.00
JH	James Houser/182	8.00
OHU	Orlando Hudson	4.00
TH	Tim Hudson	6.00
THU	Torii Hunter	6.00
KI	Kazuhisa Ishii	4.00
RJ	Reggie Jackson	10.00
DJ	Derek Jeter	20.00
AJ	Andruw Jones	6.00
CJ	Chipper Jones	8.00
AK	Al Kaline	15.00
JK	Jason Kendall	
JKE	Jeff Kent/200	8.00
HK	Harmon Killebrew	
PK	Paul Konerko	6.00
BL	Barry Larkin/200	10.00
AL	Al Leiter	4.00
SL	Steve Lerud	4.00
EL	Esteban Loaiza	4.00
PL	Paul LoDuca	4.00
JL	Javy Lopez	6.00
DL	Derek Lowe/200	4.00
CL	Chris Lubanski/209	8.00
GM	Greg Maddux	15.00
EMA	Edgar Martinez/200	6.00
PM	Pedro Martinez/200	10.00
TM	Tino Martinez	6.00
EM	Eddie Mathews/174	25.00
WM	Willie Mays	60.00
FM	Fred McGriff	6.00
KM	Kevin Millwood	4.00
MM	Mark Mulder	6.00
EMU	Eddie Murray	12.00
BM	Brett Myers	4.00
HN	Hideo Nomo/207	8.00
JO	John Olerud	6.00
MO	Magglio Ordonez	4.00
RP	Rafael Palmeiro/200	10.00
CP	Chan Ho Park	4.00
DP	Dave Parker/292	10.00
CPA	Corey Patterson/267	8.00
WP	Wily Mo Pena	8.00
TPE	Troy Percival	4.00
TP	Tony Perez	10.00
MP	Mike Piazza	10.00
JP	Jorge Posada/264	8.00
AP	Albert Pujols	15.00
ARA	Aramis Ramirez	8.00
MR	Manny Ramirez/207	8.00
JRE	Jose Reyes	6.00
CR	Cal Ripken Jr.	20.00
MRI	Mariano Rivera/239	8.00
FR	Frank Robinson	8.00
JR	Jackie Robinson/262	50.00
AR	Alex Rodriguez	10.00
IR	Ivan Rodriguez	8.00
SR	Scott Rolen	10.00
JRO	Jimmy Rollins	6.00
NR	Nolan Ryan	20.00
CS	C.C. Sabathia	4.00
TS	Tim Salmon	6.00
RSA	Ryne Sandberg	15.00
JS	Jay Sborz	6.00
CSC	Curt Schilling	8.00
MS	Mike Schmidt	15.00
RS	Richie Sexson/200	6.00
GS	Gary Sheffield	6.00
RSI	Ruben Sierra	10.00
OS	Ozzie Smith	15.00
JSM	John Smoltz	6.00
DS	Duke Snider	15.00
AS	Alfonso Soriano	6.00
SS	Sammy Sosa	12.00
WS	Willie Stargell/200	10.00
CST	Casey Stengel/217	10.00
MSW	Mike Sweeney	4.00
MTE	Miguel Tejada	6.00
MT	Mark Teixeira	6.00
FT	Frank Thomas	8.00
JT	Jim Thome	8.00
FV	Fernando Valenzuela	8.00
JVI	Jose Vidro	4.00
BWA	Billy Wagner	4.00
LW	Larry Walker	4.00
VW	Vernon Wells/200	4.00
BW	Bernie Williams	6.00
PW	Preston Wilson	4.00
JV	Javier Vazquez	6.00
CY	Carl Yastrzemski	15.00
RY	Robin Yount	12.00
BZ	Barry Zito/230	6.00

Copper

Copper: .75-1.5X
Production 99 sets

Black

Black: 2-3X
Production 25 sets

Red

Red: No Pricing
Production one set

All-Star Appeal Ball

No Pricing
Production 10 sets

All-Star Appeal Ball Auto.

		NM/M
Production 30 sets		
GA	Garret Anderson	30.00
HB	Hank Blalock	35.00
JP	Jorge Posada	50.00
GS	Gary Sheffield	

All-Star Appeal Base

		NM/M
Common Player:		5.00
Production 65 sets		
On Deck Circle:		1X
Production 90 sets		
GA	Garret Anderson	8.00
HB	Hank Blalock	8.00
BB	Bret Boone	5.00
CD	Carlos Delgado	6.00
JE	Jim Edmonds	8.00
RF	Rafael Furcal	6.00
NG	Nomar Garciaparra	15.00
JG	Jason Giambi	8.00
TG	Troy Glaus	6.00
LG	Luis Gonzalez	6.00
TH	Todd Helton	8.00
AJ	Andruw Jones	6.00
JL	Javy Lopez	8.00
ML	Mike Lowell	6.00
EM	Edgar Martinez	8.00
MO	Magglio Ordonez	6.00
JP	Jorge Posada	8.00

AP Albert Pujols 25.00
ER Edgar Renteria 8.00
AR Alex Rodriguez 15.00
SR Scott Rolen 10.00
RS Richie Sexson 6.00
GS Gary Sheffield 8.00
AS Alfonso Soriano 10.00
VW Vernon Wells 6.00
PW Preston Wilson 5.00

All-Star Appeal Base Auto.

NM/M

Production 50 sets
GA Garret Anderson 25.00
HB Hank Blalock
JP Jorge Posada 35.00
GS Gary Sheffield 25.00

All-Star Appeal On Deck Circle

NM/M

Common Player: 5.00
Production 90 sets
GA Garret Anderson 8.00
HB Hank Blalock 8.00
AB Aaron Boone 5.00
BB Bret Boone 5.00
LC Luis Castillo 5.00
CD Carlos Delgado 6.00
JE Jim Edmonds 8.00
CE Carl Everett 5.00
RF Rafael Furcal 6.00
NG Nomar Garciaparra 15.00
JG Jason Giambi 8.00
TG Troy Glaus 6.00
LG Luis Gonzalez 6.00
TH Todd Helton 8.00
AJ Andruw Jones 6.00
PL Paul LoDuca 5.00
JL Javy Lopez 8.00
ML Mike Lowell 6.00
EM Edgar Martinez 8.00
MM Melvin Mora 5.00
MO Magglio Ordonez 6.00
JP Jorge Posada 8.00
AP Albert Pujols 20.00
ER Edgar Renteria 8.00
AR Alex Rodriguez 15.00
SR Scott Rolen 10.00
RS Richie Sexson 6.00
GS Gary Sheffield 8.00
AS Alfonso Soriano 10.00
JV Jose Vidro 5.00
VW Vernon Wells 6.00
RW Rondell White 5.00
PW Preston Wilson 5.00

All-Star Appeal On Deck Auto

NM/M

Quantity produced listed
GA Garret Anderson/320 15.00
HB Hank Blalock/920 15.00
JP Jorge Posada/420 30.00
GS Gary Sheffield/170 25.00

Legends Relics

NM/M

Common Player:
BR1 Babe Ruth/60 175.00
BR2 Babe Ruth/171 150.00
BR3 Babe Ruth/45 200.00
EB1 Ernie Banks/143 15.00
EB3 Ernie Banks/47 20.00
EB6 Ernie Banks/71 15.00
LG1 Lou Gehrig/49 125.00
LG2 Lou Gehrig/184 100.00
LG3 Lou Gehrig/52 125.00
TC3 Ty Cobb/47 120.00
TC4 Ty Cobb/24
WM1 Willie Mays/52 70.00
WM2 Willie Mays/141 60.00

Play Relics

NM/M

Production 75 sets
CLE Omar Vizquel, Brandon Phillips, Travis Hafner 10.00
NYM Ty Wigginton, Jose Reyes, Mike Piazza 25.00
NYY Derek Jeter, Alex Rodriguez, Jason Giambi 50.00
PHI Jimmy Rollins, David Bell, Jim Thome 20.00
SDP Khalil Greene, Sean Burroughs, Phil Nevin 10.00

Ropes Relics

NM/M

Common Player: 5.00
Production 50 sets
BA Bobby Abreu 8.00
JB Jeff Bagwell 10.00
RB Rocco Baldelli 8.00
JBE Johnny Bench 20.00
LB Lance Berkman 5.00
CB Craig Biggio 6.00
HB Hank Blalock 10.00
WB Wade Boggs 8.00
GC Gary Carter 8.00
EC Eric Chavez 8.00
ADA Andre Dawson 8.00
AD Adam Dunn 10.00
CE Carl Everett 5.00
RF Rafael Furcal 5.00
JG Jason Giambi 8.00
LG Luis Gonzalez 5.00
SG Shawn Green 5.00
VG Vladimir Guerrero 15.00
TH Todd Helton 10.00
AH Aubrey Huff 5.00
CJ Chipper Jones 15.00
PK Paul Konerko 5.00
EM Edgar Martinez 8.00
DM Don Mattingly 40.00
DMU Dale Murphy 12.00
MO Magglio Ordonez 5.00
RP Rafael Palmeiro 10.00
MP Mike Piazza 15.00
KP Kirby Puckett 15.00
AP Albert Pujols 25.00
MR Manny Ramirez 10.00
JR Jose Reyes 8.00
BR Brooks Robinson 15.00
AR Alex Rodriguez 15.00
IR Ivan Rodriguez 10.00
RS Ryne Sandberg 40.00
MS Mike Schmidt 40.00
GS Gary Sheffield 6.00
OS Ozzie Smith 25.00
DS Duke Snider 15.00
AS Alfonso Soriano 10.00
SS Sammy Sosa 15.00
MT Miguel Tejada 8.00
JT Jim Thome 10.00
BW Bernie Williams 8.00
PW Preston Wilson 5.00
CY Carl Yastrzemski 20.00

Heart of the Line-Up Relics

NM/M

Production 100 unless noted
ARI Steve Finley, Richie Sexson, Luis Gonzalez 10.00
CHC Sammy Sosa, Moises Alou, Aramis Ramirez 35.00
CHW Magglio Ordonez, Frank Thomas, Carlos Lee/78 20.00
CIN Ken Griffey Jr., Austin Kearns, Adam Dunn 25.00
COL Todd Helton, Larry Walker, Preston Wilson 15.00
NYY Alex Rodriguez, Jason Giambi, Gary Sheffield 35.00
PHI Jim Thome, Pat Burrell, Bobby Abreu 20.00
SEA Edgar Martinez, Bret Boone, John Olerud 10.00
STL Albert Pujols, Jim Edmonds, Scott Rolen 40.00
TEX Alfonso Soriano, Mark Teixeira, Hank Blalock 20.00
TOR Vernon Wells, Carlos Delgado, Eric Hinske 10.00

Pieces Relics

NM/M

Quantity produced listed
CD Carlos Delgado/25 8.00
THU Torii Hunter/48 8.00
AJ Andruw Jones/25 10.00
PM Pedro Martinez/45 10.00
WM Willie Mays/24 85.00
BP Brad Penny/31 5.00
MP Mike Piazza/31 40.00
NR Nolan Ryan/34 50.00
CS Curt Schilling/38 8.00
BZ Barry Zito/75 6.00

Place Relics

No Pricing
Production 25 or less

2004 TOPPS CRACKER JACK

NM/M

Complete Set with SPs (250): 160.00
Common Player: .25
Common SP: 2.00
SP's inserted 1:3
Pack (8): 3.00
Box (24): 60.00
1 Jose Reyes/SP 2.00
2 Edgar Renteria .25
3 Albert Pujols 2.00
3 Albert Pujols/SP/swinging 6.00
4 Garret Anderson .50
5 Bobby Abreu .40
6 Andruw Jones .75
7 Jeff Kent .40
8 Magglio Ordonez .50
9 Kris Benson .25
10 Luis Gonzalez .40
11 Corey Patterson .50
12 Connie Mack .25
13 Vernon Wells/SP 2.00
14 Jim Edmonds .50
15 Bret Boone .50
16 Travis Lee .25
17 Alex Rodriguez/SP 6.00
No # Alex Rodriguez 2.00
18 Erubiel Durazo .25
19 Brett Myers .25
20 Scott Rolen/SP 3.00
21 Paul LoDuca .25
22 Geoff Jenkins .50
23 Charles Comiskey .25
24 Cliff Floyd .25
25 Jim Thome .75
25 Jim Thome/SP/fielding 3.00
26 Russ Ortiz .25
27 Bill Mueller .25
28 Kenny Lofton .40
29 Jay Gibbons .40
30 Ken Griffey Jr. 1.50
31 Jeff Bagwell .75
32 Jose Lima .25
33 Brad Radke .25
34 Ramon Hernandez .25
35 Brian Giles/SP 2.00
36 Jeremy Bonderman .25
37 Jerome Williams .25
38 Rafael Palmeiro .50
39 Scott Podsednik .75
40 Rafael Furcal .40
41 Roy Oswalt .40
42 Orlando Hudson .25
43 Todd Helton .75
44 Kerry Wood 1.00
45 Tom Glavine .40
46 David Eckstein .25
47 Trot Nixon .25
48 Preston Wilson .25
50 Eric Gagne/SP 3.00
51 Ichiro Suzuki/SP 5.00
52 Juan Gonzalez .75
53 Torii Hunter .50
54 Bartolo Colon .40
55 Dick Hoblitzell .25
56 Al Leiter .25
57 Johnny Damon .40
58 Larry Walker .40
59 Brian Jordan .25
60 Richie Sexson/SP 3.00
61 Orlando Cabrera .25
62 Jason Phillips .25
63 Phil Nevin .25
64 John Olerud .40
65 Miguel Tejada .50
66 Nap Lajoie .50
67 C.C. Sabathia .25
68 Ty Wigginton .25
69 Troy Glaus .50
70 Mike Piazza 1.50
71 Craig Biggio .40
72 Cristian Guzman .25
73 Dmitri Young .25
74 Roger Clemens 2.00
75 Runelvys Hernandez .25
76 Nomar Garciaparra 2.00
77 Mark Mulder .40
78 Derek Lowe .40
79 Paul Konerko .25
80 Sammy Sosa/SP 5.00
81 Vladimir Guerrero 1.00
82 Xavier Nady .25
83 Joel Pineiro .25
84 Chipper Jones 1.50
85 Manny Ramirez .75
86 Burt Shotton .25
87 Raul Ibanez/SP 2.00
88 Eric Chavez .50
89 Frank Catalanotto .25
90 Dontrelle Willis .50
91 Roy Halladay .50
92 Jermaine Dye .25
93 Jason Kendall .25
94 Jacque Jones .25
95 Gary Sheffield .50
95 Gary Sheffield/SP/Yankees 3.00
96 Mike Lieberthal .25
97 Adam Dunn .50
98 Carl Crawford .25
99 Reggie Sanders .25
100 Mark Prior/SP 6.00
101 Luis Matos .25
102 Barry Zito .50
103 Randy Johnson 1.00
104 Kevin Brown .50
105 Pat Burrell .50
106 Steve Finley .25
107 Moises Alou .50
108 David Ortiz/SP 3.00
109 Austin Kearns/SP 2.00
110 Carlos Beltran .50
111 Shawn Green .40
112 Javier Vazquez .50
113 Hideo Nomo .50
114 Kazuhisa Ishii .25
115 Corey Koskie .25
116 Kevin Millwood .50
117 Randy Wolf .40
118 Darin Erstad .25
119 Fernando Vina .25
120 Pedro J. Martinez 1.00
121 Melvin Mora .25
122 Carl Everett .25
123 Matt Morris .40
124 Greg Maddux 1.50
125 Jason Schmidt .25
126 Mark Teixeira/SP 3.00
127 Randy Winn .25
128 Rich Aurilia .25
129 Vicente Padilla .25
130 Tim Hudson .50
131 Marlon Byrd .25
132 Jae Weong Seo .25
133 Branch Rickey .25
134 A.J. Pierzynski .25
135 Ryan Klesko .40
136 Eric Hinske .25
137 Mike Cameron .25
138 Roberto Alomar .50

139 Jarrod Washburn .25
140 Curt Schilling .75
140 Curt Schilling/SP/Red Sox 3.00
141 Omar Vizquel .25
142 Mike Sweeney .25
143 Wade Miller .25
144 Jose Vidro .25
145 Rich Harden/SP 2.00
146 Eric Munson .25
147 Lance Berkman .50
148 Mark Buehrle .25
149 Carlos Delgado .75
150 Sean Burroughs .25
151 Kevin Millar .25
152 Frank Thomas .75
153 Adrian Beltre .25
154 Shannon Stewart .25
155 Johan Santana .25
156 Edgardo Alfonzo .25
157 Jose Cruz Jr. .25
158 Sidney Ponson .25
159 Edgar Martinez .50
160 Jamie Moyer .25
161 Tony Batista .25
162 Wes Helms .25
163 Brandon Webb/SP 2.00
164 Gil Meche .25
165 Marcus Giles/SP 2.00
166 Angel Berroa/SP 2.00
167 Rocco Baldelli/SP 3.00
168 Michael Young .25
169 Esteban Loaiza .25
170 Casey Blake .25
171 Jody Gerut .25
172 Bo Hart/SP 2.00
173 Kelvim Escobar .25
174 Aaron Guiel .25
175 Javy Lopez/SP 3.00
176 Aubrey Huff .25
177 Hank Blalock .50
178 Edwin Jackson .25
178 Edwin Jackson/SP/#104 2.00
179 Delmon Young/SP 3.00
180 Bobby Jenks .25
181 Felix Pie .25
181 Felix Pie/SP/#80 2.00
182 Jeremy Reed/SP 2.00
183 Aaron Hill .25
184 Casey Kotchman/SP 2.00
185 Grady Sizemore .25
186 Joe Mauer/SP 3.00
187 Ryan Harvey .25
188 Neal Cotts .25
189 Victor Martinez .25
190 Rene Reyes .25
191 Eric Duncan .25
192 B.J. Upton/SP 3.00
193 Khalil Greene/SP 2.00
194 Bobby Crosby .25
195 Rickie Weeks/SP 3.00
196 Zack Greinke/SP 2.00
197 Laynce Nix .25
198 *Vito Chiaravalloti/SP* 2.00
199 *Estee Harris* .25
200 *Jon Knott/SP* 3.00
201 *Dioner Navarro* .75
201 Dioner Navarro/SP/#236 2.00
202 *Craig Ansman* .50
203 *Travis Blackley* 1.00
204 *Yadier Molina* .50
205 *Rodney Choy Foo* .50
206 Kyle Sleeth/SP 5.00
207 Jeff Allison 1.00
208 *Josh Labandeira* .50
209 Lastings Milledge/SP 5.00
210 *Rudy Guillen/SP* 3.00
211 *Blake Hawksworth/SP* 3.00
212 David Aardsma .50
213 *Shawn Hill* .50
214 *Erick Aybar/SP* 3.00
215 *Ervin Santana* 1.00
216 Tim Stauffer/SP 3.00
217 *Merkin Valdez* 1.00
218 Jack McKeon .25
219 Derrek Lee .50
220 Josh Beckett/SP 3.00
221 Luis Castillo .25
222 Mike Lowell .50
223 Juan Pierre .40
224 Ivan Rodriguez .75
224 Ivan Rodriguez/SP/Tigers 3.00
225 A.J. Burnett .25
226 Miguel Cabrera/SP 4.00
227 Jeffrey Loria .25
228 Joe Torre .50
229 Jason Giambi .75
229 Jason Giambi/SP/fielding 3.00
230 Aaron Boone .25
231 Jose Contreras .25
232 Derek Jeter/SP 6.00
233 Nick Johnson .25
234 Mike Mussina .75
235 Andy Pettitte .50
236 Jorge Posada/SP 3.00
237 Alfonso Soriano .75
238 Bernie Williams .50

Mini

Mini: 1-2X
Mini SP: 1X
Inserted 1:pack
Mini SPs inserted 1:20
SPs are same as in base set

Mini Blue

Mini Blue: 3-6X
Mini Blue SP: 1-2X
Inserted 1:10
Mini Blue SPs inserted 1:60
SPs are same as in base set

Mini White

No Pricing
Production one set

Mini Autograph

NM/M
Common Autograph:
Inserted 1:258
95 Gary Sheffield/50 40.00
112 Javier Vazquez 15.00
163 Brandon Webb 15.00
165 Marcus Giles 12.00
221 Luis Castillo 8.00
226 Miguel Cabrera 35.00

Secret Surprise Signatures

NM/M
Common Autograph: 8.00
CF Cliff Floyd 15.00
BG Brian Giles 15.00
AH Aubrey Huff 15.00
ML Mike Lamb 8.00
DM Dustin McGowan 20.00
FP Felix Pie 20.00
SP Scott Podsednik 20.00
SR Scott Rolen 30.00
MV Merkin Valdez 15.00
JW Jerome Williams 20.00
DW Dontrelle Willis 30.00

Sticker

Stickers: 1X
SP Stickers: .5X
Inserted 1:surprise pack
SP's inserted 1:10 surprise packs

Take Me Out to/Ballgame Relics

NM/M
Common Player: 5.00
BA Bobby Abreu 5.00
MA Moises Alou 6.00
GA Garret Anderson 8.00
JB Jeff Bagwell 8.00
RB Rocco Baldelli 8.00
LB Lance Berkman 5.00
AB Angel Berroa 5.00
CB Craig Biggio 5.00
HB Hank Blalock 6.00
BB1 Bret Boone/bat 5.00
BB2 Bret Boone/jsy 5.00
PB Pat Burrell 6.00
MC Miguel Cabrera 8.00
EC Eric Chavez 5.00
AD Adam Dunn 8.00
JE Jim Edmonds 5.00
RF Rafael Furcal 6.00
NG Nomar Garciaparra/bat 10.00
NG Nomar Garciaparra/jsy 10.00
JG Jason Giambi 8.00
MG Marcus Giles 5.00
TG Troy Glaus 8.00
LG Luis Gonzalez 5.00
SG Shawn Green/bat 6.00
SG Shawn Green/jsy 6.00
TH Todd Helton 8.00
TKH Torii Hunter 6.00
CJ Chipper Jones 8.00
PL Paul LoDuca 5.00
JL Javy Lopez/bat 6.00
JL Javy Lopez/jsy 6.00
MP Mike Piazza 10.00
AP Albert Pujols/bat 15.00
AP Albert Pujols/jsy 15.00
MR Manny Ramirez 8.00
JR Jose Reyes 6.00
AR Alex Rodriguez/bat/yankees 15.00
AR Alex Rodriguez/jsy 10.00
IR Ivan Rodriguez 8.00
JRO Jimmy Rollins 5.00
AS Alfonso Soriano/bat 8.00
AS Alfonso Soriano/jsy 8.00
SS Sammy Sosa/bat 10.00
SS Sammy Sosa/jsy 10.00
MS Mike Sweeney 5.00
MT Mark Teixeira 6.00
MT Miguel Tejada 6.00
JT Jim Thome 8.00
LW Larry Walker 5.00
VW Vernon Wells 5.00
KW Kerry Wood 8.00
MY Michael Young 5.00

1,2,3 Strikes You're Out Relics

NM/M
Common Player: 4.00
JB Josh Beckett 8.00
KB Kevin Brown 6.00
EG Eric Gagne 8.00
RH Rich Harden 4.00
RJ Randy Johnson 8.00
DL Derek Lowe 6.00
PM Pedro J. Martinez 8.00
KM Kevin Millwood 6.00
MAM Mark Mulder 6.00
MM Mike Mussina 15.00
BM Brett Myers 4.00
HN Hideo Nomo 8.00
CCS C.C. Sabathia 4.00
CS Curt Schilling 15.00
JS John Smoltz 6.00
BW Billy Wagner 4.00
KW Kerry Wood 10.00
BZ Barry Zito 6.00

2004 TOPPS HERITAGE

NM/M
Complete Set (475): 400.00
Common Player: .40
Common SP (398-475): 4.00
Variations & SP's inserted 1:2
Pack (8): 5.00
Box (24): 100.00
1 Jim Thome 1.50
1 Jim Thome/SP/hitting 8.00
2 Nomar Garciaparra/SP 15.00
3 Aramis Ramirez .50
4 Rafael Palmeiro/SP 6.00
5 Danny Graves .40
6 Casey Blake .40
7 Juan Uribe .40
8 Dmitri Young .40
8 Dmitri Young/SP/old logo 4.00
9 Billy Wagner .40
10 Jason Giambi .75
10 Jason Giambi/SP/batting stance 6.00
11 Carlos Beltran 1.00
12 Chad Hermansen .40
13 B.J. Upton .75
14 Dustan Mohr .40
15 Endy Chavez .40
16 Cliff Floyd .40
17 Bernie Williams .75
18 Eric Chavez .50
19 Chase Utley .40
20 Randy Johnson 1.50
21 Vernon Wells .50
22 Juan Gonzalez .75
23 Joe Kennedy .40
24 Bengie Molina .40
25 Carlos Lee .40
26 Horacio Ramirez .40
27 *Anthony Acevedo* 1.00
28 Sammy Sosa/SP 10.00
29 Jon Garland .40
30 Adam Dunn 1.00
30 Adam Dunn/SP/hitting 6.00
31 Aaron Rowand .40
32 Jody Gerut .40
33 Chin-Hui Tsao .40
34 Alex Sanchez .40
35 A.J. Burnett .40
36 Brad Ausmus .40
37 *Blake Hawksworth* 1.50
38 Francisco Rodriguez .40
39 Alex Cintron .40
40 Chipper Jones 1.50
40 Chipper Jones/SP/fielding 6.00
41 Deivi Cruz .40
42 Bill Mueller .40
43 Joe Borowski .40
44 Jimmy Haynes .40
45 Mark Loretta .40
46 Jerome Williams .40
47 Gary Sheffield/SP 6.00
48 Richard Hidalgo .40
49 Jason Kendall .40
49 Jason Kendall/SP/old logo 4.00
50 Ichiro Suzuki/SP 8.00
51 Jim Edmonds .75
52 Frank Catalanotto .40
53 Jose Contreras .40
54 Mo Vaughn .40
55 Brendan Donnelly .40
56 Luis Gonzalez .50
57 Robert Fick .40
58 Laynce Nix .40
59 Johnny Damon .75
60 Magglio Ordonez .50
60 Magglio Ordonez/SP/hitting 6.00
61 Matt Clement .40
62 Ryan Ludwick .40
63 Luis Castillo .40
64 David Crouthers .40
65 Dave Berg .40
66 *Kyle Davies* 1.00
67 Tim Salmon .50
68 Marcus Giles .40
69 Marty Cordova .40
70 Todd Helton 1.00
70 Todd Helton/SP/purple jersey 6.00
71 Jeff Kent .50
72 Michael Tucker .40
73 Cesar Izturis .40
74 Paul Quantrill .40
75 Conor Jackson .40
76 Placido Polanco .40
77 Adam Eaton .40
78 Ramon Hernandez .40
79 Edgardo Alfonzo .40
80 *Dioner Navarro* 1.00
81 Woody Williams .40
82 Rey Ordonez .40
83 Randy Winn .40
84 *Casey Myers* 1.00
85 *Rodney Choy Foo* 2.00
85 Rodney Choy Foo/SP/old logo 6.00
86 Ray Durham .40
87 Sean Burroughs .40
88 *Tim Frend* 3.00
89 Shigetoshi Hasegawa .40
90 Jeff Allison .40
91 Orlando Hudson .40
92 *Matt Creighton/SP* 6.00

93 Tim Worrell .40
94 Kris Benson .40
95 Mike Lieberthal .40
96 Boomer Wells .40
97 Jason Phillips .40
98 Bobby Cox .40
99 Johan Santana .75
100 Alex Rodriguez 3.00
100 Alex Rodriguez/ SP/throwing 10.00
101 John Vander Wal .40
102 Orlando Cabrera .50
103 Hideo Nomo .75
104 Todd Walker .40
105 Jason Johnson .40
106 Matt Mantei .40
107 Jarrod Washburn .40
108 Preston Wilson .40
109 Carl Pavano .40
110 Geoff Blum .40
111 Eric Gagne .50
112 Geoff Jenkins .50
113 Joe Torre .50
114 *Jon Knott* 1.50
115 Hank Blalock .75
116 John Olerud .50
117 Pat Burrell .75
117 Pat Burrell/old logo 5.00
118 Aaron Boone .40
119 Zach Day .40
120 Frank Thomas 1.00
120 Frank Thomas/old logo 6.00
121 Kyle Farnsworth .40
122 Derek Lowe .50
123 *Zach Miner/SP* 6.00
124 Matt Moses/SP 8.00
125 *Jesse Roman* 1.50
126 Josh Phelps .40
127 *Nic Ungs* 1.50
128 Dan Haren .40
129 Kirk Rueter .40
130 Jack McKeon .40
131 Keith Foulke .40
132 Garrett Stephenson .40
133 Wes Helms .40
134 Raul Ibanez .50
135 Morgan Ensberg .40
136 Jay Payton .40
137 Billy Koch .40
138 Mark Grudzielanek .40
139 Rodrigo Lopez .40
140 Corey Patterson .40
141 Troy Percival .40
142 Shea Hillenbrand .40
143 Brad Fullmer .40
144 Ricky Nolasco .40
145 Mark Teixeira .75
146 *Tydus Meadows* 1.50
147 Toby Hall .40
148 Orlando Palmeiro .40
149 *Khalid Ballouli* 1.50
150 Grady Little .40
151 David Eckstein .40
152 *Kenny Perez* 1.50
153 Ben Grieve .40
154 Ismael Valdes .40
155 Bret Boone .50
156 Jesse Foppert .40
157 Vicente Padilla .40
158 Bobby Abreu .50
159 Scott Hatteberg .40
160 Carlos Quentin .40
161 *Anthony Lerew* 1.50
162 Lance Carter .40
163 Robb Nen .40
164 *Zachary Duke/SP* 20.00
165 Xavier Nady .40
166 Kip Wells .40
167 Kevin Millwood .75
168 Jon Lieber .40
169 Jose Reyes .40
170 Eric Byrnes .40
171 Paul Konerko .40
172 Chris Lubanski .40
173 Jae Weong Seo .40
174 Corey Koskie .40
175 Tim Stauffer .40
176 John Lackey .40
177 Danny Bautista .40
178 Shane Reynolds .40
179 Jorge Julio .40
180 Manny Ramirez 1.00
180 Manny Ramirez/ SP/old logo 6.00
181 Alex Gonzalez .40
182 Moises Alou .75
182 Moises Alou/ SP/old logo 6.00
183 Mark Buehrle .40
184 Carlos Guillen .40
185 Nate Cornejo .40
186 Billy Traber .40
187 Jason Jennings .40
188 Eric Munson .40
189 Braden Looper .40
190 Juan Encarnacion .40
191 Dusty Baker .40
192 Travis Lee .40
193 Miguel Cairo .40
194 Rich Aurilia/SP 5.00
195 Flash Gordon .40
196 Freddy Garcia .40
197 Brian Lawrence .40
198 Jorge Posada/SP 8.00
199 Javier Vazquez .40
200 Albert Pujols 3.00
200 Albert Pujols/ SP/old logo 12.00
201 Victor Zambrano .40
202 Eli Marrero .40
203 Joel Pineiro .40
204 Rondell White .50
205 *Craig Ansman* 2.00
206 Michael Young .40
207 Carlos Baerga .40
208 Andruw Jones 1.00
209 Jerry Hairston Jr. .40
210 Shawn Green/SP 6.00
211 Ron Gardenhire .40
212 Darin Erstad .50
213 Brandon Webb .50
213 Brandon Webb/ SP/glove in air 6.00
214 Greg Maddux 2.00
215 Reed Johnson .40
216 John Thomson .40
217 Tino Martinez .40
218 Mike Cameron .40
219 Edgar Martinez .50
220 Eric Young .40
221 Reggie Sanders .40
222 Randy Wolf .40
223 Erubiel Durazo .40
224 Mike Mussina .75
225 Tom Glavine .75
226 Troy Glaus .75
227 Oscar Villarreal .40
228 David Segui .40
229 Jeff Suppan .40
230 Kenny Lofton .50
231 Esteban Loaiza .40
232 Felipe Lopez .40
233 Matt Lawton .40
234 Mark Bellhorn .40
235 Wilfredo Ledezma .40
236 Todd Hollandsworth .40
237 Octavio Dotel .40
238 Darren Dreifort .40
239 Paul LoDuca .40
240 Richie Sexson .75
241 Doug Mientkiewicz .40
242 Luis Rivas .40
243 Claudio Vargas .40
244 Mark Ellis .40
245 Brett Myers .40
246 Jake Peavy .40
247 Marquis Grissom .40
248 Armando Benitez .40
249 Ryan Franklin .40
250 Alfonso Soriano 1.50
250 Alfonso Soriano/ SP/fielding 6.00
251 Tim Hudson .75
252 Shannon Stewart .40
253 A.J. Pierzynski .40
254 Runelvys Hernandez .40
255 Roy Oswalt .50
256 Shawn Chacon .40
257 Tony Graffanino .40
258 Tim Wakefield .40
259 Damian Miller .40
260 Joe Crede .40
261 Jason LaRue .40
262 Jose Jimenez .40
263 Juan Pierre .40
264 Wade Miller .40
265 Odalis Perez .40
266 Eddie Guardado .40
267 Rocky Biddle .40
268 Jeff Nelson .40
269 Terrence Long .40
270 Ramon Ortiz .40
271 Raul Mondesi .50
272 Ugueth Urbina .40
273 Jeromy Burnitz .40
274 Brad Radke .40
275 Jose Vidro .40
276 Bobby Jenks .40
277 Ty Wigginton .40
278 Jose Guillen .40
279 Delmon Young .75
280 Brian Giles .50
281 Jason Schmidt .50
282 Nicholas Markakis .40
283 Felipe Alou .40
284 Carl Crawford .40
285 Neifi Perez .40
286 Miguel Tejada .75
287 Victor Martinez .40
288 Adam Kennedy .40
289 Kerry Ligtenberg .40
290 Scott Williamson .40
291 Tony Womack .40
292 Travis Hafner .40
293 Bobby Crosby .40
294 Chad Billingsley .40
295 Russ Ortiz .40
296 John Burkett .40
297 Carlos Zambrano .40
298 Randall Simon .40
299 Juan Castro .40
300 Mike Lowell .40
301 Fred McGriff .50
302 Glendon Rusch .40
303 *Sung Ki Jung* .40
304 Rocco Baldelli .75
305 Fernando Vina .40
306 Gil Meche .40
307 Jose Cruz Jr. .40
308 Bernie Castro .40
309 Scott Spiezio .40
310 Paul Byrd .40
311 Jay Gibbons .50
311 Jay Gibbons/SP/ old logo 6.00
312 Trot Nixon .40
313 *Chris O'Riordan* 1.50
314 Julio Lugo .40
315 Ben Davis .40
316 Mike Williams .40
317 Trevor Hoffman .40
318 Andy Pettitte .75
319 Orlando Hernandez .40
320 Juan Rivera .40
321 Elizardo Ramirez .40
322 Junior Spivey .40
323 Tony Batista .40
324 Mike Remlinger .40
325 Alex Gonzalez .40
326 Aaron Hill .40
327 Steve Finley .40
328 Vinny Castilla .40
329 Eric Duncan .40
330 Mike Gosling .40
331 Eric Hinske .40
332 Scott Rolen 1.50
333 Benito Santiago .40
334 Jimmy Gobble .40
335 Bobby Higginson .40
336 Kelvim Escobar .40
337 Mike DeJean .40
338 Sidney Ponson .40
339 *Todd Self* 1.50
340 Jeff Cirillo .40
341 Jimmy Rollins .40
342 Barry Zito .75
342 Barry Zito/ SP/green jersey 6.00
343 Felix Pie .40
344 Matt Morris .40
345 Kazuhiro Sasaki .40
346 Jack Wilson .40
347 Nick Johnson .40
348 Wil Cordero .40
349 Ryan Madson .40
350 Torii Hunter .75
351 Andy Ashby .40
352 Aubrey Huff .40
353 Brad Lidge .40
354 Derrek Lee .40
355 *Yadier Molina* 1.50
356 Paul Wilson .40
357 Omar Vizquel .50
358 Rene Reyes .40
359 Marlon Anderson .40
360 Bobby Kielty .40
361 Ryan Wagner .40
361 Ryan Wagner/ SP/old logo 5.00
362 Justin Morneau .40
363 Shane Spencer .40
364 David Bell .40
365 Matt Stairs .40
366 Joe Borchard .40
367 Mark Redman .40
368 Dave Roberts .40
369 Desi Relaford .40
370 Rich Harden .40
371 Fernando Tatis .40
372 Eric Karros .40
373 Eric Milton .40
374 Mike Sweeney .40
375 Brian Daubach .40
376 Brian Snyder .40
377 Chris Reitsma .40
378 Kyle Lohse .40
379 Livan Hernandez .40
380 Robin Ventura .40
381 Jacque Jones .40
382 Danny Kolb .40
383 Casey Kotchman .40
384 Cristian Guzman .40
385 Josh Beckett 1.00
386 Khalil Greene .40
387 Greg Myers .40
388 Francisco Cordero .40
389 Donald Levinski .40
390 Roy Halladay .75
391 J.D. Drew .40
392 Jamie Moyer .40
393 Ken Macha .40
394 Jeff DaVanon .40
395 Matt Kata .40
396 Jack Cust .40
397 Mike Timlin .40
398 Zack Greinke 4.00
399 Byung-Hyun Kim 4.00
400 Kazuhisa Ishii 4.00
401 *Brayan Pena* 6.00
402 Garret Anderson 6.00
403 Kyle Sleeth 6.00
404 Javy Lopez 5.00
405 Damian Moss 4.00
406 David Ortiz 4.00
407 Pedro J. Martinez 8.00
408 Hee Seop Choi 4.00
409 Carl Everett 4.00
410 Dontrelle Willis 6.00
411 Ryan Harvey 5.00
412 Russell Branyan 4.00
413 Milton Bradley 4.00
414 *Marcus McBeth* 6.00
415 Carlos Pena 4.00
416 Ivan Rodriguez 6.00
417 Craig Biggio 5.00
418 Angel Berroa 4.00
419 Brian Jordan 4.00
420 Scott Podsednik 6.00
421 *Omar Falcon* 6.00
422 Joe Mays 4.00
423 Brad Wilkerson 4.00
424 Al Leiter 4.00
425 Derek Jeter 15.00
426 Mark Mulder 5.00
427 Marlon Byrd 4.00
428 David Murphy 6.00
429 Phil Nevin 4.00
430 J.T. Snow Jr. 4.00
431 Brad Sullivan 6.00
432 Bo Hart 6.00
433 *Josh Labandeira* 5.00
434 Chan Ho Park 4.00
435 Carlos Delgado 6.00
436 Curt Schilling 6.00
437 John Smoltz 5.00
438 Luis Matos 4.00
439 Mark Prior 10.00
440 Roberto Alomar 6.00
441 Coco Crisp 4.00
442 Austin Kearns 5.00
443 Larry Walker 5.00
444 Neal Cotts 4.00
445 Jeff Bagwell 6.00
446 Adrian Beltre 4.00
447 Grady Sizemore 4.00
448 Keith Ginter 4.00
449 Vladimir Guerrero 8.00
450 Lyle Overbay 4.00
451 Rafael Furcal 5.00
452 Melvin Mora 4.00
453 Kerry Wood 8.00
454 Jose Valentin 4.00
455 Ken Griffey Jr. 8.00
456 Brandon Phillips 4.00
457 Miguel Cabrera 8.00
458 Edwin Jackson 5.00
459 Eric Owens 4.00
460 Miguel Batista 4.00
461 Mike Hampton 4.00
462 Kevin Millar 4.00
463 Bartolo Colon 5.00
464 Sean Casey 4.00
465 C.C. Sabathia 4.00
466 Rickie Weeks 8.00
467 Brad Penny 4.00
468 Mike MacDougal 4.00

469 Kevin Brown 6.00
470 Lance Berkman 5.00
471 Ben Sheets 5.00
472 Mariano Rivera 5.00
473 Mike Piazza 8.00
474 Ryan Klesko 5.00
475 Edgar Renteria 5.00

Chrome

NM/M
Complete Set (110):
Common Player: 1.00
Production 1,955 sets
Refractor: 1.5-2X
Production 555 sets
Black Refractor: 2-4X
Production 55 sets
THC1 Sammy Sosa 8.00
THC2 Nomar Garciaparra 8.00
THC3 Ichiro Suzuki 6.00
THC4 Rafael Palmeiro 3.00
THC5 Carlos Delgado 2.50
THC6 Troy Glaus 2.00
THC7 Jay Gibbons 1.50
THC8 Frank Thomas 3.00
THC9 Pat Burrell 2.00
THC10 Albert Pujols 8.00
THC11 Brandon Webb 1.50
THC12 Chipper Jones 4.00
THC13 Magglio Ordonez 2.00
THC14 Adam Dunn 2.00
THC15 Todd Helton 2.50
THC16 Jason Giambi 3.00
THC17 Alfonso Soriano 3.00
THC18 Barry Zito 2.00
THC19 Jim Thome 3.00
THC20 Alex Rodriguez 8.00
THC21 Hee Seop Choi 1.00
THC22 Pedro J. Martinez 3.00
THC23 Kerry Wood 3.00
THC24 Bartolo Colon 1.50
THC25 Austin Kearns 2.00
THC26 Ken Griffey Jr. 5.00
THC27 Coco Crisp 1.00
THC28 Larry Walker 1.50
THC29 Ivan Rodriguez 2.50
THC30 Dontrelle Willis 2.00
THC31 Miguel Cabrera 2.50
THC32 Jeff Bagwell 2.50
THC33 Lance Berkman 1.50
THC34 Shawn Green 1.50
THC35 Kevin Brown 1.50
THC36 Vladimir Guerrero 3.00
THC37 Mike Piazza 5.00
THC38 Derek Jeter 10.00
THC39 John Smoltz 1.50
THC40 Mark Prior 8.00
THC41 Gary Sheffield 2.00
THC42 Curt Schilling 2.00
THC43 Randy Johnson 3.00
THC44 Luis Gonzalez 1.50
THC45 Andruw Jones 2.50
THC46 Greg Maddux 5.00
THC47 Tony Batista 1.00
THC48 Esteban Loaiza 1.00
THC49 Chin-Hui Tsao 1.00
THC50 Mike Lowell 1.50
THC51 Jeff Kent 1.50
THC52 Richie Sexson 2.00
THC53 Torii Hunter 2.00
THC54 Jose Vidro 1.00
THC55 Jose Reyes 2.00
THC56 Jimmy Rollins 1.00
THC57 Bret Boone 1.50
THC58 Rocco Baldelli 2.00
THC59 Hank Blalock 2.00
THC60 Rickie Weeks 2.00
THC61 Rodney Choy Foo 1.00
THC62 Zach Miner 1.00
THC63 Brayan Pena 1.00
THC64 David Murphy 1.00
THC65 Matt Creighton 1.00
THC66 Kyle Sleeth 1.00
THC67 Matthew Moses 1.00
THC68 Josh Labandeira 1.00
THC69 Grady Sizemore 1.00
THC70 Edwin Jackson 1.00
THC71 Marcus McBeth 1.00
THC72 Bradley Sullivan 1.00
THC73 Zachary Duke 25.00
THC74 Omar Falcon 1.00
THC75 Conor Jackson 1.00
THC76 Carlos Quentin 1.00
THC77 Craig Ansman 1.00
THC78 Mike Gosling 1.00
THC79 Kyle Davies 1.00
THC80 Anthony Lerew 1.00
THC81 Sung Jung 1.00
THC82 David Crouthers 1.00
THC83 Kenny Perez 1.00
THC84 Jeffrey Allison 1.00
THC85 Nic Ungs 1.00
THC86 Donald Levinski 1.00
THC87 Anthony Acevedo 1.00
THC88 Todd Self 1.00
THC89 Tim Frend 1.00
THC90 Tydus Meadows 1.00
THC91 Khalid Ballouli 1.00
THC92 Dioner Navarro 1.00
THC93 Casey Myers 1.00
THC94 Jon Knott 1.00
THC95 Tim Stauffer 1.00
THC96 Ricky Nolasco 1.00
THC97 Blake Hawksworth 1.00
THC98 Jesse Roman 1.00
THC99 Yadier Molina 1.00
THC100 Chris O'Riordan 1.00
THC101 Cliff Floyd 1.00
THC102 Nick Johnson 1.00
THC103 Edgar Martinez 1.50
THC104 Brett Myers 1.00
THC105 Francisco Rodriguez 1.00
THC106 Scott Rolen 3.00
THC107 Mark Teixeira 2.00
THC108 Miguel Tejada 2.00
THC109 Vernon Wells 1.50
THC110 Jerome Williams 1.00

Clubhouse Collection

NM/M
Common Player: 5.00
BA Bobby Abreu 6.00
RB Rocco Baldelli 12.00
LB Lance Berkman 6.00
YB Yogi Berra 35.00
HB Hank Blalock 8.00
BB Bret Boone 6.00
KB Kevin Brown 6.00
EC Eric Chavez 5.00
RC Roger Clemens 15.00
JD Johnny Damon 10.00
AD Adam Dunn 6.00
RF Rafael Furcal 6.00
EG Eric Gagne 8.00
NG Nomar Garciaparra 15.00
JG Jason Giambi 8.00
MG Marcus Giles 8.00
TG Troy Glaus 6.00
LG Luis Gonzalez 5.00
SG Shawn Green 6.00
TH Tim Hudson 6.00
THU Torii Hunter 8.00
KI Kazuhisa Ishii 6.00
RJ Randy Johnson 10.00
AJ Andruw Jones 6.00
CJ Chipper Jones 8.00
AK Al Kaline 25.00
HK Harmon Killebrew 30.00
PL Paul LoDuca 5.00
JL Javy Lopez 6.00
GM Greg Maddux 20.00
PM Pedro J. Martinez 10.00
WM Willie Mays 100.00
FM Fred McGriff 6.00
MM Mark Mulder 5.00
SM Stan Musial 40.00
BM Brett Myers 5.00
AP Albert Pujols 15.00
MR Manny Ramirez 8.00
JRE Jose Reyes 8.00
AR Alex Rodriguez 10.00
IR Ivan Rodriguez 6.00
SRB Scott Rolen/bat 8.00
SR Scott Rolen/jsy 8.00
JR Jimmy Rollins 5.00
CS C.C. Sabathia 5.00
GS Gary Sheffield 8.00
JS John Smoltz 8.00
DS Duke Snider 30.00
AS Alfonso Soriano 10.00
SS Sammy Sosa 15.00
MS Mike Sweeney 5.00
MTE Mark Teixeira 6.00
MT Miguel Tejada/jsy 6.00
MTB Miguel Tejada/bat 8.00
JT Jim Thome 10.00
VW Vernon Wells 6.00
KW Kerry Wood 10.00
BZ Barry Zito 6.00

Clubhouse Collection Autograph

Inserted 15,186
Production 25 sets

Clubhouse Collection - Dual

NM/M
Production 55 sets
MP Albert Pujols, Stan Musial
BC Yogi Berra, Roger Clemens 160.00
GS Shawn Green, Duke Snider 150.00

Doubleheader

NM/M
Complete Set (30): 50.00
Common Player: .75
Inserted 1:box
1 Alex Rodriguez 5.00
2 Nomar Garciaparra 4.00
3 Ichiro Suzuki 4.00
4 Albert Pujols 4.00
5 Sammy Sosa 4.00
6 Derek Jeter 6.00
7 Jim Thome 2.00
8 Adam Dunn 1.00
9 Jason Giambi 2.00
10 Ivan Rodriguez 1.50
11 Todd Helton 1.50
12 Luis Gonzalez .75
13 Jeff Bagwell 1.50
14 Lance Berkman 1.00
15 Alfonso Soriano 2.00
16 Dontrelle Willis 1.00
17 Mark Prior 4.00
18 Vladimir Guerrero 2.00
19 Mike Piazza 3.00
20 Roger Clemens 4.00
21 Randy Johnson 2.00
22 Curt Schilling 1.50
23 Gary Sheffield 1.00
24 Pedro J. Martinez 2.00
25 Carlos Delgado 1.50
26 Jimmy Rollins .75
27 Andruw Jones 1.50
28 Chipper Jones 3.00
29 Rocco Baldelli 1.50
30 Hank Blalock 1.00

Flashbacks

NM/M
Complete Set (10): 8.00
Common Player: .50
Inserted 1:12
F1 Duke Snider 1.50
F2 Johnny Podres .50
F3 Don Newcombe .50
F4 Al Kaline 1.50
F5 Willie Mays 4.00
F6 Stan Musial 3.00
F7 Harmon Killebrew 2.00
F8 Herb Score .50
F9 Whitey Ford 1.00
F10 Robin Roberts .50

Flashbacks Autograph

Inserted 1:30,373

Grandstand Glory

NM/M
Common Player: 20.00
YB Yogi Berra 20.00
AK Al Kaline 30.00
HK Harmon Killebrew 30.00
WM Willie Mays
SM Stan Musial 35.00
WS Warren Spahn 20.00

New Age Performers

NM/M
Complete Set (15): 15.00
Common Player: .75
Inserted 1:5
NAP1 Jason Giambi 1.50
NAP2 Ichiro Suzuki 2.50
NAP3 Alex Rodriguez 3.00
NAP4 Alfonso Soriano 1.50
NAP5 Albert Pujols 3.00
NAP6 Nomar Garciaparra 3.00
NAP7 Mark Prior 3.00
NAP8 Derek Jeter 4.00
NAP9 Sammy Sosa 2.50
NAP10 Carlos Delgado 1.00
NAP11 Jim Thome 1.50
NAP12 Todd Helton 1.00
NAP13 Gary Sheffield .75
NAP14 Vladimir Guerrero 1.50
NAP15 Josh Beckett 1.00

Real One Autograph

NM/M
Common Autograph: 30.00
Inserted 1:230
Red Autograph: 1.5-2X
Production 55
GA Gair Allie 50.00
EB Ernie Banks 100.00
YB Yogi Berra 100.00
BB Bob Borkowski 40.00
BC Billy Consolo 55.00
CF Cliff Floyd 30.00
BG Bill Glynn 45.00
JG Johnny Gray 45.00
AH Aubrey Huff 30.00
AK Al Kaline 100.00
HK Harmon Killebrew 85.00
TK Thornton Kipper 45.00
BK Bob Kline 45.00
SK Steve Kraly 60.00
LL Lou Limmer 60.00
ML Mike Lowell 40.00
WM Willie Mays 185.00
BM Bob Milliken 45.00
SM Stan Musial 140.00
DN Don Newcombe 65.00
MO Magglio Ordonez 35.00
JP Jim Pearce 45.00
HP Harry Perkowski 50.00
DP Duane Pillette 40.00
JPO Johnny Podres 45.00
SR Scott Rolen 45.00
FS Frank Smith 45.00
DS Duke Snider 85.00
VT "Jake" Thies 45.00
HV Harold Valentine 45.00
DW Dontrelle Willis 50.00

BW Bill Wilson 40.00
TW Tom Wright 45.00

Team Topps Legends

NM/M

Inserted 1:505
Davey Johnson 12.00
Joe Rudi 15.00

Then And Now

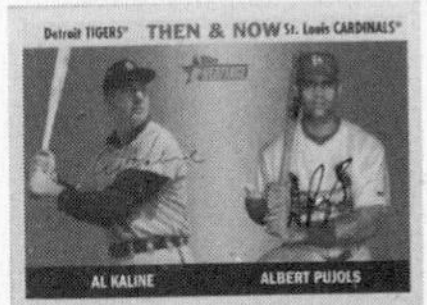

NM/M

Complete Set (6): 8.00
Common Player: 1.00
Inserted 1:15
TN1 Willie Mays, Jim Thome 4.00
TN2 Al Kaline, Albert Pujols 4.00
TN3 Duke Snider, Carlos Delgado 1.50
TN4 Robin Roberts, Roy Halladay 1.00
TN5 Don Newcombe, Johan Santana 1.00
TN6 Herb Score, Kerry Wood 1.50

2004 TOPPS OPENING DAY

NM/M

Complete Set (165): 25.00
Common Player: .10
Pack (6): 1.00
Box (36): 30.00
1 Jim Thome .50
2 Edgardo Alfonzo .10
3 Marlon Anderson .10
4 Ichiro Suzuki 1.00
5 Frank Thomas .40
6 Tom Glavine .25
7 Bo Hart .10
8 Marcus Giles .10
9 Kevin Millar .10
10 Derek Jeter 1.50
11 Corey Patterson .10
12 Jay Payton .10
13 Lance Berkman .20
14 Juan Pierre .10
15 Mike Piazza .75
16 Richie Sexson .40
17 Tim Hudson .25
18 Fred McGriff .20
19 Brad Radke .10
20 John Smoltz .20
21 Jay Gibbons .10
22 Michael Young .10
23 Steve Finley .10
24 Ramon Hernandez .10
25 Albert Pujols 1.25
26 Trot Nixon .10
27 Kevin Millwood .25
28 Mark Prior 1.00
29 Mike Lowell .20
30 Paul LoDuca .10
31 Jacque Jones .10
32 Ty Wigginton .10
33 Cliff Floyd .10
34 Marlon Byrd .10
35 Mark Mulder .20
36 Johnny Damon .20
37 Jimmy Rollins .10
38 Javy Lopez .25
39 Andruw Jones .40
40 Hank Blalock .25
41 Hee Seop Choi .10
42 Jose Vidro .10
43 Hideo Nomo .25
44 Javier Vazquez .10
45 Jorge Posada .25
46 Al Leiter .10
47 Orlando Cabrera .10
48 Mike Hampton .10
49 Esteban Loaiza .10
50 Todd Helton .40
51 Jose Contreras .20
52 Jason L. Phillips .10
53 Vernon Wells .20
54 Randy Winn .10
55 Curt Schilling .40
56 Mark Buehrle .10
57 Dmitri Young .10
58 Kazuhisa Ishii .10
59 A.J. Pierzynski .10
60 Greg Maddux .75
61 Jarrod Washburn .10
62 Omar Vizquel .10
63 Alex Gonzalez .10
64 Sean Casey .10
65 Eric Chavez .20
66 Mike Lieberthal .10
67 Jason Kendall .10
68 Mike Cameron .10
69 Woody Williams .10
70 Nomar Garciaparra 1.00
71 Bernie Williams .25
72 Darin Erstad .20
73 Bill Mueller .10
74 Damian Miller .10
75 Jason Giambi .50
76 Adam Dunn .25
77 Carlos Lee .10
78 Angel Berroa .10
79 Erubiel Durazo .10
80 Bret Boone .20
81 Aubrey Huff .20
82 Carlos Delgado .40
83 Toby Hall .10
84 Roy Halladay .25
85 Preston Wilson .10
86 Bartolo Colon .20
87 Moises Alou .20
88 Luis Castillo .10
89 Manny Ramirez .40
90 Garret Anderson .25
91 Ryan Klesko .20
92 Rich Aurilia .10
93 Rafael Furcal .20
94 Rocco Baldelli .40
95 Eric Gagne .20
96 Jeff Kent .20
97 Josh Beckett .40
98 Alex Gonzalez .10
99 Jose Cruz Jr. .10
100 Alex Rodriguez 1.25
101 Troy Glaus .25
102 Carlos Beltran .20
103 Luis Gonzalez .20
104 A.J. Burnett .10
105 Gary Sheffield .25
106 Benito Santiago .10
107 Tony Batista .10
108 David Ortiz .20
109 Shannon Stewart .10
110 Jim Edmonds .25
111 Kenny Lofton .20
112 Paul Konerko .10
113 Rafael Palmeiro .40
114 Pat Burrell .25
115 Barry Zito .25
116 Edgar Martinez .20
117 Austin Kearns .25
118 Geoff Jenkins .20
119 Mike Mussina .25
120 Alfonso Soriano .50
121 Shea Hillenbrand .10
122 Ivan Rodriguez .40
123 Kerry Wood .40
124 Scott Rolen .50
125 Jeff Bagwell .40
126 Roberto Alomar .25
127 Carl Crawford .10
128 Mike Sweeney .10
129 Melvin Mora .10
130 Larry Walker .20
131 Matt Morris .10
132 Shawn Green .20
133 Scott Podsednik .25
134 Phil Nevin .10
135 Dontrelle Willis .25
136 Torii Hunter .25
137 Carl Everett .10
138 Pedro J. Martinez .50
139 Roy Oswalt .25
140 Vladimir Guerrero .50
141 Chipper Jones .75
142 Jose Reyes .25
143 Sammy Sosa 1.00
144 Nick Johnson .10
145 Miguel Tejada .25
146 Bobby Abreu .20
147 Magglio Ordonez .25
148 Sean Burroughs .10
149 Jody Gerut .10
150 Jermaine Dye .10
151 Craig Biggio .20
152 Randy Johnson .50
153 Jeff Conine .10
154 Edgar Renteria .20
155 Mark Teixeira .25
156 Eric Hinske .10
157 Kevin Brown .20
158 Ken Griffey Jr. .75
159 Brandon Webb .10
160 Brian Giles .20
161 Jason Schmidt .20
162 Aramis Ramirez .10
163 Aaron Boone .10
164 Miguel Cabrera .40
165 Checklist .10

Autograph

NM/M

Common Autograph: 10.00
Inserted 1:629
JD Jeff Duncan 20.00
RH Rich Harden 20.00
AT Andres Torres 10.00
RW Ryan Wagner 25.00
JW Jerome Williams
DW Dontrelle Willis 30.00

2004 TOPPS ORIGINALS SIGNATURE EDITION

NM/M

Common Autograph: 10.00
Pack (4): 45.00
Box (6): 220.00
Second number reflects quantity produced
JA1 Jim Abbott 88 TR/339 20.00
SA5 Sparky Anderson 83 MG/67 15.00
SA6 Sparky Anderson 84 MG/97 15.00
SA7 Sparky Anderson 85 MG/73 15.00
LA9 Luis Aparicio 69/49 20.00
LA12 Luis Aparicio 72/15 30.00
HB2 Harold Baines 82/31 25.00
HB3 Harold Baines 83/19 30.00
HB5 Harold Baines 85/97 15.00
HB6 Harold Baines 86/93 15.00
HB7 Harold Baines 87/115 15.00
JB2 Jesse Barfield 83/45 15.00
JB4 Jesse Barfield 85/60 15.00
JB5 Jesse Barfield 86/37 15.00
JB6 Jesse Barfield 87/180 10.00
KB2 Kevin Bass 84/71 10.00
KB3 Kevin Bass 85/30 10.00
KB4 Kevin Bass 86/44 10.00
KB5 Kevin Bass 87/74 10.00
KB6 Kevin Bass 90 TR/35 10.00
BB5 Buddy Bell 79/135 15.00
BB8 Buddy Bell 82/34 15.00
BB9 Buddy Bell 83/83 10.00
BB10 Buddy Bell 84/22 15.00
BB12 Buddy Bell 86/32 15.00
GB2 George Bell 84/67 10.00
GB3 George Bell 85/32 15.00
GB4 George Bell 86/46 15.00
GB5 George Bell 87/204 10.00
JBE2 Johnny Bench 79/14 125.00
JBE5 Johnny Bench 82/16 125.00
YB10 Yogi Berra 85 MG/27 100.00
VB5 Vida Blue 79/21 20.00
VB7 Vida Blue 81/227 10.00
VB8 Vida Blue 82/53 15.00
VB9 Vida Blue 83/45 15.00
BBL4 Bert Blyleven 79/45 25.00
BBL6 Bert Blyleven 81/29 25.00
BBL8 Bert Blyleven 83/41 20.00
BBL10 Bert Blyleven 85/40 20.00
BBL11 Bert Blyleven 86/62 20.00
BBL12 Bert Blyleven 87/54 20.00
MB2 Mike Boddicker 84/56 15.00
MB3 Mike Boddicker 85/139 10.00
MB4 Mike Boddicker 86/66 10.00
MB5 Mike Boddicker 87/88 10.00
WB2 Wade Boggs 84/20 75.00
WB3 Wade Boggs 85/25 75.00
WB5 Wade Boggs 87/45 60.00
LB4 Lou Brock 70/20 50.00
LB13 Lou Brock 79/27 50.00
TB2 Tom Brunansky 83/27 15.00
TB3 Tom Brunansky 84/62 15.00
TB5 Tom Brunansky 86/28 15.00
TB6 Tom Brunansky 87/193 10.00
BU8 Bill Buckner 81/39 20.00
BU9 Bill Buckner 82/38 20.00
BU10 Bill Buckner 83/47 15.00
BU11 Bill Buckner 84/31 20.00
BU12 Bill Buckner 84 TR/24 20.00
BU13 Bill Buckner 85/80 15.00
BU14 Bill Buckner 86/63 15.00
BC5 Bert Campaneris 79/107 10.00
BC7 Bert Campaneris 84/28 15.00
JC2 John Candelaria 79/77 20.00
JC4 John Candelaria 81/19 30.00
JC5 John Candelaria 82/42 25.00
JC6 John Candelaria 83/77 20.00
JC8 John Candelaria 85/61 20.00
JC9 John Candelaria 86/36 20.00
JCA2 Jose Canseco 87/99 60.00
RC4 Rod Carew 79/29 60.00
RC6 Rod Carew 81/21 75.00
RC7 Rod Carew 82/18 75.00
GC3 Gary Carter 79/21 40.00
GC4 Gary Carter 80/24 40.00
GC5 Gary Carter 81/22 40.00
JCR2 Joe Carter 86/24 50.00
JCR3 Joe Carter 87/23 50.00
RCE3 Ron Cey 79/55 15.00
RCE6 Ron Cey 82/34 15.00
RCE7 Ron Cey 83/87 15.00
RCE8 Ron Cey 83 TR/68 15.00
RCE11 Ron Cey 86/43 15.00
VC2 Vince Coleman 87/299 15.00
VC3 Vince Coleman 88/34 20.00
VC4 Vince Coleman 91 TR/23 25.00
DC6 Dave Concepcion 80/21 40.00
DC8 Dave Concepcion 82/43 30.00
DC9 Dave Concepcion 83/34 30.00
DC10 Dave Concepcion 84/24 40.00
DC11 Dave Concepcion 85/41 30.00
DC12 Dave Concepcion 86/69 25.00
JCU8 Jose Cruz Sr. 82/28 15.00

JCU9 Jose Cruz Sr. 83/102 10.00
JCU10 Jose Cruz Sr. 84/67 10.00
JCU11 Jose Cruz Sr. 85/68 10.00
JCU12 Jose Cruz Sr. 86/31 15.00
RD3 Ron Darling 87/224 15.00
DD2 Darren Daulton 87/269 10.00
DD4 Darren Daulton 92/32 15.00
DD5 Darren Daulton 94/17 20.00
DD6 Darren Daulton 96/22 20.00
ED3 Eric Davis 87/336 15.00
AD3 Andre Dawson 80/27 25.00
AD4 Andre Dawson 81/37 25.00
AD5 Andre Dawson 82/55 20.00
AD6 Andre Dawson 83/47 20.00
AD7 Andre Dawson 84/25 25.00
AD8 Andre Dawson 85/22 25.00
AD9 Andre Dawson 86/24 25.00
DDE2 Doug DeCinces 79/38 20.00
DDE3 Doug DeCinces 80/24 20.00
DDE4 Doug DeCinces 81/24 20.00
DDE5 Doug DeCinces 82/42 20.00
DDE6 Doug DeCinces 83/75 15.00
DDE7 Doug DeCinces 84/19 20.00
DDE8 Doug DeCinces 85/54 15.00
DDE9 Doug DeCinces 86/74 15.00
BD6 Bucky Dent 82/49 20.00
BD7 Bucky Dent 83/92 15.00
BD8 Bucky Dent 84/63 15.00
RDI2 Rob Dibble 90/31 25.00
RDI3 Rob Dibble 91/62 20.00
RDI4 Rob Dibble 92/56 20.00
RDI6 Rob Dibble 93/47 15.00
RDI7 Rob Dibble 94/37 15.00
LD2 Leon Durham 82/51 10.00
LD3 Leon Durham 83/52 10.00
LD4 Leon Durham 84/151 10.00
LD7 Leon Durham 87/87 10.00
LDY2 Lenny Dykstra 87/200 15.00
LDY3 Lenny Dykstra 88/30 25.00
LDY4 Lenny Dykstra 89/17 30.00
DE3 Dennis Eckersley 79/44 40.00
DE4 Dennis Eckersley 80/40 40.00
DEV5 Darrell Evans 79/19 20.00
DEV6 Darrell Evans 80/5
DEV7 Darrell Evans 81/15 20.00
DEV8 Darrell Evans 82/25 20.00
DEV9 Darrell Evans 83/63 15.00
DEV10 Darrell Evans 84/81 10.00
DEV11 Darrell Evans 85/48 15.00
DEV12 Darrell Evans 86/82 10.00
SF2 Sid Fernandez 86/18 30.00
SF3 Sid Fernandez 87/211 15.00
SF4 Sid Fernandez 93/20 25.00
TF2 Tony Fernandez 86/41 15.00
TF3 Tony Fernandez 87/228 10.00
MF3 Mark Fidrych 79/74 25.00
MF4 Mark Fidrych 80/16 40.00
CF2 Cecil Fielder 87/208 30.00
CF3 Cecil Fielder 88/26 50.00
CF4 Cecil Fielder 89/16 50.00
RF3 Rollie Fingers 79/52 20.00
RF4 Rollie Fingers 80/15 40.00
RF5 Rollie Fingers 81/18 40.00
CFI3 Carlton Fisk 79/24 60.00
CFI4 Carlton Fisk 80/32 50.00
CFI6 Carlton Fisk 82/30 50.00
GF6 George Foster 79/20 20.00
GF10 George Foster 83/39 15.00
GF11 George Foster 84/112 10.00
GF12 George Foster 85/76 10.00
GF13 George Foster 86/64 10.00
SG4 Steve Garvey 79/26 30.00
SG7 Steve Garvey 82/122 15.00
SG9 Steve Garvey 84/32 20.00
SG10 Steve Garvey 85/129 15.00
CG3 Cesar Geronimo 79/28 15.00
CG5 Cesar Geronimo 81/21 15.00
CG6 Cesar Geronimo 82/52 10.00
CG7 Cesar Geronimo 83/67 10.00
CG8 Cesar Geronimo 84/70 10.00
KGI2 Kirk Gibson 82/35 20.00
KGI3 Kirk Gibson 83/35 20.00
KGI5 Kirk Gibson 85/44 20.00
KGI6 Kirk Gibson 86/44 20.00
KGI7 Kirk Gibson 87/65 20.00
DG3 Dwight Gooden 87/52 30.00
RG7 Rich "Goose" Gossage 81/21 20.00
RG8 Rich "Goose" Gossage 82/30 20.00
RG9 Rich "Goose" Gossage 83/34 20.00
RG10 Rich "Goose" Gossage 84/90 15.00
RG12 Rich "Goose" Gossage 86/30 15.00
BG2 Bobby Grich 79/29 20.00
BG3 Bobby Grich 80/70 15.00
BG5 Bobby Grich 82/45 15.00
BG6 Bobby Grich 83/85 10.00
BG7 Bobby Grich 84/57 15.00
BG8 Bobby Grich 85/36 15.00
KG5 Ken Griffey Sr. 80/15 30.00
KG7 Ken Griffey Sr. 82/18 30.00
KG8 Ken Griffey Sr. 83/70 15.00
KG9 Ken Griffey Sr. 84/64 15.00
KG10 Ken Griffey Sr. 85/32 20.00
KG11 Ken Griffey Sr. 86 TR/32 20.00
KGU2 Kelly Gruber 88/77 10.00
KGU3 Kelly Gruber 89/44 10.00
KGU4 Kelly Gruber 90/86 10.00
KGU5 Kelly Gruber 91/52 10.00
KGU6 Kelly Gruber 92/55 10.00
KGU7 Kelly Gruber 93/26 15.00
RGU4 Ron Guidry 80/22 40.00
RGU5 Ron Guidry 81/104 20.00
RGU6 Ron Guidry 82/53 40.00
RGU7 Ron Guidry 83/46 40.00
RGU8 Ron Guidry 84/40 40.00
RGU9 Ron Guidry 85/50 40.00
TG2 Tony Gwynn 84/95 60.00
KH3 Keith Hernandez 80/38 50.00
KH4 Keith Hernandez 81/19 50.00
KH5 Keith Hernandez 82/156 20.00
KH6 Keith Hernandez 83/17 50.00
TH2 Tom Herr 81/22 15.00
TH3 Tom Herr 82/42 15.00
TH4 Tom Herr 83/80 10.00
TH5 Tom Herr 84/30 15.00
TH6 Tom Herr 85/17 15.00
TH7 Tom Herr 86/28 15.00
TH8 Tom Herr 87/134 10.00
OH2 Orel Hershiser 86/23 40.00
OH3 Orel Hershiser 87/218 20.00
WH4 Whitey Herzog 83 MG/63 10.00
WH5 Whitey Herzog 84 MG/85 10.00
WH6 Whitey Herzog 85 MG/75 10.00
WH7 Whitey Herzog 86 MG/66 10.00
WH8 Whitey Herzog 87 MG/29 15.00
WH9 Whitey Herzog 88 MG/35 15.00
BH5 Bob Horner 83/69 15.00
BH6 Bob Horner 84/63 15.00
BH8 Bob Horner 86/118 15.00
BH9 Bob Horner 87/38 15.00
CH2 Charlie Hough 83/19 20.00
CH3 Charlie Hough 84/50 10.00
CH4 Charlie Hough 85/57 10.00
CH5 Charlie Hough 86/66 10.00
CH6 Charlie Hough 87/46 10.00
CH7 Charlie Hough 88/19 20.00
CH8 Charlie Hough 91 TR/70 10.00
CH9 Charlie Hough 92/25 15.00
AH6 Al Hrabosky 78/20 20.00
AH7 Al Hrabosky 79/40 15.00
AH8 Al Hrabosky 80/61 10.00
AH9 Al Hrabosky 81/38 15.00
AH10 Al Hrabosky 82/62 10.00
AH11 Al Hrabosky 89 Sr./20 20.00
BJ2 Bo Jackson 87/100 60.00
RJ8 Reggie Jackson 82/21 75.00
RJ11 Reggie Jackson 85/17 75.00
RJ12 Reggie Jackson 86/17 75.00
BJA2 Brook Jacoby 86/133 10.00
BJA3 Brook Jacoby 87/191 10.00
FJ8 Fergie Jenkins 78/17 40.00
FJ10 Fergie Jenkins 80/37 30.00
FJ11 Fergie Jenkins 81/32 30.00
FJ12 Fergie Jenkins 82/65 20.00
FJ13 Fergie Jenkins 83/22 30.00
FJ14 Fergie Jenkins 84/42 30.00
WJ2 Wally Joyner 87/335 15.00
DJ3 David Justice 93/32 20.00
AK10 Al Kaline 67/18 120.00
AK16 Al Kaline 73/25 140.00
JK2 Jimmy Key 86/21 20.00
JK3 Jimmy Key 87/263 10.00
JK5 Jimmy Key 92/37 20.00
DK4 Dave Kingman 81/25 30.00
DK6 Dave Kingman 83/32 30.00
DK7 Dave Kingman 86/25 30.00
RK2 Ron Kittle 85/86 10.00
RK3 Ron Kittle 86/55 15.00
RK4 Ron Kittle 87/201 10.00
RKN5 Ray Knight 82/25 20.00
RKN6 Ray Knight 83/36 20.00
RKN7 Ray Knight 84/26 20.00
RKN8 Ray Knight 85/68 15.00
RKN9 Ray Knight 86/80 15.00
RKN10 Ray Knight 87 TR/90 15.00
JKR2 John Kruk 87/214 15.00
JKR3 John Kruk 92/22 35.00
CL3 Carney Lansford 81/184 10.00
CL5 Carney Lansford 83/40 15.00
CL6 Carney Lansford 85/35 15.00
CL7 Carney Lansford 86/76 10.00
CLE3 Chet Lemon 79/24 20.00
CLE6 Chet Lemon 82/23 20.00
CLE7 Chet Lemon 83/35 15.00
CLE8 Chet Lemon 84/42 15.00
CLE9 Chet Lemon 85/32 15.00
CLE10 Chet Lemon 86/136 10.00
CLE11 Chet Lemon 87/27 20.00
JL2 Jim Leyritz 91/38 10.00
JL3 Jim Leyritz 93/49 10.00
JL4 Jim Leyritz 94/16 20.00
JL6 Jim Leyritz 97/62 10.00
JL7 Jim Leyritz 98/20 20.00
JL8 Jim Leyritz 99/124 10.00
JL9 Jim Leyritz 00/40 10.00
DL4 Davey Lopes 79/71 10.00
DL5 Davey Lopes 80/19 15.00
DL7 Davey Lopes 82/17 15.00
DL8 Davey Lopes 83/65 10.00
DL10 Davey Lopes 85/24 15.00
DL11 Davey Lopes 86/40 10.00
DL12 Davey Lopes 01 MG/67 10.00
DL13 Davey Lopes 02 MG/19 15.00
GL7 Greg Luzinski 80/21 30.00
GL9 Greg Luzinski 82/34 20.00
GL10 Greg Luzinski 83/75 10.00
GL11 Greg Luzinski 84/85 10.00
GL12 Greg Luzinski 85/92 10.00
BM7 Bill Madlock 82/26 15.00
BM8 Bill Madlock 83/55 15.00
BM9 Bill Madlock 84/69 15.00
BM10 Bill Madlock 85/60 15.00
BM11 Bill Madlock 86/63 15.00
BM12 Bill Madlock 87/42 15.00
GM3 Gary Matthews Sr. 83/20 15.00
GM4 Gary Matthews Sr. 84/43 10.00
GM5 Gary Matthews Sr. 85/39 10.00
GM6 Gary Matthews Sr. 86/38 10.00
GM7 Gary Matthews Sr. 87/82 10.00
GM8 Gary Matthews Sr. 88/30 15.00
DM3 Don Mattingly 87/84 100.00
WM9 Willie Mays 72/25 300.00
TM5 Tim McCarver 79/22 20.00
JM2 Jack McDowell 89/36 20.00
JM3 Jack McDowell 90 TR/61 15.00
JM4 Jack McDowell 91/33 20.00
JM5 Jack McDowell 92/38 20.00
JM6 Jack McDowell 93/27 20.00
JM9 Jack McDowell 96/15 25.00
JM10 Jack McDowell 97/27 20.00
WMC2 Willie McGee 84/66 25.00
WMC3 Willie McGee 85/44 25.00
WMC4 Willie McGee 86/24 40.00
WMC5 Willie McGee 87/117 25.00
PM1 Paul Molitor 79/15 60.00
PM2 Paul Molitor 80/26 50.00
PM4 Paul Molitor 82/32 50.00
JMO9 Joe Morgan 81/32 30.00
JMO10 Joe Morgan 82/18 40.00
JMO11 Joe Morgan 83/49 25.00
JMO13 Joe Morgan 84/73 15.00
JMO14 Joe Morgan 85/40 25.00
DMU2 Dale Murphy 79/38 50.00
DMU6 Dale Murphy 84/29 40.00
DMU8 Dale Murphy 86/25 50.00
DMU9 Dale Murphy 87/91 25.00
SM5 Stan Musial 62/16 150.00
AO6 Al Oliver 79/42 15.00
AO8 Al Oliver 81/54 15.00
AO9 Al Oliver 82/45 15.00
AO10 Al Oliver 83/50 15.00
AO11 Al Oliver 84/51 15.00
AO12 Al Oliver 85/46 15.00
AO13 Al Oliver 86/44 15.00
PO2 Paul O'Neill 89/24 50.00
PO3 Paul O'Neill 90/18 50.00
PO4 Paul O'Neill 91/24 50.00
PO5 Paul O'Neill 97/33 40.00
JP3 Jim Palmer 80/33 30.00
JP4 Jim Palmer 81/23 30.00
JP5 Jim Palmer 82/24 30.00
DP6 Dave Parker 82/73 20.00
DP7 Dave Parker 83/30 30.00
DP9 Dave Parker 85/45 25.00
DP10 Dave Parker 86/29 30.00
BP9 Boog Powell 73/17 50.00
BP11 Boog Powell 75/19 40.00
TR2 Tim Raines 82/43 20.00
TR3 Tim Raines 83/26 25.00
TR5 Tim Raines 85/43 20.00
TR6 Tim Raines 86/21 25.00
TR7 Tim Raines 87/211 15.00
HR2 Harold Reynolds 87/255 10.00
JR7 Jim Rice 81/123 20.00
JR8 Jim Rice 82/24 35.00
JR9 Jim Rice 83/71 25.00
CR4 Cal Ripken Jr. 86/74 120.00
MR2 Mickey Rivers 79/35 15.00
MR5 Mickey Rivers 82/49 15.00
MR6 Mickey Rivers 83/79 10.00
MR7 Mickey Rivers 84/91 10.00
MR8 Mickey Rivers 85/34 15.00
BR11 Brooks Robinson 74/20 75.00
BR13 Brooks Robinson 76/17 75.00
JRU9 Joe Rudi 79/24 15.00
JRU10 Joe Rudi 80/45 15.00
JRU11 Joe Rudi 82/26 15.00
JRU12 Joe Rudi 83/75 10.00
NR5 Nolan Ryan 83/23 200.00
NR6 Nolan Ryan 84/20 200.00
NR8 Nolan Ryan 86/20 200.00
BS2 Bret Saberhagen 86/23 25.00
BS3 Bret Saberhagen 87/230 15.00
RS2 Ryne Sandberg 84/37 100.00
RS5 Ryne Sandberg 87/32 100.00
SS2 Steve Sax 83/34 15.00
SS4 Steve Sax 85/33 15.00
SS5 Steve Sax 86/45 15.00
SS6 Steve Sax 87/215 10.00
MS2 Mike Schmidt 80/100 60.00
MSC3 Mike Scott 82/32 15.00
MSC4 Mike Scott 83/55 15.00
MSC5 Mike Scott 84/28 15.00
MSC6 Mike Scott 86/73 10.00
MSC7 Mike Scott 87/36 15.00
MSC8 Mike Scott 88/21 15.00
TS2 Tom Seaver 79/44 85.00
TS4 Tom Seaver 81/16 100.00
TS5 Tom Seaver 82/25 100.00
KS2 Kevin Seitzer 88/88 10.00
KS3 Kevin Seitzer 89/39 10.00
KS4 Kevin Seitzer 90/18 15.00
KS5 Kevin Seitzer 91/39 10.00
KS6 Kevin Seitzer 92/49 10.00
KS9 Kevin Seitzer 93/38 10.00

KS10 Kevin Seitzer 94/22 15.00
KS13 Kevin Seitzer 97/24 15.00
LS5 Lee Smith 86/29 25.00
LS6 Lee Smith 87/237 15.00
LS7 Lee Smith 88/27 25.00
OS2 Ozzie Smith 81/28 60.00
OS3 Ozzie Smith 82/27 60.00
OS5 Ozzie Smith 84/19 75.00
OS6 Ozzie Smith 85/16 75.00
RM8 Reggie Smith 79/15 25.00
RM9 Reggie Smith 80/16 25.00
RM10 Reggie Smith 81/14 25.00
RM11 Reggie Smith 82/32 15.00
RM12 Reggie Smith 83/48 15.00
DS8 Duke Snider 64/18 150.00
CS2 Cory Snyder 87/291 10.00
CS3 Cory Snyder 91/39 15.00
DSW2 Dave Stewart 83/41 15.00
DSW3 Dave Stewart 84/60 15.00
DSW4 Dave Stewart 85/24 15.00
DSW5 Dave Stewart 86/53 15.00
DSW6 Dave Stewart 87/171 10.00
DSE2 Dave Stieb 81/21 35.00
DSE3 Dave Stieb 82/34 30.00
DSE4 Dave Stieb 83/70 25.00
DSE5 Dave Stieb 84/20 35.00
DSE6 Dave Stieb 85/55 25.00
DSE7 Dave Stieb 86/69 25.00
DSE8 Dave Stieb 87/75 25.00
DSR2 Darryl Strawberry 85/32 25.00
DSR3 Darryl Strawberry 86/24 25.00
DSR4 Darryl Strawberry 87/183 20.00
DSR5 Darryl Strawberry 87 AS/110 20.00
RU3 Rick Sutcliffe 82/53 20.00
RU4 Rick Sutcliffe 83/43 20.00
RU5 Rick Sutcliffe 84/33 20.00
RU6 Rick Sutcliffe 85/82 20.00
RU8 Rick Sutcliffe 87/19 25.00
BSU6 Bruce Sutter 82/111 20.00
BSU7 Bruce Sutter 83/45 25.00
BSU8 Bruce Sutter 84/24 30.00
BSU9 Bruce Sutter 85/19 35.00
BSU10 Bruce Sutter 86/78 20.00
BSU11 Bruce Sutter 87/36 25.00
KT5 Kent Tekulve 81/17 20.00
KT6 Kent Tekulve 82/36 15.00
KT7 Kent Tekulve 83/52 15.00
KT8 Kent Tekulve 84/71 15.00
KT9 Kent Tekulve 85/43 15.00
KT10 Kent Tekulve 86/57 15.00
KT11 Kent Tekulve 87/32 15.00
KT12 Kent Tekulve 88/20 20.00
LT2 Luis Tiant 68/16 40.00
LT11 Luis Tiant 79/22 30.00
LT12 Luis Tiant 80/23 30.00
LT13 Luis Tiant 81/20 30.00
LT14 Luis Tiant 82/51 15.00
LT15 Luis Tiant 83/58 15.00
AT2 Alan Trammell 80/17 30.00
AT3 Alan Trammell 81/26 30.00
AT4 Alan Trammell 82/40 30.00
AT5 Alan Trammell 83/21 30.00
AT6 Alan Trammell 84/57 30.00
AT7 Alan Trammell 85/39 30.00
AT8 Alan Trammell 86/23 30.00
AT9 Alan Trammell 87/15 30.00
AV2 Andy Van Slyke 85/35 35.00
AV3 Andy Van Slyke 86/37 35.00
AV4 Andy Van Slyke 87/178 25.00
AV5 Andy Van Slyke 87 TR/130 25.00
FV3 Frank Viola 85/25 25.00
FV4 Frank Viola 86/99 15.00
FV5 Frank Viola 87/209 15.00
TW2 Tim Wallach 83/49 15.00
TW4 Tim Wallach 85/46 15.00
TW5 Tim Wallach 86/44 15.00
TW6 Tim Wallach 87/197 10.00
BW3 Bob Watson 79/77 10.00
BW6 Bob Watson 82/23 20.00
BW7 Bob Watson 83/93 10.00
BW8 Bob Watson 84/64 10.00
BW9 Bob Watson 85/68 10.00
EW4 Earl Weaver 78 MG/52 15.00
EW5 Earl Weaver 83 MG/38 20.00
EW7 Earl Weaver 86 MG/107 15.00
EW8 Earl Weaver 87 MG/175 10.00
WW2 Walt Weiss 89/34 10.00
WW3 Walt Weiss 91/30 10.00
WW4 Walt Weiss 92/71 10.00
WW7 Walt Weiss 97/49 10.00
WW10 Walt Weiss 99/40 10.00
WW11 Walt Weiss 01/51 10.00
MW2 Mookie Wilson 82/20 20.00
MW3 Mookie Wilson 83/41 15.00
MW5 Mookie Wilson 85/51 15.00
MW6 Mookie Wilson 86/47 15.00
MW7 Mookie Wilson 87/67 15.00
CY4 Carl Yastrzemski 80/60 100.00
CY5 Carl Yastrzemski 81/35 120.00
SY5 Steve Yeager 79/23 25.00
SY9 Steve Yeager 83/80 10.00
SY12 Steve Yeager 86/47 15.00
SY13 Steve Yeager 86 TR/100 10.00
RY5 Robin Yount 80/18 100.00
RY6 Robin Yount 81/23 100.00
RY9 Robin Yount 84/15 125.00
RY11 Robin Yount 86/21 100.00

2004 TOPPS PRISTINE

NM/M

Complete Set (190):
Common Player: 1.00
Common Rookie: 1.50
Common Uncommon RC: 3.00
Production 999
Common Rare RC: 6.00
Production 499
Pack (8): 35.00
Box (5): 140.00
1 Jim Thome 2.00
2 Ryan Klesko 1.00
3 Ichiro Suzuki 4.00
4 Rocco Baldelli 1.00
5 Vernon Wells 1.00
6 Javier Vazquez 1.00
7 Billy Wagner 1.00
8 Jose Reyes 1.00
9 Lance Berkman 1.00
10 Alex Rodriguez 6.00
11 Pat Burrell 1.00
12 Mark Mulder 1.00
13 Mike Piazza 3.00
14 Miguel Cabrera 2.00
15 Larry Walker 1.00
16 Carlos Lee 1.00
17 Mark Prior 2.00
18 Pedro J. Martinez 2.00
19 Melvin Mora 1.00
20 Sammy Sosa 4.00
21 Bartolo Colon 1.00
22 Luis Gonzalez 1.00
23 Marcus Giles 1.00
24 Ken Griffey Jr. 3.00
25 Ivan Rodriguez 1.50
26 Carlos Beltran 1.50
27 Geoff Jenkins 1.00
28 Nick Johnson 1.00
29 Gary Sheffield 1.50
30 Alfonso Soriano 2.00
31 Scott Rolen 2.00
32 Garret Anderson 1.00
33 Richie Sexson 1.00
34 Curt Schilling 1.50
35 Greg Maddux 3.00
36 Adam Dunn 1.50
37 Preston Wilson 1.00
38 Josh Beckett 1.50
39 Roy Oswalt 1.00
40 Derek Jeter 6.00
41 Jason Kendall 1.00
42 Bret Boone 1.00
43 Torii Hunter 1.00
44 Roy Halladay 1.00
45 Edgar Renteria 1.00
46 Troy Glaus 1.00
47 Chipper Jones 2.00
48 Manny Ramirez 1.50
49 C.C. Sabathia 1.00
50 Albert Pujols 5.00
51 Randy Wolf 1.00
52 Eric Chavez 1.00
53 Kevin Brown 1.00
54 Cliff Floyd 1.00
55 Jeff Bagwell 1.50
56 Frank Thomas 1.50
57 David Ortiz 1.50
58 Rafael Palmeiro 1.50
59 Randy Johnson 2.00
60 Vladimir Guerrero 2.00
61 Carlos Delgado 1.00
62 Hank Blalock 1.50
63 Jim Edmonds 1.00
64 Jason Schmidt 1.00
65 Mike Lieberthal 1.00
66 Tim Hudson 1.00
67 Jorge Posada 1.00
68 Jose Vidro 1.00
69 Eric Gagne 1.00
70 Roger Clemens 5.00
71 Mike Lowell 1.00
72 Dontrelle Willis 1.00
73 Austin Kearns 1.00
74 Kerry Wood 2.00
75 Miguel Tejada 1.50
76 Bobby Abreu 1.00
77 Edgar Martinez 1.00
78 Joe Mauer 1.00
79 Mike Sweeney 1.00
80 Jason Giambi 1.00
81 Mark Teixeira 1.00
82 Aubrey Huff 1.00
83 Brian Giles 1.00
84 Barry Zito 1.00
85 Mike Mussina 1.50
86 Brandon Webb 1.00
87 Andruw Jones 1.50
88 Javy Lopez 1.00
89 Bill Mueller 1.00
90 Scott Podsednik 1.00
91 Moises Alou 1.00
92 Esteban Loaiza 1.00
93 Magglio Ordonez 1.00
94 Jeff Kent 1.00
95 Todd Helton 1.50
96 Juan Pierre 1.00
97 Jody Gerut 1.00
98 Angel Berroa 1.00
99 Shawn Green 1.00
100 Nomar Garciaparra 3.00
101 David Aardsma/C 1.50
102 David Aardsma/U 4.00
103 David Aardsma/R 8.00
104 *Erick Aybar/C* 5.00
105 *Erick Aybar/U* 10.00
106 *Erick Aybar/R* 15.00
107 *Chad Bentz/C* 1.50
108 *Chad Bentz/U* 3.00
109 *Chad Bentz/R* 6.00
110 *Travis Blackley/C* 1.50
111 *Travis Blackley/U* 3.00
112 *Travis Blackley/R* 6.00
113 *Bobby Brownlie/C* 4.00
114 *Bobby Brownlie/U* 6.00
115 *Bobby Brownlie/R* 10.00
116 *Alberto Callaspo/C* 1.50
117 *Alberto Callaspo/U* 3.00
118 *Alberto Callaspo/R* 6.00
119 *Kazuo Matsui/C* 5.00
120 *Kazuo Matsui/U* 8.00
121 *Kazuo Matsui/R* 12.00
122 Jesse Crain/C 3.00
123 Jesse Crain/U 5.00
124 Jesse Crain/R 8.00
125 *Howard Kendrick/C* 10.00
126 *Howard Kendrick/U* 20.00
127 *Howard Kendrick/R* 30.00
128 *Blake Hawksworth/C* 1.50
129 *Blake Hawksworth/U* 3.00
130 *Blake Hawksworth/R* 6.00
131 Conor Jackson/C 1.50
132 Conor Jackson/U 3.00
133 Conor Jackson/R 6.00
134 *Paul Maholm/C* 1.50
135 *Paul Maholm/U* 3.00
136 *Paul Maholm/R* 6.00
137 Lastings Milledge/C 4.00
138 Lastings Milledge/U 8.00
139 Lastings Milledge/R 12.00
140 Matt Moses/C 4.00
141 Matt Moses/U 6.00
142 Matt Moses/R 10.00
143 David Murphy/C 1.50
144 David Murphy/U 3.00
145 David Murphy/R 6.00
146 *Dioner Navarro/C* 5.00
147 *Dioner Navarro/U* 8.00
148 *Dioner Navarro/R* 12.00
149 *Dustin Nippert/C* 1.50
150 *Dustin Nippert/U* 3.00
151 *Dustin Nippert/R* 6.00
152 *Vito Chiaravalloti/C* 3.00
153 *Vito Chiaravalloti/U* 6.00
154 *Vito Chiaravalloti/R* 8.00
155 *Akinori Otsuka/C* 3.00
156 *Akinori Otsuka/U* 5.00
157 *Akinori Otsuka/R* 8.00
158 *Casey Daigle/C* 1.50
159 *Casey Daigle/U* 3.00
160 *Casey Daigle/R* 6.00
161 Carlos Quentin/C 3.00
162 Carlos Quentin/U 5.00
163 Carlos Quentin 8.00
164 Omar Quintanilla/C 4.00
165 Omar Quintanilla/U 8.00
166 Omar Quintanilla/R 12.00
167 *Chris Saenz/C* 1.50
168 *Chris Saenz/U* 3.00
169 *Chris Saenz/R* 6.00
170 *Ervin Santana/C* 1.50
171 *Ervin Santana/U* 3.00
172 *Ervin Santana/R* 6.00
173 *Chris Shelton/C* 3.00
174 *Chris Shelton/U* 6.00
175 *Chris Shelton/R* 12.00
176 Kyle Sleeth/C 1.50
177 Kyle Sleeth/U 3.00
178 Kyle Sleeth/R 6.00
179 Brad Snyder/C 4.00
180 Brad Snyder/U 8.00
181 Brad Snyder/R 12.00
182 Tim Stauffer/C 4.00
183 Tim Stauffer/U 8.00
184 Tim Stauffer/R 12.00
185 *Shingo Takatsu/C* 4.00
186 *Shingo Takatsu/U* 8.00
187 *Shingo Takatsu/R* 12.00
188 *Merkin Valdez/C* 1.50
189 *Merkin Valdez/U* 3.00
190 *Merkin Valdez/R* 6.00

Refractors

Veterans (1-100): 4-8X
Production 49
Common RC's: .75-1.5X
Production 999
UnCommon RC's: 1-2X
Production 399
Rare RC's: 1.5-3X
Production 49

Gold Refractors

Veterans (1-100): 4-8X
Common RC's: 4-8X
Uncommon RC's: 3-5X
Rare RC's: 1.5-3X
Production 41 sets

Mini

NM/M

Common Player: 2.00
Inserted 1:5
DA David Aardsma 5.00
EA Erick Aybar 4.00
VC Vito Chiaravalloti 3.00
NG Nomar Garciaparra 4.00
JG Jason Giambi 2.00
VG Vladimir Guerrero 4.00
BH Blake Hawksworth 4.00
CJA Conor Jackson 4.00
DJ Derek Jeter 6.00
CJ Chipper Jones 3.00
HK Howard Kendrick 5.00
KM Kazuo Matsui 4.00
LM Lastings Milledge 6.00
MM Matt Moses 6.00
DM David Murphy 3.00
DN Dioner Navarro 10.00
AO Akinori Otsuka 3.00
MPI Mike Piazza 4.00
MP Mark Prior 4.00
AP Albert Pujols 6.00
AR Alex Rodriguez 6.00
KS Kyle Sleeth 4.00
SS Sammy Sosa 4.00
TS Tim Stauffer 3.00
IS Ichiro Suzuki 5.00
ST Shingo Takatsu 4.00
JT Jim Thome 3.00
MV Merkin Valdez 3.00
DW Dontrelle Willis 3.00
KW Kerry Wood 4.00

Mini Relics

		NM/M
Common Player:		5.00
Inserted 1:51		
JB	Jeff Bagwell	20.00
EG	Eric Gagne	15.00
NG	Nomar Garciaparra	12.00
CJ	Chipper Jones	10.00
PM	Pedro J. Martinez	12.00
MPI	Mike Piazza	12.00
MP	Mark Prior	12.00
AP	Albert Pujols	25.00
PW	Preston Wilson	5.00
KW	Kerry Wood	10.00

Fantasy Favorite Relics

		NM/M
Common Player:		4.00
Refractor:		2-4X
Production 25 sets		
MA	Moises Alou	6.00
JB	Jeff Bagwell	8.00
RB	Rocco Baldelli	6.00
AB	Angel Berroa	4.00
BB	Bret Boone	4.00
JD	Johnny Damon	8.00
CD	Carlos Delgado	5.00
RF	Rafael Furcal	4.00
RFJ	Rafael Furcal	4.00
EG	Eric Gagne	10.00
NG	Nomar Garciaparra	10.00
SG	Shawn Green	4.00
MG	Mark Grudzielanek	4.00
VG	Vladimir Guerrero	8.00
THE	Todd Helton	8.00
TH	Tim Hudson	6.00
DJ	Derek Jeter	20.00
AJ	Andruw Jones	6.00
CJ	Chipper Jones	8.00
CK	Corey Koskie	4.00
KL	Kenny Lofton	4.00
PM	Pedro J. Martinez	8.00
MPI	Mike Piazza	10.00
MP	Mark Prior	8.00
AP	Albert Pujols	15.00
AR	Alex Rodriguez	12.00
JR	Jimmy Rollins	4.00
MT	Mark Teixeira	4.00
FT	Frank Thomas	8.00
JT	Jim Thome	10.00
JV	Jose Vidro	4.00
LW	Larry Walker	4.00
BW	Brandon Webb	4.00
PW	Preston Wilson	4.00
KW	Kerry Wood	8.00

Going, Going, Gone! Relics

		NM/M
Common Player:		4.00
Refractor:		2-4X
Production 25 sets		
LB	Lance Berkman	4.00
BB	Bret Boone	4.00
AD	Adam Dunn	8.00
JG	Juan Gonzalez	6.00
LG	Luis Gonzalez	4.00
VG	Vladimir Guerrero	8.00
TH	Todd Helton	8.00
CJ	Chipper Jones	8.00
JJ	Jacque Jones	4.00
JK	Jeff Kent	4.00
RK	Ryan Klesko	4.00
MO	Magglio Ordonez	4.00
DO	David Ortiz	10.00
MP	Mike Piazza	10.00
AP	Albert Pujols	15.00
MR	Manny Ramirez	8.00
AR	Alex Rodriguez	12.00
SR	Scott Rolen	8.00
AS	Alfonso Soriano	8.00
SS	Sammy Sosa	10.00
FT	Frank Thomas	8.00
JT	Jim Thome	10.00
VW	Vernon Wells	4.00

Key Acquisitions Relics

		NM/M
Common Player:		4.00
Inserted 1:8		
Refractors:		2-4X
Production 25 sets		
HC	Hee Seop Choi	4.00
JG	Juan Gonzalez	6.00
VG	Vladimir Guerrero	8.00
JL	Javy Lopez	6.00
AR	Alex Rodriguez	12.00
IR	Ivan Rodriguez	8.00
GS	Gary Sheffield	6.00
AS	Alfonso Soriano	8.00

Patch Place Relics

		NM/M
Common Player:		10.00
Refractor:		No Pricing
Production 10 sets		
JB	Jeff Bagwell	20.00
RB	Rocco Baldelli	12.00
JBE	Josh Beckett	15.00
BB	Bret Boone	10.00
LC	Luis Castillo	10.00
CC	Chin-Feng Chen	40.00
CD	Carlos Delgado	10.00
AD	Adam Dunn	15.00
RF	Rafael Furcal	10.00
EG	Eric Gagne	15.00
NG	Nomar Garciaparra	40.00
LG	Luis Gonzalez	10.00
SG	Shawn Green	10.00
THE	Todd Helton	15.00
TH	Tim Hudson	10.00
RJ	Randy Johnson	20.00
AJ	Andruw Jones	10.00
CJ	Chipper Jones	15.00
AK	Austin Kearns	10.00
PL	Paul LoDuca	10.00
ML	Mike Lowell	10.00
PM	Pedro J. Martinez	20.00
MPI	Mike Piazza	35.00
MP	Mark Prior	20.00
AP	Albert Pujols	40.00
JR	Jose Reyes	10.00
JS	John Smoltz	15.00
SS	Sammy Sosa	20.00
FT	Frank Thomas	20.00
DW	Dontrelle Willis	10.00
PW	Preston Wilson	10.00
KW	Kerry Wood	20.00
BZ	Barry Zito	15.00

Personal Endorsements

		NM/M
Common Autograph:		6.00
Golds:		1.5-3X
Production 25 sets		
DA	David Aardsma	15.00
GA	Garret Anderson	10.00
LB	Lance Berkman	20.00
HB	Hank Blalock	20.00
MC	Miguel Cabrera	30.00
VC	Vito Chiaravalloti	10.00
BC	Bobby Crosby	25.00
JF	Jennie Finch	120.00
MG	Marcus Giles	10.00
VG	Vladimir Guerrero	50.00
EH	Estee Harris	8.00
AH	Aubrey Huff	8.00
CJ	Conor Jackson	20.00
CL	Chris Lubanski	10.00
JM	Joe Mauer	30.00
WM	Willie Mays	200.00
DM	Dustin McGowan	6.00
BM	Brett Myers	10.00
SP	Scott Podsednik	10.00
JP	Jorge Posada	40.00
AR	Alex Rodriguez	150.00
IR	Ivan Rodriguez	40.00
ES	Ervin Santana	10.00
GS	Gary Sheffield	40.00
GS	Grady Sizemore	15.00
JV	Javier Vazquez	15.00
BW	Brandon Webb	6.00
DY	Delmon Young	15.00

Two of a Kind Autograph

Production 13

20K-RM Alex Rodriguez, Willie Mays

1, 2, 3 Triple Relics

		NM/M
Inserted 1:171		
Refractor:		1.5-2X
Production 25 sets		
NYY	Kenny Lofton, Derek Jeter, Alex Rodriguez	50.00
CHC	Mark Grudzielanek, Alex Gonzalez, Sammy Sosa	40.00
BOS	Johnny Damon, Bill Mueller, Nomar Garciaparra	40.00

2004 TOPPS RETIRED SIGNATURE EDITION

		NM/M
Complete Set (110):		125.00
Common Player:		1.00
Pack (5):		35.00
Box (5):		140.00
1	Willie Mays	6.00
2	Tony Gwynn	3.00
3	Dale Murphy	2.00
4	Lenny Dykstra	1.00
5	Johnny Bench	4.00
6	Bill Buckner	1.00
7	Ferguson Jenkins	1.50
8	George Brett	6.00
9	Ralph Kiner	2.00
10	Ernie Banks	4.00
11	Hal McRae	1.00
12	Lou Brock	2.00
13	Keith Hernandez	1.00
14	Jose Canseco	2.00
15	Whitey Ford	2.50
16	Dave Kingman	1.00
17	Tim Raines	1.00
18	Paul O'Neill	1.50
19	Lou Whitaker	1.00
20	Mike Schmidt	5.00
21	Wally Joyner	1.00
22	Kirk Gibson	1.00
23	Ryne Sandberg	5.00
24	Luis Tiant	1.00
25	Al Kaline	4.00
26	Brooks Robinson	3.00
27	Don Zimmer	1.00
28	Nolan Ryan	6.00
29	Maury Wills	1.00
30	Stan Musial	4.00
31	Garry Maddox	1.00
32	Tom Brunansky	1.00
33	Don Mattingly	5.00
34	Earl Weaver	1.00
35	Bobby Grich	1.00
36	Orlando Cepeda	1.50
37	Alan Trammell	1.50
38	Al Hrabosky	1.00
39	Davey Lopes	1.00
40	Rod Carew	2.00
41	Robin Yount	4.00
42	Dwight Gooden	1.00
43	Andre Dawson	1.50
44	Hank Aaron	6.00
45	Norm Cash	1.00
46	Reggie Jackson	2.50
47	Jim Rice	1.00
48	Carlton Fisk	2.00
49	Dave Parker	1.00
50	Cal Ripken Jr.	6.00
51	Roy Face	1.00
52	Bob Gibson	2.50
53	Jimmy Key	1.00
54	Al Oliver	1.00
55	Don Larsen	1.50
56	Tom Seaver	3.00
57	Tony Armas	1.00
58	Dave Stieb	1.00
59	Will Clark	2.00
60	Duke Snider	2.50
61	Cesar Geronimo	1.00
62	Ron Kittle	1.00
63	Ron Santo	2.00
64	Mickey Rivers	1.00
65	Jimmy Piersall	1.00
66	Ron Swoboda	1.00
67	Kent Hrbek	1.00
68	Dennis Eckersley	2.00
69	Greg Luzinski	1.00
70	Harmon Killebrew	3.00
71	Ron Guidry	1.50
72	Steve Garvey	1.00
73	Andy Van Slyke	1.00
74	Rich "Goose" Gossage	1.00
75	Ozzie Smith	3.00
76	Richie Allen	1.00
77	Vida Blue	1.00
78	Tony Oliva	1.00
79	Darryl Strawberry	1.00
80	Frank Robinson	2.00
81	Bruce Sutter	1.50
82	Dave Concepcion	1.00
83	Darrell Evans	1.00
84	Jack Morris	1.00
85	Bo Jackson	2.00
86	Orel Hershiser	1.00
87	Rob Dibble	1.00
88	Wade Boggs	2.00
89	Fernando Valenzuela	1.00
90	Jim Palmer	2.00
91	George Foster	1.00
92	Mike Scott	1.00
93	Paul Molitor	2.50
94	Gary Carter	2.00
95	Bobby Richardson	1.00
96	Rollie Fingers	1.00
97	Tim McCarver	1.00
98	John Candelaria	1.00
99	Dave Winfield	2.00
100	Yogi Berra	3.00
101	Bill Madlock	1.00
102	Jack McDowell	1.00
103	Luis Aparicio	1.00
104	Graig Nettles	1.00
105	Dave Stewart	1.00
106	Darren Daulton	1.00
107	Gary Gaetti	1.00
108	Tony Fernandez	1.00
109	Buddy Bell	1.00
110	Carl Yastrzemski	4.00

Black

Black (1-110):	4-6X
Production 99 sets	

Chrome Autographs

		NM/M
Common Autograph:		10.00
Inserted 1:1		
Refractor:		2-4X
SP Refractor:		.75-2X
Production 25 sets		
HA	Hank Aaron/SP/50	300.00
TA	Tony Armas	10.00
EB	Ernie Banks/SP/50	180.00
BBE	Buddy Bell	12.00
JB	Johnny Bench/SP/75	80.00
YB	Yogi Berra/SP/75	80.00

VB Vida Blue 10.00
WB Wade Boggs 40.00
TB Tom Brunansky 10.00
BB Bill Buckner 12.00
JC John Candelaria 20.00
JCA Jose Canseco 35.00
RC Rod Carew 35.00
GC Gary Carter 20.00
OC Orlando Cepeda 15.00
DD Darren Daulton 10.00
BD Bucky Dent 10.00
RD Rob Dibble 12.00
DEC Dennis Eckersley 30.00
DE Darrell Evans 10.00
RF Roy Face 15.00
TF Tony Fernandez 10.00
WF Whitey Ford/SP/75 90.00
RF Rollie Fingers 15.00
CF Carlton Fisk 40.00
GF George Foster 12.00
CG Cesar Geronimo 25.00
BG Bob Gibson/SP/75 75.00
KG Kirk Gibson 20.00
DG Dwight Gooden/SP/75 40.00
GG Rich "Goose" Gossage 15.00
BGR Bobby Grich 10.00
TG Tony Gwynn/SP/75 75.00
OH Orel Hershiser 25.00
AH Al Hrabosky 10.00
FJ Ferguson Jenkins 15.00
WJ Wally Joyner 10.00
JK Jimmy Key 10.00
RK Ralph Kiner 50.00
RKI Ron Kittle 10.00
DL Davey Lopes 10.00
GL Greg Luzinski 15.00
BM Bill Madlock 10.00
DM Don Mattingly/SP/75 100.00
JM Jack McDowell 10.00
PM Paul Molitor 50.00
DM Dale Murphy 25.00
SM Stan Musial/SP/50 160.00
GN Graig Nettles 12.00
TO Tony Oliva 20.00
AO Al Oliver 12.00
PO Paul O'Neill 40.00
DP Dave Parker 20.00
JP Jimmy Piersall 15.00
BR Bobby Richardson 15.00
CR Cal Ripken Jr./SP/25 275.00
BRO Brooks Robinson/SP/75 90.00
FR Frank Robinson 30.00
NR Nolan Ryan/SP/25 300.00
RSA Ryne Sandberg 75.00
RS Ron Santo 20.00
MS Mike Schmidt/SP/75 150.00
TS Tom Seaver/SP/75 75.00
OS Ozzie Smith/SP/75 90.00
DSN Duke Snider/SP/50 90.00
DST Dave Stieb 12.00
DS Darryl Strawberry 30.00
BS Bruce Sutter 25.00
RS Ron Swoboda 10.00
LT Luis Tiant 10.00
AT Alan Trammell 20.00
EW Earl Weaver 10.00
MW Maury Wills 10.00
CY Carl Yastrzemski/SP/25 180.00
RY Robin Yount/SP/50 125.00
DZ Don Zimmer 20.00

Chrome Co-Signers

No Pricing
Production 25 sets

2004 TOPPS TOTAL

NM/M

Complete Set (880): 100.00
Common Player: .10
Pack (10): 1.00
Box (36): 30.00
1 Kevin Brown .25
2 Mike Mordecai .10
3 Seung Jun Song .10
4 Mike Maroth .10
5 Mike Lieberthal .10
6 Billy Koch .10
7 Mike Stanton .10
8 Brad Penny .10
9 Brooks Kieschnick .10
10 Carlos Delgado .40
11 Brady Clark .10
12 Ramon Martinez .10
13 Dan Wilson .10
14 Guillermo Mota .10
15 Trevor Hoffman .10
16 Tony Batista .10
17 Rusty Greer .10
18 David Weathers .10
19 Horacio Ramirez .10
20 Aubrey Huff .10
21 Casey Blake .10
22 Ryan Bukvich .10
23 Garrett Atkins .10
24 Jose Contreras .10
25 Chipper Jones .75
26 Neifi Perez .10
27 Scott Linebrink .10
28 Matt Kinney .10
29 Michael Restovich .10
30 Scott Rolen .75
31 John Franco .10
32 Toby Hall .10
33 Wily Mo Pena .10
34 Dennis Tankersley .10
35 Robb Nen .10
36 Jose Valverde .10
37 Chin-Feng Chen .10
38 Gary Knotts .10
39 Scott Elarton .10
40 Bret Boone .25
41 Josh Phelps .10
42 Jason Larue .10
43 Tim Redding .10
44 Greg Myers .10
45 Darin Erstad .25
46 Kip Wells .10
47 Matt Ford .10
48 Jerome Williams .10
49 Brian Meadows .10
50 Albert Pujols 1.50
51 Kirk Saarloos .10
52 Scott Eyre .10
53 John Flaherty .10
54 Rafael Soriano .10
55 Shea Hillenbrand .10
56 Kyle Farnsworth .10
57 Nate Cornejo .10
58 Kerry Robinson .10
59 Yan Vogelsong .10
60 Ryan Klesko .20
61 Luke Hudson .10
62 Justin Morneau .10
63 Frank Catalanotto .10
64 Derrick Turnbow .10
65 Marcus Giles .10
66 Mark Mulder .25
67 Matt Anderson .10
68 Mike Matheny .10
69 Brian Lawrence .10
70 Bobby Abreu .10
71 Damian Moss .10
72 Richard Hidalgo .10
73 Mark Kotsay .10
74 Mike Cameron .10
75 Troy Glaus .40
76 Matt Holliday .10
77 Byung-Hyun Kim .10
78 Aaron Sele .10
79 Danny Graves .10
80 Barry Zito .40
81 Matt LeCroy .10
82 Jason Isringhausen .10
83 Colby Lewis .10
84 Franklyn German .10
85 Luis Matos .10
86 Mike Timlin .10
87 Miguel Batista .10
88 John McDonald .10
89 Joey Eischen .10
90 Mike Mussina .50
91 Jack Wilson .20
92 Aaron Cook .10
93 John Parrish .10
94 Jose Valentin .10
95 Johnny Damon .20
96 Pat Burrell .25
97 Brendan Donnelly .10
98 Lance Carter .10
99 Omar Daal .10
100 Ichiro Suzuki 1.00
101 Robin Ventura .10
102 Brian Shouse .10
103 Kevin Jarvis .10
104 Jason Young .10
105 Moises Alou .25
106 Wes Obermueller .10
107 David Segui .10
108 Mike MacDougal .10
109 John Buck .10
110 Gary Sheffield .25
111 Yorvit Torrealba .10
112 Matt Kata .10
113 David Bell .10
114 Juan Gonzalez .40
115 Kelvim Escobar .10
116 Ruben Sierra .10
117 Todd Wellemeyer .10
118 Jamie Walker .10
119 Will Cunnane .10
120 Cliff Floyd .10
121 Aramis Ramirez .40
122 Damaso Marte .10
123 Juan Castro .10
124 Chris Woodward .10
125 Andruw Jones .50
126 Ben Weber .10
127 Dee Brown .10
128 Steve Reed .10
129 Gabe Kapler .10
130 Miguel Cabrera .75
131 Billy McMillon .10
132 Julio Mateo .10
133 Preston Wilson .10
134 Tony Clark .10
135 Carlos Lee .20
136 Carlos Baerga .10
137 Mike Crudale .10
138 David Ross .10
139 Josh Fogg .10
140 Dmitri Young .10
141 Cliff Lee .10
142 Mike Lowell .25
143 Jason Lane .10
144 Pedro Feliz .10
145 Ken Griffey Jr. 1.00
146 Dustin Hermanson .10
147 Scott Hodges .10
148 Aquilino Lopez .10
149 Wes Helms .10
150 Jason Giambi .50
151 Erasmo Ramirez .10
152 Sean Burroughs .10
153 J.T. Snow .10
154 Eddie Guardado .10
155 C.C. Sabathia .10
156 Kyle Lohse .10
157 Roberto Hernandez .10
158 Jason Simontacchi .10
159 Tim Spooneybarger .10
160 Alfonso Soriano .50
161 Mike Gonzalez .10
162 Alex Cora .10
163 Kevin Gryboski .10
164 Steve Cox .10
165 Luis Castillo .10
166 Odalis Perez .10
167 Alex Sanchez .10
168 Robert Mackowiak .10
169 Francisco Rodriguez .10
170 Roy Oswalt .25
171 Omar Infante .10
172 Ryan Jensen .10
173 Ben Broussard .10
174 Mark Hendrickson .10
175 Manny Ramirez .50
176 Rob Bell .10
177 Adam Everett .10
178 Chris George .10
179 Ricky Gutierrez .10
180 Eric Gagne .40
181 Scott Schoeneweis .10
182 Kris Benson .10
183 Amaury Telemaco .10
184 John Riedling .10
185 Juan Pierre .10
186 Ramon Ortiz .10
187 Luis Rivas .10
188 Larry Bigbie .10
189 Robby Hammock .10
190 Geoff Jenkins .20
191 Chad Cordero .10
192 Mark Ellis .10
193 Mark Loretta .10
194 Ryan Drese .10
195 Lance Berkman .10
196 Kevin Appier .10
197 Enrique Calero (Kiko) .10
198 Mickey Callaway .10
199 Chase Utley .10
200 Nomar Garciaparra 1.00
201 Kevin Cash .10
202 Ramiro Mendoza .10
203 Shane Reynolds .10
204 Chris Spurling .10
205 Aaron Guiel .10
206 Mark Derosa .10
207 Adam Kennedy .10
208 Andy Pettitte .25
209 Rafael Palmeiro .50
210 Luis Gonzalez .25
211 Ryan Franklin .10
212 Bob Wickman .10
213 Ron Calloway .10
214 Jae Weong Seo .10
215 Kazuhisa Ishii .10
216 Sterling Hitchcock .10
217 Jimmy Gobble .10
218 Chad Moeller .10
219 Jake Peavy .10
220 John Smoltz .25
221 Erick Almonte .10
222 David Wells .10
223 Brad Lidge .10
224 Carlos Zambrano .25
225 Kerry Wood .75
226 Alex Cintron .10
227 Javier Lopez .25
228 Jeremy Griffiths .10
229 Jon Garland .10
230 Curt Schilling .50
231 Alex Gonzalez .10
232 Jay Gibbons .10
233 Damian Jackson .10
234 Jeriome Robertson .10
235 Johan Santana .10
236 Jose Guillen .10
237 Jeff Connie .10
238 Matt Roney .10
239 Desi Relaford .10
240 Frank Thomas .50
241 Danny Patterson .10
242 Kevin Mench .10
243 Mike Redmond .10
244 Jeff Suppan .10
245 Carl Everett .10
246 Jack Cressend .10
247 Matt Mantei .10
248 Enrique Wilson .10
249 Craig Counsell .10
250 Mark Prior 1.50
251 Jared Sandberg .10
252 Scott Strickland .10
253 Lew Ford .10
254 Hee Seop Choi .10
255 Jason Phillips .10
256 Jason Jennings .10
257 Todd Pratt .10
258 Matt Herges .10
259 Kerry Ligtenberg .10
260 Austin Kearns .25
261 Jay Witasick .10
262 Tony Armas Jr. .10
263 Tom Martin .10
264 Oliver Perez .10
265 Jorge Posada .40
266 Joe Beimel .10
267 Ben Hendrickson .10
268 Reggie Sanders .10
269 Julio Lugo .10
270 Josh Beckett .40
271 Kyle Snyder .10
272 Felipe Lopez .10
273 Kevin Millar .10
274 Travis Hafner .20
275 Magglio Ordonez .25
276 Marlon Byrd .10
277 Scott Spiezio .10
278 Mark Corey .10
279 Tim Salmon .25
280 Alex Gonzalez .10
281 Marquis Grissom .20
282 Miguel Olivo .10
283 Orlando Hudson .10
284 Rondell White .20
285 Jermaine Dye .10
286 Paul Shuey .10
287 Brandon Inge .10
288 B.J. Surhoff .10
289 Edgar Gonzalez .10
290 Angel Berroa .10
291 Claudio Vargas .10
292 Cesar Izturis .10
293 Brandon Phillips .10
294 Jeff Duncan .10

No.	Player	Price
295	Randy Wolf	.10
296	Barry Larkin	.25
297	Felix Rodriguez	.10
298	Robb Quinlan	.10
299	Brian Jordan	.10
300	Dontrelle Willis	.25
301	Doug Davis	.10
302	Ricky Stone	.10
303	Travis Harper	.10
304	Jaret Wright	.10
305	Edgardo Alfonzo	.10
306	Quinton McCracken	.10
307	Jason Bay	.10
308	Joe Randa	.10
309	Steve Sparks	.10
310	Roy Halladay	.25
311	Antonio Alfonseca	.10
312	Michael Cuddyer	.10
313	John Patterson	.10
314	Chris Widger	.10
315	Shigetoshi Hasegawa	.10
316	Tim Wakefield	.10
317	Scott Hatteberg	.10
318	Mike Remlinger	.10
319	Jose Vizcaino	.10
320	Rocco Baldelli	.25
321	David Riske	.10
322	Steve Karsay	.10
323	Peter Bergeron	.10
324	Jeff Weaver	.10
325	Larry Walker	.25
326	Jack Cust	.10
327	Bo Hart	.10
328	Rod Beck	.10
329	Jose Acevedo	.10
330	Hank Blalock	.40
331	Flash Gordon	.10
332	Brian Fuentes	.10
333	Tomas Perez	.10
334	Lenny Harris	.10
335	Matt Morris	.25
336	Jeremi Gonzalez	.10
337	David Eckstein	.10
338	Aaron Rowand	.10
339	Rick Bauer	.10
340	Jim Edmonds	.25
341	Joe Borowski	.10
342	Eric Dubose	.10
343	D'Angelo Jimenez	.10
344	Tomokazu Ohka	.10
345	Victor Zambrano	.10
346	Joe McEwing	.10
347	Jorge Sosa	.10
348	Keith Ginter	.10
349	A.J. Pierzynski	.10
350	Mike Sweeney	.10
351	Shawn Chacon	.10
352	Matt Clement	.25
353	Vance Wilson	.10
354	Benito Santiago	.10
355	Eric Hinske	.10
356	Vladimir Guerrero	.75
357	Kenny Rogers	.10
358	Aaron Boone	.10
359	Jay Powell	.10
360	Phil Nevin	.10
361	Willie Harris	.10
362	Ty Wigginton	.10
363	Chad Fox	.10
364	Junior Spivey	.10
365	Brandon Webb	.10
366	Brett Myers	.10
367	Alexis Gomez	.10
368	Dave Roberts	.10
369	LaTroy Hawkins	.10
370	Kevin Millwood	.25
371	Brian Schneider	.10
372	Blaine Neal	.10
373	Jeromy Burnitz	.10
374	Ted Lilly	.10
375	Shawn Green	.25
376	Carlos Pena	.10
377	Gil Meche	.10
378	Jeff Bagwell	.50
379	Alex Escobar	.10
380	Erubiel Durazo	.10
381	Cristian Guzman	.10
382	Rocky Biddle	.10
383	Craig Wilson	.25
384	Rey Sanchez	.10
385	Russ Ortiz	.10
386	Freddy Garcia	.10
387	Luis Vizcaino	.10
388	David Ortiz	.40
389	Jose Molina	.10
390	Edgar Martinez	.25
391	Nate Bump	.10
392	Brent Mayne	.10
393	Ray King	.10
394	Paul Wilson	.10
395	Melvin Mora	.10
396	Morgan Ensberg	.10
397	Ramon Hernandez	.10
398	Juan Rincon	.10
399	Ron Mahay	.10
400	Jeff Kent	.25
401	Cal Eldred	.10
402	Mike Difelice	.10
403	Valerio De Los Santos	.10
404	Steve Finley	.10
405	Trot Nixon	.25
406	Kevin Walker	.10
407	John Vander Wal	.10
408	Ray Durham	.10
409	Aaron Heilman	.10
410	Edgar Renteria	.25
411	Mike Hampton	.10
412	Kirk Rueter	.10
413	Jim Mecir	.10
414	Brian Roberts	.10
415	Paul Konerko	.10
416	Reed Johnson	.10
417	Roger Clemens	1.50
418	Coco Crisp	.10
419	Carlos Hernandez	.10
420	Scott Podsednik	.40
421	Miguel Cairo	.10
422	Abraham Nunez	.10
423	Endy Chavez	.10
424	Eric Munson	.10
425	Torii Hunter	.25
426	Ben Howard	.10
427	Chris Gomez	.10
428	Francisco Cordero	.10
429	Jeffrey Hammonds	.10
430	Shannon Stewart	.10
431	Einar Diaz	.10
432	Eric Byrnes	.10
433	Marty Cordova	.10
434	Matt Ginter	.10
435	Victor Martinez	.10
436	Geronimo Gil	.10
437	Grant Balfour	.10
438	Ramon Vazquez	.10
439	Jose Cruz	.10
440	Orlando Cabrera	.10
441	Joe Kennedy	.10
442	Scott Williamson	.10
443	Troy Percival	.10
444	Derrek Lee	.25
445	Runelvys Hernandez	.10
446	Mark Grudzielanek	.10
447	Trey Hodges	.10
448	Jimmy Haynes	.10
449	Eric Milton	.10
450	Todd Helton	.50
451	Greg Zaun	.10
452	Woody Williams	.10
453	Todd Walker	.10
454	Gary Matthews	.10
455	Fernando Vina	.10
456	Omar Vizquel	.10
457	Roberto Alomar	.40
458	Bill Hall	.10
459	Juan Rivera	.10
460	Tom Glavine	.40
461	Ramon Castro	.10
462	Cory Vance	.10
463	Dan Miceli	.10
464	Lyle Overbay	.25
465	Craig Biggio	.25
466	Ricky Ledee	.10
467	Michael Barrett	.10
468	Jason Anderson	.10
469	Matt Stairs	.10
470	Jarrod Washburn	.10
471	Todd Hundley	.10
472	Grant Roberts	.10
473	Randy Winn	.10
474	Pat Hentgen	.10
475	Jose Vidro	.10
476	Tony Torcato	.10
477	Jeremy Affeldt	.10
478	Carlos Guillen	.10
479	Paul Quantrill	.10
480	Rafael Furcal	.10
481	Adam Melhuse	.10
482	Jerry Hairston	.10
483	Adam Bernero	.10
484	Terrence Long	.10
485	Paul Lo Duca	.10
486	Corey Koskie	.10
487	John Lackey	.10
488	Chad Zerbe	.10
489	Vinny Castilla	.10
490	Corey Patterson	.20
491	John Olerud	.20
492	Josh Bard	.10
493	Darren Dreifort	.10
494	Jason Standridge	.10
495	Ben Sheets	.25
496	Jose Castillo	.10
497	Jay Payton	.10
498	Rob Bowen	.10
499	Bobby Higginson	.10
500	Alex Rodriguez	1.50
501	Octavio Dotel	.10
502	Rheal Cormier	.10
503	Felix Heredia	.10
504	Dan Wright	.10
505	Michael Young	.10
506	Wilfredo Ledezma	.10
507	Sun-Woo Kim	.10
508	Michael Tejera	.10
509	Herbert Perry	.10
510	Esteban Loaiza	.10
511	Alan Embree	.10
512	Ben Davis	.10
513	Greg Colbrunn	.10
514	Josh Hall	.10
515	Raul Ibanez	.10
516	Jayson Werth	.10
517	Corky Miller	.10
518	Jason Marquis	.10
519	Roger Cedeno	.10
520	Adam Dunn	.50
521	Paul Byrd	.10
522	Sandy Alomar	.10
523	Salomon Torres	.10
524	John Halama	.10
525	Mike Piazza	1.00
526	Buddy Groom	.10
527	Adrian Beltre	.25
528	Chad Harville	.10
529	Javier Vazquez	.20
530	Jody Gerut	.10
531	Elmer Dessens	.10
532	B.J. Ryan	.10
533	Chad Durbin	.10
534	Doug Mirabelli	.10
535	Bernie Williams	.40
536	Jeff Davanon	.10
537	Dave Berg	.10
538	Geoff Blum	.10
539	John Thomson	.10
540	Jeremy Bonderman	.10
541	Jeff Zimmerman	.10
542	Derek Lowe	.10
543	Scot Shields	.10
544	Michael Tucker	.10
545	Tim Hudson	.40
546	Ryan Ludwick	.10
547	Rick Reed	.10
548	Placido Palanco	.10
549	Tony Graffanino	.10
550	Garret Anderson	.40
551	Timoniel Perez	.10
552	Jesus Colome	.10
553	R.A. Dickey	.10
554	Tim Worrell	.10
555	Jason Kendall	.10
556	Tom Goodwin	.10
557	Joaquin Benoit	.10
558	Stephen Randolph	.10
559	Miguel Tejada	.40
560	A.J. Burnett	.10
561	Ben Diggins	.10
562	Juan Cruz	.10
563	Zach Day	.10
564	Antonio Perez	.10
565	Jason Schmidt	.25
566	Armando Benitez	.10
567	Denny Neagle	.10
568	Eric Eckenstahler	.10
569	Chan Ho Park	.10
570	Carlos Beltran	.40
571	Brett Tomko	.10
572	Henry Mateo	.10
573	Ken Harvey	.10
574	Matt Lawton	.10
575	Mariano Rivera	.25
576	Darrell May	.10
577	Jamie Moyer	.10
578	Paul Bako	.10
579	Cory Lidle	.10
580	Jacque Jones	.10
581	Jolbert Cabrera	.10
582	Jason Grimsley	.10
583	Danny Kolb	.10
584	Billy Wagner	.10
585	Rich Aurilia	.10
586	Vicente Padilla	.10
587	Oscar Villarreal	.10
588	Rene Reyes	.10
589	Jon Lieber	.10
590	Nick Johnson	.10
591	Bobby Crosby	.10
592	Steve Trachsel	.10
593	Brian Boehringer	.10
594	Juan Uribe	.10
595	Bartolo Colon	.20
596	Bobby Hill	.10
597	Andy Van Hekken	.10
598	Carl Pavano	.10
599	Kurt Ainsworth	.10
600	Derek Jeter	2.00
601	Doug Mientkiewicz	.10
602	Orlando Pameiro	.10
603	J.C. Romero	.10
604	Scott Sullivan	.10
605	Brad Radke	.10
606	Fernando Rodney	.10
607	Jim Brower	.10
608	Josh Towers	.10
609	Brad Fullmer	.10
610	Jose Reyes	.10
611	Ryan Wagner	.10
612	Joe Mays	.10
613	Jung Bong	.10
614	Curtis Leskanic	.10
615	Al Leiter	.10
616	Wade Miller	.10
617	Keith Foulke	.10
618	Casey Fossum	.10
619	Craig Monroe	.10
620	Hideo Nomo	.25
621	Bob File	.10
622	Steve Kline	.10
623	Bobby Kielty	.10
624	Dewon Brazelton	.10
625	Eric Chavez	.25
626	Chris Carpenter	.10
627	Trever Miller	.10
628	Jason Davis	.10
629	Jose Jimenez	.10
630	Vernon Wells	.10
631	Kenny Lofton	.25
632	Chad Bradford	.10
633	Brad Wilkerson	.10
634	Pokey Reese	.10
635	Richie Sexson	.40
636	Chin-Hui Tsao	.10
637	Eli Marrero	.10
638	Chris Reitsma	.10
639	Daryle Ward	.10
640	Mark Teixeira	.25
641	Corwin Malone	.10
642	Adam Eaton	.10
643	Jimmy Rollins	.10
644	Brian Anderson	.10
645	Bill Mueller	.10
646	Jake Westbrook	.10
647	Bengie Molina	.10
648	Jorge Julio	.10
649	Billy Traber	.10
650	Randy Johnson	.75
651	Javy Lopez	.25
652	Doug Glanville	.10
653	Jeff Cirillo	.10
654	Tino Martinez	.10
655	Mark Buehrle	.10
656	Jason Michaels	.10
657	Damian Rolls	.10
658	Rosman Garcia	.10
659	Scott Hairston	.10
660	Carl Crawford	.10
661	Livan Hernandez	.10
662	Danny Bautista	.10
663	Brad Ausmus	.10
664	Juan Acevedo	.10
665	Sean Casey	.10
666	Pedro Martinez	.75
667	Milton Bradley	.10
668	Braden Looper	.10
669	Paul Abbott	.10
670	Joel Pinero	.10
671	Luis Terrero	.10
672	Rodrigo Lopez	.10
673	Joe Crede	.10
674	Mike Koplove	.10
675	Brian Giles	.25
676	Jeff Nelson	.10
677	Russell Branyan	.10
678	Mike DeJean	.10
679	Brian Daubach	.10
680	Ellis Burks	.10
681	Ryan Dempster	.10
682	Cliff Politte	.10
683	Brian Reith	.10
684	Scott Stewart	.10
685	Allan Simpson	.10
686	Shawn Estes	.10
687	Jason Johnson	.10
688	Wil Cordero	.10
689	Kelly Stinnett	.10
690	Jose Lima	.10

691	Gary Bennett	.10
692	T.J. Tucker	.10
693	Shane Spencer	.10
694	Chris Hammond	.10
695	Chris Singleton	.10
696	Xavier Nady	.10
697	Cody Ransom	.10
698	Ron Villone	.10
699	Brook Fordyce	.10
700	Sammy Sosa	1.50
701	Terry Adams	.10
702	Ricardo Rincon	.10
703	Tike Redman	.10
704	Chris Stynes	.10
705	Mark Redman	.10
706	Juan Encarnacion	.10
707	Jhonny Peralta	.10
708	Denny Hocking	.10
709	Ivan Rodriguez	.50
710	Jose Hernandez	.10
711	Brandon Duckworth	.10
712	Dave Burba	.10
713	Joe Nathan	.10
714	Dan Smith	.10
715	Karim Garcia	.10
716	Arthur Rhodes	.10
717	Shawn Wooten	.10
718	Ramon Santiago	.10
719	Luis Ugueto	.10
720	Danys Baez	.10
721	Alfredo Amezaga	.10
722	Sidney Ponson	.10
723	Joe Mauer	.40
724	Jesse Foppert	.10
725	Todd Greene	.10
726	Dan Haren	.10
727	Brandon Larson	.10
728	Bobby Jenks	.10
729	Grady Sizemore	.10
730	Ben Grieve	.10
731	Khalil Greene	.10
732	Chad Gaudin	.10
733	Johnny Estrada	.10
734	Joe Valentine	.10
735	Tim Raines	.10
736	Brandon Claussen	.10
737	Sam Marsonek	.10
738	Delmon Young	.25
739	David Dellucci	.10
740	Sergio Mitre	.10
741	Nick Neugebauer	.10
742	Laynce Nix	.10
743	Joe Thurston	.10
744	Ryan Langerhans	.10
745	Pete LaForest	.10
746	Arnie Munoz	.10
747	Rickie Weeks	.25
748	Neal Cotts	.10
749	Jonny Gomes	.10
750	Jim Thome	.75
751	Jon Rauch	.10
752	Edwin Jackson	.10
753	Ryan Madson	.10
754	Chad Tracy	.10
755	Eddie Perez	.10
756	Joe Borchard	.10
757	Jeremy Guthrie	.10
758	Jose Mesa	.10
759	Doug Waechter	.10
760	J.D. Drew	.25
761	Adam LaRoche	.10
762	Rich Harden	.10
763	Justin Speier	.10
764	Todd Zeile	.10
765	Turk Wendell	.10
766	Mark Bellhorn	.10
767	Mike Jackson	.10
768	Chone Figgins	.10
769	Mike Neu	.10
770	Greg Maddux	.10
771	Frank Brooks	.10
772	*Alec Zumwalt*	.25
773	Glendon Rusch	.10
774	Dustan Mohr	.10
775	Shane Halter	.10
776	Tom Wilson	.10
777	So Taguchi	.10
778	Eric Karros	.10
779	Ramon Nivar	.10
780	Marlon Anderson	.10
781	*Brayan Pena*	.10
782	Chris O'Riordan	.10
783	*Dioner Navarro*	1.50
784	*Alberto Callaspo*	.50
785	*Hector Gimenez*	.25
786	*Yadier Molina*	.40
787	Kevin Richardson	.25
788	Brian Pilkington	.40
789	Adam Greenberg	.50
790	*Ervin Santana*	1.00
791	Brent Colamarino	.75
792	Ben Himes	.10
793	*Todd Self*	.25
794	Brad Vericker	.25
795	*Donald Kelly*	.25
796	Brock Jacobsen	.25
797	Brock Peterson	.25
798	Carlos Sosa	.50
799	Chad Chop	.10
800	Matt Moses	1.00
801	*Chris Aguila*	.25
802	David Murphy	.50
803	*Don Sutton*	1.00
804	Jereme Milons	.10
805	Jon Coutlangus	.10
806	Greg Thissen	.10
807	*Jose Capellan*	1.00
808	*Chad Santos*	.10
809	*Wardell Starling*	.10
810	Kevin Kouzmanoff	.50
811	Kevin Davidson	.40
812	Michael Mooney	.10
813	Rodney Choy Foo	.10
814	Reid Gorecki	.10
815	*Rudy Guillen*	1.00
816	Harvey Garcia	.10
817	*Warner Madrigal*	.50
818	Kenny Perez	.10
819	*Joaquin Arias*	.10
820	Benji Dequin	.40
821	Lastings Milledge	1.50
822	*Blake Hawksworth*	.50
823	*Estee Harris*	.50
824	*Bobby Brownlie*	.75
825	*Wanell Severino*	.10
826	Bobby Madritsch	.10
827	Travis Hanson	.40
828	*Brandon Medders*	.40
829	*Kevin Howard*	.50
830	Brian Steffek	.10
831	Terry Jones	.10
832	Anthony Acevedo	.40
833	Kory Casto	.10
834	Brooks Conrad	.10
835	Juan Gutierrez	.10
836	*Charlie Zink*	.40
837	David Aardsma	.40
838	Carl Loadenthal	.10
839	Donald Levinski	.10
840	*Dustin Nippert*	.75
841	Calvin Hayes	.10
842	*Felix Hernandez*	6.00
843	Tyler Davidson	.50
844	*George Sherrill*	.10
845	*Craig Ansman*	.10
846	Jeffrey Allison	.50
847	*Tommy Murphy*	.10
848	*Jerome Gamble*	.40
849	*Jesse English*	.10
850	*Alex Romero*	.40
851	Joel Zumaya	1.50
852	Carlos Quentin	1.00
853	Jose Valdez	.25
854	J.J. Furmaniak	.75
855	*Juan Cedeno*	.25
856	Kyle Sleeth	1.00
857	*Josh Labandeira*	.25
858	Lee Gwaltney	.10
859	*Lincoln Holdzkom*	.25
860	*Ivan Ochoa*	.10
861	Luke Anderson	.10
862	Conor Jackson	1.00
863	Matt Capps	.75
864	*Merkin Valdez*	.75
865	Paul Bacot	.50
866	*Erick Aybar*	.50
867	*Scott Proctor*	1.00
868	Tim Stauffer	.50
869	*Matt Creighton*	.50
870	Zach Miner	.50
871	*Danny Gonzalez*	.10
872	Tom Farmer	.10
873	John Santor	.10
874	*Logan Kensing*	.25
875	*Vito Chiaravalloti*	.50
876	Checklist	.10
877	Checklist	.10
878	Checklist	.10
879	Checklist	.10
880	Checklist	.10

Silver

Stars: 2-3X
Inserted 1:1

Press Plates

No Pricing
Production one for each color

Autograph

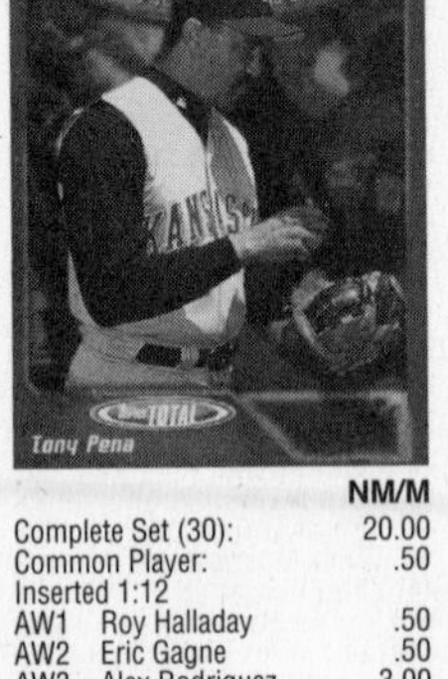

		NM/M
Inserted 1:414		8.00
GB	Grant Balfour	8.00
LB	Larry Bigbie	10.00
BC	Brandon Claussen	8.00
TH	Toby Hall	8.00
JJ	Jimmy Journell	8.00

Total Award Winners

		NM/M
Complete Set (30):		20.00
Common Player:		.50
Inserted 1:12		
AW1	Roy Halladay	.50
AW2	Eric Gagne	.50
AW3	Alex Rodriguez	3.00
AW4	Albert Pujols	3.00
AW5	Alex Rodriguez	3.00
AW6	Jorge Posada	.50
AW7	Javy Lopez	.50
AW8	Carlos Delgado	.50
AW9	Todd Helton	.75
AW10	Bret Boone	.50
AW11	Jose Vidro	.50
AW12	Bill Mueller	.50
AW13	Mike Lowell	.50
AW14	Alex Rodriguez	3.00
AW15	Edgar Renteria	.50
AW16	Garret Anderson	.50
AW17	Albert Pujols	3.00
AW18	Manny Ramirez	1.00
AW19	Vernon Wells	.50
AW20	Gary Sheffield	.50
AW21	Edgar Martinez	.50
AW22	Mike Hampton	.50
AW23	Angel Berroa	.50
AW24	Dontrelle Willis	.50
AW25	Keith Foulke	.50
AW26	Eric Gagne	.50
AW27	Alex Rodriguez	3.00
AW28	Albert Pujols	3.00
AW29	Tony Pena	.50
AW30	Jack McKeon	.50

Total Production

		NM/M
Complete Set (10):		10.00
Common Player:		.50
Inserted 1:18		
TP1	Alex Rodriguez	3.00
TP2	Albert Pujols	3.00
TP3	Sammy Sosa	2.50
TP4	Carlos Delgado	.50
TP5	Gary Sheffield	.50
TP6	Manny Ramirez	1.00
TP7	Jim Thome	1.00
TP8	Todd Helton	.75
TP9	Garret Anderson	.50
TP10	Nomar Garciaparra	2.00

Total Topps

		NM/M
Complete Set (50):		25.00
Common Player:		.50
Inserted 1:7		
TT1	Derek Jeter	3.00
TT2	Jose Reyes	.50
TT3	Miguel Tejada	.50
TT4	Larry Walker	.50
TT5	Frank Thomas	.75
TT6	Carlos Delgado	.50
TT7	Vernon Wells	.50
TT8	Jeff Bagwell	.75
TT9	Jason Giambi	.75
TT10	Mike Lowell	.50
TT11	Shannon Stewart	.50
TT12	Mike Piazza	1.50
TT13	Todd Helton	.75
TT14	Austin Kearns	.50
TT15	Jim Edmonds	.50
TT16	Jose Vidro	.50
TT17	Andruw Jones	.50
TT18	Gary Sheffield	.50
TT19	Eric Chavez	.50
TT20	Magglio Ordonez	.50
TT21	Geoff Jenkins	.50
TT22	Ken Griffey Jr.	1.50
TT23	Jeff Kent	.50
TT24	Jorge Posada	.50
TT25	Albert Pujols	2.00
TT26	Javy Lopez	.50
TT27	Alfonso Soriano	1.00
TT28	Brian Giles	.50
TT29	Mike Sweeney	.50
TT30	Miguel Cabrera	1.00
TT31	Luis Gonzalez	.50
TT32	Scott Rolen	1.00
TT33	Jim Thome	1.00
TT34	Garret Anderson	.75
TT35	Vladimir Guerrero	1.00
TT36	Shawn Green	.50
TT37	Hank Blalock	.75
TT38	Marcus Giles	.50
TT39	Torii Hunter	.50
TT40	Sammy Sosa	2.00
TT41	Nomar Garciaparra	2.00
TT42	Bobby Abreu	.50
TT43	Richie Sexson	.50
TT44	Manny Ramirez	.75
TT45	Troy Glaus	.75
TT46	Preston Wilson	.50
TT47	Ivan Rodriguez	.75
TT48	Ichiro Suzuki	1.50
TT49	Chipper Jones	1.00
TT50	Alex Rodriguez	3.00

2004 TOPPS TRIBUTE HOF

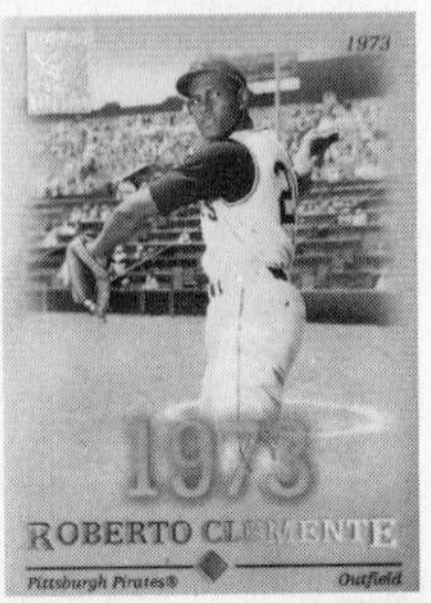

	NM/M
Complete Set (80):	120.00

Common Player: 2.00
Pack (5): 50.00
Box (6): 260.00
1 Willie Mays 8.00
2 Richie Ashburn 2.00
3 Babe Ruth 10.00
4 Lou Gehrig 8.00
5 Carl Yastrzemski 5.00
6 Fergie Jenkins 2.00
7 Cool Papa Bell 3.00
8 Johnny Bench 4.00
9 Satchel Paige 4.00
10 Ty Cobb 6.00
11 Robin Roberts 2.00
12 Eddie Mathews 3.00
13 Tom Seaver 3.00
14 Kirby Puckett 3.00
15 Stan Musial 5.00
16 Ralph Kiner 2.00
17 Reggie Jackson 3.00
18 Walter Johnson 4.00
19 Phil Niekro 2.00
20 Mike Schmidt 6.00
21 Brooks Robinson 3.00
22 Jimmie Foxx 4.00
23 Nellie Fox 2.00
24 Joe Morgan 2.00
25 Cy Young 3.00
26 Hank Greenberg 3.00
27 Josh Gibson 3.00
28 Robin Yount 5.00
29 Hoyt Wilhelm 2.00
30 Yogi Berra 3.00
31 Rollie Fingers 2.00
32 Gaylord Perry 2.00
33 Ozzie Smith 4.00
34 Jim Palmer 2.00
35 Harmon Killebrew 4.00
36 Bob Feller 2.00
37 Chuck Klein 2.00
38 Mordecai Brown 2.00
39 Napoleon Lajoie 2.00
40 Al Kaline 3.00
41 Paul Molitor 3.00
42 Jackie Robinson 5.00
43 Mel Ott 3.00
44 Hank Aaron 8.00
45 Rod Carew 2.00
46 Rogers Hornsby 3.00
47 Bob Gibson 3.00
48 Juan Marichal 2.00
49 Bill Mazeroski 2.00
50 Roberto Clemente 8.00
51 Willie McCovey 2.00
52 Red Schoendienst 2.00
53 Nolan Ryan 8.00
54 Dennis Eckersley 2.00
55 Monte Irvin 2.00
56 George Kell 2.00
57 Gary Carter 2.00
58 Tony Perez 2.00
59 Carlton Fisk 2.00
60 Duke Snider 3.00
61 Bobby Doerr 2.00
62 John McGraw 2.00
63 George Sisler 2.00
64 Orlando Cepeda 2.00
65 Earl Weaver 2.00
66 Roy Campanella 3.00
67 Tris Speaker 3.00
68 Sparky Anderson 2.00
69 Willie Stargell 2.00
70 Honus Wagner 3.00
71 Lou Brock 2.00
72 Whitey Ford 3.00
73 George Brett 8.00
74 Luis Aparicio 2.00
75 Ernie Banks 4.00
76 Jim Bunning 2.00
77 Warren Spahn 3.00
78 Jim "Catfish" Hunter 2.00
79 Pee Wee Reese 2.00
80 Frank Robinson 2.00

Gold

Gold print run 61-99: 2-3X
Gold p/r 36-60: 2-4X
#'d to last 2 digits of HOF induction yr

Cooperstown Cut Signatures

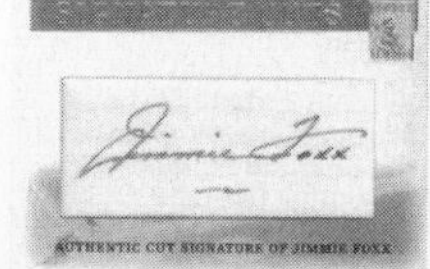

No Pricing
Production one set

Cooperstown Classmates Dual Reli

NM/M
Common Duo: 20.00
Gold: .75-1.5X
Production 25
ME Paul Molitor, Dennis Eckersley/75 35.00
KK Chuck Klein, Al Kaline/75 35.00
RB Nolan Ryan, George Brett/50 60.00
MP Joe Morgan, Jim Palmer/75 20.00
RC Babe Ruth, Ty Cobb/5
SK Duke Snider, Al Kaline/50 60.00
PC Gaylord Perry, Rod Carew/50 30.00
BY Johnny Bench, Carl Yastrzemski/75 50.00
CR Orlando Cepeda, Nolan Ryan/75 60.00
OF Mel Ott, Jimmie Foxx/5
MR Juan Marichal, Brooks Robinson/50 35.00

Cut Signatures

No Pricing
Production one set

Dual Cut Signatures

No Pricing
Production one set

Hall of Fame Patches Relics

NM/M
Common Player: 20.00
Gold: .75-1.5X
Production 1-25
No pricing for production 15 or less
GB George Brett/50 40.00
LB Lou Brock/17
RC Rod Carew/100 25.00
DE Dennis Eckersley/50 25.00
RJ Reggie Jackson/50 25.00
FR Frank Robinson/39 35.00
NR Nolan Ryan/100 50.00
MS Mike Schmidt/100 40.00
MS2 Mike Schmidt/100 40.00
OS Ozzie Smith/10
RY Robin Yount/35 40.00

Tribute Relics

NM/M
Common Player: 10.00
Golds: 1-3X
Production 25 sets
HA Hank Aaron/bat 30.00
JB Johnny Bench/jsy/250 15.00
JB2 Johnny Bench/jsy 10.00
GB George Brett/jsy 15.00
GBB George Brett/bat 15.00
LBB Lou Brock/bat 10.00
GC Gary Carter/jsy/200 10.00
GCU Gary Carter/jsy 10.00
OC Orlando Cepeda/bat/100 20.00
RC Roberto Clemente/bat 50.00
TC Ty Cobb/jsy/20 275.00
TCB Ty Cobb/bat 75.00
CF Carlton Fisk/wall/300 20.00
WF Whitey Ford/jsy/50 60.00
JF Jimmie Foxx/bat/25 100.00
LG Lou Gehrig/bat/52 300.00
BG Bob Gibson/jsy 15.00
HG Hank Greenberg/bat 20.00
RH Rogers Hornsby/bat 40.00
RJ Reggie Jackson/jsy/110 15.00
RJB Reggie Jackson/bat/200 10.00
AK Al Kaline/jsy/125 20.00
AKB Al Kaline/bat 15.00
HK Harmon Killebrew/bat/135 30.00
CK Chuck Klein/bat/107 20.00
JMA Juan Marichal/jsy/125 10.00
WM1 Willie Mays/glove/110 150.00
WM2 Willie Mays/bat 30.00
WM3 Willie Mays/bat 30.00
WM4 Willie Mays/jsy 30.00
WM5 Willie Mays/jsy 30.00
PM Paul Molitor/jsy 10.00
PMB Paul Molitor/bat 10.00
JM Joe Morgan/bat 10.00
SM Stan Musial/jsy 20.00
MO Mel Ott/bat/25 100.00
JP Jim Palmer/jsy 10.00
JP2 Jim Palmer/jsy 10.00
KP Kirby Puckett/jsy/175 15.00
KPB Kirby Puckett/bat 10.00
BRO Brooks Robinson/bat 10.00
FR Frank Robinson/jsy 10.00
FRA Frank Robinson/jsy 10.00
FRB Frank Robinson/bat 10.00
JR Jackie Robinson/bat 25.00
BR Babe Ruth/bat/163 150.00
NR Nolan Ryan/jsy 25.00
NRA Nolan Ryan/jsy/425 25.00
NRJ Nolan Ryan/jsy 25.00
MS Mike Schmidt/jsy/50 30.00
MSB Mike Schmidt/bat 15.00
TS Tom Seaver/jsy 10.00
GS George Sisler/bat/455 25.00
OS Ozzie Smith/bat 15.00
DS Duke Snider/bat 10.00
TSP Tris Speaker/bat/85 120.00
HW Honus Wagner/bat/118 120.00
EW Earl Weaver/jsy/25 20.00
CY Carl Yastrzemski/wall/300 30.00
CYU Carl Yastrzemski/jsy 15.00
RY Robin Yount/jsy/50 25.00

Tribute Relic Autographs

NM/M
Common Player: 40.00
Gold: No Pricing
Production 5 sets
AKB Al Kaline/95 60.00
BRO Brooks Robinson/95 50.00
NRJ Nolan Ryan/95 140.00
EW Earl Weaver/55 40.00
CYU Carl Yastrzemski/95 85.00

2005 TOPPS

NM/M
Complete Set (733): 75.00
Common Player: .10
Pack (10): 2.00
Box (36): 60.00
1 Alex Rodriguez 1.50
2 Placido Polanco .10
3 Torii Hunter .25
4 Lyle Overbay .10
5 Johnny Damon .40
6 Johnny Estrada .10
8 Francisco Rodriguez .10
9 Jason LaRue .10
10 Sammy Sosa 1.00
11 Randy Wolf .10
12 Jason Bay .10
13 Tom Glavine .25
14 Michael Tucker .10
15 Brian Giles .20
16 Dan Wilson .10
17 Jim Edmonds .40
18 Danys Baez .10
19 Roy Halladay .20
20 Hank Blalock .50
21 Darin Erstad .20
22 Robby Hammock .10
23 Mike Hampton .10
24 Mark Bellhorn .10
25 Jim Thome .50
26 Scott Schoeneweis .10
27 Jody Gerut .10
28 Vinny Castilla .10
29 Luis Castillo .10
30 Ivan Rodriguez .50
31 Craig Biggio .20
32 Joe Randa .10
33 Dave Roberts .10
34 Scott Podsednik .10
35 Cliff Floyd .10
36 Livan Hernandez .10
37 Eric Byrnes .10
38 Ricky Ledee .10
39 Jack Wilson .10
40 Gary Sheffield .40
41 Chan Ho Park .10
42 Carl Crawford .10
43 Miguel Batista .10
44 David Bell .10
45 Jeff DaVanon .10
46 Brandon Webb .10
47 Bronson Arroyo .10
48 Melvin Mora .10
49 David Ortiz .50
50 Andruw Jones .40
51 Chone Figgins .10
52 Danny Graves .10
53 Preston Wilson .10
54 Jeremy Bonderman .10
55 Chad Fox .10
56 Dan Miceli .10
57 Jimmy Gobble .10
58 Darren Dreifort .10
59 Matt LeCroy .10
60 Jose Vidro .10
61 Al Leiter .10
62 Javier Vazquez .10
63 Erubiel Durazo .10
64 Doug Glanville .10
65 Scot Shields .10
66 Edgardo Alfonzo .10
67 Ryan Franklin .10
68 Francisco Cordero .10
69 Brett Myers .10
70 Curt Schilling .50
71 Matt Kata .10
72 Mark DeRosa .10
73 Rodrigo Lopez .10
74 Tim Wakefield .10
75 Frank Thomas .50
76 Jimmy Rollins .10
77 Barry Zito .25
78 Hideo Nomo .25
79 Brad Wilkerson .10
80 Adam Dunn .50
81 Billy Traber .10
82 Fernando Vina .10
83 Nate Robertson .10
84 Brad Ausmus .10
85 Mike Sweeney .10
86 Kip Wells .10
87 Doug Mientkiewicz .10
88 Zach Day .10
89 Tony Clark .10
90 Bret Boone .10
91 Mark Loretta .10
92 Jerome Williams .10
93 Randy Winn .10
94 Marlon Anderson .10
95 Aubrey Huff .10
96 Kevin Mench .10
97 Frank Catalanotto .10
98 Flash Gordon .10
99 Scott Hatteberg .10
100 Albert Pujols 1.50
101 Jose Molina, Bengie Molina .10
102 Oscar Villarreal .10
103 Jay Gibbons .10

No.	Player	Price
104	Byung-Hyun Kim	.10
105	Joe Borowski	.10
106	Mark Grudzielanek	.10
107	Mark Buehrle	.10
108	Paul Wilson	.10
109	Ronnie Belliard	.10
110	Larry Walker	.40
111	Tim Redding	.10
112	Hee Seop Choi	.10
113	Darrell May	.10
114	Jose Hernandez	.10
115	Ben Sheets	.25
116	Johan Santana	.40
117	Billy Wagner	.20
118	Mariano Rivera	.25
119	Steve Trachsel	.10
120	Akinori Otsuka	.10
121	Bobby Kielty	.10
122	Felix Rodriguez	.10
123	Raul Ibanez	.10
124	Mike Matheny	.10
125	Vernon Wells	.10
126	Jason Isringhausen	.10
127	Jose Guillen	.10
128	Danny Bautista	.10
129	Marcus Giles	.10
130	Javy Lopez	.25
131	Kevin Millar	.10
132	Kyle Farnsworth	.10
133	Carl Pavano	.10
134	D'Angelo Jimenez	.10
135	Casey Blake	.10
136	Matt Holliday	.10
137	Bobby Higginson	.10
138	Ramon Castro	.10
139	Alex Gonzalez	.10
140	Jeff Kent	.20
141	Aaron Guiel	.10
142	Shawn Green	.25
143	Bill Hall	.10
144	Shannon Stewart	.10
145	Juan Rivera	.10
146	Ty Wigginton	.10
147	Mike Mussina	.50
148	Eric Chavez	.25
149	Randall Simon	.10
150	Vladimir Guerrero	.75
151	Alex Cintron	.10
152	Horacio Ramirez	.10
153	Sidney Ponson	.10
154	Trot Nixon	.10
155	Greg Maddux	1.00
156	Esteban Loaiza	.10
157	Ryan Freel	.10
158	Matt Lawton	.10
159	Shawn Chacon	.10
160	Josh Beckett	.25
161	Ken Harvey	.10
162	Juan Cruz	.10
163	Juan Encarnacion	.10
164	Wes Helms	.10
165	Brad Radke	.10
166	Claudio Vargas	.10
167	Mike Cameron	.10
168	Jose Contreras	.10
169	Bobby Crosby	.10
170	Mike Lieberthal	.10
171	Robert Mackowiak	.10
172	Sean Burroughs	.10
173	J.T. Snow Jr.	.10
174	Paul Konerko	.10
175	Luis Gonzalez	.10
176	John Lackey	.10
177	Antonio Alfonseca	.10
178	Brian Roberts	.10
179	Bill Mueller	.10
180	Carlos Lee	.10
181	Corey Patterson	.25
182	Sean Casey	.25
183	Cliff Lee	.10
184	Jason Jennings	.10
185	Dmitri Young	.10
186	Brad Penny	.10
187	Andy Pettitte	.25
188	Juan Gonzalez	.25
189	Paul LoDuca	.10
190	Jason Phillips	.10
191	Rocky Biddle	.10
192	Lew Ford	.10
193	Mark Mulder	.25
194	Bobby Abreu	.25
195	Jason Kendall	.10
196	Terrence Long	.10
197	A.J. Pierzynski	.10
198	Eddie Guardado	.10
199	So Taguchi	.10
200	Jason Giambi	.25
201	Tony Batista	.10
202	Kyle Lohse	.10
203	Trevor Hoffman	.10
204	Tike Redman	.10
205	Neifi Perez	.10
206	Gil Meche	.10
207	Chris Carpenter	.10
208	Josh Phelps	.10
209	Eric Young	.10
210	Doug Waechter	.10
211	Jarrod Washburn	.10
212	Chad Tracy	.10
213	John Smoltz	.25
214	Jorge Julio	.10
215	Alex Gonzalez	.10
216	Shingo Takatsu	.10
217	Jose Acevedo	.10
218	Jason Davis	.10
219	Shawn Estes	.10
220	Lance Berkman	.25
221	Carlos Guillen	.10
222	Jeremy Affeldt	.10
223	Cesar Izturis	.10
224	Scott Sullivan	.10
225	Kazuo Matsui	.25
226	Josh Fogg	.10
227	Jason Schmidt	.25
228	Jason Marquis	.10
229	Scott Spiezio	.10
230	Miguel Tejada	.40
231	Bartolo Colon	.10
232	Jose Valverde	.10
233	Derrek Lee	.25
234	Scott Williamson	.10
235	Joe Crede	.10
236	Cory Lidle	.10
237	Mike MacDougal	.10
238	Eric Gagne	.25
239	Alex Sanchez	.10
240	Miguel Cabrera	.75
241	Luis Rivas	.10
242	Adam Everett	.10
243	Jason Johnson	.10
244	Travis Hafner	.25
245	Jose Valentin	.10
246	Stephen Randolph	.10
247	Rafael Furcal	.25
248	Adam Kennedy	.10
249	Luis Matos	.10
250	Mark Prior	.75
251	Angel Berroa	.10
252	Phil Nevin	.10
253	Oliver Perez	.10
254	Orlando Hudson	.10
255	Victor Zambrano	.10
256	Khalil Greene	.25
257	Tim Worrell	.10
258	Carlos Zambrano	.25
259	Elmer Dessens	.10
260	Gerald Laird	.10
261	Jose Cruz Jr.	.10
262	Michael Barrett	.10
263	Michael Young (Uncorrected error - photo is Rod Barajas)	.10
264	Toby Hall	.10
265	Woody Williams	.10
266	Rich Harden	.10
267	Mike Scioscia	.10
268	Al Pedrique	.10
269	Bobby Cox	.10
270	Lee Mazzilli	.10
271	Terry Francona	.10
272	Dusty Baker	.10
273	Ozzie Guillen	.10
274	Dave Miley	.10
275	Eric Wedge	.10
276	Clint Hurdle	.10
277	Alan Trammell	.10
278	Jack McKeon	.10
279	Phil Garner	.10
280	Tony Pena	.10
281	Jim Tracy	.10
282	Ned Yost	.10
283	Ron Gardenhire	.10
284	Frank Robinson	.25
285	Art Howe	.10
286	Joe Torre	.25
287	Ken Macha	.10
288	Larry Bowa	.10
289	Lloyd McClendon	.10
290	Bruce Bochy	.10
291	Felipe Alou	.10
292	Bob Melvin	.10
293	Tony LaRussa	.10
294	Lou Piniella	.10
295	Buck Showalter	.10
296	Carlos Tosca	.10
297	*Steven Doetsch*	.10
298	*Melky Cabrera*	.75
299	*Luis Ramirez*	.10
300	*Chris Seddon*	.10
301	Nate Schierholtz	1.00
302	*Ian Kinsler*	1.50
303	*Brandon Moss*	1.50
304	*Chadd Blasko*	.10
305	*Jeremy West*	1.00
306	*Sean Marshall*	.10
307	*Matt DeSalvo*	.10
308	Ryan Sweeney	1.50
309	*Matt Lindstrom*	.10
310	*Ryan Goleski*	.50
311	*Brett Harper*	.25
312	*Chris Roberson*	.10
313	Andre Ethier	.50
314	*Chris Denorfia*	.10
315	*Ian Bladergroen*	.75
316	*Darren Fenster*	.10
317	*Kevin West*	.10
318	*Chaz Lytle*	.50
319	*James Jurries*	.10
320	*Matt Rogelstad*	.10
321	*Wade Robinson*	.10
322	Jake Dittler	.10
323	*Edgar Huerta*	.10
324	Kole Strayhorn	.10
325	*Jose Vaquedano*	.10
326	*Elvys Quezada*	.10
327	John Maine, Val Majewski	.10
328	Rickie Weeks, J.J. Hardy	.10
329	Gabe Gross, Guillermo Quiroz	.10
330	David Wright, Craig Brazell	1.50
331	Dallas McPherson, Jeff Mathis	.10
332	Randy Johnson	.10
333	Randy Johnson	.10
334	Ichiro Suzuki	.10
335	Ken Griffey Jr.	.10
336	Greg Maddux	.10
337	Ichiro Suzuki, Melvin Mora, Vladimir Guerrero	.10
338	Ichiro Suzuki, Michael Young, Vladimir Guerrero	.10
339	Manny Ramirez, Paul Konerko, David Ortiz	.10
340	Miguel Tejada, David Ortiz, Manny Ramirez	.10
341	Johan Santana, Curt Schilling, Jake Westbrook	.10
342	Johan Santana, Pedro J. Martinez, Curt Schilling	.10
343	Todd Helton, Mark Loretta, Adrian Beltre	.10
344	Juan Pierre, Mark Loretta, Jack Wilson	.10
345	Adrian Beltre, Adam Dunn, Albert Pujols	.10
346	Vinny Castilla, Scott Rolen, Albert Pujols	.10
347	Jake Peavy, Randy Johnson, Ben Sheets	.10
348	Randy Johnson, Ben Sheets, Jason Schmidt	.10
349	Postseason Highlight	.10
350	Postseason Highlight	.10
351	Postseason Highlight	.10
352	Postseason Highlight	.10
353	Postseason Highlight	.10
354	Postseason Highlight	.10
355	Postseason Highlight	.10
356	Paul Konerko	.10
357	Alfonso Soriano	.10
358	Miguel Tejada	.10
359	Melvin Mora	.10
360	Vladimir Guerrero	.10
361	Ichiro Suzuki	.10
362	Manny Ramirez	.10
363	Ivan Rodriguez	.10
364	Johan Santana	.10
365	Paul Konerko	.10
366	David Ortiz	.10
367	Bobby Crosby	.10
368	Sox Celebration WS4	1.50
369	Garret Anderson	.25
370	Randy Johnson	.75
371	Charles Thomas	.10
372	Rafael Palmeiro	.40
373	Kevin Youkilis	.10
374	Freddy Garcia	.10
375	Magglio Ordonez	.10
376	Aaron Harang	.10
377	Grady Sizemore	.10
378	Chin-Hui Tsao	.10
379	Eric Munson	.10
380	Juan Pierre	.10
381	Brad Lidge	.10
382	Brian Anderson	.10
383	Alex Cora	.10
384	Brady Clark	.10
385	Todd Helton	.40
386	Chad Cordero	.10
387	Kris Benson	.10
388	Brad Halsey	.10
389	Jermaine Dye	.10
390	Manny Ramirez	.50
391	Daryle Ward	.10
392	Adam Eaton	.10
393	Brett Tomko	.10
394	Bucky Jacobsen	.10
395	Dontrelle Willis	.40
396	B.J. Upton	.25
397	Rocco Baldelli	.10
398	Ted Lilly	.10
399	Ryan Drese	.10
400	Ichiro Suzuki	1.25
401	Brendan Donnelly	.10
402	Brandon Lyon	.10
403	Nick Green	.10
404	Jerry Hairston Jr.	.10
405	Mike Lowell	.10
406	Kerry Wood	.50
407	Carl Everett	.10
408	Hideki Matsui	1.25
409	Omar Vizquel	.25
410	Joe Kennedy	.10
411	Carlos Pena	.10
412	Armando Benitez	.10
413	Carlos Beltran	.50
414	Kevin Appier	.10
415	Jeff Weaver	.10
416	Chad Moeller	.10
417	Joe Mays	.10
418	Termel Sledge	.10
419	Richard Hidalgo	.10
420	Kenny Lofton	.10
421	Justin Duchscherer	.10
422	Eric Milton	.10
423	Jose Mesa	.10
424	Ramon Hernandez	.10
425	Jose Reyes	.10
426	Joel Pineiro	.10
427	Matt Morris	.10
428	John Halama	.10
429	Gary Matthews Jr.	.10
430	Ryan Madson	.10
431	Mark Kotsay	.10
432	Carlos Delgado	.10
433	Casey Kotchman	.10
434	Greg Aquino	.10
435	Eli Marrero	.10
436	David Newhan	.10
437	Mike Timlin	.10
438	LaTroy Hawkins	.10
439	Jose Contreras	.10
440	Ken Griffey Jr.	1.00
441	C.C. Sabathia	.10
442	Brandon Inge	.10
443	Peter Munro	.10
444	John Buck	.10
445	Hee Seop Choi	.10
446	Chris Capuano	.10
447	Jesse Crain	.10
448	Geoff Jenkins	.10
449	Brian Schneider	.10
450	Mike Piazza	1.00
451	Jorge Posada	.40
452	Nick Swisher	.10
453	Kevin Millwood	.25
454	Mike Gonzalez	.10
455	Jake Peavy	.25
456	Dustin Hermanson	.10
457	Jeremy Reed	.10
458	Julian Tavarez	.10
459	Geoff Blum	.10
460	Alfonso Soriano	.50
461	Alexis Rios	.10
462	David Eckstein	.10
463	Shea Hillenbrand	.10
464	Russ Ortiz	.10
465	Kurt Ainsworth	.10
466	Orlando Cabrera	.10
467	Carlos Silva	.10
468	Ross Gload	.10
469	Josh Phelps	.10
470	Marquis Grissom	.10
471	Mike Maroth	.10
472	Guillermo Mota	.10
473	Chris Burke	.10
474	David DeJesus	.10
475	Jose Lima	.10
476	Cristian Guzman	.10
477	Nick Johnson	.10
478	Victor Zambrano	.10

479 Rod Barajas .10
480 Damian Miller .10
481 Chase Utley .10
482 Todd Pratt .10
483 Sean Burnett .10
484 Boomer Wells .10
485 Dustan Mohr .10
486 Bobby Madritsch .10
487 Ray King .10
488 Reed Johnson .10
489 R.A. Dickey .10
490 Scott Kazmir .25
491 Tony Womack .10
492 Tomas Perez .10
493 Esteban Loaiza .10
494 Tomokazu Ohka .10
495 Mike Lamb .10
496 Ramon Ortiz .10
497 Richie Sexson .40
498 J.D. Drew .25
499 David Segui .10
500 Barry Bonds 2.00
501 Aramis Ramirez .25
502 Wily Mo Pena .10
503 Jeromy Burnitz .10
504 Craig Monroe .10
505 Nomar Garciaparra 1.00
506 Brandon Backe .10
507 Marcus Thames .10
508 Derek Lowe .10
509 Doug Davis .10
510 Joe Mauer .25
511 Endy Chavez .10
512 Bernie Williams .25
513 Mark Redman .10
514 Jason Michaels .10
515 Craig Wilson .10
516 Ryan Klesko .10
517 Ray Durham .10
518 Jose Lopez .10
519 Jeff Suppan .10
520 Julio Lugo .10
521 Mike Wood .10
522 David Bush .10
523 Juan Rincon .10
524 Paul Quantrill .10
525 Marlon Byrd .10
526 Roy Oswalt .25
527 Rondell White .10
528 Troy Glaus .25
529 Scott Hairston .10
530 Chipper Jones .75
531 Daniel Cabrera .10
532 Doug Mientkiewicz .10
533 Glendon Rusch .10
534 Jon Garland .10
535 Austin Kearns .10
536 Jake Westbrook .10
537 Aaron Miles .10
538 Omar Infante .10
539 Paul LoDuca .10
540 Morgan Ensberg .10
541 Tony Graffanino .10
542 Milton Bradley .25
543 Keith Ginter .10
544 Justin Morneau .25
545 Tony Armas Jr. .10
546 Mike Stanton .10
547 Kevin Brown .10
548 Marco Scutaro .10
549 Tim Hudson .10
550 Pat Burrell .10
551 Ty Wigginton .10
552 Jeff Cirillo .10
553 Jim Brower .10
554 Jamie Moyer .10
555 Larry Walker .10
556 Dewon Brazelton .10
557 Brian Jordan .10
558 Josh Towers .10
559 Shigetoshi Hasegawa .10
560 Octavio Dotel .10
561 Travis Lee .10
562 Michael Cuddyer .10
563 Junior Spivey .10
564 Zack Greinke .10
565 Roger Clemens 1.50
566 Chris Shelton .10
567 Ugueth Urbina .10
568 Rafael Betancourt .10
569 Willie Harris .10
570 Todd Hollandsworth .10
571 Keith Foulke .10
572 Larry Bigbie .10
573 Paul Byrd .10
574 Troy Percival .10
575 Pedro Martinez .75
576 Matt Clement .10
577 Ryan Wagner .10
578 Jeff Francis .10
579 Jeff Conine .10
580 Wade Miller .10
581 Matt Stairs .10
582 Gavin Floyd .10
583 Kazuhisa Ishii .10
584 Victor Santos .10
585 Jacque Jones .10
586 Sunny Kim .10
587 Dan Kolb .10
588 Cory Lidle .10
589 Jose Castillo .10
590 Alex Gonzalez .10
591 Kirk Rueter .10
592 Jolbert Cabrera .10
593 Erik Bedard .10
594 Ben Grieve .10
595 Ricky Ledee .10
596 Mark Hendrickson .10
597 Laynce Nix .10
598 Jason Frasor .10
599 Kevin Gregg .10
600 Derek Jeter 1.50
601 Luis Terrero .10
602 Jaret Wright .10
603 Edwin Jackson .10
604 Dave Roberts .10
605 Moises Alou .25
606 Aaron Rowand .10
607 Kazuhito Tadano .10
608 Luis Gonzalez .10
609 A.J. Burnett .25
610 Jeff Bagwell .40
611 Brad Penny .10
612 Craig Counsell .10
613 Corey Koskie .10
614 Mark Ellis .10
615 Felix Rodriguez .10
616 Jay Payton .10
617 Hector Luna .10
618 Miguel Olivo .10
619 Rob Bell .10
620 Scott Rolen .50
621 Ricardo Rodriguez .10
622 Eric Hinske .10
623 Tim Salmon .10
624 Adam LaRoche .10
625 B.J. Ryan .10
626 Roberto Alomar .25
627 Steve Finley .10
628 Joe Nathan .10
629 Scott Linebrink .10
630 Vicente Padilla .10
631 Raul Mondesi .10
632 Yadier Molina .10
633 Tino Martinez .10
634 Mark Teixeira .25
635 Kelvim Escobar .10
636 Pedro Felix .10
637 Rich Aurilia .10
638 Los Angeles Angels of Anaheim .10
639 Arizona Diamondbacks .10
640 Atlanta Braves .10
641 Baltimore Orioles .10
642 Boston Red Sox .10
643 Chicago Cubs .10
644 Chicago White Sox .10
645 Cincinnati Reds .10
646 Cleveland Indians .10
647 Colorado Rockies .10
648 Detroit Tigers .10
649 Florida Marlins .10
650 Houston Astros .10
651 Kansas City Royals .10
652 Los Angeles Dodgers .10
653 Milwaukee Brewers .10
654 Minnesota Twins .10
655 Montreal Expos .10
656 New York Mets .10
657 New York Yankees .10
658 Oakland Athletics .10
659 Philadelphia Phillies .10
660 Pittsburgh Pirates .10
661 San Diego Padres .10
662 San Francisco Giants .10
663 Seattle Mariners .10
664 St. Louis Cardinals .10
665 Tampa Bay Devil Rays .10
666 Texas Rangers .10
667 Toronto Blue Jays .10
668 *Billy Butler* 1.50
669 *Wes Swackhamer* .25
670 *Matt Campbell* .25
671 *Ryan Webb* .50
672 *Glen Perkins* .25
673 *Michael Rogers* .25
674 *Kevin Melillo* .25
675 *Erik Cordier* .50
676 *Landon Powell* .50
677 *Justin Verlander* 1.00
678 *Eric Nielsen* .25
679 *Alexander Smit* .25
680 *Ryan Garko* .50
681 *Bobby Livingston* .25
682 *Jeff Niemann* .50
683 *Wladimir Balentien* .50
684 *Chip Cannon* .25
685 *Yorman Bazardo* .50
686 Michael Bourn .10
687 *Andy LaRoche* 2.00
688 Felix Hernandez, Justin Leone .50
689 Ryan Howard, Cole Hamels .25
690 Matt Cain, Merkin Valdez .25
691 Andy Marte, Jeff Francoeur .10
692 Chad Billingsley, Joel Guzman .10
693 Jerry Hairston Jr., Scott Hairston .10
694 Miguel Tejada, Lance Berkman .25
695 Kenny Rogers .10
696 Ivan Rodriguez .25
697 Darin Erstad .10
698 Bret Boone .10
699 Eric Chavez .10
700 Derek Jeter 1.00
701 Vernon Wells .10
702 Ichiro Suzuki .75
703 Torii Hunter .10
704 Greg Maddux .50
705 Mike Matheny .10
706 Todd Helton .25
707 Luis Castillo .10
708 Scott Rolen .40
709 Cesar Izturis .10
710 Jim Edmonds .25
711 Andruw Jones .25
712 Steve Finley .10
713 Johan Santana .40
714 Roger Clemens 1.00
715 Vladimir Guerrero .40
716 Barry Bonds 1.50
717 Bobby Crosby .10
718 Jason Bay .10
719 Albert Pujols 1.00
720 Mark Loretta .10
721 Edgar Renteria .10
722 Scott Rolen .40
723 J.D. Drew .10
724 Jim Edmonds .25
725 Johnny Estrada .10
726 Jason Schmidt .10
727 Chris Carpenter .10
728 Eric Gagne .10
729 Jason Bay .10
730 Bobby Cox .10
731 Game 1 .50
732 Game 2 .50
733 Game 3 .50
734 Game 4 .50

Gold

Stars: 5-10X
Production 2,005 sets

Black

1st Edition: 20-50X
Production 54 sets

1st Edition

NM/M

Stars: 3-5X
HTA Exclusive
1st Edition Pack (10): 4.00
1st Edition Box (20): 65.00

All-Star Patches

No Pricing
Production 25 Sets

All-Stars

NM/M

Complete Set (15): 20.00
Common Player:
Inserted 1:9

TAS1 Todd Helton .75
TAS2 Albert Pujols 3.00
TAS3 Vladimir Guerrero 1.00
TAS4 Ichiro Suzuki 2.00
TAS5 Randy Johnson 1.00
TAS6 Manny Ramirez 1.00
TAS7 Sammy Sosa 2.00
TAS8 Alfonso Soriano 1.00
TAS9 Jim Thome 1.00
TAS10 Barry Bonds 3.00
TAS11 Roger Clemens 3.00
TAS12 Mike Piazza 1.50
TAS13 Derek Jeter 3.00
TAS14 Alex Rodriguez 2.50
TAS15 Carlos Beltran 1.00

All-Star Stitches Relics

NM/M

Common Player: 5.00
Inserted 1:96

BA Bobby Abreu 8.00
MA Moises Alou 10.00
RB Ronnie Belliard 5.00
CB Carlos Beltran 10.00
LB Lance Berkman 10.00
HB Hank Blalock 10.00
MC Miguel Cabrera 10.00
CC Carl Crawford 5.00
JE Johnny Estrada 8.00
EG Eric Gagne 10.00
JG Jason Giambi 10.00
TG Tom Glavine 10.00
FG Flash Gordon 5.00
VG Vladimir Guerrero 10.00
KH Ken Harvey 5.00
TH Todd Helton 10.00
JK Jeff Kent 8.00
DK Danny Kolb 8.00
BL Barry Larkin 10.00
MLA Matt Lawton 5.00
TL Ted Lilly 8.00
EL Esteban Loaiza 5.00
PL Paul LoDuca 5.00
MLO Mark Loretta 8.00
ML Mike Lowell 8.00
VM Victor Martinez 10.00
MM Mark Mulder 10.00
JN Joe Nathan 8.00
DO David Ortiz 20.00
CP Carl Pavano 10.00
MP Mike Piazza 12.00
AP Albert Pujols 25.00
MR Manny Ramirez 10.00
ER Edgar Renteria 8.00
MRI Mariano Rivera 10.00
FR Francisco Rodriguez 10.00
IR Ivan Rodriguez 10.00
SR Scott Rolen 12.00
CS C.C. Sabathia 8.00
BS Ben Sheets 10.00
GS Gary Sheffield 10.00
AS Alfonso Soriano 10.00
SS Sammy Sosa 15.00
MT Miguel Tejada 10.00
JT Jim Thome 12.00
JW Jack Wilson 10.00
MY Michael Young 15.00
CZ Carlos Zambrano 10.00

Autographs

NM/M

Common Autograph:
CB Carlos Beltran 75.00
HB Hank Blalock
MC Miguel Cabrera 40.00
JC Jose Capellan 30.00
EC Eric Chavez 25.00
DD David DeJesus 20.00
KG Khalil Greene
ZG Zack Greinke 20.00

CK Casey Kotchman 20.00
JMA John Maine 20.00
DM Dallas McPherson 25.00
LO Lyle Overbay
ARI Alexis Rios 25.00
AR Alex Rodriguez 160.00
CT Chad Tracy 20.00
VW Vernon Wells 25.00
DW David Wright 75.00
MY Michael Young
Series 2
JB Jason Bay 25.00
CB Carlos Beltran 60.00
BBO Barry Bonds/125
MB Milton Bradley 25.00
BB Billy Butler 60.00
MC Matt Campbell 15.00
EC Eric Chavez 20.00
ECO Erik Cordier 10.00
CC Carl Crawford 15.00
EG Eric Gagne 50.00
FH Felix Hernandez 30.00
SK Scott Kazmir 25.00
ML Mark Loretta 20.00
GP Glen Perkins 15.00
LP Landon Powell 20.00
AR2 Alex Rodriguez/150 250.00
IR Ivan Rodriguez 50.00
MR Michael Rogers 10.00
JS Johan Santana 50.00
TS Terrmel Sledge 15.00
CW Craig Wilson 10.00

Barry Bonds Home Run Highlights

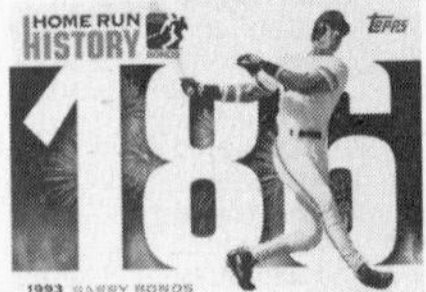

NM/M
Complete Set (330):
Common Bonds: 3.00
Inserted 1:4

Bonds MVP

NM/M
Production 25-500
BBI1 Barry Bonds/25
BBI2 Barry Bonds/50 40.00
BBI3 Barry Bonds/100 30.00
BBI4 Barry Bonds/200 25.00
BBI5 Barry Bonds/300 20.00
BBI6 Barry Bonds/400 15.00
BBI7 Barry Bonds/500 15.00

Bonds MVP Autographs

No Pricing
BBA1 Barry Bonds/1
BBA2 Barry Bonds/2
BBA3 Barry Bonds/3
BBA4 Barry Bonds/4
BBA5 Barry Bonds/5
BBA6 Barry Bonds/6
BBA7 Barry Bonds/7

Bonds MVP Relics

NM/M
Production 25-500
BBR1 Barry Bonds/25
BBR2 Barry Bonds/50
BBR3 Barry Bonds/100 50.00
BBR4 Barry Bonds/200 40.00
BBR5 Barry Bonds/300 40.00
BBR6 Barry Bonds/400 25.00
BBR7 Barry Bonds/500 25.00

Celebrity Threads Relics

NM/M
Common Player: 8.00
Inserted 1:562
CC Cesar Cedeno 8.00
CF Cecil Fielder 15.00
RF Rollie Fingers 12.00
GG Rich "Goose" Gossage 10.00
HR Harold Reynolds 8.00
MS Mike Scott 8.00
OS Ozzie Smith 25.00
DW Dave Winfield 15.00

Dem Bums

NM/M
Complete Set (13): 40.00
Common Player: 4.00
Inserted 1:12

WA Walter Alston 4.00
BB Bob Borkowski 4.00
RC Roy Campanella 6.00
RCR Roger Craig 4.00
CF Carl Furillo 4.00
JG Jim Gilliam 4.00
DH Don Hoak 4.00
JH Jim Hughes 4.00
RM Russ Meyer 4.00
JR Jackie Robinson 8.00
ER Ed Roebuck 4.00
GS George Shuba 4.00
KS Karl Spooner 4.00

Dem Bums Autographs

NM/M
Common Autograph: 30.00
CE Carl Erskine 30.00
CL Clem Labine 50.00
JP Johnny Podres 30.00
DS Duke Snider 50.00
DZ Don Zimmer 50.00

Dem Bums Cuts

No Pricing
Production one set

Derby Digs Relics

NM/M
Common Player: 15.00
Production 100 Sets
LB Lance Berkman 15.00
HB Hank Blalock 20.00
DO David Ortiz 35.00
SS Sammy Sosa 40.00
MT Miguel Tejada 15.00
JT Jim Thome 25.00
Series 2
Production 10 Sets

Grudge Match

NM/M
Complete Set (10):
Common Duo: 1.00
Inserted 1:24
GM1 Jorge Posada, Pedro J. Martinez 2.00
GM2 Mike Piazza, Roger Clemens 3.00
GM3 Mariano Rivera, Luis Gonzalez 1.00
GM4 Carlos Zambrano, Jim Edmonds 1.00
GM5 Aaron Boone, Tim Wakefield 1.00
GM6 Manny Ramirez, Roger Clemens 3.00
GM7 Michael Tucker, Eric Gagne 1.00
GM8 Ivan Rodriguez, J.T. Snow 1.00
GM9 Alex Rodriguez, Bronson Arroyo 3.00
GM10 Corky Miller, Sammy Sosa 2.50

Hit Parade

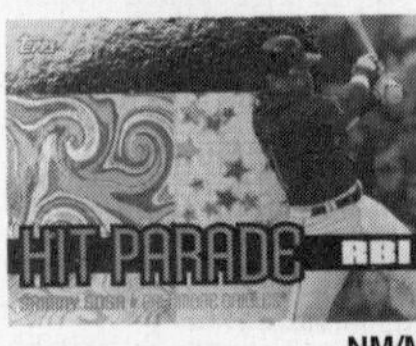

NM/M
Complete Set (30): 25.00
Common Player: .50
Inserted 1:12
HR1 Barry Bonds 4.00
HR2 Sammy Sosa 2.50
HR3 Rafael Palmeiro 1.00
HR4 Ken Griffey Jr. 2.00
HR5 Jeff Bagwell 1.00
HR6 Frank Thomas 1.00
HR7 Juan Gonzalez .75
HR8 Jim Thome 1.00
HR9 Gary Sheffield 1.00
HR10 Manny Ramirez 1.50
RBI1 Barry Bonds 4.00
RBI2 Rafael Palmeiro 1.00
RBI3 Sammy Sosa 2.50
RBI4 Jeff Bagwell 1.00
RBI5 Ken Griffey Jr. 2.00
RBI6 Frank Thomas 1.00
RBI7 Juan Gonzalez .75
RBI8 Gary Sheffield 1.00
RBI9 Ruben Sierra .50
RBI10 Manny Ramirez 1.50
HIT1 Rafael Palmeiro 1.00
HIT2 Barry Bonds 4.00
HIT3 Roberto Alomar .75
HIT4 Craig Biggio .50
HIT5 Julio Franco .50
HIT6 Steve Finley .50
HIT7 Jeff Bagwell 1.00
HIT8 B.J. Surhoff .50
HIT9 Marquis Grissom .50
HIT10 Sammy Sosa 2.50

Hobby Masters

NM/M
Complete Set (20): 25.00
Common Player: .75
Inserted 1:18
HM1 Alex Rodriguez 4.00
HM2 Sammy Sosa 2.50
HM3 Ichiro Suzuki 3.00
HM4 Albert Pujols 4.00
HM5 Derek Jeter 4.00
HM6 Jim Thome 1.50
HM7 Vladimir Guerrero 1.50
HM8 Nomar Garciaparra 2.00
HM9 Mike Piazza 2.00
HM10 Jason Giambi .75
HM11 Ivan Rodriguez 1.00
HM12 Alfonso Soriano 1.50
HM13 Dontrelle Willis .75
HM14 Chipper Jones 1.50
HM15 Mark Prior 1.50
HM16 Todd Helton 1.00
HM17 Randy Johnson 1.50
HM18 Hank Blalock 1.00
HM19 Ken Griffey Jr. 2.00
HM20 Roger Clemens 3.00

Midsummer Covers Relics

No Pricing
Production 10 Sets
Series 2
Production 10 Sets

On-Deck Relics

NM/M
Inserted 1:1,493
CB Carlos Beltran 15.00
HB Hank Blalock 12.00
TH Todd Helton 12.00
AP Albert Pujols 30.00
AR Alex Rodriguez 25.00
IR Ivan Rodriguez 15.00
SR Scott Rolen 15.00
AS Alfonso Soriano 15.00
SS Sammy Sosa 25.00
JT Jim Thome 15.00

Own The Game

NM/M
Complete Set (30): 15.00
Common Player: .50
Inserted 1:12
OG1 Ichiro Suzuki 3.00
OG2 Todd Helton 1.00
OG3 Adrian Beltre 1.00
OG4 Albert Pujols 4.00
OG5 Adam Dunn 1.00
OG6 Jim Thome 1.50
OG7 Miguel Tejada .75
OG8 David Ortiz 1.50
OG9 Manny Ramirez 1.50
OG10 Scott Rolen 1.50
OG11 Gary Sheffield .75
OG12 Vladimir Guerrero 1.50
OG13 Jim Edmonds .75
OG14 Ivan Rodriguez 1.00
OG15 Lance Berkman .50
OG16 Michael Young .50
OG17 Juan Pierre .50
OG18 Craig Biggio .50
OG19 Johnny Damon .75
OG20 Jimmy Rollins .50
OG21 Scott Podsednik .50
OG22 Bobby Abreu .50
OG23 Lyle Overbay .50
OG24 Carl Crawford .50
OG25 Mark Loretta .50
OG26 Vinny Castilla .50
OG27 Curt Schilling 1.00
OG28 Johan Santana .75
OG29 Randy Johnson 1.50
OG30 Pedro J. Martinez 1.50

Power Brokers Cut Signatures

No Pricing

Spokesman

NM/M
Complete Set (4): 10.00
Common Player: 3.00
Inserted 1:24
ARI1 Alex Rodriguez 3.00
ARI2 Alex Rodriguez 3.00
ARI3 Alex Rodriguez 3.00
ARI4 Alex Rodriguez 3.00

Spokesman Autographs

NM/M
Production 1-200
ARA1 Alex Rodriguez/1
ARA2 Alex Rodriguez/25
ARA3 Alex Rodriguez/100 200.00
ARA4 Alex Rodriguez/200 180.00

Spokesman Relics

NM/M
Production 1-800
ARR1 Alex Rodriguez/1
ARR2 Alex Rodriguez/50 30.00
ARR3 Alex Rodriguez/300 20.00
ARR4 Alex Rodriguez/800 20.00

Spokesman Relic Autographs

13 Sets

ARRA1 Alex Rodriguez
ARRA2 Alex Rodriguez
ARRA3 Alex Rodriguez
ARRA4 Alex Rodriguez

Spokesman Relic

NM/M
Inserted 1:5,627
AR Alex Rodriguez 50.00

Touch'em All Relics

Common Player:
Production 50 Sets

1955 World Series Cut Signatures

No Pricing

1955 World Series Dual Cut Signatures

Production 1 Set

2005 TOPPS ALL-TIME FAN FAVORITES

NM/M
Complete Set (142): 40.00
Common Player: .25
Pack (6): 5.00
Box (24): 110.00
1 Andy Van Slyke .25
2 Bill Freehan .25
3 Bo Jackson .75
4 Mark Grace .50
5 Chuck Knoblauch .25
6 Candy Maldonado .25
7 David Cone .25
8 Don Mattingly 1.50
9 Darryl Strawberry .25
10 Dick Williams .25
11 Frank Robinson .75
12 Glenn Hubbard .25
13 Jim Abbott .25
14 Jeff Brantley .25
15 John Elway 2.00
16 Jim Leyland .25
17 Jesse Orosco .25
18 Joe Pepitone .25
19 J.R. Richard .25
20 Jerome Walton .25
21 Kevin Maas .25
22 Lou Brock .50
23 Lou Whitaker .25
24 Carl Erskine .25
25 John Candelaria .25
26 Mike Norris .25
27 Nolan Ryan 2.00
28 Pedro Guerrero .25
29 Roger Craig .25
30 Ron Gant .25
31 Sid Bream .25
32 Sid Fernandez .25
33 Tony LaRussa .25
34 Tom Seaver .75
35 Yogi Berra .75
36 Andre Dawson .25
37 Al Kaline .75
38 Brett Butler .25
39 Bob Gibson .75
40 Bill Mazeroski .25
41 Matty Alou .25
42 Chet Lemon .25
43 Cal Ripken Jr. 2.00
44 Dusty Baker .25
45 Dwight Gooden .25
46 Dave Winfield .50
47 Ernie Banks 1.00
48 Gary Carter .50
49 Howard Johnson .25
50 Mike Schmidt 1.50
51 Matt Williams .25
52 Ozzie Smith 1.00
53 Atlee Hammaker .25
54 Cleon Jones .25
55 Dave Johnson .25
56 Denny McLain .25
57 Don Zimmer .25
58 Gregg Jefferies .25
59 Jay Buhner .25
60 Johnny Bench .75
61 George Brett 1.50
62 Dale Murphy .50
63 Bob Welch .25
64 Paul O'Neill .25
65 Mark Lemke .25
66 Kevin McReynolds .25
67 Jesus Alou .25
68 Joe Pignatano .25
69 Jim Lonborg .25
70 Jerry Grote .25
71 Joaquin Andujar .25
72 Gary Gaetti .25
73 Edgar Martinez .25
74 Ron Darling .25
75 Duke Snider .75
76 Dave Magadan .25
77 Doug Drabek .25
78 Carl Yastrzemski 1.00
79 Mitch Williams .25
80 Marvin Miller .25
81 Michael Kay .25
82 Lonnie Smith .25
83 John Wetteland .25
84 Johnny Podres .25
85 Joe Morgan .25
86 Juan Marichal .50
87 Jeffrey Leonard .25
88 Bob Feller .50
89 Brooks Robinson .75
90 Clem Labine .25
91 Barry Lyons .25
92 Harmon Killebrew .75
93 Jim Frey .25
94 John Kruk .25
95 Ed Kranepool .25
96 Jose Oquendo .25
97 Johnny Pesky .25
98 John Tudor .25
99 Keith Hernandez .25
100 Monte Irvin .50
101 Marty Barrett .25
102 Oscar Gamble .25
103 Hank Bauer .25
104 Ron Blomberg .25
105 Rod Carew .50
106 Rick Dempsey .25
107 Walt Jocketty .25
108 Tom Kelly .25
109 Steve Carlton .50
110 Rick Monday .25
111 Rob Dibble .25
112 Shawon Dunston .25
113 Tony Gwynn .75
114 Tom Niedenfuer .25
115 Bob Dernier .25
116 Anthony Young .25
117 Reggie Jackson .75
118 Steve Garvey .25
119 Tim Raines .25
120 Whitey Ford .75
121 Rafael Santana .25
122 Scott Brosius .25
123 Stan Musial 1.50
124 Ron Santo .50
125 Wade Boggs .75
126 Jose Canseco .50
127 Brady Anderson .25
128 Vida Blue .25
129 Charlie Hough .25
130 Jim Kaat .25
131 Zane Smith .25
132 Bob Boone .25
133 Travis Fryman .25
134 Harold Baines .25
135 Orlando Cepeda .25
136 Mike Cuellar .25
137 Tito Fuentes .25
138 Daryl Boston .25
139 Jim Leyritz .25
140 Bill "Moose" Skowron .25
141 Theo Epstein .25
142 Barry Bonds 3.00

Refractor

Stars (1-142): 3-5X
Production 299 sets

Gold Refractor

No Pricing
Production 25 sets

Printing Plates

No Pricing
Production one set per color (4):

Autographs

NM/M
Common Autograph: 15.00
Rainbow: No Pricing
Production 10 Sets
JA Jim Abbott 30.00
JAN Joaquin Andujar 20.00
DB Dusty Baker 25.00
EB Ernie Banks/SP/40
MB Marty Barrett 15.00
JBE Dr. Jim Beckett/SP/90 100.00
JB Johnny Bench/SP/40 125.00
YB Yogi Berra/SP/90 125.00
RB Ron Blomberg 15.00
WB Wade Boggs/SP/40
BLB Barry Bonds/SP/15
JBR Jeff Brantley 20.00
SB Sid Bream 20.00
GB George Brett/SP/40 250.00
SBR Scott Brosius/SP/90 85.00
JBU Jay Buhner 20.00
BB Brett Butler 20.00
SC Steve Carlton/SP/90 60.00
GC Gary Carter 25.00
DC David Cone 25.00
RCR Roger Craig 25.00
AD Andre Dawson/SP/40
RD Rick Dempsey 15.00
DD Doug Drabek 20.00
SD Shawon Dunston 20.00
JE John Elway/SP/40 250.00
TE Theo Epstein/SP/90
BFE Bob Feller 85.00
SF Sid Fernandez 15.00
WF Whitey Ford/SP/90 150.00
BF Bill Freehan 20.00
GG Gary Gaetti 15.00
OG Oscar Gamble 15.00
RG Ron Gant/SP/90 50.00
SG Steve Garvey 50.00
BG Bob Gibson/SP/90 100.00
DG Dwight Gooden 40.00
MG Mark Grace
JG Jerry Grote 30.00
TG Tony Gwynn/SP/90 125.00
AH Atlee Hammaker 15.00
GH Glenn Hubbard 20.00
MI Monte Irvin 50.00
BJ Bo Jackson 70.00
RJ Reggie Jackson/SP/40 100.00
GJ Gregg Jefferies 40.00
WJ Walt Jocketty/SP/90 60.00
DJ Dave Johnson 20.00
HJ Howard Johnson 20.00
CJ Cleon Jones 35.00
AK Al Kaline 60.00
MK Michael Kay/SP/90
TK Tom Kelly 25.00
HK Harmon Killebrew 85.00
CK Chuck Knoblauch 25.00
JK John Kruk 30.00
CL Clem Labine 40.00
TL Tony LaRussa 30.00
MLE Mark Lemke 15.00
CLE Chet Lemon 15.00
JL Jeffrey Leonard
JLE Jim Leyland 20.00
JLO Jim Lonborg 15.00
BL Barry Lyons 15.00
KM Kevin Maas 15.00
DMA Dave Magadan 20.00
CM Candy Maldonado 15.00
JMA Juan Marichal/SP/90 140.00
EM Edgar Martinez 30.00
DM Don Mattingly 140.00
BM Bill Mazeroski 75.00
DMC Denny McLain 30.00
KMC Kevin McReynolds 15.00
MM Marvin Miller/SP/90 80.00
RM Rick Monday 30.00
DMU Dale Murphy 30.00
SM Stan Musial/SP/40 150.00
TN Tom Niedenfuer 15.00
MNO Mike Norris 15.00
PO Paul O'Neill 60.00
JO Jesse Orosco 25.00
JOQ Jose Oquendo 15.00
JPE Joe Pepitone 25.00
JPY Johnny Pesky 65.00
JP Joe Pignatano 30.00
JPO Johnny Podres/SP/40
TR Tim Raines 25.00
JR J.R. Richard 15.00
CR Cal Ripken Jr./SP/90 200.00
BR Brooks Robinson/SP/90 125.00
FR Frank Robinson 100.00
NR Nolan Ryan/SP/40 200.00
BS Brian Sabean/SP/90
RS Rafael Santana 20.00
RSA Ron Santo/SP/90 75.00
MS Mike Schmidt/SP/40 160.00
TS Tom Seaver/SP/40
LS Lonnie Smith 15.00
OS Ozzie Smith
DSN Duke Snider/SP/40 60.00
DS Darryl Strawberry 25.00
JT John Tudor 35.00
AV Andy Van Slyke 25.00
JW Jerome Walton 15.00
BW Bob Welch 30.00
JWE John Wetteland 20.00
LW Lou Whitaker/SP/90 60.00
DWI Dick Williams/SP/90 75.00
MW Matt Williams 25.00
MWI Mitch Williams 25.00
DW Dave Winfield/SP/90 125.00
CY Carl Yastrzemski/SP/90 125.00
AY Anthony Young 15.00
DZ Don Zimmer/SP/40 50.00

Best Seat in House

NM/M
Production 125 unless noted
Rainbow: No Pricing
Production 25 Sets
MFBJ Don Mattingly, Whitey Ford, Yogi Berra, Reggie Jackson/50 50.00
RRRD Brooks Robinson, Rick Dempsey, Frank Robinson, Cal Ripken Jr. 25.00
RR Brooks Robinson, Cal Ripken Jr. 25.00
CR Cal Ripken Jr., Frank Robinson 25.00
JD Dave Johnson, Rick Dempsey 10.00
KMLW Al Kaline, Lou Whitaker, Chet Lemon, Denny McLain 20.00

Fan Favorite Relics

NM/M
Inserted 1:Box
Rainbow: No Pricing
Production 25 Sets
WB Wade Boggs/200 8.00
JCC Jose Canseco/350 8.00
RC Rod Carew/200 8.00
GC Gary Carter/350 5.00
JC Joe Carter/350 5.00
VC Vince Coleman/200 5.00
ED Eric Davis/200 5.00
AD Andre Dawson/350 5.00
BD Bucky Dent/200 5.00
LD Lenny Dykstra/200 5.00
CF Cecil Fielder/200 5.00
TG Tony Gwynn/200 15.00
KH Keith Hernandez/200 5.00
BJ Bo Jackson/200 12.00
RJ Reggie Jackson/350 10.00
WJ Wally Joyner/200 5.00
WM Willie McGee/350 5.00
DM Dale Murphy/200 10.00
SM Stan Musial/50 20.00
PO Paul O'Neill/200 15.00
JR Jim Rice/200 5.00
BR Brooks Robinson/350 10.00
NR Nolan Ryan/135 25.00
DS Darryl Strawberry/350 5.00
BS Bruce Sutter/350 7.50
MW Mookie Wilson/135 5.00
CY Carl Yastrzemski/50 25.00

Originals Relics

NM/M
Production 50 Sets
Actual vintage cards used
WB Wade Boggs Bat 15.00

RC Rod Carew Bat 20.00
GC Gary Carter Bat 10.00
AD Andre Dawson Bat 10.00
TG Tony Gwynn Jsy 20.00
BJ Bo Jackson Jsy 25.00
RJ Reggie Jackson Bat 20.00
DM Dale Murphy Bat 15.00
JR Jim Rice Bat 15.00
NR Nolan Ryan Jsy 35.00

Rookie Dual Autograph

NM/M

Production 50 Sets
SC Tom Seaver, Rod Carew 160.00
RB Nolan Ryan, Johnny Bench

2005 TOPPS BAZOOKA

NM/M

Complete Set (220): 35.00
Common Player: .15
Common (191-220): .25
Pack (8): 2.50
Box (24): 50.00
1 Eric Gagne .40
2 Aramis Ramirez .40
3 Hank Blalock .50
4 Jason Kendall .15
5 Jeromy Burnitz .15
6 Jose Guillen .15
7 Tom Glavine .40
8 Adrian Beltre .25
9 Jason Bay .25
10 Mark Teixeira .40
11 Moises Alou .25
12 Ronnie Belliard .15
13 Aaron Guiel .15
14 Vladimir Guerrero .75
15 Scott Podsednik .15
16 Alfonso Soriano .75
17 Craig Wilson .15
18 Jose Reyes .15
19 Mark Prior .75
20 Preston Wilson .15
21 Shawn Green .25
22 Troy Glaus .25
23 Dmitri Young .15
24 Garret Anderson .25
25 Kazuo Matsui .25
26 Kerry Wood .75
27 Michael Young .15
28 Oliver Perez .15
29 Bartolo Colon .15
30 Richie Sexson .40
31 Brad Penny .15
32 Carlos Guillen .15
33 Carlos Zambrano .25
34 David Wright .50
35 Al Leiter .25
36 Jack Wilson .15
37 Ryan Drese .15
38 Darin Erstad .15
39 Derrek Lee .25
40 Ivan Rodriguez .50
41 Kenny Rogers .15
42 Mike Piazza 1.00
43 Phil Nevin .15
44 Geoff Jenkins .15
45 Jorge Posada .40
46 Khalil Greene .40
47 Randy Johnson .75
48 Rondell White .15
49 Sammy Sosa 1.25
50 Vernon Wells .15
51 Ben Sheets .40
52 Brian Giles .15
53 Carlos Delgado .40
54 Derek Jeter 2.00
55 Jeremy Bonderman .15
56 Magglio Ordonez .25
57 Chad Tracy .15
58 Kevin Brown .15
59 Luis Castillo .15
60 Lyle Overbay .15
61 Mark Buehrle .15
62 Mark Loretta .15
63 Orlando Hudson .15
64 Adam Dunn .50
65 Frank Thomas .50
66 Jake Peavy .15
67 Jason Giambi .40
68 Joe Mauer .25
69 Marcus Giles .15
70 Mike Lowell .25
71 Roy Halladay .15
72 Aaron Rowand .15
73 Alex Rodriguez 1.50
74 Brian Lawrence .15
75 Gabe Gross .15
76 Johnny Estrada .25
77 Justin Morneau .25
78 Miguel Cabrera .75
79 Alex Rios .15
80 Gary Sheffield .40
81 Jason Schmidt .25
82 Juan Pierre .15
83 Paul Konerko .25
84 Jermaine Dye .15
85 Rafael Furcal .25
86 Torii Hunter .25
87 A.J. Pierzynski .15
88 Carl Pavano .25
89 Carlos Lee .25
90 J.D. Drew .25
91 Javier Vazquez .25
92 Lew Ford .15
93 Ted Lilly .15
94 Austin Kearns .15
95 Chipper Jones .75
96 Erubiel Durazo .15
97 Johan Santana .50
98 Josh Beckett .25
99 Mariano Rivera .25
100 Mark Mulder .25
101 Andruw Jones .25
102 Barry Zito .25
103 Bret Boone .15
104 Paul LoDuca .15
105 Shannon Stewart .15
106 Wily Mo Pena .25
107 Dontrelle Willis .25
108 Eric Chavez .25
109 Jamie Moyer .15
110 Joe Nathan .15
111 Sidney Ponson .15
112 John Smoltz .25
113 Ichiro Suzuki 1.50
114 Javy Lopez .25
115 Victor Martinez .25
116 Ken Griffey Jr. 1.00
117 Lance Berkman .25
118 Scott Hatteberg .15
119 Jim Edmonds .25
120 Kazuhisa Ishii .15
121 Miguel Tejada .40
122 Roger Clemens 2.00
123 Ryan Freel .15
124 Albert Pujols 2.00
125 Hideo Nomo .25
126 Mark Kotsay .15
127 Melvin Mora .15
128 Roy Oswalt .25
129 Sean Casey .25
130 Casey Blake .15
131 Edgar Renteria .25
132 Jeff Kent .25
133 Rafael Palmeiro .50
134 Tim Hudson .25
135 Tony Batista .15
136 Andy Pettitte .25
137 Brian Roberts .15
138 Jose Vidro .15
139 Omar Vizquel .15
140 Rich Harden .25
141 Scott Rolen .75
142 Carlos Beltran .50
143 Chris Carpenter .15
144 Manny Ramirez .75
145 Nick Johnson .15
146 Pat Burrell .25
147 C.C. Sabathia .15
148 Johnny Damon .50
149 Juan Rivera .15
150 Ken Harvey .15
151 Kevin Millwood .15
152 Larry Walker .50
153 Aubrey Huff .15
154 Curt Schilling .75
155 Jake Westbrook .15
156 Randy Wolf .15
157 Zach Day .15
158 Zack Greinke .15
159 Brad Wilkerson .15
160 Carl Crawford .15
161 Jim Thome .75
162 Mike Sweeney .15
163 Pedro J. Martinez .75
164 Travis Hafner .15
165 Bobby Abreu .25
166 Cliff Floyd .15
167 David DeJesus .15
168 David Ortiz .75
169 Rocco Baldelli .15
170 Todd Helton .50
171 Dallas McPherson .50
172 Kevin Youkilis .25
173 Val Majewski .15
174 Grady Sizemore .25
175 Joey Gathright .15
176 Rickie Weeks .25
177 Jason Kubel .25
178 Robinson Cano .15
179 Nick Swisher .25
180 Ryan Howard .25
181 Tim Stauffer .15
182 Merkin Valdez .15
183 B.J. Upton .40
184 Scott Kazmir .40
185 Chris Burke .25
186 Felix Hernandez .50
187 Freddy Guzman .15
188 Josh Labandeira .15
189 Willy Taveras .15
190 Casey Kotchman .25
191 *Steven Doetsch* .25
192 *Melky Cabrera* .75
193 *Luis Ramirez* .25
194 *Chris Seddon* .40
195 *Chad Orvella* .50
196 *Ian Kinsler* 1.50
197 *Brandon Moss* 1.00
198 *Chadd Blasko* .50
199 *Jeremy West* .75
200 *Sean Marshall* .25
201 *Matt DeSalvo* .25
202 Ryan Sweeney 1.50
203 *Matt Lindstrom* .50
204 *Ryan Goleski* .40
205 *Brett Harper* .25
206 *Chris Roberson* .25
207 Andre Ethier .25
208 *Chris Denorfia* .25
209 *Darren Fenster* .25
210 *Elvys Quezada* .25
211 *Kevin West* .50
212 *Chaz Lytle* .50
213 *James Jurries* .25
214 *Matt Rogelstad* .25
215 *Wade Robinson* .25
216 *Ian Bladergroen* .75
217 Jake Dittler .25
218 *Nate McLouth* .40
219 Kole Strayhorn .25
220 *Jose Vaquedano* .25

Gold Chunks

Golds: 1-2X
Inserted 1:1

Minis

Mini: 1-2x
Inserted 1:1

Blasts

NM/M

Common Bat: 4.00
RA Roberto Alomar 6.00
RB Ron Belliard 4.00

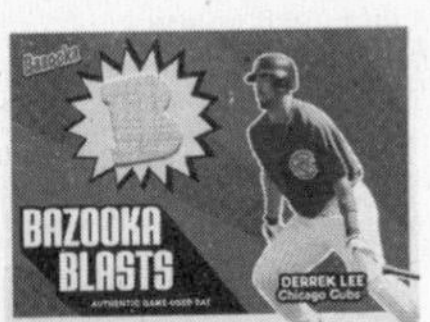

AB Angel Berroa 4.00
CB Craig Biggio 8.00
HB Hank Blalock 8.00
JB Jeromy Burnitz 4.00
SB Sean Burroughs 4.00
MC Miguel Cabrera 10.00
VC Vinny Castilla 4.00
TC Tony Clark 4.00
JC Jeff Conine 4.00
JCJ Jose Cruz Jr. 4.00
AD Adam Dunn 6.00
ME Morgan Ensberg 4.00
DE Darin Erstad 4.00
CE Carl Everett 4.00
CF Chone Figgins 4.00
JF Julio Franco 4.00
NG Nomar Garciaparra 8.00
AGO Adrian Gonzalez 4.00
AG Alex Gonzalez 4.00
LG Luis Gonzalez 4.00
VG Vladimir Guerrero 8.00
CGU Carlos Guillen 4.00
CG Cristian Guzman 4.00
TH Todd Helton 6.00
LH Livan Hernandez 4.00
RH Richard Hidalgo 4.00
JK Jeff Kent 4.00
PK Paul Konerko 4.00
DL Derrek Lee 4.00
ML Mike Lowell 6.00
PM Pedro Martinez 6.00
TM Tino Martinez 6.00
VM Victor Martinez 6.00
KM Kazuo Matsui 8.00
MO Magglio Ordonez 4.00
DO David Ortiz 10.00
ARA Aramis Ramirez 6.00
MR Manny Ramirez 6.00
AR Alex Rodriguez 20.00
CS Curt Schilling 6.00
GS Gary Sheffield 4.00
RS Ruben Sierra 4.00
MT Miguel Tejada 6.00
BU B.J. Upton 10.00
JV Jose Valentin 4.00
JVI Jose Vidro 4.00
LW Larry Walker 6.00
JW Jayson Werth 4.00
PW Preston Wilson 4.00
DW David Wright 10.00
MY Michael Young 4.00

Comics

NM/M

Complete Set (24): 8.00
Common Player: .25
Inserted 1:4
1 Randy Johnson .50
2 Gary Sheffield .25
3 Ken Griffey Jr. .75
4 Alex Rodriguez .75
5 Vladimir Guerrero .50
6 David Bell .25
7 Carlos Pena .25
8 Eric Gagne .25
9 Jim Thome .50
10 Cleveland Indians .25
11 Greg Maddux .50
12 Miguel Tejada .25
13 Ichiro Suzuki .75
14 Mariano Rivera .25
15 Juan Pierre .25
16 Carl Crawford .25
17 Mike Mussina .25
18 Vladimir Guerrero .50
19 Oliver Perez .25
20 Ichiro Suzuki .75
21 Johan Santana .25
22 Kevin Brown .25
23 Mike Piazza .50
24 Randy Johnson .50

Fun Facts Relics

NM/M

Common Relic: 4.00
HB Harold Baines 4.00
WB Wade Boggs 6.00
GB George Brett 12.00

JC	Jose Canseco	8.00
RC	Rod Carew	12.00
GC	Gary Carter	4.00
DD	Darren Daulton	4.00
DE	Darrell Evans	4.00
CF	Cecil Fielder	8.00
KG	Ken Griffey Sr.	4.00
WH	Willie Horton	4.00
WJ	Wally Joyner	4.00
DJ	David Justice	4.00
DJ2	David Justice	4.00
RK	Ron Kittle	4.00
JL	Jim Leyritz	4.00
DP	Dave Parker	4.00
HR	Harold Reynolds	4.00
MR	Mickey Rivers	4.00
MS	Mike Schmidt	10.00
OS	Ozzie Smith	20.00
CS	Cory Snyder	4.00
DS	Darryl Strawberry	4.00
WW	Walt Weiss	4.00

Moments Relics

		NM/M
Common Relic:		6.00
MB	Matt Bush	8.00
RH	Ramon Hernandez	6.00
TL	Terrence Long	6.00
MM	Mark Mulder	6.00
MP	Mike Piazza	12.00
JP	Jorge Posada	8.00
AP	Albert Pujols	25.00
AR	Alex Rodriguez	12.00
IR	Ivan Rodriguez	8.00
KR	Kenny Rogers	6.00
AS	Alfonso Soriano	6.00
MT	Mark Teixeira	6.00
FT	Frank Thomas	6.00

Tatoos

		NM/M
Common Player:		.25
Inserted 1:4		
1	Alex Rodriguez	.50
2	Randy Johnson	.50
3	Jim Thome	.25
4	Pedro Martinez	.50
5	Roger Clemens	.50
6	Troy Glaus	.25
7	Todd Helton	.25
8	Albert Pujols	.50
9	Sammy Sosa	.50
10	David Wright	.50
11	Mike Piazza	.50
12	Gary Sheffield	.25
13	David Ortiz	.50
14	Hank Blalock	.25
15	Miguel Tejada	.25
16	Dontrelle Willis	.25
17	Ivan Rodriguez	.25
18	Nomar Garciaparra	.50
19	Alfonso Soriano	.25
20	Adrian Beltre	.25
21	Torii Hunter	.25
22	Brian Giles	.25
23	Chipper Jones	.50
24	Carlos Beltran	.25
25	Manny Ramirez	.50

2005 TOPPS CHROME

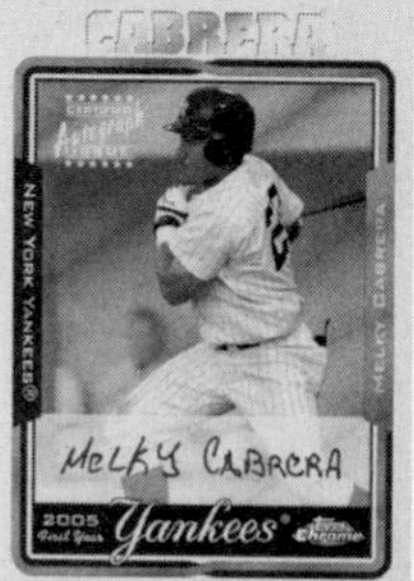

		NM/M
Complete Set (472):		
Common Player:		.25
Common Rookie Auto. (221-252):		10.00
Inserted 1:20		
Hobby pack (4):		3.00
Hobby box (20):		50.00
1	Alex Rodriguez	2.50
2	Placido Polanco	.25
3	Torii Hunter	.50
4	Lyle Overbay	.25
5	Johnny Damon	.75
6	Johnny Estrada	.25
7	Rich Harden	.25
8	Francisco Rodriguez	.25
9	Jarrod Washburn	.25
10	Sammy Sosa	2.00
11	Randy Wolf	.25
12	Jason Bay	.50
13	Tom Glavine	.50
14	Michael Tucker	.25
15	Brian Giles	.25
16	Chad Tracy	.25
17	Jim Edmonds	.50
18	John Smoltz	.50
19	Roy Halladay	.25
20	Hank Blalock	.75
21	Darin Erstad	.50
22	Todd Walker	.25
23	Mike Hampton	.25
24	Mark Bellhorn	.25
25	Jim Thome	1.00
26	Shingo Takatsu	.25
27	Jody Gerut	.25
28	Vinny Castilla	.25
29	Luis Castillo	.25
30	Ivan Rodriguez	.75
31	Craig Biggio	.50
32	Joe Randa	.25
33	Adrian Beltre	.50
34	Scott Podsednik	.25
35	Cliff Floyd	.25
36	Livan Hernandez	.25
37	Eric Byrnes	.25
38	Jose Acevedo	.25
39	Jack Wilson	.25
40	Gary Sheffield	.75
41	Chan Ho Park	.25
42	Carl Crawford	.25
43	Shawn Estes	.25
44	David Bell	.25
45	Jeff DaVanon	.25
46	Brandon Webb	.25
47	Lance Berkman	.50
48	Melvin Mora	.25
49	David Ortiz	1.00
50	Andruw Jones	.50
51	Chone Figgins	.25
52	Danny Graves	.25
53	Preston Wilson	.25
54	Jeremy Bonderman	.25
55	Carlos Guillen	.25
56	Cesar Izturis	.25
57	Kazuo Matsui	.25
58	Jason Schmidt	.50
59	Jason Marquis	.25
60	Jose Vidro	.25
61	Al Leiter	.40
62	Javier Vazquez	.25
63	Erubiel Durazo	.25
64	Scott Spiezio	.25
65	Scot Shields	.25
66	Edgardo Alfonzo	.25
67	Miguel Tejada	.50
68	Francisco Cordero	.25
69	Brett Myers	.25
70	Curt Schilling	1.00
71	Matt Kata	.25
72	Bartolo Colon	.25
73	Rodrigo Lopez	.25
74	Tim Wakefield	.25
75	Frank Thomas	.75
76	Jimmy Rollins	.25
77	Barry Zito	.50
78	Hideo Nomo	.50
79	Brad Wilkerson	.25
80	Adam Dunn	.75
81	Derrek Lee	.50
82	Joe Crede	.25
83	Nate Robertson	.25
84	John Thomson	.25
85	Mike Sweeney	.25
86	Kip Wells	.25
87	Eric Gagne	.50
88	Boomer Wells	.25
89	Alex Sanchez	.25
90	Bret Boone	.25
91	Mark Loretta	.25
92	Miguel Cabrera	1.00
93	Randy Winn	.25
94	Adam Everett	.25
95	Aubrey Huff	.25
96	Kevin Mench	.25
97	Frank Catalanotto	.25
98	Flash Gordon	.25
99	Scott Hatteberg	.25
100	Albert Pujols	3.00
101	Jose Molina, Bengie Molina	.25
102	Jason Johnson	.25
103	Jay Gibbons	.25
104	Byung-Hyun Kim	.25
105	Joe Borowski	.25
106	Mark Grudzielanek	.25
107	Mark Buehrle	.25
108	Paul Wilson	.25
109	Ronnie Belliard	.25
110	Reggie Sanders	.25
111	Tim Redding	.25
112	Brian Lawrence	.25
113	Travis Hafner	.40
114	Jose Hernandez	.25
115	Ben Sheets	.50
116	Johan Santana	.75
117	Billy Wagner	.40
118	Mariano Rivera	.50
119	Steve Trachsel	.25
120	Akinori Otsuka	.25
121	Jose Valentin	.25
122	Orlando Hernandez	.25
123	Raul Ibanez	.25
124	Mike Matheny	.25
125	Vernon Wells	.25
126	Jason Isringhausen	.25
127	Jose Guillen	.25
128	Danny Bautista	.25
129	Marcus Giles	.25
130	Javy Lopez	.40
131	Kevin Millar	.25
132	Kyle Farnsworth	.25
133	Carl Pavano	.25
134	Rafael Furcal	.25
135	Casey Blake	.25
136	Matt Holliday	.25
137	Bobby Higginson	.25
138	Adam Kennedy	.25
139	Alex Gonzalez	.25
140	Jeff Kent	.40
141	Aaron Guiel	.25
142	Shawn Green	.40
143	Bill Hall	.25
144	Shannon Stewart	.25
145	Juan Rivera	.25
146	Coco Crisp	.25
147	Mike Mussina	.50
148	Eric Chavez	.50
149	Jon Lieber	.25
150	Vladimir Guerrero	1.00
151	Alex Cintron	.25
152	Luis Matos	.25
153	Sidney Ponson	.25
154	Trot Nixon	.25
155	Greg Maddux	2.00
156	Edgar Renteria	.50
157	Ryan Freel	.25
158	Matt Lawton	.25
159	Mark Prior	1.00
160	Josh Beckett	.50
161	Ken Harvey	.25
162	Angel Berroa	.25
163	Juan Encarnacion	.25
164	Wes Helms	.25
165	Brad Radke	.25
166	Phil Nevin	.25
167	Mike Cameron	.25
168	Billy Koch	.25
169	Bobby Crosby	.50
170	Mike Lieberthal	.25
171	Robert Mackowiak	.25
172	Sean Burroughs	.25
173	J.T. Snow Jr.	.25
174	Paul Konerko	.40
175	Luis Gonzalez	.25
176	John Lackey	.25
177	Oliver Perez	.25
178	Brian Roberts	.25
179	Bill Mueller	.25
180	Carlos Lee	.25
181	Corey Patterson	.50
182	Sean Casey	.40
183	Cliff Lee	.25
184	Jason Jennings	.25
185	Dmitri Young	.25
186	Juan Uribe	.25
187	Andy Pettitte	.50
188	Juan Gonzalez	.50
189	Orlando Hudson	.25
190	Jason Phillips	.25
191	Braden Looper	.25
192	Lew Ford	.25
193	Mark Mulder	.40
194	Bobby Abreu	.40
195	Jason Kendall	.25
196	Khalil Greene	.50
197	A.J. Pierzynski	.25
198	Tim Worrell	.25
199	So Taguchi	.25
200	Jason Giambi	.50
201	Tony Batista	.25
202	Carlos Zambrano	.50
203	Trevor Hoffman	.25
204	Odalis Perez	.25
205	Jose Cruz Jr.	.25
206	Michael Barrett	.25
207	Chris Carpenter	.25
208	Michael Young	.25
209	Toby Hall	.25
210	Woody Williams	.25
211	*Chris Denorfia*	1.00
212	*Darren Fenster*	1.00
213	*Elvys Quezada*	2.00
214	*Ian Kinsler*	4.00
215	*Matt Lindstrom*	2.00
216	*Ryan Goleski*	2.00
217	Ryan Sweeney	3.00
218	*Sean Marshall*	1.00
219	*Steven Doetsch*	2.00
220	*Wade Robinson*	3.00
221	Andre Ethier	20.00
222	*Brandon Moss*	25.00
223	*Chadd Blasko*	10.00
224	*Chris Roberson*	10.00
225	*Chris Seddon*	15.00
226	*Ian Bladergroen*	20.00
227	Jake Dittler	15.00
228	*Jose Vaquedano*	15.00
229	*Jeremy West*	35.00
230	Kole Strayhorn	10.00
231	*Kevin West*	15.00
232	*Luis Ramirez*	10.00
233	*Melky Cabrera*	25.00
234	Nate Schierholtz	15.00
235	*Billy Butler*	60.00
236	*Brandon Szymanski*	20.00
237	*Chad Orvella*	25.00
238	*Chip Cannon*	20.00
239	*Eric Nielsen*	15.00
240	*Erik Cordier*	25.00
241	*Glen Perkins*	20.00
242	*Justin Verlander*	35.00
243	*Kevin Melillo*	25.00
244	*Landon Powell*	20.00
245	*Matt Campbell*	35.00
246	*Michael Rogers*	15.00
247	*Nate McLouth*	20.00
248	*Scott Mathieson*	20.00
249	Shane Costa	20.00
250	*Tony Giarratano*	25.00
251	*Tyler Pelland*	20.00
252	*Wes Swackhamer*	20.00
253	Garret Anderson	.50
254	Randy Johnson	1.00
255	Charles Thomas	.25
256	Rafael Palmeiro	.75
257	Kevin Youkilis	.25
258	Freddy Garcia	.25
259	Magglio Ordonez	.25
260	Aaron Harang	.25
261	Grady Sizemore	.25
262	Chin-Hui Tsao	.25
263	Eric Munson	.25
264	Juan Pierre	.25
265	Brad Lidge	.25
266	Brian Anderson	.25
267	Todd Helton	.75
268	Chad Cordero	.25
269	Kris Benson	.25
270	Brad Halsey	.25
271	Jermaine Dye	.25
272	Manny Ramirez	1.00
273	Adam Eaton	.25
274	Brett Tomko	.25
275	Bucky Jacobsen	.25
276	Dontrelle Willis	.50
277	B.J. Upton	.25
278	Rocco Baldelli	.25
279	Ryan Drese	.25
280	Ichiro Suzuki	2.50
281	Brandon Lyon	.25
282	Nick Green	.25
283	Jerry Hairston	.25
284	Mike Lowell	.25
285	Kerry Wood	1.00
286	Omar Vizquel	.25
287	Carlos Beltran	.50
288	Carlos Pena	.25

289	Jeff Weaver	.25
290	Chad Moeller	.25
291	Joe Mays	.25
292	Terrmel Sledge	.25
293	Richard Hidalgo	.25
294	Justin Duchscherer	.25
295	Eric Milton	.25
296	Ramon Hernandez	.25
297	Jose Reyes	.25
298	Joel Pineiro	.25
299	Matt Morris	.25
300	John Halama	.25
301	Gary Matthews	.25
302	Ryan Madson	.25
303	Mark Kotsay	.25
304	Carlos Delgado	.50
305	Casey Kotchman	.25
306	Greg Aquino	.25
307	LaTroy Hawkins	.25
308	Jose Contreras	.25
309	Ken Griffey Jr.	2.00
310	C.C. Sabathia	.25
311	Brandon Inge	.25
312	John Buck	.25
313	Hee Seop Choi	.25
314	Chris Capuano	.25
315	Jesse Crain	.25
316	Geoff Jenkins	.25
317	Mike Piazza	2.00
318	Jorge Posada	.50
319	Nick Swisher	.25
320	Kevin Millwood	.25
321	Mike Gonzalez	.25
322	Jake Peavy	.25
323	Dustin Hermanson	.25
324	Jeremy Reed	.25
325	Alfonso Soriano	1.00
326	Alexis Rios	.25
327	David Eckstein	.25
328	Shea Hillenbrand	.25
329	Russ Ortiz	.25
330	Kurt Ainsworth	.25
331	Orlando Cabrera	.25
332	Carlos Silva	.25
333	Ross Gload	.25
334	Josh Phelps	.25
335	Mike Maroth	.25
336	Guillermo Mota	.25
337	Chris Burke	.25
338	David DeJesus	.25
339	Jose Lima	.25
340	Cristian Guzman	.25
341	Nick Johnson	.25
342	Victor Zambrano	.25
343	Rod Barajas	.25
344	Damian Miller	.25
345	Chase Utley	.25
346	Sean Burnett	.25
347	Boomer Wells	.25
348	Dustan Mohr	.25
349	Bobby Madritsch	.25
350	Reed Johnson	.25
351	R.A. Dickey	.25
352	Scott Kazmir	.25
353	Tony Womack	.25
354	Thomas Perez	.25
355	Esteban Loaiza	.25
356	Tomokazu Ohka	.25
357	Ramon Ortiz	.25
358	Richie Sexson	.50
359	J.D. Drew	.40
360	Barry Bonds	4.00
361	Aramis Ramirez	.50
362	Wily Mo Pena	.25
363	Jeromy Burnitz	.25
364	Nomar Garciaparra	2.00
365	Brandon Backe	.25
366	Derek Lowe	.25
367	Doug Davis	.25
368	Joe Mauer	.50
369	Endy Chavez	.25
370	Bernie Williams	.50
371	Jason Michaels	.25
372	Craig Wilson	.25
373	Ryan Klesko	.25
374	Ray Durham	.25
375	Jose Lopez	.25
376	Jeff Suppan	.25
377	David Bush	.25
378	Marlon Byrd	.25
379	Roy Oswalt	.40
380	Rondell White	.25
381	Troy Glaus	.50
382	Scott Hairston	.25
383	Chipper Jones	1.00
384	Daniel Cabrera	.25
385	Jon Garland	.25
386	Austin Kearns	.25
387	Jake Westbrook	.25
388	Aaron Miles	.25
389	Omar Infante	.25
390	Paul LoDuca	.25
391	Morgan Ensberg	.25
392	Tony Graffanino	.25
393	Milton Bradley	.25
394	Keith Ginter	.25
395	Justin Morneau	.50
396	Tony Armas Jr.	.25
397	Kevin Brown	.25
398	Marco Scutaro	.25
399	Tim Hudson	.50
400	Pat Burrell	.40
401	Jeff Cirillo	.25
402	Larry Walker	.50
403	Dewon Brazelton	.25
404	Shigetoshi Hasegawa	.25
405	Octavio Dotel	.25
406	Michael Cuddyer	.25
407	Junior Spivey	.25
408	Zack Greinke	.25
409	Roger Clemens	3.00
410	Chris Shelton	.25
411	Ugueth Urbina	.25
412	Rafael Betancourt	.25
413	Willie Harris	.25
414	Keith Foulke	.25
415	Larry Bigbie	.25
416	Paul Byrd	.25
417	Troy Percival	.25
418	Pedro J. Martinez	1.00
419	Matt Clement	.25
420	Ryan Wagner	.25
421	Jeff Francis	.25
422	Jeff Conine	.25
423	Wade Miller	.25
424	Gavin Floyd	.25
425	Kazuhisa Ishii	.25
426	Victor Santos	.25
427	Jacque Jones	.25
428	Hideki Matsui	2.00
429	Cory Lidle	.25
430	Jose Castillo	.25
431	Alex Gonzalez	.25
432	Kirk Rueter	.25
433	Jolbert Cabrera	.25
434	Erik Bedard	.25
435	Ricky Ledee	.25
436	Mark Hendrickson	.25
437	Laynce Nix	.25
438	Jason Frasor	.25
439	Kevin Gregg	.25
440	Derek Jeter	3.00
441	Jaret Wright	.25
442	Edwin Jackson	.25
443	Moises Alou	.50
444	Aaron Rowand	.25
445	Kazuhito Tadano	.25
446	Luis Gonzalez	.40
447	A.J. Burnett	.40
448	Jeff Bagwell	.50
449	Brad Penny	.25
450	Corey Koskie	.25
451	Mark Ellis	.25
452	Hector Luna	.25
453	Miguel Olivo	.25
454	Scott Rolen	1.00
455	Ricardo Rodriguez	.25
456	Eric Hinske	.25
457	Tim Salmon	.25
458	Adam LaRoche	.25
459	B.J. Ryan	.25
460	Steve Finley	.25
461	Joe Nathan	.25
462	Vicente Padilla	.25
463	Yadier Molina	.25
464	Tino Martinez	.25
465	Mark Teixeira	.50
466	Kelvim Escobar	.25
467	Pedro Feliz	.25
468	*Ryan Garko*	4.00
469	*Bobby Livingston*	2.00
470	*Yorman Bazardo*	3.00
471	Michael Bourn	2.00
472	*Andy LaRoche*	10.00

Refractor

Cards (1-220):	2-3X
Inserted 1:6	
Rookie Auto. (221-234):	1-1.5X
Production 500	

Black Refractor

Cards (1-220):	3-5X
Production 225	
Rookie Auto. (221-234):	1.5X-3X
Production 200	

X-Fractor

Cards (1-220):	5-10X

Rookie Auto. (221-234): No Pricing
Production 25 sets

Printing Plates

No Pricing
Production one set per color

Chrome The Game Relics

		NM/M
Common Player:		5.00
Inserted 1:box		
JB	Jeff Bagwell	8.00
WB	Wade Boggs	6.00
TH	Torii Hunter	5.00
MPI	Mike Piazza	8.00
JP	Jorge Posada	6.00
MP	Mark Prior	8.00
AR	Alex Rodriguez	15.00
JS	John Smoltz	8.00
AS	Alfonso Soriano	8.00
SS	Sammy Sosa	10.00
MY	Michael Young	5.00

Chrome The Game Patch Relics

		NM/M
Common Player:		10.00
JB	Jeff Bagwell	15.00
JBE	Josh Beckett	10.00
LB	Lance Berkman	10.00
BB	Bret Boone	10.00
AD1	Adam Dunn	15.00
AD2	Adam Dunn	15.00
TG	Troy Glaus	10.00
TH	Todd Helton	15.00
KI	Kazuhisa Ishii	10.00
CJ	Chipper Jones	20.00
PL	Paul LoDuca	10.00
ML	Mike Lowell	10.00
PM	Pedro Martinez	20.00
HN	Hideo Nomo	20.00
MO	Magglio Ordonez	10.00
MPI	Mike Piazza	20.00
AP	Albert Pujols	25.00
AR	Alex Rodriguez	25.00
CS	C.C. Sabathia	10.00
SS	Sammy Sosa	20.00
MT	Mark Teixeira	15.00
FT	Frank Thomas	15.00
DW	Dontrelle Willis	10.00
KW	Kerry Wood	20.00

Dem Bums Autographs

		NM/M
Inserted 1:1,816		
CE	Carl Erskine	50.00
CL	Clem Labine	
JP	Johnny Podres	
DS	Duke Snider	85.00
DZ	Don Zimmer	

2005 TOPPS CRACKER JACK

		NM/M
Complete Set (240):		
Common Player:		.25
Common SP:		3.00
Inserted 1:3		
Pack (8):		4.00
Box (20):		70.00
1	David Wright SP	8.00
2	Rafael Furcal	.25
3	Alex Rodriguez SP	1.50
3	Alex Rodriguez/ SP fielding	5.00
4	Victor Martinez SP	3.00
5	Ken Griffey Jr.	1.50
6	Bobby Crosby SP	3.00
7	Ivan Rodriguez	.50
8	Darin Erstad	.25
9	Javy Lopez	.25
10	Brian Giles	.25
11	Aaron Rowand SP	3.00
12	Joe Torre	.25
13	Zack Greinke SP	3.00
14	Shannon Stewart	.25
15	Jack Wilson	.25
16	Jose Vidro	.25
17	Josh Beckett	.40
---	Josh Beckett (no number)	4.00
18	Barry Zito	.40
19	Bret Boone	.25
20	Greg Maddux	1.00
21	Carl Crawford SP	3.00
22	Mark Teixeira	.50
23	Jason Schmidt	.40
24	Kazuhisa Ishii	.25
25	Mike Piazza	1.00
26	Daniel Cabrera SP	3.00
27	Mike Lieberthal	.25
28	Gil Meche	.25
29	Phil Nevin	.25
30	Adrian Beltre SP	3.00
31	Chipper Jones SP	4.00
32	Zach Day	.25
33	Ben Sheets	.40
34	Carlos Zambrano	.40
35	Melvin Mora	.25
36	Joe Mauer	.50
37	Ken Harvey	.25
38	Bernie Williams	.40
39	Mike Maroth	.25
40	Eric Chavez	.40
41	Matt Lawton SP	3.00
42	Ray Durham	.25
43	Vernon Wells	.25
44	Mike Lowell	.25
45	Jim Thome	.50
46	Joel Pineiro	.25
47	Lance Berkman	.40
48	Ryan Klesko	.25
49	Adam Dunn	.50
50	Vladimir Guerrero	.75
51	Eric Gagne SP	4.00
52	Richie Sexson	.40
53	Javier Vazquez	.25
54	Roy Oswalt	.40
55	Carlos Delgado	.50
56	John Buck SP	3.00
57	Kenny Rogers	.25
58	Sidney Ponson	.25
59	Vicente Padilla	.25
60	Mark Prior SP	.75
60	Mark Prior/SP portrait	4.00
61	A.J. Pierzynski	.25
62	Aubrey Huff	.25
63	Shea Hillenbrand	.25
64	Carlos Guillen	.25
65	Lyle Overbay	.25
66	Al Leiter	.25
67	Eric Hinske	.25
68	Laynce Nix	.25
69	Scott Hairston	.25
70	Roger Clemens	2.00
71	Cesar Izturis SP	3.00
72	Shawn Green	.25

73 Marcus Giles .25
74 Rafael Palmeiro .50
75 Melky Cabrera SP 3.00
75 Gary Sheffield SP 4.00
76 Juan Pierre .25
77 Pat Burrell .40
78 Sean Burroughs .25
79 Frank Thomas .50
80 Andruw Jones .40
81 C.C. Sabathia .25
82 Jeff Bagwell .50
83 Tom Glavine .40
84 Craig Wilson SP 3.00
85 Johan Santana .75
85 Johan Santana/ SP portrait 4.00
86 Raul Ibanez .25
87 Sean Casey .25
88 Bucky Jacobsen .25
89 B.J. Upton .40
90 Bobby Abreu .40
91 Geoff Jenkins .25
92 Troy Glaus .40
93 Dontrelle Willis .40
94 Jose Lima .25
95 Rocco Baldelli .25
96 Aramis Ramirez .40
97 Paul LoDuca .25
98 Torii Hunter .40
99 Jay Payton .25
100 Carlos Beltran .50
101 Jaret Wright .25
102 Jason Bay .40
103 Cliff Floyd .25
104 Mike Sweeney .25
105 Sammy Sosa 1.50
106 Khalil Greene SP 4.00
107 David DeJesus .25
108 Jermaine Dye .25
109 Miguel Cabrera .75
110 Miguel Tejada SP 5.00
111 Johnny Estrada SP 3.00
112 Ronnie Belliard SP 3.00
113 Austin Kearns .25
114 Erubiel Durazo .25
115 Preston Wilson .25
116 Hideo Nomo .40
117 Dmitri Young .25
118 Jon Lieber .25
119 Derrek Lee .40
120 Todd Helton .50
121 Omar Vizquel .25
122 Wily Mo Pena .40
123 J.D. Drew .40
124 Matt Holliday .25
125 Ichiro Suzuki 1.50
126 Mark Buehrle SP 3.00
127 Eric Munson .25
128 Jeff Kent .25
129 Kerry Wood .75
130 Mariano Rivera .50
131 Nick Johnson .25
132 Randy Winn .25
133 Phil Garner .25
134 Jose Reyes .25
135 Michael Young SP 3.00
135 Ian Kinsler SP 4.00
136 Jose Contreras .25
137 Oliver Perez .25
138 Roy Halladay .40
139 Kevin Millwood .25
140 Jorge Posada .40
141 Mike Cameron .25
142 Edgardo Alfonzo .25
143 Chris Shelton .25
144 Luis Castillo .25
145 Alfonso Soriano .75
146 Ryan Drese SP 3.00
147 Mark Mulder .40
148 Jason Giambi .25
149 Travis Hafner .25
150 Randy Johnson .75
151 Paul Konerko SP 3.00
152 Mike Mussina .50
153 Brad Wilkerson .25
154 Tim Hudson .40
155 Garret Anderson .40
156 Chase Utley SP 3.00
157 Jamie Moyer .25
158 Scott Kazmir .40
159 Brett Myers .25
160 Kazuo Matsui .25
161 Orlando Hudson .25
162 Luis Gonzalez .25
163 Kevin Youkilis .25
164 Jason Kendall SP .25
164 Landon Powell SP 3.00
165 Hank Blalock .50
166 Mark Loretta SP 3.00
167 Miguel Cairo .25
168 Corey Patterson .40
169 Carlos Zambrano .25
170 Magglio Ordonez .25
171 J.T. Snow .25
172 Randy Wolf .25
173 Rich Harden .40
174 Bartolo Colon .25
175 Derek Jeter 2.00
176 Casey Kotchman SP 3.00
177 Val Majewski .25
178 Grady Sizemore .25
179 Rickie Weeks .25
180 Robinson Cano .25
181 Nick Swisher SP 3.00
182 Ryan Howard .50
183 John Van Benschoten .25
184 Delmon Young .50
185 Aaron Hill .25
186 Chris Burke SP 3.00
187 Merkin Valdez .25
188 Jeremy Reed .25
189 Conor Jackson .25
190 Melky Cabrera .25
191 Joey Gathright SP 3.00
192 Gavin Floyd .25
193 Joe Blanton .25
194 Jason Kubel .25
195 Jeff Francis .25
196 Angel Guzman SP 3.00
197 Dallas McPherson .25
198 *Melky Cabrera* 1.00
199 Jake Dittler .25
200 *Elvys Quezada* .50
201 *Ian Kinsler SP* 4.00
202 *Nate McLouth* .50
203 *Chris Seddon* .75
204 *Chad Orvella* .50
205 *Ian Bladergroen* 1.00
206 *James Jurries SP* 4.00
207 *Landon Powell* .75
208 *Eric Nielsen* .50
209 *Chris Roberson* .50
210 Andre Ethier .75
211 *Chris Denorfia SP* 4.00
212 *Darren Fenster* .50
213 *Jeremy West* 1.00
214 *Sean Marshall* .50
215 Ryan Sweeney 1.50
216 *Steven Doetsch SP* 3.00
217 *Kevin Melillo* .50
218 *Chip Cannon* .50
219 Tony LaRussa .25
220 Chris Carpenter .25
221 Edgar Renteria/ SP Red Sox 3.00
221 Edgar Renteria/ SP Cardinals 3.00
222 Albert Pujols 2.00
223 Jim Edmonds .40
224 Jason Marquis .25
225 Scott Rolen SP 4.00
226 Larry Walker SP 4.00
227 Matt Morris .25
228 Mike Matheny 3.00
228 Mike Matheny/ SP Cardinals 3.00
229 Jeromy Burnitz .25
230 Terry Francona .25
231 Johnny Damon SP 4.00
232 Keith Foulke .25
233 Trot Nixon .25
234 Manny Ramirez .75
235 David Ortiz SP 4.00
236 Pedro Martinez/ SP Mets 4.00
236 Pedro J. Martinez/ SP Red Sox 4.00
237 Curt Schilling .75
238 Kevin Millar .25
239 Bill Mueller .25
240 Mark Bellhorn .25
Josh Beckett SP 3.00

Mini Blue

Stars: 8-15X
SP's: 4-6X
Production 50 sets

Mini Grey

No Pricing
Production 25 sets

Mini Red

Stars: 1-2X
Inserted 1:1
SP's: .75-1.5X
Inserted 1:20

Mini White

No Pricing
Production one set

Mini Stickers

Stars: 1-2X
Inserted 1:1
SP's: .75-1.5X
Inserted 1:20

Gold Refractor

No Pricing
Production one set

A-Rod Throwbacks

NM/M

ARI1 Alex Rodriquez 3.00
ARI2 Alex Rodriquez 3.00
ARI3 Alex Rodriquez 3.00
ARI4 Alex Rodriquez 3.00

Autographs

NM/M

Production 50 Sets
Bonds Production 25
CB Carlos Beltran 80.00
EG Eric Gagne 40.00
AR Alex Rodriguez 250.00
JS Johan Santana 60.00

Secret Surprise Autographs

NM/M

GA Garret Anderson 20.00
EC Eric Chavez 20.00
EG Eric Gagne 30.00
AG Angel Guzman 8.00
SK Scott Kazmir 25.00
MK Mark Kotsay 100 15.00
ML Mark Loretta 100 30.00
DM Dallas McPherson 100 35.00
KM Kevin Millar 25.00
MM Melvin Mora 15.00
CN Chris Nelson 12.00
RR Richie Robnett 12.00
CS C.C. Sabathia 15.00
JS Johan Santana 50.00
CT Curtis Thigpen 20.00
CW Craig Wilson 10.00
DW David Wright 35.00

1,2,3 Strikes You're Out Relics

NM/M

Inserted 1:204
JB Josh Beckett 8.00
RD Ryan Drese 5.00
RO Russ Ortiz 5.00
BR Brad Radke 8.00
CS Curt Schilling 15.00
JW Jaret Wright 8.00

Take Me Out To/Ballgame Relics

NM/M

Inserted 1:16
JB Jeff Bagwell 6.00
RB Ronnie Belliard 4.00
CB Carlos Beltran 8.00
AB Adrian Beltre 6.00
LB1 Lance Berkman 6.00
LB2 Lance Berkman 6.00
AB1 Angel Berroa 4.00
AB2 Angel Berroa 4.00
CBI Craig Biggio 6.00
HB1 Hank Blalock 8.00
HB2 Hank Blalock 8.00
HB3 Hank Blalock 8.00
SB Sean Burroughs 4.00
MC Miguel Cabrera 8.00
VC Vinny Castilla 4.00
EC1 Eric Chavez 6.00
EC2 Eric Chavez 6.00
BC Bobby Cox 6.00
CC Coco Crisp 4.00
BCR Bobby Crosby 6.00
AD Adam Dunn 8.00
JE1 Jim Edmonds 6.00
JE2 Jim Edmonds 6.00
DE Darin Erstad 4.00
JE Johnny Estrada 4.00
RF Rafael Furcal 6.00
JG Jody Gerut 4.00
JGI Jay Gibbons 4.00
MG Marcus Giles 4.00
TG Troy Glaus 6.00
LG Luis Gonzalez 4.00
NG Nick Green 4.00
SG Shawn Green 4.00
VG Vladimir Guerrero 10.00
JGU Jose Guillen 6.00
CG Cristian Guzman 4.00
TH Todd Helton 8.00
THU Torii Hunter 6.00
JJ Jacque Jones 4.00
JK Jason Kendall 4.00
BK Bobby Kielty 4.00
RK Ryan Klesko 4.00
PK Paul Konerko 4.00
MK Mark Kotsay 4.00
AL Adam LaRoche 6.00
VM Victor Martinez 6.00
KME Kevin Mench 4.00
DM Doug Mientkiewicz 4.00
KM Kevin Millar 10.00
MM Melvin Mora 6.00
PN Phil Nevin 4.00
LN Laynce Nix 4.00
MO Magglio Ordonez 4.00
DO David Ortiz 10.00
RP Rafael Palmeiro 8.00
CP Corey Patterson 6.00
MP Mike Piazza 12.00
JP1 Jorge Posada 8.00
JP2 Jorge Posada 8.00
AP Albert Pujols 20.00
MR Manny Ramirez 10.00
JR Jeremy Reed 8.00
MRE Mike Restovich 4.00
AR Alex Rodriguez 15.00
ARA Aramis Ramirez 6.00
IR1 Ivan Rodriguez 8.00
IR2 Ivan Rodriguez 8.00
RS Reggie Sanders 4.00
BS Benito Santiago 4.00
GS Gary Sheffield 8.00
AS Alfonso Soriano 8.00
MT1 Mark Teixeira 8.00
MT2 Mark Teixeira 8.00
MT3 Mark Teixeira 8.00
MTE1 Miguel Tejada 8.00
MTE2 Miguel Tejada 8.00
CT Charles Thomas 4.00
JT Jim Thome 8.00
JTO Joe Torre 10.00
OV Omar Vizquel 6.00
BW Bernie Williams 6.00
DW Dontrelle Willis 8.00
MY Michael Young 6.00

2005 TOPPS GALLERY

NM/M

Complete Set (195): 175.00

Common Player:		.25
Common SP (151-195):		1.00
Inserted 1:1		
Variations 1:40		
Pack (5):		6.00
Box (20):		100.00
1	Alex Rodriguez	2.50
1	Alex Rodriguez/ SP/black bat. glove	8.00
2	Eric Chavez	.50
3	Mike Piazza	1.50
4	Bret Boone	.25
5	Albert Pujols	3.00
6	Vernon Wells	.25
7	Andruw Jones	.50
8	Miguel Tejada	.50
9	Johnny Damon	.75
10	Nomar Garciaparra	2.00
11	Pat Burrell	.40
12	Bartolo Colon	.25
13	Johnny Estrada	.25
14	Luis Gonzalez	.40
15	Jay Gibbons	.25
16	Curt Schilling	1.00
17	Aramis Ramirez	.50
18	Frank Thomas	.75
19	Adam Dunn	.75
20	Sammy Sosa	2.00
21	Matt Lawton	.25
22	Preston Wilson	.25
23	Carlos Pena	.25
24	Josh Beckett	.50
25	Carlos Beltran	.75
26	Juan Gonzalez	.50
27	Adrian Beltre	.50
28	Lyle Overbay	.25
29	Justin Morneau	.25
30	Derek Jeter	3.00
31	Barry Zito	.50
32	Bobby Abreu	.40
33	Jason Bay	.25
34	Jose Reyes	.25
35	Nick Johnson	.25
36	Lew Ford	.25
37	Scott Podsednik	.25
38	Rocco Baldelli	.40
39	Eric Hinske	.25
40	Ichiro Suzuki	2.50
40	Ichiro Suzuki/ SP/writing on wall	8.00
41	Larry Walker	.50
42	Mark Teixeira	.50
43	Khalil Greene	.50
44	Edgardo Alfonzo	.25
45	Javier Vazquez	.25
46	Cliff Floyd	.25
47	Geoff Jenkins	.25
48	Ken Griffey Jr.	2.00
49	Vinny Castilla	.25
50	Mark Prior	1.00
51	Jose Guillen	.25
52	J.D. Drew	.50
53	Rafael Palmeiro	.75
54	Kevin Youkilis	.25
55	Derrek Lee	.50
56	Freddy Garcia	.25
57	Wily Mo Pena	.25
58	C.C. Sabathia	.25
59	Craig Biggio	.40
60	Ivan Rodriguez	.75
61	Angel Berroa	.25
62	Ben Sheets	.50
63	Johan Santana	.75
64	Al Leiter	.40
65	Bernie Williams	.50
66	Bobby Crosby	.50
67	Jack Wilson	.25
68	A.J. Pierzynski	.25
69	Jimmy Rollins	.25
70	Jason Giambi	.50
71	Tom Glavine	.50
72	Kevin Brown	.25
73	B.J. Upton	.50
74	Edgar Renteria	.50
75	Alfonso Soriano	1.00
76	Mike Lieberthal	.25
77	Kazuo Matsui	.25
78	Phil Nevin	.25
79	Shawn Green	.40
80	Miguel Cabrera	1.00
81	Todd Helton	.75
82	Magglio Ordonez	.40
83	Manny Ramirez	1.00
84	Bill Mueller	.25
85	Troy Glaus	.50
86	Richie Sexson	.50
87	Javy Lopez	.40
88	David Ortiz	1.00
89	Greg Maddux	1.50
90	Vladimir Guerrero	1.00
91	Jeromy Burnitz	.25
92	Jeff Kent	.40
93	Travis Hafner	.40
94	Mark Buehrle	.25
95	Paul LoDuca	.25
96	Roy Oswalt	.40
97	Torii Hunter	.40
98	Gary Sheffield	.75
99	Erubiel Durazo	.25
100	Jim Thome	1.00
100	Jim Thome/ SP/kid's shirt is red	6.00
101	Ken Harvey	.25
102	Shannon Stewart	.25
103	Dmitri Young	.25
104	Kevin Millar	.50
105	Kerry Wood	1.00
106	Paul Konerko	.40
107	Ronnie Belliard	.25
108	Mike Lowell	.40
109	Hee Seop Choi	.25
110	Joe Mauer	.25
111	David Wright	.50
112	Jorge Posada	.50
113	Tim Hudson	.50
114	Brian Giles	.25
115	Jason Schmidt	.50
116	Aubrey Huff	.25
117	Hank Blalock	.75
118	Jim Edmonds	.50
119	Raul Ibanez	.25
120	Carlos Delgado	.50
121	Craig Wilson	.40
122	Ryan Klesko	.25
123	Mark Mulder	.50
124	Jose Vidro	.25
125	Mike Sweeney	.25
126	Lance Berkman	.50
127	Juan Pierre	.25
128	Austin Kearns	.25
129	Moises Alou	.50
130	Garret Anderson	.50
131	Pedro J. Martinez	1.00
132	Melvin Mora	.25
133	Marcus Giles	.25
134	Corey Patterson	.50
135	Carlos Lee	.25
136	Sean Casey	.40
137	Jody Gerut	.25
138	Jose Valentin	.25
139	Aaron Miles	.25
140	Randy Johnson	1.00
141	Carlos Guillen	.25
142	Dontrelle Willis	.50
143	Jeff Bagwell	.75
144	Jason Kendall	.25
145	Mark Loretta	.25
146	Scott Rolen	1.00
147	Carl Crawford	.25
148	Michael Young	.25
149	Jermaine Dye	.25
150	Chipper Jones	1.00
151	*Melky Cabrera*	3.00
152	*Chris Seddon*	4.00
153	Nate Schierholtz	4.00
154	*Ian Kinsler*	3.00
154	Ian Kinsler/ SP/gold background	8.00
155	*Brandon Moss*	4.00
155	Brandon Moss/ SP/red hat	10.00
156	*Chadd Blasko*	2.00
157	*Jeremy West*	2.00
157	Jeremy West/ SP/navy blue jersey	6.00
158	*Sean Marshall*	2.00
159	Ryan Sweeney	4.00
160	*Matt Lindstrom*	2.00
161	*Ryan Goleski*	4.00
162	*Brett Harper*	2.00
163	*Chris Roberson*	3.00
164	Andre Ethier	6.00
165	*Ian Bladergroen*	2.00
165	Ian Bladergroen/ SP/swinging	6.00
166	*James Jurries*	2.00
167	*Billy Butler*	6.00
167	Billy Butler/ SP/black jersey	15.00
168	*Michael Rogers*	3.00
168	Michael Rogers/ SP/baseball in hand	8.00
169	*Tyler Clippard*	4.00
170	*Luis Ramirez*	3.00
171	Casey Kotchman	2.00
172	Chris Burke	2.00
173	Dallas McPherson	2.00
174	Edwin Jackson	1.00
175	Felix Hernandez	4.00
176	Gavin Floyd	1.00
177	Guillermo Quiroz	1.00
178	Jason Kubel	1.00
179	Jeff Mathis	1.00
180	Rickie Weeks	1.00
181	Ryan Howard	3.00
182	Franklin Gutierrez	1.00
183	Jeremy Reed	5.00
184	Carlos Quentin	5.00
185	Jeff Francis	5.00
186	Nolan Ryan	6.00
187	Hank Aaron	6.00
187	Hank Aaron/ SP/red 755	15.00
188	Duke Snider	4.00
189	Mike Schmidt	5.00
190	Ernie Banks	4.00
191	Frank Robinson	3.00
192	Harmon Killebrew	4.00
193	Al Kaline	3.00
194	Rod Carew	3.00
195	Johnny Bench	4.00

Artist's Proof

Stars (1-150):	2-4X
SP's (151-195):	1-2X
Inserted 1:1	

Printing Plates

No Pricing
Production one for each color

Cut Signatures

No Pricing

Gallo's Gallery Sketches

		NM/M
Complete Set (20):		50.00
Common Player:		1.50
Inserted 1:15		
HA	Hank Aaron	6.00
HB	Hank Blalock	1.50
NG	Nomar Garciaparra	4.00
VG	Vladimir Guerrero	2.00
TH	Todd Helton	1.50
DJ	Derek Jeter	6.00
RJ	Randy Johnson	2.00
CJ	Chipper Jones	2.00
MPI	Mike Piazza	4.00
MP	Mark Prior	2.00
AP	Albert Pujols	6.00
AR	Alex Rodriguez	5.00
IR	Ivan Rodriguez	1.50
NR	Nolan Ryan	6.00
MS	Mike Schmidt	5.00
AS	Alfonso Soriano	2.00
SS	Sammy Sosa	4.00
IS	Ichiro Suzuki	4.00
MT	Miguel Tejada	1.50
JT	Jim Thome	2.00

Heritage Insert

		NM/M
Complete Set (25):		65.00
Common Player:		2.00
Inserted 1:15		
EB	Ernie Banks	4.00
CB	Carlos Beltran	3.00
JB	Johnny Bench	4.00
HB	Hank Blalock	2.00
GB	George Brett	6.00
JC	Jose Canseco	2.00
BG	Bob Gibson	3.00
AK	Al Kaline	3.00
DM	Don Mattingly	6.00
RP	Rafael Palmeiro	3.00
JP	Jim Palmer	2.00
AP	Albert Pujols	8.00
BR	Brooks Robinson	3.00
FR	Frank Robinson	2.00
RR	Frank Robinson, Brooks Robinson	3.00
RJ	Alex Rodriguez, Derek Jeter	8.00
IR	Ivan Rodriguez	3.00
NR	Nolan Ryan	8.00
CS	Curt Schilling	3.00
MS	Mike Schmidt	5.00
TS	Jim Thome, Mike Schmidt	5.00
OS	Ozzie Smith	3.00
DSN	Duke Snider	3.00
DS	Darryl Strawberry	2.00
DW	Dontrelle Willis	2.00

Heritage Relics

		NM/M
Common Player:		5.00
Inserted 1:40		
GB	George Brett	12.00
JC	Jose Canseco	8.00
DM	Don Mattingly	15.00
AP	Albert Pujols	15.00
AR	Alex Rodriguez	15.00
IR	Ivan Rodriguez	8.00
NR	Nolan Ryan	20.00
OS	Ozzie Smith	8.00
DS	Darryl Strawberry	5.00
DW	Dontrelle Willis	5.00

Heritage Relic Autographs

		NM/M
Production 25 sets		
DM	Don Mattingly	75.00
AR	Alex Rodriguez	300.00
IR	Ivan Rodriguez	
NR	Nolan Ryan	150.00

Originals Relics

		NM/M
Common Player:		4.00
Inserted 1:10		
JB	Jeff Bagwell	8.00
RB	Rocco Baldelli	4.00
JBE	Josh Beckett	4.00
LB	Lance Berkman	4.00
AB	Angel Berroa	4.00
HB	Hank Blalock	8.00
HBB	Hank Blalock	8.00
MC	Miguel Cabrera	8.00
JD	Johnny Damon	8.00
RD	Ryan Drese	4.00
JG	Jason Giambi	6.00
MG	Marcus Giles	4.00
VG	Vladimir Guerrero	8.00
RH	Rich Harden	4.00
TH	Todd Helton	8.00
CJ	Chipper Jones	8.00
JL	Javy Lopez	4.00
ML	Mike Lowell	4.00
PM	Pedro J. Martinez	8.00
KM	Kazuo Matsui	6.00
LN	Laynce Nix	4.00
DO	David Ortiz	8.00
MP	Mike Piazza	8.00
MPB	Mike Piazza	8.00
MPR	Mark Prior	8.00
AP	Albert Pujols	15.00
MR	Manny Ramirez	8.00
JR	Jose Reyes	4.00
AR	Alex Rodriguez	12.00
IR	Ivan Rodriguez	8.00
AS	Alfonso Soriano	8.00
SS	Sammy Sosa	10.00
MT	Mark Teixeira	4.00
MTE	Miguel Tejada	6.00
FT	Frank Thomas	8.00
BU	B.J. Upton	4.00

BW Bernie Williams 6.00
DW Dontrelle Willis 4.00
KW Kerry Wood 8.00
MY Michael Young 4.00

Penmanship Autographs

NM/M
Common Autograph: 10.00
JB Jason Bartlett 10.00
TB Taylor Buchholz 10.00
EC Eric Chavez 15.00
FH Felix Hernandez 40.00
AH Aubrey Huff 15.00
JJ Justin Jones 15.00
ML Mike Lowell
DM Dallas McPherson 25.00
JP Jorge Posada
AR Alex Rodriguez 250.00
IR Ivan Rodriguez
VW Vernon Wells 10.00

2005 TOPPS HERITAGE

NM/M
Complete Set (475): 400.00
Common Player: .40
Common SP (398-475): 4.00
SP's & Variations inserted 1:2
Pack (8): 4.75
Box (24): 100.00
1 Will Harridge .40
2 Warren Giles .40
3 Alfonso Soriano 1.00
3 Alfonso Soriano/ SP/running 5.00
4 Mark Mulder .75
5 Todd Helton/SP 5.00
6 Jason Bay .40
6 Jason Bay/SP/ 1956 Pirates Uniform 5.00
7 Ichiro Suzuki 2.50
7 Ichiro Suzuki/ SP/squatting on-deck 8.00
8 Jim Tracy .40
9 Gavin Floyd .40
10 John Smoltz .75
11 Chicago Cubs .50
12 Darin Erstad .40
13 Chad Tracy .40
14 Charles Thomas .40
15 Miguel Tejada .75
16 Andre Ethier 2.00
17 Jeff Francis .40
18 Derrek Lee .50
19 Juan Uribe .40
20 Jim Edmonds/SP 5.00
21 Kenny Lofton .40
22 Brad Ausmus .40
23 Jon Garland .40
24 Edwin Jackson .40
25 Joe Mauer .50
26 Wes Helms .40
27 Brian Schneider .40
28 Kazuo Matsui .40
29 Tom Gordon .40
30 Hideo Nomo/SP 4.00
31 Albert Pujols/SP 15.00
31 Albert Pujols/SP/ 1956 Cards uniform 15.00
32 Carl Crawford .40
33 Vladimir Guerrero/SP 6.00
34 Nick Green .40
35 Jay Gibbons .40
36 Kevin Youkilis .40
37 Billy Wagner .40
38 Terrence Long .40
39 Kevin Mench .40
40 Garret Anderson .50
41 Reed Johnson .40
42 Reggie Sanders .40
43 Kirk Rueter .40
44 Jay Payton .40
45 Tike Redman .40
46 Mike Lieberthal .40
47 Damian Miller .40
48 Zach Day .40
49 Juan Rincon .40
50 Jim Thome 1.00
50 Jim Thome/SP/Fielding 6.00
51 Jose Guillen .40
52 Richie Sexson .75
53 Juan Cruz .40
54 Byung-Hyun Kim .40
55 Carlos Zambrano .50
56 Carlos Lee .40
57 Adam Dunn .75
58 David Riske .40
59 Carlos Guillen .40
60 Larry Bowa .40
61 Barry Bonds 4.00
62 Chris Woodward .40
63 *Matt DeSalvo* 1.00
64 *Brian Stavisky* 1.00
65 Scot Shields .40
66 J.D. Drew .50
67 Erik Bedard .40
68 Scott Williamson .40
69 Mark Prior 1.00
69 Mark Prior/SP/ 1956 Cubs uniform 6.00
69 6.00
70 Ken Griffey Jr. 2.00
71 Kazuhito Tadano .40
72 Philadelphia Phillies .40
73 Jeremy Reed .40
74 Ricardo Rodriguez .40
75 Carlos Delgado .50
76 Eric Milton .40
77 Miguel Olivo .40
78 Edgardo Alfonzo .40
78 Edgardo Alfonzo/SP/ 1956 Giants uniform 4.00
79 Kazuhisa Ishii/SP 4.00
80 Jason Giambi .75
81 Cliff Floyd .40
82 Torii Hunter .50
82 Torii Hunter/SP/ 1956 Senators uniform 4.00
83 Odalis Perez .40
84 Scott Podsednik .40
85 Cleveland Indians .40
86 Jeff Suppan .40
87 Ray Durham .40
88 *Tyler Clippard* 1.00
89 Ryan Howard .75
90 Cincinnati Reds .40
91 Bengie Molina .40
92 Danny Bautista .40
93 Eli Marrero .40
94 Larry Bigbie .40
95 Atlanta Braves .40
96 Merkin Valdez .40
97 Rocco Baldelli .40
98 Woody Williams .40
99 Jason Frasor .40
100 Baltimore Orioles .40
101 Ivan Rodriguez/SP 6.00
102 Joe Kennedy .40
103 Mike Lowell .50
104 Armando Benitez .40
105 Craig Biggio .50
106 David DeJesus .40
107 Adrian Beltre .75
108 Phil Nevin .40
109 Cristian Guzman .40
110 Jorge Posada/SP 6.00
111 Boston Red Sox .75
112 Jeff Mathis .40
113 Bartolo Colon .40
114 Alex Cintron .40
115 Russ Ortiz .40
116 Doug Mientkiewicz .40
117 Placido Polanco .40
118 Magglio Ordonez .40
118 Magglio Ordonez/SP/ 1956 White Sox uni. 4.00
119 *Chris Seddon* 1.00
120 Bobby Abreu .50
121 Pittsburgh Pirates .40
122 Dallas McPherson .75
123 Rodrigo Lopez .40
124 Mark Bellhorn .40
125 Nomar Garciaparra 2.00
125 Nomar Garciaparra/ SP/1956 Cubs uniform 8.00
126 Sean Casey .40
127 Ronnie Belliard .40
128 Tom Goodwin .40
129 Preston Wilson .40
130 Andruw Jones/SP 5.00
131 Roberto Alomar .75
132 John Buck .40
133 Jason LaRue .40
134 St. Louis Cardinals .75
135 Alex Rodriguez/SP 10.00
135 Alex Rodriguez/ SP/Fielding 10.00
136 Nate Robertson .40
137 Juan Pierre .40
138 Morgan Ensberg .40
139 Vinny Castilla .40
140 Jake Dittler 1.00
141 Chan Ho Park .40
142 Felix Hernandez 2.50
143 Jason Isringhausen .40
144 Dustan Mohr .40
145 Khalil Greene .75
146 Minnesota Twins .40
147 Vicente Padilla .40
148 Oliver Perez .40
149 Brian Giles .40
150 Shawn Green .40
151 Matt Lawton .40
152 Casey Blake .40
153 Frank Thomas .75
154 Orlando Hernandez .40
155 Eric Chavez .50
155 Eric Chavez/SP/ 1956 Kansas City uni. 4.00
156 Chase Utley .40
157 John Olerud .40
158 Adam Eaton .40
159 Josh Fogg .40
160 Michael Tucker .40
161 Kevin Brown .40
162 Bobby Crosby .50
163 Jason Schmidt .50
164 Shannon Stewart .40
165 Tony Womack .40
166 Los Angeles Dodgers .40
167 Franklin Gutierrez .40
168 Ted Lilly .40
169 Mark Teixeira .50
170 Matt Morris .40
171 Bucky Jacobsen .40
172 *Steven Doetsch* 1.00
173 Jeff Weaver .40
174 Tony Graffanino .40
175 Jeff Bagwell .75
176 Carl Pavano .50
177 Junior Spivey .40
178 Carlos Silva .40
179 Tim Redding .40
180 Brett Myers .40
181 Mike Mussina .75
182 Richard Hidalgo .40
183 Nick Johnson .40
184 Lew Ford .40
185 Barry Zito .50
186 Jimmy Rollins .40
187 Jack Wilson .40
188 Chicago White Sox .40
189 Guillermo Quiroz .40
190 Mark Hendrickson .40
191 Jeremy Bonderman .40
192 Jason Jennings .40
193 Paul LoDuca .40
194 A.J. Burnett .40
195 Ken Harvey .40
196 Geoff Jenkins .40
197 Joe Mays .40
198 Jose Vidro .40
199 David Wright .75
200 Randy Johnson 1.00
201 Jeff DeVanon .40
202 Paul Byrd .40
203 David Ortiz 1.00
204 Kyle Farnsworth .40
205 Keith Foulke .40
206 Joe Crede .40
207 Austin Kearns .40
208 Jody Gerut .40
209 Shawn Chacon .40
210 Carlos Pena .40
211 Luis Castillo .40
212 *Chris Denorfia* 1.00
213 Detroit Tigers .40
214 Aubrey Huff .40
215 Brad Fullmer .40
216 Frank Catalanotto .40
217 Raul Ibanez .40
218 Ryan Klesko .40
219 Octavio Dotel .40
220 Robert Mackowiak .40
221 Scott Hatteberg .40
222 Pat Burrell .40
223 Bernie Williams .50
224 Kris Benson .40
225 Eric Gagne .50
226 San Francisco Giants .40
227 Roy Oswalt .40
228 Josh Beckett .50
229 Lee Mazzilli .40
230 Rickie Weeks .40
231 Troy Glaus .50
232 Chone Figgins .40
233 John Thomson .40
234 Trot Nixon .40
235 Brad Penny .40
236 Oakland Athletics .40
237 Miguel Batista .40
238 Ryan Drese .40
239 Aaron Miles .40
240 Randy Wolf .40
241 Brian Lawrence .40
242 A.J. Pierzynski .40
243 Jamie Moyer .40
244 Chris Carpenter .40
245 So Taguchi .40
246 Rob Bell .40
247 Francisco Cordero .40
248 Tom Glavine .50
249 Jermaine Dye .40
250 Cliff Lee .40
251 New York Yankees .75
252 Vernon Wells .40
253 R.A. Dickey .40
254 Larry Walker .50
255 Randy Winn .40
256 Pedro Feliz .40
257 Mark Loretta .40
258 Tim Worrell .40
259 Kip Wells .40
260 Cesar Izturis/SP 4.00
261 Carlos Beltran .75
261 Carlos Beltran/ SP/Batting 6.00
262 Juan Encarnacion .40
263 Luis Gonzalez .40
264 Grady Sizemore .40
265 Paul Wilson .40
266 Mark Buehrle .40
267 Todd Hollandsworth .40
268 Orlando Cabrera .50
269 Sidney Ponson .40
270 Mike Hampton .40
271 Luis Gonzalez .50
272 Brendan Donnelly .40
273 Chipper Jones 1.00
273 Chipper Jones/ SP/Blue background 6.00
274 Brandon Webb .40
275 Marty Cordova .40
276 Greg Maddux 2.00
277 Jose Contreras .40
278 Aaron Harang .40
279 Coco Crisp .40
280 Bobby Higginson .40
281 Guillermo Mota .40
282 Andy Pettitte .50
283 *Jeremy West* 3.00
284 Craig Brazell .40
285 Eric Hinske .40
286 Hank Blalock .75
286 Hank Blalock/ SP/Fielding 6.00
287 B.J. Upton .75
288 Jason Marquis .40
289 Matt Herges .40
290 Ramon Hernandez .40
291 Marlon Byrd .40
292 Ryan Sweeney/SP 8.00
293 Esteban Loaiza .40
294 Al Leiter .50
295 Alex Gonzalez .40
296 Johan Santana .75
296 Johan Santana/SP/ 1956 Senators uniform 6.00
297 Milton Bradley .40
298 Mike Sweeney .40
299 Wade Miller .40
300 Sammy Sosa 2.00
300 Sammy Sosa/ SP/Blue jersey 8.00
301 Wily Mo Pena .40
302 Tim Wakefield .40
303 Rafael Palmeiro .75
304 Rafael Furcal .40
305 David Eckstein .40
306 David Segui .40
307 Kevin Millar .40
308 Matt Clement .40
309 *Wade Robinson* 1.00
310 Brad Radke .40
311 Steve Finley .40
312 Lance Berkman .50

312 Lance Berkman/SP/Fielding 5.00
313 Joe Randa .40
314 Miguel Cabrera 1.00
315 Billy Koch .40
316 Alex Sanchez .40
317 Chin-Hui Tsao .40
318 Omar Vizquel .40
319 Ryan Freel .40
320 LaTroy Hawkins .40
321 Aaron Rowand .40
322 Paul Konerko .40
323 Joe Borowski .40
324 Jarrod Washburn .40
325 Jaret Wright .40
326 Johnny Damon .75
327 Corey Patterson .50
328 Travis Hafner .40
329 Shingo Takatsu .40
330 Dmitri Young .40
331 Matt Holliday .40
332 Jeff Kent .50
333 Desi Relaford .40
334 Jose Hernandez .40
335 Lyle Overbay .40
336 Jacque Jones .40
337 Terrmel Sledge .40
338 Victor Zambrano .40
339 Gary Sheffield .75
340 Brad Wilkerson .40
341 *Ian Kinsler* 1.00
342 Jesse Crain .40
343 Orlando Hudson .40
344 Laynce Nix .40
345 Jose Cruz Jr. .40
346 Edgar Renteria .50
347 Eddie Guardado .40
348 Jerome Williams .40
349 Trevor Hoffman .40
350 Mike Piazza 1.50
351 Jason Kendall .40
352 Kevin Millwood .40
353 Tim Hudson .50
353 Tim Hudson/SP/1956 Braves uniform 5.00
354 Paul Quantrill .40
355 Jon Lieber .40
356 Braden Looper .40
357 Chad Cordero .40
358 Joe Nathan .40
359 Doug Davis .40
360 *Ian Bladergroen* 1.00
361 Val Majewski .40
362 Francisco Rodriguez .40
363 Kelvim Escobar .40
364 Marcus Giles .40
365 *Darren Fenster* 1.00
366 David Bell .40
367 Shea Hillenbrand .40
368 Manny Ramirez 1.00
369 Ben Broussard .40
370 *Luis Ramirez* 1.00
371 Dustin Hermanson .40
372 Akinori Otsuka .40
373 *Chadd Blasko* 1.00
374 Delmon Young .75
375 Michael Young .40
376 Bret Boone .40
377 Jake Peavy .40
378 *Matt Lindstrom* 1.00
379 Sean Burroughs .40
380 Rich Harden .40
381 *Chris Roberson* 1.00
382 John Lackey .40
383 Johnny Estrada .40
384 *Matt Rogelstad* 1.00
385 Toby Hall .40
386 Adam LaRoche .40
387 Bill Hall .40
388 Tim Salmon .50
389 Curt Schilling 1.00
389 Curt Schilling/SP/Looking in 6.00
390 Michael Barrett .40
391 Jose Acevedo .40
392 Nate Schierholtz 1.00
393 J.T. Snow Jr. .40
394 Mark Redman .40
395 Ryan Madson .40
396 *Kevin West* 1.00
397 Ramon Ortiz .40
398 Derek Lowe 4.00
399 Kerry Wood 6.00
400 Derek Jeter 15.00
401 Livan Hernandez 4.00
402 Casey Kotchman 6.00
403 *Chaz Lytle* 6.00
404 Alexis Rios 5.00
405 Scott Spiezio 4.00
406 Craig Wilson 4.00
407 Felix Rodriguez 4.00
408 D'Angelo Jimenez 4.00
409 Rondell White 4.00
410 Shawn Estes 4.00
411 Troy Percival 4.00
412 Melvin Mora 4.00
413 Aramis Ramirez 6.00
414 Carl Everett 4.00
415 *Elvys Quezada* 6.00
416 Ben Sheets 5.00
417 Matt Stairs 4.00
418 Adam Everett 4.00
419 Jason Johnson 4.00
420 *Billy Butler* 8.00
421 Justin Morneau 5.00
422 Jose Reyes 5.00
423 Mariano Rivera 5.00
424 *Jose Vaquedano* 6.00
425 Gabe Gross 5.00
426 Scott Rolen 6.00
427 Ty Wigginton 4.00
428 *James Jurries* 6.00
429 Pedro J. Martinez 6.00
430 Mark Grudzielanek 4.00
431 Josh Phelps 4.00
432 *Ryan Goleski* 5.00
433 Mike Matheny 4.00
434 Bobby Kielty 4.00
435 Tony Batista 4.00
436 Corey Koskie 4.00
437 Brad Lidge 4.00
438 Dontrelle Willis 4.00
439 Angel Berroa 4.00
440 Jason Kubel 4.00
441 Roy Halladay 4.00
442 Brian Roberts 4.00
443 Bill Mueller 4.00
444 Adam Kennedy 4.00
445 *Brandon Moss* 5.00
446 Sean Burnett 4.00
447 Eric Byrnes 4.00
448 *Matt Campbell* 6.00
449 *Ryan Webb* 6.00
450 Jose Valentin 4.00
451 Jake Westbrook 4.00
452 *Glen Perkins* 6.00
453 Alex Gonzalez 4.00
454 Jeromy Burnitz 4.00
455 Zack Greinke 4.00
456 *Sean Marshall* 6.00
457 Erubiel Durazo 4.00
458 Michael Cuddyer 4.00
459 Hee Seop Choi 4.00
460 *Melky Cabrera* 6.00
461 Jerry Hairston Jr. 4.00
462 Moises Alou 5.00
463 *Michael Rogers* 6.00
464 Javy Lopez 4.00
465 Freddy Garcia 4.00
466 *Brett Harper* 5.00
467 Juan Gonzalez 5.00
468 *Kevin Melillo* 5.00
469 Todd Walker 5.00
470 C.C. Sabathia 4.00
471 Kole Strayhorn 5.00
472 Mark Kotsay 4.00
473 Javier Vazquez 4.00
474 Mike Cameron 4.00
475 *Wes Swackhamer* 6.00

Chrome Parallel

NM/M

Complete Set (110):
Common Player: 1.00
Production 1,956 sets
Refractors: 1.5-2X
Production 556 sets
Black Refractor: 3-5X
Production 56 sets
THC1 Will Harridge 2.00
THC2 Warren Giles 2.00
THC3 Alex Rodriguez 10.00
THC4 Alfonso Soriano 5.00
THC5 Barry Bonds 12.00
THC6 Todd Helton 3.00
THC7 Kazuo Matsui 2.00
THC8 Garret Anderson 1.50
THC9 Mark Prior 5.00
THC10 Jim Thome 4.00
THC11 Jason Giambi 2.00
THC12 Ivan Rodriguez 4.00
THC13 Mike Lowell 1.00
THC14 Vladimir Guerrero 5.00
THC15 Adrian Beltre 2.00
THC16 Andruw Jones 2.00
THC17 Jose Vidro 1.00
THC18 Josh Beckett 1.50
THC19 Mike Sweeney 1.00
THC20 Sammy Sosa 6.00
THC21 Scott Rolen 5.00
THC22 Javy Lopez 1.50
THC23 Albert Pujols 12.00
THC24 Adam Dunn 3.00
THC25 Ken Griffey Jr. 6.00
THC26 Torii Hunter 1.50
THC27 Jorge Posada 2.00
THC28 Magglio Ordonez 1.00
THC29 Shawn Green 1.50
THC30 Frank Thomas 3.00
THC31 Barry Zito 1.50
THC32 David Ortiz 5.00
THC33 Pat Burrell 1.50
THC34 Luis Gonzalez 1.50
THC35 Chipper Jones 5.00
THC36 Hank Blalock 3.00
THC37 Rafael Palmeiro 3.00
THC38 Lance Berkman 2.00
THC39 Miguel Cabrera 5.00
THC40 Paul Konerko 1.00
THC41 Jeff Kent 1.50
THC42 Gary Sheffield 3.00
THC43 Mike Piazza 6.00
THC44 Bret Boone 1.00
THC45 Kerry Wood 5.00
THC46 Derek Jeter 12.00
THC47 Pedro J. Martinez 5.00
THC48 Jason Bay 2.00
THC49 Ichiro Suzuki 8.00
THC50 Miguel Tejada 3.00
THC51 Richie Sexson 2.00
THC52 Jeff Bagwell 3.00
THC53 Lew Ford 1.00
THC54 Randy Johnson 5.00
THC55 Carlos Beltran 3.00
THC56 Greg Maddux 6.00
THC57 Lyle Overbay 1.00
THC58 Michael Young 1.00
THC59 Curt Schilling 5.00
THC60 Jose Reyes 2.00
THC61 Dontrelle Willis 1.50
THC62 Nomar Garciaparra 6.00
THC63 Paul LoDuca 1.00
THC64 Larry Walker 2.00
THC65 Andre Ethier 4.00
THC66 Matt DeSalvo 3.00
THC67 Brian Stavisky 2.00
THC68 Tyler Clippard 4.00
THC69 Chris Seddon 3.00
THC70 Steven Doetsch 3.00
THC71 Chris Denorfia 2.00
THC72 Jeremy West 3.00
THC73 Ryan Sweeney 5.00
THC74 Ian Kinsler 4.00
THC75 Ian Bladergroen 4.00
THC76 Darren Fenster 4.00
THC77 Luis Ramirez 2.00
THC78 Chadd Blasko 2.00
THC79 Matt Lindstrom 2.00
THC80 Chris Roberson 3.00
THC81 Matt Rogelstad 3.00
THC82 Nate Schierholtz 4.00
THC83 Kevin West 4.00
THC84 Chaz Lytle 4.00
THC85 Elvys Quezada 4.00
THC86 Billy Butler 10.00
THC87 Jose Vaquedano 4.00
THC88 James Jurries 4.00
THC89 Ryan Goleski 4.00
THC90 Brandon Moss 4.00
THC91 Matt Campbell 4.00
THC92 Ryan Webb 5.00
THC93 Glen Perkins 5.00
THC94 Sean Marshall 4.00
THC95 Melky Cabrera 4.00
THC96 Michael Rogers 4.00
THC97 Brett Harper 4.00
THC98 Kevin Melillo 4.00
THC99 Kole Strayhorn 4.00
THC100 Wes Swackhamer 4.00
THC101 Rickie Weeks 2.00
THC102 Delmon Young 4.00
THC103 Kazuhito Tadano 1.00
THC104 Kazuhisa Ishii 1.00
THC105 David Wright 4.00
THC106 Eric Gagne 3.00
THC107 So Taguchi 1.00
THC108 B.J. Upton 4.00
THC109 Shingo Takatsu 1.00
THC110 Akinori Otsuka 1.00

Clubhouse Collection Relics

NM/M

Common Player: 5.00
LA Luis Aparicio 8.00
EB Ernie Banks 15.00
LB Lance Berkman 5.00
MC Miguel Cabrera 8.00
AK Al Kaline 15.00
HK Harmon Killebrew 15.00
AP Albert Pujols 20.00
MR Manny Ramirez 8.00
AR Alex Rodriguez 15.00
RS Red Schoendienst 8.00
GS Gary Sheffield 8.00
AS Alfonso Soriano 8.00
MT Miguel Tejada 8.00
BW Bernie Williams 5.00
DW Dontrelle Willis 5.00

Clubhouse Collection Dual Relics

NM/M

Production 56 sets
MP Stan Musial, Albert Pujols 85.00
KR Al Kaline, Ivan Rodriguez 65.00
BG Ernie Banks, Nomar Garciaparra 85.00

Clubhouse Collection Relic Auto.

NM/M

Production 25 sets
LA Luis Aparicio 165.00
EB Ernie Banks 200.00
AK Al Kaline 200.00
HK Harmon Killebrew 200.00
RS Red Schoendienst 165.00

Flashbacks

NM/M

Complete Set (10): 8.00
Common Player: .50
Inserted 1:12
HA Hank Aaron 4.00
LA Luis Aparicio .50
EB Ernie Banks 2.00
BF Bob Feller .50
AK Al Kaline 1.50
DL Don Larsen .50
SM Stan Musial 2.00
FR Frank Robinson 1.00
HS Herb Score .50
DS Duke Snider 1.00

Flashbacks Autographs

NM/M

Common Player:
Production 25 sets
HA Hank Aaron
LA Luis Aparicio 125.00
EB Ernie Banks 200.00
BF Bob Feller 165.00
AK Al Kaline 165.00
DL Don Larsen 175.00
SM Stan Musial 200.00
FR Frank Robinson 200.00
HS Herb Score 150.00
DS Duke Snider

Flashbacks Relics

NM/M

Common Player: 8.00

SEPTEMBER 30, 1956
DUKE SNIDER'S 2 HOMERS LEAD DODGERS TO PENNANT ON LAST DAY OF SEASON.
YANKEE STADIUM BRONX, NY
AUTHENTIC STADIUM SEAT
OCTOBER 8, 1956
DON LARSEN PITCHES A PERFECT GAME IN THE WORLD SERIES
EBBETS FIELD, BROOKLYN, NEW YORK

Inserted 1:96

HA	Hank Aaron	15.00
LA	Luis Aparicio	8.00
EB	Ernie Banks	15.00
BF	Bob Feller	10.00
AK	Al Kaline	15.00
DL	Don Larsen	8.00
SM	Stan Musial	15.00
FR	Frank Robinson	10.00
HS	Herb Score	8.00
DS	Duke Snider	10.00

Flashbacks Relic Autographs

		NM/M
Production 25 sets		
HA	Hank Aaron	
LA	Luis Aparicio	150.00
EB	Ernie Banks	200.00
BF	Bob Feller	175.00
AK	Al Kaline	175.00
DL	Don Larsen	175.00
SM	Stan Musial	200.00
FR	Frank Robinson	200.00
HS	Herb Score	150.00
DS	Duke Snider	

New Age Performers

		NM/M
Complete Set (15):		15.00
Common Player:		1.00
Inserted 1:15		
NAP1	Alfonso Soriano	1.50
NAP2	Alex Rodriguez	3.00
NAP3	Ichiro Suzuki	3.00
NAP4	Albert Pujols	4.00
NAP5	Vladimir Guerrero	1.50
NAP6	Jim Thome	1.50
NAP7	Derek Jeter	4.00
NAP8	Sammy Sosa	2.50
NAP9	Ivan Rodriguez	1.00
NAP10	Manny Ramirez	1.50
NAP11	Todd Helton	1.00
NAP12	David Ortiz	1.50
NAP13	Gary Sheffield	1.00
NAP14	Nomar Garciaparra	2.00
NAP15	Randy Johnson	1.50

Real One Autographs

		NM/M
Production 200 sets		
Red Ink:		1.5-2X
Production 56 sets		
HA	Hank Aaron	250.00
JA	Joe Astroth	60.00
EB	Ernie Banks	125.00
YB	Yogi Berra	100.00
JB	Jim Brady	50.00
CD	Chuck Diering	60.00
BF	Bob Feller	65.00
JG	Jim Greengrass	50.00
MI	Monte Irvin	70.00
SJ	Spook Jacobs	60.00
FM	Fred Marsh	60.00
JM	Jake Martin	60.00
RM	Rudy Minarcin	50.00
PM	Paul Minner	60.00
BN	Bob Nelson	50.00
LP	Laurin Pepper	40.00
LPO	Leroy Powell	60.00
JSA	Jose Santiago	50.00
JS	Johnny Schmitz	50.00
DS	Duke Snider	85.00
AS	Art Swanson	60.00
BT	Bill Tremel	50.00
WW	Wally Westlake	50.00

Then and Now

		NM/M
Complete Set (10):		8.00
Common Duo:		.50
Inserted 1:15		
TN1	Hank Aaron, Ichiro Suzuki	4.00
TN2	Don Newcombe, Curt Schilling	1.50
TN3	Robin Roberts, Livan Hernandez	.50
TN4	Bob Friend, Livan Hernandez	.50
TN5	Herb Score, Randy Johnson	1.50
TN6	Whitey Ford, Jake Peavy	1.00
TN7	Jimmy Piersall, Lyle Overbay	.50
TN8	Clem Labine, Mariano Rivera	.75
TN9	Bill Bruton, Carl Crawford	.50
TN10	Eddie Yost, Bobby Abreu	.50

1956 Cuts - Cut Signatures

No Pricing
Production one set

2005 TOPPS OPENING DAY

		NM/M
Complete Set (165):		30.00
Common player:		.15
Pack (6):		1.00
Box (36):		30.00
1	Alex Rodriguez	1.50
2	Placido Polanco	.15
3	Torii Hunter	.25
4	Lyle Overbay	.15
5	Johnny Damon	.50
6	Mike Cameron	.15
7	Ichiro Suzuki	1.50
8	Francisco Rodriguez	.15
9	Bobby Crosby	.15
10	Sammy Sosa	1.25
11	Randy Wolf	.15
12	Jason Bay	.25
13	Mike Lieberthal	.15
14	Paul Konerko	.15
15	Brian Giles	.15
16	Luis Gonzalez	.25
17	Jim Edmonds	.40
18	Carlos Lee	.25
19	Corey Patterson	.40
20	Hank Blalock	.50
21	Sean Casey	.25
22	Dmitri Young	.25
23	Mark Mulder	.25
24	Bobby Abreu	.25
25	Jim Thome	.50
26	Jason Kendall	.15
27	Jason Giambi	.25
28	Vinny Castilla	.15
29	Tony Batista	.15
30	Ivan Rodriguez	.50
31	Craig Biggio	.25
32	Chris Carpenter	.15
33	Adrian Beltre	.40
34	Scott Podsednik	.15
35	Cliff Floyd	.15
36	Chad Tracy	.15
37	John Smoltz	.25
38	Shingo Takatsu	.15
39	Jack Wilson	.15
40	Gary Sheffield	.50
41	Lance Berkman	.25
42	Carl Crawford	.25
43	Carlos Guillen	.15
44	David Bell	.15
45	Kazuo Matsui	.15
46	Jason Schmidt	.25
47	Jason Marquis	.15
48	Melvin Mora	.15
49	David Ortiz	.50
50	Andruw Jones	.40
51	Miguel Tejada	.50
52	Bartolo Colon	.15
53	Derrek Lee	.25
54	Eric Gagne	.25
55	Miguel Cabrera	.75
56	Travis Hafner	.15
57	Jose Valentin	.15
58	Mark Prior	.75
59	Phil Nevin	.15
60	Jose Vidro	.15
61	Khalil Greene	.25
62	Carlos Zambrano	.40
63	Erubiel Durazo	.15
64	Michael Young	.15
65	Woody Williams	.15
66	Edgardo Alfonzo	.15
67	Troy Glaus	.40
68	Garret Anderson	.25
69	Richie Sexson	.40
70	Curt Schilling	.75
71	Randy Johnson	.75
72	Chipper Jones	.75
73	J.D. Drew	.25
74	Russ Ortiz	.15
75	Frank Thomas	.50
76	Jimmy Rollins	.15
77	Barry Zito	.25
78	Rafael Palmeiro	.50
79	Brad Wilkerson	.15
80	Adam Dunn	.50
81	Doug Mientkiewicz	.15
82	Manny Ramirez	.75
83	Pedro J. Martinez	.75
84	Moises Alou	.25
85	Mike Sweeney	.15
86	Boston Red Sox WC	1.00
87	Matt Clement	.15
88	Nomar Garciaparra	1.00
89	Magglio Ordonez	.15
90	Bret Boone	.15
91	Mark Loretta	.15
92	Jose Contreras	.15
93	Randy Winn	.15
94	Austin Kearns	.15
95	Ken Griffey Jr.	1.25
96	Jake Westbrook	.15
97	Kazuhito Tadano	.15
98	C.C. Sabathia	.15
99	Todd Helton	.50
100	Albert Pujols	2.00
101	Jose Molina	.15
102	Aaron Miles	.15
103	Mike Lowell	.25
104	Paul LoDuca	.15
105	Juan Pierre	.15
106	Dontrelle Willis	.40
107	Jeff Bagwell	.40
108	Carlos Beltran	.50
109	Ronnie Belliard	.15
110	Roy Oswalt	.25
111	Zack Greinke	.15
112	Steve Finley	.15
113	Kazuhisa Ishii	.15
114	Justin Morneau	.40
115	Ben Sheets	.25
116	Johan Santana	.50
117	Billy Wagner	.15
118	Mariano Rivera	.25
119	Corey Koskie	.15
120	Akinori Otsuka	.15
121	Joe Mauer	.40
122	Jacque Jones	.15
123	Joe Nathan	.15
124	Nick Johnson	.15
125	Vernon Wells	.15
126	Mike Piazza	1.00
127	Jose Guillen	.15
128	Jose Reyes	.15
129	Marcus Giles	.15
130	Javy Lopez	.25
131	Kevin Millar	.15
132	Jorge Posada	.40
133	Carl Pavano	.25
134	Bernie Williams	.40
135	Kerry Wood	.75
136	Matt Holiday	.15
137	Kevin Brown	.15
138	Derek Jeter	2.00
139	Barry Bonds	2.00
140	Jeff Kent	.25
141	Mark Kotsay	.15
142	Shawn Green	.25
143	Tim Hudson	.25
144	Shannon Stewart	.15
145	Pat Burrell	.25
146	Gavin Floyd	.15
147	Mike Mussina	.50
148	Eric Chavez	.25
149	Jon Lieber	.15
150	Vladimir Guerrero	.75
151	Vicente Padilla	.15
152	Ryan Klesko	.15
153	Jake Peavy	.25
154	Scott Rolen	.75
155	Greg Maddux	1.00
156	Edgar Renteria	.25
157	Larry Walker	.25
158	Scott Kazmir	.25
159	B.J. Upton	.25
160	Mark Teixeira	.50
161	Ken Harvey	.15
162	Alfonso Soriano	.75
163	Carlos Delgado	.40
164	Alexis Rios	.15
165	Checklist	.15

Autographs

		NM/M
Complete Set (6):		
Common Player:		
CC	Chad Cordero	10.00
FH	Felix Hernandez	30.00
AH	Aaron Hill	8.00
PM	Paul Maholm	8.00
OQ	Omar Quintanilla	15.00
AW	Anthony Whittington	8.00

MLB Game Worn Jersey Collection

		NM/M
Target Retail Exclusive		
37	Vladimir Guerrero	8.00
38	Albert Pujols	15.00
39	Torii Hunter	4.00
40	Alfonso Soriano	6.00
41	Bobby Abreu	6.00
42	Moises Alou	6.00
43	Sean Burroughs	4.00
44	Shannon Stewart	4.00
45	Troy Glaus	6.00
46	Fernando Vina	4.00
47	Dan Wilson	4.00
48	Paul Konerko	4.00
49	Jimmy Rollins	4.00
50	Livan Hernandez	4.00
51	Sean Casey	4.00
52	Paul LoDuca	4.00
53	Richie Sexson	6.00
54	Aubrey Huff	4.00

2005 TOPPS PACK WARS

		NM/M
Complete Set (175):		40.00
Common Player:		.25
Pack (7):		20.00
Box (7):		120.00
1	Alex Rodriguez	3.00
2	Eric Chavez	.40
3	Jimmy Rollins	.25
4	Jason Bay	.50
5	Nomar Carciaparra	2.00
6	Melvin Mora	.25
7	Bobby Abreu	.50
8	Bartolo Colon	.25
9	Orlando Cabrera	1.00

10 Albert Pujols 3.00
11 Barry Zito .40
12 Vernon Wells .25
13 J.D. Drew .40
14 Darin Erstad .25
15 Manny Ramirez 1.00
16 Derrek Lee .40
17 Juan Uribe .25
18 Wily Mo Pena .25
19 Jeromy Burnitz .25
20 Dontrelle Willis .25
21 Craig Biggio .40
22 Cesar Izturis .25
23 Geoff Jenkins .25
24 Joe Mauer .50
25 Derek Jeter 3.00
26 David Wright 1.00
27 Jose Vidro .25
28 Bobby Crosby .25
29 Khalil Greene .50
30 Ichiro Suzuki 2.00
31 Reggie Sanders .25
32 A.J. Pierzynski .25
33 Corey Patterson .40
34 Frank Thomas .75
35 Craig Wilson .25
36 Carl Crawford .25
37 Michael Young .25
38 Mark Kotsay .25
39 Javier Vazquez .25
40 Kazuo Matsui .25
41 Lew Ford .25
42 Corey Koskie .25
43 Larry Walker .50
44 Mike Lowell .40
45 Todd Helton .75
46 Travis Hafner .25
47 Sean Casey .25
48 Ken Griffey Jr. 1.50
49 Milton Bradley .25
50 Ivan Rodriguez .75
51 Carlos Lee .25
52 Aramis Ramirez .50
53 Curt Schilling 1.00
54 Russ Ortiz .25
55 Randy Johnson 1.00
56 Preston Wilson .25
57 Jay Gibbons .25
58 Mike Lieberthal .25
59 Johnny Damon .75
60 Mark Prior 1.00
61 Freddy Garcia .25
62 Casey Blake .25
63 Chipper Jones 1.00
64 Carlos Guillen .25
65 Juan Pierre .25
66 Tom Glavine .50
67 Alex Sanchez .25
68 Tony Batista .25
69 Paul LoDuca .25
70 Hank Blalock .75
71 Pedro Feliz .25
72 Jim Edmonds .50
73 Phil Nevin .25
74 Rocco Baldelli .25
75 Alfonso Soriano 1.00
76 David Bell .25
77 Eric Hinske .25
78 Jose Guillen .25
79 Marcus Giles .25
80 Rafael Palmeiro .75
81 Jeff Bagwell .75
82 Kerry Wood 1.00
83 Johan Santana .75
84 Troy Glaus .40
85 Andruw Jones .50
86 Barry Bonds 3.00
87 Jermaine Dye .25
88 Carlos Zambrano .50
89 Aaron Rowand .25
90 Garret Anderson .40
91 Ryan Klesko .25
92 Paul Konerko .25
93 Jeff Kent .40
94 Richie Sexson .50
95 Lyle Overbay .25
96 Torii Hunter .40
97 Mike Cameron .25
98 Eric Byrnes .25
99 Jason Kendall .25
100 Vladimir Guerrero 1.00
101 Johnny Estrada .25
102 Mark Bellhorn .25
103 Moises Alou .40
104 Ronnie Belliard .25
105 Adam Dunn .75
106 Dmitri Young .25
107 Luis Castillo .25
108 Carlos Beltran .75
109 Steve Finley .25
110 Shannon Stewart .25
111 Al Leiter .25
112 Bernie Williams .50
113 Roy Oswalt .40
114 Sean Burroughs .25
115 Randy Winn .25
116 Tony Womack .25
117 Jim Thome 1.00
118 Aubrey Huff .25
119 Bret Boone .25
120 Carlos Delgado .40
121 Jason Schmidt .50
122 Rafael Furcal .25
123 Miguel Tejada .75
124 Bill Mueller .25
125 Pedro Martinez 1.00
126 Michael Barrett .25
127 Jody Gerut .25
128 Vinny Castilla .25
129 Rondell White .25
130 Magglio Ordonez .25
131 Lance Berkman .25
132 Alex Gonzalez .25
133 Mike Sweeney .25
134 Ben Sheets .50
135 Jacque Jones .25
136 Brad Wilkerson .25
137 Cliff Floyd .25
138 Kevin Brown .25
139 Scott Hatteberg .25
140 Gary Sheffield .50
141 Justin Morneau .25
142 Scott Podsednik .25
143 Shawn Green .40
144 David Ortiz 1.00
145 Josh Beckett .50
146 Tim Hudson .50
147 Matt Lawton .25
148 Mark Buehrle .25
149 Todd Walker .25
150 Jason Giambi .50
151 Brian Giles .25
152 Erubiel Durazo .25
153 Jack Wilson .25
154 Jose Reyes .25
155 Scott Rolen 1.00
156 Raul Ibanez .25
157 Mark Teixeira .50
158 Luis Gonzalez .25
159 Javy Lopez .25
160 Greg Maddux 1.50
161 Kevin Millar .25
162 Jose Valentin .25
163 C.C. Sabathia .25
164 Carlos Pena .25
165 Miguel Cabrera 1.00
166 Adrian Beltre .50
167 Sammy Sosa 2.00
168 Nick Johnson .25
169 Jorge Posada .50
170 Mike Piazza 1.50
171 Mark Mulder .50
172 Mark Loretta .25
173 Edgardo Alfonzo .25
174 Edgar Renteria .50
175 Pat Burrell .25

Autographs

NM/M

Common Autograph: 15.00
CB Carlos Beltran 30.00
HB Hank Blalock 20.00
BB Barry Bonds
AB Aaron Boone 20.00
MC Miguel Cabrera 25.00
EC Eric Chavez 15.00
JE Johnny Estrada 10.00
KG Khalil Greene
ZG Zack Greinke 15.00
VM Victor Martinez 15.00
AR Alex Rodriguez
CS C.C. Sabathia 15.00
VW Vernon Wells 10.00
MY Michael Young 15.00

Collector Chips

NM/M

Common Player: 8.00
Inserted 1:box
Blue: No Pricing
Production 25 sets
Red: No Pricing
Production 10 sets
1 Alex Rodriquez
2 Ichiro Suzuki 30.00
3 Jim Thome 20.00
4 Albert Pujols 30.00
5 Vladimir Guerrero 15.00
6 Derek Jeter 30.00
7 Sammy Sosa 20.00
8 Barry Bonds
9 Ivan Rodriguez 10.00
10 Alfonso Soriano
11 Nomar Garciaparra 20.00
12 Ken Griffey Jr. 20.00
13 Mark Prior 15.00
14 Todd Helton 10.00
15 Mike Piazza 20.00
16 Jorge Posada 10.00
17 Chipper Jones 10.00
18 Randy Johnson 15.00
19 Gary Sheffield 8.00
20 Mike Schmidt 25.00
21 Ernie Banks 20.00
22 Frank Robinson 20.00
23 Reggie Jackson 10.00
24 George Brett 25.00
25 Nolan Ryan 30.00

Cut Signatures

No Pricing

Relics

NM/M

Common Player: 8.00
RC Roger Clemens 12.00
NG Nomar Garciaparra 15.00
VG Vladimir Guerrero 10.00
TH Todd Helton 8.00
THB Todd Helton 8.00
CJ Chipper Jones 8.00
CJB Chipper Jones 8.00
GM Greg Maddux 10.00
PM Pedro Martinez 8.00
RP Rafael Palmeiro 8.00
MP Mike Piazza 10.00
AP Albert Pujols 15.00
MR Manny Ramirez 10.00
MRB Manny Ramirez 10.00
AR Alex Rodriguez 15.00
IR Ivan Rodriguez 8.00
SR Scott Rolen 10.00
GS Gary Sheffield 8.00
AS Alfonso Soriano 8.00
SS Sammy Sosa 10.00
FT Frank Thomas 8.00
JT Jim Thome 8.00

Relic Autographs

NM/M

Common Autograph: 15.00
Production 200 sets
CB Carlos Beltran 40.00
HB Hank Blalock 25.00
MC Miguel Cabrera 30.00
EC Eric Chavez 20.00
JE Johnny Estrada 15.00
VM Victor Martinez 15.00
AR Alex Rodriguez
MY Michael Young 20.00

2005 TOPPS PRISTINE

NM/M

Common 1-100 .75
Common Rookie (101-130): 1.00
Common (131-180): 3.00
Production 500
Common (181-205): 10.00
Production 100
Common (206-210):
Production 49
Pack (8): 30.00
Box (5): 125.00
1 Alex Rodriguez 3.00
2 Jake Peavy .75
3 Bobby Crosby .75
4 J.D. Drew .75
5 Scott Rolen 1.50
6 Bobby Abreu .75
7 Ken Griffey Jr. 2.50
8 Jeremy Bonderman .75
9 Mike Sweeney .75
10 Mark Prior 1.50
11 Tim Hudson .75
12 Clint Barmes .75
13 Jeff Bagwell 1.00
14 Andruw Jones 1.50
15 Carlos Delgado .75
16 Rocco Baldelli .75
17 Adam Dunn 1.50
18 Greg Maddux 2.00
19 Torii Hunter .75
20 Miguel Tejada 1.50
21 Lyle Overbay .75
22 Craig Wilson .75
23 Scott Kazmir .75
24 Alex Rios .75
25 Ichiro Suzuki 3.00
26 Jorge Posada 1.00
27 Jose Reyes .75
28 Hank Blalock .75
29 Troy Glaus 1.00
30 Todd Helton 1.50
31 Javy Lopez .75
32 Barry Zito 1.00
33 Jimmy Rollins .75
34 Mark Loretta .75
35 Richie Sexson 1.00
36 Nick Johnson .75
37 Ivan Rodriguez 1.00
38 Jeff Kent .75
39 Jake Westbrook .75
40 Carlos Beltran 1.00
41 Rich Harden .75
42 Joe Mauer 1.00
43 Luis Gonzalez .75
44 Frank Thomas 1.00
45 Michael Young .75
46 Jason Schmidt .75
47 Eric Chavez .75
48 Vinny Castilla .75
49 John Smoltz 1.00
50 Barry Bonds 4.00
51 Jim Edmonds 1.00
52 Edgar Renteria .75
53 Jose Vidro .75
54 Chipper Jones 1.50
55 Curt Schilling 1.50
56 Victor Martinez .75
57 Josh Beckett .75
58 Derrek Lee 1.50
59 Shawn Green .75
60 Roger Clemens 4.00
61 Orlando Cabrera .75
62 Mike Piazza 2.00
63 Gary Sheffield 1.00
64 Carl Crawford .75
65 Johan Santana 1.50
66 Oliver Perez .75
67 Manny Ramirez 1.50
68 Paul Konerko 1.00
69 Preston Wilson .75
70 Sammy Sosa 2.00
71 Eric Gagne .75
72 Geoff Jenkins .75
73 Magglio Ordonez .75
74 Kerry Wood 1.00
75 Albert Pujols 4.00
76 Roy Halladay 1.00
77 Aubrey Huff .75
78 Nomar Garciaparra 1.50
79 Brian Roberts .75
80 Randy Johnson 1.50
81 Pat Burrell .75
82 Brian Giles .75
83 Mike Mussina 1.00
84 Mark Teixeira 1.00
85 Pedro Martinez 1.50
86 Jason Bay .75
87 Mark Buehrle .75
88 Rafael Furcal .75

89 Juan Pierre .75
90 Jim Thome 1.00
91 Ben Sheets 1.00
92 Alfonso Soriano 1.50
93 Adrian Beltre .75
94 Miguel Cabrera 1.50
95 Derek Jeter 4.00
96 Vernon Wells .75
97 Lance Berkman 1.00
98 Hideki Matsui 2.50
99 David Ortiz 1.50
100 Vladimir Guerrero 1.50
101 *Justin Verlander* 3.00
102 *Billy Butler* 8.00
103 *Wladimir Balentien* 2.00
104 *Jeremy West* 2.00
105 *Philip Humber* 3.00
106 *Tyler Pelland* 1.00
107 *Andy LaRoche* 5.00
108 *Hernan Iribarren* 1.00
109 *Luke Scott* 1.00
110 *Landon Powell* 1.00
111 *Alexander Smit* 1.00
112 *Ryan Garko* 1.00
113 *Bear Bay* 1.00
114 *Ian Bladergroen* 1.00
115 *Manny Parra* 1.00
116 *Andy Sides* 1.00
117 *Travis Chick* 1.00
118 *Stefan Bailie* 1.00
119 *Chuck Tiffany* 2.00
120 *Buck Coats* 1.00
121 *Jeff Niemann* 2.00
122 *Jake Postlewait* 1.00
123 *Matt Campbell* 1.00
124 *Kevin Melillo* 2.00
125 *Mike Morse* 3.00
126 *Anthony Reyes* 3.00
127 *Casey McGehee* 1.00
128 *Cody Haerther* 1.00
129 *Brandon McCarthy* 4.00
130 *Glen Perkins* 2.00
131 Moises Alou 3.00
132 Nomar Garciaparra 6.00
133 Scott Rolen 6.00
134 Miguel Tejada 4.00
135 Alex Rodriguez 10.00
136 Michael Young 3.00
137 Tim Hudson 5.00
138 Troy Glaus 3.00
139 Eric Chavez 3.00
140 David Ortiz 10.00
141 Andruw Jones 5.00
142 Richie Sexson 5.00
143 Jim Thome 5.00
144 Javy Lopez 3.00
145 Lance Berkman 3.00
146 Gary Sheffield 5.00
147 Dontrelle Willis 4.00
148 Curt Schilling 5.00
149 Jorge Posada 5.00
150 Vladimir Guerrero 8.00
151 Adam Dunn 5.00
152 Ryan Drese 3.00
153 Hank Blalock 3.00
154 Kerry Wood 4.00
155 Alfonso Soriano 5.00
156 Aramis Ramirez 4.00
157 Mark Mulder 4.00
158 Paul Konerko 4.00
159 Jim Edmonds 6.00
160 Roger Clemens 10.00
161 Mariano Rivera 6.00
162 Rafael Palmeiro 6.00
163 Mark Teixeira 6.00
164 Eric Gagne 3.00
165 Sammy Sosa 8.00
166 Brett Myers 3.00
167 Kazuhisa Ishii 3.00
168 Ken Harvey 3.00
169 Johnny Estrada 3.00
170 Todd Helton 5.00
171 Rich Harden 3.00
172 Johnny Damon 6.00
173 Manny Ramirez 6.00
174 Benito Santiago 3.00
175 Albert Pujols 15.00
176 Chipper Jones .75
177 Miguel Cabrera 8.00
178 Jeff Bagwell 5.00
179 Ivan Rodriguez 5.00
180 Mike Piazza 8.00
181 *Chip Cannon* 15.00
182 *Erik Cordier* 15.00
183 *Billy Butler* 50.00
184 *C.J. Smith* 10.00
185 Alfonso Soriano 25.00
186 *Bobby Livingston* 15.00
187 *Wladimir Balentien* 25.00
188 *Mike Morse* 30.00
189 *Wes Swackhamer* 30.00
190 *Justin Verlander* 25.00
191 *Jake Postlewait* 15.00
192 *Michael Rogers* 20.00
193 *Matt Campbell* 20.00
194 *Eric Nielsen* 15.00
195 Gary Sheffield 30.00
196 *Glen Perkins* 30.00
197 *Kevin Melillo* 30.00
198 *Chad Orvella* 10.00
199 *Jeff Niemann* 25.00
200 Alex Rodriguez 180.00
201 *Brian Stavisky* 15.00
202 *Brian Miller* 15.00
203 *Landon Powell* 25.00
204 *Philip Humber* 30.00
205 Mariano Rivera 100.00
206 Curt Schilling 50.00
207 Nolan Ryan 150.00
208 Albert Pujols
209 Stan Musial
210 Barry Bonds

Red

Red (1-130): 2-4X
Production 66
Red (131-210): No Pricing
Production three sets

Printing Plates

No Pricing
Production one set for each color

Uncirculated Bronze

Bronze (1-130): 1.5-3X
Production 375
Bronze (131-180): 1-1.5X
Production 100
Bronze (181-205): No Pricing
Production 18
Bronze (206-210): No Pricing
Production 10

Doubles Act Autographs

No Pricing
Production 5 Sets

Fielder's Choice

No Pricing
Production Nine Sets

Personal Endorsements

NM/M
Common
Production 497 Sets
Uncirculated: No Pricing
Production 3 Sets
MB Milton Bradley 10.00
BB Billy Butler 40.00
LC Lance Cormier 5.00
SE Scott Elbert 8.00
JF Josh Fields 5.00
LH Livan Hernandez 12.00
JPH J.P. Howell 8.00
PH Philip Humber 10.00
ZJ Zach Jackson 8.00
BJ Blake Johnson 5.00
BL Bobby Livingston 8.00
CO Chad Orvella 5.00
GP Glen Perkins 10.00
LP Landon Powell 8.00
MR Mike Rodriguez 5.00
MRO Mark Rogers 8.00
TS Terrmel Sledge 5.00
CJS C.J. Smith 5.00
JS Jeremy Sowers 10.00
JV Justin Verlander 15.00
Uncommon
Production 247 Sets
JB Jason Bay 25.00
AB Aaron Boone 10.00
MB Matt Bush 15.00
BB Billy Butler 40.00
CC Chip Cannon 8.00
CE Carl Erskine 10.00
HK Harmon Killebrew 25.00
BL Bobby Livingston 8.00
ML Mark Loretta 8.00
DO David Ortiz 40.00
CW Craig Wilson 10.00
DW David Wright 40.00
DZ Don Zimmer 15.00
Rare
Production 97 Sets
GA Garret Anderson 15.00
EB Ernie Banks 50.00
SM Stan Musial 50.00
MR Mariano Rivera 100.00
TS Tom Seaver 30.00
AS Alfonso Soriano 25.00
Scarce
Production 22 Sets
BB Barry Bonds
AP Albert Pujols

Personal Pieces

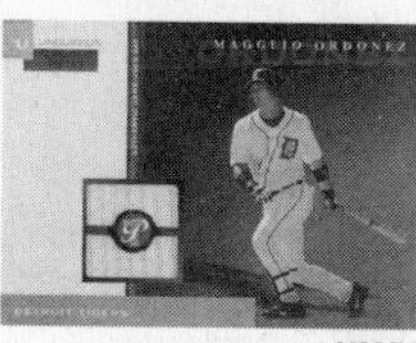

NM/M
Common
Production 425
Uncirculated: No Pricing
Production 3 Sets
JB Jeff Bagwell 5.00
RB Ronnie Belliard 3.00
AB Adrian Beltre 3.00
LB Lance Berkman 5.00
HB Hank Blalock 5.00
EC Eric Chavez 3.00
RC Roger Clemens 12.00
BC Bobby Crosby 5.00
JDD J.D. Drew 3.00
AD Adam Dunn 5.00
JE Jim Edmonds 5.00
JES Johnny Estrada 3.00
JG Jason Giambi 5.00
JGI Jay Gibbons 3.00
SG Shawn Green 3.00
VG Vladimir Guerrero 8.00
CG Cristian Guzman 3.00
THA Travis Hafner 3.00
TH Todd Helton 5.00
THU Tim Hudson 5.00
AJ Andruw Jones 5.00
CJ Chipper Jones 8.00
JL Javy Lopez 3.00
ML Mark Loretta 3.00
MLO Mike Lowell 3.00
PM Pedro Martinez 8.00
VM Victor Martinez 3.00
KM Kevin Millar 3.00
MM Mark Mulder 5.00
BM Brett Myers 3.00
LN Laynce Nix 3.00
MP Mike Piazza 8.00
MPR Mark Prior 6.00
AP Albert Pujols 15.00
BR Brad Radke 3.00
MR Manny Ramirez 8.00
ER Edgar Renteria 3.00
MRI Mariano Rivera 6.00
SR Scott Rolen 5.00
CS Curt Schilling 6.00
GS Gary Sheffield 5.00
AS Alfonso Soriano 5.00
MTE Mark Teixeira 5.00
MT Miguel Tejada 5.00
FT Frank Thomas 8.00
JT Jim Thome 5.00
BJU B.J. Upton 3.00
BW Bernie Williams 5.00
KW Kerry Wood 5.00
BZ Barry Zito 3.00
Uncommon
Production 200
CB Carlos Beltran 5.00
AB Adrian Beltre 3.00
MC Miguel Cabrera 8.00
RC Roger Clemens 12.00
JE Jim Edmonds 5.00
EG Eric Gagne 3.00
TG Troy Glaus 3.00
TH Torii Hunter 3.00
AJ Andruw Jones 5.00
CJ Chipper Jones 8.00
MM Mark Mulder 5.00
MO Magglio Ordonez 3.00
DO David Ortiz 8.00
MP Mike Piazza 8.00
JP Jorge Posada 5.00
AP Albert Pujols 15.00
MR Manny Ramirez 8.00
MRI Mariano Rivera 6.00
AR Alex Rodriguez 15.00
IR Ivan Rodriguez 5.00
SR Scott Rolen 5.00
CS Curt Schilling 6.00
AS Alfonso Soriano 5.00
SS Sammy Sosa 8.00
JT Jim Thome 5.00
Rare
CB Carlos Beltran 10.00
BB Barry Bonds 40.00
RC Roger Clemens 20.00
JD Johnny Damon 12.00
EG Eric Gagne 8.00
VG Vladimir Guerrero 10.00
TH Todd Helton 10.00
PM Pedro Martinez 10.00
AP Albert Pujols 25.00
AR Alex Rodriguez 25.00
Scarce
BB Barry Bonds
RC Roger Clemens
VG Vladimir Guerrero
AP Albert Pujols
AR Alex Rodriguez

Power Core

No Pricing
Production 3-10
Power Stick: No Pricing
Production One Set

Selective Swatch

No Pricing
Production One Set

2005 TOPPS PRISTINE LEGENDS

NM/M
Complete Set (140):
Common Player: 1.00
Common SP (101-125): 2.00
Production 1,999
Common SP (126-135): 3.00
Production 999
Common SP (136-140): 4.00
Production 499
Pack (8): 30.00
Box (5): 120.00
1 Vida Blue 1.00
2 Bert Blyleven 1.00
3 Joe Carter 1.00
4 Bill Buckner 1.00
5 Luis Aparicio 1.00
6 Ernie Banks 2.50
7 Wade Boggs 2.00
8 George Brett 4.00
9 Lou Brock 2.00
10 Rod Carew 2.00
11 Gary Carter 1.00
12 Andre Dawson 1.00
13 Dennis Eckersley 1.00
14 Rollie Fingers 1.00
15 Steve Garvey 1.00
16 Dwight Gooden 1.00
17 Rich "Goose" Gossage 1.00
18 Ron Guidry 1.00
19 Keith Hernandez 1.00
20 Charlie Hough 1.00
21 Bo Jackson 2.50
22 Monte Irvin 2.00
23 Reggie Jackson 2.00
24 Ferguson Jenkins 1.00
25 Ralph Kiner 1.00
26 Juan Marichal 1.00
27 Stan Musial 4.00
28 Tony Oliva 1.00
29 Jim Palmer 1.50
30 Dave Parker 1.00
31 Gaylord Perry 1.00
32 Jimmy Piersall 1.00
33 Johnny Podres 1.00
34 Brooks Robinson 2.00
35 Frank Robinson 2.00
36 Nolan Ryan 5.00
37 Tom Seaver 2.00
38 Ozzie Smith 3.00
39 Duke Snider 2.00
40 Bobby Thomson 1.00
41 Carl Yastrzemski 3.00

42 Maury Wills 1.00
43 Robin Yount 3.00
44 Matt Williams 1.00
45 Orel Hershiser 1.00
46 Tim McCarver 1.00
47 Don Newcombe 1.00
48 Paul O'Neill 1.00
49 Al Kaline 2.00
50 Harmon Killebrew 2.00
51 Dave Kingman 1.00
52 Ken Griffey 1.00
53 George Foster 1.00
54 Mark Fidrych 1.00
55 Orlando Cepeda 1.00
56 Don Larsen 1.00
57 Bill Madlock 1.00
58 Dale Murphy 1.50
59 Graig Nettles 1.00
60 Phil Niekro 1.00
61 Al Oliver 1.00
62 Harold Reynolds 1.00
63 Bobby Richardson 1.00
64 Mike Scott 1.00
65 Dave Stewart 1.00
66 Rick Sutcliffe 1.00
67 Bruce Sutter 1.50
68 Luis Tiant 1.00
69 Bob Watson 1.00
70 Walt Weiss 1.00
71 Don Zimmer 1.00
72 Tommy John 1.00
73 Ray Knight 1.00
74 Jack Morris 1.00
75 Mickey Rivers 1.00
76 Lee Smith 1.00
77 Darryl Strawberry 1.00
78 David Justice 1.00
79 Wally Joyner 1.00
80 Jimmy Key 1.00
81 John Kruk 1.00
82 Greg Luzinski 1.00
83 Mookie Wilson 1.00
84 Wilbur Wood 1.00
85 Tim Raines 1.00
86 Jim Rice 1.00
87 Tony Armas 1.00
88 Harold Baines 1.00
89 Bucky Dent 1.00
90 Darrell Evans 1.00
91 Cecil Fielder 1.00
92 Jose Cruz 1.00
93 Dave Concepcion 1.00
94 Ron Cey 1.00
95 Davey Lopes 1.00
96 Boog Powell 1.00
97 Buddy Bell 1.00
98 George Bell 1.00
99 Bert Campaneris 1.00
100 Chet Lemon 1.00
101 Bo Jackson 4.00
102 Will Clark 2.00
103 Cecil Fielder 2.00
104 Ron Cey 2.00
105 Tony Gwynn 5.00
106 Orel Hershiser 2.00
107 Jimmy Key 2.00
108 Paul Molitor 3.00
109 Pete Incaviglia 2.00
110 Wally Joyner 2.00
111 Dave Kingman 2.00
112 Ron Guidry 2.00
113 Ron Darling 2.00
114 Mookie Wilson 2.00
115 Reggie Jackson 3.00
116 Walt Weiss 2.00
117 Joe Carter 2.00
118 Cory Snyder 2.00
119 Dave Winfield 3.00
120 Terry Steinbach 2.00
121 Matt Williams 2.00
122 Ozzie Smith 5.00
123 Jack McDowell 2.00
124 Bob Horner 2.00
125 Don Kessinger 2.00
126 Minnie Minoso 3.00
127 Cecil Kaiser 3.00
128 Buck O'Neil 3.00
129 Monte Irvin 4.00
130 Jim Gilliam 3.00
131 Josh Gibson 4.00
132 Ernie Banks 6.00
133 Don Newcombe 3.00
134 Red Moore 3.00
135 Willie Pope 3.00
136 Gary Carter 4.00
137 Bo Jackson 6.00
138 George Brett 8.00
139 Joe Carter 4.00
140 Nolan Ryan 8.00

Refractor

Refractor (1-100): 1-1.5X
Production 549
Refractor (101-125): 1.5-2X
Production 199
Refractor (126-135): 1.5-2.5X
Production 99
Refractor (136-140): No Pricing
Production 25

Refractors Gold Die-Cut

Gold (1-100): 3-4X
Gold (101-135): 1-2.5X
Gold (136-140): 1-1.5X
Production 65 sets

SuperFractor

No Pricing
Production one set

Printing Plates

No Pricing
One set produced per color

Celebrity Threads

NM/M

Inserted 1:18
Refractor: No Pricing
Production 25 sets
MM Marilyn Monroe 75.00
EP Elvis Presley 65.00

Leading Indicators

LEADING INDICATORS
TOTAL BASES LEADER – 1978
JIM RICE
RED SOX

NM/M

Common Player: 4.00
Refractor: No Pricing
Production one or 25
WB Wade Boggs 10.00
LB Lou Brock
RC Rod Carew 8.00
AD Andre Dawson 6.00
BF Bob Feller 10.00
CF Cecil Fielder 8.00
GF George Foster 4.00
TG Tony Gwynn 10.00
AK Al Kaline 12.00
DK Dave Kingman 6.00
RM Roger Maris 35.00
DM Don Mattingly 15.00
DBM Dale Murphy 10.00
TO Tony Oliva 6.00
PO Paul O'Neill 10.00
DP Dave Parker 4.00
GP Gaylord Perry 4.00
TR Tim Raines 4.00
TR2 Tim Raines 6.00
JR Jim Rice 4.00
NR Nolan Ryan 20.00
MS Mike Scott 4.00
TS Tom Seaver 10.00
DS Darryl Strawberry 6.00
MW Maury Wills 10.00
CY Carl Yastrzemski 15.00

Personal Endorsements

NM/M

Common Autograph: 10.00
Gold: No Pricing
Production 25 sets
JA Jim Abbott 15.00

LA Luis Aparicio 15.00
BB Bert Blyleven 15.00
GB George Brett 50.00
GC Gary Carter 15.00
RD Ron Darling 15.00
AD Andre Dawson 15.00
DE Dennis Eckersley 15.00
DWE Darrell Evans 15.00
CF Carlton Fisk 25.00
GF George Foster 10.00
GG Rich "Goose" Gossage 10.00
BG Bobby Grich 10.00
KH Keith Hernandez 12.00
BJ Bo Jackson 60.00
RJ Reggie Jackson 50.00
AK Al Kaline 40.00
DL Don Larsen 15.00
JM Jack McDowell 10.00
SM Stan Musial 50.00
GN Graig Nettles 15.00
JO Jesse Orosco 10.00
JP Jim Palmer 15.00
JAP Jimmy Piersall 15.00
CR Cal Ripken Jr. 125.00
BR Brooks Robinson 30.00
NR Nolan Ryan 90.00
DS Duke Snider 40.00
EW Earl Weaver 15.00
CY Carl Yastrzemski 50.00
RY Robin Yount 50.00

Signature Marks

No Pricing
Production one set

Title Threads

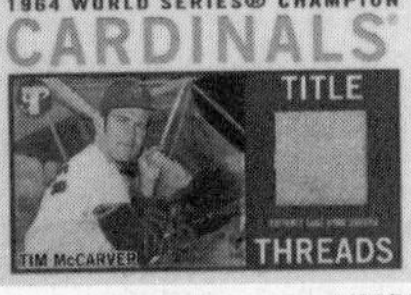

1964 WORLD SERIES CHAMPION
CARDINALS
TITLE
THREADS
TIM McCARVER

NM/M

Common Player: 4.00
Refractors: No Pricing
Production 25 sets
WB Wade Boggs 10.00
GC Gary Carter 6.00
JC Joe Carter 6.00
OC Orlando Cepeda 8.00
BD Bucky Dent 6.00
LD Lenny Dykstra 6.00
RF Rollie Fingers 8.00
GF George Foster 4.00
CS Cesar Geronimo 6.00
GG Rich "Goose" Gossage 6.00
KG Ken Griffey Sr. 6.00
OH Orel Hershiser 8.00
WH Willie Horton 10.00
MI Monte Irvin 12.00
DJ David Justice 6.00
JK Jimmy Key 6.00
EK Ed Kranepool 6.00
TM Tim McCarver 6.00
GN Graig Nettles 8.00
PO Paul O'Neill 10.00
JP Jim Palmer 8.00
DS Darryl Strawberry 6.00
MW Mookie Wilson 4.00

Valuable Performances

NM/M

Common Player: 4.00
Refractor: No Pricing
Production one or 25

YB Yogi Berra 15.00
JC Jose Canseco 10.00
RC Roberto Clemente/9
AD Andre Dawson 6.00
DE Dennis Eckersley 8.00
CF Cecil Fielder 8.00
SG Steve Garvey 6.00
KH Keith Hernandez 4.00
RJ Reggie Jackson 10.00
HK Harmon Killebrew 12.00
DBM Don Mattingly 15.00
JM Joe Morgan 6.00
DM Dale Murphy 10.00
SM Stan Musial 15.00
DP Dave Parker 4.00
JR Jim Rice 8.00
CR Cal Ripken Jr. 25.00
FR Frank Robinson 8.00
MS Mike Schmidt 15.00
CY Carl Yastrzemski 15.00
RY Robin Yount 8.00

2005 TOPPS RETIRED SIGNATURE EDITION

NM/M

Complete Set (110): 150.00
Common Player: 1.00
Pack (5): 30.00
Box (5): 125.00
1 Josh Gibson 1.00
2 Andre Dawson 1.00
3 Al Kaline 2.00
4 Andy Van Slyke 1.00
5 Brett Butler 1.00
6 Bob Gibson 1.50
7 Bo Jackson 2.00
8 Carlton Fisk 1.00
9 Chuck Knoblauch 1.00
10 Cal Ripken Jr. 6.00
11 Carl Yastrzemski 3.00
12 Tom Niedenfuer 1.00
13 Dennis Eckersley 1.00
14 Darryl Strawberry 1.00
15 Dwight Gooden 1.00
16 Davey Johnson 1.00
17 Don Mattingly 3.00
18 Dave Winfield 1.50
19 Don Zimmer 1.00
20 Ernie Banks 2.00
21 George Brett 3.00
22 Gary Carter 1.00
23 Gregg Jefferies 1.00
24 Harold Baines 1.00
25 Ryne Sandberg 2.00
26 Howard Johnson 1.00
27 Jim Abbott 1.00
28 Johnny Bench 2.00
29 Jay Buhner 1.00
30 Johnny Podres 1.00
31 Jose Canseco 1.50
32 Keith Hernandez 1.00
33 Lou Brock 1.00
34 Lou Whitaker 1.00
35 Mark Fidrych 1.00
36 Orlando Cepeda 1.00
37 Ozzie Smith 2.00
38 Paul O'Neill 1.00
39 Reggie Jackson 1.50
40 Sid Fernandez 1.00
41 Tony Gwynn 2.00
42 Tim Raines 1.00
43 Tom Seaver 1.50
44 Vida Blue 1.00
45 Brady Anderson 1.00
46 Bob Brenly 1.00
47 Bob Feller 1.50
48 Bill Mazeroski 1.00
49 Brooks Robinson 1.50
50 Harmon Killebrew 1.50

51 Bob Welch 1.00
52 Carl Erskine 1.00
53 Dale Murphy 1.00
54 Denny McClain 1.00
55 Dave Magadan 1.00
56 Duke Snider 1.50
57 Ed Kranepool 1.00
58 Frank Robinson 1.50
59 Jesus Alou 1.00
60 Joe Girardi 1.00
61 John Kruk 1.00
62 Jim Leyland 1.00
63 Juan Marichal 1.00
64 Johnny Pesky 1.00
65 Jesse Orosco 1.00
66 Ken Singleton 1.00
67 Matty Alou 1.00
68 Monte Irvin 1.00
69 Matt Williams 1.00
70 Pedro Guerrero 1.00
71 Ron Blomberg 1.00
72 Rod Carew 1.50
73 Rafael Santana 1.00
74 Ralph Kiner 1.00
75 Wade Boggs 1.50
76 Roger Craig 1.00
77 Robin Yount 2.00
78 Steve Carlton 1.00
79 Shawon Dunston 1.00
80 Steve Garvey 1.00
81 Stan Musial 3.00
82 Travis Fryman 1.00
83 Tito Fuentes 1.00
84 Mike Cuellar 1.00
85 Roberto Clemente 4.00
86 Whitey Ford 1.50
87 Yogi Berra 2.00
88 Atlee Hammaker 1.00
89 Bill Freehan 1.00
90 Brian Cashman 1.00
91 Bobby Richardson 1.00
92 Bob Boone 1.00
93 Charlie Hough 1.00
94 Glenn Hubbard 1.00
95 Grady Little 1.00
96 Jimmy Piersall 1.00
97 Jim Frey 1.00
98 Jerry Grote 1.00
99 Jim Leyritz 1.00
100 Nolan Ryan 5.00
101 Jim Kaat 1.00
102 Joe Pepitone 1.00
103 J.R. Richard 1.00
104 John Candelaria 1.00
105 Bill "Moose" Skowron 1.00
106 Rick Cerone 1.00
107 Ron Santo 1.00
108 Rick Dempsey 1.00
109 Roy White 1.00
110 Tippy Martinez 1.00

Autographs

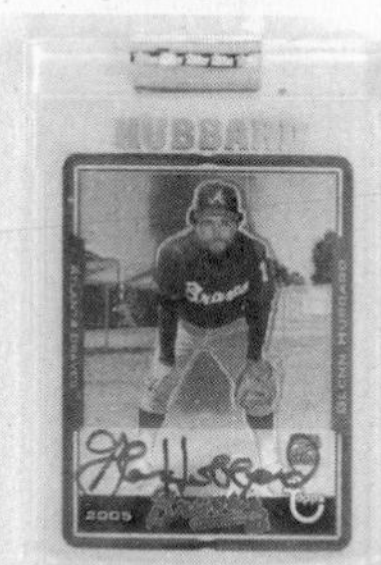

NM/M
Common Autograph: 10.00
JAA Jim Abbott 20.00
JA Jesus Alou 15.00
MA Matty Alou 15.00
BA Brady Anderson 15.00
HB Harold Baines 15.00
DB Dusty Baker
EB Ernie Banks
JB Johnny Bench 200.00
YB Yogi Berra 200.00
RB Ron Blomberg 15.00
VB Vida Blue 25.00
WB Wade Boggs 50.00
BRB Bob Boone 20.00
DLB Daryl Boston 10.00
BEB Bob Brenly 10.00
GB George Brett 150.00
LB Lou Brock 30.00
JCB Jay Buhner 25.00
BB Brett Butler 20.00
JRC John Candelaria 15.00
JC Jose Canseco 50.00
RCC Rod Carew 30.00
SC Steve Carlton 35.00
GC Gary Carter 20.00
BC Brian Cashman 85.00
OC Orlando Cepeda 15.00
RC Rick Cerone 15.00
RLC Roger Craig 15.00
MC Mike Cuellar 15.00
RD Ron Darling 15.00
AD Andre Dawson 25.00
RRD Rick Dempsey 15.00
BD Bob Dernier 20.00
SD Shawon Dunston 35.00
DE Dennis Eckersley
CE Carl Erskine 30.00
BF Bob Feller 30.00
SF Sid Fernandez 20.00
MF Mark Fidrych
CF Carlton Fisk 40.00
WF Whitey Ford
BAF Bill Freehan 10.00
JF Jim Frey 15.00
TDF Travis Fryman 15.00
TF Tito Fuentes 15.00
REG Ron Gant 40.00
SG Steve Garvey 20.00
BG Bob Gibson 150.00
JEG Joe Girardi
DG Dwight Gooden 20.00
JG Jerry Grote 20.00
PG Pedro Guerrero 15.00
TG Tony Gwynn 120.00
AH Atlee Hammaker 10.00
TH Toby Harrah 15.00
KH Keith Hernandez 20.00
CH Charlie Hough 10.00
GH Glenn Hubbard 10.00
MI Monte Irvin 75.00
BJ Bo Jackson 100.00
RJ Reggie Jackson 150.00
GJ Gregg Jefferies 20.00
DJ Davey Johnson
HJ Howard Johnson 25.00
JLK Jim Kaat 15.00
AK Al Kaline 40.00
HK Harmon Killebrew 100.00
RK Ralph Kiner 35.00
CK Chuck Knoblauch
EK Ed Kranepool 15.00
JK John Kruk 20.00
TL Tony LaRussa 20.00
JL Jim Leyland 15.00
JJL Jim Leyritz 15.00
GL Grady Little 15.00
JRL Jim Lonborg 15.00
DJM Dave Magadan 15.00
JM Juan Marichal 25.00
TM Tippy Martinez 10.00
DM Don Mattingly 140.00
BM Bill Mazeroski 40.00
DDM Denny McLain 20.00
DBM Dale Murphy 30.00
SM Stan Musial
TN Tom Niedenfuer 15.00
PO Paul O'Neill 40.00
JO Jesse Orosco 10.00
JP Joe Pepitone 15.00
JMP Johnny Pesky 25.00
JAP Jimmy Piersall 20.00
JJP Johnny Podres 50.00
TR Tim Raines 40.00
JR J.R. Richard 20.00
BCR Bobby Richardson 20.00
CR Cal Ripken Jr. 180.00
BR Brooks Robinson 80.00
FR Frank Robinson 60.00
NR Nolan Ryan 250.00
RS Ryne Sandberg 90.00
RFS Rafael Santana 10.00
RES Ron Santo 30.00
TS Tom Seaver 100.00
KS Ken Singleton
MS Bill "Moose" Skowron 15.00
OS Ozzie Smith 125.00
ZS Zane Smith 10.00
DS Duke Snider 60.00
DES Darryl Strawberry 50.00
JT Joe Torre
AV Andy Van Slyke
BW Bob Welch 15.00
LW Lou Whitaker 35.00
RW Roy White 15.00
MW Matt Williams 30.00
DW Dave Winfield 50.00
CY Carl Yastrzemski 120.00
AY Anthony Young 10.00
RY Robin Yount 125.00
DZ Don Zimmer 30.00

Co-Signers

NM/M
Some not priced
BS Wade Boggs, Ryne Sandberg/49 140.00
BF Johnny Bench, Carlton Fisk/49 125.00
GF Bob Gibson, Whitey Ford/49 100.00
SR Tom Seaver, Nolan Ryan
BJ Barry Bonds, Reggie Jackson/9
MS Stan Musial, Duke Snider

Black

Black (1-110): 4-6X
Production 54 sets

Gold

Gold (1-110): 2-4X
Production 500 sets

Holographic

No Pricing
Production one set

2005 TOPPS TOTAL

NM/M
Complete Set (770): 120.00
Common Player: .15
Pack (10): 1.00
Box (36): 35.00
1 Rafael Furcal .15
2 Tony Clark .15
3 Hideki Matsui 1.25
4 Zach Day .15
5 Garret Anderson .40
6 B.J. Surhoff .15
7 Trevor Hoffman .15
8 Kenny Lofton .15
9 Ross Gload .15
10 Jorge Cantu .15
11 Joel Pineiro .15
12 Alex Cintron .15
13 Mike Matheny .15
14 Rod Barajas .15
15 Ray Durham .15
16 Danys Baez .15
17 Brian Schneider .15
18 Tike Redman .15
19 Ricardo Rodriguez .15
20 Mike Sweeney .15
21 Greg Myers .15
22 Chone Figgins .15
23 Brian Lawrence .15
24 Joe Nathan .15
25 Placido Polanco .15
26 Yadier Molina .15
27 Gary Bennett .15
28 Yorvit Torrealba .15
29 Javier Valentin .15
30 Jason Giambi .25
31 Brandon Claussen .15
32 Miguel Olivo .15
33 Josh Bard .15
34 Ramon Hernandez .15
35 Geoff Jenkins .15
36 Bobby Kielty .15
37 Luis A. Gonzalez .15
38 Benito Santiago .15
39 Brandon Inge .15
40 Mark Prior .50
41 Mike Lieberthal .15
42 Toby Hall .15
43 Brad Ausmus .15
44 Damian Miller .15
45 Mark Kotsay .15
46 John Buck .15
47 Oliver Perez .25
48 Matt Morris .25
49 Raul Chavez .15
50 Randy Johnson .50
51 David Bush .15
52 Jose Macias .15
53 Paul Wilson .15
54 Wilfredo Ledezma .15
55 J.D. Drew .25
56 Pedro Martinez .50
57 Josh Towers .15
58 Jamie Moyer .15
59 Scott Elarton .15
60 Ken Griffey Jr. 1.00
61 Steve Trachsel .15
62 Bubba Crosby .15
63 Michael Barrett .15
64 Odalis Perez .15
65 B.J. Upton .25
66 Eric Bruntlett .15
67 Carlos Zambrano .15
68 Brandon League .15
69 Carlos Silva .15
70 Lyle Overbay .25
71 Runelvys Hernandez .15
72 Brad Penny .15
73 Ty Wigginton .15
74 Orlando Hudson .15
75 Roy Oswalt .25
76 Jason LaRue .15
77 Ismael Valdez .15
78 Calvin Pickering .15
79 Bill Hall .15
80 Carl Crawford .15
81 Tomas Perez .15
82 Joe Kennedy .15
83 Chris Woodward .15
84 Jason Lane .15
85 Steve Finley .15
86 Jeff Francis .15
87 Felipe Lopez .15
88 Chan Ho Park .15
89 Joe Crede .15
90 Jose Vidro .15
91 Casey Kotchman .25
92 Brandon Backe .15
93 Mike Hampton .15
94 Ryan Dempster .15
95 Wily Mo Pena .25
96 Matt Holliday .15
97 A.J. Pierzynski .15
98 Jason Jennings .15
99 Eli Marrero .15
100 Carlos Beltran .40
101 Scott Kazmir .25
102 Kenny Rogers .15
103 Roy Halladay .25
104 Alex Cora .15
105 Richie Sexson .25
106 Ben Sheets .25
107 Bartolo Colon .25
108 Eddie Perez .15
109 Vicente Padilla .15
110 Sammy Sosa 1.00
111 Mark Ellis .15
112 Woody Williams .15
113 Todd Greene .15
114 Nook Logan .15
115 Francisco Rodriguez .15
116 Miguel Batista .15
117 Livan Hernandez .15
118 Chris Aguila .15
119 Coco Crisp .15
120 Jose Reyes .15

121 Ricky Ledee .15
122 Brad Radke .15
123 Carlos Guillen .15
124 Paul Bako .15
125 Tom Glavine .25
126 Chad Moeller .15
127 Mark Buehrle .25
128 Casey Blake .15
129 Juan Rivera .15
130 Preston Wilson .15
131 Nate Robertson .15
132 Julio Franco .15
133 Derek Lowe .15
134 Rob Bell .15
135 Javy Lopez .25
136 Javier Vazquez .25
137 Desi Relaford .15
138 Danny Graves .15
139 Josh Fogg .15
140 Bobby Crosby .25
141 Ramon Castro .15
142 Jerry Hairston Jr. .15
143 Morgan Ensberg .15
144 Brandon Webb .25
145 Jack Wilson .15
146 Bill Mueller .15
147 Troy Glaus .25
148 Armando Benitez .15
149 Adam LaRoche .15
150 Hank Blalock .40
151 Ryan Franklin .15
152 Kevin Millwood .15
153 Jason Marquis .15
154 Dewon Brazelton .15
155 Al Leiter .15
156 Garrett Atkins .15
157 Todd Walker .15
158 Kris Benson .15
159 Eric Milton .15
160 Bret Boone .15
161 Matthew LeCroy .15
162 Chris Widger .15
163 Ruben Gotay .15
164 Craig Monroe .15
165 Travis Hafner .15
166 Vance Wilson .15
167 Jason Grabowski .15
168 Tim Salmon .25
169 Henry Blanco .15
170 Josh Beckett .25
171 Jake Westbrook .15
172 Paul LoDuca .15
173 Julio Lugo .15
174 Juan Cruz .15
175 Mark Mulder .25
176 Juan Castro .15
177 Damion Easley .15
178 LaTroy Hawkins .15
179 Jon Lieber .25
180 Vernon Wells .25
181 Jeff DaVanon .15
182 Dustan Mohr .15
183 Ryan Freel .15
184 Doug Davis .15
185 Sean Casey .25
186 Robb Quinlan .15
187 J.D. Closser .15
188 Tim Wakefield .15
189 Brian Jordan .15
190 Adam Dunn .40
191 Antonio Perez .15
192 Brett Tomko .15
193 John Flaherty .15
194 Michael Cuddyer .15
195 Ronnie Belliard .15
196 Tony Womack .15
197 Jason Johnson .15
198 Victor Santos .15
199 Dan Haren .15
200 Derek Jeter 1.50
201 Brian Anderson .15
202 Carlos Pena .15
203 Jaret Wright .15
204 Paul Byrd .15
205 Shannon Stewart .15
206 Chris Carpenter .15
207 Matt Stairs .15
208 Brad Hawpe .15
209 Bobby Higginson .15
210 Torii Hunter .25
211 Shawn Green .25
212 Todd Hollandsworth .15
213 Scott Erickson .15
214 C.C. Sabathia .15
215 Mike Mussina .40
216 Jason Kendall .15
217 Todd Pratt .15
218 Danny Kolb .15
219 Tony Armas .15
220 Edgar Renteria .25
221 Dave Roberts .15
222 Luis Rivas .15
223 Adam Everett .15
224 Jeff Cirillo .15
225 Orlando Hernandez .15
226 Ken Harvey .15
227 Corey Patterson .25
228 Humberto Cota .15
229 A.J. Burnett .25
230 Roger Clemens 1.50
231 Joe Randa .15
232 David Dellucci .15
233 Troy Percival .15
234 Dustin Hermanson .15
235 Eric Gagne .25
236 Terry Tiffee .15
237 Tony Graffanino .15
238 Jayson Werth .15
239 Michael Sweeney .15
240 Chipper Jones .75
241 Aramis Ramirez .40
242 Frank Catalanotto .15
243 Mike Maroth .15
244 Kelvim Escobar .15
245 Bobby Abreu .25
246 Kyle Lohse .15
247 Jason Isringhausen .15
248 Jose Lima .15
249 Adrian Gonzalez .15
250 Alex Rodriguez 1.50
251 Ramon Ortiz .15
252 Frank Menechino .15
253 Keith Ginter .15
254 Kip Wells .15
255 Dmitri Young .15
256 Craig Biggio .25
257 Ramon E. Martinez .15
258 Jason Bartlett .15
259 Brad Lidge .15
260 Brian Giles .25
261 Luis Terrero .15
262 Miguel Ojeda .15
263 Rich Harden .25
264 Jacque Jones .15
265 Marcus Giles .25
266 Carlos Zambrano .25
267 Michael Tucker .15
268 Wes Obermueller .15
269 Peter Orr .50
270 Jim Thome .50
271 Omar Vizquel .25
272 Jose Valentin .15
273 Juan Uribe .15
274 Doug Mirabelli .15
275 Jeff Kent .25
276 Brad Wilkerson .15
277 Chris Burke .25
278 Endy Chavez .15
279 Richard Hidalgo .15
280 John Smoltz .25
281 Jarrod Washburn .15
282 Larry Bigbie .15
283 Edgardo Alfonzo .15
284 Cliff Lee .15
285 Carlos Lee .25
286 Olmedo Saenz .15
287 Tomokazu Ohka .15
288 Ruben Sierra .15
289 Nick Swisher .15
290 Frank Thomas .40
291 Aaron Cook .15
292 Cody McKay .15
293 Hee Seop Choi .15
294 Carl Pavano .25
295 Scott Rolen .50
296 Matt Kata .15
297 Terrence Long .15
298 Jimmy Gobble .15
299 Jason Repko .15
300 Manny Ramirez .50
301 Dan Wilson .15
302 Jhonny Peralta .15
303 John Mabry .15
304 Adam Melhuse .15
305 Kerry Wood .50
306 Ryan Langerhans .15
307 Antonio Alfonseca .15
308 Marco Scutaro .15
309 Jamey Carroll .15
310 Lance Berkman .25
311 Willie Harris .15
312 Phil Nevin .25
313 Gregg Zaun .15
314 Michael Ryan .15
315 Zack Greinke .15
316 Ted Lilly .15
317 David Eckstein .15
318 Tony Torcato .15
319 Robert Mackowiak .15
320 Mark Teixeira .40
321 Jason Phillips .15
322 Jeremy Reed .15
323 Bengie Molina .15
324 Terrmel Sledge .15
325 Justin Morneau .40
326 Sandy Alomar Jr. .15
327 Jon Garland .25
328 Jay Payton .15
329 Tino Martinez .25
330 Jason Bay .25
331 Jeff Conine .15
332 Shawn Chacon .15
333 Angel Berroa .15
334 Reggie Sanders .15
335 Kevin Brown .15
336 Brady Clark .15
337 Casey Fossum .15
338 Raul Ibanez .15
339 Derrek Lee .40
340 Victor Martinez .25
341 Kazuhisa Ishii .15
342 Royce Clayton .15
343 Trot Nixon .25
344 Eric Young .15
345 Aubrey Huff .15
346 Brett Myers .25
347 Joey Gathright .15
348 Mark Grudzielanek .15
349 Scott Spiezio .15
350 Eric Chavez .25
351 Einar Diaz .15
352 Dallas McPherson .25
353 John Thomson .15
354 Neifi Perez .15
355 Larry Walker .25
356 Billy Wagner .25
357 Mike Cameron .15
358 Jimmy Rollins .15
359 Kevin Mench .15
360 Joe Mauer .25
361 Jose Molina .15
362 Joe Borchard .15
363 Kevin Cash .15
364 Jay Gibbons .15
365 Khalil Greene .25
366 Justin Leone .15
367 Eddie Guardado .15
368 Mike Lamb .15
369 Matt Riley .15
370 Luis Gonzalez .25
371 Alfredo Amezaga .15
372 J.J. Hardy .15
373 Hector Luna .15
374 Greg Aquino .15
375 Jim Edmonds .25
376 Joe Blanton .15
377 Russell Branyan .15
378 J.T. Snow .15
379 Magglio Ordonez .25
380 Rafael Palmeiro .40
381 Andruw Jones .25
382 David DeJesus .15
383 Marquis Grissom .15
384 Bobby Hill .15
385 Kazuo Matsui .15
386 Mark Loretta .15
387 Chris Shelton .15
388 Johnny Estrada .15
389 Adam Hyzdu .15
390 Nomar Garciaparra 1.00
391 Mark Teahen .15
392 Chris Capuano .15
393 Ben Broussard .15
394 Daniel Cabrera .15
395 Jeremy Bonderman .25
396 Darin Erstad .25
397 Alex S. Gonzalez .15
398 Kevin Millar .15
399 Freddy Garcia .15
400 Alfonso Soriano .50
401 Koyie Hill .15
402 Omar Infante .15
403 Alex Gonzalez .15
404 Pat Burrell .25
405 Wes Helms .15
406 Junior Spivey .15
407 Joe Mays .15
408 Jason Stanford .15
409 Gil Meche .15
410 Tim Hudson .25
411 Chase Utley .25
412 Matt Clement .25
413 Nick Green .15
414 Jose Vizcaino .15
415 Ryan Klesko .15
416 Vinny Castilla .15
417 Brian Roberts .40
418 Geronimo Gil .15
419 Gary Matthews .15
420 Jeff Weaver .15
421 Jerome Williams .15
422 Andy Pettitte .40
423 Randy Wolf .15
424 D'Angelo Jimenez .15
425 Moises Alou .25
426 Eric Byrnes .15
427 Mark Redman .15
428 Jermaine Dye .15
429 Cory Lidle .15
430 Jason Schmidt .25
431 Jason W. Smith .15
432 Jose Castillo .15
433 Pokey Reese .15
434 Matt Lawton .15
435 Jose Guillen .25
436 Craig Counsell .15
437 Jose Hernandez .15
438 Braden Looper .15
439 Scott Hatteberg .15
440 Gary Sheffield .40
441 Gabe Gross .15
442 Chris Gomez .15
443 Dontrelle Willis .40
444 Jamey Wright .15
445 Rocco Baldelli .15
446 Bernie Williams .25
447 Sean Burroughs .15
448 Willie Bloomquist .15
449 Luis Castillo .15
450 Mike Piazza 1.00
451 Ryan Drese .15
452 Pedro Feliz .15
453 Horacio Ramirez .15
454 Luis Matos .15
455 Craig Wilson .15
456 Russ Ortiz .15
457 Xavier Nady .15
458 Hideo Nomo .25
459 Miguel Cairo .15
460 Mike Lowell .25
461 Corky Miller .15
462 Bobby Madritsch .15
463 Jose Contreras .15
464 Johnny Damon .75
465 Miguel Cabrera .50
466 Eric Hinske .15
467 Marlon Byrd .15
468 Aaron Miles .15
469 Ramon Vazquez .15
470 Michael Young .15
471 Alex Sanchez .15
472 Shea Hillenbrand .15
473 Jeff Bagwell .40
474 Erik Bedard .15
475 Jake Peavy .40
476 Jody Gerut .15
477 Randy Winn .15
478 Kevin Youkilis .15
479 Eric Dubose .15
480 David Wright .75
481 Wilson Valdez .15
482 Cliff Floyd .15
483 Jose Mesa .25
484 Doug Mientkiewicz .15
485 Jorge Posada .40
486 Sidney Ponson .15
487 David Krynzel .15
488 Octavio Dotel .15
489 Matt Treanor .15
490 Johan Santana .40
491 John Patterson .15
492 So Taguchi .15
493 Carl Everett .15
494 Jason Dubois .15
495 Albert Pujols 1.50
496 Kirk Rueter .15
497 Geoff Blum .15
498 Juan Encarnacion .15
499 Mark Hendrickson .15
500 Barry Bonds 2.00
501 Cesar Izturis .15
502 David Wells .15
503 Jorge Julio .15
504 Cristian Guzman .15
505 Juan Pierre .15
506 Adam Eaton .15
507 Nick Johnson .25
508 Mike Redmond .15
509 Daryle Ward .15
510 Adrian Beltre .25
511 Laynce Nix .15
512 Reed Johnson .15
513 Jeremy Affeldt .15
514 R.A. Dickey .15
515 Alex Rios .15
516 Orlando Palmeiro .15

517 Mark Belhorn .15
518 Adam Kennedy .15
519 Curtis Granderson .15
520 Todd Helton .40
521 Aaron Boone .15
522 Milton Bradley .25
523 Timoniel Perez .15
524 Jeff Suppan .15
525 Austin Kearns .15
526 Charles Thomas .15
527 Bronson Arroyo .15
528 Roger Cedeno .15
529 Russ Adams .15
530 Barry Zito .25
531 Bob Wickman .15
532 Deivi Cruz .15
533 Mariano Rivera .40
534 J.J. Davis .15
535 Greg Maddux 1.00
536 Ryan Vogelsong .15
537 Josh Phelps .15
538 Scott Hairston .15
539 Vladimir Guerrero .75
540 Ivan Rodriguez .50
541 David Newhan .15
542 David Bell .15
543 Lew Ford .15
544 Grady Sizemore .15
545 David Ortiz .75
546 Jose Cruz Jr. .15
547 Aaron Rowand .15
548 Marcus Thames .15
549 Scott Podsednik .25
550 Ichiro Suzuki 1.25
551 Eduardo Perez .15
552 Chris Snyder .15
553 Corey Koskie .15
554 Miguel Tejada .50
555 Orlando Cabrera .25
556 Rondell White .15
557 Wade Miller .15
558 Rodrigo Lopez .15
559 Chad Tracy .15
560 Paul Konerko .25
561 Wil Cordero .15
562 John McDonald .15
563 Jason Ellison .15
564 Jason Michaels .15
565 Melvin Mora .25
566 Ryan Church .15
567 Ryan Ludwick .15
568 Erubiel Durazo .15
569 Noah Lowry .15
570 Curt Schilling .50
571 Esteban Loaiza .15
572 Freddy Sanchez .15
573 Rich Aurilia .15
574 Travis Lee .15
575 Dennis Tankersley, Chris George .15
576 Jason Christiansen, Kevin Correia .15
577 Ryan Bukvich, Randy Williams .15
578 Terry Agams, Gavin Floyd .15
579 Seth Etherton, Dan Meyer .15
580 Justin Lehr, Derrick Turnbow .15
581 Mike Gosling, Brad Halsey .15
582 Jim Mecir, Logan Kensing .15
583 Brad Hennessey, Jeff Fassero .15
584 Jason Grilli, John Adkins .15
585 Jesse Crain, Juan Rincon .15
586 Jaime Cerda, Nate Field .15
587 Bartolome Fortunato, Jae Weong Seo .15
588 Frank Brooks, Yhency Brazoban .15
589 Jamie Walker, Ugueth Urbina .15
590 Bret Prinz, Scott Proctor .15
591 Bob Howry, Jason Davis .15
592 Amaury Telemaco, Tim Worrell .15
593 Jose Acevedo, Kent Mercker .15
594 Chris Hammond, Scott Linebrink .15
595 Fernando Nieve, John Franco .15
596 Mike Lincoln, Randy Flores .15
597 Joe Borowski, Kyle Farnsworth .15
598 Jesus Colome, Lance Carter .15
599 Abe Alvarez, Lenny DiNardo .15
600 Chad Bradford, Kiko Calero .15
601 David Aardsma, Jim Brower .15
602 Geoff Geary, Ryan Madson .15
603 Ben Howard, Nate Bump .15
604 Chin-Hui Tsao, Jason Young .15
605 Aaron Harang, Ryan Wagner .15
606 Rick Bauer, Steve Kline .15
607 Lance Cormier, Randy Choate .15
608 Jon Leicester, Todd Wellemeyer .15
609 Jason Frasor, Vinnie Chulk .15
610 Brian Fuentes, Scott Dohmann .15
611 Matt Ginter, Tyler Yates .15
612 Cory Stewart, Salomon Torres .15
613 Cal Eldred, Mike Myers .15
614 Carlos Almanzar, Doug Brocail .15
615 George Sherrill, J.J. Putz .15
616 Bruce Chen, Matt Riley .15
617 Ben Weber, David Weathers .15
618 Dennys Reyes, Rudy Seanez .15
619 Ricardo Rincon, Tim Harikkala .15
620 D.J. Carrasco, Shawn Camp .15
621 Allan Simpson, Javier Lopez .15
622 Glendon Rusch, Mike Remlinger .15
623 Kevin Gryboski, Roman Colon .15
624 Chris Reitsma, Tom Martin .15
625 Chad Qualls, Dan Wheeler .15
626 Brooks Kieschnick, Matt Wise .15
627 Justin Speier, Kerry Ligtenberg .15
628 Francisco Cordero, Frank Francisco .15
629 Matt Thornton, Rafael Soriano .15
630 Mike Stanton, Steve Karsay .15
631 Mike MacDougal, Scott Sullivan .15
632 Brian Bruney, Oscar Villarreal .15
633 Jeff Bennett, Mike Adams .15
634 Dave Borkowski, Eddy Rodriguez .15
635 David Riske, Rafael Betancourt .15
636 Gary Glover, Jorge De La Rosa .15
637 Justin Wayne, Matt Perisho .15
638 Jeff Bajenaru, Luis Vizcaino .15
639 Erasmo Ramirez, Ron Mahay .15
640 John Grabow, Mike Gonzalez .15
641 J.C. Romero, Matt Guerrier .15
642 Brandon Duckworth, Tim Redding .15
643 Franklin Nunez, Travis Harper .15
644 Matt Herges, Tyler Walker .15
645 Elmer Dessens, Wilson Alvarez .15
646 Anastacio Martinez, Mark Malaska .15
647 Gary Knotts, Roberto Novoa .15
648 Jairo Garcia, Justin Duchscherer .15
649 Aaron Rakers, Todd Williams .15
650 Paul Quantrill, Tom Gordon .15
651 Brandon Lyon, Shawn Estes .15
652 Gustavo Chacin, Justin Miller .15
653 John Lackey, Scot Shields .15
654 Bobby Seay, Jorge Sosa .15
655 Chad Cordero, Luis Ayala .15
656 Julio Mateo, Ron Villone .15
657 Byung-Hyun Kim, Matt Mantei .15
658 Cliff Politte, Damaso Marte .15
659 Joe Valentine, Luke Hudson .15
660 John Riedling, Todd Jones .15
661 Aaron Heilman, Heath Bell .15
662 Akinori Otsuka, Blaine Neal .15
663 Joe Horgan, Joey Eischen .15
664 Grant Balfour, J.D. Durbin .15
665 Alan Embree, Mike Timlin .15
666 Keith Foulke .15
667 Aaron Fultz, Rheal Cormier .15
668 Kevin Gregg, Scott Dunn .15
669 Franklyn German, Steve Coyler .15
670 Scott Eyre, Wayne Franklin .15
671 Brian Meadows, Mike Johnston .15
672 Guillermo Mota, Tim Spooneybarger .15
673 B.J. Ryan, Jason Grimsley .15
674 Neal Cotts, Shingo Takatsu .15
675 Felix Heredia, Mike DeJean .15
676 Brian Shackelford, Josh Hancock .15
677 Jon Rauch, T.J. Tucker .15
678 Brian Shouse, Nick Regilio .15
679 Julian Tavarez, Ray King .15
680 Mike Wuertz, Stephen Randolph .15
681 Gabe White, Jorge Vasquez .15
682 Jose Valverde, Mike Koplove .15
683 Arthur Rhodes, Scott Sauerbeck .15
684 Felix Rodriguez, Tanyon Sturtze .15
685 Duaner Sanchez, Giovanni Carrara .15
686 Chad Harville, Mike Gallo .15
687 Dave Williams, Sean Burnett .15
688 Scott Atchison, Shigetoshi Hasegawa .15
689 Claudio Vargas, Francis Beltran .15
690 Brendan Donnelly, Esteban Yan .15
691 Ervin Santana, Jeff Mathis .15
692 Bill Bray, Clint Everts .15
693 Jason Kubel, Trevor Plouffe .15
694 Andy Marte, Jake Stevens .15
695 Aaron Hill, Chad Gaudin .15
696 Carlos Quentin, Jesus Cota .15
697 Chris Young, Thomas Diamond .15
698 Dan Johnson, Omar Quintanilla .15
699 John Maine, Val Majewski .15
700 James Houser, Jonny Gomes .15
701 David Murphy, Hanley Ramirez .15
702 Chris Lambert, Rick Ankiel .15
703 Angel Guzman, Felix Pie .15
704 Merkin Valdez, Nate Schierholtz .15
705 Arnie Munoz, Gio Gonzalez .15
706 Felix Hernandez, Travis Blackley .15
707 Edwin Encarnacion, Tony Blanco .15
708 Justin Germano, Tim Stauffer .15
709 Jeremy Guthrie, Jeremy Sowers .15
710 Jorge Cortes, Tom Gorzelanny .15
711 Logan Kensing, Taylor Tankersley .15
712 Neil Walker, Paul Maholm .15
713 Carlos Hernandez, Willy Taveras .50
714 Greg Golson, Ryan Howard .15
715 Blake DeWitt, Edwin Jackson .15
716 Dan Putnam, Huston Street .15
717 Mark Rogers, Rickie Weeks .25
718 Phillip Hughes, Robinson Cano .15
719 Jay Rainville, Kyle Waldrop .15
720 Craig Brazell, Yusmeiro Petit .15
721 *Baltazar Lopez, Matt Brown* .25
722 *Brett Price, Jerry Owens* .50
723 *Dan Uggla, Kyle Nichols* .25
724 *Francisco Rosario, Jayce Tingler* .25
725 *Eulogio de la Cruz, Tony Giarratano* .25
726 *Matt Campbell, Shane Costa* .25
727 *Bill McCarthy, Martin Prado* .25
728 *Edison Volquez, Ian Kinsler* .50
729 *Lorenzo Scott, Luis Ramirez* .25
730 *Chris Seddon, Elliot Johnson* .25
731 *Chris Dickerson, Thomas Pauly* .15
732 *Jason Motte, Stuart Pomeranz* .25
733 *Jose Vaquedano, Stefan Bailie* .25
734 *D.J. Houlton, Wade Robinson* .25
735 *Matt DeSalvo, Melky Cabrera* .50
736 *Brian Stavisky, Landon Powell* .25
737 *Scott Mathieson, Scott Mitchinson* .25
738 *Bear Bay, Sean Marshall* .25
739 *Brandon McCarthy, Pedro Lopez* 1.50
740 *Alexander Smit, Jair Jurrjens* .25
741 *Matt Rogelstad, Ryan Feierabend* .25
742 *Adam Boeve, Nate McLouth* .25
743 *Kevin Melillo, Michael Rogers* .25
744 *Heath Totten, Matthew Kemp* 1.00
745 *Trevor Hutchinson, Yorman Bazardo* .15
746 *Jesse Gutierrez, Tyler Pelland* .25
747 *Jeremy West, Willy Mota* .25
748 *Ryan Garko, Ryan Goleski* .25
749 *Bryan Triplett, Jared Gothreaux* .25
750 *Glen Perkins, Kevin West* .25
751 *Michael Esposito, Zachary Parker* .25
752 *Brian Miller, Ryan Sweeney* .25
753 *Buck Coats, Casey McGehee* .25
754 *Nate Cabrera, Zachary Cline* .15
755 *Bobby Livingston, Mike Morse* .25
756 *Brendan Ryan, Wes Swackhamer* .25
757 *John Hudgins, Nick Masset* .25
758 *George Kottaras, Peeter Ramos* .25

759 *Elvys Quezada, T.J. Beam* .25
760 *Dana Eveland, Travis Hinton* .25
761 *Chris Vines, James Jurries* .25
762 *Humberto Sanchez, Justin Verlander* 1.00
763 *Ian Bladergroen, Shawn Bowman* .50
764 *J.B. Thurmond, Pat Misch* .25
765 *Christian Colonel, Neil Wilson* .25
766 Checklist 1 .15
767 Checklist 2 .15
768 Checklist 3 .15
769 Checklist 4 .15
770 Checklist 5 .15

Press Plates

NM/M
Common Card Front P. Plate: 25.00
Common Card Back P. Plate: 15.00
Stars not priced
Production one set per color (4):

Silver

Stars: 1-3X
Inserted 1:1

Award Winners

NM/M
Complete Set (30): 15.00
Common Player: .25
Inserted 1:10
AW1 Barry Bonds 2.00
AW2 Vladimir Guerrero .75
AW3 Roger Clemens 2.00
AW4 Johan Santana .75
AW5 Jason Bay .25
AW6 Bobby Crosby .25
AW7 Eric Gagne .40
AW8 Mariano Rivera .50
AW9 Albert Pujols 2.00
AW10 Mark Teixeira .50
AW11 Mark Loretta .25
AW12 Alfonso Soriano .75
AW13 Jack Wilson .25
AW14 Miguel Tejada .50
AW15 Adrian Beltre .40
AW16 Melvin Mora .25
AW17 Barry Bonds 2.00
AW18 Jim Edmonds .50
AW19 Bobby Abreu .40
AW20 Manny Ramirez .75
AW21 Gary Sheffield .50
AW22 Vladimir Guerrero .75
AW23 Johnny Estrada .25
AW24 Victor Martinez .25
AW25 Ivan Rodriguez .50
AW26 Livan Hernandez .25
AW27 David Ortiz .75
AW28 Bobby Cox .25
AW29 Buck Showalter .25
AW30 Barry Bonds 2.00

Domination

NM/M
Complete Set (30): 15.00
Common Player: .25
Inserted 1:10
40 Mark Prior .75
50 Randy Johnson .75
56 Pedro Martinez .75
60 Ken Griffey Jr. 1.00
100 Carlos Beltran .50
110 Sammy Sosa 1.50
147 Troy Glaus .50
150 Hank Blalock .50
180 Vernon Wells .25
190 Adam Dunn .50
200 Derek Jeter 2.00
230 Roger Clemens 2.00
250 Alex Rodriguez 1.50
260 Brian Giles .25
270 Jim Thome .75
290 Frank Thomas .50
300 Manny Ramirez .75
345 Aubrey Huff .25
350 Eric Chavez .25
400 Alfonso Soriano .75
465 Miguel Cabrera .75
490 Johan Santana .50
495 Albert Pujols 2.00
500 Barry Bonds 2.00
510 Adrian Beltre .40
520 Todd Helton .50
575 Vladimir Guerrero .75
540 Ivan Rodriguez .50
545 David Ortiz .75
554 Miguel Tejada .50

Domination Autograph

Production 10
500 Barry Bonds

Production

NM/M
Complete Set (10): 8.00
Common Player: .40
Inserted 1:15
AB Adrian Beltre .40
BB Barry Bonds 2.00
VG Vladimir Guerrero .75
TH Todd Helton .50
AP Albert Pujols 2.00
MR Manny Ramirez .75
AR Alex Rodriguez 1.50
AS Alfonso Soriano .75
MT Miguel Tejada .50
JT Jim Thome .75

Signatures

NM/M
Common Autograph: 8.00
BB Brian Bruney 8.00
RC Robinson Cano 25.00
JG Joey Gathright 10.00
ZG Zack Greinke 12.00
BM Brett Myers 12.00
TT Terry Tiffee 15.00
DW David Wright 35.00

Total Topps

NM/M
Complete Set (20): 12.00
Common Player: .25
Inserted 1:15
CB Carlos Beltran .50
AB Adrian Beltre .40
BB Barry Bonds 2.00
EC Eric Chavez .25
RC Roger Clemens 2.00
VG Vladimir Guerrero .75
TH Todd Helton .50
DJ Derek Jeter 2.00
RJ Randy Johnson .75
GM Greg Maddux 1.00
MP Mike Piazza 1.00
AP Albert Pujols 2.00
MR Manny Ramirez .75
AR Alex Rodriguez 1.50
IR Ivan Rodriguez .50
JS Johan Santana .50
AS Alfonso Soriano .75
SS Sammy Sosa 1.50
MT Miguel Tejada .50
JT Jim Thome .50

2005 TOPPS TURKEY RED

NM/M
Complete Set (315):
Common Player: .25
Common SP: 4.00
Inserted 1:4
Pack (8): 5.00
Box (24): 100.00
1 Barry Bonds Grey Uni SP 15.00
1 Barry Bonds 4.00
2 Michael Young .25
3 Jim Edmonds .50
4 Cliff Floyd .25
5 Roger Clemens Blue Sky SP 12.00
5 Roger Clemens Yellow Sky SP 12.00
6 Hal Chase .25
7 Shannon Stewart .25
8 Fred Clarke .25
9 Travis Hafner .50
10 Sammy Sosa w/Name SP 6.00
10 Sammy Sosa w/o Name SP 6.00
11 Jermaine Dye .25
12 Lyle Overbay .25
13 Oliver Perez .25
14 Red Dooin .25
15 Kid Elberfeld .25
16 Mike Piazza Blue Uni SP 6.00
16 Mike Piazza Pinstripe 1.50
17 Bret Boone .25
18 Hughie Jennings .25
19 Jeff Francis .25
20 Manny Ramirez SP 6.00
21 Russ Ortiz .25
22 Carlos Zambrano .50
23 Luis Castillo .25
24 David DeJesus .25
25 Carlos Beltran SP 5.00
26 Doug Davis .25
27 Bobby Abreu .50
28 Rich Harden SP 4.00
29 Brian Giles .25
30 Richie Sexson SP 4.00
31 Nick Johnson .25
32 Roy Halladay .50
33 Andy Pettitte .50
34 Miguel Cabrera 1.00
35 Jeff Kent .25
36 Chone Figgins .25
37 Carlos Lee .50
38 Greg Maddux 2.00
39 Preston Wilson .25
40 Chipper Jones 1.00
41 Coco Crisp .25
42 Adam Dunn .75
43 Miguel Tejada CL .50
44 Gary Sheffield CL .50
45 Javy Lopez CL .25
46 Scott Rolen CL .50
47 Todd Helton CL .50
48 Roger Clemens CL 1.00
49 Jimmy Rollins CL .25
50 Ichiro Suzuki CL 1.00
51 Cliff Floyd CL .25
52 Johan Santana CL .50
53 Mark Teixeira .75
54 Chris Carpenter .25
55 Roy Oswalt SP 4.00
56 Casey Kotchman .25
57 Torii Hunter .25
58 Jose Reyes .25
59 Wily Mo Pena SP 4.00
60 Magglio Ordonez SP 4.00
61 Aaron Miles .25
62 Dallas McPherson .25
63 Javy Lopez .25
64 Luis Gonzalez .25
65 David Ortiz 1.00
66 Jorge Posada .50
67 Xavier Nady .25
68 Larry Walker .50
69 Mark Loretta .25
70 Jim Thome SP 5.00
71 Livan Hernandez .25
72 Garrett Atkins .25
73 Milton Bradley .25
74 B.J. Upton .25
75 Ichiro Suzuki w/Name SP 8.00
75 Ichiro Suzuki w/o Name SP 8.00
76 Aramis Ramirez .25
77 Eric Milton .25
78 Troy Glaus SP 4.00
79 David Newhan .25
80 Delmon Young .50
81 Justin Morneau .25
82 Ramon Ortiz .25
83 Eric Chavez Blue Sky .25
83 Eric Chavez Purple Sky SP 4.00
84 Sean Burroughs .25
85 Scott Rolen SP 6.00
86 Rocco Baldelli .25
87 Joe Mauer SP 5.00
88 Tony Womack .25
89 Ken Griffey Jr. 2.00
90 Alfonso Soriano SP 6.00
91 Paul Konerko .25
92 Guillermo Mota .25
93 Lance Berkman .50
94 Mark Buehrle .25
95 Matt Clement .25
96 Melvin Mora .25
97 Khalil Greene .50
98 David Wright 1.50
99 Jack Wilson .25
100 Alex Rodriguez w/Bat SP 10.00
100 Alex Rodriguez w/Glove SP 10.00
101 Joe Nathan .25
102 Adrian Beltre Grey Uni SP 4.00
102 Adrian Beltre White Uni .25
103 Mike Sweeney .25
104 Brad Lidge .25
105 Shawn Green .25
106 Miguel Tejada SP 5.00
107 Derrek Lee .75
108 Eric Hinske .25
109 Eric Byrnes .25
110 Hideki Matsui SP 8.00
111 Tom Glavine .50
112 Jimmy Rollins .25
113 Ryan Drese .25
114 Josh Beckett .25
115 Curt Schilling SP 6.00
116 Jeremy Bonderman .25
117 Hideki Matsui .25
118 Chase Utley .50
119 Troy Percival .25
120 Vladimir Guerrero w/Bat SP 6.00
120 Vladimir Guerrero w/Glove SP 6.00
121 Gary Sheffield .50
122 Jeromy Burnitz .25
123 Javier Vazquez .25
124 Kevin Millar .25
125 Randy Johnson Blue Sky 1.00
125 Randy Johnson Purple Sky SP 5.00

126 Pat Burrell .25
127 Jason Schmidt .25
128 Jose Vidro .25
129 Kip Wells .25
130 Ivan Rodriguez w/Cap .75
130 Ivan Rodriguez w/Helmet SP 6.00
131 C.C. Sabathia .25
132 Carlos Delgado SP 4.00
133 Bartolo Colon .25
134 Andruw Jones .50
135 Kerry Wood .50
136 Sidney Ponson .25
137 Eric Gagne .25
138 Rickie Weeks .50
139 Mariano Rivera .50
140 Bobby Crosby .25
141 Jamie Moyer .25
142 Corey Koskie .25
143 John Smoltz .50
144 Frank Thomas .75
145 Cristian Guzman .25
146 Paul LoDuca .25
147 Geoff Jenkins .25
148 Nick Swisher .25
149 Jason Bay SP 4.00
150 Albert Pujols SP 10.00
151 Edwin Jackson .25
152 Carl Crawford .25
153 Mark Mulder .50
154 Rafael Palmeiro .75
155 Pedro Martinez SP 6.00
156 Jake Westbrook .25
157 Sean Casey .25
158 Aaron Rowand .25
159 J.D. Drew .25
160 Johan Santana Glove on Knee SP 5.00
160 Johan Santana Throwing SP 5.00
161 Gavin Floyd .25
162 Vernon Wells .25
163 Aubrey Huff .25
164 Jeff Bagwell .50
165 Boomer Wells .25
166 Brad Penny .25
167 Austin Kearns .25
168 Mike Mussina .50
169 Randy Wolf .25
170 Tim Hudson SP 4.00
171 Casey Blake .25
172 Edgar Renteria .50
173 Ben Sheets .50
174 Kevin Brown .25
175 Nomar Garciaparra SP 8.00
176 Armando Benitez .25
177 Jody Gerut .25
178 Craig Biggio .50
179 Omar Vizquel .25
180 Jake Peavy .50
181 Gustavo Chacin SP 4.00
182 Johnny Damon .75
183 Mike Lieberthal .25
184 Felix Hernandez SP 15.00
185 Zach Day SP 4.00
186 Matt Cain .25
187 Erubiel Durazo .25
188 Zack Greinke .25
189 Matt Morris .25
190 Billy Wagner .25
191 Al Leiter .25
192 Miguel Olivo .25
193 Jose Capellan SP 4.00
194 Adam Eaton .25
195 Steven White SP 4.00
196 Joe Randa .25
197 Richard Hidalgo .25
198 Orlando Cabrera .25
199 Joel Guzman SP 6.00
200 Garret Anderson .50
201 Endy Chavez .25
202 Andy Marte .25
203 Jose Guillen .25
204 Victor Martinez .25
205 Johnny Estrada .25
206 Damian Miller .25
207 Ken Harvey .25
208 Ronnie Belliard .25
209 Chan Ho Park .25
210 Laynce Nix .25
211 Lew Ford .25
212 Moises Alou .50
213 Kris Benson .25
214 Mike Gonzalez SP 4.00
215 Chris Burke .25
216 Juan Pierre .25
217 Phil Nevin .25
218 Jerry Hairston Jr. .25
219 Jeremy Reed .25
220 Scott Kazmir SP 4.00
221 Mike Maroth .25
222 Alex Rios .25
223 Esteban Loaiza .25
224 Terrmel Sledge .25
225 Mark Prior Blue Sky SP 6.00
225 Mark Prior Yellow Sky SP 6.00
226 Hank Blalock .50
227 Craig Wilson .25
228 Cesar Izturis .25
229 Dmitri Young .25
230 Derek Jeter Blue Sky SP 15.00
230 Derek Jeter Purple Sky SP 15.00
231 Mark Kotsay .25
232 Darin Erstad .25
233 Brandon Backe SP 4.00
234 Mike Lowell .25
235 Scott Podsednik .25
236 Michael Barrett .25
237 Chad Tracy .25
238 David Dellucci .25
239 Brady Clark .25
240 Jorge Cantu .25
241 Wilfredo Ledezma .25
242 Morgan Ensberg .25
243 Omar Infante .25
244 Corey Patterson .25
245 Matt Holliday .25
246 Vinny Castilla .25
247 Jason Bartlett .25
248 Noah Lowry .25
249 Huston Street .25
250 Russell Branyan .25
251 Juan Uribe .25
252 Larry Bigbie .25
253 Grady Sizemore .25
254 Pedro Feliz .25
255 Brad Wilkerson .25
256 Brandon Inge .25
257 Dewon Brazelton .25
258 Rodrigo Lopez .25
259 Jacque Jones .25
260 Jason Giambi .50
261 Clint Barmes .25
262 Willy Taveras .25
263 Marcus Giles .25
264 Joe Blanton .25
265 John Thomson .25
266 Steve Finley SP 4.00
267 Kevin Millwood .25
268 David Eckstein .25
269 Barry Zito .50
270 Todd Helton Purple Sky SP 5.00
270 Todd Helton Yellow Sky SP 5.00
271 *Landon Powell* 1.00
272 *Justin Verlander* 3.00
273 *Wes Swackhamer* 1.00
274 *Wladimir Balentien* 2.00
275 *Philip Humber* 1.00
276 *Kevin Melillo* 2.00
277 *Billy Butler* 5.00
278 *Michael Rogers* 1.00
279 *Bobby Livingston* 1.00
280 *Glen Perkins* 1.00
281 *Michael Bourn* 1.00
282 *Tyler Pelland* 1.00
283 *Jeremy West* 2.00
284 *Brandon McCarthy* 4.00
285 *Ian Kinsler* 1.00
286 *Chris Roberson* 1.00
287 *Melky Cabrera* 2.00
288 *Ryan Sweeney* 1.00
289 *Chip Cannon* 1.00
290 *Andy LaRoche* 5.00
291 *Chuck Tiffany* 1.00
292 *Ian Bladergroen* 1.00
293 *Bear Bay* 1.00
294 *Hernan Iribarren* 1.00
295 *Stuart Pomeranz* 1.00
296 *Luke Scott* 1.00
297 *Chuck James* 1.00
298 *Kennard Bibbs* 1.00
299 Steve Bondurant 1.50
300 *Tom Oldham* 1.00
301 Nolan Ryan 3.00
302 Reggie Jackson 1.00
303 Tom Seaver 1.00
304 Al Kaline 1.50
305 Cal Ripken Jr. 4.00
306 Josh Gibson 1.50
307 Frank Robinson 1.00
308 Duke Snider 1.00
309 Wade Boggs 1.50
310 Tony Gwynn 2.00
311 Carl Yastrzemski 2.00
312 Ryne Sandberg 2.00
313 Gary Carter 1.00
314 Brooks Robinson 1.50
315 Ernie Banks 1.50

Black

Stars (1-315): 3-5X
SP's: 1.5-2X
Inserted 1:20

White

Stars (1-315): 2-3X
SP's: 1-1.5X
Inserted 1:4

Red

Stars (1-315): 1-2X
SP's: .5-1X

Gold

Stars (1-315): 5-10X
SP's: 3-5X
Production 50 sets

Suede

No Pricing
Production one set

Autographs

NM/M

BB Barry Bonds
MB Matt Bush 30.00
CC Carl Crawford 25.00
SE Scott Elbert 20.00
JF Josh Fields 15.00
EG Eric Gagne 35.00
JG Jody Gerut 10.00
JPH J.P. Howell 15.00
ZJ Zach Jackson 12.00
JJ Jason Jaramillo 12.00
BJ Blake Johnson 15.00
MK Mark Kotsay
BM Brett Myers
CN Chris Nelson 10.00
DO David Ortiz 50.00
ZP Zachary Parker 12.00
DP Dustin Pedroia 20.00
MR Mariano Rivera 60.00
AR Alex Rodriguez
MRO Mike Rodriguez 10.00
GS Gary Sheffield 40.00
AS Alfonso Soriano 40.00
JS Jeremy Sowers 20.00

Cabinet Boxloaders

NM/M

Inserted 1:box
BB Barry Bonds 25.00
GB George W. Bush 10.00
RJ Randy Johnson 12.00
MP Mike Piazza 12.00
AP Albert Pujols 20.00
MR Manny Ramirez 12.00
AR Alex Rodriguez 20.00
SR Scott Rolen 10.00
JS Johan Santana 12.00
SS Sammy Sosa 15.00
WT William H. Taft 15.00
MT Miguel Tejada 10.00
JT Jim Thome 10.00
GW George Washington 25.00

Cabinet Auto Relics

NM/M

Production 5-450
BB Barry Bonds/5
MB Matt Bush/450 30.00
CC Carl Crawford/450 25.00
EG Eric Gagne/75
JG Jody Gerut/450 20.00
MK Mark Kotsay/450 30.00
BM Brett Myers/150 40.00
DO David Ortiz/75 100.00
MR Mariano Rivera/25 90.00
AR Alex Rodriguez/25 400.00
GS Gary Sheffield/25 100.00
AS Alfonso Soriano/75 75.00

Cut Signatures

Production one set

Relics

NM/M

Common Player: 4.00
JB Jeff Bagwell 6.00
CB Carlos Beltran 6.00
AB Adrian Beltre 6.00
HB Hank Blalock 6.00
BB Barry Bonds 20.00
MC Miguel Cabrera 8.00
RC Roger Clemens 15.00
RC2 Roger Clemens 15.00
JD Johnny Damon 10.00
JD2 Johnny Damon 10.00
VG Vladimir Guerrero 8.00
TH Todd Helton 6.00
CJ Chipper Jones 8.00
ML Mike Lowell 4.00
MM Mark Mulder 4.00
MO Magglio Ordonez 4.00
DO David Ortiz 8.00
RP Rafael Palmeiro 6.00
MP Mike Piazza 8.00
MPR Mark Prior 8.00
AP Albert Pujols 15.00
MR Manny Ramirez 8.00
AR Alex Rodriguez 12.00
AR2 Alex Rodriguez 12.00
CS Curt Schilling 8.00
GS Gary Sheffield 6.00
AS Alfonso Soriano 8.00
SS Sammy Sosa 10.00
MTE Mark Teixeira 6.00
MT Miguel Tejada 8.00
JT Jim Thome 6.00
LW Larry Walker 4.00

B-18 Blanket Boxloaders

NM/M

Common Blanket 8.00
Barry Bonds 20.00
Roger Clemens 20.00
Todd Helton 8.00
Derek Jeter 20.00
Alex Rodriguez 15.00
Curt Schilling 12.00
Alfonso Soriano 8.00
Ichiro Suzuki 15.00

2005 TOPPS UPDATE

NM/M

Complete Set (330): 35.00
Complete Factory Set (330): 40.00
Common Player: .10
Pack (10): 2.00
Box (36): 60.00
1 Sammy Sosa 1.00
2 Jeff Francoeur .25
3 Tony Clark .10
4 Michael Tucker .10
5 Mike Matheny .10
6 Eric Young .10
7 Jose Valentin .10
8 Matt Lawton .10
9 Juan Rivera .10
10 Shawn Green .25
11 Aaron Boone .10
12 Woody Williams .10
13 Brad Wilkerson .10
14 *Anthony Reyes* .75
15 Russ Adams .10
16 Gustavo Chacin .10
17 Mike Restovich .10
18 Humberto Quintero .10
19 Matt Ginter .10
20 Scott Podsednik .25
21 Byung-Hyun Kim .10
22 Orlando Hernandez .10
23 Mark Grudzielanek .10
24 Jody Gerut .10
25 Adrian Beltre .25

26 Scott Schoeneweis .10
27 Marlon Anderson .10
28 Jason Vargas .10
29 Claudio Vargas .10
30 Jason Kendall .10
31 Aaron Small .10
32 Juan Cruz .10
33 Placido Polanco .10
34 Jorge Sosa .10
35 John Olerud .10
36 Ryan Langerhans .10
37 Randy Winn .10
38 Zachary Duke .25
39 Garrett Atkins .10
40 Al Leiter .10
41 Shawn Chacon .10
42 Mark DeRosa .10
43 Miguel Ojeda .10
44 A.J. Pierzynski .10
45 Carlos Lee .10
46 LaTroy Hawkins .10
47 Nick Green .10
48 Shawn Estes .10
49 Eli Marrero .10
50 Jeff Kent .10
51 Joe Randa .10
52 Jose Hernandez .10
53 Joe Blanton .10
54 Huston Street .10
55 Marlon Byrd .10
56 Alex Sanchez .10
57 Livan Hernandez .10
58 Chris Young .10
59 Brad Eldred .10
60 Terrence Long .10
61 Phil Nevin .10
62 Kyle Farnsworth .10
63 Jon Lieber .10
64 Antonio Alfonseca .10
65 Tony Graffanino .10
66 *Tadahito Iguchi* 1.00
67 Brad Thompson .10
68 Jose Vidro .10
69 Jason Phillips .10
70 Carl Pavano .10
71 Pokey Reese .10
72 Jerome Williams .10
73 Kazuhisa Ishii .10
74 Zach Day .10
75 Edgar Renteria .25
76 Mike Myers .10
77 Jeff Cirillo .10
78 Endy Chavez .10
79 Jose Guillen .10
80 Ugueth Urbina .10
81 Vinny Castilla .10
82 Javier Vazquez .10
83 Willy Taveras .10
84 Mark Mulder .25
85 Mike Hargrove .10
86 Buddy Bell .10
87 Charlie Manuel .10
88 Willie Randolph .10
89 Bob Melvin .10
90 Chris Lambert .10
91 Homer Bailey .10
92 Ervin Santana .10
93 Bill Bray .10
94 Thomas Diamond .10
95 Trevor Plouffe .10
96 James Houser .10
97 Jake Stevens .10
98 Anthony Whittington .10
99 Phillip Hughes .10
100 Greg Golson .10
101 Paul Maholm .10
102 Carlos Quentin .10
103 Dan Johnson .10
104 Mark Rogers .10
105 Neil Walker .10
106 Omar Quintanilla .10
107 Blake DeWitt .10
108 Taylor Tankersley .10
109 David Murphy .10
110 Felix Hernandez .50
111 Craig Biggio .10
112 Greg Maddux .50
113 Bobby Abreu .10
114 Alex Rodriguez .75
115 Trevor Hoffman .10
116 A.J. Pierzynski, Tadahito Iguchi .25
117 Reggie Sanders .10
118 Bengie Molina, Ervin Santana .10
119 Chris Burke, Lance Berkman, Adam LaRoche .10
120 Garret Anderson .25
121 A.J. Pierzynski .10
122 Paul Konerko .25
123 Joe Crede .10
124 Mark Buehrle, Jon Garland .10
125 Freddy Garcia, Jose Contreras .10
126 Reggie Sanders .10
127 Roy Oswalt .10
128 Roger Clemens .75
129 Albert Pujols .75
130 Roy Oswalt .25
131 Joe Crede, Bobby Jenks .10
132 Paul Konerko, Scott Podsednik .25
133 Geoff Blum .10
134 White Sox Sweep .10
135 Alex Rodriguez, David Ortiz, Manny Ramirez .50
136 Michael Young, Alex Rodriguez, Vladimir Guerrero .50
137 David Ortiz, Mark Teixeira, Manny Ramirez .25
138 Bartolo Colon, Jon Garland, Cliff Lee .10
139 Kevin Millwood, Johan Santana, Mark Buehrle .10
140 Johan Santana, Randy Johnson, John Lackey .25
141 Andruw Jones, Derrek Lee, Albert Pujols .50
142 Derek Lee, Albert Pujols, Miguel Cabrera .50
143 Andruw Jones, Albert Pujols, Pat Burrell .50
144 Dontrelle Willis, Chris Carpenter, Roy Oswalt .25
145 Roger Clemens, Andy Pettitte, Dontrelle Willis .50
146 Jake Peavy, Chris Carpenter, Pedro Martinez .25
147 Mark Teixeira .25
148 Brian Roberts .10
149 Michael Young .10
150 Alex Rodriguez 1.00
151 Johnny Damon .25
152 Vladimir Guerrero .25
153 Manny Ramirez .25
154 David Ortiz .25
155 Mariano Rivera .25
156 Joe Nathan .10
157 Albert Pujols 1.00
158 Jeff Kent .10
159 Felipe Lopez .10
160 Morgan Ensberg .10
161 Miguel Cabrera .25
162 Ken Griffey Jr. .50
163 Andruw Jones .25
164 Paul LoDuca .10
165 Chad Cordero .10
166 Ken Griffey Jr. .50
167 Jason Giambi .10
168 Willy Taveras .10
169 Huston Street .10
170 Chris Carpenter .10
171 Bartolo Colon .10
172 Bobby Cox .10
173 Ozzie Guillen .10
174 Andruw Jones .25
175 Johnny Damon .25
176 Alex Rodriguez 1.00
177 David Ortiz .25
178 Manny Ramirez .25
179 Miguel Tejada .25
180 Vladimir Guerrero .25
181 Mark Teixeira .25
182 Ivan Rodriguez .25
183 Brian Roberts .10
184 Mark Buehrle .10
185 Bobby Abreu .25
186 Carlos Beltran .25
187 Albert Pujols 1.00
188 Derrek Lee .25
189 Jim Edmonds .25
190 Aramis Ramirez .10
191 Mike Piazza .50
192 Jeff Kent .10
193 David Eckstein .10
194 Chris Carpenter .10
195 Bobby Abreu .25
196 Ivan Rodriguez .25
197 Carlos Lee .10
198 David Ortiz .25
199 Hee Seop Choi .10
200 Andruw Jones .25
201 Mark Teixeira .25
202 Jason Bay .10
203 Hanley Ramirez .10
204 Shin-Soo Choo .10
205 Justin Huber .10
206 *Nelson Cruz* .50
207 Edwin Encarnacion .10
208 *Miguel Montero* .10
209 William Bergolla .10
210 Luis Montanez .10
211 Francisco Liriano .10
212 Kevin Thompson .10
213 B.J. Upton .10
214 Conor Jackson .10
215 Delmon Young .25
216 Andy LaRoche .50
217 Ryan Garko .10
218 Josh Barfield .10
219 Chris Young .10
220 Justin Verlander .25
221 *Drew Anderson* .25
222 *Luis Hernandez* .25
223 *Jim Burt* .25
224 *Mike Morse* .25
225 *Elliot Johnson* .25
226 *C.J. Smith* .25
227 *Casey McGehee* .25
228 *Brian Miller* .15
229 *Chris Vines* .40
230 *D.J. Houlton* .25
231 *Chuck Tiffany* .40
232 *Humberto Sanchez* .25
233 *Baltazar Lopez* .25
234 *Russell Martin* .25
235 *Dana Eveland* .25
236 *Johan Silva* .25
237 *Adam Harben* 1.00
238 *Brian Bannister* .25
239 *Adam Boeve* .25
240 *Tom Oldham* .25
241 *Cody Haerther* .25
242 *Dan Santin* .25
243 *Daniel Haigwood* .25
244 *Craig Tatum* .25
245 *Martin Prado* .40
246 *Errol Simonitsch* .40
247 *Lorenzo Scott* .25
248 *Hayden Penn* .25
249 *Heath Totten* .25
250 *Nick Masset* .25
251 *Pedro Lopez* .25
252 Benjamin Harrison .15
253 *Michael Spidale* .25
254 *Jeremy Harts* .25
255 *Danny Zell* .40
256 *Kevin Collins* .15
257 *Tony Arnerich* .15
258 *Matt Albers* .15
259 *Ricky Barrett* .25
260 *Hernan Iribarren* .40
261 *Sean Tracey* .25
262 *Jerry Owens* .40
263 *Steve Nelson* .25
264 *Brandon McCarthy* 1.00
265 *David Shepard* .25
266 *Steve Bondurant* .25
267 *Billy Sadler* .15
268 *Ryan Feierabend* .25
269 *Stuart Pomeranz* .40
270 Shaun Marcum .25
271 *Erik Schindewolf* .25
272 *Stefan Bailie* .15
273 *Mike Esposito* .25
274 *Buck Coats* .40
275 *Andy Sides* .25
276 *Micah Schnurstein* .40
277 *Jesse Gutierrez* .25
278 *Jake Postlewait* .25
279 *Willy Mota* .50
280 *Ryan Speier* .25
281 *Frank Mata* .25
282 *Jair Jurrjens* .50
283 *Nick Touchstone* .25
284 *Matthew Kemp* .75
285 *Vinny Rottino* .40
286 *J.B. Thurmond* .40
287 *Kelvin Pichardo* .25
288 *Scott Mitchinson* .25
289 *Darwinson Salazar* .25
290 *George Kottaras* .50
291 *Ken Durost* .40
292 *Jonathan Sanchez* .40
293 *Brandon Moorhead* .25
294 *Kennard Bibbs* .25
295 *David Gassner* .40
296 *Micah Furtado* .25
297 *Ismael Ramirez* .25
298 *Carlos Gonzalez* 1.00
299 *Brandon Sing* .50
300 *Jason Motte* .25
301 *Chuck James* .75
302 *Andy Santana* .25
303 *Manny Parra* .40
304 *Chris Young* .40
305 *Juan Senreiso* .25
306 *Franklin Morales* .25
307 *Jared Gothreaux* .15
308 *Jayce Tingler* .25
309 *Matt Brown* .25
310 *Frank Diaz* .40
311 *Stephen Drew* 2.00
312 *Jered Weaver* .75
313 *Ryan Braun* 1.00
314 *John Mayberry* .50
315 *Aaron Thompson* 1.00
316 *Cesar Carrillo* .50
317 *Jacoby Ellsbury* 1.00
318 *Matt Garza* .50
319 *Cliff Pennington* .75
320 *Colby Rasmus* 1.50
321 *Chris Volstad* 1.00
322 *Ricky Romero* .50
323 *Ryan Zimmerman* 3.00
324 *C.J. Henry* .75
325 *Jay Bruce* .75
326 *Beau Jones* .50
327 *Mark McCormick* .50
328 *Eli Iorg* .50
329 *Andrew McCutchen* 1.00
330 *Mike Costanzo* .50

Blue

No Pricing
Production one set

Gold

Gold Rookies: 2-4X
Gold Stars: 4-8X
Production 2,005 Sets

Printing Plates

No Pricing
Production one set per color

All-Star Stitches

		NM/M
Common Player:		4.00
BA	Bobby Abreu B	4.00
MA	Moises Alou C	6.00
	Danys Baez	
JB	Jason Bay C	4.00
CB	Carlos Beltran D	6.00
MB	Mark Buehrle B	4.00
MC	Miguel Cabrera E	8.00
CC	Chris Carpenter E	4.00
LC	Luis Castillo B	4.00
	Hee Seop Choi	
MCL	Matt Clement B	4.00
BC	Bartolo Colon D	4.00
CCO	Chad Cordero D	4.00
JD	Johnny Damon B	8.00
	Justin Duchscherer	
DE	David Eckstein B	4.00
JE	Jim Edmonds A	6.00
ME	Morgan Ensberg B	4.00
	Brian Fuentes	
JG	Jon Garland E	4.00
LG	Luis Gonzalez C	4.00
LH	Livan Hernandez	4.00
	Shea Hillenbrand	
JI	Jason Isringhausen E	4.00
AJ	Andruw Jones C	6.00
JK	Jeff Kent C	4.00
PK	Paul Konerko A	4.00
CL	Carlos Lee E	4.00
DL	Derrek Lee F	6.00
BL	Brad Lidge D	4.00
	Paul LoDuca	
FL	Felipe Lopez B	4.00
MM	Melvin Mora B	4.00
JN	Joe Nathan D	4.00
DO	David Ortiz E	8.00
RO	Roy Oswalt A	4.00
JP	Jake Peavy D	4.00
MP	Mike Piazza E	8.00
SP	Scott Podsednik A	4.00
AP	Albert Pujols E	20.00
ARA	Aramis Ramirez E	4.00
MR	Manny Ramirez E	8.00
MRI	Mariano Rivera	6.00
BR	Brian Roberts C	4.00
AR	Alex Rodriguez D	15.00
IR	Ivan Rodriguez A	6.00
KR	Kenny Rogers A	4.00
	B.J. Ryan	
JS	Johan Santana C	6.00
GS	Gary Sheffield D	6.00
JSM	John Smoltz D	6.00
IS	Ichiro Suzuki A	20.00
MTE	Mark Teixeira C	6.00

MT Miguel Tejada B 6.00
BW Billy Wagner C 4.00
Bob Wickman
DW Dontrelle Willis F 6.00
MY Michael Young A 4.00

Derby Digs Jersey

Production 100 sets
BA Bobby Abreu
JB Jason Bay
HSC Hee Seop Choi
AJ Andruw Jones
CL Carlos Lee
DO David Ortiz
IR Ivan Rodriguez
MT Mark Teixeira

Hall of Fame Bat

NM/M
Complete Set (2):
WB Wade Boggs A
RS Ryne Sandberg B 12.00

Hall of Fame Dual Bat

Production 200 Sets
BS Wade Boggs, Ryne Sandberg

Legendary Sacks

NM/M
Production 300 Sets
JA Jim Abbott 6.00
AD Andre Dawson 6.00
MF Mark Fidrych 4.00
RF Rollie Fingers 4.00
BJ Bo Jackson 8.00
HR Harold Reynolds 4.00
OS Ozzie Smith 8.00
LW Lou Whitaker 4.00
DW Dave Winfield 8.00

Midsummer Covers

NM/M
Production 150 Sets
CB Carlos Beltran 10.00
RC Roger Clemens 20.00
VG Vladimir Guerrero 15.00
DL Derrek Lee 10.00
AP Albert Pujols 25.00
BR Brian Roberts 8.00
AR Alex Rodriguez 20.00
IS Ichiro Suzuki
MT Miguel Tejada 10.00
DW Dontrelle Willis 10.00

Signature Moves

NM/M
Production 15-475 Sets
Red Foil: No Pricing
Production 25 Sets
MA Matt Albers/475 10.00
BB Barry Bonds/15
TC Travis Chick/475 8.00
TG Troy Glaus/275 20.00
TH Tim Hudson/275 25.00
KI Kazuhisa Ishii/275 15.00
GK George Kottaras/475 15.00
BL Bobby Livingston/475 10.00
PM Pedro Martinez/25
MM Mark Mulder/275 25.00
GP Glen Perkins/275 10.00
JP Jake Postlewait/275 10.00
HS Humberto Sanchez 10.00
BS Benito Santiago 20.00
RS Richie Sexson/275 25.00
CJS C.J. Smith/475 10.00
JV Justin Verlander/275 25.00
TW Tony Womack 15.00

Touch Em All Base

NM/M
Production 1,000 Sets
VG Vladimir Guerrero 10.00
DL Derrek Lee 8.00
DO David Ortiz 10.00
AP Albert Pujols 20.00
MR Manny Ramirez 10.00
AR Alex Rodriguez 15.00
IR Ivan Rodriguez 8.00
GS Gary Sheffield 6.00
IS Ichiro Suzuki 20.00
MT Miguel Tejada 10.00

Washington Nationals Inaugural Lineup

NM/M
Inserted 1:10
Ball Relics: No Pricing
Production 5 Sets
VC Vinny Castilla .50
JG Jose Guillen 1.00
CG Cristian Guzman .50
LH Livan Hernandez .50
NJ Nick Johnson .50
BS Brian Schneider .50
TS Terrmel Sledge .50
JV Jose Vidro .50
BW Brad Wilkerson .50
TEAM Team Photo 1.00

U

1991 ULTRA

NM/M
Complete Set (400): 12.00
Common Player: .05
Wax Pack (14): .50
Wax Box (36): 9.00
1 Steve Avery .05
2 Jeff Blauser .05
3 Francisco Cabrera .05
4 Ron Gant .05
5 Tom Glavine .25
6 Tommy Gregg .05
7 Dave Justice .05
8 Oddibe McDowell .05
9 Greg Olson .05
10 Terry Pendleton .05
11 Lonnie Smith .05
12 John Smoltz .05
13 Jeff Treadway .05
14 Glenn Davis .05
15 Mike Devereaux .05
16 Leo Gomez .05
17 Chris Hoiles .05
18 Dave Johnson .05
19 Ben McDonald .05
20 Randy Milligan .05
21 Gregg Olson .05
22 Joe Orsulak .05
23 Bill Ripken .05
24 Cal Ripken, Jr. 1.50
25 David Segui .05
26 Craig Worthington .05
27 Wade Boggs .60
28 Tom Bolton .05
29 Tom Brunansky .05
30 Ellis Burks .05
31 Roger Clemens .65
32 Mike Greenwell .05
33 Greg Harris .05
34 Daryl Irvine .05
35 Mike Marshall .05
36 Tim Naehring .05
37 Tony Pena .05
38 *Phil Plantier* .05
39 Carlos Quintana .05
40 Jeff Reardon .05
41 Jody Reed .05
42 Luis Rivera .05
43 Jim Abbott .05
44 Chuck Finley .05
45 Bryan Harvey .05
46 Donnie Hill .05
47 Jack Howell .05
48 Wally Joyner .05
49 Mark Langston .05
50 Kirk McCaskill .05
51 Lance Parrish .05
52 Dick Schofield .05
53 Lee Stevens .05
54 Dave Winfield .50
55 George Bell .05
56 Damon Berryhill .05
57 Mike Bielecki .05
58 Andre Dawson .25
59 Shawon Dunston .05
60 Joe Girardi .05
61 Mark Grace .05
62 Mike Harkey .05
63 Les Lancaster .05
64 Greg Maddux .60
65 Derrick May .05
66 Ryne Sandberg .60
67 Luis Salazar .05
68 Dwight Smith .05
69 Hector Villanueva .05
70 Jerome Walton .05
71 Mitch Williams .05
72 Carlton Fisk .50
73 Scott Fletcher .05
74 Ozzie Guillen .05
75 Greg Hibbard .05
76 Lance Johnson .05
77 Steve Lyons .05
78 Jack McDowell .05
79 Dan Pasqua .05
80 Melido Perez .05
81 Tim Raines .05
82 Sammy Sosa .60
83 Cory Snyder .05
84 Bobby Thigpen .05
85 Frank Thomas .50
86 Robin Ventura .05
87 Todd Benzinger .05
88 Glenn Braggs .05
89 Tom Browning .05
90 Norm Charlton .05
91 Eric Davis .05
92 Rob Dibble .05
93 Bill Doran .05
94 Mariano Duncan .05
95 Billy Hatcher .05
96 Barry Larkin .05
97 Randy Myers .05
98 Hal Morris .05
99 Joe Oliver .05
100 Paul O'Neill .05
101a Jeff Reed .05
101b Beau Allred (Should be #104) .05
102 Jose Rijo .05
103a Chris Sabo .05
103b Carlos Baerga (Should be #106) .05
104 Not Issued (See #101b)
105 Sandy Alomar,Jr. .05
106 Not Issued (See #103b)
107 Albert Belle .05
108 Jerry Browne .05
109 Tom Candiotti .05
110 Alex Cole .05
111a John Farrell .05
111b Chris James (Should be #114) .05
112 Felix Fermin .05
113 Brook Jacoby .05
114 Not Issued (See #111b)
115 Doug Jones .05
116a Steve Olin .05
116b Mitch Webster (Should be #119) .05
117 Greg Swindell .05
118 Turner Ward .05
119 Not Issued (See #116b)
120 Dave Bergman .05
121 Cecil Fielder .05
122 Travis Fryman .05
123 Mike Henneman .05
124 Lloyd Moseby .05
125 Dan Petry .05
126 Tony Phillips .05
127 Mark Salas .05
128 Frank Tanana .05
129 Alan Trammell .05
130 Lou Whitaker .05
131 Eric Anthony .05
132 Craig Biggio .05
133 Ken Caminiti .05
134 Casey Candaele .05
135 Andujar Cedeno .05
136 Mark Davidson .05
137 Jim Deshaies .05
138 Mark Portugal .05
139 Rafael Ramirez .05
140 Mike Scott .05
141 Eric Yelding .05
142 Gerald Young .05
143 Kevin Appier .05
144 George Brett .65
145 *Jeff Conine* .40
146 Jim Eisenreich .05
147 Tom Gordon .05
148 Mark Gubicza .05
149 Bo Jackson .10
150 Brent Mayne .05
151 Mike Macfarlane .05
152 *Brian McRae* .10
153 Jeff Montgomery .05
154 Bret Saberhagen .05
155 Kevin Seitzer .05
156 Terry Shumpert .05
157 Kurt Stillwell .05
158 Danny Tartabull .05
159 Tim Belcher .05
160 Kal Daniels .05
161 Alfredo Griffin .05
162 Lenny Harris .05
163 Jay Howell .05
164 Ramon Martinez .05
165 Mike Morgan .05
166 Eddie Murray .50
167 Jose Offerman .05
168 Juan Samuel .05
169 Mike Scioscia .05
170 Mike Sharperson .05
171 Darryl Strawberry .05
172 Greg Brock .05
173 Chuck Crim .05
174 Jim Gantner .05
175 Ted Higuera .05
176 Mark Knudson .05
177 Tim McIntosh .05
178 Paul Molitor .50
179 Dan Plesac .05
180 Gary Sheffield .35
181 Bill Spiers .05
182 B.J. Surhoff .05
183 Greg Vaughn .05
184 Robin Yount .50
185 Rick Aguilera .05
186 Greg Gagne .05
187 Dan Gladden .05
188 Brian Harper .05
189 Kent Hrbek .05
190 Gene Larkin .05
191 Shane Mack .05
192 Pedro Munoz .05
193 Al Newman .05
194 Junior Ortiz .05
195 Kirby Puckett .60
196 Kevin Tapani .05
197 Dennis Boyd .05
198 Tim Burke .05
199 Ivan Calderon .05
200 Delino DeShields .05
201 Mike Fitzgerald .05
202 Steve Frey .05
203 Andres Galarraga .05
204 Marquis Grissom .05
205 Dave Martinez .05
206 Dennis Martinez .05
207 Junior Noboa .05
208 Spike Owen .05
209 Scott Ruskin .05
210 Tim Wallach .05
211 Daryl Boston .05
212 Vince Coleman .05
213 David Cone .05
214 Ron Darling .05
215 Kevin Elster .05
216 Sid Fernandez .05
217 John Franco .05
218 Dwight Gooden .05
219 Tom Herr .05
220 Todd Hundley .05
221 Gregg Jefferies .05
222 Howard Johnson .05
223 Dave Magadan .05
224 Kevin McReynolds .05
225 Keith Miller .05
226 Mackey Sasser .05
227 Frank Viola .05
228 Jesse Barfield .05
229 Greg Cadaret .05
230 Alvaro Espinoza .05
231 Bob Geren .05
232 Lee Guetterman .05
233 Mel Hall .05
234 Andy Hawkins .05
235 Roberto Kelly .05
236 Tim Leary .05
237 Jim Leyritz .05
238 Kevin Maas .05
239 Don Mattingly .65
240 Hensley Meulens .05
241 Eric Plunk .05
242 Steve Sax .05
243 Todd Burns .05
244 Jose Canseco .35
245 Dennis Eckersley .40
246 Mike Gallego .05
247 Dave Henderson .05
248 Rickey Henderson .50
249 Rick Honeycutt .05
250 Carney Lansford .05
251 Mark McGwire 1.00
252 Mike Moore .05

253	Terry Steinbach	.05
254	Dave Stewart	.05
255	Walt Weiss	.05
256	Bob Welch	.05
257	Curt Young	.05
258	Wes Chamberlain	.05
259	Pat Combs	.05
260	Darren Daulton	.05
261	Jose DeJesus	.05
262	Len Dykstra	.05
263	Charlie Hayes	.05
264	Von Hayes	.05
265	Ken Howell	.05
266	John Kruk	.05
267	Roger McDowell	.05
268	Mickey Morandini	.05
269	Terry Mulholland	.05
270	Dale Murphy	.15
271	Randy Ready	.05
272	Dickie Thon	.05
273	Stan Belinda	.05
274	Jay Bell	.05
275	Barry Bonds	1.50
276	Bobby Bonilla	.05
277	Doug Drabek	.05
278	*Carlos Garcia*	.05
279	Neal Heaton	.05
280	Jeff King	.05
281	Bill Landrum	.05
282	Mike LaValliere	.05
283	Jose Lind	.05
284	*Orlando Merced*	.10
285	Gary Redus	.05
286	Don Slaught	.05
287	Andy Van Slyke	.05
288	Jose DeLeon	.05
289	Pedro Guerrero	.05
290	Ray Lankford	.05
291	Joe Magrane	.05
292	Jose Oquendo	.05
293	Tom Pagnozzi	.05
294	Bryn Smith	.05
295	Lee Smith	.05
296	Ozzie Smith	.60
297	Milt Thompson	.05
298	*Craig Wilson*	.05
299	Todd Zeile	.05
300	Shawn Abner	.05
301	Andy Benes	.05
302	Paul Faries	.05
303	Tony Gwynn	.60
304	Greg Harris	.05
305	Thomas Howard	.05
306	Bruce Hurst	.05
307	Craig Lefferts	.05
308	Fred McGriff	.05
309	Dennis Rasmussen	.05
310	Bip Roberts	.05
311	Benito Santiago	.05
312	Garry Templeton	.05
313	Ed Whitson	.05
314	Dave Anderson	.05
315	Kevin Bass	.05
316	Jeff Brantley	.05
317	John Burkett	.05
318	Will Clark	.05
319	Steve Decker	.05
320	Scott Garrelts	.05
321	Terry Kennedy	.05
322	Mark Leonard	.05
323	Darren Lewis	.05
324	Greg Litton	.05
325	Willie McGee	.05
326	Kevin Mitchell	.05
327	Don Robinson	.05
328	Andres Santana	.05
329	Robby Thompson	.05
330	Jose Uribe	.05
331	Matt Williams	.05
332	Scott Bradley	.05
333	Henry Cotto	.05
334	Alvin Davis	.05
335	Ken Griffey, Sr.	.05
336	Ken Griffey, Jr.	.75
337	Erik Hanson	.05
338	Brian Holman	.05
339	Randy Johnson	.50
340	Edgar Martinez	.05
341	Tino Martinez	.05
342	Pete O'Brien	.05
343	Harold Reynolds	.05
344	David Valle	.05
345	Omar Vizquel	.05
346	Brad Arnsberg	.05
347	Kevin Brown	.05
348	Julio Franco	.05
349	Jeff Huson	.05
350	Rafael Palmeiro	.40
351	Geno Petralli	.05
352	Gary Pettis	.05
353	Kenny Rogers	.05
354	Jeff Russell	.05
355	Nolan Ryan	1.50
356	Ruben Sierra	.05
357	Bobby Witt	.05
358	Roberto Alomar	.15
359	Pat Borders	.05
360	Joe Carter	.05
361	Kelly Gruber	.05
362	Tom Henke	.05
363	Glenallen Hill	.05
364	Jimmy Key	.05
365	Manny Lee	.05
366	Rance Mulliniks	.05
367	John Olerud	.05
368	Dave Stieb	.05
369	Duane Ward	.05
370	David Wells	.05
371	Mark Whiten	.05
372	Mookie Wilson	.05
373	Willie Banks	.05
374	Steve Carter	.05
375	Scott Chiamparino	.05
376	Steve Chitren	.05
377	Darrin Fletcher	.05
378	Rich Garces	.05
379	Reggie Jefferson	.05
380	*Eric Karros*	.50
381	Pat Kelly	.05
382	Chuck Knoblauch	.05
383	Denny Neagle	.05
384	Dan Opperman	.05
385	John Ramos	.05
386	*Henry Rodriguez*	.05
387	Mo Vaughn	.05
388	Gerald Williams	.05
389	Mike York	.05
390	Eddie Zosky	.05
391	Barry Bonds (Great Performer)	.75
392	Cecil Fielder (Great Performer)	.05
393	Rickey Henderson (Great Performer)	.25
394	Dave Justice (Great Performer)	.05
395	Nolan Ryan (Great Performer)	.75
396	Bobby Thigpen (Great Performer)	.05
397	Checklist	.05
398	Checklist	.05
399	Checklist	.05
400	Checklist	.05

Gold

		NM/M
Complete Set (10):		5.00
Common Player:		.15
1	Barry Bonds	2.50
2	Will Clark	.15
3	Doug Drabek	.15
4	Ken Griffey, Jr.	1.50
5	Rickey Henderson	.75
6	Bo Jackson	.25
7	Ramon Martinez	.15
8	Kirby Puckett	1.00
9	Chris Sabo	.15
10	Ryne Sandberg	1.00

Update

		NM/M
Complete Set (120):		15.00
Common Player:		.05
1	Dwight Evans	.05
2	Chito Martinez	.05
3	Bob Melvin	.05
4	*Mike Mussina*	3.00
5	Jack Clark	.05
6	Dana Kiecker	.05
7	Steve Lyons	.05
8	Gary Gaetti	.05
9	Dave Gallagher	.05
10	Dave Parker	.05
11	Luis Polonia	.05
12	Luis Sojo	.05
13	Wilson Alvarez	.05
14	Alex Fernandez	.05
15	Craig Grebeck	.05
16	Ron Karkovice	.05
17	Warren Newson	.05
18	Scott Radinsky	.05
19	Glenallen Hill	.05
20	Charles Nagy	.05
21	Mark Whiten	.05
22	Milt Cuyler	.05
23	Paul Gibson	.05
24	Mickey Tettleton	.05
25	Todd Benzinger	.05
26	Storm Davis	.05
27	Kirk Gibson	.05
28	Bill Pecota	.05
29	Gary Thurman	.05
30	Darryl Hamilton	.05
31	Jaime Navarro	.05
32	Willie Randolph	.05
33	Bill Wegman	.05
34	Randy Bush	.05
35	Chili Davis	.05
36	Scott Erickson	.05
37	Chuck Knoblauch	.05
38	Scott Leius	.05
39	Jack Morris	.05
40	John Habyan	.05
41	Pat Kelly	.05
42	Matt Nokes	.05
43	Scott Sanderson	.05
44	Bernie Williams	.05
45	Harold Baines	.05
46	Brook Jacoby	.05
47	Ernest Riles	.05
48	Willie Wilson	.05
49	Jay Buhner	.05
50	Rich DeLucia	.05
51	Mike Jackson	.05
52	Bill Krueger	.05
53	Bill Swift	.05
54	Brian Downing	.05
55	Juan Gonzalez	.75
56	Dean Palmer	.05
57	Kevin Reimer	.05
58	*Ivan Rodriguez*	6.00
59	Tom Candiotti	.05
60	Juan Guzman	.05
61	Bob MacDonald	.05
62	Greg Myers	.05
63	Ed Sprague	.05
64	Devon White	.05
65	Rafael Belliard	.05
66	Juan Berenguer	.05
67	Brian Hunter	.05
68	Kent Mercker	.05
69	Otis Nixon	.05
70	Danny Jackson	.05
71	Chuck McElroy	.05
72	Gary Scott	.05
73	Heathcliff Slocumb	.05
74	Chico Walker	.05
75	Rick Wilkins	.05
76	Chris Hammond	.05
77	Luis Quinones	.05
78	Herm Winningham	.05
79	*Jeff Bagwell*	6.00
80	Jim Corsi	.05
81	Steve Finley	.05
82	*Luis Gonzalez*	1.00
83	Pete Harnisch	.05
84	Darryl Kile	.05
85	Brett Butler	.05
86	Gary Carter	1.00
87	Tim Crews	.05
88	Orel Hershiser	.05
89	Bob Ojeda	.05
90	Bret Barberie	.05
91	Barry Jones	.05
92	Gilberto Reyes	.05
93	Larry Walker	.05
94	Hubie Brooks	.05
95	Tim Burke	.05
96	Rick Cerone	.05
97	Jeff Innis	.05
98	Wally Backman	.05
99	Tommy Greene	.05
100	Ricky Jordan	.05
101	Mitch Williams	.05
102	John Smiley	.05
103	Randy Tomlin	.05
104	Gary Varsho	.05
105	Cris Carpenter	.05
106	Ken Hill	.05
107	Felix Jose	.05
108	*Omar Oliveras*	.05
109	Gerald Perry	.05
110	Jerald Clark	.05
111	Tony Fernandez	.05
112	Darrin Jackson	.05
113	Mike Maddux	.05
114	Tim Teufel	.05
115	Bud Black	.05
116	Kelly Downs	.05
117	Mike Felder	.05
118	Willie McGee	.05
119	Trevor Wilson	.05
120	Checklist	.05

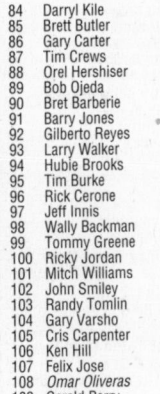

1992 ULTRA

		NM/M
Complete Set (600):		12.00
Common Player:		.05
Ser. 1 or 2 Pack (14):		.60
Ser. 1 or 2 Box (36):		12.50
Tony Gwynn auto.		60.00
1	Glenn Davis	.05
2	Mike Devereaux	.05
3	Dwight Evans	.05
4	Leo Gomez	.05
5	Chris Hoiles	.05
6	Sam Horn	.05
7	Chito Martinez	.05
8	Randy Milligan	.05
9	Mike Mussina	.30
10	Billy Ripken	.05
11	Cal Ripken, Jr.	1.00
12	Tom Brunansky	.05
13	Ellis Burks	.05
14	Jack Clark	.05
15	Roger Clemens	.60
16	Mike Greenwell	.05
17	Joe Hesketh	.05
18	Tony Pena	.05
19	Carlos Quintana	.05
20	Jeff Reardon	.05
21	Jody Reed	.05
22	Luis Rivera	.05
23	Mo Vaughn	.05
24	Gary DiSarcina	.05
25	Chuck Finley	.05
26	Gary Gaetti	.05
27	Bryan Harvey	.05
28	Lance Parrish	.05
29	Luis Polonia	.05
30	Dick Schofield	.05
31	Luis Sojo	.05
32	Wilson Alvarez	.05
33	Carlton Fisk	.40
34	Craig Grebeck	.05

35	Ozzie Guillen	.05
36	Greg Hibbard	.05
37	Charlie Hough	.05
38	Lance Johnson	.05
39	Ron Karkovice	.05
40	Jack McDowell	.05
41	Donn Pall	.05
42	Melido Perez	.05
43	Tim Raines	.05
44	Frank Thomas	.40
45	Sandy Alomar, Jr.	.05
46	Carlos Baerga	.05
47	Albert Belle	.05
48	Jerry Browne	.05
49	Felix Fermin	.05
50	Reggie Jefferson	.05
51	Mark Lewis	.05
52	Carlos Martinez	.05
53	Steve Olin	.05
54	Jim Thome	.35
55	Mark Whiten	.05
56	Dave Bergman	.05
57	Milt Cuyler	.05
58	Rob Deer	.05
59	Cecil Fielder	.05
60	Travis Fryman	.05
61	Scott Livingstone	.05
62	Tony Phillips	.05
63	Mickey Tettleton	.05
64	Alan Trammell	.05
65	Lou Whitaker	.05
66	Kevin Appier	.05
67	Mike Boddicker	.05
68	George Brett	.60
69	Jim Eisenreich	.05
70	Mark Gubicza	.05
71	David Howard	.05
72	Joel Johnston	.05
73	Mike Macfarlane	.05
74	Brent Mayne	.05
75	Brian McRae	.05
76	Jeff Montgomery	.05
77	Terry Shumpert	.05
78	Don August	.05
79	Dante Bichette	.05
80	Ted Higuera	.05
81	Paul Molitor	.40
82	Jamie Navarro	.05
83	Gary Sheffield	.30
84	Bill Spiers	.05
85	B.J. Surhoff	.05
86	Greg Vaughn	.05
87	Robin Yount	.40
88	Rick Aguilera	.05
89	Chili Davis	.05
90	Scott Erickson	.05
91	Brian Harper	.05
92	Kent Hrbek	.05
93	Chuck Knoblauch	.05
94	Scott Leius	.05
95	Shane Mack	.05
96	Mike Pagliarulo	.05
97	Kirby Puckett	.50
98	Kevin Tapani	.05
99	Jesse Barfield	.05
100	Alvaro Espinoza	.05
101	Mel Hall	.05
102	Pat Kelly	.05
103	Roberto Kelly	.05
104	Kevin Maas	.05
105	Don Mattingly	.60
106	Hensley Meulens	.05
107	Matt Nokes	.05
108	Steve Sax	.05
109	Harold Baines	.05
110	Jose Canseco	.30
111	Ron Darling	.05
112	Mike Gallego	.05
113	Dave Henderson	.05
114	Rickey Henderson	.40
115	Mark McGwire	.75
116	Terry Steinbach	.05
117	Dave Stewart	.05
118	Todd Van Poppel	.05
119	Bob Welch	.05
120	Greg Briley	.05
121	Jay Buhner	.05
122	Rich DeLucia	.05
123	Ken Griffey, Jr.	.65
124	Erik Hanson	.05
125	Randy Johnson	.40
126	Edgar Martinez	.05
127	Tino Martinez	.05
128	Pete O'Brien	.05
129	Harold Reynolds	.05
130	Dave Valle	.05
131	Julio Franco	.05
132	Juan Gonzalez	.20
133	Jeff Huson	.05
134	Mike Jeffcoat	.05
135	Terry Mathews	.05
136	Rafael Palmeiro	.35
137	Dean Palmer	.05
138	Geno Petralli	.05
139	Ivan Rodriguez	.35
140	Jeff Russell	.05
141	Nolan Ryan	1.00
142	Ruben Sierra	.05
143	Roberto Alomar	.15
144	Pat Borders	.05
145	Joe Carter	.05
146	Kelly Gruber	.05
147	Jimmy Key	.05
148	Manny Lee	.05
149	Rance Mulliniks	.05
150	Greg Myers	.05
151	John Olerud	.05
152	Dave Stieb	.05
153	Todd Stottlemyre	.05
154	Duane Ward	.05
155	Devon White	.05
156	Eddie Zosky	.05
157	Steve Avery	.05
158	Rafael Belliard	.05
159	Jeff Blauser	.05
160	Sid Bream	.05
161	Ron Gant	.05
162	Tom Glavine	.25
163	Brian Hunter	.05
164	Dave Justice	.05
165	Mark Lemke	.05
166	Greg Olson	.05
167	Terry Pendleton	.05
168	Lonnie Smith	.05
169	John Smoltz	.05
170	Mike Stanton	.05
171	Jeff Treadway	.05
172	Paul Assenmacher	.05
173	George Bell	.05
174	Shawon Dunston	.05
175	Mark Grace	.05
176	Danny Jackson	.05
177	Les Lancaster	.05
178	Greg Maddux	.50
179	Luis Salazar	.05
180	Rey Sanchez	.05
181	Ryne Sandberg	.50
182	Jose Vizcaino	.05
183	Chico Walker	.05
184	Jerome Walton	.05
185	Glenn Braggs	.05
186	Tom Browning	.05
187	Rob Dibble	.05
188	Bill Doran	.05
189	Chris Hammond	.05
190	Billy Hatcher	.05
191	Barry Larkin	.05
192	Hal Morris	.05
193	Joe Oliver	.05
194	Paul O'Neill	.05
195	Jeff Reed	.05
196	Jose Rijo	.05
197	Chris Sabo	.05
198	Jeff Bagwell	.40
199	Craig Biggio	.05
200	Ken Caminiti	.05
201	Andujar Cedeno	.05
202	Steve Finley	.05
203	Luis Gonzalez	.05
204	Pete Harnisch	.05
205	Xavier Hernandez	.05
206	Darryl Kile	.05
207	Al Osuna	.05
208	Curt Schilling	.25
209	Brett Butler	.05
210	Kal Daniels	.05
211	Lenny Harris	.05
212	Stan Javier	.05
213	Ramon Martinez	.05
214	Roger McDowell	.05
215	Jose Offerman	.05
216	Juan Samuel	.05
217	Mike Scioscia	.05
218	Mike Sharperson	.05
219	Darryl Strawberry	.05
220	Delino DeShields	.05
221	Tom Foley	.05
222	Steve Frey	.05
223	Dennis Martinez	.05
224	Spike Owen	.05
225	Gilberto Reyes	.05
226	Tim Wallach	.05
227	Daryl Boston	.05
228	Tim Burke	.05
229	Vince Coleman	.05
230	David Cone	.05
231	Kevin Elster	.05
232	Dwight Gooden	.05
233	Todd Hundley	.05
234	Jeff Innis	.05
235	Howard Johnson	.05
236	Dave Magadan	.05
237	Mackey Sasser	.05
238	Anthony Young	.05
239	Wes Chamberlain	.05
240	Darren Daulton	.05
241	Len Dykstra	.05
242	Tommy Greene	.05
243	Charlie Hayes	.05
244	Dave Hollins	.05
245	Ricky Jordan	.05
246	John Kruk	.05
247	Mickey Morandini	.05
248	Terry Mulholland	.05
249	Dale Murphy	.25
250	Jay Bell	.05
251	Barry Bonds	1.00
252	Steve Buechele	.05
253	Doug Drabek	.05
254	Mike LaValliere	.05
255	Jose Lind	.05
256	Lloyd McClendon	.05
257	Orlando Merced	.05
258	Don Slaught	.05
259	John Smiley	.05
260	Zane Smith	.05
261	Randy Tomlin	.05
262	Andy Van Slyke	.05
263	Pedro Guerrero	.05
264	Felix Jose	.05
265	Ray Lankford	.05
266	Omar Olivares	.05
267	Jose Oquendo	.05
268	Tom Pagnozzi	.05
269	Bryn Smith	.05
270	Lee Smith	.05
271	Ozzie Smith	.50
272	Milt Thompson	.05
273	Todd Zeile	.05
274	Andy Benes	.05
275	Jerald Clark	.05
276	Tony Fernandez	.05
277	Tony Gwynn	.50
278	Greg Harris	.05
279	Thomas Howard	.05
280	Bruce Hurst	.05
281	Mike Maddux	.05
282	Fred McGriff	.05
283	Benito Santiago	.05
284	Kevin Bass	.05
285	Jeff Brantley	.05
286	John Burkett	.05
287	Will Clark	.05
288	Royce Clayton	.05
289	Steve Decker	.05
290	Kelly Downs	.05
291	Mike Felder	.05
292	Darren Lewis	.05
293	Kirt Manwaring	.05
294	Willie McGee	.05
295	Robby Thompson	.05
296	Matt Williams	.05
297	Trevor Wilson	.05
298	Sandy Alomar, Jr. Checklist 1-108	.05
299	Rey Sanchez Checklist 109-208	.05
300	Nolan Ryan Checklist 209-300	.25
301	Brady Anderson	.05
302	Todd Frohwirth	.05
303	Ben McDonald	.05
304	Mark McLemore	.05
305	Jose Mesa	.05
306	Bob Milacki	.05
307	Gregg Olson	.05
308	David Segui	.05
309	Rick Sutcliffe	.05
310	Jeff Tackett	.05
311	Wade Boggs	.50
312	Scott Cooper	.05
313	John Flaherty	.05
314	Wayne Housie	.05
315	Peter Hoy	.05
316	John Marzano	.05
317	Tim Naehring	.05
318	Phil Plantier	.05
319	Frank Viola	.05
320	Matt Young	.05
321	Jim Abbott	.05
322	Hubie Brooks	.05
323	*Chad Curtis*	.25
324	Alvin Davis	.05
325	Junior Felix	.05
326	Von Hayes	.05
327	Mark Langston	.05
328	Scott Lewis	.05
329	Don Robinson	.05
330	Bobby Rose	.05
331	Lee Stevens	.05
332	George Bell	.05
333	Esteban Beltre	.05
334	Joey Cora	.05
335	Alex Fernandez	.05
336	Roberto Hernandez	.05
337	Mike Huff	.05
338	Kirk McCaskill	.05
339	Dan Pasqua	.05
340	Scott Radinsky	.05
341	Steve Sax	.05
342	Bobby Thigpen	.05
343	Robin Ventura	.05
344	Jack Armstrong	.05
345	Alex Cole	.05
346	Dennis Cook	.05
347	Glenallen Hill	.05
348	Thomas Howard	.05
349	Brook Jacoby	.05
350	Kenny Lofton	.05
351	Charles Nagy	.05
352	Rod Nichols	.05
353	Junior Ortiz	.05
354	Dave Otto	.05
355	Tony Perezchica	.05
356	Scott Scudder	.05
357	Paul Sorrento	.05
358	Skeeter Barnes	.05
359	Mark Carreon	.05
360	John Doherty	.05
361	Dan Gladden	.05
362	Bill Gullickson	.05
363	Shawn Hare	.05
364	Mike Henneman	.05
365	Chad Kreuter	.05
366	Mark Leiter	.05
367	Mike Munoz	.05
368	Kevin Ritz	.05
369	Mark Davis	.05
370	Tom Gordon	.05
371	Chris Gwynn	.05
372	Gregg Jefferies	.05
373	Wally Joyner	.05
374	Kevin McReynolds	.05
375	Keith Miller	.05
376	Rico Rossy	.05
377	Curtis Wilkerson	.05
378	Ricky Bones	.05
379	Chris Bosio	.05
380	Cal Eldred	.05
381	Scott Fletcher	.05
382	Jim Gantner	.05
383	Darryl Hamilton	.05
384	Doug Henry	.05
385	*Pat Listach*	.05
386	Tim McIntosh	.05
387	Edwin Nunez	.05
388	Dan Plesac	.05
389	Kevin Seitzer	.05
390	Franklin Stubbs	.05
391	William Suero	.05
392	Bill Wegman	.05
393	Willie Banks	.05
394	Jarvis Brown	.05
395	Greg Gagne	.05
396	Mark Guthrie	.05
397	Bill Krueger	.05
398	*Pat Mahomes*	.05
399	Pedro Munoz	.05
400	John Smiley	.05
401	Gary Wayne	.05
402	Lenny Webster	.05
403	Carl Willis	.05
404	Greg Cadaret	.05
405	Steve Farr	.05
406	Mike Gallego	.05
407	Charlie Hayes	.05
408	Steve Howe	.05
409	Dion James	.05
410	Jeff Johnson	.05
411	Tim Leary	.05
412	Jim Leyritz	.05
413	Melido Perez	.05
414	Scott Sanderson	.05
415	Andy Stankiewicz	.05
416	Mike Stanley	.05
417	Danny Tartabull	.05
418	Lance Blankenship	.05
419	Mike Bordick	.05
420	*Scott Brosius*	.05
421	Dennis Eckersley	.35
422	Scott Hemond	.05
423	Carney Lansford	.05
424	Henry Mercedes	.05
425	Mike Moore	.05
426	Gene Nelson	.05
427	Randy Ready	.05

428	Bruce Walton	.05
429	Willie Wilson	.05
430	Rich Amaral	.05
431	Dave Cochrane	.05
432	Henry Cotto	.05
433	Calvin Jones	.05
434	Kevin Mitchell	.05
435	Clay Parker	.05
436	Omar Vizquel	.05
437	Floyd Bannister	.05
438	Kevin Brown	.05
439	John Cangelosi	.05
440	Brian Downing	.05
441	Monty Fariss	.05
442	Jose Guzman	.05
443	Donald Harris	.05
444	Kevin Reimer	.05
445	Kenny Rogers	.05
446	Wayne Rosenthal	.05
447	Dickie Thon	.05
448	Derek Bell	.05
449	Juan Guzman	.05
450	Tom Henke	.05
451	Candy Maldonado	.05
452	Jack Morris	.05
453	David Wells	.05
454	Dave Winfield	.40
455	Juan Berenguer	.05
456	Damon Berryhill	.05
457	Mike Bielecki	.05
458	Marvin Freeman	.05
459	Charlie Leibrandt	.05
460	Kent Mercker	.05
461	Otis Nixon	.05
462	Alejandro Pena	.05
463	Ben Rivera	.05
464	Deion Sanders	.10
465	Mark Wohlers	.05
466	Shawn Boskie	.05
467	Frank Castillo	.05
468	Andre Dawson	.25
469	Joe Girardi	.05
470	Chuck McElroy	.05
471	Mike Morgan	.05
472	Ken Patterson	.05
473	Bob Scanlan	.05
474	Gary Scott	.05
475	Dave Smith	.05
476	Sammy Sosa	.50
477	Hector Villanueva	.05
478	Scott Bankhead	.05
479	Tim Belcher	.05
480	Freddie Benavides	.05
481	Jacob Brumfield	.05
482	Norm Charlton	.05
483	Dwayne Henry	.05
484	Dave Martinez	.05
485	Bip Roberts	.05
486	Reggie Sanders	.05
487	Greg Swindell	.05
488	Ryan Bowen	.05
489	Casey Candaele	.05
490	Juan Guerrero	.05
491	Pete Incaviglia	.05
492	Jeff Juden	.05
493	Rob Murphy	.05
494	Mark Portugal	.05
495	Rafael Ramirez	.05
496	Scott Servais	.05
497	Ed Taubensee	.05
498	Brian Williams	.05
499	Todd Benzinger	.05
500	John Candelaria	.05
501	Tom Candiotti	.05
502	Tim Crews	.05
503	Eric Davis	.05
504	Jim Gott	.05
505	Dave Hansen	.05
506	Carlos Hernandez	.05
507	Orel Hershiser	.05
508	Eric Karros	.05
509	Bob Ojeda	.05
510	Steve Wilson	.05
511	Moises Alou	.05
512	Bret Barberie	.05
513	Ivan Calderon	.05
514	Gary Carter	.40
515	Archi Cianfrocco	.05
516	Jeff Fassero	.05
517	Darrin Fletcher	.05
518	Marquis Grissom	.05
519	Chris Haney	.05
520	Ken Hill	.05
521	Chris Nabholz	.05
522	Bill Sampen	.05
523	John VanderWal	.05
524	David Wainhouse	.05
525	Larry Walker	.05
526	John Wetteland	.05
527	Bobby Bonilla	.05
528	Sid Fernandez	.05
529	John Franco	.05
530	Dave Gallagher	.05
531	Paul Gibson	.05
532	Eddie Murray	.40
533	Junior Noboa	.05
534	Charlie O'Brien	.05
535	Bill Pecota	.05
536	Willie Randolph	.05
537	Bret Saberhagen	.05
538	Dick Schofield	.05
539	Pete Schourek	.05
540	Ruben Amaro	.05
541	Andy Ashby	.05
542	Kim Batiste	.05
543	Cliff Brantley	.05
544	Mariano Duncan	.05
545	Jeff Grotewold	.05
546	Barry Jones	.05
547	Julio Peguero	.05
548	Curt Schilling	.25
549	Mitch Williams	.05
550	Stan Belinda	.05
551	Scott Bullett	.05
552	Cecil Espy	.05
553	Jeff King	.05
554	Roger Mason	.05
555	Paul Miller	.05
556	Denny Neagle	.05
557	Vocente Palacios	.05
558	Bob Patterson	.05
559	Tom Prince	.05
560	Gary Redus	.05
561	Gary Varsho	.05
562	Juan Agosto	.05
563	Cris Carpenter	.05
564	*Mark Clark*	.05
565	Jose DeLeon	.05
566	Rich Gedman	.05
567	Bernard Gilkey	.05
568	Rex Hudler	.05
569	Tim Jones	.05
570	Donovan Osborne	.05
571	Mike Perez	.05
572	Gerald Perry	.05
573	Bob Tewksbury	.05
574	Todd Worrell	.05
575	Dave Eiland	.05
576	Jeremy Hernandez	.05
577	Craig Lefferts	.05
578	Jose Melendez	.05
579	Randy Myers	.05
580	Gary Pettis	.05
581	Rich Rodriguez	.05
582	Gary Sheffield	.30
583	Craig Shipley	.05
584	Kurt Stillwell	.05
585	Tim Teufel	.05
586	*Rod Beck*	.05
587	Dave Burba	.05
588	Craig Colbert	.05
589	Bryan Hickerson	.05
590	Mike Jackson	.05
591	Mark Leonard	.05
592	Jim McNamara	.05
593	John Patterson	.05
594	Dave Righetti	.05
595	Cory Snyder	.05
596	Bill Swift	.05
597	Ted Wood	.05
598	Scott Sanderson Checklist 301-403	.05
599	Junior Ortiz Checklist 404-498	.05
600	Mike Morgan Checklist 499-600	.05

All-Rookies

		NM/M
Complete Set (10):		2.00
Common Player:		.25
1	Eric Karros	.35
2	Andy Stankiewicz	.25
3	Gary DiSarcina	.25
4	Archi Cianfrocco	.25
5	Jim McNamara	.25
6	Chad Curtis	.25
7	Kenny Lofton	.35
8	Reggie Sanders	.25
9	Pat Mahomes	.25
10	Donovan Osborne	.25

All-Stars

		NM/M
Complete Set (20):		7.50
Common Player:		.15
1	Mark McGwire	1.25
2	Roberto Alomar	.30
3	Cal Ripken, Jr.	1.50
4	Wade Boggs	.75
5	Mickey Tettleton	.15
6	Ken Griffey, Jr.	1.00
7	Roberto Kelly	.15
8	Kirby Puckett	.75
9	Frank Thomas	.65
10	Jack McDowell	.15
11	Will Clark	.15
12	Ryne Sandberg	.75
13	Barry Larkin	.15
14	Gary Sheffield	.35
15	Tom Pagnozzi	.15
16	Barry Bonds	1.50
17	Deion Sanders	.15
18	Darryl Strawberry	.15
19	David Cone	.15
20	Tom Glavine	.30

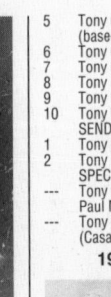

Award Winners

		NM/M
Complete Set (26):		10.00
Common Player:		.20
1	Jack Morris	.20
2	Chuck Knoblauch	.20
3	Jeff Bagwell	.75
4	Terry Pendleton	.20
5	Cal Ripken, Jr.	2.00
6	Roger Clemens	1.25
7	Tom Glavine	.35
8	Tom Pagnozzi	.20
9	Ozzie Smith	1.00
10	Andy Van Slyke	.20
11	Barry Bonds	2.00
12	Tony Gwynn	1.00
13	Matt Williams	.20
14	Will Clark	.20
15	Robin Ventura	.20
16	Mark Langston	.20
18	Devon White	.20
19	Don Mattingly	1.25
20	Roberto Alomar	.40
21a	Cal Ripken, Jr. (reversed negative)	2.00
21b	Cal Ripken, Jr. (correct)	2.00
22	Ken Griffey, Jr.	1.50
23	Kirby Puckett	1.00
24	Greg Maddux	1.00
25	Ryne Sandberg	1.00

Tony Gwynn

		NM/M
Complete Set (12):		9.00
Common Card:		.75
Certified Autograph Card:		60.00
	INSERT CARDS	
1	Tony Gwynn (fielding)	.75
2	Tony Gwynn (batting)	.75
3	Tony Gwynn (fielding)	.75
4	Tony Gwynn (batting)	.75
5	Tony Gwynn (base-running)	.75
6	Tony Gwynn (awards)	.75
7	Tony Gwynn (bunting)	.75
8	Tony Gwynn (batting)	.75
9	Tony Gwynn (running)	.75
10	Tony Gwynn (batting)	.75
	SEND-AWAY CARDS	
1	Tony Gwynn (batting)	2.00
2	Tony Gwynn (fielding)	2.00
	SPECIAL CARDS	
---	Tony Gwynn, Paul Mullan	3.00
---	Tony Gwynn (Casa de Amparo)	7.50

1993 ULTRA

		NM/M
Complete Set (650):		15.00
Common Player:		.05
Series 1 or 2 Pack (14):		.75
Series 1 or 2 Wax Box (36):		15.00
1	Steve Avery	.05
2	Rafael Belliard	.05
3	Damon Berryhill	.05
4	Sid Bream	.05
5	Ron Gant	.05
6	Tom Glavine	.20
7	Ryan Klesko	.05
8	Mark Lemke	.05
9	Javier Lopez	.05
10	Greg Olson	.05
11	Terry Pendleton	.05
12	Deion Sanders	.05
13	Mike Stanton	.05
14	Paul Assenmacher	.05
15	Steve Buechele	.05
16	Frank Castillo	.05
17	Shawon Dunston	.05
18	Mark Grace	.05
19	Derrick May	.05
20	Chuck McElroy	.05
21	Mike Morgan	.05
22	Bob Scanlan	.05
23	Dwight Smith	.05
24	Sammy Sosa	.60
25	Rick Wilkins	.05
26	Tim Belcher	.05
27	Jeff Branson	.05
28	Bill Doran	.05
29	Chris Hammond	.05
30	Barry Larkin	.05
31	Hal Morris	.05
32	Joe Oliver	.05
33	Jose Rijo	.05
34	Bip Roberts	.05
35	Chris Sabo	.05
36	Reggie Sanders	.05
37	Craig Biggio	.05
38	Ken Caminiti	.05
39	Steve Finley	.05
40	Luis Gonzalez	.05
41	Juan Guerrero	.05
42	Pete Harnisch	.05
43	Xavier Hernandez	.05
44	Doug Jones	.05
45	Al Osuna	.05
46	Eddie Taubensee	.05
47	Scooter Tucker	.05
48	Brian Williams	.05
49	Pedro Astacio	.05
50	Rafael Bournigal	.05
51	Brett Butler	.05
52	Tom Candiotti	.05
53	Eric Davis	.05
54	Lenny Harris	.05
55	Orel Hershiser	.05
56	Eric Karros	.05
57	Pedro Martinez	.50

58 Roger McDowell .05
59 Jose Offerman .05
60 Mike Piazza .75
61 Moises Alou .05
62 Kent Bottenfield .05
63 Archi Cianfrocco .05
64 Greg Colbrunn .05
65 Wil Cordero .05
66 Delino DeShields .05
67 Darrin Fletcher .05
68 Ken Hill .05
69 Chris Nabholz .05
70 Mel Rojas .05
71 Larry Walker .05
72 Sid Fernandez .05
73 John Franco .05
74 Dave Gallagher .05
75 Todd Hundley .05
76 Howard Johnson .05
77 Jeff Kent .05
78 Eddie Murray .50
79 Bret Saberhagen .05
80 Chico Walker .05
81 Anthony Young .05
82 Kyle Abbott .05
83 Ruben Amaro Jr. .05
84 Juan Bell .05
85 Wes Chamberlain .05
86 Darren Daulton .05
87 Mariano Duncan .05
88 Dave Hollins .05
89 Ricky Jordan .05
90 John Kruk .05
91 Mickey Morandini .05
92 Terry Mulholland .05
93 Ben Rivera .05
94 Mike Williams .05
95 Stan Belinda .05
96 Jay Bell .05
97 Jeff King .05
98 Mike LaValliere .05
99 Lloyd McClendon .05
100 Orlando Merced .05
101 Zane Smith .05
102 Randy Tomlin .05
103 Andy Van Slyke .05
104 Tim Wakefield .05
105 John Wehner .05
106 Bernard Gilkey .05
107 Brian Jordan .05
108 Ray Lankford .05
109 Donovan Osborne .05
110 Tom Pagnozzi .05
111 Mike Perez .05
112 Lee Smith .05
113 Ozzie Smith .60
114 Bob Tewksbury .05
115 Todd Zeile .05
116 Andy Benes .05
117 Greg Harris .05
118 Darrin Jackson .05
119 Fred McGriff .05
120 Rich Rodriguez .05
121 Frank Seminara .05
122 Gary Sheffield .35
123 Craig Shipley .05
124 Kurt Stillwell .05
125 Dan Walters .05
126 Rod Beck .05
127 Mike Benjamin .05
128 Jeff Brantley .05
129 John Burkett .05
130 Will Clark .05
131 Royce Clayton .05
132 Steve Hosey .05
133 Mike Jackson .05
134 Darren Lewis .05
135 Kirt Manwaring .05
136 Bill Swift .05
137 Robby Thompson .05
138 Brady Anderson .05
139 Glenn Davis .05
140 Leo Gomez .05
141 Chito Martinez .05
142 Ben McDonald .05
143 Alan Mills .05
144 Mike Mussina .30
145 Gregg Olson .05
146 David Segui .05
147 Jeff Tackett .05
148 Jack Clark .05
149 Scott Cooper .05
150 Danny Darwin .05
151 John Dopson .05
152 Mike Greenwell .05
153 Tim Naehring .05
154 Tony Pena .05
155 Paul Quantrill .05
156 Mo Vaughn .05
157 Frank Viola .05
158 Bob Zupcic .05
159 Chad Curtis .05
160 Gary DiScarcina .05
161 Damion Easley .05
162 Chuck Finley .05
163 Tim Fortugno .05
164 Rene Gonzales .05
165 Joe Grahe .05
166 Mark Langston .05
167 John Orton .05
168 Luis Polonia .05
169 Julio Valera .05
170 Wilson Alvarez .05
171 George Bell .05
172 Joey Cora .05
173 Alex Fernandez .05
174 Lance Johnson .05
175 Ron Karkovice .05
176 Jack McDowell .05
177 Scott Radinsky .05
178 Tim Raines .05
179 Steve Sax .05
180 Bobby Thigpen .05
181 Frank Thomas .50
182 Sandy Alomar Jr. .05
183 Carlos Baerga .05
184 Felix Fermin .05
185 Thomas Howard .05
186 Mark Lewis .05
187 Derek Lilliquist .05
188 Carlos Martinez .05
189 Charles Nagy .05
190 Scott Scudder .05
191 Paul Sorrento .05
192 Jim Thome .40
193 Mark Whiten .05
194 Milt Cuyler .05
195 Rob Deer .05
196 John Doherty .05
197 Travis Fryman .05
198 Dan Gladden .05
199 Mike Henneman .05
200 John Kiely .05
201 Chad Kreuter .05
202 Scott Livingstone .05
203 Tony Phillips .05
204 Alan Trammell .05
205 Mike Boddicker .05
206 George Brett .65
207 Tom Gordon .05
208 Mark Gubicza .05
209 Gregg Jefferies .05
210 Wally Joyner .05
211 Kevin Koslofski .05
212 Brent Mayne .05
213 Brian McRae .05
214 Kevin McReynolds .05
215 Rusty Meacham .05
216 Steve Shifflett .05
217 James Austin .05
218 Cal Eldred .05
219 Darryl Hamilton .05
220 Doug Henry .05
221 John Jaha .05
222 Dave Nilsson .05
223 Jesse Orosco .05
224 B.J. Surhoff .05
225 Greg Vaughn .05
226 Bill Wegman .05
227 Robin Yount .50
228 Rick Aguilera .05
229 J.T. Bruett .05
230 Scott Erickson .05
231 Kent Hrbek .05
232 Terry Jorgensen .05
233 Scott Leius .05
234 Pat Mahomes .05
235 Pedro Munoz .05
236 Kirby Puckett .60
237 Kevin Tapani .05
238 Lenny Webster .05
239 Carl Willis .05
240 Mike Gallego .05
241 John Habyan .05
242 Pat Kelly .05
243 Kevin Maas .05
244 Don Mattingly .65
245 Hensley Meulens .05
246 Sam Militello .05
247 Matt Nokes .05
248 Melido Perez .05
249 Andy Stankiewicz .05
250 Randy Velarde .05
251 Bob Wickman .05
252 Bernie Williams .05
253 Lance Blankenship .05
254 Mike Bordick .05
255 Jerry Browne .05
256 Ron Darling .05
257a Dennis Eckersley .40
257b Dennis Eckersley (Wt. 195; no "MLBPA" on back - unmarked sample card) 1.50
257c Dennis Eckersley (Wt, 195; no "Printed in USA" on back - unmarked sample card) 1.50
258 Rickey Henderson .50
259 Vince Horsman .05
260 Troy Neel .05
261 Jeff Parrett .05
262 Terry Steinbach .05
263 Bob Welch .05
264 Bobby Witt .05
265 Rich Amaral .05
266 Bret Boone .05
267 Jay Buhner .05
268 Dave Fleming .05
269 Randy Johnson .50
270 Edgar Martinez .05
271 Mike Schooler .05
272 Russ Swan .05
273 Dave Valle .05
274 Omar Vizquel .05
275 Kerry Woodson .05
276 Kevin Brown .05
277 Julio Franco .05
278 Jeff Frye .05
279 Juan Gonzalez .25
280 Jeff Huson .05
281 Rafael Palmeiro .40
282 Dean Palmer .05
283 Roger Pavlik .05
284 Ivan Rodriguez .40
285 Kenny Rogers .05
286 Derek Bell .05
287 Pat Borders .05
288 Joe Carter .05
289 Bob MacDonald .05
290 Jack Morris .05
291 John Olerud .05
292 Ed Sprague .05
293 Todd Stottlemyre .05
294 Mike Timlin .05
295 Duane Ward .05
296 David Wells .05
297 Devon White .05
298 Ray Lankford Checklist .05
299 Bobby Witt Checklist .05
300 Mike Piazza Checklist .40
301 Steve Bedrosian .05
302 Jeff Blauser .05
303 Francisco Cabrera .05
304 Marvin Freeman .05
305 Brian Hunter .05
306 Dave Justice .05
307 Greg Maddux .60
308 *Greg McMichael* .05
309 Kent Mercker .05
310 Otis Nixon .05
311 Pete Smith .05
312 John Smoltz .05
313 Jose Guzman .05
314 Mike Harkey .05
315 Greg Hibbard .05
316 Candy Maldonado .05
317 Randy Myers .05
318 Dan Plesac .05
319 Rey Sanchez .05
320 Ryne Sandberg .60
321 *Tommy Shields* .05
322 Jose Vizcaino .05
323 *Matt Walbeck* .05
324 Willie Wilson .05
325 Tom Browning .05
326 Tim Costo .05
327 Rob Dibble .05
328 Steve Foster .05
329 Roberto Kelly .05
330 Randy Milligan .05
331 Kevin Mitchell .05
332 *Tim Pugh* .05
333 Jeff Reardon .05
334 *John Roper* .05
335 Juan Samuel .05
336 John Smiley .05
337 San Wilson .05
338 Scott Aldred .05
339 Andy Ashby .05
340 Freddie Benavides .05
341 Dante Bichette .05
342 Willie Blair .05
343 Daryl Boston .05
344 Vinny Castilla .05
345 Jerald Clark .05
346 Alex Cole .05
347 Andres Galarraga .05
348 Joe Girardi .05
349 *Ryan Hawblitzel* .05
350 Charlie Hayes .05
351 Butch Henry .05
352 Darren Holmes .05
353 Dale Murphy .20
354 David Nied .05
355 Jeff Parrett .05
356 *Steve Reed* .05
357 Bruce Ruffin .05
358 *Danny Sheaffer* .05
359 Bryn Smith .05
360 *Jim Tatum* .05
361 Eric Young .05
362 Gerald Young .05
363 Luis Aquino .05
364 *Alex Arias* .05
365 Jack Armstrong .05
366 Bret Barberie .05
367 Ryan Bowen .05
368 Greg Briley .05
369 Cris Carpenter .05
370 Chuck Carr .05
371 *Jeff Conine* .25
372 Steve Decker .05
373 Orestes Destrade .05
374 Monty Fariss .05
375 Junior Felix .05
376 Chris Hammond .05
377 Bryan Harvey .05
378 *Trevor Hoffman* .25
379 Charlie Hough .05
380 Joe Klink .05
381 *Richie Lewis* .05
382 Dave Magadan .05
383 Bob McCLure .05
384 *Scott Pose* .05
385 *Rich Renteria* .05
386 Benito Santiago .05
387 Walt Weiss .05
388 Nigel Wilson .05
389 Eric Anthony .05
390 Jeff Bagwell .50
391 Andujar Cedeno .05
392 Doug Drabek .05
393 Darryl Kile .05
394 Mark Portugal .05
395 Karl Rhodes .05
396 Scott Servais .05
397 Greg Swindell .05
398 Tom Goodwin .05
399 Kevin Gross .05
400 Carlos Hernandez .05
401 Ramon Martinez .05
402 Raul Mondesi .05
403 Jody Reed .05
404 Mike Sharperson .05
405 Cory Snyder .05
406 Darryl Strawberry .05
407 *Rick Trlicek* .05
408 Tim Wallach .05
409 Todd Worrell .05
410 Tavo Alvarez .05
411 *Sean Berry* .05
412 *Frank Bolick* .05
413 Cliff Floyd .05
414 Mike Gardiner .05
415 Marquis Grissom .05
416 *Tim Laker* .05
417 *Mike Lansing* .10
418 Dennis Martinez .05
419 John Vander Wal .05
420 John Wetteland .05
421 Rondell White .05
422 Bobby Bonilla .05
423 Jeromy Burnitz .05
424 *Vince Burnitz* .05
425 *Mike Draper* .05
426 Tony Fernandez .05
427 Dwight Gooden .05
428 Jeff Innis .05
429 Bobby Jones .05
430 Mike Maddux .05
431 Charlie O'Brien .05
432 Joe Orsulak .05
433 Pete Schourek .05
434 Frank Tanana .05
435 *Ryan Thompson* .05
436 Kim Batiste .05
437 Mark Davis .05
438 Jose DeLeon .05
439 Len Dykstra .05
440 Jim Eisenreich .05
441 Tommy Greene .05
442 Pete Incaviglia .05
443 Danny Jackson .05
444 *Todd Pratt* .05
445 Curt Schilling .20
446 Milt Thompson .05
447 David West .05

No.	Player	NM/M
448	Mitch Williams	.05
449	Steve Cooke	.05
450	Carlos Garcia	.05
451	Al Martin	.05
452	*Blas Minor*	.05
453	Dennis Moeller	.05
454	Denny Neagle	.05
455	Don Slaught	.05
456	Lonnie Smith	.05
457	Paul Wagner	.05
458	Bob Walk	.05
459	Kevin Young	.05
460	*Rene Arocha*	.05
461	Brian Barber	.05
462	Rheal Cormier	.05
463	Gregg Jefferies	.05
464	Joe Magrane	.05
465	Omar Olivares	.05
466	Geronimo Pena	.05
467	Allen Watson	.05
468	Mark Whiten	.05
469	Derek Bell	.05
470	Phil Clark	.05
471	*Pat Gomez*	.05
472	Tony Gwynn	.60
473	Jeremy Hernandez	.05
474	Bruce Hurst	.05
475	Phil Plantier	.05
476	*Scott Sanders*	.05
477	*Tim Scott*	.05
478	*Darrell Sherman*	.05
479	Guillermo Velasquez	.05
480	*Tim Worrell*	.05
481	Todd Benzinger	.05
482	Bud Black	.05
483	Barry Bonds	1.50
484	Dave Burba	.05
485	Bryan Hickerson	.05
486	Dave Martinez	.05
487	Willie McGee	.05
488	Jeff Reed	.05
489	Kevin Rogers	.05
490	Matt Williams	.05
491	Trevor Wilson	.05
492	Harold Baines	.05
493	Mike Devereaux	.05
494	Todd Frohwirth	.05
495	Chris Hoiles	.05
496	Luis Mercedes	.05
497	*Sherman Obando*	.05
498	*Brad Pennington*	.05
499	Harold Reynolds	.05
500	Arthur Rhodes	.05
501	Cal Ripken, Jr.	1.50
502	Rick Sutcliffe	.05
503	Fernando Valenzuela	.05
504	Mark Williamson	.05
505	Scott Bankhead	.05
506	Greg Blosser	.05
507	Ivan Calderon	.05
508	Roger Clemens	.65
509	Andre Clemens	.05
510	Scott Fletcher	.05
511	Greg Harris	.05
512	Billy Hatcher	.05
513	Bob Melvin	.05
514	Carlos Quintana	.05
515	Luis Rivera	.05
516	Jeff Russell	.05
517	*Ken Ryan*	.05
518	Chili Davis	.05
519	*Jim Edmonds*	1.50
520	Gary Gaetti	.05
521	Torey Lovullo	.05
522	*Tony Percival*	.05
523	Tim Salmon	.05
524	Scott Sanderson	.05
525	*J.T. Snow*	.75
526	Jerome Walton	.05
527	Jason Bere	.05
528	*Rod Bolton*	.05
529	Ellis Burks	.05
530	Carlton Fisk	.50
531	Craig Grebeck	.05
532	Ozzie Guillen	.05
533	Roberto Hernandez	.05
534	Bo Jackson	.10
535	Kirk McCaskill	.05
536	Dave Stieb	.05
537	Robin Ventura	.05
538	Albert Belle	.05
539	Mike Bielecki	.05
540	Glenallen Hill	.05
541	Reggie Jefferson	.05
542	Kenny Lofton	.05
543	*Jeff Mutis*	.05
544	Junior Ortiz	.05
545	Manny Ramirez	.50
546	Jeff Treadway	.05
547	Kevin Wickander	.05
548	Cecil Fielder	.05
549	Kirk Gibson	.05
550	*Greg Gohr*	.05
551	David Haas	.05
552	Bill Krueger	.05
553	Mike Moore	.05
554	Mickey Tettleton	.05
555	Lou Whitaker	.05
556	Kevin Appier	.05
557	*Billy Brewer*	.05
558	David Cone	.05
559	Greg Gagne	.05
560	Mark Gardner	.05
561	Phil Hiatt	.05
562	Felix Jose	.05
563	Jose Lind	.05
564	Mike Macfarlane	.05
565	Keith Miller	.05
566	Jeff Montgomery	.05
567	Hipolito Pechardo	.05
568	Ricky Bones	.05
569	Tom Brunansky	.05
570	*Joe Kmak*	.05
571	Pat Listach	.05
572	*Graeme Lloyd*	.05
573	*Carlos Maldonado*	.05
574	Josias Manzanillo	.05
575	Matt Mieske	.05
576	Kevin Reimer	.05
577	Bill Spiers	.05
578	Dickie Thon	.05
579	Willie Banks	.05
580	Jim Deshaies	.05
581	Mark Guthrie	.05
582	Brian Harper	.05
583	Chuck Knoblauch	.05
584	Gene Larkin	.05
585	Shane Mack	.05
586	David McCarty	.05
587	Mike Pagliarulo	.05
588	Mike Trombley	.05
589	Dave Winfield	.50
590	Jim Abbott	.05
591	Wade Boggs	.60
592	*Russ Davis*	.05
593	Steve Farr	.05
594	Steve Howe	.05
595	*Mike Humphreys*	.05
596	Jimmy Key	.05
597	Jim Leyritz	.05
598	*Bobby Munoz*	.05
599	Paul O'Neill	.05
600	Spike Owen	.05
601	Mike Stanley	.05
602	Danny Tartabull	.05
603	Scott Brosius	.05
604	Storm Davis	.05
605	Eric Fox	.05
606	Goose Gossage	.05
607	Scott Hammond	.05
608	Dave Henderson	.05
609	Mark McGwire	1.00
610	*Mike Mohler*	.05
611	Edwin Nunez	.05
612	Kevin Seitzer	.05
613	Ruben Sierra	.05
614	Chris Bosio	.05
615	Norm Charlton	.05
616	*Jim Converse*	.05
617	*John Cummings*	.05
618	Mike Felder	.05
619	Ken Griffey, Jr.	.75
620	Mike Hampton	.05
621	Erik Hanson	.05
622	Bill Haselman	.05
623	Tino Martinez	.05
624	Lee Tinsley	.05
625	*Fernando Vina*	.05
626	*David Wainhouse*	.05
627	Jose Canseco	.30
628	Benji Gil	.05
629	Tom Henke	.05
630	*David Hulse*	.05
631	Manuel Lee	.05
632	Craig Lefferts	.05
633	*Robb Nen*	.05
634	Gary Redus	.05
635	Bill Ripken	.05
636	Nolan Ryan	1.50
637	Dan Smith	.05
638	*Matt Whiteside*	.05
639	Roberto Alomar	.25
640	Juan Guzman	.05
641	Pat Hentgen	.05
642	Darrin Jackson	.05
643	Randy Knorr	.05
644	*Domingo Martinez*	.05
645	Paul Molitor	.50
646	Dick Schofield	.05
647	Dave Stewart	.05
648	Rey Sanchez Checklist	.05
649	Jeremy Hernandez Checklist	.05
650	Junior Ortiz Checklist	.05

All-Rookies

		NM/M
Complete Set (10):		4.00
Common Player:		.25
1	Rene Arocha	.25
2	Jeff Conine	.25
3	Phil Hiatt	.25
4	Mike Lansing	.25
5	Al Martin	.25
6	David Nied	.25
7	Mike Piazza	3.00
8	Tim Salmon	.50
9	J.T. Snow	.45
10	Kevin Young	.25

All-Stars

		NM/M
Complete Set (20):		17.50
Common Player:		.25
1	Darren Daulton	.25
2	Will Clark	.35
3	Ryne Sandberg	1.50
4	Barry Larkin	.25
5	Gary Sheffield	.40
6	Barry Bonds	3.00
7	Ray Lankford	.25
8	Larry Walker	.25
9	Greg Maddux	1.50
10	Lee Smith	.25
11	Ivan Rodriguez	.75
12	Mark McGwire	2.50
13	Carlos Baerga	.25
14	Cal Ripken, Jr.	3.00
15	Edgar Martinez	.25
16	Juan Gonzalez	1.00
17	Ken Griffey, Jr.	2.00
18	Kirby Puckett	1.50
19	Frank Thomas	1.25
20	Mike Mussina	.65

Award Winners

		NM/M
Complete Set (25):		12.00
Common Player:		.25
1	Greg Maddux	.75
2	Tom Pagnozzi	.25
3	Mark Grace	.25
4	Jose Lind	.25
5	Terry Pendleton	.25
6	Ozzie Smith	.75
7	Barry Bonds	2.00
8	Andy Van Slyke	.25
9	Larry Walker	.25
10	Mark Langston	.25
11	Ivan Rodriguez	.60
12	Don Mattingly	.75
13	Roberto Alomar	.35
14	Robin Ventura	.25
15	Cal Ripken, Jr.	2.00
16	Ken Griffey, Jr.	1.00
17	Kirby Puckett	.75
18	Devon White	.25
19	Pat Listach	.25
20	Eric Karros	.25
21	Pat Borders	.25
22	Greg Maddux	.75
23	Dennis Eckersley	.60
24	Barry Bonds	2.00
25	Gary Sheffield	.45

Dennis Eckersley Career Highlights

	NM/M
Complete Set (12):	6.00
Common Card:	.50
Autographed Card:	35.00

Home Run Kings

		NM/M
Complete Set (10):		8.00
Common Player:		.50
1	Juan Gonzalez	.65
2	Mark McGwire	2.50
3	Cecil Fielder	.50
4	Fred McGriff	.50
5	Albert Belle	.50
6	Barry Bonds	2.50
7	Joe Carter	.50
8	Gary Sheffield	.65
9	Darren Daulton	.50
10	Dave Hollins	.50

Performers

		NM/M
Complete Set (10):		5.00
Common Player:		.25
1	Barry Bonds	2.50
2	Juan Gonzalez	.30
3	Ken Griffey, Jr.	1.00
4	Eric Karros	.25
5	Pat Listach	.25
6	Greg Maddux	.75
7	David Nied	.25
8	Gary Sheffield	.40
9	J.T. Snow	.25
10	Frank Thomas	.65

Strikeout Kings

		NM/M
Complete Set (5):		7.50
Common Player:		.25
1	Roger Clemens	2.50
2	Juan Guzman	.25
3	Randy Johnson	1.25
4	Nolan Ryan	5.00
5	John Smoltz	.50

1994 ULTRA

	NM/M
Complete Set (600):	15.00
Common Player:	.05

Series 1 or 2 Pack (14): .50
Series 1 or 2 Wax Box (36): 15.00

1 Jeffrey Hammonds .05
2 Chris Hoiles .05
3 Ben McDonald .05
4 Mark McLemore .05
5 Alan Mills .05
6 Jamie Moyer .05
7 Brad Pennington .05
8 Jim Poole .05
9 Cal Ripken, Jr. 1.50
10 Jack Voigt .05
11 Roger Clemens .65
12 Danny Darwin .05
13 Andre Dawson .25
14 Scott Fletcher .05
15 Greg Harris .05
16 Billy Hatcher .05
17 Jeff Russell .05
18 Aaron Sele .05
19 Mo Vaughn .05
20 Mike Butcher .05
21 Rod Correia .05
22 Steve Frey .05
23 *Phil Leftwich* .05
24 Torey Lovullo .05
25 Ken Patterson .05
26 Eduardo Perez .05
27 Tim Salmon .05
28 J.T. Snow .05
29 Chris Turner .05
30 Wilson Alvarez .05
31 Jason Bere .05
32 Joey Cora .05
33 Alex Fernandez .05
34 Roberto Hernandez .05
35 Lance Johnson .05
36 Ron Karkovice .05
37 Kirk McCaskill .05
38 Jeff Schwarz .05
39 Frank Thomas .50
40 Sandy Alomar Jr. .05
41 Albert Belle .05
42 Felix Fermin .05
43 Wayne Kirby .05
44 Tom Kramer .05
45 Kenny Lofton .05
46 Jose Mesa .05
47 Eric Plunk .05
48 Paul Sorrento .05
49 Jim Thome .35
50 Bill Wertz .05
51 John Doherty .05
52 Cecil Fielder .05
53 Travis Fryman .05
54 Chris Gomez .05
55 Mike Henneman .05
56 Chad Kreuter .05
57 Bob MacDonald .05
58 Mike Moore .05
59 Tony Phillips .05
60 Lou Whitaker .05
61 Kevin Appier .05
62 Greg Gagne .05
63 Chris Gwynn .05
64 Bob Hamelin .05
65 Chris Haney .05
66 Phil Hiatt .05
67 Felix Jose .05
68 Jose Lind .05
69 Mike Macfarlane .05
70 Jeff Montgomery .05
71 Hipolito Pichardo .05
72 Juan Bell .05
73 Cal Eldred .05
74 Darryl Hamilton .05
75 Doug Henry .05
76 Mike Ignasiak .05
77 John Jaha .05
78 Graeme Lloyd .05
79 Angel Miranda .05
80 Dave Nilsson .05
81 Troy O'Leary .05
82 Kevin Reimer .05
83 Willie Banks .05
84 Larry Casian .05
85 Scott Erickson .05
86 Eddie Guardado .05
87 Kent Hrbek .05
88 Terry Jorgensen .05
89 Chuck Knoblauch .05
90 Pat Meares .05
91 Mike Trombley .05
92 Dave Winfield .50
93 Wade Boggs .60
94 Scott Kamieniecki .05
95 Pat Kelly .05
96 Jimmy Key .05
97 Jim Leyritz .05
98 Bobby Munoz .05
99 Paul O'Neill .05
100 Melido Perez .05
101 Mike Stanley .05
102 Danny Tartabull .05
103 Bernie Williams .05
104 *Kurt Abbott* .05
105 Mike Bordick .05
106 Ron Darling .05
107 Brent Gates .05
108 Miguel Jimenez .05
109 Steve Karsay .05
110 Scott Lydy .05
111 Mark McGwire 1.00
112 Troy Neel .05
113 Craig Paquette .05
114 Bob Welch .05
115 Bobby Witt .05
116 Rich Amaral .05
117 Mike Blowers .05
118 Jay Buhner .05
119 Dave Fleming .05
120 Ken Griffey, Jr. .75
121 Tino Martinez .05
122 Marc Newfield .05
123 Ted Power .05
124 Mackey Sasser .05
125 Omar Vizquel .05
126 Kevin Brown .05
127 Juan Gonzalez .25
128 Tom Henke .05
129 David Hulse .05
130 Dean Palmer .05
131 Roger Pavlik .05
132 Ivan Rodriguez .40
133 Kenny Rogers .05
134 Doug Strange .05
135 Pat Borders .05
136 Joe Carter .05
137 Darnell Coles .05
138 Pat Hentgen .05
139 Al Leiter .05
140 Paul Molitor .50
141 John Olerud .05
142 Ed Sprague .05
143 Dave Stewart .05
144 Mike Timlin .05
145 Duane Ward .05
146 Devon White .05
147 Steve Avery .05
148 Steve Bedrosian .05
149 Damon Berryhill .05
150 Jeff Blauser .05
151 Tom Glavine .20
152 Chipper Jones .60
153 Mark Lemke .05
154 Fred McGriff .05
155 Greg McMichael .05
156 Deion Sanders .05
157 John Smoltz .05
158 Mark Wohlers .05
159 Jose Bautista .05
160 Steve Buechele .05
161 Mike Harkey .05
162 Greg Hibbard .05
163 Chuck McElroy .05
164 Mike Morgan .05
165 Kevin Roberson .05
166 Ryne Sandberg .60
167 Jose Vizcaino .05
168 Rick Wilkins .05
169 Willie Wilson .05
170 Willie Greene .05
171 Roberto Kelly .05
172 Larry Luebbers .05
173 Kevin Mitchell .05
174 Joe Oliver .05
175 John Roper .05
176 Johnny Ruffin .05
177 Reggie Sanders .05
178 John Smiley .05
179 Jerry Spradlin .05
180 Freddie Benavides .05
181 Dante Bichette .05
182 Willie Blair .05
183 Kent Bottenfield .05
184 Jerald Clark .05
185 Joe Girardi .05
186 Roberto Mejia .05
187 Steve Reed .05
188 Armando Reynoso .05
189 Bruce Ruffin .05
190 Eric Young .05
191 Luis Aquino .05
192 Bret Barberie .05
193 Ryan Bowen .05
194 Chuck Carr .05
195 Orestes Destrade .05
196 Richie Lewis .05
197 Dave Magadan .05
198 Bob Natal .05
199 Gary Sheffield .30
200 Matt Turner .05
201 Darrell Whitmore .05
202 Eric Anthony .05
203 Jeff Bagwell .50
204 Andujar Cedeno .05
205 Luis Gonzalez .05
206 Xavier Hernandez .05
207 Doug Jones .05
208 Darryl Kile .05
209 Scott Servais .05
210 Greg Swindell .05
211 Brian Williams .05
212 Pedro Astacio .05
213 Brett Butler .05
214 Omar Daal .05
215 Jim Gott .05
216 Raul Mondesi .05
217 Jose Offerman .05
218 Mike Piazza .75
219 Cory Snyder .05
220 Tim Wallach .05
221 Todd Worrell .05
222 Moises Alou .05
223 Sean Berry .05
224 Wil Cordero .05
225 Jeff Fassero .05
226 Darrin Fletcher .05
227 Cliff Floyd .05
228 Marquis Grissom .05
229 Ken Hill .05
230 Mike Lansing .05
231 Kirk Rueter .05
232 John Wetteland .05
233 Rondell White .05
234 Tim Bogar .05
235 Jeromy Burnitz .05
236 Dwight Gooden .05
237 Todd Hundley .05
238 Jeff Kent .05
239 Josias Manzanillo .05
240 Joe Orsulak .05
241 Ryan Thompson .05
242 Kim Batiste .05
243 Darren Daulton .05
243a Darren Daulton ("PROMOTIONAL SAMPLE") 1.00
244 Tommy Greene .05
245 Dave Hollins .05
246 Pete Incaviglia .05
247 Danny Jackson .05
248 Ricky Jordan .05
249 John Kruk .05
249a John Kruk ("PROMOTIONAL SAMPLE") 1.00
250 Mickey Morandini .05
251 Terry Mulholland .05
252 Ben Rivera .05
253 Kevin Stocker .05
254 Jay Bell .05
255 Steve Cooke .05
256 Jeff King .05
257 Al Martin .05
258 Danny Miceli .05
259 Blas Minor .05
260 Don Slaught .05
261 Paul Wagner .05
262 Tim Wakefield .05
263 Kevin Young .05
264 Rene Arocha .05
265 *Richard Batchelor* .05
266 Gregg Jefferies .05
267 Brian Jordan .05
268 Jose Oquendo .05
269 Donovan Osborne .05
270 Erik Pappas .05
271 Mike Perez .05
272 Bob Tewksbury .05
273 Mark Whiten .05
274 Todd Zeile .05
275 Andy Ashby .05
276 Brad Ausmus .05
277 Phil Clark .05
278 Jeff Gardner .05
279 Ricky Gutierrez .05
280 Tony Gwynn .60
281 Tim Mauser .05
282 Scott Sanders .05
283 Frank Seminara .05
284 Wally Whitehurst .05
285 Rod Beck .05
286 Barry Bonds 1.50
287 Dave Burba .05
288 Mark Carreon .05
289 Royce Clayton .05
290 Mike Jackson .05
291 Darren Lewis .05
292 Kirt Manwaring .05
293 Dave Martinez .05
294 Billy Swift .05
295 Salomon Torres .05
296 Matt Williams .05
297 Checklist 1-103 (Joe Orsulak) .05
298 Checklist 104-201 (Pete Incaviglia) .05
299 Checklist 202-300 (Todd Hundley) .05
300 Checklist - Inserts (John Doherty) .05
301 Brady Anderson .05
302 Harold Baines .05
303 Damon Buford .05
304 Mike Devereaux .05
305 Sid Fernandez .05
306 Rick Krivda .05
307 Mike Mussina .30
308 Rafael Palmeiro .40
309 Arthur Rhodes .05
310 Chris Sabo .05
311 Lee Smith .05
312 *Gregg Zaun* .05
313 Scott Cooper .05
314 Mike Greenwell .05
315 Tim Naehring .05
316 Otis Nixon .05
317 Paul Quantrill .05
318 John Valentin .05
319 Dave Valle .05
320 Frank Viola .05
321 *Brian Anderson* .10
322 Garret Anderson .05
323 Chad Curtis .05
324 Chili Davis .05
325 Gary DiSarcina .05
326 Damion Easley .05
327 Jim Edmonds .05
328 Chuck Finley .05
329 Joe Grahe .05
330 Bo Jackson .10
331 Mark Langston .05
332 Harold Reynolds .05
333 James Baldwin .05
334 *Ray Durham* .50
335 Julio Franco .05
336 Craig Grebeck .05
337 Ozzie Guillen .05
338 Joe Hall .05
339 Darrin Jackson .05
340 Jack McDowell .05
341 Tim Raines .05
342 Robin Ventura .05
343 Carlos Baerga .05
344 Derek Lilliquist .05
345 Dennis Martinez .05
346 Jack Morris .05
347 Eddie Murray .50
348 Chris Nabholz .05
349 Charles Nagy .05
350 Chad Ogea .05
351 Manny Ramirez .50
352 Omar Vizquel .05
353 Tim Belcher .05
354 Eric Davis .05
355 Kirk Gibson .05
356 Rick Greene .05
357 Mickey Tettleton .05
358 Alan Trammell .05
359 David Wells .05
360 Stan Belinda .05
361 Vince Coleman .05
362 David Cone .05
363 Gary Gaetti .05
364 Tom Gordon .05
365 Dave Henderson .05

366	Wally Joyner	.05
367	Brent Mayne	.05
368	Brian McRae	.05
369	Michael Tucker	.05
370	Ricky Bones	.05
371	Brian Harper	.05
372	Tyrone Hill	.05
373	Mark Kiefer	.05
374	Pat Listach	.05
375	*Mike Matheny*	.10
376	*Jose Mercedes*	.05
377	Jody Reed	.05
378	Kevin Seitzer	.05
379	B.J. Surhoff	.05
380	Greg Vaughn	.05
381	Turner Ward	.05
382	*Wes Weger*	.05
383	Bill Wegman	.05
384	Rick Aguilera	.05
385	Rich Becker	.05
386	Alex Cole	.05
387	Steve Dunn	.05
388	*Keith Garagozzo*	.05
389	*LaTroy Hawkins*	.05
390	Shane Mack	.05
391	David McCarty	.05
392	Pedro Munoz	.05
393	*Derek Parks*	.05
394	Kirby Puckett	.60
395	Kevin Tapani	.05
396	Matt Walbeck	.05
397	Jim Abbott	.05
398	Mike Gallego	.05
399	Xavier Hernandez	.05
400	Don Mattingly	.65
401	Terry Mulholland	.05
402	Matt Nokes	.05
403	Luis Polonia	.05
404	Bob Wickman	.05
405	Mark Acre	.05
406	*Fausto Cruz*	.05
407	Dennis Eckersley	.45
408	Rickey Henderson	.50
409	Stan Javier	.05
410	*Carlos Reyes*	.05
411	Ruben Sierra	.05
412	Terry Steinbach	.05
413	Bill Taylor	.05
414	Todd Van Poppel	.05
415	Eric Anthony	.05
416	Bobby Ayala	.05
417	Chris Bosio	.05
418	Tim Davis	.05
419	Randy Johnson	.50
420	Kevin King	.05
421	*Anthony Manahan*	.05
422	Edgar Martinez	.05
423	Keith Mitchell	.05
424	Roger Salkeld	.05
425	*Mac Suzuki*	.05
426	Dan Wilson	.05
427	*Duff Brumley*	.05
428	Jose Canseco	.30
429	Will Clark	.05
430	Steve Dreyer	.05
431	Rick Helling	.05
432	Chris James	.05
433	Matt Whiteside	.05
434	Roberto Alomar	.20
435	Scott Brow	.05
436	*Domingo Cedeno*	.05
437	Carlos Delgado	.35
438	Juan Guzman	.05
439	Paul Spoljaric	.05
440	Todd Stottlemyre	.05
441	Woody Williams	.05
442	Dave Justice	.05
443	Mike Kelly	.05
444	Ryan Klesko	.05
445	Javier Lopez	.05
446	Greg Maddux	.60
447	Kent Mercker	.05
448	Charlie O'Brien	.05
449	Terry Pendleton	.05
450	Mike Stanton	.05
451	Tony Tarasco	.05
452	*Terrell Wade*	.05
453	Willie Banks	.05
454	Shawon Dunston	.05
455	Mark Grace	.05
456	Jose Guzman	.05
457	Jose Hernandez	.05
458	Glenallen Hill	.05
459	Blaise Ilsley	.05
460	*Brooks Kieschnick*	.05
461	Derrick May	.05
462	Randy Myers	.05
463	Karl Rhodes	.05
464	Sammy Sosa	.60
465	*Steve Trachsel*	.10
466	Anthony Young	.05
467	*Eddie Zambrano*	.05
468	Bret Boone	.05
469	Tom Browning	.05
470	*Hector Carrasco*	.05
471	Rob Dibble	.05
472	Erik Hanson	.05
473	Thomas Howard	.05
474	Barry Larkin	.05
475	Hal Morris	.05
476	Jose Rijo	.05
477	John Burke	.05
478	Ellis Burks	.05
479	Marvin Freeman	.05
480	Andres Galarraga	.05
481	Greg Harris	.05
482	Charlie Hayes	.05
483	Darren Holmes	.05
484	Howard Johnson	.05
485	*Marcus Moore*	.05
486	David Nied	.05
487	Mark Thompson	.05
488	Walt Weiss	.05
489	Kurt Abbott	.05
490	Matias Carrillo	.05
491	Jeff Conine	.05
492	Chris Hammond	.05
493	Bryan Harvey	.05
494	Charlie Hough	.05
495	*Yorkis Perez*	.05
496	Pat Rapp	.05
497	Benito Santiago	.05
498	David Weathers	.05
499	Craig Biggio	.05
500	Ken Caminiti	.05
501	Doug Drabek	.05
502	*Tony Eusebio*	.10
503	Steve Finley	.05
504	Pete Harnisch	.05
505	Brian Hunter	.05
506	Domingo Jean	.05
507	Todd Jones	.05
508	Orlando Miller	.05
509	James Mouton	.05
510	Roberto Petagine	.05
511	Shane Reynolds	.05
512	Mitch Williams	.05
513	Billy Ashley	.05
514	Tom Candiotti	.05
515	Delino DeShields	.05
516	Kevin Gross	.05
517	Orel Hershiser	.05
518	Eric Karros	.05
519	Ramon Martinez	.05
520	*Chan Ho Park*	.75
521	Henry Rodriguez	.05
522	Joey Eischen	.05
523	Rod Henderson	.05
524	Pedro Martinez	.50
525	Mel Rojas	.05
526	Larry Walker	.05
527	*Gabe White*	.10
528	Bobby Bonilla	.05
529	Jonathan Hurst	.05
530	Bobby Jones	.05
531	Kevin McReynolds	.05
532	Bill Pulsipher	.05
533	Bret Saberhagen	.05
534	David Segui	.05
535	Pete Smith	.05
536	*Kelly Stinnett*	.05
537	Dave Telgheder	.05
538	*Quilvio Veras*	.05
539	Jose Vizcaino	.05
540	Pete Walker	.05
541	Ricky Bottalico	.05
542	Wes Chamberlain	.05
543	Mariano Duncan	.05
544	Len Dykstra	.05
545	Jim Eisenreich	.05
546	*Phil Geisler*	.05
547	*Wayne Gomes*	.10
548	Doug Jones	.05
549	Jeff Juden	.05
550	Mike Lieberthal	.05
551	*Tony Longmire*	.05
552	Tom Marsh	.05
553	Bobby Munoz	.05
554	Curt Schilling	.15
555	Carlos Garcia	.05
556	*Ravelo Manzanillo*	.05
557	Orlando Merced	.05
558	*Will Pennyfeather*	.05
559	Zane Smith	.05
560	Andy Van Slyke	.05
561	Rick White	.05
562	Luis Alicea	.05
563	*Brian Barber*	.05
564	*Clint Davis*	.05
565	Bernard Gilkey	.05
566	Ray Lankford	.05
567	Tom Pagnozzi	.05
568	Ozzie Smith	.60
569	Rick Sutcliffe	.05
570	Allen Watson	.05
571	Dmitri Young	.05
572	Derek Bell	.05
573	Andy Benes	.05
574	Archi Cianfrocco	.05
575	Joey Hamilton	.05
576	Gene Harris	.05
577	Trevor Hoffman	.05
578	*Tim Hyers*	.05
579	*Brian Johnson*	.05
580	*Keith Lockhart*	.05
581	Pedro Martinez	.05
582	Ray McDavid	.05
583	Phil Plantier	.05
584	Bip Roberts	.05
585	Dave Staton	.05
586	Todd Benzinger	.05
587	John Burkett	.05
588	Bryan Hickerson	.05
589	Willie McGee	.05
590	John Patterson	.05
591	Mark Portugal	.05
592	Kevin Rogers	.05
593	*Joe Rosselli*	.05
594	*Steve Soderstrom*	.05
595	Robby Thompson	.05
596	125th Anniversary card	.05
597	Checklist	.05
598	Checklist	.05
599	Checklist	.05
600	Checklist	.05

All-Rookie Team

		NM/M
Complete Set (10):		4.00
Common Player:		.35
1	Kurt Abbott	.35
2	Carlos Delgado	3.00
3	Cliff Floyd	.35
4	Jeffrey Hammonds	.35
5	Ryan Klesko	.35
6	Javier Lopez	.35
7	Raul Mondesi	.35
8	James Mouton	.35
9	Chan Ho Park	.50
10	Dave Staton	.35

All-Stars

		NM/M
Complete Set (20):		5.00
Common Player:		.15
1	Chris Hoiles	.15
2	Frank Thomas	.35
3	Roberto Alomar	.20
4	Cal Ripken, Jr.	1.00
5	Robin Ventura	.15
6	Albert Belle	.15
7	Juan Gonzalez	.20
8	Ken Griffey, Jr.	.50
9	John Olerud	.15
10	Jack McDowell	.15
11	Mike Piazza	.50
12	Fred McGriff	.15
13	Ryne Sandberg	.40
14	Jay Bell	.15
15	Matt Williams	.15
16	Barry Bonds	1.00
17	Len Dykstra	.15
18	Dave Justice	.15
19	Tom Glavine	.20
20	Greg Maddux	.40

Award Winners

		NM/M
Complete Set (25):		5.00
Common Player:		.10
1	Ivan Rodriguez	.25
2	Don Mattingly	.45
3	Roberto Alomar	.20
4	Robin Ventura	.10
5	Omar Vizquel	.10
6	Ken Griffey, Jr.	.50
7	Kenny Lofton	.10
8	Devon White	.10
9	Mark Langston	.10
10	Kirt Manwaring	.10
11	Mark Grace	.10
12	Robby Thompson	.10
13	Matt Williams	.10
14	Jay Bell	.10
15	Barry Bonds	.60
16	Marquis Grissom	.10
17	Larry Walker	.10
18	Greg Maddux	.40
19	Frank Thomas	.35
20	Barry Bonds	.60
21	Paul Molitor	.35
22	Jack McDowell	.10
23	Greg Maddux	.40
24	Tim Salmon	.10
25	Mike Piazza	.50

Career Achievement Awards

		NM/M
Complete Set (5):		4.00
Common Player:		.50
1	Joe Carter	.50
2	Paul Molitor	.75
3	Cal Ripken, Jr.	2.00
4	Ryne Sandberg	1.00
5	Dave Winfield	.75

Firemen

		NM/M
Complete Set (10):		2.00
Common Player:		.25
1	Jeff Montgomery	.25
2	Duane Ward	.25
3	Tom Henke	.25
4	Roberto Hernandez	.25
5	Dennis Eckersley	1.25
6	Randy Myers	.25
7	Rod Beck	.25
8	Bryan Harvey	.25
9	John Wetteland	.25
10	Mitch Williams	.25

Hitting Machines

		NM/M
Complete Set (10):		4.00

Common Player:		.15
1	Roberto Alomar	.25
2	Carlos Baerga	.15
3	Barry Bonds	2.00
4	Andres Galarraga	.15
5	Juan Gonzalez	.25
6	Tony Gwynn	.50
7	Paul Molitor	.40
8	John Olerud	.15
9	Mike Piazza	.75
10	Frank Thomas	.40

Home Run Kings

		NM/M
Complete Set (12):		15.00
Common Player:		.75
1	Juan Gonzalez	1.00
2	Ken Griffey, Jr.	2.50
3	Frank Thomas	2.00
4	Albert Belle	.75
5	Rafael Palmeiro	1.50
6	Joe Carter	.75
7	Barry Bonds	4.00
8	Dave Justice	.75
9	Matt Williams	.75
10	Fred McGriff	.75
11	Ron Gant	.75
12	Mike Piazza	2.50

League Leaders

		NM/M
Complete Set (10):		3.00
Common Player:		.25
1	John Olerud	.25
2	Rafael Palmeiro	1.00
3	Kenny Lofton	.25
4	Jack McDowell	.25
5	Randy Johnson	1.50
6	Andres Galarraga	.25
7	Len Dykstra	.25
8	Chuck Carr	.25
9	Tom Glavine	.35
10	Jose Rijo	.25

On-Base Leaders

		NM/M
Complete Set (12):		25.00
Common Player:		1.50
1	Roberto Alomar	2.00
2	Barry Bonds	6.50
3	Len Dykstra	1.50
4	Andres Galarraga	1.50
5	Mark Grace	1.50
6	Ken Griffey, Jr.	5.00
7	Gregg Jefferies	1.50
8	Orlando Merced	1.50
9	Paul Molitor	3.50
10	John Olerud	1.50
11	Tony Phillips	1.50
12	Frank Thomas	3.50

Phillies Finest

		NM/M
Complete Set (24):		4.00
Common Player:		.25
Autographed Daulton:		45.00
Autographed Kruk:		30.00
1-5	Darren Daulton	.25
6-10	John Kruk	.25
11-15	Darren Daulton	.25
16-20	John Kruk	.25
9a	John Kruk ("PROMOTIONAL SAMPLE")	1.50
	MAIL-IN CARDS	
1M, 3M	Darren Daulton	.75
2M, 4M	John Kruk	.75

Rising Stars

		NM/M
Complete Set (12):		15.00
Common Player:		1.00
1	Carlos Baerga	1.00
2	Jeff Bagwell	5.00
3	Albert Belle	1.00
4	Cliff Floyd	1.00
5	Travis Fryman	1.00
6	Marquis Grissom	1.00
7	Kenny Lofton	1.00
8	John Olerud	1.00
9	Mike Piazza	7.50
10	Kirk Rueter	1.00
11	Tim Salmon	1.00
12	Aaron Sele	1.00

RBI Kings

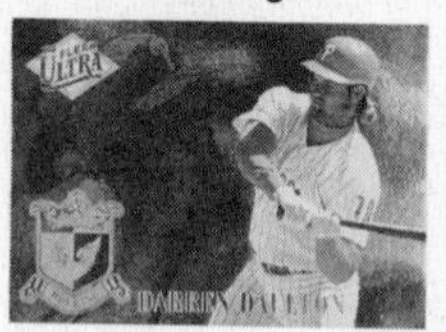

		NM/M
Complete Set (12):		16.00
Common Player:		1.00
1	Albert Belle	1.00
2	Frank Thomas	2.50
3	Joe Carter	1.00
4	Juan Gonzalez	1.25
5	Cecil Fielder	1.00
6	Carlos Baerga	1.00
7	Barry Bonds	5.00
8	David Justice	1.00
9	Ron Gant	1.00
10	Mike Piazza	3.50
11	Matt Williams	1.00
12	Darren Daulton	1.00

Second Year Standouts

		NM/M
Complete Set (10):		5.00
Common Player:		.25
1	Jason Bere	.25
2	Brent Gates	.25
3	Jeffrey Hammonds	.25
4	Tim Salmon	.50
5	Aaron Sele	.25
6	Chuck Carr	.25
7	Jeff Conine	.25
8	Greg McMichael	.25
9	Mike Piazza	4.00
10	Kevin Stocker	.25

Strikeout Kings

		NM/M
Complete Set (5):		2.00
Common Player:		.25
1	Randy Johnson	.75
2	Mark Langston	.25
3	Greg Maddux	1.00
4	Jose Rijo	.25
5	John Smoltz	.25

1995 ULTRA

		NM/M
Complete Set (450):		10.00
Common Player:		.05
Gold Medallion:		2X
Series 1 or 2 Pack (12):		.50
Series 1 or 2 Wax Box (36):		12.50
1	Brady Anderson	.05
2	Sid Fernandez	.05
3	Jeffrey Hammonds	.05
4	Chris Hoiles	.05
5	Ben McDonald	.05
6	Mike Mussina	.35
7	Rafael Palmeiro	.65
8	Jack Voigt	.05
9	Wes Chamberlain	.05
10	Roger Clemens	1.00
11	Chris Howard	.05
12	Tim Naehring	.05
13	Otis Nixon	.05
14	Rich Rowland	.05
15	Ken Ryan	.05
16	John Valentin	.05
17	Mo Vaughn	.05
18	Brian Anderson	.05
19	Chili Davis	.05
20	Damion Easley	.05
21	Jim Edmonds	.05
22	Mark Langston	.05
23	Tim Salmon	.05
24	J.T. Snow	.05
25	Chris Turner	.05
26	Wilson Alvarez	.05
27	Joey Cora	.05
28	Alex Fernandez	.05
29	Roberto Hernandez	.05
30	Lance Johnson	.05
31	Ron Karkovice	.05
32	Kirk McCaskill	.05
33	Tim Raines	.05
34	Frank Thomas	.75
35	Sandy Alomar	.05
36	Albert Belle	.05
37	Mark Clark	.05
38	Kenny Lofton	.05
39	Eddie Murray	.75
40	Eric Plunk	.05
41	Manny Ramirez	.75
42	Jim Thome	.60
43	Omar Vizquel	.05
44	Danny Bautista	.05
45	Junior Felix	.05
46	Cecil Fielder	.05
47	Chris Gomez	.05
48	Chad Kreuter	.05
49	Mike Moore	.05
50	Tony Phillips	.05
51	Alan Trammell	.05
52	David Wells	.05
53	Kevin Appier	.05
54	Billy Brewer	.05
55	David Cone	.05
56	Greg Gagne	.05
57	Bob Hamelin	.05
58	Jose Lind	.05
59	Brent Mayne	.05
60	Brian McRae	.05
61	Terry Shumpert	.05
62	Ricky Bones	.05
63	Mike Fetters	.05
64	Darryl Hamilton	.05
65	John Jaha	.05
66	Graeme Lloyd	.05
67	Matt Mieske	.05
68	Kevin Seitzer	.05
69	Jose Valentin	.05
70	Turner Ward	.05
71	Rick Aguilera	.05
72	Rich Becker	.05
73	Alex Cole	.05
74	Scott Leius	.05
75	Pat Meares	.05
76	Kirby Puckett	1.00
77	Dave Stevens	.05
78	Kevin Tapani	.05
79	Matt Walbeck	.05
80	Wade Boggs	1.00
81	Scott Kamieniecki	.05
82	Pat Kelly	.05
83	Jimmy Key	.05
84	Paul O'Neill	.05
85	Luis Polonia	.05
86	Mike Stanley	.05
87	Danny Tartabull	.05
88	Bob Wickman	.05
89	Mark Acre	.05
90	Geronimo Berroa	.05
91	Mike Bordick	.05
92	Ron Darling	.05
93	Stan Javier	.05
94	Mark McGwire	1.50
95	Troy Neel	.05
96	Ruben Sierra	.05
97	Terry Steinbach	.05
98	Eric Anthony	.05
99	Chris Bosio	.05
100	Dave Fleming	.05
101	Ken Griffey Jr.	1.25
102	Reggie Jefferson	.05
103	Randy Johnson	.75
104	Edgar Martinez	.05
105	Bill Risley	.05
106	Dan Wilson	.05
107	Cris Carpenter	.05
108	Will Clark	.05
109	Juan Gonzalez	.40
110	Rusty Greer	.05
111	David Hulse	.05
112	Roger Pavlik	.05
113	Ivan Rodriguez	.75
114	Doug Strange	.05
115	Matt Whiteside	.05
116	Roberto Alomar	.20
117	Brad Cornett	.05
118	Carlos Delgado	.45
119	Alex Gonzalez	.05
120	Darren Hall	.05
121	Pat Hentgen	.05
122	Paul Molitor	.75
123	Ed Sprague	.05
124	Devon White	.05
125	Tom Glavine	.25
126	Dave Justice	.05
127	Roberto Kelly	.05
128	Mark Lemke	.05
129	Greg Maddux	1.00
130	Charles Johnson	.05
131	Kent Mercker	.05
132	Charlie O'Brien	.05
133	John Smoltz	.05
134	Willie Banks	.05
135	Steve Buechele	.05
136	Kevin Foster	.05
137	Glenallen Hill	.05
138	Ray Sanchez	.05
139	Sammy Sosa	1.00
140	Steve Trachsel	.05
141	Rick Wilkins	.05
142	Jeff Brantley	.05
143	Hector Carrasco	.05
144	Kevin Jarvis	.05
145	Barry Larkin	.05
146	Chuck McElroy	.05
147	Jose Rijo	.05
148	Johnny Ruffin	.05
149	Deion Sanders	.05
150	Eddie Taubensee	.05
151	Dante Bichette	.05
152	Ellis Burks	.05
153	Joe Girardi	.05
154	Charlie Hayes	.05
155	Mike Kingery	.05
156	Steve Reed	.05
157	Kevin Ritz	.05
158	Bruce Ruffin	.05
159	Eric Young	.05
160	Kurt Abbott	.05
161	Chuck Carr	.05
162	Chris Hammond	.05
163	Bryan Harvey	.05
164	Terry Mathews	.05
165	Yorkis Perez	.05
166	Pat Rapp	.05
167	Gary Sheffield	.40
168	Dave Weathers	.05
169	Jeff Bagwell	.75
170	Ken Caminiti	.05
171	Doug Drabek	.05
172	Steve Finley	.05
173	John Hudek	.05
174	Todd Jones	.05

#	Player	Price
175	James Mouton	.05
176	Shane Reynolds	.05
177	Scott Servais	.05
178	Tom Candiotti	.05
179	Omar Daal	.05
180	Darren Dreifort	.05
181	Eric Karros	.05
182	Ramon Martinez	.05
183	Raul Mondesi	.05
184	Henry Rodriguez	.05
185	Todd Worrell	.05
186	Moises Alou	.05
187	Sean Berry	.05
188	Wil Cordero	.05
189	Jeff Fassero	.05
190	Darrin Fletcher	.05
191	Butch Henry	.05
192	Ken Hill	.05
193	Mel Rojas	.05
194	John Wetteland	.05
195	Bobby Bonilla	.05
196	Rico Brogna	.05
197	Bobby Jones	.05
198	Jeff Kent	.05
199	Josias Manzanillo	.05
200	Kelly Stinnett	.05
201	Ryan Thompson	.05
202	Jose Vizcaino	.05
203	Lenny Dykstra	.05
204	Jim Eisenreich	.05
205	Dave Hollins	.05
206	Mike Lieberthal	.05
207	Mickey Morandini	.05
208	Bobby Munoz	.05
209	Curt Schilling	.20
210	Heathcliff Slocumb	.05
211	David West	.05
212	Dave Clark	.05
213	Steve Cooke	.05
214	Midre Cummings	.05
215	Carlos Garcia	.05
216	Jeff King	.05
217	Jon Lieber	.05
218	Orlando Merced	.05
219	Don Slaught	.05
220	Rick White	.05
221	Rene Arocha	.05
222	Bernard Gilkey	.05
223	Brian Jordan	.05
224	Tom Pagnozzi	.05
225	Vicente Palacios	.05
226	Geronimo Pena	.05
227	Ozzie Smith	1.00
228	Allen Watson	.05
229	Mark Whiten	.05
230	Brad Ausmus	.05
231	Derek Bell	.05
232	Andy Benes	.05
233	Tony Gwynn	1.00
234	Joey Hamilton	.05
235	Luis Lopez	.05
236	Pedro A. Martinez	.05
237	Scott Sanders	.05
238	Eddie Williams	.05
239	Rod Beck	.05
240	Dave Burba	.05
241	Darren Lewis	.05
242	Kirt Manwaring	.05
243	Mark Portugal	.05
244	Darryl Strawberry	.05
245	Robby Thompson	.05
246	William VanLandingham	.05
247	Matt Williams	.05
248	Checklist	.05
249	Checklist	.05
250	Checklist	.05
251	Harold Baines	.05
252	Bret Barberie	.05
253	Armando Benitez	.05
254	Mike Devereaux	.05
255	Leo Gomez	.05
256	Jamie Moyer	.05
257	Arthur Rhodes	.05
258	Cal Ripken Jr.	2.00
259	Luis Alicea	.05
260	Jose Canseco	.45
261	Scott Cooper	.05
262	Andre Dawson	.25
263	Mike Greenwell	.05
264	Aaron Sele	.05
265	Garret Anderson	.05
266	Chad Curtis	.05
267	Gary DiSarcina	.05
268	Chuck Finley	.05
269	Rex Hudler	.05
270	Andrew Lorraine	.05
271	Spike Owen	.05
272	Lee Smith	.05
273	Jason Bere	.05
274	Ozzie Guillen	.05
275	Norberto Martin	.05
276	Scott Ruffcorn	.05
277	Robin Ventura	.05
278	Carlos Baerga	.05
279	Jason Grimsley	.05
280	Dennis Martinez	.05
281	Charles Nagy	.05
282	Paul Sorrento	.05
283	Dave Winfield	.75
284	John Doherty	.05
285	Travis Fryman	.05
286	Kirk Gibson	.05
287	Lou Whitaker	.05
288	Gary Gaetti	.05
289	Tom Gordon	.05
290	Mark Gubicza	.05
291	Wally Joyner	.05
292	Mike Macfarlane	.05
293	Jeff Montgomery	.05
294	Jeff Cirillo	.05
295	Cal Eldred	.05
296	Pat Listach	.05
297	Jose Mercedes	.05
298	Dave Nilsson	.05
299	Duane Singleton	.05
300	Greg Vaughn	.05
301	Scott Erickson	.05
302	Denny Hocking	.05
303	Chuck Knoblauch	.05
304	Pat Mahomes	.05
305	Pedro Munoz	.05
306	Erik Schullstrom	.05
307	Jim Abbott	.05
308	Tony Fernandez	.05
309	Sterling Hitchcock	.05
310	Jim Leyritz	.05
311	Don Mattingly	1.00
312	Jack McDowell	.05
313	Melido Perez	.05
314	Bernie Williams	.05
315	Scott Brosius	.05
316	Dennis Eckersley	.65
317	Brent Gates	.05
318	Rickey Henderson	.75
319	Steve Karsay	.05
320	Steve Ontiveros	.05
321	Bill Taylor	.05
322	Todd Van Poppel	.05
323	Bob Welch	.05
324	Bobby Ayala	.05
325	Mike Blowers	.05
326	Jay Buhner	.05
327	Felix Fermin	.05
328	Tino Martinez	.05
329	Marc Newfield	.05
330	Greg Pirkl	.05
331	Alex Rodriguez	1.50
332	Kevin Brown	.05
333	John Burkett	.05
334	Jeff Frye	.05
335	Kevin Gross	.05
336	Dean Palmer	.05
337	Joe Carter	.05
338	Shawn Green	.35
339	Juan Guzman	.05
340	Mike Huff	.05
341	Al Leiter	.05
342	John Olerud	.05
343	Dave Stewart	.05
344	Todd Stottlemyre	.05
345	Steve Avery	.05
346	Jeff Blauser	.05
347	Chipper Jones	1.00
348	Mike Kelly	.05
349	Ryan Klesko	.05
350	Javier Lopez	.05
351	Fred McGriff	.05
352	Jose Oliva	.05
353	Terry Pendleton	.05
354	Mike Stanton	.05
355	Tony Tarasco	.05
356	Mark Wohlers	.05
357	Jim Bullinger	.05
358	Shawon Dunston	.05
359	Mark Grace	.05
360	Derrick May	.05
361	Randy Myers	.05
362	Karl Rhodes	.05
363	Bret Boone	.05
364	Brian Dorsett	.05
365	Ron Gant	.05
366	Brian R. Hunter	.05
367	Hal Morris	.05
368	Jack Morris	.05
369	John Roper	.05
370	Reggie Sanders	.05
371	Pete Schourek	.05
372	John Smiley	.05
373	Marvin Freeman	.05
374	Andres Galarraga	.05
375	Mike Munoz	.05
376	David Nied	.05
377	Walt Weiss	.05
378	Greg Colbrunn	.05
379	Jeff Conine	.05
380	Charles Johnson	.05
381	Kurt Miller	.05
382	Robb Nen	.05
383	Benito Santiago	.05
384	Craig Biggio	.05
385	Tony Eusebio	.05
386	Luis Gonzalez	.05
387	Brian L. Hunter	.05
388	Darryl Kile	.05
389	Orlando Miller	.05
390	Phil Plantier	.05
391	Greg Swindell	.05
392	Billy Ashley	.05
393	Pedro Astacio	.05
394	Brett Butler	.05
395	Delino DeShields	.05
396	Orel Hershiser	.05
397	Garey Ingram	.05
398	Chan Ho Park	.05
399	Mike Piazza	1.25
400	Ismael Valdes	.05
401	Tim Wallach	.05
402	Cliff Floyd	.05
403	Marquis Grissom	.05
404	Mike Lansing	.05
405	Pedro Martinez	.75
406	Kirk Rueter	.05
407	Tim Scott	.05
408	Jeff Shaw	.05
409	Larry Walker	.05
410	Rondell White	.05
411	John Franco	.05
412	Todd Hundley	.05
413	Jason Jacome	.05
414	Joe Orsulak	.05
415	Bret Saberhagen	.05
416	David Segui	.05
417	Darren Daulton	.05
418	Mariano Duncan	.05
419	Tommy Greene	.05
420	Gregg Jefferies	.05
421	John Kruk	.05
422	Kevin Stocker	.05
423	Jay Bell	.05
424	Al Martin	.05
425	Denny Neagle	.05
426	Zane Smith	.05
427	Andy Van Slyke	.05
428	Paul Wagner	.05
429	Tom Henke	.05
430	Danny Jackson	.05
431	Ray Lankford	.05
432	John Mabry	.05
433	Bob Tewksbury	.05
434	Todd Zeile	.05
435	Andy Ashby	.05
436	Andujar Cedeno	.05
437	Donnie Elliott	.05
438	Bryce Florie	.05
439	Trevor Hoffman	.05
440	Melvin Nieves	.05
441	Bip Roberts	.05
442	Barry Bonds	2.00
443	Royce Clayton	.05
444	Mike Jackson	.05
445	John Patterson	.05
446	J.R. Phillips	.05
447	Bill Swift	.05
448	Checklist	.05
449	Checklist	.05
450	Checklist	.05

Gold Medallion

NM/M

Complete Set (450): 60.00
Common Player: .25
Stars/Rookies: 2X

(See 1995 Ultra for checklist and base card values.)

All-Rookies

		NM/M
Complete Set (10):		2.25
Common Player:		.15
Gold Medallion:		2X
1	Cliff Floyd	.15
2	Chris Gomez	.15
3	Rusty Greer	.15
4	Bob Hamelin	.15
5	Joey Hamilton	.15
6	John Hudek	.15
7	Ryan Klesko	.15
8	Raul Mondesi	.15
9	Manny Ramirez	2.00
10	Steve Trachsel	.15

All-Stars

		NM/M
Complete Set (20):		7.50
Common Player:		.15
Gold Medallion:		2X
1	Moises Alou	.15
2	Albert Belle	.15
3	Craig Biggio	.15
4	Wade Boggs	.60
5	Barry Bonds	1.50
6	David Cone	.15
7	Ken Griffey Jr.	.75
8	Tony Gwynn	.60
9	Chuck Knoblauch	.15
10	Barry Larkin	.15
11	Kenny Lofton	.15
12	Greg Maddux	.60
13	Fred McGriff	.15
14	Paul O'Neill	.15
15	Mike Piazza	.75
16	Kirby Puckett	.60
17	Cal Ripken Jr.	1.50
18	Ivan Rodriguez	.45
19	Frank Thomas	.50
20	Matt Williams	.15

Award Winners

		NM/M
Complete Set (25):		6.00
Common Player:		.10
Gold Medallion:		2X
1	Ivan Rodriguez	.30
2	Don Mattingly	.65
3	Roberto Alomar	.20
4	Wade Boggs	.60
5	Omar Vizquel	.10
6	Ken Griffey Jr.	.75
7	Kenny Lofton	.10
8	Devon White	.10
9	Mark Langston	.10
10	Tom Pagnozzi	.10
11	Jeff Bagwell	.45
12	Craig Biggio	.10
13	Matt Williams	.10
14	Barry Larkin	.10
15	Barry Bonds	1.00
16	Marquis Grissom	.10
17	Darren Lewis	.10
18	Greg Maddux	.60
19	Frank Thomas	.45
20	Jeff Bagwell	.45
21	David Cone	.10
22	Greg Maddux	.60
23	Bob Hamelin	.10
24	Raul Mondesi	.10
25	Moises Alou	.10

Golden Prospects

		NM/M
Complete Set (10):		5.00
Common Player:		.10
Gold Medallion:		2X
1	James Baldwin	.10
2	Alan Benes	.10
3	Armando Benitez	.10
4	Ray Durham	.10

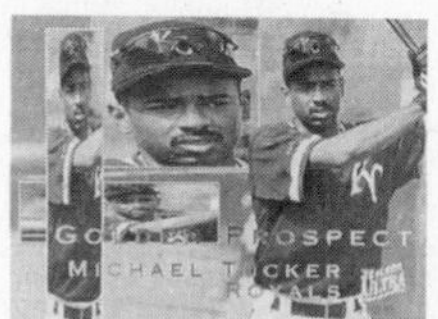

5	LaTroy Hawkins	.10
6	Brian Hunter	.10
7	Derek Jeter	3.00
8	Charles Johnson	.10
9	Alex Rodriguez	2.00
10	Michael Tucker	.10

Hitting Machines

		NM/M
Complete Set (10):		6.00
Common Player:		.40
Gold Medallion:		2X
1	Jeff Bagwell	.65
2	Albert Belle	.25
3	Dante Bichette	.25
4	Barry Bonds	2.50
5	Jose Canseco	.50
6	Ken Griffey Jr.	1.00
7	Tony Gwynn	.75
8	Fred McGriff	.25
9	Mike Piazza	1.00
10	Frank Thomas	.65

Home Run Kings

		NM/M
Complete Set (10):		7.50
Common Player:		.25
Gold Medallion:		2X
1	Ken Griffey Jr.	2.00
2	Frank Thomas	.75
3	Albert Belle	.25
4	Jose Canseco	.50
5	Cecil Fielder	.25
6	Matt Williams	.25
7	Jeff Bagwell	.75
8	Barry Bonds	3.00
9	Fred McGriff	.25
10	Andres Galarraga	.25

League Leaders

		NM/M
Complete Set (10):		2.50
Common Player:		.15
Gold Medallion:		2X
1	Paul O'Neill	.15
2	Kenny Lofton	.15
3	Jimmy Key	.15
4	Randy Johnson	.50
5	Lee Smith	.15
6	Tony Gwynn	.75
7	Craig Biggio	.15
8	Greg Maddux	.75
9	Andy Benes	.15
10	John Franco	.15

On-Base Leaders

		NM/M
Complete Set (10):		15.00
Common Player:		1.00
Gold Medallion:		2X
1	Jeff Bagwell	2.00
2	Albert Belle	1.00
3	Craig Biggio	1.00
4	Wade Boggs	2.50
5	Barry Bonds	6.00
6	Will Clark	1.00
7	Tony Gwynn	2.50
8	Dave Justice	1.00
9	Paul O'Neill	1.00
10	Frank Thomas	2.00

Power Plus

		NM/M
Complete Set (6):		7.50
Common Player:		.50
Gold Medallion:		2X
1	Albert Belle	.50
2	Ken Griffey Jr.	2.00
3	Frank Thomas	1.00
4	Jeff Bagwell	1.00
5	Barry Bonds	4.00
6	Matt Williams	.50

Rising Stars

		NM/M
Complete Set (9):		7.00
Common Player:		.50
Gold Medallion:		2X
1	Moises Alou	.50
2	Jeff Bagwell	1.50
3	Albert Belle	.65
4	Juan Gonzalez	1.50
5	Chuck Knoblauch	.50
6	Kenny Lofton	.50
7	Raul Mondesi	.50
8	Mike Piazza	2.50
9	Frank Thomas	1.50

RBI Kings

		NM/M
Complete Set (10):		12.00
Common Player:		.50
Gold Medallion:		2X
1	Kirby Puckett	3.00
2	Joe Carter	.50
3	Albert Belle	.50
4	Frank Thomas	2.00
5	Julio Franco	.50
6	Jeff Bagwell	2.00
7	Matt Williams	.50
8	Dante Bichette	.50
9	Fred McGriff	.50
10	Mike Piazza	4.00

Second Year Standouts

		NM/M
Complete Set (15):		3.50
Common Player:		.15
Gold Medallion:		2X
1	Cliff Floyd	.15
2	Chris Gomez	.15
3	Rusty Greer	.15
4	Darren Hall	.15
5	Bob Hamelin	.15
6	Joey Hamilton	.15
7	Jeffrey Hammonds	.15
8	John Hudek	.15
9	Ryan Klesko	.15
10	Raul Mondesi	.15
11	Manny Ramirez	3.00
12	Bill Risley	.15
13	Steve Trachsel	.15
14	William Van Landingham	.15
15	Rondell White	.15

Strikeout Kings

		NM/M
Complete Set (6):		3.00
Common Player:		.10
Gold Medallion:		2X
1	Andy Benes	.10
2	Roger Clemens	1.50
3	Randy Johnson	.75
4	Greg Maddux	1.00
5	Pedro Martinez	.75
6	Jose Rijo	.10

1996 ULTRA

		NM/M
Complete Set (600):		22.50
Common Player:		.05
Series 1 or 2 Pack (12):		1.25
Series 1 or 2 Wax Box (24):		20.00
1	Manny Alexander	.05
2	Brady Anderson	.05
3	Bobby Bonilla	.05
4	Scott Erickson	.05
5	Curtis Goodwin	.05
6	Chris Hoiles	.05
7	Doug Jones	.05
8	Jeff Manto	.05
9	Mike Mussina	.35
10	Rafael Palmeiro	.50
11	Cal Ripken Jr.	1.50
12	Rick Aguilera	.05
13	Luis Alicea	.05
14	Stan Belinda	.05
15	Jose Canseco	.40
16	Roger Clemens	.85
17	Mike Greenwell	.05
18	Mike Macfarlane	.05
19	Tim Naehring	.05
20	Troy O'Leary	.05
21	John Valentin	.05
22	Mo Vaughn	.05
23	Tim Wakefield	.05
24	Brian Anderson	.05
25	Garret Anderson	.05
26	Chili Davis	.05
27	Gary DiSarcina	.05
28	Jim Edmonds	.05
29	Jorge Fabregas	.05
30	Chuck Finley	.05
31	Mark Langston	.05
32	Troy Percival	.05
33	Tim Salmon	.05
34	Lee Smith	.05
35	Wilson Alvarez	.05
36	Ray Durham	.05
37	Alex Fernandez	.05
38	Ozzie Guillen	.05
39	Roberto Hernandez	.05
40	Lance Johnson	.05
41	Ron Karkovice	.05
42	Lyle Mouton	.05
43	Tim Raines	.05
44	Frank Thomas	.60
45	Carlos Baerga	.05
46	Albert Belle	.05
47	Orel Hershiser	.05
48	Kenny Lofton	.05
49	Dennis Martinez	.05
50	Jose Mesa	.05
51	Eddie Murray	.60
52	Chad Ogea	.05
53	Manny Ramirez	.60
54	Jim Thome	.50
55	Omar Vizquel	.05
56	Dave Winfield	.60
57	Chad Curtis	.05
58	Cecil Fielder	.05
59	John Flaherty	.05
60	Travis Fryman	.05
61	Chris Gomez	.05
62	Bob Higginson	.05
63	Felipe Lira	.05
64	Brian Maxcy	.05
65	Alan Trammell	.05
66	Lou Whitaker	.05
67	Kevin Appier	.05
68	Gary Gaetti	.05
69	Tom Goodwin	.05
70	Tom Gordon	.05
71	Jason Jacome	.05
72	Wally Joyner	.05
73	Brent Mayne	.05
74	Jeff Montgomery	.05
75	Jon Nunnally	.05
76	Joe Vitiello	.05
77	Ricky Bones	.05
78	Jeff Cirillo	.05
79	Mike Fetters	.05
80	Darryl Hamilton	.05
81	David Hulse	.05
82	Dave Nilsson	.05
83	Kevin Seitzer	.05
84	Steve Sparks	.05
85	B.J. Surhoff	.05
86	Jose Valentin	.05
87	Greg Vaughn	.05
88	Marty Cordova	.05
89	Chuck Knoblauch	.05
90	Pat Meares	.05
91	Pedro Munoz	.05
92	Kirby Puckett	.75
93	Brad Radke	.05
94	Scott Stahoviak	.05
95	Dave Stevens	.05
96	Mike Trombley	.05
97	Matt Walbeck	.05
98	Wade Boggs	.75
99	Russ Davis	.05
100	Jim Leyritz	.05
101	Don Mattingly	.85
102	Jack McDowell	.05
103	Paul O'Neill	.05
104	Andy Pettitte	.30
105	Mariano Rivera	.15
106	Ruben Sierra	.05
107	Darryl Strawberry	.05
108	John Wetteland	.05
109	Bernie Williams	.05
110	Geronimo Berroa	.05
111	Scott Brosius	.05
112	Dennis Eckersley	.50
113	Brent Gates	.05
114	Rickey Henderson	.60
115	Mark McGwire	1.25
116	Ariel Prieto	.05
117	Terry Steinbach	.05
118	Todd Stottlemyre	.05
119	Todd Van Poppel	.05
120	Steve Wojciechowski	.05
121	Rich Amaral	.05
122	Bobby Ayala	.05
123	Mike Blowers	.05
124	Chris Bosio	.05
125	Joey Cora	.05
126	Ken Griffey Jr.	1.00
127	Randy Johnson	.60
128	Edgar Martinez	.05
129	Tino Martinez	.05
130	Alex Rodriguez	1.25
131	Dan Wilson	.05
132	Will Clark	.05
133	Jeff Frye	.05
134	Benji Gil	.05
135	Juan Gonzalez	.30
136	Rusty Greer	.05
137	Mark McLemore	.05
138	Roger Pavlik	.05
139	Ivan Rodriguez	.50
140	Kenny Rogers	.05
141	Mickey Tettleton	.05
142	Roberto Alomar	.20
143	Joe Carter	.05
144	Tony Castillo	.05
145	Alex Gonzalez	.05
146	Shawn Green	.35
147	Pat Hentgen	.05
148	*Sandy Martinez*	.05
149	Paul Molitor	.60
150	John Olerud	.05
151	Ed Sprague	.05
152	Jeff Blauser	.05

153 Brad Clontz .05
154 Tom Glavine .30
155 Marquis Grissom .05
156 Chipper Jones .75
157 David Justice .05
158 Ryan Klesko .05
159 Javier Lopez .05
160 Greg Maddux .75
161 John Smoltz .05
162 Mark Wohlers .05
163 Jim Bullinger .05
164 Frank Castillo .05
165 Shawon Dunston .05
166 Kevin Foster .05
167 Luis Gonzalez .05
168 Mark Grace .05
169 Rey Sanchez .05
170 Scott Servais .05
171 Sammy Sosa .75
172 Ozzie Timmons .05
173 Steve Trachsel .05
174 Bret Boone .05
175 Jeff Branson .05
176 Jeff Brantley .05
177 Dave Burba .05
178 Ron Gant .05
179 Barry Larkin .05
180 Darren Lewis .05
181 Mark Portugal .05
182 Reggie Sanders .05
183 Pete Schourek .05
184 John Smiley .05
185 Jason Bates .05
186 Dante Bichette .05
187 Ellis Burks .05
188 Vinny Castilla .05
189 Andres Galarraga .05
190 Darren Holmes .05
191 Armando Reynoso .05
192 Kevin Ritz .05
193 Bill Swift .05
194 Larry Walker .05
195 Kurt Abbott .05
196 John Burkett .05
197 Greg Colbrunn .05
198 Jeff Conine .05
199 Andre Dawson .25
200 Chris Hammond .05
201 Charles Johnson .05
202 Robb Nen .05
203 Terry Pendleton .05
204 Quilvio Veras .05
205 Jeff Bagwell .60
206 Derek Bell .05
207 Doug Drabek .05
208 Tony Eusebio .05
209 Mike Hampton .05
210 Brian Hunter .05
211 Todd Jones .05
212 Orlando Miller .05
213 James Mouton .05
214 Shane Reynolds .05
215 Dave Veres .05
216 Billy Ashley .05
217 Brett Butler .05
218 Chad Fonville .05
219 Todd Hollandsworth .05
220 Eric Karros .05
221 Ramon Martinez .05
222 Raul Mondesi .05
223 Hideo Nomo .30
224 Mike Piazza 1.00
225 Kevin Tapani .05
226 Ismael Valdes .05
227 Todd Worrell .05
228 Moises Alou .05
229 Wil Cordero .05
230 Jeff Fassero .05
231 Darrin Fletcher .05
232 Mike Lansing .05
233 Pedro Martinez .60
234 Carlos Perez .05
235 Mel Rojas .05
236 David Segui .05
237 Tony Tarasco .05
238 Rondell White .05
239 Edgardo Alfonzo .05
240 Rico Brogna .05
241 Carl Everett .05
242 Todd Hundley .05
243 Butch Huskey .05
244 Jason Isringhausen .05
245 Bobby Jones .05
246 Jeff Kent .05
247 Bill Pulsipher .05
248 Jose Vizcaino .05
249 Ricky Bottalico .05
250 Darren Daulton .05
251 Jim Eisenreich .05
252 Tyler Green .05
253 Charlie Hayes .05
254 Gregg Jefferies .05
255 Tony Longmire .05
256 Michael Mimbs .05
257 Mickey Morandini .05
258 Paul Quantrill .05
259 Heathcliff Slocumb .05
260 Jay Bell .05
261 Jacob Brumfield .05
262 *Angelo Encarnacion* .05
263 John Ericks .05
264 Mark Johnson .05
265 Esteban Loaiza .05
266 Al Martin .05
267 Orlando Merced .05
268 Dan Miceli .05
269 Denny Neagle .05
270 Brian Barber .05
271 Scott Cooper .05
272 Tripp Cromer .05
273 Bernard Gilkey .05
274 Tom Henke .05
275 Brian Jordan .05
276 John Mabry .05
277 Tom Pagnozzi .05
278 *Mark Petkovsek* .05
279 Ozzie Smith .75
280 Andy Ashby .05
281 Brad Ausmus .05
282 Ken Caminiti .05
283 Glenn Dishman .05
284 Tony Gwynn .75
285 Joey Hamilton .05
286 Trevor Hoffman .05
287 Phil Plantier .05
288 Jody Reed .05
289 Eddie Williams .05
290 Barry Bonds 1.50
291 Jamie Brewington .05
292 Mark Carreon .05
293 Royce Clayton .05
294 Glenallen Hill .05
295 Mark Leiter .05
296 Kirt Manwaring .05
297 J.R. Phillips .05
298 Deion Sanders .05
299 William VanLandingham .05
300 Matt Williams .05
301 Roberto Alomar .20
302 Armando Benitez .05
303 Mike Devereaux .05
304 Jeffrey Hammonds .05
305 Jimmy Haynes .05
306 *Scott McClain* .05
307 Kent Mercker .05
308 Randy Myers .05
309 B.J. Surhoff .05
310 Tony Tarasco .05
311 David Wells .05
312 Wil Cordero .05
313 Alex Delgado .05
314 Tom Gordon .05
315 Dwayne Hosey .05
316 Jose Malave .05
317 Kevin Mitchell .05
318 Jamie Moyer .05
319 Aaron Sele .05
320 Heathcliff Slocumb .05
321 Mike Stanley .05
322 Jeff Suppan .05
323 Jim Abbott .05
324 George Arias .05
325 Todd Greene .05
326 Bryan Harvey .05
327 J.T. Snow .05
328 Randy Velarde .05
329 Tim Wallach .05
330 Harold Baines .05
331 Jason Bere .05
332 Darren Lewis .05
333 Norberto Martin .05
334 Tony Phillips .05
335 Bill Simas .05
336 Chris Snopek .05
337 Kevin Tapani .05
338 Danny Tartabull .05
339 Robin Ventura .05
340 Sandy Alomar .05
341 Julio Franco .05
342 Jack McDowell .05
343 Charles Nagy .05
344 Julian Tavarez .05
345 Kimera Bartee .05
346 Greg Keagle .05
347 Mark Lewis .05
348 Jose Lima .05
349 Melvin Nieves .05
350 Mark Parent .05
351 Eddie Williams .05
352 Johnny Damon .30
353 Sal Fasano .05
354 Mark Gubicza .05
355 Bob Hamelin .05
356 Chris Haney .05
357 Keith Lockhart .05
358 Mike Macfarlane .05
359 Jose Offerman .05
360 Bip Roberts .05
361 Michael Tucker .05
362 Chuck Carr .05
363 Bobby Hughes .05
364 John Jaha .05
365 Mark Loretta .05
366 Mike Matheny .05
367 Ben McDonald .05
368 Matt Mieske .05
369 Angel Miranda .05
370 Fernando Vina .05
371 Rick Aguilera .05
372 Rich Becker .05
373 LaTroy Hawkins .05
374 Dave Hollins .05
375 Roberto Kelly .05
376 *Matt Lawton* .25
377 Paul Molitor .60
378 *Dan Naulty* .05
379 Rich Robertson .05
380 Frank Rodriguez .05
381 David Cone .05
382 Mariano Duncan .05
383 *Andy Fox* .05
384 Joe Girardi .05
385 Dwight Gooden .05
386 Derek Jeter 1.50
387 Pat Kelly .05
388 Jimmy Key .05
389 *Matt Luke* .05
390 Tino Martinez .05
391 Jeff Nelson .05
392 Melido Perez .05
393 Tim Raines .05
394 Ruben Rivera .05
395 Kenny Rogers .05
396 *Tony Batista* .25
397 Allen Battle .05
398 Mike Bordick .05
399 Steve Cox .05
400 Jason Giambi .40
401 Doug Johns .05
402 Pedro Munoz .05
403 Phil Plantier .05
404 Scott Spiezio .05
405 George Williams .05
406 Ernie Young .05
407 Darren Bragg .05
408 Jay Buhner .05
409 Norm Charlton .05
410 Russ Davis .05
411 Sterling Hitchcock .05
412 Edwin Hurtado .05
413 *Raul Ibanez* .05
414 Mike Jackson .05
415 Luis Sojo .05
416 Paul Sorrento .05
417 Bob Wolcott .05
418 Damon Buford .05
419 Kevin Gross .05
420 Darryl Hamilton .05
421 Mike Henneman .05
422 Ken Hill .05
423 Dean Palmer .05
424 Bobby Witt .05
425 Tilson Brito .05
426 Giovanni Carrara .05
427 Domingo Cedeno .05
428 Felipe Crespo .05
429 Carlos Delgado .40
430 Juan Guzman .05
431 Erik Hanson .05
432 *Marty Janzen* .05
433 Otis Nixon .05
434 Robert Perez .05
435 Paul Quantrill .05
436 Bill Risley .05
437 Steve Avery .05
438 Jermaine Dye .05
439 Mark Lemke .05
440 *Marty Malloy* .05
441 Fred McGriff .05
442 Greg McMichael .05
443 Wonderful Monds .05
444 Eddie Perez .05
445 Jason Schmidt .05
446 Terrell Wade .05
447 Terry Adams .05
448 Scott Bullett .05
449 *Robin Jennings* .05
450 Doug Jones .05
451 Brooks Kieschnick .05
452 Dave Magadan .05
453 *Jason Maxwell* .05
454 Brian McRae .05
455 Rodney Myers .05
456 Jaime Navarro .05
457 Ryne Sandberg .75
458 Vince Coleman .05
459 Eric Davis .05
460 Steve Gibralter .05
461 Thomas Howard .05
462 Mike Kelly .05
463 Hal Morris .05
464 Eric Owens .05
465 Jose Rijo .05
466 Chris Sabo .05
467 Eddie Taubensee .05
468 Trenidad Hubbard .05
469 Curt Leskanic .05
470 Quinton McCracken .05
471 Jayhawk Owens .05
472 Steve Reed .05
473 Bryan Rekar .05
474 Bruce Ruffin .05
475 Bret Saberhagen .05
476 Walt Weiss .05
477 Eric Young .05
478 Kevin Brown .05
479 Al Leiter .05
480 Pat Rapp .05
481 Gary Sheffield .35
482 Devon White .05
483 Bob Abreu .05
484 Sean Berry .05
485 Craig Biggio .05
486 Jim Dougherty .05
487 Richard Hidalgo .05
488 Darryl Kile .05
489 Derrick May .05
490 Greg Swindell .05
491 Rick Wilkins .05
492 Mike Blowers .05
493 Tom Candiotti .05
494 Roger Cedeno .05
495 Delino DeShields .05
496 Greg Gagne .05
497 Karim Garcia .10
498 *Wilton Guerrero* .05
499 Chan Ho Park .05
500 Israel Alcantara .05
501 Shane Andrews .05
502 Yamil Benitez .05
503 Cliff Floyd .05
504 Mark Grudzielanek .05
505 Ryan McGuire .05
506 Sherman Obando .05
507 Jose Paniagua .05
508 Henry Rodriguez .05
509 Kirk Rueter .05
510 Juan Acevedo .05
511 John Franco .05
512 Bernard Gilkey .05
513 Lance Johnson .05
514 Rey Ordonez .05
515 Robert Person .05
516 Paul Wilson .05
517 Toby Borland .05
518 *David Doster* .05
519 Lenny Dykstra .05
520 Sid Fernandez .05
521 *Mike Grace* .05
522 *Rich Hunter* .05
523 Benito Santiago .05
524 Gene Schall .05
525 Curt Schilling .15
526 *Kevin Sefcik* .05
527 Lee Tinsley .05
528 David West .05
529 Mark Whiten .05
530 Todd Zeile .05
531 Carlos Garcia .05
532 Charlie Hayes .05
533 Jason Kendall .05
534 Jeff King .05
535 Mike Kingery .05
536 Nelson Liriano .05
537 Dan Plesac .05
538 Paul Wagner .05
539 Luis Alicea .05
540 David Bell .05
541 Alan Benes .05
542 Andy Benes .05
543 *Mike Busby* .05
544 Royce Clayton .05
545 Dennis Eckersley .50
546 Gary Gaetti .05
547 Ron Gant .05
548 Aaron Holbert .05

549	Ray Lankford	.05
550	T.J. Mathews	.05
551	Willie McGee	.05
552	*Miguel Mejia*	.05
553	Todd Stottlemyre	.05
554	Sean Bergman	.05
555	Willie Blair	.05
556	Andujar Cedeno	.05
557	Steve Finley	.05
558	Rickey Henderson	.60
559	Wally Joyner	.05
560	Scott Livingstone	.05
561	Marc Newfield	.05
562	Bob Tewksbury	.05
563	Fernando Valenzuela	.05
564	Rod Beck	.05
565	Doug Creek	.05
566	Shawon Dunston	.05
567	*Osvaldo Fernandez*	.20
568	Stan Javier	.05
569	Marcus Jensen	.05
570	Steve Scarsone	.05
571	Robby Thompson	.05
572	Allen Watson	.05
573	Roberto Alomar	.10
574	Jeff Bagwell	.30
575	Albert Belle	.05
576	Wade Boggs	.40
577	Barry Bonds	.75
578	Juan Gonzalez	.15
579	Ken Griffey Jr.	.50
580	Tony Gwynn	.40
581	Randy Johnson	.30
582	Chipper Jones	.40
583	Barry Larkin	.05
584	Kenny Lofton	.05
585	Greg Maddux	.40
586	Raul Mondesi	.05
587	Mike Piazza	.50
588	Cal Ripken Jr.	.75
589	Tim Salmon	.05
590	Frank Thomas	.35
591	Mo Vaughn	.05
592	Matt Williams	.05
593	Marty Cordova	.05
594	Jim Edmonds	.05
595	Cliff Floyd	.05
596	Chipper Jones	.40
597	Ryan Klesko	.05
598	Raul Mondesi	.05
599	Manny Ramirez	.30
600	Ruben Rivera	.05

Gold Medallion

	NM/M
Complete Set (600):	75.00
Common Player:	.25

(Star cards valued at 2X regular edition Fleer Ultra.)

Call to the Hall

#	Player	NM/M
	Complete Set (10):	10.00
	Common Player:	1.00
	Gold Medallion Edition:	2X
1	Barry Bonds	3.00
2	Ken Griffey Jr.	2.00
3	Tony Gwynn	1.25
4	Rickey Henderson	1.00
5	Greg Maddux	1.25
6	Eddie Murray	1.00
7	Cal Ripken Jr.	3.00
8	Ryne Sandberg	1.25
9	Ozzie Smith	1.25
10	Frank Thomas	1.00

Diamond Producers

#	Player	NM/M
	Complete Set (12):	15.00
	Common Player:	.50
	Gold Medallions:	2X
1	Albert Belle	.50
2	Barry Bonds	3.00
3	Ken Griffey Jr.	2.00
4	Tony Gwynn	1.50
5	Greg Maddux	1.50
6	Hideo Nomo	.75
7	Mike Piazza	2.00
8	Kirby Puckett	1.50
9	Cal Ripken Jr.	3.00
10	Frank Thomas	1.25
11	Mo Vaughn	.50
12	Matt Williams	.50

Fresh Foundations

#	Player	NM/M
	Complete Set (10):	2.00
	Common Player:	.15
	Gold Medallions:	2X
1	Garret Anderson	.15
2	Marty Cordova	.15
3	Jim Edmonds	.15
4	Brian Hunter	.15
5	Chipper Jones	.50
6	Ryan Klesko	.15
7	Raul Mondesi	.15
8	Hideo Nomo	.25
9	Manny Ramirez	.40
10	Rondell White	.15

Golden Prospects, Series 1

#	Player	NM/M
	Complete Set (10):	7.00
	Common Player:	.25
	Gold Medallions:	2X
1	Yamil Benitez	.25
2	Alberto Castillo	.25
3	Roger Cedeno	.25
4	Johnny Damon	1.00
5	Micah Franklin	.25
6	Jason Giambi	1.00
7	Jose Herrera	.25
8	Derek Jeter	5.00
9	Kevin Jordan	.25
10	Ruben Rivera	.25

Golden Prospects, Series 2

#	Player	NM/M
	Complete Set (15):	10.00
	Common Player:	1.00
	Gold Medallions:	2X
1	Bob Abreu	1.50
2	Israel Alcantara	1.00
3	Tony Batista	1.00
4	Mike Cameron	1.00
5	Steve Cox	1.00
6	Jermaine Dye	1.00
7	Wilton Guerrero	1.00
8	Richard Hidalgo	1.00
9	Raul Ibanez	1.00
10	Marty Janzen	1.00
11	Robin Jennings	1.00
12	Jason Maxwell	1.00
13	Scott McClain	1.00
14	Wonderful Monds	1.00
15	Chris Singleton	1.00

Hitting Machines

#	Player	NM/M
	Complete Set (10):	35.00
	Common Player:	2.00
	Gold Medallion:	2X
1	Albert Belle	2.00
2	Barry Bonds	12.00
3	Juan Gonzalez	2.50
4	Ken Griffey Jr.	6.00
5	Edgar Martinez	2.00
6	Rafael Palmeiro	3.00
7	Mike Piazza	6.00
8	Tim Salmon	2.00
9	Frank Thomas	4.00
10	Matt Williams	2.00

Home Run Kings

#	Player	NM/M
	Complete Set (12):	50.00
	Common Player:	2.50
	Gold Medallions:	2X
1	Albert Belle	2.50
2	Dante Bichette	2.50
3	Barry Bonds	12.50
4	Jose Canseco	5.00
5	Juan Gonzalez	3.00
6	Ken Griffey Jr.	9.00
7	Mark McGwire	10.00
8	Manny Ramirez	6.50
9	Tim Salmon	2.50
10	Frank Thomas	6.50
11	Mo Vaughn	2.50
12	Matt Williams	2.50

On-Base Leaders

#	Player	NM/M
	Complete Set (10):	4.50
	Common Player:	.25
	Gold Medallion:	2X
1	Wade Boggs	.75
2	Barry Bonds	2.00
3	Tony Gwynn	.75
4	Rickey Henderson	.60
5	Chuck Knoblauch	.25
6	Edgar Martinez	.25
7	Mike Piazza	1.00
8	Tim Salmon	.25
9	Frank Thomas	.60
10	Jim Thome	.50

Power Plus

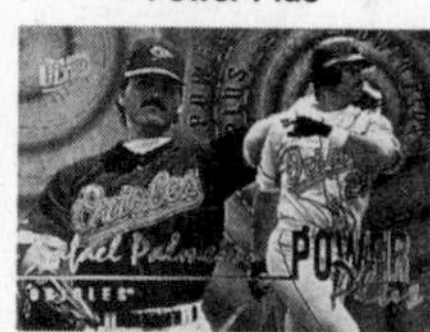

#	Player	NM/M
	Complete Set (12):	10.00
	Common Player:	.40
	Gold Medallions:	2X
1	Jeff Bagwell	1.25
2	Barry Bonds	3.00
3	Ken Griffey Jr.	2.00
4	Raul Mondesi	.40
5	Rafael Palmeiro	1.00
6	Mike Piazza	2.00
7	Manny Ramirez	1.25
8	Tim Salmon	.40
9	Reggie Sanders	.40
10	Frank Thomas	1.25
11	Larry Walker	.40
12	Matt Williams	.40

Prime Leather

#	Player	NM/M
	Complete Set (18):	17.50
	Common Player:	.50
	Gold Medallions:	2X
1	Ivan Rodriguez	1.50
2	Will Clark	.50
3	Roberto Alomar	.65
4	Cal Ripken Jr.	4.00
5	Wade Boggs	2.00
6	Ken Griffey Jr.	2.50
7	Kenny Lofton	.50
8	Kirby Puckett	2.00
9	Tim Salmon	.65
10	Mike Piazza	2.50
11	Mark Grace	.50
12	Craig Biggio	.50
13	Barry Larkin	.50
14	Matt Williams	.50
15	Barry Bonds	4.00
16	Tony Gwynn	2.00
17	Brian McRae	.50
18	Raul Mondesi	.50

R-E-S-P-E-C-T

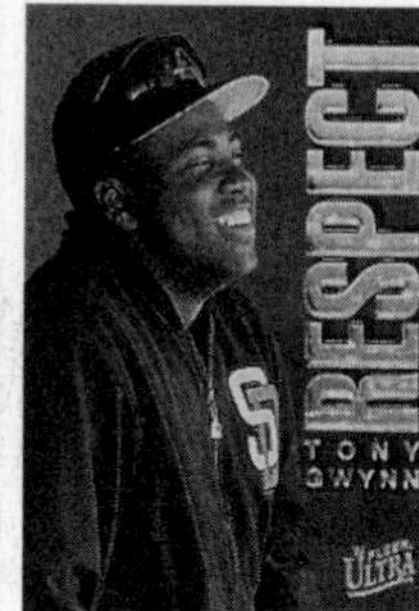

#	Player	NM/M
	Complete Set (10):	20.00
	Common Player:	.50
	Gold Medallion:	2X
1	Joe Carter	.50
2	Ken Griffey Jr.	3.00
3	Tony Gwynn	2.50
4	Greg Maddux	2.50
5	Eddie Murray	2.00
6	Kirby Puckett	2.50
7	Cal Ripken Jr.	5.00
8	Ryne Sandberg	2.50
9	Frank Thomas	2.00
10	Mo Vaughn	.50

Rawhide

#	Player	NM/M
	Complete Set (10):	10.00
	Common Player:	.45
	Gold Medallion:	2X
1	Roberto Alomar	.65
2	Barry Bonds	3.00
3	Mark Grace	.45
4	Ken Griffey Jr.	1.50
5	Kenny Lofton	.45
6	Greg Maddux	1.00
7	Raul Mondesi	.45
8	Mike Piazza	1.50
9	Cal Ripken Jr.	3.00
10	Matt Williams	.45

Rising Stars

#	Player	NM/M
	Complete Set (10):	4.00
	Common Player:	.20
	Gold Medallion:	2X
1	Garret Anderson	.20
2	Marty Cordova	.20
3	Jim Edmonds	.35
4	Cliff Floyd	.20
5	Brian Hunter	.20
6	Chipper Jones	2.00
7	Ryan Klesko	.20
8	Hideo Nomo	.65
9	Manny Ramirez	1.25
10	Rondell White	.20

RBI Kings

		NM/M
Complete Set (10):		4.00
Common Player:		.10
Gold Medallions:		2X
1	Derek Bell	.10
2	Albert Belle	.10
3	Dante Bichette	.10
4	Barry Bonds	2.00
5	Jim Edmonds	.15
6	Manny Ramirez	1.00
7	Reggie Sanders	.10
8	Sammy Sosa	1.50
9	Frank Thomas	1.00
10	Mo Vaughn	.10

Season Crowns

		NM/M
Complete Set (10):		12.50
Common Player:		.75
Gold Medallions:		2X
1	Barry Bonds	4.00
2	Tony Gwynn	2.00
3	Randy Johnson	1.25
4	Kenny Lofton	.75
5	Greg Maddux	2.00
6	Edgar Martinez	.75
7	Hideo Nomo	1.00
8	Cal Ripken Jr.	4.00
9	Frank Thomas	1.25
10	Tim Wakefield	.75

Thunderclap

		NM/M
Complete Set (20):		45.00
Common Player:		1.00
Gold Medallion:		2X
1	Albert Belle	1.00
2	Barry Bonds	7.50
3	Bobby Bonilla	1.00
4	Jose Canseco	1.50
5	Joe Carter	1.00
6	Will Clark	1.00
7	Andre Dawson	1.50
8	Cecil Fielder	1.00
9	Andres Galarraga	1.00
10	Juan Gonzalez	1.50
11	Ken Griffey Jr.	5.00
12	Fred McGriff	1.00
13	Mark McGwire	6.00
14	Eddie Murray	2.50
15	Rafael Palmeiro	2.00
16	Kirby Puckett	4.00
17	Cal Ripken Jr.	7.50
18	Ryne Sandberg	4.00
19	Frank Thomas	2.50
20	Matt Williams	1.00

Diamond Dust

	NM/M
Cal Ripken Jr. (numbered)	40.00
Cal Ripken Jr. (unnumbered)	20.00

1997 ULTRA

		NM/M
Complete Set (553):		30.00
Common Player:		.05
Series 1 or 2 Pack (10):		1.25
Series 1 or 2 Wax Box (24):		20.00
1	Roberto Alomar	.25
2	Brady Anderson	.05
3	Rocky Coppinger	.05
4	Jeffrey Hammonds	.05
5	Chris Hoiles	.05
6	Eddie Murray	.75
7	Mike Mussina	.45
8	Jimmy Myers	.05
9	Randy Myers	.05
10	Arthur Rhodes	.05
11	Cal Ripken Jr.	2.50
12	Jose Canseco	.50
13	Roger Clemens	1.25
14	Tom Gordon	.05
15	Jose Malave	.05
16	Tim Naehring	.05
17	Troy O'Leary	.05
18	Bill Selby	.05
19	Heathcliff Slocumb	.05
20	Mike Stanley	.05
21	Mo Vaughn	.05
22	Garret Anderson	.05
23	George Arias	.05
24	Chili Davis	.05
25	Jim Edmonds	.05
26	Darin Erstad	.25
27	Chuck Finley	.05
28	Todd Greene	.05
29	Troy Percival	.05
30	Tim Salmon	.05
31	Jeff Schmidt	.05
32	Randy Velarde	.05
33	Shad Williams	.05
34	Wilson Alvarez	.05
35	Harold Baines	.05
36	James Baldwin	.05
37	Mike Cameron	.05
38	Ray Durham	.05
39	Ozzie Guillen	.05
40	Roberto Hernandez	.05
41	Darren Lewis	.05
42	Jose Munoz	.05
43	Tony Phillips	.05
44	Frank Thomas	.75
45	Sandy Alomar Jr.	.05
46	Albert Belle	.05
47	Mark Carreon	.05
48	Julio Franco	.05
49	Orel Hershiser	.05
50	Kenny Lofton	.05
51	Jack McDowell	.05
52	Jose Mesa	.05
53	Charles Nagy	.05
54	Manny Ramirez	.75
55	Julian Tavarez	.05
56	Omar Vizquel	.05
57	Raul Casanova	.05
58	Tony Clark	.05
59	Travis Fryman	.05
60	Bob Higginson	.05
61	Melvin Nieves	.05
62	Curtis Pride	.05
63	Justin Thompson	.05
64	Alan Trammell	.05
65	Kevin Appier	.05
66	Johnny Damon	.35
67	Keith Lockhart	.05
68	Jeff Montgomery	.05
69	Jose Offerman	.05
70	Bip Roberts	.05
71	Jose Rosado	.05
72	Chris Stynes	.05
73	Mike Sweeney	.05
74	Jeff Cirillo	.05
75	Jeff D'Amico	.05
76	John Jaha	.05
77	Scott Karl	.05
78	Mike Matheny	.05
79	Ben McDonald	.05
80	Matt Mieske	.05
81	Marc Newfield	.05
82	Dave Nilsson	.05
83	Jose Valentin	.05
84	Fernando Vina	.05
85	Rick Aguilera	.05
86	Marty Cordova	.05
87	Chuck Knoblauch	.05
88	Matt Lawton	.05
89	Pat Meares	.05
90	Paul Molitor	.75
91	Greg Myers	.05
92	Dan Naulty	.05
93	Kirby Puckett	1.00
94	Frank Rodriguez	.05
95	Wade Boggs	1.00
96	Cecil Fielder	.05
97	Joe Girardi	.05
98	Dwight Gooden	.05
99	Derek Jeter	2.50
100	Tino Martinez	.05
101	*Ramiro Mendoza*	.05
102	Andy Pettitte	.20
103	Mariano Rivera	.15
104	Ruben Rivera	.05
105	Kenny Rogers	.05
106	Darryl Strawberry	.05
107	Bernie Williams	.05
108	Tony Batista	.05
109	Geronimo Berroa	.05
110	Bobby Chouinard	.05
111	Brent Gates	.05
112	Jason Giambi	.60
113	*Damon Mashore*	.05
114	Mark McGwire	2.00
115	Scott Spiezio	.05
116	John Wasdin	.05
117	Steve Wojciechowski	.05
118	Ernie Young	.05
119	Norm Charlton	.05
120	Joey Cora	.05
121	Ken Griffey Jr.	1.50
122	Sterling Hitchcock	.05
123	Raul Ibanez	.05
124	Randy Johnson	.75
125	Edgar Martinez	.05
126	Alex Rodriguez	2.00
127	Matt Wagner	.05
128	Bob Wells	.05
129	Dan Wilson	.05
130	Will Clark	.05
131	Kevin Elster	.05
132	Juan Gonzalez	.40
133	Rusty Greer	.05
134	Darryl Hamilton	.05
135	Mike Henneman	.05
136	Ken Hill	.05
137	Mark McLemore	.05
138	Dean Palmer	.05
139	Roger Pavlik	.05
140	Ivan Rodriguez	.65
141	Joe Carter	.05
142	Carlos Delgado	.50
143	Alex Gonzalez	.05
144	Juan Guzman	.05
145	Pat Hentgen	.05
146	Marty Janzen	.05
147	Otis Nixon	.05
148	Charlie O'Brien	.05
149	John Olerud	.05
150	Robert Perez	.05
151	Jermaine Dye	.05
152	Tom Glavine	.30
153	Andruw Jones	.75
154	Chipper Jones	1.00
155	Ryan Klesko	.05
156	Javier Lopez	.05
157	Greg Maddux	1.00
158	Fred McGriff	.05
159	Wonderful Monds	.05
160	John Smoltz	.05
161	Terrell Wade	.05
162	Mark Wohlers	.05
163	Brant Brown	.05
164	Mark Grace	.05
165	Tyler Houston	.05
166	Robin Jennings	.05
167	Jason Maxwell	.05
168	Ryne Sandberg	1.00
169	Sammy Sosa	1.00
170	Amaury Telemaco	.05
171	Steve Trachsel	.05
172	*Pedro Valdes*	.05
173	Tim Belk	.05
174	Bret Boone	.05
175	Jeff Brantley	.05
176	Eric Davis	.05
177	Barry Larkin	.05
178	Chad Mottola	.05
179	Mark Portugal	.05
180	Reggie Sanders	.05
181	John Smiley	.05
182	Eddie Taubensee	.05
183	Dante Bichette	.05
184	Ellis Burks	.05
185	Andres Galarraga	.05
186	Curt Leskanic	.05
187	Quinton McCracken	.05
188	Jeff Reed	.05
189	Kevin Ritz	.05
190	Walt Weiss	.05
191	Jamey Wright	.05
192	Eric Young	.05
193	Kevin Brown	.05
194	Luis Castillo	.05
195	Jeff Conine	.05
196	Andre Dawson	.25
197	Charles Johnson	.05
198	Al Leiter	.05
199	Ralph Milliard	.05
200	Robb Nen	.05
201	Edgar Renteria	.05
202	Gary Sheffield	.40
203	Bob Abreu	.10
204	Jeff Bagwell	.75
205	Derek Bell	.05
206	Sean Berry	.05
207	Richard Hidalgo	.05
208	Todd Jones	.05
209	Darryl Kile	.05
210	Orlando Miller	.05
211	Shane Reynolds	.05
212	Billy Wagner	.05
213	Donne Wall	.05
214	Roger Cedeno	.05
215	Greg Gagne	.05
216	Karim Garcia	.10
217	Wilton Guerrero	.05
218	Todd Hollandsworth	.05
219	Ramon Martinez	.05
220	Raul Mondesi	.05
221	Hideo Nomo	.40
222	Chan Ho Park	.05
223	Mike Piazza	1.50
224	Ismael Valdes	.05
225	Moises Alou	.05
226	Derek Aucoin	.05
227	Yamil Benitez	.05
228	Jeff Fassero	.05
229	Darrin Fletcher	.05
230	Mark Grudzielanek	.05
231	Barry Manuel	.05
232	Pedro Martinez	.75
233	Henry Rodriguez	.05
234	Ugueth Urbina	.05
235	Rondell White	.05
236	Carlos Baerga	.05
237	John Franco	.05
238	Bernard Gilkey	.05
239	Todd Hundley	.05
240	Butch Huskey	.05
241	Jason Isringhausen	.05
242	Lance Johnson	.05
243	Bobby Jones	.05
244	Alex Ochoa	.05
245	Rey Ordonez	.05
246	Paul Wilson	.05
247	Ron Blazier	.05
248	David Doster	.05
249	Jim Eisenreich	.05
250	Mike Grace	.05
251	Mike Lieberthal	.05
252	Wendell Magee	.05
253	Mickey Morandini	.05
254	Ricky Otero	.05
255	Scott Rolen	.60
256	Curt Schilling	.20
257	Todd Zeile	.05
258	Jermaine Allensworth	.05
259	Trey Beamon	.05
260	Carlos Garcia	.05
261	Mark Johnson	.05
262	Jason Kendall	.05
263	Jeff King	.05
264	Al Martin	.05
265	Denny Neagle	.05
266	Matt Ruebel	.05
267	*Marc Wilkins*	.05
268	Alan Benes	.05
269	Dennis Eckersley	.65
270	Ron Gant	.05
271	Aaron Holbert	.05
272	Brian Jordan	.05
273	Ray Lankford	.05
274	John Mabry	.05
275	T.J. Mathews	.05
276	Ozzie Smith	1.00
277	Todd Stottlemyre	.05
278	Mark Sweeney	.05
279	Andy Ashby	.05
280	Steve Finley	.05
281	John Flaherty	.05
282	Chris Gomez	.05
283	Tony Gwynn	1.00
284	Joey Hamilton	.05
285	Rickey Henderson	.75
286	Trevor Hoffman	.05
287	Jason Thompson	.05
288	Fernando Valenzuela	.05
289	Greg Vaughn	.05
290	Barry Bonds	2.50
291	Jay Canizaro	.05
292	Jacob Cruz	.05
293	Shawon Dunston	.05
294	Shawn Estes	.05
295	Mark Gardner	.05

296	Marcus Jensen	.05
297	*Bill Mueller*	.35
298	Chris Singleton	.05
299	Allen Watson	.05
300	Matt Williams	.05
301	Rod Beck	.05
302	Jay Bell	.05
303	Shawon Dunston	.05
304	Reggie Jefferson	.05
305	Darren Oliver	.05
306	Benito Santiago	.05
307	Gerald Williams	.05
308	Damon Buford	.05
309	Jeromy Burnitz	.05
310	Sterling Hitchcock	.05
311	Dave Hollins	.05
312	Mel Rojas	.05
313	Robin Ventura	.05
314	David Wells	.05
315	Cal Eldred	.05
316	Gary Gaetti	.05
317	John Hudek	.05
318	Brian Johnson	.05
319	Denny Neagle	.05
320	Larry Walker	.05
321	Russ Davis	.05
322	Delino DeShields	.05
323	Charlie Hayes	.05
324	Jermaine Dye	.05
325	John Ericks	.05
326	Jeff Fassero	.05
327	Nomar Garciaparra	1.00
328	Willie Greene	.05
329	Greg McMichael	.05
330	Damion Easley	.05
331	Ricky Bones	.05
332	John Burkett	.05
333	Royce Clayton	.05
334	Greg Colbrunn	.05
335	Tony Eusebio	.05
336	Gregg Jefferies	.05
337	Wally Joyner	.05
338	Jim Leyritz	.05
339	Paul O'Neill	.05
340	Bruce Ruffin	.05
341	Michael Tucker	.05
342	Andy Benes	.05
343	Craig Biggio	.05
344	Rex Hudler	.05
345	Brad Radke	.05
346	Deion Sanders	.05
347	Moises Alou	.05
348	Brad Ausmus	.05
349	Armando Benitez	.05
350	Mark Gubicza	.05
351	Terry Steinbach	.05
352	Mark Whiten	.05
353	Ricky Bottalico	.05
354	*Brian Giles*	.75
355	Eric Karros	.05
356	Jimmy Key	.05
357	Carlos Perez	.05
358	Alex Fernandez	.05
359	J.T. Snow	.05
360	Bobby Bonilla	.05
361	Scott Brosius	.05
362	Greg Swindell	.05
363	Jose Vizcaino	.05
364	Matt Williams	.05
365	Darren Daulton	.05
366	Shane Andrews	.05
367	Jim Eisenreich	.05
368	Ariel Prieto	.05
369	Bob Tewksbury	.05
370	Mike Bordick	.05
371	Rheal Cormier	.05
372	Cliff Floyd	.05
373	David Justice	.05
374	John Wetteland	.05
375	Mike Blowers	.05
376	Jose Canseco	.50
377	Roger Clemens	1.25
378	Kevin Mitchell	.05
379	Todd Zeile	.05
380	Jim Thome	.60
381	Turk Wendell	.05
382	Rico Brogna	.05
383	Eric Davis	.05
384	Mike Lansing	.05
385	Devon White	.05
386	Marquis Grissom	.05
387	Todd Worrell	.05
388	Jeff Kent	.05
389	Mickey Tettleton	.05
390	Steve Avery	.05
391	David Cone	.05
392	Scott Cooper	.05
393	Lee Stevens	.05
394	Kevin Elster	.05
395	Tom Goodwin	.05
396	Shawn Green	.25
397	Pete Harnisch	.05
398	Eddie Murray	.75
399	Joe Randa	.05
400	Scott Sanders	.05
401	John Valentin	.05
402	Todd Jones	.05
403	Terry Adams	.05
404	Brian Hunter	.05
405	Pat Listach	.05
406	Kenny Lofton	.05
407	Hal Morris	.05
408	Ed Sprague	.05
409	Rich Becker	.05
410	Edgardo Alfonzo	.05
411	Albert Belle	.05
412	Jeff King	.05
413	Kirt Manwaring	.05
414	Jason Schmidt	.05
415	Allen Watson	.05
416	Lee Tinsley	.05
417	Brett Butler	.05
418	Carlos Garcia	.05
419	Mark Lemke	.05
420	Jaime Navarro	.05
421	David Segui	.05
422	Ruben Sierra	.05
423	B.J. Surhoff	.05
424	Julian Tavarez	.05
425	Billy Taylor	.05
426	Ken Caminiti	.05
427	Chuck Carr	.05
428	Benji Gil	.05
429	Terry Mulholland	.05
430	Mike Stanton	.05
431	Wil Cordero	.05
432	Chili Davis	.05
433	Mariano Duncan	.05
434	Orlando Merced	.05
435	Kent Mercker	.05
436	John Olerud	.05
437	Quilvio Veras	.05
438	Mike Fetters	.05
439	Glenallen Hill	.05
440	Bill Swift	.05
441	Tim Wakefield	.05
442	Pedro Astacio	.05
443	Vinny Castilla	.05
444	Doug Drabek	.05
445	Alan Embree	.05
446	Lee Smith	.05
447	Darryl Hamilton	.05
448	Brian McRae	.05
449	Mike Timlin	.05
450	Bob Wickman	.05
451	Jason Dickson	.05
452	Chad Curtis	.05
453	Mark Leiter	.05
454	Damon Berryhill	.05
455	Kevin Orie	.05
456	Dave Burba	.05
457	Chris Holt	.05
458	*Ricky Ledee*	.10
459	Mike Devereaux	.05
460	Pokey Reese	.05
461	Tim Raines	.05
462	Ryan Jones	.05
463	Shane Mack	.05
464	Darren Dreifort	.05
465	Mark Parent	.05
466	Mark Portugal	.05
467	Dante Powell	.05
468	Craig Grebeck	.05
469	Ron Villone	.05
470	Dmitri Young	.05
471	Shannon Stewart	.05
472	Rick Helling	.05
473	Bill Haselman	.05
474	Albie Lopez	.05
475	Glendon Rusch	.05
476	Derrick May	.05
477	Chad Ogea	.05
478	Kirk Reuter	.05
479	Chris Hammond	.05
480	Russ Johnson	.05
481	James Mouton	.05
482	Mike Macfarlane	.05
483	Scott Ruffcorn	.05
484	Jeff Frye	.05
485	Richie Sexson	.05
486	*Emil Brown*	.05
487	Desi Wilson	.05
488	Brent Gates	.05
489	Tony Graffanino	.05
490	Dan Miceli	.05
491	*Orlando Cabrera*	.65
492	*Tony Womack*	.20
493	Jerome Walton	.05
494	Mark Thompson	.05
495	Jose Guillen	.05
496	Willie Blair	.05
497	*T.J. Staton*	.05
498	Scott Kamieniecki	.05
499	Vince Coleman	.05
500	Jeff Abbott	.05
501	Chris Widger	.05
502	Kevin Tapani	.05
503	*Carlos Castillo*	.05
504	Luis Gonzalez	.05
505	Tim Belcher	.05
506	Armando Reynoso	.05
507	Jamie Moyer	.05
508	*Randall Simon*	.05
509	Vladimir Guerrero	.75
510	*Wady Almonte*	.05
511	Dustin Hermanson	.05
512	*Deivi Cruz*	.25
513	Luis Alicea	.05
514	*Felix Heredia*	.15
515	Don Slaught	.05
516	Shigetosi Hasegawa	.05
517	Matt Walbeck	.05
518	*David Arias* (last name actually Ortiz)	35.00
519	*Brady Raggio*	.05
520	Rudy Pemberton	.05
521	Wayne Kirby	.05
522	Calvin Maduro	.05
523	Mark Lewis	.05
524	Mike Jackson	.05
525	Sid Fernandez	.05
526	Mike Bielecki	.05
527	*Bubba Trammell*	.05
528	*Brent Brede*	.05
529	Matt Morris	.05
530	Joe Borowski	.05
531	Orlando Miller	.05
532	Jim Bullinger	.05
533	Robert Person	.05
534	Doug Glanville	.05
535	Terry Pendleton	.05
536	Jorge Posada	.05
537	*Marc Sagmoen*	.05
538	*Fernando Tatis*	.20
539	Aaron Sele	.05
540	Brian Banks	.05
541	Derrek Lee	.50
542	John Wasdin	.05
543	*Justin Towle*	.05
544	Pat Cline	.05
545	Dave Magadan	.05
546	Jeff Blauser	.05
547	Phil Nevin	.05
548	Todd Walker	.05
549	Elieser Marrero	.05
550	Bartolo Colon	.05
551	*Jose Cruz Jr.*	.50
552	Todd Dunwoody	.05
553	*Hideki Irabu*	.25

Gold Medallion Edition

	NM/M
Complete Set (553):	100.00
Common Player:	.25
Stars/Rookies:	3X

(See 1997 Ultra for checklist and base card values.)

Platinum Medallion Edition

	NM/M
Common Player:	2.00
Stars/Rookies:	25X

(See 1997 Ultra for checklist and base card values.)

Baseball Rules!

		NM/M
Complete Set (10):		45.00

Common Player:		.50
1	Barry Bonds	10.00
2	Ken Griffey Jr.	6.00
3	Derek Jeter	10.00
4	Chipper Jones	5.00
5	Greg Maddux	5.00
6	Mark McGwire	7.50
7	Troy Percival	.50
8	Mike Piazza	6.00
9	Cal Ripken Jr.	10.00
10	Frank Thomas	4.00

Diamond Producers

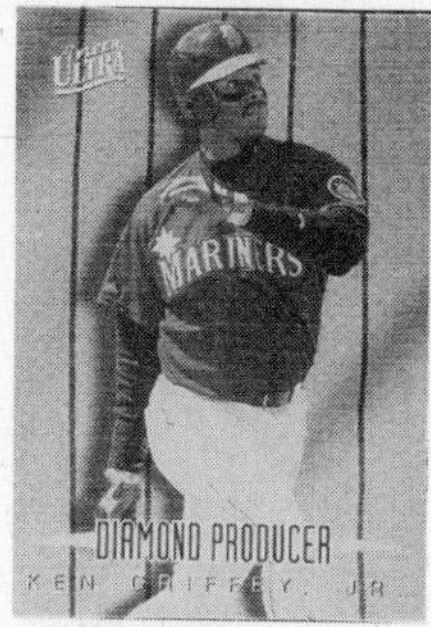

		NM/M
Complete Set (12):		110.00
Common Player:		2.50
1	Jeff Bagwell	7.00
2	Barry Bonds	20.00
3	Ken Griffey Jr.	12.50
4	Chipper Jones	10.00
5	Kenny Lofton	2.50
6	Greg Maddux	10.00
7	Mark McGwire	15.00
8	Mike Piazza	12.50
9	Cal Ripken Jr.	20.00
10	Alex Rodriguez	15.00
11	Frank Thomas	7.50
12	Matt Williams	2.50

Double Trouble

		NM/M
Complete Set (20):		10.00
Common Player:		.15
1	Roberto Alomar, Cal Ripken Jr.	1.50
2	Mo Vaughn, Jose Canseco	.40
3	Jim Edmonds, Tim Salmon	.15
4	Harold Baines, Frank Thomas	.50
5	Albert Belle, Kenny Lofton	.15
6	Chuck Knoblauch, Marty Cordova	.15
7	Andy Pettitte, Derek Jeter	1.50
8	Jason Giambi, Mark McGwire	1.00

9	Ken Griffey Jr., Alex Rodriguez	1.00
10	Juan Gonzalez, Will Clark	.30
11	Greg Maddux, Chipper Jones	.60
12	Mark Grace, Sammy Sosa	.60
13	Dante Bichette, Andres Galarraga	.15
14	Jeff Bagwell, Derek Bell	.50
15	Hideo Nomo, Mike Piazza	.75
16	Henry Rodriguez, Moises Alou	.15
17	Rey Ordonez, Alex Ochoa	.15
18	Ray Lankford, Ron Gant	.15
19	Tony Gwynn, Rickey Henderson	.60
20	Barry Bonds, Matt Williams	1.50

Fame Game

		NM/M
Complete Set (18):		20.00
Common Player:		.35
1	Ken Griffey Jr.	1.75
2	Frank Thomas	1.00
3	Alex Rodriguez	2.00
4	Cal Ripken Jr.	3.00
5	Mike Piazza	1.75
6	Greg Maddux	1.25
7	Derek Jeter	3.00
8	Jeff Bagwell	1.00
9	Juan Gonzalez	.50
10	Albert Belle	.35
11	Tony Gwynn	1.25
12	Mark McGwire	2.00
13	Andy Pettitte	.45
14	Kenny Lofton	.35
15	Roberto Alomar	.40
16	Ryne Sandberg	1.25
17	Barry Bonds	3.00
18	Eddie Murray	1.00

Fielder's Choice

		NM/M
Complete Set (18):		80.00
Common Player:		1.00
1	Roberto Alomar	1.50
2	Jeff Bagwell	6.00
3	Wade Boggs	7.50
4	Barry Bonds	15.00
5	Mark Grace	1.00
6	Ken Griffey Jr.	10.00
7	Marquis Grissom	1.00
8	Charles Johnson	1.00
9	Chuck Knoblauch	1.00
10	Barry Larkin	1.00
11	Kenny Lofton	1.00
12	Greg Maddux	7.50
13	Raul Mondesi	1.00
14	Rey Ordonez	1.00
15	Cal Ripken Jr.	15.00
16	Alex Rodriguez	12.50
17	Ivan Rodriguez	5.00
18	Matt Williams	1.00

Golden Prospects

		NM/M
Complete Set (10):		3.00
Common Player:		.25
1	Andruw Jones	1.50
2	Vladimir Guerrero	1.50
3	Todd Walker	.25
4	Karim Garcia	.25
5	Kevin Orie	.25
6	Brian Giles	.25
7	Jason Dickson	.25
8	Jose Guillen	.25
9	Ruben Rivera	.25
10	Derrek Lee	1.00

Hitting Machines

		NM/M
Complete Set (18):		60.00
Common Player:		1.00
1	Andruw Jones	3.00
2	Ken Griffey Jr.	5.00
3	Frank Thomas	3.00
4	Alex Rodriguez	6.50
5	Cal Ripken Jr.	9.00
6	Mike Piazza	5.00
7	Derek Jeter	9.00
8	Albert Belle	1.00
9	Tony Gwynn	4.00
10	Jeff Bagwell	3.00
11	Mark McGwire	6.50
12	Kenny Lofton	1.00
13	Manny Ramirez	3.00
14	Roberto Alomar	1.25
15	Ryne Sandberg	4.00
16	Eddie Murray	3.00
17	Sammy Sosa	4.00
18	Ken Caminiti	1.00

HR Kings

		NM/M
Complete Set (12):		30.00
Common Player:		1.00
1	Albert Belle	1.00
2	Barry Bonds	7.50
3	Juan Gonzalez	1.50
4	Ken Griffey Jr.	4.50
5	Todd Hundley	1.00
6	Ryan Klesko	1.00
7	Mark McGwire	6.00
8	Mike Piazza	4.50
9	Sammy Sosa	3.50
10	Frank Thomas	2.50
11	Mo Vaughn	1.00
12	Matt Williams	1.00

Leather Shop

		NM/M
Complete Set (12):		9.00
Common Player:		.25
1	Ken Griffey Jr.	1.25
2	Alex Rodriguez	1.50
3	Cal Ripken Jr.	2.00
4	Derek Jeter	2.00
5	Juan Gonzalez	.45
6	Tony Gwynn	1.00
7	Jeff Bagwell	.75
8	Roberto Alomar	.40
9	Ryne Sandberg	1.00
10	Ken Caminiti	.25
11	Kenny Lofton	.25
12	John Smoltz	.25

Power Plus Series 2

		NM/M
Complete Set (12):		6.50
Common Player:		.25
1	Ken Griffey Jr.	.75
2	Frank Thomas	.50
3	Alex Rodriguez	1.00
4	Cal Ripken Jr.	1.50
5	Mike Piazza	.75
6	Chipper Jones	.65
7	Albert Belle	.25
8	Juan Gonzalez	.35
9	Jeff Bagwell	.50
10	Mark McGwire	1.00
11	Mo Vaughn	.25
12	Barry Bonds	1.50

Power Plus Series 1

		NM/M
Complete Set (12):		15.00
Common Player:		.50
1	Jeff Bagwell	.75
2	Barry Bonds	3.00
3	Juan Gonzalez	.60
4	Ken Griffey Jr.	1.50
5	Chipper Jones	1.00
6	Mark McGwire	2.00
7	Mike Piazza	1.50
8	Cal Ripken Jr.	3.00
9	Alex Rodriguez	2.00
10	Sammy Sosa	1.00
11	Frank Thomas	.75
12	Matt Williams	.50

Rookie Reflections

		NM/M
Complete Set (10):		3.50
Common Player:		.25
1	James Baldwin	.25
2	Jermaine Dye	.25
3	Darin Erstad	.40
4	Todd Hollandsworth	.25
5	Derek Jeter	3.00
6	Jason Kendall	.25
7	Alex Ochoa	.25
8	Rey Ordonez	.25
9	Edgar Renteria	.25
10	Scott Rolen	.50

RBI Kings

		NM/M
Complete Set (10):		12.50
Common Player:		.75
1	Jeff Bagwell	1.50
2	Albert Belle	.75
3	Dante Bichette	.75
4	Barry Bonds	4.00
5	Jay Buhner	.75
6	Juan Gonzalez	1.00
7	Ken Griffey Jr.	2.50
8	Sammy Sosa	2.00
9	Frank Thomas	1.50
10	Mo Vaughn	.75

Season Crowns

		NM/M
Complete Set (12):		10.00
Common Player:		.50
1	Albert Belle	.50
2	Dante Bichette	.50
3	Barry Bonds	3.00
4	Kenny Lofton	.50
5	Edgar Martinez	.50
6	Mark McGwire	2.00
7	Andy Pettitte	.50
8	Mike Piazza	1.50
9	Alex Rodriguez	2.00
10	John Smoltz	.50
11	Sammy Sosa	1.25
12	Frank Thomas	1.00

Starring Role

		NM/M
Complete Set (12):		175.00
Common Player:		7.50
1	Andruw Jones	12.00
2	Ken Griffey Jr.	20.00
3	Frank Thomas	12.00
4	Alex Rodriguez	25.00
5	Cal Ripken Jr.	30.00
6	Mike Piazza	20.00
7	Greg Maddux	15.00
8	Chipper Jones	15.00
9	Derek Jeter	30.00
10	Juan Gonzalez	9.00
11	Albert Belle	7.50
12	Tony Gwynn	15.00

Thunderclap

		NM/M
Complete Set (10):		20.00
Common Player:		.75
1	Barry Bonds	5.00
2	Mo Vaughn	.75
3	Mark McGwire	4.00
4	Jeff Bagwell	1.50
5	Juan Gonzalez	1.00
6	Alex Rodriguez	4.00
7	Chipper Jones	2.50
8	Ken Griffey Jr.	3.00
9	Mike Piazza	3.00
10	Frank Thomas	2.00

Top 30

		NM/M
Complete Set (30):		12.00
Common Player:		.20
Gold Medallions:		6X
1	Andruw Jones	.75
2	Ken Griffey Jr.	1.25
3	Frank Thomas	.75
4	Alex Rodriguez	1.50
5	Cal Ripken Jr.	2.00
6	Mike Piazza	1.25
7	Greg Maddux	1.00
8	Chipper Jones	1.00
9	Derek Jeter	2.00
10	Juan Gonzalez	.40
11	Albert Belle	.20
12	Tony Gwynn	1.00
13	Jeff Bagwell	.75
14	Mark McGwire	1.50
15	Andy Pettitte	.30
16	Mo Vaughn	.20
17	Kenny Lofton	.20
18	Manny Ramirez	.75
19	Roberto Alomar	.40
20	Ryne Sandberg	1.00
21	Hideo Nomo	.40
22	Barry Bonds	2.00
23	Eddie Murray	.75
24	Ken Caminiti	.20
25	John Smoltz	.20
26	Pat Hentgen	.20
27	Todd Hollandsworth	.20
28	Matt Williams	.20
29	Bernie Williams	.20
30	Brady Anderson	.20

1998 ULTRA

		NM/M
Complete Set (501):		75.00

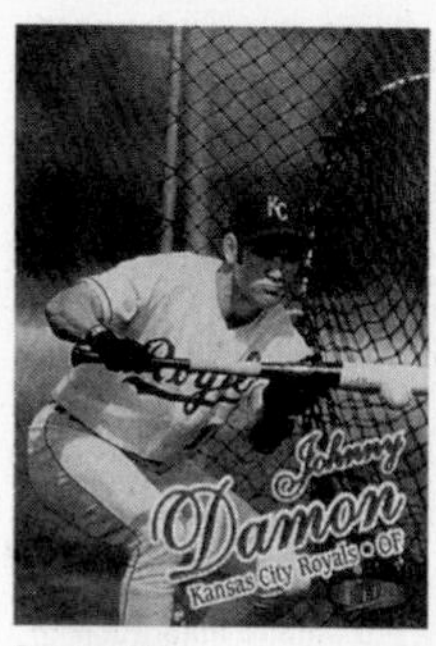

Common Player: .05
Alex Rodriguez Autograph (750): 50.00
Pack (10): 1.25
Wax Box (24): 20.00

1 Ken Griffey Jr. 1.25
2 Matt Morris .05
3 Roger Clemens 1.00
4 Matt Williams .05
5 Roberto Hernandez .05
6 Rondell White .05
7 Tim Salmon .05
8 Brad Radke .05
9 Brett Butler .05
10 Carl Everett .05
11 Chili Davis .05
12 Chuck Finley .05
13 Darryl Kile .05
14 Deivi Cruz .05
15 Gary Gaetti .05
16 Matt Stairs .05
17 Pat Meares .05
18 Will Cunnane .05
19 *Steve Woodard* .15
20 Andy Ashby .05
21 Bobby Higginson .05
22 Brian Jordan .05
23 Craig Biggio .05
24 Jim Edmonds .05
25 Ryan McGuire .05
26 Scott Hatteberg .05
27 Willie Greene .05
28 Albert Belle .05
29 Ellis Burks .05
30 Hideo Nomo .40
31 Jeff Bagwell .75
32 Kevin Brown .05
33 Nomar Garciaparra 1.00
34 Pedro Martinez .75
35 Raul Mondesi .05
36 Ricky Bottalico .05
37 Shawn Estes .05
38 Shawon Dunston .05
39 Terry Steinbach .05
40 Tom Glavine .25
41 Todd Dunwoody .05
42 Deion Sanders .05
43 Gary Sheffield .45
44 Mike Lansing .05
45 Mike Lieberthal .05
46 Paul Sorrento .05
47 Paul O'Neill .05
48 Tom Goodwin .05
49 Andruw Jones .75
50 Barry Bonds 2.00
51 Bernie Williams .05
52 Jeremi Gonzalez .05
53 Mike Piazza 1.25
54 Russ Davis .05
55 Vinny Castilla .05
56 Rod Beck .05
57 Andres Galarraga .05
58 Ben McDonald .05
59 Billy Wagner .05
60 Charles Johnson .05
61 Fred McGriff .05
62 Dean Palmer .05
63 Frank Thomas .75
64 Ismael Valdes .05
65 Mark Bellhorn .05
66 Jeff King .05
67 John Wetteland .05
68 Mark Grace .05
69 Mark Kotsay .05
70 Scott Rolen .60
71 Todd Hundley .05
72 Todd Worrell .05
73 Wilson Alvarez .05
74 Bobby Jones .05
75 Jose Canseco .50
76 Kevin Appier .05
77 Neifi Perez .05
78 Paul Molitor .75
79 Quilvio Veras .05
80 Randy Johnson .75
81 Glendon Rusch .05
82 Curt Schilling .15
83 Alex Rodriguez 1.50
84 Rey Ordonez .05
85 Jeff Juden .05
86 Mike Cameron .05
87 Ryan Klesko .05
88 Trevor Hoffman .05
89 Chuck Knoblauch .05
90 Larry Walker .05
91 Mark McLemore .05
92 B.J. Surhoff .05
93 Darren Daulton .05
94 Ray Durham .05
95 Sammy Sosa 1.00
96 Eric Young .05
97 Gerald Williams .05
98 Javy Lopez .05
99 John Smiley .05
100 Juan Gonzalez .40
101 Shawn Green .30
102 Charles Nagy .05
103 David Justice .05
104 Joey Hamilton .05
105 Pat Hentgen .05
106 Raul Casanova .05
107 Tony Phillips .05
108 Tony Gwynn 1.00
109 Will Clark .05
110 Jason Giambi .50
111 Jay Bell .05
112 Johnny Damon .30
113 Alan Benes .05
114 Jeff Suppan .05
115 *Kevin Polcovich* .05
116 Shigetosi Hasegawa .05
117 Steve Finley .05
118 Tony Clark .05
119 David Cone .05
120 Jose Guillen .05
121 *Kevin Millwood* 1.00
122 Greg Maddux 1.00
123 Dave Nilsson .05
124 Hideki Irabu .05
125 Jason Kendall .05
126 Jim Thome .60
127 Delino DeShields .05
128 Edgar Renteria .05
129 Edgardo Alfonzo .05
130 J.T. Snow .05
131 Jeff Abbott .05
132 Jeffrey Hammonds .05
133 Rich Loiselle .05
134 Vladimir Guerrero .75
135 Jay Buhner .05
136 Jeff Cirillo .05
137 Jeromy Burnitz .05
138 Mickey Morandini .05
139 Tino Martinez .05
140 Jeff Shaw .05
141 Rafael Palmeiro .65
142 Bobby Bonilla .05
143 Cal Ripken Jr. 2.00
144 *Chad Fox* .05
145 Dante Bichette .05
146 Dennis Eckersley .65
147 Mariano Rivera .15
148 Mo Vaughn .05
149 Reggie Sanders .05
150 Derek Jeter 2.00
151 Rusty Greer .05
152 Brady Anderson .05
153 Brett Tomko .05
154 Jaime Navarro .05
155 Kevin Orie .05
156 Roberto Alomar .20
157 Edgar Martinez .05
158 John Olerud .05
159 John Smoltz .05
160 Ryne Sandberg 1.00
161 Billy Taylor .05
162 Chris Holt .05
163 Damion Easley .05
164 Darin Erstad .25
165 Joe Carter .05
166 Kelvim Escobar .05
167 Ken Caminiti .05
168 Pokey Reese .05
169 Ray Lankford .05
170 Livan Hernandez .05
171 Steve Kline .05
172 Tom Gordon .05
173 Travis Fryman .05
174 Al Martin .05
175 Andy Pettitte .25
176 Jeff Kent .05
177 Jimmy Key .05
178 Mark Grudzielanek .05
179 Tony Saunders .05
180 Barry Larkin .05
181 Bubba Trammell .05
182 Carlos Delgado .50
183 Carlos Baerga .05
184 Derek Bell .05
185 Henry Rodriguez .05
186 Jason Dickson .05
187 Ron Gant .05
188 Tony Womack .05
189 Justin Thompson .05
190 Fernando Tatis .05
191 Mark Wohlers .05
192 Takashi Kashiwada .05
193 Garret Anderson .05
194 Jose Cruz, Jr. .05
195 Ricardo Rincon .05
196 Tim Naehring .05
197 Moises Alou .05
198 Eric Karros .05
199 John Jaha .05
200 Marty Cordova .05
201 Travis Lee .10
202 Mark Davis .05
203 Vladimir Nunez .05
204 Stanton Cameron .05
205 *Mike Stoner* .05
206 *Rolando Arrojo* .40
207 Rick White .05
208 Luis Polonia .05
209 Greg Blosser .05
210 Cesar Devarez .05
211 Jeff Bagwell 1.00
212 Barry Bonds 3.00
213 Roger Clemens 1.75
214 Nomar Garciaparra 1.50
215 Ken Griffey Jr. 2.00
216 Tony Gwynn 1.50
217 Randy Johnson 1.00
218 Mark McGwire 3.00
219 Scott Rolen .75
220 Frank Thomas 1.25
221 Matt Perisho .25
222 Wes Helms .25
223 *David Dellucci* .25
224 Todd Helton 1.00
225 Brian Rose .25
226 Aaron Boone .25
227 Keith Foulke .25
228 Homer Bush .25
229 Shannon Stewart .25
230 Richard Hidalgo .25
231 Russ Johnson .25
232 *Henry Blanco* .25
233 Paul Konerko .35
234 Antone Williamson .25
235 *Shane Bowers* .25
236 Jose Vidro .25
237 Derek Wallace .25
238 Ricky Ledee .25
239 Ben Grieve .25
240 Lou Collier .25
241 Derrek Lee .65
242 Ruben Rivera .25
243 Jorge Velandia .25
244 Andrew Vessel .25
245 Chris Carpenter .25
246 Ken Griffey Jr. Checklist .65
247 Andruw Jones Checklist .50
248 Alex Rodriguez Checklist .75
249 Frank Thomas Checklist .60
250 Cal Ripken Jr. Checklist 1.00
251 Carlos Perez .05
252 Larry Sutton .05
253 Brad Rigby .05
254 Wally Joyner .05
255 Todd Stottlemyre .05
256 Nerio Rodriguez .05
257 Jeff Frye .05
258 Pedro Astacio .05
259 Cal Eldred .05
260 Chili Davis .05
261 Freddy Garcia .05
262 Bobby Witt .05
263 Michael Coleman .05
264 Mike Caruso .05
265 Mike Lansing .05
266 Dennis Reyes .05
267 F.P. Santangelo .05
268 Darryl Hamilton .05
269 Mike Fetters .05
270 Charlie Hayes .05
271 Royce Clayton .05
272 Doug Drabek .05
273 James Baldwin .05
274 Brian Hunter .05
275 Chan Ho Park .05
276 John Franco .05
277 David Wells .05
278 Eli Marrero .05
279 Kerry Wood .40
280 Donnie Sadler .05
281 *Scott Winchester* .05
282 Hal Morris .05
283 Brad Fullmer .05
284 Bernard Gilkey .05
285 Ramiro Mendoza .05
286 Kevin Brown .05
287 David Segui .05
288 Willie McGee .05
289 Darren Oliver .05
290 Antonio Alfonseca .05
291 Eric Davis .05
292 Mickey Morandini .05
293 *Frank Catalanotto* .20
294 Derrek Lee .50
295 Todd Zeile .05
296 Chuck Knoblauch .05
297 Wilson Delgado .05
298 Raul Ibanez .05
299 Orel Hershiser .05
300 Ozzie Guillen .05
301 Aaron Sele .05
302 Joe Carter .05
303 Darryl Kile .05
304 Shane Reynolds .05
305 Todd Dunn .05
306 Bob Abreu .10
307 Doug Strange .05
308 Jose Canseco .50
309 Lance Johnson .05
310 Harold Baines .05
311 Todd Pratt .05
312 Greg Colbrunn .05
313 *Masato Yoshii* .25
314 Felix Heredia .05
315 Dennis Martinez .05
316 Geronimo Berroa .05
317 Darren Lewis .05
318 Billy Ripken .05
319 Enrique Wilson .05
320 Alex Ochoa .05
321 Doug Glanville .05
322 Mike Stanley .05
323 Gerald Williams .05
324 Pedro Martinez .75
325 Jaret Wright .05
326 Terry Pendleton .05
327 LaTroy Hawkins .05
328 Emil Brown .05
329 Walt Weiss .05
330 Omar Vizquel .05
331 Carl Everett .05
332 Fernando Vina .05
333 Mike Blowers .05
334 Dwight Gooden .05
335 Mark Lewis .05
336 Jim Leyritz .05
337 Kenny Lofton .05
338 *John Halama* .05
339 Jose Valentin .05
340 Desi Relaford .05
341 Dante Powell .05
342 Ed Sprague .05
343 Reggie Jefferson .05
344 Mike Hampton .05
345 Marquis Grissom .05
346 Heathcliff Slocumb .05
347 Francisco Cordova .05
348 Ken Cloude .05
349 Benito Santiago .05
350 Denny Neagle .05
351 Sean Casey .15
352 Robb Nen .05
353 Orlando Merced .05
354 Adrian Brown .05
355 Gregg Jefferies .05
356 Otis Nixon .05
357 Michael Tucker .05
358 Eric Milton .05
359 Travis Fryman .05
360 Gary DiSarcina .05
361 Mario Valdez .05
362 Craig Counsell .05
363 Jose Offerman .05
364 Tony Fernandez .05
365 Jason McDonald .05
366 Sterling Hitchcock .05
367 Donovan Osborne .05
368 Troy Percival .05
369 Henry Rodriguez .05
370 Dmitri Young .05
371 Jay Powell .05

372	Jeff Conine	.05
373	Orlando Cabrera	.10
374	Butch Huskey	.05
375	*Mike Lowell*	.50
376	Kevin Young	.05
377	Jamie Moyer	.05
378	Jeff D'Amico	.05
379	Scott Erickson	.05
380	*Magglio Ordonez*	1.50
381	Melvin Nieves	.05
382	Ramon Martinez	.05
383	A.J. Hinch	.05
384	Jeff Brantley	.05
385	Kevin Elster	.05
386	Allen Watson	.05
387	Moises Alou	.05
388	Jeff Blauser	.05
389	Pete Harnisch	.05
390	Shane Andrews	.05
391	Rico Brogna	.05
392	Stan Javier	.05
393	David Howard	.05
394	Darryl Strawberry	.05
395	Kent Mercker	.05
396	Juan Encarnacion	.05
397	Sandy Alomar	.05
398	Al Leiter	.05
399	Tony Graffanino	.05
400	Terry Adams	.05
401	Bruce Aven	.05
402	Derrick Gibson	.05
403	Jose Cabrera	.05
404	Rich Becker	.05
405	David Ortiz	.50
406	Brian McRae	.05
407	Bobby Estalella	.05
408	Bill Mueller	.05
409	Dennis Eckersley	.65
410	Sandy Martinez	.05
411	Jose Vizcaino	.05
412	Jermaine Allensworth	.05
413	Miguel Tejada	.20
414	Turner Ward	.05
415	Glenallen Hill	.05
416	Lee Stevens	.05
417	Cecil Fielder	.05
418	Ruben Sierra	.05
419	Jon Nunnally	.05
420	Rod Myers	.05
421	Dustin Hermanson	.05
422	James Mouton	.05
423	Dan Wilson	.05
424	Roberto Kelly	.05
425	Antonio Osuna	.05
426	Jacob Cruz	.05
427	Brent Mayne	.05
428	Matt Karchner	.05
429	Damian Jackson	.05
430	Roger Cedeno	.05
431	Rickey Henderson	.75
432	Joe Randa	.05
433	Greg Vaughn	.05
434	Andres Galarraga	.05
435	Rod Beck	.05
436	Curtis Goodwin	.05
437	Brad Ausmus	.05
438	Bob Hamelin	.05
439	Todd Walker	.05
440	Scott Brosius	.05
441	Lenny Dykstra	.05
442	Abraham Nunez	.05
443	Brian Johnson	.05
444	Randy Myers	.05
445	Bret Boone	.15
446	Oscar Henriquez	.05
447	Mike Sweeney	.05
448	Kenny Rogers	.05
449	Mark Langston	.05
450	Luis Gonzalez	.05
451	John Burkett	.05
452	Bip Roberts	.05
453	Travis Lee	.15
454	Felix Rodriguez	.05
455	Andy Benes	.05
456	Willie Blair	.05
457	Brian Anderson	.05
458	Jay Bell	.05
459	Matt Williams	.05
460	Devon White	.05
461	Karim Garcia	.10
462	Jorge Fabregas	.05
463	Wilson Alvarez	.05
464	Roberto Hernandez	.05
465	Tony Saunders	.05
466	*Rolando Arrojo*	.35
467	Wade Boggs	1.00
468	Fred McGriff	.05
469	Paul Sorrento	.05
470	Kevin Stocker	.05
471	Bubba Trammell	.05
472	Quinton McCracken	.05
473	Ken Griffey Jr. Checklist	.65
474	Cal Ripken Jr. Checklist	1.00
475	Frank Thomas Checklist	.60
476	Ken Griffey Jr.	1.75
477	Cal Ripken Jr.	3.00
478	Frank Thomas	1.25
479	Alex Rodriguez	2.00
480	Nomar Garciaparra	1.50
481	Derek Jeter	3.00
482	Andruw Jones	1.00
483	Chipper Jones	1.50
484	Greg Maddux	1.50
485	Mike Piazza	1.75
486	Juan Gonzalez	.60
487	Jose Cruz	.50
488	Jaret Wright	.50
489	Hideo Nomo	.60
490	Scott Rolen	.65
491	Tony Gwynn	1.50
492	Roger Clemens	1.60
493	Darin Erstad	.50
494	Mark McGwire	2.00
495	Jeff Bagwell	1.00
496	Mo Vaughn	.50
497	Albert Belle	.50
498	Kenny Lofton	.50
499	Ben Grieve	.50
500	Barry Bonds	2.50
501	Mike Piazza	1.50

Gold Medallion

	NM/M
Common Player:	.25
Stars/RCs:	2X
Checklists:	2X
Season Crowns:	1X
Prospects:	1X
Pizzazz:	1X

(See 1998 Ultra for checklist and base card values.)

Platinum Medallion

	NM/M
Common Player:	5.00
Stars/RCs:	25X
Checklists:	25X
Season Crowns:	8X
Prospects:	8X
Pizzazz:	8X

(See 1998 Ultra for checklist and base card values.)

Masterpiece

	NM/M
Common Player:	50.00

(Individual players cannot be priced due to scarcity and fluctuating demand.)

Artistic Talents

		NM/M
Complete Set (18):		12.00
Common Player:		.40
Inserted 1:8		
1	Ken Griffey Jr.	1.00
2	Andruw Jones	.60
3	Alex Rodriguez	1.25
4	Frank Thomas	.60
5	Cal Ripken Jr.	1.50
6	Derek Jeter	1.50
7	Chipper Jones	.75
8	Greg Maddux	.75
9	Mike Piazza	1.00
10	Albert Belle	.40
11	Darin Erstad	.50
12	Juan Gonzalez	.50
13	Jeff Bagwell	.60
14	Tony Gwynn	.75
15	Mark McGwire	1.25
16	Scott Rolen	.50
17	Barry Bonds	1.50
18	Kenny Lofton	.40

Back to the Future

		NM/M
Complete Set (15):		4.00
Common Player:		.10
Inserted 1:6		
1	Andruw Jones	.50
2	Alex Rodriguez	1.00
3	Derek Jeter	1.50
4	Darin Erstad	.25
5	Mike Cameron	.10
6	Scott Rolen	.35
7	Nomar Garciaparra	.75
8	Hideki Irabu	.10
9	Jose Cruz, Jr.	.10
10	Vladimir Guerrero	.50
11	Mark Kotsay	.10
12	Tony Womack	.10
13	Jason Dickson	.10
14	Jose Guillen	.10
15	Tony Clark	.10

Big Shots

		NM/M
Complete Set (15):		4.00
Common Player:		.10
Inserted 1:4		
1	Ken Griffey Jr.	.75
2	Frank Thomas	.35
3	Chipper Jones	.50
4	Albert Belle	.10
5	Juan Gonzalez	.25
6	Jeff Bagwell	.35
7	Mark McGwire	1.00
8	Barry Bonds	1.50
9	Manny Ramirez	.35
10	Mo Vaughn	.10
11	Matt Williams	.10
12	Jim Thome	.30
13	Tino Martinez	.10
14	Mike Piazza	.75
15	Tony Clark	.10

Diamond Producers

		NM/M
Complete Set (15):		180.00
Common Player:		7.50
Inserted 1:288		
1	Ken Griffey Jr.	30.00
2	Andruw Jones	12.50
3	Alex Rodriguez	40.00
4	Frank Thomas	12.50
5	Cal Ripken Jr.	50.00
6	Derek Jeter	50.00
7	Chipper Jones	20.00
8	Greg Maddux	20.00
9	Mike Piazza	30.00
10	Juan Gonzalez	9.00
11	Jeff Bagwell	12.50
12	Tony Gwynn	20.00
13	Mark McGwire	40.00
14	Barry Bonds	50.00
15	Jose Cruz, Jr.	7.50

Diamond Immortals

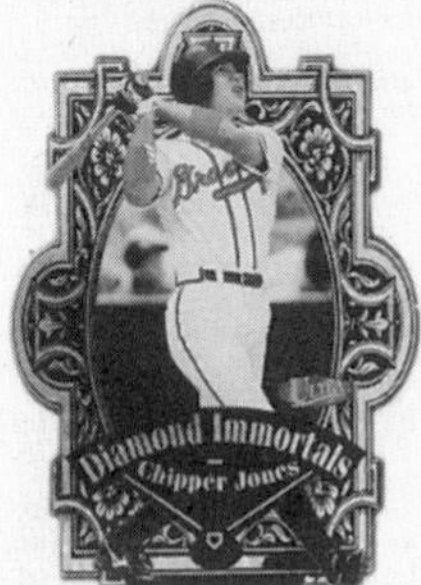

		NM/M
Complete Set (15):		330.00
Common Player:		7.50
Inserted 1:288		
1	Ken Griffey Jr.	30.00
2	Frank Thomas	12.50
3	Alex Rodriguez	40.00
4	Cal Ripken Jr.	50.00
5	Mike Piazza	30.00
6	Mark McGwire	40.00
7	Greg Maddux	20.00
8	Andruw Jones	12.50
9	Chipper Jones	20.00
10	Derek Jeter	50.00
11	Tony Gwynn	20.00
12	Juan Gonzalez	9.00
13	Jose Cruz	7.50
14	Roger Clemens	25.00
15	Barry Bonds	50.00

Double Trouble

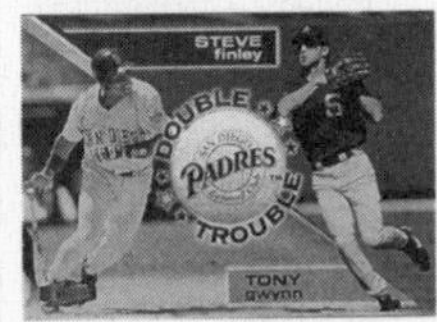

		NM/M
Complete Set (20):		12.00
Common Player:		.15
Inserted 1:4		
1	Ken Griffey Jr., Alex Rodriguez	1.25
2	Vladimir Guerrero, Pedro Martinez	.60
3	Andruw Jones, Kenny Lofton	.60
4	Chipper Jones, Greg Maddux	.65
5	Derek Jeter, Tino Martinez	1.50
6	Frank Thomas, Albert Belle	.60
7	Cal Ripken Jr., Roberto Alomar	1.50
8	Mike Piazza, Hideo Nomo	1.00
9	Darin Erstad, Jason Dickson	.15
10	Juan Gonzalez, Ivan Rodriguez	.25
11	Jeff Bagwell, Darryl Kile	.60
12	Tony Gwynn, Steve Finley	.65

13	Mark McGwire, Ray Lankford	1.00
14	Barry Bonds, Jeff Kent	1.50
15	Andy Pettitte, Bernie Williams	.25
16	Mo Vaughn, Nomar Garciaparra	.65
17	Matt Williams, Jim Thome	.15
18	Hideki Irabu, Mariano Rivera	.25
19	Roger Clemens, Jose Cruz, Jr.	.75
20	Manny Ramirez, David Justice	.60

Fall Classics

		NM/M
Complete Set (15):		35.00
Common Player:		1.00
Inserted 1:18		
1	Ken Griffey Jr.	3.00
2	Andruw Jones	1.50
3	Alex Rodriguez	4.00
4	Frank Thomas	1.50
5	Cal Ripken Jr.	5.00
6	Derek Jeter	5.00
7	Chipper Jones	2.00
8	Greg Maddux	2.00
9	Mike Piazza	4.00
10	Albert Belle	1.00
11	Juan Gonzalez	1.00
12	Jeff Bagwell	1.50
13	Tony Gwynn	2.00
14	Mark McGwire	3.00
15	Barry Bonds	5.00

Kid Gloves

		NM/M
Complete Set (12):		9.00
Common Player:		.25
Inserted 1:8		
1	Andruw Jones	.75
2	Alex Rodriguez	2.00
3	Derek Jeter	3.00
4	Chipper Jones	1.00
5	Darin Erstad	.35
6	Todd Walker	.25
7	Scott Rolen	.65
8	Nomar Garciaparra	1.00
9	Jose Cruz, Jr.	.25
10	Charles Johnson	.25
11	Rey Ordonez	.25
12	Vladimir Guerrero	.75

Millennium Men

		NM/M
Complete Set (15):		30.00
Common Player:		.75
Inserted 1:35		
1	Jose Cruz	.75
2	Ken Griffey Jr.	3.50
3	Cal Ripken Jr.	6.00
4	Derek Jeter	6.00
5	Andruw Jones	2.00
6	Alex Rodriguez	4.50
7	Chipper Jones	2.50
8	Scott Rolen	1.00
9	Nomar Garciaparra	2.50
10	Frank Thomas	2.00
11	Mike Piazza	3.50
12	Greg Maddux	2.50
13	Juan Gonzalez	1.00
14	Ben Grieve	.75
15	Jaret Wright	.75

Notables

		NM/M
Complete Set (20):		13.50
Common Player:		.20
Inserted 1:4		
1	Frank Thomas	.50
2	Ken Griffey Jr.	1.25
3	Edgar Renteria	.20
4	Albert Belle	.20
5	Juan Gonzalez	.30
6	Jeff Bagwell	.50
7	Mark McGwire	1.50
8	Barry Bonds	2.25
9	Scott Rolen	.40
10	Mo Vaughn	.20
11	Andruw Jones	.50
12	Chipper Jones	.75
13	Tino Martinez	.20
14	Mike Piazza	1.25
15	Tony Clark	.20
16	Jose Cruz	.20
17	Nomar Garciaparra	.75
18	Cal Ripken Jr.	2.25
19	Alex Rodriguez	1.50
20	Derek Jeter	2.25

Power Plus

		NM/M
Complete Set (10):		16.00
Common Player:		1.00
Inserted 1:36		
1	Ken Griffey Jr.	4.00
2	Andruw Jones	2.00
3	Alex Rodriguez	3.00
4	Frank Thomas	2.00
5	Mike Piazza	3.00
6	Albert Belle	1.00
7	Juan Gonzalez	1.25
8	Jeff Bagwell	2.00
9	Barry Bonds	5.00
10	Jose Cruz, Jr.	1.00

Prime Leather

		NM/M
Complete Set (18):		135.00
Common Player:		2.00
Inserted 1:144		
1	Ken Griffey Jr.	12.50
2	Andruw Jones	7.50
3	Alex Rodriguez	15.00
4	Frank Thomas	7.50
5	Cal Ripken Jr.	20.00
6	Derek Jeter	20.00
7	Chipper Jones	10.00
8	Greg Maddux	10.00
9	Mike Piazza	12.50
10	Albert Belle	2.00
11	Darin Erstad	3.00
12	Juan Gonzalez	3.00
13	Jeff Bagwell	7.50
14	Tony Gwynn	10.00
15	Roberto Alomar	2.50
16	Barry Bonds	20.00
17	Kenny Lofton	2.00
18	Jose Cruz, Jr.	2.00

Rocket to Stardom

		NM/M
Complete Set (15):		15.00
Common Player:		.75
Inserted 1:20		
1	Ben Grieve	.75
2	Magglio Ordonez	4.00
3	Travis Lee	1.00
4	Carl Pavano	.75
5	Brian Rose	.75
6	Brad Fullmer	.75
7	Michael Coleman	.75
8	Juan Encarnacion	.75
9	Karim Garcia	1.00
10	Todd Helton	7.50
11	Richard Hildalgo	.75
12	Paul Konerko	1.50
13	Rod Myers	.75
14	Jaret Wright	.75
15	Miguel Tejada	1.50

Ticket Studs

		NM/M
Complete Set (15):		150.00
Common Player:		2.50
Inserted 1:144		
1	Travis Lee	3.00
2	Tony Gwynn	12.00
3	Scott Rolen	6.00
4	Nomar Garciaparra	12.00
5	Mike Piazza	15.00
6	Mark McGwire	17.50
7	Ken Griffey Jr.	15.00
8	Juan Gonzalez	5.00
9	Jose Cruz	2.50
10	Frank Thomas	9.00
11	Derek Jeter	20.00
12	Chipper Jones	12.00
13	Cal Ripken Jr.	20.00
14	Andruw Jones	9.00
15	Alex Rodriguez	17.50

Top 30

		NM/M
Complete Set (30):		20.00
Common Player:		.15
Inserted 1:1 R		
1	Barry Bonds	2.00
2	Ivan Rodriguez	.65
3	Kenny Lofton	.15
4	Albert Belle	.15
5	Mo Vaughn	.15
6	Jeff Bagwell	.75
7	Mark McGwire	1.50
8	Darin Erstad	.35
9	Roger Clemens	1.00
10	Tony Gwynn	1.00
11	Scott Rolen	.45
12	Hideo Nomo	.35
13	Juan Gonzalez	.35
14	Mike Piazza	1.25
15	Greg Maddux	1.00
16	Chipper Jones	1.00
17	Andruw Jones	.75
18	Derek Jeter	2.00
19	Nomar Garciaparra	1.00
20	Alex Rodriguez	1.50
21	Frank Thomas	.75
22	Cal Ripken Jr.	2.00
23	Ken Griffey Jr.	1.25
24	Jose Cruz Jr.	.15
25	Jaret Wright	.15
26	Travis Lee	.30
27	Wade Boggs	1.00
28	Chuck Knoblauch	.15
29	Joe Carter	.15
30	Ben Grieve	.15

Win Now

		NM/M
Complete Set (20):		100.00
Common Player:		2.50
Inserted 1:72		
1	Alex Rodriguez	10.00
2	Andruw Jones	4.00
3	Cal Ripken Jr.	12.50
4	Chipper Jones	5.00
5	Darin Erstad	3.00
6	Derek Jeter	12.50
7	Frank Thomas	4.00
8	Greg Maddux	5.00
9	Hideo Nomo	3.00
10	Jeff Bagwell	4.00
11	Jose Cruz	2.50
12	Juan Gonzalez	3.00
13	Ken Griffey Jr.	7.50
14	Mark McGwire	10.00
15	Mike Piazza	7.50
16	Mo Vaughn	2.50
17	Nomar Garciaparra	5.00
18	Roger Clemens	6.00
19	Scott Rolen	3.00
20	Tony Gwynn	5.00

1999 ULTRA

		NM/M
Complete Set (250):		35.00
Common Player:		.05
Common Season Crown:		.25
Inserted 1:8		
Common Prospect:		.25
Inserted 1:4		
Pack (10):		1.50
Wax Box (24):		25.00
1	Greg Maddux	1.00
2	Greg Vaughn	.05
3	John Wetteland	.05
4	Tino Martinez	.05
5	Todd Walker	.05
6	Troy O'Leary	.05
7	Barry Larkin	.05
8	Mike Lansing	.05
9	Delino DeShields	.05
10	Brett Tomko	.05
11	Carlos Perez	.05
12	Mark Langston	.05
13	Jamie Moyer	.05
14	Jose Guillen	.05
15	Bartolo Colon	.05
16	Brady Anderson	.05
17	Walt Weiss	.05
18	Shane Reynolds	.05
19	David Segui	.05
20	Vladimir Guerrero	.75
21	Freddy Garcia	.05
22	Carl Everett	.05

23	Jose Cruz Jr.	.05
24	David Ortiz	.40
25	Andruw Jones	.75
26	Darren Lewis	.05
27	Ray Lankford	.05
28	Wally Joyner	.05
29	Charles Johnson	.05
30	Derek Jeter	2.00
31	Sean Casey	.10
32	Bobby Bonilla	.05
33	Todd Zelle	.05
34	Todd Helton	.65
35	David Wells	.05
36	Darin Erstad	.30
37	Ivan Rodriguez	.65
38	Antonio Osuna	.05
39	Mickey Morandini	.05
40	Rusty Greer	.05
41	Rod Beck	.05
42	Larry Sutton	.05
43	Edgar Renteria	.05
44	Otis Nixon	.05
45	Eli Marrero	.05
46	Reggie Jefferson	.05
47	Trevor Hoffman	.05
48	Andres Galarraga	.05
49	Scott Brosius	.05
50	Vinny Castilla	.05
51	Bret Boone	.05
52	Masato Yoshii	.05
53	Matt Williams	.05
54	Robin Ventura	.05
55	Jay Powell	.05
56	Dean Palmer	.05
57	Eric Milton	.05
58	Willie McGee	.05
59	Tony Gwynn	1.00
60	Tom Gordon	.05
61	Dante Bichette	.05
62	Jaret Wright	.05
63	Devon White	.05
64	Frank Thomas	.75
65	Mike Piazza	1.25
66	Jose Offerman	.05
67	Pat Meares	.05
68	Brian Meadows	.05
69	Nomar Garciaparra	1.00
70	Mark McGwire	1.50
71	Tony Graffanino	.05
72	Ken Griffey Jr.	1.25
73	Ken Caminiti	.05
74	Todd Jones	.05
75	A.J. Hinch	.05
76	Marquis Grissom	.05
77	Jay Buhner	.05
78	Albert Belle	.05
79	Brian Anderson	.05
80	Quinton McCracken	.05
81	Omar Vizquel	.05
82	Todd Stottlemyre	.05
83	Cal Ripken Jr.	2.00
84	Magglio Ordonez	.30
85	John Olerud	.05
86	Hal Morris	.05
87	Derrek Lee	.40
88	Doug Glanville	.05
89	Marty Cordova	.05
90	Kevin Brown	.05
91	Kevin Young	.05
92	Rico Brogna	.05
93	Wilson Alvarez	.05
94	Bob Wickman	.05
95	Jim Thome	.50
96	Mike Mussina	.35
97	Al Leiter	.05
98	Travis Lee	.10
99	Jeff King	.05
100	Kerry Wood	.40
101	Cliff Floyd	.05
102	Jose Valentin	.05
103	Manny Ramirez	.75
104	Butch Huskey	.05
105	Scott Erickson	.05
106	Ray Durham	.05
107	Johnny Damon	.30
108	Craig Counsell	.05
109	Rolando Arrojo	.05
110	Bob Abreu	.05
111	Tony Womack	.05
112	Mike Stanley	.05
113	Kenny Lofton	.05
114	Eric Davis	.05
115	Jeff Conine	.05
116	Carlos Baerga	.05
117	Rondell White	.05
118	Billy Wagner	.05
119	Ed Sprague	.05
120	Jason Schmidt	.05
121	Edgar Martinez	.05
122	Travis Fryman	.05
123	Armando Benitez	.05
124	Matt Stairs	.05
125	Roberto Hernandez	.05
126	Jay Bell	.05
127	Justin Thompson	.05
128	John Jaha	.05
129	Mike Caruso	.05
130	Miguel Tejada	.20
131	Geoff Jenkins	.05
132	Wade Boggs	1.00
133	Andy Benes	.05
134	Aaron Sele	.05
135	Bret Saberhagen	.05
136	Mariano Rivera	.15
137	Neifi Perez	.05
138	Paul Konerko	.15
139	Barry Bonds	2.00
140	Garret Anderson	.05
141	Bernie Williams	.05
142	Gary Sheffield	.40
143	Rafael Palmeiro	.65
144	Orel Hershiser	.05
145	Craig Biggio	.05
146	Dmitri Young	.05
147	Damion Easley	.05
148	Henry Rodriguez	.05
149	Brad Radke	.05
150	Pedro Martinez	.75
151	Mike Lieberthal	.05
152	Jim Leyritz	.05
153	Chuck Knoblauch	.05
154	Darryl Kile	.05
155	Brian Jordan	.05
156	Chipper Jones	1.00
157	Pete Harnisch	.05
158	Moises Alou	.05
159	Ismael Valdes	.05
160	Stan Javier	.05
161	Mark Grace	.05
162	Jason Giambi	.40
163	Chuck Finley	.05
164	Juan Encarnacion	.05
165	Chan Ho Park	.05
166	Randy Johnson	.75
167	J.T. Snow	.05
168	Tim Salmon	.05
169	Brian Hunter	.05
170	Rickey Henderson	.75
171	Cal Eldred	.05
172	Curt Schilling	.25
173	Alex Rodriguez	1.50
174	Dustin Hermanson	.05
175	Mike Hampton	.05
176	Shawn Green	.30
177	Roberto Alomar	.20
178	Sandy Alomar Jr.	.05
179	Larry Walker	.05
180	Mo Vaughn	.05
181	Raul Mondesi	.05
182	Hideki Irabu	.05
183	Jim Edmonds	.05
184	Shawn Estes	.05
185	Tony Clark	.05
186	Dan Wilson	.05
187	Michael Tucker	.05
188	Jeff Shaw	.05
189	Mark Grudzielanek	.05
190	Roger Clemens	1.00
191	Juan Gonzalez	.40
192	Sammy Sosa	1.00
193	Troy Percival	.05
194	Robb Nen	.05
195	Bill Mueller	.05
196	Ben Grieve	.05
197	Luis Gonzalez	.05
198	Will Clark	.05
199	Jeff Cirillo	.05
200	Scott Rolen	.50
201	Reggie Sanders	.05
202	Fred McGriff	.05
203	Denny Neagle	.05
204	Brad Fullmer	.05
205	Royce Clayton	.05
206	Jose Canseco	.50
207	Jeff Bagwell	.75
208	Hideo Nomo	.40
209	Karim Garcia	.15
210	Kenny Rogers	.05
211	Kerry Wood Checklist	.25
212	Alex Rodriguez Checklist	.75
213	Cal Ripken Jr. Checklist	1.00
214	Frank Thomas Checklist	.50
215	Ken Griffey Jr. Checklist	.65
216	Alex Rodriguez	1.00
217	Greg Maddux	.50
218	Juan Gonzalez	.20
219	Ken Griffey Jr.	.75
220	Kerry Wood	.25
221	Mark McGwire	1.00
222	Mike Piazza	.75
223	Rickey Henderson	.40
224	Sammy Sosa	.50
225	Travis Lee	.25
226	Gabe Alvarez	.25
227	Matt Anderson	.25
228	Adrian Beltre	.35
229	Orlando Cabrera	.35
230	Orlando Hernandez	.25
231	Aramis Ramirez	.25
232	Troy Glaus	1.00
233	Gabe Kapler	.25
234	Jeremy Giambi	.25
235	Derrick Gibson	.25
236	Carlton Loewer	.25
237	Mike Frank	.25
238	Carlos Guillen	.25
239	Alex Gonzalez	.25
240	Enrique Wilson	.25
241	J.D. Drew	.75
242	Bruce Chen	.25
243	Ryan Minor	.25
244	Preston Wilson	.35
245	Josh Booty	.25
246	Luis Ordaz	.25
247	George Lombard	.25
248	Matt Clement	.25
249	Eric Chavez	.35
250	Corey Koskie	.30

Gold Medallion

	NM/M
Common Player (1-215):	.25
Stars/RCs 2X	
Season Crowns (216-225):	4X
Prospects (226-250):	3X

(See 1999 Ultra for checklist and base card values.)

Platinum Medallion

	NM/M
Common Player (1-215):	5.00
Stars/RCs:	25X
Season Crowns (216-225):	20X
Prospects (226-250):	6X

(See 1999 Ultra for checklist and base card values.)

Masterpiece

	NM/M
Common Player:	50.00

(Individual player cards cannot be valueddue to scarcity and fluctuating demand.)

Book On

		NM/M
Complete Set (20):		13.50
Common Player:		.25
Inserted 1:6		
1	Kerry Wood	.35
2	Ken Griffey Jr.	1.00
3	Frank Thomas	.65
4	Albert Belle	.25
5	Juan Gonzalez	.35
6	Jeff Bagwell	.65
7	Mark McGwire	1.25
8	Barry Bonds	1.50
9	Andruw Jones	.65
10	Mo Vaughn	.25
11	Scott Rolen	.40
12	Travis Lee	.25
13	Tony Gwynn	.75
14	Greg Maddux	.75
15	Mike Piazza	1.00
16	Chipper Jones	.75
17	Nomar Garciaparra	.75
18	Cal Ripken Jr.	1.50
19	Derek Jeter	1.50
20	Alex Rodriguez	1.25

Damage Inc.

		NM/M
Complete Set (15):		50.00
Common Player:		1.00
Inserted 1:72		
1	Alex Rodriguez	5.00
2	Greg Maddux	3.50
3	Cal Ripken Jr.	7.50
4	Chipper Jones	3.50
5	Derek Jeter	7.50
6	Frank Thomas	2.50
7	Juan Gonzalez	1.50
8	Ken Griffey Jr.	4.00
9	Kerry Wood	1.25
10	Mark McGwire	5.00
11	Mike Piazza	4.00
12	Nomar Garciaparra	3.50
13	Scott Rolen	1.50
14	Tony Gwynn	3.50
15	Travis Lee	1.00

Diamond Producers

		NM/M
Complete Set (10):		140.00
Common Player:		6.00
Inserted 1:288		
1	Ken Griffey Jr.	17.50
2	Frank Thomas	12.00
3	Alex Rodriguez	20.00
4	Cal Ripken Jr.	25.00
5	Mike Piazza	17.50
6	Mark McGwire	20.00
7	Greg Maddux	15.00
8	Kerry Wood	6.00
9	Chipper Jones	15.00
10	Derek Jeter	25.00

RBI Kings

		NM/M
Complete Set (30):		12.00
Common Player:		.15
Inserted 1:1 R		
1	Rafael Palmeiro	.40
2	Mo Vaughn	.15
3	Ivan Rodriguez	.40
4	Barry Bonds	1.25
5	Albert Belle	.15
6	Jeff Bagwell	.45
7	Mark McGwire	1.00
8	Darin Erstad	.25
9	Manny Ramirez	.45
10	Chipper Jones	.60
11	Jim Thome	.40
12	Scott Rolen	.35
13	Tony Gwynn	.60
14	Juan Gonzalez	.25
15	Mike Piazza	.75
16	Sammy Sosa	.60
17	Andruw Jones	.45
18	Derek Jeter	1.25
19	Nomar Garciaparra	.60
20	Alex Rodriguez	1.00
21	Frank Thomas	.45
22	Cal Ripken Jr.	1.25
23	Ken Griffey Jr.	.75
24	Travis Lee	.25
25	Paul O'Neill	.15
26	Greg Vaughn	.15

#	Player	Price
27	Andres Galarraga	.15
28	Tino Martinez	.15
29	Jose Canseco	.30
30	Ben Grieve	.15

Thunderclap

		NM/M
Complete Set (15):		35.00
Common Player:		.75
Inserted 1:36		
1	Alex Rodriguez	4.00
2	Andruw Jones	1.50
3	Cal Ripken Jr.	6.00
4	Chipper Jones	2.50
5	Darin Erstad	.75
6	Derek Jeter	6.00
7	Frank Thomas	1.50
8	Jeff Bagwell	1.50
9	Juan Gonzalez	.75
10	Ken Griffey Jr.	3.00
11	Mark McGwire	4.00
12	Mike Piazza	3.00
13	Travis Lee	.75
14	Nomar Garciaparra	2.50
15	Scott Rolen	1.00

World Premiere

		NM/M
Complete Set (15):		8.00
Common Player:		.50
Inserted 1:18		
1	Gabe Alvarez	.50
2	Kerry Wood	1.50
3	Orlando Hernandez	.60
4	Mike Caruso	.50
5	Matt Anderson	.50
6	Randall Simon	.50
7	Adrian Beltre	.65
8	Scott Elarton	.50
9	Karim Garcia	.60
10	Mike Frank	.50
11	Richard Hidalgo	.50
12	Paul Konerko	.60
13	Travis Lee	.65
14	J.D. Drew	1.50
15	Miguel Tejada	.75

2000 ULTRA

		NM/M
Complete Set (300):		35.00
Common Player:		.10
Common Player (251-300):		.50
Inserted 1:4		
Pack (10):		2.00
Wax Box (24):		35.00
1	Alex Rodriguez	1.50
2	Shawn Green	.25
3	Magglio Ordonez	.25
4	Tony Gwynn	.75
5	Joe McEwing	.10
6	Jose Rosado	.10
7	Sammy Sosa	1.00
8	Gary Sheffield	.25
9	Mickey Morandini	.10
10	Mo Vaughn	.15
11	Todd Hollandsworth	.10
12	Tom Gordon	.10
13	Charles Johnson	.10
14	Derek Bell	.10
15	Kevin Young	.10
16	Jay Buhner	.15
17	J.T. Snow	.10
18	Jay Bell	.10
19	John Rocker	.10
20	Ivan Rodriguez	.40
21	Pokey Reese	.10
22	Paul O'Neill	.20
23	Ronnie Belliard	.10
24	Ryan Rupe	.10
25	Travis Fryman	.20
26	Trot Nixon	.10
27	Wally Joyner	.10
28	Andy Pettitte	.25
29	Dan Wilson	.10
30	Orlando Hernandez	.20
31	Dmitri Young	.10
32	Edgar Renteria	.10
33	Eric Karros	.20
34	Fernando Seguignol	.10
35	Jason Kendall	.20
36	Jeff Shaw	.10
37	Matt Lawton	.10
38	Robin Ventura	.20
39	Scott Williamson	.10
40	Ben Grieve	.10
41	Billy Wagner	.10
42	Javy Lopez	.20
43	Joe Randa	.10
44	Neifi Perez	.10
45	David Justice	.20
46	Ray Durham	.10
47	Dustin Hermanson	.10
48	Andres Galarraga	.20
49	Brad Fullmer	.10
50	Nomar Garciaparra	1.50
51	David Cone	.15
52	David Nilsson	.10
53	David Wells	.10
54	Miguel Tejada	.25
55	Ismael Valdes	.10
56	Jose Lima	.10
57	Juan Encarnacion	.10
58	Fred McGriff	.20
59	Kenny Rogers	.10
60	Vladimir Guerrero	.75
61	Benito Santiago	.10
62	Chris Singleton	.10
63	Carlos Lee	.10
64	Sean Casey	.20
65	Tom Goodwin	.10
66	Todd Hundley	.10
67	Ellis Burks	.10
68	Tim Hudson	.25
69	Matt Stairs	.10
70	Chipper Jones	1.00
71	Craig Biggio	.20
72	Brian Rose	.10
73	Carlos Delgado	.40
74	Eddie Taubensee	.10
75	John Smoltz	.20
76	Ken Caminiti	.15
77	Rafael Palmeiro	.40
78	Sidney Ponson	.10
79	Todd Helton	.50
80	Juan Gonzalez	.50
81	Bruce Aven	.10
82	Desi Relaford	.10
83	Johnny Damon	.20
84	Albert Belle	.15
85	Mark McGwire	1.50
86	Rico Brogna	.10
87	Tom Glavine	.25
88	Harold Baines	.10
89	Chad Allen	.10
90	Barry Bonds	2.00
91	Mark Grace	.25
92	Paul Byrd	.10
93	Roberto Alomar	.40
94	Roberto Hernandez	.10
95	Steve Finley	.10
96	Bret Boone	.20
97	Charles Nagy	.10
98	Eric Chavez	.20
99	Jamie Moyer	.10
100	Ken Griffey Jr.	1.00
101	J.D. Drew	.20
102	Todd Stottlemyre	.10
103	Tony Fernandez	.10
104	Jeromy Burnitz	.10
105	Jeremy Giambi	.10
106	Livan Hernandez	.10
107	Marlon Anderson	.10
108	Troy Glaus	.50
109	Troy O'Leary	.10
110	Scott Rolen	.50
111	Bernard Gilkey	.10
112	Brady Anderson	.15
113	Chuck Knoblauch	.10
114	Jeff Weaver	.10
115	B.J. Surhoff	.10
116	Alex Gonzalez	.10
117	Vinny Castilla	.10
118	Tim Salmon	.20
119	Brian Jordan	.10
120	Corey Koskie	.10
121	Dean Palmer	.10
122	Gabe Kapler	.15
123	Jim Edmonds	.25
124	John Jaha	.10
125	Mark Grudzielanek	.10
126	Mike Bordick	.10
127	Mike Lieberthal	.10
128	Pete Harnisch	.10
129	Russ Ortiz	.10
130	Kevin Brown	.20
131	Troy Percival	.10
132	Alex Gonzalez	.10
133	Bartolo Colon	.10
134	John Valentin	.10
135	Jose Hernandez	.10
136	Marquis Grissom	.10
137	Wade Boggs	.25
138	Dante Bichette	.10
139	Bobby Higginson	.10
140	Frank Thomas	.50
141	Geoff Jenkins	.20
142	Jason Giambi	.50
143	Jeff Cirillo	.10
144	Sandy Alomar Jr.	.10
145	Luis Gonzalez	.20
146	Preston Wilson	.20
147	Carlos Beltran	.10
148	Greg Vaughn	.10
149	Carlos Febles	.10
150	Jose Canseco	.40
151	Kris Benson	.10
152	Chuck Finley	.10
153	Michael Barrett	.10
154	Rey Ordonez	.10
155	Adrian Beltre	.20
156	Andruw Jones	.50
157	Barry Larkin	.20
158	Brian Giles	.20
159	Carl Everett	.10
160	Manny Ramirez	.50
161	Darryl Kile	.10
162	Edgar Martinez	.15
163	Jeff Kent	.20
164	Matt Williams	.20
165	Mike Piazza	1.00
166	Pedro J. Martinez	.75
167	Ray Lankford	.10
168	Roger Cedeno	.10
169	Ron Coomer	.10
170	Cal Ripken Jr.	2.00
171	Jose Offerman	.10
172	Kenny Lofton	.20
173	Kent Bottenfield	.10
174	Kevin Millwood	.20
175	Omar Daal	.10
176	Orlando Cabrera	.20
177	Pat Hentgen	.10
178	Tino Martinez	.20
179	Tony Clark	.10
180	Roger Clemens	1.25
181	Brad Radke	.10
182	Darin Erstad	.20
183	Jose Jimenez	.10
184	Jim Thome	.50
185	John Wetteland	.10
186	Justin Thompson	.10
187	John Hamala	.10
188	Lee Stevens	.10
189	Miguel Cairo	.10
190	Mike Mussina	.40
191	Raul Mondesi	.15
192	Armando Rios	.10
193	Trevor Hoffman	.10
194	Tony Batista	.10
195	Will Clark	.40
196	Brad Ausmus	.10
197	Chili Davis	.10
198	Cliff Floyd	.10
199	Curt Schilling	.25
200	Derek Jeter	2.00
201	Henry Rodriguez	.10
202	Jose Cruz Jr.	.10
203	Omar Vizquel	.20
204	Randy Johnson	.75
205	Reggie Sanders	.10
206	Al Leiter	.10
207	Damion Easley	.10
208	David Bell	.10
209	Fernando Tatis	.10
210	Kerry Wood	.25
211	Kevin Appier	.10
212	Mariano Rivera	.20
213	Mike Caruso	.10
214	Moises Alou	.20
215	Randy Winn	.10
216	Roy Halladay	.20
217	Shannon Stewart	.10
218	Todd Walker	.10
219	Jim Parque	.10
220	Travis Lee	.10
221	Andy Ashby	.10
222	Ed Sprague	.10
223	Larry Walker	.20
224	Rick Helling	.10
225	Rusty Greer	.10
226	Todd Zeile	.10
227	Freddy Garcia	.15
228	Hideo Nomo	.40
229	Marty Cordova	.10
230	Greg Maddux	1.00
231	Rondell White	.20
232	Paul Konerko	.15
233	Warren Morris	.10
234	Bernie Williams	.40
235	Bobby Abreu	.20
236	John Olerud	.25
237	Doug Glanville	.10
238	Eric Young	.10
239	Robb Nen	.10
240	Jeff Bagwell	.50
241	Sterling Hitchcock	.10
242	Todd Greene	.10
243	Bill Mueller	.10
244	Rickey Henderson	.25
245	Chan Ho Park	.10
246	Jason Schmidt	.10
247	Jeff Zimmerman	.10
248	Jermaine Dye	.10
249	Randall Simon	.10
250	Richie Sexson	.40
251	Micah Bowie	.50
252	Joe Nathan	.50
253	Chris Woodward	.50
254	Lance Berkman	.75
255	Ruben Mateo	.50
256	Russell Branyan	.50
257	Randy Wolf	.75
258	A.J. Burnett	.75
259	Mark Quinn	.50
260	Buddy Carlyle	.50
261	Ben Davis	.50
262	Yamid Haad	.50
263	Mike Colangelo	.50
264	Rick Ankiel	.75
265	Jacque Jones	.75
266	Kelly Dransfeldt	.50
267	Matt Riley	.50
268	Adam Kennedy	.50
269	Octavio Dotel	.50
270	Francisco Cordero	.50
271	Wilton Veras	.50
272	Calvin Pickering	.50
273	Alex Sanchez	.50
274	Tony Armas Jr.	.50
275	Pat Burrell	1.00
276	Chad Meyers	.50
277	Ben Petrick	.50
278	Ramon Hernandez	.50
279	Ed Yarnall	.50
280	Erubiel Durazo	.50
281	Vernon Wells	1.00

282	Gary Matthews	.50
283	Kip Wells	.50
284	Peter Bergeron	.50
285	Travis Dawkins	.50
286	Jorge Toca	.50
287	Cole Liniak	.50
288	Chad Hermansen	.50
289	Eric Gagne	.50
290	Chad Hutchinson	.50
291	Eric Munson	.50
292	Wiki Gonzalez	.50
293	Alfonso Soriano	1.50
294	Trent Durrington	.50
295	Ben Molina	.50
296	Aaron Myette	.50
297	Willi Mo Pena	.75
298	Kevin Barker	.50
299	Geoff Blum	.50
300	Josh Beckett	.75

Gold Medallion

Stars:	2X
Inserted 1:1	
Prospects (251-300):	2X to 4X
Inserted 1:24	

(See 2000 Ultra for checklist and base card values.)

Platinum Medallion

	NM/M
Stars:	15X to 30X
Production 50 sets	
Prospects (251-300):	4X to 8X
Production 25 sets	

(See 2000 Ultra for checklist and base card values.)

Masterpiece Edition

(Star card values undetermined because ofunique status.)

Club 3000

	NM/M
Common Player:	3.00
Inserted 1:24	
Wade Boggs	2.00
Tony Gwynn	3.00
Carl Yastrzemski	3.00

Club 3000 Memorabilia

	NM/M
Wade Boggs - bat/250	20.00
Wade Boggs - hat/100	40.00
Wade Boggs - jersey/440	20.00
Wade Boggs - bat, jersey/100	40.00
Wade Boggs - bat, hat, jersey/25	150.00
Tony Gwynn - bat/260	40.00
Tony Gwynn - hat/115	60.00
Tony Gwynn - jersey/450	25.00
Tony Gwynn - bat, jersey/100	65.00
Tony Gwynn - bat, hat, jersey/25	375.00
Carl Yastrzemski - bat/250	40.00
Carl Yastrzemski - hat/100	60.00
Carl Yastrzemski - jersey/440	25.00
Carl Yastrzemski - bat, jersey/100	75.00
Carl Yastrzemski - bat, hat, jersey/25	300.00

Crunch Time

		NM/M
Complete Set (15):		50.00
Common Player:		2.00
Inserted 1:72		
1	Nomar Garciaparra	8.00
2	Ken Griffey Jr.	5.00
3	Mark McGwire	8.00
4	Alex Rodriguez	8.00
5	Derek Jeter	8.00
6	Sammy Sosa	6.00
7	Mike Piazza	5.00
8	Cal Ripken Jr.	10.00
9	Frank Thomas	3.00
10	Juan Gonzalez	3.00
11	J.D. Drew	2.00
12	Greg Maddux	5.00
13	Tony Gwynn	3.00
14	Vladimir Guerrero	3.00
15	Ben Grieve	2.00

Diamond Mine

		NM/M
Complete Set (15):		20.00
Common Player:		1.00
Inserted 1:6		
1	Greg Maddux	1.50
2	Mark McGwire	2.00
3	Ken Griffey Jr.	1.50
4	Cal Ripken Jr.	3.00
5	Nomar Garciaparra	2.50
6	Mike Piazza	2.00
7	Alex Rodriguez	2.50
8	Frank Thomas	1.00
9	Juan Gonzalez	1.00
10	Derek Jeter	2.50
11	Tony Gwynn	1.00
12	Chipper Jones	1.50
13	Sammy Sosa	2.00
14	Roger Clemens	1.50
15	Vladimir Guerrero	1.00

Feel the Game

	NM/M
Common Player:	5.00
Roberto Alomar	10.00
J.D. Drew	5.00
Tony Gwynn/SP	40.00
Randy Johnson	20.00
Greg Maddux	20.00
Edgar Martinez	10.00
Pedro Martinez	20.00
Kevin Millwood	10.00
Cal Ripken Jr.	40.00
Alex Rodriguez	25.00
Scott Rolen	10.00
Curt Schilling	10.00
Chipper Jones	20.00
Frank Thomas/SP	40.00
Robin Ventura	5.00

Fresh Ink

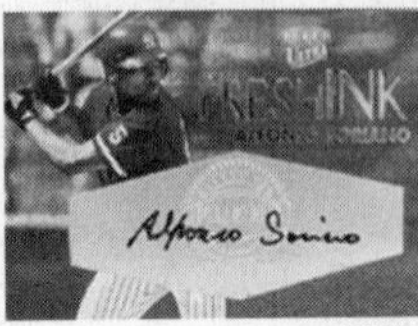

		NM/M
Common Player:		5.00
1	Bobby Abreu (400)	10.00
2	Chad Allen (1,000)	5.00
3	Marlon Anderson (1,000)	5.00
4	Glen Barker (1,000)	5.00
5	Michael Barrett (1,000)	5.00
6	Carlos Beltran (1,000)	15.00
7	Adrian Beltre (1,000)	8.00
8	Wade Boggs (250)	40.00
9	Barry Bonds (250)	150.00
10	Peter Bergeron (1,000)	5.00
11	Pat Burrell (500)	20.00
12	Roger Cedeno (500)	5.00
13	Eric Chavez (750)	10.00
14	Bruce Chen (600)	5.00
15	Johnny Damon (750)	8.00
16	Ben Davis (1,000)	5.00
17	Carlos Delgado (300)	10.00
18	Einar Diaz (1,000)	5.00
19	Octavio Dotel (1,000)	6.00
20	J.D. Drew (600)	8.00
21	Scott Elarton (1,000)	5.00
22	Freddy Garcia (500)	8.00
23	Jeremy Giambi (1,000)	5.00
24	Troy Glaus (500)	20.00
25	Shawn Green (350)	30.00
26	Tony Gwynn (250)	50.00
27	Richard Hidalgo (500)	8.00
28	Bobby Higginson (1,000)	6.00
29	Tim Hudson (1,000)	10.00
30	Norm Hutchins (1,000)	5.00
31	Derek Jeter (95)	200.00
32	Randy Johnson (150)	50.00
33	Gabe Kapler (750)	8.00
34	Jason Kendall (400)	8.00
35	Paul Konerko (500)	8.00
36	Matt Lawton (1,000)	6.00
37	Carlos Lee (1,000)	8.00
38	Jose Macias (1,000)	5.00
39	Greg Maddux (250)	65.00
40	Ruben Mateo (250)	8.00
41	Kevin Millwood (500)	10.00
42	Warren Morris (1,000)	5.00
43	Eric Munson (1,000)	6.00
44	Heath Murray (1,000)	5.00
45	Joe Nathan (1,000)	5.00
46	Magglio Ordonez (350)	10.00
47	Angel Pena (1,000)	5.00
48	Cal Ripken Jr. (350)	125.00
49	Alex Rodriguez (350)	80.00
50	Scott Rolen (250)	35.00
51	Ryan Rupe (1,000)	5.00
52	Curt Schilling (375)	25.00
53	Randall Simon (1,000)	5.00
54	Alfonso Soriano (1,000)	60.00
55	Shannon Stewart (300)	5.00
56	Miguel Tejada (1,000)	25.00
57	Frank Thomas (150)	60.00
58	Jeff Weaver (1,000)	6.00
59	Randy Wolf (1,000)	8.00
60	Ed Yarnall (1,000)	5.00
61	Kevin Young (1,000)	5.00
62	Tony Gwynn, Wade Boggs, Nolan Ryan (100)	450.00
63	Rick Ankiel (500)	5.00

Swing King

		NM/M
Complete Set (10):		20.00
Common Player:		1.00
Inserted 1:24		
1	Cal Ripken Jr.	4.00
2	Nomar Garciaparra	3.00
3	Frank Thomas	1.00
4	Tony Gwynn	1.50
5	Ken Griffey Jr.	2.00
6	Chipper Jones	2.00
7	Mark McGwire	3.00
8	Sammy Sosa	2.50
9	Derek Jeter	3.00
10	Alex Rodriguez	3.00

Ultra Talented

		NM/M
Common Player:		5.00
Production 100 sets		
1	Sammy Sosa	15.00
2	Derek Jeter	20.00
3	Alex Rodriguez	20.00
4	Mike Piazza	15.00
5	Ken Griffey Jr.	15.00
6	Nomar Garciaparra	20.00
7	Mark McGwire	20.00
8	Cal Ripken Jr.	25.00
9	Frank Thomas	8.00
10	J.D. Drew	5.00

World Premiere

		NM/M
Complete Set (10):		5.00
Common Player:		.50
Inserted 1:12		
1	Ruben Mateo	.50
2	Lance Berkman	1.00
3	Octavio Dotel	.50
4	Ben Davis	.50
5	Warren Morris	.50
6	Carlos Beltran	.75
7	Rick Ankiel	.50
8	Adam Kennedy	.50
9	Tim Hudson	1.00
10	Jorge Toca	.50

2001 ULTRA

		NM/M
Complete Set (275):		65.00
Common Player:		.15
Common Prospect (251-275):		1.00
Inserted 1:4		
Pack (10):		3.00
Box (24):		55.00
1	Pedro Martinez	.75
2	Derek Jeter	2.00
3	Cal Ripken Jr.	2.00
4	Alex Rodriguez	1.50
5	Vladimir Guerrero	.75
6	Troy Glaus	.40
7	Sammy Sosa	1.25
8	Mike Piazza	1.00
9	Tony Gwynn	.75
10	Tim Hudson	.25

#	Player	Price
11	John Flaherty	.15
12	Jeff Cirillo	.15
13	Ellis Burks	.15
14	Carlos Lee	.15
15	Carlos Beltran	.25
16	Ruben Rivera	.15
17	Richard Hidalgo	.15
18	Omar Vizquel	.25
19	Michael Barrett	.15
20	Jose Canseco	.40
21	Jason Giambi	.50
22	Greg Maddux	1.00
23	Charles Johnson	.15
24	Sandy Alomar	.15
25	Rick Ankiel	.15
26	Richie Sexson	.40
27	Matt Williams	.25
28	Joe Girardi	.15
29	Jason Kendall	.25
30	Brad Fullmer	.15
31	Alex Gonzalez	.15
32	Rick Helling	.15
33	Mike Mussina	.50
34	Joe Randa	.15
35	J.T. Snow	.15
36	Edgardo Alfonzo	.15
37	Dante Bichette	.15
38	Brad Ausmus	.15
39	Bobby Abreu	.25
40	Warren Morris	.15
41	Tony Womack	.15
42	Russell Branyan	.15
43	Mike Lowell	.15
44	Mark Grace	.40
45	Jeromy Burnitz	.15
46	J.D. Drew	.25
47	David Justice	.25
48	Alex Gonzalez	.15
49	Tino Martinez	.25
50	Raul Mondesi	.25
51	Rafael Furcal	.25
52	Marquis Grissom	.15
53	Kevin Young	.15
54	Jon Lieber	.15
55	Henry Rodriguez	.15
56	Dave Burba	.15
57	Shannon Stewart	.15
58	Preston Wilson	.15
59	Paul O'Neill	.25
60	Jimmy Haynes	.15
61	Darryl Kile	.15
62	Bret Boone	.25
63	Bartolo Colon	.25
64	Andres Galarraga	.25
65	Trot Nixon	.15
66	Steve Finley	.15
67	Shawn Green	.30
68	Robert Person	.15
69	Kenny Rogers	.15
70	Bobby Higginson	.15
71	Barry Larkin	.30
72	Al Martin	.15
73	Tom Glavine	.40
74	Rondell White	.15
75	Ray Lankford	.15
76	Moises Alou	.25
77	Matt Clement	.15
78	Geoff Jenkins	.25
79	David Wells	.15
80	Chuck Finley	.15
81	Andy Pettitte	.25
82	Travis Fryman	.25
83	Ron Coomer	.15
84	Mark McGwire	1.50
85	Kerry Wood	.50
86	Jorge Posada	.40
87	Jeff Bagwell	.50
88	Andruw Jones	.50
89	Ryan Klesko	.25
90	Mariano Rivera	.25
91	Lance Berkman	.25
92	Kenny Lofton	.25
93	Jacque Jones	.15
94	Eric Young	.15
95	Edgar Renteria	.15
96	Chipper Jones	1.00
97	Todd Helton	.50
98	Shawn Estes	.15
99	Mark Mulder	.25
100	Lee Stevens	.15
101	Jermaine Dye	.15
102	Greg Vaughn	.15
103	Chris Singleton	.15
104	Brady Anderson	.15
105	Terrence Long	.15
106	Quilvio Veras	.15
107	Magglio Ordonez	.40
108	Johnny Damon	.25
109	Jeffrey Hammonds	.15
110	Fred McGriff	.25
111	Carl Pavano	.15
112	Bobby Estalella	.15
113	Todd Hundley	.15
114	Scott Rolen	.75
115	Robin Ventura	.25
116	Pokey Reese	.15
117	Luis Gonzalez	.25
118	Jose Offerman	.15
119	Edgar Martinez	.25
120	Dean Palmer	.15
121	David Segui	.15
122	Troy O'Leary	.15
123	Tony Batista	.15
124	Todd Zeile	.15
125	Randy Johnson	.75
126	Luis Castillo	.15
127	Kris Benson	.15
128	John Olerud	.25
129	Eric Karros	.25
130	Eddie Taubensee	.15
131	Neifi Perez	.15
132	Matt Stairs	.15
133	Luis Alicea	.15
134	Jeff Kent	.25
135	Javier Vazquez	.15
136	Garret Anderson	.25
137	Frank Thomas	.50
138	Carlos Febles	.15
139	Albert Belle	.15
140	Tony Clark	.15
141	Pat Burrell	.50
142	Mike Sweeney	.15
143	Jay Buhner	.15
144	Gabe Kapler	.15
145	Derek Bell	.15
146	B.J. Surhoff	.15
147	Adam Kennedy	.15
148	Aaron Boone	.15
149	Todd Stottlemyre	.15
150	Roberto Alomar	.40
151	Orlando Hernandez	.25
152	Jason Varitek	.15
153	Gary Sheffield	.40
154	Cliff Floyd	.15
155	Chad Hermansen	.15
156	Carlos Delgado	.50
157	Aaron Sele	.15
158	Sean Casey	.15
159	Ruben Mateo	.15
160	Mike Bordick	.15
161	Mike Cameron	.15
162	Doug Glanville	.15
163	Damion Easley	.15
164	Carl Everett	.15
165	Bengie Molina	.15
166	Adrian Beltre	.25
167	Tom Goodwin	.15
168	Rickey Henderson	.40
169	Mo Vaughn	.25
170	Mike Lieberthal	.15
171	Ken Griffey Jr.	1.00
172	Juan Gonzalez	.50
173	Ivan Rodriguez	.50
174	Al Leiter	.25
175	Vinny Castilla	.15
176	Peter Bergeron	.15
177	Pedro Astacio	.15
178	Paul Konerko	.15
179	Mitch Meluskey	.15
180	Kevin Millwood	.25
181	Ben Grieve	.15
182	Barry Bonds	2.00
183	Rusty Greer	.15
184	Miguel Tejada	.40
185	Mark Quinn	.15
186	Larry Walker	.25
187	Jose Valentin	.15
188	Jose Vidro	.15
189	Delino DeShields	.15
190	Darin Erstad	.25
191	Bill Mueller	.15
192	Ray Durham	.15
193	Ken Caminiti	.15
194	Jim Thome	.75
195	Javy Lopez	.25
196	Fernando Vina	.15
197	Eric Chavez	.25
198	Eric Owens	.15
199	Brad Radke	.15
200	Travis Lee	.15
201	Tim Salmon	.25
202	Rafael Palmeiro	.50
203	Nomar Garciaparra	1.50
204	Mike Hampton	.15
205	Kevin Brown	.25
206	Juan Encarnacion	.15
207	Danny Graves	.15
208	Carlos Guillen	.15
209	Phil Nevin	.15
210	Matt Lawton	.15
211	Manny Ramirez	.50
212	James Baldwin	.15
213	Fernando Tatis	.15
214	Craig Biggio	.25
215	Brian Jordan	.15
216	Bernie Williams	.40
217	Ryan Dempster	.15
218	Roger Clemens	1.50
219	Jose Cruz Jr.	.15
220	John Valentin	.15
221	Dmitri Young	.15
222	Curt Schilling	.40
223	Jim Edmonds	.30
224	Chan Ho Park	.15
225	Brian Giles	.25
226	Jimmy Anderson	.15
227	Adam Piatt	.15
228	Kenny Kelly	.15
229	Randy Choate	.15
230	Eric Cammack	.15
231	Yovanny Lara	.15
232	Wayne Franklin	.15
233	Cameron Cairncross	.15
234	J.C. Romero	.15
235	Geraldo Guzman	.15
236	Morgan Burkhart	.15
237	Pascual Coco	.15
238	John Parrish	.15
239	Keith McDonald	.15
240	Carlos Casimiro	.15
241	Daniel Garibay	.15
242	Sang-Hoon Lee	.15
243	Hector Ortiz	.15
244	Jeff Sparks	.15
245	Jason Boyd	.15
246	Mark Buehrle	.15
247	Adam Melhuse	.15
248	Kane Davis	.15
249	Mike Darr	.15
250	Vicente Padilla	.15
251	Barry Zito	4.00
252	Tim Drew	1.00
253	Luis Matos	2.00
254	Alex Cabrera	1.00
255	Jon Garland	1.00
256	Milton Bradley	1.50
257	Juan Pierre	2.00
258	Ismael Villegas	1.00
259	Eric Munson	1.00
260	Tomas De La Rosa	1.00
261	Chris Richard	1.00
262	Jason Tyner	1.00
263	B.J. Waszgis	1.00
264	Jason Marquis	1.00
265	Dusty Allen	1.00
266	Corey Patterson	2.00
267	Eric Byrnes	2.00
268	Xavier Nady	2.00
269	George Lombard	1.00
270	Timoniel Perez	1.00
271	Gary Matthews Jr.	1.00
272	Chad Durbin	1.00
273	Tony Armas Jr.	2.00
274	Francisco Cordero	1.00
275	Alfonso Soriano	5.00

Gold Medallion

Stars (1-250): 1-2X
Inserted 1:1
Prospects (251-275): 1-2X
Inserted 1:24

Platinum Medallion

Stars (1-250): 15-25X
Production 50 sets
Prospects (251-275): 5-10X
Production 25 sets

Autographics

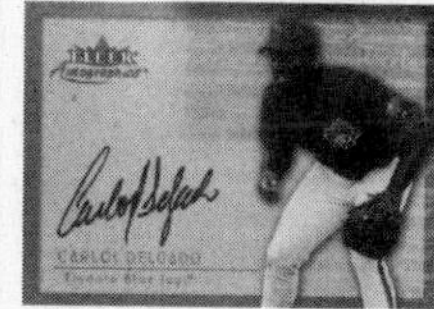

		NM/M
Common Player:		5.00
Inserted 1:48		
Silvers:		1-1.5X
Production 250 sets		
1	Roberto Alomar	30.00
2	Jimmy Anderson	5.00
3	Lance Berkman	8.00
4	Barry Bonds	75.00
5	Roosevelt Brown	5.00
6	Jeromy Burnitz	5.00
7	Pat Burrell	10.00
8	Alex Cabrera	5.00
9	Eric Chavez	10.00
10	Joe Crede	5.00
11	Johnny Damon	8.00
12	Carlos Delgado	10.00
13	Adam Dunn	10.00
14	Jim Edmonds	10.00
15	Chad Green	5.00
16	Dustin Hermanson	5.00
17	Randy Johnson	40.00
18	Corey Lee	5.00
19	Derrek Lee	15.00
20	Terrence Long	5.00
21	Julio Lugo	5.00
22	Edgar Martinez	10.00
23	Justin Miller	5.00
24	Russ Ortiz	5.00
25	Pablo Ozuna	5.00
26	Adam Piatt	5.00
27	Mark Redman	5.00
28	Richie Sexson	10.00
29	Gary Sheffield	10.00
30	Alfonso Soriano	40.00
31	Jose Vidro	8.00
32	Vernon Wells	8.00
33	Preston Wilson	8.00
34	Jamey Wright	5.00
35	Julio Zuleta	5.00

Decade of Dominance

		NM/M
Complete Set (15):		15.00
Common Player:		.50
Inserted 1:8		
1	Barry Bonds	3.00
2	Mark McGwire	2.00
3	Sammy Sosa	2.00
4	Ken Griffey Jr.	1.50
5	Cal Ripken Jr.	3.00
6	Tony Gwynn	1.00
7	Albert Belle	.50
8	Frank Thomas	1.00
9	Randy Johnson	1.00
10	Juan Gonzalez	.75
11	Greg Maddux	1.50
12	Craig Biggio	.50
13	Edgar Martinez	.50
14	Roger Clemens	2.00
15	Andres Galarraga	.50

Fall Classics

		NM/M
Complete Set (37):		150.00
Common Player:		2.00
Inserted 1:20		
1	Jackie Robinson	8.00
2	Enos Slaughter	2.00
3	Mariano Rivera	2.00
4	Hank Bauer	2.00
5	Cal Ripken Jr.	12.00
6	Babe Ruth	15.00
7	Thurman Munson	5.00
8	Tom Glavine	3.00
9	Fred Lynn	2.00
10	Johnny Bench	6.00
11	Tony Lazzeri	2.00

12	Al Kaline	5.00
13	Reggie Jackson	5.00
14	Derek Jeter	10.00
15	Willie Stargell	3.00
16	Roy Campanella	4.00
17	Phil Rizzuto	4.00
18	Roberto Clemente	12.00
19	Carlton Fisk	4.00
20	Duke Snider	4.00
21	Ted Williams	12.00
22	Bill Skowron	2.00
23	Bucky Dent	2.00
24	Mike Schmidt	8.00
25	Lou Brock	3.00
26	Whitey Ford	5.00
27	Brooks Robinson	4.00
28	Roberto Alomar	4.00
29	Yogi Berra	5.00
30	Joe Carter	2.00
31	Bill Mazeroski	2.00
32	Bob Gibson	3.00
33	Hank Greenberg	4.00
34	Andruw Jones	4.00
35	Bernie Williams	3.00
36	Don Larsen	3.00
37	Billy Martin	3.00

Fall Classics Memorabilia

		NM/M
Common Player:		10.00
Inserted 1:288		
1	Jackie Robinson pants	80.00
2	Enos Slaughter bat	15.00
3	Mariano Rivera jersey	15.00
4	Hank Bauer bat	10.00
5	Cal Ripken Jr. jersey	40.00
6	Thurman Munson bat	25.00
7	Tom Glavine jersey	15.00
8	Fred Lynn bat	10.00
9	Babe Ruth bat	200.00
10	Tony Lazzeri bat	10.00
11	Al Kaline jersey	20.00
12	Reggie Jackson jersey	20.00
13	Derek Jeter jersey	40.00
14	Willie Stargell bat	15.00
15	Roy Campanella bat	50.00
16	Phil Rizzuto bat	20.00
17	Roberto Clemente bat	120.00
18	Carlton Fisk jersey	20.00
19	Duke Snider bat	25.00
20	Ted Williams bat	120.00
21	Bill Skowron bat	10.00
22	Bucky Dent bat	10.00
23	Mike Schmidt jersey	40.00
24	Lou Brock jersey	15.00
25	Brooks Robinson bat	20.00
26	Johnny Bench jersey	25.00

Fall Classics Memorabilia Autographs

No pricing due to scarcity

1	Enos Slaughter/9
2	Cal Ripken Jr./8
3	Al Kaline/7
4	Reggie Jackson/44
5	Carlton Fisk/27
6	Mike Schmidt/20

Feel the Game

		NM/M
Common Player:		5.00
Inserted 1:48		
Golds:		2X
Production 50 sets		
1	Moises Alou	5.00
2	Brady Anderson	5.00
3	Adrian Beltre	5.00
4	Carlos Delgado	8.00

5	J.D. Drew	5.00
6	Jermaine Dye	5.00
7	Jason Giambi	8.00
8	Richard Hidalgo	5.00
9	Chipper Jones	10.00
10	Eric Karros	5.00
11	Raul Mondesi	5.00
12	Chan Ho Park	5.00
13	Ivan Rodriguez	8.00
14	Matt Stairs	5.00
15	Frank Thomas	8.00
16	Jose Vidro	5.00
17	Matt Williams	5.00
18	Preston Wilson	5.00

Power Plus

		NM/M
Complete Set (10):		15.00
Common Player:		1.00
Inserted 1:24		
1	Vladimir Guerrero	1.50
2	Mark McGwire	3.00
3	Mike Piazza	2.00
4	Derek Jeter	4.00
5	Chipper Jones	2.00
6	Carlos Delgado	1.00
7	Sammy Sosa	2.00
8	Ken Griffey Jr.	2.00
9	Nomar Garciaparra	2.50
10	Alex Rodriguez	3.00

The Greatest Hits of ...

		NM/M
Complete Set (10):		10.00
Common Player:		.50
Inserted 1:12		
1	Mark McGwire	2.00
2	Alex Rodriguez	2.00
3	Ken Griffey Jr.	1.50
4	Ivan Rodriguez	.75
5	Cal Ripken Jr.	3.00
6	Todd Helton	.75
7	Derek Jeter	3.00
8	Pedro Martinez	1.00
9	Tony Gwynn	1.00
10	Jim Edmonds	.50

Tomorrow's Legends

		NM/M
Complete Set (15):		10.00
Common Player:		.25
Inserted 1:4		
1	Rick Ankiel	.25
2	J.D. Drew	.40
3	Carlos Delgado	.75
4	Todd Helton	.75
5	Andruw Jones	.75
6	Troy Glaus	.75
7	Jermaine Dye	.25
8	Vladimir Guerrero	1.00
9	Brian Giles	.25
10	Scott Rolen	.75
11	Darin Erstad	.40
12	Derek Jeter	3.00
13	Alex Rodriguez	3.00
14	Pat Burrell	.50
15	Nomar Garciaparra	2.00

2002 ULTRA

		NM/M
Complete Set (285):		100.00
Common Player:		.15
Common SP (201-285):		.50
Inserted 1:4		
Pack (10):		2.00
Box (24):		40.00
1	Jeff Bagwell	.50
2	Derek Jeter	2.00

3	Alex Rodriguez	1.50
4	Eric Chavez	.40
5	Tsuyoshi Shinjo	.15
6	Chris Stynes	.15
7	Ivan Rodriguez	.50
8	Cal Ripken Jr.	2.00
9	Freddy Garcia	.15
10	Chipper Jones	.75
11	Hideo Nomo	.40
12	Rafael Furcal	.25
13	Preston Wilson	.15
14	Jimmy Rollins	.15
15	Cristian Guzman	.15
16	Garret Anderson	.40
17	Todd Helton	.50
18	Moises Alou	.25
19	Tony Gwynn	.75
20	Jorge Posada	.40
21	Sean Casey	.25
22	Kazuhiro Sasaki	.15
23	Ray Lankford	.15
24	Manny Ramirez	.50
25	Barry Bonds	2.00
26	Fred McGriff	.25
27	Vladimir Guerrero	.75
28	Jermaine Dye	.15
29	Adrian Beltre	.25
30	Ken Griffey Jr.	1.00
31	Ramon Hernandez	.15
32	Kerry Wood	.75
33	Greg Maddux	1.00
34	Rondell White	.15
35	Mike Mussina	.50
36	Jim Edmonds	.40
37	Scott Rolen	.75
38	Mike Lowell	.25
39	Al Leiter	.25
40	Tony Clark	.15
41	Joe Mays	.15
42	Mo Vaughn	.25
43	Geoff Jenkins	.25
44	Curt Schilling	.50
45	Pedro Martinez	.75
46	Andy Pettitte	.40
47	Tim Salmon	.25
48	Carl Everett	.15
49	Lance Berkman	.25
50	Troy Glaus	.40
51	Ichiro Suzuki	1.00
52	Alfonso Soriano	.75
53	Tomo Ohka	.15
54	Dean Palmer	.15
55	Kevin Brown	.25
56	Albert Pujols	1.50
57	Homer Bush	.15
58	Tim Hudson	.40
59	Frank Thomas	.50
60	Joe Randa	.15
61	Chan Ho Park	.15
62	Bobby Higginson	.15
63	Bartolo Colon	.15
64	Aramis Ramirez	.40
65	Jeff Cirillo	.15
66	Roberto Alomar	.50
67	Mark Kotsay	.15
68	Mike Cameron	.15
69	Mike Hampton	.15
70	Trot Nixon	.15
71	Juan Gonzalez	.50
72	Damian Rolls	.15
73	Brad Fullmer	.15
74	David Ortiz	.25
75	Brandon Inge	.15
76	Orlando Hernandez	.15
77	Matt Stairs	.15
78	Jay Gibbons	.15
79	Greg Vaughn	.15
80	Brady Anderson	.15
81	Jim Thome	.75
82	Ben Sheets	.40
83	Rafael Palmeiro	.50
84	Edgar Renteria	.25
85	Doug Mientkiewicz	.15
86	Raul Mondesi	.15
87	Shane Reynolds	.15
88	Steve Finley	.15
89	Jose Cruz Jr.	.15
90	Edgardo Alfonzo	.15
91	Jose Valentin	.15
92	Mark McGwire	2.00
93	Mark Grace	.40
94	Mike Lieberthal	.15
95	Barry Larkin	.25
96	Chuck Knoblauch	.15
97	Deivi Cruz	.15
98	Jeromy Burnitz	.15
99	Shannon Stewart	.15
100	David Wells	.15
101	Brook Fordyce	.15
102	Rusty Greer	.15
103	Andruw Jones	.50
104	Jason Kendall	.15
105	Nomar Garciaparra	1.25
106	Shawn Green	.25
107	Craig Biggio	.25
108	Masato Yoshii	.15
109	Ben Petrick	.15
110	Gary Sheffield	.40
111	Travis Lee	.15
112	Matt Williams	.25
113	Billy Wagner	.15
114	Robin Ventura	.15
115	Jerry Hairston Jr.	.15
116	Paul LoDuca	.15
117	Darin Erstad	.25
118	Ruben Sierra	.15
119	Ricky Gutierrez	.15
120	Bret Boone	.25
121	John Rocker	.15
122	Roger Clemens	1.50
123	Eric Karros	.15
124	J.D. Drew	.25
125	Carlos Delgado	.40
126	Jeffrey Hammonds	.15
127	Jeff Kent	.25
128	David Justice	.25
129	Cliff Floyd	.15
130	Omar Vizquel	.25
131	Matt Morris	.25
132	Rich Aurilia	.15
133	Larry Walker	.25
134	Miguel Tejada	.25
135	Eric Young	.15
136	Aaron Sele	.15
137	Eric Milton	.15
138	Travis Fryman	.15
139	Magglio Ordonez	.25
140	Sammy Sosa	1.50
141	Pokey Reese	.15
142	Adam Eaton	.15
143	Adam Kennedy	.15
144	Mike Piazza	1.00
145	Larry Barnes	.15
146	Darryl Kile	.15
147	Tom Glavine	.25
148	Ryan Klesko	.15
149	Jose Vidro	.15
150	Joe Kennedy	.15
151	Bernie Williams	.40
152	C.C. Sabathia	.15
153	Alex Ochoa	.15
154	A.J. Pierzynski	.15
155	Johnny Damon	.25
156	Omar Daal	.15
157	A.J. Burnett	.15
158	Eric Munson	.15
159	Fernando Vina	.15
160	Chris Singleton	.15
161	Juan Pierre	.15
162	John Olerud	.25
163	Randy Johnson	.75
164	Paul Konerko	.25
165	Tino Martinez	.25
166	Richard Hidalgo	.15
167	Luis Gonzalez	.25
168	Ben Grieve	.15
169	Matt Lawton	.15
170	Gabe Kapler	.25
171	Mariano Rivera	.25
172	Kenny Lofton	.25
173	Brian Jordan	.15
174	Brian Giles	.25
175	Mark Quinn	.15
176	Neifi Perez	.15
177	Ellis Burks	.15
178	Bobby Abreu	.40
179	Jeff Weaver	.15
180	Andres Galarraga	.25
181	Javy Lopez	.25

No.	Player	Price
182	Todd Walker	.15
183	Fernando Tatis	.15
184	Charles Johnson	.15
185	Pat Burrell	.40
186	Jay Bell	.15
187	Aaron Boone	.15
188	Jason Giambi	.50
189	Jay Payton	.15
190	Carlos Lee	.15
191	Phil Nevin	.15
192	Mike Sweeney	.15
193	J.T. Snow	.15
194	Dmitri Young	.15
195	Richie Sexson	.40
196	Derrek Lee	.25
197	Corey Koskie	.15
198	Edgar Martinez	.25
199	Wade Miller	.15
200	Tony Batista	.15
201	John Olerud	.50
202	Bret Boone	.50
203	Cal Ripken Jr.	3.00
204	Alex Rodriguez	2.50
205	Ichiro Suzuki	2.00
206	Manny Ramirez	.75
207	Juan Gonzalez	.75
208	Ivan Rodriguez	.75
209	Roger Clemens	2.00
210	Edgar Martinez	.50
211	Todd Helton	.75
212	Jeff Kent	.50
213	Chipper Jones	1.00
214	Rich Aurilia	.50
215	Barry Bonds	3.00
216	Sammy Sosa	2.00
217	Luis Gonzalez	.50
218	Mike Piazza	2.00
219	Randy Johnson	1.00
220	Larry Walker	.50
221	Todd Helton, Juan Uribe	.50
222	Pat Burrell, Eric Valent	.50
223	Edgar Martinez, Ichiro Suzuki	2.00
224	Ben Grieve, Jason Tyner	.50
225	Mark Quinn, Dee Brown	.50
226	Cal Ripken Jr., Brian Roberts	3.00
227	Cliff Floyd, Abraham Nunez	.50
228	Jeff Bagwell, Adam Everett	.75
229	Mark McGwire, Albert Pujols	3.00
230	Doug Mientkiewicz, Luis Rivas	.50
231	Juan Gonzalez, Danny Peoples	.75
232	Kevin Brown, Luke Prokopec	.50
233	Richie Sexson, Ben Sheets	.50
234	Jason Giambi, Jason Hart	.75
235	Barry Bonds, Carlos Valderrama	3.00
236	Tony Gwynn, Cesar Crespo	1.00
237	Ken Griffey Jr., Adam Dunn	1.50
238	Frank Thomas, Joe Crede	.75
239	Derek Jeter, Drew Henson	3.00
240	Chipper Jones, Wilson Betemit	1.00
241	Luis Gonzalez, Junior Spivey	.50
242	Bobby Higginson, Andres Torres	.50
243	Carlos Delgado, Vernon Wells	.50
244	Sammy Sosa, Corey Patterson	2.00
245	Nomar Garciaparra, Shea Hillenbrand	2.00
246	Alex Rodriguez, Jason Romano	2.50
247	Troy Glaus, David Eckstein	.75
248	Mike Piazza, Alex Escobar	2.00
249	Brian Giles, Jack Wilson	.50
250	Vladimir Guerrero, Scott Hodges	1.00
251	Bud Smith	1.00
252	Juan Diaz	1.00
253	Wilkin Ruan	1.00
254	*Chris Spurling*	1.00
255	Toby Hall	1.00
256	Jason Jennings	1.00
257	George Perez	1.00
258	D'Angelo Jimenez	1.00
259	Jose Acevedo	1.00
260	Josue Perez	1.00
261	Brian Rogers	1.00
262	Carlos Maldonado	1.00
263	Travis Phelps	1.00
264	Rob Mackowiak	1.50
265	Ryan Drese	1.00
266	Carlos Garcia	1.00
267	Alexis Gomez	1.00
268	Jeremy Affeldt	1.00
269	Scott Podsednik	3.00
270	Adam Johnson	1.00
271	Pedro Santana	1.00
272	Les Walrond	1.00
273	Jackson Melian	1.00
274	Carlos Hernandez	1.00
275	*Mark Nussbeck*	1.00
276	Cory Aldridge	1.00
277	Troy Mattes	1.00
278	Brent Abernathy	1.00
279	J.J. Davis	1.00
280	Brandon Duckworth	1.00
281	Kyle Lohse	1.00
282	Justin Kaye	1.00
283	Cody Ransom	1.00
284	Dave Williams	1.00
285	Luis Lopez	1.00

Gold Medallion

Stars (1-200):	2-3X
Inserted 1:1	
Stars (201-250):	2-4X
Inserted 1:24	
Prospects (251-285):	4-8X
Production 100	

Fall Classic

		NM/M
Complete Set (39):		180.00
Common Player:		2.50
Inserted 1:20		
1FC	Ty Cobb	10.00
2FC	Lou Gehrig	10.00
3FC	Babe Ruth	15.00
4FC	Stan Musial	8.00
5FC	Ted Williams	12.00
6FC	Dizzy Dean	6.00
7FC	Mickey Cochrane	2.50
8FC	Jimmie Foxx	8.00
9FC	Mel Ott	5.00
10FC	Rogers Hornsby	6.00
11FC	Hank Aaron	10.00
12FC	Clete Boyer	2.50
13FC	George Brett	10.00
14FC	Bob Gibson	5.00
15FC	Carlton Fisk	4.00
16FC	Johnny Bench	8.00
17FC	Rusty Staub	2.50
18FC	Willie McCovey	2.50
19FC	Paul Molitor	5.00
20FC	Jim Palmer	4.00
21FC	Frank Robinson	5.00
22FC	Derek Jeter	10.00
23FC	Earl Weaver	2.50
24FC	Lefty Grove	2.50
25FC	Tony Perez	2.50
26FC	Reggie Jackson	5.00
27FC	Sparky Anderson	2.50
28FC	Casey Stengel	2.50
29FC	Roy Campanella	6.00
30FC	Roberto Clemente	10.00
31FC	Don Drysdale	6.00
32FC	Joe Morgan	4.00
33FC	Eddie Murray	5.00
34FC	Nolan Ryan	15.00
35FC	Tom Seaver	8.00
36FC	Bill Mazeroski	2.50
37FC	Jackie Robinson	8.00
38FC	Kirk Gibson	2.50
39FC	Robin Yount	8.00

Fall Classic Game Used

	NM/M
Inserted 1:113	
Sparky Anderson/pants	5.00
Johnny Bench/jersey	15.00
Johnny Bench/pants	10.00
George Brett/bat	15.00
George Brett/ blue jersey/65	45.00
George Brett/ white jersey	15.00
Roy Campanella/ bat/21	225.00
Carlton Fisk/bat/42	35.00
Carlton Fisk/jersey	8.00
Jimmie Foxx/bat	35.00
Bob Gibson/jersey	10.00
Kirk Gibson/bat	5.00
Reggie Jackson/bat	10.00
Reggie Jackson/ jersey/73	20.00
Derek Jeter/pants	30.00
Willie McCovey/jersey	5.00
Paul Molitor/bat	10.00
Paul Molitor/jersey	10.00
Joe Morgan/bat	8.00
Joe Morgan/jersey	8.00
Eddie Murray/bat	10.00
Eddie Murray/jersey/91	35.00
Jim Palmer/ gray jersey/85	20.00
Jim Palmer/white jersey	5.00
Tony Perez/bat	8.00
Frank Robinson/bat/40	25.00
Jackie Robinson/jersey	50.00
Babe Ruth/bat/44	200.00
Nolan Ryan/pants	30.00
Tom Seaver/jersey	10.00
Earl Weaver/jersey	5.00
Ted Williams/bat/30	200.00
Ted Williams/jersey	75.00
Robin Yount/bat	10.00
Robin Yount/ gray jersey	10.00
Robin Yount/ white jersey/30	30.00

Fall Classic Autographs

		NM/M
Common Autograph:		10.00
Inserted 1:240		
1	Sparky Anderson	15.00
2	Johnny Bench SP	40.00
3	George Brett SP	80.00
4	Carlton Fisk	25.00
5	Bob Gibson	25.00
6	Kirk Gibson	15.00
7	Reggie Jackson SP	40.00
8	Derek Jeter SP	
9	Bill Mazeroski	20.00
10	Willie McCovey SP	30.00
11	Joe Morgan	15.00
12	Eddie Murray SP	40.00
13	Stan Musial SP	
14	Jim Palmer	15.00
15	Tony Perez	15.00
16	Frank Robinson	20.00
17	Nolan Ryan SP	175.00
18	Tom Seaver SP	30.00
19	Earl Weaver	10.00
20	Robin Yount SP	50.00

Glove Works

		NM/M
Complete Set (15):		25.00
Common Player:		1.00
Inserted 1:20		
1GW	Andruw Jones	1.50
2GW	Derek Jeter	6.00
3GW	Cal Ripken Jr.	8.00
4GW	Larry Walker	1.00
5GW	Chipper Jones	2.00
6GW	Barry Bonds	6.00
7GW	Scott Rolen	2.00
8GW	Jim Edmonds	1.00
9GW	Robin Ventura	1.00
10GW	Darin Erstad	1.00
11GW	Barry Larkin	1.00
12GW	Raul Mondesi	1.00
13GW	Mark Grace	1.50
14GW	Bernie Williams	1.00
15GW	Ivan Rodriguez	1.50

Glove Works Game Worn

	NM/M
Common Player:	10.00
Production 450 sets	
Platinum (25 sets) randomly inserted	
Derek Jeter	35.00
Andruw Jones/SP/100	
Cal Ripken Jr.	50.00
Chipper Jones/SP/100	
Barry Bonds	40.00
Robin Ventura	10.00
Barry Larkin/SP	15.00
Raul Mondesi	10.00
Ivan Rodriguez	15.00

Hitting Machine

		NM/M
Complete Set (25):		60.00
Common Player:		1.00
Inserted 1:20		
1HM	Frank Thomas	2.00
2HM	Derek Jeter	8.00
3HM	Vladimir Guerrero	3.00
4HM	Jim Edmonds	1.50
5HM	Mike Piazza	5.00
6HM	Ivan Rodriguez	2.00
7HM	Chipper Jones	3.00
8HM	Tony Gwynn	3.00
9HM	Manny Ramirez	2.00
10HM	Andruw Jones	2.00
11HM	Carlos Delgado	1.50
12HM	Bernie Williams	1.50
13HM	Larry Walker	1.00
14HM	Juan Gonzalez	2.00
15HM	Ichiro Suzuki	5.00
16HM	Albert Pujols	6.00
17HM	Barry Bonds	8.00
18HM	Cal Ripken Jr.	8.00
19HM	Edgar Martinez	1.50
20HM	Luis Gonzalez	1.00
21HM	Moises Alou	1.50
22HM	Roberto Alomar	2.00
23HM	Todd Helton	2.00
24HM	Rafael Palmeiro	2.00
25HM	Bobby Abreu	1.50

Hitting Machine Game Worn

	NM/M
Common Player:	8.00
Inserted 1:81	
Platinum (25 sets) randomly inserted	

Frank Thomas	15.00
Derek Jeter	25.00
Jim Edmonds	10.00
Mike Piazza	15.00
Ivan Rodriguez	15.00
Chipper Jones	15.00
Tony Gwynn	15.00
Manny Ramirez	10.00
Andruw Jones	10.00
Carlos Delgado	10.00
Bernie Williams	10.00
Larry Walker	8.00
Juan Gonzalez	10.00
Albert Pujols	30.00
Barry Bonds	25.00
Cal Ripken Jr.	40.00
Edgar Martinez	10.00
Luis Gonzalez	8.00
Moises Alou	10.00
Roberto Alomar	15.00
Todd Helton	15.00
Rafael Palmeiro	10.00
Bobby Abreu	10.00

On the Road Game Used

	NM/M
Common Player:	10.00
Inserted 1:93	
Platinum (25 sets) randomly inserted	
Derek Jeter	30.00
Ivan Rodriguez	10.00
Carlos Delgado	8.00
Larry Walker	8.00
Roberto Alomar	15.00
Tony Gwynn	15.00
Greg Maddux	20.00
Barry Bonds	30.00
Todd Helton	15.00
Kazuhiro Sasaki	10.00
Jeff Bagwell	15.00
Omar Vizquel	8.00
Chan Ho Park	10.00
Tom Glavine	10.00

Rising Stars

		NM/M
Complete Set (15):		15.00
Common Player:		.50
Inserted 1:12		
1RS	Ichiro Suzuki	2.50
2RS	Derek Jeter	4.00
3RS	Albert Pujols	3.00
4RS	Jimmy Rollins	.75
5RS	Adam Dunn	1.00
6RS	Sean Casey	1.00
7RS	Kerry Wood	2.00
8RS	Tsuyoshi Shinjo	.50
9RS	Shea Hillenbrand	.50
10RS	Pat Burrell	1.00
11RS	Ben Sheets	1.00
12RS	Alfonso Soriano	1.50
13RS	J.D. Drew	1.00
14RS	Kazuhiro Sasaki	.50
15RS	Corey Patterson	.75

Rising Stars Game Worn

	NM/M
Common Player:	20.00
Production 100 sets	
Platinum (25 sets) randomly seeded	
Derek Jeter	75.00
Albert Pujols	50.00
Tsuyoshi Shinjo	25.00
Alfonso Soriano	25.00
J.D. Drew	25.00
Kazuhiro Sasaki	20.00

2003 ULTRA

		NM/M
Complete Set (250):		75.00
Common Player:		.15
Common SP (201-250):		.50
Inserted 1:4		
Hobby pack (10):		2.00
Hobby Box (24):		35.00
1	Barry Bonds	2.00
2	Derek Jeter	2.50
3	Ichiro Suzuki	1.50
4	Mike Lowell	.15
5	Hideo Nomo	.50
6	Javier Vazquez	.15
7	Jeremy Giambi	.15
8	Jamie Moyer	.15
9	Rafael Palmeiro	.40
10	Magglio Ordonez	.25
11	Trot Nixon	.15
12	Luis Castillo	.15
13	Paul Byrd	.15
14	Adam Kennedy	.15
15	Trevor Hoffman	.15
16	Matt Morris	.15
17	Nomar Garciaparra	1.50
18	Matt Lawton	.15
19	Carlos Beltran	.15
20	Jason Giambi	1.25
21	Brian Giles	.25
22	Jim Edmonds	.25
23	Garret Anderson	.25
24	Tony Batista	.15
25	Aaron Boone	.15
26	Mike Hampton	.15
27	Billy Wagner	.15
28	Kazuhisa Ishii	.15
29	Al Leiter	.25
30	Pat Burrell	.40
31	Jeff Kent	.25
32	Randy Johnson	.75
33	Ray Durham	.15
34	Josh Beckett	.15
35	Cristian Guzman	.15
36	Roger Clemens	1.25
37	Freddy Garcia	.15
38	Roy Halladay	.15
39	David Eckstein	.15
40	Jerry Hairston Jr.	.15
41	Barry Larkin	.25
42	Larry Walker	.25
43	Craig Biggio	.25
44	Edgardo Alfonzo	.15
45	Marlon Byrd	.15
46	J.T. Snow	.15
47	Juan Gonzalez	.50
48	Ramon Ortiz	.15
49	Jay Gibbons	.15
50	Adam Dunn	.60
51	Juan Pierre	.15
52	Jeff Bagwell	.60
53	Kevin Brown	.15
54	Pedro Astacio	.15
55	Mike Lieberthal	.15
56	Johnny Damon	.15
57	Tim Salmon	.25
58	Mike Bordick	.15
59	Ken Griffey Jr.	1.50
60	Jason Jennings	.15
61	Lance Berkman	.50
62	Jeromy Burnitz	.15
63	Jimmy Rollins	.15
64	Tsuyoshi Shinjo	.15
65	Alex Rodriguez	2.00
66	Greg Maddux	1.25
67	Mark Prior	.40
68	Mike Maroth	.15
69	Geoff Jenkins	.15
70	Tony Armas Jr.	.15
71	Jermaine Dye	.15
72	Albert Pujols	.75
73	Shannon Stewart	.15
74	Troy Glaus	.60
75	Brook Fordyce	.15
76	Juan Encarnacion	.15
77	Todd Hollandsworth	.15
78	Roy Oswalt	.25
79	Paul LoDuca	.15
80	Mike Piazza	1.50
81	Bobby Abreu	.15
82	Sean Burroughs	.15
83	Randy Winn	.15
84	Curt Schilling	.50
85	Chris Singleton	.15
86	Sean Casey	.25
87	Todd Zeile	.15
88	Richard Hidalgo	.15
89	Roberto Alomar	.50
90	Tim Hudson	.25
91	Ryan Klesko	.15
92	Greg Vaughn	.15
93	Tony Womack	.15
94	Fred McGriff	.25
95	Tom Glavine	.40
96	Todd Walker	.15
97	Travis Fryman	.15
98	Shane Reynolds	.15
99	Shawn Green	.25
100	Mo Vaughn	.25
101	Adam Piatt	.15
102	Deivi Cruz	.15
103	Steve Cox	.15
104	Luis Gonzalez	.25
105	Russell Branyan	.15
106	Daryle Ward	.15
107	Mariano Rivera	.25
108	Phil Nevin	.15
109	Ben Grieve	.15
110	Moises Alou	.15
111	Omar Vizquel	.25
112	Joe Randa	.15
113	Jorge Posada	.40
114	Mark Kotsay	.15
115	Ryan Rupe	.15
116	Javy Lopez	.15
117	Corey Patterson	.15
118	Bobby Higginson	.15
119	Jose Vidro	.15
120	Barry Zito	.25
121	Matt Morris	.15
122	Gary Sheffield	.25
123	Kerry Wood	.15
124	Brandon Inge	.15
125	Jose Hernandez	.15
126	Michael Barrett	.15
127	Miguel Tejada	.40
128	Edgar Renteria	.15
129	Junior Spivey	.15
130	Jose Valentin	.15
131	Derrek Lee	.15
132	A.J. Pierzynski	.15
133	Mike Mussina	.50
134	Bret Boone	.15
135	Chan Ho Park	.15
136	Steve Finley	.15
137	Mark Buehrle	.15
138	A.J. Burnett	.15
139	Ben Sheets	.15
140	David Ortiz	.15
141	Nick Johnson	.15
142	Randall Simon	.15
143	Carlos Delgado	.40
144	Darin Erstad	.25
145	Shea Hillenbrand	.15
146	Todd Helton	.40
147	Preston Wilson	.15
148	Eric Gagne	.15
149	Vladimir Guerrero	.75
150	Brandon Duckworth	.15
151	Rich Aurilia	.15
152	Ivan Rodriguez	.50
153	Andruw Jones	.50
154	Carlos Lee	.15
155	Robert Fick	.15
156	Jacque Jones	.15
157	Bernie Williams	.50
158	John Olerud	.25
159	Eric Hinske	.15
160	Matt Clement	.15
161	Dmitri Young	.15
162	Torii Hunter	.15
163	Carlos Pena	.15
164	Mike Cameron	.15
165	Raul Mondesi	.15
166	Pedro J. Martinez	.75
167	Bob Wickman	.15
168	Mike Sweeney	.15
169	David Wells	.15
170	Jason Kendall	.15
171	Tino Martinez	.15
172	Matt Williams	.15
173	Frank Thomas	.60
174	Cliff Floyd	.15
175	Corey Koskie	.15
176	Orlando Hernandez	.15
177	Edgar Martinez	.15
178	Richie Sexson	.25
179	Manny Ramirez	.60
180	Jim Thome	.50
181	Andy Pettitte	.40
182	Aramis Ramirez	.15
183	J.D. Drew	.25
184	Brian Jordan	.15
185	Sammy Sosa	1.25
186	Jeff Weaver	.15
187	Jeffrey Hammonds	.15
188	Eric Milton	.15
189	Eric Chavez	.25
190	Kazuhiro Sasaki	.15
191	Jose Cruz Jr.	.15
192	Derek Lowe	.15
193	C.C. Sabathia	.15
194	Adrian Beltre	.15
195	Alfonso Soriano	1.00
196	Jack Wilson	.15
197	Fernando Vina	.15
198	Chipper Jones	1.25
199	Paul Konerko	.15
200	Rusty Greer	.15
201	Jason Giambi	2.00
202	Alfonso Soriano	2.00
203	Shea Hillenbrand	.50
204	Alex Rodriguez	3.00
205	Jorge Posada	.60
206	Ichiro Suzuki	3.00
207	Manny Ramirez	1.00
208	Torii Hunter	.50
209	Todd Helton	.75
210	Roberto Alomar	.75
211	Scott Rolen	.75
212	Jimmy Rollins	.50
213	Mike Piazza	3.00
214	Barry Bonds	3.00
215	Sammy Sosa	2.00
216	Vladimir Guerrero	1.50
217	Lance Berkman	.75
218	Derek Jeter	4.00
219	Nomar Garciaparra	3.00
220	Luis Gonzalez	.75
221	Kazuhisa Ishii	1.00
222	Satoru Komiyama	.50
223	So Taguchi	.50
224	Jorge Padilla	.50
225	Ben Howard	.50
226	Jason Simontacchi	.50
227	Barry Wesson	.50
228	Howie Clark	.50
229	Aaron Guiel	.50
230	Oliver Perez	.75
231	David Ross	.50
232	Julius Matos	.50
233	Chris Snelling	.50
234	Rodrigo Lopez	.50
235	Wilbert Nieves	.50
236	Brendan Donnelly	.50
237	Aaron Cook	.50
238	Anderson Machado	.50
239	Corey Thurman	.50
240	Tyler Yates	.50
241	Coco Crisp	4.00
242	Andy Van Hekken	1.50
243	Jim Rushford	2.00
244	Jeriome Robertson	1.00
245	Shane Nance	1.00
246	Kevin Cash	.50
247	Kirk Saarloos	1.50
248	Josh Bard	2.00
249	*David Pember*	1.00
250	Freddy Sanchez	1.50

Gold Medallion

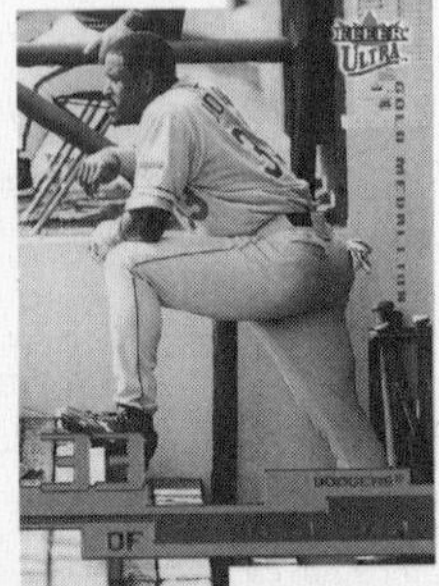

Stars (1-200): 2-3X
Inserted 1:1
Stars (201-220): 3-4X
Inserted 1:24
Rookies (221-250): 1-3X
Inserted 1:24

Back 2 Back

NM/M
Complete Set (17): 60.00
Common Player: 2.00
Production 1,000 sets
1B2B Derek Jeter 10.00
2B2B Barry Bonds 8.00
3B2B Mike Piazza 6.00
4B2B Alex Rodriguez 8.00
5B2B Todd Helton 2.00
6B2B Edgar Martinez 2.00
7B2B Chipper Jones 5.00
8B2B Shawn Green 2.00
9B2B Chan Ho Park 2.00
10B2B Preston Wilson 2.00
11B2B Manny Ramirez 3.00
12B2B Aramis Ramirez 2.00
13B2B Pedro J. Martinez 4.00
14B2B Ivan Rodriguez 2.00
15B2B Ichiro Suzuki 6.00
16B2B Sammy Sosa 5.00
17B2B Jason Giambi 5.00

Back 2 Back Memorabilia

NM/M
Common Player: 5.00
Production 500 sets
Golds: 1.5-3X
Production 50 sets
Derek Jeter
Barry Bonds/bat 20.00
Mike Piazza/jsy 12.00
Alex Rodriguez/jsy 12.00
Todd Helton/jsy 8.00
Edgar Martinez/jsy 6.00
Chipper Jones/jsy 15.00
Shawn Green/jsy 6.00
Chan Ho Park/bat 6.00
Preston Wilson/jsy 5.00
Manny Ramirez/jsy 8.00
Aramis Ramirez/jsy 5.00
Pedro Martinez/jsy 10.00
Ivan Rodriguez/jsy 8.00
Ichiro Suzuki/base 15.00
Sammy Sosa/base 10.00
Jason Giambi/base 8.00

Double Up

NM/M
Complete Set (16): 30.00
Common Card: 1.00
Inserted 1:8
1DU Derek Jeter, Mike Piazza 4.00
2DU Alex Rodriguez, Rafael Palmeiro 3.00
3DU Chipper Jones, Andruw Jones 2.00
4DU Derek Jeter, Alex Rodriguez 4.00
5DU Nomar Garciaparra, Derek Jeter 4.00
6DU Barry Bonds, Jason Giambi 3.00
7DU Ichiro Suzuki, Hideo Nomo 3.00
8DU Randy Johnson, Curt Schilling 1.00
9DU Pedro J. Martinez, Nomar Garciaparra 2.50
10DU Roger Clemens, Kevin Brown 2.00
11DU Nomar Garciaparra, Manny Ramirez 2.50
12DU Kazuhiro Sasaki, Hideo Nomo 1.00
13DU Mike Piazza, Ivan Rodriguez 3.00
14DU Ichiro Suzuki, Ken Griffey Jr. 3.00
15DU Barry Bonds, Sammy Sosa 3.00
16DU Alfonso Soriano, Roberto Alomar 2.00

Double Up Memorabilia

NM/M
Common Card: 15.00
Production 100 sets
Derek Jeter, Mike Piazza 50.00
Alex Rodriguez, Rafael Palmeiro 25.00
Chipper Jones, Andruw Jones 15.00
Derek Jeter, Alex Rodriguez 50.00
Nomar Garciaparra, Derek Jeter 50.00
Barry Bonds, Jason Giambi 30.00
Ichiro Suzuki, Hideo Nomo 80.00
Randy Johnson, Curt Schilling 20.00
Pedro J. Martinez, Nomar Garciaparra 30.00
Roger Clemens, Kevin Brown 25.00
Nomar Garciaparra, Manny Ramirez 25.00
Kazuhiro Sasaki, Hideo Nomo 50.00
Mike Piazza, Ivan Rodriguez 25.00
Ichiro Suzuki, Ken Griffey Jr. 50.00
Barry Bonds, Sammy Sosa 40.00
Alfonso Soriano, Roberto Alomar 25.00

Moonshots

NM/M
Complete Set (20): 30.00
Common Player: .75
Inserted 1:12
1M Mike Piazza 4.00
2M Alex Rodriguez 4.00
3M Manny Ramirez 1.50
4M Ivan Rodriguez 1.00
5M Luis Gonzalez .75
6M Shawn Green .75
7M Barry Bonds 5.00
8M Jason Giambi 3.00
9M Nomar Garciaparra 4.00
10M Edgar Martinez .75
11M Mo Vaughn .75
12M Chipper Jones 3.00
13M Todd Helton 1.00
14M Raul Mondesi .75
15M Preston Wilson .75
16M Rafael Palmeiro 1.00
17M Jim Edmonds .75
18M Bernie Williams 1.00
19M Vladimir Guerrero 2.00
20M Alfonso Soriano 2.00

Moonshots Memorabilia

NM/M
Common Player: 4.00
Inserted 1:20
Mike Piazza/jsy 12.00
Alex Rodriguez/jsy 12.00
Manny Ramirez/jsy 5.00
Ivan Rodriguez/jsy 5.00
Luis Gonzalez/jsy 4.00
Shawn Green/jsy 4.00
Barry Bonds/jsy 12.00
Jason Giambi/base 8.00
Nomar Garciaparra/jsy 12.00
Edgar Martinez/jsy 5.00
Mo Vaughn/jsy 4.00
Chipper Jones/jsy 8.00
Todd Helton/jsy 6.00
Raul Mondesi/jsy 5.00
Preston Wilson/jsy 4.00
Rafael Palmeiro/jsy 5.00
Jim Edmonds/jsy 5.00
Bernie Williams/jsy 6.00
Vladimir Guerrero/base 5.00
Alfonso Soriano/jsy 8.00

Photo Effex

NM/M
Complete Set (20): 45.00
Common Player: 1.00
Inserted 1:12
Golds: 6-12X
Production 25 sets
1PE Derek Jeter 6.00
2PE Barry Bonds 5.00
3PE Sammy Sosa 3.00
4PE Troy Glaus 1.50
5PE Albert Pujols 2.00
6PE Alex Rodriguez 5.00
7PE Ichiro Suzuki 4.00
8PE Greg Maddux 3.00
9PE Nomar Garciaparra 4.00
10PE Jeff Bagwell 1.50
11PE Chipper Jones 3.00
12PE Mike Piazza 4.00
13PE Randy Johnson 2.00
14PE Vladimir Guerrero 2.00
15PE Alfonso Soriano 3.00
16PE Lance Berkman 1.00
17PE Todd Helton 1.00
18PE Mike Lowell 1.00
19PE Carlos Delgado 1.00
20PE Jason Giambi 3.00

When it was a Game

NM/M
Complete Set (40): 125.00
Common Player: 2.00
Inserted 1:20
1WG Derek Jeter 10.00
2WG Barry Bonds 8.00
3WG Luis Aparicio 2.00
4WG Richie Ashburn 2.00
5WG Ernie Banks 5.00
6WG Enos Slaughter 3.00
7WG Yogi Berra 5.00
8WG Lou Boudreau 2.00
9WG Lou Brock 4.00
10WG Jim Bunning 2.00
11WG Rod Carew 4.00
12WG Orlando Cepeda 2.00
13WG Larry Doby 4.00
14WG Bobby Doerr 2.00
15WG Bob Feller 3.00
16WG Brooks Robinson 5.00
17WG Rollie Fingers 2.00
18WG Whitey Ford 3.00
19WG Bob Gibson 4.00
20WG Jim "Catfish" Hunter 3.00
21WG Nolan Ryan 15.00
22WG Reggie Jackson 5.00
23WG Fergie Jenkins 3.00
24WG Al Kaline 6.00
25WG Mike Schmidt 8.00
26WG Harmon Killebrew 8.00
27WG Ralph Kiner 4.00
28WG Willie Stargell 4.00
29WG Billy Williams 2.00
30WG Tom Seaver 5.00
31WG Juan Marichal 3.00
32WG Eddie Mathews 6.00
33WG Willie McCovey 4.00
34WG Joe Morgan 4.00
35WG Stan Musial 8.00
36WG Robin Roberts 4.00
37WG Robin Yount 8.00
38WG Jim Palmer 3.00
39WG Phil Rizzuto 4.00
40WG Pee Wee Reese 4.00

When it was a Game Autograph

No Pricing
DJ Derek Jeter
BB Barry Bonds

When it was a Game Memorabilia

NM/M
Common Player:
Varying quantities produced
Derek Jeter/jsy/200 35.00
Barry Bonds/bat/200 25.00
Yogi Berra/100 35.00
Larry Doby/bat/150 20.00
Catfish Hunter/jsy 8.00
Reggie Jackson/bat 12.00
Tom Seaver/jsy 15.00
Juan Marichal/jsy 8.00
Eddie Mathews/bat 25.00
Willie McCovey/jsy/150 15.00
Joe Morgan/jsy/200 10.00
Jim Palmer/jsy/300 10.00

2004 ULTRA

NM/M
Complete Set (220): 45.00
Common Player: .15
Common All-Rookie (201-220): .50
Common Player (221-295): .25
Common Player (296-382): 2.00
Inserted 2:1
Common Player (383-395): 15.00
Production 500 Sets
Pack (8): 3.00
Box (24): 60.00
1 Magglio Ordonez .40
2 Bobby Abreu .25
3 Eric Munson .15
4 Eric Byrnes .15
5 Bartolo Colon .25
6 Juan Encarnacion .15
7 Jody Gerut .15
8 Eddie Guardado .15
9 Shea Hillenbrand .15
10 Andruw Jones .50
11 Carlos Lee .15
12 Pedro J. Martinez .75
13 Barry Larkin .25
14 Angel Berroa .15
15 Edgar Martinez .25
16 Sidney Ponson .15
17 Mariano Rivera .25

No.	Player	Price
18	Richie Sexson	.40
19	Frank Thomas	.50
20	Jerome Williams	.15
21	Barry Zito	.40
22	Roberto Alomar	.50
23	Rocky Biddle	.15
24	Orlando Cabrera	.25
25	Placido Polanco	.15
26	Morgan Ensberg	.15
27	Jason Giambi	.75
28	Jim Thome	.75
29	Vladimir Guerrero	.75
30	Tim Hudson	.40
31	Jacque Jones	.15
32	Derrek Lee	.25
33	Rafael Palmeiro	.40
34	Mike Mussina	.40
35	Corey Patterson	.15
36	Mike Cameron	.15
37	Ivan Rodriguez	.50
38	Ben Sheets	.15
39	Woody Williams	.15
40	Ichiro Suzuki	1.00
41	Moises Alou	.25
42	Craig Biggio	.25
43	Jorge Posada	.40
44	Craig Monroe	.15
45	Darin Erstad	.25
46	Jay Gibbons	.25
47	Aaron Guiel	.15
48	Travis Lee	.15
49	Jorge Julio	.15
50	Torii Hunter	.25
51	Luis Matos	.15
52	Brett Myers	.15
53	Sean Casey	.25
54	Mark Prior	1.50
55	Alex Rodriguez	1.50
56	Gary Sheffield	.40
57	Jason Varitek	.15
58	Dontrelle Willis	.40
59	Garret Anderson	.25
60	Casey Blake	.15
61	Jay Payton	.15
62	Carl Crawford	.15
63	Carl Everett	.15
64	Marcus Giles	.15
65	Jose Guillen	.15
66	Eric Karros	.15
67	Mike Lieberthal	.15
68	Hideki Matsui	3.00
69	Xavier Nady	.15
70	Hank Blalock	.40
71	Albert Pujols	1.50
72	Jose Cruz Jr.	.15
73	Randall Simon	.15
74	Javier Vazquez	.15
75	Preston Wilson	.15
76	Danys Baez	.15
77	Alex Cintron	.15
78	Jake Peavy	.15
79	Scott Rolen	.50
80	Robert Fick	.15
81	Brian Giles	.25
82	Roy Halladay	.25
83	Kazuhisa Ishii	.15
84	Austin Kearns	.40
85	Paul LoDuca	.15
86	Darrell May	.15
87	Phil Nevin	.15
88	Carlos Pena	.15
89	Manny Ramirez	.50
90	C.C. Sabathia	.15
91	John Smoltz	.25
92	Jose Vidro	.15
93	Randy Wolf	.15
94	Jeff Bagwell	.50
95	Barry Bonds	2.00
96	Frank Catalanotto	.15
97	Zach Day	.15
98	David Ortiz	.15
99	Troy Glaus	.40
100	Bo Hart	.15
101	Geoff Jenkins	.25
102	Jason Kendall	.15
103	Esteban Loiaza	.15
104	Doug Mientkiewicz	.15
105	Trot Nixon	.15
106	Troy Percival	.15
107	Aramis Ramirez	.15
108	Alex Sanchez	.15
109	Alfonso Soriano	.75
110	Omar Vizquel	.25
111	Kerry Wood	.50
112	Rocco Baldelli	.15
113	Bret Boone	.25
114	Shawn Chacon	.15
115	Carlos Delgado	.50
116	Shawn Green	.40
117	Tim Worrell	.15
118	Tom Glavine	.25
119	Shigetoshi Hasegawa	.15
120	Derek Jeter	2.00
121	Jeff Kent	.25
122	Braden Looper	.15
123	Kevin Millwood	.25
124	Hideo Nomo	.40
125	Jason Phillips	.15
126	Tim Redding	.15
127	Reggie Sanders	.15
128	Sammy Sosa	1.25
129	Billy Wagner	.25
130	Miguel Batista	.15
131	Milton Bradley	.15
132	Eric Chavez	.25
133	J.D. Drew	.15
134	Keith Foulke	.15
135	Luis Gonzalez	.25
136	LaTroy Hawkins	.15
137	Randy Johnson	.75
138	Byung-Hyun Kim	.15
139	Javy Lopez	.25
140	Melvin Mora	.15
141	Aubrey Huff	.15
142	Mike Piazza	1.00
143	Mark Redman	.15
144	Kazuhiro Sasaki	.15
145	Shannon Stewart	.15
146	Larry Walker	.25
147	Dmitri Young	.15
148	Josh Beckett	.50
149	Jae Weong Seo	.15
150	Hee Seop Choi	.15
151	Adam Dunn	.40
152	Rafael Furcal	.25
153	Juan Gonzalez	.50
154	Todd Helton	.50
155	Carlos Zambrano	.15
156	Ryan Klesko	.25
157	Mike Lowell	.25
158	Jamie Moyer	.15
159	Russ Ortiz	.15
160	Juan Pierre	.15
161	Edgar Renteria	.15
162	Curt Schilling	.40
163	Mike Sweeney	.15
164	Brandon Webb	.15
165	Michael Young	.15
166	Carlos Beltran	.25
167	Sean Burroughs	.15
168	Luis Castillo	.15
169	David Eckstein	.15
170	Eric Gagne	.25
171	Chipper Jones	1.00
172	Livan Hernandez	.15
173	Nick Johnson	.15
174	Corey Koskie	.15
175	Jason Schmidt	.15
176	Bill Mueller	.15
177	Steve Finley	.15
178	A.J. Pierzynski	.15
179	Rene Reyes	.15
180	Jason Johnson	.15
181	Mark Teixeira	.15
182	Kip Wells	.15
183	Mike MacDougal	.15
184	Lance Berkman	.25
185	Victor Zambrano	.15
186	Roger Clemens	1.50
187	Jim Edmonds	.25
188	Nomar Garciaparra	1.50
189	Ken Griffey Jr.	1.00
190	Richard Hidalgo	.15
191	Cliff Floyd	.15
192	Greg Maddux	1.00
193	Mark Mulder	.25
194	Roy Oswalt	.25
195	Marlon Byrd	.15
196	Jose Reyes	.15
197	Kevin Brown	.25
198	Miguel Tejada	.25
199	Vernon Wells	.25
200	Joel Pineiro	.15
201	Rickie Weeks	5.00
202	Chad Gaudin	1.50
203	Ryan Wagner	1.50
204	Chris Bootcheck	.50
205	Koyie Hill	.50
206	Jeff Duncan	1.00
207	Rich Harden	1.00
208	Edwin Jackson	.50
209	Robby Hammock	.50
210	Khalil Greene	.50
211	Chien-Ming Wang	.50
212	Prentice Redman	.50
213	Todd Wellemeyer	.50
214	Clint Barmes	1.00
215	Matt Kata	.50
216	Jon Leicester	.50
217	Jeremy Guthrie	.50
218	Chin-Hui Tsao	1.50
219	Dan Haren	1.00
220	Delmon Young	5.00
221	Vladimir Guerrero	1.00
222	Andy Pettitte	.60
223	Gary Sheffield	.60
224	Javier Vazquez	.25
225	Alex Rodriguez	2.50
226	Billy Wagner	.25
227	Miguel Tejada	.60
228	Greg Maddux	1.50
229	Ivan Rodriguez	.60
230	Roger Clemens	2.50
231	Alfonso Soriano	1.00
232	Miguel Cabrera	.75
233	Javy Lopez	.40
234	David Wells	.25
235	Eric Milton	.25
236	Armando Benitez	.25
237	Mike Cameron	.25
238	J.D. Drew	.40
239	Carlos Beltran	.60
240	Bartolo Colon	.40
241	Jose Guillen	.25
242	Kevin Brown	.40
243	Carlos Guillen	.25
244	Kenny Lofton	.25
245	Pokey Reese	.25
246	Rafael Palmeiro	.75
247	Nomar Garciaparra	2.50
248	Hee Seop Choi	.25
249	Juan Uribe	.25
250	Nick Johnson	.25
251	Scott Podsednik	.25
252	Richie Sexson	.60
253	Keith Foulke	.25
254	Jaret Wright	.25
255	Johnny Estrada	.25
256	Michael Barrett	.25
257	Bernie Williams	.60
258	Octavio Dotel	.25
259	Jeromy Burnitz	.25
260	Kevin Youkilis	.25
261	Derrek Lee	.40
262	Jack Wilson	.25
263	Craig Wilson	.25
264	Richard Hidalgo	.25
265	Royce Clayton	.25
266	Curt Schilling	.60
267	Joe Mauer	.60
268	Bobby Crosby	.25
269	Zack Greinke	.25
270	Victor Martinez	.25
271	Pedro Feliz	.25
272	Tony Batista	.25
273	Casey Kotchman	.25
274	Freddy Garcia	.25
275	Adam Everett	.25
276	Alexis Rios	.25
277	Lew Ford	.25
278	Adam LaRoche	.25
279	Lyle Overbay	.25
280	Juan Gonzalez	.40
281	A.J. Pierzynski	.25
282	Scott Hairston	.25
283	Danny Bautista	.25
284	Brad Penny	.25
285	Paul Konerko	.25
286	Matt Lawton	.25
287	Carl Pavano	.25
288	Pat Burrell	.40
289	Kenny Rogers	.25
290	Laynce Nix	.25
291	Johnny Damon	.40
292	Paul Wilson	.25
293	Vinny Castilla	.25
294	Aaron Miles	.25
295	Ken Harvey	.25
296	*Onil Joseph*	2.00
297	*Kazuhito Tadano*	3.00
298	*Jeff Bennett*	2.00
299	*Chad Bentz*	3.00
300	*Akinori Otsuka*	2.00
301	*Jon Knott*	3.00
302	*Ian Snell*	2.00
303	*Fernando Nieve*	2.00
304	Mike Rouse	2.00
305	*Dennis Sarfate*	2.00
306	*Josh Labandeira*	3.00
307	*Chris Oxspring*	2.00
308	*Alfredo Simon*	2.00
309	*Rusty Tucker*	2.00
310	*Lincoln Holdzkom*	2.00
311	*Justin Leone*	2.00
312	*Jorge Sequea*	2.00
313	*Brian Dallimore*	2.00
314	*Tim Bittner*	2.00
315	*Ronny Cedeno*	2.00
316	*Justin Hampson*	2.00
317	*Ryan Wing*	2.00
318	*Mariano Gomez*	2.00
319	*Carlos Vasquez*	2.00
320	*Casey Daigle*	2.00
321	*Renyel Pinto*	2.00
322	*Chris Shelton*	3.00
323	*Mike Gosling*	2.00
324	*Aarom Baldiris*	2.00
325	*Ramon Ramirez*	2.00
326	*Roberto Novoa*	2.00
327	Sean Henn	2.00
328	*Nick Regilio*	2.00
329	*David Crouthers*	2.00
330	*Greg Dobbs*	2.00
331	*Angel Chavez*	2.00
332	*Luis A. Gonzalez*	2.00
333	*Justin Knoedler*	2.00
334	*Jason Frasor*	2.00
335	*Jerry Gil*	2.00
336	*Carlos Hines*	2.00
337	*Ivan Ochoa*	3.00
338	*Jose Capellan*	3.00
339	*Hector Gimenez*	2.00
340	*Shawn Hill*	3.00
341	*Freddy Guzman*	2.00
342	*Scott Proctor*	2.00
343	*Frank Francisco*	2.00
344	*Brandon Medders*	2.00
345	*Andy Green*	2.00
346	*Eddy Rodriguez*	2.00
347	*Tim Hamulack*	2.00
348	*Mike Wuertz*	2.00
349	Arnie Munoz	2.00
350	*Enemencio Pacheco*	2.00
351	*Dusty Bergman*	2.00
352	*Charles Thomas*	5.00
353	*William Bergolla*	2.00
354	*Ramon Castro*	2.00
355	*Justin Lehr*	2.00
356	*Lino Urdaneta*	2.00
357	*Donnie Kelly*	2.00
358	*Kevin Cave*	2.00
359	*Franklyn Gracesqui*	2.00
360	*Chris Aguila*	2.00
361	*Jorge Vasquez*	2.00
362	*Andres Blanco*	2.00
363	*Orlando Rodriguez*	2.00
364	*Colby Miller*	2.00
365	*Shawn Camp*	2.00
366	Jake Woods	2.00
367	*George Sherrill*	2.00
368	*Justin Huisman*	2.00
369	*Jimmy Serrano*	3.00
370	*Mike Johnston*	3.00
371	*Ryan Meaux*	2.00
372	*Scott Dohmann*	2.00
373	*Brad Halsey*	5.00
374	*Joey Gathright*	3.00
375	*Yadier Molina*	3.00
376	*Travis Blackley*	2.00
377	*Steve Andrade*	2.00
378	*Phil Stockman*	2.00
379	*Roman Colon*	2.00
380	Jesse Crain	2.00
381	*Edwardo Sierra*	2.00
382	*Justin Germano*	2.00
383	*Kazuo Matsui*	30.00
384	*Shingo Takatsu*	20.00
385	*John Gall*	15.00
386	*Chris Saenz*	15.00
387	*Merkin Valdez*	20.00
388	*Jamie Brown*	15.00
389	*Jason Bartlett*	20.00
390	*David Aardsma*	20.00
391	Scott Kazmir	30.00
392	David Wright	40.00
393	*Dioner Navarro*	30.00
394	B.J. Upton	25.00
395	Gavin Floyd	30.00

Gold Medallion

Cards (1-200):	2-3X
Inserted 1:1	
All-Rookies (201-220):	3-4X
Inserted 1:8	
Cards (221-295):	.75X-1.5X
Inserted 1:1	
Cards (296-382):	.75X-1.25X
Cards (383-395):	.25X-.75X
Inserted 1:4	

Platinum Medallion

Cards (1-200):	8-15X
All-Rookies (201-220):	5-10X
Production 66 sets	
Cards (221-295):	4-8X
Cards (296-382):	2-4X
Production 100 Sets	
Cards (383-395):	No Pricing
Production 13 Sets	

Diamond Producers

		NM/M
Complete Set (10):		60.00
Common Player:		4.00
Inserted 1:144		
1DP	Greg Maddux	8.00
2DP	Dontrelle Willis	4.00
3DP	Jim Thome	5.00
4DP	Alfonso Soriano	6.00
5DP	Alex Rodriguez	10.00
6DP	Sammy Sosa	10.00
7DP	Nomar Garciaparra	10.00
8DP	Derek Jeter	15.00
9DP	Adam Dunn	4.00
10DP	Mark Prior	10.00

Diamond Producers Memorabilia

	NM/M
Production 1,000 sets	
Dontrelle Willis	15.00
Alfonso Soriano	10.00
Alex Rodriguez	10.00
Sammy Sosa	10.00
Nomar Garciaparra	10.00
Derek Jeter	15.00
Mark Prior	15.00

Diamond Producers UltraSwatch

	NM/M
Numbered to Jersey #	
Dontrelle Willis/35	25.00
Alfonso Soriano/12	
Alex Rodriguez/2	
Sammy Sosa/21	
Nomar Garciaparra/5	
Derek Jeter/2	
Mark Prior/22	

HR Kings

		NM/M
Complete Set (10):		35.00
Inserted 1:96		
Golds:		2-3X
Production 50 sets		
1HK	Barry Bonds	8.00
2HK	Albert Pujols	6.00
3HK	Jason Giambi	3.00
4HK	Jeff Bagwell	2.00
5HK	Ken Griffey Jr.	4.00
6HK	Alex Rodriguez	6.00
7HK	Sammy Sosa	5.00
8HK	Alfonso Soriano	3.00
9HK	Chipper Jones	4.00
10HK	Mike Piazza	4.00

Hitting Machines

		NM/M
Common Player:		3.00
Inserted 1:12		
Die-Cut:		1X-2X
1HM	Albert Pujols	6.00
2HM	Ken Griffey Jr.	4.00
3HM	Vladimir Guerrero	3.50
4HM	Mike Piazza	4.00
5HM	Ichiro Suzuki	5.00
6HM	Miguel Cabrera	3.00
7HM	Hideki Matsui	6.00
8HM	Nomar Garciaparra	6.00
9HM	Derek Jeter	8.00
10HM	Chipper Jones	4.00

Hitting Machines Game-Used Silver

		NM/M
Common Player:		8.00
Inserted 1:74		
Gold:		1X-3X
Production 50 Sets		
Platinum:		No Pricing
Production 10 Sets		
JB	Jeff Bagwell	10.00
MC	Miguel Cabrera	10.00
AD	Adam Dunn	8.00
VG	Vladimir Guerrero	10.00
TH	Todd Helton	10.00
CJ	Chipper Jones	12.00
HM	Hideki Matsui	20.00
MP	Mike Piazza	12.00
AP	Albert Pujols	12.00
FT	Frank Thomas	10.00

Performers

		NM/M
Complete Set (15):		12.00
Common Player:		.50
Inserted 1:6		
1UP	Ichiro Suzuki	1.50
2UP	Albert Pujols	2.00
3UP	Barry Bonds	3.00
4UP	Hideki Matsui	2.00
5UP	Randy Johnson	1.00
6UP	Jason Giambi	1.00
7UP	Pedro J. Martinez	1.00
8UP	Hank Blalock	.50
9UP	Chipper Jones	1.50
10UP	Mike Piazza	1.50
11UP	Derek Jeter	3.00
12UP	Vladimir Guerrero	1.00
13UP	Barry Zito	.75
14UP	Rocco Baldelli	.50
15UP	Hideo Nomo	.75

Performers Memorabilia

	NM/M
Common Player:	6.00
Production 500 sets	
Albert Pujols	15.00
Barry Bonds/base	15.00
Randy Johnson	8.00
Jason Giambi	8.00
Pedro J. Martinez	10.00
Hank Blalock	6.00
Chipper Jones	10.00
Mike Piazza	10.00
Derek Jeter	15.00
Vladimir Guerrero	8.00
Rocco Baldelli	10.00
Hideo Nomo	15.00

Performers UltraSwatch

	NM/M
Numbered to Jersey #	
Albert Pujols/5	
Barry Bonds/base/25	
Randy Johnson/51	15.00
Jason Giambi/25	
Pedro Martinez/45	20.00
Hank Blalock/9	
Chipper Jones/10	
Mike Piazza/31	25.00
Derek Jeter/2	
Vladimir Guerrero/27	20.00
Rocco Baldelli/5	
Hideo Nomo/10	

RBI Kings

		NM/M
Complete Set (10):		15.00
Inserted 1:32		
Golds:		3-4X
Production 50 sets		
1RK	Hideki Matsui	4.00
2RK	Albert Pujols	4.00
3RK	Todd Helton	1.50
4RK	Jim Thome	1.50
5RK	Carlos Delgado	1.50
6RK	Alex Rodriguez	4.00
7RK	Barry Bonds	5.00
8RK	Manny Ramirez	1.50
9RK	Vladimir Guerrero	1.50
10RK	Nomar Garciaparra	4.00

Season Crowns Memorabilia

	NM/M
Common Player:	4.00
Production 399 sets	
Golds:	1-2X
Production 99 sets	
Platinums:	No Pricing
Production 25 sets	
Adam Dunn	6.00
Carlos Pena	4.00
Torii Hunter	8.00
Gary Sheffield	8.00
Sean Casey	4.00
Lance Berkman	4.00
Tom Glavine	6.00
Sean Burroughs	4.00
Shawn Green	6.00
Jason Kendall	4.00
Vladimir Guerrero	10.00
Todd Helton	8.00
Tim Hudson	8.00
Troy Glaus	6.00
Larry Walker	4.00
Carlos Beltran	6.00
Hideo Nomo	10.00
Kazuhiro Sasaki	4.00
Mike Piazza	10.00
Scott Rolen	8.00
Carlos Delgado	6.00
Andruw Jones	8.00
Alfonso Soriano	10.00
Angel Berroa	4.00
Brandon Webb	6.00
Jason Giambi	8.00
Pedro J. Martinez	10.00
Manny Ramirez	8.00
Alex Rodriguez	10.00
Derek Jeter	15.00
Mark Mulder	6.00
Greg Maddux	10.00
Sammy Sosa	15.00
Jim Thome	10.00
Hank Blalock	6.00
Roberto Alomar	8.00
Omar Vizquel	5.00
Austin Kearns	8.00
Jeff Bagwell	8.00
Frank Thomas	8.00
Randy Johnson	8.00
Rocco Baldelli	12.00
Albert Pujols	15.00
Jose Reyes	8.00
Dontrelle Willis	12.00
Hideki Matsui/base	20.00
Barry Bonds/base	15.00
Ichiro Suzuki/base	15.00
Chipper Jones	10.00
Roger Clemens	15.00

Season Crowns Autograph

	NM/M
Common Player:	15.00
Production 150 sets	
Golds:	No Pricing
Production 25 sets	
Rocco Baldelli	35.00
Hank Blalock	15.00
Bo Hart	30.00
Aubrey Huff	15.00
Chipper Jones	60.00
Austin Kearns	15.00
Mike Lowell	15.00
Corey Patterson	20.00
Carlos Pena	15.00
Jose Reyes	25.00
Scott Rolen	20.00
Miguel Tejada	25.00
Brandon Webb	15.00
Rickie Weeks	50.00
Dontrelle Willis	35.00

Strikeout Kings

		NM/M
Complete Set (10):		10.00
Common Player:		.75
Inserted 1:24		
Golds:		3-5X
Production 50 sets		
1KK	Randy Johnson	1.50
2KK	Pedro J. Martinez	1.50
3KK	Curt Schilling	1.00
4KK	Roger Clemens	3.00
5KK	Mike Mussina	1.00
6KK	Roy Halladay	.75
7KK	Kerry Wood	1.00
8KK	Dontrelle Willis	1.00
9KK	Greg Maddux	2.00
10KK	Mark Prior	3.00

Turn Back the Clock

		NM/M
Common Player:		1.50
Inserted 1:6		
1	Roger Clemens	5.00
2	Alex Rodriguez	5.00
3	Randy Johnson	2.00
4	Pedro Martinez	2.00
5	Alfonso Soriano	2.00
6	Curt Schilling	1.50
7	Miguel Tejada	1.50
8	Scott Rolen	2.00
9	Jim Thome	2.00
10	Manny Ramirez	1.50
11	Vladimir Guerrero	2.00
12	Tom Glavine	1.50
13	Andy Pettitte	1.50
14	Ivan Rodriguez	1.50
15	Jason Giambi	2.00
16	Rafael Palmeiro	2.00
17	Greg Maddux	3.00
18	Hideo Nomo	1.50
19	Mike Mussina	1.50
20	Sammy Sosa	4.00

Turn Back the Clock Game-Used Copper

	NM/M
Common Player:	8.00

Production 399 Sets
Silver: .75X-1.5X
Production 199 Sets
Gold: 1X-2X
Production 99 Sets
Platinum Patch: 2X-5X
Production 29 Sets
RC Roger Clemens 12.00
JG Jason Giambi 10.00
TG Tom Glavine 8.00
VG Vladimir Guerrero 10.00
RJ Randy Johnson 10.00
GM Greg Maddux 12.00
PR Pedro Martinez 10.00
MM Mike Mussina 8.00
HM Hideo Nomo 8.00
RP Rafael Palmeiro 10.00
AP Andy Pettitte 8.00
MR Manny Ramirez 10.00
IR Ivan Rodriguez 8.00
SR Scott Rolen 10.00
CS Curt Schilling 8.00
AS Alfonso Soriano 10.00
SS Sammy Sosa 12.00
MT Miguel Tejada 8.00
JT Jim Thome 10.00

3 Kings

NM/M

Production 33 sets
Mike Piazza, Roger Clemens, Alex Rodriguez 70.00
Albert Pujols, Mark Prior, Todd Helton 65.00
Alfonso Soriano, Dontrelle Willis, Albert Pujols 60.00
P. Martinez, Sammy Sosa, Albert Pujols 70.00
Randy Johnson, Albert Pujols, Todd Helton 50.00
Dontrelle Willis, Chipper Jones, Albert Pujols 60.00
Dontrelle Willis, Jeff Bagwell, Jim Thome 40.00
Greg Maddux, Jason Giambi, Manny Ramirez 50.00

2005 ULTRA

NM/M

Common Player (1-200): .15
Common Player (201-220): 2.00
Inserted 1:4
Pack (8): 3.50
Box (24): 75.00
1 Andy Pettitte .40
2 Jose Cruz .15
3 Cliff Floyd .25
4 Paul Konerko .15
5 Joe Mauer .60
6 Scott Spiezio .15
7 Ben Sheets .25
8 Kerry Wood .50
9 Carl Pavano .15
10 Matt Morris .15
11 Kazuo Matsui .75
12 Ivan Rodriguez .40
13 Victor Martinez .15
14 Justin Morneau .15
15 Adam Everett .15
16 Carl Crawford .15
17 David Ortiz .25
18 Jason Giambi .75
19 Derrek Lee .25
20 Magglio Ordonez .25
21 Bobby Abreu .25
22 Milton Bradley .15
23 Jeff Bagwell .50
24 Jim Edmonds .25
25 Garret Anderson .25
26 Jacque Jones .15
27 Ted Lilly .15
28 Greg Maddux 1.00
29 Jermaine Dye .15
30 Bill Mueller .15
31 Roy Oswalt .25
32 Tony Womack .15
33 Andruw Jones .50
34 Tom Glavine .25
35 Mariano Rivera .25
36 Sean Casey .15
37 Edgardo Alfonzo .15
38 Brad Penny .15
39 Johan Santana .15
40 Mark Teixeira .25
41 Manny Ramirez .50
42 Gary Sheffield .40
43 Matt Lawton .15
44 Troy Percival .15
45 Rocco Baldelli .40
46 Doug Mientkiewicz .15
47 Corey Patterson .15
48 Austin Kearns .15
49 Edgar Martinez .25
50 Brad Radke .15
51 Barry Larkin .25
52 Chone Figgins .15
53 Alexis Rios .15
54 Alex Rodriguez 1.50
55 Vinny Castilla .15
56 Javier Vazquez .15
57 Javy Lopez .25
58 Mike Cameron .15
59 Brian Giles .25
60 Dontrelle Willis .25
61 Rafael Furcal .15
62 Trot Nixon .15
63 Mark Mulder .25
64 Josh Beckett .50
65 J.D. Drew .25
66 Brandon Webb .15
67 Wade Miller .15
68 Lyle Overbay .15
69 Pedro J. Martinez .75
70 Rich Harden .15
71 Al Leiter .15
72 Adam Eaton .15
73 Mike Sweeney .15
74 Steve Finley .15
75 Kris Benson .15
76 Jim Thome .75
77 Juan Pierre .15
78 Bartolo Colon .25
79 Carlos Delgado .50
80 Jack Wilson .15
81 Ken Harvey .15
82 Nomar Garciaparra 1.50
83 Paul LoDuca .15
84 Cesar Izturis .15
85 Adrian Beltre .25
86 Brian Roberts .15
87 David Eckstein .15
88 Jimmy Rollins .15
89 Roger Clemens 1.00
90 Randy Johnson .75
91 Orlando Hudson .15
92 Tim Hudson .25
93 Dmitri Young .15
94 Chipper Jones 1.00
95 John Smoltz .25
96 Billy Wagner .15
97 Hideo Nomo .25
98 Sammy Sosa 1.25
99 Darin Erstad .25
100 Todd Helton .50
101 Aubrey Huff .15
102 Alfonso Soriano .75
103 Jose Vidro .15
104 Carlos Lee .15
105 Corey Koskie .15
106 Bret Boone .25
107 Torii Hunter .40
108 Aramis Ramirez .15
109 Chase Utley .15
110 Reggie Sanders .15
111 Livan Hernandez .15
112 Jeromy Burnitz .15
113 Carlos Zambrano .15
114 Hank Blalock .40
115 Sidney Ponson .15
116 Zack Greinke .15
117 Trevor Hoffman .15
118 Jeff Kent .25
119 Richie Sexson .40
120 Melvin Mora .15
121 Eric Chavez .25
122 Miguel Cabrera .50
123 Ryan Freel .15
124 Russ Ortiz .15
125 Craig Wilson .15
126 Craig Biggio .25
127 Curt Schilling .40
128 Kazuhisa Ishii .15
129 Marquis Grissom .15
130 Bernie Williams .40
131 Travis Hafner .15
132 Hee Seop Choi .15
133 Scott Rolen .15
134 Tony Batista .75
135 Frank Thomas .15
136 Jason Varitek .50
137 Ichiro Suzuki 1.25
138 Junior Spivey .15
139 Adam Dunn .40
140 Jorge Posada .40
141 Edgar Renteria .15
142 Hideki Matsui 1.50
143 Carlos Guillen .15
144 Jody Gerut .15
145 Wily Mo Pena .15
146 Derek Jeter 2.00
147 C.C. Sabathia .15
148 Geoff Jenkins .25
149 Albert Pujols 1.50
150 Eric Munson .15
151 Moises Alou .25
152 Jerry Hairston .15
153 Ray Durham .15
154 Mike Piazza 1.00
155 Omar Vizquel .25
156 A.J. Pierzynski .15
157 Michael Young .15
158 Jason Bay .15
159 Mark Loretta .15
160 Shawn Green .25
161 Luis Gonzalez .25
162 Johnny Damon .25
163 Eric Milton .15
164 Mike Lowell .15
165 Jose Guillen .15
166 Eric Hinske .15
167 Jason Kendall .25
168 Carlos Beltran .40
169 Johnny Estrada .15
170 Scott Hatteberg .15
171 Laynce Nix .15
172 Eric Gagne .25
173 Richard Hidalgo .15
174 Bobby Crosby .15
175 Woody Williams .15
176 Justin Leone .15
177 Orlando Cabrera .15
178 Mark Prior 1.50
179 Jorge Julio .15
180 Jamie Moyer .15
181 Jose Reyes .15
182 Ken Griffey Jr. 1.00
183 Mike Lieberthal .15
184 Kenny Rogers .15
185 Mike Mussina .40
186 Preston Wilson .15
187 Khalil Greene .50
188 Angel Berroa .15
189 Miguel Tejada .40
190 Freddy Garcia .15
191 Pat Burrell .25
192 Luis Castillo .15
193 Vladimir Guerrero .75
194 Roy Halladay .25
195 Barry Zito .40
196 Lance Berkman .25
197 Rafael Palmeiro .50
198 Nate Robertson .15
199 Jason Schmidt .25
200 Scott Podsednik .15
201 Casey Kotchman 3.00
202 Scott Kazmir 4.00
203 Bucky Jacobsen 4.00
204 Jeff Keppinger 3.00
205 David Bush 2.00
206 Gavin Floyd 5.00
207 David Wright 8.00
208 B.J. Upton 3.00
209 David Aardsma 2.00
210 Jason Bartlett 3.00
211 Dioner Navarro 3.00
212 Jason Kubel 3.00
213 Ryan Howard 3.00
214 *Charles Thomas* 2.00
215 Freddy Guzman 2.00
216 Brad Halsey 3.00
217 Joey Gathright 2.00
218 Jeff Francis 2.00
219 Terry Tiffee 2.00
220 Nick Swisher 5.00

Gold

Cards 1-200: 1X-3X
Inserted 1:1
Cards 201-220: .5X-1X
Inserted 1:8

Platinum

Cards 1-200: 5X-8X
Cards 201-220: 3X-5X
Production 50 Sets

Follow the Leader

NM/M

Common Player: 1.50
Inserted 1:6
Copper Game-Used: 3X-5X
Inserted 1:72 (hobby only)
Red Game-Used: 2X-4X
Inserted 1:48 (retail only)
Gold Game-Used: 4X-6X
Production 250 Sets
Platinum Game-Used: 5X-8X
Production 99 Sets
Ultra Game-Used:
Numbered 26-51: 5X-10X
Numbered 25 or less: No Pricing
Production to player's jersey number
1 Roger Clemens 3.00
2 Albert Pujols 3.00
3 Sammy Sosa 2.50
4 Manny Ramirez 1.50
5 Vladimir Guerrero 2.00
6 Ivan Rodriguez 1.50
7 Mike Piazza 2.00
8 Scott Rolen 2.00
9 Ichiro Suzuki 2.50
10 Randy Johnson 2.00
11 Mark Prior 3.00
12 Jim Thome 2.00
13 Greg Maddux 2.00
14 Pedro J. Martinez 2.00
15 Miguel Cabrera 1.50

HR Kings

NM/M

Common Player: 2.50
Inserted 1:96
Ultra Kings Gold: 1X-3X
Production 50 Sets
1 Jim Thome 4.00
2 David Ortiz 3.00
3 Adam Dunn 3.00
4 Albert Pujols 8.00
5 Manny Ramirez 3.50
6 Vladimir Guerrero 4.00
7 Miguel Tejada 3.00
8 Rafael Palmeiro 3.50
9 Mark Teixeira 2.50
10 Sammy Sosa 6.00
11 Frank Thomas 3.50
12 Pat Burrell 2.50
13 Adrian Beltre 2.50
14 Miguel Cabrera 3.50
15 Gary Sheffield 3.00

RBI Kings

NM/M

Common Player: 2.50
Inserted 1:32

Ultra Kings Gold: 2X-4X
Production 50 Sets
1 Sean Casey 2.50
2 Ivan Rodriguez 2.50
3 Mike Piazza 4.00
4 Todd Helton 3.00
5 Scott Rolen 3.50
6 Hideki Matsui 6.00
7 Gary Sheffield 2.50
8 Alfonso Soriano 3.50
9 Bobby Abreu 2.50
10 Lance Berkman 2.50
11 Miguel Tejada 2.50
12 Travis Hafner 2.50
13 Hank Blalock 2.50
14 Jeff Bagwell 3.00
15 Chipper Jones 4.00

Season Crowns Copper Game-Used

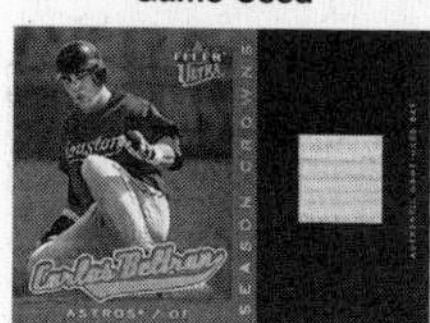

NM/M
Common Player: 5.00
Production 399 Sets
Gold: .75X-1.5X
Production 99 Sets
Platinum: No Pricing
Production 25 Sets
1 Andy Pettitte/Jersey 8.00
3 Cliff Floyd/Jersey 5.00
7 Ben Sheets/Jersey 5.00
8 Kerry Wood/Jersey 8.00
11 Kazuo Matsui/Bat 15.00
13 Victor Martinez/Jersey 5.00
17 David Carr/Jersey 8.00
20 Magglio Ordonez/Bat 5.00
21 Bobby Abreu/Bat 5.00
24 Jim Edmonds/Jersey 5.00
31 Roy Oswalt/Jersey 5.00
33 Andruw Jones/Jersey 8.00
34 Tom Glavine/Bat 5.00
36 Sean Casey/Jersey 5.00
37 Edgardo Alfonzo/Bat 5.00
41 Manny Ramirez/Bat 8.00
42 Gary Sheffield/Bat 8.00
45 Rocco Baldelli/Jersey 8.00
48 Austin Kearns/Jersey 5.00
49 Edgar Martinez/Jersey 5.00
60 Dontrelle Willis/Jersey 5.00
65 J.D. Drew/Jersey 5.00
70 Rich Harden/Jersey 5.00
71 Al Leiter/Jersey 5.00
80 Jack Wilson/Bat 5.00
93 Dmitri Young/Bat 5.00
94 Chipper Jones/Bat 10.00
97 Hideo Nomo/Jersey 8.00
98 Sammy Sosa/Bat 12.00
100 Todd Helton/Bat 8.00
102 Alfonso Soriano/Bat 8.00
107 Torii Hunter/Jersey 8.00
114 Hank Blalock/Bat 8.00
119 Richie Sexson/Jersey 8.00
121 Eric Chavez/Jersey 5.00
130 Bernie Williams/Bat 8.00
135 Frank Thomas/Bat 8.00
139 Adam Dunn/Bat 8.00
142 Hideki Matsui/Bat 15.00
144 Jody Gerut/Bat 8.00
154 Mike Piazza/Bat 10.00
158 Jason Bay/Bat 8.00
162 Johnny Damon/Jersey 10.00
168 Carlos Beltran/Bat 8.00
173 Richard Hidalgo/Jersey 5.00
181 Jose Reyes/Bat 5.00
187 Khalil Greene/Jersey 15.00
191 Pat Burrell/Bat 8.00
193 Vladimir Guerrero/Bat 8.00
197 Rafael Palmeiro/Jersey 8.00

Season Crown Autographs Copper

NM/M
Common Player: 20.00
Stated Production 199 Sets
All 199 cards not released for same players
31 Roy Oswalt/50 25.00
80 Jack Wilson/199 20.00
125 Craig Wilson/130 20.00
157 Michael Young/150 20.00
200 Scott Podsednik/22

Season Crown Autographs Gold

NM/M
Common Player: 20.00
Stated Production 99 Sets
All 99 cards not released for same players
20 Magglio Ordonez/13
21 Roy Oswalt/99 20.00
40 Mark Teixeira/25
50 Brad Radke/89 20.00
51 Barry Larkin/99 25.00
62 Trot Nixon/37 25.00
70 Rich Harden/41 20.00
80 Jack Wilson/99 20.00
88 Jimmy Rollins/45 25.00
121 Eric Chavez/69 20.00
125 Craig Wilson/99 20.00
157 Michael Young/99 20.00
200 Scott Podsednik/99 20.00
201 Casey Kotchman/21

Season Crown Autographs Platinum

NM/M
Common Player: 25.00
Stated Production 50 Sets
All 50 cards not released for some players
Masterpiece: No Pricing
Production 1 Set
8 Kerry Wood/7
12 Ivan Rodriguez/25
20 Magglio Ordonez/50 25.00
25 Garret Anderson/50 25.00
31 Roy Oswalt/50 25.00
35 Mariano Rivera/25
40 Mark Teixeira/50 30.00
41 Manny Ramirez/25
50 Brad Radke/50 25.00
51 Barry Larkin/50 30.00
62 Trot Nixon/50 25.00
65 J.D. Drew/19
70 Rich Harden/50 25.00
80 Jack Wilson/50 25.00
87 David Eckstein/45 25.00
88 Jimmy Rollins/50 25.00
90 Randy Johnson/10
94 Chipper Jones/19
95 John Smoltz/23
96 Billy Wagner/50 30.00
116 Zack Greinke/49 25.00
121 Eric Chavez/50 25.00
125 Craig Wilson/50 25.00
130 Bernie Williams/15
136 Jason Varitek/19
149 Albert Pujols/10
154 Mike Piazza/10
157 Michael Young/50 25.00
161 Luis Gonzalez/50 25.00
185 Mike Mussina/50 30.00
195 Barry Zito/50 25.00
199 Jason Schmidt/50 25.00
200 Scott Podsednik/50 25.00
201 Casey Kotchman/50 25.00

Strikeout Kings

NM/M
Common Player: 2.50
Inserted 1:24
Ultra Kings Gold: 2X-4X
Production 50 Sets
1 Pedro J. Martinez 3.50
2 Randy Johnson 3.50
3 Mark Mulder 2.50
4 Barry Zito 2.50
5 Roger Clemens 6.00
6 Mark Prior 6.00
7 Ben Sheets 2.50
8 Curt Schilling 2.50
9 Billy Wagner 2.50
10 Eric Gagne 2.50
11 Josh Beckett 3.00
12 Kerry Wood 3.00
13 Jason Schmidt 2.50
14 Roy Halladay 2.50
15 Greg Maddux 4.00

Ultra Kings Game-Used Gold

NM/M
Common Player: 8.00
Production 150 Sets
Ultra Swatch
Numbered 51-75: .75X-1.5X
Numbered 26-50: 1X-2X
Numbered 25 or less: No Pricing
Production to player's jersey number
Platinum: No Pricing
Production 25 Sets
1 Pedro J. Martinez 12.00
2 Randy Johnson 12.00
3 Mark Mulder 8.00
4 Barry Zito 8.00
5 Roger Clemens 25.00
6 Mark Prior 25.00
7 Ben Sheets 8.00
8 Curt Schilling 8.00
9 Billy Wagner 8.00
10 Eric Gagne 8.00
11 Josh Beckett 10.00
12 Kerry Wood 10.00
13 Jason Schmidt 8.00
14 Roy Halladay 8.00
15 Greg Maddux 15.00
16 Sean Casey 8.00
17 Ivan Rodriguez 8.00
18 Mike Piazza 15.00
19 Todd Helton 10.00
20 Scott Rolen 12.00
21 Hideki Matsui 30.00
22 Gary Sheffield 8.00
23 Alfonso Soriano 12.00
24 Bobby Abreu 8.00
25 Lance Berkman 8.00
26 Miguel Tejada 8.00
27 Travis Hafner 8.00
28 Hank Blalock 8.00
29 Jeff Bagwell 10.00
30 Chipper Jones 15.00
31 Jim Thome 12.00
32 David Ortiz 8.00
33 Adam Dunn 8.00
34 Albert Pujols 25.00
35 Manny Ramirez 10.00
36 Vladimir Guerrero 12.00
37 Miguel Tejada 8.00
38 Rafael Palmeiro 10.00
39 Mark Teixeira 8.00
40 Sammy Sosa 20.00
41 Frank Thomas 10.00
42 Pat Burrell 8.00
43 Adrian Beltre 8.00
44 Miguel Cabrera 10.00
45 Gary Sheffield 8.00

Ultra 3 Kings Triple Swatch

NM/M
Common Card: 40.00
Production 33 Sets
1 Greg Maddux, Mark Prior, Kerry Wood 75.00
2 Mark Teixeira, Hank Blalock, Alfonso Soriano 40.00
3 Jeff Bagwell, Roger Clemens, Lance Berkman 60.00
4 Jim Thome, Pat Burrell, Billy Wagner 40.00
5 Gary Sheffield, Hideki Matsui, Mike Piazza 75.00
6 Scott Rolen, Chipper Jones, Adrian Beltre 40.00
7 Albert Pujols, Adam Dunn, Miguel Cabrera 50.00
8 Curt Schilling, Pedro J. Martinez, Manny Ramirez 60.00
9 Randy Johnson, Greg Maddux, Pedro J. Martinez 50.00
10 Josh Beckett, Miguel Cabrera, Ivan Rodriguez 40.00

1989 UPPER DECK

NM/M
Unopened Fact. Set (800): 75.00
Complete Set (800): 50.00
Complete Low Set (700): 50.00
Complete High Set (100): 3.00
Common Player: .05
Low Foil Pack (15): 5.00
Low Foil Box (36): 100.00
High Foil Pack (15): 2.00
High Foil Box (36): 65.00
1 *Ken Griffey, Jr.* 45.00
2 *Luis Medina* .05
3 *Tony Chance* .05
4 *Dave Otto* .05
5 *Sandy Alomar, Jr.* 1.00
6 *Rolando Roomes* .05
7 *David West* .05
8 *Cris Carpenter* .05
9 Gregg Jefferies .25
10 *Doug Dascenzo* .05
11 *Ron Jones* .05
12 *Luis de los Santos* .05
13a *Gary Sheffield* ("SS" upside-down) 8.00
13b *Gary Sheffield* ("SS" correct) 8.00
14 *Mike Harkey* .05
15 *Lance Blankenship* .05
16 *William Brennan* .05
17 John Smoltz .05
18 *Ramon Martinez* .25
19 *Mark Lemke* .05
20 *Juan Bell* .05
21 *Rey Palacios* .05
22 *Felix Jose* .05
23 *Van Snider* .05
24 *Dante Bichette* .75
25 *Randy Johnson* 15.00
26 *Carlos Quintana* .05
27 Star Rookie Checklist 1-26 .05
28 *Mike Schooler* .05
29 Randy St. Claire .05
30 *Jerald Clark* .05
31 Kevin Gross .05
32 *Dan Firova* .05
33 Jeff Calhoun .05
34 Tommy Hinzo .05
35 *Ricky Jordan* .05
36 Larry Parrish .05
37 Bret Saberhagen .05
38 Mike Smithson .05
39 Dave Dravecky .05
40 Ed Romero .05
41 Jeff Musselman .05
42 Ed Hearn .05
43 Rance Mulliniks .05
44 Jim Eisenreich .05
45 *Sil Campusano* .05
46 Mike Krukow .05
47 *Paul Gibson* .05
48 Mike LaCoss .05
49 Larry Herndon .05
50 Scott Garrelts .05
51 Dwayne Henry .05
52 Jim Acker .05
53 Steve Sax .05
54 Pete O'Brien .05

No.	Player	Value
55	Paul Runge	.05
56	Rick Rhoden	.05
57	*John Dopson*	.05
58	Casey Candaele	.05
59	Dave Righetti	.05
60	Joe Hesketh	.05
61	Frank DiPino	.05
62	Tim Laudner	.05
63	Jamie Moyer	.05
64	Fred Toliver	.05
65	Mitch Webster	.05
66	John Tudor	.05
67	John Cangelosi	.05
68	Mike Devereaux	.05
69	Brian Fisher	.05
70	Mike Marshall	.05
71	Zane Smith	.05
72a	Brian Holton (ball not visible on card front, photo actually Shawn Hillegas)	.75
72b	Brian Holton (ball visible, correct photo)	.05
73	Jose Guzman	.05
74	Rick Mahler	.05
75	John Shelby	.05
76	Jim Deshaies	.05
77	Bobby Meacham	.05
78	Bryn Smith	.05
79	Joaquin Andujar	.05
80	Richard Dotson	.05
81	Charlie Lea	.05
82	Calvin Schiraldi	.05
83	Les Straker	.05
84	Les Lancaster	.05
85	Allan Anderson	.05
86	Junior Ortiz	.05
87	Jesse Orosco	.05
88	Felix Fermin	.05
89	Dave Anderson	.05
90	Rafael Belliard	.05
91	Franklin Stubbs	.05
92	Cecil Espy	.05
93	Albert Hall	.05
94	Tim Leary	.05
95	Mitch Williams	.05
96	Tracy Jones	.05
97	Danny Darwin	.05
98	Gary Ward	.05
99	Neal Heaton	.05
100	Jim Pankovits	.05
101	Bill Doran	.05
102	Tim Wallach	.05
103	Joe Magrane	.05
104	Ozzie Virgil	.05
105	Alvin Davis	.05
106	Tom Brookens	.05
107	Shawon Dunston	.05
108	Tracy Woodson	.05
109	Nelson Liriano	.05
110	Devon White	.05
111	Steve Balboni	.05
112	Buddy Bell	.05
113	*German Jimenez*	.05
114	Ken Dayley	.05
115	Andres Galarraga	.05
116	Mike Scioscia	.05
117	Gary Pettis	.05
118	Ernie Whitt	.05
119	Bob Boone	.05
120	Ryne Sandberg	1.50
121	Bruce Benedict	.05
122	Hubie Brooks	.05
123	Mike Moore	.05
124	Wallace Johnson	.05
125	Bob Horner	.05
126	Chili Davis	.05
127	Manny Trillo	.05
128	Chet Lemon	.05
129	John Cerutti	.05
130	Orel Hershiser	.05
131	Terry Pendleton	.05
132	Jeff Blauser	.05
133	Mike Fitzgerald	.05
134	Henry Cotto	.05
135	Gerald Young	.05
136	Luis Salazar	.05
137	Alejandro Pena	.05
138	Jack Howell	.05
139	Tony Fernandez	.05
140	Mark Grace	.05
141	Ken Caminiti	.05
142	Mike Jackson	.05
143	Larry McWilliams	.05
144	Andres Thomas	.05
145	Nolan Ryan	2.00
146	Mike Davis	.05
147	DeWayne Buice	.05
148	Jody Davis	.05
149	Jesse Barfield	.05
150	Matt Nokes	.05
151	Jerry Reuss	.05
152	Rick Cerone	.05
153	Storm Davis	.05
154	Marvell Wynne	.05
155	Will Clark	.05
156	Luis Aguayo	.05
157	Willie Upshaw	.05
158	Randy Bush	.05
159	Ron Darling	.05
160	Kal Daniels	.05
161	Spike Owen	.05
162	Luis Polonia	.05
163	Kevin Mitchell	.05
164	*Dave Gallagher*	.05
165	Benito Santiago	.05
166	Greg Gagne	.05
167	Ken Phelps	.05
168	Sid Fernandez	.05
169	Bo Diaz	.05
170	Cory Snyder	.05
171	Eric Show	.05
172	Robby Thompson	.05
173	Marty Barrett	.05
174	Dave Henderson	.05
175	Ozzie Guillen	.05
176	Barry Lyons	.05
177	*Kelvin Torve*	.05
178	Don Slaught	.05
179	Steve Lombardozzi	.05
180	*Chris Sabo*	.05
181	Jose Uribe	.05
182	Shane Mack	.05
183	Ron Karkovice	.05
184	Todd Benzinger	.05
185	Dave Stewart	.05
186	Julio Franco	.05
187	Ron Robinson	.05
188	Wally Backman	.05
189	Randy Velarde	.05
190	Joe Carter	.05
191	Bob Welch	.05
192	Kelly Paris	.05
193	Chris Brown	.05
194	Rick Reuschel	.05
195	Roger Clemens	1.60
196	Dave Concepcion	.05
197	Al Newman	.05
198	Brook Jacoby	.05
199	Mookie Wilson	.05
200	Don Mattingly	1.60
201	Dick Schofield	.05
202	Mark Gubicza	.05
203	Gary Gaetti	.05
204	Dan Pasqua	.05
205	Andre Dawson	.35
206	Chris Speier	.05
207	Kent Tekulve	.05
208	Rod Scurry	.05
209	Scott Bailes	.05
210	Rickey Henderson	1.00
211	Harold Baines	.05
212	Tony Armas	.05
213	Kent Hrbek	.05
214	Darrin Jackson	.05
215	George Brett	1.60
216	Rafael Santana	.05
217	Andy Allanson	.05
218	Brett Butler	.05
219	Steve Jeltz	.05
220	Jay Buhner	.05
221	Bo Jackson	.15
222	Angel Salazar	.05
223	Kirk McCaskill	.05
224	Steve Lyons	.05
225	Bert Blyleven	.05
226	Scott Bradley	.05
227	Bob Melvin	.05
228	Ron Kittle	.05
229	Phil Bradley	.05
230	Tommy John	.05
231	Greg Walker	.05
232	Juan Berenguer	.05
233	Pat Tabler	.05
234	*Terry Clark*	.05
235	Rafael Palmeiro	.75
236	Paul Zuvella	.05
237	Willie Randolph	.05
238	Bruce Fields	.05
239	Mike Aldrete	.05
240	Lance Parrish	.05
241	Greg Maddux	1.50
242	John Moses	.05
243	Melido Perez	.05
244	Willie Wilson	.05
245	Mark McLemore	.05
246	Von Hayes	.05
247	Matt Williams	.05
248	John Candelaria	.05
249	Harold Reynolds	.05
250	Greg Swindell	.05
251	Juan Agosto	.05
252	Mike Felder	.05
253	Vince Coleman	.05
254	Larry Sheets	.05
255	George Bell	.05
256	Terry Steinbach	.05
257	*Jack Armstrong*	.05
258	Dickie Thon	.05
259	Ray Knight	.05
260	Darryl Strawberry	.05
261	Doug Sisk	.05
262	Alex Trevino	.05
263	Jeff Leonard	.05
264	Tom Henke	.05
265	Ozzie Smith	1.50
266	Dave Bergman	.05
267	Tony Phillips	.05
268	Mark Davis	.05
269	Kevin Elster	.05
270	Barry Larkin	.05
271	Manny Lee	.05
272	Tom Brunansky	.05
273	Craig Biggio	.05
274	Jim Gantner	.05
275	Eddie Murray	1.00
276	Jeff Reed	.05
277	Tim Teufel	.05
278	Rick Honeycutt	.05
279	Guillermo Hernandez	.05
280	John Kruk	.05
281	*Luis Alicea*	.15
282	Jim Clancy	.05
283	Billy Ripken	.05
284	Craig Reynolds	.05
285	Robin Yount	1.00
286	Jimmy Jones	.05
287	Ron Oester	.05
288	Terry Leach	.05
289	Dennis Eckersley	.75
290	Alan Trammell	.05
291	Jimmy Key	.05
292	Chris Bosio	.05
293	Jose DeLeon	.05
294	Jim Traber	.05
295	Mike Scott	.05
296	Roger McDowell	.05
297	Garry Templeton	.05
298	Doyle Alexander	.05
299	Nick Esasky	.05
300	Mark McGwire	1.75
301	*Darryl Hamilton*	.05
302	Dave Smith	.05
303	Rick Sutcliffe	.05
304	Dave Stapleton	.05
305	Alan Ashby	.05
306	Pedro Guerrero	.05
307	Ron Guidry	.05
308	Steve Farr	.05
309	Curt Ford	.05
310	Claudell Washington	.05
311	Tom Prince	.05
312	*Chad Kreuter*	.15
313	Ken Oberkfell	.05
314	Jerry Browne	.05
315	R.J. Reynolds	.05
316	Scott Bankhead	.05
317	Milt Thompson	.05
318	Mario Diaz	.05
319	Bruce Ruffin	.05
320	Dave Valle	.05
321a	*Gary Varsho* (batting righty on card back, photo actually Mike Bielecki)	1.00
321b	*Gary Varsho* (batting lefty on card back, correct photo)	.05
322	Paul Mirabella	.05
323	Chuck Jackson	.05
324	Drew Hall	.05
325	Don August	.05
326	*Israel Sanchez*	.05
327	Denny Walling	.05
328	Joel Skinner	.05
329	Danny Tartabull	.05
330	Tony Pena	.05
331	Jim Sundberg	.05
332	Jeff Robinson	.05
333	Odibbe McDowell	.05
334	Jose Lind	.05
335	Paul Kilgus	.05
336	Juan Samuel	.05
337	Mike Campbell	.05
338	Mike Maddux	.05
339	Darnell Coles	.05
340	Bob Dernier	.05
341	Rafael Ramirez	.05
342	Scott Sanderson	.05
343	B.J. Surhoff	.05
344	Billy Hatcher	.05
345	Pat Perry	.05
346	Jack Clark	.05
347	Gary Thurman	.05
348	*Timmy Jones*	.05
349	Dave Winfield	1.00
350	Frank White	.05
351	Dave Collins	.05
352	Jack Morris	.05
353	Eric Plunk	.05
354	Leon Durham	.05
355	Ivan DeJesus	.05
356	*Brian Holman*	.05
357a	Dale Murphy (reversed negative)	17.50
357b	Dale Murphy (corrected)	.25
358	Mark Portugal	.05
359	Andy McGaffigan	.05
360	Tom Glavine	.25
361	Keith Moreland	.05
362	Todd Stottlemyre	.05
363	Dave Leiper	.05
364	Cecil Fielder	.05
365	Carmelo Martinez	.05
366	Dwight Evans	.05
367	Kevin McReynolds	.05
368	Rich Gedman	.05
369	Len Dykstra	.05
370	Jody Reed	.05
371	Jose Canseco	.60
372	Rob Murphy	.05
373	Mike Henneman	.05
374	Walt Weiss	.05
375	*Rob Dibble*	.05
376	Kirby Puckett	1.50
377	Denny Martinez	.05
378	Ron Gant	.05
379	Brian Harper	.05
380	*Nelson Santovenia*	.05
381	Lloyd Moseby	.05
382	Lance McCullers	.05
383	Dave Stieb	.05
384	Tony Gwynn	1.50
385	Mike Flanagan	.05
386	Bob Ojeda	.05
387	Bruce Hurst	.05
388	Dave Magadan	.05
389	Wade Boggs	1.50
390	Gary Carter	1.00
391	Frank Tanana	.05
392	Curt Young	.05
393	Jeff Treadway	.05
394	Darrell Evans	.05
395	Glenn Hubbard	.05
396	Chuck Cary	.05
397	Frank Viola	.05
398	Jeff Parrett	.05
399	*Terry Blocker*	.05
400	Dan Gladden	.05
401	*Louie Meadows*	.05
402	Tim Raines	.05
403	Joey Meyer	.05
404	Larry Andersen	.05
405	Rex Hudler	.05
406	Mike Schmidt	1.60
407	John Franco	.05
408	Brady Anderson	.05
409	Don Carman	.05
410	Eric Davis	.05
411	Bob Stanley	.05
412	Pete Smith	.05
413	Jim Rice	.25
414	Bruce Sutter	.75
415	Oil Can Boyd	.05
416	Ruben Sierra	.05
417	Mike LaValliere	.05
418	Steve Buechele	.05
419	Gary Redus	.05
420	Scott Fletcher	.05
421	Dale Sveum	.05
422	Bob Knepper	.05
423	Luis Rivera	.05
424	Ted Higuera	.05
425	Kevin Bass	.05
426	Ken Gerhart	.05
427	Shane Rawley	.05
428	Paul O'Neill	.05
429	Joe Orsulak	.05
430	Jackie Gutierrez	.05
431	Gerald Perry	.05
432	Mike Greenwell	.05
433	Jerry Royster	.05
434	Ellis Burks	.05
435	Ed Olwine	.05
436	Dave Rucker	.05
437	Charlie Hough	.05
438	Bob Walk	.05
439	Bob Brower	.05
440	Barry Bonds	2.00

No.	Player	Price
441	Tom Foley	.05
442	Rob Deer	.05
443	Glenn Davis	.05
444	Dave Martinez	.05
445	Bill Wegman	.05
446	Lloyd McClendon	.05
447	Dave Schmidt	.05
448	Darren Daulton	.05
449	Frank Williams	.05
450	Don Aase	.05
451	Lou Whitaker	.05
452	Goose Gossage	.05
453	Ed Whitson	.05
454	Jim Walewander	.05
455	Damon Berryhill	.05
456	Tim Burke	.05
457	Barry Jones	.05
458	Joel Youngblood	.05
459	Floyd Youmans	.05
460	Mark Salas	.05
461	Jeff Russell	.05
462	Darrell Miller	.05
463	Jeff Kunkel	.05
464	*Sherman Corbett*	.05
465	Curtis Wilkerson	.05
466	Bud Black	.05
467	Cal Ripken, Jr.	2.00
468	John Farrell	.05
469	Terry Kennedy	.05
470	Tom Candiotti	.05
471	Roberto Alomar	.20
472	Jeff Robinson	.05
473	Vance Law	.05
474	Randy Ready	.05
475	Walt Terrell	.05
476	Kelly Downs	.05
477	*Johnny Paredes*	.05
478	Shawn Hillegas	.05
479	Bob Brenly	.05
480	Otis Nixon	.05
481	Johnny Ray	.05
482	Geno Petralli	.05
483	Stu Cliburn	.05
484	Pete Incaviglia	.05
485	Brian Downing	.05
486	Jeff Stone	.05
487	Carmen Castillo	.05
488	Tom Niedenfuer	.05
489	Jay Bell	.05
490	Rick Schu	.05
491	*Jeff Pico*	.05
492	*Mark Parent*	.05
493	Eric King	.05
494	Al Nipper	.05
495	Andy Hawkins	.05
496	Daryl Boston	.05
497	Ernie Riles	.05
498	Pascual Perez	.05
499	Bill Long	.05
500	Kirt Manwaring	.05
501	Chuck Crim	.05
502	Candy Maldonado	.05
503	Dennis Lamp	.05
504	Glenn Braggs	.05
505	Joe Price	.05
506	Ken Williams	.05
507	Bill Pecota	.05
508	Rey Quinones	.05
509	*Jeff Bittiger*	.05
510	Kevin Seitzer	.05
511	Steve Bedrosian	.05
512	Todd Worrell	.05
513	Chris James	.05
514	Jose Oquendo	.05
515	David Palmer	.05
516	John Smiley	.05
517	Dave Clark	.05
518	Mike Dunne	.05
519	Ron Washington	.05
520	Bob Kipper	.05
521	Lee Smith	.05
522	Juan Castillo	.05
523	Don Robinson	.05
524	Kevin Romine	.05
525	Paul Molitor	1.00
526	Mark Langston	.05
527	Donnie Hill	.05
528	Larry Owen	.05
529	Jerry Reed	.05
530	Jack McDowell	.05
531	Greg Mathews	.05
532	John Russell	.05
533	Dan Quisenberry	.05
534	Greg Gross	.05
535	Danny Cox	.05
536	Terry Francona	.05
537	Andy Van Slyke	.05
538	Mel Hall	.05
539	Jim Gott	.05
540	Doug Jones	.05
541	Criag Lefferts	.05
542	Mike Boddicker	.05
543	Greg Brock	.05
544	Atlee Hammaker	.05
545	Tom Bolton	.05
546	*Mike Macfarlane*	.25
547	*Rich Renteria*	.05
548	John Davis	.05
549	Floyd Bannister	.05
550	Mickey Brantley	.05
551	Duane Ward	.05
552	Dan Petry	.05
553	Mickey Tettleton	.05
554	Rick Leach	.05
555	Mike Witt	.05
556	Sid Bream	.05
557	Bobby Witt	.05
558	Tommy Herr	.05
559	Randy Milligan	.05
560	*Jose Cecena*	.05
561	Mackey Sasser	.05
562	Carney Lansford	.05
563	Rick Aguilera	.05
564	Ron Hassey	.05
565	Dwight Gooden	.05
566	Paul Assenmacher	.05
567	Neil Allen	.05
568	Jim Morrison	.05
569	Mike Pagliarulo	.05
570	Ted Simmons	.05
571	Mark Thurmond	.05
572	Fred McGriff	.05
573	Wally Joyner	.05
574	*Jose Bautista*	.05
575	Kelly Gruber	.05
576	Cecilio Guante	.05
577	Mark Davidson	.05
578	Bobby Bonilla	.05
579	Mike Stanley	.05
580	Gene Larkin	.05
581	Stan Javier	.05
582	Howard Johnson	.05
583a	Mike Gallego (photo on card back reversed)	.75
583b	Mike Gallego (correct photo)	.05
584	David Cone	.05
585	*Doug Jennings*	.05
586	Charlie Hudson	.05
587	Dion James	.05
588	Al Leiter	.05
589	Charlie Puleo	.05
590	Roberto Kelly	.05
591	Thad Bosley	.05
592	Pete Stanicek	.05
593	*Pat Borders*	.25
594	*Bryan Harvey*	.05
595	Jeff Ballard	.05
596	Jeff Reardon	.05
597	Doug Drabek	.05
598	Edwin Correa	.05
599	Keith Atherton	.05
600	Dave LaPoint	.05
601	Don Baylor	.05
602	Tom Pagnozzi	.05
603	Tim Flannery	.05
604	Gene Walter	.05
605	Dave Parker	.05
606	Mike Diaz	.05
607	Chris Gwynn	.05
608	Odell Jones	.05
609	Carlton Fisk	1.00
610	Jay Howell	.05
611	Tim Crews	.05
612	Keith Hernandez	.05
613	Willie Fraser	.05
614	Jim Eppard	.05
615	Jeff Hamilton	.05
616	Kurt Stillwell	.05
617	Tom Browning	.05
618	Jeff Montgomery	.05
619	Jose Rijo	.05
620	Jamie Quirk	.05
621	Willie McGee	.05
622	Mark Grant	.05
623	Bill Swift	.05
624	Orlando Mercado	.05
625	*John Costello*	.05
626	Jose Gonzalez	.05
627a	Bill Schroeder (putting on shin guards on card back, photo actually Ronn Reynolds)	.75
627b	Bill Schroeder (arms crossed on card back, correct photo)	.05
628a	Fred Manrique (throwing on card back, photo actually Ozzie Guillen)	.75
628b	Fred Manrique (batting on card back, correct photo)	.05
629	Ricky Horton	.05
630	Dan Plesac	.05
631	Alfredo Griffin	.05
632	Chuck Finley	.05
633	Kirk Gibson	.05
634	Randy Myers	.05
635	Greg Minton	.05
636	Herm Winningham	.05
637	Charlie Leibrandt	.05
638	Tim Birtsas	.05
639	Bill Buckner	.05
640	Danny Jackson	.05
641	Greg Booker	.05
642	Jim Presley	.05
643	Gene Nelson	.05
644	Rod Booker	.05
645	Dennis Rasmussen	.05
646	Juan Nieves	.05
647	Bobby Thigpen	.05
648	Tim Belcher	.05
649	Mike Young	.05
650	Ivan Calderon	.05
651	*Oswaldo Peraza*	.05
652a	Pat Sheridan (no position on front)	8.00
652b	Pat Sheridan (position on front)	.05
653	Mike Morgan	.05
654	Mike Heath	.05
655	Jay Tibbs	.05
656	Fernando Valenzuela	.05
657	Lee Mazzilli	.05
658	Frank Viola	.05
659	Jose Canseco	.60
660	Walt Weiss	.05
661	Orel Hershiser	.05
662	Kirk Gibson	.05
663	Chris Sabo	.05
664	Dennis Eckersley	.75
665	Orel Hershiser	.05
666	Kirk Gibson	.05
667	Orel Hershiser	.05
668	Wally Joyner (TC)	.05
669	Nolan Ryan (TC)	1.00
670	Jose Canseco (TC)	.30
671	Fred McGriff (TC)	.05
672	Dale Murphy (TC)	.20
673	Paul Molitor (TC)	.50
674	Ozzie Smith (TC)	.75
675	Ryne Sandberg (TC)	.40
676	Kirk Gibson (TC)	.05
677	Andres Galarraga (TC)	.05
678	Will Clark (TC)	.05
679	Cory Snyder (TC)	.05
680	Alvin Davis (TC)	.05
681	Darryl Strawberry (TC)	.05
682	Cal Ripken, Jr. (TC)	1.00
683	Tony Gwynn (TC)	.40
684	Mike Schmidt (TC)	.85
685	Andy Van Slyke (TC)	.05
686	Ruben Sierra (TC)	.05
687	Wade Boggs (TC)	.40
688	Eric Davis (TC)	.05
689	George Brett (TC)	.85
690	Alan Trammell (TC)	.05
691	Frank Viola (TC)	.05
692	Harold Baines (TC)	.05
693	Don Mattingly (TC)	.85
694	Checklist 1-100	.05
695	Checklist 101-200	.05
696	Checklist 201-300	.05
697	Checklist 301-400	.05
698	Checklist 401-500	.05
699	Checklist 501-600	.05
700	Checklist 601-700	.05
701	Checklist 701-800	.05
702	Jessie Barfield	.05
703	Walt Terrell	.05
704	Dickie Thon	.05
705	Al Leiter	.05
706	Dave LaPoint	.05
707	*Charlie Hayes*	.05
708	Andy Hawkins	.05
709	Mickey Hatcher	.05
710	Lance McCullers	.05
711	Ron Kittle	.05
712	Bert Blyleven	.05
713	Rick Dempsey	.05
714	Ken Williams	.05
715	Steve Rosenberg	.05
716	Joe Skalski	.05
717	Spike Owen	.05
718	Todd Burns	.05
719	Kevin Gross	.05
720	Tommy Herr	.05
721	Rob Ducey	.05
722	Gary Green	.05
723	*Gregg Olson*	.10
724	Greg Harris	.05
725	Craig Worthington	.05
726	Tom Howard	.05
727	Dale Mohorcic	.05
728	Rich Yett	.05
729	Mel Hall	.05
730	Floyd Youmans	.05
731	Lonnie Smith	.05
732	Wally Backman	.05
733	Trevor Wilson	.05
734	Jose Alvarez	.05
735	Bob Milacki	.05
736	*Tom Gordon*	.50
737	Wally Whitehurst	.05
738	Mike Aldrete	.05
739	Keith Miller	.05
740	Randy Milligan	.05
741	Jeff Parrett	.05
742	*Steve Finley*	.75
743	*Junior Felix*	.05
744	*Pete Harnisch*	.25
745	Bill Spiers	.05
746	Hensley Meulens	.05
747	Juan Bell	.05
748	Steve Sax	.05
749	Phil Bradley	.05
750	Rey Quinones	.05
751	Tommy Gregg	.05
752	Kevin Brown	.25
753	Derek Lilliquist	.05
754	*Todd Zeile*	.75
755	Jim Abbott	.05
756	*Ozzie Canseco*	.05
757	Nick Esasky	.05
758	Mike Moore	.05
759	Rob Murphy	.05
760	Rick Mahler	.05
761	Fred Lynn	.05
762	*Kevin Blankenship*	.05
763	Eddie Murray	1.00
764	*Steve Searcy*	.05
765	*Jerome Walton*	.05
766	*Erik Hanson*	.05
767	Bob Boone	.05
768	Edgar Martinez	.05
769	*Jose DeJesus*	.05
770	*Greg Briley*	.05
771	*Steve Peters*	.05
772	Rafael Palmeiro	.75
773	Jack Clark	.05
774	Nolan Ryan	2.00
775	Lance Parrish	.05
776	*Joe Girardi*	.30
777	Willie Randolph	.05
778	Mitch Williams	.05
779	*Dennis Cook*	.05
780	*Dwight Smith*	.05
781	*Lenny Harris*	.10
782	*Torey Lovullo*	.05
783	*Norm Charlton*	.15
784	Chris Brown	.05
785	Todd Benzinger	.05
786	Shane Rawley	.05
787	*Omar Vizquel*	2.00
788	*LaVel Freeman*	.05
789	Jeffrey Leonard	.05
790	*Eddie Williams*	.05
791	Jamie Moyer	.05
792	Bruce Hurst	.05
793	Julio Franco	.05
794	Claudell Washington	.05
795	Jody Davis	.05
796	Oddibe McDowell	.05
797	Paul Kilgus	.05
798	Tracy Jones	.05
799	Steve Wilson	.05
800	Pete O'Brien	.05

1990 UPPER DECK

Tom Gordon

	NM/M
Unopened Factory Set (800):	20.00
Complete Set (800):	15.00
Complete Low Set (700):	12.00
Complete High Set (100):	5.00
Common Player:	.05
Low or High Foil Pack (15):	.50
Low or High Foil Box (36):	12.00

1 Star Rookie Checklist .05
2 *Randy Nosek* .05
3 *Tom Drees* .05
4 Curt Young .05
5 Devon White Angels checklist .05
6 Luis Salazar .05
7 Von Hayes Phillies checklist .05
8 Jose Bautista .05
9 *Marquis Grissom* .50
10 Orel Hershiser Dodgers checklist .05
11 Rick Aguilera .05
12 Benito Santiago Padres checklist .05
13 Deion Sanders .10
14 Marvell Wynne .05
15 David West .05
16 Bobby Bonilla Pirates checklist .05
17 *Sammy Sosa* 5.00
18 Steve Sax Yankees checklist .05
19 Jack Howell .05
20 Mike Schmidt Mike Schmidt Retires .75
21 Robin Ventura .05
22 Brian Meyer .05
23 *Blaine Beatty* .05
24 Ken Griffey, Jr. Mariners checklist .50
25 Greg Vaughn .05
26 *Xavier Hernandez* .05
27 *Jason Grimsley* .05
28 *Eric Anthony* .05
29 Tim Raines Expos checklist .05
30 David Wells .05
31 Hal Morris .05
32 Bo Jackson Royals checklist .10
33 *Kelly Mann* .05
34 Nolan Ryan Nolan Ryan 5000 Strikeouts 1.00
35 *Scott Service* .05
36 Mark McGwire Athletics checklist .50
37 Tino Martinez .05
38 Chili Davis .05
39 Scott Sanderson .05
40 Kevin Mitchell Giants checklist .05
41 Lou Whitaker Tigers checklist .05
42 *Scott Coolbaugh* .05
43 *Jose Cano* .05
44 *Jose Vizcaino* .10
45 *Bob Hamelin* .05
46 *Jose Offerman* .15
47 Kevin Blankenship .05
48 Kirby Puckett Twins checklist .40
49 *Tommy Greene* .05
50 Will Clark N.L. Top Vote Getter .05
51 Rob Nelson .05
52 *Chris Hammond* .15
53 Joe Carter Indians checklist .05
54a *Ben McDonald* (Orioles Logo) 1.00
54b *Ben McDonald* (Star Rookie logo) .25
55 Andy Benes .05
56 *John Olerud* 1.00
57 Roger Clemens Red Sox checklist .45
58 Tony Armas .05
59 *George Canale* .05
60a Mickey Tettleton Orioles checklist (#683 Jamie Weston) 1.00
60b Mickey Tettleton Orioles checklist (#683 Mickey Weston) .05
61 *Mike Stanton* .05
62 Dwight Gooden Mets checklist .05
63 *Kent Mercker* .10
64 *Francisco Cabrera* .05
65 Steve Avery .05
66 Jose Canseco .35
67 *Matt Merullo* .05
68 Vince Coleman Cardinals checklist .05
69 Ron Karkovice .05
70 *Kevin Maas* .05
71 Dennis Cook .05
72 *Juan Gonzalez* 2.00
73 Andre Dawson Cubs checklist .10
74 *Dean Palmer* .25
75 Bo Jackson A.L. Top Vote Getter .10
76 *Rob Richie* .05
77 *Bobby Rose* .05
78 *Brian DuBois* .05
79 Ozzie Guillen White Sox checklist .05
80 Gene Nelson .05
81 Bob McClure .05
82 Julio Franco Rangers checklist .05
83 Greg Minton .05
84 John Smoltz Braves checklist .05
85 Willie Fraser .05
86 Neal Heaton .05
87 *Kevin Tapani* .05
88 Mike Scott Astros checklist .05
89a Jim Gott (incorrect photo) 1.00
89b Jim Gott (correct photo) .05
90 Lance Johnson .05
91 Robin Yount Brewers checklist .35
92 Jeff Parrett .05
93 *Julio Machado* .05
94 Ron Jones .05
95 George Bell Blue Jays checklist .05
96 Jerry Reuss .05
97 Brian Fisher .05
98 *Kevin Ritz* .05
99 Barry Larkin Reds checklist .05
100 Checklist 1-100 .05
101 Gerald Perry .05
102 Kevin Appier .05
103 Julio Franco .05
104 Craig Biggio .05
105 Bo Jackson .10
106 *Junior Felix* .05
107 Mike Harkey .05
108 Fred McGriff .05
109 Rick Sutcliffe .05
110 Pete O'Brien .05
111 Kelly Gruber .05
112 Pat Borders .05
113 Dwight Evans .05
114 Dwight Gooden .05
115 *Kevin Batiste* .05
116 Eric Davis .05
117 Kevin Mitchell .05
118 Ron Oester .05
119 Brett Butler .05
120 Danny Jackson .05
121 Tommy Gregg .05
122 Ken Caminiti .05
123 Kevin Brown .05
124 George Brett .85
125 Mike Scott .05
126 Cory Snyder .05
127 George Bell .05
128 Mark Grace .05
129 Devon White .05
130 Tony Fernandez .05
131 Don Aase .05
132 Rance Mulliniks .05
133 Marty Barrett .05
134 Nelson Liriano .05
135 Mark Carreon .05
136 Candy Maldonado .05
137 Tim Birtsas .05
138 Tom Brookens .05
139 John Franco .05
140 Mike LaCoss .05
141 Jeff Treadway .05
142 Pat Tabler .05
143 Darrell Evans .05
144 Rafael Ramirez .05
145 Oddibe McDowell .05
146 Brian Downing .05
147 Curtis Wilkerson .05
148 Ernie Whitt .05
149 Bill Schroeder .05
150 Domingo Ramos .05
151 Rick Honeycutt .05
152 Don Slaught .05
153 Mitch Webster .05
154 Tony Phillips .05
155 Paul Kilgus .05
156 Ken Griffey, Jr. 1.50
157 Gary Sheffield .35
158 Wally Backman .05
159 B.J. Surhoff .05
160 Louie Meadows .05
161 Paul O'Neill .05
162 *Jeff McKnight* .05
163 Alvaro Espinoza .05
164 *Scott Scudder* .05
165 Jeff Reed .05
166 Gregg Jefferies .05
167 Barry Larkin .05
168 Gary Carter .60
169 Robby Thompson .05
170 Rolando Roomes .05
171 Mark McGwire 1.50
172 Steve Sax .05
173 Mark Williamson .05
174 Mitch Williams .05
175 Brian Holton .05
176 Rob Deer .05
177 Tim Raines .05
178 Mike Felder .05
179 Harold Reynolds .05
180 Terry Francona .05
181 Chris Sabo .05
182 Darryl Strawberry .05
183 Willie Randolph .05
184 Billy Ripken .05
185 Mackey Sasser .05
186 Todd Benzinger .05
187 Kevin Elster .05
188 Jose Uribe .05
189 Tom Browning .05
190 Keith Miller .05
191 Don Mattingly .85
192 Dave Parker .05
193 Roberto Kelly .05
194 Phil Bradley .05
195 Ron Hassey .05
196 Gerald Young .05
197 Hubie Brooks .05
198 Bill Doran .05
199 Al Newman .05
200 Checklist 101-200 .05
201 Terry Puhl .05
202 Frank DiPino .05
203 Jim Clancy .05
204 Bob Ojeda .05
205 Alex Trevino .05
206 Dave Henderson .05
207 Henry Cotto .05
208 Rafael Belliard .05
209 Stan Javier .05
210 Jerry Reed .05
211 Doug Dascenzo .05
212 Andres Thomas .05
213 Greg Maddux .75
214 Mike Schooler .05
215 Lonnie Smith .05
216 Jose Rijo .05
217 Greg Gagne .05
218 Jim Gantner .05
219 Allan Anderson .05
220 Rick Mahler .05
221 Jim Deshaies .05
222 Keith Hernandez .05
223 Vince Coleman .05
224 David Cone .05
225 Ozzie Smith .75
226 Matt Nokes .05
227 Barry Bonds 2.00
228 Felix Jose .05
229 Dennis Powell .05
230 Mike Gallego .05
231 Shawon Dunston .05
232 Ron Gant .05
233 Omar Vizquel .05
234 Derek Lilliquist .05
235 Erik Hanson .05
236 Kirby Puckett .75
237 Bill Spiers .05
238 Dan Gladden .05
239 Bryan Clutterbuck .05
240 John Moses .05
241 Ron Darling .05
242 Joe Magrane .05
243 Dave Magadan .05
244 Pedro Guerrero .05
245 Glenn Davis .05
246 Terry Steinbach .05
247 Fred Lynn .05
248 Gary Redus .05
249 Kenny Williams .05
250 Sid Bream .05
251 Bob Welch .05
252 Bill Buckner .05
253 Carney Lansford .05
254 Paul Molitor .60
255 Jose DeJesus .05
256 Orel Hershiser .05
257 Tom Brunansky .05
258 Mike Davis .05
259 Jeff Ballard .05
260 Scott Terry .05
261 Sid Fernandez .05
262 Mike Marshall .05
263 Howard Johnson .05
264 Kirk Gibson .05
265 Kevin McReynolds .05
266 Cal Ripken, Jr. 2.00
267 Ozzie Guillen .05
268 Jim Traber .05
269 Bobby Thigpen .05
270 Joe Orsulak .05
271 Bob Boone .05
272 Dave Stewart .05
273 Tim Wallach .05
274 Luis Aquino .05
275 Mike Moore .05
276 Tony Pena .05
277 Eddie Murray .60
278 Milt Thompson .05
279 Alejandro Pena .05
280 Ken Dayley .05
281 Carmen Castillo .05
282 Tom Henke .05
283 Mickey Hatcher .05
284 Roy Smith .05
285 Manny Lee .05
286 Dan Pasqua .05
287 Larry Sheets .05
288 Garry Templeton .05
289 Eddie Williams .05
290 Brady Anderson .05
291 Spike Owen .05
292 Storm Davis .05
293 Chris Bosio .05
294 Jim Eisenreich .05
295 Don August .05
296 Jeff Hamilton .05
297 Mickey Tettleton .05
298 Mike Scioscia .05
299 Kevin Hickey .05
300 Checklist 201-300 .05
301 Shawn Abner .05
302 Kevin Bass .05
303 Bip Roberts .05
304 Joe Girardi .05
305 Danny Darwin .05
306 Mike Heath .05
307 Mike Macfarlane .05
308 Ed Whitson .05
309 Tracy Jones .05
310 Scott Fletcher .05
311 Darnell Coles .05
312 Mike Brumley .05
313 Bill Swift .05
314 Charlie Hough .05
315 Jim Presley .05
316 Luis Polonia .05
317 Mike Morgan .05
318 Lee Guetterman .05
319 Jose Oquendo .05
320 Wayne Tollenson .05
321 Jody Reed .05
322 Damon Berryhill .05
323 Roger Clemens .85
324 Ryne Sandberg .75
325 Benito Santiago .05
326 Bret Saberhagen .05
327 Lou Whitaker .05
328 Dave Gallagher .05
329 Mike Pagliarulo .05
330 Doyle Alexander .05
331 Jeffrey Leonard .05
332 Torey Lovullo .05
333 Pete Incaviglia .05
334 Rickey Henderson .60
335 Rafael Palmeiro .50
336 Ken Hill .05
337 Dave Winfield .60
338 Alfredo Griffin .05
339 Andy Hawkins .05
340 Ted Power .05
341 Steve Wilson .05
342 Jack Clark .05
343 Ellis Burks .05
344 Tony Gwynn .75
345 Jerome Walton .05
346 Roberto Alomar .20
347 *Carlos Martinez* .05
348 Chet Lemon .05
349 Willie Wilson .05

No.	Player	Value
350	Greg Walker	.05
351	Tom Bolton	.05
352	German Gonzalez	.05
353	Harold Baines	.05
354	Mike Greenwell	.05
355	Ruben Sierra	.05
356	Andres Galarraga	.05
357	Andre Dawson	.25
358	*Jeff Brantley*	.05
359	Mike Bielecki	.05
360	Ken Oberkfell	.05
361	Kurt Stillwell	.05
362	Brian Holman	.05
363	Kevin Seitzer	.05
364	Alvin Davis	.05
365	Tom Gordon	.05
366	Bobby Bonilla	.05
367	Carlton Fisk	.60
368	*Steve Carter*	.05
369	Joel Skinner	.05
370	John Cangelosi	.05
371	Cecil Espy	.05
372	*Gary Wayne*	.05
373	Jim Rice	.20
374	*Mike Dyer*	.05
375	Joe Carter	.05
376	Dwight Smith	.05
377	*John Wetteland*	.15
378	Ernie Riles	.05
379	Otis Nixon	.05
380	Vance Law	.05
381	Dave Bergman	.05
382	Frank White	.05
383	Scott Bradley	.05
384	Israel Sanchez	.05
385	Gary Pettis	.05
386	Donn Pall	.05
387	John Smiley	.05
388	Tom Candiotti	.05
389	Junior Ortiz	.05
390	Steve Lyons	.05
391	Brian Harper	.05
392	Fred Manrique	.05
393	Lee Smith	.05
394	Jeff Kunkel	.05
395	Claudell Washington	.05
396	John Tudor	.05
397	Terry Kennedy	.05
398	Lloyd McClendon	.05
399	Craig Lefferts	.05
400	Checklist 301-400	.05
401	Keith Moreland	.05
402	Rich Gedman	.05
403	Jeff Robinson	.05
404	Randy Ready	.05
405	Rick Cerone	.05
406	Jeff Blauser	.05
407	Larry Andersen	.05
408	Joe Boever	.05
409	Felix Fermin	.05
410	Glenn Wilson	.05
411	Rex Hudler	.05
412	Mark Grant	.05
413	Dennis Martinez	.05
414	Darrin Jackson	.05
415	Mike Aldrete	.05
416	Roger McDowell	.05
417	Jeff Reardon	.05
418	Darren Daulton	.05
419	Tim Laudner	.05
420	Don Carman	.05
421	Lloyd Moseby	.05
422	Doug Drabek	.05
423	Lenny Harris	.05
424	Jose Lind	.05
425	*Dave Johnson*	.05
426	Jerry Browne	.05
427	*Eric Yelding*	.05
428	Brad Komminsk	.05
429	Jody Davis	.05
430	Mariano Duncan	.05
431	Mark Davis	.05
432	Nelson Santovenia	.05
433	Bruce Hurst	.05
434	*Jeff Huson*	.05
435	Chris James	.05
436	*Mark Guthrie*	.05
437	Charlie Hayes	.05
438	Shane Rawley	.05
439	Dickie Thon	.05
440	Juan Berenguer	.05
441	Kevin Romine	.05
442	Bill Landrum	.05
443	Todd Frohwirth	.05
444	Craig Worthington	.05
445	Fernando Valenzuela	.05
446	Albert Belle	.05
447	*Ed Whited*	.05
448	Dave Smith	.05
449	Dave Clark	.05
450	Juan Agosto	.05
451	Dave Valle	.05
452	Kent Hrbek	.05
453	Von Hayes	.05
454	Gary Gaetti	.05
455	Greg Briley	.05
456	Glenn Braggs	.05
457	Kirt Manwaring	.05
458	Mel Hall	.05
459	Brook Jacoby	.05
460	Pat Sheridan	.05
461	Rob Murphy	.05
462	Jimmy Key	.05
463	Nick Esasky	.05
464	Rob Ducey	.05
465	Carlos Quintana	.05
466	*Larry Walker*	1.00
467	Todd Worrell	.05
468	Kevin Gross	.05
469	Terry Pendleton	.05
470	Dave Martinez	.05
471	Gene Larkin	.05
472	Len Dykstra	.05
473	Barry Lyons	.05
474	Terry Mulholland	.05
475	*Chip Hale*	.05
476	Jesse Barfield	.05
477	Dan Plesac	.05
478a	Scott Garrelts (Photo actually Bill Bathe)	1.00
478b	Scott Garrelts (Correct photo)	.05
479	Dave Righetti	.05
480	Gus Polidor	.05
481	Mookie Wilson	.05
482	Luis Rivera	.05
483	Mike Flanagan	.05
484	Dennis "Oil Can" Boyd	.05
485	John Cerutti	.05
486	John Costello	.05
487	Pascual Perez	.05
488	Tommy Herr	.05
489	Tom Foley	.05
490	Curt Ford	.05
491	Steve Lake	.05
492	Tim Teufel	.05
493	Randy Bush	.05
494	Mike Jackson	.05
495	Steve Jeltz	.05
496	Paul Gibson	.05
497	Steve Balboni	.05
498	Bud Black	.05
499	Dale Sveum	.05
500	Checklist 401-500	.05
501	Timmy Jones	.05
502	Mark Portugal	.05
503	Ivan Calderon	.05
504	Rick Rhoden	.05
505	Willie McGee	.05
506	Kirk McCaskill	.05
507	Dave LaPoint	.05
508	Jay Howell	.05
509	Johnny Ray	.05
510	Dave Anderson	.05
511	Chuck Crim	.05
512	Joe Hesketh	.05
513	Dennis Eckersley	.40
514	Greg Brock	.05
515	Tim Burke	.05
516	Frank Tanana	.05
517	Jay Bell	.05
518	Guillermo Hernandez	.05
519	Randy Kramer	.05
520	Charles Hudson	.05
521	Jim Corsi	.05
522	Steve Rosenberg	.05
523	Cris Carpenter	.05
524	*Matt Winters*	.05
525	Melido Perez	.05
526	Chris Gwynn	.05
527	Bert Blyleven	.05
528	Chuck Cary	.05
529	Daryl Boston	.05
530	Dale Mohorcic	.05
531	Geronimo Berroa	.05
532	Edgar Martinez	.05
533	Dale Murphy	.20
534	Jay Buhner	.05
535	John Smoltz	.05
536	Andy Van Slyke	.05
537	Mike Henneman	.05
538	Miguel Garcia	.05
539	Frank Williams	.05
540	R.J. Reynolds	.05
541	Shawn Hillegas	.05
542	Walt Weiss	.05
543	*Greg Hibbard*	.05
544	Nolan Ryan	2.00
545	Todd Zeile	.05
546	Hensley Meulens	.05
547	Tim Belcher	.05
548	Mike Witt	.05
549	Greg Cadaret	.05
550	Franklin Stubbs	.05
551	*Tony Castillo*	.05
552	Jeff Robinson	.05
553	*Steve Olin*	.05
554	Alan Trammell	.05
555	Wade Boggs	.75
556	Will Clark	.05
557	Jeff King	.05
558	Mike Fitzgerald	.05
559	Ken Howell	.05
560	Bob Kipper	.05
561	Scott Bankhead	.05
562a	*Jeff Innis* (Photo actually David West)	1.00
562b	*Jeff Innis* (Correct photo)	.05
563	Randy Johnson	.60
564	*Wally Whithurst*	.05
565	*Gene Harris*	.05
566	Norm Charlton	.05
567	Robin Yount	.60
568	*Joe Oliver*	.05
569	Mark Parent	.05
570	John Farrell	.05
571	Tom Glavine	.20
572	Rod Nichols	.05
573	Jack Morris	.05
574	Greg Swindell	.05
575	Steve Searcy	.05
576	Ricky Jordan	.05
577	Matt Williams	.05
578	Mike LaValliere	.05
579	Bryn Smith	.05
580	Bruce Ruffin	.05
581	Randy Myers	.05
582	*Rick Wrona*	.05
583	Juan Samuel	.05
584	Les Lancaster	.05
585	Jeff Musselman	.05
586	Rob Dibble	.05
587	Eric Show	.05
588	Jesse Orosco	.05
589	Herm Winningham	.05
590	Andy Allanson	.05
591	Dion James	.05
592	Carmelo Martinez	.05
593	Luis Quinones	.05
594	Dennis Rasmussen	.05
595	Rich Yett	.05
596	Bob Walk	.05
597a	Andy McGaffigan (player #48, photo actually Rich Thompson)	.75
597b	Andy McGaffigan (player #27, correct photo)	.05
598	Billy Hatcher	.05
599	Bob Knepper	.05
600	Checklist 501-600	.05
601	Joey Cora	.05
602	*Steve Finley*	.20
603	Kal Daniels	.05
604	Gregg Olson	.05
605	Dave Steib	.05
606	*Kenny Rogers*	.05
607	Zane Smith	.05
608	*Bob Geren*	.05
609	Chad Kreuter	.05
610	Mike Smithson	.05
611	*Jeff Wetherby*	.05
612	*Gary Mielke*	.05
613	Pete Smith	.05
614	*Jack Daugherty*	.05
615	Lance McCullers	.05
616	Don Robinson	.05
617	Jose Guzman	.05
618	Steve Bedrosian	.05
619	Jamie Moyer	.05
620	Atlee Hammaker	.05
621	*Rick Luecken*	.05
622	Greg W. Harris	.05
623	Pete Harnisch	.05
624	Jerald Clark	.05
625	Jack McDowell	.05
626	Frank Viola	.05
627	Ted Higuera	.05
628	*Marty Pevey*	.05
629	Bill Wegman	.05
630	Eric Plunk	.05
631	Drew Hall	.05
632	Doug Jones	.05
633	Geno Petralli	.05
634	Jose Alvarez	.05
635	Bob Milacki	.05
636	Bobby Witt	.05
637	Trevor Wilson	.05
638	Jeff Russell	.05
639	Mike Krukow	.05
640	Rick Leach	.05
641	Dave Schmidt	.05
642	Terry Leach	.05
643	Calvin Schiraldi	.05
644	Bob Melvin	.05
645	Jim Abbott	.05
646	*Jaime Navarro*	.05
647	Mark Langston	.05
648	Juan Nieves	.05
649	Damaso Garcia	.05
650	Charlie O'Brien	.05
651	Eric King	.05
652	Mike Boddicker	.05
653	Duane Ward	.05
654	Bob Stanley	.05
655	Sandy Alomar, Jr.	.05
656	Danny Tartabull	.05
657	Randy McCament	.05
658	Charlie Leibrandt	.05
659	Dan Quisenberry	.05
660	Paul Assenmacher	.05
661	Walt Terrell	.05
662	Tim Leary	.05
663	Randy Milligan	.05
664	Bo Diaz	.05
665	Mark Lemke	.05
666	Jose Gonzalez	.05
667	Chuck Finley	.05
668	John Kruk	.05
669	Dick Schofield	.05
670	Tim Crews	.05
671	John Dopson	.05
672	*John Orton*	.05
673	Eric Hetzel	.05
674	Lance Parrish	.05
675	Ramon Martinez	.05
676	Mark Gubicza	.05
677	Greg Litton	.05
678	Greg Mathews	.05
679	Dave Dravecky	.05
680	Steve Farr	.05
681	Mike Devereaux	.05
682	Ken Griffey, Sr.	.05
683a	*Jamie Weston* (first name incorrect)	1.00
683b	*Mickey Weston* (corrected)	.05
684	Jack Armstrong	.05
685	Steve Buechele	.05
686	Bryan Harvey	.05
687	Lance Blankenship	.05
688	Dante Bichette	.05
689	Todd Burns	.05
690	Dan Petry	.05
691	*Kent Anderson*	.05
692	Todd Stottlemyre	.05
693	Wally Joyner	.05
694	Mike Rochford	.05
695	Floyd Bannister	.05
696	Rick Reuschel	.05
697	Jose DeLeon	.05
698	Jeff Montgomery	.05
699	Kelly Downs	.05
700a	Checklist 601-700 (#683 Jamie Weston)	.05
700b	Checklist 601-700 (# 683 Mickey Weston)	.05
701	Jim Gott	.05
702	Delino DeShields, Larry Walker, Marquis Grissom "Rookie Threats"	.25
703	Alejandro Pena	.05
704	Willie Randolph	.05
705	Tim Leary	.05
706	Chuck McElroy	.05
707	Gerald Perry	.05
708	Tom Brunansky	.05
709	John Franco	.05
710	Mark Davis	.05
711	*Dave Justice*	1.50
712	Storm Davis	.05
713	Scott Ruskin	.05
714	Glenn Braggs	.05
715	Kevin Bearse	.05
716	Jose Nunez	.05
717	Tim Layana	.05
718	Greg Myers	.05
719	Pete O'Brien	.05
720	John Candelaria	.05
721	Craig Grebeck	.05
722	Shawn Boskie	.05
723	Jim Leyritz	.10
724	Bill Sampen	.05
725	Scott Radinsky	.05
726	*Todd Hundley*	.25
727	Scott Hemond	.05

#	Player	NM/M
728	Lenny Webster	.05
729	Jeff Reardon	.05
730	Mitch Webster	.05
731	Brian Bohanon	.05
732	Rick Parker	.05
733	Terry Shumpert	.05
734a	Nolan Ryan (300-win stripe on front)	1.50
734b	Nolan Ryan (no stripe)	4.00
735	John Burkett	.05
736	*Derrick May*	.05
737	*Carlos Baerga*	.05
738	Greg Smith	.05
739	Joe Kraemer	.05
740	Scott Sanderson	.05
741	Hector Villanueva	.05
742	Mike Fetters	.05
743	Mark Gardner	.05
744	Matt Nokes	.05
745	Dave Winfield	.60
746	*Delino DeShields*	.15
747	Dann Howitt	.05
748	Tony Pena	.05
749	Oil Can Boyd	.05
750	Mike Benjamin	.05
751	Alex Cole	.05
752	Eric Gunderson	.05
753	Howard Farmer	.05
754	Joe Carter	.05
755	*Ray Lankford*	.25
756	Sandy Alomar,Jr.	.05
757	Alex Sanchez	.05
758	Nick Esasky	.05
759	Stan Belinda	.05
760	Jim Presley	.05
761	Gary DiSarcina	.05
762	Wayne Edwards	.05
763	Pat Combs	.05
764	Mickey Pina	.05
765	*Wilson Alvarez*	.25
766	Dave Parker	.05
767	Mike Blowers	.05
768	Tony Phillips	.05
769	Pascual Perez	.05
770	Gary Pettis	.05
771	Fred Lynn	.05
772	*Mel Rojas*	.10
773	David Segui	.25
774	Gary Carter	.60
775	Rafael Valdez	.05
776	Glenallen Hill	.05
777	Keith Hernandez	.05
778	Billy Hatcher	.05
779	Marty Clary	.05
780	Candy Maldonado	.05
781	Mike Marshall	.05
782	Billy Jo Robidoux	.05
783	Mark Langston	.05
784	*Paul Sorrento*	.05
785	*Dave Hollins*	.05
786	Cecil Fielder	.05
787	Matt Young	.05
788	Jeff Huson	.05
789	Lloyd Moseby	.05
790	Ron Kittle	.05
791	Hubie Brooks	.05
792	Craig Lefferts	.05
793	Kevin Bass	.05
794	Bryn Smith	.05
795	Juan Samuel	.05
796	Sam Horn	.05
797	Randy Myers	.05
798	Chris James	.05
799	Bill Gullickson	.05
800	Checklist 701-800	.05

Baseball Heroes Reggie Jackson

	NM/M
Complete Set (10):	5.00
Common Player:	.50
Autographed Card:	100.00

1991 UPPER DECK

	NM/M
Unopened Factory Set (800):	13.50
Complete Set (800):	10.00
Complete Low Series (700):	9.00
Complete High Series (100):	1.00
Common Player:	.05
Low or High Wax Pack (15):	.60
Low or High Wax Box (36):	13.50

#	Player	NM/M
1	Star Rookie Checklist	.05
2	*Phil Plantier*	.05
3	*D.J. Dozier*	.05
4	Dave Hansen	.05
5	Mo Vaughn	.10
6	*Leo Gomez*	.05
7	*Scott Aldred*	.05
8	*Scott Chiamparino*	.05
9	*Lance Dickson*	.05
10	*Sean Berry*	.05
11	Bernie Williams	.25
12	*Brian Barnes*	.05
13	*Narciso Elvira*	.05
14	*Mike Gardiner*	.05
15	*Greg Colbrunn*	.05
16	*Bernard Gilkey*	.05
17	Mark Lewis	.05
18	*Mickey Morandini*	.05
19	Charles Nagy	.05
20	*Geronimo Pena*	.05
21	*Henry Rodriguez*	.05
22	Scott Cooper	.05
23	*Andujar Cedeno*	.05
24	*Eric Karros*	.25
25	*Steve Decker*	.05
26	*Kevin Belcher*	.05
27	*Jeff Conine*	.25
28	Dave Stewart Oakland Athletics checklist	.05
29	Carlton Fisk Chicago White Sox checklist	.20
30	Rafael Palmeiro Texas Rangers checklist	.20
31	Chuck Finley California Angels checklist	.05
32	Harold Reynolds Seattle Mariners checklist	.05
33	Bret Saberhagen Kansas City Royals checklist	.05
34	Gary Gaetti Minnesota Twins checklist	.05
35	Scott Leius	.05
36	Neal Heaton	.05
37	*Terry Lee*	.05
38	Gary Redus	.05
39	Barry Jones	.05
40	Chuck Knoblauch	.05
41	Larry Andersen	.05
42	Darryl Hamilton	.05
43	Mike Greenwell Boston Red Sox checklist	.05
44	Kelly Gruber Toronto Blue Jays checklist	.05
45	Jack Morris Detroit Tigers checklist	.05
46	Sandy Alomar Jr. Cleveland Indians checklist	.05
47	Gregg Olson Baltimore Orioles checklist	.05
48	Dave Parker Milwaukee Brewers checklist	.05
49	Roberto Kelly New York Yankees checklist	.05
50	Top Prospect '91 checklist	.05
51	*Kyle Abbott*	.10
52	Jeff Juden	.05
53	*Todd Van Poppel*	.10
54	*Steve Karsay*	.10
55	*Chipper Jones*	2.00
56	*Chris Johnson*	.05
57	*John Ericks*	.05
58	*Gary Scott*	.05
59	Kiki Jones	.05
60	*Wil Cordero*	.05
61	*Royce Clayton*	.05
62	*Tim Costo*	.05
63	Roger Salkeld	.05
64	*Brook Fordyce*	.05
65	*Mike Mussina*	1.00
66	*Dave Staton*	.05
67	*Mike Lieberthal*	.50
68	*Kurt Miller*	.05
69	*Dan Peltier*	.05
70	Greg Blosser	.05
71	*Reggie Sanders*	.25
72	Brent Mayne	.05
73	*Rico Brogna*	.05
74	*Willie Banks*	.05
75	*Len Brutcher*	.05
76	*Pat Kelly*	.05
77	Chris Sabo Cincinnati Reds checklist	.05
78	Ramon Martinez Los Angeles Dodgers checklist	.05
79	Matt Williams San Francisco Giants checklist	.05
80	Roberto Alomar San Diego Padres checklist	.05
81	Glenn Davis Houston Astros checklist	.05
82	Ron Gant Atlanta Braves checklist	.05
83	Cecil Fielder "Fielder's Feat"	.05
84	*Orlando Merced*	.10
85	Domingo Ramos	.05
86	Tom Bolton	.05
87	*Andres Santana*	.05
88	John Dopson	.05
89	Kenny Williams	.05
90	Marty Barrett	.05
91	Tom Pagnozzi	.05
92	Carmelo Martinez	.05
93	Bobby Thigpen "Save Master"	.05
94	Barry Bonds Pittsburgh Pirates checklist	.50
95	Gregg Jefferies New York Mets checklist	.05
96	Tim Wallach Montreal Expos checklist	.05
97	Lenny Dykstra Philadelphia Phillies checklist	.05
98	Pedro Guerrero St. Louis Cardinals checklist	.05
99	Mark Grace Chicago Cubs checklist	.05
100	Checklist 1-100	.05
101	Kevin Elster	.05
102	Tom Brookens	.05
103	Mackey Sasser	.05
104	Felix Fermin	.05
105	Kevin McReynolds	.05
106	Dave Steib	.05
107	Jeffrey Leonard	.05
108	Dave Henderson	.05
109	Sid Bream	.05
110	Henry Cotto	.05
111	Shawon Dunston	.05
112	Mariano Duncan	.05
113	Joe Girardi	.05
114	Billy Hatcher	.05
115	Greg Maddux	.50
116	Jerry Browne	.05
117	Juan Samuel	.05
118	Steve Olin	.05
119	Alfredo Griffin	.05
120	Mitch Webster	.05
121	Joel Skinner	.05
122	Frank Viola	.05
123	Cory Snyder	.05
124	Howard Johnson	.05
125	Carlos Baerga	.05
126	Tony Fernandez	.05
127	Dave Stewart	.05
128	Jay Buhner	.05
129	Mike LaValliere	.05
130	Scott Bradley	.05
131	Tony Phillips	.05
132	Ryne Sandberg	.50
133	Paul O'Neill	.05
134	Mark Grace	.05
135	Chris Sabo	.05
136	Ramon Martinez	.05
137	Brook Jacoby	.05
138	Candy Maldonado	.05
139	Mike Scioscia	.05
140	Chris James	.05
141	Craig Worthington	.05
142	Manny Lee	.05
143	Tim Raines	.05
144	Sandy Alomar, Jr.	.05
145	John Olerud	.05
146	*Ozzie Canseco*	.05
147	Pat Borders	.05
148	Harold Reynolds	.05
149	Tom Henke	.05
150	R.J. Reynolds	.05
151	Mike Gallego	.05
152	Bobby Bonilla	.05
153	Terry Steinbach	.05
154	Barry Bonds	1.00
155	Jose Canseco	.30
156	Gregg Jefferies	.05
157	Matt Williams	.05
158	Craig Biggio	.05
159	Daryl Boston	.05
160	Ricky Jordan	.05
161	Stan Belinda	.05
162	Ozzie Smith	.50
163	Tom Brunansky	.05
164	Todd Zeile	.05
165	Mike Greenwell	.05
166	Kal Daniels	.05
167	Kent Hrbek	.05
168	Franklin Stubbs	.05
169	Dick Schofield	.05
170	Junior Ortiz	.05
171	*Hector Villanueva*	.05
172	Dennis Eckersley	.35
173	Mitch Williams	.05
174	Mark McGwire	.75
175	Fernando Valenzuela	.05
176	Gary Carter	.40
177	Dave Magadan	.05
178	Robby Thompson	.05
179	Bob Ojeda	.05
180	Ken Caminiti	.05
181	Don Slaught	.05
182	Luis Rivera	.05
183	Jay Bell	.05
184	Jody Reed	.05
185	Wally Backman	.05
186	Dave Martinez	.05
187	Luis Polonia	.05
188	Shane Mack	.05
189	Spike Owen	.05
190	Scott Bailes	.05
191	John Russell	.05
192	Walt Weiss	.05
193	Jose Oquendo	.05
194	Carney Lansford	.05
195	Jeff Huson	.05
196	Keith Miller	.05
197	Eric Yelding	.05
198	Ron Darling	.05
199	John Kruk	.05
200	Checklist 101-200	.05
201	John Shelby	.05
202	Bob Geren	.05
203	Lance McCullers	.05
204	Alvaro Espinoza	.05
205	Mark Salas	.05
206	Mike Pagliarulo	.05
207	Jose Uribe	.05
208	Jim Deshaies	.05
209	Ron Karkovice	.05
210	Rafael Ramirez	.05
211	Donnie Hill	.05
212	Brian Harper	.05
213	Jack Howell	.05
214	Wes Gardner	.05
215	Tim Burke	.05
216	Doug Jones	.05
217	Hubie Brooks	.05
218	Tom Candiotti	.05
219	Gerald Perry	.05
220	Jose DeLeon	.05
221	Wally Whitehurst	.05
222	*Alan Mills*	.05
223	Alan Trammell	.05
224	Dwight Gooden	.05
225	Travis Fryman	.05
226	Joe Carter	.05
227	Julio Franco	.05
228	Craig Lefferts	.05
229	Gary Pettis	.05
230	Dennis Rasmussen	.05
231a	Brian Downing (no position on front)	2.00
231b	Brian Downing (DH on front)	.05

232 Carlos Quintana .05
233 Gary Gaetti .05
234 Mark Langston .05
235 Tim Wallach .05
236 Greg Swindell .05
237 Eddie Murray .40
238 Jeff Manto .05
239 Lenny Harris .05
240 Jesse Orosco .05
241 Scott Lusader .05
242 Sid Fernandez .05
243 Jim Leyritz .05
244 Cecil Fielder .05
245 Darryl Strawberry .05
246 Frank Thomas .50
247 Kevin Mitchell .05
248 Lance Johnson .05
249 Rick Rueschel .05
250 Mark Portugal .05
251 Derek Lilliquist .05
252 Brian Holman .05
253 Rafael Valdez .05
254 B.J. Surhoff .05
255 Tony Gwynn .50
256 Andy Van Slyke .05
257 Todd Stottlemyre .05
258 Jose Lind .05
259 Greg Myers .05
260 Jeff Ballard .05
261 Bobby Thigpen .05
262 *Jimmy Kremers* .05
263 Robin Ventura .05
264 John Smoltz .05
265 Sammy Sosa .50
266 Gary Sheffield .30
267 Len Dykstra .05
268 Bill Spiers .05
269 Charlie Hayes .05
270 Brett Butler .05
271 Bip Roberts .05
272 Rob Deer .05
273 Fred Lynn .05
274 Dave Parker .05
275 Andy Benes .05
276 Glenallen Hill .05
277 *Steve Howard* .05
278 Doug Drabek .05
279 Joe Oliver .05
280 Todd Benzinger .05
281 Eric King .05
282 Jim Presley .05
283 Ken Patterson .05
284 Jack Daugherty .05
285 Ivan Calderon .05
286 *Edgar Diaz* .05
287 Kevin Bass .05
288 Don Carman .05
289 Greg Brock .05
290 John Franco .05
291 Joey Cora .05
292 Bill Wegman .05
293 Eric Show .05
294 Scott Bankhead .05
295 Garry Templeton .05
296 Mickey Tettleton .05
297 Luis Sojo .05
298 Jose Rijo .05
299 Dave Johnson .05
300 Checklist 201-300 .05
301 Mark Grant .05
302 Pete Harnisch .05
303 Greg Olson .05
304 *Anthony Telford* .05
305 Lonnie Smith .05
306 Chris Hoiles .05
307 Bryn Smith .05
308 Mike Devereaux .05
309a Milt Thompson ("86" in stats obscured by "bull's eye") .50
309b Milt Thompson ("86" visible) .05
310 Bob Melvin .05
311a Luis Salazar (circled dot over "i" in Luis on back) 2.00
311b Luis Salazar (corrected) .05
312 Ed Whitson .05
313 Charlie Hough .05
314 Dave Clark .05
315 *Eric Gunderson* .05
316 Dan Petry .05
317 Dante Bichette .05
318 Mike Heath .05
319 Damon Berryhill .05
320 Walt Terrell .05
321 Scott Fletcher .05
322 Dan Plesac .05
323 Jack McDowell .05
324 Paul Molitor .40
325 Ozzie Guillen .05
326 Gregg Olson .05
327 Pedro Guerrero .05
328 Bob Milacki .05
329 John Tudor .05
330 Steve Finley .05
331 Jack Clark .05
332 Jerome Walton .05
333 Andy Hawkins .05
334 Derrick May .05
335 Roberto Alomar .20
336 Jack Morris .05
337 Dave Winfield .40
338 Steve Searcy .05
339 Chili Davis .05
340 Larry Sheets .05
341 Ted Higuera .05
342 *David Segui* .10
343 Greg Cadaret .05
344 Robin Yount .40
345 Nolan Ryan 1.00
346 Ray Lankford .05
347 Cal Ripken, Jr. 1.00
348 Lee Smith .05
349 Brady Anderson .05
350 Frank DiPino .05
351 Hal Morris .05
352 Deion Sanders .10
353 Barry Larkin .05
354 Don Mattingly .60
355 Eric Davis .05
356 Jose Offerman .05
357 Mel Rojas .05
358 Rudy Seanez .05
359 Oil Can Boyd .05
360 Nelson Liriano .05
361 Ron Gant .05
362 *Howard Farmer* .05
363 Dave Justice .05
364 Delino DeShields .05
365 Steve Avery .05
366 David Cone .05
367 Lou Whitaker .05
368 Von Hayes .05
369 Frank Tanana .05
370 Tim Teufel .05
371 Randy Myers .05
372 Roberto Kelly .05
373 Jack Armstrong .05
374 Kelly Gruber .05
375 Kevin Maas .05
376 Randy Johnson .40
377 David West .05
378 *Brent Knackert* .05
379 Rick Honeycutt .05
380 Kevin Gross .05
381 Tom Foley .05
382 Jeff Blauser .05
383 *Scott Ruskin* .05
384 Andres Thomas .05
385 Dennis Martinez .05
386 Mike Henneman .05
387 Felix Jose .05
388 Alejandro Pena .05
389 Chet Lemon .05
390 *Craig Wilson* .05
391 Chuck Crim .05
392 Mel Hall .05
393 Mark Knudson .05
394 Norm Charlton .05
395 Mike Felder .05
396 *Tim Layana* .05
397 Steve Frey .05
398 Bill Doran .05
399 Dion James .05
400 Checklist 301-400 .05
401 Ron Hassey .05
402 Don Robinson .05
403 Gene Nelson .05
404 Terry Kennedy .05
405 Todd Burns .05
406 Roger McDowell .05
407 Bob Kipper .05
408 Darren Daulton .05
409 Chuck Cary .05
410 Bruce Ruffin .05
411 Juan Berenguer .05
412 Gary Ward .05
413 Al Newman .05
414 Danny Jackson .05
415 Greg Gagne .05
416 Tom Herr .05
417 Jeff Parrett .05
418 Jeff Reardon .05
419 Mark Lemke .05
420 Charlie O'Brien .05
421 Willie Randolph .05
422 Steve Bedrosian .05
423 Mike Moore .05
424 Jeff Brantley .05
425 Bob Welch .05
426 Terry Mulholland .05
427 *Willie Blair* .05
428 Darrin Fletcher .05
429 Mike Witt .05
430 Joe Boever .05
431 Tom Gordon .05
432 *Pedro Munoz* .05
433 Kevin Seitzer .05
434 Kevin Tapani .05
435 Bret Saberhagen .05
436 Ellis Burks .05
437 Chuck Finley .05
438 Mike Boddicker .05
439 Francisco Cabrera .05
440 Todd Hundley .05
441 Kelly Downs .05
442 *Dann Howitt* .05
443 Scott Garrelts .05
444 Rickey Henderson .40
445 Will Clark .05
446 Ben McDonald .05
447 Dale Murphy .20
448 Dave Righetti .05
449 Dickie Thon .05
450 Ted Power .05
451 Scott Coolbaugh .05
452 Dwight Smith .05
453 Pete Incaviglia .05
454 Andre Dawson .25
455 Ruben Sierra .05
456 Andres Galarraga .05
457 Alvin Davis .05
458 Tony Castillo .05
459 Pete O'Brien .05
460 Charlie Leibrandt .05
461 Vince Coleman .05
462 Steve Sax .05
463 *Omar Oliveras* .05
464 *Oscar Azocar* .05
465 Joe Magrane .05
466 *Karl Rhodes* .05
467 Benito Santiago .05
468 *Joe Klink* .05
469 Sil Campusano .05
470 Mark Parent .05
471 *Shawn Boskie* .05
472 Kevin Brown .05
473 Rick Sutcliffe .05
474 Rafael Palmeiro .35
475 Mike Harkey .05
476 Jaime Navarro .05
477 Marquis Grissom .05
478 Marty Clary .05
479 Greg Briley .05
480 Tom Glavine .25
481 Lee Guetterman .05
482 Rex Hudler .05
483 Dave LaPoint .05
484 Terry Pendleton .05
485 Jesse Barfield .05
486 Jose DeJesus .05
487 *Paul Abbott* .05
488 Ken Howell .05
489 Greg W. Harris .05
490 Roy Smith .05
491 Paul Assenmacher .05
492 Geno Petralli .05
493 Steve Wilson .05
494 Kevin Reimer .05
495 Bill Long .05
496 Mike Jackson .05
497 Oddibe McDowell .05
498 Bill Swift .05
499 Jeff Treadway .05
500 Checklist 401-500 .05
501 Gene Larkin .05
502 Bob Boone .05
503 Allan Anderson .05
504 Luis Aquino .05
505 Mark Guthrie .05
506 Joe Orsulak .05
507 *Dana Kiecker* .05
508 Dave Gallagher .05
509 Greg A. Harris .05
510 Mark Williamson .05
511 Casey Candaele .05
512 Mookie Wilson .05
513 Dave Smith .05
514 *Chuck Carr* .05
515 Glenn Wilson .05
516 Mike Fitzgerald .05
517 Devon White .05
518 Dave Hollins .05
519 Mark Eichhorn .05
520 Otis Nixon .05
521 *Terry Shumpert* .05
522 *Scott Erickson* .15
523 Danny Tartabull .05
524 Orel Hershiser .05
525 George Brett .60
526 Greg Vaughn .05
527 Tim Naehring .05
528 Curt Schilling .25
529 Chris Bosio .05
530 Sam Horn .05
531 Mike Scott .05
532 George Bell .05
533 Eric Anthony .05
534 *Julio Valera* .05
535 Glenn Davis .05
536 Larry Walker .05
537 Pat Combs .05
538 *Chris Nabholz* .05
539 Kirk McCaskill .05
540 Randy Ready .05
541 Mark Gubicza .05
542 Rick Aguilera .05
543 *Brian McRae* .05
544 Kirby Puckett .50
545 Bo Jackson .10
546 Wade Boggs .50
547 Tim McIntosh .05
548 Randy Milligan .05
549 Dwight Evans .05
550 Billy Ripken .05
551 Erik Hanson .05
552 Lance Parrish .05
553 Tino Martinez .05
554 Jim Abbott .05
555 Ken Griffey, Jr. .65
556 Milt Cuyler .05
557 *Mark Leonard* .05
558 Jay Howell .05
559 Lloyd Moseby .05
560 Chris Gwynn .05
561 *Mark Whiten* .05
562 Harold Baines .05
563 Junior Felix .05
564 Darren Lewis .05
565 Fred McGriff .05
566 Kevin Appier .05
567 *Luis Gonzalez* 1.00
568 Frank White .05
569 Juan Agosto .05
570 Mike Macfarlane .05
571 Bert Blyleven .05
572 Ken Griffey, Sr. .05
573 Lee Stevens .05
574 Edgar Martinez .05
575 Wally Joyner .05
576 Tim Belcher .05
577 John Burkett .05
578 Mike Morgan .05
579 Paul Gibson .05
580 Jose Vizcaino .05
581 Duane Ward .05
582 Scott Sanderson .05
583 David Wells .05
584 Willie McGee .05
585 John Cerutti .05
586 Danny Darwin .05
587 Kurt Stillwell .05
588 Rich Gedman .05
589 Mark Davis .05
590 Bill Gullickson .05
591 Matt Young .05
592 Bryan Harvey .05
593 Omar Vizquel .05
594 *Scott Lewis* .05
595 Dave Valle .05
596 Tim Crews .05
597 Mike Bielecki .05
598 Mike Sharperson .05
599 Dave Bergman .05
600 Checklist 501-600 .05
601 Steve Lyons .05
602 Bruce Hurst .05
603 Donn Pall .05
604 *Jim Vatcher* .05
605 Dan Pasqua .05
606 Kenny Rogers .05
607 *Jeff Schulz* .05
608 Brad Arnsberg .05
609 Willie Wilson .05
610 Jamie Moyer .05
611 Ron Oester .05
612 Dennis Cook .05
613 Rick Mahler .05
614 Bill Landrum .05
615 Scott Scudder .05
616 *Tom Edens* .05
617 "1917 Revisited" (Chicago White Sox team photo) .05
618 Jim Gantner .05
619 Darrel Akerfelds .05
620 Ron Robinson .05
621 Scott Radinsky .05

622 Pete Smith .05
623 Melido Perez .05
624 Jerald Clark .05
625 Carlos Martinez .05
626 *Wes Chamberlain* .05
627 Bobby Witt .05
628 Ken Dayley .05
629 *John Barfield* .05
630 Bob Tewksbury .05
631 Glenn Braggs .05
632 *Jim Neidlinger* .05
633 Tom Browning .05
634 Kirk Gibson .05
635 Rob Dibble .05
636 Lou Brock, Rickey Henderson "Stolen Base Leaders" .15
637 Jeff Montgomery .05
638 Mike Schooler .05
639 Storm Davis .05
640 *Rich Rodriguez* .05
641 Phil Bradley .05
642 Kent Mercker .05
643 Carlton Fisk .40
644 Mike Bell .05
645 *Alex Fernandez* .05
646 Juan Gonzalez .30
647 Ken Hill .05
648 Jeff Russell .05
649 *Chuck Malone* .05
650 Steve Buechele .05
651 Mike Benjamin .05
652 Tony Pena .05
653 Trevor Wilson .05
654 Alex Cole .05
655 Roger Clemens .60
656 Mark McGwire "The Bashing Years" .50
657 *Joe Grahe* .05
658 Jim Eisenreich .05
659 Dan Gladden .05
660 Steve Farr .05
661 *Bill Sampen* .05
662 *Dave Rohde* .05
663 Mark Gardner .05
664 *Mike Simms* .05
665 Moises Alou .05
666 Mickey Hatcher .05
667 Jimmy Key .05
668 John Wetteland .05
669 John Smiley .05
670 Jim Acker .05
671 Pascual Perez .05
672 *Reggie Harris* .05
673 Matt Nokes .05
674 *Rafael Novoa* .05
675 Hensley Meulens .05
676 Jeff M. Robinson .05
677 "Ground Breaking" (New Comiskey Park) .15
678 Johnny Ray .05
679 Greg Hibbard .05
680 Paul Sorrento .05
681 Mike Marshall .05
682 Jim Clancy .05
683 Rob Murphy .05
684 Dave Schmidt .05
685 *Jeff Gray* .05
686 Mike Hartley .05
687 Jeff King .05
688 Stan Javier .05
689 Bob Walk .05
690 Jim Gott .05
691 Mike LaCoss .05
692 John Farrell .05
693 Tim Leary .05
694 *Mike Walker* .05
695 Eric Plunk .05
696 Mike Fetters .05
697 Wayne Edwards .05
698 Tim Drummond .05
699 Willie Fraser .05
700 Checklist 601-700 .05
701 Mike Heath .05
702 Luis Gonzalez, Karl Rhodes, Jeff Bagwell "Rookie Threats" .45
703 Jose Mesa .05
704 Dave Smith .05
705 Danny Darwin .05
706 Rafael Belliard .05
707 Rob Murphy .05
708 Terry Pendleton .05
709 Mike Pagliarulo .05
710 Sid Bream .05
711 Junior Felix .05
712 Dante Bichette .05
713 Kevin Gross .05
714 Luis Sojo .05
715 Bob Ojeda .05
716 Julio Machado .05
717 Steve Farr .05
718 Franklin Stubbs .05
719 Mike Boddicker .05
720 Willie Randolph .05
721 Willie McGee .05
722 Chili Davis .05
723 Danny Jackson .05
724 Cory Snyder .05
725 Andre Dawson, George Bell, Ryne Sandberg "MVP Lineup" .20
726 Rob Deer .05
727 Rich DeLucia .05
728 Mike Perez .05
729 Mickey Tettleton .05
730 Mike Blowers .05
731 Gary Gaetti .05
732 Brett Butler .05
733 Dave Parker .05
734 Eddie Zosky .05
735 Jack Clark .05
736 Jack Morris .05
737 Kirk Gibson .05
738 Steve Bedrosian .05
739 Candy Maldonado .05
740 Matt Young .05
741 Rich Garces .05
742 George Bell .05
743 Deion Sanders .10
744 Bo Jackson .10
745 Luis Mercedes .05
746 Reggie Jefferson .05
747 Pete Incaviglia .05
748 Chris Hammond .05
749 Mike Stanton .05
750 Scott Sanderson .05
751 Paul Faries .05
752 Al Osuna .05
753 Steve Chitren .05
754 Tony Fernandez .05
755 *Jeff Bagwell* 1.50
756 Kirk Dressendorfer .05
757 Glenn Davis .05
758 Gary Carter .40
759 Zane Smith .05
760 Vance Law .05
761 Denis Boucher .05
762 Turner Ward .05
763 Roberto Alomar .20
764 Albert Belle .05
765 Joe Carter .05
766 Pete Schourek .05
767 Heathcliff Slocumb .05
768 Vince Coleman .05
769 Mitch Williams .05
770 Brian Downing .05
771 Dana Allison .05
772 Pete Harnisch .05
773 Tim Raines .05
774 Darryl Kile .05
775 Fred McGriff .05
776 Dwight Evans .05
777 Joe Slusarski .05
778 Dave Righetti .05
779 Jeff Hamilton .05
780 Ernest Riles .05
781 Ken Dayley .05
782 Eric King .05
783 Devon White .05
784 Beau Allred .05
785 Mike Timlin .05
786 Ivan Calderon .05
787 Hubie Brooks .05
788 Juan Agosto .05
789 Barry Jones .05
790 Wally Backman .05
791 Jim Presley .05
792 Charlie Hough .05
793 Larry Andersen .05
794 Steve Finley .05
795 Shawn Abner .05
796 Jeff M. Robinson .05
797 Joe Bitker .05
798 Eric Show .05
799 Bud Black .05
800 Checklist 701-800 .05
SP1 Michael Jordan 3.00
SP2 Rickey Henderson, Nolan Ryan "A Day to Remember" 1.00
HH1 Hank Aaron (hologram) 1.00

Rookie cards are in *Italic.*

Baseball Heroes Hank Aaron

	NM/M
Complete Set (10):	4.00
Common Aaron:	.50
Autographed Card:	160.00
Aaron Header:	1.00

BASEBALL HEROES NOLAN RYAN

	NM/M
Complete Set (10):	3.00
Common Player:	.50
Ryan header Card:	1.00
Autographed Card:	200.00
"Strike Out King" Auto.:	575.00

1991 UPPER DECK HEROES OF BASEBALL

	NM/M
Complete Set (4):	7.00
Common Card:	2.00

1 Harmon Killebrew 2.00
1a Harmon Killebrew (autographed) 10.00
2 Gaylord Perry 2.00
2a Gaylord Perry (autographed) 10.00
3 Ferguson Jenkins 2.00
3a Ferguson Jenkins (autographed) 10.00
4 Gaylord Perry, Ferguson Jenkins, Harmon Killebrew 2.00

Silver Sluggers

	NM/M
Complete Set (18):	5.00
Common Player:	.15

1 Julio Franco .15
2 Alan Trammell .15
3 Rickey Henderson .75
4 Jose Canseco .50
5 Barry Bonds 2.00
6 Eddie Murray .75
7 Kelly Gruber .15
8 Ryne Sandberg 1.00
9 Darryl Strawberry .15
10 Ellis Burks .15
11 Lance Parrish .15
12 Cecil Fielder .15
13 Matt Williams .15
14 Dave Parker .15
15 Bobby Bonilla .15
16 Don Robinson .15
17 Benito Santiago .15
18 Barry Larkin .15

Final Edition

	NM/M
Complete Set (100):	9.00
Common Player:	.05

1 Ryan Klesko, Reggie Sanders (Minor League Diamond Skills Checklist) .10
2 *Pedro Martinez* 5.00
3 Lance Dickson .05
4 Royce Clayton .05
5 Scott Bryant .05
6 Dan Wilson .05
7 *Dmitri Young* .50
8 *Ryan Klesko* .50
9 Tom Goodwin .05
10 *Rondell White* .25
11 Reggie Sanders .05
12 Todd Van Poppel .05
13 Arthur Rhodes .05
14 Eddie Zosky .05
15 Gerald Williams .05
16 Robert Eenhoorn .05
17 *Jim Thome* 1.50
18 *Marc Newfield* .05
19 Kerwin Moore .05
20 Jeff McNeely .05
21 Frankie Rodriguez .05
22 Andy Mota .05
23 Chris Haney .05
24 *Kenny Lofton* .25
25 Dave Nilsson .05
26 Derek Bell .05
27 Frank Castillo .05
28 Candy Maldonado .05
29 Chuck McElroy .05
30 Chito Martinez .05
31 Steve Howe .05
32 Freddie Benavides .05
33 Scott Kamieniecki .05
34 Denny Neagle .05
35 Mike Humphreys .05
36 Mike Remlinger .05
37 Scott Coolbaugh .05
38 Darren Lewis .05
39 Thomas Howard .05
40 John Candelaria .05
41 Todd Benzinger .05
42 Wilson Alvarez .05
43 Patrick Lennon .05
44 Rusty Meacham .05
45 *Ryan Bowen* .05
46 *Rick Wilkins* .10
47 *Ed Sprague* .05
48 *Bob Scanlan* .05
49 Tom Candiotti .05
50 Dennis Martinez (Perfecto) .05
51 Oil Can Boyd .05
52 Glenallen Hill .05
53 *Scott Livingstone* .05
54 *Brian Hunter* .05
55 *Ivan Rodriguez* 1.50
56 *Keith Mitchell* .05
57 Roger McDowell .05
58 Otis Nixon .05
59 *Juan Bell* .05
60 Bill Krueger .05
61 *Chris Donnels* .05

62	Tommy Greene	.05
63	Doug Simons	.05
64	*Andy Ashby*	.15
65	*Anthony Young*	.05
66	*Kevin Morton*	.05
67	*Bret Barberie*	.05
68	*Scott Servais*	.05
69	Ron Darling	.05
70	Vicente Palacios	.05
71	*Tim Burke*	.05
72	*Gerald Alexander*	.05
73	Reggie Jefferson	.05
74	Dean Palmer	.05
75	Mark Whiten	.05
76	Randy Tomlin	.05
77	*Mark Wohlers*	.05
78	Brook Jacoby	.05
79	Ken Griffey Jr., Ryne Sandberg (All-Star Checklist)	.25
80	Jack Morris (AS)	.05
81	Sandy Alomar, Jr. (AS)	.05
82	Cecil Fielder (AS)	.05
83	Roberto Alomar (AS)	.10
84	Wade Boggs (AS)	.25
85	Cal Ripken, Jr. (AS)	.60
86	Rickey Henderson (AS)	.15
87	Ken Griffey, Jr. (AS)	.60
88	Dave Henderson (AS)	.05
89	Danny Tartabull (AS)	.05
90	Tom Glavine (AS)	.10
91	Benito Santiago (AS)	.05
92	Will Clark (AS)	.05
93	Ryne Sandberg (AS)	.50
94	Chris Sabo (AS)	.05
95	Ozzie Smith (AS)	.50
96	Ivan Calderon (AS)	.05
97	Tony Gwynn (AS)	.25
98	Andre Dawson (AS)	.05
99	Bobby Bonilla (AS)	.05
100	Checklist	.05

1992 UPPER DECK

	NM/M
Unopened Fact. Set (800):	12.50
Complete Set (800):	8.00
Common Player:	.05
Low or High Pack (15):	.50
Low or High Box (36):	12.50
Jumbo Pack (27):	1.00
Jumbo Box (20):	16.00
Bench/Morgan auto.	75.00
Ted Williams auto.	425.00

1	Ryan Klesko, Jim Thome Star Rookie Checklist	.25
2	Royce Clayton	.05
3	*Brian Jordan*	.30
4	*Dave Fleming*	.05
5	Jim Thome	.40
6	Jeff Juden	.05
7	*Roberto Hernandez*	.15
8	Kyle Abbott	.05
9	*Chris George*	.05
10	*Rob Maurer*	.05
11	*Donald Harris*	.05
12	*Ted Wood*	.05
13	*Patrick Lennon*	.05
14	Willie Banks	.05
15	Roger Salkeld	.05
16	Wil Cordero	.05
17	*Arthur Rhodes*	.05
18	Pedro Martinez	.40
19	*Andy Ashby*	.10
20	Tom Goodwin	.05
21	*Braulio Castillo*	.05
22	Todd Van Poppel	.05
23	*Brian Williams*	.05
24	Ryan Klesko	.05
25	Kenny Lofton	.05
26	Derek Bell	.05
27	Reggie Sanders	.05
28	Dave Winfield	.25
29	Dave Justice Atlanta Braves Checklist	.05
30	Rob Dibble Cincinnati Reds Checklist	.05
31	Craig Biggio Houston Astros Checklist	.05
32	Eddie Murray Los Angeles Dodgers Checklist	.20
33	Fred McGriff San Diego Padres Checklist	.05
34	Willie McGee San Francisco Giants Checklist	.05
35	Shawon Dunston Chicago Cubs Checklist	.05
36	Delino DeShields Montreal Expos Checklist	.05
37	Howard Johnson New York Mets Checklist	.05
38	John Kruk Philadelphia Phillies Checklist	.05
39	Doug Drabek Pittsburgh Pirates Checklist	.05
40	Todd Zeile St. Louis Cardinals Checklist	.05
41	Steve Avery	.05
42	*Jeremy Hernandez*	.05
43	*Doug Henry*	.05
44	*Chris Donnels*	.05
45	*Mo Sanford*	.05
46	*Scott Kamieniecki*	.10
47	Mark Lemke	.05
48	Steve Farr	.05
49	Francisco Oliveras	.05
50	*Ced Landrum*	.05
51	Rondell White, Marc Newfield Top Prospect Checklist	.05
52	*Eduardo Perez*	.10
53	*Tom Nevers*	.05
54	*David Zancanaro*	.05
55	*Shawn Green*	1.50
56	*Mark Wohlers*	.05
57	Dave Nilsson	.05
58	Dmitri Young	.05
59	*Ryan Hawblitzel*	.05
60	Raul Mondesi	.05
61	Rondell White	.05
62	Steve Hosey	.05
63	*Manny Ramirez*	2.00
64	Marc Newfield	.05
65	Jeromy Burnitz	.05
66	*Mark Smith*	.05
67	*Joey Hamilton*	.10
68	*Tyler Green*	.05
69	*John Farrell*	.05
70	*Kurt Miller*	.05
71	*Jeff Plympton*	.05
72	Dan Wilson	.05
73	*Joe Vitiello*	.05
74	Rico Brogna	.05
75	*David McCarty*	.05
76	*Bob Wickman*	.05
77	*Carlos Rodriguez*	.05
78	Jim Abbott	.05
79	Pedro Martinez, Ramon Martinez Bloodlines	.25
80	Kevin Mitchell, Keith Mitchell Bloodlines	.05
81	Sandy Jr. & Roberto Alomar, Sandy Jr. & Roberto Alomar Bloodlines	.10
82	Cal Jr. & Billy Ripken, Cal Jr. & Billy Ripken Bloodlines	.40
83	Tony & Chris Gwynn, Tony & Chris Gwynn Bloodlines	.20
84	Dwight Gooden, Gary Sheffield Bloodlines	.15
85	Ken, Sr.; Ken, Jr.; & Craig Griffey, Ken, Sr.; Ken, Jr.; & Craig Griffey, Ken, Sr.; Ken, Jr.; & Craig Griffey Bloodlines	.30
86	Jim Abbott California Angels Checklist	.05
87	Frank Thomas Chicago White Sox Checklist	.25
88	Danny Tartabull Kansas City Royals Checklist	.05
89	Scott Erickson Minnesota Twins Checklist	.05
90	Rickey Henderson Oakland Athletics Checklist	.25
91	Edgar Martinez Seattle Mariners Checklist	.05
92	Nolan Ryan Texas Rangers Checklist	.50
93	Ben McDonald Baltimore Orioles Checklist	.05
94	Ellis Burks Boston Red Sox Checklist	.05
95	Greg Swindell Cleveland Indians Checklist	.05
96	Cecil Fielder Detroit Tigers Checklist	.05
97	Greg Vaughn Milwaukee Brewers Checklist	.05
98	Kevin Maas New York Yankees Checklist	.05
99	Dave Steib Toronto Blue Jays Checklist	.05
100	Checklist 1-100	.05
101	Joe Oliver	.05
102	Hector Villanueva	.05
103	Ed Whitson	.05
104	Danny Jackson	.05
105	Chris Hammond	.05
106	Ricky Jordan	.05
107	Kevin Bass	.05
108	Darrin Fletcher	.05
109	Junior Ortiz	.05
110	Tom Bolton	.05
111	Jeff King	.05
112	Dave Magadan	.05
113	Mike LaValliere	.05
114	Hubie Brooks	.05
115	Jay Bell	.05
116	David Wells	.05
117	Jim Leyritz	.05
118	Manuel Lee	.05
119	Alvaro Espinoza	.05
120	B.J. Surhoff	.05
121	Hal Morris	.05
122	Shawon Dunston	.05
123	Chris Sabo	.05
124	Andre Dawson	.25
125	Eric Davis	.05
126	Chili Davis	.05
127	Dale Murphy	.15
128	Kirk McCaskill	.05
129	Terry Mulholland	.05
130	Rick Aguilera	.05
131	Vince Coleman	.05
132	Andy Van Slyke	.05
133	Gregg Jefferies	.05
134	Barry Bonds	1.00
135	Dwight Gooden	.05
136	Dave Stieb	.05
137	Albert Belle	.05
138	Teddy Higuera	.05
139	Jesse Barfield	.05
140	Pat Borders	.05
141	Bip Roberts	.05
142	Rob Dibble	.05
143	Mark Grace	.05
144	Barry Larkin	.05
145	Ryne Sandberg	.50
146	Scott Erickson	.05
147	Luis Polonia	.05
148	John Burkett	.05
149	Luis Sojo	.05
150	Dickie Thon	.05
151	Walt Weiss	.05
152	Mike Scioscia	.05
153	Mark McGwire	.75
154	Matt Williams	.05
155	Rickey Henderson	.40
156	Sandy Alomar, Jr.	.05
157	Brian McRae	.05
158	Harold Baines	.05
159	Kevin Appier	.05
160	Felix Fermin	.05
161	Leo Gomez	.05
162	Craig Biggio	.05
163	Ben McDonald	.05
164	Randy Johnson	.40
165	Cal Ripken, Jr.	1.00
166	Frank Thomas	.40
167	Delino DeShields	.05
168	Greg Gagne	.05
169	Ron Karkovice	.05
170	Charlie Leibrandt	.05
171	Dave Righetti	.05
172	Dave Henderson	.05
173	Steve Decker	.05
174	Darryl Strawberry	.05
175	Will Clark	.05
176	Ruben Sierra	.05
177	Ozzie Smith	.50
178	Charles Nagy	.05
179	Gary Pettis	.05
180	Kirk Gibson	.05
181	Randy Milligan	.05
182	Dave Valle	.05
183	Chris Hoiles	.05
184	Tony Phillips	.05
185	Brady Anderson	.05
186	Scott Fletcher	.05
187	Gene Larkin	.05
188	Lance Johnson	.05
189	Greg Olson	.05
190	Melido Perez	.05
191	Lenny Harris	.05
192	Terry Kennedy	.05
193	Mike Gallego	.05
194	Willie McGee	.05
195	Juan Samuel	.05
196	Jeff Huson	.05
197	Alex Cole	.05
198	Ron Robinson	.05
199	Joel Skinner	.05
200	Checklist 101-200	.05
201	Kevin Reimer	.05
202	Stan Belinda	.05
203	Pat Tabler	.05
204	Jose Guzman	.05
205	Jose Lind	.05
206	Spike Owen	.05
207	Joe Orsulak	.05
208	Charlie Hayes	.05
209	Mike Devereaux	.05
210	Mike Fitzgerald	.05
211	Willie Randolph	.05
212	Rod Nichols	.05
213	Mike Boddicker	.05
214	Bill Spiers	.05
215	Steve Olin	.05
216	*David Howard*	.05
217	Gary Varsho	.05
218	Mike Harkey	.05
219	Luis Aquino	.05
220	Chuck McElroy	.05
221	Doug Drabek	.05
222	Dave Winfield	.40
223	Rafael Palmeiro	.35
224	Joe Carter	.05
225	Bobby Bonilla	.05
226	Ivan Calderon	.05
227	Gregg Olson	.05
228	Tim Wallach	.05
229	Terry Pendleton	.05
230	Gilberto Reyes	.05
231	Carlos Baerga	.05
232	Greg Vaughn	.05
233	Bret Saberhagen	.05
234	Gary Sheffield	.30
235	Mark Lewis	.05
236	George Bell	.05
237	Danny Tartabull	.05
238	Willie Wilson	.05
239	Doug Dascenzo	.05
240	Bill Pecota	.05
241	Julio Franco	.05
242	Ed Sprague	.05
243	Juan Gonzalez	.20
244	Chuck Finley	.05
245	Ivan Rodriguez	.35
246	Len Dykstra	.05
247	Deion Sanders	.10
248	Dwight Evans	.05
249	Larry Walker	.05
250	Billy Ripken	.05
251	Mickey Tettleton	.05
252	Tony Pena	.05
253	Benito Santiago	.05
254	Kirby Puckett	.50
255	Cecil Fielder	.05
256	Howard Johnson	.05
257	Andujar Cedeno	.05
258	Jose Rijo	.05
259	Al Osuna	.05
260	Todd Hundley	.05
261	Orel Hershiser	.05
262	Ray Lankford	.05
263	Robin Ventura	.05
264	Felix Jose	.05
265	Eddie Murray	.40
266	Kevin Mitchell	.05
267	Gary Carter	.40
268	Mike Benjamin	.05
269	Dick Schofield	.05
270	Jose Uribe	.05
271	Pete Incaviglia	.05
272	Tony Fernandez	.05
273	Alan Trammell	.05
274	Tony Gwynn	.50
275	Mike Greenwell	.05
276	Jeff Bagwell	.40
277	Frank Viola	.05
278	Randy Myers	.05
279	Ken Caminiti	.05
280	Bill Doran	.05
281	Dan Pasqua	.05

No.	Player	Price
282	Alfredo Griffin	.05
283	Jose Oquendo	.05
284	Kal Daniels	.05
285	Bobby Thigpen	.05
286	Robby Thompson	.05
287	Mark Eichhorn	.05
288	Mike Felder	.05
289	Dave Gallagher	.05
290	Dave Anderson	.05
291	Mel Hall	.05
292	Jerald Clark	.05
293	Al Newman	.05
294	Rob Deer	.05
295	Matt Nokes	.05
296	Jack Armstrong	.05
297	Jim Deshaies	.05
298	Jeff Innis	.05
299	Jeff Reed	.05
300	Checklist 201-300	.05
301	Lonnie Smith	.05
302	Jimmy Key	.05
303	Junior Felix	.05
304	Mike Heath	.05
305	Mark Langston	.05
306	Greg W. Harris	.05
307	Brett Butler	.05
308	Luis Rivera	.05
309	Bruce Ruffin	.05
310	Paul Faries	.05
311	Terry Leach	.05
312	*Scott Brosius*	.10
313	Scott Leius	.05
314	Harold Reynolds	.05
315	Jack Morris	.05
316	David Segui	.05
317	Bill Gullickson	.05
318	Todd Frohwirth	.05
319	*Mark Leiter*	.05
320	Jeff M. Robinson	.05
321	Gary Gaetti	.05
322	John Smoltz	.05
323	Andy Benes	.05
324	Kelly Gruber	.05
325	Jim Abbott	.05
326	John Kruk	.05
327	Kevin Seitzer	.05
328	Darrin Jackson	.05
329	Kurt Stillwell	.05
330	Mike Maddux	.05
331	Dennis Eckersley	.35
332	Dan Gladden	.05
333	Jose Canseco	.30
334	Kent Hrbek	.05
335	Ken Griffey, Sr.	.05
336	Greg Swindell	.05
337	Trevor Wilson	.05
338	Sam Horn	.05
339	Mike Henneman	.05
340	Jerry Browne	.05
341	Glenn Braggs	.05
342	Tom Glavine	.20
343	Wally Joyner	.05
344	Fred McGriff	.05
345	Ron Gant	.05
346	Ramon Martinez	.05
347	Wes Chamberlain	.05
348	Terry Shumpert	.05
349	Tim Teufel	.05
350	Wally Backman	.05
351	Joe Girardi	.05
352	Devon White	.05
353	Greg Maddux	.50
354	*Ryan Bowen*	.05
355	Roberto Alomar	.20
356	Don Mattingly	.60
357	Pedro Guerrero	.05
358	Steve Sax	.05
359	Joey Cora	.05
360	Jim Gantner	.05
361	Brian Barnes	.05
362	Kevin McReynolds	.05
363	*Bret Barberie*	.05
364	David Cone	.05
365	Dennis Martinez	.05
366	*Brian Hunter*	.05
367	Edgar Martinez	.05
368	Steve Finley	.05
369	Greg Briley	.05
370	Jeff Blauser	.05
371	Todd Stottlemyre	.05
372	Luis Gonzalez	.05
373	Rick Wilkins	.05
374	*Darryl Kile*	.05
375	John Olerud	.05
376	Lee Smith	.05
377	Kevin Maas	.05
378	Dante Bichette	.05
379	Tom Pagnozzi	.05
380	Mike Flanagan	.05
381	Charlie O'Brien	.05
382	Dave Martinez	.05
383	Keith Miller	.05
384	Scott Ruskin	.05
385	Kevin Elster	.05
386	Alvin Davis	.05
387	Casey Candaele	.05
388	Pete O'Brien	.05
389	Jeff Treadway	.05
390	Scott Bradley	.05
391	Mookie Wilson	.05
392	Jimmy Jones	.05
393	Candy Maldonado	.05
394	Eric Yelding	.05
395	Tom Henke	.05
396	Franklin Stubbs	.05
397	Milt Thompson	.05
398	Mark Carreon	.05
399	Randy Velarde	.05
400	Checklist 301-400	.05
401	Omar Vizquel	.05
402	Joe Boever	.05
403	Bill Krueger	.05
404	Jody Reed	.05
405	Mike Schooler	.05
406	Jason Grimsley	.05
407	Greg Myers	.05
408	Randy Ready	.05
409	*Mike Timlin*	.15
410	Mitch Williams	.05
411	Garry Templeton	.05
412	Greg Cadaret	.05
413	Donnie Hill	.05
414	Wally Whitehurst	.05
415	Scott Sanderson	.05
416	Thomas Howard	.05
417	Neal Heaton	.05
418	Charlie Hough	.05
419	Jack Howell	.05
420	Greg Hibbard	.05
421	Carlos Quintana	.05
422	*Kim Batiste*	.05
423	Paul Molitor	.40
424	Ken Griffey, Jr.	.65
425	Phil Plantier	.05
426	Denny Neagle	.05
427	Von Hayes	.05
428	Shane Mack	.05
429	Darren Daulton	.05
430	Dwayne Henry	.05
431	Lance Parrish	.05
432	*Mike Humphreys*	.05
433	Tim Burke	.05
434	Bryan Harvey	.05
435	Pat Kelly	.05
436	Ozzie Guillen	.05
437	Bruce Hurst	.05
438	Sammy Sosa	.50
439	Dennis Rasmussen	.05
440	Ken Patterson	.05
441	Jay Buhner	.05
442	Pat Combs	.05
443	Wade Boggs	.50
444	George Brett	.60
445	Mo Vaughn	.05
446	Chuck Knoblauch	.05
447	Tom Candiotti	.05
448	Mark Portugal	.05
449	Mickey Morandini	.05
450	Duane Ward	.05
451	Otis Nixon	.05
452	Bob Welch	.05
453	Rusty Meacham	.05
454	Keith Mitchell	.05
455	Marquis Grissom	.05
456	Robin Yount	.40
457	*Harvey Pulliam*	.05
458	Jose DeLeon	.05
459	Mark Gubicza	.05
460	Darryl Hamilton	.05
461	Tom Browning	.05
462	Monty Fariss	.05
463	Jerome Walton	.05
464	Paul O'Neill	.05
465	Dean Palmer	.05
466	Travis Fryman	.05
467	John Smiley	.05
468	Lloyd Moseby	.05
469	*John Wehner*	.05
470	Skeeter Barnes	.05
471	Steve Chitren	.05
472	Kent Mercker	.05
473	Terry Steinbach	.05
474	Andres Galarraga	.05
475	Steve Avery	.05
476	Tom Gordon	.05
477	Cal Eldred	.05
478	Omar Olivares	.05
479	Julio Machado	.05
480	Bob Milacki	.05
481	Les Lancaster	.05
482	John Candelaria	.05
483	Brian Downing	.05
484	Roger McDowell	.05
485	Scott Scudder	.05
486	Zane Smith	.05
487	John Cerutti	.05
488	Steve Buechele	.05
489	Paul Gibson	.05
490	Curtis Wilkerson	.05
491	Marvin Freeman	.05
492	Tom Foley	.05
493	Juan Berenguer	.05
494	Ernest Riles	.05
495	Sid Bream	.05
496	Chuck Crim	.05
497	Mike Macfarlane	.05
498	Dale Sveum	.05
499	Storm Davis	.05
500	Checklist 401-500	.05
501	Jeff Reardon	.05
502	Shawn Abner	.05
503	Tony Fossas	.05
504	Cory Snyder	.05
505	Matt Young	.05
506	Allan Anderson	.05
507	Mark Lee	.05
508	Gene Nelson	.05
509	Mike Pagliarulo	.05
510	Rafael Belliard	.05
511	Jay Howell	.05
512	Bob Tewksbury	.05
513	Mike Morgan	.05
514	John Franco	.05
515	Kevin Gross	.05
516	Lou Whitaker	.05
517	Orlando Merced	.05
518	Todd Benzinger	.05
519	Gary Redus	.05
520	Walt Terrell	.05
521	Jack Clark	.05
522	Dave Parker	.05
523	Tim Naehring	.05
524	Mark Whiten	.05
525	Ellis Burks	.05
526	*Frank Castillo*	.05
527	Brian Harper	.05
528	Brook Jacoby	.05
529	Rick Sutcliffe	.05
530	Joe Klink	.05
531	Terry Bross	.05
532	Jose Offerman	.05
533	Todd Zeile	.05
534	Eric Karros	.05
535	*Anthony Young*	.05
536	Milt Cuyler	.05
537	Randy Tomlin	.05
538	*Scott Livingstone*	.05
539	Jim Eisenreich	.05
540	Don Slaught	.05
541	Scott Cooper	.05
542	Joe Grahe	.05
543	Tom Brunansky	.05
544	Eddie Zosky	.05
545	Roger Clemens	.60
546	Dave Justice	.05
547	Dave Stewart	.05
548	David West	.05
549	Dave Smith	.05
550	Dan Plesac	.05
551	Alex Fernandez	.05
552	Bernard Gilkey	.05
553	Jack McDowell	.05
554	Tino Martinez	.05
555	Bo Jackson	.10
556	Bernie Williams	.05
557	Mark Gardner	.05
558	Glenallen Hill	.05
559	Oil Can Boyd	.05
560	Chris James	.05
561	*Scott Servais*	.05
562	*Rey Sanchez*	.05
563	*Paul McClellan*	.05
564	*Andy Mota*	.05
565	Darren Lewis	.05
566	*Jose Melendez*	.05
567	Tommy Greene	.05
568	Rich Rodriguez	.05
569	*Heathcliff Slocumb*	.05
570	Joe Hesketh	.05
571	Carlton Fisk	.40
572	Erik Hanson	.05
573	Wilson Alvarez	.05
574	*Rheal Cormier*	.05
575	Tim Raines	.05
576	Bobby Witt	.05
577	Roberto Kelly	.05
578	Kevin Brown	.05
579	Chris Nabholz	.05
580	Jesse Orosco	.05
581	Jeff Brantley	.05
582	Rafael Ramirez	.05
583	Kelly Downs	.05
584	Mike Simms	.05
585	*Mike Remlinger*	.05
586	Dave Hollins	.05
587	Larry Andersen	.05
588	Mike Gardiner	.05
589	Craig Lefferts	.05
590	Paul Assenmacher	.05
591	Bryn Smith	.05
592	Donn Pall	.05
593	Mike Jackson	.05
594	Scott Radinsky	.05
595	Brian Holman	.05
596	Geronimo Pena	.05
597	Mike Jeffcoat	.05
598	Carlos Martinez	.05
599	Geno Petralli	.05
600	Checklist 501-600	.05
601	Jerry Don Gleaton	.05
602	Adam Peterson	.05
603	Craig Grebeck	.05
604	Mark Guthrie	.05
605	Frank Tanana	.05
606	Hensley Meulens	.05
607	Mark Davis	.05
608	Eric Plunk	.05
609	Mark Williamson	.05
610	Lee Guetterman	.05
611	Bobby Rose	.05
612	Bill Wegman	.05
613	Mike Hartley	.05
614	*Chris Beasley*	.05
615	Chris Bosio	.05
616	Henry Cotto	.05
617	*Chico Walker*	.05
618	Russ Swan	.05
619	Bob Walk	.05
620	Billy Swift	.05
621	*Warren Newson*	.05
622	Steve Bedrosian	.05
623	*Ricky Bones*	.05
624	Kevin Tapani	.05
625	*Juan Guzman*	.05
626	*Jeff Johnson*	.05
627	Jeff Montgomery	.05
628	Ken Hill	.05
629	Gary Thurman	.05
630	Steve Howe	.05
631	Jose DeJesus	.05
632	Bert Blyleven	.05
633	Jaime Navarro	.05
634	Lee Stevens	.05
635	Pete Harnisch	.05
636	Bill Landrum	.05
637	Rich DeLucia	.05
638	Luis Salazar	.05
639	Rob Murphy	.05
640	Rickey Henderson, Jose Canseco A.L. Diamond Skills Checklist	.05
641	Roger Clemens	.40
642	Jim Abbott	.05
643	Travis Fryman	.05
644	Jesse Barfield	.05
645	Cal Ripken, Jr.	.50
646	Wade Boggs	.35
647	Cecil Fielder	.05
648	Rickey Henderson	.20
649	Jose Canseco	.15
650	Ken Griffey, Jr.	.45
651	Kenny Rogers	.05
652	*Luis Mercedes*	.05
653	Mike Stanton	.05
654	Glenn Davis	.05
655	Nolan Ryan	1.00
656	Reggie Jefferson	.05
657	*Javier Ortiz*	.05
658	Greg A. Harris	.05
659	Mariano Duncan	.05
660	Jeff Shaw	.05
661	Mike Moore	.05
662	*Chris Haney*	.05
663	*Joe Slusarski*	.05
664	*Wayne Housie*	.05
665	Carlos Garcia	.05
666	Bob Ojeda	.05
667	*Bryan Hickerson*	.05
668	Tim Belcher	.05
669	Ron Darling	.05
670	Rex Hudler	.05
671	Sid Fernandez	.05
672	*Chito Martinez*	.05
673	*Pete Schourek*	.05
674	*Armando Renoso*	.05
675	Mike Mussina	.30

676	Kevin Morton	.05
677	Norm Charlton	.05
678	Danny Darwin	.05
679	Eric King	.05
680	Ted Power	.05
681	Barry Jones	.05
682	Carney Lansford	.05
683	Mel Rojas	.05
684	Rick Honeycutt	.05
685	*Jeff Fassero*	.05
686	Cris Carpenter	.05
687	Tim Crews	.05
688	Scott Terry	.05
689	Chris Gwynn	.05
690	Gerald Perry	.05
691	John Barfield	.05
692	Bob Melvin	.05
693	Juan Agosto	.05
694	Alejandro Pena	.05
695	Jeff Russell	.05
696	Carmelo Martinez	.05
697	Bud Black	.05
698	Dave Otto	.05
699	Billy Hatcher	.05
700	Checklist 601-700	.05
701	Clemente Nunez	.05
702	Donovan Osborne, Brian Jordan, Mark Clark "Rookie Threats"	.05
703	Mike Morgan	.05
704	Keith Miller	.05
705	Kurt Stillwell	.05
706	Damon Berryhill	.05
707	Von Hayes	.05
708	Rick Sutcliffe	.05
709	Hubie Brooks	.05
710	Ryan Turner	.05
711	Barry Bonds, Andy Van Slyke N.L. Diamond Skills Checklist	.30
712	Jose Rijo	.05
713	Tom Glavine	.05
714	Shawon Dunston	.05
715	Andy Van Slyke	.05
716	Ozzie Smith	.35
717	Tony Gwynn	.35
718	Will Clark	.05
719	Marquis Grissom	.05
720	Howard Johnson	.05
721	Barry Bonds	.50
722	Kirk McCaskill	.05
723	Sammy Sosa	.50
724	George Bell	.05
725	Gregg Jefferies	.05
726	Gary DiSarcina	.05
727	Mike Bordick	.05
728	Eddie Murray (400 Home Run Club)	.20
729	Rene Gonzales	.05
730	Mike Bielecki	.05
731	Calvin Jones	.05
732	Jack Morris	.05
733	Frank Viola	.05
734	Dave Winfield	.40
735	Kevin Mitchell	.05
736	Billy Swift	.05
737	Dan Gladden	.05
738	Mike Jackson	.05
739	Mark Carreon	.05
740	Kirt Manwaring	.05
741	Randy Myers	.05
742	Kevin McReynolds	.05
743	Steve Sax	.05
744	Wally Joyner	.05
745	Gary Sheffield	.25
746	Danny Tartabull	.05
747	Julio Valera	.05
748	Denny Neagle	.05
749	Lance Blankenship	.05
750	Mike Gallego	.05
751	Bret Saberhagen	.05
752	Ruben Amaro	.05
753	Eddie Murray	.40
754	Kyle Abbott	.05
755	Bobby Bonilla	.05
756	Eric Davis	.05
757	Eddie Taubensee	.05
758	Andres Galarraga	.05
759	Pete Incaviglia	.05
760	Tom Candiotti	.05
761	Tim Belcher	.05
762	Ricky Bones	.05
763	Bip Roberts	.05
764	Pedro Munoz	.05
765	Greg Swindell	.05
766	Kenny Lofton	.05
767	Gary Carter	.40
768	Charlie Hayes	.05
769	Dickie Thon	.05
770	Donovan Osborne Diamond Debuts Checklist	.05
771	Bret Boone	.10
772	*Archi Cianfrocco*	.05
773	*Mark Clark*	.05
774	*Chad Curtis*	.20
775	*Pat Listach*	.05
776	*Pat Mahomes*	.05
777	*Donovan Osborne*	.05
778	*John Patterson*	.05
779	*Andy Stankiewicz*	.05
780	*Turk Wendell*	.10
781	Bill Krueger	.05
782	Rickey Henderson	.20
783	Kevin Seitzer	.05
784	Dave Martinez	.05
785	John Smiley	.05
786	Matt Stairs	.05
787	Scott Scudder	.05
788	John Wetteland	.05
789	Jack Armstrong	.05
790	Ken Hill	.05
791	Dick Schofield	.05
792	Mariano Duncan	.05
793	Bill Pecota	.05
794	*Mike Kelly*	.05
795	Willie Randolph	.05
796	*Butch Henry*	.05
797	*Carlos Hernandez*	.05
798	Doug Jones	.05
799	Melido Perez	.05
800	Checklist	.05
SP3	Deion Sanders "Prime Time's Two"	.25
SP4	Tom Selleck, Frank Thomas "Mr. Baseball"	2.00
HH2	Ted Williams (hologram)	2.00

Baseball Heroes Bench/Morgan

		NM/M
Complete Set (10):		4.00
Common Card:		.50
Autographed Card:		65.00
---	Header Card	.75
37	Johnny Bench 1968 Rookie of the Year	.75
38	Johnny Bench 1968-77 Ten Straight Gold Gloves	.75
39	Johnny Bench 1970 & 1972 MVP	.75
40	Joe Morgan 1965 Rookie Year	.50
41	Joe Morgan 1975-76 Back-to-Back MVP	.50
42	Joe Morgan 1980-83 The Golden Years	.50
43	Johnny Bench, Joe Morgan 1972-79 Big Red Machine	.60
44	Johnny Bench, Joe Morgan 1989 & 1990 Hall of Fame	.60
45	Johnny Bench, Joe Morgan Checklist - Heroes 37-45	.60

Baseball Heroes Ted Williams

		NM/M
Complete Set (10):		3.00
Common Player:		.50
Autographed Card:		425.00
---	Header Card	.75
28	Ted Williams 1939 Rookie Year	.50
29	Ted Williams 1941 .406!	.50
30	Ted Williams 1942 Triple Crown Year	.50
31	Ted Williams 1946 & 1949 MVP	.50
32	Ted Williams 1947 Second Triple Crown	.50
33	Ted Williams 1950s Player of the Decade	.50
34	Ted Williams 1960 500 Home Run Club	.50
35	Ted Williams 1966 Hall of Fame	.50
36	Ted Williams Checklist - Heroes 28-36	.50

Hall of Fame Heroes

		NM/M
Complete Set (4):		2.50
Common Player:		.50
5	Vida Blue	.50
5a	Vida Blue (autographed)	20.00
6	Lou Brock	1.00
6a	Lou Brock (autographed)	35.00
7	Rollie Fingers	.50
7a	Rollie Fingers (autographed)	30.00
8	Vida Blue, Lou Brock, Rollie Fingers	1.00

Heroes Highlights

		NM/M
Complete Set (10):		4.00
Common Player:		.45
1	Bobby Bonds	.45
2	Lou Brock	.45
3	Rollie Fingers	.45
4	Bob Gibson	.45
5	Reggie Jackson	.75
6	Gaylord Perry	.45
7	Robin Roberts	.45
8	Brooks Robinson	.45
9	Billy Williams	.45
10	Ted Williams	2.00

Home Run Heroes

		NM/M
Complete Set (26):		5.00
Common Player:		.15
1	Jose Canseco	.45
2	Cecil Fielder	.15
3	Howard Johnson	.15
4	Cal Ripken, Jr.	1.50
5	Matt Williams	.15
6	Joe Carter	.15
7	Ron Gant	.15
8	Frank Thomas	.75
9	Andre Dawson	.40
10	Fred McGriff	.15
11	Danny Tartabull	.15
12	Chili Davis	.15
13	Albert Belle	.15
14	Jack Clark	.15
15	Paul O'Neill	.15
16	Darryl Strawberry	.15
17	Dave Winfield	.75
18	Jay Buhner	.15
19	Juan Gonzalez	.25
20	Greg Vaughn	.15
21	Barry Bonds	1.50
22	Matt Nokes	.15
23	John Kruk	.15
24	Ivan Calderon	.15
25	Jeff Bagwell	.75
26	Todd Zeile	.15

Scouting Report

		NM/M
Complete Set (25):		2.00
Common Player:		.25
1	Andy Ashby	.25
2	Willie Banks	.25
3	Kim Batiste	.25
4	Derek Bell	.25
5	Archi Cianfrocco	.25
6	Royce Clayton	.25
7	Gary DiSarcina	.25
8	Dave Fleming	.25
9	Butch Henry	.25
10	Todd Hundley	.25
11	Brian Jordan	.25
12	Eric Karros	.25
13	Pat Listach	.25
14	Scott Livingstone	.25
15	Kenny Lofton	.25
16	Pat Mahomes	.25
17	Denny Neagle	.25
18	Dave Nilsson	.25
19	Donovan Osborne	.25
20	Reggie Sanders	.25
21	Andy Stankiewicz	.25
22	Jim Thome	1.50
23	Julio Valera	.25
24	Mark Wohlers	.25
25	Anthony Young	.25

1993 UPPER DECK

	NM/M
Unopened Fact. Set (840):	30.00

Complete Set (840): 25.00
Common Player: .05
Gold Hologram: 4X
Series 1 or 2 Pack (15): .75
Series 1 or 2 Wax Box (36): 17.50
Jumbo Pack, USA (27): 1.50
Jumbo Box, USA (20): 17.50
Jumbo Pack, Canada (23): 2.00
Jumbo Box, Canada (20): 20.00
1 Tim Salmon (Checklist) .05
2 Mike Piazza 1.25
3 *Rene Arocha* .05
4 *Willie Greene* .05
5 *Manny Alexander* .05
6 Dan Wilson .05
7 *Dan Smith* .05
8 *Kevin Rogers* .05
9 *Nigel Wilson* .05
10 *Joe Vitko* .05
11 Tim Costo .05
12 Alan Embree .05
13 *Jim Tatum* .05
14 *Cris Colon* .05
15 Steve Hosey .05
16 *Sterling Hitchcock* .15
17 *Dave Mlicki* .05
18 *Jessie Hollins* .05
19 *Bobby J. Jones* .05
20 *Kurt Miller* .05
21 *Melvin Nieves* .05
22 *Billy Ashley* .05
23 *J.T. Snow* .50
24 Chipper Jones .85
25 Tim Salmon .25
26 *Tim Pugh* .05
27 David Nied .05
28 *Mike Trombley* .05
29 Javier Lopez .05
30 Jim Abbott Community Heroes Checklist .05
31 Jim Abbott .05
32 Dale Murphy .10
33 Tony Pena .05
34 Kirby Puckett .40
35 Harold Reynolds .05
36 Cal Ripken, Jr. .65
37 Nolan Ryan .65
38 Ryne Sandberg .35
39 Dave Stewart .05
40 Dave Winfield .25
41 Joe Carter, Mark McGwire Teammates Checklist .50
42 Joe Carter, Roberto Alomar Blockbuster Trade .05
43 Pat Listach, Robin Yount, Paul Molitor Brew Crew .15
44 Brady Anderson, Cal Ripken, Jr. Iron and Steal .45
45 Albert Belle, Sandy Alomar Jr., Jim Thome, Carlos Baerga, Kenny Lofton Youthful Tribe .25
46 Cecil Fielder, Mickey Tettleton Motown Mashers .05
47 Roberto Kelly, Don Mattingly Yankee Pride .45
48 Frank Viola, Roger Clemens Boston Cy Sox .30
49 Ruben Sierra, Mark McGwire Bash Brothers .50
50 Kent Hrbek, Kirby Puckett Twin Titles .35
51 Robin Ventura, Frank Thomas Southside Sluggers .35
52 Jose Canseco, Ivan Rodriguez, Rafael Palmeiro, Juan Gonzalez Latin Stars .35
53 Mark Langston, Jim Abbott, Chuck Finley Lethal Lefties .05
54 Gregg Jefferies, George Brett, Wally Joyner Royal Family .35
55 Kevin Mitchell, Jay Buhner, Ken Griffey, Jr. Pacific Sox Exchange .40
56 George Brett .85
57 Scott Cooper .05
58 Mike Maddux .05
59 *Rusty Meacham* .05
60 Wil Cordero .05
61 Tim Teufel .05
62 Jeff Montgomery .05
63 Scott Livingstone .05
64 Doug Dascenzo .05
65 Bret Boone .05
66 *Tim Wakefield* .10
67 Curt Schilling .20
68 Frank Tanana .05
69 Len Dykstra .05
70 Derek Lilliquist .05
71 Anthony Young .05
72 *Hipolito Pichardo* .05
73 Rod Beck .05
74 Kent Hrbek .05
75 Tom Glavine .20
76 Kevin Brown .05
77 Chuck Finley .05
78 Bob Walk .05
79 Rheal Cormier .05
80 Rick Sutcliffe .05
81 Harold Baines .05
82 Lee Smith .05
83 Geno Petralli .05
84 Jose Oquendo .05
85 Mark Gubicza .05
86 Mickey Tettleton .05
87 Bobby Witt .05
88 Mark Lewis .05
89 Kevin Appier .05
90 Mike Stanton .05
91 Rafael Belliard .05
92 Kenny Rogers .05
93 Randy Velarde .05
94 Luis Sojo .05
95 Mark Leiter .05
96 Jody Reed .05
97 Pete Harnisch .05
98 Tom Candiotti .05
99 Mark Portugal .05
100 Dave Valle .05
101 Shawon Dunston .05
102 B.J. Surhoff .05
103 Jay Bell .05
104 Sid Bream .05
105 Frank Thomas Checklist 1-105 .35
106 Mike Morgan .05
107 Bill Doran .05
108 Lance Blankenship .05
109 Mark Lemke .05
110 Brian Harper .05
111 Brady Anderson .05
112 Bip Roberts .05
113 Mitch Williams .05
114 Craig Biggio .05
115 Eddie Murray .65
116 Matt Nokes .05
117 Lance Parrish .05
118 Bill Swift .05
119 Jeff Innis .05
120 Mike LaValliere .05
121 Hal Morris .05
122 Walt Weiss .05
123 Ivan Rodriguez .60
124 Andy Van Slyke .05
125 Roberto Alomar .20
126 Robby Thompson .05
127 Sammy Sosa .75
128 Mark Langston .05
129 Jerry Browne .05
130 Chuck McElroy .05
131 Frank Viola .05
132 Leo Gomez .05
133 Ramon Martinez .05
134 Don Mattingly .85
135 Roger Clemens .85
136 Rickey Henderson .65
137 Darren Daulton .05
138 Ken Hill .05
139 Ozzie Guillen .05
140 Jerald Clark .05
141 Dave Fleming .05
142 Delino DeShields .05
143 Matt Williams .05
144 Larry Walker .05
145 Ruben Sierra .05
146 Ozzie Smith .75
147 Chris Sabo .05
148 *Carlos Hernandez* .05
149 Pat Borders .05
150 Orlando Merced .05
151 Royce Clayton .05
152 Kurt Stillwell .05
153 Dave Hollins .05
154 Mike Greenwell .05
155 Nolan Ryan 1.50
156 Felix Jose .05
157 Junior Felix .05
158 Derek Bell .05
159 Steve Buechele .05
160 John Burkett .05
161 *Pat Howell* .05
162 Milt Cuyler .05
163 Terry Pendleton .05
164 Jack Morris .05
165 Tony Gwynn .75
166 Deion Sanders .10
167 Mike Devereaux .05
168 Ron Darling .05
169 Orel Hershiser .05
170 Mike Jackson .05
171 Doug Jones .05
172 *Dan Walters* .05
173 Darren Lewis .05
174 Carlos Baerga .05
175 Ryne Sandberg .75
176 Gregg Jefferies .05
177 John Jaha .05
178 Luis Polonia .05
179 Kirt Manwaring .05
180 Mike Magnante .05
181 Billy Ripken .05
182 Mike Moore .05
183 Eric Anthony .05
184 Lenny Harris .05
185 Tony Pena .05
186 Mike Felder .05
187 Greg Olson .05
188 Rene Gonzales .05
189 Mike Bordick .05
190 Mel Rojas .05
191 Todd Frohwirth .05
192 Darryl Hamilton .05
193 Mike Fetters .05
194 Omar Olivares .05
195 Tony Phillips .05
196 Paul Sorrento .05
197 Trevor Wilson .05
198 Kevin Gross .05
199 Ron Karkovice .05
200 Brook Jacoby .05
201 Mariano Duncan .05
202 Dennis Cook .05
203 Daryl Boston .05
204 Mike Perez .05
205 Manuel Lee .05
206 Steve Olin .05
207 Charlie Hough .05
208 Scott Scudder .05
209 Charlie O'Brien .05
210 Barry Bonds Checklist 106-210 .60
211 Jose Vizcaino .05
212 Scott Leius .05
213 Kevin Mitchell .05
214 Brian Barnes .05
215 Pat Kelly .05
216 Chris Hammond .05
217 Rob Deer .05
218 Cory Snyder .05
219 Gary Carter .65
220 Danny Darwin .05
221 Tom Gordon .05
222 Gary Sheffield .40
223 Joe Carter .05
224 Jay Buhner .05
225 Jose Offerman .05
226 Jose Rijo .05
227 Mark Whiten .05
228 Randy Milligan .05
229 Bud Black .05
230 Gary DiSarcina .05
231 Steve Finley .05
232 Dennis Martinez .05
233 Mike Mussina .30
234 Joe Oliver .05
235 Chad Curtis .05
236 Shane Mack .05
237 Jaime Navarro .05
238 Brian McRae .05
239 Chili Davis .05
240 Jeff King .05
241 Dean Palmer .05
242 Danny Tartabull .05
243 Charles Nagy .05
244 Ray Lankford .05
245 Barry Larkin .05
246 Steve Avery .05
247 John Kruk .05
248 Derrick May .05
249 Stan Javier .05
250 Roger McDowell .05
251 Dan Gladden .05
252 Wally Joyner .05
253 Pat Listach .05
254 Chuck Knoblauch .05
255 Sandy Alomar Jr. .05
256 Jeff Bagwell .65
257 Andy Stankiewicz .05
258 Darrin Jackson .05
259 Brett Butler .05
260 Joe Orsulak .05
261 Andy Benes .05
262 Kenny Lofton .05
263 Robin Ventura .05
264 Ron Gant .05
265 Ellis Burks .05
266 Juan Guzman .05
267 Wes Chamberlain .05
268 John Smiley .05
269 Franklin Stubbs .05
270 Tom Browning .05
271 Dennis Eckersley .60
272 Carlton Fisk .65
273 Lou Whitaker .05
274 Phil Plantier .05
275 Bobby Bonilla .05
276 Ben McDonald .05
277 Bob Zupcic .05
278 Terry Steinbach .05
279 Terry Mulholland .05
280 Lance Johnson .05
281 Willie McGee .05
282 Bret Saberhagen .05
283 Randy Myers .05
284 Randy Tomlin .05
285 Mickey Morandini .05
286 Brian Williams .05
287 Tino Martinez .05
288 Jose Melendez .05
289 Jeff Huson .05
290 Joe Grahe .05
291 Mel Hall .05
292 Otis Nixon .05
293 Todd Hundley .05
294 Casey Candaele .05
295 Kevin Seitzer .05
296 Eddie Taubensee .05
297 Moises Alou .05
298 Scott Radinsky .05
299 Thomas Howard .05
300 Kyle Abbott .05
301 Omar Vizquel .05
302 Keith Miller .05
303 Rick Aguilera .05
304 Bruce Hurst .05
305 Ken Caminiti .05
306 Mike Pagiarulo .05
307 Frank Seminara .05
308 Andre Dawson .30
309 Jose Lind .05
310 Joe Boever .05
311 Jeff Parrett .05
312 Alan Mills .05
313 Kevin Tapani .05
314 Darryl Kile .05
315 Will Clark Checklist 211-315 .05
316 Mike Sharperson .05
317 John Orton .05
318 Bob Tewksbury .05
319 Xavier Hernandez .05
320 Paul Assenmacher .05
321 John Franco .05
322 Mike Timlin .05
323 Jose Guzman .05
324 Pedro Martinez .65
325 Bill Spiers .05
326 Melido Perez .05
327 Mike Macfarlane .05
328 Ricky Bones .05
329 Scott Bankhead .05
330 Rich Rodriguez .05
331 Geronimo Pena .05
332 Bernie Williams .05
333 Paul Molitor .65
334 Roger Mason .05
335 David Cone .05
336 Randy Johnson .65
337 Pat Mahomes .05
338 Erik Hanson .05
339 Duane Ward .05
340 Al Martin .05
341 Pedro Munoz .05
342 Greg Colbrunn .05
343 Julio Valera .05
344 John Olerud .05
345 George Bell .05
346 Devon White .05
347 Donovan Osborne .05
348 Mark Gardner .05
349 Zane Smith .05
350 Wilson Alvarez .05
351 *Kevin Koslofski* .05
352 Roberto Hernandez .05
353 Glenn Davis .05
354 Reggie Sanders .05
355 Ken Griffey, Jr. 1.00
355a Ken Griffey Jr. (promo, 1992-dated hologram on back) 3.00

355b Ken Griffey, Jr. (8-1/2" x 11" limited edition of 1,000) 15.00
356 Marquis Grissom .05
357 Jack McDowell .05
358 Jimmy Key .05
359 Stan Belinda .05
360 Gerald Williams .05
361 Sid Fernandez .05
362 Alex Fernandez .05
363 John Smoltz .05
364 Travis Fryman .05
365 Jose Canseco .50
366 Dave Justice .05
367 *Pedro Astacio* .10
368 Tim Belcher .05
369 Steve Sax .05
370 Gary Gaetti .05
371 Jeff Frye .05
372 Bob Wickman .05
373 *Ryan Thompson* .05
374 *David Hulse* .05
375 Cal Eldred .05
376 Ryan Klesko .05
377 *Damion Easley* .10
378 *John Kiely* .05
379 *Jim Bullinger* .05
380 Brian Bohanon .05
381 Rod Brewer .05
382 *Fernando Ramsey* .05
383 Sam Militello .05
384 Arthur Rhodes .05
385 Eric Karros .05
386 Rico Brogna .05
387 *John Valentin* .10
388 *Kerry Woodson* .05
389 *Ben Rivera* .05
390 *Matt Whiteside* .05
391 Henry Rodriguez .05
392 John Wetteland .05
393 Kent Mercker .05
394 Bernard Gilkey .05
395 Doug Henry .05
396 Mo Vaughn .05
397 Scott Erickson .05
398 Bill Gullickson .05
399 Mark Guthrie .05
400 Dave Martinez .05
401 *Jeff Kent* .50
402 Chris Hoiles .05
403 Mike Henneman .05
404 Chris Nabholz .05
405 Tom Pagnozzi .05
406 Kelly Gruber .05
407 Bob Welch .05
408 Frank Castillo .05
409 John Dopson .05
410 Steve Farr .05
411 Henry Cotto .05
412 Bob Patterson .05
413 Todd Stottlemyre .05
414 Greg A. Harris .05
415 Denny Neagle .05
416 Bill Wegman .05
417 Willie Wilson .05
418 Terry Leach .05
419 Willie Randolph .05
420 Mark McGwire Checklist 316-420 .65
421 Calvin Murray .05
422 *Pete Janicki* .05
423 Todd Jones .05
424 Mike Neill .05
425 Carlos Delgado .40
426 Jose Oliva .05
427 Tyrone Hill .05
428 Dmitri Young .05
429 *Derek Wallace* .05
430 *Michael Moore* .05
431 Cliff Floyd .05
432 Calvin Murray .05
433 Manny Ramirez .75
434 Marc Newfield .05
435 Charles Johnson .05
436 Butch Huskey .05
437 Brad Pennington .05
438 *Ray McDavid* .05
439 Chad McConnell .05
440 *Midre Cummings* .05
441 Benji Gil .05
442 Frank Rodriguez .05
443 *Chad Mottola* .05
444 *John Burke* .05
445 Michael Tucker .05
446 Rick Greene .05
447 Rich Becker .05
448 Mike Robertson .05
449 *Derek Jeter* 8.00
450 David McCarty, Ivan Rodriguez Checklist 451-470 Inside the Numbers .05
451 Jim Abbott .05
452 Jeff Bagwell .40
453 Jason Bere .05
454 Delino DeShields .05
455 Travis Fryman .05
456 Alex Gonzalez .05
457 Phil Hiatt .05
458 Dave Hollins .05
459 Chipper Jones .65
460 Dave Justice .05
461 Ray Lankford .05
462 David McCarty .05
463 Mike Mussina .15
464 Jose Offerman .05
465 Dean Palmer .05
466 Geronimo Pena .05
467 Eduardo Perez .05
468 Ivan Rodriguez .25
469 Reggie Sanders .05
470 Bernie Williams .05
471 Barry Bonds, Matt Williams, Will Clark Checklist 472-485 Team Stars .45
472 John Smoltz, Steve Avery, Greg Maddux, Tom Glavine Strike Force .10
473 Jose Rijo, Rob Dibble, Roberto Kelly, Reggie Sanders, Barry Larkin Red October .10
474 Gary Sheffield, Phil Plantier, Tony Gwynn, Fred McGriff Four Corners .20
475 Doug Drabek, Craig Biggio, Jeff Bagwell Shooting Stars .15
476 Will Clark, Barry Bonds, Matt Williams Giant Sticks .40
477 Darryl Strawberry, Eric Davis Boyhood Friends .05
478 Dante Bichette, David Nied, Andres Galarraga Rock Solid .05
479 Dave Magadan, Orestes Destrade, Bret Barbarie, Jeff Conine Inaugural Catch .05
480 Tim Wakefield, Andy Van Slyke, Jay Bell Steel City Champions .05
481 Marquis Grissom, Delino DeShields, Dennis Martinez, Larry Walker "Les Grandes Etoiles" .05
482 Geronimo Pena, Ray Lankford, Ozzie Smith, Bernard Gilkey Runnin' Redbirds .10
483 Ryne Sandberg, Mark Grace, Randy Myers Ivy Leaguers .15
484 Eddie Murray, Bobby Bonilla, Howard Johnson Big Apple Power Switch .10
485 John Kruk, Dave Hollins, Darren Daulton, Len Dykstra Hammers & Nails .05
486 Barry Bonds .60
487 Dennis Eckersley .30
488 Greg Maddux .40
489 Dennis Eckersley .30
490 Eric Karros .05
491 Pat Listach .05
492 Gary Sheffield .10
493 Mark McGwire .75
494 Gary Sheffield .10
495 Edgar Martinez .05
496 Fred McGriff .05
497 Juan Gonzalez .20
498 Darren Daulton .05
499 Cecil Fielder .05
500 Brent Gates Checklist 501-510 Diamond Debuts .05
501 Tavo Alvarez .05
502 Rod Bolton .05
503 *John Cummings* .05
504 Brent Gates .05
505 Tyler Green .05
506 *Jose Martinez* .05
507 Troy Percival .05
508 Kevin Stocker .05
509 *Matt Walbeck* .10
510 Rondell White .05
511 Billy Ripken .05
512 Mike Moore .05
513 Jose Lind .05
514 Chito Martinez .05
515 Jose Guzman .05
516 Kim Batiste .05
517 Jeff Tackett .05
518 Charlie Hough .05
519 Marvin Freeman .05
520 Carlos Martinez .05
521 Eric Young .05
522 Pete Incaviglia .05
523 Scott Fletcher .05
524 Orestes Destrade .05
525 Ken Griffey, Jr. Checklist 421-525 .40
526 Ellis Burks .05
527 Juan Samuel .05
528 Dave Magadan .05
529 Jeff Parrett .05
530 Bill Krueger .05
531 Frank Bolick .05
532 Alan Trammell .05
533 Walt Weiss .05
534 David Cone .05
535 Greg Maddux .75
536 Kevin Young .05
537 Dave Hansen .05
538 Alex Cole .05
539 Greg Hibbard .05
540 Gene Larkin .05
541 Jeff Reardon .05
542 Felix Jose .05
543 Jimmy Key .05
544 Reggie Jefferson .05
545 Gregg Jefferies .05
546 Dave Stewart .05
547 Tim Wallach .05
548 Spike Owen .05
549 Tommy Greene .05
550 Fernando Valenzuela .05
551 Rich Amaral .05
552 Bret Barberie .05
553 Edgar Martinez .05
554 Jim Abbott .05
555 Frank Thomas .65
556 Wade Boggs .75
557 Tom Henke .05
558 Milt Thompson .05
559 Lloyd McClendon .05
560 Vinny Castilla .05
561 Ricky Jordan .05
562 Andujar Cedeno .05
563 Greg Vaughn .05
564 Cecil Fielder .05
565 Kirby Puckett .75
566 Mark McGwire 1.25
567 Barry Bonds 1.50
568 Jody Reed .05
569 Todd Zeile .05
570 Mark Carreon .05
571 Joe Girardi .05
572 Luis Gonzalez .05
573 Mark Grace .05
574 Rafael Palmeiro .60
575 Darryl Strawberry .05
576 Will Clark .05
577 Fred McGriff .05
578 Kevin Reimer .05
579 Dave Righetti .05
580 Juan Bell .05
581 Jeff Brantley .05
582 Brian Hunter .05
583 Tim Naehring .05
584 Glenallen Hill .05
585 Cal Ripken, Jr. 1.50
586 Albert Belle .05
587 Robin Yount .65
588 Chris Bosio .05
589 Pete Smith .05
590 Chuck Carr .05
591 Jeff Blauser .05
592 Kevin McReynolds .05
593 Andres Galarraga .05
594 Kevin Maas .05
595 Eric Davis .05
596 Brian Jordan .05
597 Tim Raines .05
598 Rick Wilkins .05
599 Steve Cooke .05
600 Mike Gallego .05
601 Mike Munoz .05
602 Luis Rivera .05
603 Junior Ortiz .05
604 Brent Mayne .05
605 Luis Alicea .05
606 Damon Berryhill .05
607 Dave Henderson .05
608 Kirk McCaskill .05
609 Jeff Fassero .05
610 Mike Harkey .05
611 Francisco Cabrera .05
612 Rey Sanchez .05
613 Scott Servais .05
614 Darrin Fletcher .05
615 Felix Fermin .05
616 Kevin Seitzer .05
617 Bob Scanlan .05
618 Billy Hatcher .05
619 John Vander Wal .05
620 Joe Hesketh .05
621 Hector Villanueva .05
622 Randy Milligan .05
623 *Tony Tarasco* .05
624 Russ Swan .05
625 Willie Wilson .05
626 Frank Tanana .05
627 Pete O'Brien .05
628 Lenny Webster .05
629 Mark Clark .05
630 Roger Clemens Checklist 526-630 .40
631 Alex Arias .05
632 Chris Gwynn .05
633 Tom Bolton .05
634 Greg Briley .05
635 Kent Bottenfield .05
636 Kelly Downs .05
637 Manuel Lee .05
638 Al Leiter .05
639 Jeff Gardner .05
640 Mike Gardiner .05
641 Mark Gardner .05
642 Jeff Branson .05
643 Paul Wagner .05
644 Sean Berry .05
645 Phil Hiatt .05
646 Kevin Mitchell .05
647 Charlie Hayes .05
648 Jim Deshaies .05
649 Dan Pasqua .05
650 Mike Maddux .05
651 *Domingo Martinez* .05
652 *Greg McMichael* .05
653 *Eric Wedge* .05
654 Mark Whiten .05
655 Bobby Kelly .05
656 Julio Franco .05
657 Gene Harris .05
658 Pete Schourek .05
659 Mike Bielecki .05
660 Ricky Gutierrez .05
661 Chris Hammond .05
662 Tim Scott .05
663 Norm Charlton .05
664 Doug Drabek .05
665 Dwight Gooden .05
666 Jim Gott .05
667 Randy Myers .05
668 Darren Holmes .05
669 Tim Spehr .05
670 Bruce Ruffin .05
671 Bobby Thigpen .05
672 Tony Fernandez .05
673 Darrin Jackson .05
674 Gregg Olson .05
675 Rob Dibble .05
676 Howard Johnson .05
677 *Mike Lansing* .15
678 Charlie Leibrandt .05
679 Kevin Bass .05
680 Hubie Brooks .05
681 Scott Brosius .05
682 Randy Knorr .05
683 Dante Bichette .05
684 Bryan Harvey .05
685 Greg Gohr .05
686 Willie Banks .05
687 Robb Nen .05
688 Mike Scioscia .05
689 John Farrell .05
690 John Candelaria .05
691 Damon Buford .05
692 Todd Worrell .05
693 Pat Hentgen .05
694 John Smiley .05
695 Greg Swindell .05
696 Derek Bell .05
697 Terry Jorgensen .05
698 Jimmy Jones .05
699 David Wells .05
700 Dave Martinez .05
701 Steve Bedrosian .05
702 Jeff Russell .05
703 Joe Magrane .05
704 Matt Mieske .05
705 Paul Molitor .65
706 Dale Murphy .15
707 Steve Howe .05

708 Greg Gagne .05
709 Dave Eiland .05
710 David West .05
711 Luis Aquino .05
712 Joe Orsulak .05
713 Eric Plunk .05
714 Mike Felder .05
715 Joe Klink .05
716 Lonnie Smith .05
717 Monty Fariss .05
718 Craig Lefferts .05
719 John Habyan .05
720 Willie Blair .05
721 Darnell Coles .05
722 Mark Williamson .05
723 Bryn Smith .05
724 Greg W. Harris .05
725 *Graeme Lloyd* .05
726 Cris Carpenter .05
727 Chico Walker .05
728 Tracy Woodson .05
729 Jose Uribe .05
730 Stan Javier .05
731 Jay Howell .05
732 Freddie Benavides .05
733 Jeff Reboulet .05
734 Scott Sanderson .05
735 Ryne Sandberg Checklist 631-735 .20
736 Archi Cianfrocco .05
737 Daryl Boston .05
738 Craig Grebeck .05
739 Doug Dascenzo .05
740 Gerald Young .05
741 Candy Maldonado .05
742 Joey Cora .05
743 Don Slaught .05
744 Steve Decker .05
745 Blas Minor .05
746 Storm Davis .05
747 Carlos Quintana .05
748 Vince Coleman .05
749 Todd Burns .05
750 Steve Frey .05
751 Ivan Calderon .05
752 *Steve Reed* .05
753 Danny Jackson .05
754 Jeff Conine .05
755 Juan Gonzalez .35
756 Mike Kelly .05
757 John Doherty .05
758 Jack Armstrong .05
759 John Wehner .05
760 Scott Bankhead .05
761 Jim Tatum .05
762 *Scott Pose* .05
763 Andy Ashby .05
764 Ed Sprague .05
765 Harold Baines .05
766 Kirk Gibson .05
767 Troy Neel .05
768 Dick Schofield .05
769 Dickie Thon .05
770 Butch Henry .05
771 Junior Felix .05
772 *Ken Ryan* .05
773 Trevor Hoffman .05
774 Phil Plantier .05
775 Bo Jackson .10
776 Benito Santiago .05
777 Andre Dawson .25
778 Bryan Hickerson .05
779 Dennis Moeller .05
780 Ryan Bowen .05
781 Eric Fox .05
782 Joe Kmak .05
783 Mike Hampton .05
784 *Darrell Sherman* .05
785 J.T. Snow .05
786 Dave Winfield .65
787 Jim Austin .05
788 Craig Shipley .05
789 Greg Myers .05
790 Todd Benzinger .05
791 Cory Snyder .05
792 David Segui .05
793 Armando Reynoso .05
794 Chili Davis .05
795 Dave Nilsson .05
796 Paul O'Neill .05
797 Jerald Clark .05
798 Jose Mesa .05
799 Brian Holman .05
800 Jim Eisenreich .05
801 Mark McLemore .05
802 Luis Sojo .05
803 Harold Reynolds .05
804 Dan Plesac .05
805 Dave Stieb .05
806 Tom Brunansky .05
807 Kelly Gruber .05
808 Bob Ojeda .05
809 Dave Burba .05
810 Joe Boever .05
811 Jeremy Hernandez .05
812 Tim Salmon Angels Checklist .05
813 Jeff Bagwell Astros Checklist .35
814 Mark McGwire Athletics Checklist .75
815 Roberto Alomar Blue Jays Checklist .10
816 Steve Avery Braves Checklist .05
817 Pat Listach Brewers Checklist .05
818 Gregg Jefferies Cardinals Checklist .05
819 Sammy Sosa Cubs Checklist .40
820 Darryl Strawberry Dodgers Checklist .05
821 Dennis Martinez Expos Checklist .05
822 Robby Thompson Giants Checklist .05
823 Albert Belle Indians Checklist .05
824 Randy Johnson Mariners Checklist .30
825 Nigel Wilson Marlins Checklist .05
826 Bobby Bonilla Mets Checklist .05
827 Glenn Davis Orioles Checklist .05
828 Gary Sheffield Padres Checklist .10
829 Darren Daulton Phillies Checklist .05
830 Jay Bell Pirates Checklist .05
831 Juan Gonzalez Rangers Checklist .20
832 Andre Dawson Red Sox Checklist .10
833 Hal Morris Reds Checklist .05
834 David Nied Rockies Checklist .05
835 Felix Jose Royals Checklist .05
836 Travis Fryman Tigers Checklist .05
837 Shane Mack Twins Checklist .05
838 Robin Ventura White Sox Checklist .05
839 Danny Tartabull Yankees Checklist .05
840 Roberto Alomar Checklist 736-840 .10
SP5 Robin Yount, George Brett 3,000 Hits .50
SP6 Nolan Ryan 1.50

1993 UPPER DECK ALL-TIME HEROES

NM/M

Complete Set (165): 35.00
Common Player: .10
Wax Pack (12): 2.00
Wax Box (24): 30.00

1 Hank Aaron 2.00
2 Tommie Agee .10
3 Bob Allison .10
4 Matty Alou .10
5 Sal Bando .10
6 Hank Bauer .15
7 Don Baylor .10
8 Glenn Beckert .10
9 Yogi Berra .50
10 Buddy Biancalana .10
11 Jack Billingham .10
12 Joe Black .10
13 Paul Blair .10
14 Steve Blass .10
15 Ray Boone .10
16 Lou Boudreau .10
17 Ken Brett .10
18 Nellie Briles .10
19 Bobby Brown .10
20 Bill Buckner .10
21 Don Buford .10
22 Al Bumbry .10
23 Lew Burdette .10
24 Jeff Burroughs .10
25 Johnny Callison .10
26 Bert Campaneris .10
27 Rico Carty .10
28 Dave Cash .10
29 Cesar Cedeno .10
30 Frank Chance .25
31 Joe Charboneau .15
32 Ty Cobb 2.00
33 Jerry Coleman .10
34 Cecil Cooper .10
35 Frankie Crossetti .10
36 Alvin Dark .10
37 Tommy Davis .10
38 Dizzy Dean .25
39 Doug DeCinces .10
40 Bucky Dent .10
41 Larry Dierker .10
42 Larry Doby .20
43 Moe Drabowsky .10
44 Dave Dravecky .10
45 Del Ennis .10
46 Carl Erskine .10
47 Johnny Evers .25
48 Elroy Face .10
49 Rick Ferrell .10
50 Mark Fidrych .15
51 Curt Flood .10
52 Whitey Ford .50
53 George Foster .10
54 Jimmie Foxx .25
55 Jim Fregosi .10
56 Phil Garner .10
57 Ralph Garr .10
58 Lou Gehrig 2.00
59 Bobby Grich .10
60 Jerry Grote .10
61 Harvey Haddix .10
62 Toby Harrah .10
63 Bud Harrelson .10
64 Jim Hegan .10
65 Gil Hodges .25
66 Ken Holtzman .10
67 Bob Horner .10
68 Rogers Hornsby .25
69 Carl Hubbell .25
70 Ron Hunt .10
71 Monte Irvin .10
72a Reggie Jackson (regular issue, black printing on back) .50
72b Reggie Jackson (dealer promo, red printing on back) 6.00
73 Larry Jansen .10
74 Ferguson Jenkins .10
75 Tommy John .10
76 Cliff Johnson .10
77 Davey Johnson .10
78 Walter Johnson .45
79 George Kell .10
80 Don Kessinger .10
81 Vern Law .10
82 Dennis Leonard .10
83 Johnny Logan .10
84 Mickey Lolich .10
85 Jim Lonborg .10
86 Bill Madlock .10
87 Mickey Mantle 4.00
88 Billy Martin .25
89 Christy Mathewson .45
90 Lee May .10
91 Willie Mays 2.00
92 Bill Mazeroski .25
93 Gil McDougald .15
94 Sam McDowell .10
95 Minnie Minoso .15
96 Johnny Mize .25
97 Rick Monday .10
98 Wally Moon .10
99 Manny Mota .10
100 Bobby Murcer .10
101 Ron Necciai .10
102 Al Oliver .10
103 Mel Ott .15
104 Mel Parnell .10
105 Jimmy Piersall .10
106 Johnny Podres .15
107 Bobby Richardson .15
108 Robin Roberts .15
109 Al Rosen .10
110 Babe Ruth 3.00
111 Joe Sambito .10
112 Manny Sanguillen .10
113 Ron Santo .10
114 Bill Skowron .15
115 Enos Slaughter .15
116 Warren Spahn .20
117 Tris Speaker .20
118 Frank Thomas .10
119 Bobby Thomson .10
120 Andre Thornton .10
121 Marv Throneberry .10
122 Luis Tiant .10
123 Joe Tinker .25
124 Honus Wagner .50
125 Bill White .10
126 Ted Williams 1.00
127 Earl Wilson .10
128 Joe Wood .10
129 Cy Young .40
130 Richie Zisk .10
131 Babe Ruth, Lou Gehrig 2.00
132 Ted Williams, Rogers Hornsby 1.00
133 Lou Gehrig, Babe Ruth 2.00
134 Babe Ruth, Mickey Mantle 3.00
135 Mickey Mantle, Reggie Jackson 1.00
136 Mel Ott, Carl Hubbell .15
137 Mickey Mantle, Willie Mays 2.00
138 Cy Young, Walter Johnson .25
139 Honus Wagner, Rogers Hornsby .25
140 Mickey Mantle, Whitey Ford 2.00
141 Mickey Mantle, Billy Martin 2.00
142 Cy Young, Walter Johnson .25
143 Christy Mathewson, Walter Johnson .25
144 Warren Spahn, Christy Mathewson .15
145 Honus Wagner, Ty Cobb .50
146 Babe Ruth, Ty Cobb 1.00
147 Joe Tinker, Johnny Evers .15
148 Johnny Evers, Frank Chance .15
149 Hank Aaron, Babe Ruth 1.00
150 Willie Mays, Hank Aaron 1.00
151 Babe Ruth, Willie Mays 1.00
152 Babe Ruth, Whitey Ford 1.00
153 Larry Doby, Minnie Minoso .25
154 Joe Black, Monte Irvin .10
155 Joe Wood, Christy Mathewson .15
156 Christy Mathewson, Cy Young .25
157 Cy Young, Joe Wood .15
158 Cy Young, Whitey Ford .20
159 Cy Young, Ferguson Jenkins .15
160 Ty Cobb, Rogers Hornsby .45
161 Tris Speaker, Ted Williams 1.00
162 Rogers Hornsby, Ted Williams 1.00
163 Willie Mays, Monte Irvin .50
164 Willie Mays, Bobby Thomson .50
165 Reggie Jackson, Mickey Mantle 2.00

Baseball Heroes Willie Mays

NM/M

Complete Set (10): 4.00
Common Card: .50
Header Card: 1.00

Clutch Performers

NM/M

Complete Set (20): 8.00
Common Player: .25

1 Roberto Alomar .30
2 Wade Boggs 1.00
3 Barry Bonds 2.50
4 Jose Canseco .40
5 Joe Carter .25

6 Will Clark .25
7 Roger Clemens 1.25
8 Dennis Eckersley .60
9 Cecil Fielder .25
10 Juan Gonzalez .60
11 Ken Griffey, Jr. 2.00
12 Rickey Henderson .75
13 Barry Larkin .25
14 Don Mattingly 1.25
15 Fred McGriff .25
16 Terry Pendleton .25
17 Kirby Puckett 1.00
18 Ryne Sandberg 1.00
19 John Smoltz .25
20 Frank Thomas .75

Diamond Gallery

NM/M
Complete Set (36): 6.00
Common Player: .10
1 Tim Salmon .10
2 Jeff Bagwell .30
3 Mark McGwire .75
4 Roberto Alomar .25
5 Terry Pendleton .10
6 Robin Yount .30
7 Ray Lankford .10
8 Ryne Sandberg .40
9 Darryl Strawberry .10
10 Marquis Grissom .10
11 Barry Bonds 1.00
12 Carlos Baerga .10
13 Ken Griffey, Jr. .65
14 Benito Santiago .10
15 Dwight Gooden .10
16 Cal Ripken, Jr. 1.00
17 Tony Gwynn .40
18 Dave Hollins .10
19 Andy Van Slyke .10
20 Juan Gonzalez .25
21 Roger Clemens .50
22 Barry Larkin .10
23 Dave Nied .10
24 George Brett .50
25 Travis Fryman .10
26 Kirby Puckett .40
27 Frank Thomas .30
28 Don Mattingly .50
29 Rickey Henderson .30
30 Nolan Ryan 1.00
31 Ozzie Smith .40
32 Wil Cordero .10
33 Phil Hiatt .10
34 Mike Piazza .65
35 J.T. Snow .10
36 Kevin Young .10

Future Heroes

NM/M
Complete Set (10): 5.00
Common Player: .50
Header Card: .25
55 Roberto Alomar .50
56 Barry Bonds 2.50
57 Roger Clemens 1.00
58 Juan Gonzalez .50
59 Ken Griffey, Jr. 1.50
60 Mark McGwire 2.00
61 Kirby Puckett .85
62 Frank Thomas .75
63 Checklist .05

Highlights

NM/M
Complete Set (20): 20.00
Common Player: .25
1 Roberto Alomar .50
2 Steve Avery .25
3 Harold Baines .25
4 Damon Berryhill .25
5 Barry Bonds 7.50
6 Bret Boone .25
7 George Brett 4.00
8 Francisco Cabrera .25
9 Ken Griffey, Jr. 5.00
10 Rickey Henderson 2.00
11 Kenny Lofton .25
12 Mickey Morandini .25
13 Eddie Murray 2.00
14 David Nied .25
15 Jeff Reardon .25
16 Bip Roberts .25
17 Nolan Ryan 7.50
18 Ed Sprague .25
19 Dave Winfield 2.00
20 Robin Yount 2.00

Home Run Heroes

NM/M
Complete Set (28): 7.50
Common Player: .15
1 Juan Gonzalez .50
2 Mark McGwire 2.25
3 Cecil Fielder .15
4 Fred McGriff .15
5 Albert Belle .15
6 Barry Bonds 2.50
7 Joe Carter .15
8 Darren Daulton .15
9 Ken Griffey, Jr. 2.00
10 Dave Hollins .15
11 Ryne Sandberg 1.00
12 George Bell .15
13 Danny Tartabull .15
14 Mike Devereaux .15
15 Greg Vaughn .15
16 Larry Walker .15
17 Dave Justice .15
18 Terry Pendleton .15
19 Eric Karros .15
20 Ray Lankford .15
21 Matt Williams .15
22 Eric Anthony .15
23 Bobby Bonilla .15
24 Kirby Puckett 1.00
25 Mike Macfarlane .15
26 Tom Brunansky .15
27 Paul O'Neill .15
28 Gary Gaetti .15

Iooss Collection

NM/M
Complete Set (27): 10.00
Common Player: .25
Header Card: .25
1 Tim Salmon .25
2 Jeff Bagwell .75
3 Mark McGwire 1.50
4 Roberto Alomar .35
5 Steve Avery .25
6 Paul Molitor .75
7 Ozzie Smith 1.00
8 Mark Grace .25
9 Eric Karros .25
10 Delino DeShields .25
11 Will Clark .25
12 Albert Belle .35
13 Ken Griffey, Jr. 1.50

14 Howard Johnson .25
15 Cal Ripken, Jr. 2.00
16 Fred McGriff .25
17 Darren Daulton .25
18 Andy Van Slyke .25
19 Nolan Ryan 2.00
20 Wade Boggs 1.00
21 Barry Larkin .25
22 George Brett 1.25
23 Cecil Fielder .25
24 Kirby Puckett 1.00
25 Frank Thomas .75
26 Don Mattingly 1.25

On Deck

NM/M
Complete Set (25): 10.00
Common Player: .15
1 Jim Abbott .15
2 Roberto Alomar .25
3 Carlos Baerga .15
4 Albert Belle .15
5 Wade Boggs 1.00
6 George Brett 1.25
7 Jose Canseco .45
8 Will Clark .15
9 Roger Clemens 1.25
10 Dennis Eckersley .65
11 Cecil Fielder .15
12 Juan Gonzalez .40
13 Ken Griffey, Jr. 1.50
14 Tony Gwynn 1.00
15 Bo Jackson .20
16 Chipper Jones 1.00
17 Eric Karros .15
18 Mark McGwire 2.00
19 Kirby Puckett 1.00
20 Nolan Ryan 2.50
21 Tim Salmon .15
22 Ryne Sandberg 1.00
23 Darryl Strawberry .15
24 Frank Thomas .75
25 Andy Van Slyke .15

Then And Now

NM/M
Complete Set (18): 30.00
Common Player: .75
1 Wade Boggs 2.00
2 George Brett 2.50
3 Rickey Henderson 1.25
4 Cal Ripken, Jr. 4.00
5 Nolan Ryan 4.00
6 Ryne Sandberg 2.00
7 Ozzie Smith 2.00
8 Darryl Strawberry .75
9 Dave Winfield 1.25
10 Dennis Eckersley 1.00
11 Tony Gwynn 2.00
12 Howard Johnson .75
13 Don Mattingly 2.50
14 Eddie Murray 1.25
15 Robin Yount 1.25
16 Reggie Jackson 2.00
17 Mickey Mantle 6.00
17a Mickey Mantle (5" x 7") 13.50
18 Willie Mays 3.00

Triple Crown Contenders

NM/M
Complete Set (10): 6.00
Common Player: .25
1 Barry Bonds 1.50
2 Jose Canseco .45
3 Will Clark .25
4 Ken Griffey, Jr. 1.25
5 Fred McGriff .25
6 Kirby Puckett .75
7 Cal Ripken, Jr. 1.50
8 Gary Sheffield .35
9 Frank Thomas .60
10 Larry Walker .25

5th Anniversary

NM/M
Complete Set (15): 7.00
Common Player: .25
1 Ken Griffey, Jr. 1.50
2 Gary Sheffield .35
3 Roberto Alomar .35
4 Jim Abbott .25
5 Nolan Ryan 2.00
6 Juan Gonzalez .35
7 Dave Justice .25
8 Carlos Baerga .25
9 Reggie Jackson 1.00
10 Eric Karros .25
11 Chipper Jones 1.00
12 Ivan Rodriguez .50
13 Pat Listach .25
14 Frank Thomas .90
15 Tim Salmon .25

1994 UPPER DECK

NM/M
Complete Set (550): 30.00
Complete Series 1 (280): 25.00

Complete Series 2 (270):		5.00
Common Player:		.05
Series 1 Hobby Pack (12):		2.50
Series 1 Hobby Box (36):		65.00
Series 1 Retail Pack (12):		2.00
Series 1 Retail Box (36):		40.00
Series 2 Hobby Pack (12):		.75
Series 2 Hobby Box (36):		20.00
Series 2 Retail Pack (12):		1.25
Series 2 Retail Box (36):		25.00
1	*Brian Anderson*	.15
2	Shane Andrews	.05
3	James Baldwin	.05
4	Rich Becker	.05
5	Greg Blosser	.05
6	*Ricky Bottalico*	.05
7	Midre Cummings	.05
8	Carlos Delgado	.50
9	*Steve Dreyer*	.05
10	*Joey Eischen*	.05
11	Carl Everett	.05
12	Cliff Floyd	.05
13	Alex Gonzalez	.05
14	Jeff Granger	.05
15	Shawn Green	.35
16	Brian Hunter	.05
17	Butch Huskey	.05
18	Mark Hutton	.05
19	*Michael Jordan*	5.00
20	Steve Karsay	.05
21	Jeff McNeely	.05
22	Marc Newfield	.05
23	Manny Ramirez	.60
24	*Alex Rodriguez*	15.00
25	Scott Ruffcorn	.05
26	Paul Spoljaric	.05
27	*Salomon Torres*	.05
28	Steve Trachsel	.05
29	*Chris Turner*	.05
30	Gabe White	.05
31	Randy Johnson	.40
32	John Wetteland	.05
33	Mike Piazza	.65
34	Rafael Palmeiro	.35
35	Roberto Alomar	.10
36	Matt Williams	.05
37	Travis Fryman	.05
38	Barry Bonds	1.00
39	Marquis Grissom	.05
40	Albert Belle	.05
41	Steve Avery	.05
42	Jason Bere	.05
43	Alex Fernandez	.05
44	Mike Mussina	.15
45	Aaron Sele	.05
46	Rod Beck	.05
47	Mike Piazza	.65
48	John Olerud	.05
49	Carlos Baerga	.05
50	Gary Sheffield	.20
51	Travis Fryman	.05
52	Juan Gonzalez	.20
53	Ken Griffey, Jr.	.65
54	Tim Salmon	.05
55	Frank Thomas	.45
56	Tony Phillips	.05
57	Julio Franco	.05
58	Kevin Mitchell	.05
59	Raul Mondesi	.05
60	Rickey Henderson	.75
61	Jay Buhner	.05
62	Bill Swift	.05
63	Brady Anderson	.05
64	Ryan Klesko	.05
65	Darren Daulton	.05
66	Damion Easley	.05
67	Mark McGwire	1.50
68	John Roper	.05
69	Dave Telgheder	.05
70	Dave Nied	.05
71	Mo Vaughn	.05
72	Tyler Green	.05
73	Dave Magadan	.05
74	Chili Davis	.05
75	Archi Cianfrocco	.05
76	Joe Girardi	.05
77	Chris Hoiles	.05
78	Ryan Bowen	.05
79	Greg Gagne	.05
80	Aaron Sele	.05
81	Dave Winfield	.75
82	Chad Curtis	.05
83	Andy Van Slyke	.05
84	Kevin Stocker	.05
85	Deion Sanders	.05
86	Bernie Williams	.05
87	John Smoltz	.05
88	*Ruben Santana*	.05
89	Dave Stewart	.05
90	Don Mattingly	1.00
91	Joe Carter	.05
92	Ryne Sandberg	.90
93	Chris Gomez	.05
94	Tino Martinez	.05
95	Terry Pendleton	.05
96	Andre Dawson	.25
97	Wil Cordero	.05
98	Kent Hrbek	.05
99	John Olerud	.05
100	Kirt Manwaring	.05
101	Tim Bogar	.05
102	Mike Mussina	.30
103	Nigel Wilson	.05
104	Ricky Gutierrez	.05
105	Roberto Mejia	.05
106	Tom Pagnozzi	.05
107	Mike Macfarlane	.05
108	Jose Bautista	.05
109	Luis Ortiz	.05
110	Brent Gates	.05
111	Tim Salmon	.05
112	Wade Boggs	.90
113	*Tripp Cromer*	.05
114	Denny Hocking	.05
115	Carlos Baerga	.05
116	*J.R. Phillips*	.05
117	Bo Jackson	.10
118	Lance Johnson	.05
119	Bobby Jones	.05
120	Bobby Witt	.05
121	Ron Karkovice	.05
122	Jose Vizcaino	.05
123	Danny Darwin	.05
124	Eduardo Perez	.05
125	Brian Looney	.05
126	Pat Hentgen	.05
127	Frank Viola	.05
128	Darren Holmes	.05
129	Wally Whitehurst	.05
130	Matt Walbeck	.05
131	Albert Belle	.05
132	Steve Cooke	.05
133	Kevin Appier	.05
134	Joe Oliver	.05
135	Benji Gil	.05
136	Steve Buechele	.05
137	Devon White	.05
138	Sterling Hitchcock	.05
139	*Phil Leftwich*	.05
140	Jose Canseco	.45
141	Rick Aguilera	.05
142	Rod Beck	.05
143	Jose Rijo	.05
144	Tom Glavine	.25
145	Phil Plantier	.05
146	Jason Bere	.05
147	Jamie Moyer	.05
148	Wes Chamberlain	.05
149	Glenallen Hill	.05
150	Mark Whiten	.05
151	Bret Barberie	.05
152	Chuck Knoblauch	.05
153	Trevor Hoffman	.05
154	Rick Wilkins	.05
155	Juan Gonzalez	.40
156	Ozzie Guillen	.05
157	Jim Eisenreich	.05
158	Pedro Astacio	.05
159	Joe Magrane	.05
160	Ryan Thompson	.05
161	Jose Lind	.05
162	Jeff Conine	.05
163	Todd Benzinger	.05
164	Roger Salkeld	.05
165	Gary DiSarcina	.05
166	Kevin Gross	.05
167	Charlie Hayes	.05
168	Tim Costo	.05
169	Wally Joyner	.05
170	Johnny Ruffin	.05
171	*Kirk Rueter*	.10
172	Len Dykstra	.05
173	Ken Hill	.05
174	Mike Bordick	.05
175	Billy Hall	.05
176	Rob Butler	.05
177	Jay Bell	.05
178	Jeff Kent	.05
179	David Wells	.05
180	Dean Palmer	.05
181	Mariano Duncan	.05
182	Orlando Merced	.05
183	Brett Butler	.05
184	Milt Thompson	.05
185	Chipper Jones	.90
186	Paul O'Neill	.05
187	Mike Greenwell	.05
188	Harold Baines	.05
189	Todd Stottlemyre	.05
190	Jeromy Burnitz	.05
191	Rene Arocha	.05
192	Jeff Fassero	.05
193	Robby Thompson	.05
194	Greg W. Harris	.05
195	Todd Van Poppel	.05
196	Jose Guzman	.05
197	Shane Mack	.05
198	Carlos Garcia	.05
199	Kevin Roberson	.05
200	David McCarty	.05
201	Alan Trammell	.05
202	Chuck Carr	.05
203	Tommy Greene	.05
204	Wilson Alvarez	.05
205	Dwight Gooden	.05
206	Tony Tarasco	.05
207	Darren Lewis	.05
208	Eric Karros	.05
209	Chris Hammond	.05
210	Jeffrey Hammonds	.05
211	Rich Amaral	.05
212	Danny Tartabull	.05
213	Jeff Russell	.05
214	Dave Staton	.05
215	Kenny Lofton	.05
216	Manuel Lee	.05
217	Brian Koelling	.05
218	Scott Lydy	.05
219	Tony Gwynn	.90
220	Cecil Fielder	.05
221	Royce Clayton	.05
222	Reggie Sanders	.05
223	Brian Jordan	.05
224	Ken Griffey, Jr.	1.25
224a	Ken Griffey, Jr. (promo card)	3.00
225	Fred McGriff	.05
226	Felix Jose	.05
227	Brad Pennington	.05
228	Chris Bosio	.05
229	Mike Stanley	.05
230	Willie Greene	.05
231	Alex Fernandez	.05
232	Brad Ausmus	.05
233	Darrell Whitmore	.05
234	Marcus Moore	.05
235	Allen Watson	.05
236	Jose Offerman	.05
237	Rondell White	.05
238	Jeff King	.05
239	Luis Alicea	.05
240	Dan Wilson	.05
241	Ed Sprague	.05
242	Todd Hundley	.05
243	Al Martin	.05
244	Mike Lansing	.05
245	Ivan Rodriguez	.65
246	Dave Fleming	.05
247	John Doherty	.05
248	Mark McLemore	.05
249	Bob Hamelin	.05
250	*Curtis Pride*	.05
251	Zane Smith	.05
252	Eric Young	.05
253	Brian McRae	.05
254	Tim Raines	.05
255	Javier Lopez	.05
256	Melvin Nieves	.05
257	Randy Myers	.05
258	Willie McGee	.05
259	Jimmy Key	.05
260	Tom Candiotti	.05
261	Eric Davis	.05
262	Craig Paquette	.05
263	Robin Ventura	.05
264	Pat Kelly	.05
265	Gregg Jefferies	.05
266	Cory Snyder	.05
267	Dave Justice	.05
268	Sammy Sosa	.45
269	Barry Larkin	.05
270	Andres Galarraga	.05
271	Gary Sheffield	.20
272	Jeff Bagwell	.40
273	Mike Piazza	.65
274	Larry Walker	.05
275	Bobby Bonilla	.05
276	John Kruk	.05
277	Jay Bell	.05
278	Ozzie Smith	.45
279	Tony Gwynn	.45
280	Barry Bonds	1.00
281	Cal Ripken, Jr.	1.00
282	Mo Vaughn	.05
283	Tim Salmon	.05
284	Frank Thomas	.40
285	Albert Belle	.05
286	Cecil Fielder	.05
287	Wally Joyner	.05
288	Greg Vaughn	.05
289	Kirby Puckett	.45
290	Don Mattingly	.50
291	Terry Steinbach	.05
292	Ken Griffey, Jr.	.90
293	Juan Gonzalez	.20
294	Paul Molitor	.40
295	Tavo Alvarez	.05
296	Matt Brunson	.05
297	Shawn Green	.20
298	Alex Rodriguez	2.00
299	Shannon Stewart	.05
300	Frank Thomas	.75
301	Mickey Tettleton	.05
302	Pedro Munoz	.05
303	Jose Valentin	.05
304	Orestes Destrade	.05
305	Pat Listach	.05
306	Scott Brosius	.05
307	*Kurt Miller*	.05
308	Rob Dibble	.05
309	Mike Blowers	.05
310	Jim Abbott	.05
311	Mike Jackson	.05
312	Craig Biggio	.05
313	*Kurt Abbott*	.05
314	Chuck Finley	.05
315	Andres Galarraga	.05
316	Mike Moore	.05
317	Doug Strange	.05
318	Pedro J. Martinez	.75
319	Kevin McReynolds	.05
320	Greg Maddux	.90
321	Mike Henneman	.05
322	Scott Leius	.05
323	John Franco	.05
324	Jeff Blauser	.05
325	Kirby Puckett	.90
326	Darryl Hamilton	.05
327	John Smiley	.05
328	Derrick May	.05
329	Jose Vizcaino	.05
330	Randy Johnson	.75
331	Jack Morris	.05
332	Graeme Lloyd	.05
333	Dave Valle	.05
334	Greg Myers	.05
335	John Wetteland	.05
336	Jim Gott	.05
337	Tim Naehring	.05
338	Mike Kelly	.05
339	Jeff Montgomery	.05
340	Rafael Palmeiro	.65
341	Eddie Murray	.75
342	Xavier Hernandez	.05
343	Bobby Munoz	.05
344	Bobby Bonilla	.05
345	Travis Fryman	.05
346	Steve Finley	.05
347	Chris Sabo	.05
348	Armando Reynoso	.05
349	Ramon Martinez	.05
350	Will Clark	.05
351	Moises Alou	.05
352	Jim Thome	.50
353	Bob Tewksbury	.05
354	Andujar Cedeno	.05
355	Orel Hershiser	.05
356	Mike Devereaux	.05
357	Mike Perez	.05
358	Dennis Martinez	.05
359	Dave Nilsson	.05
360	Ozzie Smith	.90
361	Eric Anthony	.05
362	Scott Sanders	.05
363	Paul Sorrento	.05
364	Tim Belcher	.05
365	Dennis Eckersley	.60
366	Mel Rojas	.05
367	Tom Henke	.05
368	Randy Tomlin	.05
369	B.J. Surhoff	.05
370	Larry Walker	.05
371	Joey Cora	.05
372	Mike Harkey	.05
373	John Valentin	.05
374	Doug Jones	.05
375	Dave Justice	.05
376	Vince Coleman	.05
377	David Hulse	.05
378	Kevin Seitzer	.05
379	Pete Harnisch	.05
380	Ruben Sierra	.05
381	Mark Lewis	.05
382	Bip Roberts	.05
383	Paul Wagner	.05
384	Stan Javier	.05

385	Barry Larkin	.05
386	Mark Portugal	.05
387	Roberto Kelly	.05
388	Andy Benes	.05
389	Felix Fermin	.05
390	Marquis Grissom	.05
391	Troy Neel	.05
392	Chad Kreuter	.05
393	Gregg Olson	.05
394	Charles Nagy	.05
395	Jack McDowell	.05
396	Luis Gonzalez	.05
397	Benito Santiago	.05
398	Chris James	.05
399	Terry Mulholland	.05
400	Barry Bonds	2.00
401	Joe Grahe	.05
402	Duane Ward	.05
403	John Burkett	.05
404	Scott Servais	.05
405	Bryan Harvey	.05
406	Bernard Gilkey	.05
407	Greg McMichael	.05
408	Tim Wallach	.05
409	Ken Caminiti	.05
410	John Kruk	.05
411	Darrin Jackson	.05
412	Mike Gallego	.05
413	David Cone	.05
414	Lou Whitaker	.05
415	Sandy Alomar Jr.	.05
416	Bill Wegman	.05
417	Pat Borders	.05
418	Roger Pavlik	.05
419	Pete Smith	.05
420	Steve Avery	.05
421	David Segui	.05
422	Rheal Cormier	.05
423	Harold Reynolds	.05
424	Edgar Martinez	.05
425	Cal Ripken, Jr.	2.00
426	Jaime Navarro	.05
427	Sean Berry	.05
428	Bret Saberhagen	.05
429	Bob Welch	.05
430	Juan Guzman	.05
431	Cal Eldred	.05
432	Dave Hollins	.05
433	Sid Fernandez	.05
434	Willie Banks	.05
435	Darryl Kile	.05
436	Henry Rodriguez	.05
437	Tony Fernandez	.05
438	Walt Weiss	.05
439	Kevin Tapani	.05
440	Mark Grace	.05
441	Brian Harper	.05
442	Kent Mercker	.05
443	Anthony Young	.05
444	Todd Zeile	.05
445	Greg Vaughn	.05
446	Ray Lankford	.05
447	David Weathers	.05
448	Bret Boone	.05
449	Charlie Hough	.05
450	Roger Clemens	1.00
451	Mike Morgan	.05
452	Doug Drabek	.05
453	Danny Jackson	.05
454	Dante Bichette	.05
455	Roberto Alomar	.20
456	Ben McDonald	.05
457	Kenny Rogers	.05
458	Bill Gullickson	.05
459	Darrin Fletcher	.05
460	Curt Schilling	.20
461	Billy Hatcher	.05
462	Howard Johnson	.05
463	Mickey Morandini	.05
464	Frank Castillo	.05
465	Delino DeShields	.05
466	Gary Gaetti	.05
467	Steve Farr	.05
468	Roberto Hernandez	.05
469	Jack Armstrong	.05
470	Paul Molitor	.75
471	Melido Perez	.05
472	Greg Hibbard	.05
473	Jody Reed	.05
474	Tom Gordon	.05
475	Gary Sheffield	.35
476	John Jaha	.05
477	Shawon Dunston	.05
478	Reggie Jefferson	.05
479	Don Slaught	.05
480	Jeff Bagwell	.75
481	Tim Pugh	.05
482	Kevin Young	.05
483	Ellis Burks	.05
484	Greg Swindell	.05
485	Mark Langston	.05
486	Omar Vizquel	.05
487	Kevin Brown	.05
488	Terry Steinbach	.05
489	Mark Lemke	.05
490	Matt Williams	.05
491	Pete Incaviglia	.05
492	Karl Rhodes	.05
493	Shawn Green	.30
494	Hal Morris	.05
495	Derek Bell	.05
496	Luis Polonia	.05
497	Otis Nixon	.05
498	Ron Darling	.05
499	Mitch Williams	.05
500	Mike Piazza	1.25
501	Pat Meares	.05
502	Scott Cooper	.05
503	Scott Erickson	.05
504	Jeff Juden	.05
505	Lee Smith	.05
506	Bobby Ayala	.05
507	Dave Henderson	.05
508	Erik Hanson	.05
509	Bob Wickman	.05
510	Sammy Sosa	.90
511	Hector Carrasco	.05
512	Tim Davis	.05
513	Joey Hamilton	.05
514	Robert Eenhoorn	.05
515	Jorge Fabregas	.05
516	Tim Hyers	.05
517	John Hudek	.05
518	*James Mouton*	.05
519	Herbert Perry	.05
520	*Chan Ho Park*	.75
521	Bill VanLandingham	.05
522	Paul Shuey	.05
523	*Ryan Hancock*	.05
524	*Billy Wagner*	.25
525	Jason Giambi	.50
526	*Jose Silva*	.05
527	*Terrell Wade*	.05
528	Todd Dunn	.05
529	*Alan Benes*	.05
530	*Brooks Kieschnick*	.05
531	Todd Hollandsworth	.05
532	*Brad Fullmer*	.15
533	*Steve Soderstrom*	.05
534	Daron Kirkreit	.05
535	*Arquimedez Pozo*	.05
536	Charles Johnson	.05
537	Preston Wilson	.10
538	Alex Ochoa	.05
539	*Derrek Lee*	3.00
540	*Wayne Gomes*	.05
541	*Jermaine Allensworth*	.05
542	*Mike Bell*	.05
543	*Trot Nixon*	1.25
544	Pokey Reese	.05
545	*Neifi Perez*	.05
546	Johnny Damon	.30
547	Matt Brunson	.05
548	*LaTroy Hawkins*	.05
549	*Eddie Pearson*	.05
550	Derek Jeter	2.00

Electric Diamond

	NM/M
Complete Set (550):	75.00
Common Player:	.25
Stars:	1.5X

(See 1994 Upper Deck for checklist and base card values.)

All-Stars

		NM/M
Complete Set (48):		9.00
Common Player:		.15

Gold:		4X
1	Ken Griffey, Jr.	1.00
2	Ruben Sierra, Todd Van Poppel	.15
3	Bryan Harvey, Gary Sheffield	.35
4	Gregg Jefferies, Brian Jordan	.15
5	Ryne Sandberg	.75
6	Matt Williams, John Burkett	.15
7	Darren Daulton, John Kruk	.15
8	Don Mattingly, Wade Boggs	.75
9	Pat Listach, Greg Vaughn	.15
10	Tim Salmon, Eduardo Perez	.25
11	Fred McGriff, Tom Glavine	.25
12	Mo Vaughn, Andre Dawson	.35
13	Brian McRae, Kevin Appier	.15
14	Kirby Puckett, Kent Hrbek	.75
15	Cal Ripken, Jr.	2.00
16	Roberto Alomar, Paul Molitor	.65
17	Tony Gwynn, Phil Plantier	.75
18	Greg Maddux, Steve Avery	.75
19	Mike Mussina, Chris Hoiles	.50
20	Randy Johnson	.65
21	Roger Clemens, Aaron Sele	.75
22	Will Clark, Dean Palmer	.25
23	Cecil Fielder, Travis Fryman	.15
24	John Olerud, Joe Carter	.15
25	Juan Gonzalez	.65
26	Jose Rijo, Barry Larkin	.15
27	Andy Van Slyke, Jeff King	.15
28	Larry Walker, Marquis Grissom	.15
29	Kenny Lofton, Albert Belle	.25
30	Mark Grace, Sammy Sosa	1.00
31	Mike Piazza	1.00
32	Ramon Martinez, Orel Hershiser	.15
33	Dave Justice, Terry Pendleton	.15
34	Ivan Rodriguez, Jose Canseco	.50
35	Barry Bonds	2.00
36	Jeff Bagwell, Craig Biggio	.65
37	Jay Bell, Orlando Merced	.15
38	Jeff Kent, Dwight Gooden	.15
39	Andres Galarraga, Charlie Hayes	.15
40	Frank Thomas	.70
41	Bobby Bonilla	.15
42	Jack McDowell, Tim Raines	.15
43	1869 Red Stockings	.15
44	Ty Cobb	.50
45	Babe Ruth	1.50
46	Mickey Mantle	2.50
47	Reggie Jackson	.50
48	Ken Griffey, Jr.	1.00
48a	Ken Griffey Jr. (promo card)	1.00

Alex Rodriguez Autograph

	NM/M
A298 Alex Rodriguez (Classic Alumni, autographed)	300.00

Baseball Heroes Mickey Mantle

	NM/M
Complete Set (10):	25.00
Common Card:	3.00

Diamond Collection

		NM/M
Complete Set (30):		40.00
Common Player:		.25
Complete Central (10):		18.00
1	Michael Jordan	10.00
2	Jeff Bagwell	2.00
3	Barry Larkin	.25
4	Kirby Puckett	2.50
5	Manny Ramirez	2.00
6	Ryne Sandberg	2.50
7	Ozzie Smith	2.50
8	Frank Thomas	2.00
9	Andy Van Slyke	.25
10	Robin Yount	2.00
Complete East (10):		11.00
1	Roberto Alomar	1.00
2	Roger Clemens	2.50
3	Len Dykstra	.25
4	Cecil Fielder	.25
5	Cliff Floyd	.25
6	Dwight Gooden	.25
7	Dave Justice	.25
8	Don Mattingly	2.50
9	Cal Ripken, Jr.	6.00
10	Gary Sheffield	.50
Complete West (10):		14.00
1	Barry Bonds	4.00
2	Andres Galarraga	.25
3	Juan Gonzalez	1.50
4	Ken Griffey, Jr.	3.00
5	Tony Gwynn	2.00
6	Rickey Henderson	1.50
7	Bo Jackson	.50
8	Mark McGwire	4.00
9	Mike Piazza	4.00
10	Tim Salmon	.50

Ken Griffey Jr. 5th Anniversary Jumbo

	NM/M
Ken Griffey Jr.	20.00

Mickey Mantle's Long Shots

	NM/M
Complete Set (21):	20.00

Common Player:		.50
Electric Diamonds:		1X
(1)	Mickey Mantle Trade Card (silver): (Redeemable for 21-card Mantle Long Shots set)	4.00
(2)	Mickey Mantle Trade Card (blue): (Redeemable for Electric Diamond version Mantle Long Shots set)	4.00
1	Jeff Bagwell	1.50
2	Albert Belle	.50
3	Barry Bonds	4.00
4	Jose Canseco	.75
5	Joe Carter	.50
6	Carlos Delgado	.75
7	Cecil Fielder	.50
8	Cliff Floyd	.50
9	Juan Gonzalez	.75
10	Ken Griffey Jr.	2.50
11	David Justice	.50
12	Fred McGriff	.50
13	Mark McGwire	3.00
14	Dean Palmer	.50
15	Mike Piazza	2.50
16	Manny Ramirez	1.50
17	Tim Salmon	.50
18	Frank Thomas	1.50
19	Mo Vaughn	.50
20	Matt Williams	.50
21	Mickey Mantle Header	4.00

Mantle-Griffey Autographed Inserts

		NM/M
KG1	Ken Griffey Jr., Mickey Mantle (Griffey autograph)	250.00
MM1	Ken Griffey Jr., Mickey Mantle (Mantle autograph)	650.00
GM1	Ken Griffey Jr., Mickey Mantle (both autographs)	1,150

Next Generation

		NM/M
Complete Set (18):		100.00
Common Player:		1.50
1	Roberto Alomar	2.50
2	Carlos Delgado	4.00
3	Cliff Floyd	1.50
4	Alex Gonzalez	1.50
5	Juan Gonzalez	3.00
6	Ken Griffey, Jr.	10.00
7	Jeffrey Hammonds	1.50
8	Michael Jordan	30.00
9	Dave Justice	1.50
10	Ryan Klesko	1.50
11	Javier Lopez	1.50
12	Raul Mondesi	1.50
13	Mike Piazza	10.00
14	Kirby Puckett	7.50
15	Manny Ramirez	6.50
16	Alex Rodriguez	30.00
17	Tim Salmon	1.50
18	Gary Sheffield	4.00

SP Insert

		NM/M
Complete Set (15):		60.00
Common Player:		.50
EASTERN REGION		
1	Roberto Alomar	1.00
2	Cliff Floyd	.50
3	Javier Lopez	.50
4	Don Mattingly	6.00
5	Cal Ripken, Jr.	10.00

CENTRAL REGION		
1	Jeff Bagwell	3.00
2	Michael Jordan	10.00
3	Kirby Puckett	6.00
4	Manny Ramirez	3.00
5	Frank Thomas	4.00
WESTERN REGION		
1	Barry Bonds	10.00
2	Juan Gonzalez	1.50
3	Ken Griffey, Jr.	5.00
4	Mike Piazza	5.00
5	Tim Salmon	.50

1995 UPPER DECK

		NM/M
Complete Set (450):		20.00
Common Player:		.05
Electric Diamond:		2X
Electric Diamond Golds:		8X
Series 1 or 2 Pack (12):		.85
Series 1 or 2 Wax Box (36):		20.00
1	Ruben Rivera	.05
2	Bill Pulsipher	.05
3	Ben Grieve	.05
4	Curtis Goodwin	.05
5	Damon Hollins	.05
6	Todd Greene	.05
7	Glenn Williams	.05
8	Bret Wagner	.05
9	*Karim Garcia*	.50
10	Nomar Garciaparra	1.00
11	*Raul Casanova*	.10
12	Matt Smith	.05
13	Paul Wilson	.05
14	Jason Isringhausen	.05
15	Reid Ryan	.05
16	Lee Smith	.05
17	Chili Davis	.05
18	Brian Anderson	.05
19	Gary DiSarcina	.05
20	Bo Jackson	.10
21	Chuck Finley	.05
22	Darryl Kile	.05
23	Shane Reynolds	.05
24	Tony Eusebio	.05
25	Craig Biggio	.05
26	Doug Drabek	.05
27	Brian L. Hunter	.05
28	James Mouton	.05
29	Geronimo Berroa	.05
30	Rickey Henderson	.75
31	Steve Karsay	.05
32	Steve Ontiveros	.05
33	Ernie Young	.05
34	Dennis Eckersley	.65
35	Mark McGwire	1.50
36	Dave Stewart	.05
37	Pat Hentgen	.05
38	Carlos Delgado	.45
39	Joe Carter	.05
40	Roberto Alomar	.20
41	John Olerud	.05
42	Devon White	.05
43	Roberto Kelly	.05
44	Jeff Blauser	.05
45	Fred McGriff	.05
46	Tom Glavine	.25
47	Mike Kelly	.05
48	Javy Lopez	.05
49	Greg Maddux	1.00
50	Matt Mieske	.05
51	Troy O'Leary	.05
52	Jeff Cirillo	.05
53	Cal Eldred	.05
54	Pat Listach	.05
55	Jose Valentin	.05
56	John Mabry	.05
57	Bob Tewksbury	.05
58	Brian Jordan	.05
59	Gregg Jefferies	.05
60	Ozzie Smith	1.00
61	Geronimo Pena	.05
62	Mark Whiten	.05
63	Rey Sanchez	.05
64	Willie Banks	.05
65	Mark Grace	.05
66	Randy Myers	.05
67	Steve Trachsel	.05
68	Derrick May	.05
69	Brett Butler	.05
70	Eric Karros	.05
71	Tim Wallach	.05
72	Delino DeShields	.05
73	Darren Dreifort	.05
74	Orel Hershiser	.05
75	Billy Ashley	.05
76	Sean Berry	.05
77	Ken Hill	.05
78	John Wetteland	.05
79	Moises Alou	.05
80	Cliff Floyd	.05
81	Marquis Grissom	.05
82	Larry Walker	.05
83	Rondell White	.05
84	William VanLandingham	.05
85	Matt Williams	.05
86	Rod Beck	.05
87	Darren Lewis	.05
88	Robby Thompson	.05
89	Darryl Strawberry	.05
90	Kenny Lofton	.05
91	Charles Nagy	.05
92	Sandy Alomar Jr.	.05
93	Mark Clark	.05
94	Dennis Martinez	.05
95	Dave Winfield	.75
96	Jim Thome	.60
97	Manny Ramirez	.75
98	Goose Gossage	.05
99	Tino Martinez	.05
100	Ken Griffey Jr.	1.25
100a	Ken Griffey Jr. (overprinted "For Promotional Use Only")	2.00
101	Greg Maddux	.50
102	Randy Johnson	.40
103	Barry Bonds	1.00
104	Juan Gonzalez	.20
105	Frank Thomas	.40
106	Matt Williams	.05
107	Paul Molitor	.40
108	Fred McGriff	.05
109	Carlos Baerga	.05
110	Ken Griffey Jr.	.65
111	Reggie Jefferson	.05
112	Randy Johnson	.75
113	Marc Newfield	.05
114	Robb Nen	.05
115	Jeff Conine	.05
116	Kurt Abbott	.05
117	Charlie Hough	.05
118	Dave Weathers	.05
119	Juan Castillo	.05
120	Bret Saberhagen	.05
121	Rico Brogna	.05
122	John Franco	.05
123	Todd Hundley	.05
124	Jason Jacome	.05
125	Bobby Jones	.05
126	Bret Barberie	.05
127	Ben McDonald	.05
128	Harold Baines	.05
129	Jeffrey Hammonds	.05
130	Mike Mussina	.30
131	Chris Hoiles	.05
132	Brady Anderson	.05
133	Eddie Williams	.05
134	Andy Benes	.05
135	Tony Gwynn	1.00
136	Bip Roberts	.05
137	Joey Hamilton	.05
138	Luis Lopez	.05
139	Ray McDavid	.05
140	Lenny Dykstra	.05
141	Mariano Duncan	.05
142	Fernando Valenzuela	.05
143	Bobby Munoz	.05
144	Kevin Stocker	.05
145	John Kruk	.05
146	Jon Lieber	.05
147	Zane Smith	.05
148	Steve Cooke	.05
149	Andy Van Slyke	.05
150	Jay Bell	.05
151	Carlos Garcia	.05
152	John Dettmer	.05
153	Darren Oliver	.05
154	Dean Palmer	.05
155	Otis Nixon	.05
156	Rusty Greer	.05
157	Rick Helling	.05
158	Jose Canseco	.40
159	Roger Clemens	1.00
160	Andre Dawson	.25
161	Mo Vaughn	.05
162	Aaron Sele	.05
163	John Valentin	.05
164	Brian Hunter	.05
165	Bret Boone	.05
166	Hector Carrasco	.05
167	Pete Schourek	.05
168	Willie Greene	.05
169	Kevin Mitchell	.05
170	Deion Sanders	.05
171	John Roper	.05
172	Charlie Hayes	.05
173	David Nied	.05
174	Ellis Burks	.05
175	Dante Bichette	.05
176	Marvin Freeman	.05
177	Eric Young	.05
178	David Cone	.05
179	Greg Gagne	.05
180	Bob Hamelin	.05
181	Wally Joyner	.05
182	Jeff Montgomery	.05
183	Jose Lind	.05
184	Chris Gomez	.05
185	Travis Fryman	.05
186	Kirk Gibson	.05
187	Mike Moore	.05
188	Lou Whitaker	.05
189	Sean Bergman	.05
190	Shane Mack	.05
191	Rick Aguilera	.05
192	Denny Hocking	.05
193	Chuck Knoblauch	.05
194	Kevin Tapani	.05
195	Kent Hrbek	.05
196	Ozzie Guillen	.05
197	Wilson Alvarez	.05
198	Tim Raines	.05
199	Scott Ruffcorn	.05
200	Michael Jordan	2.00
201	Robin Ventura	.05
202	Jason Bere	.05
203	Darrin Jackson	.05
204	Russ Davis	.05
205	Jimmy Key	.05
206	Jack McDowell	.05
207	Jim Abbott	.05
208	Paul O'Neill	.05
209	Bernie Williams	.05
210	Don Mattingly	1.00
211	Orlando Miller	.05
212	Alex Gonzalez	.05
213	Terrell Wade	.05
214	Jose Oliva	.05
215	Alex Rodriguez	1.50
216	Garret Anderson	.05
217	Alan Benes	.05
218	Armando Benitez	.05
219	Dustin Hermanson	.05
220	Charles Johnson	.05
221	Julian Tavarez	.05
222	Jason Giambi	.50
223	LaTroy Hawkins	.05
224	Todd Hollandsworth	.05
225	Derek Jeter	2.00
226	*Hideo Nomo*	2.00
227	Tony Clark	.05
228	Roger Cedeno	.05
229	Scott Stahoviak	.05
230	Michael Tucker	.05
231	Joe Rosselli	.05
232	Antonio Osuna	.05
233	*Bobby Higginson*	.25

234 *Mark Grudzielanek* .25
235 Ray Durham .05
236 Frank Rodriguez .05
237 Quilvio Veras .05
238 Darren Bragg .05
239 Ugueth Urbina .05
240 Jason Bates .05
241 David Bell .05
242 Ron Villone .05
243 Joe Randa .05
244 *Carlos Perez* .05
245 Brad Clontz .05
246 Steve Rodriguez .05
247 Joe Vitiello .05
248 Ozzie Timmons .05
249 Rudy Pemberton .05
250 Marty Cordova .05
251 Tony Graffanino .05
252 *Mark Johnson* .05
253 *Tomas Perez* .05
254 Jimmy Hurst .05
255 Edgardo Alfonzo .05
256 Jose Malave .05
257 *Brad Radke* .30
258 Jon Nunnally .05
259 Dilson Torres .05
260 Esteban Loaiza .05
261 *Freddy Garcia* .05
262 Don Wengert .05
263 *Robert Person* .05
264 *Tim Unroe* .05
265 Juan Acevedo .05
266 Eduardo Perez .05
267 Tony Phillips .05
268 Jim Edmonds .05
269 Jorge Fabregas .05
270 Tim Salmon .05
271 Mark Langston .05
272 J.T. Snow .05
273 Phil Plantier .05
274 Derek Bell .05
275 Jeff Bagwell .75
276 Luis Gonzalez .05
277 John Hudek .05
278 Todd Stottlemyre .05
279 Mark Acre .05
280 Ruben Sierra .05
281 Mike Bordick .05
282 Ron Darling .05
283 Brent Gates .05
284 Todd Van Poppel .05
285 Paul Molitor .75
286 Ed Sprague .05
287 Juan Guzman .05
288 David Cone .05
289 Shawn Green .30
290 Marquis Grissom .05
291 Kent Mercker .05
292 Steve Avery .05
293 Chipper Jones 1.00
294 John Smoltz .05
295 Dave Justice .05
296 Ryan Klesko .05
297 Joe Oliver .05
298 Ricky Bones .05
299 John Jaha .05
300 Greg Vaughn .05
301 Dave Nilsson .05
302 Kevin Seitzer .05
303 Bernard Gilkey .05
304 Allen Battle .05
305 Ray Lankford .05
306 Tom Pagnozzi .05
307 Allen Watson .05
308 Danny Jackson .05
309 Ken Hill .05
310 Todd Zeile .05
311 Kevin Roberson .05
312 Steve Buechele .05
313 Rick Wilkins .05
314 Kevin Foster .05
315 Sammy Sosa 1.00
316 Howard Johnson .05
317 Greg Hansell .05
318 Pedro Astacio .05
319 Rafael Bournigal .05
320 Mike Piazza 1.25
321 Ramon Martinez .05
322 Raul Mondesi .05
323 Ismael Valdes .05
324 Wil Cordero .05
325 Tony Tarasco .05
326 Roberto Kelly .05
327 Jeff Fassero .05
328 Mike Lansing .05
329 Pedro J. Martinez .75
330 Kirk Rueter .05
331 Glenallen Hill .05
332 Kirt Manwaring .05
333 Royce Clayton .05
334 J.R. Phillips .05
335 Barry Bonds 2.00
336 Mark Portugal .05
337 Terry Mulholland .05
338 Omar Vizquel .05
339 Carlos Baerga .05
340 Albert Belle .05
341 Eddie Murray .75
342 Wayne Kirby .05
343 Chad Ogea .05
344 Tim Davis .05
345 Jay Buhner .05
346 Bobby Ayala .05
347 Mike Blowers .05
348 Dave Fleming .05
349 Edgar Martinez .05
350 Andre Dawson .30
351 Darrell Whitmore .05
352 Chuck Carr .05
353 John Burkett .05
354 Chris Hammond .05
355 Gary Sheffield .40
356 Pat Rapp .05
357 Greg Colbrunn .05
358 David Segui .05
359 Jeff Kent .05
360 Bobby Bonilla .05
361 Pete Harnisch .05
362 Ryan Thompson .05
363 Jose Vizcaino .05
364 Brett Butler .05
365 Cal Ripken Jr. 2.00
366 Rafael Palmeiro .65
367 Leo Gomez .05
368 Andy Van Slyke .05
369 Arthur Rhodes .05
370 Ken Caminiti .05
371 Steve Finley .05
372 Melvin Nieves .05
373 Andujar Cedeno .05
374 Trevor Hoffman .05
375 Fernando Valenzuela .05
376 Ricky Bottalico .05
377 Dave Hollins .05
378 Charlie Hayes .05
379 Tommy Greene .05
380 Darren Daulton .05
381 Curt Schilling .25
382 Midre Cummings .05
383 Al Martin .05
384 Jeff King .05
385 Orlando Merced .05
386 Denny Neagle .05
387 Don Slaught .05
388 Dave Clark .05
389 Kevin Gross .05
390 Will Clark .05
391 Ivan Rodriguez .65
392 Benji Gil .05
393 Jeff Frye .05
394 Kenny Rogers .05
395 Juan Gonzalez .40
396 Mike Macfarlane .05
397 Lee Tinsley .05
398 Tim Naehring .05
399 Tim Vanegmond .05
400 Mike Greenwell .05
401 Ken Ryan .05
402 John Smiley .05
403 Tim Pugh .05
404 Reggie Sanders .05
405 Barry Larkin .05
406 Hal Morris .05
407 Jose Rijo .05
408 Lance Painter .05
409 Joe Girardi .05
410 Andres Galarraga .05
411 Mike Kingery .05
412 Roberto Mejia .05
413 Walt Weiss .05
414 Bill Swift .05
415 Larry Walker .05
416 Billy Brewer .05
417 Pat Borders .05
418 Tom Gordon .05
419 Kevin Appier .05
420 Gary Gaetti .05
421 Greg Gohr .05
422 Felipe Lira .05
423 John Doherty .05
424 Chad Curtis .05
425 Cecil Fielder .05
426 Alan Trammell .05
427 David McCarty .05
428 Scott Erickson .05
429 Pat Mahomes .05
430 Kirby Puckett 1.00
431 Dave Stevens .05
432 Pedro Munoz .05
433 Chris Sabo .05
434 Alex Fernandez .05
435 Frank Thomas .75
436 Roberto Hernandez .05
437 Lance Johnson .05
438 Jim Abbott .05
439 John Wetteland .05
440 Melido Perez .05
441 Tony Fernandez .05
442 Pat Kelly .05
443 Mike Stanley .05
444 Danny Tartabull .05
445 Wade Boggs 1.00
446 Robin Yount .75
447 Ryne Sandberg 1.00
448 Nolan Ryan 2.00
449 George Brett 1.00
450 Mike Schmidt 1.00

Electric Diamond

	NM/M
Complete Set (1-450):	60.00
Common Player:	.25
Stars/Rookies:	2X

(See 1995 Upper Deck for checklist and base card values.)

Autograph Redemption Cards

	NM/M
Complete Set (5):	220.00
Common Player:	15.00
AC1 Reggie Jackson	20.00
AC2 Willie Mays	100.00
AC3 Frank Robinson	30.00
AC4 Roger Clemens	125.00
AC5 Raul Mondesi	10.00

Autographed Jumbos

	NM/M
Complete Set (2):	100.00
(1) Roger Clemens	50.00
(2) Alex Rodriguez	75.00

Baseball Heroes Babe Ruth

	NM/M
Complete Set (10):	45.00
Common Card:	6.00
73 Babe Ruth 1914-18 Pitching Career	6.00
74 Babe Ruth 1919 - Move to Outfield	6.00
75 Babe Ruth 1920 - Renaissance Man	6.00
76 Babe Ruth 1923 - House That Ruth Built	6.00
77 Babe Ruth 1927 - 60-Homer Season	6.00
78 Babe Ruth 1928 - Three-homer Game	6.00
79 Babe Ruth 1932 - The Called Shot	6.00
80 Babe Ruth 1930-35 - Milestones	6.00
81 Babe Ruth 1935 - The Last Hurrah	6.00
--- Header card	7.50

Special Edition

	NM/M
Complete Set (270):	60.00
Common Player:	.10
Gold:	3X

1 Cliff Floyd .10
2 Wil Cordero .10
3 Pedro Martinez 1.50
4 Larry Walker .10
5 Derek Jeter 4.00
6 Mike Stanley .10
7 Melido Perez .10
8 Jim Leyritz .10
9 Danny Tartabull .10
10 Wade Boggs 2.00
11 Ryan Klesko .10
12 Steve Avery .10
13 Damon Hollins .10
14 Chipper Jones 2.00
15 Dave Justice .10
16 Glenn Williams .10
17 Jose Oliva .10
18 Terrell Wade .10
19 Alex Fernandez .10
20 Frank Thomas 1.50
21 Ozzie Guillen .10
22 Roberto Hernandez .10
23 Albie Lopez .10
24 Eddie Murray 1.50
25 Albert Belle .10
26 Omar Vizquel .10
27 Carlos Baerga .10
28 Jose Rijo .10
29 Hal Morris .10
30 Reggie Sanders .10
31 Jack Morris .10
32 Raul Mondesi .10
33 Karim Garcia .15
34 Todd Hollandsworth .10
35 Mike Piazza 2.50
36 Chan Ho Park .10
37 Ramon Martinez .10
38 Kenny Rogers .10
39 Will Clark .10
40 Juan Gonzalez .75
41 Ivan Rodriguez 1.25
42 Orlando Miller .10
43 John Hudek .10
44 Luis Gonzalez .10
45 Jeff Bagwell 1.50
46 Cal Ripken Jr. 4.00
47 Mike Oquist .10
48 Armando Benitez .10
49 Ben McDonald .10
50 Rafael Palmeiro 1.25
51 Curtis Goodwin .10
52 Vince Coleman .10
53 Tom Gordon .10
54 Mike Macfarlane .10

#	Player	NM/M
55	Brian McRae	.10
56	Matt Smith	.10
57	David Segui	.10
58	Paul Wilson	.10
59	Bill Pulsipher	.10
60	Bobby Bonilla	.10
61	Jeff Kent	.10
62	Ryan Thompson	.10
63	Jason Isringhausen	.10
64	Ed Sprague	.10
65	Paul Molitor	1.50
66	Juan Guzman	.10
67	Alex Gonzalez	.10
68	Shawn Green	.50
69	Mark Portugal	.10
70	Barry Bonds	4.00
71	Robby Thompson	.10
72	Royce Clayton	.10
73	Ricky Bottalico	.10
74	Doug Jones	.10
75	Darren Daulton	.10
76	Gregg Jefferies	.10
77	Scott Cooper	.10
78	Nomar Garciaparra	2.00
79	Ken Ryan	.10
80	Mike Greenwell	.10
81	LaTroy Hawkins	.10
82	Rich Becker	.10
83	Scott Erickson	.10
84	Pedro Munoz	.10
85	Kirby Puckett	2.00
86	Orlando Merced	.10
87	Jeff King	.10
88	Midre Cummings	.10
89	Bernard Gilkey	.10
90	Ray Lankford	.10
91	Todd Zeile	.10
92	Alan Benes	.10
93	Bret Wagner	.10
94	Rene Arocha	.10
95	Cecil Fielder	.10
96	Alan Trammell	.10
97	Tony Phillips	.10
98	Junior Felix	.10
99	Brian Harper	.10
100	Greg Vaughn	.10
101	Ricky Bones	.10
102	Walt Weiss	.10
103	Lance Painter	.10
104	Roberto Mejia	.10
105	Andres Galarraga	.10
106	Todd Van Poppel	.10
107	Ben Grieve	.10
108	Brent Gates	.10
109	Jason Giambi	1.00
110	Ruben Sierra	.10
111	Terry Steinbach	.10
112	Chris Hammond	.10
113	Charles Johnson	.10
114	Jesus Tavarez	.10
115	Gary Sheffield	.40
116	Chuck Carr	.10
117	Bobby Ayala	.10
118	Randy Johnson	1.50
119	Edgar Martinez	.10
120	Alex Rodriguez	3.00
121	Kevin Foster	.10
122	Kevin Roberson	.10
123	Sammy Sosa	2.00
124	Steve Trachsel	.10
125	Eduardo Perez	.10
126	Tim Salmon	.10
127	Todd Greene	.10
128	Jorge Fabregas	.10
129	Mark Langston	.10
130	Mitch Williams	.10
131	Raul Casanova	.10
132	Mel Nieves	.10
133	Andy Benes	.10
134	Dustin Hermanson	.10
135	Trevor Hoffman	.10
136	Mark Grudzielanek	.10
137	Ugueth Urbina	.10
138	Moises Alou	.10
139	Roberto Kelly	.10
140	Rondell White	.10
141	Paul O'Neill	.10
142	Jimmy Key	.10
143	Jack McDowell	.10
144	Ruben Rivera	.10
145	Don Mattingly	2.25
146	John Wetteland	.10
147	Tom Glavine	.25
148	Marquis Grissom	.10
149	Javy Lopez	.10
150	Fred McGriff	.10
151	Greg Maddux	2.00
152	Chris Sabo	.10
153	Ray Durham	.10
154	Robin Ventura	.10
155	Jim Abbott	.10
156	Jimmy Hurst	.10
157	Tim Raines	.10
158	Dennis Martinez	.10
159	Kenny Lofton	.10
160	Dave Winfield	1.50
161	Manny Ramirez	1.50
162	Jim Thome	1.00
163	Barry Larkin	.10
164	Bret Boone	.10
165	Deion Sanders	.10
166	Ron Gant	.10
167	Benito Santiago	.10
168	Hideo Nomo	.75
169	Billy Ashley	.10
170	Roger Cedeno	.10
171	Ismael Valdes	.10
172	Eric Karros	.10
173	Rusty Greer	.10
174	Rick Helling	.10
175	Nolan Ryan	4.00
176	Dean Palmer	.10
177	Phil Plantier	.10
178	Darryl Kile	.10
179	Derek Bell	.10
180	Doug Drabek	.10
181	Craig Biggio	.10
182	Kevin Brown	.10
183	Harold Baines	.10
184	Jeffrey Hammonds	.10
185	Chris Hoiles	.10
186	Mike Mussina	.50
187	Bob Hamelin	.10
188	Jeff Montgomery	.10
189	Michael Tucker	.10
190	George Brett	2.25
191	Edgardo Alfonzo	.10
192	Brett Butler	.10
193	Bobby Jones	.10
194	Todd Hundley	.10
195	Bret Saberhagen	.10
196	Pat Hentgen	.10
197	Roberto Alomar	.30
198	David Cone	.10
199	Carlos Delgado	1.00
200	Joe Carter	.10
201	William Van Landingham	.10
202	Rod Beck	.10
203	J.R. Phillips	.10
204	Darren Lewis	.10
205	Matt Williams	.10
206	Lenny Dykstra	.10
207	Dave Hollins	.10
208	Mike Schmidt	2.25
209	Charlie Hayes	.10
210	Mo Vaughn	.10
211	Jose Malave	.10
212	Roger Clemens	2.25
213	Jose Canseco	.75
214	Mark Whiten	.10
215	Marty Cordova	.10
216	Rick Aguilera	.10
217	Kevin Tapani	.10
218	Chuck Knoblauch	.10
219	Al Martin	.10
220	Jay Bell	.10
221	Carlos Garcia	.10
222	Freddy Garcia	.10
223	Jon Lieber	.10
224	Danny Jackson	.10
225	Ozzie Smith	2.00
226	Brian Jordan	.10
227	Ken Hill	.10
228	Scott Cooper	.10
229	Chad Curtis	.10
230	Lou Whitaker	.10
231	Kirk Gibson	.10
232	Travis Fryman	.10
233	Jose Valentin	.10
234	Dave Nilsson	.10
235	Cal Eldred	.10
236	Matt Mieske	.10
237	Bill Swift	.10
238	Marvin Freeman	.10
239	Jason Bates	.10
240	Larry Walker	.10
241	David Nied	.10
242	Dante Bichette	.10
243	Dennis Eckersley	1.25
244	Todd Stottlemyre	.10
245	Rickey Henderson	1.50
246	Geronimo Berroa	.10
247	Mark McGwire	3.00
248	Quilvio Veras	.10
249	Terry Pendleton	.10
250	Andre Dawson	.30
251	Jeff Conine	.10
252	Kurt Abbott	.10
253	Jay Buhner	.10
254	Darren Bragg	.10
255	Ken Griffey Jr.	2.50
256	Tino Martinez	.10
257	Mark Grace	.10
258	Ryne Sandberg	2.00
259	Randy Myers	.10
260	Howard Johnson	.10
261	Lee Smith	.10
262	J.T. Snow	.10
263	Chili Davis	.10
264	Chuck Finley	.10
265	Eddie Williams	.10
266	Joey Hamilton	.10
267	Ken Caminiti	.10
268	Andujar Cedeno	.10
269	Steve Finley	.10
270	Tony Gwynn	2.00

Steal of a Deal

		NM/M
Complete Set (15):		25.00
Common Player:		1.00
1	Mike Piazza	6.00
2	Fred McGriff	1.00
3	Kenny Lofton	1.00
4	Jose Oliva	1.00
5	Jeff Bagwell	3.00
6	Roberto Alomar, Joe Carter	1.00
7	Steve Karsay	1.00
8	Ozzie Smith	4.00
9	Dennis Eckersley	2.00
10	Jose Canseco	1.50
11	Carlos Baerga	1.00
12	Cecil Fielder	1.00
13	Don Mattingly	5.00
14	Bret Boone	1.00
15	Michael Jordan	10.00

Update

		NM/M
Complete Set (45):		7.50
Common Player:		.25
451	Jim Abbott	.25
452	Danny Tartabull	.25
453	Ariel Prieto	.25
454	Scott Cooper	.25
455	Tom Henke	.25
456	Todd Zeile	.25
457	Brian McRae	.25
458	Luis Gonzalez	.25
459	Jaime Navarro	.25
460	Todd Worrell	.25
461	Roberto Kelly	.25
462	Chad Fonville	.25
463	Shane Andrews	.25
464	David Segui	.25
465	Deion Sanders	.50
466	Orel Hershiser	.25
467	Ken Hill	.25
468	Andy Benes	.25
469	Terry Pendleton	.25
470	Bobby Bonilla	.25
471	Scott Erickson	.25
472	Kevin Brown	.25
473	Glenn Dishman	.25
474	Phil Plantier	.25
475	Gregg Jefferies	.25
476	Tyler Green	.25
477	Heathcliff Slocumb	.25
478	Mark Whiten	.25
479	Mickey Tettleton	.25
480	Tim Wakefield	.25
481	Vaughn Eshelman	.25
482	Rick Aguilera	.25
483	Erik Hanson	.25
484	Willie McGee	.25
485	Troy O'Leary	.25
486	Benito Santiago	.25
487	Darren Lewis	.25
488	Dave Burba	.25
489	Ron Gant	.25
490	Bret Saberhagen	.25
491	Vinny Castilla	.25
492	Frank Rodriguez	.25
493	Andy Pettitte	5.00
494	Ruben Sierra	.25
495	David Cone	.25

1996 UPPER DECK

		NM/M
Unopened Wood Box Set (510):		40.00
Unopened Fact. Set (510):		35.00
Complete Set (480):		20.00
Common Player:		.05
Wax Pack (10):		.75
Wax Box (32):		17.50
1	Cal Ripken Jr. (Milestones)	1.00
2	Eddie Murray (Milestones)	.40
3	Mark Wohlers	.05
4	Dave Justice	.05
5	Chipper Jones	1.00
6	Javier Lopez	.05
7	Mark Lemke	.05
8	Marquis Grissom	.05
9	Tom Glavine	.25
10	Greg Maddux	1.00
11	Manny Alexander	.05
12	Curtis Goodwin	.05
13	Scott Erickson	.05
14	Chris Hoiles	.05
15	Rafael Palmeiro	.65
16	Rick Krivda	.05
17	Jeff Manto	.05
18	Mo Vaughn	.05
19	Tim Wakefield	.05
20	Roger Clemens	1.00
21	Tim Naehring	.05
22	Troy O'Leary	.05
23	Mike Greenwell	.05
24	Stan Belinda	.05
25	John Valentin	.05
26	J.T. Snow	.05
27	Gary DiSarcina	.05
28	Mark Langston	.05
29	Brian Anderson	.05
30	Jim Edmonds	.05
31	Garret Anderson	.05
32	Orlando Palmeiro	.05
33	Brian McRae	.05
34	Kevin Foster	.05
35	Sammy Sosa	1.00
36	Todd Zeile	.05
37	Jim Bullinger	.05
38	Luis Gonzalez	.05
39	Lyle Mouton	.05
40	Ray Durham	.05
41	Ozzie Guillen	.05
42	Alex Fernandez	.05
43	Brian Keyser	.05
44	Robin Ventura	.05
45	Reggie Sanders	.05
46	Pete Schourek	.05
47	John Smiley	.05

No.	Player	Price
48	Jeff Brantley	.05
49	Thomas Howard	.05
50	Bret Boone	.05
51	Kevin Jarvis	.05
52	Jeff Branson	.05
53	Carlos Baerga	.05
54	Jim Thome	.50
55	Manny Ramirez	.75
56	Omar Vizquel	.05
57	Jose Mesa	.05
58	Julian Tavarez	.05
59	Orel Hershiser	.05
60	Larry Walker	.05
61	Bret Saberhagen	.05
62	Vinny Castilla	.05
63	Eric Young	.05
64	Bryan Rekar	.05
65	Andres Galarraga	.05
66	Steve Reed	.05
67	Chad Curtis	.05
68	Bobby Higginson	.05
69	Phil Nevin	.05
70	Cecil Fielder	.05
71	Felipe Lira	.05
72	Chris Gomez	.05
73	Charles Johnson	.05
74	Quilvio Veras	.05
75	Jeff Conine	.05
76	John Burkett	.05
77	Greg Colbrunn	.05
78	Terry Pendleton	.05
79	Shane Reynolds	.05
80	Jeff Bagwell	.75
81	Orlando Miller	.05
82	Mike Hampton	.05
83	James Mouton	.05
84	Brian L. Hunter	.05
85	Derek Bell	.05
86	Kevin Appier	.05
87	Joe Vitiello	.05
88	Wally Joyner	.05
89	Michael Tucker	.05
90	Johnny Damon	.20
91	Jon Nunnally	.05
92	Jason Jacome	.05
93	Chad Fonville	.05
94	Chan Ho Park	.05
95	Hideo Nomo	.40
96	Ismael Valdes	.05
97	Greg Gagne	.05
98	Diamondbacks-Devil Rays	.10
99	Raul Mondesi	.05
100	Dave Winfield	.75
101	Dennis Eckersley	.35
102	Andre Dawson	.15
103	Dennis Martinez	.05
104	Lance Parrish	.05
105	Eddie Murray	.40
106	Alan Trammell	.05
107	Lou Whitaker	.05
108	Ozzie Smith	.50
109	Paul Molitor	.40
110	Rickey Henderson	.40
111	Tim Raines	.05
112	Harold Baines	.05
113	Lee Smith	.05
114	Fernando Valenzuela	.05
115	Cal Ripken Jr.	1.00
116	Tony Gwynn	.50
117	Wade Boggs	.50
118	Todd Hollandsworth	.05
119	Dave Nilsson	.05
120	*Jose Valentin*	.05
121	Steve Sparks	.05
122	Chuck Carr	.05
123	John Jaha	.05
124	Scott Karl	.05
125	Chuck Knoblauch	.05
126	Brad Radke	.05
127	Pat Meares	.05
128	Ron Coomer	.05
129	Pedro Munoz	.05
130	Kirby Puckett	1.00
131	David Segui	.05
132	Mark Grudzielanek	.05
133	Mike Lansing	.05
134	Sean Berry	.05
135	Rondell White	.05
136	Pedro Martinez	.75
137	Carl Everett	.05
138	Dave Mlicki	.05
139	Bill Pulsipher	.05
140	Jason Isringhausen	.05
141	Rico Brogna	.05
142	Edgardo Alfonzo	.05
143	Jeff Kent	.05
144	Andy Pettitte	.25
145	Mike Piazza	.65
146	Cliff Floyd	.05
147	Jason Isringhausen	.05
148	Tim Wakefield	.05
149	Chipper Jones	.50
150	Hideo Nomo	.20
151	Mark McGwire	.75
152	Ron Gant	.05
153	Gary Gaetti	.05
154	Don Mattingly	1.00
155	Paul O'Neill	.05
156	Derek Jeter	2.00
157	Joe Girardi	.05
158	Ruben Sierra	.05
159	Jorge Posada	.05
160	Geronimo Berroa	.05
161	Steve Ontiveros	.05
162	George Williams	.05
163	Doug Johns	.05
164	Ariel Prieto	.05
165	Scott Brosius	.05
166	Mike Bordick	.05
167	Tyler Green	.05
168	Mickey Morandini	.05
169	Darren Daulton	.05
170	Gregg Jefferies	.05
171	Jim Eisenreich	.05
172	Heathcliff Slocumb	.05
173	Kevin Stocker	.05
174	Esteban Loaiza	.05
175	Jeff King	.05
176	Mark Johnson	.05
177	Denny Neagle	.05
178	Orlando Merced	.05
179	Carlos Garcia	.05
180	Brian Jordan	.05
181	Mike Morgan	.05
182	Mark Petkovsek	.05
183	Bernard Gilkey	.05
184	John Mabry	.05
185	Tom Henke	.05
186	Glenn Dishman	.05
187	Andy Ashby	.05
188	Bip Roberts	.05
189	Melvin Nieves	.05
190	Ken Caminiti	.05
191	Brad Ausmus	.05
192	Deion Sanders	.05
193	Jamie Brewington	.05
194	Glenallen Hill	.05
195	Barry Bonds	2.00
196	William VanLandingham	.05
197	Mark Carreon	.05
198	Royce Clayton	.05
199	Joey Cora	.05
200	Ken Griffey Jr.	1.25
201	Jay Buhner	.05
202	Alex Rodriguez	1.50
203	Norm Charlton	.05
204	Andy Benes	.05
205	Edgar Martinez	.05
206	Juan Gonzalez	.40
207	Will Clark	.05
208	Kevin Gross	.05
209	Roger Pavlik	.05
210	Ivan Rodriguez	.65
211	Rusty Greer	.05
212	Angel Martinez	.05
213	Tomas Perez	.05
214	Alex Gonzalez	.05
215	Joe Carter	.05
216	Shawn Green	.30
217	Edwin Hurtado	.05
218	Edgar Martinez, Tony Pena	.05
219	Chipper Jones, Barry Larkin	.05
220	Orel Hershiser	.05
221	Mike Devereaux	.05
222	Tom Glavine	.05
223	Karim Garcia	.10
224	Arquimedez Pozo	.05
225	Billy Wagner	.05
226	John Wasdin	.05
227	Jeff Suppan	.05
228	Steve Gibralter	.05
229	Jimmy Haynes	.05
230	Ruben Rivera	.05
231	Chris Snopek	.05
232	Alex Ochoa	.05
233	Shannon Stewart	.05
234	Quinton McCracken	.05
235	Trey Beamon	.05
236	Billy McMillon	.05
237	Steve Cox	.05
238	George Arias	.05
239	Yamil Benitez	.05
240	Todd Greene	.05
241	Jason Kendall	.05
242	Brooks Kieschnick	.05
243	*Osvaldo Fernandez*	.15
244	*Livan Hernandez*	.35
245	Rey Ordonez	.05
246	*Mike Grace*	.05
247	Jay Canizaro	.05
248	Bob Wolcott	.05
249	Jermaine Dye	.05
250	Jason Schmidt	.05
251	*Mike Sweeney*	1.00
252	Marcus Jensen	.05
253	Mendy Lopez	.05
254	*Wilton Guerrero*	.10
255	Paul Wilson	.05
256	Edgar Renteria	.05
257	Richard Hidalgo	.05
258	Bob Abreu	.10
259	*Robert Smith*	.05
260	Sal Fasano	.05
261	Enrique Wilson	.05
262	*Rich Hunter*	.05
263	Sergio Nunez	.05
264	Dan Serafini	.05
265	*David Doster*	.05
266	Ryan McGuire	.05
267	Scott Spiezio	.05
268	Rafael Orellano	.05
269	Steve Avery	.05
270	Fred McGriff	.05
271	John Smoltz	.05
272	Ryan Klesko	.05
273	Jeff Blauser	.05
274	Brad Clontz	.05
275	Roberto Alomar	.20
276	B.J. Surhoff	.05
277	Jeffrey Hammonds	.05
278	Brady Anderson	.05
279	Bobby Bonilla	.05
280	Cal Ripken Jr.	2.00
281	Mike Mussina	.30
282	Wil Cordero	.05
283	Mike Stanley	.05
284	Aaron Sele	.05
285	Jose Canseco	.40
286	Tom Gordon	.05
287	Heathcliff Slocumb	.05
288	Lee Smith	.05
289	Troy Percival	.05
290	Tim Salmon	.05
291	Chuck Finley	.05
292	Jim Abbott	.05
293	Chili Davis	.05
294	Steve Trachsel	.05
295	Mark Grace	.05
296	Rey Sanchez	.05
297	Scott Servais	.05
298	Jaime Navarro	.05
299	Frank Castillo	.05
300	Frank Thomas	.75
301	Jason Bere	.05
302	Danny Tartabull	.05
303	Darren Lewis	.05
304	Roberto Hernandez	.05
305	Tony Phillips	.05
306	Wilson Alvarez	.05
307	Jose Rijo	.05
308	Hal Morris	.05
309	Mark Portugal	.05
310	Barry Larkin	.05
311	Dave Burba	.05
312	Eddie Taubensee	.05
313	Sandy Alomar Jr.	.05
314	Dennis Martinez	.05
315	Albert Belle	.15
316	Eddie Murray	.75
317	Charles Nagy	.05
318	Chad Ogea	.05
319	Kenny Lofton	.05
320	Dante Bichette	.05
321	Armando Reynoso	.05
322	Walt Weiss	.05
323	Ellis Burks	.05
324	Kevin Ritz	.05
325	Bill Swift	.05
326	Jason Bates	.05
327	Tony Clark	.05
328	Travis Fryman	.05
329	Mark Parent	.05
330	Alan Trammell	.05
331	C.J. Nitkowski	.05
332	Jose Lima	.05
333	Phil Plantier	.05
334	Kurt Abbott	.05
335	Andre Dawson	.25
336	Chris Hammond	.05
337	Robb Nen	.05
338	Pat Rapp	.05
339	Al Leiter	.05
340	Gary Sheffield	.35
341	Todd Jones	.05
342	Doug Drabek	.05
343	Greg Swindell	.05
344	Tony Eusebio	.05
345	Craig Biggio	.05
346	Darryl Kile	.05
347	Mike Macfarlane	.05
348	Jeff Montgomery	.05
349	Chris Haney	.05
350	Bip Roberts	.05
351	Tom Goodwin	.05
352	Mark Gubicza	.05
353	Joe Randa	.05
354	Ramon Martinez	.05
355	Eric Karros	.05
356	Delino DeShields	.05
357	Brett Butler	.05
358	Todd Worrell	.05
359	Mike Blowers	.05
360	Mike Piazza	1.25
361	Ben McDonald	.05
362	Ricky Bones	.05
363	Greg Vaughn	.05
364	Matt Mieske	.05
365	Kevin Seitzer	.05
366	Jeff Cirillo	.05
367	LaTroy Hawkins	.05
368	Frank Rodriguez	.05
369	Rick Aguilera	.05
370	Roberto Alomar	.15
371	Albert Belle	.05
372	Wade Boggs	.50
373	Barry Bonds	1.00
374	Roger Clemens	.65
375	Dennis Eckersley	.35
376	Ken Griffey Jr.	.65
377	Tony Gwynn	.50
378	Rickey Henderson	.40
379	Greg Maddux	.50
380	Fred McGriff	.05
381	Paul Molitor	.40
382	Eddie Murray	.40
383	Mike Piazza	.65
384	Kirby Puckett	.50
385	Cal Ripken Jr.	1.00
386	Ozzie Smith	.50
387	Frank Thomas	.45
388	Matt Walbeck	.05
389	Dave Stevens	.05
390	Marty Cordova	.05
391	Darrin Fletcher	.05
392	Cliff Floyd	.05
393	Mel Rojas	.05
394	Shane Andrews	.05
395	Moises Alou	.05
396	Carlos Perez	.05
397	Jeff Fassero	.05
398	Bobby Jones	.05
399	Todd Hundley	.05
400	John Franco	.05
401	Jose Vizcaino	.05
402	Bernard Gilkey	.05
403	Pete Harnisch	.05
404	Pat Kelly	.05
405	David Cone	.05
406	Bernie Williams	.05
407	John Wetteland	.05
408	Scott Kamieniecki	.05
409	Tim Raines	.05
410	Wade Boggs	1.00
411	Terry Steinbach	.05
412	Jason Giambi	.40
413	Todd Van Poppel	.05
414	Pedro Munoz	.05
415	Eddie Murray-1990	.40
416	Dennis Eckersley-1990	.35
417	Bip Roberts-1992	.05
418	Glenallen Hill-1992	.05
419	John Hudek-1994	.05
420	Derek Bell-1995	.05
421	Larry Walker-1995	.05
422	Greg Maddux-1995	.50
423	Ken Caminiti-1995	.05
424	Brent Gates	.05
425	Mark McGwire	1.50
426	Mark Whiten	.05
427	Sid Fernandez	.05
428	Ricky Bottalico	.05
429	Mike Mimbs	.05
430	Lenny Dykstra	.05
431	Todd Zeile	.05
432	Benito Santiago	.05
433	Danny Miceli	.05
434	Al Martin	.05
435	Jay Bell	.05
436	Charlie Hayes	.05
437	Mike Kingery	.05
438	Paul Wagner	.05
439	Tom Pagnozzi	.05
440	Ozzie Smith	1.00

441	Ray Lankford	.05
442	Dennis Eckersley	.65
443	Ron Gant	.05
444	Alan Benes	.05
445	Rickey Henderson	.75
446	Jody Reed	.05
447	Trevor Hoffman	.05
448	Andujar Cedeno	.05
449	Steve Finley	.05
450	Tony Gwynn	1.00
451	Joey Hamilton	.05
452	Mark Leiter	.05
453	Rod Beck	.05
454	Kirt Manwaring	.05
455	Matt Williams	.05
456	Robby Thompson	.05
457	Shawon Dunston	.05
458	Russ Davis	.05
459	Paul Sorrento	.05
460	Randy Johnson	.75
461	Chris Bosio	.05
462	Luis Sojo	.05
463	Sterling Hitchcock	.05
464	Benji Gil	.05
465	Mickey Tettleton	.05
466	Mark McLemore	.05
467	Darryl Hamilton	.05
468	Ken Hill	.05
469	Dean Palmer	.05
470	Carlos Delgado	.40
471	Ed Sprague	.05
472	Otis Nixon	.05
473	Pat Hentgen	.05
474	Juan Guzman	.05
475	John Olerud	.05
476	Buck Showalter Checklist	.05
477	Bobby Cox Checklist	.05
478	Tommy Lasorda Checklist	.05
479	Jim Leyland Checklist	.05
480	Sparky Anderson Checklist	.05

Blue Chip Prospects

		NM/M
Complete Set (20):		50.00
Common Player:		1.00
1	Hideo Nomo	4.00
2	Johnny Damon	3.50
3	Jason Isringhausen	1.00
4	Bill Pulsipher	1.00
5	Marty Cordova	1.00
6	Michael Tucker	1.00
7	John Wasdin	1.00
8	Karim Garcia	1.50
9	Ruben Rivera	1.00
10	Chipper Jones	10.00
11	Billy Wagner	1.00
12	Brooks Kieschnick	1.00
13	Alex Ochoa	1.00
14	Roger Cedeno	1.00
15	Alex Rodriguez	15.00
16	Jason Schmidt	1.00
17	Derek Jeter	20.00
18	Brian L. Hunter	1.00
19	Garret Anderson	1.00
20	Manny Ramirez	7.50

Cal Ripken Collection

		NM/M
Complete Set (8):		12.50
Common Card:		2.00
Header:		2.00
5	Cal Ripken Jr.	2.00
6	Cal Ripken Jr.	2.00
7	Cal Ripken Jr.	2.00
8	Cal Ripken Jr.	2.00
13	Cal Ripken Jr.	2.00
14	Cal Ripken Jr.	2.00
15	Cal Ripken Jr.	2.00

16	Cal Ripken Jr.	2.00
17	Cal Ripken Jr.	2.00

Diamond Destiny

		NM/M
Complete Set (Bronze):		35.00
Common Player (Bronze):		.30
Silver:		6X
Gold:		12X
1	Chipper Jones	1.50
2	Fred McGriff	.30
3	Ryan Klesko	.30
4	John Smoltz	.30
5	Greg Maddux	1.50
6	Cal Ripken Jr.	3.00
7	Roberto Alomar	.45
8	Eddie Murray	1.25
9	Brady Anderson	.30
10	Mo Vaughn	.30
11	Roger Clemens	1.75
12	Darin Erstad	.60
13	Sammy Sosa	1.50
14	Frank Thomas	1.25
15	Barry Larkin	.30
16	Albert Belle	.30
17	Manny Ramirez	1.25
18	Kenny Lofton	.30
19	Dante Bichette	.30
20	Gary Sheffield	.75
21	Jeff Bagwell	1.25
22	Hideo Nomo	.65
23	Mike Piazza	2.00
24	Kirby Puckett	1.50
25	Paul Molitor	1.25
26	Chuck Knoblauch	.30
27	Wade Boggs	1.50
28	Derek Jeter	3.00
29	Rey Ordonez	.30
30	Mark McGwire	2.50
31	Ozzie Smith	1.50
32	Tony Gwynn	1.50
33	Barry Bonds	3.00
34	Matt Williams	.30
35	Ken Griffey Jr.	2.00
36	Jay Buhner	.30
37	Randy Johnson	1.25
38	Alex Rodriguez	2.00
39	Juan Gonzalez	.65
40	Joe Carter	.30

Future Stock

		NM/M
Complete Set (20):		4.00
Common Player:		.25
1	George Arias	.25
2	Brian Barnes	.25
3	Trey Beamon	.25
4	Yamil Benitez	.25
5	Jamie Brewington	.25
6	Tony Clark	.25
7	Steve Cox	.25
8	Carlos Delgado	.75
9	Chad Fonville	.25
10	Steve Gibralter	.25
11	Curtis Goodwin	.25
12	Todd Greene	.25
13	Jimmy Haynes	.25
14	Quinton McCracken	.25
15	Billy McMillon	.25
16	Chan Ho Park	.25
17	Arquimedez Pozo	.25
18	Chris Snopek	.25
19	Shannon Stewart	.25
20	Jeff Suppan	.25

Gameface

		NM/M
Complete Set (10):		6.00
Common Player:		.15
1	Ken Griffey Jr.	1.00
2	Frank Thomas	.65
3	Barry Bonds	1.50
4	Albert Belle	.15
5	Cal Ripken Jr.	1.50
6	Mike Piazza	1.00
7	Chipper Jones	.75
8	Matt Williams	.15
9	Hideo Nomo	.40
10	Greg Maddux	.75

Hideo Nomo R.O.Y.

	NM/M
Hideo Nomo	15.00

Hot Commodities

		NM/M
Complete Set (20):		30.00
Common Player:		.75
1	Ken Griffey Jr.	3.00
2	Hideo Nomo	1.50
3	Roberto Alomar	1.50
4	Paul Wilson	.75
5	Albert Belle	.75
6	Manny Ramirez	2.25
7	Kirby Puckett	2.50
8	Johnny Damon	2.00
9	Randy Johnson	2.25
10	Greg Maddux	2.50
11	Chipper Jones	2.50
12	Barry Bonds	5.00
13	Mo Vaughn	.75
14	Mike Piazza	3.00
15	Cal Ripken Jr.	5.00
16	Tim Salmon	.75
17	Sammy Sosa	2.50
18	Kenny Lofton	.75
19	Tony Gwynn	2.50
20	Frank Thomas	2.25

Lovero Collection

		NM/M
Complete Set (20):		17.50
Common Player:		.25
1	Rod Carew	1.00
2	Hideo Nomo	.50
3	Derek Jeter	3.00
4	Barry Bonds	3.00
5	Greg Maddux	1.50
6	Mark McGwire (w/ Will Clark)	2.50
7	Jose Canseco	.50
8	Ken Caminiti	.25
9	Raul Mondesi	.25
10	Ken Griffey Jr.	2.50
11	Jay Buhner	.25
12	Randy Johnson	1.00
13	Roger Clemens	2.00
14	Brady Anderson	.25
15	Frank Thomas	1.00
16	Angels Outfielders	.25
17	Mike Piazza	2.50
18	Dante Bichette	.25
19	Tony Gwynn	1.50
20	Jim Abbott	.25

1996 UPPER DECK NATIONAL HEROES

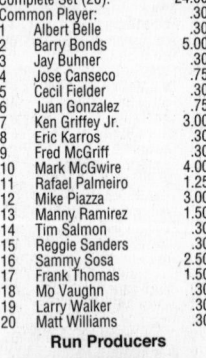

		NM/M
Complete Set (2):		20.00
Complete Set, Autographed (2):		190.00
(1)	Ken Griffey Jr.	7.50
(1a)	Ken Griffey Jr. (autographed)	90.00
(2)	Cal Ripken Jr.	10.00
(2a)	Cal Ripken Jr. (autographed)	100.00

Nomo Highlights

	NM/M
Complete Set (5):	3.00
Common Card:	.75

Power Driven

		NM/M
Complete Set (20):		24.00
Common Player:		.30
1	Albert Belle	.30
2	Barry Bonds	5.00
3	Jay Buhner	.30
4	Jose Canseco	.75
5	Cecil Fielder	.30
6	Juan Gonzalez	.75
7	Ken Griffey Jr.	3.00
8	Eric Karros	.30
9	Fred McGriff	.30
10	Mark McGwire	4.00
11	Rafael Palmeiro	1.25
12	Mike Piazza	3.00
13	Manny Ramirez	1.50
14	Tim Salmon	.30
15	Reggie Sanders	.30
16	Sammy Sosa	2.50
17	Frank Thomas	1.50
18	Mo Vaughn	.30
19	Larry Walker	.30
20	Matt Williams	.30

Run Producers

		NM/M
Complete Set (20):		50.00
Common Player:		1.00
1	Albert Belle	1.00
2	Dante Bichette	1.00
3	Barry Bonds	10.00
4	Jay Buhner	1.00
5	Jose Canseco	2.00
6	Juan Gonzalez	1.50
7	Ken Griffey Jr.	6.00
8	Tony Gwynn	5.00
9	Kenny Lofton	1.00
10	Edgar Martinez	1.00
11	Fred McGriff	1.00
12	Mark McGwire	7.50
13	Rafael Palmeiro	2.50
14	Mike Piazza	6.00
15	Manny Ramirez	3.00
16	Tim Salmon	1.00
17	Sammy Sosa	5.00
18	Frank Thomas	3.00
19	Mo Vaughn	1.00
20	Matt Williams	1.00

1996 UPPER DECK UPDATE

		NM/M
Complete Set (30):		8.00
Common Player:		.25
481	Randy Myers	.25
482	Kent Mercker	.25
483	David Wells	.35
484	Kevin Mitchell	.25
485	Randy Velarde	.25
486	Ryne Sandberg	4.00
487	Doug Jones	.25
488	Terry Adams	.25
489	Kevin Tapani	.25
490	Harold Baines	.25
491	Eric Davis	.25
492	Julio Franco	.25
493	Jack McDowell	.25
494	Devon White	.25
495	Kevin Brown	.35
496	Rick Wilkins	.25
497	Sean Berry	.25
498	Keith Lockhart	.25
499	Mark Loretta	.25
500	Paul Molitor	2.50
501	Roberto Kelly	.25
502	Lance Johnson	.25
503	Tino Martinez	.25
504	Kenny Rogers	.25
505	Todd Stottlemyre	.25
506	Gary Gaetti	.25
507	Royce Clayton	.25
508	Andy Benes	.25
509	Wally Joyner	.25
510	Erik Hanson	.25

1997 UPPER DECK

		NM/M
Complete Set (550):		75.00
Complete Series 1 Set (240):		35.00
Complete Update Set (241-270):		5.00
Complete Series 2 Set (271-520):		35.00
Complete Update Set (521-550):		7.50
Common Player:		.05
Series 1 or 2 Pack (12):		1.50
Series 1 or 2 Wax Box (28):		25.00
1	Jackie Robinson	.50
2	Jackie Robinson	.50
3	Jackie Robinson	.50
4	Jackie Robinson	.50
5	Jackie Robinson	.50
6	Jackie Robinson	.50
7	Jackie Robinson	.50
8	Jackie Robinson	.50
9	Jackie Robinson	.50
10	Chipper Jones	1.00
11	Marquis Grissom	.05
12	Jermaine Dye	.05
13	Mark Lemke	.05
14	Terrell Wade	.05
15	Fred McGriff	.05
16	Tom Glavine	.20
17	Mark Wohlers	.05
18	Randy Myers	.05
19	Roberto Alomar	.25
20	Cal Ripken Jr.	2.00
21	Rafael Palmeiro	.65
22	Mike Mussina	.30
23	Brady Anderson	.05
24	Jose Canseco	.50
25	Mo Vaughn	.05
26	Roger Clemens	1.00
27	Tim Naehring	.05
28	Jeff Suppan	.05
29	Troy Percival	.05
30	Sammy Sosa	1.00
31	Amaury Telemaco	.05
32	Rey Sanchez	.05
33	Scott Servais	.05
34	Steve Trachsel	.05
35	Mark Grace	.05
36	Wilson Alvarez	.05
37	Harold Baines	.05
38	Tony Phillips	.05
39	James Baldwin	.05
40	Frank Thomas (wrong (Ken Griffey Jr.'s) vital data)	.85
41	Lyle Mouton	.05
42	Chris Snopek	.05
43	Hal Morris	.05
44	Eric Davis	.05
45	Barry Larkin	.05
46	Reggie Sanders	.05
47	Pete Schourek	.05
48	Lee Smith	.05
49	Charles Nagy	.05
50	Albert Belle	.05
51	Julio Franco	.05
52	Kenny Lofton	.05
53	Orel Hershiser	.05
54	Omar Vizquel	.05
55	Eric Young	.05
56	Curtis Leskanic	.05
57	Quinton McCracken	.05
58	Kevin Ritz	.05
59	Walt Weiss	.05
60	Dante Bichette	.05
61	Marc Lewis	.05
62	Tony Clark	.05
63	Travis Fryman	.05
64	John Smoltz	.05
65	Greg Maddux	.50
66	Tom Glavine	.10
67	Mike Mussina	.15
68	Andy Pettitte	.15
69	Mariano Rivera	.10
70	Hideo Nomo	.20
71	Kevin Brown	.05
72	Randy Johnson	.40
73	Felipe Lira	.05
74	Kimera Bartee	.05
75	Alan Trammell	.05
76	Kevin Brown	.05
77	Edgar Renteria	.05
78	Al Leiter	.05
79	Charles Johnson	.05
80	Andre Dawson	.25
81	Billy Wagner	.05
82	Donne Wall	.05
83	Jeff Bagwell	.75
84	Keith Lockhart	.05
85	Jeff Montgomery	.05
86	Tom Goodwin	.05
87	Tim Belcher	.05
88	Mike Macfarlane	.05
89	Joe Randa	.05
90	Brett Butler	.05
91	Todd Worrell	.05
92	Todd Hollandsworth	.05
93	Ismael Valdes	.05
94	Hideo Nomo	.40
95	Mike Piazza	1.25
96	Jeff Cirillo	.05
97	Ricky Bones	.05
98	Fernando Vina	.05
99	Ben McDonald	.05
100	John Jaha	.05
101	Mark Loretta	.05
102	Paul Molitor	.75
103	Rick Aguilera	.05
104	Marty Cordova	.05
105	Kirby Puckett	1.00
106	Dan Naulty	.05
107	Frank Rodriguez	.05
108	Shane Andrews	.05
109	Henry Rodriguez	.05
110	Mark Grudzielanek	.05
111	Pedro Martinez	.75
112	Ugueth Urbina	.05
113	David Segui	.05
114	Rey Ordonez	.05
115	Bernard Gilkey	.05
116	Butch Huskey	.05
117	Paul Wilson	.05
118	Alex Ochoa	.05
119	John Franco	.05
120	Dwight Gooden	.05
121	Ruben Rivera	.05
122	Andy Pettitte	.20
123	Tino Martinez	.05
124	Bernie Williams	.05
125	Wade Boggs	1.00
126	Paul O'Neill	.05
127	Scott Brosius	.05
128	Ernie Young	.05
129	Doug Johns	.05
130	Geronimo Berroa	.05
131	Jason Giambi	.50
132	John Wasdin	.05
133	Jim Eisenreich	.05
134	Ricky Otero	.05
135	Ricky Bottalico	.05
136	Mark Langston	.05
137	Greg Maddux	.50
138	Ivan Rodriguez	.35
139	Charles Johnson	.05
140	J.T. Snow	.05
141	Mark Grace	.05
142	Roberto Alomar	.15
143	Craig Biggio	.05
144	Ken Caminiti	.05
145	Matt Williams	.05
146	Omar Vizquel	.05
147	Cal Ripken Jr.	1.00
148	Ozzie Smith	.40
149	Rey Ordonez	.05
150	Ken Griffey Jr.	.65
151	Devon White	.05
152	Barry Bonds	1.00
153	Kenny Lofton	.05
154	Mickey Morandini	.05
155	Gregg Jefferies	.05
156	Curt Schilling	.20
157	Jason Kendall	.05
158	Francisco Cordova	.05
159	Dennis Eckersley	.65
160	Ron Gant	.05
161	Ozzie Smith	1.00
162	Brian Jordan	.05
163	John Mabry	.05
164	Andy Ashby	.05
165	Steve Finley	.05
166	Fernando Valenzuela	.05
167	Archi Cianfrocco	.05
168	Wally Joyner	.05
169	Greg Vaughn	.05
170	Barry Bonds	2.00
171	William VanLandingham	.05
172	Marvin Benard	.05
173	Rich Aurilia	.05
174	Jay Canizaro	.05
175	Ken Griffey Jr.	1.25
176	Bob Wells	.05
177	Jay Buhner	.05
178	Sterling Hitchcock	.05
179	Edgar Martinez	.05
180	Rusty Greer	.05
181	Dave Nilsson	.05
182	Larry Walker	.05
183	Edgar Renteria	.05
184	Rey Ordonez	.05
185	Rafael Palmeiro	.35
186	Osvaldo Fernandez	.05
187	Raul Mondesi	.05
188	Manny Ramirez	.40
189	Sammy Sosa	.50
190	Robert Eenhoorn	.05
191	Devon White	.05
192	Hideo Nomo	.20
193	Mac Suzuki	.05
194	Chan Ho Park	.05
195	Fernando Valenzuela	.05
196	Andruw Jones	.40
197	Vinny Castilla	.05
198	Dennis Martinez	.05
199	Ruben Rivera	.05
200	Juan Gonzalez	.20
201	Roberto Alomar	.30
202	Edgar Martinez	.05
203	Ivan Rodriguez	.35
204	Carlos Delgado	.20
205	Andres Galarraga	.05
206	Ozzie Guillen	.05
207	Midre Cummings	.05
208	Roger Pavlik	.05
209	Darren Oliver	.05
210	Dean Palmer	.05
211	Ivan Rodriguez	.65
212	Otis Nixon	.05
213	Pat Hentgen	.05
214	Ozzie Smith, Andre Dawson, Kirby Puckett CL	.10
215	Barry Bonds, Gary Sheffield, Brady Anderson	.25
216	Ken Caminiti	.05
217	John Smoltz	.05
218	Eric Young	.05
219	Juan Gonzalez	.10
220	Eddie Murray	.15
221	Tommy Lasorda	.05
222	Paul Molitor	.15
223	Luis Castillo	.05
224	Justin Thompson	.05
225	Rocky Coppinger	.05
226	Jermaine Allensworth	.05
227	Jeff D'Amico	.05
228	Jamey Wright	.05
229	Scott Rolen	.60
230	Darin Erstad	.25
231	Marty Janzen	.05
232	Jacob Cruz	.05
233	Raul Ibanez	.05
234	Nomar Garciaparra	1.00
235	Todd Walker	.05
236	*Brian Giles*	.75
237	Matt Beech	.05
238	Mike Cameron	.05
239	Jose Paniagua	.05
240	Andruw Jones	.75
241	Brant Brown	.25
242	Robin Jennings	.25
243	Willie Adams	.25
244	Ken Caminiti	.25
245	Brian Jordan	.25
246	Chipper Jones	2.50
247	Juan Gonzalez	1.00
248	Bernie Williams	.25
249	Roberto Alomar	.30
250	Bernie Williams	.25
251	David Wells	.25
252	Cecil Fielder	.25
253	Darryl Strawberry	.25
254	Andy Pettitte	.40
255	Javier Lopez	.25
256	Gary Gaetti	.25
257	Ron Gant	.25
258	Brian Jordan	.25
259	John Smoltz	.25
260	Greg Maddux	2.50
261	Tom Glavine	.45
262	Chipper Jones	2.50
263	Greg Maddux	2.50
264	David Cone	.25
265	Jim Leyritz	.25
266	Andy Pettitte	.40
267	John Wetteland	.25
268	*Dario Veras*	.25
269	Neifi Perez	.25
270	Bill Mueller	.25
271	Vladimir Guerrero	.75
272	Dmitri Young	.05
273	*Nerio Rodriguez*	.05
274	Kevin Orie	.05
275	Felipe Crespo	.05
276	Danny Graves	.05
277	Roderick Myers	.05
278	*Felix Heredia*	.25
279	Ralph Milliard	.05
280	Greg Norton	.05
281	Derek Wallace	.05
282	Trot Nixon	.10
283	Bobby Chouinard	.05
284	Jay Witasick	.05
285	Travis Miller	.05
286	Brian Bevil	.05
287	Bobby Estalella	.05
288	Steve Soderstrom	.05
289	Mark Langston	.05
290	Tim Salmon	.05
291	Jim Edmonds	.05
292	Garret Anderson	.05
293	George Arias	.05
294	Gary DiSarcina	.05
295	Chuck Finley	.05
296	Todd Greene	.05
297	Randy Velarde	.05
298	David Justice	.05
299	Ryan Klesko	.05
300	John Smoltz	.05

301	Javier Lopez	.05
302	Greg Maddux	1.00
303	Denny Neagle	.05
304	B.J. Surhoff	.05
305	Chris Hoiles	.05
306	Eric Davis	.05
307	Scott Erickson	.05
308	Mike Bordick	.05
309	John Valentin	.05
310	Heathcliff Slocumb	.05
311	Tom Gordon	.05
312	Mike Stanley	.05
313	Reggie Jefferson	.05
314	Darren Bragg	.05
315	Troy O'Leary	.05
316	John Mabry	.05
317	Mark Whiten	.05
318	Edgar Martinez	.05
319	Alex Rodriguez	.75
320	Mark McGwire	.75
321	Hideo Nomo	.20
322	Todd Hundley	.05
323	Barry Bonds	1.00
324	Andruw Jones	.40
325	Ryne Sandberg	1.00
326	Brian McRae	.05
327	Frank Castillo	.05
328	Shawon Dunston	.05
329	Ray Durham	.05
330	Robin Ventura	.05
331	Ozzie Guillen	.05
332	Roberto Hernandez	.05
333	Albert Belle	.25
334	Dave Martinez	.05
335	Willie Greene	.05
336	Jeff Brantley	.05
337	Kevin Jarvis	.05
338	John Smiley	.05
339	Eddie Taubensee	.05
340	Bret Boone	.05
341	Kevin Seitzer	.05
342	Jack McDowell	.05
343	Sandy Alomar Jr.	.05
344	Chad Curtis	.05
345	Manny Ramirez	.75
346	Chad Ogea	.05
347	Jim Thome	.05
348	Mark Thompson	.05
349	Ellis Burks	.05
350	Andres Galarraga	.05
351	Vinny Castilla	.05
352	Kirt Manwaring	.05
353	Larry Walker	.05
354	Omar Olivares	.05
355	Bobby Higginson	.05
356	Melvin Nieves	.05
357	Brian Johnson	.05
358	Devon White	.05
359	Jeff Conine	.05
360	Gary Sheffield	.35
361	Robb Nen	.05
362	Mike Hampton	.05
363	Bob Abreu	.10
364	Luis Gonzalez	.05
365	Derek Bell	.05
366	Sean Berry	.05
367	Craig Biggio	.05
368	Darryl Kile	.05
369	Shane Reynolds	.05
370	Jeff Bagwell	.40
371	Ron Gant	.05
372	Andy Benes	.05
373	Gary Gaetti	.05
374a	Ramon Martinez	.05
374b	Ramon Martinez	.05
375	Raul Mondesi	.05
376a	Steve Finley	.05
376b	Steve Finley	.05
377	Ken Caminiti	.05
378	Tony Gwynn	.40
379	Dario Veras	.05
380	Andy Pettitte	.10
381	Ruben Rivera	.05
382	David Cone	.05
383	Roberto Alomar	.20
384	Edgar Martinez	.05
385	Ken Griffey Jr.	.65
386	Mark McGwire	.75
387	Rusty Greer	.05
388	Jose Rosado	.05
389	Kevin Appier	.05
390	Johnny Damon	.25
391	Jose Offerman	.05
392	Michael Tucker	.05
393	Craig Paquette	.05
394	Bip Roberts	.05
395	Ramon Martinez	.05
396	Greg Gagne	.05
397	Chan Ho Park	.05
398	Karim Garcia	.10
399	Wilton Guerrero	.05
400	Eric Karros	.05
401	Raul Mondesi	.05
402	Matt Mieske	.05
403	Mike Fetters	.05
404	Dave Nilsson	.05
405	Jose Valentin	.05
406	Scott Karl	.05
407	Marc Newfield	.05
408	Cal Eldred	.05
409	Rich Becker	.05
410	Terry Steinbach	.05
411	Chuck Knoblauch	.05
412	Pat Meares	.05
413	Brad Radke	.05
414	Not Issued	
415a	Kirby Puckett (should be #414)	1.00
415b	Andruw Jones	1.50
416	Chipper Jones	2.00
417	Mo Vaughn	.50
418	Frank Thomas	1.50
419	Albert Belle	.50
420	Mark McGwire	3.00
421	Derek Jeter	4.50
422	Alex Rodriguez	3.00
423	Juan Gonzalez	.75
424	Ken Griffey Jr.	2.50
425	Rondell White	.05
426	Darrin Fletcher	.05
427	Cliff Floyd	.05
428	Mike Lansing	.05
429	F.P. Santangelo	.05
430	Todd Hundley	.05
431	Mark Clark	.05
432	Pete Harnisch	.05
433	Jason Isringhausen	.05
434	Bobby Jones	.05
435	Lance Johnson	.05
436	Carlos Baerga	.05
437	Mariano Duncan	.05
438	David Cone	.05
439	Mariano Rivera	.15
440	Derek Jeter	2.00
441	Joe Girardi	.05
442	Charlie Hayes	.05
443	Tim Raines	.05
444	Darryl Strawberry	.05
445	Cecil Fielder	.05
446	Ariel Prieto	.05
447	Tony Batista	.05
448	Brent Gates	.05
449	Scott Spiezio	.05
450	Mark McGwire	1.50
451	Don Wengert	.05
452	Mike Lieberthal	.05
453	Lenny Dykstra	.05
454	Rex Hudler	.05
455	Darren Daulton	.05
456	Kevin Stocker	.05
457	Trey Beamon	.05
458	Midre Cummings	.05
459	Mark Johnson	.05
460	Al Martin	.05
461	Kevin Elster	.05
462	Jon Lieber	.05
463	Jason Schmidt	.05
464	Paul Wagner	.05
465	Andy Benes	.05
466	Alan Benes	.05
467	Royce Clayton	.05
468	Gary Gaetti	.05
469	Curt Lyons	.05
470	Eugene Kingsale	.05
471	Damian Jackson	.05
472	Wendell Magee	.05
473	Kevin L. Brown	.05
474	Raul Casanova	.05
475	*Ramiro Mendoza*	.25
476	Todd Dunn	.05
477	Chad Mottola	.05
478	Andy Larkin	.05
479	Jaime Bluma	.05
480	Mac Suzuki	.05
481	Brian Banks	.05
482	Desi Wilson	.05
483	Einar Diaz	.05
484	Tom Pagnozzi	.05
485	Ray Lankford	.05
486	Todd Stottlemyre	.05
487	Donovan Osborne	.05
488	Trevor Hoffman	.05
489	Chris Gomez	.05
490	Ken Caminiti	.05
491	John Flaherty	.05
492	Tony Gwynn	1.00
493	Joey Hamilton	.05
494	Rickey Henderson	.75
495	Glenallen Hill	.05
496	Rod Beck	.05
497	Osvaldo Fernandez	.05
498	Rick Wilkins	.05
499	Joey Cora	.05
500	Alex Rodriguez	1.50
501	Randy Johnson	.75
502	Paul Sorrento	.05
503	Dan Wilson	.05
504	Jamie Moyer	.05
505	Will Clark	.05
506	Mickey Tettleton	.05
507	John Burkett	.05
508	Ken Hill	.05
509	Mark McLemore	.05
510	Juan Gonzalez	.40
511	Bobby Witt	.05
512	Carlos Delgado	.40
513	Alex Gonzalez	.05
514	Shawn Green	.25
515	Joe Carter	.05
516	Juan Guzman	.05
517	Charlie O'Brien	.05
518	Ed Sprague	.05
519	Mike Timlin	.05
520	Roger Clemens	1.00
521	Eddie Murray	2.00
522	Jason Dickson	.25
523	Jim Leyritz	.25
524	Michael Tucker	.25
525	Kenny Lofton	.25
526	Jimmy Key	.25
527	Mel Rojas	.25
528	Deion Sanders	.25
529	Bartolo Colon	.25
530	Matt Williams	.25
531	Marquis Grissom	.25
532	David Justice	.25
533	*Bubba Trammell*	.35
534	Moises Alou	.25
535	Bobby Bonilla	.25
536	Alex Fernandez	.25
537	Jay Bell	.25
538	Chili Davis	.25
539	Jeff King	.25
540	Todd Zeile	.25
541	John Olerud	.25
542	Jose Guillen	.25
543	Derrek Lee	1.00
544	Dante Powell	.25
545	J.T. Snow	.25
546	Jeff Kent	.25
547	*Jose Cruz Jr.*	.75
548	John Wetteland	.25
549	Orlando Merced	.25
550	*Hideki Irabu*	.50

Amazing Greats

		NM/M
Complete Set (20):		140.00
Common Player:		2.50
1	Ken Griffey Jr.	12.50
2	Roberto Alomar	3.00
3	Alex Rodriguez	15.00
4	Paul Molitor	7.50
5	Chipper Jones	10.00
6	Tony Gwynn	10.00
7	Kenny Lofton	2.50
8	Albert Belle	2.50
9	Matt Williams	2.50
10	Frank Thomas	7.50
11	Greg Maddux	10.00
12	Sammy Sosa	10.00
13	Kirby Puckett	10.00
14	Jeff Bagwell	7.50
15	Cal Ripken Jr.	20.00
16	Manny Ramirez	7.50
17	Barry Bonds	20.00
18	Mo Vaughn	2.50
19	Eddie Murray	7.50
20	Mike Piazza	12.50

Blue Chip Prospects

		NM/M
Common Player:		6.00
Production 500 sets		
1	Andruw Jones	25.00
2	Derek Jeter	60.00
3	Scott Rolen	15.00
4	Manny Ramirez	25.00
5	Todd Walker	6.00
6	Rocky Coppinger	6.00
7	Nomar Garciaparra	30.00
8	Darin Erstad	7.50
9	Jermaine Dye	6.00
10	Vladimir Guerrero	25.00
11	Edgar Renteria	6.00
12	Bob Abreu	7.50
13	Karim Garcia	6.00
14	Jeff D'Amico	6.00
15	Chipper Jones	30.00
16	Todd Hollandsworth	6.00
17	Andy Pettitte	9.00
18	Ruben Rivera	6.00
19	Jason Kendall	6.00
20	Alex Rodriguez	40.00

Game Jersey

		NM/M
Complete Set (3):		160.00
Common Player:		15.00
GJ1	Ken Griffey Jr.	135.00
GJ2	Tony Gwynn	25.00
GJ3	Rey Ordonez	15.00

Home Team Heroes

		NM/M
Complete Set (12):		10.00
Common Player:		.50
1	Alex Rodriguez, Ken Griffey Jr.	2.00
2	Bernie Williams, Derek Jeter	2.50
3	Bernard Gilkey, Randy Hundley	.50
4	Hideo Nomo, Mike Piazza	1.50
5	Andruw Jones, Chipper Jones	1.00
6	John Smoltz, Greg Maddux	1.00
7	Mike Mussina, Cal Ripken Jr.	2.50
8	Andres Galarraga, Dante Bichette	.50
9	Juan Gonzalez, Ivan Rodriguez	.65
10	Albert Belle, Frank Thomas	.75
11	Jim Thome, Manny Ramirez	.75
12	Ken Caminiti, Tony Gwynn	1.00

Hot Commodities

		NM/M
Complete Set (20):		20.00

Common Player: .30
1 Alex Rodriguez 2.00
2 Andruw Jones 1.00
3 Derek Jeter 2.50
4 Frank Thomas 1.00
5 Ken Griffey Jr. 1.50
6 Chipper Jones 1.25
7 Juan Gonzalez .50
8 Cal Ripken Jr. 2.50
9 John Smoltz .30
10 Mark McGwire 2.00
11 Barry Bonds 2.50
12 Albert Belle .30
13 Mike Piazza 1.50
14 Manny Ramirez 1.00
15 Mo Vaughn .30
16 Tony Gwynn 1.25
17 Vladimir Guerrero 1.00
18 Hideo Nomo .50
19 Greg Maddux 1.25
20 Kirby Puckett 1.25

Jackie Robinson Tribute

NM/M
Jackie Robinson 3.50

Long Distance Connection

NM/M
Complete Set (20): 32.50
Common Player: .60
1 Mark McGwire 4.00
2 Brady Anderson .60
3 Ken Griffey Jr. 3.00
4 Albert Belle .60
5 Juan Gonzalez 1.25
6 Andres Galarraga .60
7 Jay Buhner .60
8 Mo Vaughn .60
9 Barry Bonds 5.00
10 Gary Sheffield 1.25
11 Todd Hundley .60
12 Frank Thomas 2.00
13 Sammy Sosa 2.50
14 Rafael Palmeiro 1.75
15 Alex Rodriguez 4.00
16 Mike Piazza 3.00
17 Ken Caminiti .60
18 Chipper Jones 2.50
19 Manny Ramirez 2.00
20 Andruw Jones 2.00

Memorable Moments

Braves / P
Maddux wins four NL Cy Young Awards in a row (1992-95).

NM/M
Complete Set (20): 20.00
Common Player: .50
SERIES 1
1 Andruw Jones .75
2 Chipper Jones 1.00
3 Cal Ripken Jr. 2.50
4 Frank Thomas .75
5 Manny Ramirez .75
6 Mike Piazza 1.50
7 Mark McGwire 2.00
8 Barry Bonds 2.50
9 Ken Griffey Jr. 1.50
10 Alex Rodriguez 2.00
SERIES 2
1 Ken Griffey Jr. 1.50
2 Albert Belle .50
3 Derek Jeter 2.50
4 Greg Maddux 1.00
5 Tony Gwynn 1.00
6 Ryne Sandberg 1.00
7 Juan Gonzalez .60
8 Roger Clemens 1.25
9 Jose Cruz Jr. .50
10 Mo Vaughn .50

Power Package

NM/M
Complete Set (20): 30.00
Common Player: 1.00
1 Ken Griffey Jr. 3.50
2 Joe Carter 1.00
3 Rafael Palmeiro 1.75
4 Jay Buhner 1.00
5 Sammy Sosa 3.00
6 Fred McGriff 1.00
7 Jeff Bagwell 2.00
8 Albert Belle 1.00
9 Matt Williams 1.00
10 Mark McGwire 4.00
11 Gary Sheffield 1.25
12 Tim Salmon 1.00
13 Ryan Klesko 1.00
14 Manny Ramirez 2.00
15 Mike Piazza 3.50
16 Barry Bonds 5.00
17 Mo Vaughn 1.00
18 Jose Canseco 1.25
19 Juan Gonzalez 1.25
20 Frank Thomas 2.00

Rock Solid Foundation

NM/M
Complete Set (20): 7.50
Common Player: .15
1 Alex Rodriguez 1.50
2 Rey Ordonez .15
3 Derek Jeter 2.00
4 Darin Erstad .35
5 Chipper Jones 1.25
6 Johnny Damon .35
7 Ryan Klesko .15
8 Charles Johnson .15
9 Andy Pettitte .30
10 Manny Ramirez .75
11 Ivan Rodriguez .65
12 Jason Kendall .15
13 Rondell White .15
14 Alex Ochoa .15
15 Javy Lopez .15
16 Pedro Martinez .75
17 Carlos Delgado .50
18 Paul Wilson .15
19 Alan Benes .15
20 Raul Mondesi .15

Run Producers

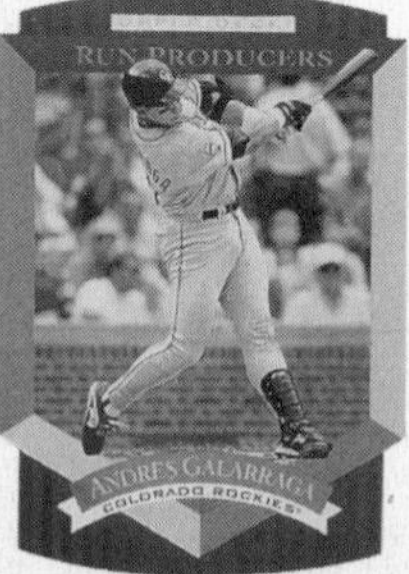

NM/M
Complete Set (24): 45.00
Common Player: .50
1 Ken Griffey Jr. 5.00
2 Barry Bonds 7.50
3 Albert Belle .50
4 Mark McGwire 6.00
5 Frank Thomas 3.00
6 Juan Gonzalez 1.50
7 Brady Anderson .50
8 Andres Galarraga .50
9 Rafael Palmeiro 2.50
10 Alex Rodriguez 6.00
11 Jay Buhner .50
12 Gary Sheffield 1.50
13 Sammy Sosa 4.00
14 Dante Bichette .50
15 Mike Piazza 5.00
16 Manny Ramirez 3.00
17 Kenny Lofton .50
18 Mo Vaughn .50
19 Tim Salmon .50
20 Chipper Jones 4.00
21 Jim Thome 2.00
22 Ken Caminiti .50
23 Jeff Bagwell 3.00
24 Paul Molitor 3.00

1997 UPPER DECK STAR ATTRACTIONS

NM/M
Complete Set (20): 30.00
Common Player: .30
Gold: 1.5X
1 Ken Griffey Jr. 3.00
2 Barry Bonds 5.00
3 Jeff Bagwell 2.00
4 Nomar Garciaparra 2.50
5 Tony Gwynn 2.50
6 Roger Clemens 2.75
7 Chipper Jones 2.50
8 Tino Martinez .30
9 Albert Belle .30
10 Kenny Lofton .30
11 Alex Rodriguez 4.00
12 Mark McGwire 4.00
13 Cal Ripken Jr. 5.00
14 Larry Walker .30
15 Mike Piazza 3.00
16 Frank Thomas 2.00
17 Juan Gonzalez .65
18 Greg Maddux 2.50
19 Jose Cruz Jr. .30
20 Mo Vaughn .30

Ticket to Stardom

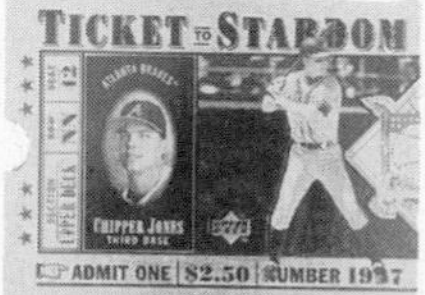

NM/M
Complete Set (20): 35.00
Common Player: .75
1 Chipper Jones 5.00
2 Jermaine Dye .75
3 Rey Ordonez .75
4 Alex Ochoa .75
5 Derek Jeter 7.50
6 Ruben Rivera .75
7 Billy Wagner .75
8 Jason Kendall .75
9 Darin Erstad 1.00
10 Alex Rodriguez 6.00
11 Bob Abreu .75
12 Richard Hidalgo .75
13 Karim Garcia 1.00
14 Andruw Jones 4.00
15 Carlos Delgado 1.50
16 Rocky Coppinger .75
17 Jeff D'Amico .75
18 Johnny Damon 2.00
19 John Wasdin .75
20 Manny Ramirez 4.00

Tony Gwynn Commemorative

NM/M
Tony Gwynn 7.50

1997 UPPER DECK UD3

NM/M
Complete Set (60): 30.00
Common Player: .15
Pack (3): 1.50
Wax Box (24): 30.00
1 Mark McGwire 2.50
2 Brady Anderson .15
3 Ken Griffey Jr. 2.00
4 Albert Belle .15
5 Andres Galarraga .15
6 Juan Gonzalez .40
7 Jay Buhner .15
8 Mo Vaughn .15
9 Barry Bonds 3.00
10 Gary Sheffield .40
11 Todd Hundley .15
12 Ellis Burks .15
13 Ken Caminiti .15
14 Vinny Castilla .15
15 Sammy Sosa 1.50
16 Frank Thomas .75
17 Rafael Palmeiro .65
18 Mike Piazza 2.00
19 Matt Williams .15
20 Eddie Murray .75
21 Roger Clemens 1.75
22 Tim Salmon .15
23 Robin Ventura .15
24 Ron Gant .15
25 Cal Ripken Jr. 3.00
26 Bernie Williams .15
27 Hideo Nomo .40
28 Ivan Rodriguez .65
29 John Smoltz .15
30 Paul Molitor .75
31 Greg Maddux 1.50
32 Raul Mondesi .15
33 Roberto Alomar .25
34 Barry Larkin .15
35 Tony Gwynn 1.50
36 Jim Thome .60
37 Kenny Lofton .15
38 Jeff Bagwell .75
39 Ozzie Smith 1.50
40 Kirby Puckett 1.50
41 Andruw Jones .75
42 Vladimir Guerrero .75
43 Edgar Renteria .15
44 Luis Castillo .15
45 Darin Erstad .30
46 Nomar Garciaparra 1.50
47 Todd Greene .15

48 Jason Kendall .15
49 Rey Ordonez .15
50 Alex Rodriguez 2.50
51 Manny Ramirez .75
52 Todd Walker .15
53 Ruben Rivera .15
54 Andy Pettitte .30
55 Derek Jeter 3.00
56 Todd Hollandsworth .15
57 Rocky Coppinger .15
58 Scott Rolen .60
59 Jermaine Dye .15
60 Chipper Jones 1.50

Superb Signatures

NM/M
Complete Set (4): 400.00
Common Autograph: 15.00
1 Ken Caminiti 25.00
2 Ken Griffey Jr. 150.00
3 Vladimir Guerrero 50.00
4 Derek Jeter 225.00

Marquee Attraction

NM/M
Complete Set (10): 40.00
Common Player: 1.25
1 Ken Griffey Jr. 6.00
2 Mark McGwire 7.50
3 Juan Gonzalez 1.75
4 Barry Bonds 9.00
5 Frank Thomas 2.50
6 Albert Belle 1.25
7 Mike Piazza 6.00
8 Cal Ripken Jr. 9.00
9 Mo Vaughn 1.25
10 Alex Rodriguez 7.50

Generation Next

NM/M
Complete Set (20): 35.00
Common Player: 1.00
1 Alex Rodriguez 5.00
2 Vladimir Guerrero 2.50
3 Luis Castillo 1.00
4 Rey Ordonez 1.00
5 Andruw Jones 2.50
6 Darin Erstad 1.25
7 Edgar Renteria 1.00
8 Jason Kendall 1.00
9 Jermaine Dye 1.00
10 Chipper Jones 3.00
11 Rocky Coppinger 1.00
12 Andy Pettitte 1.25
13 Todd Greene 1.00
14 Todd Hollandsworth 1.00
15 Derek Jeter 6.00
16 Ruben Rivera 1.00
17 Todd Walker 1.00
18 Nomar Garciaparra 3.00
19 Scott Rolen 2.00
20 Manny Ramirez 2.50

1998 UPPER DECK

NM/M
Complete Set (750): 100.00
Complete Series 1 Set (270): 25.00
Complete Series 2 Set (270): 25.00
Complete Series 3 Set (210): 75.00
Common Emminent Prestige (601-630): .25
Common Player: .05
Series 1 or 2 Pack (12): 1.50
Series 3 Pack (10): 1.50
Series 1 or 2 Wax Box (24): 35.00
Series 3 Wax Box (24): 35.00
1 Tino Martinez .05
2 Jimmy Key .05
3 Jay Buhner .05
4 Mark Gardner .05
5 Greg Maddux .25
6 Pedro Martinez .20
7 Hideo Nomo, Shigetosi Hasegawa .25
8 Sammy Sosa .35
9 Mark McGwire .50
10 Ken Griffey Jr. .45
11 Larry Walker .05
12 Tino Martinez .05
13 Mike Piazza .40
14 Jose Cruz, Jr. .05
15 Tony Gwynn .25
16 Greg Maddux .25
17 Roger Clemens .35
18 Alex Rodriguez .50
19 Shigetosi Hasegawa .05
20 Eddie Murray .50
21 Jason Dickson .05
22 Darin Erstad .25
23 Chuck Finley .05
24 Dave Hollins .05
25 Garret Anderson .05
26 Michael Tucker .05
27 Kenny Lofton .05
28 Javier Lopez .05
29 Fred McGriff .05
30 Greg Maddux .65
31 Jeff Blauser .05
32 John Smoltz .05
33 Mark Wohlers .05
34 Scott Erickson .05
35 Jimmy Key .05
36 Harold Baines .05
37 Randy Myers .05
38 B.J. Surhoff .05
39 Eric Davis .05
40 Rafael Palmeiro .35
41 Jeffrey Hammonds .05
42 Mo Vaughn .05
43 Tom Gordon .05
44 Tim Naehring .05
45 Darren Bragg .05
46 Aaron Sele .05
47 Troy O'Leary .05
48 John Valentin .05
49 Doug Glanville .05
50 Ryne Sandberg .65
51 Steve Trachsel .05
52 Mark Grace .05
53 Kevin Foster .05
54 Kevin Tapani .05
55 Kevin Orie .05
56 Lyle Mouton .05
57 Ray Durham .05
58 Jaime Navarro .05
59 Mike Cameron .05
60 Albert Belle .05
61 Doug Drabek .05
62 Chris Snopek .05
63 Eddie Taubensee .05
64 Terry Pendleton .05
65 Barry Larkin .05
66 Willie Greene .05
67 Deion Sanders .05
68 Pokey Reese .05
69 Jeff Shaw .05
70 Jim Thome .35
71 Orel Hershiser .05
72 Omar Vizquel .05
73 Brian Giles .05
74 David Justice .05
75 Bartolo Colon .05
76 Sandy Alomar Jr. .05
77 Neifi Perez .05
78 Eric Young .05
79 Vinny Castilla .05
80 Dante Bichette .05
81 Quinton McCracken .05
82 Jamey Wright .05
83 John Thomson .05
84 Damion Easley .05
85 Justin Thompson .05
86 Willie Blair .05
87 Raul Casanova .05
88 Bobby Higginson .05
89 Bubba Trammell .05
90 Tony Clark .05
91 Livan Hernandez .05
92 Charles Johnson .05
93 Edgar Renteria .05
94 Alex Fernandez .05
95 Gary Sheffield .30
96 Moises Alou .05
97 Tony Saunders .05
98 Robb Nen .05
99 Darryl Kile .05
100 Craig Biggio .05
101 Chris Holt .05
102 Bob Abreu .10
103 Luis Gonzalez .05
104 Billy Wagner .05
105 Brad Ausmus .05
106 Chili Davis .05
107 Tim Belcher .05
108 Dean Palmer .05
109 Jeff King .05
110 Jose Rosado .05
111 Mike Macfarlane .05
112 Jay Bell .05
113 Todd Worrell .05
114 Chan Ho Park .05
115 Raul Mondesi .05
116 Brett Butler .05
117 Greg Gagne .05
118 Hideo Nomo .25
119 Todd Zeile .05
120 Eric Karros .05
121 Cal Eldred .05
122 Jeff D'Amico .05
123 Antone Williamson .05
124 Doug Jones .05
125 Dave Nilsson .05
126 Gerald Williams .05
127 Fernando Vina .05
128 Ron Coomer .05
129 Matt Lawton .05
130 Paul Molitor .50
131 Todd Walker .05
132 Rick Aguilera .05
133 Brad Radke .05
134 Bob Tewksbury .05
135 Vladimir Guerrero .50
136 Tony Gwynn .25
137 Roger Clemens .35
138 Dennis Eckersley .15
139 Brady Anderson .05
140 Ken Griffey Jr. .40
141 Derek Jeter .75
142 Ken Caminiti .05
143 Frank Thomas .20
144 Barry Bonds .75
145 Cal Ripken Jr. .75
146 Alex Rodriguez .50
147 Greg Maddux .25
148 Kenny Lofton .05
149 Mike Piazza .40
150 Mark McGwire .50
151 Andruw Jones .20
152 Rusty Greer .05
153 F.P. Santangelo .05
154 Mike Lansing .05
155 Lee Smith .05
156 Carlos Perez .05
157 Pedro Martinez .50
158 Ryan McGuire .05
159 F.P. Santangelo .05
160 Rondell White .05
161 *Takashi Kashiwada* .05
162 Butch Huskey .05
163 Edgardo Alfonzo .05
164 John Franco .05
165 Todd Hundley .05
166 Rey Ordonez .05
167 Armando Reynoso .05
168 John Olerud .05
169 Bernie Williams .05
170 Andy Pettitte .15
171 Wade Boggs .65
172 Paul O'Neill .05
173 Cecil Fielder .05
174 Charlie Hayes .05
175 David Cone .05
176 Hideki Irabu .05
177 Mark Bellhorn .05
178 Steve Karsay .05
179 Damon Mashore .05
180 Jason McDonald .05
181 Scott Spiezio .05
182 Ariel Prieto .05
183 Jason Giambi .30
184 Wendell Magee .05
185 Rico Brogna .05
186 Garrett Stephenson .05
187 Wayne Gomes .05
188 Ricky Bottalico .05
189 Mickey Morandini .05
190 Mike Lieberthal .05
191 *Kevin Polcovich* .05
192 Francisco Cordova .05
193 Kevin Young .05
194 Jon Lieber .05
195 Kevin Elster .05
196 Tony Womack .05
197 Lou Collier .05
198 *Mike Defelice* .05
199 Gary Gaetti .05
200 Dennis Eckersley .40
201 Alan Benes .05
202 Willie McGee .05
203 Ron Gant .05
204 Fernando Valenzuela .05
205 Mark McGwire 1.00
206 Archi Cianfrocco .05
207 Andy Ashby .05
208 Steve Finley .05
209 Quilvio Veras .05
210 Ken Caminiti .05
211 Rickey Henderson .50
212 Joey Hamilton .05
213 Derrek Lee .30
214 Bill Mueller .05
215 Shawn Estes .05
216 J.T. Snow .05
217 Mark Gardner .05
218 Terry Mulholland .05
219 Dante Powell .05
220 Jeff Kent .05
221 Jamie Moyer .05
222 Joey Cora .05
223 Jeff Fassero .05
224 Dennis Martinez .05
225 Ken Griffey Jr. .75
226 Edgar Martinez .05
227 Russ Davis .05
228 Dan Wilson .05
229 Will Clark .05
230 Ivan Rodriguez .40
231 Benji Gil .05
232 Lee Stevens .05
233 Mickey Tettleton .05
234 Julio Santana .05
235 Rusty Greer .05
236 Bobby Witt .05
237 Ed Sprague .05
238 Pat Hentgen .05
239 Kevin Escobar .05
240 Joe Carter .05
241 Carlos Delgado .25
242 Shannon Stewart .05
243 Benito Santiago .05
244 Tino Martinez .05
245 Ken Griffey Jr. .40
246 Kevin Brown .05
247 Ryne Sandberg .35
248 Mo Vaughn .05
249 Darryl Hamilton .05
250 Randy Johnson .20
251 Steve Finley .05
252 Bobby Higginson .05
253 Brett Tomko .05
254 Mark Kotsay .05
255 Jose Guillen .05
256 Elieser Marrero .05
257 Dennis Reyes .05
258 Richie Sexson .05
259 Pat Cline .05
260 Todd Helton .50
261 Juan Melo .05
262 Matt Morris .05
263 Jeremi Gonzalez .05
264 Jeff Abbott .05
265 Aaron Boone .05
266 Todd Dunwoody .05
267 Jaret Wright .05
268 Derrick Gibson .05

269 Mario Valdez .05
270 Fernando Tatis .05
271 Craig Counsell .05
272 Brad Rigby .05
273 Danny Clyburn .05
274 Brian Rose .05
275 Miguel Tejada .15
276 Jason Varitek .05
277 *David Dellucci* .15
278 Michael Coleman .05
279 Adam Riggs .05
280 Ben Grieve .05
281 Brad Fullmer .05
282 Ken Cloude .05
283 Tom Evans .05
284 *Kevin Millwood* .75
285 Paul Konerko .15
286 Juan Encarnacion .05
287 Chris Carpenter .05
288 Tom Fordham .05
289 Gary DiSarcina .05
290 Tim Salmon .05
291 Troy Percival .05
292 Todd Greene .05
293 Ken Hill .05
294 Dennis Springer .05
295 Jim Edmonds .05
296 Allen Watson .05
297 Brian Anderson .05
298 Keith Lockhart .05
299 Tom Glavine .20
300 Chipper Jones .65
301 Randall Simon .05
302 Mark Lemke .05
303 Ryan Klesko .05
304 Denny Neagle .05
305 Andruw Jones .50
306 Mike Mussina .30
307 Brady Anderson .05
308 Chris Hoiles .05
309 Mike Bordick .05
310 Cal Ripken Jr. 1.50
311 Geronimo Berroa .05
312 Armando Benitez .05
313 Roberto Alomar .25
314 Tim Wakefield .05
315 Reggie Jefferson .05
316 Jeff Frye .05
317 Scott Hatteberg .05
318 Steve Avery .05
319 Robinson Checo .05
320 Nomar Garciaparra .65
321 Lance Johnson .05
322 Tyler Houston .05
323 Mark Clark .05
324 Terry Adams .05
325 Sammy Sosa .65
326 Scott Servais .05
327 Manny Alexander .05
328 Norberto Martin .05
329 *Scott Eyre* .05
330 Frank Thomas .50
331 Robin Ventura .05
332 Matt Karchner .05
333 Keith Foulke .05
334 James Baldwin .05
335 Chris Stynes .05
336 Bret Boone .05
337 Jon Nunnally .05
338 Dave Burba .05
339 Eduardo Perez .05
340 Reggie Sanders .05
341 Mike Remlinger .05
342 Pat Watkins .05
343 Chad Ogea .05
344 John Smiley .05
345 Kenny Lofton .05
346 Jose Mesa .05
347 Charles Nagy .05
348 Bruce Aven .05
349 Enrique Wilson .05
350 Manny Ramirez .50
351 Jerry DiPoto .05
352 Ellis Burks .05
353 Kirt Manwaring .05
354 Vinny Castilla .05
355 Larry Walker .05
356 Kevin Ritz .05
357 Pedro Astacio .05
358 Scott Sanders .05
359 Deivi Cruz .05
360 Brian L. Hunter .05
361 Pedro Martinez .20
362 Tom Glavine .05
363 Willie McGee .05
364 J.T. Snow .05
365 Rusty Greer .05
366 Mike Grace .05
367 Tony Clark .05
368 Ben Grieve .05
369 Gary Sheffield .10
370 Joe Oliver .05
371 Todd Jones .05
372 *Frank Catalanotto* .10
373 Brian Moehler .05
374 Cliff Floyd .05
375 Bobby Bonilla .05
376 Al Leiter .05
377 Josh Booty .05
378 Darren Daulton .05
379 Jay Powell .05
380 Felix Heredia .05
381 Jim Eisenreich .05
382 Richard Hidalgo .05
383 Mike Hampton .05
384 Shane Reynolds .05
385 Jeff Bagwell .50
386 Derek Bell .05
387 Ricky Gutierrez .05
388 Bill Spiers .05
389 Jose Offerman .05
390 Johnny Damon .25
391 Jermaine Dye .05
392 Jeff Montgomery .05
393 Glendon Rusch .05
394 Mike Sweeney .05
395 Kevin Appier .05
396 Joe Vitiello .05
397 Ramon Martinez .05
398 Darren Dreifort .05
399 Wilton Guerrero .05
400 Mike Piazza .75
401 Eddie Murray .50
402 Ismael Valdes .05
403 Todd Hollandsworth .05
404 Mark Loretta .05
405 Jeromy Burnitz .05
406 Jeff Cirillo .05
407 Scott Karl .05
408 Mike Matheny .05
409 Jose Valentin .05
410 John Jaha .05
411 Terry Steinbach .05
412 Torii Hunter .05
413 Pat Meares .05
414 Marty Cordova .05
415 Jaret Wright .05
416 Mike Mussina .10
417 John Smoltz .05
418 Devon White .05
419 Denny Neagle .05
420 Livan Hernandez .05
421 Kevin Brown .05
422 Marquis Grissom .05
423 Mike Mussina .10
424 Eric Davis .05
425 Tony Fernandez .05
426 Moises Alou .05
427 Sandy Alomar Jr. .05
428 Gary Sheffield .10
429 Jaret Wright .05
430 Livan Hernandez .05
431 Chad Ogea .05
432 Edgar Renteria .05
433 LaTroy Hawkins .05
434 Rich Robertson .05
435 Chuck Knoblauch .05
436 Jose Vidro .05
437 Dustin Hermanson .05
438 Jim Bullinger .05
439 Orlando Cabrera .10
440 Vladimir Guerrero .50
441 Ugueth Urbina .05
442 Brian McRae .05
443 Matt Franco .05
444 Bobby Jones .05
445 Bernard Gilkey .05
446 Dave Mlicki .05
447 Brian Bohanon .05
448 Mel Rojas .05
449 Tim Raines .05
450 Derek Jeter 1.50
451 Roger Clemens .35
452 Nomar Garciaparra .35
453 Mike Piazza .40
454 Mark McGwire .50
455 Ken Griffey Jr. .40
456 Larry Walker .05
457 Alex Rodriguez .50
458 Tony Gwynn .25
459 Frank Thomas .20
460 Tino Martinez .05
461 Chad Curtis .05
462 Ramiro Mendoza .05
463 Joe Girardi .05
464 David Wells .05
465 Mariano Rivera .15
466 Willie Adams .05
467 George Williams .05
468 Dave Telgheder .05
469 Dave Magadan .05
470 Matt Stairs .05
471 Billy Taylor .05
472 Jimmy Haynes .05
473 Gregg Jefferies .05
474 Midre Cummings .05
475 Curt Schilling .15
476 Mike Grace .05
477 Mark Leiter .05
478 Matt Beech .05
479 Scott Rolen .35
480 Jason Kendall .05
481 Esteban Loaiza .05
482 Jermaine Allensworth .05
483 Mark Smith .05
484 Jason Schmidt .05
485 Jose Guillen .05
486 Al Martin .05
487 Delino DeShields .05
488 Todd Stottlemyre .05
489 Brian Jordan .05
490 Ray Lankford .05
491 Matt Morris .05
492 Royce Clayton .05
493 John Mabry .05
494 Wally Joyner .05
495 Trevor Hoffman .05
496 Chris Gomez .05
497 Sterling Hitchcock .05
498 Pete Smith .05
499 Greg Vaughn .05
500 Tony Gwynn .65
501 Will Cunnane .05
502 Darryl Hamilton .05
503 Brian Johnson .05
504 Kirk Rueter .05
505 Barry Bonds 1.50
506 Osvaldo Fernandez .05
507 Stan Javier .05
508 Julian Tavarez .05
509 Rich Aurilia .05
510 Alex Rodriguez 1.00
511 David Segui .05
512 Rich Amaral .05
513 Raul Ibanez .05
514 Jay Buhner .05
515 Randy Johnson .50
516 Heathcliff Slocumb .05
517 Tony Saunders .05
518 Kevin Elster .05
519 John Burkett .05
520 Juan Gonzalez .25
521 John Wetteland .05
522 Domingo Cedeno .05
523 Darren Oliver .05
524 Roger Pavlik .05
525 Jose Cruz Jr. .05
526 Woody Williams .05
527 Alex Gonzalez .05
528 Robert Person .05
529 Juan Guzman .05
530 Roger Clemens .70
531 Shawn Green .20
532 Cordova, Ricon, Smith .05
533 Nomar Garciaparra .35
534 Roger Clemens .35
535 Mark McGwire .50
536 Larry Walker .05
537 Mike Piazza .40
538 Curt Schilling .05
539 Tony Gwynn .25
540 Ken Griffey Jr. .40
541 Carl Pavano .05
542 Shane Monahan .05
543 *Gabe Kapler* .25
544 Eric Milton .05
545 *Gary Matthews Jr.* .05
546 *Mike Kinkade* .25
547 *Ryan Christenson* .10
548 *Corey Koskie* .25
549 Norm Hutchins .05
550 Russell Branyan .05
551 *Masato Yoshii* .25
552 *Jesus Sanchez* .05
553 Anthony Sanders .05
554 Edwin Diaz .05
555 Gabe Alvarez .05
556 *Carlos Lee* .25
557 Mike Darr .05
558 Kerry Wood .20
559 Carlos Guillen .05
560 Sean Casey .15
561 *Manny Aybar* .05
562 Octavio Dotel .05
563 Jarrod Washburn .05
564 Mark L. Johnson .05
565 Ramon Hernandez .05
566 *Rich Butler* .05
567 Mike Caruso .05
568 Cliff Politte .05
569 Scott Elarton .05
570 *Magglio Ordonez* 1.50
571 *Adam Butler* .05
572 Marlon Anderson .05
573 *Julio Ramirez* .05
574 *Darron Ingram* .05
575 Bruce Chen .05
576 *Steve Woodard* .05
577 Hiram Bocachica .05
578 Kevin Witt .05
579 Javier Vazquez .10
580 Alex Gonzalez .05
581 Brian Powell .05
582 Wes Helms .05
583 Ron Wright .05
584 Rafael Medina .05
585 Daryle Ward .05
586 Geoff Jenkins .05
587 Preston Wilson .10
588 *Jim Chamblee* .05
589 *Mike Lowell* .25
590 A.J. Hinch .05
591 *Francisco Cordero* .10
592 *Rolando Arrojo* .25
593 Braden Looper .05
594 Sidney Ponson .05
595 Matt Clement .05
596 Carlton Loewer .05
597 Brian Meadows .05
598 Danny Klassen .05
599 Larry Sutton .05
600 Travis Lee .15
601 Randy Johnson 1.50
602 Greg Maddux 2.00
603 Roger Clemens 2.25
604 Jaret Wright .25
605 Mike Piazza 2.50
606 Tino Martinez .25
607 Frank Thomas 1.50
608 Mo Vaughn .25
609 Todd Helton 1.00
610 Mark McGwire 3.00
611 Jeff Bagwell 1.50
612 Travis Lee .40
613 Scott Rolen 1.00
614 Cal Ripken Jr. 4.00
615 Chipper Jones 2.00
616 Nomar Garciaparra 2.00
617 Alex Rodriguez 3.00
618 Derek Jeter 4.00
619 Tony Gwynn 2.00
620 Ken Griffey Jr. 2.50
621 Kenny Lofton .25
622 Juan Gonzalez .75
623 Jose Cruz Jr. .25
624 Larry Walker .25
625 Barry Bonds 4.00
626 Ben Grieve .25
627 Andruw Jones 1.50
628 Vladimir Guerrero 1.50
629 Paul Konerko .50
630 Paul Molitor 1.50
631 Cecil Fielder .05
632 Jack McDowell .05
633 Mike James .05
634 Brian Anderson .05
635 Jay Bell .05
636 Devon White .05
637 Andy Stankiewicz .05
638 Tony Batista .05
639 Omar Daal .05
640 Matt Williams .05
641 Brent Brede .05
642 Jorge Fabregas .05
643 Karim Garcia .10
644 Felix Rodriguez .05
645 Andy Benes .05
646 Willie Blair .05
647 Jeff Suppan .05
648 Yamil Benitez .05
649 Walt Weiss .05
650 Andres Galarraga .05
651 Doug Drabek .05
652 Ozzie Guillen .05
653 Joe Carter .05
654 Dennis Eckersley .40
655 Pedro Martinez .50
656 Jim Leyritz .05
657 Henry Rodriguez .05
658 Rod Beck .05
659 Mickey Morandini .05
660 Jeff Blauser .05
661 Ruben Sierra .05
662 Mike Sirotka .05
663 Pete Harnisch .05
664 Damian Jackson .05

No.	Player	Price
665	Dmitri Young	.05
666	Steve Cooke	.05
667	Geronimo Berroa	.05
668	Shawon Dunston	.05
669	Mike Jackson	.05
670	Travis Fryman	.05
671	Dwight Gooden	.05
672	Paul Assenmacher	.05
673	Eric Plunk	.05
674	Mike Lansing	.05
675	Darryl Kile	.05
676	Luis Gonzalez	.05
677	Frank Castillo	.05
678	Joe Randa	.05
679	Bip Roberts	.05
680	Derrek Lee	.30
681a	Mike Piazza (Marlins)	2.00
681b	Mike Piazza (Mets)	1.00
682	Sean Berry	.05
683	Ramon Garcia	.05
684	Carl Everett	.05
685	Moises Alou	.05
686	Hal Morris	.05
687	Jeff Conine	.05
688	Gary Sheffield	.25
689	Jose Vizcaino	.05
690	Charles Johnson	.05
691	Bobby Bonilla	.05
692	Marquis Grissom	.05
693	Alex Ochoa	.05
694	Mike Morgan	.05
695	Orlando Merced	.05
696	David Ortiz	.30
697	Brent Gates	.05
698	Otis Nixon	.05
699	Trey Moore	.05
700	Derrick May	.05
701	Rich Becker	.05
702	Al Leiter	.05
703	Chili Davis	.05
704	Scott Brosius	.05
705	Chuck Knoblauch	.05
706	Kenny Rogers	.05
707	Mike Blowers	.05
708	Mike Fetters	.05
709	Tom Candiotti	.05
710	Rickey Henderson	.50
711	Bob Abreu	.05
712	Mark Lewis	.05
713	Doug Glanville	.05
714	Desi Relaford	.05
715	Kent Mercker	.05
716	J. Kevin Brown	.05
717	James Mouton	.05
718	Mark Langston	.05
719	Greg Myers	.05
720	Orel Hershiser	.05
721	Charlie Hayes	.05
722	Robb Nen	.05
723	Glenallen Hill	.05
724	Tony Saunders	.05
725	Wade Boggs	.65
726	Kevin Stocker	.05
727	Wilson Alvarez	.05
728	Albie Lopez	.05
729	Dave Martinez	.05
730	Fred McGriff	.05
731	Quinton McCracken	.05
732	Bryan Rekar	.05
733	Paul Sorrento	.05
734	Roberto Hernandez	.05
735	Bubba Trammell	.05
736	Miguel Cairo	.05
737	John Flaherty	.05
738	Terrell Wade	.05
739	Roberto Kelly	.05
740	Mark Mclemore (McLemore)	.05
741	Danny Patterson	.05
742	Aaron Sele	.05
743	Tony Fernandez	.05
744	Randy Myers	.05
745	Jose Canseco	.30
746	Darrin Fletcher	.05
747	Mike Stanley	.05
748	Marquis Grissom	.05
749	Fred McGriff	.05
750	Travis Lee	.05

Amazing Greats

		NM/M
Complete Set (30):		75.00
Common Player:		.60
Die-Cuts (250):		8X
1	Ken Griffey Jr.	5.00
2	Derek Jeter	7.50
3	Alex Rodriguez	6.00
4	Paul Molitor	3.00
5	Jeff Bagwell	3.00
6	Larry Walker	.60
7	Kenny Lofton	.60
8	Cal Ripken Jr.	7.50
9	Juan Gonzalez	1.50
10	Chipper Jones	4.00
11	Greg Maddux	4.00
12	Roberto Alomar	1.25
13	Mike Piazza	5.00
14	Andres Galarraga	.60
15	Barry Bonds	7.50
16	Andy Pettitte	1.25
17	Nomar Garciaparra	4.00
18	Hideki Irabu	.60
19	Tony Gwynn	4.00
20	Frank Thomas	3.00
21	Roger Clemens	4.50
22	Sammy Sosa	5.00
23	Jose Cruz, Jr.	.60
24	Manny Ramirez	3.00
25	Mark McGwire	6.00
26	Randy Johnson	3.00
27	Mo Vaughn	.60
28	Gary Sheffield	1.50
29	Andruw Jones	3.00
30	Albert Belle	.60

A Piece of the Action

		NM/M
Complete Set (14):		250.00
Common Player:		5.00
Inserted 1:2,500		
	SERIES 1	
(1)	Jay Buhner (bat)	25.00
(2)	Tony Gwynn (bat)	20.00
(3)	Tony Gwynn (jersey)	25.00
(4)	Todd Hollandsworth (bat)	5.00
(5)	Todd Hollandsworth (jersey)	5.00
(6)	Greg Maddux (jersey)	17.50
(7)	Alex Rodriguez (bat)	30.00
(8)	Alex Rodriguez (jersey)	35.00
(9)	Gary Sheffield (bat)	7.50
(10)	Gary Sheffield (jersey)	7.50
	SERIES 2	
RA	Roberto Alomar	35.00
JB	Jay Buhner	10.00
AJ	Andruw Jones	35.00
GS	Gary Sheffield	15.00

Blue Chip Prospects

		NM/M
Complete Set (30):		75.00
Common Player:		2.00
1	Nomar Garciaparra	9.00
2	Scott Rolen	5.00
3	Jason Dickson	2.00
4	Darin Erstad	3.00
5	Brad Fullmer	2.00
6	Jaret Wright	2.00
7	Justin Thompson	2.00
8	Matt Morris	2.00
9	Fernando Tatis	2.00
10	Alex Rodriguez	12.50
11	Todd Helton	6.50
12	Andy Pettitte	2.50
13	Jose Cruz Jr.	2.00
14	Mark Kotsay	2.00
15	Derek Jeter	15.00
16	Paul Konerko	3.00
17	Todd Dunwoody	2.00
18	Vladimir Guerrero	7.50
19	Miguel Tejada	5.00
20	Chipper Jones	9.00
21	Kevin Orie	2.00
22	Juan Encarnacion	2.00
23	Brian Rose	2.00
24	Andruw Jones	7.50
25	Livan Hernandez	2.00
26	Brian Giles	2.00
27	Brett Tomko	2.00
28	Jose Guillen	2.00
29	Aaron Boone	2.00
30	Ben Grieve	2.00

Clearly Dominant

		NM/M
Complete Set (30):		300.00
Common Player:		3.00
Production 250 sets		
1	Mark McGwire	25.00
2	Derek Jeter	30.00
3	Alex Rodriguez	25.00
4	Paul Molitor	12.00
5	Jeff Bagwell	12.00
6	Ivan Rodriguez	10.00
7	Kenny Lofton	3.00
8	Cal Ripken Jr.	30.00
9	Albert Belle	3.00
10	Chipper Jones	15.00
11	Gary Sheffield	5.00
12	Roberto Alomar	4.00
13	Mo Vaughn	3.00
14	Andres Galarraga	3.00
15	Nomar Garciaparra	15.00
16	Randy Johnson	12.00
17	Mike Mussina	6.00
18	Greg Maddux	15.00
19	Tony Gwynn	15.00
20	Frank Thomas	12.00
21	Roger Clemens	17.50
22	Dennis Eckersley	10.00
23	Juan Gonzalez	6.00
24	Tino Martinez	3.00
25	Andruw Jones	12.00
26	Larry Walker	3.00
27	Ken Caminiti	3.00
28	Mike Piazza	20.00
29	Barry Bonds	30.00
30	Ken Griffey Jr.	20.00

Ken Griffey Jr.'s HR Chronicles

	NM/M
Complete Set (56):	45.00
Common Card:	1.00
Inserted 1:9	
1-56 Ken Griffey Jr.	

Rookie cards are in *Italic*.

Mark McGwire's Chase for 62

		NM/M
Complete Boxed Set:		7.50
Common Card:		.50
1-30	Mark McGwire	.50
---	Mark McGwire (3-1/2" x 5" HR #61/62)	3.00

National Pride

		NM/M
Complete Set (42):		65.00
Common Player:		.75
1	Dave Nilsson	.75
2	Larry Walker	.75
3	Edgar Renteria	.75
4	Jose Canseco	1.25
5	Rey Ordonez	.75
6	Rafael Palmeiro	2.50
7	Livan Hernandez	.75
8	Andruw Jones	3.00
9	Manny Ramirez	3.00
10	Sammy Sosa	4.00
11	Raul Mondesi	.75
12	Moises Alou	.75
13	Pedro Martinez	3.00
14	Vladimir Guerrero	3.00
15	Chili Davis	.75
16	Hideo Nomo	1.50
17	Hideki Irabu	.75
18	Shigetosi Hasegawa	.75
19	Takashi Kashiwada	.75
20	Chan Ho Park	.75
21	Fernando Valenzuela	.75
22	Vinny Castilla	.75
23	Armando Reynoso	.75
24	Karim Garcia	1.00
25	Marvin Benard	.75
26	Mariano Rivera	1.00
27	Juan Gonzalez	1.50
28	Roberto Alomar	1.00
29	Ivan Rodriguez	2.50
30	Carlos Delgado	1.00
31	Bernie Williams	.75
32	Edgar Martinez	.75
33	Frank Thomas	3.00
34	Barry Bonds	7.50
35	Mike Piazza	5.00
36	Chipper Jones	4.00
37	Cal Ripken Jr.	7.50
38	Alex Rodriguez	6.00
39	Ken Griffey Jr.	5.00
40	Andres Galarraga	.75
41	Omar Vizquel	.75
42	Ozzie Guillen	.75

Prime Nine

	NM/M
Complete Set (60):	50.00
Common Griffey:	1.00
Common Piazza:	1.25
Common Thomas:	.60
Common McGwire:	1.25
Common Ripken:	1.75
Common Gonzalez:	.50
Common Gwynn:	.70
Common Bonds:	1.75

Common Maddux:		.70
Inserted 1:5		
PN11	Mike Piazza (1994)	1.00

Tape Measure Titans

		NM/M
Complete Set (30):		45.00
Common Player:		.40
Inserted 1:23		
Gold:		1.5X
1	Mark McGwire	5.00
2	Andres Galarraga	.40
3	Jeff Bagwell	2.00
4	Larry Walker	.40
5	Frank Thomas	2.50
6	Rafael Palmeiro	1.50
7	Nomar Garciaparra	4.00
8	Mo Vaughn	.40
9	Albert Belle	.60
10	Ken Griffey Jr.	4.00
11	Manny Ramirez	2.00
12	Jim Thome	.40
13	Tony Clark	.40
14	Juan Gonzalez	2.00
15	Mike Piazza	4.00
16	Jose Canseco	1.00
17	Jay Buhner	.40
18	Alex Rodriguez	5.00
19	Jose Cruz Jr.	.40
20	Tino Martinez	.40
21	Carlos Delgado	.75
22	Andruw Jones	2.00
23	Chipper Jones	3.00
24	Fred McGriff	.40
25	Matt Williams	.40
26	Sammy Sosa	4.00
27	Vinny Castilla	.40
28	Tim Salmon	.60
29	Ken Caminiti	.40
30	Barry Bonds	6.00

Rookie Edition Preview

		NM/M
Complete Set (10):		5.00
Common Player:		.50
1	Nomar Garciaparra	2.00
2	Scott Rolen	1.00
3	Mark Kotsay	.50
4	Todd Helton	1.50
5	Paul Konerko	.60
6	Juan Encarnacion	.50
7	Brad Fullmer	.50
8	Miguel Tejada	.65
9	Richard Hidalgo	.50
10	Ben Grieve	.50

Rookie Edition A Piece of the Action

		NM/M
Common Card:		15.00

KG	Ken Griffey Jr. (300)	100.00
KGS	Ken Griffey Jr. (24) (Signed)	300.00
BG	Ben Grieve (200)	15.00
JC	Jose Cruz Jr. (200)	15.00
TL	Travis Lee (200)	15.00

Rookie Edition Eminent Prestige 5x7

		NM/M
Complete Set (10):		25.00
Common Player:		2.00
605	Mike Piazza	3.50
607	Frank Thomas	2.50
610	Mark McGwire	4.00
611	Jeff Bagwell	2.50
612	Travis Lee	2.00
614	Cal Ripken Jr.	5.00
616	Nomar Garciaparra	3.00
617	Alex Rodriguez	4.00
619	Tony Gwynn	3.00
620	Ken Griffey Jr.	3.50

Rookie Edition All-Star Credentials

		NM/M
Complete Set (30):		25.00
Common Player:		.25
Inserted 1:9		
AS1	Ken Griffey Jr.	1.50
AS2	Travis Lee	.40
AS3	Ben Grieve	.25
AS4	Jose Cruz Jr.	.25
AS5	Andruw Jones	.75
AS6	Craig Biggio	.25
AS7	Hideo Nomo	.40
AS8	Cal Ripken Jr.	2.50
AS9	Jaret Wright	.25
AS10	Mark McGwire	2.00
AS11	Derek Jeter	2.50
AS12	Scott Rolen	.60
AS13	Jeff Bagwell	.75
AS14	Manny Ramirez	.75
AS15	Alex Rodriguez	2.00
AS16	Chipper Jones	1.00
AS17	Larry Walker	.25
AS18	Barry Bonds	2.50
AS19	Tony Gwynn	1.00
AS20	Mike Piazza	1.50
AS21	Roger Clemens	1.25
AS22	Greg Maddux	1.00
AS23	Jim Thome	.60
AS24	Tino Martinez	.25
AS25	Nomar Garciaparra	1.00
AS26	Juan Gonzalez	.40
AS27	Kenny Lofton	.25
AS28	Randy Johnson	.75
AS29	Todd Helton	.65
AS30	Frank Thomas	.75

Rookie Edition Destination Stardom

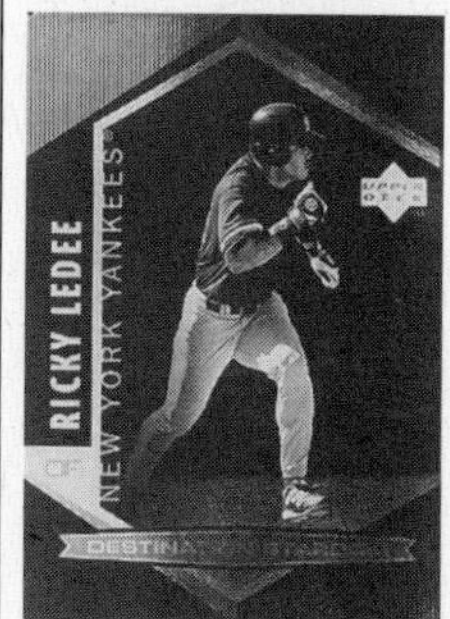

		NM/M
Complete Set (60):		40.00
Common Player:		.50
Inserted 1:5		
1	Travis Lee	.75
2	Nomar Garciaparra	3.50
3	Alex Gonzalez	.50
4	Richard Hidalgo	.50
5	Jaret Wright	.50
6	Mike Kinkade	.50
7	Matt Morris	.50
8	Gary Mathews Jr.	.50
9	Brett Tomko	.50
10	Todd Helton	2.00
11	Scott Elarton	.50
12	Scott Rolen	1.50
13	Jose Cruz Jr.	.50
14	Jarrod Washburn	.50
15	Sean Casey	.50
16	Magglio Ordonez	2.00
17	Gabe Alvarez	.50
18	Todd Dunwoody	.50
19	Kevin Witt	.50
20	Ben Grieve	.50
21	Daryle Ward	.50
22	Matt Clement	.50
23	Carlton Loewer	.50
24	Javier Vazquez	.50
25	Paul Konerko	.75
26	Preston Wilson	.60
27	Wes Helms	.50
28	Derek Jeter	5.00
29	Corey Koskie	.50
30	Russell Branyan	.50
31	Vladimir Guerrero	2.50
32	Ryan Christenson	.50
33	Carlos Lee	.60
34	David Dellucci	.50
35	Bruce Chen	.50
36	Ricky Ledee	.50
37	Ron Wright	.50
38	Derrek Lee	1.50
39	Miguel Tejada	.75
40	Brad Fullmer	.50
41	Rich Butler	.50
42	Chris Carpenter	.50
43	Alex Rodriguez	4.00
44	Darron Ingram	.50
45	Kerry Wood	1.50
46	Jason Varitek	.50
47	Ramon Hernandez	.50
48	Aaron Boone	.50
49	Juan Encarnacion	.50
50	A.J. Hinch	.50
51	Mike Lowell	.60
52	Fernando Tatis	.50
53	Jose Guillen	.50
54	Mike Caruso	.50
55	Carl Pavano	.50
56	Chris Clemons	.50
57	Mark L. Johnson	.50
58	Ken Cloude	.50
59	Rolando Arrojo	.50
60	Mark Kotsay	.50

Rookie Edition Unparalleled

		NM/M
Complete Set (20):		75.00
Common Player:		1.00
Inserted 1:72		
1	Ken Griffey Jr.	6.00
2	Travis Lee	1.50
3	Ben Grieve	1.00
4	Jose Cruz Jr.	1.00
5	Nomar Garciaparra	5.00
6	Hideo Nomo	1.75
7	Kenny Lofton	1.00
8	Cal Ripken Jr.	10.00
9	Roger Clemens	5.50
10	Mike Piazza	6.00
11	Jeff Bagwell	3.50
12	Chipper Jones	5.00
13	Greg Maddux	5.00
14	Randy Johnson	3.50
15	Alex Rodriguez	7.50
16	Barry Bonds	10.00
17	Frank Thomas	3.50
18	Juan Gonzalez	1.75
19	Tony Gwynn	5.00
20	Mark McGwire	7.50

Rookie Edition Retrospectives

		NM/M
Complete Set (30):		55.00
Common Player:		.50
Inserted 1:24		
1	Dennis Eckersley	2.50
2	Rickey Henderson	3.00
3	Harold Baines	.50
4	Cal Ripken Jr.	7.50
5	Tony Gwynn	4.00
6	Wade Boggs	4.00
7	Orel Hershiser	.50
8	Joe Carter	.50
9	Roger Clemens	4.50
10	Barry Bonds	7.50
11	Mark McGwire	6.00
12	Greg Maddux	4.00
13	Fred McGriff	.50
14	Rafael Palmeiro	3.00
15	Craig Biggio	.50
16	Brady Anderson	.50
17	Randy Johnson	3.00
18	Gary Sheffield	1.00
19	Albert Belle	.50
20	Ken Griffey Jr.	5.00
21	Juan Gonzalez	1.50
22	Larry Walker	.50
23	Tino Martinez	.50
24	Frank Thomas	3.00
25	Jeff Bagwell	3.00
26	Kenny Lofton	.50
27	Mo Vaughn	.50
28	Mike Piazza	5.00
29	Alex Rodriguez	6.00
30	Chipper Jones	4.00

1998 UPPER DECK SPECIAL F/X

		NM/M
Complete Set (150):		30.00
Common Player:		.05
1	Ken Griffey Jr.	1.00
2	Mark McGwire	1.25
3	Alex Rodriguez	2.50
4	Larry Walker	.05
5	Tino Martinez	.05
6	Mike Piazza	2.50
7	Jose Cruz Jr.	.05
8	Greg Maddux	.75
9	Tony Gwynn	.75

10	Roger Clemens	1.75
11	Jason Dickson	.05
12	Darin Erstad	.25
13	Chuck Finley	.05
14	Dave Hollins	.05
15	Garret Anderson	.05
16	Michael Tucker	.05
17	Javier Lopez	.05
18	John Smoltz	.05
19	Mark Wohlers	.05
20	Greg Maddux	1.50
21	Scott Erickson	.05
22	Jimmy Key	.05
23	B.J. Surhoff	.05
24	Eric Davis	.05
25	Rafael Palmeiro	.75
26	Tim Naehring	.05
27	Darren Bragg	.05
28	Troy O'Leary	.05
29	John Valentin	.05
30	Mo Vaughn	.05
31	Mark Grace	.05
32	Kevin Foster	.05
33	Kevin Tapani	.05
34	Kevin Orie	.05
35	Albert Belle	.05
36	Ray Durham	.05
37	Jaime Navarro	.05
38	Mike Cameron	.05
39	Eddie Taubensee	.05
40	Barry Larkin	.05
41	Willie Greene	.05
42	Jeff Shaw	.05
43	Omar Vizquel	.05
44	Brian Giles	.05
45	Jim Thome	.60
46	David Justice	.05
47	Sandy Alomar Jr.	.05
48	Neifi Perez	.05
49	Dante Bichette	.05
50	Vinny Castilla	.05
51	John Thomson	.05
52	Damion Easley	.05
53	Justin Thompson	.05
54	Bobby Higginson	.05
55	Tony Clark	.05
56	Charles Johnson	.05
57	Edgar Renteria	.05
58	Alex Fernandez	.05
59	Gary Sheffield	.50
60	Livan Hernandez	.05
61	Craig Biggio	.05
62	Chris Holt	.05
63	Billy Wagner	.05
64	Brad Ausmus	.05
65	Dean Palmer	.05
66	Tim Belcher	.05
67	Jeff King	.05
68	Jose Rosado	.05
69	Chan Ho Park	.05
70	Raul Mondesi	.05
71	Hideo Nomo	.50
72	Todd Zeile	.05
73	Eric Karros	.05
74	Cal Eldred	.05
75	Jeff D'Amico	.05
76	Doug Jones	.05
77	Dave Nilsson	.05
78	Todd Walker	.05
79	Rick Aguilera	.05
80	Paul Molitor	1.00
81	Brad Radke	.05
82	Vladimir Guerrero	1.00
83	Carlos Perez	.05
84	F.P. Santangelo	.05
85	Rondell White	.05
86	Butch Huskey	.05
87	Edgardo Alfonzo	.05
88	John Franco	.05
89	John Olerud	.05
90	Todd Hundley	.05
91	Bernie Williams	.05
92	Andy Pettitte	.30
93	Paul O'Neill	.05
94	David Cone	.05
95	Jason Giambi	.50
96	Damon Mashore	.05
97	Scott Spiezio	.05
98	Ariel Prieto	.05
99	Rico Brogna	.05
100	Mike Lieberthal	.05
101	Garrett Stephenson	.05
102	Ricky Bottalico	.05
103	Kevin Polcovich	.05
104	Jon Lieber	.05
105	Kevin Young	.05
106	Tony Womack	.05
107	Gary Gaetti	.05
108	Alan Benes	.05
109	Willie McGee	.05
110	Mark McGwire	2.50
111	Ron Gant	.05
112	Andy Ashby	.05
113	Steve Finley	.05
114	Quilvio Veras	.05
115	Ken Caminiti	.05
116	Joey Hamilton	.05
117	Bill Mueller	.05
118	Mark Gardner	.05
119	Shawn Estes	.05
120	J.T. Snow	.05
121	Dante Powell	.05
122	Jeff Kent	.05
123	Jamie Moyer	.05
124	Joey Cora	.05
125	Ken Griffey Jr.	2.00
126	Jeff Fassero	.05
127	Edgar Martinez	.05
128	Will Clark	.05
129	Lee Stevens	.05
130	Ivan Rodriguez	.75
131	Rusty Greer	.05
132	Ed Sprague	.05
133	Pat Hentgen	.05
134	Shannon Stewart	.05
135	Carlos Delgado	.40
136	Brett Tomko	.05
137	Jose Guillen	.05
138	Elieser Marrero	.05
139	Dennis Reyes	.05
140	Mark Kotsay	.05
141	Richie Sexson	.05
142	Todd Helton	.75
143	Jeremi Gonzalez	.05
144	Jeff Abbott	.05
145	Matt Morris	.05
146	Aaron Boone	.05
147	Todd Dunwoody	.05
148	Mario Valdez	.05
149	Fernando Tatis	.05
150	Jaret Wright	.05

Power Zone

		NM/M
Complete Set (20):		40.00
Common Player:		.50
Inserted 1:7		
PZ1	Jose Cruz Jr.	.50
PZ2	Frank Thomas	2.50
PZ3	Juan Gonzalez	1.25
PZ4	Mike Piazza	4.50
PZ5	Mark McGwire	4.50
PZ6	Barry Bonds	6.00
PZ7	Greg Maddux	3.00
PZ8	Alex Rodriguez	4.50
PZ9	Nomar Garciaparra	3.00
PZ10	Ken Griffey Jr.	3.50
PZ11	John Smoltz	.50
PZ12	Andruw Jones	2.50
PZ13	Sandy Alomar Jr.	.50
PZ14	Roberto Alomar	1.00
PZ15	Chipper Jones	3.00
PZ16	Kenny Lofton	.50
PZ17	Larry Walker	.50
PZ18	Jeff Bagwell	2.50
PZ19	Mo Vaughn	.50
PZ20	Tom Glavine	1.00

OctoberBest

		NM/M
Complete Set (15):		40.00
Common Player:		1.00
Inserted 1:34		
PZ1	Frank Thomas	3.00
PZ2	Juan Gonzalez	1.50
PZ3	Mike Piazza	5.00
PZ4	Mark McGwire	6.00
PZ5	Jeff Bagwell	3.00
PZ6	Barry Bonds	7.50
PZ7	Ken Griffey Jr.	5.00
PZ8	John Smoltz	1.00
PZ9	Andruw Jones	3.00
PZ10	Greg Maddux	4.00
PZ11	Sandy Alomar Jr.	1.00
PZ12	Roberto Alomar	1.25
PZ13	Chipper Jones	4.00
PZ14	Kenny Lofton	1.00
PZ15	Tom Glavine	1.25

Power Driven

		NM/M
Complete Set (10):		40.00
Common Player:		1.50
Inserted 1:69		
PZ1	Frank Thomas	4.50
PZ2	Juan Gonzalez	2.50
PZ3	Mike Piazza	6.00
PZ4	Larry Walker	1.50
PZ5	Mark McGwire	7.50
PZ6	Jeff Bagwell	4.50
PZ7	Mo Vaughn	1.50
PZ8	Barry Bonds	10.00
PZ9	Tino Martinez	1.50
PZ10	Ken Griffey Jr.	6.00

Superstar Xcitement

		NM/M
Complete Set (10):		275.00
Common Player:		10.00
Production 250 sets		
PZ1	Jose Cruz Jr.	10.00
PZ2	Frank Thomas	25.00
PZ3	Juan Gonzalez	10.00
PZ4	Mike Piazza	40.00
PZ5	Mark McGwire	45.00
PZ6	Barry Bonds	50.00
PZ7	Greg Maddux	35.00
PZ8	Alex Rodriguez	45.00
PZ9	Nomar Garciaparra	35.00
PZ10	Ken Griffey Jr.	40.00

1998 UPPER DECK UD 3

		NM/M
Complete Set (270):		200.00
Common Future Impact (1-30):		.50
Inserted 1:12		
Die-Cuts (2,000 sets):		1X
Common Power Corps (31-60):		.25
Inserted 1:1		
Die-Cuts (2,000 sets):		3X
Common Establishment (61-90):		.25
Inserted 1:6		
Die-Cuts (2,000 sets):		2X
Common Future Impact Embossed (91-120):		.25
Inserted 1:6		
Die-Cuts (1,000 sets):		3X
Common Power Corps Embossed (121-150):		.25
Inserted 1:4		
Die-Cuts (1,000 sets):		6X
Common Establishment Embossed (151-180):		.25
Inserted 1:1		
Die-Cuts (1,000 sets):		12X
Common Future Impact Rainbow (181-210):		.25
Inserted 1:1		
Die-Cuts (100 sets):		15X
Common Power Corps Rainbow (211-240):		.50
Inserted 1:12		
Die-Cuts (100 sets):		8X
Common Establishment Rainbow (241-270):		.75
Inserted 1:24		
Die-Cuts (100 sets):		5X
Pack (3):		1.00
Wax Box (24):		20.00
	LIGHT FX FUTURE IMPACT (1:12)	
1	Travis Lee	.50
2	A.J. Hinch	.50
3	Mike Caruso	.50
4	Miguel Tejada	.75
5	Brad Fullmer	.50
6	Eric Milton	.50
7	Mark Kotsay	.50
8	Darin Erstad	.75
9	Magglio Ordonez	1.00
10	Ben Grieve	.50
11	Brett Tomko	.50
12	*Mike Kinkade*	.75
13	Rolando Arrojo	.50
14	Todd Helton	1.00
15	Scott Rolen	1.00
16	Bruce Chen	.50
17	Daryle Ward	.50
18	Jaret Wright	.50
19	Sean Casey	.65
20	Paul Konerko	.65
21	Kerry Wood	1.00
22	Russell Branyan	.50
23	Gabe Alvarez	.50
24	Juan Encarnacion	.50
25	Andruw Jones	1.50
26	Vladimir Guerrero	1.50
27	Eli Marrero	.50
28	Matt Clement	.50
29	Gary Matthews Jr.	.50
30	Derrek Lee	1.50
	LIGHT FX POWER CORPS (1:1)	
31	Ken Caminiti	.25
32	Gary Sheffield	.50
33	Jay Buhner	.25
34	Ryan Klesko	.25
35	Nomar Garciaparra	.75
36	Vinny Castilla	.25
37	Tony Clark	.25
38	Sammy Sosa	.75
39	Tino Martinez	.25
40	Mike Piazza	1.00
41	Manny Ramirez	.65
42	Larry Walker	.25
43	Jose Cruz Jr.	.25
44	Matt Williams	.25
45	Frank Thomas	.65
46	Jim Edmonds	.25
47	Raul Mondesi	.25
48	Alex Rodriguez	1.50
49	Albert Belle	.25
50	Mark McGwire	1.50
51	Tim Salmon	.25
52	Andres Galarraga	.25
53	Jeff Bagwell	.65
54	Jim Thome	.50
55	Barry Bonds	2.50
56	Carlos Delgado	.40
57	Mo Vaughn	.25
58	Chipper Jones	.75
59	Juan Gonzalez	.40
60	Ken Griffey Jr.	1.00
	LIGHT FX THE ESTABLISHMENT (1:6)	
61	David Cone	.25

62 Hideo Nomo .75
63 Edgar Martinez .25
64 Fred McGriff .25
65 Cal Ripken Jr. 4.00
66 Todd Hundley .25
67 Barry Larkin .25
68 Dennis Eckersley 1.00
69 Randy Johnson 1.50
70 Paul Molitor 1.50
71 Eric Karros .25
72 Rafael Palmeiro 1.00
73 Chuck Knoblauch .25
74 Ivan Rodriguez 1.25
75 Greg Maddux 2.00
76 Dante Bichette .25
77 Brady Anderson .25
78 Craig Biggio .25
79 Derek Jeter 4.00
80 Roger Clemens 2.25
81 Roberto Alomar .40
82 Wade Boggs 2.00
83 Charles Johnson .25
84 Mark Grace .25
85 Kenny Lofton .25
86 Mike Mussina 1.00
87 Pedro Martinez 1.50
88 Curt Schilling .50
89 Bernie Williams .25
90 Tony Gwynn 2.00

EMBOSSED FUTURE IMPACT (1:6)

91 Travis Lee .40
92 A.J. Hinch .25
93 Mike Caruso .25
94 Miguel Tejada .40
95 Brad Fullmer .25
96 Eric Milton .25
97 Mark Kotsay .25
98 Darin Erstad 1.00
99 Magglio Ordonez 1.00
100 Ben Grieve .25
101 Brett Tomko .25
102 *Mike Kinkade* .40
103 Rolando Arrojo .25
104 Todd Helton 1.00
105 Scott Rolen 1.00
106 Bruce Chen .25
107 Daryle Ward .25
108 Jaret Wright .25
109 Sean Casey .25
110 Paul Konerko .40
111 Kerry Wood 1.00
112 Russell Branyan .25
113 Gabe Alvarez .25
114 Juan Encarnacion .25
115 Andruw Jones 1.50
116 Vladimir Guerrero 1.50
117 Eli Marrero .25
118 Matt Clement .25
119 Gary Matthews Jr. .25
120 Derrek Lee 1.00

EMBOSSED POWER CORPS (1:4)

121 Ken Caminiti .25
122 Gary Sheffield .50
123 Jay Buhner .25
124 Ryan Klesko .25
125 Nomar Garciaparra 1.50
126 Vinny Castilla .25
127 Tony Clark .25
128 Sammy Sosa 1.50
129 Tino Martinez .25
130 Mike Piazza 2.00
131 Manny Ramirez 1.00
132 Larry Walker .25
133 Jose Cruz Jr. .25
134 Matt Williams .25
135 Frank Thomas 1.00
136 Jim Edmonds .25
137 Raul Mondesi .25
138 Alex Rodriguez 3.00
139 Albert Belle .25
140 Mark McGwire 3.00
141 Tim Salmon .25
142 Andres Galarraga .25
143 Jeff Bagwell 1.00
144 Jim Thome .75
145 Barry Bonds 5.00
146 Carlos Delgado .50
147 Mo Vaughn .25
148 Chipper Jones 1.50
149 Juan Gonzalez .50
150 Ken Griffey Jr. 2.00

EMBOSSED THE ESTABLISHMENT (1:1)

151 David Cone .25
152 Hideo Nomo .40
153 Edgar Martinez .25
154 Fred McGriff .25
155 Cal Ripken Jr. 2.00
156 Todd Hundley .25
157 Barry Larkin .25
158 Dennis Eckersley .65
159 Randy Johnson .75
160 Paul Molitor .75
161 Eric Karros .25
162 Rafael Palmeiro .65
163 Chuck Knoblauch .25
164 Ivan Rodriguez .65
165 Greg Maddux 1.00
166 Dante Bichette .25
167 Brady Anderson .25
168 Craig Biggio .25
169 Derek Jeter 2.00
170 Roger Clemens 1.25
171 Roberto Alomar .30
172 Wade Boggs 1.00
173 Charles Johnson .25
174 Mark Grace .25
175 Kenny Lofton .25
176 Mike Mussina .40
177 Pedro Martinez .75
178 Curt Schilling .40
179 Bernie Williams .25
180 Tony Gwynn 1.00

RAINBOW FUTURE IMPACT (1:1)

181 Travis Lee .40
182 A.J. Hinch .25
183 Mike Caruso .25
184 Miguel Tejada .40
185 Brad Fullmer .25
186 Eric Milton .25
187 Mark Kotsay .25
188 Darin Erstad .50
189 Magglio Ordonez 1.25
190 Ben Grieve .25
191 Brett Tomko .25
192 *Mike Kinkade* .40
193 Rolando Arrojo .25
194 Todd Helton .65
195 Scott Rolen .60
196 Bruce Chen .25
197 Daryle Ward .25
198 Jaret Wright .25
199 Sean Casey .40
200 Paul Konerko .40
201 Kerry Wood .60
202 Russell Branyan .25
203 Gabe Alvarez .25
204 Juan Encarnacion .25
205 Andruw Jones 1.50
206 Vladimir Guerrero 1.50
207 Eli Marrero .25
208 Matt Clement .25
209 Gary Matthews Jr. .25
210 Derrek Lee 1.00

RAINBOW POWER CORPS (1:12)

211 Ken Caminiti .50
212 Gary Sheffield 1.00
213 Jay Buhner .50
214 Ryan Klesko .50
215 Nomar Garciaparra 3.00
216 Vinny Castilla .50
217 Tony Clark .50
218 Sammy Sosa 3.00
219 Tino Martinez .50
220 Mike Piazza 4.00
221 Manny Ramirez 2.00
222 Larry Walker .50
223 Jose Cruz Jr. .50
224 Matt Williams .50
225 Frank Thomas 2.00
226 Jim Edmonds .50
227 Raul Mondesi .50
228 Alex Rodriguez 6.00
229 Albert Belle .50
230 Mark McGwire 6.00
231 Tim Salmon .50
232 Andres Galarraga .50
233 Jeff Bagwell 2.00
234 Jim Thome 1.50
235 Barry Bonds 9.00
236 Carlos Delgado .75
267 Mo Vaughn .50
238 Chipper Jones 3.00
239 Juan Gonzalez 1.00
240 Ken Griffey Jr. 4.00

RAINBOW THE ESTABLISHMENT (1:24)

241 David Cone .75
242 Hideo Nomo 1.50
243 Edgar Martinez .75
244 Fred McGriff .75
245 Cal Ripken Jr. 12.00
246 Todd Hundley .75
247 Barry Larkin .75
248 Dennis Eckersley 3.00
249 Randy Johnson 4.50
250 Paul Molitor 4.50
251 Eric Karros .75
252 Rafael Palmeiro 3.50
253 Chuck Knoblauch .75
254 Ivan Rodriguez 4.00
255 Greg Maddux 6.00
256 Dante Bichette .75
257 Brady Anderson .75
258 Craig Biggio .75
259 Derek Jeter 12.00
260 Roger Clemens 6.50
261 Roberto Alomar 1.25
262 Wade Boggs 6.00
263 Charles Johnson .75
264 Mark Grace .75
265 Kenny Lofton .75
266 Mike Mussina 1.25
267 Pedro Martinez 4.50
268 Curt Schilling 1.50
269 Bernie Williams .75
270 Tony Gwynn 6.00

Power Corps Jumbos

		NM/M
Complete Set (10):		60.00
Common Player:		2.50
35	Ken Griffey Jr.	7.50
38	Sammy Sosa	6.00
40	Mike Piazza	7.50
45	Frank Thomas	5.00
48	Alex Rodriguez	10.00
50	Mark McGwire	10.00
55	Barry Bonds	12.50
58	Chipper Jones	6.00
59	Juan Gonzalez	2.50
60	Ken Griffey Jr.	7.50

1998 UD RETRO

		NM/M
Complete Set (129):		15.00
Common Player:		.05
Pack (6):		2.25
Lunchbox (24):		40.00

1 Jim Edmonds .05
2 Darin Erstad .25
3 Tim Salmon .05
4 Jay Bell .05
5 Matt Williams .05
6 Andres Galarraga .05
7 Andruw Jones .60
8 Chipper Jones .75
9 Greg Maddux .75
10 Rafael Palmeiro .50
11 Cal Ripken Jr. 2.00
12 Brooks Robinson .15
13 Nomar Garciaparra .75
14 Pedro Martinez .60
15 Mo Vaughn .05
16 Ernie Banks .50
17 Mark Grace .05
18 Gary Matthews .05
19 Sammy Sosa .75
20 Albert Belle .05
21 Carlton Fisk .15
22 Frank Thomas .60
23 Ken Griffey Sr. .05
24 Paul Konerko .15
25 Barry Larkin .05
26 Sean Casey .10
27 Tony Perez .05
28 Bob Feller .15
29 Kenny Lofton .05
30 Manny Ramirez .60
31 Jim Thome .45
32 Omar Vizquel .05
33 Dante Bichette .05
34 Larry Walker .05
35 Tony Clark .05
36 Damion Easley .05
37 Cliff Floyd .05
38 Livan Hernandez .05
39 Jeff Bagwell .60
40 Craig Biggio .05
41 Al Kaline .15
42 Johnny Damon .20
43 Dean Palmer .05
44 Charles Johnson .05
45 Eric Karros .05
46 Gaylord Perry .05
47 Raul Mondesi .05
48 Gary Sheffield .30
49 Eddie Mathews .15
50 Warren Spahn .15
51 Jeromy Burnitz .05
52 Jeff Cirillo .05
53 Marquis Grissom .05
54 Paul Molitor .60
55 Kirby Puckett .75
56 Brad Radke .05
57 Todd Walker .05
58 Vladimir Guerrero .60
59 Brad Fullmer .05
60 Rondell White .05
61 Bobby Jones .05
62 Hideo Nomo .30
63 Mike Piazza 1.00
64 Tom Seaver .15
65 Frank J. Thomas .05
66 Yogi Berra .50
67 Derek Jeter 2.00
68 Tino Martinez .05
69 Paul O'Neill .05
70 Andy Pettitte .20
71 Rollie Fingers .05
72 Rickey Henderson .60
73 Matt Stairs .05
74 Scott Rolen .50
75 Curt Schilling .25
76 Jose Guillen .05
77 Jason Kendall .05
78 Lou Brock .10
79 Bob Gibson .10
80 Ray Lankford .05
81 Mark McGwire 1.50
82 NOT ISSUED
83 Kevin Brown .05
84 Ken Caminiti .05
85 Tony Gwynn .75
86 Greg Vaughn .05
87 Barry Bonds 2.00
88 Willie Stargell .10
89 Willie McCovey .10
90 Ken Griffey Jr. 1.00
91 Randy Johnson .60
92 Alex Rodriguez 1.50
93 Quinton McCracken .05
94 Fred McGriff .05
95 Juan Gonzalez .30
96 Ivan Rodriguez .50
97 Nolan Ryan 1.50
98 Jose Canseco .45
99 Roger Clemens .90
100 Jose Cruz Jr. .05
101 *Justin Baughman* .05
102 *David Dellucci* .15
103 Travis Lee .15
104 *Troy Glaus* 1.00
105 Kerry Wood .40
106 Mike Caruso .05
107 *Jim Parque* .10
108 Brett Tomko .05
109 Russell Branyan .05
110 Jaret Wright .05
111 Todd Helton .60
112 Gabe Alvarez .05
113 *Matt Anderson* .10
114 Alex Gonzalez .05
115 Mark Kotsay .10
116 Derrek Lee .50
117 Richard Hidalgo .05
118 Adrian Beltre .10
119 Geoff Jenkins .05
120 Eric Milton .05
121 Brad Fullmer .05
122 Vladimir Guerrero .60
123 Carl Pavano .05
124 *Orlando Hernandez* .25
125 Ben Grieve .05

126	A.J. Hinch	.05
127	Matt Clement	.05
128	*Gary Matthews Jr.*	.05
129	Aramis Ramirez	.05
130	Rolando Arrojo	.05

Big Boppers

		NM/M
Complete Set (30):		80.00
Common Player:		1.00
Production 500 sets		
B1	Darin Erstad	1.50
B2	Rafael Palmeiro	3.00
B3	Cal Ripken Jr.	10.00
B4	Nomar Garciaparra	5.00
B5	Mo Vaughn	1.00
B6	Frank Thomas	4.00
B7	Albert Belle	1.00
B8	Jim Thome	2.50
B9	Manny Ramirez	4.00
B10	Tony Clark	1.00
B11	Tino Martinez	1.00
B12	Ben Grieve	1.00
B13	Ken Griffey Jr.	6.00
B14	Alex Rodriguez	7.50
B15	Jay Buhner	1.00
B16	Juan Gonzalez	2.00
B17	Jose Cruz Jr.	1.00
B18	Jose Canseco	2.50
B19	Travis Lee	1.50
B20	Chipper Jones	5.00
B21	Andres Galarraga	1.00
B22	Andruw Jones	4.00
B23	Sammy Sosa	5.00
B24	Vinny Castilla	1.00
B25	Larry Walker	1.00
B26	Jeff Bagwell	4.00
B27	Gary Sheffield	2.00
B28	Mike Piazza	6.00
B29	Mark McGwire	7.50
B30	Barry Bonds	10.00

Groovy Kind of Glove

		NM/M
Complete Set (30):		50.00
Common Player:		.60
Inserted 1:7		
G1	Roberto Alomar	1.00
G2	Cal Ripken Jr.	7.50
G3	Nomar Garciaparra	3.50
G4	Frank Thomas	2.25
G5	Robin Ventura	.60
G6	Omar Vizquel	.60
G7	Kenny Lofton	.60
G8	Ben Grieve	.60
G9	Alex Rodriguez	6.00
G10	Ken Griffey Jr.	5.00
G11	Ivan Rodriguez	1.50
G12	Travis Lee	.75
G13	Matt Williams	.60
G14	Greg Maddux	3.50
G15	Andres Galarraga	.60
G16	Andruw Jones	2.25
G17	Kerry Wood	1.25
G18	Mark Grace	.60
G19	Craig Biggio	.60
G20	Charles Johnson	.60
G21	Raul Mondesi	.60
G22	Mike Piazza	5.00
G23	Rey Ordonez	.60
G24	Derek Jeter	7.50
G25	Scott Rolen	1.25
G26	Mark McGwire	6.00
G27	Ken Caminiti	.60
G28	Tony Gwynn	3.50
G29	J.T. Snow	.60
G30	Barry Bonds	7.50

New Frontier

		NM/M
Complete Set (30):		45.00
Common Player:		1.00
Production 1,000 sets		
NF1	Justin Baughman	1.00
NF2	David Dellucci	1.00
NF3	Travis Lee	1.50
NF4	Troy Glaus	6.00
NF5	Mike Caruso	1.00
NF6	Jim Parque	1.00
NF7	Kerry Wood	2.00
NF8	Brett Tomko	1.00
NF9	Russell Branyan	1.00
NF10	Jaret Wright	1.00
NF11	Todd Helton	5.00
NF12	Gabe Alvarez	1.00
NF13	Matt Anderson	1.00
NF14	Alex Gonzalez	1.00
NF15	Mark Kotsay	1.00
NF16	Derrek Lee	3.00
NF17	Richard Hidalgo	1.00
NF18	Adrian Beltre	2.00
NF19	Geoff Jenkins	1.00
NF20	Eric Milton	1.00
NF21	Brad Fullmer	1.00
NF22	Vladimir Guerrero	6.00
NF23	Carl Pavano	1.00
NF24	Orlando Hernandez	1.25
NF25	Ben Grieve	1.00
NF26	A.J. Hinch	1.00
NF27	Matt Clement	1.00
NF28	Gary Matthews	1.00
NF29	Aramis Ramirez	1.00
NF30	Rolando Arrojo	1.00

Lunchbox

	NM/M
Complete Set (6):	40.00
Common Lunchbox:	4.00
Nomar Garciaparra	6.00
Ken Griffey Jr.	7.50
Chipper Jones	6.00
Travis Lee	4.00
Mark McGwire	10.00
Cal Ripken Jr.	12.00

Quantum Leap

		NM/M
Common Player:		15.00
Production 50 sets		
Q1	Darin Erstad	20.00
Q2	Cal Ripken Jr.	100.00
Q3	Nomar Garciaparra	50.00
Q4	Frank Thomas	40.00
Q5	Kenny Lofton	15.00
Q6	Ben Grieve	15.00
Q7	Ken Griffey Jr.	60.00
Q8	Alex Rodriguez	75.00
Q9	Juan Gonzalez	20.00
Q10	Jose Cruz Jr.	15.00
Q11	Roger Clemens	55.00
Q12	Travis Lee	15.00
Q13	Chipper Jones	50.00
Q14	Greg Maddux	50.00
Q15	Kerry Wood	20.00
Q16	Jeff Bagwell	40.00
Q17	Mike Piazza	60.00
Q18	Scott Rolen	30.00
Q19	Mark McGwire	75.00
Q20	Tony Gwynn	50.00
Q21	Larry Walker	15.00
Q22	Derek Jeter	100.00
Q23	Sammy Sosa	50.00
Q24	Barry Bonds	100.00
Q25	Mo Vaughn	15.00
Q26	Roberto Alomar	20.00
Q27	Todd Helton	30.00
Q28	Ivan Rodriguez	30.00
Q29	Vladimir Guerrero	40.00
Q30	Albert Belle	15.00

Time Capsule

		NM/M
Complete Set (50):		35.00
Common Player:		.25
Inserted 1:2		
TC1	Mike Mussina	.50
TC2	Rafael Palmeiro	.65
TC3	Cal Ripken Jr.	3.00
TC4	Nomar Garciaparra	1.50
TC5	Pedro Martinez	1.00
TC6	Mo Vaughn	.25
TC7	Albert Belle	.25
TC8	Frank Thomas	1.00
TC9	David Justice	.25
TC10	Kenny Lofton	.25
TC11	Manny Ramirez	1.00
TC12	Jim Thome	.60
TC13	Derek Jeter	3.00
TC14	Tino Martinez	.25
TC15	Ben Grieve	.25
TC16	Rickey Henderson	1.00
TC17	Ken Griffey Jr.	2.00
TC18	Randy Johnson	1.00
TC19	Alex Rodriguez	2.50
TC20	Wade Boggs	1.50
TC21	Fred McGriff	.25
TC22	Juan Gonzalez	.50
TC23	Ivan Rodriguez	.75
TC24	Nolan Ryan	2.50
TC25	Jose Canseco	.50
TC26	Roger Clemens	1.75
TC27	Jose Cruz Jr.	.25
TC28	Travis Lee	.40
TC29	Matt Williams	.25
TC30	Andres Galarraga	.25
TC31	Andruw Jones	1.00
TC32	Chipper Jones	1.50
TC33	Greg Maddux	1.50
TC34	Kerry Wood	.50
TC35	Barry Larkin	.25
TC36	Dante Bichette	.25
TC37	Larry Walker	.25
TC38	Livan Hernandez	.25
TC39	Jeff Bagwell	1.00
TC40	Craig Biggio	.25
TC41	Charles Johnson	.25
TC42	Gary Sheffield	.50
TC43	Marquis Grissom	.25
TC44	Mike Piazza	2.00
TC45	Scott Rolen	.65
TC46	Curt Schilling	.40
TC47	Mark McGwire	2.50
TC48	Ken Caminiti	.25
TC49	Tony Gwynn	1.50
TC50	Barry Bonds	3.00

Legendary Cut

		NM/M
LC	Babe Ruth (3 issued; 1/04 auction)	9,500

Sign of the Times

		NM/M
Common Autograph:		7.50
Inserted 1:36		
EB	Ernie Banks (300)	30.00
YB	Yogi Berra (150)	45.00
RB	Russell Branyan (750)	7.50
LB	Lou Brock (300)	15.00
JC	Jose Cruz Jr. (300)	7.50
RF	Rollie Fingers (600)	7.50

BF	Bob Feller (600)	17.50
CF	Carlton Fisk (600)	25.00
BGi	Bob Gibson (300)	25.00
BGr	Ben Grieve (300)	7.50
KGj	Ken Griffey Jr. (100)	185.00
KGs	Ken Griffey Sr. (600)	7.50
TG	Tony Gwynn (200)	35.00
AK	Al Kaline (600)	17.50
PK	Paul Konerko (750)	7.50
TLe	Travis Lee (300)	7.50
EM	Eddie Mathews (600)	25.00
GMj	Gary Matthews Jr. (750)	7.50
GMs	Gary Matthews (600)	7.50
WM	Willie McCovey (600)	25.00
TP	Tony Perez (600)	17.50
GP	Gaylord Perry (1,000)	7.50
KP	Kirby Puckett (450)	50.00
BR	Brooks Robinson (300)	17.50
SR	Scott Rolen (300)	10.00
NR	Nolan Ryan (500)	100.00
TS	Tom Seaver (300)	30.00
WS	Warren Spahn (600)	25.00
WiS	Willie Stargell (600)	25.00
FT	Frank Thomas (600)	7.50
KW	Kerry Wood (200)	30.00

1999 UPPER DECK

		NM/M
Complete Set (525):		45.00
Complete Series 1 (255):		25.00
Complete Series 2 (270):		20.00
Common Player:		.05
Exclusive Stars/RCs:		15X
Production 100 each		
Pack (10):		1.50
Wax Box (24):		35.00
1	Troy Glaus	.60
2	Adrian Beltre	.25
3	Matt Anderson	.05
4	Eric Chavez	.15
5	Jin Cho	.05
6	*Robert Smith*	.05
7	George Lombard	.05
8	Mike Kinkade	.05
9	Seth Greisinger	.05
10	J.D. Drew	.50
11	Aramis Ramirez	.05
12	Carlos Guillen	.05
13	Justin Baughman	.05
14	Jim Parque	.05
15	Ryan Jackson	.05
16	Ramon Martinez	.05
17	Orlando Hernandez	.05
18	Jeremy Giambi	.05
19	Gary DiSarcina	.05
20	Darin Erstad	.25
21	Troy Glaus	.50
22	Chuck Finley	.05
23	Dave Hollins	.05

24 Troy Percival .05
25 Tim Salmon .05
26 Brian Anderson .05
27 Jay Bell .05
28 Andy Benes .05
29 Brent Brede .05
30 David Dellucci .05
31 Karim Garcia .10
32 Travis Lee .20
33 Andres Galarraga .05
34 Ryan Klesko .05
35 Keith Lockhart .05
36 Kevin Millwood .05
37 Denny Neagle .05
38 John Smoltz .05
39 Michael Tucker .05
40 Walt Weiss .05
41 Dennis Martinez .05
42 Javy Lopez .05
43 Brady Anderson .05
44 Harold Baines .05
45 Mike Bordick .05
46 Roberto Alomar .20
47 Scott Erickson .05
48 Mike Mussina .30
49 Cal Ripken Jr. 2.00
50 Darren Bragg .05
51 Dennis Eckersley .50
52 Nomar Garciaparra .75
53 Scott Hatteberg .05
54 Troy O'Leary .05
55 Bret Saberhagen .05
56 John Valentin .05
57 Rod Beck .05
58 Jeff Blauser .05
59 Brant Brown .05
60 Mark Clark .05
61 Mark Grace .05
62 Kevin Tapani .05
63 Henry Rodriguez .05
64 Mike Cameron .05
65 Mike Caruso .05
66 Ray Durham .05
67 Jaime Navarro .05
68 Magglio Ordonez .30
69 Mike Sirotka .05
70 Sean Casey .15
71 Barry Larkin .05
72 Jon Nunnally .05
73 Paul Konerko .15
74 Chris Stynes .05
75 Brett Tomko .05
76 Dmitri Young .05
77 Sandy Alomar .05
78 Bartolo Colon .05
79 Travis Fryman .05
80 Brian Giles .05
81 David Justice .05
82 Omar Vizquel .05
83 Jaret Wright .05
84 Jim Thome .40
85 Charles Nagy .05
86 Pedro Astacio .05
87 Todd Helton .50
88 Darryl Kile .05
89 Mike Lansing .05
90 Neifi Perez .05
91 John Thomson .05
92 Larry Walker .05
93 Tony Clark .05
94 Deivi Cruz .05
95 Damion Easley .05
96 Brian L. Hunter .05
97 Todd Jones .05
98 Brian Moehler .05
99 Gabe Alvarez .05
100 Craig Counsell .05
101 Cliff Floyd .05
102 Livan Hernandez .05
103 Andy Larkin .05
104 Derrek Lee .35
105 Brian Meadows .05
106 Moises Alou .05
107 Sean Berry .05
108 Craig Biggio .05
109 Ricky Gutierrez .05
110 Mike Hampton .05
111 Jose Lima .05
112 Billy Wagner .05
113 Hal Morris .05
114 Johnny Damon .30
115 Jeff King .05
116 Jeff Montgomery .05
117 Glendon Rusch .05
118 Larry Sutton .05
119 Bobby Bonilla .05
120 Jim Eisenreich .05
121 Eric Karros .05
122 Matt Luke .05

123 Ramon Martinez .05
124 Gary Sheffield .40
125 Eric Young .05
126 Charles Johnson .05
127 Jeff Cirillo .05
128 Marquis Grissom .05
129 Jeromy Burnitz .05
130 Bob Wickman .05
131 Scott Karl .05
132 Mark Loretta .05
133 Fernando Vina .05
134 Matt Lawton .05
135 Pat Meares .05
136 Eric Milton .05
137 Paul Molitor .60
138 David Ortiz .35
139 Todd Walker .05
140 Shane Andrews .05
141 Brad Fullmer .05
142 Vladimir Guerrero .60
143 Dustin Hermanson .05
144 Ryan McGuire .05
145 Ugueth Urbina .05
146 John Franco .05
147 Butch Huskey .05
148 Bobby Jones .05
149 John Olerud .05
150 Rey Ordonez .05
151 Mike Piazza 1.25
152 Hideo Nomo .30
153 Masato Yoshii .05
154 Derek Jeter 2.00
155 Chuck Knoblauch .05
156 Paul O'Neill .05
157 Andy Pettitte .20
158 Mariano Rivera .15
159 Darryl Strawberry .05
160 David Wells .05
161 Jorge Posada .05
162 Ramiro Mendoza .05
163 Miguel Tejada .15
164 Ryan Christenson .05
165 Rickey Henderson .60
166 A.J. Hinch .05
167 Ben Grieve .05
168 Kenny Rogers .05
169 Matt Stairs .05
170 Bob Abreu .05
171 Rico Brogna .05
172 Doug Glanville .05
173 Mike Grace .05
174 Desi Relaford .05
175 Scott Rolen .40
176 Jose Guillen .05
177 Francisco Cordova .05
178 Al Martin .05
179 Jason Schmidt .05
180 Turner Ward .05
181 Kevin Young .05
182 Mark McGwire 1.50
183 Delino DeShields .05
184 Eli Marrero .05
185 Tom Lampkin .05
186 Ray Lankford .05
187 Willie McGee .05
188 Matt Morris .05
189 Andy Ashby .05
190 Kevin Brown .05
191 Ken Caminiti .05
192 Trevor Hoffman .05
193 Wally Joyner .05
194 Greg Vaughn .05
195 Danny Darwin .05
196 Shawn Estes .05
197 Orel Hershiser .05
198 Jeff Kent .05
199 Bill Mueller .05
200 Robb Nen .05
201 J.T. Snow .05
202 Ken Cloude .05
203 Russ Davis .05
204 Jeff Fassero .05
205 Ken Griffey Jr. 1.00
206 Shane Monahan .05
207 David Segui .05
208 Dan Wilson .05
209 Wilson Alvarez .05
210 Wade Boggs .75
211 Miguel Cairo .05
212 Bubba Trammell .05
213 Quinton McCracken .05
214 Paul Sorrento .05
215 Kevin Stocker .05
216 Will Clark .05
217 Rusty Greer .05
218 Rick Helling .05
219 Mike McLemore .05
220 Ivan Rodriguez .50
221 John Wetteland .05

222 Jose Canseco .40
223 Roger Clemens .85
224 Carlos Delgado .25
225 Darrin Fletcher .05
226 Alex Gonzalez .05
227 Jose Cruz Jr. .05
228 Shannon Stewart .05
229 Rolando Arrojo .05
230 Livan Hernandez .05
231 Orlando Hernandez .05
232 Raul Mondesi .05
233 Moises Alou .05
234 Pedro Martinez .30
235 Sammy Sosa .50
236 Vladimir Guerrero .40
237 Bartolo Colon .05
238 Miguel Tejada .05
239 Ismael Valdes .05
240 Mariano Rivera .05
241 Jose Cruz Jr. .05
242 Juan Gonzalez .20
243 Ivan Rodriguez .15
244 Sandy Alomar .05
245 Roberto Alomar .10
246 Magglio Ordonez .05
247 Kerry Wood .10
248 Mark McGwire .75
249 David Wells .05
250 Rolando Arrojo .05
251 Ken Griffey Jr. .65
252 Trevor Hoffman .05
253 Travis Lee .05
254 Roberto Alomar .10
255 Sammy Sosa .50
266 *Pat Burrell* 2.00
267 *Shea Hillenbrand* .65
268 Robert Fick .05
269 Roy Halladay .05
270 Ruben Mateo .05
271 Bruce Chen .05
272 Angel Pena .05
273 Michael Barrett .05
274 Kevin Witt .05
275 Damon Minor .05
276 Ryan Minor .05
277 A.J. Pierzynski .05
278 *A.J. Burnett* .50
279 Dermal Brown .05
280 Joe Lawrence .05
281 Derrick Gibson .05
282 Carlos Febles .05
283 Chris Haas .05
284 Cesar King .05
285 Calvin Pickering .05
286 Mitch Meluskey .05
287 Carlos Beltran .50
288 Ron Belliard .05
289 Jerry Hairston Jr. .05
290 Fernando Seguignol .05
291 Kris Benson .05
292 *Chad Hutchinson* .05
293 Jarrod Washburn .05
294 Jason Dickson .05
295 Mo Vaughn .05
296 Garrett Anderson .05
297 Jim Edmonds .05
298 Ken Hill .05
299 Shigetosi Hasegawa .05
300 Todd Stottlemyre .05
301 Randy Johnson .60
302 Omar Daal .05
303 Steve Finley .05
304 Matt Williams .05
305 Danny Klassen .05
306 Tony Batista .05
307 Brian Jordan .05
308 Greg Maddux .75
309 Chipper Jones .75
310 Bret Boone .05
311 Ozzie Guillen .05
312 John Rocker .05
313 Tom Glavine .25
314 Andruw Jones .60
315 Albert Belle .05
316 Charles Johnson .05
317 Will Clark .05
318 B.J. Surhoff .05
319 Delino DeShields .05
320 Heathcliff Slocumb .05
321 Sidney Ponson .05
322 Juan Guzman .05
323 Reggie Jefferson .05
324 Mark Portugal .05
325 Tim Wakefield .05
326 Jason Varitek .05
327 Jose Offerman .05
328 Pedro Martinez .60
329 Trot Nixon .05
330 Kerry Wood .30

331 Sammy Sosa .75
332 Glenallen Hill .05
333 Gary Gaetti .05
334 Mickey Morandini .05
335 Benito Santiago .05
336 Jeff Blauser .05
337 Frank Thomas .65
338 Paul Konerko .15
339 Jaime Navarro .05
340 Carlos Lee .05
341 Brian Simmons .05
342 Mark Johnson .05
343 Jeff Abbot .05
344 Steve Avery .05
345 Mike Cameron .05
346 Michael Tucker .05
347 Greg Vaughn .05
348 Hal Morris .05
349 Pete Harnisch .05
350 Denny Neagle .05
351 Manny Ramirez .60
352 Roberto Alomar .20
353 Dwight Gooden .05
354 Kenny Lofton .05
355 Mike Jackson .05
356 Charles Nagy .05
357 Enrique Wilson .05
358 Russ Branyan .05
359 Richie Sexson .05
360 Vinny Castilla .05
361 Dante Bichette .05
362 Kirt Manwaring .05
363 Darryl Hamilton .05
364 Jamey Wright .05
365 Curt Leskanic .05
366 Jeff Reed .05
367 Bobby Higginson .05
368 Justin Thompson .05
369 Brad Ausmus .05
370 Dean Palmer .05
371 Gabe Kapler .05
372 Juan Encarnacion .05
373 Karim Garcia .10
374 Alex Gonzalez .05
375 Braden Looper .05
376 Preston Wilson .05
377 Todd Dunwoody .05
378 Alex Fernandez .05
379 Mark Kotsay .05
380 Mark Mantei .05
381 Ken Caminiti .05
382 Scott Elarton .05
383 Jeff Bagwell .60
384 Derek Bell .05
385 Ricky Gutierrez .05
386 Richard Hildalgo .05
387 Shane Reynolds .05
388 Carl Everett .05
389 Scott Service .05
390 Jeff Suppan .05
391 Joe Randa .05
392 Kevin Appier .05
393 Shane Halter .05
394 Chad Kreuter .05
395 Mike Sweeney .05
396 Kevin Brown .05
397 Devon White .05
398 Todd Hollandsworth .05
399 Todd Hundley .05
400 Chan Ho Park .05
401 Mark Grudzielanek .05
402 Raul Mondesi .05
403 Ismael Valdes .05
404 Rafael Roque .05
405 Sean Berry .05
406 Kevin Barker .05
407 Dave Nilsson .05
408 Geoff Jenkins .05
409 Jim Abbott .05
410 Bobby Hughes .05
411 Corey Koskie .05
412 Rick Aguilera .05
413 LaTroy Hawkins .05
414 Ron Coomer .05
415 Denny Hocking .05
416 Marty Cordova .05
417 Terry Steinbach .05
418 Rondell White .05
419 Wilton Guerrero .05
420 Shane Andrews .05
421 Orlando Cabrera .05
422 Carl Pavano .05
423 Jeff Vasquez .05
424 Chris Widger .05
425 Robin Ventura .05
426 Rickey Henderson .60
427 Al Leiter .05
428 Bobby Jones .05
429 Brian McRae .05

430 Roger Cedeno .05
431 Bobby Bonilla .05
432 Edgardo Alfonzo .05
433 Bernie Williams .05
434 Ricky Ledee .05
435 Chili Davis .05
436 Tino Martinez .05
437 Scott Brosius .05
438 David Cone .05
439 Joe Girardi .05
440 Roger Clemens .85
441 Chad Curtis .05
442 Hideki Irabu .05
443 Jason Giambi .40
444 Scott Spezio .05
445 Tony Phillips .05
446 Ramon Hernandez .05
447 Mike Macfarlane .05
448 Tom Candiotti .05
449 Billy Taylor .05
450 Bobby Estella .05
451 Curt Schilling .25
452 Carlton Loewer .05
453 Marlon Anderson .05
454 Kevin Jordan .05
455 Ron Gant .05
456 Chad Ogea .05
457 Abraham Nunez .05
458 Jason Kendall .05
459 Pat Meares .05
460 Brant Brown .05
461 Brian Giles .05
462 Chad Hermansen .05
463 Freddy Garcia .05
464 Edgar Renteria .05
465 Fernando Tatis .05
466 Eric Davis .05
467 Darren Bragg .05
468 Donovan Osborne .05
469 Manny Aybar .05
470 Jose Jimenez .05
471 Kent Mercker .05
472 Reggie Sanders .05
473 Ruben Rivera .05
474 Tony Gwynn .75
475 Jim Leyritz .05
476 Chris Gomez .05
477 Matt Clement .05
478 Carlos Hernandez .05
479 Sterling Hitchcock .05
480 Ellis Burks .05
481 Barry Bonds 2.00
482 Marvin Bernard .05
483 Kirk Rueter .05
484 F.P. Santangelo .05
485 Stan Javier .05
486 Jeff Kent .05
487 Alex Rodriguez 1.50
488 Tom Lampkin .05
489 Jose Mesa .05
490 Jay Buhner .05
491 Edgar Martinez .05
492 Butch Huskey .05
493 John Mabry .05
494 Jamie Moyer .05
495 Roberto Hernandez .05
496 Tony Saunders .05
497 Fred McGriff .05
498 Dave Martinez .05
499 Jose Canseco .40
500 Rolando Arrojo .05
501 Esteban Yan .05
502 Juan Gonzalez .30
503 Rafael Palmeiro .50
504 Aaron Sele .05
505 Royce Clayton .05
506 Todd Zeile .05
507 Tom Goodwin .05
508 Lee Stevens .05
509 Esteban Loaiza .05
510 Joey Hamilton .05
511 Homer Bush .05
512 Willie Greene .05
513 Shawn Green .25
514 David Wells .05
515 Kelvim Escobar .05
516 Tony Fernandez .05
517 Pat Hentgen .05
518 Mark McGwire .75
519 Ken Griffey Jr. .65
520 Sammy Sosa .50
521 Juan Gonzalez .20
522 J.D. Drew .10
523 Chipper Jones .40
524 Alex Rodriguez .75
525 Mike Piazza .65
526 Nomar Garciaparra .50
527 Mark McGwire Season Highlights Checklist .75
528 Sammy Sosa Season Highlights Checklist .50
529 Scott Brosius Season Highlights Checklist .05
530 Cal Ripken Jr. Season Highlights Checklist 1.00
531 Barry Bonds Season Highlights Checklist 1.00
532 Roger Clemens Season Highlights Checklist .40
533 Ken Griffey Jr. Season Highlights Checklist .65
534 Alex Rodriguez Season Highlights Checklist .75
535 Curt Schilling Season Highlights Checklist .05

Exclusives

NM/M

Common Player: 3.00
Stars/Rookies: 15X
Greens (1-255): Values Undetermined
Greens (266-535): 100X
(See 1999 Upper Deck for checklist and base card values.)

Babe Ruth Piece of History Bat

NM/M

PH Babe Ruth (bat card) 900.00
PHLC Babe Ruth (Legendary Cut autograph) 25,000

Crowning Glory

NM/M

Complete Set (3): 22.50
Common Player: 3.00
Inserted 1:23
Doubles (1,000 sets): 2X
Triples (25 sets): 8X
Home Runs (1 set): Values Undetermined
CG1 Roger Clemens, Kerry Wood 6.00
CG2 Mark McGwire, Barry Bonds 12.00
CG3 Ken Griffey Jr., Mark McGwire 7.50

Forte

NM/M

Complete Set (30): 50.00
Common Player: .50
Inserted 1:23
Doubles (2,000 sets): 3X
Triples (100): 15X
Quadruples (10): 40X
1 Darin Erstad 1.50
2 Troy Glaus 1.50
3 Mo Vaughn .50
4 Greg Maddux 2.50
5 Andres Galarraga .50
6 Chipper Jones 2.50
7 Cal Ripken Jr. 5.00
8 Albert Belle .50
9 Nomar Garciaparra 2.50
10 Sammy Sosa 2.50
11 Kerry Wood 1.00
12 Frank Thomas 2.00
13 Jim Thome 1.50
14 Jeff Bagwell 2.00
15 Vladimir Guerrero 2.00
16 Mike Piazza 3.00
17 Derek Jeter 5.00
18 Ben Grieve .50
19 Eric Chavez .50
20 Scott Rolen 1.50
21 Mark McGwire 4.00
22 J.D. Drew 1.00
23 Tony Gwynn 2.50
24 Barry Bonds 5.00
25 Alex Rodriguez 4.00
26 Ken Griffey Jr. 3.00
27 Ivan Rodriguez 1.50
28 Juan Gonzalez 1.00
29 Roger Clemens 2.75
30 Andruw Jones 2.00

Game Jersey

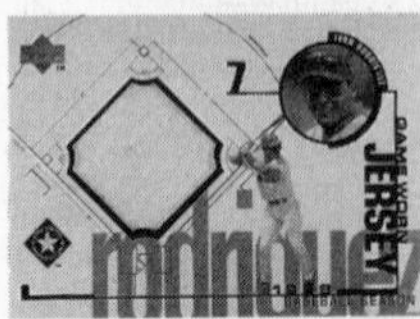

NM/M

Common Player: 6.00
AB Adrian Beltre (H1) 10.00
EC Eric Chavez (H2) 6.00
JD J.D. Drew (H2) 10.00
JDs J.D. Drew (autographed/8)(H2) 150.00
DE Darin Erstad (H1) 10.00
BF Brad Fullmer (H2) 4.50
JG Juan Gonzalez (HR1) 15.00
BG Ben Grieve (H1) 6.00
KG Ken Griffey Jr. (H1) 20.00
KGs Ken Griffey Jr. (autographed/24)(H1) 150.00
JR Ken Griffey Jr. (HR2) 20.00
JRs Ken Griffey Jr. (autographed/24) (HR2) 150.00
TGw Tony Gwynn (H2) 15.00
TH Todd Helton (H2) 15.00
CJ Charles Johnson (HR1) 6.00
CJ Chipper Jones (H2) 15.00
TL Travis Lee (H1) 6.00
GM Greg Maddux (HR2) 15.00
MP Mike Piazza (HR1) 20.00
MR Manny Ramirez (H2) 10.00
AR Alex Rodriguez (HR1) 25.00
IR Ivan Rodriguez (H1) 7.50
NRa Nolan Ryan (Astros)(H2) 25.00
NRas Nolan Ryan (autographed/34)(H2) 450.00
NRb Nolan Ryan (Rangers)(HR2) 25.00
SS Sammy Sosa (H2) 20.00
BT Bubba Trammell (H2) 6.00
FT Frank Thomas (HR2) 15.00
KW Kerry Wood (HR1) 15.00
KWs Kerry Wood (autographed/34) (HR1) 150.00

Homerun Heroes

NM/M

Complete Set (10): 10.00
Common Player: .50
Complete Set Cans (6): 10.00
Common Player Can: 2.00
H1 Ken Griffey Jr. 1.25
H2 Mark McGwire 2.00
H3 Sammy Sosa 1.00
H4 Troy Glaus .75
H5 Mike Piazza 2.00
H6 Chipper Jones 1.00
H7 Vladimir Guerrero .75
H8 Frank Thomas .75
H9 Juan Gonzalez .50
H10 Alex Rodriguez 2.00
SEALED CANS
1 Ken Griffey Jr. 2.50
2 Mark McGwire 2.50
3 Sammy Sosa 2.00
4 Troy Glaus 1.50
5 Mike Piazza 2.50
6 Chipper Jones 2.00

Immaculate Perception

NM/M

Complete Set (27): 45.00
Common Player: .25
Inserted 1:23
Doubles (1,000 sets): 1.5X
Triples (25): 8X
Home Runs (1): Values Undetermined
I1 Jeff Bagwell 2.00
I2 Craig Biggio .25
I3 Barry Bonds 5.00
I4 Roger Clemens 2.75
I5 Jose Cruz Jr. .25
I6 Nomar Garciaparra 2.50
I7 Tony Clark .25
I8 Ben Grieve .25
I9 Ken Griffey Jr. 3.00
I10 Tony Gwynn 2.50
I11 Randy Johnson 2.00
I12 Chipper Jones 2.50
I13 Travis Lee .40
I14 Kenny Lofton .25
I15 Greg Maddux 2.50
I16 Mark McGwire 4.00
I17 Hideo Nomo 1.00
I18 Mike Piazza 3.00
I19 Manny Ramirez 2.00
I20 Cal Ripken Jr. 5.00
I21 Alex Rodriguez 4.00
I22 Scott Rolen 1.50
I23 Frank Thomas 2.00
I24 Kerry Wood 1.00
I25 Larry Walker .25
I26 Vinny Castilla .25
I27 Derek Jeter 5.00

Ken Griffey Jr. 1989 Buyback Autograph

NM/M

Ken Griffey Jr. (100) 900.00

Mark McGwire 500 Home Run Card Set

NM/M

Complete Boxed Set (30): 7.00
Common Card: .35
1-30 Mark McGwire .35

Piece of History 500 Club Babe Ruth

		NM/M
BR	Babe Ruth	4,000

Textbook Excellence

		NM/M
Complete Set (30):		12.50
Common Player:		.25
Inserted 1:4		
Doubles (2,000 sets):		1.5X
Triples (100):		5X
Quadruples (10):		40X
T1	Mo Vaughn	.25
T2	Greg Maddux	.75
T3	Chipper Jones	.75
T4	Andruw Jones	.60
T5	Cal Ripken Jr.	2.00
T6	Albert Belle	.25
T7	Roberto Alomar	.30
T8	Nomar Garciaparra	.75
T9	Kerry Wood	.30
T10	Sammy Sosa	.75
T11	Greg Vaughn	.25
T12	Jeff Bagwell	.60
T13	Kevin Brown	.25
T14	Vladimir Guerrero	.60
T15	Mike Piazza	1.00
T16	Bernie Williams	.25
T17	Derek Jeter	2.00
T18	Ben Grieve	.25
T19	Eric Chavez	.25
T29	Scott Rolen	.50
T21	Mark McGwire	1.50
T22	David Wells	.25
T23	J.D. Drew	.50
T24	Tony Gwynn	.75
T25	Barry Bonds	2.00
T26	Alex Rodriguez	1.50
T27	Ken Griffey Jr.	1.00
T28	Juan Gonzalez	.30
T29	Ivan Rodriguez	.50
T30	Roger Clemens	.85

View to a Thrill

		NM/M
Complete Set (30):		25.00
Common Player:		.35
Inserted 1:7		
Doubles (2,000 sets):		1.5X
Triples (100):		4X
Quadruples (10):		30X
V1	Mo Vaughn	.35
V2	Darin Erstad	.40
V3	Travis Lee	.40
V4	Chipper Jones	1.50
V5	Greg Maddux	1.50
V6	Gabe Kapler	.35
V7	Cal Ripken Jr.	3.00
V8	Nomar Garciaparra	1.50
V9	Kerry Wood	.40
V10	Frank Thomas	1.00
V11	Manny Ramirez	1.00
V12	Larry Walker	.35
V13	Tony Clark	.35
V14	Jeff Bagwell	1.00
V15	Craig Biggio	.35
V16	Vladimir Guerrero	1.00
V17	Mike Piazza	2.00
V18	Bernie Williams	.35
V19	Derek Jeter	3.00
V20	Ben Grieve	.35
V21	Eric Chavez	.35
V22	Scott Rolen	.65
V23	Mark McGwire	2.50
V24	Tony Gwynn	1.50
V25	Barry Bonds	3.00
V26	Ken Griffey Jr.	2.00
V27	Alex Rodriguez	2.50
V28	J.D. Drew	.65
V29	Juan Gonzalez	.50
V30	Roger Clemens	1.75

Wonder Years

		NM/M
Complete Set (30):		30.00
Common Player:		.50
Inserted 1:7		
Doubles (2,000):		2.5X
Triples (50):		10X
Home Runs (1):		
VALUES UNDETERMINED		
WY1	Kerry Wood	.75
WY2	Travis Lee	.65
WY3	Jeff Bagwell	1.50
WY4	Barry Bonds	4.00
WY5	Roger Clemens	2.25
WY6	Jose Cruz Jr.	.50
WY7	Andres Galarraga	.50
WY8	Nomar Garciaparra	2.00
WY9	Juan Gonzalez	.75
WY10	Ken Griffey Jr.	2.50
WY11	Tony Gwynn	2.00
WY12	Derek Jeter	4.00
WY13	Randy Johnson	1.50
WY14	Andruw Jones	1.50
WY15	Chipper Jones	2.00
WY16	Kenny Lofton	.50
WY17	Greg Maddux	2.00
WY18	Tino Martinez	.50
WY19	Mark McGwire	3.00
WY20	Paul Molitor	1.50
WY21	Mike Piazza	2.50
WY22	Manny Ramirez	1.50
WY23	Cal Ripken Jr.	4.00
WY24	Alex Rodriguez	3.00
WY25	Sammy Sosa	2.00
WY26	Frank Thomas	1.50
WY27	Mo Vaughn	.50
WY28	Larry Walker	.50
WY29	Scott Rolen	1.00
WY30	Ben Grieve	.50

10th Anniversary Team

		NM/M
Complete Set (30):		20.00
Common Player:		.15
Inserted 1:4		
Doubles (4,000 sets):		2X
Triples (100):		6X
Home Runs (1):		Values
Undetermined		
X1	Mike Piazza	1.50
X2	Mark McGwire	2.00
X3	Roberto Alomar	.30
X4	Chipper Jones	1.00
X5	Cal Ripken Jr.	3.00
X6	Ken Griffey Jr.	1.50
X7	Barry Bonds	3.00
X8	Tony Gwynn	1.00
X9	Nolan Ryan	3.00
X10	Randy Johnson	.75
X11	Dennis Eckersley	.65
X12	Ivan Rodriguez	.65
X13	Frank Thomas	.75
X14	Craig Biggio	.15
X15	Wade Boggs	1.00
X16	Alex Rodriguez	2.00
X17	Albert Belle	.15
X18	Juan Gonzalez	.40
X19	Rickey Henderson	.75
X20	Greg Maddux	1.00
X21	Tom Glavine	.35
X22	Randy Myers	.15
X23	Sandy Alomar	.15
X24	Jeff Bagwell	.75
X25	Derek Jeter	3.00
X26	Matt Williams	.15
X27	Kenny Lofton	.15
X28	Sammy Sosa	1.00
X29	Larry Walker	.15
X30	Roger Clemens	1.25

1999 UPPER DECK BLACK DIAMOND

		NM/M
Complete Set (120):		30.00
Common Player:		.10
Common Diamond Debut (91-120):		.25
Inserted 1:4		
Pack (6):		2.00
Wax Box (30):		40.00
1	Darin Erstad	.25
2	Tim Salmon	.10
3	Jim Edmonds	.10
4	Matt Williams	.10
5	David Dellucci	.10
6	Jay Bell	.10
7	Andres Galarraga	.10
8	Chipper Jones	1.00
9	Greg Maddux	1.00
10	Andruw Jones	.75
11	Cal Ripken Jr.	2.50
12	Rafael Palmeiro	.65
13	Brady Anderson	.10
14	Mike Mussina	.40
15	Nomar Garciaparra	1.00
16	Mo Vaughn	.10
17	Pedro Martinez	.75
18	Sammy Sosa	1.00
19	Henry Rodriguez	.10
20	Frank Thomas	.75
21	Magglio Ordonez	.40
22	Albert Belle	.10
23	Paul Konerko	.20
24	Sean Casey	.10
25	Jim Thome	.60
26	Kenny Lofton	.10
27	Sandy Alomar Jr.	.10
28	Jaret Wright	.10
29	Larry Walker	.10
30	Todd Helton	.65
31	Vinny Castilla	.10
32	Tony Clark	.10
33	Damion Easley	.10
34	Mark Kotsay	.10
35	Derrek Lee	.50
36	Moises Alou	.10
37	Jeff Bagwell	.75
38	Craig Biggio	.10
39	Randy Johnson	.75
40	Dean Palmer	.10
41	Johnny Damon	.35
42	Chan Ho Park	.10
43	Raul Mondesi	.10
44	Gary Sheffield	.40
45	Jeromy Burnitz	.10
46	Marquis Grissom	.10
47	Jeff Cirillo	.10
48	Paul Molitor	.75
49	Todd Walker	.10
50	Vladimir Guerrero	.75
51	Brad Fullmer	.10
52	Mike Piazza	1.50
53	Hideo Nomo	.40
54	Carlos Baerga	.10
55	John Olerud	.10
56	Derek Jeter	2.50
57	Hideki Irabu	.10
58	Tino Martinez	.10
59	Bernie Williams	.10
60	Miguel Tejada	.25
61	Ben Grieve	.10
62	Jason Giambi	.55
63	Scott Rolen	.60
64	Doug Glanville	.10
65	Desi Relaford	.10
66	Tony Womack	.10
67	Jason Kendall	.10
68	Jose Guillen	.10
69	Tony Gwynn	1.00
70	Ken Caminiti	.10
71	Greg Vaughn	.10
72	Kevin Brown	.10
73	Barry Bonds	2.50
74	J.T. Snow	.10
75	Jeff Kent	.10
76	Ken Griffey Jr.	1.50
77	Alex Rodriguez	2.00
78	Edgar Martinez	.10
79	Jay Buhner	.10
80	Mark McGwire	2.00
81	Delino DeShields	.10
82	Brian Jordan	.10
83	Quinton McCracken	.10
84	Fred McGriff	.10
85	Juan Gonzalez	.40
86	Ivan Rodriguez	.65
87	Will Clark	.10
88	Roger Clemens	1.25
89	Jose Cruz Jr.	.10
90	Babe Ruth	2.00
91	Troy Glaus	1.00
92	Jarrod Washburn	.25
93	Travis Lee	.75
94	Bruce Chen	.25
95	Mike Caruso	.25
96	Jim Parque	.25
97	Kerry Wood	.50
98	Jeremy Giambi	.25
99	Matt Anderson	.25
100	Seth Greisinger	.25
101	Gabe Alvarez	.25
102	Rafael Medina	.25
103	Daryle Ward	.25
104	Alex Cora	.25
105	Adrian Beltre	.50
106	Geoff Jenkins	.25
107	Eric Milton	.25
108	Carl Pavano	.25
109	Eric Chavez	.50
110	Orlando Hernandez	.25
111	A.J. Hinch	.25
112	Carlton Loewer	.25
113	Aramis Ramirez	.25
114	Cliff Politte	.25
115	Matt Clement	.25
116	Alex Gonzalez	.25
117	J.D. Drew	.75
118	Shane Monahan	.25
119	Rolando Arrojo	.25
120	George Lombard	.25

Double Diamond

		NM/M
Complete Set (120):		200.00

Common Player (1-90): .25
Common Diamond Debut (91-120): 1.00
Stars (1-90): 3X
Diamond Debuts (91-120): 2X
(See 1999 Upper Deck Black Diamond for checklist and base card values.)

Triple Diamond

	NM/M
Common Player (1-90):	1.00
Common Diamond Debut (91-120):	1.50
Stars (1-90):	6X
Diamond Debuts (91-120):	3X

(See 1999 Upper Deck Black Diamond for checklist and base card values.)

Quadruple Diamond

		NM/M
Common Player (1-90):		4.00
Production 150 each		
Common Diamond Debut (91-120):		6.00
Production 100 each		
Stars (1-90):		25X
Diamond Debuts (91-120):		8X
18	Sammy Sosa/66	50.00
76	Ken Griffey Jr. /56	60.00
80	Mark McGwire/70	75.00

(See 1999 Upper Deck Black Diamond for checklist and base card values.)

A Piece of History

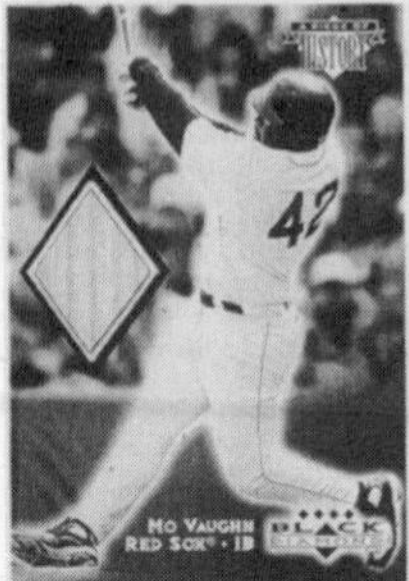

		NM/M
Common Player:		5.00
JG	Juan Gonzalez	7.50
TG	Tony Gwynn	10.00
BW	Bernie Williams	5.00
MM	Mark McGwire	200.00
MV	Mo Vaughn	5.00
SS	Sammy Sosa	25.00

Diamond Dominance

		NM/M
Complete Set (30):		65.00
Common Player:		.50
Production 1,500 sets		
D01	Kerry Wood	1.00
D02	Derek Jeter	6.00
D03	Alex Rodriguez	5.00
D04	Frank Thomas	2.00
D05	Jeff Bagwell	2.00
D06	Mo Vaughn	.50
D07	Ivan Rodriguez	1.50
D08	Cal Ripken Jr.	6.00
D09	Rolando Arrojo	.50
D10	Chipper Jones	3.00
D11	Kenny Lofton	.50
D12	Paul Konerko	.75
D13	Mike Piazza	4.00
D14	Ben Grieve	.50
D15	Nomar Garciaparra	3.00
D16	Travis Lee	.65
D17	Scott Rolen	1.00
D18	Juan Gonzalez	1.00
D19	Tony Gwynn	3.00
D20	Tony Clark	.50
D21	Roger Clemens	3.50
D22	Sammy Sosa	3.00
D23	Larry Walker	.50
D24	Ken Griffey Jr.	4.00
D25	Mark McGwire	5.00
D26	Barry Bonds	6.00
D27	Vladimir Guerrero	2.00
D28	Tino Martinez	.50
D29	Greg Maddux	3.00
D30	Babe Ruth	5.00

Mystery Numbers

		NM/M
Complete Set (30):		100.00
Common Player:		.75
M1	Babe Ruth (100)	25.00
M2	Ken Griffey Jr. (200)	12.50
M3	Kerry Wood (300)	4.00
M4	Mark McGwire (400)	12.50
M5	Alex Rodriguez (500)	12.50
M6	Chipper Jones (600)	6.00
M7	Nomar Garciaparra (700)	6.00
M8	Derek Jeter (800)	10.00
M9	Mike Piazza (900)	6.00
M10	Roger Clemens (1,000)	4.50
M11	Greg Maddux (1,100)	4.00
M12	Scott Rolen (1,200)	1.25
M13	Cal Ripken Jr. (1,300)	7.50
M14	Ben Grieve (1,400)	.75
M15	Troy Glaus (1,500)	3.00
M16	Sammy Sosa (1,600)	4.50
M17	Darin Erstad (1,700)	1.25
M18	Juan Gonzalez (1,800)	1.25
M19	Pedro Martinez (1,900)	1.50
M20	Larry Walker (2,000)	.75
M21	Vladimir Guerrero (2,100)	1.50
M22	Jeff Bagwell (2,200)	1.50
M23	Jaret Wright (2,300)	.75
M24	Travis Lee (2,400)	.75
M25	Barry Bonds (2,500)	6.00
M26	Orlando Hernandez (2,600)	.75
M27	Frank Thomas (2,700)	1.50
M28	Tony Gwynn (2,800)	2.00
M29	Andres Galarraga (2,900)	.75
M30	Craig Biggio (3,000)	.75

Piece of History 500 Club

	NM/M
Reggie Jackson	165.00
Reggie Jackson Auto.	400.00

1999 UPPER DECK CENTURY LEGENDS

		NM/M
Complete Set (131):		20.00
Common Player:		.10
Century Collection:		20X
Production 100 sets		
Pack (5):		3.00
Wax Box (24):		60.00
1	Babe Ruth	2.00
1	Babe Ruth (SAMPLE overprint on back)	2.00
2	Willie Mays	1.00
3	Ty Cobb	1.00
4	Walter Johnson	.40
5	Hank Aaron	1.00
6	Lou Gehrig	1.50
7	Christy Mathewson	.40
8	Ted Williams	1.25
9	Rogers Hornsby	.25
10	Stan Musial	.65
12	Grover Alexander	.25
13	Honus Wagner	.40
14	Cy Young	.40
15	Jimmie Foxx	.25
16	Johnny Bench	.50
17	Mickey Mantle	2.00
18	Josh Gibson	.25
19	Satchel Paige	.50
20	Roberto Clemente	1.50
21	Warren Spahn	.20
22	Frank Robinson	.20
23	Lefty Grove	.20
24	Eddie Collins	.10
27	Tris Speaker	.25
28	Mike Schmidt	.50
29	Napoleon LaJoie	.20
30	Steve Carlton	.25
31	Bob Gibson	.25
32	Tom Seaver	.25
33	George Sisler	.10
34	Barry Bonds	1.50
35	Joe Jackson	1.25
36	Bob Feller	.25
37	Hank Greenberg	.25
38	Ernie Banks	.40
39	Greg Maddux	.75
40	Yogi Berra	.40
41	Nolan Ryan	2.00
42	Mel Ott	.25
43	Al Simmons	.10
44	Jackie Robinson	1.25
45	Carl Hubbell	.25
46	Charley Gehringer	.10
47	Buck Leonard	.10
48	Reggie Jackson	.40
49	Tony Gwynn	.75
50	Roy Campanella	.40
51	Ken Griffey Jr.	1.00
52	Barry Bonds	1.50
53	Roger Clemens	.85
54	Tony Gwynn	.75
55	Cal Ripken Jr.	1.50
56	Greg Maddux	.75
57	Frank Thomas	.65
58	Mark McGwire	1.25
59	Mike Piazza	1.00
60	Wade Boggs	.75
61	Alex Rodriguez	1.25
62	Juan Gonzalez	.30
63	Mo Vaughn	.10
64	Albert Belle	.10
65	Sammy Sosa	.75
66	Nomar Garciaparra	.75
67	Derek Jeter	1.50
68	Kevin Brown	.10
69	Jose Canseco	.35
70	Randy Johnson	.60
71	Tom Glavine	.25
72	Barry Larkin	.10
73	Curt Schilling	.25
74	Moises Alou	.10
75	Fred McGriff	.10
76	Pedro Martinez	.65
77	Andres Galarraga	.10
78	Will Clark	.10
79	Larry Walker	.10
80	Ivan Rodriguez	.50
81	Chipper Jones	.75
82	Jeff Bagwell	.60
83	Craig Biggio	.10
84	Kerry Wood	.35
85	Roberto Alomar	.20
86	Vinny Castilla	.10
87	Kenny Lofton	.10
88	Rafael Palmeiro	.50
89	Manny Ramirez	.60
90	David Wells	.10
91	Mark Grace	.10
92	Bernie Williams	.10
93	David Cone	.10
94	John Olerud	.10
95	John Smoltz	.10
96	Tino Martinez	.10
97	Raul Mondesi	.10
98	Gary Sheffield	.35
99	Orel Hershiser	.10
100	Rickey Henderson	.65
101	J.D. Drew	.50
102	Troy Glaus	.50
103	Nomar Garciaparra	.75
104	Scott Rolen	.45
105	Ryan Minor	.10
106	Travis Lee	.20
107	Roy Halladay	.10
108	Carlos Beltran	.50
109	Alex Rodriguez)	1.25
110	Eric Chavez	.20
111	Vladimir Guerrero	.60
112	Ben Grieve	.15
113	Kerry Wood	.30
114	Alex Gonzalez	.10
115	Darin Erstad	.30
116	Derek Jeter	1.50
117	Jaret Wright	.10
118	Jose Cruz Jr.	.10
119	Chipper Jones	.75
120	Gabe Kapler	.10
121	Satchel Paige	.50
122	Willie Mays	1.00
123	Roberto Clemente	1.50
124	Lou Gehrig	1.50
125	Mark McGwire	1.25
127	Bob Gibson	.25
128	Johnny Vander Meer	.10
129	Walter Johnson	.25
130	Ty Cobb	.75
131	Don Larsen	.20
132	Jackie Robinson	1.00
133	Tom Seaver	.25
134	Johnny Bench	.35
135	Frank Robinson	.25

Century Collection

	NM/M
Common Player:	2.00
Stars:	30X

(See 1999 Upper Deck Century Legends for checklist and base card values.)

All-Century Team

		NM/M
Complete Set (10):		30.00
Common Player:		2.50
Inserted 1:23		
1	Babe Ruth	7.50
2	Ty Cobb	3.50
3	Willie Mays	3.50
4	Lou Gehrig	6.00
5	Jackie Robinson	5.00
6	Mike Schmidt	2.50
7	Ernie Banks	2.50
8	Johnny Bench	2.50
9	Cy Young	2.50
10	Lineup Sheet	.25

Century MVPs

One Set Produced
VALUES UNDETERMINED

Epic Signatures

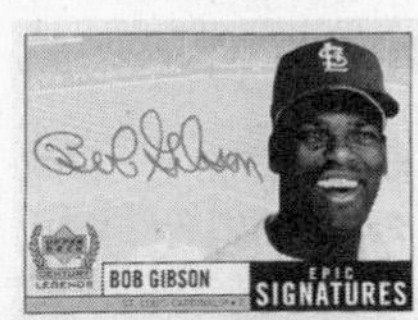

		NM/M
Common Player:		10.00
Inserted 1:24		
EB	Ernie Banks	65.00
JB	Johnny Bench	40.00
YB	Yogi Berra	50.00
BB	Barry Bonds	250.00
SC	Steve Carlton	20.00
BD	Bucky Dent	10.00
BF	Bob Feller	15.00
CF	Carlton Fisk	25.00
BG	Bob Gibson	25.00
JG	Juan Gonzalez	20.00
Jr.	Ken Griffey Jr.	100.00
Sr.	Ken Griffey Sr.	10.00
VG	Vladimir Guerrero	30.00
TG	Tony Gwynn	40.00
RJ	Reggie Jackson	40.00
HK	Harmon Killebrew	30.00
DL	Don Larsen	15.00
GM	Greg Maddux	100.00
EMa	Eddie Mathews	80.00
BM	Bill Mazeroski	30.00
WMc	Willie McCovey	20.00
SM	Stan Musial	80.00
FR	Frank Robinson	30.00
AR	Alex Rodriguez	150.00
NR	Nolan Ryan	150.00
MS	Mike Schmidt	50.00
TS	Tom Seaver	40.00
WS	Warren Spahn	60.00
FT	Frank Thomas	50.00
BT	Bobby Thomson	10.00

Century Epic Signatures

		NM/M
Common Player:		20.00
Production 100 sets		
EB	Ernie Banks	85.00
JB	Johnny Bench	90.00
YB	Yogi Berra	75.00
BB	Barry Bonds	300.00
SC	Steve Carlton	50.00
BD	Bucky Dent	20.00
BF	Bob Feller	50.00
CF	Carlton Fisk	40.00
BG	Bob Gibson	60.00
JG	Juan Gonzalez	60.00
Jr.	Ken Griffey Jr.	165.00
Sr.	Ken Griffey Sr.	20.00
VG	Vladimir Guerrero	70.00
TG	Tony Gwynn	90.00
RJ	Reggie Jackson	60.00
HK	Harmon Killebrew	75.00
DL	Don Larsen	30.00
GM	Greg Maddux	150.00
EMa	Eddie Mathews	90.00
WM	Willie Mays	300.00
BM	Bill Mazeroski	25.00
WMc	Willie McCovey	50.00
SM	Stan Musial	100.00
FR	Frank Robinson	50.00
AR	Alex Rodriguez	200.00
NR	Nolan Ryan	200.00
MS	Mike Schmidt	125.00
TS	Tom Seaver	75.00
WS	Warren Spahn	80.00
FT	Frank Thomas	80.00
BT	Bobby Thomson	20.00
TW	Ted Williams	750.00

Epic Milestones

		NM/M
Complete Set (9):		5.00
Common Player:		.25
Inserted 1:12		
2	Jackie Robinson	.75
3	Nolan Ryan	1.00
4	Mark McGwire	.75
5	Roger Clemens	.60
6	Sammy Sosa	.50
7	Cal Ripken Jr.	1.00
8	Rickey Henderson	.25
9	Hank Aaron	.75
10	Barry Bonds	1.00

Jerseys of the Century

		NM/M
Common Player:		12.50

Inserted 1:418		
GB	George Brett	25.00
RC	Roger Clemens	25.00
TG	Tony Gwynn	20.00
GM	Greg Maddux	20.00
EM	Eddie Murray	15.00
NR	Nolan Ryan	90.00
MS	Mike Schmidt	25.00
OZ	Ozzie Smith	20.00
DW	Dave Winfield	15.00

Legendary Cuts

		NM/M
Values Undetermined		
CY	Cy Young (11/00 auction)	1,850

Memorable Shots

		NM/M
Complete Set (10):		15.00
Common Player:		.50
Inserted 1:12		
1	Babe Ruth	5.00
2	Bobby Thomson	1.00
3	Kirk Gibson	.50
4	Carlton Fisk	.50
5	Bill Mazeroski	1.00
6	Bucky Dent	.50
7	Mark McGwire	2.00
8	Mickey Mantle	5.00
9	Joe Carter	.50
10	Mark McGwire	2.00

500 Club Piece History

		NM/M
JF	Jimmie Foxx	150.00

1999 UPPER DECK CHALLENGERS FOR 70

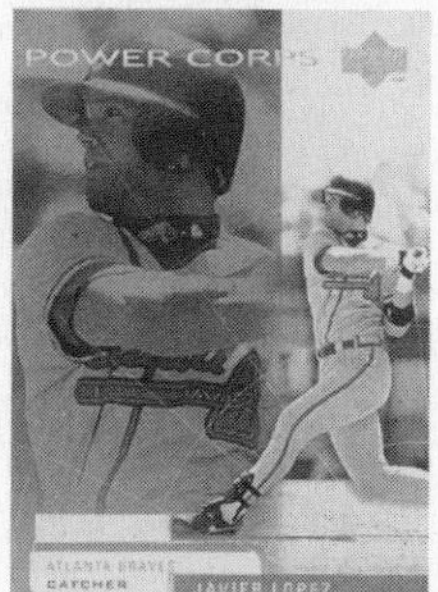

		NM/M
Complete Set (90):		15.00
Common Player:		.05
Challenger's Edition (600 sets):		5X
Pack (5):		2.00
Wax Box (20):		25.00
1	Mark McGwire	1.50
2	Sammy Sosa	1.00
3	Ken Griffey Jr.	1.25
4	Alex Rodriguez	1.50
5	Albert Belle	.05
6	Mo Vaughn	.05
7	Mike Piazza	1.25
8	Frank Thomas	.75
9	Juan Gonzalez	.35
10	Barry Bonds	2.00
11	Rafael Palmeiro	.60
12	Jose Canseco	.50
13	Nomar Garciaparra	1.00
14	Carlos Delgado	.20
15	Brian Jordan	.05
16	Vladimir Guerrero	.65
17	Vinny Castilla	.05
18	Chipper Jones	1.00
19	Jeff Bagwell	.65
20	Moises Alou	.05
21	Tony Clark	.05
22	Jim Thome	.50
23	Tino Martinez	.05
24	Greg Vaughn	.05
25	Javy Lopez	.05
26	Jeromy Burnitz	.05
27	Cal Ripken Jr.	2.00
28	Manny Ramirez	.65
29	Darin Erstad	.25
30	Ken Caminiti	.05
31	Edgar Martinez	.05
32	Ivan Rodriguez	.60
33	Larry Walker	.05
34	Todd Helton	.60
35	Andruw Jones	.65
36	Ray Lankford	.05
37	Travis Lee	.10
38	Raul Mondesi	.05
39	Scott Rolen	.50
40	Ben Grieve	.05
41	J.D. Drew	.50
42	Troy Glaus	.60
43	Eric Chavez	.10
44	Gabe Kapler	.05
45	Michael Barrett	.05
46	Mark McGwire	.75
47	Jose Canseco	.25
48	Greg Vaughn	.05
49	Albert Belle	.05
50	Mark McGwire	.75
51	Vinny Castilla	.05
52	Vladimir Guerrero	.35
53	Andres Galarraga	.05
54	Rafael Palmeiro	.30
55	Juan Gonzalez	.20
56	Ken Griffey Jr.	.60
57	Barry Bonds	1.00
58	Mo Vaughn	.05
59	Nomar Garciaparra	.50
60	Tino Martinez	.05
61	Mark McGwire	.75
62	Mark McGwire	.75
63	Mark McGwire	.75
64	Mark McGwire	.75
65	Mark McGwire	.75
66	Sammy Sosa	.50
67	Mark McGwire	.75
68	Mark McGwire	.75
69	Mark McGwire	.75
70	Mark McGwire	.75
71	Mark McGwire	.75
72	Scott Brosius	.05
73	Tony Gwynn	.40
74	Chipper Jones	.50
75	Jeff Bagwell	.35
76	Moises Alou (HR Highlights)	.05
77	Manny Ramirez	.35
78	Carlos Delgado	.05
79	Kerry Wood	.20
80	Ken Griffey Jr.	.60
81	Cal Ripken Jr.	1.00
82	Alex Rodriguez	.75
83	Barry Bonds	1.00
84	Ken Griffey Jr.	.60
85	Travis Lee	.15
86	George Lombard	.05
87	Michael Barrett	.05
88	Jeremy Giambi	.05
89	Troy Glaus	.30
90	J.D. Drew	.25

Swinging/Fences

		NM/M
Complete Set (15):		15.00
Common Player:		.50
1	Ken Griffey Jr.	1.50
2	Mark McGwire	2.00
3	Sammy Sosa	1.25
4	Alex Rodriguez	2.00
5	Nomar Garciaparra	1.25
6	J.D. Drew	.75
7	Vladimir Guerrero	1.00
8	Ben Grieve	.50
9	Chipper Jones	1.25
10	Gabe Kapler	.50
11	Travis Lee	.60
12	Todd Helton	.75
13	Juan Gonzalez	.60
14	Mike Piazza	1.50
15	Mo Vaughn	.50

Autographed Swinging

		NM/M
Complete Set (6):		200.00
Common Player:		5.00
JR	Ken Griffey Jr.	95.00
VG	Vladimir Guerrero	25.00
TH	Todd Helton	15.00
GK	Gabe Kapler	5.00
TL	Travis Lee	7.50
AR	Alex Rodriguez	90.00

Challengers Insert

		NM/M
Complete Set (30):		9.00
Common Player:		.15
Parallel Edition (70 sets):		15X
1	Mark McGwire	1.00
2	Sammy Sosa	.65
3	Ken Griffey Jr.	.75
4	Alex Rodriguez	1.00
5	Albert Belle	.15
6	Mo Vaughn	.15
7	Mike Piazza	.75
8	Frank Thomas	.50
9	Juan Gonzalez	.25
10	Barry Bonds	1.50
11	Rafael Palmeiro	.35
12	Nomar Garciaparra	.65
13	Vladimir Guerrero	.45
14	Vinny Castilla	.15
15	Chipper Jones	.60
16	Jeff Bagwell	.45
17	Moises Alou	.15
18	Tony Clark	.15
19	Jim Thome	.35
20	Tino Martinez	.15
21	Greg Vaughn	.15
22	Manny Ramirez	.45
23	Darin Erstad	.25
24	Ken Caminiti	.15
25	Ivan Rodriguez	.35
26	Andruw Jones	.45
27	Travis Lee	.25
28	Scott Rolen	.35
29	Ben Grieve	.15
30	J.D. Drew	.35

Longball Legends

		NM/M
Complete Set (30):		20.00
Common Player:		.50
1	Ken Griffey Jr.	1.50
2	Mark McGwire	2.00
3	Sammy Sosa	1.00
4	Cal Ripken Jr.	2.50
5	Barry Bonds	2.50
6	Larry Walker	.50
7	Fred McGriff	.50
8	Alex Rodriguez	2.00

9	Frank Thomas	.75
10	Juan Gonzalez	.60
11	Jeff Bagwell	.75
12	Mo Vaughn	.50
13	Albert Belle	.50
14	Mike Piazza	1.50
15	Vladimir Guerrero	.75
16	Chipper Jones	1.00
17	Ken Caminiti	.50
18	Rafael Palmeiro	.65
19	Nomar Garciaparra	1.00
20	Jim Thome	.60
21	Edgar Martinez	.50
22	Ivan Rodriguez	.65
23	Andres Galarraga	.50
24	Scott Rolen	.60
25	Darin Erstad	.65
26	Moises Alou	.50
27	J.D. Drew	.65
28	Andruw Jones	.75
29	Manny Ramirez	.75
30	Tino Martinez	.50

Mark on History

	NM/M
Complete Set (25):	25.00
Common McGwire:	1.50
Parallel:	8X

Piece of History 500

	NM/M
Harmon Killebrew	120.00
Harmon Killebrew (autographed)	450.00

1999 UPPER DECK ENCORE

	NM/M
Complete Set (180):	75.00
Common Player (1-90):	.05
Common Player (91-135):	.25
Inserted 1:4	
Common Player (136-165):	.35
Inserted 1:6	
Common Player (166-180):	.50
Inserted 1:8	
Pack (6):	1.50
Wax Box (24):	25.00

1	Darin Erstad	.25
2	Mo Vaughn	.05
3	Travis Lee	.15
4	Randy Johnson	.60
5	Matt Williams	.05
6	John Smoltz	.05
7	Greg Maddux	.75
8	Chipper Jones	.75
9	Tom Glavine	.25
10	Andruw Jones	.60
11	Cal Ripken Jr.	1.50
12	Mike Mussina	.30
13	Albert Belle	.05
14	Nomar Garciaparra	.75
15	Jose Offerman	.05
16	Pedro Martinez	.60
17	Trot Nixon	.10
18	Kerry Wood	.40
19	Sammy Sosa	.75
20	Frank Thomas	.60
21	Paul Konerko	.15
22	Sean Casey	.15
23	Barry Larkin	.05
24	Greg Vaughn	.05
25	Travis Fryman	.05
26	Jaret Wright	.05
27	Jim Thome	.45
28	Manny Ramirez	.60
29	Roberto Alomar	.20
30	Kenny Lofton	.05
31	Todd Helton	.60
32	Larry Walker	.05
33	Vinny Castilla	.05
34	Dante Bichette	.05
35	Tony Clark	.05
36	Dean Palmer	.05
37	Gabe Kapler	.05
38	Juan Encarnacion	.05
39	Alex Gonzalez	.05
40	Preston Wilson	.05
41	Mark Kotsay	.05
42	Moises Alou	.05
43	Craig Biggio	.05
44	Ken Caminiti	.05
45	Jeff Bagwell	.60
46	Johnny Damon	.30
47	Gary Sheffield	.25
48	Kevin Brown	.05
49	Raul Mondesi	.05
50	Jeff Cirillo	.05
51	Jeromy Burnitz	.05
52	Todd Walker	.05
53	Corey Koskie	.05
54	Brad Fullmer	.05
55	Vladimir Guerrero	.60
56	Mike Piazza	1.25
57	Robin Ventura	.05
58	Rickey Henderson	.60
59	Derek Jeter	1.50
60	Paul O'Neill	.05
61	Bernie Williams	.05
62	Tino Martinez	.05
63	Roger Clemens	.85
64	Ben Grieve	.05
65	Jason Giambi	.35
66	Bob Abreu	.10
67	Scott Rolen	.40
68	Curt Schilling	.25
69	Marlon Anderson	.05
70	Kevin Young	.05
71	Jason Kendall	.05
72	Brian Giles	.05
73	Mark McGwire	1.25
74	Fernando Tatis	.05
75	Eric Davis	.05
76	Trevor Hoffman	.05
77	Tony Gwynn	.75
78	Matt Clement	.05
79	Robb Nen	.05
80	Barry Bonds	1.50
81	Ken Griffey Jr.	1.00
82	Alex Rodriguez	1.25
83	Wade Boggs	.75
84	Fred McGriff	.05
85	Jose Canseco	.30
86	Ivan Rodriguez	.50
87	Juan Gonzalez	.30
88	Rafael Palmeiro	.50
89	Carlos Delgado	.25
90	David Wells	.05
91	Troy Glaus	1.00
92	Adrian Beltre	.50
93	Matt Anderson	.25
94	Eric Chavez	.40
95	*Jeff Weaver*	.50
96	Warren Morris	.25
97	George Lombard	.25
98	Mike Kinkade	.25
99	*Kyle Farnsworth*	.25
100	J.D. Drew	.50
101	*Joe McEwing*	.50
102	Carlos Guillen	.25
103	*Kelly Dransfeldt*	.25
104	*Eric Munson*	.50
105	Armando Rios	.25
106	Ramon Martinez	.25
107	Orlando Hernandez	.45
108	Jeremy Giambi	.25
109	*Pat Burrell*	2.50
110	*Shea Hillenbrand*	1.00
111	Billy Koch	.25
112	Roy Halladay	.35
113	Ruben Mateo	.25
114	Bruce Chen	.25
115	Angel Pena	.25
116	Michael Barrett	.25
117	Kevin Witt	.25
118	Damon Minor	.25
119	Ryan Minor	.25
120	A.J. Pierzynski	.25
121	*A.J. Burnett*	.50
122	Christian Guzman	.25
123	Joe Lawrence	.25
124	Derrick Gibson	.25
125	Carlos Febles	.25
126	Chris Haas	.25
127	Cesar King	.25
128	Calvin Pickering	.25
129	Mitch Meluskey	.25
130	Carlos Beltran	1.00
131	Ron Belliard	.25
132	Jerry Hairston Jr.	.25
133	Fernando Seguignol	.25
134	Kris Benson	.25
135	*Chad Hutchinson*	.25
136	Ken Griffey Jr.	1.50
137	Mark McGwire	2.00
138	Sammy Sosa	1.25
139	Albert Belle	.35
140	Mo Vaughn	.35
141	Alex Rodriguez	2.00
142	Manny Ramirez	.75
143	J.D. Drew	.50
144	Juan Gonzalez	.45
145	Vladimir Guerrero	.75
146	Fernando Tatis	.35
147	Mike Piazza	2.00
148	Barry Bonds	2.50
149	Ivan Rodriguez	.60
150	Jeff Bagwell	.75
151	Raul Mondesi	.35
152	Nomar Garciaparra	1.25
153	Jose Canseco	.50
154	Greg Vaughn	.35
155	Scott Rolen	.50
156	Vinny Castilla	.35
157	Troy Glaus	.65
158	Craig Biggio	.35
159	Tino Martinez	.35
160	Jim Thome	.60
161	Frank Thomas	1.00
162	Tony Clark	.35
163	Ben Grieve	.35
164	Matt Williams	.35
165	Derek Jeter	2.50
166	Ken Griffey Jr.	2.00
167	Tony Gwynn	1.50
168	Mike Piazza	2.00
169	Mark McGwire	2.50
170	Sammy Sosa	1.50
171	Juan Gonzalez	.60
172	Mo Vaughn	.50
173	Derek Jeter	3.00
174	Bernie Williams	.50
175	Ivan Rodriguez	.75
176	Barry Bonds	3.00
177	Scott Rolen	.75
178	Larry Walker	.50
179	Chipper Jones	1.50
180	Alex Rodriguez	2.50

FX Gold

	NM/M
Common Player:	1.00
Gold (1-90):	10X
Gold (91-135):	1.5X
Gold (136-165):	3X
Gold (166-180):	4X

(See 1999 Upper Deck Encore for checklist and base card values.)

Batting Practice Caps

		NM/M
Complete Set (15):		85.00
Common Player:		4.00
Inserted 1:750		
CB	Carlos Beltran	8.00
BB	Barry Bonds	30.00
VC	Vinny Castilla	4.00
EC	Eric Chavez	6.00
TC	Tony Clark	4.00
JD	J.D. Drew	6.00
VG	Vladimir Guerrero	8.00
TG	Tony Gwynn	15.00
TH	Todd Helton	8.00
GK	Gabe Kapler	4.00
JK	Jason Kendall	4.00
DP	Dean Palmer	4.00
BH	Frank Thomas	8.00
GV	Greg Vaughn	4.00
TW	Todd Walker	4.00

Driving Forces

		NM/M
Complete Set (15):		30.00
Common Player:		1.00
Inserted 1:23		
Gold (10 sets):		30X
D1	Ken Griffey Jr.	3.00
D2	Mark McGwire	4.00
D3	Sammy Sosa	2.50
D4	Albert Belle	1.00
D5	Alex Rodriguez	4.00
D6	Mo Vaughn	1.00
D7	Juan Gonzalez	1.00
D8	Jeff Bagwell	2.00
D9	Mike Piazza	3.00
D10	Frank Thomas	2.00
D11	Barry Bonds	5.00
D12	Vladimir Guerrero	2.00
D13	Chipper Jones	2.50
D14	Tony Gwynn	2.50
D15	J.D. Drew	1.50

McGwired!

		NM/M
Complete Set (10):		12.50
Common Card:		1.50
Inserted 1:23		
Parallel:		2X
Production 500 sets		
1	Mark McGwire, Carl Pavano	1.50
2	Mark McGwire, Michael Morgan	1.50
3	Mark McGwire, Steve Trachsel	1.50
4	Mark McGwire	2.50
5	Mark McGwire	2.50
6	Mark McGwire, Scott Elarton	1.50

7	Mark McGwire, Jim Parque	1.50
8	Mark McGwire	2.50
9	Mark McGwire, Rafael Roque	1.50
10	Mark McGwire, Jaret Wright	1.50

Rookie Encore

		NM/M
Complete Set (10):		17.50
Common Player:		1.00
Inserted 1:23		
FX Gold:		2X
Production 500 sets		
1	J.D. Drew	2.00
2	Eric Chavez	1.00
3	Gabe Kapler	1.00
4	Bruce Chen	1.00
5	Carlos Beltran	3.00
6	Troy Glaus	5.00
7	Roy Halladay	1.00
8	Adrian Beltre	2.00
9	Michael Barrett	1.00
10	Pat Burrell	5.00

UD Authentics

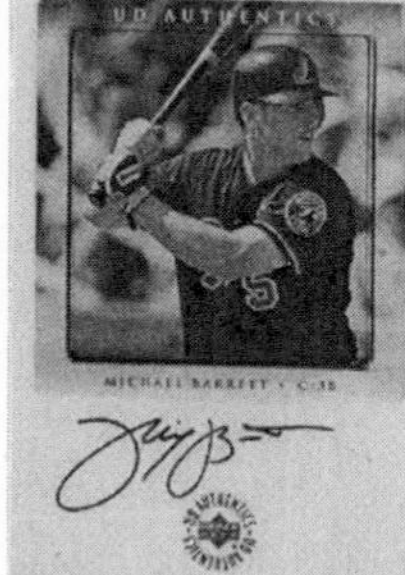

		NM/M
Complete Set (6):		130.00
Common Player:		5.00
Inserted 1:288		
MB	Michael Barrett	4.00
PB	Pat Burrell	10.00
JD	J.D. Drew	12.00
NG	Nomar Garciaparra	70.00
TG	Troy Glaus	12.00
JR	Ken Griffey Jr.	90.00

Upper Realm

		NM/M
Complete Set (15):		13.00
Common Player:		.30
Inserted 1:11		
1	Ken Griffey Jr.	1.25
2	Mark McGwire	1.50
3	Sammy Sosa	.75
4	Tony Gwynn	.75
5	Alex Rodriguez	1.50
6	Juan Gonzalez	.40
7	J.D. Drew	.50
8	Roger Clemens	.85
9	Greg Maddux	.75
10	Randy Johnson	.60
11	Mo Vaughn	.30
12	Derek Jeter	2.00
13	Vladimir Guerrero	.60
14	Cal Ripken Jr.	2.00
15	Nomar Garciaparra	.75

2K Countdown

		NM/M
Complete Set (10):		16.00
Common Player:		.75
Inserted 1:11		
1	Ken Griffey Jr.	2.00
2	Derek Jeter	3.00
3	Mike Piazza	2.00
4	J.D. Drew	.75
5	Vladimir Guerrero	1.00
6	Chipper Jones	1.50
7	Alex Rodriguez	2.50
8	Nomar Garciaparra	1.50
9	Mark McGwire	2.50
10	Sammy Sosa	1.50

1999 UPPER DECK HOLOGRFX

		NM/M
Complete Set (60):		12.00
Common Player:		.10
AUsome:		1.5X
Inserted 1:8		
Pack (3):		1.00
Wax Box (36):		20.00
1	Mo Vaughn	.10
2	Troy Glaus	.60
3	Tim Salmon	.10
4	Randy Johnson	.65
5	Travis Lee	.25
6	Chipper Jones	.75
7	Greg Maddux	.75
8	Andruw Jones	.65
9	Tom Glavine	.25
10	Cal Ripken Jr.	1.50
11	Albert Belle	.10
12	Nomar Garciaparra	.75
13	Pedro J. Martinez	.65
14	Sammy Sosa	.75
15	Frank Thomas	.65
16	Greg Vaughn	.10
17	Kenny Lofton	.10
18	Jim Thome	.50
19	Manny Ramirez	.65
20	Todd Helton	.60
21	Larry Walker	.10
22	Tony Clark	.10
23	Juan Encarnacion	.10
24	Mark Kotsay	.10
25	Jeff Bagwell	.65
26	Craig Biggio	.10
27	Ken Caminiti	.10
28	Carlos Beltran	.50
29	Jeremy Giambi	.10
30	Raul Mondesi	.10
31	Kevin Brown	.10
32	Jeromy Burnitz	.10
33	Corey Koskie	.10
34	Todd Walker	.10
35	Vladimir Guerrero	.65
36	Mike Piazza	1.00
37	Robin Ventura	.10
38	Derek Jeter	1.50
39	Roger Clemens	.85
40	Bernie Williams	.10
41	Orlando Hernandez	.10
42	Ben Grieve	.10
43	Eric Chavez	.15
44	Scott Rolen	.45
45	*Pat Burrell*	1.50
46	Warren Morris	.10
47	Jason Kendall	.10
48	Mark McGwire	1.25
49	J.D. Drew	.50
50	Tony Gwynn	.75
51	Trevor Hoffman	.10
52	Barry Bonds	1.50
53	Ken Griffey Jr.	1.00
54	Alex Rodriguez	1.25
55	Jose Canseco	.35
56	Juan Gonzalez	.30
57	Ivan Rodriguez	.60
58	Rafael Palmeiro	.60
59	David Wells	.10
60	Carlos Delgado	.25

Future Fame

		NM/M
Complete Set (6):		15.00
Common Player:		2.50
Inserted 1:34		
Gold:		2X
Inserted 1:210		
1	Tony Gwynn	2.50
2	Cal Ripken Jr.	5.00
3	Mark McGwire	4.00
4	Ken Griffey Jr.	3.50
5	Greg Maddux	2.50
6	Roger Clemens	3.00

Launchers

		NM/M
Complete Set (15):		20.00
Common Player:		.50
Inserted 1:3		
Gold:		2X
Inserted 1:105		
1	Mark McGwire	3.00
2	Ken Griffey Jr.	2.50
3	Sammy Sosa	2.00
4	J.D. Drew	.75
5	Mo Vaughn	.50
6	Juan Gonzalez	.50
7	Mike Piazza	2.50
8	Alex Rodriguez	3.00
9	Chipper Jones	2.00
10	Nomar Garciaparra	2.00
11	Vladimir Guerrero	1.00
12	Albert Belle	.50
13	Barry Bonds	4.00
14	Frank Thomas	1.00
15	Jeff Bagwell	1.00

StarView

		NM/M
Complete Set (9):		25.00
Common Player:		2.50
Inserted 1:17		
Gold:		2X
Inserted 1:210		
1	Mark McGwire	5.00
2	Ken Griffey Jr.	4.00
3	Sammy Sosa	2.50
4	Nomar Garciaparra	2.50
5	Roger Clemens	3.00
6	Greg Maddux	2.50
7	Mike Piazza	4.00
8	Alex Rodriguez	5.00
9	Chipper Jones	2.50

UD Authentics

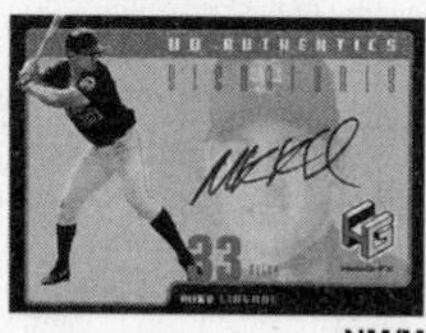

		NM/M
Common Player:		4.00
Inserted 1:431		
CB	Carlos Beltran	25.00
BC	Bruce Chen	4.00
JD	J.D. Drew	12.00
AG	Alex Gonzalez	4.00
JR	Ken Griffey Jr.	80.00
CJ	Chipper Jones	50.00
GK	Gabe Kapler	6.00
MK	Mike Kinkade	4.00
CK	Corey Koskie	7.50
GL	George Lombard	4.00
RM	Ryan Minor	4.00
SM	Shane Monahan	4.00

500 Club Piece of History

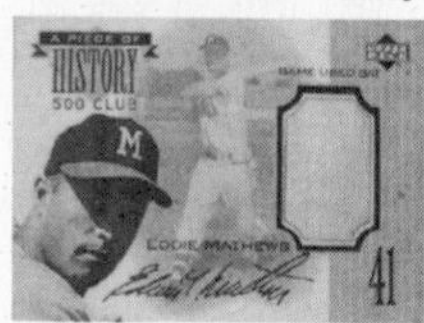

	NM/M
Eddie Mathews (350)	150.00
Eddie Mathews (autographed/41)	550.00
Willie McCovey (350)	120.00
Willie McCovey (autographed/44)	650.00

1999 UPPER DECK MVP

		NM/M
Complete Set (220):		10.00
Common Player:		.05
Pack (10):		1.00
Wax Box (36):		20.00
1	Mo Vaughn	.05
2	Tim Belcher	.05
3	Jack McDowell	.05
4	Troy Glaus	.60
5	Darin Erstad	.40
6	Tim Salmon	.15
7	Jim Edmonds	.05
8	Randy Johnson	.60
9	Steve Finley	.05
10	Travis Lee	.15
11	Matt Williams	.05
12	Todd Stottlemyre	.05
13	Jay Bell	.05
14	David Dellucci	.05
15	Chipper Jones	.75
16	Andruw Jones	.60
17	Greg Maddux	.75
18	Tom Glavine	.25
19	Javy Lopez	.05
20	Brian Jordan	.05
21	George Lombard	.05
22	John Smoltz	.05
23	Cal Ripken Jr.	1.50
24	Charles Johnson	.05
25	Albert Belle	.15
26	Brady Anderson	.05
27	Mike Mussina	.35
28	Calvin Pickering	.05
29	Ryan Minor	.05
30	Jerry Hairston Jr.	.05
31	Nomar Garciaparra	1.00
32	Pedro Martinez	.60
33	Jason Varitek	.05
34	Troy O'Leary	.05
35	Donnie Sadler	.05
36	Mark Portugal	.05
37	John Valentin	.05
38	Kerry Wood	.35
39	Sammy Sosa	1.00
40	Mark Grace	.10
41	Henry Rodriguez	.05
42	Rod Beck	.05
43	Benito Santiago	.05
44	Kevin Tapani	.05
45	Frank Thomas	.60

46	Mike Caruso	.05
47	Magglio Ordonez	.40
48	Paul Konerko	.05
49	Ray Durham	.05
50	Jim Parque	.05
51	Carlos Lee	.05
52	Denny Neagle	.05
53	Pete Harnisch	.05
54	Michael Tucker	.05
55	Sean Casey	.15
56	Eddie Taubensee	.05
57	Barry Larkin	.05
58	Pokey Reese	.05
59	Sandy Alomar	.05
60	Roberto Alomar	.25
61	Bartolo Colon	.05
62	Kenny Lofton	.05
63	Omar Vizquel	.05
64	Travis Fryman	.05
65	Jim Thome	.05
66	Manny Ramirez	.60
67	Jaret Wright	.05
68	Darryl Kile	.05
69	Kirt Manwaring	.05
70	Vinny Castilla	.05
71	Todd Helton	.60
72	Dante Bichette	.05
73	Larry Walker	.05
74	Derrick Gibson	.05
75	Gabe Kapler	.05
76	Dean Palmer	.05
77	Matt Anderson	.05
78	Bobby Higginson	.05
79	Damion Easley	.05
80	Tony Clark	.05
81	Juan Encarnacion	.05
82	Livan Hernandez	.05
83	Alex Gonzalez	.05
84	Preston Wilson	.05
85	Derrek Lee	.05
86	Mark Kotsay	.05
87	Todd Dunwoody	.05
88	Cliff Floyd	.05
89	Ken Caminiti	.05
90	Jeff Bagwell	.60
91	Moises Alou	.05
92	Craig Biggio	.05
93	Billy Wagner	.05
94	Richard Hidalgo	.05
95	Derek Bell	.05
96	Hipolito Pichardo	.05
97	Jeff King	.05
98	Carlos Beltran	.40
99	Jeremy Giambi	.05
100	Larry Sutton	.05
101	Johnny Damon	.20
102	Dee Brown	.05
103	Kevin Brown	.10
104	Chan Ho Park	.05
105	Raul Mondesi	.05
106	Eric Karros	.05
107	Adrian Beltre	.15
108	Devon White	.05
109	Gary Sheffield	.35
110	Sean Berry	.05
111	Alex Ochoa	.05
112	Marquis Grissom	.05
113	Fernando Vina	.05
114	Jeff Cirillo	.05
115	Geoff Jenkins	.05
116	Jeromy Burnitz	.05
117	Brad Radke	.05
118	Eric Milton	.05
119	A.J. Pierzynski	.05
120	Todd Walker	.05
121	David Ortiz	.05
122	Corey Koskie	.05
123	Vladimir Guerrero	.60
124	Rondell White	.05
125	Brad Fullmer	.05
126	Ugueth Urbina	.05
127	Dustin Hermanson	.05
128	Michael Barrett	.05
129	Fernando Seguignol	.05
130	Mike Piazza	1.00
131	Rickey Henderson	.60
132	Rey Ordonez	.05
133	John Olerud	.05
134	Robin Ventura	.05
135	Hideo Nomo	.60
136	Mike Kinkade	.05
137	Al Leiter	.05
138	Brian McRae	.05
139	Derek Jeter	1.50
140	Bernie Williams	.15
141	Paul O'Neill	.05
142	Scott Brosius	.05
143	Tino Martinez	.05
144	Roger Clemens	.85
145	Orlando Hernandez	.10
146	Mariano Rivera	.10
147	Ricky Ledee	.05
148	A.J. Hinch	.05
149	Ben Grieve	.10
150	Eric Chavez	.15
151	Miguel Tejada	.15
152	Matt Stairs	.05
153	Ryan Christenson	.05
154	Jason Giambi	.35
155	Curt Schilling	.25
156	Scott Rolen	.45
157	*Pat Burrell*	1.50
158	Doug Glanville	.05
159	Bobby Abreu	.05
160	Rico Brogna	.05
161	Ron Gant	.05
162	Jason Kendall	.05
163	Aramis Ramirez	.05
164	Jose Guillen	.05
165	Emil Brown	.05
166	Pat Meares	.05
167	Kevin Young	.05
168	Brian Giles	.05
169	Mark McGwire	1.25
170	J.D. Drew	.40
171	Edgar Renteria	.05
172	Fernando Tatis	.05
173	Matt Morris	.05
174	Eli Marrero	.05
175	Ray Lankford	.05
176	Tony Gwynn	.75
177	Sterling Hitchcock	.05
178	Ruben Rivera	.05
179	Wally Joyner	.05
180	Trevor Hoffman	.05
181	Jim Leyritz	.05
182	Carlos Hernandez	.05
183	Barry Bonds	1.50
184	Ellis Burks	.05
185	F.P. Santangelo	.05
186	J.T. Snow	.05
187	Ramon Martinez	.05
188	Jeff Kent	.05
189	Robb Nen	.05
190	Ken Griffey Jr.	1.00
191	Alex Rodriguez	1.25
192	Shane Monahan	.05
193	Carlos Guillen	.05
194	Edgar Martinez	.05
195	David Segui	.05
196	Jose Mesa	.05
197	Jose Canseco	.35
198	Rolando Arrojo	.05
199	Wade Boggs	.75
200	Fred McGriff	.05
201	Quinton McCracken	.05
202	Bobby Smith	.05
203	Bubba Trammell	.05
204	Juan Gonzalez	.60
205	Ivan Rodriguez	.45
206	Rafael Palmeiro	.45
207	Royce Clayton	.05
208	Rick Helling	.05
209	Todd Zeile	.05
210	Rusty Greer	.05
211	David Wells	.05
212	Roy Halladay	.05
213	Carlos Delgado	.25
214	Darrin Fletcher	.05
215	Shawn Green	.15
216	Kevin Witt	.05
217	Jose Cruz Jr.	.05
218	Ken Griffey Jr. Checklist	.45
219	Sammy Sosa Checklist	.45
220	Mark McGwire Checklist	.50

Scripts/Super Scripts

Silver Script:	1X
Gold Script:	10X
Super Script:	30X

(See 1999 UD MVP for checklist and base card values.)

All-Star Game

		NM/M
Complete Set (30):		12.50
Common Player:		.25
1	Mo Vaughn	.25
2	Randy Johnson	.60
3	Chipper Jones	.75
4	Greg Maddux	.75
5	Cal Ripken Jr.	2.00
6	Albert Belle	.35
7	Nomar Garciaparra	1.00
8	Pedro Martinez	.60
9	Sammy Sosa	1.00
10	Frank Thomas	.60
11	Sean Casey	.35
12	Roberto Alomar	.30

13	Manny Ramirez	.60
14	Larry Walker	.25
15	Jeff Bagwell	.60
16	Craig Biggio	.25
17	Raul Mondesi	.25
18	Vladimir Guerrero	.60
19	Mike Piazza	1.00
20	Derek Jeter	2.00
21	Roger Clemens	.85
22	Scott Rolen	.40
23	Mark McGwire	1.50
24	Tony Gwynn	.75
25	Barry Bonds	2.00
26	Ken Griffey Jr.	1.00
27	Alex Rodriguez	1.50
28	Jose Canseco	.40
29	Juan Gonzalez	.60
30	Ivan Rodriguez	.50

Dynamics

		NM/M
Complete Set (15):		17.50
Common Player:		.60
Inserted 1:28		
1	Ken Griffey Jr.	2.00
2	Alex Rodriguez	2.50
3	Nomar Garciaparra	2.00
4	Mike Piazza	2.00
5	Mark McGwire	2.25
6	Sammy Sosa	2.00
7	Chipper Jones	1.50
8	Mo Vaughn	.60
9	Tony Gwynn	1.50
10	Vladimir Guerrero	1.25
11	Derek Jeter	3.00
12	Jeff Bagwell	1.25
13	Cal Ripken Jr.	3.00
14	Juan Gonzalez	1.25
15	J.D. Drew	.90

Game Used Souvenirs

		NM/M
Complete Set (9):		75.00
Common Player:		5.00
Inserted 1:144		
JB	Jeff Bagwell	8.00
BB	Barry Bonds	20.00
JD	J.D. Drew	8.00
KGj	Ken Griffey Jr.	15.00
CJ	Chipper Jones	10.00
MP	Mike Piazza	15.00
CR	Cal Ripken Jr.	20.00
SR	Scott Rolen	8.00
MV	Mo Vaughn	5.00

Signed Game Used Souvenirs

		NM/M
KGj	Ken Griffey Jr.	300.00
CJ	Chipper Jones	200.00

ProSign

		NM/M
Common Autograph:		5.00
Inserted 1:216 R		
MA	Matt Anderson	5.00
CB	Carlos Beltran	15.00
RB	Russ Branyan	5.00
EC	Eric Chavez	10.00
BC	Bruce Chen	5.00
BF	Brad Fuller	5.00
NG	Nomar Garciaparra	80.00
JG	Jeremy Giambi	5.00
DG	Derrick Gibson	5.00
CG	Chris Gomez	5.00
AG	Alex Gonzalez	5.00
BG	Ben Grieve	5.00
JR.	Ken Griffey Jr.	80.00
RH	Richard Hidalgo	5.00
SH	Shea Hillenbrand	10.00
CJ	Chipper Jones/SP	50.00
GK	Gabe Kapler	6.00
SK	Scott Karl	5.00
CK	Corey Koskie	7.50
RL	Ricky Ledee	5.00
ML	Mike Lincoln	5.00
GL	George Lombard	5.00
MLo	Mike Lowell	7.50
RM	Ryan Minor	5.00
SM	Shane Monahan	5.00
AN	Abraham Nunez	5.00
JP	Jim Parque	5.00
CP	Calvin Pickering	5.00
JRa	Jason Rakers	5.00
RR	Ruben Rivera	5.00
IR	Ivan Rodriguez/SP	50.00
KW	Kevin Witt	5.00

Power Surge

		NM/M
Complete Set (15):		12.50
Common Player:		.50
Inserted 1:9		
1	Mark McGwire	1.50
2	Sammy Sosa	1.25

3	Ken Griffey Jr.	1.25
4	Alex Rodriguez	1.50
5	Juan Gonzalez	.75
6	Nomar Garciaparra	1.25
7	Vladimir Guerrero	.75
8	Chipper Jones	1.00
9	Albert Belle	.50
10	Frank Thomas	.75
11	Mike Piazza	1.25
12	Jeff Bagwell	.75
13	Manny Ramirez	.75
14	Mo Vaughn	.50
15	Barry Bonds	2.00

Scout's Choice

		NM/M
Complete Set (15):		5.00
Common Player:		.25
Inserted 1:9		
1	J.D. Drew	.65
2	Ben Grieve	.35
3	Troy Glaus	1.50
4	Gabe Kapler	.25
5	Carlos Beltran	.45
6	Aramis Ramirez	.25
7	Pat Burrell	1.00
8	Kerry Wood	.65
9	Ryan Minor	.25
10	Todd Helton	1.00
11	Eric Chavez	.35
12	Russ Branyon	.25
13	Travis Lee	.35
14	Ruben Mateo	.25
15	Roy Halladay	.35

Super Tools

		NM/M
Complete Set (15):		25.00
Common Player:		.50
Inserted 1:14		
1	Ken Griffey Jr.	2.50
2	Alex Rodriguez	3.00
3	Sammy Sosa	2.00
4	Derek Jeter	4.00
5	Vladimir Guerrero	1.50
6	Ben Grieve	.50
7	Mike Piazza	2.50
8	Kenny Lofton	.50
9	Barry Bonds	4.00
10	Darin Erstad	1.00
11	Nomar Garciaparra	2.00
12	Cal Ripken Jr.	4.00
13	J.D. Drew	1.00
14	Larry Walker	.50
15	Chipper Jones	2.00

Swing Time

		NM/M
Complete Set (12):		5.00
Common Player:		.35
Inserted 1:6		
1	Ken Griffey Jr.	.75
2	Mark McGwire	1.00
3	Sammy Sosa	.60
4	Tony Gwynn	.60
5	Alex Rodriguez	1.00
6	Nomar Garciaparra	.60
7	Barry Bonds	1.50
8	Frank Thomas	.45
9	Chipper Jones	.60
10	Ivan Rodriguez	.35
11	Mike Piazza	.75
12	Derek Jeter	1.50

500 Club Piece of History

	NM/M
Mike Schmidt/350	160.00
Mike Schmidt/auto/20	1,250

1999 UPPER DECK OVATION

		NM/M
Complete Set (90):		20.00
Common Player:		.05
Common World Premiere:		.15
Inserted 1:3.5		
Common Superstar Spotlight:		.60
Inserted 1:6		
Pack (5):		2.00
Box (20):		30.00
1	Ken Griffey Jr.	1.50
2	Rondell White	.05
3	Tony Clark	.05
4	Barry Bonds	2.50
5	Larry Walker	.05
6	Greg Vaughn	.05
7	Mark Grace	.05
8	John Olerud	.05
9	Matt Williams	.05
10	Craig Biggio	.05
11	Quinton McCracken	.05
12	Kerry Wood	.35
13	Derek Jeter	2.50
14	Frank Thomas	.75
15	Tino Martinez	.05
16	Albert Belle	.05
17	Ben Grieve	.05
18	Cal Ripken Jr.	2.50
19	Johnny Damon	.30
20	Jose Cruz Jr.	.05
21	Barry Larkin	.05
22	Jason Giambi	.45
23	Sean Casey	.10
24	Scott Rolen	.60
25	Jim Thome	.45
26	Curt Schilling	.25
27	Moises Alou	.05
28	Alex Rodriguez	2.00
29	Mark Kotsay	.05
30	Darin Erstad	.25
31	Mike Mussina	.30
32	Todd Walker	.05
33	Nomar Garciaparra	1.00
34	Vladimir Guerrero	.75
35	Jeff Bagwell	.75
36	Mark McGwire	2.00
37	Travis Lee	.15
38	Dean Palmer	.05
39	Fred McGriff	.05
40	Sammy Sosa	1.00
41	Mike Piazza	1.50
42	Andres Galarraga	.05
43	Pedro Martinez	.75
44	Juan Gonzalez	.40
45	Greg Maddux	1.00
46	Jeromy Burnitz	.05
47	Roger Clemens	1.25
48	Vinny Castilla	.05
49	Kevin Brown	.05
50	Mo Vaughn	.05
51	Raul Mondesi	.05
52	Randy Johnson	.75
53	Ray Lankford	.05
54	Jaret Wright	.05
55	Tony Gwynn	1.00
56	Chipper Jones	1.00
57	Gary Sheffield	.40
58	Ivan Rodriguez	.65
59	Kenny Lofton	.05
60	Jason Kendall	.05
61	J.D. Drew	.75
62	Gabe Kapler	.15
63	Adrian Beltre	.40
64	Carlos Beltran	.50
65	Eric Chavez	.35
66	Mike Lowell	.25
67	Troy Glaus	1.00
68	George Lombard	.15
69	Alex Gonzalez	.15
70	Mike Kinkade	.15
71	Jeremy Giambi	.15
72	Bruce Chen	.15
73	Preston Wilson	.25
74	Kevin Witt	.15
75	Carlos Guillen	.15
76	Ryan Minor	.15
77	Corey Koskie	.15
78	Robert Fick	.15
79	Michael Barrett	.15
80	Calvin Pickering	.15
81	Ken Griffey Jr.	1.00
82	Mark McGwire	1.50
83	Cal Ripken Jr.	2.00
84	Derek Jeter	2.00
85	Chipper Jones	.75
86	Nomar Garciapparra	.75
87	Sammy Sosa	.75
88	Juan Gonzalez	.30
89	Mike Piazza	1.00
90	Alex Rodriguez	1.50

Standing Ovation

Stars (1-60):	3X
World Premiere (61-80):	1.5X
Superstar Spotlight (81-90):	2X

Production 500 sets
(See 1999 Upper Deck Ovation for checklist and base card values.)

Curtain Calls

		NM/M
Complete Set (20):		20.00
Common Player:		.25
Inserted 1:8		
R1	Mark McGwire	2.00
R2	Sammy Sosa	1.00
R3	Ken Griffey Jr.	1.50
R4	Alex Rodriguez	2.00
R5	Roger Clemens	1.25
R6	Cal Ripken Jr.	2.50
R7	Barry Bonds	2.50
R8	Kerry Wood	.40
R9	Nomar Garciaparra	1.00
R10	Derek Jeter	2.50
R11	Juan Gonzalez	.50
R12	Greg Maddux	1.00
R13	Pedro Martinez	1.00
R14	David Wells	.25
R15	Moises Alou	.25
R16	Tony Gwynn	1.00
R17	Albert Belle	.25
R18	Mike Piazza	1.50
R19	Ivan Rodriguez	.65
R20	Randy Johnson	.75

Major Production

		NM/M
Complete Set (20):		45.00
Common Player:		.75
Inserted 1:45		
S1	Mike Piazza	4.00
S2	Mark McGwire	5.00
S3	Chipper Jones	3.00
S4	Cal Ripken Jr.	6.00
S5	Ken Griffey Jr.	4.00
S6	Barry Bonds	6.00
S7	Tony Gwynn	3.00
S8	Randy Johnson	2.50
S9	Ivan Rodriguez	2.00
S10	Frank Thomas	2.50
S11	Alex Rodriguez	5.00
S12	Albert Belle	.75
S13	Juan Gonzalez	1.25
S14	Greg Maddux	3.00
S15	Jeff Bagwell	2.50
S16	Derek Jeter	6.00
S17	Matt Williams	.75
S18	Kenny Lofton	.75
S19	Sammy Sosa	3.00
S20	Roger Clemens	3.50

Piece of History

		NM/M
Common Player:		5.00
Inserted 1:247		
BB	Barry Bonds	25.00
CJ	Chipper Jones	15.00
BW	Bernie Williams	5.00
KGj	Ken Griffey Jr.	20.00
NG	Nomar Garciaparra	15.00
JG	Juan Gonzalez	5.00
DJ	Derek Jeter	25.00
SS	Sammy Sosa	15.00
TG	Tony Gwynn	15.00
AR	Alex Rodriguez	20.00
CR	Cal Ripken Jr.	25.00
BG	Ben Grieve	5.00
VG	Vladimir Guerrero	10.00
MP	Mike Piazza	20.00
BGAU	Ben Grieve (autographed/25)	30.00
KWAU	Kerry Wood (autographed/25)	50.00

ReMarkable

		NM/M
Complete Set (15):		20.00
Common #1-5:		1.50
Inserted 1:9		
Common #6-10:		2.25
Inserted 1:25		
Common # 11-15		3.00
Inserted 1:99		
MM1	Mark McGwire	1.50
MM2	Mark McGwire	1.50
MM3	Mark McGwire	1.50
MM4	Mark McGwire	1.50
MM5	Mark McGwire	1.50
MM6	Mark McGwire	2.25
MM7	Mark McGwire	2.25
MM8	Mark McGwire	2.25
MM9	Mark McGwire	2.25
MM10	Mark McGwire	2.25
MM11	Mark McGwire	3.00
MM12	Mark McGwire	3.00
MM13	Mark McGwire	3.00
MM14	Mark McGwire	3.00
MM15	Mark McGwire	3.00

500 Club Piece of History

	NM/M
MIC-PMickey Mantle (350)	600.00
Mickey Mantle (bat/autograph, 6/01 auction)	8,000

1999 UPPER DECK POWERDECK

		NM/M
Complete Set (25):		20.00
Common Player:		.50
Pack (3):		1.50
Wax Box (24):		20.00
1	Ken Griffey Jr.	2.00
2	Mark McGwire	2.50
3	Cal Ripken Jr.	3.00
4	Sammy Sosa	1.50
5	Derek Jeter	3.00
6	Mike Piazza	2.00
7	Nomar Garciaparra	1.50
8	Greg Maddux	1.50
9	Tony Gwynn	1.50
10	Roger Clemens	1.75
11	Scott Rolen	1.00

12	Alex Rodriguez	2.50
13	Manny Ramirez	1.25
14	Chipper Jones	1.50
15	Juan Gonzalez	.65
16	Ivan Rodriguez	1.00
17	Frank Thomas	1.25
18	Mo Vaughn	.50
19	Barry Bonds	3.00
20	Vladimir Guerrero	1.25
21	Jose Canseco	.65
22	Jeff Bagwell	1.25
23	Pedro Martinez	1.25
24	Gabe Kapler	.50
25	J.D. Drew	.75
---	Checklist	.10

Auxiliary Power

		NM/M
Complete Set (25):		6.00
Common Player:		.10
1	Ken Griffey Jr.	.50
2	Mark McGwire	.60
3	Cal Ripken Jr.	.75
4	Sammy Sosa	.40
5	Derek Jeter	.75
6	Mike Piazza	.50
7	Nomar Garciaparra	.40
8	Greg Maddux	.40
9	Tony Gwynn	.40
10	Roger Clemens	.45
11	Scott Rolen	.25
12	Alex Rodriguez	.60
13	Manny Ramirez	.30
14	Chipper Jones	.40
15	Juan Gonzalez	.15
16	Ivan Rodriguez	.25
17	Frank Thomas	.30
18	Mo Vaughn	.10
19	Barry Bonds	.75
20	Vladimir Guerrero	.30
21	Jose Canseco	.20
22	Jeff Bagwell	.30
23	Pedro Martinez	.30
24	Gabe Kapler	.10
25	J.D. Drew	.25

A Season to Remember

	NM/M
Mark McGwire	3.00

Most Valuable Performances

		NM/M
Complete Set (7):		75.00
Common Player:		6.00
Inserted 1:287		
1	Sammy Sosa	10.00
2	Barry Bonds	20.00
3	Cal Ripken Jr.	20.00
4	Juan Gonzalez	6.00
5	Ken Griffey Jr.	12.50
6	Roger Clemens	10.00
7	Mark McGwire, Sammy Sosa	12.50

MVP Auxiliary

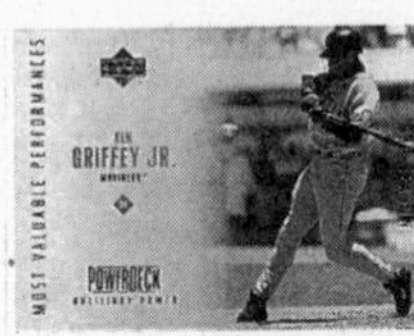

		NM/M
Complete Set (7):		60.00
Common Player:		4.00
Inserted 1:287		
1	Sammy Sosa	7.50
2	Barry Bonds	15.00
3	Cal Ripken Jr.	15.00
4	Juan Gonzalez	4.00
5	Ken Griffey Jr.	10.00
6	Roger Clemens	7.50
7	Mark McGwire, Sammy Sosa	12.50

Powerful Moments

		NM/M
Complete Set (6):		10.00
Common Player:		1.00
Inserted 1:7		
1	Mark McGwire	2.00
2	Sammy Sosa	1.00
3	Cal Ripken Jr.	3.00
4	Ken Griffey Jr.	1.50
5	Derek Jeter	3.00
6	Alex Rodriguez	2.00

Powerful Moments Auxiliary

		NM/M
Complete Set (6):		10.00
Common Player:		1.00
Inserted 1:7		
Gold (one each): VALUE UNDETERMINED		
1	Mark McGwire	2.00
2	Sammy Sosa	1.00
3	Cal Ripken Jr.	3.00
4	Ken Griffey Jr.	1.50
5	Derek Jeter	3.00
6	Alex Rodriguez	2.00

Time Capsule

		NM/M
Complete Set (6):		12.50
Common Player:		1.00
Inserted 1:23		
1	Ken Griffey Jr.	2.50
2	Mike Piazza	2.50
3	Mark McGwire	3.00
4	Derek Jeter	4.00
5	Jose Canseco	1.00
6	Nomar Garciaparra	2.00

Time Capsule-Auxiliary Power

		NM/M
Complete Set (6):		15.00
Common Player:		1.00
Inserted 1:23		
Gold (one of each): VALUES UNDETERMINED		
1	Ken Griffey Jr.	2.50
2	Mike Piazza	2.50
3	Mark McGwire	3.00
4	Derek Jeter	4.00
5	Jose Canseco	1.00
6	Nomar Garciaparra	2.00

1999 UPPER DECK ULTIMATE VICTORY

		NM/M
Complete Set (180):		150.00
Common Player:		.10
Common 99 Rookie (121-150):		.50
Common McGwire Magic (151-180):		1.00
Victory (1-120):		3.5X
Victory SP (121-180):		2X
Inserted 1:12		
Ultimate (1-120):		12X
Ultimate SP (121-180):		5X
Production 100 sets		
Pack (5):		5.00
Wax Box (24):		100.00
1	Troy Glaus	.65
2	Tim Salmon	.10
3	Mo Vaughn	.10
4	Garret Anderson	.10
5	Darin Erstad	.30
6	Randy Johnson	.75
7	Matt Williams	.10
8	Travis Lee	.25
9	Jay Bell	.10
10	Steve Finley	.10
11	Luis Gonzalez	.10
12	Greg Maddux	1.00
13	Chipper Jones	1.00
14	Javy Lopez	.10
15	Tom Glavine	.35
16	John Smoltz	.10
17	Cal Ripken Jr.	3.00
18	Charles Johnson	.10
19	Albert Belle	.10
20	Mike Mussina	.40
21	Pedro Martinez	.75
22	Nomar Garciaparra	1.00
23	Jose Offerman	.10
24	Sammy Sosa	1.00
25	Mark Grace	.10
26	Kerry Wood	.35
27	Frank Thomas	.75
28	Ray Durham	.10
29	Paul Konerko	.20
30	Pete Harnisch	.10
31	Greg Vaughn	.10
32	Sean Casey	.20
33	Manny Ramirez	.75
34	Jim Thome	.65
35	Sandy Alomar	.10
36	Roberto Alomar	.30
37	Travis Fryman	.10
38	Kenny Lofton	.10
39	Omar Vizquel	.10
40	Larry Walker	.10
41	Todd Helton	.65
42	Vinny Castilla	.10
43	Tony Clark	.10
44	Juan Encarnacion	.10
45	Dean Palmer	.10
46	Damion Easley	.10
47	Mark Kotsay	.10
48	Cliff Floyd	.10
49	Jeff Bagwell	.75
50	Ken Caminiti	.10
51	Craig Biggio	.10
52	Moises Alou	.10
53	Johnny Damon	.35
54	Larry Sutton	.10
55	Kevin Brown	.10
56	Adrian Beltre	.25
57	Raul Mondesi	.10
58	Gary Sheffield	.50
59	Jeromy Burnitz	.10
60	Sean Berry	.10
61	Jeff Cirillo	.10
62	Brad Radke	.10
63	Todd Walker	.10
64	Matt Lawton	.10
65	Vladimir Guerrero	.75
66	Rondell White	.10
67	Dustin Hermanson	.10
68	Mike Piazza	2.00
69	Rickey Henderson	.75
70	Robin Ventura	.10
71	John Olerud	.10
72	Derek Jeter	3.00
73	Roger Clemens	1.25
74	Orlando Hernandez	.10
75	Paul O'Neill	.10
76	Bernie Williams	.10
77	Chuck Knoblauch	.10
78	Tino Martinez	.10
79	Jason Giambi	.50
80	Ben Grieve	.10
81	Matt Stairs	.10
82	Scott Rolen	.60
83	Ron Gant	.10
84	Bobby Abreu	.10
85	Curt Schilling	.35
86	Brian Giles	.10
87	Jason Kendall	.10
88	Kevin Young	.10
89	Mark McGwire	2.00
90	Fernando Tatis	.10
91	Ray Lankford	.10
92	Eric Davis	.10
93	Tony Gwynn	1.00
94	Reggie Sanders	.10
95	Wally Joyner	.10
96	Trevor Hoffman	.10
97	Robb Nen	.10
98	Barry Bonds	3.00
99	Jeff Kent	.10
100	J.T. Snow	.10
101	Ellis Burks	.10
102	Ken Griffey Jr.	1.50
103	Alex Rodriguez	2.00
104	Jay Buhner	.10
105	Edgar Martinez	.10
106	David Bell	.10
107	Bobby Smith	.10
108	Wade Boggs	1.00
109	Fred McGriff	.10
110	Rolando Arrojo	.10
111	Jose Canseco	.50
112	Ivan Rodriguez	.65
113	Juan Gonzalez	.40
114	Rafael Palmeiro	.65
115	Rusty Greer	.10
116	Todd Zeile	.10
117	Jose Cruz Jr.	.10
118	Carlos Delgado	.35
119	Shawn Green	.30
120	David Wells	.10
121	*Eric Munson*	2.50
122	Lance Berkman	2.00
123	Ed Yarnall	.50
124	Jacque Jones	1.00
125	Kyle Farnsworth	1.00
126	Ryan Rupe	1.00
127	*Jeff Weaver*	2.00
128	Gabe Kapler	.50
129	Alex Gonzalez	.50
130	Randy Wolf	1.00
131	Ben Davis	.50
132	Carlos Beltran	2.00
133	Jim Morris	2.00
134	Jeff Zimmerman	2.00
135	Bruce Aven	.50
136	*Alfonso Soriano*	45.00
137	*Tim Hudson*	25.00
138	*Josh Beckett*	30.00
139	Michael Barrett	.50
140	Eric Chavez	1.00
141	*Pat Burrell*	15.00
142	Kris Benson	1.00
143	J.D. Drew	2.00
144	Matt Clement	1.00
145	*Rick Ankiel*	4.00
146	Vernon Wells	1.00
147	Ruben Mateo	.50
148	Roy Halladay	1.00
149	Joe McEwing	.50
150	*Freddy Garcia*	8.00
151	Mark McGwire	1.00
152	Mark McGwire	1.00
153	Mark McGwire	1.00
154	Mark McGwire	1.00
155	Mark McGwire	1.00

156 Mark McGwire 1.00
157 Mark McGwire 1.00
158 Mark McGwire 1.00
159 Mark McGwire 1.00
160 Mark McGwire 1.00
161 Mark McGwire 1.00
162 Mark McGwire 1.00
163 Mark McGwire 1.00
164 Mark McGwire 1.00
165 Mark McGwire 1.00
166 Mark McGwire 1.00
167 Mark McGwire 1.00
168 Mark McGwire 1.00
169 Mark McGwire 1.00
170 Mark McGwire 1.00
171 Mark McGwire 1.00
172 Mark McGwire 1.00
173 Mark McGwire 1.00
174 Mark McGwire 1.00
175 Mark McGwire 1.00
176 Mark McGwire 1.00
177 Mark McGwire 1.00
178 Mark McGwire 1.00
179 Mark McGwire 1.00
180 Mark McGwire 1.00

Victory Collection

NM/M

Common Player (1-120, 151-180): 1.00
Common Player (121-150): 5.00
Stars (1-120): 3.5X
Stars (121-150): 2X
(See 1999 Ultimate Victory for checklist and base card values.)

Ultimate Collection

NM/M

Common Player (1-120, 151-180): 2.00
Common Player (121-150): 12.00
Stars (1-120): 12X
Stars (121-150): 5X
(See 1999 Upper Deck Ultimate Victory forchecklist and base card values.)

Fame-Used Combo

NM/M

Edition of 99:
HOF Nolan Ryan, George Brett, Robin Yount, Orlando Cepeda 250.00

Fame-Used Memorabilia

NM/M

Complete Set (4): 50.00
Common Player: 7.50
Production 350 cards
GB George Brett 20.00
OC Orlando Cepeda 7.50
NR Nolan Ryan 25.00
RY Robin Yount 10.00

Frozen Ropes

NM/M

Complete Set (10): 15.00
Common Player: .50
Inserted 1:23

1 Ken Griffey Jr. 2.00
2 Mark McGwire 2.50
3 Sammy Sosa 1.50
4 Derek Jeter 3.00
5 Tony Gwynn 1.50
6 Nomar Garciaparra 1.50
7 Alex Rodriguez 2.50
8 Mike Piazza 2.00
9 Mo Vaughn .50
10 Craig Biggio .50

STATure

NM/M

Complete Set (15): 9.00
Common Player: .30
Inserted 1:6
1 Ken Griffey Jr. .75
2 Mark McGwire 1.00
3 Sammy Sosa .65
4 Nomar Garciaparra .65
5 Roger Clemens .65
6 Greg Maddux .65
7 Alex Rodriguez 1.00
8 Derek Jeter 1.50
9 Juan Gonzalez .30
10 Manny Ramirez .50
11 Mike Piazza .75
12 Tony Gwynn .65
13 Chipper Jones .65
14 Pedro Martinez .50
15 Frank Thomas .50

Tribute 1999

NM/M

Complete Set (4): 5.00
Common Player: 1.00
Inserted 1:11
1 Nolan Ryan 2.00
2 Robin Yount 1.50
3 George Brett 1.50
4 Orlando Cepeda 1.00

Ultimate Competitors

NM/M

Complete Set (12): 20.00
Common Player: .60
Inserted 1:23
1 Ken Griffey Jr. 3.00
2 Roger Clemens 2.50
3 Scott Rolen 1.00
4 Greg Maddux 2.00
5 Mark McGwire 4.00
6 Derek Jeter 5.00
7 Randy Johnson 1.50
8 Cal Ripken Jr. 5.00
9 Craig Biggio .50
10 Kevin Brown .50
11 Chipper Jones 2.00
12 Vladimir Guerrero 1.50

Ultimate Hit Men

NM/M

Complete Set (8): 15.00
Common Player: 1.00
Inserted 1:23
1 Tony Gwynn 2.00
2 Cal Ripken Jr. 4.00
3 Wade Boggs 2.00
4 Larry Walker 1.00
5 Alex Rodriguez 3.00
6 Derek Jeter 4.00
7 Ivan Rodriguez 1.25
8 Ken Griffey Jr. 2.50

1999 UPPER DECK UD CHOICE

NM/M

Complete Set (155): 7.50
Common Player: .03
Prime Choice Reserve Stars: 10X
Production 100 sets
Pack (12): .50
Wax Box (36): 10.00
1 Gabe Kapler .05
2 Jin Ho Cho .05
3 Matt Anderson .05
4 Ricky Ledee .05
5 Bruce Chen .05
6 Alex Gonzalez .05
7 Ryan Minor .05
8 Michael Barrett .05
9 Carlos Beltran .50
10 Ramon Martinez .05
11 Dermal Brown .05
12 Robert Fick .05
13 Preston Wilson .05
14 Orlando Hernandez .05
15 Troy Glaus .65
16 Calvin Pickering .05
17 Corey Koskie .05
18 Fernando Seguignol .05
19 Carlos Guillen .05
20 Kevin Witt .05
21 Mike Kinkade .05
22 Eric Chavez .15
23 Mike Lowell .10
24 Adrian Beltre .10
25 George Lombard .05
26 Jeremy Giambi .05
27 J.D. Drew .40
28 Mark McGwire .60
29 Kerry Wood .15
30 David Wells .05
31 Juan Gonzalez .15
32 Randy Johnson .35
33 Derek Jeter .75
34 Tony Gwynn .45
35 Greg Maddux .45
36 Cal Ripken Jr. .75
37 Ken Griffey Jr. .50
38 Bartolo Colon .05
39 Troy Glaus .30
40 Ben Grieve .05
41 Roger Clemens .50
42 Chipper Jones .45
43 Scott Rolen .25
44 Nomar Garciaparra .45
45 Sammy Sosa .45
46 Tim Salmon .05
47 Darin Erstad .25
48 Chuck Finley .05
49 Garrett Anderson .05
50 Matt Williams .05
51 Jay Bell .05
52 Travis Lee .10
53 Andruw Jones .65
54 Andres Galarraga .05
55 Chipper Jones .75
56 Greg Maddux .75
57 Javy Lopez .05
58 Cal Ripken Jr. 1.50
59 Brady Anderson .05
60 Rafael Palmeiro .50
61 B.J. Surhoff .05
62 Nomar Garciaparra .75
63 Troy O'Leary .05
64 Pedro Martinez .65
65 Jason Varitek .05
66 Kerry Wood .35
67 Sammy Sosa .75
68 Mark Grace .05
69 Mickey Morandini .05
70 Albert Belle .05
71 Mike Caruso .05
72 Frank Thomas .65
73 Sean Casey .10
74 Pete Harnisch .05
75 Dmitri Young .05
76 Manny Ramirez .65
77 Omar Vizquel .05
78 Travis Fryman .05
79 Jim Thome .40
80 Kenny Lofton .05
81 Todd Helton .50
82 Larry Walker .05
83 Vinny Castilla .05
84 Gabe Alvarez .05
85 Tony Clark .05
86 Damion Easley .05
87 Livan Hernandez .05
88 Mark Kotsay .05
89 Cliff Floyd .05
90 Jeff Bagwell .65
91 Moises Alou .05
92 Randy Johnson .65
93 Craig Biggio .05
94 Larry Sutton .05
95 Dean Palmer .05
96 Johnny Damon .20
97 Charles Johnson .05
98 Gary Sheffield .25
99 Raul Mondesi .05
100 Mark Grudzielanek .05
101 Jeromy Burnitz .05
102 Jeff Cirillo .05
103 Jose Valentin .05
104 Mark Loretta .05
105 Todd Walker .05
106 David Ortiz .35
107 Brad Radke .05
108 Brad Fullmer .05
109 Rondell White .05
110 Vladimir Guerrero .65
111 Mike Piazza 1.00
112 Brian McRae .05
113 John Olerud .05
114 Rey Ordonez .05
115 Derek Jeter 1.50
116 Bernie Williams .05
117 David Wells .05
118 Paul O'Neill .05
119 Tino Martinez .05
120 A.J. Hinch .05
121 Jason Giambi .30
122 Miguel Tejada .10
123 Ben Grieve .05
124 Scott Rolen .50
125 Desi Relaford .05
126 Bobby Abreu .10
127 Jose Guillen .05
128 Jason Kendall .05
129 Aramis Ramirez .05
130 Mark McGwire 1.25
131 Ray Lankford .05
132 Eli Marrero .05
133 Wally Joyner .05
134 Greg Vaughn .05
135 Trevor Hoffman .05
136 Kevin Brown .05
137 Tony Gwynn .75
138 Bill Mueller .05
139 Ellis Burks .05
140 Barry Bonds 1.50
141 Robb Nen .05
142 Ken Griffey Jr. 1.00
143 Alex Rodriguez 1.25
144 Jay Buhner .05
145 Edgar Martinez .05
146 Rolando Arrojo .05
147 Robert Smith .05
148 Quinton McCracken .05
149 Ivan Rodriguez .50
150 Will Clark .05
151 Mark McLemore .05
152 Juan Gonzalez .35
153 Jose Cruz Jr. .05
154 Carlos Delgado .25
155 Roger Clemens .85

Prime Choice Reserve

NM/M
Common Player: 2.50
Stars: 10X
(See 1999 UD Choice for checklist and base card values.)

Mini Bobbing Head

		NM/M
Complete Set (30):		15.00
Common Player:		.25
Inserted 1:5		
B1	Randy Johnson	.50
B2	Troy Glaus	.50
B3	Chipper Jones	.65
B4	Cal Ripken Jr.	1.50
B5	Nomar Garciaparra	.65
B6	Pedro Martinez	.50
B7	Kerry Wood	.35
B8	Sammy Sosa	.65
B9	Frank Thomas	.50
B10	Paul Konerko	.35
B11	Omar Vizquel	.25
B12	Kenny Lofton	.25
B13	Gabe Kapler	.25
B14	Adrian Beltre	.35
B15	Orlando Hernandez	.25
B16	Derek Jeter	1.50
B17	Mike Piazza	.75
B18	Tino Martinez	.25
B19	Ben Grieve	.25
B20	Rickey Henderson	.50
B21	Scott Rolen	.40
B22	Aramis Ramirez	.25
B23	Greg Vaughn	.25
B24	Tony Gwynn	.65
B25	Barry Bonds	1.50
B26	Alex Rodriguez	1.00
B27	Ken Griffey Jr.	.75
B28	Mark McGwire	1.00
B29	J.D. Drew	.45
B30	Juan Gonzalez	.30

Piece of History 500 Club

		NM/M
EM	Eddie Murray (350)	150.00

StarQuest

		NM/M
Complete Set (30):		7.50
Common Player:		.10
Inserted 1:1		
Green (1:8):		1.5X
Red (1:23):		3X
Gold (100 sets):		50X
SQ1	Ken Griffey Jr.	.60
SQ2	Sammy Sosa	.50
SQ3	Alex Rodriguez	.75
SQ4	Derek Jeter	1.00
SQ5	Troy Glaus	.35
SQ6	Mike Piazza	.60
SQ7	Barry Bonds	1.00
SQ8	Tony Gwynn	.50
SQ9	Juan Gonzalez	.20
SQ10	Chipper Jones	.50
SQ11	Greg Maddux	.50
SQ12	Randy Johnson	.40
SQ13	Roger Clemens	.55
SQ14	Ben Grieve	.10
SQ15	Nomar Garciaparra	.50
SQ16	Travis Lee	.15
SQ17	Frank Thomas	.40
SQ18	Vladimir Guerrero	.40
SQ19	Scott Rolen	.30
SQ20	Ivan Rodriguez	.35
SQ21	Cal Ripken Jr.	1.00
SQ22	Mark McGwire	.75
SQ23	Jeff Bagwell	.40
SQ24	Tony Clark	.10
SQ25	Kerry Wood	.25
SQ26	Kenny Lofton	.10
SQ27	Adrian Beltre	.15
SQ28	Larry Walker	.10
SQ29	Curt Schilling	.25
SQ30	Jim Thome	.40

Yard Work

		NM/M
Complete Set (30):		20.00
Common Player:		.35
Inserted 1:13		
Y1	Andres Galarraga	.35
Y2	Chipper Jones	1.50
Y3	Rafael Palmeiro	.75
Y4	Nomar Garciaparra	1.50
Y5	Sammy Sosa	1.50
Y6	Frank Thomas	1.00
Y7	J.D. Drew	.75
Y8	Albert Belle	.35
Y9	Jim Thome	.60
Y10	Manny Ramirez	1.00
Y11	Larry Walker	.35
Y12	Vinny Castilla	.35
Y13	Tony Clark	.35
Y14	Jeff Bagwell	1.00
Y15	Moises Alou	.35
Y16	Dean Palmer	.35
Y17	Gary Sheffield	.50
Y18	Vladimir Guerrero	1.00
Y19	Mike Piazza	1.75
Y20	Tino Martinez	.35
Y21	Ben Grieve	.35
Y22	Greg Vaughn	.35
Y23	Ken Caminiti	.35
Y24	Barry Bonds	3.00
Y25	Ken Griffey Jr.	1.75
Y26	Alex Rodriguez	2.25
Y27	Mark McGwire	2.25
Y28	Juan Gonzalez	.50
Y29	Jose Canseco	.50
Y30	Jose Cruz Jr.	.35

1999 UD IONIX

		NM/M
Complete Set (90):		45.00
Common Player (1-60):		.25
Common Techno (61-90):		.50
Inserted 1:4		
Reciprocals (1-60):		3X
Production 750 sets		
Techno Reciprocals (61-90):		1.5X
Production 100 sets		
Pack (4):		2.00
Wax Box (20):		25.00
1	Troy Glaus	.60
2	Darin Erstad	.50
3	Travis Lee	.35
4	Matt Williams	.25
5	Chipper Jones	.75
6	Greg Maddux	.75
7	Andruw Jones	.65
8	Andres Galarraga	.25
9	Tom Glavine	.35
10	Cal Ripken Jr.	2.00
11	Ryan Minor	.25
12	Nomar Garciaparra	1.00
13	Mo Vaughn	.25
14	Pedro Martinez	.65
15	Sammy Sosa	.75
16	Kerry Wood	.50
17	Albert Belle	.25
18	Frank Thomas	.65
19	Sean Casey	.25
20	Kenny Lofton	.25
21	Manny Ramirez	.65
22	Jim Thome	.60
23	Bartolo Colon	.25
24	Jaret Wright	.25
25	Larry Walker	.25
26	Tony Clark	.25
27	Gabe Kapler	.25
28	Edgar Renteria	.25
29	Randy Johnson	.65
30	Craig Biggio	.25
31	Jeff Bagwell	.65
32	Moises Alou	.25
33	Johnny Damon	.50
34	Adrian Beltre	.35
35	Jeromy Burnitz	.25
36	Todd Walker	.25
37	Corey Koskie	.25
38	Vladimir Guerrero	.65
39	Mike Piazza	1.00
40	Hideo Nomo	.35
41	Derek Jeter	2.00
42	Tino Martinez	.25
43	Orlando Hernandez	.25
44	Ben Grieve	.25
45	Rickey Henderson	.65
46	Scott Rolen	.60
47	Curt Schilling	.35
48	Aramis Ramirez	.25
49	Tony Gwynn	.75
50	Kevin Brown	.25
51	Barry Bonds	2.00
52	Ken Griffey Jr.	1.00
53	Alex Rodriguez	1.50
54	Mark McGwire	1.50
55	J.D. Drew	.60
56	Rolando Arrojo	.25
57	Ivan Rodriguez	.60
58	Juan Gonzalez	.35
59	Roger Clemens	.85
60	Jose Cruz Jr.	.25
61	Travis Lee	.65
62	Andres Galarraga	.50
63	Andruw Jones	1.50
64	Chipper Jones	2.00
65	Greg Maddux	2.00
66	Cal Ripken Jr.	4.00
67	Nomar Garciaparra	2.00
68	Mo Vaughn	.50
69	Sammy Sosa	2.00
70	Frank Thomas	1.50
71	Kerry Wood	.75
72	Kenny Lofton	.50
73	Manny Ramirez	1.50
74	Larry Walker	.50
75	Jeff Bagwell	1.50
76	Randy Johnson	1.50
77	Paul Molitor	1.50
78	Derek Jeter	4.00
79	Tino Martinez	.50
80	Mike Piazza	2.50
81	Ben Grieve	.50
82	Scott Rolen	.75
83	Mark McGwire	3.00
84	Tony Gwynn	2.00
85	Barry Bonds	4.00
86	Ken Griffey Jr.	2.50
87	Alex Rodriguez	3.00
88	Juan Gonzalez	.75
89	Roger Clemens	2.25
90	J.D. Drew	1.00
100	Ken Griffey Jr. (SAMPLE)	2.50

Reciprocal

Stars (1-60): 3X
Stars (61-90): 1.5X
(See 1999 UD Ionix for checklist and base card values.)

Cyber

		NM/M
Complete Set (25):		125.00
Common Player:		2.00
C01	Ken Griffey Jr.	8.00
C02	Cal Ripken Jr.	12.50
C03	Frank Thomas	5.00
C04	Greg Maddux	6.50
C05	Mike Piazza	8.00
C06	Alex Rodriguez	10.00
C07	Chipper Jones	6.50
C08	Derek Jeter	12.50
C09	Mark McGwire	10.00
C10	Juan Gonzalez	2.50
C11	Kerry Wood	2.50
C12	Tony Gwynn	6.50
C13	Scott Rolen	4.00
C14	Nomar Garciaparra	6.50
C15	Roger Clemens	7.00
C16	Sammy Sosa	6.50
C17	Travis Lee	2.00
C18	Ben Grieve	2.00
C19	Jeff Bagwell	5.00
C20	Ivan Rodriguez	4.00
C21	Barry Bonds	12.50
C22	J.D. Drew	4.00
C23	Kenny Lofton	2.00
C24	Andruw Jones	5.00
C25	Vladimir Guerrero	5.00

HoloGrFX

		NM/M
Complete Set (10):		800.00
Common Player:		50.00
Inserted 1:1,500		
HG01	Ken Griffey Jr.	100.00
HG02	Cal Ripken Jr.	150.00
HG03	Frank Thomas	75.00
HG04	Greg Maddux	90.00
HG05	Mike Piazza	100.00
HG06	Alex Rodriguez	125.00
HG07	Chipper Jones	90.00
HG08	Derek Jeter	150.00
HG09	Mark McGwire	125.00
HG10	Juan Gonzalez	50.00

Hyper

		NM/M
Complete Set (20):		37.00
Common Player:		.75
Inserted 1:9		
H01	Ken Griffey Jr.	3.00
H02	Cal Ripken Jr.	4.50
H03	Frank Thomas	1.50
H04	Greg Maddux	2.25
H05	Mike Piazza	3.00
H06	Alex Rodriguez	3.75
H07	Chipper Jones	2.25
H08	Derek Jeter	4.50
H09	Mark McGwire	3.75
H10	Juan Gonzalez	.75
H11	Kerry Wood	1.00
H12	Tony Gwynn	2.25

H13	Scott Rolen	1.00
H14	Nomar Garciaparra	2.25
H15	Roger Clemens	2.75
H16	Sammy Sosa	2.25
H17	Travis Lee	1.00
H18	Ben Grieve	.75
H19	Jeff Bagwell	1.50
H20	J.D. Drew	1.00

Nitro

		NM/M
Complete Set (10):		18.00
Common Player:		1.00
Inserted 1:18		
N01	Ken Griffey Jr.	2.50
N02	Cal Ripken Jr.	4.00
N03	Frank Thomas	1.50
N04	Greg Maddux	2.00
N05	Mike Piazza	2.50
N06	Alex Rodriguez	3.00
N07	Chipper Jones	2.00
N08	Derek Jeter	4.00
N09	Mark McGwire	3.00
N10	J.D. Drew	1.00

Warp Zone

		NM/M
Complete Set (15):		195.00
Common Player:		6.00
Inserted 1:216		
WZ1	Ken Griffey Jr.	20.00
WZ2	Cal Ripken Jr.	30.00
WZ3	Frank Thomas	10.00
WZ4	Greg Maddux	15.00
WZ5	Mike Piazza	20.00
WZ6	Alex Rodriguez	25.00
WZ7	Chipper Jones	15.00
WZ8	Derek Jeter	30.00
WZ9	Mark McGwire	25.00
WZ10	Juan Gonzalez	6.00
WZ11	Kerry Wood	6.00
WZ12	Tony Gwynn	15.00
WZ13	Scott Rolen	6.00
WZ14	Nomar Garciaparra	15.00
WZ15	J.D. Drew	6.00

500 Club Piece of History

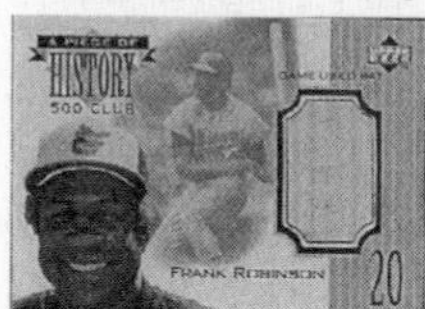

		NM/M
FR	Frank Robinson (350)	165.00
FRA	Frank Robinson (autographed/20)	650.00

1999 UD RETRO

		NM/M
Complete Set (110):		15.00
Common Player:		.05
Wax Pack (6):		2.50
Lunchbox (24):		45.00
1	Mo Vaughn	.05
2	Troy Glaus	.65
3	Tim Salmon	.05
4	Randy Johnson	.75
5	Travis Lee	.15
6	Matt Williams	.05
7	Greg Maddux	.85
8	Chipper Jones	.85
9	Andruw Jones	.75
10	Tom Glavine	.25
11	Javy Lopez	.05
12	Albert Belle	.05
13	Cal Ripken Jr.	2.00
14	Brady Anderson	.05
15	Nomar Garciaparra	.85
16	Pedro J. Martinez	.75
17	Sammy Sosa	.85
18	Mark Grace	.05
19	Frank Thomas	.75
20	Ray Durham	.05
21	Sean Casey	.10
22	Greg Vaughn	.05
23	Barry Larkin	.05
24	Manny Ramirez	.75
25	Jim Thome	.50
26	Jaret Wright	.05
27	Kenny Lofton	.05
28	Larry Walker	.05
29	Todd Helton	.65
30	Vinny Castilla	.05
31	Tony Clark	.05
32	Juan Encarnacion	.05
33	Dean Palmer	.05
34	Mark Kotsay	.05
35	Alex Gonzalez	.05
36	Shane Reynolds	.05
37	Ken Caminiti	.05
38	Jeff Bagwell	.75
39	Craig Biggio	.05
40	Carlos Febles	.05
41	Carlos Beltran	.35
42	Jeremy Giambi	.05
43	Raul Mondesi	.05
44	Adrian Beltre	.10
45	Kevin Brown	.05
46	Jeromy Burnitz	.05
47	Jeff Cirillo	.05
48	Corey Koskie	.05
49	Todd Walker	.05
50	Vladimir Guerrero	.75
51	Michael Barrett	.05
52	Mike Piazza	1.00
53	Robin Ventura	.05
54	Edgardo Alfonzo	.05
55	Derek Jeter	2.00
56	Roger Clemens	.90
57	Tino Martinez	.05
58	Orlando Hernandez	.05
59	Chuck Knoblauch	.05
60	Bernie Williams	.05
61	Eric Chavez	.10
62	Ben Grieve	.05
63	Jason Giambi	.40
64	Scott Rolen	.60
65	Curt Schilling	.25
66	Bobby Abreu	.10
67	Jason Kendall	.05
68	Kevin Young	.05
69	Mark McGwire	1.50
70	J.D. Drew	.60
71	Eric Davis	.05
72	Tony Gwynn	.85
73	Trevor Hoffman	.05
74	Barry Bonds	2.00
75	Robb Nen	.05
76	Ken Griffey Jr.	1.00
77	Alex Rodriguez	1.50
78	Jay Buhner	.05
79	Carlos Guillen	.05
80	Jose Canseco	.40
81	Bobby Smith	.05
82	Juan Gonzalez	.40
83	Ivan Rodriguez	.65
84	Rafael Palmeiro	.65
85	Rick Helling	.05
86	Jose Cruz Jr.	.05
87	David Wells	.05
88	Carlos Delgado	.20
89	Nolan Ryan	1.50
90	George Brett	.90
91	Robin Yount	.50
92	Paul Molitor	.50
93	Dave Winfield	.50
94	Steve Garvey	.25
95	Ozzie Smith	.85
96	Ted Williams	1.50
97	Don Mattingly	.90
98	Mickey Mantle	2.50
99	Harmon Killebrew	.25
100	Rollie Fingers	.10
101	Kirk Gibson	.05
102	Bucky Dent	.05
103	Willie Mays	1.00
104	Babe Ruth	1.50
105	Gary Carter	.50
106	Reggie Jackson	.85
107	Frank Robinson	.25
108	Ernie Banks	.50
109	Eddie Murray	.50
110	Mike Schmidt	.90

Gold/Platinum

	NM/M
Common Gold:	1.00
Gold Stars:	15X
Platinum 1/1:	

VALUES UNDETERMINED
(See 1999 UD Retro for checklist and base card values.)

Distant Replay

		NM/M
Complete Set (15):		30.00
Common Player:		1.00
Inserted 1:8		
Level 2:		6X
Production 100 sets		
1	Ken Griffey Jr.	2.50
2	Mark McGwire	3.00
3	Cal Ripken Jr.	4.00
4	Greg Maddux	2.00
5	Nomar Garciaparra	2.00
6	Roger Clemens	2.25
7	Alex Rodriguez	3.00
8	Frank Thomas	1.50
9	Mike Piazza	2.50
10	Chipper Jones	2.00
11	Juan Gonzalez	1.00
12	Tony Gwynn	2.00
13	Barry Bonds	4.00
14	Ivan Rodriguez	1.00
15	Derek Jeter	4.00

INKredible

		NM/M
Common Player:		4.00
Inserted 1:23		
CBe	Carlos Beltran	30.00
GB	George Brett/SP	80.00
PB	Pat Burrell	10.00
SC	Sean Casey	10.00
TC	Tony Clark	4.00
BD	Bucky Dent	8.00
DE	Darin Erstad	15.00
RF	Rollie Fingers	8.00
SG	Steve Garvey	10.00
KG	Kirk Gibson	10.00
RG	Rusty Greer	4.00
JR	Ken Griffey Jr.	80.00
TG	Tony Gwynn	30.00
CJ	Chipper Jones	30.00
GK	Gabe Kapler	5.00
HK	Harmon Killebrew	30.00
FL	Fred Lynn	10.00
DM	Don Mattingly	50.00
PM	Paul Molitor	20.00
EM	Eddie Murray/SP	50.00
PO	Paul O'Neill	15.00
AP	Angel Pena	4.00
MR	Manny Ramirez	30.00
IR	Ivan Rodriguez	25.00
NR	Nolan Ryan	150.00
OZ	Ozzie Smith	30.00
DWe	David Wells	15.00
BW	Bernie Williams	40.00
DW	Dave Winfield	20.00
RY	Robin Yount	35.00

INKredible Level 2

		NM/M
Common Player:		10.00
Limited to player's jersey #		
CBe	Carlos Beltran (36)	60.00
GB	George Brett (5)	
PB	Pat Burrell (76)	50.00
SC	Sean Casey (21)	40.00
TC	Tony Clark (17)	20.00
BD	Bucky Dent (20)	25.00
DE	Darin Erstad (17)	50.00
RF	Rollie Fingers (34)	25.00
SG	Steve Garvey (6)	
KG	Kirk Gibson (23)	30.00
RG	Rusty Greer (29)	20.00
JR	Ken Griffey Jr. (24)	200.00
TG	Tony Gwynn (19)	150.00
CJ	Chipper Jones (10)	
GK	Gabe Kapler (23)	40.00
HK	Harmon Killebrew (3)	
FL	Fred Lynn (19)	30.00
DM	Don Mattingly (23)	200.00
PM	Paul Molitor (4)	
EM	Eddie Murray (33)	80.00
PO	Paul O'Neill (21)	50.00
AP	Angel Pena (36)	10.00
MR	Manny Ramirez (24)	80.00
IR	Ivan Rodriguez (7)	
NR	Nolan Ryan (34)	400.00
OZ	Ozzie Smith (1)	
DWe	David Wells (33)	25.00
BW	Bernie Williams (51)	60.00
DW	Dave Winfield (31)	60.00
RY	Robin Yount (19)	90.00

Lunchbox

	NM/M
Complete Set (17):	140.00
Common Lunchbox:	7.50
1 dual-player per case	
Roger Clemens	7.50
Ken Griffey Jr.	7.50
Mickey Mantle	10.00
Mark McGwire	10.00
Mike Piazza	7.50
Alex Rodriguez	7.50
Babe Ruth	10.00
Sammy Sosa	7.50
Ted Williams	10.00
Ken Griffey Jr., Mark McGwire	12.50
Ken Griffey Jr., Babe Ruth	12.50
Ken Griffey Jr., Ted Williams	12.50
Mickey Mantle, Babe Ruth	15.00
Mark McGwire, Mickey Mantle	15.00
Mark McGwire, Babe Ruth	15.00
Mark McGwire, Ted Williams	15.00

Old/New School

		NM/M
Complete Set (30):		35.00
Common Player:		.40
Production 1,000 sets		
Level 2:		5X
Production 50 sets		
1	Ken Griffey Jr.	2.50
2	Alex Rodriguez	3.00
3	Frank Thomas	1.50
4	Cal Ripken Jr.	4.00

5 Chipper Jones 2.00
6 Craig Biggio .40
7 Greg Maddux 2.00
8 Jeff Bagwell 1.50
9 Juan Gonzalez .75
10 Mark McGwire 3.00
11 Mike Piazza 2.50
12 Mo Vaughn .40
13 Roger Clemens 2.25
14 Sammy Sosa 2.00
15 Tony Gwynn 2.00
16 Gabe Kapler .40
17 J.D. Drew 1.00
18 Pat Burrell 1.00
19 Roy Halladay .40
20 Jeff Weaver .40
21 Troy Glaus 1.00
22 Vladimir Guerrero 1.50
23 Michael Barrett .40
24 Carlos Beltran .40
25 Scott Rolen 1.00
26 Nomar Garciaparra 2.00
27 Warren Morris .40
28 Alex Gonzalez .40
29 Kyle Farnsworth .40
30 Derek Jeter 4.00

Piece of History 500 Club

NM/M

TW Ted Williams (edition of 350) 250.00
TWA Ted Williams (autographed/9)

Throwback Attack

NM/M

Complete Set (15): 20.00
Common Player: .50
Inserted 1:5
Level 2: 3X
Production 500 sets
1 Ken Griffey Jr. 2.00
2 Mark McGwire 2.50
3 Sammy Sosa 1.25
4 Roger Clemens 1.50
5 J.D. Drew .75
6 Alex Rodriguez 2.50
7 Greg Maddux 1.25
8 Mike Piazza 2.00
9 Juan Gonzalez .50
10 Mo Vaughn .50
11 Cal Ripken Jr. 3.00
12 Frank Thomas 1.00
13 Nomar Garciaparra 1.25
14 Vladimir Guerrero 1.00
15 Tony Gwynn 1.25

2000 UPPER DECK

NM/M

Complete Set (540): 40.00
Complete Series I (270): 20.00
Complete Series II (270): 20.00
Common Player: .15
Silver Stars: 5X to 10X
Rookies: 2X to 4X
Hobby Pack (10): 3.00
Hobby Box (24): 55.00
1 Rick Ankiel .20
2 Vernon Wells .50

3 Ryan Anderson .15
4 Ed Yarnall .15
5 Brian McNichol .15
6 Ben Petrick .15
7 Kip Wells .15
8 Eric Munson .20
9 Matt Riley .15
10 Peter Bergeron .15
11 Eric Gagne .25
12 Ramon Ortiz .25
13 Josh Beckett .50
14 Alfonso Soriano 1.50
15 Jorge Toca .15
16 Buddy Carlyle .15
17 Chad Hermansen .15
18 Matt Perisho .15
19 *Tomokazu Ohka* .75
20 Jacque Jones .15
21 Josh Paul .15
22 Dermal Brown .15
23 Adam Kennedy .15
24 Chad Harville .15
25 Calvin Murray .15
26 Chad Meyers .15
27 Brian Cooper .15
28 Troy Glaus .50
29 Ben Molina .15
30 Troy Percival .15
31 Ken Hill .15
32 Chuck Finley .15
33 Todd Greene .15
34 Tim Salmon .25
35 Gary DiSarcina .15
36 Luis Gonzalez .25
37 Tony Womack .15
38 Omar Daal .15
39 Randy Johnson .50
40 Erubiel Durazo .20
41 Jay Bell .15
42 Steve Finley .15
43 Travis Lee .15
44 Greg Maddux 1.00
45 Bret Boone .25
46 Brian Jordan .15
47 Kevin Millwood .25
48 Odalis Perez .15
49 Javy Lopez .25
50 John Smoltz .25
51 Bruce Chen .15
52 Albert Belle .15
53 Jerry Hairston Jr. .15
54 Will Clark .40
55 Sidney Ponson .15
56 Charles Johnson .15
57 Cal Ripken Jr. 2.00
58 Ryan Minor .15
59 Mike Mussina .40
60 Tom Gordon .15
61 Jose Offerman .15
62 Trot Nixon .15
63 Pedro Martinez .75
64 John Valentin .15
65 Jason Varitek .15
66 Juan Pena .15
67 Troy O'Leary .15
68 Sammy Sosa 1.25
69 Henry Rodriguez .15
70 Kyle Farnsworth .15
71 Glenallen Hill .15
72 Lance Johnson .15
73 Mickey Morandini .15
74 Jon Lieber .15
75 Kevin Tapani .15
76 Carlos Lee .15
77 Ray Durham .15
78 Jim Parque .15
79 Bob Howry .15
80 Magglio Ordonez .25
81 Paul Konerko .20
82 Mike Caruso .15
83 Chris Singleton .15
84 Sean Casey .20
85 Barry Larkin .25
86 Pokey Reese .15
87 Eddie Taubensee .15
88 Scott Williamson .15
89 Jason LaRue .15
90 Aaron Boone .20
91 Jeffrey Hammonds .15
92 Omar Vizquel .20
93 Manny Ramirez .50
94 Kenny Lofton .20
95 Jaret Wright .15
96 Einar Diaz .15
97 Charles Nagy .15
98 David Justice .25
99 Richie Sexson .25
100 Steve Karsay .15
101 Todd Helton .50
102 Dante Bichette .15
103 Larry Walker .25
104 Pedro Astacio .15
105 Neifi Perez .15
106 Brian Bohanon .15
107 Edgard Clemente .15
108 Dave Veres .15
109 Gabe Kapler .15
110 Juan Encarnacion .15
111 Jeff Weaver .15
112 Damion Easley .15
113 Justin Thompson .15
114 Brad Ausmus .15
115 Frank Catalanotto .15
116 Todd Jones .15
117 Preston Wilson .25
118 Cliff Floyd .15
119 Mike Lowell .15
120 Jorge Fabregas .15
121 Alex Gonzalez .15
122 Braden Looper .15
123 Bruce Aven .15
124 Richard Hidalgo .15
125 Mitch Meluskey .15
126 Jeff Bagwell .50
127 Jose Lima .15
128 Derek Bell .15
129 Billy Wagner .15
130 Shane Reynolds .15
131 Moises Alou .25
132 Carlos Beltran .25
133 Carlos Febles .15
134 Jermaine Dye .15
135 Jeremy Giambi .15
136 Joe Randa .15
137 Jose Rosado .15
138 Chad Kreuter .15
139 Jose Vizcaino .15
140 Adrian Beltre .25
141 Kevin Brown .25
142 Ismael Valdes .15
143 Angel Pena .15
144 Chan Ho Park .15
145 Mark Grudzielanek .15
146 Jeff Shaw .15
147 Geoff Jenkins .20
148 Jeromy Burnitz .15
149 Hideo Nomo .25
150 Ron Belliard .15
151 Sean Berry .15
152 Mark Loretta .15
153 Steve Woodard .15
154 Joe Mays .15
155 Eric Milton .15
156 Corey Koskie .15
157 Ron Coomer .15
158 Brad Radke .15
159 Terry Steinbach .15
160 Christian Guzman .15
161 Vladimir Guerrero .50
162 Wilton Guerrero .15
163 Michael Barrett .15
164 Chris Widger .15
165 Fernando Seguignol .15
166 Ugueth Urbina .15
167 Dustin Hermanson .15
168 Kenny Rogers .15
169 Edgardo Alfonzo .15
170 Orel Hershiser .15
171 Robin Ventura .20
172 Octavio Dotel .15
173 Rickey Henderson .25
174 Roger Cedeno .15
175 John Olerud .25
176 Derek Jeter 2.00
177 Tino Martinez .25
178 Orlando Hernandez .20
179 Chuck Knoblauch .15
180 Bernie Williams .40
181 Chili Davis .15
182 David Cone .20
183 Ricky Ledee .15
184 Paul O'Neill .25
185 Jason Giambi .50
186 Eric Chavez .25
187 Matt Stairs .15
188 Miguel Tejada .25
189 Olmedo Saenz .15
190 Tim Hudson .40
191 John Jaha .15
192 Randy Velarde .15
193 Rico Brogna .15
194 Mike Lieberthal .20
195 Marlon Anderson .15
196 Bobby Abreu .25
197 Ron Gant .15
198 Randy Wolf .15
199 Desi Relaford .15
200 Doug Glanville .15
201 Warren Morris .15
202 Kris Benson .15
203 Kevin Young .15
204 Brian Giles .25
205 Jason Schmidt .15
206 Ed Sprague .15
207 Francisco Cordova .15
208 Mark McGwire 2.00
209 Jose Jimenez .15
210 Fernando Tatis .15
211 Kent Bottenfield .15
212 Eli Marrero .15
213 Edgar Renteria .15
214 Joe McEwing .15
215 J.D. Drew .20
216 Tony Gwynn .75
217 Gary Matthews Jr. .15
218 Eric Owens .15
219 Damian Jackson .15
220 Reggie Sanders .15
221 Trevor Hoffman .15
222 Ben Davis .15
223 Shawn Estes .15
224 F.P. Santangelo .15
225 Livan Hernandez .15
226 Ellis Burks .15
227 J.T. Snow .15
228 Jeff Kent .25
229 Robb Nen .15
230 Marvin Benard .15
231 Ken Griffey Jr. 1.00
232 John Halama .15
233 Gil Meche .15
234 David Bell .15
235 Brian L. Hunter .15
236 Jay Buhner .25
237 Edgar Martinez .25
238 Jose Mesa .15
239 Wilson Alvarez .15
240 Wade Boggs .40
241 Fred McGriff .25
242 Jose Canseco .40
243 Kevin Stocker .15
244 Roberto Hernandez .15
245 Bubba Trammell .15
246 John Flaherty .15
247 Ivan Rodriguez .40
248 Rusty Greer .15
249 Rafael Palmeiro .40
250 Jeff Zimmerman .15
251 Royce Clayton .15
252 Todd Zeile .15
253 John Wetteland .15
254 Ruben Mateo .15
255 Kelvim Escobar .15
256 David Wells .15
257 Shawn Green .40
258 Homer Bush .15
259 Shannon Stewart .15
260 Carlos Delgado .50
261 Roy Halladay .25
262 Fernando Tatis CL .15
263 Jose Jimenez CL .15
264 Tony Gwynn CL .40
265 Wade Boggs CL .25
266 Cal Ripken Jr. CL 1.00
267 David Cone CL .15
268 Mark McGwire CL .75
269 Pedro Martinez CL .40
270 Nomar Garciaparra CL .75
271 Nick Johnson .40
272 Mark Quinn .15
273 Roosevelt Brown .15
274 Adam Everett .15
275 Jason Marquis .15
276 *Kazuhiro Sasaki* 1.50
277 Aaron Myette .15
278 *Danys Baez* .50
279 Travis Dawkins .15

280	Mark Mulder	.25
281	Chris Haas	.15
282	Milton Bradley	.15
283	Brad Penny	.15
284	Rafael Furcal	.25
285	*Luis Matos*	1.00
286	Victor Santos	.15
287	*Rico Washington*	.15
288	Rob Bell	.15
289	Joe Crede	.15
290	Pablo Ozuna	.15
291	*Wascar Serrano*	.15
292	*Sang-Hoon Lee*	.25
293	Chris Wakeland	.15
294	Luis Rivera	.15
295	*Mike Lamb*	.20
296	Wily Pena	.20
297	*Mike Meyers*	.15
298	Mo Vaughn	.20
299	Darin Erstad	.25
300	Garret Anderson	.25
301	Tim Belcher	.15
302	Scott Spiezio	.15
303	Kent Bottenfield	.15
304	Orlando Palmeiro	.15
305	Jason Dickson	.15
306	Matt Williams	.20
307	Brian Anderson	.15
308	Hanley Frias	.15
309	Todd Stottlemyre	.15
310	Matt Mantei	.15
311	David Dellucci	.15
312	Armando Reynoso	.15
313	Bernard Gilkey	.15
314	Chipper Jones	1.00
315	Tom Glavine	.25
316	Quilvio Veras	.15
317	Andruw Jones	.50
318	Bobby Bonilla	.15
319	Reggie Sanders	.15
320	Andres Galarraga	.20
321	George Lombard	.15
322	John Rocker	.15
322	Wally Joyner	.15
324	B.J. Surhoff	.15
325	Scott Erickson	.15
326	Delino DeShields	.15
327	Jeff Conine	.15
328	Mike Timlin	.15
329	Brady Anderson	.15
330	Mike Bordick	.15
331	Harold Baines	.15
332	Nomar Garciaparra	1.50
333	Bret Saberhagen	.15
334	Ramon Martinez	.15
335	Donnie Sadler	.15
336	Wilton Veras	.15
337	Mike Stanley	.15
338	Brian Rose	.15
339	Carl Everett	.15
340	Tim Wakefield	.15
341	Mark Grace	.25
342	Kerry Wood	.30
343	Eric Young	.15
344	Jose Nieves	.15
345	Ismael Valdes	.15
346	Joe Girardi	.15
347	Damon Buford	.15
348	Ricky Gutierrez	.15
349	Frank Thomas	.50
350	Brian Simmons	.15
351	James Baldwin	.15
352	Brook Fordyce	.15
353	Jose Valentin	.15
354	Mike Sirotka	.15
355	Greg Norton	.15
356	Dante Bichette	.15
357	Deion Sanders	.25
358	Ken Griffey Jr.	1.00
359	Denny Neagle	.15
360	Dmitri Young	.15
361	Pete Harnisch	.15
362	Michael Tucker	.15
363	Roberto Alomar	.40
364	Dave Roberts	.15
365	Jim Thome	.50
366	Bartolo Colon	.15
367	Travis Fryman	.20
368	Chuck Finley	.15
369	Russell Branyan	.15
370	Alex Ramirez	.15
371	Jeff Cirillo	.15
372	Jeffrey Hammonds	.15
373	Scott Karl	.15
374	Brent Mayne	.15
375	Tom Goodwin	.15
376	Jose Jimenez	.15
377	Rolando Arrojo	.15
378	Terry Shumpert	.15
379	Juan Gonzalez	.50
380	Bobby Higginson	.15
381	Tony Clark	.15
382	Dave Mlicki	.15
383	Deivi Cruz	.15
384	Brian Moehler	.15
385	Dean Palmer	.15
386	Luis Castillo	.15
387	Mike Redmond	.15
388	Alex Fernandez	.15
389	Brant Brown	.15
390	Dave Berg	.15
391	A.J. Burnett	.15
392	Mark Kotsay	.15
393	Craig Biggio	.20
394	Daryle Ward	.15
395	Lance Berkman	.25
396	Roger Cedeno	.15
397	Scott Elarton	.15
398	Octavio Dotel	.15
399	Ken Caminiti	.15
400	Johnny Damon	.25
401	Mike Sweeney	.15
402	Jeff Suppan	.15
403	Rey Sanchez	.15
404	Blake Stein	.15
405	Ricky Bottalico	.15
406	Jay Witasick	.15
407	Shawn Green	.40
408	Orel Hershiser	.15
409	Gary Sheffield	.40
410	Todd Hollandsworth	.15
411	Terry Adams	.15
412	Todd Hundley	.15
413	Eric Karros	.15
414	F.P. Santangelo	.15
415	Alex Cora	.15
416	Marquis Grissom	.15
417	Henry Blanco	.15
418	Jose Hernandez	.15
419	Kyle Peterson	.15
420	*John Snyder*	.15
421	Bob Wickman	.15
422	Jamey Wright	.15
423	Chad Allen	.15
424	Todd Walker	.15
425	*J.C. Romero*	.15
426	Butch Huskey	.15
427	Jacque Jones	.15
428	Matt Lawton	.15
429	Rondell White	.25
430	Jose Vidro	.15
431	Hideki Irabu	.15
432	Javier Vazquez	.15
433	Lee Stevens	.15
434	Mike Thurman	.15
435	Geoff Blum	.15
436	Mike Hampton	.15
437	Mike Piazza	1.00
438	Al Leiter	.15
439	Derek Bell	.15
440	Armando Benitez	.15
441	Rey Ordonez	.15
442	Todd Zeile	.15
443	Roger Clemens	1.25
444	Ramiro Mendoza	.15
445	Andy Pettitte	.25
446	Scott Brosius	.15
447	Mariano Rivera	.25
448	Jim Leyritz	.15
449	Jorge Posada	.25
450	Omar Olivares	.15
451	Ben Grieve	.15
452	A.J. Hinch	.15
453	Gil Heredia	.15
454	Kevin Appier	.15
455	Ryan Christenson	.15
456	Ramon Hernandez	.15
457	Scott Rolen	.50
458	Alex Arias	.15
459	Andy Ashby	.15
460	(Not issued, see #474)	
461	Robert Person	.15
462	Paul Byrd	.15
463	Curt Schilling	.25
464	Mike Jackson	.15
465	Jason Kendall	.25
466	Pat Meares	.15
467	Bruce Aven	.15
468	Todd Ritchie	.15
469	Wil Cordero	.15
470	Aramis Ramirez	.15
471	Andy Benes	.15
472	Ray Lankford	.15
473	Fernando Vina	.15
474a	Jim Edmonds	.25
474b	Kevin Jordan (should be #460)	.15
475	Craig Paquette	.15
476	Pat Hentgen	.15
477	Darryl Kile	.15
478	Sterling Hitchcock	.15
479	Ruben Rivera	.15
480	Ryan Klesko	.15
481	Phil Nevin	.15
482	Woody Williams	.15
483	Carlos Hernandez	.15
484	Brian Meadows	.15
485	Bret Boone	.25
486	Barry Bonds	1.50
487	Russ Ortiz	.15
488	Bobby Estalella	.15
489	Rich Aurilia	.15
490	Bill Mueller	.15
491	Joe Nathan	.15
492	Russ Davis	.15
493	John Olerud	.25
494	Alex Rodriguez	1.50
495	Fred Garcia	.15
496	Carlos Guillen	.15
497	Aaron Sele	.15
498	Brett Tomko	.15
499	Jamie Moyer	.15
500	Mike Cameron	.15
501	Vinny Castilla	.15
502	Gerald Williams	.15
503	Mike DiFelice	.15
504	Ryan Rupe	.15
505	Greg Vaughn	.15
506	Miguel Cairo	.15
507	*Juan Guzman*	.15
508	Jose Guillen	.15
509	Gabe Kapler	.15
510	Rick Helling	.15
511	David Segui	.15
512	Doug Davis	.15
513	Justin Thompson	.15
514	Chad Curtis	.15
515	Tony Batista	.15
516	Billy Koch	.15
517	Raul Mondesi	.20
518	Joey Hamilton	.15
519	Darrin Fletcher	.15
520	Brad Fullmer	.15
521	Jose Cruz Jr.	.15
522	Kevin Witt	.15
523	Mark McGwire	1.00
524	Roberto Alomar	.25
525	Chipper Jones	.50
526	Derek Jeter	1.00
527	Ken Griffey Jr.	.50
528	Sammy Sosa	.75
529	Manny Ramirez	.40
530	Ivan Rodriguez	.25
531	Pedro J. Martinez	.40
532	Mariano Rivera	.15
533	Sammy Sosa	.75
534	Cal Ripken Jr.	1.00
535	Vladimir Guerrero	.40
536	Tony Gwynn	.25
537	Mark McGwire	1.00
538	Bernie Williams	.25
539	Pedro J. Martinez	.40
540	Ken Griffey Jr.	.50

Exclusives

	NM/M
Common Silver Exclusive:	1.00
Silver Stars/Rookies:	8X

(See 2000 Upper Deck for checklist and base card values.)

Cooperstown Calling

		NM/M
Complete Set (15):		25.00
Common Player:		.75
Inserted 1:23		
1	Roger Clemens	3.00
2	Cal Ripken Jr.	5.00
3	Ken Griffey Jr.	3.00
4	Mike Piazza	3.00
5	Tony Gwynn	2.00
6	Sammy Sosa	2.50
7	Jose Canseco	1.00
8	Larry Walker	.75
9	Barry Bonds	4.00

10	Greg Maddux	2.50
11	Derek Jeter	5.00
12	Mark McGwire	4.00
13	Randy Johnson	2.00
14	Frank Thomas	1.50
15	Jeff Bagwell	1.50

e-Card

		NM/M
Complete Set (6):		10.00
Common Player:		1.00
Inserted 1:12		
1	Ken Griffey Jr.	2.00
2	Alex Rodriguez	3.00
3	Cal Ripken Jr.	3.00
4	Jeff Bagwell	1.00
5	Barry Bonds	3.00
6	Manny Ramirez	1.00

eVolve Signature

		NM/M
Common Player:		40.00
Production 200 sets		
1	Ken Griffey Jr.	85.00
2	Alex Rodriguez	85.00
3	Cal Ripken Jr.	150.00
4	Jeff Bagwell	40.00
5	Barry Bonds	120.00
6	Manny Ramirez	40.00

eVolve Jersey

		NM/M
Common Player:		15.00
Production 300 sets		
1	Ken Griffey Jr.	40.00
2	Alex Rodriguez	40.00
3	Cal Ripken Jr.	65.00

4	Jeff Bagwell	20.00
5	Barry Bonds	50.00
6	Manny Ramirez	20.00

eVolve Signed Jersey

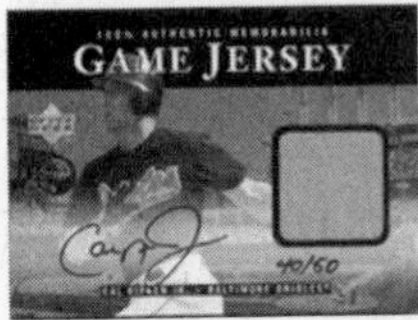

		NM/M
Common Player:		80.00
Production 50 sets		
1	Ken Griffey Jr.	150.00
2	Alex Rodriguez	150.00
3	Cal Ripken Jr.	200.00
4	Jeff Bagwell	60.00
5	Barry Bonds	250.00
6	Manny Ramirez	60.00

Game Balls

		NM/M
Common Player:		10.00
JB	Jeff Bagwell	10.00
RC	Roger Clemens	30.00
KG	Ken Griffey Jr.	25.00
VG	Vladimir Guerrero	15.00
TG	Tony Gwynn	25.00
DJ	Derek Jeter	40.00
CJ	Chipper Jones	20.00
GM	Greg Maddux	20.00
MM	Mark McGwire	50.00
AR	Alex Rodriguez	30.00
BW	Bernie Williams	10.00

Game Jersey

		NM/M
Common Player:		10.00
Inserted 1:2,500		
JC	Jose Canseco	15.00
JG	Juan Gonzalez	15.00
VG	Vladimir Guerrero	20.00
TH	Todd Helton	15.00
CJ	Chipper Jones	25.00
GK	Gabe Kapler	10.00
GM	Greg Maddux	35.00
MR	Manny Ramirez	20.00
CR	Cal Ripken Jr.	60.00
GV	Greg Vaughn	10.00

Game Jersey Hobby

		NM/M
Common Player:		10.00
Inserted 1:288		
JB	Jeff Bagwell	15.00
TG	Troy Glaus	15.00
CY	Tom Glavine	10.00
Jr.	Ken Griffey Jr.	25.00
DJ	Derek Jeter	40.00
PM	Pedro J. Martinez	20.00
MP	Mike Piazza	30.00
AR	Alex Rodriguez	30.00
FT	Frank Thomas	15.00
LW	Larry Walker	10.00

Game Jersey Patch

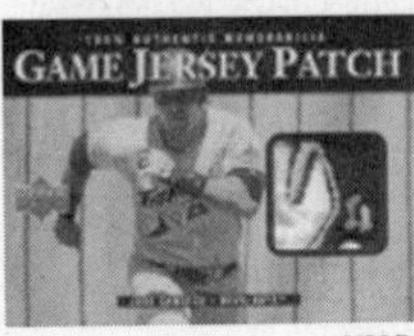

		NM/M
Common Player:		40.00
Inserted 1:10,000		
JB	Jeff Bagwell	60.00
JC	Jose Canseco	60.00
TG	Troy Glaus	50.00
CY	Tom Glavine	60.00
Jr.	Ken Griffey Jr.	100.00
VG	Vladimir Guerrero	100.00
TH	Todd Helton	60.00
DJ	Derek Jeter	150.00
CJ	Chipper Jones	75.00
GK	Gabe Kapler	40.00
GM	Greg Maddux	100.00
PM	Pedro J. Martinez	100.00
MP	Mike Piazza	100.00
MR	Manny Ramirez	80.00
CR	Cal Ripken Jr.	200.00
AR	Alex Rodriguez	125.00
FT	Frank Thomas	80.00
GV	Greg Vaughn	40.00
LW	Larry Walker	50.00

Game Jersey Series 2

		NM/M
Common Player:		10.00
AR	Alex Rodriguez	30.00
TG	Tony Gwynn	20.00
FT	Frank Thomas	15.00
MW	Matt Williams	10.00
JT	Jim Thome	15.00
MV	Mo Vaughn	10.00
TGl	Tom Glavine	15.00
BG	Ben Grieve	10.00
TrG	Troy Glaus	15.00
RJ	Randy Johnson	20.00
KM	Kevin Millwood	10.00
KG	Ken Griffey Jr.	25.00
AB	Albert Belle	10.00
DC	David Cone	10.00
MH	Mike Hampton	10.00
EC	Eric Chavez	10.00
EM	Edgar Martinez	15.00
PW	Preston Wilson	10.00
RV	Robin Ventura	10.00

Game Jersey Auto. Hobby Series 2

		NM/M
Common Player:		30.00
H-KG	Ken Griffey Jr.	100.00
H-CR	Cal Ripken Jr.	150.00
H-DJ	Derek Jeter	150.00
H-IR	Ivan Rodriguez	40.00
H-AR	Alex Rodriguez	100.00
H-MR	Manny Ramirez	50.00
H-JC	Jose Canseco	30.00
H-BB	Barry Bonds	250.00
H-SR	Scott Rolen	40.00
H-PO	Paul O'Neill	40.00
H-JK	Jason Kendall	30.00
H-VG	Vladimir Guerrero	50.00
H-JB	Jeff Bagwell	40.00

Game Jersey Patch Series 2

		NM/M
Common Player:		50.00
JB	Jeff Bagwell	75.00
BB	Barry Bonds	250.00
JC	Jose Canseco	75.00
TGl	Troy Glaus	75.00
KG	Ken Griffey Jr.	125.00
VG	Vladimir Guerrero	100.00
TG	Tony Gwynn	100.00
DJ	Derek Jeter	150.00
RJ	Randy Johnson	100.00
AJ	Andruw Jones	80.00
CJ	Chipper Jones	100.00
GM	Greg Maddux	100.00
PM	Pedro Martinez	100.00
MR	Manny Ramirez	100.00
CR	Cal Ripken Jr.	200.00
SR	Scott Rolen	75.00
AR	Alex Rodriguez	150.00
IR	Ivan Rodriguez	90.00
FT	Frank Thomas	100.00
MV	Mo Vaughn	50.00
MW	Matt Williams	50.00

Faces of the Game

		NM/M
Complete Set (20):		30.00
Common Player:		.75
Inserted 1:11		
Silver:		4X to 8X
Production 100 sets		
1	Ken Griffey Jr.	2.50
2	Mark McGwire	3.00
3	Sammy Sosa	2.00
4	Alex Rodriguez	3.00
5	Manny Ramirez	1.00
6	Derek Jeter	4.00
7	Jeff Bagwell	1.00
8	Roger Clemens	2.00
9	Scott Rolen	.75
10	Tony Gwynn	1.50
11	Nomar Garciaparra	2.50
12	Randy Johnson	1.50
13	Greg Maddux	2.00
14	Mike Piazza	2.50
15	Frank Thomas	1.00
16	Cal Ripken Jr.	4.00
17	Ivan Rodriguez	.75
18	Mo Vaughn	.75
19	Chipper Jones	2.00
20	Sean Casey	.75

Five-Tool Talents

		NM/M
Complete Set (15):		15.00
Common Player:		.50
Inserted 1:11		
1	Vladimir Guerrero	1.50
2	Barry Bonds	3.00
3	Jason Kendall	.50
4	Derek Jeter	4.00
5	Ken Griffey Jr.	2.50
6	Andruw Jones	.75
7	Bernie Williams	.75
8	Jose Canseco	.75
9	Scott Rolen	.75
10	Shawn Green	.50
11	Nomar Garciaparra	2.50
12	Jeff Bagwell	1.00
13	Larry Walker	.75
14	Chipper Jones	2.00
15	Alex Rodriguez	3.00

Hit Brigade

		NM/M
Complete Set (15):		15.00
Common Player:		.50
Inserted 1:8		
Silver:		5X to 10X
Production 100 sets		
1	Ken Griffey Jr.	2.00
2	Tony Gwynn	1.00
3	Alex Rodriguez	2.50
4	Derek Jeter	3.00
5	Mike Piazza	2.00
6	Sammy Sosa	1.50
7	Juan Gonzalez	.75
8	Scott Rolen	.50
9	Nomar Garciaparra	2.00
10	Barry Bonds	2.50
11	Craig Biggio	.50
12	Chipper Jones	1.50
13	Frank Thomas	.75
14	Larry Walker	.50
15	Mark McGwire	2.50

Hot Properties

		NM/M
Complete Set (15):		10.00
Common Player:		.50
Inserted 1:11		
1	Carlos Beltran	1.00
2	Rick Ankiel	.50
3	Sean Casey	1.00
4	Preston Wilson	1.00
5	Vernon Wells	1.00
6	Pat Burrell	1.50
7	Eric Chavez	1.00
8	J.D. Drew	1.00
9	Alfonso Soriano	2.00
10	Gabe Kapler	.50
11	Rafael Furcal	1.00
12	Ruben Mateo	.50
13	Corey Koskie	.75
14	Kip Wells	.50
15	Ramon Ortiz	.75

Pennant Driven

		NM/M
Complete Set (10):		8.00
Common Player:		.50
Inserted 1:4		
1	Derek Jeter	2.00
2	Roberto Alomar	.50
3	Chipper Jones	1.50
4	Jeff Bagwell	.75
5	Roger Clemens	1.00
6	Nomar Garciaparra	1.50
7	Manny Ramirez	.75
8	Mike Piazza	1.50
9	Ivan Rodriguez	.75
10	Randy Johnson	.75

Piece of History-500 Club

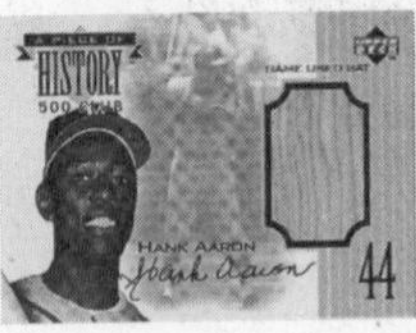

		NM/M
755HR	Hank Aaron	275.00
HAAU	Hank Aaron Auto./44	900.00

Power Deck

		NM/M
Complete Set (11):		60.00
Common Player:		2.50
Inserted 1:23		
1	Ken Griffey Jr.	5.00
2	Cal Ripken Jr.	7.50
3	Mark McGwire	6.00
4	Tony Gwynn	3.50
5	Roger Clemens	3.50
6	Alex Rodriguez	6.00
7	Sammy Sosa	3.50
8	Derek Jeter	7.50

9 Ken Griffey Jr. 25.00
10 Mark McGwire 30.00
11 Reggie Jackson 15.00

Power MARK

NM/M
Complete Set (10): 25.00
Common McGwire: 3.00
Inserted 1:23
Silver: 5X to 10X
Production 100 sets

1 Mark McGwire 3.00
2 Mark McGwire 3.00
3 Mark McGwire 3.00
4 Mark McGwire 3.00
5 Mark McGwire 3.00
6 Mark McGwire 3.00
7 Mark McGwire 3.00
8 Mark McGwire 3.00
9 Mark McGwire 3.00
10 Mark McGwire 3.00

Power Rally

NM/M
Complete Set (15): 20.00
Common Player: .75
Inserted 1:11
Silver: 4X to 8X
Production 100 sets

1 Ken Griffey Jr. 2.50
2 Mark McGwire 3.00
3 Sammy Sosa 2.00
4 Jose Canseco .75
5 Juan Gonzalez 1.00
6 Bernie Williams .75
7 Jeff Bagwell 1.00
8 Chipper Jones 2.00
9 Vladimir Guerrero 1.50
10 Mo Vaughn .75
11 Derek Jeter 4.00
12 Mike Piazza 2.50
13 Barry Bonds 3.00
14 Alex Rodriguez 3.00
15 Nomar Garciaparra 2.50

Prime Performers

NM/M
Complete Set (10): 10.00
Common Player: .50
Inserted 1:8

1 Manny Ramirez .75
2 Pedro Martinez 1.00
3 Carlos Delgado .50
4 Ken Griffey Jr. 2.00
5 Derek Jeter 3.00
6 Chipper Jones 1.50
7 Sean Casey .50
8 Shawn Green .50
9 Sammy Sosa 1.50
10 Alex Rodriguez 2.50

STATitude

NM/M
Complete Set (30): 25.00
Common Player: .40
Inserted 1:4
Silver: 5X-10X
Production 100 sets

1 Mo Vaughn .40
2 Matt Williams .40

3 Travis Lee .40
4 Chipper Jones 1.50
5 Greg Maddux 1.50
6 Gabe Kapler .40
7 Cal Ripken Jr. 3.00
8 Nomar Garciaparra 2.00
9 Sammy Sosa 1.50
10 Frank Thomas .75
11 Manny Ramirez .75
12 Larry Walker .50
13 Ivan Rodriguez .50
14 Jeff Bagwell .75
15 Craig Biggio .50
16 Vladimir Guerrero 1.00
17 Mike Piazza 2.00
18 Bernie Williams .50
19 Derek Jeter 3.00
20 Jose Canseco .50
21 Eric Chavez .50
22 Scott Rolen .50
23 Mark McGwire 2.50
24 Tony Gwynn 1.00
25 Barry Bonds 2.50
26 Ken Griffey Jr. 2.00
27 Alex Rodriguez 2.50
28 J.D. Drew .50
29 Juan Gonzalez .50
30 Roger Clemens 1.50

The People's Choice

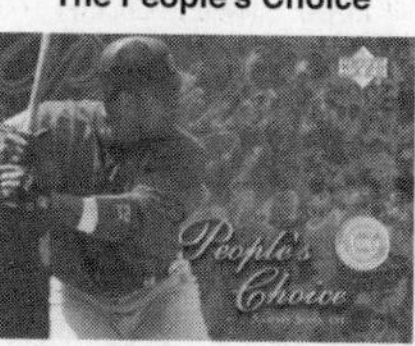

NM/M
Complete Set (15): 20.00
Common Player: .75
Inserted 1:23

1 Mark McGwire 3.00
2 Nomar Garciaparra 3.00
3 Derek Jeter 3.00
4 Shawn Green .75
5 Manny Ramirez 1.00
6 Pedro Martinez 1.50
7 Ivan Rodriguez .75
8 Alex Rodriguez 3.00
9 Juan Gonzalez 1.00
10 Ken Griffey Jr. 2.00
11 Sammy Sosa 2.50
12 Jeff Bagwell 1.00
13 Chipper Jones 2.00
14 Cal Ripken Jr. 4.00
15 Mike Piazza 2.00

3,000 Hit Club Series 2

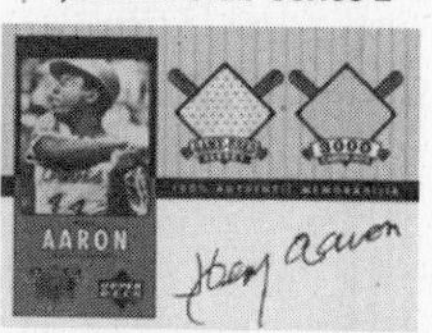

NM/M
HA-B Hank Aaron bat/350 50.00
HA-JB Hank Aaron bat/jersey/100 100.00
HA-J Hank Aaron jersey/350 50.00
HA-JBS Hank Aaron Auto. bat/jersey/44 700.00

3,000 Hit Club Series 1

NM/M
CR-B Cal Ripken Jr. (bat/350) 25.00
CR-J Cal Ripken Jr. (jersey/350) 25.00
CR-JB Cal Ripken Jr. (jersey, bat/100) 150.00

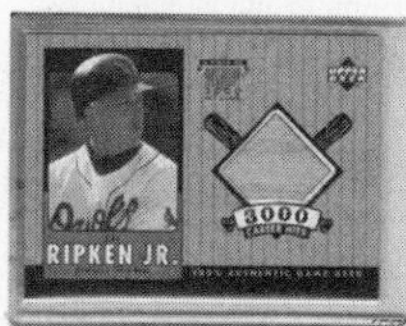

CR-JBS Cal Ripken Jr. (jersey, bat, autographed/8)
EM-B Eddie Murray (bat/350) 10.00
EM-J Eddie Murray (jersey/350) 8.00
EM-JB Eddie Murray (jersey, bat/100) 60.00
EM-JBS Eddie Murray (jersey, bat, autographed/33)

2000 UPPER DECK BLACK DIAMOND

NM/M
Complete Set (120): 25.00
Common Player: .15
Common Diamond Debut: .50
Pack (6): 1.50
Wax Box (24): 30.00

1 Darin Erstad .25
2 Tim Salmon .25
3 Mo Vaughn .20
4 Matt Williams .25
5 Travis Lee .15
6 Randy Johnson .75
7 Tom Glavine .40
8 Chipper Jones 1.50
9 Greg Maddux 1.50
10 Andruw Jones .50
11 Brian Jordan .15
12 Cal Ripken Jr. 2.50
13 Albert Belle .20
14 Mike Mussina .50
15 Nomar Garciaparra 2.00
16 Troy O'Leary .15
17 Pedro J. Martinez 1.00
18 Sammy Sosa 1.50
19 Henry Rodriguez .15
20 Frank Thomas .75
21 Magglio Ordonez .40
22 Greg Vaughn .15
23 Barry Larkin .25
24 Sean Casey .25
25 Jim Thome .75
26 Kenny Lofton .25
27 Roberto Alomar .50
28 Manny Ramirez .75
29 Larry Walker .25
30 Todd Helton .75
31 Gabe Kapler .15
32 Tony Clark .15
33 Dean Palmer .15
34 Cliff Floyd .15
35 Alex Gonzalez .15
36 Moises Alou .25
37 Jeff Bagwell .75
38 Craig Biggio .25
39 Richard Hidalgo .15
40 Carlos Beltran .25
41 Johnny Damon .25
42 Adrian Beltre .25
43 Gary Sheffield .40
44 Kevin Brown .25
45 Jeromy Burnitz .15
46 Jeff Cirillo .15
47 Joe Mays .15
48 Todd Walker .15
49 Vladimir Guerrero .75
50 Michael Barrett .15
51 Rickey Henderson .40
52 Mike Piazza 1.50
53 Robin Ventura .25
54 John Olerud .25
55 Edgardo Alfonzo .15
56 Derek Jeter 2.00
57 Orlando Hernandez .15
58 Tino Martinez .25
59 Bernie Williams .50
60 Roger Clemens 1.50
61 Eric Chavez .25
62 Ben Grieve .15
63 Jason Giambi 1.00
64 Scott Rolen .50
65 Bobby Abreu .25
66 Curt Schilling .40
67 Mike Lieberthal .15
68 Warren Morris .15
69 Brian Giles .25
70 Eric Owens .15
71 Tony Gwynn 1.00
72 Reggie Sanders .15
73 Barry Bonds 2.00
74 J.T. Snow .15
75 Jeff Kent .25
76 Ken Griffey Jr. 1.50
77 Alex Rodriguez 2.00
78 Edgar Martinez .15
79 Jay Buhner .15
80 Mark McGwire 2.00
81 J.D. Drew .25
82 Eric Davis .15
83 Fernando Tatis .15
84 Wade Boggs .50
85 Fred McGriff .25
86 Juan Gonzalez .75
87 Ivan Rodriguez .50
88 Rafael Palmeiro .50
89 Shawn Green .40
90 Carlos Delgado .60
91 Pat Burrell 1.00
92 Eric Munson .50
93 Jorge Toca .50
94 Rick Ankiel .50
95 Tony Armas Jr. .75
96 Byung-Hyun Kim .75
97 Alfonso Soriano 3.00
98 Mark Quinn .50
99 Ryan Rupe .50
100 Adam Kennedy .50
101 Jeff Weaver .75
102 Ramon Ortiz .75
103 Eugene Kingsale .50
104 Josh Beckett 1.00
105 Eric Gagne 1.00
106 Peter Bergeron .50
107 Erubiel Durazo .75
108 Chad Meyers .50
109 Kip Wells .50
110 Chad Harville .50
111 Matt Riley .50
112 Ben Petrick .50
113 Ed Yarnall .50
114 Calvin Murray .50
115 Vernon Wells 1.00
116 A.J. Burnett .75
117 Jacque Jones .75
118 Francisco Cordero .50
119 *Tomokazu Ohka* 1.50
120 Julio Ramirez .50

Final Cut

Stars (1-90): 5X to 10X
Diamond Debuts: 2X to 4X
Production 100 sets
(See 2000 UD Black Diamond for checklist and base card values.)

Reciprocal Cut

NM/M
Stars (1-90): 2X to 5X
Diamond Debuts 1X to 1.5X
1-90 inserted 1:7
Diamond Debuts inserted 1:12
(See 2000 UD Black Diamond for checklist and base card values.)

A Piece of History Double

NM/M
Common Player: 10.00
Inserted 1:1079

AB Albert Belle 10.00
BB Barry Bonds 75.00
JC Jose Canseco 20.00
DE Darin Erstad 15.00
JR Ken Griffey Jr. 50.00

VG	Vladimir Guerrero	30.00
TG	Tony Gwynn	40.00
TH	Todd Helton	15.00
DJ	Derek Jeter	75.00
AJ	Andruw Jones	15.00
CJ	Chipper Jones	40.00
TL	Travis Lee	10.00
RM	Raul Mondesi	10.00
MP	Mike Piazza	50.00
CAL	Cal Ripken Jr.	80.00
AR	Alex Rodriguez	50.00
IR	Ivan Rodriguez	15.00
SR	Scott Rolen	15.00
MV	Mo Vaughn	10.00

A Piece of History Single

		NM/M
Common Player:		8.00
Inserted 1:179		
AB	Albert Belle	8.00
BB	Barry Bonds	40.00
JC	Jose Canseco	10.00
DE	Darin Erstad	8.00
JR	Ken Griffey Jr.	25.00
VG	Vladimir Guerrero	15.00
TG	Tony Gwynn	20.00
TH	Todd Helton	10.00
DJ	Derek Jeter	40.00
AJ	Andruw Jones	10.00
CJ	Chipper Jones	20.00
TL	Travis Lee	8.00
RM	Raul Mondesi	8.00
MP	Mike Piazza	25.00
CAL	Cal Ripken Jr.	50.00
AR	Alex Rodriguez	25.00
IR	Ivan Rodriguez	10.00
SR	Scott Rolen	10.00
MV	Mo Vaughn	8.00

Barrage

		NM/M
Complete Set (10):		15.00
Common Player:		1.00
Inserted 1:29		
1	Mark McGwire	3.00
2	Ken Griffey Jr.	2.00
3	Sammy Sosa	2.50
4	Jeff Bagwell	1.00
5	Juan Gonzalez	1.00
6	Alex Rodriguez	3.00
7	Manny Ramirez	1.00
8	Ivan Rodriguez	1.00
9	Chipper Jones	2.00
10	Mike Piazza	2.00

Constant Threat

		NM/M
Complete Set (10):		20.00
Common Player:		1.00
Inserted 1:29		
1	Ken Griffey Jr.	2.00
2	Vladimir Guerrero	1.00
3	Alex Rodriguez	3.00
4	Sammy Sosa	2.50
5	Juan Gonzalez	1.00
6	Derek Jeter	3.00
7	Nomar Garciaparra	3.00
8	Barry Bonds	4.00
9	Chipper Jones	2.00
10	Mike Piazza	2.00

Diamond Gallery

		NM/M
Complete Set (10):		20.00
Common Player:		1.50
Inserted 1:14		
1	Derek Jeter	3.00
2	Alex Rodriguez	3.00
3	Nomar Garciaparra	3.00
4	Cal Ripken Jr.	4.00
5	Sammy Sosa	2.50
6	Tony Gwynn	1.50
7	Mark McGwire	3.00
8	Roger Clemens	2.50
9	Greg Maddux	2.00
10	Pedro Martinez	1.50

DiamondMight

		NM/M
Complete Set (10):		15.00
Common Player:		1.00
Inserted 1:14		
1	Ken Griffey Jr.	2.00
2	Mark McGwire	3.00
3	Sammy Sosa	2.50
4	Manny Ramirez	1.00
5	Jeff Bagwell	1.00
6	Frank Thomas	1.00
7	Mike Piazza	2.00
8	Juan Gonzalez	1.00
9	Barry Bonds	4.00
10	Alex Rodriguez	3.00

Diamonds in the Rough

		NM/M
Complete Set (10):		8.00
Common Player:		.75
Inserted 1:9		
1	Pat Burrell	2.00
2	Eric Munson	.75
3	Alfonso Soriano	3.00
4	Ruben Mateo	.75
5	A.J. Burnett	1.00
6	Ben Davis	.75
7	Lance Berkman	1.50
8	Ed Yarnall	.75
9	Rick Ankiel	.75
10	Ryan Bradley	.75

Diamonation

		NM/M
Complete Set (10):		6.00
Common Player:		.50
Inserted 1:4		
1	Ken Griffey Jr.	1.00
2	Randy Johnson	1.00
3	Mark McGwire	1.50
4	Manny Ramirez	.75
5	Scott Rolen	.75
6	Bernie Williams	.75
7	Roger Clemens	1.50
8	Mo Vaughn	.50
9	Frank Thomas	.75
10	Sean Casey	.50

500 Club Piece of History

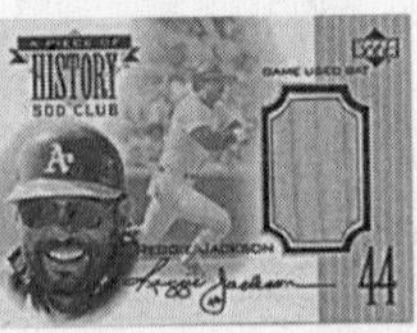

	NM/M
Reggie Jackson	100.00
Reggie Jackson Autograph/44	600.00

2000 UPPER DECK BLACK DIAMOND ROOKIE EDITION

		NM/M
Complete Set (154):		200.00
Common Player:		.15
Common Rookie Gem (91-120):		4.00
Production 1,000		
Rookie Jersey Gems (121-136):		
Inserted 1:24		
USA Authentics (137-154):		
Inserted 1:96		
Golds (1-90):		2-4X
Gold Gems (91-120):		1X
Gold Jerseys (121-136):		1-2X
Pack (6):		2.00
Box (24):		40.00
1	Troy Glaus	.75
2	Mo Vaughn	.40
3	Darin Erstad	.40
4	Jason Giambi	.40
5	Tim Hudson	.25
6	Ben Grieve	.25
7	Eric Chavez	.25
8	Tony Batista	.15
9	Carlos Delgado	.60
10	David Wells	.15
11	Greg Vaughn	.15
12	Fred McGriff	.25
13	Manny Ramirez	.75
14	Roberto Alomar	.60
15	Jim Thome	.40
16	Alex Rodriguez	2.50
17	Edgar Martinez	.15
18	John Olerud	.20
19	Albert Belle	.40
20	Mike Mussina	.40
21	Cal Ripken Jr.	2.50
22	Ivan Rodriguez	.75
23	Rafael Palmeiro	.40
24	Pedro J. Martinez	.75
25	Nomar Garciaparra	2.00
26	Carl Everett	.15
27	Jermaine Dye	.15
28	Mike Sweeney	.15
29	Juan Gonzalez	.75
30	Bobby Higginson	.15
31	Dean Palmer	.15
32	Jacque Jones	.15
33	Eric Milton	.15
34	Matt Lawton	.15
35	Magglio Ordonez	.25
36	Paul Konerko	.15
37	Frank Thomas	1.00
38	Ray Durham	.15
39	Roger Clemens	1.00
40	Derek Jeter	2.50
41	Bernie Williams	.50
42	Jose Canseco	.40
43	Craig Biggio	.25
44	Richard Hidalgo	.15
45	Jeff Bagwell	.75
46	Greg Maddux	1.50
47	Chipper Jones	1.50
48	Rafael Furcal	.25
49	Andruw Jones	.50
50	Geoff Jenkins	.25
51	Jeromy Burnitz	.15
52	Mark McGwire	3.00
53	Rick Ankiel	.50
54	Jim Edmonds	.25
55	Kerry Wood	.25
56	Sammy Sosa	2.00
57	Matt Williams	.25
58	Randy Johnson	.75
59	Steve Finley	.15
60	Curt Schilling	.15
61	Kevin Brown	.15
62	Gary Sheffield	.30
63	Shawn Green	.30
64	Jose Vidro	.15
65	Vladimir Guerrero	1.00
66	Jeff Kent	.15
67	Barry Bonds	1.00
68	Ryan Dempster	.15
69	Cliff Floyd	.15
70	Preston Wilson	.15
71	Mike Piazza	2.00
72	Al Leiter	.15
73	Edgardo Alfonzo	.25
74	Derek Bell	.15
75	Ryan Klesko	.15
76	Tony Gwynn	1.00
77	Bobby Abreu	.15
78	Pat Burrell	.50
79	Scott Rolen	.50
80	Mike Lieberthal	.15
81	Jason Kendall	.15
82	Brian Giles	.25
83	Ken Griffey Jr.	2.00
84	Pokey Reese	.15
85	Dmitri Young	.15
86	Sean Casey	.15
87	Jeff Cirillo	.15
88	Todd Helton	.75
89	Jeffrey Hammonds	.15
90	Larry Walker	.30
91	*Barry Zito*	15.00
92	*Keith Ginter*	6.00
93	*Dane Sardinha*	4.00
94	*Kenny Kelly*	4.00
95	*Ryan Kohlmeier*	4.00
96	*Leo Estrella*	4.00
97	*Danys Baez*	4.00
98	*Paul Rigdon*	4.00
99	*Mike Lamb*	4.00
100	*Aaron McNeal*	4.00
101	*Juan Pierre*	6.00
102	*Rico Washington*	4.00
103	*Luis Matos*	8.00
104	*Adam Bernero*	4.00
105	*Wascar Serrano*	4.00
106	*Chris Richard*	4.00
107	*Justin Miller*	4.00
108	*Julio Zuleta*	4.00
109	*Alex Cabrera*	4.00
110	*Gene Stechschulte*	4.00
111	*Tony Mota*	4.00
112	*Tomokazu Ohka*	4.00
113	*Geraldo Guzman*	4.00
114	*Scott Downs*	4.00
115	*Timoniel Perez*	4.00
116	*Chad Durbin*	4.00
117	*Sun-Woo Kim*	4.00
118	*Tomas de la Rosa*	4.00
119	*Javier Cardona*	4.00
120	*Kazuhiro Sasaki*	6.00

121	*Brad Cresse*	5.00
122	*Matt Wheatland*	5.00
123	*Joe Torres*	5.00
124	*Dave Krynzel*	5.00
125	*Ben Diggins*	5.00
126	*Sean Burnett*	8.00
127	*David Espinosa*	5.00
128	*Scott Heard*	5.00
129	*Daylan Holt*	5.00
130	*Koyie Hill*	5.00
131	*Mark Buehrle*	15.00
132	*Xavier Nady*	8.00
133	*Mike Tonis*	5.00
134	*Matt Ginter*	5.00
135	*Lorenzo Barcelo*	5.00
136	*Cory Vance*	5.00
137	Sean Burroughs	8.00
138	Todd Williams	5.00
139	*Brad Wilkerson*	5.00
140	*Ben Sheets*	20.00
141	*Kurt Ainsworth*	8.00
142	Anthony Sanders	5.00
143	Ryan Franklin	5.00
144	*Shane Heams*	5.00
145	*Roy Oswalt*	20.00
146	*Jon Rauch*	5.00
147	*Brent Abernathy*	5.00
148	Ernie Young	5.00
149	Chris George	5.00
150	Gookie Dawkins	5.00
151	Adam Everett	5.00
152	*John Cotton*	5.00
153	Pat Borders	5.00
154	Doug Mientkiewicz	5.00

Combos

NM/M

Random game-used inserts
25 produced of each combo bat
100 produced of combo jersey

DJ-JD	Derek Jeter, Joe DiMaggio bat	
DJ-MM	Derek Jeter, Mickey Mantle bat	
JDM	Derek Jeter, Joe DiMaggio, Mickey Mantle bat	925.00
JWO	Derek Jeter, Bernie Williams, Paul O'Neill jersey	150.00

2000 UPPER DECK GOLD RESERVE

NM/M

Complete Set (300):	75.00
Common Player:	.15
Common 268-297:	3.00
Production 2,500 sets	
Pack (10):	2.00
Box (24):	40.00

1	Mo Vaughn	.20
2	Darin Erstad	.25
3	Garret Anderson	.25
4	Troy Glaus	.50
5	Troy Percival	.15
6	Kent Bottenfield	.15
7	Orlando Palmeiro	.15
8	Tim Salmon	.25
9	Jason Giambi	.75
10	Eric Chavez	.25
11	Matt Stairs	.15
12	Miguel Tejada	.40
13	Tim Hudson	.25
14	John Jaha	.15
15	Ben Grieve	.15
16	Kevin Appier	.15
17	David Wells	.15
18	Jose Cruz Jr.	.15
19	Homer Bush	.15
20	Shannon Stewart	.15
21	Carlos Delgado	.50
22	Roy Halladay	.25
23	Tony Batista	.15
24	Raul Mondesi	.25
25	Fred McGriff	.25
26	Jose Canseco	.40
27	Roberto Hernandez	.15
28	Vinny Castilla	.15
29	Gerald Williams	.15
30	Ryan Rupe	.15
31	Greg Vaughn	.15
32	Miguel Cairo	.15
33	Roberto Alomar	.40
34	Jim Thome	.50
35	Bartolo Colon	.15
36	Omar Vizquel	.25
37	Manny Ramirez	.50
38	Chuck Finley	.15
39	Travis Fryman	.25
40	Kenny Lofton	.25
41	Richie Sexson	.40
42	Charles Nagy	.15
43	John Halama	.15
44	David Bell	.15
45	Jay Buhner	.15
46	Edgar Martinez	.15
47	Alex Rodriguez	1.50
48	Fred Garcia	.15
49	Aaron Sele	.15
50	Jamie Moyer	.15
51	Mike Cameron	.15
52	Albert Belle	.20
53	Jerry Hairston Jr.	.15
54	Sidney Ponson	.15
55	Cal Ripken Jr.	2.00
56	Mike Mussina	.40
57	B.J. Surhoff	.15
58	Brady Anderson	.15
59	Mike Bordick	.15
60	Ivan Rodriguez	.40
61	Rusty Greer	.15
62	Rafael Palmeiro	.40
63	John Wetteland	.15
64	Ruben Mateo	.15
65	Gabe Kapler	.15
66	David Segui	.15
67	Justin Thompson	.15
68	Rick Helling	.15
69	Jose Offerman	.15
70	Trot Nixon	.15
71	Pedro Martinez	.75
72	Jason Varitek	.15
73	Troy O'Leary	.15
74	Nomar Garciaparra	1.50
75	Carl Everett	.15
76	Wilton Veras	.15
77	Tim Wakefield	.15
78	Ramon Martinez	.15
79	Johnny Damon	.25
80	Mike Sweeney	.15
81	Rey Sanchez	.15
82	Carlos Beltran	.25
83	Carlos Febles	.15
84	Jermaine Dye	.15
85	Joe Randa	.15
86	Jose Rosado	.15
87	Jeff Suppan	.15
88	Juan Encarnacion	.15
89	Damion Easley	.15
90	Brad Ausmus	.15
91	Todd Jones	.15
92	Juan Gonzalez	.50
93	Bobby Higginson	.15
94	Tony Clark	.15
95	Brian Moehler	.15
96	Dean Palmer	.15
97	Joe Mays	.15
98	Eric Milton	.15
99	Corey Koskie	.15
100	Ron Coomer	.15
101	Brad Radke	.15
102	Todd Walker	.15
103	Butch Huskey	.15
104	Jacque Jones	.15
105	Frank Thomas	.50
106	Mike Sirotka	.15
107	Carlos Lee	.15
108	Ray Durham	.15
109	Bob Howry	.15
110	Magglio Ordonez	.25
111	Paul Konerko	.15
112	Chris Singleton	.15
113	James Baldwin	.15
114	Derek Jeter	2.00
115	Tino Martinez	.25
116	Orlando Hernandez	.25
117	Chuck Knoblauch	.15
118	Bernie Williams	.50
119	David Cone	.25
120	Paul O'Neill	.25
121	Roger Clemens	1.25
122	Mariano Rivera	.25
123	Ricky Ledee	.15
124	Richard Hidalgo	.25
125	Jeff Bagwell	.50
126	Jose Lima	.15
127	Billy Wagner	.15
128	Shane Reynolds	.15
129	Moises Alou	.25
130	Craig Biggio	.25
131	Roger Cedeno	.15
132	Octavio Dotel	.15
133	Greg Maddux	1.00
134	Brian Jordan	.15
135	Kevin Millwood	.25
136	Javy Lopez	.25
137	Bruce Chen	.15
138	Chipper Jones	1.00
139	Tom Glavine	.40
140	Andruw Jones	.40
141	Andres Galarraga	.25
142	Reggie Sanders	.15
143	Geoff Jenkins	.25
144	Jeromy Burnitz	.15
145	Ron Belliard	.15
146	Mark Loretta	.15
147	Steve Woodard	.15
148	Marquis Grissom	.15
149	Bob Wickman	.15
150	Mark McGwire	1.50
151	Fernando Tatis	.15
152	Edgar Renteria	.15
153	J.D. Drew	.20
154	Ray Lankford	.15
155	Fernando Vina	.15
156	Pat Hentgen	.15
157	Jim Edmonds	.25
158	Mark Grace	.25
159	Kerry Wood	.40
160	Eric Young	.15
161	Ismael Valdes	.15
162	Sammy Sosa	1.25
163	Henry Rodriguez	.15
164	Kyle Farnsworth	.15
165	Glenallen Hill	.15
166	Jon Lieber	.15
167	Luis Gonzalez	.25
168	Tony Womack	.15
169	Omar Daal	.15
170	Randy Johnson	.75
171	Erubiel Durazo	.15
172	Jay Bell	.15
173	Steve Finley	.15
174	Travis Lee	.15
175	Matt Williams	.25
176	Matt Mantei	.15
177	Adrian Beltre	.25
178	Kevin Brown	.25
179	Chan Ho Park	.15
180	Mark Grudzielanek	.15
181	Jeff Shaw	.15
182	Shawn Green	.25
183	Gary Sheffield	.40
184	Todd Hundley	.15
185	Eric Karros	.25
186	Kevin Elster	.15
187	Vladimir Guerrero	.75
188	Michael Barrett	.15
189	Chris Widger	.15
190	Ugueth Urbina	.15
191	Dustin Hermanson	.15
192	Rondell White	.15
193	Jose Vidro	.15
194	Hideki Irabu	.15
195	Lee Stevens	.15
196	Livan Hernandez	.15
197	Ellis Burks	.15
198	J.T. Snow	.15
199	Jeff Kent	.25
200	Robb Nen	.15
201	Marvin Benard	.15
202	Barry Bonds	1.50
203	Russ Ortiz	.15
204	Rich Aurilia	.15
205	Joe Nathan	.15
206	Preston Wilson	.25
207	Cliff Floyd	.15
208	Mike Lowell	.15
209	Ryan Dempster	.15
210	Luis Castillo	.15
211	Alex Fernandez	.15
212	Mark Kotsay	.15
213	Brant Brown	.15
214	Edgardo Alfonzo	.15
215	Robin Ventura	.25
216	Rickey Henderson	.25
217	Mike Hampton	.15
218	Mike Piazza	1.00
219	Al Leiter	.15
220	Derek Bell	.15
221	Armando Benitez	.15
222	Rey Ordonez	.15
223	Todd Zeile	.15
224	Tony Gwynn	.75
225	Eric Owens	.15
226	Damian Jackson	.15
227	Trevor Hoffman	.15
228	Ben Davis	.15
229	Sterling Hitchcock	.15
230	Ruben Rivera	.15
231	Ryan Klesko	.15
232	Phil Nevin	.15
233	Mike Lieberthal	.15
234	Bobby Abreu	.25
235	Doug Glanville	.15
236	Rico Brogna	.15
237	Scott Rolen	.50
238	Andy Ashby	.15
239	Robert Person	.15
240	Curt Schilling	.25
241	Mike Jackson	.15
242	Warren Morris	.15
243	Kris Benson	.15
244	Kevin Young	.15
245	Brian Giles	.25
246	Jason Schmidt	.15
247	Jason Kendall	.25
248	Todd Ritchie	.15
249	Wil Cordero	.15
250	Aramis Ramirez	.15
251	Sean Casey	.25
252	Barry Larkin	.25
253	Pokey Reese	.15
254	Scott Williamson	.15
255	Aaron Boone	.25
256	Dante Bichette	.15
257	Ken Griffey Jr.	1.00
258	Denny Neagle	.15
259	Dmitri Young	.15
260	Todd Helton	.50
261	Larry Walker	.25
262	Pedro Astacio	.15
263	Neifi Perez	.15
264	Jeff Cirillo	.15
265	Jeffrey Hammonds	.15
266	Tom Goodwin	.15
267	Rolando Arrojo	.15
268	Rick Ankiel	3.00
269	Pat Burrell	4.00
270	Eric Munson	3.00
271	Rafael Furcal	3.00
272	Brad Penny	3.00
273	Adam Kennedy	3.00
274	*Mike Lamb*	3.00
275	Matt Riley	3.00
276	Eric Gagne	5.00
277	*Kazuhiro Sasaki*	3.00
278	Julio Lugo	3.00
279	Kip Wells	3.00
280	*Danys Baez*	3.00
281	Josh Beckett	4.00
282	Alfonso Soriano	4.00
283	Vernon Wells	4.00
284	Nick Johnson	3.00
285	Ramon Ortiz	3.00
286	Peter Bergeron	3.00
287	*Wascar Serrano*	3.00
288	Josh Paul	3.00
289	Mark Quinn	3.00
290	Jason Marquis	3.00
291	Rob Bell	3.00
292	Pablo Ozuna	3.00
293	Milton Bradley	3.00
294	Roosevelt Brown	3.00
295	Terrence Long	3.00
296	*Chad Durbin*	3.00
297	Matt LeCroy	3.00
298	Ken Griffey Jr.	.50
299	Mark McGwire	.75
300	Derek Jeter	1.00

Game-used Ball

NM/M

Common Player:		10.00
Inserted 1:480		
JB	Jeff Bagwell	25.00

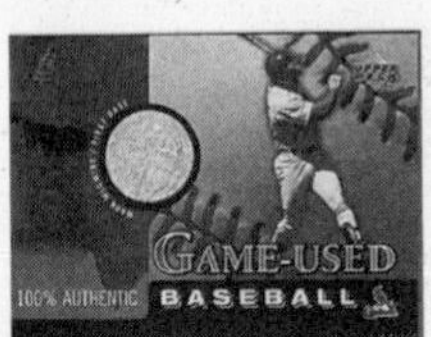

BB	Barry Bonds	70.00
SC	Sean Casey	10.00
RC	Roger Clemens	35.00
NG	Nomar Garciaparra	40.00
SG	Shawn Green	10.00
KG	Ken Griffey Jr.	30.00
TG	Tony Gwynn	25.00
DJ	Derek Jeter	60.00
AJ	Andruw Jones	15.00
CJ	Chipper Jones	30.00
GM	Greg Maddux	30.00
MM	Mark McGwire	60.00
MP	Mike Piazza	30.00
MR	Manny Ramirez	15.00
IR	Ivan Rodriguez	15.00
SR	Scott Rolen	10.00
GS	Gary Sheffield	10.00
SS	Sammy Sosa	30.00
BW	Bernie Williams	10.00

Setting the Standard

		NM/M
Complete Set (15):		25.00
Common Player:		.50
Inserted 1:11		
1	Tony Gwynn	1.50
2	Manny Ramirez	1.00
3	Derek Jeter	3.00
4	Cal Ripken Jr.	4.00
5	Mo Vaughn	.50
6	Jose Canseco	.75
7	Barry Bonds	4.00
8	Nomar Garciaparra	3.00
9	Juan Gonzalez	1.00
10	Mark McGwire	3.00
11	Alex Rodriguez	3.00
12	Jeff Bagwell	1.00
13	Ken Griffey Jr.	2.00
14	Frank Thomas	1.00
15	Sammy Sosa	2.50

Solid Gold Gallery

		NM/M
Complete Set (12):		20.00
Common Player:		1.00
Inserted 1:13		
1	Ken Griffey Jr.	2.00
2	Alex Rodriguez	3.00
3	Mike Piazza	2.00
4	Sammy Sosa	2.50
5	Derek Jeter	3.00
6	Jeff Bagwell	1.00
7	Mark McGwire	3.00
8	Cal Ripken Jr.	4.00
9	Pedro Martinez	1.50
10	Chipper Jones	2.00
11	Ivan Rodriguez	1.00
12	Vladimir Guerrero	1.00

UD Authentics

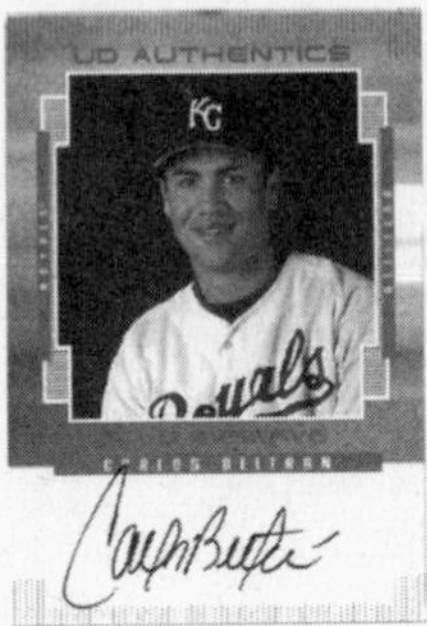

		NM/M
Inserted 1:480		
CB	Carlos Beltran	40.00
JC	Jose Canseco	35.00
SG	Shawn Green	20.00
KG	Ken Griffey Jr.	
TG	Tony Gwynn	30.00
CJ	Chipper Jones	60.00
MR	Manny Ramirez	25.00
CR	Cal Ripken Jr.	100.00
AR	Alex Rodriguez	80.00
IR	Ivan Rodriguez	20.00

24-Karat Gems

		NM/M
Complete Set (15):		12.00
Common Player:		.50
Inserted 1:7		
1	Pedro Martinez	1.50
2	Scott Rolen	1.00
3	Jason Giambi	1.50
4	Jeromy Burnitz	.50
5	Rafael Palmeiro	1.00
6	Rick Ankiel	.50
7	Carlos Beltran	.75
8	Derek Jeter	3.00
9	Jason Kendall	.50
10	Chipper Jones	2.00
11	Carlos Delgado	1.00
12	Alex Rodriguez	3.00
13	Randy Johnson	1.50
14	Tony Gwynn	1.50
15	Shawn Green	.75

3,000 Hit Club

		NM/M
AK-B	Al Kaline bat/400	20.00
AK-BS	Al Kaline bat/auto/6	

2000 UPPER DECK HITTER'S CLUB

		NM/M
Complete Set (90):		20.00
Common Player:		.15
Pack (5):		1.50
Wax Box (24):		25.00
1	Mo Vaughn	.20
2	Troy Glaus	.40
3	Jeff Bagwell	.50
4	Craig Biggio	.25
5	Jason Giambi	.75
6	Eric Chavez	.25
7	Carlos Delgado	.50
8	Chipper Jones	1.00
9	Andruw Jones	.50
10	Andres Galarraga	.20
11	Jeromy Burnitz	.15
12	Mark McGwire	1.50
13	Mark Grace	.25
14	Sammy Sosa	1.25
15	Jose Canseco	.40
16	Vinny Castilla	.15
17	Matt Williams	.25
18	Gary Sheffield	.25
19	Shawn Green	.25
20	Vladimir Guerrero	.50
21	Barry Bonds	1.50
22	Manny Ramirez	.50
23	Roberto Alomar	.40
24	Jim Thome	.50
25	Ken Griffey Jr.	1.00
26	Alex Rodriguez	1.50
27	Edgar Martinez	.15
28	Preston Wilson	.25
29	Mike Piazza	1.00
30	Robin Ventura	.25
31	Albert Belle	.20
32	Cal Ripken Jr.	2.00
33	Tony Gwynn	.75
34	Scott Rolen	.50
35	Bob Abreu	.25
36	Brian Giles	.25
37	Ivan Rodriguez	.40
38	Rafael Palmeiro	.40
39	Nomar Garciaparra	1.50
40	Sean Casey	.20
41	Larry Walker	.25
42	Todd Helton	.50
43	Carlos Beltran	.25
44	Dean Palmer	.15
45	Juan Gonzalez	.50
46	Corey Koskie	.15
47	Frank Thomas	.50
48	Magglio Ordonez	.25
49	Derek Jeter	2.00
50	Bernie Williams	.40
51	Paul Waner	.25
52	Honus Wagner	.50
53	Tris Speaker	.25
54	Nap Lajoie	.25
55	Eddie Collins	.25
56	Roberto Clemente	1.00
57	Ty Cobb	1.50
58	Cap Anson	.50
59	Robin Yount	.50
60	Carl Yastrzemski	.50
61	Dave Winfield	.25
62	Stan Musial	1.00
63	Eddie Murray	.40
64	Paul Molitor	.50
65	Willie Mays	1.50
66	Al Kaline	.50
67	Tony Gwynn	.75
68	Rod Carew	.40
69	Lou Brock	.25
70	George Brett	1.00
71	Wade Boggs	.25
72	Hank Aaron	1.50
73	Jorge Luis Toca	.15
74	J.D. Drew	.15
75	Pat Burrell	.25
76	Vernon Wells	.25
77	Julio Ramirez	.15
78	Gabe Kapler	.15
79	Erubiel Durazo	.15
80	Lance Berkman	.25
81	Peter Bergeron	.15
82	Alfonso Soriano	.75
83	Jacque Jones	.15
84	Ben Petrick	.15
85	Jerry Hairston Jr.	.15
86	Kevin Witt	.15
87	Dermal Brown	.15
88	Chad Hermansen	.15
89	Ruben Mateo	.15
90	Ken Griffey Jr. Checklist	.50

Accolades

		NM/M
Complete Set (10):		12.00
Common Player:		.75
Inserted 1:11		
1	Robin Yount	1.00
2	Tony Gwynn	1.00
3	Sammy Sosa	2.00
4	Mike Piazza	1.50
5	Cal Ripken Jr.	3.00
6	Mark McGwire	2.50
7	Barry Bonds	2.50
8	Wade Boggs	.75
9	Ken Griffey Jr.	1.50
10	Willie Mays	2.00

Autographs

		NM/M
Common Player:		15.00
Inserted 1:215		
HA	Hank Aaron #44	220.00
WB	Wade Boggs #12	30.00
GB	George Brett #5	80.00
Lou	Lou Brock #20	15.00
Rod	Rod Carew #29	15.00
TG	Tony Gwynn #19	40.00
AI	Al Kaline #6	30.00
WM	Willie Mays #24	150.00
PM	Paul Molitor #4	30.00
EM	Eddie Murray #33	30.00
Man	Stan Musial #6	75.00
Cal	Cal Ripken Jr. #8	150.00
DW	Dave Winfield #31	20.00
Yaz	Carl Yastrzemski #7	60.00
RY	Robin Yount #19	40.00

Epic Performances

		NM/M
Complete Set (10):		12.00
Common Player:		1.00
Inserted 1:3		
1	Mark McGwire	2.50
3	Sammy Sosa	2.00
4	Ken Griffey Jr.	1.50
5	Carl Yastrzemski	1.00
6	Tony Gwynn	1.00
7	Nomar Garciaparra	2.50
8	Cal Ripken Jr.	3.00
9	George Brett	1.50
10	Hank Aaron	2.00
11	Wade Boggs	1.00

Eternals

		NM/M
Complete Set (10):		20.00
Common Player:		1.00
Inserted 1:23		
1	Cal Ripken Jr.	4.00
2	Mark McGwire	3.00
3	Ken Griffey Jr.	2.00
4	Nomar Garciaparra	3.00
5	Tony Gwynn	1.50
6	Derek Jeter	3.00
7	Jose Canseco	1.00
8	Mike Piazza	2.00
9	Alex Rodriguez	3.00
10	Barry Bonds	4.00

Generations of Excellence

		NM/M
Complete Set (10):		15.00
Common Card:		1.00
Inserted 1:6		
1	Cal Ripken Jr., Eddie Murray	3.00
2	Vladimir Guerrero, Roberto Clemente	2.00
3	George Brett, Robin Yount	2.00
4	Barry Bonds, Willie Mays	3.00
5	Chipper Jones, Hank Aaron	2.00
6	Mark McGwire, Sammy Sosa	2.00
7	Tony Gwynn, Wade Boggs	1.00
8	Rickey Henderson, Lou Brock	1.00

9	Derek Jeter, Nomar Garciaparra	3.00
10	Alex Rodriguez, Ken Griffey Jr.	2.50

On Target

		NM/M
Complete Set (10):		12.00
Common Player:		.50
Inserted 1:23		
1	Nomar Garciaparra	3.00
2	Sean Casey	.50
3	Alex Rodriguez	3.00
4	Troy Glaus	1.00
5	Ivan Rodriguez	1.00
6	Chipper Jones	2.00
7	Manny Ramirez	1.00
8	Derek Jeter	3.00
9	Vladimir Guerrero	1.00
10	Scott Rolen	1.00

The Hitters' Club

		NM/M
Complete Set (10):		60.00
Common Player:		3.00
1	Rod Carew	5.00
2	Alex Rodriguez	15.00
3	Willie Mays	10.00
4	George Brett	10.00
5	Tony Gwynn	8.00
6	Stan Musial	8.00
7	Frank Thomas	5.00
8	Wade Boggs	3.00
9	Larry Walker	3.00
10	Nomar Garciaparra	15.00

3,000 Hit Club

		NM/M
Common Player:		25.00
WB	Wade Boggs bat/350	25.00
WB	Wade Boggs bat & cap/50	65.00
WB	Wade Boggs AU/12	
TG	Tony Gwynn bat/350	25.00
TG	Tony Gwynn bat & cap/50	100.00
TG	Tony Gwynn AU/19	550.00
GB	Tony Gwynn, Wade Boggs bat/99	85.00

2000 UPPER DECK HOLOGRFX

		NM/M
Complete Set (90):		20.00
Common Player:		.15
Pack (4):		1.50
Wax Box (32):		25.00
1	Mo Vaughn	.20
2	Troy Glaus	.50
3	Daryle Ward	.15
4	Jeff Bagwell	.50
5	Craig Biggio	.25
6	Jose Lima	.15
7	Jason Giambi	.75
8	Eric Chavez	.25
9	Tim Hudson	.25
10	Raul Mondesi	.25
11	Carlos Delgado	.50
12	David Wells	.15
13	Chipper Jones	1.00
14	Greg Maddux	1.00
15	Andruw Jones	.50
16	Brian Jordan	.15
17	Jeromy Burnitz	.15
18	Ron Belliard	.15
19	Mark McGwire	1.50
20	Fernando Tatis	.15
21	J.D. Drew	.25
22	Sammy Sosa	1.00
23	Mark Grace	.40
24	Greg Vaughn	.15
25	Jose Canseco	.40
26	Vinny Castilla	.15
27	Fred McGriff	.25
28	Matt Williams	.25
29	Randy Johnson	.75
30	Erubiel Durazo	.15
31	Shawn Green	.25
32	Gary Sheffield	.40
33	Kevin Brown	.25
34	Vladimir Guerrero	.50
35	Michael Barrett	.15
36	Russ Ortiz	.15
37	Barry Bonds	1.50
38	Jeff Kent	.25
39	Kenny Lofton	.25
40	Manny Ramirez	.50
41	Roberto Alomar	.40
42	Richie Sexson	.25
43	Edgar Martinez	.25
44	Alex Rodriguez	1.50
45	Fred Garcia	.15
46	Preston Wilson	.15
47	Alex Gonzalez	.15
48	Mike Hampton	.15
49	Mike Piazza	1.00
50	Robin Ventura	.25
51	Edgardo Alfonzo	.15
52	Albert Belle	.15
53	Cal Ripken Jr.	2.00
54	B.J. Surhoff	.15
55	Tony Gwynn	.75
56	Trevor Hoffman	.15
57	Mike Lieberthal	.15
58	Scott Rolen	.50
59	Bob Abreu	.25
60	Curt Schilling	.40
61	Jason Kendall	.25
62	Brian Giles	.25
63	Kris Benson	.15
64	Rafael Palmeiro	.40
65	Ivan Rodriguez	.50
66	Gabe Kapler	.40
67	Nomar Garciaparra	1.50
68	Pedro Martinez	.75
69	Troy O'Leary	.15
70	Barry Larkin	.25
71	Dante Bichette	.15
72	Sean Casey	.20
73	Ken Griffey Jr.	1.00
74	Jeff Cirillo	.15
75	Todd Helton	.50
76	Larry Walker	.25
77	Carlos Beltran	.25
78	Jermaine Dye	.15
79	Juan Gonzalez	.50
80	Juan Encarnacion	.15
81	Dean Palmer	.15
82	Corey Koskie	.15
83	Eric Milton	.15
84	Frank Thomas	.50
85	Magglio Ordonez	.25
86	Carlos Lee	.15
87	Derek Jeter	2.00
88	Tino Martinez	.25
89	Bernie Williams	.50
90	Roger Clemens	1.50

A Piece of the Series

		NM/M
Common Player:		5.00
Inserted 1:215		
1	Derek Jeter	40.00
2	Chipper Jones	20.00
3	Roger Clemens	30.00
4	Greg Maddux	30.00
5	Bernie Williams	10.00
6	Andruw Jones	10.00
7	Tino Martinez	8.00
8	Brian Jordan	5.00
9	Mariano Rivera	8.00
11	Paul O'Neill	8.00
12	Tom Glavine	10.00

A Piece of Series Autograph

		NM/M
Common Player:		40.00
Production 25 sets		

PSA1	Derek Jeter	300.00
PSA2	Chipper Jones	125.00
PSA3	Roger Clemens	220.00
PSA4	Greg Maddux	220.00
PSA6	Andruw Jones	85.00
PSA7	Tino Martinez	65.00
PSA8	Brian Jordan	40.00
PSA11	Paul O'Neill	75.00
PSA12	Tom Glavine	100.00

Bomb Squad

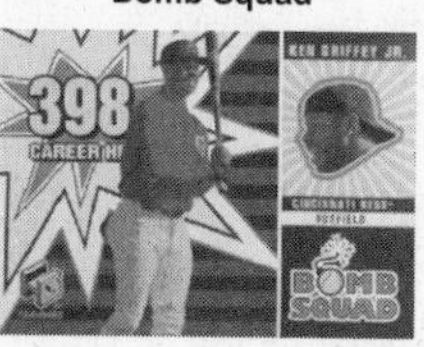

		NM/M
Complete Set (6):		15.00
Common Player:		2.00
Inserted 1:34		
1	Ken Griffey Jr.	2.00
2	Mark McGwire	3.00
3	Chipper Jones	2.00
4	Alex Rodriguez	3.00
5	Sammy Sosa	2.50
6	Barry Bonds	4.00

Future Fame

		NM/M
Complete Set (6):		10.00
Common Player:		2.00
Inserted 1:34		
1	Cal Ripken Jr.	4.00
2	Mark McGwire	3.00
3	Greg Maddux	2.00
4	Tony Gwynn	1.50
5	Ken Griffey Jr.	2.00
6	Roger Clemens	2.50

Longball Legacy

		NM/M
Complete Set (15):		15.00
Common Player:		.50
Inserted 1:6		
1	Mike Piazza	2.00
2	Ivan Rodriguez	.75
3	Jeff Bagwell	1.00
4	Alex Rodriguez	3.00
5	Jose Canseco	.75
6	Mark McGwire	3.00
7	Scott Rolen	.75
8	Carlos Delgado	.75
9	Mo Vaughn	.50
10	Manny Ramirez	1.00
11	Matt Williams	.50
12	Sammy Sosa	2.50
13	Ken Griffey Jr.	2.00
14	Nomar Garciaparra	3.00
15	Larry Walker	.50

Stars of the System

		NM/M
Complete Set (10):		8.00
Common Player:		.75
Inserted 1:8		
1	Rick Ankiel	.75
2	Alfonso Soriano	2.00
3	Vernon Wells	1.00
4	Ben Petrick	.75
5	Francisco Cordero	.75
6	Matt Riley	.75
7	A.J. Burnett	1.00
8	Pat Burrell	1.50
9	Ed Yarnall	.75
10	Dermal Brown	.75

StarView

		NM/M
Complete Set (8):		15.00
Common Player:		2.00
Inserted 1:11		
1	Ken Griffey Jr.	2.00
2	Nomar Garciaparra	3.00
3	Chipper Jones	2.00
4	Mark McGwire	3.00
5	Sammy Sosa	2.50
6	Derek Jeter	4.00
7	Mike Piazza	2.00
8	Alex Rodriguez	3.00

3,000 Hit Club

		NM/M
Common Card:		20.00
RY	Robin Yount bat/350	20.00
RYJ	Robin Yount jersey/350	20.00
GB	George Brett bat/350	35.00
GBJ	George Brett jersey/350	35.00
BY	George Brett, Robin Yount bat/99	120.00
BYA	George Brett, Robin Yount AU/10	
BYJ	George Brett, Robin Yount jersey/99	120.00

2000 UPPER DECK LEGENDS

		NM/M
Complete Set (135):		80.00

Common Player:		.15
Common Y2K:		.75
Inserted 1:9		
Common 20th Century Legend		1.00
Inserted 1:5		
Pack (7):		5.00
Box (24):		90.00
1	Darin Erstad	.25
2	Troy Glaus	.75
3	Mo Vaughn	.20
4	Craig Biggio	.25
5	Jeff Bagwell	.75
6	Reggie Jackson	1.00
7	Tim Hudson	.25
8	Jason Giambi	1.00
9	Hank Aaron	2.00
10	Greg Maddux	1.50
11	Chipper Jones	1.50
12	Andres Galarraga	.25
13	Robin Yount	.50
14	Jeromy Burnitz	.15
15	Paul Molitor	.50
16	David Wells	.15
17	Carlos Delgado	.75
18	Ernie Banks	.75
19	Sammy Sosa	2.00
20	Kerry Wood	.40
21	Stan Musial	.75
22	Bob Gibson	.50
23	Mark McGwire	2.00
24	Fernando Tatis	.15
25	Randy Johnson	1.00
26	Matt Williams	.40
27	Jackie Robinson	2.00
28	Sandy Koufax	1.50
29	Shawn Green	.40
30	Kevin Brown	.25
31	Gary Sheffield	.40
32	Greg Vaughn	.15
33	Jose Canseco	.50
34	Gary Carter	.15
35	Vladimir Guerrero	.75
36	Willie Mays	2.00
37	Barry Bonds	2.00
38	Jeff Kent	.25
39	Bob Feller	.40
40	Roberto Alomar	.50
41	Jim Thome	.75
42	Manny Ramirez	.75
43	Alex Rodriguez	2.00
44	Preston Wilson	.15
45	Tom Seaver	.75
46	Robin Ventura	.15
47	Mike Piazza	1.50
48	Mike Hampton	.15
49	Brooks Robinson	.75
50	Frank Robinson	.75
51	Cal Ripken Jr.	2.50
52	Albert Belle	.20
53	Eddie Murray	.40
54	Tony Gwynn	1.00
55	Roberto Clemente	1.50
56	Willie Stargell	.25
57	Brian Giles	.25
58	Jason Kendall	.25
59	Mike Schmidt	1.00
60	Bob Abreu	.25
61	Scott Rolen	.50
62	Curt Schilling	.40
63	Johnny Bench	1.00
64	Sean Casey	.15
65	Barry Larkin	.25
66	Ken Griffey Jr.	1.50
67	George Brett	1.50
68	Carlos Beltran	.15
69	Nolan Ryan	3.00
70	Ivan Rodriguez	.75
71	Rafael Palmeiro	.40
72	Larry Walker	.25
73	Todd Helton	.75
74	Jeff Cirillo	.15
75	Carl Everett	.15
76	Nomar Garciaparra	2.00
77	Pedro Martinez	1.00
78	Harmon Killebrew	.50
79	Corey Koskie	.15
80	Ty Cobb	2.00
81	Dean Palmer	.15
82	Juan Gonzalez	.75
83	Carlton Fisk	.15
84	Frank Thomas	.75
85	Magglio Ordonez	.25
86	Lou Gehrig	2.00
87	Babe Ruth	3.00
88	Derek Jeter	2.50
89	Roger Clemens	1.50
90	Bernie Williams	.50
91	Rick Ankiel	.75
92	Kip Wells	.75
93	Pat Burrell	1.50
94	Mark Quinn	.75
95	Ruben Mateo	.75
96	Adam Kennedy	.75
97	Brad Penny	.75
98	*Kazuhiro Sasaki*	2.00
99	Peter Bergeron	.75
100	Rafael Furcal	1.00
101	Eric Munson	.75
102	Nick Johnson	1.00
103	Rob Bell	.75
104	Vernon Wells	1.00
105	Ben Petrick	.75
106	Babe Ruth	8.00
107	Mark McGwire	6.00
108	Nolan Ryan	8.00
109	Hank Aaron	5.00
110	Barry Bonds	6.00
111	Nomar Garciaparra	5.00
112	Roger Clemens	5.00
113	Johnny Bench	2.50
114	Alex Rodriguez	6.00
115	Cal Ripken Jr.	8.00
116	Willie Mays	6.00
117	Mike Piazza	4.00
118	Reggie Jackson	2.00
119	Tony Gwynn	3.00
120	Cy Young	2.00
121	George Brett	4.00
122	Greg Maddux	4.00
123	Yogi Berra	2.00
124	Sammy Sosa	5.00
125	Randy Johnson	2.50
126	Bob Gibson	2.00
127	Lou Gehrig	6.00
128	Ken Griffey Jr.	4.00
129	Derek Jeter	6.00
130	Mike Schmidt	3.00
131	Pedro Martinez	2.50
132	Jackie Robinson	5.00
133	Jose Canseco	1.00
134	Ty Cobb	5.00
135	Stan Musial	3.00

Commemorative Collection

Stars (1-90):	4-8X
Y2K:	1-2X
20th Century Legends:	2-3X
Production 100 sets	

(See 2000 Upper Deck Legends for checklist and base card values.)

Defining Moments

		NM/M
Complete Set (10):		20.00
Common Player:		1.00
Inserted 1:12		
1	Reggie Jackson	1.50
2	Hank Aaron	3.00
3	Babe Ruth	4.00
4	Cal Ripken Jr.	4.00
5	Carlton Fisk	1.00
6	Ken Griffey Jr.	2.00
7	Nolan Ryan	4.00
8	Roger Clemens	2.50
9	Willie Mays	3.00
10	Mark McGwire	3.00

Eternal Glory

		NM/M
Complete Set (7):		15.00
Common Player:		2.00
Inserted 1:24		
1	Nolan Ryan	4.00
2	Ken Griffey Jr.	2.00
4	Sammy Sosa	2.50
5	Derek Jeter	4.00
6	Willie Mays	3.00
7	Roger Clemens	3.00

Legendary Jerseys

		NM/M
Common Player:		8.00
Inserted 1:48		
HA	Hank Aaron	40.00
JB	Jeff Bagwell	10.00
JB	Johnny Bench	20.00
WB	Wade Boggs	10.00
BaB	Barry Bonds	40.00
BoB	Bobby Bonds	8.00
GB	George Brett	30.00
LB	Lou Brock	8.00
JC	Jose Canseco	10.00
RC	Roger Clemens	30.00
DC	Dave Concepcion	8.00
DD	Don Drysdale	25.00
RF	Rollie Fingers	8.00
LG	Lou Gehrig pants	250.00
BG	Bob Gibson pants	20.00
KG	Ken Griffey Jr.	35.00
TG	Tony Gwynn	20.00
RJ	Reggie Jackson	10.00
DJ	Derek Jeter	40.00
RaJ	Randy Johnson	20.00
CJ	Chipper Jones	20.00
SK	Sandy Koufax	250.00
SK	Sandy Koufax auto/32	1,200
GM	Greg Maddux	30.00
MM	Mickey Mantle	150.00
RM	Roger Maris pants	60.00
EM	Eddie Mathews	20.00
WM	Willie Mays SP/29	675.00
BM	Bill Mazeroski	8.00
WMc	Willie McCovey	10.00
TM	Thurman Munson	30.00
DM	Dale Murphy	10.00
SM	Stan Musial SP/28	650.00
JP	Jim Palmer	8.00
GP	Gaylord Perry	8.00
MR	Manny Ramirez	10.00
CR	Cal Ripken Jr.	40.00
BR	Brooks Robinson	20.00
FR	Frank Robinson	10.00
AR	Alex Rodriguez	35.00
NR	Nolan Ryan	40.00
MS	Mike Schmidt	25.00
TS	Tom Seaver	20.00
OS	Ozzie Smith	20.00
WS	Willie Stargell	8.00
FT	Frank Thomas	10.00
JT	Joe Torre	8.00
EW	Earl Weaver	8.00
MW	Matt Williams	8.00
MW	Maury Wills	8.00
DW	Dave Winfield	10.00

Legendary Signatures

		NM/M
Common Player:		8.00
Inserted 1:23		
Golds:		1-2X
Production 50 sets		
HA	Hank Aaron SP/94	275.00
JB	Johnny Bench	30.00
BB	Bobby Bonds	8.00
LB	Lou Brock	8.00
GB	George Brett	60.00
JC	Jose Canseco	20.00
GC	Gary Carter	10.00
SC	Sean Casey	8.00
RC	Roger Clemens	80.00
DC	Dave Concepcion	8.00
AD	Andre Dawson	10.00
KG	Ken Griffey Jr.	85.00
VG	Vladimir Guerrero	30.00
TG	Tony Gwynn	40.00
RJ	Reggie Jackson	20.00
DJ	Derek Jeter SP/61	400.00
RaJ	Randy Johnson	50.00
CJ	Chipper Jones	35.00
HK	Harmon Killebrew	25.00
FL	Fred Lynn	8.00
DM	Dale Murphy	15.00
SM	Stan Musial	50.00
PN	Phil Niekro	8.00
JP	Jim Palmer	10.00
MP	Mike Piazza	120.00
MR	Manny Ramirez SP/141	60.00
CR	Cal Ripken Jr.	120.00
AR	Alex Rodriguez	85.00
IR	Ivan Rodriguez	25.00
NR	Nolan Ryan	85.00
MS	Mike Schmidt	50.00
TS	Tom Seaver	30.00
OS	Ozzie Smith	40.00
WS	Willie Stargell	60.00
FT	Frank Thomas	30.00
AT	Alan Trammell	10.00
BW	Matt Williams	8.00

Ones for the Ages

		NM/M
Complete Set (7):		15.00
Inserted 1:24		
01	Ty Cobb	2.50
02	Cal Ripken Jr.	4.00
03	Babe Ruth	4.00
04	Jackie Robinson	2.50
05	Mark McGwire	3.00
06	Alex Rodriguez	3.00
07	Mike Piazza	4.00

Reflections in Time

		NM/M
Complete Set (10):		25.00
Common Player:		2.00
Inserted 1:12		
1	Ken Griffey Jr., Hank Aaron	3.00
2	Sammy Sosa, Roberto Clemente	3.00
3	Roger Clemens, Nolan Ryan	4.00
4	Ivan Rodriguez, Johnny Bench	2.00
5	Alex Rodriguez, Ernie Banks	3.00
6	Tony Gwynn, Stan Musial	2.00
7	Barry Bonds, Willie Mays	4.00
8	Cal Ripken Jr., Lou Gehrig	4.00
9	Chipper Jones, Mike Schmidt	2.50
10	Mark McGwire, Babe Ruth	4.00

UD Millennium Team

		NM/M
Complete Set (10):		15.00
Common Player:		1.50
Inserted 1:4		
1	Mark McGwire	2.00
2	Jackie Robinson	2.00
3	Mike Schmidt	1.50
4	Cal Ripken Jr.	3.00
5	Babe Ruth	3.00
7	Willie Mays	2.00
8	Johnny Bench	1.50
9	Nolan Ryan	3.00
10	Ken Griffey Jr.	1.50

3,000 Hit Club

		NM/M
CY	Carl Yastrzemski bat/350	30.00

CY Carl Yastrzemski jersey/350 30.00
CY Carl Yastrzemski bat/jersey/100 80.00
CY Carl Yastrzemski auto/bat/jersey/8

2000 UPPER DECK MVP

NM/M

Complete Set (220): 20.00
Common Player: .10
Pack (10): 1.25
Wax Box (28): 25.00

1 Garret Anderson .25
2 Mo Vaughn .15
3 Tim Salmon .20
4 Ramon Ortiz .10
5 Darin Erstad .25
6 Troy Glaus .50
7 Troy Percival .10
8 Jeff Bagwell .50
9 Ken Caminiti .10
10 Daryle Ward .10
11 Craig Biggio .25
12 Jose Lima .10
13 Moises Alou .20
14 Octavio Dotel .10
15 Ben Grieve .10
16 Jason Giambi .50
17 Tim Hudson .20
18 Eric Chavez .20
19 Matt Stairs .10
20 Miguel Tejada .25
21 John Jaha .10
22 Chipper Jones 1.00
23 Kevin Millwood .20
24 Brian Jordan .10
25 Andruw Jones .25
26 Andres Galarraga .20
27 Greg Maddux 1.00
28 Reggie Sanders .10
29 Javy Lopez .20
30 Jeromy Burnitz .10
31 Kevin Barker .10
32 Jose Hernandez .10
33 Ron Belliard .10
34 Henry Blanco .10
35 Marquis Grissom .10
36 Geoff Jenkins .20
37 Carlos Delgado .50
38 Raul Mondesi .20
39 Roy Halladay .20
40 Tony Batista .10
41 David Wells .10
42 Shannon Stewart .10
43 Vernon Wells .20
44 Sammy Sosa 1.00
45 Ismael Valdes .10
46 Joe Girardi .10
47 Mark Grace .20
48 Henry Rodriguez .10
49 Kerry Wood .25
50 Eric Young .10
51 Mark McGwire 2.00
52 Daryle Kile .10
53 Fernando Vina .10
54 Ray Lankford .10
55 J.D. Drew .20
56 Fernando Tatis .10
57 Rick Ankiel .10
58 Matt Williams .20
59 Erubiel Durazo .15
60 Tony Womack .10
61 Jay Bell .10
62 Randy Johnson .75
63 Steve Finley .10
64 Matt Mantei .10
65 Luis Gonzalez .20
66 Gary Sheffield .25
67 Eric Gagne .10
68 Adrian Beltre .20
69 Mark Grudzielanek .10
70 Kevin Brown .20
71 Chan Ho Park .10
72 Shawn Green .40
73 Vinny Castilla .15
74 Fred McGriff .25
75 Wilson Alvarez .10
76 Greg Vaughn .10
77 Gerald Williams .10
78 Ryan Rupe .10
79 Jose Canseco .25
80 Vladimir Guerrero .50
81 Dustin Hermanson .10
82 Michael Barrett .10
83 Rondell White .20
84 Tony Armas Jr. .10
85 Wilton Guerrero .10
86 Jose Vidro .10
87 Barry Bonds 1.50
88 Russ Ortiz .10
89 Ellis Burks .10
90 Jeff Kent .20
91 Russ Davis .10
92 J.T. Snow .10
93 Roberto Alomar .40
94 Manny Ramirez .50
95 Chuck Finley .10
96 Kenny Lofton .20
97 Jim Thome .50
98 Bartolo Colon .20
99 Omar Vizquel .20
100 Richie Sexson .25
101 Mike Cameron .10
102 Brett Tomko .10
103 Edgar Martinez .20
104 Alex Rodriguez 1.50
105 John Olerud .20
106 Fred Garcia .10
107 *Kazuhiro Sasaki* 1.00
108 Preston Wilson .20
109 Luis Castillo .10
110 A.J. Burnett .10
111 Mike Lowell .10
112 Cliff Floyd .10
113 Brad Penny .10
114 Alex Gonzalez .10
115 Mike Piazza 1.00
116 Derek Bell .10
117 Edgardo Alfonzo .10
118 Rickey Henderson .20
119 Todd Zeile .10
120 Mike Hampton .10
121 Al Leiter .20
122 Robin Ventura .20
123 Cal Ripken Jr. 1.50
124 Mike Mussina .40
125 B.J. Surhoff .10
126 Jerry Hairston Jr. .10
127 Brady Anderson .10
128 Albert Belle .10
129 Sidney Ponson .10
130 Tony Gwynn .75
131 Ryan Klesko .10
132 Sterling Hitchcock .10
133 Eric Owens .10
134 Trevor Hoffman .10
135 Al Martin .10
136 Bret Boone .25
137 Brian Giles .25
138 Chad Hermansen .10
139 Kevin Young .10
140 Kris Benson .10
141 Warren Morris .10
142 Jason Kendall .20
143 Wil Cordero .10
144 Scott Rolen .50
145 Curt Schilling .40
146 Doug Glanville .10
147 Mike Lieberthal .10
148 Mike Jackson .10
149 Rico Brogna .10
150 Andy Ashby .10
151 Bob Abreu .20
152 Sean Casey .20
153 Pete Harnisch .10
154 Dante Bichette .10
155 Pokey Reese .10
156 Aaron Boone .20
157 Ken Griffey Jr. 1.00
158 Barry Larkin .25
159 Scott Williamson .10
160 Carlos Beltran .20
161 Jermaine Dye .10
162 Jose Rosado .10
163 Joe Randa .10
164 Johnny Damon .20
165 Mike Sweeney .10
166 Mark Quinn .10
167 Ivan Rodriguez .40
168 Rusty Greer .10
169 Ruben Mateo .10
170 Doug Davis .10
171 Gabe Kapler .10
172 Justin Thompson .10
173 Rafael Palmeiro .40
174 Larry Walker .20
175 Neifi Perez .10
176 Rolando Arrojo .10
177 Jeffrey Hammonds .10
178 Todd Helton .50
179 Pedro Astacio .10
180 Jeff Cirillo .10
181 Pedro Martinez .75
182 Carl Everett .10
183 Troy O'Leary .10
184 Nomar Garciaparra 1.25
185 Jose Offerman .10
186 Bret Saberhagen .10
187 Trot Nixon .10
188 Jason Varitek .10
189 Todd Walker .10
190 Eric Milton .10
191 Chad Allen .10
192 Jacque Jones .10
193 Brad Radke .10
194 Corey Koskie .10
195 Joe Mays .10
196 Juan Gonzalez .50
197 Jeff Weaver .10
198 Juan Encarnacion .10
199 Deivi Cruz .10
200 Damion Easley .10
201 Tony Clark .10
202 Dean Palmer .10
203 Frank Thomas .50
204 Carlos Lee .10
205 Mike Sirotka .10
206 Kip Wells .10
207 Magglio Ordonez .20
208 Paul Konerko .20
209 Chris Singleton .10
210 Derek Jeter 1.50
211 Tino Martinez .25
212 Mariano Rivera .20
213 Roger Clemens .75
214 Nick Johnson .25
215 Paul O'Neill .20
216 Bernie Williams .40
217 David Cone .20
218 Ken Griffey Jr. Checklist .50
219 Sammy Sosa Checklist .50
220 Mark McGwire Checklist .75

Silver

Stars: 1-2X
Inserted 1:2

Gold

Stars: 10-20X
Production 50 sets

Rookie cards are in *Italic*.

Super

Stars: 15-30X
Production 25 sets

Drawing Power

NM/M

Complete Set (7): 12.00
Common Player: 1.00
Inserted 1:28

1 Mark McGwire 3.00
2 Ken Griffey Jr. 2.00
3 Mike Piazza 2.00
4 Chipper Jones 2.00
5 Nomar Garciaparra 3.00
6 Sammy Sosa 2.50
7 Jose Canseco 1.00

Game Used Souvenirs - Bats

NM/M

Common Bat: 8.00
Inserted 1:130

BB Barry Bonds 40.00
JC Jose Canseco 8.00
KG Ken Griffey Jr. 20.00
VG Vladimir Guerrero 10.00
TG Tony Gwynn 15.00
CJ Chipper Jones 15.00
MR Manny Ramirez 10.00
AR Alex Rodriguez 20.00
IR Ivan Rodriguez 8.00
BW Bernie Williams 10.00

Game Used Souvenirs

NM/M

Common Glove: 8.00
Inserted 1:130

RA Roberto Alomar 15.00
JB Jeff Bagwell 20.00
AB Albert Belle 8.00
BB Barry Bonds 65.00
JC Jose Canseco 15.00
WC Will Clark 20.00
AF Alex Fernandez 8.00
JG Jason Giambi 15.00
TGl Troy Glaus 15.00
AG Alex Gonzalez 8.00

BG Ben Grieve 8.00
KG Ken Griffey Jr. 40.00
VG Vladimir Guerrero 15.00
TG Tony Gwynn 30.00
AJ Andruw Jones 15.00
CJ Chipper Jones 30.00
KL Kenny Lofton 8.00
RM Raul Mondesi 8.00
PO Paul O'Neill 10.00
RP Rafael Palmeiro 15.00
MR Manny Ramirez 15.00
CR Cal Ripken Jr. 65.00
AR Alex Rodriguez 40.00
IR Ivan Rodriguez 15.00
NR Nolan Ryan 65.00
TS Tim Salmon 8.00
LW Larry Walker 8.00
BW Bernie Williams 15.00
MW Matt Williams 8.00

PROLIFICS

NM/M
Complete Set (7): 10.00
Common Player: .50
Inserted 1:28
1 Manny Ramirez 1.00
2 Vladimir Guerrero 1.00
3 Derek Jeter 3.00
4 Pedro Martinez 1.50
5 Shawn Green .50
6 Alex Rodriguez 3.00
7 Cal Ripken Jr. 4.00

ProSign

NM/M
Common Player: 5.00
Inserted 1:216 R
RA Rick Ankiel 5.00
MB Michael Barrett 5.00
RB Rob Bell 5.00
CB Carlos Beltran 20.00
LB Lance Berkman 15.00
RB Rico Brogna 5.00
SC Sean Casey 8.00
DD Doug Davis 5.00
ED Erubiel Durazo 8.00
RF Robert Fick 8.00
NG Nomar Garciaparra 65.00
AG Alex Gonzalez 8.00
KG Ken Griffey Jr. 60.00
TG Tony Gwynn 40.00
TH Tim Hudson 15.00
DJ Derek Jeter 80.00
CJ Chipper Jones 50.00
MM Mike Meyers 5.00
EM Eric Milton 8.00
JM Jim Morris 5.00
WM Warren Morris 5.00
TN Trot Nixon 8.00
BP Ben Petrick 5.00
AP Adam Piatt 5.00
MP Mike Piazza 60.00
MQ Mark Quinn 5.00
MR Manny Ramirez 25.00
RR Rob Ramsay 5.00
MRe Mike Redmond 5.00
MRi Mariano Rivera 15.00
AR Alex Rodriguez 65.00
MS Mike Sweeney 8.00
BT Bubba Trammell 5.00
JV Jose Vidro 8.00
DW Daryle Ward 5.00
KW Kip Wells 8.00
SW Scott Williamson 5.00
PW Preston Wilson 8.00
KW Kevin Witt 5.00
TW Tony Womack 8.00
EY Ed Yarnall 5.00
JZ Jeff Zimmerman 5.00

Pure Grit

NM/M
Complete Set (10): 10.00
Common Player: .50
Inserted 1:6
1 Derek Jeter 2.00
2 Kevin Brown .50
3 Craig Biggio .50
4 Ivan Rodriguez .75
5 Scott Rolen .75
6 Carlos Beltran .50
7 Ken Griffey Jr. 1.50
8 Cal Ripken Jr. 2.50
9 Nomar Garciaparra 2.00
10 Randy Johnson 1.00

Scout's Choice

NM/M
Complete Set (10): 8.00
Common Player: .50
Inserted 1:14
1 Rick Ankiel .50
2 Vernon Wells 1.00
3 Pat Burrell 1.50
4 Travis Dawkins .50
5 Eric Munson .50
6 Nick Johnson 1.00
7 Dermal Brown .50
8 Alfonso Soriano 2.00
9 Ben Petrick .50
10 Adam Everett .50

Second Season Standouts

NM/M
Complete Set (10): 6.00
Common Player: .25
Inserted 1:6
1 Pedro Martinez 1.00
2 Mariano Rivera .40
3 Orlando Hernandez .25
4 Ken Caminiti .25
5 Bernie Williams .50
6 Jim Thome .75
7 Nomar Garciaparra 2.00
8 Edgardo Alfonzo .25
9 Derek Jeter 2.50
10 Kevin Millwood .40

3,000 Hit Club

NM/M
Common Player:
SM Stan Musial jersey-350 30.00
SM Stan Musial bat-350 30.00
SM Stan Musial jersey/bat-100 80.00
SM Stan Musial J/B/Auto-6

2000 UPPER DECK OVATION

NM/M
Complete Set (90): 65.00
Common Player: .25
Common World Prem. (61-80): 1.00
Inserted 1:3
Common Super. Spot (81-90): 1.50
Inserted 1:6
Pack (5): 2.00
Wax Box (20): 30.00
1 Mo Vaughn .25
2 Troy Glaus .75
3 Jeff Bagwell .75
4 Craig Biggio .40
5 Mike Hampton .25
6 Jason Giambi .75
7 Tim Hudson .40
8 Chipper Jones 1.50
9 Greg Maddux 1.50
10 Kevin Millwood .40
11 Brian Jordan .25
12 Jeromy Burnitz .25
13 David Wells .25
14 Carlos Delgado .75
15 Sammy Sosa 2.50
16 Mark McGwire 3.00
17 Matt Williams .25
18 Randy Johnson .75
19 Erubiel Durazo .40
20 Kevin Brown .40
21 Shawn Green .75
22 Gary Sheffield .50
23 Jose Canseco .50
24 Vladimir Guerrero 1.00
25 Barry Bonds 3.00
26 Manny Ramirez .75
27 Roberto Alomar .75
28 Richie Sexson .40
29 Jim Thome .75
30 Alex Rodriguez 2.50
31 Ken Griffey Jr. 1.50
32 Preston Wilson .25
33 Mike Piazza 1.50
34 Al Leiter .25
35 Robin Ventura .25
36 Cal Ripken Jr. 3.00
37 Albert Belle .25
38 Tony Gwynn 1.00
39 Brian Giles .40
40 Jason Kendall .40
41 Scott Rolen .75
42 Bob Abreu .40
43 Ken Griffey Jr. 1.50
44 Sean Casey .25
45 Carlos Beltran .40
46 Gabe Kapler .25
47 Ivan Rodriguez .75
48 Rafael Palmeiro .50
49 Larry Walker .40
50 Nomar Garciaparra 2.00
51 Pedro J. Martinez 1.00
52 Eric Milton .25
53 Juan Gonzalez .75
54 Tony Clark .25
55 Frank Thomas .75
56 Magglio Ordonez .40
57 Roger Clemens 1.50
58 Derek Jeter 2.50
59 Bernie Williams .50
60 Orlando Hernandez .40
61 Rick Ankiel 1.00
62 Josh Beckett 1.50
63 Vernon Wells 1.50
64 Alfonso Soriano 3.00
65 Pat Burrell 2.00
66 Eric Munson 1.00
67 Chad Hutchinson 1.00
68 Eric Gagne 1.00
69 Peter Bergeron 1.00
70 Ryan Anderson (Supposed to have been withdrawn, all known cards have embossed UD racing mark.) 300.00
71 A.J. Burnett 1.00
72 Jorge Luis Toca 1.00
73 Matt Riley 1.00
74 Chad Hermansen 1.00
75 Doug Davis 1.00
76 Jim Morris 1.00
77 Ben Petrick 1.00
78 Mark Quinn 1.00
79 Ed Yarnall 1.00
80 Ramon Ortiz 1.00
81 Ken Griffey Jr. 3.00
82 Mark McGwire 5.00
83 Derek Jeter 5.00
84 Jeff Bagwell 1.50
85 Nomar Garciaparra 5.00
86 Sammy Sosa 4.00
87 Mike Piazza 3.00
88 Alex Rodriguez 5.00
89 Cal Ripken Jr. 6.00
90 Pedro Martinez 2.00

Standing Ovation

Stars (1-60): 8X-15X
World Prem. (61-80): 2X-3X
Super. Spot. (81-90): 3X-5X
Production 50 sets
(See 2000 UD Ovation for checklist and base card values.)

A Piece of History

NM/M
Common Player: 5.00
Production 400 sets
JB Jeff Bagwell 10.00
CB Carlos Beltran 10.00
SC Sean Casey 5.00
KG Ken Griffey Jr. 25.00
DJ Derek Jeter 35.00
TG Tony Gwynn 15.00
AJ Andruw Jones 10.00
CJ Chipper Jones 20.00
RP Rafael Palmeiro 10.00
MP Mike Piazza 20.00
MR Manny Ramirez 10.00
CR Cal Ripken Jr. 35.00
AR Alex Rodriguez 25.00
SR Scott Rolen 15.00
SS Sammy Sosa 25.00
FT Frank Thomas 10.00

A Piece of History - Signed

VALUES UNDETERMINED

Center Stage

NM/M
Complete Set (10): 20.00
Common Player: 1.00
Inserted 1:9
Gold: 2X
Inserted 1:39
Rainbow: 3X-4X
Inserted 1:99
1 Jeff Bagwell 1.00
2 Ken Griffey Jr. 2.00
3 Nomar Garciaparra 3.00
4 Mike Piazza 2.00
5 Mark McGwire 3.00
6 Alex Rodriguez 3.00
7 Cal Ripken Jr. 4.00
8 Derek Jeter 3.00
9 Chipper Jones 2.00
10 Sammy Sosa 2.50

Curtain Calls

NM/M
Complete Set (20): 15.00
Common Player: .50
Inserted 1:3
1 David Cone .50
2 Mark McGwire 2.00
3 Sammy Sosa 2.00
4 Eric Milton .50
5 Bernie Williams .75
6 Tony Gwynn 1.00
7 Nomar Garciaparra 2.00
8 Manny Ramirez 1.00

9	Wade Boggs	.50
10	Randy Johnson	1.00
11	Cal Ripken Jr.	3.00
12	Pedro J. Martinez	1.00
13	Alex Rodriguez	2.00
14	Fernando Tatis	.50
15	Vladimir Guerrero	1.00
16	Robin Ventura	.50
17	Larry Walker	.50
18	Carlos Beltran	.50
19	Jose Canseco	.75
20	Ken Griffey Jr.	1.50

Diamond Futures

		NM/M
Complete Set (10):		8.00
Common Player:		.50
Inserted 1:6		
1	J.D. Drew	.75
2	Alfonso Soriano	2.50
3	Preston Wilson	1.00
4	Erubiel Durazo	.75
5	Rick Ankiel	.50
6	Octavio Dotel	.50
7	A.J. Burnett	.50
8	Carlos Beltran	.75
9	Vernon Wells	1.00
10	Troy Glaus	2.00

Lead Performers

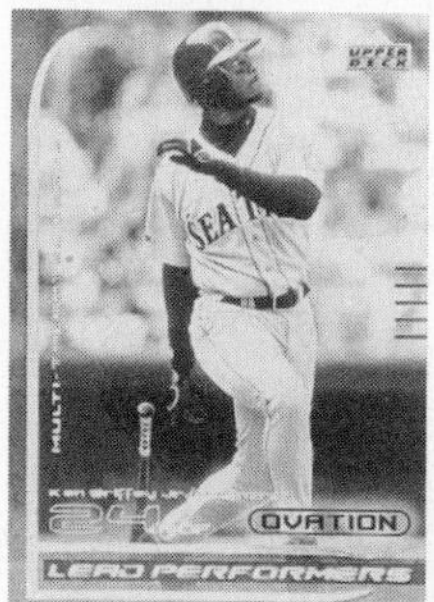

		NM/M
Complete Set (10):		20.00
Common Player:		1.00
Inserted 1:19		
1	Mark McGwire	3.00
2	Derek Jeter	3.00
3	Vladimir Guerrero	1.00
4	Mike Piazza	2.00
5	Cal Ripken Jr.	4.00
6	Sammy Sosa	2.50
7	Jeff Bagwell	1.00
8	Nomar Garciaparra	3.00
9	Chipper Jones	2.00
10	Ken Griffey Jr.	2.00

Superstar Theatre

		NM/M
Complete Set (20):		20.00
Common Player:		.50
Inserted 1:19		
1	Ivan Rodriguez	1.00
2	Brian Giles	.50
3	Bernie Williams	1.00
4	Greg Maddux	2.00
5	Frank Thomas	1.00
6	Sean Casey	.50
7	Mo Vaughn	.50
8	Carlos Delgado	1.00
9	Tony Gwynn	1.50
10	Pedro Martinez	1.50
11	Scott Rolen	1.00
12	Mark McGwire	3.00
13	Manny Ramirez	1.00
14	Rafael Palmeiro	.75
15	Jose Canseco	.75
16	Randy Johnson	1.50
17	Gary Sheffield	.75
18	Larry Walker	.50
19	Barry Bonds	4.00
20	Roger Clemens	3.00

Super Signatures

		NM/M
Common Card:		
Jr	Ken Griffey Rainbow/10	
KG	Ken Griffey Gold/50	180.00
KG	Ken Griffey Silver/100	100.00
MP	Mike Piazza Rainbow/10	
MP	Mike Piazza Gold/50	180.00
MP	Mike Piazza Silver/100	150.00

3,000 Hit Club

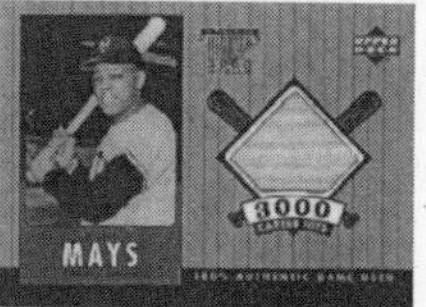

		NM/M
1	Willie Mays (Jersey Card/350)	40.00
2	Willie Mays (Bat Card/300)	40.00
3	Willie Mays (Jersey+Bat Card/50)	180.00
4	Willie Mays (Signed Jersey+Bat Card/24)	675.00

2000 UPPER DECK PROS AND PROSPECTS

		NM/M
Complete Set (132):		300.00
Common Player (1-90):		.15
Common (91-120):		5.00
Production 1,350 sets		
Common (121-132):		4.00
Production 1,000 sets		
Pack (5):		2.50
Box (24):		40.00
1	Darin Erstad	.40
2	Troy Glaus	.75
3	Mo Vaughn	.20
4	Jason Giambi	.75
5	Tim Hudson	.25
6	Ben Grieve	.15
7	Eric Chavez	.25
8	Shannon Stewart	.15
9	Raul Mondesi	.25
10	Carlos Delgado	.75
11	Jose Canseco	.40
12	Fred McGriff	.25
13	Greg Vaughn	.15
14	Manny Ramirez	.75
15	Roberto Alomar	.50
16	Jim Thome	.75
17	Alex Rodriguez	2.50
18	Fred Garcia	.15
19	John Olerud	.25
20	Cal Ripken Jr.	2.50
21	Albert Belle	.20
22	Mike Mussina	.40
23	Ivan Rodriguez	.50
24	Rafael Palmeiro	.50
25	Ruben Mateo	.15
26	Gabe Kapler	.15
27	Pedro Martinez	1.00
28	Nomar Garciaparra	2.00
29	Carl Everett	.15
30	Carlos Beltran	.25
31	Jermaine Dye	.15
32	Johnny Damon	.25
33	Juan Gonzalez	.75
34	Juan Encarnacion	.15
35	Dean Palmer	.15
36	Jacque Jones	.15
37	Matt Lawton	.15
38	Frank Thomas	.75
39	Paul Konerko	.15
40	Magglio Ordonez	.25
41	Derek Jeter	2.00
42	Bernie Williams	.50
43	Mariano Rivera	.25
44	Roger Clemens	1.50
45	Jeff Bagwell	.75
46	Craig Biggio	.25
47	Richard Hidalgo	.25
48	Chipper Jones	1.50
49	Andres Galarraga	.25
50	Andruw Jones	.50
51	Greg Maddux	1.50
52	Jeromy Burnitz	.15
53	Geoff Jenkins	.25
54	Mark McGwire	2.00
55	Jim Edmonds	.25
56	Fernando Tatis	.15
57	J.D. Drew	.15
58	Sammy Sosa	2.00
59	Kerry Wood	.50
60	Randy Johnson	.75
61	Matt Williams	.25
62	Erubiel Durazo	.15
63	Shawn Green	.25
64	Kevin Brown	.25
65	Gary Sheffield	.25
66	Adrian Beltre	.25
67	Vladimir Guerrero	.75
68	Jose Vidro	.15
69	Barry Bonds	2.00
70	Jeff Kent	.25
71	Preston Wilson	.15
72	Ryan Dempster	.15
73	Mike Lowell	.15
74	Mike Piazza	1.50
75	Robin Ventura	.25
76	Edgardo Alfonzo	.15
77	Derek Bell	.15
78	Tony Gwynn	1.00
79	Matt Clement	.15
80	Scott Rolen	.75
81	Bobby Abreu	.25
82	Curt Schilling	.40
83	Brian Giles	.25
84	Jason Kendall	.25
85	Kris Benson	.15
86	Ken Griffey Jr.	1.50
87	Sean Casey	.25
88	Pokey Reese	.15
89	Larry Walker	.25
90	Todd Helton	.75
91	Rick Ankiel	5.00
92	Milton Bradley	5.00
93	Vernon Wells	6.00
94	Rafael Furcal	6.00
95	*Kazuhiro Sasaki*	8.00
96	*Joe Torres*	5.00
97	Adam Kennedy	5.00
98	Adam Piatt	5.00
99	*Matt Wheatland*	5.00
100	*Alex Cabrera*	5.00
101	*Barry Zito*	25.00
102	*Mike Lamb*	5.00
103	*Scott Heard*	5.00
104	*Danys Baez*	8.00
105	Matt Riley	5.00
106	Mark Mulder	6.00
107	*Wilfredo Rodriguez*	5.00
108	*Luis Matos*	10.00
109	Alfonso Soriano	8.00
110	Pat Burrell	6.00
111	*Mike Tonis*	5.00
112	*Aaron McNeal*	5.00
113	*Dave Krynzel*	8.00
114	Josh Beckett	5.00
115	*Sean Burnett*	8.00
116	Eric Munson	5.00
117	*Scott Downs*	5.00
118	*Brian Tollberg*	5.00
119	Nick Johnson	5.00
120	*Leo Estrella*	5.00
121	Ken Griffey Jr.	8.00
122	Frank Thomas	4.00
123	Cal Ripken Jr.	15.00
124	Ivan Rodriguez	4.00
125	Derek Jeter	12.00
126	Mark McGwire	12.00
127	Pedro Martinez	5.00
128	Chipper Jones	8.00
129	Sammy Sosa	10.00
130	Alex Rodriguez	10.00
131	Vladimir Guerrero	4.00
132	Jeff Bagwell	4.00

Future Forces

		NM/M
Complete Set (10):		5.00
Common Player:		.50
Inserted 1:6		
1	Pat Burrell	2.00
2	Brad Penny	.50
3	Rick Ankiel	.50
4	Adam Kennedy	.50
5	Eric Munson	.50
6	Rafael Furcal	.75
7	Mark Mulder	.75
8	Vernon Wells	.75
9	Matt Riley	.50
10	Nick Johnson	.75

ProMotion

		NM/M
Complete Set (10):		15.00
Common Player:		.75
Inserted 1:6		
1	Derek Jeter	3.00
2	Mike Piazza	1.50
3	Mark McGwire	2.50
4	Ivan Rodriguez	.75
5	Kerry Wood	.75
6	Nomar Garciaparra	2.00
7	Sammy Sosa	2.00
8	Alex Rodriguez	2.50
9	Ken Griffey Jr.	1.50
10	Vladimir Guerrero	1.00

Rare Breed

		NM/M
Complete Set (12):		15.00
Common Player:		.50
Inserted 1:12		
1	Mark McGwire	3.00
2	Frank Thomas	1.00
3	Mike Piazza	2.00
4	Barry Bonds	4.00
5	Manny Ramirez	1.00
6	Ken Griffey Jr.	2.00
7	Nomar Garciaparra	3.00
8	Randy Johnson	1.50
9	Vladimir Guerrero	1.00
10	Jeff Bagwell	1.00
11	Rick Ankiel	.50
12	Alex Rodriguez	3.00

The Best in the Bigs

		NM/M
Complete Set (10):		15.00
Common Player:		1.00
Inserted 1:12		
1	Sammy Sosa	2.50
2	Tony Gwynn	1.50
3	Pedro Martinez	1.50
4	Mark McGwire	3.00
5	Chipper Jones	2.00
6	Derek Jeter	3.00
7	Ken Griffey Jr.	2.00
8	Cal Ripken Jr.	4.00

9	Greg Maddux	2.00
10	Ivan Rodriguez	1.00

Signed Game-Worn Jerseys

		NM/M
Common Player:		25.00
Inserted 1:96		
BB	Barry Bonds	250.00
JC	Jose Canseco	40.00
JD	J.D. Drew	25.00
TG	Tom Glavine	40.00
LG	Luis Gonzalez	25.00
KG	Ken Griffey Jr.	100.00
TG	Tony Gwynn	50.00
DJ	Derek Jeter/SP	350.00
RJ	Randy Johnson	80.00
CJ	Chipper Jones	50.00
KL	Kenny Lofton	25.00
CR	Cal Ripken Jr.	140.00
AR	Alex Rodriguez	120.00
IR	Ivan Rodriguez	40.00
SR	Scott Rolen	50.00
GS	Gary Sheffield	40.00
FT	Frank Thomas	40.00
MV	Mo Vaughn	25.00
RV	Robin Ventura	25.00
MW	Matt Williams	25.00
PW	Preston Wilson	25.00

3,000 Hit Club

	NM/M
Lou Brock bat/350	20.00
Lou Brock jersey/350	20.00
Lou Brock bat/jersey/100	40.00
Lou Brock auto./bat/jersey/20	
Rod Carew bat/350	20.00
Rod Carew jersey/350	20.00
Rod Carew bat/jersey/100	40.00
Rod Carew auto./bat/jersey/29	

2000 UPPER DECK POWERDECK

		NM/M
Complete Set (12):		50.00
Common Card:		3.00
Pack (1):		4.00
Box:		40.00
1	Sammy Sosa	6.00
2	Ken Griffey Jr.	6.00
3	Mark McGwire	8.00
4	Derek Jeter	6.00
5	Alex Rodriguez	8.00
6	Nomar Garciaparra	6.00
7	Mike Piazza	5.00
8	Cal Ripken Jr.	8.00

9	Ivan Rodriguez	3.00
10	Chipper Jones	5.00
11	Pedro Martinez	3.00
12	Manny Ramirez	3.00

Power Trio

		NM/M
Complete Set (3):		15.00
Common Player:		5.00
Inserted 1:7		
PT1	Derek Jeter	6.00
PT2	Ken Griffey Jr.	5.00
PT3	Mark McGwire	6.00

Magical Moments

		NM/M
Inserted 1:10 H		
KG	Ken Griffey Jr.	6.00
CR	Cal Ripken Jr.	10.00

Magical Moments Autograph

		NM/M
Each signed 50 cards		
KG	Ken Griffey Jr.	180.00
CR	Cal Ripken Jr.	275.00

2000 UPPER DECK ROOKIE UPDATE

		NM/M
Common Player:		.25
Common Rookie:		5.00
Pack (4):		4.50
Box (15):		50.00
SP Authentic Update (136-164) production 1,700		
136	*Barry Zito*	40.00
137	*Aaron McNeal*	5.00
138	Teofilo Perez	5.00
139	*Sun-Woo Kim*	6.00
140	*Xavier Nady*	8.00
141	*Matt Wheatland*	5.00
142	*Brent Abernathy*	5.00
143	*Cory Vance*	5.00
144	*Scott Heard*	5.00
145	*Mike Meyers*	5.00
146	*Ben Diggins*	5.00
147	*Luis Matos*	8.00
148	*Ben Sheets*	20.00
149	*Kurt Ainsworth*	10.00
150	*Dave Krynzel*	8.00
151	*Alex Cabrera*	5.00
152	*Mike Tonis*	5.00
153	*Dane Sardinha*	5.00
154	*Keith Ginter*	8.00
155	*David Espinosa*	5.00
156	*Joe Torres*	8.00
157	*Daylan Holt*	5.00
158	*Koyie Hill*	5.00
159	*Brad Wilkerson*	10.00
160	*Juan Pierre*	10.00
161	*Matt Ginter*	8.00
162	*Dane Artman*	5.00
163	*Jon Rauch*	5.00
164	*Sean Burnett*	8.00
166	Darin Erstad	.50
167	Ben Grieve	.25
168	David Wells	.25
169	Fred McGriff	.40
170	Bob Wickman	.25
171	Al Martin	.25
172	Melvin Mora	.25
173	Ricky Ledee	.25
174	Dante Bichette	.25
175	Mike Sweeney	.25
176	Bobby Higginson	.25
177	Matt Lawton	.25
178	Charles Johnson	.25
179	David Justice	.50
180	Richard Hidalgo	.40
181	B.J. Surhoff	.25
182	Richie Sexson	.50
183	Jim Edmonds	.50
184	Rondell White	.25
185	Curt Schilling	.50
186	Tom Goodwin	.25
187	Jose Vidro	.25
188	Ellis Burks	.25
189	Henry Rodriguez	.25
190	Mike Bordick	.25
191	Eric Owens	.25
192	Travis Lee	.25
193	Kevin Young	.25
194	Aaron Boone	.40
195	Todd Hollandsworth	.25
SPx Update (121-135, 182-196) 1,600 (136-151) production 1,500		
Common Autograph		10.00
121	*Brad Wilkerson*	12.00
122	*Roy Oswalt*	75.00
123	*Wascar Serrano*	5.00
124	*Sean Burnett*	10.00
125	*Alex Cabrera*	5.00
126	*Timoniel Perez*	5.00
127	*Juan Pierre*	10.00
128	*Daylan Holt*	5.00
129	*Tomokazu Ohka*	5.00
130	*Kazuhiro Sasaki*	10.00
131	*Kurt Ainsworth*	10.00
132	*Brent Abernathy*	5.00
133	*Danys Baez*	5.00
134	*Brad Cresse*	5.00
135	Ryan Franklin	5.00
136	*Mike Lamb*	10.00
137	*David Espinosa*	5.00
138	*Matt Wheatland*	5.00
139	*Xavier Nady*	40.00
140	*Scott Heard*	5.00
141	*Pascual Coco*	5.00
142	*Justin Miller*	5.00
143	*Dave Krynzel*	10.00
144	*Dane Sardinha*	5.00
145	*Ben Sheets*	80.00
146	*Leo Estrella*	10.00
147	*Ben Diggins*	10.00
148	*Barry Zito*	65.00
149	*Joe Torres*	10.00
150	*Mike Meyers*	10.00
151	*Kris Wilson*	10.00
152	Darin Erstad	.50
153	Richard Hidalgo	.40
154	Eric Chavez	.50
155	B.J. Surhoff	.25
156	Richie Sexson	.75
157	Raul Mondesi	.50
158	Rondell White	.50
159	Jim Edmonds	.75
160	Curt Schilling	.75
161	Tom Goodwin	.25
162	Fred McGriff	.50
163	Jose Vidro	.25
164	Ellis Burks	.25
165	David Segui	.25
166	Aaron Sele	.25
167	Henry Rodriguez	.25
168	Mike Bordick	.25
169	Mike Mussina	1.00
170	Ryan Klesko	.25
171	Kevin Young	.25
172	Travis Lee	.25
173	Aaron Boone	.50
174	Jermaine Dye	.25
175	Ricky Ledee	.25
176	Jeffrey Hammonds	.25
177	Carl Everett	.25
178	Matt Lawton	.25
179	Bobby Higginson	.25
180	Charles Johnson	.25
181	David Justice	.75
182	*Joey Nation*	4.00
183	*Rico Washington*	4.00
184	*Luis Matos*	15.00
185	Chris Wakeland	4.00
186	*Sun-Woo Kim*	4.00
187	*Keith Ginter*	5.00
188	*Geraldo Guzman*	4.00
189	*Jay Spurgeon*	4.00
190	*Jace Brewer*	4.00
191	*Juan Guzman*	4.00
192	*Ross Gload*	4.00
193	*Paxton Crawford*	4.00
194	*Ryan Kohlmeier*	4.00
195	*Julio Zuleta*	4.00
196	*Matt Ginter*	4.00
UD Pros & Prospects Update (133-162) production 1,600		
133	*Dane Artman*	5.00
134	*Juan Pierre*	8.00
135	*Jace Brewer*	5.00
136	*Sun-Woo Kim*	6.00
137	*Jon Rauch*	6.00
138	*Juan Guzman*	5.00
139	*Daylan Holt*	5.00
140	*Rico Washington*	5.00
141	*Ben Diggins*	8.00
142	*Mike Meyers*	5.00
143	Chris Wakeland	5.00
144	*Cory Vance*	5.00
145	*Keith Ginter*	8.00
146	*Koyie Hill*	8.00
147	*Julio Zuleta*	5.00
148	*Geraldo Guzman*	5.00
149	*Jay Spurgeon*	5.00
150	*Ross Gload*	5.00
151	*Ben Sheets*	20.00
152	*Josh Kalinowski*	6.00
153	*Kurt Ainsworth*	5.00
154	*Paxton Crawford*	5.00
155	*Xavier Nady*	8.00
156	*Brad Wilkerson*	10.00
157	*Kris Wilson*	5.00
158	*Paul Rigdon*	5.00
159	*Ryan Kohlmeier*	5.00
160	*Dane Sardinha*	5.00
161	*Javier Cardona*	5.00
162	*Brad Cresse*	5.00
163	Ron Gant	.25
164	Mark Mulder	.50
165	David Wells	.25
166	Jason Tyner	.25
167	David Segui	.25
168	Al Martin	.25
169	Melvin Mora	.25
170	Ricky Ledee	.25
171	Rolando Arrojo	.25
172	Mike Sweeney	.25
173	Bobby Higginson	.25
174	Eric Milton	.25
175	Charles Johnson	.25
176	David Justice	.50
177	Moises Alou	.50
178	Andy Ashby	.25
179	Richie Sexson	.75
180	Will Clark	.75
181	Rondell White	.40
182	Curt Schilling	.75
183	Tom Goodwin	.25
184	Lee Stevens	.25
185	Ellis Burks	.25
186	Henry Rodriguez	.25
187	Mike Bordick	.25
188	Ryan Klesko	.50
189	Travis Lee	.25
190	Kevin Young	.25
191	Barry Larkin	.75
192	Jeff Cirillo	.25

Winning Materials

		NM/M
Common Card:		10.00
Inserted 1:15		
NG-PM	Nomar Garciaparra, Pedro Martinez	40.00
DJ-AR	Derek Jeter, Alex Rodriguez	40.00
DJ-NG	Derek Jeter, Nomar Garciaparra	40.00
MM-KG	Mark McGwire, Ken Griffey Jr.	40.00
MM-SS	Mark McGwire, Sammy Sosa	40.00
MM-RA	Mark McGwire, Rick Ankiel	30.00
KG-SS	Ken Griffey Jr., Sammy Sosa	25.00

RC-PM Roger Clemens, Pedro Martinez 30.00
CR-TG Cal Ripken Jr., Tony Gwynn 40.00
JC-BB Jose Canseco, Barry Bonds 30.00
FT-MO Frank Thomas, Magglio Ordonez 10.00
JB-CB Jeff Bagwell, Craig Biggio 10.00
MP-RV Mike Piazza, Robin Ventura 25.00
IR-RP Ivan Rodriguez, Rafael Palmeiro 10.00
J-G-R Derek Jeter, Nomar Garciaparra, Alex Rodriguez 75.00
G-S-R Ken Griffey Jr., Sammy Sosa, Alex Rodriguez 40.00

Winning Materials Gold

NM/M
Common Player: 5.00
JC John Cotton 5.00
BS Ben Sheets 15.00
SB Sean Burroughs 8.00
MN Mike Neill 5.00
DM Doug Mientkiewicz 8.00
EY Ernie Young 5.00
GD Travis Dawkins, Mike Kinkade 5.00
BS Sean Burroughs, Ben Sheets 15.00
AE Brent Abernathy, Adam Everett 5.00
EY Brad Wilkerson, Ernie Young 8.00

2000 UPPER DECK ULTIMATE VICTORY

NM/M
Complete Set (120): 200.00
Common Player: .15
Common Ultimate Rookie (91-120): 4.00
Varying production levels
Pack (5): 1.50
Box (24): 25.00
1 Mo Vaughn .20
2 Darin Erstad .40
3 Troy Glaus .75
4 Adam Kennedy .15
5 Jason Giambi .75
6 Ben Grieve .15
7 Terrence Long .15
8 Tim Hudson .25
9 David Wells .15
10 Carlos Delgado .75
11 Shannon Stewart .15
12 Greg Vaughn .15
13 Gerald Williams .15
14 Manny Ramirez .75
15 Roberto Alomar .60
16 Jim Thome .75
17 Edgar Martinez .25
18 Alex Rodriquez 2.50
19 Matt Riley .15
20 Cal Ripken Jr. 2.50
21 Mike Mussina .50
22 Albert Belle .20
23 Ivan Rodriguez .75
24 Rafael Palmeiro .50
25 Nomar Garciaparra 2.00
26 Pedro Martinez 1.00
27 Carl Everett .15
28 *Tomokazu Ohka* .40
29 Jermaine Dye .15
30 Johnny Damon .25
31 Dean Palmer .15
32 Juan Gonzalez .75
33 Eric Milton .15
34 Matt Lawton .15
35 Frank Thomas .75
36 Paul Konerko .15
37 Magglio Ordonez .25
38 Jon Garland .15
39 Derek Jeter 2.50
40 Roger Clemens 1.50
41 Bernie Williams .50
42 Nick Johnson .15
43 Julio Lugo .15
44 Jeff Bagwell .75
45 Richard Hidalgo .15
46 Chipper Jones 1.50
47 Greg Maddux 1.50
48 Andruw Jones .50
49 Andres Galarraga .25
50 Rafael Furcal .50
51 Jeromy Burnitz .15
52 Geoff Jenkins .25
53 Mark McGwire 2.00
54 Jim Edmonds .25
55 Rick Ankiel .15
56 Sammy Sosa 2.00
57 *Julio Zuleta* .25
58 Kerry Wood .40
59 Randy Johnson .75
60 Matt Williams .25
61 Steve Finley .15
62 Gary Sheffield .40
63 Kevin Brown .25
64 Shawn Green .25
65 Milton Bradley .15
66 Vladimir Guerrero .75
67 Jose Vidro .15
68 Barry Bonds 2.00
69 Jeff Kent .25
70 Preston Wilson .15
71 Mike Lowell .15
72 Mike Piazza 2.00
73 Robin Ventura .25
74 Edgardo Alfonzo .15
75 Jay Payton .15
76 Tony Gwynn 1.00
77 Adam Eaton .15
78 Phil Nevin .15
79 Scott Rolen .75
80 Bob Abreu .25
81 Pat Burrell .50
82 Brian Giles .25
83 Jason Kendall .25
84 Kris Benson .15
85 Gookie Dawkins .15
86 Ken Griffey Jr. 1.50
87 Barry Larkin .40
88 Larry Walker .25
89 Todd Helton .75
90 Ben Petrick .15
91 *Alex Cabrera 3,500* 4.00
92 *Matt Wheatland 1,000* 4.00
93 *Joe Torres 1,000* 4.00
94 *Xavier Nady 1,000* 8.00
95 *Kenny Kelly 3,500* 4.00
96 *Matt Ginter 3,500* 4.00
97 *Ben Diggins 1,000* 8.00
98 *Danys Baez 3,500* 6.00
99 *Daylan Holt 2,500* 4.00
100 *Kazuhiro Sasaki 3,500* 5.00
101 *Dane Artman 2,500* 4.00
102 *Mike Tonis 1,000* 4.00
103 *Timoniel Perez 2,500* 4.00
104 *Barry Zito 2,500* 20.00
105 *Koyie Hill 2,500* 4.00
106 *Brad Wilkerson 2,500* 8.00
107 *Juan Pierre 3,500* 8.00
108 *Aaron McNeal 3,500* 4.00
109 *Jay Spurgeon 3,500* 4.00
110 *Sean Burnett 1,000* 10.00
111 *Luis Matos 3,500* 10.00
112 *Dave Krynzel 1,000* 6.00
113 *Scott Heard 1,000* 4.00
114 *Ben Sheets 2,500* 20.00
115 *Dane Sardinha 1,000* 4.00
116 *David Espinosa 1,000* 4.00
117 *Leo Estrella 3,500* 4.00
118 *Kurt Ainsworth 2,500* 4.00
119 *Jon Rauch 2,500* 4.00
120 Ryan Franklin 2,500 4.00

Collection

Parallel 25 Stars: 20-40X
Rookies (91-120): 2-4X
Production 25 sets
Parallel 100 Stars: 4-8X
Rookies (91-120): 1-2X
Production 100 sets
Parallel 250 Stars: 2-4X
Rookies (91-120): 1-2X
Production 250 sets

Diamond Dignitaries

NM/M
Complete Set (10): 20.00
Common Player: 1.00
Inserted 1:23
1 Ken Griffey Jr. 2.00
2 Nomar Garciaparra 3.00
3 Chipper Jones 2.00
4 Ivan Rodriguez 1.00
5 Mark McGwire 3.00
6 Cal Ripken Jr. 4.00
7 Vladimir Guerrero 1.00
8 Alex Rodriguez 3.00
9 Sammy Sosa 2.50
10 Derek Jeter 3.00

HOF Game Jersey

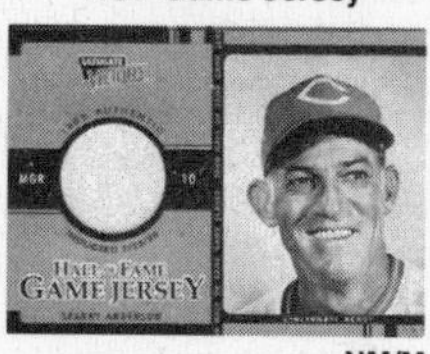

NM/M
Common Card: 8.00
SA Sparky Anderson 8.00
CF Carlton Fisk 10.00
TP Tony Perez 8.00

HOF Game Jersey Combo

NM/M
UV-C Sparky Anderson, Carlton Fisk, Tony Perez 40.00

Lasting Impressions

NM/M
Complete Set (10): 15.00
Common Player: 1.00
Inserted 1:11
1 Barry Bonds 3.00
2 Mike Piazza 2.00
3 Manny Ramirez 1.00
4 Pedro J. Martinez 1.50
5 Mark McGwire 2.00
6 Ken Griffey Jr. 2.00
7 Ivan Rodriguez 1.00
8 Jeff Bagwell 1.00
9 Randy Johnson 1.50
10 Alex Rodriguez 3.00

Starstruck

NM/M
Complete Set (10): 20.00
Common Player: 1.00
Inserted 1:11
1 Alex Rodriguez 3.00
2 Frank Thomas 1.00
3 Derek Jeter 3.00
4 Mark McGwire 3.00
5 Nomar Garciaparra 3.00
6 Chipper Jones 2.00
7 Cal Ripken Jr. 4.00
8 Sammy Sosa 2.00
9 Vladimir Guerrero 1.00
10 Ken Griffey Jr. 2.00

2000 UPPER DECK VICTORY

NM/M
Complete Set (440): 25.00
Complete Factory Set (466): 35.00
Common Player: .10

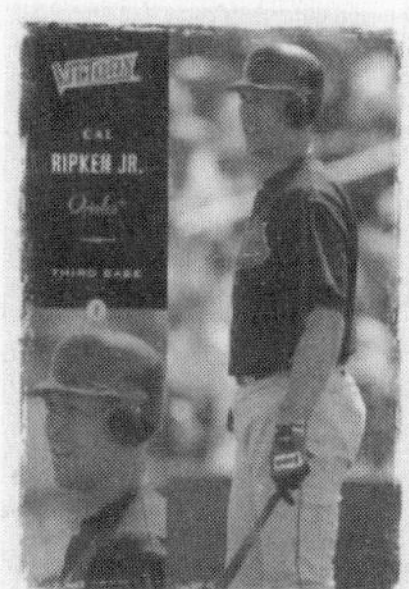

Common Griffey (391-440): .50
Common USA (441-466): .40
Pack (12): 1.00
Wax Box (36): 25.00
1 Mo Vaughn .15
2 Garret Anderson .20
3 Tim Salmon .20
4 Troy Percival .10
5 Orlando Palmeiro .10
6 Darin Erstad .20
7 Ramon Ortiz .10
8 Ben Molina .10
9 Troy Glaus .40
10 Jim Edmonds .20
11 Mo Vaughn, Troy Percival .15
12 Craig Biggio .25
13 Roger Cedeno .10
14 Shane Reynolds .10
15 Jeff Bagwell .50
16 Octavio Dotel .10
17 Moises Alou .20
18 Jose Lima .10
19 Ken Caminiti .15
20 Richard Hidalgo .10
21 Billy Wagner .10
22 Lance Berkman .20
23 Jeff Bagwell, Jose Lima .25
24 Jason Giambi .50
25 Randy Velarde .10
26 Miguel Tejada .25
27 Matt Stairs .10
28 A.J. Hinch .10
29 Olmedo Saenz .10
30 Ben Grieve .10
31 Ryan Christenson .10
32 Eric Chavez .20
33 Tim Hudson .20
34 John Jaha .10
35 Jason Giambi, Matt Stairs .25
36 Raul Mondesi .20
37 Tony Batista .10
38 David Wells .10
39 Homer Bush .10
40 Carlos Delgado .40
41 Billy Koch .10
42 Darrin Fletcher .10
43 Tony Fernandez .10
44 Shannon Stewart .10
45 Roy Halladay .20
46 Chris Carpenter .10
47 Carlos Delgado, David Wells .20
48 Chipper Jones 1.00
49 Greg Maddux 1.00
50 Andruw Jones .40
51 Andres Galarraga .20
52 Tom Glavine .20
53 Brian Jordan .10
54 John Smoltz .15
55 John Rocker .10
56 Javy Lopez .15
57 Eddie Perez .10
58 Kevin Millwood .20
59 Chipper Jones, Greg Maddux .50
60 Jeromy Burnitz .10
61 Steve Woodard .10
62 Ron Belliard .10
63 Geoff Jenkins .20
64 Bob Wickman .10
65 Marquis Grissom .10
66 Henry Blanco .10
67 Mark Loretta .10
68 Alex Ochoa .10
69 Marquis Grissom, Jeromy Burnitz .10
70 Mark McGwire 1.50

No.	Player	Price
71	Edgar Renteria	.10
72	Dave Veres	.10
73	Eli Marrero	.10
74	Fernando Tatis	.10
75	J.D. Drew	.20
76	Ray Lankford	.10
77	Daryle Kile	.10
78	Kent Bottenfield	.10
79	Joe McEwing	.10
80	Mark McGwire, Ray Lankford	.75
81	Sammy Sosa	1.25
82	Jose Nieves	.10
83	Jon Lieber	.10
84	Henry Rodriguez	.10
85	Mark Grace	.20
86	Eric Young	.10
87	Kerry Wood	.25
88	Ismael Valdes	.10
89	Glenallen Hill	.10
90	Sammy Sosa, Mark Grace	.60
91	Greg Vaughn	.10
92	Fred McGriff	.20
93	Ryan Rupe	.10
94	Bubba Trammell	.10
95	Miguel Cairo	.10
96	Roberto Hernandez	.10
97	Jose Canseco	.40
98	Wilson Alvarez	.10
99	John Flaherty	.10
100	Vinny Castilla	.15
101	Jose Canseco, Roberto Hernandez	.25
102	Randy Johnson	.50
103	Matt Williams	.15
104	Matt Mantei	.10
105	Steve Finley	.10
106	Luis Gonzalez	.20
107	Travis Lee	.10
108	Omar Daal	.10
109	Jay Bell	.10
110	Erubiel Durazo	.10
111	Tony Womack	.10
112	Todd Stottlemyre	.10
113	Randy Johnson, Matt Williams	.25
114	Gary Sheffield	.25
115	Adrian Beltre	.10
116	Kevin Brown	.20
117	Todd Hundley	.10
118	Eric Karros	.20
119	Shawn Green	.40
120	Chan Ho Park	.10
121	Mark Grudzielanek	.10
122	Todd Hollandsworth	.10
123	Jeff Shaw	.10
124	Darren Dreifort	.10
125	Gary Sheffield, Kevin Brown	.15
126	Vladimir Guerrero	.50
127	Michael Barrett	.10
128	Dustin Hermanson	.10
129	Jose Vidro	.10
130	Chris Widger	.10
131	Mike Thurman	.10
132	Wilton Guerrero	.10
133	Brad Fullmer	.10
134	Rondell White	.20
135	Ugueth Urbina	.10
136	Vladimir Guerrero, Rondell White	.40
137	Barry Bonds	1.50
138	Russ Ortiz	.10
139	J.T. Snow	.10
140	Joe Nathan	.10
141	Rich Aurilia	.10
142	Jeff Kent	.20
143	Armando Rios	.10
144	Ellis Burks	.10
145	Robb Nen	.10
146	Marvin Benard	.10
147	Barry Bonds, Russ Ortiz	.75
148	Manny Ramirez	.50
149	Bartolo Colon	.10
150	Kenny Lofton	.20
151	Sandy Alomar Jr.	.10
152	Travis Fryman	.15
153	Omar Vizquel	.15
154	Roberto Alomar	.40
155	Richie Sexson	.25
156	David Justice	.20
157	Jim Thome	.50
158	Manny Ramirez, Roberto Alomar	.25
159	Ken Griffey Jr.	1.00
160	Edgar Martinez	.15
161	Fred Garcia	.10
162	Alex Rodriguez	1.50
163	John Halama	.10
164	Russ Davis	.10
165	David Bell	.10
166	Gil Meche	.10
167	Jamie Moyer	.10
168	John Olerud	.20
169	Ken Griffey Jr., Fred Garcia	.50
170	Preston Wilson	.20
171	Antonio Alfonseca	.10
172	A.J. Burnett	.10
173	Luis Castillo	.10
174	Mike Lowell	.10
175	Alex Fernandez	.10
176	Mike Redmond	.10
177	Alex Gonzalez	.10
178	Vladimir Nunez	.10
179	Mark Kotsay	.10
180	Preston Wilson, Luis Castillo	.10
181	Mike Piazza	1.00
182	Darryl Hamilton	.10
183	Al Leiter	.20
184	Robin Ventura	.20
185	Rickey Henderson	.20
186	Rey Ordonez	.10
187	Edgardo Alfonzo	.10
188	Derek Bell	.10
189	Mike Hampton	.10
190	Armando Benitez	.10
191	Mike Piazza, Rickey Henderson	.50
192	Cal Ripken Jr.	1.50
193	B.J. Surhoff	.10
194	Mike Mussina	.40
195	Albert Belle	.15
196	Jerry Hairston Jr.	.10
197	Will Clark	.20
198	Sidney Ponson	.10
199	Brady Anderson	.10
200	Scott Erickson	.10
201	Ryan Minor	.10
202	Cal Ripken Jr., Albert Belle	.75
203	Tony Gwynn	.75
204	Bret Boone	.20
205	Ryan Klesko	.10
206	Ben Davis	.10
207	Matt Clement	.10
208	Eric Owens	.10
209	Trevor Hoffman	.10
210	Sterling Hitchcock	.10
211	Phil Nevin	.10
212	Tony Gwynn, Trevor Hoffman	.40
213	Scott Rolen	.50
214	Bob Abreu	.20
215	Curt Schilling	.25
216	Rico Brogna	.10
217	Robert Person	.10
218	Doug Glanville	.10
219	Mike Lieberthal	.10
220	Andy Ashby	.10
221	Randy Wolf	.10
222	Bob Abreu, Curt Schilling	.20
223	Brian Giles	.20
224	Jason Kendall	.20
225	Kris Benson	.10
226	Warren Morris	.10
227	Kevin Young	.10
228	Al Martin	.10
229	Wil Cordero	.10
230	Bruce Aven	.10
231	Todd Ritchie	.10
232	Jason Kendall, Brian Giles	.10
233	Ivan Rodriguez	.50
234	Rusty Greer	.10
235	Ruben Mateo	.10
236	Justin Thompson	.10
237	Rafael Palmeiro	.25
238	Chad Curtis	.10
239	Royce Clayton	.10
240	Gabe Kapler	.10
241	Jeff Zimmerman	.10
242	John Wetteland	.10
243	Ivan Rodriguez, Rafael Palmeiro	.25
244	Nomar Garciaparra	1.25
245	Pedro Martinez	.75
246	Jose Offerman	.10
247	Jason Varitek	.10
248	Troy O'Leary	.10
249	John Valentin	.10
250	Trot Nixon	.10
251	Carl Everett	.10
252	Wilton Veras	.10
253	Bret Saberhagen	.10
254	Nomar Garciaparra, Pedro J. Martinez	.60
255	Sean Casey	.10
256	Barry Larkin	.25
257	Pokey Reese	.10
258	Pete Harnisch	.10
259	Aaron Boone	.20
260	Dante Bichette	.10
261	Scott Williamson	.10
262	Steve Parris	.10
263	Dmitri Young	.10
264	Mike Cameron	.10
265	Sean Casey, Scott Williamson	.10
266	Larry Walker	.25
267	Rolando Arrojo	.10
268	Pedro Astacio	.10
269	Todd Helton	.50
270	Jeff Cirillo	.10
271	Neifi Perez	.10
272	Brian Bohanon	.10
273	Jeffrey Hammonds	.10
274	Tom Goodwin	.10
275	Larry Walker, Todd Helton	.25
276	Carlos Beltran	.15
277	Jermaine Dye	.10
278	Mike Sweeney	.10
279	Joe Randa	.10
280	Jose Rosado	.10
281	Carlos Febles	.10
282	Jeff Suppan	.10
283	Johnny Damon	.20
284	Jeremy Giambi	.10
285	Mike Sweeney, Carlos Beltran	.10
286	Tony Clark	.10
287	Damion Easley	.10
288	Jeff Weaver	.10
289	Dean Palmer	.10
290	Juan Gonzalez	.50
291	Juan Encarnacion	.10
292	Todd Jones	.10
293	Karim Garcia	.10
294	Deivi Cruz	.10
295	Dean Palmer, Juan Encarnacion	.10
296	Corey Koskie	.10
297	Brad Radke	.10
298	Doug Mientkiewicz	.10
299	Ron Coomer	.10
300	Joe Mays	.10
301	Eric Milton	.10
302	Jacque Jones	.10
303	Chad Allen	.10
304	Cristian Guzman	.10
305	Jason Ryan	.10
306	Todd Walker	.10
307	Corey Koskie, Eric Milton	.10
308	Frank Thomas	.50
309	Paul Konerko	.10
310	Mike Sirotka	.10
311	Jim Parque	.10
312	Magglio Ordonez	.25
313	Bob Howry	.10
314	Carlos Lee	.10
315	Ray Durham	.10
316	Chris Singleton	.10
317	Brook Fordyce	.10
318	Frank Thomas, Magglio Ordonez	.25
319	Derek Jeter	1.50
320	Roger Clemens	1.00
321	Paul O'Neill	.20
322	Bernie Williams	.40
323	Mariano Rivera	.20
324	Tino Martinez	.20
325	David Cone	.20
326	Chuck Knoblauch	.10
327	Darryl Strawberry	.20
328	Orlando Hernandez	.10
329	Ricky Ledee	.10
330	Derek Jeter, Bernie Williams	.75
331	Pat Burrell	.50
332	Alfonso Soriano	.75
333	Josh Beckett	.25
334	Matt Riley	.15
335	Brian Cooper	.10
336	Eric Munson	.20
337	Vernon Wells	.25
338	Juan Pena	.10
339	Mark DeRosa	.10
340	Kip Wells	.10
341	Roosevelt Brown	.10
342	Jason LaRue	.10
343	Ben Petrick	.10
344	Mark Quinn	.10
345	Julio Ramirez	.10
346	Rod Barajas	.10
347	Robert Fick	.10
348	David Newhan	.10
349	Eric Gagne	.15
350	Jorge Toca	.10
351	Mitch Meluskey	.10
352	Ed Yarnall	.10
353	Chad Hermansen	.10
354	Peter Bergeron	.10
355	Dermal Brown	.10
356	Adam Kennedy	.10
357	Kevin Barker	.10
358	Francisco Cordero	.10
359	Travis Dawkins	.10
360	Jeff Williams	.10
361	Chad Hutchinson	.10
362	D'Angelo Jimenez	.10
363	Derrick Gibson	.10
364	Calvin Murray	.10
365	Doug Davis	.10
366	*Rob Ramsay*	.20
367	Mark Redman	.10
368	Rick Ankiel	.10
369	Domingo Guzman	.10
370	Eugene Kingsale	.10
371	Nomar Garciaparra	.75
372	Ken Griffey Jr.	.50
373	Randy Johnson	.25
374	Jeff Bagwell	.25
375	Ivan Rodriguez	.25
376	Derek Jeter	.75
377	Carlos Beltran	.10
378	Vladimir Guerrero	.40
379	Sammy Sosa	.60
380	Barry Bonds	.75
381	Pedro Martinez	.40
382	Chipper Jones	.50
383	Mo Vaughn	.10
384	Mike Piazza	.50
385	Alex Rodriguez	.75
386	Manny Ramirez	.25
387	Mark McGwire	.75
388	Tony Gwynn	.40
389	Sean Casey	.10
390	Cal Ripken Jr.	.75
391	Ken Griffey Jr.	.40
392	Ken Griffey Jr.	.40
393	Ken Griffey Jr.	.40
394	Ken Griffey Jr.	.40
395	Ken Griffey Jr.	.40
396	Ken Griffey Jr.	.40
397	Ken Griffey Jr.	.40
398	Ken Griffey Jr.	.40
399	Ken Griffey Jr.	.40
400	Ken Griffey Jr.	.40
401	Ken Griffey Jr.	.40
402	Ken Griffey Jr.	.40
403	Ken Griffey Jr.	.40
404	Ken Griffey Jr.	.40
405	Ken Griffey Jr.	.40
406	Ken Griffey Jr.	.40
407	Ken Griffey Jr.	.40
408	Ken Griffey Jr.	.40
409	Ken Griffey Jr.	.40
410	Ken Griffey Jr.	.40
411	Ken Griffey Jr.	.40
412	Ken Griffey Jr.	.40
413	Ken Griffey Jr.	.40
414	Ken Griffey Jr.	.40
415	Ken Griffey Jr.	.40
416	Ken Griffey Jr.	.40
417	Ken Griffey Jr.	.40
418	Ken Griffey Jr.	.40
419	Ken Griffey Jr.	.40
420	Ken Griffey Jr.	.40
421	Ken Griffey Jr.	.40
422	Ken Griffey Jr.	.40
423	Ken Griffey Jr.	.40
424	Ken Griffey Jr.	.40
425	Ken Griffey Jr.	.40
426	Ken Griffey Jr.	.40
427	Ken Griffey Jr.	.40
428	Ken Griffey Jr.	.40
429	Ken Griffey Jr.	.40
430	Ken Griffey Jr.	.40
431	Ken Griffey Jr.	.40
432	Ken Griffey Jr.	.40
433	Ken Griffey Jr.	.40
434	Ken Griffey Jr.	.40
435	Ken Griffey Jr.	.40
436	Ken Griffey Jr.	.40
437	Ken Griffey Jr.	.40
438	Ken Griffey Jr.	.40
439	Ken Griffey Jr.	.40
440	Ken Griffey Jr.	.40
441	Tommy Lasorda	.50
442	Sean Burroughs	.75
443	Rick Krivda	.40
444	*Ben Sheets*	1.50
445	Pat Borders	.40
446	*Brent Abernathy*	.75

447 Tim Young .40
448 Adam Everett .50
449 Anthony Sanders .40
450 Ernie Young .40
451 *Brad Wilkerson* 1.50
452 Kurt Ainsworth 1.00
453 Ryan Franklin .40
454 Todd Williams .40
455 *Jon Rauch* .50
456 *Roy Oswalt* 5.00
457 Shane Heams .50
458 Chris George .50
459 Bobby Seay .40
460 Mike Kinkade .40
461 Marcus Jensen .40
462 Travis Dawkins .50
463 Doug Mientkiewicz .40
464 John Cotton .40
465 Mike Neill .40
466 Team Photo USA 2.50

2000 UPPER DECK YANKEES LEGENDS

	NM/M
Complete Set (90):	20.00
Common Player:	.15
Pack (5):	6.00
Box (24):	120.00
1 Babe Ruth	2.00
2 Mickey Mantle	2.00
3 Lou Gehrig	2.00
4 Joe DiMaggio	2.00
5 Yogi Berra	.75
6 Don Mattingly	1.00
7 Reggie Jackson	.75
8 Dave Winfield	.40
9 Bill Skowron	.15
10 Willie Randolph	.15
11 Phil Rizzuto	.50
12 Tony Kubek	.15
13 Thurman Munson	1.00
14 Roger Maris	1.00
15 Billy Martin	.40
16 Elston Howard	.15
17 Graig Nettles	.15
18 Whitey Ford	.50
19 Earl Combes	.15
20 Tony Lazzeri	.15
21 Bob Meusel	.15
22 Joe Gordon	.15
23 Jerry Coleman	.15
24 Joe Torre	.50
25 Bucky Dent	.15
26 Don Larsen	.40
27 Bobby Richardson	.15
28 Ron Guidry	.15
29 Bobby Murcer	.15
30 Tommy Henrich	.15
31 Hank Bauer	.15
32 Joe Pepitone	.15
33 Clete Boyer	.15
34 Chris Chambliss	.15
35 Tommy John	.15
36 Goose Gossage	.15
37 Red Ruffing	.15
38 Charlie Keller	.15
39 Billy Gardner	.15
40 Hector Lopez	.15
41 Cliff Johnson	.15
42 Oscar Gamble	.15
43 Allie Reynolds	.15
44 Mickey Rivers	.15
45 Bill Dickey	.40
46 Dave Righetti	.15
47 Mel Stottlemyre	.15
48 Waite Hoyt	.15
49 Lefty Gomez	.15
50 Wade Boggs	.50
51 Billy Martin	.25
52 Babe Ruth	1.00
53 Lou Gehrig	1.00
54 Joe DiMaggio	1.00
55 Mickey Mantle	1.00
56 Yogi Berra	.40
57 Bill Dickey	.25
58 Roger Maris	.50
59 Phil Rizzuto	.25
60 Thurman Munson	.50
61 Whitey Ford	.25
62 Don Mattingly	.50
63 Elston Howard	.15
64 Casey Stengel	.15
65 Reggie Jackson	.50
66 Babe Ruth (1923)	1.00
67 Lou Gehrig (1927)	1.00
68 Tony Lazzeri (1928)	.15
69 Babe Ruth (1932)	1.00
70 Lou Gehrig (1936)	1.00
71 Lefty Gomez (1937)	.15
72 Bill Dickey (1938)	.25
73 Tommy Henrich (1939)	.15
74 Joe DiMaggio (1941)	1.00
75 Spud Chandler (1943)	.15
76 Tommy Henrich (1947)	.15
77 Phil Rizzuto (1949)	.25
78 Whitey Ford (1950)	.25
79 Yogi Berra (1951)	.40
80 Casey Stengel (1952)	.15
81 Billy Martin (1953)	.25
82 Don Larsen (1956)	.25
83 Elston Howard (1958)	.15
84 Roger Maris (1961)	.50
85 Mickey Mantle (1962)	1.00
86 Reggie Jackson (1977)	.50
87 Bucky Dent (1978)	.15
88 Wade Boggs (1996)	.25
89 Joe Torre (1998)	.25
90 Joe Torre (1999)	.25

DiMaggio Memorabilia

	NM/M
YLB-JD Joe DiMaggio (bat)	125.00
YLG-JD Joe DiMaggio (gold bat/56)	200.00
YLC-JD Joe DiMaggio (bat, cut sig./5)	650.00

Legendary Lumber

	NM/M
Common Player:	8.00
Inserted 1:23	
HB Hank Bauer	10.00
YB Yogi Berra	20.00
PB Paul Blair	8.00
CB Clete Boyer	8.00
CC Chris Chambliss	8.00
JC Joe Collins	8.00
BD Bucky Dent	10.00
JD Joe DiMaggio	150.00
OG Oscar Gamble	8.00
BG Billy Gardner	8.00
TH Tommy Henrich	8.00
RH Ralph Houk	10.00
EH Elston Howard	10.00
RJ Reggie Jackson	20.00
TJ Tommy John	8.00
CJ Cliff Johnson	8.00
CK Charlie Keller	8.00
TK Tony Kubek	10.00
HL Hector Lopez	8.00
MM Mickey Mantle	180.00
RM Roger Maris	75.00
DM Don Mattingly	50.00
TM Thurman Munson	40.00
BM Bobby Murcer	10.00
GN Graig Nettles	8.00
JP Joe Pepitone	8.00
WR Willie Randolph	10.00
MR Mickey Rivers	8.00
BR Babe Ruth	200.00
MS Moose Skowron	8.00
DW Dave Winfield	15.00

Leg. Lumber/Sign. Cut

	NM/M
BM-LC Billy Martin (1)	
BR-LC Babe Ruth (3)	
MM-LC Mickey Mantle (7)	4,000
RM-LC Roger Maris (9)	
TM-LC Thurman Munson (15)	

Legendary Pinstripes

	NM/M
Common Player:	20.00
Inserted 1:144	
BD Bucky Dent	20.00
WF Whitey Ford	50.00
LG Lou Gehrig	300.00
GG Goose Gossage	20.00
RG Ron Guidry	20.00
TH Tommy Henrich	20.00
EH Elston Howard	20.00
RJ Reggie Jackson	40.00
HL Hector Lopez	20.00
MM Mickey Mantle	250.00
RM Roger Maris	75.00
BM Billy Martin	40.00
DM Don Mattingly	60.00
TM Thurman Munson	75.00
JP Joe Pepitone	20.00
AR Allie Reynolds	20.00
BR Bobby Richardson	20.00
PR Phil Rizzuto	40.00
DW Dave Winfield	40.00

Auto. Legend. Pinstripe

	NM/M
Common Player:	40.00
BD Bucky Dent	40.00
WF Whitey Ford	75.00
GG Goose Gossage	40.00
RG Ron Guidry	50.00
TH Tommy Henrich	40.00
GM Gil MacDougald	40.00
DM Don Mattingly	100.00
JP Joe Pepitone	40.00
PR Phil Rizzuto	60.00
DW Dave Winfield	50.00

Monument Park

	NM/M
Complete Set (6):	20.00
Common Player:	1.00
Inserted 1:23	2.50
1 Lou Gehrig	5.00
2 Babe Ruth	5.00
3 Mickey Mantle	5.00
4 Joe DiMaggio	5.00
5 Thurman Munson	2.50
6 Elston Howard	1.00

Murderer's Row

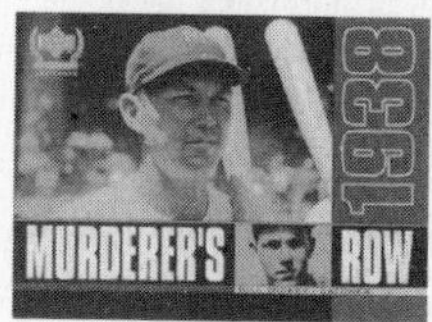

	NM/M
Complete Set (10):	15.00
Common Player:	1.00
Inserted 1:11	
1 Tony Lazzeri	1.00
2 Babe Ruth	5.00
3 Bob Meusel	1.00
4 Lou Gehrig	5.00
5 Joe Dugan	1.00
6 Bill Dickey	1.50
7 Waite Hoyt	1.00
8 Red Ruffing	1.00
9 Earl Combes	1.00
10 Lefty Gomez	1.00

Pride of the Pinstripes

	NM/M
Complete Set (6):	15.00
Common Player:	2.00
Inserted 1:23	
1 Babe Ruth	5.00
2 Mickey Mantle	5.00
3 Joe DiMaggio	4.00
4 Lou Gehrig	4.00
5 Reggie Jackson	2.00
6 Yogi Berra	2.00

The Golden Years

	NM/M
Complete Set (10):	15.00
Common Player:	1.00
Inserted 1:11	
1 Joe DiMaggio	4.00
2 Phil Rizzuto	1.50
3 Yogi Berra	2.00
4 Billy Martin	1.50
5 Whitey Ford	1.50
6 Roger Maris	3.00
7 Mickey Mantle	5.00
8 Elston Howard	1.00
9 Tommy Henrich	1.00
10 Joe Gordon	1.00

The New Dynasty

	NM/M
Complete Set (10):	10.00
Common Player:	1.00
Inserted 1:11	
1 Reggie Jackson	2.00
2 Graig Nettles	1.00
3 Don Mattingly	4.00
4 Goose Gossage	1.00
5 Dave Winfield	2.00
6 Chris Chambliss	1.00
7 Thurman Munson	2.50

8 Willie Randolph 1.00
9 Ron Guidry 1.50
10 Bucky Dent 1.50

2000 UD IONIX

NM/M
Complete Set (90): 50.00
Common Player: .15
Common Futuristic: 1.00
Inserted 1:4
Reciprocal (1-60): 1.5X-2X
Reciprocal (61-90): 1X-1.5X
Inserted 1:4
Future Recip. 1:11
Pack (4): 2.00
Wax Box (24): 35.00
1 Mo Vaughn .20
2 Troy Glaus .75
3 Jeff Bagwell .75
4 Craig Biggio .40
5 Jose Lima .15
6 Jason Giambi 1.00
7 Tim Hudson .40
8 Shawn Green .50
9 Carlos Delgado .75
10 Chipper Jones 1.50
11 Andruw Jones .75
12 Greg Maddux 1.50
13 Jeromy Burnitz .15
14 Mark McGwire 2.00
15 J.D. Drew .25
16 Sammy Sosa 2.00
17 Jose Canseco .50
18 Fred McGriff .40
19 Randy Johnson .75
20 Matt Williams .25
21 Kevin Brown .40
22 Gary Sheffield .40
23 Vladimir Guerrero .75
24 Barry Bonds 2.50
25 Jim Thome .75
26 Manny Ramirez .75
27 Roberto Alomar .50
28 Kenny Lofton .25
29 Ken Griffey Jr. 1.50
30 Alex Rodriguez 2.50
31 Alex Gonzalez .15
32 Preston Wilson .15
33 Mike Piazza 1.50
34 Robin Ventura .25
35 Cal Ripken Jr. 2.50
36 Albert Belle .20
37 Tony Gwynn 1.00
38 Scott Rolen .75
39 Curt Schilling .50
40 Brian Giles .25
41 Juan Gonzalez .75
42 Ivan Rodriguez .75
43 Rafael Palmeiro .60
44 Pedro J. Martinez 1.00
45 Nomar Garciaparra 2.00
46 Sean Casey .25
47 Aaron Boone .25
48 Barry Larkin .40
49 Larry Walker .25
50 Vinny Castilla .20
51 Carlos Beltran .25
52 Gabe Kapler .15
53 Dean Palmer .15
54 Eric Milton .15
55 Corey Koskie .15
56 Frank Thomas .75
57 Magglio Ordonez .40
58 Roger Clemens 2.00
59 Bernie Williams .75
60 Derek Jeter 2.50
61 Josh Beckett 1.50
62 Eric Munson 1.00
63 Rick Ankiel 1.00
64 Matt Riley 1.00
65 Robert Ramsay 1.00
66 Vernon Wells 2.00
67 Eric Gagne 1.50
68 Robert Fick 1.50
69 Mark Quinn 1.00
70 Kip Wells 1.00
71 Peter Bergeron 1.00
72 Ed Yarnall 1.00
73 Jorge Luis Toca 1.00
74 Alfonso Soriano 4.00
75 Calvin Murray 1.00
76 Ramon Ortiz 1.50
77 Chad Meyers 1.00
78 Jason LaRue 1.00
79 Pat Burrell 2.00
80 Chad Hermansen 1.00
81 Lance Berkman 1.50
82 Erubiel Durazo 1.50
83 Juan Pena 1.00
84 Adam Kennedy 1.00
85 Ben Petrick 1.00
86 Kevin Barker 1.00
87 Bruce Chen 1.00
88 Jerry Hairston Jr. 1.00
89 A.J. Burnett 1.00
90 Gary Matthews Jr. 1.00

Atomic

NM/M
Complete Set (15): 25.00
Common Player: 1.00
Inserted 1:8
1 Pedro J. Martinez 1.50
2 Mark McGwire 3.00
3 Ken Griffey Jr. 2.00
4 Jeff Bagwell 1.00
5 Greg Maddux 2.00
6 Derek Jeter 3.00
7 Cal Ripken Jr. 4.00
8 Manny Ramirez 1.00
9 Randy Johnson 1.50
10 Nomar Garciaparra 3.00
11 Tony Gwynn 1.50
12 Bernie Williams 1.00
13 Mike Piazza 2.00
14 Roger Clemens 3.00
15 Alex Rodriguez 3.00

Awesome Powers

NM/M
Complete Set (15): 50.00
Common Player: 1.00
Inserted 1:23
1 Ken Griffey Jr. 4.00
2 Mike Piazza 4.00
3 Carlos Delgado 2.00
4 Mark McGwire 6.00
5 Chipper Jones 4.00
6 Scott Rolen 2.00
7 Cal Ripken Jr. 8.00
8 Alex Rodriguez 6.00
9 Larry Walker 1.00
10 Sammy Sosa 5.00
11 Barry Bonds 6.00
12 Nomar Garciaparra 6.00
13 Jose Canseco 1.50
14 Manny Ramirez 2.00
15 Jeff Bagwell 2.00

BIOrhythm

NM/M
Complete Set (15): 25.00
Common Player: .50
Inserted 1:11
1 Randy Johnson 1.50
2 Derek Jeter 3.00
3 Sammy Sosa 2.50
4 Jose Lima .50
5 Chipper Jones 2.00
6 Barry Bonds 4.00
7 Ken Griffey Jr. 2.00
8 Nomar Garciaparra 3.00
9 Frank Thomas 1.00
10 Pedro Martinez 1.50
11 Larry Walker .50
12 Greg Maddux 2.00
13 Alex Rodriguez 3.00
14 Mark McGwire 3.00
15 Cal Ripken Jr. 4.00

Pyrotechnics

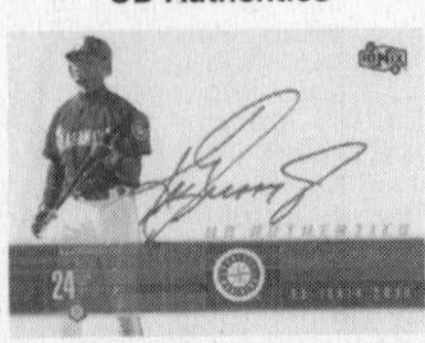

NM/M
Complete Set (15): 125.00
Common Player: 5.00
Inserted 1:72
1 Roger Clemens 12.00
2 Chipper Jones 10.00
3 Alex Rodriguez 15.00
4 Jeff Bagwell 5.00
5 Mark McGwire 15.00
6 Pedro Martinez 6.00
7 Manny Ramirez 5.00
8 Cal Ripken Jr. 20.00
9 Mike Piazza 10.00
10 Derek Jeter 15.00
11 Ken Griffey Jr. 10.00
12 Frank Thomas 5.00
13 Sammy Sosa 12.00
14 Nomar Garciaparra 15.00
15 Greg Maddux 10.00

Shockwave

NM/M
Complete Set (15): 15.00
Common Player: .50
Inserted 1:4
1 Mark McGwire 2.00
2 Sammy Sosa 2.00
3 Manny Ramirez 1.00
4 Ken Griffey Jr. 1.50
5 Vladimir Guerrero 1.00
6 Barry Bonds 2.50
7 Albert Belle .50
8 Ivan Rodriguez 1.00
9 Chipper Jones 1.50
10 Mo Vaughn .50
11 Jose Canseco .75
12 Jeff Bagwell 1.00
13 Matt Williams .50
14 Alex Rodriguez 2.50
15 Carlos Delgado .75

UD Authentics

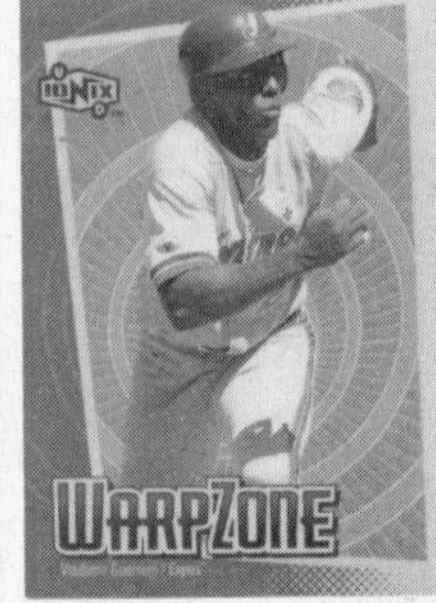

NM/M
Common Player: 10.00
Inserted 1:144
CBE Carlos Beltran 30.00
AB Adrian Beltre 15.00
PB Pat Burrell 15.00
JC Jose Canseco 25.00
SC Sean Casey 15.00
BD Ben Davis 10.00
SG Shawn Green 20.00
JR Ken Griffey Jr. 100.00
VG Vladimir Guerrero 30.00
DJ Derek Jeter 100.00
GK Gabe Kapler 10.00
PM Pedro Martinez
RM Ruben Mateo 10.00
RB Joe McEwing 10.00
MR Manny Ramirez 35.00
SR Scott Rolen 30.00
MW Matt Williams 15.00

Warp Zone

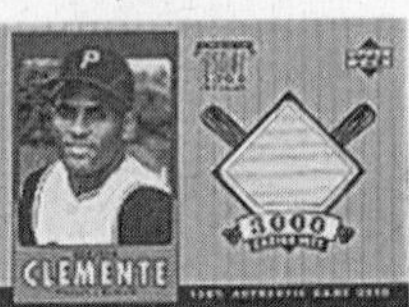

NM/M
Complete Set (15): 250.00
Common Player: 8.00
Inserted 1:288
1 Cal Ripken Jr. 30.00
2 Barry Bonds 30.00
3 Ken Griffey Jr. 20.00
4 Nomar Garciaparra 25.00
5 Chipper Jones 20.00
6 Ivan Rodriguez 8.00
7 Greg Maddux 20.00
8 Derek Jeter 25.00
9 Mike Piazza 20.00
10 Sammy Sosa 20.00
11 Roger Clemens 20.00
12 Alex Rodriguez 25.00
13 Vladimir Guerrero 10.00
14 Pedro Martinez 10.00
15 Mark McGwire 25.00

3,000 Hit Club

NM/
RC1 Roberto Clemente 75.00
RC2 Roberto Clemente Bat/Cut/5
RC3 Roberto Clemente Cut/4

2001 UPPER DECK

NM/M
Complete Set (450): 75.00
Complete Series 1 (270): 25.00

Complete Series 2 (180):		50.00
Common Player:		.15
Series 1 Pack (10):		2.00
Series 1 Box (24):		35.00
Series 2 Pack (10):		6.00
Series 2 Box (24):		120.00
1	Jeff DaVanon	.25
2	Aubrey Huff	.25
3	Pascual Coco	.25
4	Barry Zito	.75
5	Augie Ojeda	.25
6	Chris Richard	.25
7	Josh Phelps	.25
8	Kevin Nicholson	.25
9	Juan Guzman	.25
10	Brandon Kolb	.25
11	Johan Santana	4.00
12	Josh Kalinowski	.25
13	Tike Redman	.25
14	Ivanon Coffie	.25
15	Chad Durbin	.25
16	Derrick Turnbow	.25
17	Scott Downs	.25
18	Jason Grilli	.25
19	Mark Buehrle	.25
20	Paxton Crawford	.25
21	Bronson Arroyo	.25
22	Tomas de la Rosa	.25
23	Paul Rigdon	.25
24	Rob Ramsay	.25
25	Damian Rolls	.25
26	Jason Conti	.25
27	John Parrish	.25
28	Geraldo Guzman	.25
29	Tony Mota	.25
30	Luis Rivas	.25
31	Brian Tollberg	.25
32	Adam Bernero	.25
33	Michael Cuddyer	.25
34	Josue Espada	.25
35	Joe Lawrence	.25
36	Chad Moeller	.25
37	Nick Bierbrodt	.25
38	Dewayne Wise	.25
39	Javier Cardona	.25
40	Hiram Bocachica	.25
41	Giuseppe Chiaramonte	.25
42	Alex Cabrera	.25
43	Jimmy Rollins	.25
44	*Pat Flury*	.25
45	Leo Estrella	.25
46	Darin Erstad	.40
47	Seth Etherton	.15
48	Troy Glaus	.40
49	Brian Cooper	.15
50	Tim Salmon	.25
51	Adam Kennedy	.15
52	Bengie Molina	.15
53	Jason Giambi	.50
54	Miguel Tejada	.40
55	Tim Hudson	.25
56	Eric Chavez	.25
57	Terrence Long	.15
58	Jason Isringhausen	.15
59	Ramon Hernandez	.15
60	Raul Mondesi	.25
61	David Wells	.15
62	Shannon Stewart	.15
63	Tony Batista	.15
64	Brad Fullmer	.15
65	Chris Carpenter	.15
66	Homer Bush	.15
67	Gerald Williams	.15
68	Miguel Cairo	.15
69	Ryan Rupe	.15
70	Greg Vaughn	.15
71	John Flaherty	.15
72	Dan Wheeler	.15
73	Fred McGriff	.25
74	Roberto Alomar	.40
75	Bartolo Colon	.25
76	Kenny Lofton	.25
77	David Segui	.15
78	Omar Vizquel	.25
79	Russ Branyan	.15
80	Chuck Finley	.15
81	Manny Ramirez	.50
82	Alex Rodriguez	1.50
83	John Halama	.15
84	Mike Cameron	.15
85	David Bell	.15
86	Jay Buhner	.15
87	Aaron Sele	.15
88	Rickey Henderson	.40
89	Brook Fordyce	.15
90	Cal Ripken Jr.	2.00
91	Mike Mussina	.40
92	Delino DeShields	.15
93	Melvin Mora	.15
94	Sidney Ponson	.15
95	Brady Anderson	.15
96	Ivan Rodriguez	.50
97	Ricky Ledee	.15
98	Rick Helling	.15
99	Ruben Mateo	.15
100	Luis Alicea	.15
101	John Wetteland	.15
102	Mike Lamb	.15
103	Carl Everett	.15
104	Troy O'Leary	.15
105	Wilton Veras	.15
106	Pedro Martinez	.75
107	Rolando Arrojo	.15
108	Scott Hatteberg	.15
109	Jason Varitek	.15
110	Jose Offerman	.15
111	Carlos Beltran	.25
112	Johnny Damon	.25
113	Mark Quinn	.15
114	Rey Sanchez	.15
115	Mac Suzuki	.15
116	Jermaine Dye	.15
117	Chris Fussell	.15
118	Jeff Weaver	.15
119	Dean Palmer	.15
120	Robert Fick	.15
121	Brian Moehler	.15
122	Damion Easley	.15
123	Juan Encarnacion	.15
124	Tony Clark	.15
125	Cristian Guzman	.15
126	Matt LeCroy	.15
127	Eric Milton	.15
128	Jay Canizaro	.15
129	David Ortiz	.15
130	Brad Radke	.15
131	Jacque Jones	.15
132	Magglio Ordonez	.25
133	Carlos Lee	.15
134	Mike Sirotka	.15
135	Ray Durham	.15
136	Paul Konerko	.15
137	Charles Johnson	.15
138	James Baldwin	.15
139	Jeff Abbott	.15
140	Roger Clemens	1.50
141	Derek Jeter	2.00
142	David Justice	.25
143	Ramiro Mendoza	.15
144	Chuck Knoblauch	.15
145	Orlando Hernandez	.25
146	Alfonso Soriano	.75
147	Jeff Bagwell	.50
148	Julio Lugo	.15
149	Mitch Meluskey	.15
150	Jose Lima	.15
151	Richard Hidalgo	.15
152	Moises Alou	.25
153	Scott Elarton	.15
154	Andruw Jones	.50
155	Quilvio Veras	.15
156	Greg Maddux	1.00
157	Brian Jordan	.15
158	Andres Galarraga	.20
159	Kevin Millwood	.25
160	Rafael Furcal	.25
161	Jeromy Burnitz	.15
162	Jimmy Haynes	.15
163	Mark Loretta	.15
164	Ron Belliard	.15
165	Richie Sexson	.40
166	Kevin Barker	.15
167	Jeff D'Amico	.15
168	Rick Ankiel	.15
169	Mark McGwire	1.50
170	J.D. Drew	.25
171	Eli Marrero	.15
172	Darryl Kile	.15
173	Edgar Renteria	.15
174	Will Clark	.40
175	Eric Young	.15
176	Mark Grace	.40
177	Jon Lieber	.15
178	Damon Buford	.15
179	Kerry Wood	.50
180	Rondell White	.15
181	Joe Girardi	.15
182	Curt Schilling	.40
183	Randy Johnson	.75
184	Steve Finley	.15
185	Kelly Stinnett	.15
186	Jay Bell	.15
187	Matt Mantei	.15
188	Luis Gonzalez	.25
189	Shawn Green	.25
190	Todd Hundley	.15
191	Chan Ho Park	.15
192	Adrian Beltre	.25
193	Mark Grudzielanek	.15
194	Gary Sheffield	.40
195	Tom Goodwin	.15
196	Lee Stevens	.15
197	Javier Vazquez	.15
198	Milton Bradley	.15
199	Vladimir Guerrero	.75
200	Carl Pavano	.15
201	Orlando Cabrera	.15
202	Tony Armas Jr.	.15
203	Jeff Kent	.25
204	Calvin Murray	.15
205	Ellis Burks	.15
206	Barry Bonds	2.00
207	Russ Ortiz	.15
208	Marvin Benard	.15
209	Joe Nathan	.15
210	Preston Wilson	.15
211	Cliff Floyd	.15
212	Mike Lowell	.15
213	Ryan Dempster	.15
214	Brad Penny	.15
215	Mike Redmond	.15
216	Luis Castillo	.15
217	Derek Bell	.15
218	Mike Hampton	.25
219	Todd Zeile	.15
220	Robin Ventura	.25
221	Mike Piazza	1.00
222	Al Leiter	.25
223	Edgardo Alfonzo	.15
224	Mike Bordick	.15
225	Phil Nevin	.15
226	Ryan Klesko	.25
227	Adam Eaton	.15
228	Eric Owens	.15
229	Tony Gwynn	.75
230	Matt Clement	.15
231	Wiki Gonzalez	.15
232	Robert Person	.15
233	Doug Glanville	.15
234	Scott Rolen	.50
235	Mike Lieberthal	.15
236	Randy Wolf	.15
237	Bobby Abreu	.25
238	Pat Burrell	.40
239	Bruce Chen	.15
240	Kevin Young	.15
241	Todd Ritchie	.15
242	Adrian Brown	.15
243	Chad Hermansen	.15
244	Warren Morris	.15
245	Kris Benson	.15
246	Jason Kendall	.25
247	Pokey Reese	.15
248	Rob Bell	.15
249	Ken Griffey Jr.	1.00
250	Sean Casey	.15
251	Aaron Boone	.15
252	Pete Harnisch	.15
253	Barry Larkin	.40
254	Dmitri Young	.15
255	Todd Hollandsworth	.15
256	Pedro Astacio	.15
257	Todd Helton	.50
258	Terry Shumpert	.15
259	Neifi Perez	.15
260	Jeffrey Hammonds	.15
261	Ben Petrick	.15
262	Mark McGwire	.75
263	Derek Jeter	1.00
264	Sammy Sosa	.75
265	Cal Ripken Jr.	1.00
266	Pedro J. Martinez	.40
267	Barry Bonds	1.00
268	Fred McGriff	.20
269	Randy Johnson	.40
270	Darin Erstad	.25
271	*Ichiro Suzuki*	15.00
272	*Wilson Betemit*	.50
273	Corey Patterson	.25
274	*Sean Douglass*	.25
275	*Mike Penney*	.25
276	*Nate Teut*	.25
277	*Ricardo Rodriguez*	.25
278	*Brandon Duckworth*	.50
279	*Rafael Soriano*	.75
280	*Juan Diaz*	.25
281	*Horacio Ramirez*	.75
282	*Tsuyoshi Shinjo*	.50
283	Keith Ginter	.25
284	*Esix Snead*	.25
285	*Erick Almonte*	.25
286	*Travis Hafner*	1.00
287	*Jason Smith*	.25
288	*Jackson Melian*	.25
289	*Tyler Walker*	.25
290	Jason Standridge	.25
291	*Juan Uribe*	.50
292	*Adrian Hernandez*	.25
293	*Jason Michaels*	.25
294	Jason Hart	.15
295	*Albert Pujols*	50.00
296	*Morgan Ensberg*	3.00
297	Brandon Inge	.25
298	Jesus Colome	.25
299	*Kyle Kessel*	.25
300	Timo Perez	.25
301	Mo Vaughn	.20
302	Ismael Valdes	.15
303	Glenallen Hill	.15
304	Garret Anderson	.40
305	Johnny Damon	.25
306	Jose Ortiz	.15
307	Mark Mulder	.25
308	Adam Piatt	.15
309	Gil Heredia	.15
310	Mike Sirotka	.15
311	Carlos Delgado	.50
312	Alex Gonzalez	.15
313	Jose Cruz Jr.	.15
314	Darrin Fletcher	.15
315	Ben Grieve	.15
316	Vinny Castilla	.15
317	Wilson Alvarez	.15
318	Brent Abernathy	.15
319	Ellis Burks	.15
320	Jim Thome	.75
321	Juan Gonzalez	.50
322	Ed Taubensee	.15
323	Travis Fryman	.15
324	John Olerud	.25
325	Edgar Martinez	.25
326	Fred Garcia	.15
327	Bret Boone	.25
328	Kazuhiro Sasaki	.15
329	Albert Belle	.15
330	Mike Bordick	.15
331	David Segui	.15
332	Pat Hentgen	.15
333	Alex Rodriguez	1.50
334	Andres Galarraga	.25
335	Gabe Kapler	.15
336	Ken Caminiti	.15
337	Rafael Palmeiro	.50
338	Manny Ramirez	.50
339	David Cone	.15
340	Nomar Garciaparra	1.50
341	Trot Nixon	.15
342	Derek Lowe	.15
343	Roberto Hernandez	.15
344	Mike Sweeney	.15
345	Carlos Febles	.15
346	Jeff Suppan	.15
347	Roger Cedeno	.15
348	Bobby Higginson	.15
349	Deivi Cruz	.15
350	Mitch Meluskey	.15
351	Matt Lawton	.15
352	Mark Redman	.15
353	Jay Canizaro	.15
354	Corey Koskie	.15
355	Matt Kinney	.15
356	Frank Thomas	.50
357	Sandy Alomar Jr.	.15
358	David Wells	.15
359	Jim Parque	.15
360	Chris Singleton	.15
361	Tino Martinez	.15
362	Paul O'Neill	.25
363	Mike Mussina	.40
364	Bernie Williams	.50
365	Andy Pettitte	.40
366	Mariano Rivera	.25
367	Brad Ausmus	.15
368	Craig Biggio	.25
369	Lance Berkman	.25
370	Shane Reynolds	.15
371	Chipper Jones	1.00
372	Tom Glavine	.40
373	B.J. Surhoff	.15
374	John Smoltz	.25
375	Rico Brogna	.15
376	Geoff Jenkins	.25
377	Jose Hernandez	.15
378	Tyler Houston	.15
379	Henry Blanco	.15
380	Jeffrey Hammonds	.15
381	Jim Edmonds	.25
382	Fernando Vina	.15
383	Andy Benes	.15
384	Ray Lankford	.15
385	Dustin Hermanson	.15
386	Todd Hundley	.15
387	Sammy Sosa	1.50
388	Tom Gordon	.15
389	Bill Mueller	.15
390	Ron Coomer	.15

391 Matt Stairs .15
392 Mark Grace .40
393 Matt Williams .25
394 Todd Stottlemyre .15
395 Tony Womack .15
396 Erubiel Durazo .15
397 Reggie Sanders .15
398 Andy Ashby .15
399 Eric Karros .15
400 Kevin Brown .25
401 Darren Dreifort .15
402 Fernando Tatis .15
403 Jose Vidro .15
404 Peter Bergeron .15
405 Geoff Blum .15
406 J.T. Snow .15
407 Livan Hernandez .15
408 Robb Nen .15
409 Bobby Estalella .15
410 Rich Aurilia .15
411 Eric Davis .15
412 Charles Johnson .15
413 Alex Gonzalez .15
414 A.J. Burnett .15
415 Antonio Alfonseca .15
416 Derek Lee .15
417 Jay Payton .15
418 Kevin Appier .15
419 Steve Trachsel .15
420 Rey Ordonez .15
421 Darryl Hamilton .15
422 Ben Davis .15
423 Damian Jackson .15
424 Mark Kotsay .15
425 Trevor Hoffman .15
426 Travis Lee .15
427 Omar Daal .15
428 Paul Byrd .15
429 Reggie Taylor .15
430 Brian Giles .25
431 Derek Bell .15
432 Francisco Cordova .15
433 Pat Meares .15
434 Scott Williamson .15
435 Jason LaRue .15
436 Michael Tucker .15
437 Wilton Guerrero .15
438 Mike Hampton .15
439 Ron Gant .15
440 Jeff Cirillo .15
441 Denny Neagle .15
442 Larry Walker .40
443 Juan Pierre .15
444 Todd Walker .15
445 Jason Giambi .40
446 Jeff Kent .15
447 Mariano Rivera .15
448 Edgar Martinez .15
449 Troy Glaus .25
450 Alex Rodriguez .75

Exclusives

Silver Stars: 8-15X
Production 100 sets
Gold Stars: 15-30X
Production 25 sets

All-Star Heroes Base Cards

NM/M
Quantity produced listed
DJ Derek Jeter/2000 20.00
MP Mike Piazza/1996 10.00

All-Star Heroes Jersey Cards

NM/M
Common Player: 10.00
RC Roger Clemens/1986 20.00
JD Joe DiMaggio/36 300.00
TG Tony Gwynn/1994 10.00
RJ Randy Johnson/1993 10.00
ASH-MM Mickey Mantle/54 400.00
ASH-SS Sammy Sosa - 2000 20.00

All-Star Heroes Bat Cards

NM/M
Common Player: 10.00

RoC Roberto Clemente/1961 75.00
KG Ken Griffey Jr/1992 20.00
TP Tony Perez/1967 10.00
CR Cal Ripken Jr/1991 40.00
AR Alex Rodriguez/1998 20.00
BR Babe Ruth/1933 175.00

All-Star Salute

NM/M
Common Player: 10.00
Inserted 1:288
HA Hank Aaron/bat 35.00
HA Hank Aaron/jersey 35.00
LA Luis Aparicio/jersey 10.00
JB Johnny Bench/bat 20.00
JB Johnny Bench/jersey 20.00
LB Lou Brock/bat 15.00
RC Roberto Clemente/jersey 125.00
RJ Reggie Jackson/jersey 20.00
TM Thurman Munson/jersey 35.00
BR Brooks Robinson/bat 20.00
FR Frank Robinson/jersey 15.00
TS Tom Seaver/jersey 20.00

Big League Beat

NM/M
Complete Set (20): 15.00
Common Player: .50
Inserted 1:3
1 Barry Bonds 2.00
2 Nomar Garciaparra 1.50
3 Mark McGwire 1.50
4 Roger Clemens 1.25
5 Chipper Jones 1.00
6 Jeff Bagwell .50
7 Sammy Sosa 1.50
8 Cal Ripken Jr. 2.00
9 Randy Johnson .75
10 Carlos Delgado .50
11 Manny Ramirez .50
12 Derek Jeter 2.00
13 Tony Gwynn .75
14 Pedro J. Martinez .75
15 Jose Canseco .50
16 Frank Thomas .75
17 Alex Rodriguez 1.50
18 Bernie Williams .50
19 Greg Maddux 1.00
20 Rafael Palmeiro .50

Big League Challenge Jerseys

NM/M
Common Player: 5.00
Inserted 1:288
BB Barry Bonds 40.00
JC Jose Canseco 8.00
JE Jim Edmonds 8.00
TF Steve Finley 5.00
TG Troy Glaus 8.00
TH Todd Helton 10.00
RH Richard Hidalgo 5.00
RP Rafael Palmeiro 10.00
MP Mike Piazza 20.00
GS Gary Sheffield 8.00
FT Frank Thomas 10.00

Classic Midsummer Moments

NM/M
Complete Set (20): 25.00
Common Player: .50
Inserted 1:12
CM1 Joe DiMaggio - 1936 3.00
CM2 Joe DiMaggio - 1951 3.00

CM3 Mickey Mantle - 1952 4.00
CM4 Mickey Mantle - 1968 4.00
CM5 Roger Clemens - 1986 2.50
CM6 Mark McGwire - 1987 2.50
CM7 Cal Ripken Jr. - 1991 3.00
CM8 Ken Griffey Jr. - 1992 1.50
CM9 Randy Johnson - 1993 1.00
CM10 Tony Gwynn - 1994 1.00
CM11 Fred McGriff - 1994 .50
CM12 Hideo Nomo - 1995 .75
CM13 Jeff Conine - 1995 .50
CM14 Mike Piazza - 1996 1.50
CM15 Sandy Alomar Jr. - 1997 .50
CM16 Alex Rodriguez - 1998 2.50
CM17 Roberto Alomar - 1998 .75
CM18 Pedro Martinez - 1999 1.00
CM19 Andres Galarraga - 2000 .50
CM20 Derek Jeter - 2000 2.50

e-Card

NM/M
Complete Set (6): 10.00
Common Player: 1.00
Inserted 1:12
1 Andruw Jones 1.00
2 Alex Rodriguez 3.00
3 Frank Thomas 1.50
4 Todd Helton 1.50
5 Troy Glaus 1.00
6 Barry Bonds 4.00

eVolve Signature

NM/M
Common Player: 35.00
BB Barry Bonds 200.00
TG Troy Glaus 35.00
TH Todd Helton 35.00
AJ Andruw Jones 35.00
AR Alex Rodriguez 75.00
SS Sammy Sosa 150.00
IS Ichiro Suzuki 250.00
FT Frank Thomas 40.00

Evolve Jersey

NM/M
Common Player: 10.00
BB Barry Bonds 60.00

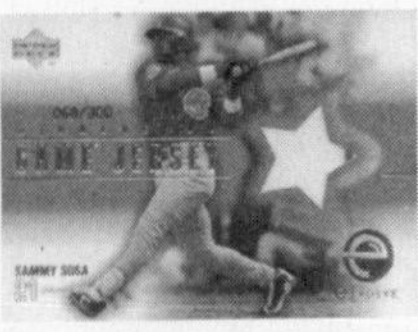

TG Troy Glaus 10.00
TH Todd Helton 15.00
AJ Andruw Jones 15.00
AR Alex Rodriguez 30.00
SS Sammy Sosa 40.00
IS Ichiro Suzuki 65.00
FT Frank Thomas 15.00

eVolve Jersey Autograph

NM/M
Common Player: 50.00
BB Barry Bonds 250.00
TG Troy Glaus 50.00
TH Todd Helton 50.00
AJ Andruw Jones 50.00
AR Alex Rodriguez 120.00
SS Sammy Sosa 180.00
IS Ichiro Suzuki 300.00
FT Frank Thomas 75.00

Game Jersey

NM/M
Common Player: 8.00
Inserted 1:288
KG Ken Griffey Jr. 30.00
TG Tony Gwynn 20.00
TH Todd Helton 12.00
TiH Tim Hudson 10.00
DJ Derek Jeter 50.00
AJ Andruw Jones 10.00
SK Sandy Koufax 100.00
PO Paul O'Neill 10.00
MR Manny Ramirez 10.00
CR Cal Ripken Jr. 60.00
AR Alex Rodriguez 40.00
IR Ivan Rodriguez 10.00
NRa Nolan Ryan 65.00
NRr Nolan Ryan 65.00
FT Fernando Tatis 8.00
RV Robin Ventura 8.00
BW Bernie Williams 10.00
MW Matt Williams 8.00

Game Jersey Autograph

NM/M
Print Runs listed
KG Ken Griffey/30 250.00
RA Rick Ankiel/66 25.00
TG Tony Gwynn/19
TH Todd Helton/17
TiH Tim Hudson/15
AJ Andruw Jones/25
SK Sandy Koufax/32 900.00
PO Paul O'Neill/21
JP Javy Lopez/8 110.00
AR Alex Rodriguez/3
IR Ivan Rodriguez/7
NRa Nolan Ryan Mets/30 350.00
NRr Nolan Ryan Angels/30 350.00
RV Robin Ventura/4 50.00
MW Matt Williams/9 200.00

Game Jersey Hobby Autograph

NM/M
Common Player: 15.00
Inserted 1:288

RA	Rick Ankiel	15.00
JB	Jeff Bagwell	40.00
BB	Barry Bonds	275.00
JC	Jose Canseco	50.00
SC	Sean Casey	25.00
JD	J.D. Drew	30.00
JG	Jason Giambi	30.00
SG	Shawn Green	30.00
KG	Ken Griffey Jr.	100.00
MH	Mike Hampton	20.00
RJ	Randy Johnson	75.00
JL	Javy Lopez	20.00
GM	Greg Maddux	125.00
RP	Rafael Palmeiro	40.00
AR	Alex Rodriguez	125.00
NRm	Nolan Ryan	125.00
NRa	Nolan Ryan	125.00
FT	Frank Thomas	50.00

Game Jersey Auto. Series 2

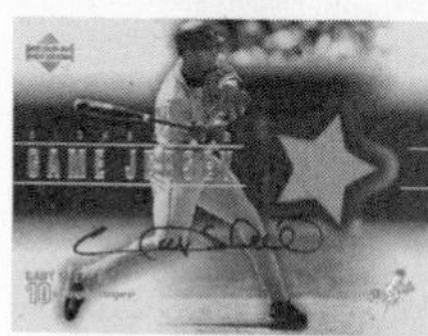

NM/M

Common Player: 30.00
Inserted 1:288 H

JB	Johnny Bench	50.00
BB	Barry Bonds	275.00
JC	Jose Canseco	40.00
RC	Roger Clemens	125.00
TG	Troy Glaus	30.00
KG	Ken Griffey Jr.	100.00
AJ	Andruw Jones	40.00
CJ	Chipper Jones	50.00
CR	Cal Ripken Jr. SP	200.00
AR	Alex Rodriguez	100.00
IR	Ivan Rodriguez SP	75.00
NR	Nolan Ryan	150.00
GS	Gary Sheffield	30.00
SS	Sammy Sosa SP	150.00

Game Jersey Combo

NM/M

Production 50 sets

BB-KG	Barry Bonds, Ken Griffey Jr.	100.00
IR-RP	Ivan Rodriguez, Rafael Palmeiro	25.00
DJ-AR	Derek Jeter, Alex Rodriguez	100.00
MM-KG	Mickey Mantle, Ken Griffey Jr.	250.00
TG-CR	Tony Gwynn, Cal Ripken Jr.	100.00
NR-AR	Nolan Ryan Astros/Rangers	100.00
NR-MA	Nolan Ryan Mets/Astros	100.00
RJ-GM	Randy Johnson, Greg Maddux	50.00
VG-MR	Vladimir Guerrero, Manny Ramirez	40.00
BB-JC	Barry Bonds, Jose Canseco	80.00
FT-JB	Frank Thomas, Jeff Bagwell	40.00
AJ-KG	Andruw Jones, Ken Griffey Jr.	60.00

Game Jersey Combo Autograph

Production 10 Sets
VALUES UNDETERMINED

Game Jersey Patch

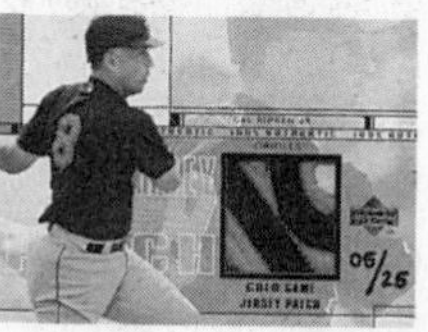

NM/M

Common Player: 40.00
Production 25 sets

RA	Rick Ankiel	40.00
JB	Jeff Bagwell	60.00
BB	Barry Bonds	150.00
JC	Jose Canseco	50.00
JG	Jason Giambi	50.00
KG	Ken Griffey Jr.	75.00
TG	Tony Gwynn	75.00
DJ	Derek Jeter	125.00
RP	Rafael Palmeiro	60.00
CR	Cal Ripken Jr.	150.00
AR	Alex Rodriguez	100.00
IR	Ivan Rodriguez	60.00
NRa	Nolan Ryan	150.00
NRr	Nolan Ryan	150.00
FT	Frank Thomas	60.00

Game Jersey Patch Gold

NM/M

Production 25 sets

BB	Barry Bonds	200.00
JC	Jose Canseco	100.00
JG	Jason Giambi	100.00
KG	Ken Griffey Jr.	150.00
TG	Tony Gwynn	100.00
DJ	Derek Jeter	200.00
CR	Cal Ripken Jr.	200.00
AR	Alex Rodriguez	
NRa	Nolan Ryan	200.00
NRr	Nolan Ryan	200.00
FT	Frank Thomas	90.00

Game Jersey Patch Autograph

NM/M

Print Runs listed

RA	Rick Ankiel /66	65.00
KG	Ken Griffey Jr /30	600.00
AR	Alex Rodriguez /3	

Game-Used Ball

NM/M

Common Player: 10.00
Production 100 sets

RA	Rick Ankiel	10.00
JB	Jeff Bagwell	15.00
BB	Barry Bonds	50.00
JG	Jason Giambi	15.00
SG	Shawn Green	10.00
KG	Ken Griffey Jr.	35.00
ToG	Tony Gwynn	25.00
DJ	Derek Jeter	60.00
RJ	Randy Johnson	25.00
AJ	Andruw Jones	15.00
MM	Mark McGwire	75.00
AR	Alex Rodriguez	40.00
IR	Ivan Rodriguez	15.00
SS	Sammy Sosa	40.00

Game-Used Ball Autographs

NM/M

Production 25 Sets

RA	Rick Ankiel	40.00
JB	Jeff Bagwell	60.00
BB	Barry Bonds	150.00
JG	Jason Giambi	75.00
KG	Ken Griffey Jr.	90.00
SG	Shawn Green	60.00
TH	Todd Helton	60.00
RJ	Randy Johnson	90.00
AR	Alex Rodriguez	80.00

Game-Used Ball Series 2

NM/M

Common Player: 5.00
Inserted 1:288

JB	Jeff Bagwell	10.00
BB	Barry Bonds	30.00
RC	Roger Clemens	20.00
NG	Nomar Garciaparra	30.00
KG	Ken Griffey Jr.	20.00
VG	Vladimir Guerrero	10.00
DJ	Derek Jeter	30.00
AJ	Andruw Jones	8.00
CJ	Chipper Jones	10.00
JK	Jeff Kent	5.00
MM	Mark McGwire	40.00
MP	Mike Piazza	20.00
CR	Cal Ripken Jr.	25.00
MR	Mariano Rivera	8.00
AR	Alex Rodriguez	20.00
GS	Gary Sheffield	8.00
SS	Sammy Sosa	20.00
BW	Bernie Williams	10.00

Home Run Explosion

NM/M

Complete Set (15): 20.00
Common Player: .50
Inserted 1:12

1	Mark McGwire	3.00
2	Chipper Jones	2.00
3	Jeff Bagwell	1.00
4	Carlos Delgado	1.00
5	Barry Bonds	4.00
6	Troy Glaus	1.00
7	Sammy Sosa	2.50
8	Alex Rodriguez	3.00
9	Mike Piazza	2.00
10	Vladimir Guerrero	1.50
11	Ken Griffey Jr.	2.00
12	Frank Thomas	1.00
13	Ivan Rodriguez	1.00
14	Jason Giambi	1.00
15	Carl Everett	.50

Home Run Derby Heroes

NM/M

Complete Set (10): 25.00
Common Player: 1.00
Inserted 1:36

HD1	Mark McGwire - 1999	5.00
HD2	Sammy Sosa - 2000	3.00
HD3	Frank Thomas - 1996	2.00
HD4	Cal Ripken Jr. - 1991	5.00
HD5	Tino Martinez - 1997	1.00
HD6	Ken Griffey Jr. - 1999	3.00
HD7	Barry Bonds - 1996	5.00
HD8	Albert Belle - 1995	1.00
HD9	Mark McGwire - 1992	5.00
HD10	Juan Gonzalez - 1993	2.00

Midseason Superstar Summit

NM/M

Complete Set (15): 25.00

Common Player: .75
Inserted 1:24

MS1	Derek Jeter	5.00
MS2	Sammy Sosa	3.00
MS3	Jeff Bagwell	1.50
MS4	Tony Gwynn	1.50
MS5	Alex Rodriguez	4.00
MS6	Greg Maddux	2.50
MS7	Jason Giambi	1.50
MS8	Mark McGwire	4.00
MS9	Barry Bonds	5.00
MS10	Ken Griffey Jr.	3.00
MS11	Carlos Delgado	1.50
MS12	Troy Glaus	1.00
MS13	Todd Helton	1.50
MS14	Manny Ramirez	1.50
MS15	Jeff Kent	.75

Most Wanted

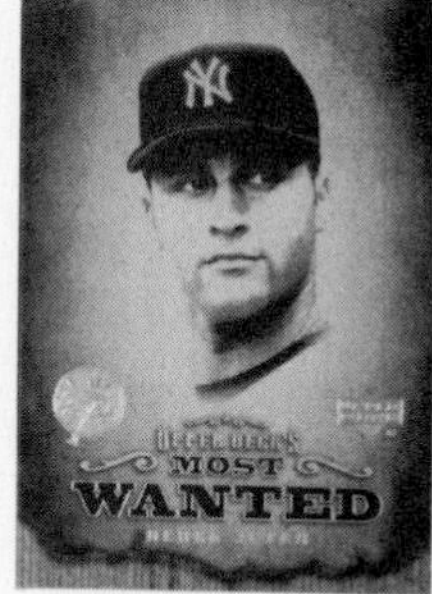

NM/M

Complete Set (15): 20.00
Common Player: .75
Inserted 1:14 Series 1

MW1	Mark McGwire	2.50
MW2	Cal Ripken Jr.	3.00
MW3	Ivan Rodriguez	.75
MW4	Pedro Martinez	1.00
MW5	Sammy Sosa	2.00
MW6	Tony Gwynn	1.00
MW7	Vladimir Guerrero	1.00
MW8	Derek Jeter	3.00
MW9	Mike Piazza	1.50
MW10	Chipper Jones	1.50
MW11	Alex Rodriguez	2.50
MW12	Barry Bonds	3.00
MW13	Jeff Bagwell	.75
MW14	Frank Thomas	.75
MW15	Nomar Garciaparra	2.00

Rookie Roundup

NM/M

Complete Set (10): 5.00
Common Player: .50
Inserted 1:6

1	Rick Ankiel	.50
2	Adam Kennedy	.50
3	Mike Lamb	.50
4	Adam Eaton	.50
5	Rafael Furcal	.75
6	Pat Burrell	1.50
7	Adam Piatt	.50
8	Eric Munson	.50
9	Brad Penny	.50
10	Mark Mulder	.75

Superstar Summit

NM/M

Complete Set (15): 25.00

Common Player: 1.00
Inserted 1:12
1 Derek Jeter 4.00
2 Randy Johnson 1.50
3 Barry Bonds 4.00
4 Frank Thomas 1.00
5 Cal Ripken Jr. 4.00
6 Pedro J. Martinez 1.50
7 Ivan Rodriguez 1.00
8 Mike Piazza 2.00
9 Mark McGwire 3.00
10 Manny Ramirez 1.00
11 Ken Griffey Jr. 2.00
12 Sammy Sosa 2.50
13 Alex Rodriguez 3.00
14 Chipper Jones 2.00
15 Nomar Garciaparra 2.50

Subway Series Jersey Cards

NM/M
Common Player: 5.00
Inserted 1:144
SS-EA Edgardo Alfonzo 5.00
SS-RC Roger Clemens 40.00
SS-JF John Franco 5.00
SS-OH Orlando Hernandez 8.00
SS-AL Al Leiter 5.00
SS-PO Paul O'Neill 10.00
SS-JP Jay Payton 5.00
SS-TP Timo Perez 5.00
SS-AP Andy Pettitte 15.00
SS-BW Bernie Williams 15.00

The Franchise

NM/M
Complete Set (10): 25.00
Common Player: 1.50
Inserted 1:36
F1 Frank Thomas 1.50
F2 Mark McGwire 5.00
F3 Ken Griffey Jr. 3.00
F4 Manny Ramirez 1.50
F5 Alex Rodriguez 5.00
F6 Greg Maddux 3.00
F7 Sammy Sosa 4.00
F8 Derek Jeter 6.00
F9 Mike Piazza 3.00
F10 Vladimir Guerrero 2.00

The People's Choice

NM/M
Complete Set (15): 35.00
Common Player: 1.50
Inserted 1:24
PC1 Alex Rodriguez 5.00
PC2 Ken Griffey Jr. 3.00
PC3 Mark McGwire 5.00
PC4 Todd Helton 1.50
PC5 Manny Ramirez 1.50
PC6 Mike Piazza 3.00
PC7 Vladimir Guerrero 2.00
PC8 Randy Johnson 2.00
PC9 Cal Ripken Jr. 6.00
PC10 Andruw Jones 1.50
PC11 Sammy Sosa 4.00
PC12 Derek Jeter 6.00
PC13 Pedro Martinez 2.00
PC14 Frank Thomas 1.50
PC15 Nomar Garciaparra 4.00

UD Game-Worn Patch

NM/M
Common Player: 40.00
P-JB Johnny Bench 120.00
P-BB Barry Bonds 150.00
P-KG Ken Griffey Jr. 100.00
P-CJ Chipper Jones 60.00
P-CR Cal Ripken Jr. 150.00
P-AR Alex Rodriguez 125.00
P-IR Ivan Rodriguez 60.00
P-NR Nolan Ryan 150.00
P-SS Sammy Sosa 100.00

2001 UPPER DECK DECADE

NM/M
Complete Set (180): 25.00
Common Player: .15
Pack (5): 1.50
Box (24): 30.00
1 Nolan Ryan 3.00
2 Don Baylor .15
3 Bobby Grich .15
4 Reggie Jackson .50
5 Jim "Catfish" Hunter .25
6 Gene Tenace .15
7 Rollie Fingers .25
8 Sal Bando .15
9 Bert Campaneris .15
10 John Mayberry .15
11 Rico Carty .15
12 Gaylord Perry .25
13 Andre Thornton .15
14 Buddy Bell .15
15 Dennis Eckersley .25
16 Ruppert Jones .15
17 Brooks Robinson .75
18 Tommy Davis .15
19 Eddie Murray .25
20 Boog Powell .15
21 Al Oliver .15
22 Jeff Burroughs .15
23 Mike Hargrove .15
24 Dwight Evans .15
25 Fred Lynn .15
26 Rico Petrocelli .15
27 Carlton Fisk .50
28 Luis Aparicio .15
29 Amos Otis .15
30 Hal McRae .15
31 Jason Thompson .15
32 Al Kaline .75
33 Jim Perry .15
34 Bert Blyleven .15
35 Harmon Killebrew 1.00
36 Wilbur Wood .15
37 Jim Kaat .15
38 Ron Guidry .15
39 Thurman Munson 1.00
40 Graig Nettles .15
41 Bobby Murcer .15
42 Chris Chambliss .15
43 Roy White .15
44 J.R. Richard .15
45 Jose Cruz .15
46 Hank Aaron 2.00
47 Phil Niekro .15
48 Bob Horner .15
49 Darryl Evans .15
50 Gorman Thomas .15
51 Don Money .15
52 Robin Yount .75
53 Joe Torre .25
54 Tim McCarver .15
55 Lou Brock .40
56 Keith Hernandez .15
57 Bill Madlock .15
58 Ron Santo .15
59 Billy Williams .15
60 Ferguson Jenkins .25
61 Steve Garvey .15
62 Bill Russell .15
63 Maury Wills .25
64 Ron Cey .15
65 Manny Mota .15
66 Ron Fairly .15
67 Steve Rogers .15
68 Gary Carter .15
69 Andre Dawson .25
70 Bobby Bonds .25
71 Jack Clark .15
72 Willie McCovey .15
73 Tom Seaver 1.00
74 Bud Harrelson .15
75 Dave Kingman .15
76 Jerry Koosman .15
77 Jon Matlack .15
78 Randy Jones .15
79 Ozzie Smith 1.00
80 Garry Maddox .15
81 Mike Schmidt 1.00
82 Greg Luzinski .15
83 Tug McGraw .15
84 Willie Stargell .75
85 Dave Parker .15
86 Roberto Clemente 2.00
87 Johnny Bench 1.50
88 Joe Morgan .40
89 George Foster .15
90 Ken Griffey Sr. .15
91 Carlton Fisk 1972 .50
92 Andre Dawson 1977 .25
93 Fred Lynn 1975 .15
94 Eddie Murray 1977 .25
95 Bob Horner 1978 .15
96 Jon Matlack 1972 .15
97 Mike Hargrove 1974 .15
98 Robin Yount 1974 .50
99 Mike Schmidt 1972 .50
100 Gary Carter 1974 .15
101 Ozzie Smith 1978 .50
102 Paul Molitor 1978 .50
103 Dennis Eckersley 1975 .25
104 Dale Murphy 1976 .15
105 Bert Blyleven 1970 .15
106 Thurman Munson 1970 .75
107 Dave Parker 1973 .15
108 Jack Clark 1975 .15
109 Keith Hernandez 1974 .15
110 Ron Cey 1971 .15
111 Billy Williams 1970 .15
112 Tom Seaver 1970 .75
113 Reggie Jackson 1971 .75
114 Barry Bonds 1971 .15
115 Willie Stargell 1971 .40
116 Harmon Killebrew 1971 .50
117 Roberto Clemente 1972 1.00
118 Wilbur Wood 1972 .15
119 Billy Williams 1972 .15
120 Nolan Ryan 1973 1.50
121 Ron Blomberg 1973 .15
122 Hank Aaron 1974 1.00
123 Lou Brock 1974 .25
124 Al Kaline 1974 .40
125 Brooks Robinson 1975 .40
126 Bill Madlock 1975 .15
127 Rennie Stennett 1975 .15
128 Carlton Fisk 1975 .40
129 Chris Chambliss 1976 .15
130 Ruppert Jones 1977 .15
131 Ron Fairly 1977 .15
132 George Foster 1977 .15
133 Reggie Jackson 1977 .75
134 Ron Guidry 1978 .15
135 Gaylord Perry 1978 .15
136 Bucky Dent 1978 .15
137 Dave Kingman 1979 .15
138 Lou Brock 1979 .15
139 Thurman Munson 1979 .75
140 Willie Stargell 1979 .40
141 Johnny Bench 1970 NL MVP .75
142 Boog Powell 1970 AL MVP .15
143 Jim Perry 1970 AL CY .15
144 Joe Torre 1971 NL MVP .15
145 Chris Chambliss 1971 AL ROY .15
146 Ferguson Jenkins 1971 NL CY .15
147 Carlton Fisk 1972 AL ROY .40
148 Gaylord Perry 1972 AL CY .15
149 Johnny Bench 1972 NL MVP .75
150 Reggie Jackson 1973 AL MVP .75
151 Tom Seaver 1973 NL CY .75
152 Thurman Munson 1973 AL GG .75
153 Steve Garvey 1974 NL MVP .15
154 Jim "Catfish" Hunter 1974 AL CY .15
155 Mike Hargrove 1974 AL ROY .15
156 Joe Morgan 1975 NL MVP .15
157 Fred Lynn 1975 AL MVP & ROY .15
158 Tom Seaver 1975 NL CY .75
159 Thurman Munson 1976 AL MVP .75
160 Randy Jones 1976 NL CY .15
161 Joe Morgan 1976 NL ROY .15
162 George Foster 1977 NL MVP .15
163 Eddie Murray 1977 AL ROY .25
164 Andre Dawson 1977 NL ROY .25
165 Gaylord Perry 1978 NL CY .15
166 Ron Guidry 1978 AL CY .15
167 Dave Parker 1978 NL MVP .15
168 Don Baylor 1979 AL MVP .15
169 Bruce Sutter 1979 NL CY .30
170 Willie Stargell 1979 NL co-MVP .40
171 Brooks Robinson 1970 .50
172 Roberto Clemente 1971 1.00
173 Gene Tenace 1972 .15
174 Reggie Jackson 1973 .75
175 Rollie Fingers 1974 .15
176 Carlton Fisk 1975 .40
177 Johnny Bench 1976 .75
178 Reggie Jackson 1977 .75
179 Bucky Dent 1978 .15
180 Willie Stargell 1979 .40

Bellbottomed Bashers

NM/M
Complete Set (10): 12.00
Common Player: 1.00
Inserted 1:14
BB1 Reggie Jackson 2.00
BB2 Gorman Thomas 1.00
BB3 Willie McCovey 1.50
BB4 Willie Stargell 1.50
BB5 Mike Schmidt 3.00
BB6 George Foster 1.00
BB7 Johnny Bench 2.50
BB8 Dave Kingman 1.00
BB9 Graig Nettles 1.00
BB10 Steve Garvey 1.00

Decade Dynasties

NM/M
Complete Set (10): 15.00

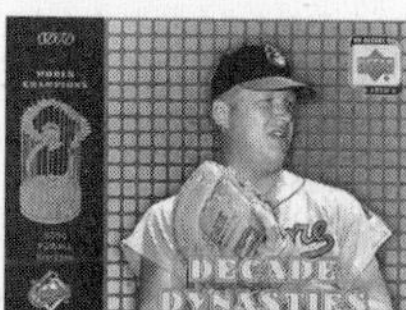

Common Player: 1.00
Inserted 1:14
D1 Boog Powell 1.00
D2 Johnny Bench 3.00
D3 Willie Stargell 1.50
D4 Jim "Catfish" Hunter 1.00
D5 Steve Garvey 1.00
D6 Carlton Fisk 2.00
D7 Mike Schmidt 4.00
D8 Hal McRae 1.00
D9 Tom Seaver 3.00
D10 Reggie Jackson 2.50

Game-Used Bat

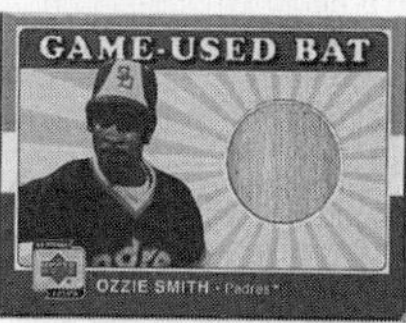

NM/M
Common Player: 5.00
Inserted 1:24 H
HA Hank Aaron 40.00
DB Don Baylor 5.00
BB Bobby Bonds 5.00
GC Gary Carter 8.00
JaC Jack Clark 5.00
RC Roberto Clemente/243 100.00
DC Dave Concepcion 5.00
JoC Jose Cruz 5.00
TD Tommy Davis 5.00
AD Andre Dawson 8.00
DaE Darryl Evans 5.00
DwE Dwight Evans 5.00
CF Carlton Fisk 10.00
GF George Foster 5.00
SG Steve Garvey 5.00
BG Bobby Grich 5.00
KG Ken Griffey Sr. 5.00
BH Bud Harrelson/290 5.00
KH Keith Hernandez/243 20.00
RH Ron Hunt 5.00
ReJ Reggie Jackson 15.00
RaJ Randy Jones 5.00
GL Greg Luzinski 5.00
FL Fred Lynn 5.00
GM Garry Maddox 5.00
BiM Bill Madlock 5.00
TiM Tim McCarver 5.00
TuM Tug McGraw/97 25.00
HM Hal McRae 5.00
RM Rick Monday 5.00
WM Willie Montanez 5.00
JM Joe Morgan 5.00
BoM Bobby Murcer 20.00
EM Eddie Murray 10.00
GN Graig Nettles/219 15.00
AO Al Oliver 5.00
DP Dave Parker 5.00
BP Boog Powell 5.00
WR Willie Randolph 5.00
BR Bill Russell 5.00
NR Nolan Ryan 50.00
RS Ron Santo 5.00
ToS Tom Seaver/121 30.00
OS Ozzie Smith 15.00
RW Roy White 5.00
MW Maury Wills 5.00
DW Dave Winfield 8.00

Game-Used Bat Combo

NM/M
Common Card: 20.00
Inserted 1:336
NYY Reggie Jackson, Graig Nettles, Chris Chambliss, Roy White 40.00
LA Steve Garvey, Ron Cey, Bill Russell, Rick Monday 25.00
NYM Tom Seaver, Bud Harrelson, Ron Hunt, Tug McGraw 50.00
CIN Johnny Bench, George Foster, Ken Griffey Sr., Joe Morgan 50.00
ROY Andre Dawson, Fred Lynn, Carlton Fisk, Eddie Murray 40.00
MVPN Johnny Bench, Steve Garvey, Willie Stargell, George Foster 50.00
BAT Keith Hernandez, Bill Madlock, Fred Lynn, Dave Parker 20.00
GGA Carlton Fisk, Graig Nettles, Bobby Grich, Fred Lynn 25.00
GGN Johnny Bench, Roberto Clemente, Dave Concepcion, Garry Maddox 100.00
WS72 Reggie Jackson, Bert Campaneris, Dave Concepcion, Johnny Bench/97 80.00
WS73 Reggie Jackson, Bert Campaneris, Tom Seaver, Bud Harrelson 40.00
WS74 Reggie Jackson, Bert Campaneris, Steve Garvey, Ron Cey 40.00
WS75 Carlton Fisk, Fred Lynn, George Foster, Joe Morgan 40.00
WS76 Chris Chambliss, Graig Nettles, Johnny Bench, Ken Griffey Sr/97 80.00
WS77 Reggie Jackson, Graig Nettles, Steve Garvey, Ron Cey 40.00
WS78 Graig Nettles, Chris Chambliss, Bill Russell, Ron Cey/238 50.00
ASMV Bill Madlock, Joe Morgan, Steve Garvey, Dave Parker 40.00
RY Chris Chambliss, Reggie Jackson, Roy White, Hal McRae/238 40.00
RD George Foster, Joe Morgan, Ron Cey, Bill Russell 25.00

Game-Used Jersey

NM/M
Common Player: 8.00
Inserted 1:168
HA Hank Aaron 40.00
LA Luis Aparicio 8.00
SB Sal Bando/15
JB Johnny Bench 20.00
RC Roberto Clemente 100.00
WD Willie Davis 8.00
RF Rollie Fingers 8.00
CF Carlton Fisk 10.00
KG Ken Griffey Sr/15
RG Ron Guidry 8.00
BH Burt Hooton 8.00
CH Jim "Catfish" Hunter 10.00
RJ Reggie Jackson 15.00
JKa Jim Kaat 8.00
JKo Jerry Koosman 8.00
BM Bill Madlock 8.00
JM Jon Matlack 8.00
TM Tug McGraw 8.00
BM Bobby Murcer 15.00
JP Jim Perry 8.00
RP Rico Petrocelli/15
LP Lou Piniella 10.00
WR Willie Randolph 8.00
NR Nolan Ryan/50 75.00
TS Tom Seaver 20.00
WS Willie Stargell 10.00
MW Maury Wills 8.00

Game-Used Jersey Autograph

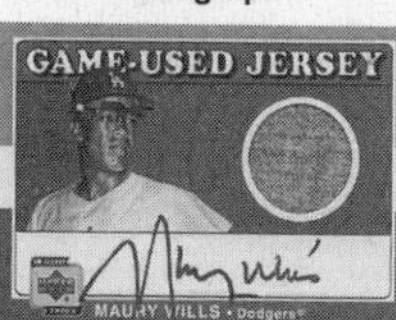

NM/M
Common Autograph: 20.00
Inserted 1:168 H
HA Hank Aaron/97 150.00
LA Luis Aparicio 30.00
SB Sal Bando 20.00
JB Johnny Bench 70.00
RF Rollie Fingers 25.00
CF Carlton Fisk/243 40.00
KG Ken Griffey Sr. 20.00
RG Ron Guidry 30.00
BH Burt Hooton 20.00
RJ Reggie Jackson/291 65.00
JKa Jim Kaat 25.00
JKo Jerry Koosman 20.00
BM Bill Madlock 20.00
TM Tug McGraw 20.00
BM Bobby Murcer 50.00
RP Rico Petrocelli 25.00
NR Nolan Ryan/291 125.00
MW Maury Wills 20.00

Game-Used Patch

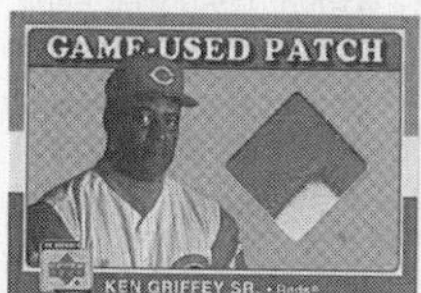

Inserted 1:7,500
No pricing due to scarcity

The Arms Race

NM/M
Complete Set (10): 10.00
Common Player: .50
Inserted 1:14
AR1 Nolan Ryan 4.00
AR2 Ferguson Jenkins 1.00
AR3 Jim "Catfish" Hunter 1.00
AR4 Tom Seaver 2.00
AR5 Randy Jones .50
AR6 J.R. Richard .50
AR7 Rollie Fingers 1.00
AR8 Gaylord Perry .75
AR9 Ron Guidry .75
AR10 Phil Niekro .75

70s Super Powers

NM/M
Complete Set (6): 12.00
Common Player: 1.50
Inserted 1:24
SP1 Reggie Jackson 3.00
SP2 Joe Morgan 1.50
SP3 Willie Stargell 2.00
SP4 Willie McCovey 1.50
SP5 Mike Schmidt 4.00
SP6 Nolan Ryan 5.00

70s Disco Era Dandies

NM/M
Complete Set (6): 5.00
Common Player: .50
Inserted 1:23
DE1 Mike Schmidt 2.00
DE2 Johnny Bench 1.00
DE3 Lou Brock .50
DE4 Reggie Jackson 2.00
DE5 Willie Stargell .50
DE6 Tom Seaver 1.00

2001 UPPER DECK EVOLUTION

NM/M
Complete Set (120): 125.00
Common Player: .15
Common SP (91-120): 3.00
Production 2,250
Pack (5): 2.00
Box (24): 40.00
1 Darin Erstad .25
2 Troy Glaus .50
3 Jason Giambi .50
4 Tim Hudson .40
5 Jermaine Dye .15
6 Barry Zito .40
7 Carlos Delgado .50
8 Shannon Stewart .15
9 Jose Cruz Jr. .15
10 Greg Vaughn .15
11 Juan Gonzalez .50
12 Roberto Alomar .50
13 Omar Vizquel .25
14 Jim Thome .50
15 Edgar Martinez .25
16 John Olerud .25
17 Kazuhiro Sasaki .15
18 Cal Ripken Jr. 2.00
19 Alex Rodriguez 1.50
20 Ivan Rodriguez .50
21 Rafael Palmeiro .50
22 Pedro Martinez .75
23 Nomar Garciaparra 1.50
24 Manny Ramirez .50
25 Carl Everett .15
26 Mark Quinn .15
27 Mike Sweeney .15
28 Neifi Perez .15
29 Tony Clark .15
30 Eric Milton .15
31 Doug Mientkiewicz .15
32 Corey Koskie .15
33 Frank Thomas .50
34 David Wells .15
35 Magglio Ordonez .40
36 Derek Jeter 2.00
37 Mike Mussina .40
38 Bernie Williams .50
39 Roger Clemens 1.50
40 David Justice .25
41 Jeff Bagwell .50
42 Richard Hidalgo .25
43 Wade Miller .15
44 Chipper Jones 1.00
45 Greg Maddux 1.00
46 Andruw Jones .50
47 Rafael Furcal .25
48 Geoff Jenkins .25
49 Jeromy Burnitz .15
50 Ben Sheets .25

51 Richie Sexson .40
52 Mark McGwire 1.50
53 Jim Edmonds .40
54 Darryl Kile .15
55 J.D. Drew .25
56 Sammy Sosa 1.50
57 Kerry Wood .50
58 Randy Johnson .75
59 Luis Gonzalez .25
60 Matt Williams .25
61 Kevin Brown .25
62 Gary Sheffield .40
63 Shawn Green .40
64 Chan Ho Park .15
65 Vladimir Guerrero .75
66 Jose Vidro .15
67 Fernando Tatis .15
68 Barry Bonds 2.00
69 Jeff Kent .25
70 Russ Ortiz .15
71 Preston Wilson .15
72 Ryan Dempster .15
73 Charles Johnson .15
74 Mike Piazza 1.00
75 Edgardo Alfonzo .15
76 Robin Ventura .25
77 Jay Payton .15
78 Tony Gwynn .75
79 Phil Nevin .15
80 Pat Burrell .40
81 Scott Rolen .50
82 Bob Abreu .25
83 Brian Giles .25
84 Jason Kendall .25
85 Ken Griffey Jr. 1.00
86 Barry Larkin .40
87 Sean Casey .25
88 Todd Helton .50
89 Larry Walker .25
90 Mike Hampton .15
91 *Ichiro Suzuki* 20.00
92 *Albert Pujols* 40.00
93 *Wilson Betemit* 3.00
94 *Jay Gibbons* 8.00
95 *Juan Uribe* 5.00
96 *Morgan Ensberg* 8.00
97 *Christian Parker* 3.00
98 *Tsuyoshi Shinjo* 4.00
99 *Jack Wilson* 8.00
100 *Donaldo Mendez* 3.00
101 *Ryan Freel* 4.00
102 *Juan Diaz* 3.00
103 *Horacio Ramirez* 8.00
104 *Ricardo Rodriguez* 3.00
105 *Erick Almonte* 3.00
106 *Josh Towers* 3.00
107 *Adrian Hernandez* 3.00
108 *Brandon Duckworth* 4.00
109 *Travis Hafner* 8.00
110 *Martin Vargas* 3.00
111 *Kris Keller* 3.00
112 *Brian Lawrence* 3.00
113 *Esix Snead* 3.00
114 *Wilken Ruan* 3.00
115 *Jose Mieses* 3.00
116 *Johnny Estrada* 8.00
117 *Elpidio Guzman* 3.00
118 *Sean Douglass* 3.00
119 *Billy Sylvester* 3.00
120 *Bret Prinz* 3.00

Autographed Bat/Jersey

NM/M
Common Player: 25.00
RB Russell Branyan 25.00
PB Pat Burrell 40.00
CD Carlos Delgado 40.00
JD J.D. Drew 25.00
JaG Jason Giambi 65.00
SG Shawn Green 40.00
KG Ken Griffey Jr. 100.00
AJ Andruw Jones 50.00
CJ Chipper Jones 60.00
JK Jason Kendall 30.00
CR Cal Ripken Jr. 150.00
AR Alex Rodriguez 150.00
GS Gary Sheffield 50.00
SS Sammy Sosa 200.00
IS Ichiro Suzuki 300.00

Game-Used Bat Cards

NM/M
Common Player: 5.00
Winners evolve into Bat/Jrsy Auto.
Inserted 1:120
RB Russell Branyan 5.00
PB Pat Burrell 8.00
CD Carlos Delgado 8.00
JD J.D. Drew 5.00
JaG Jason Giambi 8.00
KG Ken Griffey Jr. 20.00
AJ Andruw Jones 8.00
JK Jason Kendall 5.00
AR Alex Rodriguez 15.00
GS Gary Sheffield 6.00

Game-Used Jersey Cards

NM/M
Common Player: 5.00
Inserted 1:120
RB Russell Branyan 5.00
PB Pat Burrell 8.00
JD J.D. Drew 5.00
JaG Jason Giambi 10.00
BG Brian Giles 6.00
TG Troy Glaus 8.00
SG Shawn Green 6.00
KG Ken Griffey Jr. 20.00
AJ Andruw Jones 8.00
CJ Chipper Jones 10.00
JK Jason Kendall 5.00
CR Cal Ripken Jr. 30.00
AR Alex Rodriguez 15.00
GS Gary Sheffield 8.00
SS Sammy Sosa 15.00

Ichiro Suzuki All-Star Game

NM/M
Random inserts
51B Ichiro Suzuki Bronze 8.00
51S Ichiro Suzuki Silver/2001 20.00
51G Ichiro Suzuki Gold/51 120.00
51G Ichiro Suzuki Gold not #'d

UD Classics

NM/M
Complete Set (15): 15.00
Common Player: .50
Prices for unscratched cards
Winners evolve into Game Jersey
Inserted 1:4
EC1 Ken Griffey Jr. 3.00
EC2 Gary Sheffield .75
EC3 Randy Johnson 1.50
EC4 Sammy Sosa 3.00
EC5 Carlos Delgado 1.00
EC6 Ichiro Suzuki 3.00
EC7 Andruw Jones 1.00
EC8 Chipper Jones 2.00
EC9 Kazuhiro Sasaki .50
EC10 Shawn Green .75
EC11 Alex Rodriguez 3.00
EC12 Brian Giles .75
EC13 J.D. Drew .50
EC14 Pat Burrell 1.00
EC15 Ivan Rodriguez 1.00

2001 UPPER DECK GOLD GLOVE

NM/M
Common Player: .25
Common SP (91-129): 4.00
Production 1,000
Common SP (130-135): 8.00
Production 500
Pack (4): 8.00
Box (20): 140.00
1 Troy Glaus 1.00
2 Darin Erstad .50
3 Jason Giambi 1.00
4 Tim Hudson .50
5 Jermaine Dye .25
6 Raul Mondesi .25
7 Carlos Delgado 1.00
8 Shannon Stewart .25
9 Greg Vaughn .25
10 Aubrey Huff .25
11 Juan Gonzalez 1.00
12 Roberto Alomar 1.00
13 Omar Vizquel .25
14 Jim Thome 1.00
15 John Olerud .50
16 Edgar Martinez .50
17 Kazuhiro Sasaki .25
18 Aaron Sele .25
19 Cal Ripken Jr. 4.00
20 Chris Richard .25
21 Ivan Rodriguez 1.00
22 Rafael Palmeiro .75
23 Alex Rodriguez 3.00
24 Pedro Martinez 1.50
25 Nomar Garciaparra 3.00
26 Manny Ramirez 1.00
27 Neifi Perez .25
28 Mike Sweeney .25
29 Bobby Higginson .25
30 Dean Palmer .25
31 Tony Clark .25
32 Doug Mientkiewicz .25
33 Brad Radke .25
34 Joe Mays .25
35 Frank Thomas 1.00
36 Magglio Ordonez .50
37 Carlos Lee .25
38 Bernie Williams 1.00
39 Mike Mussina 1.00
40 Derek Jeter 4.00
41 Roger Clemens 2.50
42 Craig Biggio .40
43 Jeff Bagwell 1.00
44 Lance Berkman .50
45 Andruw Jones 1.00
46 Greg Maddux 2.00
47 Chipper Jones 2.00
48 Geoff Jenkins .40
49 Ben Sheets .25
50 Jeromy Burnitz .25
51 Jim Edmonds .50
52 Mark McGwire 3.00
53 Mike Matheny .25
54 J.D. Drew .50
55 Sammy Sosa 2.50
56 Kerry Wood .75
57 Fred McGriff .40
58 Randy Johnson 1.50
59 Steve Finley .25
60 Mark Grace .75
61 Matt Williams .40
62 Luis Gonzalez .40
63 Shawn Green .40
64 Kevin Brown .40
65 Gary Sheffield .50
66 Vladimir Guerrero 1.25
67 Tony Armas Jr. .25
68 Barry Bonds 4.00
69 J.T. Snow .25
70 Jeff Kent .25
71 Charles Johnson .25
72 Preston Wilson .25
73 Cliff Floyd .25
74 Robin Ventura .25
75 Mike Piazza 2.00
76 Edgardo Alfonzo .25
77 Tony Gwynn 1.50
78 Ryan Klesko .50
79 Scott Rolen 1.00
80 Mike Lieberthal .25
81 Pat Burrell .75
82 Jason Kendall .25
83 Brian Giles .50
84 Ken Griffey Jr. 2.50
85 Barry Larkin .50
86 Pokey Reese .25
87 Larry Walker .40
88 Mike Hampton .25
89 Juan Pierre .25
90 Todd Helton 1.00
91 *Mike Penney* 4.00
92 *Wilkin Ruan* 4.00
93 *Greg Miller* 4.00
94 *Johnny Estrada* 8.00
95 *Tsuyoshi Shinjo* 4.00
96 *Josh Towers* 4.00
97 *Horacio Ramirez* 6.00
98 *Ryan Freel* 4.00
99 *Morgan Ensberg* 15.00
100 *Adrian Hernandez* 8.00
101 *Juan Uribe* 6.00
102 *Jose Mieses* 4.00
103 *Jack Wilson* 8.00
104 *Cesar Crespo* 4.00
105 *Bud Smith* 4.00
106 *Erick Almonte* 4.00
107 *Elpidio Guzman* 4.00
108 *Brandon Duckworth* 4.00
109 *Juan Diaz* 4.00
110 *Kris Keller* 4.00
111 *Jason Michaels* 4.00
112 *Bret Prinz* 4.00
113 *Henry Mateo* 4.00
114 *Ricardo Rodriguez* 4.00
115 *Travis Hafner* 15.00
116 *Nate Teut* 4.00
117 *Alexis Gomez* 4.00
118 *Billy Sylvester* 4.00
119 *Adam Pettyjohn* 4.00
120 *Josh Fogg* 4.00
121 *Juan Cruz* 4.00
122 *Carlos Valderrama* 4.00
123 *Jay Gibbons* 10.00
124 *Donaldo Mendez* 4.00
125 *William Ortega* 4.00
126 *Sean Douglass* 4.00
127 *Christian Parker* 4.00
128 *Grant Balfour* 4.00
129 *Joe Kennedy* 4.00
130 *Albert Pujols* 120.00
131 *Wilson Betemit* 10.00
132 *Mark Teixeira* 50.00
133 *Mark Prior* 40.00
134 *Dewon Brazelton* 10.00
135 *Ichiro Suzuki* 50.00

Limited

Stars (1-90): 4-8X
Rookies (91-135): .75-1.5X
Production 100 sets
(See 2001 Upper Deck Gold Glove for checklist and base card values.)

Finite

NM/M
Common Player: 9.00
Stars (1-90): 15-25X
Rookies (91-135): 3-5X
Production 25 Sets
(See 2001 Upper Deck Gold Glove for checklist and base card values.)

Game-Used Ball

NM/M
Common Player: 5.00
Inserted 1:20
GC Ken Griffey Jr., Sean Casey 20.00

RR	Alex Rodriguez, Ivan Rodriguez	20.00
SW	Sammy Sosa, Rondell White	15.00
MP	Mark McGwire, Albert Pujols	75.00
JW	Derek Jeter, Bernie Williams	
RE	Manny Ramirez, Carl Everett	15.00
GE	Troy Glaus, Darin Erstad	8.00
GT	Jason Giambi, Miguel Tejada	10.00
IO	Ichiro Suzuki, John Olerud	40.00
RP	Ivan Rodriguez, Rafael Palmeiro	10.00
GV	Vladimir Guerrero, Jose Vidro	10.00
PS	Mike Piazza, Tsuyoshi Shinjo	20.00
JJ	Chipper Jones, Andruw Jones	15.00
RB	Scott Rolen, Pat Burrell	10.00
WF	Preston Wilson, Cliff Floyd	5.00
JF	Andruw Jones, Rafael Furcal	10.00
BB	Jeff Bagwell, Lance Berkman	15.00
PE	Albert Pujols, Jim Edmonds	35.00
JB	Geoff Jenkins, Jeromy Burnitz	5.00
KG	Jason Kendall, Brian Giles	5.00
BK	Barry Bonds, Jeff Kent	25.00
NK	Phil Nevin, Ryan Klesko	5.00
SG	Gary Sheffield, Shawn Green	8.00
GG	Luis Gonzalez, Mark Grace	10.00
HW	Todd Helton, Larry Walker	10.00
WP	Larry Walker, Juan Pierre	5.00
AG	Roberto Alomar, Juan Gonzalez	10.00
VM	Greg Vaughn, Fred McGriff	5.00
WP	Bernie Williams, Jorge Posada	
RB	Cal Ripken Jr., Tony Batista	30.00
DM	Carlos Delgado, Raul Mondesi	8.00
MG	Doug Mientkiewicz, Cristian Guzman	5.00
TO	Frank Thomas, Magglio Ordonez	10.00
HC	Bobby Higginson, Tony Clark	5.00
SB	Mike Sweeney, Carlos Beltran	5.00
MO	Edgar Martinez, John Olerud	8.00
EA	Darin Erstad, Garret Anderson	8.00
TC	Miguel Tejada, Eric Chavez	8.00
PR	Rafael Palmeiro, Alex Rodriguez	20.00
BA	Pat Burrell, Bobby Abreu	8.00
FJ	Cliff Floyd, Charles Johnson	5.00
VP	Robin Ventura, Mike Piazza	15.00
WS	Kerry Wood, Sammy Sosa	20.00
DP	J.D. Drew, Albert Pujols	40.00
BH	Lance Berkman, Richard Hidalgo	8.00
BS	Jeromy Burnitz, Richie Sexson	5.00
LG	Barry Larkin, Ken Griffey Jr.	20.00
GR	Brian Giles, Aramis Ramirez	5.00
JG	Randy Johnson, Luis Gonzalez	15.00
GB	Shawn Green, Adrian Beltre	8.00
KA	Jeff Kent, Rich Aurilia	5.00
GK	Tony Gwynn, Ryan Klesko	15.00
MJ	Greg Maddux, Chipper Jones	20.00
HH	Mike Hampton, Todd Helton	10.00
SV	Tsuyoshi Shinjo, Robin Ventura	5.00
GJ	Cristian Guzman, Jacque Jones	5.00
CJ	Roger Clemens, Derek Jeter	125.00

Fielder's Gloves

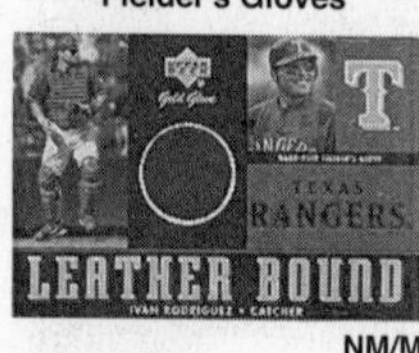

		NM/M
Common Player:		6.00
Inserted 1:60		
GA	Garret Anderson/100	15.00
CB	Craig Biggio	15.00
JBi	Johnny Blanchard	10.00
BB	Barry Bonds	50.00
JBu	Jay Buhner/100	
KC	Ken Caminiti	10.00
RCa	Roy Campanella	60.00
GC	Gary Carter	10.00
RCe	Roger Cedeno	10.00
JD	Johnny Damon	15.00
LD	Leon Day/100	60.00
OD	Octavio Dotel	6.00
JE	Jim Edmonds	15.00
DE	Dock Ellis	10.00
AF	Alex Fernandez	6.00
CF	Cliff Floyd	10.00
NF	Nellie Fox	25.00
RF	Rafael Furcal	10.00
AG	Alex Gonzalez	6.00
BG	Ben Grieve	8.00
KG	Ken Griffey Jr.	30.00
MG	Marquis Grissom	8.00
LG	Lefty Grove	100.00
THe	Todd Helton	20.00
OH	Orlando Hernandez	8.00
THo	Todd Hollandsworth	8.00
HI	Hideki Irabu	8.00
JI	Jason Isringhausen	10.00
RJ	Reggie Jackson	20.00
CJ	Chipper Jones	25.00
JKa	Jim Kaat	10.00
JKe	Jason Kendall	10.00
RK	Ryan Klesko	8.00
HK	Harvey Kuenn	15.00
CL	Carlos Lee	8.00
KL	Kenny Lofton	10.00
JL	Javy Lopez	10.00
GL	Greg Luzinski	10.00
EM	Edgar Martinez	15.00
PM	Pedro Martinez	25.00
JM	Jose Mesa	
JO	John Olerud	10.00
PO	Paul O'Neill	15.00
RP	Rafael Palmeiro	15.00
CP	Chan Ho Park	10.00
MP	Mike Piazza	30.00
MR	Manny Ramirez	25.00
FR	Frank Robinson	15.00
AR	Alex Rodriguez	30.00
IR	Ivan Rodriguez	15.00
TS	Tim Salmon	8.00
AS	Aaron Sele	6.00
GS	Gary Sheffield	10.00
OS	Ozzie Smith	40.00
SS	Sammy Sosa	30.00
I	Ichiro Suzuki	250.00
FT	Frank Thomas	20.00
OV	Omar Vizquel	15.00
DW	Dave Winfield	20.00
MY	Masato Yoshii	10.00

Fielder's Gloves Autograph

		NM/M
Inserted 1:240		
BB	Barry Bonds	
JD	Johnny Damon	50.00
JE	Jim Edmonds	
CF	Cliff Floyd	20.00
RF	Rafael Furcal	25.00
RP	Ken Griffey Jr./49	150.00
TH	Todd Helton	
RJ	Reggie Jackson/68	60.00
CJ	Chipper Jones	
JK	Jim Kaat	25.00
JK	Jason Kendall	20.00
RK	Ryan Klesko	20.00
KL	Kenny Lofton	20.00
JL	Javy Lopez	20.00
GL	Greg Luzinski	20.00
EM	Edgar Martinez	50.00
PM	Pedro Martinez	
JO	John Olerud	25.00
PO	Paul O'Neill	50.00
RP	Rafael Palmeiro	
MP	Mike Piazza	
FR	Frank Robinson	50.00
AR	Alex Rodriguez/29	
IR	Ivan Rodriguez	60.00
AS	Aaron Sele	
GS	Gary Sheffield	
OS	Ozzie Smith	85.00
SS	Sammy Sosa	
I	Ichiro Suzuki/50	
FT	Frank Thomas	60.00
DW	Dave Winfield	50.00

Jerseys

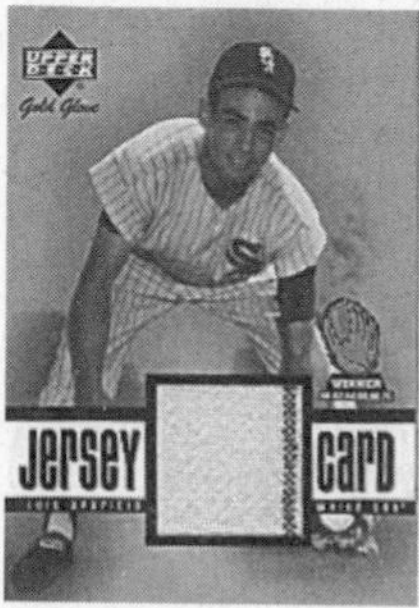

		NM/M
Common Player:		5.00
Inserted 1:20		
LA	Luis Aparicio	5.00
JB	Jeff Bagwell	8.00
BB	Barry Bonds	25.00
GC	Gary Carter	5.00
CC	Cesar Cedeno	5.00
DE	Darin Erstad	6.00
CF	Carlton Fisk	8.00
MG	Mark Grace	8.00
SG	Shawn Green	5.00
KG	Ken Griffey Jr.	20.00
RG	Ron Guidry	5.00
AJ	Andruw Jones	8.00
JK	Jim Kaat	5.00
GM	Greg Maddux	15.00
MM	Mickey Mantle	175.00
RM	Roger Maris	75.00
DM	Don Mattingly	30.00
TM	Thurman Munson	60.00
MM	Mike Mussina	10.00
RP	Rafael Palmeiro	10.00
BR	Bobby Richardson	8.00
CR	Cal Ripken Jr.	35.00
IR	Ivan Rodriguez	10.00
OS	Ozzie Smith	15.00
IS	Ichiro Suzuki	65.00
OV	Omar Vizquel	8.00
BW	Bernie Williams	8.00

Batting Gloves

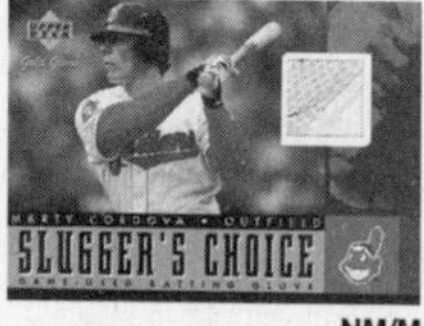

		NM/M
Common Player:		5.00
Inserted 1:20		
BA	Bobby Abreu	8.00
BA	Brady Anderson	5.00
TB	Tony Batista	5.00
BB	Barry Bonds	30.00
MC	Marty Cordova	5.00
JC	Jose Cruz	5.00
RF	Rafael Furcal	8.00
AG	Andres Galarraga	5.00
JG	Juan Gonzalez	8.00
KGR	Ken Griffey Jr Reds	20.00
KGM	Ken Griffey Jr.	20.00
CJ	Chipper Jones	10.00
EM	Edgar Martinez	8.00
PO	Paul O'Neill	8.00
RP	Rafael Palmeiro	10.00
NP	Neifi Perez	5.00
MR	Manny Ramirez	8.00
ARR	Alex Rodriguez Rangers	20.00
ARM	Alex Rodriguez M's	20.00
HR	Henry Rodriguez	5.00
IR	Ivan Rodriguez	8.00
GS	Gary Sheffield	8.00
SS	Sammy Sosa	15.00
FT	Fernando Tatis	5.00
MT	Miguel Tejada	8.00

2001 UPPER DECK HALL OF FAMERS

		NM/M
Complete Set (90):		25.00
Common Player:		.15
Hobby Pack (5):		4.00
Box (24):		80.00
1	Reggie Jackson	.75
2	Hank Aaron	1.50
3	Eddie Mathews	.75
4	Warren Spahn	.40
5	Robin Yount	.40
6	Lou Brock	.25
7	Dizzy Dean	.15
8	Bob Gibson	.40
9	Stan Musial	.75
10	Enos Slaughter	.15
11	Rogers Hornsby	.40
12	Ernie Banks	.50
13	Ferguson Jenkins	.15
14	Roy Campanella	.75
15	Pee Wee Reese	.15
16	Jackie Robinson	1.50
17	Juan Marichal	.15
18	Christy Mathewson	.15
19	Willie Mays	1.50
20	Hoyt Wilhelm	.15
21	Buck Leonard	.15
22	Bob Feller	.40
23	Cy Young	.40
24	Satchel Paige	.40
25	Tom Seaver	.50
26	Brooks Robinson	.40
27	Mike Schmidt	.75
28	Roberto Clemente	1.50
29	Ralph Kiner	.15
30	Willie Stargell	.50
31	Honus Wagner	.75
32	Josh Gibson	.40
33	Nolan Ryan	1.50
34	Carlton Fisk	.15
35	Jimmie Foxx	.75
36	Johnny Bench	.75
37	Joe Morgan	.40
38	George Brett	.75
39	Walter Johnson	.40
40	Cool Papa Bell	.15
41	Ty Cobb	1.00
42	Al Kaline	.15
43	Harmon Killebrew	.15
44	Luis Aparicio	.15
45	Yogi Berra	.75
46	Joe DiMaggio	1.50

47	Whitey Ford	.25
48	Lou Gehrig	2.00
49	Mickey Mantle	2.00
50	Babe Ruth	2.00
51	Josh Gibson	.15
52	Honus Wagner	.20
53	Hoyt Wilhelm	.15
54	Cy Young	.20
55	Walter Johnson	.20
56	Satchel Paige	.25
57	Rogers Hornsby	.20
58	Christy Mathewson	.15
59	Tris Speaker	.20
60	Nap Lajoie	.15
61	Mickey Mantle	1.00
62	Jackie Robinson	.75
63	Nolan Ryan	.75
64	Josh Gibson	.20
65	Yogi Berra	.40
66	Brooks Robinson	.20
67	Stan Musial	.40
68	Mike Schmidt	.40
69	Joe DiMaggio	1.00
70	Ernie Banks	.25
71	Willie Stargell	.25
72	Johnny Bench	.40
73	Willie Mays	.75
74	Satchel Paige	.25
75	Bob Gibson	.20
76	Harmon Killebrew	.15
77	Al Kaline	.15
78	Carlton Fisk	.15
79	Tom Seaver	.25
80	Reggie Jackson	.40
81	Bob Gibson	.20
82	Nolan Ryan	.75
83	Walter Johnson	.20
84	Stan Musial	.40
85	Josh Gibson	.20
86	Cy Young	.20
87	Joe DiMaggio	1.00
88	Hoyt Wilhelm	.15
89	Lou Brock	.15
90	Mickey Mantle	1.00

Coop. Coll. Game Bat

		NM/M
Common Player:		5.00
Inserted 1:24		
HA	Hank Aaron.	30.00
LA	Luis Aparicio.	5.00
EB	Ernie Banks.	15.00
JB	Johnny Bench.	15.00
YB	Yogi Berra.	10.00
JBo	Jim Bottomley.	5.00
GB	George Brett.	20.00
RC	Roy Campanella.	30.00
OC	Orlando Cepeda.	5.00
RC	Roberto Clemente SP/409.	120.00
JD	Joe DiMaggio.	100.00
CF	Carlton Fisk.	10.00
RF	Rollie Fingers.	5.00
JF	Jimmie Foxx.	50.00
HG	Hank Greenberg.	40.00
RH	Rogers Hornsby.	100.00
RJ	Reggie Jackson	15.00
GK	George Kell	5.00
RK	Ralph Kiner	10.00
MM	Mickey Mantle	125.00
WM	Willie Mays	30.00
JM	Johnny Mize	10.00
JMo	Joe Morgan	5.00
MO	Mel Ott	50.00
JP	Jim Palmer SP/372	50.00
TP	Tony Perez	5.00
BR	Brooks Robinson	10.00
FR	Frank Robinson	10.00
JR	Jackie Robinson SP/371	175.00
BR	Babe Ruth	200.00
NR	Nolan Ryan	50.00
RS	Red Schoendienst	5.00
ES	Enos Slaughter	5.00
DS	Duke Snider	10.00
WS	Willie Stargell	5.00
BW	Billy Williams	5.00
EW	Early Wynn	5.00
RY	Robin Yount	15.00

Coop. Coll. Game Jersey

		NM/M
Common Player:		10.00
Inserted 1:168		
LA	Luis Aparicio	10.00
OC	Orlando Cepeda	10.00
RC	Roberto Clemente	100.00
JD	Joe DiMaggio	100.00
DD	Don Drysdale SP/49	200.00
LG	Lou Gehrig SP/194	250.00
MM	Mickey Mantle SP/216	250.00
WM	Willie Mays	80.00
JM	Joe Morgan	10.00
TP	Tony Perez	10.00
PW	Pee Wee Reese	15.00
BR	Brooks Robinson	20.00
FR	Frank Robinson	10.00
NR	Nolan Ryan	30.00
TS	Tom Seaver	15.00
DS	Duke Snider SP/267	50.00
WS	Willie Stargell	15.00
DSu	Don Sutton	10.00

Coop. Coll. Jersey Auto.

		NM/M
Common Autograph:		40.00
Inserted 1:504		
LA	Luis Aparicio	40.00
OC	Orlando Cepeda	40.00
RJ	Reggie Jackson	75.00
EB	Ernie Banks	90.00
JM	Joe Morgan	40.00
TP	Tony Perez	40.00
GB	George Brett	125.00
BR	Brooks Robinson	80.00
FR	Frank Robinson	60.00
NR	Nolan Ryan	175.00
TS	Tom Seaver	75.00
DS	Duke Snider	65.00
WS	Willie Stargell	75.00
DSu	Don Sutton	40.00

Hall of Fame Gallery

		NM/M
Complete Set (15):		25.00
Common Player:		1.00
Inserted 1:6		
1	Reggie Jackson	1.50
2	Tom Seaver	1.50
3	Bob Gibson	1.50
4	Jackie Robinson	3.00
5	Joe DiMaggio	3.00
6	Ernie Banks	1.50
7	Mickey Mantle	4.00
8	Willie Mays	3.00
9	Cy Young	1.50
10	Nolan Ryan	4.00
11	Johnny Bench	1.50
12	Yogi Berra	1.50
13	Satchel Paige	1.00
14	George Brett	2.00
15	Stan Musial	2.00

Values quoted in this guide reflect the retail price of a card, the price a collector can expect to pay when buying a card from a dealer.

Mantle Pinstripes Excl.

	NM/M
Complete Set (56):	75.00
Common Mantle:	2.00
One pack/box	

Mantle Pinstripe Memor.

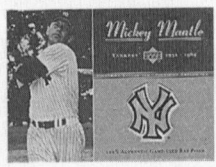

		NM/M
Print Runs listed:		
MMBC	Mickey Mantle bat/cut/7	
MMB	Mickey Mantle bat/100	100.00
MMCJ	Mickey Mantle, Joe DiMaggio jsy/50	300.00
MMC	Mickey Mantle cut/7	
MMJ	Mickey Mantle jsy/100	125.00

The Class of '36

		NM/M
Complete Set (5):		8.00
Common Player:		1.50
Inserted 1:17		
1	Ty Cobb	2.00
2	Babe Ruth	5.00
3	Christy Mathewson	1.50
4	Walter Johnson	1.50
5	Honus Wagner	1.50

The Endless Summer

		NM/M
Complete Set (11):		15.00
Common Player:		1.00
Inserted 1:8		
1	Mickey Mantle	4.00
2	Yogi Berra	1.00
3	Mike Schmidt	2.50
4	Jackie Robinson	2.50
5	Johnny Bench	1.50
6	Tom Seaver	1.50
7	Ernie Banks	1.50
8	Harmon Killebrew	1.00
9	Joe DiMaggio	3.00
10	Willie Mays	3.00
11	Brooks Robinson	1.00

20th Century Showcase

		NM/M
Complete Set (11):		15.00
Common Player:		1.00
Inserted 1:8		
1	Cy Young	1.00
2	Joe DiMaggio	3.00
3	Harmon Killebrew	1.00
4	Stan Musial	2.00
5	Mickey Mantle	4.00
6	Satchel Paige	1.00
7	Nolan Ryan	4.00
8	Bob Gibson	1.00
9	Ernie Banks	1.50
10	Mike Schmidt	2.00
11	Willie Mays	3.00

2001 UPPER DECK LEGENDS

		NM/M
Complete Set (90):		20.00
Common Player:		.20
Pack (5):		4.00
Box (24):		80.00
1	Darin Erstad	.40
2	Troy Glaus	.75
3	Nolan Ryan	3.00
4	Reggie Jackson	.50
5	Jim "Catfish" Hunter	.20
6	Jason Giambi	.50
7	Tim Hudson	.30
8	Miguel Tejada	.30
9	Carlos Delgado	.50
10	Shannon Stewart	.20
11	Greg Vaughn	.20
12	Larry Doby	.20
13	Jim Thome	.40
14	Juan Gonzalez	.75
15	Roberto Alomar	.50
16	Edgar Martinez	.20
17	John Olerud	.40
18	Eddie Murray	.40
19	Cal Ripken Jr.	2.50
20	Alex Rodriguez	2.00
21	Ivan Rodriguez	.75
22	Rafael Palmeiro	.40
23	Jimmie Foxx	.50
24	Cy Young	.50
25	Manny Ramirez	.75
26	Pedro Martinez	1.00
27	Nomar Garciaparra	2.00
28	George Brett	1.00
29	Mike Sweeney	.20
30	Jermaine Dye	.20
31	Ty Cobb	1.50
32	Dean Palmer	.20
33	Harmon Killebrew	.50
34	Matt Lawton	.20
35	Luis Aparicio	.20
36	Frank Thomas	.75
37	Magglio Ordonez	.20
38	David Wells	.20
39	Mickey Mantle	3.00
40	Joe DiMaggio	3.00

41	Roger Maris	.75
42	Babe Ruth	3.00
43	Derek Jeter	2.50
44	Roger Clemens	1.00
45	Bernie Williams	.50
46	Jeff Bagwell	.75
47	Richard Hidalgo	.40
48	Warren Spahn	.40
49	Greg Maddux	1.50
50	Chipper Jones	1.50
51	Andruw Jones	.50
52	Robin Yount	.50
53	Jeromy Burnitz	.20
54	Jeffrey Hammonds	.20
55	Ozzie Smith	.50
56	Stan Musial	1.00
57	Mark McGwire	2.50
58	Jim Edmonds	.30
59	Sammy Sosa	1.50
60	Ernie Banks	.50
61	Kerry Wood	.20
62	Randy Johnson	.75
63	Luis Gonzalez	.40
64	Don Drysdale	.50
65	Jackie Robinson	2.00
66	Gary Sheffield	.20
67	Kevin Brown	.20
68	Vladimir Guerrero	1.00
69	Willie Mays	1.50
70	Mel Ott	.20
71	Jeff Kent	.20
72	Barry Bonds	1.00
73	Preston Wilson	.20
74	Ryan Dempster	.20
75	Tom Seaver	.40
76	Mike Piazza	2.00
77	Robin Ventura	.20
78	Dave Winfield	.40
79	Tony Gwynn	1.00
80	Bob Abreu	.20
81	Scott Rolen	.40
82	Mike Schmidt	.75
83	Roberto Clemente	1.50
84	Brian Giles	.20
85	Ken Griffey Jr.	2.00
86	Frank Robinson	.40
87	Johnny Bench	.75
88	Todd Helton	.75
89	Larry Walker	.40
90	Mike Hampton	.20

Fiorentino Collection

		NM/M
Complete Set (14):		40.00
Common Player:		1.50
Inserted 1:12		
F1	Babe Ruth	6.00
F2	Satchel Paige	1.50
F3	Joe DiMaggio	5.00
F4	Willie Mays	4.00
F5	Ty Cobb	3.00
F6	Nolan Ryan	5.00
F7	Lou Gehrig	5.00
F8	Jackie Robinson	4.00
F9	Hank Aaron	4.00
F10	Roberto Clemente	4.00
F11	Stan Musial	3.00
F12	Johnny Bench	2.00
F13	Honus Wagner	1.50
F14	Reggie Jackson	1.50

Legendary Game Jerseys

		NM/M
Common Player:		5.00
Inserted 1:24		
HA	Hank Aaron	40.00
JB	Jeff Bagwell	8.00
EB	Ernie Banks	15.00

YB	Yogi Berra	10.00
BB	Barry Bonds	25.00
JC	Jose Canseco	10.00
RCl	Roger Clemens	20.00
RoC	Roberto Clemente/195	170.00
JD	Joe DiMaggio/245	175.00
KG	Ken Griffey Jr.	15.00
TG	Tony Gwynn	10.00
RJa	Reggie Jackson	10.00
RJo	Randy Johnson	10.00
CJ	Chipper Jones	10.00
GM	Greg Maddux	15.00
MM	Mickey Mantle/245	200.00
RM	Roger Maris/343	65.00
PM	Pedro Martinez	10.00
WM	Willie Mays	30.00
SM	Stan Musial/490	30.00
MP	Mike Piazza	20.00
MR	Manny Ramirez	8.00
CR	Cal Ripken Jr.	30.00
AR	Alex Rodriguez	20.00
IR	Ivan Rodriguez	8.00
NR	Nolan Ryan	50.00
KS	Kazuhiro Sasaki	5.00
TS	Tom Seaver	15.00
GS	Gary Sheffield	5.00
OS	Ozzie Smith	15.00
SS	Sammy Sosa	15.00
DW	Dave Winfield	5.00
RY	Robin Yount	12.00

Legendary Jerseys Gold

		NM/M
Common Player:		30.00
Production 25 sets		
RCl	Roger Clemens	75.00
RoC	Roberto Clemente	180.00
KG	Ken Griffey Jr.	75.00
RJ	Reggie Jackson	40.00
WM	Willie Mays	120.00
AR	Alex Rodriguez	75.00
NR	Nolan Ryan	100.00
SS	Sammy Sosa	75.00
DW	Dave Winfield	30.00

Legendary Jerseys Auto.

		NM/M
Inserted 1:288		
EB	Ernie Banks	75.00
RC	Roger Clemens/211	100.00
KG	Ken Griffey Jr.	80.00
RJ	Reggie Jackson/224	60.00
SM	Stan Musial/266	100.00
AR	Alex Rodriguez	85.00
NR	Nolan Ryan	125.00
TS	Tom Seaver	60.00
OS	Ozzie Smith	60.00
SS	Sammy Sosa/91	175.00

Legendary Jerseys Gold Auto.

No pricing due to scarcity
Production 25 sets

Legendary Lumber

		NM/M
Common Player:		5.00
Inserted 1:24		
HA	Hank Aaron	30.00
LA	Luis Aparicio	5.00
EB	Ernie Banks/80	50.00
JB	Johnny Bench	15.00
BB	Barry Bonds	25.00
RCa	Roy Campanella/335	40.00
JC	Jose Canseco	8.00
RCl	Roger Clemens	20.00
RoC	Roberto Clemente/170	120.00
JD	Joe DiMaggio	85.00
JF	Jimmie Foxx/351	50.00
KG	Ken Griffey Jr.	15.00
TG	Tony Gwynn	10.00
RJ	Reggie Jackson	10.00
RJ	Randy Johnson	10.00
AJ	Andruw Jones	8.00
CJ	Chipper Jones	10.00
MM	Mickey Mantle	150.00
RM	Roger Maris	40.00
WM	Willie Mays	30.00
EM	Eddie Murray	8.00
MO	Mel Ott/355	40.00
MP	Mike Piazza	15.00
AP	Albert Pujols	45.00
MR	Manny Ramirez	8.00
FR	Frank Robinson	8.00
CR	Cal Ripken Jr.	40.00
AR	Alex Rodriguez	15.00
IR	Ivan Rodriguez	8.00
GS	Gary Sheffield	5.00
OS	Ozzie Smith	10.00
SS	Sammy Sosa	15.00

Legendary Lumber Gold

		NM/M
Common Player:		25.00
Production 25 sets		
RC	Roger Clemens	75.00
RC	Roberto Clemente	180.00
KG	Ken Griffey Jr.	75.00
RJ	Reggie Jackson	40.00
WM	Willie Mays	120.00
PW	Pee Wee Reese	
AR	Alex Rodriguez	75.00
GS	Gary Sheffield	25.00
SS	Sammy Sosa	75.00

Legendary Lumber Auto.

		NM/M
Common Player:		25.00
Inserted 1:288		
LA	Luis Aparicio	25.00
EB	Ernie Banks	65.00
RC	Roger Clemens/227	100.00
KG	Ken Griffey Jr.	80.00
TG	Tony Gwynn	60.00
RJ	Reggie Jackson/211	65.00
EM	Eddie Murray	40.00
AR	Alex Rodriguez	100.00
SS	Sammy Sosa/66	240.00

Legendary Cuts

		NM/M
Most not priced due to scarcity		
C-TC	Ty Cobb (3)	3,150
C-WJ	Walter Johnson (3)	
C-CM	Christy Mathewson	
C-BRu	Babe Ruth (7)	6,000
C-HW	Honus Wagner	

Reflections

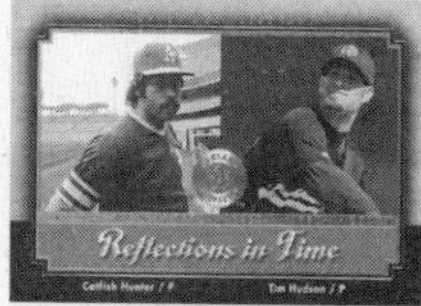

		NM/M
Complete Set (10):		25.00
Common Card:		1.00
Inserted 1:18		
R1	Bernie Williams, Mickey Mantle	6.00
R2	Pedro Martinez, Cy Young	2.00
R3	Barry Bonds, Willie Mays	5.00
R4	Scott Rolen, Mike Schmidt	3.00
R5	Mark McGwire, Stan Musial	4.00
R6	Ken Griffey Jr., Frank Robinson	3.00
R7	Sammy Sosa, Andre Dawson	3.00
R8	Kevin Brown, Don Drysdale	1.50
R9	Jason Giambi, Reggie Jackson	1.50
R10	Tim Hudson, Jim "Catfish" Hunter	1.00

2001 UPPER DECK LEGENDS OF NEW YORK

		NM/M
Complete Set (200):		40.00
Common Player:		.20
Pack (5):		2.50
Box (24):		50.00
1	Billy Herman	.20

LEGENDS OF NEW YORK
1952
DEM BUMS
GIL HODGES POWERS DODGERS TO PENNANT

2 Carl Erskine .20
3 Burleigh Grimes .20
4 Don Newcombe .20
5 Gil Hodges .75
6 Pee Wee Reese .75
7 Jackie Robinson 2.00
8 Duke Snider 1.00
9 Jim Gilliam .20
10 Roy Campanella 1.50
11 Carl Furillo .20
12 Casey Stengel .75
13 Casey Stengel .40
14 Billy Herman .20
15 Jackie Robinson 1.00
16 Jackie Robinson 1.00
17 Gil Hodges .40
18 Carl Furillo .20
19 Roy Campanella .50
20 Don Newcombe .40
21 Duke Snider .75
22 Casey Stengel .40
23 Burleigh Grimes .20
24 Pee Wee Reese .50
25 Jackie Robinson 1.00
26 Jackie Robinson 1.00
27 Carl Erskine .20
28 Roy Campanella .75
29 Duke Snider .75
30 Rube Marquard .20
31 Ross Youngs .20
32 Bobby Thomson .20
33 Christy Mathewson 1.00
34 Carl Hubbell .20
35 Hoyt Wilhelm .20
36 Johnny Mize .40
37 John McGraw .20
38 Monte Irvin .50
39 Travis Jackson .20
40 Mel Ott 1.00
41 Dusty Rhodes .20
42 Leo Durocher .50
43 John McGraw .20
44 Christy Mathewson .50
45 The Polo Grounds .20
46 Travis Jackson .20
47 Mel Ott .50
48 Johnny Mize .20
49 Leo Durocher .30
50 Bobby Thomson .20
51 Monte Irvin .30
52 Bobby Thomson .20
53 Christy Mathewson .50
54 Christy Mathewson .50
55 Christy Mathewson .50
56 John McGraw .20
57 John McGraw .20
58 John McGraw .20
59 Travis Jackson .20
60 Mel Ott .50
61 Mel Ott .50
62 Carl Hubbell .20
63 Bobby Thomson .20
64 Monte Irvin .20
65 Al Weis .20
66 Donn Clendenon .20
67 Ed Kranepool .20
68 Gary Carter .20
69 Tommie Agee .20
70 Jon Matlack .20
71 Ken Boswell .20
72 Len Dykstra .20
73 Nolan Ryan 3.00
74 Ray Sadecki .20
75 Ron Darling .20
76 Ron Swoboda .20
77 Dwight Gooden .20
78 Tom Seaver 1.00
79 Wayne Garrett .20
80 Casey Stengel .50
81 Tom Seaver .50
82 Tommie Agee .20
83 Tom Seaver .50
84 Yogi Berra .50
85 Yogi Berra .50
86 Tom Seaver .50
87 Dwight Gooden .20
88 Gary Carter .20
89 Ron Darling .20
90 Tommie Agee .20
91 Tom Seaver .50
92 Gary Carter .20
93 Len Dykstra .20
94 Babe Ruth 3.00
95 Bill Dickey .50
96 Rich "Goose" Gossage .20
97 Casey Stengel .50
98 Jim "Catfish" Hunter .75
99 Charlie Keller .20
100 Chris Chambliss .20
101 Don Larsen .40
102 Dave Winfield .75
103 Don Mattingly 2.00
104 Elston Howard .20
105 Frankie Crosetti .20
106 Hank Bauer .20
107 Joe DiMaggio 3.00
108 Graig Nettles .20
109 Lefty Gomez .20
110 Phil Rizzuto 1.00
111 Lou Gehrig 2.00
112 Lou Piniella .20
113 Mickey Mantle 3.00
114 Red Rolfe .20
115 Reggie Jackson 1.00
116 Roger Maris 1.50
117 Ray White .20
118 Thurman Munson 1.50
119 Tom Tresh .20
120 Tommy Henrich .20
121 Waite Hoyt .20
122 Willie Randolph .20
123 Whitey Ford .75
124 Yogi Berra 1.00
125 Babe Ruth 1.50
126 Babe Ruth 1.50
127 Lou Gehrig 1.25
128 Babe Ruth 1.50
129 Joe DiMaggio 1.50
130 Joe DiMaggio 1.50
131 Mickey Mantle 1.50
132 Roger Marris .75
133 Mickey Mantle 1.50
134 Reggie Jackson .75
135 Babe Ruth 1.50
136 Babe Ruth 1.50
137 Babe Ruth 1.50
138 Lefty Gomez .20
139 Lou Gehrig 1.25
140 Lou Gehrig 1.25
141 Joe DiMaggio 1.50
142 Joe DiMaggio 1.50
143 Casey Stengel .40
144 Mickey Mantle 1.50
145 Yogi Berra .50
146 Mickey Mantle 1.50
147 Elston Howard .40
148 Whitey Ford .50
149 Reggie Jackson .50
150 Reggie Jackson .50
151 John McGraw, Babe Ruth 1.00
152 Babe Ruth, John McGraw 1.00
153 Lou Gehrig, Mel Ott .75
154 Joe DiMaggio, Mel Ott 1.00
155 Joe DiMaggio, Billy Herman 1.00
156 Joe DiMaggio, Jackie Robinson 1.50
157 Mickey Mantle, Bobby Thomson 1.00
158 Yogi Berra, Pee Wee Reese .75
159 Roy Campanella, Mickey Mantle 1.00
160 Don Larsen, Duke Snider .50
161 Christy Mathewson .75
162 Christy Mathewson .50
163 Rube Marquard .20
164 Christy Mathewson .50
165 John McGraw .20
166 Burleigh Grimes .20
167 Babe Ruth 1.50
168 Burleigh Grimes .20
169 Babe Ruth 1.50
170 John McGraw .40
171 Lou Gehrig 1.25
172 Babe Ruth 1.50
173 Babe Ruth 1.50
174 Carl Hubbell .20
175 Joe DiMaggio 1.50
176 Lou Gehrig 1.25
177 Leo Durocher .40
178 Mel Ott .50
179 Joe DiMaggio 1.50
180 Jackie Robinson 1.00
181 Babe Ruth 1.50
182 Bobby Thomson .20
183 Joe DiMaggio 1.50
184 Mickey Mantle 1.50
185 Monte Irvin .20
186 Roy Campanella .50
187 Duke Snider .50
188 Dusty Rhodes .20
189 Yogi Berra .50
190 Mickey Mantle 1.50
191 Mickey Mantle 1.50
192 Casey Stengel .40
193 Tom Seaver .50
194 Mickey Mantle 1.50
195 Tommie Agee .20
196 Tom Seaver .50
197 Chris Chambliss .20
198 Reggie Jackson .50
199 Reggie Jackson .50
200 Gary Carter .20

Dodgers Game Jersey

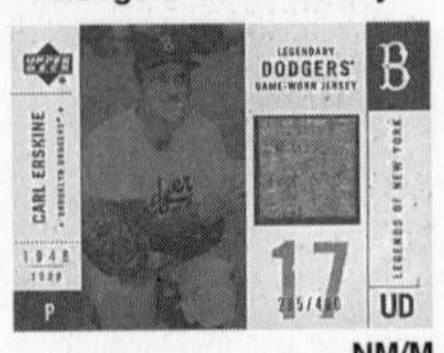

NM/M
Common Player: 5.00
Gold Edition of 400: 1.25X
HB Hank Behrman 5.00
CD Chuck Dressen 5.00
CE Carl Erskine 10.00
SJ Spider Jurgenson 5.00
JR Jackie Robinson/126 120.00

Giants Game Jersey

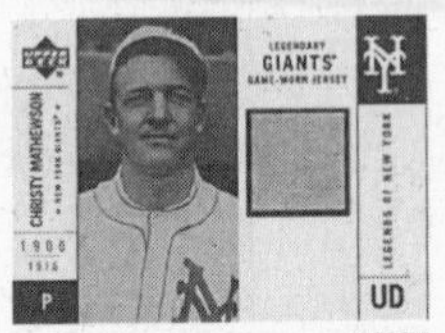

NM/M
Complete Set (1):
CM Christy Mathewson/63 350.00

Mets Game Jersey

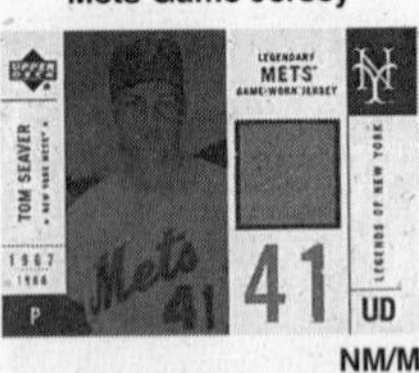

NM/M
Common Player: 5.00
Gold Edition of 400: 1.25X
RD Ron Darling 5.00
JM Jon Matlack 5.00
RS Ray Sadecki 5.00
TS Tom Seaver 15.00
CS Casey Stengel 8.00
JT Joe Torre 5.00

Signed Game Jersey

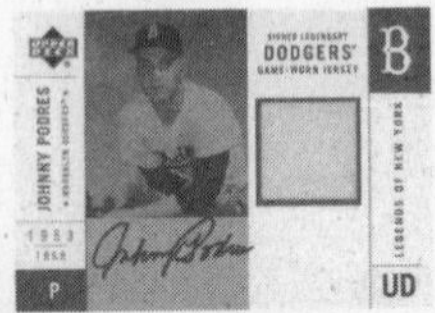

NM/M
Common Autograph: 15.00
DODGERS
CE Carl Erskine 50.00
JG Jim Gilliam/49
JP Johnny Podres/193 50.00
METS
GF George Foster/196 30.00
NR Nolan Ryan/47 200.00
TS Tom Seaver/60
CS Craig Swan 30.00
YANKEES
YG Yogi Berra/73 125.00
BD Bucky Dent 30.00
RG Rich Gossage/145 40.00
RG Ron Guidry 50.00
RJ Reggie Jackson/47
TJ Tommy John 30.00
DL Don Larsen 60.00
HL Hector Lopez/195 15.00
SL Sparky Lyle 30.00
DM Don Mattingly/72 125.00
PN Phil Niekro/195 40.00
GN Graig Nettles 30.00
JP Joe Pepitone 30.00
WR Willie Randolph 30.00
DR Dave Righetti

Yankees Game Jersey

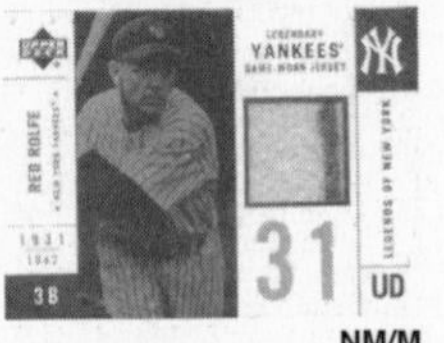

NM/M
Common Player: 5.00
Gold Edition of 400: 1.25X
HB Hank Bauer 8.00
FC Frank Crosetti 10.00
JD Joe DiMaggio/63
TH Tommy Henrich 10.00
EH Elston Howard 10.00
CH Jim "Catfish" Hunter 10.00
DM Duke Maas 5.00
MM Mickey Mantle/63 250.00
RM Roger Maris/63
LM Lindy McDaniel 5.00
TM Thurman Munson 30.00
GN Graig Nettles 10.00
PN Phil Niekro 10.00
JP Joe Pepitone 5.00
WR Willie Randolph 8.00
RR Red Rolfe 5.00
BT Bob Turley 8.00
DW Dave Winfield 15.00

Signatures

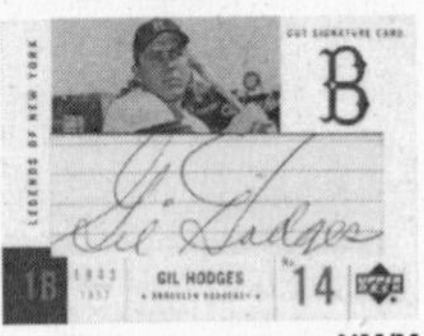

NM/M
Most not priced due to scarcity
LC-JD Joe DiMaggio (38 issued) 1,000
LC-GH Gil Hodges (1 issued)
LC-MO Mel Ott (2 issued)
LC-JR Jackie Robinson (3 issued)
LC-BR Babe Ruth (5 issued)

Ebbets Field G-U Base

NM/M
Complete Set (1):
JR Jackie Robinson (100) 50.00
JR Jackie Robinson (Silver/50) 60.00

JR Jackie Robinson (Gold/25) 75.00

Shea Stadium G-U Base

NM/M
Quantity produced listed
TS Tom Seaver (100) 25.00
TS Tom Seaver (Silver/50) 40.00
TS Tom Seaver (Gold/25) 50.00

Ebbets Field Seat

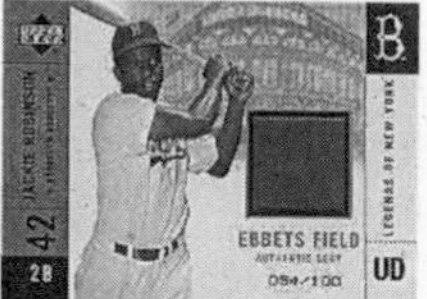

NM/M
Complete Set (1):
JR Jackie Robinson 50.00

Yankee Stadium Seat

Complete Set (1):
MM Mickey Mantle

Combination Signatures

NM/M
Common Card: 75.00
NP Don Newcombe, Johnny Podres 85.00
WM Dave Winfield, Don Mattingly 200.00
RS Nolan Ryan, Tom Seaver 400.00
LB Don Larsen, Yogi Berra 150.00
GJ Ron Guidry, Tommy John 60.00
CN Chris Chambliss, Graig Nettles 60.00
RD Willie Randolph, Bucky Dent 60.00
RW Mickey Rivers, Roy White 60.00
WJ Dave Winfield, Reggie Jackson 150.00

Bat Cards

NM/M
Common Player: 5.00
Inserted 1:24
DODGERS
JG Jim Gilliam 10.00
BH Billy Herman 8.00
DN Don Newcombe/67 40.00
GIANTS
BTh Bobby Thomson 25.00
METS
KB Ken Boswell 5.00
GC Gary Carter 15.00
DC Donn Clendenon/60
LD Len Dykstra 5.00
WG Wayne Garrett 8.00
EK Ed Kranepool 10.00
JM J.C. Martin 8.00
NR Nolan Ryan 40.00
TS Tom Seaver 20.00
RSw Ron Swoboda 8.00
AW Al Weis 5.00
YANKEES
HB Hank Bauer 10.00
YB Yogi Berra 15.00
CC Chris Chambliss/130 15.00
BD Bill Dickey 15.00
JD Joe DiMaggio/43
TH Tommy Henrich 8.00
EH Elston Howard 10.00
RJ Reggie Jackson 15.00
CK Charlie Keller 8.00
MM Mickey Mantle/134 200.00
RM Roger Maris/60 85.00
DM Don Mattingly 30.00
TM Thurman Munson 20.00
LP Lou Piniella 8.00
MR Mickey Rivers 5.00
BR Babe Ruth/107 250.00
JT Joe Torre
TT Tom Tresh 10.00
RW Roy White
DW Dave Winfield 10.00

Bat Autographs

NM/M
Common Autograph:
DODGERS
JG Jim Gilliam
DN Don Newcombe 30.00
METS
GC Gary Carter 40.00
DC Donn Clendenon 30.00
NR Nolan Ryan/129 200.00
TS Tom Seaver/89 100.00
RS Ron Swoboda
YANKEES
YB Yogi Berra 75.00
CC Chris Chambliss 30.00
RJ Reggie Jackson/123 75.00
DM Don Mattingly 100.00
MR Mickey Rivers 25.00
RW Roy White 25.00
DW Dave Winfield/167

United We Stand

NM/M
Complete Set (15): 10.00
Common Card: 1.00
Inserted 1:12

2001 UPPER DECK MVP

NM/M
Complete Set (330): 35.00
Common Player: .10
Pack (8): 1.50
Box (24): 30.00
1 Mo Vaughn .10
2 Troy Percival .10
3 Adam Kennedy .10
4 Darin Erstad .25
5 Tim Salmon .10
6 Bengie Molina .10
7 Troy Glaus .40
8 Garret Anderson .25

9 Ismael Valdes .10
10 Glenallen Hill .10
11 Tim Hudson .25
12 Eric Chavez .20
13 Johnny Damon .20
14 Barry Zito .40
15 Jason Giambi .40
16 Terrence Long .10
17 Jason Hart .10
18 Jose Ortiz .10
19 Miguel Tejada .25
20 Jason Isringhausen .10
21 Adam Piatt .10
22 Jeremy Giambi .10
23 Tony Batista .10
24 Darrin Fletcher .10
25 Mike Sirotka .10
26 Carlos Delgado .40
27 Billy Koch .10
28 Shannon Stewart .10
29 Raul Mondesi .15
30 Brad Fullmer .10
31 Jose Cruz Jr. .10
32 Kelvim Escobar .10
33 Greg Vaughn .10
34 Aubrey Huff .10
35 Albie Lopez .10
36 Gerald Williams .10
37 Ben Grieve .10
38 John Flaherty .10
39 Fred McGriff .15
40 Ryan Rupe .10
41 Travis Harper .10
42 Steve Cox .10
43 Roberto Alomar .40
44 Jim Thome .50
45 Russell Branyan .10
46 Bartolo Colon .20
47 Omar Vizquel .15
48 Travis Fryman .15
49 Kenny Lofton .15
50 Chuck Finley .10
51 Ellis Burks .10
52 Eddie Taubensee .10
53 Juan Gonzalez .40
54 Edgar Martinez .20
55 Aaron Sele .10
56 John Olerud .20
57 Jay Buhner .10
58 Mike Cameron .10
59 John Halama .10
60 *Ichiro Suzuki* 8.00
61 David Bell .10
62 Freddy Garcia .10
63 Carlos Guillen .10
64 Bret Boone .20
65 Al Martin .10
66 Cal Ripken Jr. 1.50
67 Delino DeShields .10
68 Chris Richard .10
69 *Sean Douglass* .25
70 Melvin Mora .10
71 Luis Matos .10
72 Sidney Ponson .10
73 Mike Bordick .10
74 Brady Anderson .10
75 David Segui .10
76 Jeff Conine .10
77 Alex Rodriguez 1.25
78 Gabe Kapler .10
79 Ivan Rodriguez .40
80 Rick Helling .10
81 Kenny Rogers .10
82 Andres Galarraga .15
83 Rusty Greer .10
84 Justin Thompson .10
85 Ken Caminiti .10
86 Rafael Palmeiro .40
87 Ruben Mateo .10
88 *Travis Hafner* .50
89 Manny Ramirez .40
90 Pedro Martinez .50
91 Carl Everett .10
92 Dante Bichette .10
93 Derek Lowe .10
94 Jason Varitek .10
95 Nomar Garciaparra 1.25
96 David Cone .10
97 Tomokazu Ohka .10
98 Troy O'Leary .10
99 Trot Nixon .10
100 Jermaine Dye .10
101 Joe Randa .10
102 Jeff Suppan .10
103 Roberto Hernandez .10
104 Mike Sweeney .10
105 Mac Suzuki .10
106 Carlos Febles .10
107 Jose Rosado .10
108 Mark Quinn .10
109 Carlos Beltran .20
110 Dean Palmer .10
111 Mitch Meluskey .10
112 Bobby Higginson .10
113 Brandon Inge .10
114 Tony Clark .10
115 Brian Moehler .10
116 Juan Encarnacion .10
117 Damion Easley .10
118 Roger Cedeno .10
119 Jeff Weaver .10
120 Matt Lawton .10
121 Jay Canizaro .10
122 Eric Milton .10
123 Corey Koskie .10
124 Mark Redman .10
125 Jacque Jones .10
126 Brad Radke .10
127 Cristian Guzman .10
128 Joe Mays .10
129 Denny Hocking .10
130 Frank Thomas .40
131 David Wells .10
132 Ray Durham .10
133 Paul Konerko .10
134 Joe Crede .10
135 Jim Parque .10
136 Carlos Lee .10
137 Magglio Ordonez .25
138 Sandy Alomar Jr. .10
139 Chris Singleton .10
140 Jose Valentin .10
141 Roger Clemens 1.00
142 Derek Jeter 1.50
143 Orlando Hernandez .15
144 Tino Martinez .10
145 Bernie Williams .40
146 Jorge Posada .25
147 Mariano Rivera .20
148 David Justice .20
149 Paul O'Neill .15
150 Mike Mussina .25
151 *Christian Parker* .10
152 Andy Pettitte .25
153 Alfonso Soriano .50
154 Jeff Bagwell .40
155 *Morgan Ensberg* .50
156 Daryle Ward .10
157 Craig Biggio .20
158 Richard Hidalgo .10
159 Shane Reynolds .10
160 Scott Elarton .10
161 Julio Lugo .10
162 Moises Alou .20
163 Lance Berkman .20
164 Chipper Jones .75
165 Greg Maddux 1.00
166 Javy Lopez .15
167 Andruw Jones .40
168 Rafael Furcal .25
169 Brian Jordan .10
170 Wes Helms .10
171 Tom Glavine .25
172 B.J. Surhoff .10
173 John Smoltz .10
174 Quilvio Veras .10
175 Rico Brogna .10
176 Jeromy Burnitz .10
177 Jeff D'Amico .10
178 Geoff Jenkins .20
179 Henry Blanco .10
180 Mark Loretta .10
181 Richie Sexson .25
182 Jimmy Haynes .10
183 Jeffrey Hammonds .10
184 Ron Belliard .10
185 Tyler Houston .10
186 Mark McGwire 1.00

187 Rick Ankiel .10
188 Darryl Kile .10
189 Jim Edmonds .25
190 Mike Matheny .10
191 Edgar Renteria .10
192 Ray Lankford .10
193 Garrett Stephenson .10
194 J.D. Drew .20
195 Fernando Vina .10
196 Dustin Hermanson .10
197 Sammy Sosa 1.00
198 Corey Patterson .25
199 Jon Lieber .10
200 Kerry Wood .40
201 Todd Hundley .10
202 Kevin Tapani .10
203 Rondell White .10
204 Eric Young .10
205 Matt Stairs .10
206 Bill Mueller .10
207 Randy Johnson .50
208 Mark Grace .25
209 Jay Bell .10
210 Curt Schilling .25
211 Erubiel Durazo .10
212 Luis Gonzalez .20
213 Steve Finley .10
214 Matt Williams .20
215 Reggie Sanders .10
216 Tony Womack .10
217 Gary Sheffield .25
218 Kevin Brown .15
219 Adrian Beltre .20
220 Shawn Green .20
221 Darren Dreifort .10
222 Chan Ho Park .10
223 Eric Karros .15
224 Alex Cora .10
225 Mark Grudzielanek .10
226 Andy Ashby .10
227 Vladimir Guerrero .75
228 Tony Armas Jr. .10
229 Fernando Tatis .10
230 Jose Vidro .10
231 Javier Vazquez .10
232 Lee Stevens .10
233 Milton Bradley .10
234 Carl Pavano .10
235 Peter Bergeron .10
236 Wilton Guerrero .10
237 Ugueth Urbina .10
238 Barry Bonds 1.50
239 Livan Hernandez .10
240 Jeff Kent .15
241 Pedro Feliz .10
242 Bobby Estalella .10
243 J.T. Snow .10
244 Shawn Estes .10
245 Robb Nen .10
246 Rich Aurilia .10
247 Russ Ortiz .10
248 Preston Wilson .10
249 Brad Penny .10
250 Cliff Floyd .10
251 A.J. Burnett .10
252 Mike Lowell .10
253 Luis Castillo .10
254 Ryan Dempster .10
255 Derrek Lee .10
256 Charles Johnson .10
257 Pablo Ozuna .10
258 Antonio Alfonseca .10
259 Mike Piazza 1.00
260 Robin Ventura .10
261 Al Leiter .15
262 Timoniel Perez .10
263 Edgardo Alfonzo .10
264 Jay Payton .10
265 *Tsuyoshi Shinjo* .75
266 Todd Zeile .10
267 Armando Benitez .10
268 Glendon Rusch .10
269 Rey Ordonez .10
270 Kevin Appier .10
271 Tony Gwynn .50
272 Phil Nevin .10
273 Mark Kotsay .10
274 Ryan Klesko .20
275 Adam Eaton .10
276 Mike Darr .10
277 Damian Jackson .10
278 Woody Williams .10
279 Chris Gomez .10
280 Trevor Hoffman .10
281 Xavier Nady .15
282 Scott Rolen .40
283 Bruce Chen .10
284 Pat Burrell .30
285 Mike Lieberthal .10
286 *Brandon Duckworth* .40
287 Travis Lee .10
288 Bobby Abreu .10
289 Jimmy Rollins .10
290 Robert Person .10
291 Randy Wolf .10
292 Jason Kendall .10
293 Derek Bell .10
294 Brian Giles .25
295 Kris Benson .10
296 John Vander Wal .10
297 Todd Ritchie .10
298 Warren Morris .10
299 Kevin Young .10
300 Francisco Cordova .10
301 Aramis Ramirez .10
302 Ken Griffey Jr. 1.00
303 Pete Harnisch .10
304 Aaron Boone .10
305 Sean Casey .20
306 *Jackson Melian* .40
307 Rob Bell .10
308 Barry Larkin .25
309 Dmitri Young .10
310 Danny Graves .10
311 Pokey Reese .10
312 Leo Estrella .10
313 Todd Helton .40
314 Mike Hampton .15
315 Juan Pierre .10
316 Brent Mayne .10
317 Larry Walker .25
318 Denny Neagle .10
319 Jeff Cirillo .10
320 Pedro Astacio .10
321 Todd Hollandsworth .10
322 Neifi Perez .10
323 Ron Gant .10
324 Todd Walker .10
325 Alex Rodriguez CL .50
326 Ken Griffey Jr. CL .50
327 Mark McGwire CL .50
328 Pedro Martinez CL .30
329 Derek Jeter CL .75
330 Mike Piazza CL .40

Drawing Power

NM/M

Complete Set (10): 10.00
Common Player: .75
Inserted 1:12

DP1 Mark McGwire 2.00
DP2 Vladimir Guerrero 1.00
DP3 Manny Ramirez .75
DP4 Frank Thomas .75
DP5 Ken Griffey Jr. 1.50
DP6 Alex Rodriguez 2.50
DP7 Mike Piazza 1.50
DP8 Derek Jeter 3.00
DP9 Sammy Sosa 2.00
DP10 Todd Helton .75

Authentic Griffey

NM/M

Inserted 1:288

AGS Ken Griffey Jr. Auto. 125.00
AGJ Ken Griffey Jr. jersey 15.00
AGC Ken Griffey Jr. Cap 40.00
AGB Ken Griffey Jr. bat 15.00
AGU Ken Griffey Jr. uniform 15.00
AGGS Ken Griffey Gold Auto/30 250.00
AGGJ Ken Griffey Jr. Gold jsy/30 75.00
AGGC Ken Griffey Gold cap/30 75.00
AGGB Ken Griffey Gold bat/30 75.00

CGR Ken Griffey Jr., Alex Rodriguez/100 35.00
CGS Ken Griffey Jr., Sammy Sosa/100 35.00
CGT Ken Griffey Jr., Frank Thomas/100 25.00

Mantle Pinstripes Exclusive

NM/M

Complete Set (56): 75.00
Common Mantle: 2.00
One pack/box

Mantle Pinstripes Excl. Memorabilia

NM/M

Print Runs listed

MMCJ3 Mickey Mantle, Ken Griffey Jr./50 200.00
MMJ3 Mickey Mantle jsy/100 125.00

Souvenirs Two-Player Bat Combo

NM/M

Common Combo: 10.00
Inserted 1:144

TS Frank Thomas, Sammy Sosa 25.00
RR Alex Rodriguez, Ivan Rodriguez 25.00
TG Jim Thome, Ken Griffey Jr. 25.00
GS Ken Griffey Jr., Sammy Sosa 30.00
WA Kerry Wood, Rick Ankiel 10.00
3K Tony Gwynn, Cal Ripken Jr. 40.00
DV Carlos Delgado, Jose Vidro 10.00
JJ Andruw Jones, Chipper Jones 20.00
HR Jose Canseco, Ken Griffey Jr. 20.00
JF Chipper Jones, Rafael Furcal 15.00
OW Paul O'Neill, Bernie Williams 10.00
TO Frank Thomas, Magglio Ordonez 15.00
RM Alex Rodriguez, Edgar Martinez 20.00
RP Ivan Rodriguez, Rafael Palmeiro 15.00

Souvenirs Three Player Bat Combo

No pricing due to scarcity
Production 25 sets

Souvenirs Two-Player Bat Autograph

NM/M

Production 25 sets

RG Alex Rodriguez, Ken Griffey Jr. 250.00
SG Sammy Sosa, Ken Griffey Jr. 300.00
RR Alex Rodriguez, Ivan Rodriguez 200.00
JG Chipper Jones, Troy Glaus 125.00
TS Frank Thomas, Sammy Sosa 275.00
GD Jason Giambi, Carlos Delgado 75.00
3K Cal Ripken Jr., Tony Gwynn 300.00
TG Frank Thomas, Jason Giambi 85.00
HH Todd Helton, Mike Hampton 60.00

Souvenirs Batting Gloves

NM/M

Common Player: 8.00
Inserted 1:96 H 20.00

BB Barry Bonds 40.00
TrG Troy Glaus 10.00
JG Juan Gonzalez 10.00
KG Ken Griffey Jr. 20.00
ToG Tony Gwynn/200 30.00
CJ Chipper Jones 15.00
JL Javy Lopez 8.00
GM Greg Maddux/95 60.00
EM Edgar Martinez 8.00
FM Fred McGriff 8.00
RP Rafael Palmeiro 15.00
CR Cal Ripken Jr. 50.00
AR Alex Rodriguez 20.00
IR Ivan Rodriguez 10.00
SS Sammy Sosa 20.00
MT Miguel Tejada 8.00
FT Frank Thomas 10.00
MV Mo Vaughn 8.00

Souvenirs Batting Gloves Autographs

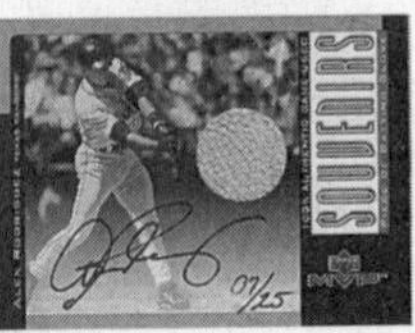

NM/M

Production 25 sets

TrG Troy Glaus
KG Ken Griffey Jr. 150.00
ToG Tony Gwynn 80.00
CJ Chipper Jones
CR Cal Ripken Jr. 250.00
AR Alex Rodriguez 150.00
IR Ivan Rodriguez 80.00
SS Sammy Sosa 250.00
FT Frank Thomas 80.00

Super Tools

		NM/M
Complete Set (20):		20.00
Common Player:		.50
Inserted 1:6		
ST1	Ken Griffey Jr.	1.50
ST2	Carlos Delgado	.75
ST3	Alex Rodriguez	2.50
ST4	Troy Glaus	.75
ST5	Jeff Bagwell	.75
ST6	Ichiro Suzuki	3.00
ST7	Derek Jeter	3.00
ST8	Jim Edmonds	.50
ST9	Vladimir Guerrero	1.00
ST10	Jason Giambi	.75
ST11	Todd Helton	.75
ST12	Cal Ripken Jr.	3.00
ST13	Barry Bonds	3.00
ST14	Nomar Garciaparra	2.00
ST15	Randy Johnson	1.00
ST16	Jermaine Dye	.50
ST17	Andruw Jones	.75
ST18	Ivan Rodriguez	.75
ST19	Sammy Sosa	2.00
ST20	Pedro Martinez	1.00

2001 UPPER DECK OVATION

		NM/M
Complete Set (90):		150.00
Common Player:		.20
Common WP (61-90):		3.00
WP Production 2,000		
Pack (5):		5.00
Box (20):		80.00
1	Troy Glaus	.50
2	Darin Erstad	.40
3	Jason Giambi	.50
4	Tim Hudson	.40
5	Eric Chavez	.30
6	Carlos Delgado	.50
7	David Wells	.20
8	Greg Vaughn	.20
9	Omar Vizquel	.20
10	Jim Thome	.50
11	Roberto Alomar	.40
12	John Olerud	.30
13	Edgar Martinez	.20
14	Cal Ripken Jr.	2.00
15	Alex Rodriguez	1.50
16	Ivan Rodriguez	.50
17	Manny Ramirez	.50
18	Nomar Garciaparra	1.50
19	Pedro Martinez	.75
20	Jermaine Dye	.20
21	Juan Gonzalez	.50
22	Matt Lawton	.20
23	Frank Thomas	.50
24	Magglio Ordonez	.40
25	Bernie Williams	.40
26	Derek Jeter	2.00
27	Roger Clemens	1.50
28	Jeff Bagwell	.50
29	Richard Hidalgo	.20
30	Chipper Jones	1.00
31	Greg Maddux	1.00
32	Andruw Jones	.50
33	Jeromy Burnitz	.20
34	Mark McGwire	1.50
35	Jim Edmonds	.40
36	Sammy Sosa	1.50
37	Kerry Wood	.50
38	Randy Johnson	.75
39	Steve Finley	.20
40	Gary Sheffield	.40
41	Kevin Brown	.40
42	Shawn Green	.40
43	Vladimir Guerrero	.75
44	Jose Vidro	.20
45	Barry Bonds	2.00
46	Jeff Kent	.30
47	Preston Wilson	.20
48	Luis Castillo	.20
49	Mike Piazza	1.00
50	Edgardo Alfonzo	.20
51	Tony Gwynn	.75
52	Ryan Klesko	.30
53	Scott Rolen	.50
54	Bob Abreu	.30
55	Jason Kendall	.20
56	Brian Giles	.30
57	Ken Griffey Jr.	1.00
58	Barry Larkin	.40
59	Todd Helton	.50
60	Mike Hampton	.20
61	Corey Patterson	3.00
62	Timoniel Perez	3.00
63	Toby Hall	3.00
64	Brandon Inge	3.00
65	Joe Crede	3.00
66	Xavier Nady	3.00
67	*Adam Pettyjohn*	3.00
68	Keith Ginter	3.00
69	Brian Cole	3.00
70	*Tyler Walker*	3.00
71	*Juan Uribe*	5.00
72	Alex Hernandez	3.00
73	Leo Estrella	3.00
74	Joey Nation	3.00
75	Aubrey Huff	3.00
76	*Ichiro Suzuki*	75.00
77	Jay Spurgeon	3.00
78	Sun-Woo Kim	3.00
79	Pedro Feliz	3.00
80	Pablo Ozuna	3.00
81	Hiram Bocachica	3.00
82	Brad Wilkerson	3.00
83	Rocky Biddle	3.00
84	Aaron McNeal	3.00
85	Adam Bernero	3.00
86	Danys Baez	3.00
87	Dee Brown	3.00
88	Jimmy Rollins	3.00
89	Jason Hart	3.00
90	Ross Gload	3.00

A Piece of History

		NM/M
Common Player:		5.00
Inserted 1:40		
RA	Rick Ankiel	5.00
JB	Johnny Bench	15.00
BB	Barry Bonds	30.00
KB	Kevin Brown	5.00
JC	Jose Canseco	8.00
RC	Roger Clemens	15.00
DC	David Cone	5.00
CD	Carlos Delgado	8.00
JD	Joe DiMaggio	100.00
DD	Don Drysdale SP	25.00
DE	Darin Erstad	5.00
RF	Rollie Fingers SP	8.00
CF	Carlton Fisk	10.00
RF	Rafael Furcal	5.00
TrG	Troy Glaus	8.00
TG	Tom Glavine	8.00
SG	Shawn Green	5.00
KG	Ken Griffey Jr.	15.00
KGs	Ken Griffey Sr.	5.00
MH	Mike Hampton	5.00
RJ	Randy Johnson	10.00
AJ	Andruw Jones	8.00
CJ	Chipper Jones	10.00
GM	Greg Maddux	15.00
MM	Mickey Mantle	125.00
JP	Jim Palmer	10.00
CR	Cal Ripken Jr.	30.00
BR	Brooks Robinson	15.00
AR	Alex Rodriguez	15.00
IR	Ivan Rodriguez	8.00
NR	Nolan Ryan/SP	120.00
TS	Tom Seaver	10.00
GS	Gary Sheffield	5.00
OS	Ozzie Smith SP	20.00
SS	Sammy Sosa	15.00
FT	Frank Thomas	8.00
BW	Bernie Williams	8.00
MW	Matt Williams	5.00
EW	Early Wynn	5.00

A Piece of History Autograph

VALUES UNDETERMINED

BB	Barry Bonds/25
CD	Carlos Delgado/25
KG	Ken Griffey Jr/30
CJ	Chipper Jones/10
AR	Alex Rodriguez/3
IR	Ivan Rodriguez/7
FT	Frank Thomas/35

Curtain Calls

		NM/M
Complete Set (10):		10.00
Common Player:		.50
Inserted 1:7		
1	Sammy Sosa	2.00
2	Darin Erstad	.50
3	Barry Bonds	2.50
4	Todd Helton	.75
5	Mike Piazza	1.50
6	Ken Griffey Jr.	1.50
7	Nomar Garciaparra	2.00
8	Carlos Delgado	.75
9	Jason Giambi	.75
10	Alex Rodriguez	2.00

DiMaggio Pinstripes Exclusive

	NM/M
Complete Set (56):	60.00
Common DiMaggio:	1.50
One pack/box	

DiMaggio Pinstripes Memorabilia

		NM/M
Print Runs listed:		150.00
JDB	Joe DiMaggio bat/100	75.00
JDBC	Joe DiMaggio bat/cut/5	
JDCJ	Joe DiMaggio, Mickey Mantle jsy/50	300.00
JDJ	Joe DiMaggio jsy/100	100.00

Lead Performers

		NM/M
Complete Set (11):		15.00
Common Player:		1.00
Inserted 1:12		
1	Mark McGwire	3.00
2	Derek Jeter	4.00
3	Alex Rodriguez	3.00
4	Frank Thomas	1.00
5	Sammy Sosa	2.50
6	Mike Piazza	2.00
7	Vladimir Guerrero	1.50
8	Pedro Martinez	1.50
9	Carlos Delgado	1.00
10	Ken Griffey Jr.	2.00
11	Jeff Bagwell	1.00

Rookie cards are in *Italic*.

POH Combo Cards

Production 25 sets
VALUES UNDETERMINED

Superstar Theatre

		NM/M
Complete Set (11):		20.00
Common Player:		1.00
Inserted 1:12		
1	Nomar Garciaparra	2.50
2	Ken Griffey Jr.	2.00
3	Frank Thomas	1.00
4	Derek Jeter	4.00
5	Mike Piazza	2.00
6	Sammy Sosa	2.50
7	Barry Bonds	4.00
8	Alex Rodriguez	3.00
9	Todd Helton	1.00
10	Mark McGwire	3.00
11	Jason Giambi	1.00

2001 UPPER DECK PROS & PROSPECTS

		NM/M
Complete Set (141):		
Common Player:		.15
Common (91-135):		4.00
Production 1,250		
Common (136-141):		8.00
Production 500		
Pack (5):		6.00
Box (24):		120.00
1	Troy Glaus	.50
2	Darin Erstad	.25
3	Tim Hudson	.40
4	Jason Giambi	.50
5	Jermaine Dye	.15
6	Barry Zito	.40
7	Carlos Delgado	.50
8	Shannon Stewart	.15
9	Raul Mondesi	.15
10	Greg Vaughn	.15
11	Ben Grieve	.15
12	Roberto Alomar	.40
13	Juan Gonzalez	.50
14	Jim Thome	.50
15	C.C. Sabathia	.15
16	Edgar Martinez	.25

17	Kazuhiro Sasaki	.15
18	Aaron Sele	.15
19	John Olerud	.25
20	Cal Ripken Jr.	2.00
21	Rafael Palmeiro	.50
22	Ivan Rodriguez	.50
23	Alex Rodriguez	1.50
24	Manny Ramirez	.50
25	Pedro Martinez	.75
26	Carl Everett	.15
27	Nomar Garciaparra	1.50
28	Neifi Perez	.15
29	Mike Sweeney	.15
30	Bobby Higginson	.15
31	Tony Clark	.15
32	Doug Mientkiewicz	.15
33	Cristian Guzman	.15
34	Brad Radke	.15
35	Magglio Ordonez	.40
36	Carlos Lee	.15
37	Frank Thomas	.50
38	Roger Clemens	1.50
39	Bernie Williams	.50
40	Derek Jeter	2.00
41	Tino Martinez	.25
42	Wade Miller	.15
43	Jeff Bagwell	.50
44	Lance Berkman	.25
45	Richard Hidalgo	.15
46	Greg Maddux	1.00
47	Andruw Jones	.50
48	Chipper Jones	1.00
49	Rafael Furcal	.25
50	Jeromy Burnitz	.15
51	Geoff Jenkins	.25
52	Ben Sheets	.25
53	Mark McGwire	1.50
54	Jim Edmonds	.40
55	J.D. Drew	.25
56	Fred McGriff	.25
57	Sammy Sosa	1.50
58	Kerry Wood	.50
59	Randy Johnson	.75
60	Luis Gonzalez	.25
61	Curt Schilling	.40
62	Kevin Brown	.25
63	Shawn Green	.25
64	Gary Sheffield	.40
65	Vladimir Guerrero	.75
66	Jose Vidro	.15
67	Barry Bonds	2.00
68	Jeff Kent	.25
69	Rich Aurilia	.15
70	Preston Wilson	.15
71	Charles Johnson	.15
72	Cliff Floyd	.15
73	Mike Piazza	1.00
74	Al Leiter	.25
75	Matt Lawton	.15
76	Tony Gwynn	.75
77	Ryan Klesko	.25
78	Phil Nevin	.15
79	Scott Rolen	.50
80	Pat Burrell	.40
81	Jimmy Rollins	.15
82	Jason Kendall	.25
83	Brian Giles	.25
84	Aramis Ramirez	.15
85	Ken Griffey Jr.	1.00
86	Barry Larkin	.40
87	Sean Casey	.25
88	Larry Walker	.25
89	Todd Helton	.50
90	Mike Hampton	.15
91	*Juan Cruz*	4.00
92	*Brian Lawrence*	4.00
93	*Brandon Lyon*	4.00
94	*Adrian Hernandez*	4.00
95	*Jose Mieses*	4.00
96	Juan Uribe	4.00
97	*Morgan Ensberg*	12.00
98	*Wilson Betemit*	8.00
99	*Ryan Freel*	4.00
100	*Jack Wilson*	8.00
101	*Cesar Crespo*	4.00
102	*Bret Prinz*	4.00
103	*Horacio Ramirez*	8.00
104	*Elpidio Guzman*	4.00
105	*Josh Towers*	4.00
106	*Brandon Duckworth*	4.00
107	*Esix Snead*	4.00
108	*Billy Sylvester*	4.00
109	*Alexis Gomez*	4.00
110	*Johnny Estrada*	8.00
111	*Joe Kennedy*	4.00
112	*Travis Hafner*	10.00
113	*Martin Vargas*	4.00
114	*Jay Gibbons*	10.00
115	*Andres Torres*	4.00
116	*Sean Douglass*	4.00
117	*Juan Diaz*	4.00
118	*Greg Miller*	4.00
119	*Carlos Valderrama*	4.00
120	*William Ortega*	4.00
121	*Josh Fogg*	4.00
122	*Wilken Ruan*	4.00
123	*Kris Keller*	4.00
124	*Erick Almonte*	4.00
125	*Ricardo Rodriguez*	4.00
126	*Grant Balfour*	4.00
127	*Nick Maness*	4.00
128	*Jeremy Owens*	4.00
129	*Doug Nickle*	4.00
130	*Bert Snow*	4.00
131	*Jason Smith*	4.00
132	*Henry Mateo*	4.00
133	*Mike Penney*	4.00
134	*Bud Smith*	4.00
135	*Junior Spivey*	8.00
136	*Ichiro Suzuki*	90.00
137	*Albert Pujols*	150.00
138	*Mark Teixeira*	90.00
139	*Dewon Brazelton*	8.00
140	*Mark Prior*	75.00
141	*Tsuyoshi Shinjo*	8.00

Bats

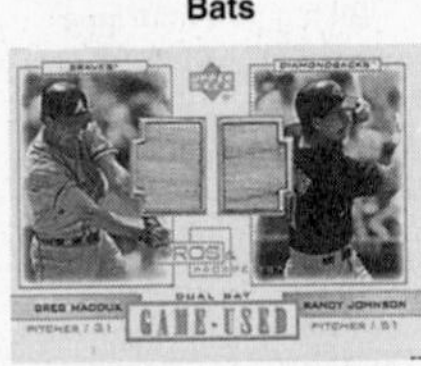

		NM/M
	Common Card:	4.00
	Inserted 1:24	
	Golds:	3-5X
	Production 25 sets	
WI	Bernie Williams, Ichiro Suzuki	35.00
RG	Manny Ramirez, Juan Gonzalez	8.00
RP	Ivan Rodriguez, Mike Piazza	15.00
BT	Jeff Bagwell, Frank Thomas	8.00
GBo	Ken Griffey Jr., Barry Bonds	35.00
SG	Sammy Sosa, Luis Gonzalez	15.00
KA	Jeff Kent, Roberto Alomar	4.00
RF	Alex Rodriguez, Rafael Furcal	15.00
PT	Rafael Palmeiro, Jim Thome	10.00
JP	Chipper Jones, Albert Pujols	40.00
GBu	Shawn Green, Jeromy Burnitz	4.00
JL	Andruw Jones, Kenny Lofton	6.00
MJ	Greg Maddux, Randy Johnson	15.00

Ichiro World Tour

	NM/M
Complete Set (15):	25.00
Common Ichiro:	2.00
Inserted 1:12	

Legends Bats

		NM/M
	Common Card:	15.00
	Inserted 1:216	
	Gold:	3-5X
	Production 25 sets	
RF	Manny Ramirez, Carlton Fisk	15.00
BY	Jeromy Burnitz, Robin Yount	15.00
WJ	Bernie Williams, Reggie Jackson	15.00
RG	Cal Ripken Jr., Tony Gwynn	50.00

Specialty Jersey

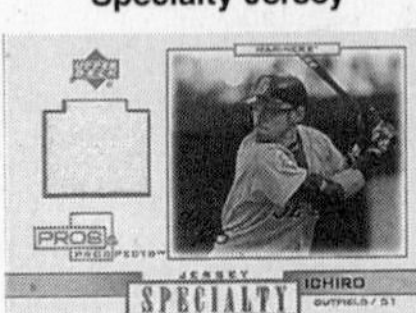

		NM/M
	Common Player:	4.00
	Inserted 1:24	
	Golds:	3-5X
	Production 25 sets	
RA	Roberto Alomar	6.00
BB	Barry Bonds	25.00
JE	Jim Edmonds	4.00
JG	Juan Gonzalez	6.00
SG	Shawn Green	4.00
TG	Tony Gwynn	10.00
RJ	Randy Johnson	10.00
CR	Cal Ripken Jr.	30.00
AR	Alex Rodriguez	15.00
SR	Scott Rolen	8.00
SS	Sammy Sosa	15.00
I	Ichiro	60.00
JT	Jim Thome	8.00
LW	Larry Walker	4.00

Then & Now Jersey

		NM/M
	Common Player:	4.00
	Inserted 1:24	
	Golds:	3-5X
	Production 25 sets	
RA	Rick Ankiel	4.00
BB	Barry Bonds	30.00
KB	Kevin Brown	6.00
RC	Roger Clemens	20.00
JE	Jim Edmonds	6.00
FG	Freddy Garcia	4.00
JGi	Jason Giambi	8.00
JGo	Juan Gonzalez	8.00
KG	Ken Griffey Jr.	20.00
RJ	Randy Johnson	10.00
GM	Greg Maddux	20.00
PM	Pedro Martinez	10.00
XN	Xavier Nady	4.00
PN	Phil Nevin	4.00
MP	Mike Piazza	15.00
MR	Manny Ramirez	8.00
AR	Alex Rodriguez	15.00
CS	Curt Schilling	6.00
GS	Gary Sheffield	6.00
RV	Robin Ventura	4.00

2001 UPPER DECK PROSPECT PREMIERES

		NM/M
	Complete Set (90):	25.00
	Common Player:	.25
	Common Auto. SP (91-102):	10.00
	Auto. Production 1,000	
	Pack (4):	5.00
	Box (18):	80.00
1	*Jeff Mathis*	1.00
2	*Jake Woods*	.25
3	*Dallas McPherson*	6.00
4	*Steven Shell*	.25
5	*Ryan Budde*	.25
6	*Kirk Saarloos*	.40
7	*Ryan Stegall*	.25
8	*Bobby Crosby*	4.00
9	*J.T. Stotts*	.25

10	*Neal Cotts*	.75
11	*Jeremy Bonderman*	2.50
12	*Brandon League*	.40
13	*Tyrell Godwin*	.25
14	*Gabe Gross*	1.50
15	*Chris Neylan*	.25
16	*Michael Rouse*	.25
17	*MaCay McBride*	.25
18	*Josh Burrus*	.25
19	*Adam Stern*	.25
20	*Richard Lewis*	.40
21	*Cole Barthel*	.50
22	*Mike Jones*	.25
23	*J.J. Hardy*	1.50
24	*Brad Nelson*	1.00
25	*Justin Pope*	.25
26	*Dan Haren*	.75
27	*Andy Sisco*	.50
28	*Ryan Theriot*	.25
29	*Ricky Nolasco*	.25
30	*Jon Switzer*	.25
31	*Justin Wechsler*	.25
32	*Mike Gosling*	.25
33	*Scott Hairston*	.75
34	*Brian Pilkington*	.25
35	*Kole Strayhorn*	.25
36	*David Taylor*	.25
37	*Donald Levinski*	.25
38	*Mike Hinckley*	.50
39	*Nick Long*	.25
40	*Brad Hennessey*	.25
41	*Noah Lowry*	2.00
42	*Josh Cram*	.25
43	*Jesse Foppert*	.50
44	*Julian Benavidez*	.25
45	*Daniel Denham*	.25
46	*Travis Foley*	.40
47	*Mike Conroy*	.25
48	*Jake Dittler*	.25
49	*Rene Rivera*	.25
50	*John Cole*	.25
51	*Lazaro Abreu*	.25
52	*David Wright*	15.00
53	*Aaron Heilman*	.40
54	*Lenny DiNardo*	.25
55	*Alhaji Turay*	.40
56	*Chris Smith*	.25
57	*Rommie Lewis*	.25
58	*Bryan Bass*	.25
59	*David Crouthers*	.25
60	*Josh Barfield*	1.50
61	*Jake Peavy*	3.00
62	*Ryan Howard*	6.00
63	*Gavin Floyd*	1.50
64	*Mike Floyd*	.25
65	*Stefan Bailie*	.25
66	*Jon DeVries*	.25
67	*Steve Kelly*	.25
68	*Alan Moye*	.25
69	*Justin Gillman*	.25
70	*Jayson Nix*	1.00
71	*John Draper*	.25
72	*Kenny Baugh*	.25
73	*Michael Woods*	.25
74	*Preston Larrison*	.25
75	*Matt Coenen*	.25
76	*Scott Tyler*	.50
77	*Jose Morales*	.25
78	*Corwin Malone*	.50
79	*Dennis Ulacia*	.40
80	*Andy Gonzalez*	.25
81	*Kris Honel*	1.00
82	*Wyatt Allen*	.25
83	*Ryan Wing*	.25
84	*Sean Henn*	.40
85	*John-Ford Griffin*	.50
86	*Bronson Sardinha*	.50
87	*Jon Skaggs*	.25
88	*Shelley Duncan*	.25

89 *Jason Arnold* .75
90 *Aaron Rifkin* .50
91 *Colt Griffin* 15.00
92 *J.D. Martin* 10.00
93 *Justin Wayne* 20.00
94 *John VanBenschotten* 20.00
95 *Chris Burke* 40.00
96 *Casey Kotchman* 60.00
97 *Michael Garciaparra* 15.00
98 *Jake Gautreau* 10.00
99 *Jerome Williams* 20.00
100 *Greg Nash* 10.00
101 *Joe Borchard* 15.00
102 *Mark Prior* 120.00

HOB Bat Autograph

Production 25 sets
VALUES UNDETERMINED

MJ Grandslam Bat

	NM/M
Common MJ:	25.00
MJ1 Michael Jordan	25.00
MJ2 Michael Jordan	25.00
MJ3 Michael Jordan	25.00
MJ4 Michael Jordan	25.00
MJ5 Michael Jordan (White Sox)	40.00

Tribute to 42

	NM/M
Inserted 1:750	
42-B Jackie Robinson bat	40.00
42-J Jackie Robinson jersey	60.00
42-C Jackie Robinson cut	500.00
42-BC Jackie Robinson bat/cut	
42-JC Jackie Robinson jsy/cut	
42-B Jackie Robinson bat/42	100.00
42-J Jackie Robinson jsy/42	100.00

2001 UPPER DECK ROOKIE UPDATE

	NM/M
Common Player:	.25
Common Rookie:	
Pack (4):	15.00
Box (18):	220.00
Sweet Spot	
Common SP (121-150):	3.00
Production 1,500	
91 Garret Anderson	.50
92 Jermaine Dye	.25
93 Shannon Stewart	.25
94 Ben Grieve	.25
95 Juan Gonzalez	.75
96 Bret Boone	.50
97 Tony Batista	.25
98 Rafael Palmeiro	1.00
99 Carl Everett	.25
100 Mike Sweeney	.25
101 Tony Clark	.25
102 Doug Mientkiewicz	.25
103 Jose Canseco	.50
104 Mike Mussina	.75
105 Lance Berkman	.50
106 Andruw Jones	.75
107 Geoff Jenkins	.40
108 Matt Morris	.25
109 Fred McGriff	.40
110 Luis Gonzalez	.50
111 Kevin Brown	.25
112 Tony Armas Jr.	.25
113 John Vander Wal	.25
114 Cliff Floyd	.25
115 Matt Lawton	.25
116 Phil Nevin	.25
117 Pat Burrell	.50
118 Aramis Ramirez	.25
119 Sean Casey	.40
120 Larry Walker	.40
121 *Albert Pujols*	200.00
122 *Johnny Estrada*	8.00
123 *Wilson Betemit*	3.00
124 *Adrian Hernandez*	3.00
125 *Morgan Ensberg*	20.00
126 *Horacio Ramirez*	6.00
127 *Josh Towers*	6.00
128 *Juan Uribe*	5.00
129 *Wilken Ruan*	3.00
130 *Andres Torres*	3.00
131 *Brian Lawrence*	4.00
132 *Ryan Freel*	4.00
133 *Brandon Duckworth*	4.00
134 *Juan Diaz*	3.00
135 *Rafael Soriano*	6.00
136 *Ricardo Rodriguez*	3.00
137 *Bud Smith*	3.00
138 *Mark Teixeira*	65.00
139 *Mark Prior*	50.00
140 *Jackson Melian*	3.00
141 *Dewon Brazelton*	3.00
142 *Greg Miller*	3.00
143 *Billy Sylvester*	3.00
144 *Elpidio Guzman*	3.00
145 *Jack Wilson*	8.00
146 *Jose Mieses*	3.00
147 *Brandon Lyon*	3.00
148 *Tsuyoshi Shinjo*	4.00
149 *Juan Cruz*	3.00
150 *Jay Gibbons*	8.00
SPx	
Common (181-205)	3.00
Production 1,500	
Cards (206-210) Autographed	
151 Garret Anderson	.50
152 Jermaine Dye	.25
153 Shannon Stewart	.25
154 Toby Hall	.25
155 C.C. Sabathia	.25
156 Bret Boone	.50
157 Tony Batista	.25
158 Gabe Kapler	.25
159 Carl Everett	.25
160 Mike Sweeney	.25
161 Dean Palmer	.25
162 Doug Mientkiewicz	.25
163 Carlos Lee	.25
164 Mike Mussina	.75
165 Lance Berkman	.50
166 Ken Caminiti	.25
167 Ben Sheets	.40
168 Matt Morris	.25
169 Fred McGriff	.40
170 Curt Schilling	.50
171 Paul LoDuca	.25
172 Javier Vazquez	.25
173 Rich Aurilia	.25
174 A.J. Burnett	.25
175 Al Leiter	.40
176 Mark Kotsay	.25
177 Jimmy Rollins	.25
178 Aramis Ramirez	.25
179 Aaron Boone	.25
180 Jeff Cirillo	.25
181 *Johnny Estrada*	10.00
182 *Dave Williams*	3.00
183 *Donaldo Mendez*	3.00
184 *Junior Spivey*	8.00
185 *Jay Gibbons*	10.00
186 *Kyle Lohse*	8.00
187 *Willie Harris*	3.00
188 *Juan Cruz*	5.00
189 *Joe Kennedy*	3.00
190 *Duaner Sanchez*	3.00
191 *Jorge Julio*	5.00
192 *Cesar Crespo*	3.00
193 *Casey Fossum*	5.00
194 *Brian Roberts*	20.00
195 *Troy Mattes*	3.00
196 *Rob Mackowiak*	3.00
197 *Tsuyoshi Shinjo*	8.00
198 *Nick Punto*	3.00
199 *Wilmy Caceres*	3.00
200 *Jeremy Affeldt*	3.00
201 *Bret Prinz*	3.00
202 *Delvin James*	3.00
203 *Luis Pineda*	3.00
204 *Matt White*	3.00
205 *Brandon Knight*	3.00
206 *Albert Pujols*	500.00
207 *Mark Teixeira*	200.00
208 *Mark Prior*	125.00
209 *Dewon Brazelton*	10.00
210 *Bud Smith*	8.00
SP Authentic	
Common (211-240):	4.00
Production 1,500	
181 Garrett Anderson	.50
182 Jermaine Dye	.25
183 Shannon Stewart	.25
184 Ben Grieve	.25
185 Ellis Burks	.25
186 John Olerud	.50
187 Tony Batista	.25
188 Ruben Sierra	.25
189 Carl Everett	.25
190 Neifi Perez	.25
191 Tony Clark	.25
192 Doug Mientkiewicz	.25
193 Carlos Lee	.25
194 Jorge Posada	.50
195 Lance Berkman	.50
196 Ken Caminiti	.25
197 Ben Sheets	.50
198 Matt Morris	.25
199 Fred McGriff	.40
200 Mark Grace	.50
201 Paul LoDuca	.25
202 Tony Armas, Jr.	.25
203 Andres Galarraga	.40
204 Cliff Floyd	.25
205 Matt Lawton	.25
206 Ryan Klesko	.40
207 Jimmy Rollins	.25
208 Aramis Ramirez	.25
209 Aaron Boone	.25
210 Jose Ortiz	.25
211 *Mark Prior*	90.00
212 *Mark Teixeira*	100.00
213 *Bud Smith*	4.00
214 *Wilmy Caceres*	4.00
215 *Dave Williams*	4.00
216 *Delvin James*	4.00
217 *Endy Chavez*	4.00
218 *Doug Nickle*	4.00
219 *Bret Prinz*	4.00
220 *Troy Mattes*	4.00
221 *Duaner Sanchez*	4.00
222 *Dewon Brazelton*	4.00
223 *Brian Bowles*	4.00
224 *Donaldo Mendez*	4.00
225 *Jorge Julio*	6.00
226 *Matt White*	4.00
227 *Casey Fossum*	6.00
228 *Mike Rivera*	4.00
229 *Joe Kennedy*	4.00
230 *Kyle Lohse*	6.00
231 *Juan Cruz*	4.00
232 *Jeremy Affeldt*	4.00
233 *Brandon Lyon*	4.00
234 *Brian Roberts*	50.00
235 *Willie Harris*	4.00
236 *Pedro Santana*	4.00
237 *Rafael Soriano*	6.00
238 *Steve Green*	4.00
239 *Junior Spivey*	6.00
240 *Rob Mackowiak*	4.00

Ichiro ROY

	NM/M
Complete Set (51):	35.00
Common Ichiro:	1.00

Ichiro ROY Game Jersey

	NM/M
Numbers 1-12 production 100	50.00
Numbers 13-17 production 50	75.00
Numbers 18-19 production 25	150.00
J-I1 Ichiro Suzuki	50.00
J-I2 Ichiro Suzuki	50.00
J-I3 Ichiro Suzuki	50.00
J-I4 Ichiro Suzuki	50.00
J-I5 Ichiro Suzuki	50.00
J-I6 Ichiro Suzuki	50.00
J-I7 Ichiro Suzuki	50.00
J-I8 Ichiro Suzuki	50.00
J-I9 Ichiro Suzuki	50.00
J-I10 Ichiro Suzuki	50.00
J-I11 Ichiro Suzuki	50.00
J-I12 Ichiro Suzuki	50.00
J-I13 Ichiro Suzuki	75.00
J-I14 Ichiro Suzuki	75.00
J-I15 Ichiro Suzuki	75.00
J-I16 Ichiro Suzuki	75.00
J-I17 Ichiro Suzuki	75.00
J-I18 Ichiro Suzuki	150.00
J-I19 Ichiro Suzuki	150.00
J-I20 Ichiro Suzuki /1	

Ichiro ROY Game-Used Bat

	NM/M
Numbers 1-12 production 100	50.00
Numbers 13-17 production 50	75.00
Numbers 18-19 production 25	150.00
B-I1 Ichiro Suzuki	50.00
B-I2 Ichiro Suzuki	50.00
B-I3 Ichiro Suzuki	50.00
B-I4 Ichiro Suzuki	50.00
B-I5 Ichiro Suzuki	50.00
B-I6 Ichiro Suzuki	50.00
B-I7 Ichiro Suzuki	50.00
B-I8 Ichiro Suzuki	50.00
B-I9 Ichiro Suzuki	50.00
B-I10 Ichiro Suzuki	50.00
B-I11 Ichiro Suzuki	50.00
B-I12 Ichiro Suzuki	50.00
B-I13 Ichiro Suzuki	75.00
B-I14 Ichiro Suzuki	75.00
B-I15 Ichiro Suzuki	75.00
B-I16 Ichiro Suzuki	75.00
B-I17 Ichiro Suzuki	75.00
B-I18 Ichiro Suzuki	150.00
B-I19 Ichiro Suzuki	150.00
B-I20 Ichiro Suzuki/1	

SP Chirography

	NM/M
Common Autograph:	15.00
Production 250	
Silver:	.75-1.5X

Production 100
Gold: No Pricing
Production 25 sets

LB	Lance Berkman/100	10.00
KG	Ken Griffey Jr/250	90.00
TG	Tony Gwynn/250	30.00
TG	Tony Gwynn/100	40.00
MS	Doug Mientkiewicz/100	15.00
JP	Jorge Posada/250	25.00
JP	Jorge Posada/100	30.00
CR	Cal Ripken Jr.	100.00
MS	Mike Sweeney/100	15.00

SP Chirography - Ichiro

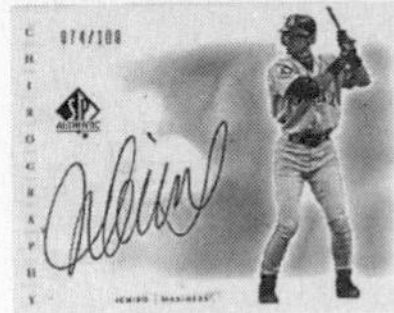

	NM/M
Ichiro (unnumbered)	300.00
Ichiro (Silver/100)	500.00
Ichiro (Gold/25)	

USA Touch of Gold

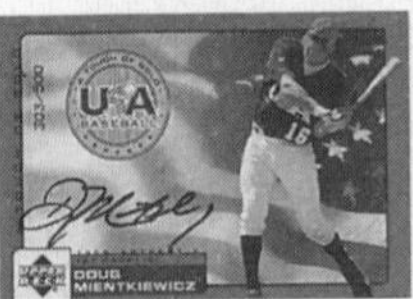

		NM/M
Common Autograph:		8.00
Production 500 sets		
BA	Brent Abernathy	8.00
KU	Kurt Ainsworth	10.00
PB	Pat Borders	8.00
SB	Sean Burroughs	12.00
JC	John Cotton	8.00
TD	Gookie Dawkins	8.00
AE	Adam Everett	8.00
RF	Ryan Franklin	8.00
CG	Chris George	8.00
SH	Shane Heams	8.00
MJ	Marcus Jensen	8.00
MK	Mike Kinkade	8.00
RK	Rick Krivda	8.00
DM	Doug Mientkiewicz	12.00
MN	Mike Neill	8.00
RO	Roy Oswalt	20.00
JR	Jon Rauch	8.00
AS	Anthony Sanders	8.00
BSe	Bobby Seay	8.00
BSh	Ben Sheets	12.00
BW	Brad Wilkerson	8.00
TW	Todd Williams	8.00
EY	Ernie Young	8.00
TY	Tim Young	8.00

Materials 2-Player

		NM/M
Common Card:		10.00
Inserted 1:15		
BB-LG	Barry Bonds, Luis Gonzalez	25.00
JG-BB	Jason Giambi, Barry Bonds	25.00
IR-AR	Ivan Rodriguez, Alex Rodriguez	25.00
AP-JE	Albert Pujols, Jim Edmonds	35.00
GS-SG	Gary Sheffield, Shawn Green	15.00
MP-EA	Mike Piazza, Edgardo Alfonzo	20.00
LW-TH	Larry Walker, Todd Helton	15.00
MR-JG	Manny Ramirez, Juan Gonzalez	15.00
TG-CR	Tony Gwynn, Cal Ripken Jr.	40.00
SR-BA	Scott Rolen, Bobby Abreu	15.00
JB-CB	Jeff Bagwell, Craig Biggio	20.00
KG-SC	Ken Griffey Jr., Sean Casey	25.00
EM-JM	Eric Milton, Joe Mays	10.00
HN-MY	Hideo Nomo, Masato Yoshii	20.00
TS-HN	Tsuyoshi Shinjo, Hideo Nomo	15.00
CS-RJ	Curt Schilling, Randy Johnson	20.00
AS-KS	Aaron Sele, Kazuhiro Sasaki	10.00
PM-RJ	Pedro Martinez, Randy Johnson	15.00
BW-MR	Bernie Williams, Mariano Rivera	15.00
TG-X2	Tony Gwynn	15.00
CR-X2	Cal Ripken Jr.	40.00
JB-RY	Jeromy Burnitz, Robin Yount	15.00
CR-EM	Cal Ripken Jr., Eddie Murray	30.00
TG-DW	Tony Gwynn, Dave Winfield	15.00
FT-MO	Frank Thomas, Magglio Ordonez	15.00
PM-GM	Pedro Martinez, Greg Maddux	20.00
BW-RJ	Bernie Williams, Reggie Jackson	20.00
SS-EB	Sammy Sosa, Ernie Banks	30.00
CP-FV	Chan Ho Park, Fernando Valenzuela	10.00

Materials 3-Player Jersey

		NM/M
Common Card:		10.00
Inserted 1:15		
KBA	Jeff Kent, Barry Bonds, Rich Aurilia	25.00
JAF	Chipper Jones, Andruw Jones, Rafael Furcal	15.00
GZH	Jason Giambi, Barry Zito, Tim Hudson	15.00
SKB	Gary Sheffield, Eric Karros, Kevin Brown	10.00
SSM	Aaron Sele, Ichiro Suzuki, Edgar Martinez	40.00
HDG	Todd Helton, Carlos Delgado, Jason Giambi	15.00
VRF	Omar Vizquel, Alex Rodriguez, Rafael Furcal	25.00
SYN	Kazuhiro Sasaki, Masato Yoshii, Hideo Nomo	20.00
BTD	Jeff Bagwell, Frank Thomas, Carlos Delgado	15.00
BGG	Barry Bonds, Luis Gonzalez, Ken Griffey Jr.	30.00
RPK	Ivan Rodriguez, Mike Piazza, Jason Kendall	20.00
PPV	Jay Payton, Mike Piazza, Robin Ventura	15.00
CHN	Roger Clemens, Tim Hudson, Hideo Nomo	20.00
PWO	Andy Pettitte, Bernie Williams, Paul O'Neill	20.00
TDK	Frank Thomas, Ray Durham, Paul Konerko	15.00
SJC	Curt Schilling, Randy Johnson, Roger Clemens	20.00
DEA	J.D. Drew, Jim Edmonds, Bobby Abreu	15.00
DOP	Carlos Delgado, Magglio Ordonez, Albert Pujols	35.00
TGA	Jim Thome, Juan Gonzalez, Roberto Alomar	15.00
GWS	Luis Gonzalez, Matt Williams, Curt Schilling	20.00
MGJ	Greg Maddux, Tom Glavine, Andruw Jones	20.00

2001 UPPER DECK SWEET SPOT

		NM/M
Complete Set (90):		300.00
Common Player:		.25
Common Sweet Beginnings:		5.00
(61-90) Production 1,000		
Pack (4):		15.00
Box (18):		250.00
1	Troy Glaus	.75
2	Darin Erstad	.50
3	Jason Giambi	.75
4	Tim Hudson	.50
5	Ben Grieve	.25
6	Carlos Delgado	.75
7	David Wells	.25
8	Greg Vaughn	.25
9	Roberto Alomar	.75
10	Jim Thome	.75
11	John Olerud	.50
12	Edgar Martinez	.40
13	Cal Ripken Jr.	3.00
14	Albert Belle	.25
15	Ivan Rodriguez	.75
16	Alex Rodriguez	2.50
17	Pedro Martinez	1.00
18	Nomar Garciaparra	2.00
19	Manny Ramirez	.75
20	Jermaine Dye	.25
21	Juan Gonzalez	.75
22	Dean Palmer	.25
23	Matt Lawton	.25
24	Eric Milton	.25
25	Frank Thomas	.75
26	Magglio Ordonez	.50
27	Derek Jeter	3.00
28	Bernie Williams	.75
29	Roger Clemens	2.00
30	Jeff Bagwell	.75
31	Richard Hidalgo	.25
32	Chipper Jones	1.50
33	Greg Maddux	1.50
34	Richie Sexson	.50
35	Jeromy Burnitz	.25
36	Mark McGwire	2.50
37	Jim Edmonds	.50
38	Sammy Sosa	2.00
39	Randy Johnson	1.00
40	Steve Finley	.25
41	Gary Sheffield	.50
42	Shawn Green	.50
43	Vladimir Guerrero	1.00
44	Jose Vidro	.25
45	Barry Bonds	3.00
46	Jeff Kent	.40
47	Preston Wilson	.25
48	Luis Castillo	.25
49	Mike Piazza	1.50
50	Edgardo Alfonzo	.25
51	Tony Gwynn	1.00
52	Ryan Klesko	.40
53	Scott Rolen	.75
54	Bob Abreu	.40
55	Jason Kendall	.40
56	Brian Giles	.40
57	Ken Griffey Jr.	1.50
58	Barry Larkin	.50
59	Todd Helton	.75
60	Mike Hampton	.25
61	Corey Patterson	5.00
62	*Ichiro Suzuki*	200.00
63	Jason Grilli	5.00
64	Brian Cole	5.00
65	Juan Pierre	5.00
66	Matt Ginter	5.00
67	Jimmy Rollins	5.00
68	*Jason Smith*	5.00
69	Israel Alcantara	5.00
70	*Adam Pettyjohn*	5.00
71	Luke Prokopec	5.00
72	Barry Zito	5.00
73	Keith Ginter	5.00
74	Sun-Woo Kim	5.00
75	Ross Gload	5.00
76	Matt Wise	5.00
77	Aubrey Huff	5.00
78	Ryan Franklin	5.00
79	Brandon Inge	5.00
80	Wes Helms	5.00
81	*Junior Spivey*	8.00
82	Ryan Vogelsong	5.00
83	John Parrish	5.00
84	Joe Crede	5.00
85	Damian Rolls	5.00
86	*Esix Snead*	5.00
87	Rocky Biddle	5.00
88	Brady Clark	5.00
89	Timoniel Perez	5.00
90	Jay Spurgeon	5.00

Big League Challenge

		NM/M
Complete Set (20):		20.00
Common Player:		.50
Inserted 1:6		
1	Mark McGwire	2.50
2	Richard Hidalgo	.50
3	Alex Rodriguez	2.50
4	Shawn Green	.75
5	Frank Thomas	1.00
6	Chipper Jones	1.50
7	Rafael Palmeiro	1.00
8	Troy Glaus	1.00
9	Mike Piazza	1.50
10	Andruw Jones	1.00
11	Todd Helton	1.00
12	Jason Giambi	1.00
13	Sammy Sosa	2.00
14	Carlos Delgado	1.00
15	Barry Bonds	3.00
16	Jose Canseco	.75
17	Jim Edmonds	.75
18	Manny Ramirez	1.00
19	Gary Sheffield	.75
20	Nomar Garciaparra	2.00

DiMaggio Pinstripes Excl.

	NM/M
Complete Set (56):	60.00
Common DiMaggio:	1.50
One pack/box	

DiMaggio Pinstripes Memor.

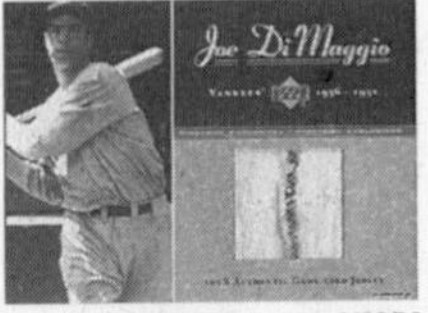

		NM/M
Print Runs listed:		150.00
JDB	Joe DiMaggio bat/100	80.00
JDBC	Joe DiMaggio bat/cut/5	
JDCJ	Joe DiMaggio, Lou Gehrig jsy/50	600.00
JDJ	Joe DiMaggio jsy/100	100.00

Game-Used Bat

	NM/M
Common Player:	5.00

Inserted 1:18

HA	Hank Aaron	60.00
RA	Rick Ankiel	5.00
BB	Barry Bonds	25.00
JC	Jose Canseco	8.00
TC	Ty Cobb	175.00
JD	Joe DiMaggio	80.00
KG	Ken Griffey Jr.	15.00
RJ	Reggie Jackson	10.00
AJ	Andruw Jones	10.00
MM	Mickey Mantle	140.00
WM	Willie Mays	75.00
SM	Stan Musial	50.00
CR	Cal Ripken Jr.	40.00
AR	Alex Rodriguez	20.00
IR	Ivan Rodriguez	8.00
NR	Nolan Ryan	65.00
GS	Gary Sheffield	8.00
SS	Sammy Sosa	20.00
FT	Frank Thomas	10.00

Game Jerseys

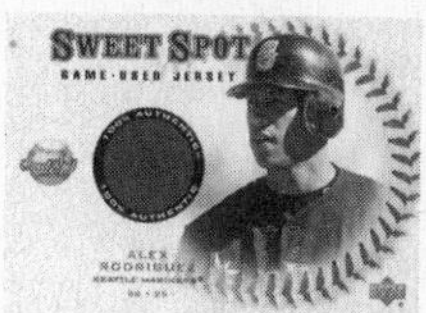

		NM/M
Common Player:		8.00
Inserted 1:18		
BB	Barry Bonds	25.00
JC	Jose Canseco	8.00
RC	Roger Clemens	20.00
RC	Roberto Clemente	125.00
JD	Joe DiMaggio	80.00
KG	Ken Griffey Jr.	20.00
RJ	Randy Johnson	10.00
AJ	Andruw Jones	8.00
CJ	Chipper Jones	10.00
MM	Mickey Mantle	150.00
WM	Willie Mays	100.00
SM	Stan Musial	65.00
CR	Cal Ripken Jr.	40.00
AR	Alex Rodriguez	20.00
IR	Ivan Rodriguez	8.00
NR	Nolan Ryan	65.00
DS	Duke Snider	10.00
SS	Sammy Sosa	20.00
IS	Ichiro Suzuki	100.00
FT	Frank Thomas	10.00

Players Party

		NM/M
Complete Set (10):		10.00
Common Player:		.75
Inserted 1:12		
1	Derek Jeter	3.00
2	Randy Johnson	1.00
3	Frank Thomas	1.00
4	Nomar Garciaparra	2.00
5	Ken Griffey Jr.	1.50
6	Carlos Delgado	.75
7	Mike Piazza	1.50
8	Barry Bonds	3.00
9	Sammy Sosa	2.00
10	Pedro Martinez	1.00

Signatures

		NM/M
Common Player:		20.00
RAl	Roberto Alomar	40.00
RAn	Rick Ankiel	20.00
JB	Jeff Bagwell SP/214	120.00
DB	Dusty Baker	20.00
DB	Don Baylor	20.00
BB	Buddy Bell	20.00
AB	Albert Belle	25.00
MB	Milton Bradley	20.00
PB	Pat Burrell	30.00
JC	Jose Canseco	60.00
CB	Chris Chambliss	20.00
RC	Roger Clemens	140.00
TC	Ty Cobb/1	
CD	Carlos Delgado	30.00
JD	Joe DiMaggio SP/150	600.00
DE	Darin Erstad	25.00
RF	Rafael Furcal	25.00
JG	Joe Garagiola	50.00
JG	Jason Giambi	50.00
TGl	Troy Glaus	40.00
SG	Shawn Green	30.00
KG	Ken Griffey SP/100	350.00
TGw	Tony Gwynn	110.00
AH	Art Howe	20.00
TH	Tim Hudson	30.00
DJ	Davey Johnson	20.00
RJ	Randy Johnson	85.00
AJ	Andruw Jones	50.00
CJ	Chipper Jones	80.00
ML	Mike Lamb	20.00
TL	Tony LaRussa	20.00
DL	Davey Lopes	20.00
BM	Bill Madlock	20.00
MM	Mickey Mantle SP/10	3,500
WM	Willie Mays	200.00
HM	Hal McRae	20.00
SM	Stan Musial	120.00
PO	Paul O'Neill	50.00
LP	Lou Piniella	25.00
JR	Jim Rice	25.00
AR	Alex Rodriguez SP/154	200.00
IR	Ivan Rodriguez SP/150	100.00
BR	Babe Ruth SP/1 (8/03 auction)	12,000
NR	Nolan Ryan	200.00
GS	Gary Sheffield	30.00
SS	Sammy Sosa SP/148	250.00
FT	Frank Thomas	60.00
AT	Alan Trammell	25.00
BV	Bobby Valentine	20.00
RV	Robin Ventura	20.00
MW	Matt Williams	25.00

S.S. Game-Used Bases Tier 1

		NM/M
Common Card:		5.00
BH	Barry Bonds, Todd Helton	25.00
MG	Mark McGwire, Ken Griffey Jr.	60.00
JG	Chipper Jones, Nomar Garciaparra	20.00
GD	Vladimir Guerrero, Carlos Delgado	8.00
ST	Sammy Sosa, Frank Thomas	20.00
SR	Gary Sheffield, Alex Rodriguez	15.00
GR	Tony Gwynn, Ivan Rodriguez	10.00
PJ	Mike Piazza, Derek Jeter	30.00
HG	Jeffrey Hammonds, Troy Glaus	5.00
JGi	Randy Johnson, Jason Giambi	8.00
BD	Jeff Bagwell, Jermaine Dye	8.00
RR	Scott Rolen, Cal Ripken Jr.	25.00
GR	Ken Griffey Jr., Manny Ramirez	15.00
RJ	Alex Rodriguez, Derek Jeter	40.00
MP	Mark McGwire, Timoniel Perez	35.00
CP	Roger Clemens, Mike Piazza	20.00

S.S. Game-Used Bases Tier 2

		NM/M
Common Card:		20.00
Production 50 sets		
BHK	Barry Bonds, Todd Helton, Jeff Kent	75.00
MGE	Mark McGwire, Ken Griffey Jr., Bobby Edmonds	120.00
JGJ	Chipper Jones, Nomar Garciaparra, Andruw Jones	60.00
GDM	Vladimir Guerrero, Carlos Delgado, Raul Mondesi	20.00
STO	Sammy Sosa, Frank Thomas, Magglio Ordonez	50.00
SRM	Gary Sheffield, Alex Rodriguez, Edgar Martinez	50.00
GRP	Tony Gwynn, Ivan Rodriguez, Rafael Palmeiro	40.00
PJW	Mike Piazza, Derek Jeter, Bernie Williams	75.00
HGH	Jeffrey Hammonds, Troy Glaus, Todd Helton	20.00
JGC	Randy Johnson, Jason Giambi, Eric Chavez	25.00
BDH	Jeff Bagwell, Jermaine Dye, Richard Hidalgo	20.00
RRB	Scott Rolen, Cal Ripken Jr., Albert Belle	75.00
GRT	Ken Griffey Jr., Manny Ramirez, Jim Thome	50.00

2001 UPPER DECK ULTIMATE COLLECTION

		NM/M
Common Player:		1.00
Common SP (91-100):		5.00
Production 1,000		
Common SP (101-110):		5.00
Production 750		
Common (111-120):		20.00
Production 250		
Pack (4):		160.00
Box (4):		575.00
1	Troy Glaus	2.50
2	Darin Erstad	1.50
3	Jason Giambi	3.00
4	Barry Zito	2.00
5	Tim Hudson	2.00
6	Miguel Tejada	1.50
7	Carlos Delgado	2.50
8	Shannon Stewart	1.00
9	Greg Vaughn	1.00
10	Toby Hall	1.00
11	Roberto Alomar	2.00
12	Juan Gonzalez	2.50
13	Jim Thome	3.00
14	Edgar Martinez	1.50
15	Freddy Garcia	1.00
16	Bret Boone	1.50
17	Kazuhiro Sasaki	1.00
18	Cal Ripken Jr.	10.00
19	Tim Raines Jr.	1.00
20	Alex Rodriguez	8.00
21	Ivan Rodriguez	2.50
22	Rafael Palmeiro	2.50
23	Pedro Martinez	3.00
24	Nomar Garciaparra	6.00
25	Manny Ramirez	2.50
26	Hideo Nomo	2.00
27	Mike Sweeney	1.00
28	Carlos Beltran	1.50
29	Tony Clark	1.00
30	Dean Palmer	1.00
31	Doug Mientkiewicz	1.00
32	Cristian Guzman	1.00
33	Corey Koskie	1.00
34	Frank Thomas	3.00
35	Magglio Ordonez	1.50
36	Jose Canseco	2.00
37	Roger Clemens	6.00
38	Derek Jeter	10.00
39	Bernie Williams	2.00
40	Mike Mussina	2.00
41	Tino Martinez	1.00
42	Jeff Bagwell	2.50
43	Lance Berkman	2.00
44	Roy Oswalt	1.50
45	Chipper Jones	5.00
46	Greg Maddux	5.00
47	Andruw Jones	2.50
48	Tom Glavine	2.00
49	Richie Sexson	2.00
50	Jeromy Burnitz	1.00
51	Ben Sheets	1.00
52	Mark McGwire	8.00
53	Matt Morris	1.00
54	Jim Edmonds	2.00
55	J.D. Drew	1.50
56	Sammy Sosa	6.00
57	Fred McGriff	1.00
58	Kerry Wood	2.50
59	Randy Johnson	3.00
60	Luis Gonzalez	2.00
61	Curt Schilling	2.00
62	Shawn Green	1.50
63	Kevin Brown	1.50
64	Gary Sheffield	2.00
65	Vladimir Guerrero	3.00
66	Barry Bonds	10.00
67	Jeff Kent	1.50
68	Rich Aurilia	1.00
69	Cliff Floyd	1.00
70	Charles Johnson	1.00
71	Josh Beckett	2.00
72	Mike Piazza	5.00
73	Edgardo Alfonzo	1.00
74	Robin Ventura	1.00
75	Tony Gwynn	2.50
76	Ryan Klesko	1.50
77	Phil Nevin	1.00
78	Scott Rolen	2.50
79	Bobby Abreu	1.00
80	Jimmy Rollins	1.00
81	Brian Giles	1.50
82	Jason Kendall	1.00
83	Aramis Ramirez	1.00
84	Ken Griffey Jr.	6.00
85	Adam Dunn	2.00
86	Sean Casey	1.50
87	Barry Larkin	2.00
88	Larry Walker	1.50
89	Mike Hampton	1.00
90	Todd Helton	2.50
91	Ken Harvey	5.00
92	*William Ortega*	5.00
93	*Juan Diaz*	5.00
94	*Greg Miller*	5.00
95	*Brandon Berger*	5.00
96	*Brandon Lyon*	5.00
97	*Jay Gibbons*	20.00
98	*Rob Mackowiak*	5.00
99	*Erick Almonte*	5.00
100	*Jason Middlebrook*	5.00
101	*Johnny Estrada*	10.00
102	*Juan Uribe*	10.00
103	*Travis Hafner*	25.00
104	*Morgan Ensberg*	30.00
105	*Mike Rivera*	5.00
106	*Josh Towers*	5.00
107	*Adrian Hernandez*	5.00
108	*Rafael Soriano*	10.00
109	*Jackson Melian*	5.00
110	*Wilken Ruan*	5.00
111	*Albert Pujols*	375.00
112	*Tsuyoshi Shinjo*	20.00
113	*Brandon Duckworth*	20.00
114	*Juan Cruz*	20.00
115	*Dewon Brazelton*	20.00
116	*Mark Prior Auto*	400.00
117	*Mark Teixeira Auto*	450.00
118	*Wilson Betemit Auto*	25.00
119	*Bud Smith Auto*	25.00
120	*Ichiro Suzuki Auto*	750.00

Game Jersey

		NM/M
Common Player:		10.00
Inserted 1:2		
RA	Roberto Alomar	20.00
JB	Jeff Bagwell	20.00

BB Barry Bonds 50.00
JC Jose Canseco 10.00
RC Roger Clemens 40.00
CD Carlos Delgado 10.00
DE Darin Erstad 10.00
JaG Jason Giambi 20.00
JG Juan Gonzalez 20.00
LG Luis Gonzalez 10.00
SG Shawn Green 10.00
KG Ken Griffey Jr. 40.00
TG Tony Gwynn 20.00
TH Todd Helton 15.00
RJ Randy Johnson 15.00
AJ Andruw Jones 10.00
CJ Chipper Jones 15.00
GM Greg Maddux 40.00
MO Magglio Ordonez 10.00
MP Mike Piazza 30.00
AP Albert Pujols 75.00
CR Cal Ripken Jr. 75.00
AR Alex Rodriguez 40.00
IR Ivan Rodriguez 15.00
SR Scott Rolen 15.00
GS Gary Sheffield 10.00
SS Sammy Sosa 40.00
FT Frank Thomas 15.00
LW Larry Walker 10.00
BW Bernie Williams 10.00

Ichiro

NM/M

Pricing not available for all Ichiro's
B-IA Ichiro Suzuki/bat away 65.00
B-IH Ichiro Suzuki/bat home 65.00
B-IS Ichiro Suzuki/bat/250 80.00
B-IG Ichiro Suzuki/bat/200 90.00
SB-I Ichiro Suzuki/bat/auto/50 675.00
J-IA Ichiro Suzuki/jsy/away 50.00
J-IH Ichiro Suzuki/jsy/home 50.00
J-IS Ichiro Suzuki/jsy/250 75.00
J-IG Ichiro Suzuki/jsy/200 85.00
SJ-I Ichiro Suzuki/jsy/auto/50 675.00
UB-I Ichiro Suzuki/base 25.00
UB-IC Ichiro Suzuki/base/150 80.00
UB-IS Ichiro Suzuki/base/50 100.00
UB-IG Ichiro Suzuki/base/25
SUB-I Ichiro Suzuki/base/auto/25
BB-I Ichiro Suzuki/ball 60.00
BB-IC Ichiro Suzuki/ball/150 85.00
BB-IS Ichiro Suzuki/ball/50 100.00
BB-IG Ichiro Suzuki/ball/25
SBB-I Ichiro Suzuki/ball/auto/25 675.00
C-I Ichiro Suzuki/glove/75 180.00
C-IG Ichiro Suzuki/glove/25
BG-I Ichiro Suzuki/batglove/75 180.00
BG-IG Ichiro Suzuki/batglove/25

Magic Numbers

NM/M

Common Player: 10.00
Production 150
Coppers #'d to 24 not priced
Silvers #'d to 20 not priced
Golds #'d to 15 not priced
RA Roberto Alomar 20.00
JB Jeff Bagwell 20.00
BB Barry Bonds 50.00
JC Jose Canseco 15.00
RC Roger Clemens 50.00
CD Carlos Delgado 15.00
DE Darin Erstad 10.00
JaG Jason Giambi 20.00
JG Juan Gonzalez 15.00
LG Luis Gonzalez 10.00
SG Shawn Green 10.00
KG Ken Griffey Jr. 40.00
TG Tony Gwynn 20.00
TH Todd Helton 15.00
RJ Randy Johnson 15.00
AJ Andruw Jones 10.00
CJ Chipper Jones 15.00
GM Greg Maddux 40.00
MO Magglio Ordonez 10.00
MP Mike Piazza 30.00
AP Albert Pujols 75.00
CR Cal Ripken Jr. 90.00
AR Alex Rodriguez 40.00
IR Ivan Rodriguez 15.00
SR Scott Rolen 15.00
GS Gary Sheffield 10.00
SS Sammy Sosa 40.00
FT Frank Thomas 15.00
LW Larry Walker 10.00
BW Bernie Williams 10.00

Ultimate Signatures

NM/M

Common Autograph: 20.00
Inserted 1:4
Silvers #'d to 24 not priced
Golds #'d to 15 not priced
RA Roberto Alomar 40.00
EB Ernie Banks 50.00
BaB Barry Bonds 200.00
RC Roger Clemens 100.00
CD Carlos Delgado 25.00
CF Carlton Fisk 40.00
JaG Jason Giambi 25.00
TGl Tom Glavine 40.00
LG Luis Gonzalez 25.00
KG Ken Griffey Jr. 100.00
TG Tony Gwynn 60.00
RK Ryan Klesko 20.00
SK Sandy Koufax 275.00
EM Edgar Martinez 30.00
HN Hideo Nomo
TP Tony Perez 20.00
KP Kirby Puckett 50.00
CR Cal Ripken Jr. 125.00
AR Alex Rodriguez 80.00
IR Ivan Rodriguez 50.00
TS Tom Seaver 40.00
GS Gary Sheffield 30.00
DS Duke Snider 35.00
SS Sammy Sosa 120.00
FT Frank Thomas 40.00
JT Jim Thome 50.00
RY Robin Yount 60.00

2001 UPPER DECK VICTORY

NM/M

Complete Set (660): 50.00
Common Player: .15
1 Troy Glaus .50
2 Scott Spiezio .15
3 Gary DiSarcina .15
4 Darin Erstad .20
5 Tim Salmon .20
6 Troy Percival .15
7 Ramon Ortiz .15
8 Orlando Palmeiro .15
9 Tim Belcher .15

10 Mo Vaughn .15
11 Bengie Molina .15
12 Benji Gil .15
13 Scott Schoeneweis .15
14 Garret Anderson .15
15 Matt Wise .15
16 Adam Kennedy .15
17 Jarrod Washburn .15
18 Darin Erstad, Troy Percival .15
19 Jason Giambi .20
20 Tim Hudson .20
21 Ramon Hernandez .15
22 Eric Chavez .15
23 Gil Heredia .15
24 Jason Isringhausen .15
25 Jeremy Giambi .15
26 Miguel Tejada .15
27 Barry Zito .50
28 Terrence Long .15
29 Ryan Christenson .15
30 Mark Mulder .15
31 Olmedo Saenz .15
32 Adam Piatt .15
33 Ben Grieve .20
34 Omar Olivares .15
35 John Jaha .15
36 Jason Giambi, Tim Hudson .15
37 Carlos Delgado .40
38 Esteban Loaiza .15
39 Brad Fullmer .15
40 David Wells .15
41 Chris Woodward .15
42 Billy Koch .15
43 Shannon Stewart .15
44 Chris Carpenter .15
45 Steve Parris .15
46 Darrin Fletcher .15
47 Joey Hamilton .15
48 Jose Cruz Jr. .15
49 Vernon Wells .15
50 Raul Mondesi .15
51 Kelvim Escobar .15
52 Tony Batista .15
53 Alex Gonzalez .15
54 Carlos Delgado, David Wells .20
55 Greg Vaughn .15
56 Albie Lopez .15
57 Randy Winn .15
58 Ryan Rupe .15
59 Steve Cox .15
60 Vinny Castilla .15
61 Jose Guillen .15
62 Wilson Alvarez .15
63 Bryan Rekar .15
64 Gerald Williams .15
65 Esteban Yan .15
66 Felix Martinez .15
67 Fred McGriff .20
68 John Flaherty .15
69 Jason Tyner .15
70 Russ Johnson .15
71 Roberto Hernandez .15
72 Greg Vaughn, Albie Lopez .15
73 Eddie Taubensee .15
74 Bob Wickman .15
75 Ellis Burks .15
76 Kenny Lofton .20
77 Einar Diaz .15
78 Travis Fryman .15
79 Omar Vizquel .15
80 Jason Bere .15
81 Bartolo Colon .15
82 Jim Thome .20
83 Roberto Alomar .40
84 Chuck Finley .15
85 Steve Woodard .15
86 Russ Branyan .15
87 Dave Burba .15
88 Jaret Wright .15
89 Jacob Cruz .15
90 Steve Karsay .15
91 Manny Ramirez, Bartolo Colon .20
92 Raul Ibanez .15
93 Freddy Garcia .15
94 Edgar Martinez .15
95 Jay Buhner .15
96 Jamie Moyer .15
97 John Olerud .20
98 Aaron Sele .15
99 Kazuhiro Sasaki .20
100 Mike Cameron .15
101 John Halama .15
102 David Bell .15
103 Gil Meche .15
104 Carlos Guillen .15
105 Mark McLemore .15
106 Stan Javier .15
107 Al Martin .15
108 Dan Wilson .15
109 Alex Rodriguez, Kazuhiro Sasaki .50
110 Cal Ripken Jr. 1.50
111 Delino DeShields .15
112 Sidney Ponson .15
113 Albert Belle .15
114 Jose Mercedes .15
115 Scott Erickson .15
116 Jerry Hairston Jr. .15
117 Brook Fordyce .15
118 Luis Matos .15
119 Eugene Kingsale .15
120 Jeff Conine .15
121 Chris Richard .15
122 Fernando Lunar .15
123 John Parrish .15
124 Brady Anderson .15
125 Ryan Kohlmeier .15
126 Melvin Mora .15
127 Albert Belle, Jose Mercedes .15
128 Ivan Rodriguez .50
129 Justin Thompson .15
130 Kenny Rogers .15
131 Rafael Palmeiro .30
132 Rusty Greer .15
133 Gabe Kapler .15
134 John Wetteland .15
135 Mike Lamb .15
136 Doug Davis .15
137 Ruben Mateo .15
138 Alex Rodriguez 1.25
139 Chad Curtis .15
140 Rick Helling .15
141 Ryan Glynn .15
142 Andres Galarraga .25
143 Ricky Ledee .15
144 Frank Catalanotto .15
145 Rafael Palmeiro, Rick Helling .20
146 Pedro Martinez .60
147 Wilton Veras .15
148 Manny Ramirez .50
149 Rolando Arrojo .15
150 Nomar Garciaparra 1.00
151 Darren Lewis .15
152 Troy O'Leary .15
153 Tomokazu Ohka .15
154 Carl Everett .15
155 Jason Varitek .15
156 Frank Castillo .15
157 Pete Schourek .15
158 Jose Offerman .15
159 Derek Lowe .15
160 John Valentin .15
161 Dante Bichette .15
162 Trot Nixon .15
163 Nomar Garciaparra, Pedro Martinez .25
164 Jermaine Dye .15
165 Dave McCarty .15
166 Jose Rosado .15
167 Mike Sweeney .15
168 Rey Sanchez .15
169 Jeff Suppan .15
170 Chad Durbin .15
171 Carlos Beltran .15
172 Brian Meadows .15
173 Todd Dunwoody .15
174 Johnny Damon .15
175 Blake Stein .15
176 Carlos Febles .15
177 Joe Randa .15
178 Makoto Suzuki .15
179 Mark Quinn .15

180 Greg Zaun .15
181 Mike Sweeney, Jeff Suppan .15
182 Juan Gonzalez .50
183 Dean Palmer .15
184 Wendell Magee .15
185 Todd Jones .15
186 Bobby Higginson .15
187 Brian Moehler .15
188 Juan Encarnacion .15
189 Tony Clark .15
190 Rich Becker .15
191 Roger Cedeno .15
192 Mitch Meluskey .15
193 Shane Halter .15
194 Jeff Weaver .15
195 Deivi Cruz .15
196 Damion Easley .15
197 Robert Fick .15
198 Matt Anderson .15
199 Bobby Higginson, Brian Moehler .15
200 Brad Radke .15
201 Mark Redman .15
202 Corey Koskie .15
203 Matt Lawton .15
204 Eric Milton .15
205 Chad Moeller .15
206 Jacque Jones .15
207 Matt Kinney .15
208 Jay Canizaro .15
209 Torii Hunter .15
210 Ron Coomer .15
211 Chad Allen .15
212 Denny Hocking .15
213 Cristian Guzman .15
214 LaTroy Hawkins .15
215 Joe Mays .15
216 David Ortiz .15
217 Matt Lawton, Eric Milton .15
218 Frank Thomas .60
219 Jose Valentin .15
220 Mike Sirotka .15
221 Kip Wells .15
222 Magglio Ordonez .25
223 Herbert Perry .15
224 James Baldwin .15
225 Jon Garland .15
226 Sandy Alomar .15
227 Chris Singleton .15
228 Keith Foulke .15
229 Paul Konerko .15
230 Jim Parque .15
231 Greg Norton .15
232 Carlos Lee .15
233 Cal Eldred .15
234 Ray Durham .15
235 Jeff Abbott .15
236 Frank Thomas, Mike Sirotka .20
237 Derek Jeter 1.50
238 Glenallen Hill .15
239 Roger Clemens 1.00
240 Bernie Williams .40
241 David Justice .25
242 Luis Sojo .15
243 Orlando Hernandez .20
244 Mike Mussina .25
245 Jorge Posada .20
246 Andy Pettitte .20
247 Paul O'Neill .20
248 Scott Brosius .15
249 Alfonso Soriano .50
250 Mariano Rivera .20
251 Chuck Knoblauch .20
252 Ramiro Mendoza .15
253 Tino Martinez .15
254 David Cone .15
255 Derek Jeter, Andy Pettitte .40
256 Jeff Bagwell .50
257 Lance Berkman .15
258 Craig Biggio .20
259 Scott Elarton .15
260 Bill Spiers .15
261 Moises Alou .15
262 Billy Wagner .15
263 Shane Reynolds .15
264 Tony Eusebio .15
265 Julio Lugo .15
266 Jose Lima .15
267 Octavio Dotel .15
268 Brad Ausmus .15
269 Daryle Ward .15
270 Glen Barker .15
271 Wade Miller .15
272 Richard Hidalgo .25
273 Chris Truby .15
274 Jeff Bagwell, Scott Elarton .25
275 Greg Maddux .75
276 Chipper Jones .75
277 Tom Glavine .25
278 Brian Jordan .15
279 Andruw Jones .40
280 Kevin Millwood .15
281 Rico Brogna .15
282 George Lombard .15
283 Reggie Sanders .15
284 John Rocker .15
285 Rafael Furcal .25
286 John Smoltz .15
287 Javy Lopez .15
288 Walt Weiss .15
289 Quilvio Veras .15
290 Eddie Perez .15
291 B.J. Surhoff .15
292 Chipper Jones, Tom Glavine .25
293 Jeromy Burnitz .15
294 Charlie Hayes .15
295 Jeff D'Amico .15
296 Jose Hernandez .15
297 Richie Sexson .15
298 Tyler Houston .15
299 Paul Rigdon .15
300 Jamey Wright .15
301 Mark Loretta .15
302 Geoff Jenkins .20
303 Luis Lopez .15
304 John Snyder .15
305 Henry Blanco .15
306 Curtis Leskanic .15
307 Ron Belliard .15
308 Jimmy Haynes .15
309 Marquis Grissom .15
310 Geoff Jenkins, Jeff D'Amico .15
311 Mark McGwire 1.00
312 Rick Ankiel .20
313 Dave Veres .15
314 Carlos Hernandez .15
315 Jim Edmonds .20
316 Andy Benes .15
317 Garrett Stephenson .15
318 Ray Lankford .15
319 Dustin Hermanson .15
320 Steve Kline .15
321 Mike Matheny .15
322 Edgar Renteria .15
323 J.D. Drew .15
324 Craig Paquette .15
325 Darryl Kile .15
326 Fernando Vina .15
327 Eric Davis .15
328 Placido Polanco .15
329 Jim Edmonds, Darryl Kile .15
330 Sammy Sosa 1.00
331 Rick Aguilera .15
332 Willie Greene .15
333 Kerry Wood .20
334 Todd Hundley .15
335 Rondell White .20
336 Julio Zuleta .15
337 Jon Lieber .15
338 Joe Girardi .15
339 Damon Buford .15
340 Kevin Tapani .15
341 Ricky Gutierrez .15
342 Bill Mueller .15
343 Ruben Quevedo .15
344 Eric Young .15
345 Gary Matthews Jr. .15
346 Daniel Garibay .15
347 Sammy Sosa, Jon Lieber .30
348 Randy Johnson .50
349 Matt Williams .20
350 Kelly Stinnett .15
351 Brian Anderson .15
352 Steve Finley .15
353 Curt Schilling .20
354 Erubiel Durazo .15
355 Todd Stottlemyre .15
356 Mark Grace .20
357 Luis Gonzalez .20
358 Danny Bautista .15
359 Matt Mantei .15
360 Tony Womack .15
361 Armando Reynoso .15
362 Greg Colbrunn .15
363 Jay Bell .15
364 Byung-Hyun Kim .15
365 Luis Gonzalez, Randy Johnson .20
366 Gary Sheffield .20
367 Eric Karros .15
368 Jeff Shaw .15
369 Jim Leyritz .15
370 Kevin Brown .20
371 Alex Cora .15
372 Andy Ashby .15
373 Eric Gagne .15
374 Chan Ho Park .15
375 Shawn Green .20
376 Kevin Elster .15
377 Mark Grudzielanek .15
378 Darren Dreifort .15
379 Dave Hansen .15
380 Bruce Aven .15
381 Adrian Beltre .20
382 Tom Goodwin .15
383 Gary Sheffield, Chan Ho Park .15
384 Vladimir Guerrero .60
385 Ugueth Urbina .15
386 Michael Barrett .15
387 Geoff Blum .15
388 Fernando Tatis .15
389 Carl Pavano .15
390 Jose Vidro .15
391 Orlando Cabrera .15
392 Terry Jones .15
393 Mike Thurman .15
394 Lee Stevens .15
395 Tony Armas Jr. .15
396 Wilton Guerrero .15
397 Peter Bergeron .15
398 Milton Bradley .15
399 Javier Vazquez .15
400 Fernando Seguignol .15
401 Vladimir Guerrero, Dustin Hermanson .25
402 Barry Bonds .60
403 Russ Ortiz .15
404 Calvin Murray .15
405 Armando Rios .15
406 Livan Hernandez .15
407 Jeff Kent .20
408 Bobby Estalella .15
409 Felipe Crespo .15
410 Shawn Estes .15
411 J.T. Snow .15
412 Marvin Benard .15
413 Joe Nathan .15
414 Robb Nen .15
415 Shawon Dunston .15
416 Mark Gardner .15
417 Kirk Rueter .15
418 Rich Aurilia .15
419 Doug Mirabelli .15
420 Russ Davis .15
421 Barry Bonds, Livan Hernandez .30
422 Cliff Floyd .15
423 Luis Castillo .15
424 Antonio Alfonseca .15
425 Preston Wilson .15
426 Ryan Dempster .15
427 Jesus Sanchez .15
428 Derrek Lee .15
429 Brad Penny .15
430 Mark Kotsay .15
431 Alex Fernandez .15
432 Mike Lowell .15
433 Chuck Smith .15
434 Alex Gonzalez .15
435 Dave Berg .15
436 A.J. Burnett .15
437 Charles Johnson .15
438 Reid Cornelius .15
439 Mike Redmond .15
440 Preston Wilson, Ryan Dempster .15
441 Mike Piazza .75
442 Kevin Appier .15
443 Jay Payton .15
444 Steve Trachsel .15
445 Al Leiter .20
446 Joe McEwing .15
447 Armando Benitez .15
448 Edgardo Alfonzo .15
449 Glendon Rusch .15
450 Mike Bordick .15
451 Lenny Harris .15
452 Matt Franco .15
453 Darryl Hamilton .15
454 Bobby J. Jones .15
455 Robin Ventura .15
456 Todd Zeile .15
457 John Franco .15
458 Mike Piazza, Al Leiter .40
459 Tony Gwynn .75
460 John Mabry .15
461 Trevor Hoffman .15
462 Phil Nevin .15
463 Ryan Klesko .15
464 Wiki Gonzalez .15
465 Matt Clement .15
466 Alex Arias .15
467 Woody Williams .15
468 Ruben Rivera .15
469 Sterling Hitchcock .15
470 Ben Davis .15
471 Bubba Trammell .15
472 Jay Witasick .15
473 Eric Owens .15
474 Damian Jackson .15
475 Adam Eaton .15
476 Mike Darr .15
477 Phil Nevin, Trevor Hoffman .15
478 Scott Rolen .25
479 Robert Person .15
480 Mike Lieberthal .15
481 Reggie Taylor .15
482 Paul Byrd .15
483 Bruce Chen .15
484 Pat Burrell .25
485 Kevin Jordan .15
486 Bobby Abreu .15
487 Randy Wolf .15
488 Kevin Sefcik .15
489 Brian Hunter .15
490 Doug Glanville .15
491 Kent Bottenfield .15
492 Travis Lee .15
493 Jeff Brantley .15
494 Omar Daal .15
495 Bobby Abreu, Randy Wolf .15
496 Jason Kendall .15
497 Adrian Brown .15
498 Warren Morris .15
499 Brian Giles .20
500 Jimmy Anderson .15
501 John Vander Wal .15
502 Mike Williams .15
503 Aramis Ramirez .15
504 Pat Meares .15
505 Jason Schmidt .15
506 Todd Ritchie .15
507 Abraham Nunez .15
508 Jose Silva .15
509 Francisco Cordova .15
510 Kevin Young .15
511 Derek Bell .15
512 Kris Benson .15
513 Brian Giles, Jose Silva .15
514 Ken Griffey Jr. 1.00
515 Scott Williamson .15
516 Dmitri Young .15
517 Sean Casey .20
518 Barry Larkin .25
519 Juan Castro .15
520 Danny Graves .15
521 Aaron Boone .15
522 Pokey Reese .15
523 Elmer Dessens .15
524 Michael Tucker .15
525 Benito Santiago .15
526 Pete Harnisch .15
527 Alex Ochoa .15
528 Gookie Dawkins .15
529 Seth Etherton .15
530 Rob Bell .15
531 Ken Griffey Jr., Steve Parris .50
532 Todd Helton .50
533 Jose Jimenez .15
534 Todd Walker .15
535 Ron Gant .15
536 Neifi Perez .15
537 Butch Huskey .15
538 Pedro Astacio .15
539 Juan Pierre .15
540 Jeff Cirillo .15
541 Ben Petrick .15
542 Brian Bohanon .15
543 Larry Walker .25
544 Masato Yoshii .15
545 Denny Neagle .15
546 Brent Mayne .15
547 Mike Hampton .20
548 Todd Hollandsworth .15
549 Brian Rose .15
550 Todd Helton, Pedro Astacio .20
551 Jason Hart .15
552 Joe Crede .15
553 Timoniel Perez .15
554 Brady Clark .15
555 *Adam Pettyjohn* .15
556 Jason Grilli .15
557 Paxton Crawford .15
558 Jay Spurgeon .15
559 Hector Ortiz .15
560 Vernon Wells .15

561	Aubrey Huff	.15
562	Xavier Nady	.25
563	Billy McMillon	.15
564	*Ichiro Suzuki*	8.00
565	Tomas de la Rosa	.15
566	Matt Ginter	.15
567	Sun-Woo Kim	.15
568	Nick Johnson	.15
569	Pablo Ozuna	.15
570	Tike Redman	.15
571	Brian Cole	.15
572	Ross Gload	.15
573	Dee Brown	.15
574	Tony McKnight	.15
575	Allen Levrault	.15
576	Lesli Brea	.15
577	Adam Bernero	.15
578	Tom Davey	.15
579	Morgan Burkhart	.15
580	Britt Reames	.15
581	Dave Coggin	.15
582	Trey Moore	.15
583	Matt Kinney	.15
584	Pedro Feliz	.15
585	Brandon Inge	.15
586	Alex Hernandez	.15
587	Toby Hall	.15
588	Grant Roberts	.15
589	Brian Sikorski	.15
590	Aaron Myette	.15
591	Derek Jeter	1.00
592	Ivan Rodriguez	.40
593	Alex Rodriguez	.75
594	Carlos Delgado	.30
595	Mark McGwire	.75
596	Troy Glaus	.40
597	Sammy Sosa	.75
598	Vladimir Guerrero	.50
599	Manny Ramirez	.40
600	Pedro J. Martinez	.50
601	Chipper Jones	.75
602	Jason Giambi	.20
603	Frank Thomas	.50
604	Ken Griffey Jr.	.75
605	Nomar Garciaparra	.75
606	Randy Johnson	.40
607	Mike Piazza	.75
608	Barry Bonds	.50
609	Todd Helton	.40
610	Jeff Bagwell	.40
611	Ken Griffey Jr.	.75
612	Carlos Delgado	.40
613	Jeff Bagwell	.40
614	Jason Giambi	.20
615	Cal Ripken Jr.	1.00
616	Brian Giles	.15
617	Bernie Williams	.30
618	Greg Maddux	.75
619	Troy Glaus	.40
620	Greg Vaughn	.15
621	Sammy Sosa	.75
622	Pat Burrell	.20
623	Ivan Rodriguez	.40
624	Chipper Jones	.75
625	Barry Bonds	.50
626	Roger Clemens	.50
627	Jim Edmonds	.15
628	Nomar Garciaparra	.75
629	Frank Thomas	.50
630	Mike Piazza	.75
631	Randy Johnson	.40
632	Andruw Jones	.30
633	David Wells	.15
634	Manny Ramirez	.40
635	Preston Wilson	.15
636	Todd Helton	.40
637	Kerry Wood	.15
638	Albert Belle	.15
639	Juan Gonzalez	.40
640	Vladimir Guerrero	.50
641	Gary Sheffield	.15
642	Larry Walker	.15
643	Magglio Ordonez	.15
644	Jermaine Dye	.15
645	Scott Rolen	.20
646	Tony Gwynn	.50
647	Shawn Green	.15
648	Roberto Alomar	.30
649	Eric Milton	.15
650	Mark McGwire	.75
651	Tim Hudson	.15
652	Jose Canseco	.20
653	Tom Glavine	.20
654	Derek Jeter	1.00
655	Alex Rodriguez	.75
656	Darin Erstad	.15
657	Jason Kendall	.15
658	Pedro Martinez	.50
659	Richie Sexson	.15
660	Rafael Palmeiro	.20

2001 UPPER DECK VINTAGE

		NM/M
Complete Set (400):		30.00
Common Player:		.10
Pack (10):		2.00
Box (24):		40.00
1	Darin Erstad	.25
2	Seth Etherton	.10
3	Troy Glaus	.50
4	Bengie Molina	.10
5	Mo Vaughn	.20
6	Tim Salmon	.25
7	Ramon Ortiz	.10
8	Adam Kennedy	.10
9	Garret Anderson	.25
10	Troy Percival	.10
11	2000 Angels Lineup	.10
12	Jason Giambi	.50
13	Tim Hudson	.25
14	Adam Piatt	.10
15	Miguel Tejada	.25
16	Mark Mulder	.25
17	Eric Chavez	.25
18	Ramon Hernandez	.10
19	Terrence Long	.10
20	Jason Isringhausen	.10
21	Barry Zito	.50
22	Ben Grieve	.10
23	2000 Athletics Lineup	.10
24	David Wells	.10
25	Raul Mondesi	.20
26	Darrin Fletcher	.10
27	Shannon Stewart	.10
28	Kelvim Escobar	.10
29	Tony Batista	.10
30	Carlos Delgado	.50
31	Brad Fullmer	.10
32	Billy Koch	.10
33	Jose Cruz Jr.	.10
34	2000 Blue Jays Lineup	.10
35	Greg Vaughn	.10
36	Roberto Hernandez	.10
37	Vinny Castilla	.10
38	Gerald Williams	.10
39	Aubrey Huff	.10
40	Bryan Rekar	.10
41	Albie Lopez	.10
42	Fred McGriff	.25
43	Miguel Cairo	.10
44	Ryan Rupe	.10
45	2000 Devil Rays Lineup	.10
46	Jim Thome	.50
47	Roberto Alomar	.50
48	Bartolo Colon	.25
49	Omar Vizquel	.20
50	Travis Fryman	.20
51	Manny Ramirez	.50
52	Dave Burba	.10
53	Chuck Finley	.10
54	Russ Branyan	.10
55	Kenny Lofton	.25
56	2000 Indians Lineup	.10
57	Alex Rodriguez	1.50
58	Jay Buhner	.10
59	Aaron Sele	.10
60	Kazuhiro Sasaki	.20
61	Edgar Martinez	.20
62	John Halama	.10
63	Mike Cameron	.10
64	Fred Garcia	.10
65	John Olerud	.20
66	Jamie Moyer	.10
67	Gil Meche	.10
68	2000 Mariners Lineup	.10
69	Cal Ripken Jr.	2.00
70	Sidney Ponson	.10
71	Chris Richard	.10
72	Jose Mercedes	.10
73	Albert Belle	.15
74	Mike Mussina	.50
75	Brady Anderson	.15
76	Delino DeShields	.10
77	Melvin Mora	.10
78	Luis Matos	.10
79	Brook Fordyce	.10
80	2000 Orioles Lineup	.10
81	Rafael Palmeiro	.50
82	Rick Helling	.10
83	Ruben Mateo	.10
84	Rusty Greer	.10
85	Ivan Rodriguez	.50
86	Doug Davis	.10
87	Gabe Kapler	.15
88	Mike Lamb	.10
89	Alex Rodriguez	1.50
90	Kenny Rogers	.10
91	2000 Rangers Lineup	.10
92	Nomar Garciaparra	1.50
93	Trot Nixon	.10
94	Tomokazu Ohka	.10
95	Pedro Martinez	.75
96	Dante Bichette	.10
97	Jason Varitek	.10
98	Rolando Arrojo	.10
99	Carl Everett	.10
100	Derek Lowe	.10
101	Troy O'Leary	.10
102	Tim Wakefield	.10
103	2000 Red Sox Lineup	.10
104	Mike Sweeney	.10
105	Carlos Febles	.10
106	Joe Randa	.10
107	Jeff Suppan	.10
108	Mac Suzuki	.10
109	Jermaine Dye	.10
110	Carlos Beltran	.25
111	Mark Quinn	.10
112	Johnny Damon	.20
113	2000 Royals Lineup	.10
114	Tony Clark	.10
115	Dean Palmer	.10
116	Brian Moehler	.10
117	Brad Ausmus	.10
118	Juan Gonzalez	.50
119	Juan Encarnacion	.10
120	Jeff Weaver	.10
121	Bobby Higginson	.10
122	Todd Jones	.10
123	Deivi Cruz	.10
124	2000 Tigers Lineup	.10
125	Corey Koskie	.10
126	Matt Lawton	.10
127	Mark Redman	.10
128	David Ortiz	.10
129	Jay Canizaro	.10
130	Eric Milton	.10
131	Jacque Jones	.10
132	J.C. Romero	.10
133	Ron Coomer	.10
134	Brad Radke	.10
135	2000 Twins Lineup	.10
136	Carlos Lee	.10
137	Frank Thomas	.75
138	Mike Sirotka	.10
139	Charles Johnson	.10
140	James Baldwin	.10
141	Magglio Ordonez	.25
142	Jon Garland	.10
143	Paul Konerko	.10
144	Ray Durham	.10
145	Keith Foulke	.10
146	Chris Singleton	.10
147	2000 White Sox Lineup	.10
148	Bernie Williams	.50
149	Orlando Hernandez	.15
150	David Justice	.25
151	Andy Pettitte	.25
152	Mariano Rivera	.25
153	Derek Jeter	2.00
154	Jorge Posada	.25
155	Jose Canseco	.50
156	Glenallen Hill	.10
157	Paul O'Neill	.25
158	Denny Neagle	.10
159	Chuck Knoblauch	.10
160	Roger Clemens	1.50
161	2000 Yankees Lineup	.10
162	Jeff Bagwell	.50
163	Moises Alou	.20
164	Lance Berkman	.40
165	Shane Reynolds	.10
166	Ken Caminiti	.10
167	Craig Biggio	.25
168	Jose Lima	.10
169	Octavio Dotel	.10
170	Richard Hidalgo	.20
171	Scott Elarton	.10
172	2000 Astros Lineup	.10
173	Rafael Furcal	.25
174	Greg Maddux	1.00
175	Quilvio Veras	.10
176	Chipper Jones	1.00
177	Andres Galarraga	.25
178	Brian Jordan	.10
179	Tom Glavine	.25
180	Kevin Millwood	.25
181	Javier Lopez	.25
182	B.J. Surhoff	.10
183	Andruw Jones	.50
184	Andy Ashby	.10
185	2000 Braves Lineup	.10
186	Richie Sexson	.40
187	Jeff D'Amico	.10
188	Ron Belliard	.10
189	Jeromy Burnitz	.10
190	Jimmy Haynes	.10
191	Marquis Grissom	.10
192	Jose Hernandez	.10
193	Geoff Jenkins	.20
194	Jamey Wright	.10
195	Mark Loretta	.10
196	2000 Brewers Lineup	.10
197	Rick Ankiel	.10
198	Mark McGwire	1.50
199	Fernando Vina	.10
200	David Renteria	.10
201	Darryl Kile	.10
202	Jim Edmonds	.25
203	Ray Lankford	.10
204	Garrett Stephenson	.10
205	Fernando Tatis	.10
206	Will Clark	.40
207	J.D. Drew	.15
208	2000 Cardinals Lineup	.10
209	Mark Grace	.25
210	Eric Young	.10
211	Sammy Sosa	1.50
212	Jon Lieber	.10
213	Joe Girardi	.10
214	Kevin Tapani	.10
215	Ricky Gutierrez	.10
216	Kerry Wood	.50
217	Rondell White	.20
218	Damon Buford	.10
219	2000 Cubs Lineup	.10
220	Luis Gonzalez	.25
221	Randy Johnson	.75
222	Jay Bell	.10
223	Erubiel Durazo	.10
224	Matt Williams	.25
225	Steve Finley	.10
226	Curt Schilling	.40
227	Todd Stottlemyre	.10
228	Tony Womack	.10
229	Brian Anderson	.10
230	2000 Diamondbacks Lineup	.10
231	Gary Sheffield	.40
232	Adrian Beltre	.25
233	Todd Hundley	.10
234	Chan Ho Park	.10
235	Shawn Green	.25
236	Kevin Brown	.25
237	Tom Goodwin	.10
238	Mark Grudzielanek	.10
239	Ismael Valdes	.10
240	Eric Karros	.10
241	2000 Dodgers Lineup	.10
242	Jose Vidro	.10
243	Javier Vazquez	.20
244	Orlando Cabrera	.10
245	Peter Bergeron	.10
246	Vladimir Guerrero	.75
247	Dustin Hermanson	.10
248	Tony Armas Jr.	.10
249	Lee Stevens	.10
250	Milton Bradley	.10
251	Carl Pavano	.10
252	2000 Expos Lineup	.10
253	Ellis Burks	.10
254	Robb Nen	.10
255	J.T. Snow	.10
256	Barry Bonds	2.00
257	Shawn Estes	.10
258	Jeff Kent	.20
259	Kirk Rueter	.10
260	Bill Mueller	.10
261	Livan Hernandez	.10
262	Rich Aurilia	.10
263	2000 Giants Lineup	.10
264	Ryan Dempster	.10
265	Cliff Floyd	.10
266	Mike Lowell	.10
267	A.J. Burnett	.10
268	Preston Wilson	.10

269	Luis Castillo	.10
270	Henry Rodriguez	.10
271	Antonio Alfonseca	.10
272	Derek Lee	.10
273	Mark Kotsay	.10
274	Brad Penny	.10
275	2000 Marlins Lineup	.10
276	Mike Piazza	1.00
277	Jay Payton	.10
278	Al Leiter	.15
279	Mike Bordick	.10
280	Armando Benitez	.10
281	Todd Zeile	.10
282	Mike Hampton	.20
283	Edgardo Alfonzo	.10
284	Derek Bell	.10
285	Robin Ventura	.20
286	2000 Mets Lineup	.10
287	Tony Gwynn	.75
288	Trevor Hoffman	.10
289	Ryan Klesko	.20
290	Phil Nevin	.10
291	Matt Clement	.10
292	Ben Davis	.10
293	Ruben Rivera	.10
294	Bret Boone	.25
295	Adam Eaton	.10
296	Eric Owens	.10
297	2000 Padres Lineup	.10
298	Bob Abreu	.20
299	Mike Lieberthal	.10
300	Robert Person	.10
301	Scott Rolen	.50
302	Randy Wolf	.10
303	Bruce Chen	.10
304	Travis Lee	.10
305	Kent Bottenfield	.10
306	Pat Burrell	.50
307	Doug Glanville	.10
308	2000 Phillies Lineup	.10
309	Brian Giles	.25
310	Todd Ritchie	.10
311	Warren Morris	.10
312	John Vander Wal	.10
313	Kris Benson	.10
314	Jason Kendall	.10
315	Kevin Young	.10
316	Francisco Cordova	.10
317	Jimmy Anderson	.10
318	2000 Pirates Lineup	.10
319	Ken Griffey Jr.	1.00
320	Pokey Reese	.10
321	Chris Stynes	.10
322	Barry Larkin	.40
323	Steve Parris	.10
324	Michael Tucker	.10
325	Dmitri Young	.10
326	Pete Harnisch	.10
327	Adam Graves	.10
328	Aaron Boone	.10
329	Sean Casey	.10
330	2000 Reds Lineup	.10
331	Todd Helton	.50
332	Pedro Astacio	.10
333	Larry Walker	.25
334	Ben Petrick	.10
335	Brian Bohanon	.10
336	Juan Pierre	.10
337	Jeffrey Hammonds	.10
338	Jeff Cirillo	.10
339	Todd Hollandsworth	.10
340	2000 Rockies Lineup	.10
341	Matt Wise, Keith Luuloa, Derrick Turnbow	.10
342	Jason Hart, Jose Ortiz, Mario Encarnacion	.10
343	Vernon Wells, Pascual Coco, Josh Phelps	.25
344	Travis Harper, Kenny Kelley, Toby Hall	.10
345	*Danys Baez, Tim Drew, Martin Vargas*	.10
346	Ichiro Suzuki, Ryan Franklin, Ryan Christianson	10.00
347	Jay Spurgeon, Lesli Brea, Carlos Casimiro	.10
348	B.J. Waszgis, Brian Sikorski, Joaquin Benoit	.10
349	Sun-Woo Kim, Paxton Crawford, Steve Lomasney	.10
350	Kris Wilson, Orber Moreno, Dee Brown	.10
351	Mark Johnson, Brandon Inge, Adam Bernero	.10
352	Danny Ardoin, Matt Kinney, Jason Ryan	.10
353	Rocky Biddle, Joe Crede, Aaron Myette	.10
354	Nick Johnson, D'Angelo Jimenez, Willi Mo Pena	.10
355	Tony McKnight, Aaron McNeal, Keith Ginter	.10
356	Mark DeRosa, Jason Marquis, Wes Helms	.10
357	Allen Levrault, Horacio Estrada, Santiago Perez	.10
358	Luis Saturria, Gene Stechschulte, Britt Reames	.10
359	Joey Nation, Corey Patterson, Cole Liniak	.25
360	Alex Cabrera, Geraldo Guzman, Nelson Figueroa	.10
361	Hiram Bocachica, Mike Judd, Luke Prokopec	.10
362	Tomas de la Rosa, Yohanny Valera, Talmadge Nunnari	.10
363	Ryan Vogelsong, Juan Melo, Chad Zerbe	.10
364	Jason Grilli, Pablo Ozuna, Ramon Castro	.10
365	Timoniel Perez, Grant Roberts, Brian Cole	.10
366	Tom Davey, Xavier Nady, Dave Maurer	.50
367	Jimmy Rollins, Mark Brownson, Reggie Taylor	.10
368	Alex Hernandez, Adam Hyzdu, Tike Redman	.10
369	Brady Clark, John Riedling, Mike Bell	.10
370	Giovanni Carrara, Josh Kalinowski, Elvis Pena	.10
371	Jim Edmonds	.10
372	Edgar Martinez	.10
373	Rickey Henderson	.10
374	Barry Zito	.25
375	Tino Martinez	.10
376	J.T. Snow	.10
377	Bobby Jones	.10
378	Alex Rodriguez	1.00
379	Mike Hampton	.10
380	Roger Clemens	.50
381	Jay Payton	.10
382	John Olerud	.10
383	David Justice	.25
384	Mike Hampton	.10
385	Yankees Celebrate	.75
386	Jose Vizcaino	.10
387	Roger Clemens	.75
388	Todd Zeile	.10
389	Derek Jeter	1.25
390	Yankees Celebrate	.50
391	Nomar Garciaparra - AL Batting	.75
392	Todd Helton - NL Batting	.25
393	Troy Glaus - AL HR	.25
394	Sammy Sosa - NL HR	.50
395	Edgar Martinez - AL RBI	.10
396	Todd Helton - NL RBI	.25
397	Pedro Martinez - AL ERA	.40
398	Kevin Brown - NL ERA	.10
399	David Wells, Tim Hudson - AL Wins	.10
400	Tom Glavine - NL Wins	.10

All-Star Tributes

		NM/M
Complete Set (10):		20.00
Common Player:		1.00
Inserted 1:23		
1	Derek Jeter	4.00
2	Mike Piazza	2.00
3	Carlos Delgado	1.00
4	Pedro Martinez	1.50
5	Vladimir Guerrero	1.50
6	Mark McGwire	3.00
7	Alex Rodriguez	3.00
8	Barry Bonds	4.00
9	Chipper Jones	2.00
10	Sammy Sosa	2.50

Glory Days

		NM/M
Complete Set (15):		15.00
Common Player:		.50
Inserted 1:15		
1	Jermaine Dye	.50
2	Chipper Jones	2.00
3	Todd Helton	1.00
4	Magglio Ordonez	.75
5	Tony Gwynn	1.50
6	Jim Edmonds	.75
7	Rafael Palmeiro	1.00
8	Barry Bonds	4.00
9	Carl Everett	.50
10	Mike Piazza	2.00
11	Brian Giles	.50
12	Tony Batista	.50
13	Jeff Bagwell	1.00
14	Ken Griffey Jr.	2.00
15	Troy Glaus	1.00

Fantasy Outfield Combo Jersey

		NM/M
Production 25 cards		
FO-CJ	Joe DiMaggio, Mickey Mantle, Ken Griffey Jr.	1,000

Matinee Idols

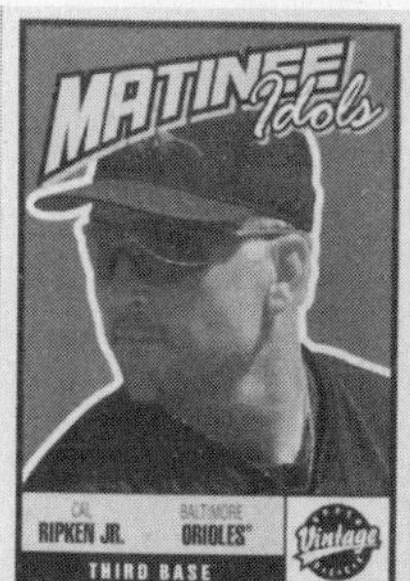

		NM/M
Complete Set (20):		10.00
Common Player:		.50
Inserted 1:4		
1	Ken Griffey Jr.	1.00
2	Derek Jeter	2.00
3	Barry Bonds	2.00
4	Chipper Jones	1.00
5	Mike Piazza	1.00
6	Todd Helton	.50
7	Randy Johnson	.75
8	Alex Rodriguez	1.50
9	Sammy Sosa	1.50
10	Cal Ripken Jr.	2.00
11	Nomar Garciaparra	1.50
12	Carlos Delgado	.50
13	Jason Giambi	.50
14	Ivan Rodriguez	.50
15	Vladimir Guerrero	.75
16	Gary Sheffield	.50
17	Frank Thomas	.50
18	Jeff Bagwell	.50
19	Pedro Martinez	.75
20	Mark McGwire	1.50

Mantle Pinstripes Exclusive

	NM/M
Complete Set (56):	75.00
Common Mantle:	2.00
One pack/box	

Mantle Pinstripes Memorabilia

		NM/M
Print Runs listed:		
MMBC	Mickey Mantle bat/cut/7	
MMB	Mickey Mantle bat/100	100.00
MMCJ	Mickey Mantle, Roger Maris jsy/50	300.00
MMC	Mickey Mantle cut/7	
MMJ	Mickey Mantle jsy/100	125.00

Retro Rules

		NM/M
Complete Set (15):		20.00
Common Player:		.50
Inserted 1:15		
1	Nomar Garciaparra	3.00
2	Frank Thomas	1.00
3	Jeff Bagwell	1.00
4	Sammy Sosa	2.50
5	Derek Jeter	4.00
6	David Wells	.50
7	Vladimir Guerrero	1.50
8	Jim Thome	1.00
9	Mark McGwire	3.00
10	Todd Helton	1.00
11	Tony Gwynn	1.50
12	Bernie Williams	.75
13	Cal Ripken Jr.	4.00
14	Brian Giles	.75
15	Jason Giambi	1.50

Timeless Teams Bat

		NM/M
Common Player:		8.00
Inserted 1:72		
NYY-JD	Joe DiMaggio	150.00
NYY-TH	Tommy Henrich	8.00
NYY-CK	Charlie Keller	8.00
NYY-BD	Bill Dickey	20.00
BK-JR	Jackie Robinson	90.00
BK-RC	Roy Campanella	50.00
BK-GH	Gil Hodges	25.00
BK-DN	Don Newcombe	8.00
LA-SG	Steve Garvey	8.00
LA-RC	Ron Cey	8.00
LA-BR	Bill Russell	8.00
LA-DB	Dusty Baker	8.00
BA-BP	Boog Powell	8.00
BA-BR	Brooks Robinson	25.00
BA-FR	Frank Robinson	20.00
BA-MB	Mark Belanger	8.00
PI-RC	Roberto Clemente	100.00
PI-WS	Willie Stargell	20.00
PI-MS	Manny Sanguillen	8.00
PI-AO	Al Oliver	8.00
OA-RJ	Reggie Jackson	20.00
OA-SB	Sal Bando	8.00
OA-GT	Gene Tenace	8.00
OA-JR	Joe Rudi	8.00
CI2-JB	Johnny Bench	25.00
CI2-TP	Tony Perez	15.00
CI2-JM	Joe Morgan	8.00
CI2-KG	Ken Griffey Sr.	8.00
NYM-NR	Nolan Ryan	40.00
NYM-RS	Ron Swoboda	8.00
NYM-EK	Ed Kranepool	8.00
NYM-TA	Tommie Agee	8.00

Timeless Teams Jersey

	NM/M
Common Player:	15.00

Inserted 1:288
NYY-MM Mickey Mantle 160.00
NYY-RM Roger Maris 50.00
NYY-BR Bobby Richardson 15.00
CI-DC Dave Concepcion 15.00
CI-TP Tony Perez 20.00
CI-KG Ken Griffey Sr. 15.00
CI-JM Joe Morgan 20.00

Timeless Teams Combo Bat

NM/M
Common Card: 75.00
Production 100 sets
NYY41 Joe DiMaggio, Tommy Henrich, Bill Dickey, Charlie Keller 200.00
BKN55 Jackie Robinson, Roy Campanella, Gil Hodges, Don Newcombe 175.00
BAL70 Frank Robinson, Brooks Robinson, Mark Belanger, Boog Powell 120.00
LA81 Steve Garvey, Ron Cey, Dusty Baker, Bill Russell 75.00
PIT71 Roberto Clemente, Willie Stargell, Bill Mazeroski, Al Oliver 200.00
OAK72 Reggie Jackson, Sal Bando, Gene Tenace, Joe Rudi 80.00
CIN75 Johnny Bench, Tony Perez, Joe Morgan, Ken Griffey Sr. 120.00
NYM69 Nolan Ryan, Ron Swoboda, Ed Kranepool, Tommie Agee 200.00

Timeless Teams Combo Jersey

NM/M
Production 100 sets
NYY61 Mickey Mantle, Roger Maris, Bobby Richardson 250.00
CIN75 Dave Concepcion, Tony Perez, Ken Griffey Sr. 120.00

2001 UD RESERVE

NM/M
Complete Set (210):
Common Player: .15
Common SP (181-210): 3.00
Production 2,500
Pack (5): 3.00
Box (24): 60.00
1 Darin Erstad .25
2 Tim Salmon .25
3 Bengie Molina .15
4 Troy Glaus .50
5 Glenallen Hill .15

6 Garret Anderson .25
7 Jason Giambi .50
8 Johnny Damon .25
9 Eric Chavez .25
10 Tim Hudson .25
11 Miguel Tejada .25
12 Barry Zito .25
13 Jose Ortiz .15
14 Tony Batista .15
15 Carlos Delgado .50
16 Shannon Stewart .15
17 Raul Mondesi .15
18 Ben Grieve .15
19 Aubrey Huff .15
20 Greg Vaughn .15
21 Fred McGriff .25
22 Gerald Williams .15
23 Bartolo Colon .25
24 Roberto Alomar .40
25 Jim Thome .50
26 Omar Vizquel .25
27 Juan Gonzalez .50
28 Ellis Burks .15
29 Edgar Martinez .25
30 Aaron Sele .15
31 Jay Buhner .15
32 Mike Cameron .15
33 Kazuhiro Sasaki .15
34 John Olerud .25
35 Cal Ripken Jr. 2.00
36 Brady Anderson .15
37 Pat Hentgen .15
38 Chris Richard .15
39 Jerry Hairston Jr. .15
40 Mike Bordick .15
41 Ivan Rodriguez .50
42 Rick Helling .15
43 Rafael Palmeiro .50
44 Alex Rodriguez 1.50
45 Andres Galarraga .25
46 Rusty Greer .15
47 Ruben Mateo .15
48 Ken Caminiti .15
49 Nomar Garciaparra 1.50
50 Pedro Martinez .75
51 Manny Ramirez .50
52 Carl Everett .15
53 Dante Bichette .15
54 Hideo Nomo .40
55 Mike Sweeney .15
56 Carlos Beltran .25
57 Jeff Suppan .15
58 Jermaine Dye .15
59 Mark Quinn .15
60 Joe Randa .15
61 Bobby Higginson .15
62 Tony Clark .15
63 Brian Moehler .15
64 Dean Palmer .15
65 Brandon Inge .15
66 Damion Easley .15
67 Brad Radke .15
68 Corey Koskie .15
69 Cristian Guzman .15
70 Eric Milton .15
71 Jacque Jones .15
72 Matt Lawton .15
73 Frank Thomas .50
74 David Wells .15
75 Magglio Ordonez .25
76 Paul Konerko .15
77 Sandy Alomar Jr. .15
78 Ray Durham .15
79 Roger Clemens 1.50
80 Bernie Williams .50
81 Derek Jeter 2.00
82 David Justice .25
83 Paul O'Neill .25
84 Mike Mussina .40
85 Jorge Posada .40
86 Jeff Bagwell .50
87 Richard Hidalgo .15
88 Craig Biggio .25
89 Scott Elarton .15
90 Moises Alou .25
91 Greg Maddux 1.00
92 Rafael Furcal .25
93 Andruw Jones .50
94 Tom Glavine .25
95 Chipper Jones 1.00
96 Javy Lopez .25
97 Richie Sexson .40
98 Jeromy Burnitz .15
99 Jeff D'Amico .15
100 Jeffrey Hammonds .15
101 Geoff Jenkins .25
102 Ben Sheets .25
103 Mark McGwire 1.50
104 Rick Ankiel .15
105 Darryl Kile .15
106 Edgar Renteria .15
107 Jim Edmonds .25
108 J.D. Drew .25
109 Sammy Sosa 1.50
110 Corey Patterson .25
111 Kerry Wood .50
112 Todd Hundley .15
113 Rondell White .15
114 Matt Stairs .15
115 Randy Johnson .75
116 Mark Grace .40
117 Steve Finley .15
118 Luis Gonzalez .25
119 Matt Williams .25
120 Curt Schilling .40
121 Gary Sheffield .40
122 Kevin Brown .25
123 Shawn Green .25
124 Eric Karros .15
125 Chan Ho Park .15
126 Adrian Beltre .25
127 Vladimir Guerrero .75
128 Fernando Tatis .15
129 Lee Stevens .15
130 Jose Vidro .15
131 Peter Bergeron .15
132 Michael Barrett .15
133 Jeff Kent .25
134 Russ Ortiz .15
135 Barry Bonds 2.00
136 J.T. Snow .15
137 Livan Hernandez .15
138 Rich Aurilia .15
139 Preston Wilson .15
140 Mike Lowell .15
141 Ryan Dempster .15
142 Charles Johnson .15
143 Matt Clement .15
144 Luis Castillo .15
145 Mike Piazza 1.00
146 Al Leiter .15
147 Robin Ventura .25
148 Jay Payton .15
149 Todd Zeile .15
150 Edgardo Alfonzo .15
151 Tony Gwynn .75
152 Ryan Klesko .25
153 Phil Nevin .15
154 Mark Kotsay .15
155 Trevor Hoffman .15
156 Damian Jackson .15
157 Scott Rolen .50
158 Mike Lieberthal .15
159 Bruce Chen .15
160 Bobby Abreu .25
161 Pat Burrell .40
162 Travis Lee .15
163 Jason Kendall .15
164 Derek Bell .15
165 Kris Benson .15
166 Kevin Young .15
167 Brian Giles .25
168 Pat Meares .15
169 Sean Casey .25
170 Pokey Reese .15
171 Pete Harnisch .15
172 Barry Larkin .25
173 Ken Griffey Jr. 1.00
174 Dmitri Young .15
175 Mike Hampton .15
176 Todd Helton .50
177 Jeff Cirillo .15
178 Denny Neagle .15
179 Larry Walker .25
180 Todd Hollandsworth .15
181 *Ichiro Suzuki* 35.00
182 *Wilson Betemit* 6.00
183 *Adrian Hernandez* 3.00
184 *Travis Hafner* 10.00
185 *Sean Douglass* 3.00
186 *Juan Diaz* 3.00
187 *Horacio Ramirez* 5.00
188 *Morgan Ensberg* 10.00
189 *Brandon Duckworth* 3.00
190 *Jack Wilson* 8.00
191 *Erick Almonte* 3.00
192 *Ricardo Rodriguez* 3.00
193 *Elpidio Guzman* 3.00
194 *Juan Uribe* 5.00
195 *Ryan Freel* 4.00
196 *Christian Parker* 3.00
197 *Jackson Melian* 3.00
198 *Jose Mieses* 3.00
199 *Andres Torres* 3.00
200 *Jason Smith* 3.00
201 *Johnny Estrada* 6.00
202 *Cesar Crespo* 3.00
203 *Carlos Valderrama* 3.00
204 *Albert Pujols* 65.00
205 *Wilken Ruan* 3.00
206 *Josh Fogg* 4.00
207 *Bert Snow* 3.00
208 *Brian Lawrence* 5.00
209 *Esix Snead* 3.00
210 *Tsuyoshi Shinjo* 4.00

Big Game Reserve

NM/M
Complete Set (10): 15.00
Common Player: 1.00
Inserted 1:24
BG1 Alex Rodriguez 3.00
BG2 Ken Griffey Jr. 2.00
BG3 Mark McGwire 3.00
BG4 Derek Jeter 4.00
BG5 Sammy Sosa 2.50
BG6 Pedro Martinez 1.50
BG7 Jason Giambi 1.00
BG8 Todd Helton 1.00
BG9 Carlos Delgado 1.00
BG10 Mike Piazza 2.00

Jerseys duo

NM/M
Common Duo: 15.00
Inserted 1:240
HG Tim Hudson, Jason Giambi 25.00
BK Barry Bonds, Jeff Kent 40.00
JJ Andruw Jones, Chipper Jones 25.00
GE Troy Glaus, Darin Erstad 15.00
WO David Wells, Magglio Ordonez 15.00
WE Bernie Williams, Jim Edmonds 15.00
DG Carlos Delgado, Jason Giambi 20.00
GK Jason Giambi, Jeff Kent 20.00
JW Randy Johnson, David Wells 25.00
JG Chipper Jones, Troy Glaus 25.00
SB Gary Sheffield, Barry Bonds 40.00
HE Todd Helton, Darin Erstad 20.00
RB Alex Rodriguez, Tony Batista 25.00
GW Brian Giles, Bernie Williams 15.00
SG Sammy Sosa, Troy Glaus 30.00

Jerseys trio

NM/M
Common Trio: 25.00

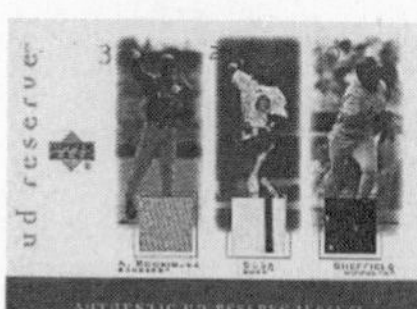

Inserted 1:480
GHD Jason Giambi, Todd Helton, Carlos Delgado 30.00
RSS Alex Rodriguez, Sammy Sosa, Gary Sheffield 50.00
WEJ Bernie Williams, Jim Edmonds, Andruw Jones 25.00
HJW Tim Hudson, Randy Johnson, David Wells 30.00
SOD Sammy Sosa, Magglio Ordonez, Carlos Delgado 40.00
GGR Jason Giambi, Troy Glaus, Alex Rodriguez 40.00
BWD Tony Batista, Bernie Williams, Carlos Delgado 25.00
BSH Barry Bonds, Gary Sheffield, Todd Helton 50.00
WSH David Wells, Sammy Sosa, Todd Helton 40.00
EKE Darin Erstad, Jeff Kent, Jim Edmonds 25.00

Jerseys quad

NM/M
Common Quad: 25.00
Production 50 sets
DRGS Carlos Delgado, Alex Rodriguez, Troy Glaus, Sammy Sosa 40.00
GWBG Jason Giambi, Bernie Williams, Barry Bonds, Brian Giles 75.00
HKEJ Todd Helton, Jeff Kent, Jim Edmonds, Chipper Jones 40.00
HKEJ Gary Sheffield, Magglio Ordonez, Darin Erstad, Tony Batista 25.00
JRSB Andruw Jones, Alex Rodriguez, Sammy Sosa, Barry Bonds 100.00

G-U Reserve Base/Ball duo

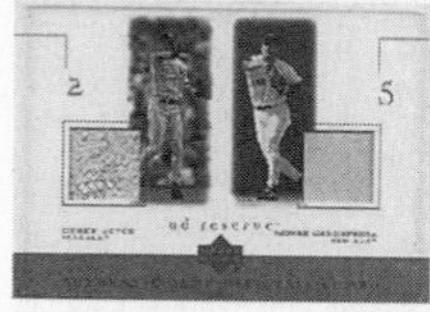

NM/M
Inserted 1:240
JR Derek Jeter, Alex Rodriguez 50.00
JP Derek Jeter, Mike Piazza 60.00
MP Mark McGwire, Mike Piazza 100.00
MJ Mark McGwire, Derek Jeter 100.00
RM Alex Rodriguez, Mark McGwire 100.00
CR Roger Clemens, Alex Rodriguez 40.00
ST Sammy Sosa, Frank Thomas 40.00
GD Vladimir Guerrero, Carlos Delgado 20.00
BH Barry Bonds, Todd Helton 35.00
MG Mark McGwire, Ken Griffey Jr. 40.00
GS Ken Griffey Jr., Sammy Sosa 20.00
GJ Ken Griffey Jr., Derek Jeter 35.00
JN Chipper Jones, Nomar Garciaparra 20.00
NJ Nomar Garciaparra, Derek Jeter 35.00
GR Nomar Garciaparra, Alex Rodriguez 30.00

G-U Reserve Base/Ball trio

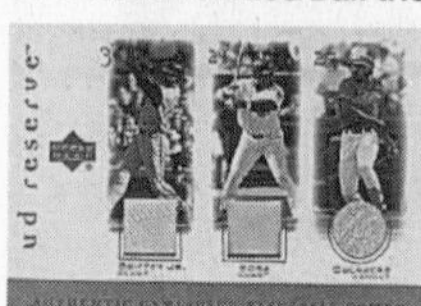

NM/M
Inserted 1:480
JRG Derek Jeter, Alex Rodriguez, Nomar Garciaparra 50.00
SGM Sammy Sosa, Ken Griffey Jr., Mark McGwire 65.00
PRS Mike Piazza, Alex Rodriguez, Sammy Sosa 40.00
GSG Ken Griffey Jr., Sammy Sosa, Vladimir Guerrero 30.00
THM Frank Thomas, Todd Helton, Mark McGwire 65.00
CMJ Roger Clemens, Pedro Martinez, Derek Jeter 45.00
BSH Barry Bonds, Gary Sheffield, Todd Helton 40.00
GPJ Vladimir Guerrero, Mike Piazza, Chipper Jones 30.00
MJR Mark McGwire, Derek Jeter, Alex Rodriguez 75.00
JGS Derek Jeter, Ken Griffey Jr., Sammy Sosa 45.00

G-U Reserve Base/Ball quad

NM/M
Production 50 sets
SGRM Sammy Sosa, Ken Griffey Jr., Alex Rodriguez, Mark McGwire 175.00
GPJG Vladimir Guerrero, Mike Piazza, Chipper Jones, Nomar Garciaparra 65.00
THMJ Frank Thomas, Todd Helton, Mark McGwire, Derek Jeter 90.00
GBJE Ken Griffey Jr., Barry Bonds, Andruw Jones, Jim Edmonds 75.00
PMJR Mike Piazza, Mark McGwire, Derek Jeter, Alex Rodriguez 150.00

The New Order

NM/M
Complete Set (10): 15.00
Common Player: .75
Inserted 1:24
NO1 Vladimir Guerrero 1.50
NO2 Andruw Jones 1.00
NO3 Corey Patterson .75
NO4 Derek Jeter 4.00
NO5 Alex Rodriguez 3.00
NO6 Pat Burrell .75
NO7 Ichiro Suzuki 5.00
NO8 Barry Zito .75
NO9 Rafael Furcal .75
NO10 Troy Glaus 1.00

UD Royalty

NM/M
Complete Set (10): 15.00
Common Player: 1.00
Inserted 1:24
R1 Ken Griffey Jr. 2.00
R2 Derek Jeter 4.00
R3 Alex Rodriguez 3.00
R4 Sammy Sosa 2.50
R5 Mark McGwire 3.00

R6 Mike Piazza 2.00
R7 Vladimir Guerrero 1.50
R8 Chipper Jones 2.00
R9 Frank Thomas 1.00
R10 Nomar Garciaparra 3.00

2002 UPPER DECK

NM/M
Complete Set (745): 100.00
Complete Series I (500): 60.00
Complete Series II (245): 40.00
Common Player: .15
Series 1 Hobby Pack (8): 4.00
Series 1 Hobby Box (24): 75.00
Series 2 Hobby Pack (8): 1.25
Series 2 Hobby Box (24): 25.00
1 Mark Prior 4.00
2 Mark Teixeira 1.50
3 Brian Roberts .25
4 Jason Romano .25
5 *Dennis Stark* .50
6 Oscar Salazar .50
7 John Patterson .25
8 Shane Loux .25
9 Marcus Giles .40
10 Juan Cruz .25
11 Jorge Julio .25
12 Adam Dunn .50
13 Delvin James .25
14 Jeremy Affeldt .25
15 Tim Raines Jr. .25
16 Luke Hudson .25
17 Todd Sears .25
18 George Perez .25
19 Wilmy Caceres .25
20 Abraham Nunez .25
21 Mike Amrhein .25
22 Carlos Hernandez .25
23 Scott Hodges .25
24 Brandon Knight .25
25 Geoff Goetz .25
26 Carlos Garcia .25
27 Luis Pineda .25
28 Chris Gissell .25
29 Jae Weong .25
30 Paul Phillips .25
31 Cory Aldridge .25
32 *Aaron Cook* .50
33 Rendy Espina .25
34 Jason Phillips .25
35 Carlos Silva .25
36 Ryan Mills .25
37 Pedro Santana .25
38 John Grabow .25
39 Cody Ransom .15
40 Orlando Woodlands .25
41 Bud Smith .25
42 Junior Guerrero .25
43 David Brous .25
44 Steve Green .25
45 Brian Rogers .25
46 Juan Figueroa .25
47 Nick Punto .25
48 Junior Herndon .25
49 Justin Kaye .25
50 Jason Karnuth .25
51 Troy Glaus .40
52 Bengie Molina .15
53 Ramon Ortiz .15
54 Adam Kennedy .15
55 Jarrod Washburn .15
56 Troy Percival .15
57 David Eckstein .15
58 Ben Weber .15
59 Larry Barnes .15
60 Ismael Valdes .15
61 Benji Gil .15
62 Scott Schoeneweis .15
63 Pat Rapp .15
64 Jason Giambi .50
65 Mark Mulder .25
66 Ron Gant .15
67 Johnny Damon .25
68 Adam Piatt .15
69 Jermaine Dye .25
70 Jason Hart .15
71 Eric Chavez .40
72 Jim Mecir .15
73 Barry Zito .40
74 Jason Isringhausen .15
75 Jeremy Giambi .15
76 Olmedo Saenz .15
77 Terrence Long .15
78 Ramon Hernandez .15
79 Chris Carpenter .15
80 Raul Mondesi .15
81 Carlos Delgado .50
82 Billy Koch .15
83 Vernon Wells .25
84 Darrin Fletcher .15
85 Homer Bush .15
86 Pasqual Coco .15
87 Shannon Stewart .15
88 Chris Woodward .15
89 Joe Lawrence .15
90 Esteban Loaiza .15
91 Cesar Izturis .15
92 Kelvim Escobar .15
93 Greg Vaughn .15
94 Brent Abernathy .15
95 Tanyon Sturtze .15
96 Steve Cox .15
97 Aubrey Huff .15
98 Jesus Colome .15
99 Ben Grieve .15
100 Esteban Yan .15
101 Joe Kennedy .15
102 Felix Martinez .15
103 Nick Bierbrodt .15
104 Damian Rolls .15
105 Russ Johnson .15
106 Toby Hall .15
107 Roberto Alomar .40
108 Bartolo Colon .25
109 John Rocker .15
110 Juan Gonzalez .50
111 Einar Diaz .15
112 Chuck Finley .15
113 Kenny Lofton .25
114 Danys Baez .15
115 Travis Fryman .25
116 C.C. Sabathia .25
117 Paul Shuey .15
118 Marty Cordova .15
119 Ellis Burks .15
120 Bob Wickman .15
121 Edgar Martinez .25
122 Freddy Garcia .15
123 Ichiro Suzuki 1.50
124 John Olerud .25
125 Gil Meche .15
126 Dan Wilson .15
127 Aaron Sele .15
128 Kazuhiro Sasaki .15
129 Mark McLemore .15
130 Carlos Guillen .15
131 Al Martin .15
132 David Bell .15
133 Jay Buhner .15
134 Stan Javier .15
135 Tony Batista .15
136 Jason Johnson .15
137 Brook Fordyce .15
138 Mike Kinkade .15
139 Willis Roberts .15
140 David Segui .15
141 Josh Towers .15
142 Jeff Conine .15

No.	Player	Price
143	Chris Richard	.15
144	Pat Hentgen	.15
145	Melvin Mora	.15
146	Jerry Hairston Jr.	.15
147	Calvin Maduro	.15
148	Brady Anderson	.15
149	Alex Rodriguez	1.50
150	Kenny Rogers	.15
151	Chad Curtis	.15
152	Ricky Ledee	.15
153	Rafael Palmeiro	.50
154	Rob Bell	.15
155	Rick Helling	.15
156	Doug Davis	.15
157	Mike Lamb	.15
158	Gabe Kapler	.15
159	Jeff Zimmerman	.15
160	Bill Haselman	.15
161	Tim Crabtree	.15
162	Carlos Pena	.15
163	Nomar Garciaparra	1.00
164	Shea Hillenbrand	.15
165	Hideo Nomo	.40
166	Manny Ramirez	.50
167	Jose Offerman	.15
168	Scott Hatteberg	.15
169	Trot Nixon	.25
170	Darren Lewis	.15
171	Derek Lowe	.25
172	Troy O'Leary	.15
173	Tim Wakefield	.15
174	Chris Stynes	.15
175	John Valentin	.15
176	David Cone	.15
177	Neifi Perez	.15
178	Brent Mayne	.15
179	Dan Reichert	.15
180	A.J. Hinch	.15
181	Chris George	.15
182	Mike Sweeney	.15
183	Jeff Suppan	.15
184	Roberto Hernandez	.15
185	Joe Randa	.15
186	Paul Byrd	.15
187	Luis Ordaz	.15
188	Kris Wilson	.15
189	Dee Brown	.15
190	Tony Clark	.15
191	Matt Anderson	.15
192	Robert Fick	.15
193	Juan Encarnacion	.15
194	Dean Palmer	.15
195	Victor Santos	.15
196	Damion Easley	.15
197	Jose Lima	.15
198	Deivi Cruz	.15
199	Roger Cedeno	.15
200	Jose Macias	.15
201	Jeff Weaver	.15
202	Brandon Inge	.15
203	Brian Moehler	.15
204	Brad Radke	.15
205	Doug Mientkiewicz	.15
206	Cristian Guzman	.15
207	Corey Koskie	.15
208	LaTroy Hawkins	.15
209	J.C. Romero	.15
210	Chad Allen	.15
211	Torii Hunter	.25
212	Travis Miller	.15
213	Joe Mays	.15
214	Todd Jones	.15
215	David Ortiz	.40
216	Brian Buchanan	.15
217	A.J. Pierzynski	.15
218	Carlos Lee	.15
219	Gary Glover	.15
220	Jose Valentin	.15
221	Aaron Rowand	.15
222	Sandy Alomar Jr.	.15
223	Herbert Perry	.15
224	Jon Garland	.15
225	Mark Buehrle	.15
226	Chris Singleton	.15
227	Kip Wells	.15
228	Ray Durham	.15
229	Joe Crede	.15
230	Keith Foulke	.15
231	Royce Clayton	.15
232	Andy Pettitte	.40
233	Derek Jeter	2.00
234	Jorge Posada	.40
235	Roger Clemens	1.50
236	Paul O'Neill	.25
237	Nick Johnson	.15
238	Gerald Williams	.15
239	Mariano Rivera	.25
240	Alfonso Soriano	.50
241	Ramiro Mendoza	.15
242	Mike Mussina	.50
243	Luis Sojo	.15
244	Scott Brosius	.15
245	David Justice	.25
246	Wade Miller	.15
247	Brad Ausmus	.15
248	Jeff Bagwell	.50
249	Daryle Ward	.15
250	Shane Reynolds	.15
251	Chris Truby	.15
252	Billy Wagner	.15
253	Craig Biggio	.25
254	Moises Alou	.25
255	Vinny Castilla	.15
256	Tim Redding	.15
257	Roy Oswalt	.40
258	Julio Lugo	.15
259	Chipper Jones	.75
260	Greg Maddux	1.00
261	Ken Caminiti	.15
262	Kevin Millwood	.25
263	Keith Lockhart	.15
264	Rey Sanchez	.15
265	Jason Marquis	.15
266	Brian Jordan	.15
267	Steve Karsay	.15
268	Wes Helms	.15
269	B.J. Surhoff	.15
270	Wilson Betemit	.15
271	John Smoltz	.25
272	Rafael Furcal	.25
273	Jeromy Burnitz	.15
274	Jimmy Haynes	.15
275	Mark Loretta	.15
276	Jose Hernandez	.15
277	Paul Rigdon	.15
278	Alex Sanchez	.15
279	Chad Fox	.15
280	Devon White	.15
281	Tyler Houston	.15
282	Ronnie Belliard	.15
283	Luis Lopez	.15
284	Ben Sheets	.40
285	Curtis Leskanic	.15
286	Henry Blanco	.15
287	Mark McGwire	2.00
288	Edgar Renteria	.25
289	Matt Morris	.25
290	Gene Stechschulte	.15
291	Dustin Hermanson	.15
292	Eli Marrero	.15
293	Albert Pujols	1.50
294	Luis Saturria	.15
295	Bobby Bonilla	.15
296	Garrett Stephenson	.15
297	Jim Edmonds	.40
298	Rick Ankiel	.15
299	Placido Polanco	.15
300	Dave Veres	.15
301	Sammy Sosa	1.50
302	Eric Young	.15
303	Kerry Wood	.75
304	Jon Lieber	.15
305	Joe Girardi	.15
306	Fred McGriff	.25
307	Jeff Fassero	.15
308	Julio Zuleta	.15
309	Kevin Tapani	.15
310	Rondell White	.15
311	Julian Tavarez	.15
312	Tom Gordon	.15
313	Corey Patterson	.25
314	Bill Mueller	.15
315	Randy Johnson	.75
316	Chad Moeller	.15
317	Tony Womack	.15
318	Erubiel Durazo	.15
319	Luis Gonzalez	.25
320	Brian Anderson	.15
321	Reggie Sanders	.15
322	Greg Colbrunn	.15
323	Robert Ellis	.15
324	Jack Cust	.15
325	Bret Prinz	.15
326	Steve Finley	.15
327	Byung-Hyun Kim	.15
328	Albie Lopez	.15
329	Gary Sheffield	.40
330	Mark Grudzielanek	.15
331	Paul LoDuca	.15
332	Tom Goodwin	.15
333	Andy Ashby	.15
334	Hiram Bocachica	.15
335	Dave Hansen	.15
336	Kevin Brown	.25
337	Marquis Grissom	.15
338	Terry Adams	.15
339	Chan Ho Park	.15
340	Adrian Beltre	.25
341	Luke Prokopec	.15
342	Jeff Shaw	.15
343	Vladimir Guerrero	.75
344	Orlando Cabrera	.15
345	Tony Armas Jr.	.15
346	Michael Barrett	.15
347	Geoff Blum	.15
348	Ryan Minor	.15
349	Peter Bergeron	.15
350	Graeme Lloyd	.15
351	Jose Vidro	.15
352	Javier Vazquez	.15
353	Matt Blank	.15
354	Masato Yoshii	.15
355	Carl Pavano	.15
356	Barry Bonds	2.00
357	Shawon Dunston	.15
358	Livan Hernandez	.15
359	Felix Rodriguez	.15
360	Pedro Feliz	.15
361	Calvin Murray	.15
362	Robb Nen	.15
363	Marvin Benard	.15
364	Russ Ortiz	.15
365	Jason Schmidt	.25
366	Rich Aurilia	.15
367	John Vander Wal	.15
368	Benito Santiago	.15
369	Ryan Dempster	.15
370	Charles Johnson	.15
371	Alex Gonzalez	.15
372	Luis Castillo	.15
373	Mike Lowell	.25
374	Antonio Alfonseca	.15
375	A.J. Burnett	.15
376	Brad Penny	.15
377	Jason Grilli	.15
378	Derrek Lee	.25
379	Matt Clement	.15
380	Eric Owens	.15
381	Vladimir Nunez	.15
382	Cliff Floyd	.15
383	Mike Piazza	1.25
384	Lenny Harris	.15
385	Glendon Rusch	.15
386	Todd Zeile	.15
387	Al Leiter	.25
388	Armando Benitez	.15
389	Alex Escobar	.15
390	Kevin Appier	.15
391	Matt Lawton	.15
392	Bruce Chen	.15
393	John Franco	.15
394	Tsuyoshi Shinjo	.15
395	Rey Ordonez	.15
396	Joe McEwing	.15
397	Ryan Klesko	.15
398	Brian Lawrence	.15
399	Kevin Walker	.15
400	Phil Nevin	.15
401	Bubba Trammell	.15
402	Wiki Gonzalez	.15
403	D'Angelo Jimenez	.15
404	Rickey Henderson	.40
405	Mike Darr	.15
406	Trevor Hoffman	.15
407	Damian Jackson	.15
408	Santiago Perez	.15
409	Cesar Crespo	.15
410	Robert Person	.15
411	Travis Lee	.15
412	Scott Rolen	.75
413	Turk Wendell	.15
414	Randy Wolf	.15
415	Kevin Jordan	.15
416	Jose Mesa	.15
417	Mike Lieberthal	.15
418	Bobby Abreu	.25
419	Tomas Perez	.15
420	Doug Glanville	.15
421	Reggie Taylor	.15
422	Jimmy Rollins	.15
423	Brian Giles	.25
424	Rob Mackowiak	.15
425	Bronson Arroyo	.15
426	Kevin Young	.15
427	Jack Wilson	.15
428	Adam Brown	.15
429	Chad Hermansen	.15
430	Jimmy Anderson	.15
431	Aramis Ramirez	.25
432	Todd Ritchie	.15
433	Pat Meares	.15
434	Warren Morris	.15
435	Derek Bell	.15
436	Ken Griffey Jr.	1.00
437	Elmer Dessens	.15
438	Ruben Rivera	.15
439	Jason LaRue	.15
440	Sean Casey	.25
441	Pete Harnisch	.15
442	Danny Graves	.15
443	Aaron Boone	.15
444	Dmitri Young	.15
445	Brandon Larson	.15
446	Pokey Reese	.15
447	Todd Walker	.15
448	Juan Castro	.15
449	Todd Helton	.50
450	Ben Petrick	.15
451	Juan Pierre	.15
452	Jeff Cirillo	.15
453	Juan Uribe	.15
454	Brian Bohanon	.15
455	Terry Shumpert	.15
456	Mike Hampton	.15
457	Shawn Chacon	.15
458	Adam Melhuse	.15
459	Greg Norton	.15
460	Gabe White	.15
461	Ichiro Suzuki	1.50
462	Carlos Delgado	.40
463	Manny Ramirez	.50
464	Miguel Tejada	.25
465	Tsuyoshi Shinjo	.15
466	Bernie Williams	.40
467	Juan Gonzalez	.50
468	Andruw Jones	.40
469	Ivan Rodriguez	.50
470	Larry Walker	.25
471	Hideo Nomo	.25
472	Albert Pujols	1.00
473	Pedro Martinez	.75
474	Vladimir Guerrero	.75
475	Tony Batista	.15
476	Kazuhiro Sasaki	.15
477	Richard Hidalgo	.15
478	Carlos Lee	.15
479	Roberto Alomar	.40
480	Rafael Palmeiro	.50
481	Ken Griffey Jr.	.50
482	Ken Griffey Jr.	.50
483	Ken Griffey Jr.	.50
484	Ken Griffey Jr.	.50
485	Ken Griffey Jr.	.50
486	Ken Griffey Jr.	.50
487	Ken Griffey Jr.	.50
488	Ken Griffey Jr.	.50
489	Ken Griffey Jr.	.50
490	Ken Griffey Jr.	.50
491	Barry Bonds	.75
492	Hideo Nomo	.15
493	Ichiro Suzuki	.50
494	Cal Ripken Jr.	.75
495	Tony Gwynn	.40
496	Randy Johnson	.40
497	A.J. Burnett	.15
498	Rickey Henderson	.15
499	Albert Pujols	.75
500	Luis Gonzalez	.25
501	*Brandon Puffer*	.50
502	*Rodrigo Rosario*	.50
503	*Tom Shearn*	.50
504	*Reed Johnson*	.50
505	*Chris Baker*	.50
506	*John Ennis*	.50
507	*Luis Martinez*	.50
508	*So Taguchi*	.75
509	*Scotty Layfield*	.50
510	*Francis Beltran*	.50
511	*Brandon Backe*	.50
512	*Doug Devore*	.50
513	*Jeremy Ward*	.50
514	*Jose Vaverde*	.50
515	*P.J. Bevis*	.50
516	*Victor Alvarez*	.50
517	*Kazuhisa Ishii*	2.00
518	*Jorge Nunez*	.50
519	*Eric Good*	.50
520	*Ron Calloway*	.50
521	Valentino Pasucci	.25
522	*Nelson Castro*	.50
523	Deivis Santos	.25
524	*Luis Ugueto*	.50
525	Matt Thornton	.25
526	*Hansel Izquierdo*	.75
527	*Tyler Yates*	.50
528	*Mark Corey*	.50
529	*Jaime Cerda*	.50
530	*Satoru Komiyama*	.50
531	*Steve Bechler*	.50
532	*Ben Howard*	.50
533	*Anderson Machado*	.50
534	*Jorge Padilla*	.50
535	*Eric Junge*	.50
536	*Adrian Burnside*	.50
537	*Mike Gonzalez*	.50
538	*Josh Hancock*	.50

539 *Colin Young* .50
540 *Rene Reyes* .50
541 *Cam Esslinger* .50
542 *Tim Kalita* .50
543 *Kevin Frederick* .50
544 *Kyle Kane* .50
545 *Edwin Almonte* .50
546 Aaron Sele .15
547 Garret Anderson .40
548 Darin Erstad .25
549 Brad Fullmer .15
550 Kevin Appier .15
551 Tim Salmon .25
552 David Justice .25
553 Billy Koch .15
554 Scott Hatteberg .15
555 Tim Hudson .25
556 Miguel Tejada .25
557 Carlos Pena .15
558 Mike Sirotka .15
559 Jose Cruz Jr. .15
560 Josh Phelps .15
561 Brandon Lyon .15
562 Luke Prokopec .15
563 Felipe Lopez .15
564 Jason Standridge .15
565 Chris Gomez .15
566 John Flaherty .15
567 Jason Tyner .15
568 Bobby Smith .15
569 Wilson Alvarez .15
570 Matt Lawton .15
571 Omar Vizquel .25
572 Jim Thome .75
573 Brady Anderson .15
574 Alex Escobar .15
575 Russell Branyan .15
576 Bret Boone .25
577 Ben Davis .15
578 Mike Cameron .15
579 Jamie Moyer .15
580 Ruben Sierra .15
581 Jeff Cirillo .15
582 Marty Cordova .15
583 Mike Bordick .15
584 Brian Roberts .15
585 Luis Matos .15
586 Geronimo Gil .15
587 Jay Gibbons .15
588 Carl Everett .15
589 Ivan Rodriguez .50
590 Chan Ho Park .15
591 Juan Gonzalez .50
592 Hank Blalock .40
593 Todd Van Poppel .15
594 Pedro J. Martinez .75
595 Jason Varitek .15
596 Tony Clark .15
597 Johnny Damon .25
598 Dustin Hermanson .15
599 John Burkett .15
600 Carlos Beltran .40
601 Mark Quinn .15
602 Chuck Knoblauch .15
603 Michael Tucker .15
604 Carlos Febles .15
605 Jose Rosado .15
606 Dmitri Young .15
607 Bobby Higginson .15
608 Craig Paquette .15
609 Mitch Meluskey .15
610 Wendell Magee .15
611 Mike Rivera .15
612 Jacque Jones .15
613 Luis Rivas .15
614 Eric Milton .15
615 Eddie Guardado .15
616 Matt LeCroy .15
617 Mike Jackson .15
618 Magglio Ordonez .25
619 Frank Thomas .50
620 Rocky Biddle .15
621 Paul Konerko .25
622 Todd Ritchie .15
623 Jon Rauch .15
624 John Vander Wal .15
625 Rondell White .15
626 Jason Giambi .50
627 Robin Ventura .25
628 David Wells .15
629 Bernie Williams .50
630 Lance Berkman .25
631 Richard Hidalgo .15
632 Greg Zaun .15
633 Jose Vizcaino .15
634 Octavio Dotel .15
635 Morgan Ensberg .15
636 Andruw Jones .50
637 Tom Glavine .40
638 Gary Sheffield .40
639 Vinny Castilla .15
640 Javy Lopez .25
641 Albie Lopez .15
642 Geoff Jenkins .25
643 Jeffrey Hammonds .15
644 Alex Ochoa .15
645 Richie Sexson .40
646 Eric Young .15
647 Glendon Rusch .15
648 Tino Martinez .25
649 Fernando Vina .15
650 J.D. Drew .25
651 Woody Williams .15
652 Darryl Kile .15
653 Jason Isringhausen .15
654 Moises Alou .25
655 Alex Gonzalez .15
656 Delino DeShields .15
657 Todd Hundley .15
658 Chris Stynes .15
659 Jason Bere .15
660 Curt Schilling .40
661 Craig Counsell .15
662 Mark Grace .40
663 Matt Williams .25
664 Jay Bell .15
665 Rick Helling .15
666 Shawn Green .40
667 Eric Karros .15
668 Hideo Nomo .40
669 Omar Daal .15
670 Brian Jordan .15
671 Cesar Izturis .15
672 Fernando Tatis .15
673 Lee Stevens .15
674 Tomokazu Ohka .15
675 Brian Schneider .15
676 Brad Wilkerson .15
677 Bruce Chen .15
678 Tsuyoshi Shinjo .15
679 Jeff Kent .25
680 Kirk Rueter .15
681 J.T. Snow .15
682 David Bell .15
683 Reggie Sanders .15
684 Preston Wilson .15
685 Vic Darensbourg .15
686 Josh Beckett .40
687 Pablo Ozuna .15
688 Mike Redmond .15
689 Scott Strickland .15
690 Mo Vaughn .25
691 Roberto Alomar .50
692 Edgardo Alfonzo .15
693 Shawn Estes .15
694 Roger Cedeno .15
695 Jeromy Burnitz .15
696 Ray Lankford .15
697 Mark Kotsay .15
698 Kevin Jarvis .15
699 Bobby Jones .15
700 Sean Burroughs .15
701 Ramon Vazquez .15
702 Pat Burrell .40
703 Marlon Byrd .15
704 Brandon Duckworth .15
705 Marlon Anderson .15
706 Vicente Padilla .15
707 Kip Wells .15
708 Jason Kendall .15
709 Pokey Reese .15
710 Pat Meares .15
711 Kris Benson .15
712 Armando Rios .15
713 Mike Williams .15
714 Barry Larkin .40
715 Adam Dunn .50
716 Juan Encarnacion .15
717 Scott Williamson .15
718 Wilton Guerrero .15
719 Chris Reitsma .15
720 Larry Walker .25
721 Denny Neagle .15
722 Todd Zeile .15
723 Jose Ortiz .15
724 Jason Jennings .15
725 Tony Eusebio .15
726 Ichiro Suzuki 1.00
727 Barry Bonds 1.50
728 Randy Johnson .50
729 Albert Pujols 1.00
730 Roger Clemens .50
731 Sammy Sosa .50
732 Alex Rodriguez .50
733 Chipper Jones .40
734 Rickey Henderson .25
735 Marioners Team Photo .15
736 Luis Gonzalez .25
737 Derek Jeter 1.50
738 Ichiro Suzuki 1.00
739 Barry Bonds 1.50
740 Curt Schilling .25
741 Shawn Green .25
742 Jason Giambi .50
743 Roberto Alomar .25
744 Larry Walker .15
745 Mark McGwire .75

AL Centennial G-U Jerseys Autograph

No Pricing
Production 25 sets

AL Centennial Jerseys

NM/M
Common Player: 10.00
Inserted 1:144
PM Pedro Martinez 10.00
CR Cal Ripken Jr. 40.00
AR Alex Rodriguez 15.00
IR Ivan Rodriguez 10.00
NR Nolan Ryan 40.00
FT Frank Thomas 10.00

AL Centennial Bats

NM/M
Inserted 1:144
JD Joe DiMaggio 125.00
MM Mickey Mantle 150.00
BR Babe Ruth 150.00

All-Star Salute Game Jerseys

NM/M
Common Player: 10.00
Inserted 1:288
SA Sparky Anderson 10.00
LB Lou Boudreau 10.00
DE Dennis Eckersley 10.00
NF Nellie Fox 15.00
KG Ken Griffey Jr. 25.00
AR Alex Rodriguez 25.00
DS Don Sutton 10.00
IS Ichiro Suzuki 40.00

Big Fly Zone

NM/M
Complete Set (10): 15.00
Common Player: .50
Inserted 1:14
Z1 Mark McGwire 4.00
Z2 Ken Griffey Jr. 3.00
Z3 Manny Ramirez 1.00
Z4 Sammy Sosa 3.00
Z5 Todd Helton 1.00
Z6 Barry Bonds 4.00
Z7 Luis Gonzalez .50
Z8 Alex Rodriguez 4.00
Z9 Carlos Delgado 1.00
Z10 Chipper Jones 1.50

Breakout Performers

NM/M
Complete Set (10): 10.00
Common Player: .50
Inserted 1:14
BP1 Ichiro Suzuki 3.00
BP2 Albert Pujols 4.00
BP3 Doug Mientkiewicz .50
BP4 Lance Berkman 1.00
BP5 Tsuyoshi Shinjo .50
BP6 Ben Sheets 1.00
BP7 Jimmy Rollins .50
BP8 J.D. Drew .75
BP9 Bret Boone .50
BP10 Alfonso Soriano 1.00

Championship Caliber

NM/M
Complete Set (6): 10.00
Common Player: 1.00
Inserted 1:23
CC1 Derek Jeter 5.00
CC2 Roberto Alomar 1.00
CC3 Chipper Jones 2.00
CC4 Gary Sheffield 1.00
CC5 Roger Clemens 3.00
CC6 Greg Maddux 2.50

Championship Caliber Swatches

NM/M
Common Player: 8.00
Inserted 1:288
RA Roberto Alomar/SP 20.00
KB Kevin Brown/SP 10.00
CF Cliff Floyd 10.00
ChJ Charles Johnson 8.00
RJ Randy Johnson 10.00
CJo Chipper Jones/SP 25.00
BL Barry Larkin 10.00
GM Greg Maddux/SP 40.00
TM Tino Martinez 8.00
JO John Olerud 8.00
AP Andy Pettitte 10.00
JP Jorge Posada 10.00
CS Curt Schilling 10.00
BW Bernie Williams 10.00

Chasing History

NM/M
Complete Set (15): 12.00
Common Player: .50
Inserted 1:11
CH1 Sammy Sosa 2.00
CH2 Ken Griffey Jr. 1.50
CH3 Roger Clemens 2.00
CH4 Barry Bonds 3.00
CH5 Rafael Palmeiro 1.00
CH6 Andres Galarraga .50
CH7 Juan Gonzalez 1.00
CH8 Roberto Alomar 1.00
CH9 Randy Johnson 1.00
CH10 Jeff Bagwell 1.00
CH11 Fred McGriff .50
CH12 Matt Williams .50
CH13 Greg Maddux 1.50
CH14 Robb Nen .50
CH15 Kenny Lofton .50

Combo Jersey

NM/M
Common Duo: 10.00
Inserted 1:288
RS Alex Rodriguez, Sammy Sosa 30.00
RM Nolan Ryan, Pedro Martinez 40.00
RC Nolan Ryan, Roger Clemens 50.00
BS Barry Bonds, Sammy Sosa 40.00
HK Shigetoshi Hasegawa, Byung-Hun Kim 10.00

Combo Bat

NM/M
Inserted 1:288
CB-RG Alex Rodriguez, Ken Griffey Jr. 30.00
CB-DM Joe DiMaggio, Mickey Mantle 200.00

Double Game-Worn Gems

NM/M
Common Card: 8.00
Production 450 sets
Golds: 1-2X
Production 100 sets
NK Phil Nevin, Ryan Klesko 8.00
VB Omar Vizquel, Russell Branyan 10.00
DH Jermaine Dye, Tim Hudson 10.00
TO Frank Thomas, Magglio Ordonez 15.00

MI Edgar Martinez, Ichiro Suzuki/150 80.00
GS Luis Gonzalez, Curt Schilling 15.00
AP Roberto Alomar, Mike Piazza 20.00
PL Robert Person, Mike Lieberthal 8.00
MM Kevin Millwood, Greg Maddux 20.00
KG Jason Kendall, Brian Giles 10.00
DF Carlos Delgado, Shannon Stewart 10.00
PN Chan Ho Park, Hideo Nomo 30.00

Game Jersey Autograph

NM/M
Common Player: 20.00
Production 200 sets
BB Barry Bonds 250.00
CD Carlos Delgado 25.00
RF Rafael Furcal 20.00
JGi Jason Giambi 35.00
KG Ken Griffey Jr. 125.00
AJ Andruw Jones 35.00
AP Albert Pujols 125.00
CR Cal Ripken Jr. 200.00
NR Nolan Ryan 140.00
GS Gary Sheffield 20.00
IS Ichiro Suzuki 300.00
PW Preston Wilson 20.00

Game Jerseys

NM/M
Common Player: 8.00
Production 350 sets
Golds: .75-1.5X
Production 100
TB Tony Batista 8.00
AB Adrian Beltre 8.00
JC Jeff Cirillo 8.00
KG Ken Griffey Jr. 20.00
TH Tim Hudson 10.00
MP Mike Piazza 15.00
SR Scott Rolen 15.00
CS Curt Schilling 15.00
SS Sammy Sosa 25.00
FT Frank Thomas 12.00
PW Preston Wilson 8.00

Game-Used Base Combo

NM/M
Common Combo: 40.00
Inserted 1:288
RG Alex Rodriguez, Ken Griffey Jr. 40.00
MJ Mark McGwire, Derek Jeter 60.00

Game-Used Base

NM/M
Common Player: 5.00
Inserted 1:288
BB Barry Bonds 20.00
RC Roger Clemens 20.00
CD Carlos Delgado 5.00
JG Jason Giambi 10.00
TG Troy Glaus 8.00
JG Juan Gonzalez 10.00
LG Luis Gonzalez 5.00
SG Shawn Green 5.00
KG Ken Griffey Jr. 15.00
DJ Derek Jeter 25.00
AJ Andruw Jones 8.00
CJ Chipper Jones 10.00
MM Mark McGwire 40.00
MP Mike Piazza 15.00
CR Cal Ripken Jr. 40.00
AR Alex Rodriguez 15.00
IR Ivan Rodriguez 8.00
KS Kazuhiro Sasaki 5.00
SS Sammy Sosa 20.00
IS Ichiro Suzuki 50.00

Game-Used Base Autograph

Production 25
SB-KGKen Griffey Jr.

Game-Worn Gems

NM/M
Common Player: 5.00
Inserted 1:48
Golds: 1-2X
Production 100 sets
RA Roberto Alomar 8.00
EC Eric Chavez 6.00
CD Carlos Delgado 8.00
DE Darin Erstad/SP 10.00
FG Freddy Garcia/SP 8.00
TG Tom Glavine 8.00
JG Juan Gonzalez 8.00
LG Luis Gonzalez/SP 10.00
MH Mike Hampton/SP 8.00
CJ Chipper Jones 10.00
JK Jason Kendall 5.00
RK Ryan Klesko/SP 8.00
GM Greg Maddux 15.00
EM Edgar Martinez 8.00
PM Pedro Martinez/SP 15.00
TM Tino Martinez 8.00
JM Joe Mays 5.00
EM Eric Milton 5.00
PN Phil Nevin 5.00
HN Hideo Nomo/SP 30.00
JO John Olerud/SP 8.00
RP Robert Person 5.00
CR Cal Ripken Jr. 40.00
IR Ivan Rodriguez 10.00
SR Scott Rolen 15.00
CS Curt Schilling 10.00
AS Aaron Sele 5.00
GS Gary Sheffield/SP 8.00
FT Frank Thomas 10.00
OV Omar Vizquel/SP 10.00
RY Robin Yount 15.00

Global Swatch Jerseys

NM/M
Common Player: 5.00
Inserted 1:144
CD Carlos Delgado 8.00
SH Shigetoshi Hasegawa 5.00
BK Byung-Hun Kim 5.00
HN Hideo Nomo 35.00
CP Chan Ho Park 5.00
MR Manny Ramirez 10.00
KS Kazuhiro Sasaki 5.00
TS Tsuyoshi Shinjo 5.00
IS Ichiro Suzuki 50.00
MY Masato Yoshii 5.00

Global Swatch Jerseys Autograph

No Pricing
Production 25 sets
SGS-CD Carlos Delgado
SGS-BK Byun-Hun Kim

First Timers Jerseys Autograph

No Pricing
Production 25 sets
SFT-FG Freddy Garcia
SFT-JM Joe Mays
SFT-AP Albert Pujols
SFT-SS Shannon Stewart

First Timers Jerseys

NM/M
Common Player: 8.00
Inserted 1:288
RB Russell Branyan 8.00
OD Omar Daal 8.00
FG Freddy Garcia 8.00
ML Matt Lawton 8.00
JM Joe Mays 8.00
EM Eric Milton 8.00
CP Corey Patterson 10.00
AP Albert Pujols 50.00
SS Shannon Stewart 8.00

McGwire Memorabilia

NM/M
Common Card:
AM-J Mark McGwire/jsy/70 150.00
AM-B Mark McGwire/bat/70 150.00
MMc Mark McGwire/500 HR Club bat/350 300.00
S-MMc Mark McGwire/500 HR Auto./25
MM-SS Mark McGwire, Sammy Sosa/25 (combo jersey) 300.00
MM-KG Mark McGwire, Ken Griffey Jr/25 (combo jersey) 300.00
MM-JG Mark McGwire, Jason Giambi/25 (combo jersey) 250.00

Patch Numbers

No Pricing
SPN-BB Barry Bonds
SPN-KG Ken Griffey Jr.
SPN-CR Cal Ripken Jr.

Return of the Ace

NM/M
Complete Set (15): 15.00
Common Player: 1.00
Inserted 1:11
RA1 Randy Johnson 2.00
RA2 Greg Maddux 3.00
RA3 Pedro Martinez 2.00
RA4 Freddy Garcia 1.00
RA5 Matt Morris 1.00
RA6 Mark Mulder 1.00
RA7 Wade Miller 1.00
RA8 Kevin Brown 1.00
RA9 Roger Clemens 4.00
RA10 Jon Lieber 1.00
RA11 C.C. Sabathia 1.00
RA12 Tim Hudson 1.50
RA13 Curt Schilling 2.00
RA14 Al Leiter 1.00
RA15 Mike Mussina 1.50

Sons of Summer Game Jerseys

NM/M
Common Player: 10.00
Inserted 1:288
RA Roberto Alomar 10.00
JB Jeff Bagwell 10.00
RC Roger Clemens 15.00
JG Juan Gonzalez 10.00
GM Greg Maddux 15.00
PM Pedro Martinez/SP 15.00
MP Mike Piazza 15.00
AR Alex Rodriguez 15.00

Superstar Summit

NM/M
Complete Set (6): 15.00
Common Player: 1.50
Inserted 1:23
SS1 Sammy Sosa 3.00
SS2 Alex Rodriguez 4.00
SS3 Mark McGwire 4.00
SS4 Barry Bonds 4.00
SS5 Mike Piazza 3.00
SS6 Ken Griffey Jr. 2.50

Superstar Summit II

NM/M
Complete Set (15): 25.00
Common Player: 1.00
Inserted 1:11
SS1 Alex Rodriguez 4.00
SS2 Jason Giambi 1.00
SS3 Vladimir Guerrero 1.50
SS4 Randy Johnson 1.50
SS5 Chipper Jones 1.50
SS6 Ichiro Suzuki 3.00
SS7 Sammy Sosa 2.50
SS8 Greg Maddux 2.00
SS9 Ken Griffey Jr. 2.50
SS10 Todd Helton 1.00
SS11 Barry Bonds 4.00
SS12 Derek Jeter 4.00
SS13 Mike Piazza 3.00
SS14 Ivan Rodriguez 1.00
SS15 Frank Thomas 1.00

The People's Choice Game Jerseys

NM/M
Common Player: 5.00
Inserted 1:24
Golds: 1-2X
Production 100 sets
JBa Jeff Bagwell 10.00
EB Ellis Burks/SP 10.00
JBu Jeromy Burnitz 5.00
OD Omar Daal 5.00
CD Carlos Delgado 8.00
RF Rafael Furcal 6.00
AG Andres Galarraga/SP 10.00
BG Brian Giles 5.00
JG Juan Gonzalez 10.00
KG Ken Griffey Jr. 20.00
TG Tony Gwynn 12.00
SH Sterling Hitchcock 5.00
HI Hideki Irabu 5.00
CJ Charles Johnson 5.00
DL Derek Lowe 8.00
GM Greg Maddux 15.00
TM Tino Martinez 10.00
JN Jeff Nelson 5.00
RO Rey Ordonez 5.00
RP Rafael Palmeiro/SP 15.00
RP Robert Person/SP 10.00
AP Andy Pettitte 10.00
MP Mike Piazza 15.00
TR Tim Raines 5.00
MRa Manny Ramirez 10.00
MRi Mariano Rivera 8.00
AR Alex Rodriguez 15.00
TS Tim Salmon 6.00
CS Curt Schilling 10.00
TSh Tsuyoshi Shinjo 5.00
JS J.T. Snow 5.00
SS Sammy Sosa 20.00
MS Mike Stanton 5.00
FT Frank Thomas 10.00
RV Robin Ventura 6.00
OV Omar Vizquel 6.00
DW David Wells 6.00
BW Bernie Williams 8.00
MW Matt Williams/SP 10.00

UD Patch Logo

NM/M
Common Player: 60.00
Inserted 1:2,500
Prices for Stripes & Numbers identical
BB Barry Bonds 125.00
JG Jason Giambi 60.00
KG Ken Griffey Jr. 100.00
PM Pedro Martinez 80.00
CR Cal Ripken Jr. 150.00
AR Alex Rodriguez 125.00
SS Sammy Sosa 100.00

UD-Plus

NM/M
Common Player: 2.00
Production 1,125 sets
1 two-card pack per Series 2 H pack
Comp. Set can be exchanged for Jsy cards
Redemption Deadline 5-16-03
UD1 Darin Erstad 3.00

UD2 Troy Glaus 3.00
UD3 Tim Hudson 3.00
UD4 Jermaine Dye 2.00
UD5 Barry Zito 2.00
UD6 Carlos Delgado 3.00
UD7 Shannon Stewart 2.00
UD8 Greg Vaughn 2.00
UD9 Jim Thome 5.00
UD10 C.C. Sabathia 2.00
UD11 Ichiro Suzuki 10.00
UD12 Edgar Martinez 2.00
UD13 Bret Boone 2.00
UD14 Freddy Garcia 2.00
UD15 Matt Thornton 2.00
UD16 Jeff Conine 2.00
UD17 Steve Bechler 2.00
UD18 Rafael Palmeiro 4.00
UD19 Juan Gonzalez 4.00
UD20 Alex Rodriguez 10.00
UD21 Ivan Rodriguez 4.00
UD22 Carl Everett 2.00
UD23 Manny Ramirez 4.00
UD24 Nomar Garciaparra 10.00
UD25 Pedro J. Martinez 4.00
UD26 Mike Sweeney 2.00
UD27 Chuck Knoblauch 2.00
UD28 Dmitri Young 2.00
UD29 Bobby Higginson 2.00
UD30 Dean Palmer 2.00
UD31 Doug Mientkiewicz 2.00
UD32 Corey Koskie 2.00
UD33 Brad Radke 2.00
UD34 Cristian Guzman 2.00
UD35 Frank Thomas 4.00
UD36 Magglio Ordonez 3.00
UD37 Carlos Lee 2.00
UD38 Roger Clemens 10.00
UD39 Bernie Williams 3.00
UD40 Derek Jeter 15.00
UD41 Jason Giambi 4.00
UD42 Mike Mussina 3.00
UD43 Jeff Bagwell 4.00
UD44 Lance Berkman 3.00
UD45 Wade Miller 2.00
UD46 Greg Maddux 8.00
UD47 Chipper Jones 5.00
UD48 Andruw Jones 4.00
UD49 Gary Sheffield 3.00
UD50 Richie Sexson 3.00
UD51 Albert Pujols 10.00
UD52 J.D. Drew 3.00
UD53 Matt Morris 2.00
UD54 Jim Edmonds 3.00
UD55 So Taguchi 2.00
UD56 Sammy Sosa 10.00
UD57 Fred McGriff 3.00
UD58 Kerry Wood 5.00
UD59 Moises Alou 3.00
UD60 Randy Johnson 5.00
UD61 Luis Gonzalez 3.00
UD62 Mark Grace 3.00
UD63 Curt Schilling 4.00
UD64 Matt Williams 2.00
UD65 Kevin Brown 3.00
UD66 Brian Jordan 2.00
UD67 Shawn Green 3.00
UD68 Hideo Nomo 3.00
UD69 Kazuhisa Ishii 4.00
UD70 Vladimir Guerrero 4.00
UD71 Jose Vidro 2.00
UD72 Eric Good 2.00
UD73 Barry Bonds 15.00
UD74 Jeff Kent 3.00
UD75 Rich Aurilia 2.00
UD76 Deivis Santos 2.00
UD77 Preston Wilson 2.00
UD78 Cliff Floyd 2.00
UD79 Josh Beckett 4.00
UD80 Hansel Izquierdo 2.00
UD81 Mike Piazza 10.00
UD82 Roberto Alomar 3.00
UD83 Mo Vaughn 3.00
UD84 Jeromy Burnitz 2.00
UD85 Phil Nevin 2.00
UD86 Ryan Klesko 2.00
UD87 Bobby Abreu 3.00
UD88 Scott Rolen 5.00
UD89 Jimmy Rollins 2.00
UD90 Jason Kendall 2.00
UD91 Brian Giles 3.00
UD92 Aramis Ramirez 3.00
UD93 Ken Griffey Jr. 10.00
UD94 Sean Casey 2.00
UD95 Barry Larkin 3.00
UD96 Adam Dunn 4.00
UD97 Todd Helton 4.00
UD98 Larry Walker 3.00
UD99 Mike Hampton 2.00
UD100 Rene Reyes 2.00

UD-Plus Milestone Game Jerseys

No Pricing
M-JD1 Joe DiMaggio
M-JD2 Joe DiMaggio
M-JD3 Joe DiMaggio
M-JD4 Joe DiMaggio
M-JD5 Joe DiMaggio
M-MM1 Mickey Mantle
M-MM2 Mickey Mantle
M-MM3 Mickey Mantle
M-MM4 Mickey Mantle
M-MM5 Mickey Mantle

UD-Plus Memorabila Moments Jerseys

NM/M
Common DiMaggio (1-5): 125.00
Common Mantle: (1-5): 200.00
MM-JD1 Joe DiMaggio 125.00
MM-JD2 Joe DiMaggio 125.00
MM-JD3 Joe DiMaggio 125.00
MM-JD4 Joe DiMaggio 125.00
MM-JD5 Joe DiMaggio 125.00
MM-MM1 Mickey Mantle/25 (pants) 200.00
MM-MM2 Mickey Mantle 200.00
MM-MM3 Mickey Mantle 200.00
MM-MM4 Mickey Mantle 200.00
MM-MM5 Mickey Mantle 200.00

Yankees Dynasty Jerseys

NM/M
Common Combo: 20.00
Inserted 1:288
PR Andy Pettitte, Mariano Rivera 25.00
BT Wade Boggs, Joe Torre 25.00
CP Roger Clemens, Jorge Posada 50.00
DM Joe DiMaggio, Mickey Mantle 300.00
RK Willie Randolph, Chuck Knoblauch 20.00
BJ Scott Brosius, David Justice 20.00
OM Paul O'Neill, Tino Martinez 25.00
WO Bernie Williams, Paul O'Neill 25.00
WG David Wells, Dwight Gooden 25.00
GC Joe Girardi, David Cone 25.00
KR Chuck Knoblauch, Tim Raines 25.00

Yankees Dynasty Combo Base

NM/M
Common Combo: 50.00
JW Derek Jeter, Bernie Williams 60.00
CJ Roger Clemens, Derek Jeter 75.00

2001 All-Star HR Derby Jerseys

NM/M
Common Player: 10.00
Inserted 1:288
BrB Bret Boone 10.00
JG Jason Giambi 15.00
TH Todd Helton 15.00
AR Alex Rodriguez 20.00
SS Sammy Sosa 25.00

2001'S GREATEST HITS

NM/M
Complete Set (10): 20.00
Common Player: 1.00
Inserted 1:14
GH1 Barry Bonds 4.00
GH2 Ichiro Suzuki 3.00
GH3 Albert Pujols 3.00
GH4 Mike Piazza 2.50
GH5 Alex Rodriguez 3.00
GH6 Mark McGwire 3.00
GH7 Manny Ramirez 1.00
GH8 Ken Griffey Jr. 2.00
GH9 Sammy Sosa 3.00
GH10 Derek Jeter 4.00

2002 UPPER DECK BALLPARK IDOLS

NM/M
Complete Set (245): 125.00
Common Player: .15
Common (201-245): 3.00
Production 1,750
Pack (5): 2.00
Box (24 + bobber): 50.00
1 Troy Glaus .40
2 Kevin Appier .15
3 Darin Erstad .25
4 Garret Anderson .25
5 Brad Fullmer .15
6 Tim Salmon .25
7 Eric Chavez .25
8 Tim Hudson .25
9 David Justice .25
10 Barry Zito .25
11 Miguel Tejada .40
12 Mark Mulder .40
13 Jermaine Dye .15
14 Carlos Delgado .40
15 Jose Cruz Jr. .15
16 Brandon Lyon .15
17 Shannon Stewart .15
18 Eric Hinske .25
19 Chris Carpenter .15
20 Greg Vaughn .15
21 Tanyon Sturtze .15
22 Jason Tyner .15
23 Toby Hall .15
24 Ben Grieve .15
25 Jim Thome .75
26 Omar Vizquel .25
27 Ricky Gutierrez .15
28 C.C. Sabathia .15
29 Ellis Burks .15
30 Matt Lawton .15
31 Milton Bradley .15
32 Edgar Martinez .25
33 Ichiro Suzuki 1.50
34 Bret Boone .25
35 Freddy Garcia .25
36 Mike Cameron .15
37 John Olerud .25
38 Kazuhiro Sasaki .15
39 Jeff Cirillo .15
40 Jeff Conine .15
41 Marty Cordova .15
42 Tony Batista .15
43 Jerry Hairston Jr. .15
44 Jason Johnson .15
45 David Segui .15
46 Alex Rodriguez 2.00
47 Rafael Palmeiro .50
48 Carl Everett .15
49 Chan Ho Park .15
50 Ivan Rodriguez .50
51 Juan Gonzalez .50
52 Hank Blalock .50
53 Manny Ramirez .50
54 Pedro J. Martinez .75
55 Tony Clark .15
56 Nomar Garciaparra 1.25
57 Johnny Damon .25
58 Trot Nixon .25
59 Rickey Henderson .50
60 Mike Sweeney .15
61 Neifi Perez .15
62 Joe Randa .15
63 Carlos Beltran .25
64 Chuck Knoblauch .15
65 Michael Tucker .15
66 Dean Palmer .15
67 Bobby Higginson .15
68 Dmitri Young .15
69 Randall Simon .15
70 Mitch Meluskey .15
71 Damion Easley .15
72 Joe Mays .15
73 Doug Mientkiewicz .15
74 Corey Koskie .15
75 Brad Radke .15
76 Cristian Guzman .15
77 Torii Hunter .25
78 Eric Milton .15
79 Frank Thomas .50
80 Paul Konerko .25
81 Mark Buehrle .15
82 Magglio Ordonez .25
83 Carlos Lee .15
84 Joe Crede .15
85 Derek Jeter 2.00
86 Bernie Williams .50
87 Mike Mussina .50
88 Jorge Posada .40
89 Roger Clemens 1.50
90 Jason Giambi .50
91 Alfonso Soriano .75
92 Rondell White .15
93 Jeff Bagwell .50
94 Lance Berkman .40
95 Roy Oswalt .25
96 Richard Hidalgo .15
97 Wade Miller .15
98 Craig Biggio .25
99 Greg Maddux 1.00
100 Chipper Jones .75
101 Gary Sheffield .40
102 Rafael Furcal .15
103 Andruw Jones .50
104 Vinny Castilla .15
105 Marcus Giles .15
106 Tom Glavine .40
107 Richie Sexson .40
108 Geoff Jenkins .15
109 Glendon Rusch .15
110 Eric Young .15
111 Ben Sheets .25
112 Alex Sanchez .15
113 Albert Pujols 1.50
114 J.D. Drew .25
115 Matt Morris .25
116 Jim Edmonds .40
117 Tino Martinez .15
118 Scott Rolen .75
119 Edgar Renteria .25
120 Sammy Sosa 1.50
121 Kerry Wood .75
122 Moises Alou .25
123 Jon Lieber .15
124 Fred McGriff .25
125 Juan Cruz .15
126 Alex Gonzalez .15
127 Corey Patterson .25
128 Randy Johnson .75
129 Luis Gonzalez .25
130 Steve Finley .15

131	Matt Williams	.15
132	Curt Schilling	.50
133	Mark Grace	.40
134	Craig Counsell	.15
135	Shawn Green	.25
136	Kevin Brown	.25
137	Hideo Nomo	.40
138	Paul LoDuca	.15
139	Brian Jordan	.15
140	Eric Karros	.15
141	Adrian Beltre	.25
142	Vladimir Guerrero	.75
143	Fernando Tatis	.15
144	Javier Vazquez	.15
145	Orlando Cabrera	.15
146	Tony Armas Jr.	.15
147	Jose Vidro	.15
148	Barry Bonds	2.00
149	Rich Aurilia	.15
150	Tsuyoshi Shinjo	.15
151	Jeff Kent	.25
152	Russ Ortiz	.15
153	Jason Schmidt	.25
154	Reggie Sanders	.15
155	Preston Wilson	.15
156	Luis Castillo	.15
157	Charles Johnson	.15
158	Josh Beckett	.40
159	Derrek Lee	.25
160	Mike Lowell	.25
161	Mike Piazza	1.00
162	Roberto Alomar	.40
163	Al Leiter	.25
164	Mo Vaughn	.25
165	Jeromy Burnitz	.15
166	Edgardo Alfonzo	.15
167	Roger Cedeno	.15
168	Ryan Klesko	.25
169	Brian Lawrence	.15
170	Sean Burroughs	.15
171	Phil Nevin	.15
172	Ramon Vazquez	.15
173	Mark Kotsay	.15
174	Marlon Anderson	.15
175	Mike Lieberthal	.15
176	Bobby Abreu	.25
177	Pat Burrell	.40
178	Robert Person	.15
179	Brandon Duckworth	.15
180	Jimmy Rollins	.15
181	Brian Giles	.25
182	Pokey Reese	.15
183	Kris Benson	.15
184	Aramis Ramirez	.25
185	Jason Kendall	.15
186	Kip Wells	.15
187	Ken Griffey Jr.	1.00
188	Adam Dunn	.50
189	Barry Larkin	.40
190	Sean Casey	.25
191	Austin Kearns	.25
192	Aaron Boone	.15
193	Todd Helton	.50
194	Juan Pierre	.15
195	Mike Hampton	.15
196	Jose Ortiz	.15
197	Larry Walker	.25
198	Juan Uribe	.15
199	Ichiro Suzuki (Checklist)	.75
200	Jason Giambi (Checklist)	.25
201	*Franklyn German*	3.00
202	*Rodrigo Rosario*	3.00
203	*Brandon Puffer*	3.00
204	Kirk Saarloos	3.00
205	*Chris Baker*	3.00
206	*John Ennis*	3.00
207	*Luis Martinez*	3.00
208	*So Taguchi*	6.00
209	*Michael Crudale*	3.00
210	*Francis Beltran*	3.00
211	*Brandon Backe*	3.00
212	*Felix Escalona*	3.00
213	*Jose Valverde*	4.00
214	*Doug Devore*	3.00
215	*Kazuhisa Ishii*	6.00
216	*Victor Alvarez*	3.00
217	*Ron Calloway*	3.00
218	*Eric Good*	3.00
219	Jorge Nunez	3.00
220	Deivis Santos	3.00
221	*Nelson Castro*	3.00
222	Matt Thornton	3.00
223	*Jason Simontacchi*	3.00
224	*Hansel Izquierdo*	3.00
225	*Tyler Yates*	4.00
226	*Jaime Cerda*	3.00
227	*Satoru Komiyama*	3.00
228	*Steve Bechler*	3.00
229	*Ben Howard*	3.00
230	*Todd Donovan*	3.00
231	*Jorge Padilla*	3.00
232	*Eric Junge*	3.00
233	*Anderson Machado*	3.00
234	*Adrian Burnside*	3.00
235	*Mike Gonzalez*	3.00
236	*Josh Hancock*	3.00
237	*Anastacio Martinez*	3.00
238	*Chris Booker*	3.00
239	*Rene Reyes*	3.00
240	*Cam Esslinger*	3.00
241	*Oliver Perez*	10.00
242	*Tim Kalita*	3.00
243	*Kevin Frederick*	3.00
244	*Mitch Wylie*	3.00
245	*Edwin Almonte*	3.00

Bronze

Stars (1-200): 5-10X
SP's (201-245): .75-1.5X
Production 100 sets

Gold

No pricing due to scarcity
Production 25 sets

Bobbers

	NM/M
Inserted 1:box	
Roberto Alomar	10.00
Jeff Bagwell	15.00
Josh Beckett	10.00
Barry Bonds	30.00
Sean Burroughs	8.00
Roger Clemens	20.00
Joe DiMaggio/555/Away	40.00
Joe DiMaggio/361/Home	50.00
Nomar Garciaparra	20.00
Jason Giambi	10.00
Luis Gonzalez	8.00
Ken Griffey Jr.	20.00
Vladimir Guerrero	15.00
Kazuhisa Ishii	10.00
Derek Jeter/SP/Away	40.00
Randy Johnson/D'backs	15.00
Randy Johnson/Expos	15.00
Chipper Jones	15.00
Greg Maddux	20.00
Mickey Mantle/777/Away	50.00
Mickey Mantle/536/Home	60.00
Mark McGwire/Cards	35.00
Mike Piazza/Mets	20.00
Mark Prior	20.00
Albert Pujols	25.00
Albert Pujols/SP	
Alex Rodriguez	20.00
Ivan Rodriguez	10.00
Curt Schilling/D'backs	10.00
Sammy Sosa/Cubs/Away	25.00
Ichiro Suzuki/SP/Away	30.00
Frank Thomas	10.00
Jim Thome	15.00

Bobbers Gold

	NM/M
Amount produced listed	
Joe DiMaggio/56/Away	100.00
Joe DiMaggio/41/Home	125.00
Mickey Mantle/77/Away	140.00
Mickey Mantle/61/Home	125.00

Bobbers Autograph

	NM/M
Inserted 1:14 boxes	
Josh Beckett	60.00

Field Garb Jerseys

		NM/M
Common Player:		4.00
Inserted 1:72		
TB	Tony Batista	4.00
BG	Brian Giles	4.00
RJ	Randy Johnson	10.00
JK	Jeff Kent	4.00
TM	Tino Martinez	4.00
JO	John Olerud	4.00
AR	Alex Rodriguez	12.00
IR	Ivan Rodriguez	6.00
MS	Mike Sweeney	4.00
RV	Robin Ventura	4.00
LW	Larry Walker	4.00
BZ	Barry Zito	6.00

Figure Heads

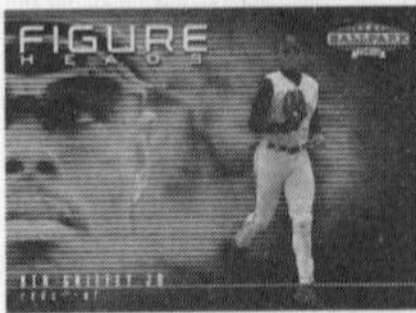

		NM/M
Complete Set (10):		20.00
Common Player:		1.00
Inserted 1:12		
F1	Ichiro Suzuki	3.00
F2	Sammy Sosa	2.50
F3	Alex Rodriguez	4.00
F4	Jason Giambi	1.00
F5	Barry Bonds	4.00
F6	Chipper Jones	1.50
F7	Mike Piazza	2.00
F8	Derek Jeter	4.00
F9	Nomar Garciaparra	2.50
F10	Ken Griffey Jr.	2.00

Player's Club Jerseys

		NM/M
Common Player:		6.00
Inserted 1:72		
KB	Kevin Brown	6.00
DE	Darin Erstad	8.00
RF	Rafael Furcal	6.00
TH	Tim Hudson	6.00
AJ	Andruw Jones	8.00
JK	Jason Kendall	6.00
MM	Mark McGwire/SP	70.00
PN	Phil Nevin	6.00
HN	Hideo Nomo	20.00
MO	Maggio Ordonez	6.00
CS	Curt Schilling	8.00
IS	Ichiro Suzuki/SP	40.00
JT	Jim Thome	12.00

Playmakers 2002

		NM/M
Complete Set (20):		25.00
Common Player:		.75
Inserted 1:6		
P1	Ken Griffey Jr.	2.00
P2	Alex Rodriguez	4.00
P3	Sammy Sosa	2.50
P4	Derek Jeter	4.00
P5	Mike Piazza	2.00
P6	Jason Giambi	1.00
P7	Barry Bonds	4.00
P8	Frank Thomas	1.00
P9	Randy Johnson	1.50
P10	Chipper Jones	1.50
P11	Jeff Bagwell	1.00
P12	Vladimir Guerrero	1.50
P13	Albert Pujols	3.00
P14	Nomar Garciaparra	2.50
P15	Ichiro Suzuki	3.00
P16	Troy Glaus	1.00
P17	Ivan Rodriguez	1.00
P18	Carlos Delgado	.75
P19	Greg Maddux	2.00
P20	Todd Helton	1.00

Uniform Sluggers

		NM/M
Common Player:		5.00
Inserted 1:72		
JB	Jeff Bagwell	8.00
JGi	Jason Giambi	8.00
JGo	Juan Gonzalez	8.00
SG	Shawn Green	5.00
KG	Ken Griffey Jr./SP	25.00
TH	Todd Helton	8.00
CJ	Chipper Jones	10.00
MM	Mickey Mantle/SP	100.00
MP	Mike Piazza	15.00
AR	Alex Rodriguez	12.00
SS	Sammy Sosa/95	
BW	Bernie Williams	8.00

2002 UPPER DECK DIAMOND CONNECTION

		NM/M
Complete Set (550):		
Common Player:		.15
Common Rk (91-200):		4.00
Production 1,500		
Common Jersey (201-270):		4.00
Production 775		
Common Jersey (271-320):		5.00
Production 200		
Common Jersey (321-353):		5.00
Production 150		
Common Jersey (354-368):		6.00
Production 100		
Common Bat (369-438):		5.00
Production 775		
Common Bat (439-488):		5.00
Production 200		
Common Bat (489-521):		5.00
Production 150		
Common Bat (522-536):		10.00
Production 100		
Pack (5):		4.00
Box (14):		50.00
1	Troy Glaus	.50
2	Darin Erstad	.40
3	Barry Zito	.40
4	Eric Chavez	.40
5	Tim Hudson	.40
6	Miguel Tejada	.40
7	Carlos Delgado	.40
8	Shannon Stewart	.15
9	Greg Vaughn	.15
10	Jim Thome	.75
11	C.C. Sabathia	.15
12	Ichiro Suzuki	1.50
13	Edgar Martinez	.25
14	Bret Boone	.25
15	Freddy Garcia	.15
16	Jeff Conine	.15
17	Alex Rodriguez	2.00
18	Rafael Palmeiro	.50
19	Ivan Rodriguez	.50
20	Juan Gonzalez	.50
21	Pedro J. Martinez	.75
22	Nomar Garciaparra	1.50
23	Manny Ramirez	.50
24	Carlos Beltran	.25
25	Mike Sweeney	.15
26	Dmitri Young	.15
27	Bobby Higginson	.15
28	Corey Koskie	.15
29	Cristian Guzman	.15
30	Doug Mientkiewicz	.15
31	Torii Hunter	.25
32	Frank Thomas	.50
33	Mark Buehrle	.15
34	Carlos Lee	.15
35	Magglio Ordonez	.40
36	Roger Clemens	1.50
37	Bernie Williams	.50
38	Jason Giambi	.75
39	Derek Jeter	2.00
40	Mike Mussina	.50
41	Jeff Bagwell	.50
42	Richard Hidalgo	.15
43	Lance Berkman	.40
44	Roy Oswalt	.40
45	Chipper Jones	.75
46	Gary Sheffield	.40
47	Andruw Jones	.50
48	Greg Maddux	1.00
49	Geoff Jenkins	.15
50	Ben Sheets	.25
51	Richie Sexson	.40
52	Albert Pujols	1.50
53	Matt Morris	.25

54	J.D. Drew	.40
55	Tino Martinez	.25
56	Sammy Sosa	1.50
57	Kerry Wood	.75
58	Moises Alou	.25
59	Fred McGriff	.25
60	Randy Johnson	.75
61	Luis Gonzalez	.25
62	Curt Schilling	.50
63	Kevin Brown	.25
64	Shawn Green	.40
65	Paul LoDuca	.15
66	Vladimir Guerrero	.75
67	Jose Vidro	.15
68	Barry Bonds	2.00
69	Jeff Kent	.25
70	Rich Aurilia	.15
71	Preston Wilson	.15
72	Josh Beckett	.40
73	Cliff Floyd	.25
74	Mike Piazza	1.00
75	Mo Vaughn	.25
76	Roberto Alomar	.40
77	Jeromy Burnitz	.15
78	Phil Nevin	.15
79	Sean Burroughs	.15
80	Scott Rolen	.75
81	Bobby Abreu	.25
82	Pat Burrell	.40
83	Brian Giles	.40
84	Jason Kendall	.15
85	Ken Griffey Jr.	1.00
86	Adam Dunn	.50
87	Aaron Boone	.15
88	Larry Walker	.25
89	Todd Helton	.50
90	Mike Hampton	.15
91	*Brandon Puffer*	4.00
92	*Rodrigo Rosario*	4.00
93	*Tom Shearn*	4.00
94	Morgan Ensberg	4.00
95	Jason Lane	4.00
96	*Franklyn German*	4.00
97	Carlos Pena	4.00
98	*Joe Orloski*	4.00
99	*Reed Johnson*	6.00
100	*Chris Baker*	4.00
101	*Corey Thurman*	4.00
102	*Gustavo Chacin*	4.00
103	Eric Hinske	4.00
104	*John Foster*	4.00
105	*John Ennis*	4.00
106	*Kevin Gryboski*	4.00
107	Jung Bong	4.00
108	Travis Wilson	4.00
109	*Luis Martinez*	4.00
110	*Brian Mallette*	4.00
111	*Takahito Nomura*	4.00
112	Bill Hall	4.00
113	*Jeff Deardorff*	4.00
114	Cristian Guerrero	4.00
115	*Scotty Layfield*	4.00
116	*Michael Crudale*	4.00
117	*So Taguchi*	6.00
118	*Jeremy Lambert*	4.00
119	Jimmy Journell	4.00
120	*Francis Beltran*	4.00
121	Mark Prior	8.00
122	Ben Christensen	4.00
123	*Jorge Sosa*	4.00
124	*Brandon Backe*	4.00
125	*Steve Kent*	4.00
126	*Felix Escalona*	4.00
127	*P.J. Bevis*	4.00
128	*Jose Valverde*	4.00
129	*Doug Devore*	4.00
130	*Jeremy Ward*	4.00
131	Mike Koplove	4.00
132	Luis Terrero	4.00
133	John Patterson	4.00
134	*Victor Alvarez*	4.00
135	Kirk Saarloos	4.00
136	*Kazuhisa Ishii*	8.00
137	Steve Colyer	4.00
138	Cesar Izturis	4.00
139	*Ron Calloway*	4.00
140	*Eric Good*	4.00
141	*Jorge Nunez*	4.00
142	Ron Chiavacci	4.00
143	Donnie Bridges	4.00
144	*Nelson Castro*	4.00
145	Deivis Santos	4.00
146	Kurt Ainsworth	4.00
147	Arturo McDowell	4.00
148	*Allan Simpson*	4.00
149	Matt Thornton	4.00
150	*Luis Ugueto*	4.00
151	*J.J. Putz*	4.00
152	*Hansel Izquierdo*	4.00
153	*Oliver Perez*	4.00
154	*Jaime Cerda*	4.00
155	*Mark Corey*	4.00
156	*Tyler Yates*	6.00
157	*Satoru Komiyama*	4.00
158	*Adam Walker*	4.00
159	*Steve Bechler*	6.00
160	Erik Bedard	4.00
161	*Todd Donovan*	4.00
162	*Clifford Bartosh*	4.00
163	*Ben Howard*	8.00
164	*Andy Shibilo*	4.00
165	Dennis Tankersley	4.00
166	Mike Bynum	4.00
167	*Anderson Machado*	4.00
168	*Peter Zamora*	5.00
169	*Eric Junge*	4.00
170	*Elio Serrano*	4.00
171	*Jorge Padilla*	4.00
172	Marlon Byrd	4.00
173	*Adrian Burnside*	4.00
174	*Mike Gonzalez*	4.00
175	J.R. House	4.00
176	Hank Blalock	6.00
177	*Travis Hughes*	4.00
178	Mark Teixeira	6.00
179	*Josh Hancock*	4.00
180	*Anastacio Martinez*	4.00
181	*Jorge de la Rosa*	4.00
182	Ben Broussard	4.00
183	Austin Kearns	4.00
184	Corky Miller	4.00
185	*Colin Young*	4.00
186	*Cam Esslinger*	4.00
187	*Rene Reyes*	4.00
188	*Aaron Cook*	4.00
189	Alexis Gomez	4.00
190	*Nate Field*	4.00
191	*Miguel Asencio*	4.00
192	Brandon Berger	4.00
193	Fernando Rodney	4.00
194	Andy Van Hekken	4.00
195	*Kevin Frederick*	4.00
196	Todd Sears	4.00
197	*Edwin Almonte*	4.00
198	*Kyle Kane*	4.00
199	*Mitch Wylie*	4.00
200	Mike Porzio	4.00
201	Darin Erstad	6.00
202	Tim Salmon	6.00
203	Jeff Bagwell	10.00
204	Lance Berkman	6.00
205	Eric Chavez	6.00
206	Tim Hudson	6.00
207	Carlos Delgado	6.00
208	Chipper Jones	10.00
209	Gary Sheffield	6.00
210	Greg Maddux	15.00
211	Tom Glavine	6.00
212	Mike Mussina	10.00
213	J.D. Drew	6.00
214	Rick Ankiel	4.00
215	Sammy Sosa	15.00
216	Mike Lieberthal	6.00
217	Fred McGriff	8.00
218	David Wells	4.00
219	Curt Schilling	10.00
220	Luis Gonzalez	6.00
221	Mark Grace	10.00
222	Kevin Brown	4.00
223	Hideo Nomo	20.00
224	Jose Vidro	4.00
225	Jeff Kent	4.00
226	Rich Aurilia	4.00
227	Kenny Lofton	4.00
228	C.C. Sabathia	4.00
229	Edgar Martinez	8.00
230	Freddy Garcia	4.00
231	Cliff Floyd	4.00
232	Preston Wilson	4.00
233	Mike Piazza	10.00
234	Roberto Alomar	8.00
235	Trevor Hoffman	4.00
236	Ryan Klesko	5.00
237	Sean Burroughs	4.00
238	Scott Rolen	10.00
239	Pat Burrell	8.00
240	Edgardo Alfonzo	4.00
241	Brian Giles	8.00
242	Jason Kendall	5.00
243	Alex Rodriguez	15.00
244	Juan Gonzalez	8.00
245	Ivan Rodriguez	8.00
246	Rafael Palmeiro	8.00
247	Ken Griffey Jr.	12.00
248	Adam Dunn	15.00
249	Barry Larkin	5.00
250	Manny Ramirez	10.00
251	Pedro Martinez	10.00
252	Todd Helton	8.00
253	Larry Walker	6.00
254	Randy Johnson	10.00
255	Mike Sweeney	4.00
256	Carlos Beltran	6.00
257	Dmitri Young	4.00
258	Joe Mays	4.00
259	Doug Mientkiewicz	4.00
260	Corey Koskie	4.00
261	Magglio Ordonez	8.00
262	Frank Thomas	8.00
263	Ray Durham	4.00
264	Jason Giambi	10.00
265	Bernie Williams	8.00
266	Roger Clemens	15.00
267	Mariano Rivera	6.00
268	Robin Ventura	6.00
269	Andy Pettitte	10.00
270	Jorge Posada	8.00
271	Mike Piazza	15.00
272	Alex Rodriguez	15.00
273	Ken Griffey Jr.	15.00
274	Jason Giambi	10.00
275	Frank Thomas	8.00
276	Greg Maddux	15.00
277	Sammy Sosa	15.00
278	Roger Clemens	15.00
279	Jeff Bagwell	10.00
280	Todd Helton	8.00
281	Ichiro Suzuki	40.00
282	Randy Johnson	10.00
283	Jim Thome	15.00
284	Ivan Rodriguez	8.00
285	Darin Erstad	6.00
286	Eric Chavez	8.00
287	Barry Zito	10.00
288	Carlos Delgado	8.00
289	Omar Vizquel	6.00
290	Edgar Martinez	8.00
291	Manny Ramirez	10.00
292	Mike Sweeney	6.00
293	Tom Glavine	8.00
294	Joe Mays	6.00
295	Eric Milton	6.00
296	Magglio Ordonez	8.00
297	Bernie Williams	8.00
298	Trevor Hoffman	6.00
299	Andruw Jones	8.00
300	Aubrey Huff	5.00
301	Jim Edmonds	8.00
302	Kerry Wood	10.00
303	Luis Gonzalez	8.00
304	Shawn Green	6.00
305	Jose Vidro	5.00
306	Jeff Kent	5.00
307	Edgardo Alfonzo	5.00
308	Preston Wilson	5.00
309	Roberto Alomar	10.00
310	Jeromy Burnitz	5.00
311	Phil Nevin	5.00
312	Ryan Klesko	5.00
313	Bobby Abreu	6.00
314	Scott Rolen	12.00
315	Kazuhiro Sasaki	5.00
316	Jason Kendall	5.00
317	Sean Casey	5.00
318	Larry Walker	5.00
319	Mike Hampton	5.00
320	Juan Gonzalez	8.00
321	Darin Erstad	8.00
322	Tim Hudson	8.00
323	Carlos Delgado	8.00
324	Greg Vaughn	5.00
325	Jim Thome	15.00
326	Ichiro Suzuki	40.00
327	Rafael Palmeiro	8.00
328	Alex Rodriguez	15.00
329	Juan Gonzalez	8.00
330	Manny Ramirez	10.00
331	Carlos Beltran	6.00
332	Eric Milton	5.00
333	Frank Thomas	8.00
334	Roger Clemens	15.00
335	Jason Giambi	10.00
336	Lance Berkman	8.00
337	Greg Maddux	15.00
338	Chipper Jones	10.00
339	Sean Casey	8.00
340	Jim Edmonds	8.00
341	Kerry Wood	10.00
342	Sammy Sosa	15.00
343	Luis Gonzalez	8.00
344	Shawn Green	6.00
345	Jeff Kent	6.00
346	Preston Wilson	5.00
347	Roberto Alomar	10.00
348	Phil Nevin	5.00
349	Scott Rolen	12.00
350	Mike Sweeney	5.00
351	Ken Griffey Jr.	15.00
352	Todd Helton	8.00
353	Larry Walker	5.00
354	Alex Rodriguez	15.00
355	Pedro J. Martinez	10.00
356	Frank Thomas	10.00
357	Jason Giambi	10.00
358	Bernie Williams	10.00
359	Jeff Bagwell	10.00
360	Chipper Jones	10.00
361	Sammy Sosa	20.00
362	Randy Johnson	10.00
363	Shawn Green	6.00
364	Mike Piazza	15.00
365	Ichiro Suzuki	50.00
366	Ken Griffey Jr.	15.00
367	Larry Walker	8.00
368	Jim Edmonds	8.00
369	Darin Erstad	8.00
370	Tim Salmon	8.00
371	Mark Kotsay	5.00
372	Craig Biggio	8.00
373	Eric Chavez	10.00
374	David Justice	8.00
375	Carlos Delgado	8.00
376	Chipper Jones	15.00
377	Gary Sheffield	6.00
378	Greg Maddux	10.00
379	Eric Karros	5.00
380	Fred McGriff	8.00
381	J.D. Drew	8.00
382	Rick Ankiel	5.00
383	Sammy Sosa	15.00
384	Moises Alou	5.00
385	Ben Grieve	5.00
386	Greg Vaughn	5.00
387	Jay Payton	5.00
388	Luis Gonzalez	6.00
389	Ray Durham	5.00
390	Shawn Green	8.00
391	Hideo Nomo	20.00
392	Jose Vidro	5.00
393	Jeff Kent	5.00
394	Adrian Beltre	5.00
395	Jim Thome	15.00
396	Bobby Abreu	5.00
397	Edgar Martinez	10.00
398	Carl Everett	5.00
399	Luis Castillo	5.00
400	Preston Wilson	5.00
401	Jermaine Dye	8.00
402	Roberto Alomar	8.00
403	Todd Hundley	5.00
404	Ryan Klesko	5.00
405	Phil Nevin	5.00
406	Scott Rolen	10.00
407	Rafael Furcal	5.00
408	Miguel Tejada	8.00
409	Brian Giles	6.00
410	Jason Kendall	5.00
411	Alex Rodriguez	15.00
412	Juan Gonzalez	8.00
413	Ivan Rodriguez	8.00
414	Rafael Palmeiro	8.00
415	Ken Griffey Jr.	15.00
416	Edgardo Alfonzo	5.00
417	Barry Larkin	8.00
418	Manny Ramirez	8.00
419	Pedro J. Martinez	12.00
420	Todd Helton	8.00
421	Larry Walker	8.00
422	Garret Anderson	6.00
423	Mike Sweeney	5.00
424	Carlos Beltran	5.00
425	Javier Lopez	5.00
426	J.T. Snow	5.00
427	Doug Mientkiewicz	5.00
428	John Olerud	5.00
429	Magglio Ordonez	6.00
430	Frank Thomas	10.00
431	Kenny Lofton	5.00
432	Al Leiter	5.00
433	Bernie Williams	8.00
434	Roger Clemens	15.00
435	Tom Glavine	8.00
436	Robin Ventura	6.00
437	Chan Ho Park	5.00
438	Jorge Posada	8.00
439	Charles Johnson	5.00
440	Alex Rodriguez	20.00
441	Ken Griffey Jr.	15.00
442	Mark Kotsay	5.00
443	Frank Thomas	10.00
444	Greg Maddux	20.00
445	Sammy Sosa	20.00
446	Tom Glavine	10.00
447	Chipper Jones	15.00
448	Todd Helton	10.00
449	Jeff Cirillo	5.00

450	Steve Finley	8.00
451	Jim Thome	15.00
452	Ivan Rodriguez	8.00
453	Darin Erstad	8.00
454	Eric Chavez	8.00
455	Miguel Tejada	8.00
456	Carlos Delgado	8.00
457	Omar Vizquel	5.00
458	Edgar Martinez	10.00
459	Johnny Damon	8.00
460	Russell Branyan	5.00
461	Kenny Lofton	5.00
462	Jermaine Dye	5.00
463	Ellis Burks	5.00
464	Magglio Ordonez	8.00
465	Bernie Williams	10.00
466	Tim Salmon	5.00
467	Andruw Jones	8.00
468	Jeffrey Hammonds	5.00
469	Jim Edmonds	10.00
470	Kerry Wood	15.00
471	Luis Gonzalez	8.00
472	Shawn Green	8.00
473	Jose Vidro	5.00
474	Jeff Kent	6.00
475	Javier Lopez	5.00
476	Preston Wilson	5.00
477	Roberto Alomar	10.00
478	Robin Ventura	6.00
479	Phil Nevin	5.00
480	Ryan Klesko	8.00
481	Bobby Abreu	6.00
482	Scott Rolen	10.00
483	Brian Giles	8.00
484	Jason Kendall	5.00
485	Tsuyoshi Shinjo	5.00
486	Larry Walker	6.00
487	Mike Lieberthal	5.00
488	Juan Gonzalez	8.00
489	Darin Erstad	6.00
490	Tom Glavine	10.00
491	Carlos Delgado	6.00
492	Greg Vaughn	5.00
493	Jim Thome	15.00
494	Mark Grace	15.00
495	Rafael Palmeiro	8.00
496	Alex Rodriguez	20.00
497	Juan Gonzalez	10.00
498	Miguel Tejada	8.00
499	Carlos Beltran	5.00
500	Andruw Jones	8.00
501	Frank Thomas	10.00
502	Andres Galarraga	5.00
503	Gary Sheffield	8.00
504	Craig Biggio	8.00
505	Greg Maddux	20.00
506	Chipper Jones	20.00
507	Pat Burrell	10.00
508	Jim Edmonds	10.00
509	Kerry Wood	15.00
510	Sammy Sosa	20.00
511	Luis Gonzalez	8.00
512	Shawn Green	8.00
513	Edgardo Alfonzo	5.00
514	Preston Wilson	5.00
515	Roberto Alomar	10.00
516	Phil Nevin	5.00
517	Scott Rolen	15.00
518	Brian Giles	8.00
519	Jorge Posada	10.00
520	Todd Helton	12.00
521	Larry Walker	8.00
522	Alex Rodriguez	25.00
523	Pedro J. Martinez	20.00
524	Frank Thomas	12.00
525	Jason Giambi	15.00
526	Bernie Williams	10.00
527	J.D. Drew	10.00
528	Chipper Jones	20.00
529	Sammy Sosa	25.00
530	Randy Johnson	15.00
531	Shawn Green	10.00
532	Kevin Brown	10.00
533	Brian Giles	10.00
534	Ken Griffey Jr.	20.00
535	Larry Walker	10.00
536	Jim Edmonds	10.00
537	Sean Casey/jsy/775	8.00
538	Ichiro Suzuki/jsy/775	40.00
539	Pat Burrell/jsy/200	10.00
540	Adam Dunn//jsy/200	20.00
541	Lance Berkman/jsy/200	10.00
542	Cliff Floyd/jsy/150	8.00
543	Roger Clemens/jsy/100	20.00
544	Kerry Wood/bat/775	15.00
545	Andruw Jones/bat/775	8.00
546	Manny Ramirez/bat/200	10.00
547	Jorge Posada/bat/200	10.00
548	Fred McGriff/bat/200	8.00
549	Mike Sweeney/bat/150	6.00
550	Todd Helton/bat/100	12.00

Great Connections

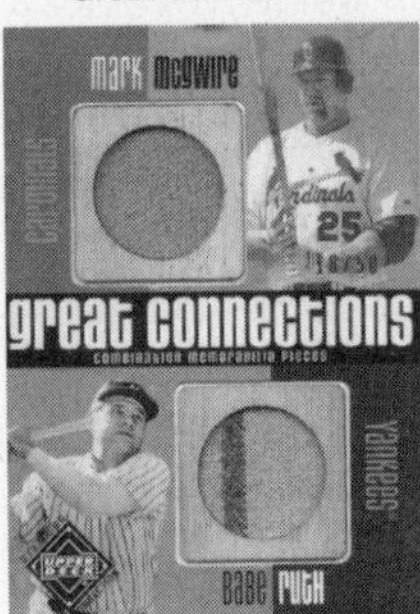

		NM/M
Production 50 sets		
GC-GR	Jason Giambi, Babe Ruth	350.00
GC-MD	Mickey Mantle, Joe DiMaggio	350.00
GC-MR	Mark McGwire, Babe Ruth	350.00
GC-MS	Mark McGwire, Sammy Sosa	200.00
GC-RR	Alex Rodriguez, Nolan Ryan	150.00
GC-IG	Ichiro Suzuki, Ken Griffey Jr.	150.00

Mem. Signatures Bat

		NM/M
Varying quantities produced		
JD	Joe DiMaggio/20	600.00
JG	Jason Giambi/49	60.00
KG	Ken Griffey Jr/49	150.00
MMc	Mark McGwire/49	300.00
JM	Joe Morgan/99	35.00
KP	Kirby Puckett/145	75.00
CR	Cal Ripken Jr/145	150.00
AR	Alex Rodriguez/145	100.00
BR	Babe Ruth/3	
NR	Nolan Ryan/99	150.00
SS	Sammy Sosa/99	150.00
IS	Ichiro Suzuki/99	250.00

Mem. Signatures Jsy

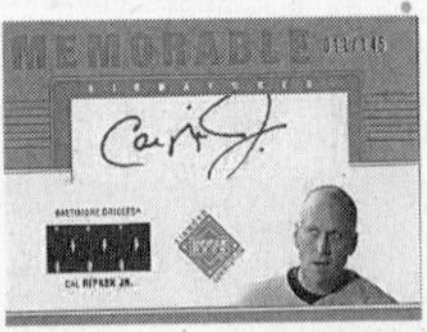

		NM/M
Varying quantities produced		
Gold:		.75-1X
Production 150		
EB	Ernie Banks/150	80.00
JD	Joe DiMaggio/20	550.00
JG	Jason Giambi/49	
KG	Ken Griffey Jr/49	150.00
SK	Sandy Koufax/150	300.00
MMa	Mickey Mantle/1	
MMc	Mark McGwire/49	300.00
JM	Joe Morgan/99	35.00
CR	Cal Ripken Jr/145	150.00
AR	Alex Rodriguez/145	100.00
BR	Babe Ruth/3	
NR	Nolan Ryan/99	150.00
SS	Sammy Sosa/99	200.00
IS	Ichiro Suzuki/99	250.00

2002 UPPER DECK HONOR ROLL

		NM/M
Complete Set (100):		25.00
Common Player:		.15
Pack (5):		2.00
Box (24):		30.00
1	Randy Johnson	.50
2	Mike Piazza	.75
3	Albert Pujols	1.00
4	Roberto Alomar	.25
5	Chipper Jones	.50
6	Rich Aurilia	.15
7	Barry Bonds	1.00
8	Ken Griffey Jr.	.75
9	Sammy Sosa	.75
10	Roger Clemens	.75
11	Ivan Rodriguez	.40
12	Jason Giambi	.40
13	Bret Boone	.15
14	Troy Glaus	.25
15	Alex Rodriguez	.75
16	Manny Ramirez	.40
17	Bernie Williams	.40
18	Ichiro Suzuki	.75
19	Matt Thornton	.25
20	*Chris Baker*	.25
21	*Tyler Yates*	.50
22	*Jorge Nunez*	.50
23	*Rene Reyes*	.50
24	*Ben Howard*	.50
25	*Ron Calloway*	.40
26	Danny Wright	.15
27	*Reed Johnson*	.50
28	Randy Johnson	.25
29	Randy Johnson	.25
30	Randy Johnson	.25
31	Randy Johnson	.25
32	Mike Piazza	.50
33	Mike Piazza	.50
34	Mike Piazza	.50
35	Mike Piazza	.50
36	Albert Pujols	.75
37	Albert Pujols	.75
38	Albert Pujols	.75
39	Albert Pujols	.75
40	Roberto Alomar	.20
41	Roberto Alomar	.20
42	Roberto Alomar	.20
43	Roberto Alomar	.20
44	Chipper Jones	.50
45	Chipper Jones	.50
46	Chipper Jones	.50
47	Chipper Jones	.50
48	Rich Aurilia	.15
49	Rich Aurilia	.15
50	Rich Aurilia	.15
51	Rich Aurilia	.15
52	Barry Bonds	1.00
53	Barry Bonds	1.00
54	Barry Bonds	1.00
55	Barry Bonds	1.00
56	Ken Griffey Jr.	.75
57	Ken Griffey Jr.	.75
58	Ken Griffey Jr.	.75
59	Ken Griffey Jr.	.75
60	Sammy Sosa	.50
61	Sammy Sosa	.50
62	Sammy Sosa	.50
63	Sammy Sosa	.50
64	Roger Clemens	.75
65	Roger Clemens	.75
66	Roger Clemens	.75
67	Roger Clemens	.75
68	Ivan Rodriguez	.25
69	Ivan Rodriguez	.25
70	Ivan Rodriguez	.25
71	Ivan Rodriguez	.25
72	Jason Giambi	.25
73	Jason Giambi	.25
74	Jason Giambi	.25
75	Jason Giambi	.25
76	Bret Boone	.15
77	Bret Boone	.15
78	Bret Boone	.15
79	Bret Boone	.15
80	Troy Glaus	.20
81	Troy Glaus	.20
82	Troy Glaus	.20
83	Troy Glaus	.20
84	Alex Rodriguez	.75
85	Alex Rodriguez	.75
86	Alex Rodriguez	.75
87	Alex Rodriguez	.75
88	Manny Ramirez	.25
89	Manny Ramirez	.25
90	Manny Ramirez	.25
91	Manny Ramirez	.25
92	Bernie Williams	.20
93	Bernie Williams	.20
94	Bernie Williams	.20
95	Bernie Williams	.20
96	Ichiro Suzuki	1.00
97	Ichiro Suzuki	1.00
98	Ichiro Suzuki	1.00
99	Ichiro Suzuki	1.00
100	Checklist (Original nine players) (Nine team names)	.25

Silver

Stars:	4-8X
Production 100 sets	

Gold

Gold Stars (1-100):	15-25X
Production 25 sets	

Batting Glove

		NM/M
Numbered to 250		
BB	Bret Boone/89	20.00
JG	Jason Giambi	20.00
KG	Ken Griffey Jr.	40.00
AR	Alex Rodriguez	25.00
IR1	Ivan Rodriguez	20.00
IR2	Ivan Rodriguez	20.00
SS	Sammy Sosa	30.00
I	Ichiro Suzuki/46	150.00

Game-Used Bat

		NM/M
Common Player:		10.00
Numbered to 99		
Each player has multiple versions		
BB	Bret Boone	10.00
RC	Roger Clemens	30.00
JG	Jason Giambi	15.00
KG	Ken Griffey Jr.	40.00
CJ	Chipper Jones	20.00
AR	Alex Rodriguez	20.00
IR	Ivan Rodriguez	15.00
SS	Sammy Sosa	30.00
I	Ichiro Suzuki	40.00

Game Jersey

		NM/M
Common Player:		10.00
Inserted 1:90		
Golds:		2-3X
Production 99 sets		
Each player has multiple versions		
BB	Bret Boone/SP/45	10.00
RC	Roger Clemens	20.00
JG	Jason Giambi/SP	15.00
KG	Ken Griffey Jr.	25.00
CJ	Chipper Jones	15.00
AR	Alex Rodriguez	15.00

IR	Ivan Rodriguez	10.00
SS	Sammy Sosa/SP	25.00
I	Ichiro Suzuki/SP	40.00

Star Swatches Game Jersey

		NM/M
Common Player:		10.00
Inserted 1:90		
Golds:		2-5X
Production 24		
BB	Bret Boone/45	10.00
RC	Roger Clemens/29	40.00
JG	Jason Giambi	10.00
KG	Ken Griffey Jr/SP	25.00
CJ	Chipper Jones	15.00
AR	Alex Rodriguez	15.00
IR	Ivan Rodriguez	10.00
SS	Sammy Sosa	20.00
I	Ichiro Suzuki/SP	40.00

Stitch of Nine Game Jersey

		NM/M
Common Player:		10.00
Inserted 1:90		
Golds:		2-5X
Production 24 sets		
BB	Bret Boone/45	10.00
RC	Roger Clemens	20.00
JG	Jason Giambi/SP	10.00
KG	Ken Griffey Jr.	15.00
CJ	Chipper Jones	10.00
AR	Alex Rodriguez	15.00
IR	Ivan Rodriguez	10.00
SS	Sammy Sosa	20.00
I	Ichiro Suzuki/85	40.00

Time Capsule Game Jersey

		NM/M
Common Player:		8.00
Inserted 1:90		
Golds:		2-3X
Production 99 sets		
BB	Bret Boone	8.00
RC	Roger Clemens	20.00
JG	Jason Giambi/52	15.00
KG	Ken Griffey Jr./5	
CJ	Chipper Jones	10.00
AR	Alex Rodriguez	15.00
IR	Ivan Rodriguez/SP	15.00
SS	Sammy Sosa	20.00
I	Ichiro Suzuki	40.00

2002 UPPER DECK MVP

		NM/M
Complete Set (300):		20.00
Common Player:		.10
Pack (8):		1.50
Box (24):		25.00
1	Darin Erstad	.20
2	Ramon Ortiz	.10
3	Garret Anderson	.20
4	Jarrod Washburn	.10
5	Troy Glaus	.20
6	*Brendan Donnelly*	.10
7	Troy Percival	.10
8	Tim Salmon	.15
9	Aaron Sele	.10
10	Brad Fullmer	.10
11	Scott Hatteberg	.10
12	Barry Zito	.20
13	Tim Hudson	.20
14	Miguel Tejada	.25
15	Jermaine Dye	.10
16	Mark Mulder	.20
17	Eric Chavez	.15
18	Terrence Long	.10
19	Carlos Pena	.20
20	David Justice	.20
21	Jeremy Giambi	.10
22	Shannon Stewart	.10
23	Raul Mondesi	.15
24	Chris Carpenter	.10
25	Carlos Delgado	.20
26	Mike Sirotka	.10
27	*Reed Johnson*	.15
28	Darrin Fletcher	.10
29	Jose Cruz Jr.	.10
30	Vernon Wells	.10
31	Tanyon Sturtze	.10
32	Toby Hall	.10
33	Brent Abernathy	.10
34	Ben Grieve	.10
35	Joe Kennedy	.10
36	Dewon Brazelton	.10
37	Aubrey Huff	.10
38	Steve Cox	.10
39	Greg Vaughn	.10
40	Brady Anderson	.10
41	Chuck Finley	.10
42	Jim Thome	.40
43	Russell Branyan	.10
44	C.C. Sabathia	.10
45	Matt Lawton	.10
46	Omar Vizquel	.10
47	Bartolo Colon	.15
48	Alex Escobar	.10
49	Ellis Burks	.10
50	Bret Boone	.10
51	John Olerud	.20
52	Jeff Cirillo	.10
53	Ichiro Suzuki	1.00
54	Kazuhiro Sasaki	.10
55	Freddy Garcia	.10
56	Edgar Martinez	.15
57	Matt Thornton	.10
58	Mike Cameron	.10
59	Carlos Guillen	.10
60	Jeff Conine	.10
61	Tony Batista	.10
62	Jason Johnson	.10
63	Melvin Mora	.10
64	Brian Roberts	.10
65	Josh Towers	.10
66	*Steve Bechler*	.10
67	Jerry Hairston Jr.	.10
68	Chris Richard	.10
69	Alex Rodriguez	1.00
70	Chan Ho Park	.10
71	Ivan Rodriguez	.25
72	Jeff Zimmerman	.10
73	Mark Teixeira	.20
74	Gabe Kapler	.10
75	Frank Catalanotto	.10
76	Rafael Palmeiro	.25
77	Doug Davis	.10
78	Carl Everett	.10
79	Pedro J. Martinez	.40
80	Nomar Garciaparra	.75
81	Tony Clark	.10
82	Trot Nixon	.10
83	Manny Ramirez	.25
84	*Josh Hancock*	.10
85	Johnny Damon	.20
86	Jose Offerman	.10
87	Rich Garces	.10
88	Shea Hillenbrand	.10
89	Carlos Beltran	.20
90	Mike Sweeney	.10
91	Jeff Suppan	.10
92	Joe Randa	.10
93	Chuck Knoblauch	.10
94	Mark Quinn	.10
95	Neifi Perez	.10
96	Carlos Febles	.10
97	*Miguel Asencio*	.10
98	Michael Tucker	.10
99	Dean Palmer	.10
100	Jose Lima	.10
101	Craig Paquette	.10
102	Dmitri Young	.10
103	Bobby Higginson	.10
104	Jeff Weaver	.10
105	Matt Anderson	.10
106	Damion Easley	.10
107	Eric Milton	.10
108	Doug Mientkiewicz	.10
109	Cristian Guzman	.10
110	Brad Radke	.10
111	Torii Hunter	.20
112	Corey Koskie	.10
113	Joe Mays	.10
114	Jacque Jones	.10
115	David Ortiz	.20
116	*Kevin Frederick*	.20
117	Magglio Ordonez	.20
118	Ray Durham	.10
119	Mark Buehrle	.10
120	Jon Garland	.10
121	Paul Konerko	.10
122	Todd Ritchie	.10
123	Frank Thomas	.25
124	*Edwin Almonte*	.10
125	Carlos Lee	.10
126	Kenny Lofton	.15
127	Roger Clemens	.75
128	Derek Jeter	1.00
129	Jorge Posada	.20
130	Bernie Williams	.25
131	Mike Mussina	.25
132	Alfonso Soriano	.40
133	Robin Ventura	.15
134	John Vander Wal	.10
135	Jason Giambi	.25
136	Mariano Rivera	.20
137	Rondell White	.10
138	Jeff Bagwell	.25
139	Wade Miller	.10
140	Richard Hidalgo	.10
141	Julio Lugo	.10
142	Roy Oswalt	.20
143	*Rodrigo Rosario*	.10
144	Lance Berkman	.20
145	Craig Biggio	.20
146	Shane Reynolds	.10
147	John Smoltz	.20
148	Chipper Jones	.40
149	Gary Sheffield	.20
150	Rafael Furcal	.10
151	Greg Maddux	.50
152	Tom Glavine	.20
153	Andruw Jones	.25
154	*John Ennis*	.20
155	Vinny Castilla	.10
156	Marcus Giles	.10
157	Javy Lopez	.10
158	Richie Sexson	.20
159	Geoff Jenkins	.20
160	Jeffrey Hammonds	.10
161	Alex Ochoa	.10
162	Ben Sheets	.20
163	Jose Hernandez	.10
164	Eric Young	.10
165	Luis Montanez	.10
166	Albert Pujols	.75
167	Darryl Kile	.10
168	*So Taguchi*	.50
169	Jim Edmonds	.20
170	Fernando Vina	.10
171	Matt Morris	.10
172	J.D. Drew	.20
173	Bud Smith	.10
174	Edgar Renteria	.20
175	Placido Polanco	.10
176	Tino Martinez	.10
177	Sammy Sosa	.75
178	Moises Alou	.20
179	Kerry Wood	.40
180	Delino DeShields	.10
181	Alex Gonzalez	.10
182	Jon Lieber	.10
183	Fred McGriff	.15
184	Corey Patterson	.15
185	Mark Prior	.75
186	Tom Gordon	.10
187	*Francis Beltran*	.10
188	Randy Johnson	.40
189	Luis Gonzalez	.20
190	Matt Williams	.15
191	Mark Grace	.25
192	Curt Schilling	.25
193	*Doug Devore*	.20
194	Erubiel Durazo	.10
195	Steve Finley	.15
196	Craig Counsell	.10
197	Shawn Green	.25
198	Kevin Brown	.20
199	Paul LoDuca	.10
200	Brian Jordan	.15
201	Andy Ashby	.10
202	Darren Dreifort	.10
203	Adrian Beltre	.15
204	*Victor Alvarez*	.10
205	Eric Karros	.10
206	Hideo Nomo	.25
207	Vladimir Guerrero	.40
208	Javier Vazquez	.10
209	Michael Barrett	.10
210	Jose Vidro	.10
211	Brad Wilkerson	.10
212	Tony Armas Jr.	.10
213	*Eric Good*	.10
214	Orlando Cabrera	.10
215	Lee Stevens	.10
216	Jeff Kent	.10
217	Rich Aurilia	.10
218	Robb Nen	.10
219	Calvin Murray	.10
220	Russ Ortiz	.10
221	Deivis Santos	.10
222	Marvin Benard	.10
223	Jason Schmidt	.10
224	Reggie Sanders	.10
225	Barry Bonds	1.00
226	Brad Penny	.10
227	Cliff Floyd	.10
228	Mike Lowell	.20
229	Derrek Lee	.10
230	Ryan Dempster	.10
231	Josh Beckett	.20
232	*Hansel Izquierdo*	.10
233	Preston Wilson	.10
234	A.J. Burnett	.10
235	Charles Johnson	.10
236	Mike Piazza	.50
237	Al Leiter	.20
238	Jay Payton	.10
239	Roger Cedeno	.10
240	Jeromy Burnitz	.10
241	Roberto Alomar	.20
242	Mo Vaughn	.20
243	Shawn Estes	.10
244	Armando Benitez	.10
245	*Tyler Yates*	.10
246	Phil Nevin	.10
247	D'Angelo Jimenez	.10
248	Ramon Vazquez	.10
249	Bubba Trammell	.10
250	Trevor Hoffman	.10
251	*Ben Howard*	.20
252	Mark Kotsay	.10
253	Ray Lankford	.10
254	Ryan Klesko	.10
255	Scott Rolen	.40
256	Robert Person	.10

257	Jimmy Rollins	.10
258	Pat Burrell	.20
259	*Anderson Machado*	.10
260	Randy Wolf	.10
261	Travis Lee	.10
262	Mike Lieberthal	.10
263	Doug Glanville	.10
264	Bobby Abreu	.10
265	Brian Giles	.15
266	Kris Benson	.10
267	Aramis Ramirez	.10
268	Kevin Young	.10
269	Jack Wilson	.10
270	Mike Williams	.10
271	Jimmy Anderson	.10
272	Jason Kendall	.10
273	Pokey Reese	.10
274	Robert Mackowiak	.10
275	Sean Casey	.20
276	Juan Encarnacion	.10
277	Austin Kearns	.20
278	Danny Graves	.10
279	Ken Griffey Jr.	.50
280	Barry Larkin	.20
281	Todd Walker	.10
282	Elmer Dessens	.10
283	Aaron Boone	.10
284	Adam Dunn	.40
285	Larry Walker	.15
286	*Rene Reyes*	.20
287	Juan Uribe	.10
288	Mike Hampton	.10
289	Todd Helton	.40
290	Juan Pierre	.10
291	Denny Neagle	.10
292	Jose Ortiz	.10
293	Todd Zeile	.10
294	Ben Petrick	.10
295	Ken Griffey Jr. Checklist 1-50	.25
296	Derek Jeter Checklist 51-100	.50
297	Sammy Sosa Checklist 101-150	.30
298	Ichiro Suzuki Checklist 151-200	.50
299	Barry Bonds Checklist 201-250	.50
300	Alex Rodriguez Checklist 251-300	.40

Gold

No Pricing
Production 25 sets

Silver

Stars: 5-10X
Production 100 sets

Ichiro - A Season to Remember

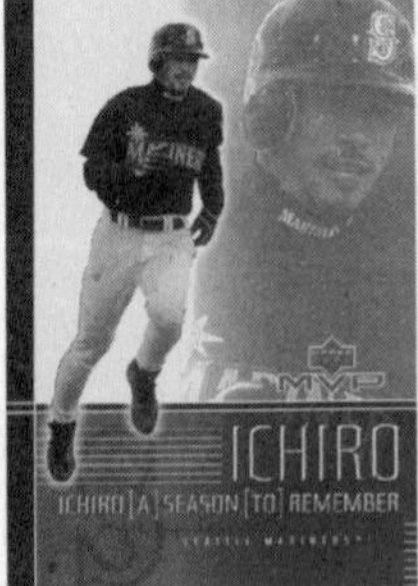

	NM/M
Complete Set (10):	15.00
Ichiro's (1-10):	2.00
Inserted 1:10	

A Season to Remember Jersey

I-J Ichiro Suzuki

Souvenirs Bats

		NM/M
Common Player:		8.00
Inserted 1:144		
RA	Roberto Alomar	20.00
CD	Carlos Delgado	8.00
BG	Brian Giles	8.00
LG	Luis Gonzalez	8.00
SG	Shawn Green	8.00
KG	Ken Griffey Jr.	25.00
TH	Todd Helton	15.00
DJ	David Justice	8.00
JK	Jeff Kent	8.00
RK	Ryan Klesko	8.00
GM	Greg Maddux	20.00
EM	Edgar Martinez	10.00
DM	Doug Mientkiewicz	8.00
MO	Magglio Ordonez	8.00
RP	Rafael Palmeiro/97	18.00
MP	Mike Piazza/97	25.00
AR	Alex Rodriguez	15.00
IR	Ivan Rodriguez	10.00
SR	Scott Rolen	10.00
GS	Gary Sheffield	8.00
SS	Sammy Sosa	20.00
MS	Mike Sweeney	8.00
FT	Frank Thomas/97	25.00
JT	Jim Thome	10.00
GV	Greg Vaughn	8.00
LW	Larry Walker	8.00
BW	Bernie Williams	10.00

Souvenirs Jerseys

		NM/M
Common Player:		5.00
Inserted 1:48		
RA	Roberto Alomar	10.00
GA	Garret Anderson	10.00
JB	Jeff Bagwell	10.00
AB	Adrian Beltre	8.00
JB	Jeromy Burnitz	5.00
RC	Roger Clemens	15.00
CD	Carlos Delgado	8.00
DE	Darin Erstad	8.00
RF	Rafael Furcal	8.00
JG	Juan Gonzalez	10.00
THo	Trevor Hoffman	5.00
THu	Tim Hudson	8.00
JK	Jeff Kent	8.00
PK	Paul Konerko/SP	10.00
MK	Mark Kotsay	5.00
KL	Kenny Lofton	8.00
EM	Edgar Martinez	10.00
JP	Jay Payton/SP	10.00
MP	Mike Piazza	15.00
AR	Alex Rodriguez	15.00
IR	Ivan Rodriguez	10.00
SR	Scott Rolen	10.00
TS	Tim Salmon	10.00
FT	Frank Thomas	15.00
JT	Jim Thome/SP	15.00
RV	Robin Ventura	5.00
OV	Omar Vizquel	8.00
PW	Preston Wilson	5.00
TZ	Todd Zeile	5.00

Ichiro - A Season to Remember Bat

No Pricing
Production 25
I-B Ichiro Suzuki

Souvenirs Bat/Jersey Combos

		NM/M
Common Card:		10.00
Inserted 1:144		
Gold:		No Pricing
Production 25 sets		
EA	Edgardo Alfonzo	10.00
RA	Roberto Alomar	15.00
JB	Jeff Bagwell	20.00
AB	Adrian Beltre	15.00
PB	Pat Burrell/97	
CD	Carlos Delgado	15.00
DE	Darin Erstad	20.00
JG	Jason Giambi	20.00
BG	Brian Giles	15.00
LG	Luis Gonzalez	15.00
SG	Shawn Green	15.00
KG	Ken Griffey Jr.	40.00
TH	Todd Helton	20.00
RJ	Randy Johnson	25.00
CJ	Chipper Jones	20.00
JK	Jeff Kent	15.00
MO	Magglio Ordonez	15.00
RP	Rafael Palmeiro	20.00
MP	Mike Piazza	15.00
AR	Alex Rodriguez	25.00
IR	Ivan Rodriguez	15.00
SR	Scott Rolen	15.00
SS	Sammy Sosa	15.00
JT	Jim Thome	25.00
RV	Robin Ventura	10.00
OV	Omar Vizquel/97	20.00
BW	Bernie Williams/97	25.00
TZ	Todd Zeile	10.00

2002 UPPER DECK OVATION

		NM/M
Complete Set (120):		120.00
Common Player:		.25
Common (61-89, 120):		3.00
Production 2,002		
Pack (5):		1.50
Box (24):		30.00
1	Troy Glaus	.40
2	David Justice	.40
3	Tim Hudson	.40
4	Jermaine Dye	.25
5	Carlos Delgado	.40
6	Greg Vaughn	.25
7	Jim Thome	.75
8	C.C. Sabathia	.25
9	Ichiro Suzuki	1.50
10	Edgar Martinez	.40
11	Chris Richard	.25
12	Rafael Palmeiro	.50
13	Alex Rodriguez	2.00
14	Ivan Rodriguez	.50
15	Nomar Garciaparra	1.50
16	Manny Ramirez	.50
17	Pedro J. Martinez	.75
18	Mike Sweeney	.25
19	Dmitri Young	.25
20	Doug Mientkiewicz	.25
21	Brad Radke	.25
22	Cristian Guzman	.25
23	Frank Thomas	.50
24	Magglio Ordonez	.40
25	Bernie Williams	.50
26	Derek Jeter	2.00
27	Jason Giambi	.50
28	Roger Clemens	1.50
29	Jeff Bagwell	.50
30	Lance Berkman	.40
31	Chipper Jones	.75
32	Gary Sheffield	.40
33	Greg Maddux	1.00
34	Richie Sexson	.40
35	Albert Pujols	1.50
36	Tino Martinez	.25
37	J.D. Drew	.40
38	Sammy Sosa	1.50
39	Moises Alou	.40
40	Randy Johnson	.75
41	Luis Gonzalez	.40
42	Shawn Green	.40
43	Kevin Brown	.25
44	Vladimir Guerrero	.75
45	Barry Bonds	2.00
46	Jeff Kent	.40
47	Cliff Floyd	.25
48	Josh Beckett	.50
49	Mike Piazza	1.00
50	Mo Vaughn	.25
51	Jeromy Burnitz	.25
52	Roberto Alomar	.40
53	Phil Nevin	.25
54	Scott Rolen	.75
55	Jimmy Rollins	.25
56	Brian Giles	.40
57	Ken Griffey Jr.	1.00
58	Sean Casey	.40
59	Larry Walker	.40
60	Todd Helton	.50
61	*Rodrigo Rosario*	5.00
62	*Reed Johnson*	8.00
63	*John Ennis*	3.00
64	*Luis Martinez*	3.00
65	*So Taguchi*	6.00
66	*Brandon Backe*	3.00
67	*Doug Devore*	3.00
68	*Victor Alvarez*	3.00
69	*Kazuhisa Ishii*	8.00
70	*Eric Good*	3.00
71	Deivis Santos	3.00
72	Matt Thornton	3.00
73	*Hansel Izquierdo*	3.00
74	*Tyler Yates*	6.00
75	*Jaime Cerda*	3.00
76	*Satoru Komiyama*	3.00
77	*Steve Bechler*	3.00
78	*Ben Howard*	3.00
79	*Jorge Padilla*	3.00
80	*Eric Junge*	3.00
81	*Anderson Machado*	3.00
82	*Adrian Burnside*	3.00
83	*Josh Hancock*	3.00
84	*Anastacio Martinez*	3.00
85	*Rene Reyes*	3.00
86	*Nate Field*	3.00
87	*Tim Kalita*	3.00
88	*Kevin Frederick*	3.00
89	*Edwin Almonte*	3.00
90	Ichiro Suzuki	.75
91	Ichiro Suzuki	.75
92	Ichiro Suzuki	.75
93	Ichiro Suzuki	.75
94	Ichiro Suzuki	.75
95	Ken Griffey Jr.	.75
96	Ken Griffey Jr.	.75
97	Ken Griffey Jr.	.75
98	Ken Griffey Jr.	.75
99	Ken Griffey Jr.	.75
100	Jason Giambi	.40
101	Jason Giambi	.40
102	Jason Giambi	.40
103	Jason Giambi	.40
104	Jason Giambi	.40
105	Sammy Sosa	.75
106	Sammy Sosa	.75
107	Sammy Sosa	.75
108	Sammy Sosa	.75
109	Sammy Sosa	.75
110	Alex Rodriguez	.75
111	Alex Rodriguez	.75
112	Alex Rodriguez	.75
113	Alex Rodriguez	.75
114	Alex Rodriguez	.75
115	Mark McGwire	.75
116	Mark McGwire	.75
117	Mark McGwire	.75
118	Mark McGwire	.75
119	Mark McGwire	.75
120	Alex Rodriguez, Ken Griffey Jr., Mark McGwire, Sammy Sosa, Jason Giambi, Ichiro Suzuki	15.00

Gold

(1-60) print run 25-50:	8-15X
(1-60) p/r 51-75:	4-8X
(1-60) p/r 76-90:	3-5X
(61-120) 25 of each produced	
Print runs based on stats	

Silver

(1-60):	1-3X
(61-89, 120):	.5-1X
(90-119):	2-4X

Authentic McGwire

		NM/M
Varying quantities produced		
AM-B	Mark McGwire/bat/70	100.00
AM-BG	Mark McGwire/bat/50	100.00
AM-SB	Mark McGwire/bat/auto/25	
AM-J	Mark McGwire/jsy/70	100.00
AM-JG	Mark McGwire/jsy/50	100.00
AM-SJ	Mark McGwire/jsy/auto/25	

Diamond Futures Jersey

		NM/M
Common Player:		5.00
Inserted 1:72		
Golds production 25 no pricing		
LB	Lance Berkman	8.00
RB	Russell Branyan	5.00
PB	Pat Burrell	8.00
FG	Freddy Garcia	5.00
TH	Tim Hudson	6.00
JK	Jason Kendall	8.00
JP	Jorge Posada	10.00
IR	Ivan Rodriguez	10.00
JR	Jimmy Rollins	5.00
KS	Kazuhiro Sasaki	5.00
JV	Jose Vidro	5.00
BZ	Barry Zito	8.00

Lead Performer Jersey

		NM/M
Common Player:		5.00
Inserted 1:72		
Golds:		No Pricng
Production 25 sets		
JB	Jeff Bagwell	8.00
CD	Carlos Delgado	6.00
JGi	Jason Giambi	10.00
JG	Juan Gonzalez	8.00
LG	Luis Gonzalez	5.00
KG	Ken Griffey Jr/SP	20.00
MP	Mike Piazza	15.00
AR	Alex Rodriguez	15.00
IR	Ivan Rodriguez	8.00
SS	Sammy Sosa/SP	15.00
IS	Ichiro Suzuki	40.00
FT	Frank Thomas	8.00

Swatches Jersey

		NM/M
Common Player:		5.00
Inserted 1:72		
Golds: 25 sets produced no pricing		
RA	Roberto Alomar/SP	20.00
EB	Ellis Burks	5.00
JB	Jeromy Burnitz	5.00
EC	Eric Chavez	6.00
CD	Carlos Delgado	6.00
DE	Darin Erstad	5.00
MG	Mark Grace	10.00
CJ	Chipper Jones	12.00
GM	Greg Maddux	15.00
PM	Pedro J. Martinez	10.00
AR	Alex Rodriguez	15.00
BW	Bernie Williams	10.00

2002 UPPER DECK PIECE OF HISTORY

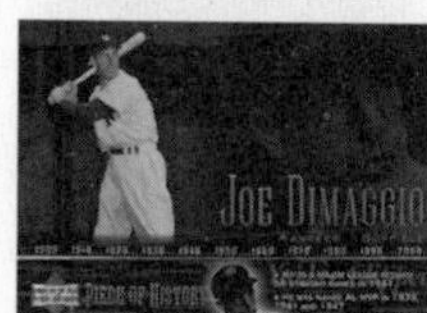

		NM/M
Complete Set (132):		200.00
Common Player:		.15
Common SP (91-132):		5.00
Production 625		
Pack (5):		2.00
Box (24):		40.00
1	Troy Glaus	.40
2	Darin Erstad	.25
3	Reggie Jackson	.50
4	Miguel Tejada	.40
5	Tim Hudson	.25
6	Jim "Catfish" Hunter	.25
7	Joe Carter	.15
8	Carlos Delgado	.40
9	Greg Vaughn	.15
10	Early Wynn	.15
11	Omar Vizquel	.15
12	Jim Thome	.75
13	Ichiro Suzuki	1.50
14	Edgar Martinez	.25
15	Freddy Garcia	.15
16	Cal Ripken Jr/SP	15.00
17	Jeff Conine	.15
18	Juan Gonzalez	.50
19	Nolan Ryan/SP	15.00
20	Alex Rodriguez/SP	10.00
21	Rafael Palmeiro	.50
22	Ivan Rodriguez	.50
23	Carlton Fisk	.25
24	Wade Boggs	.30
25	Pedro J. Martinez	.75
26	Nomar Garciaparra	1.50
27	Manny Ramirez	.50
28	Mike Sweeney	.15
29	Bobby Higginson	.15
30	Kirby Puckett	.75
31	Doug Mientkiewicz	.15
32	Corey Koskie	.15
33	Joe Mays	.15
34	Frank Thomas	.50
35	Magglio Ordonez	.25
36	Jason Giambi/SP	5.00
37	Derek Jeter/SP	10.00
38	Mickey Mantle/SP	15.00
39	Joe DiMaggio	2.00
40	Roger Maris	1.00
41	Roger Clemens	1.50
42	Bernie Williams	.50
43	Jeff Bagwell	.50
44	Lance Berkman	.25
45	Eddie Mathews	.50
46	Andruw Jones	.40
47	Phil Niekro	.15
48	Gary Sheffield	.25
49	Chipper Jones	.75
50	Greg Maddux	1.00
51	Robin Yount	.50
52	Richie Sexson	.25
53	Jim Edmonds	.25
54	J.D. Drew	.25
55	Albert Pujols	1.50
56	Andre Dawson	.25
57	Billy Williams	.15
58	Ernie Banks	.50
59	Sammy Sosa/SP	10.00
60	Randy Johnson	.75
61	Curt Schilling	.50
62	Luis Gonzalez	.25
63	Kirk Gibson	.15
64	Steve Garvey	.15
65	Sandy Koufax/SP	15.00
66	Shawn Green	.25
67	Hideo Nomo	.25
68	Kevin Brown	.15
69	Vladimir Guerrero	.75
70	Tim Raines	.15
71	Gaylord Perry	.15
72	Mel Ott	.25
73	Willie McCovey	.15
74	Barry Bonds/SP	10.00
75	Jeff Kent	.15
76	Cliff Floyd	.15
77	Dwight Gooden	.15
78	Tom Seaver	.50
79	Mike Piazza	1.00
80	Roberto Alomar	.50
81	Dave Winfield	.25
82	Tony Gwynn	.75
83	Scott Rolen	.75
84	Bill Mazeroski	.15
85	Willie Stargell	.25
86	Brian Giles	.25
87	Ken Griffey Jr/SP	10.00
88	Sean Casey	.25
89	Todd Helton	.50
90	Larry Walker	.25
91	*Brendan Donnelly*	5.00
92	*Tom Shearn*	5.00
93	*Brandon Puffer*	5.00
94	*Corey Thurman*	5.00
95	*Reed Johnson*	8.00
96	*Gustavo Chacin*	5.00
97	*Chris Baker*	5.00
98	*John Ennis*	5.00
99	*So Taguchi*	8.00
100	*Michael Crudale*	5.00
101	*Francis Beltran*	5.00
102	*Jose Valverde*	8.00
103	*Doug Devore*	5.00
104	*Jeremy Ward*	5.00
105	*P.J. Bevis*	5.00
106	*Steve Kent*	5.00
107	*Brandon Backe*	5.00
108	*Jorge Nunez*	5.00
109	*Kazuhisa Ishii*	10.00
110	*Ron Calloway*	5.00
111	Valentino Pasucci	5.00
112	*J.J. Putz*	5.00
113	Matt Thornton	5.00
114	*Allan Simpson*	5.00
115	*Jaime Cerda*	5.00
116	*Mark Corey*	5.00
117	*Tyler Yates*	8.00
118	*Steve Bechler*	5.00
119	*Ben Howard*	5.00
120	*Clifford Bartosh*	5.00
121	*Todd Donovan*	5.00
122	*Eric Junge*	5.00
123	*Adrian Burnside*	5.00
124	*Andy Pratt*	5.00
125	*Josh Hancock*	5.00
126	*Rene Reyes*	5.00
127	*Cam Esslinger*	5.00
128	*Colin Young*	5.00
129	*Kevin Frederick*	5.00
130	*Kyle Kane*	5.00
131	*Mitch Wylie*	5.00
132	Danny Wright	5.00

Batting Champs

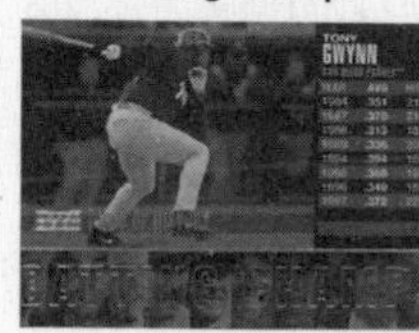

		NM/M
Complete Set (10):		18.00
Common Player:		1.50
Inserted 1:30		
B1	Tony Gwynn	2.00
B2	Frank Thomas	2.00
B3	Billy Williams	1.50
B4	Edgar Martinez	1.50
B5	Bernie Williams	1.50
B6	Mickey Mantle	6.00
B7	Larry Walker	1.50
B8	Gary Sheffield	1.50
B9	Wade Boggs	1.50
B10	Alex Rodriguez	4.00

Batting Champ Jerseys

		NM/M
Common Player:		8.00
Inserted 1:96		
WB	Wade Boggs	10.00
AG	Andres Galarraga	5.00
TG	Tony Gwynn	15.00
MM	Mickey Mantle/50	200.00
EM	Edgar Martinez	10.00
JO	John Olerud	8.00
PO	Paul O'Neil	10.00
TR	Tim Raines	8.00
AR	Alex Rodriguez	15.00
GS	Gary Sheffield/SP	8.00
FT	Frank Thomas	10.00
LW	Larry Walker/SP	8.00
BeW	Bernie Williams	10.00

Champ Jerseys Auto.

SBC-TG Tony Gwynn Auto/24
SBC-JO John Olerud Auto/24
SBC-PO Paul O'Neill Auto/24
SBC-AR Alex Rodriguez Auto/24
SBC-FT Frank Thomas Auto/24

ERA Leaders

		NM/M
Complete Set (10):		18.00
Common Player:		1.00
Inserted 1:30		
E1	Greg Maddux	3.00
E2	Pedro J. Martinez	2.00
E3	Freddy Garcia	1.00
E4	Randy Johnson	2.00
E5	Tom Seaver	2.00
E6	Early Wynn	1.00
E7	Dwight Gooden	1.00
E8	Kevin Brown	1.00
E9	Roger Clemens	3.00
E10	Nolan Ryan	6.00

ERA Leaders Jerseys

		NM/M
Common Player:		8.00
Inserted 1:96		
KB	Kevin Brown	8.00
RC	Roger Clemens	15.00
FG	Freddy Garcia	8.00
DG	Dwight Gooden	8.00
CH	"Catfish" Hunter/SP	15.00
RJ	Randy Johnson	15.00
SK	Sandy Koufax/SP	100.00
GM	Greg Maddux	15.00
PM	Pedro Martinez	15.00
PN	Phil Niekro	8.00
NR	Nolan Ryan/SP	50.00
TS	Tom Seaver	15.00

ERA Leaders Jerseys Autographs

		NM/M
production 24 sets		
RC	Roger Clemens	200.00
FG	Freddy Garcia	
SK	Sandy Koufax	750.00

Hitting for the Cycle

		NM/M
Complete Set (20):		35.00
Common Player:		1.00
Inserted 1:15		
H1	Alex Rodriguez	4.00
H2	Andre Dawson	1.00
H3	Cal Ripken Jr.	6.00
H4	Carlton Fisk	1.50
H5	Dante Bichette	1.00
H6	Dave Winfield	1.50
H7	Eric Chavez	1.00
H8	Robin Yount	2.00
H9	Jason Kendall	1.00
H10	Jay Buhner	1.00
H11	Jeff Kent	1.00
H12	Joe DiMaggio	6.00
H13	John Olerud	1.00
H14	Kirby Puckett	3.00
H15	Luis Gonzalez	1.50
H16	Mark Grace	1.50
H17	Mickey Mantle	6.00
H18	Miguel Tejada	1.00
H19	Rondell White	1.00
H20	Todd Helton	2.00

Hitting for the Cycle Bats

		NM/M
Inserted 1:576		
DB	Dante Bichette	10.00
JB	Jay Buhner	10.00
EC	Eric Chavez	10.00
AD	Andre Dawson	10.00
CF	Carlton Fisk	25.00
LG	Luis Gonzalez	10.00
MM	Mickey Mantle/50	200.00
CR	Cal Ripken Jr/SP	75.00
AR	Alex Rodriguez	25.00
DW	Dave Winfield	15.00

Hitting for the Cycle Bats Autograph

No Pricing
Production 10 sets
SHC-LG Luis Gonzalez
SHC-CR Cal Ripken Jr.
SHC-AR Alex Rodriguez

MVP Club Jerseys

		NM/M
Common Player:		8.00
Inserted 1:96		
JB	Jeff Bagwell	10.00
RC	Roger Clemens	15.00
SG	Steve Garvey	8.00
JGi	Jason Giambi	10.00
KGi	Kirk Gibson	10.00
JGo	Juan Gonzalez	10.00
KGr	Ken Griffey Jr.	15.00
RJ	Reggie Jackson	15.00
CJ	Chipper Jones	15.00
JK	Jeff Kent	8.00
BL	Barry Larkin/SP	25.00
MM	Mickey Mantle/50	200.00
RM	Roger Maris/50	100.00
CR	Cal Ripken Jr.	35.00
IR	Ivan Rodriguez	10.00
SS	Sammy Sosa	15.00
FT	Frank Thomas	10.00
RY	Robin Yount/SP	25.00

MVP Club Jerseys Auto.

No Pricing
Production 10 sets
SM-KG Ken Griffey Jr.
SM-CR Cal Ripken Jr.
SM-SS Sammy Sosa

The 500 Home Run Club

		NM/M
Complete Set (9):		25.00
Common Player:		1.50
Inserted 1:9		
HR1	Harmon Killebrew	3.00
HR2	Jimmie Foxx	3.00
HR3	Reggie Jackson	3.00
HR4	Mickey Mantle	8.00
HR5	Ernie Banks	3.00
HR6	Eddie Mathews	3.00
HR7	Mark McGwire	6.00
HR8	Willie McCovey	1.50
HR9	Mel Ott	3.00

500 HR Club Jerseys

		NM/M
Inserted 1:336		
HA	Hank Aaron	40.00
EB	Ernie Banks/SP	40.00
JF	Jimmie Foxx	40.00
RJ	Reggie Jackson	25.00
MM	Mickey Mantle/50	200.00
EM	Eddie Mathews	30.00
WM	Willie McCovey	20.00
MO	Mel Ott	40.00

300 Game Winners

		NM/M
Complete Set (6):		12.00
Common Player:		1.00
Inserted 1:50		
GW1	Nolan Ryan	6.00
GW2	Tom Seaver	3.00
GW3	Cy Young	3.00
GW4	Gaylord Perry	1.00
GW5	Early Wynn	1.00
GW6	Phil Niekro	1.00

300 Game Winners Jerseys

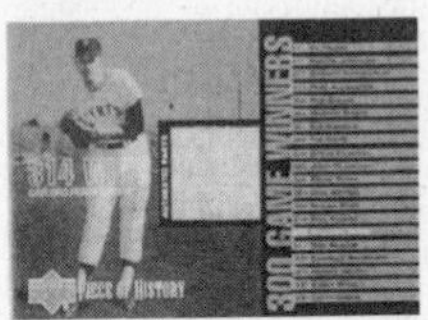

		NM/M
Common Player:		15.00
Inserted 1:576		
PN	Phil Niekro	10.00
GP	Gaylord Perry	10.00
NR	Nolan Ryan/SP	50.00
TS	Tom Seaver/SP	20.00

Tape Measure Heroes

		NM/M
Complete Set (30):		50.00
Common Player:		1.00
Inserted 1:10		
TM1	Joe Carter	1.00
TM2	Cal Ripken Jr.	6.00
TM3	Mike Piazza	4.00
TM4	Shawn Green	1.25
TM5	Mark McGwire	5.00
TM6	Reggie Jackson	1.50
TM7	Mickey Mantle	6.00
TM8	Manny Ramirez	2.00
TM9	Mo Vaughn	1.00
TM10	Jeff Bagwell	2.00
TM11	Sammy Sosa	3.00
TM12	Tony Gwynn	2.00
TM13	Bill Mazeroski	1.00
TM14	Jose Canseco	1.50
TM15	Brian Giles	1.00
TM16	Kirk Gibson	1.00
TM17	Kirby Puckett	3.00
TM18	Wade Boggs	1.50
TM19	Albert Pujols	3.00
TM20	David Justice	1.00
TM21	Steve Garvey	1.00
TM22	Luis Gonzalez	1.50
TM23	Derek Jeter	6.00
TM24	Robin Yount	2.00
TM25	Barry Bonds	3.00
TM26	Alex Rodriguez	4.00
TM27	Willie Stargell	1.50
TM28	Carlton Fisk	1.50
TM29	Carlos Delgado	1.50
TM30	Ken Griffey Jr.	5.00

The MVP Club

		NM/M
Complete Set (14):		30.00
Common Player:		1.00
Inserted 1:22		
M1	Jason Giambi	2.00
M2	Sammy Sosa	3.00
M3	Cal Ripken Jr.	6.00
M4	Robin Yount	2.00
M5	Ken Griffey Jr.	5.00
M6	Kirk Gibson	1.00
M7	Mickey Mantle	6.00
M8	Barry Bonds	3.00
M9	Frank Thomas	2.00
M10	Reggie Jackson	2.00
M11	Jeff Bagwell	2.00
M12	Roger Clemens	3.00
M13	Steve Garvey	1.00
M14	Chipper Jones	3.00

500 Hom Run Club Jerseys Auto.

No Pricing
Production 10 sets
SHR-EB Ernie Banks
SHR-RJ Reggie Jackson

Tape Measure Heroes Jerseys

		NM/M
Common Player:		5.00
Inserted 1:96		
JB	Jeff Bagwell	12.00
WB	Wade Boggs	15.00
JCa	Jose Canseco	10.00
JoC	Joe Carter	5.00
CD	Carlos Delgado	8.00
CF	Carlton Fisk	10.00
SGa	Steve Garvey	5.00
KGi	Kirk Gibson	8.00
BG	Brian Giles	5.00
SGr	Shawn Green	8.00
KGr	Ken Griffey Jr/90	40.00
TG	Tony Gwynn/SP	
RJ	Reggie Jackson/23	
MMa	Mickey Mantle/50	200.00
RM	Roger Maris/50	100.00
BM	Bill Mazeroski	10.00
MP	Mike Piazza	15.00
MR	Manny Ramirez	10.00
CR	Cal Ripken Jr.	30.00
AR	Alex Rodriguez	15.00
SS	Sammy Sosa	15.00
WS	Willie Stargell	15.00
RY	Robin Yount/SP	25.00

2002 UPPER DECK PROSPECT PREMIERES

		NM/M
Complete Set (109):		
Common Player (1-60):		.40
Common (61-85):		5.00

Inserted 1:18		
Common (86-97):		10.00
Inserted 1:18		
Pack (4):		5.00
Box (18):		80.00
1	*Josh Rupe*	.40
2	*Blair Johnson*	.40
3	*Jason Pridie*	.75
4	*Tim Gilhooly*	.40
5	*Kennard Jones*	.40
6	*Darrell Rasner*	.40
7	*Adam Donachie*	.75
8	*Josh Murray*	.40
9	*Brian Dopirak*	1.00
10	*Jason Cooper*	.50
11	*Zach Hammes*	.40
12	*Jon Lester*	2.00
13	*Kevin Jepsen*	.40
14	*Curtis Granderson*	.50
15	*David Bush*	.75
16	*Joel Guzman*	.50
17a	*Matt Pender* (black, photo is Curtis Granderson)	.40
17b	Matt Pender (white, correct photo)	2.00
18	*Derick Grigsby*	.40
19	*Jeremy Reed*	3.00
20	*Jonathan Broxton*	.40
21	*Jesse Crain*	.40
22	*Justin Jones*	1.00
23	*Brian Slocum*	.50
24	*Brian McCann*	.75
25	*Francisco Liriano*	2.00
26	*Fred Lewis*	.50
27	*Steve Stanley*	.40
28	*Chris Snyder*	.40
29	*Daniel Cevette*	.40
30	*Kiel Fisher*	.40
31	*Brandon Wheeder*	.40
32	*Pat Osborn*	.40
33	*Taber Lee*	.40
34	*Dan Ortmeyer*	.75
35	*Josh Johnson*	.40
36	*Val Majewski*	.75
37	*Larry Broadway*	.50
38	*Joey Gomes*	.50
39	*Eric Thomas*	.40
40	*James Loney*	2.00
41	*Charlie Morton*	.40
42	Mark McLemore	.40
43	*Matt Craig*	.40
44	*Ryan Rodriguez*	.40
45	*Rich Hill*	.40
46	*Bob Malek*	.40
47	*Justin Maureau*	.40
48	*Randy Braun*	.40
49	*Brian Grant*	.50
50	*Tyler Davidson*	.50
51	*Travis Hanson*	.50
52	*Kyle Boyer*	.40
53	*James Holcomb*	.40
54	*Ryan Williams*	.40
55	*Ben Crockett*	.40
56	*Adam Greenberg*	.75
57	*John Baker*	.40
58	*Matt Carson*	.40
59	*Jonathan George*	.40
60	*David Jensen*	.40
61	*Nick Swisher*	15.00
62	*Brent Cleven*	8.00
63	*Royce Ring*	8.00
64	*Mike Nixon*	5.00
65	*Ricky Barrett*	5.00
66	*Russ Adams*	8.00
67	*Joe Mauer*	25.00
68	*Jeff Francoeur*	50.00
69	*Joseph Blanton*	10.00
70	*Micah Schilling*	8.00
71	*John McCurdy*	5.00
72	*Sergio Santos*	8.00
73	*Josh Womack*	5.00
74	*Jared Doyle*	5.00
75	*Ben Fritz*	5.00
76	Greg Miller	10.00
77	*Luke Hagerty*	8.00
78	*Matt Whitney*	10.00
79	*Dan Meyer*	5.00
80	*Bill Murphy*	5.00
81	*Zach Segovia*	8.00
82	*Steve Obenchain*	8.00
83	*Matt Clanton*	8.00
84	*Mark Teahen*	10.00
85	*Kyle Pawelczyk*	8.00
86	*Khalil Greene/auto*	50.00
87	*Joe Saunders/auto*	10.00
88	*Jeremy Hermida/auto*	75.00
89	*Drew Meyer/auto*	10.00
90	*Jeff Francis/auto*	20.00
91	*Scott Moore/auto*	10.00
92	*Prince Fielder/auto*	120.00
93	*Zack Greinke/auto*	25.00
94	*Chris Gruler/auto*	10.00
95	*Scott Kazmir/auto*	60.00
96	*B.J. Upton/auto*	50.00
97	*Clint Everts/auto*	15.00
98	Cal Ripken Jr.	1.00
99	Cal Ripken Jr.	1.00
100	Mark McGwire	1.00
101	Mark McGwire	1.00
102	Mark McGwire	1.00
103	Mark McGwire	1.00
104	Mark McGwire	1.00
105	Joe DiMaggio	1.00
106	Joe DiMaggio	1.00
107	Joe DiMaggio	1.00
108	Joe DiMaggio	1.00
109	Joe DiMaggio	1.00

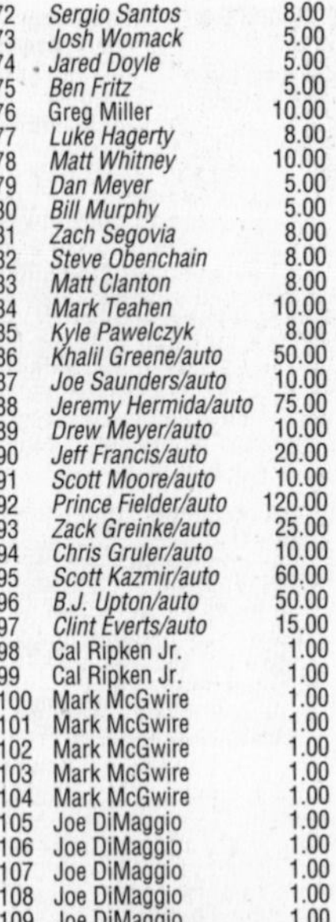

Heroes of Baseball

	NM/M
Complete Ripken set (10):	15.00
Common Ripken:	2.00
Complete Morgan set (10):	4.00
Common Morgan:	.50
Complete Stargell set (10):	5.00
Common Stargell:	.50
Complete Seaver set (10):	10.00
Common Seaver:	1.25
Complete Mantle set (10):	15.00
Common Mantle:	2.00
Complete DiMaggio set (10):	12.00
Common DiMaggio:	1.50
Complete Gwynn set (10):	10.00
Common Gwynn:	1.25
Complete McGwire set (10):	12.00
Common McGwire:	1.50
Complete Ozzie Smith (10):	8.00
Common Ozzie:	1.00
Sets include Headers	
Inserted 1:1	

Future Gems Quads

		NM/M
Common Card:		4.00
Inserted 1:box		
1	David Bush, Matt Craig, Blair Johnson, Brian McCann	4.00
2	Jason Cooper, Jonathan George, Larry Broadway, Joel Guzman	4.00
3	Matt Craig, Josh Murray, Brian McCann, Jason Pridie	4.00
4	Jesse Crain, Brian Grant, Curtis Granderson, Joey Gomes	4.00

5 Tyler Davidson, Val Majewski, Kennard Jones, Daniel Cevette 4.00
6 Joe DiMaggio, Jon Lester, Mac, Mark McLemore 4.00
7 Jonathan George, Jeremy Reed, Adam Donachie, Matt Carson 4.00
8 Jonathan George, Eric Thomas, Joel Guzman, Kiel Fisher 4.00
9 Tim Gilhooly, Brandon Wheeder, Brian Slocum, Brian Dopirak 4.00
10 Brian Grant, Rich Hill, Joey Gomes, Joe DiMaggio 4.00
11 Derick Grigsby, Bob Malek, James Loney, Fred Lewis 4.00
12 Zach Hammes, James Holcomb, Cal Ripken Jr., Kennard Jones 4.00
13 Rich Hill, Mark McGwire, Brian Grant, Matt Carson 4.00
14 James Holcomb, David Jensen, Kennard Jones, Ryan Williams 4.00
15 David Jensen, Francisco Liriano, Ryan Williams, Travis Hanson 4.00
16 Blair Johnson, Jesse Crain, Adam Greenberg, Curtis Granderson 4.00
17 Jon Lester, Jonathan George, Adam Donachie, Mark McLemore 4.00
18 Francisco Liriano, Mark McGwire, Travis Hanson, Taber Lee 4.00
19 Val Majewski, Charlie Morton, Daniel Cevette, Joey Gomes 4.00
20 Bob Malek, Zach Hammes, Fred Lewis, Cal Ripken Jr. 4.00
21 Justin Maureau, Joe DiMaggio, Chris Snyder, Mark McGwire 4.00
22 Mark McGwire, Bob Malek, Joe DiMaggio, Kyle Boyer 4.00
23 Charlie Morton, David Bush, Joey Gomes, Blair Johnson 4.00
24 Josh Murray, Mark McGwire, Jason Pridie, Joe DiMaggio 4.00
25 Matt Pender, Mark McGwire, Mark McLemore, Ryan Rodriguez 4.00
26 Jason Pridie, Josh Murray, Matt Craig, Brian McCann 4.00
27 Jeremy Reed, Blair Johnson, Matt Carson, Adam Greenberg 4.00
28 Cal Ripken Jr., Jason Cooper, Matt Carson, Larry Broadway 4.00
29 Ryan Rodriguez, Eric Thomas, Pat Osborn, Randy Braun 4.00
30 Josh Rupe, Tyler Davidson, John Baker, Kennard Jones 4.00
31 Eric Thomas, Derick Grigsby, Randy Braun, James Loney 4.00
32 Eric Thomas, Matt Pender, Kiel Fisher, Mark McLemore 4.00
33 Brandon Wheeder, Rich Hill, Brian Dopirak, Brian Grant 4.00

Heroes of Baseball Quads

NM/M

Common Quad: 10.00
Production 85 sets
1 Joe DiMaggio, Tony Gwynn 15.00
2 Joe DiMaggio, Tony Gwynn, Cal Ripken Jr. 20.00
3 Joe DiMaggio, Mickey Mantle, Willie Stargell 20.00
4 Tony Gwynn, Ozzie Smith, Willie Stargell 10.00
5 Tony Gwynn, Willie Stargell, Joe DiMaggio, Joe Morgan 15.00
6 Tony Gwynn, Willie Stargell, Cal Ripken Jr., Ozzie Smith 15.00
7 Mickey Mantle, Mark McGwire, Joe Morgan, Tom Seaver 20.00
8 Mickey Mantle, Tom Seaver 20.00
9 Mark McGwire, Joe Morgan 20.00
10 Mark McGwire, Cal Ripken Jr., Tony Gwynn, Joe DiMaggio 25.00
11 Mark McGwire, Tom Seaver, Joe Morgan, Ozzie Smith 15.00
12 Joe Morgan, Tony Gwynn 10.00
13 Joe Morgan, Joe DiMaggio, Mickey Mantle, Cal Ripken Jr. 25.00
14 Joe Morgan, Joe DiMaggio, Willie Stargell, Tony Gwynn 15.00
15 Ozzie Smith, Joe DiMaggio, Ozzie Smith, Willie Stargell 15.00
16 Ozzie Smith, Mark McGwire, Willie Stargell, Tony Gwynn 15.00
17 Ozzie Smith, Tom Seaver, Mark McGwire 15.00
18 Cal Ripken Jr., Mickey Mantle, Joe DiMaggio, Joe Morgan 20.00
19 Cal Ripken Jr., Mark McGwire, Cal Ripken Jr. 20.00
20 Tom Seaver, Joe DiMaggio, Tom Seaver, Joe DiMaggio 15.00
21 Tom Seaver, Joe Morgan, Ozzie Smith, Willie Stargell 10.00
22 Tom Seaver, Cal Ripken Jr., Mark McGwire, Mickey Mantle 20.00
23 Willie Stargell, Ozzie Smith 10.00
24 Willie Stargell, Ozzie Smith, Tom Seaver, Joe Morgan 10.00

2002 UPPER DECK ROOKIE DEBUT

NM/M

Common Player: .10
Pack (5): 1.50
Box (24): 30.00
Honor Roll
Common Honor Roll Rk (131-190): .25
Golds (131-190): 5-10X
Production 50
101 Curt Schilling .40
102 Geronimo Gil .10

103 Cliff Floyd .10
104 Derek Lowe .10
105 Hee Seop Choi .10
106 Mark Prior .75
107 Joe Borchard .10
108 Austin Kearns .40
109 Adam Dunn .50
110 Brandon Phillips .10
111 Carlos Pena .10
112 Andy Van Hekken .10
113 Juan Encarnacion .10
114 Lance Berkman .25
115 Torii Hunter .25
116 Bartolo Colon .10
117 Raul Mondesi .20
118 Alfonso Soriano .75
119 Miguel Tejada .40
120 Ray Durham .10
121 Eric Chavez .20
122 Brett Myers .10
123 Marlon Byrd .10
124 Sean Burroughs .10
125 Kenny Lofton .10
126 Scott Rolen .50
127 Carl Crawford .10
128 Josh Phelps .10
129 Eric Hinske .10
130 Orlando Hudson .10
131 Barry Wesson .40
132 *Jose Valverde* .25
133 *Kevin Gryboski* .25
134 *Trey Hodges* .25
135 *Howie Clark* .25
136 *Josh Hancock* .25
137 *Freddy Sanchez* .25
138 *Francis Beltran* .10
139 Mike Mahoney .10
140 Brian Tallet .10
141 *Jason Davis* .50
142 *Carl Sadler* .25
143 *Jason Beverlin* .25
144 *Josh Bard* .25
145 *Aaron Cook* .25
146 *Eric Eckenstahler* .25
147 *Tim Kalita* .25
148 *Franklyn German* .25
149 *Hansel Izquierdo* .25
150 *Brandon Puffer* .25
151 *Rodrigo Rosario* .25
152 Kirk Saarloos .10
153 *Jeriome Robertson* .25
154 *Jeremy Hill* .25
155 *Wes Obermueller* .25
156 *Aaron Guiel* .25
157 *Kazuhisa Ishii* 1.00
158 David Ross .10
159 *Jayson Durocher* .25
160 *Luis Martinez* .25
161 *Shane Nance* .25
162 *Eric Good* .25
163 *Jamey Carroll* .25
164 *Jaime Cerda* .25
165 *Satoru Komiyama* .25
166 *Adam Walker* .25
167 *Nate Field* .25
168 *Cody McKay* .25
169 *Jose Flores* .25
170 *Eric Junge* .25
171 *Jorge Padilla* .25
172 *Oliver Perez* 1.00
173 *Julius Matos* .25
174 *Wilbert Nieves* .25
175 *Clay Condrey* .25
176 *Mike Crudale* .25
177 *Jason Simontacchi* .50
178 *So Taguchi* .50
179 Jose Rodriguez .10
180 *Jorge Sosa* .25
181 *Felix Escalona* .25
182 *Lance Carter* .25
183 Travis Hughes .10
184 *Reynaldo Garcia* .25
185 Mike Smith .10
186 *Corey Thurman* .25
187 *Ken Huckaby* .25
188 *Reed Johnson* .50
189 *Kevin Cash* .25
190 *Scott Wiggins* .25
Ovation
Common SP (151-180): 3.00
Production 2,002
Golds (151-180): 2-4X
Production 50
121 Curt Schilling .50
122 Cliff Floyd .15
123 Derek Lowe .15
124 Hee Seop Choi .25
125 Mark Prior 1.00
126 Joe Borchard .15
127 Austin Kearns .50
128 Adam Dunn .75
129 Jay Payton .15
130 Carlos Pena .15
131 Andy Van Hekken .15
132 Andres Torres .15
133 Ben Diggins .15
134 Torii Hunter .40
135 Bartolo Colon .25
136 Raul Mondesi .25
137 Alfonso Soriano 1.00
138 Miguel Tejada .75
139 Ray Durham .15
140 Eric Chavez .40
141 Marlon Byrd .15
142 Brett Myers .15
143 Sean Burroughs .15
144 Kenny Lofton .15
145 Scott Rolen .75
146 Carl Crawford .15
147 Jayson Werth .15
148 Josh Phelps .15
149 Eric Hinske .15
150 Orlando Hudson .15
151 *Jose Valverde* 5.00
152 *Trey Hodges* 3.00
153 Joey Dawley 3.00
154 *Travis Driskill* 3.00
155 Howie Clark 3.00
156 *Jorge De La Rosa* 3.00
157 Freddy Sanchez 3.00
158 *Earl Snyder* 5.00
159 *Cliff Lee* 8.00
160 *Josh Bard* 3.00
161 *Aaron Cook* 3.00
162 *Franklyn German* 3.00
163 *Brandon Puffer* 3.00
164 Kirk Saarloos 3.00
165 *Jeriome Robertson* 3.00
166 *Miguel Asencio* 3.00
167 Shawn Sedlacek 3.00
168 *Jayson Durocher* 3.00
169 *Shane Nance* 3.00
170 *Jamey Carroll* 8.00
171 *Oliver Perez* 10.00
172 Wilbert Nieves 3.00
173 *Clay Condrey* 3.00
174 *Chris Snelling* 5.00
175 *Mike Crudale* 3.00
176 *Jason Simontacchi* 3.00
177 *Felix Escalona* 3.00
178 *Lance Carter* 3.00
179 *Scott Wiggins* 3.00
180 *Kevin Cash* 3.00
Victory
Common Rk (606-660): .20
551 John Lackey .25
552 Francisco Rodriguez .50
553 Cliff Floyd .10
554 Derek Lowe .10
555 Mark Bellhorn .10
556 Matt Clement .10
557 Hee Seop Choi .25
558 Joe Borchard .10
559 Ryan Dempster .10
560 Russell Branyan .10
561 Brandon Larson .10
562 Coco Crisp .10
563 Karim Garcia .10
564 Brandon Phillips .10
565 Jay Payton .10
566 Gabe Kapler .10
567 Carlos Pena .10
568 George Lombard .10
569 Andy Van Hekken .10
570 Andres Torres .10
571 Justin Wayne .10
572 Juan Encarnacion .10
573 Abraham Nunez .10

574 Peter Munro .10
575 Jason Lane .10
576 Dave Roberts .10
577 Eric Gagne .10
578 Alex Sanchez .10
579 *Jim Rushford* .10
580 Ben Diggins .10
581 Eddie Guardado .10
582 Bartolo Colon .20
583 Endy Chavez .10
584 Raul Mondesi .20
585 Jeff Weaver .10
586 Marcus Thames .10
587 Ted Lilly .10
588 Ray Durham .10
589 Jeremy Giambi .10
590 Vicente Padilla .10
591 Brett Myers .10
592 Josh Fogg .10
593 Tony Alvarez .10
594 Jake Peavy .10
595 Dennis Tankersley .10
596 Sean Burroughs .10
597 Kenny Lofton .10
598 Scott Rolen .50
599 Chuck Finley .10
600 Carl Crawford .10
601 Kevin Mench .10
602 Juan Gonzalez .50
603 Jayson Werth .10
604 Eric Hinske .10
605 Josh Phelps .10
606 *Jose Valverde* .20
607 *John Ennis* .20
608 *Trey Hodges* .20
609 *Kevin Gryboski* .20
610 *Travis Driskill* .20
611 *Howie Clark* .20
612 *Freddy Sanchez* .20
613 *Josh Hancock* .20
614 *Jorge De La Rosa* .20
615 Mike Mahoney .10
616 *Jason Davis* .20
617 *Josh Bard* .20
618 *Jason Beverlin* .20
619 *Carl Sadler* .20
620 *Earl Snyder* .50
621 *Aaron Cook* .20
622 *Eric Eckenstahler* .20
623 *Franklyn German* .20
624 Kirk Saarloos .50
625 *Rodrigo Rosario* .20
626 *Jeriome Robertson* .20
627 *Brandon Puffer* .20
628 *Miguel Asencio* .20
629 *Aaron Guiel* .30
630 *Ryan Bukvich* .20
631 *Jeremy Hill* .20
632 *Kazuhisa Ishii* .75
633 *Jayson Durocher* .20
634 *Shane Nance* .20
635 *Eric Good* .20
636 *Jamey Carroll* .50
637 *Jaime Cerda* .20
638 *Nate Field* .20
639 *Cody McKay* .20
640 *Jose Flores* .20
641 *Jorge Padilla* .20
642 *Anderson Machado* .20
643 *Eric Junge* .20
644 *Oliver Perez* .75
645 *Julius Matos* .20
646 *Ben Howard* .20
647 *Julio Mateo* .20
648 Matt Thornton .10
649 *Chris Snelling* .50
650 *Jason Simontacchi* .50
651 *So Taguchi* .40
652 *Mike Crudale* .20
653 Mike Coolbaugh .10
654 *Felix Escalona* .20
655 *Jorge Sosa* .20
656 *Lance Carter* .20
657 *Reynaldo Garcia* .20
658 *Kevin Cash* .40
659 *Ken Huckaby* .20
660 *Scott Wiggins* .20

Solid Contact

NM/M
Common Player: 4.00
Inserted 1:24
BA Bobby Abreu 4.00
EA Edgardo Alfonzo 4.00
RA Roberto Alomar 10.00
MA Moises Alou 6.00
JC Jose Cruz Jr. 6.00
CD Carlos Delgado/SP 8.00
JE Jim Edmonds 6.00
CE Carl Everett 4.00
JG Jason Giambi/50 15.00
BG Brian Giles 6.00
KG Ken Griffey Jr. 15.00
TH Todd Helton 8.00
JK Jason Kendall 4.00
BL Barry Larkin 10.00
EM Edgar Martinez 8.00
FM Fred McGriff 8.00
DM Doug Mientkiewicz 6.00
JO John Olerud 6.00
MO Magglio Ordonez 6.00
JP Jorge Posada 10.00
AR Alex Rodriguez 15.00
IR Ivan Rodriguez 6.00
GS Gary Sheffield 6.00
SS Sammy Sosa 15.00
TA Fernando Tatis 4.00
FT Frank Thomas 8.00
JT Jim Thome 12.00
OV Omar Vizquel 6.00
BW Bernie Williams 8.00
MW Matt Williams 4.00

2002 UPPER DECK ROOKIE UPDATE

NM/M
Common Player: .25
Pack (5): 3.00
Box (15): 35.00
SP Authentic
Common SP (201-230): 5.00
Production 1,999
171 Erubiel Durazo .25
172 Junior Spivey .25
173 Geronimo Gil .25
174 Cliff Floyd .25
175 Brandon Larsen .25
176 Aaron Boone .25
177 Shawn Estes .25
178 Austin Kearns .75
179 Joe Borchard .25
180 Russell Branyan .25
181 Jay Payton .25
182 Andres Torres .25
183 Andy Van Hekken .25
184 Alex Sanchez .25
185 Endy Chavez .25
186 Bartolo Colon .25
187 Raul Mondesi .40
188 Robin Ventura .25
189 Mike Mussina .75
190 Jorge Posada .75
191 Ted Lilly .25
192 Ray Durham .25
193 Brett Myers .25
194 Marlon Byrd .25
195 Vicente Padilla .25
196 Josh Fogg .25
197 Kenny Lofton .25
198 Scott Rolen 1.00
199 Jason Lane .25
200 Josh Phelps .25
201 *Travis Driskill* 5.00
202 *Howie Clark* 5.00
203 Mike Mahoney 5.00
204 Brian Tallet 5.00
205 Kirk Saarloos 5.00
206 Barry Wesson 5.00
207 *Aaron Guiel* 5.00
208 Shawn Sedlacek 5.00
209 Jose Diaz 5.00
210 Jorge Nunez 5.00
211 Danny Mota 5.00
212 David Ross 5.00
213 *Jayson Durocher* 5.00
214 *Shane Nance* 5.00
215 *Wilbert Nieves* 5.00
216 *Freddy Sanchez* 5.00
217 Alex Pelaez 5.00
218 *Jamey Carroll* 5.00
219 J.J. Trujillo 5.00
220 Kevin Pickford 5.00
221 *Clay Condrey* 5.00
222 *Chris Snelling* 5.00
223 *Cliff Lee* 8.00
224 *Jeremy Hill* 5.00
225 Jose Rodriguez 5.00
226 *Lance Carter* 5.00
227 *Ken Huckaby* 5.00
228 *Scott Wiggins* 5.00
229 *Corey Thurman* 5.00
230 *Kevin Cash* 5.00
SPx
Common SPx Auto. (221-250): 10.00
Production 825
191 Tom Glavine .75
192 Cliff Floyd .25
193 Mark Prior 1.50
194 Corey Patterson .50
195 Paul Konerko .50
196 Adam Dunn 1.00
197 Joe Borchard .25
198 Carlos Pena .25
199 Juan Encarnacion .25
200 Luis Castillo .25
201 Torii Hunter .50
202 Hee Seop Choi .50
203 Bartolo Colon .40
204 Raul Mondesi .40
205 Jeff Weaver .25
206 Eric Munson .25
207 Alfonso Soriano 1.00
208 Ray Durham .25
209 Eric Chavez .50
210 Brett Myers .25
211 Jeremy Giambi .25
212 Vicente Padilla .25
213 Felipe Lopez .25
214 Sean Burroughs .25
215 Kenny Lofton .25
216 Scott Rolen 1.00
217 Carl Crawford .25
218 Juan Gonzalez .75
219 Orlando Hudson .25
220 Eric Hinske .25
221 *Adam Walker* 10.00
222 *Aaron Cook* 10.00
223 *Cam Esslinger* 10.00
224 Kirk Saarloos 10.00
225 Jose Diaz 10.00
226 David Ross 10.00
227 *Jayson Durocher* 10.00
228 Brian Mallette 10.00
229 *Aaron Guiel* 10.00
230 Jorge Nunez 10.00
231 *Satoru Komiyama* 20.00
232 *Tyler Yates* 15.00
233 *Peter Zamora* 10.00
234 *Mike Gonzalez* 10.00
235 *Oliver Perez* 40.00
236 *Julius Matos* 10.00
237 Andy Shibilo 10.00
238 *Jason Simontacchi* 10.00
239 Ron Chiavacci 10.00
240 Deivis Santos 10.00
241 *Travis Driskill* 10.00
242 *Jorge De La Rosa* 10.00
243 *Anastacio Martinez* 10.00
244 *Earl Snyder* 10.00
245 *Freddy Sanchez* 10.00
246 *Miguel Asencio* 10.00
247 Juan Brito 10.00
248 *Franklyn German* 10.00
249 *Chris Snelling* 10.00
250 *Ken Huckaby* 10.00
Diamond Connection
Common SP (601-630): 4.00
Production 1,999
571 Erubiel Durazo .25
572 Geronimo Gil .25
573 Shea Hillenbrand .50
574 Cliff Floyd .25
575 Corey Patterson .50
576 Joe Borchard .25
577 Austin Kearns .75
578 Ryan Dempster .25
579 Brandon Larsen .25
580 Luis Castillo .25
581 Juan Encarnacion .25
582 Chin-Feng Chen .25
583 Hideo Nomo .75
584 Bartolo Colon .40
585 Raul Mondesi .40
586 Eric Munson .25
587 Alfonso Soriano 1.00
588 Ted Lilly .25
589 Ray Durham .25
590 Brett Myers .25
591 Brandon Phillips .25
592 Kenny Lofton .25
593 Scott Rolen 1.00
594 Jim Edmonds .50
595 Carl Crawford .25
596 Hank Blalock .50
597 Kevin Mench .25
598 Josh Phelps .25
599 Orlando Hudson .25
600 Eric Hinske .25
601 Mike Mahoney 4.00
602 *Jason Davis* 8.00
603 *Trey Hodges* 4.00
604 *Josh Bard* 4.00
605 *Jeriome Robertson* 4.00
606 Jose Diaz 4.00
607 Jorge Nunez 4.00
608 Danny Mota 4.00
609 David Ross 4.00
610 *Jayson Durocher* 4.00
611 *Freddy Sanchez* 4.00
612 *Julius Matos* 4.00
613 *Wilbert Nieves* 4.00
614 Brian Kozlowski 4.00
615 *Jason Simontacchi* 4.00
616 Mike Coolbaugh 4.00
617 *Travis Driskill* 4.00
618 *Howie Clark* 4.00
619 *Earl Snyder* 6.00
620 *Carl Sadler* 4.00
621 *Jason Beverlin* 4.00
622 Terry Pearson 4.00
623 *Eric Eckenstahler* 4.00
624 Shawn Sedlacek 4.00
625 *Aaron Guiel* 5.00
626 *Ryan Bukvich* 4.00
627 *Julio Mateo* 4.00
628 *Chris Snelling* 6.00
629 *Lance Carter* 4.00
630 *Scott Wiggins* 4.00

Star Tributes

NM/M
Common Player: 5.00
Inserted 1:15
JB Josh Beckett 8.00
LB Lance Berkman 6.00
RC Roger Clemens 15.00
CD Carlos Delgado 5.00
JD Joe DiMaggio/SP 75.00
AD Adam Dunn 8.00
JG Jason Giambi 10.00
TG Tom Glavine 8.00
LG Luis Gonzalez/SP 8.00
SG Shawn Green 5.00
KG Ken Griffey Jr. 12.00
KI Kazuhisa Ishii 8.00
RJ Randy Johnson 10.00
CJ Chipper Jones 10.00
PM Pedro J. Martinez 8.00
MM Mark McGwire/SP 50.00
RP Rafael Palmeiro 8.00
MPi Mike Piazza 10.00
MPr Mark Prior 8.00
AR Alex Rodriguez 10.00
IR Ivan Rodriguez 8.00
KS Kazuhiro Sasaki 5.00
CS Curt Schilling 8.00
TS Tsuyoshi Shinjo 5.00
AS Alfonso Soriano 10.00
SS Sammy Sosa 12.00
IS Ichiro Suzuki/19
MS Mike Sweeney 5.00
FT Frank Thomas 8.00

Signed Star Tributes

NM/M
Production 50 sets

Copper & Silver No Pricing
Production 25
Gold No Pricing
Production 5
SS-MM Mark McGwire 350.00

USA Future Watch Swatches

NM/M
Common Player: 5.00
Inserted 1:15
Red: 1.5-2X
Production 50
Copper: No Pricing
Production 25
Gold: No Pricing
Production 5
AA Abe Alvarez 5.00
MA Michael Aubrey 10.00
KB Kyle Bakker 8.00
CC Chad Cordero 5.00
SC Shane Costa 5.00
SF Sam Fuld 8.00
AH Aaron Hill 8.00
PH Philip Humber 8.00
CJ Conor Jackson 5.00
GJ Grant Johnson 5.00
MJ Mark Jurich 5.00
WL Wes Littleton 8.00
EP Eric Patterson 5.00
DP Dustin Pedroia 5.00
LP Landon Powell 5.00
CQ Carlos Quentin 8.00
CS Clint Sammons 5.00
KS Kyle Sleeth 10.00
HS Huston Street 5.00
BS Brad Sullivan 8.00
RW Rickie Weeks 15.00
BZ Bob Zimmermann 5.00

2002 UPPER DECK SWEET SPOT

NM/M
Complete Set (175):
Common Player: .25
Common (91-130): 4.00
Production 1,300
Common Auto. (131-145): 15.00
Production 750 or 100
Common Game Faces
(146-175): 3.00
Inserted 1:24
Parallel (146-175): 1.5X-3X
Production 100
Pack (4): 8.00
Box (12): 90.00
1 Troy Glaus .50
2 Darin Erstad .50
3 Tim Hudson .50
4 Eric Chavez .50
5 Barry Zito .50
6 Miguel Tejada .50
7 Carlos Delgado .50
8 Eric Hinske .25
9 Ben Grieve .25
10 Jim Thome 1.00
11 C.C. Sabathia .25
12 Omar Vizquel .40
13 Ichiro Suzuki 2.00
14 Edgar Martinez .40
15 Bret Boone .40
16 Freddy Garcia .25
17 Tony Batista .25
18 Geronimo Gil .25
19 Alex Rodriguez 2.50
20 Rafael Palmeiro .75
21 Ivan Rodriguez .75
22 Hank Blalock .50
23 Juan Gonzalez .75
24 Nomar Garciaparra 2.00
25 Pedro J. Martinez 1.00
26 Manny Ramirez 1.00
27 Mike Sweeney .25
28 Carlos Beltran .50
29 Dmitri Young .25
30 Torii Hunter .50
31 Eric Milton .25
32 Corey Koskie .25
33 Frank Thomas .75
34 Mark Buehrle .25
35 Magglio Ordonez .50
36 Roger Clemens 2.00
37 Derek Jeter 3.00
38 Jason Giambi .75
39 Alfonso Soriano 1.00
40 Bernie Williams .50
41 Jeff Bagwell .75
42 Roy Oswalt .50
43 Lance Berkman .50
44 Greg Maddux 1.50
45 Chipper Jones 1.00
46 Gary Sheffield .50
47 Andruw Jones .75
48 Richie Sexson .50
49 Ben Sheets .50
50 Albert Pujols 2.00
51 Matt Morris .40
52 J.D. Drew .50
53 Sammy Sosa 2.00
54 Kerry Wood 1.00
55 Mark Prior 1.50
56 Moises Alou .50
57 Corey Patterson .50
58 Randy Johnson 1.00
59 Luis Gonzalez .40
60 Curt Schilling .75
61 Shawn Green .50
62 Kevin Brown .40
63 Paul LoDuca .25
64 Adrian Beltre .50
65 Vladimir Guerrero 1.00
66 Jose Vidro .25
67 Javier Vazquez .25
68 Barry Bonds 3.00
69 Jeff Kent .40
70 Rich Aurilia .25
71 Mike Lowell .40
72 Josh Beckett .50
73 Brad Penny .25
74 Roberto Alomar .50
75 Mike Piazza 1.50
76 Jeromy Burnitz .25
77 Mo Vaughn .25
78 Phil Nevin .25
79 Sean Burroughs .25
80 Jeremy Giambi .25
81 Bobby Abreu .50
82 Jimmy Rollins .25
83 Pat Burrell .50
84 Brian Giles .50
85 Aramis Ramirez .50
86 Ken Griffey Jr. 1.50
87 Adam Dunn .75
88 Austin Kearns .50
89 Todd Helton .75
90 Larry Walker .50
91 *Earl Snyder* 6.00
92 *Jorge Padilla* 4.00
93 *Felix Escalona* 4.00
94 *John Foster* 4.00
95 *Brandon Puffer* 4.00
96 *Steve Bechler* 4.00
97 *Hansel Izquierdo* 4.00
98 *Chris Baker* 4.00
99 *Jeremy Ward* 4.00
100 *Kevin Frederick* 4.00
101 *Josh Hancock* 4.00
102 *Allan Simpson* 4.00
103 *Mitch Wylie* 4.00
104 *Mark Corey* 4.00
105 *Victor Alvarez* 4.00
106 *Todd Donovan* 4.00
107 *Nelson Castro* 4.00
108 *Chris Booker* 4.00
109 *Corey Thurman* 4.00
110 Kirk Saarloos 4.00
111 *Michael Crudale* 4.00
112 *Jason Simontacchi* 4.00
113 *Ron Calloway* 4.00
114 *Brandon Backe* 4.00
115 *Tom Shearn* 4.00
116 *Oliver Perez* 8.00
117 *Kyle Kane* 4.00
118 *Francis Beltran* 4.00
119 *So Taguchi* 8.00
120 *Doug Devore* 4.00
121 *Juan Brito* 4.00
122 *Clifford Bartosh* 4.00
123 *Eric Junge* 4.00
124 *Joe Orloski* 4.00
125 *Scotty Layfield* 4.00
126 *Jorge Sosa* 4.00
127 *Satoru Komiyama* 4.00
128 *Edwin Almonte* 4.00
129 *Takahito Nomura* 4.00
130 *John Ennis* 4.00
131 *Kazuhisa Ishii/Auto/100* 90.00
132 *Ben Howard/Auto/100* 20.00
133 *Aaron Cook/Auto/750* 15.00
134 *Anderson Machado/Auto/750* 15.00
135 *Luis Ugueto/Auto/750* 15.00
136 *Tyler Yates/Auto/750* 20.00
137 *Rodrigo Rosario/Auto/750* 15.00
138 *Jaime Cerda/Auto/750* 15.00
139 *Luis Martinez/Auto/750* 15.00
140 *Rene Reyes/Auto/750* 15.00
141 *Eric Good/Auto/750* 15.00
142 Matt Thornton/Auto/100 25.00
143 *Steve Kent/Auto/750* 15.00
144 *Jose Valverde/Auto/750* 15.00
145 *Adrian Burnside/Auto/750* 15.00
146 Barry Bonds 15.00
147 Ken Griffey Jr. 10.00
148 Alex Rodriguez 12.00
149 Jason Giambi 4.00
150 Chipper Jones 5.00
151 Nomar Garciaparra 10.00
152 Mike Piazza 10.00
153 Sammy Sosa 10.00
154 Derek Jeter 15.00
155 Jeff Bagwell 4.00
156 Albert Pujols 10.00
157 Ichiro Suzuki 10.00
158 Randy Johnson 5.00
159 Frank Thomas 4.00
160 Greg Maddux 8.00
161 Jim Thome 5.00
162 Scott Rolen 6.00
163 Shawn Green 3.00
164 Vladimir Guerrero 6.00
165 Troy Glaus 3.00
166 Carlos Delgado 4.00
167 Luis Gonzalez 3.00
168 Roger Clemens 10.00
169 Todd Helton 4.00
170 Eric Chavez 3.00
171 Rafael Palmeiro 4.00
172 Pedro J. Martinez 5.00
173 Lance Berkman 3.00
174 Josh Beckett 4.00
175 Sean Burroughs 3.00

Bat Barrels

No Pricing
100 Total Produced

Legendary Signatures

NM/M
Common Autograph: 20.00
Inserted 1:72
LA Luis Aparicio/485 25.00
JD Joe DiMaggio/50
RF Rollie Fingers/866 20.00
SG Steve Garvey/871 20.00
KH Keith Hernandez/906 20.00
FJ Ferguson Jenkins/857 20.00
AK Al Kaline/835 40.00
SK Sandy Koufax/485 200.00
FL Fred Lynn/853 20.00
MM Mark McGwire/90 575.00
PM Paul Molitor/852 30.00
GP Gaylord Perry/921 25.00
BP Boog Powell/944 20.00
CR Cal Ripken Jr./194 175.00
BR Brooks Robinson 35.00
AT Alan Trammell/843 25.00

Mark Gwire Priority Signing Redem.

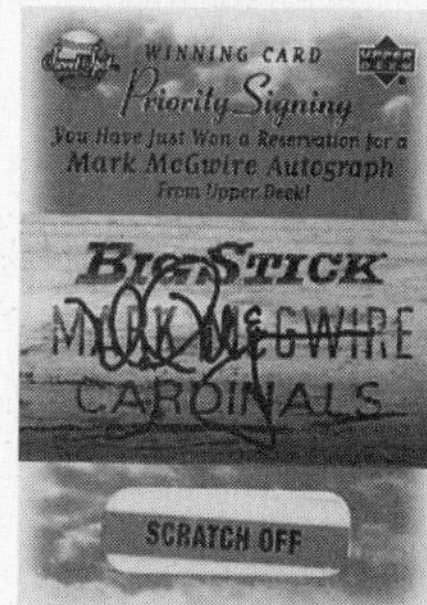

NM/M
100 Produced
MM Mark McGwire 500.00

Signatures

NM/M
Common Autograph: 25.00
Inserted 1:72
LB Lance Berkman/291 35.00
HB Hank Blalock/291 40.00
BB Barry Bonds/380 275.00
JB Jeromy Burnitz/291 20.00
SB Sean Burroughs/291 20.00
RC Roger Clemens/194 150.00
CD Carlos Delgado/291 25.00
AD Adam Dunn/291 40.00
FG Freddy Garcia/145 25.00
JG Jason Giambi/291 40.00
BG Brian Giles/291 25.00
TG Tom Glavine/291 40.00
LG Luis Gonzalez/291 20.00
KG Ken Griffey Jr./291 125.00
AJ Andruw Jones/291 25.00
RO Roy Oswalt/291 20.00
MPr Mark Prior/291 100.00
AR Alex Rodriguez/291 160.00
SR Scott Rolen/291 40.00
SS Sammy Sosa/145 200.00
MS Mike Sweeney/291 20.00
IS Ichiro Suzuki/145 400.00
FT Frank Thomas/291 60.00
JT Jim Thome/291 50.00
BZ Barry Zito/291 30.00

Sweet Swatches

NM/M
Common Player: 5.00
Inserted 1:12

JBa	Jeff Bagwell	8.00
JBe	Josh Beckett	6.00
SB	Sean Burroughs	5.00
EC	Eric Chavez	6.00
JE	Jim Edmonds	8.00
DE	Darin Erstad	5.00
JGi	Jason Giambi	8.00
BG	Brian Giles	5.00
JGo	Juan Gonzalez	6.00
LG	Luis Gonzalez	5.00
SG	Shawn Green	5.00
KG	Ken Griffey Jr.	15.00
KI	Kazuhisa Ishii	10.00
CJ	Chipper Jones	10.00
GM	Greg Maddux	12.00
PM	Pedro J. Martinez	10.00
MP	Mike Piazza	15.00
AR	Alex Rodriguez	15.00
IR	Ivan Rodriguez	8.00
SR	Scott Rolen	8.00
SS	Sammy Sosa	15.00
IS	Ichiro Suzuki	40.00
FT	Frank Thomas	8.00
OV	Omar Vizquel	5.00
BW	Bernie Williams	8.00

USA Jerseys

		NM/M
Common Player:		5.00
Inserted 1:12		
BA	Brent Abernathy	5.00
TB	Taggert Bozied	8.00
DB	Dewon Brazelton	5.00
AE	Adam Everett	5.00
DG	Danny Graves	5.00
JG	Jake Gautreau	5.00
JK	Josh Karp	5.00
AK	Adam Kennedy	8.00
JM	Joe Mauer	20.00
DM	Doug Mientkiewicz	6.00
EM	Eric Munson	5.00
XN	Xavier Nady	5.00
RO	Roy Oswalt	8.00
MP	Mark Prior	15.00
JR	Jon Rauch	5.00
MT	Mark Teixeira	8.00
JW	Justin Wayne	5.00

2002 UPPER DECK SWEET SPOT CLASSICS

		NM/M
Complete Set (90):		40.00
Common Player:		.40
Pack (4):		20.00
Box (12):		200.00
1	Mickey Mantle	4.00
2	Joe DiMaggio	3.00
3	Babe Ruth	3.00
4	Ty Cobb	1.50
5	Nolan Ryan	3.00
6	Sandy Koufax	2.00
7	Cy Young	1.00
8	Roberto Clemente	2.00
9	Lefty Grove	.50
10	Lou Gehrig	2.50
11	Walter Johnson	1.00
12	Honus Wagner	1.00
13	Christy Mathewson	.75
14	Jackie Robinson	1.50
15	Joe Morgan	.50
16	Reggie Jackson	.75
17	Eddie Collins	.40
18	Cal Ripken Jr.	3.00
19	Hank Greenberg	.40
20	Harmon Killebrew	.75
21	Johnny Bench	1.00
22	Ernie Banks	1.00
23	Willie McCovey	.40
24	Mel Ott	.40
25	Tom Seaver	1.00
26	Tony Gwynn	.75
27	Dave Winfield	.50
28	Willie Stargell	.40
29	Mark McGwire	2.00
30	Al Kaline	.75
31	Jimmie Foxx	.75
32	Satchel Paige	1.50
33	Eddie Murray	.40
34	Lou Boudreau	.40
35	"Shoeless" Joe Jackson	1.50
36	Luke Appling	.40
37	Ralph Kiner	.40
38	Robin Yount	.75
39	Paul Molitor	.75
40	Juan Marichal	.40
41	Brooks Robinson	.75
42	Wade Boggs	.50
43	Kirby Puckett	1.00
44	Yogi Berra	1.00
45	George Sisler	.40
46	Buck Leonard	.40
47	Billy Williams	.40
48	Duke Snider	.75
49	Don Drysdale	.60
50	Bill Mazeroski	.40
51	Tony Oliva	.40
52	Luis Aparicio	.40
53	Carlton Fisk	.40
54	Kirk Gibson	.40
55	Jim "Catfish" Hunter	.40
56	Joe Carter	.40
57	Gaylord Perry	.40
58	Don Mattingly	2.00
59	Eddie Mathews	1.25
60	Ferguson Jenkins	.40
61	Roy Campanella	1.00
62	Orlando Cepeda	.40
63	Tony Perez	.40
64	Dave Parker	.40
65	Richie Ashburn	.40
66	Andre Dawson	.40
67	Dwight Evans	.40
68	Rollie Fingers	.40
69	Dale Murphy	.40
70	Ron Santo	.40
71	Steve Garvey	.40
72	Monte Irvin	.40
73	Alan Trammell	.40
74	Ryne Sandberg	1.00
75	Gary Carter	.40
76	Fred Lynn	.40
77	Maury Wills	.40
78	Ozzie Smith	1.00
79	Bobby Bonds	.40
80	Mickey Cochrane	.60
81	Dizzy Dean	.60
82	Graig Nettles	.40
83	Keith Hernandez	.40
84	Boog Powell	.40
85	Jack Clark	.40
86	Dave Stewart	.40
87	Tommy Lasorda	.40
88	Dennis Eckersley	.40
89	Ken Griffey Sr.	.40
90	Bucky Dent	.40

Bat Barrels

VALUES UNDETERMINED DUE TO SCARCITY

Game Jersey

		NM/M
Common Player:		5.00
Inserted 1:8		
WB	Wade Boggs	12.00
GC	Gary Carter	10.00
JC	Joe Carter	5.00
JD	Joe DiMaggio/53	180.00
RF	Rollie Fingers	5.00
SG	Steve Garvey	5.00
TG	Tony Gwynn	15.00
RJ	Reggie Jackson	15.00
SK	Sandy Koufax/SP	125.00
BM	Bill Madlock	5.00
MM	Mickey Mantle/53	250.00
JMa	Juan Marichal	10.00
DM	Don Mattingly	25.00
PM	Paul Molitor	15.00
EM	Eddie Murray	10.00
GN	Graig Nettles	8.00
DP	Dave Parker	5.00
CR	Cal Ripken Jr.	25.00
NR	Nolan Ryan	40.00
RS	Ryne Sandberg	15.00
TS	Tom Seaver	15.00
OS	Ozzie Smith	15.00
DSn	Duke Snider/53	80.00
WS	Willie Stargell	10.00
DSt	Dave Stewart	5.00
BW	Billy Williams	8.00
RY	Robin Yount	15.00

Game Jersey Gold

No Pricing
Production 25 sets

Game-Used Bats

		NM/M
Common Player:		5.00
Inserted 1:8		
JB	Johnny Bench	15.00
YB	Yogi Berra	15.00
WB	Wade Boggs	12.00
BBo	Bob Boone	5.00
BBu	Bill Buckner	5.00
GC	Gary Carter	10.00
RC	Roberto Clemente	50.00
BD	Bucky Dent	8.00
JD	Joe DiMaggio/40	180.00
DE	Dwight Evans	8.00
SG	Steve Garvey	8.00
HG	Hank Greenberg/SP	50.00
KG	Ken Griffey Sr.	5.00
TG	Tony Gwynn	15.00
RJ	Reggie Jackson	10.00
FJ	Ferguson Jenkins	10.00
AK	Al Kaline	15.00
FL	Fred Lynn	5.00
BM	Bill Madlock	5.00
DM	Don Mattingly	25.00
PM	Paul Molitor	15.00
TM	Thurman Munson	35.00
GN	Graig Nettles	8.00
DP	Dave Parker	5.00
KP	Kirby Puckett	15.00
CR	Cal Ripken Jr.	25.00
BR	Brooks Robinson	15.00
NR	Nolan Ryan	40.00
BW	Billy Williams	8.00
DW	Dave Winfield	10.00

Game-Used Bats Gold

		NM/M
Common Player:		25.00
JB	Johnny Bench	100.00
YB	Yogi Berra	125.00
WB	Wade Boggs	100.00
BBo	Bob Boone	40.00
BBu	Bill Buckner	35.00
GC	Gary Carter	40.00
RC	Roberto Clemente	250.00
BD	Bucky Dent	25.00
JD	Joe DiMaggio	250.00
DE	Dwight Evans	25.00
SG	Steve Garvey	35.00
HG	Hank Greenberg	125.00
KG	Ken Griffey Sr.	25.00
TG	Tony Gwynn	150.00
RJ	Reggie Jackson	150.00
FJ	Ferguson Jenkins	45.00
AK	Al Kaline	75.00
FL	Fred Lynn	25.00
BM	Bill Madlock	25.00
DM	Don Mattingly	125.00
PM	Paul Molitor	40.00
TM	Thurman Munson	150.00
GN	Graig Nettles	25.00
DP	Dave Parker	25.00
KP	Kirby Puckett	125.00
CR	Cal Ripken Jr.	225.00
BR	Brooks Robinson	75.00
NR	Nolan Ryan	175.00
BW	Billy Williams	45.00
DW	Dave Winfield	45.00

Signatures

		NM/M
Common Autograph:		20.00
Inserted 1:24		
EB	Ernie Banks	60.00
JB	Johnny Bench	60.00
YB	Yogi Berra/100	150.00
AD	Andre Dawson/100	100.00
BD	Bucky Dent	20.00
DeE	Dennis Eckersley	40.00
RF	Rollie Fingers	25.00
CF	Carlton Fisk/100	125.00
SG	Steve Garvey	25.00
KG	Kirk Gibson/SP	50.00
KH	Keith Hernandez	30.00
RJ	Reggie Jackson/SP	100.00
FJ	Ferguson Jenkins	25.00
AK	Al Kaline	40.00
SK	Sandy Koufax/SP	250.00
TL	Tommy Lasorda	35.00
FL	Fred Lynn	25.00
DoM	Don Mattingly	100.00
BM	Bill Mazeroski	40.00
WM	Willie McCovey/SP	75.00
PM	Paul Molitor	40.00
JM	Joe Morgan	25.00
DaM	Dale Murphy	50.00
GP	Gaylord Perry	25.00
BP	Boog Powell	25.00
KP	Kirby Puckett	180.00
CR	Cal Ripken Jr.	180.00
BR	Brooks Robinson	50.00
NR	Nolan Ryan/74	300.00
TS	Tom Seaver	50.00
OS	Ozzie Smith/137	200.00
DaS	Dave Stewart	25.00
AT	Alan Trammell	30.00
DW	Dave Winfield/70	125.00

Signatures Gold

No Pricing
Production 25 sets

2002 UPPER DECK ULTIMATE COLLECTION

		NM/M
Complete Set (120):		
Common Player (1-60):		2.00
Production 799		
Common Player (61-110, 114-120):		10.00
Production 550		
Common (111-113):		25.00
Production 330		
Pack (4):		100.00
Box (4):		350.00
1	Troy Glaus	2.50
2	Luis Gonzalez	2.00
3	Curt Schilling	2.50
4	Randy Johnson	4.00
5	Andruw Jones	2.50
6	Greg Maddux	6.00
7	Chipper Jones	5.00
8	Gary Sheffield	2.00
9	Cal Ripken Jr.	12.00
10	Manny Ramirez	3.00
11	Pedro J. Martinez	4.00
12	Nomar Garciaparra	8.00
13	Sammy Sosa	6.00
14	Kerry Wood	4.00
15	Mark Prior	5.00
16	Magglio Ordonez	2.00
17	Frank Thomas	3.00
18	Adam Dunn	3.00
19	Ken Griffey Jr.	8.00
20	Jim Thome	4.00
21	Larry Walker	2.00
22	Todd Helton	3.00
23	Nolan Ryan	12.00
24	Jeff Bagwell	3.00
25	Roy Oswalt	2.00
26	Lance Berkman	2.00
27	Mike Sweeney	2.00
28	Shawn Green	2.00
29	Hideo Nomo	2.00
30	Torii Hunter	2.00
31	Vladimir Guerrero	5.00
32	Tom Seaver	4.00
33	Mike Piazza	8.00
34	Roberto Alomar	2.00
35	Derek Jeter	12.00
36	Alfonso Soriano	5.00
37	Jason Giambi	4.00
38	Roger Clemens	8.00
39	Mike Mussina	2.50
40	Bernie Williams	2.50
41	Joe DiMaggio	10.00
42	Mickey Mantle	15.00
43	Miguel Tejada	3.00
44	Eric Chavez	2.00
45	Barry Zito	2.00
46	Pat Burrell	2.50
47	Jason Kendall	2.00
48	Brian Giles	2.00
49	Barry Bonds	15.00
50	Ichiro Suzuki	8.00
51	Stan Musial	8.00
52	J.D. Drew	2.00
53	Scott Rolen	5.00
54	Albert Pujols	10.00
55	Mark McGwire	10.00
56	Alex Rodriguez	10.00
57	Ivan Rodriguez	3.00
58	Juan Gonzalez	2.50
59	Rafael Palmeiro	3.00
60	Carlos Delgado	2.50
61	*Jose Valverde*	10.00
62	*Doug Devore*	10.00
63	*John Ennis*	10.00
64	Joey Dawley	10.00
65	*Trey Hodges*	10.00
66	Mike Mahoney	10.00
67	*Aaron Cook*	10.00
68	*Rene Reyes*	10.00
69	Mark Corey	10.00
70	*Hansel Izquierdo*	10.00
71	*Brandon Puffer*	10.00
72	*Jeriome Robertson*	10.00
73	Jose Diaz	10.00
74	David Ross	10.00
75	*Jayson Durocher*	10.00
76	*Eric Good*	10.00
77	*Satoru Komiyama*	10.00
78	*Tyler Yates*	10.00
79	*Eric Junge*	10.00
80	*Anderson Machado*	10.00
81	*Adrian Burnside*	10.00
82	*Ben Howard*	10.00
83	*Clay Condrey*	10.00
84	*Nelson Castro*	10.00
85	*So Taguchi*	15.00
86	*Mike Crudale*	10.00
87	*Scotty Layfield*	10.00
88	*Steve Bechler*	10.00
89	*Travis Driskill*	10.00
90	*Howie Clark*	10.00
91	*Josh Hancock*	10.00
92	*Jorge De La Rosa*	10.00
93	*Anastacio Martinez*	10.00
94	Brian Tallet	10.00
95	*Carl Sadler*	10.00
96	*Cliff Lee*	15.00
97	*Josh Bard*	10.00
98	*Wes Obermueller*	10.00
99	Juan Brito	10.00
100	*Aaron Guiel*	10.00
101	*Jeremy Hill*	10.00
102	*Kevin Frederick*	10.00
103	*Nate Field*	10.00
104	*Julio Mateo*	10.00
105	*Chris Snelling*	15.00
106	*Felix Escalona*	10.00
107	*Reynaldo Garcia*	10.00
108	*Mike Smith*	10.00
109	*Ken Huckaby*	10.00
110	*Kevin Cash*	10.00
111	*Kazuhisa Ishii/auto*	50.00
112	*Freddy Sanchez/auto*	25.00
113	*Jason Simontacchi/auto*	25.00
114	*Jorge Padilla/auto*	15.00
115	Kirk Saarloos/auto	15.00
116	*Rodrigo Rosario/auto*	15.00
117	*Oliver Perez/auto*	60.00
118	*Miguel Asencio/auto*	15.00
119	*Franklyn German/auto*	15.00
120	*Jaime Cerda/auto*	15.00

Double Barrel

		NM/M
Most not priced due to scarcity		
DB-RI	Ivan Rodriguez, Alex Rodriguez/5	2,225
DB-RR	Cal Ripken Jr., Alex Rodriguez/9	1,625
DB-TO	Magglio Ordonez, Frank Thomas/4	950.00

Double Patches

		NM/M
Production 100 sets		
Golds:		.75-1.5X
Production 50 sets		
DE	J.D. Drew, Jim Edmonds	60.00
GC	Jason Giambi, Roger Clemens	80.00
IG	Ken Griffey Jr., Ichiro Suzuki	125.00
JS	Randy Johnson, Curt Schilling	60.00
MG	Tom Glavine, Greg Maddux	75.00
MS	Sammy Sosa, Mark McGwire	150.00
PA	Mike Piazza, Roberto Alomar	80.00
RG	Alex Rodriguez, Juan Gonzalez	80.00
RM	Manny Ramirez, Pedro J. Martinez	50.00

Jerseys Tier 1

		NM/M
Common Player:		10.00
Production 99 sets		
Golds:		.75-1.5X
Production 50 sets		
RC	Roger Clemens	20.00
JD	Joe DiMaggio	100.00
AD	Adam Dunn	15.00
JG	Jason Giambi	15.00
KG	Ken Griffey Jr.	20.00
KI	Kazuhisa Ishii	10.00
RJ	Randy Johnson	15.00
AJ	Andruw Jones	10.00
CJ	Chipper Jones	15.00
MM	Mickey Mantle	125.00
PM	Pedro J. Martinez	15.00
MC	Mark McGwire	60.00
MP	Mike Piazza	15.00
PR	Mark Prior	25.00
MR	Manny Ramirez	10.00
CR	Cal Ripken Jr.	40.00
AR	Alex Rodriguez	25.00
IR	Ivan Rodriguez	15.00
AS	Alfonso Soriano	20.00
SS	Sammy Sosa	25.00
IS	Ichiro Suzuki	45.00

Jerseys Tier 2

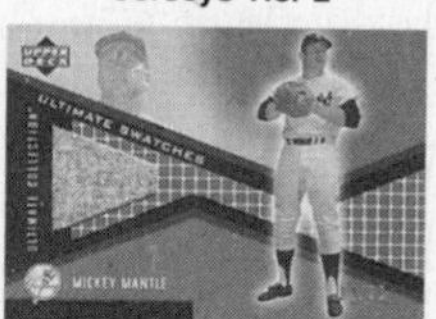

		NM/M
Same price as Tier 1		
Production 99 sets		
Golds:		1.5-2X
Production 25 sets		
JF-RC	Roger Clemens	20.00
JF-JD	Joe DiMaggio	100.00
JF-AD	Adam Dunn	15.00
JF-JG	Jason Giambi	15.00
JF-KG	Ken Griffey Jr.	20.00
JF-KI	Kazuhisa Ishii	10.00
JF-RJ	Randy Johnson	15.00
JF-AJ	Andruw Jones	10.00
JF-CJ	Chipper Jones	15.00
JF-MM	Mickey Mantle	125.00
JF-PM	Pedro J. Martinez	15.00
JF-MC	Mark McGwire	60.00
JF-MP	Mike Piazza	15.00
JF-PR	Mark Prior	25.00
JF-MR	Manny Ramirez	10.00
JF-CR	Cal Ripken Jr.	40.00
JF-AR	Alex Rodriguez	25.00
JF-IR	Ivan Rodriguez	15.00
JF-AS	Alfonso Soriano	20.00
JF-SS	Sammy Sosa	25.00
JF-IS	Ichiro Suzuki	45.00

Jerseys Tier 3

		NM/M
Common Player:		8.00
Stars:		.4-.6X Tier 1 price
Production 199 sets		
JP-RC	Roger Clemens	15.00
JP-AD	Adam Dunn	10.00
JP-JG	Jason Giambi	10.00
JP-KG	Ken Griffey Jr.	15.00
JP-KI	Kazuhisa Ishii	8.00
JP-RJ	Randy Johnson	12.00
JP-AJ	Andruw Jones	8.00
JP-CJ	Chipper Jones	12.00
JP-MM	Mickey Mantle	75.00
JP-PM	Pedro J. Martinez	10.00
JP-MC	Mark McGwire	40.00
JP-MP	Mike Piazza	15.00
JP-PR	Mark Prior	15.00
JP-MR	Manny Ramirez	8.00
JP-CR	Cal Ripken Jr.	30.00
JP-AR	Alex Rodriguez	15.00
JP-IR	Ivan Rodriguez	8.00
JP-AS	Alfonso Soriano	12.00
JP-SS	Sammy Sosa	20.00
JP-IS	Ichiro Suzuki	30.00
JP-BW	Bernie Williams	8.00

Jerseys Tier 4

		NM/M
Common Player:		8.00
Stars:		.4-.6X Tier 1 price
Production 199 sets		
JR-RC	Roger Clemens	15.00
JR-AD	Adam Dunn	10.00
JR-JG	Jason Giambi	10.00
JR-KG	Ken Griffey Jr.	15.00
JR-KI	Kazuhisa Ishii	8.00
JR-RJ	Randy Johnson	10.00
JR-AJ	Andruw Jones	8.00
JR-CJ	Chipper Jones	10.00
JR-MM	Mickey Mantle	75.00
JR-PM	Pedro J. Martinez	10.00
JR-MC	Mark McGwire	40.00
JR-MP	Mike Piazza	15.00
JR-PR	Mark Prior	15.00
JR-MR	Manny Ramirez	8.00
JR-CR	Cal Ripken Jr.	25.00
JR-AR	Alex Rodriguez	15.00
JR-IR	Ivan Rodriguez	8.00
JR-AS	Alfonso Soriano	15.00
JR-SS	Sammy Sosa	20.00
JR-IS	Ichiro Suzuki	30.00
JR-BW	Bernie Williams	8.00

Patch

		NM/M
Common Player:		25.00
Production 100 sets		
LG	Luis Gonzalez	25.00
SG	Shawn Green	25.00
TH	Todd Helton	40.00
KI	Kazuhisa Ishii	40.00
CJ	Chipper Jones	40.00
MM	Mark McGwire	125.00
MP	Mark Prior	50.00
IR	Ivan Rodriguez	40.00
SS	Sammy Sosa	65.00
IS	Ichiro Suzuki	150.00

Signed Excellence

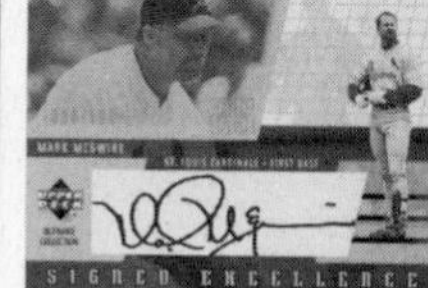

		NM/M
Quantity produced listed		
Golds:		No Pricing
Production 1 set		
I1	Ichiro Suzuki/56	375.00
I2	Ichiro Suzuki/51	375.00
I3	Ichiro Suzuki/23	

I4 Ichiro Suzuki/12
I5 Ichiro Suzuki/ batting 250.00
I6 Ichiro Suzuki/ throwing 250.00
MM1 Mark McGwire/70 275.00
MM2 Mark McGwire/65 275.00
MM3 Mark McGwire/49 300.00
MM4 Mark McGwire/25
MM5 Mark McGwire/ standing 220.00
MM6 Mark McGwire/ waving 220.00
MM7 Mark McGwire/ fielding 220.00
SS1 Sammy Sosa/66 175.00
SS2 Sammy Sosa/64 175.00
SS3 Sammy Sosa/54 175.00
SS4 Sammy Sosa/21
SS5 Sammy Sosa/ running 150.00
SS6 Sammy Sosa/ holding bat 150.00
SS7 Sammy Sosa/150 150.00

Excellence Gold

No Pricing

Signatures Tier 1

NM/M

Common Autograph: 20.00
Quantity produced listed
Golds: No Pricing
Production 25 sets

RA1 Roberto Alomar/155 45.00
LB1 Lance Berkman/179 25.00
PB1 Pat Burrell/95 25.00
RC1 Roger Clemens/320 80.00
CD1 Carlos Delgado/95 25.00
JD1 J.D. Drew/220 25.00
AD1 Adam Dunn/125 45.00
JG1 Jason Giambi/295 25.00
BG1 Brian Giles/220 20.00
LG1 Luis Gonzalez/199 20.00
KG1 Ken Griffey Jr./195 100.00
JK1 Jason Kendall/220 20.00
MP1 Mark Prior/160 60.00
CR1 Cal Ripken Jr./75 165.00
AR1 Alex Rodriguez/329 100.00
SR1 Scott Rolen/160 30.00
GS1 Gary Sheffield/95 20.00
JT1 Jim Thome/95 60.00
BZ1 Barry Zito/199 25.00

Signatures Tier 2

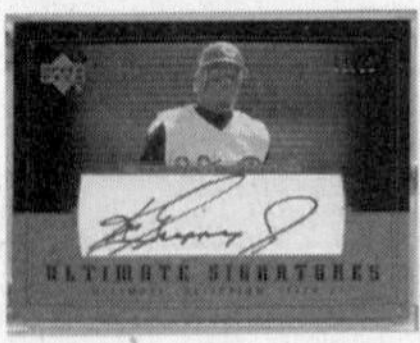

NM/M

Quantity produced listed
Golds: No Pricing
Production 10 sets

JB2 Jeff Bagwell/51 55.00
LB2 Lance Berkman/85 40.00
JG2 Jason Giambi/50 60.00
LG2 Luis Gonzalez/70 25.00
KG2 Ken Griffey Jr./30 150.00
TG2 Tony Gwynn/51 75.00
TH2 Todd Helton/51 60.00
AJ2 Andruw Jones/51 50.00
MP2 Mark Prior/60 80.00
KP2 Kirby Puckett/75 60.00
AR2 Alex Rodriguez/75 100.00
SR2 Scott Rolen/60 50.00
DS2 Duke Snider/51 60.00
FT2 Frank Thomas/51 65.00
KW2 Kerry Wood/51 75.00
BZ2 Barry Zito/70 40.00

Mark McGwire Signing Redem.

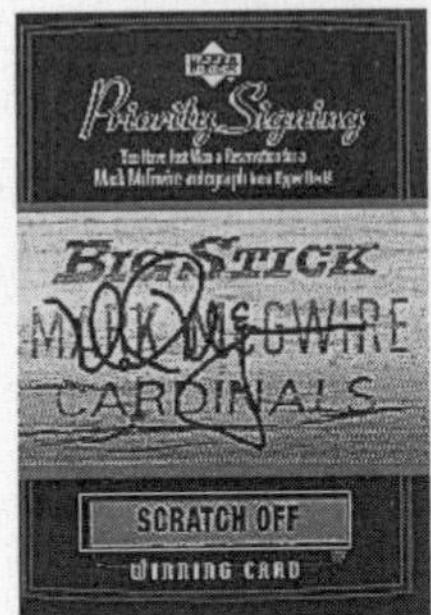

NM/M

Exchange Card 1:500 Packs:
1-MM Mark McGwire 600.00

2002 Upper Deck Victory

NM/M

Complete Set (550): 40.00
Common Player: .10
Pack (10): 1.00
Box (36): 25.00

1 Troy Glaus .30
2 Tim Salmon .20
3 Troy Percival .10
4 Darin Erstad .25
5 Adam Kennedy .10
6 Scott Spiezio .10
7 Ramon Ortiz .10
8 Ismael Valdes .10
9 Jarrod Washburn .10
10 Garret Anderson .10
11 David Eckstein .10
12 Mo Vaughn .25
13 Benji Gil .10
14 Bengie Molina .10
15 Scott Schoeneweis .10
16 Troy Glaus, Ramon Ortiz .20
17 David Justice .25
18 Jermaine Dye .10
19 Eric Chavez .25
20 Jeremy Giambi .10
21 Terrence Long .10
22 Miguel Tejada .20
23 Johnny Damon .10
24 Jason Hart .10
25 Adam Piatt .10
26 Billy Koch .10
27 Ramon Hernandez .10
28 Eric Byrnes .10
29 Olmedo Saenz .10
30 Barry Zito .20
31 Tim Hudson .25
32 Mark Mulder .20
33 Jason Giambi, Mark Mulder .25
34 Carlos Delgado .40
35 Shannon Stewart .10
36 Vernon Wells .10
37 Homer Bush .10
38 Brad Fullmer .10
39 Jose Cruz .10
40 Felipe Lopez .10
41 Raul Mondesi .20
42 Esteban Loaiza .10
43 Darrin Fletcher .10
44 Mike Sirotka .10
45 Luke Prokopec .10
46 Chris Carpenter .10
47 Roy Halladay .10
48 Kelvim Escobar .10
49 Carlos Delgado, Billy Koch .20
50 Nick Bierbrodt .10
51 Greg Vaughn .10
52 Ben Grieve .10
53 Damian Rolls .10
54 Russ Johnson .10
55 Brent Abernathy .10
56 Steve Cox .10
57 Aubrey Huff .10
58 Randy Winn .10
59 Jason Tyner .10
60 Tanyon Sturtze .10
61 Joe Kennedy .10
62 Jared Sandberg .10
63 Esteban Yan .10
64 Ryan Rupe .10
65 Toby Hall .10
66 Greg Vaughn, Tanyon Sturtze .10
67 Matt Lawton .10
68 Juan Gonzalez .40
69 Jim Thome .25
70 Einar Diaz .10
71 Ellis Burks .10
72 Kenny Lofton .10
73 Omar Vizquel .10
74 Russell Branyan .10
75 Brady Anderson .10
76 John Rocker .10
77 Travis Fryman .10
78 Wil Cordero .10
79 Chuck Finley .10
80 C.C. Sabathia .10
81 Bartolo Colon .10
82 Bob Wickman .10
83 Roberto Alomar, C.C. Sabathia .20
84 Ichiro Suzuki 1.50
85 Edgar Martinez .10
86 Aaron Sele .10
87 Carlos Guillen .10
88 Bret Boone .10
89 John Olerud .20
90 Jamie Moyer .10
91 Ben Davis .10
92 Dan Wilson .10
93 Jeff Cirillo .10
94 John Halama .10
95 Freddy Garcia .10
96 Kazuhiro Sasaki .10
97 Mike Cameron .10
98 Paul Abbott .10
99 Mark McLemore .10
100 Ichiro Suzuki, Freddy Garcia .50
101 Jeff Conine .10
102 David Segui .10
103 Marty Cordova .10
104 Tony Batista .10
105 Chris Richard .10
106 Willis Roberts .10
107 Melvin Mora .10
108 Mike Bordick .10
109 Jay Gibbons .10
110 Mike Kinkade .10
111 Brian Roberts .10
112 Jerry Hairston Jr. .10
113 Jason Johnson .10
114 Josh Towers .10
115 Calvin Maduro .10
116 Sidney Ponson .10
117 Jeff Conine, Jason Johnson .10
118 Alex Rodriguez 1.00
119 Ivan Rodriguez .40
120 Frank Catalanotto .10
121 Mike Lamb .10
122 Ruben Sierra .10
123 Rusty Greer .10
124 Rafael Palmeiro .20
125 Gabe Kapler .15
126 Aaron Myette .10
127 Kenny Rogers .10
128 Carl Everett .10
129 Rick Helling .10
130 Ricky Ledee .10
131 Michael Young .10
132 Doug Davis .10
133 Jeff Zimmerman .10
134 Alex Rodriguez, Rick Helling .40
135 Manny Ramirez .40
136 Nomar Garciaparra 1.00
137 Jason Varitek .10
138 Dante Bichette .10
139 Tony Clark .10
140 Scott Hatteberg .10
141 Trot Nixon .10
142 Hideo Nomo .25
143 Dustin Hermanson .10
144 Chris Stynes .10
145 Jose Offerman .10
146 Pedro Martinez .50
147 Shea Hillenbrand .10
148 Tim Wakefield .10
149 Troy O'Leary .10
150 Ugueth Urbina .10
151 Manny Ramirez, Hideo Nomo .25
152 Carlos Beltran .10
153 Dee Brown .10
154 Mike Sweeney .10
155 Luis Alicea .10
156 Raul Ibanez .10
157 Mark Quinn .10
158 Joe Randa .10
159 Roberto Hernandez .10
160 Neifi Perez .10
161 Carlos Febles .10
162 Jeff Suppan .10
163 Dave McCarty .10
164 Blake Stein .10
165 Chad Durbin .10
166 Paul Byrd .10
167 Carlos Beltran, Jeff Suppan .10
168 Craig Paquette .10
169 Dean Palmer .10
170 Shane Halter .10
171 Bobby Higginson .10
172 Robert Fick .10
173 Jose Macias .10
174 Deivi Cruz .10
175 Damion Easley .10
176 Brandon Inge .10
177 Mark Redman .10
178 Dmitri Young .10
179 Steve Sparks .10
180 Jeff Weaver .10
181 Victor Santos .10
182 Jose Lima .10
183 Matt Anderson .10
184 Roger Cedeno, Steve Sparks .10
185 Doug Mientkiewicz .10
186 Cristian Guzman .10
187 Torii Hunter .10
188 Matt LeCroy .10
189 Corey Koskie .10
190 Jacque Jones .10
191 Luis Rivas .10
192 David Ortiz .10
193 A.J. Pierzynski .10
194 Brian Buchanan .10
195 Joe Mays .10
196 Brad Radke .10
197 Denny Hocking .10
198 Eric Milton .10
199 LaTroy Hawkins .10
200 Doug Mientkiewicz, Joe Mays .10
201 Magglio Ordonez .20
202 Jose Valentin .10
203 Chris Singleton .10
204 Aaron Rowand .10
205 Paul Konerko .10
206 Carlos Lee .10
207 Ray Durham .10
208 Keith Foulke .10
209 Todd Ritchie .10
210 Royce Clayton .10
211 Jose Canseco .20
212 Frank Thomas .40
213 David Wells .10
214 Mark Buehrle .10
215 Jon Garland .10
216 Magglio Ordonez, Mark Buehrle .15
217 Derek Jeter 1.50
218 Bernie Williams .30
219 Rondell White .10
220 Jorge Posada .20
221 Alfonso Soriano .50
222 Ramiro Mendoza .10
223 Jason Giambi .75
224 John Vander Wal .10
225 Steve Karsay .10
226 Nick Johnson .10
227 Mariano Rivera .20
228 Orlando Hernandez .10
229 Andy Pettitte .20
230 Robin Ventura .10
231 Roger Clemens .60
232 Mike Mussina .40

233 Derek Jeter, Roger Clemens .50
234 Moises Alou .20
235 Lance Berkman .20
236 Craig Biggio .20
237 Octavio Dotel .10
238 Jeff Bagwell .40
239 Richard Hidalgo .10
240 Morgan Ensberg .10
241 Julio Lugo .10
242 Daryle Ward .10
243 Roy Oswalt .20
244 Billy Wagner .10
245 Brad Ausmus .10
246 Jose Vizcaino .10
247 Wade Miller .10
248 Shane Reynolds .10
249 Jeff Bagwell, Wade Miller .20
250 Chipper Jones .75
251 Brian Jordan .10
252 B.J. Surhoff .10
253 Rafael Furcal .10
254 Julio Franco .10
255 Javy Lopez .10
256 John Burkett .10
257 Andruw Jones .20
258 Marcus Giles .10
259 Wes Helms .10
260 Greg Maddux .75
261 John Smoltz .10
262 Tom Glavine .20
263 Vinny Castilla .10
264 Kevin Millwood .10
265 Jason Marquis .10
266 Chipper Jones, Greg Maddux .40
267 Tyler Houston .10
268 Mark Loretta .10
269 Richie Sexson .20
270 Jeromy Burnitz .10
271 Jimmy Haynes .10
272 Geoff Jenkins .20
273 Ron Belliard .10
274 Jose Hernandez .10
275 Jeffrey Hammonds .10
276 Curtis Leskanic .10
277 Devon White .10
278 Ben Sheets .20
279 Henry Blanco .10
280 Jamey Wright .10
281 Allen Levrault .10
282 Jeff D'Amico .10
283 Richie Sexson, Jimmy Haynes .10
284 Albert Pujols .75
285 Jason Isringhausen .10
286 J.D. Drew .25
287 Placido Polanco .10
288 Jim Edmonds .20
289 Fernando Vina .10
290 Edgar Renteria .10
291 Mike Matheny .10
292 Bud Smith .10
293 Mike Defelice .10
294 Woody Williams .10
295 Eli Marrero .10
296 Matt Morris .10
297 Darryl Kile .10
298 Kerry Robinson .10
299 Luis Saturria .10
300 Albert Pujols, Matt Morris .40
301 Sammy Sosa .75
302 Michael Tucker .10
303 Bill Mueller .10
304 Ricky Gutierrez .10
305 Fred McGriff .20
306 Eric Young .10
307 Corey Patterson .10
308 Alex Gonzalez .10
309 Ron Coomer .10
310 Kerry Wood .20
311 Delino DeShields .10
312 Jon Lieber .10
313 Tom Gordon .10
314 Todd Hundley .10
315 Jason Bere .10
316 Kevin Tapani .10
317 Sammy Sosa, Jon Lieber .40
318 Steve Finley .10
319 Luis Gonzalez .25
320 Mark Grace .25
321 Craig Counsell .10
322 Matt Williams .20
323 Tony Womack .10
324 Junior Spivey .10
325 David Dellucci .10
326 Jay Bell .10
327 Curt Schilling .25
328 Randy Johnson .40
329 Danny Bautista .10
330 Miguel Batista .10
331 Erubiel Durazo .10
332 Brian Anderson .10
333 Byung-Hyun Kim .10
334 Luis Gonzalez, Curt Schilling .20
335 Paul LoDuca .10
336 Gary Sheffield .20
337 Shawn Green .25
338 Adrian Beltre .20
339 Darren Dreifort .10
340 Mark Grudzielanek .10
341 Eric Karros .10
342 Cesar Izturis .10
343 Tom Goodwin .10
344 Marquis Grissom .10
345 Kevin Brown .20
346 James Baldwin .10
347 Terry Adams .10
348 Alex Cora .10
349 Andy Ashby .10
350 Chan Ho Park .20
351 Shawn Green, Chan Ho Park .20
352 Jose Vidro .10
353 Vladimir Guerrero .40
354 Orlando Cabrera .10
355 Fernando Tatis .10
356 Michael Barrett .10
357 Lee Stevens .10
358 Geoff Blum .10
359 Brad Wilkerson .10
360 Peter Bergeron .10
361 Javier Vazquez .10
362 Tony Armas Jr. .10
363 Tomokazu Ohka .10
364 Scott Strickland .10
365 Vladimir Guerrero, Javier Vazquez .20
366 Barry Bonds .75
367 Rich Aurilia .10
368 Jeff Kent .10
369 Andres Galarraga .20
370 Desi Relaford .10
371 Shawon Dunston .10
372 Benito Santiago .10
373 Tsuyoshi Shinjo .10
374 Calvin Murray .10
375 Marvin Benard .10
376 J.T. Snow .10
377 Livan Hernandez .10
378 Russ Ortiz .10
379 Robb Nen .10
380 Jason Schmidt .10
381 Barry Bonds, Russ Ortiz .30
382 Cliff Floyd .10
383 Antonio Alfonseca .10
384 Mike Redmond .10
385 Mike Lowell .10
386 Derrek Lee .10
387 Preston Wilson .10
388 Luis Castillo .10
389 Charles Johnson .10
390 Eric Owens .10
391 Alex Gonzalez .10
392 Josh Beckett .10
393 Brad Penny .10
394 Ryan Dempster .10
395 Matt Clement .10
396 A.J. Burnett .10
397 Cliff Floyd, Ryan Dempster .10
398 Mike Piazza 1.00
399 Joe McEwing .10
400 Todd Zeile .10
401 Jay Payton .10
402 Roger Cedeno .10
403 Rey Ordonez .10
404 Edgardo Alfonzo .10
405 Roberto Alomar .30
406 Glendon Rusch .10
407 Timo Perez .10
408 Al Leiter .15
409 Lenny Harris .10
410 Shawn Estes .10
411 Armando Benitez .10
412 Kevin Appier .10
413 Bruce Chen .10
414 Mike Piazza, Al Leiter .40
415 Phil Nevin .10
416 Ryan Klesko .10
417 Mark Kotsay .10
418 Ray Lankford .10
419 Mike Darr .10
420 D'Angelo Jimenez .10
421 Bubba Trammell .10
422 Adam Eaton .10
423 Ramon Vazquez .10
424 Cesar Crespo .10
425 Trevor Hoffman .10
426 Kevin Jarvis .10
427 Wiki Gonzalez .10
428 Damian Jackson .10
429 Brian Lawrence .10
430 Phil Nevin, Trevor Hoffman .10
431 Scott Rolen .25
432 Marlon Anderson .10
433 Bobby Abreu .10
434 Jimmy Rollins .10
435 Doug Glanville .10
436 Travis Lee .10
437 Brandon Duckworth .10
438 Pat Burrell .25
439 Kevin Jordan .10
440 Robert Person .10
441 Johnny Estrada .10
442 Randy Wolf .10
443 Jose Mesa .10
444 Mike Lieberthal .10
445 Bobby Abreu, Robert Person .10
446 Brian Giles .20
447 Jason Kendall .10
448 Aramis Ramirez .10
449 Rob Mackowiak .10
450 Abraham Nunez .10
451 Pat Meares .10
452 Craig Wilson .10
453 Jack Wilson .10
454 Gary Matthews Jr. .10
455 Kevin Young .10
456 Derek Bell .10
457 Kip Wells .10
458 Jimmy Anderson .10
459 Kris Benson .10
460 Brian Giles, Todd Ritchie .10
461 Sean Casey .20
462 Wilton Guerrero .10
463 Jason LaRue .10
464 Juan Encarnacion .10
465 Todd Walker .10
466 Aaron Boone .10
467 Pete Harnisch .10
468 Ken Griffey Jr. 1.00
469 Adam Dunn .40
470 Barry Larkin .20
471 Kelly Stinnett .10
472 Pokey Reese .10
473 Brady Clark .10
474 Scott Williamson .10
475 Danny Graves .10
476 Ken Griffey Jr., Elmer Dessens .10
477 Larry Walker .25
478 Todd Helton .40
479 Juan Pierre .10
480 Juan Uribe .10
481 Mario Encarnacion .10
482 Jose Ortiz .10
483 Todd Hollandsworth .10
484 Alex Ochoa .10
485 Mike Hampton .10
486 Terry Shumpert .10
487 Denny Neagle .10
488 Jose Jimenez .10
489 Jason Jennings .10
490 Todd Helton, Mike Hampton .20
491 Tim Redding .10
492 Mark Teixeira 2.00
493 Alex Cintron .10
494 Tim Raines Jr. .10
495 Juan Cruz .20
496 Joe Crede .10
497 Steve Green .10
498 Mike Rivera .10
499 Mark Prior 1.50
500 Ken Harvey .10
501 Tim Spooneybarger .10
502 Adam Everett .10
503 Jason Standridge .10
504 Nick Neugebauer .10
505 Adam Johnson .10
506 Sean Douglass .10
507 Brandon Berger .10
508 Alex Escobar .10
509 Doug Nickle .10
510 Jason Middlebrook .10
511 Dewon Brazelton .10
512 Yorvit Torrealba .10
513 Henry Mateo .10
514 Dennis Tankersley .10
515 Marlon Byrd .75
516 Andy Barkett .10
517 Orlando Hudson .10
518 Josh Fogg .10
519 Ryan Drese .10
520 Mike MacDougal .10
521 Luis Pineda .10
522 Jack Cust .10
523 Kurt Ainsworth .10
524 Bart Miadich .10
525 Dernell Stenson .10
526 Carlos Zambrano .10
527 Austin Kearns .50
528 Larry Barnes .10
529 Mike Cuddyer .10
530 Carlos Pena .75
531 Derek Jeter 1.00
532 Ken Griffey Jr. .75
533 Manny Ramirez .25
534 Luis Gonzalez .20
535 Sammy Sosa .50
536 Roger Clemens .40
537 Phil Nevin .10
538 Mike Piazza .75
539 Alex Rodriguez .75
540 Jason Giambi .50
541 Randy Johnson .25
542 Albert Pujols .50
543 Jeff Bagwell .25
544 Shawn Green .15
545 Carlos Delgado .15
546 Pedro Martinez .25
547 Todd Helton .25
548 Roberto Alomar .20
549 Barry Bonds .40
550 Ichiro Suzuki 1.00

Gold

Stars: 3-6X
Inserted 1:2

2002 UPPER DECK VINTAGE

NM/M

Complete Set (300): 30.00
Common Player: .10
Pack (10): 2.00
Box (24): 35.00
1 Darin Erstad .20
2 Mo Vaughn .20
3 Ramon Ortiz .10
4 Garret Anderson .25
5 Troy Glaus .40
6 Troy Percival .10
7 Tim Salmon .20
8 Wilmy Caceres, Elpidio Guzman .10
9 2001 Anaheim Angels .10
10 Jason Giambi .50
11 Mark Mulder .25
12 Jermaine Dye .10
13 Miguel Tejada .40
14 Tim Hudson .25
15 Eric Chavez .25
16 Barry Zito .25
17 Oscar Salazar, Juan Pena .10
18 2001 Oakland Athletics .10
19 Carlos Delgado .40
20 Raul Mondesi .15
21 Chris Carpenter .10
22 Jose Cruz Jr. .10
23 Alex Gonzalez .10
24 Brad Fullmer .10
25 Shannon Stewart .10
26 Brandon Lyon, Vernon Wells .10
27 2001 Toronto Blue Jays .10
28 Greg Vaughn .10
29 Toby Hall .10
30 Ben Grieve .10
31 Aubrey Huff .10
32 Tanyon Sturtze .10

33 Brent Abernathy .10
34 Dewon Brazelton, Delvin James .10
35 2001 Tampa Bay Devil Rays .10
36 Roberto Alomar .40
37 Juan Gonzalez .50
38 Bartolo Colon .25
39 C.C. Sabathia .10
40 Jim Thome .75
41 Omar Vizquel .20
42 Russell Branyan .10
43 Ryan Drese, Roy Smith .10
44 2001 Cleveland Indians .10
45 Edgar Martinez .20
46 Bret Boone .20
47 Freddy Garcia .10
48 John Olerud .25
49 Kazuhiro Sasaki .10
50 Ichiro Suzuki 1.50
51 Mike Cameron .10
52 Rafael Soriano, Dennis Stark .10
53 2001 Seattle Mariners .10
54 Tony Batista .10
55 Jeff Conine .10
56 Jason Johnson .10
57 Jay Gibbons .10
58 Chris Richard .10
59 Josh Towers .10
60 Jerry Hairston Jr. .10
61 Sean Douglass, Tim Raines Jr. .10
62 2001 Baltimore Orioles .10
63 Alex Rodriguez 1.50
64 Ruben Sierra .10
65 Ivan Rodriguez .50
66 Gabe Kapler .20
67 Rafael Palmeiro .50
68 Frank Catalanotto .10
69 Mark Teixeira, Carlos Pena .40
70 2001 Texas Rangers .10
71 Nomar Garciaparra 1.50
72 Pedro Martinez .75
73 Trot Nixon .10
74 Dante Bichette .10
75 Manny Ramirez .50
76 Carl Everett .10
77 Hideo Nomo .40
78 Dernell Stenson, Juan Diaz .10
79 2001 Boston Red Sox .10
80 Mike Sweeney .10
81 Carlos Febles .10
82 Dee Brown .10
83 Neifi Perez .10
84 Mark Quinn .10
85 Carlos Beltran .25
86 Joe Randa .10
87 Ken Harvey, Mike MacDougal .10
88 2001 Kansas City Royals .10
89 Dean Palmer .10
90 Jeff Weaver .10
91 Jose Lima .10
92 Tony Clark .10
93 Damion Easley .10
94 Bobby Higginson .10
95 Robert Fick .10
96 Pedro Santana, Mike Rivera .10
97 2001 Detroit Tigers .10
98 Doug Mientkiewicz .10
99 David Ortiz .25
100 Joe Mays .10
101 Corey Koskie .10
102 Eric Milton .10
103 Cristian Guzman .10
104 Brad Radke .10
105 Adam Johnson, Juan Rincon .10
106 2001 Minnesota Twins .10
107 Frank Thomas .50
108 Carlos Lee .10
109 Mark Buehrle .10
110 Jose Canseco .25
111 Magglio Ordonez .25
112 Jon Garland .10
113 Ray Durham .10
114 Joe Crede, Josh Fogg .10
115 2001 Chicago White Sox .10
116 Derek Jeter 2.00
117 Roger Clemens 1.50
118 Alfonso Soriano .75
119 Paul O'Neill .25
120 Jorge Posada .25
121 Bernie Williams .40
122 Mariano Rivera .25
123 Tino Martinez .20
124 Mike Mussina .50
125 Nick Johnson, Erick Almonte .10
126 2001 New York Yankees .10
127 Jeff Bagwell .50
128 Wade Miller .10
129 Lance Berkman .25
130 Moises Alou .25
131 Craig Biggio .20
132 Roy Oswalt .20
133 Richard Hidalgo .15
134 Morgan Ensberg, Tim Redding .10
135 2001 Houston Astros .10
136 Greg Maddux 1.00
137 Chipper Jones .75
138 Brian Jordan .10
139 Marcus Giles .10
140 Andruw Jones .40
141 Tom Glavine .40
142 Rafael Furcal .25
143 Wilson Betemit, Horacio Ramirez .10
144 2001 Atlanta Braves .10
145 Jeromy Burnitz .10
146 Ben Sheets .25
147 Geoff Jenkins .20
148 Devon White .10
149 Jimmy Haynes .10
150 Richie Sexson .40
151 Jose Hernandez .10
152 Jose Mieses, Alex Sanchez .10
153 2001 Milwaukee Brewers .10
154 Mark McGwire 2.00
155 Albert Pujols 1.50
156 Matt Morris .20
157 J.D. Drew .25
158 Jim Edmonds .25
159 Bud Smith .10
160 Darryl Kile .10
161 William Ortega, Luis Saturria .10
162 2001 St. Louis Cardinals .10
163 Sammy Sosa 1.25
164 Jon Lieber .10
165 Eric Young .10
166 Kerry Wood .75
167 Fred McGriff .25
168 Corey Patterson .25
169 Rondell White .15
170 Juan Cruz, Mark Prior 1.00
171 2001 Chicago Cubs .10
172 Luis Gonzalez .25
173 Randy Johnson .75
174 Matt Williams .20
175 Mark Grace .25
176 Steve Finley .10
177 Reggie Sanders .10
178 Curt Schilling .40
179 Alex Cintron, Jack Cust .10
180 2001 Arizona Diamondbacks .10
181 Gary Sheffield .25
182 Paul LoDuca .10
183 Chan Ho Park .10
184 Shawn Green .25
185 Eric Karros .15
186 Adrian Beltre .25
187 Kevin Brown .25
188 Ricardo Rodriguez, Carlos Garcia .10
189 2001 Los Angeles Dodgers .10
190 Vladimir Guerrero .75
191 Javier Vazquez .10
192 Jose Vidro .10
193 Fernando Tatis .10
194 Orlando Cabrera .10
195 Lee Stevens .10
196 Tony Armas Jr. .10
197 Donnie Bridges, Henry Mateo .10
198 2001 Montreal Expos .10
199 Barry Bonds 2.00
200 Rich Aurilia .10
201 Russ Ortiz .10
202 Jeff Kent .20
203 Jason Schmidt .25
204 John Vander Wal .10
205 Robb Nen .10
206 Yorvit Torrealba, Kurt Ainsworth .10
207 2001 San Francisco Giants .10
208 Preston Wilson .10
209 Brad Penny .10
210 Cliff Floyd .10
211 Luis Castillo .10
212 Ryan Dempster .10
213 Charles Johnson .10
214 A.J. Burnett .10
215 Abraham Nunez, Josh Beckett .20
216 2001 Florida Marlins .10
217 Mike Piazza 1.00
218 Al Leiter .20
219 Edgardo Alfonzo .10
220 Tsuyoshi Shinjo .10
221 Matt Lawton .10
222 Robin Ventura .15
223 Jay Payton .10
224 Alex Escobar, Jae Weong Seo .10
225 2001 New York Mets .10
226 Ryan Klesko .20
227 D'Angelo Jimenez .10
228 Trevor Hoffman .10
229 Phil Nevin .10
230 Mark Kotsay .10
231 Brian Lawrence .10
232 Bubba Trammell .10
233 Jason Middlebrook, Xavier Nady .10
234 2001 San Diego Padres .10
235 Scott Rolen .75
236 Jimmy Rollins .10
237 Mike Lieberthal .10
238 Bobby Abreu .25
239 Brandon Duckworth .10
240 Robert Person .10
241 Pat Burrell .20
242 Nick Punto, Carlos Silva .10
243 2001 Philadelphia Phillies .10
244 Brian Giles .20
245 Jack Wilson .10
246 Kris Benson .10
247 Jason Kendall .20
248 Aramis Ramirez .25
249 Todd Ritchie .10
250 Robert Mackowiak .10
251 John Grabow, Humberto Cota .10
252 2001 Pittsburgh Pirates .10
253 Ken Griffey Jr. 1.00
254 Barry Larkin .25
255 Sean Casey .25
256 Aaron Boone .10
257 Dmitri Young .10
258 Pokey Reese .10
259 Adam Dunn .50
260 David Espinosa, Dane Sardinha .10
261 2001 Cincinnati Reds .10
262 Todd Helton .50
263 Mike Hampton .20
264 Juan Pierre .10
265 Larry Walker .25
266 Juan Uribe .10
267 Jose Ortiz .10
268 Jeff Cirillo .10
269 Jason Jennings, Luke Hudson .10
270 2001 Colorado Rockies .10
271 Ichiro Suzuki 1.50
272 Larry Walker .20
273 Alex Rodriguez .75
274 Barry Bonds 1.00
275 Roger Clemens .75
276 Curt Schilling .15
277 Freddy Garcia .10
278 Randy Johnson .25
279 Mariano Rivera .15
280 Robb Nen .10
281 Jason Giambi .25
282 Jorge Posada .15
283 Jim Thome .25
284 Edgar Martinez .10
285 Andruw Jones .20
286 Chipper Jones .50
287 Matt Williams .15
288 Curt Schilling .20
289 Derek Jeter 1.00
290 Mike Mussina .25
291 Bret Boone .10
292 Alfonso Soriano .40
293 Randy Johnson .25
294 Tom Glavine .20
295 Curt Schilling .25
296 Randy Johnson .40
297 Derek Jeter 1.00
298 Tino Martinez .10
299 Curt Schilling .20
300 Luis Gonzalez .20

Day at the Park

NM/M

Complete Set (6): 15.00
Inserted 1:23
DP1 Ichiro Suzuki 3.00
DP2 Derek Jeter 5.00
DP3 Alex Rodriguez 4.00
DP4 Mark McGwire 4.00
DP5 Barry Bonds 5.00
DP6 Sammy Sosa 3.00

Night-Gamers

NM/M

Complete Set (12): 10.00
Common Player: .50
Inserted 1:11
NG1 Todd Helton .75
NG2 Manny Ramirez .75
NG3 Ivan Rodriguez .50
NG4 Albert Pujols 2.50
NG5 Greg Maddux 1.50
NG6 Carlos Delgado .50
NG7 Frank Thomas .75
NG8 Derek Jeter 3.00
NG9 Troy Glaus .50
NG10 Jeff Bagwell .75
NG11 Juan Gonzalez .75
NG12 Randy Johnson 1.00

Sandlot Stars

NM/M

Complete Set (12): 15.00
Common Player: .75
Inserted 1:11
SS1 Ken Griffey Jr. 1.50
SS2 Derek Jeter 3.00
SS3 Ichiro Suzuki 2.00
SS4 Nomar Garciaparra 2.00
SS5 Sammy Sosa 2.00
SS6 Chipper Jones 1.00
SS7 Jason Giambi .75
SS8 Alex Rodriguez 2.50
SS9 Mark McGwire 2.50
SS10 Barry Bonds 3.00
SS11 Mike Piazza 2.00
SS12 Vladimir Guerrero 1.00

Special Collection Jerseys

NM/M

Common Player: 8.00
Inserted 1:144
StB Stan Bahnsen 8.00
SaB Sal Bando 10.00
BC Bert Campaneris 10.00
AD Andre Dawson 15.00
RF Rollie Fingers 15.00
MG Mark Grace 15.00
MH Mike Hegan 8.00
CH "Catfish" Hunter 20.00
RJ Reggie Jackson 15.00
FJ Ferguson Jenkins 15.00
PL Paul Linblad 8.00
JR Joe Rudi 10.00
RS Ryne Sandberg 50.00
SS Sammy Sosa 25.00
BW Billy Williams 10.00

Timeless Teams Jerseys

NM/M

Common Player: 10.00
Inserted 1:144
JB Johnny Bench 20.00
DE Dwight Evans 15.00
RF Rollie Fingers 15.00
CH "Catfish" Hunter 15.00
RJ Reggie Jackson 15.00
AJ Andruw Jones 15.00
CJ Chipper Jones 15.00
FL Fred Lynn 15.00
GM Greg Maddux SP
EMa Edgar Martinez 15.00
WM Willie McCovey 15.00

EMu Eddie Murray 15.00
KS Kazuhiro Sasaki 10.00
IS Ichiro Suzuki SP

Timeless Teams Combos

NM/M

Inserted 1:288
NYY00 Roger Clemens, Mariano Rivera, Bernie Williams 40.00
ATL96 Greg Maddux, Chipper Jones, Andruw Jones 40.00
OAK74 Rollie Fingers, Jim "Catfish" Hunter, Reggie Jackson 40.00
HOF36 Ty Cobb, Babe Ruth, Honus Wagner (pants) 1,500

Timeless Teams Bat

NM/M

Inserted 1:288
SEA Ichiro Suzuki, Edgar Martinez, John Olerud, Bret Boone 75.00
NYY Mariano Rivera, Bernie Williams, Paul O'Neill, Jorge Posada 40.00
ATL Tom Glavine, Greg Maddux, Chipper Jones, Andruw Jones 40.00
CLE Juan Gonzalez, Jim Thome, Roberto Alomar, Kenny Lofton 30.00
OAK Jose Canseco, Ricky Henderson, Dave Parker, Don Baylor 30.00
OF Mickey Mantle, Joe DiMaggio, Reggie Jackson, Babe Ruth 300.00
1B Willie McCovey, Frank Thomas, Hank Greenberg, Eddie Murray 30.00
OF Ken Griffey Jr., Barry Bonds, Ricky Henderson, Tony Gwynn 50.00

Vintage Aces Jerseys

NM/M

Common Player: 8.00
Inserted 1:144
RC Roger Clemens SP
JD John Denny 8.00
TH Tim Hudson 10.00
FJ Ferguson Jenkins 10.00
RJ Randy Johnson 20.00
GM Greg Maddux 25.00
JM Juan Marichal 15.00
MMa Mike Marshall 8.00
PM Pedro Martinez 20.00
MMu Mike Mussina 25.00
HN Hideo Nomo 20.00
NR Nolan Ryan 100.00
JS Johnny Sain 20.00
MT Mike Torrez 8.00

Vintage Signature Combos

NM/M

Production 100 sets
FB Carlton Fisk, Johnny Bench 100.00
JM Reggie Jackson, Willie McCovey 80.00
SD Ryne Sandberg, Andre Dawson 100.00
BR Sal Bando, Joe Rudi 40.00
EL Dwight Evans, Fred Lynn 60.00
AT Roberto Alomar, Jim Thome 75.00
BB Yogi Berra, Johnny Bench 100.00
GR Ken Griffey Jr., Alex Rodriguez 300.00
JO Edgar Martinez, John Olerud 60.00

2002 UPPER DECK WORLD SERIES HEROES

NM/M

Complete Set (180): 20.00
Common Player: .15
Common RC (91-135): 1.50
Common (136-180): 1.00
Inserted 1:10
Pack (5): 2.00
Box (24): 40.00

1 Jim "Catfish" Hunter .15
2 Jimmie Foxx .50
3 Mark McGwire 2.00
4 Rollie Fingers .25
5 Rickey Henderson .40
6 Joe Carter .15
7 John Olerud .15
8 Roberto Alomar .50
9 Pat Hentgen .15
10 Devon White .15
11 Eddie Mathews .50
12 Greg Maddux 1.00
13 Chipper Jones .75
14 Tom Glavine .25
15 Andruw Jones .50
16 David Justice .25
17 Fred McGriff .15
18 Ryan Klesko .15
19 John Smoltz .25
20 Javy Lopez .25
21 Marquis Grissom .15
22 Robin Yount .75
23 Ozzie Smith .75
24 Frankie Frisch .15
25 Stan Musial 1.00
26 Randy Johnson .75
27 Luis Gonzalez .25
28 Matt Williams .15
29 Steve Finley .15
30 Sandy Koufax 1.50
31 Duke Snider .50
32 Kirk Gibson .15
33 Steve Garvey .15
34 Jackie Robinson 1.50
35 Don Drysdale .50
36 Juan Marichal .50
37 Mel Ott .50
38 Orlando Cepeda .15
39 Jim Thome .75
40 Manny Ramirez .50
41 Omar Vizquel .15
42 Lou Boudreau .15
43 Gary Sheffield .25
44 Moises Alou .25
45 Livan Hernandez .15
46 Edgar Renteria .25
47 Al Leiter .15
48 Tom Seaver .75
49 Gary Carter .15
50 Mike Piazza 1.00
51 Nolan Ryan 2.00
52 Robin Ventura .15
53 Mike Hampton .15
54 Jesse Orosco .15
55 Cal Ripken Jr. 2.00
56 Brooks Robinson .75
57 Tony Gwynn .75
58 Kevin Brown .15
59 Curt Schilling .50
60 Cy Young .50
61 Honus Wagner .75
62 Willie Stargell .40
63 Wade Boggs .40
64 Carlton Fisk .40
65 Ken Griffey Sr. .15
66 Joe Morgan .15
67 Johnny Bench 1.00
68 Barry Larkin .40
69 Jose Rijo .15
70 Ty Cobb 1.50
71 Kirby Puckett 1.00
72 Chuck Knoblauch .15
73 Harmon Killebrew .50
74 Mickey Mantle 2.50
75 Joe DiMaggio 2.00
76 Don Larsen .40
77 Thurman Munson .75
78 Roger Maris 1.50
79 Phil Rizzuto .50
80 Babe Ruth 2.50
81 Lou Gehrig 2.00
82 Billy Martin .40
83 Derek Jeter 2.00
84 Roger Clemens 1.50
85 Tino Martinez .15
86 Bernie Williams .50
87 Mariano Rivera .25
88 Andy Pettitte .40
89 David Wells .15
90 Jorge Posada .25
91 *Rodrigo Rosario* 1.50
92 *Brandon Puffer* 1.50
93 *Franklyn German* 1.50
94 *Reed Johnson* 1.50
95 *Chris Baker* 1.50
96 *John Ennis* 1.50
97 *Luis Martinez* 1.50
98 *Takaki Nomura* 1.50
99 *So Taguchi* 4.00
100 *Michael Crudale* 1.50
101 *Francis Beltran* 1.50
102 *Steve Kent* 1.50
103 *Jorge Sosa* 1.50
104 *Felix Escalona* 1.50
105 *Jose Valverde* 1.50
106 *Doug Devore* 1.50
107 *Kazuhisa Ishii* 4.00
108 *Victor Alvarez* 1.50
109 *Eric Good* 1.50
110 *Jorge Nunez* 1.50
111 *Ron Calloway* 1.50
112 *Nelson Castro* 1.50
113 Matt Thornton 1.50
114 *Luis Ugueto* 1.50
115 *Hansel Izquierdo* 1.50
116 *Jaime Cerda* 1.50
117 *Mark Corey* 1.50
118 *Tyler Yates* 2.50
119 *Satoru Komiyama* 1.50
120 *Steve Bechler* 1.50
121 *Ben Howard* 1.50
122 *Anderson Machado* 1.50
123 *Jorge Padilla* 1.50
124 *Eric Junge* 1.50
125 *Adrian Burnside* 1.50
126 *Mike Gonzalez* 1.50
127 *Anastacio Martinez* 1.50
128 *Josh Hancock* 1.50
129 *Rene Reyes* 1.50
130 *Aaron Cook* 1.50
131 *Cam Esslinger* 1.50
132 *Juan Brito* 1.50
133 *Miguel Ascencio* 1.50
134 *Kevin Frederick* 1.50
135 *Edwin Almonte* 1.50
136 Troy Glaus 1.00
137 Darin Erstad 1.00
138 Jeff Bagwell 1.50
139 Lance Berkman 1.50
140 Tim Hudson 1.25
141 Eric Chavez 1.25
142 Barry Zito 1.50
143 Carlos Delgado 1.00
144 Richie Sexson 1.50
145 Albert Pujols 4.00
146 Sammy Sosa 4.00
147 Kerry Wood 2.00
148 Greg Vaughn 1.00
149 Shawn Green 1.00
150 Vladimir Guerrero 2.50
151 Barry Bonds 6.00
152 C.C. Sabathia 1.00
153 Ichiro Suzuki 5.00
154 Freddy Garcia 1.00
155 Edgar Martinez 1.00
156 Josh Beckett 1.00
157 Cliff Floyd 1.00
158 Mo Vaughn 1.00
159 Jeromy Burnitz 1.00
160 Sean Burroughs 1.00
161 Phil Nevin 1.00
162 Scott Rolen 2.00
163 Brian Giles 1.25
164 Alex Rodriguez 5.00
165 Ivan Rodriguez 1.50
166 Juan Gonzalez 1.25
167 Rafael Palmeiro 1.50
168 Nomar Garciaparra 4.00
169 Pedro J. Martinez 2.00
170 Ken Griffey Jr. 4.00
171 Adam Dunn 1.50
172 Todd Helton 1.50
173 Mike Sweeney 1.00
174 Carlos Beltran 1.00
175 Dmitri Young 1.00
176 Doug Mientkiewicz 1.00
177 Torii Hunter 1.00
178 Frank Thomas 1.50
179 Magglio Ordonez 1.00
180 Jason Giambi 1.50

World Series Heroes Base

NM/M

DJ Derek Jeter 35.00

World Series Heroes Bats

NM/M

Common Player: 15.00
Inserted 1:288
JD Joe DiMaggio/SP 100.00
MM Mickey Mantle 125.00
KP Kirby Puckett 25.00
ES Enos Slaughter 15.00

World Series Heroes Jerseys

NM/M

Common Player: 10.00
Inserted 1:288
JC Joe Carter 10.00
CF Carlton Fisk 15.00
DL Don Larsen 20.00
BM Bill Mazeroski 15.00

World Series Heroes Jerseys Autograph

No Pricing
Production 25 sets

Match-ups Memorabilia

NM/M

Common Card: 8.00
Inserted 1:24
MU00 Mike Piazza, Roger Clemens 15.00
MU00a Andy Pettitte, Mike Piazza 15.00
MU00b Al Leiter, Derek Jeter 10.00
MU00d Edgardo Alfonzo, Mariano Rivera 8.00
MU00e John Franco, Derek Jeter 10.00
MU00c Robin Ventura, Roger Clemens 8.00
MU01 Mariano Rivera, Luis Gonzalez 8.00
MU01a Paul O'Neill, Curt Schilling 8.00
MU01b Bernie Williams, Randy Johnson 8.00
MU01c David Justice, Curt Schilling 8.00
MU01d Randy Johnson, Bernie Williams 8.00
MU01e Curt Schilling, Tino Martinez 8.00
MU01f Roger Clemens, Luis Gonzalez 15.00
MU01g Paul O'Neill, Byung-Hyun Kim 10.00
MU01h Luis Gonzalez, Mariano Rivera/97 12.00
MU03 Honus Wagner, Cy Young 100.00

MU09 Ty Cobb, Honus Wagner/SP 125.00
MU30 Jimmie Foxx 25.00
MU36 Joe DiMaggio, Mel Ott/SP 80.00
MU49 Duke Snider, Joe DiMaggio 25.00
MU53 Jackie Robinson, Billy Martin 25.00
MU55 Mickey Mantle, Jackie Robinson 110.00
MU56 Don Larsen, Duke Snider 25.00
MU56a Don Larsen, Jackie Robinson 20.00
MU57 Eddie Mathews, Yogi Berra 15.00
MU58 Yogi Berra, Eddie Mathews 15.00
MU62 Roger Maris, Juan Marichal 40.00
MU63 Sandy Koufax, Mickey Mantle 100.00
MU66 Don Drysdale, Brooks Robinson/SP 40.00
MU69 Nolan Ryan, Brooks Robinson 50.00
MU72 Joe Morgan, Jim "Catfish" Hunter 8.00
MU72a Rollie Fingers, Johnny Bench 10.00
MU73 Tom Seaver, "Catfish" Hunter 15.00
MU74 Jim "Catfish" Hunter, Steve Garvey 8.00
MU74a Davey Lopes, Jim "Catfish" Hunter 8.00
MU76 Ken Griffey Sr., Thurman Munson 12.00
MU76a Thurman Munson, Johnny Bench 20.00
MU78 Thurman Munson, Steve Garvey 15.00
MU78a Bill Russell, Thurman Munson 12.00
MU81 Steve Garvey, Dave Winfield 8.00
MU82 Robin Yount, Ozzie Smith 15.00
MU83 Cal Ripken Jr., Joe Morgan 25.00
MU84 Jack Morris, Tony Gwynn 12.00
MU86 Jesse Orosco, Roger Clemens 15.00
MU87 Ozzie Smith, Kirby Puckett 15.00
MU88 Mark McGwire, Kirk Gibson/SP 60.00
MU90 Barry Larkin, Mark McGwire/SP 20.00
MU91 Tom Glavine, Kirby Puckett 15.00
MU93 Joe Carter, Curt Schilling 8.00
MU95 Dennis Martinez, David Justice 8.00
MU96 Andruw Jones, Andy Pettitte 8.00
MU96a Tim Raines, Tom Glavine 10.00
MU96b Kenny Rogers, Chipper Jones 8.00
MU95a Kenny Lofton, John Smoltz 8.00
MU97 Jim Thome, Kevin Brown 10.00
MU98 Tony Gwynn, Bernie Williams 10.00
MU98a Trevor Hoffman, Bernie Williams/SP 8.00
MU99 Jorge Posada, Greg Maddux 15.00
MU99a Greg Maddux, Derek Jeter 15.00
MU99b Paul O'Neill, John Smoltz 8.00
MU99c Chipper Jones, Mariano Rivera 15.00

Patch Collection

NM/M

Common Patch: 15.00
Inserted 1:hobby box
WS03 1903 World Series 25.00
WS05 1905 World Series 25.00
WS06 1906 World Series 20.00
WS07 1907 World Series 20.00
WS08 1908 World Series 25.00
WS09 1909 World Series 20.00

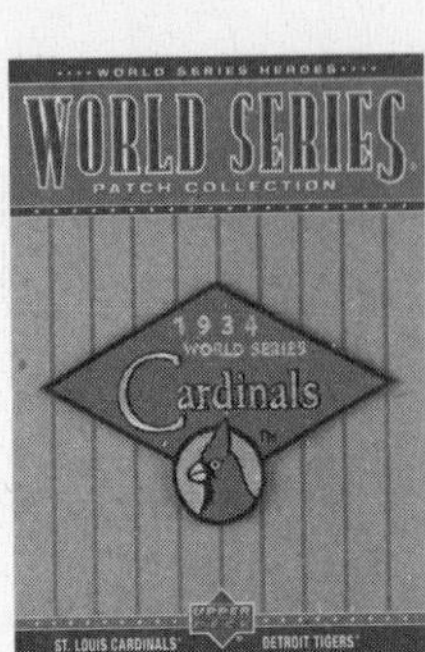

WS10 1910 World Series 20.00
WS11 1911 World Series 20.00
WS12 1912 World Series 30.00
WS13 1913 World Series 20.00
WS14 1914 World Series 25.00
WS15 1915 World Series 20.00
WS16 1916 World Series 25.00
WS17 1917 World Series 20.00
WS18 1918 World Series 30.00
WS19 1919 World Series 25.00
WS20 1920 World Series 20.00
WS21 1921 World Series 15.00
WS22 1922 World Series 20.00
WS23 1923 World Series 20.00
WS24 1924 World Series 20.00
WS25 1925 World Series 25.00
WS26 1926 World Series 25.00
WS27 1927 World Series 30.00
WS28 1928 World Series 25.00
WS29 1929 World Series 20.00
WS30 1930 World Series 20.00
WS31 1931 World Series 25.00
WS32 1932 World Series 30.00
WS33 1933 World Series 20.00
WS34 1934 World Series 20.00
WS35 1935 World Series 20.00
WS36 1936 World Series 20.00
WS37 1937 World Series 20.00
WS38 1938 World Series 25.00
WS39 1939 World Series 20.00
WS40 1940 World Series 20.00
WS41 1941 World Series 20.00
WS42 1942 World Series 20.00
WS43 1943 World Series 20.00
WS44 1944 World Series 30.00
WS45 1945 World Series 20.00
WS46 1946 World Series 25.00
WS47 1947 World Series 25.00
WS48 1948 World Series 30.00
WS49 1949 World Series 25.00
WS50 1950 World Series 25.00
WS51 1951 World Series 25.00
WS52 1952 World Series 20.00
WS53 1953 World Series 25.00
WS54 1954 World Series 15.00
WS55 1955 World Series 25.00
WS56 1956 World Series 25.00
WS57 1957 World Series 25.00
WS58 1958 World Series 20.00
WS59 1959 World Series 20.00
WS60 1960 World Series 20.00
WS61 1961 World Series 35.00
WS62 1962 World Series 20.00
WS63 1963 World Series 20.00
WS64 1964 World Series 20.00
WS65 1965 World Series 20.00
WS66 1966 World Series 20.00
WS67 1967 World Series 20.00
WS68 1968 World Series 20.00
WS69 1969 World Series 35.00
WS70 1970 World Series 20.00
WS71 1971 World Series 20.00
WS72 1972 World Series 20.00
WS73 1973 World Series 20.00
WS74 1974 World Series 20.00
WS75 1975 World Series 30.00
WS76 1976 World Series 30.00
WS77 1977 World Series 20.00
WS78 1978 World Series 20.00
WS79 1979 World Series 20.00
WS80 1980 World Series 20.00
WS81 1981 World Series 20.00
WS82 1982 World Series 25.00
WS83 1983 World Series 25.00
WS84 1984 World Series 20.00
WS85 1985 World Series 20.00
WS86 1986 World Series 20.00
WS87 1987 World Series 20.00
WS88 1988 World Series 20.00
WS89 1989 World Series 20.00
WS90 1990 World Series 20.00
WS91 1991 World Series 20.00
WS92 1992 World Series 20.00
WS93 1993 World Series 20.00
WS95 1995 World Series 20.00
WS96 1996 World Series 20.00
WS97 1997 World Series 20.00
WS98 1998 World Series 15.00
WS99 1999 World Series 20.00
WS00 2000 World Series
WS01 2001 World Series 20.00

Patch Collection Autographs

NM/M

Inserted 1:336
WS93 Joe Carter 40.00
WS99 Roger Clemens 100.00
WS74 Rollie Fingers 30.00
WS75 Carlton Fisk 60.00
WS81 Steve Garvey 35.00
WS65 Sandy Koufax 250.00
WS56 Don Larsen 60.00
WS89 Mark McGwire 275.00
WS76 Joe Morgan 40.00
WS91 Kirby Puckett 60.00
WS83 Cal Ripken Jr. 175.00
WS70 Brooks Robinson 80.00
WS69 Nolan Ryan 200.00
WS73 Tom Seaver 60.00
WS55 Duke Snider 75.00
WS82 Ozzie Smith 90.00

2002 UPPER DECK 40-MAN

NM/M

Complete Set (1182): 200.00
Common Player: .15
Silvers: 1-3X
Inserted 1:4
Rainbows: 5-10X
Production 40 sets
Hobby Pack (10): 1.75
Hobby Box (24): 30.00
1 Darin Erstad .40
2 Kevin Appier .15
3 Scott Schoeneweis .15
4 Bengie Molina .15
5 Troy Glaus .50
6 Adam Kennedy .15
7 Aaron Sele .15
8 Garret Anderson .25
9 Ramon Ortiz .15
10 Dennis Cook .15
11 Scott Spiezio .15
12 Orlando Palmeiro .15
13 Troy Percival .15
14 David Eckstein .15
15 Jarrod Washburn .40
16 Nathan Haynes .15
17 Benji Gil .15
18 Alfredo Amezega .15
19 Ben Weber .15
20 Al Levine .15
21 Brad Fullmer .15
22 Elpidio Guzman .15
23 Tim Salmon .25
24 Jose Nieves .15
25 Shawn Wooten .15
26 Lou Pote .15
27 Mickey Callaway .15
28 Steve Green .15
29 John Lackey .15
30 Mark Lukasiewicz .15
31 Jorge Fabregas .15
32 Jeff Da Vanon .15
33 Elvin Nina .15
34 Donne Wall .15
35 Eric Chavez .50
36 Jermaine Dye .15
37 Scott Hatteberg .15
38 Mark Mulder .50
39 Ramon Hernandez .15
40 Jim Mecir .15
41 Barry Zito .50
42 Greg Myers .15
43 David Justice .50
44 Mike Magnante .15
45 Terrence Long .15
46 Tim Hudson .50
47 Olmedo Saenz .15
48 Billy Koch .15
49 Carlos Pena .50
50 Mike Venafro .15
51 Mark Ellis .15
52 Randy Velarde .15
53 Jeremy Giambi .15
54 Mike Colagelo .15
55 Mike Holtz .15
56 Chad Bradford .15
57 Miguel Tejada .50
58 Mike Fyhrie .15
59 Eric Hiljus .15
60 Juan Pena .15
61 Mario Valdez .15
62 *Franklyn German* .50
63 Carlos Delgado .50
64 Orlando Hudson .15
65 Chris Carpenter .15
66 Kelvim Escobar .15
67 Felipe Lopez .15
68 Brandon Lyon .15
69 Jose Cruz Jr. .15
70 Luke Prokopec .15
71 Darrin Fletcher .15
72 Bob File .15
73 Felix Heredia .15
74 Mike Sirotka .15
75 Shannon Stewart .15
76 Joe Lawrence .15
77 Chris Woodward .15
78 Dan Plesac .15
79 Pedro Borbon .15
80 Roy Halladay .40
81 Raul Mondesi .40
82 Steve Parris .15
83 Homer Bush .15
84 Esteban Loaiza .15
85 Vernon Wells .15
86 Justin Miller .15
87 Scott Eyre .15
88 Dave Berg .15
89 *Gustavo Chacin* .15
90 *Joe Orloski* .40
91 *Corey Thurman* .15
92 Tom Wilson .15
93 Eric Hinske .50
94 *Chris Baker* .40
95 *Reed Johnson* .40
96 Greg Vaughn .15
97 Toby Hall .15
98 Brent Abernathy .15
99 Bobby Smith .15
100 Tanyon Sturtze .15
101 Chris Gomez .15
102 Joe Kennedy .15
103 Ben Grieve .15
104 Aubrey Huff .15
105 Jesus Colome .15
106 *Felix Escalona* .40
107 Paul Wilson .15
108 Ryan Rupe .15
109 Jason Tyner .15
110 Esteban Yan .15
111 Russ Johnson .15
112 Randy Winn .15
113 Wilson Alvarez .15
114 Wilmy Caceres .15
115 Steve Cox .15
116 Dewon Brazelton .15
117 Doug Creek .15
118 Jason Conti .15
119 John Flaherty .15
120 Delvin James .15
121 *Steve Kent* .15
122 Kevin McGlinchy .15
123 Travis Phelps .15
124 Bobby Seay .15
125 Travis Harper .15
126 Victor Zambrano .15
127 Jace Brewer .15
128 Jason Smith .15
129 Ramon Soler .15
130 *Brandon Backe* .50
131 *Jorge Sosa* .25
132 Jim Thome .75
133 Brady Anderson .15

No.	Player	Price
134	C.C. Sabathia	.15
135	Einar Diaz	.15
136	Ricky Gutierrez	.15
137	Danys Baez	.15
138	Bob Wickman	.15
139	Milton Bradley	.15
140	Bartolo Colon	.40
141	Jolbert Cabrera	.15
142	Eddie Taubensee	.15
143	Ellis Burks	.15
144	Omar Vizquel	.40
145	Eddie Perez	.15
146	Jaret Wright	.15
147	Chuck Finley	.15
148	Paul Shuey	.15
149	Travis Fryman	.15
150	Wil Cordero	.15
151	Ricardo Rincon	.15
152	Victor Martinez	.15
153	Charles Nagy	.15
154	Alex Escobar	.15
155	Russell Branyan	.15
156	Matt Lawton	.15
157	Ryan Drese	.15
158	Jerrod Riggan	.15
159	David Riske	.15
160	Jake Westbrook	.15
161	Mark Wohlers	.15
162	John McDonald	.15
163	Ichiro Suzuki	1.50
164	Freddy Garcia	.15
165	Edgar Martinez	.15
166	Ben Davis	.15
167	Shigetoshi Hasegawa	.15
168	Carlos Guillen	.15
169	Ruben Sierra	.15
170	Joel Pineiro	.15
171	Norm Charlton	.15
172	Bret Boone	.15
173	Jamie Moyer	.15
174	Jeff Nelson	.15
175	Kazuhiro Sasaki	.50
176	Jeff Cirillo	.15
177	Mark McLemore	.15
178	Paul Abbott	.15
179	Mike Cameron	.15
180	Dan Wilson	.15
181	John Olerud	.50
182	Arthur Rhodes	.15
183	Desi Relaford	.15
184	John Halama	.15
185	Antonio Perez	.15
186	Ryan Anderson	.15
187	James Baldwin	.15
188	Ryan Franklin	.15
189	Justin Kaye	.15
190	*J.J. Putz*	.40
191	*Allan Simpson*	.40
192	Matt Thornton	.15
193	*Luis Ugueto*	.40
194	Chris Richard	.15
195	Sidney Ponson	.15
196	Brook Fordyce	.15
197	Luis Matos	.15
198	Josh Towers	.15
199	David Segui	.15
200	Chris Brock	.15
201	Tony Batista	.15
202	Erik Bedard	.15
203	Marty Cordova	.15
204	Jerry Hairston Jr.	.15
205	Jason Johnson	.15
206	Buddy Groom	.15
207	Mike Bordick	.15
208	Melvin Mora	.15
209	Calvin Maduro	.15
210	Jeff Conine	.15
211	Luis Rivera	.15
212	Jay Gibbons	.15
213	B.J. Ryan	.15
214	Sean Douglass	.15
215	Rodrigo Lopez	.15
216	Rick Bauer	.15
217	Scott Erickson	.15
218	Jorge Julio	.15
219	Willis Roberts	.15
220	John Stephens	.15
221	Geronimo Gil	.15
222	Chris Singleton	.15
223	Mike Paradis	.15
224	John Parrish	.15
225	*Steve Bechler*	.50
226	*Mike Moriarty*	.15
227	Luis Garcia	.15
228	Alex Rodriguez	1.50
229	Mark Teixeira	.50
230	Chan Ho Park	.15
231	Todd Van Poppel	.15
232	Mike Young	.15
233	Kenny Rogers	.15
234	Rusty Greer	.15
235	Rafael Palmeiro	.50
236	Francisco Cordero	.15
237	John Rocker	.15
238	Dave Burba	.15
239	Travis Hafner	.15
240	Kevin Mench	.15
241	Carl Everett	.15
242	Ivan Rodriguez	.50
243	Jeff Zimmerman	.15
244	Juan Gonzalez	.50
245	Herbert Perry	.15
246	Rob Bell	.15
247	Doug Davis	.15
248	Frank Catalanotto	.15
249	Jay Powell	.15
250	Gabe Kapler	.15
251	Joaquin Benoit	.15
252	Jovanny Cedeno	.15
253	Hideki Irabu	.15
254	Dan Miceli	.15
255	Danny Kolb	.15
256	Colby Lewis	.15
257	Rich Rodriguez	.15
258	Ismael Valdes	.15
259	Bill Haselman	.15
260	Jason Hart	.15
261	Rudy Seanez	.15
262	*Travis Hughes*	.40
263	Hank Blalock	.50
264	Steve Woodard	.15
265	Nomar Garciaparra	1.50
266	Pedro J. Martinez	.75
267	Frank Castillo	.15
268	Johnny Damon	.15
269	Doug Mirabelli	.15
270	Derek Lowe	.40
271	Shea Hillenbrand	.50
272	Paxton Crawford	.15
273	Tony Clark	.15
274	Dustin Hermanson	.15
275	Trot Nixon	.15
276	John Burkett	.15
277	Rich Garces	.15
278	*Josh Hancock*	.15
279	Michael Coleman	.15
280	Darren Oliver	.15
281	Jason Varitek	.15
282	Jose Offerman	.15
283	Tim Wakefield	.15
284	Rolando Arrojo	.15
285	Rickey Henderson	.50
286	Ugueth Urbina	.15
287	Casey Fossum	.15
288	Manny Ramirez	.50
289	Sun-Woo Kim	.15
290	Juan Diaz	.15
291	Willie Banks	.15
292	*Jorge De La Rosa*	.50
293	Juan Pena	.15
294	Jeff Wallace	.15
295	Calvin Pickering	.15
296	*Anastacio Martinez*	.40
297	Carlos Baerga	.15
298	Rey Sanchez	.15
299	Mike Sweeney	.15
300	Jeff Suppan	.15
301	Brent Mayne	.15
302	Chad Durbin	.15
303	Dan Reichert	.15
304	Raul Ibanez	.15
305	Joe Randa	.15
306	Chris George	.15
307	Michael Tucker	.15
308	Paul Byrd	.15
309	Kris Wilson	.15
310	Luis Alicea	.15
311	Neifi Perez	.15
312	Brian Shouse	.15
313	Chuck Knoblauch	.15
314	Dave McCarty	.15
315	Blake Stein	.15
316	Alexis Gomez	.15
317	Mark Quinn	.15
318	A.J. Hinch	.15
319	Carlos Febles	.15
320	Roberto Hernandez	.15
321	Brandon Berger	.15
322	*Jeff Austin*	.40
323	Corey Bailey	.15
324	Tony Cogan	.15
325	*Nate Field*	.40
326	Jason Grimsley	.15
327	Darrell May	.15
328	Donnie Sadler	.15
329	Carlos Beltran	.15
330	*Miguel Asencio*	.40
331	Jeff Weaver	.15
332	Bobby Higginson	.15
333	Mike Rivera	.15
334	Matt Anderson	.15
335	Craig Paquette	.15
336	Jose Lima	.15
337	Juan Acevedo	.15
338	Danny Patterson	.15
339	Andres Torres	.15
340	Dean Palmer	.15
341	Randall Simon	.15
342	Craig Monroe	.15
343	Damion Easley	.15
344	Robert Fick	.15
345	Steve Sparks	.15
346	Dmitri Young	.15
347	Nate Cornejo	.15
348	Matt Miller	.15
349	Wendell Magee	.15
350	Shane Halter	.15
351	Brian Moehler	.15
352	Mitch Meluskey	.15
353	Jose Macias	.15
354	Mark Redman	.15
355	Jeff Farnsworth	.15
356	Kris Keller	.15
357	Adam Pettyjohn	.15
358	Fernando Rodney	.15
359	Andy Van Hekken	.15
360	Damian Jackson	.15
361	Jose Paniagua	.15
362	Jacob Cruz	.15
363	Doug Mientkiewicz	.15
364	Torii Hunter	.15
365	Brad Radke	.15
366	Denny Hocking	.15
367	Mike Jackson	.15
368	Eddie Guardado	.15
369	Jacque Jones	.15
370	Joe Mays	.15
371	Matt Kinney	.15
372	Kyle Lohse	.15
373	David Ortiz	.15
374	Luis Rivas	.15
375	Jay Canizaro	.15
376	Dustan Mohr	.15
377	LaTroy Hawkins	.15
378	Warren Morris	.15
379	A.J. Pierzynski	.15
380	Eric Milton	.15
381	Bob Wells	.15
382	Cristian Guzman	.15
383	Brian Buchanan	.15
384	Bobby Kielty	.15
385	Corey Koskie	.15
386	J.C. Romero	.15
387	Jack Cressend	.15
388	Mike Duvall	.15
389	Tony Fiore	.15
390	Tom Prince	.15
391	Todd Sears	.15
392	*Kevin Frederick*	.40
393	Frank Thomas	.50
394	Mark Buehrle	.15
395	Jon Garland	.15
396	Jeff Liefer	.15
397	Magglio Ordonez	.50
398	Rocky Biddle	.15
399	Lorenzo Barcelo	.15
400	Ray Durham	.15
401	Bob Howry	.15
402	Aaron Rowand	.15
403	Keith Foulke	.15
404	Paul Konerko	.50
405	Sandy Alomar Jr.	.15
406	Mark Johnson	.15
407	Carlos Lee	.15
408	Jose Valentin	.15
409	Jon Rauch	.15
410	Royce Clayton	.15
411	Kenny Lofton	.40
412	Tony Graffanino	.15
413	Todd Ritchie	.15
414	Antonio Osuna	.15
415	Gary Glover	.15
416	Mike Porzio	.15
417	Danny Wright	.15
418	Kelly Wunsch	.15
419	Miguel Olivo	.15
420	*Edwin Almonte*	.15
421	*Kyle Kane*	.50
422	*Mitch Wylie*	.15
423	Derek Jeter	2.00
424	Jason Giambi	.50
425	Roger Clemens	1.50
426	Enrique Wilson	.15
427	David Wells	.15
428	Mike Mussina	.50
429	Bernie Williams	.50
430	Mike Stanton	.15
431	Sterling Hitchcock	.15
432	Alex Graman	.15
433	Robin Ventura	.50
434	Mariano Rivera	.50
435	Jay Tessmer	.15
436	Andy Pettitte	.50
437	John Vander Wal	.15
438	Adrian Hernandez	.15
439	Alberto Castillo	.15
440	Steve Karsay	.15
441	Alfonso Soriano	.75
442	Rondell White	.15
443	Nick Johnson	.50
444	Jorge Posada	.50
445	Ramiro Mendoza	.15
446	Gerald Williams	.15
447	Orlando Hernandez	.15
448	Randy Choate	.15
449	Randy Keisler	.15
450	Ted Lilly	.15
451	Christian Parker	.15
452	Ron Coomer	.15
453	Marcus Thames	.15
454	Drew Henson	.50
455	Jeff Bagwell	.50
456	Wade Miller	.15
457	Lance Berkman	.50
458	Julio Lugo	.15
459	Roy Oswalt	.40
460	Nelson Cruz	.15
461	Morgan Ensberg	.15
462	Geoff Blum	.15
463	*Ryan Jamison*	.50
464	Billy Wagner	.15
465	Dave Mlicki	.15
466	Brad Ausmus	.15
467	Jose Vizcaino	.15
468	Craig Biggio	.50
469	Shane Reynolds	.15
470	Gregg Zaun	.15
471	Octavio Dotel	.15
472	Carlos Hernandez	.15
473	Richard Hidalgo	.15
474	Daryle Ward	.15
475	Orlando Merced	.15
476	John Buck	.15
477	Adam Everett	.15
478	Doug Brocail	.15
479	Brad Lidge	.15
480	Scott Linebrink	.15
481	T.J. Mathews	.15
482	Greg Miller	.15
483	Hipolito Pichardo	.15
484	*Brandon Puffer*	.15
485	Ricky Stone	.15
486	Jason Lane	.15
487	Brian L. Hunter	.15
488	*Rodrigo Rosario*	.50
489	*Tom Shearn*	.50
490	Gary Sheffield	.40
491	Tom Glavine	.40
492	Mike Remlinger	.15
493	Henry Blanco	.15
494	Vinny Castilla	.15
495	Chris Hammond	.15
496	Kevin Millwood	.50
497	Darren Holmes	.15
498	Cory Aldridge	.15
499	Tim Spooneybarger	.15
500	Rafael Furcal	.50
501	Albie Lopez	.15
502	Javy Lopez	.40
503	Greg Maddux	1.00
504	Andruw Jones	.50
505	Steve Torrealba	.15
506	George Lombard	.15
507	B.J. Surhoff	.15
508	Marcus Giles	.15
509	Derrick Lewis	.15
510	Wes Helms	.15
511	John Smoltz	.50
512	Chipper Jones	.75
513	Jason Marquis	.15
514	Mark DeRosa	.15
515	Jung Bong	.15
516	*Kevin Gryboski*	.15
517	Damian Moss	.15
518	Horacio Ramirez	.15
519	Scott Sobkowiak	.15
520	Billy Sylvester	.15
521	Nick Green	.15
522	Travis Wilson	.15
523	Ryan Langerhans	.15
524	*John Ennis*	.50
525	*John Foster*	.15
526	Keith Lockhart	.15
527	Julio Franco	.15
528	Richie Sexson	.50
529	Jeffrey Hammonds	.15

No.	Player	Price
530	Ben Sheets	.50
531	Mike DeJean	.15
532	Mark Loretta	.15
533	Alex Ochoa	.15
534	Jamey Wright	.15
535	Jose Hernandez	.15
536	Glendon Rusch	.15
537	Geoff Jenkins	.50
538	Luis S. Lopez	.15
539	Curtis Leskanic	.15
540	Chad Fox	.15
541	Tyler Houston	.15
542	Nick Neugebauer	.15
543	Matt Stairs	.15
544	Paul Rigdon	.15
545	Bill Hall	.15
546	Luis Vizcaino	.15
547	Lenny Harris	.15
548	Alex Sanchez	.15
549	Raul Casanova	.15
550	Eric Young	.15
551	*Jeff Deardorff*	.15
552	Nelson Figueroa	.15
553	Ron Belliard	.15
554	Mike Buddie	.15
555	Jose Cabrera	.15
556	J.M. Gold	.15
557	Ray King	.15
558	Jose Mieses	.15
559	*Takahito Nomura*	.50
560	Ruben Quevedo	.15
561	Jackson Melian	.15
562	Cristian Guerrero	.15
563	Paul Bako	.15
564	*Luis Martinez*	.50
565	*Brian Mallette*	.50
566	Matt Morris	.50
567	Tino Martinez	.40
568	Fernando Vina	.15
569	Gene Stechschulte	.15
570	Andy Benes	.15
571	Placido Polanco	.15
572	Luis Garcia	.15
573	Jim Edmonds	.50
574	Bud Smith	.15
575	Mike Matheny	.15
576	Garrett Stephenson	.15
577	Miguel Cairo	.15
578	Darryl Kile	.15
579	Mike Timlin	.15
580	Rick Ankiel	.15
581	Jason Isringhausen	.15
582	Albert Pujols	1.50
583	Eli Marrero	.15
584	Steve Kline	.15
585	J.D. Drew	.50
586	Mike DiFelice	.15
587	Dave Veres	.15
588	Kerry Robinson	.15
589	Edgar Renteria	.15
590	Woody Williams	.15
591	Chance Caple	.15
592	*Michael Crudale*	.15
593	Luther Hackman	.15
594	Josh Pearce	.15
595	Kevin Joseph	.15
596	Jimmy Journell	.15
597	*Jeremy Lambert*	.40
598	Mike Matthews	.15
599	Les Walrond	.15
600	Keith McDonald	.15
601	William Ortega	.15
602	*Scotty Layfield*	.50
603	*So Taguchi*	1.00
604	Eduardo Perez	.15
605	Sammy Sosa	1.50
606	Kerry Wood	.75
607	Kyle Farnsworth	.15
608	Alex Gonzalez	.15
609	Tom Gordon	.15
610	Carlos Zambrano	.15
611	Roosevelt Brown	.15
612	Bill Mueller	.15
613	Mark Prior	1.50
614	Darren Lewis	.15
615	Joe Girardi	.15
616	Fred McGriff	.50
617	Jon Lieber	.15
618	Robert Machado	.15
619	Corey Patterson	.50
620	Joe Borowski	.15
621	Todd Hundley	.15
622	Jason Bere	.15
623	Moises Alou	.40
624	Jeff Fassero	.15
625	Jesus Sanchez	.15
626	Chris Stynes	.15
627	Delino DeShields	.15
628	Augie Ojeda	.15
629	Juan Cruz	.15
630	Ben Christensen	.15
631	Mike Meyers	.15
632	Will Ohman	.15
633	Steve Smyth	.15
634	Mark Bellhorn	.15
635	Nate Frese	.15
636	David Kelton	.15
637	*Francis Beltran*	.40
638	Antonio Alfonseca	.15
639	Donovan Osborne	.15
640	Shawn Sonnier	.15
641	Matt Clement	.15
642	Luis Gonzalez	.25
643	Brian Anderson	.15
644	Randy Johnson	.75
645	Mark Grace	.50
646	Danny Bautista	.15
647	Junior Spivey	.15
648	Jay Bell	.15
649	Miguel Batista	.15
650	Tony Womack	.15
651	Byung-Hyun Kim	.15
652	Steve Finley	.40
653	Rick Helling	.15
654	Curt Schilling	.50
655	Erubiel Durazo	.15
656	Chris Donnels	.15
657	Greg Colbrunn	.15
658	Mike Morgan	.15
659	Jose Guillen	.15
660	Matt Williams	.50
661	Craig Counsell	.15
662	Greg Swindell	.15
663	Rod Barajas	.15
664	David Dellucci	.15
665	Todd Stottlemyre	.15
666	*P.J. Bevis*	.15
667	Mike Koplove	.15
668	Mike Myers	.15
669	John Patterson	.15
670	Bret Prinz	.15
671	*Jeremy Ward*	.50
672	Danny Klassen	.15
673	Luis Terrero	.15
674	*Jose Valverde*	.50
675	*Doug Devore*	.50
676	Quinton McCracken	.15
677	Paul LoDuca	.15
678	Mark Grudzielanek	.15
679	Kevin Brown	.50
680	Paul Quantrill	.15
681	Shawn Green	.50
682	Hideo Nomo	.50
683	Eric Gagne	.15
684	Giovanni Carrara	.15
685	Marquis Grissom	.15
686	Hiram Bocachica	.15
687	Guillermo Mota	.15
688	Alex Cora	.15
689	Odalis Perez	.15
690	Brian Jordan	.15
691	Andy Ashby	.15
692	Eric Karros	.40
693	Chad Krueter	.15
694	Dave Roberts	.15
695	Omar Daal	.15
696	Dave Hansen	.15
697	Adrian Beltre	.50
698	Terry Mulholland	.15
699	Cesar Izturis	.15
700	Steve Colyer	.15
701	Carlos Garcia	.15
702	Ricardo Rodriguez	.15
703	Darren Dreifort	.15
704	Jeff Reboulet	.15
705	*Victor Alvarez*	.50
706	*Kazuhisa Ishii*	2.00
707	Jose Vidro	.15
708	Henry Mateo	.15
709	Tony Armas Jr.	.15
710	Carl Pavano	.15
711	Peter Bergeron	.15
712	Bruce Chen	.15
713	Orlando Cabrera	.15
714	Britt Reames	.15
715	Masato Yoshii	.15
716	Fernando Tatis	.15
717	Graeme Lloyd	.15
718	Scott Stewart	.15
719	Lou Collier	.15
720	Michael Barrett	.15
721	Vladimir Guerrero	.75
722	Troy Mattes	.15
723	Brian Schneider	.15
724	Lee Stevens	.15
725	Javier Vazquez	.15
726	Brad Wilkerson	.15
727	Zach Day	.15
728	Ed Vosberg	.15
729	Tomokazu Ohka	.15
730	Mike Mordecai	.15
731	Donnie Bridges	.15
732	Ron Chiavacci	.15
733	T.J. Tucker	.15
734	Scott Hodges	.15
735	Valentino Pascucci	.15
736	Andres Galarraga	.15
737	Scott Downs	.15
738	*Eric Good*	.15
739	*Ron Calloway*	.50
740	*Jorge Nunez*	.15
741	Henry Rodriguez	.15
742	Jeff Kent	.15
743	Russ Ortiz	.15
744	Felix Rodriguez	.15
745	Benito Santiago	.15
746	Tsuyoshi Shinjo	.50
747	Tim Worrell	.15
748	Marvin Benard	.15
749	Kurt Ainsworth	.15
750	Edwards Guzman	.15
751	J.T. Snow	.15
752	Jason Christiansen	.15
753	Robb Nen	.15
754	Barry Bonds	2.00
755	Shawon Dunston	.15
756	Chad Zerbe	.15
757	Ramon E. Martinez	.15
758	Calvin Murray	.15
759	Pedro Feliz	.15
760	Jason Schmidt	.15
761	Damon Minor	.15
762	Reggie Sanders	.15
763	Rich Aurilia	.15
764	Kirk Rueter	.15
765	David Bell	.15
766	Yorvit Torrealba	.15
767	Livan Hernandez	.15
768	Felix Diaz	.15
769	Aaron Fultz	.15
770	Ryan Jensen	.15
771	Arturo McDowell	.15
772	Carlos Valderrama	.15
773	*Nelson Castro*	.50
774	Jay Witasick	.15
775	Deivis Santos	.15
776	Josh Beckett	.15
777	Charles Johnson	.15
778	Derrek Lee	.15
779	A.J. Burnett	.15
780	Vic Darensbourg	.15
781	Cliff Floyd	.50
782	Jose Cueto	.15
783	Nate Teut	.15
784	Alex Gonzalez	.15
785	Brad Penny	.15
786	Kevin Olsen	.15
787	Mike Lowell	.15
788	Mike Redmond	.15
789	Braden Looper	.15
790	Eric Owens	.15
791	Andy Fox	.15
792	Vladimir Nunez	.15
793	Luis Castillo	.15
794	Ryan Dempster	.15
795	Armando Almanza	.15
796	Preston Wilson	.15
797	Pablo Ozuna	.15
798	Gary Knotts	.15
799	Ramon Castro	.15
800	Benito Baez	.15
801	Michael Tejera	.15
802	Claudio Vargas	.15
803	Chip Ambres	.15
804	*Hansel Izquierdo*	.50
805	Tim Raines	.15
806	Marty Malloy	.15
807	Julian Tavarez	.15
808	Roberto Alomar	.50
809	Al Leiter	.50
810	Jeromy Burnitz	.15
811	John Franco	.15
812	Edgardo Alfonzo	.15
813	Mike Piazza	1.00
814	Shawn Estes	.15
815	Joe McEwing	.15
816	David Weathers	.15
817	Pedro Astacio	.15
818	Timoniel Perez	.15
819	Grant Roberts	.15
820	Rey Ordonez	.15
821	Steve Trachsel	.15
822	Roger Cedeno	.15
823	Mark Johnson	.15
824	Armando Benitez	.15
825	Vance Wilson	.15
826	Jay Payton	.15
827	Mo Vaughn	.50
828	Scott Strickland	.15
829	Mark Guthrie	.15
830	Jeff D'Amico	.15
831	*Mark Corey*	.50
832	Kane Davis	.15
833	Jae Weong Seo	.15
834	Pat Strange	.15
835	*Adam Walker*	.15
836	Tyler Walker	.15
837	Gary Matthews Jr.	.15
838	*Jaime Cerda*	.25
839	*Satoru Komiyama*	.50
840	*Tyler Yates*	.50
841	John Valentin	.15
842	Ryan Klesko	.40
843	Wiki Gonzalez	.15
844	Trevor Hoffman	.15
845	Sean Burroughs	.40
846	Alan Embree	.15
847	Dennis Tankersley	.15
848	D'Angelo Jimenez	.15
849	Kevin Jarvis	.15
850	Mark Kotsay	.15
851	Phil Nevin	.25
852	Jeremy Fikac	.15
853	Brett Tomko	.15
854	Brian Lawrence	.15
855	Steve Reed	.15
856	Bubba Trammell	.15
857	Tom Davey	.15
858	Ramon Vazquez	.15
859	Tom Lampkin	.15
860	Bobby Jones	.15
861	Ray Lankford	.15
862	Mark Sweeney	.15
863	Adam Eaton	.15
864	Trenidad Hubbard	.15
865	Jason Boyd	.15
866	Javier Cardona	.15
867	*Clifford Bartosh*	.50
868	Mike Bynum	.15
869	*Eric Cyr*	.50
870	Jose Nunez	.15
871	Ron Gant	.15
872	Deivi Cruz	.15
873	*Ben Howard*	.50
874	*Todd Donovan*	.25
875	*Andy Shibilo*	.15
876	Scott Rolen	.75
877	Jose Mesa	.15
878	Rheal Cormier	.15
879	Travis Lee	.15
880	Mike Lieberthal	.15
881	Brandon Duckworth	.15
882	David Coggin	.15
883	Bobby Abreu	.50
884	Turk Wendell	.15
885	Marlon Byrd	.15
886	Jason Michaels	.15
887	Robert Person	.15
888	Tomas Perez	.15
889	Jimmy Rollins	.15
890	Vicente Padilla	.15
891	Pat Burrell	.50
892	Dave Hollins	.15
893	Randy Wolf	.15
894	Jose Santiago	.15
895	Doug Glanville	.15
896	Cliff Politte	.15
897	Marlon Anderson	.15
898	Ricky Bottalico	.15
899	Terry Adams	.15
900	Brad Baisley	.15
901	Hector Mercado	.15
902	*Elio Serrano*	.50
903	Todd Pratt	.15
904	*Peter Zamora*	.50
905	Nick Punto	.15
906	Ricky Ledee	.15
907	*Eric Junge*	.50
908	*Anderson Machado*	.50
909	*Jorge Padilla*	.50
910	John Mabry	.15
911	Brian Giles	.50
912	Jason Kendall	.40
913	Jack Wilson	.15
914	Kris Benson	.15
915	Aramis Ramirez	.15
916	Mike Fetters	.15
917	Adrian Brown	.15
918	Pokey Reese	.15
919	Dave Williams	.15
920	Mike Benjamin	.15
921	Kip Wells	.15
922	Mike Williams	.15
923	Pat Meares	.15
924	Ron Villone	.15
925	Armando Rios	.15

No.	Player	Price
926	Jimmy Anderson	.15
927	Robert Mackowiak	.15
928	Kevin Young	.15
929	Brian Boehringer	.15
930	Joe Beimel	.15
931	Chad Hermansen	.15
932	Scott Sauerbeck	.15
933	Josh Fogg	.15
934	*Mike Gonzalez*	.15
935	Mike Lincoln	.15
936	Sean Lowe	.15
937	Matt Guerrier	.15
938	Ryan Vogelsong	.15
939	J.R. House	.15
940	Craig Wilson	.15
941	Tony Alvarez	.15
942	J.J. Davis	.15
943	Abraham Nunez	.15
944	*Adrian Burnside*	.50
945	Ken Griffey Jr.	1.00
946	Jimmy Haynes	.15
947	Juan Castro	.15
948	Jose Rijo	.15
949	Corky Miller	.15
950	Elmer Dessens	.15
951	Aaron Boone	.15
952	Juan Encarnacion	.15
953	Chris Reitsma	.15
954	Wilton Guerrero	.15
955	Danny Graves	.15
956	Jim Brower	.15
957	Barry Larkin	.50
958	Todd Walker	.15
959	Gabe White	.15
960	Adam Dunn	.50
961	Jason LaRue	.15
962	Reggie Taylor	.15
963	Sean Casey	.40
964	Scott Williamson	.15
965	Austin Kearns	.50
966	Kelly Stinnett	.15
967	Jose Acevedo	.15
968	Gookie Dawkins	.15
969	Brady Clark	.15
970	Scott Sullivan	.15
971	Ricardo Aramboles	.15
972	Lance Davis	.15
973	Seth Etherton	.15
974	Luke Hudson	.15
975	Joey Hamilton	.15
976	Luis Pineda	.15
977	John Riedling	.15
978	Jose Silva	.15
979	Dane Sardinha	.15
980	Ben Broussard	.15
981	David Espinosa	.15
982	Ruben Mateo	.15
983	Larry Walker	.50
984	Juan Uribe	.15
985	Mike Hampton	.15
986	*Aaron Cook*	.15
987	Jose Ortiz	.15
988	Todd Jones	.15
989	Todd Helton	.50
990	Shawn Chacon	.15
991	Jason Jennings	.15
992	Todd Zeile	.15
993	Ben Petrick	.15
994	Denny Neagle	.15
995	Jose Jimenez	.15
996	Juan Pierre	.15
997	Todd Hollandsworth	.15
998	Kent Mercker	.15
999	Greg Norton	.15
1000	Terry Shumpert	.15
1001	Mark Little	.15
1002	Gary Bennett	.15
1003	Dennys Reyes	.15
1004	Justin Speier	.15
1005	John Thomson	.15
1006	Rick White	.15
1007	*Colin Young*	.40
1008	*Cam Esslinger*	.50
1009	*Rene Reyes*	.50
1010	Mike James	.15
1011	Morgan Ensberg	.15
1012	Adam Everett	.15
1013	Rodrigo Rosario	.15
1014	Carlos Pena	.15
1015	Eric Hinske	.50
1016	Orlando Hudson	.15
1017	Reed Johnson	.15
1018	Jung Bong	.15
1019	Bill Hall	.15
1020	Mark Prior	1.50
1021	Francis Beltran	.15
1022	David Kelton	.15
1023	Felix Escalona	.15
1024	Jorge Sosa	.15
1025	Dewon Brazelton	.15
1026	Jose Valverde	.15
1027	Luis Terrero	.15
1028	Kazuhisa Ishii	1.00
1029	Cesar Izturis	.15
1030	Ryan Jensen	.15
1031	Matt Thornton	.15
1032	Hansel Izquierdo	.15
1033	Jaime Cerda	.15
1034	Erik Bedard	.15
1035	Sean Burroughs	.15
1036	Ben Howard	.15
1037	Ramon Vazquez	.15
1038	Marlon Byrd	.15
1039	Josh Fogg	.15
1040	Hank Blalock	.50
1041	Mark Teixeira	.50
1042	Kevin Mench	.15
1043	Dane Sardinha	.15
1044	Austin Kearns	.50
1045	Anastacio Martinez	.15
1046	Eric Munson	.15
1047	Jon Rauch	.15
1048	Nick Johnson	.50
1049	Alex Graman	.15
1050	Drew Henson	.50
1051	Darin Erstad	.50
1052	Garret Anderson	.15
1053	Craig Biggio	.50
1054	Lance Berkman	.50
1055	Jeff Bagwell	.50
1056	Shannon Stewart	.15
1057	Chipper Jones	.75
1058	J.D. Drew	.50
1059	Moises Alou	.15
1060	Mark Grace	.50
1061	Jose Vidro Expos	.15
1062	Vladimir Guerrero	.75
1063	Matt Lawton	.15
1064	Ichiro Suzuki	1.50
1065	Edgar Martinez	.15
1066	John Olerud	.50
1067	Jeff Cirillo	.15
1068	Mike Lowell	.15
1069	Mike Piazza	1.00
1070	Roberto Alomar	.50
1071	Bobby Abreu	.15
1072	Jason Kendall	.15
1073	Brian Giles	.50
1074	Rafael Palmeiro	.50
1075	Ivan Rodriguez	.50
1076	Alex Rodriguez	1.50
1077	Juan Gonzalez	.50
1078	Nomar Garciaparra	1.50
1079	Manny Ramirez	.50
1080	Sean Casey	.25
1081	Barry Larkin	.25
1082	Larry Walker	.40
1083	Carlos Beltran	.15
1084	Corey Koskie	.15
1085	Magglio Ordonez	.25
1086	Frank Thomas	.50
1087	Kenny Lofton	.25
1088	Derek Jeter	2.00
1089	Bernie Williams	.50
1090	Jason Giambi	.50
1091	Troy Glaus	.50
1092	Jeff Bagwell	.50
1093	Lance Berkman	.50
1094	David Justice	.25
1095	Eric Chavez	.25
1096	Carlos Delgado	.40
1097	Gary Sheffield	.40
1098	Chipper Jones	.75
1099	Andruw Jones	.50
1100	Richie Sexson	.40
1101	Albert Pujols	1.50
1102	Sammy Sosa	1.50
1103	Fred McGriff	.40
1104	Greg Vaughn	.15
1105	Matt Williams	.25
1106	Luis Gonzalez	.40
1107	Shawn Green	.40
1108	Andres Galarraga	.15
1109	Vladimir Guerrero	.75
1110	Barry Bonds	2.00
1111	Rich Aurilia	.15
1112	Ellis Burks	.15
1113	Jim Thome	.50
1114	Bret Boone	.15
1115	Cliff Floyd	.15
1116	Mike Piazza	1.00
1117	Jeromy Burnitz	.15
1118	Phil Nevin	.15
1119	Brian Giles	.50
1120	Rafael Palmeiro	.50
1121	Juan Gonzalez	.50
1122	Alex Rodriguez	1.50
1123	Manny Ramirez	.50
1124	Ken Griffey Jr.	1.00
1125	Larry Walker	.40
1126	Todd Helton	.50
1127	Mike Sweeney	.15
1128	Frank Thomas	.50
1129	Paul Konerko	.40
1130	Jason Giambi	.50
1131	Aaron Sele	.15
1132	Roy Oswalt	.40
1133	Wade Miller	.15
1134	Tim Hudson	.40
1135	Barry Zito	.40
1136	Mark Mulder	.25
1137	Greg Maddux	1.00
1138	Tom Glavine	.40
1139	Ben Sheets	.40
1140	Darryl Kile	.15
1141	Matt Morris	.15
1142	Kerry Wood	.40
1143	Jon Lieber	.15
1144	Juan Cruz	.15
1145	Randy Johnson	.75
1146	Curt Schilling	.50
1147	Kevin Brown	.15
1148	Javier Vazquez	.15
1149	Russ Ortiz	.15
1150	C.C. Sabathia	.15
1151	Bartolo Colon	.15
1152	Freddy Garcia	.15
1153	Jamie Moyer	.15
1154	Josh Beckett	.50
1155	Brad Penny	.15
1156	Al Leiter	.40
1157	Brandon Duckworth	.15
1158	Robert Person	.15
1159	Kris Benson	.15
1160	Chan Ho Park	.15
1161	Pedro J. Martinez	.75
1162	Mike Hampton	.15
1163	Jeff Weaver	.15
1164	Joe Mays	.15
1165	Brad Radke	.15
1166	Eric Milton	.15
1167	Roger Clemens	1.00
1168	Mike Mussina	.50
1169	Andy Pettitte	.50
1170	David Wells	.15
1171	Ken Griffey Jr.	1.00
1172	Ichiro Suzuki	1.00
1173	Jason Giambi	.50
1174	Alex Rodriguez	1.00
1175	Sammy Sosa	.75
1176	Nomar Garciaparra	1.00
1177	Barry Bonds	1.00
1178	Mike Piazza	.75
1179	Derek Jeter	1.50
1180	Randy Johnson	.40
1181	Jeff Bagwell	.40
1182	Albert Pujols	1.00

Gargantuan Gear

		NM/M
Common Player:		3.00
Gold:		2X
Production 100 sets		
G-JB	James Baldwin	3.00
G-BC	Bruce Chen	3.00
G-JD	Jermaine Dye/SP	5.00
G-JG	Juan Gonzalez	6.00
G-BG	Ben Grieve	3.00
G-KG	Ken Griffey Jr.	10.00
G-TH	Tim Hudson	6.00
G-AJ	Andruw Jones	6.00
G-JK	Jeff Kent	3.00
G-ML	Mike Lieberthal	3.00
G-TM	Tino Martinez	3.00
G-JO	John Olerud	3.00
G-MO	Magglio Ordonez	5.00
G-MP	Mike Piazza	15.00
G-JP	Jorge Posada	8.00
G-AP	Andy Pettitte	6.00
G-BR	Brad Radke	3.00
G-AR	Alex Rodriguez	10.00
G-SR	Scott Rolen	10.00
G-CS	Curt Schilling	8.00
G-AS	Aaron Sele	3.00
G-IS	Ichiro Suzuki/SP	30.00
G-BW	Bernie Williams	8.00
G-DY	Dmitri Young	3.00
G-TZ	Todd Zeile	3.00

Looming Large Jerseys

		NM/M
Common Player:		8.00
Production 250 sets		
Gold:		2X
Production 40 sets		
LBa	Jeff Bagwell	10.00
LB	Lance Berkman	10.00
JBu	John Burkett	8.00
SC	Sean Casey	10.00
TC	Tony Clark	8.00
RC	Roger Clemens	20.00
JC	Jeff Cirillo	8.00
JD	J.D. Drew	10.00
CE	Carl Everett	8.00
CF	Chuck Finley	8.00
TF	Travis Fryman	8.00
JGi	Jason Giambi	10.00
BG	Brian Giles	10.00
TG	Tom Glavine	10.00
JGo	Juan Gonzalez	10.00
KG	Ken Griffey Jr.	20.00
TH	Todd Helton	15.00
RJ	Randy Johnson	15.00
DK	Darryl Kile	8.00
AL	Al Leiter	8.00
ML	Mike Lieberthal	8.00
KL	Kenny Lofton	8.00
GM	Greg Maddux	15.00
EM	Edgar Martinez	10.00
FM	Fred McGriff	10.00
MO	Magglio Ordonez	8.00
HN	Hideo Nomo	50.00
RP	Rafael Palmeiro	10.00
JP	Jorge Posada	10.00
SR	Shane Reynolds	8.00
AR	Alex Rodriguez	15.00
JR	Jimmy Rollins	8.00
KS	Kazuhiro Sasaki	8.00
CS	Curt Schilling	10.00
JS	J.T. Snow	8.00
SS	Sammy Sosa	20.00
FT	Frank Thomas	10.00
IV	Ismael Valdes	8.00
RV	Randy Velarde	8.00
RV	Ron Villone	8.00
BZ	Barry Zito	10.00

Lumber Yard

		NM/M
Common Player:		10.00
Inserted 1:168		
LY1	Chipper Jones	15.00
LY2	Joe DiMaggio	40.00
LY3	Albert Pujols	20.00
LY4	Mark McGwire	30.00
LY5	Sammy Sosa	15.00
LY6	Vladimir Guerrero	15.00
LY7	Barry Bonds	25.00
LY8	Mickey Mantle	50.00
LY9	Mike Piazza	15.00
LY10	Alex Rodriguez	15.00
LY11	Nomar Garciaparra	15.00
LY12	Ken Griffey Jr.	20.00
LY13	Frank Thomas	10.00
LY14	Jason Giambi	15.00
LY15	Derek Jeter	25.00
LY16	Luis Gonzalez	10.00
LY17	Jeff Bagwell	10.00
LY18	Todd Helton	10.00

Mark McGwire Flashbacks

	NM/M
Complete Set (40):	120.00
Common McGwire:	4.00
Inserted 1:24	

Super Swatches

	NM/M
Common Player:	5.00

Production 250 sets
Gold: 1-2X
Production 40 sets
EA Edgardo Alfonzo 5.00
RA Rich Aurilia 5.00
JB Jeff Bagwell 15.00
SC Sean Casey 8.00
CD Carlos Delgado 8.00
RD Ray Durham 5.00
DE Darin Erstad 8.00
JG Juan Gonzalez 8.00
MG Mark Grace 8.00
SG Shawn Green 8.00
KG Ken Griffey Jr. 20.00
TG Tony Gwynn 15.00
MH Mike Hampton 5.00
TH Trevor Hoffman 5.00
CJ Chipper Jones 10.00
DJ David Justice 8.00
KL Kenny Lofton 5.00
JM Joe Mays 5.00
EM Eric Milton 5.00
MM Matt Morris 5.00
HN Hideo Nomo 50.00
JP Jorge Posada 10.00
MR Manny Ramirez 12.00
MR Mariano Rivera 10.00
AR Alex Rodriguez 15.00
IR Ivan Rodriguez 10.00
KS Kazuhiro Sasaki 5.00
CS Curt Schilling 10.00
BS Ben Sheets 8.00
SS Sammy Sosa 20.00
IS Ichiro Suzuki 40.00
MS Mike Sweeney 5.00
FT Frank Thomas 10.00
GV Greg Vaughn 5.00
JV Jose Vidro 5.00
DW David Wells 5.00
MY Masato Yoshii 5.00

2002 UD AUTHENTICS

Kazuhisa Ishii

NM/M
Complete Set (200): 50.00
Common Player: .25
Reversed Negatives: 1-2.5X
Inserted 1:9
Pack (5): 2.50
Box (18): 35.00
1 Brad Fullmer .25
2 Garret Anderson .40
3 Darin Erstad .40
4 Jarrod Washburn .25
5 Troy Glaus .50
6 Barry Zito .40
7 David Justice .40
8 Eric Chavez .40
9 Tim Hudson .40
10 Miguel Tejada .40
11 Jermaine Dye .25
12 Mark Mulder .40
13 Carlos Delgado .50
14 Jose Cruz Jr. .25
16 Shannon Stewart .25
17 Raul Mondesi .25
18 Tanyon Sturtze .25
19 Toby Hall .25
20 Greg Vaughn .25
21 Aubrey Huff .25
22 Ben Grieve .25
23 Brent Abernathy .25
24 Jim Thome .75
25 C.C. Sabathia .25
26 Matt Lawton .25
27 Omar Vizquel .25
28 Ellis Burks .25
29 Russ Branyan .25
30 Bartolo Colon .40
31 Ichiro Suzuki 1.50
32 John Olerud .40
33 Freddy Garcia .25
34 Mike Cameron .25
35 Jeff Cirillo .25
36 Kazuhiro Sasaki .25
37 Edgar Martinez .40
38 Bret Boone .25
39 Jeff Conine .25
40 Melvin Mora .25
41 Jason Johnson .25
42 Chris Richard .25
43 Tony Batista .25
44 Ivan Rodriguez .50
45 Gabe Kapler .25
46 Rafael Palmeiro .50
47 Alex Rodriguez 1.50
48 Juan Gonzalez .50
49 Carl Everett .25
50 Nomar Garciaparra 1.50
51 Trot Nixon .25
52 Manny Ramirez .50
53 Pedro J. Martinez .75
54 Johnny Damon .40
55 Shea Hillenbrand .25
56 Mike Sweeney .25
57 Mark Quinn .25
58 Joe Randa .25
59 Carlos Beltran .40
60 Chuck Knoblauch .25
61 Robert Fick .25
62 Jeff Weaver .25
63 Bobby Higginson .25
64 Dean Palmer .25
65 Dmitri Young .25
66 Corey Koskie .25
67 Doug Mientkiewicz .25
68 Joe Mays .25
69 Torii Hunter .40
70 Cristian Guzman .25
71 Jacque Jones .25
72 Magglio Ordonez .40
73 Paul Konerko .25
74 Carlos Lee .25
75 Mark Buehrle .25
76 Jose Canseco .50
77 Frank Thomas .50
78 Roger Clemens 1.50
79 Derek Jeter 2.00
80 Jason Giambi .50
81 Rondell White .25
82 Bernie Williams .50
83 Jorge Posada .50
84 Mike Mussina .50
85 Alfonso Soriano .75
86 Wade Miller .25
87 Jeff Bagwell .50
88 Craig Biggio .40
89 Roy Oswalt .40
90 Lance Berkman .40
91 Daryle Ward .25
92 Chipper Jones .75
93 Greg Maddux 1.00
94 Marcus Giles .25
95 Gary Sheffield .50
96 Tom Glavine .50
97 Andruw Jones .50
98 Rafael Furcal .25
99 Richie Sexson .40
100 Ben Sheets .40
101 Jose Hernandez .25
102 Geoff Jenkins .40
103 Jeffrey Hammonds .25
104 Edgar Renteria .40
105 Matt Morris .40
106 Tino Martinez .25
107 Jim Edmonds .40
108 Albert Pujols 1.50
109 J.D. Drew .40
110 Fernando Vina .25
111 Darryl Kile .25
112 Sammy Sosa 1.50
113 Fred McGriff .40
114 Kerry Wood .75
115 Moises Alou .40
116 Jon Lieber .25
117 Mark Grace .50
118 Randy Johnson .75
119 Curt Schilling .50
120 Luis Gonzalez .40
121 Steve Finley .25
122 Matt Williams .40
123 Shawn Green .40
124 Kevin Brown .40
125 Adrian Beltre .40
126 Paul LoDuca .25
127 Hideo Nomo .50
128 Brian Jordan .25
129 Vladimir Guerrero .75
130 Javier Vazquez .25
131 Jose Vidro .25
132 Orlando Cabrera .25
133 Jeff Kent .25
134 Rich Aurilia .25
135 Russ Ortiz .25
136 Barry Bonds 2.00
137 Preston Wilson .25
138 Ryan Dempster .25
139 Cliff Floyd .25
140 Josh Beckett .40
141 Mike Lowell .40
142 Mike Piazza 1.00
143 Roberto Alomar .50
144 Al Leiter .40
145 Edgardo Alfonzo .25
146 Roger Cedeno .25
147 Jeromy Burnitz .25
148 Phil Nevin .25
149 Mark Kotsay .25
150 Ryan Klesko .25
151 Trevor Hoffman .25
152 Bobby Abreu .40
153 Scott Rolen .75
154 Jimmy Rollins .25
155 Robert Person .25
156 Pat Burrell .40
157 Randy Wolf .25
158 Brian Giles .40
159 Aramis Ramirez .50
160 Kris Benson .25
161 Jason Kendall .25
162 Ken Griffey Jr. 1.00
163 Sean Casey .40
164 Adam Dunn .50
165 Barry Larkin .50
166 Todd Helton .50
167 Mike Hampton .25
168 Larry Walker .40
169 Juan Pierre .25
170 Juan Uribe .25
171 *So Taguchi* 2.00
172 *Brendan Donnelly* .75
173 *Chris Baker* .50
174 *John Ennis* .75
175 *Francis Beltran* .75
176 Danny Wright .50
177 *Brandon Backe* .75
178 *Mark Corey* .75
179 *Kazuhisa Ishii* 3.00
180 *Ron Calloway* .50
181 *Kevin Frederick* .75
182 *Jaime Cerda* .75
183 *Doug Devore* .50
184 *Brandon Puffer* .75
185 *Andy Pratt* .50
186 *Adrian Burnside* .50
187 *Josh Hancock* .75
188 *Jorge Nunez* .50
189 *Tyler Yates* 1.00
190 *Kyle Kane* .75
191 *Jose Valverde* 1.00
192 Matt Thornton .50
193 *Ben Howard* .50
194 *Reed Johnson* 1.50
195 *Rene Reyes* .50
196 *Jeremy Ward* .50
197 *Steve Bechler* .50
198 *Cam Esslinger* .50
199 *Michael Crudale* .50
200 *Todd Donovan* .50

Retro UD Star Rookie Jerseys

NM/M
Common Player: 5.00
Inserted 1:16
Golds: 1-2X
Production 275 sets
CB Craig Biggio 8.00
PB Pat Burrell 8.00
BG Brian Giles 5.00
JG Juan Gonzalez 8.00
LG Luis Gonzalez 8.00
SG Shawn Green 8.00
KG Ken Griffey Jr. 20.00
RJ Randy Johnson 10.00
CJ Chipper Jones 10.00
DJ David Justice 5.00
GK Gabe Kapler/SP
RK Ryan Klesko 5.00
KL Kenny Lofton 5.00
PM Pedro J. Martinez 15.00
HN Hideo Nomo 15.00
JO John Olerud 5.00
MO Magglio Ordonez 8.00
RP Robert Person 5.00
AP Albert Pujols 20.00
MR Manny Ramirez/SP 15.00
AR Alex Rodriguez 20.00
IR Ivan Rodriguez 10.00
KS Kazuhiro Sasaki 5.00
GS Gary Sheffield 8.00
SS Sammy Sosa/SP 20.00
I Ichiro Suzuki 40.00
JT Jim Thome 12.00
LW Larry Walker 5.00

Retro UD Jerseys

NM/M
Common Player: 5.00
Inserted 1:16
Golds: 1-2X
Production 275 sets
Reverse Neg.: 1-2X
Production 350 sets
JB Jeff Bagwell 15.00
KB Kevin Brown 8.00
EC Eric Chavez 5.00
RC Roger Clemens/SP 25.00
CD Carlos Delgado 8.00
JD J.D. Drew 10.00
JE Jim Edmonds 8.00
DE Darin Erstad 5.00
RF Rafael Furcal 5.00
JG Jason Giambi 10.00
TG Tom Glavine 10.00
LG Luis Gonzalez 5.00
KG Ken Griffey Jr. 20.00
TH Todd Helton 12.00
RJ Randy Johnson 12.00
AJ Andruw Jones 8.00
CJ Chipper Jones 15.00
GM Greg Maddux 15.00
TM Tino Martinez/SP/25
MP Mike Piazza 15.00
MR Manny Ramirez 10.00
AR Alex Rodriguez 15.00
IR Ivan Rodriguez 10.00
SR Scott Rolen/SP/25
SS Sammy Sosa/SP 20.00
MS Mike Sweeney 5.00
FT Frank Thomas 10.00
BW Bernie Williams 10.00
BZ Barry Zito 8.00

Signed Retro UD Star Rookie Jerseys

NM/M
Production 40 sets
KG Ken Griffey Jr. 100.00
AR Alex Rodriguez 150.00
JT Jim Thome 75.00

Stars of '89 Jerseys

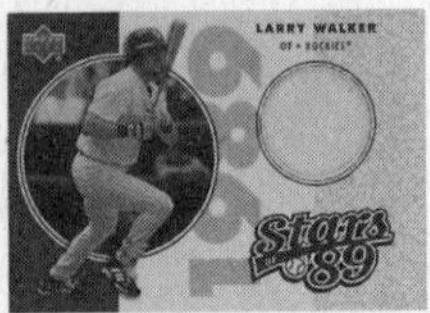

NM/M
Common Player: 5.00
Inserted 1:16
RA Roberto Alomar 8.00
KB Kevin Brown 8.00
EB Ellis Burks 5.00
JC Jose Canseco 8.00
RC Roger Clemens 15.00
DC David Cone 5.00
AG Andres Galarraga 5.00
TG Tom Glavine 10.00
JG Juan Gonzalez 10.00
MG Mark Grace 8.00

KG	Ken Griffey Jr.	20.00
RH	Rickey Henderson	10.00
RJ	Randy Johnson	10.00
DJ	David Justice	5.00
BL	Barry Larkin/SP	15.00
AL	Al Leiter	5.00
GM	Greg Maddux	15.00
EM	Edgar Martinez	8.00
FM	Fred McGriff	5.00
JO	John Olerud	5.00
PO	Paul O'Neill	8.00
RP	Rafael Palmeiro	8.00
CS	Curt Schilling	8.00
GS	Gary Sheffield	8.00
SS	Sammy Sosa	15.00
RV	Robin Ventura	5.00
LW	Larry Walker	5.00
MW	Matt Williams	5.00

UD Heroes of Baseball

		NM/M
Complete Set (30):		150.00
Ichiro:		8.00
Griffey Jr.:		6.00
Alex Rodriguez:		8.00
Production 1,989 sets		
HB-I1	Ichiro Suzuki	8.00
HB-I2	Ichiro Suzuki	8.00
HB-I3	Ichiro Suzuki	8.00
HB-I4	Ichiro Suzuki	8.00
HB-I5	Ichiro Suzuki	8.00
HB-I6	Ichiro Suzuki	8.00
HB-I7	Ichiro Suzuki	8.00
HB-I8	Ichiro Suzuki	8.00
HB-I9	Ichiro Suzuki	8.00
HB-I10	Ichiro Suzuki	8.00
HB-G1	Ken Griffey Jr.	6.00
HB-G2	Ken Griffey Jr.	6.00
HB-G3	Ken Griffey Jr.	6.00
HB-G4	Ken Griffey Jr.	6.00
HB-G5	Ken Griffey Jr.	6.00
HB-G6	Ken Griffey Jr.	6.00
HB-G7	Ken Griffey Jr.	6.00
HB-G8	Ken Griffey Jr.	6.00
HB-G9	Ken Griffey Jr.	6.00
HB-G10	Ken Griffey Jr.	6.00
HB-R1	Alex Rodriguez	8.00
HB-R2	Alex Rodriguez	8.00
HB-R3	Alex Rodriguez	8.00
HB-R4	Alex Rodriguez	8.00
HB-R5	Alex Rodriguez	8.00
HB-R6	Alex Rodriguez	8.00
HB-R7	Alex Rodriguez	8.00
HB-R8	Alex Rodriguez	8.00
HB-R9	Alex Rodriguez	8.00
HB-R10	Alex Rodriguez	8.00

1989 FLASHBACKS

		NM/M
Complete Set (12):		30.00
Common Player:		1.50
Production 4,225 sets		
F1	Ken Griffey Jr.	8.00
F2	Gary Sheffield	1.50
F3	Randy Johnson	3.00
F4	Roger Clemens	4.00
F5	Greg Maddux	5.00
F6	Mark Grace	2.00
F7	Barry Bonds	5.00
F8	Roberto Alomar	2.00
F9	Sammy Sosa	5.00
F10	Rafael Palmeiro	2.00
F11	Edgar Martinez	1.50
F12	Jose Canseco	2.00

2003 UPPER DECK

		NM/M
Complete Set (540):		75.00
Common Player:		.15
Common RC (501-529):		.50
Series 1 or 2 Pack (8):		2.50
Series 1 or 2 Box (24):		45.00
1	John Lackey	.15
2	Alex Cintron	.15
3	Jose Leon	.15
4	Bobby Hill	.15
5	Brandon Larson	.15
6	Raul Gonzalez	.15
7	Ben Broussard	.15
8	Earl Snyder	.15
9	Ramon Santiago	.15
10	Jason Lane	.15
11	Keith Ginter	.15
12	Kirk Saarloos	.15
13	Juan Brito	.15
14	Runelvys Hernandez	.15
15	Shawn Sedlacek	.15
16	Jayson Durocher	.15
17	Kevin Frederick	.15
18	Zach Day	.15
20	Marcus Thames	.15
21	Esteban German	.15
22	Brett Myers	.15
23	Oliver Perez	.25
24	Dennis Tankersley	.15
25	Julius Matos	.15
26	Jake Peavy	.15
27	Eric Cyr	.15
28	Mike Crudale	.15
29	Josh Pearce	.15
30	Carl Crawford	.15
31	Tim Salmon	.25
32	Troy Glaus	.50
33	Adam Kennedy	.15
34	David Eckstein	.15
35	Bengie Molina	.15
36	Jarrod Washburn	.15
37	Ramon Ortiz	.15
38	Eric Chavez	.40
39	Miguel Tejada	.50
40	Adam Piatt	.15
41	Jermaine Dye	.15
42	Olmedo Saenz	.15
43	Tim Hudson	.25
44	Barry Zito	.25
45	Billy Koch	.15
46	Shannon Stewart	.15
47	Kelvim Escobar	.15
48	Jose Cruz Jr.	.15
49	Vernon Wells	.15
50	Roy Halladay	.15
51	Esteban Loaiza	.15
52	Eric Hinske	.15
53	Steve Cox	.15
54	Brent Abernathy	.15
55	Ben Grieve	.15
56	Aubrey Huff	.15
57	Jared Sandberg	.15
58	Paul Wilson	.15
59	Tanyon Sturtze	.15
60	Jim Thome	.60
61	Omar Vizquel	.25
62	C.C. Sabathia	.15
63	Chris Magruder	.15
64	Ricky Gutierrez	.15
65	Einar Diaz	.15
66	Danys Baez	.15
67	Ichiro Suzuki	2.00
68	Ruben Sierra	.15
69	Carlos Guillen	.15
70	Mark McLemore	.15
71	Dan Wilson	.15
72	Jamie Moyer	.15
73	Joel Pineiro	.15
74	Edgar Martinez	.25
75	Tony Batista	.15
76	Jay Gibbons	.15
77	Chris Singleton	.15
78	Melvin Mora	.15
79	Geronimo Gil	.15
80	Rodrigo Lopez	.15
81	Jorge Julio	.15
82	Rafael Palmeiro	.50
83	Juan Gonzalez	.50
84	Mike Young	.15
85	Hideki Irabu	.15
86	Chan Ho Park	.15
87	Kevin Mench	.15
88	Doug Davis	.15
89	Pedro Martinez	.75
90	Shea Hillenbrand	.15
91	Derek Lowe	.15
92	Jason Varitek	.25
93	Tony Clark	.15
94	John Burkett	.15
95	Frank Castillo	.15
96	Nomar Garciaparra	2.00
97	Rickey Henderson	.40
98	Mike Sweeney	.15
99	Carlos Febles	.15
100	Mark Quinn	.15
101	Raul Ibanez	.15
102	A.J. Hinch	.15
103	Paul Byrd	.15
104	Chuck Knoblauch	.15
105	Dmitri Young	.15
106	Randall Simon	.15
107	Brandon Inge	.15
108	Damion Easley	.15
109	Carlos Pena	.15
110	George Lombard	.15
111	Juan Acevedo	.15
112	Torii Hunter	.25
113	Doug Mientkiewicz	.15
114	David Ortiz	.50
115	Eric Milton	.15
116	Eddie Guardado	.15
117	Cristian Guzman	.15
118	Corey Koskie	.15
119	Magglio Ordonez	.25
120	Mark Buehrle	.15
121	Todd Ritchie	.15
122	Jose Valentin	.15
123	Paul Konerko	.25
124	Carlos Lee	.15
125	Jon Garland	.15
126	Jason Giambi	.40
127	Derek Jeter	2.00
128	Roger Clemens	1.50
129	Raul Mondesi	.15
130	Jorge Posada	.25
131	Rondell White	.15
132	Robin Ventura	.25
133	Mike Mussina	.50
134	Jeff Bagwell	.50
135	Craig Biggio	.25
136	Morgan Ensberg	.15
137	Richard Hidalgo	.15
138	Brad Ausmus	.15
139	Roy Oswalt	.25
140	Carlos Hernandez	.15
141	Shane Reynolds	.15
142	Gary Sheffield	.25
143	Andruw Jones	.50
144	Tom Glavine	.40
145	Rafael Furcal	.25
146	Javy Lopez	.25
147	Vinny Castilla	.15
148	Marcus Giles	.15
149	Kevin Millwood	.15
150	Jason Marquis	.15
151	Ruben Quevedo	.15
152	Ben Sheets	.25
153	Geoff Jenkins	.15
154	Jose Hernandez	.15
155	Glendon Rusch	.15
156	Jeffrey Hammonds	.15
157	Alex Sanchez	.15
158	Jim Edmonds	.25
159	Tino Martinez	.25
160	Albert Pujols	1.50
161	Eli Marrero	.15
162	Woody Williams	.15
163	Fernando Vina	.15
164	Jason Isringhausen	.15
165	Jason Simontacchi	.15
166	Kerry Robinson	.15
167	Sammy Sosa	1.25
168	Juan Cruz	.15
169	Fred McGriff	.25
170	Antonio Alfonseca	.15
171	Jon Lieber	.15
172	Mark Prior	.75
173	Moises Alou	.25
174	Matt Clement	.15
175	Mark Bellhorn	.15
176	Randy Johnson	.75
177	Luis Gonzalez	.25
178	Tony Womack	.15
179	Mark Grace	.30
180	Junior Spivey	.15
181	Byung-Hyun Kim	.15
182	Danny Bautista	.15
183	Brian Anderson	.15
184	Shawn Green	.25
185	Brian Jordan	.15
186	Eric Karros	.15
187	Andy Ashby	.15
188	Cesar Izturis	.15
189	Dave Roberts	.15
190	Eric Gagne	.40
191	Kazuhisa Ishii	.15
192	Adrian Beltre	.25
193	Vladimir Guerrero	.75
194	Tony Armas Jr.	.15
195	Bartolo Colon	.15
196	Troy O'Leary	.15
197	Tomokazu Ohka	.15
198	Brad Wilkerson	.15
199	Orlando Cabrera	.15
200	Barry Bonds	2.00
201	David Bell	.15
202	Tsuyoshi Shinjo	.15
203	Benito Santiago	.15
204	Livan Hernandez	.15
205	Jason Schmidt	.40
206	Kirk Reuter	.15
207	Ramon E. Martinez	.15
208	Mike Lowell	.25
209	Luis Castillo	.15
210	Derrek Lee	.25
211	Andy Fox	.15
212	Eric Owens	.15
213	Charles Johnson	.15
214	Brad Penny	.15
215	A.J. Burnett	.15
216	Edgardo Alfonzo	.15
217	Roberto Alomar	.50
218	Rey Ordonez	.15
219	Al Leiter	.15
220	Roger Cedeno	.15
221	Timoniel Perez	.15
222	Jeromy Burnitz	.15
223	Pedro Astacio	.15
224	Joe McEwing	.15
225	Ryan Klesko	.15
226	Ramon Vazquez	.15
227	Mark Kotsay	.15
228	Bubba Trammell	.15
229	Wiki Gonzalez	.15
230	Trevor Hoffman	.15
231	Ron Gant	.15
232	Bobby Abreu	.25
233	Marlon Anderson	.15
234	Jeremy Giambi	.15
235	Jimmy Rollins	.15
236	Mike Lieberthal	.15
237	Vicente Padilla	.15
238	Randy Wolf	.15
239	Pokey Reese	.15
240	Brian Giles	.25
241	Jack Wilson	.15
242	Mike Williams	.15
243	Kip Wells	.15
244	Robert Mackowiak	.15
245	Craig Wilson	.15
246	Adam Dunn	.60
247	Sean Casey	.25
248	Todd Walker	.15
249	Corky Miller	.15
250	Ryan Dempster	.15
251	Reggie Taylor	.15
252	Aaron Boone	.15
253	Larry Walker	.30
254	Jose Ortiz	.15
255	Todd Zeile	.15
256	Bobby Estalella	.15
257	Juan Pierre	.15
258	Terry Shumpert	.15
259	Mike Hampton	.15
260	Denny Stark	.15
261	Shawn Green	.25
262	Derek Lowe	.15
263	Barry Bonds	1.00
264	Mike Cameron	.15

265	Luis Castillo	.15
266	Vladimir Guerrero	.40
267	Jason Giambi	.25
268	Eric Gagne	.25
269	Magglio Ordonez	.20
270	Jim Thome	.40
271	Garret Anderson	.40
272	Tony Percival	.15
273	Brad Fullmer	.15
274	Scott Spezio	.15
275	Darin Erstad	.40
276	Francisco Rodriguez	.15
277	Kevin Appier	.15
278	Shawn Wooten	.15
279	Eric Owens	.15
280	Scott Hatteberg	.15
281	Terrence Long	.15
282	Mark Mulder	.25
283	Ramon Hernandez	.15
284	Ted Lilly	.15
285	Erubiel Durazo	.15
286	Mark Ellis	.15
287	Carlos Delgado	.50
288	Orlando Hudson	.15
289	Chris Woodward	.15
290	Mark Hendrickson	.15
291	Josh Phelps	.15
292	Ken Huckaby	.15
293	Justin Miller	.15
294	Travis Lee	.15
295	Jorge Sosa	.15
296	Joe Kennedy	.15
297	Carl Crawford	.15
298	Toby Hall	.15
299	Rey Ordonez	.15
300	Brandon Phillips	.15
301	Matt Lawton	.15
302	Ellis Burks	.15
303	Bill Selby	.15
304	Travis Hafner	.15
305	Milton Bradley	.15
306	Karim Garcia	.15
307	Cliff Lee	.15
308	Jeff Cirillo	.15
309	John Olerud	.25
310	Kazuhiro Sasaki	.15
311	Freddy Garcia	.15
312	Bret Boone	.25
313	Mike Cameron	.15
314	Ben Davis	.15
315	Randy Winn	.15
316	Gary Matthews Jr.	.15
317	Jeff Conine	.15
318	Sidney Ponson	.15
319	Jerry Hairston	.15
320	David Segui	.15
321	Scott Erickson	.15
322	Marty Cordova	.15
323	Hank Blalock	.50
324	Herbert Perry	.15
325	Alex Rodriguez	2.00
326	Carl Everett	.15
327	Einar Diaz	.15
328	Ugueth Urbina	.15
329	Mark Teixeira	.40
330	Manny Ramirez	.75
331	Johnny Damon	.50
332	Trot Nixon	.15
333	Tim Wakefield	.15
334	Casey Fossum	.15
335	Todd Walker	.15
336	Jeremy Giambi	.15
337	Bill Mueller	.15
338	Ramiro Mendoza	.15
339	Carlos Beltran	.50
340	Jason Grimsley	.15
341	Brent Mayne	.15
342	Angel Berroa	.15
343	Albie Lopez	.15
344	Michael Tucker	.15
345	Bobby Higginson	.15
346	Shane Halter	.15
347	Jeremy Bonderman	.40
348	Eric Munson	.15
349	Andy Van Hekken	.15
350	Matt Anderson	.15
351	Jacque Jones	.15
352	A.J. Pierzynski	.15
353	Joe Mays	.15
354	Brad Radke	.15
355	Dustan Mohr	.15
356	Bobby Kielty	.15
357	Michael Cuddyer	.15
358	Luis Rivas	.15
359	Frank Thomas	.75
360	Joe Borchard	.15
361	D'Angelo Jimenez	.15
362	Bartolo Colon	.25
363	Joe Crede	.15
364	Miguel Olivo	.15
365	Billy Koch	.15
366	Bernie Williams	.50
367	Nick Johnson	.15
368	Andy Pettitte	.40
369	Mariano Rivera	.25
370	Alfonso Soriano	.75
371	David Wells	.15
372	Drew Henson	.15
373	Juan Rivera	.15
374	Steve Karsay	.15
375	Jeff Kent	.25
376	Lance Berkman	.50
377	Octavio Dotel	.15
378	Julio Lugo	.15
379	Jason Lane	.15
380	Wade Miller	.15
381	Billy Wagner	.15
382	Brad Ausmus	.15
383	Mike Hampton	.15
384	Chipper Jones	.75
385	John Smoltz	.25
386	Greg Maddux	1.25
387	Javy Lopez	.25
388	Robert Fick	.15
389	Mark DeRosa	.15
390	Russ Ortiz	.15
391	Julio Franco	.15
392	Richie Sexson	.50
393	Eric Young	.15
394	Robert Machado	.15
395	Mike DeJean	.15
396	Todd Ritchie	.15
397	Royce Clayton	.15
398	Nick Neugebauer	.15
399	J.D. Drew	.25
400	Edgar Renteria	.25
401	Scott Rolen	.75
402	Matt Morris	.25
403	Garrett Stephenson	.15
404	Eduardo Perez	.15
405	Mike Matheny	.15
406	Miguel Cairo	.15
407	Brett Tomko	.15
408	Bobby Hill	.15
409	Troy O'Leary	.15
410	Corey Patterson	.40
411	Kerry Wood	.75
412	Eric Karros	.15
413	Hee Seop Choi	.15
414	Alex Gonzalez	.15
415	Matt Clement	.15
416	Mark Grudzielanek	.15
417	Curt Schilling	.50
418	Steve Finley	.15
419	Craig Counsell	.15
420	Matt Williams	.15
421	Quinton McCracken	.15
422	Chad Moeller	.15
423	Lyle Overbay	.15
424	Miguel Batista	.15
425	Paul LoDuca	.15
426	Kevin Brown	.25
427	Hideo Nomo	.40
428	Fred McGriff	.25
429	Joe Thurston	.15
430	Odalis Perez	.15
431	Darren Dreifort	.15
432	Todd Hundley	.15
433	Dave Roberts	.15
434	Jose Vidro	.15
435	Javier Vazquez	.15
436	Michael Barrett	.15
437	Fernando Tatis	.15
438	Peter Bergeron	.15
439	Endy Chavez	.15
440	Orlando Hernandez	.15
441	Marvin Bernard	.15
442	Rich Aurilia	.15
443	Pedro Feliz	.15
444	Robb Nen	.15
445	Ray Durham	.15
446	Marquis Grissom	.15
447	Damian Moss	.15
448	Edgardo Alfonzo	.15
449	Juan Pierre	.15
450	Braden Looper	.15
451	Alex Gonzalez	.15
452	Justin Wayne	.15
453	Josh Beckett	.25
454	Juan Encarnacion	.15
455	Ivan Rodriguez	.50
456	Todd Hollandsworth	.15
457	Cliff Floyd	.15
458	Rey Sanchez	.15
459	Mike Piazza	1.50
460	Mo Vaughn	.15
461	Armando Benitez	.15
462	Tsuyoshi Shinjo	.15
463	Tom Glavine	.40
464	David Cone	.15
465	Phil Nevin	.15
466	Sean Burroughs	.15
467	Jake Peavy	.15
468	Brian Lawrence	.15
469	Mark Loretta	.15
470	Dennis Tankersley	.15
471	Jesse Orosco	.15
472	Jim Thome	.75
473	Kevin Millwood	.40
474	David Bell	.15
475	Pat Burrell	.40
476	Brandon Duckworth	.15
477	Jose Mesa	.15
478	Marlon Byrd	.15
479	Reggie Sanders	.15
480	Jason Kendall	.25
481	Aramis Ramirez	.40
482	Kris Benson	.15
483	Matt Stairs	.15
484	Kevin Young	.15
485	Kenny Lofton	.25
486	Austin Kearns	.40
487	Barry Larkin	.25
488	Jason LaRue	.15
489	Ken Griffey Jr.	1.25
490	Danny Graves	.15
491	Russell Branyan	.15
492	Reggie Taylor	.15
493	Jimmy Haynes	.15
494	Charles Johnson	.15
495	Todd Helton	.75
496	Juan Uribe	.15
497	Preston Wilson	.15
498	Chris Stynes	.15
499	Jason Jennings	.15
500	Jay Payton	.15
501	*Hideki Matsui*	5.00
502	*Jose Contreras*	2.00
503	*Brandon Webb*	1.50
504	*Robby Hammock*	.50
505	*Matt Kata*	.50
506	*Tim Olson*	.50
507	*Michael Hessman*	.50
508	*Jon Leicester*	.50
509	*Todd Wellemeyer*	.50
510	*David Sanders*	.50
511	*Josh Stewart*	.50
512	*Luis Ayala*	.50
513	*Clint Barmes*	2.00
514	*Josh Willingham*	.50
515	*Alejandro Machado*	.50
516	*Felix Sanchez*	.50
517	*Willie Eyre*	.50
518	*Brent Hoard*	.50
519	*Lew Ford*	1.50
520	*Terrmel Sledge*	.50
521	Jeremy Griffiths	.15
522	*Phil Seibel*	.50
523	*Craig Brazell*	.50
524	*Prentice Redman*	.50
525	*Jeff Duncan*	.50
526	*Shane Bazzell*	.75
527	*Bernie Castro*	.50
528	*Rett Johnson*	.50
529	*Bobby Madritsch*	3.00
530	Rocco Baldelli	.40
531	Alex Rodriguez	1.00
532	Eric Chavez	.25
533	Miguel Tejada	.25
534	Ichiro Suzuki	.75
535	Sammy Sosa	.75
536	Barry Zito	.25
537	Darin Erstad	.25
538	Alfonso Soriano	.50
539	Troy Glaus	.25
540	Nomar Garciaparra	.75

AL All-Star Swatch

		NM/M
Common Player:		5.00
Inserted 1:144 Retail		
MC	Mike Cameron	5.00
RD	Ray Durham	5.00
CE	Carl Everett	5.00
CF	Chuck Finley	5.00
TF	Travis Fryman	6.00
JG	Juan Gonzalez	8.00
JM	Joe Mays	5.00
MO	Magglio Ordonez	8.00
AP	Andy Pettitte	8.00
JP	Jorge Posada	8.00
MR	Mariano Rivera	10.00
AS	Aaron Sele	5.00
MS	Mike Sweeney	5.00

Big League Breakdown

		NM/M
Complete Set (15):		20.00
Common Player:		.50
Inserted 1:8		
BL1	Troy Glaus	.75
BL2	Miguel Tejada	.75
BL3	Chipper Jones	1.50
BL4	Torii Hunter	.50
BL5	Nomar Garciaparra	3.00
BL6	Sammy Sosa	2.50
BL7	Todd Helton	1.00
BL8	Lance Berkman	.75
BL9	Shawn Green	.50
BL10	Vladimir Guerrero	1.50
BL11	Jason Giambi	.50
BL12	Derek Jeter	4.00
BL13	Barry Bonds	4.00
BL14	Ichiro Suzuki	3.00
BL15	Alex Rodriguez	4.00

Game Swatches Hobby

		NM/M
Common Player:		5.00
Inserted 1:72		
SB	Sean Burroughs/SP	8.00
CD	Carlos Delgado/SP	8.00
GM	Greg Maddux	15.00
MM	Mike Mussina	10.00
MO	Magglio Ordonez	5.00
CP	Carlos Pena	5.00
MP	Mike Piazza/SP	15.00
AR	Alex Rodriguez	15.00
CC	C.C. Sabathia	5.00
CS	Curt Schilling/100	10.00
SS	Sammy Sosa	15.00
BW	Bernie Williams	10.00

Game Jersey Autograph

		NM/M
Golds:		1.5-2X
Production 25 or 75		
RC	Roger Clemens/350	100.00
JG	Jason Giambi/350	40.00
KG	Ken Griffey Jr/350	110.00
MM	Mark McGwire/150	350.00
CR	Cal Ripken Jr/350	140.00
AR	Alex Rodriguez/350	120.00
SS	Sammy Sosa/150	140.00

Game Swatches Retail

		NM/M
Common Player:		5.00
Inserted 1:72		
RC	Roger Clemens	15.00
JD	J.D. Drew	5.00
AD	Adam Dunn	8.00
JE	Jim Edmonds	8.00
DE	Darin Erstad	8.00
JG	Jason Giambi	8.00
KG	Ken Griffey Jr.	12.00
TH	Tim Hudson	6.00
RJ	Randy Johnson	8.00
JK	Jeff Kent	5.00
EM	Edgar Martinez	6.00
IR	Ivan Rodriguez	6.00
FT	Frank Thomas	8.00

Lineup Time Jerseys

		NM/M
Common Player:		6.00

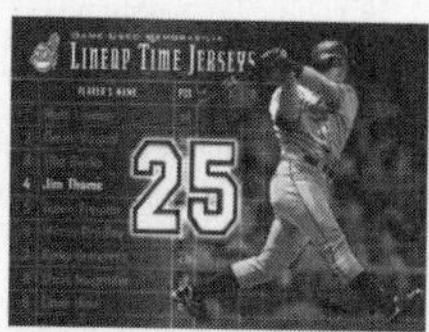

Inserted 1:96

RC	Roger Clemens/SP	20.00
CD	Carlos Delgado	8.00
JD	J.D. Drew	6.00
SG	Shawn Green	8.00
TH	Todd Helton	8.00
RJ	Randy Johnson/SP	15.00
GM	Greg Maddux	10.00
IS	Ichiro Suzuki	40.00
JT	Jim Thome	10.00
BW	Bernie Williams	10.00

Leading Swatches

NM/M

Common Player: 4.00
Inserted 1:24
Golds: 1-2X
Production 100 sets

BA	Bobby Abreu	6.00
GA	Garret Anderson	6.00
JB	Jeff Bagwell	6.00
JB1	Jeff Bagwell	6.00
TB	Tony Batista	4.00
AB	Adrian Beltre	6.00
LB	Lance Berkman	4.00
PB	Pat Burrell	6.00
PB1	Pat Burrell	6.00
EC	Eric Chavez	6.00
RC	Roger Clemens	10.00
RC1	Roger Clemens	10.00
CD	Carlos Delgado	6.00
JD	J.D. Drew	4.00
AD	Adam Dunn	8.00
AD1	Adam Dunn	8.00
JE	Jim Edmonds	4.00
JG	Jason Giambi	6.00
JG1	Jason Giambi	6.00
BG	Brian Giles	4.00
TG	Troy Glaus	4.00
GO	Juan Gonzalez	6.00
LG	Luis Gonzalez	4.00
SG	Shawn Green	4.00
SG1	Shawn Green	4.00
KG	Ken Griffey Jr.	12.00
KG1	Ken Griffey Jr.	12.00
VG	Vladimir Guerrero	8.00
THe	Todd Helton	6.00
THu	Tim Hudson	4.00
TH1	Tim Hudson	4.00
KI	Kazuhisa Ishii	4.00
RJ	Randy Johnson	8.00
RJ1	Randy Johnson	8.00
AJ	Andruw Jones	6.00
AJ1	Andruw Jones	6.00
CJ	Chipper Jones	8.00
KE	Jason Kendall	4.00
JL	Javy Lopez	4.00
GM	Greg Maddux	10.00
GM1	Greg Maddux	10.00
PM	Pedro J. Martinez	8.00
HM	Hideki Matsui	40.00
HM1	Hideki Matsui	50.00
HN	Hideo Nomo	8.00
RO	Roy Oswalt	4.00
RO1	Roy Oswalt	4.00
RP	Rafael Palmeiro	6.00
RP1	Rafael Palmeiro	6.00
CP	Corey Patterson	6.00
JP	Jay Payton	4.00
TP	Troy Percival	4.00
AP	Andy Pettitte	6.00
MP	Mike Piazza	10.00
MP1	Mike Piazza	10.00
MR	Manny Ramirez	8.00
AR	Alex Rodriguez	10.00
AR1	Alex Rodriguez	10.00
IR	Ivan Rodriguez	6.00
SR	Scott Rolen	8.00
KS	Kazuhiro Sasaki	4.00
CS	Curt Schilling	8.00
AS	Aaron Sele	4.00
JS	J.T. Snow	4.00
AS	Alfonso Soriano	8.00
AS1	Alfonso Soriano	8.00
SS	Sammy Sosa	12.00
SS1	Sammy Sosa	12.00
MS	Mike Stanton	4.00
IS	Ichiro Suzuki	25.00
IS1	Ichiro Suzuki	25.00
MS	Mike Sweeney	4.00
MT	Miguel Tejada	6.00
MT1	Miguel Tejada	6.00
JT	Jim Thome	8.00
JT1	Jim Thome	8.00
OV	Omar Vizquel	4.00
LW	Larry Walker	4.00
BW	Bernie Williams	6.00
BW1	Bernie Williams	6.00
KW	Kerry Wood	8.00
BZ	Barry Zito	6.00

Mark of Greatness

NM/M

400 Total cards produced

MoG	Mark McGwire	350.00
MoG	Mark McGwire/Gold/25	
MoG	Mark McGwire/ Silver/70	400.00

Mid-Summer Stars

NM/M

Common Player: 5.00
Inserted 1:72

RC	Roger Clemens	12.00
CD	Carlos Delgado	8.00
JE	Jim Edmonds	8.00
DE	Darin Erstad	8.00
FG	Freddy Garcia	5.00
TG	Tom Glavine	8.00
JG	Juan Gonzalez	8.00
SG	Shawn Green/SP	8.00
RJ	Randy Johnson	10.00
AJ	Andruw Jones	6.00
EM	Edgar Martinez	10.00
HN	Hideo Nomo	20.00
MP	Mike Piazza	15.00
MR	Manny Ramirez	8.00
AR	Alex Rodriguez	15.00
KS	Kazuhiro Sasaki	8.00
CS	Curt Schilling	10.00
SS	Sammy Sosa	15.00
IS	Ichiro Suzuki/SP	40.00
FT	Frank Thomas	8.00
RV	Robin Ventura	8.00
DW	David Wells	5.00
BZ	Barry Zito	8.00

Magical Performances

NM/M

Common Player: 8.00
Inserted 1:96
Golds: 1-2X
Production 50 sets

MP1	Hideki Matsui	20.00
MP2	Ken Griffey Jr.	15.00
MP3	Ichiro Suzuki	15.00
MP4	Ken Griffey Jr.	15.00
MP5	Hideo Nomo	8.00
MP6	Mickey Mantle	40.00
MP7	Ken Griffey Jr.	15.00
MP8	Barry Bonds	20.00
MP9	Mickey Mantle	40.00
MP10	Tom Seaver	8.00
MP11	Mike Piazza	15.00
MP12	Roger Clemens	12.00
MP13	Nolan Ryan	30.00
MP14	Nomar Garciaparra	15.00
MP15	Ernie Banks	15.00
MP16	Stan Musial	25.00
MP17	Mickey Mantle	40.00
MP18	Nolan Ryan	30.00
MP19	Nolan Ryan	30.00
MP20	Mickey Mantle	40.00
MP21	Ichiro Suzuki	15.00
MP22	Nolan Ryan	30.00
MP23	Tom Seaver	8.00
MP24	Ken Griffey Jr.	15.00
MP25	Hideo Nomo	8.00
MP26	Ken Griffey Jr.	15.00
MP27	Mark McGwire	30.00
MP28	Barry Bonds	20.00
MP29	Alex Rodriguez	20.00
MP30	Nolan Ryan	30.00
MP31	Mark McGwire	30.00
MP32	Nolan Ryan	30.00
MP33	Sammy Sosa	15.00
MP34	Ichiro Suzuki	15.00
MP35	Barry Bonds	20.00
MP36	Derek Jeter	20.00
MP37	Roger Clemens	15.00
MP38	Jason Giambi	8.00
MP39	Mickey Mantle	40.00
MP40	Ted Williams	40.00
MP41	Ted Williams	40.00
MP42	Ted Williams	40.00

Masters with the Leather

NM/M

Complete Set (12): 20.00
Common Player: .75
Inserted 1:12

L1	Darin Erstad	.75
L2	Andruw Jones	1.50
L3	Greg Maddux	3.00
L4	Nomar Garciaparra	3.00
L5	Torii Hunter	1.00
L6	Roberto Alomar	1.00
L7	Derek Jeter	5.00
L8	Eric Chavez	1.00
L9	Ichiro Suzuki	3.00
L10	Jim Edmonds	1.00
L11	Scott Rolen	1.50
L12	Alex Rodriguez	4.00

NL All-Star Swatch

NM/M

Common Player: 5.00
Inserted 1:72

SC	Sean Casey	5.00
CF	Cliff Floyd	5.00
TGl	Tom Glavine	8.00
TGw	Tony Gwynn	12.00
MH	Mike Hampton	5.00
TH	Trevor Hoffman	5.00
RK	Ryan Klesko	5.00
AL	Al Leiter	5.00
FM	Fred McGriff	5.00
MM	Matt Morris	8.00
CS	Curt Schilling	8.00
JV	Jose Vidro	5.00

National Pride

NM/M

Common Player: 3.00
Inserted 1:24

AA	Abe Alvarez	3.00
MA	Michael Aubrey	15.00
KB	Kyle Bakker	3.00
SB	Sean Burroughs	5.00
CC	Chad Cordero	3.00
SC	Shane Costa	3.00
RF	Robert Fick	3.00
SF	Sam Fuld	3.00
AH	Aaron Hill	8.00
BH	Bobby Hill	3.00
BH1	Bobby Hill	3.00
AJ	A.J. Hinch	3.00
PH	Philip Humber	5.00
CJ	Conor Jackson	3.00
JJe	Jason Jennings	3.00
GJ	Grant Johnson	3.00
JJ	Jacque Jones	8.00
JJ1	Jacque Jones	8.00
MJ	Mark Jurich	3.00
AK	Austin Kearns	12.00
AK1	Austin Kearns	12.00
WL	Wes Littleton	3.00
EM	Eric Milton	5.00
EM1	Eric Milton	5.00
RO	Roy Oswalt	6.00
RO1	Roy Oswalt	6.00
EP	Eric Patterson	3.00
DP	Dustin Pedroia	3.00
LP	Landon Powell	3.00
MP	Mark Prior	20.00
MP1	Mark Prior	20.00
CQ	Carlos Quentin	3.00
KSa	Kirk Saarloos	3.00
KSa1	Kirk Saarloos	3.00
CS	Clint Sammons	3.00
KSl	Kyle Sleeth	5.00
HS	Huston Street	5.00
BS	Brad Sullivan	3.00
BS1	Brad Sullivan	3.00
RW	Rickie Weeks	15.00
RW1	Rickie Weeks	15.00
BZ	Bob Zimmermann	3.00

Patch Logo

NM/M

Quantity produced listed

PL-JB	Jeff Bagwell/41	60.00
PLE-RC	Roger Clemens/34	
PLE-JD	Joe DiMaggio/9	
PLE-JG	Jason Giambi/34	
PLE-KG	Ken Griffey Jr./50	100.00
PL-TH	Todd Helton/41	50.00
PL-KI	Kazuhisa Ishii/54	40.00
PL-RJ	Randy Johnson/50	75.00
PL-CJ	Chipper Jones/52	80.00
PL-GM	Greg Maddux/50	100.00
PLE-MM	Mickey Mantle/10	
PLE-MG	Mark McGwire/43	
PLE-MP	Mike Piazza/61	120.00
PLE-AR	Alex Rodriguez/34	
PLE-SS	Sammy Sosa/60	100.00
PLE-IS	Ichiro Suzuki/46	
PL-FT	Frank Thomas/52	60.00
PL-BW	Bernie Williams/42	40.00

Patch Number

NM/M

Quantity produced listed

PNE-JG	Jason Giambi/68	40.00
PNE-KG	Ken Griffey Jr./97	70.00
PN-TH	Todd Helton/27	
PN-KI	Kazuhisa Ishii/63	40.00
PN-RJ	Randy Johnson/90	75.00
PN-CJ	Chipper Jones/44	
PNE-MG	Mark McGwire/60	180.00
PNE-AR	Alex Rodriguez/56	90.00
PNE-SS	Sammy Sosa/100	80.00
PN-FT	Frank Thomas/91	60.00
PN-BW	Bernie Williams/66	50.00

Patch Stripes

NM/M

Quantity produced listed

PS-JB	Jeff Bagwell/73	60.00
PSE-JG	Jason Giambi/66	40.00
PSE-KG	Ken Griffey Jr./63	75.00
PS-TH	Todd Helton/43	
PS-KI	Kazuhisa Ishii/58	40.00
PS-RJ	Randy Johnson/58	65.00
PS-CJ	Chipper Jones/58	60.00
PSE-MG	Mark McGwire/63	180.00
PSE-AR	Alex Rodriguez/63	80.00
PSE-SS	Sammy Sosa/63	100.00
PSE-IS	Ichiro Suzuki/63	180.00
PS-FT	Frank Thomas/58	60.00
PS-BW	Bernie Williams/58	50.00

Piece of the Action

NM/M

Common Player: 5.00
Inserted 1:288
Cards are not serial numbered
Print runs provided by Upper Deck

BA	Bobby Abreu/125	5.00
GA	Garret Anderson/150	5.00
AB	Adrian Beltre/100	10.00
BB	Barry Bonds/125	30.00
KB	Kevin Brown/100	5.00
PB	Pat Burrell/150	8.00
DE	Darin Erstad/125	5.00
FG	Freddy Garcia/100	5.00
BG	Brian Giles/100	5.00
TG	Troy Glaus/150	6.00
JG	Juan Gonzalez/100	8.00
LG	Luis Gonzalez/100	5.00
SG	Shawn Green/175	5.00
VG	Vladimir Guerrero/50	15.00
THe	Todd Helton/100	10.00
THo	Trevor Hoffman/150	5.00
DJ	Derek Jeter/65	40.00
RJ	Randy Johnson/100	10.00
CJ	Chipper Jones/62	15.00
JK	Jason Kendall/100	5.00
KE	Jeff Kent/150	5.00
RK	Ryan Klesko/75	6.00
EM	Edgar Martinez/125	5.00
PM	Pedro Martinez/150	10.00
PN	Phil Nevin/75	5.00
HN	Hideo Nomo/100	20.00
RP	Rafael Palmeiro/150	10.00
Ara	Aramis Ramirez/100	8.00
MP	Mike Piazza/150	15.00
ARo	Alex Rodriguez/100	15.00
IR	Ivan Rodriguez/10	
KS	Kazuhiro Sasaki/100	5.00
CS	Curt Schilling/100	10.00
RS	Richie Sexson/160	8.00
GS	Gary Sheffield/100	6.00
SS	Sammy Sosa/85	20.00
IS	Ichiro Suzuki/25	
FT	Frank Thomas/150	8.00
JT	Jim Thome/125	10.00
JV	Jose Vidro/100	5.00
LW	Larry Walker/150	5.00
BW	Bernie Williams/125	6.00

Slammin' Sammy Tribute Jersey

NM/M

384 Total produced

SST	Sammy Sosa	175.00
SST	Sammy Sosa/Gold/25	290.00
SST	Sammy Sosa/ Silver/66	240.00

Star-Spangled Swatches

		NM/M
Common Player:		4.00
Inserted 1:72		
MA	Michael Aubrey	8.00
KB	Kyle Bakker	4.00
CC	Chad Cordero	4.00
SC	Shane Costa	6.00
AH	Aaron Hill	4.00
PH	Philip Humber	6.00
CJ	Conor Jackson	8.00
GJ	Grant Johnson	4.00
EP	Eric Patterson	8.00
DP	Dustin Pedroia	6.00
LP	Landon Powell	6.00
CQ	Carlos Quentin	8.00
KS	Kyle Sleeth	6.00
HS	Huston Street	10.00
BS	Brad Sullivan	4.00
RW	Rickie Weeks	15.00

The Chase for 755

		NM/M
Complete Set (15):		15.00
Common Player:		.75
Inserted 1:8		
C1	Troy Glaus	.75
C2	Andruw Jones	1.00
C3	Manny Ramirez	1.25
C4	Sammy Sosa	2.50
C5	Ken Griffey Jr.	3.00
C6	Adam Dunn	1.25
C7	Todd Helton	1.00
C8	Lance Berkman	.75
C9	Jeff Bagwell	1.00
C10	Shawn Green	.75
C11	Vladimir Guerrero	1.50
C12	Barry Bonds	4.00
C13	Alex Rodriguez	3.00
C14	Juan Gonzalez	.75
C15	Carlos Delgado	.75

Triple Game Jersey

		NM/M
Quantity produced listed		
Golds:		1.5-2X
Production 50, 25 or 10		
ARZ	Randy Johnson, Curt Schilling, Luis Gonzalez/150	40.00
CIN	Ken Griffey Jr., Sean Casey, Adam Dunn/150	40.00
HOU	Jeff Bagwell, Lance Berkman, Craig Biggio/150	40.00
TEX	Rafael Palmeiro, Alex Rodriguez, Juan Gonzalez/150	40.00
ATL	Chipper Jones, Greg Maddux, Gary Sheffield/75	65.00
CHC	Sammy Sosa, Moises Alou, Kerry Wood/75	50.00
NYM	Mike Piazza, Roberto Alomar, Mo Vaughn/75	40.00
SEA	Ichiro Suzuki, Freddy Garcia, Bret Boone/75	80.00
NYY	Roger Clemens, Jason Giambi, Bernie Williams/75	

Superstar Slam Jerseys

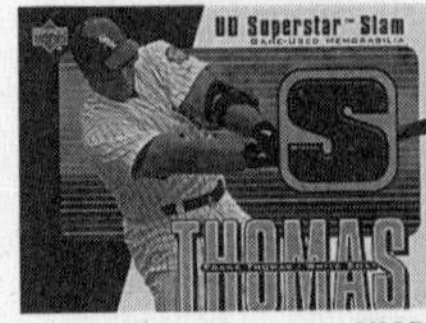

		NM/M
Common Player:		4.00
Inserted 1:48		
JB	Jeff Bagwell	8.00
JG	Jason Giambi	6.00
JGo	Juan Gonzalez	6.00
LG	Luis Gonzalez	4.00
KG	Ken Griffey Jr.	15.00
CJ	Chipper Jones	10.00
MP	Mike Piazza	10.00
AR	Alex Rodriguez	15.00
SS	Sammy Sosa	15.00
FT	Frank Thomas	8.00

Superior Sluggers

		NM/M
Complete Set (18):		30.00
Common Player:		1.00
Inserted 1:8		
S1	Troy Glaus	1.00
S2	Chipper Jones	1.50
S3	Manny Ramirez	1.50
S4	Ken Griffey Jr.	2.50
S5	Jim Thome	1.50
S6	Todd Helton	1.00
S7	Lance Berkman	1.00
S8	Derek Jeter	4.00
S9	Vladimir Guerrero	1.50
S10	Mike Piazza	2.50
S11	Hideki Matsui	3.00
S12	Barry Bonds	4.00
S13	Mickey Mantle	5.00
S14	Alex Rodriguez	3.00
S15	Ted Williams	3.00
S16	Carlos Delgado	1.00
S17	Frank Thomas	1.00
S18	Adam Dunn	1.50

Super Patch Logos

Common Player:
Inserted 1:7,500
No Pricing

500 HR Club

		NM/M
Production 350 cards		
SS	Sammy Sosa	150.00
SS	Sammy Sosa (autographed/21)	2,300

2003 UPPER DECK YANKEES 100TH ANNIVERSARY

		NM/M
Complete Set (30):		15.00
Common Player:		.50
1	Babe Ruth	2.00
2	Tony Lazzeri	.50
3	Lou Gehrig	1.50
4	Lou Gehrig	1.50
5	Red Rolfe	.50
6	Lou Gehrig	1.50
7	Bill Dickey	.50
8	Joe DiMaggio	1.50
9	Charlie Keller	.50
10	Frank Crosetti	.50
11	Phil Rizzuto	.50
12	Joe DiMaggio	1.50
13	Joe DiMaggio	1.50
14	Phil Rizzuto	.50
15	Mickey Mantle	2.00
16	Yogi Berra	.75
17	Yogi Berra	.75
18	Mickey Mantle	2.00
19	Whitey Ford	.50
20	Mickey Mantle	2.00
21	Thurman Munson	.75
22	Thurman Munson	.75
23	Bernie Williams	.50
24	Jorge Posada	.50
25	Mariano Rivera	.50
26	Derek Jeter	1.50
27	Hideki Matsui	1.00
28	Hideki Matsui	1.00
29	Roger Clemens	1.50
30	Yankee Stadium	.50

2003 UD AUTHENTICS

		NM/M
Complete Set (130):		
Common Player:		.25
Common Rk Hype (101-130):		4.00
Production 999		
Pack (4):		10.00
Box (10 + framed auto.):		170.00
1	Pee Wee Reese	.25
2	Richie Ashburn	.25
3	Derek Jeter	2.50
4	Alex Rodriguez	2.00
5	Jose Vidro	.25
6	Miguel Tejada	.50
7	Nomar Garciaparra	2.00
8	Pat Burrell	.50
9	Albert Pujols	2.00
10	Jeff Bagwell	.75
11	Stan Musial	1.00
12	Mickey Mantle	3.00
13	J.D. Drew	.25
14	Ivan Rodriguez	.75
15	Joe Morgan	.25
16	Ted Williams	2.00
17	Travis Hafner	.25
18	Chipper Jones	1.50
19	Hideo Nomo	.50
20	Gary Sheffield	.50
21	Jacque Jones	.25
22	Alfonso Soriano	1.50
23	Roberto Alomar	.50
24	Jeff Kent	.40
25	Omar Vizquel	.40
26	Ernie Banks	1.00
27	Shawn Green	.50
28	Tim Hudson	.50
29	Jim Edmonds	.50
30	Brandon Larson	.25
31	Doug Mientkiewicz	.25
32	Darin Erstad	.50
33	Bobby Hill	.25
34	Todd Helton	.75
35	Kazuhisa Ishii	.25
36	Lance Berkman	.50
37	Eric Hinske	.25
38	Jason Kendall	.25
39	Bob Feller	.50
40	Luis Gonzalez	.40
41	Sammy Sosa	2.00
42	Mike Piazza	1.50
43	Roger Clemens	2.00
44	Jose Cruz Jr.	.25
45	Mark Prior	2.00
46	Mark Teixeira	.40
47	Phil Nevin	.25
48	Lyle Overbay	.25
49	Manny Ramirez	.75
50	Brian Giles	.40
51	Preston Wilson	.25
52	Jermaine Dye	.25
53	Troy Glaus	.50
54	Frank Thomas	.75
55	Jim Thome	.75
56	Barry Bonds	2.50
57	Carlos Delgado	.75
58	Jason Giambi	1.00
59	Joe Mays	.25
60	Andruw Jones	.75
61	Billy Williams	.25
62	Vladimir Guerrero	.75
63	Scott Rolen	.75
64	Juan Marichal	.25
65	Austin Kearns	.50
66	Kerry Wood	.75
67	Bret Boone	.25
68	Shea Hillenbrand	.25
69	Mike Sweeney	.25
70	Rocco Baldelli	.25
71	Ken Griffey Jr.	1.50
72	Cliff Floyd	.25
73	Greg Maddux	1.50
74	Mike Hampton	.25
75	Larry Walker	.40
76	Nolan Ryan	3.00
77	Rollie Fingers	.25
78	Mike Mussina	.75
79	Matt Morris	.25
80	Robin Roberts	.25
81	Barry Zito	.50
82	Curt Schilling	.50
83	Ken Harvey	.25
84	Troy Percival	.25
85	Tom Seaver	1.00
86	Mariano Rivera	.40
87	Raul Mondesi	.25
88	Adam Dunn	.50
89	Roy Oswalt	.25
90	Pedro J. Martinez	1.00
91	Andy Pettitte	.50
92	Tom Glavine	.50
93	Torii Hunter	.50
94	Joe Thurston	.25
95	Runelvys Hernandez	.25
96	Randy Johnson	1.00
97	Bernie Williams	.75
98	Ichiro Suzuki	1.50
99	C.C. Sabathia	.25
100	Bobby Abreu	.40
101	*Jose Contreras*	6.00
102	*Hideki Matsui*	15.00
103	*Chris Capuano*	4.00
104	*Willie Eyre*	4.00
105	*Lew Ford*	6.00
106	*Shane Bazzell*	6.00
107	*Guillermo Quiroz*	6.00
108	*Fernando Cabrera*	4.00
109	*Francisco Cruceta*	4.00
110	Jhonny Peralta	4.00
111	*Bobby Madritsch*	8.00
112	*Diegomar Markwell*	4.00
113	*Matt Bruback*	4.00
114	*Matt Kata*	6.00
115	*Rob Hammock*	4.00
116	*Brandon Webb*	8.00
117	*Jon Leicester*	4.00
118	*Josh Willingham*	6.00
119	*Prentice Redman*	4.00
120	*Jeff Duncan*	4.00
121	*Craig Brazell*	6.00
122	*Jeremy Griffiths*	4.00
123	*Phil Seibel*	4.00
124	*Luis Ayala*	4.00
125	*Miguel Ojeda*	6.00
126	*Jeremy Wedel*	4.00
127	*Josh Hall*	6.00
128	*Oscar Villarreal*	4.00
129	*Clint Barmes*	8.00
130	*Nook Logan*	4.00

Cut Signatures

Mickey Mantle/7
Ted Williams/9

Framed Autograph

	NM/M
Common Framed Autograph:	40.00
Inserted 1:box	
Lance Berkman/150	40.00
Lance Berkman/50	60.00
Lance Berkman/17	
Hank Blalock/325	45.00
Hank Blalock/300	45.00
Hank Blalock/200	45.00
Hank Blalock/175	45.00
Hank Blalock/12	
Pat Burrell/330	40.00
Pat Burrell/240	40.00
Pat Burrell/150	40.00
Pat Burrell/5	
Gary Carter/225	50.00
Gary Carter/75	60.00
Gary Carter/8	
Jose Contreras/350	50.00
Jose Contreras/120	50.00
Carlton Fisk/250	50.00
Carlton Fisk/125	75.00

Carlton Fisk/70	80.00
Carlton Fisk/27	
Nomar Garciaparra/250	100.00
Nomar Garciaparra/150	100.00
Nomar Garciaparra/75	120.00
Nomar Garciaparra/5	
Jason Giambi/350	40.00
Jason Giambi/300	40.00
Jason Giambi/200	40.00
Jason Giambi/150	40.00
Jason Giambi/100	40.00
Jason Giambi/75	40.00
Jason Giambi/25	
Bob Gibson/200	60.00
Bob Gibson/50	120.00
Bob Gibson/45	120.00
Troy Glaus/350	40.00
Troy Glaus/200	40.00
Troy Glaus/100	50.00
Troy Glaus/25	
Tom Glavine/275	50.00
Tom Glavine/150	50.00
Tom Glavine/47	75.00
Ken Griffey Jr/325	90.00
Ken Griffey Jr./200	90.00
Ken Griffey Jr/75	100.00
Ken Griffey Jr./30	120.00
Vladimir Guerrero/150	60.00
Vladimir Guerrero/27	125.00
Drew Henson/350	40.00
Drew Henson/300	40.00
Drew Henson/250	40.00
Drew Henson/100	40.00
Chipper Jones/350	70.00
Chipper Jones/200	70.00
Chipper Jones/100	85.00
Chipper Jones/10	
Austin Kearns/325	40.00
Austin Kearns/300	40.00
Austin Kearns/200	40.00
Austin Kearns/175	40.00
Austin Kearns/28	80.00
Mickey Mantle/25	
Mickey Mantle/7	
Hideki Matsui/75	300.00
Hideki Matsui/55	300.00
Mark Prior/300	75.00
Mark Prior/250	75.00
Mark Prior/175	75.00
Mark Prior/100	75.00
Mark Prior/25	
Mark Prior/22	
Cal Ripken Jr/125	175.00
Cal Ripken Jr./50	200.00
Cal Ripken Jr./8	
Phil Rizzuto/350	50.00
Phil Rizzuto/200	60.00
Phil Rizzuto/100	75.00
Phil Rizzuto/10	
Scott Rolen/300	50.00
Scott Rolen/100	65.00
Scott Rolen/27	120.00
Nolan Ryan/150	125.00
Nolan Ryan/100	180.00
Nolan Ryan/50	200.00
Nolan Ryan/34	240.00
Tom Seaver/100	75.00
Tom Seaver/50	100.00
Tom Seaver/41	100.00
Ozzie Smith/150	85.00
Ozzie Smith/50	120.00
Ozzie Smith/1	
Duke Snider/150	60.00
Duke Snider/50	100.00
Duke Snider/4	
Ichiro Suzuki/75	300.00
Ichiro Suzuki/51	350.00
Mark Teixeira/325	60.00
Mark Teixeira/200	60.00
Mark Teixeira/175	60.00
Mark Teixeira/150	60.00
Mark Teixeira/23	
Ted Williams/25	
Ted Williams/9	

Rookie Hype Gold

Cards (101-130): 1-2X
Production 50

Star Quality

NM/M

Common Player: 4.00
Production 350 unless noted
Golds: 1-2X
Production 50, 25 or 10
No pricing for #'d to 25 or less

RA	Roberto Alomar	6.00
JB	Jeff Bagwell	8.00
JO	Josh Beckett	4.00
LB	Lance Berkman	5.00
RC	Roger Clemens	15.00
RC1	Roger Clemens	15.00
CD	Carlos Delgado	5.00
JD	J.D. Drew	4.00
AD	Adam Dunn	6.00
JG	Jason Giambi	4.00
TR	Troy Glaus	5.00
TG	Tom Glavine	4.00
SG	Shawn Green	4.00
KG	Ken Griffey Jr./250	12.00
VG	Vladimir Guerrero	6.00
TH	Todd Helton	6.00
EH	Eric Hinske	4.00
CJ	Chipper Jones	8.00
AK	Austin Kearns	6.00
JK	Jeff Kent	4.00
MM	Mickey Mantle/250	100.00
HM	Hideki Matsui/250	25.00
PM	Paul Molitor/250	8.00
MU	Mike Mussina	6.00
HN	Hideo Nomo	8.00
RO	Roy Oswalt	4.00
RP	Rafael Palmeiro	6.00
MP	Mark Prior	15.00
AP	Albert Pujols	20.00
AP1	Albert Pujols	20.00
CR	Cal Ripken Jr./250	25.00
NR	Nolan Ryan/130	50.00
TS	Tom Seaver	8.00
GS	Gary Sheffield	4.00
AS	Alfonso Soriano	10.00
SS	Sammy Sosa/250	12.00
CS	Casey Stengel	15.00
JT	Jim Thome	8.00
BW	Bernie Williams	8.00
TW	Ted Williams/250	65.00
KW	Kerry Wood	8.00

Threads of Time

NM/M

Common Player: 4.00
Production 350, unless noted
Golds: 1-2X
Production 50, 25 or 10
No pricing for #'d to 25 or less

JB	Johnny Bench	10.00
GC	Gary Carter	4.00
RC	Roger Clemens	15.00
TC	Ty Cobb	100.00
DD	Don Drysdale	15.00
DE	Dennis Eckersley	4.00
RF	Rollie Fingers	4.00
LG	Lou Gehrig/250	140.00
JG	Jason Giambi/250	6.00
JU	Juan Gonzalez	5.00
KG	Ken Griffey Jr./250	12.00
VG	Vladimir Guerrero	6.00
RJ	Randy Johnson	8.00
CJ	Chipper Jones	8.00
HK	Harmon Killebrew	12.00
GM	Greg Maddux	8.00
MM	Mickey Mantle/250	100.00
RM	Roger Maris	40.00
PM	Pedro J. Martinez	8.00
DM	Don Mattingly	20.00
HN	Hideo Nomo	8.00
AP	Andy Pettitte	6.00
MP	Mike Piazza	10.00
AP	Albert Pujols	20.00
CR	Cal Ripken Jr.	25.00
FR	Frank Robinson	8.00
AR	Alex Rodriguez	12.00
IR	Ivan Rodriguez	5.00
NR	Nolan Ryan	30.00
RS	Ryne Sandberg	12.00
TS	Tom Seaver	8.00
OS	Ozzie Smith	10.00
SS	Sammy Sosa/250	12.00
IS	Ichiro Suzuki/250	30.00
FT	Frank Thomas	6.00
JT	Jim Thome	8.00
HW	Honus Wagner	75.00
TW	Ted Williams/250	65.00
MW	Maury Wills	4.00
DW	Dave Winfield/250	6.00

2003 UPPER DECK CLASSIC PORTRAITS

NM/M

Complete Set (232):
Common Player: .15
Common SP (101-145): 2.00
Inserted 1:4
Common SP (145-190): 3.00
Production 2,003
Common Royalty (191-232): 2.00
Production 1,200
Pack (5): 3.00
Box (18 + Bust): 75.00

1	Ken Griffey Jr.	1.50
2	Randy Johnson	1.00
3	Rafael Furcal	.25
4	Omar Vizquel	.25
5	Shawn Green	.40
6	Roy Oswalt	.40
7	Hideo Nomo	.40
8	Jason Giambi	.40
9	Barry Bonds	2.50
10	Mike Piazza	1.50
11	Ichiro Suzuki	2.00
12	Carlos Delgado	.40
13	Preston Wilson	.15
14	Lance Berkman	.25
15	Magglio Ordonez	.25
16	Kerry Wood	.75
17	Ivan Rodriguez	.75
18	Chipper Jones	1.00
19	Adam Dunn	.75
20	C.C. Sabathia	.15
21	Mike MacDougal	.15
22	Torii Hunter	.40
23	Jim Thome	.75
24	Hank Blalock	.40
25	Johnny Damon	.50
26	Troy Glaus	.40
27	Manny Ramirez	.75
28	Mark Prior	1.00
29	Brent Mayne	.15
30	Derek Jeter	2.50
31	Tim Hudson	.40
32	Mike Cameron	.15
33	Mark Teixeira	.40
34	Shannon Stewart	.15
35	Tim Salmon	.25
36	Luis Gonzalez	.25
37	Jason Johnson	.15
38	Shea Hillenbrand	.15
39	Bartolo Colon	.25
40	Austin Kearns	.40
41	Vladimir Guerrero	1.00
42	Tom Glavine	.40
43	Andres Galarraga	.25
44	Kazuhiro Sasaki	.15
45	Juan Gonzalez	.75
46	Vernon Wells	.25
47	Jeff Bagwell	.75
48	Mike Sweeney	.15
49	Carlos Beltran	.50
50	Dave Roberts	.15
51	Todd Helton	.75
52	Carlos Pena	.15
53	Darin Erstad	.25
54	Gary Sheffield	.40
55	Lyle Overbay	.15
56	Sammy Sosa	1.50
57	Mike Mussina	.50
58	Matt Morris	.25
59	Roberto Alomar	.50
60	Larry Walker	.25
61	Jacque Jones	.15
62	Josh Beckett	.40
63	Richie Sexson	.50
64	Derek Lowe	.15
65	Pedro J. Martinez	1.00
66	Moises Alou	.25
67	Craig Biggio	.25
68	Curt Schilling	.75
69	Jesse Foppert	.15
70	Nomar Garciaparra	1.50
71	Barry Zito	.40
72	Alfonso Soriano	.75
73	Miguel Tejada	.50
74	Rafael Palmeiro	.50
75	Albert Pujols	2.00
76	Mariano Rivera	.25
77	Bobby Abreu	.25
78	Alex Rodriguez	2.00
79	Andruw Jones	.50
80	Frank Thomas	.75
81	Greg Maddux	1.50
82	Jim Edmonds	.40
83	Bernie Williams	.50
84	Roger Clemens	2.00
85	Eric Chavez	.25
86	Scott Rolen	1.00
87	Jorge Posada	.50
88	Bret Boone	.25
89	Ben Sheets	.25
90	John Olerud	.15
91	J.D. Drew	.25
92	Aaron Boone	.15
93	Corey Koskie	.15
94	Sean Casey	.25
95	Jose Cruz Jr.	.15
96	Pat Burrell	.40
97	Jose Guillen	.15
98	Mark Mulder	.25
99	Garret Anderson	.25
100	Kazuhisa Ishii	.15
101	*Dave Matranga*	2.00
102	*Colin Porter*	2.00
103	*Jason Gilfillan*	2.00
104	*Carlos Mendez*	2.00
105	*Jason Shiell*	2.00
106	*Kevin Tolar*	2.00
107	*Terrmel Sledge*	3.00
108	*Craig Brazell*	4.00
109	*Bernie Castro*	2.00
110	*Tim Olson*	3.00
111	*Kevin Ohme*	2.00
112	Pedro Liriano	2.00
113	Joe Borowski	2.00
114	*Edgar Gonzalez*	3.00
115	Joe Thurston	2.00
116	Bobby Hill	2.00
117	*Michel Hernandez*	2.00
118	*Arnie Munoz*	2.00
119	*David Sanders*	2.00
120	*Willie Eyre*	3.00
121	*Brent Hoard*	2.00
122	*Lew Ford*	4.00
123	*Beau Kemp*	2.00
124	*Jonathan Pridie*	2.00
125	*Mike Ryan*	4.00
126	*Richard Fischer*	2.00
127	*Luis Ayala*	2.00
128	*Mike Neu*	2.00
129	*Joe Valentine*	2.00
130	*Nate Bland*	2.00
131	*Shane Bazzell*	2.00
132	*Jason Roach*	2.00
133	*Diegomar Markwell*	2.00
134	*Francisco Rosario*	2.00
135	*Guillermo Quiroz*	4.00
136	Jerome Williams	2.00
137	*Fernando Cabrera*	2.00
138	*Francisco Cruceta*	2.00
139	Jhonny Peralta	4.00
140	*Rett Johnson*	2.00
141	*Aaron Looper*	2.00
142	*Bobby Madritsch*	6.00
143	Dan Haren	2.00
144	Jose Castillo	2.00
145	*Chris Waters*	3.00
146	*Hideki Matsui*	10.00
147	*Jose Contreras*	4.00
148	*Felix Sanchez*	3.00
149	*Jon Leicester*	3.00
150	*Todd Wellemeyer*	3.00
151	*Matt Bruback*	3.00
152	*Chris Capuano*	3.00
153	*Oscar Villarreal*	3.00
154	*Matt Kata*	3.00
155	*Robby Hammock*	3.00
156	Gerald Laird	3.00
157	*Brandon Webb*	4.00
158	*Tommy Whiteman*	3.00
159	*Andrew Brown*	3.00
160	*Alfredo Gonzalez*	3.00
161	Carlos Rivera	3.00
162	*Rick Roberts*	3.00
163	Dontrelle Willis	3.00
164	*Josh Willingham*	4.00

165	*Prentice Redman*	3.00
166	*Jeff Duncan*	4.00
167	Jose Reyes	3.00
168	Jeremy Griffiths	3.00
169	*Phil Seibel*	3.00
170	*Heath Bell*	3.00
171	*Anthony Ferrari*	3.00
172	*Mike Nicolas*	3.00
173	*Cory Stewart*	3.00
174	*Miguel Ojeda*	5.00
175	*Rickie Weeks*	10.00
176	*Delmon Young*	10.00
177	Tommy Phelps	3.00
178	*Josh Hall*	4.00
179	*Ryan Cameron*	3.00
180	Garrett Atkins	3.00
181	*Clint Barmes*	6.00
182	*Michael Hessman*	3.00
183	Chin-Hui Tsao	3.00
184	Rocco Baldelli	3.00
185	*Bo Hart*	3.00
186	*Wilfredo Ledezma*	3.00
187	Miguel Cabrera	5.00
188	*Ian Ferguson*	3.00
189	*Micheal Nakamura*	3.00
190	*Alejandro Machado*	3.00
191	Mickey Mantle	12.00
192	Ted Williams	10.00
193	Mark Prior	8.00
194	Stan Musial	6.00
195	Phil Rizzuto	3.00
196	Nolan Ryan	12.00
197	Tom Seaver	4.00
198	Robin Yount	5.00
199	Yogi Berra	3.00
200	Ernie Banks	8.00
201	Willie McCovey	3.00
202	Ralph Kiner	3.00
203	Ken Griffey Jr.	4.00
204	Sammy Sosa	5.00
205	Derek Jeter	8.00
206	Nomar Garciaparra	6.00
207	Alex Rodriguez	6.00
208	Ichiro Suzuki	4.00
209	Mike Piazza	4.00
210	Jackie Robinson	6.00
211	Roberto Clemente	8.00
212	Babe Ruth	12.00
213	Duke Snider	3.00
214	Greg Maddux	4.00
215	Juan Marichal	3.00
216	Joe Morgan	2.00
217	Rollie Fingers	2.00
218	Warren Spahn	4.00
219	Pee Wee Reese	2.00
220	Troy Glaus	2.00
221	Jason Giambi	2.00
222	Roger Clemens	6.00
223	Pedro J. Martinez	3.00
224	Chipper Jones	4.00
225	Randy Johnson	3.00
226	Jim Thome	3.00
227	Barry Bonds	8.00
228	Hideo Nomo	2.00
229	Whitey Ford	3.00
230	Bob Gibson	4.00
231	Alfonso Soriano	4.00
232	Richie Ashburn	3.00

Gold

No pricing due to scarcity
Production 25 sets

Stitches Jersey

		NM/M
Common Player:		4.00
Production 299 sets		
Golds:		No Pricing
Production 25 sets		
JB	Jeff Bagwell	6.00
RB	Rocco Baldelli	4.00
HB	Hank Blalock	6.00
HC	Hee Seop Choi	4.00
RC	Roger Clemens	15.00
JD	J.D. Drew	4.00
AD	Adam Dunn	8.00
JE	Jim Edmonds	6.00
RF	Rafael Furcal	4.00
JG	Jason Giambi	6.00
TG	Troy Glaus	6.00
SG	Shawn Green	4.00
KG	Ken Griffey Jr.	10.00
VG	Vladimir Guerrero	8.00
TH	Torii Hunter	6.00
RJ	Randy Johnson	8.00
AJ	Andruw Jones	6.00
CJ	Chipper Jones	8.00
JK	Jeff Kent	4.00
ML	Mike Lowell	4.00
GM	Greg Maddux	10.00
PM	Pedro J. Martinez	8.00
HM	Hideki Matsui	40.00
MM	Matt Morris	6.00
HN	Hideo Nomo	8.00
MO	Magglio Ordonez	4.00
RO	Roy Oswalt	4.00
CP	Corey Patterson	6.00
AP	Andy Pettitte	6.00
MI	Mike Piazza	8.00
MP	Mark Prior	10.00
AL	Albert Pujols	15.00
AR	Alex Rodriguez	10.00
IR	Ivan Rodriguez	6.00
CS	Curt Schilling	8.00
GS	Gary Sheffield	6.00
AS	Alfonso Soriano	8.00
SS	Sammy Sosa	15.00
IS	Ichiro Suzuki	25.00
JT	Jim Thome	8.00
DW	Dontrelle Willis	8.00
KW	Kerry Wood	8.00

Stitches Patch

		NM/M
Common Player:		15.00
Production 99 sets		
Golds:		No Pricing
Production 10 sets		
JB	Jeff Bagwell	25.00
RB	Rocco Baldelli	15.00
HB	Hank Blalock	25.00
HC	Hee Seop Choi	15.00
RC	Roger Clemens	40.00
JD	J.D. Drew	15.00
AD	Adam Dunn	15.00
JE	Jim Edmonds	20.00
RF	Rafael Furcal	15.00
JG	Jason Giambi	15.00
TG	Troy Glaus	15.00
SG	Shawn Green	15.00
KG	Ken Griffey Jr.	50.00
VG	Vladimir Guerrero	25.00
TH	Torii Hunter	15.00
RJ	Randy Johnson	30.00
AJ	Andruw Jones	15.00
CJ	Chipper Jones	25.00
JK	Jeff Kent	15.00
ML	Mike Lowell	15.00
GM	Greg Maddux	35.00
PM	Pedro J. Martinez	25.00
HM	Hideki Matsui	85.00
MM	Matt Morris	15.00
HN	Hideo Nomo	40.00
MO	Maggiio Ordonez	15.00
RO	Roy Oswalt	15.00
CP	Corey Patterson	20.00
AP	Andy Pettitte	20.00
MI	Mike Piazza	40.00
MP	Mark Prior	25.00
AL	Albert Pujols	40.00
AR	Alex Rodriguez	50.00
IR	Ivan Rodriguez	20.00
CS	Curt Schilling	20.00
GS	Gary Sheffield	15.00
AS	Alfonso Soriano	20.00
SS	Sammy Sosa	35.00
IS	Ichiro Suzuki	120.00
JT	Jim Thome	20.00
DW	Dontrelle Willis	20.00
KW	Kerry Wood	25.00

Bronze Bust

		NM/M
Common Player:		
YB	Yogi Berra	25.00
RC	Roberto Clemente	60.00
NG	Nomar Garciaparra	40.00
JG	Jason Giambi	25.00
BG	Bob Gibson	25.00
KG	Ken Griffey Jr./300	40.00
MM	Mickey Mantle	70.00
HM	Hideki Matsui	30.00
SM	Stan Musial	40.00
BRS	Babe Ruth Sox/300	60.00
BRY	Babe Ruth Yanks	60.00
NRA	Nolan Ryan Astros	50.00
NRA	Nolan Ryan Astros/300	50.00
NRM	Nolan Ryan Mets	50.00
TSM	Tom Seaver Mets	25.00
TSR	Tom Seaver Reds/300	25.00
TSR	Tom Seaver Reds	25.00
DS	Duke Snider	25.00
SS	Sammy Sosa/300	40.00
IS	Ichiro Suzuki/300	40.00
TW	Ted Williams	50.00

Bronze Bust Autograph

		NM/M
Some not priced due to scarcity		
YB	Yogi Berra	100.00
NG	Nomar Garciaparra/106	125.00
BG	Bob Gibson	60.00
KG	Ken Griffey Jr.	100.00
HM	Hideki Matsui	250.00
SM	Stan Musial/62	120.00
DS	Duke Snider	90.00
IS	Ichiro Suzuki/62	275.00

Bust Signature

No Pricing

Marble Bust

		NM/M
Common Player:		
YB	Yogi Berra/125	40.00
YB	Yogi Berra/250	25.00
RC	Roberto Clemente/250	70.00
NG	Nomar Garciaparra/250	40.00
JG	Jason Giambi	25.00
BG	Bob Gibson/125	30.00
BG	Bob Gibson/250	25.00
KG	Ken Griffey Jr./250	40.00
MM	Mickey Mantle/80	80.00
MM	Mickey Mantle/125	80.00
HM	Hideki Matsui/250	60.00
SM	Stan Musial/250	50.00
BRS	Babe Ruth Sox/250	60.00
BRY	Babe Ruth Yanks/125	75.00
BRY	Babe Ruth Yanks/250	65.00
NRA	Nolan Ryan Astros/125	60.00
NRA	Nolan Ryan Astros/250	50.00
NRM	Nolan Ryan Mets/125	60.00
NRM	Nolan Ryan Mets/250	50.00
TSM	Tom Seaver Mets/125	40.00
TSM	Tom Seaver Mets/250	30.00
TSR	Tom Seaver Reds/125	40.00
TSR	Tom Seaver Reds/250	30.00
DS	Duke Snider/100	40.00
DS	Duke Snider/250	40.00
SS	Sammy Sosa/250	40.00
IS	Ichiro Suzuki/250	50.00
TW	Ted Williams/125	65.00
TW	Ted Williams/250	50.00

Pewter Bust

		NM/M
Common Player:		
YB	Yogi Berra/75	40.00
YB	Yogi Berra/100	40.00
RC	Roberto Clemente/100	100.00
NG	Nomar Garciaparra/100	60.00
JG	Jason Giambi/100	40.00
BG	Bob Gibson/75	40.00
BG	Bob Gibson/100	40.00
KG	Ken Griffey Jr./100	70.00
MM	Mickey Mantle/75	125.00
MM	Mickey Mantle/100	125.00
HM	Hideki Matsui/100	50.00
SM	Stan Musial/100	60.00
BRS	Babe Ruth Sox/100	80.00
BRY	Babe Ruth Yanks/75	90.00
BRY	Babe Ruth Yanks/100	90.00
NRA	Nolan Ryan Astros/75	80.00
NRA	Nolan Ryan Astros/100	80.00
NRM	Nolan Ryan Mets/75	80.00
NRM	Nolan Ryan Mets/100	80.00
TSM	Tom Seaver Mets/75	40.00
TSM	Tom Seaver Mets/100	40.00
TSR	Tom Seaver Reds/100	40.00
TSR	Tom Seaver Reds/75	40.00
DS	Duke Snider/75	40.00
DS	Duke Snider/100	40.00
SS	Sammy Sosa/100	60.00
IS	Ichiro Suzuki/100	65.00
TW	Ted Williams/75	100.00
TW	Ted Williams/100	100.00

Signs of Success

		NM/M
Common Player:		6.00
MI	Milton Bradley/220	10.00
DB	Dewon Brazelton/299	6.00
JB	John Buck/98	8.00
MB	Mark Buehrle/220	10.00
BR	Brandon Claussen/121	6.00
BC	Brad Cresse/121	10.00
JD	Johnny Damon/297	30.00
BD	Ben Diggins/299	6.00
JI	Jay Gibbons/22	
AG	Alex Graman/215	10.00
KG	Ken Griffey Jr./299	90.00
TG	Tony Gwynn/49	80.00
DH	Drew Henson/246	15.00
BH	Ben Howard/299	6.00
HI	Hansel Izquierdo/299	8.00
JJ	Jimmy Journell/98	8.00
DK	David Kelton/102	8.00
KL	Kenny Lofton/296	15.00
CM	Corwin Malone/103	8.00
BP	Brandon Phillips/131	10.00
SR	Scott Rolen/100	20.00
CC	C.C. Sabathia/106	15.00
MT	Mark Teixeira/280	25.00
TH	Matt Thornton/298	6.00
AH	Andy Van Hekken/299	8.00
JU	Justin Wayne/299	8.00
JW	Jayson Werth/299	8.00
JE	Jerome Williams/103	15.00

Marble Autograph

No pricing due to scarcity

2003 UPPER DECK FINITE

	NM/M
Complete Set (380):	
Common Player (1-100):	1.00
Production 1,999	
Common (101-150):	1.00
Production 1,599	
Common (151-180):	2.00
Production 499	
Common (181-200):	2.50
Production 299	
Common (201-300):	1.50
Production 1,299	
Common (301-330):	3.00
Production 599	
Common (331-360):	3.00
Production 299	
Common (361-380):	5.00
Production 150	

Pack (3): 9.00
Box (10): 80.00
1 Darin Erstad 1.00
2 Garret Anderson 1.50
3 Tim Salmon 1.00
4 Troy Glaus 1.50
5 Luis Gonzalez 1.00
6 Randy Johnson 2.00
7 Curt Schilling 1.50
8 Andruw Jones 1.50
9 Gary Sheffield 1.50
10 Rafael Furcal 1.00
11 Greg Maddux 3.00
12 Chipper Jones 2.50
13 Tony Batista 1.00
14 Jay Gibbons 1.00
15 Johnny Damon 1.00
16 Derek Lowe 1.00
17 Nomar Garciaparra 3.00
18 Pedro J. Martinez 2.00
19 Manny Ramirez 1.50
20 Mark Prior 3.00
21 Kerry Wood 1.50
22 Corey Patterson 1.00
23 Sammy Sosa 3.00
24 Moises Alou 1.00
25 Magglio Ordonez 1.00
26 Frank Thomas 1.50
27 Paul Konerko 1.00
28 Bartolo Colon 1.00
29 Adam Dunn 1.00
30 Austin Kearns 1.00
31 Aaron Boone 1.00
32 Ken Griffey Jr. 2.50
33 Omar Vizquel 1.00
34 C.C. Sabathia 1.00
35 Brandon Phillips 1.00
36 Larry Walker 1.00
37 Preston Wilson 1.00
38 Todd Helton 1.50
39 Eric Munson 1.00
40 Ivan Rodriguez 1.50
41 Josh Beckett 1.50
42 Roy Oswalt 1.00
43 Craig Biggio 1.00
44 Jeff Bagwell 1.50
45 Dontrelle Willis 1.00
46 Carlos Beltran 1.00
47 Brent Mayne 1.00
48 Hideo Nomo 1.00
49 Rickey Henderson 1.00
50 Adrian Beltre 1.00
51 Miguel Cabrera 2.00
52 Kazuhisa Ishii 1.00
53 Richie Sexson 1.00
54 Torii Hunter 1.00
55 Jacque Jones 1.00
56 A.J. Pierzynski 1.00
57 Jose Vidro 1.00
58 Vladimir Guerrero 2.00
59 Tom Glavine 1.00
60 Jose Reyes 1.00
61 Mike Piazza 2.50
62 Jorge Posada 1.50
63 Mike Mussina 1.50
64 Robin Ventura 1.00
65 Mariano Rivera 1.00
66 Roger Clemens 3.00
67 Jason Giambi 2.00
68 Bernie Williams 1.50
69 Alfonso Soriano 2.00
70 Derek Jeter 5.00
71 Miguel Tejada 1.50
72 Eric Chavez 1.00
73 Tim Hudson 1.00
74 Barry Zito 1.50
75 Pat Burrell 1.00
76 Jim Thome 2.00
77 Bobby Abreu 1.00
78 Brian Giles 1.00
79 Reggie Sanders 1.00
80 Ryan Klesko 1.00
81 Edgardo Alfonzo 1.00
82 Rich Aurilia 1.00
83 Barry Bonds 5.00
84 Mike Cameron 1.00
85 Kazuhiro Sasaki 1.00
86 Bret Boone 1.00
87 Ichiro Suzuki 3.00
88 J.D. Drew 1.00
89 Jim Edmonds 1.00
90 Scott Rolen 2.00
91 Matt Morris 1.00
92 Tino Martinez 1.00
93 Albert Pujols 3.00
94 Rocco Baldelli 1.00
95 Hank Blalock 1.50
96 Alex Rodriguez 3.00
97 Rafael Palmeiro 1.50
98 Eric Hinske 1.00
99 Orlando Hudson 1.00
100 Carlos Delgado 1.50
101 Albert Pujols 3.00
102 Alex Rodriguez 3.00
103 Alfonso Soriano 2.00
104 Andruw Jones 1.50
105 Barry Zito 1.50
106 Bernie Williams 1.50
107 Carlos Delgado 1.50
108 Chipper Jones 2.50
109 Curt Schilling 1.50
110 Doug Mientkiewicz 1.00
111 Frank Thomas 1.50
112 Garret Anderson 1.50
113 Gary Sheffield 1.50
114 Greg Maddux 3.00
115 Hank Blalock 1.00
116 Hideki Matsui 4.00
117 Hideo Nomo 1.00
118 Ichiro Suzuki 3.00
119 Ivan Rodriguez 1.50
120 Jason Giambi 2.00
121 Jeff Bagwell 1.50
122 Jeff Kent 1.00
123 Jerome Williams 1.00
124 Jeromy Burnitz 1.00
125 Jim Thome 2.00
126 Jose Cruz Jr. 1.00
127 Ken Griffey Jr. 2.50
128 Kerry Wood 1.50
129 Lance Berkman 1.00
130 Luis Gonzalez 1.00
131 Manny Ramirez 1.50
132 Mark Prior 3.00
133 Miguel Cabrera 2.00
134 Miguel Tejada 1.50
135 Mike Piazza 2.50
136 Pat Burrell 1.00
137 Pedro J. Martinez 2.00
138 Rafael Furcal 1.00
139 Randy Johnson 2.00
140 Rich Harden 1.00
141 Rickey Henderson 1.50
142 Roberto Alomar 1.50
143 Roger Clemens 3.00
144 Sammy Sosa 3.00
145 Shawn Green 1.00
146 Todd Helton 1.50
147 Tom Glavine 1.00
148 Torii Hunter 1.00
149 Troy Glaus 1.00
150 Vladimir Guerrero 2.00
151 Adam Dunn 2.00
152 Albert Pujols 6.00
153 Alex Rodriguez 6.00
154 Alfonso Soriano 3.00
155 Andruw Jones 2.50
156 Barry Bonds 8.00
157 Carlos Delgado 2.50
158 Chipper Jones 3.00
159 Derek Jeter 8.00
160 Gary Sheffield 2.50
161 Hank Blalock 2.50
162 Hideki Matsui 6.00
163 Ichiro Suzuki 4.00
164 J.D. Drew 2.00
165 Jason Giambi 3.00
166 Jeff Bagwell 3.00
167 Jeff Kent 2.00
168 Jim Edmonds 2.00
169 Jim Thome 3.00
170 Ken Griffey Jr. 5.00
171 Luis Gonzalez 2.00
172 Magglio Ordonez 2.00
173 Manny Ramirez 2.50
174 Mike Lowell 2.00
175 Mike Piazza 4.00
176 Nomar Garciaparra 6.00
177 Rafael Palmeiro 2.50
178 Shawn Green 2.00
179 Troy Glaus 2.00
180 Vladimir Guerrero 3.00
181 Albert Pujols 8.00
182 Alex Rodriguez 8.00
183 Alfonso Soriano 4.00
184 Bernie Williams 2.50
185 Chipper Jones 4.00
186 Derek Jeter 10.00
187 Hideki Matsui 8.00
188 Ichiro Suzuki 6.00
189 Jim Thome 3.00
190 Joe DiMaggio 8.00
191 Ken Griffey Jr. 6.00
192 Mickey Mantle 12.00
193 Mike Piazza 5.00
194 Pedro J. Martinez 4.00
195 Randy Johnson 4.00
196 Roger Clemens 6.00
197 Sammy Sosa 6.00
198 Ted Williams 8.00
199 Troy Glaus 2.50
200 Vladimir Guerrero 3.00
201 *Aaron Looper* 2.00
202 Alejandro Machado 1.50
203 *Alfredo Gonzalez* 2.00
204 *Andrew Brown* 2.00
205 Anthony Ferrari 1.50
206 *Aquilino Lopez* 2.00
207 *Beau Kemp* 2.00
208 Bernie Castro 1.50
209 *Bobby Madritsch* 8.00
210 Brandon Villafuerte 1.50
211 *Brent Hoard* 2.00
212 Brian Stokes 1.50
213 Carlos Mendez 1.50
214 *Chris Capuano* 2.00
215 Chris Waters 1.50
216 *Clint Barmes* 5.00
217 *Colin Porter* 1.50
218 Cory Stewart 1.50
219 *Craig Brazell* 3.00
220 *D.J. Carrasco* 1.50
221 *Daniel Cabrera* 1.50
222 *Dave Matranga* 2.00
223 David Sanders 1.50
224 Diegomar Markwell 1.50
225 *Edgar Gonzalez* 2.00
226 Felix Sanchez 1.50
227 *Fernando Cabrera* 2.00
228 *Francisco Cruceta* 2.00
229 *Francisco Rosario* 2.00
230 Garrett Atkins 1.50
231 Gerald Laird 1.50
232 *Guillermo Quiroz* 4.00
233 *Heath Bell* 2.00
234 *Delmon Young* 10.00
235 *Jason Shiell* 2.00
236 Jeremy Bonderman 6.00
237 Jeremy Griffiths 1.50
238 Jeremy Guthrie 1.50
239 *Jeremy Wedel* 2.00
240 Carlos Rivera 1.50
241 Joe Valentine 1.50
242 Jon Leicester 1.50
243 Jonathan Pridie 1.50
244 Jorge Cordova 1.50
245 Jose Castillo 1.50
246 *Josh Hall* 2.00
247 *Josh Stewart* 1.50
248 *Josh Willingham* 3.00
249 *Julio Manon* 1.50
250 *Kevin Correia* 1.50
251 *Kevin Ohme* 2.00
252 Kevin Tolar 1.50
253 Luis De Los Santos 1.50
254 Jermaine Clark 1.50
255 *Mark Malaska* 2.00
256 Juan Dominguez 1.50
257 *Michael Hessman* 1.50
258 *Micheal Nakamura* 2.00
259 *Miguel Ojeda* 1.50
260 Mike Gallo 1.50
261 *Edwin Jackson* 6.00
262 *Mike Ryan* 1.50
263 *Nate Bland* 1.50
264 Nate Robertson 3.00
265 *Nook Logan* 2.00
266 *Phil Seibel* 1.50
267 *Prentice Redman* 2.00
268 Rafael Betancourt 1.50
269 *Rett Johnson* 2.00
270 Richard Fischer 1.50
271 *Rick Roberts* 2.00
272 Roger Deago 1.50
273 *Ryan Cameron* 1.50
274 Shane Bazzell 2.00
275 Erasmo Ramirez 1.50
276 *Termel Sledge* 2.00
277 *Tim Olson* 3.00
278 Tommy Phelps 1.50
279 Tommy Whiteman 1.50
280 *Willie Eyre* 2.00
281 *Alex Prieto* 2.00
282 *Michel Hernandez* 1.50
283 *Greg Jones* 1.50
284 Victor Martinez 1.50
285 *Tom Gregorio* 2.00
286 Marcus Thames 1.50
287 *Jorge DePaula* 1.50
288 *Aaron Miles* 3.00
289 Reynaldo Garcia 1.50
290 *Brian Sweeney* 1.50
291 *Pete LaForest* 2.00
292 *Pete Zoccolilo* 1.50
293 *Danny Garcia* 1.50
294 Jonny Gomes 1.50
295 *Rosman Garcia* 1.50
296 Mike Edwards 1.50
297 Marlon Byrd 1.50
298 Khalil Greene 4.00
299 Jose Valverde 1.50
300 Drew Henson 1.50
301 Chris Bootcheck 3.00
302 Matt Belisle 3.00
303 Kevin Gregg 3.00
304 Bobby Jenks 3.00
305 Jason Young 3.00
306 Laynce Nix 3.00
307 Robb Quinlan 3.00
308 Chase Utley 3.00
309 *Humberto Quintero* 4.00
310 Tim Raines Jr. 3.00
311 Stephen Smitherman 3.00
312 Jason Anderson 3.00
313 Joe Dawley 3.00
314 *Chad Cordero* 3.00
315 Victor Alvarez 3.00
316 Jimmy Gobble 3.00
317 Jared Fernandez 3.00
318 Eric Bruntlett 3.00
319 Neal Cotts 3.00
320 Ryan Madson 3.00
321 Rocco Baldelli 3.00
322 *Graham Koonce* 3.00
323 Bobby Crosby 3.00
324 Mike Wood 3.00
325 Jesse Garcia 3.00
326 Noah Lowry 6.00
327 Edwin Almonte 3.00
328 Justin Morneau 3.00
329 Steve Colyer 3.00
330 Vinnie Chulk 3.00
331 Brian Schmack 3.00
332 *Stephen Randolph* 3.00
333 Pedro Feliciano 3.00
334 Koyie Hill 3.00
335 *Geoff Geary* 3.00
336 Jon Switzer 3.00
337 Xavier Nady 3.00
338 Rich Harden 4.00
339 Dontrelle Willis 4.00
340 Angel Berroa 3.00
341 Jerome Williams 3.00
342 Brandon Claussen 3.00
343 Kurt Ainsworth 3.00
344 Horacio Ramirez 3.00
345 Hee Seop Choi 3.00
346 Billy Traber 3.00
347 Brandon Phillips 3.00
348 Jody Gerut 3.00
349 Mark Teixeira 4.00
350 Javier Lopez 3.00
351 Miguel Cabrera 5.00
352 Brad Lidge 3.00
353 Mike MacDougal 3.00
354 Ken Harvey 3.00
355 *Chien-Ming Wang* 25.00
356 Aaron Heilman 3.00
357 Jason Phillips 3.00
358 Jason Bay 3.00
359 Arnie Munoz 3.00
360 *Ian Ferguson* 3.00
361 *Ryan Wagner* 8.00
362 *Rickie Weeks* 40.00
363 *Chad Gaudin* 8.00
364 *Jason Gilfillan* 5.00
365 Jason Roach 5.00
366 Jhonny Peralta 6.00
367 *Mike Neu* 5.00
368 *Jose Contreras* 10.00
369 *Wilfredo Ledezma* 5.00
370 *Lew Ford* 8.00
371 *Luis Ayala* 5.00
372 *Bo Hart* 5.00
373 *Brandon Webb* 15.00
374 Dan Haren 8.00
375 *Hideki Matsui* 50.00
376 *Jeff Duncan* 8.00
377 *Matt Kata* 5.00
378 *Oscar Villarreal* 5.00
379 *Rob Hammock* 5.00
380 *Todd Wellemeyer* 5.00

Game Face (193-217):
Common Rookie: 5.00
Production 299
193 *Aaron Looper* 5.00
194 *Alex Prieto* 5.00
195 *Bo Hart* 5.00
196 *Chad Gaudin* 5.00
197 *Colin Porter* 5.00
198 *D.J. Carrasco* 5.00
199 Dan Haren 5.00
200 *Delmon Young* 30.00
201 Dontrelle Willis 5.00
202 Jon Switzer 5.00
203 *Edwin Jackson* 15.00

204 *Fernando Cabrera* 5.00
205 Garrett Atkins 5.00
206 Jeremy Bonderman 10.00
207 *Kevin Ohme* 5.00
208 Khalil Greene 10.00
209 *Luis Ayala* 5.00
210 *Matt Kata* 5.00
211 Noah Lowry 10.00
212 Rich Harden 5.00
213 *Rickie Weeks* 20.00
214 *Rosman Garcia* 5.00
215 *Ryan Wagner* 5.00
216 *Tom Gregorio* 5.00
217 *Wilfredo Ledezma* 5.00
SP Authentic (190-239):
Common SP Authentic Rookie: 4.00
Production 699
190 Aaron Looper 4.00
191 Alex Prieto 4.00
192 *Alfredo Gonzalez* 4.00
193 *Andrew Brown* 4.00
194 Anthony Ferrari 4.00
195 *Aquilino Lopez* 4.00
196 *Beau Kemp* 4.00
197 *Bo Hart* 4.00
198 *Chad Gaudin* 4.00
199 *Colin Porter* 4.00
200 *D.J. Carrasco* 4.00
201 Dan Haren 8.00
202 *Danny Garcia* 4.00
203 Jon Switzer 4.00
204 *Edwin Jackson* 15.00
205 *Fernando Cabrera* 4.00
206 Garrett Atkins 4.00
207 Gerald Laird 4.00
208 *Greg Jones* 4.00
209 *Ian Ferguson* 4.00
210 Jason Roach 4.00
211 *Jason Shiell* 4.00
212 Jeremy Bonderman 10.00
213 *Jeremy Wedel* 4.00
214 Jhonny Peralta 4.00
215 *Delmon Young* 40.00
216 *Jorge DePaula* 4.00
217 *Josh Hall* 4.00
218 *Julio Manon* 4.00
219 *Kevin Correia* 4.00
220 *Kevin Ohme* 4.00
221 Kevin Tolar 4.00
222 *Luis Ayala* 4.00
223 Luis De Los Santos 4.00
224 *Chad Cordero* 4.00
225 *Mark Malaska* 4.00
226 Khalil Greene 10.00
227 *Micheal Nakamura* 4.00
228 *Michel Hernandez* 4.00
229 *Miguel Ojeda* 4.00
230 *Mike Neu* 4.00
231 *Nate Bland* 4.00
232 *Pete LaForest* 4.00
233 *Rickie Weeks* 25.00
234 *Rosman Garcia* 4.00
235 *Ryan Wagner* 4.00
236 Lance Niekro 4.00
237 *Tom Gregorio* 4.00
238 Tommy Phelps 4.00
239 *Wilfredo Ledezma* 4.00
SPX (179-193, 381-387):
179 *Chad Gaudin/150* 8.00
180 *Chris Capuano/150* 10.00
181 *Danny Garcia/150* 8.00
182 *Delmon Young/150* 60.00
183 *Edwin Jackson/150* 20.00
184 *Greg Jones/150* 8.00
185 Jeremy Bonderman/150 20.00
186 *Jorge DePaula/150* 8.00
187 Khalil Greene/150 25.00
188 *Chad Cordero/150* 8.00
189 Miguel Cabrera/150 10.00
190 Rich Harden/150 10.00
191 *Rickie Weeks/150* 40.00
192 *Rosman Garcia/150* 8.00
193 *Tom Gregorio/150* 8.00
381 *Andrew Brown/jsy/auto/355* 25.00
382 *Delmon Young/jsy/auto/355* 375.00
383 *Colin Porter/jsy/auto/355* 15.00
385 *Rickie Weeks/jsy/auto/355* 200.00
386 *Dave Matranga/jsy/auto/355* 20.00
387 *Bo Hart/jsy/auto/355* 15.00
UD Authentics (131-140):
Common Authentics: 5.00
Production 150
131 Dan Haren 6.00
132 *Delmon Young* 35.00
133 Dontrelle Willis 6.00
134 *Edwin Jackson* 15.00
135 Jeremy Bonderman 12.00
136 Khalil Greene 15.00
137 Rich Harden 5.00
138 *Rickie Weeks* 35.00
139 *Rosman Garcia* 5.00
140 *Ryan Wagner* 5.00

Gold

Gold (1-150): 1-2X
Gold (151-180): 1X
Production 199
Gold (181-200): 1-2X
Production 99

Elements Jersey

NM/M
Common Player: 4.00
JB Jeff Bagwell 8.00
RB Rocco Baldelli 6.00
HB Hank Blalock 6.00
HC Hee Seop Choi 4.00
JD J.D. Drew 4.00
AD Adam Dunn 6.00
JE Jim Edmonds 5.00
SG Shawn Green 5.00
KG Ken Griffey Jr./SP 15.00
TH Torii Hunter 6.00
CJ Chipper Jones 6.00
JK Jeff Kent 4.00
ML Mike Lowell 4.00
GM Greg Maddux 8.00
HM Hideki Matsui 25.00
MM Matt Morris 5.00
RO Roy Oswalt 5.00
CP Corey Patterson 5.00
AP Andy Pettitte 6.00
MI Mike Piazza 8.00
MP Mark Prior 15.00
AL Albert Pujols 15.00
AR Alex Rodriguez 10.00
AS Alfonso Soriano 6.00
IS Ichiro Suzuki 15.00
JT Jim Thome 10.00
RW Rickie Weeks/SP 15.00
DW Dontrelle Willis 6.00
KW Kerry Wood 8.00
DY Delmon Young/SP 20.00

Elements Patch

No pricing due to scarcity
Production 25 sets
Patch Gold: No Pricing
Production 10 sets

First Class Jersey

NM/M
Common Player: 4.00

RC Roger Clemens 10.00
JD Joe DiMaggio/SP 80.00
TG Troy Glaus 5.00
LG Luis Gonzalez 4.00
KG Ken Griffey Jr. 12.00
VG Vladimir Guerrero 8.00
RJ Randy Johnson 8.00
CJ Chipper Jones 6.00
MM Mickey Mantle/SP 100.00
PM Pedro J. Martinez 8.00
HM Hideki Matsui 25.00
MP Mike Piazza 8.00
AP Albert Pujols 20.00
AR Alex Rodriguez 10.00
AS Alfonso Soriano 6.00
SS Sammy Sosa 10.00
IS Ichiro Suzuki 15.00
JT Jim Thome 10.00
BW Bernie Williams 6.00
TW Ted Williams/SP 75.00

Signatures

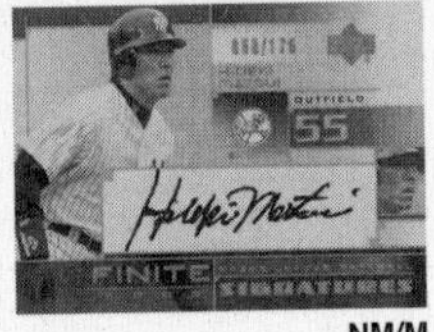

NM/M
Common Auto: 6.00
Varying quantities produced
EA Erick Almonte/355 6.00
SZ Shane Bazzell/250 6.00
MC Miguel Cabrera/100 50.00
RC Roger Clemens/50 150.00
WE Willie Eyre/200 6.00
NG Nomar Garciaparra/50 120.00
RK Rob Hammock/200 6.00
RN Rich Harden/150 25.00
BH Bo Hart/150 8.00
HM Hideki Matsui/99 250.00
MP Mark Prior/75 60.00
JR Jose Reyes/100 15.00
SR Scott Rolen/100 40.00
CS C.C. Sabathia/50 15.00
DS David Sanders/150 6.00
PS Phil Seibel/200 6.00
IS Ichiro Suzuki/25 350.00
MT Mark Teixeira/200 25.00
BW Brandon Webb/150 15.00
RW Rickie Weeks/25
JW Jerome Williams/150 15.00
DW Dontrelle Willis/50 40.00
DY Delmon Young/50 100.00

SPX Jersey Autograph

NM/M
Production 355
DW Dontrelle Willis 40.00
KG Khalil Greene 60.00
RH Rich Harden 35.00

Stars and Stripes

NM/M
Common Player: 2.00
Production 299 sets
USA-1 Justin Orenduff 2.00
USA-2 Micah Owings 2.00
USA-3 Steven Register 2.00
USA-4 Huston Street 6.00
USA-5 Justin Verlander 8.00
USA-6 Jered Weaver 8.00
USA-7 Matt Campbell 4.00
USA-8 Stephen Head 2.00
USA-9 Mark Romanczuk 2.00
USA-10 Jeff Clement 10.00
USA-11 Mike Nickeas 2.00
USA-12 Tyler Greene 2.00
USA-13 Paul Janish 2.00
USA-14 Jeff Larish 2.00
USA-15 Eric Patterson 2.00
USA-16 Dustin Pedroia 4.00
USA-17 Michael Griffin 2.00
USA-18 Brent Lillibridge 2.00
USA-19 Danny Putnam 5.00
USA-20 Seth Smith 5.00

Stars and Stripes Jersey

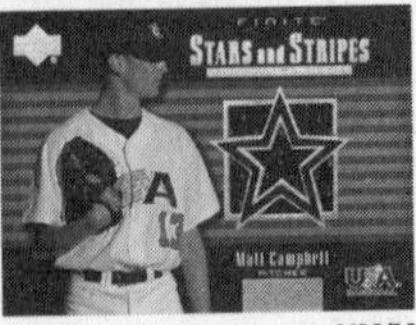

NM/M
Common Player: 4.00
J1 Justin Orenduff 4.00
J2 Micah Owings 4.00
J3 Steven Register 4.00
J4 Huston Street 8.00
J5 Justin Verlander 8.00
J6 Jered Weaver 8.00
J7 Matt Campbell 6.00
J8 Stephen Head 4.00
J9 Mark Romanczuk 4.00
J10 Jeff Clement 10.00
J11 Mike Nickeas 4.00
J12 Tyler Greene 4.00
J13 Paul Janish 4.00
J14 Jeff Larish 4.00
J15 Eric Patterson 4.00
J16 Dustin Pedroia 6.00
J17 Michael Griffin 4.00
J18 Brent Lillibridge 4.00
J19 Danny Putnam 6.00
J20 Seth Smith 6.00

2003 UPPER DECK FIRST PITCH

NM/M
Complete Set (300): 50.00
Common Player: .10
Common SP (271-300): 1.00
Inserted 1:4
Pack (5): 1.00
Box (36): 25.00
1 John Lackey .10
2 Alex Cintron .10
3 Jose Leon .10
4 Bobby Hill .10
5 Brandon Larson .10
6 Raul Gonzalez .10
7 Ben Broussard .10
8 Earl Snyder .10
9 Ramon Santiago .10
10 Jason Lane .10
11 *Rob Hammock* .50
12 Kirk Saarloos .10
13 Juan Brito .10
14 Runelvys Hernandez .10
15 Shawn Sedlacek .10
16 Jayson Durocher .10
17 Kevin Frederick .10
18 Zach Day .10
19 Marco Scutaro .10
20 Marcus Thames .10
21 Esteban German .10
22 Brett Myers .10

No.	Player	Price
23	Oliver Perez	.10
24	Dennis Tankersley	.10
25	Julius Matos	.10
26	Jake Peavy	.10
27	Eric Cyr	.10
28	Mike Crudale	.10
29	Josh Pearce	.10
30	Carl Crawford	.10
31	Tim Salmon	.25
32	Troy Glaus	.50
33	Adam Kennedy	.10
34	David Eckstein	.10
35	Bengie Molina	.10
36	Jarrod Washburn	.10
37	Ramon Ortiz	.10
38	Eric Chavez	.25
39	Miguel Tejada	.25
40	Adam Piatt	.10
41	Jermaine Dye	.10
42	Olmedo Saenz	.10
43	Tim Hudson	.20
44	Barry Zito	.25
45	Billy Koch	.10
46	Shannon Stewart	.10
47	Kelvim Escobar	.10
48	Jose Cruz Jr.	.10
49	Vernon Wells	.10
50	Roy Halladay	.10
51	Esteban Loaiza	.10
52	Eric Hinske	.10
53	Steve Cox	.10
54	Brent Abernathy	.10
55	Ben Grieve	.10
56	Aubrey Huff	.10
57	Jared Sandberg	.10
58	Paul Wilson	.10
59	Tanyon Sturtze	.10
60	Jim Thome	.50
61	Omar Vizquel	.20
62	C.C. Sabathia	.10
63	Chris Magruder	.10
64	Ricky Gutierrez	.10
65	Einar Diaz	.10
66	Danys Baez	.10
67	Ichiro Suzuki	.75
68	Ruben Sierra	.10
69	Carlos Guillen	.10
70	Mark McLemore	.10
71	Dan Wilson	.10
72	Jamie Moyer	.10
73	Joel Pineiro	.10
74	Edgar Martinez	.10
75	Tony Batista	.10
76	Jay Gibbons	.10
77	Chris Singleton	.10
78	Melvin Mora	.10
79	Geronimo Gil	.10
80	Rodrigo Lopez	.10
81	Jorge Julio	.10
82	Rafael Palmeiro	.40
83	Juan Gonzalez	.40
84	Mike Young	.10
85	Hideki Irabu	.10
86	Chan Ho Park	.10
87	Kevin Mench	.10
88	Doug Davis	.10
89	Pedro J. Martinez	.75
90	Shea Hillenbrand	.10
91	Derek Lowe	.10
92	Jason Varitek	.10
93	Tony Clark	.10
94	John Burkett	.10
95	Frank Castillo	.10
96	Nomar Garciaparra	1.00
97	Rickey Henderson	.25
98	Mike Sweeney	.10
99	Carlos Febles	.10
100	Mark Quinn	.10
101	Raul Ibanez	.10
102	A.J. Hinch	.10
103	Paul Byrd	.10
104	Chuck Knoblauch	.10
105	Dmitri Young	.10
106	Randall Simon	.10
107	Brandon Inge	.10
108	Damion Easley	.10
109	Carlos Pena	.10
110	George Lombard	.10
111	Juan Acevedo	.10
112	Torii Hunter	.25
113	Doug Mientkiewicz	.10
114	David Ortiz	.10
115	Eric Milton	.10
116	Eddie Guardado	.10
117	Cristian Guzman	.10
118	Corey Koskie	.10
119	Magglio Ordonez	.25
120	Mark Buehrle	.10
121	Todd Ritchie	.10
122	Jose Valentin	.10
123	Paul Konerko	.10
124	Carlos Lee	.10
125	Jon Garland	.10
126	Jason Giambi	.75
127	Derek Jeter	1.50
128	Roger Clemens	1.00
129	Raul Mondesi	.25
130	Jorge Posada	.25
131	Rondell White	.10
132	Robin Ventura	.20
133	Mike Mussina	.40
134	Jeff Bagwell	.50
135	Craig Biggio	.20
136	Morgan Ensberg	.10
137	Richard Hidalgo	.10
138	Brad Ausmus	.10
139	Roy Oswalt	.20
140	Carlos Hernandez	.10
141	Shane Reynolds	.10
142	Gary Sheffield	.25
143	Andruw Jones	.25
144	Tom Glavine	.25
145	Rafael Furcal	.20
146	Javy Lopez	.10
147	Vinny Castilla	.10
148	Marcus Giles	.10
149	Kevin Millwood	.20
150	Jason Marquis	.10
151	Ruben Quevedo	.10
152	Ben Sheets	.10
153	Geoff Jenkins	.10
154	Jose Hernandez	.10
155	Glendon Rusch	.10
156	Jeffrey Hammonds	.10
157	Alex Sanchez	.10
158	Jim Edmonds	.25
159	Tino Martinez	.10
160	Albert Pujols	.75
161	Eli Marrero	.10
162	Woody Williams	.10
163	Fernando Vina	.10
164	Jason Isringhausen	.10
165	Jason Simontacchi	.10
166	Kerry Robinson	.10
167	Sammy Sosa	.75
168	Juan Cruz	.10
169	Fred McGriff	.20
170	Antonio Alfonseca	.10
171	Jon Lieber	.10
172	Mark Prior	.50
173	Moises Alou	.20
174	Matt Clement	.10
175	Mark Bellhorn	.10
176	Randy Johnson	.50
177	Luis Gonzalez	.20
178	Tony Womack	.10
179	Mark Grace	.25
180	Junior Spivey	.10
181	Byung-Hyun Kim	.10
182	Danny Bautista	.10
183	Brian Anderson	.10
184	Shawn Green	.25
185	Brian Jordan	.10
186	Eric Karros	.10
187	Andy Ashby	.10
188	Cesar Izturis	.10
189	Dave Roberts	.10
190	Eric Gagne	.10
191	Kazuhisa Ishii	.10
192	Adrian Beltre	.10
193	Vladimir Guerrero	.50
194	Tony Armas Jr.	.10
195	Bartolo Colon	.10
196	Troy O'Leary	.10
197	Tomokazu Ohka	.10
198	Brad Wilkerson	.10
199	Orlando Cabrera	.10
200	Barry Bonds	1.50
201	David Bell	.10
202	Tsuyoshi Shinjo	.10
203	Benito Santiago	.10
204	Livan Hernandez	.10
205	Jason Schmidt	.10
206	Kirk Rueter	.10
207	Ramon E. Martinez	.10
208	Mike Lowell	.10
209	Luis Castillo	.10
210	Derek Lee	.10
211	Andy Fox	.10
212	Eric Owens	.10
213	Charles Johnson	.10
214	Brad Penny	.10
215	A.J. Burnett	.10
216	Edgardo Alfonzo	.10
217	Roberto Alomar	.40
218	Rey Ordonez	.10
219	Al Leiter	.10
220	Roger Cedeno	.10
221	Timoniel Perez	.10
222	Jeromy Burnitz	.10
223	Pedro Astacio	.10
224	Joe McEwing	.10
225	Ryan Klesko	.20
226	Ramon Vazquez	.10
227	Mark Kotsay	.10
228	Bubba Trammell	.10
229	Wiki Gonzalez	.10
230	Trevor Hoffman	.10
231	Ron Gant	.10
232	Bobby Abreu	.20
233	Marlon Anderson	.10
234	Jeremy Giambi	.10
235	Jimmy Rollins	.10
236	Mike Lieberthal	.10
237	Vicente Padilla	.10
238	Randy Wolf	.10
239	Pokey Reese	.10
240	Brian Giles	.25
241	Jack Wilson	.10
242	Mike Williams	.10
243	Kip Wells	.10
244	Robert Mackowiak	.10
245	Craig Wilson	.10
246	Adam Dunn	.50
247	Sean Casey	.10
248	Todd Walker	.10
249	Corky Miller	.10
250	Ryan Dempster	.10
251	Reggie Taylor	.10
252	Aaron Boone	.10
253	Larry Walker	.10
254	Jose Ortiz	.10
255	Todd Zeile	.10
256	Bobby Estalella	.10
257	Juan Pierre	.10
258	Terry Shumpert	.10
259	Mike Hampton	.10
260	Denny Stark	.10
261	Shawn Green	.20
262	Derek Lowe	.10
263	Barry Bonds	.50
264	Mike Cameron	.10
265	Luis Castillo	.10
266	Vladimir Guerrero	.40
267	Jason Giambi	.40
268	Eric Gagne	.10
269	Magglio Ordonez	.20
270	Jim Thome	.25
271	*Hideki Matsui*	20.00
272	*Jose Contreras*	4.00
273	Robert Madritsch	1.00
274	*Shane Bazzell*	1.50
275	*Felix Sanchez*	2.00
276	*Todd Wellemeyer*	2.00
277	*Lew Ford*	2.00
278	Jeremy Griffiths	1.00
279	*Oscar Villarreal*	1.00
280	*Brandon Webb*	3.00
281	Delvis Lantigua	3.00
282	*Josh Willingham*	1.00
283	*Mike Nicolas*	1.00
284	Mike Hampton	1.00
285	Jim Thome	2.00
286	Bartolo Colon	1.00
287	Orlando Hernandez	1.00
288	Jeremy Giambi	1.00
289	Jeff Kent	1.50
290	Tom Glavine	1.50
291	Cliff Floyd	1.00
292	Tsuyoshi Shinjo	1.00
293	Jose Cruz Jr.	1.00
294	Edgardo Alfonzo	1.00
295	Andres Galarraga	1.00
296	Troy O'Leary	1.00
297	Eric Karros	1.00
298	Ivan Rodriguez	1.50
299	Fred McGriff	1.50
300	Preston Wilson	1.00

Signature Stars

NM/M

Print Runs listed:

Code	Player	Price
NM	Nomar Garciaparra/100	100.00
JG	Jason Giambi/100	30.00
KG	Ken Griffey Jr./100	75.00
KGS	Ken Griffey Sr./800	6.00
SS	Sammy Sosa/50	175.00
IS	Ichiro Suzuki/50	375.00

2003 UPPER DECK GAME FACE

	NM/M
Complete Set (192):	
Common Player:	.25
Common Base SP:	1.00
Inserted 1:4	
Common SP (121-150):	2.00
Inserted 1:8	
Common SP (151-192):	3.00
Inserted 1:16	
Pack (4):	4.00
Box (24):	75.00

No.	Player	Price
1	Darin Erstad	.50
2	Garret Anderson	.50
3	Tim Salmon	.50
4	Jarrod Washburn	.25
5	Troy Glaus/SP	1.50
6	Luis Gonzalez	.50
7	Junior Spivey	.25
8	Randy Johnson/SP	2.00
9	Curt Schilling/SP	1.50
10	Andruw Jones	.75
11	Gary Sheffield	.50
12	Rafael Furcal	.25
13	Greg Maddux/SP	3.00
14	Chipper Jones/SP	3.00
15	Tony Batista	.25
16	Rodrigo Lopez	.25
17	Jay Gibbons	.25
18	Shea Hillenbrand	.25
19	Johnny Damon	.25
20	Derek Lowe	.25
21	Nomar Garciaparra	2.50
22	Pedro J. Martinez/SP	2.00
23	Manny Ramirez/SP	1.50
24	Mark Prior	1.00
25	Kerry Wood	.75
26	Corey Patterson	.25
27	Sammy Sosa	2.00
28	Magglio Ordonez	.50
29	Frank Thomas	1.00
30	Paul Konerko	.25
31	Adam Dunn	1.00
32	Austin Kearns	1.00
33	Aaron Boone	.25
34	Ken Griffey Jr./SP	3.00
35	Omar Vizquel	.40
36	C.C. Sabathia	.25
37	Karim Garcia/SP	1.00
38	Larry Walker	.40
39	Preston Wilson	.25
40	Jay Payton	.25
41	Todd Helton/SP	1.50
42	Carlos Pena	.25
43	Eric Munson	.25
44	Mike Lowell	.25
45	Josh Beckett	.25
46	A.J. Burnett	.25
47	Roy Oswalt	.50
48	Craig Biggio	.50
49	Jeff Bagwell/SP	1.50
50	Lance Berkman/SP	1.25
51	Mike Sweeney	.25
52	Carlos Beltran	.25
53	Hideo Nomo	.75
54	Odalis Perez	.25
55	Adrian Beltre	.25
56	Shawn Green/SP	1.00
57	Kazuhisa Ishii/SP	1.00
58	Ben Sheets	.50
59	Richie Sexson	.50
60	Torii Hunter	.50
61	Jacque Jones	.25
62	Eric Milton	.25
63	Corey Koskie	.25

#	Player	Price
64	A.J. Pierzynski	.25
65	Jose Vidro	.25
66	Bartolo Colon	.25
67	Vladimir Guerrero/SP	1.50
68	Tom Glavine	.50
69	Mike Piazza/SP	3.00
70	Roberto Alomar/SP	1.50
71	Jorge Posada	.75
72	Mike Mussina	.75
73	Robin Ventura	.25
74	Raul Mondesi	.50
75	Roger Clemens/SP	3.00
76	Jason Giambi/SP	2.00
77	Bernie Williams/SP	1.50
78	Alfonso Soriano/SP	2.00
79	Derek Jeter/SP	6.00
80	Miguel Tejada	.75
81	Eric Chavez	.50
82	Tim Hudson	.50
83	Barry Zito	.50
84	Mark Mulder	.50
85	Pat Burrell	1.00
86	Jim Thome	1.00
87	Bobby Abreu	.50
88	Brian Giles	.50
89	Jason Kendall	.40
90	Aramis Ramirez	.25
91	Ryan Klesko	.25
92	Phil Nevin	.25
93	Sean Burroughs	.25
94	J.T. Snow	.25
95	Rich Aurilia	.25
96	Benito Santiago	.25
97	Barry Bonds/SP	6.00
98	Edgar Martinez	.25
99	John Olerud	.50
100	Bret Boone	.25
101	Ichiro Suzuki/SP	3.00
102	J.D. Drew	.50
103	Jim Edmonds	.50
104	Scott Rolen	1.00
105	Matt Morris	.50
106	Tino Martinez	.25
107	Albert Pujols/SP	2.00
108	Aubrey Huff	.25
109	Carl Crawford	.25
110	Rafael Palmeiro	.75
111	Hank Blalock	.50
112	Alex Rodriguez/SP	5.00
113	Kevin Mench/SP	1.00
114	Juan Gonzalez/SP	1.50
115	Shannon Stewart	.25
116	Vernon Wells	.25
117	Josh Phelps	.25
118	Eric Hinske	.25
119	Orlando Hudson	.25
120	Carlos Delgado/SP	1.00
121	*David Sanders*	2.00
122	*Rob Hammock*	2.00
123	*Rett Johnson*	2.00
124	*Mike Nicolas*	2.00
125	*Terrmel Sledge*	3.00
126	*Ryan Cameron*	4.00
127	*Prentice Redman*	2.00
128	*Clint Barmes*	6.00
129	*Brent Hoard*	2.00
130	*Willie Eyre*	2.00
131	*Phil Seibel*	2.00
132	*Chris Capuano*	5.00
133	*Bobby Madritsch*	8.00
134	*Shane Bazzell*	2.00
135	Jeremy Griffiths	3.00
136	*Jon Leicester*	3.00
137	*Brandon Webb*	5.00
138	*Todd Wellemeyer*	2.00
139	*Jose Contreras*	5.00
140	*Felix Sanchez*	2.00
141	*Arnie Munoz*	2.00
142	*Delvis Lantigua*	2.00
143	*Francisco Cruceta*	2.00
144	*Josh Willingham*	3.00
145	*Oscar Villarreal*	2.00
146	*Ian Ferguson*	2.00
147	Pedro Liriano	2.00
148	*Lew Ford*	5.00
149	*Jeff Duncan*	2.00
150	*Richard Fischer*	2.00
151	Troy Glaus	3.00
152	Randy Johnson	5.00
153	*Hideki Matsui*	15.00
154	Chipper Jones	6.00
155	Nomar Garciaparra	10.00
156	Pedro J. Martinez	5.00
157	Ted Williams	15.00
158	Sammy Sosa	8.00
159	Ken Griffey Jr.	8.00
160	Vladimir Guerrero	5.00
161	Mike Piazza	8.00
162	Mickey Mantle	30.00
163	Alfonso Soriano	6.00
164	Derek Jeter	15.00
165	Roger Clemens	8.00
166	Jason Giambi	4.00
167	Barry Bonds	15.00
168	Ichiro Suzuki	8.00
169	Albert Pujols	8.00
170	Mark McGwire	15.00
171	Alex Rodriguez	10.00
172	Ken Griffey Jr., Roy Oswalt	6.00
173	Barry Zito, Troy Glaus	3.00
174	Tim Hudson, Ichiro Suzuki	8.00
175	Alex Rodriguez, Mark Mulder	10.00
176	Tom Glavine, Vladimir Guerrero	4.00
177	Mike Piazza, Greg Maddux	6.00
178	Mark McGwire, Sammy Sosa	10.00
179	Lance Berkman, Mark Prior	5.00
180	Albert Pujols, Kerry Wood	6.00
181	Randy Johnson, Jeff Bagwell	4.00
182	Derek Jeter, Curt Schilling	10.00
183	Barry Bonds, Hideo Nomo	10.00
184	Todd Helton, Kazuhisa Ishii	4.00
185	Freddy Garcia, Eric Chavez	3.00
186	Al Leiter, Chipper Jones	6.00
187	Ted Williams, Nomar Garciaparra	10.00
188	Pedro J. Martinez, Hideki Matsui	15.00
189	Derek Lowe, Bernie Williams	3.00
190	Roger Clemens, Mike Piazza	10.00
191	Mike Mussina, Manny Ramirez	4.00
192	Jason Giambi, Mickey Mantle	20.00

Autograph

NM/M

Inserted 1:576
Golds: Not Priced
Production 25

	Player	Price
LB	Lance Berkman/SP	50.00
JG	Jason Giambi	40.00
KG	Ken Griffey Jr.	125.00
TH	Todd Helton/SP	45.00
AJ	Andruw Jones/SP	40.00
HM	Hideki Matsui/SP	250.00
MM	Mark McGwire/SP	350.00
MP	Mark Prior/SP	90.00
SS	Sammy Sosa	120.00
IS	Ichiro Suzuki/SP	300.00
BZ	Barry Zito	40.00

Gear

NM/M

Common Player: 4.00
Inserted 1:8
Patches: 3-5X
Production 100 sets

	Player	Price
BA	Bobby Abreu	4.00
EA	Edgardo Alfonzo	4.00
JB	Jeff Bagwell	8.00
CB	Carlos Beltran	6.00
LB	Lance Berkman	6.00
AB	Aaron Boone/SP	8.00
PB	Pat Burrell	6.00
EC	Eric Chavez	4.00
RC	Roger Clemens	15.00
CD	Carlos Delgado	4.00
DR	J.D. Drew	4.00
DR2	J.D. Drew	4.00
AD	Adam Dunn	8.00
JE	Jim Edmonds	6.00
DE	Darin Erstad	4.00
DE2	Darin Erstad	4.00
JG	Jason Giambi	6.00
BG	Brian Giles	4.00
TG	Tom Glavine	6.00
GO	Juan Gonzalez	6.00
LG	Luis Gonzalez	4.00
LG2	Luis Gonzalez	4.00
SG	Shawn Green	4.00
KG	Ken Griffey Jr./SP	
TH	Todd Helton/SP	8.00
TI	Tim Hudson	4.00
HU	Torii Hunter	4.00
KI	Kazuhisa Ishii	4.00
RJ	Randy Johnson	8.00
AJ	Andruw Jones	6.00
CJ	Chipper Jones	8.00
JJ	Jacque Jones	4.00
AK	Austin Kearns	4.00
JK	Jason Kendall	4.00
KE	Jeff Kent	6.00
RK	Ryan Klesko	4.00
ML	Mike Lowell	4.00
GM	Greg Maddux	10.00
GM2	Greg Maddux	10.00
EM	Edgar Martinez	6.00
PM	Pedro J. Martinez	8.00
MM	Mike Mussina	8.00
HN	Hideo Nomo	8.00
MO	Magglio Ordonez	4.00
RO	Roy Oswalt	4.00
RP	Rafael Palmeiro	8.00
MiP	Mike Piazza	10.00
JP	Jorge Posada	8.00
MaP	Mark Prior	10.00
MR	Manny Ramirez	8.00
AR	Alex Rodriguez	10.00
AR2	Alex Rodriguez	10.00
IR	Ivan Rodriguez	8.00
SR	Scott Rolen	8.00
CS	Curt Schilling	8.00
RS	Richie Sexson	6.00
AS	Alfonso Soriano	8.00
SS	Sammy Sosa	10.00
IS	Ichiro Suzuki/SP	50.00
MS	Mike Sweeney	4.00
MT	Miguel Tejada	6.00
FT	Frank Thomas	8.00
JT	Jim Thome	8.00
JV	Jose Vidro	4.00
OV	Omar Vizquel	4.00
LW	Larry Walker	4.00
BW	Bernie Williams	6.00
PW	Preston Wilson	4.00
KW	Kerry Wood	8.00
BZ	Barry Zito	4.00
BZ2	Barry Zito	4.00

2003 UPPER DECK HONOR ROLL

NM/M

Complete Set (161):
Common Player: .20
Common Even # SP (2-60): 1.00
Inserted 1:6
Common SP (131-161): 3.00
Production 2,500
Pack (5): 1.50
Box (24): 30.00

#	Player	Price
1	Derek Jeter	2.00
2	Derek Jeter/SP	5.00
3	Alex Rodriguez	1.50
4	Alex Rodriguez/SP	5.00
5	Roger Clemens	1.50
6	Roger Clemens/SP	4.00
7	Mike Piazza	1.00
8	Mike Piazza/SP	3.00
9	Jeff Bagwell	.50
10	Jeff Bagwell/SP	1.50
11	Vladimir Guerrero	.75
12	Vladimir Guerrero/SP	2.00
13	Ken Griffey Jr.	1.00
14	Ken Griffey Jr./SP	3.00
15	Greg Maddux	1.00
16	Greg Maddux/SP	3.00
17	Chipper Jones	.75
18	Chipper Jones/SP	2.00
19	Randy Johnson	.75
20	Randy Johnson/SP	2.00
21	Miguel Tejada	.50
22	Miguel Tejada/SP	1.50
23	Nomar Garciaparra	1.50
24	Nomar Garciaparra/SP	4.00
25	Ichiro Suzuki	1.50
26	Ichiro Suzuki/SP	4.00
27	Sammy Sosa	1.00
28	Sammy Sosa/SP	3.00
29	Albert Pujols	2.00
30	Albert Pujols/SP	5.00
31	Alfonso Soriano	.75
32	Alfonso Soriano/SP	2.00
33	Barry Bonds	2.00
34	Barry Bonds/SP	6.00
35	Jeff Kent	.30
36	Jeff Kent/SP	1.00
37	Jim Thome	.50
38	Jim Thome/SP	1.50
39	Pedro J. Martinez	.75
40	Pedro J. Martinez/SP	2.00
41	Todd Helton	.50
42	Todd Helton/SP	1.50
43	Troy Glaus	.50
44	Troy Glaus/SP	1.50
45	Mark Prior	.75
46	Mark Prior/SP	3.00
47	Tom Glavine	.40
48	Tom Glavine/SP	1.00
49	Pat Burrell	.40
50	Pat Burrell/SP	1.00
51	Barry Zito	.40
52	Barry Zito/SP	1.00
53	Bernie Williams	.50
54	Bernie Williams/SP	1.50
55	Curt Schilling	.50
56	Curt Schilling/SP	1.50
57	Darin Erstad	.30
58	Darin Erstad/SP	1.00
59	Carlos Delgado	.50
60	Carlos Delgado/SP	1.50
61	Gary Sheffield	.40
62	Gary Sheffield	.40
63	Frank Thomas	.50
64	Frank Thomas	.50
65	Lance Berkman	.40
66	Lance Berkman	.40
67	Shawn Green	.40
68	Shawn Green	.40
69	Hideo Nomo	.40
70	Hideo Nomo	.40
71	Torii Hunter	.40
72	Torii Hunter	.40
73	Roberto Alomar	.50
74	Roberto Alomar	.50
75	Andruw Jones	.50
76	Andruw Jones	.50
77	Scott Rolen	.75
78	Scott Rolen	.75
79	Eric Chavez	.40
80	Eric Chavez	.40
81	Rafael Palmeiro	.50
82	Rafael Palmeiro	.50
83	Bobby Abreu	.20
84	Bobby Abreu	.20
85	Craig Biggio	.20
86	Craig Biggio	.20
87	Rafael Furcal	.20
88	Rafael Furcal	.20
89	Jose Vidro	.20
90	Jose Vidro	.20
91	Luis Gonzalez	.20
92	Luis Gonzalez	.20
93	Roy Oswalt	.20
94	Roy Oswalt	.20
95	Cliff Floyd	.20
96	Cliff Floyd	.20
97	Larry Walker	.20
98	Larry Walker	.20
99	Jim Edmonds	.30
100	Jim Edmonds	.30
101	Adam Dunn	.40
102	Adam Dunn	.40
103	J.D. Drew	.20
104	J.D. Drew	.20
105	Josh Beckett	.20
106	Josh Beckett	.20
107	Brian Giles	.20
108	Brian Giles	.20
109	Magglio Ordonez	.40
110	Magglio Ordonez	.40
111	Edgardo Alfonzo	.20

112	Edgardo Alfonzo	.20
113	Bartolo Colon	.20
114	Bartolo Colon	.20
115	Roy Halladay	.20
116	Roy Halladay	.20
117	Joe Thurston	.20
118	Joe Thurston	.20
119	Brandon Phillips	.20
120	Brandon Phillips	.20
121	Kazuhisa Ishii	.20
122	Kazuhisa Ishii	.20
123	Mike Mussina	.40
124	Mike Mussina	.40
125	Tim Hudson	.40
126	Tim Hudson	.40
127	Mariano Rivera	.20
128	Mariano Rivera	.20
129	Travis Hafner	.20
130	Travis Hafner	.20
131	*Hideki Matsui*	20.00
132	*Jose Contreras*	5.00
133	Jason Anderson	3.00
134	*Willie Eyre*	3.00
135	*Shane Bazzell*	3.00
136	*Guillermo Quiroz*	5.00
137	*Francisco Cruceta*	3.00
138	Jhonny Peralta	4.00
139	*Aaron Looper*	3.00
140	*Bobby Madritsch*	6.00
141	*Michael Hessman*	3.00
142	*Todd Wellemeyer*	3.00
143	*Matt Bruback*	3.00
144	*Chris Capuano*	3.00
145	*Oscar Villarreal*	3.00
146	*Prentice Redman*	3.00
147	*Jeff Duncan*	5.00
148	*Phil Seibel*	3.00
149	Arnaldo Munoz	3.00
150	*David Sanders*	3.00
151	*Rick Roberts*	3.00
152	*Terrmel Sledge*	4.00
153	Franklin Perez	3.00
154	*Jeremy Wedel*	3.00
155	*Ian Ferguson*	3.00
156	*Josh Hall*	4.00
157	Rocco Baldelli	3.00
158	*Alejandro Machado*	3.00
159	*Jorge Cordova*	3.00
160	*Wilfredo Ledezma*	3.00
161	*Luis Ayala*	3.00

Gold

Production 25 sets:
No pricing due to scarcity

Silver

Even # SP's (2-60):	1-2X
Non-SP's (1-130):	4-8X
SP's (132-161):	.5-1X

Production 150 sets

Dean's List

		NM/M
Common Player:		4.00
Inserted 1:24		
RC	Roger Clemens	10.00
RC1	Roger Clemens	10.00
JG1	Jason Giambi	4.00
JG1	Jason Giambi	4.00
TG	Troy Glaus	4.00
TG1	Troy Glaus	4.00
NG	Shawn Green	4.00
NG1	Shawn Green	4.00
VG	Vladimir Guerrero	6.00
VG	Vladimir Guerrero	6.00
KG	Ken Griffey Jr.	10.00
KG1	Ken Griffey Jr.	10.00
CJ	Chipper Jones	8.00
CJ1	Chipper Jones	8.00
HM	Hideki Matsui	20.00
HM1	Hideki Matsui	20.00
HN	Hideo Nomo	10.00
HN1	Hideo Nomo	10.00
MP	Mike Piazza	10.00
MP1	Mike Piazza	10.00
MA	Mark Prior	10.00
MA1	Mark Prior	10.00
AP	Albert Pujols	15.00
AP1	Albert Pujols	15.00
AR	Alex Rodriguez	10.00
AR1	Alex Rodriguez	10.00
SS	Sammy Sosa	10.00
IS	Ichiro Suzuki	20.00
IS1	Ichiro Suzuki	20.00

Grade A Batting Gloves

		NM/M
Most not priced due to scarcity		
Inserted 1:960		
RA	Roberto Alomar/65	20.00
CD	Carlos Delgado/65	15.00
RF	Rafael Furcal/45	
TG	Troy Glaus/60	15.00
TG1	Troy Glaus/25	
JG	Juan Gonzalez/65	15.00
KG	Ken Griffey Jr./65	
KG1	Ken Griffey Jr./25	
RM	Raul Mondesi/65	10.00
RP	Rafael Palmeiro/65	20.00
RP1	Rafael Palmeiro/25	
MR	Manny Ramirez/69	20.00
AR	Alex Rodriguez/67	25.00
AR1	Alex Rodriguez/25	
IR	Ivan Rodriguez/70	20.00
IR1	Ivan Rodriguez/25	
SS	Sammy Sosa/65	
SS1	Sammy Sosa/25	
MT	Miguel Tejada/70	10.00
MT1	Miguel Tejada/25	
FT	Frank Thomas/70	20.00

Leather of Distinction

		NM/M
Most not priced due to scarcity		
Inserted 1:960		
JG	Jason Giambi/65	
KG	Ken Griffey Jr./70	30.00
KG1	Ken Griffey Jr./25	
CJ	Chipper Jones/70	
PM	Pedro Martinez/70	
PM1	Pedro Martinez/25	
RP	Rafael Palmeiro/70	20.00
MP	Mike Piazza/50	40.00
MP1	Mike Piazza/25	
MR	Manny Ramirez/70	20.00
AR	Alex Rodriguez/70	25.00
AR1	Alex Rodriguez/25	
IR	Ivan Rodriguez/69	20.00
TS	Tim Salmon/70	10.00
GS	Gary Sheffield/70	10.00
SS	Sammy Sosa/70	
SS1	Sammy Sosa/25	
IS	Ichiro Suzuki/9	
FT	Frank Thomas/70	20.00
OV	Omar Vizquel/65	10.00

2003 UPPER DECK MVP

		NM/M
Complete Set (220):		20.00
Complete Factory Set (330):		30.00
Common Player:		.10
Pack (8):		1.50
Box (24):		25.00
1	Troy Glaus	.40
2	Darin Erstad	.25
3	Jarrod Washburn	.10
4	Francisco Rodriguez	.10
5	Garret Anderson	.20
6	Tim Salmon	.20
7	Adam Kennedy	.10
8	Randy Johnson	.50
9	Luis Gonzalez	.20
10	Curt Schilling	.50
11	Junior Spivey	.10
12	Craig Counsell	.10
13	Mark Grace	.25
14	Steve Finley	.10
15	Javy Lopez	.10
16	Rafael Furcal	.10
17	John Smoltz	.15
18	Greg Maddux	.75
19	Chipper Jones	.50
20	Gary Sheffield	.20
21	Andruw Jones	.20
22	Tony Batista	.10
23	Geronimo Gil	.10
24	Jay Gibbons	.10
25	Rodrigo Lopez	.10
26	Chris Singleton	.10
27	Melvin Mora	.10
28	Jeff Conine	.10
29	Nomar Garciaparra	1.00
30	Pedro J. Martinez	.50
31	Manny Ramirez	.50
32	Shea Hillenbrand	.10
33	Johnny Damon	.40
34	Jason Varitek	.25
35	Derek Lowe	.10
36	Trot Nixon	.10
37	Sammy Sosa	.75
38	Kerry Wood	.50
39	Mark Prior	.50
40	Moises Alou	.20
41	Corey Patterson	.25
42	Hee Seop Choi	.10
43	Mark Bellhorn	.10
44	Frank Thomas	.40
45	Mark Buehrle	.20
46	Magglio Ordonez	.20
47	Carlos Lee	.20
48	Paul Konerko	.20
49	Joe Borchard	.10
50	Joe Crede	.10
51	Ken Griffey Jr.	.75
52	Adam Dunn	.40
53	Austin Kearns	.40
54	Aaron Boone	.10
55	Sean Casey	.10
56	Danny Graves	.10
57	Russell Branyan	.10
58	Matt Lawton	.10
59	C.C. Sabathia	.10
60	Omar Vizquel	.20
61	Brandon Phillips	.10
62	Karim Garcia	.10
63	Ellis Burks	.10
64	Cliff Lee	.10
65	Todd Helton	.40
66	Larry Walker	.20
67	Jay Payton	.10
68	Brent Butler	.10
69	Juan Uribe	.10
70	Jason Jennings	.10
71	Denny Stark	.10
72	Dmitri Young	.10
73	Carlos Pena	.10
74	Andres Torres	.10
75	Andy Van Hekken	.10
76	George Lombard	.10
77	Eric Munson	.10
78	Bobby Higginson	.10
79	Luis Castillo	.10
80	A.J. Burnett	.10
81	Juan Encarnacion	.10
82	Ivan Rodriguez	.40
83	Mike Lowell	.10
84	Josh Beckett	.25
85	Brad Penny	.10
86	Craig Biggio	.25
87	Jeff Kent	.20
88	Morgan Ensberg	.10
89	Daryle Ward	.10
90	Jeff Bagwell	.40
91	Roy Oswalt	.20
92	Lance Berkman	.25
93	Mike Sweeney	.10
94	Carlos Beltran	.40
95	Raul Ibanez	.10
96	Carlos Febles	.10
97	Joe Randa	.10
98	Shawn Green	.25
99	Kevin Brown	.15
100	Paul LoDuca	.10
101	Adrian Beltre	.25
102	Eric Gagne	.20
103	Kazuhisa Ishii	.10
104	Odalis Perez	.10
105	Brian Jordan	.10
106	Geoff Jenkins	.10
107	Richie Sexson	.25
108	Ben Sheets	.20
109	Alex Sanchez	.10
110	Eric Young	.10
111	Jose Hernandez	.10
112	Torii Hunter	.25
113	Eric Milton	.10
114	Corey Koskie	.10
115	Doug Mientkiewicz	.10
116	A.J. Pierzynski	.10
117	Jacque Jones	.10
118	Cristian Guzman	.10
119	Bartolo Colon	.10
120	Brad Wilkerson	.10
121	Michael Barrett	.10
122	Vladimir Guerrero	.50
123	Jose Vidro	.10
124	Javier Vazquez	.10
125	Endy Chavez	.10
126	Roberto Alomar	.25
127	Mike Piazza	1.00
128	Jeromy Burnitz	.10
129	Mo Vaughn	.15
130	Tom Glavine	.25
131	Al Leiter	.15
132	Armando Benitez	.10
133	Timoniel Perez	.10
134	Roger Clemens	1.00
135	Derek Jeter	1.50
136	Jason Giambi	.25
137	Alfonso Soriano	.50
138	Bernie Williams	.25
139	Mike Mussina	.25
140	Jorge Posada	.20
141	*Hideki Matsui*	4.00
142	Robin Ventura	.10
143	David Wells	.10
144	Nick Johnson	.10
145	Tim Hudson	.20
146	Eric Chavez	.20
147	Barry Zito	.25
148	Miguel Tejada	.40
149	Jermaine Dye	.10
150	Mark Mulder	.20
151	Terrence Long	.10
152	Scott Hatteberg	.10
153	Marlon Byrd	.10
154	Jim Thome	.40
155	Marlon Anderson	.10
156	Vicente Padilla	.10
157	Bobby Abreu	.20
158	Jimmy Rollins	.10
159	Pat Burrell	.40
160	Brian Giles	.20
161	Aramis Ramirez	.20
162	Jason Kendall	.20
163	Josh Fogg	.10
164	Kip Wells	.10
165	Pokey Reese	.10
166	Kris Benson	.10
167	Ryan Klesko	.20
168	Brian Lawrence	.10
169	Mark Kotsay	.10
170	Jake Peavy	.20
171	Phil Nevin	.10
172	Sean Burroughs	.10
173	Trevor Hoffman	.10
174	Jason Schmidt	.20
175	Kirk Rueter	.10
176	Barry Bonds	1.50
177	Pedro Feliz	.10
178	Rich Aurilia	.10
179	Benito Santiago	.10
180	J.T. Snow	.10
181	Robb Nen	.10
182	Ichiro Suzuki	1.00
183	Edgar Martinez	.10
184	Bret Boone	.10
185	Freddy Garcia	.10
186	John Olerud	.20
187	Mike Cameron	.10
188	Joel Pineiro	.10
189	Albert Pujols	1.25
190	Matt Morris	.20
191	J.D. Drew	.20
192	Scott Rolen	.50
193	Tino Martinez	.20
194	Jim Edmonds	.20
195	Edgar Renteria	.20
196	Fernando Vina	.10
197	Jason Isringhausen	.10
198	Ben Grieve	.10
199	Carl Crawford	.10
200	Dewon Brazelton	.10
201	Aubrey Huff	.10
202	Jared Sandberg	.10
203	Steve Cox	.10

204	Carl Everett	.10
205	Kevin Mench	.10
206	Alex Rodriguez	1.00
207	Rafael Palmeiro	.40
208	Michael Young	.10
209	Hank Blalock	.40
210	Juan Gonzalez	.25
211	Carlos Delgado	.20
212	Eric Hinske	.20
213	Josh Phelps	.10
214	Mark Hendrickson	.10
215	Roy Halladay	.10
216	Orlando Hudson	.10
217	Shannon Stewart	.10
218	Vernon Wells	.10
219	Ichiro Suzuki	.40
220	Jason Giambi	.25
221	Scott Spiezio	.10
222	Rich Fischer	.10
223	Bengie Molina	.10
224	David Eckstein	.10
225	*Brandon Webb*	1.50
226	Oscar Villarreal	.10
227	*Rob Hammock*	.40
228	*Matt Kata*	.40
229	Lyle Overbay	.10
230	*Chris Capuano*	.25
231	Horacio Ramirez	.10
232	Shane Reynolds	.10
233	Russ Ortiz	.10
234	Mike Hampton	.10
235	Mike Hessman	.10
236	Byung-Hyun Kim	.10
237	Freddy Sanchez	.10
238	Jason Shiell	.10
239	Ryan Cameron	.10
240	*Todd Wellemeyer*	.40
241	Joe Borowski	.10
242	Alex Gonzalez	.10
243	Jon Leicester	.10
244	David Sanders	.10
245	Roberto Alomar	.25
246	Barry Larkin	.25
247	Jhonny Peralta	.10
248	Zach Sorensen	.10
249	Jason Davis	.10
250	Coco Crisp	.10
251	Greg Vaughn	.10
252	Preston Wilson	.10
253	Denny Neagle	.10
254	*Clint Barmes*	1.00
255	Jeremy Bonderman	.50
256	*Wilfredo Ledezma*	.10
257	Dontrelle Willis	.25
258	Alex Gonzalez	.10
259	Tommy Phelps	.10
260	Kirk Saarloos	.10
261	*Colin Porter*	.10
262	Nate Bland	.10
263	Jason Gilfillan	.10
264	Mike MacDougal	.10
265	Ken Harvey	.10
266	Brent Mayne	.10
267	Miguel Cabrera	.40
268	Hideo Nomo	.25
269	Dave Roberts	.10
270	Fred McGriff	.20
271	Joe Thurston	.10
272	Royce Clayton	.10
273	Micheal Nakamura	.10
274	Brad Radke	.10
275	Joe Mays	.10
276	*Lew Ford*	1.00
277	Michael Cuddyer	.10
278	Luis Ayala	.10
279	Julio Manon	.10
280	Anthony Ferrari	.10
281	Livan Hernandez	.10
282	Jae Weong Seo	.10
283	Jose Reyes	.20
284	Tony Clark	.10
285	Ty Wigginton	.10
286	Cliff Floyd	.10
287	Jeremy Griffiths	.10
288	Jason Roach	.10
289	Jeff Duncan	.10
290	Phil Seibel	.10
291	*Prentice Redman*	.25
292	*Jose Contreras*	1.00
293	Ruben Sierra	.10
294	Andy Pettitte	.25
295	Aaron Boone	.10
296	Mariano Rivera	.20
297	Michel Hernandez	.10
298	Mike Neu	.10
299	Erubiel Durazo	.10
300	Billy McMillon	.10
301	Rich Harden	.10
302	David Bell	.10
303	Kevin Millwood	.20
304	Mike Lieberthal	.10
305	Jeremy Wedel	.10
306	Kenny Lofton	.10
307	Reggie Sanders	.10
308	Randall Simon	.10
309	Xavier Nady	.10
310	Rod Beck	.10
311	Miguel Ojeda	.10
312	Mark Loretta	.10
313	Edgardo Alfonzo	.10
314	Andres Galarraga	.10
315	Jose Cruz Jr.	.10
316	Jesse Foppert	.10
317	Kurt Ainsworth	.10
318	Dan Wilson	.10
319	Ben Davis	.10
320	Rocco Baldelli	.25
321	Al Martin	.10
322	Runelvys Hernandez	.10
323	Dan Haren	.50
324	*Bo Hart*	.25
325	Einar Diaz	.10
326	Mike Lamb	.10
327	Aquilino Lopez	.10
328	Reed Johnson	.10
329	Diegomar Markwell	.10
330	Hideki Matsui	.75

Gold

Stars (1-220): 6-12X
Production 150 sets
Black Stars: 10-20X
Production 50 sets
Silver Stars: 1-2X
Inserted 1:2

Base-to-Base

NM/M

Inserted 1:488

CP	Roger Clemens, Mike Piazza	25.00
IG	Ichiro Suzuki, Ken Griffey Jr.	40.00
IJ	Ichiro Suzuki, Derek Jeter	45.00
JW	Derek Jeter, Bernie Williams	25.00
MB	Mark McGwire, Barry Bonds	60.00
RJ	Alex Rodriguez, Derek Jeter	40.00

Covering the Bases

NM/M

Common Player: 4.00
Inserted 1:125

BB	Barry Bonds	15.00
CD	Carlos Delgado	4.00
JD	J.D. Drew	4.00
DE	Darin Erstad	6.00
TG	Troy Glaus	6.00
LG	Luis Gonzalez	4.00
SG	Shawn Green	6.00
DJ	Derek Jeter	15.00
MP	Mike Piazza	12.00
AR	Alex Rodriguez	12.00
IR	Ivan Rodriguez	4.00
IS	Ichiro Suzuki	15.00
MT	Miguel Tejada	6.00
FT	Frank Thomas	8.00
JT	Jim Thome	10.00

Covering the Plate Bat

NM/M

Common Player: 6.00
Inserted 1:160

RA	Roberto Alomar	15.00
RF	Rafael Furcal	8.00
VG	Vladimir Guerrero	8.00
FM	Fred McGriff	6.00
MM	Mark McGwire	60.00
JT	Jim Thome	12.00

Dual Aces

NM/M

Common Card: 8.00
Inserted 1:488

BS	Kevin Brown, Curt Schilling	10.00
CJ	Roger Clemens, Randy Johnson	20.00
CL	Roger Clemens, Al Leiter	15.00
ML	Matt Morris, Al Leiter	8.00
SJ	Curt Schilling, Randy Johnson	12.00
SM	Curt Schilling, Andy Pettitte	10.00

Express Delivery

NM/M

Complete Set (15): 10.00
Common Player: .50
Inserted 1:12

ED1	Randy Johnson	2.00
ED2	Curt Schilling	1.00
ED3	Pedro J. Martinez	2.00
ED4	Kerry Wood	1.00
ED5	Mark Prior	1.50
ED6	A.J. Burnett	.50
ED7	Josh Beckett	.50
ED8	Roy Oswalt	.75
ED9	Hideo Nomo	.75
ED10	Ben Sheets	.50
ED11	Bartolo Colon	.50
ED12	Roger Clemens	2.50
ED13	Mike Mussina	.75
ED14	Tim Hudson	.75
ED15	Matt Morris	.50

MVP Celebration

NM/M

Common Player: 1.50
#'d to yr. MVP was won

MVP1	Yogi Berra	4.00
MVP2	Mickey Mantle	15.00
MVP3	Mickey Mantle	15.00
MVP4	Mickey Mantle	15.00
MVP5	Roger Clemens	5.00
MVP6	Rickey Henderson	4.00
MVP7	Frank Thomas	4.00
MVP8	Mo Vaughn	1.50
MVP9	Juan Gonzalez	3.00
MVP10	Ken Griffey Jr.	6.00
MVP11	Juan Gonzalez	3.00
MVP12	Ivan Rodriguez	2.00
MVP13	Jason Giambi	4.00
MVP14	Ichiro Suzuki	6.00
MVP15	Miguel Tejada	2.00
MVP16	Barry Bonds	8.00
MVP17	Barry Bonds	8.00
MVP18	Barry Bonds	8.00
MVP19	Jeff Bagwell	4.00
MVP20	Barry Larkin	1.50
MVP21	Larry Walker	1.50
MVP22	Sammy Sosa	6.00
MVP23	Chipper Jones	5.00
MVP24	Jeff Kent	1.50
MVP25	Barry Bonds	8.00
MVP26	Barry Bonds	8.00
MVP27	Ken Griffey Sr.	1.50
MVP28	Roger Clemens	5.00
MVP29	Ken Griffey Jr.	6.00
MVP30	Fred McGriff	1.50
MVP31	Jeff Conine	1.50
MVP32	Mike Piazza	6.00
MVP33	Sandy Alomar Jr.	1.50
MVP34	Roberto Alomar	2.50
MVP35	Pedro J. Martinez	4.00
MVP36	Derek Jeter	8.00
MVP37	Rickey Henderson	4.00
MVP38	Roberto Alomar	2.50
MVP39	Bernie Williams	3.00
MVP40	Marquis Grissom	1.50
MVP41	David Wells	1.50
MVP42	Orlando Hernandez	1.50
MVP43	David Justice	1.50
MVP44	Andy Pettitte	2.00
MVP45	Adam Kennedy	1.50
MVP46	John Smoltz	1.50
MVP47	Curt Schilling	2.00
MVP48	Javy Lopez	1.50
MVP49	Livan Hernandez	1.50
MVP50	Sterling Hitchcock	1.50
MVP51	Mike Hampton	1.50
MVP52	Craig Counsell	1.50
MVP53	Benito Santiago	1.50
MVP54	Tom Glavine	2.00
MVP55	Livan Hernandez	1.50
MVP56	Mariano Rivera	1.50
MVP57	Derek Jeter	8.00
MVP58	Randy Johnson	4.00
MVP59	Curt Schilling	2.50
MVP60	Troy Glaus	3.00
MVP61	Yogi Berra	4.00
MVP62	Yogi Berra	4.00
MVP63	Mickey Mantle	15.00
MVP64	Mickey Mantle	15.00
MVP65	Ken Griffey Sr.	1.50
MVP66	Rickey Henderson	4.00
MVP67	Roberto Alomar	2.50
MVP68	Bernie Williams	3.00
MVP69	Livan Hernandez	1.50
MVP70	Sammy Sosa	6.00
MVP71	Sterling Hitchcock	1.50
MVP72	David Wells	1.50
MVP73	Mariano Rivera	1.50
MVP74	Chipper Jones	5.00
MVP75	Ivan Rodriguez	2.00
MVP76	Derek Jeter	8.00
MVP77	Jason Giambi	4.00
MVP78	Jeff Kent	1.50
MVP79	Mike Hampton	1.50
MVP80	Randy Johnson	4.00
MVP81	Curt Schilling	2.50
MVP82	Barry Bonds	8.00
MVP83	Ichiro Suzuki	6.00
MVP84	Ichiro Suzuki	6.00
MVP85	Adam Kennedy	1.50
MVP86	Benito Santiago	1.50
MVP87	Troy Glaus	3.00
MVP88	Troy Glaus	3.00
MVP89	Miguel Tejada	2.00
MVP90	Barry Bonds	8.00

Pro View

NM/M

Complete Set (45): 65.00
Common Player: .75
Inserted 2:box
Golds: 2-3X

PV1	Troy Glaus	1.50
PV2	Darin Erstad	1.00
PV3	Randy Johnson	2.00
PV4	Curt Schilling	1.50
PV5	Luis Gonzalez	.75
PV6	Chipper Jones	2.00
PV7	Andruw Jones	1.00
PV8	Greg Maddux	3.00
PV9	Pedro J. Martinez	2.00
PV10	Manny Ramirez	2.00
PV11	Sammy Sosa	3.00
PV12	Mark Prior	2.00
PV13	Magglio Ordonez	1.00
PV14	Frank Thomas	1.50
PV15	Ken Griffey Jr.	3.00
PV16	Adam Dunn	1.50
PV17	Jim Thome	1.50
PV18	Todd Helton	1.00
PV19	Jeff Bagwell	1.50
PV20	Lance Berkman	1.00
PV21	Shawn Green	.75
PV22	Hideo Nomo	1.00
PV23	Vladimir Guerrero	2.00
PV24	Roberto Alomar	1.00
PV25	Mike Piazza	4.00
PV26	Jason Giambi	1.00
PV27	Roger Clemens	3.00
PV28	Alfonso Soriano	2.00
PV29	Derek Jeter	6.00
PV30	Miguel Tejada	1.50
PV31	Eric Chavez	.75
PV32	Barry Zito	1.00
PV33	Pat Burrell	1.50
PV34	Brian Giles	.75
PV35	Barry Bonds	6.00
PV36	Ichiro Suzuki	4.00
PV37	Albert Pujols	5.00
PV38	Scott Rolen	1.50
PV39	J.D. Drew	.75
PV40	Mark McGwire	5.00
PV41	Alex Rodriguez	5.00
PV42	Rafael Palmeiro	1.00
PV43	Juan Gonzalez	1.00
PV44	Eric Hinske	.75
PV45	Carlos Delgado	.75

SportsNut Fantasy

NM/M
Complete Set (90): 45.00
Common Player: .40
Inserted 1:3
Prices for unscratched cards
SN1 Troy Glaus 1.00
SN2 Darin Erstad .50
SN3 Luis Gonzalez .50
SN4 Andruw Jones .75
SN5 Chipper Jones 2.00
SN6 Gary Sheffield .50
SN7 Jay Gibbons .40
SN8 Manny Ramirez 1.00
SN9 Shea Hillenbrand .40
SN10 Johnny Damon .40
SN11 Nomar Garciaparra 2.50
SN12 Sammy Sosa 2.00
SN13 Magglio Ordonez .75
SN14 Frank Thomas .75
SN15 Ken Griffey Jr. 1.50
SN16 Adam Dunn 1.00
SN17 Matt Lawton .40
SN18 Larry Walker .40
SN19 Todd Helton .75
SN20 Carlos Pena .40
SN21 Mike Lowell .40
SN22 Jeff Bagwell 1.00
SN23 Lance Berkman .75
SN24 Mike Sweeney .50
SN25 Carlos Beltran .40
SN26 Shawn Green .75
SN27 Richie Sexson .50
SN28 Torii Hunter .40
SN29 Jacque Jones .40
SN30 Vladimir Guerrero 1.50
SN31 Jose Vidro .40
SN32 Roberto Alomar .50
SN33 Mike Piazza 2.00
SN34 Alfonso Soriano 1.50
SN35 Derek Jeter 3.00
SN36 Jason Giambi 2.00
SN37 Bernie Williams .75
SN38 Eric Chavez .75
SN39 Miguel Tejada .75
SN40 Jim Thome 1.00
SN41 Pat Burrell 1.00
SN42 Bobby Abreu .50
SN43 Brian Giles .50
SN44 Jason Kendall .40
SN45 Ryan Klesko .40
SN46 Phil Nevin .40
SN47 Barry Bonds 4.00
SN48 Rich Aurilia .40
SN49 Ichiro Suzuki 2.00
SN50 Bret Boone .40
SN51 J.D. Drew .40
SN52 Jim Edmonds .75
SN53 Albert Pujols 1.50
SN54 Scott Rolen 1.00
SN55 Ben Grieve .40
SN56 Alex Rodriguez 3.00
SN57 Rafael Palmeiro .75
SN58 Juan Gonzalez .50
SN59 Carlos Delgado .40
SN60 Josh Phelps .40
SN61 Jarrod Washburn .40
SN62 Randy Johnson 1.00
SN63 Curt Schilling .75
SN64 Greg Maddux 1.50
SN65 Mike Hampton .40
SN66 Rodrigo Lopez .40
SN67 Pedro J. Martinez 1.50
SN68 Derek Lowe .40
SN69 Mark Prior 1.00
SN70 Kerry Wood .75
SN71 Mark Buehrle .40
SN72 Roy Oswalt .50
SN73 Wade Miller .40
SN74 Odalis Perez .40
SN75 Hideo Nomo .50
SN76 Ben Sheets .40
SN77 Eric Milton .40
SN78 Bartolo Colon .40
SN79 Tom Glavine .40
SN80 Al Leiter .40
SN81 Roger Clemens 2.00
SN82 Mike Mussina .75
SN83 Tim Hudson .75
SN84 Barry Zito .75
SN85 Mark Mulder .50
SN86 Vicente Padilla .40
SN87 Jason Schmidt .40
SN88 Freddy Garcia .40
SN89 Matt Morris .40
SN90 Roy Halladay .40

Talk of the Town

NM/M
Complete Set (15): 20.00
Common Player: .75
Inserted 1:12
TT1 Hideki Matsui 3.00
TT2 Chipper Jones 1.00
TT3 Manny Ramirez 1.50
TT4 Sammy Sosa 2.00
TT5 Ken Griffey Jr. 2.00
TT6 Lance Berkman .75
TT7 Shawn Green .75
TT8 Vladimir Guerrero 1.50
TT9 Mike Piazza 2.50
TT10 Jason Giambi .75
TT11 Alfonso Soriano 1.50
TT12 Ichiro Suzuki 2.50
TT13 Albert Pujols 3.00
TT14 Alex Rodriguez 3.00
TT15 Eric Hinske .75

Three Bagger

NM/M
Inserted 1:488
BMP Barry Bonds, Mark McGwire, Mike Piazza 80.00
GIB Ken Griffey Jr., Ichiro Suzuki, Barry Bonds 60.00
GTD Troy Glaus, Frank Thomas, Carlos Delgado 10.00
IBJ Ichiro Suzuki, Barry Bonds, Derek Jeter 80.00
JWP Derek Jeter, Bernie Williams, Jorge Posada 35.00
SCB Curt Schilling, Roger Clemens, Kevin Brown 20.00

Total Bases

NM/M
Production 150 sets
BB Barry Bonds 20.00
RC Roger Clemens 20.00
TG Troy Glaus 8.00
KG Ken Griffey Jr. 15.00
DJ Derek Jeter 20.00
MM Mark McGwire 25.00
MP Mike Piazza 15.00
AR Alex Rodriguez 15.00
IS Ichiro Suzuki 30.00

2003 UPPER DECK PATCH COLLECTION

NM/M
Complete Set (161):
Common Player: .25
Common SP Patch (121-161): 4.00
All-Star & HOF Patches (121-150):
Inserted 1:40
Rookie Patches (151-161):
Inserted 1:20
Pack (5): 4.75
Box (20): 80.00
1 Darin Erstad .40
2 Troy Glaus .75
3 *Robby Hammock* .25
4 Luis Gonzalez .50
5 Randy Johnson/SP 3.00
6 Curt Schilling/SP 2.50
7 *Oscar Villarreal* .25
8 Gary Sheffield .50
9 Mike Hampton .25
10 Greg Maddux 1.50
11 Chipper Jones 1.50
12 Tony Batista .25
13 Rodrigo Lopez .25
14 Jay Gibbons .25
15 Shea Hillenbrand .25
16 Johnny Damon .25
17 Derek Lowe .25
18 Nomar Garciaparra 2.00
19 Pedro J. Martinez 1.00
20 Manny Ramirez .75
21 Mark Prior 1.00
22 Kerry Wood .50
23 Corey Patterson .25
24 Sammy Sosa 1.50
25 Troy O'Leary .25
26 Frank Thomas .75
27 Magglio Ordonez .40
28 Bartolo Colon .25
29 Austin Kearns .75
30 Aaron Boone .25
31 Ken Griffey Jr. 1.50
32 Adam Dunn .75
33 C.C. Sabathia .25
34 Karim Garcia .25
35 Larry Walker .40
36 Preston Wilson .40
37 Jason Jennings .25
38 Todd Helton .75
39 Carlos Pena .25
40 Eric Munson .25
41 Ivan Rodriguez .50
42 Josh Beckett .25
43 A.J. Burnett .25
44 Roy Oswalt .25
45 Craig Biggio .40
46 Jeff Bagwell .75
47 Lance Berkman .50
48 Jeff Kent .40
49 Carlos Beltran .25
50 Mike Sweeney .25
51 Hideo Nomo .50
52 Adrian Beltre .25
53 Shawn Green .50
54 Kazuhisa Ishii .25
55 Ben Sheets .25
56 Richie Sexson .50
57 Torii Hunter .50
58 Doug Mientkiewicz .25
59 Eric Milton .25
60 Corey Koskie .25
61 Joe Mays .25
62 Jose Vidro .25
63 Vladimir Guerrero .75
64 *Luis Ayala* .25
65 Cliff Floyd .25
66 Tom Glavine .50
67 Mike Piazza 2.00
68 Roberto Alomar .50
69 Al Leiter .25
70 Mike Mussina .50
71 Mariano Rivera .40
72 Drew Henson .25
73 Roger Clemens 1.50
74 Jason Giambi 1.00
75 Bernie Williams .50
76 Alfonso Soriano 1.50
77 Derek Jeter 3.00
78 Miguel Tejada .50
79 Jermaine Dye .25
80 Tim Hudson .50
81 Barry Zito .50
82 Mark Mulder .40
83 Pat Burrell .50
84 Jim Thome .75
85 Bobby Abreu .40
86 Kevin Millwood .40
87 Jason Kendall .40
88 Brian Giles .40
89 Phil Nevin .25
90 Sean Burroughs .25
91 Oliver Perez .25
92 Jose Cruz Jr. .25
93 Rich Aurilia .25
94 Edgardo Alfonzo .25
95 Barry Bonds 3.00
96 J.T. Snow .25
97 Mike Cameron .25
98 John Olerud .50
99 Bret Boone .25
100 Ichiro Suzuki 1.50
101 J.D. Drew .40
102 Jim Edmonds .50
103 Scott Rolen .75
104 Matt Morris .40
105 Tino Martinez .40
106 Albert Pujols 1.50
107 Rocco Baldelli .25
108 Carl Crawford .25
109 Mark Teixeira .50
110 Rafael Palmeiro .50
111 Hank Blalock .50
112 Alex Rodriguez 2.50
113 Kevin Mench .25
114 Juan Gonzalez .75
115 Shannon Stewart .25
116 Vernon Wells .40
117 Josh Phelps .25
118 Eric Hinske .25
119 Orlando Hudson .25
120 Carlos Delgado .50
121 Alex Rodriguez 10.00
122 Nomar Garciaparra 10.00
123 Miguel Tejada 4.00
124 Jim Thome 8.00
125 Alfonso Soriano 6.00
126 Vladimir Guerrero 6.00
127 Derek Jeter 15.00
128 Mike Piazza 8.00
129 Ichiro Suzuki 12.00
130 Pedro J. Martinez 8.00
131 Luis Gonzalez 4.00
132 Adam Dunn 6.00
133 Shawn Green 4.00
134 Barry Zito 4.00
135 Torii Hunter 5.00
136 Ted Williams 20.00
137 Mickey Mantle 25.00
138 Ernie Banks 10.00
139 Yogi Berra 8.00
140 Rollie Fingers 4.00
141 Jim "Catfish" Hunter 4.00
142 Juan Marichal 8.00
143 Eddie Mathews 10.00
144 Willie McCovey 10.00
145 Joe Morgan 5.00
146 Stan Musial 12.00
147 Pee Wee Reese 10.00
148 Phil Rizzuto 6.00
149 Nolan Ryan 20.00
150 Tom Seaver 8.00
151 *Hideki Matsui* 15.00
152 *Jose Contreras* 5.00
153 *Lew Ford* 5.00
154 Jeremy Griffiths 4.00
155 *Guillermo Quiroz* 4.00
156 *Ryan Cameron* 4.00
157 *Jon Leicester* 4.00
158 *Josh Willingham* 4.00
159 *Shane Bazzell* 4.00
160 *Willie Eyre* 4.00
161 *Prentice Redman* 4.00

All-Star Game History Patches

NM/M
Common Patch: 8.00
Inserted 2:box
1 1933 All-Star Game 12.00
2 1934 All-Star Game 15.00
3 1935 All-Star Game 15.00
4 1936 All-Star Game 10.00
5 1937 All-Star Game 10.00
6 1938 All-Star Game 10.00
7 1939 All-Star Game 15.00
8 1940 All-Star Game 15.00

9	1941 All-Star Game	10.00
10	1942 All-Star Game	15.00
11	1943 All-Star Game	12.00
12	1944 All-Star Game	12.00
13	1946 All-Star Game	15.00
14	1947 All-Star Game	15.00
15	1948 All-Star Game	15.00
16	1949 All-Star Game	15.00
17	1950 All-Star Game	12.00
18	1951 All-Star Game	12.00
19	1952 All-Star Game	15.00
20	1953 All-Star Game	12.00
21	1954 All-Star Game	12.00
22	1955 All-Star Game	10.00
23	1956 All-Star Game	12.00
24	1957 All-Star Game	15.00
25	1958 All-Star Game	12.00
26	1959 All-Star Game	15.00
27	1959 All-Star Game	15.00
28	1960 All-Star Game	10.00
29	1960 All-Star Game	15.00
30	1961 All-Star Game	10.00
31	1961 All-Star Game	15.00
32	1962 All-Star Game	8.00
33	1962 All-Star Game	12.00
34	1963 All-Star Game	10.00
35	1964 All-Star Game	15.00
36	1965 All-Star Game	10.00
37	1966 All-Star Game	15.00
38	1967 All-Star Game	12.00
39	1968 All-Star Game	8.00
40	1969 All-Star Game	10.00
41	1970 All-Star Game	15.00
42	1971 All-Star Game	10.00
43	1972 All-Star Game	10.00
44	1973 All-Star Game	10.00
45	1974 All-Star Game	10.00
46	1975 All-Star Game	10.00
47	1976 All-Star Game	15.00
48	1977 All-Star Game	12.00
49	1978 All-Star Game	10.00
50	1979 All-Star Game	8.00
51	1980 All-Star Game	8.00
52	1981 All-Star Game	10.00
53	1982 All-Star Game	8.00
54	1983 All-Star Game	10.00
55	1984 All-Star Game	10.00
56	1985 All-Star Game	10.00
57	1986 All-Star Game	10.00
58	1987 All-Star Game	8.00
59	1988 All-Star Game	10.00
60	1989 All-Star Game	8.00
61	1990 All-Star Game	15.00
62	1991 All-Star Game	8.00
63	1992 All-Star Game	8.00
64	1993 All-Star Game	10.00
65	1994 All-Star Game	15.00
66	1995 All-Star Game	8.00
67	1996 All-Star Game	12.00
68	1997 All-Star Game	10.00
69	1998 All-Star Game	8.00
70	1999 All-Star Game	15.00
71	2000 All-Star Game	10.00
72	2001 All-Star Game	10.00
73	2002 All-Star Game	12.00

MVPs Patches

		NM/M
Common Player:		5.00
Inserted 1:20		
1	Derek Jeter	15.00
2	Randy Johnson	8.00
3	Curt Schilling	6.00
4	Troy Glaus	5.00
5	Ted Williams	15.00
6	Ted Williams	15.00
7	Mickey Mantle	20.00
8	Mickey Mantle	20.00
9	Phil Rizzuto	5.00
10	Roger Clemens	10.00
11	Ken Griffey Jr.	10.00
12	Jason Giambi	5.00
13	Ichiro Suzuki	15.00
14	Roger Clemens	10.00
15	Yogi Berra	6.00
16	Sammy Sosa	10.00
17	Derek Jeter	15.00
18	Mike Piazza	10.00
19	Barry Bonds	15.00
20	Stan Musial	12.00
21	Joe Morgan	5.00

Signature Patches

		NM/M
Common Autograph:		25.00
Inserted 1:320		
JB	Jeff Bagwell	50.00
LB	Lance Berkman	50.00
RC	Roger Clemens	160.00
AD	Adam Dunn	60.00
FG	Freddy Garcia	30.00
JG	Jason Giambi	40.00
LG	Luis Gonzalez	40.00
KG	Ken Griffey Jr.	100.00
DH	Drew Henson	40.00
EH	Eric Hinske	25.00
HM	Hideki Matsui	
TP	Troy Percival	25.00
SR	Scott Rolen	50.00
CS	Curt Schilling	50.00
GS	Gary Sheffield	50.00
SS	Sammy Sosa	
IS	Ichiro Suzuki	300.00
MT	Miguel Tejada	50.00
BZ	Barry Zito	40.00

2003 UPPER DECK PLAY BALL

		NM/M
Complete Set (104):		
Common Player:		.25
Common Summer of '41 (74-88):		4.00
Inserted 1:24		
Common Ted Williams (89-103):		10.00
Inserted 1:24		
Pack (5):		2.50
Box (24):		40.00
1	Troy Glaus	.40
2	Darin Erstad	.25
3	Randy Johnson	.75
4	Luis Gonzalez	.40
5	Curt Schilling	.75
6	Tom Glavine	.40
7	Chipper Jones	.75
8	Greg Maddux	1.00
9	Andruw Jones	.40
10	Pedro J. Martinez	.75
11	Manny Ramirez	.75
12	Nomar Garciaparra	1.00
13	Billy Williams	.25
14	Sammy Sosa	1.00
15	Kerry Wood	.75
16	Mark Prior	.75
17	Ernie Banks	1.00
18	Frank Thomas	.75
19	Joe Morgan	.25
20	Ken Griffey Jr.	1.25
21	Adam Dunn	.50
22	Jim Thome	.75
23	Todd Helton	.50
24	Larry Walker	.40
25	Lance Berkman	.40
26	Roy Oswalt	.40
27	Jeff Bagwell	.50
28	Nolan Ryan	2.00
29	Mike Sweeney	.25
30	Shawn Green	.40
31	Hideo Nomo	.40
32	Kazuhisa Ishii	.25
33	Richie Sexson	.40
34	Robin Yount	.75
35	Harmon Killebrew	.75
36	Torii Hunter	.50
37	Vladimir Guerrero	.75
38	Roberto Alomar	.50
39	Mike Piazza	1.00
40	Tom Seaver	.75
41	Phil Rizzuto	.50
42	Yogi Berra	.75
43	Mike Mussina	.50
44	Roger Clemens	1.50
45	Derek Jeter	2.00
46	Jason Giambi	.25
47	Bernie Williams	.50
48	Alfonso Soriano	.75
49	Jim "Catfish" Hunter	.25
50	Barry Zito	.40
51	Eric Chavez	.40
52	Tim Hudson	.40
53	Rollie Fingers	.25
54	Miguel Tejada	.50
55	Pat Burrell	.40
56	Brian Giles	.40
57	Willie Stargell	.50
58	Phil Nevin	.25
59	Orlando Cepeda	.25
60	Barry Bonds	2.00
61	Jeff Kent	.40
62	Willie McCovey	.25
63	Ichiro Suzuki	1.50
64	Stan Musial	1.50
65	Albert Pujols	2.00
66	J.D. Drew	.40
67	Scott Rolen	.75
68	Mark McGwire	1.00
69	Alex Rodriguez	1.00
70	Juan Gonzalez	.40
71	Ivan Rodriguez	.50
72	Rafael Palmeiro	.50
73	Carlos Delgado	.40
74	Ted Williams	15.00
75	Hank Greenberg	6.00
76	Joe DiMaggio	15.00
77	Lefty Gomez	6.00
78	Tommy Henrich	4.00
79	Pee Wee Reese	5.00
80	Mel Ott	6.00
81	Carl Hubbell	6.00
82	Jimmie Foxx	8.00
83	Joe Cronin	4.00
84	Charlie Gehringer	5.00
85	Frank Hayes	5.00
86	Babe Dahlgren	4.00
87	Dolph Camilli	4.00
88	Johnny Vander Meer	4.00
89	Ted Williams	10.00
90	Ted Williams	10.00
91	Ted Williams	10.00
92	Ted Williams	10.00
93	Ted Williams	10.00
94	Ted Williams	10.00
95	Ted Williams	10.00
96	Ted Williams	10.00
97	Ted Williams	10.00
98	Ted Williams	10.00
99	Ted Williams	10.00
100	Ted Williams	10.00
101	Ted Williams	10.00
102	Ted Williams	10.00
103	Ted Williams	10.00
104	*Hideki Matsui*	5.00

Mini

		NM/M
Complete Set (73):		40.00
Common Player:		.50
Inserted 1:2		
1	Troy Glaus	.50
2	Darin Erstad	.50
3	Randy Johnson	1.00
4	Luis Gonzalez	.50
5	Curt Schilling	.75
6	Tom Glavine	.50
7	Chipper Jones	1.00
8	Greg Maddux	1.50
9	Andruw Jones	.75
10	Pedro J. Martinez	1.00
11	Manny Ramirez	1.00
12	Nomar Garciaparra	2.00
13	Billy Williams	.50
14	Sammy Sosa	2.00
15	Kerry Wood	1.00
16	Mark Prior	1.00
17	Ernie Banks	1.50
18	Frank Thomas	1.00
19	Joe Morgan	.50
20	Ken Griffey Jr.	2.00
21	Adam Dunn	1.00
22	Jim Thome	1.00
23	Todd Helton	.75
24	Larry Walker	.50
25	Lance Berkman	.75
26	Roy Oswalt	.50
27	Jeff Bagwell	1.00
28	Nolan Ryan	3.00
29	Mike Sweeney	.50
30	Shawn Green	.50
31	Hideo Nomo	.75
32	Kazuhisa Ishii	.50
33	Richie Sexson	.50
34	Robin Yount	1.00
35	Harmon Killebrew	1.00
36	Torii Hunter	.75
37	Vladimir Guerrero	1.00
38	Roberto Alomar	.75
39	Mike Piazza	2.00
40	Tom Seaver	1.00
41	Phil Rizzuto	.75
42	Yogi Berra	1.50
43	Mike Mussina	.75
44	Roger Clemens	2.00
45	Derek Jeter	3.00
46	Jason Giambi	.50
47	Bernie Williams	.75
48	Alfonso Soriano	1.00
49	Jim "Catfish" Hunter	.50
50	Barry Zito	.50
51	Eric Chavez	.50
52	Tim Hudson	.50
53	Rollie Fingers	.50
54	Miguel Tejada	1.00
55	Pat Burrell	1.00
56	Brian Giles	.50
57	Willie Stargell	.75
58	Phil Nevin	.50
59	Orlando Cepeda	.50
60	Barry Bonds	3.00
61	Jeff Kent	.50
62	Willie McCovey	.50
63	Ichiro Suzuki	2.50
64	Stan Musial	2.00
65	Albert Pujols	3.00
66	J.D. Drew	.50
67	Scott Rolen	1.00
68	Mark McGwire	2.00
69	Alex Rodriguez	2.50
70	Juan Gonzalez	1.00
71	Ivan Rodriguez	1.00
72	Rafael Palmeiro	.75
73	Carlos Delgado	.50

Red Back

	NM/M
Stars (1-73):	1.5-2X
SP's (74-103):	1-1.5X
Matsui Red #104:	10.00
Inserted 1:2	

Game-Used Memorabilia Tier 1

		NM/M
Common Player:		5.00
Inserted 1:82		
Golds:		Not Priced
Production 25 sets		
RC1	Roger Clemens	20.00
CD1	Carlos Delgado	5.00
DR1	J.D. Drew	5.00
AD1	Adam Dunn	10.00
JG1	Jason Giambi	5.00
LG1	Luis Gonzalez	5.00
KG1	Ken Griffey Jr.	15.00
TH1	Tommy Henrich	5.00
KI1	Kazuhisa Ishii	5.00
CJ1	Chipper Jones	10.00
MM1	Mark McGwire	50.00
RP1	Rafael Palmeiro	8.00
MP1	Mike Piazza	10.00
PR1	Mark Prior	10.00
IR1	Ivan Rodriguez	8.00
CS1	Curt Schilling	8.00
AS1	Alfonso Soriano	8.00
SS1	Sammy Sosa	10.00
IS1	Ichiro Suzuki	30.00
MS1	Mike Sweeney	5.00
BW1	Bernie Williams	5.00

Game-Used Memorabilia Tier 2

		NM/M
Common Player:		5.00
Production 150 sets		
JB2	Jeff Bagwell	10.00
LB2	Lance Berkman	5.00
JD2	Joe DiMaggio	100.00
DE2	Darin Erstad	5.00
JG2	Jason Giambi	5.00
SG2	Shawn Green	5.00
KG2	Ken Griffey Jr.	15.00
RJ2	Randy Johnson	10.00
AJ2	Andruw Jones	8.00
CJ2	Chipper Jones	10.00
GM2	Greg Maddux	15.00
PM2	Pedro J. Martinez	10.00
MM2	Mark McGwire	60.00
MP2	Mike Piazza	10.00
MR2	Manny Ramirez	10.00
AR2	Alex Rodriguez	15.00
CS2	Curt Schilling	10.00
SS2	Sammy Sosa	15.00
IS2	Ichiro Suzuki	50.00
JT2	Jim Thome	10.00
KW2	Kerry Wood	10.00

Game-Used Memorabilia Auto.

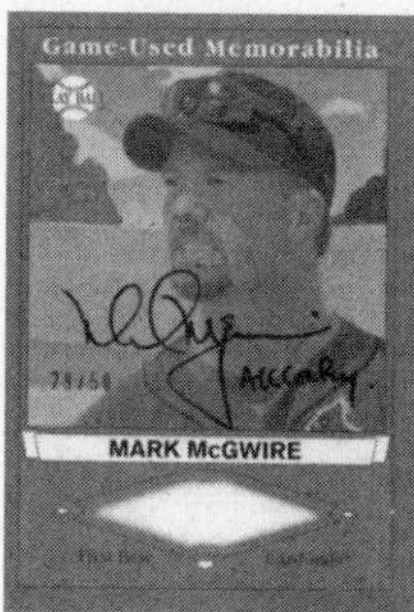

		NM/M
Production 50 except A-Rod		
JB2	Jeff Bagwell	75.00
LB2	Lance Berkman	75.00
JG2	Jason Giambi	50.00
KG2	Ken Griffey Jr.	125.00
AJ2	Andruw Jones	50.00
MM2	Mark McGwire	350.00
AR2	Alex Rodriguez/285	100.00
CS2	Curt Schilling	75.00
SS2	Sammy Sosa	180.00
IS2	Ichiro Suzuki	375.00
JT2	Jim Thome	75.00
KW2	Kerry Wood	75.00

Reprint Series Original 1941

		NM/M
Complete Set (25):		15.00
Common Player:		.75
Inserted 1:2		
R1	Ted Williams	2.50
R2	Hank Greenberg	.75
R3	Joe DiMaggio	2.50
R4	Lefty Gomez	.75
R5	Tommy Henrich	.75
R6	Pee Wee Reese	.75
R7	Mel Ott	1.00
R8	Carl Hubbell	.75
R9	Jimmie Foxx	1.00
R10	Joe Cronin	.75
R11	Charley Gehringer	.75
R12	Frank Hayes	.75
R13	Babe Dahlgren	.75
R14	Dolph Camilli	.75
R15	Johnny Vander Meer	.75
R16	Bucky Walters	.75
R17	Red Ruffing	.75
R18	Charlie Keller	.75
R19	Bob Johnson	.75
R20	Emil "Dutch" Leonard	.75
R21	Barney McCosky	.75
R22	Soupy Campbell	.75
R23	Roy Weatherly	.75
R24	Bobby Doerr	.75
R25	Bill Dickey	.75

Yankee Clipper: 1941 Streak

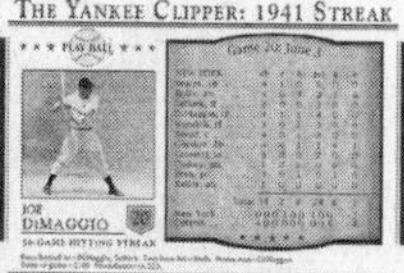

	NM/M
Complete Set (56):	250.00
Common DiMaggio (1-41):	5.00
Inserted 1:12	
Common DiMaggio (42-56):	8.00
Inserted 1:24	

2003 UPPER DECK PROSPECT PREMIERES

		NM/M
Complete Set (90):		30.00
Common Player:		.25
Pack (4):		5.00
Box (18):		75.00
1	*Bryan Opdyke*	.25
2	*Gabriel Sosa*	.25
3	*Tila Reynolds*	.25
4	*Aaron Hill*	1.00
5	*Aaron Marsden*	.25
6	*Abe Alvarez*	.75
7	*Adam Jones*	.50
8	*Adam Miller*	2.00
9	*Andre Ethier*	1.00
10	*Anthony Gwynn*	.75
11	*Brad Snyder*	1.00
12	*Brad Sullivan*	.75
13	*Brian Anderson*	1.00
14	*Brian Buscher*	.25
15	*Brian Snyder*	.75
16	*Carlos Quentin*	2.00
17	*Chad Billingsley*	.75
18	*Fraser Dizard*	.50
19	*Chris Durbin*	.50
20	*Chris Ray*	.50
21	*Conor Jackson*	2.00
22	*Kory Casto*	.50
23	*Craig Whitaker*	.75
24	*Daniel Moore*	.25
25	*Daric Barton*	2.00
26	*Darin Downs*	.75
27	*David Murphy*	1.00
28	*Dustin Majewski*	.50
29	*Edgardo Baez*	.25
30	*Jake Fox*	.50
31	*Jake Stevens*	.50
32	*Jamie D'Antona*	.75
33	*James Houser*	.50
34	*Jarrod Saltalamacchia*	1.50
35	*Jason Hirsh*	.50
36	*Javi Herrera*	1.00
37	*Jeff Allison*	.75
38	*John Hudgins*	.50
39	*Jo Jo Reyes*	.50
40	*Justin James*	.50
41	*Kurt Isenberg*	.50
42	*Kyle Boyer*	.75
43	*Lastings Milledge*	2.00
44	*Luis Atilano*	.50
45	*Matt Murton*	1.50
46	*Matt Moses*	1.00
47	*Matt Harrison*	.50
48	*Michael Bourn*	.50
49	*Miguel Vega*	.50
50	*Mitch Maier*	1.00
51	*Omar Quintanilla*	.50
52	*Ryan Sweeney*	1.50
53	*Scott Baker*	.75
54	*Sean Rodriguez*	.75
55	*Steve Lerud*	.25
56	*Thomas Pauly*	.25
57	*Tom Gorzelanny*	.50
58	*Tim Moss*	.25
59	*Robbie Wooley*	.50
60	*Trey Webb*	.25
61	*Wes Littleton*	.50
62	*Beau Vaughan*	.25
63	*Willy Jo Ronda*	.50
64	*Chris Lubanski*	1.00
65	*Ian Stewart*	8.00
66	*John Danks*	1.00
67	*Kyle Sleeth*	1.00
68	*Michael Aubrey*	1.50
69	*Kevin Kouzmanoff*	.50
70	*Ryan Harvey*	1.50
71	*Tim Stauffer*	1.00
72	*Tony Richie*	.25
73	*Brandon Wood*	3.00
74	*David Aardsma*	.75
75	*David Shinskie*	.50
76	*Dennis Dove*	.25
77	*Eric Sultemeier*	.25
78	*Jay Sborz*	.25
79	*Jimmy Barthmaier*	.25
80	*Josh Whitesell*	.25
81	*Josh Anderson*	.25
82	*Kenny Lewis*	.50
83	*Mateo Miramontes*	.50
84	*Nicholas Markakis*	1.00
85	*Paul Bacot*	.50
86	*Peter Stonard*	.25
87	*Reggie Willits*	.25
88	*Shane Costa*	.50
89	*Billy Sadler*	.25
90	*Delmon Young*	3.00

Star Rookie Jersey

		NM/M
Common Player:		4.00
Inserted 1:18		
P72	Tony Richie	4.00
P73	Brandon Wood	12.00
P74	David Aardsma	5.00
P75	David Shinskie	4.00
P76	Dennis Dove	6.00
P77	Eric Sultemeier	4.00
P78	Jay Sborz	4.00
P79	Jimmy Barthmaier	4.00
P80	Josh Whitesell	4.00
P81	Josh Anderson	8.00
P82	Kenny Lewis	8.00
P83	Mateo Miramontes	8.00
P84	Nicholas Markakis	10.00
P85	Paul Bacot	4.00
P86	Peter Stonard	4.00
P87	Reggie Willits	8.00
P88	Shane Costa	4.00
P89	Billy Sadler	4.00
P91	Kyle Sleeth	8.00
P92	Ian Stewart	25.00
P93	Fraser Dizard	6.00
P94	Abe Alvarez	6.00
P95	Adam Jones	4.00
P96	Brian Anderson	8.00
P97	Chris Durbin	4.00
P98	Craig Whitaker	8.00
P99	Jake Fox	4.00
P100	Kurt Isenberg	4.00
P101	Luis Atilano	4.00
P102	Miguel Vega	4.00
P103	Mitch Maier	8.00
P104	Ryan Sweeney	10.00
P105	Scott Baker	4.00
P106	Sean Rodriguez	8.00
P108	Trey Webb	4.00
P109	Willy Jo Ronda	6.00
P110	John Danks	8.00
P111	Michael Aubrey	10.00
P112	Lastings Milledge	20.00
P113	Chris Lubanski	8.00

Star Rookie Signature

		NM/M
Common Autograph:		5.00
Inserted 1:9		
P1	Bryan Opdyke	10.00
P2	Gabriel Sosa	8.00
P3	Tila Reynolds	5.00
P4	Aaron Hill	15.00
P5	Aaron Marsden	10.00
P6	Abe Alvarez	15.00
P7	Adam Jones	20.00
P8	Adam Miller	30.00
P9	Andre Ethier	30.00
P10	Anthony Gwynn	20.00
P11	Brad Snyder	25.00
P12	Brad Sullivan	15.00
P13	Brian Anderson	35.00
P14	Brian Buscher	8.00
P15	Brian Snyder	10.00
P16	Carlos Quentin	50.00
P17	Chad Billingsley	25.00
P19	Chris Durbin	10.00
P20	Chris Ray	8.00
P21	Conor Jackson	65.00
P22	Kory Casto	8.00
P23	Craig Whitaker	10.00
P24	Daniel Moore	10.00
P25	Daric Barton	65.00
P26	Darin Downs	15.00
P27	David Murphy	15.00
P29	Edgardo Baez	12.00
P30	Jake Fox	8.00
P31	Jake Stevens	20.00
P32	Jamie D'Antona	20.00
P33	James Houser	15.00
P34	Jarrod Saltalamacchia	30.00
P35	Jason Hirsh	8.00
P36	Javi Herrera	10.00
P37	Jeff Allison	25.00
P38	John Hudgins	10.00
P39	Jo Jo Reyes	10.00
P40	Justin James	10.00
P41	Kurt Isenberg	10.00
P42	Kyle Boyer	12.00
P43	Lastings Milledge	70.00
P44	Luis Atilano	8.00
P45	Matt Murton	25.00
P46	Matt Moses	35.00
P48	Michael Bourn	15.00
P49	Miguel Vega	15.00
P50	Mitch Maier	25.00
P51	Omar Quintanilla	15.00

P52 Ryan Sweeney 40.00
P53 Scott Baker 15.00
P55 Steve Lerud 15.00
P56 Thomas Pauly 10.00
P57 Tom Gorzelanny 15.00
P58 Tim Moss 10.00
P60 Trey Webb 10.00
P61 Wes Littleton 15.00
P62 Beau Vaughan 10.00
P63 Willy Jo Ronda 10.00
P64 Chris Lubanski 20.00
P65 Ian Stewart 100.00
P66 John Danks 25.00
P67 Kyle Sleeth 20.00
P68 Michael Aubrey 40.00
P70 Ryan Harvey 30.00
P71 Tim Stauffer 30.00

2003 UPPER DECK SWEET SPOT

NM/M

Complete Set (232):
Common Player: .25
Common SP: 1.00
Inserted 1:4
Common SP (131-190): 3.00
Production 2,003
Common SP (191-232): 4.00
Production 1,430 unless noted
Pack (4): 9.00
Box (12): 90.00
1 Darin Erstad .50
2 Garret Anderson .50
3 Tim Salmon .50
4 Troy Glaus .75
5 Luis Gonzalez .50
6 Randy Johnson 1.00
7 Curt Schilling .50
8 Lyle Overbay .25
9 Andruw Jones/SP 2.00
10 Gary Sheffield/SP 1.50
11 Rafael Furcal/SP 1.00
12 Greg Maddux/SP 4.00
13 Chipper Jones/SP 4.00
14 Tony Batista .25
15 Rodrigo Lopez .25
16 Jay Gibbons .25
17 Jason Johnson .25
18 Byung-Hyun Kim/SP 1.00
19 Johnny Damon/SP 2.50
20 Derek Lowe/SP 1.00
21 Nomar Garciaparra/SP 5.00
22 Pedro Martinez/SP 3.00
23 Manny Ramirez/SP 2.50
24 Mark Prior 1.50
25 Kerry Wood 1.00
26 Corey Patterson .50
27 Sammy Sosa 2.00
28 Moises Alou .40
29 Magglio Ordonez .40
30 Frank Thomas .75
31 Paul Konerko .25
32 Roberto Alomar .50
33 Adam Dunn .75
34 Austin Kearns .50
35 *Ryan Wagner* .25
36 Ken Griffey Jr. 1.50
37 Sean Casey .25
38 Omar Vizquel .40
39 C.C. Sabathia .25
40 Jason Davis .25
41 Travis Hafner .25
42 Brandon Phillips .25
43 Larry Walker .40
44 Preston Wilson .25
45 Jay Payton .25
46 Todd Helton .75
47 Carlos Pena .25
48 Eric Munson .25
49 Ivan Rodriguez .75
50 Josh Beckett .50
51 Alex Gonzalez .25
52 Roy Oswalt .40
53 Craig Biggio .40
54 Jeff Bagwell .75
55 Lance Berkman .50
56 Mike Sweeney .25
57 Carlos Beltran .75
58 Brent Mayne .25
59 Mike MacDougal .25
60 Hideo Nomo .50
61 Dave Roberts .25
62 Adrian Beltre .50
63 Shawn Green .50
64 Kazuhisa Ishii .25
65 Rickey Henderson .50
66 Richie Sexson .50
67 Torii Hunter .50
68 Jacque Jones .25
69 Joe Mays .25
70 Corey Koskie .25
71 A.J. Pierzynski .25
72 Jose Vidro .25
73 Vladimir Guerrero .75
74 Tom Glavine .50
75 Mike Piazza 1.50
76 Jose Reyes .50
77 Jae Weong Seo .25
78 Jorge Posada/SP 2.00
79 Mike Mussina/SP 2.00
80 Robin Ventura/SP 1.00
81 Mariano Rivera/SP 1.50
82 Roger Clemens/SP 6.00
83 Jason Giambi/SP 1.50
84 Bernie Williams/SP 2.00
85 Alfonso Soriano/SP 3.00
86 Derek Jeter 2.50
87 Miguel Tejada .75
88 Eric Chavez .50
89 Tim Hudson .50
90 Barry Zito .50
91 Mark Mulder .50
92 Erubiel Durazo .25
93 Pat Burrell .50
94 Jim Thome .75
95 Bobby Abreu .50
96 Brian Giles .40
97 Reggie Sanders .25
98 Jose Hernandez .25
99 Ryan Klesko .25
100 Sean Burroughs .25
101 Edgardo Alfonzo/SP 1.00
102 Rich Aurilia/SP 1.00
103 Jose Cruz Jr./SP 1.00
104 Barry Bonds/SP 6.00
105 Andres Galarraga/SP 1.00
106 Mike Cameron .25
107 Kazuhiro Sasaki .25
108 Bret Boone .40
109 Ichiro Suzuki 2.00
110 John Olerud .40
111 J.D. Drew/SP 1.50
112 Jim Edmonds/SP 2.00
113 Scott Rolen/SP 3.00
114 Matt Morris/SP 1.00
115 Tino Martinez/SP 1.00
116 Albert Pujols/SP 6.00
117 Jared Sandberg .25
118 Carl Crawford .25
119 Rafael Palmeiro .50
120 Hank Blalock .50
121 Alex Rodriguez 2.50
122 Kevin Mench .25
123 Juan Gonzalez .75
124 Mark Teixeira .50
125 Shannon Stewart .25
126 Vernon Wells .50
127 Josh Phelps .25
128 Eric Hinske .25
129 Orlando Hudson .25
130 Carlos Delgado .75
131 *Jason Shiell* 3.00
132 *Kevin Tolar* 3.00
133 *Nate Bland* 3.00
134 *Brent Hoard* 3.00
135 *Jonathan Pridie* 3.00
136 *Mike Ryan* 4.00
137 *Francisco Rosario* 3.00
138 Runelvys Hernandez 3.00
139 *Guillermo Quiroz* 4.00
140 Chin-Hui Tsao 3.00
141 *Rett Johnson* 3.00
142 *Colin Porter* 3.00
143 Jose Castillo 3.00
144 *Chris Waters* 3.00
145 Jeremy Guthrie 3.00
146 Pedro Liriano 3.00
147 Joe Borowski 3.00
148 *Felix Sanchez* 3.00
149 *Todd Wellemeyer* 3.00
150 Gerald Laird 3.00
151 *Brandon Webb* 5.00
152 *Tommy Whiteman* 3.00
153 Carlos Rivera 3.00
154 *Rick Roberts* 3.00
155 *Terrmel Sledge* 3.00
156 *Jeff Duncan* 3.00
157 *Craig Brazell* 3.00
158 *Bernie Castro* 3.00
159 *Cory Stewart* 3.00
160 *Brandon Villafuerte* 3.00
161 Tommy Phelps 3.00
162 *Josh Hall* 3.00
163 *Ryan Cameron* 3.00
164 Garrett Atkins 3.00
165 *Brian Stokes* 3.00
166 *Rafael Betancourt* 3.00
167 Jaime Cerda 3.00
168 *Danny Carrasco* 3.00
169 *Ian Ferguson* 3.00
170 *Jorge Cordova* 3.00
171 Eric Munson 3.00
172 *Nook Logan* 3.00
173 Jeremy Bonderman 8.00
174 Kyle Snyder 3.00
175 Rich Harden 5.00
176 *Kevin Ohme* 3.00
177 *Roger Deago* 3.00
178 Marlon Byrd 3.00
179 Dontrelle Willis 5.00
180 Bobby Hill 3.00
181 Jesse Foppert 3.00
182 Andrew Good 3.00
183 Chase Utley 3.00
184 *Bo Hart* 3.00
185 Dan Haren 3.00
186 *Tim Olson* 3.00
187 Joe Thurston 3.00
188 Jason Anderson 3.00
189 *Jason Gilfillan* 3.00
190 *Rickie Weeks* 12.00
191 *Hideki Matsui/500* 25.00
192 *Jose Contreras* 8.00
193 *Willie Eyre* 4.00
194 *Matt Bruback* 4.00
195 *Heath Bell* 4.00
196 *Lew Ford* 8.00
197 Jeremy Griffiths 5.00
198 *Oscar Villarreal/500* 5.00
199 *Francisco Cruceta* 5.00
200 *Fernando Cabrera* 5.00
201 Jhonny Peralta 4.00
202 *Shane Bazzell* 4.00
203 *Bobby Madritsch/500* 15.00
204 *Phil Seibel* 4.00
205 *Josh Willingham* 6.00
206 *Robby Hammock/500* 5.00
207 *Alejandro Machado* 5.00
208 *David Sanders* 4.00
209 *Mike Neu/500* 5.00
210 *Andrew Brown* 4.00
211 *Nathan Robertson* 6.00
212 *Miguel Ojeda* 4.00
213 *Beau Kemp* 4.00
214 *Aaron Looper* 4.00
215 *Alfredo Gonzalez* 4.00
216 *Richard Fischer/500* 5.00
218 *Jeremy Wedel* 6.00
219 *Prentice Redman* 4.00
220 *Michel Hernandez* 6.00
221 Rocco Baldelli/500 5.00
222 *Luis Ayala* 5.00
223 *Arnie Munoz* 4.00
224 *Wilfredo Ledezma* 4.00
225 *Chris Capuano* 5.00
226 *Aquilino Lopez* 4.00
227 *Joe Valentine/500* 5.00
228 *Matt Kata/1,200* 5.00
229 *Diegomar Markwell/1,200* 4.00
230 *Clint Barmes/1,200* 15.00
231 *Mike Nicolas/500* 5.00
232 *Jon Leicester/1,200* 5.00

Autographs Black Ink

NM/M

Common Player:
Red & Blue Ink variations exist
Reds not priced due to scarcity
Mirror Parallel: No Pricing
Production 25
HB Hank Blalock 30.00
HB Hank Blalock/blue/40 40.00
PB Pat Burrell 30.00
PB Pat Burrell/blue/40 40.00
RC Roger Clemens/73 125.00
RC Roger Clemens/blue/40 150.00
JC Jose Contreras 40.00
JC Jose Contreras/blue/40 50.00
AD Adam Dunn 30.00
AD Adam Dunn/blue/40 50.00
NG Nomar Garciaparra 75.00
NG Nomar Garciaparra/blue/40 100.00
JG Jason Giambi 20.00
JG Jason Giambi/blue/40 30.00
TR Troy Glaus 35.00
TR Troy Glaus/blue/40 50.00
GL Tom Glavine 30.00
GL Tom Glavine/blue/40 50.00
KG Ken Griffey Jr. 75.00
KG Ken Griffey Jr./blue/40 100.00
KGs Ken Griffey Sr. 15.00
KGs Ken Griffey Sr./blue/40 20.00
VG Vladimir Guerrero 50.00
VG Vladimir Guerrero/blue/40 65.00
TG Tony Gwynn 40.00
HA Travis Hafner 15.00
HA Travis Hafner/blue/40 25.00
BH Bo Hart 10.00
BH Bo Hart/blue/40 15.00
TH Todd Helton/45 75.00
TH Todd Helton/blue/40 75.00
DH Drew Henson 25.00
DH Drew Henson/blue/40 40.00
KI Kazuhisa Ishii 35.00
KI Kazuhisa Ishii/blue/40 50.00
AK Austin Kearns 20.00
AK Austin Kearns/blue/40 25.00
MM Mickey Mantle/7
HM Hideki Matsui 300.00
HM Hideki Matsui/blue/40 375.00
RO Roy Oswalt 25.00
RO Roy Oswalt/Blue/40 35.00
LO Lyle Overbay 15.00
LO Lyle Overbay/blue/40 20.00
BP Brandon Phillips 10.00
BP Brandon Phillips/blue/40 15.00
MP Mark Prior 50.00
MP Mark Prior/blue/40 60.00
JR Jose Reyes 25.00
JR Jose Reyes/blue/40 40.00
CR Cal Ripken Jr. 165.00
CR Cal Ripken Jr./blue/40 220.00
NR Nolan Ryan 120.00
NR Nolan Ryan/blue/40 165.00
TS Tim Salmon 25.00
TS Tim Salmon/blue/40 35.00
CS Curt Schilling 40.00
CS Curt Schilling/blue/40 75.00
GS Gary Sheffield 30.00
GS Gary Sheffield/blue/40 40.00
SS Sammy Sosa/7
SS Sammy Sosa/blue/40 200.00
IS Ichiro Suzuki/blue/40 400.00
IS Ichiro Suzuki/red/35 400.00
MT Mark Teixeira 40.00
MT Mark Teixeira/blue/40 50.00
JT Jim Thome 40.00
JT Jim Thome/blue/40 60.00
BW Brandon Webb 35.00
BW Brandon Webb/blue/40 50.00
RW Rickie Weeks 70.00
JW Jerome Williams 25.00
JW Jerome Williams/blue/40 35.00
TW Ted Williams/9
DW Dontrelle Willis 45.00
DW Dontrelle Willis/blue/40 75.00

Barrel Autographs

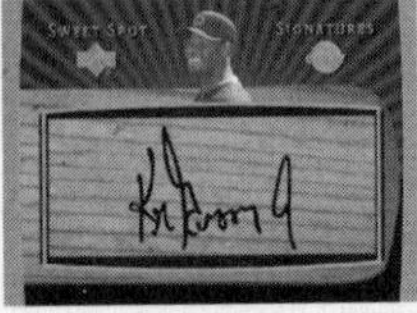

NM/M

Quantity produced listed
HB Hank Blalock/420 35.00
PB Pat Burrell/345 35.00
RC Roger Clemens/49 220.00
AD Adam Dunn/345 40.00
TR Troy Glaus/345 40.00
TG Tom Glavine/345 45.00
KG Ken Griffey Jr./295 125.00
HM Hideki Matsui/124 400.00
CR Cal Ripken Jr./149 180.00

NR Nolan Ryan/445 150.00
JT Jim Thome/345 65.00

Game-Used Barrel

NM/M

No pricing due to scarcity
KW-BB Kerry Wood/2 (2/04 auction) 1,000

Game-Used Patch

Production 25 or 10
No pricing due to scarcity

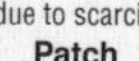

Patch

NM/M

Common Player: 4.00
Inserted 1:6
Logo Patch Parallel: 1-2X
Production 75 sets
JB1 Jeff Bagwell 6.00
LB1 Lance Berkman 5.00
BB1 Barry Bonds 15.00
PB1 Pat Burrell 5.00
RC1 Roger Clemens 12.00
CD1 Carlos Delgado 4.00
AD1 Adam Dunn 5.00
JE1 Jim Edmonds 4.00
DE1 Darin Erstad 4.00
NG1 Nomar Garciaparra 10.00
JG1 Jason Giambi 4.00
TG1 Troy Glaus 5.00
TO1 Tom Glavine 5.00
LG1 Luis Gonzalez 4.00
SG1 Shawn Green 5.00
KG1 Ken Griffey Jr. 8.00
VG1 Vladimir Guerrero 6.00
TH1 Torii Hunter 5.00
KI1 Kazuhisa Ishii 4.00
DJ1 Derek Jeter 15.00
RJ1 Randy Johnson 6.00
AJ1 Andruw Jones 5.00
CJ1 Chipper Jones 10.00
JK1 Jeff Kent 4.00
GM1 Greg Maddux 10.00
PM1 Pedro J. Martinez 6.00
HN1 Hideo Nomo 5.00
MO1 Magglio Ordonez 4.00
CP1 Corey Patterson 6.00
MP1 Mike Piazza 10.00
MA1 Mark Prior 10.00
AP1 Albert Pujols 15.00
AR1 Alex Rodriguez 10.00
CS1 Curt Schilling 6.00
GS1 Gary Sheffield 6.00
AS1 Alfonso Soriano 8.00
SS1 Sammy Sosa 10.00
IS1 Ichiro Suzuki 10.00
MT1 Miguel Tejada 6.00
JT1 Jim Thome 6.00
BW1 Bernie Williams 5.00
BZ1 Barry Zito 4.00

Swatches

NM/M

Common Player: 4.00
Inserted 1:24
Tier 2: 1-2X
Production 75
RA Roberto Alomar 4.00

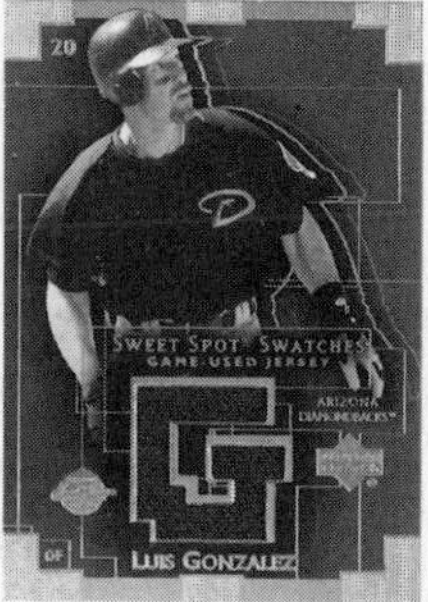

PB Pat Burrell 6.00
RC Roger Clemens 10.00
NM Nomar Garciaparra 15.00
NG1 Nomar Garciaparra 4.00
JG Jason Giambi 8.00
TG Troy Glaus 4.00
TG1 Troy Glaus 5.00
TO Tom Glavine 4.00
LG Luis Gonzalez 4.00
KG Ken Griffey Jr. 10.00
VG Vladimir Guerrero 6.00
TH Torii Hunter 5.00
RJ Randy Johnson 6.00
AJ Andruw Jones 5.00
CJ Chipper Jones 8.00
AK Austin Kearns 6.00
GM Greg Maddux 10.00
MM Mickey Mantle 120.00
HM Hideki Matsui 45.00
HM1 Hideki Matsui 4.00
RO Roy Oswalt 4.00
RO1 Roy Oswalt 4.00
MP Mike Piazza 10.00
MA Mark Prior 4.00
AP Albert Pujols 15.00
AR Alex Rodriguez 10.00
CS Curt Schilling 5.00
GS Gary Sheffield 4.00
AS Alfonso Soriano 10.00
AS1 Alfonso Soriano 4.00
SS Sammy Sosa 12.00
IS Ichiro Suzuki 20.00
MT Miguel Tejada 4.00
FT Frank Thomas 6.00
JT Jim Thome 8.00
BW Bernie Williams 4.00
TW Ted Williams 60.00
BZ Barry Zito 4.00

2003 UPPER DECK SWEET SPOT CLASSIC

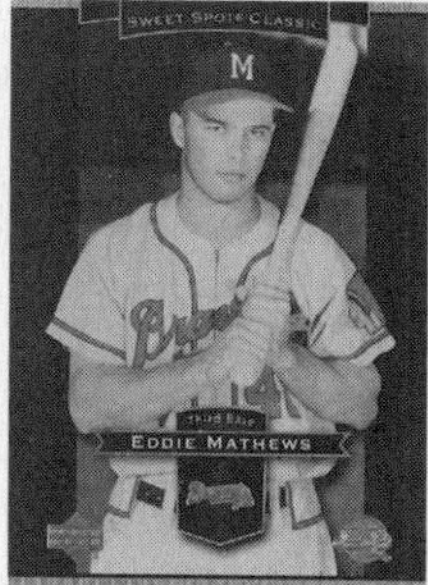

NM/M

Complete Set (150):
Common Player: .40
Common Ted Williams (91-120): 5.00
Production 1,941
Common Yankee Heritage (121-150): 2.00
Production 1,500
Pack (4): 12.00
Box (12): 120.00
1 Al Hrabosky .40
2 Al Lopez .40
3 Andre Dawson .75
4 Bill Buckner .40
5 Billy Williams .50
6 Bob Feller .75
7 Bob Lemon .40
8 Bobby Doerr .40
9 Cecil Cooper .40
10 Cal Ripken Jr. 2.50
11 Carlton Fisk .60
12 Jim "Catfish" Hunter .40
13 Chris Chambliss .40
14 Dale Murphy .75
15 Gaylord Perry .40
16 Dave Kingman .40
17 Dave Parker .40
18 Dave Stewart .40
19 David Cone .40
20 Dennis Eckersley .60
21 Don Baylor .40
22 Don Sutton .40
23 Duke Snider 1.00
24 Dwight Evans .40
25 Dwight Gooden .40
26 Earl Weaver .40
27 Early Wynn .40
28 Eddie Mathews 1.50
29 Enos Slaughter .40
30 Ernie Banks 1.50
31 Fred Lynn .40
32 Fred Stanley .40
33 Gary Carter .75
34 George Foster .40
35 Hal Newhouser .40
36 George Kell .40
37 Harmon Killebrew 1.50
38 Hoyt Wilhelm .40
39 Jack Morris .40
40 Jim Bunning .40
41 Jim Gilliam .40
42 Jim Leyritz .40
43 Jimmy Key .40
44 Joe Carter .40
45 Joe Morgan .40
46 John Montefusco .40
47 Johnny Bench 2.00
48 Johnny Podres .40
49 Jose Canseco .75
50 Juan Marichal .40
51 Keith Hernandez .40
52 Ken Griffey Sr. .40
53 Kirby Puckett 1.50
54 Kirk Gibson .40
55 Larry Doby .40
56 Lee May .40
57 Lee Mazzilli .40
58 Lou Boudreau .40
59 Mark McGwire 3.00
60 Maury Wills .40
61 Mike Pagliarulo .40
62 Monte Irvin .75
63 Nolan Ryan 3.00
64 Orlando Cepeda .40
65 Ozzie Smith 1.50
66 Paul O'Neill .40
67 Pee Wee Reese .40
68 Phil Niekro .40
69 Ralph Kiner .40
70 Red Schoendienst .40
71 Richie Ashburn .40
72 Rick Ferrell .40
73 Robin Roberts .40
74 Robin Yount 1.50
75 *Hideki Matsui/1,999* 20.00
75 Hideki Matsui/Red/500 25.00
75 Hideki Matsui/Blue/250 30.00
75 Hideki Matsui/Silver/25 200.00
76 Rollie Fingers .40
77 Ron Cey .40
78 Tom Seaver 1.00
79 Sparky Anderson .40
80 Stan Musial 2.00
81 Steve Garvey .40
82 Ted Williams 3.00
83 Tommy Lasorda .40
84 Tony Gwynn 1.00
85 Tony Perez .40
86 Vida Blue .40
87 Warren Spahn .75
88 Bob Gibson 1.00
89 Willie McCovey .40
90 Willie Stargell .75
91 Ted Williams 5.00
92 Ted Williams 5.00
93 Ted Williams 5.00
94 Ted Williams 5.00
95 Ted Williams 5.00
96 Ted Williams 5.00
97 Ted Williams 5.00
98 Ted Williams 5.00
99 Ted Williams 5.00
100 Ted Williams 5.00
101 Ted Williams 5.00
102 Ted Williams 5.00
103 Ted Williams 5.00
104 Ted Williams 5.00
105 Ted Williams 5.00
106 Ted Williams 5.00
107 Ted Williams 5.00
108 Ted Williams 5.00
109 Ted Williams 5.00
110 Ted Williams 5.00
111 Ted Williams 5.00
112 Ted Williams 5.00
113 Ted Williams 5.00
114 Ted Williams 5.00
115 Ted Williams 5.00
116 Ted Williams 5.00
117 Ted Williams 5.00
118 Ted Williams 5.00
119 Ted Williams 5.00
120 Ted Williams 5.00
121 Babe Ruth 8.00
122 Bucky Dent 2.00
123 Casey Stengel 3.00
124 Dave Righetti 2.00
125 Dave Winfield 3.00
126 Dick Tidrow 2.00
127 Dock Ellis 2.00
128 Don Mattingly 8.00
129 Hank Bauer 2.00
130 Jim Bouton 2.00
131 Jim Kaat 2.00
132 Joe DiMaggio 6.00
133 Joe Torre 3.00
134 Lou Piniella 2.00
135 Mel Stottlemyre 2.00
136 Mickey Mantle 15.00
137 Mickey Rivers 2.00
138 Phil Rizzuto 4.00
139 Ralph Branca 2.00
140 Ralph Houk 2.00
141 Roger Maris 6.00
142 Ron Guidry 2.00
143 Ruben Amaro Jr. 2.00
144 Sparky Lyle 2.00
145 Thurman Munson 5.00
146 Tommy Henrich 2.00
147 Tommy John 2.00
148 Tony Kubek 2.00
149 Whitey Ford 4.00
150 Yogi Berra 4.00

Greats Autograph

NM/M

Common Autograph:
Blue, Black and Red ink variations exist
Listings without notations are blue ink
EB Ernie Banks/black/73 80.00
DB Don Baylor 25.00
DB Don Baylor/black/50 35.00
JB Johnny Bench/black/73 100.00
BB Bill Buckner 20.00
BB Bill Buckner/black/85 25.00
BB Bill Buckner/red/25
GC Gary Carter/black/173 40.00
GC Gary Carter/red/25
JC Joe Carter/black/173 35.00
JC Joe Carter/red/25
OC Orlando Cepeda 20.00
OC Orlando Cepeda/black/34 35.00
OC Orlando Cepeda/red/25
AD Andre Dawson 20.00
AD Andre Dawson/black/75 30.00
AD Andre Dawson/red/25
DEc Dennis Eckersley 25.00
DE Dwight Evans 20.00
DE Dwight Evans/black/100 30.00
DE Dwight Evans/red/25
RF Rollie Fingers/black/73 30.00
RF Rollie Fingers/red/25 90.00
CF Carlton Fisk 50.00
GF George Foster/black/173 35.00
SG Steve Garvey/black/174 30.00

GI Kirk Gibson/black/173 30.00
GI Kirk Gibson/red/25
KG Ken Griffey Sr. 20.00
KG Ken Griffey Sr/black/100 25.00
KG Ken Griffey Sr/red/25
TG Tony Gwynn 45.00
TG Tony Gwynn/black/101 60.00
TG Tony Gwynn/red/25
KH Keith Hernandez/black/173 40.00
KH Keith Hernandez/red/25 110.00
AH Al Hrabosky 25.00
AH Al Hrabosky/black/100 35.00
AH Al Hrabosky/red/25
HK Harmon Killebrew/black/73 80.00
HK Harmon Killebrew/red/25
FL Fred Lynn
MM Mark McGwire/black/73 425.00
MM Mark McGwire/red/25
JoM Joe Morgan/black/169 40.00
JoM Joe Morgan/red/25
JMo Jack Morris/black/123 40.00
JMo Jack Morris/red/25
DM Dale Murphy 30.00
PN Phil Niekro/black/173 30.00
PN Phil Niekro/red/25 75.00
DP Dave Parker/black/113 30.00
DP Dave Parker/red/25
TP Tony Perez/black/51 65.00
TP Tony Perez/red/25
JP Johnny Podres/black/173 30.00
JP Johnny Podres/red/25 80.00
KP Kirby Puckett 45.00
KP Kirby Puckett/b lack/174 60.00
KP Kirby Puckett/red/25
CR Cal Ripken Jr. 150.00
CR Cal Ripken Jr/black/38 250.00
CR Cal Ripken Jr/red/25
RR Robin Roberts/black/173 40.00
TS Tom Seaver/black/74 80.00
TS Tom Seaver/red/25 135.00
SN Duke Snider 40.00
SN Duke Snider/black/100 50.00
SN Duke Snider/red/25
DSt Dave Stewart 15.00
DSu Don Sutton/black/123 30.00
AT Alan Trammell/black/173 35.00
AT Alan Trammell/red/25
BW Billy Williams/black/173 35.00
BW Billy Williams/red/25
TW Ted Williams/9 3,650
MW Maury Wills/black/173 30.00
RY Robin Yount/black/73 100.00
RY Robin Yount/red/25 200.00

Game Jersey

NM/M

Common Player: 5.00
Inserted 1:16
EB Ernie Banks 15.00
JB Johnny Bench 15.00
JC Jose Canseco 6.00
GC Gary Carter 6.00
RC Ron Cey 5.00
CC Cecil Cooper 6.00
AD Andre Dawson 6.00
RF Rollie Fingers 5.00
CF Carlton Fisk 8.00
GF George Foster 5.00
SG Steve Garvey 5.00
JG Jim Gilliam 6.00
TG Tony Gwynn 8.00
HK Harmon Killebrew 12.00
FL Fred Lynn 5.00
LM Lee May 5.00
MM Mark McGwire 30.00
JM Joe Morgan 6.00
DM Dale Murphy 10.00
SM Stan Musial 25.00
DP Dave Parker 5.00
JP Johnny Podres 5.00
KP Kirby Puckett 12.00
CR Cal Ripken Jr. 20.00
NR Nolan Ryan 30.00
OS Ozzie Smith 10.00
DS Duke Snider 12.00
WS Willie Stargell/SP 15.00
TW Ted Williams/SP 100.00
RY Robin Yount 10.00

Patch Logo

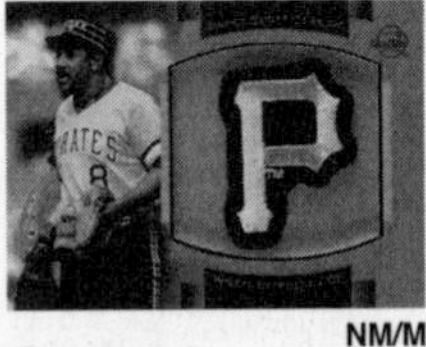

NM/M

Common Player: 5.00
Note: some are actual game-used Patches
EB1 Ernie Banks 12.00
JB1 Johnny Bench 12.00
JB2 Johnny Bench/150 50.00
JB3 Johnny Bench/150 35.00
YB1 Yogi Berra 12.00
YB2 Yogi Berra/350 25.00
YB3 Yogi Berra/150 35.00
JD1 Joe DiMaggio 20.00
JD2 Joe DiMaggio/50 85.00
JD3 Joe DiMaggio/350 30.00
JD4 Joe DiMaggio/150 40.00
CF1 Carlton Fisk 8.00
CF2 Carlton Fisk/150 10.00
GF1 George Foster/350 10.00
GF2 George Foster 5.00
SG1 Steve Garvey 5.00
SG2 Steve Garvey/350 10.00
SG3 Steve Garvey/150 30.00
SG4 Steve Garvey/50 25.00
SG5 Steve Garvey/50 25.00
KG1 Kirk Gibson 5.00
KG2 Kirk Gibson/350 12.00
TG1 Tony Gwynn 8.00
TG2 Tony Gwynn/150 50.00
TG3 Tony Gwynn/350 25.00
CH1 Catfish Hunter/350 10.00
CH2 Catfish Hunter 5.00
CH3 Catfish Hunter/39
CH4 Catfish Hunter/50 30.00
FL1 Fred Lynn 5.00
FL2 Fred Lynn/350 10.00
FL3 Fred Lynn/150 15.00
FL4 Fred Lynn/50 20.00
MM1 Mickey Mantle 35.00
MM2 Mickey Mantle/150 85.00
MM3 Mickey Mantle/150 85.00
MM4 Mickey Mantle/150 75.00
RM1 Roger Maris 15.00
RM2 Roger Maris/350 25.00
RM3 Roger Maris/150 40.00
RM4 Roger Maris/50 60.00
HM1 Hideki Matsui 25.00
MC1 Mark McGwire 20.00
MC2 Mark McGwire/350 50.00
MC3 Mark McGwire/9
JM1 Joe Morgan 6.00
JM2 Joe Morgan/350 8.00
JM3 Joe Morgan/150 15.00
JM4 Joe Morgan/150 30.00
JM5 Joe Morgan/100 15.00
KP1 Kirby Puckett 10.00
KP2 Kirby Puckett/40 100.00
CR1 Cal Ripken Jr. 25.00
CR2 Cal Ripken Jr/75 100.00
CR3 Cal Ripken Jr./150 50.00
BR1 Babe Ruth/350 40.00
BR2 Babe Ruth 30.00
BR3 Babe Ruth/150 50.00
NR1 Nolan Ryan 25.00
NR2 Nolan Ryan/350 40.00
NR3 Nolan Ryan/150 50.00
NR4 Nolan Ryan/105 100.00
OS1 Ozzie Smith 10.00
OS2 Ozzie Smith/350 20.00
OS3 Ozzie Smith/150 60.00
OS4 Ozzie Smith/100 40.00
OS5 Ozzie Smith/100 35.00
DS1 Duke Snider 8.00
DS2 Duke Snider/150 25.00
DS3 Duke Snider/350 15.00
DS4 Duke Snider/25
DS5 Duke Snider/150 20.00
DS6 Duke Snider/150 20.00
WS1 Willie Stargell 5.00
WS2 Willie Stargell/137 50.00
WS3 Willie Stargell/150 25.00
WS4 Willie Stargell/50 40.00
BW1 Billy Williams 6.00
TW1 Ted Williams 20.00
TW2 Ted Williams/350 40.00
RY1 Robin Yount 8.00
RY2 Robin Yount/150 40.00
RY3 Robin Yount/350 20.00

Pinstripes

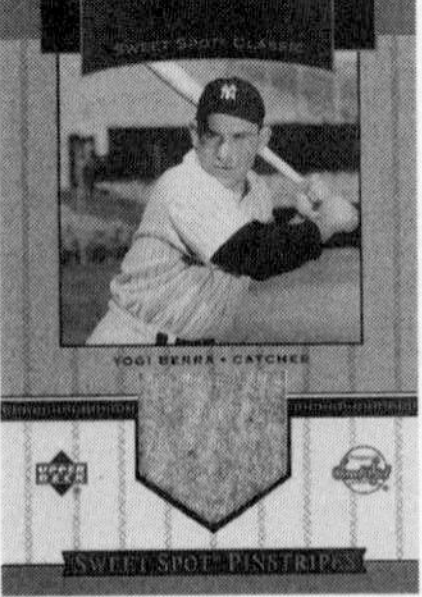

NM/M

Common Player: 5.00
Inserted 1:40
YB Yogi Berra 15.00
JB Jim Bouton 5.00
DE Bucky Dent 8.00
JD Joe DiMaggio 100.00
DG Dwight Gooden 5.00
MM Mickey Mantle 140.00
DM Don Mattingly 25.00
TM Thurman Munson 30.00
DR Dave Righetti 5.00
PR Phil Rizzuto 15.00
BR Babe Ruth 250.00
CS Casey Stengel 12.00

Yankee Greats Auto.

NM/M

Common Autograph:
RA Ruben Amaro Sr. 25.00
RA Ruben Amaro Sr/black/100 30.00
RA Ruben Amaro Sr/red/25 60.00
HB Hank Bauer 30.00
HB Hank Bauer/black/75 40.00
YB Yogi Berra/black/73 100.00
YB Yogi Berra/red/25
JB Jim Bouton 25.00
JB Jim Bouton/black/100 30.00
RB Ralph Branca 25.00
RB Ralph Branca/black/100 30.00
RB Ralph Branca/red/25
JC Jose Canseco/black/73 90.00
JC Jose Canseco/red/25 150.00
CC Chris Chambliss 30.00
CC Chris Chambliss/black/101 35.00
CC Chris Chambliss/red/25 75.00
DC David Cone/black/74 75.00
DC David Cone/red/25 110.00
BD Bucky Dent 20.00
JD Joe DiMaggio/5 2,325
DE Dock Ellis/black/174 25.00
DE Dock Ellis/red/25 65.00
DG Dwight Gooden/black/74 70.00
GU Ron Guidry 35.00
GU Ron Guidry/black/100 45.00
GU Ron Guidry/red/25
TH Tommy Henrich 35.00
TH Tommy Henrich/black/100 40.00
TH Tommy Henrich/red/25 125.00
RH Ralph Houk 25.00
RH Ralph Houk/black/100 30.00
RH Ralph Houk/red/25
TJ Tommy John 30.00
TJ Tommy John/black/100 35.00
TJ Tommy John/red/25
JKa Jim Kaat 20.00
JKa Jim Kaat/black/25 25.00
JKa Jim Kaat/red/25
JKe Jimmy Key 40.00
JKe Jimmy Key/black/100 50.00
JKe Jimmy Key/red/25
DK Dave Kingman 25.00
DK Dave Kingman/black/100 30.00
DK Dave Kingman/red/25
TK Tony Kubek/black/123 15.00
JL Jim Leyritz 25.00
JL Jim Leyritz/black/100 35.00
JL Jim Leyritz/red/25 65.00
SL Sparky Lyle 30.00
SL Sparky Lyle/black/100 40.00
SL Sparky Lyle/red/25
MM Mickey Mantle/blue/7 2,850
HM Hideki Matsui/redemp.
DM Don Mattingly/black/74 100.00
DM Don Mattingly/red/25 340.00
LM Lee Mazzilli 30.00
JM John Montefusco 20.00
JM John Montefusco/black/100 25.00
JM John Montefusco/red/25 50.00
PO Paul O'Neill 50.00
PO Paul O'Neill/black/100 65.00
PO Paul O'Neill/red/25 100.00
MP Mike Pagliarulo 20.00
MP Mike Pagliarulo/black/99 25.00
MP Mike Pagliarulo/red/25 60.00
LP Lou Piniella 40.00
LP Lou Piniella/black/100 45.00
LP Lou Piniella/red/25
DR Dave Righetti/black/173 40.00
DR Dave Righetti/red/25 85.00
MR Mickey Rivers/black/73 40.00
MR Mickey Rivers/red/25
PR Phil Rizzuto/black/173 55.00
PR Phil Rizzuto/red/25
FS Fred Stanley 25.00
FS Fred Stanley/black/101 25.00
FS Fred Stanley/red/25
MS Mel Stottlemyre/black/73 85.00
MS Mel Stottlemyre/red/25
DT Dick Tidrow 20.00
DT Dick Tidrow/black/101 25.00
DT Dick Tidrow/red/25 70.00
JT Joe Torre/black/73 60.00
JT Joe Torre/red/25 140.00
DW Dave Winfield/black/25 165.00

2003 UPPER DECK ULTIMATE COLLECTION

NM/M

Complete Set (181):
Common Player (1-84): 2.00
Production 850
Common (85-117): 3.00
Production 625
Common (118-140): 3.00
Production 399
Common (141-158): 4.00
Production 250
Common (159-168): 6.00

Production 100
Common (169-174): 25.00
Common (175-180): 10.00
169-180 production 250
Pack (4): 90.00
Box (4): 300.00
1 Ichiro Suzuki 8.00
2 Ken Griffey Jr. 6.00
3 Sammy Sosa 6.00
4 Jason Giambi 2.00
5 Mike Piazza 5.00
6 Derek Jeter 10.00
7 Randy Johnson 4.00
8 Barry Bonds 10.00
9 Carlos Delgado 3.00
10 Mark Prior 4.00
11 Vladimir Guerrero 4.00
12 Alfonso Soriano 4.00
13 Jim Thome 4.00
14 Pedro J. Martinez 4.00
15 Nomar Garciaparra 5.00
16 Chipper Jones 4.00
17 Rocco Baldelli 2.00
18 Dontrelle Willis 2.00
19 Garret Anderson 2.00
20 Jeff Bagwell 2.00
21 Jim Edmonds 2.50
22 Rickey Henderson 3.00
23 Torii Hunter 2.50
24 Tom Glavine 2.50
25 Hideo Nomo 2.50
26 Luis Gonzalez 2.50
27 Alex Rodriguez 8.00
28 Albert Pujols 10.00
29 Manny Ramirez 4.00
30 Rafael Palmeiro 3.00
31 Bernie Williams 3.00
32 Curt Schilling 3.00
33 Roger Clemens 8.00
34 Andruw Jones 2.00
35 J.D. Drew 2.00
36 Kerry Wood 3.00
37 Scott Rolen 3.00
38 Darin Erstad 2.00
39 Joe DiMaggio 8.00
40 Magglio Ordonez 2.00
41 Todd Helton 3.00
42 Barry Zito 2.00
43 Mickey Mantle 10.00
44 Miguel Tejada 3.00
45 Troy Glaus 2.00
46 Kazuhisa Ishii 2.00
47 Adam Dunn 3.00
48 Ted Williams 8.00
49 Mike Mussina 3.00
50 Ivan Rodriguez 3.00
51 Jacque Jones 2.00
52 Stan Musial 6.00
53 Mariano Rivera 2.50
54 Larry Walker 2.50
55 Aaron Boone 2.00
56 Hank Blalock 2.50
57 Rich Harden 2.00
58 Lance Berkman 2.00
59 Eric Chavez 2.00
60 Carlos Beltran 3.00
61 Roy Oswalt 2.00
62 Moises Alou 2.00
63 Nolan Ryan 10.00
64 Jeff Kent 2.00
65 Roberto Alomar 2.00
66 Runelvys Hernandez 2.00
67 Roy Halladay 3.00
68 Tim Hudson 2.50
69 Tom Seaver 4.00
70 Edgardo Alfonzo 2.00
71 Andy Pettitte 2.00
72 Preston Wilson 2.00
73 Frank Thomas 3.00
74 Jerome Williams 2.00
75 Shawn Green 2.50
76 David Wells 2.00
77 John Smoltz 2.00
78 Jorge Posada 3.00
79 Marlon Byrd 2.00
80 Austin Kearns 2.00
81 Bret Boone 2.00
82 Rafael Furcal 2.50
83 Jay Gibbons 2.00
84 Shane Reynolds 2.00
85 *Nate Bland* 3.00
86 *Willie Eyre* 3.00
87 Jeremy Guthrie 3.00
88 *Jeremy Wedel* 3.00
89 Jhonny Peralta 6.00
90 *Luis Ayala* 3.00
91 *Michael Hessman* 3.00
92 *Micheal Nakamura* 3.00
93 *Nook Logan* 3.00
94 *Rett Johnson* 5.00
95 *Josh Hall* 4.00
96 *Julio Manon* 3.00
97 *Heath Bell* 3.00
98 *Ian Ferguson* 3.00
99 *Jason Gilfillan* 3.00
100 Jason Roach 3.00
101 *Jason Shiell* 3.00
102 *Terrmel Sledge* 5.00
103 *Phil Seibel* 3.00
104 *Jeff Duncan* 6.00
105 *Mike Neu* 3.00
106 *Colin Porter* 3.00
107 *Dave Matranga* 3.00
108 *Aaron Looper* 3.00
109 Jeremy Bonderman 15.00
110 *Miguel Ojeda* 3.00
111 *Chad Cordero* 3.00
112 *Shane Bazell* 4.00
113 *Tim Olson* 5.00
114 *Michel Hernandez* 3.00
115 *Chien-Ming Wang* 20.00
116 *Josh Stewart* 3.00
117 *Clint Barmes* 10.00
118 *Craig Brazell* 5.00
119 *Josh Willingham* 8.00
120 *Brent Hoard* 3.00
121 *Francisco Rosario* 3.00
122 *Rick Roberts* 3.00
123 *Geoff Geary* 3.00
124 *Edgar Gonzalez* 3.00
125 *Kevin Correia* 3.00
126 *Ryan Cameron* 3.00
127 *Beau Kemp* 3.00
128 Tommy Phelps 3.00
129 *Mark Malaska* 3.00
130 *Kevin Ohme* 3.00
131 *Humberto Quintero* 3.00
132 *Aquilino Lopez* 3.00
133 *Andrew Brown* 3.00
134 *Wilfredo Ledezma* 3.00
135 Luis De Los Santos 3.00
136 Garrett Atkins 3.00
137 *Fernando Cabrera* 3.00
138 *D.J. Carrasco* 3.00
139 *Alfredo Gonzalez* 3.00
140 *Alex Prieto* 3.00
141 *Matt Kata* 5.00
142 *Chris Capuano* 4.00
143 *Bobby Madritsch* 20.00
144 *Greg Jones* 4.00
145 *Pete Zoccolillo* 4.00
146 *Chad Gaudin* 4.00
147 *Rosman Garcia* 4.00
148 Gerald Laird 4.00
149 *Danny Garcia* 4.00
150 *Stephen Randolph* 4.00
151 *Pete LaForest* 8.00
152 *Brian Sweeney* 4.00
153 *Aaron Miles* 4.00
154 *Jorge DePaula* 4.00
155 *Graham Koonce* 10.00
156 *Tom Gregorio* 4.00
157 Javier Lopez 4.00
158 *Oscar Villarreal* 4.00
159 *Prentice Redman* 6.00
160 *Francisco Cruceta* 6.00
161 *Guillermo Quiroz* 20.00
162 Jeremy Griffiths 10.00
163 *Lew Ford* 20.00
164 *Rob Hammock* 10.00
165 *Todd Wellemeyer* 10.00
166 *Ryan Wagner* 10.00
167 *Edwin Jackson* 20.00
168 Dan Haren 15.00
169 *Hideki Matsui/auto* 275.00
170 Jose Contreras/auto 30.00
171 *Delmon Young/auto* 275.00
172 *Rickie Weeks/auto* 150.00
173 *Brandon Webb/auto* 30.00
174 *Bo Hart/auto* 15.00
175 Rocco Baldelli/auto 25.00
176 Jose Reyes/auto 25.00
177 Dontrelle Willis/auto 50.00
178 Bobby Hill/auto 10.00
179 Jae Weong Seo/auto 25.00
180 Jesse Foppert/auto 25.00
CL Checklist 2.00

Gold

Stars (1-184): 1.5-3X
(85-117): 1-2X
Production 50
(118-140): 1-2X
Production 35
(141-158): 1-2X
Production 25
(159-168): No Pricing
Production 10
(169-180): No Pricing
Production 25

Buybacks

NM/M

Production 1-75
Hank Blalock/35 40.00
Hank Blalock 03 40M/25 40.00
Hank Blalock 03 GF/25 40.00
Hank Blalock 03 Patch/25 40.00
Hank Blalock 03 SPA/20 40.00
Hank Blalock 03 SPA/25 40.00
Hank Blalock 03 VIN/25 40.00
Luis Gonzalez 03 40M HR/25 40.00
Luis Gonzalez 03 SPA/25 40.00
Luis Gonzalez 03 VIN/25 40.00
Ken Griffey Jr. 02-3 SUP/75 80.00
Ken Griffey Jr. 02-3 SUP Spok/50 80.00
Ken Griffey Jr. 03 40M/50 80.00
Ken Griffey Jr. 03 40M/50 80.00
Ken Griffey Jr. 03 40M/50 80.00
Ken Griffey Jr. 03 40M/50 80.00
Ken Griffey Jr. 03 40M T40/50 80.00
Ken Griffey Jr. 03 GF/50 80.00
Ken Griffey Jr. 03 HON/50 80.00
Ken Griffey Jr. 03 HON SP/30 100.00
Ken Griffey Jr. 03 Patch/75 80.00
Ken Griffey Jr. 03 PB/75 80.00
Ken Griffey Jr. 03 SPA/50 80.00
Ken Griffey Jr. 03 SPA/75 80.00
Ken Griffey Jr. 03 SPx/75 80.00
Ken Griffey Jr. 03 SWS/75 80.00
Ken Griffey Jr. 03 UDA/75 80.00
Ken Griffey Jr. 03 VIN/50 80.00
Torii Hunter 03 Patch/25 40.00
Torii Hunter 03 PB/50 30.00
Torii Hunter 03 VIN/25 40.00
Austin Kearns 03 40M/33 30.00
Hideki Matsui 03 40M/20 250.00
Hideki Matsui 03 40M Flag/20 250.00
Hideki Matsui 03 GF/18 250.00
Hideki Matsui 03 PB/17 250.00
Hideki Matsui 03 UD/25 250.00
Hideki Matsui 03 VIN/25 250.00
Stan Musial 02 SPLC/30 75.00
Stan Musial 02 WSH/25 75.00
Stan Musial 03 PB/50 60.00
Stan Musial 03 SWSC/37 75.00
Stan Musial 03 VIN/50 60.00
Sammy Sosa 02-3 SUP/25 120.00
Sammy Sosa 03 PB/25 120.00
Sammy Sosa 03 SPA/25 120.00
Sammy Sosa 03 VIN/25 120.00
Mark Teixeira 03 40M/50 40.00
Mark Teixeira 03 Patch/50 40.00
Mark Teixeira 03 SPA RA/25 50.00
Mark Teixeira 03 SWS/23 50.00
Mark Teixeira 03 UD/25 50.00
Mark Teixeira 03 VIN/25 50.00

Double Barrel

NM/M

No pricing due to scarcity
DB-AE Darin Erstad, Garret Anderson/3 (3/04 auction) 645.00
DB-GS Tom Seaver, Tom Glavine/2 (3/04 auction) 700.00

Dual Jersey

NM/M

Common Duo: 10.00
Production 50 sets
Gold: 1-1.25X
Production 25 sets
AH Alfonso Soriano, Hideki Matsui 40.00
AI Albert Pujols, Ichiro Suzuki 50.00
BK Jeff Kent, Jeff Bagwell 15.00
CA Chipper Jones, Andruw Jones 15.00
CJ Carlos Delgado, Jason Giambi 15.00
DE Jim Edmonds, J.D. Drew 10.00
DG Carlos Delgado, Vladimir Guerrero 15.00
DM Mickey Mantle, Joe DiMaggio 250.00
DP Carlos Delgado, Rafael Palmeiro 15.00
DW Joe DiMaggio, Ted Williams 150.00
GB Shawn Green, Kevin Brown 10.00
GD Adam Dunn, Ken Griffey Jr. 25.00
GE Darin Erstad, Troy Glaus 10.00
GP Rafael Palmeiro, Ken Griffey Jr. 25.00
GR Alex Rodriguez, Nomar Garciaparra 25.00
GS Vladimir Guerrero, Sammy Sosa 25.00
HJ Torii Hunter, Jacque Jones 10.00
HZ Roy Halladay, Barry Zito 10.00
IG Ken Griffey Jr., Ichiro Suzuki 50.00
IN Ichiro Suzuki, Hideo Nomo 50.00
IS Sammy Sosa, Ichiro Suzuki 45.00
JF Andruw Jones, Rafael Furcal 15.00
JM Mike Piazza, Jorge Posada 20.00
MC Greg Maddux, Roger Clemens 30.00
MW Ted Williams, Mickey Mantle 250.00
NI Hideo Nomo, Kazuhisa Ishii 30.00
NM Hideki Matsui, Hideo Nomo 60.00
PC Roger Clemens, Pedro J. Martinez 25.00
PM Mike Mussina, Andy Pettitte 15.00
PS Sammy Sosa, Mark Prior 40.00

RM Pedro J. Martinez, Manny Ramirez 15.00
RP Rafael Palmeiro, Alex Rodriguez 20.00
SA Albert Pujols, Scott Rolen 40.00
SB Alfonso Soriano, Bernie Williams 15.00
SJ Randy Johnson, Curt Schilling 20.00
SM Greg Maddux, John Smoltz 25.00
TB Mark Teixeira, Hank Blalock 15.00
TH Todd Helton, Jim Thome 15.00
TR Alex Rodriguez, Miguel Tejada 20.00
WL Mike Lowell, Dontrelle Willis 15.00
YW Delmon Young, Rickie Weeks 35.00

Dual Patch

NM/M
Common Duo: 20.00
Production 99 unless noted
Gold: .75-1.25X
Production 35

AI Ichiro Suzuki, Albert Pujols 100.00
AM Andy Pettitte, Mike Mussina 25.00
BK Jeff Bagwell, Jeff Kent 25.00
CA Andruw Jones, Chipper Jones 30.00
CV Carlos Delgado, Vladimir Guerrero 35.00
DE Jim Edmonds, J.D. Drew 25.00
DG Carlos Delgado, Jason Giambi 25.00
DP Carlos Delgado, Rafael Palmeiro/14
DP Carlos Delgado, Rafael Palmeiro/35 40.00
GB Shawn Green, Kevin Brown 20.00
GD Adam Dunn, Ken Griffey Jr. 45.00
GE Darin Erstad, Troy Glaus 30.00
GP Ken Griffey Jr., Rafael Palmeiro/14
GP Ken Griffey Jr., Rafael Palmeiro/35 50.00
GR Alex Rodriguez, Nomar Garciaparra 75.00
GS Vladimir Guerrero, Sammy Sosa 40.00
HJ Torii Hunter, Jacque Jones/83 20.00
HZ Roy Halladay, Barry Zito 35.00
IG Ken Griffey Jr., Ichiro Suzuki 90.00
IN Ichiro Suzuki, Hideo Nomo 140.00
IS Sammy Sosa, Ichiro Suzuki 90.00
JF Rafael Furcal, Andruw Jones 25.00
JG John Smoltz, Greg Maddux 40.00
MC Greg Maddux, Roger Clemens/75 60.00
NI Hideo Nomo, Kazuhisa Ishii/63 65.00
NM Hideki Matsui, Hideo Nomo/35 180.00
PM Mike Piazza, Jorge Posada/73 35.00
PR Roger Clemens, Pedro Martinez/35 60.00
PS Sammy Sosa, Mark Prior 50.00
RM Pedro J. Martinez, Manny Ramirez 40.00
RP Rafael Palmeiro, Alex Rodriguez/35 40.00
SA Albert Pujols, Scott Rolen 75.00
SB Alfonso Soriano, Bernie Williams/21
SJ Randy Johnson, Curt Schilling 40.00
SM Alfonso Soriano, Hideki Matsui 80.00
TB Mark Teixeira, Hank Blalock 40.00
TH Jim Thome, Todd Helton 35.00
TR Alex Rodriguez, Miguel Tejada 50.00
WL Mike Lowell, Dontrelle Willis/85 35.00
YW Delmon Young, Rickie Weeks/28 75.00

Game Jersey Tier 1

NM/M
Common Player: 8.00
Production 99 sets
Copper: No Pricing
Production 10 sets
Gold: .75-2X
No pricing production of 20 or less

RB Rocco Baldelli 8.00
PB Pat Burrell 8.00
RC Roger Clemens 20.00
CD Carlos Delgado 10.00
AD Adam Dunn 10.00
JE Jim Edmonds 8.00
RF Rafael Furcal 8.00
JG Jason Giambi 8.00
TR Troy Glaus 10.00
TG Tom Glavine 10.00
SG Shawn Green 8.00
KG Ken Griffey Jr. 20.00
VG Vladimir Guerrero 10.00
TH Torii Hunter 8.00
KI Kazuhisa Ishii 8.00
RJ Randy Johnson 12.00
AJ Andruw Jones 10.00
CJ Chipper Jones 15.00
GM Greg Maddux 15.00
HM Hideki Matsui 50.00
MM Mike Mussina 8.00
HN Hideo Nomo 15.00
MI Mike Piazza 15.00
MP Mark Prior 20.00
AP Albert Pujols 25.00
MR Manny Ramirez 12.00
JR Jose Reyes 10.00
AR Alex Rodriguez 15.00
CS Curt Schilling 10.00
GS Gary Sheffield 8.00
AS Alfonso Soriano 10.00
SS Sammy Sosa 25.00
IS Ichiro Suzuki 50.00
MT Miguel Tejada 10.00
FT Frank Thomas 10.00
JT Jim Thome 10.00
RW Rickie Weeks 15.00
BW Bernie Williams 10.00
DW Dontrelle Willis 10.00
KW Kerry Wood 10.00
DY Delmon Young 15.00
BZ Barry Zito 8.00

Game Jersey Tier 2

Tier 2: 1X Tier 1 price
Production 75 sets

Game Used Patch

NM/M
Common Player: 15.00
Production 99 sets
Copper: 1-1.5X
Production 35 sets
Gold: 1-1.5X
Production 25 sets

RB Rocco Baldelli 20.00
PB Pat Burrell 20.00
RC Roger Clemens 50.00
CD Carlos Delgado 15.00
AD Adam Dunn 20.00
JE Jim Edmonds 20.00
RF Rafael Furcal 15.00
JG Jason Giambi 20.00
TR Troy Glaus 25.00
TG Tom Glavine 25.00
SG Shawn Green 15.00
KG Ken Griffey Jr. 45.00
VG Vladimir Guerrero 30.00
RH Roy Halladay 20.00
TH Torii Hunter 20.00
KI Kazuhisa Ishii 20.00
RJ Randy Johnson 25.00
AJ Andruw Jones 25.00
CJ Chipper Jones 30.00
GM Greg Maddux 40.00
HM Hideki Matsui 85.00
MM Mike Mussina 25.00
HN Hideo Nomo 40.00
MI Mike Piazza 35.00
MP Mark Prior 40.00
AP Albert Pujols 50.00
MR Manny Ramirez 30.00
JR Jose Reyes 25.00
AR Alex Rodriguez 50.00
CS Curt Schilling 25.00
AS Alfonso Soriano/42 25.00
SS Sammy Sosa 35.00
IS Ichiro Suzuki 75.00
MT Miguel Tejada 25.00
FT Frank Thomas 25.00
JT Jim Thome 30.00
RW Rickie Weeks 25.00
BW Bernie Williams 20.00
DW Dontrelle Willis 30.00
KW Kerry Wood 40.00
DY Delmon Young 35.00
BZ Barry Zito 20.00

Ultimate Signature Tier 1

NM/M
Common Player: 20.00

AP1 Albert Pujols/40 160.00
AP2 Albert Pujols/35 160.00
AR1 Alex Rodriguez/75 EXCH 120.00
AR2 Alex Rodriguez/60 EXCH 120.00
BG1 Bob Gibson/299 20.00
BG2 Bob Gibson/199 20.00
CD1 Carlos Delgado/150 20.00
CR1 Cal Ripken Jr./85 150.00
CR2 Cal Ripken Jr./85 150.00
CY1 Carl Yastrzemski/199 60.00
DY1 Delmon Young/300 50.00
DY2 Delmon Young/300 50.00
EG1 Eric Gagne/350 40.00
GC1 Gary Carter/199 20.00
GM1 Greg Maddux/250 60.00
GM2 Greg Maddux/140 80.00
HM1 Hideki Matsui/250 250.00
HM2 Hideki Matsui/240 250.00
IS1 Ichiro Suzuki/199 280.00
IS2 Ichiro Suzuki/99 350.00
JG1 Jason Giambi/35 40.00
JG2 Jason Giambi/35 40.00
KG1 Ken Griffey Jr./350 75.00
KG2 Ken Griffey Jr./350 75.00
KW1 Kerry Wood/170 40.00
KW2 Kerry Wood/85 50.00
MP1 Mark Prior/299 60.00
MP2 Mark Prior/225 60.00
NG1 Nomar Garciaparra/125 EXCH 90.00
NG2 Nomar Garciaparra/180 90.00
NR1 Nolan Ryan/85 100.00
NR2 Nolan Ryan/75 100.00
OS1 Ozzie Smith/199 50.00
RC1 Roger Clemens/70 125.00
RC2 Roger Clemens/30 150.00
RJ1 Randy Johnson/75 75.00
RJ2 Randy Johnson/50 85.00
RS1 Ryne Sandberg/240 50.00
RS2 Ryne Sandberg/200 50.00
RW1 Rickie Weeks/300 40.00
RW2 Rickie Weeks/300 40.00
TS1 Tom Seaver/75 50.00
TS2 Tom Seaver/60 50.00
VG1 Vladimir Guerrero/75 60.00
VG2 Vladimir Guerrero/50 60.00

Ultimate Signatures Tier 2

NM/M
Production 25 sets 40.00

GC Gary Carter 50.00
RC Roger Clemens 200.00
CD Carlos Delgado 40.00
EG Eric Gagne 75.00
NG Nomar Garciaparra 120.00
JG Jason Giambi 50.00
BG Bob Gibson 60.00
KG Ken Griffey Jr. 120.00
VG Vladimir Guerrero 90.00
RJ Randy Johnson 100.00
GM Greg Maddux 200.00
HM Hideki Matsui 380.00
MP Mark Prior 120.00
AP Albert Pujols 250.00
CR Cal Ripken Jr. 250.00
AR Alex Rodriguez 200.00
NR Nolan Ryan 165.00
RS Ryne Sandberg 120.00
TS Tom Seaver 65.00
OS Ozzie Smith 100.00
IS Ichiro Suzuki 400.00
RW Rickie Weeks 100.00
KW Kerry Wood 75.00
CY Carl Yastrzemski 125.00
DY Delmon Young 125.00

2003 UPPER DECK VICTORY

NM/M
Complete Set (200): 40.00
Common Player (1-100): .10
Common (101-200): .40
Cards (101-128): Inserted 1:4
(129-168): 1:5
(169-188): 1:10
(189-200): 1:20
Pack (6): .75
Box (36): 20.00

1 Troy Glaus .40
2 Garret Anderson .20
3 Tim Salmon .20
4 Darin Erstad .20
5 Luis Gonzalez .20
6 Curt Schilling .25
7 Randy Johnson .50
8 Junior Spivey .10
9 Andruw Jones .25
10 Greg Maddux .75
11 Chipper Jones .75
12 Gary Sheffield .20
13 John Smoltz .10
14 Geronimo Gil .10
15 Tony Batista .10
16 Trot Nixon .10
17 Manny Ramirez .40
18 Pedro J. Martinez .50
19 Nomar Garciaparra 1.00
20 Derek Lowe .10
21 Shea Hillenbrand .10
22 Sammy Sosa .75
23 Kerry Wood .25
24 Mark Prior .40
25 Magglio Ordonez .20
26 Frank Thomas .40
27 Mark Buehrle .10
28 Paul Konerko .10
29 Adam Dunn .40
30 Ken Griffey Jr. .75
31 Austin Kearns .25
32 Matt Lawton .10
33 Larry Walker .20
34 Todd Helton .25
35 Jeff Bagwell .40
36 Roy Oswalt .20
37 Lance Berkman .25
38 Mike Sweeney .10
39 Carlos Beltran .10
40 Kazuhisa Ishii .10
41 Shawn Green .20
42 Hideo Nomo .25
43 Adrian Beltre .20
44 Richie Sexson .25
45 Ben Sheets .20
46 Torii Hunter .25
47 Jacque Jones .10
48 Corey Koskie .10

49	Vladimir Guerrero	.50
50	Jose Vidro	.10
51	Mo Vaughn	.20
52	Mike Piazza	1.00
53	Roberto Alomar	.25
54	Derek Jeter	1.50
55	Alfonso Soriano	.75
56	Jason Giambi	.75
57	Roger Clemens	.75
58	Mike Mussina	.25
59	Bernie Williams	.25
60	Jorge Posada	.20
61	Nick Johnson	.10
62	*Hideki Matsui*	4.00
63	Eric Chavez	.20
64	Barry Zito	.20
65	Miguel Tejada	.25
66	Tim Hudson	.20
67	Pat Burrell	.40
68	Bobby Abreu	.20
69	Jimmy Rollins	.10
70	Brett Myers	.10
71	Jim Thome	.40
72	Jason Kendall	.20
73	Brian Giles	.20
74	Aramis Ramirez	.10
75	Sean Burroughs	.10
76	Ryan Klesko	.20
77	Phil Nevin	.10
78	Barry Bonds	1.50
79	J.T. Snow	.10
80	Rich Aurilia	.10
81	Ichiro Suzuki	1.00
82	Edgar Martinez	.10
83	Freddy Garcia	.10
84	Jim Edmonds	.20
85	J.D. Drew	.10
86	Scott Rolen	.40
87	Albert Pujols	.50
88	Mark McGwire	1.25
89	Matt Morris	.20
90	Ben Grieve	.10
91	Carl Crawford	.10
92	Alex Rodriguez	1.25
93	Carl Everett	.10
94	Juan Gonzalez	.25
95	Rafael Palmeiro	.20
96	Hank Blalock	.20
97	Carlos Delgado	.20
98	Josh Phelps	.10
99	Eric Hinske	.10
100	Shannon Stewart	.10
101	Albert Pujols	1.00
102	Alex Rodriguez	2.50
103	Alfonso Soriano	1.00
104	Barry Bonds	3.00
105	Bernie Williams	.50
106	Brian Giles	.50
107	Chipper Jones	.75
108	Darin Erstad	.50
109	Derek Jeter	3.00
110	Eric Chavez	.50
111	Miguel Tejada	.50
112	Ichiro Suzuki	1.50
113	Rafael Palmeiro	.40
114	Jason Giambi	1.50
115	Jeff Bagwell	.75
116	Jim Thome	.75
117	Ken Griffey Jr.	1.50
118	Lance Berkman	.50
119	Luis Gonzalez	.40
120	Manny Ramirez	.75
121	Mike Piazza	2.00
122	J.D. Drew	.40
123	Sammy Sosa	1.50
124	Scott Rolen	.75
125	Shawn Green	.50
126	Todd Helton	.50
127	Troy Glaus	.75
128	Vladimir Guerrero	1.00
129	Albert Pujols	1.00
130	Brian Giles	.50
131	Carlos Delgado	.50
132	Curt Schilling	.50
133	Derek Jeter	3.00
134	Frank Thomas	.75
135	Greg Maddux	1.50
136	Jeff Bagwell	.75
137	Jim Thome	.75
138	Jorge Posada	.50
139	Kazuhisa Ishii	.40
140	Larry Walker	.40
141	Luis Gonzalez	.40
142	Miguel Tejada	.50
143	Pat Burrell	.75
144	Pedro J. Martinez	1.00
145	Rafael Palmeiro	.50
146	Roger Clemens	1.50
147	Tim Hudson	.50
148	Troy Glaus	.75
149	Alfonso Soriano	1.00
150	Andruw Jones	.50
151	Barry Zito	.50
152	Darin Erstad	.50
153	Eric Chavez	.50
154	Alex Rodriguez	2.50
155	J.D. Drew	.40
156	Jason Giambi	1.50
157	Jason Kendall	.40
158	Ken Griffey Jr.	1.50
159	Lance Berkman	.50
160	Mike Mussina	.50
161	Mike Piazza	2.00
162	Nomar Garciaparra	2.00
163	Randy Johnson	1.00
164	Roberto Alomar	.50
165	Scott Rolen	.75
166	Shawn Green	.50
167	Torii Hunter	.50
168	Vladimir Guerrero	1.00
169	Alex Rodriguez	2.50
170	Andruw Jones	.50
171	Bernie Williams	.50
172	Ichiro Suzuki	1.50
173	Miguel Tejada	.50
174	Nomar Garciaparra	2.00
175	Pedro J. Martinez	1.00
176	Randy Johnson	1.00
177	Todd Helton	.50
178	Vladimir Guerrero	1.00
179	Barry Bonds	3.00
180	Carlos Delgado	.50
181	Chipper Jones	1.50
182	Frank Thomas	.75
183	Lance Berkman	.50
184	Larry Walker	.40
185	Manny Ramirez	.75
186	Mike Piazza	2.00
187	Sammy Sosa	1.50
188	Shawn Green	.50
189	Chipper Jones	1.50
190	Curt Schilling	.50
191	Derek Jeter	3.00
192	Ken Griffey Jr.	1.50
193	Sammy Sosa	1.50
194	Vladimir Guerrero	1.00
195	Alex Rodriguez	2.50
196	Barry Bonds	3.00
197	Greg Maddux	1.50
198	Ichiro Suzuki	1.50
199	Jason Giambi	1.50
200	Mike Piazza	2.00

Parallels

Tier 1 Green:	1-2X
Inserted 1:1	
Tier 2 Orange:	2-4X
Inserted 1:8	
Tier 3 Blue:	3-6X
Production 650	
Tier 4 Purple:	10-25X
Production 50 sets	
Tier 5 Red:	No Pricing
Production 25 sets	

2003 UPPER DECK VINTAGE

	NM/M
Complete Set (280):	
Common Player:	.15
Common SP (223-232):	1.50
Inserted 1:7	
Common SP (233-247):	.50
Inserted 1:5	
Common 3D SP (248-277):	6.00
Inserted 1:48	
Pack (8):	2.00
Box (24):	45.00

1	Troy Glaus	.25
2	Darin Erstad	.25
3	Garret Anderson	.25
4	Jarrod Washburn	.15
5	Nolan Ryan	2.00
6	Tim Salmon	.25
7	Troy Percival	.15
8	Alex Ochoa/SP	4.00
9	Daryle Ward	.15
10	Jeff Bagwell	.50
11	Roy Oswalt	.25
12	Lance Berkman	.40
13	Craig Biggio	.25
14	Richard Hidalgo	.15
15	Tim Hudson	.25
16	Eric Chavez	.25
17	Barry Zito	.25
18	Miguel Tejada	.50
19	Mark Mulder	.25
20	Rollie Fingers	.15
21	Jim "Catfish" Hunter	.25
22	Jermaine Dye	.15
23	Ray Durham/SP	4.00
24	Carlos Delgado	.25
25	Eric Hinske	.15
26	Josh Phelps	.15
27	Shannon Stewart	.15
28	Vernon Wells	.15
29	John Smoltz	.25
30	Greg Maddux	1.00
31	Chipper Jones	.75
32	Gary Sheffield	.25
33	Andruw Jones	.40
34	Tom Glavine	.25
35	Rafael Furcal	.15
36	Phil Niekro	.15
37	Eddie Mathews	.50
38	Robin Yount	.75
39	Richie Sexson	.25
40	Ben Sheets	.15
41	Geoff Jenkins	.15
42	Alex Sanchez	.15
43	Jason Isringhausen	.15
44	Albert Pujols	1.50
45	Matt Morris	.15
46	J.D. Drew	.25
47	Jim Edmonds	.25
48	Stan Musial	1.00
49	Red Schoendienst	.15
50	Edgar Renteria	.25
51	Mark McGwire/SP	10.00
52	Scott Rolen/SP	5.00
53	Mark Bellhorn	.15
54	Kerry Wood	.50
55	Mark Prior	.50
56	Moises Alou	.25
57	Corey Patterson	.25
58	Ernie Banks	.75
59	Hee Seop Choi	.15
60	Billy Williams	.15
61	Sammy Sosa/SP	8.00
62	Ben Grieve	.15
63	Jared Sandberg	.15
64	Carl Crawford	.15
65	Randy Johnson	.75
66	Luis Gonzalez	.25
67	Steve Finley	.15
68	Junior Spivey	.15
69	Erubiel Durazo	.15
70	Curt Schilling/SP	8.00
71	Al Lopez	.15
72	Pee Wee Reese	.15
73	Eric Gagne	.25
74	Shawn Green	.25
75	Kevin Brown	.15
76	Paul LoDuca	.15
77	Adrian Beltre	.25
78	Hideo Nomo	.40
79	Eric Karros	.15
80	Odalis Perez	.15
81	Kazuhisa Ishii/SP	5.00
82	Tommy Lasorda	.15
83	Fernando Tatis	.15
84	Vladimir Guerrero	.75
85	Jose Vidro	.15
86	Javier Vazquez	.15
87	Brad Wilkerson	.15
88	Bartolo Colon/SP	4.00
89	Monte Irvin	.15
90	Robb Nen	.15
91	Reggie Sanders	.15
92	Jeff Kent	.25
93	Rich Aurilia	.15
94	Orlando Cepeda	.15
95	Juan Marichal	.25
96	Willie McCovey	.25
97	David Bell	.15
98	Barry Bonds/SP	10.00
99	Kenny Lofton/SP	4.00
100	Jim Thome	.50
101	C.C. Sabathia	.15
102	Omar Vizquel	.25
103	Lou Boudreau	.15
104	Larry Doby	.25
105	Bob Lemon	.15
106	John Olerud	.25
107	Edgar Martinez	.15
108	Bret Boone	.15
109	Freddy Garcia	.15
110	Mike Cameron	.15
111	Kazuhiro Sasaki	.15
112	Ichiro Suzuki/SP	8.00
113	Mike Lowell	.15
114	Josh Beckett	.25
115	A.J. Burnett	.15
116	Juan Pierre	.15
117	Derrek Lee	.25
118	Luis Castillo	.15
119	Juan Encarnacion/SP	4.00
120	Roberto Alomar	.40
121	Edgardo Alfonzo	.15
122	Jeromy Burnitz	.15
123	Mo Vaughn	.25
124	Tom Seaver	.50
125	Al Leiter	.15
126	Mike Piazza/SP	8.00
127	Tony Batista	.15
128	Geronimo Gil	.15
129	Chris Singleton	.15
130	Rodrigo Lopez	.15
131	Jay Gibbons	.15
132	Melvin Mora	.15
133	Earl Weaver	.15
134	Trevor Hoffman	.15
135	Phil Nevin	.15
136	Sean Burroughs	.15
137	Ryan Klesko	.15
138	Mark Kotsay	.15
139	Mike Lieberthal	.15
140	Bobby Abreu	.25
141	Jimmy Rollins	.15
142	Pat Burrell	.40
143	Vicente Padilla	.15
144	Richie Ashburn	.15
145	Jeremy Giambi/SP	4.00
146	Josh Fogg	.15
147	Brian Giles	.25
148	Aramis Ramirez	.25
149	Jason Kendall	.15
150	Ralph Kiner	.15
151	Willie Stargell	.25
152	Kevin Mench	.15
153	Rafael Palmeiro	.25
154	Ivan Rodriguez	.40
155	Hank Blalock	.25
156	Juan Gonzalez	.40
157	Carl Everett	.15
158	Alex Rodriguez/SP	10.00
159	Nomar Garciaparra	1.25
160	Derek Lowe	.15
161	Manny Ramirez	.50
162	Shea Hillenbrand	.25
163	Bobby Doerr	.15
164	Johnny Damon	.40
165	Jason Varitek	.25
166	Pedro Martinez/SP	8.00
167	Cliff Floyd/SP	4.00
168	Ken Griffey Jr.	1.25
169	Adam Dunn	.50
170	Austin Kearns	.25
171	Aaron Boone	.15
172	Joe Morgan	.25
173	Sean Casey	.15
174	Todd Walker	.15
175	Ryan Dempster/SP	4.00
176	Shawn Estes/SP	4.00
177	Gabe Kapler/SP	4.00
178	Jason Jennings	.15
179	Todd Helton	.40
180	Larry Walker	.25
181	Preston Wilson	.15
182	Jay Payton/SP	4.00
183	Mike Sweeney	.15
184	Carlos Beltran	.50
185	Paul Byrd	.15
186	Raul Ibanez	.15
187	Rick Ferrell	.15
188	Early Wynn	.15
189	Dmitri Young	.15
190	Jim Bunning	.15
191	George Kell	.15
192	Hal Newhouser	.15
193	Bobby Higginson	.15
194	Carlos Pena/SP	4.00
195	Sparky Anderson	.15
196	Torii Hunter	.25
197	Eric Milton	.15
198	Corey Koskie	.15

199 Jacque Jones .15
200 Harmon Killebrew .50
201 Doug Mientkiewicz .15
202 Frank Thomas .50
203 Mark Buehrle .15
204 Magglio Ordonez .25
205 Paul Konerko .25
206 Joe Borchard .15
207 Hoyt Wilhelm .15
208 Carlos Lee .15
209 Roger Clemens 1.50
210 Nick Johnson .15
211 Jason Giambi .25
212 Alfonso Soriano .75
213 Bernie Williams .40
214 Robin Ventura .15
215 Jorge Posada .25
216 Mike Mussina .40
217 Yogi Berra .75
218 Phil Rizzuto .40
219 Mariano Rivera .25
220 Derek Jeter/SP 12.00
221 Jeff Weaver/SP 4.00
222 Raul Mondesi/SP 4.00
223 Freddy Sanchez, Josh Hancock 2.00
224 Joe Borchard, Miguel Olivo 2.00
225 Brandon Phillips, Josh Bard 1.50
226 Andy Van Hekken, Andres Torres 1.50
227 Jason Lane, Jeriome Robertson 1.50
228 Chin-Feng Chen, Joe Thurston 1.50
229 Endy Chavez, Jamey Carroll 1.50
230 Drew Henson, Alex Graman 2.50
231 Dewon Brazelton, Lance Carter 1.50
232 Jayson Werth, Kevin Cash 1.50
233 Randy Johnson, Curt Schilling, Barry Zito 1.00
234 Pedro J. Martinez, Randy Johnson, Derek Lowe 1.00
235 Randy Johnson, Curt Schilling, Pedro J. Martinez 1.00
236 John Smoltz, Eric Gagne, Mike Williams .50
237 Randy Johnson, Bartolo Colon, A.J. Burnett 1.00
238 Alfonso Soriano, Ichiro Suzuki, Vladimir Guerrero 1.50
239 Alex Rodriguez, Jim Thome, Sammy Sosa 2.00
240 Barry Bonds, Manny Ramirez, Mike Sweeney 2.00
241 Alfonso Soriano, Alex Rodriguez, Derek Jeter 2.00
242 Alex Rodriguez, Magglio Ordonez, Miguel Tejada 2.00
243 Luis Castillo, Juan Pierre, Dave Roberts .50
244 Nomar Garciaparra, Garret Anderson, Alfonso Soriano 1.00
245 Johnny Damon, Jimmy Rollins, Kenny Lofton .50
246 Barry Bonds, Jim Thome, Manny Ramirez 2.00
247 Barry Bonds, Brian Giles, Manny Ramirez 2.00
248 Troy Glaus 10.00
249 Luis Gonzalez 6.00
250 Chipper Jones 15.00
251 Nomar Garciaparra 15.00
252 Manny Ramirez 10.00
253 Sammy Sosa 15.00
254 Frank Thomas 10.00
255 Magglio Ordonez 6.00
256 Adam Dunn 10.00
257 Ken Griffey Jr. 15.00
258 Jim Thome 10.00
259 Todd Helton 8.00
260 Larry Walker 6.00
261 Lance Berkman 6.00
262 Jeff Bagwell 10.00
263 Mike Sweeney 6.00
264 Shawn Green 6.00
265 Vladimir Guerrero 12.00
266 Mike Piazza 15.00
267 Jason Giambi 15.00
268 Pat Burrell 20.00
269 Barry Bonds 15.00
270 Mark McGwire 20.00
271 Alex Rodriguez 15.00
272 Carlos Delgado 6.00
273 Richie Sexson 6.00
274 Andruw Jones 8.00
275 Derek Jeter 20.00
276 Juan Gonzalez 8.00
277 Albert Pujols 12.00
278 Jason Giambi/CL .75
279 Sammy Sosa/CL .75
280 Ichiro Suzuki/CL .75

All Caps

NM/M
Common Player: 8.00
Production 250 sets
JB Jeff Bagwell 15.00
LB Lance Berkman 8.00
DE Darin Erstad 8.00
RF Rafael Furcal 8.00
JG Juan Gonzalez 10.00
LG Luis Gonzalez 8.00
TG Tony Gwynn 25.00
TH Tim Hudson 10.00
GM Greg Maddux 30.00
RP Rafael Palmeiro 10.00
CP Chan Ho Park 8.00
MP Mike Piazza 35.00
KS Kazuhiro Sasaki 8.00
MV Mo Vaughn 8.00
RV Robin Ventura 8.00

Capping the Action

NM/M
Common Player: 10.00
Quantity produced listed
RA Roberto Alomar/101 20.00
CD Carlos Delgado/91 10.00
JG Juan Gonzalez/99 20.00
SG Shawn Green/125 20.00
KG Ken Griffey Jr/102 40.00
TH Todd Helton/99 20.00
PM Pedro Martinez/125 25.00
MM Mike Mussina/109 40.00
HM Hideo Nomo/117 45.00
RP Rafael Palmeiro/125 20.00
AR Alex Rodriguez/110 25.00
IR Ivan Rodriguez/125 15.00
SR Scott Rolen/109 25.00
AS Alfonso Soriano/109 20.00
SS Sammy Sosa/125 40.00

Crackin the Lumber

NM/M
Production 25
Golds: No Pricing
Production 5
JG Jason Giambi 25.00
IS Ichiro Suzuki 125.00

Dropping the Hammer

NM/M
Common Player: 6.00
Inserted 1:130
Golds: 1.5-2X
Production 100 sets
BA Bobby Abreu 8.00
RA Roberto Alomar 10.00
LB Lance Berkman 8.00
RF Rafael Furcal 6.00
JG Jason Giambi 6.00
SG Shawn Green 6.00
KG Ken Griffey Jr. 15.00
TH Todd Helton 8.00
AJ Andruw Jones 8.00
DJ David Justice 8.00
KL Kenny Lofton 6.00
FM Fred McGriff 8.00
MO Magglio Ordonez 6.00
RP Rafael Palmeiro 8.00
MP Mike Piazza 15.00
AR Alex Rodriguez 15.00
SS Sammy Sosa 20.00
TA Fernando Tatis 6.00
MT Miguel Tejada 8.00
FT Frank Thomas 10.00
JT Jim Thome 10.00
RV Robin Ventura 6.00
OV Omar Vizquel 6.00
LW Larry Walker 8.00
PW Preston Wilson 6.00

Men with Hats

NM/M
Common Player: 8.00
Inserted 1:285
VC Vinny Castilla 8.00
EC Eric Chavez 10.00
JD Johnny Damon 15.00
AD Adam Dunn 15.00
JG Jason Giambi 8.00
TH Todd Helton 10.00
HU Tim Hudson 10.00
AJ Andruw Jones 10.00
JK Jason Kendall 8.00
KL Kenny Lofton 8.00
AR Alex Rodriguez 20.00
MT Miguel Tejada 12.00
FT Frank Thomas 12.00
TW Todd Walker 8.00
BW Bernie Williams 10.00

Slugfest

NM/M
Common Player: 8.00
Production 200 sets
Golds: 1.5-2.5X
Production 50 sets
CD Carlos Delgado 8.00
SG Shawn Green 8.00
AJ Andruw Jones 8.00
RP Rafael Palmeiro 8.00
MP Mike Piazza 20.00
AR Alex Rodriguez 15.00
FT Frank Thomas 10.00
JT Jim Thome 10.00
LW Larry Walker 8.00
BW Bernie Williams 10.00

Timeless Teams Bat

NM/M
Common Card: 20.00
Production 175 sets
BLAR Pat Burrell, Mike Lieberthal, Bobby Abreu, Jimmy Rollins 25.00
CTDJ Eric Chavez, Miguel Tejada, Jermaine Dye, David Justice 25.00
DEMR J.D. Drew, Jim Edmonds, Tino Martinez, Scott Rolen 40.00
DGCL Adam Dunn, Ken Griffey Jr., Sean Casey, Barry Larkin 40.00
GNBL Shawn Green, Hideo Nomo, Adrian Beltre, Paul LoDuca 40.00
GPMS Jason Giambi, Jorge Posada, Raul Mondesi, Alfonso Soriano 30.00
GWVS Jason Giambi, Bernie Williams, Robin Ventura, Alfonso Soriano 40.00
HWPZ Todd Helton, Larry Walker, Juan Pierre, Todd Zeile 25.00
IMBC Ichiro Suzuki, Edgar Martinez, Bret Boone, Mike Cameron 90.00
JGSW Randy Johnson, Luis Gonzalez, Curt Schilling, Matt Williams 40.00
JJSF Chipper Jones, Andruw Jones, Gary Sheffield, Rafael Furcal 40.00
KNKB Ryan Klesko, Phil Nevin, Mark Kotsay, Sean Burroughs 20.00
MGLJ Greg Maddux, Tom Glavine, Javy Lopez, Chipper Jones 40.00
OTLK Magglio Ordonez, Frank Thomas, Carlos Lee, Paul Konerko 30.00
PVAA Mike Piazza, Mo Vaughn, Roberto Alomar, Edgardo Alfonzo 40.00
RGRP Alex Rodriguez, Juan Gonzalez, Ivan Rodriguez, Rafael Palmeiro 40.00
RMHN Manny Ramirez, Pedro J. Martinez, Shea Hillenbrand, Trot Nixon 30.00
SMAP Sammy Sosa, Fred McGriff, Moises Alou, Corey Patterson 40.00

UD Giants

NM/M
Complete Set (42): 45.00
Common Player: .75
Inserted 1:box
RA Roberto Alomar 1.00
JB Jeff Bagwell 1.00
LB Lance Berkman 1.00
BB Barry Bonds 4.00
PB Pat Burrell 1.00
RC Roger Clemens 4.00
CD Carlos Delgado .75
JD J.D. Drew .75
AD Adam Dunn 1.50
NG Nomar Garciaparra 3.00
JG Jason Giambi .75
BG Brian Giles .75
GO Juan Gonzalez 1.00
LG Luis Gonzalez .75
SG Shawn Green .75
KG Ken Griffey Jr. 3.00
VG Vladimir Guerrero 1.50
TH Todd Helton 1.00
KI Kazuhisa Ishii .75
RJ Randy Johnson 1.50
AJ Andruw Jones 1.00
CJ Chipper Jones 2.50
GM Greg Maddux 2.50
PM Pedro J. Martinez 1.50
MM Mike Mussina 1.00
HN Hideo Nomo 1.00
MO Magglio Ordonez .75
RP Rafael Palmeiro 1.00
MP Mike Piazza 3.00
PR Mark Prior 1.50
AP Albert Pujols 4.00
MR Manny Ramirez 1.50
AR Alex Rodriguez 4.00
IR Ivan Rodriguez 1.50
SR Scott Rolen 1.50
CS Curt Schilling 1.50
SS Sammy Sosa 2.50
IS Ichiro Suzuki 3.00
FT Frank Thomas 1.00
JT Jim Thome 1.50
BW Bernie Williams 1.00
KW Kerry Wood 1.50

Vintage Hitmen

NM/M
Production 150 sets
Golds: Not Priced
Production 10 sets
JG Jason Giambi 10.00
KG Ken Griffey Jr. 30.00
MM Mark McGwire 60.00
IS Ichiro Suzuki 60.00

Vintage Hitmen Double Signed

NM/M
Production 75
Gold: Not Priced
Production 5
MS Mark McGwire, Sammy Sosa 600.00

2003 UPPER DECK 40-MAN

NM/M
Complete Set (990): 200.00
Common Player: .25
Common Rk (877-960): .40
Pack (10): 2.00
Box (24): 35.00

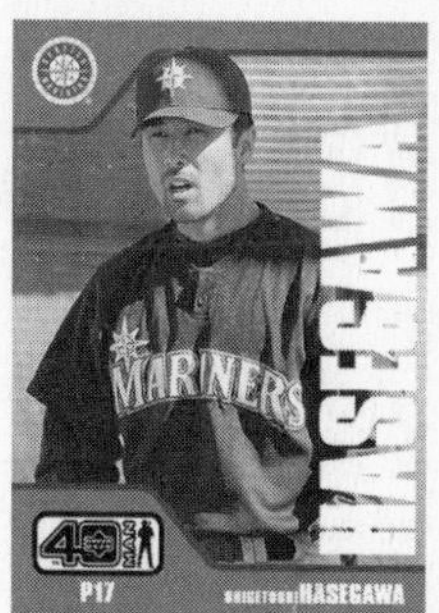

No.	Player	Value
1	Troy Glaus	.50
2	Darin Erstad	.40
3	Garret Anderson	.50
4	Aaron Sele	.25
5	Adam Kennedy	.25
6	Scott Spiezio	.25
7	Troy Percival	.25
8	David Eckstein	.25
9	Ramon Ortiz	.25
10	Bengie Molina	.25
11	Tim Salmon	.50
12	John Lackey	.25
13	Brad Fullmer	.25
14	Jarrod Washburn	.25
15	Shawn Wooten	.25
16	Kevin Appier	.25
17	Ben Weber	.25
18	Eric Owens	.25
19	Matt Wise	.25
20	Francisco Rodriguez	.25
21	Scot Shields	.25
22	Jose Molina	.25
23	Scott Schoeneweis	.25
24	Derrick Turnbow	.25
25	Benji Gil	.25
26	Julio Ramirez	.25
27	Mickey Callaway	.25
28	Barry Zito	.50
29	Tim Hudson	.50
30	Mark Mulder	.40
31	Eric Chavez	.40
32	Miguel Tejada	.50
33	Terrence Long	.25
34	Jermaine Dye	.25
35	Erubiel Durazo	.25
36	Scott Hatteberg	.25
37	Chris Singleton	.25
38	Keith Foulke	.25
39	John Halama	.25
40	Mark Ellis	.25
41	Ted Lilly	.25
42	Jim Mecir	.25
43	Adam Piatt	.25
44	Freddie Bynum	.25
45	Adam Morrissey	.25
46	Jeremy Fikac	.25
47	Ricardo Rincon	.25
48	Ramon Hernandez	.25
49	Micah Bowie	.25
50	Chad Bradford	.25
51	Eric Byrnes	.25
52	Ron Gant	.25
53	Jose Flores	.25
54	Mark Johnson	.25
55	Carlos Delgado	.75
56	Orlando Hudson	.25
57	Kelvim Escobar	.25
58	Eric Hinske	.25
59	Doug Creek	.25
60	Josh Phelps	.25
61	Shannon Stewart	.25
62	Roy Halladay	.40
63	Vernon Wells	.40
64	Mark Henrickson	.25
65	Mike Bordick.	.25
66	Jayson Werth.	.25
67	Chris Woodward.	.25
68	Ken Huckaby.	.25
69	Frank Catalanotto.	.25
70	Jason Kershner.	.25
71	Greg Myers.	.25
72	Tanyon Sturtze.	.25
73	Trever Miller.	.25
74	Pete Walker	.25
75	Alexis Rios	.25
76	Tom Wilson	.25
77	Dave Berg	.25
78	Doug Linton	.25
79	Cliff Politte	.25
80	Damion Easley	.25
81	Toby Hall	.25
82	George Lombard	.25
83	Ben Grieve	.25
84	Aubrey Huff	.25
85	Jesus Colome	.25
86	Dewon Brazelton	.25
87	Rey Ordonez	.25
88	Al Martin	.25
89	Carl Crawford	.25
90	Travis Lee	.25
91	Marlon Anderson	.25
92	Javier Valentin	.25
93	Joe Kennedy	.25
94	Jorge Sosa	.25
95	Travis Harper	.25
96	Bobby Seay	.25
97	Seth McClung	.25
98	Delvin James	.25
99	Victor Zambrano	.25
100	Terry Shumpert	.25
101	Josh Hamilton	.25
102	Jared Sandberg	.25
103	Steve Parris	.25
104	C.C. Sabathia	.25
105	Omar Vizquel	.40
106	Milton Bradley	.25
107	Ellis Burks	.25
108	Danys Baez	.25
109	Jason Davis	.25
110	Terry Mulholland	.25
111	Matt Lawton	.25
112	Alex Escobar	.25
113	Mark Wohlers	.25
114	Josh Bard	.25
115	Bill Selby	.25
116	Brandon Phillips	.25
117	Jason Bere	.25
118	Casey Blake	.25
119	Travis Hafner	.25
120	Brian Anderson	.25
121	David Riske	.25
122	Karim Garcia	.25
123	Ricardo Rodriguez	.25
124	Carl Sadler	.25
125	Jose Santiago	.25
126	Tim Laker	.25
127	John McDonald	.25
128	Jake Westbrook	.25
129	Ichiro Suzuki	1.00
130	Freddy Garcia	.25
131	Edgar Martinez	.40
132	Ben Davis	.25
133	Shigetoshi Hasegawa	.25
134	Carlos Guillen	.25
135	Randy Winn	.25
136	John Mabry	.25
137	Matt Thornton	.25
138	Bret Boone	.40
139	Jamie Moyer	.25
140	Giovanni Carrara	.25
141	Kazuhiro Sasaki	.25
142	Jeff Cirillo	.25
143	Mark McLemore	.25
144	Pat Borders	.25
145	Mike Cameron	.25
146	Dan Wilson	.25
147	John Olerud	.40
148	Arthur Rhodes	.25
149	Rafael Soriano	.25
150	Greg Colbrunn	.25
151	Ryan Franklin	.25
152	Joel Pineiro	.25
153	Jeff Nelson	.25
154	Jerry Hairston	.25
155	Rick Helling	.25
156	Gary Matthews Jr.	.25
157	Jeff Conine	.25
158	Sidney Ponson	.25
159	Tony Batista	.25
160	Jay Gibbons	.40
161	Marty Cordova	.25
162	Geronimo Gil	.25
163	Deivi Cruz	.25
164	B.J. Ryan	.25
165	Jason Johnson	.25
166	Buddy Groom	.25
167	Pat Hentgen	.25
168	Omar Daal	.25
169	Willis Roberts	.25
170	Scott Erickson	.25
171	David Segui	.25
172	Brook Fordyce	.25
173	Rodrigo Lopez	.25
174	Jose Leon	.25
175	Jose Morban	.25
176	Melvin Mora	.25
177	B.J. Surhoff	.25
178	Jorge Julio	.25
179	Alex Rodriguez	2.00
180	Mark Teixeira	.40
181	Chan Ho Park	.25
182	Todd Van Poppel	.25
183	Todd Greene	.25
184	Ismael Valdes	.25
185	Rusty Greer	.25
186	Rafael Palmeiro	.50
187	Francisco Cordero	.25
188	Einar Diaz	.25
189	Doug Glanville	.25
190	Michael Young	.25
191	Kevin Mench	.25
192	Carl Everett	.25
193	Herbert Perry	.25
194	Jeff Zimmerman	.25
195	Juan Gonzalez	.50
196	Ugueth Urbina	.25
197	Jermaine Clark	.25
198	John Thomson	.25
199	Hank Blalock	.50
200	Jay Powell	.25
201	Mike Lamb	.25
202	Aaron Fultz	.25
203	Esteban Yan	.25
204	Nomar Garciaparra	2.00
205	Pedro J. Martinez	.75
206	John Burkett	.25
207	Johnny Damon	.40
208	Doug Mirabelli	.25
209	Derek Lowe	.25
210	Shea Hillenbrand	.25
211	Brandon Lyon	.25
212	Trot Nixon	.25
213	Jason Varitek	.25
214	Tim Wakefield	.25
215	Manny Ramirez	.75
216	Todd Walker	.25
217	Jeremy Giambi	.25
218	Ramiro Mendoza	.25
219	Bill Mueller	.25
220	David Ortiz	.25
221	Mike Timlin	.25
222	Alan Embree	.25
223	Bob Howry	.25
224	Chad Fox	.25
225	Damian Jackson	.25
226	Casey Fossum	.25
227	Steve Woodard	.25
228	Freddy Sanchez	.25
229	Mike Sweeney	.25
230	Desi Relaford	.25
231	Brent Mayne	.25
232	Angel Berroa	.25
233	Albie Lopez	.25
234	Raul Ibanez	.25
235	Joe Randa	.25
236	Chris George	.25
237	Michael Tucker	.25
238	Mendy Lopez	.25
239	Kris Wilson	.25
240	Jason Grimsley	.25
241	Carlos Febles	.25
242	Runelvys Hernandez	.25
243	Mike MacDougal	.25
244	Carlos Beltran	.40
245	Brandon Berger	.25
246	Darrell May	.25
247	Miguel Asencio	.25
248	Ryan Bukvich	.25
249	Dee Brown	.25
250	Jeremy Hill	.25
251	Jeremy Affeldt	.25
252	Ken Harvey	.25
253	Bobby Higginson	.25
254	Matt Anderson	.25
255	Dmitri Young	.25
256	Gene Kingsdale	.25
257	Craig Paquette	.25
258	Adam Bernero	.25
259	Andres Torres	.25
260	Carlos Pena	.25
261	Dean Palmer	.25
262	Eric Munson	.25
263	Omar Infante	.25
264	Shane Halter	.25
265	Jeremy Bonderman	.25
266	Steve Sparks	.25
267	Gary Knotts	.25
268	Mike Maroth	.25
269	Nate Cornejo	.25
270	Matt Roney	.25
271	Franklyn German	.25
272	Matt Walbeck	.25
273	Brandon Inge	.25
274	Hiram Bocachica	.25
275	Chris Spurling	.25
276	Craig Monroe	.25
277	Ramon Santiago	.25
278	Doug Mientkiewicz	.25
279	Torii Hunter	.50
280	Brad Radke	.25
281	Denny Hocking	.25
282	Tom Prince	.25
283	Eddie Guardado	.25
284	Jacque Jones	.25
285	Joe Mays	.25
286	Mike Fetters	.25
287	LaTroy Hawkins	.25
288	A.J. Pierzynski	.25
289	Eric Milton	.25
290	Cristian Guzman	.25
291	Bobby Kielty	.25
292	Corey Koskie	.25
293	J.C. Romero	.25
294	Mike Cuddyer	.25
295	Luis Rivas	.25
296	Matt LeCroy	.25
297	Tony Fiore	.25
298	Dustan Mohr	.25
299	Chris Gomez	.25
300	Johan Santana	.25
301	Kyle Lohse	.25
302	Frank Thomas	.75
303	Mark Buehrle	.25
304	Jon Garland	.25
305	Magglio Ordonez	.50
306	Paul Konerko	.25
307	Sandy Alomar Jr.	.25
308	Carlos Lee	.25
309	Jon Rauch	.25
310	Esteban Loaiza	.25
311	Gary Glover	.25
312	Kelly Wunsch	.25
313	Tony Graffanino	.25
314	Aaron Rowand	.25
315	Armando Rios	.25
316	Jose Valentin	.25
317	D'Angelo Jimenez	.25
318	Joe Crede	.25
319	Miguel Olivo	.25
320	Rick White	.25
321	Billy Koch	.25
322	Tom Gordon	.25
323	Bartolo Colon	.40
324	Josh Paul	.25
325	Joe Borchard	.25
326	Damaso Marte	.25
327	Derek Jeter	2.00
328	Jason Giambi	.75
329	Roger Clemens	2.00
330	Enrique Wilson	.25
331	Dave Wells	.25
332	Mike Mussina	.50
333	Bernie Williams	.50
334	Todd Zeile	.25
335	Sterling Hitchcock	.25
336	Juan Acevedo	.25
337	Robin Ventura	.25
338	Mariano Rivera	.40
339	John Flaherty	.25
340	Andy Pettitte	.50
341	Antonio Osuna	.25
342	Erick Almonte	.25
343	Chris Hammond	.25
344	Steve Karsay	.25
345	Alfonso Soriano	1.00
346	Bubba Trammell	.25
347	Nick Johnson	.25
348	Jorge Posada	.50
349	Jeff Weaver	.25
350	Raul Mondesi	.25
351	Randy Choate	.25
352	Drew Henson	.25
353	Jeff Bagwell	.75
354	Wade Miller	.25
355	Lance Berkman	.40
356	Julio Lugo	.25
357	Roy Oswalt	.40
358	Bruce Chen	.25
359	Morgan Ensberg	.25
360	Geoff Blum	.25
361	Brian Moehler	.25
362	Billy Wagner	.40
363	Peter Munro	.25
364	Brad Ausmus	.25
365	Jose Vizcaino	.25
366	Craig Biggio	.40
367	Tim Redding	.25
368	Gregg Zaun	.25
369	Octavio Dotel	.25
370	Carlos Hernandez	.25
371	Richard Hidalgo	.25
372	Jeriome Robertson	.25
373	Orlando Merced	.25
374	John Buck	.25
375	Adam Everett	.25
376	Raul Chavez	.25

No.	Player	Value
377	Brad Lidge	.25
378	Jeff Kent	.40
379	Scott Linebrink	.25
380	Greg Miller	.25
381	Kirk Saarloos	.25
382	Brandon Puffer	.25
383	Ricky Stone	.25
384	Jason Lane	.25
385	Brian L. Hunter	.25
386	Rodrigo Rosario	.25
387	Horacio Ramirez	.25
388	Gary Sheffield	.50
389	Mike Hampton	.25
390	Robert Fick	.25
391	Henry Blanco	.25
392	Vinny Castilla	.25
393	Joe Dawley	.25
394	Jung Bong	.25
395	Rafael Furcal	.40
396	Javy Lopez	.40
397	Greg Maddux	1.25
398	Andruw Jones	.50
399	John Smoltz	.40
400	Chipper Jones	1.00
401	Mark DeRosa	.25
402	Shane Reynolds	.25
403	Kevin Gryboski	.25
404	Russ Ortiz	.25
405	Roberto Hernandez	.25
406	Ray King	.25
407	Matt Franco	.25
408	Marcus Giles	.25
409	Trey Hodges	.25
410	Darren Holmes	.25
411	Julio Franco	.25
412	Darren Bragg	.25
413	Richie Sexson	.50
414	Jeffrey Hammonds	.25
415	Ben Sheets	.25
416	Mike DeJean	.25
417	Royce Clayton	.25
418	Wes Helms	.25
419	Valerio de los Santos	.25
420	Brady Clark	.25
421	Glendon Rusch	.25
422	Geoff Jenkins	.40
423	John Foster	.25
424	Curtis Leskanic	.25
425	Todd Ritchie	.25
426	Enrique Cruz	.25
427	Wayne Franklin	.25
428	Matt Ford	.25
429	Matt Kinney	.25
430	Scott Podsednik	2.00
431	Luis Vizcaino	.25
432	Shane Nance	.25
433	Alex Sanchez	.25
434	John Vander Wal	.25
435	Eric Young	.25
436	Eddie Perez	.25
437	Jason Conti	.25
438	Matt Morris	.25
439	Tino Martinez	.25
440	Fernando Vina	.25
441	Kiko Calero	.25
442	Cal Eldred	.25
443	Jimmy Journell	.25
444	Jim Edmonds	.40
445	Jeff Fassero	.25
446	Mike Matheny	.25
447	Garrett Stephenson	.25
448	Brett Tomko	.25
449	So Taguchi	.25
450	Eduardo Perez	.25
451	Lance Painter	.25
452	Jason Isringhausen	.25
453	Albert Pujols	2.00
454	Eli Marrero	.25
455	Jason Simontacchi	.25
456	J.D. Drew	.25
457	Scott Rolen	.75
458	Orlando Palmeiro	.25
459	Dustin Hermanson	.25
460	Edgar Renteria	.25
461	Woody Williams	.25
462	Chris Carpenter	.25
463	Sammy Sosa	1.50
464	Kerry Wood	.75
465	Kyle Farnsworth	.25
466	Alex Gonzalez	.25
467	Eric Karros	.25
468	Troy O'Leary	.25
469	Mark Grudzielanek	.25
470	Alan Benes	.25
471	Mark Prior	2.00
472	Paul Bako	.25
473	Shawn Estes	.25
474	Matt Clement	.25
475	Ramon Martinez	.25
476	Tom Goodwin	.25
477	Corey Patterson	.25
478	Moises Alou	.40
479	Juan Cruz	.25
480	Bobby Hill	.25
481	Mark Bellhorn	.25
482	Mark Guthrie	.25
483	Mike Remlinger	.25
484	Lenny Harris	.25
485	Antonio Alfonseca	.25
486	Dave Veres	.25
487	Hee Seop Choi	.25
488	Luis Gonzalez	.40
489	Lyle Overbay	.25
490	Randy Johnson	.75
491	Mark Grace	.50
492	Danny Bautista	.25
493	Junior Spivey	.25
494	Matt Williams	.25
495	Miguel Batista	.25
496	Tony Womack	.25
497	Byung-Hyun Kim	.25
498	Steve Finley	.25
499	Craig Counsell	.25
500	Curt Schilling	.50
501	Elmer Dessens	.25
502	Rod Barajas	.25
503	David Dellucci	.25
504	Mike Koplove	.25
505	Mike Myers	.25
506	Matt Mantei	.25
507	*Stephen Randolph*	.40
508	Chad Moeller	.25
509	Carlos Baerga	.25
510	Andrew Good	.25
511	Quinton McCracken	.25
512	Jason Romano	.25
513	Jolbert Cabrera	.25
514	Darren Dreifort	.25
515	Kevin Brown	.40
516	Paul Quantrill	.25
517	Shawn Green	.40
518	Hideo Nomo	.40
519	Eric Gagne	.25
520	Troy Brohawn	.25
521	Kazuhisa Ishii	.25
522	Guillermo Mota	.25
523	Alex Cora	.25
524	Odalis Perez	.25
525	Brian Jordan	.25
526	Andy Ashby	.25
527	Fred McGriff	.40
528	Adrian Beltre	.40
529	Daryle Ward	.25
530	Todd Hundley	.25
531	David Ross	.25
532	Paul Shuey	.25
533	Paul LoDuca	.25
534	Dave Roberts	.25
535	Mike Kinkade	.25
536	Cesar Izturis	.25
537	Ron Coomer	.25
538	Jose Vidro	.25
539	Henry Mateo	.25
540	Tony Armas Jr.	.25
541	Joey Eischen	.25
542	Orlando Cabrera	.25
543	Jose Macias	.25
544	Fernando Tatis	.25
545	Jeff Liefer	.25
546	Michael Barrett	.25
547	Vladimir Guerrero	.75
548	Javier Vazquez	.25
549	Brad Wilkerson	.25
550	Zach Day	.25
551	Tomokazu Ohka	.25
552	Livan Hernandez	.25
553	Endy Chavez	.25
554	Dan Smith	.25
555	Scott Stewart	.25
556	T.J. Tucker	.25
557	Jamey Carroll	.25
558	Ron Calloway	.25
559	Brian Schneider	.25
560	Orlando Hernandez	.25
561	Wil Cordero	.25
562	Rocky Biddle	.25
563	Edgardo Alfonzo	.25
564	Andres Galarraga	.25
565	Felix Rodriguez	.25
566	Benito Santiago	.25
567	Jose Cruz	.25
568	Tim Worrell	.25
569	Marvin Benard	.25
570	Kurt Ainsworth	.25
571	Jim Brower	.25
572	J.T. Snow	.25
573	Scott Eyre	.25
574	Robb Nen	.25
575	Barry Bonds	2.50
576	Ray Durham	.25
577	Marquis Grissom	.25
578	Pedro Feliz	.25
579	Jason Schmidt	.25
580	Rich Aurilia	.25
581	Kirk Rueter	.25
582	Chad Zerbe	.25
583	Damian Moss	.25
584	Neifi Perez	.25
585	Joe Nathan	.25
586	Ruben Rivera	.25
587	Yorvit Torrealba	.25
588	Josh Beckett	.50
589	Todd Hollandsworth	.25
590	Derrek Lee	.25
591	A.J. Burnett	.25
592	Juan Pierre	.25
593	Mark Redman	.25
594	Blaine Neal	.25
595	Mike Mordecai	.25
596	Alex Gonzalez	.25
597	Brad Penny	.25
598	Tim Spooneybarger	.25
599	Mike Lowell	.25
600	Mike Redmond	.25
601	Braden Looper	.25
602	Ivan Rodriguez	.50
603	Andy Fox	.25
604	Vladimir Nunez	.25
605	Luis Castillo	.25
606	Juan Encarnacion	.25
607	Armando Almanza	.25
608	Gerald Williams	.25
609	Carl Pavano	.25
610	Michael Tejera	.25
611	Ramon Castro	.25
612	Brian Banks	.25
613	Roberto Alomar	.50
614	Al Leiter	.25
615	Jeromy Burnitz	.25
616	John Franco	.25
617	Tom Glavine	.40
618	Mike Piazza	1.00
619	Cliff Floyd	.25
620	Joe McEwing	.25
621	David Weathers	.25
622	Pedro Astacio	.25
623	Timoniel Perez	.25
624	Jason Phillips	.25
625	Ty Wigginton	.25
626	Steve Trachsel	.25
627	Roger Cedeno	.25
628	Tsuyoshi Shinjo	.25
629	Armando Benitez	.25
630	Vance Wilson	.25
631	Mike Stanton	.25
632	Mo Vaughn	.25
633	Scott Strickland	.25
634	Rey Sanchez	.25
635	Jay Bell	.25
636	David Cone	.25
637	Jae Weong So	.25
638	Ryan Klesko	.40
639	Wiki Gonzalez	.25
640	Trevor Hoffman	.25
641	Sean Burroughs	.25
642	Mike Bynum	.25
643	Clay Condrey	.25
644	Gary Bennett	.25
645	Kevin Jarvis	.25
646	Mark Kotsay	.25
647	Phil Nevin	.25
648	Dave Hansen	.25
649	Keith Lockhart	.25
650	Brian Lawrence	.25
651	Jay Witasick	.25
652	Rondell White	.25
653	Jaret Wright	.25
654	Luther Hackman	.25
655	Jake Peavy	.25
656	Brian Buchanan	.25
657	Mark Loretta	.25
658	Oliver Perez	.25
659	Adam Eaton	.25
660	Xavier Nady	.25
661	Jesse Orosco	.25
662	Ramon Vazquez	.25
663	Jim Thome	.75
664	Jose Mesa	.25
665	Rheal Cormier	.25
666	David Bell	.25
667	Mike Lieberthal	.25
668	Brandon Duckworth	.25
669	David Coggin	.25
670	Bobby Abreu	.40
671	Turk Wendell	.25
672	Marlon Byrd	.25
673	Jason Michaels	.25
674	Kevin Millwood	.40
675	Tomas Perez	.25
676	Jimmy Rollins	.25
677	Vicente Padilla	.25
678	Pat Burrell	.50
679	Tyler Houston	.25
680	Hector Mercado	.25
681	Carlos Silva	.25
682	Nick Punto	.25
683	Ricky Ledee	.25
684	Randy Wolf	.25
685	Todd Pratt	.25
686	Placido Polanco	.25
687	Chase Utley	.25
688	Brian Giles	.25
689	Jason Kendall	.40
690	Matt Stairs	.25
691	Kris Benson	.25
692	Julian Tavarez	.25
693	Reggie Sanders	.25
694	Jeff D'Amico	.25
695	Pokey Reese	.25
696	Kenny Lofton	.25
697	Mike Williams	.25
698	David Williams	.25
699	Kevin Young	.25
700	Brian Boehringer	.25
701	Scott Sauerbeck	.25
702	Josh Fogg	.25
703	Joe Beimel	.25
704	Dennys Reyes	.25
705	Jeff Suppan	.25
706	Solomon Torres	.25
707	Kip Wells	.25
708	Craig Wilson	.25
709	Jack Wilson	.25
710	Robert Mackowiak	.25
711	Abraham Nunez	.25
712	Randall Simon	.25
713	Josias Manzanillo	.25
714	Ken Griffey Jr.	1.00
715	Jimmy Haynes	.25
716	Felipe Lopez	.25
717	Jimmy Anderson	.25
718	Ryan Dempster	.25
719	Russell Branyan	.25
720	Aaron Boone	.25
721	Luke Prokopec	.25
722	Felix Heredia	.25
723	Scott Sullivan	.25
724	Danny Graves	.25
725	Kent Mercker	.25
726	Barry Larkin	.40
727	Jason LaRue	.25
728	Gabe White	.25
729	Adam Dunn	.50
730	Brandon Larson	.25
731	Reggie Taylor	.25
732	Sean Casey	.25
733	Scott Williamson	.25
734	Austin Kearns	.50
735	Kelly Stinnett	.25
736	Ruben Mateo	.25
737	Wily Mo Pena	.25
738	Larry Walker	.40
439	Juan Uribe	.25
740	Denny Neagle	.25
741	Darren Oliver	.25
742	Charles Johnson	.25
743	Todd Jones	.25
744	Todd Helton	.75
745	Shawn Chacon	.25
746	Jason Jennings	.25
747	Preston Wilson	.25
748	Chris Richard	.25
749	Chris Stynes	.25
750	Jose Jimenez	.25
751	Gabe Kapler	.25
752	Jay Payton	.25
753	Aaron Cook	.25
754	Greg Norton	.25
755	Scott Elarton	.25
756	Brian Fuentes	.25
757	Jose Hernandez	.25
758	Nelson Cruz	.25
759	Justin Speier	.25
760	Javier Lopez	.40
761	Garret Anderson	.40
762	Tony Batista	.25
763	Mark Buehrle	.25
764	Johnny Damon	.40
765	Freddy Garcia	.25
766	Nomar Garciaparra	.75
767	Jason Giambi	.50
768	Roy Halladay	.25
769	Shea Hillenbrand	.25
770	Torii Hunter	.40
771	Derek Jeter	1.00
772	Paul Konerko	.25

773 Derek Lowe .25
774 Pedro J. Martinez .50
775 A.J. Pierzynski .25
776 Jorge Posada .40
777 Manny Ramirez .40
778 Mariano Rivera .25
779 Alex Rodriguez 1.00
780 Kazuhiro Sasaki .25
781 Alfonso Soriano .50
782 Ichiro Suzuki .50
783 Mike Sweeney .25
784 Miguel Tejada .40
785 Ugueth Urbina .25
786 Robin Ventura .25
787 Omar Vizquel .25
788 Randy Winn .25
789 Barry Zito .40
790 Lance Berkman .25
791 Barry Bonds 1.00
792 Adam Dunn .40
793 Tom Glavine .25
794 Luis Gonzalez .25
795 Shawn Green .25
796 Vladimir Guerrero .40
797 Todd Helton .40
798 Trevor Hoffman .25
799 Randy Johnson .50
800 Andruw Jones .40
801 Byung-Hyun Kim .25
802 Mike Lowell .25
803 Eric Gagne .25
804 Matt Morris .25
805 Robb Nen .25
806 Vicente Padilla .25
807 Odalis Perez .25
808 Mike Piazza .50
809 Mike Remlinger .25
810 Scott Rolen .40
811 Jimmy Rollins .25
812 Benito Santiago .25
813 Curt Schilling .40
814 Richie Sexson .40
815 John Smoltz .25
816 Sammy Sosa .75
817 Junior Spivey .25
818 Jose Vidro .25
819 Mike Williams .25
820 Luis Castillo .25
821 Jason Giambi .40
822 Luis Gonzalez .25
823 Sammy Sosa .75
824 Ken Griffey Jr. .75
825 Ken Griffey Jr. .75
826 Tino Martinez .25
827 Barry Bonds 1.00
828 Frank Thomas .40
829 Ken Griffey Jr. .75
830 Barry Bonds 1.00
831 Tim Salmon .25
832 Troy Glaus .25
833 Robb Nen .25
834 Jeff Kent .25
835 Scott Spiezio .25
836 Darin Erstad .25
837 Randy Johnson .50
838 Chipper Jones .50
839 Greg Maddux .75
840 Nomar Garciaparra .75
841 Manny Ramirez .40
842 Pedro J. Martinez .50
843 Sammy Sosa .75
844 Ken Griffey Jr. .75
845 Jim Thome .40
846 Vladimir Guerrero .50
847 Mike Piazza .50
848 Derek Jeter 1.00
849 Jason Giambi .40
850 Roger Clemens 1.00
851 Alfonso Soriano .50
852 Hideki Matsui 4.00
853 Barry Bonds 1.00
854 Ichiro Suzuki .50
855 Albert Pujols .75
856 Alex Rodriguez .75
857 Darin Erstad .25
858 Troy Glaus .25
859 Curt Schilling .25
860 Luis Gonzalez .25
861 Tom Glavine .25
862 Andruw Jones .40
863 Gary Sheffield .25
864 Frank Thomas .40
865 Mark Prior 1.00
866 Ivan Rodriguez .40
867 Jeff Bagwell .40
868 Lance Berkman .25
869 Shawn Green .25
870 Hideo Nomo .40
871 Torii Hunter .25
872 Bernie Williams .25
873 Barry Zito .25
874 Pat Burrell .25
875 Carlos Delgado .25
876 Miguel Tejada .25
877 *Hideki Matsui* 4.00
878 *Jose Contreras* 2.00
879 Jason Anderson .40
880 *Jason Shiell* .40
881 *Kevin Tolar* .40
882 *Michel Hernandez* .40
883 *Arnie Munoz* .40
884 *David Sanders* .40
885 *Willie Eyre* .40
886 *Brent Hoard* .40
887 *Lew Ford* 2.00
888 *Beau Kemp* .75
889 *Jonathan Pridie* .40
890 *Mike Ryan* .40
891 *Richard Fischer* .40
892 *Luis Ayala* .40
893 *Mike Neu* .40
894 *Joe Valentine* .40
895 *Nate Bland* .40
896 *Shane Bazzell* .75
897 *Aquilino Lopez* .40
898 *Diegomar Markwell* .40
899 *Francisco Rosario* .40
900 *Guillermo Quiroz* .75
901 Luis De Los Santos .40
902 *Fernando Cabrera* .40
903 *Francisco Cruceta* .40
904 Jhonny Peralta .50
905 *Rett Johnson* .50
906 *Aaron Looper* .40
907 *Bobby Madritsch* .40
908 Luis Matos .40
909 Jose Castillo .25
910 *Chris Waters* .40
911 Jeremy Guthrie .25
912 Pedro Liriano .25
913 Joe Borowski .25
914 *Felix Sanchez* .40
915 *Jon Leicester* .40
916 *Todd Wellemeyer* .75
917 *Matt Bruback* .25
918 *Chris Capuano* .50
919 *Oscar Villarreal* .25
920 *Matt Kata* .75
921 *Robby Hammock* .75
922 Gerald Laird .25
923 *Brandon Webb* 3.00
924 *Tommy Whiteman* .40
925 *Andrew Brown* .40
926 *Alfredo Gonzalez* .40
927 Carlos Rivera .25
928 *Rick Roberts* .40
929 *Terrmel Sledge* .40
930 *Josh Willingham* .40
931 *Prentice Redman* .50
932 *Jeff Duncan* 1.50
933 *Craig Brazell* 1.00
934 Jeremy Griffiths .25
935 *Phil Seibel* .40
936 *Heath Bell* .40
937 *Bernie Castro* .40
938 *Mike Nicolas* .40
939 *Cory Stewart* .40
940 *Shane Victorino* .40
941 *Brandon Villafuerte* .40
942 *Jeremy Wedel* .40
943 Tommy Phelps .25
944 *Josh Hall* .75
945 *Ryan Cameron* .40
946 Garrett Atkins .25
947 *Clint Barmes* .75
948 *Michael Hessman* .40
949 *Brian Stokes* .40
950 Rocco Baldelli 1.00
951 Hector Luna .25
952 Jaime Cerda .25
953 *D.J. Carrasco* .40
954 *Ian Ferguson* .40
955 *Tim Olson* .75
956 *Alejandro Machado* .40
957 *Jorge Cordova* .40
958 *Wilfredo Ledezma* .40
959 *Nathan Robertson* .40
960 *Nook Logan* .40
961 Anaheim Angels .25
962 Baltimore Orioles .25
963 Boston Red Sox .25
964 Chicago White Sox .25
965 Cleveland Indians .25
966 Detroit Tigers .25
967 Kansas City Royals .25
968 Minnesota Twins .25
969 New York Yankees .25
970 Oakland Athletics .25
971 Seattle Mariners .25
972 Tampa Bay Devil Rays .25
973 Texas Rangers .25
974 Toronto Blue Jays .25
975 Arizona Diamondbacks .25
976 Atlanta Braves .25
977 Chicago Cubs .25
978 Cincinnati Reds .25
979 Colorado Rockies .25
980 Florida Marlins .25
981 Houston Astros .25
982 Los Angeles Dodgers .25
983 Milwaukee Brewers .25
984 Montreal Expos .25
985 New York Mets .25
986 Philadelphia Phillies .25
987 Pittsburgh Pirates .25
988 San Diego Padres .25
989 San Francisco Giants .25
990 St. Louis Cardinals .25

Rainbow

Stars (1-990): 10-20X
Rookies: 4-8X
Production 40 sets

Red, White & Blue

Stars (1-990): 1-3X
Rookies: 1-2X
#'s 1-752 inserted 1:6
#'s 877-960 1:36

Endorsements

NM/M

Inserted 1:500
Some not priced due to scarcity

RA Rick Ankiel 20.00
DB Dewon Brazelton/50 15.00
BD Ben Diggins 15.00
AG Alex Graman/50 15.00
KGS Ken Griffey Sr. 15.00
HI Hansel Izquierdo/50 15.00
JL Jon Lieber 15.00
CM Corwin Malone/50 15.00
TO Tomokazu Ohka 20.00

Vintage Update

NM/M

Complete Set (61): 15.00
Common Player: .40
Inserted 1:pack

281 Tom Glavine 1.00
282 Josh Stewart .40
283 Aquilino Lopez .40
284 Horacio Ramirez .40
285 Brandon Phillips .40
286 Kirk Saarloos .40
287 Runelvys Hernandez .40
288 Hideki Matsui 5.00
289 Jeremy Bonderman 1.00
290 Russ Ortiz .40
291 Ken Harvey .40
292 Edgardo Alfonzo .40
293 Oscar Villarreal .40
294 Marlon Byrd .40
295 Josh Bard .40
296 David Cone .40
297 Mike Neu .40
298 Cliff Floyd .40
299 Travis Lee .40
300 Jeff Kent .50
301 Ron Calloway .40
302 Bartolo Colon .40
303 Jose Contreras 1.50
304 Mark Teixeira 1.00
305 Ivan Rodriguez 1.00
306 Jim Thome 1.00
307 Shane Reynolds .40
308 Luis Ayala .40
309 Lyle Overbay .40
310 Travis Hafner .40
311 Wilfredo Ledezma .40
312 Rocco Baldelli 1.50
313 Jason Anderson .40
314 Kenny Lofton .75
315 Brandon Larson .40
316 Ty Wigginton .40
317 Fred McGriff .40
318 Antonio Osuna .40
319 Corey Patterson .40
320 Erubiel Durazo .40
321 Mike MacDougal .40
322 Sammy Sosa 2.00
323 Mike Hampton .40
324 Ramiro Mendoza .40
325 Kevin Millwood .75
326 Dave Roberts .40
327 Todd Zeile .40
328 Reggie Sanders .40
329 Billy Koch .40
330 Mike Stanton .40
331 Orlando Hernandez .40
332 Tony Clark .40
333 Chris Hammond .40
334 Michael Cuddyer .40
335 Sandy Alomar .40
336 Jose Cruz Jr. .40
337 Omar Daal .40
338 Robert Fick .40
339 Daryle Ward .40
340 David Bell .40
341 Checklist .40

2003 UD YANKEES SIGNATURE SERIES

NM/M

Complete Set (90): 65.00
Common Player: .50
Pack (3): 17.00
Box (10): 140.00

1 Al Downing .50
2 Allen Gettel .50
3 Art Ditmar .50
4 Babe Ruth 6.00
5 Bill Virdon .50
6 Billy Martin 2.00
7 Bob Cerv .50
8 Bob Turley .50
9 Bobby Cox .75
10 Bobby Richardson 1.00
11 Bobby Shantz .50
12 Bucky Dent .75
13 Bud Metheny .50
14 Casey Stengel 2.00
15 Charlie Hayes .50
16 Charlie Silvera .50
17 Chris Chambliss .50
18 Danny Cater .50
19 Dave Kingman .75
20 Dave Righetti .75
21 Dave Winfield 2.00
22 David Cone .75
23 Dick Tidrow .50
24 Doc Medich .50
25 Dock Ellis .50
26 Don Gullett .50
27 Don Mattingly 5.00
28 Dwight Gooden .75
29 Eddie Robinson .50
30 Felipe Alou .50
31 Fred Sanford .50
32 Fred Stanley .50
33 Gene Michael .50
34 Hank Bauer .50
35 Hector Lopez .50
36 Horace Clarke .50
37 Jake Gibbs .50
38 Jerry Coleman .50
39 Jerry Lumpe .50
40 Jim Bouton .50
41 Jim Kaat 1.00
42 Jim Mason .50
43 Jimmy Key .50
44 Joe DiMaggio 5.00
45 Joe Torre 1.00
46 John Montefusco .50
47 Johnny Blanchard .50
48 Johnny Callison .50
49 Lew Burdette .50
50 Johnny Kucks .50
51 Steve Balboni .50
52 Ken Singleton .50
53 Lee Mazzilli .50
54 Lou Gehrig 5.00
55 Lou Piniella 1.00
56 Luis Tiant .50
57 Marius Russo .50
58 Mel Stottlemyre .75
59 Mickey Mantle 6.00
60 Mike Pagliarulo .50

61 Mike Torrez .50
62 Miller Huggins .50
63 Norm Siebern .50
64 Paul O'Neill .75
65 Phil Niekro .50
66 Phil Rizzuto 3.00
67 Ralph Branca .50
68 Ralph Houk .50
69 Ralph Terry .50
70 Randy Gumpert .50
71 Roger Maris 5.00
72 Ron Blomberg .50
73 Ron Guidry 1.00
74 Ruben Amaro .50
75 Ryne Duren .50
76 Sam McDowell .50
77 Sparky Lyle .50
78 Thurman Munson 3.00
79 Tom Sturdivant .50
80 Tom Tresh .50
81 Tommy Byrne .50
82 Tommy Henrich .50
83 Tommy John .75
84 Tony Kubek .75
85 Tony Lazzeri .50
86 Virgil Trucks .50
87 Wade Boggs 1.00
88 Whitey Ford 3.00
89 Willie Randolph .75
90 Yogi Berra 3.00

Monumental Cuts

NM/M

30 total cards produced:
MC-JD Joe DiMaggio/4
MC-LG Lou Gehrig/1
(6/03 auction) 17,600
MC-MH Miller Huggins/2
MC-TL Tony Lazzeri/2
MC-MM Mickey Mantle/1
(1/04 auction) 10,000
MC-RM Roger Maris/6
MC-BM Billy Martin/9 825.00
MC-TM Thurman Munson/1
(3/04 auction) 2,605
MC-BR Babe Ruth/1
(4/04 auction) 12,600
MC-CS Casey Stengel/3

Pinstripe Excell. Dual

NM/M

Common Dual Autograph: 20.00
Some not priced yet
Production 125 sets
AA Felipe Alou, Ruben Amaro 50.00
BA Hank Bauer, Felipe Alou 50.00
BP Wade Boggs, Mike Pagliarulo 60.00
BT Jim Bouton, Ralph Terry 50.00
CK Chris Chambliss, Dave Kingman 60.00
DC Bucky Dent, Chris Chambliss 50.00
DR Bucky Dent, Willie Randolph 80.00
DS Ryne Duren, Tom Sturdivant 35.00
FB Whitey Ford, Yogi Berra 150.00
GB Jake Gibbs, Johnny Blanchard 40.00
GM Ron Guidry, John Montefusco 80.00
GR Ron Guidry, Willie Randolph 80.00
JK Tommy John, Jim Kaat 60.00
LG Sparky Lyle, Ron Guidry 75.00
LM Jerry Lumpe, Jim Mason 25.00
MC John Montefusco, Chris Chambliss 60.00
MK Gene Michael, Tony Kubek 60.00
ML Sam McDowell, Sparky Lyle 50.00
MR Don Mattingly, Dave Righetti 150.00
NT Phil Niekro, Luis Tiant 50.00
RB Bobby Richardson, Hank Bauer 75.00
RC Bobby Richardson, Jerry Coleman 50.00
SC Ken Singleton, Jerry Coleman 60.00
ST Tom Sturdivant, Bob Turley 40.00
TK Luis Tiant, Jim Kaat 60.00
TM Mike Torrez, Lee Mazzilli 50.00
BRi Hank Bauer, Phil Rizzuto 75.00
BRu Tommy Byrne, Marius Russo 30.00

Pride of New York Auto.

NM/M

Common Autograph: 8.00
Inserted 1:1
JA Jason Alexander SP 600.00
FA Felipe Alou 15.00
RA Ruben Amaro 8.00
SB Steve Balboni 8.00
HB Hank Bauer 10.00
YB Yogi Berra 85.00
BL Johnny Blanchard 15.00
RBl Ron Blomberg 10.00
WB Wade Boggs 40.00
JB Jim Bouton 10.00
RBr Ralph Branca 8.00
LB Lew Burdette 10.00
TB Tommy Byrne 10.00
CAS Johnny Callison 8.00
TC Tom Carroll 8.00
CAL Brian Cashman SP 250.00
DC Danny Cater 8.00
CE Bob Cerv 8.00
CC Chris Chambliss 12.00
HC Horace Clarke 10.00
JC Jerry Coleman 10.00
CO David Cone 25.00
CX Bobby Cox 12.00
DE Bucky Dent 12.00
DI Art Ditmar 10.00
AD Al Downing 8.00
BD Brian Doyle 8.00
RD Ryne Duren 10.00
EL Dock Ellis 10.00
WF Whitey Ford 50.00
AG Allen Gettel 8.00
JG Jake Gibbs 8.00
GO Dwight Gooden 15.00
JO John Goodman 300.00
RaG Ron Guidry 15.00
DG Don Gullett 8.00
RoG Randy Gumpert 8.00
CH Charlie Hayes 10.00
TH Tommy Henrich 30.00
RH Ralph Houk 12.00
TJ Tommy John 10.00
JK Jim Kaat 15.00
KE Jimmy Key 15.00
DK Dave Kingman 15.00
TK Tony Kubek 25.00
KU Johnny Kucks 10.00
HL Hector Lopez 10.00
JL Jerry Lumpe 8.00
SL Sparky Lyle 10.00
JM Jim Mason 8.00
MA Don Mattingly 80.00
LM Lee Mazzilli 10.00
SM Sam McDowell 8.00
DM Doc Medich 8.00
BM Bud Metheny
GM Gene Michael 10.00
MO John Montefusco 8.00
PN Phil Niekro 15.00
PO Paul O'Neill SP 25.00
MP Mike Pagliarulo 8.00
LP Lou Piniella SP 20.00
WR Willie Randolph SP 15.00
HR Hal Reniff 10.00
BR Bobby Richardson 15.00
DR Dave Righetti 15.00
PR Phil Rizzuto 40.00
ER Eddie Robinson 8.00
MR Marius Russo 10.00
FS Fred Sanford 8.00
BS Bobby Shantz 10.00
NS Norm Siebern 8.00
CS Charlie Silvera 10.00
KS Ken Singleton 10.00
ST Fred Stanley 8.00
MS Mel Stottlemyre 15.00
TS Tom Sturdivant 8.00
RT Ralph Terry 10.00
LT Luis Tiant 10.00
DT Dick Tidrow 10.00
JT Joe Torre 35.00
MT Mike Torrez 8.00
TT Tom Tresh 15.00
VT Virgil Trucks 10.00
BT Bob Turley 12.00
BV Bill Virdon 8.00
DW Dave Winfield SP 75.00
JW Jim Wynn 8.00
DZ Don Zimmer 40.00

Yankees Forever Triple

NM/M

Common Triple Auto.:
Production 50 sets
ALB Felipe Alou, Hector Lopez, Hank Bauer 120.00
AOM Felipe Alou, Paul O'Neill, Lee Mazzilli 150.00
BSB Yogi Berra, Bobby Shantz, Hank Bauer 200.00
DFB Al Downing, Whitey Ford, Yogi Berra 240.00
DRC Bucky Dent, Willie Randolph, Chris Chambliss 125.00
EMG Dock Ellis, Doc Medich, Don Gullett 125.00
FKB Whitey Ford, Johnny Kucks, Jim Bouton 150.00
GCK Dwight Gooden, David Cone, Jimmy Key 150.00
GRJ Ron Guidry, Dave Righetti, Tommy John 150.00
HMC Ralph Houk, Gene Michael, Bobby Cox 120.00
HRB Tommy Henrich, Phil Rizzuto, Ralph Branca 150.00
JKL Tommy John, Jim Kaat, Sparky Lyle 120.00
KCC Dave Kingman, Chris Chambliss, Danny Cater 120.00
KGT Jim Kaat, Don Gullett, Mike Torrez 120.00
KJB Jim Kaat, Tommy John, Jim Bouton 120.00
MTT John Montefusco, Mike Torrez, Dick Tidrow 120.00
OBK Paul O'Neill, Wade Boggs, Jimmy Key 175.00
PTV Lou Piniella, Joe Torre, Bill Virdon 150.00
RBC Phil Rizzuto, Yogi Berra, Jerry Coleman 220.00
RKD Phil Rizzuto, Tony Kubek, Bucky Dent 150.00
RRC Bobby Richardson, Willie Randolph, Jerry Coleman 150.00
RSB Marius Russo, Tom Sturdivant, Tommy Byrne 120.00
SSB Fred Stanley, Charlie Silvera, Johnny Blanchard 120.00
STE Mel Stottlemyre, Luis Tiant, Dock Ellis 120.00
TCO Joe Torre, David Cone, Paul O'Neill 175.00
TLN Luis Tiant, Sparky Lyle, Phil Niekro 120.00
TMT Luis Tiant, Sam McDowell, Ralph Terry 120.00
WHM Dave Winfield, Tommy Henrich, Lee Mazzilli 160.00
WMG Dave Winfield, Don Mattingly, Ron Guidry 300.00
WPC Dave Winfield, Lou Piniella, Chris Chambliss 100.00

2004 UPPER DECK

NM/M

Complete Set (540): 75.00
Common Player: .15
Hobby Pack (8): 2.00
Hobby Box (24): 40.00
1 Dontrelle Willis .40
2 Edgar Gonzalez .15
3 Jose Reyes .25
4 Jae Weong Seo .15
5 Miguel Cabrera .25
6 Jesse Foppert .15
7 Mike Neu .15
8 Micheal Nakamura .15
9 Luis Ayala .15
10 Jared Sandberg .15
11 Jhonny Peralta .15
12 Wilfredo Ledezma .15
13 Jason Roach .15
14 Kirk Saarloos .15
15 Cliff Lee .15
16 Bobby Hill .15
17 Lyle Overbay .15
18 Josh Hall .15
19 Joe Thurston .15
20 Matt Kata .15
21 Jeremy Bonderman .15
22 Julio Manon .15
23 Rodrigo Rosario .15
24 Robby Hammock .15
25 David Sanders .15
26 Miguel Ojeda .15
27 Mark Teixeira .25
28 Franklyn German .15
29 Ken Harvey .15
30 Xavier Nady .15
31 Tim Salmon .25
32 Troy Glaus .40
33 Adam Kennedy .15
34 David Eckstein .15
35 Bengie Molina .15
36 Jarrod Washburn .15
37 Ramon Ortiz .15
38 Eric Chavez .25
39 Miguel Tejada .25
40 Chris Singleton .15
41 Jermaine Dye .15
42 John Halama .15
43 Tim Hudson .40
44 Barry Zito .40
45 Ted Lilly .15
46 Bobby Kielty .15
47 Kelvim Escobar .15
48 Josh Phelps .15
49 Vernon Wells .25
50 Roy Halladay .25
51 Orlando Hudson .15
52 Eric Hinske .15
53 Brandon Backe .15
54 Dewon Brazelton .15
55 Ben Grieve .15
56 Aubrey Huff .15
57 Toby Hall .15
58 Rocco Baldelli .40
59 Al Martin .15
60 Brandon Phillips .15
61 Omar Vizquel .25
62 C.C. Sabathia .15
63 Milton Bradley .15

#	Player	Value
64	Ricky Gutierrez	.15
65	Matt Lawton	.15
66	Danys Baez	.15
67	Ichiro Suzuki	1.00
68	Randy Winn	.15
69	Carlos Guillen	.15
70	Mark McLemore	.15
71	Dan Wilson	.15
72	Jamie Moyer	.15
73	Joel Pineiro	.15
74	Edgar Martinez	.25
75	Tony Batista	.15
76	Jay Gibbons	.15
77	Jeff Conine	.15
78	Melvin Mora	.15
79	Geronimo Gil	.15
80	Rodrigo Lopez	.15
81	Jorge Julio	.15
82	Rafael Palmeiro	.50
83	Juan Gonzalez	.40
84	Mike Young	.15
85	Alex Rodriguez	1.50
86	Einar Diaz	.15
87	Kevin Mench	.15
88	Hank Blalock	.40
89	Pedro J. Martinez	.75
90	Byung-Hyun Kim	.15
91	Derek Lowe	.25
92	Jason Varitek	.15
93	Manny Ramirez	.50
94	John Burkett	.15
95	Todd Walker	.15
96	Nomar Garciaparra	1.50
97	Trot Nixon	.15
98	Mike Sweeney	.15
99	Carlos Febles	.15
100	Mike MacDougal	.15
101	Raul Ibanez	.15
102	Jason Grimsley	.15
103	Chris George	.15
104	Brent Mayne	.15
105	Dmitri Young	.15
106	Eric Munson	.15
107	A.J. Hinch	.15
108	Andres Torres	.15
109	Bobby Higginson	.15
110	Shane Halter	.15
111	Matt Walbeck	.15
112	Torii Hunter	.40
113	Doug Mientkiewicz	.15
114	Lew Ford	.15
115	Eric Milton	.15
116	Eddie Guardado	.15
117	Cristian Guzman	.15
118	Corey Koskie	.15
119	Maggilo Ordonez	.40
120	Mark Buehrle	.15
121	Billy Koch	.15
122	Jose Valentin	.15
123	Paul Konerko	.15
124	Carlos Lee	.15
125	Jon Garland	.15
126	Jason Giambi	.75
127	Derek Jeter	1.50
128	Roger Clemens	1.50
129	Andy Pettitte	.40
130	Jorge Posada	.40
131	David Wells	.15
132	Hideki Matsui	1.50
133	Mike Mussina	.50
134	Jeff Bagwell	.50
135	Craig Biggio	.25
136	Morgan Ensberg	.15
137	Richard Hidalgo	.15
138	Brad Ausmus	.15
139	Roy Oswalt	.25
140	Billy Wagner	.25
141	Octavio Dotel	.15
142	Gary Sheffield	.40
143	Andruw Jones	.40
144	John Smoltz	.25
145	Rafael Furcal	.25
146	Javy Lopez	.25
147	Shane Reynolds	.15
148	Horacio Ramirez	.15
149	Mike Hampton	.15
150	Jung Bong	.15
151	Ruben Quevedo	.15
152	Ben Sheets	.15
153	Geoff Jenkins	.25
154	Royce Clayton	.15
155	Glendon Rusch	.15
156	John Vander Wal	.15
157	Scott Podsednik	.40
158	Jim Edmonds	.40
159	Tino Martinez	.15
160	Albert Pujols	1.50
161	Matt Morris	.15
162	Woody Williams	.15

#	Player	Value
163	Edgar Renteria	.15
164	Jason Isringhausen	.15
165	Jason Simontacchi	.15
166	Kerry Robinson	.15
167	Sammy Sosa	1.25
168	Joe Borowski	.15
169	Tony Womack	.15
170	Antonio Alfonseca	.15
171	Corey Patterson	.15
172	Mark Prior	1.50
173	Moises Alou	.25
174	Matt Clement	.15
175	Randall Simon	.15
176	Randy Johnson	.75
177	Luis Gonzalez	.25
178	Craig Counsell	.15
179	Miguel Batista	.15
180	Steve Finley	.15
181	Brandon Webb	.15
182	Danny Bautista	.15
183	Oscar Villarreal	.15
184	Shawn Green	.25
185	Brian Jordan	.15
186	Fred McGriff	.25
187	Andy Ashby	.15
188	Rickey Henderson	.50
189	Dave Roberts	.15
190	Eric Gagne	.15
191	Kazuhisa Ishii	.15
192	Adrian Beltre	.15
193	Vladimir Guerrero	.75
194	Livan Hernandez	.15
195	Ron Calloway	.15
196	Sun-Woo Kim	.15
197	Wil Cordero	.15
198	Brad Wilkerson	.15
199	Orlando Cabrera	.15
200	Barry Bonds	2.00
201	Ray Durham	.15
202	Andres Galarraga	.15
203	Benito Santiago	.15
204	Jose Cruz Jr.	.15
205	Jason Schmidt	.15
206	Kirk Rueter	.15
207	Felix Rodriguez	.15
208	Mike Lowell	.15
209	Luis Castillo	.15
210	Derrek Lee	.25
211	Andy Fox	.15
212	Tommy Phelps	.15
213	Todd Hollandsworth	.15
214	Brad Penny	.15
215	Juan Pierre	.15
216	Mike Piazza	1.00
217	Jae Weong Seo	.15
218	Ty Wigginton	.15
219	Al Leiter	.15
220	Roger Cedeno	.15
221	Timoniel Perez	.15
222	Aaron Heilman	.15
223	Pedro Astacio	.15
224	Joe McEwing	.15
225	Ryan Klesko	.15
226	Brian Giles	.25
227	Mark Kotsay	.15
228	Brian Lawrence	.15
229	Rod Beck	.15
230	Trevor Hoffman	.15
231	Sean Burroughs	.15
232	Bobby Abreu	.25
233	Jim Thome	.50
234	David Bell	.15
235	Jimmy Rollins	.15
236	Mike Lieberthal	.15
237	Vicente Padilla	.15
238	Randy Wolf	.15
239	Reggie Sanders	.15
240	Jason Kendall	.15
241	Jack Wilson	.15
242	Jose Hernandez	.15
243	Kip Wells	.15
244	Carlos Rivera	.15
245	Craig Wilson	.15
246	Adam Dunn	.40
247	Sean Casey	.15
248	Danny Graves	.15
249	Ryan Dempster	.15
250	Barry Larkin	.40
251	Reggie Taylor	.15
252	Wily Mo Pena	.15
253	Larry Walker	.25
254	Mark Sweeney	.15
255	Preston Wilson	.15
256	Jason Jennings	.15
257	Charles Johnson	.15
258	Jay Payton	.15
259	Chris Stynes	.15
260	Juan Uribe	.15
261	Hideki Matsui	1.00

#	Player	Value
262	Barry Bonds	1.00
263	Dontrelle Willis	.25
264	Kevin Millwood	.15
265	Billy Wagner	.15
266	Rocco Baldelli	.25
267	Roger Clemens	.75
268	Rafael Palmeiro	.25
269	Miguel Cabrera	.25
270	Jose Contreras	.15
271	Aaron Sele	.15
272	Bartolo Colon	.25
273	Darin Erstad	.25
274	Francisco Rodriguez	.15
275	Garret Anderson	.40
276	Jose Guillen	.15
277	Troy Percival	.15
278	Alex Cintron	.15
279	Casey Fossum	.15
280	Elmer Dessens	.15
281	Jose Valverde	.15
282	Matt Mantei	.15
283	Richie Sexson	.40
284	Roberto Alomar	.40
285	Shea Hillenbrand	.15
286	Chipper Jones	.75
287	Greg Maddux	1.00
288	J.D. Drew	.25
289	Marcus Giles	.15
290	Mike Hessman	.15
291	John Thomson	.15
292	Russ Ortiz	.15
293	Adam Loewen	.15
294	Jack Cust	.15
295	Jerry Hairston	.15
296	Kurt Ainsworth	.15
297	Luis Matos	.15
298	Marty Cordova	.15
299	Sidney Ponson	.15
300	Bill Mueller	.15
301	Curt Schilling	.50
302	David Ortiz	.50
303	Johnny Damon	.25
304	Keith Foulke	.15
305	Pokey Reese	.15
306	Scott Williamson	.15
307	Tim Wakefield	.15
308	Alex Gonzalez	.15
309	Aramis Ramirez	.40
310	Carlos Zambrano	.40
311	Juan Cruz	.15
312	Kerry Wood	.75
313	Kyle Farnsworth	.15
314	Aaron Rowand	.15
315	Esteban Loaiza	.15
316	Frank Thomas	.50
317	Joe Borchard	.15
318	Joe Crede	.15
319	Miguel Olivo	.15
320	Willie Harris	.15
321	Aaron Harang	.15
322	Austin Kearns	.25
323	Brandon Claussen	.15
324	Brandon Larson	.15
325	Ryan Freel	.15
326	Ken Griffey Jr.	1.00
327	Ryan Wagner	.15
328	Alex Escobar	.15
329	Coco Crisp	.15
330	David Riske	.15
331	Jody Gerut	.15
332	Josh Bard	.15
333	Travis Hafner	.25
334	Chin-Hui Tsao	.15
335	Denny Stark	.15
336	Jeromy Burnitz	.15
337	Shawn Chacon	.15
338	Todd Helton	.50
339	Vinny Castilla	.15
340	Alex Sanchez	.15
341	Carlos Pena	.15
342	Fernando Vina	.15
343	Jason Johnson	.15
344	Matt Anderson	.15
345	Mike Maroth	.15
346	Rondell White	.15
347	A.J. Burnett	.15
348	Alex Gonzalez	.15
349	Armando Benitez	.15
350	Carl Pavano	.15
351	Hee Seop Choi	.15
352	Ivan Rodriguez	.50
353	Josh Beckett	.50
354	Josh Willingham	.15
355	Adam Everett	.15
356	Brandon Duckworth	.15
357	Jason Lane	.15
358	Jeff Kent	.25
359	Jeriome Robertson	.15
360	Lance Berkman	.25

#	Player	Value
361	Wade Miller	.15
362	Aaron Guiel	.15
363	Angel Berroa	.15
364	Carlos Beltran	.50
365	David DeJesus	.15
366	Desi Relaford	.15
367	Joe Randa	.15
368	Runelvys Hernandez	.15
369	Edwin Jackson	.15
370	Hideo Nomo	.40
371	Jeff Weaver	.15
372	Juan Encarnacion	.15
373	Odalis Perez	.15
374	Paul LoDuca	.15
375	Robin Ventura	.15
376	Bill Hall	.15
377	Chad Moeller	.15
378	Chris Capuano	.15
379	Junior Spivey	.15
380	Rickie Weeks	.25
381	Wes Helms	.15
382	Brad Radke	.15
383	Jacque Jones	.15
384	Joe Mays	.15
385	Joe Nathan	.15
386	Johan Santana	.15
387	Nick Punto	.15
388	Shannon Stewart	.15
389	Carl Everett	.15
390	Claudio Vargas	.15
391	Jose Vidro	.15
392	Nick Johnson	.15
393	Rocky Biddle	.15
394	Tony Armas	.15
395	Braden Looper	.15
396	Cliff Floyd	.15
397	Jason Phillips	.15
398	Mike Cameron	.15
399	Tom Glavine	.40
400	Kenny Lofton	.25
401	Alfonso Soriano	.50
402	Bernie Williams	.40
403	Javier Vazquez	.15
404	Jon Lieber	.15
405	Jose Contreras	.15
406	Kevin Brown	.25
407	Mariano Rivera	.25
408	Arthur Rhodes	.15
409	Eric Byrnes	.15
410	Erubiel Durazo	.15
411	Graham Koonce	.15
412	Marco Scutaro	.15
413	Mark Mulder	.15
414	Mark Redman	.15
415	Rich Harden	.15
416	Brett Myers	.15
417	Chase Utley	.15
418	Kevin Millwood	.25
419	Marlon Byrd	.15
420	Pat Burrell	.25
421	Placido Polanco	.15
422	Tim Worrell	.15
423	Jason Bay	.15
424	Josh Fogg	.15
425	Kris Benson	.15
426	Mike Gonzalez	.15
427	Oliver Perez	.15
428	Tike Redman	.15
429	Adam Eaton	.15
430	Ismael Valdez	.15
431	Jake Peavy	.15
432	Khalil Greene	.15
433	Mark Loretta	.15
434	Phil Nevin	.15
435	Ramon Hernandez	.15
436	A.J. Pierzynski	.15
437	Edgardo Alfonzo	.15
438	J.T. Snow	.15
439	Jerome Williams	.15
440	Marquis Grissom	.15
441	Robb Nen	.15
442	Bret Boone	.25
443	Freddy Garcia	.15
444	Gil Meche	.15
445	John Olerud	.25
446	Rich Aurilia	.15
447	Shigetoshi Hasegawa	.15
448	Bo Hart	.15
449	Dan Haren	.15
450	Jason Marquis	.15
451	Marlon Anderson	.15
452	Scott Rolen	.75
453	So Taguchi	.15
454	Carl Crawford	.15
455	Delmon Young	.25
456	Geoff Blum	.15
457	Jesus Colome	.15
458	Jonny Gomes	.15
459	Lance Carter	.15

460 Robert Fick .15
461 Chan Ho Park .15
462 Francisco Cordero .15
463 Jeff Nelson .15
464 Jeff Zimmerman .15
465 Kenny Rogers .15
466 Aquilino Lopez .15
467 Carlos Delgado .50
468 Frank Catalanotto .15
469 Reed Johnson .15
470 Pat Hentgen .15
471 Curt Schilling .25
472 Gary Sheffield .25
473 Javier Vazquez .15
474 Kazuo Matsui 1.00
475 Kevin Brown .25
476 Rafael Palmeiro .25
477 Richie Sexson .25
478 Roger Clemens .75
479 Vladimir Guerrero .50
480 Alex Rodriguez 1.00
481 Jake Woods .25
482 Tim Bittner .25
483 Brandon Medders .50
484 Casey Daigle .25
485 Jerry Gil .25
486 Mike Gosling .25
487 Jose Capellan 1.00
488 Onil Joseph .25
489 Roman Colon .25
490 David Crouthers .25
491 Eddy Rodriguez .25
492 Franklyn Gracesqui .50
493 Jamie Brown .25
494 Jerome Gamble .25
495 Tim Hamulack .25
496 Carlos Vasquez .25
497 Renyel Pinto .50
498 Ronny Cedeno .25
499 Enemencio Pacheco .25
500 Ryan Meaux .25
501 Ryan Wing .25
502 Shingo Takatsu 1.00
503 William Bergolla .25
504 Ivan Ochoa .25
505 Mariano Gomez .25
506 Justin Hampson .25
507 Justin Huisman .25
508 Scott Dohmann .25
509 Donnie Kelly .50
510 Chris Aguila .25
511 *Lincoln Holdzkom* .25
512 Freddy Guzman .25
513 Hector Gimenez .25
514 Jorge Vasquez .25
515 Jason Frasor .25
516 Chris Saenz .50
517 Dennis Sarfate .25
518 Colby Miller .25
519 Jason Bartlett .25
520 Chad Bentz .25
521 Josh Labandeira .25
522 Shawn Hill .25
523 *Kazuo Matsui* 3.00
524 Carlos Hines .25
525 Michael Vento 2.00
526 Scott Proctor .50
527 Sean Henn .50
528 David Aardsma .25
529 Ian Snell .25
530 Mike Johnson .25
531 Akinori Otsuka .75
532 Rusty Tucker .25
533 Justin Knoedler .25
534 Merkin Valdez 1.00
535 Greg Dobbs .25
536 Justin Leone .25
537 Shawn Camp .25
538 Edwin Moreno .25
539 Angel Chavez .25
540 Jesse Harper .25
Reflections Update Set (50): 30.00
341 Shingo Takatsu 3.00
342 Franklyn Gracesqui .75
343 Angel Chavez .75
344 Jorge Sequea .75
345 David Aardsma .75
346 *Ramon Ramirez* .75
347 Lino Urdaneta .75
348 Orlando Rodriguez .75
349 Jason Szuminski .75
350 Luis Gonzalez .75
351 John Gall 1.00
352 Kevin Cave .75
353 Chris Oxspring .75
354 Freddy Guzman .75
355 Jeff Bennett .75
356 Jorge Vasquez .75
357 Merkin Valdez 2.00
358 Tim Hamulack .75
359 Hector Gimenez .75
360 Jerry Gil .75
361 Ryan Wing .75
362 Shawn Hill .75
363 Jason Bartlett .75
364 Renyel Pinto .75
365 Carlos Vasquez .75
366 Mike Vento 1.50
367 Casey Daigle .75
368 Chad Bentz 1.00
369 Chris Saenz .75
370 Shawn Camp .75
371 Carlos Hines .75
372 Edwin Moreno .75
373 Mike Wuertz .75
374 *Aarom Baldiris* 1.50
375 Ronny Cedeno .75
376 Akinori Otsuka 1.50
377 Jose Capellan 2.00
378 Justin Germano .75
379 Justin Knoedler .75
380 Mariano Gomez .75
381 Fernando Nieve 1.50
382 Scott Proctor .75
383 Roman Colon .75
384 Onil Joseph .75
385 Eddy Rodriguez .75
386 Enemencio Pacheco .75
387 William Bergolla .75
388 Ivan Ochoa .75
389 Rusty Tucker .75
390 Roberto Novoa .75
SPGU Patch Edition Update Set (50): 85.00
121 Richie Sexson 3.00
122 Javier Vazquez 2.00
123 Alex Rodriguez 8.00
124 Javy Lopez 3.00
125 Miguel Tejada 3.00
126 Bartolo Colon 2.00
127 Ivan Rodriguez 4.00
128 Rafael Palmeiro 3.00
129 Kevin Brown 3.00
130 Gary Sheffield 3.00
131 Greg Maddux 5.00
132 Curt Schilling 4.00
133 Roger Clemens 8.00
134 Alfonso Soriano 3.00
135 Vladimir Guerrero 4.00
136 Carlos Vasquez 2.00
137 Roman Colon 2.00
138 William Bergolla 2.00
139 Jason Bartlett 2.00
140 Casey Daigle 2.00
141 Ryan Wing 2.00
142 Chris Saenz 2.00
143 Edwin Moreno 2.00
144 Shawn Hill 2.00
145 Eddy Rodriguez 2.00
146 Justin Knoedler 2.00
147 Renyel Pinto 2.00
148 Kevin Cave 2.00
149 Carlos Hines 2.00
150 *Merkin Valdez* 4.00
151 *Tim Hamulack* 2.00
152 *Hector Gimenez* 2.00
153 *Mike Vento* 5.00
154 *Scott Proctor* 3.00
155 *Rusty Tucker* 2.00
156 *Akinori Otsuka* 4.00
157 *Ronny Cedeno* 2.00
158 *Jose Capellan* 6.00
159 Justin Germano 2.00
160 *Shingo Takatsu* 5.00
161 Fernando Nieve 2.00
162 Mike Wuertz 2.00
163 Jerry Gil 2.00
164 Jorge Vasquez 2.00
165 Chad Bentz 4.00
166 Luis Gonzalez 2.00
167 Ivan Ochoa 2.00
168 Onil Joseph 2.00
169 Enemencio Pacheco 2.00
170 *Kazuo Matsui* 8.00
Play Ball Update Set (50): 20.00
183 *Kazuo Matsui* 3.00
184 Jerry Gil .50
185 *Jose Capellan* 2.00
186 Tim Hamulack .50
187 Renyel Pinto .50
188 Carlos Vasquez .50
189 Enemencio Pacheco .50
190 Ronny Cedeno .50
191 Mariano Gomez .50
192 Carlos Hines .50
193 Michael Vento .50
194 David Aardsma .50
195 Hector Gimenez .50
196 Fernando Nieve .50
197 Chris Saenz .50
198 Shawn Hill .50
199 Angel Chavez .50
200 Scott Proctor .50
201 William Bergolla .50
202 Justin Germano .50
203 Onil Joseph .50
204 Rusty Tucker .50
205 Justin Knoedler .50
206 Casey Daigle .50
207 Edwin Moreno .50
208 Chad Bentz .50
209 Ryan Wing .50
210 Shawn Camp .50
211 Eddy Rodriguez .50
212 Roman Colon .50
213 Jason Bartlett .50
214 Jorge Vasquez .50
215 Ivan Ochoa .50
216 Akinori Otsuka .50
217 *Merkin Valdez* 2.00
218 *Shingo Takatsu* 2.00
219 Chris Oxspring .50
220 Kevin Cave .50
221 Ramon Ramirez .50
222 Orlando Rodriguez .50
223 Lino Urdaneta .50
224 Franklyn Gracesqui .50
225 Mike Wuertz .50
226 Jorge Sequea .50
227 Luis Gonzalez .50
228 Jason Szuminski .50
229 John Gall .50
230 Freddy Guzman .50
231 Jeff Bennett .50
232 Roberto Novoa .50
Vintage Update Set (50): 10.00
451 Alex Rodriguez 1.50
452 Javy Lopez .40
453 Alfonso Soriano .50
454 Vladimir Guerrero .50
455 Rafael Palmeiro .50
456 Gary Sheffield .50
457 Curt Schilling .50
458 Miguel Tejada .50
459 Kevin Brown .40
460 Richie Sexson .50
461 Roger Clemens 1.50
462 Javier Vazquez .25
463 Bartolo Colon .25
464 Ivan Rodriguez .50
465 Greg Maddux 1.00
466 Jamie Brown .25
467 David Crouthers .25
468 Jason Frasor .25
469 Greg Dobbs .25
470 Jesse Harper .25
471 *Nick Regilio* .25
472 Ryan Wing .25
473 *Akinori Otsuka* 1.00
474 *Shingo Takatsu* 1.50
475 *Kazuo Matsui* 3.00
476 *Michael Vento* 1.00
477 Mike Gosling .25
478 Justin Huisman .25
479 Justin Hampson .25
480 Dennis Sarfate .25
481 *Ian Snell* .25
482 *Tim Bausher* .25
483 Donnie Kelly .25
484 Jerome Gamble .25
485 *Mike Rouse* .50
486 *Merkin Valdez* .75
487 *Lincoln Holdzkom* .25
488 *Justin Leone* .25
489 *Sean Henn* .25
490 *Brandon Medders* .25
491 *Mike Johnston* .25
492 Tim Bittner .25
493 Mike Wuertz .25
494 Chad Bentz .50
495 *Ryan Meaux* .25
496 *Chris Aguila* .25
497 *Jake Woods* .25
498 *Scott Dohmann* .25
499 Colby Miller .25
500 Josh Labandeira .25

Glossy

NM/M
Complete Factory Set (590): 85.00
Glossy: 1-2X
Issued only in Factory Sets

Authentic Stars Jersey

NM/M
Common Player: 4.00
Inserted 1:48
Golds: 1-2X

Production 100 sets
BA Bobby Abreu 6.00
RO Roberto Alomar 6.00
JB Jeff Bagwell 6.00
RB Rocco Baldelli 10.00
JH Josh Beckett 5.00
HB Hank Blalock 5.00
EC Eric Chavez 4.00
RC Roger Clemens 15.00
CD Carlos Delgado 5.00
JD J.D. Drew 4.00
DE Darin Erstad 4.00
JG Jason Giambi 8.00
TG Troy Glaus 5.00
TL Tom Glavine 6.00
VG Vladimir Guerrero 8.00
SG Shawn Green 5.00
KG Ken Griffey Jr. 15.00
TH Todd Helton 8.00
TO Torii Hunter 6.00
RJ Randy Johnson 8.00
AJ Andruw Jones 6.00
CJ Chipper Jones 8.00
JK Jeff Kent 4.00
GM Greg Maddux 10.00
PM Pedro J. Martinez 8.00
TM Tino Martinez 4.00
HM Hideki Matsui 35.00
PN Phil Nevin 4.00
MI Mike Piazza 10.00
MP Mark Prior 15.00
AP Albert Pujols 15.00
AR Alex Rodriguez 12.00
IR Ivan Rodriguez 8.00
CS Curt Schilling 5.00
AS Alfonso Soriano 10.00
SS Sammy Sosa 12.00
IS Ichiro Suzuki 30.00
MT Mark Teixeira 8.00
FT Frank Thomas 8.00
LW Larry Walker 4.00
BW Bernie Williams 6.00
BZ Barry Zito 6.00

Awesome Honors

NM/M
5.00
1 Albert Pujols 5.00
2 Alex Rodriguez 5.00
3 Angel Berroa 5.00
4 Dontrelle Willis 1.00
5 Eric Gagne 1.50
6 Garret Anderson 1.00
7 Ivan Rodriguez 1.50
8 Josh Beckett 1.50
9 Mariano Rivera 1.00
10 Roy Halladay .75

Awesome Honors Jersey

		NM/M
Golds:		1.5-2X
Production 165		
GA	Garret Anderson	5.00
JB	Josh Beckett	6.00
BB	Bret Boone	5.00
MC	Mike Cameron	4.00
LC	Luis Castillo	4.00
EC	Eric Chavez	5.00
JE	Jim Edmonds	6.00
EG	Eric Gagne	12.00
EG1	Eric Gagne	12.00
JG	Jason Giambi	8.00
VG	Vladimir Guerrero	8.00
RH	Roy Halladay	6.00
MH	Mike Hampton	4.00
TH	Todd Helton	6.00
HU	Torii Hunter	5.00
AJ	Andruw Jones	6.00
DL	Derrek Lee	5.00
EM	Edgar Martinez	5.00
BM	Bengie Molina	4.00
JM	Jamie Moyer	4.00
MU	Mike Mussina	8.00
JO	John Olerud	5.00
MO	Magglio Ordonez	5.00
AP	Albert Pujols	10.00
AP1	Albert Pujols	
AP2	Albert Pujols	10.00
MR	Mariano Rivera	5.00
AR	Alex Rodriguez	10.00
AR3	Alex Rodriguez	10.00
IR	Ivan Rodriguez	8.00
SR	Scott Rolen	8.00
JS	John Smoltz	5.00
AS	Alfonso Soriano	8.00
IS	Ichiro Suzuki	20.00
JT	Jim Thome	8.00
DW	Dontrelle Willis	6.00

First Pitch

		NM/M
Common Player:		
Inserted 1:72		
SP7	LeBron James	20.00
SP8	Mr. Hockey	10.00
SP10	Ernie Banks	10.00
SP11	General Tommy Franks	5.00
SP12	Ben Affleck	10.00
SP13	Halle Berry	10.00
SP14	George H.W. Bush	5.00
SP15	George W. Bush	5.00

Game Winners

		NM/M
Common Player:		5.00
Golds:		1-1.5X
Production 50 Sets		
GW-BA	Bobby Abreu	8.00
GW-GA	Garret Anderson	
GW-JB	Jeff Bagwell	8.00
GW-HB	Hank Blalock	8.00
GW-MC	Miguel Cabrera	8.00
GW-JE	Jim Edmonds	5.00
GW-DE	Darin Erstad	5.00
GW-RF	Rafael Furcal (Gold parallel only)	5.00
GW-JG	Jason Giambi	8.00
GW-TG	Troy Glaus	5.00
GW-AG	Alex Gonzalez	5.00
GW-SG	Shawn Green	5.00
GW-KG	Ken Griffey Jr.	
GW-VG	Vladimir Guerrero	10.00
GW-TH	Todd Helton	8.00
GW-RH	Ramon Hernandez	5.00
GW-HU	Torii Hunter	5.00
GW-DJ	Derek Jeter	25.00
GW-AJ	Andruw Jones	8.00
GW-CJ	Chipper Jones	8.00
GW-RK	Ryan Klesko	5.00
GW-JL	Javy Lopez	
GW-ML	Mike Lowell	5.00
GW-HM	Hideki Matsui	25.00
GW-TN	Trot Nixon (Gold parallel only)	10.00
GW-MO	Magglio Ordonez	5.00
GW-CP	Corey Patterson	5.00
GW-MP	Mike Piazza	10.00
GW-JP	Jorge Posada	8.00
GW-AP	Albert Pujols	15.00
GW-IR	Ivan Rodriguez	8.00
GW-SR	Scott Rolen	10.00
GW-GS	Gary Sheffield	5.00
GW-AS	Alfonso Soriano	8.00
GW-MT	Mark Teixeira	5.00
GW-TE	Miguel Tejada	5.00
GW-JT	Jim Thome	10.00
GW-BW	Bernie Williams	8.00

Going Deep Bat

		NM/M
Common Player:		6.00
Inserted 1:288		
Some not priced yet due to scarcity		
Golds:		1-2X
Production 50 sets		
BA	Bobby Abreu	6.00
RO	Roberto Alomar	8.00
SC	Sandy Alomar Jr.	6.00
GA	Garret Anderson	8.00
RA	Rich Aurilia	
JB	Jeff Bagwell	10.00
RB	Rocco Baldelli	15.00
CB	Craig Biggio	6.00
JE	Jim Edmonds	8.00
DE	Darin Erstad	6.00
RF	Rafael Furcal	6.00
TG	Troy Glaus	8.00
SG	Shawn Green	8.00
KG	Ken Griffey Jr.	15.00
RH	Rickey Henderson	10.00
TH	Torii Hunter	8.00
AJ	Andruw Jones	8.00
CJ	Chipper Jones	15.00
JL	Javy Lopez	8.00
HM	Hideki Matsui	45.00
DM	Doug Mientkiewicz	6.00
HN	Hideo Nomo	15.00
MO	Magglio Ordonez	6.00
CP	Corey Patterson	
PO	Jay Payton	6.00
MP	Mike Piazza	
JP	Jorge Posada	8.00
AP	Albert Pujols	20.00
SR	Scott Rolen	10.00
CS	Curt Schilling	8.00
AS	Alfonso Soriano	
MT	Miguel Tejada	6.00
JT	Jim Thome	10.00
OV	Omar Vizquel	6.00
BW	Bernie Williams	8.00
KW	Kerry Wood	10.00

Headliners Jersey

		NM/M
Common Player:		4.00
Inserted 1:48		
Golds:		1-2X
Production 100 sets		
TB	Tony Batista	4.00
JB	Josh Beckett	8.00
LB	Lance Berkman	4.00
MB	Mark Buehrle	4.00
LC	Luis Castillo	4.00
JD	Joe DiMaggio/SP	
AD	Adam Dunn	6.00
JE	Jim Edmonds	6.00
RF	Robert Fick	4.00
TG	Tom Glavine	6.00
LG	Luis Gonzalez	4.00
SG	Shawn Green	4.00
KG	Ken Griffey Jr.	15.00
VG	Vladimir Guerrero	8.00
RH	Roy Halladay	4.00
JH	Jose Hernandez	4.00
TH	Trevor Hoffman	4.00
BK	Byung-Hyun Kim	4.00
RK	Ryan Klesko	4.00
PK	Paul Konerko	4.00
ML	Mike Lowell	4.00
GM	Greg Maddux	12.00
MM	Mickey Mantle/SP	
PM	Pedro J. Martinez	8.00
HM	Hideki Matsui	35.00
MY	Matt Morris	4.00
MU	Mike Mussina	8.00
MO	Magglio Ordonez	4.00
RO	Roy Oswalt	4.00
MR	Manny Ramirez	6.00
MA	Mariano Rivera	6.00
JR	Jimmy Rollins	4.00
BS	Benito Santiago	4.00
CS	Curt Schilling	6.00
JS	Junior Spivey	4.00
IS	Ichiro Suzuki	25.00
MS	Mike Sweeney	4.00
MT	Miguel Tejada	6.00
JT	Jim Thome	8.00
JV	Jose Vidro	4.00
TW	Ted Williams	75.00

Famous Quotes

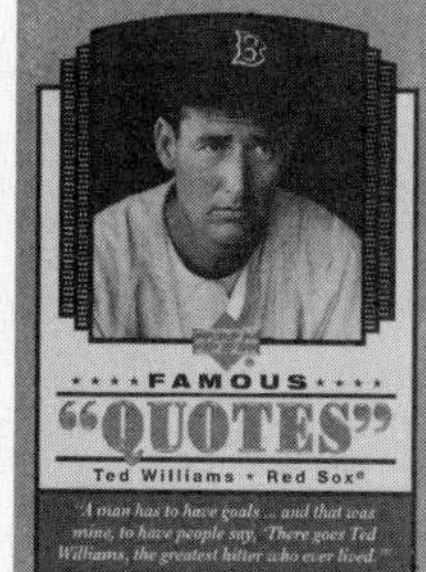

		NM/M
Q-1	Al Lopez	.75
Q-2	Bob Feller	1.00
Q-3	Bob Gibson	1.50
Q-4	Brooks Robinson	1.50
Q-5	Cal Ripken Jr.	5.00
Q-6	Carl Yastrzemski	2.00
Q-7	Earl Weaver	.75
Q-8	Eddie Mathews	2.00
Q-9	Ernie Banks	2.00
Q-10	Greg Maddux	2.00
Q-11	Joe DiMaggio	4.00
Q-12	Mickey Mantle	6.00
Q-13	Nolan Ryan	6.00
Q-14	Stan Musial	4.00
Q-15	Ted Williams	5.00
Q-16	Tom Seaver	2.00
Q-17	Tommy Lasorda	.75
Q-18	Warren Spahn	2.00
Q-19	Whitey Ford	1.50
Q-20	Yogi Berra	2.00

Magical Performances

		NM/M
Common Player:		6.00
Inserted 1:96		
Golds:		1-1.5X
Production 50 sets		
MP1	Mickey Mantle	35.00
MP2	Mickey Mantle	35.00
MP3	Joe DiMaggio	25.00
MP4	Joe DiMaggio	25.00
MP5	Derek Jeter	25.00
MP6	Derek Jeter	25.00
MP7	Roger Clemens	20.00
MP8	Roger Clemens	20.00
MP9	Alfonso Soriano	10.00
MP10	Andy Pettitte	8.00
MP11	Hideki Matsui	30.00
MP12	Mike Mussina	10.00
MP13	Jorge Posada	10.00
MP14	Jason Giambi	10.00
MP15	David Wells	6.00
MP16	Mariano Rivera	10.00
MP17	Yogi Berra	15.00
MP18	Phil Rizzuto	10.00
MP19	Whitey Ford	10.00
MP20	Jose Contreras	8.00
MP21	Jim "Catfish" Hunter	6.00
MP22	Mickey Mantle	35.00
MP23	Mickey Mantle	35.00
MP24	Joe DiMaggio	25.00
MP25	Joe DiMaggio	25.00
MP26	Derek Jeter	25.00
MP27	Derek Jeter	25.00
MP28	Roger Clemens	20.00
MP29	Roger Clemens	20.00
MP30	Alfonso Soriano	10.00
MP31	Andy Pettitte	8.00
MP32	Hideki Matsui	30.00
MP33	Mike Mussina	10.00
MP34	Jorge Posada	10.00
MP35	Jason Giambi	10.00
MP36	David Wells	6.00
MP37	Mariano Rivera	10.00
MP38	Yogi Berra	15.00
MP39	Phil Rizzuto	10.00
MP40	Whitey Ford	10.00
MP41	Jose Contreras	10.00
MP42	Jim "Catfish" Hunter	6.00

National Pride

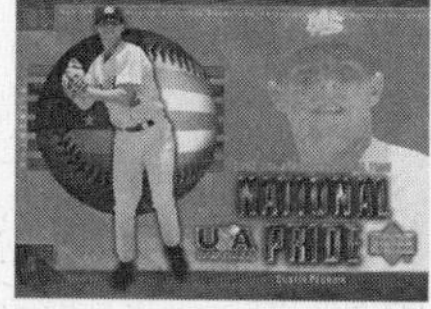

		NM/M
Complete Set (20):		25.00
Common Player:		1.00
Inserted 1:6		
USA1	Justin Orenduff	1.00
USA2	Micah Owings	2.00
USA3	Steven Register	2.00
USA4	Huston Street	1.00
USA5	Justin Verlander	2.00
USA6	Jered Weaver	1.00
USA7	Matt Campbell	1.00
USA8	Stephen Head	1.00
USA9	Mark Romanczuk	1.00
USA10	Jeff Clement	6.00
USA11	Mike Nickeas	2.00
USA12	Tyler Greene	1.00
USA13	Paul Janish	2.00
USA14	Jeff Larish	1.00
USA15	Eric Patterson	1.00
USA16	Dustin Pedroia	1.00
USA17	Michael Griffin	1.00
USA18	Brent Lillibridge	1.00
USA19	Danny Putnam	1.00
USA20	Seth Smith	1.00

National Pride Jersey

		NM/M
Common Player:		4.00
Inserted 1:24		
USA1	Justin Orenduff	4.00
USA2	Micah Owings	4.00
USA3	Steven Register	4.00
USA4	Huston Street	4.00
USA5	Justin Verlander	6.00
USA6	Jered Weaver	6.00
USA7	Matt Campbell	8.00
USA8	Stephen Head	4.00
USA9	Mark Romanczuk	4.00
USA10	Jeff Clement	15.00
USA11	Mike Nickeas	4.00
USA12	Tyler Greene	4.00
USA13	Paul Janish	4.00
USA14	Jeff Larish	6.00
USA15	Eric Patterson	4.00
USA16	Dustin Pedroia	4.00
USA17	Michael Griffin	4.00
USA18	Brent Lillibridge	6.00
USA19	Danny Putnam	4.00
USA20	Seth Smith	6.00
USA21	Justin Orenduff	4.00

USA22 Micah Owings 4.00
USA23 Steven Register 4.00
USA24 Huston Street 4.00
USA25 Justin Verlander 6.00
USA26 Jered Weaver 6.00
USA27 Matt Campbell 8.00
USA28 Stephen Head 4.00
USA29 Mark Romanczuk 4.00
USA30 Jeff Clement 15.00
USA31 Mike Nickeas 4.00
USA32 Tyler Greene 4.00
USA33 Paul Janish 4.00
USA34 Jeff Larish 6.00
USA35 Eric Patterson 4.00
USA36 Dustin Pedroia 4.00
USA37 Michael Griffin 4.00
USA38 Brent Lillibridge 6.00
USA39 Danny Putnam 4.00
USA40 Seth Smith 6.00
USA41 Delmon Young 35.00
USA42 Rickie Weeks 12.00
Series 2
TB Thad Bosley 4.00
BB Brian Bruney 6.00
CB Chris Burke 9.00
JC Jesse Crain 8.00
DU Justin Duchscherer 6.00
JD J.D. Durbin 4.00
JG John Grabow 6.00
GG Gabe Gross 4.00
JH J.J. Hardy 6.00
GK Graham Koonce 6.00
GL Gerald Laird 6.00
ML Mike Lamb 4.00
JL Justin Leone 8.00
JM Joe Mauer 15.00
HR Horacio Ramirez 8.00
JR Jeremy Reed 10.00
RR Royce Ring 6.00
ER Eddie Rodriguez 5.00
MR Mike Rouse 8.00
GS Grady Sizemore 8.00
JS Jason Stanford 6.00
JB John Van Benschoten 8.00
TW Todd Williams 4.00
EY Ernie Young 4.00

National Pride Pants

NM/M

CB Chris Burke 9.00
JC Jesse Crain 4.00
DU Justin Duchscherer 6.00
GK Graham Koonce 6.00
JL Justin Leone 8.00
RM Ryan Madson 6.00
JM Joe Mauer 15.00
HR Horacio Ramirez 8.00
RR Royce Ring 6.00
ER Eddie Rodriguez 5.00
MR Mike Rouse 8.00
GS Grady Sizemore 8.00
JS Jason Stanford 6.00
JB John Van Benschoten 8.00

Peak Performers

NM/M

Golds: 1.5X-2X
Production 165
PP-JB Jeff Bagwell 8.00
PP-BE Josh Beckett 6.00
PP-LB Lance Berkman 5.00
PP-CB Craig Biggio 5.00
PP-HB Hank Blalock 8.00
PP-PB Pat Burrell 6.00
PP-LC Luis Castillo 4.00
PP-CD Carlos Delgado 6.00
PP-RF Rafael Furcal 4.00
PP-EG Eric Gagne 12.00
PP-SG Shawn Green 5.00
PP-KG Ken Griffey Jr. 15.00
PP-VG Vladimir Guerrero 8.00
PP-TH Todd Helton 8.00
PP-PL Paul LoDuca 4.00
PP-PM Pedro J. Martinez 8.00
PP-HM Hideki Matsui 25.00
PP-MM Mike Mussina 8.00
PP-HN Hideo Nomo 8.00
PP-MO Magglio Ordonez 5.00
PP-RP Rafael Palmeiro 6.00
PP-PE Andy Pettitte 6.00
PP-BP Brandon Phillips 4.00
PP-MP Mark Prior 15.00
PP-AP Albert Pujols 10.00
PP-JR Jose Reyes 5.00
PP-IR Ivan Rodriguez 8.00
PP-SR Scott Rolen 8.00
PP-SA C.C. Sabathia 4.00
PP-CS Curt Schilling 8.00
PP-AS Alfonso Soriano 8.00
PP-IS Ichiro Suzuki 20.00
PP-MT Miguel Tejada 5.00
PP-FT Frank Thomas 8.00
PP-JT Jim Thome 8.00
PP-DV Omar Vizquel 4.00
PP-VW Vernon Wells 4.00
PP-KW Kerry Wood 10.00

Signature Stars Black Ink

NM/M

Some not priced due to lack of info.
Inserted 1:288
RA Rich Aurilia/479 8.00
RC Roger Clemens/19
AG Andres Galarraga/248 10.00
NG Nomar Garciaparra/69 85.00
BG Bob Gibson/19
VG Vladimir Guerrero/68 40.00
RH Rich Harden/163 8.00
AH Aaron Heilman/49 15.00
TH Torii Hunter/374 10.00
KI Kazuhisa Ishii/58 15.00
BK Billy Koch/429 8.00
HM Hideki Matsui/25 325.00
MU Mike Mussina/68 60.00
MO Magglio Ordonez/377 20.00
RP Rafael Palmeiro/18
JRa Joe Randa/271 10.00
CR Cal Ripken Jr./69 200.00
DR Dave Roberts/278 8.00
NR Nolan Ryan/69 100.00
IS Ichiro Suzuki/19
Series 2
SS-BB Bret Boone/43 20.00
SS-DB Dewon Brazelton/96 8.00
SS-JC Jose Canseco/160 50.00
SS-EC Eric Chavez/60 20.00
SS-EG Eric Gagne/160 40.00
SS-KG Ken Griffey Jr./450 90.00
SS-RH Rich Harden/65 15.00
SS-AK Al Kaline/60
SS-CL Cliff Lee/160
SS-DR Dave Roberts/450 5.00
SS-NR Nolan Ryan/95 100.00
SS-TS Tom Seaver SP
SS-DS Darryl Strawberry/160 8.00
SS-IS Ichiro Suzuki SP
SS-MT Mark Teixeira/200
SS-JV Javier Vazquez/60 20.00
SS-BW Brandon Webb/60 15.00
SS-RW Rickie Weeks/65 30.00
SS-DW Dontrelle Willis/160 15.00

Signature Stars Blue Ink

NM/M

No Pricing
Production 25 sets
Matsui #'d to 324
BB Bret Boone/25
JC Jose Canseco/25
EC Eric Chavez/25
EG Eric Gagne/25
KG Ken Griffey Jr./25
RH2 Rich Harden/25
AK Al Kaline/25
CL Cliff Lee/25
HM Hideki Matsui/324 180.00
DR2 Dave Roberts/25
TS Tom Seaver/20
DS Darryl Strawberry
IS2 Ichiro Suzuki/20
JV Javier Vazquez/25
BW Brandon Webb/25
RW Rickie Weeks/25
DW Dontrelle Willis/25

Signature Stars Red Ink

No Pricing
Production 10 sets
Series 2

Signature Stars Gold Ink

Gold Ink: 1-2X black ink
Production 99 sets

Super Patches Logos

No pricing due to scarcity
Inserted 1:7,500

Super Sluggers

NM/M

Complete Set (30): 15.00
Common Player: .50
Inserted 1:1 Retail
SL-1 Albert Pujols 2.00
SL-2 Alex Rodriguez 2.00
SL-3 Alfonso Soriano .75
SL-4 Andruw Jones .75
SL-5 Bret Boone .50
SL-6 Carlos Delgado .50
SL-7 Edgar Renteria .50
SL-8 Eric Chavez .50
SL-9 Frank Thomas .75
SL-10 Garret Anderson .50
SL-11 Gary Sheffield .50
SL-12 Jason Giambi .75
SL-13 Javy Lopez .50
SL-14 Jeff Bagwell .75
SL-15 Jim Edmonds .50
SL-16 Jim Thome 1.00
SL-17 Jorge Posada .50
SL-18 Lance Berkman .50
SL-19 Magglio Ordonez .50
SL-20 Manny Ramirez .75
SL-21 Mike Lowell .50
SL-22 Nomar Garciaparra 1.50
SL-23 Preston Wilson .50
SL-24 Rafael Palmeiro .75
SL-25 Richie Sexson .50
SL-26 Sammy Sosa 2.00
SL-27 Shawn Green .50
SL-28 Todd Helton .75
SL-29 Vernon Wells .50
SL-30 Vladimir Guerrero 1.00

Twenty-Five Salute

NM/M

Common Player: 6.00
Inserted 1:12
S1 Barry Bonds 3.00
S2 Troy Glaus .75
S3 Andruw Jones .75
S4 Jay Gibbons .75
S5 Jeremy Giambi .75
S6 Jason Giambi 1.00
S7 Jim Thome 1.00
S8 Rafael Palmeiro 1.00
S9 Carlos Delgado 1.00
S10 Dmitri Young .75

SPGU Patch Edition Update Patch

NM/M

Production 20 unless noted
BA Bobby Abreu 40.00
GA Garret Anderson 40.00
RB Rocco Baldelli 30.00
LB Lance Berkman 40.00
HB Hank Blalock 40.00
BB Bret Boone 30.00
BC Bartolo Colon 25.00
JE Jim Edmonds 35.00
EG Eric Gagne 75.00
TG Troy Glaus 35.00
VG Vladimir Guerrero 50.00
TH Torii Hunter 25.00
JJ Jacque Jones 25.00
AK Austin Kearns 30.00
JK Jeff Kent 25.00
RK Ryan Klesko 25.00
EM Edgar Martinez 50.00
KM Kevin Millwood 30.00
MM Mark Mulder 40.00
HN Hideo Nomo 40.00
RO Roy Oswalt 35.00
CP Corey Patterson 30.00
JR Jose Reyes 30.00
RS Richie Sexson 40.00
MS Mike Sweeney 25.00
BW Brandon Webb 25.00
VW Vernon Wells/21 25.00
KW Kerry Wood 50.00

500 HR Club

NM/M

Production 350
RP Rafael Palmeiro 180.00
RPAU Rafael Palmeiro/auto/25

2003 UPDATE

NM/M

Complete Set (60): 18.00
Common Player: .15
One set per hobby box
541 Bo Hart 1.50
542 Dan Haren .50
543 Ryan Wagner 1.00
544 Rich Harden .50
545 Dontrelle Willis .75
546 Jerome Williams .25
547 Bobby Crosby 1.00
548 Greg Jones .25
549 Todd Linden .25
550 Byung-Hyun Kim .25
551 Rickie Weeks 4.00
552 Jason Roach .25
553 Oscar Villarreal .25
554 Justin Duchscherer .15
555 Chris Capuano .15
556 Josh Hall .50
557 Luis Matos .15
558 Miguel Ojeda .15
559 Kevin Ohme .15
560 Julio Manon .15
561 Kevin Correia .15
562 Delmon Young 5.00
563 Aaron Boone .15
564 Aaron Looper .15
565 Mike Neu .15
566 Aquilino Lopez .15
567 Jhonny Peralta .15
568 Duaner Sanchez .15
569 Stephen Randolph .15
570 Nate Bland .15
571 Chin-Hui Tsao .15
572 Michel Hernandez .15
573 Rocco Baldelli 1.00
574 Robb Quinlan .15
575 Aaron Heilman .15
576 Jae Weong Seo .15
577 Joe Borowski .15
578 Chris Bootcheck .15
579 Michael Ryan .15
580 Mark Malaska .15
581 Jose Guillen .15
582 Josh Towers .15
583 Tom Gregorio .15
584 Edwin Jackson .15
585 Jason Anderson .15
586 Jose Reyes .50
587 Miguel Cabrera 1.00
588 Nate Bump .15
589 Jeromy Burnitz .15
590 David Ross .15
591 Chase Utley .15
592 Brandon Webb 1.00
593 Masao Kida .15
594 Jimmy Journell .15
595 Eric Young .15
596 Tony Womack .15
597 Amaury Telemaco .15
598 Rickey Henderson .50
599 Esteban Loaiza .15
600 Sidney Ponson .15

2004 UPPER DECK DIAMOND COLLECTION

NM/M

Complete Set (120): 70.00

Common Player: .15
Common (91-120): 2.00
Inserted 1:6
Pack (6): 2.00
Box (24): 40.00
1 Garret Anderson .25
2 Darin Erstad .25
3 Troy Glaus .40
4 Curt Schilling .50
5 Brandon Webb .15
6 Randy Johnson .75
7 Andruw Jones .50
8 Chipper Jones .75
9 Gary Sheffield .40
10 Jay Gibbons .25
11 Miguel Tejada .40
12 Tony Batista .15
13 Nomar Garciaparra 1.25
14 Manny Ramirez .50
15 Pedro J. Martinez .75
16 Mark Prior 1.50
17 Kerry Wood .75
18 Sammy Sosa 1.25
19 Bartolo Colon .25
20 Magglio Ordonez .25
21 Frank Thomas .50
22 Adam Dunn .40
23 Austin Kearns .25
24 Ken Griffey Jr. 1.00
25 Brandon Phillips .15
26 Milton Bradley .15
27 Jody Gerut .15
28 Todd Helton .50
29 Larry Walker .25
30 Preston Wilson .25
31 Jeremy Bonderman .15
32 Carlos Pena .15
33 Dmitri Young .15
34 Dontrelle Willis .40
35 Miguel Cabrera .50
36 Mike Lowell .25
37 Jeff Bagwell .50
38 Roy Oswalt .25
39 Lance Berkman .25
40 Carlos Beltran .40
41 Mike Sweeney .15
42 Rondell White .25
43 Hideo Nomo .40
44 Kevin Brown .25
45 Shawn Green .25
46 Ben Sheets .25
47 Geoff Jenkins .25
48 Richie Sexson .40
49 Jacque Jones .15
50 Johan Santana .15
51 Torii Hunter .25
52 Javier Vazquez .25
53 Jose Vidro .15
54 Vladimir Guerrero .75
55 Cliff Floyd .15
56 Mike Piazza 1.00
57 Jose Reyes .25
58 Derek Jeter 2.00
59 Jason Giambi .50
60 Alfonso Soriano .50
61 Eric Chavez .25
62 Barry Zito .25
63 Tim Hudson .25
64 Bobby Abreu .25
65 Jim Thome .75
66 Kevin Millwood .25
67 Roger Clemens 1.50
68 Jason Kendall .15
69 Reggie Sanders .15
70 Phil Nevin .15
71 Ryan Klesko .25
72 Brian Giles .25
73 A.J. Pierzynski .15
74 Jason Schmidt .25
75 Sidney Ponson .15
76 Edgar Martinez .25
77 Ichiro Suzuki 1.00
78 Bret Boone .25
79 Albert Pujols 1.50
80 Scott Rolen .75
81 Jim Edmonds .25
82 Aubrey Huff .15
83 Delmon Young .40
84 Rocco Baldelli .40
85 Alex Rodriguez 1.50
86 Mark Teixeira .25
87 Rafael Palmeiro .50
88 Carlos Delgado .50
89 Vernon Wells .25
90 Roy Halladay .25
91 *Brandon Medders* 2.00
92 *Colby Miller* 2.00
93 David Crouthers 2.00
94 *Dennis Sarfate* 3.00
95 *Donald Kelly* 2.00
96 *Alec Zumwalt* 2.00
97 *Frank Brooks* 2.00
98 *Greg Dobbs* 2.00
99 *Ian Snell* 3.00
100 Jake Woods 2.00
101 *Jamie Brown* 2.00
102 *Jason Frasor* 2.00
103 *Jerome Gamble* 2.00
104 *Jesse Harper* 2.00
105 *Josh Labandeira* 2.00
106 *Justin Hampson* 2.00
107 *Justin Huisman* 2.00
108 *Justin Leone* 2.00
109 *Chris Aguila* 2.00
110 *Lincoln Holdzkom* 2.00
111 *Mike Bumatay* 2.00
112 Mike Gosling 2.00
113 *Mike Johnston* 2.00
114 Mike Rouse 2.00
115 *Nick Regilio* 2.00
116 *Ryan Meaux* 2.00
117 *Scott Dohmann* 2.00
118 Sean Henn 2.00
119 *Tim Bausher* 2.00
120 *Tim Bittner* 2.00

Class of 2004 Autograph

NM/M

Quantity produced listed
MC Miguel Cabrera/50 40.00
KG Ken Griffey Jr./100 75.00
VG Vladimir Guerrero/100 40.00
RH Rich Harden/100 15.00
HM Hideki Matsui/100 250.00
MP Mark Prior/100 80.00
JR Jose Reyes/100 25.00
DW Dontrelle Willis/100 40.00
BZ Barry Zito/100 25.00

Silver Honors

Silver (1-90): 2-4X
Silver (91-120): .75-1X
1-90 inserted 1:6
91-120 inserted 1:48

Gold Honors

Gold (1-90): 5-10X
Gold (91-120): 1-2X
Production 50 sets

Dean's List Jersey

NM/M

Common Player: 4.00
Inserted 1:72
BA Jeff Bagwell 8.00
HB Hank Blalock 6.00
JG Jason Giambi 6.00
GL Troy Glaus 6.00
LG Luis Gonzalez 4.00
SG Shawn Green 4.00
KG Ken Griffey Jr. 10.00
VG Vladimir Guerrero 8.00
GM Greg Maddux 10.00
HM Hideki Matsui 20.00
HN Hideo Nomo 8.00
PI Mike Piazza 8.00
MP Mark Prior 10.00
AP Albert Pujols 15.00
AR Alex Rodriguez 10.00
AS Alfonso Soriano 8.00
SS Sammy Sosa 10.00
IS Ichiro Suzuki 20.00
JT Jim Thome 8.00
DW Dontrelle Willis 6.00

Future Gems Jersey

NM/M

Common Player: 4.00
Inserted 1:72
BA Josh Bard 4.00

JB Josh Beckett 8.00
SB Sean Burroughs 6.00
MC Mike Cameron 4.00
AE Adam Eaton 4.00
WE Willie Eyre 4.00
LF Lew Ford 4.00
GU Jeremy Guthrie 4.00
TH Travis Hafner 6.00
RH Roy Halladay 4.00
AH Aaron Heilman 4.00
IS Kazuhisa Ishii 4.00
JJ Jason Jennings 4.00
KA Matt Kata 4.00
MK Mark Kotsay 4.00
JL Jon Leicester 4.00
EM Eric Milton 4.00
JR Jose Reyes 8.00
RR Rick Roberts 4.00
PS Phil Seibel 4.00
BS Ben Sheets 6.00
MT Mark Teixeira 6.00
TW Todd Wellemeyer 6.00
WI Josh Willingham 4.00

Pick the All Star MVP

NM/M

Common Player: .50
Inserted 1:1
BA Bobby Abreu .50
GA Garret Anderson .50
JB Jeff Bagwell .50
BE Josh Beckett .50
CB Carlos Beltran .50
HB Hank Blalock .50
BO Bret Boone .50
OC Orlando Cabrera .50
EC Eric Chavez .50
BC Bartolo Colon .50
JD Johnny Damon .50
CD Carlos Delgado .50
AD Adam Dunn .50
JE Jim Edmonds .50
RF Rafael Furcal .50
NG Nomar Garciaparra 1.50
JG Jason Giambi .75
MG Marcus Giles .50
TG Troy Glaus .50
SG Shawn Green .50
KG Ken Griffey Jr. 1.00
VG Vladimir Guerrero .75
RH Roy Halladay .50
TH Todd Helton .75
HU Tim Hudson .50
TH Torii Hunter .50
DJ Derek Jeter 2.50
RJ Randy Johnson .75
AJ Andruw Jones .50
CJ Chipper Jones .75
JJ Jacque Jones .50
AK Austin Kearns .50
JK Jeff Kent .50
JL Javy Lopez .50
ML Mike Lowell .50
PM Pedro J. Martinez .75
HM Hideki Matsui 1.50
MM Mark Mulder .50
MU Mike Mussina .75
MO Magglio Ordonez .50
RP Rafael Palmeiro .75
PI Mike Piazza 1.00
JP Jorge Posada .50
MP Mark Prior 1.50
AP Albert Pujols 2.00
MR Manny Ramirez .75
ER Edgar Renteria .50
AR Alex Rodriguez 2.00
IR Ivan Rodriguez .75
SR Scott Rolen .75
CS Curt Schilling .75
JS Jason Schmidt .50
RS Richie Sexson .50
GS Gary Sheffield .50
AS Alfonso Soriano .75
SS Sammy Sosa 1.50
IS Ichiro Suzuki 1.50
MS Mike Sweeney .50
MT Mark Teixeira .50
TE Miguel Tejada .50
FT Frank Thomas .75
JT Jim Thome .75
JV Jason Varitek .50
VI Jose Vidro .50
VW Vernon Wells .50
DW Dontrelle Willis .50
PW Preston Wilson .50
KW Kerry Wood 1.00
BZ Barry Zito .50

Premium Stars

No Pricing

2004 UPPER DECK ETCHINGS

NM/M

Complete Set (150):
Common Player: .15
Common SP (91-120): 4.00
Production 2,004
Common SP Black Auto (121-150): 8.00
Production 700
Blue Auto (121-150): .75-1.5X
Production 200
Red Auto (121-150): No Pricing
Production 25
Pack (5): 12.00
Box (12): 120.00
1 Albert Pujols 1.50
2 Torii Hunter .40
3 Jim Edmonds .40
4 Alex Rodriguez 1.50
5 Rafael Palmeiro .50
6 Ken Griffey Jr. 1.00
7 Adam Dunn .50
8 Andruw Jones .50
9 Carlos Lee .15
10 Mike Piazza 1.00
11 Jeff Bagwell .50
12 Hideki Matsui 1.50
13 Gary Sheffield .40
14 Edgar Renteria .40
15 Shawn Green .25
16 Kerry Wood .75
17 Ivan Rodriguez .50
18 Josh Beckett .40
19 Scott Rolen .75
20 Brian Giles .25
21 Derrek Lee .25
22 Mike Lowell .25
23 Mike Mussina .40
24 Sammy Sosa 1.50
25 Brandon Webb .15
26 Jacque Jones .15
27 Randy Johnson 1.00
28 Luis Gonzalez .25
29 Eric Chavez .25
30 Carlos Delgado .40
31 Phil Nevin .15
32 Ichiro Suzuki 1.50
33 Roy Oswalt .25
34 Tim Hudson .25
35 Juan Gonzalez .50
36 Frank Thomas .50
37 Mark Mulder .40
38 Mark Teixeira .40
39 Miguel Tejada .40
40 Jeff Kent .25
41 Andy Pettitte .25
42 Barry Zito .40
43 Roy Halladay .25
44 Rocco Baldelli .25
45 Derek Jeter 2.00
46 Corey Patterson .40
47 Javy Lopez .40
48 A.J. Burnett .15
49 Chipper Jones .75
50 Curt Schilling .50
51 Todd Helton .50

52	Pedro J. Martinez	.75
53	Hideo Nomo	.40
54	Jose Reyes	.40
55	Vernon Wells	.15
56	Geoff Jenkins	.15
57	Troy Glaus	.25
58	Greg Maddux	1.00
59	Jason Schmidt	.40
60	Preston Wilson	.15
61	Miguel Cabrera	.75
62	Hank Blalock	.50
63	Rafael Furcal	.15
64	Vladimir Guerrero	.75
65	Lance Berkman	.15
66	Javier Vazquez	.15
67	Bret Boone	.15
68	Mark Prior	1.00
69	Magglio Ordonez	.15
70	Dontrelle Willis	.25
71	Richie Sexson	.25
72	Alfonso Soriano	.75
73	Edwin Jackson	.15
74	Jose Vidro	.15
75	Jason Giambi	.50
76	Kevin Brown	.25
77	Orlando Cabrera	.15
78	Nomar Garciaparra	1.00
79	Bobby Abreu	.25
80	Manny Ramirez	.50
81	J.D. Drew	.15
82	Roger Clemens	1.50
83	Pat Burrell	.15
84	Ryan Klesko	.15
85	Garret Anderson	.40
86	Johan Santana	.15
87	Kevin Millwood	.25
88	Austin Kearns	.25
89	Jim Thome	.75
90	Carlos Beltran	.40
91	*Kazuo Matsui*	15.00
92	*Jamie Brown*	4.00
93	*Brandon Medders*	4.00
94	*Carlos Vasquez*	4.00
95	*Chris Aguila*	4.00
96	David Aardsma	4.00
97	*Justin Leone*	4.00
98	*Mike Johnston*	4.00
99	*Tim Bittner*	4.00
100	Mike Rouse	4.00
101	*Dennis Sarfate*	4.00
102	*Jason Frasor*	4.00
103	*Jorge Vasquez*	4.00
104	Mike Gosling	4.00
105	Jake Woods	4.00
106	*Akinori Otsuka*	8.00
107	*Lincoln Holdzkom*	4.00
108	*Jesse Harper*	4.00
109	*Edwin Moreno*	4.00
110	*Shingo Takatsu*	6.00
111	*Ryan Meaux*	4.00
112	*Donnie Kelly*	4.00
113	*Jerome Gamble*	4.00
114	*Josh Labandeira*	4.00
115	*Ian Snell*	6.00
116	*Mike Wuertz*	4.00
117	*Greg Dobbs*	4.00
118	Sean Henn	4.00
119	David Crouthers	4.00
120	*Hector Gimenez*	4.00
121	*Renyel Pinto*	10.00
122	Tim Hamulack	8.00
123	*Chris Saenz*	8.00
124	*Carlos Hines*	8.00
125	*Justin Knoedler*	10.00
126	*Onil Joseph*	10.00
127	Ryan Wing	8.00
128	*Scott Proctor*	10.00
129	*Rusty Tucker*	8.00
130	*Fernando Nieve*	8.00
131	*Chad Bentz*	10.00
132	*Jerry Gil*	8.00
133	*Mariano Gomez*	10.00
134	*Justin Germano*	10.00
135	*Jason Bartlett*	10.00
136	Ronald Belisario	8.00
137	Enemencio Pacheco	8.00
138	*Justin Hampson*	8.00
139	Michael Vento	8.00
140	*Merkin Valdez*	10.00
141	*Casey Daigle*	8.00
142	Eddy Rodriguez	8.00
143	*William Bergolla*	25.00
144	*Jose Capellan*	8.00
145	*Ronny Cedeno*	8.00
146	*Franklyn Gracesqui*	8.00
147	*Roman Colon*	10.00
148	*Roberto Novoa*	8.00
149	*Ivan Ochoa*	10.00
150	*Shawn Hill*	8.00

Dual Etchings

NM/M

Production 150 Sets

RJ	Alex Rodriguez, Derek Jeter	60.00
WP	Kerry Wood, Mark Prior	35.00
RP	Jose Reyes, Mike Piazza	30.00
PG	Albert Pujols, Vladimir Guerrero	30.00
MM	Hideki Matsui, Kazuo Matsui	40.00
MW	Mickey Mantle, Ted Williams	180.00

Combo Etchings

NM/M

Production 5-115
Gold Foil: .75-1.5X
Production 1-50
Silver Foil: .75-1X
Production 4-50
No pricing 15 oror Less

JB	Josh Beckett/25	60.00
MC	Miguel Cabrera/23	50.00
KG	Ken Griffey Jr./100	90.00
KG1	Ken Griffey Jr./90	90.00
KG2	Ken Griffey Jr./90	90.00
VG	Vladimir Guerrero/60	65.00
DJ1	Derek Jeter/25	200.00
MR	Manny Ramirez/60	65.00
MR1	Manny Ramirez/60	65.00
CR	Cal Ripken Jr./15	250.00
CR1	Cal Ripken Jr./15	250.00
AR	Alex Rodriguez/15	200.00
AR1	Alex Rodriguez/15	200.00
AR2	Alex Rodriguez/115	150.00
KW	Kerry Wood/20	65.00
KW1	Kerry Wood/20	65.00
KW2	Kerry Wood/30	50.00

Etched in Time Black Ink

NM/M

Quantity produced listed
Common Autograph: 6.00

AA	Alfredo Amezaga/375	6.00
SA	Sparky Anderson/375	15.00
TA	Tony Armas/325	6.00
BA	Dusty Baker/150	15.00
JB	Jason Bay/375	15.00
BE	Carlos Beltran/150	30.00
AB	Angel Berroa/1,325	6.00
HB	Hank Blalock/375	15.00
GB	Geoff Blum/375	6.00
BB	Bert Blyleven/375	8.00
CB	Chris Bootcheck/375	8.00
DB	Dewon Brazelton/375	8.00
MB	Marlon Byrd/1,025	8.00
EB	Eric Byrnes/Redemp.	8.00
MC	Miguel Cabrera/1,025	15.00
CA	Chris Capuano/375	8.00
EC	Eric Chavez/375	15.00
AC	Alex Cintron/375	8.00
WC	Will Clark/150	30.00
CL	Brandon Claussen/375	8.00
CC	Chad Cordero/375	6.00
BC	Bobby Crosby/1,325	15.00
AD	Andre Dawson/375	10.00
BD	Brandon Duckworth/375	8.00
ME	Morgan Ensberg/1,325	8.00
DE	Dwight Evans/375	15.00
AE	Adam Everett/325	6.00
WE	Willie Eyre/375	6.00
KF	Kyle Farnsworth/1,325	8.00
PF	Pedro Feliz/325	8.00
RF	Rollie Fingers/375	10.00
JF	Josh Fogg/325	8.00
LF	Lew Ford/375	20.00
NG	Nomar Garciaparra/100	75.00
CG	Chad Gaudin/375	6.00
BG	Brian Giles/375	10.00
MG	Marcus Giles/325	10.00
GO	Jonny Gomes/325	6.00
AG	Adrian Gonzalez/325	6.00
DG	Dwight Gooden/375	10.00
KG	Ken Griffey Jr./1,625	60.00
GR	Ken Griffey Sr./375	8.00
VG	Vladimir Guerrero	
TG	Tony Gwynn/150	40.00
SH	Scott Hairston/375	8.00
RH	Rob Hammock/325	8.00
AH	Aaron Harang/375	12.00
HA	Rich Harden/325	10.00
HE	Ramon Hernandez/325	8.00
RI	Raul Ibanez/325	8.00
EJ	Edwin Jackson/325	8.00
DJ	Derek Jeter	100.00
JJ	Jacque Jones/375	10.00
KA	Al Kaline/375	25.00
MK	Matt Kata/325	8.00
AK	Adam Kennedy/375	6.00
BK	Bobby Kielty/1,325	6.00
HK	Harmon Killebrew/Redemp.	35.00
DK	Dave Kingman/375	8.00
GK	Graham Koonce/375	8.00
LA	Adam LaRoche/1,325	8.00
CS	Carlos Lee/325	10.00
LE	Cliff Lee/1,325	8.00
TL	Ted Lilly/325	8.00
AL	Adam Loewen/375	6.00
ML	Mike Lowell/375	10.00
LM	Luis Matos/325	8.00
DM	Don Mattingly/150	50.00
MA	Joe Mauer/375	30.00
JM	Justin Miller/325	8.00
MO	Jack Morris/375	10.00
MM	Mark Mulder/375	20.00
MU	Dale Murphy/375	25.00
MN	Mike Neu/325	6.00
LN	Laynce Nix/Redemp.	15.00
RO	Roy Oswalt/375	12.00
LO	Lyle Overbay/1,325	8.00
PA	Jim Palmer/375	15.00
CP	Corey Patterson/375	20.00
BP	Brad Penny/375	8.00
JP	Jason Phillips/375	8.00
LP	Lou Piniella	
PO	Boog Powell/375	15.00
MP	Mark Prior/150	40.00
JR	Jose Reyes/325	12.00
JI	Jim Rice/375	10.00
CR	Cal Ripken Jr./100	120.00
BR	Brooks Robinson/375	25.00
RS	Ryne Sandberg/150	50.00
SO	Ron Santo/375	25.00
SS	Steve Sax/375	10.00
MS	Mike Scioscia/375	12.00
BS	Ben Sheets/375	15.00
TS	Terrmel Sledge/325	6.00
DS	Darryl Strawberry/150	15.00
MT	Mark Teixeira/325	20.00
LT	Luis Tiant/375	10.00
AT	Alan Trammell/375	15.00
CU	Chase Utley/375	25.00
RW	Ryan Wagner/1,325	8.00
WK	Rickie Weeks/Redemp.	20.00
JW	Jerome Williams/1,325	8.00
WI	Josh Willingham/1,325	6.00
RA	Randy Winn/375	8.00
KW	Kerry Wood/150	35.00
DY	Delmon Young/375	20.00
MY	Michael Young/1,325	15.00
CZ	Carlos Zambrano/375	25.00

Etched in Time Blue Ink

NM/M

Quantity produced listed
Common Autograph: 6.00

AA	Alfredo Amezaga/100	8.00
SA	Sparky Anderson/250	15.00
TA	Tony Armas/150	6.00
JB	Jason Bay/250	15.00
AB	Angel Berroa/150	8.00
HB	Hank Blalock/250	15.00
GB	Geoff Blum/250	6.00
BB	Bert Blyleven/250	8.00
CB	Chris Bootcheck/100	8.00
DB	Dewon Brazelton/250	8.00
MB	Marlon Byrd/150	8.00
EB	Eric Byrnes/Redemp.	8.00
MC	Miguel Cabrera/150	25.00
CA	Chris Capuano/100	8.00
EC	Eric Chavez/250	15.00
AC	Alex Cintron/100	10.00
WC	Will Clark/50	40.00
CL	Brandon Claussen/100	8.00
CC	Chad Cordero/100	6.00
BC	Bobby Crosby/150	15.00
AD	Andre Dawson/250	10.00
BD	Brandon Duckworth/100	8.00
ME	Morgan Ensberg/150	8.00
DE	Dwight Evans/250	15.00
AE	Adam Everett/150	8.00
WE	Willie Eyre/100	8.00
KF	Kyle Farnsworth/150	8.00
PF	Pedro Feliz/150	8.00
RF	Rollie Fingers/250	10.00
JF	Josh Fogg/150	8.00
LF	Lew Ford/200	20.00
NG	Nomar Garciaparra/50	85.00
CG	Chad Gaudin/100	6.00
BG	Brian Giles/250	10.00
MG	Marcus Giles/150	10.00
GO	Jonny Gomes/150	6.00
AG	Adrian Gonzalez/150	6.00
DG	Dwight Gooden/250	10.00
KG	Ken Griffey Jr./150	75.00
GR	Ken Griffey Sr./250	8.00
VG	Vladimir Guerrero/50	50.00
TG	Tony Gwynn/50	50.00
SH	Scott Hairston/100	8.00
RH	Rob Hammock/150	8.00
AH	Aaron Harang/100	15.00
HA	Rich Harden/150	15.00
HE	Ramon Hernandez/150	8.00
RI	Raul Ibanez/150	8.00
EJ	Edwin Jackson/100	8.00
DJ	Derek Jeter/50	120.00
JJ	Jacque Jones/250	10.00
KA	Al Kaline/250	25.00
MK	Matt Kata/150	8.00
AK	Adam Kennedy/100	8.00
BK	Bobby Kielty/150	8.00
DK	Dave Kingman/250	8.00
GK	Graham Koonce/250	8.00
LA	Adam LaRoche/150	10.00
LE	Cliff Lee/150	10.00
TL	Ted Lilly/150	8.00
ML	Mike Lowell/250	10.00
LM	Luis Matos/150	8.00
DM	Don Mattingly/50	60.00
MA	Joe Mauer/250	30.00
JM	Justin Miller/150	8.00
MO	Jack Morris/250	10.00
MM	Mark Mulder/250	20.00
MU	Dale Murphy/250	25.00
MN	Mike Neu/150	6.00
RO	Roy Oswalt/250	12.00
LO	Lyle Overbay/150	15.00
PA	Jim Palmer/250	15.00
CP	Corey Patterson/250	20.00
BP	Brad Penny/100	8.00
JP	Jason Phillips/250	8.00
LP	Lou Piniella/50	15.00
PO	Boog Powell/250	15.00
MP	Mark Prior/50	50.00
JR	Jose Reyes/150	15.00
JI	Jim Rice/250	10.00
CR	Cal Ripken Jr./50	150.00
BR	Brooks Robinson/250	25.00
RS	Ryne Sandberg/50	60.00
SO	Ron Santo/250	25.00
SS	Steve Sax/250	10.00
MS	Mike Scioscia/250	12.00
BS	Ben Sheets/250	15.00
TS	Terrmel Sledge/150	6.00
MT	Mark Teixeira/150	25.00
LT	Luis Tiant/250	10.00
AT	Alan Trammell/250	15.00
CU	Chase Utley/100	25.00
RW	Ryan Wagner/150	10.00
JW	Jerome Williams/150	10.00
WI	Josh Willingham/150	6.00
RA	Randy Winn/100	10.00
KW	Kerry Wood/50	50.00
DY	Delmon Young/250	20.00
MY	Michael Young/150	15.00
CZ	Carlos Zambrano/250	25.00

Etched in Time Red Ink

No Pricing
Production 25 sets

Game Bat Blue

NM/M

Common Player:
Purple: 1X
Production 250
Red: 1X
Production 150
Green: 1-2X
Production 50

BA	Bobby Abreu	6.00

RA	Roberto Alomar	6.00
GA	Garret Anderson	6.00
CB	Carlos Beltran	6.00
AB	Adrian Beltre	6.00
LB	Lance Berkman	4.00
HB	Hank Blalock	6.00
BB	Bret Boone	4.00
SC	Sean Casey	4.00
EC	Eric Chavez	6.00
JC	Jose Cruz Jr.	4.00
CD	Carlos Delgado	6.00
JD	J.D. Drew	4.00
AD	Adam Dunn	8.00
JE	Jim Edmonds	6.00
CF	Cliff Floyd	4.00
RF	Rafael Furcal	4.00
NG	Nomar Garciaparra	10.00
JG	Jason Giambi	6.00
BG	Brian Giles	4.00
TG	Troy Glaus	6.00
LG	Luis Gonzalez	4.00
SG	Shawn Green	6.00
KG	Ken Griffey Jr.	12.00
VG	Vladimir Guerrero	10.00
TH	Todd Helton	8.00
HU	Torii Hunter	6.00
GJ	Geoff Jenkins	4.00
DJ	Derek Jeter	20.00
RJ	Randy Johnson	8.00
AJ	Andruw Jones	8.00
CJ	Chipper Jones	8.00
JL	Javy Lopez	6.00
ML	Mike Lowell	6.00
KM	Kazuo Matsui	10.00
MO	Magglio Ordonez	4.00
RP	Rafael Palmeiro	8.00
JP	Jay Payton	4.00
PI	Mike Piazza	10.00
AP	Albert Pujols	15.00
MR	Manny Ramirez	8.00
JR	Jose Reyes	6.00
AR	Alex Rodriguez	15.00
IR	Ivan Rodriguez	8.00
SR	Scott Rolen	15.00
TS	Tim Salmon	6.00
CS	Curt Schilling	6.00
GS	Gary Sheffield	6.00
AS	Alfonso Soriano	8.00
SS	Sammy Sosa	10.00
IS	Ichiro Suzuki	15.00
MT	Mark Teixeira	6.00
TE	Miguel Tejada	6.00
FT	Frank Thomas	8.00
JT	Jim Thome	8.00
OV	Omar Vizquel	4.00
LW	Larry Walker	4.00
VW	Vernon Wells	4.00
BW	Bernie Williams	8.00
KW	Kerry Wood	8.00

Master Etchings

No Pricing
Production One Set

Star Etchings

NM/M

Quantity produced listed

BA	Bobby Abreu/50	20.00
GA	Garret Anderson/50	20.00
JB	Josh Beckett/50	20.00
CB	Carlos Beltran/50	50.00
LB	Lance Berkman/15	
HB	Hank Blalock/50	25.00
BB	Bret Boone/50	
MC	Miguel Cabrera/50	
EC	Eric Chavez/50	20.00
JD	J.D. Drew/50	30.00
AD	Adam Dunn/50	30.00
NG	Nomar Garciaparra/15	100.00
BG	Brian Giles/50	
KG	Ken Griffey Jr./50	85.00
KG1	Ken Griffey Jr./50	85.00
VG	Vladimir Guerrero/15	80.00
RH	Roy Halladay/50	15.00
HE	Todd Helton/15	
TH	Tim Hudson/50	30.00
GJ	Geoff Jenkins/50	15.00
DJ	Derek Jeter/10	
DL	Derrek Lee/50	35.00
JL	Javy Lopez/50	
ML	Mike Lowell/50	15.00
MU	Mark Mulder/50	25.00
MM	Mike Mussina/15	
MO	Magglio Ordonez/50	15.00
RO	Roy Oswalt/50	
MP	Mike Piazza/10	
PR	Mark Prior/50	60.00
MR	Manny Ramirez/15	
IR	Ivan Rodriguez/15	
JS	Jason Schmidt/50	40.00
MT	Mark Teixeira/50	40.00
TE	Miguel Tejada/50	25.00
FT	Frank Thomas/15	
BW	Brandon Webb/50	15.00
VW	Vernon Wells/50	15.00
DW	Dontrelle Willis/50	25.00
KW	Kerry Wood/50	40.00

Triple Etchings

NM/M

Production 50 Sets

RJM	Alex Rodriguez, Derek Jeter, Hideki Matsui	125.00
PER	Albert Pujols, Jim Edmonds, Scott Rolen	90.00
SRG	Curt Schilling, Manny Ramirez, Nomar Garciaparra	40.00
SBT	Alfonso Soriano, Hank Blalock, Mark Teixeira	40.00
WPS	Kerry Wood, Mark Prior, Sammy Sosa	60.00
DMW	Joe DiMaggio, Mickey Mantle, Ted Williams	400.00

2004 UPPER DECK FIRST PITCH

NM/M

Complete Set (300): 40.00
Common Player: .10
Common SP (271-300): 1.00
Inserted 1:4
Pack (5): 1.00
Box (36): 25.00

1	Dontrelle Willis	.50
2	Edgar Gonzalez	.25
3	Jose Reyes	.50
4	Jae Weong Seo	.25
5	Miguel Cabrera	.75
6	Jesse Foppert	.25
7	Mike Neu	.25
8	Micheal Nakamura	.25
9	Luis Ayala	.25
10	Jared Sandberg	.25
11	Jhonny Peralta	.25
12	Wilfredo Ledezma	.25
13	Jason Roach	.25
14	Kirk Saarloos	.25
15	Cliff Lee	.25
16	Bobby Hill	.25
17	Lyle Overbay	.25
18	Josh Hall	.25
19	Joe Thurston	.25
20	Matt Kata	.25
21	Jeremy Bonderman	.25
22	Julio Manon	.25
23	Rodrigo Rosario	.25
24	Robby Hammock	.25
25	David Sanders	.25
26	Miguel Ojeda	.25
27	Mark Teixeira	.50
28	Franklyn German	.25
29	Ken Harvey	.25
30	Xavier Nady	.25
31	Tim Salmon	.25
32	Troy Glaus	.25
33	Adam Kennedy	.10
34	David Eckstein	.10
35	Bengie Molina	.10
36	Jarrod Washburn	.10
37	Ramon Ortiz	.10
38	Eric Chavez	.25
39	Miguel Tejada	.25
40	Chris Singleton	.10
41	Jermaine Dye	.10
42	John Halama	.10
43	Tim Hudson	.25
44	Barry Zito	.25
45	Ted Lilly	.10
46	Bobby Kielty	.10
47	Kelvim Escobar	.10
48	Josh Phelps	.10
49	Vernon Wells	.20
50	Roy Halladay	.20
51	Orlando Hudson	.10
52	Eric Hinske	.10
53	Brandon Backe	.10
54	Dewon Brazelton	.10
55	Ben Grieve	.10
56	Aubrey Huff	.10
57	Toby Hall	.10
58	Rocco Baldelli	.50
59	Al Martin	.10
60	Brandon Phillips	.10
61	Omar Vizquel	.10
62	C.C. Sabathia	.10
63	Milton Bradley	.10
64	Ricky Gutierrez	.10
65	Matt Lawton	.10
66	Danys Baez	.10
67	Ichiro Suzuki	1.00
68	Randy Winn	.10
69	Carlos Guillen	.10
70	Mark McLemore	.10
71	Dan Wilson	.10
72	Jamie Moyer	.10
73	Joel Pineiro	.10
74	Edgar Martinez	.20
75	Tony Batista	.10
76	Jay Gibbons	.10
77	Jeff Conine	.10
78	Melvin Mora	.10
79	Geronimo Gil	.10
80	Rodrigo Lopez	.10
81	Jorge Julio	.10
82	Rafael Palmeiro	.40
83	Juan Gonzalez	.40
84	Mike Young	.10
85	Alex Rodriguez	1.00
86	Einar Diaz	.10
87	Kevin Mench	.10
88	Hank Blalock	.25
89	Pedro J. Martinez	.50
90	Byung-Hyun Kim	.10
91	Derek Lowe	.20
92	Jason Varitek	.10
93	Manny Ramirez	.40
94	John Burkett	.10
95	Todd Walker	.10
96	Nomar Garciaparra	1.00
97	Trot Nixon	.10
98	Mike Sweeney	.10
99	Carlos Febles	.10
100	Mike MacDougal	.10
101	Raul Ibanez	.10
102	Jason Grimsley	.10
103	Chris George	.10
104	Brent Mayne	.10
105	Dmitri Young	.10
106	Eric Munson	.10
107	A.J. Hinch	.10
108	Andres Torres	.10
109	Bobby Higginson	.10
110	Shane Halter	.10
111	Matt Walbeck	.10
112	Torii Hunter	.25
113	Doug Mientkiewicz	.10
114	Lew Ford	.10
115	Eric Milton	.10
116	Eddie Guardado	.10
117	Cristian Guzman	.10
118	Corey Koskie	.10
119	Magglio Ordonez	.25
120	Mark Buehrle	.10
121	Billy Koch	.10
122	Jose Valentin	.10
123	Paul Konerko	.10
124	Carlos Lee	.10
125	Jon Garland	.10
126	Jason Giambi	.50
127	Derek Jeter	1.50
128	Roger Clemens	1.00
129	Andy Pettitte	.25
130	Jorge Posada	.25
131	David Wells	.10
132	Hideki Matsui	1.25
133	Mike Mussina	.40
134	Jeff Bagwell	.40
135	Craig Biggio	.20
136	Morgan Ensberg	.10
137	Richard Hidalgo	.10
138	Brad Ausmus	.10
139	Roy Oswalt	.25
140	Billy Wagner	.20
141	Octavio Dotel	.10
142	Gary Sheffield	.25
143	Andruw Jones	.40
144	John Smoltz	.20
145	Rafael Furcal	.20
146	Javy Lopez	.25
147	Shane Reynolds	.10
148	Horacio Ramirez	.10
149	Mike Hampton	.10
150	Jung Bong	.10
151	Ruben Quevedo	.10
152	Ben Sheets	.20
153	Geoff Jenkins	.20
154	Royce Clayton	.10
155	Glendon Rusch	.10
156	John Vander Wal	.10
157	Scott Podsednik	.25
158	Jim Edmonds	.25
159	Tino Martinez	.20
160	Albert Pujols	1.00
161	Matt Morris	.10
162	Woody Williams	.10
163	Edgar Renteria	.10
164	Jason Isringhausen	.10
165	Jason Simontacchi	.10
166	Kerry Robinson	.10
167	Sammy Sosa	1.00
168	Joe Borowski	.10
169	Tony Womack	.10
170	Antonio Alfonseca	.10
171	Corey Patterson	.10
172	Mark Prior	1.00
173	Moises Alou	.20
174	Matt Clement	.10
175	Randall Simon	.10
176	Randy Johnson	.50
177	Luis Gonzalez	.20
178	Craig Counsell	.10
179	Miguel Batista	.10
180	Steve Finley	.10
181	Brandon Webb	.10
182	Danny Bautista	.10
183	Oscar Villarreal	.10
184	Shawn Green	.25
185	Brian Jordan	.10
186	Fred McGriff	.20
187	Andy Ashby	.10
188	Rickey Henderson	.25
189	Dave Roberts	.10
190	Eric Gagne	.20
191	Kazuhisa Ishii	.10
192	Adrian Beltre	.10
193	Vladimir Guerrero	.50
194	Livan Hernandez	.10
195	Ron Calloway	.10
196	Sun-Woo Kim	.10
197	Wil Cordero	.10
198	Brad Wilkerson	.10
199	Orlando Cabrera	.10
200	Sidney Ponson	.10
201	Ray Durham	.10
202	Andres Galarraga	.10
203	Benito Santiago	.10
204	Jose Cruz Jr.	.10
205	Jason Schmidt	.10
206	Kirk Rueter	.10
207	Felix Rodriguez	.10
208	Mike Lowell	.10
209	Luis Castillo	.10
210	Derrek Lee	.10
211	Andy Fox	.10
212	Tommy Phelps	.10
213	Todd Hollandsworth	.10
214	Brad Penny	.10
215	Juan Pierre	.10
216	Mike Piazza	.75
217	Jae Weong Seo	.10
218	Ty Wigginton	.10
219	Al Leiter	.10
220	Roger Cedeno	.10
221	Timoniel Perez	.10

222	Aaron Heilman	.10
223	Pedro Astacio	.10
224	Joe McEwing	.10
225	Ryan Klesko	.20
226	Brian Giles	.20
227	Mark Kotsay	.10
228	Brian Lawrence	.10
229	Rod Beck	.10
230	Trevor Hoffman	.10
231	Sean Burroughs	.10
232	Bobby Abreu	.20
233	Jim Thome	.50
234	David Bell	.10
235	Jimmy Rollins	.10
236	Mike Lieberthal	.10
237	Vicente Padilla	.10
238	Randy Wolf	.10
239	Reggie Sanders	.10
240	Jason Kendall	.10
241	Jack Wilson	.10
242	Jose Hernandez	.10
243	Kip Wells	.10
244	Carlos Rivera	.10
245	Craig Wilson	.10
246	Adam Dunn	.25
247	Sean Casey	.10
248	Danny Graves	.10
249	Ryan Dempster	.10
250	Barry Larkin	.25
251	Reggie Taylor	.10
252	Wily Mo Pena	.10
253	Larry Walker	.20
254	Mark Sweeney	.10
255	Preston Wilson	.10
256	Jason Jennings	.10
257	Charles Johnson	.10
258	Jay Payton	.10
259	Chris Stynes	.10
260	Juan Uribe	.10
261	Hideki Matsui/CL	.50
262	Josh Beckett/CL	.20
263	Dontrelle Willis/CL	.20
264	Kevin Millwood/CL	.20
265	Billy Wagner/CL	.10
266	Rocco Baldelli/CL	.25
267	Roger Clemens/CL	.50
268	Rafael Palmeiro/CL	.20
269	Miguel Cabrera/CL	.25
270	Jose Contreras/CL	.10
271	Rickie Weeks	3.00
272	Delmon Young	4.00
273	Chien-Ming Wang	1.00
274	Rich Harden	1.00
275	Edwin Jackson	1.50
276	Dan Haren	1.00
277	Todd Wellemeyer	1.00
278	Prentice Redman	1.00
279	Ryan Wagner	1.50
280	Aaron Looper	1.00
281	Rick Roberts	1.00
282	Josh Willingham	1.00
283	David Crouthers	1.00
284	Chris Capuano	1.00
285	Mike Gosling	1.00
286	Brian Sweeney	1.00
287	*Donald Kelly*	1.00
288	*Ryan Meaux*	1.50
289	Colin Porter	1.00
290	*Jerome Gamble*	1.50
291	*Colby Miller*	1.50
292	Ian Ferguson	1.00
293	*Tim Bittner*	1.00
294	*Jason Frasor*	1.00
295	*Brandon Medders*	1.00
296	*Mike Johnston*	1.00
297	*Tim Bausher*	1.00
298	*Justin Leone*	1.00
299	Sean Henn	1.00
300	Michel Hernandez	1.00

First and Foremost

		NM/M
Complete Set (14):		40.00
Common Player:		3.00
Inserted 1:Blaster Box		
EB	Ernie Banks	5.00
GH	George H.W. Bush	5.00
GW	George W. Bush	5.00
JC	Jose Contreras	3.00
WF	Whitey Ford	4.00
RH	Rich Harden	3.00
DH	Dan Haren	3.00
HR	Horacio Ramirez	3.00
MS	Mike Schmidt	5.00
LT	Luis Tiant	3.00
RW	Ryan Wagner	3.00
BW	Brandon Webb	3.00
JW	Jerome Williams	3.00
DW	Dontrelle Willis	3.00

2004 UPPER DECK PLAY BALL

		NM/M
Complete Set (183):		
Common Player:		.15
Common SP (133-162):		3.00
Production 2,004		
Common Classic Combo (163-183):		2.00
Production 1,999		
Pack (5):		3.00
Box (24):		65.00
1	Hideo Nomo	.25
2	Curt Schilling	.50
3	Barry Zito	.40
4	Nomar Garciaparra	1.50
5	Yogi Berra	.50
6	Randy Johnson	.75
7	Jason Giambi	.75
8	Sammy Sosa	1.25
9	David Ortiz	.40
10	Derek Jeter	2.00
11	Warren Spahn	.50
12	Mark Prior	1.50
13	Roger Clemens	1.50
14	Mike Piazza	1.00
15	Nolan Ryan	2.00
16	Joe DiMaggio	1.50
17	Alfonso Soriano	.75
18	Brandon Webb	.25
19	Shawn Green	.25
20	Bob Feller	.25
21	Mike Schmidt	.75
22	Mark Teixeira	.25
23	Pedro J. Martinez	.75
24	Vladimir Guerrero	.75
25	Rafael Furcal	.25
26	Derrek Lee	.25
27	Carlos Delgado	.50
28	Mickey Mantle	3.00
29	Dontrelle Willis	.25
30	Ted Williams	1.50
31	Vernon Wells	.25
32	Alex Rodriguez	1.50
33	Brooks Robinson	.50
34	Tom Seaver	.50
35	Ernie Banks	.50
36	Bob Gibson	.50
37	Jim Thome	.75
38	Mike Mussina	.50
39	Eric Chavez	.25
40	Roy Halladay	.25
41	Eric Gagne	.40
42	Jose Reyes	.15
43	Jeff Bagwell	.50
44	Rich Harden	.15
45	Jeff Kent	.25
46	Lance Berkman	.25
47	Adam Dunn	.40
48	Richie Sexson	.40
49	Andruw Jones	.50
50	Ichiro Suzuki	1.25
51	Edgar Renteria	.25
52	Rocco Baldelli	.25
53	Jim Edmonds	.25
54	Magglio Ordonez	.25
55	Austin Kearns	.25
56	Garret Anderson	.40
57	Manny Ramirez	.50
58	Roy Oswalt	.25
59	Gary Sheffield	.40
60	Mark Mulder	.25
61	Ben Sheets	.25
62	Scott Rolen	.75
63	Greg Maddux	1.00
64	Jose Contreras	.15
65	Miguel Cabrera	.50
66	Hank Blalock	.40
67	Miguel Tejada	.40
68	Albert Pujols	1.50
69	Hideki Matsui	1.50
70	Mike Lowell	.25
71	Tim Hudson	.25
72	Bret Boone	.25
73	Ivan Rodriguez	.50
74	Josh Beckett	.50
75	Todd Helton	.50
76	Brian Giles	.25
77	Orlando Cabrera	.15
78	Carlos Beltran	.40
79	Jason Schmidt	.25
80	Kerry Wood	.75
81	Preston Wilson	.15
82	Troy Glaus	.40
83	Kevin Brown	.25
84	Rafael Palmeiro	.50
85	Chipper Jones	1.00
86	Reggie Sanders	.15
87	Cliff Floyd	.15
88	Corey Patterson	.25
89	Kevin Millwood	.25
90	Aaron Boone	.15
91	Darin Erstad	.25
92	Richard Hidalgo	.15
93	Dmitri Young	.15
94	Jeremy Bonderman	.15
95	Larry Walker	.25
96	Edgar Martinez	.25
97	Jerome Williams	.15
98	Luis Gonzalez	.25
99	Roberto Alomar	.40
100	Jerry Hairston Jr.	.15
101	Luis Matos	.15
102	Andy Pettitte	.40
103	Frank Thomas	.50
104	Rondell White	.25
105	Jody Gerut	.15
106	Bartolo Colon	.25
107	Johnny Damon	.25
108	Ryan Klesko	.25
109	Geoff Jenkins	.25
110	Jorge Posada	.40
111	Melvin Mora	.15
112	Bernie Williams	.40
113	Shannon Stewart	.15
114	Bobby Abreu	.25
115	Jose Guillen	.25
116	Brandon Phillips	.15
117	Jose Vidro	.15
118	Mike Sweeney	.15
119	Jacque Jones	.15
120	Josh Phelps	.15
121	Milton Bradley	.15
122	Torii Hunter	.25
123	Carl Crawford	.15
124	Javier Vazquez	.25
125	Juan Gonzalez	.50
126	Travis Hafner	.15
127	Ken Griffey Jr.	1.00
128	Phil Nevin	.15
129	Trot Nixon	.15
130	Carlos Lee	.15
131	Javy Lopez	.25
132	Jay Gibbons	.15
133	*Brandon Medders*	3.00
134	*Colby Miller*	3.00
135	David Crouthers	3.00
136	*Dennis Sarfate*	5.00
137	*Donald Kelly*	3.00
138	*Frank Brooks*	5.00
139	*Chris Aguila*	3.00
140	*Greg Dobbs*	3.00
141	*Ian Snell*	5.00
142	Jake Woods	3.00
143	*Jamie Brown*	3.00
144	*Jason Frasor*	4.00
145	*Jerome Gamble*	4.00
146	*Jesse Harper*	5.00
147	*Josh Labandeira*	4.00
148	*Justin Hampson*	4.00
149	*Justin Huisman*	4.00
150	*Justin Leone*	5.00
151	*Lincoln Holdzkom*	3.00
152	*Mike Bumatay*	5.00
153	Mike Gosling	5.00
154	*Mike Johnston*	3.00
155	Mike Rouse	3.00
156	*Nick Regilio*	3.00
157	*Ryan Meaux*	3.00
158	*Scott Dohmann*	3.00
159	Sean Henn	6.00
160	*Tim Bausher*	3.00
161	*Tim Bittner*	3.00
162	*Alec Zumwalt*	3.00
163	Aaron Boone, Bret Boone, Geoff Jenkins, Mark Prior, Barry Zito	4.00
164	Albert Pujols, Edgar Renteria, Alex Rodriguez	5.00
165	Alfonso Soriano, Sammy Sosa	4.00
166	Bobby Abreu, Jim Thome	2.00
167	Bret Boone, John Olerud, Ichiro Suzuki	4.00
168	Derek Jeter, Alfonso Soriano	6.00
169	Eric Chavez, Miguel Tejada	2.00
170	Garret Anderson, Jim Edmonds, Troy Glaus	2.00
171	Hank Blalock, Alex Rodriguez	5.00
172	Alex Rodriguez, Mark Teixeira, Michael Young, Rafael Palmeiro	5.00
173	Ivan Rodriguez, Dontrelle Willis	2.00
174	Jason Giambi, Derek Jeter	6.00
175	Joe DiMaggio, Mickey Mantle	8.00
176	Joe DiMaggio, Mickey Mantle, Ted Williams	8.00
177	Joe DiMaggio, Ted Williams	6.00
178	Nomar Garciaparra, Alfonso Soriano	4.00
179	Nomar Garciaparra, Jason Giambi	4.00
180	Paul LoDuca, Hideo Nomo	2.00
181	Rafael Palmeiro, Alex Rodriguez, Michael Young	4.00
182	Ralph Kiner, Ted Williams	5.00
183	Aaron Boone, Derek Jeter	6.00

Blue

Blue (1-132): 2-3X
Inserted 1:6

Green

No Pricing
Production 15 sets

Purple

No Pricing
Production one set

Die-Cut

Die-Cut (1-132): 3-6X
Production 175

Apparel Collection

		NM/M
Common Player:		4.00
Inserted 1:24		
JB	Jeff Bagwell	6.00
RB	Rocco Baldelli	8.00
BE	Josh Beckett	6.00
LB	Lance Berkman	4.00
CD	Carlos Delgado	5.00
JD	Joe DiMaggio	75.00
AD	Adam Dunn	6.00
RF	Rafael Furcal	5.00
JG	Jason Giambi	6.00
TG	Troy Glaus	6.00
KG	Ken Griffey Jr.	15.00
HA	Roy Halladay	5.00
RH	Rich Harden	
BH	Bo Hart	4.00
TH	Torii Hunter	4.00
DJ	Derek Jeter	15.00
RJ	Randy Johnson	8.00
CJ	Chipper Jones	8.00
ML	Mike Lowell	5.00
MM	Mickey Mantle	90.00
PM	Pedro J. Martinez	8.00
HM	Hideki Matsui	20.00
MU	Mike Mussina	6.00
HN	Hideo Nomo	6.00
RO	Roy Oswalt	4.00

RP	Rafael Palmeiro	6.00
PI	Mike Piazza	10.00
JP	Jorge Posada	8.00
MP	Mark Prior	12.00
AP	Albert Pujols	10.00
MR	Manny Ramirez	6.00
AR	Alex Rodriguez	8.00
CS	Curt Schilling	6.00
AS	Alfonso Soriano	6.00
SS	Sammy Sosa	10.00
IS	Ichiro Suzuki	15.00
JT	Jim Thome	8.00
BW	Bernie Williams	5.00
TW	Ted Williams	70.00
DW	Dontrelle Willis	5.00
KW	Kerry Wood	8.00
BZ	Barry Zito	5.00

Artist's Touch

		NM/M
Common Player:		4.00
Production 250		
Parallel:		1-2X
Production 50		
RB	Rocco Baldelli	8.00
JB	Josh Beckett	8.00
LB	Lance Berkman	5.00
CD	Carlos Delgado	6.00
RF	Rafael Furcal	5.00
JG	Jason Giambi	8.00
TG	Troy Glaus	6.00
KG	Ken Griffey Jr.	15.00
HA	Roy Halladay	5.00
BH	Bo Hart	4.00
TH	Torii Hunter	5.00
DJ	Derek Jeter	15.00
RJ	Randy Johnson	8.00
CJ	Chipper Jones	8.00
ML	Mike Lowell	
PM	Pedro J. Martinez	8.00
HM	Hideki Matsui	20.00
MM	Mike Mussina	8.00
HN	Hideo Nomo	8.00
RO	Roy Oswalt	4.00
RP	Rafael Palmeiro	8.00
PI	Mike Piazza	10.00
JP	Jorge Posada	8.00
MP	Mark Prior	15.00
AP	Albert Pujols	10.00
MR	Manny Ramirez/50	10.00
AR	Alex Rodriguez	
AS	Alfonso Soriano	15.00
SS	Sammy Sosa	15.00
IS	Ichiro Suzuki	20.00
JT	Jim Thome	10.00
BW	Bernie Williams	6.00
DW	Dontrelle Willis	5.00
KW	Kerry Wood	8.00
BZ	Barry Zito	6.00

Home Run Heroics

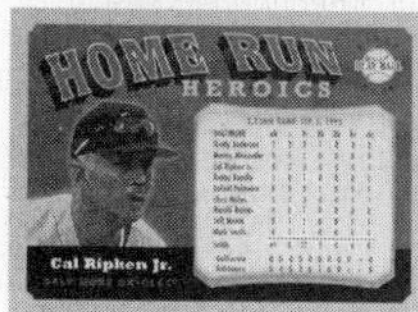

		NM/M
Common Player:		2.00
Inserted 1:24		
EB	Ernie Banks	4.00
HB	Hank Blalock	3.00
AB	Aaron Boone	2.00
MC	Miguel Cabrera	4.00
CD	Carlos Delgado	3.00
JD	Joe DiMaggio	8.00
JD1	Joe DiMaggio	8.00
JG	Jason Giambi	3.00
SG	Shawn Green	2.00
KG	Ken Griffey Jr.	6.00
KG1	Ken Griffey Jr.	6.00
RH	Rickey Henderson	2.00
RJ	Randy Johnson	3.00
HK	Harmon Killebrew	4.00
MM	Mickey Mantle	15.00
MM1	Mickey Mantle	15.00
MM2	Mickey Mantle	15.00
EM	Eddie Mathews	4.00
HM	Hideki Matsui	6.00
HM1	Hideki Matsui	6.00
WM	Willie McCovey	2.00
BM	Bill Mueller	2.00
SM	Stan Musial	5.00
RP	Rafael Palmeiro	3.00
CR	Cal Ripken Jr.	10.00
CR1	Cal Ripken Jr.	10.00
AR	Alex Rodriguez	6.00
AR1	Alex Rodriguez	6.00
FR	Frank Robinson	3.00
MS	Mike Schmidt	5.00
RS	Red Schoendienst	2.00
AS	Alfonso Soriano	4.00
SS	Sammy Sosa	6.00
SS1	Sammy Sosa	6.00
SS2	Sammy Sosa	6.00
SS3	Sammy Sosa	6.00
TW	Ted Williams	10.00
TW1	Ted Williams	10.00
TW2	Ted Williams	10.00
TW3	Ted Williams	10.00

Rookie Signature Portfolio

		NM/M
Common Player:		5.00
Inserted 1:30		
CA	Chris Aguila	6.00
TB	Tim Bausher	8.00
BI	Tim Bittner	8.00
FB	Frank Brooks	8.00
JB	Jamie Brown	5.00
MB	Mike Bumatay	8.00
DC	David Crouthers	8.00
GD	Greg Dobbs	6.00
SD	Scott Dohmann	8.00
JF	Jason Frasor	8.00
JG	Jerome Gamble	8.00
MG	Mike Gosling	8.00
HA	Justin Hampson	6.00
JH	Jesse Harper	8.00
SH	Sean Henn	15.00
LH	Lincoln Holdzkom	5.00
HU	Justin Huisman	5.00
MJ	Mike Johnston	10.00
DK	Donald Kelly	5.00
JL	Josh Labandeira	8.00
LE	Justin Leone	10.00
RM	Ryan Meaux	5.00
BM	Brandon Medders	5.00
CM	Colby Miller	5.00
NR	Nick Regilio	5.00
MR	Mike Rouse	6.00
DS	Dennis Sarfate	8.00
IS	Ian Snell	8.00
JW	Jake Woods	5.00
AZ	Alec Zumwalt	8.00

Signature Portfolio

		NM/M
Production 100		
Parallel:		No Pricing
Production 25 or 10		
KG	Ken Griffey Jr.	100.00
HM	Hideki Matsui	250.00
CR	Cal Ripken Jr.	120.00
TS	Tom Seaver	40.00
CY	Carl Yastrzemski	50.00
BZ	Barry Zito	30.00

Tools of the Stars

		NM/M
Common Player:		6.00
Inserted 1:48		
Level 1 Parallel:		1-1.5X
Production 250		
Level 2 Parallel:		No Pricing
Production 25		
JB	Josh Beckett	6.00
CD	Carlos Delgado	6.00
KG	Ken Griffey Jr./SP	15.00
DJ	Derek Jeter	15.00
CJ	Chipper Jones	8.00
HM	Hideki Matsui	15.00
HN	Hideo Nomo	6.00
PI	Mike Piazza	10.00
AP	Albert Pujols	15.00
AR	Alex Rodriguez	10.00
AS	Alfonso Soriano	6.00
IS	Ichiro Suzuki	15.00
JT	Jim Thome	8.00
KW	Kerry Wood	8.00

2004 UPPER DECK POWER UP

		NM/M
Complete Set (100):		20.00
Common Player:		.15
Pack (9):		1.50
Box (24):		25.00
1	Austin Kearns	.25
2	Rafael Furcal	.25
3	Larry Walker	.25
4	Jeremy Bonderman	.15
5	Scott Rolen	.50
6	Nomar Garciaparra	1.00
7	Jody Gerut	.15
8	Troy Glaus	.25
9	Roy Halladay	.25
10	Barry Zito	.40
11	Gary Sheffield	.40
12	Ichiro Suzuki	1.00
13	Juan Gonzalez	.25
14	Jim Edmonds	.25
15	Hank Blalock	.40
16	Roy Oswalt	.25
17	Magglio Ordonez	.25
18	Garret Anderson	.40
19	Mark Teixeira	.25
20	Mike Sweeney	.15
21	Reggie Sanders	.15
22	Rafael Palmeiro	.40
23	Orlando Cabrera	.15
24	Edgar Renteria	.25
25	Ryan Klesko	.25
26	Torii Hunter	.25
27	Bret Boone	.25
28	Roberto Alomar	.25
29	Frank Thomas	.50
30	Chipper Jones	.50
31	Eric Chavez	.25
32	Miguel Tejada	.40
33	Carlos Beltran	.40
34	Geoff Jenkins	.25
35	Hideki Matsui	1.00
36	Jason Kendall	.15
37	Adam Dunn	.40
38	Jay Gibbons	.15
39	Ivan Rodriguez	.50
40	Sidney Ponson	.15
41	Albert Pujols	1.00
42	Bartolo Colon	.25
43	Lance Berkman	.25
44	Brandon Webb	.15
45	Shannon Stewart	.15
46	Josh Beckett	.50
47	Jason Schmidt	.25
48	Luis Gonzalez	.25
49	Jacque Jones	.15
50	Andruw Jones	.40
51	Todd Helton	.50
52	Javier Vazquez	.25
53	Alfonso Soriano	.50
54	Manny Ramirez	.50
55	Bobby Abreu	.25
56	Rocco Baldelli	.25
57	Kerry Wood	.50
58	Derek Jeter	1.50
59	Phil Nevin	.15
60	Jeff Bagwell	.40
61	Sammy Sosa	1.00
62	Tom Glavine	.25
63	Miguel Cabrera	.50
64	Shawn Green	.25
65	Mark Prior	1.00
66	Jose Reyes	.25
67	Curt Schilling	.40
68	Hideo Nomo	.25
69	Mike Lowell	.25
70	Randy Johnson	.50
71	Edgar Martinez	.25
72	Dontrelle Willis	.25
73	Milton Bradley	.15
74	Preston Wilson	.15
75	Mike Piazza	.75
76	Mike Mussina	.40
77	Darin Erstad	.25
78	Greg Maddux	.75
79	Tim Hudson	.25
80	Kevin Millwood	.25
81	Dmitri Young	.15
82	Ben Sheets	.25
83	Alex Rodriguez	1.00
84	Johan Santana	.15
85	Jeff Kent	.25
86	Pedro Martinez	.50
87	Carlos Delgado	.40
88	Jim Thome	.50
89	Aubrey Huff	.15
90	Ken Griffey Jr.	1.00
91	Kevin Brown	.25
92	Tony Batista	.15
93	Richie Sexson	.25
94	Cliff Floyd	.15
95	Jose Vidro	.15
96	Brian Giles	.25
97	Jorge Posada	.40
98	Vernon Wells	.25
99	Vladimir Guerrero	.50
100	Jason Giambi	.50

Mega Rare

No Pricing
Inserted 1:240

Super Rare

Stars:	5-10X
Inserted 1:96	

Rare

Stars:	3-4X
Inserted 1:6	

Ultra Rare

Stars:	4-6X
Inserted 1:24	

Stickers

		NM/M
1	Hideo Nomo	.50
2	Mark Prior	3.00
3	Scott Rolen	1.50
4	Luis Gonzalez	.50
5	Miguel Tejada	.75
6	Richie Sexson	.75
7	Jim Edmonds	.75
8	Carlos Beltran	.75
9	Manny Ramirez	1.00
10	Torii Hunter	.75
11	Garret Anderson	.75
12	Eric Chavez	.75
13	Juan Gonzalez	.75
14	Albert Pujols	3.00
15	Tim Hudson	.75
16	Roy Halladay	.75
17	Roy Oswalt	.50
18	Andruw Jones	1.00
19	Gary Sheffield	.75
20	Magglio Ordonez	.75
21	Jason Giambi	1.50
22	Brian Giles	.75
23	Barry Zito	.75
24	Todd Helton	1.00
25	Randy Johnson	1.50
26	Pedro Martinez	1.50
27	Vernon Wells	.50
28	Lance Berkman	.75
29	Mike Mussina	.75
30	Carlos Delgado	.75
31	Ivan Rodriguez	1.00
32	Kevin Brown	.75
33	Kerry Wood	1.50
34	Mark Teixeira	.75
35	Hideki Matsui	2.50
36	Troy Glaus	.75
37	Mike Piazza	2.00
38	Nomar Garciaparra	3.00
39	Vladimir Guerrero	1.50
40	Derek Jeter	4.00
41	Jason Schmidt	.50
42	Alex Rodriguez	3.00
43	Jeff Bagwell	1.00
44	Shawn Green	.75
45	Sammy Sosa	2.50
46	Josh Beckett	1.00

47 Bret Boone .50
48 Ichiro Suzuki 2.00
49 Jeff Kent .75
50 Rafael Palmeiro 1.00
51 Curt Schilling 1.00
52 Greg Maddux 2.00
53 Mike Lowell .75
54 Dontrelle Willis .75
55 Alfonso Soriano 1.00
56 Preston Wilson .50
57 Jorge Posada .75
58 Frank Thomas 1.00
59 Jim Thome 1.50
60 Ken Griffey Jr. 2.00
61 Rocco Baldelli .75
62 Jose Vidro .50
63 Austin Kearns .50
64 Phil Nevin .50
65 Darin Erstad .50
66 Johan Santana .50
67 Chipper Jones 1.50
68 Brandon Webb .50
69 Hank Blalock .75
70 Adam Dunn .75
71 Javier Vazquez .75
72 Jacque Jones .50
73 Bobby Abreu .75
74 Edgar Renteria .75
75 Rafael Furcal .75
76 Mike Sweeney .50
77 Geoff Jenkins .50
78 Shannon Stewart .50
79 Ryan Klesko .75
80 Edgar Martinez .75
81 Kevin Millwood .75
82 Bartolo Colon .75
83 Tom Glavine .75
84 Miguel Cabrera 1.50
85 Jose Reyes .75
86 Padres/Astros/ A's/Angels/Cubs/D-Rays .50
87 Pirates/M's/ Expos/Twins/Reds/Phils .50
88 Royals/O's/W.Sox/ Dodgers/Marlins/Yanks .50
89 Giants/Mets/Cards/ Indians/Braves/Rangers .50
90 Tigers/R.Sox/Rockies/ D-Backs/Brewers/Jay .50

Shining Through

NM/M

1 Hideo Nomo .25
2 Mark Prior 1.50
3 Scott Rolen .75
4 Luis Gonzalez .25
5 Miguel Tejada .40
6 Richie Sexson .40
7 Jim Edmonds .40
8 Carlos Beltran .40
9 Manny Ramirez .50
10 Torii Hunter .40
11 Garret Anderson .40
12 Eric Chavez .40
13 Juan Gonzalez .40
14 Albert Pujols 1.50
15 Tim Hudson .40
16 Roy Halladay .40
17 Roy Oswalt .25
18 Andruw Jones .50
19 Gary Sheffield .40
20 Magglio Ordonez .40
21 Jason Giambi .75
22 Brian Giles .40
23 Barry Zito .40
24 Todd Helton .50
25 Randy Johnson .75
26 Pedro Martinez .75
27 Vernon Wells .25
28 Lance Berkman .40
29 Mike Mussina .50
30 Carlos Delgado .40
31 Ivan Rodriguez .50
32 Kevin Brown .40
33 Kerry Wood .75
34 Mark Teixeira .40
35 Hideki Matsui 1.50
36 Troy Glaus .40
37 Mike Piazza 1.00
38 Nomar Garciaparra 1.50
39 Vladimir Guerrero .75
40 Derek Jeter 2.00
41 Jason Schmidt .40
42 Alex Rodriguez Yanks 1.50
43 Jeff Bagwell .50
44 Shawn Green .40
45 Sammy Sosa 1.50
46 Josh Beckett .75
47 Bret Boone .40
48 Ichiro Suzuki 1.00
49 Jeff Kent .40
50 Rafael Palmeiro .50
51 Curt Schilling .50
52 Greg Maddux 1.00
53 Mike Lowell .40
54 Dontrelle Willis .40
55 Alfonso Soriano .50
56 Preston Wilson .25
57 Jorge Posada .40
58 Frank Thomas .50
59 Jim Thome .75
60 Ken Griffey Jr. 1.00
61 Rocco Baldelli .40
62 Jose Vidro .25
63 Austin Kearns .25
64 Cliff Floyd .25
65 Phil Nevin .25
66 Darin Erstad .25
67 Johan Santana .25
68 Chipper Jones .75
69 Brandon Webb .25
70 Hank Blalock .40
71 Adam Dunn .40
72 Javier Vazquez .25
73 Jacque Jones .25
74 Bobby Abreu .40
75 Edgar Renteria .40
76 Roger Clemens 1.50
77 Rafael Furcal .40
78 Mike Sweeney .25
79 Geoff Jenkins .25
80 Orlando Cabrera .25
81 Ben Sheets .40
82 Shannon Stewart .25
83 Ryan Klesko .40
84 Edgar Martinez .40
85 Kevin Millwood .40
86 Bartolo Colon .40
87 Larry Walker .25
88 Tom Glavine .40
89 Miguel Cabrera .75
90 Jose Reyes .40

2004 UPPER DECK REFLECTIONS

NM/M

Complete Set (340):
Common (1-100): .50
Common SP (101-130): 4.00
Production 1,250
Common Jersey (131-214): 4.00
Common Jersey (215-298): 5.00
Production 100 (215-298):
Common Auto. (299-340): 15.00
Production 35
Pack (4): 10.00
Box (8): 70.00

1 Adam Dunn 1.00
2 Albert Pujols 3.00
3 Alex Rodriguez 3.00
4 Alfonso Soriano 1.00
5 Andruw Jones 1.00
6 Austin Kearns .50
7 Rafael Furcal .50
8 Barry Zito .75
9 Bartolo Colon .50
10 Ben Sheets .50
11 Bernie Williams .75
12 Bobby Abreu .50
13 Brandon Webb .50
14 Bret Boone .50
15 Brian Giles .50
16 Carlos Beltran .50
17 Carlos Delgado .75
18 Carlos Lee .50
19 Chipper Jones 1.50
20 Corey Patterson .50
21 Curt Schilling .75
22 Delmon Young .50
23 Derek Jeter 4.00
24 Dmitri Young .50
25 Dontrelle Willis .50
26 Edgar Martinez .50
27 Edgar Renteria .50
28 Eric Chavez .50
29 Eric Gagne .75
30 Frank Thomas 1.50
31 Garret Anderson .50
32 Gary Sheffield .50
33 Geoff Jenkins .50
34 Greg Maddux 2.00
35 Hank Blalock .75
36 Hideki Matsui 3.00
37 Hideo Nomo .75
38 Ichiro Suzuki 2.50
39 Ivan Rodriguez 1.00
40 Jacque Jones .50
41 Jason Giambi 1.50
42 Jason Schmidt .75
43 Javy Lopez .75
44 Jay Gibbons .50
45 Jeff Bagwell 1.00
46 Jeff Kent .50
47 Jeremy Bonderman .50
48 Jim Edmonds .75
49 Jim Thome 1.50
50 Johnny Damon .50
51 Jorge Posada .75
52 Jose Contreras .50
53 Jose Reyes .50
54 Jose Vidro .50
55 Josh Beckett 1.00
56 Juan Gonzalez 1.00
57 Ken Griffey Jr. 2.50
58 Kerry Wood 1.50
59 Kevin Brown .50
60 Kevin Millwood .50
61 Lance Berkman .50
62 Larry Walker .50
63 Luis Gonzalez .50
64 Magglio Ordonez .50
65 Manny Ramirez 1.00
66 Mark Mulder .50
67 Mark Prior 2.50
68 Mark Teixeira .50
69 Miguel Cabrera 1.50
70 Miguel Tejada .75
71 Mike Lowell .75
72 Mike Mussina .75
73 Mike Piazza 2.00
74 Mike Sweeney .50
75 Milton Bradley .50
76 Nomar Garciaparra 2.00
77 Orlando Cabrera .50
78 Pedro Martinez 1.50
79 Phil Nevin .50
80 Preston Wilson .50
81 Rafael Palmeiro 1.00
82 Randy Johnson 1.50
83 Rich Harden .50
84 Richie Sexson .50
85 Rickie Weeks .50
86 Rocco Baldelli .75
87 Roy Halladay .75
88 Roy Oswalt .75
89 Ryan Klesko .50
90 Sammy Sosa 2.50
91 Scott Rolen 1.50
92 Shannon Stewart .50
93 Shawn Green .50
94 Tim Hudson .75
95 Todd Helton 1.00
96 Torii Hunter .75
97 Trot Nixon .50
98 Troy Glaus .75
99 Vernon Wells .50
100 Vladimir Guerrero 1.50
101 *Brandon Medders* 4.00
102 *Colby Miller* 4.00
103 David Crouthers 4.00
104 *Dennis Sarfate* 4.00
105 *Donnie Kelly* 4.00
106 *Alec Zumwalt* 4.00
107 *Chris Aguila* 4.00
108 *Greg Dobbs* 4.00
109 *Ian Snell* 8.00
110 Jake Woods 4.00
111 *Jamie Brown* 4.00
112 *Jason Frasor* 4.00
113 *Jerome Gamble* 4.00
114 *Jesse Harper* 4.00
115 *Josh Labandeira* 5.00
116 *Justin Hampson* 4.00
117 *Justin Huisman* 4.00
118 *Justin Leone* 8.00
119 *Kazuo Matsui* 15.00
120 *Lincoln Holdzkom* 4.00
121 *Mike Bumatay* 4.00
122 Mike Gosling 4.00
123 *Mike Johnston* 4.00
124 Mike Rouse 4.00
125 *Nick Regilio* 4.00
126 *Ryan Meaux* 4.00
127 *Scott Dohmann* 4.00
128 Sean Henn 6.00
129 *Tim Bausher* 4.00
130 *Tim Bittner* 4.00
131 Adam Dunn 6.00
132 Andruw Jones 6.00
133 Austin Kearns 4.00
134 Bartolo Colon 4.00
135 Ben Sheets 5.00
136 Bernie Williams 5.00
137 Bobby Abreu 4.00
138 Brian Giles 4.00
139 Carlos Lee 4.00
140 Chipper Jones 8.00
141 Corey Patterson 5.00
142 Darin Erstad 4.00
143 Edgar Martinez 5.00
144 Vladimir Guerrero 8.00
145 Eric Gagne 8.00
146 Frank Thomas 8.00
147 Garret Anderson 5.00
148 Roger Clemens 12.00
149 Greg Maddux 8.00
150 Jacque Jones 4.00
151 Randy Johnson 8.00
152 Javy Lopez 6.00
153 Mike Piazza 8.00
154 Albert Pujols 12.00
155 Jim Edmonds 5.00
156 Eric Milton 4.00
157 Jorge Posada 6.00
158 J.D. Drew 5.00
159 Jose Vidro 4.00
160 Kevin Millwood 5.00
161 Larry Walker 4.00
162 Luis Gonzalez 5.00
163 Mike Sweeney 4.00
164 Kerry Wood 10.00
165 Mike Cameron 4.00
166 Phil Nevin 4.00
167 Rocco Baldelli 6.00
168 Ryan Klesko 4.00
169 Shannon Stewart 4.00
170 Torii Hunter 6.00
171 Trot Nixon 6.00
172 Vernon Wells 4.00
173 Alfonso Soriano 6.00
174 Andruw Jones 6.00
175 Barry Zito 6.00
176 Brandon Webb 4.00
177 Bret Boone 4.00
178 Scott Rolen 10.00
179 Carlos Delgado 4.00
180 Curt Schilling 8.00
181 Dontrelle Willis 6.00
182 Eric Chavez 5.00
183 Frank Thomas 8.00
184 Gary Sheffield 6.00
185 Greg Maddux 8.00
186 Hank Blalock 6.00
187 Hideki Matsui 15.00
188 Hideo Nomo 8.00
189 Ichiro Suzuki 15.00
190 Ivan Rodriguez 8.00
191 Jason Giambi 6.00
192 Rafael Furcal 5.00
193 Jeff Bagwell 6.00
194 Jeff Kent 4.00
195 Jim Thome 8.00
196 Jose Reyes 4.00
197 Josh Beckett 6.00
198 Juan Gonzalez 6.00

199	Ken Griffey Jr.	15.00
200	Kevin Brown	4.00
201	Lance Berkman	6.00
202	Magglio Ordonez	5.00
203	Mark Mulder	4.00
204	Mark Teixeira	6.00
205	Miguel Tejada	6.00
206	Mike Mussina	6.00
207	Preston Wilson	4.00
208	Rafael Palmeiro	6.00
209	Alex Rodriguez	15.00
210	Richie Sexson	5.00
211	Roy Halladay	6.00
212	Roy Oswalt	5.00
213	Tim Hudson	5.00
214	Troy Glaus	6.00
215	Adam Dunn	8.00
216	Austin Kearns	6.00
217	Bartolo Colon	5.00
218	Ben Sheets	6.00
219	Bernie Williams	6.00
220	Bobby Abreu	5.00
221	Bret Boone	5.00
222	Todd Helton	8.00
223	Chipper Jones	8.00
224	Corey Patterson	6.00
225	Darin Erstad	5.00
226	Dontrelle Willis	6.00
227	Edgar Martinez	6.00
228	Eric Gagne	10.00
229	Garret Anderson	6.00
230	Roger Clemens	20.00
231	Hank Blalock	6.00
232	Jacque Jones	5.00
233	Jeff Bagwell	10.00
234	Jeff Kent	5.00
235	Jeremy Bonderman	5.00
236	Jim Edmonds	8.00
237	Jorge Posada	8.00
238	J.D. Drew	8.00
239	Jose Reyes	5.00
240	Jose Vidro	5.00
241	Kevin Millwood	6.00
242	Luis Gonzalez	6.00
243	Mike Sweeney	5.00
244	Jason Giambi	8.00
245	Manny Ramirez	10.00
246	Phil Nevin	5.00
247	Preston Wilson	5.00
248	Alex Rodriguez	20.00
249	Richie Sexson	6.00
250	Rocco Baldelli	5.00
251	Ryan Klesko	5.00
252	Sammy Sosa	20.00
253	Torii Hunter	6.00
254	Mike Lowell	8.00
255	Troy Glaus	8.00
256	Vernon Wells	6.00
257	Albert Pujols	25.00
258	Alex Rodriguez	20.00
259	Alfonso Soriano	8.00
260	Roger Clemens	20.00
261	Barry Zito	6.00
262	Brandon Webb	6.00
263	Carlos Delgado	6.00
264	Curt Schilling	10.00
265	Derek Jeter	30.00
266	Eric Chavez	8.00
267	Gary Sheffield	8.00
268	Hideki Matsui	25.00
269	Hideo Nomo	10.00
270	Ichiro Suzuki	25.00
271	Ivan Rodriguez	10.00
272	Jason Giambi	8.00
273	Jim Thome	10.00
274	Josh Beckett	10.00
275	Juan Gonzalez	8.00
276	Ken Griffey Jr.	20.00
277	Kerry Wood	15.00
278	Kevin Brown	5.00
279	Lance Berkman	8.00
280	Magglio Ordonez	8.00
281	Manny Ramirez	10.00
282	Mark Mulder	8.00
283	Mark Prior	15.00
284	Mark Teixeira	5.00
285	Miguel Tejada	8.00
286	Mike Mussina	8.00
287	Mike Piazza	15.00
288	Pedro Martinez	10.00
289	Rafael Palmeiro	10.00
290	Randy Johnson	12.00
291	Roy Halladay	6.00
292	Roy Oswalt	6.00
293	Sammy Sosa	20.00
294	Scott Rolen	12.00
295	Shawn Green	6.00
296	Tim Hudson	6.00
297	Todd Helton	8.00
298	Vladimir Guerrero	10.00
299	Bret Boone	35.00
300	Alex Rodriguez	200.00
301	Dontrelle Willis	30.00
302	Barry Larkin	30.00
303	Barry Zito	
304	Eric Chavez	35.00
305	Bernie Williams	85.00
306	Brandon Webb	20.00
307	Cal Ripken Jr.	
308	Carl Yastrzemski	65.00
309	Carlos Delgado	30.00
310	Shawn Green	25.00
311	Eric Gagne	55.00
312	Frank Thomas	40.00
313	Carlos Lee	
314	Garret Anderson	20.00
315	Hideki Matsui	300.00
316	Jim Edmonds	40.00
317	Jeff Bagwell	40.00
318	Luis Gonzalez	25.00
319	Mike Mussina	40.00
320	John Smoltz	60.00
321	Jose Reyes	30.00
322	Josh Beckett	45.00
323	Juan Gonzalez	35.00
324	Ken Griffey Jr.	140.00
325	Rich Harden	20.00
326	Pat Burrell	
327	Mark Teixeira	25.00
328	Roy Oswalt	30.00
329	Miguel Tejada	40.00
330	Mike Hampton	
331	Mike Piazza	175.00
332	Nolan Ryan	110.00
333	Orlando Hernandez	
334	Paul Lo Duca	30.00
335	Roberto Alomar	45.00
336	Rocco Baldelli	40.00
337	Trevor Hoffman	
338	Tom Glavine	50.00
339	Tom Seaver	60.00
340	Mark Prior	75.00

Blue

Blue (1-100):	2-4X
Production 250	
Blue (215-256):	1-2X
Production 15	

Red

Red (1-100):	4-6X
Production 50	
Red Jersey (131-214):	1.5-2X
Production 50	
Red Jersey (215-256):	1-1.5X
Production 50	

Gold

Gold (1-100):	5-10X
Production 15	
Gold Auto. (101-130):	2X
Production 250	
Gold Auto. parallel (101-130):	2X
Production 125	
Gold Jersey (131-172):	1.5-3X
Production 15	
Gold Jersey (257-298):	No Pricing
Production 5	
Gold Jsy Auto. (299-340):	1X
Production 15	

Black

Black (1-100):	No Pricing
Production one set	
Black Auto. (101-130):	No Pricing
Production one set	
Black Jersey (173-214):	No Pricing
Production one set	
Black Jersey (257-298):	No Pricing
Production one set	
Black Jsy Auto. (299-340):	No Pricing
Production one set	

2004 UPPER DECK RIVALS: YANKEES VS RED SOX

		NM/M
Complete Sealed Set (32):		25.00
Common Player (1-30):		.50
1	Alex Rodriguez	2.00
2	Bobby Doerr	.75
3	Don Mattingly	1.50
4	Dwight Evans	.50
5	Fred Lynn	.50
6	Jason Giambi	.50
7	Jim Rice	.50
8	Lou Gehrig	2.00
9	Luis Tiant	.50
10	Manny Ramirez	1.00

11	Mike Mussina	.75
12	Pedro Martinez	1.00
13	Phil Rizzuto	.75
14	Whitey Ford	.75
15	Yogi Berra	1.00
16	Tim Wakefield	.50
17	Billy Martin	.75
18	Mike Torrez, Bucky Dent	.50
19	Nomar Garciaparra, Derek Jeter	2.00
20	Gary Sheffield, Curt Schilling	1.00
21	Joe DiMaggio, Dick Newsome	1.50
22	Joe DiMaggio, Lefty Grove	1.50
23	Joe DiMaggio, Ted Williams	1.50
24	Jorge Posada, Jason Varitek	.50
25	Mickey Mantle, Carl Yastrzemski	2.00
26	Tracy Stallard, Roger Maris	1.00
27	Carlton Fisk, Thurman Munson	1.00
28	Babe Ruth	2.00
29	Roger Clemens	1.50
30	Wade Boggs	.50

"What If"

		NM/M
Common Player:		4.00
Production 2,150 sets		
1	Aaron Boone	4.00
2	Alex Rodriguez	10.00
3	Babe Ruth	10.00
4	Babe Ruth	10.00
5	Billy Martin	4.00
6	Bucky Dent	4.00
7	Carl Yastrzemski	8.00
8	Carlton Fisk	5.00
9	Derek Jeter	10.00
10	Hideki Matsui	8.00
11	Joe DiMaggio	8.00
12	Joe Torre	4.00
13	Mickey Mantle	15.00
14	Pedro Martinez	6.00
15	Pee Wee Reese	4.00
16	Roger Clemens	8.00
17	Roger Maris	8.00
18	Ted Williams	8.00
19	Ted Williams	8.00
20	Carl Yastrzemski	8.00

What If Auto

No Pricing

Commemorative

	NM/M
Complete Set (5):	10.00
One oversized card per set	
Babe Ruth	4.00
Ted Williams	3.00
Derek Jeter	3.00
Nomar Garciaparra	2.00
Mickey Mantle	5.00

2004 UPPER DECK R CLASS

		NM/M
Complete Set (180):		50.00
Common Player:		.10
Pack (6):		2.50
Box (24):		50.00
1	Adam Dunn	.50
2	Jose Vidro	.10
3	Vladimir Guerrero	.75
4	Hideo Nomo	.25
5	Eric Chavez	.25
6	Carlos Delgado	.40
7	Javy Lopez	.25
8	Javier Vazquez	.25
9	Miguel Cabrera	.75
10	Manny Ramirez	.50
11	Scott Rolen	.75
12	Rafael Furcal	.10
13	Jim Thome	.75
14	Edgar Renteria	.25
15	Jason Kendall	.10
16	Alfonso Soriano	.75
17	Troy Glaus	.40
18	Vernon Wells	.10
19	Todd Helton	.50
20	Mark Mulder	.25
21	Albert Pujols	2.00
22	Andy Pettitte	.25
23	Kevin Millwood	.10
24	Bret Boone	.10
25	Ken Griffey Jr.	1.00
26	Kevin Brown	.20
27	J.D. Drew	.25
28	Corey Patterson	.40
29	Jason Giambi	.40
30	Jason Schmidt	.25
31	Jose Reyes	.25
32	Torii Hunter	.25
33	Brian Giles	.25
34	Garret Anderson	.25
35	Mark Teixeira	.40
36	Sammy Sosa	1.50
37	Rocco Baldelli	.25
38	Jeff Bagwell	.50
39	Rafael Palmeiro	.50
40	Derrek Lee	.25
41	Randy Johnson	.75
42	Roger Clemens	1.50
43	Austin Kearns	.25
44	Dontrelle Willis	.10
45	Lance Berkman	.25
46	Juan Gonzalez	.40
47	Ichiro Suzuki	1.50
48	Pat Burrell	.25
49	Miguel Tejada	.40
50	Mike Piazza	1.00
51	Mark Prior	.75
52	C.C. Sabathia	.10
53	Jacque Jones	.10
54	Carlos Beltran	.75
55	Mike Mussina	.40
56	Mike Lowell	.25
57	Phil Nevin	.10
58	Andruw Jones	.40
59	Barry Zito	.25
60	Magglio Ordonez	.25
61	Carlos Lee	.20
62	Nomar Garciaparra	1.00
63	Kerry Wood	.75
64	Luis Gonzalez	.20
65	Derek Jeter	2.00
66	Preston Wilson	.10
67	Greg Maddux	1.00
68	Pedro J. Martinez	.75
69	Richie Sexson	.25
70	Hank Blalock	.50
71	Chipper Jones	.75
72	Ivan Rodriguez	.50
73	Roy Halladay	.25
74	Tim Hudson	.25
75	Ryan Klesko	.10
76	Hideki Matsui	1.50

77	Josh Beckett	.40
78	Brandon Webb	.10
79	Alex Rodriguez	2.00
80	Jim Edmonds	.40
81	Jeff Kent	.10
82	Bobby Abreu	.25
83	Curt Schilling	.75
84	Roy Oswalt	.25
85	Orlando Cabrera	.75
86	Johan Santana	.50
87	Geoff Jenkins	.10
88	Gary Sheffield	.40
89	Shawn Green	.25
90	Frank Thomas	.50
91	Tim Hamulack	.25
92	*Shingo Takatsu*	.50
93	Justin Huisman	.25
94	Sean Henn	.50
95	Jamie Brown	.25
96	*Dennis Sarfate*	.25
97	*Lincoln Holdzkom*	.25
98	*Roman Colon*	.25
99	*Scott Dohmann*	.25
100	Ivan Ochoa	.25
101	*Akinori Otsuka*	.50
102	*Fernando Nieve*	.25
103	*Mike Johnston*	.25
104	*Mariano Gomez*	.25
105	*Justin Leone*	.25
106	*Evan Rust*	.25
107	Mike Rouse	.25
108	*Ian Snell*	.50
109	Jason Bartlett	.25
110	Ryan Wing	.25
111	*Nick Regilio*	.25
112	*Merkin Valdez*	.50
113	*Josh Labandeira*	.25
114	David Aardsma	.75
115	*Justin Knoedler*	.25
116	*Shawn Hill*	.25
117	*Casey Daigle*	.25
118	*Donnie Kelly*	.25
119	*Justin Germano*	.25
120	Eddy Rodriguez	.25
121	*Onil Joseph*	.25
122	Mike Wuertz	.50
123	*Roberto Novoa*	.25
124	*Jerome Gamble*	.50
125	*Justin Hampson*	.25
126	Ronald Belisario	.25
127	*Tim Bausher*	.25
128	*Chris Saenz*	.25
129	*Hector Gimenez*	.25
130	*Ronny Cedeno*	.25
131	*Jason Frasor*	.25
132	*Kazuo Matsui*	2.00
133	Mike Gosling	.25
134	*Jerry Gil*	.25
135	*Orlando Rodriguez*	.25
136	*Jorge Vasquez*	.50
137	*Chris Aguila*	.25
138	*Tim Bittner*	.25
139	Jake Woods	.25
140	Enemencio Pacheco	.25
141	David Crouthers	.25
142	*Jose Capellan*	1.00
143	*Chad Bentz*	.25
144	Michael Vento	.75
145	*Scott Proctor*	.50
146	*Edwin Moreno*	.25
147	*Brandon Medders*	.25
148	*Renyel Pinto*	.25
149	*Rusty Tucker*	.25
150	*Ryan Meaux*	.25
151	William Bergolla	.25
152	Angel Chavez	.25
153	*Colby Miller*	.25
154	*John Gall*	.25
155	*Carlos Hines*	.25
156	*Carlos Vasquez*	.50
157	*Justin Lehr*	.25
158	*Kevin Cave*	.25
159	*Jeff Bennett*	.25
160	*Greg Dobbs*	.25
161	*Jorge Sequea*	.25
162	*Chris Oxspring*	.25
163	*Franklyn Gracesqui*	.25
164	*Shawn Camp*	.25
165	Lino Urdaneta	.25
166	Luis Gonzalez	.25
167	*Ramon Ramirez*	.50
168	*Freddy Guzman*	.25
169	*Chris Shelton*	1.00
170	Andres Blanco	.25
171	*Aarom Baldiris*	.25
172	*Kazuhito Tadano*	.50
173	*Brian Dallimore*	.25
174	Eduardo Villacis	.25
175	*Frank Francisco*	.25
176	Edwin Jackson	.25
177	Bobby Crosby	.50
178	Joe Mauer	.50
179	Rickie Weeks	.50
180	Delmon Young	.50

First Class Black Ink Auto

NM/M

No Pricing
Inserted 1:2,880

SA	Sandy Alomar	20.00
PB	Pat Burrell	30.00
MC	Miguel Cabrera	40.00
CD	Carlos Delgado	30.00
EG	Eric Gagne	50.00
KG	Ken Griffey Jr.	80.00
TH	Trevor Hoffman	30.00
BL	Barry Larkin	40.00
PL	Paul LoDuca	30.00
EM	Edgar Martinez	40.00
MP	Mark Prior	50.00
HR	Horacio Ramirez	20.00
DW	Dontrelle Willis	30.00

First Class Blue Ink Auto

No Pricing
Production 3 Sets

Taking Over!

NM/M

Common Player: 3.00
1-20 production 650
21-30 production 150

TO-1	Richie Sexson, Lyle Overbay	3.00
TO-2	Jason Phillips, Mike Piazza	6.00
TO-3	Barry Larkin, William Bergolla	4.00
TO-4	Jason Dubois, Moises Alou	3.00
TO-5	Nook Logan, Alex Sanchez	3.00
TO-6	Merkin Valdez, Robb Nen	4.00
TO-7	Troy Percival, Francisco Rodriguez	3.00
TO-8	Carlos Beltran, David DeJesus	4.00
TO-9	Alex Rodriguez, Michael Young	6.00
TO-10	Alexis Rios, Vernon Wells	3.00
TO-11	Matt Lawton, Grady Sizemore	3.00
TO-12	Danny Graves, Ryan Wagner	3.00
TO-13	Miguel Cabrera, Jeff Conine	4.00
TO-14	Josh Willingham, Ramon Castro	3.00
TO-15	Junior Spivey, Rickie Weeks	3.00
TO-16	Guillermo Quiroz, Greg Myers	3.00
TO-17	Scott Hatteberg, Graham Koonce	3.00
TO-18	Rene Reyes, Larry Walker	4.00
TO-19	Khalil Greene, Ramon Vazquez	4.00
TO-20	Billy Wagner, Octavio Dotel	3.00
TO-21	Joe Mauer, A.J. Pierzynski	8.00
TO-22	Javier Vazquez, Roger Clemens	10.00
TO-23	Curt Schilling, Brandon Webb	3.00
TO-24	Delmon Young, Cirilo Cruz Jr.	8.00
TO-25	Vladimir Guerrero, Tim Salmon	8.00
TO-26	Gary Sheffield, J.D. Drew	3.00
TO-27	Miguel Tejada, Bobby Crosby	8.00
TO-28	Edwin Jackson, Kevin Brown	3.00
TO-29	Kazuo Matsui, Jose Reyes	10.00
TO-30	Wily Mo Pena, Ken Griffey Jr.	10.00

2004 UPPER DECK SWEET SPOT

NM/M

Complete Set (262):	
Common Player:	.25
Common (91-170):	3.00
Production 799	
Common SP (171-230):	1.50
Production 399	
Common SP (231-250):	1.50
Production 299	
Common SP (251-260):	3.00
Production 199	
Pack (4):	10.00
Box (12):	100.00

1	Albert Pujols	3.00
2	Alex Rodriguez	3.00
3	Alfonso Soriano	1.00
4	Andruw Jones	.50
5	Andy Pettitte	.50
6	Aubrey Huff	.25
7	Austin Kearns	.50
8	Barry Zito	.50
9	Bobby Abreu	.50
10	Brandon Webb	.25
11	Bret Boone	.25
12	Brian Giles	.25
13	C.C. Sabathia	.25
14	Carlos Beltran	1.00
15	Carlos Delgado	.50
16	Chipper Jones	1.00
17	Cliff Floyd	.25
18	Curt Schilling	1.00
19	Delmon Young	.50
20	Derek Jeter	3.00
21	Dontrelle Willis	.25
22	Edgar Martinez	.50
23	Edgar Renteria	.50
24	Eric Chavez	.50
25	Eric Gagne	.50
26	Frank Thomas	.75
27	Garret Anderson	.50
28	Gary Sheffield	.75
29	Geoff Jenkins	.25
30	Greg Maddux	1.50
31	Hank Blalock	.75
32	Hideo Nomo	.50
33	Ichiro Suzuki	2.00
34	Ivan Rodriguez	.75
35	Jacque Jones	.25
36	Jason Giambi	.50
37	Jason Schmidt	.50
38	Javier Vazquez	.25
39	Javy Lopez	.50
40	Jeff Bagwell	.75
41	Jim Edmonds	.50
42	Jim Thome	.75
43	Joe Mauer	.50
44	John Smoltz	.50
45	Jose Cruz Jr.	.25
46	Jose Reyes	.25
47	Jose Vidro	.25
48	Josh Beckett	.50
49	Ken Griffey Jr.	1.50
50	Kerry Wood	1.00
51	Kevin Brown	.25
52	Larry Walker	.50
53	Magglio Ordonez	.25
54	Manny Ramirez	.75
55	Mark Mulder	.50
56	Mark Prior	1.00
57	Mark Teixeira	.50
58	Miguel Cabrera	1.00
59	Miguel Tejada	.50
60	Mike Lowell	.40
61	Mike Mussina	.75
62	Mike Piazza	1.50
63	Nomar Garciaparra	1.50
64	Orlando Cabrera	.40
65	Pat Burrell	.25
66	Pedro J. Martinez	1.00
67	Phil Nevin	.25
68	Preston Wilson	.25
69	Rafael Furcal	.25
70	Rafael Palmeiro	.75
71	Randy Johnson	1.00
72	Craig Wilson	.25
73	Rich Harden	.25
74	Richie Sexson	.50
75	Rickie Weeks	.50
76	Rocco Baldelli	.50
77	Roger Clemens	2.50
78	Roy Halladay	.25
79	Roy Oswalt	.50
80	Ryan Klesko	.25
81	Sammy Sosa	2.00
82	Scott Podsednik	.25
83	Scott Rolen	1.00
84	Shawn Green	.40
85	Tim Hudson	.40
86	Todd Helton	.75
87	Torii Hunter	.40
88	Troy Glaus	.25
89	Vernon Wells	.25
90	Vladimir Guerrero	1.00
91	*Aarom Baldiris*	3.00
92	*Akinori Otsuka*	8.00
93	*Andres Blanco*	5.00
94	*Angel Chavez*	3.00
95	*Brian Dallimore*	8.00
96	*Carlos Hines*	5.00
97	*Carlos Vasquez*	5.00
98	*Casey Daigle*	3.00
99	*Chad Bentz*	3.00
100	*Chris Aguila*	3.00
101	*Chris Oxspring*	5.00
102	*Chris Saenz*	3.00
103	*Chris Shelton*	8.00
104	*Colby Miller*	5.00
105	*David Crouthers*	3.00
106	*David Aardsma*	5.00
107	*Dennis Sarfate*	3.00
108	*Donnie Kelly*	3.00
109	*Eddy Rodriguez*	3.00
110	*Eduardo Villacis*	3.00
111	*Edwin Moreno*	5.00
112	*Enemencio Pacheco*	5.00
113	*Fernando Nieve*	3.00
114	*Franklyn Gracesqui*	3.00
115	*Freddy Guzman*	3.00
116	*Greg Dobbs*	3.00
117	*Hector Gimenez*	3.00
118	*Ian Snell*	3.00
119	*Ivan Ochoa*	5.00
120	Jake Woods	5.00
121	*Jamie Brown*	5.00
122	*Jason Bartlett*	3.00
123	*Jason Frasor*	3.00
124	*Jeff Bennett*	3.00
125	*Jerome Gamble*	5.00
126	*Jerry Gil*	3.00
127	*Brandon Medders*	3.00
128	*Ryan Meaux*	3.00
129	*John Gall*	3.00
130	*Jorge Sequea*	3.00
131	*Jorge Vasquez*	5.00
132	*Jose Capellan*	8.00
133	*Josh Labandeira*	3.00
134	*Justin Germano*	8.00
135	*Justin Hampson*	5.00
136	*Justin Huisman*	5.00
137	*Justin Knoedler*	5.00
138	*Justin Leone*	5.00
139	*Kazuhito Tadano*	5.00
140	*Kazuo Matsui*	10.00
141	*Kevin Cave*	5.00
142	*Lincoln Holdzkom*	3.00
143	*Lino Urdaneta*	3.00
144	*Luis A. Gonzalez*	5.00
145	*Mariano Gomez*	5.00
146	*Merkin Valdez*	5.00
147	*Michael Vento*	8.00
148	*Mike Wuertz*	5.00
149	*Mike Gosling*	5.00
150	*Mike Johnston*	3.00
151	Mike Rouse	5.00
152	*Nick Regilio*	5.00
153	*Onil Joseph*	3.00
154	*Orlando Rodriguez*	5.00
155	*Ramon Ramirez*	5.00
156	*Renyel Pinto*	5.00
157	*Roberto Novoa*	5.00
158	*Roman Colon*	3.00
159	*Ronald Belisario*	5.00
160	*Ronny Cedeno*	8.00
161	*Rusty Tucker*	5.00
162	*Ryan Wing*	3.00
163	*Scott Dohmann*	3.00
164	*Scott Proctor*	5.00
165	*Sean Henn*	5.00
166	*Shawn Camp*	5.00
167	*Shawn Hill*	3.00
168	*Shingo Takatsu*	8.00
169	*Tim Hamulack*	3.00

170 *William Bergolla* 3.00
171 Adam Dunn 2.00
172 Albert Pujols 8.00
173 Alex Rodriguez 8.00
174 Alfonso Soriano 3.00
175 Andruw Jones 2.00
176 Bret Boone 1.50
177 Brian Giles 1.50
178 Carlos Delgado 2.00
179 Derrek Lee 2.00
180 Eric Chavez 1.50
181 Frank Thomas 2.00
182 Garret Anderson 1.50
183 Gary Sheffield 2.00
184 Hank Blalock 2.00
185 Jason Giambi 1.50
186 Javy Lopez 1.50
187 Jeff Bagwell 2.00
188 Jim Edmonds 2.00
189 Jim Thome 2.00
190 Ken Griffey Jr. 4.00
191 Lance Berkman 1.50
192 Magglio Ordonez 1.50
193 Manny Ramirez 3.00
194 Mike Lowell 1.50
195 Mike Piazza 5.00
196 Preston Wilson 1.50
197 Rafael Palmeiro 2.00
198 Richie Sexson 1.50
199 Sammy Sosa 5.00
200 Scott Rolen 4.00
201 Shawn Green 1.50
202 Todd Helton 2.00
203 Troy Glaus 1.50
204 Vernon Wells 1.50
205 Vladimir Guerrero 3.00
206 Garret Anderson, Vladimir Guerrero 3.00
207 Luis Gonzalez, Richie Sexson 2.00
208 Andruw Jones, Chipper Jones 3.00
209 Javy Lopez, Miguel Tejada 2.00
210 Manny Ramirez, David Ortiz 5.00
211 Derrek Lee, Sammy Sosa 5.00
212 Frank Thomas, Magglio Ordonez 2.00
213 Austin Kearns, Ken Griffey Jr. 4.00
214 Preston Wilson, Todd Helton 2.00
215 Delmon Young, Ivan Rodriguez 2.00
216 Miguel Cabrera, Mike Lowell 3.00
217 Jeff Bagwell, Lance Berkman 2.00
218 Lyle Overbay, Geoff Jenkins 1.50
219 Adrian Beltre, Shawn Green 2.00
220 Jacque Jones, Torii Hunter 1.50
221 Jose Vidro, N. Johnson 1.50
222 Kazuo Matsui, Mike Piazza 5.00
223 Alex Rodriguez, Jason Giambi 6.00
224 Eric Chavez, Jermaine Dye 1.50
225 Jim Thome, Pat Burrell 2.50
226 Brian Giles, Phil Nevin 1.50
227 Bret Boone, Ichiro Suzuki 6.00
228 Albert Pujols, Scott Rolen 8.00
229 Hank Blalock, Mark Teixeira 3.00
230 Carlos Delgado, Vernon Wells 2.00
231 Albert Pujols 8.00
232 Alex Rodriguez 8.00
233 Chipper Jones 3.00
234 Craig Biggio 1.50
235 Curt Schilling 2.00
236 Derek Jeter 8.00
237 Ivan Rodriguez 2.00
238 Jeff Bagwell 2.00
239 Jim Edmonds 2.00
240 Jim Thome 2.00
241 Josh Beckett 2.00
242 Kerry Wood 3.00
243 Kevin Brown 1.50
244 Mark Prior 3.00
245 Miguel Tejada 2.00
246 Mike Mussina 2.00
247 Nomar Garciaparra 4.00
248 Pedro J. Martinez 3.00
249 Randy Johnson 3.00
250 Roger Clemens 6.00
251 Alex Rodriguez, Derek Jeter 12.00
252 Alfonso Soriano, Hank Blalock 4.00
253 Bobby Abreu, Pat Burrell 3.00
254 Edgar Renteria, Scott Rolen 4.00
255 Garret Anderson, Vladimir Guerrero 4.00
256 Jeff Bagwell, Jeff Kent 3.00
257 Jose Reyes, Kazuo Matsui 4.00
258 K. Greene, S. Burroughs 4.00
259 Marcus Giles, Rafael Furcal 3.00
260 Manny Ramirez, Johnny Damon 6.00
261 *Tim Bausher* 3.00
262 *Tim Bittner* 5.00

Wood

Stars (1-90): 3-6X
SP's (91-262): .75-1.5X
Production 99 sets

Limited

No Pricing
Production 10 sets

Diamond Champs Jersey

NM/M
Common Player: 5.00
Production 150 sets
GA Garret Anderson 5.00
JB Josh Beckett 8.00
RC Roger Clemens 12.00
EG Eric Gagne 8.00
KG Ken Griffey Jr. 12.00
RH Roy Halladay 5.00
DJ Derek Jeter 20.00
RJ Randy Johnson 10.00
CJ Chipper Jones 8.00
GM Greg Maddux 10.00
PM Pedro J. Martinez 8.00
PE Andy Pettitte 5.00
MP Mike Piazza 10.00
AP Albert Pujols 20.00
AR Alex Rodriguez Yanks 15.00
IR Ivan Rodriguez 8.00
CS Curt Schilling 8.00
IS Ichiro Suzuki 30.00
MT Miguel Tejada 6.00
BZ Barry Zito 5.00

Home Run Heroes Jersey

NM/M
Common Player: 5.00
Production 199 sets
GA Garret Anderson 5.00
JB Jeff Bagwell 8.00
CB Carlos Beltran 8.00
AB Adrian Beltre 8.00
LB Lance Berkman 5.00
HB Hank Blalock 8.00
BB Bret Boone 5.00
PB Pat Burrell 5.00
MC Miguel Cabrera 10.00
EC Eric Chavez 5.00
CD Carlos Delgado 5.00
JD J.D. Drew 5.00
AD Adam Dunn 8.00
JE Jim Edmonds 8.00
JG Jason Giambi 5.00
BG Brian Giles 5.00
TG Troy Glaus 5.00
LG Luis Gonzalez 5.00
SG Shawn Green 5.00
KG Ken Griffey Jr. Bat Up 12.00
KG1 Ken Griffey Jr. Swing 12.00
VG Vladimir Guerrero 10.00
HA Travis Hafner 5.00
TH Todd Helton 8.00
DJ Derek Jeter 20.00
AJ Andruw Jones 6.00
CJ Chipper Jones 8.00
JK Jeff Kent 5.00
DL Derrek Lee 5.00
ML Mike Lowell 5.00
HM Hideki Matsui 25.00
JM Joe Mauer 8.00
FM Fred McGriff 5.00
MO Magglio Ordonez 5.00
DO David Ortiz 15.00
RP Rafael Palmeiro 8.00
MP Mike Piazza 10.00
JP Jorge Posada 5.00
AP Albert Pujols 20.00
MR Manny Ramirez 8.00
AR Alex Rodriguez Yanks Bat Up 15.00
AR1 Alex Rodriguez Yanks Swing 15.00
IR Ivan Rodriguez 8.00
SR Scott Rolen 10.00
RS Richie Sexson 5.00
GS Gary Sheffield 8.00
AS Alfonso Soriano 8.00
SS Sammy Sosa 12.00
MT Mark Teixeira 6.00
TE Miguel Tejada 6.00
FT Frank Thomas 8.00
JT Jim Thome 10.00
VW Vernon Wells 5.00
BW Bernie Williams 8.00
PW Preston Wilson 5.00

Marquee Attractions Jersey

NM/M
Common Player: 5.00
Production 199 sets
HB Hank Blalock 8.00
MC Miguel Cabrera 10.00
EC Eric Chavez 5.00
RC Roger Clemens 12.00
CD Carlos Delgado 5.00
EG Eric Gagne 8.00
BG Brian Giles 5.00
KG Ken Griffey Jr. 12.00
VG Vladimir Guerrero 10.00
TH Todd Helton 8.00
HU Torii Hunter 5.00
DJ Derek Jeter 20.00
RJ Randy Johnson 10.00
AJ Andruw Jones 5.00
PI Mike Piazza 10.00
MP Mark Prior 10.00
AP Albert Pujols 20.00
AR Alex Rodriguez 15.00
IR Ivan Rodriguez 8.00
CS Curt Schilling 10.00
JS Jason Schmidt 8.00
BS Ben Sheets 8.00
IS Ichiro Suzuki 30.00
MS Mike Sweeney 5.00
MT Miguel Tejada 8.00
FT Frank Thomas 8.00
JT Jim Thome 10.00

Signatures

NM/M
Common Player: 10.00
Black Stitch: No Pricing
Production one set
GA Garret Anderson 20.00
RB Rocco Baldelli 30.00
BE Josh Beckett 25.00
CB Carlos Beltran 50.00
AB Angel Berroa 10.00
HB Hank Blalock 25.00
BB Bret Boone 15.00
PB Pat Burrell 25.00
SB Sean Burroughs 15.00
MC Miguel Cabrera 40.00
EC Eric Chavez 20.00
WC Will Clark 30.00
RC Roger Clemens 150.00
JD J.D. Drew 40.00
AD Adam Dunn 30.00
NG Nomar Garciaparra 80.00
BG Brian Giles 12.00
MG Marcus Giles 15.00
GL Tom Glavine 40.00
JG Juan Gonzalez 35.00
LG Luis Gonzalez 20.00
KG Ken Griffey Jr. 75.00
VG Vladimir Guerrero 75.00
TG Tony Gwynn 40.00
HA Roy Halladay 20.00
RH Rich Harden 20.00
TH Todd Helton 50.00
HI Richard Hidalgo 10.00
HO Trevor Hoffman 20.00
TI Tim Hudson 30.00
HU Torii Hunter 20.00
EJ Edwin Jackson
GJ Geoff Jenkins 15.00
DJ Derek Jeter 160.00
JJ Jacque Jones 15.00
AK Austin Kearns 20.00
RK Ryan Klesko 15.00
CL Carlos Lee 15.00
DL Derrek Lee 25.00
ML Mike Lieberthal 20.00
EL Esteban Loaiza 10.00
LO Mike Lowell 20.00
MA Mike Marshall 150.00
EM Edgar Martinez 50.00
DM Don Mattingly 65.00
JM Joe Mauer 25.00
MU Mark Mulder 20.00
MM Mike Mussina 40.00
RO Roy Oswalt 20.00
CP Corey Patterson 35.00
OP Odalis Perez 15.00
PI Mike Piazza
SP Scott Podsednik 15.00
MP Mark Prior 60.00
AP Albert Pujols 200.00
MR Manny Ramirez 80.00
JR Jose Reyes 15.00
CR Cal Ripken Jr. 180.00
AR Alex Rodriguez/27
IR Ivan Rodriguez 60.00
SR Scott Rolen 40.00
NR Nolan Ryan 150.00
RS Ryne Sandberg 75.00
SA Johan Santana 50.00
JS Jason Schmidt 25.00
TS Tom Seaver 40.00
BS Ben Sheets 20.00
GS Gary Sheffield 35.00
SM John Smoltz
IS Ichiro Suzuki 250.00
MT Mark Teixeira 30.00
TE Miguel Tejada 50.00
FT Frank Thomas 50.00
JV Javier Vazquez 20.00
WA Billy Wagner 15.00
BW Brandon Webb 15.00
WE Rickie Weeks 20.00
VW Vernon Wells/30 30.00
DW Dontrelle Willis 25.00
RW Randy Wolf 15.00
KW Kerry Wood 40.00
DY Delmon Young 25.00
CZ Carlos Zambrano 40.00

Signatures Red-Blue Stitch

NM/M
Quantity produced listed
GA Garret Anderson/45 25.00
RB Rocco Baldelli/35 40.00
BE Josh Beckett/45 30.00
CB Carlos Beltran/45 65.00
AB Angel Berroa/45 20.00
HB Hank Blalock/45 40.00
BB Bret Boone/45 20.00
PB Pat Burrell/35 40.00
SB Sean Burroughs/45 20.00
MC Miguel Cabrera/45 40.00
EC Eric Chavez/45 35.00
WC Will Clark/45
RC Roger Clemens/30 175.00
JD J.D. Drew/40 50.00
AD Adam Dunn/45 40.00
NG Nomar Garciaparra/45
BG Brian Giles/45 15.00
MG Marcus Giles/45 20.00
GL Tom Glavine/45 60.00
JG Juan Gonzalez/45
LG Luis Gonzalez/45 25.00
KG Ken Griffey Jr./44 100.00
VG Vladimir Guerrero/45 85.00
TG Tony Gwynn/45 65.00
HA Roy Halladay/35 25.00
RH Rich Harden/45 25.00
TH Todd Helton/45 70.00
HI Richard Hidalgo/45 15.00
HO Trevor Hoffman/45 30.00
TI Tim Hudson/45 40.00
HU Torii Hunter/45 30.00
EJ Edwin Jackson/45
GJ Geoff Jenkins/45 15.00
DJ Derek Jeter/35 275.00
JJ Jacque Jones/45 20.00
AK Austin Kearns/45 40.00
RK Ryan Klesko/45 20.00
CL Carlos Lee/45 20.00
DL Derrek Lee/45 35.00
ML Mike Lieberthal/45 25.00
EL Esteban Loaiza/45 15.00
LO Mike Lowell/35
MA Mike Marshall/25
EM Edgar Martinez/30
DM Don Mattingly/45

JM Joe Mauer/45 35.00
MU Mark Mulder/45
MM Mike Mussina/40
RO Roy Oswalt/45 25.00
CP Corey Patterson/45 40.00
OP Odalis Perez/45 20.00
PI Mike Piazza/20
SP Scott Podsednik/45 20.00
MP Mark Prior/45 80.00
AP Albert Pujols/45 250.00
MR Manny Ramirez/40
JR Jose Reyes/45 25.00
CR Cal Ripken Jr./35 250.00
AR Alex Rodriguez/10
IR Ivan Rodriguez/45
SR Scott Rolen/15
NR Nolan Ryan/40
RS Ryne Sandberg/40
SA Johan Santana/45 65.00
JS Jason Schmidt/45 40.00
TS Tom Seaver/35 75.00
BS Ben Sheets/55 25.00
GS Gary Sheffield/45 50.00
SM John Smoltz/40 80.00
IS Ichiro Suzuki/25
MT Mark Teixeira/45 40.00
TE Miguel Tejada/25 60.00
FT Frank Thomas/25
JV Javier Vazquez/45
WA Billy Wagner/45 20.00
BW Brandon Webb/45 20.00
WE Rickie Weeks/45 30.00
VW Vernon Wells/29 35.00
DW Dontrelle Willis/45 40.00
RW Randy Wolf/45 20.00
KW Kerry Wood/45 50.00
DY Delmon Young/45 35.00
CZ Carlos Zambrano/30

Signatures Glove

NM/M

Quantity produced listed
GA Garret Anderson/25
RB Rocco Baldelli/25 75.00
BE Josh Beckett/25
CB Carlos Beltran/25
AB Angel Berroa/25 40.00
HB Hank Blalock/25 60.00
BB Bret Boone/25
PB Pat Burrell/15
SB Sean Burroughs/25 60.00
MC Miguel Cabrera/25 100.00
EC Eric Chavez/25
WC Will Clark/25 120.00
JD J.D. Drew/5
AD Adam Dunn/25 80.00
NG Nomar Garciaparra/25 160.00
BG Brian Giles/25 35.00
MG Marcus Giles/25
GL Tom Glavine/25
JG Juan Gonzalez/25
LG Luis Gonzalez/25
KG Ken Griffey Jr./25
VG Vladimir Guerrero/25 175.00
TG Tony Gwynn/25
HA Roy Halladay/24
RH Rich Harden/25 80.00
TH Todd Helton/25 80.00
HI Richard Hidalgo/15
HO Trevor Hoffman/15
TI Tim Hudson/25
HU Torii Hunter/25 40.00
EJ Edwin Jackson/25
GJ Geoff Jenkins/25
DJ Derek Jeter/5
JJ Jacque Jones/25 20.00
AK Austin Kearns/25 60.00
RK Ryan Klesko/15
CL Carlos Lee/25
DL Derrek Lee/25 65.00
ML Mike Lieberthal/25 40.00
EL Esteban Loaiza/25
LO Mike Lowell/5
MA Mike Marshall/25 150.00
EM Edgar Martinez/25 85.00
DM Don Mattingly/25 180.00
JM Joe Mauer/25
MU Mark Mulder/25
MM Mike Mussina/25 100.00
RO Roy Oswalt/25 65.00
CP Corey Patterson/25
OP Odalis Perez/25
PI Mike Piazza/5
SP Scott Podsednik/25 40.00
MP Mark Prior/25
AP Albert Pujols/25 300.00
MR Manny Ramirez/25
JR Jose Reyes/25 65.00
CR Cal Ripken Jr./25
AR Alex Rodriguez/5
IR Ivan Rodriguez/25
NR Nolan Ryan/25
RS Ryne Sandberg/20
SA Johan Santana/25 85.00
JS Jason Schmidt/25
TS Tom Seaver/15
BS Ben Sheets/25
GS Gary Sheffield/20
SM John Smoltz/5
IS Ichiro Suzuki/15
MT Mark Teixeira/25 100.00
TE Miguel Tejada/25 75.00
FT Frank Thomas/15
JV Javier Vazquez/25
WA Billy Wagner/25
BW Brandon Webb/25
WE Rickie Weeks/25 35.00
VW Vernon Wells/5
DW Dontrelle Willis/25 70.00
RW Randy Wolf/15
KW Kerry Wood/25
DY Delmon Young/25 50.00
CZ Carlos Zambrano/15

Signatures Dual

No Pricing
Production 10 sets

Signatures Barrel

NM/M

Cards not serial numbered, quantity produced provided by Upper Deck
GA Garret Anderson/74 40.00
RB Rocco Baldelli/19
BE Josh Beckett/65 35.00
CB Carlos Beltran/55
AB Angel Berroa/64
HB Hank Blalock/74 50.00
BB Bret Boone/64
PB Pat Burrell/13
SB Sean Burroughs/64
MC Miguel Cabrera/64
EC Eric Chavez/74
WC Will Clark/13
JD J.D. Drew/13
AD Adam Dunn/74 40.00
NG Nomar Garciaparra/38 120.00
BG Brian Giles/64 20.00
MG Marcus Giles/64
GL Tom Glavine/64
JG Juan Gonzalez/13
LG Luis Gonzalez/13
KG Ken Griffey Jr./64
VG Vladimir Guerrero/38
TG Tony Gwynn/15
HA Roy Halladay/64 25.00
RH Rich Harden/64
TH Todd Helton/38 65.00
HI Richard Hidalgo/64
HO Trevor Hoffman/68
TI Tim Hudson/64 40.00
HU Torii Hunter/64 30.00
EJ Edwin Jackson/64 Exch
GJ Geoff Jenkins/64 30.00
DJ Derek Jeter/53
JJ Jacque Jones/64 20.00
AK Austin Kearns/64
RK Ryan Klesko/64 25.00
CL Carlos Lee/64 35.00
DL Derrek Lee/64
ML Mike Lieberthal/64
EL Esteban Loaiza/64 25.00
LO Mike Lowell/64 35.00
MA Mike Marshall/13
EM Edgar Martinez/64 60.00
DM Don Mattingly/38
JM Joe Mauer/72 50.00
MU Mark Mulder/64 50.00
MM Mike Mussina/64 50.00
RO Roy Oswalt/64
CP Corey Patterson/74 Exch
OP Odalis Perez/64
PI Mike Piazza/38 150.00
SP Scott Podsednik/64 25.00
MP Mark Prior/64
AP Albert Pujols/64
MR Manny Ramirez/63 85.00
JR Jose Reyes/49
CR Cal Ripken Jr./38
AR Alex Rodriguez/28
IR Ivan Rodriguez/64
NR Nolan Ryan/38
RS Ryne Sandberg/14
SA Johan Santana/64 60.00
JS Jason Schmidt/64
TS Tom Seaver/38
BS Ben Sheets/64 35.00
GS Gary Sheffield/38
SM John Smoltz/13
IS Ichiro Suzuki/64
MT Mark Teixeira/64
TE Miguel Tejada/64 60.00
FT Frank Thomas/13
JV Javier Vazquez/64 50.00
WA Billy Wagner/64 20.00
BW Brandon Webb/64 35.00
WE Rickie Weeks/64
VW Vernon Wells/33 25.00
DW Dontrelle Willis/64 40.00
RW Randy Wolf/64 25.00
KW Kerry Wood/64
DY Delmon Young/74
CZ Carlos Zambrano/38 40.00

Sweet Impressions Plates

No Pricing
Production one set

Sweet Sticks

NM/M

Common Player: 4.00
Production 199 sets
BA Bobby Abreu 6.00
MA Moises Alou 6.00
GA Garret Anderson 4.00
JB Jeff Bagwell 8.00
BE Carlos Beltran 8.00
AB Adrian Beltre 4.00
LB Lance Berkman 4.00
CB Craig Biggio 4.00
HB Hank Blalock 8.00
BB Bret Boone 4.00
PB Pat Burrell 4.00
MC Miguel Cabrera 8.00
EC Eric Chavez 6.00
RC Roger Clemens 15.00
CD Carlos Delgado 6.00
JD J.D. Drew 6.00
AD Adam Dunn
JE Jim Edmonds 6.00
RF Rafael Furcal 4.00
NG Nomar Garciaparra 12.00
JG Jason Giambi 6.00
BG Brian Giles 4.00
MG Marcus Giles 4.00
TG Troy Glaus 4.00
GL Tom Glavine 6.00
LG Luis Gonzalez 4.00
SG Shawn Green 4.00
KG Ken Griffey Jr. 15.00
VG Vladimir Guerrero 8.00
TH Todd Helton 8.00
DJ Derek Jeter 25.00
RJ Randy Johnson 8.00
CJ Chipper Jones 10.00
AJ Andruw Jones 6.00
JK Jeff Kent 4.00
DL Derrek Lee 4.00
ML Mike Lowell 4.00
GM Greg Maddux 10.00
HM Hideki Matsui 35.00
KM Kazuo Matsui 15.00
MO Maggio Ordonez 4.00
RP Rafael Palmeiro 8.00
MP Mike Piazza 10.00
PR Mark Prior 8.00
AP Albert Pujols 20.00
MR Manny Ramirez 8.00
ER Edgar Renteria 6.00
JR Jose Reyes 6.00
CR Cal Ripken Jr. 30.00
AR Alex Rodriguez 15.00
IR Ivan Rodriguez 8.00
SR Scott Rolen 10.00
CS Curt Schilling 6.00
RS Richie Sexson 6.00
GS Gary Sheffield 8.00
AS Alfonso Soriano 8.00
SS Sammy Sosa 10.00
IS Ichiro Suzuki 40.00
MT Mark Teixeira 6.00
TE Miguel Tejada 6.00
FT Frank Thomas 8.00
JT Jim Thome 8.00
LW Larry Walker 6.00
TW Ted Williams 60.00
PW Preston Wilson 4.00

Sweet Sticks Dual

NM/M

Common Duo: 10.00
Production 100 sets
BT Hank Blalock, Mark Teixeira 10.00
CL Miguel Cabrera, Mike Lowell 10.00
JC Randy Johnson, Roger Clemens 25.00
JG Derek Jeter, Nomar Garciaparra 25.00
JM Jose Reyes, Kazuo Matsui 25.00
MM Hideki Matsui, Kazuo Matsui 40.00
PR Albert Pujols, Scott Rolen 40.00
RG Manny Ramirez, Nomar Garciaparra 15.00
RJ Alex Rodriguez, Derek Jeter 50.00
RP Ivan Rodriguez, Mike Piazza
TB Jim Thome, Pat Burrell 20.00
WP Kerry Wood, Mark Prior

Sweet Sticks Quad

NM/M

Production 25 sets
RGDM Babe Ruth, Lou Gehrig, Joe DiMaggio, Mickey Mantle 1,500

Sweet Sticks Triple

NM/M

Production 50 sets
GPS Ken Griffey Jr., Rafael Palmeiro, Sammy Sosa 40.00
JJD Andruw Jones, Chipper Jones, J.D. Drew 25.00
JSG Derek Jeter, Ichiro Suzuki, Ken Griffey Jr. 120.00
MWP Greg Maddux, Kerry Wood, Mark Prior 30.00

Sweet Threads

NM/M

Common Player: 4.00
Patch: 1.5-2.5X
Production 85 sets
JB Jeff Bagwell 8.00
CB Carlos Beltran 8.00
LB Lance Berkman 4.00
HB Hank Blalock 8.00
BB Bret Boone 4.00
MC Miguel Cabrera 8.00
EC Eric Chavez 4.00
BC Bartolo Colon 4.00
CD Carlos Delgado 4.00
JG Jason Giambi 6.00
BG Brian Giles 4.00
TG Troy Glaus 4.00
SG Shawn Green 4.00
VG Vladimir Guerrero 8.00
RH Rich Harden 4.00
HE Todd Helton 8.00
TH Tim Hudson 4.00
ML Mike Lowell 4.00

EM Edgar Martinez 4.00
KM Kazuo Matsui SP 15.00
JM Joe Mauer 8.00
MM Mark Mulder 4.00
HN Hideo Nomo 8.00
MO Magglio Ordonez 4.00
RO Roy Oswalt 4.00
MP Mark Prior 8.00
MR Manny Ramirez 8.00
JR Jose Reyes 4.00
SS Sammy Sosa 10.00
JS Jason Schmidt 6.00
RS Richie Sexson 4.00
GS Gary Sheffield 6.00
AS Alfonso Soriano 8.00
MT Mark Teixeira 6.00
FT Frank Thomas 8.00
JT Jim Thome 8.00
RW Rickie Weeks 4.00
VW Vernon Wells 4.00
DW Dontrelle Willis 4.00
PW Preston Wilson 4.00
KW Kerry Wood 8.00
DY Delmon Young 8.00

Sweet Threads Dual

NM/M
Common Duo: 5.00
Production 150 sets
Patch: 1.5-2X
Production 60 sets
BP Angel Berroa, Scott Podsednik 4.00
BT Hank Blalock, Mark Teixeira 10.00
CK Curt Schilling, Kevin Brown 10.00
CS Roger Clemens, Sammy Sosa 20.00
DT Carlos Delgado, Jim Thome 8.00
GH Eric Gagne, Roy Halladay 8.00
HG Tim Hudson, Vladimir Guerrero 10.00
JC Randy Johnson, Roger Clemens 25.00
JH Andruw Jones, Torii Hunter 8.00
JJ Andruw Jones, Chipper Jones 10.00
MM Hideki Matsui, Kazuo Matsui 50.00
MP Joe Mauer, Mark Prior 15.00
PC Andy Pettitte, Roger Clemens 20.00
PP Jorge Posada, Mike Piazza 15.00
PS Albert Pujols, Ichiro Suzuki 50.00
PW Albert Pujols, Kerry Wood 15.00
RJ Alex Rodriguez, Derek Jeter 50.00
RM Jose Reyes, Kazuo Matsui 15.00
SB Alfonso Soriano, Bret Boone 8.00
SM Gary Sheffield, Pedro J. Martinez 12.00
WP Kerry Wood, Mark Prior 15.00
YW Delmon Young, Rickie Weeks 10.00

Sweet Threads Quad

NM/M
Common Quad: 20.00
Production 99 sets
Quad Patch: No Pricing
Production 1-15
BADH Carlos Beltran, Garret Anderson, Johnny Damon, Torii Hunter 30.00
BBGS Angel Berroa, Carlos Beltran, Alex Gonzalez, Mike Sweeney 20.00
BPJC Josh Beckett, Mark Prior, Randy Johnson, Roger Clemens 35.00
BWRC Josh Beckett, Kerry Wood, Nolan Ryan, Roger Clemens 50.00
CAGG Bartolo Colon, Garret Anderson, Troy Glaus, Vladimir Guerrero 25.00
DHHW Carlos Delgado, Eric Hinske, Roy Halladay, Vernon Wells 20.00
DOGP Carlos Delgado, David Ortiz, Jason Giambi, Rafael Palmeiro 25.00
GNKB Brian Giles, Phil Nevin, Ryan Klesko, Sean Burroughs 25.00
GNLG Eric Gagne, Hideo Nomo, Paul LoDuca, Shawn Green 30.00
JBGB Chipper Jones, Lance Berkman, Luis Gonzalez, Pat Burrell 25.00
JEGW Andruw Jones, Jim Edmonds, Ken Griffey Jr., Preston Wilson 35.00
JJDF Andruw Jones, Chipper Jones, J.D. Drew, Rafael Furcal 25.00
JMSH Jacque Jones, Joe Mauer, Shannon Stewart, Torii Hunter 35.00
JRMT Derek Jeter, Edgar Renteria, Kazuo Matsui, Miguel Tejada 40.00
KGCS Austin Kearns, Brian Giles, Miguel Cabrera, Sammy Sosa 25.00
LMRS Carlos Lee, Hideki Matsui, Manny Ramirez, Shannon Stewart 75.00
LTOK Carlos Lee, Frank Thomas, Magglio Ordonez, Paul Konerko 25.00
LTPP Javy Lopez, Miguel Tejada, Raffy, Sidney Ponson 25.00
MMMH Mark Mulder, Mike Mussina, Pedro J. Martinez, Roy Halladay 25.00
MTTS Edgar Martinez, Jim Thome, Mark Teixeira, Mike Sweeney 20.00
NSGH Phil Nevin, Richie Sexson, Shawn Green, Todd Helton 20.00
PBBC Andy Pettitte, Craig Biggio, Jeff Bagwell, Roger Clemens 40.00
PLBT Albert Pujols, Lee, Jeff Bagwell, Jim Thome 40.00
PRER Albert Pujols, Edgar Renteria, Jim Edmonds, Scott Rolen 70.00
PWPS Corey Patterson, Kerry Wood, Mark Prior, Sammy Sosa 50.00
RCBG Alex Rodriguez, Eric Chavez, Hank Blalock, Troy Glaus 30.00
RJDM Alex Rodriguez, Derek Jeter, Joe DiMaggio, Mickey Mantle 275.00
RLPM Ivan Rodriguez, Javy Lopez, Jorge Posada, Joe Mauer 40.00
RMPG Jose Reyes, Kazuo Matsui, Mike Piazza, Tom Glavine 30.00
SBKV Alfonso Soriano, Bret Boone, Jeff Kent, Jose Vidro 20.00
SBMM Curt Schilling, Kevin Brown, Mike Mussina, Pedro J. Martinez 40.00
SDRM Curt Schilling, Johnny Damon, Manny Ramirez, Pedro J. Martinez 60.00
SSOG Gary Sheffield, Ichiro Suzuki, Magglio Ordonez, Vladimir Guerrero 50.00
VCBM Javier Vazquez, Jose Contreras, Kevin Brown, Mike Mussina 25.00
WATM Billy Wagner, Bobby Abreu, Jim Thome, Kevin Millwood 30.00
WBCL Dontrelle Willis, Josh Beckett, Miguel Cabrera, Mike Lowell 20.00
WGJS Brandon Webb, Luis Gonzalez, Randy Johnson, Richie Sexson 25.00
ZMHH Barry Zito, Mark Mulder, Rich Harden, Tim Hudson 35.00

Sweet Threads Triple

NM/M
Common Trio: 10.00
Production 99 sets
Triple Patch: 2X
No pricing 15 or less
AGG Garret Anderson, Troy Glaus, Vladimir Guerrero 20.00
BKE Jeff Bagwell, Jeff Kent, Morgan Ensberg 15.00
BLR Adrian Beltre, Mike Lowell, Scott Rolen 20.00
BMS Bret Boone, Edgar Martinez, Ichiro Suzuki 50.00
BWC Josh Beckett, Kerry Wood, Roger Clemens 30.00
CMM Bobby Crosby, Joe Mauer, Kazuo Matsui 30.00
DHW Carlos Delgado, Roy Halladay, Vernon Wells 15.00
DKG Adam Dunn, Austin Kearns, Ken Griffey Jr. 20.00
DMJ Joe DiMaggio, Mickey Mantle, Derek Jeter 220.00
DMW Joe DiMaggio, Mickey Mantle, Ted Williams 250.00
DRN Johnny Damon, Manny Ramirez, Trot Nixon 40.00
FRP Keith Foulke, Mariano Rivera, Troy Percival 25.00
GPS Ken Griffey Jr., Rafael Palmeiro, Sammy Sosa 35.00
JJD Andruw Jones, Chipper Jones, J.D. Drew 20.00
JTG Derek Jeter, Miguel Tejada, Nomar Garciaparra 40.00
JWH Edwin Jackson, Jerome Williams, Rich Harden 10.00
KVG Jeff Kent, Jose Vidro, Marcus Giles 10.00
LTO Carlos Lee, Frank Thomas, Maggio Ordonez 20.00
LTP Javy Lopez, Miguel Tejada, Rafael Palmeiro 20.00
MCF Kazuo Matsui, Miguel Cabrera, Rafael Furcal 20.00
MMH Mike Mussina, Pedro J. Martinez, Tim Hudson 25.00
MSH Joe Mauer, Johan Santana, Torii Hunter 35.00
MWP Greg Maddux, Kerry Wood, Mark Prior 35.00
PAS Corey Patterson, Moises Alou, Sammy Sosa 30.00
PCO Andy Pettitte, Roger Clemens, Roy Oswalt 25.00
PRR Albert Pujols, Edgar Renteria, Scott Rolen 40.00
PTH Albert Pujols, Jim Thome, Todd Helton 30.00
RCB Alex Rodriguez, Eric Chavez, Hank Blalock 30.00
RGJ Alex Rodriguez, Ken Griffey Jr., Randy Johnson 35.00
RGW Jose Reyes, Khalil Greene, Rickie Weeks 30.00
RJG Alex Rodriguez, Derek Jeter, Jason Giambi 60.00
RMP Jose Reyes, Kazuo Matsui, Mike Piazza 25.00
SBK Alfonso Soriano, Bret Boone, Jeff Kent 20.00
SBP Jason Schmidt, Josh Beckett, Mark Prior 20.00
SBT Alfonso Soriano, Hank Blalock, Mark Teixeira 20.00
SLM Curt Schilling, Derek Lowe, Pedro J. Martinez 40.00
VBM Javier Vazquez, Kevin Brown, Mike Mussina 20.00
WBP Brandon Webb, Josh Beckett, Mark Prior 20.00
WGS Billy Wagner, Eric Gagne, John Smoltz 20.00
WRC Kerry Wood, Nolan Ryan, Roger Clemens 60.00
YCW Delmon Young, Miguel Cabrera, Rickie Weeks 20.00
ZMH Barry Zito, Mark Mulder, Tim Hudson 10.00

2004 UPPER DECK SWEET SPOT CLASSIC

NM/M
Complete Set (161):
Common Player (1-90): .40
Common (91-161): 2.00
Production 1,910-1,999
Pack (4): 15.00
Box (12): 150.00
1 Al Kaline 1.00
2 Andre Dawson .40
3 Bert Blyleven .40
4 Bill Dickey .40
5 Bill Mazeroski .40
6 Billy Martin .40
7 Bob Feller .50
8 Bob Gibson 1.00
9 Bob Lemon .40
10 George Kell .40
11 Bobby Doerr .40
12 Brooks Robinson 1.00
13 Cal Ripken Jr. 4.00
14 Carl Hubbell .40
15 Carl Yastrzemski 1.50
16 Charlie Keller .40
17 Chuck Dressen .40
18 Cy Young 1.00
19 Dave Winfield .75
20 Dizzy Dean .75
21 Don Drysdale .75
22 Don Larsen .75
23 Don Mattingly 2.50
24 Don Newcombe .40
25 Duke Snider .75
26 Early Wynn .40
27 Eddie Mathews 1.00
28 Elston Howard .40
29 Frank Robinson .75
30 Gary Carter .40
31 Gil Hodges .40
32 Gil McDougald .40
33 Hank Greenberg .75
34 Harmon Killebrew 1.50
35 Harry Caray .40
36 Honus Wagner 1.00
37 Hoyt Wilhelm .40
38 Jackie Robinson 2.00
39 Jim Bunning .40
40 Jim Palmer .75
41 Jimmie Foxx 1.00
42 Jimmy Wynn .40
43 Joe DiMaggio 3.00
44 Joe Torre .40
45 Johnny Mize .40

46	Juan Marichal	.75
47	Larry Doby	.40
48	Lefty Gomez	.40
49	Lefty Grove	.40
50	Leo Durocher	.40
51	Lou Boudreau	.40
52	Lou Brock	.50
53	Lou Gehrig	3.00
54	Luis Aparicio	.40
55	Maury Wills	.40
56	Mel Allen	.40
57	Mel Ott	.40
58	Mickey Cochrane	.40
59	Mickey Mantle	4.00
60	Mike Schmidt	2.00
61	Monte Irvin	.40
62	Nolan Ryan	4.00
63	Pee Wee Reese	.40
64	Phil Rizzuto	.50
65	Ralph Kiner	.40
66	Richie Ashburn	.40
67	Rick Ferrell	.40
68	Roberto Clemente	2.50
69	Robin Roberts	.40
70	Robin Yount	1.00
71	Rogers Hornsby	.75
72	Rollie Fingers	.40
73	Roy Campanella	.75
74	Ryne Sandberg	1.50
75	Tony Gwynn	1.00
76	Satchel Paige	.75
77	Shoeless Joe Jackson	2.00
78	Stan Musial	2.00
79	Ted Williams	3.00
80	Thurman Munson	.75
81	Tom Seaver	1.50
82	Tommy Henrich	.40
83	Tony Perez	.40
84	Tris Speaker	.40
85	Vida Blue	.40
86	Wade Boggs	.50
87	Walter Johnson	.75
88	Warren Spahn	1.00
89	Whitey Ford	.75
90	Willie McCovey	.40
91	Andre Dawson	2.50
92	Andre Dawson	2.50
93	Ernie Banks	4.00
94	Bob Lemon	2.00
95	Cal Ripken Jr.	8.00
96	Cal Ripken Jr.	8.00
97	Carl Yastrzemski	3.00
98	Carlton Fisk	2.50
99	Cy Young	4.00
100	Don Larsen	2.50
101	Don Newcombe	2.00
102	Don Newcombe	2.00
103	Dwight Evans	2.00
104	Elston Howard	2.50
105	Frank Robinson	3.00
106	Frank Robinson	3.00
107	Frank Robinson	3.00
108	Gil McDougald	2.00
109	Hank Greenberg	4.00
110	Harmon Killebrew	4.00
111	Hoyt Wilhelm	2.00
112	Hoyt Wilhelm	2.00
113	Jackie Robinson	5.00
114	Jackie Robinson	5.00
115	Jackie Robinson	5.00
116	Jackie Robinson	5.00
117	Jim Bunning	2.00
118	Joe DiMaggio	6.00
119	Joe Morgan	2.00
120	Johnny Mize	2.50
121	Johnny Mize	2.50
122	Juan Marichal	3.00
123	Ken Griffey Sr.	2.00
124	Larry Doby	2.50
125	Lefty Gomez	2.00
126	Lou Boudreau	2.00
127	Lou Gehrig	6.00
128	Lou Gehrig	6.00
129	Mark McGwire	6.00
130	Mark McGwire	6.00
131	Maury Wills	2.00
132	Mel Ott	3.00
133	Mike Schmidt	5.00
134	Nolan Ryan	8.00
135	Nolan Ryan	8.00
136	Pee Wee Reese	2.00
137	Nolan Ryan	8.00
138	Richie Ashburn	2.50
139	Roberto Clemente	8.00
140	Roberto Clemente	8.00
141	Robin Roberts	2.00
142	Robin Yount	3.00
143	Roger Clemens	2.00
144	Rollie Fingers	2.00
145	Rollie Fingers	2.00
146	Roy Campanella	3.00
147	Ryne Sandberg	4.00
149	Satchel Paige	4.00
150	Stan Musial	5.00
151	Stan Musial	5.00
152	Stan Musial	5.00
153	Ted Williams	6.00
154	Ted Williams	6.00
155	Tom Seaver	3.00
156	Tom Seaver	3.00
157	Wade Boggs	2.50
158	Warren Spahn	3.00
159	Warren Spahn	3.00
160	Joe DiMaggio	6.00
161	Yogi Berra	4.00

Game Used Patch

NM/M

Some not priced due to scarcity
Holofoil: No Pricing
Production 10

BB	Bert Blyleven/113	25.00
WB	Wade Boggs/90	30.00
AD	Andre Dawson/100	20.00
TG	Tony Gwynn/100	35.00
EH	Elston Howard/23	
CK	Charlie Keller/55	30.00
ML	Mickey Lolich/115	15.00
DM	Don Mattingly/176	40.00
GM	Gil McDougald/31	25.00
TM	Thurman Munson/100	30.00
CR	Cal Ripken Jr./17	
FR	Frank Robinson/50	30.00
NR	Nolan Ryan/96	65.00
TS	Tom Seaver/94	30.00
MW	Maury Wills/78	25.00
CY	Carl Yastrzemski/20	65.00
RY	Robin Yount/100	30.00

Jersey

NM/M

Common Player: 5.00
Production 275 sets
Holofoils: 1.5-2X
Production 50

SA	Sparky Anderson	6.00
SB	Sal Bando	5.00
RB	Ron Blomberg	5.00
BB	Bert Blyleven	5.00
WB	Wade Boggs	8.00
WB1	Wade Boggs	8.00
JB	Jim Bunning	5.00
GC	Gary Carter	6.00
RC	Roberto Clemente	65.00
AD	Andre Dawson	5.00
AD1	Andre Dawson	5.00
JD	Joe DiMaggio	70.00
CD	Chuck Dressen	5.00
KG	Ken Griffey Sr.	5.00
TG	Tony Gwynn	10.00
EH	Elston Howard	8.00
CK	Charlie Keller	15.00
ML	Mickey Lolich	6.00
MM	Mickey Mantle	125.00
JM	Juan Marichal	8.00
RM	Roger Maris	45.00
BM	Billy Martin	8.00
EM	Eddie Mathews	10.00
DM	Don Mattingly	20.00
GM	Gil McDougald	8.00
JO	Johnny Mize	10.00
TM	Thurman Munson	20.00
SM	Stan Musial	25.00
JP	Jim Palmer	8.00
CR	Cal Ripken Jr.	20.00
PR	Phil Rizzuto	15.00
FR	Frank Robinson	8.00
JR	Jackie Robinson	40.00
NR	Nolan Ryan	25.00
TS	Tom Seaver	15.00
OS	Ozzie Smith	10.00
JT	Joe Torre	8.00
TW	Ted Williams	70.00
MW	Maury Wills	5.00
CY	Carl Yastrzemski	15.00
RY	Robin Yount	10.00

Logo Patch

NM/M

Common Level 1: 5.00
Production 300
Level 2: 1X
Production 230
Level 3: 1X
Production 200
Level 4: 1-1.5X
Production 150
Level 5: 1-1.5X
Production 125
Level 6: 1-2X
Production 75
Level 7: 1.5-2.5X
Production 50
Level 8: No Pricing
Production 25

AL	Mel Allen	5.00
LA	Luis Aparicio	5.00
RA	Richie Ashburn	6.00
WB	Wade Boggs	8.00
LB	Lou Boudreau	5.00
BR	Lou Brock	8.00
JB	Jim Bunning	5.00
CA	Roy Campanella	8.00
GC	Gary Carter	5.00
HC	Harry Caray	10.00
RC	Roberto Clemente	25.00
TC	Ty Cobb	12.00
CO	Mickey Cochrane	5.00
AD	Andre Dawson	8.00
DD	Dizzy Dean	8.00
BD	Bill Dickey	5.00
JD	Joe DiMaggio	15.00
LD	Larry Doby	6.00
DO	Bobby Doerr	6.00
DR	Don Drysdale	6.00
DU	Leo Durocher	5.00
BF	Bob Feller	8.00
RF	Rick Ferrell	5.00
FI	Rollie Fingers	6.00
WF	Whitey Ford	6.00
JF	Jimmie Foxx	8.00
FF	Frankie Frisch	5.00
GE	Lou Gehrig	15.00
CG	Charlie Gehringer	8.00
BG	Bob Gibson	8.00
LG	Lefty Gomez	5.00
HG	Hank Greenberg	10.00
GR	Lefty Grove	6.00
TH	Tommy Henrich	5.00
GH	Gil Hodges	8.00
RH	Rogers Hornsby	8.00
CH	Carl Hubbell	5.00
IR	Monte Irvin	5.00
JJ	Shoeless Joe Jackson	20.00
FJ	Ferguson Jenkins	6.00
WJ	Walter Johnson	8.00
AK	Al Kaline	15.00
HK	Harmon Killebrew	15.00
RK	Ralph Kiner	8.00
DL	Don Larsen	6.00
TL	Tommy Lasorda	5.00
BL	Bob Lemon	5.00
ML	Mickey Lolich	5.00
MI	Mickey Mantle	40.00
MA	Juan Marichal	6.00
BM	Billy Martin	8.00
EM	Eddie Mathews	8.00
CM	Christy Mathewson	10.00
DM	Don Mattingly	20.00
WM	Willie McCovey	8.00
JM	Johnny Mize	6.00
TM	Thurman Munson	10.00
SM	Stan Musial	10.00
DN	Don Newcombe	5.00
MO	Mel Ott	6.00
SP	Satchel Paige	10.00
JP	Jim Palmer	8.00
TP	Tony Perez	5.00
GP	Gaylord Perry	5.00
PR	Pee Wee Reese	6.00
CR	Cal Ripken Jr.	30.00
RI	Phil Rizzuto	8.00
RR	Robin Roberts	6.00
RO	Brooks Robinson	12.00
FR	Frank Robinson	8.00
JR	Jackie Robinson	12.00
RU	Babe Ruth	20.00
NR	Nolan Ryan	25.00
RS	Ryne Sandberg	20.00
MS	Mike Schmidt	15.00
TS	Tom Seaver	10.00
SK	Bill "Moose" Skowron	5.00
ES	Enos Slaughter	5.00
DS	Duke Snider	8.00
WS	Warren Spahn	10.00
TR	Tris Speaker	8.00
JT	Joe Torre	5.00
HW	Honus Wagner	10.00
WI	Hoyt Wilhelm	5.00
TW	Ted Williams	20.00
MW	Maury Wills	5.00
DW	Dave Winfield	6.00
EW	Early Wynn	5.00
YA	Carl Yastrzemski	12.00
CY	Cy Young	10.00

Signature Black Ink

NM/M

Common Autograph: 15.00

SSA-2	Preacher Roe/225	25.00
SSA-4	Bob Feller/65	45.00
SSA-5	Bob Gibson/50	50.00
SSA-6	Harry Kalas/100	45.00
SSA-7	Bobby Doerr/100	25.00
SSA-8	Cal Ripken Jr./50	165.00
SSA-9	Carl Yastrzemski/35	110.00
SSA-10	Carlton Fisk/100	45.00
SSA-11	Chuck Tanner/150	15.00
SSA-12	Cito Gaston/150	15.00
SSA-13	Danny Ozark/150	15.00
SSA-14	Dave Winfield/80	50.00
SSA-15	Davey Johnson/175	15.00
SSA-16	Ernie Harwell/100	50.00
SSA-17	Dick Williams/150	15.00
SSA-18	Don Mattingly/40	100.00
SSA-19	Don Newcombe/40	35.00
SSA-20	Duke Snider/35	60.00
SSA-21	Steve Carlton/150	35.00
SSA-22	Felipe Alou/175	20.00
SSA-23	Frank Robinson/65	40.00
SSA-24	Gary Carter/100	35.00
SSA-25	Gene Mauch/225	15.00
SSA-26	George Bamberger/225	15.00
SSA-28	Gus Suhr/100	30.00
SSA-30	Harmon Killebrew/50	70.00
SSA-31	Jack McKeon/225	20.00
SSA-32	Jim Bunning/100	25.00
SSA-33	Jimmy Piersall/212	20.00
SSA-35	Johnny Bench/50	75.00
SSA-36	Juan Marichal/50	40.00
SSA-37	Lou Brock/50	50.00
SSA-38	George Kell/40	50.00
SSA-39	Maury Wills/40	30.00
SSA-41	Mike Schmidt/40	100.00
SSA-42	Nolan Ryan/50	135.00
SSA-43	Ozzie Smith/65	75.00
SSA-44	Eddie Mayo/140	15.00
SSA-45	Phil Rizzuto/50	50.00
SSA-46	Ralph Kiner/40	45.00
SSA-47	Lonny Frey/114	15.00
SSA-48	Bill Mazeroski/50	40.00
SSA-49	Robin Roberts/40	40.00
SSA-50	Robin Yount/40	75.00
SSA-52	Roger Craig/175	15.00
SSA-55	Tony Perez/40	70.00
SSA-56	Sparky Anderson/175	20.00
SSA-57	Stan Musial/40	100.00
SSA-58	Ted Radcliffe/225	25.00
SSA-60	Tom Seaver/25	70.00
SSA-61	Tony Gwynn/65	75.00
SSA-62	Tony LaRussa/275	15.00
SSA-63	Tony Oliva/150	20.00
SSA-64	Tony Pena/150	15.00
SSA-66	Whitey Ford/45	65.00
SSA-67	Yogi Berra/65	60.00

Signature Blue Ink

		NM/M
Common Autograph:		15.00
Some not priced due to scarcity		
SSA-2	Preacher Roe/150	25.00
SSA-4	Bob Feller/50	45.00
SSA-5	Bob Gibson/25	60.00
SSA-6	Harry Kalas/50	45.00
SSA-7	Bobby Doerr/50	30.00
SSA-8	Cal Ripken Jr./25	200.00
SSA-10	Carlton Fisk/50	50.00
SSA-11	Chuck Tanner/125	15.00
SSA-12	Cito Gaston/125	15.00
SSA-13	Danny Ozark/125	15.00
SSA-14	Dave Winfield/35	55.00
SSA-15	Davey Johnson/150	15.00
SSA-16	Ernie Harwell/50	50.00
SSA-17	Dick Williams/125	15.00
SSA-21	Steve Carlton/100	35.00
SSA-22	Felipe Alou/150	20.00
SSA-23	Frank Robinson/50	40.00
SSA-24	Gary Carter/75	35.00
SSA-25	Gene Mauch/150	15.00
SSA-26	George Bamberger/150	15.00
SSA-28	Gus Suhr/85	30.00
SSA-31	Jack McKeon/150	20.00
SSA-32	Jim Bunning/65	30.00
SSA-33	Jimmy Piersall/150	25.00
SSA-35	Johnny Bench/20	90.00
SSA-38	George Kell/25	50.00
SSA-39	Maury Wills/25	40.00
SSA-42	Nolan Ryan/25	175.00
SSA-43	Ozzie Smith/50	75.00
SSA-44	Eddie Mayo/50	20.00
SSA-45	Phil Rizzuto/25	60.00
SSA-46	Ralph Kiner/25	
SSA-47	Lonny Frey/75	15.00
SSA-48	Bill Mazeroski/25	40.00
SSA-49	Robin Roberts/25	40.00
SSA-50	Robin Yount/25	75.00
SSA-52	Roger Craig/150	15.00
SSA-56	Sparky Anderson/150	20.00
SSA-57	Stan Musial/25	120.00
SSA-58	Ted Radcliffe/150	25.00
SSA-62	Tony LaRussa/145	15.00
SSA-63	Tony Oliva/125	20.00
SSA-64	Tony Pena/115	15.00
SSA-67	Yogi Berra/50	60.00

Signature Holofoil

		NM/M
Many not priced due to scarcity		
SSA-4	Bob Feller/25	70.00
SSA-5	Bob Gibson/25	60.00
SSA-11	Chuck Tanner/100	15.00
SSA-12	Cito Gaston/100	15.00
SSA-13	Danny Ozark/100	15.00
SSA-15	Davey Johnson/50	20.00
SSA-17	Dick Williams/100	15.00
SSA-22	Felipe Alou/50	30.00
SSA-24	Gary Carter/50	45.00
SSA-45	Phil Rizzuto/25	60.00
SSA-49	Robin Roberts/25	40.00
SSA-50	Robin Yount/25	75.00
SSA-52	Roger Craig/50	20.00
SSA-56	Sparky Anderson/50	30.00
SSA-57	Stan Musial/25	120.00
SSA-62	Tony LaRussa/50	20.00
SSA-63	Tony Oliva/100	25.00
SSA-64	Tony Pena/100	15.00

Signature Red Ink

		NM/M
Many not priced due to scarcity		
SSA-14	Dave Winfield/25	65.00
SSA-25	Gene Mauch/25	25.00
SSA-26	George Bamberger/25	30.00

Wood Barrel Auto.

		NM/M
Varying quantities produced		
Some not priced due to scarcity		
HB	Harold Baines/200	35.00
JB	Johnny Bench/50	120.00
WB	Wade Boggs/200	55.00
LB	Lou Brock/50	
BM	Bill Mazeroski/24	
SM	Stan Musial/25	185.00
CR	Cal Ripken Jr./25	300.00
NR	Nolan Ryan/25	200.00
RS	Ron Santo/203	45.00
TS	Tom Seaver/25	140.00
BW	Billy Williams/200	35.00

2004 UPPER DECK ULTIMATE COLLECTION

		NM/M
Complete Set (222):		
Common Player (1-126):		2.00
Production 675		
Common (127-168):		4.00
Production 525		
Common (169-194):		6.00
Production 299		
Common (195-209, 222)		8.00
Production 199		
Common (210-221):		15.00
Production 75		
Pack (4):		80.00
Box (4):		275.00
1	Al Kaline	4.00
2	Billy Williams	2.00
3	Bob Feller	2.00
4	Bob Gibson	4.00
5	Bob Lemon	2.00
6	Bobby Doerr	2.00
7	Brooks Robinson	3.00
8	Cal Ripken Jr.	10.00
9	Jim "Catfish" Hunter	2.00
10	Eddie Mathews	4.00
11	Enos Slaughter	2.00
12	Ernie Banks	4.00
13	Fergie Jenkins	2.00
14	Gaylord Perry	2.00
15	Harmon Killebrew	4.00
16	Jim Bunning	2.00
17	Joe DiMaggio	6.00
18	Joe Morgan	2.00
19	Juan Marichal	2.00
20	Lou Brock	2.00
21	Luis Aparicio	2.00
22	Mickey Mantle	12.00
23	Mike Schmidt	6.00
24	Monte Irvin	2.00
25	Nolan Ryan	8.00
26	Pee Wee Reese	2.00
27	Phil Niekro	2.00
28	Phil Rizzuto	3.00
29	Ralph Kiner	3.00
30	Richie Ashburn	2.00
31	Robin Roberts	3.00
32	Robin Yount	5.00
33	Rod Carew	2.00
34	Rollie Fingers	2.00
35	Stan Musial	6.00
36	Ted Williams	8.00
37	Tom Seaver	4.00
38	Warren Spahn	4.00
39	Whitey Ford	3.00
40	Willie McCovey	3.00
41	Willie Stargell	3.00
42	Yogi Berra	4.00
43	Adrian Beltre	2.00
44	Albert Pujols	8.00
45	Alex Rodriguez	6.00
46	Alfonso Soriano	3.00
47	Andruw Jones	2.00
48	Andy Pettitte	2.00
49	Aubrey Huff	2.00
50	Barry Larkin	2.00
51	Ben Sheets	2.00
52	Bernie Williams	2.00
53	Bobby Abreu	2.00
54	Brad Penny	2.00
55	Bret Boone	2.00
56	Brian Giles	2.00
57	Carlos Beltran	3.00
58	Carlos Delgado	2.00
59	Carlos Guillen	2.00
60	Carlos Lee	2.00
61	Carlos Zambrano	2.00
62	Chipper Jones	4.00
63	Craig Biggio	2.00
64	Craig Wilson	2.00
65	Curt Schilling	4.00
66	David Ortiz	4.00
67	Derek Jeter	10.00
68	Eric Chavez	2.00
69	Eric Gagne	3.00
70	Frank Thomas	3.00
71	Garret Anderson	2.00
72	Gary Sheffield	3.00
73	Greg Maddux	5.00
74	Hank Blalock	3.00
75	Hideki Matsui	6.00
76	Ichiro Suzuki	6.00
77	Ivan Rodriguez	3.00
78	J.D. Drew	2.00
79	Jake Peavy	2.00
80	Jason Schmidt	2.00
81	Jeff Bagwell	3.00
82	Jeff Kent	2.00
83	Jim Thome	4.00
84	Joe Mauer	2.00
85	Johan Santana	3.00
86	Jose Reyes	2.00
87	Jose Vidro	2.00
88	Ken Griffey Jr.	5.00
89	Kerry Wood	4.00
90	Larry Walker	2.00
91	Luis Gonzalez	2.00
92	Lyle Overbay	2.00
93	Magglio Ordonez	2.00
94	Manny Ramirez	4.00
95	Mark Mulder	2.00
96	Mark Prior	4.00
97	Mark Teixeira	2.00
98	Melvin Mora	2.00
99	Michael Young	2.00
100	Miguel Cabrera	4.00
101	Miguel Tejada	3.00
102	Mike Lowell	2.00
103	Mike Piazza	6.00
104	Mike Sweeney	2.00
105	Nomar Garciaparra	6.00
106	Oliver Perez	2.00
107	Pedro J. Martinez	4.00
108	Preston Wilson	2.00
109	Rafael Palmeiro	4.00
110	Randy Johnson	4.00
111	Roger Clemens	10.00
112	Roy Halladay	2.00
113	Roy Oswalt	2.00
114	Sammy Sosa	6.00
115	Scott Podsednik	2.00
116	Scott Rolen	4.00
117	Shawn Green	2.00
118	Tim Hudson	2.00
119	Todd Helton	3.00
120	Tom Glavine	3.00
121	Torii Hunter	2.00
122	Travis Hafner	2.00
123	Troy Glaus	2.00
124	Vernon Wells	2.00
125	Victor Martinez	2.00
126	Vladimir Guerrero	4.00
127	*Aarom Baldiris*	8.00
128	*Alfredo Simon*	4.00
129	*Andres Blanco*	4.00
130	*Jeff Bajenaru*	4.00
131	*Bartolome Fortunato*	4.00
132	*Brandon Medders*	4.00
133	*Brian Dallimore*	4.00
134	*Carlos Hines*	4.00
135	*Carlos Vasquez*	8.00
136	*Casey Daigle*	4.00
137	*Chad Bentz*	4.00
138	*Chris Aguila*	4.00
139	*Chris Saenz*	4.00
140	*Chris Shelton*	20.00
141	*Colby Miller*	4.00
142	*David Crouthers*	4.00
143	*David Aardsma*	4.00
144	*Dennis Sarfate*	4.00
145	*Donnie Kelly*	4.00
146	*Eddy Rodriguez*	8.00
147	*Eduardo Villacis*	4.00
148	*Edwardo Sierra*	6.00
149	*Edwin Moreno*	6.00
150	*Kyle Denney*	4.00
151	*Evan Rust*	4.00
152	*Fernando Nieve*	4.00
153	*Frank Francisco*	4.00
154	*Franklyn Gracesqui*	4.00
155	*Freddy Guzman*	4.00
156	*Greg Dobbs*	4.00
157	*Hector Gimenez*	4.00
158	*Jason Alfaro*	4.00
159	*Jake Woods*	4.00
160	*Andy Green*	4.00
161	*Jason Bartlett*	8.00
162	*Jason Frasor*	4.00
163	*Jeff Bennett*	4.00
164	*Jerome Gamble*	4.00
165	*Jerry Gil*	4.00
166	*Joe Hietpas*	4.00
167	*Jorge Sequea*	4.00
168	*Jorge Vasquez*	6.00
169	*Josh Labandeira*	6.00
170	*Justin Germano*	6.00
171	*Justin Hampson*	6.00
172	*Chris Young*	6.00
173	*Justin Knoedler*	6.00
174	*Justin Lehr*	6.00
175	*Justin Leone*	10.00
176	*Kazuhito Tadano*	8.00
177	*Kevin Cave*	6.00
178	*Lincoln Holdzkom*	6.00
179	*Mike Rose*	6.00
180	*Luis Gonzalez*	6.00
181	*Mariano Gomez*	6.00
182	*Rene Rivera*	6.00
183	*Mike Wuertz*	8.00
184	*Mike Gosling*	6.00
185	*Mike Johnston*	6.00
186	*Mike Rouse*	6.00
187	*Nick Regilio*	6.00
188	*Onil Joseph*	6.00
189	*Orlando Rodriguez*	6.00
190	*Phil Stockman*	6.00
191	*Renyel Pinto*	10.00
192	*Roberto Novoa*	12.00
193	*Roman Colon*	6.00
194	*Ronald Belisario*	6.00
195	*Ronny Cedeno*	8.00
196	*Ryan Meaux*	8.00
197	*Ryan Wing*	8.00
198	*Scott Dohmann*	8.00
199	*Joey Gathright*	10.00
200	*Shawn Camp*	8.00
201	*Shawn Hill*	8.00
202	*Steve Andrade*	8.00
203	*Tim Bausher*	8.00
204	*Tim Bittner*	8.00
205	*Brad Halsey*	10.00
206	*William Bergolla*	8.00
207	*Kameron Loe*	8.00
208	*Jesse Crain*	10.00
209	*Scott Kazmir*	25.00
210	*Akinori Otsuka/auto*	60.00
211	*Chris Oxspring/auto*	15.00
212	*Ian Snell/auto*	25.00
213	*John Gall/auto*	20.00
214	*Jose Capellan/auto*	50.00
215	*Yadier Molina/auto*	40.00
216	*Merkin Valdez/auto*	25.00
217	*Ramon Ramirez/auto*	15.00
218	*Rusty Tucker/auto*	20.00
219	*Scott Proctor/auto*	25.00
220	*Sean Henn/auto*	15.00
221	*Shingo Takatsu/auto*	75.00
222	*Kazuo Matsui*	30.00

Gold

Gold (1-194): 1-2X
Production 50
Gold (195-222): No Pricing
Production 25
Gold 210-221 production 15

Platinum

Platinum (1-126): No Pricing
Production 10
Platinum (210-221): No Pricing
Production One

Rainbow

Rainbows: No Pricing
Production one set

Achievement Material

		NM/M
Common Player:		
EB	Ernie Banks/58	25.00
JB	Johnny Bench/68	15.00
YB	Yogi Berra/51	20.00
GB	George Brett/80	25.00
CA	Roy Campanella/51	25.00
RO	Rod Carew/77	15.00
SC	Steve Carlton/72	10.00
OC	Orlando Cepeda/58	10.00
CL	Roger Clemens/86	25.00
RC	Roberto Clemente/66	100.00
TC	Ty Cobb/9	
JD	Joe DiMaggio/39	100.00
DD	Don Drysdale/62	15.00
BG	Bob Gibson/68	15.00
KG	Ken Griffey Jr./97	25.00
DJ	Derek Jeter/96	40.00
RJ	Randy Johnson/99	15.00
HK	Harmon Killebrew/69	15.00
GM	Greg Maddux/92	20.00

MA Mickey Mantle/56 200.00
RM Roger Maris/61 80.00
PM Pedro J. Martinez/99 15.00
DM Don Mattingly/85 20.00
MC Willie McCovey/59 15.00
TM Thurman Munson/70 15.00
EM Eddie Murray/77 15.00
JP Jim Palmer/73 10.00
MP Mike Piazza/93 20.00
CR Cal Ripken Jr./82 50.00
BR Brooks Robinson/64 15.00
FR Frank Robinson/66 10.00
JR Jackie Robinson/47 65.00
RS Ryne Sandberg/84 40.00
MS Mike Schmidt/80 25.00
TS Tom Seaver/69 15.00
SS Sammy Sosa/98 20.00
WS Warren Spahn/57
TW Ted Williams/42 100.00
CY Carl Yastrzemski/67 25.00
RY Robin Yount/82 25.00

All-Stars Signatures

NM/M

Most not priced
RC Rod Carew/18 40.00
SM Stan Musial/24 75.00
BR Brooks Robinson/15 60.00
CY Carl Yastrzemski/18 80.00

Bat Barrel Signatures

No Pricing
Production 1-5

Dual Game Patch

NM/M

Production 25 sets
BB Carlos Beltran, Jeff Bagwell 40.00
BC Josh Beckett, Miguel Cabrera 40.00
BG Lou Brock, Tony Gwynn 75.00
BM Yogi Berra, Roger Maris
BS Mike Schmidt, George Brett 100.00
BT Hank Blalock, Mark Teixeira 40.00
CG Rod Carew, Tony Gwynn 50.00
CP Mike Piazza, Gary Carter 50.00
CR Eric Chavez, Scott Rolen 50.00
FB Johnny Bench, Carlton Fisk 50.00
FR Nolan Ryan, Bob Feller 100.00
GC Will Clark, Mark Grace 40.00
GG Ken Griffey Sr., Ken Griffey Jr. 75.00
GM Stan Musial, Bob Gibson 60.00
GS Mark Grace, Ryne Sandberg 100.00
HF Rollie Fingers, Jim "Catfish" Hunter 30.00
JC Roger Clemens, Randy Johnson 75.00
JJ Chipper Jones, Andruw Jones 40.00
JM Derek Jeter, Hideki Matsui 125.00
KC Rod Carew, Harmon Killebrew 60.00
KM Willie McCovey, Harmon Killebrew 50.00
KS Sammy Sosa, Ken Griffey Jr. 75.00
LS Fred Lynn, Ichiro Suzuki 100.00
MG Greg Maddux, Tom Glavine 50.00
MJ Chipper Jones, Eddie Mathews 75.00
MM Kazuo Matsui, Hideki Matsui 120.00
MY Robin Yount, Paul Molitor 60.00
PC Will Clark, Rafael Palmeiro 40.00
PR Scott Rolen, Albert Pujols 100.00
RC Nolan Ryan, Roger Clemens 100.00
RM Cal Ripken Jr., Eddie Murray 150.00
RP Cal Ripken Jr., Jim Palmer 125.00
RR Jackie Robinson, Pee Wee Reese 150.00
RS Nolan Ryan, Tom Seaver 100.00
RT Cal Ripken Jr., Miguel Tejada 75.00
SB Jim Bunning, Mike Schmidt 75.00
SM Pedro J. Martinez, Curt Schilling 60.00
ST Mike Schmidt, Jim Thome 75.00
WM Don Mattingly, Dave Winfield 75.00
WP Mark Prior, Kerry Wood 60.00
WS Billy Williams, Sammy Sosa 60.00
YR Carl Yastrzemski, Jim Rice 75.00

Dual Legendary Materials

NM/M

Common Player:
Production 50 sets
BM Willie McCovey, Ernie Banks 40.00
BR Roger Maris, Babe Ruth 300.00
CB Yogi Berra, Roy Campanella 35.00
CM Roberto Clemente, Thurman Munson 100.00
CS Duke Snider, Roy Campanella 40.00
DM Mickey Mantle, Joe DiMaggio 200.00
DW Joe DiMaggio, Ted Williams 150.00
FD Don Drysdale, Bob Feller 25.00
MB Yogi Berra, Thurman Munson 50.00
MC Mickey Mantle, Roberto Clemente 180.00
MM Mickey Mantle, Roger Maris 220.00
MW Mickey Mantle, Ted Williams 200.00
RB Ernie Banks, Jackie Robinson 75.00
RC Jackie Robinson, Roy Campanella 75.00
RD Joe DiMaggio, Babe Ruth 275.00
RM Babe Ruth, Mickey Mantle 400.00
RP Jackie Robinson, Satchel Paige 100.00
RW Roberto Clemente, Willie McCovey 100.00
WM Eddie Mathews, Ted Williams 125.00

Dual Materials

NM/M

Common Player:
Production 60 sets
BC Brooks Robinson, Cal Ripken Jr. 50.00
BM Yogi Berra, Thurman Munson 40.00
BP Johnny Bench, Mike Piazza 25.00
BS Mike Schmidt, George Brett 40.00
CK Harmon Killebrew, Rod Carew 30.00
CM Willie McCovey, Will Clark 30.00
ER Ryne Sandberg, Ernie Banks 60.00
GS Sammy Sosa, Ken Griffey Jr. 40.00
JC Randy Johnson, Roger Clemens 40.00
JM Derek Jeter, Don Mattingly 60.00
MB Johnny Bench, Thurman Munson 40.00
MC Don Mattingly, Will Clark 40.00
MP Mark Prior, Joe Mauer 30.00
MR Bill Mazeroski, Jackie Robinson 60.00
MT Kazuo Matsui, Shingo Takatsu 30.00
MY Robin Yount, Paul Molitor 40.00
PR Manny Ramirez, Albert Pujols 50.00
RC Nolan Ryan, Roger Clemens 60.00
RP Mike Piazza, Ivan Rodriguez 20.00
RR Brooks Robinson, Frank Robinson 25.00
RT Thurman Munson, Roy Campanella 30.00
SG Ken Griffey Jr., Ichiro Suzuki 60.00
SP Mark Prior, Ben Sheets 15.00
SR Duke Snider, Pee Wee Reese 30.00
SS Sammy Sosa, Ryne Sandberg 50.00
TS Jim Thome, Mike Schmidt 35.00
WM Don Mattingly, Dave Winfield 40.00
WP Mark Prior, Kerry Wood 25.00
WR Kerry Wood, Nolan Ryan 50.00
YR Manny Ramirez, Carl Yastrzemski 35.00

Dual Materials Signature

NM/M

Production 25 sets
AB Luis Aparicio, Ernie Banks 100.00
BB Wade Boggs, Hank Blalock 80.00
BC Brooks Robinson, Cal Ripken Jr. 250.00
BF Carlton Fisk, Johnny Bench 100.00
BG Carlos Beltran, Ken Griffey Jr. 150.00
BJ Derek Jeter, Yogi Berra 200.00
BM Brian Giles, Marcus Giles 35.00
BP Johnny Bench, Mike Piazza 160.00
BR Jim Bunning, Robin Roberts 40.00
BT Hank Blalock, Mark Teixeira 60.00
CB Hank Blalock, Eric Chavez 50.00
CC Steve Carlton, Roger Clemens 150.00
CJ Roger Clemens, Randy Johnson 300.00
CK Harmon Killebrew, Rod Carew 80.00
CL Miguel Cabrera, Mike Lowell 75.00
CM Miguel Cabrera, Carlos Beltran 125.00
DD Derek Jeter, Don Mattingly 300.00
DG Gaylord Perry, Don Sutton 50.00
DJ Jim Rice, Dave Parker 80.00
DS Ryne Sandberg, Andre Dawson 125.00
DW Andre Dawson, Billy Williams 50.00
ER Ryne Sandberg, Ernie Banks 160.00
FC Bob Feller, Rocky Colavito 75.00
FR Bob Feller, Nolan Ryan 180.00
GB Brooks Robinson, George Brett 140.00
GC Ron Guidry, Steve Carlton 50.00
GG Ken Griffey Sr., Ken Griffey Jr. 150.00
GM Mike Schmidt, George Brett 150.00
GP Rafael Palmeiro, Ken Griffey Jr. 150.00
GR Greg Maddux, Roger Clemens 300.00
GS John Smoltz, Eric Gagne 75.00
IV Ivan Rodriguez, Victor Martinez 65.00
JB Ernie Banks, Fergie Jenkins 100.00
JC Randy Johnson, Steve Carlton 125.00
JD Johnny Podres, Don Sutton 50.00
JG Randy Johnson, Ken Griffey Jr. 200.00
JM Chipper Jones, Dale Murphy 150.00
JP Jim Palmer, Fergie Jenkins 50.00
JR Cal Ripken Jr., Derek Jeter 500.00
KG Ken Griffey Jr., Harmon Killebrew 150.00
KN Kerry Wood, Nolan Ryan 175.00
KT Scott Kazmir, Shingo Takatsu 75.00
LB Yogi Berra, Don Larsen 180.00
MB Johnny Bench, Joe Morgan 80.00
MC Don Mattingly, Will Clark 125.00
MH Mark Mulder, Tim Hudson 50.00
MP Mark Prior, Joe Mauer 100.00
MS Bill Mazeroski, Ryne Sandberg 150.00
MW Will Clark, Mark Grace 75.00
MY Robin Yount, Paul Molitor 150.00
NR Roger Clemens, Nolan Ryan 300.00
OR Manny Ramirez, David Ortiz 200.00
OS Stan Musial, Ozzie Smith 150.00
PC Will Clark, Rafael Palmeiro 100.00
PN Phil Niekro, Gaylord Perry 50.00
PS Johnny Podres, Duke Snider 60.00
RB Rod Carew, Bill Mazeroski 75.00
RC Eric Chavez, Brooks Robinson 60.00
RM Eddie Murray, Cal Ripken Jr. 275.00
RP Brooks Robinson, Jim Palmer 65.00
RR Brooks Robinson, Frank Robinson 75.00
RS Robin Roberts, Steve Carlton 60.00
RT Miguel Tejada, Cal Ripken Jr. 200.00
RW Jose Reyes, David Wright
SB Ernie Banks, Ron Santo/12
SC Mike Schmidt, Steve Carlton 150.00
SF Ben Sheets, Bob Feller 50.00
SG Eric Gagne, Bruce Sutter 75.00
SO Ben Sheets, Roy Oswalt 50.00
SP Mark Prior, Ben Sheets 100.00
SR Brooks Robinson, Mike Schmidt 150.00
SS Tom Seaver, Ben Sheets 75.00
TB Tony Gwynn, Brian Giles 75.00
TC Mark Teixeira, Miguel Cabrera 75.00
WM Dave Winfield, Don Mattingly 150.00
WO Orlando Cepeda, Willie McCovey 75.00
WP Mark Prior, Kerry Wood
WW Will Clark, Willie McCovey 75.00
YR Carl Yastrzemski, Manny Ramirez 160.00

Game Materials

NM/M

Common Player: 8.00
Production 99 sets
EB Ernie Banks 15.00
JB Johnny Bench 10.00
WB Wade Boggs 8.00
GB George Brett 20.00
LB Lou Brock 8.00
RC Rod Carew 8.00
SC Steve Carlton 8.00
WC Will Clark 8.00
CL Roger Clemens 20.00
TC Ty Cobb 100.00
DD Don Drysdale 8.00
BF Bob Feller 8.00
CF Carlton Fisk 10.00
BG Bob Gibson 10.00

KG	Ken Griffey Jr.	20.00
TG	Tony Gwynn	10.00
DJ	Derek Jeter	30.00
RJ	Randy Johnson	15.00
AK	Al Kaline	15.00
HK	Harmon Killebrew	10.00
MA	Juan Marichal	8.00
RM	Roger Maris	50.00
ED	Eddie Mathews	15.00
DM	Don Mattingly	25.00
BM	Bill Mazeroski	8.00
WM	Willie McCovey	8.00
PM	Paul Molitor	10.00
TM	Thurman Munson	15.00
EM	Eddie Murray	15.00
SM	Stan Musial	25.00
JP	Jim Palmer	8.00
PI	Mike Piazza	15.00
MP	Mark Prior	15.00
AP	Albert Pujols	25.00
CR	Cal Ripken Jr.	40.00
BR	Brooks Robinson	10.00
FR	Frank Robinson	8.00
JR	Jackie Robinson	40.00
RS	Ryne Sandberg	25.00
MS	Mike Schmidt	15.00
TS	Tom Seaver	10.00
OS	Ozzie Smith	15.00
DS	Duke Snider	10.00
WS	Warren Spahn	15.00
WSt	Willie Stargell	8.00
IS	Ichiro Suzuki	60.00
DW	Dave Winfield	8.00
KW	Kerry Wood	10.00
CY	Carl Yastrzemski	20.00
RY	Robin Yount	20.00

Game Patch

		NM/M
Common Player:		
Production 75 unless noted		
5 Color +:		1.5X
BA	Jeff Bagwell	25.00
BE	Josh Beckett	15.00
CB	Carlos Beltran	25.00
JB	Johnny Bench	50.00
YB	Yogi Berra	50.00
HB	Hank Blalock	15.00
WB	Wade Boggs	20.00
GB	George Brett	50.00
LB	Lou Brock	40.00
BU	Jim Bunning/66	30.00
CA	Miguel Cabrera	30.00
RC	Rod Carew	30.00
RO	Rod Carew	30.00
GC	Gary Carter	30.00
EC	Eric Chavez	15.00
WC	Will Clark	30.00
WC1	Will Clark	30.00
RC	Roger Clemens	40.00
RB	Roberto Clemente	200.00
CO1	Rocky Colavito	80.00
JD	Joe DiMaggio	180.00
BF	Bob Feller	40.00
CF	Carlton Fisk/18	
CF1	Carlton Fisk/10	
NF	Nellie Fox/55	125.00
GL	Troy Glaus	20.00
KG	Ken Griffey Jr.	50.00
VG	Vladimir Guerrero	30.00
RG	Ron Guidry	30.00
TG	Tony Gwynn	30.00
TH	Todd Helton	25.00
CH	Jim "Catfish" Hunter	30.00
DJ	Derek Jeter	40.00
RJ	Randy Johnson	25.00
RJ1	Randy Johnson	25.00
CJ	Chipper Jones	25.00
AK	Al Kaline/21	
HK	Harmon Killebrew	40.00
GM	Greg Maddux	35.00
GM1	Greg Maddux	35.00
MA	Juan Marichal	25.00
PE	Pedro J. Martinez	25.00
EM	Eddie Mathews/17	
HM	Hideki Matsui/44	100.00
KM	Kazuo Matsui	50.00
DM	Don Mattingly	40.00
JM	Joe Mauer	30.00
BM	Bill Mazeroski/55	60.00
WM	Willie McCovey	35.00
PM	Paul Molitor	30.00
MO	Joe Morgan	20.00
TM	Thurman Munson	40.00
MU	Eddie Murray	40.00
SM	Stan Musial	75.00
RP	Rafael Palmeiro	25.00
JP	Jim Palmer	25.00
PI	Mike Piazza	30.00
PO	Johnny Podres	30.00
MP	Mark Prior	25.00
AP	Albert Pujols	50.00
MR	Manny Ramirez	25.00
CR	Cal Ripken Jr.	60.00
BR	Brooks Robinson	40.00
IR	Ivan Rodriguez	25.00
SR	Scott Rolen	25.00
NR	Nolan Ryan/51	50.00
NR1	Nolan Ryan	50.00
NR2	Nolan Ryan	50.00
RS	Ryne Sandberg	50.00
CS	Curt Schilling	25.00
MS	Mike Schmidt	40.00
TS	Tom Seaver	20.00
BS	Ben Sheets	25.00
GS	Gary Sheffield	20.00
OS	Ozzie Smith	40.00
AS	Alfonso Soriano	25.00
SS	Sammy Sosa	35.00
SP	Warren Spahn/62	60.00
WS	Willie Stargell	30.00
IS	Ichiro Suzuki	120.00
MT	Mark Teixeira	15.00
TE	Miguel Tejada	25.00
JT	Jim Thome	35.00
BW	Bernie Williams	20.00
WI	Billy Williams	20.00
DW	Dave Winfield	35.00
KW	Kerry Wood	25.00
CY	Carl Yastrzemski	50.00
RY	Robin Yount	40.00

Game Patch Signatures

		NM/M
Common Player:		
Production 30 sets		
EB	Ernie Banks	75.00
CB	Carlos Beltran	65.00
JB	Johnny Bench	65.00
HB	Hank Blalock	50.00
WB	Wade Boggs	65.00
GB	George Brett	100.00
MC	Miguel Cabrera	65.00
RC	Rod Carew	50.00
EC	Eric Chavez	40.00
WC	Will Clark	60.00
AD	Andre Dawson	40.00
CF	Carlton Fisk/10	
BG	Bob Gibson	50.00
KG	Ken Griffey Jr.	125.00
TG	Tony Gwynn	65.00
DJ	Derek Jeter	200.00
RJ	Randy Johnson	125.00
AK	Al Kaline	75.00
HK	Harmon Killebrew	75.00
GM	Greg Maddux	150.00
MA	Juan Marichal	50.00
DM	Don Mattingly	100.00
JM	Joe Mauer	60.00
WM	Willie McCovey	50.00
PM	Paul Molitor	60.00
MU	Mark Mulder	40.00
EM	Eddie Murray	80.00
SM	Stan Musial	120.00
RO	Roy Oswalt	50.00
JP	Jim Palmer	50.00
PI	Mike Piazza	125.00
MP	Mark Prior	80.00
JR	Jim Rice	50.00
CR	Cal Ripken Jr.	200.00
BR	Brooks Robinson	60.00
FR	Frank Robinson	50.00
NR	Nolan Ryan	150.00
RS	Ryne Sandberg	150.00
MS	Mike Schmidt	125.00
SC	Red Schoendienst	40.00
TS	Tom Seaver	75.00
BS	Ben Sheets	50.00
OS	Ozzie Smith	75.00
MT	Mark Teixeira	50.00
KW	Kerry Wood	75.00
CY	Carl Yastrzemski	100.00
RY	Robin Yount	80.00

Gold Glove Sign. Materials

No Pricing
Production 1-16

Game Jersey Sign.

		NM/M
Quantity produced listed		
EB	Ernie Banks/19	85.00
JB	Johnny Bench/17	
GB	George Brett/21	100.00
TG	Tony Gwynn/20	70.00
HK	Harmon Killebrew/21	75.00
CR	Cal Ripken Jr./21	200.00
BR	Brooks Robinson/23	50.00
MS	Mike Schmidt/18	100.00
CY	Carl Yastrzemski/23	85.00
RY	Robin Yount/20	85.00

Materials Signatures

		NM/M
Production 50 sets		
BA	Bobby Abreu	25.00
JE	Jeff Bagwell	50.00
EB	Ernie Banks	75.00
BE	Josh Beckett	25.00
CB	Carlos Beltran	60.00
JB	Johnny Bench	60.00
HB	Hank Blalock	30.00
WB	Wade Boggs	50.00
WB1	Wade Boggs	50.00
GB	George Brett	80.00
LB	Lou Brock	40.00
LB1	Lou Brock	40.00
BU	Jim Bunning	30.00
CA	Miguel Cabrera	40.00
RC	Rod Carew	40.00
RC1	Rod Carew	40.00
SC	Steve Carlton	35.00
SC1	Steve Carlton	35.00
GC	Gary Carter	30.00
GC1	Gary Carter	30.00
JC	Joe Carter	30.00
OC	Orlando Cepeda	35.00
OC1	Orlando Cepeda	35.00
EC	Eric Chavez	30.00
WC	Will Clark	40.00
WC1	Will Clark	40.00
WC2	Will Clark	40.00
WC3	Will Clark	40.00
CL	Roger Clemens	125.00
CL1	Roger Clemens	125.00
CL2	Roger Clemens	125.00
CO	Rocky Colavito	75.00
CO1	Rocky Colavito	75.00
AD	Andre Dawson	30.00
AD1	Andre Dawson	30.00
DE	Dennis Eckersley	30.00
DE1	Dennis Eckersley	30.00
BF	Bob Feller	30.00
RF	Rollie Fingers	30.00
RF1	Rollie Fingers	30.00
CF	Carlton Fisk	40.00
CF1	Carlton Fisk	40.00
EG	Eric Gagne	50.00
NG	Nomar Garciaparra	125.00
NG1	Nomar Garciaparra	125.00
BG	Bob Gibson	40.00
MG	Mark Grace	40.00
KG	Ken Griffey Jr.	100.00
KG1	Ken Griffey Jr.	100.00
VG	Vladimir Guerrero	65.00
RG	Ron Guidry	40.00
TG	Tony Gwynn	50.00
HE	Todd Helton	40.00
TH	Tim Hudson	30.00
FJ	Fergie Jenkins	30.00
DJ	Derek Jeter	150.00
RJ	Randy Johnson	100.00
RJ1	Randy Johnson	100.00
CJ	Chipper Jones	50.00
AK	Al Kaline	50.00
HK	Harmon Killebrew	60.00
DL	Don Larsen	50.00
ML	Mike Lowell	20.00
GM	Greg Maddux	100.00
GM1	Greg Maddux	100.00
JU	Juan Marichal	30.00
DO	Don Mattingly	80.00
JM	Joe Mauer	40.00
JM1	Joe Mauer	40.00
BM	Bill Mazeroski	40.00
MC	Willie McCovey	40.00
PM	Paul Molitor	50.00
PM1	Paul Molitor	50.00
PM2	Paul Molitor	50.00
MO	Joe Morgan	30.00
MU	Mark Mulder	30.00
DM	Dale Murphy	40.00
EM	Eddie Murray	80.00
EM1	Eddie Murray	80.00
RO	Roy Oswalt	25.00
RP	Rafael Palmeiro	50.00
JP	Jim Palmer	30.00
TP	Tony Perez	30.00
GP	Gaylord Perry	25.00
GP1	Gaylord Perry	25.00
PI	Mike Piazza	100.00
PI1	Mike Piazza	100.00
PO	Johnny Podres	30.00
MP	Mark Prior	80.00
MP1	Mark Prior	80.00
MR	Manny Ramirez	75.00
JR	Jim Rice	30.00
CR	Cal Ripken Jr.	180.00
RR	Robin Roberts	30.00
BR	Brooks Robinson	40.00
FR	Frank Robinson	35.00
FR1	Frank Robinson	35.00
IR	Ivan Rodriguez	50.00
SR	Scott Rolen	50.00
NR	Nolan Ryan	120.00
NR1	Nolan Ryan	120.00
NR2	Nolan Ryan	120.00
NR3	Nolan Ryan	120.00
SA	Ryne Sandberg	100.00
MS	Mike Schmidt	75.00
RS	Red Schoendienst	30.00
TS	Tom Seaver	50.00
TS1	Tom Seaver	50.00
BS	Ben Sheets	30.00
BS1	Ben Sheets	30.00
OS	Ozzie Smith	60.00
JS	John Smoltz	50.00
SN	Duke Snider	40.00
SN1	Duke Snider	40.00
AS	Alfonso Soriano	40.00
DS	Don Sutton	30.00
MT	Mark Teixeira	40.00
TE	Miguel Tejada	40.00
TE1	Miguel Tejada/34	40.00
FT	Frank Thomas	60.00
RW	Rickie Weeks	30.00
RW1	Rickie Weeks	30.00
BW	Billy Williams	30.00
DW	Dave Winfield	40.00
DW1	Dave Winfield	40.00
KW	Kerry Wood	50.00
CY	Carl Yastrzemski	75.00
DY	Delmon Young	40.00
DY1	Delmon Young	40.00
RY	Robin Yount	60.00

Legendary Materials

		NM/M
Common Player:		10.00
Production 50 sets		
EB	Ernie Banks	20.00
YB	Yogi Berra	20.00
CA	Roy Campanella	15.00
RC	Roberto Clemente	100.00
TC	Ty Cobb	100.00
JD	Joe DiMaggio	100.00
DD	Don Drysdale	15.00
BF	Bob Feller	10.00
MM	Mickey Mantle	200.00
RM	Roger Maris	60.00
EM	Eddie Mathews	20.00
WM	Willie McCovey	15.00
TM	Thurman Munson	25.00
SM	Stan Musial	40.00
SP	Satchel Paige	50.00
JR	Jackie Robinson	60.00
BR	Babe Ruth	250.00
DS	Duke Snider	15.00
TW	Ted Williams	80.00

Stat Patch

		NM/M
Quantity produced listed		
5+ color patch:		1.5X
JB	Jeff Bagwell/47	25.00
CB	Carlos Beltran/29	35.00
CB1	Carlos Beltran/41	30.00
BE	Johnny Bench/45	50.00
HB	Hank Blalock/29	20.00
GB	George Brett/20	80.00
GB1	George Brett/30	75.00
WC	Will Clark/35	50.00
CL1	Roger Clemens/24	50.00
DD	Don Drysdale/25	50.00
EG	Eric Gagne/55	25.00
VG	Vladimir Guerrero/44	25.00
VG1	Vladimir Guerrero/40	25.00
TG	Tony Gwynn/56	40.00
TG1	Tony Gwynn/25	50.00
DJ	Derek Jeter/32	60.00
DJ1	Derek Jeter/24	60.00
RJ	Randy Johnson/20	40.00
CJ	Chipper Jones/45	25.00
HK	Harmon Killebrew/49	50.00
GM1	Greg Maddux/20	40.00
GM2	Greg Maddux/17	40.00
JM	Juan Marichal/26	30.00
MA	Pedro Martinez/23	35.00
HM	Hideki Matsui/31	120.00
DM	Don Mattingly/35	75.00
PM	Paul Molitor/39	40.00
TM	Thurman Munson/20	75.00
PN	Phil Niekro/23	30.00
PN1	Phil Niekro/23	30.00
RP	Rafael Palmeiro/47	25.00
JP1	Jim Palmer/23	30.00
PI	Mike Piazza/40	40.00
AP	Albert Pujols/43	60.00
AP1	Albert Pujols/51	50.00
MR	Manny Ramirez/45	25.00
JR1	Jim Rice/46	25.00

CR Cal Ripken Jr./34 100.00
CR1 Cal Ripken Jr./47 75.00
IR Ivan Rodriguez/35 30.00
IR1 Ivan Rodriguez/25 30.00
SR Scott Rolen/31 35.00
RS Ryne Sandberg/40 65.00
RS1 Ryne Sandberg/19 100.00
MS Mike Schmidt/48 65.00
TS Tom Seaver/25 50.00
JS John Smoltz/24 30.00
JS1 John Smoltz/55 25.00
AS Alfonso Soriano/39 20.00
AS1 Alfonso Soriano/43 20.00
SS1 Sammy Sosa/66 30.00
WS Willie Stargell/48 50.00
IS Ichiro Suzuki/56 120.00
MT Miguel Tejada/34 25.00
JT Jim Thome/52 25.00
CY Carl Yastrzemski/44 50.00
RY Robin Yount/49 50.00
DW Dave Winfield/37 25.00

Quadruple Materials

No Pricing
Production 15 sets

Signatures

NM/M
Common Player: 20.00
Production 25 unless noted
Gold: 1-1.5X
Production 10-25
No pricing 20 or less
Platinum: No Pricing
Production one set
LA1 Luis Aparicio 20.00
BE Johnny Bench 50.00
YB Yogi Berra 50.00
WB Wade Boggs 50.00
MC1 Miguel Cabrera 50.00
CW Rod Carew 40.00
CA1 Steve Carlton 30.00
CL Roger Clemens 125.00
BF1 Bob Feller 35.00
RF1 Rollie Fingers 25.00
WF Whitey Ford 50.00
NG Nomar Garciaparra 100.00
GI Bob Gibson 40.00
VG Vladimir Guerrero 50.00
RJ Randy Johnson 100.00
AK1 Al Kaline 50.00
HK1 Harmon Killebrew 60.00
RK1 Ralph Kiner 40.00
GM Greg Maddux 80.00
WI Willie McCovey 40.00
MO Joe Morgan 25.00
EM Eddie Murray 75.00
MU Stan Musial 75.00
JP1 Jim Palmer 30.00
PI Mike Piazza 100.00
MP Mark Prior 60.00
KP Kirby Puckett 65.00
CR Cal Ripken Jr. 160.00
RR1 Robin Roberts 30.00
BR1 Brooks Robinson 50.00
RY Ryne Sandberg 75.00
TS Tom Seaver 50.00
OS Ozzie Smith 60.00
SN Duke Snider 40.00
DW Dave Winfield 35.00
CY Carl Yastrzemski 75.00

Signatures Tier B

NM/M
Common Player:
BA Bobby Abreu/25 30.00
LA Luis Aparicio/25 25.00
CB Carlos Beltran/25 50.00
BI Craig Biggio/25 40.00
HB Hank Blalock/25 35.00
BL Bert Blyleven/99 20.00
JB Jim Bunning/99 20.00
MC Miguel Cabrera/99 30.00
SC Sean Casey/99 20.00
OC Orlando Cepeda/25 25.00
EC Eric Chavez/25 30.00
WC Will Clark/25 40.00
RC Rocky Colavito/99 50.00
DC David Cone/99 20.00
CC Carl Crawford/99 10.00
AD Andre Dawson/25 25.00
BD Bobby Doerr/99 25.00
DE Dennis Eckersley/25 35.00
BF Bob Feller/25 30.00
RF Rollie Fingers/25 25.00
GF George Foster/25 20.00
EG Eric Gagne/25 50.00
BG Brian Giles/99 10.00
MG Marcus Giles/99 10.00
DG Dwight Gooden/99 20.00
GG Rich "Goose" Gossage/99 10.00
GR Mark Grace/99 30.00
KG Ken Griffey Sr./69 15.00
RG Ron Guidry/25 40.00
TH Travis Hafner/99 20.00
KH Keith Hernandez/99 15.00
FH Frank Howard/99 15.00
MI Monte Irvin/25 25.00
JK Jim Kaat/99 20.00
AK Al Kaline/25 60.00
GK George Kell/99 20.00
HK Harmon Killebrew/25 60.00
RK Ralph Kiner/25 40.00
ML Mike Lowell/99 10.00
SL Sparky Lyle/99 10.00
FL Fred Lynn/25 20.00
VM Victor Martinez/99 20.00
JM Joe Mauer/99 25.00
BM Bill Mazeroski/25 50.00
MM Mark Mulder/99 20.00
DM Dale Murphy/99 30.00
GN Graig Nettles/99 15.00
DN Don Newcombe/25 25.00
RO Roy Oswalt/99 20.00
AO Akinori Otsuka/99 40.00
JP Jim Palmer/99 20.00
DP Dave Parker/25 25.00
CP Corey Patterson/99 20.00
TP Tony Perez/25 35.00
GP Gaylord Perry/25 20.00
PO Johnny Podres/99 25.00
RR Robin Roberts/25 30.00
BR Brooks Robinson/25 50.00
AR Al Rosen/99 20.00
SA Ron Santo/99 25.00
JS Jason Schmidt/99 25.00
RS Red Schoendienst/25 30.00
BS Ben Sheets/99 25.00
SM John Smoltz/25 50.00
SU Bruce Sutter/99 25.00
ST Shingo Takatsu/99 40.00
MT Mark Teixeira/25 40.00
LT Luis Tiant/99 10.00
RW Rickie Weeks/99 20.00
BW Billy Williams/25 30.00
MW Maury Wills/25 20.00
DY Delmon Young/99 25.00
CZ Carlos Zambrano/99

Signatures Duals

NM/M
Production 25 sets
BB Wade Boggs, Hank Blalock 80.00
BC Miguel Cabrera, Carlos Beltran 120.00
BG Carlos Beltran, Ken Griffey Jr. 175.00
BP Mike Piazza, Johnny Bench
BR Jim Bunning, Robin Roberts 75.00
BS George Brett, Mike Schmidt 150.00
BT Hank Blalock, Mark Teixeira 70.00
CB Hank Blalock, Eric Chavez 50.00
CG Ron Guidry, Steve Carlton
CJ Roger Clemens, Randy Johnson 300.00
CL Mike Lowell, Miguel Cabrera 50.00
CR Eric Chavez, Brooks Robinson 65.00
DW Billy Williams, Andre Dawson 40.00
EF Rollie Fingers, Dennis Eckersley 50.00
FR Bob Feller, Nolan Ryan 160.00
GC Will Clark, Mark Grace 65.00
GG Marcus Giles, Brian Giles 40.00
GK Ken Griffey Jr., Harmon Killebrew 150.00
GS John Smoltz, Eric Gagne 85.00
IC Monte Irvin, Orlando Cepeda 50.00
JC Steve Carlton, Randy Johnson 125.00
JM Derek Jeter, Don Mattingly 300.00
JP Jim Palmer, Fergie Jenkins 50.00
JT Fergie Jenkins, Luis Tiant 50.00
KG Ken Griffey Sr., Ken Griffey Jr. 175.00
KK Al Kaline, Harmon Killebrew 80.00
MC Don Mattingly, Will Clark 125.00
MH Mark Mulder, Tim Hudson 40.00
MK Ralph Kiner, Bill Mazeroski
MP Joe Mauer, Mark Prior 80.00
NR Roger Clemens, Nolan Ryan 400.00
NS Don Sutton, Don Newcombe 40.00
PC Rafael Palmeiro, Will Clark 120.00
PN Phil Niekro, Gaylord Perry 40.00
PR Jim Rice, Dave Parker 60.00
PS Ben Sheets, Mark Prior 80.00
RC Steve Carlton, Robin Roberts 40.00
RJ Derek Jeter, Cal Ripken Jr. 500.00
RM Cal Ripken Jr., Eddie Murray
RP Brooks Robinson, Jim Palmer 75.00
SF Ben Sheets, Bob Feller 40.00
SG Eric Gagne, Bruce Sutter 60.00
SO Ben Sheets, Roy Oswalt 40.00
SP Don Sutton, Gaylord Perry 40.00
TC Mark Teixeira, Miguel Cabrera 80.00
VM Miguel Cabrera, Vladimir Guerrero 100.00
WS Billy Williams, Ron Santo 60.00

Signatures Six

No Pricing
Production 5 sets

Signatures Triple

No Pricing
Production 20 sets

Signature Numbers Patch

NM/M
Quantity produced listed
WB Wade Boggs/26 65.00
LB Lou Brock/20 50.00
MC Miguel Cabrera/24 60.00
BF Bob Feller/19 50.00
EG Eric Gagne/38 50.00
KG Ken Griffey Jr./30 120.00
VG Vladimir Guerrero/27 80.00
DM Don Mattingly/23 100.00
WM Willie McCovey/44 60.00
RO Roy Oswalt/44 30.00
PI Mike Piazza/31 120.00
MP Mark Prior/22 80.00
RS Ryne Sandberg/23 125.00
MS Mike Schmidt/20 100.00
MT Mark Teixeira/23 40.00
BW Billy Williams/26 40.00
DW Dave Winfield/31 50.00
RY Robin Yount/19 100.00

2004 UPPER DECK USA

NM/M
Complete Factory Set (204): 50.00
Complete Set (200): 25.00
Common Player: .15
1 Jim Abbott .25
2 Brent Abernathy .15
3 Kurt Ainsworth .15
4 Abe Alvarez .15
5 Matt Anderson .15
6 Jeff Austin .15
7 Justin Wayne .15
8 Scott Bankhead .15
9 Josh Bard .15
10 Michael Barrett .15
11 Mark Bellhorn .25
12 Buddy Bell .15
13 Andy Benes .25
14 Kris Benson .25
15 Peter Bergeron .15
16 Rocky Biddle .15
17 Casey Blake .15
18 Willie Bloomquist .25
19 Jeremy Bonderman .25
20 Jeff Weaver .25
21 Joe Borchard .15
22 Rickie Weeks .50
23 Rob Bowen .15
24 Milton Bradley .25
25 Dan Wheeler .15
26 Ben Broussard .15
27 Brian Bruney .15
28 Mark Budzinski .15
29 Kirk Bullinger .15
30 Chris Burke .25
31 Sean Burnett .15
32 Jeromy Burnitz .25
33 Pat Burrell .50
34 Sean Burroughs .50
35 Paul Byrd .25
36 Chris Capuano .25
37 Scott Cassidy .15
38 Will Clark .75
39 Chad Cordero .15
40 Carl Crawford .25
41 Bobby Crosby .75
42 Brad Wilkerson .15
43 Michael Cuddyer .25
44 Ben Davis .15
45 Gookie Dawkins .15
46 Rod Dedeaux .15
47 R.A. Dickey .15
48 Ben Diggins .15
49 Lenny DiNardo .15
50 Ryan Drese .15
51 Tim Drew .15
52 Todd Williams .15
53 Justin Duchscherer .15
54 J.D. Durbin .15
55 Scott Elarton .15
56 Adam Everett .15
57 Dan Wilson .15
58 Steve Finley .25
59 Casey Fossum .15
60 Terry Francona .15
61 Ryan Franklin .15
62 Ryan Freel .15
63 John Van Benschoten .15
64 Nomar Garciaparra 1.00
65 Chris George .15
66 Jody Gerut .15
67 Jason Giambi .40
68 Matt Ginter .15
69 Troy Glaus .50
70 Tom Goodwin .15
71 Mike Gosling .15
72 Danny Graves .15
73 Shawn Green .50
74 Khalil Greene .75
75 Todd Greene .15
76 Seth Greisinger .15
77 Gabe Gross .15
78 Jeffrey Hammonds .25
79 Aaron Heilman .15
80 Paul Wilson .15
81 Todd Helton .75
82 Dustin Hermanson .15
83 Bobby Hill .15
84 Koyie Hill .15
85 A.J. Hinch .15
86 Matt Holliday .15
87 Ted Wood .15
88 Ken Huckaby .15
89 Orlando Hudson .15
90 Ernie Young .15
91 Jason Jennings .25
92 Charles Johnson .25
93 Jacque Jones .15
94 Matt Kata .15
95 Austin Kearns .25
96 Adam Kennedy .25
97 Brooks Kieschnick .25
98 Jesse Crain .15
99 Scott Kazmir 1.50
100 Billy Koch .25
101 Paul Konerko .25
102 Graham Koonce .15
103 Casey Kotchman .50
104 Chris Snyder .15
105 Nick Swisher .50
106 Gerald Laird .15
107 Barry Larkin .50
108 Mike Lamb .15
109 Tommy Lasorda .25
110 Matt LeCroy .15
111 Travis Lee .25
112 Justin Leone .15
113 John Vander Wal .15
114 Braden Looper .15
115 Shane Loux .15
116 Ryan Ludwick .25
117 Jason Varitek .40
118 Ryan Madson .15
119 Dave Magadan .15
120 Tino Martinez .25
121 Joe Mauer .50
122 David McCarty .15
123 Robin Ventura .25
124 Jack McDowell .25
125 Todd Walker .25
126 Mark McGwire 1.50

127 Gil Meche .15
128 Doug Mientkiewicz .25
129 Matt Morris .25
130 Warren Morris .15
131 Mark Mulder .50
132 Calvin Murray .15
133 Eric Munson .25
134 Mike Mussina .50
135 Xavier Nady .15
136 Shane Nance .15
137 Mike Neill .15
138 Augie Ojeda .15
139 John Olerud .25
140 Gregg Olson .15
141 Roy Oswalt .50
142 Jim Parque .15
143 John Patterson .15
144 Brad Penny .15
145 Jay Powell .15
146 Mark Prior .75
147 Horacio Ramirez .15
148 Jon Rauch .15
149 Jeremy Reed .15
150 Bob Watson .15
151 Matt Riley .15
152 Brian Roberts .15
153 Dave Roberts .15
154 Frank Robinson .15
155 J.C. Romero .15
156 David Ross .15
157 Cory Vance .15
158 Kirk Saarloos .15
159 Anthony Sanders .15
160 Dane Sardinha .15
161 Bobby Seay .15
162 Phil Seibel .15
163 Aaron Sele .15
164 Ben Sheets .50
165 Paul Shuey .15
166 Grady Sizemore .25
167 Reggie Smith .15
168 John Smoltz .50
169 Zach Sorensen .15
170 Scott Spezio .25
171 Ed Sprague .15
172 Jason Stanford .15
173 Dave Stewart .15
174 Scott Stewart .15
175 B.J. Surhoff .15
176 Bill Swift .15
177 Mike Tonis .15
178 Jason Tyner .15
179 Michael Tucker .15
180 B.J. Upton .75
181 Eric Valent .15
182 Ron Villone .15
183 2000: Team USA Shocks Cuba .15
184 1984: Abbott halts Japan .15
185 1996: Berman's Boys Take Third .15
186 1984: Team USA Takes Second .15
187 2000: Home Run Heroics .15
188 1999: Neill's Hit Boosts Team USA .15
189 1996: High Five for Team USA .15
190 1992: Garciaparra Makes the Roster .50
191 2003: USA Rolls to Record .15
192 1995: Juniors Are Golden In Boston .15
193 1999: The Streak Goes On .15
194 1998: Perfect Finish in St. Louis .15
195 1999: McGwire's Number Retired 1.00
196 2000: Filled with Firsts .15
197 Red, White and Blue Cardinal .15
198 2000: Quick Start for Neill .15
199 1999: Jensen Goes Deep vs. Cuba .15
200 2000: Mauer on the Mark .25

Team USA Jersey

NM/M
Common Player: 4.00
Inserted 1:Factory Set
KA Kurt Ainsworth 4.00
BB Brian Bruney 4.00
CB Chris Burke 4.00
SB Sean Burroughs 4.00
JD Justin Duchscherer 4.00
AE Adam Everett 4.00
JG Jason Giambi 6.00
GG Gabe Gross 4.00
DH Dustin Hermanson 4.00
MH Matt Holliday 4.00
GK Graham Koonce 4.00
GL Gerald Laird 4.00
JL Justin Leone 6.00
JM Joe Mauer 10.00
DM Doug Mientkiewicz 6.00
EM Eric Munson 8.00
XN Xavier Nady 4.00
RO Roy Oswalt 6.00
MP Mark Prior 10.00
HR Horacio Ramirez 4.00
JR Jon Rauch 4.00
RE Jeremy Reed 4.00
FR Frank Robinson 8.00
MR Mike Rouse 4.00
BS Ben Sheets 8.00
GS Grady Sizemore 8.00
DS Dave Stewart 6.00
JV John Van Benschoten 4.00
JW Jeff Weaver 4.00
BW Brad Wilkerson 4.00

Team USA Signature Black Ink

NM/M
Common Autograph: 5.00
Signatures Inserted 3:Factory Set
ABB Jim Abbott/180 20.00
ABE Brent Abernathy/360 5.00
AIN Kurt Ainsworth/360 8.00
ALV Abe Alvarez/360 10.00
AND Matt Anderson/360 5.00
AUS Jeff Austin/360 5.00
BANK Scott Bankhead/360 5.00
BARD Josh Bard/350 5.00
BARR Michael Barrett/360 10.00
BELL Buddy Bell/81 25.00
BEN Andy Benes/350 10.00
BENS Kris Benson/180 15.00
BERG Peter Bergeron/360 5.00
BLA Casey Blake/180 10.00
BLO Willie Bloomquist/175 15.00
BON Jeremy Bonderman/150 10.00
BOR Joe Borchard/350 10.00
BRAD Milton Bradley/360 15.00
BRO Ben Broussard/210 5.00
BRU Brian Bruney/160 5.00
BUD Mark Budzinski/360 5.00
BULL Kirk Bullinger/360 5.00
BURK Chris Burke/350 8.00
BU Sean Burnett/180 5.00
BURN Jeromy Burnitz/360 15.00
BUR Pat Burrell/360 15.00
BURR Sean Burroughs/360 10.00
BYRD Paul Byrd/360 10.00
CAP Chris Capuano/150 8.00
CASS Scott Cassidy/360 5.00
CLA Will Clark/60 75.00
COR Chad Cordero/360 5.00
CR Jesse Crain/180 10.00
CRA Carl Crawford/60 35.00
CUD Michael Cuddyer/370 8.00
DAV Ben Davis/344 5.00
DED Rod Dedeaux/29 40.00
DIC R.A. Dickey/180 5.00
DIG Ben Diggins/180 8.00
DIN Lenny DiNardo/150 5.00
DRE Ryan Drese/180 8.00
DREW Tim Drew/360 5.00
DUCH Justin Duchscherer/210 8.00
DUR J.D. Durbin/180 5.00
ELAR Scott Elarton/180 8.00
EVER Adam Everett/360 8.00
FIN Steve Finley/360 10.00
FOSS Casey Fossum/320 8.00
FRAN Terry Francona/150 40.00
FRA Ryan Franklin/360 5.00
FRE Ryan Freel/360 5.00
GEO Chris George/360 5.00
GER Jody Gerut/350 5.00
GIAM Jason Giambi/60 50.00
GIN Matt Ginter/179 8.00
GLA Troy Glaus/120 35.00
GOS Mike Gosling/150 8.00
DRA Danny Graves/360 8.00
GR Shawn Green/150 40.00
GRE Khalil Greene/180 40.00
GREE Todd Greene/120 10.00
GREI Seth Greisinger/360 5.00
GRO Gabe Gross/150 5.00
HAM Jeffrey Hammonds/150 10.00
HEIL Aaron Heilman/350 5.00
HELT Todd Helton/71 50.00
HERM Dustin Hermanson/150 10.00
HI Bobby Hill/360 5.00
HILL Koyie Hill/150 5.00
HIN A.J. Hinch/360 5.00
HUCK Ken Huckaby/360 5.00
HUD Orlando Hudson/360 5.00
JENN Jason Jennings/350 8.00
JON Jacque Jones/150 10.00
KATA Matt Kata/350 8.00
KAZ Scott Kazmir/360 30.00
KENN Adam Kennedy/150 8.00
KIES Brooks Kieschnick/360 8.00
KOCH Billy Koch/71 20.00
KON Paul Konerko/179 15.00
KOO Graham Koonce/360 8.00
KOTC Casey Kotchman/150 20.00
LAMB Mike Lamb/360 5.00
LAR Barry Larkin/60 75.00
LEC Matt LeCroy/360 5.00
LEE Travis Lee/360 8.00
LEO Justin Leone/150 10.00
LOO Braden Looper/360 5.00
LOUX Shane Loux/360 5.00
MAD Ryan Madson/360 8.00
MAG Dave Magadan/360 8.00
MART Tino Martinez/360 20.00
MAU Joe Mauer/360 35.00
MCC David McCarty/360 10.00
MCDO Jack McDowell/60 20.00
MC Mark McGwire/20
MEC Gil Meche/360 5.00
MIE Doug Mientkiewicz/300 10.00
MOR Matt Morris/150 10.00
MORR Warren Morris/360 5.00
MUL Mark Mulder/180 10.00
MUN Eric Munson/510 8.00
MURR Calvin Murray/360 5.00
MUSS Mike Mussina/60 50.00
NADY Xavier Nady/360 5.00
NAN Shane Nance/150 5.00
NEI Mike Neill/360 5.00
OJE Augie Ojeda/360 5.00
OLE John Olerud/360 20.00
OLS Gregg Olson/180 5.00
OSW Roy Oswalt/350 15.00
PARQ Jim Parque/360 5.00
PATT John Patterson/210 5.00
PEN Brad Penny/360 8.00
POW Jay Powell/180 5.00
PRI Mark Prior/350 50.00
RAM Horacio Ramirez/150 10.00
RAU Jon Rauch/359 5.00
REED Jeremy Reed/180 10.00
RIL Matt Riley/60 15.00
ROB Brian Roberts/60 20.00
ROBE Dave Roberts/360 10.00
ROM J.C. Romero/360 5.00
ROSS David Ross/360 5.00
SAAR Kirk Saarloos/360 5.00
SAND Anthony Sanders/360 5.00
SAR Dane Sardinha/360 5.00
SEAY Bobby Seay/360 5.00
SEI Phil Seibel/150 8.00
SELE Aaron Sele/360 10.00
SHE Ben Sheets/143 25.00
SHU Paul Shuey/360 5.00
SIZE Grady Sizemore/160 15.00
SMI Reggie Smith/360 10.00
SMO John Smoltz/360 35.00
SNY Chris Snyder/360 5.00
SPI Scott Spiezio/360 10.00
SPR Ed Sprague/360 10.00
STE Dave Stewart/180 15.00
STEW Scott Stewart/360 5.00
SUR B.J. Surhoff/60 30.00
SWIF Bill Swift/360 5.00
SWI Nick Swisher/360 5.00
TON Mike Tonis/350 5.00
TUCK Michael Tucker/150 10.00
TYN Jason Tyner/360 8.00
VAL Eric Valent/360 8.00
VANB John Van Benschoten/180 10.00
VAN Cory Vance/360 5.00
VAND John Vander Wal/360 10.00
VAR Jason Varitek/360 40.00
VENT Robin Ventura/360 15.00
VILL Ron Villone/359 5.00
WALK Todd Walker/60 20.00
WAT Bob Watson/150 8.00
WAY Justin Wayne/150 8.00
WEA Jeff Weaver/360 10.00
WEEK Rickie Weeks/360 15.00
WHEE Dan Wheeler/360 5.00
WILL Todd Williams/360 5.00
WI Dan Wilson/360 10.00
WIL Paul Wilson/360 5.00
WOOD Ted Wood/330 5.00
YOUN Ernie Young/350 8.00

Team USA Signature Blue Ink

NM/M
Common Autograph: 8.00
ABB Jim Abbott/60 30.00
ABE Brent Abernathy/120 8.00
AIN Kurt Ainsworth/120 8.00
ALV Abe Alvarez/120 10.00
AND Matt Anderson/110 8.00
AUS Jeff Austin/120 8.00
BANK Scott Bankhead/120 8.00
BARD Josh Bard/100 8.00
BARR Michael Barrett/120 8.00
BELL Buddy Bell/29 25.00
BEN Andy Benes/100 10.00
BENS Kris Benson/60 25.00
BERG Peter Bergeron/120 8.00
BLA Casey Blake/60 20.00
BLO Willie Bloomquist/51 20.00
BON Jeremy Bonderman/90 10.00
BOR Joe Borchard/100 8.00
BOW Rob Bowen/510 8.00
BRAD Milton Bradley/120 15.00
BRO Ben Broussard/150 8.00
BRU Brian Bruney/60 10.00
BUD Mark Budzinski/120 8.00
BULL Kirk Bullinger/120 8.00
BURK Chris Burke/110 8.00
BU Sean Burnett/60 10.00
BURN Jeromy Burnitz/120 15.00
BUR Pat Burrell/80 15.00
BURR Sean Burroughs/142 8.00
BYRD Paul Byrd/120 8.00
CAP Chris Capuano/90 8.00
CASS Scott Cassidy/120 8.00
CLA Will Clark/30 80.00
COR Chad Cordero/120 8.00
CR Jesse Crain/60 15.00
CUD Michael Cuddyer/89 8.00
DAV Ben Davis/100 8.00
DED Rod Dedeaux/25 30.00
DIC R.A. Dickey/60 10.00
DIG Ben Diggins/30 15.00
DIN Lenny DiNardo/60 10.00
DRE Ryan Drese/60 10.00
DREW Tim Drew/120 8.00
DUCH Justin Duchscherer/110 8.00
DUR J.D. Durbin/60 10.00
ELAR Scott Elarton/60 10.00
EVER Adam Everett/120 8.00
FIN Steve Finley/120 15.00
FOSS Casey Fossum/100 8.00
FRAN Terry Francona/40 40.00
FRA Ryan Franklin/120 8.00
FRE Ryan Freel/110 8.00
GAR Nomar Garciaparra/60 100.00
GEO Chris George/120 8.00
GER Jody Gerut/100 8.00
GIAM Jason Giambi/30 50.00
GIN Matt Ginter/42 10.00
GLA Troy Glaus/60 30.00
GOS Mike Gosling/60 10.00
DRA Danny Graves/120 8.00
GR Shawn Green/90 30.00
GRE Khalil Greene/60 50.00
GREE Todd Greene/60 10.00
GREI Seth Greisinger/120 8.00
GRO Gabe Gross/90 8.00
HAM Jeffrey Hammonds/90 10.00
HEIL Aaron Heilman/100 8.00
HELT Todd Helton/20 65.00
HERM Dustin Hermanson/90 10.00
HI Bobby Hill/120 8.00
HILL Koyie Hill/90 8.00
HIN A.J. Hinch/120 8.00
HUCK Ken Huckaby/120 8.00
HUD Orlando Hudson/110 8.00
JENN Jason Jennings/100 8.00
JON Jacque Jones/60 20.00
KATA Matt Kata/100 8.00
KAZ Scott Kazmir/110 35.00
KEAR Austin Kearns/110 20.00
KENN Adam Kennedy/90 8.00
KIES Brooks Kieschnick/120 8.00
KOCH Billy Koch/18 25.00
KON Paul Konerko/52 20.00
KOO Graham Koonce/120 8.00
KOTC Casey Kotchman/60 30.00
LAMB Mike Lamb/120 8.00
LAR Barry Larkin/20 80.00
LAS Tommy Lasorda/30 60.00
LEC Matt LeCroy/120 8.00
LEE Travis Lee/120 8.00

LEO	Justin Leone/60	15.00
LOO	Braden Looper/120	8.00
LOUX	Shane Loux/110	8.00
LUD	Ryan Ludwick/450	8.00
MAD	Ryan Madson/110	8.00
MAG	Dave Magadan/120	8.00
MART	Tino Martinez/120	20.00
MAU	Joe Mauer/120	35.00
MCC	David McCarty/120	10.00
MCDO	Jack McDowell/30	20.00
MC	Mark McGwire/6	
MEC	Gil Meche/120	8.00
MIE	Doug Mientkiewicz/120	10.00
MOR	Matt Morris/90	15.00
MORR	Warren Morris/120	8.00
MUL	Mark Mulder/110	15.00
MURR	Calvin Murray/120	8.00
MUSS	Mike Mussina/30	50.00
NADY	Xavier Nady/120	8.00
NAN	Shane Nance/60	10.00
NEI	Mike Neill/110	8.00
OJE	Augie Ojeda/119	8.00
OLE	John Olerud/120	20.00
OLS	Gregg Olson/60	10.00
OSW	Roy Oswalt/100	15.00
PARQ	Jim Parque/120	8.00
PATT	John Patterson/120	8.00
PEN	Brad Penny/110	8.00
POW	Jay Powell/60	10.00
PRI	Mark Prior/108	50.00
RAM	Horacio Ramirez/90	8.00
RAU	Jon Rauch/100	8.00
REED	Jeremy Reed/45	20.00
ROBE	Dave Roberts/120	10.00
ROBI	Frank Robinson/30	90.00
ROM	J.C. Romero/120	8.00
ROSS	David Ross/120	8.00
SAAR	Kirk Saarloos/120	8.00
SAND	Anthony Sanders/120	8.00
SAR	Dane Sardinha/110	8.00
SEAY	Bobby Seay/120	8.00
SEI	Phil Seibel/90	8.00
SELE	Aaron Sele/120	10.00
SHU	Paul Shuey/120	8.00
SIZE	Grady Sizemore/60	20.00
SMI	Reggie Smith/120	10.00
SMO	John Smoltz/120	40.00
SNY	Chris Snyder/120	8.00
SOR	Zach Sorensen/450	8.00
SPI	Scott Spiezio/120	8.00
SPR	Ed Sprague/120	8.00
STAN	Jason Stanford/450	8.00
STE	Dave Stewart/90	10.00
STEW	Scott Stewart/119	8.00
SWIF	Bill Swift/120	8.00
SWI	Nick Swisher/110	20.00
TON	Mike Tonis/100	8.00
TUCK	Michael Tucker/90	10.00
TYN	Jason Tyner/120	8.00
UPT	B.J. Upton/120	30.00
VAL	Eric Valent/120	8.00
VANB	John Van Benschoten/60	20.00
VAN	Cory Vance/120	8.00
VAND	John Vander Wal/120	8.00
VAR	Jason Varitek/100	40.00
VENT	Robin Ventura/120	15.00
VILL	Ron Villone/120	8.00
WAT	Bob Watson/60	10.00
WAY	Justin Wayne/60	10.00
WEA	Jeff Weaver/120	8.00
WEEK	Rickie Weeks/120	15.00
WHEE	Dan Wheeler/120	8.00
WILL	Todd Williams/90	8.00
WI	Dan Wilson/120	10.00
WIL	Paul Wilson/110	8.00
WOOD	Ted Wood/120	8.00
YOUN	Ernie Young/130	10.00

Team USA Signature Red Ink

		NM/M
Common Autograph:		10.00
Some not priced due to scarcity		
ABE	Brent Abernathy/20	15.00
AIN	Kurt Ainsworth/20	15.00
AND	Matt Anderson/30	15.00
AUS	Jeff Austin/20	15.00
BARD	Josh Bard/50	10.00
BARR	Michael Barrett/20	20.00
BEN	Andy Benes/50	15.00
BLO	Willie Bloomquist/25	25.00
BOR	Joe Borchard/50	10.00
BRAD	Milton Bradley/20	25.00
BRO	Ben Broussard/40	15.00
BRU	Brian Bruney/30	15.00
BURK	Chris Burke/50	10.00
BURN	Jeromy Burnitz/20	25.00
BUR	Pat Burrell/29	25.00
BYRD	Paul Byrd/20	20.00
CRO	Bobby Crosby/60	50.00
CUD	Michael Cuddyer/40	10.00
DAV	Ben Davis/50	10.00
DIN	Lenny DiNardo/40	10.00
EVER	Adam Everett/20	15.00
FIN	Steve Finley/20	25.00
FOSS	Casey Fossum/42	10.00
FRE	Ryan Freel/30	15.00
GAR	Nomar Garciaparra/30	125.00
GER	Jody Gerut/50	10.00
GLA	Troy Glaus/20	60.00
GOS	Mike Gosling/40	10.00
HEIL	Aaron Heilman/50	10.00
HIN	A.J. Hinch/20	15.00
HUD	Orlando Hudson/30	20.00
JENN	Jason Jennings/50	15.00
JON	Jacque Jones/40	20.00
KATA	Matt Kata/50	15.00
KAZ	Scott Kazmir/30	75.00
KEAR	Austin Kearns/30	35.00
KON	Paul Konerko/23	25.00
KOO	Graham Koonce/20	15.00
KOTC	Casey Kotchman/40	35.00
LEC	Matt LeCroy/20	15.00
LEE	Travis Lee/20	15.00
LEO	Justin Leone/40	20.00
LOUX	Shane Loux/30	15.00
LUD	Ryan Ludwick/50	10.00
MAD	Ryan Madson/30	15.00
MART	Tino Martinez/20	40.00
MAU	Joe Mauer/20	65.00
MCC	David McCarty/20	25.00
MIE	Doug Mientkiewicz/20	25.00
NADY	Xavier Nady/20	15.00
NAN	Shane Nance/40	10.00
NEI	Mike Neill/30	15.00
OSW	Roy Oswalt/50	20.00
PARQ	Jim Parque/20	15.00
PATT	John Patterson/20	15.00
PEN	Brad Penny/30	15.00
PRI	Mark Prior/48	75.00
RAU	Jon Rauch/53	10.00
REED	Jeremy Reed/25	25.00
ROM	J.C. Romero/20	15.00
SAR	Dane Sardinha/30	15.00
SIZE	Grady Sizemore/30	25.00
SMO	John Smoltz/20	65.00
SOR	Zach Sorensen/50	10.00
SPR	Ed Sprague/20	15.00
STAN	Jason Stanford/50	10.00
STE	Dave Stewart/30	25.00
SWI	Nick Swisher/30	40.00
TON	Mike Tonis/50	10.00
UPT	B.J. Upton/20	40.00
VAR	Jason Varitek/30	70.00
VENT	Robin Ventura/20	25.00
WAT	Bob Watson/30	15.00
WAY	Justin Wayne/40	10.00
WEA	Jeff Weaver/20	25.00
WEEK	Rickie Weeks/20	25.00
WILL	Todd Williams/50	10.00
WIL	Paul Wilson/30	15.00
WOOD	Ted Wood/30	15.00
YOUN	Ernie Young/50	10.00

Team USA Signature Green Ink

No Pricing
Production 1-3

2004 UPPER DECK VINTAGE

		NM/M
Complete Set (450):		
Common Player:		.15
Common SP (301-315):		.50
Inserted 1:5		
Common SP (316-325):		.40
Inserted 1:7		
Common SP (326-350):		.40
Inserted 1:5		
Common 3D SP (351-440):		2.00
Inserted 1:12		
Old Judge (441-450) found in bonus packs		
Pack (8):		2.50
Box (24 + 1 bonus pack):		50.00
1	Albert Pujols	1.50
2	Carlos Delgado	.50
3	Todd Helton	.50
4	Nomar Garciaparra	1.50
5	Vladimir Guerrero	.75
6	Alfonso Soriano	.75
7	Alex Rodriguez	1.50
8	Jason Giambi	.75
9	Derek Jeter	2.00
10	Pedro J. Martinez	.75
11	Ivan Rodriguez	.50
12	Mark Prior	1.50
13	Marquis Grissom	.15
14	Barry Zito	.25
15	Alex Cintron	.15
16	Wade Miller	.15
17	Eric Chavez	.25
18	Matt Clement	.15
19	Orlando Cabrera	.15
20	Odalis Perez	.15
21	Lance Berkman	.25
22	Keith Foulke	.15
23	Shawn Green	.25
24	Byung-Hyun Kim	.15
25	Geoff Jenkins	.25
26	Torii Hunter	.40
27	Richard Hidalgo	.15
28	Edgar Martinez	.25
29	Placido Polanco	.15
30	Brad Lidge	.15
31	Alex Escobar	.15
32	Garret Anderson	.25
33	Larry Walker	.25
34	Ken Griffey Jr.	1.00
35	Junior Spivey	.15
36	Carlos Beltran	.25
37	Bartolo Colon	.25
38	Ichiro Suzuki	1.00
39	Ramon Ortiz	.15
40	Roy Oswalt	.25
41	Mike Piazza	1.00
42	Benito Santiago	.15
43	Mike Mussina	.50
44	Jeff Kent	.25
45	Curt Schilling	.50
46	Adam Dunn	.40
47	Mike Sweeney	.15
48	Chipper Jones	1.00
49	Frank Thomas	.50
50	Kerry Wood	.50
51	Rod Beck	.15
52	Brian Giles	.25
53	Hank Blalock	.25
54	Andruw Jones	.50
55	Dmitri Young	.15
56	Juan Pierre	.15
57	Jacque Jones	.15
58	Phil Nevin	.15
59	Rocco Baldelli	.25
60	Greg Maddux	1.00
61	Eric Gagne	.15
62	Tim Hudson	.25
63	Brian Lawrence	.15
64	Sammy Sosa	1.00
65	Corey Koskie	.15
66	Bobby Abreu	.25
67	Preston Wilson	.15
68	Jay Gibbons	.15
69	Dontrelle Willis	.25
70	Richie Sexson	.40
71	Kevin Millwood	.25
72	Randy Johnson	.75
73	Jack Cust	.15
74	Randy Wolf	.15
75	Johan Santana	.15
76	Magglio Ordonez	.25
77	Sean Casey	.15
78	Billy Wagner	.25
79	Javier Vazquez	.15
80	Jorge Posada	.40
81	Jason Schmidt	.15
82	Bret Boone	.25
83	Jeff Bagwell	.50
84	Rickie Weeks	.25
85	Troy Percival	.15
86	Jose Vidro	.15
87	Freddy Garcia	.15
88	Manny Ramirez	.50
89	John Smoltz	.25
90	Moises Alou	.25
91	Ugueth Urbina	.15
92	Bobby Hill	.15
93	Marcus Giles	.15
94	Aramis Ramirez	.25
95	Brad Wilkerson	.15
96	Ray Durham	.15
97	David Wells	.15
98	Paul LoDuca	.15
99	Danny Graves	.15
100	Jason Kendall	.25
101	Carlos Lee	.25
102	Rafael Furcal	.25
103	Mike Lowell	.15
104	Kevin Brown	.25
105	Vicente Padilla	.15
106	Miguel Tejada	.40
107	Bernie Williams	.40
108	Octavio Dotel	.15
109	Steve Finley	.15
110	Lyle Overbay	.15
111	Delmon Young	.25
112	Bo Hart	.15
113	Jason Lane	.15
114	Matt Roney	.15
115	Brian Roberts	.15
116	Tom Glavine	.25
117	Rich Aurilia	.15
118	Adam Kennedy	.15
119	Hee Seop Choi	.15
120	Trot Nixon	.15
121	Gary Sheffield	.40
122	Jay Payton	.15
123	Brad Penny	.15
124	Garrett Atkins	.15
125	Aubrey Huff	.15
126	Juan Gonzalez	.40
127	Jason Jennings	.15
128	Luis Gonzalez	.25
129	Vinny Castilla	.15
130	Esteban Loaiza	.15
131	Erubiel Durazo	.15
132	Eric Hinske	.15
133	Scott Rolen	.75
134	Craig Biggio	.25
135	Tim Wakefield	.15
136	Darin Erstad	.25
137	Denny Stark	.15
138	Ben Sheets	.25
139	Hideo Nomo	.40
140	Derrek Lee	.25
141	Matt Mantei	.15
142	Reggie Sanders	.15
143	Jose Guillen	.15
144	Joe Mays	.15
145	Jimmy Rollins	.15
146	Juan Encarnacion	.15
147	Joe Crede	.15
148	Aaron Guiel	.15
149	Mark Mulder	.25
150	Travis Lee	.15
151	Josh Phelps	.15
152	Michael Young	.15
153	Paul Konerko	.15
154	John Lackey	.15
155	Damian Moss	.15
156	Javy Lopez	.25
157	Joe Borowski	.15
158	Jose Cruz Jr.	.15
159	Ramon Hernandez	.15
160	Raul Ibanez	.15
161	Adrian Beltre	.15
162	Bobby Higginson	.15
163	Jorge Julio	.15
164	Miguel Batista	.15
165	Luis Castillo	.15
166	Aaron Harang	.15
167	Ken Harvey	.15
168	Rocky Biddle	.15
169	Mariano Rivera	.25
170	Matt Morris	.15
171	Laynce Nix	.15
172	Mike Maroth	.15
173	Francisco Rodriguez	.15
174	Livan Hernandez	.15
175	Aaron Heilman	.15
176	Nick Johnson	.15
177	Woody Williams	.15
178	Joe Kennedy	.15
179	Jesse Foppert	.15
180	Ryan Franklin	.15
181	Endy Chavez	.15
182	Chin-Hui Tsao	.15
183	Todd Walker	.15
184	Edgardo Alfonzo	.15
185	Edgar Renteria	.15

No.	Player	Price
186	Matt LeCroy	.15
187	Carl Everett	.15
188	Jeff Conine	.15
189	Jason Varitek	.15
190	Russ Ortiz	.15
191	Melvin Mora	.15
192	Mark Buehrle	.15
193	Bill Mueller	.15
194	Miguel Cabrera	.25
195	Carlos Zambrano	.15
196	Jose Valverde	.15
197	Danys Baez	.15
198	Mike MacDougal	.15
199	Zach Day	.15
200	Roy Halladay	.25
201	Jerome Williams	.15
202	Josh Fogg	.15
203	Mark Kotsay	.15
204	Pat Burrell	.40
205	A.J. Pierzynski	.15
206	Fred McGriff	.25
207	Brandon Larson	.15
208	Robb Quinlan	.15
209	David Ortiz	.15
210	A.J. Burnett	.15
211	John Vander Wal	.15
212	Jim Thome	.75
213	Matt Kata	.15
214	Kip Wells	.15
215	Scott Podsednik	.40
216	Rickey Henderson	.25
217	Travis Hafner	.15
218	Tony Batista	.15
219	Robert Fick	.15
220	Derek Lowe	.25
221	Ryan Klesko	.25
222	Joe Beimel	.15
223	Doug Mientkiewicz	.15
224	Angel Berroa	.15
225	Adam Eaton	.15
226	C.C. Sabathia	.15
227	Wilfredo Ledezma	.15
228	Jason Johnson	.15
229	Ryan Wagner	.15
230	Al Leiter	.15
231	Joel Pineiro	.15
232	Jason Isringhausen	.15
233	John Olerud	.25
234	Ron Calloway	.15
235	Jose Reyes	.15
236	J.D. Drew	.15
237	Jared Sandberg	.15
238	Gil Meche	.15
239	Jose Contreras	.15
240	Eric Milton	.15
241	Jason L. Phillips	.15
242	Luis Ayala	.15
243	Bobby Kielty	.15
244	Jose Lima	.15
245	Brooks Kieschnick	.15
246	Xavier Nady	.15
247	Dan Haren	.15
248	Victor Zambrano	.15
249	Kelvim Escobar	.15
250	Oliver Perez	.15
251	Jamie Moyer	.15
252	Orlando Hudson	.15
253	Danny Kolb	.15
254	Jake Peavy	.15
255	Kris Benson	.15
256	Roger Clemens	1.50
257	Jim Edmonds	.40
258	Rafael Palmeiro	.50
259	Jae Weong Seo	.15
260	Chase Utley	.15
261	Rich Harden	.15
262	Mark Teixeira	.25
263	Johnny Damon	.25
264	Luis Matos	.15
265	Shigetoshi Hasegawa	.15
266	Alfredo Amezaga	.15
267	Tim Worrell	.15
268	Kazuhisa Ishii	.15
269	Miguel Ojeda	.15
270	Kazuhiro Sasaki	.15
271	Hideki Matsui	2.00
272	Troy Glaus	.40
273	Michael Tucker	.15
274	Lew Ford	.15
275	Brian Jordan	.15
276	David Eckstein	.15
277	Robby Hammock	.15
278	Corey Patterson	.25
279	Wes Helms	.15
280	Jermaine Dye	.15
281	Cliff Floyd	.15
282	Dustan Mohr	.15
283	Kevin Mench	.15
284	Ellis Burks	.15
285	Jerry Hairston Jr.	.15
286	Tim Salmon	.25
287	Omar Vizquel	.25
288	Andy Pettitte	.40
289	Guillermo Mota	.15
290	Tino Martinez	.15
291	Lance Carter	.15
292	Francisco Cordero	.15
293	Robb Nen	.15
294	Mike Cameron	.15
295	Jhonny Peralta	.15
296	Braden Looper	.15
297	Jarrod Washburn	.15
298	Mark Prior	.50
299	Alfonso Soriano	.25
300	Rocco Baldelli	.25
301	Pedro J. Martinez	1.50
302	Mark Prior	2.50
303	Barry Zito	.75
304	Roger Clemens	2.50
305	Randy Johnson	1.50
306	Roy Halladay	.50
307	Hideo Nomo	.75
308	Roy Oswalt	.50
309	Kerry Wood	1.00
310	Dontrelle Willis	.75
311	Mark Mulder	.50
312	Brandon Webb	.50
313	Mike Mussina	.75
314	Curt Schilling	.75
315	Tim Hudson	.75
316	Dontrelle Willis	.75
317	Juan Pierre	.40
318	Hideki Matsui	4.00
319	Andy Pettitte	.75
320	Mike Mussina	.75
321	Roger Clemens	2.50
322	Alex Gonzalez	.40
323	Brad Penny	.40
324	Ivan Rodriguez	.75
325	Josh Beckett	1.00
326	Aaron Boone	.40
327	Jeff Suppan	.40
328	Shea Hillenbrand	.40
329	Jeromy Burnitz	.40
330	Sidney Ponson	.40
331	Rondell White	.50
332	Shannon Stewart	.40
333	Armando Benitez	.40
334	Roberto Alomar	1.00
335	Raul Mondesi	.50
336	Morgan Ensberg	.40
337	Milton Bradley	.40
338	Brandon Webb	.50
339	Marlon Byrd	.40
340	Carlos Pena	.40
341	Brandon Phillips	.40
342	Josh Beckett	1.00
343	Eric Munson	.40
344	Brett Myers	.40
345	Austin Kearns	1.00
346	Jody Gerut	.40
347	Vernon Wells	.50
348	Jeff Duncan	.40
349	Sean Burroughs	.40
350	Jeremy Bonderman	.40
351	Hideki Matsui	15.00
352	Jason Giambi	8.00
353	Alfonso Soriano	6.00
354	Derek Jeter	15.00
355	Aaron Boone	3.00
356	Jorge Posada	5.00
357	Bernie Williams	5.00
358	Manny Ramirez	5.00
359	Nomar Garciaparra	12.00
360	Johnny Damon	3.00
361	Jason Varitek	2.50
362	Carlos Delgado	5.00
363	Vernon Wells	4.00
364	Jay Gibbons	4.00
365	Tony Batista	2.00
366	Rocco Baldelli	5.00
367	Aubrey Huff	2.00
368	Carlos Beltran	4.00
369	Mike Sweeney	3.00
370	Magglio Ordonez	4.00
371	Frank Thomas	6.00
372	Carlos Lee	2.00
373	Roberto Alomar	4.00
374	Jacque Jones	2.00
375	Torii Hunter	4.00
376	Milton Bradley	2.00
377	Travis Hafner	2.00
378	Jody Gerut	2.00
379	Dmitri Young	2.00
380	Carlos Pena	2.00
381	Ichiro Suzuki	10.00
382	Bret Boone	3.00
383	Edgar Martinez	3.00
384	Eric Chavez	3.00
385	Miguel Tejada	3.00
386	Erubiel Durazo	2.00
387	Jose Guillen	2.00
388	Garret Anderson	3.00
389	Troy Glaus	4.00
390	Alex Rodriguez	10.00
391	Rafael Palmeiro	5.00
392	Hank Blalock	4.00
393	Mark Teixeira	4.00
394	Gary Sheffield	4.00
395	Andruw Jones	5.00
396	Chipper Jones	8.00
397	Javy Lopez	3.00
398	Marcus Giles	2.00
399	Rafael Furcal	3.00
400	Jim Thome	5.00
401	Bobby Abreu	3.00
402	Pat Burrell	4.00
403	Mike Lowell	3.00
404	Ivan Rodriguez	5.00
405	Derrek Lee	3.00
406	Miguel Cabrera	5.00
407	Vladimir Guerrero	6.00
408	Orlando Cabrera	2.00
409	Jose Vidro	2.00
410	Mike Piazza	8.00
411	Cliff Floyd	3.00
412	Albert Pujols	15.00
413	Scott Rolen	6.00
414	Jim Edmonds	4.00
415	Edgar Renteria	3.00
416	Lance Berkman	3.00
417	Jeff Bagwell	5.00
418	Jeff Kent	3.00
419	Richard Hidalgo	2.00
420	Morgan Ensberg	2.00
421	Sammy Sosa	10.00
422	Moises Alou	3.00
423	Ken Griffey Jr.	10.00
424	Adam Dunn	4.00
425	Austin Kearns	4.00
426	Richie Sexson	4.00
427	Geoff Jenkins	3.00
428	Brian Giles	3.00
429	Reggie Sanders	2.00
430	Rich Aurilia	2.00
431	Jose Cruz Jr.	2.00
432	Shawn Green	3.00
433	Jeromy Burnitz	2.00
434	Luis Gonzalez	3.00
435	Todd Helton	5.00
436	Preston Wilson	2.00
437	Larry Walker	3.00
438	Ryan Klesko	3.00
439	Phil Nevin	2.00
440	Sean Burroughs	2.00
441	Sammy Sosa	3.00
442	Albert Pujols	4.00
443	Magglio Ordonez	.50
444	Vladimir Guerrero	1.50
445	Todd Helton	1.00
446	Jason Giambi	1.50
447	Ichiro Suzuki	3.00
448	Alex Rodriguez	3.00
449	Carlos Delgado	.75
450	Manny Ramirez	1.00

Black & White

Cards (1-300): 1-2X
Inserted 1:6
SP's (301-325): 1-2X
Inserted 1:24
SP's (326-350): 1-2X
Inserted 1:20
B/W Color Variations: 6-10X
Inserted 1:48

Old Judge

NM/M

Complete Set (20): 15.00
Common Player: .40
Inserted 3:bonus pack
Blue Back: 1-2X
Inserted 1:4 bonus packs
Red Back: 2-3X
Inserted 1:12 bonus packs

No.	Player	Price
11	Randy Johnson	1.50
12	Pedro J. Martinez	1.50
13	Mark Prior	3.00
14	Barry Zito	.50
15	Roy Oswalt	.40
16	Roy Halladay	.50
17	Curt Schilling	.75
18	Mike Mussina	.75
19	Kevin Brown	.40
20	Roger Clemens	2.50
21	Eric Gagne	.50
22	Mariano Rivera	.50
23	Mike Piazza	2.00
24	Jorge Posada	.75
25	Jeff Kent	.50
26	Alfonso Soriano	1.00
27	Scott Rolen	1.00
28	Eric Chavez	.50
29	Edgar Renteria	.40
30	Hideki Matsui	4.00

Stellar Signatures

NM/M

Some not priced due to scarcity
Inserted 1:600

Code	Player	Price
HM	Hideki Matsui	300.00
MP	Mike Piazza	
AR	Alex Rodriguez	
TS	Tom Seaver	60.00
IS	Ichiro Suzuki	185.00
CY	C. Yastrzemski/125	75.00
BZ	Barry Zito	50.00

Stellar Stat Men

NM/M

Common Player: 4.00
Inserted 1:24

No.	Player	Price
1	Jose Reyes	6.00
2	Bo Hart	8.00
3	Hideki Matsui	30.00
4	Dontrelle Willis	6.00
5	Rocco Baldelli	6.00
6	Ichiro Suzuki	20.00
7	Mike Lowell	6.00
8	Derek Jeter	20.00
9	Ken Griffey Jr.	15.00
10	Sammy Sosa	12.00
11	Kerry Wood	10.00
12	Chipper Jones	6.00
13	Alfonso Soriano	8.00
14	Khalil Greene	6.00
15	Jim Thome	8.00
16	Rafael Furcal	5.00
17	Andrew Brown	4.00
18	Mark Prior	15.00
19	Barry Zito	6.00
20	Al Leiter	4.00
21	Carlos Delgado	6.00
22	Pedro J. Martinez	8.00
23	Alex Rodriguez	10.00
24	Lance Berkman	5.00
25	Jeff Bagwell	6.00
26	Bernie Williams	6.00
27	Hideo Nomo	8.00
28	Randy Johnson	8.00
29	Curt Schilling	8.00
30	Mike Piazza	10.00
31	Albert Pujols	12.00
32	Joe DiMaggio	100.00
33	Ted Williams	60.00
34	Mickey Mantle	100.00
35	Mike Mussina	8.00
36	Rich Harden	5.00
37	Roy Oswalt	4.00
38	Torii Hunter	8.00
39	Jorge Posada	6.00
40	Troy Glaus	6.00
41	Manny Ramirez	6.00
42	Roy Halladay	5.00

Timeless Teams

NM/M

Common Quad: 15.00

Inserted 1:400
Production 175 sets

1 Derek Jeter, Jason Giambi, Alfonso Soriano, Hideki Matsui 90.00
2 Randy Johnson, Luis Gonzalez, Steve Finley, Curt Schilling 20.00
4 Johnny Damon, Manny Ramirez, Nomar Garciaparra, Trot Nixon 35.00
5 Alex Rodriguez, Rafael Palmeiro, Mark Teixeira, Hank Blalock 35.00
6 Roberto Alomar, Frank Thomas, Magglio Ordonez, Carl Everett 20.00
7 Shannon Stewart, Torii Hunter, Jacque Jones, Doug Mientkiewicz 15.00
8 Jim Edmonds, Scott Rolen, J.D. Drew, Albert Pujols 40.00
9 Bret Boone, John Olerud, Mike Cameron, Ichiro Suzuki 45.00
10 Jeff Bagwell, Craig Biggio, Jeff Kent, Lance Berkman 20.00
11 Tim Salmon, Garret Anderson, Darin Erstad, Troy Glaus 15.00
12 Bernie Williams, Alfonso Soriano, Jorge Posada, Hideki Matsui 85.00
13 Carlos Beltran, Michael Tucker, Mike Sweeney, Brent Mayne 15.00
14 Jim Thome, Mike Lieberthal, Bobby Abreu, Marlon Byrd 30.00
15 Ivan Rodriguez, Juan Encarnacion, Mike Lowell, Miguel Cabrera 25.00
16 Sammy Sosa, Kerry Wood, Moises Alou, Corey Patterson 50.00
17 Andres Galarraga, Edgardo Alfonzo, Jose Cruz Jr., Rich Aurilia 15.00
18 Derek Jeter, Bernie Williams, Alfonso Soriano, Hideki Matsui 90.00

2004 UPPER DECK YANKEES CLASSICS

NM/M

Complete Set (90): 20.00
Common Player: .25
Pack (5): 6.00
Box (24): 120.00

1 Bill "Moose" Skowron .50
2 Bob Cerv .25
3 Bobby Murcer .50
4 Bobby Richardson .25
5 Brian Doyle .25
6 Bucky Dent .25
7 Chris Chambliss .25
8 Clete Boyer .25
9 Dave Kingman .25
10 Dave Righetti .25
11 Dave Winfield .50
12 David Cone .25
13 Red Ruffing .25
14 Dock Ellis .25
15 Don Baylor .25
16 Don Larsen .75
17 Don Mattingly 1.50
18 Dwight Gooden .40
19 Ed Figueroa .25
20 Joe Torre .50
21 Darryl Strawberry .40
22 Horace Clarke .25
23 Gaylord Perry .25
24 Phil Linz .25
25 Gil McDougald .25
26 Rich "Goose" Gossage .25
27 Graig Nettles .25
28 Hank Bauer .25
29 Jack Clark .25
30 Don Gullett .25
31 Jim Abbott .25
32 Jim Bouton .25
33 Jim Kaat .40
34 Jim Leyritz .25
35 Jim Wynn .25
36 Jimmy Key .25
37 Joe Niekro .25
38 Joe Pepitone .25
39 John Wetteland .25
40 Ken Griffey Sr. .25
41 Felipe Alou .25
42 Kevin Maas .25
43 Lindy McDaniel .25
44 Lou Piniella .50
45 Luis Tiant .25
46 Mel Stottlemyre .25
47 Mickey Rivers .25
48 Oscar Gamble .25
49 Pat Dobson .25
50 Paul O'Neill .50
51 Phil Niekro .25
52 Phil Rizzuto .75
53 Doc Medich .25
54 Rick Cerone .25
55 Ron Blomberg .25
56 Ron Guidry .50
57 Roy White .25
58 Rudy May .25
59 Sam McDowell .25
60 Sparky Lyle .25
61 Steve Balboni .25
62 Steve Sax .25
63 Jerry Coleman .25
64 Tom Tresh .25
65 Tommy John .25
66 Tony Kubek .50
67 Wade Boggs .50
68 Whitey Ford .75
69 Willie Randolph .25
70 Yogi Berra 1.00
71 Babe Ruth 3.00
72 Bill Dickey .50
73 Billy Martin .50
74 Bob Meusel .25
75 Casey Stengel .50
76 Elston Howard .25
77 Jim "Catfish" Hunter .50
78 Joe DiMaggio 2.00
79 Lefty Gomez .50
80 Lou Gehrig 2.00
81 Mickey Mantle 3.00
82 Miller Huggins .25
83 Roger Maris 1.50
84 Thurman Munson .75
85 Tony Lazzeri .50
86 Yankee Stadium .75
87 Times Square .50
88 Central Park .50
89 Empire State Building .50
90 Statue of Liberty .50

Bronze

Bronze: 4-8X
Production 99 sets

Gold

Gold: 8-15X
Production 30 sets

Silver

Silver: No Pricing

Scripts Single Auto

NM/M

Common Autograph: 10.00
Inserted 1:8

AU-1 Bill "Moose" Skowron 15.00
AU-2 Bob Cerv 10.00
AU-3 Bobby Murcer/SP 60.00
AU-4 Bobby Richardson 15.00
AU-5 Brian Doyle 10.00
AU-6 Bucky Dent 10.00
AU-7 Chris Chambliss 12.00
AU-8 Clete Boyer 15.00
AU-9 Dave Kingman 10.00
AU-10 Dave Righetti 10.00
AU-11 Dave Winfield/SP 75.00
AU-12 David Cone 10.00
AU-14 Dock Ellis 10.00
AU-15 Don Baylor/SP 25.00
AU-16 Don Larsen/SP 50.00
AU-17 Don Mattingly/SP 85.00
AU-18 Dwight Gooden 15.00
AU-19 Ed Figueroa 10.00
AU-20 Joe Torre/SP 75.00
AU-21 Darryl Strawberry 20.00
AU-23 Gaylord Perry 20.00
AU-24 Phil Linz 10.00
AU-25 Gil McDougald 15.00
AU-26 Rich "Goose" Gossage 20.00
AU-27 Graig Nettles 15.00
AU-28 Hank Bauer 15.00
AU-29 Jack Clark 15.00
AU-31 Jim Abbott 15.00
AU-32 Jim Bouton 15.00
AU-33 Jim Kaat 15.00
AU-34 Jim Leyritz/SP 25.00
AU-35 Jim Wynn 10.00
AU-36 Jimmy Key 10.00
AU-37 Joe Niekro 10.00
AU-38 Joe Pepitone 15.00
AU-39 John Wetteland/SP 20.00
AU-40 Ken Griffey Sr. 12.00
AU-42 Kevin Maas 10.00
AU-43 Lindy McDaniel 10.00
AU-44 Lou Piniella/SP 35.00
AU-45 Luis Tiant 20.00
AU-46 Mel Stottlemyre 15.00
AU-47 Mickey Rivers 15.00
AU-48 Oscar Gamble 15.00
AU-49 Pat Dobson 15.00
AU-50 Paul O'Neill/SP 40.00
AU-51 Phil Niekro 15.00
AU-52 Phil Rizzuto/SP 75.00
AU-53 Doc Medich 10.00
AU-54 Rick Cerone 15.00
AU-55 Ron Blomberg 10.00
AU-56 Ron Guidry 25.00
AU-57 Roy White 12.00
AU-58 Rudy May 10.00
AU-59 Sam McDowell 10.00
AU-60 Sparky Lyle 12.00
AU-61 Steve Balboni 10.00
AU-62 Steve Sax 10.00
AU-63 Jerry Coleman 15.00
AU-64 Tom Tresh 15.00
AU-65 Tommy John 15.00
AU-66 Tony Kubek/SP
AU-67 Wade Boggs/SP 60.00
AU-68 Whitey Ford/SP 60.00
AU-69 Willie Randolph/SP 40.00
AU-70 Yogi Berra/SP 75.00

Scripts Dual Auto

NM/M

Production 100 sets

SC Bill "Moose" Skowron, Bob Cerv 50.00
MP Bobby Murcer, Lou Piniella 65.00
CB Chris Chambliss, Ron Blomberg 50.00
BN Clete Boyer, Graig Nettles 50.00
RC Dave Righetti, Rick Cerone 60.00
ED Dock Ellis, Pat Dobson 70.00
BG Don Baylor, Ken Griffey Sr. 65.00
MW Don Mattingly, Dave Winfield 150.00

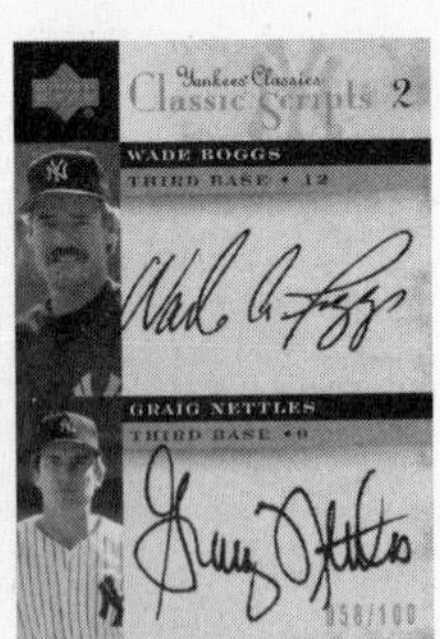

FG Ed Figueroa, Ron Guidry 60.00
MB Bobby Murcer, Hank Bauer 75.00
GL Rich "Goose" Gossage, Sparky Lyle 50.00
NB Graig Nettles, Wade Boggs 80.00
KJ Jim Kaat, Tommy John 60.00
KA Jimmy Key, Jim Abbott 50.00
PS Joe Pepitone, Bill "Moose" Skowron 50.00
MM Kevin Maas, Don Mattingly 100.00
RW Mickey Rivers, Roy White 50.00
OL Paul O'Neil, Jim Leyritz 75.00
RM Phil Rizzuto, Gil McDougald 100.00
GK Ron Guidry, Jim Kaat
SD Steve Sax, Brian Doyle 40.00
KR Tony Kubek, Bobby Richardson 100.00
FL Whitey Ford, Don Larsen 125.00
BL Yogi Berra, Don Larsen 150.00
BH Yogi Berra, Joe Torre 100.00
BF Yogi Berra, Whitey Ford 150.00
KC Dave Kingman, Jack Clark
WM Bobby Murcer, Roy White 75.00
DN Bucky Dent, Graig Nettles 50.00
CN Chris Chambliss, Graig Nettles 50.00
CL David Cone, Don Larsen 100.00
MC Don Mattingly, Jack Clark 85.00
MO Bobby Murcer, Paul O'Neill
BM Don Mattingly, Wade Boggs 150.00
SG Darryl Strawberry, Dwight Gooden 75.00
CG David Cone, Dwight Gooden 70.00

Classic Cuts

No Pricing
Production one set

Mitchell & Ness Pennant

NM/M

Inserted 1:box
Cards: .3X

P2 1927 World Series/96 25.00
P3 1928 World Series/96 25.00
P4 1932 World Series/96 25.00
P6 1937 World Series/96 25.00
P8 1939 World Series/96 25.00
P10 1943 World Series/97 25.00
P11 1947 World Series/97 25.00
P13 1950 World Series/97 25.00
P15 1952 World Series/97 25.00
P17 1956 World Series/97 25.00
P18 1958 World Series/97 25.00
P23 1996 World Series/99 25.00
P24 1998 World Series/99 25.00
P25 1999 World Series/99 25.00
P26 2000 World Series/100 25.00
MM57 Mickey Mantle - 1957 MVP/97 30.00
MM62 Mickey Mantle - 1962 MVP/98 30.00

Mitchell & Ness Pennant Card

		NM/M
Inserted 1:box		
P2	1927 World Series/1927	5.00
P3	1928 World Series/1,928	5.00
P4	1932 World Series/1,932	5.00
P5	1936 World Series/36	10.00
P6	1937 World Series/1,937	5.00
P7	1938 World Series/38	10.00
P8	1939 World Series/1,939	5.00
P9	1941 World Series/41	10.00
P10	1943 World Series/1,943	5.00
P11	1947 World Series/1,947	5.00
P12	1949 World Series/49	10.00
P13	1950 World Series/1,950	5.00
P14	1951 World Series/51	10.00
P15	1952 World Series/1,952	5.00
P16	1953 World Series/53	10.00
P17	1956 World Series/1,956	5.00
P18	1958 World Series/1,958	5.00
P19	1961 World Series/61	10.00
P20	1962 World Series/62	10.00
P21	1977 World Series/77	8.00
P22	1978 World Series/78	8.00
P23	1996 World Series/1,996	5.00
P24	1998 World Series/1,998	5.00
P25	1999 World Series/1,999	5.00
P26	2000 World Series/2,000	5.00
MM57	Mickey Mantle - 1957 MVP/1,957	8.00
MM62	Mickey Mantle - 1962 MVP/1,962	8.00

Mitchell & Ness Jersey Redempt

		NM/M
Inserted 1:384		
Production 40-99		
MNJ1	Babe Ruth/40	350.00
MNJ2	Bill Dickey/75	120.00
MNJ3	Billy Martin/99	150.00
MNJ4	Bobby Murcer/99	100.00
MNJ5	Bucky Dent/92	100.00
MNJ6	Casey Stengel/65	120.00
MNJ7	"Catfish" Hunter/92	120.00
MNJ8	Chris Chambliss/99	80.00
MNJ9	Don Larsen/75	120.00
MNJ10	Don Mattingly/92	150.00
MNJ11	Elston Howard/88	100.00
MNJ12	Rich "Goose" Gossage/92	100.00
MNJ13	Graig Nettles/99	100.00
MNJ14	Joe DiMaggio/55	200.00
MNJ15	Lefty Gomez/81	120.00
MNJ16	Lou Gehrig/40	200.00
MNJ17	Lou Piniella/92	120.00
MNJ18	Mickey Mantle/50	275.00
MNJ19	Bill "Moose" Skowron/85	125.00
MNJ20	Phil Rizzuto/40	150.00
MNJ21	Roy White/50	100.00
MNJ22	Roger Maris/92	200.00
MNJ23	Ron Guidry/99	100.00
MNJ24	Sparky Lyle/99	100.00
MNJ25	Thurman Munson/91	200.00
MNJ26	Tony Kubek/75	150.00
MNJ27	Tony Lazzeri/79	120.00
MNJ28	Whitey Ford/43	180.00
MNJ29	Willie Randolph/92	100.00
MNJ30	Yogi Berra/50	200.00

2004 UD DIAMOND COLLECTION PRO SIGS

		NM/M
Complete Set (1-240):		
Common Player (1-90):		.15
Common SP (91-150):		2.00
Inserted 1:6		
Common Auto. (151-240):		5.00
Inserted 1:24		
Pack (6):		2.00
Box (24):		40.00
1	Alfonso Soriano	.50
2	Josh Beckett	.50
3	Kerry Wood	.75
4	Brandon Webb	.15
5	Shannon Stewart	.15
6	Larry Walker	.25
7	Tim Hudson	.25
8	Carlos Lee	.25
9	Austin Kearns	.25
10	Vernon Wells	.25
11	Jeff Bagwell	.50
12	Hideo Nomo	.40
13	Jerome Williams	.15
14	Kevin Brown	.25
15	Jose Vidro	.15
16	Rocco Baldelli	.25
17	Frank Thomas	.50
18	Albert Pujols	1.50
19	Bartolo Colon	.25
20	C.C. Sabathia	.15
21	Andruw Jones	.50
22	Reggie Sanders	.15
23	Carlos Beltran	.40
24	Curt Schilling	.50
25	Miguel Tejada	.40
26	Barry Zito	.40
27	Pedro Martinez	.75
28	Sean Burroughs	.15
29	Sammy Sosa	1.50
30	Eric Chavez	.25
31	Roy Halladay	.25
32	Todd Helton	.50
33	Mark Prior	1.00
34	Mike Mussina	.50
35	Alex Rodriguez	2.00
36	Ivan Rodriguez	.50
37	Mike Piazza	1.00
38	Angel Berroa	.15
39	Orlando Cabrera	.25
40	Jim Thome	.75
41	Brian Giles	.25
42	Ichiro Suzuki	1.00
43	Edgar Renteria	.25
44	Eric Gagne	.25
45	Gary Sheffield	.40
46	Torii Hunter	.25
47	Roger Clemens	1.50
48	Scott Rolen	.75
49	Johan Santana	.15
50	Jacque Jones	.15
51	Hank Blalock	.40
52	Rafael Palmeiro	.50
53	Dmitri Young	.15
54	Ryan Klesko	.25
55	Mark Teixeira	.25
56	Nomar Garciaparra	1.50
57	Jose Reyes	.25
58	Vladimir Guerrero	.75
59	Mike Sweeney	.15
60	Jorge Posada	.40
61	Derek Jeter	2.00
62	Milton Bradley	.15
63	Bobby Abreu	.25
64	Greg Maddux	1.00
65	Adam Dunn	.50
66	Troy Glaus	.40
67	Luis Gonzalez	.25
68	Shawn Green	.25
69	Bret Boone	.25
70	Mark Mulder	.25
71	Lance Berkman	.25
72	Preston Wilson	.15
73	Phil Nevin	.15
74	Chipper Jones	.75
75	Garret Anderson	.40
76	Jason Giambi	.75
77	Magglio Ordonez	.25
78	Jeff Kent	.25
79	Richie Sexson	.40
80	Mike Lowell	.25
81	Ben Sheets	.25
82	Randy Johnson	.75
83	Dontrelle Willis	.25
84	Javier Vazquez	.25
85	Geoff Jenkins	.25
86	Manny Ramirez	.50
87	Jim Edmonds	.40
88	Roy Oswalt	.25
89	Edgar Martinez	.25
90	Carlos Delgado	.40
91	*Chris Saenz*	5.00
92	*Justin Leone*	2.00
93	*Shawn Hill*	4.00
94	*Chad Bentz*	4.00
95	*Jesse Harper*	2.00
96	David Crouthers	2.00
97	*Justin Germano*	2.00
98	*Tim Bausher*	2.00
99	*Greg Dobbs*	5.00
100	*Enemencio Pacheco*	8.00
101	*Dennis Sarfate*	2.00
102	*Edwin Moreno*	4.00
103	*Colby Miller*	2.00
104	Mike Rouse	2.00
105	*Fernando Nieve*	2.00
106	Tim Hamulack	6.00
107	*Jason Frasor*	2.00
108	*Jose Capellan*	5.00
109	*Jamie Brown*	3.00
110	*Mariano Gomez*	2.00
111	Mike Vento	8.00
112	*Josh Labandeira*	3.00
113	Mike Gosling	2.00
114	*Shingo Takatsu*	8.00
115	*Justin Hampson*	2.00
116	*Tim Bittner*	2.00
117	*Jerry Gil*	2.00
118	*Carlos Vasquez*	5.00
119	*Lincoln Holdzkom*	2.00
120	*Mike Johnston*	4.00
121	*William Bergolla*	2.00
122	Luis Gonzalez	2.00
123	*Ivan Ochoa*	4.00
124	*Roman Colon*	2.00
125	*Renyel Pinto*	6.00
126	*Donnie Kelly*	4.00
127	*Chris Oxspring*	2.00
128	Sean Henn	5.00
129	*Ryan Meaux*	2.00
130	*Shawn Camp*	2.00
131	*Brandon Medders*	2.00
132	*Rusty Tucker*	2.00
133	*Kazuo Matsui*	10.00
134	*Jorge Sequea*	2.00
135	*Hector Gimenez*	4.00
136	*Casey Daigle*	2.00
137	*Ian Snell*	3.00
138	*Scott Dohmann*	2.00
139	*Ronny Cedeno*	2.00
140	*Jorge Vasquez*	4.00
141	David Aardsma	4.00
142	*Carlos Hines*	2.00
143	*Scott Proctor*	3.00
144	*Jerome Gamble*	5.00
145	*Jason Bartlett*	6.00
146	*Akinori Otsuka*	8.00
147	*Merkin Valdez*	2.00
148	Jake Woods	4.00
149	*Chris Aguila*	2.00
150	*John Gall*	2.00
151	Aaron Miles	10.00
152	Aquilino Lopez	10.00
153	Bill Hall	10.00
154	Billy Traber	15.00
155	Brad Lidge	12.00
156	Brady Clark	10.00
157	Brandon Duckworth	8.00
158	Brett Tomko	6.00
159	Brian Fuentes	6.00
161	Brooks Kieschnick	8.00
162	Carlos Rivera	6.00
163	Chad Cordero	6.00
164	Chad Tracy	10.00
165	Claudio Vargas	5.00
166	D.J. Carrasco	5.00
167	Damian Rolls	6.00
168	David Sanders	5.00
170	Derrick Turnbow	5.00
171	Desi Relaford	5.00
172	Doug Davis	8.00
173	Dustan Mohr	6.00
176	Frank Catalanotto	8.00
178	Franklyn German	5.00
179	Ron Belliard	5.00
180	Geoff Geary	15.00
181	Greg Colbrunn	5.00
182	Henry Mateo	5.00
183	Brent Mayne	5.00
184	Horacio Ramirez	15.00
185	J.C. Romero	5.00
186	J.J. Putz	8.00
187	Ferdin Tejeda	8.00
188	Jaime Cerda	8.00
189	Jason Michaels	10.00
190	Jason Simontacchi	8.00
191	Jay Witasick	5.00
192	Joe Valentine	8.00
193	Joey Eischen	5.00
194	Johnny Estrada	8.00
195	Jon Garland	5.00
196	Jon Switzer	5.00
197	Jorge Julio	5.00
198	Jorge Sosa	8.00
199	Jose Castillo	5.00
200	Jose Macias	8.00
201	Josh Bard	5.00
202	Juan Cruz	5.00
203	Juan Rivera	5.00
204	Ken Griffey Jr.	150.00
205	Kevin Hooper	5.00
206	*Kiko Calero*	15.00
207	Chad Gaudin	5.00
208	Luis Rivas	5.00
209	Mark Corey	5.00
210	Matt Ford	8.00
211	Matt Herges	8.00
212	Miguel Cairo	15.00
213	Fernando Cabrera	5.00
214	Mike MacDougal	5.00
215	Mike Neu	8.00
216	Lew Ford	15.00
217	Mike Wood	8.00
218	Nate Robertson	5.00
219	Nick Punto	5.00
221	Oscar Villarreal	5.00
222	Ramon Vazquez	10.00
223	Randall Simon	5.00
225	Ricky Stone	5.00
229	Ryan Drese	5.00
230	Ryan Ludwick	8.00
231	Scot Shields	5.00
232	Shane Nance	5.00
233	Steve Colyer	5.00
234	Tony Armas	5.00
235	Robby Hammock	5.00
236	Travis Hafner	8.00
237	Victor Martinez	8.00
238	Wilfredo Ledezma	5.00
239	Willie Bloomquist	5.00
240	Yorvit Torrealba	8.00

Gold

Gold (1-90): 3-6X
Overall odds for parallel 1:6

Silver

Silver (1-90): 2-3X
Overall odds for parallel 1:6

Blue Ink Autograph

No Pricing
Production 25 sets

Red Signature

No Pricing
Production 10 sets

2004 UD LEGENDS TIMELESS TEAMS

		NM/M
Complete Set (300):		40.00
Common Player:		.15
Pack (5):		5.00
Box (18):		75.00
1	Bob Gibson	.50
2	Lou Brock	.50
3	Ray Washburn	.15
4	Tim McCarver	.15
5	Harmon Killebrew	1.00
6	Jim Kaat	.25
7	Jim Perry	.15
8	Jim "Mudcat" Grant	.15
9	Boog Powell	.15
10	Brooks Robinson	.50
11	Frank Robinson	.50
12	Jim Palmer	.25
13	Carl Yastrzemski	1.00
14	Jim Lonborg	.15
15	George Scott	.15
16	Sparky Lyle	.15
17	Rico Petrocelli	.15
18	Bob Gibson	.50
19	Julian Javier	.15
20	Lou Brock	.50
21	Orlando Cepeda	.15
22	Ray Washburn	.15
23	Steve Carlton	.50
24	Tim McCarver	.15
25	Al Kaline	.50
26	Bill Freehan	.15
27	Denny McLain	.15
28	Dick McAuliffe	.15
29	Jim Northrup	.15
30	John Hiller	.15
31	Mickey Lolich	.15
32	Mickey Stanley	.15
33	Willie Horton	.15
34	Bob Gibson	.50
35	Julian Javier	.15
36	Lou Brock	.50
37	Orlando Cepeda	.25
38	Steve Carlton	.50
39	Boog Powell	.15
40	Brooks Robinson	.50
41	Davey Johnson	.15
42	Merv Rettenmund	.15
43	Eddie Watt	.15
44	Frank Robinson	.50
45	Jim Palmer	.25
46	Mike Cuellar	.15
47	Paul Blair	.15
48	Pete Richert	.15
49	Ellie Hendricks	.15
50	Billy Williams	.25
51	Randy Hundley	.15
52	Ernie Banks	1.00
53	Fergie Jenkins	.25
54	Jim Hickman	.15
55	Ken Holtzman	.15
56	Ron Santo	.25
57	Ed Kranepool	.15
58	Jerry Koosman	.15
59	Nolan Ryan	2.00
60	Tom Seaver	.50
61	Boog Powell	.15
62	Brooks Robinson	.50
63	Davey Johnson	.15
64	Merv Rettenmund	.15
65	Eddie Watt	.15
66	Frank Robinson	.50
67	Jim Palmer	.25
68	Mike Cuellar	.15
69	Paul Blair	.15
70	Pete Richert	.15
71	Ellie Hendricks	.15
72	Al Kaline	.50
73	Bill Freehan	.15
74	Dick McAuliffe	.15
75	Jim Northrup	.15
76	John Hiller	.15
77	Mickey Lolich	.15
78	Mickey Stanley	.15
79	Willie Horton	.15
80	Bert Campaneris	.15
81	Blue Moon Odom	.15
82	Sal Bando	.15
83	Joe Rudi	.15
84	Ken Holtzman	.15
85	Bill North	.15
86	Blue Moon Odom	.15
87	Gene Tenace	.15
88	Manny Trillo	.15
89	Dick Green	.15
90	Rollie Fingers	.25
91	Sal Bando	.15
92	Vida Blue	.15
93	Bill Buckner	.15
94	Davey Lopes	.15
95	Don Sutton	.25
96	Al Downing	.15
97	Ron Cey	.15
98	Steve Garvey	.15
99	Tommy John	.15
100	Bert Campaneris	.15
101	Bill North	.15
102	Joe Rudi	.15
103	Sal Bando	.15
104	Vida Blue	.15
105	Carl Yastrzemski	.75
106	Carlton Fisk	.25
107	Cecil Cooper	.15
108	Dwight Evans	.15
109	Fred Lynn	.15
110	Jim Rice	.25
111	Luis Tiant	.15
112	Rick Burleson	.15
113	Rico Petrocelli	.15
114	Pedro Borbon	.15
115	Dave Concepcion	.15
116	Don Gullett	.15
117	George Foster	.15
118	Joe Morgan	.25
119	Johnny Bench	.50
120	Rawly Eastwick	.15
121	Sparky Anderson	.15
122	Tony Perez	.25
123	Billy Williams	.25
124	Gene Tenace	.15
125	Jim Perry	.15
126	Vida Blue	.15
127	Pedro Borbon	.15
128	Dave Concepcion	.15
129	Don Gullett	.15
130	George Foster	.15
131	Joe Morgan	.25
132	Johnny Bench	.50
133	Ken Griffey Sr.	.15
134	Rawly Eastwick	.15
135	Tony Perez	.25
136	Bill Russell	.15
137	Burt Hooton	.15
138	Davey Lopes	.15
139	Don Sutton	.25
140	Dusty Baker	.15
141	Steve Yeager	.15
142	Ron Cey	.15
143	Steve Garvey	.15
144	Tommy John	.15
145	Bucky Dent	.15
146	Chris Chambliss	.15
147	Ed Figueroa	.15
148	Graig Nettles	.15
149	Lou Piniella	.25
150	Roy White	.15
151	Don Gullett	.15
152	Sparky Lyle	.15
153	Brian Doyle	.15
154	Bucky Dent	.15
155	Chris Chambliss	.15
156	Ed Figueroa	.15
157	Graig Nettles	.15
158	Lou Piniella	.25
159	Roy White	.15
160	Rich "Goose" Gossage	.15
161	Sparky Lyle	.15
162	Bobby Grich	.15
163	Brian Downing	.15
164	Dan Ford	.15
165	Nolan Ryan	2.00
166	Dave Concepcion	.15
167	George Foster	.15
168	Johnny Bench	.50
169	Ray Knight	.15
170	Tom Seaver	.50
171	Bert Blyleven	.15
172	Bill Madlock	.15
173	Dave Parker	.25
174	Phil Garner	.15
175	Bill Russell	.15
176	Steve Yeager	.15
177	Don Sutton	.25
178	Dusty Baker	.25
179	Jerry Reuss	.15
180	Mickey Hatcher	.15
181	Pedro Guerrero	.15
182	Ron Cey	.15
183	Steve Garvey	.15
184	Rudy May	.15
185	Brian Doyle	.15
186	Bucky Dent	.15
187	Jim Kaat	.15
188	Lou Piniella	.15
189	Luis Tiant	.15
190	Tommy John	.15
191	Bake McBride	.15
192	Bob Boone	.15
193	Dickie Noles	.15
194	Manny Trillo	.15
195	Mike Schmidt	1.00
196	Sparky Lyle	.15
197	Steve Carlton	.50
198	Steve Yeager	.15
199	Burt Hooton	.15
200	Dusty Baker	.15
201	Jerry Reuss	.15
202	Mike Scioscia	.15
203	Pedro Guerrero	.15
204	Ron Cey	.15
205	Steve Garvey	.15
206	Alejandro Pena	.15
207	Steve Sax	.15
208	Cecil Cooper	.15
209	Gorman Thomas	.15
210	Paul Molitor	.50
211	Robin Yount	1.00
212	Rollie Fingers	.25
213	Don Money	.15
214	Rudy May	.15
215	Bucky Dent	.15
216	Dave Winfield	.50
217	Lou Piniella	.25
218	Rich "Goose" Gossage	.15
219	Tommy John	.15
220	Cecil Cooper	.15
221	Gorman Thomas	.15
222	Paul Molitor	.50
223	Robin Yount	1.00
224	Don Money	.15
225	Cal Ripken Jr.	2.00
226	Dan Ford	.15
227	Jim Palmer	.25
228	John Shelby	.15
229	Alan Trammell	.25
230	Chet Lemon	.15
231	Howard Johnson	.15
232	Jack Morris	.15
233	Kirk Gibson	.25
234	Lou Whitaker	.15
235	Sparky Anderson	.15
236	Dave Winfield	.50
237	Don Mattingly	1.00
238	Ken Griffey Sr.	.15
239	Phil Niekro	.15
240	Yogi Berra	.75
241	Bill Buckner	.15
242	Bruce Hurst	.15
243	Dave Henderson	.15
244	Dwight Evans	.15
245	Jim Rice	.15
246	Tom Seaver	.50
247	Wade Boggs	.50
248	Bob Boone	.15
249	Bobby Grich	.15
250	Brian Downing	.15
251	Don Sutton	.25
252	Terry Forster	.15
253	Rick Burleson	.15
254	Wally Joyner	.15
255	Darryl Strawberry	.15
256	Dwight Gooden	.15
257	Gary Carter	.15
258	Jesse Orosco	.15
259	Keith Hernandez	.15
260	Lenny Dykstra	.15
261	Mookie Wilson	.15
262	Ray Knight	.15
263	Wally Backman	.15
264	Sid Fernandez	.15
265	Alan Trammell	.25
266	Dan Petry	.15
267	Chet Lemon	.15
268	Sparky Anderson	.15
269	Jack Morris	.15
270	Kirk Gibson	.15
271	Lou Whitaker	.15
272	Bert Blyleven	.15
273	Kent Hrbek	.15
274	Kirby Puckett	.75
275	Alejandro Pena	.15
276	Jesse Orosco	.15
277	John Shelby	.15
278	Kirk Gibson	.15
279	Mickey Hatcher	.15
280	Mike Scioscia	.15
281	Steve Sax	.15
282	Darryl Strawberry	.15
283	Dwight Gooden	.15
284	Gary Carter	.15
285	Howard Johnson	.15
286	Keith Hernandez	.15
287	Lenny Dykstra	.15
288	Mookie Wilson	.15
289	Wally Backman	.15
290	Sid Fernandez	.15
291	Jack Morris	.15
292	Kent Hrbek	.15
293	Kirby Puckett	.75
294	Dave Winfield	.50
295	Jack Morris	.15
296	Joe Carter	.15
297	Don Mattingly	1.00
298	Paul O'Neill	.15
299	Jack McDowell	.15
300	Wade Boggs	.50

Gold

No Pricing
Production 5 sets

Autographs

		NM/M
Common Autograph:		10.00
Golds:		No Pricing
Production 5 sets		
Platinum:		No Pricing
Production one set		
1	Bob Gibson SP/50	
2	Lou Brock MM SP/75	20.00
3	Ray Washburn	10.00
4	Tim McCarver	15.00
5	Harmon Killebrew	40.00
6	Jim Kaat	10.00
7	Jim Perry	12.00
8	Jim "Mudcat" Grant	
9	Boog Powell	10.00
10	Brooks Robinson	35.00
11	Frank Robinson SP/35	
12	Jim Palmer SP/50	20.00
13	Carl Yastrzemski SP/25	80.00
14	Jim Lonborg	10.00
15	George Scott	10.00
16	Sparky Lyle	10.00
17	Rico Petrocelli	10.00
18	Bob Gibson SP/35	40.00
19	Julian Javier	10.00
20	Lou Brock SP/60	20.00
21	Orlando Cepeda SP/50	20.00
22	Ray Washburn	10.00
23	Steve Carlton SP/25	
24	Tim McCarver	12.00
25	Al Kaline	25.00
26	Bill Freehan	10.00
27	Denny McLain	20.00
28	Dick McAuliffe	10.00
29	Jim Northrup	15.00
30	John Hiller	10.00
31	Mickey Lolich	15.00
32	Mickey Stanley	10.00
33	Willie Horton	10.00
34	Bob Gibson SP/25	
35	Julian Javier	10.00
36	Lou Brock SP/50	20.00
37	Orlando Cepeda SP/25	
38	Steve Carlton SP/35	30.00
39	Boog Powell	10.00
40	Brooks Robinson SP/100	40.00
41	Davey Johnson	10.00
42	Merv Rettenmund	10.00
43	Eddie Watt	10.00
44	Frank Robinson SP/25	
45	Jim Palmer SP/25	
46	Mike Cuellar	10.00
47	Paul Blair	10.00
48	Pete Richert	10.00
49	Ellie Hendricks	10.00
50	Billy Williams SP/75	25.00
51	Randy Hundley	10.00
52	Ernie Banks SP/50	
53	Fergie Jenkins	15.00
54	Jim Hickman	20.00
55	Ken Holtzman	15.00
56	Ron Santo	25.00
57	Ed Kranepool	10.00
58	Jerry Koosman	15.00

59 Nolan Ryan SP/50 175.00
60 Tom Seaver SP/50 50.00
61 Boog Powell 12.00
62 Brooks Robinson SP/35 50.00
63 Davey Johnson 10.00
64 Merv Rettenmund 10.00
65 Eddie Watt 10.00
66 Frank Robinson SP/50 30.00
67 Jim Palmer SP/75 20.00
68 Mike Cuellar 12.00
69 Paul Blair 10.00
70 Pete Richert 10.00
71 Ellie Hendricks 10.00
72 Al Kaline 25.00
73 Bill Freehan 10.00
74 Dick McAuliffe 15.00
75 Jim Northrup 15.00
76 John Hiller 10.00
77 Mickey Lolich 15.00
78 Mickey Stanley 10.00
79 Willie Horton 12.00
80 Bert Campaneris 10.00
81 Blue Moon Odom 15.00
82 Sal Bando Exch 10.00
83 Joe Rudi 10.00
84 Ken Holtzman 10.00
85 Bill North 10.00
86 Blue Moon Odom 15.00
87 Gene Tenace 10.00
88 Manny Trillo 15.00
89 Dick Green 10.00
90 Rollie Fingers 15.00
91 Sal Bando 10.00
92 Vida Blue 15.00
93 Bill Buckner 15.00
94 Davey Lopes 10.00
95 Don Sutton 15.00
96 Al Downing MM 10.00
97 Ron Cey SP/25
98 Steve Garvey SP/25
99 Tommy John SP/25
100 Bert Campaneris 10.00
101 Bill North 10.00
102 Joe Rudi 10.00
103 Sal Bando 10.00
104 Vida Blue SP/100 15.00
105 Carl Yastrzemski SP/50 60.00
106 Carlton Fisk SP/100 30.00
107 Cecil Cooper SP/75 15.00
108 Dwight Evans SP/75 10.00
109 Fred Lynn 10.00
110 Jim Rice SP/100 Exch 20.00
111 Luis Tiant Exch 10.00
112 Rick Burleson 10.00
113 Rico Petrocelli 10.00
114 Pedro Borbon 10.00
115 Dave Concepcion Exch 10.00
116 Don Gullett 15.00
117 George Foster SP/50 15.00
118 Joe Morgan SP/25
119 Johnny Bench SP/85 50.00
120 Rawly Eastwick 10.00
121 Sparky Anderson 10.00
122 Tony Perez 30.00
123 Billy Williams SP/50 20.00
124 Gene Tenace 10.00
125 Jim Perry 10.00
126 Vida Blue SP/75 20.00
127 Pedro Borbon 10.00
128 Dave Concepcion Exch 10.00
129 Don Gullett 15.00
130 George Foster SP/35
131 Joe Morgan SP/50
132 Johnny Bench SP/50
133 Ken Griffey Sr. 10.00
134 Rawly Eastwick 10.00
135 Tony Perez 30.00
136 Bill Russell 10.00
137 Burt Hooton 10.00
138 Davey Lopes 10.00
139 Don Sutton 15.00
140 Dusty Baker Exch 15.00
141 Steve Yeager SP/75 Exch 10.00
142 Ron Cey SP/35
143 Steve Garvey SP/35
144 Tommy John SP/35 15.00
145 Bucky Dent SP/75 15.00
146 Chris Chambliss 15.00
147 Ed Figueroa 10.00
148 Graig Nettles 15.00
149 Lou Piniella SP/25
150 Roy White 10.00
151 Don Gullett 15.00
152 Sparky Lyle 10.00
153 Brian Doyle 10.00
154 Bucky Dent SP/75
155 Chris Chambliss 15.00
156 Ed Figueroa 10.00
157 Graig Nettles 15.00
158 Lou Piniella SP/35
159 Roy White 10.00
160 Rich "Goose" Gossage 15.00
161 Sparky Lyle 10.00
162 Bobby Grich 10.00
163 Brian Downing 10.00
164 Dan Ford 10.00
165 Nolan Ryan SP/25
166 Dave Concepcion SP/75 Exch 10.00
167 George Foster SP/25
168 Johnny Bench SP/25
169 Ray Knight 10.00
170 Tom Seaver SP/35
171 Bert Blyleven 15.00
172 Bill Madlock 10.00
173 Dave Parker 12.00
174 Phil Garner 10.00
175 Bill Russell 10.00
176 Steve Yeager 10.00
177 Don Sutton SP/50 20.00
178 Dusty Baker 15.00
179 Jerry Reuss 10.00
180 Mickey Hatcher 10.00
181 Pedro Guerrero 10.00
182 Ron Cey SP/50 15.00
183 Steve Garvey SP/50 15.00
184 Rudy May 10.00
185 Brian Doyle 10.00
186 Bucky Dent SP/60 15.00
187 Jim Kaat 10.00
188 Lou Piniella SP/50 15.00
189 Luis Tiant 10.00
190 Tommy John SP/50 15.00
191 Bake McBride 15.00
192 Bob Boone 10.00
193 Dickie Noles 10.00
194 Manny Trillo 15.00
195 Mike Schmidt SP/50 75.00
196 Sparky Lyle 10.00
197 Steve Carlton SP/50 20.00
198 Steve Yeager 10.00
199 Burt Hooton 10.00
200 Dusty Baker Exch 15.00
201 Jerry Reuss 10.00
202 Mike Scioscia 10.00
203 Pedro Guerrero 10.00
204 Ron Cey SP/75 10.00
205 Steve Garvey SP/75 15.00
206 Alejandro Pena 10.00
207 Steve Sax SP/100 10.00
208 Cecil Cooper SP/85 15.00
209 Gorman Thomas Exch 10.00
210 Paul Molitor SP/25
211 Robin Yount SP/25
212 Rollie Fingers 15.00
213 Don Money 10.00
214 Rudy May 10.00
215 Bucky Dent SP/25
216 Dave Winfield SP/50 30.00
217 Lou Piniella SP/75 15.00
218 Rich "Goose" Gossage 15.00
219 Tommy John SP/75 10.00
220 Cecil Cooper 15.00
221 Gorman Thomas Exch 10.00
222 Paul Molitor SP/50 45.00
223 Robin Yount SP/50 75.00
224 Don Money 10.00
225 Cal Ripken Jr. SP/50 180.00
226 Dan Ford 10.00
227 Jim Palmer SP/35
228 John Shelby 10.00
229 Alan Trammell 15.00
230 Chet Lemon 10.00
231 Howard Johnson 15.00
232 Jack Morris SP/35 15.00
233 Kirk Gibson 15.00
234 Lou Whitaker SP/100 15.00
235 Sparky Anderson 10.00
236 Dave Winfield SP/25
237 Don Mattingly SP/50 60.00
238 Ken Griffey Sr. 10.00
239 Phil Niekro 15.00
240 Yogi Berra SP/47 50.00
241 Bill Buckner 15.00
242 Bruce Hurst 15.00
243 Dave Henderson 10.00
244 Dwight Evans SP/50
245 Jim Rice SP/75 Exch 20.00
246 Tom Seaver SP/25
247 Wade Boggs SP/50 30.00
248 Bob Boone 10.00
249 Bobby Grich 10.00
250 Brian Downing 10.00
251 Don Sutton SP/75 15.00
252 Terry Forster 10.00
253 Rick Burleson 10.00
254 Wally Joyner 15.00
255 Darryl Strawberry 15.00
256 Dwight Gooden 15.00
257 Gary Carter SP/75 20.00
258 Jesse Orosco 10.00
259 Keith Hernandez 15.00
260 Lenny Dykstra 10.00
261 Mookie Wilson 10.00
262 Ray Knight 10.00
263 Wally Backman 10.00
264 Sid Fernandez Exch 10.00
265 Alan Trammell 15.00
266 Dan Petry 10.00
267 Chet Lemon 10.00
268 Sparky Anderson 10.00
269 Jack Morris SP/25
270 Kirk Gibson 15.00
271 Lou Whitaker SP/50 20.00
272 Bert Blyleven 10.00
273 Kent Hrbek 15.00
274 Kirby Puckett SP/25
275 Alejandro Pena 10.00
276 Jesse Orosco 10.00
277 John Shelby 10.00
278 Kirk Gibson SP/50 20.00
279 Mickey Hatcher 10.00
280 Mike Scioscia 10.00
281 Steve Sax 10.00
282 Darryl Strawberry 15.00
283 Dwight Gooden 15.00
284 Gary Carter SP/50 20.00
285 Howard Johnson 10.00
286 Keith Hernandez 15.00
287 Lenny Dykstra 10.00
288 Mookie Wilson 10.00
289 Wally Backman 10.00
290 Sid Fernandez Exch 10.00
291 Jack Morris SP/50 15.00
292 Kent Hrbek 15.00
293 Kirby Puckett SP/50 50.00
294 Dave Winfield SP/35 35.00
295 Jack Morris SP/75 15.00
296 Joe Carter SP/100
297 Don Mattingly SP/25
298 Paul O'Neill 40.00
299 Jack McDowell 10.00
300 Wade Boggs SP/75 25.00

Legendary Sign. Dual

NM/M

Quantity produced listed

BC Lou Brock, Orlando Cepeda/75 40.00
BJ Lou Brock, Julian Javier/150 25.00
BM Wade Boggs, Don Mattingly/50 140.00
BO Vida Blue, Blue Moon Odom/150 25.00
BW Ernie Banks, Billy Williams/25 100.00
CB Steve Carlton, Bret Boone/150 50.00
CG Ron Cey, Steve Garvey/150 40.00
CH Gary Carter, Keith Hernandez/150 30.00
CM Dave Concepcion, Joe Morgan/75 Exch 35.00
CW Joe Carter, Dave Winfield/25
DD Bucky Dent, Brian Doyle/150 25.00
FR Fred Lynn, Jim Rice/150 40.00
GA Kirk Gibson, Sparky Anderson/150 40.00
GB Bob Gibson, Lou Brock/50 75.00
GC Dwight Gooden, Gary Carter/150 30.00
GL Rich "Goose" Gossage, Sparky Lyle/150 Exch 25.00
GM Bob Gibson, Tim McCarver/50
HJ Ken Holtzman, Fergie Jenkins/150 40.00
HK Keith Hernandez, Ray Knight/150 30.00
JH Fergie Jenkins, Randy Hundley/150 40.00
JS Tommy John, Don Sutton/150 25.00
KH Al Kaline, Willie Horton/150 40.00
KK Harmon Killebrew, Jim Kaat/150 50.00
LM Mickey Lolich, Denny McLain/75 60.00
MB Joe Morgan, Johnny Bench/25 80.00
MF Denny McLain, Bill Freehan/150 40.00
NC Graig Nettles, Chris Chambliss/150 30.00
OM Paul O'Neill, Don Mattingly/75 140.00
PC Jim Palmer, Mike Cuellar/150 30.00
PF Tony Perez, George Foster/150 40.00
PH Kirby Puckett, Kent Hrbek/50 65.00
PN Lou Piniella, Graig Nettles/150 30.00
PR Jim Palmer, Merv Rettenmund/150 35.00
RL Bill Russell, Davey Lopes/150 30.00
RR Brooks Robinson, Frank Robinson/50 70.00
RS Nolan Ryan, Tom Seaver/25 250.00
SD Steve Garvey, Davey Lopes/150 25.00
SG Darryl Strawberry, Dwight Gooden/150 40.00
SY Don Sutton, Steve Yeager/150 30.00
TF Luis Tiant, Carlton Fisk/50 45.00
TM Gorman Thomas, Paul Molitor/150 Exch 35.00
WB Mookie Wilson, Bill Buckner/150 30.00
WT Lou Whitaker, Alan Trammell/75 75.00
YM Robin Yount, Paul Molitor/50 120.00
YP Carl Yastrzemski, Rico Petrocelli/50 75.00

Legendary Sign. Triple

NM/M

Quantity produced listed

BRB Sal Bando, Joe Rudi, Vida Blue/75 50.00
BSW Ernie Banks, Ron Santo, Billy Williams/25 140.00
CDK Gary Carter, Lenny Dykstra, Ray Knight/50 75.00
GBC Steve Garvey, Dusty Baker, Ron Cey/50 75.00
GBM Bob Gibson, Lou Brock, Tim McCarver/25 100.00
GDR Bobby Grich, Al Downing, Nolan Ryan/25 175.00
GHS Kirk Gibson, Mickey Hatcher, Mike Scioscia/75 85.00
GMP Phil Garner, Bill Madlock, Dave Parker/50 75.00
HHS Jim Hickman, Ken Holtzman, Ron Santo/75 60.00
HSJ Burt Hooton, Don Sutton, Tommy John/50 50.00
JHH Fergie Jenkins, Randy Hundley, Ken Holtzman/75 50.00
KKP Harmon Killebrew, Jim Kaat, Jim Perry/50 65.00
KPG Jim Kaat, Jim Perry, Jim "Mudcat" Grant/75 Exch 40.00
KSR Jerry Koosman, Tom Seaver, Nolan Ryan/25 250.00
MHP Jack Morris, Kent Hrbek, Kirby Puckett/50 100.00
MLF Denny McLain, Mickey Lolich, Bill Freehan/50 60.00
NKH Jim Northrup, Al Kaline, Willie Horton/75 65.00
PBH Kirby Puckett, Bert Blyleven, Kent Hrbek/50 90.00
PCR Jim Palmer, Mike Cuellar, Pete Richert/75 45.00
PPW Jim Palmer, Boog Powell, Earl Weaver/75 60.00
RWP Cal Ripken Jr., Earl Weaver, Jim Palmer/25 250.00
SCB Mike Schmidt, Steve Carlton, Bob Boone/50 125.00
SGS Steve Sax, Pedro Guerrero, Mike Scioscia/75 60.00
TWA Alan Trammell, Lou Whitaker, Sparky Anderson/50 75.00
YCT Robin Yount, Cecil Cooper, Gorman Thomas/50 Exch 120.00

YFT Carl Yastrzemski, Carlton Fisk, Luis Tiant/25 140.00

Team Terrific GU Stats

No Pricing
Production 1-5

Team Terrific GU Team Logo

NM/M

Quantity produced listed
BO Baltimore Orioles/85 60.00
BR Boston Red Sox/85 50.00
CR Cincinnati Reds/85 75.00
LD Los Angeles Dodgers/85 50.00
MB Milwaukee Brewers/100 30.00
NM New York Mets/85 30.00
NY New York Yankees/30
OA Oakland A's/100 30.00
SC St. Louis Cardinals/100 50.00

Team Terrific GU League

No Pricing
Production 15 Sets
BO Baltimore Orioles/15
BR Boston Red Sox/15
CR Cincinnati Reds/15
LD Los Angeles Dodgers/15
MB Milwaukee Brewers/15
NM New York Mets/15
NY New York Yankees/5
OA Oakland A's/15
SC St. Louis Cardinals/15

Team Terrific GU Hat Logo

NM/M

Quantity produced listed
BO Baltimore Orioles/50 90.00
BR Boston Red Sox/50 80.00
CR Cincinnati Reds/50 80.00
LD Los Angeles Dodgers/50 60.00
MB Milwaukee Brewers/82 40.00
NM New York Mets/50 50.00
NY New York Yankees/15
OA Oakland A's/50 40.00
SC St. Louis Cardinals/50 75.00

Team Terrific GU Brand Logo

NM/M

Quantity produced listed
BO Baltimore Orioles/35 90.00
BR Boston Red Sox/35 80.00
CR Cincinnati Reds/35 80.00
LD Los Angeles Dodgers/35 60.00
MB Milwaukee Brewers/41 50.00
NM New York Mets/35 50.00
NY New York Yankees/10
OA Oakland A's/39 40.00
SC St. Louis Cardinals/35 75.00

2005 UPPER DECK

NM/M

Complete Set (500): 75.00
Common Player: .15
Common (211-250): .50
Hobby Pack (8): 3.00
Hobby Box (24): 65.00
1 Casey Kotchman .15
2 Chone Figgins .15
3 David Eckstein .15
4 Jarrod Washburn .15
5 Robb Quinlan .15
6 Troy Glaus .25
7 Vladimir Guerrero .75
8 Brandon Webb .15
9 Danny Bautista .15
10 Luis Gonzalez .15
11 Matt Kata .15
12 Randy Johnson .75
13 Robby Hammock .15
14 Shea Hillenbrand .15
15 Adam LaRoche .15
16 Andruw Jones .25
17 Horacio Ramirez .15
18 John Smoltz .25
19 Johnny Estrada .15
20 Mike Hampton .15
21 Rafael Furcal .15
22 Brian Roberts .15
23 Javy Lopez .25
24 Jay Gibbons .15
25 Jorge Julio .15
26 Melvin Mora .15
27 Miguel Tejada .25
28 Rafael Palmeiro .50
29 Derek Lowe .25
30 Jason Varitek .25
31 Kevin Youkilis .15
32 Manny Ramirez .75
33 Curt Schilling .75
34 Pedro Martinez .75
35 Trot Nixon .15
36 Corey Patterson .25
37 Derrek Lee .25
38 LaTroy Hawkins .15
39 Mark Prior .75
40 Matt Clement .15
41 Moises Alou .25
42 Sammy Sosa 1.50
43 Aaron Rowand .15
44 Carlos Lee .15
45 Jose Valentin .15
46 Juan Uribe .15
47 Magglio Ordonez .25
48 Mark Buehrle .15
49 Paul Konerko .25
50 Adam Dunn .50
51 Barry Larkin .25
52 D'Angelo Jimenez .15
53 Danny Graves .15
54 Paul Wilson .15
55 Sean Casey .25
56 Wily Mo Pena .25
57 Ben Broussard .15
58 C.C. Sabathia .15
59 Casey Blake .15
60 Cliff Lee .15
61 Matt Lawton .15
62 Omar Vizquel .15
63 Victor Martinez .15
64 Charles Johnson .15
65 Joe Kennedy .15
66 Jeromy Burnitz .15
67 Matt Holliday .15
68 Preston Wilson .15
69 Royce Clayton .15
70 Shawn Estes .15
71 Bobby Higginson .15
72 Brandon Inge .15
73 Carlos Guillen .15
74 Dmitri Young .15
75 Eric Munson .15
76 Jeremy Bonderman .15
77 Ugueth Urbina .15
78 Josh Beckett .40
79 Dontrelle Willis .15
80 Jeff Conine .15
81 Juan Pierre .15
82 Luis Castillo .15
83 Miguel Cabrera .75
84 Mike Lowell .25
85 Andy Pettitte .25
86 Brad Lidge .15
87 Carlos Beltran .50
88 Craig Biggio .25
89 Jeff Bagwell .50
90 Roger Clemens 1.50
91 Roy Oswalt .25
92 Benito Santiago .15
93 Jeremy Affeldt .15
94 Juan Gonzalez .25
95 Ken Harvey .15
96 Mike MacDougal .15
97 Mike Sweeney .15
98 Zack Greinke .15
99 Adrian Beltre .40
100 Alex Cora .15
101 Cesar Izturis .15
102 Eric Gagne .40
103 Kazuhisa Ishii .15
104 Milton Bradley .15
105 Shawn Green .25
106 Danny Kolb .15
107 Ben Sheets .25
108 Brooks Kieschnick .15
109 Craig Counsell .15
110 Geoff Jenkins .15
111 Lyle Overbay .15
112 Scott Podsednik .15
113 Corey Koskie .15
114 Johan Santana .40
115 Joe Mauer .25
116 Justin Morneau .15
117 Lew Ford .15
118 Matt LeCroy .15
119 Torii Hunter .25
120 Brad Wilkerson .15
121 Chad Cordero .15
122 Livan Hernandez .15
123 Jose Vidro .15
124 Termel Sledge .15
125 Tony Batista .15
126 Zach Day .15
127 Al Leiter .25
128 Jae Weong Seo .15
129 Jose Reyes .15
130 Kazuo Matsui .15
131 Mike Piazza 1.00
132 Todd Zeile .15
133 Cliff Floyd .15
134 Alex Rodriguez 2.00
135 Derek Jeter 2.00
136 Gary Sheffield .40
137 Hideki Matsui 1.50
138 Jason Giambi .25
139 Jorge Posada .25
140 Mike Mussina .40
141 Barry Zito .25
142 Bobby Crosby .25
143 Octavio Dotel .15
144 Eric Chavez .25
145 Jermaine Dye .15
146 Mark Kotsay .15
147 Tim Hudson .25
148 Billy Wagner .15
149 Bobby Abreu .25
150 David Bell .15
151 Jim Thome .50
152 Jimmy Rollins .15
153 Mike Lieberthal .15
154 Randy Wolf .15
155 Craig Wilson .15
156 Daryle Ward .15
157 Jack Wilson .15
158 Jason Kendall .15
159 Kip Wells .15
160 Oliver Perez .15
161 Robert Mackowiak .15
162 Brian Giles .25
163 Brian Lawrence .15
164 David Wells .15
165 Jay Payton .15
166 Ryan Klesko .15
167 Sean Burroughs .15
168 Trevor Hoffman .15
169 Brett Tomko .15
170 J.T. Snow .15
171 Jason Schmidt .25
172 Kirk Rueter .15
173 A.J. Pierzynski .15
174 Pedro Feliz .15
175 Ray Durham .15
176 Eddie Guardado .15
177 Edgar Martinez .15
178 Ichiro Suzuki 1.50
179 Jamie Moyer .15
180 Joel Pineiro .15
181 Randy Winn .15
182 Raul Ibanez .15
183 Albert Pujols 2.00
184 Edgar Renteria .25
185 Jason Isringhausen .15
186 Jim Edmonds .40
187 Matt Morris .15
188 Reggie Sanders .15
189 Tony Womack .15
190 Aubrey Huff .15
191 Danys Baez .15
192 Carl Crawford .15
193 Jose Cruz Jr. .15
194 Rocco Baldelli .15
195 Tino Martinez .15
196 Dewon Brazelton .15
197 Alfonso Soriano .75
198 Brad Fullmer .15
199 Gerald Laird .15
200 Hank Blalock .50
201 Laynce Nix .15
202 Mark Teixeira .25
203 Mike Young .15
204 Alexis Rios .15
205 Eric Hinske .15
206 Miguel Batista .15
207 Orlando Hudson .15
208 Roy Halladay .15
209 Ted Lilly .15
210 Vernon Wells .15
211 Aarom Baldiris .50
212 B.J. Upton 1.00
213 Dallas McPherson .50
214 Brian Dallimore .50
215 Chris Oxspring .50
216 Chris Shelton .50
217 David Wright 1.50
218 Edwardo Sierra .50
219 Fernando Nieve .50
220 Frank Francisco .50
221 Jeff Bennett .50
222 Justin Lehr .50
223 John Gall .50
224 Jorge Sequea .50
225 Justin Germano .50
226 Kazuhito Tadano .50
227 Kevin Cave .50
228 Joe Blanton .50
229 Luis Gonzalez .50
230 Mike Wuertz .50
231 Mike Rouse .50
232 Nick Regilio .50
233 Orlando Rodriguez .50
234 Phil Stockman .50
235 Ramon Ramirez .50
236 Roberto Novoa .50
237 Dioner Navarro .50
238 Tim Bausher .50
239 Logan Kensing .50
240 Andy Green .50
241 Brad Halsey .50
242 Charles Thomas .50
243 George Sherrill .50
244 Jesse Crain .50
245 Jimmy Serrano .50
246 Joe Horgan .50
247 *Chris Young* .50
248 Joey Gathright .50
249 Gavin Floyd .50
250 Ryan Howard .75
251 Lance Cormier .15
252 Matt Treanor .15
253 Jeff Francis .15
254 Nick Swisher .15
255 Scott Atchison .15
256 Travis Blackley .15
257 Travis Smith .15
258 Yadier Molina .15
259 Jeff Keppinger .15
260 Scott Kazmir 1.00
261 Garret Anderson, Vladimir Guerrero .40
262 Luis Gonzalez, Randy Johnson .40
263 Andruw Jones, Chipper Jones .40
264 Miguel Tejada, Rafael Palmeiro .40
265 Curt Schilling, Manny Ramirez .50
266 Mark Prior, Sammy Sosa .75
267 Frank Thomas, Magglio Ordonez .25
268 Barry Larkin, Ken Griffey Jr. .75
269 C.C. Sabathia, Victor Martinez .15
270 Jeromy Burnitz, Todd Helton .25
271 Dmitri Young, Ivan Rodriguez .40
272 Josh Beckett, Miguel Cabrera .25
273 Jeff Bagwell, Roger Clemens .75
274 Ken Harvey, Mike Sweeney .15
275 Adrian Beltre, Eric Gagne .25
276 Ben Sheets, Geoff Jenkins .15
277 Joe Mauer, Torii Hunter .15
278 Jose Vidro, Livan Hernandez .15
279 Kazuo Matsui, Mike Piazza .50
280 Alex Rodriguez, Derek Jeter 1.00
281 Eric Chavez, Tim Hudson .15
282 Bobby Abreu, Jim Thome .40
283 Craig Wilson, Jason Kendall .15
284 Brian Giles, Phil Nevin .15
285 A.J. Pierzynski, Jason Schmidt .15
286 Bret Boone, Ichiro Suzuki .75

287 Albert Pujols, Scott Rolen .75
288 Aubrey Huff, Tino Martinez .15
289 Hank Blalock, Mark Teixeira .15
290 Carlos Delgado, Roy Halladay .15
291 Vladimir Guerrero .40
292 Curt Schilling .25
293 Mark Prior .40
294 Josh Beckett .15
295 Roger Clemens .75
296 Derek Jeter .75
297 Eric Chavez .15
298 Jim Thome .25
299 Albert Pujols .75
300 Hank Blalock .25
301 Bartolo Colon .25
302 Darin Erstad .15
303 Garret Anderson .25
304 Orlando Cabrera .15
305 Steve Finley .15
306 Javier Vazquez .15
307 Russ Ortiz .15
308 Chipper Jones .75
309 Marcus Giles .15
310 Raul Mondesi .15
311 B.J. Ryan .15
312 Luis Matos .15
313 Sidney Ponson .15
314 Bill Mueller .15
315 David Ortiz .75
316 Johnny Damon .75
317 Keith Foulke .15
318 Mark Bellhorn .15
319 Wade Miller .15
320 Aramis Ramirez .40
321 Carlos Zambrano .40
322 Greg Maddux 1.25
323 Kerry Wood .50
324 Nomar Garciaparra 1.00
325 Todd Walker .15
326 Frank Thomas .50
327 Freddy Garcia .15
328 Joe Crede .15
329 Jose Contreras .15
330 Orlando Hernandez .15
331 Shingo Takatsu .15
332 Austin Kearns .15
333 Eric Milton .15
334 Ken Griffey Jr. 1.00
335 Aaron Boone .15
336 David Riske .15
337 Jake Westbrook .15
338 Kevin Millwood .15
339 Travis Hafner .25
340 Aaron Miles .15
341 Jeff Baker .15
342 Todd Helton .50
343 Garrett Atkins .15
344 Carlos Pena .15
345 Ivan Rodriguez .50
346 Rondell White .15
347 Troy Percival .15
348 A.J. Burnett .25
349 Carlos Delgado .40
350 Guillermo Mota .15
351 Paul LoDuca .15
352 Jason Lane .15
353 Lance Berkman .25
354 Angel Berroa .15
355 David DeJesus .15
356 Ruben Gotay .15
357 Jose Lima .15
358 Brad Penny .15
359 J.D. Drew .25
360 Jayson Werth .15
361 Jeff Kent .25
362 Odalis Perez .15
363 Brady Clark .15
364 Junior Spivey .15
365 Rickie Weeks .25
366 Jacque Jones .15
367 Joe Nathan .15
368 Nick Punto .15
369 Shannon Stewart .15
370 Doug Mientkiewicz .15
371 Kris Benson .15
372 Tom Glavine .25
373 Victor Zambrano .15
374 Bernie Williams .40
375 Carl Pavano .15
376 Jaret Wright .15
377 Kevin Brown .25
378 Mariano Rivera .25
379 Dan Haren .15
380 Eric Byrnes .15
381 Erubiel Durazo .15
382 Rich Harden .25
383 Brett Myers .15
384 Chase Utley .25
385 Marlon Byrd .15
386 Pat Burrell .25
387 Placido Polanco .15
388 Freddy Sanchez .15
389 Jason Bay .25
390 Josh Fogg .15
391 Adam Eaton .15
392 Jake Peavy .40
393 Khalil Greene .40
394 Mark Loretta .15
395 Phil Nevin .15
396 Ramon Hernandez .15
397 Woody Williams .15
398 Armando Benitez .15
399 Edgardo Alfonzo .15
400 Marquis Grissom .15
401 Mike Matheny .15
402 Richie Sexson .40
403 Bret Boone .15
404 Gil Meche .15
405 Chris Carpenter .40
406 Jeff Suppan .15
407 Larry Walker .40
408 Mark Grudzielanek .15
409 Mark Mulder .25
410 Scott Rolen .75
411 Josh Phelps .15
412 Jonny Gomes .15
413 Francisco Cordero .15
414 Kenny Rogers .15
415 Richard Hidalgo .15
416 David Bush .15
417 Frank Catalanotto .15
418 Gabe Gross .15
419 Guillermo Quiroz .15
420 Reed Johnson .15
421 Cristian Guzman .15
422 Esteban Loaiza .15
423 Jose Guillen .25
424 Nick Johnson .25
425 Vinny Castilla .15
426 *Peter Orr* .50
427 *Tadahito Iguchi* 4.00
428 Jeff Baker .15
429 *Marcos Carvajal* .50
430 *Justin Verlander* 3.00
431 *Luke Scott* .50
432 Willy Taveras .15
433 *Ambiorix Burgos* .50
434 Andy Sisco .15
435 Denny Bautista .15
436 Mark Teahen .15
437 Ervin Santana .15
438 *Dennis Houlton* .50
439 *Philip Humber* 1.00
440 *Steve Schmoll* .50
441 J.J. Hardy .15
442 *Ambiorix Concepcion* .50
443 *Dae-Sung Koo* .50
444 Andy Phillips .15
445 Dan Meyer .15
446 Huston Street .15
447 *Keiichi Yabu* .50
448 *Jeff Niemann* 1.00
449 Jeremy Reed .15
450 Tony Blanco .15
451 Albert Pujols .75
452 Alex Rodriguez .75
453 Curt Schilling .40
454 Derek Jeter .75
455 Greg Maddux .50
456 Ichiro Suzuki .50
457 Ivan Rodriguez .25
458 Jeff Bagwell .25
459 Jim Thome .25
460 Ken Griffey Jr. .50
461 Manny Ramirez .40
462 Mike Mussina .25
463 Mike Piazza .40
464 Pedro Martinez .40
465 Rafael Palmeiro .25
466 Randy Johnson .40
467 Roger Clemens .75
468 Sammy Sosa .50
469 Todd Helton .25
470 Vladimir Guerrero .40
471 Vladimir Guerrero .25
472 Shawn Green .15
473 John Smoltz .15
474 Miguel Tejada .25
475 Curt Schilling .25
476 Mark Prior .40
477 Frank Thomas .25
478 Ken Griffey Jr. .50
479 C.C. Sabathia .15
480 Todd Helton .25
481 Ivan Rodriguez .25
482 Miguel Cabrera .40
483 Roger Clemens .50
484 Mike Sweeney .15
485 Eric Gagne .15
486 Ben Sheets .15
487 Johan Santana .25
488 Mike Piazza .40
489 Derek Jeter .50
490 Eric Chavez .15
491 Jim Thome .25
492 Craig Wilson .15
493 Jake Peavy .15
494 Jason Schmidt .15
495 Ichiro Suzuki .50
496 Albert Pujols .50
497 Carl Crawford .15
498 Mark Teixeira .25
499 Vernon Wells .15
500 Jose Vidro .15

Blue

Stars (301-500): 4X-6X
Production 150 Sets
Exclusive to Series 2

Gold

Stars (301-500): 4X-8X
Production 99 Sets
Exclusive to Series 2

Emerald

Stars (301-500): 10X-20X
Production 25 Sets
Exclusive to Series 2

Platinum

No Pricing
Production 5 Sets
Exclusive to Series 2

Retro

Retro: 2X-3X
One Retro Box per Hobby Case

Plates

No Pricing
Production One Set Per Color

American Flag

No Pricing
Production 15 sets

Game Jersey

NM/M
Common Jersey: 5.00
Inserted 1:8
JB Jeff Bagwell SP 8.00
CB Carlos Beltran SP 8.00
AB Adrian Beltre 5.00
LB Lance Berkman 5.00
HB Hank Blalock 5.00
MC Miguel Cabrera 8.00
EC Eric Chavez 5.00
EG Eric Gagne 5.00
TG Troy Glaus 5.00
KG Ken Griffey Jr. SP 15.00
VG Vladimir Guerrero 8.00
HE Todd Helton 8.00
TH Tim Hudson 5.00
HU Torii Hunter 5.00
DJ Derek Jeter 25.00
RJ Randy Johnson SP 10.00
CJ Chipper Jones 8.00
JK Jeff Kent 5.00
GM Greg Maddux SP 10.00
PM Pedro Martinez 8.00
MM Mark Mulder 5.00
DO David Ortiz SP 10.00
PI Mike Piazza 8.00
MP Mark Prior 8.00
AP Albert Pujols 20.00
MR Manny Ramirez SP 10.00
IR Ivan Rodriguez 8.00
SR Scott Rolen 8.00
JS Johan Santana SP 10.00
CS Curt Schilling 8.00
SM John Smoltz 8.00
AS Alfonso Soriano 8.00
SS Sammy Sosa 10.00
MT Mark Teixeira SP 8.00
TE Miguel Tejada 8.00
FT Frank Thomas 8.00
JT Jim Thome SP 8.00
KW Kerry Wood 8.00
DW David Wright 10.00

Game Patch

NM/M
Inserted 1:288
DJ Derek Jeter 75.00
CR Cal Ripken Jr. 75.00

Hall of Fame Plaques

NM/M
Complete Set (10): 40.00
Common Player: 3.00
Inserted 1:36
SP-16 Ernie Banks 4.00
SP-17 Yogi Berra 4.00
SP-18 Whitey Ford 3.00
SP-19 Bob Gibson 3.00
SP-20 Willie McCovey 3.00
SP-21 Stan Musial 6.00
SP-22 Nolan Ryan 12.00
SP-23 Mike Schmidt 8.00
SP-24 Tom Seaver 4.00
SP-25 Robin Yount 4.00

Lasting Impressions

No Pricing
Production One Set
One press plate per color

Marquee Attractions

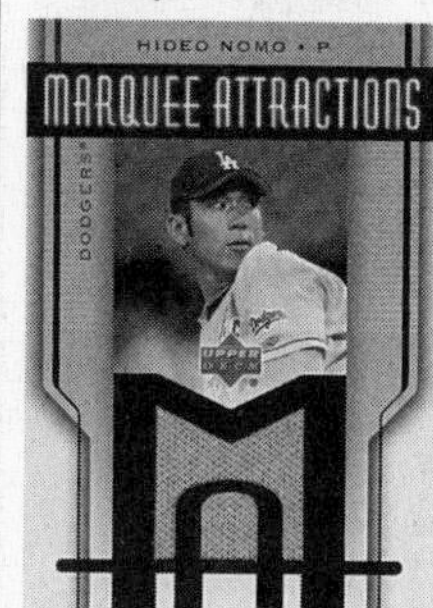

NM/M
Common Player: 4.00
Inserted 1:12
GA Garret Anderson 4.00
JB Jeff Bagwell 8.00
BE Josh Beckett 4.00
KB Kevin Brown 4.00
MC Miguel Cabrera 8.00
RC Roger Clemens 15.00
CD Carlos Delgado 4.00
AD Adam Dunn 8.00
EG Eric Gagne 6.00
JG Jason Giambi 4.00
BG Brian Giles 4.00
SG Shawn Green 4.00
KG Ken Griffey Jr. 12.00
VG Vladimir Guerrero 8.00
TH Todd Helton 8.00
HO Trevor Hoffman 4.00
DJ Derek Jeter 20.00
RJ Randy Johnson 10.00
AJ Andruw Jones 6.00
CJ Chipper Jones 8.00
GM Greg Maddux 10.00
PM Pedro Martinez 10.00
HM Hideki Matsui 30.00
KM Kazuo Matsui 8.00
JM Joe Mauer 8.00
HN Hideo Nomo 10.00
RO Roy Oswalt 4.00
PE Andy Pettitte 6.00
PI Mike Piazza 10.00
MP Mark Prior 8.00
AP Albert Pujols 15.00
IR Ivan Rodriguez 8.00
CS Curt Schilling 8.00
JS Jason Schmidt 6.00

SS	Sammy Sosa	12.00
IS	Ichiro Suzuki	25.00
MT	Miguel Tejada	6.00
JT	Jim Thome	8.00
BW	Billy Wagner	4.00
DW	Dontrelle Willis	4.00
PW	Preston Wilson	4.00
KW	Kerry Wood	8.00

Matinee Idols

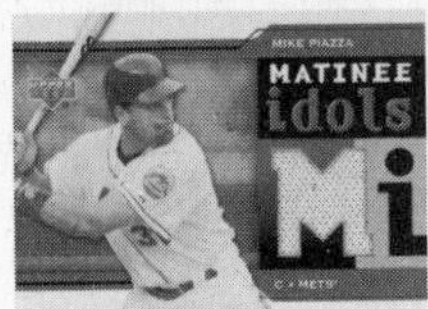

		NM/M
Common Player:		4.00
Inserted 1:12 Hobby		
JB	Jeff Bagwell	8.00
RB	Rocco Baldelli	4.00
BE	Josh Beckett	6.00
HB	Hank Blalock	8.00
BB	Bret Boone/SP	6.00
PB	Pat Burrell	6.00
SB	Sean Burroughs	4.00
EC	Eric Chavez	6.00
RC	Roger Clemens	15.00
CD	Carlos Delgado	4.00
JE	Jim Edmonds	6.00
JG	Jason Giambi	4.00
TG	Troy Glaus	4.00
KG	Ken Griffey Jr.	12.00
VG	Vladimir Guerrero	8.00
RH	Roy Halladay	4.00
TH	Todd Helton	8.00
HU	Torii Hunter	4.00
DJ	Derek Jeter	20.00
RJ	Randy Johnson	8.00
CJ	Chipper Jones	8.00
ML	Mike Lowell	4.00
MM	Mike Mussina	6.00
PI	Mike Piazza	10.00
MP	Mark Prior	8.00
CR	Cal Ripken Jr.	25.00
SR	Scott Rolen	8.00
NR	Nolan Ryan	25.00
CS	Curt Schilling	8.00
TS	Tom Seaver	8.00
GS	Gary Sheffield	6.00
SS	Sammy Sosa	12.00
MT	Mark Teixeira	6.00
JT	Jim Thome	8.00
BW	Billy Wagner	4.00
RW	Rickie Weeks	4.00
VW	Vernon Wells	4.00
DW	Dontrelle Willis	4.00
KW	Kerry Wood	8.00
BZ	Barry Zito	4.00

Milestone Materials

		NM/M
Common Jersey:		5.00
BA	Jeff Bagwell	8.00
JB	Jason Bay	5.00
CB	Carlos Beltran	8.00
BC	Bobby Crosby	5.00
EG	Eric Gagne	5.00
KG	Ken Griffey Jr.	15.00
VG	Vladimir Guerrero	8.00
RJ	Randy Johnson	8.00
GM	Greg Maddux	10.00
DO	David Ortiz	8.00
RP	Rafael Palmeiro	8.00
JP	Jake Peavy	8.00

AP	Albert Pujols	20.00
MR	Manny Ramirez	8.00
JS	Johan Santana	8.00
CS	Curt Schilling	8.00
MT	Mark Teixeira	5.00
TE	Miguel Tejada	8.00
JT	Jim Thome	8.00

Origins

		NM/M
Common Player:		4.00
Inserted 1:12 Hobby		
Inserted 1:24 Retail		
GA	Garret Anderson	4.00
CB	Carlos Beltran	10.00
AB	Adrian Beltre	6.00
LB	Lance Berkman	4.00
MC	Miguel Cabrera	8.00
RF	Rafael Furcal	4.00
EG	Eric Gagne	6.00
BG	Brian Giles	4.00
JG	Juan Gonzalez	8.00
LG	Luis Gonzalez	4.00
VG	Vladimir Guerrero	8.00
TH	Tim Hudson	4.00
AJ	Andruw Jones	6.00
JK	Jeff Kent	4.00
JL	Javy Lopez	4.00
GM	Greg Maddux	10.00
PM	Pedro Martinez	10.00
HM	Hideki Matsui	30.00
KM	Kazuo Matsui	8.00
MM	Mark Mulder	4.00
HN	Hideo Nomo	10.00
MO	Magglio Ordonez	4.00
RP	Rafael Palmeiro	8.00
PE	Jake Peavy	4.00
JP	Jorge Posada	4.00
AP	Albert Pujols	15.00
MR	Manny Ramirez	8.00
JR	Jose Reyes	4.00
IR	Ivan Rodriguez	8.00
JS	Jason Schmidt	4.00
RS	Richie Sexson	4.00
AS	Alfonso Soriano	8.00
SS	Sammy Sosa	12.00
IS	Ichiro Suzuki	25.00
MT	Miguel Tejada	6.00
BU	B.J. Upton	8.00
JV	Javier Vazquez	4.00
PW	Preston Wilson	4.00

Rewind to 1997 Jersey

		NM/M
Common Jersey:		
Inserted 1:288		
JB	Jeff Bagwell	25.00
WC	Will Clark	20.00
KG	Ken Griffey Jr.	40.00
VG	Vladimir Guerrero	25.00
TG	Tony Gwynn	30.00
DJ	Derek Jeter	40.00
RJ	Randy Johnson	25.00
AJ	Andruw Jones	20.00
CJ	Chipper Jones	30.00
GM	Greg Maddux	40.00
PM	Pedro Martinez	25.00
MP	Mike Piazza	30.00
MR	Manny Ramirez	30.00
CR	Cal Ripken Jr.	40.00
IR	Ivan Rodriguez	20.00
SR	Scott Rolen	25.00
CS	Curt Schilling	20.00
JS	John Smoltz	25.00
FT	Frank Thomas	25.00
JT	Jim Thome	25.00

Signature Stars

		NM/M
Common Player:		
Inserted 1:288 hobby		
CB	Carlos Beltran/SP	40.00
HB	Hank Blalock	25.00
MC	Miguel Cabrera	35.00
BC	Bobby Crosby	30.00
LF	Lew Ford	10.00
KG	Ken Griffey Jr.	80.00
JL	Javy Lopez	15.00
JM	Joe Mauer	20.00

OP	Odalis Perez	20.00
CR	Cal Ripken Jr./SP	180.00
BS	Ben Sheets	15.00
DW	Dontrelle Willis	20.00
KW	Kerry Wood	40.00
DY	Delmon Young	25.00

Super Patch - Logos

No Pricing
Cards are not serial numbered

World Series Heroes

		NM/M
Complete Set (45):		20.00
Common Player:		.25
Inserted 1:1 Retail		
WS-1	Garret Anderson	.50
WS-2	Troy Glaus	.50
WS-3	Vladimir Guerrero	1.00
WS-4	Andruw Jones	.50
WS-5	Chipper Jones	1.00
WS-6	Curt Schilling	1.00
WS-7	Keith Foulke	.25
WS-8	Manny Ramirez	.75
WS-9	Nomar Garciaparra	1.50
WS-10	Pedro Martinez	1.00
WS-11	Kerry Wood	1.00
WS-12	Mark Prior	1.00
WS-13	Sammy Sosa	2.00
WS-14	Frank Thomas	.75
WS-15	Magglio Ordonez	.25
WS-16	Dontrelle Willis	.25
WS-17	Josh Beckett	.50
WS-18	Miguel Cabrera	.75
WS-19	Jeff Bagwell	.75
WS-20	Lance Berkman	.25
WS-21	Roger Clemens	2.00
WS-22	Eric Gagne	.50
WS-23	Torii Hunter	.50
WS-24	Mike Piazza	1.50
WS-25	Alex Rodriguez	2.00
WS-26	Derek Jeter	2.00
WS-27	Gary Sheffield	.50
WS-28	Hideki Matsui	1.50
WS-29	Jason Giambi	.50
WS-30	Jorge Posada	.50
WS-31	Kevin Brown	.25
WS-32	Mariano Rivera	.50
WS-33	Mike Mussina	.50
WS-34	Eric Chavez	.25
WS-35	Mark Mulder	.25
WS-36	Tim Hudson	.25
WS-37	Billy Wagner	.25
WS-38	Jim Thome	.75
WS-39	Brian Giles	.25
WS-40	Jason Schmidt	.25
WS-41	Albert Pujols	2.00
WS-42	Scott Rolen	.75
WS-43	Alfonso Soriano	.75
WS-44	Hank Blalock	.75
WS-45	Mark Teixeira	.50

2004 Update Set

		NM/M
Complete Set (50):		10.00
Common Player:		.15
Inserted 1:Hobby Box		
541	Alex Rodriguez	1.50
542	Roger Clemens	1.50
543	Andy Pettitte	.25
544	Vladimir Guerrero	.75
545	David Wells	.15
546	Derek Lee	.25
547	Carlos Beltran	.50
548	Orlando Cabrera	.25
549	Paul LoDuca	.15
550	Dave Roberts	.15
551	Guillermo Mota	.15
552	Steve Finley	.15

553	Juan Encarnacion	.15
554	Larry Walker	.50
555	Ty Wigginton	.15
556	Doug Mientkiewicz	.15
557	Roberto Alomar	.40
558	B.J. Upton	.50
559	Brad Penny	.15
560	Hee Seop Choi	.15
561	David Wright	1.00
562	Nomar Garciaparra	1.00
563	Felix Rodriguez	.15
564	Victor Zambrano	.15
565	Kris Benson	.15
566	Aarom Baldiris	.15
567	Joey Gathright	.15
568	Charles Thomas	.15
569	Brian Dallimore	.15
570	Chris Oxspring	.15
571	Chris Shelton	.15
572	Dioner Navarro	.25
573	Edwardo Sierra	.15
574	Fernando Nieve	.15
575	Frank Francisco	.15
576	Jeff Bennett	.15
577	Justin Lehr	.15
578	John Gall	.15
579	Jorge Sequea	.15
580	Justin Germano	.15
581	Kazuhito Tadano	.15
582	Kevin Cave	.15
583	Jesse Crain	.15
584	Luis Gonzalez	.15
585	Mike Wuertz	.15
586	Orlando Rodriguez	.15
587	Phil Stockman	.15
588	Ramon Ramirez	.15
589	Roberto Novoa	.15
590	Scott Kazmir	1.50

2004 Update - Awesome Honors

		NM/M
Common Player:		8.00
1:12 '04 Update Set		
Production 75 Sets		
BE	Adrian Beltre	10.00
AB	Angel Berroa	8.00
KB	Kevin Brown	8.00
MC	Miguel Cabrera	15.00
RC	Roger Clemens	20.00
EG	Eric Gagne	12.00
BG	Brian Giles	8.00
DL	Derrek Lee	8.00
KM	Kazuo Matsui	20.00
JM	Joe Mauer	10.00
PE	Andy Pettitte	10.00
SP	Scott Podsednik	8.00
AP	Albert Pujols	25.00
IR	Ivan Rodriguez	12.00
SC	Curt Schilling	12.00
RS	Richie Sexson	8.00
GS	Gary Sheffield	8.00
AS	Alfonso Soriano	15.00
VA	Javier Vazquez	8.00

2004 Update - Authentic Stars

		NM/M
Common Player:		8.00
1:12 '04 Update Sets		
Production 75 Sets		
CB	Carlos Beltran	15.00
LB	Lance Berkman	8.00
JE	Jim Edmonds	8.00
RF	Rafael Furcal	8.00
HA	Roy Halladay	8.00
RH	Rich Harden	8.00
HU	Tim Hudson	8.00
DJ	Derek Jeter	35.00

AK Austin Kearns 8.00
HN Hideo Nomo 20.00
MO Maggilo Ordonez 8.00
OS Roy Oswalt 8.00
RP Rafael Palmeiro 12.00
MR Manny Ramirez 15.00
JR Jose Reyes 8.00
SR Scott Rolen 15.00
TE Miguel Tejada 8.00
JT Jim Thome 12.00
WE Brandon Webb 8.00
VW Vernon Wells 8.00
PW Preston Wilson 8.00
KW Kerry Wood 8.00

4,000-Strikeout Commemorative

NM/M

Production 4,000
Steve Carlton, Nolan Ryan, Roger Clemens, Randy Johnson 12.00

4,000 Strikeout Autographs

Production 50 sets
Quad Signature: No Pricing
Production 10

2005 UPPER DECK ARTIFACTS

NM/M

Complete Set (200):
Common Player (1-100): .25
Common (101-150): 2.00
Production 1,350
Common (151-200): 2.00
Production 1,999
Pack (4): 10.00
Box (10): 90.00
1 Adam Dunn .75
2 Adrian Beltre .75
3 Albert Pujols 3.00
4 Alex Rodriguez 2.50
5 Alfonso Soriano 1.00
6 Andruw Jones .50
7 Andy Pettitte .50
8 Aramis Ramirez .50
9 Aubrey Huff .25
10 Barry Larkin .50
11 Ben Sheets .50
12 Bernie Williams .50
13 Bobby Abreu .50
14 Brad Penny .25
15 Bret Boone .25
16 Brian Giles .25
17 Carl Crawford .25
18 Carl Pavano .50
19 Carlos Beltran .75
20 Carlos Delgado .75
21 Carlos Guillen .25
22 Carlos Lee .50
23 Carlos Zambrano .50
24 Chipper Jones 1.00
25 Craig Biggio .50
26 Craig Wilson .25
27 Curt Schilling 1.00
28 David Ortiz 1.00
29 Derek Jeter 3.00
30 Eric Chavez .50
31 Eric Gagne .50
32 Frank Thomas .75
33 Garret Anderson .50
34 Gary Sheffield .50
35 Greg Maddux 1.50
36 Hank Blalock .75
37 Hideki Matsui 2.00
38 Ichiro Suzuki 2.50
39 Ivan Rodriguez .75
40 J.D. Drew .50
41 Jake Peavy .50
42 Jason Kendall .25
43 Jason Schmidt .50
44 Jeff Bagwell .75
45 Jeff Kent .50
46 Jim Edmonds .50
47 Jim Thome 1.00
48 Joe Mauer .75
49 Johan Santana .75
50 John Smoltz .50
51 Jose Reyes .25
52 Jose Vidro .25
53 Josh Beckett .50
54 Ken Griffey Jr. 1.50
55 Kerry Wood 1.00
56 Kevin Brown .25
57 Lance Berkman .50
58 Larry Walker .50
59 Livan Hernandez .25
60 Luis Gonzalez .25
61 Lyle Overbay .25
62 Magglio Ordonez .25
63 Manny Ramirez 1.00
64 Mark Mulder .50
65 Mark Prior 1.00
66 Mark Teixeira .50
67 Melvin Mora .25
68 Michael Young .25
69 Miguel Cabrera 1.00
70 Miguel Tejada .75
71 Mike Lowell .25
72 Mike Mussina .50
73 Mike Piazza 1.50
74 Mike Sweeney .25
75 Nomar Garciaparra 2.00
76 Oliver Perez .25
77 Paul Konerko .25
78 Pedro Martinez 1.00
79 Preston Wilson .25
80 Rafael Furcal .25
81 Rafael Palmeiro .75
82 Randy Johnson 1.00
83 Richie Sexson .50
84 Roger Clemens 3.00
85 Roy Halladay .50
86 Roy Oswalt .50
87 Sammy Sosa 2.00
88 Scott Podsednik .25
89 Scott Rolen 1.00
90 Shawn Green .25
91 Steve Finley .25
92 Tim Hudson .50
93 Todd Helton .75
94 Tom Glavine .50
95 Torii Hunter .25
96 Travis Hafner .25
97 Troy Glaus .50
98 Vernon Wells .25
99 Victor Martinez .50
100 Vladimir Guerrero 1.00
101 Aaron Rowand 2.00
102 Adam LaRoche 2.00
103 Adrian Gonzalez 2.00
104 Alexis Rios 2.00
105 Angel Guzman 2.00
106 B.J. Upton 3.00
107 Bobby Crosby 3.00
108 Bobby Madritsch 2.00
109 Brandon Claussen 2.00
110 Bucky Jacobsen 2.00
111 Casey Kotchman 2.00
112 Chad Cordero 2.00
113 Chase Utley 2.00
114 Chris Burke 2.00
115 Dallas McPherson 4.00
116 Daniel Cabrera 2.00
117 David DeJesus 2.00
118 David Wright 6.00
119 Eddy Rodriguez 2.00
120 Edwin Jackson 2.00
121 Gabe Gross 2.00
122 Garrett Atkins 2.00
123 Gavin Floyd 2.00
124 Gerald Laird 2.00
125 Guillermo Quiroz 2.00
126 J.D. Closser 2.00
127 Jason Bay 4.00
128 Jason Dubois 2.00
129 Jason Lane 2.00
130 Jayson Werth 2.00
131 Jeff Francis 2.00
132 Jesse Crain 2.00
133 Joe Blanton 2.00
134 Joe Mauer 4.00
135 Jose Capellan 2.00
136 Kevin Youkilis 2.00
137 Khalil Greene 3.00
138 Laynce Nix 2.00
139 Nick Swisher 2.00
140 Oliver Perez 2.00
141 Rickie Weeks 2.00
142 Robb Quinlan 2.00
143 Roman Colon 2.00
144 Ryan Howard 4.00
145 Ryan Wagner 2.00
146 Scott Kazmir 4.00
147 Scott Proctor 2.00
148 Wily Mo Pena 2.00
149 Yhency Brazoban 2.00
150 Zack Greinke 2.00
151 Al Kaline 5.00
152 Babe Ruth 8.00
153 Billy Williams 2.00
154 Bob Feller 3.00
155 Bob Gibson 4.00
156 Bob Lemon 2.00
157 Bobby Doerr 2.00
158 Brooks Robinson 4.00
159 Cal Ripken Jr. 10.00
160 Christy Mathewson 4.00
161 Cy Young 5.00
162 Dizzy Dean 5.00
163 Don Drysdale 2.00
164 Eddie Mathews 4.00
165 Enos Slaughter 2.00
166 Ernie Banks 5.00
167 Fergie Jenkins 2.00
168 George Sisler 2.00
169 Harmon Killebrew 4.00
170 Honus Wagner 5.00
171 Jackie Robinson 5.00
172 Jimmie Foxx 4.00
173 Joe DiMaggio 6.00
174 Joe Morgan 2.00
175 Juan Marichal 2.00
176 Lou Brock 2.00
177 Lou Gehrig 6.00
178 Luis Aparicio 2.00
179 Mel Ott 4.00
180 Mickey Cochrane 2.00
181 Mickey Mantle 10.00
182 Mike Schmidt 6.00
183 Nolan Ryan 8.00
184 Pee Wee Reese 2.00
185 Phil Rizzuto 2.00
186 Ralph Kiner 2.00
187 Rogers Hornsby 3.00
188 Roy Campanella 3.00
189 Satchel Paige 4.00
190 Stan Musial 5.00
191 Rick Ferrell 2.00
192 Thurman Munson 5.00
193 Tom Seaver 4.00
194 Ty Cobb 6.00
195 Walter Johnson 5.00
196 Warren Spahn 4.00
197 Whitey Ford 4.00
198 Willie McCovey 3.00
199 Willie Stargell 3.00
200 Yogi Berra 4.00

Rainbow Blue

Blue (1-100): 3X-5X
Blue (101-200): 1X-2X
Production 100 sets

Rainbow Gold

Gold (1-100): 6X-10X
Gold (101-200): 2X-3X
Production 25 Sets

Rainbow Platinum

No Pricing
Production One Set

Rainbow Red

Red (1-100): 4X-8X
Red (101-200): 1.5X-3X
Production 50 Sets

AL/NL Artifacts

NM/M

Common Player:
Production 325 unless noted
Rainbow: .75X-1.5X
Production 99 Sets
BA Bobby Abreu Jsy 6.00
JB Jason Bay Jsy 6.00
CB Carlos Beltran Jsy 8.00
AB Adrian Beltre Jsy 6.00
BE Johnny Bench Jsy 10.00
YB Yogi Berra Pants 15.00
HB Hank Blalock Jsy 8.00
BB Bert Blyleven Jsy 6.00
WB Wade Boggs Jsy 8.00
GB George Brett Jsy 15.00
MC Miguel Cabrera Jsy 10.00
RCA Rod Carew Jsy 8.00
CA Steve Carlton Jsy 6.00
SC Sean Casey Jsy 4.00
OC Orlando Cepeda Jsy/185 8.00
EC Eric Chavez Jsy 4.00
WC Will Clark Jsy/100 10.00
RCN Roger Clemens Jsy 15.00
BC Bobby Crosby Jsy 6.00
AD Andre Dawson Jsy 6.00
BD Bobby Doerr Bat 6.00
BF Bob Feller Pants 10.00
EG Eric Gagne Jsy 8.00
BG Bob Gibson Pants 10.00
GI Brian Giles Jsy 4.00
MG Marcus Giles Jsy 4.00
DG Dwight Gooden Pants 6.00
MK Mark Grace Jsy/175 8.00
KG Ken Griffey Jr. Jsy 15.00
GR Ken Griffey Sr. Jsy 4.00
TG Tony Gwynn Jsy 10.00
TH Travis Hafner Jsy 4.00
RH Rich Harden Jsy 8.00
KHN Keith Hernandez Bat 4.00
KHA Kent Hrbek Jsy 4.00
AH Aubrey Huff Jsy 4.00
DJ Derek Jeter Jsy 20.00
RJ Randy Johnson Jsy 10.00
JK Jim Kaat Jsy 6.00
AK Al Kaline Jsy 10.00
GK George Kell Bat 6.00
HK Harmon Killebrew Jsy 10.00
RK Ralph Kiner Bat 6.00
DK Dave Kingman Bat 4.00
CK Casey Kotchman Jsy 4.00
DL Derrek Lee Jsy 6.00
ML Mike Lowell Jsy 4.00
SL Sparky Lyle Pants 4.00
FL Fred Lynn Bat 4.00
GM Greg Maddux Jsy/275 12.00
VM Victor Martinez Jsy 6.00
MA Don Mattingly Jsy 20.00
JM Joe Mauer Jsy 10.00
WM Willie McCovey Jsy 8.00
DMA Dallas McPherson Jsy 8.00
PM Paul Molitor Jsy 8.00
MM Mark Mulder Jsy 6.00
DMN Dale Murphy Jsy/150 8.00
GN Graig Nettles Jsy 4.00
PN Phil Niekro Jsy 4.00
LN Laynce Nix Jsy 4.00
DO David Ortiz Jsy 10.00
RO Roy Oswalt Jsy 4.00
AO Akinori Otsuka Jsy 4.00
JPA Jim Palmer Jsy 8.00
CP Corey Patterson Jsy 6.00
JPN Jake Peavy Jsy 6.00
BPN Brad Penny Jsy 4.00
RP Rico Petrocelli Pants 8.00
SP Scott Podsednik Jsy 4.00
BPA Boog Powell Jsy 6.00
MP Mark Prior Jsy 10.00
AP Albert Pujols Jsy 25.00
JRN Jose Reyes Jsy/250 8.00
JRA Jim Rice Jsy 8.00
CR Cal Ripken Jr. Jsy 25.00
BR Brooks Robinson Jsy 8.00
FR Frank Robinson Jsy 8.00
SR Scott Rolen Jsy 10.00
NR Nolan Ryan Jsy 25.00
JSA Johan Santana Jsy 10.00
JSN Jason Schmidt Jsy 6.00
MS Mike Schmidt Jsy 15.00
TS Tom Seaver Jsy 8.00
BS Ben Sheets Jsy 6.00
SM John Smoltz Jsy 8.00
SU Bruce Sutter Jsy 6.00
ST Shingo Takatsu Jsy 6.00
MT Mark Teixeira Jsy 8.00
BU B.J. Upton Jsy 6.00
RW Rickie Weeks Jsy 6.00
MW Maury Wills Jsy 6.00
KW Kerry Wood Jsy 8.00
DW David Wright Jsy 10.00
CY Carl Yastrzemski Jsy 15.00
MY Michael Young Jsy 6.00
RY Robin Yount Jsy 15.00
CZ Carlos Zambrano Jsy 6.00

AL/NL Artifacts Signatures

NM/M

Production 30 Sets
Rare Artifacts: No Pricing
Production One Set
BA Bobby Abreu Jsy Redemp.
JB Jason Bay Jsy 30.00
CB Carlos Beltran Jsy Redemp.
AB Adrian Beltre Jsy 30.00
BE Johnny Bench Jsy 65.00
YB Yogi Berra Pants 60.00
HB Hank Blalock Jsy 35.00
BB Bert Blyleven Jsy 30.00
WB Wade Boggs Jsy 50.00
GB George Brett Jsy 120.00
MC Miguel Cabrera Jsy 40.00
RCA Rod Carew Jsy 40.00
SC Sean Casey Jsy 30.00
CA Steve Carlton Jsy 40.00
OC Orlando Cepeda Jsy 35.00
EC Eric Chavez Jsy 30.00
WC Will Clark Jsy 50.00
RCN Roger Clemens Jsy Redemp. 100.00
BC Bobby Crosby Jsy Redemp.
AD Andre Dawson Jsy 30.00
BD Bobby Doerr Bat 35.00
BF Bob Feller Pants 40.00
EG Eric Gagne Jsy Redemp. 50.00
BG Bob Gibson Pants 50.00
GI Brian Giles Jsy 20.00
MG Marcus Giles Jsy 20.00
DG Dwight Gooden Pants 30.00
MK Mark Grace Jsy 50.00
KL Khalil Greene Jsy 50.00
KG Ken Griffey Jr. Jsy 120.00
GR Ken Griffey Sr. Jsy 25.00
TG Tony Gwynn Jsy 90.00
TH Travis Hafner Jsy 20.00
RH Rich Harden Jsy 40.00
KHN Keith Hernandez Bat 20.00
KHA Kent Hrbek Jsy 50.00
AH Aubrey Huff Jsy 25.00
DJ Derek Jeter Jsy 200.00
RJ Randy Johnson Jsy Redemp.
JK Jim Kaat Jsy 25.00
AK Al Kaline Jsy 50.00
GK George Kell Bat 30.00
HK Harmon Killebrew Jsy 60.00
RK Ralph Kiner Bat 50.00
DK Dave Kingman Bat 25.00
CK Casey Kotchman Jsy 25.00
DL Derrek Lee Jsy 40.00
ML Mike Lowell Jsy 20.00
SL Sparky Lyle Pants 20.00
FL Fred Lynn Bat 25.00
GM Greg Maddux Jsy Redemp. 150.00
VM Victor Martinez Jsy 30.00
MA Don Mattingly Jsy 100.00
JM Joe Mauer Jsy Redemp. 35.00
BM Bill Mazeroski Jsy Redemp. 30.00
WM Willie McCovey Jsy 50.00
DMA Dallas McPherson Jsy Redemp. 30.00
PM Paul Molitor Jsy 40.00
MM Mark Mulder Jsy
DMN Dale Murphy Jsy 35.00
GN Graig Nettles Jsy 35.00
PN Phil Niekro Jsy 25.00
LN Laynce Nix Jsy 20.00
DO David Ortiz Jsy 50.00
RO Roy Oswalt Jsy 25.00
AO Akinori Otsuka Jsy 40.00
JPA Jim Palmer Jsy 40.00
CP Corey Patterson Jsy Redemp. 30.00
JPN Jake Peavy Jsy 50.00
BPN Brad Penny Jsy 20.00
RP Rico Petrocelli Pants 25.00
SP Scott Podsednik Jsy 25.00
MP Mark Prior Jsy 70.00
AP Albert Pujols Jsy Redemp.
JRN Jose Reyes Jsy Redemp. 35.00
JRA Jim Rice Jsy 40.00
CR Cal Ripken Jr. Jsy 200.00
BR Brooks Robinson Jsy 50.00
FR Frank Robinson Jsy 40.00
SR Scott Rolen Jsy Redemp. 75.00
NR Nolan Ryan Jsy 125.00
JSA Johan Santana Jsy Redemp. 65.00
JSN Jason Schmidt Jsy 50.00
MS Mike Schmidt Jsy 60.00
TS Tom Seaver Jsy 50.00
BS Ben Sheets Jsy Redemp. 30.00
SM John Smoltz Jsy Redemp.
SU Bruce Sutter Jsy 20.00
ST Shingo Takatsu Jsy 50.00
MT Mark Teixeira Jsy 45.00
BU B.J. Upton Jsy 25.00
RW Rickie Weeks Jsy 25.00
MW Maury Wills Jsy 25.00
KW Kerry Wood Jsy 50.00
DW David Wright Jsy 60.00
CY Carl Yastrzemski Jsy 85.00
MY Michael Young Jsy Redemp. 25.00
RY Robin Yount Jsy 75.00
CZ Carlos Zambrano Jsy 35.00

Autofacts

NM/M

Production 15-699
Rainbow: No Pricing
Production One Set
JB Jason Bay/599 15.00
AB Adrian Beltre/75 Redemp. 25.00
BE Johnny Bench/15 75.00
HB Hank Blalock/25 35.00
GB George Brett/15 140.00
MI Miguel Cabrera/25 40.00
OC Orlando Cepeda/25 35.00
EC Eric Chavez/25 30.00
RC Rocky Colavito/75 75.00
BC Bobby Crosby/350 Redemp. 15.00
AD Andre Dawson/25 30.00
BF Bob Feller/25 40.00
SF Sid Fernandez/599 10.00
LD1 Lenny Dykstra Mets/599 10.00
LD2 Lenny Dykstra Phils/599 10.00
FR Bill Freehan/599 Redemp. 10.00
GI Marcus Giles/350 12.00
DG1 Dwight Gooden Mets/350 15.00
DG2 Dwight Gooden Yanks/350 15.00
GR Khalil Greene/599 25.00
JR Ken Griffey Jr./699 75.00
KG1 Ken Griffey Sr. Reds/699 10.00
KG2 Ken Griffey Sr. Yanks/699 10.00
TH Travis Hafner/599 12.00
RH Rich Harden/599 20.00
KH1 Keith Hernandez Mets/350 15.00
KH2 Keith Hernandez Cards/350 15.00
HO Ken Holtzman/599 10.00
BH Burt Hooton/599 8.00
HR Kent Hrbek/599 15.00
AH Aubrey Huff/350 8.00
DJ Derek Jeter/350 150.00
JK1 Jim Kaat Cards/458 15.00
JK2 Jim Kaat Twins/458 15.00
AK Al Kaline/15 80.00
DK Dave Kingman/75 25.00
CK Casey Kotchman/599 10.00
EK Ed Kranepool 12.00
JL Jim Lonborg/599 15.00
ML Mike Lowell/75 15.00
SL1 Sparky Lyle Sox/599 8.00
SL2 Sparky Lyle Yanks/599 8.00
FL Fred Lynn/25 25.00
VM Victor Martinez/599 15.00
JM Joe Mauer/25 Redemp. 30.00
MC Dallas McPherson/599 Redemp. 20.00
DM Dale Murphy/75 25.00
GN Graig Nettles/75 25.00
PN1 Phil Niekro Braves/75 20.00
PN2 Phil Niekro Yanks/75 20.00
LN Laynce Nix/599 10.00
RO Roy Oswalt/350 15.00
AO Akinori Otsuka/599 25.00
JP Jim Palmer/25 35.00
CP Corey Patterson/75 Redemp. 25.00
JA Jake Peavy/75 30.00
BP Brad Penny/599 15.00
OP Oliver Perez/350 20.00
PE Jim Perry/599 10.00
RP Rico Petrocelli/599 15.00
SP Scott Podsednik/75 15.00
PO Boog Powell/350 15.00
MP Mark Prior/15 75.00
CR Cal Ripken Jr./15 200.00
BR Brooks Robinson/25 50.00
NR Nolan Ryan/15 175.00
JS Johan Santana/350 Redemp. 40.00
BS Ben Sheets/75 Redemp. 20.00
SU Bruce Sutter/350 12.00
ST Shingo Takatsu/599 20.00
MT Mark Teixeira/25 40.00
LT Luis Tiant/75 20.00
BU B.J. Upton/599 15.00
RW Rickie Weeks/75 15.00
KW Kerry Wood/15 50.00
DW David Wright/599 40.00
MY Michael Young/599 Redemp. 12.00

Dual Artifacts

NM/M

Production 99 Sets
Rainbow: 1X-2X
Production 25 Sets
AB Bobby Abreu Jsy, Carlos Beltran Jsy 15.00
AD Adrian Beltre Jsy, Dallas McPherson Jsy 15.00
AG Bobby Abreu Jsy, Ken Griffey Jr. Jsy 15.00
BB George Brett Jsy, Wade Boggs Jsy 20.00
BC Adrian Beltre Jsy, Eric Chavez Jsy 8.00
BD Bob Gibson Pants, Dwight Gooden Pants 8.00
BE Bobby Crosby Jsy, Eric Chavez Jsy 10.00
BJ Brooks Robinson Jsy, Jim Palmer Jsy 20.00
BK Jason Bay Jsy, Ralph Kiner Bat 10.00
BM Brian Giles Jsy, Marcus Giles Jsy 8.00
BN Hank Blalock Jsy, Laynce Nix Jsy 8.00
BP Carlos Beltran Jsy, Corey Patterson Jsy 12.00
BR Ernie Banks Pants, Frank Robinson Jsy 20.00
BS Ben Sheets Jsy, Scott Podsednik Jsy 8.00
CB Jason Bay Jsy, Bobby Crosby Jsy 8.00
CC Miguel Cabrera Jsy, Orlando Cepeda Jsy 12.00
CG Dwight Gooden Pants, Gary Carter Jsy 10.00
CH Sean Casey Jsy, Travis Hafner Jsy 8.00
CK Harmon Killebrew Jsy, Rod Carew Jsy 25.00
CL Miguel Cabrera Jsy, Mike Lowell Jsy 10.00
CM Will Clark Jsy, Willie McCovey Jsy/56 25.00
CN Eric Chavez Jsy, Graig Nettles Jsy 8.00
CO Roger Clemens Jsy, Roy Oswalt Jsy 15.00
CR Bobby Crosby Jsy, Cal Ripken Jr. Jsy 40.00
DC Andre Dawson Jsy, Orlando Cepeda Jsy 10.00
DK Bobby Doerr Bat, George Kell Bat 10.00
FB Carlton Fisk Jsy, Johnny Bench Jsy 20.00
FW Bob Feller Pants, Kerry Wood Jsy 15.00
GB Brian Giles Jsy, Jason Bay Jsy 8.00
GC Ken Griffey Jr. Jsy, Sean Casey Jsy 15.00
GG Ken Griffey Sr. Jsy, Ken Griffey Jr. Jsy 15.00
GK Ken Griffey Jr. Jsy, Ralph Kiner Bat 20.00
GL Eric Gagne Jsy, Sparky Lyle Pants 10.00
GS Dwight Gooden Pants, Tom Seaver Jsy 15.00
HC Bobby Crosby Jsy, Rich Harden Jsy 8.00
HG Keith Hernandez Bat, Mark Grace Jsy 10.00
HH Aubrey Huff Jsy, Travis Hafner Jsy 8.00
HM Travis Hafner Jsy, Victor Martinez Jsy 8.00
HU Aubrey Huff Jsy, B.J. Upton Jsy 10.00
HW Harmon Killebrew Jsy, Willie McCovey Jsy/44 25.00
JG Derek Jeter Jsy, Khalil Greene Jsy 35.00
JJ Joe Mauer Jsy, Johan Santana Jsy 15.00
JR Jim Rice Jsy, Rico Petrocelli Pants 8.00
JW Derek Jeter Jsy, Maury Wills Jsy 35.00
JY Johnny Bench Jsy, Yogi Berra Pants 25.00
KB Jim Kaat Jsy, Bert Blyleven Jsy 10.00
KC Jim Kaat Jsy, Steve Carlton Jsy 10.00
KD Keith Hernandez Bat, Don Mattingly Jsy 20.00
KK Al Kaline Jsy, Ralph Kiner Bat 15.00
KM Al Kaline Jsy, Dale Murphy Jsy 15.00
KN Jim Kaat Jsy, Phil Niekro Jsy 10.00
LC Derrek Lee Jsy, Sean Casey Jsy 10.00
LG Derrek Lee Jsy, Mark Grace Jsy 10.00
LP Fred Lynn Bat, Rico Petrocelli Pants 10.00
LR Fred Lynn Bat, Jim Rice Jsy 10.00
MC Don Mattingly Jsy, Will Clark Jsy 20.00
MD Bill Mazeroski Jsy, Bobby Doerr Bat 10.00
MH Mark Mulder Jsy, Rich Harden Jsy 10.00
MK Bill Mazeroski Jsy, Ralph Kiner Bat 20.00
MM Joe Mauer Jsy, Victor Martinez Jsy 8.00
MS Dale Murphy Jsy, Mike Schmidt Jsy 20.00
MW Paul Molitor Jsy, Rickie Weeks Jsy 15.00
NL Graig Nettles Jsy, Sparky Lyle Pants 15.00
NT Laynce Nix Jsy, Mark Teixeira Jsy 10.00
NY Laynce Nix Jsy, Michael Young Jsy 10.00
OF David Ortiz Jsy, Carlton Fisk Jsy 20.00
OG Akinori Otsuka Jsy, Khalil Greene Jsy 15.00
OP Akinori Otsuka Jsy, Jake Peavy Jsy 15.00
OT Akinori Otsuka Jsy, Shingo Takatsu Jsy 20.00
PD Andre Dawson Jsy, Corey Patterson Jsy 15.00
PG Brad Penny Jsy, Eric Gagne Jsy 10.00
PH Jake Peavy Jsy, Rich Harden Jsy 12.00
PP Boog Powell Jsy, Jim Palmer Jsy 15.00
PR Boog Powell Jsy, Brooks Robinson Jsy 20.00
PS Brad Penny Jsy, Jason Schmidt Jsy 8.00
RB Ernie Banks Pants, Cal Ripken Jr. Jsy 40.00
RC Nolan Ryan Jsy, Steve Carlton Jsy 30.00
RJ Jose Reyes Jsy, Rickie Weeks Jsy 8.00
RP Frank Robinson Jsy, Boog Powell Jsy 25.00
RR Frank Robinson Jsy, Brooks Robinson Jsy 25.00
RW David Wright Jsy, Scott Rolen Jsy 15.00

SB Bert Blyleven Jsy, Johan Santana Jsy 15.00
SC Johan Santana Jsy, Roger Clemens Jsy 20.00
SF Ben Sheets Jsy, Bob Feller Pants 15.00
SG Bruce Sutter Jsy, Eric Gagne Jsy 15.00
SM Jason Schmidt Jsy, Mark Mulder Jsy 10.00
SO Ben Sheets Jsy, Roy Oswalt Jsy 10.00
SP Ben Sheets Jsy, Brad Penny Jsy 10.00
TH Mark Teixeira Jsy, Travis Hafner Jsy 10.00
TL Shingo Takatsu Jsy, Sparky Lyle Pants 10.00
TY Mark Teixeira Jsy, Michael Young Jsy 10.00
UJ B.J. Upton Jsy, Derek Jeter Jsy 30.00
WL David Wright Jsy, Mike Lowell Jsy 10.00
WR David Wright Jsy, Jose Reyes Jsy 10.00
YM Robin Yount Jsy, Paul Molitor Jsy 25.00
YP Carl Yastrzemski Jsy, Rico Petrocelli Pants 15.00
ZM Carlos Zambrano Jsy, Greg Maddux Jsy 15.00
ZP Carlos Zambrano Jsy, Mark Prior Jsy 15.00
ZW Carlos Zambrano Jsy, Kerry Wood Jsy 20.00

Dual Artifacts Bat

NM/M

Production 25 Sets
BC Josh Beckett, Miguel Cabrera 20.00
BW Josh Beckett, Kerry Wood 20.00
DR Carlos Delgado, Manny Ramirez 20.00
GS Ken Griffey Sr., Ichiro Suzuki 70.00
JP Derek Jeter, Mike Piazza 60.00
JR Derek Jeter, Manny Ramirez 70.00
RJ Cal Ripken Jr., Derek Jeter 100.00
RT Cal Ripken Jr., Miguel Tejada 60.00
SG Ichiro Suzuki, Vladimir Guerrero 60.00
WP Kerry Wood, Mark Prior 30.00

Dual Artifacts Signatures

No Pricing
Production 10 Sets

MLB Apparel

NM/M

Production 325 unless noted
Rainbow: 1X-2X
Production 99 Sets
BA Bobby Abreu Jsy 6.00
GA Garret Anderson Jsy 6.00
JB Jason Bay Jsy 6.00
CB Carlos Beltran Jsy 8.00
AB Adrian Beltre Jsy 6.00
BE Johnny Bench Jsy 10.00
YB Yogi Berra Pants 15.00
HB Hank Blalock Jsy 8.00
BB Bert Blyleven Jsy/150 8.00
WB Wade Boggs Jsy 8.00
BO Bret Boone Jsy 4.00
GB George Brett Jsy 15.00
MI Miguel Cabrera Jsy 10.00
RC Rod Carew Jsy 8.00
CA Steve Carlton Jsy 6.00
GC Gary Carter Jsy 8.00
SC Sean Casey Jsy 4.00
OC Orlando Cepeda Jsy 8.00
EC Eric Chavez Jsy 4.00
WC Will Clark Jsy/100 10.00
CL Roger Clemens Jsy 15.00
BC Bobby Crosby Jsy 6.00
AD Andre Dawson Jsy 6.00
BF Bob Feller Pants 10.00
CF Carlton Fisk R. Sox Jsy/175 10.00
CF1 Carlton Fisk W. Sox Jsy/175 10.00
EG Eric Gagne Jsy 8.00
BG Bob Gibson Pants 10.00
GI Brian Giles Jsy 4.00
GS Marcus Giles Jsy 4.00
DG Dwight Gooden Pants 6.00
MK Mark Grace Jsy/175 8.00
KL Khalil Greene Jsy 8.00
KG Ken Griffey Jr. Jsy 15.00
GR Ken Griffey Sr. Jsy 4.00
TG Tony Gwynn Jsy 10.00
TH Travis Hafner Jsy 4.00
RH Rich Harden Jsy 8.00
KH Kent Hrbek Jsy 4.00
HU Tim Hudson Jsy 6.00
AH Aubrey Huff Jsy 4.00
TO Torii Hunter Jsy 4.00
DJ Derek Jeter Jsy 20.00
JJ Jacque Jones Jsy 4.00
JK Jim Kaat Jsy 6.00
AK Al Kaline Jsy 10.00
HK Harmon Killebrew Jsy 10.00
CK Casey Kotchman Jsy 4.00
DL Derrek Lee Jsy 6.00
ML Mike Lowell Jsy 4.00
SL Sparky Lyle Pants 4.00
VM Victor Martinez Jsy 6.00
MA Don Mattingly Jsy 20.00
JM Joe Mauer Jsy 10.00
BM Bill Mazeroski Jsy/100 12.00
WM Willie McCovey Jsy 8.00
MC Dallas McPherson Jsy 8.00
PM Paul Molitor Jsy 8.00
MM Mark Mulder Jsy 6.00
DM Dale Murphy Jsy/150 8.00
GN Graig Nettles Jsy 4.00
PN Phil Niekro Jsy 4.00
LN Laynce Nix Jsy 4.00
DO David Ortiz Jsy 10.00
RO Roy Oswalt Jsy 4.00
AO Akinori Otsuka Jsy 4.00
PA Jim Palmer Jsy 8.00
CP Corey Patterson Jsy 6.00
JP Jake Peavy Jsy 6.00
PE Brad Penny Jsy 4.00
RP Rico Petrocelli Pants 8.00
SP Scott Podsednik Jsy 4.00
BP Boog Powell Jsy 6.00
MP Mark Prior Jsy 10.00
RE Jose Reyes Jsy 8.00
JR Jim Rice Jsy 8.00
CR Cal Ripken Jr. Jsy 25.00
BR Brooks Robinson Jsy 8.00
FR Frank Robinson Jsy 8.00
SR Scott Rolen Jsy 10.00
NR Nolan Ryan Jsy 25.00
SA Johan Santana Jsy 10.00
JS Jason Schmidt Jsy 6.00
MS Mike Schmidt Jsy 15.00
TS Tom Seaver Jsy/300 8.00
BS Ben Sheets Jsy 6.00
SM John Smoltz Jsy 8.00
SU Bruce Sutter Jsy 6.00
ST Shingo Takatsu Jsy 6.00
MT Mark Teixeira Jsy 8.00
BU B.J. Upton Jsy 6.00
JV Jose Vidro Jsy 4.00
RW Rickie Weeks Jsy 6.00
MW Maury Wills Jsy 6.00
KW Kerry Wood Jsy 8.00
DW David Wright Jsy 10.00
CY Carl Yastrzemski Jsy 15.00
MY Michael Young Jsy 6.00
RY Robin Yount Jsy 15.00
CZ Carlos Zambrano Jsy 6.00

MLB Apparel Autographs

NM/M

Production 30 Sets
Rare: No Pricing
Production One Set
JB Jason Bay Jsy 30.00
AB Adrian Beltre Jsy 30.00
BE Johnny Bench Jsy 65.00
YB Yogi Berra Pants 60.00
HB Hank Blalock Jsy 35.00
BB Bert Blyleven Jsy 30.00
WB Wade Boggs Jsy 50.00
GB George Brett Jsy 120.00
MI Miguel Cabrera Jsy 40.00
RC Rod Carew Jsy 40.00
CA Steve Carlton Jsy 40.00
GC Gary Carter Jsy 35.00
SC Sean Casey Jsy 30.00
OC Orlando Cepeda Jsy 35.00
EC Eric Chavez Jsy Redemp. 30.00
WC Will Clark Jsy 50.00
CL Roger Clemens Jsy Redemp. 100.00
AD Andre Dawson Jsy 30.00
BF Bob Feller Pants 40.00
CF Carlton Fisk R. Sox Jsy 40.00
CF1 Carlton Fisk W. Sox Jsy 40.00
EG Eric Gagne Jsy 50.00
BG Bob Gibson Pants 50.00
GI Brian Giles Jsy 20.00
GS Marcus Giles Jsy 20.00
DG Dwight Gooden Pants 30.00
MK Mark Grace Jsy 50.00
KL Khalil Greene Jsy 50.00
KG Ken Griffey Jr. Jsy 120.00
GR Ken Griffey Sr. Jsy 25.00
TG Tony Gwynn Jsy 90.00
TH Travis Hafner Jsy 20.00
RH Rich Harden Jsy 40.00
KH Kent Hrbek Jsy 50.00
HU Tim Hudson Jsy 40.00
AH Aubrey Huff Jsy 25.00
DJ Derek Jeter Jsy 200.00
JJ Jacque Jones Jsy 20.00
JK Jim Kaat Jsy 25.00
AK Al Kaline Jsy 50.00
HK Harmon Killebrew Jsy 60.00
CK Casey Kotchman Jsy 25.00
DL Derrek Lee Jsy 40.00
ML Mike Lowell Jsy 20.00
SL Sparky Lyle Pants 20.00
VM Victor Martinez Jsy 30.00
MA Don Mattingly Jsy 100.00
JM Joe Mauer Jsy Redemp. 35.00
BM Bill Mazeroski Jsy 30.00
WM Willie McCovey Jsy 50.00
MC Dallas McPherson Jsy Redemp. 30.00
PM Paul Molitor Jsy 40.00
DM Dale Murphy Jsy 35.00
GN Graig Nettles Jsy 35.00
PN Phil Niekro Jsy 25.00
LN Laynce Nix Jsy 20.00
DO David Ortiz Jsy 50.00
RO Roy Oswalt Jsy 25.00
AO Akinori Otsuka Jsy 40.00
PA Jim Palmer Jsy 40.00
CP Corey Patterson Jsy Redemp. 30.00
JP Jake Peavy Jsy 50.00
PE Brad Penny Jsy 20.00
RP Rico Petrocelli Pants 25.00
SP Scott Podsednik Jsy 25.00
BP Boog Powell Jsy 25.00
MP Mark Prior Jsy 70.00
RE Jose Reyes Jsy Redemp. 35.00
JR Jim Rice Jsy 40.00
CR Cal Ripken Jr. Jsy 200.00
BR Brooks Robinson Jsy 50.00
FR Frank Robinson Jsy 40.00
SR Scott Rolen Jsy Redemp. 75.00
NR Nolan Ryan Jsy 125.00
SA Johan Santana Jsy Redemp. 65.00
JS Jason Schmidt Jsy 50.00
MS Mike Schmidt Jsy 60.00
TS Tom Seaver Jsy 50.00
BS Ben Sheets Jsy Redemp. 30.00
SU Bruce Sutter Jsy 20.00
ST Shingo Takatsu Jsy 50.00
MT Mark Teixeira Jsy 45.00
BU B.J. Upton Jsy 25.00
JV Jose Vidro Jsy 20.00
RW Rickie Weeks Jsy 25.00
MW Maury Wills Jsy 25.00
KW Kerry Wood Jsy 50.00
DW David Wright Jsy 60.00
CY Carl Yastrzemski Jsy 85.00
MY Michael Young Jsy Redemp. 25.00
RY Robin Yount 75.00
CZ Carlos Zambrano Jsy 35.00

Patches

NM/M

Production 50 unless noted
BA Bobby Abreu 15.00
GA Garret Anderson 15.00
JB Jason Bay 20.00
CB Carlos Beltran 20.00
AB Adrian Beltre 20.00
BE Johnny Bench 25.00
HB Hank Blalock 20.00
BB Bert Blyleven 20.00
WB Wade Boggs 20.00
BO Bret Boone 12.00
GB George Brett 40.00
MI Miguel Cabrera 25.00
RC Rod Carew 25.00
CA Steve Carlton/30 25.00
GC Gary Carter 30.00
SC Sean Casey 12.00
EC Eric Chavez 15.00
WC Will Clark/20 50.00
CL Roger Clemens 30.00
BC Bobby Crosby 20.00
AD Andre Dawson 20.00
EG Eric Gagne 20.00
GI Brian Giles 12.00
GS Marcus Giles 12.00
DG Dwight Gooden 20.00
MK Mark Grace 35.00
KL Khalil Greene 25.00
KG Ken Griffey Jr. 40.00
GR Ken Griffey Sr. 12.00
TG Tony Gwynn 25.00
TH Travis Hafner 15.00
RH Rich Harden 20.00
KH Kent Hrbek 35.00
HU Tim Hudson 20.00
AH Aubrey Huff 12.00
TO Torii Hunter 15.00
DJ Derek Jeter 65.00
RJ Randy Johnson 25.00
JJ Jacque Jones 15.00
JK Jim Kaat 20.00
HK Harmon Killebrew 40.00
CK Casey Kotchman 20.00
DL Derrek Lee 15.00
ML Mike Lowell 12.00
GM Greg Maddux 35.00
VM Victor Martinez 15.00
MA Don Mattingly 40.00
JM Joe Mauer 30.00
WM Willie McCovey 25.00
MC Dallas McPherson 20.00
MM Mark Mulder 20.00
DM Dale Murphy 25.00
GN Graig Nettles 20.00
PN Phil Niekro 20.00
LN Laynce Nix 12.00
DO David Ortiz 25.00
RO Roy Oswalt 15.00
AO Akinori Otsuka 25.00
PA Jim Palmer 20.00
CP Corey Patterson 25.00
JP Jake Peavy 20.00
PE Brad Penny 12.00
SP Scott Podsednik 12.00
BP Boog Powell 20.00
MP Mark Prior 25.00
RE Jose Reyes 20.00
CR Cal Ripken Jr. 60.00
BR Brooks Robinson/35 40.00
FR Frank Robinson 20.00
SR Scott Rolen 25.00
NR Nolan Ryan 50.00
SA Johan Santana 25.00
JS Jason Schmidt 25.00
MS Mike Schmidt 30.00
BS Ben Sheets 20.00
SM John Smoltz 30.00
SU Bruce Sutter 15.00
ST Shingo Takatsu 20.00
MT Mark Teixeira 20.00
BU B.J. Upton 20.00
JV Jose Vidro 12.00
RW Rickie Weeks 20.00
MW Maury Wills/20 20.00
KW Kerry Wood 25.00
DW David Wright 35.00
CY Carl Yastrzemski 40.00
MY Michael Young 15.00
RY Robin Yount 30.00
CZ Carlos Zambrano 25.00

Signature Patches

No Pricing
Production 10 unless noted

2005 UPPER DECK BASEBALL HEROES

		NM/M
Complete Set (200):		
Common (1-100):		2.00
Common (101-200):		2.00
Production 575		
Tin (8):		50.00
1	Bob Feller	3.00
2	Bob Feller	3.00
3	Bob Feller	3.00
4	Bob Feller	3.00
5	Bob Feller	3.00
6	Brooks Robinson	3.00
7	Brooks Robinson	3.00
8	Brooks Robinson	3.00
9	Brooks Robinson	3.00
10	Brooks Robinson	3.00
11	Cal Ripken Jr.	8.00
12	Cal Ripken Jr.	8.00
13	Cal Ripken Jr.	8.00
14	Cal Ripken Jr.	8.00
15	Cal Ripken Jr.	8.00
16	Carl Yastrzemski	5.00
17	Carl Yastrzemski	5.00
18	Carl Yastrzemski	5.00
19	Carl Yastrzemski	5.00
20	Carl Yastrzemski	5.00
21	Don Mattingly	6.00
22	Don Mattingly	6.00
23	Don Mattingly	6.00
24	Don Mattingly	6.00
25	Don Mattingly	6.00
26	Tom Seaver	3.00
27	Tom Seaver	3.00
28	Tom Seaver	3.00
29	Tom Seaver	3.00
30	Tom Seaver	3.00
31	Harmon Killebrew	3.00
32	Harmon Killebrew	3.00
33	Harmon Killebrew	3.00
34	Harmon Killebrew	3.00
35	Harmon Killebrew	3.00
36	Jim Palmer	2.00
37	Jim Palmer	2.00
38	Jim Palmer	2.00
39	Jim Palmer	2.00
40	Jim Palmer	2.00
41	Mike Schmidt	6.00
42	Mike Schmidt	6.00
43	Mike Schmidt	6.00
44	Mike Schmidt	6.00
45	Mike Schmidt	6.00
46	Ozzie Smith	4.00
47	Ozzie Smith	4.00
48	Ozzie Smith	4.00
49	Ozzie Smith	4.00
50	Ozzie Smith	4.00
51	Paul Molitor	3.00
52	Paul Molitor	3.00
53	Paul Molitor	3.00
54	Paul Molitor	3.00
55	Paul Molitor	3.00
56	Al Kaline	3.00
57	Al Kaline	3.00
58	Al Kaline	3.00
59	Al Kaline	3.00
60	Al Kaline	3.00
61	Robin Yount	4.00
62	Robin Yount	4.00
63	Robin Yount	4.00
64	Robin Yount	4.00
65	Robin Yount	4.00
66	Ryne Sandberg	4.00
67	Ryne Sandberg	4.00
68	Ryne Sandberg	4.00
69	Ryne Sandberg	4.00
70	Ryne Sandberg	4.00
71	Stan Musial	5.00
72	Stan Musial	5.00
73	Stan Musial	5.00
74	Stan Musial	5.00
75	Stan Musial	5.00
76	Steve Carlton	2.00
77	Steve Carlton	2.00
78	Steve Carlton	2.00
79	Steve Carlton	2.00
80	Steve Carlton	2.00
81	Tony Gwynn	3.00
82	Tony Gwynn	3.00
83	Tony Gwynn	3.00
84	Tony Gwynn	3.00
85	Tony Gwynn	3.00
86	Wade Boggs	3.00
87	Wade Boggs	3.00
88	Wade Boggs	3.00
89	Wade Boggs	3.00
90	Wade Boggs	3.00
91	Will Clark	3.00
92	Will Clark	3.00
93	Will Clark	3.00
94	Will Clark	3.00
95	Will Clark	3.00
96	Yogi Berra	4.00
97	Yogi Berra	4.00
98	Yogi Berra	4.00
99	Yogi Berra	4.00
100	Yogi Berra	4.00
101	Babe Ruth	8.00
102	Babe Ruth	8.00
103	Babe Ruth	8.00
104	Babe Ruth	8.00
105	Babe Ruth	8.00
106	Roger Maris	6.00
107	Roger Maris	6.00
108	Roger Maris	6.00
109	Roger Maris	6.00
110	Roger Maris	6.00
111	Don Drysdale	2.00
112	Don Drysdale	2.00
113	Don Drysdale	2.00
114	Don Drysdale	2.00
115	Don Drysdale	2.00
116	Eddie Mathews	4.00
117	Eddie Mathews	4.00
118	Eddie Mathews	4.00
119	Eddie Mathews	4.00
120	Eddie Mathews	4.00
121	Honus Wagner	6.00
122	Honus Wagner	6.00
123	Honus Wagner	6.00
124	Honus Wagner	6.00
125	Honus Wagner	6.00
126	Jackie Robinson	5.00
127	Jackie Robinson	5.00
128	Jackie Robinson	5.00
129	Jackie Robinson	5.00
130	Jackie Robinson	5.00
131	Jimmie Foxx	5.00
132	Jimmie Foxx	5.00
133	Jimmie Foxx	5.00
134	Jimmie Foxx	5.00
135	Jimmie Foxx	5.00
136	Joe DiMaggio	6.00
137	Joe DiMaggio	6.00
138	Joe DiMaggio	6.00
139	Joe DiMaggio	6.00
140	Joe DiMaggio	6.00
141	Johnny Mize	4.00
142	Johnny Mize	4.00
143	Johnny Mize	4.00
144	Johnny Mize	4.00
145	Johnny Mize	4.00
146	Lefty Grove	3.00
147	Lefty Grove	3.00
148	Lefty Grove	3.00
149	Lefty Grove	3.00
150	Lefty Grove	3.00
151	Lou Gehrig	6.00
152	Lou Gehrig	6.00
153	Lou Gehrig	6.00
154	Lou Gehrig	6.00
155	Lou Gehrig	6.00
156	Mel Ott	4.00
157	Mel Ott	4.00
158	Mel Ott	4.00
159	Mel Ott	4.00
160	Mel Ott	4.00
161	Mickey Mantle	12.00
162	Mickey Mantle	12.00
163	Mickey Mantle	12.00
164	Mickey Mantle	12.00
165	Mickey Mantle	12.00
166	Roberto Clemente	8.00
167	Roberto Clemente	8.00
168	Roberto Clemente	8.00
169	Roberto Clemente	8.00
170	Roberto Clemente	8.00
171	Rogers Hornsby	6.00
172	Rogers Hornsby	6.00
173	Rogers Hornsby	6.00
174	*Rogers Hornsby*	6.00
175	*Rogers Hornsby*	6.00
176	Roy Campanella	3.00
177	Roy Campanella	3.00
178	Roy Campanella	3.00
179	Roy Campanella	3.00
180	Roy Campanella	3.00
181	Satchel Paige	6.00
182	Satchel Paige	6.00
183	Satchel Paige	6.00
184	Satchel Paige	6.00
185	Satchel Paige	6.00
186	Ted Williams	8.00
187	Ted Williams	8.00
188	Ted Williams	8.00
189	Ted Williams	8.00
190	Ted Williams	8.00
191	Thurman Munson	5.00
192	Thurman Munson	5.00
193	Thurman Munson	5.00
194	Thurman Munson	5.00
195	Thurman Munson	5.00
196	Ty Cobb	5.00
197	Ty Cobb	5.00
198	Ty Cobb	5.00
199	Ty Cobb	5.00
200	Ty Cobb	5.00

Blue

No Pricing
Production 10 sets

Emerald

Emerald (1-100): 1-1.5X
Emerald (101-200): 1-1.5X
Production 199 sets

Gold

No Pricing
Production one set

Red

Red (1-200): 1-2X
Production 75 sets

Baseball Heroes Jeter

		NM/M
Complete Set (9):		25.00
Common Jeter:		3.00
Inserted 1:6		
91	Derek Jeter	3.00
92	Derek Jeter	3.00
93	Derek Jeter	3.00
94	Derek Jeter	3.00
95	Derek Jeter	3.00
96	Derek Jeter	3.00
97	Derek Jeter	3.00
98	Derek Jeter	3.00
99	Derek Jeter	3.00
	Derek Jeter	3.00

Baseball Heroes Jeter Jersey

No Pricing
Production 75 Sets

Baseball Heroes Jeter Signature

No Pricing
Production 2 Sets

Memorabilia

No Pricing
Production 10 Sets

Memorabilia Emerald

		NM/M
Production 99 Sets		
Blue:		1X
Production 99 Sets		
Bronze:		1X-1.5X
Production 50 Sets		
Gold:		No Pricing
Production 1 Set		
Red:		1X
Production 99 Sets		
Silver:		No Pricing
Production 15 Sets		
1	Bob Feller	10.00
2	Bob Feller	10.00
3	Bob Feller	10.00
4	Bob Feller	10.00
5	Bob Feller	10.00
6	Brooks Robinson	10.00
7	Brooks Robinson	10.00
8	Brooks Robinson	10.00
9	Brooks Robinson	10.00
10	Brooks Robinson	10.00
11	Cal Ripken Jr.	25.00
12	Cal Ripken Jr.	25.00
13	Cal Ripken Jr.	25.00
14	Cal Ripken Jr.	25.00
15	Cal Ripken Jr.	25.00
16	Carl Yastrzemski	15.00
17	Carl Yastrzemski	15.00
18	Carl Yastrzemski	15.00
19	Carl Yastrzemski	15.00
20	Carl Yastrzemski	15.00
21	Don Mattingly	20.00
22	Don Mattingly	20.00
23	Don Mattingly	20.00
24	Don Mattingly	20.00
25	Don Mattingly	20.00
26	Tom Seaver	10.00
27	Tom Seaver	10.00
28	Tom Seaver	10.00
29	Tom Seaver	10.00
30	Tom Seaver	10.00
31	Harmon Killebrew	10.00
32	Harmon Killebrew	10.00
33	Harmon Killebrew	10.00
34	Harmon Killebrew	10.00
35	Harmon Killebrew	10.00
36	Jim Palmer	8.00
37	Jim Palmer	8.00
38	Jim Palmer	8.00
39	Jim Palmer	8.00
40	Jim Palmer	8.00
41	Mike Schmidt	20.00
42	Mike Schmidt	20.00
43	Mike Schmidt	20.00
44	Mike Schmidt	20.00
45	Mike Schmidt	20.00
46	Ozzie Smith	20.00
47	Ozzie Smith	20.00
48	Ozzie Smith	20.00
49	Ozzie Smith	20.00
50	Ozzie Smith	20.00
51	Paul Molitor	10.00
52	Paul Molitor	10.00
53	Paul Molitor	10.00
54	Paul Molitor	10.00
55	Paul Molitor	10.00
56	Al Kaline	12.00
57	Al Kaline	12.00
58	Al Kaline	12.00
59	Al Kaline	12.00
60	Al Kaline	12.00
61	Robin Yount	15.00
62	Robin Yount	15.00
63	Robin Yount	15.00
64	Robin Yount	15.00
65	Robin Yount	15.00
66	Ryne Sandberg	15.00
67	Ryne Sandberg	15.00
68	Ryne Sandberg	15.00
69	Ryne Sandberg	15.00
70	Ryne Sandberg	15.00
71	Stan Musial	20.00
72	Stan Musial	20.00
73	Stan Musial	20.00
74	Stan Musial	20.00
75	Stan Musial	20.00
76	Steve Carlton	10.00
77	Steve Carlton	10.00
78	Steve Carlton	10.00
79	Steve Carlton	10.00
80	Steve Carlton	10.00
81	Tony Gwynn	20.00
82	Tony Gwynn	20.00
83	Tony Gwynn	20.00
84	Tony Gwynn	20.00
85	Tony Gwynn	20.00
86	Wade Boggs	10.00
87	Wade Boggs	10.00
88	Wade Boggs	10.00
89	Wade Boggs	10.00
90	Wade Boggs	10.00
91	Will Clark	10.00
92	Will Clark	10.00
93	Will Clark	10.00
94	Will Clark	10.00
95	Will Clark	10.00
96	Yogi Berra	15.00

97 Yogi Berra 15.00
98 Yogi Berra 15.00
99 Yogi Berra 15.00
100 Yogi Berra 15.00

Signature Cuts

No Pricing
Production 1-10

Signature Emerald

NM/M

Production 99 Sets
Blue: 1X-1.5X
Production 20 Sets
Red: 1X
Production 49 Sets
Gold: No Pricing
Production 1 Set
Patches: No Pricing
Production 5 Sets

1 Bob Feller 35.00
2 Bob Feller 35.00
3 Bob Feller 35.00
4 Bob Feller 35.00
5 Bob Feller 35.00
6 Brooks Robinson 35.00
7 Brooks Robinson 35.00
8 Brooks Robinson 35.00
9 Brooks Robinson 35.00
10 Brooks Robinson 35.00
11 Cal Ripken Jr. 125.00
12 Cal Ripken Jr. 125.00
13 Cal Ripken Jr. 125.00
14 Cal Ripken Jr. 125.00
15 Cal Ripken Jr. 125.00
16 Carl Yastrzemski 65.00
17 Carl Yastrzemski 65.00
18 Carl Yastrzemski 65.00
19 Carl Yastrzemski 65.00
20 Carl Yastrzemski 65.00
21 Don Mattingly 60.00
22 Don Mattingly 60.00
23 Don Mattingly 60.00
24 Don Mattingly 60.00
25 Don Mattingly 60.00
26 Tom Seaver 50.00
27 Tom Seaver 50.00
28 Tom Seaver 50.00
29 Tom Seaver 50.00
30 Tom Seaver 50.00
31 Harmon Killebrew 40.00
32 Harmon Killebrew 40.00
33 Harmon Killebrew 40.00
34 Harmon Killebrew 40.00
35 Harmon Killebrew 40.00
36 Jim Palmer 25.00
37 Jim Palmer 25.00
38 Jim Palmer 25.00
39 Jim Palmer 25.00
40 Jim Palmer 25.00
41 Mike Schmidt 50.00
42 Mike Schmidt 50.00
43 Mike Schmidt 50.00
44 Mike Schmidt 50.00
45 Mike Schmidt 50.00
46 Ozzie Smith 50.00
47 Ozzie Smith 50.00
48 Ozzie Smith 50.00
49 Ozzie Smith 50.00
50 Ozzie Smith 50.00
51 Paul Molitor 30.00
52 Paul Molitor 30.00
53 Paul Molitor 30.00
54 Paul Molitor 30.00
55 Paul Molitor 30.00
56 Al Kaline 40.00
57 Al Kaline 40.00
58 Al Kaline 40.00
59 Al Kaline 40.00
60 Al Kaline 40.00
61 Robin Yount 40.00
62 Robin Yount 40.00
63 Robin Yount 40.00
64 Robin Yount 40.00
65 Robin Yount 40.00
66 Ryne Sandberg 50.00
67 Ryne Sandberg 50.00
68 Ryne Sandberg 50.00
69 Ryne Sandberg 50.00
70 Ryne Sandberg 50.00
71 Stan Musial 75.00
72 Stan Musial 75.00
73 Stan Musial 75.00
74 Stan Musial 75.00
75 Stan Musial 75.00
76 Steve Carlton 25.00
77 Steve Carlton 25.00
78 Steve Carlton 25.00
79 Steve Carlton 25.00
80 Steve Carlton 25.00
81 Tony Gwynn 40.00
82 Tony Gwynn 40.00
83 Tony Gwynn 40.00
84 Tony Gwynn 40.00
85 Tony Gwynn 40.00
86 Wade Boggs 35.00
87 Wade Boggs 35.00
88 Wade Boggs 35.00
89 Wade Boggs 35.00
90 Wade Boggs 35.00
91 Will Clark 30.00
92 Will Clark 30.00
93 Will Clark 30.00
94 Will Clark 30.00
95 Will Clark 30.00
96 Yogi Berra 60.00
97 Yogi Berra 60.00
98 Yogi Berra 60.00
99 Yogi Berra 60.00
100 Yogi Berra 60.00

Signature Memorabilia

No Pricing
Production 15 Sets

2005 UPPER DECK CLASSICS

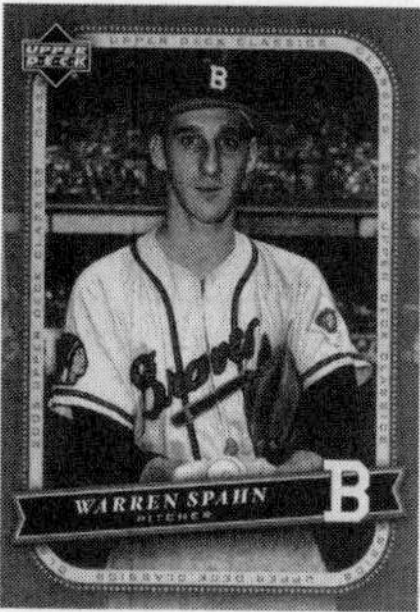

NM/M

Complete Set (130): 50.00
Common Player: .15
Common SP (101-130): 1.00
Inserted 1:4
Pack (8): 3.00
Hobby Box (28): 60.00

1 Al Kaline .50
2 Al Lopez .15
3 Allie Reynolds .15
4 Babe Herman .15
5 Bill Mazeroski .15
6 Bill Russell .15
7 Billy Herman .15
8 Billy Williams .25
9 Bob Feller .50
10 Bob Gibson .75
11 Bob Lemon .15
12 Bobby Doerr .15
13 Boog Powell .15
14 Ken Hubbs .15
15 Brooks Robinson .75
16 Buck Leonard .15
17 Cal Ripken Jr. 2.00
18 Carl Hubbell .15
19 Jim "Catfish" Hunter .25
20 Johnny Hopp .15
21 Charlie Gehringer .15
22 Curt Flood .15
23 Jimmie Foxx .75
24 Dave McNally .15
25 Davey Lopes .15
26 Don Drysdale .50
27 Don Sutton .50
28 Earl Weaver .15
29 Early Wynn .15
30 Edd Roush .15
31 Eddie Mathews .75
32 Enos Slaughter .15
33 Fergie Jenkins .50
34 Frank Howard .15
35 Leon Wagner .15
36 Frank Crosetti .15
37 Gaylord Perry .15
38 George Bell .15
39 George Kell .15
40 Graig Nettles .15
41 Hal Newhouser .15
42 Harmon Killebrew .75
43 Harvey Kuenn .15
44 Howard Johnson .15
45 Hoyt Wilhelm .15
46 Jack Clark .15
47 Jack Morris .15
48 Jim Bunning .15
49 Jim Palmer .50
50 Joe Adcock .15
51 Joe Carter .15
52 Casey Stengel .50
53 Joe Morgan .50
54 Joe Sewell .15
55 "Smoky" Joe Wood .15
56 Johnny Bench .75
57 Johnny Mize .15
58 Jose Canseco .50
59 Juan Marichal .50
60 Keith Hernandez .15
61 Ken Griffey Sr. .15
62 Kent Hrbek .15
63 Kevin Mitchell .15
64 Kirk Gibson .25
65 Larry Doby .15
66 Lou Boudreau .15
67 Lou Brock .50
68 Luis Aparicio .15
69 Luke Appling .15
70 Monte Irvin .50
71 Nellie Fox .15
72 Norm Cash .15
73 Orlando Cepeda .25
74 Pedro Guerrero .15
75 Pee Wee Reese .15
76 Phil Niekro .15
77 Phil Rizzuto .50
78 Ralph Kiner .15
79 Ray Dandridge .15
80 Red Schoendienst .15
81 Richie Ashburn .15
82 Rick Ferrell .15
83 Robin Roberts .50
84 Rollie Fingers .15
85 Ron Cey .15
86 Sparky Anderson .15
87 Stan Coveleski .15
88 Ted Kluszewski .15
89 Ted Lyons .15
90 Tom Seaver .50
91 Tommie Agee .15
92 Tommy Lasorda .15
93 Tony Perez .25
94 Vada Pinson .15
95 Waite Hoyt .15
96 Warren Spahn .75
97 Willie McCovey .50
98 Lyman Bostock .15
99 Willie Stargell .50
100 Yogi Berra .75
101 Andre Dawson 1.00
102 Andy Van Slyke 1.00
103 Bret Saberhagen 1.00
104 Carl Yastrzemski 2.50
105 Carlton Fisk 1.50
106 Dale Murphy 1.50
107 Darryl Strawberry 1.00
108 David Cone 1.00
109 Dennis Eckersley 1.50
110 Don Mattingly 2.50
111 Dwight Gooden 1.00
112 Eddie Murray 1.50
113 Eric Davis 1.00
114 Fred Lynn 1.00
115 George Brett 3.00
116 Jim Rice 1.00
117 John Kruk 1.50
118 Lenny Dykstra 1.00
119 Mickey Mantle 4.00
120 Mike Schmidt 3.00
121 Nolan Ryan 3.00
122 Ozzie Smith 2.00
123 Paul Molitor 2.00
124 Robin Yount 2.00
125 Ryne Sandberg 2.00
126 Steve Carlton 1.50
127 Ted Williams 3.00
128 Tony Gwynn 2.00
129 Wade Boggs 2.00
130 Will Clark 2.00

Gold

Gold (1-100): 2X-4X
Gold (101-130): 1X-2X
Production 199 sets

Platinum

Platinum (1-100): 5X-10X
Platinum (101-130): 3X-5X
Production 25 sets

Silver

Silver (1-100): 2X-3X
Silver (101-130): 1x-2X
Production 399 Sets

Classic Counterparts

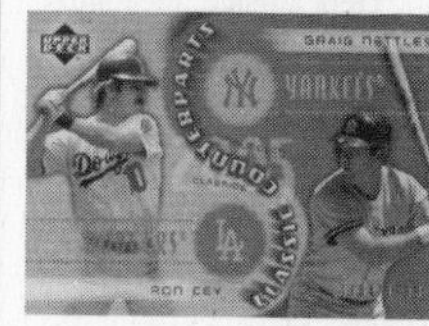

NM/M

Common Duo: 2.00
Production 1,999 Sets

CC Will Clark, Jack Clark 2.00
CG David Cone, Dwight Gooden 2.00
DS Darryl Strawberry, Lenny Dykstra 2.00
GB Wade Boggs, Tony Gwynn 4.00
GP Ken Griffey Sr., Tony Perez 2.00
KD John Kruk, Lenny Dykstra 2.00
KH John Kruk, Kent Hrbek 2.00
LR Jim Rice, Fred Lynn 2.00
MC Kevin Mitchell, Will Clark 2.00
MH Don Mattingly, Keith Hernandez 6.00
MY Robin Yount, Paul Molitor 5.00
NC Ron Cey, Graig Nettles 2.00
PH Boog Powell, Frank Howard 2.00
RC Steve Carlton, Nolan Ryan 8.00
RL Bill Russell, Davey Lopes 2.00
RS Tom Seaver, Nolan Ryan 8.00
SD Darryl Strawberry, Eric Davis 2.00
SG Dwight Gooden, Darryl Strawberry 2.00
SR Cal Ripken Jr., Mike Schmidt 10.00
VC Andy Van Slyke, Jack Clark 2.00

Classic Counterparts Materials

NM/M

CC Jack Clark, Will Clark 8.00
CG David Cone, Dwight Gooden 8.00
DS Darryl Strawberry, Lenny Dykstra 8.00
GB Wade Boggs, Tony Gwynn 20.00
GP Ken Griffey Sr., Tony Perez 8.00
KD John Kruk, Lenny Dykstra 15.00
KH John Kruk, Kent Hrbek 8.00
LR Jim Rice, Fred Lynn 8.00
MC Kevin Mitchell, Will Clark 8.00
MH Don Mattingly, Keith Hernandez 15.00
MY Robin Yount, Paul Molitor 15.00
NC Graig Nettles, Ron Cey 8.00
PH Boog Powell, Frank Howard 10.00
RC Steve Carlton, Nolan Ryan 40.00
RL Bill Russell, Davey Lopes 8.00
RS Tom Seaver, Nolan Ryan 50.00
SD Darryl Strawberry, Eric Davis 10.00
SG Dwight Gooden, Darryl Strawberry 8.00
SR Cal Ripken Jr., Mike Schmidt 50.00
VC Andy Van Slyke, Jack Clark 10.00

Classic Counterparts Sign.

NM/M

DS Darryl Strawberry, Lenny Dykstra 20.00
GB Wade Boggs, Tony Gwynn
GP Ken Griffey Sr., Tony Perez 30.00

KD John Kruk,
Lenny Dykstra 40.00
KH John Kruk, Kent Hrbek 40.00
LR Jim Rice, Fred Lynn 40.00
NC Graig Nettles, Ron Cey 35.00
RL Bill Russell,
Davey Lopes 25.00

Classic Cuts

NM/M

Quantity produced listed
JA Joe Adcock/38
LA Luke Appling/10
RA Richie Ashburn/5
LB Lou Boudreau/25
NC Norm Cash/5
SC Stan Coveleski/10
FC Frankie Crosetti/84 100.00
RD Ray Dandridge/5
JD Joe DiMaggio/5
LD Larry Doby/2
DD Don Drysdale/1
RF Rick Ferrell/25
CF Curt Flood/1
NF Nellie Fox/1
CG Charlie Gehringer/5
BH Babe Herman/50 150.00
HE Billy Herman/32
JH Johnny Hopp/35
DH Dick Howser/5
WH Waite Hoyt/10
CH Carl Hubbell/25 150.00
HU Jim "Catfish" Hunter/4
TK Ted Kluszewski/2
HK Harvey Kuenn/5
BL Bob Lemon/32
TL Ted Lyons/83 120.00
MM Mickey Mantle/1
EM Eddie Mathews/10
DM Dave McNally/1
JM Johnny Mize/5
HN Hal Newhouser/5
VP Vada Pinson/15
PW Pee Wee Reese/5
AR Allie Reynolds/14
ER Edd Roush/15
JS Joe Sewell/15
SH Eric Show/24
ES Enos Slaughter/10
WS Warren Spahn/5
ST Willie Stargell/10
LW Leon Wagner/3
HW Hoyt Wilhelm/17
TW Ted Williams/3
JW "Smoky" Joe Wood/2
EW Early Wynn/5

Classic Materials

NM/M

Common Player: 5.00
WB Wade Boggs 10.00
GB George Brett 10.00
CA Jose Canseco 10.00
JO Joe Carter 5.00
RC Ron Cey 5.00
JC Jack Clark 5.00
WC Will Clark 8.00
DC David Cone 8.00
ED Eric Davis 10.00
AD Andre Dawson 8.00
AD1 Andre Dawson 8.00
LD Lenny Dykstra 5.00
DE Dennis Eckersley 8.00
FI Carlton Fisk 8.00
GI Kirk Gibson 5.00
DG Dwight Gooden 5.00
GG Rich "Goose" Gossage 5.00
KG Ken Griffey Jr. 5.00
PG Pedro Guerrero 5.00
TG Tony Gwynn 10.00
KH Keith Hernandez 5.00
FH Frank Howard 8.00
HR Kent Hrbek 8.00
DL Davey Lopes 5.00
FL Fred Lynn 5.00
MA Don Mattingly 15.00
PM Paul Molitor 10.00
PM1 Paul Molitor SP 10.00
JM Jack Morris 5.00
DM Dale Murphy 8.00
GN Graig Nettles 10.00
BP Boog Powell SP 8.00
JR Jim Rice 5.00
CR Cal Ripken Jr. 25.00
BR Bill Russell 5.00
NR Nolan Ryan 20.00
RS Ryne Sandberg 15.00
MS Mike Schmidt 15.00
DS Darryl Strawberry 5.00
AV Andy Van Slyke 20.00
CY Carl Yastrzemski 20.00
RY Robin Yount 10.00

Classic Moments

NM/M

Common Player: 2.00
Production 1,999 Sets
WB Wade Boggs 4.00
SC Steve Carlton 2.00
CA Joe Carter 2.00
JC Jack Clark 2.00
LD Lenny Dykstra 2.00
FI Carlton Fisk 3.00
KG Kirk Gibson 2.00
TG Tony Gwynn 4.00
WJ Wally Joyner 2.00
KM Kevin Mitchell 2.00
PM Paul Molitor 4.00
JM Jack Morris 2.00
GP Gaylord Perry 2.00
CR Cal Ripken Jr. 10.00
NR Nolan Ryan 8.00
BS Bret Saberhagen 2.00
RS Ryne Sandberg 5.00
MS Mike Schmidt 6.00
DS Don Sutton 2.00
RY Robin Yount 5.00

Classic Moments Materials

NM/M

Common Player: 5.00
WB Wade Boggs 10.00
SC Steve Carlton 8.00
CA Joe Carter 5.00
JC Jack Clark 5.00
LD Lenny Dykstra 5.00
FI Carlton Fisk 8.00
KG Kirk Gibson 5.00
TG Tony Gwynn 10.00
WJ Wally Joyner 5.00
KM Kevin Mitchell 5.00
PM Paul Molitor 10.00
JM Jack Morris 5.00
GP Gaylord Perry 5.00
CR Cal Ripken Jr. 25.00
NR Nolan Ryan 20.00
RS Ryne Sandberg 15.00
MS Mike Schmidt 15.00
DS Don Sutton 5.00
RY Robin Yount 12.00

Classic Moments Signatures

NM/M

Common Autograph: 10.00
SC Steve Carlton 20.00
JC Jack Clark 15.00
LD Lenny Dykstra 15.00
FI Carlton Fisk 40.00
KG Kirk Gibson 25.00
WJ Wally Joyner 20.00
KM Kevin Mitchell 10.00
PM Paul Molitor 25.00
JM Jack Morris 20.00
GP Gaylord Perry 15.00
BS Bret Saberhagen 15.00
MS Mike Schmidt 60.00
DS Don Sutton 15.00

Classic Seasons

NM/M

Common Player: 2.00
Production 1,999 Sets
BE George Bell 2.00
JC Jose Canseco 3.00
CL Jack Clark 2.00
WC Will Clark 3.00
DC David Cone 2.00
ED Eric Davis 2.00
AD Andre Dawson 2.00
KG Kirk Gibson 2.00
DG Dwight Gooden 2.00
FL Fred Lynn 2.00
MA Don Mattingly 6.00
KM Kevin Mitchell 2.00
DM Dale Murphy 3.00
JR Jim Rice 2.00
CR Cal Ripken Jr. 10.00
NR Nolan Ryan 8.00
BS Bret Saberhagen 2.00
RS Ryne Sandberg 5.00
MS Mike Schmidt 6.00
CY Carl Yastrzemski 6.00

Classic Seasons Materials

NM/M

Common Player: 5.00
BE George Bell 5.00
JC Jose Canseco 10.00
CL Jack Clark 5.00
WC Will Clark 8.00
DC David Cone 5.00
ED Eric Davis SP 8.00
AD Andre Dawson 8.00
KG Kirk Gibson 5.00
DG Dwight Gooden 5.00
FL Fred Lynn 5.00
MA Don Mattingly 15.00
KM Kevin Mitchell 5.00
DM Dale Murphy 8.00
JR Jim Rice 5.00
CR Cal Ripken Jr. 25.00
NR Nolan Ryan 20.00
RS Ryne Sandberg 15.00
MS Mike Schmidt 15.00
CY Carl Yastrzemski 20.00

Classic Seasons Signatures

NM/M

Common Auto.: 10.00
BE George Bell 15.00
JC Jose Canseco 40.00
CL Jack Clark 15.00
WC Will Clark 40.00
DC David Cone 15.00
ED Eric Davis 20.00
AD Andre Dawson 20.00
KG Kirk Gibson 25.00
DG Dwight Gooden 12.00
FL Fred Lynn 15.00
MA Don Mattingly 60.00
KM Kevin Mitchell 10.00
DM Dale Murphy 20.00
JR Jim Rice
CR Cal Ripken Jr.
NR Nolan Ryan
BS Bret Saberhagen 15.00
RS Ryne Sandberg
MS Mike Schmidt 60.00
CY Carl Yastrzemski

League Leaders

NM/M

Common Player: 2.00
Production 999 Sets
GB George Bell 2.00
WB Wade Boggs 4.00
JC Jack Clark 2.00
WC Will Clark 3.00
AD Andre Dawson 3.00
LD Lenny Dykstra 2.00
DE Dennis Eckersley 3.00
DG Dwight Gooden
GG Rich "Goose" Gossage 2.00
PG Pedro Guerrero 2.00
TG Tony Gwynn 4.00
KH Keith Hernandez 2.00
FH Frank Howard 2.00
HJ Howard Johnson 2.00
MA Don Mattingly 8.00
KM Kevin Mitchell 2.00
PM Paul Molitor 4.00
DM Dale Murphy 3.00
JR Jim Rice 2.00
AV Andy Van Slyke 2.00

League Leaders Materials

NM/M

Common Player: 5.00
GB George Bell 5.00
WB Wade Boggs 10.00
JC Jack Clark 5.00
WC Will Clark 8.00
AD Andre Dawson 8.00
LD Lenny Dykstra 5.00
DE Dennis Eckersley 8.00
DG Dwight Gooden 5.00
GG Rich "Goose" Gossage 5.00
PG Pedro Guerrero 5.00
TG Tony Gwynn SP 10.00
KH Keith Hernandez 5.00
FH Frank Howard 8.00
HJ Howard Johnson 5.00
MA Don Mattingly 15.00
KM Kevin Mitchell 5.00
PM Paul Molitor 10.00
DM Dale Murphy 8.00
JR Jim Rice 5.00
AV Andy Van Slyke 20.00

League Leaders Signatures

NM/M

Common Auto.: 10.00
GB George Bell 10.00
JC Jack Clark 15.00
WC Will Clark 40.00
AD Andre Dawson 20.00
LD Lenny Dykstra 15.00
DG Dwight Gooden 15.00
GG Rich "Goose" Gossage 15.00
PG Pedro Guerrero 10.00
KH Keith Hernandez 15.00
FH Frank Howard 15.00
HJ Howard Johnson 15.00
MA Don Mattingly 60.00
KM Kevin Mitchell 10.00
PM Paul Molitor 25.00
DM Dale Murphy 20.00
JR Jim Rice 15.00

Post Season Performers

NM/M

Common Player: 2.00
Production 999 Sets
JO Jose Canseco 3.00
CA Joe Carter 2.00
JC Jack Clark 2.00
WC Will Clark 3.00

DC	David Cone	2.00
ED	Eric Davis	2.00
LD	Lenny Dykstra	2.00
CF	Carlton Fisk	3.00
DG	Dwight Gooden	2.00
PG	Pedro Guerrero	2.00
KH	Kent Hrbek	2.00
JK	John Kruk	3.00
KM	Kevin Mitchell	2.00
PM	Paul Molitor	4.00
JM	Jack Morris	2.00
CR	Cal Ripken Jr.	10.00
BR	Brooks Robinson	4.00
BS	Bret Saberhagen	2.00
MS	Mike Schmidt	6.00
DS	Darryl Strawberry	2.00

2005 UPPER DECK ESPN

		NM/M
Complete Set (90):		20.00
Common Player:		.15
Pack (9):		3.00
Box (24):		60.00
1	Garret Anderson	.25
2	Troy Glaus	.25
3	Vladimir Guerrero	.75
4	Luis Gonzalez	.25
5	Randy Johnson	.75
6	Andruw Jones	.40
7	Chipper Jones	.75
8	J.D. Drew	.25
9	John Smoltz	.25
10	Miguel Tejada	.50
11	Rafael Palmeiro	.50
12	Curt Schilling	.75
13	David Ortiz	.75
14	Manny Ramirez	.75
15	Pedro J. Martinez	.75
16	Carlos Zambrano	.25
17	Greg Maddux	1.00
18	Kerry Wood	.75
19	Mark Prior	.75
20	Nomar Garciaparra	1.50
21	Sammy Sosa	1.50
22	Carlos Lee	.25
23	Frank Thomas	.50
24	Magglio Ordonez	.25
25	Paul Konerko	.15
26	Adam Dunn	.50
27	Ken Griffey Jr.	1.00
28	Travis Hafner	.15
29	Victor Martinez	.25
30	Todd Helton	.50
31	Ivan Rodriguez	.50
32	Carl Pavano	.15
33	Josh Beckett	.25
34	Miguel Cabrera	.75
35	Mike Lowell	.15
36	Carlos Beltran	.50
37	Craig Biggio	.25
38	Jeff Bagwell	.50
39	Lance Berkman	.25
40	Roger Clemens	2.00
41	Roy Oswalt	.25
42	Mike Sweeney	.15
43	Adrian Beltre	.25
44	Brad Penny	.15
45	Eric Gagne	.40
46	Shawn Green	.25
47	Steve Finley	.15
48	Ben Sheets	.25
49	Scott Podsednik	.15
50	Joe Mauer	.25
51	Johan Santana	.50
52	Torii Hunter	.25
53	Jose Vidro	.15
54	Livan Hernandez	.15
55	Jose Reyes	.15
56	Mike Piazza	1.00
57	Tom Glavine	.25
58	Alex Rodriguez	1.50
59	Bernie Williams	.25
60	Derek Jeter	2.00
61	Gary Sheffield	.50
62	Hideki Matsui	1.50
63	Kevin Brown	.15
64	Mike Mussina	.25
65	Eric Chavez	.25
66	Mark Mulder	.25
67	Tim Hudson	.25
68	Bobby Abreu	.25
69	Jim Thome	.75
70	Craig Wilson	.15
71	Jason Kendall	.15
72	Oliver Perez	.15
73	Brian Giles	.15
74	Jake Peavy	.15
75	Jason Schmidt	.25
76	Bret Boone	.15
77	Ichiro Suzuki	1.50
78	Albert Pujols	2.00
79	Jim Edmonds	.25
80	Larry Walker	.40
81	Scott Rolen	.75
82	Aubrey Huff	.15
83	Carl Crawford	.15
84	Alfonso Soriano	.75
85	Hank Blalock	.50
86	Mark Teixeira	.50
87	Michael Young	.25
88	Carlos Delgado	.40
89	Roy Halladay	.25
90	Vernon Wells	.25

Award Winners

		NM/M
Inserted 1:5		
25th Anniv.:		4X-8X
Production 25 Sets		
AW-1	Gary Sheffield	1.00
AW-2	Greg Maddux	2.00
AW-3	Mike Piazza	2.00
AW-4	Jeff Bagwell	1.00
AW-5	Kenny Rogers	.50
AW-6	Cal Ripken Jr.	4.00
AW-7	Greg Maddux	2.00
AW-8	Hideo Nomo	.75
AW-9	Javier Lopez	.50
AW-10	Jim Edmonds	.75
AW-11	Ken Griffey Jr.	2.00
AW-12	Larry Walker	.75
AW-13	Nomar Garciaparra	2.50
AW-14	Roger Clemens	4.00
AW-15	David Wells	.50
AW-16	Sammy Sosa	2.50
AW-17	Pedro J. Martinez	1.50
AW-18	Andres Galarraga	.50
AW-19	Derek Jeter	4.00
AW-20	Alfonso Soriano	1.50

Ink

Inserted 1:480

Sports Center Swatches

		NM/M
Common Player:		4.00
Inserted 1:12		
GA	Garret Anderson	4.00
RB	Rocco Baldelli	4.00

CB	Carlos Beltran	8.00
AB	Adrian Beltre	8.00
LB	Lance Berkman	4.00
BI	Craig Biggio	4.00
HB	Hank Blalock	8.00
BB	Bret Boone	4.00
MG	Miguel Cabrera	8.00
EC	Eric Chavez	4.00
BC	Bartolo Colon	4.00
CC	Carl Crawford	4.00
JD	J.D. Drew	4.00
AD	Adam Dunn	8.00
JE	Jim Edmonds	6.00
EG	Eric Gagne	6.00
TG	Troy Glaus	6.00
KG	Ken Griffey Jr.	15.00
TH	Tim Hudson	4.00
AH	Aubrey Huff	4.00
DJ	Derek Jeter	20.00
JK	Jeff Kent	4.00
PK	Paul Konerko	4.00
DL	Derrek Lee	4.00
LO	Derek Lowe	4.00
MM	Mark Mulder	4.00
CP	Corey Patterson	6.00
AP	Albert Pujols	20.00
IR	Ivan Rodriguez	8.00
SA	Johan Santana	8.00
JS	Jason Schmidt	6.00
BS	Ben Sheets	4.00
AS	Alfonso Soriano	8.00
IS	Ichiro Suzuki	25.00
MS	Mike Sweeney	4.00
MT	Mark Teixeira	6.00
JT	Jim Thome	10.00
BU	B.J. Upton	6.00
VW	Vernon Wells	4.00
DW	David Wright SP	15.00
MY	Mike Young SP	10.00

Sports Century

		NM/M
Inserted 1:5		
25th Anniv.:		4X-8X
Production 25 Sets		
SC-1	Babe Ruth	4.00
SC-2	Jackie Robinson	2.00
SC-4	Ty Cobb	2.00
SC-5	Joe DiMaggio	3.00
SC-6	Lou Gehrig	3.00
SC-7	Mickey Mantle	5.00
SC-8	Walter Johnson	1.00
SC-9	Stan Musial	2.00
SC-10	Satchel Paige	1.00
SC-11	Bob Gibson	1.00
SC-12	Roberto Clemente	3.00
SC-13	Cy Young	1.00
SC-14	Honus Wagner	2.00
SC-15	Rogers Hornsby	1.00

Sports Century Signatures

Inserted 1:480

The Magazine Covers

		NM/M
Inserted 1:5		
25th Anniv.:		4X-8X
Production 25 Sets		
MC-1	Roger Clemens	4.00
MC-2	Derek Jeter	4.00
MC-3	Randy Johnson, Pedro J. Martinez	1.50
MC-4	Nomar Garciaparra	2.50
MC-5	Manny Ramirez	1.50
MC-6	Ken Griffey Jr.	2.00
MC-7	Mike Piazza	2.00
MC-8	Ichiro Suzuki	3.00
MC-9	Vladimir Guerrero	1.50
MC-10	Randy Johnson	1.50
MC-11	A.J. Pierzynski, Doug Mientkiewicz, Jacque Jones, Torii Hunter	.50
MC-12	Jason Giambi	.50
MC-13	Jeff Kent	.50
MC-14	Albert Pujols	4.00
MC-15	Kazuo Matsui	.50
MC-16	Miguel Cabrera	1.50
MC-17	Alex Rodriguez	3.00
MC-18	Ivan Rodriguez	1.00
MC-19	Eric Gagne	1.00
MC-20	Jim Edmonds, Albert Pujols, Scott Rolen	.75

This Day in Baseball History

		NM/M
Inserted 1:5		
25th Anniv.:		4X-8X
Production 25 Sets		
BH-1	Cal Ripken Jr.	4.00
BH-2	Nolan Ryan	4.00
BH-3	Nolan Ryan	4.00
BH-4	Roger Clemens	4.00
BH-5	Thurman Munson	2.00
BH-6	Mickey Mantle	5.00
BH-7	Ernie Banks	2.00
BH-8	Roy Campanella	1.00
BH-9	Yogi Berra	2.00
BH-10	Mickey Mantle	5.00
BH-11	Jackie Robinson	3.00
BH-12	Joe DiMaggio	3.00
BH-13	Bob Feller	1.00
BH-14	Lou Gehrig	3.00
BH-15	Ty Cobb	2.00
BH-16	Babe Ruth	4.00
BH-17	Walter Johnson	1.00
BH-18	Rogers Hornsby	1.00
BH-19	George Sisler	1.00
BH-20	Cy Young	1.00

Web Gems

NM/M
Inserted 1:5
25th Anniv.: 4X-8X
Production 25 Sets
WG-1 Adrian Beltre .75
WG-2 Alex Rodriguez 3.00
WG-3 Andruw Jones .75
WG-4 Bernie Williams .75
WG-5 Bret Boone .50
WG-6 Cesar Izturis .50
WG-7 Darin Erstad .50
WG-8 Derek Jeter 4.00
WG-9 Derrek Lee .75
WG-10 Eric Chavez .75
WG-11 Greg Maddux 2.00
WG-12 Ichiro Suzuki 3.00
WG-13 Ivan Rodriguez 1.00
WG-14 Jim Edmonds .75
WG-15 Ken Griffey Jr. 2.00
WG-16 Larry Walker .75
WG-17 Miguel Tejada .75
WG-18 Mike Mussina .75
WG-19 Nomar Garciaparra 2.50
WG-20 Scott Rolen 1.50
WG-21 Steve Finley .50
WG-22 Todd Helton 1.00
WG-23 Torii Hunter .50
WG-24 Vernon Wells .50
WG-25 Vladimir Guerrero 1.50

2005 UPPER DECK FIRST PITCH

NM/M
Complete Set (330):
Common (1-330): .10
Common (301-330): 1.00
Inserted 1:4
Common (321-330): 2.00
Inserted 1:36
Pack (5): 1.00
Box (36): 30.00
1 Casey Kotchman .10
2 Chone Figgins .10
3 David Eckstein .10
4 Jarrod Washburn .10
5 Robb Quinlan .10
6 Troy Glaus .25
7 Vladimir Guerrero .50
8 Brandon Webb .10
9 Danny Bautista .10
10 Luis Gonzalez .25
11 Matt Kata .10
12 Randy Johnson .50
13 Robby Hammock .10
14 Shea Hillenbrand .10
15 Adam LaRoche .10
16 Andruw Jones .40
17 Horacio Ramirez .10
18 John Smoltz .25
19 Johnny Estrada .10
20 Mike Hampton .10
21 Rafael Furcal .10
22 Brian Roberts .10
23 Javy Lopez .25
24 Jay Gibbons .10
25 Jorge Julio .10
26 Melvin Mora .10
27 Miguel Tejada .40
28 Rafael Palmeiro .40
29 Derek Lowe .10
30 Jason Varitek .25
31 Kevin Youkilis .10
32 Manny Ramirez .50
33 Curt Schilling .50
34 Pedro J. Martinez .50
35 Trot Nixon .10
36 Corey Patterson .25
37 Derrek Lee .25
38 LaTroy Hawkins .10
39 Mark Prior .50
40 Matt Clement .10
41 Moises Alou .25
42 Sammy Sosa 1.00
43 Aaron Rowand .10
44 Carlos Lee .10
45 Jose Valentin .10
46 Juan Uribe .10
47 Magglio Ordonez .10
48 Mark Buehrle .10
49 Paul Konerko .10
50 Adam Dunn .40
51 Barry Larkin .25
52 D'Angelo Jimenez .10
53 Danny Graves .10
54 Paul Wilson .10
55 Sean Casey .10
56 Wily Mo Pena .10
57 Ben Broussard .10
58 C.C. Sabathia .10
59 Casey Blake .10
60 Cliff Lee .10
61 Matt Lawton .10
62 Omar Vizquel .10
63 Victor Martinez .25
64 Charles Johnson .10
65 Joe Kennedy .10
66 Jeromy Burnitz .10
67 Matt Holliday .10
68 Preston Wilson .10
69 Royce Clayton .10
70 Shawn Estes .10
71 Bobby Higginson .10
72 Brandon Inge .10
73 Carlos Guillen .10
74 Dmitri Young .10
75 Eric Munson .10
76 Jeremy Bonderman .10
77 Ugueth Urbina .10
78 Josh Beckett .25
79 Dontrelle Willis .25
80 Jeff Conine .10
81 Juan Pierre .10
82 Luis Castillo .10
83 Miguel Cabrera .50
84 Mike Lowell .10
85 Andy Pettitte .25
86 Brad Lidge .10
87 Carlos Beltran .40
88 Craig Biggio .25
89 Jeff Bagwell .40
90 Roger Clemens 1.50
91 Roy Oswalt .25
92 Benito Santiago .10
93 Jeremy Affeldt .10
94 Juan Gonzalez .25
95 Ken Harvey .10
96 Mike MacDougal .10
97 Mike Sweeney .10
98 Zack Greinke .10
99 Adrian Beltre .25
100 Alex Cora .10
101 Cesar Izturis .10
102 Eric Gagne .25
103 Kazuhisa Ishii .10
104 Milton Bradley .10
105 Shawn Green .25
106 Danny Kolb .10
107 Ben Sheets .25
108 Brooks Kieschnick .10
109 Craig Counsell .10
110 Geoff Jenkins .10
111 Lyle Overbay .10
112 Scott Podsednik .10
113 Corey Koskie .10
114 Johan Santana .50
115 Joe Mauer .25
116 Justin Morneau .10
117 Lew Ford .10
118 Matt LeCroy .10
119 Torii Hunter .10
120 Brad Wilkerson .10
121 Chad Cordero .10
122 Livan Hernandez .10
123 Jose Vidro .10
124 Terrmel Sledge .10
125 Tony Batista .10
126 Zach Day .10
127 Al Leiter .10
128 Jae Weong Seo .10
129 Jose Reyes .10
130 Kazuo Matsui .10
131 Mike Piazza .75
132 Todd Zeile .10
133 Cliff Floyd .10
134 Alex Rodriguez 1.50
135 Derek Jeter 1.50
136 Gary Sheffield .40
137 Hideki Matsui 1.00
138 Jason Giambi .25
139 Jorge Posada .25
140 Mike Mussina .25
141 Barry Zito .25
142 Bobby Crosby .25
143 Octavio Dotel .10
144 Eric Chavez .25
145 Jermaine Dye .10
146 Mark Kotsay .10
147 Tim Hudson .25
148 Billy Wagner .10
149 Bobby Abreu .25
150 David Bell .10
151 Jim Thome .50
152 Jimmy Rollins .10
153 Mike Lieberthal .10
154 Randy Wolf .10
155 Craig Wilson .10
156 Daryle Ward .10
157 Jack Wilson .10
158 Jason Kendall .10
159 Kip Wells .10
160 Oliver Perez .25
161 Robert Mackowiak .10
162 Brian Giles .10
163 Brian Lawrence .10
164 David Wells .10
165 Jay Payton .10
166 Ryan Klesko .10
167 Sean Burroughs .10
168 Trevor Hoffman .10
169 Brett Tomko .10
170 J.T. Snow .10
171 Jason Schmidt .25
172 Kirk Rueter .10
173 A.J. Pierzynski .10
174 Pedro Feliz .10
175 Ray Durham .10
176 Eddie Guardado .10
177 Edgar Martinez .10
178 Ichiro Suzuki 1.00
179 Jamie Moyer .10
180 Joel Pineiro .10
181 Randy Winn .10
182 Raul Ibanez .10
183 Albert Pujols 1.50
184 Edgar Renteria .25
185 Jason Isringhausen .10
186 Jim Edmonds .25
187 Matt Morris .10
188 Reggie Sanders .10
189 Tony Womack .10
190 Aubrey Huff .10
191 Danys Baez .10
192 Carl Crawford .10
193 Jose Cruz Jr. .10
194 Rocco Baldelli .10
195 Tino Martinez .10
196 Dewon Brazelton .10
197 Alfonso Soriano .50
198 Brad Fullmer .10
199 Gerald Laird .10
200 Hank Blalock .50
201 Laynce Nix .10
202 Mark Teixeira .40
203 Mike Young .25
204 Alexis Rios .10
205 Eric Hinske .10
206 Miguel Batista .10
207 Orlando Hudson .10
208 Roy Halladay .10
209 Ted Lilly .10
210 Vernon Wells .10
211 Aarom Baldiris .10
212 B.J. Upton .25
213 Dallas McPherson .25
214 Brian Dallimore .10
215 Chris Oxspring .10
216 Chris Shelton .10
217 David Wright .75
218 Edwardo Sierra .10
219 Fernando Nieve .10
220 Frank Francisco .10
221 Jeff Bennett .10
222 Justin Lehr .10
223 John Gall .10
224 Jorge Sequea .10
225 Justin Germano .10
226 Kazuhito Tadano .10
227 Kevin Cave .10
228 Joe Blanton .10
229 Luis Gonzalez .10
230 Mike Wuertz .10
231 Mike Rouse .10
232 Nick Regilio .10
233 Orlando Rodriguez .10
235 Ramon Ramirez .10
236 Roberto Novoa .10
237 Dioner Navarro .10
238 Tim Bausher .10
239 Logan Kensing .10
240 Andy Green .10
241 Brad Halsey .10
242 Charles Thomas .10
243 George Sherrill .10
244 Jesse Crain .10
245 Jimmy Serrano .10
246 Joe Horgan .10
247 Chris Young .10
248 Joey Gathright .10
249 Gavin Floyd .10
250 Ryan Howard .40
251 Lance Cormier .10
252 Matt Treanor .10
253 Jeff Francis .10
254 Nick Swisher .10
255 Scott Atchison .10
256 Travis Blackley .10
257 Travis Smith .10
258 Yadier Molina .10
259 Jeff Keppinger .10
260 Scott Kazmir .50
261 Garret Anderson, Vladimir Guerrero .25
262 Luis Gonzalez, Randy Johnson .25
263 Chipper Jones, Andruw Jones .25
264 Miguel Tejada, Rafael Palmeiro .25
265 Manny Ramirez, Curt Schilling .25
266 Mark Prior, Sammy Sosa .50
267 Frank Thomas, Magglio Ordonez .25
268 Barry Larkin, Ken Griffey Jr. .50
269 C.C. Sabathia, Victor Martinez .10
270 Jeromy Burnitz, Todd Helton .25
271 Ivan Rodriguez, Dmitri Young .25
272 Josh Beckett, Miguel Cabrera .25
273 Jeff Bagwell, Roger Clemens .50
274 Mike Sweeney, Ken Harvey .10
275 Eric Gagne, Adrian Beltre .25
276 Ben Sheets, Geoff Jenkins .10
277 Torii Hunter, Joe Mauer .10
278 Jose Vidro, Livan Hernandez .10
279 Mike Piazza, Kazuo Matsui .25
280 Alex Rodriguez, Derek Jeter .75
281 Eric Chavez, Tim Hudson .10
282 Bobby Abreu, Jim Thome .25
283 Jason Kendall, C raig Wilson .10
284 Phil Nevin, Brian Giles .10
285 Jason Schmidt, A.J. Pierzynski .10
286 Bret Boone, Ichiro Suzuki .50
287 Albert Pujols, Scott Rolen .75
288 Aubrey Huff, Tino Martinez .10
289 Hank Blalock, Mark Teixeira .25
290 Roy Halladay, Carlos Delgado .10
291 Vladimir Guerrero .50
292 Curt Schilling .50
293 Mark Prior .50
294 Josh Beckett .25
295 Roger Clemens 1.00
296 Derek Jeter 1.00
297 Eric Chavez .10
298 Jim Thome .50
299 Albert Pujols 1.00
300 Hank Blalock .25
301 Guillermo Quiroz 1.00
302 Jeff Bajenaru 1.00
303 Bartolome Fortunato 1.00
304 Jason Alfaro 1.00
305 Mike Rose 1.00
306 Joe Hietpas 1.00
307 Kyle Denney 1.00
308 Rene Rivera 1.00
309 Kameron Loe 1.00
310 Rickie Weeks 1.50
311 Gustavo Chacin 1.00
312 Chris Burke 1.00
313 Yhency Brazoban 1.00
314 Brandon League 1.00
315 Jose Capellan 1.00
316 Russ Adams 1.00
317 Adrian Gonzalez 1.00
318 Jason Dubois 1.00
319 Abe Alvarez 1.00
320 Eric Crozier 1.00
321 Bengie Molina, Bartolo Colon 2.00
322 C.C. Sabathia, Victor Martinez 2.00

323 Jake Peavy, Ramon Hernandez 2.00
324 A.J. Pierzynski, Jason Schmidt 3.00
325 Joe Mauer, Johan Santana 3.00
326 Mark Prior, Michael Barrett 3.00
327 Jorge Posada, Mike Mussina 3.00
328 Roger Clemens, Brad Ausmus 4.00
329 Roy Halladay, Guillermo Quiroz 2.00
330 Mike Piazza, Tom Glavine 3.00

Jumbos

NM/M

Common Player: 1.00
FP-1 Shingo Takatsu 1.00
FP-2 Jeff Francis 1.00
FP-3 Jesse Crain 1.00
FP-4 Jose Capellan 1.00
FP-5 Zack Greinke 1.00
FP-6 Scott Proctor 1.00
FP-7 Scott Kazmir 3.00
FP-8 Gavin Floyd 1.00
FP-9 Joe Blanton 1.00
FP-10 Akinori Otsuka 1.00

Fabric

NM/M

Common Player:
Inserted 1:180
JB Jeff Bagwell 8.00
BE Josh Beckett 5.00
BB Bret Boone 5.00
EC Eric Chavez 5.00
JE Jim Edmonds 5.00
EG Eric Gagne 8.00
TG Troy Glaus 5.00
KG Ken Griffey Jr. SP 20.00
TH Torii Hunter 5.00
DJ Derek Jeter 20.00
AJ Andruw Jones 5.00
CJ Chipper Jones 8.00
MM Mark Mulder 5.00
MO Magglio Ordonez 5.00
SR Scott Rolen 8.00
CS Curt Schilling 8.00
GS Gary Sheffield SP 8.00
AS Alfonso Soriano 8.00
SS Sammy Sosa 10.00
IS Ichiro Suzuki SP 25.00

Signature Stars

Inserted 1:720

2005 UPPER DECK MVP

NM/M

Complete Set (90): 20.00
Common Player: .10
Pack (6): 1.50
Box (24): 30.00
1 Adam Dunn .40
2 Adrian Beltre .40
3 Albert Pujols 1.50
4 Alex Rodriguez 1.50
5 Alfonso Soriano .50
6 Andruw Jones .40
7 Aubrey Huff .10
8 Barry Zito .25
9 Ben Sheets .25
10 Bobby Abreu .25
11 Bobby Crosby .25
12 Bret Boone .10
13 Brian Giles .10
14 Carlos Beltran .40
15 Carlos Delgado .25
16 Carlos Lee .25
17 Chipper Jones .50
18 Craig Biggio .25
19 Curt Schilling .40
20 Dallas McPherson .10
21 David Ortiz .50
22 David Wright .50
23 Derek Jeter 1.50
24 Derek Lowe .10
25 Eric Chavez .25
26 Eric Gagne .25
27 Frank Thomas .40
28 Garret Anderson .25
29 Gary Sheffield .40
30 Greg Maddux 1.00
31 Hank Blalock .25
32 Hideki Matsui 1.00
33 Ichiro Suzuki 1.00
34 Ivan Rodriguez .40
35 J.D. Drew .10
36 Jake Peavy .25
37 Jason Bay .10
38 Jason Giambi .25
39 Jason Schmidt .25
40 Jeff Bagwell .40
41 Jeff Kent .25
42 Jim Edmonds .25
43 Jim Thome .40
44 Joe Mauer .25
45 Johan Santana .50
46 John Smoltz .25
47 Johnny Damon .50
48 Jorge Posada .25
49 Jose Vidro .10
50 Josh Beckett .25
51 Kazuo Matsui .10
52 Ken Griffey Jr. 1.00
53 Kerry Wood .25
54 Khalil Greene .25
55 Lance Berkman .25
56 Livan Hernandez .10
57 Luis Gonzalez .10
58 Magglio Ordonez .10
59 Manny Ramirez .50
60 Mark Mulder .25
61 Mark Prior .50
62 Mark Teixeira .40
63 Miguel Cabrera .50
64 Miguel Tejada .40
65 Mike Mussina .25
66 Mike Piazza 1.00
67 Mike Sweeney .10
68 Moises Alou .25
69 Nomar Garciaparra .75
70 Oliver Perez .10
71 Paul Konerko .25
72 Pedro Martinez .50
73 Rafael Palmeiro .25
74 Randy Johnson .50
75 Richie Sexson .25
76 Roger Clemens 1.50
77 Roy Halladay .25
78 Roy Oswalt .25
79 Sammy Sosa .75
80 Scott Rolen .50
81 Shawn Green .10
82 Steve Finley .10
83 Tim Hudson .25
84 Todd Helton .40
85 Tom Glavine .25
86 Torii Hunter .25
87 Travis Hafner .10
88 Troy Glaus .25
89 Victor Martinez .25
90 Vladimir Guerrero .50

All-Star Signatures

No Pricing
Inserted 1:480

Batter Up!

NM/M

Common Player: .25
Inserted 1:1
BU-1 Al Kaline .50
BU-2 Bill Mazeroski .25
BU-3 Billy Williams .25
BU-4 Bob Feller .50
BU-5 Bob Gibson .50
BU-6 Bob Lemon .25
BU-7 Brooks Robinson .50
BU-8 Carlton Fisk .50
BU-9 Jim "Catfish" Hunter .25
BU-10 Dennis Eckersley .25
BU-11 Eddie Mathews .75
BU-12 Eddie Murray .50
BU-13 Fergie Jenkins .25
BU-14 Gaylord Perry .25
BU-15 Harmon Killebrew .75
BU-16 Jim Bunning .25
BU-17 Jim Palmer .50
BU-18 Joe DiMaggio 1.50
BU-19 Joe Morgan .25
BU-20 Johnny Bench .75
BU-21 Juan Marichal .50
BU-22 Lou Brock .50
BU-23 Luis Aparicio .25
BU-24 Mike Schmidt 1.50
BU-25 Monte Irvin .50
BU-26 Nolan Ryan 2.00
BU-27 Orlando Cepeda .25
BU-28 Ozzie Smith .75
BU-29 Pee Wee Reese .25
BU-30 Phil Niekro .25
BU-31 Phil Rizzuto .50
BU-32 Ralph Kiner .25
BU-33 Richie Ashburn .25
BU-34 Robin Roberts .25
BU-35 Robin Yount .75
BU-36 Rollie Fingers .25
BU-37 Tom Seaver .75
BU-38 Tony Perez .25
BU-39 Warren Spahn .75
BU-40 Willie McCovey .50
BU-41 Willie Stargell .50
BU-42 Yogi Berra .75

Jersey

NM/M

Common Jersey: 4.00
Inserted 1:24
CB Carlos Beltran 6.00
AB Adrian Beltre 4.00
HB Hank Blalock 4.00
SB Sean Burroughs 4.00
MC Miguel Cabrera 6.00
EC Eric Chavez 4.00
EG Eric Gagne 4.00
KG Ken Griffey Jr. 10.00
VG Vladimir Guerrero 6.00
TH Todd Helton 6.00
DJ Derek Jeter 15.00
RJ Randy Johnson 6.00
CJ Chipper Jones 6.00
GM Greg Maddux 8.00
PI Mike Piazza 8.00
MP Mark Prior 6.00
AP Albert Pujols 15.00
MR Manny Ramirez 6.00
IR Ivan Rodriguez 6.00
SR Scott Rolen 6.00
JS Johan Santana 6.00
CS Curt Schilling 6.00
AS Alfonso Soriano 6.00
SS Sammy Sosa 8.00
MT Mark Teixeira 6.00
TE Miguel Tejada 6.00
JT Jim Thome 6.00
KW Kerry Wood 4.00

2005 UPPER DECK PORTRAITS

NM/M

Complete Set (100): 25.00
Common Player: .25
Box (7 cards + 8x10): 100.00
1 Dallas McPherson .25
2 Steve Finley .25
3 Vladimir Guerrero .75
4 Troy Glaus .25
5 Andruw Jones .50
6 Chipper Jones .75
7 John Smoltz .50
8 Marcus Giles .25
9 Tim Hudson .50
10 Cal Ripken Jr. 3.00
11 Miguel Tejada .50
12 Curt Schilling .75
13 David Ortiz .75
14 Edgar Renteria .25
15 Jason Varitek .50
16 Jim Rice .50
17 Johnny Damon .75
18 Matt Clement .25
19 Wade Boggs .75
20 Aramis Ramirez .50
21 Carlos Zambrano .50
22 Corey Patterson .25
23 Fergie Jenkins .25
24 Greg Maddux 1.50
25 Kerry Wood .50
26 Mark Prior .75
27 Nomar Garciaparra .75
28 Ryne Sandberg 1.50
29 Frank Thomas .50
30 Adam Dunn .50
31 Barry Larkin .50
32 Ken Griffey Jr. 1.50
33 Sean Casey .25
34 Travis Hafner .25
35 Victor Martinez .25
36 Todd Helton .50
37 Ivan Rodriguez .50
38 Magglio Ordonez .25
39 Josh Beckett .25
40 Miguel Cabrera .75
41 Mike Lowell .25
42 Craig Biggio .50
43 Jeff Bagwell .50
44 Roger Clemens 2.00
45 Roy Oswalt .25
46 Bo Jackson .50
47 Prince Fielder 5.00
48 Eric Gagne .25
49 J.D. Drew .25
50 Ben Sheets .50
51 Robin Yount .75
52 Jacque Jones .25
53 Joe Mauer .50
54 Johan Santana .75
55 Justin Morneau .25
56 Torii Hunter .25
57 Dontrelle Willis .50
58 David Wright 1.00
59 Gary Carter .25
60 Jose Reyes .25
61 Keith Hernandez .25
62 Mike Piazza 1.00
63 Pedro Martinez .75
64 Tom Glavine .50
65 Carl Pavano .25
66 Derek Jeter 2.00
67 Don Mattingly 1.00
68 Mike Mussina .50
69 Randy Johnson .75
70 Bobby Crosby .25
71 Eric Chavez .25
72 Rich Harden .25
73 Bobby Abreu .50
74 Mike Schmidt 1.00
75 Jason Bay .25
76 Oliver Perez .25
77 Brian Giles .25
78 Jake Peavy .50
79 Khalil Greene .25
80 Tony Gwynn .75
81 Jason Schmidt .25
82 Will Clark .50
83 Adrian Beltre .25
84 Justin Verlander 2.00
85 Albert Pujols 2.00
86 Jim Edmonds .50
87 Mark Mulder .50
88 Scott Rolen .75
89 Aubrey Huff .25
90 B.J. Upton .25
91 Carl Crawford .25
92 Tadahito Iguchi 4.00
93 Scott Kazmir .25
94 Alfonso Soriano .75
95 Hank Blalock .25
96 Mark Teixeira .50
97 Michael Young .25
98 Nolan Ryan 2.00
99 Roy Halladay .50
100 Jose Vidro .25

Scrapbook Materials

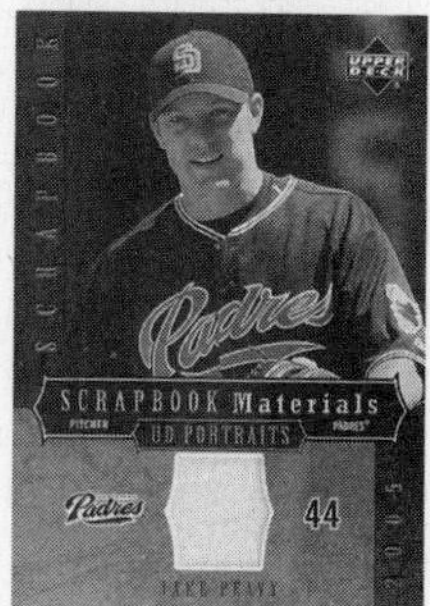

NM/M

Complete Set (59):
Common Player:
BA Bobby Abreu 4.00
JB Jeff Bagwell 6.00
BE Josh Beckett 4.00
AB Adrian Beltre 4.00
BI Craig Biggio 6.00
CA Miguel Cabrera 8.00
WC Will Clark 6.00

CL Matt Clement 4.00
BC Bobby Crosby 4.00
JE Jim Edmonds 6.00
PF Prince Fielder
SF Steve Finley 4.00
BG Brian Giles 4.00
GR Khalil Greene 6.00
KG Ken Griffey Jr. 15.00
TG Tony Gwynn 8.00
RH Roy Halladay 4.00
TH Todd Helton 6.00
KH Keith Hernandez 4.00
HU Torii Hunter 4.00
BJ Bo Jackson 10.00
DJ Derek Jeter 20.00
AJ Andruw Jones 6.00
CJ Chipper Jones 8.00
JJ Jacque Jones 4.00
SK Scott Kazmir 4.00
BL Barry Larkin 6.00
ML Mike Lowell 4.00
VM Victor Martinez 4.00
MA Don Mattingly 15.00
JM Joe Mauer 6.00
MC Dallas McPherson 4.00
MO Justin Morneau 4.00
DM Dale Murphy 6.00
MM Mike Mussina 6.00
OR Magglio Ordonez 4.00
DO David Ortiz 8.00
PA Corey Patterson 4.00
CP Carl Pavano 4.00
JP Jake Peavy 6.00
OP Oliver Perez 4.00
MP Mark Prior 6.00
AP Albert Pujols 15.00
JR Jim Rice 6.00
CR Cal Ripken Jr. 20.00
NR Nolan Ryan 15.00
RS Ryne Sandberg 10.00
SA Johan Santana 6.00
JS Jason Schmidt 4.00
MS Mike Schmidt 10.00
SM John Smoltz 6.00
MT Mark Teixeira 6.00
FT Frank Thomas 6.00
BU B.J. Upton 4.00
VE Justin Verlander
JV Jose Vidro 4.00
WI Dontrelle Willis 6.00
DW David Wright 10.00
CZ Carlos Zambrano 6.00

Scrapbook Moments

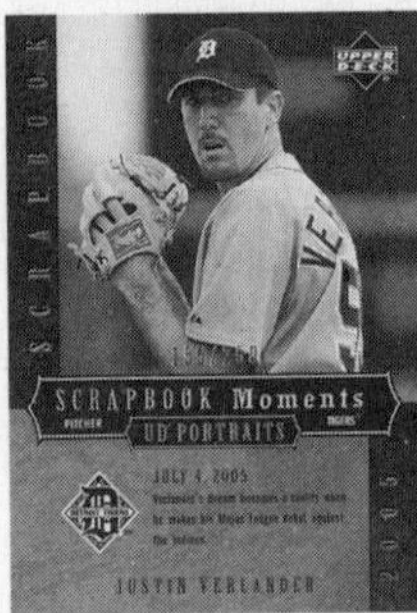

NM/M
Common Player: 1.00
Production 250 Sets
BA Bobby Abreu 1.50
JB Jeff Bagwell 1.50
BE Josh Beckett 1.50
AB Adrian Beltre 1.50
BI Craig Biggio 1.50
CA Miguel Cabrera 2.00
WC Will Clark 1.50
RC Roger Clemens 6.00
CL Matt Clement 1.00
BC Bobby Crosby 1.00
JE Jim Edmonds 1.50
PF Prince Fielder 6.00
SF Steve Finley 1.00
BG Brian Giles 1.00
GR Khalil Greene 1.50
KG Ken Griffey Jr. 4.00
TG Tony Gwynn 2.00
RH Roy Halladay 1.00
TH Todd Helton 1.50
KH Keith Hernandez 1.00
HU Torii Hunter 1.00
BJ Bo Jackson 2.00

DJ Derek Jeter 6.00
AJ Andruw Jones 1.50
CJ Chipper Jones 2.00
JJ Jacque Jones 1.00
SK Scott Kazmir 1.00
BL Barry Larkin 1.50
ML Mike Lowell 1.00
VM Victor Martinez 1.00
MA Don Mattingly 4.00
JM Joe Mauer 1.50
MC Dallas McPherson 1.00
MO Justin Morneau 1.00
DM Dale Murphy 2.00
MM Mike Mussina 1.50
OR Magglio Ordonez 1.00
DO David Ortiz 2.00
PA Corey Patterson 1.00
CP Carl Pavano 1.00
JP Jake Peavy 1.50
OP Oliver Perez 1.00
MP Mark Prior 2.00
AP Albert Pujols 6.00
JR Jim Rice 1.50
CR Cal Ripken Jr. 8.00
NR Nolan Ryan 6.00
RS Ryne Sandberg 4.00
SA Johan Santana 2.00
JS Jason Schmidt 1.00
MS Mike Schmidt 4.00
SM John Smoltz 1.50
MT Mark Teixeira 1.50
FT Frank Thomas 1.50
BU B.J. Upton 1.00
VE Justin Verlander 2.00
JV Jose Vidro 1.00
WI Dontrelle Willis 1.50
DW David Wright 3.00
CZ Carlos Zambrano 1.50

Scrapbook Signatures

No Pricing
Production 20 Sets

Signature Portraits 8x10

NM/M
DB Dusty Baker 100 25.00
JB Jason Bay 25.00
HB Hank Blalock 25.00
WB Wade Boggs 40
CA Miguel Cabrera 40.00
RC Roger Clemens 25
JD Johnny Damon 99 50.00
NG Nomar Garciaparra 25
GR Khalil Greene 35.00
VG Vladimir Guerrero 40 75.00
KH Keith Hernandez 20.00
DJ Derek Jeter 150 200.00
SK Scott Kazmir 25.00
PM Pedro Martinez
VM Victor Martinez 25.00
MA Don Mattingly 65.00
JM Joe Mauer 30.00
DM Dale Murphy 30.00
SM Stan Musial 40 80.00
JN Jeff Niemann 15.00
RO Roy Oswalt 30.00
PI Mike Piazza 35
MP Mark Prior 50 40.00
AP Albert Pujols SP
CR Cal Ripken Jr. 50 160.00
BR Brooks Robinson 50.00
NR Nolan Ryan 25 140.00
RS Ryne Sandberg 99 100.00
MS Mike Schmidt 50.00
BS Ben Sheets 25.00
OS Ozzie Smith 50.00
DS Duke Snider 150 60.00
MT Mark Teixeira 35.00
BU B.J. Upton 20.00
VE Justin Verlander 25.00
DW David Wright 75.00

Sig. Portraits Cuts 8x10 Card

No Pricing

Signature Portraits Dual 8x10

NM/M
Production 25-99
BT Mark Teixeira, Hank Blalock 99 50.00
CO Roy Oswalt, Roger Clemens 25
GC Ken Griffey Jr., Miguel Cabrera 25
HS Rich Harden, Ben Sheets 99 40.00
JJ Randy Johnson, Derek Jeter 25
NV Justin Verlander, Jeff Niemann 99 30.00
SB Mike Schmidt, Pat Burrell 50
SH Tim Hudson, John Smoltz 75
WP Kerry Wood, Mark Prior 99 85.00
WR David Wright, Jose Reyes 99 140.00

Emerald Jersey

NM/M
Common Player: 4.00
Production 99 Sets
Blue: 1X-1.5X
Production 25 Sets
Gold: 1X-2X
Production 15 Sets
1 Dallas McPherson 4.00
2 Steve Finley 4.00
3 Vladimir Guerrero 8.00
4 Troy Glaus 4.00
5 Andruw Jones 6.00
6 Chipper Jones 8.00
7 John Smoltz 6.00
8 Marcus Giles 4.00
9 Tim Hudson 6.00
10 Cal Ripken Jr. 25.00
11 Miguel Tejada 8.00
12 Curt Schilling 8.00
13 David Ortiz 8.00
14 Edgar Renteria 4.00
15 Jason Varitek 8.00
16 Jim Rice 6.00
17 Johnny Damon 8.00
18 Matt Clement 4.00
19 Wade Boggs 8.00
20 Aramis Ramirez 6.00
21 Carlos Zambrano 6.00
22 Corey Patterson 4.00
23 Fergie Jenkins 6.00
24 Greg Maddux 10.00
25 Kerry Wood 6.00
26 Mark Prior 8.00
27 Nomar Garciaparra 8.00
28 Ryne Sandberg 12.00
29 Frank Thomas 6.00
30 Adam Dunn 6.00
31 Barry Larkin 6.00
32 Ken Griffey Jr. 15.00
33 Sean Casey 4.00
34 Travis Hafner 4.00
35 Victor Martinez 4.00
36 Todd Helton 6.00
37 Ivan Rodriguez 6.00
38 Magglio Ordonez 4.00
39 Josh Beckett 4.00
40 Miguel Cabrera 8.00
41 Mike Lowell 4.00
42 Craig Biggio 6.00
43 Jeff Bagwell 8.00
44 Roger Clemens 15.00
45 Roy Oswalt 4.00
46 Bo Jackson 10.00
48 Eric Gagne 6.00
49 J.D. Drew 4.00
50 Ben Sheets 4.00
51 Robin Yount 15.00
52 Jacque Jones 4.00
53 Joe Mauer 6.00
54 Johan Santana 6.00
55 Justin Morneau 4.00
56 Torii Hunter 4.00
57 Dontrelle Willis 6.00
58 David Wright 10.00
59 Gary Carter 6.00
60 Jose Reyes 6.00
61 Keith Hernandez 4.00
62 Mike Piazza 8.00
63 Pedro Martinez 8.00
64 Tom Glavine 6.00
65 Carl Pavano 4.00
66 Derek Jeter 15.00
67 Don Mattingly 15.00
68 Mike Mussina 6.00
69 Randy Johnson 8.00
70 Bobby Crosby 4.00
71 Eric Chavez 4.00
72 Rich Harden 4.00
73 Bobby Abreu 6.00
74 Mike Schmidt 10.00
75 Jason Bay 4.00
76 Oliver Perez 4.00
77 Brian Giles 4.00
78 Jake Peavy 6.00
79 Khalil Greene 6.00
80 Tony Gwynn 8.00
81 Jason Schmidt 4.00
82 Will Clark 8.00
83 Adrian Beltre 4.00
85 Albert Pujols 15.00
86 Jim Edmonds 6.00
87 Mark Mulder 6.00
88 Scott Rolen 6.00
89 Aubrey Huff 4.00
90 B.J. Upton 4.00
91 Carl Crawford 4.00
92 Tadahito Iguchi 15.00
93 Scott Kazmir 4.00
94 Alfonso Soriano 6.00
95 Hank Blalock 6.00
96 Mark Teixeira 6.00
97 Michael Young 6.00
98 Nolan Ryan 15.00
99 Roy Halladay 6.00
100 Jose Vidro 4.00

Jersey Auto. Platinum

No Pricing
Production 10 Sets

2005 UPPER DECK PRO SIGS

NM/M
Complete Set (132): 25.00
Common Player: .10
Common Rookie (91-132): .25
Inserted 1:1
Pack (6): 2.00
Box (24): 40.00
1 Dallas McPherson .10
2 Garret Anderson .25
3 Steve Finley .10
4 Vladimir Guerrero .50
5 Luis Gonzalez .10
6 Shawn Green .10
7 Troy Glaus .25
8 Andruw Jones .40
9 Chipper Jones .50
10 John Smoltz .25
11 Tim Hudson .40
12 Miguel Tejada .40
13 Rafael Palmeiro .25
14 Sammy Sosa .75
15 Curt Schilling .50
16 David Ortiz .50
17 Johnny Damon .50
18 Manny Ramirez .50
19 Greg Maddux 1.00
20 Kerry Wood .25
21 Mark Prior .50
22 Nomar Garciaparra .50
23 Frank Thomas .40
24 Paul Konerko .25
25 Adam Dunn .40
26 Ken Griffey Jr. 1.00
27 Travis Hafner .10
28 Victor Martinez .10
29 Todd Helton .40
30 Ivan Rodriguez .40
31 Magglio Ordonez .10
32 Carlos Delgado .25
33 Josh Beckett .25
34 Miguel Cabrera .50
35 Craig Biggio .25
36 Jeff Bagwell .40
37 Lance Berkman .25
38 Roger Clemens 1.50
39 Roy Oswalt .25
40 Mike Sweeney .10
41 Derek Lowe .10
42 Eric Gagne .25
43 J.D. Drew .10
44 Jeff Kent .10
45 Ben Sheets .25
46 Carlos Lee .25
47 Joe Mauer .25
48 Johan Santana .50
49 Torii Hunter .25
50 Carlos Beltran .40

51 David Wright 1.00
52 Kazuo Matsui .10
53 Mike Piazza .75
54 Pedro Martinez .50
55 Tom Glavine .25
56 Alex Rodriguez 1.50
57 Derek Jeter 1.50
58 Gary Sheffield .40
59 Hideki Matsui 1.00
60 Jason Giambi .25
61 Jorge Posada .25
62 Mike Mussina .25
63 Randy Johnson .50
64 Barry Zito .25
65 Bobby Crosby .25
66 Eric Chavez .25
67 Bobby Abreu .25
68 Jim Thome .40
69 Jason Bay .25
70 Oliver Perez .10
71 Brian Giles .10
72 Jake Peavy .25
73 Khalil Greene .25
74 Jason Schmidt .10
75 Moises Alou .25
76 Adrian Beltre .25
77 Bret Boone .10
78 Ichiro Suzuki 1.00
79 Richie Sexson .25
80 Albert Pujols 1.50
81 Jim Edmonds .25
82 Mark Mulder .25
83 Scott Rolen .50
84 Aubrey Huff .10
85 Alfonso Soriano .50
86 Hank Blalock .25
87 Mark Teixeira .25
88 Roy Halladay .25
89 Jose Vidro .10
90 Livan Hernandez .10
91 *Tony Pena* .25
92 *Luis Hernandez* .25
93 *Peter Orr* .25
94 *Anibal Sanchez* .50
95 *Luis Mendoza* .25
96 *Stephen Drew* 8.00
97 *Russel Rohlicek* .25
98 *Casey Rogowski* .25
99 *Pedro Lopez* .25
100 *Tadahito Iguchi* 2.00
101 *Daylan Childress* .25
102 *Juan Morillo* .50
103 *Marcos Carvajal* .25
104 *Ubaldo Jimenez* .25
105 *Justin Verlander* 2.00
106 *Chris Resop* .25
107 *Yorman Bazardo* .25
108 *Jared Gothreaux* .25
109 *Luke Scott* .50
110 *Ambiorix Burgos* .50
111 *Prince Fielder* 4.00
112 *Dennis Houlton* .25
113 *Franquelis Osoria* .25
114 *Norihiro Nakamura* 1.00
115 *Oscar Robles* .25
116 *Steve Schmoll* .25
117 *Luis Pena* .25
118 *David Gassner* .25
119 *Ambiorix Concepcion* .50
120 *Dae-Sung Koo* .25
121 *Matt Lindstrom* .25
122 *Colter Bean* .25
123 *Keiichi Yabu* .25
124 *Philip Humber* 1.00
125 *Wladimir Balentien* 1.00
126 *Tony Giarratano* .25
127 *Shane Costa* .25
128 *Jeff Niemann* 1.00
129 *Nick Masset* .25
130 *Ismael Ramirez* .25
131 *John Hattig Jr.* .25
132 *Brandon McCarthy* 1.50

Gold

Gold: 2-4X
Production 350 sets

Silver

Silver: 1-3X
Inserted 1:5

Signature Sensations

NM/M
Inserted 1:24
Silver: 1X-2X
Production 50 Sets
Gold: No Pricing
Production 5 Sets
AA Abe Alvarez 10.00
BA Bronson Arroyo 20.00
GA Garrett Atkins 8.00
DB Denny Bautista 5.00
RB Russell Branyan 5.00
MC Miguel Cabrera 30.00
KC Kiko Calero 5.00
CC Chad Cordero 10.00
JC Juan Cruz 5.00
BD Brandon Duckworth 5.00
JE Johnny Estrada 8.00
LF Lew Ford SP 10.00
TH Travis Hafner 15.00
OH Orlando Hernandez 75.00
OI Omar Infante 5.00
DJ Derek Jeter SP 150.00
JJ Jorge Julio 5.00
AM Aaron Miles 5.00
YM Yadier Molina 15.00
RN Roberto Novoa 5.00
NP Nick Punto 5.00
HR Horacio Ramirez SP 10.00
AR Aaron Rowand 20.00
CS Cory Sullivan 8.00
JS Jeff Suppan 8.00
BT Brett Tomko 5.00
MV Merkin Valdez 5.00
DW David Wright 50.00

2005 UPPER DECK PROS & PROSPECTS

NM/M
Complete Set (200):
Common Player (1-100): .15
Common SP (101-150): 3.00
Production 999
Common SP (151-175): 4.00
Production 499
Common SP (176-200): 5.00
Production 199
Pack (6): 2.75
Box (24): 60.00
1 Adam Dunn .40
2 Aramis Ramirez .40
3 Bobby Abreu .25
4 Mike Lowell .15
5 Josh Beckett .25
6 Derek Jeter 1.50
7 Alex Rodriguez 1.25
8 Andruw Jones .25
9 Brian Giles .15
10 Ivan Rodriguez .40
11 Aubrey Huff .15
12 Jake Peavy .25
13 Hank Blalock .25
14 Curt Schilling .50
15 Carlos Zambrano .40
16 Mike Mussina .40
17 Travis Hafner .15
18 Scott Rolen .50
19 Luis Gonzalez .25
20 Torii Hunter .25
21 Greg Maddux 1.00
22 J.D. Drew .25
23 Kevin Brown .15
24 Carl Pavano .25
25 David Ortiz .50
26 Jose Reyes .15
27 Johan Santana .50
28 Todd Helton .40
29 Jason Kendall .15
30 Pedro Martinez .50
31 Chipper Jones .50
32 Ben Sheets .25
33 Garret Anderson .25
34 Carl Crawford .15
35 Jason Schmidt .25
36 Johnny Damon .50
37 Richie Sexson .25
38 Brad Penny .15
39 Carlos Delgado .40
40 Gary Sheffield .40
41 John Smoltz .25
42 Eric Chavez .25
43 Carlos Guillen .15
44 Jeff Kent .25
45 Miguel Tejada .40
46 Shawn Green .25
47 Vernon Wells .15
48 Albert Pujols 1.50
49 Alfonso Soriano .50
50 Eric Gagne .40
51 Mark Prior .50
52 Rafael Furcal .25
53 Preston Wilson .15
54 Barry Larkin .25
55 Randy Johnson .50
56 Craig Wilson .15
57 Victor Martinez .15
58 Jim Thome .50
59 Paul Konerko .15
60 Jeff Bagwell .40
61 Lyle Overbay .15
62 Miguel Cabrera .50
63 Melvin Mora .15
64 Scott Podsednik .25
65 Mark Mulder .25
66 Mark Teixeira .40
67 Tom Glavine .25
68 Frank Thomas .40
69 Livan Hernandez .15
70 Kazuo Matsui .15
71 Jose Vidro .15
72 Ichiro Suzuki 1.25
73 Roger Clemens 1.50
74 Manny Ramirez .50
75 Michael Young .15
76 Rafael Palmeiro .40
77 Steve Finley .15
78 Andy Pettitte .25
79 Lance Berkman .25
80 Adrian Beltre .25
81 Carlos Lee .25
82 Bret Boone .15
83 Magglio Ordonez .15
84 Sammy Sosa 1.00
85 Tim Hudson .25
86 Vladimir Guerrero .50
87 Carlos Beltran .40
88 Kerry Wood .50
89 Jim Edmonds .25
90 Mike Sweeney .15
91 Nomar Garciaparra 1.00
92 Mike Piazza 1.00
93 Roy Halladay .25
94 Troy Glaus .25
95 Bernie Williams .25
96 Larry Walker .25
97 Craig Biggio .25
98 Roy Oswalt .25
99 Ken Griffey Jr. 1.00
100 Hideki Matsui 1.00
101 Bucky Jacobsen 3.00
102 J.D. Closser 3.00
103 Antonio Perez 3.00
104 Chris Shelton 3.00
105 David Aardsma 3.00
106 Jake Woods 3.00
107 Jung Bong 3.00
108 Kazuhito Tadano 3.00
109 John Van Benschoten 3.00
110 Jesse Foppert 3.00
111 Joe Borchard 3.00
112 Brandon Phillips 3.00
113 J.D. Durbin 3.00
114 Brandon Claussen 3.00
115 Robb Quinlan 3.00
116 Aaron Harang 3.00
117 Chris Burke 3.00
118 Sergio Mitre 3.00
119 David DeJesus 3.00
120 Gustavo Chacin 3.00
121 Xavier Nady 3.00
122 Garrett Atkins 3.00
123 Jimmy Gobble 3.00
124 Yhency Brazoban 3.00
125 David Kelton 3.00
126 Dewon Brazelton 3.00
127 Koyie Hill 3.00
128 Roman Colon 3.00
129 Daniel Cabrera 3.00
130 Chris Bootcheck 3.00
131 Brad Halsey 3.00
132 Bobby Madritsch 3.00
133 Grady Sizemore 3.00
134 Akinori Otsuka 3.00
135 Wilfredo Ledezma 3.00
136 Russ Adams 3.00
137 Joe Crede 3.00
138 Chad Cordero 3.00
139 Willie Harris 3.00
140 Joey Gathright 3.00
141 Logan Kensing 3.00
142 Jon Leicester 3.00
143 Freddy Guzman 3.00
144 Jonny Gomes 3.00
145 Jeff Bajenaru 3.00
146 Andres Blanco 3.00
147 Jhonny Peralta 3.00
148 Jayson Werth 3.00
149 Bill Hall 3.00
150 Jason Davis 3.00
151 Gabe Gross 4.00
152 Abe Alvarez 4.00
153 Josh Willingham 4.00
154 Merkin Valdez 4.00
155 *Jeff Niemann* 8.00
156 Yadier Molina 4.00
157 Guillermo Quiroz 4.00
158 Ian Snell 4.00
159 Dan Meyer 4.00
160 Jason Lane 4.00
161 Adrian Gonzalez 4.00
162 Eddy Rodriguez 4.00
163 Jason Dubois 4.00
164 Juan Rincon 4.00
165 Ryan Wagner 4.00
166 Nick Swisher 4.00
167 Chad Tracy 4.00
168 Dioner Navarro 4.00
169 Gerald Laird 4.00
170 Alexis Rios 4.00
171 Aaron Rowand 4.00
172 Adam LaRoche 4.00
173 Kevin Youkilis 4.00
174 *Philip Humber* 6.00
175 Chin-Hui Tsao 4.00
176 Jeff Francis 5.00
177 Chase Utley 5.00
178 Gavin Floyd 5.00
179 David Wright 10.00
180 B.J. Upton 5.00
181 Laynce Nix 5.00
182 Joe Mauer 8.00
183 Justin Morneau 5.00
184 Zack Greinke 5.00
185 Jose Capellan 5.00
186 Khalil Greene 5.00
187 Oliver Perez 5.00
188 Joe Blanton 5.00
189 Wily Mo Pena 5.00
190 Dallas McPherson 6.00
191 Edwin Jackson 5.00
192 Casey Kotchman 5.00
193 Jesse Crain 5.00
194 Ryan Howard 6.00
195 Bobby Crosby 5.00
196 Jason Bay 5.00
197 Rickie Weeks 5.00
198 Scott Proctor 5.00
199 Dan Haren 5.00
200 Scott Kazmir 5.00

Gold

Gold (1-100): 4-8X
Production 125
Gold (101-150): 1X
Production 150
Gold (151-175): 1X
Production 99
Gold (176-200): No Pricing
Production 25

Future Fabrics

NM/M
Common Player: 4.00
Gold: 1X-2X
Production 75 Sets
MC Miguel Cabrera 8.00
BC Bobby Crosby 6.00
KG Khalil Greene 6.00
RH Rich Harden 4.00
EH Eric Hinske 4.00
JJ Jacque Jones 4.00
KE Austin Kearns 4.00
AK Adam Kennedy 4.00
CK Casey Kotchman 4.00
VM Victor Martinez 4.00
KM Kazuo Matsui 4.00
JM Joe Mauer 8.00
DM Dallas McPherson 6.00
TN Trot Nixon 4.00
SP Sidney Ponson 4.00
JR Jose Reyes 4.00
CS C.C. Sabathia 4.00
SS Shannon Stewart 4.00
BU B.J. Upton 4.00
JW Jayson Werth 4.00
DW David Wright 15.00

Pro Material

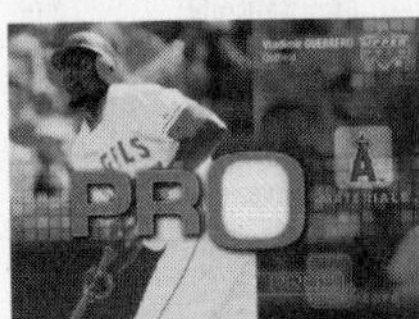

		NM/M
Common Player:		6.00
Gold:		1X-2X
Production 50 Sets		
JB	Jeff Bagwell	6.00
CB	Carlos Beltran	8.00
AB	Adrian Beltre	6.00
HB	Hank Blalock	6.00
EC	Eric Chavez	6.00
KG	Ken Griffey Jr.	10.00
VG	Vladimir Guerrero	8.00
TH	Todd Helton	8.00
DJ	Derek Jeter	20.00
RJ	Randy Johnson	8.00
CJ	Chipper Jones	8.00
PI	Mike Piazza	8.00
MP	Mark Prior	8.00
AP	Albert Pujols	15.00
MR	Manny Ramirez	8.00
SR	Scott Rolen	8.00
CS	Curt Schilling	8.00
SS	Sammy Sosa	8.00
IS	Ichiro Suzuki	25.00
MT	Miguel Tejada	8.00
JT	Jim Thome	8.00

Signs of Stardom

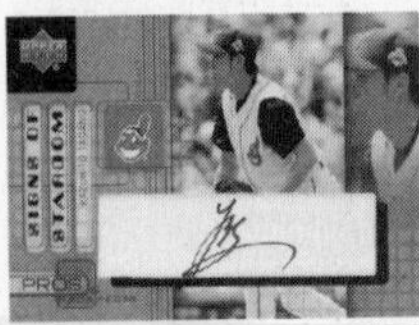

		NM/M
Common Autograph:		8.00
RB	Rocco Baldelli	15.00
JB	Josh Beckett	15.00
AB	Angel Berroa	8.00
HB	Hank Blalock	20.00
SB	Sean Burroughs	8.00
MC	Miguel Cabrera	30.00
CC	Chad Cordero	8.00
BC	Bobby Crosby	15.00
AE	Adam Eaton	12.00
FF	Frank Francisco	8.00
JF	Jason Frasor	8.00
GA	John Gall	8.00
MG	Marcus Giles	15.00
GR	Khalil Greene	25.00
RH	Rich Harden	20.00
MJ	Mike Johnston	8.00
SK	Scott Kazmir	20.00
JK	Jeff Keppinger	8.00
CK	Casey Kotchman	15.00
CL	Cliff Lee	8.00
JL	Justin Leone	8.00
MA	Joe Mauer	25.00
AO	Akinori Otsuka	20.00
LO	Lyle Overbay	10.00
CP	Corey Patterson	15.00
PE	Jake Peavy	30.00
OP	Oliver Perez	20.00
SP	Scott Podsednik	15.00
HR	Horacio Ramirez	8.00
JR	Jose Reyes	15.00
MR	Mike Rouse	8.00
BS	Ben Sheets	15.00
TS	Terrmel Sledge	10.00
KT	Kazuhito Tadano	20.00
ST	Shingo Takatsu	25.00
MT	Mark Teixeira	30.00
WA	Ryan Wagner	10.00
WE	Brandon Webb	10.00
RW	Rickie Weeks	15.00
JW	Jerome Williams	8.00
DW	Dontrelle Willis	25.00

Stardom Signatures

		NM/M
EB	Ernie Banks/240	50.00
BE	Josh Beckett/50	20.00
BL	Hank Blalock/50	20.00
JG	Jason Giambi/100	15.00
KG	Ken Griffey Jr./198	75.00
AK	Al Kaline/99	50.00
JM	Joe Morgan/194	25.00
KP	Kirby Puckett/156	50.00

2005 UPPER DECK REFLECTIONS

		NM/M
Complete Set (200):		
Common (1-100):		.50
Common SP (101-150):		1.00
Inserted 1:2		
Common SP (151-200):		2.00
Inserted 1:2		
Pack (4):		12.00
Box (12):		120.00
1	Corey Patterson	.50
2	Curt Schilling	1.00
3	Todd Helton	.75
4	Johnny Damon	1.00
5	Alex Rodriguez	2.50
6	Vladimir Guerrero	1.00
7	John Smoltz	.50
8	Ivan Rodriguez	.75
9	Roy Halladay	.50
10	Carlos Beltran	.75
11	Ichiro Suzuki	2.00
12	Jim Edmonds	.50
13	Andruw Jones	.50
14	Scott Podsednik	.50
15	Troy Glaus	.50
16	Miguel Cabrera	1.00
17	Adrian Beltre	.50
18	Ben Sheets	.50
19	Alfonso Soriano	1.00
20	Brian Giles	.50
21	Carl Crawford	.50
22	Frank Thomas	.75
23	Jeff Kent	.50
24	Eric Gagne	.50
25	Shawn Green	.50
26	Sammy Sosa	2.00
27	Carlos Lee	.50
28	Ken Griffey Jr.	2.00
29	Mike Lowell	.50
30	Magglio Ordonez	.50
31	Aubrey Huff	.50
32	Travis Hafner	.50
33	Albert Pujols	3.00
34	Vernon Wells	.50
35	Roy Oswalt	.50
36	Jose Guillen	.50
37	Jim Thome	.75
38	Bobby Abreu	.50
39	Bret Boone	.50
40	Mark Teixeira	.50
41	Garret Anderson	.50
42	Jose Reyes	.50
43	Bernie Williams	.50
44	Greg Maddux	1.50
45	Gary Sheffield	.50
46	Josh Beckett	.50
47	Chipper Jones	1.00
48	Hank Blalock	.50
49	C.C. Sabathia	.50
50	Manny Ramirez	1.00
51	Pedro Martinez	1.00
52	Michael Young	.50
53	Jacque Jones	.50
54	Marcus Giles	.50
55	Steve Finley	.50
56	Miguel Tejada	.75
57	Mike Sweeney	.50
58	Lance Berkman	.50
59	J.D. Drew	.50
60	Jeromy Burnitz	.50
61	Johan Santana	.75
62	Victor Martinez	.50
63	Carl Pavano	.50
64	Roger Clemens	3.00
65	Richie Sexson	.50
66	Tim Hudson	.50
67	Melvin Mora	.50
68	Angel Berroa	.50
69	Rafael Palmeiro	.75
70	Randy Johnson	1.00
71	Torii Hunter	.50
72	Luis Gonzalez	.50
73	Kazuo Matsui	.50
74	Hideki Matsui	2.00
75	Mark Prior	1.00
76	Jeff Bagwell	.75
77	Eric Chavez	.50
78	Mark Loretta	.50
79	Adam Dunn	.75
80	Kerry Wood	1.00
81	Jose Vidro	.50
82	Jason Schmidt	.50
83	Carlos Delgado	.50
84	Scott Rolen	1.00
85	David Ortiz	1.00
86	Edgar Renteria	.50
87	Nomar Garciaparra	1.50
88	Mike Piazza	1.50
89	Mark Mulder	.50
90	Tom Glavine	.50
91	Paul Konerko	.50
92	Larry Walker	.50
93	Derek Jeter	3.00
94	Jake Peavy	.50
95	Carlos Zambrano	.50
96	Russ Ortiz	.50
97	Barry Zito	.50
98	Austin Kearns	.50
99	Pedro Feliz	.50
100	Rich Harden	.50
101	Adam LaRoche	1.00
102	Brandon Claussen	1.00
103	Gavin Floyd	1.00
104	Daniel Cabrera	1.00
105	Joe Mauer	2.00
106	Khalil Greene	2.00
107	David Wright	3.00
108	Rickie Weeks	2.00
109	Robb Quinlan	1.00
110	Bucky Jacobsen	1.00
111	Ryan Howard	2.00
112	Jeff Francis	1.00
113	Jason Lane	1.00
114	Alexis Rios	1.00
115	Bobby Madritsch	1.00
116	Jesse Crain	1.00
117	Oliver Perez	1.00
118	Garrett Atkins	1.00
119	Casey Kotchman	2.00
120	B.J. Upton	1.00
121	Laynce Nix	1.00
122	Adrian Gonzalez	1.00
123	Joe Blanton	1.00
124	Gabe Gross	1.00
125	Scott Kazmir	2.00
126	Zack Greinke	1.00
127	Edwin Jackson	1.00
128	Jason Bay	1.00
129	J.D. Closser	1.00
130	Jason Dubois	1.00
131	Dallas McPherson	2.00
132	Chad Cordero	1.00
133	Angel Guzman	1.00
134	Jayson Werth	1.00
135	Ryan Wagner	1.00
136	Guillermo Quiroz	1.00
137	Scott Proctor	1.00
138	Chris Burke	1.00
139	Nick Swisher	1.00
140	David DeJesus	1.00
141	Yhency Brazoban	1.00
142	Bobby Crosby	1.00
143	Chase Utley	1.00
144	Wily Mo Pena	1.00
145	Roman Colon	1.00
146	Eddy Rodriguez	1.00
147	Gerald Laird	1.00
148	Jose Capellan	1.00
149	Aaron Rowand	1.00
150	Kevin Youkilis	1.00
151	Bob Feller	2.00
152	Robin Yount	4.00
153	Willie Stargell	2.00
154	Cal Ripken Jr.	8.00
155	Monte Irvin	2.00
156	Nolan Ryan	6.00
157	Bob Lemon	2.00
158	Richie Ashburn	2.00
159	Billy Williams	2.00
160	Luis Aparicio	2.00
161	Phil Niekro	2.00
162	Bobby Doerr	2.00
163	Mike Schmidt	6.00
164	Stan Musial	4.00
165	George Kell	2.00
166	Joe Morgan	2.00
167	Whitey Ford	3.00
168	Rick Ferrell	2.00
169	Jim "Catfish" Hunter	2.00
170	Red Schoendienst	2.00
171	Tom Seaver	4.00
172	Pee Wee Reese	2.00
173	Lou Boudreau	2.00
174	Hal Newhouser	2.00
175	Harmon Killebrew	3.00
176	Jim Bunning	2.00
177	Willie McCovey	3.00
178	Bob Gibson	3.00
179	Juan Marichal	2.00
180	Robin Roberts	2.00
181	Gaylord Perry	2.00
182	Brooks Robinson	4.00
183	Al Lopez	2.00
184	Joe DiMaggio	6.00
185	Al Kaline	3.00
186	Rollie Fingers	2.00
187	Mickey Mantle	10.00
188	Enos Slaughter	2.00
189	Ernie Banks	4.00
190	Eddie Mathews	3.00
191	Tommy Lasorda	2.00
192	Fergie Jenkins	2.00
193	Lou Brock	2.00
194	Larry Doby	2.00
195	Phil Rizzuto	3.00
196	Warren Spahn	4.00
197	Ralph Kiner	2.00
198	Hoyt Wilhelm	2.00
199	Early Wynn	2.00
200	Yogi Berra	4.00

Red

Red (1-100):	2X-4X
Red (101-200):	1X-2.5X
Production 99 Sets	

Purple

Purple (1-100):	2X-4X
Purple (101-200):	1X-2.5X
Production 99 Sets	

Blue

Blue (1-100):	2X-4X
Blue (101-200):	1X-2.5X
Production 75 Sets	

Turquoise

Turquoise (1-100):	3X-5X
Turquoise (101-200):	1.5X-3X
Production 50 Sets	

Emerald

Emerald (1-100):	4X-8X
Emerald (101-200):	3X-5X
Production 25 Sets	

Platinum

Platinum (1-200):	No Pricing
Production One Set	

Cut From the Same Cloth

		NM/M
Common Duo:		8.00
Production 225 Sets		
Red:		1X-1.5X
Production 99 Sets		
Blue:		1X-2X
Production 50 Sets		
Platinum:		No Pricing
Production One Set		
AA	Albert Pujols, Adrian Beltre	20.00
AB	Carlos Beltran, Bobby Abreu	10.00
AG	Garret Anderson, Vladimir Guerrero	10.00
AH	Alfonso Soriano, Hank Blalock	10.00
AJ	Albert Pujols, Jim Thome	20.00
AM	Adrian Beltre, Miguel Cabrera	10.00
AT	Jim Thome, Bobby Abreu	10.00
AW	Albert Pujols, Will Clark	20.00
BB	Jeff Bagwell, Craig Biggio	10.00
BG	Carlos Beltran, Ken Griffey Jr.	15.00
BM	Paul Molitor, George Brett	20.00
BO	Josh Beckett, Roy Oswalt	8.00

BP Johnny Bench, Mike Piazza 15.00
BR Adrian Beltre, Scott Rolen 10.00
BS George Brett, Mike Schmidt 25.00
BT Mark Teixeira, Hank Blalock 10.00
BW Hank Blalock, David Wright 15.00
CB Bobby Crosby, Jason Bay 8.00
CC Bobby Crosby, Eric Chavez 8.00
CG Bobby Crosby, Khalil Greene 8.00
CL Miguel Cabrera, Mike Lowell 10.00
CP Carl Crawford, Scott Podsednik 8.00
CR Scott Rolen, Eric Chavez 10.00
CT Miguel Tejada, Bobby Crosby 10.00
DM Mike Schmidt, Dale Murphy 15.00
DR Manny Ramirez, Johnny Damon 15.00
GI Brian Giles, Marcus Giles 8.00
GS Sammy Sosa, Ken Griffey Jr. 20.00
GV Jose Guillen, Jose Vidro 8.00
HH Tim Hudson, Rich Harden 8.00
HK Kent Hrbek, Harmon Killebrew 20.00
JD J.D. Drew, Chipper Jones 10.00
JH Torii Hunter, Jacque Jones 8.00
JJ Chipper Jones, Andruw Jones 10.00
JM Don Mattingly, Derek Jeter 30.00
JR Randy Johnson, Nolan Ryan 30.00
JS Steve Carlton, Johan Santana 10.00
JT Miguel Tejada, Derek Jeter 25.00
KH Jason Kendall, Tim Hudson 8.00
KM Dallas McPherson, Casey Kotchman 10.00
MB Wade Boggs, Don Mattingly 20.00
MC Don Mattingly, Will Clark 20.00
MH Mark Mulder, Tim Hudson 8.00
MJ Dale Murphy, Chipper Jones 15.00
MK Harmon Killebrew, Justin Morneau 15.00
MM Kazuo Matsui, Hideki Matsui 30.00
MS Johan Santana, Joe Mauer 12.00
MW Dallas McPherson, David Wright 20.00
MY Robin Yount, Paul Molitor 20.00
OD Johnny Damon, David Ortiz 15.00
OT Shingo Takatsu, Akinori Otsuka 15.00
PB Jim Bunning, Jim Palmer 10.00
PC Miguel Cabrera, Albert Pujols 20.00
PG Albert Pujols, Vladimir Guerrero 25.00
PP Mike Piazza, Jorge Posada 15.00
PR Albert Pujols, Scott Rolen 25.00
PS Tom Seaver, Mark Prior 15.00
PT Mark Teixeira, Albert Pujols 20.00
RJ Cal Ripken Jr., Derek Jeter 40.00
RM Ivan Rodriguez, Victor Martinez 8.00
RO Manny Ramirez, David Ortiz 20.00
RP Ivan Rodriguez, Mike Piazza 15.00
RR Cal Ripken Jr., Brooks Robinson 35.00
RT Miguel Tejada, Cal Ripken Jr. 30.00
RW Scott Rolen, David Wright 15.00
SB Ryne Sandberg, Wade Boggs 25.00
SM Pedro J. Martinez, Curt Schilling 15.00
SO Curt Schilling, David Ortiz 15.00
SP Ben Sheets, Mark Prior 15.00
SR Scott Rolen, Mike Schmidt 15.00
ST Alfonso Soriano, Mark Teixeira 15.00
TC Mark Teixeira, Miguel Cabrera 15.00
TH Todd Helton, Jim Thome 10.00
TP Rafael Palmeiro, Miguel Tejada 10.00
TR Manny Ramirez, Jim Thome 12.00
TS Jim Thome, Mike Schmidt 15.00
UJ Derek Jeter, B.J. Upton 25.00
UK B.J. Upton, Scott Kazmir 8.00
UW B.J. Upton, David Wright 15.00
VJ Jose Vidro, Nick Johnson 8.00
WB Bernie Williams, Carlos Beltran 10.00
WJ Bernie Williams, Derek Jeter 25.00
WM Bernie Williams, Hideki Matsui 30.00
WP Mark Prior, Kerry Wood 15.00
WR Kerry Wood, Nolan Ryan 30.00
YR Manny Ramirez, Carl Yastrzemski 20.00
ZM Mark Mulder, Barry Zito 8.00
BD1 Carlos Beltran, Johnny Damon 10.00
BD2 Johnny Damon, Carlos Beltran 10.00
GG1 Ken Griffey Jr., Ken Griffey Sr. 15.00
GG2 Ken Griffey Sr., Ken Griffey Jr. 15.00

Cut From the Same Cloth Auto Patch

NM/M
Production 25 Sets
BT Mark Teixeira, Hank Blalock 120.00
DG Ken Griffey Jr., Adam Dunn 240.00
GC Miguel Cabrera, Ken Griffey Jr. 240.00
JR Derek Jeter, Cal Ripken Jr. 500.00
MJ Chipper Jones, Dale Murphy 140.00
PC Albert Pujols, Miguel Cabrera 350.00
RP Mike Piazza, Ivan Rodriguez 140.00
SB Ryne Sandberg, Wade Boggs 160.00
TO Mark Teixeira, David Ortiz 100.00
WB David Wright, Hank Blalock 100.00
WR David Wright, Scott Rolen 100.00

Cut From Same Cloth Patch

NM/M
Production 99 Sets
AM Adrian Beltre, Miguel Cabrera 25.00
BR Adrian Beltre, Scott Rolen 25.00
BS George Brett, Mike Schmidt 40.00
BT Mark Teixeira, Hank Blalock 20.00
CB Jason Bay, Bobby Crosby 20.00
CG Bobby Crosby, Khalil Greene 20.00
CP Gary Carter, Mike Piazza 35.00
CR Eric Chavez, Scott Rolen 25.00
DG Ken Griffey Jr., Adam Dunn 40.00
GC Miguel Cabrera, Ken Griffey Jr. 40.00
GI Brian Giles, Marcus Giles 15.00
JM Derek Jeter, Don Mattingly 60.00
JR Cal Ripken Jr., Derek Jeter 80.00
KM Dallas McPherson, Casey Kotchman 25.00
MJ Chipper Jones, Dale Murphy 30.00
MP Mike Piazza, Joe Mauer 30.00
MW Dallas McPherson, David Wright 30.00
MY Robin Yount, Paul Molitor 40.00
OB Wade Boggs, David Ortiz 30.00
OT Shingo Takatsu, Akinori Otsuka 30.00
PB Albert Pujols, Adrian Beltre 40.00
PC Albert Pujols, Miguel Cabrera 40.00
PR Albert Pujols, Scott Rolen 40.00
RJ Randy Johnson, Nolan Ryan 40.00
RP Ivan Rodriguez, Mike Piazza 30.00
RR Cal Ripken Jr., Brooks Robinson 50.00
RW Nolan Ryan, Kerry Wood 40.00
SB Ryne Sandberg, Wade Boggs 50.00
SP Ben Sheets, Mark Prior 25.00
TC Mark Teixeira, Miguel Cabrera 30.00
TO Mark Teixeira, David Ortiz 25.00
UJ Derek Jeter, B.J. Upton 40.00
UW B.J. Upton, David Wright 25.00
WB David Wright, Hank Blalock 30.00
WP Mark Prior, Kerry Wood 35.00
WR David Wright, Scott Rolen 30.00
YO David Ortiz, Carl Yastrzemski 50.00
GG1 Ken Griffey Sr., Ken Griffey Jr. 40.00
GG2 Ken Griffey Jr., Ken Griffey Sr. 40.00

Dual Signature

NM/M
Red: 1X-1.5X
Production 99 Sets
Blue: 1.5X-2X
Production 35 Sets
Platinum: No Pricing
Production One Set
ABAR Al Rosen, Adrian Beltre 30.00
ABDM Adrian Beltre, Dallas McPherson 30.00
ABDW David Wright, Adrian Beltre 30.00
ABEC Adrian Beltre, Eric Chavez 30.00
ABJL Adrian Beltre, Justin Leone 30.00
ABSR Adrian Beltre, Scott Rolen 30.00
AHBU Aubrey Huff, B.J. Upton 25.00
AHCC Carl Crawford, Aubrey Huff 25.00
AKDM Al Kaline, Dale Murphy 50.00
AOST Akinori Otsuka, Shingo Takatsu 40.00
ARCC Alexis Rios, Carl Crawford 20.00
ARKG Alexis Rios, Ken Griffey Jr. 65.00
ARTH Al Rosen, Travis Hafner 25.00
BAKY Kevin Youkilis, Bronson Arroyo 50.00
BCCR Bobby Crosby, Cal Ripken Jr. 160.00
BCDJ Derek Jeter, Bobby Crosby 125.00
BCEC Bobby Crosby, Eric Chavez 25.00
BCJB Bobby Crosby, Jason Bay 35.00
BCKG Khalil Greene, Bobby Crosby 35.00
BDWB Bobby Doerr, Wade Boggs 50.00
BGMG Brian Giles, Marcus Giles 25.00
BPFH Frank Howard, Boog Powell 30.00
BRRS Brooks Robinson, Ron Santo 40.00
BSJC Ben Sheets, Jose Capellan 20.00
BSRW Rickie Weeks, Ben Sheets 35.00
BSSK Ben Sheets, Scott Kazmir 20.00
BUDJ B.J. Upton, Derek Jeter 125.00
BURW B.J. Upton, Rickie Weeks 30.00
BUSK B.J. Upton, Scott Kazmir 25.00
BWKG Billy Williams, Ken Griffey Jr. 80.00
CCNJ Nick Johnson, Chad Cordero 25.00
CKDM Casey Kotchman, Dallas McPherson 35.00
CKKH Keith Hernandez, Casey Kotchman 20.00
CKMT Casey Kotchman, Mark Teixeira 35.00
CTDM Charles Thomas, Dale Murphy 30.00
CTJC Charles Thomas, Jose Capellan 15.00
CTRH Charles Thomas, Ryan Howard 20.00
CZJS Johan Santana, Carlos Zambrano 60.00
CZLT Carlos Zambrano, Luis Tiant 20.00
DGDB Dwight Gooden, Dewon Brazelton 20.00
DGJB Jim Bouton, Dwight Gooden 20.00
DGJS Dwight Gooden, Johan Santana 50.00
DJDM Derek Jeter, Don Mattingly 200.00
DJKG Derek Jeter, Khalil Greene 140.00
DKFH Frank Howard, Dave Kingman 25.00
DMDW David Wright, Dallas McPherson 40.00
DMJL Justin Leone, Dallas McPherson 20.00
DMKY Dallas McPherson, Kevin Youkilis 20.00
DMMS Dallas McPherson, Mike Schmidt 75.00
DMRH Dallas McPherson, Ryan Howard 20.00
DOKY David Ortiz, Kevin Youkilis 60.00
DWJL Justin Leone, David Wright 30.00
DWKH David Wright, Keith Hernandez 40.00
DWKY David Wright, Kevin Youkilis 40.00
DWMS David Wright, Mike Schmidt 90.00
DWSR David Wright, Scott Rolen 50.00
ECSR Scott Rolen, Eric Chavez 50.00
FHMT Mark Teixeira, Frank Howard 40.00
FHNJ Frank Howard, Nick Johnson 25.00
GPJP Gaylord Perry, Jake Peavy 30.00
ISJC Jose Capellan, Ian Snell 15.00
ISMV Ian Snell, Merkin Valdez 15.00
ISSK Ian Snell, Scott Kazmir 20.00

JBIS Ian Snell, Joe Blanton 20.00
JBJP Jim Bunning, Jim Palmer 30.00
JBMV Merkin Valdez, Joe Blanton 15.00
JBRH Joe Blanton, Rich Harden 20.00
JBSK Scott Kazmir, Joe Blanton 20.00
JCMV Merkin Valdez, Jose Capellan 15.00
JLRH Justin Leone, Ryan Howard 20.00
JPJB Jake Peavy, Joe Blanton 25.00
JPKG Jake Peavy, Khalil Greene 50.00
JPRH Jake Peavy, Rich Harden 40.00
JPSK Jake Peavy, Scott Kazmir 30.00
JRDW Jose Reyes, David Wright 65.00
JSMP Johan Santana, Mark Prior 100.00
JSSC Johan Santana, Steve Carlton 50.00
JSSK Johan Santana, Scott Kazmir 40.00
JVMG Marcus Giles, Jose Vidro 20.00
KGKG Ken Griffey Sr., Ken Griffey Jr. 100.00
KGMC Ken Griffey Jr., Miguel Cabrera 100.00
KYWB Kevin Youkilis, Wade Boggs 50.00
MCRH Ryan Howard, Miguel Cabrera 40.00
MGRW Rickie Weeks, Marcus Giles 35.00
MTHB Hank Blalock, Mark Teixeira 50.00
MTMC Miguel Cabrera, Mark Teixeira 60.00
MTRH Mark Teixeira, Ryan Howard 40.00
MVRH Merkin Valdez, Rich Harden 20.00
PBKG Pat Burrell, Ken Griffey Jr. 85.00
PBMC Pat Burrell, Miguel Cabrera 40.00
RHDO Ryan Howard, David Ortiz 40.00
RHRO Roy Oswalt, Rich Harden 30.00
RHSK Rich Harden, Scott Kazmir 25.00
THVM Victor Martinez, Travis Hafner 20.00
TOKH Kent Hrbek, Tony Oliva 30.00
VMYM Victor Martinez, Yadier Molina 20.00

Fabric Jersey

NM/M

Common Player:
Inserted 1:12
CB Carlos Beltran 8.00
AB Adrian Beltre 6.00
HB Hank Blalock 6.00
WB Wade Boggs SP 10.00
GB George Brett SP 15.00
MC Miguel Cabrera 8.00
EC Eric Chavez 4.00
WC Will Clark SP 10.00
JD Johnny Damon 10.00
KG Ken Griffey Jr. 15.00
VG Vladimir Guerrero 8.00
TH Todd Helton 6.00
DJ Derek Jeter SP 20.00
RJ Randy Johnson 8.00
CJ Chipper Jones 8.00
GM Greg Maddux 10.00
HM Hideki Matsui 20.00
DM Don Mattingly SP 20.00
PM Paul Molitor SP 8.00
DO David Ortiz 8.00
PI Mike Piazza 10.00
MP Mark Prior 8.00
AP Albert Pujols 15.00
MR Manny Ramirez 8.00
CR Cal Ripken Jr. SP 25.00
IR Ivan Rodriguez 8.00
SR Scott Rolen 8.00
NR Nolan Ryan SP 25.00
JS Johan Santana 8.00
CS Curt Schilling 8.00
MS Mike Schmidt SP 15.00
AS Alfonso Soriano 8.00
MT Mark Teixeira 6.00
TE Miguel Tejada 8.00
JT Jim Thome 8.00
BW Bernie Williams 6.00
KW Kerry Wood 8.00
DW David Wright 10.00
CY Carl Yastrzemski SP 25.00
RY Robin Yount SP 10.00

Reflections Auto Patch

NM/M

Production 50 Sets
JB Jason Bay 50.00
HB Hank Blalock 50.00
WB Wade Boggs 60.00
DG Dwight Gooden 40.00
GR Khalil Greene 75.00
DJ Derek Jeter 275.00
RJ Randy Johnson 100.00
AJ Andruw Jones 75.00
SK Scott Kazmir 40.00
MA Don Mattingly 140.00
MC Dallas McPherson 50.00
PM Paul Molitor 60.00
DO David Ortiz 75.00
RO Roy Oswalt 50.00
JP Jake Peavy 60.00
PI Mike Piazza 120.00
MP Mark Prior 75.00
AP Albert Pujols 300.00
SR Scott Rolen 60.00
NR Nolan Ryan 180.00
MS Mike Schmidt 100.00
ST Shingo Takatsu 75.00
MT Mark Teixeira 75.00
DW David Wright 100.00
CZ Carlos Zambrano 40.00

Fabric Reflections Patch

NM/M

Production 99 Sets
JB Jason Bay 15.00
AB Adrian Beltre 10.00
HB Hank Blalock 15.00
WB Wade Boggs 20.00
GB George Brett 50.00
PB Pat Burrell 15.00
CA Miguel Cabrera 20.00
EC Eric Chavez 10.00
BC Bobby Crosby 10.00
MG Marcus Giles 10.00
DG Dwight Gooden 15.00
GR Khalil Greene 20.00
KG Ken Griffey Jr. 40.00
RH Rich Harden 15.00
DJ Derek Jeter 50.00
RJ Randy Johnson 20.00
AJ Andruw Jones 15.00
SK Scott Kazmir 10.00
MA Don Mattingly 30.00
MC Dallas McPherson 15.00
PM Paul Molitor 20.00
DM Dale Murphy 15.00
DO David Ortiz 20.00
RO Roy Oswalt 10.00
JP Jake Peavy 15.00
GP Gaylord Perry 10.00
MP Mark Prior 25.00
AP Albert Pujols 50.00
CR Cal Ripken Jr. 60.00
SR Scott Rolen 20.00
NR Nolan Ryan 40.00
JS Johan Santana 20.00
MS Mike Schmidt 25.00
BS Ben Sheets 15.00
ST Shingo Takatsu 20.00
MT Mark Teixeira 15.00
BU B.J. Upton 10.00
DW David Wright 20.00
RY Robin Yount 30.00
CZ Carlos Zambrano 15.00

Super Swatch

NM/M

Production 50 Sets
Red: 1X-1.5X
Production 25 Sets
Blue: No Pricing
Production 10 Sets
BO Bobby Abreu 15.00
RA Roberto Alomar 15.00
MA Moises Alou 10.00
GA Garret Anderson 10.00
BA Jeff Bagwell 15.00
RB Rocco Baldelli 10.00
JB Jason Bay 15.00
BE Josh Beckett 10.00
CB Carlos Beltran 15.00
AB Adrian Beltre 8.00
LB Lance Berkman 10.00
BI Craig Biggio 10.00
HB Hank Blalock 10.00
BB Bret Boone 8.00
KB Kevin Brown 8.00
MC Miguel Cabrera 15.00
EC Eric Chavez 10.00
CC Carl Crawford 10.00
BC Bobby Crosby 10.00
DA Johnny Damon 20.00
CD Carlos Delgado 15.00
JD J.D. Drew 10.00
AD Adam Dunn 15.00
JE Jim Edmonds 15.00
KF Keith Foulke 10.00
EG Eric Gagne 10.00
JG Jason Giambi 10.00
BG Brian Giles 8.00
MG Marcus Giles 8.00
TG Tom Glavine 10.00
LG Luis Gonzalez 10.00
SG Shawn Green 10.00
GR Khalil Greene 12.00
KG Ken Griffey Jr. 40.00
VG Vladimir Guerrero 15.00
HA Roy Halladay 10.00
RH Rich Harden 10.00
HE Todd Helton 10.00
HO Trevor Hoffman 10.00
TH Tim Hudson 12.00
AH Aubrey Huff 8.00
HU Torii Hunter 10.00
DJ Derek Jeter 40.00
RJ Randy Johnson 15.00
AJ Andruw Jones 15.00
CJ Chipper Jones 15.00
JJ Jacque Jones 8.00
SK Scott Kazmir 8.00
JK Jason Kendall 8.00
ML Mike Lowell 8.00
GM Greg Maddux 30.00
PM Pedro Martinez 15.00
VM Victor Martinez 8.00
HM Hideki Matsui 50.00
KM Kazuo Matsui 25.00
DM Dallas McPherson 12.00
JM Justin Morneau 20.00
MM Mark Mulder 10.00
MU Mike Mussina 15.00
HN Hideo Nomo 40.00
MO Magglio Ordonez 8.00
DO David Ortiz 15.00
RO Roy Oswalt 10.00
AO Akinori Otsuka 15.00
RP Rafael Palmeiro 15.00
CP Corey Patterson 10.00
PI Mike Piazza 20.00
SP Scott Podsednik 10.00
JP Jorge Posada 15.00
MP Mark Prior 20.00
AP Albert Pujols 35.00
MR Manny Ramirez 20.00
ER Edgar Renteria 10.00
JR Jose Reyes 12.00
IR Ivan Rodriguez 12.00
SR Scott Rolen 15.00
CS C.C. Sabathia 8.00
SA Johan Santana 15.00
SC Curt Schilling 15.00
JS Jason Schmidt 12.00
RS Richie Sexson 10.00
BS Ben Sheets 10.00
GS Gary Sheffield 15.00
AS Alfonso Soriano 15.00
SS Sammy Sosa 20.00
MS Mike Sweeney 8.00
ST Shingo Takatsu 20.00
MT Mark Teixeira 15.00
TE Miguel Tejada 15.00
JT Jim Thome 15.00
JV Jose Vidro 8.00
WA Billy Wagner 10.00
VW Vernon Wells 8.00
BW Bernie Williams 10.00
KW Kerry Wood 15.00
DW David Wright 20.00
BZ Barry Zito 10.00

2005 UPPER DECK SWEET SPOT

NM/M

Complete Set (90): 20.00
Common Player: .25
Pack (5): 12.00
Box (12): 120.00
1 Magglio Ordonez .25
2 Craig Biggio .50
3 Hank Blalock .40
4 Nomar Garciaparra .75
5 Ken Griffey Jr. 1.50
6 Khalil Greene .40
7 Andruw Jones .50
8 Ichiro Suzuki 1.50
9 *Philip Humber* 1.50
10 Vladimir Guerrero .75
11 Carlos Delgado .40
12 *Jeff Niemann* 1.50
13 Chipper Jones .75
14 Jose Vidro .25
15 Miguel Cabrera .75
16 Albert Pujols 2.00
17 *Tadahito Iguchi* 2.50
18 *Norihiro Nakamura* 1.50
19 Jeff Bagwell .50
20 Troy Glaus .40
21 Scott Rolen .75
22 Derek Lowe .25
23 Mark Prior .75
24 Bobby Abreu .40
25 David Wright 1.00
26 Barry Zito .40
27 Livan Hernandez .25
28 Mark Teixeira .50
29 Manny Ramirez .75
30 Paul Konerko .40
31 Victor Martinez .25
32 Greg Maddux 1.50
33 Jim Thome .50
34 Miguel Tejada .50
35 Ivan Rodriguez .50
36 Carlos Beltran .50
37 Steve Finley .25
38 Torii Hunter .25
39 Bobby Crosby .25
40 Jorge Posada .40
41 Ben Sheets .40
42 Mike Piazza 1.00
43 Luis Gonzalez .25
44 Joe Mauer .40
45 Shawn Green .25
46 Eric Gagne .40
47 Kerry Wood .40
48 Derek Jeter 2.00
49 Josh Beckett .25
50 Alex Rodriguez 1.50
51 Aubrey Huff .25
52 Eric Chavez .40
53 Sammy Sosa 1.00
54 Roger Clemens 2.00
55 Mike Mussina .50
56 Mike Sweeney .25
57 Oliver Perez .25
58 Tim Hudson .40
59 *Justin Verlander* 2.00
60 Johan Santana .50
61 Hideki Matsui 1.50
62 Mark Mulder .40
63 Jake Peavy .40
64 Adam Dunn .50
65 Dallas McPherson .25
66 Jeff Kent .25
67 Pedro Martinez .75
68 J.D. Drew .25
69 Frank Thomas .50
70 Kazuo Matsui .25
71 Travis Hafner .40
72 John Smoltz .40
73 Jason Schmidt .25
74 Carlos Lee .25
75 Todd Helton .50
76 David Ortiz .75
77 Roy Oswalt .40
78 Brian Giles .25
79 Gary Sheffield .50
80 Jason Bay .40
81 Alfonso Soriano .75
82 Randy Johnson .75

83 Tom Glavine .40
84 Richie Sexson .40
85 Curt Schilling .75
86 Adrian Beltre .40
87 Jim Edmonds .40
88 Roy Halladay .40
89 Johnny Damon .75
90 Lance Berkman .40

Gold

Gold (1-90): 1-2X
Production 599 sets

Platinum

Platinum (1-90): 2-4X
Production 99 sets

Plutonium

No Pricing
Production one set

Majestic Materials

NM/M

Common Player:
Gold: 1X-1.5X
Production 75 Sets
Platinum: No Pricing
Production 10 Sets
Plutonium: No Pricing
Production 1 Set
Patch: 2X-3X
Production 35 Sets
BA Bobby Abreu 4.00
MA Moises Alou 6.00
JB Jason Bay 4.00
BE Josh Beckett 4.00
LB Lance Berkman 4.00
CB Craig Biggio 6.00
BB Bret Boone 4.00
BC Bobby Crosby 4.00
CD Carlos Delgado 4.00
JD J.D. Drew 4.00
AD Adam Dunn 6.00
JE Jim Edmonds 6.00
JG Jason Giambi 6.00
BG Brian Giles 4.00
TG Troy Glaus 4.00
LG Luis Gonzalez 4.00
SG Shawn Green 4.00
KG Khalil Greene 6.00
HA Travis Hafner 4.00
RH Roy Halladay 4.00
TH Tim Hudson 4.00
HU Torii Hunter 4.00
TI Tadahito Iguchi 5.00
AJ Andruw Jones 6.00
SK Scott Kazmir 4.00
JK Jeff Kent 4.00
VM Victor Martinez 4.00
KM Kazuo Matsui 4.00
JM Joe Mauer 6.00
DM Dallas McPherson 4.00
MM Mark Mulder 4.00
MU Mike Mussina 6.00
MO Magglio Ordonez 4.00
RO Roy Oswalt 4.00
JP Jake Peavy 6.00
OP Oliver Perez 4.00
AP Andy Pettitte 6.00
PO Jorge Posada 6.00
ER Edgar Renteria 4.00
JR Jose Reyes 4.00
JS Jason Schmidt 4.00
RS Richie Sexson 6.00
BS Ben Sheets 4.00
GS Gary Sheffield 6.00
ST Shingo Takatsu 4.00
BU B.J. Upton 4.00
JV Jose Vidro 4.00
VW Vernon Wells 4.00
DW David Wright 10.00
BZ Barry Zito 4.00

Majestic Materials Dual

NM/M

Production 25 Sets
Gold: No Pricing
Production 5 Sets
Plutonium: No Pricing
Production 1 Set
Patch: No Pricing
Production 5 Sets
BB Craig Biggio, Jeff Bagwell 15.00
BP Jason Bay, Oliver Perez 10.00
BS Adrian Beltre, Richie Sexson 10.00
BT Hank Blalock, Mark Teixeira 12.00
CC Bobby Crosby, Eric Chavez 10.00
DG Adam Dunn, Ken Griffey Jr. 25.00
DK J.D. Drew, Jeff Kent 10.00
DR Johnny Damon, Manny Ramirez 15.00
GG Shawn Green, Troy Glaus 10.00
GR Eric Gagne, Mariano Rivera 15.00
HM Travis Hafner, Victor Martinez 10.00
JJ Andruw Jones, Chipper Jones 15.00
MC Don Mattingly, Will Clark 25.00
MW Dallas McPherson, David Wright 15.00
PC Albert Pujols, Miguel Cabrera 25.00
PG Jake Peavy, Khalil Greene 12.00
PL Albert Pujols, Derrek Lee 25.00
RM Jose Reyes, Kazuo Matsui 10.00
RO Ivan Rodriguez, Magglio Ordonez 10.00
RT Brian Roberts, Miguel Tejada 15.00
SH John Smoltz, Tim Hudson 12.00
SM Joe Mauer, Johan Santana 15.00
TI Shingo Takatsu, Tadahito Iguchi 20.00
UK B.J. Upton, Scott Kazmir 10.00
WC David Wright, Miguel Cabrera 15.00

Majestic Materials Quad

NM/M

Production 25 Sets
Gold: No Pricing
Production 5 Sets
Plutonium: No Pricing
Production 1 Set
Patch: No Pricing
Production 5 Sets
JJSH Andruw Jones, Chipper Jones, John Smoltz, Tim Hudson 25.00
JSJP Derek Jeter, Gary Sheffield, Randy Johnson, Jorge Posada 60.00
OVDR David Ortiz, Jason Varitek, Johnny Damon, Manny Ramirez 40.00
PEWR Albert Pujols, Jim Edmonds, Larry Walker, Scott Rolen 50.00
ZMWP Carlos Zambrano, Greg Maddux, Kerry Wood, Mark Prior 30.00

Majestic Materials Triple

NM/M

Production 25 Sets
Gold: No Pricing
Production 5 Sets
Plutonium: No Pricing
Production 1 Set
Patch: No Pricing
Production 5 Sets
BPO Josh Beckett, Mark Prior, Roy Oswalt 15.00
BSB George Brett, Mike Schmidt, Wade Boggs 30.00
BTH Jeff Bagwell, Jim Thome, Todd Helton 20.00
HRG Torii Hunter, Manny Ramirez, Vladimir Guerrero 20.00
JCG Andruw Jones, Miguel Cabrera, Vladimir Guerrero 15.00
JRT Derek Jeter, Edgar Renteria, Miguel Tejada 25.00
MMP Greg Maddux, Pedro Martinez, Jake Peavy 25.00
MSG Greg Maddux, John Smoltz, Tom Glavine 40.00
OGP David Ortiz, Jason Giambi, Rafael Palmeiro 20.00
PBC Albert Pujols, Carlos Beltran, Miguel Cabrera 40.00
RBW Nolan Ryan, Josh Beckett, Kerry Wood 40.00
RGB Cal Ripken Jr., Tony Gwynn, Wade Boggs 50.00
SSJ Curt Schilling, Johan Santana, Randy Johnson 25.00
VPP Jason Varitek, Jorge Posada, Mike Piazza 20.00
WRG David Wright, Scott Rolen, Troy Glaus 25.00

Signatures Barrel Black Ink

NM/M

Production 25-50
JB Jason Bay/50 20.00
HB Hank Blalock/25 25.00
CA Miguel Cabrera/25 70.00
SC Steve Carlton/25 25.00
SE Sean Casey/50 20.00
WC Will Clark/25 25.00
CC Carl Crawford/50 15.00
BC Bobby Crosby/50 30.00
DA Andre Dawson/25 25.00
AD Adam Dunn/25 40.00
GF Gavin Floyd/50 20.00
NG Nomar Garciaparra/25 80.00
MG Marcus Giles/50 15.00
GL Tom Glavine/50 30.00
GR Khalil Greene/50 35.00
KG Ken Griffey Jr./25 85.00
HA Travis Hafner/50 25.00
RH Rich Harden/50 20.00
KH Keith Hernandez/50 20.00
HO Ryan Howard/50 40.00
AH Aubrey Huff/50 15.00
PH Philip Humber/50 25.00
BJ Bo Jackson/25 75.00
DJ Derek Jeter/25 250.00
RJ Randy Johnson/25 125.00
AJ Andruw Jones/25 50.00
SK Scott Kazmir/50 20.00
BL Barry Larkin/25 40.00
EM Edgar Martinez/25 40.00
MA Don Mattingly/25 85.00
PM Paul Molitor/25 40.00
MO Justin Morneau/50 15.00
MM Mark Mulder/50 25.00
JN Jeff Niemann/50 20.00
RO Roy Oswalt/50 35.00
LO Lyle Overbay/50 15.00
JP Jake Peavy/50 25.00
PI Mike Piazza/25 100.00
MP Mark Prior/25 50.00
AP Albert Pujols/25 220.00
AR Aramis Ramirez/50 30.00
CR Cal Ripken Jr./25 180.00
NR Nolan Ryan/25 100.00
RS Ryne Sandberg/25 75.00
MS Mike Schmidt/25 70.00
MT Mark Teixeira/25 40.00
BU B.J. Upton/50 20.00
JV Justin Verlander/50 30.00
DW David Wright/50 75.00
RY Robin Yount/25 90.00
CZ Carlos Zambrano/50 30.00

Sign. Black Stitch Black Ink

No Pricing
Production 1 Set
Blue Ink: No Pricing
Production 1 Set
Red Ink: No Pricing
Production 1 Set

Signatures Dual Barrel

No Pricing
Production 15 Sets

Signatures Dual Red Stitch

NM/M

Production 25 Sets
BJ Bobby Crosby, Jason Bay 40.00
BW Adrian Beltre, David Wright 75.00
CG Bobby Crosby, Khalil Greene 50.00
DC Adam Dunn, Sean Casey 50.00
FH Gavin Floyd, Ryan Howard 75.00
GC Ken Griffey Jr., Miguel Cabrera 120.00
GL Khalil Greene, Mark Loretta 60.00
JG Andruw Jones, Ken Griffey Jr. 150.00
LG Barry Larkin, Ken Griffey Jr. 120.00
MG Greg Maddux, Tom Glavine 150.00
MJ Pedro Martinez, Randy Johnson 125.00
NH Jeff Niemann, Philip Humber 50.00
PB Jason Bay, Oliver Perez 40.00
PO Jake Peavy, Roy Oswalt 75.00
SB Ryne Sandberg, Wade Boggs 125.00
SG Nomar Garciaparra, Ryne Sandberg 150.00
SP Ben Sheets, Jake Peavy 50.00
WC David Wright, Miguel Cabrera 100.00
WR David Wright, Jose Reyes 100.00

Signatures Glove Black Ink

NM/M

Production 15-30
JB Jason Bay/30 40.00
SE Sean Casey/30 35.00
CC Carl Crawford/30 30.00
BC Bobby Crosby/30 40.00
GF Gavin Floyd/30 30.00
MG Marcus Giles/30 25.00
GL Tom Glavine/30 50.00
GR Khalil Greene/30 50.00
HA Travis Hafner/30 40.00
RH Rich Harden/30 35.00
KH Keith Hernandez/30 30.00
HO Ryan Howard/30 60.00
AH Aubrey Huff/30 25.00
PH Philip Humber/30 40.00
SK Scott Kazmir/30 30.00
MO Justin Morneau/30 30.00
MM Mark Mulder/30 40.00
JN Jeff Niemann/30 30.00
RO Roy Oswalt/30 50.00
LO Lyle Overbay/30 20.00
CP Corey Patterson/30 25.00
JP Jake Peavy/30 40.00
AR Aramis Ramirez/30 50.00
BU B.J. Upton/30 35.00
JV Justin Verlander/30 40.00
DW David Wright/30 100.00
CZ Carlos Zambrano/30 40.00

Sign. Red Stitch Black Ink

NM/M

Production 58-350
JB Jason Bay/350 20.00
HB Hank Blalock/175 20.00
WB Wade Boggs/175 40.00
CA Miguel Cabrera/175 40.00
SC Steve Carlton/58 25.00
SE Sean Casey/350 15.00
WC Will Clark/175 25.00
RC Roger Clemens/175 120.00
CC Carl Crawford/350 15.00
BC Bobby Crosby/350 20.00
DA Andre Dawson/175 20.00
AD Adam Dunn/175 25.00
GF Gavin Floyd/350 15.00
NG Nomar Garciaparra/175 60.00
MG Marcus Giles/350 15.00
GR Khalil Greene/350 20.00
KG Ken Griffey Jr./175 75.00
RH Rich Harden/350 15.00
KH Keith Hernandez/350 15.00
HO Ryan Howard/350 30.00
AH Aubrey Huff/350 15.00
PH Philip Humber/350 15.00

BJ Bo Jackson/175 70.00
DJ Derek Jeter/175 150.00
RJ Randy Johnson/175 75.00
AJ Andruw Jones/175 40.00
SK Scott Kazmir/350 15.00
BL Barry Larkin/175 25.00
EM Edgar Martinez/175 30.00
MA Don Mattingly/175 60.00
PM Paul Molitor/175 25.00
MO Justin Morneau/350 15.00
MM Mark Mulder/350 20.00
JN Jeff Niemann/350 15.00
RO Roy Oswalt/350 25.00
LO Lyle Overbay/350 12.00
JP Jake Peavy/350 20.00
PI Mike Piazza/175 80.00
MP Mark Prior/175 40.00
AP Albert Pujols/175 160.00
AR Aramis Ramirez/350 25.00
RE Jose Reyes/350 20.00
CR Cal Ripken Jr./175 120.00
NR Nolan Ryan/175 80.00
RS Ryne Sandberg/175 65.00
MS Mike Schmidt/175 50.00
MT Mark Teixeira/175 40.00
BU B.J. Upton/350 15.00
JV Justin Verlander/350 20.00
DW David Wright/350 50.00
RY Robin Yount/175 50.00
CZ Carlos Zambrano/350 20.00

Sign. Red Stitch Blue Ink

NM/M

Production 75-135
JB Jason Bay 25.00
HB Hank Blalock/75 20.00
WB Wade Boggs/75 40.00
CA Miguel Cabrera/75 40.00
SE Sean Casey/135 15.00
WC Will Clark/75 25.00
RC Roger Clemens/75 120.00
CC Carl Crawford/135 15.00
BC Bobby Crosby/135 20.00
DA Andre Dawson/75 20.00
AD Adam Dunn/75 30.00
GF Gavin Floyd/135 15.00
NG Nomar Garciaparra/75 65.00
MG Marcus Giles/135 15.00
GL Tom Glavine/135 25.00
GR Khalil Greene/135 25.00
KG Ken Griffey Jr./75 80.00
HA Travis Hafner/135 20.00
RH Rich Harden/135 15.00
KH Keith Hernandez/135 15.00
HO Ryan Howard/135 35.00
AH Aubrey Huff/135 15.00
PH Philip Humber/135 15.00
BJ Bo Jackson/75 75.00
DJ Derek Jeter/75 150.00
RJ Randy Johnson/75 85.00
AJ Andruw Jones/75 40.00
SK Scott Kazmir/135 15.00
BL Barry Larkin/75 30.00
EM Edgar Martinez/75 35.00
MA Don Mattingly/75 70.00
PM Paul Molitor/75 25.00
MO Justin Morneau/135 20.00
MM Mark Mulder/135 25.00
JN Jeff Niemann/135 15.00
RO Roy Oswalt/135 25.00
LO Lyle Overbay/135 12.00
CP Corey Patterson/135 15.00
JP Jake Peavy/135 25.00
PI Mike Piazza/75 80.00
MP Mark Prior/75 50.00
AP Albert Pujols/75 160.00
AR Aramis Ramirez/135 25.00
RE Jose Reyes/135 20.00
CR Cal Ripken Jr./75 120.00
NR Nolan Ryan/75 80.00
RS Ryne Sandberg/75 65.00
MS Mike Schmidt/75 50.00
MT Mark Teixeira/75 40.00
BU B.J. Upton/135 15.00
JV Justin Verlander/135 20.00
DW David Wright/135 50.00
RY Robin Yount/75 50.00
CZ Carlos Zambrano/135 20.00

Sign. Red Stitch Red Ink

NM/M

Production 15-35
JB Jason Bay/35 25.00
SE Sean Casey/35 25.00
CC Carl Crawford/35 20.00
BC Bobby Crosby 35.00
AD Adam Dunn/15 60.00
GF Gavin Floyd/35 25.00
MG Marcus Giles/35 15.00
GL Tom Glavine/35 40.00
GR Khalil Greene/35 40.00
HA Travis Hafner/35 30.00
RH Rich Harden/35 30.00
KH Keith Hernandez/35 25.00
HO Ryan Howard/35 50.00
AH Aubrey Huff/35 20.00
PH Philip Humber/35 30.00
SK Scott Kazmir/35 20.00
MO Justin Morneau/35 20.00
MM Mark Mulder/35 30.00
JN Jeff Niemann/35 25.00
RO Roy Oswalt/35 40.00
LO Lyle Overbay/35 15.00
CP Corey Patterson/35 20.00
JP Jake Peavy/35 30.00
AP Albert Pujols/15 250.00
AR Aramis Ramirez/35 40.00
BU B.J. Upton/35 25.00
JV Justin Verlander/35 35.00
DW David Wright/35 90.00
CZ Carlos Zambrano/35 35.00

Red-Blue Stitch Black Ink

NM/M

Production 25-50
JB Jason Bay/50 25.00
HB Hank Blalock/25 25.00
WB Wade Boggs/25 50.00
CA Miguel Cabrera/25 65.00
SC Steve Carlton/25 25.00
SE Sean Casey/50 20.00
WC Will Clark/25 35.00
RC Roger Clemens/25 160.00
CC Carl Crawford/50 15.00
BC Bobby Crosby/50 35.00
DA Andre Dawson/25 25.00
AD Adam Dunn/25 40.00
GF Gavin Floyd/50 15.00
NG Nomar Garciaparra/25 65.00
MG Marcus Giles/50 15.00
GR Khalil Greene/50 30.00
KG Ken Griffey Jr./25 120.00
RH Rich Harden/50 20.00
KG Keith Hernandez/50 20.00
HO Ryan Howard/50 40.00
AH Aubrey Huff/50 20.00
PH Philip Humber/50 20.00
BJ Bo Jackson/25 90.00
DJ Derek Jeter/25 250.00
RJ Randy Johnson/25 120.00
AJ Andruw Jones/25 50.00
SK Scott Kazmir/50 20.00
BL Barry Larkin/25 40.00
EM Edgar Martinez/25 40.00
MA Don Mattingly/25 90.00
PM Paul Molitor/25 40.00
MO Justin Morneau/50 15.00
MM Mark Mulder/50 25.00
JN Jeff Niemann/50 20.00
RO Roy Oswalt/50 35.00
LO Lyle Overbay/50 12.00
JP Jake Peavy/50 25.00
PI Mike Piazza/25 100.00
MP Mark Prior/25 60.00
AP Albert Pujols/25 220.00
RE Jose Reyes/50 30.00
CR Cal Ripken Jr./25 165.00
NR Nolan Ryan/25 100.00
RS Ryne Sandberg/25 80.00
JS Johan Santana/25 50.00
MS Mike Schmidt/25 75.00
MT Mark Teixeira/25 50.00
BU B.J. Upton/50 20.00
JV Justin Verlander/50 30.00
DW David Wright/50 75.00
RY Robin Yount/25 65.00
CZ Carlos Zambrano/50 30.00

Sweet Threads

NM/M

Common Player: 4.00
Gold: 1X-1.5X
Production 75 Sets
Platinum: No Pricing
Production 10 Sets
Plutonium: No Pricing
Production 1 Set
Patch: 2X-4X
Production 35 Sets
JB Jeff Bagwell 6.00
CB Carlos Beltran 6.00
AB Adrian Beltre 4.00
HB Hank Blalock 4.00
WB Wade Boggs 8.00
GB George Brett 10.00
MC Miguel Cabrera 8.00
EC Eric Chavez 4.00
WC Will Clark 6.00
BC Bartolo Colon 4.00
JD Johnny Damon 6.00
EG Eric Gagne 4.00
TG Tom Glavine 6.00
KG Ken Griffey Jr. 12.00
VG Vladimir Guerrero 8.00
GW Tony Gwynn 8.00
TH Todd Helton 6.00
HO Trevor Hoffman 4.00
BJ Bo Jackson 8.00
DJ Derek Jeter 20.00
RJ Randy Johnson 8.00
CJ Chipper Jones 8.00
CL Carlos Lee 4.00
GM Greg Maddux 10.00
PM Pedro Martinez 8.00
DM Don Mattingly 10.00
DO David Ortiz 8.00
RP Rafael Palmeiro 6.00
PI Mike Piazza 8.00
MP Mark Prior 6.00
AP Albert Pujols 15.00
MR Manny Ramirez 8.00
CR Cal Ripken Jr. 20.00
IR Ivan Rodriguez 6.00
SR Scott Rolen 6.00
NR Nolan Ryan 12.00
RS Ryne Sandberg 8.00
JS Johan Santana 6.00
CS Curt Schilling 6.00
MS Mike Schmidt 10.00
SM John Smoltz 6.00
AS Alfonso Soriano 6.00
SS Sammy Sosa 8.00
MT Mark Teixeira 6.00
TE Miguel Tejada 6.00
FT Frank Thomas 6.00
JT Jim Thome 6.00
JV Jason Varitek 10.00
BW Bernie Williams 6.00
KW Kerry Wood 4.00

Sweet Threads Dual

NM/M

Production 25 Sets
Gold: No Pricing
Production 5 Sets
Patch: No Pricing
Production 5 Sets
Plutonium: No Pricing
Production 1 Set
BG Carlos Beltran, Ken Griffey Jr. 25.00
BM Carlos Beltran, Pedro Martinez 15.00
DC Carlos Delgado, Miguel Cabrera 15.00
GC Ken Griffey Jr., Miguel Cabrera 25.00
GM Dallas McPherson, Vladimir Guerrero 15.00
JB Bo Jackson, George Brett 25.00
JJ Randy Johnson, Derek Jeter 40.00
JM Derek Jeter, Don Mattingly 50.00
JS Jim Thome, Mike Schmidt 30.00
MG Greg Maddux, Tom Glavine 25.00
MJ Mike Mussina, Randy Johnson 20.00
MP Greg Maddux, Mark Prior 25.00
OR David Ortiz, Manny Ramirez 20.00
PO Andy Pettitte, Roy Oswalt 10.00
PR Pedro Martinez, Randy Johnson 20.00
PS Rafael Palmeiro, Sammy Sosa 20.00
PW David Wright, Mike Piazza 30.00
RJ Cal Ripken Jr., Derek Jeter 70.00
RP Albert Pujols, Scott Rolen 30.00
RT Cal Ripken Jr., Miguel Tejada 40.00
SB Ryne Sandberg, Wade Boggs 30.00
SJ Curt Schilling, Randy Johnson 20.00
SV Curt Schilling, Jason Varitek 20.00
WP Kerry Wood, Mark Prior 15.00

Sweet Threads Quad

NM/M

Production 25 Sets
Gold: No Pricing
Production 5 Sets
Plutonium: No Pricing
Production 1 Set
Patch: No Pricing
Production 5 Sets
BMCB Adrian Beltre, Dallas McPherson, Eric Chavez, Hank Blalock 25.00
BRGG Carlos Beltran, Manny Ramirez, Ken Griffey Jr., Vladimir Guerrero 40.00
POTH Albert Pujols, David Ortiz, Jim Thome, Todd Helton 40.00
RBGB Cal Ripken Jr., Brett George, Tony Gwynn, Wade Boggs 90.00
RVMP Ivan Rodriguez, Jason Varitek, Joe Mauer, Jorge Posada 30.00

Sweet Threads Triple

NM/M

Production 25 Sets
Gold: No Pricing
Production 5 Sets
Plutonium: No Pricing
Production 1 Set
Patch: No Pricing
Production 5 Sets
BBB Craig Biggio, Jeff Bagwell, Lance Berkman 20.00
BWP Carlos Beltran, David Wright, Mike Piazza 25.00
GGG Luis Gonzalez, Shawn Green, Troy Glaus 10.00
JMB Randy Johnson, Mike Mussina, Kevin Brown 25.00
JWS Derek Jeter, Bernie Williams, Gary Sheffield 50.00
KGD Austin Kearns, Ken Griffey Jr., Adam Dunn 30.00
LOP Brad Lidge, Roy Oswalt, Andy Pettitte 15.00
ODR David Ortiz, Johnny Damon, Manny Ramirez 25.00
PER Albert Pujols, Jim Edmonds, Scott Rolen 40.00
PWM Mark Prior, Kerry Wood, Greg Maddux 30.00
RDN Manny Ramirez, Johnny Damon, Trot Nixon 30.00
SBT Alfonso Soriano, Hank Blalock, Mark Teixeira 20.00
SMJ Curt Schilling, Pedro Martinez, Randy Johnson 25.00
TPS Miguel Tejada, Rafael Palmeiro, Sammy Sosa 20.00

Signatures Barrel Blue Ink

NM/M

Production 15-30
JB Jason Bay/30 25.00
SE Sean Casey/30 25.00
CC Carl Crawford/30 20.00
BC Bobby Crosby/30 35.00
AD Adam Dunn/15 60.00
GF Gavin Floyd/30 25.00
MG Marcus Giles/30 15.00

GL Tom Glavine/30 40.00
GR Khalil Greene/30 40.00
HA Travis Hafner/30 30.00
RH Rich Harden/30 25.00
KH Keith Hernandez/30 25.00
HO Ryan Howard/30 50.00
AH Aubrey Huff/30 20.00
PH Philip Humber/30 30.00
SK Scott Kazmir/30 20.00
MO Justin Morneau/30 20.00
MM Mark Mulder/30 30.00
JN Jeff Niemann/30 25.00
RO Roy Oswalt/30 40.00
LO Lyle Overbay/30 15.00
CP Corey Patterson/30 20.00
JP Jake Peavy/30 30.00
AP Albert Pujols/15 250.00
AR Aramis Ramirez/30 40.00
BU B.J. Upton/30 25.00
JV Justin Verlander/30 35.00
DW David Wright/30 90.00
CZ Carlos Zambrano/30 35.00

Signatures Barrel Red Ink

No Pricing
Production 5-10

Signatures Glove Blue Ink

No Pricing
Production 5-10
Red Ink: No Pricing
Production 2-5

Red-Blue Stitch Blue Ink

NM/M
Production 15-30
Red Ink: No Pricing
Production 5-10
JB Jason Bay/30 25.00
SE Sean Casey/30 25.00
CC Carl Crawford/30 20.00
BC Bobby Crosby/30 35.00
GF Gavin Floyd/30 25.00
MG Marcus Giles/30 15.00
GL Tom Glavine/30 40.00
GR Khalil Greene/30 40.00
HA Travis Hafner/30 30.00
RH Rich Harden/30 25.00
KH Keith Hernandez/30 25.00
HO Ryan Howard/30 50.00
PH Philip Humber/30 30.00
SK Scott Kazmir/30 20.00
MO Justin Morneau/30 20.00
MM Mark Mulder/30 30.00
JN Jeff Niemann/30 25.00
RO Roy Oswalt/30 40.00
LO Lyle Overbay/30 15.00
CP Corey Patterson/30 20.00
JP Jake Peavy/30 30.00
AR Aramis Ramirez/30 40.00
RE Jose Reyes/30 40.00
BU B.J. Upton/30 25.00
JV Justin Verlander/30 35.00
DW David Wright/30 90.00
CZ Carlos Zambrano/30 35.00

2005 UPPER DECK SWEET SPOT CLASSIC

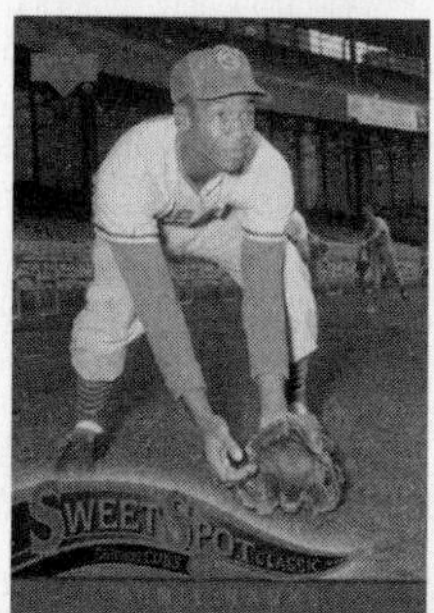

NM/M
Complete Set (100): 30.00
Common Player: .40
Pack (4): 12.00
Box (12): 120.00
1 Al Kaline 1.00
2 Al Rosen .40
3 Babe Ruth 4.00
4 Bill Mazeroski .40
5 Billy Williams .40
6 Bob Feller .75
7 Bob Gibson 1.00
8 Bobby Doerr .40
9 Brooks Robinson 1.00
10 Cal Ripken Jr. 4.00
11 Carl Yastrzemski 2.00
12 Carlton Fisk .40
13 Casey Stengel .40
14 Christy Mathewson 2.00
15 Cy Young 1.50
16 Dale Murphy .75
17 Dave Winfield .75
18 Dennis Eckersley .40
19 Dizzy Dean 1.00
20 Don Drysdale .75
21 Don Mattingly 3.00
22 Don Newcombe .40
23 Don Sutton .40
24 Duke Snider 1.00
25 Dwight Evans .40
26 Eddie Mathews 1.50
27 Eddie Murray 1.00
28 Enos Slaughter .40
29 Ernie Banks 2.00
30 Frank Howard .40
31 Frank Robinson .75
32 Gary Carter .40
33 Gaylord Perry .40
34 George Brett 3.00
35 George Kell .40
36 George Sisler .40
37 Larry Doby .40
38 Harmon Killebrew 1.50
39 Honus Wagner 2.00
40 Jackie Robinson 2.00
41 Jim Bunning .40
42 Jim Palmer .75
43 Jim Rice .40
44 Jimmie Foxx .40
45 Joe DiMaggio 3.00
46 Joe Morgan .40
47 Johnny Bench 2.00
48 Johnny Mize .40
49 Johnny Podres .40
50 Juan Marichal .40
51 Keith Hernandez .40
52 Kirby Puckett 1.00
53 Lefty Grove .40
54 Lou Brock .75
55 Lou Gehrig 4.00
56 Luis Aparicio .40
57 Fergie Jenkins .40
58 Maury Wills .40
59 Mel Ott 1.50
60 Mickey Cochrane 1.00
61 Mickey Mantle 4.00
62 Mike Schmidt 3.00
63 Monte Irvin .75
64 Nolan Ryan 4.00
65 Orlando Cepeda .40
66 Ozzie Smith 1.50
67 Paul Molitor 1.00
68 Pee Wee Reese .40
69 Phil Niekro .40
70 Phil Rizzuto 1.00
71 Ralph Kiner .40
72 Richie Ashburn .40
73 Roberto Clemente 4.00
74 Robin Roberts .40
75 Robin Yount 2.00
76 Rocky Colavito 1.00
77 Rod Carew .75
78 Rogers Hornsby 1.00
79 Rollie Fingers .40
80 Roy Campanella 1.00
81 Bob Lemon .40
82 Red Schoendienst .40
83 Satchel Paige 2.00
84 Stan Musial 2.50
85 Steve Carlton .75
86 Ted Williams 3.00
87 Thurman Munson 1.50
88 Tom Seaver 1.00
89 Tony Gwynn 1.50
90 Tony Perez .40
91 Ty Cobb 2.00
92 Wade Boggs 1.00
93 Walter Johnson 1.00
94 Warren Spahn 1.50
95 Whitey Ford 1.00
96 Will Clark .75
97 Jim "Catfish" Hunter .40
98 Willie McCovey .75
99 Willie Stargell 1.00
100 Yogi Berra 1.50

Gold

Cards (1-100): 4X-8X
Production 50 Sets

Silver

Cards (1-100): 2X-4X
Production 100 Sets

Classic Materials

NM/M
Common Player: 6.00
BE Johnny Bench 15.00
YB Yogi Berra 20.00
WB Wade Boggs 10.00
GB George Brett 10.00
GB1 George Brett 10.00
LB Lou Brock 8.00
JB Jim Bunning 10.00
CP Roy Campanella 12.00
CA Rod Carew 8.00
SC Steve Carlton 8.00
GC Gary Carter 6.00
OC Orlando Cepeda 8.00
WC Will Clark 10.00
WC1 Will Clark 10.00
RC Roberto Clemente 60.00
TC Ty Cobb SP 100.00
CO Rocky Colavito 25.00
DC David Cone 6.00
AD Andre Dawson 6.00
JD Joe DiMaggio 80.00
DD Don Drysdale 10.00
BF Bob Feller 12.00
CF Carlton Fisk 8.00
LG Lou Gehrig SP 160.00
BG Bob Gibson 10.00
MG Mark Grace 8.00
RG Ron Guidry 8.00
TG Tony Gwynn 12.00
CH Jim "Catfish" Hunter 8.00
FJ Fergie Jenkins 8.00
AK Al Kaline 10.00
HK Harmon Killebrew 12.00
MM Mickey Mantle SP 120.00
MA Juan Marichal 8.00
EM Eddie Mathews 10.00
DM Don Mattingly 15.00
DM1 Don Mattingly 15.00
BM Bill Mazeroski 10.00
WI Willie McCovey 10.00
PM Paul Molitor 10.00
JM Joe Morgan 6.00
JM1 Joe Morgan 6.00
TM Thurman Munson SP 25.00
MU Dale Murphy 10.00
ED Eddie Murray 8.00
ED1 Eddie Murray 8.00
SM Stan Musial SP 20.00
PN Phil Niekro 6.00
SP Satchel Paige SP 50.00
JP Jim Palmer 8.00
TP Tony Perez 8.00
GP Gaylord Perry 6.00
RE Pee Wee Reese SP 15.00
RI Jim Rice 8.00
CR Cal Ripken Jr. 20.00
CR1 Cal Ripken Jr. 20.00
PR Phil Rizzuto 15.00
RR Robin Roberts 10.00
RO Brooks Robinson 10.00
FR Frank Robinson 8.00
JR Jackie Robinson 50.00
BR Babe Ruth SP 275.00
NR Nolan Ryan 25.00
NR1 Nolan Ryan 25.00
MS Mike Schmidt 15.00
MS1 Mike Schmidt 15.00
SD Red Schoendienst 8.00
TS Tom Seaver 10.00
OS Ozzie Smith SP 15.00
SN Duke Snider 10.00
WS Warren Spahn 15.00
ST Willie Stargell SP
DS Don Sutton 6.00
DS1 Don Sutton 6.00
FV Fernando Valenzuela 6.00
TW Ted Williams SP 75.00
MW Maury Wills 6.00
MW1 Maury Wills 6.00
DW Dave Winfield 6.00
DW1 Dave Winfield 6.00
EW Early Wynn 10.00
CY Carl Yastrzemski 15.00
RY Robin Yount 12.00

Patch

NM/M
Some not priced due to scarcity
LA Luis Aparicio/19 150.00
BE Johnny Bench/32 100.00
WB Wade Boggs/25 60.00
WB1 Wade Boggs/34 60.00
GB George Brett/38 80.00
GB1 George Brett/50 80.00
LB Lou Brock/34 90.00
SC Steve Carlton/50 60.00
GC Gary Carter/47 50.00
GC1 Gary Carter/34 50.00
OC Orlando Cepeda/40 50.00
DC David Cone/39
AD Andre Dawson/7
JD Joe DiMaggio/38 250.00
CF1 Carlton Fisk/50 70.00
BG Bob Gibson/1
RG Ron Guidry/30
TG Tony Gwynn/34 120.00
TG1 Tony Gwynn/30 120.00
FH Frank Howard/34 85.00
FJ Fergie Jenkins/34 65.00
MM Mickey Mantle/19
DM Don Mattingly/9
DM1 Don Mattingly/9
WI Willie McCovey/50 60.00
PM Paul Molitor/13
PM1 Paul Molitor/12
JM Joe Morgan/50 60.00
MU Dale Murphy/34 80.00
ED Eddie Murray/34 70.00
ED1 Eddie Murray/50 70.00
SM Stan Musial/3
PN Phil Niekro/44 50.00
TP Tony Perez/34 75.00
GP Gaylord Perry/34 50.00
PO Johnny Podres/50 60.00
RE Pee Wee Reese/10
RI Jim Rice/34 50.00
CR Cal Ripken Jr./34 150.00
CR1 Cal Ripken Jr./34 150.00
RO Brooks Robinson/50 85.00
RO1 Brooks Robinson/43 85.00
FR Frank Robinson/34 80.00
JR Jackie Robinson/12 250.00
NR Nolan Ryan/16
NR1 Nolan Ryan/3
NR2 Nolan Ryan/15
MS Mike Schmidt/6
MS1 Mike Schmidt/5
SD Red Schoendienst/42 60.00
TS Tom Seaver/50 50.00
TS1 Tom Seaver/50 50.00
OS Ozzie Smith/34 100.00
ST Willie Stargell/50 65.00
BS Bruce Sutter/50 50.00
DS Don Sutton/34 40.00
DS1 Don Sutton/50 40.00
MW Maury Wills/50 60.00
MW1 Maury Wills/47 60.00
DW Dave Winfield/3
DW1 Dave Winfield/50 75.00
CY Carl Yastrzemski/35 100.00
RY Robin Yount/34
RY1 Robin Yount/19

Leather Signatures

No Pricing
Production 25 Sets

Sweet Spot Signatures

NM/M
Common Autograph: 20.00
Inserted 1:12
Blue/Red Stitch: 1.5X-2X
Production 40 Sets
Black Stitch: No Pricing
Production 1 Set
LA Luis Aparicio 25.00

HB Harold Baines 20.00
EB Ernie Banks 75.00
BE Johnny Bench 60.00
YB Yogi Berra SP 60.00
WB Wade Boggs 50.00
GB George Brett 85.00
JB Jim Bunning 20.00
JC Jose Canseco 40.00
CA Rod Carew 50.00
SC Steve Carlton 40.00
GC Gary Carter 25.00
OC Orlando Cepeda 25.00
WC Will Clark 30.00
RC Rocky Colavito SP 85.00
DC David Cone 20.00
AD Andre Dawson 20.00
JD Joe DiMaggio/25
BD Bobby Doerr 25.00
DE Dennis Eckersley 25.00
EV Dwight Evans 20.00
BF Bob Feller 40.00
RF Rollie Fingers 20.00
CF Carlton Fisk 40.00
WF Whitey Ford 60.00
BG Bob Gibson 40.00
MG Mark Grace 40.00
TG Tony Gwynn 50.00
EH Ernie Harwell SP 40.00
KH Keith Hernandez 20.00
FH Frank Howard 25.00
MI Monte Irvin 25.00
BJ Bo Jackson 75.00
DJ David Justice 20.00
KA Harry Kalas 25.00
AK Al Kaline 40.00
GK George Kell 25.00
HK Harmon Killebrew 50.00
RK Ralph Kiner SP 50.00
MA Juan Marichal 25.00
DM Don Mattingly 80.00
BM Bill Mazeroski 40.00
MC Willie McCovey SP 60.00
PM Paul Molitor 40.00
JM Joe Morgan SP 35.00
MU Dale Murphy 25.00
SM Stan Musial 100.00
DN Don Newcombe 25.00
PN Phil Niekro 25.00
JP Jim Palmer 25.00
TP Tony Perez 25.00
GP Gaylord Perry 25.00
PO Johnny Podres 20.00
KP Kirby Puckett SP 50.00
JR Jim Rice 25.00
CR Cal Ripken Jr. 160.00
PR Phil Rizzuto 50.00
RR Robin Roberts 30.00
BR Brooks Robinson 40.00
FR Frank Robinson 40.00
AR Al Rosen 20.00
NR Nolan Ryan 125.00
RS Ron Santo 35.00
MS Mike Schmidt 80.00
RE Red Schoendienst 30.00
TS Tom Seaver 60.00
OS Ozzie Smith 60.00
SN Duke Snider 40.00
ST Rusty Staub 20.00
SU Bruce Sutter 20.00
DS Don Sutton 20.00
LT Luis Tiant 20.00
FV Fernando Valenzuela 30.00
BW Billy Williams 25.00
MW Matt Williams 20.00
WI Maury Wills 20.00
CY Carl Yastrzemski 100.00
RY Robin Yount SP 85.00

Dual Signatures

No Pricing
Production 15 Sets

Sweet Sticks Signatures

NM/M

Production 35 Sets
LA Luis Aparicio 50.00
HB Harold Baines 40.00
EB Ernie Banks 125.00
BE Johnny Bench 75.00
YB Yogi Berra 80.00
WB Wade Boggs 100.00
GB George Brett 140.00
JC Jose Canseco 75.00
CA Rod Carew 75.00
SC Steve Carlton 60.00
OC Orlando Cepeda 50.00
RC Rocky Colavito 120.00
DC David Cone 50.00
AD Andre Dawson 50.00
BD Bobby Doerr 50.00
RF Rollie Fingers 45.00
WF Whitey Ford 85.00
BG Bob Gibson 50.00
TG Tony Gwynn 85.00
KH Keith Hernandez 40.00
FH Frank Howard 50.00
MI Monte Irvin 50.00
HK Harmon Killebrew 80.00
RK Ralph Kiner 75.00
MA Juan Marichal 40.00
DM Don Mattingly 125.00
MC Willie McCovey 85.00
PM Paul Molitor 60.00
MU Dale Murphy 50.00
SM Stan Musial 140.00
DN Don Newcombe 50.00
PN Phil Niekro 40.00
JP Jim Palmer 50.00
TP Tony Perez 50.00
GP Gaylord Perry 40.00
JR Jim Rice 50.00
CR Cal Ripken Jr. 240.00
RR Robin Roberts 50.00
BR Brooks Robinson 65.00
FR Frank Robinson 60.00
AR Al Rosen 60.00
NR Nolan Ryan 150.00
RS Ron Santo 65.00
MS Mike Schmidt 125.00
RE Red Schoendienst 50.00
TS Tom Seaver 85.00
SN Duke Snider 75.00
SU Bruce Sutter 30.00
DS Don Sutton 40.00
MW Matt Williams 50.00
CY Carl Yastrzemski 140.00

Wingfield Classic Collection

NM/M

Common Player: 4.00
Inserted 1:Box
WCC-1 Al Kaline 4.00
WCC-2 Pee Wee Reese 4.00
WCC-3 Stan Musial, Ted Williams 6.00
WCC-4 Bill Dickey 4.00
WCC-5 Frank Robinson 5.00
WCC-6 Billy Martin 4.00
WCC-7 Casey Stengel, Joe DiMaggio 6.00
WCC-8 Bob Feller, Dwight D. Eisenhower 4.00
WCC-9 Duke Snider 5.00
WCC-10 Carl Yastrzemski 8.00
WCC-11 Honus Wagner 6.00
WCC-12 Dwight D. Eisenhower, Clark Griffith 4.00
WCC-13 Mickey Mantle, Joe DiMaggio 15.00
WCC-14 Don Drysdale 4.00
WCC-15 Ted Williams 8.00
WCC-16 Al Kaline, Mickey Mantle 15.00
WCC-17 Ernie Banks 6.00
WCC-18 Lou Boudreau 4.00
WCC-19 George Sisler, Harmon Killebrew 6.00
WCC-20 Gil Hodges 4.00
WCC-21 Rogers Hornsby 6.00
WCC-22 Luis Aparicio 4.00
WCC-23 Jackie Robinson 10.00
WCC-24 Joe Morgan 4.00
WCC-25 Enos Slaughter 4.00
WCC-26 Joe DiMaggio 8.00
WCC-27 Mickey Mantle, Ted Kluszewski 15.00
WCC-28 John F. Kennedy 6.00
WCC-29 Johnny Bench 8.00
WCC-30 Juan Marichal 4.00
WCC-31 Larry Doby 4.00
WCC-32 Don Newcombe, Elston Howard 4.00
WCC-33 Harmon Killebrew, Dwight D. Eisenhower 6.00
WCC-34 Roger Maris, Mickey Mantle 20.00
WCC-35 Mickey Mantle, Stan Musial 15.00
WCC-36 Ted Williams, Mickey Mantle, Yogi Berra 15.00
WCC-37 Nellie Fox 6.00
WCC-38 Richie Ashburn 4.00
WCC-39 Roberto Clemente 15.00
WCC-40 Stan Musial, Robin Roberts 8.00
WCC-41 Tommy Heinrich, Joe DiMaggio 8.00
WCC-42 Roy Campanella 6.00
WCC-43 Rocky Colavito, Harmon Killebrew 6.00
WCC-44 Steve Carlton 4.00
WCC-45 Thurman Munson 6.00
WCC-46 Luis Aparicio, Ernie Banks 6.00
WCC-47 Gil Hodges, Yogi Berra, Dwight D. Eisenhower 6.00
WCC-48 Whitey Ford 6.00
WCC-49 Mickey Mantle, Yogi Berra, Joe DiMaggio 15.00
WCC-50 Yogi Berra 8.00

2005 UD ALL-STAR CLASSICS

NM/M

Complete Set (100): 25.00
Common Player: .15
Pack (8): 3.00
Box (24): 60.00
1 Albert Pujols 2.00
2 Alex Rodriguez 1.50
3 Alfonso Soriano .75
4 Barry Zito .25
5 Bobby Abreu .40
6 Carlos Beltran .50
7 Carlos Delgado .40
8 Chipper Jones .75
9 Curt Schilling .75
10 David Ortiz .75
11 Derek Jeter 2.00
12 Edgar Renteria .25
13 Eric Gagne .25
14 Frank Thomas .50
15 Gary Sheffield .40
16 Greg Maddux 1.00
17 Hank Blalock .40
18 Hideki Matsui 1.50
19 Ichiro Suzuki 1.50
20 Ivan Rodriguez .50
21 Jason Schmidt .25
22 Jason Varitek .25
23 Jeff Kent .25
24 Jim Thome .75
25 Jorge Posada .25
26 Ken Griffey Jr. 1.00
27 Kerry Wood .75
28 Lance Berkman .25
29 Manny Ramirez .75
30 Mariano Rivera .40
31 Mark Mulder .25
32 Mark Prior .75
33 Miguel Cabrera .75
34 Miguel Tejada .50
35 Mike Piazza 1.00
36 Nomar Garciaparra 1.00
37 Pedro Martinez .75
38 Randy Johnson .75
39 Richie Sexson .25
40 Roger Clemens 2.00
41 Roy Halladay .25
42 Sammy Sosa 1.50
43 Scott Rolen .75
44 Sean Casey .25
45 Tim Hudson .25
46 Todd Helton .50
47 Tom Glavine .40
48 Torii Hunter .25
49 Troy Glaus .25
50 Vladimir Guerrero .75
51 Adrian Beltre .25
52 Alexis Rios .15
53 Aubrey Huff .15
54 Brandon Webb .25
55 Dallas McPherson .25
56 David Wright .75
57 Edwin Jackson .15
58 Grady Sizemore .15
59 *Tadahito Iguchi* 3.00
60 Jake Peavy .40
61 Jake Westbrook .15
62 Jason Bay .25
63 Jeff Francis .15
64 Jeremy Reed .15
65 Joe Mauer .40
66 Johan Santana .50
67 Jose Capellan .15
68 Jose Reyes .15
69 Justin Morneau .40
70 Mark Teixeira .40
71 Oliver Perez .25
72 Rich Harden .25
73 Rickie Weeks .25
74 Ryan Howard .15
75 Scott Kazmir .15
76 Al Kaline .75
77 Bill Mazeroski .25
78 Bob Feller .50
79 Bob Gibson .50
80 Brooks Robinson .75
81 Cal Ripken Jr. 3.00
82 Carlton Fisk .25
83 Eddie Murray .50
84 Gaylord Perry .25
85 Harmon Killebrew .75
86 Jim Palmer .50
87 Joe DiMaggio 1.50
88 Joe Morgan .25
89 Johnny Bench .75
90 Juan Marichal .25
91 Lou Brock .25
92 Mike Schmidt 1.00
93 Nolan Ryan 2.00
94 Ozzie Smith .75
95 Phil Niekro .25
96 Robin Yount .50
97 Rollie Fingers .25
98 Tom Seaver .50
99 Willie McCovey .50
100 Yogi Berra .75

Gold

Stars (1-100): 4X-8X
Production 499 Sets

Box Scores

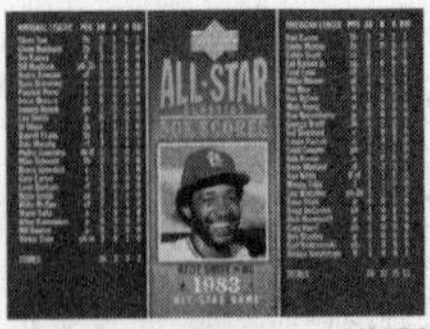

NM/M

Complete Set (20): 50.00
Common Player: 1.50
Inserted 1:24
1 Juan Marichal 2.00
2 Brooks Robinson 3.00
3 Tony Perez 1.50
4 Willie McCovey 2.00
5 Harmon Killebrew 3.00
6 Johnny Bench 3.00
7 Joe Morgan 1.50
8 Lou Brock 1.50
9 Jim Palmer 1.50
10 Mike Schmidt 5.00
11 Ozzie Smith 4.00
12 Roger Clemens 6.00
13 Cal Ripken Jr. 8.00
14 Ken Griffey Jr. 4.00
15 Greg Maddux 4.00
16 Alex Rodriguez 5.00
17 Derek Jeter 6.00
18 Johnny Damon 3.00
19 Garret Anderson 1.50
20 Alfonso Soriano 2.00

Matchups

NM/M

Complete Set (20): 40.00
Common Player: 1.50

Inserted 1:24

1	Hank Blalock	2.00
2	Curt Schilling	3.00
3	Manny Ramirez	3.00
4	Ken Griffey Jr.	4.00
5	Brooks Robinson	3.00
6	Harmon Killebrew	3.00
7	Carl Yastrzemski	4.00
8	Cal Ripken Jr.	8.00
9	Trevor Hoffman	1.50
10	Eric Gagne	2.00
11	Alfonso Soriano	2.00
12	David Ortiz	3.00
13	Andruw Jones	1.50
14	Garret Anderson	1.50
15	Magglio Ordonez	1.50
16	Derek Jeter	6.00
17	Chipper Jones	3.00
18	Roberto Alomar	2.00
19	Mike Piazza	3.00
20	Alex Rodriguez	5.00

Midsummer Classics

NM/M

Complete Set (20): 40.00
Common Player: 1.50
Inserted 1:24

1	Derek Jeter	6.00
2	Pedro Martinez	2.00
3	Mike Piazza	3.00
4	Randy Johnson	2.00
5	Gary Sheffield	2.00
6	Albert Pujols	6.00
7	David Ortiz	3.00
8	Manny Ramirez	3.00
9	Garret Anderson	1.50
10	Andruw Jones	1.50
11	Todd Helton	2.00
12	Paul Konerko	1.50
13	Alfonso Soriano	2.00
14	Magglio Ordonez	1.50
15	Cal Ripken Jr.	8.00
16	Ken Griffey Jr.	3.00
17	Harmon Killebrew	3.00
18	Mike Schmidt	5.00
19	Frank Thomas	2.00
20	Alex Rodriguez	5.00

Midsummer Swatches

NM/M

Common Player: 4.00
Inserted 1:12
Patches: No Pricing
Production 25 Sets

MA	Moises Alou Jsy	6.00
JB	Jeff Bagwell Jsy	6.00
CB	Carlos Beltran Jsy	8.00
CI	Craig Biggio Jsy	6.00
BB	Bret Boone Jsy	4.00
CD	Carlos Delgado Jsy	6.00
JE	Jim Edmonds Jsy	6.00
KF	Keith Foulke Jsy	
RF	Rafael Furcal Jsy	4.00
EG	Eric Gagne Jsy	8.00
SG	Shawn Green Jsy	4.00
KG	Ken Griffey Jr. Jsy	25.00
TH	Todd Helton Jsy	8.00
TI	Torii Hunter Jsy	6.00
AJ	Andruw Jones Pants	6.00
CJ	Chipper Jones Jsy	8.00
JK	Jeff Kent Jsy	4.00
RK	Ryan Klesko	4.00
ML	Matt Lawton Jsy	4.00
PL	Paul LoDuca Jsy	4.00
JL	Javy Lopez Jsy	4.00
PM	Pedro Martinez Jsy	8.00
VM	Victor Martinez Jsy	4.00
DO	David Ortiz Pants	8.00
RP	Rafael Palmeiro Jsy	8.00
MP	Mike Piazza Jsy	15.00
ER	Edgar Renteria Jsy	6.00
CR	Cal Ripken Jr. Pants	35.00
CC	C.C. Sabathia Jsy	4.00
SC	Jason Schmidt Jsy	4.00
BS	Ben Sheets Jsy	6.00
GS	Gary Sheffield Jsy	8.00
JS	John Smoltz Jsy	10.00
SS	Sammy Sosa Jsy	10.00
IS	Ichiro Suzuki Jsy	30.00
MS	Mike Sweeney Jsy	4.00
MT	Miguel Tejada Jsy	8.00
FT	Frank Thomas Jsy	8.00
JT	Jim Thome Jsy	8.00
OM	Omar Vizquel Jsy	6.00
WE	David Wells Jsy	4.00
DW	Dontrelle Willis Jsy	8.00

MVP's

NM/M

Complete Set (20): 45.00
Common Player: 1.00
Inserted 1:24

1	Alfonso Soriano	2.00
2	Ken Griffey Sr.	4.00
3	Brooks Robinson	3.00
4	Cal Ripken Jr.	8.00
5	Cal Ripken Jr.	8.00
6	Derek Jeter	6.00
7	Carl Yastrzemski	4.00
8	Garret Anderson	1.50
9	Jeff Conine	1.00
10	Joe Morgan	1.50
11	Juan Marichal	2.00
12	Julio Franco	1.00
13	Ken Griffey Jr.	4.00
14	Mike Piazza	3.00
15	Pedro Martinez	3.00
16	Roberto Alomar	2.00
17	Roger Clemens	6.00
18	Sandy Alomar Jr.	1.00
19	Tony Perez	1.50
20	Willie McCovey	2.00

Perennial All-Stars

NM/M

Complete Set (20): 40.00
Common Player: 2.00
Inserted 1:24

1	Albert Pujols	6.00
2	Alex Rodriguez	5.00
3	Alfonso Soriano	2.00
4	Curt Schilling	3.00
5	Derek Jeter	6.00
6	Eric Gagne	2.00
7	Greg Maddux	4.00
8	Ichiro Suzuki	5.00
9	Ivan Rodriguez	2.00
10	Jim Thome	2.00
11	Ken Griffey Jr.	4.00
12	Mariano Rivera	2.00
13	Miguel Tejada	2.00
14	Mike Piazza	3.00
15	Randy Johnson	2.00
16	Roger Clemens	6.00
17	Sammy Sosa	4.00
18	Scott Rolen	3.00
19	Todd Helton	2.00
20	Vladimir Guerrero	2.00

2005 UD HALL OF FAME

NM/M

Complete Set (100):
Common Player: 3.00
Production 550 sets
Tin (4): 125.00

1	Al Kaline	4.00
2	Al Lopez	3.00
3	Bill Mazeroski	3.00

4	Billy Williams	3.00
5	Bob Feller	4.00
6	Bob Gibson	4.00
7	Bob Lemon	3.00
8	Bobby Doerr	3.00
9	Brooks Robinson	5.00
10	Buck Leonard	3.00
11	Carl Yastrzemski	5.00
12	Carlton Fisk	4.00
13	Casey Stengel	4.00
14	Jim "Catfish" Hunter	3.00
15	Dave Winfield	4.00
16	Dennis Eckersley	3.00
17	Dizzy Dean	4.00
18	Don Drysdale	4.00
19	Don Sutton	3.00
20	Duke Snider	4.00
21	Early Wynn	3.00
22	Eddie Mathews	5.00
23	Eddie Murray	4.00
24	Enos Slaughter	3.00
25	Ernie Banks	5.00
26	Fergie Jenkins	3.00
27	Frank Robinson	4.00
28	Gary Carter	3.00
29	Gaylord Perry	3.00
30	George Brett	8.00
31	George Kell	3.00
32	George Sisler	3.00
33	Hal Newhouser	3.00
34	Harmon Killebrew	5.00
35	Hoyt Wilhelm	3.00
36	Jackie Robinson	5.00
37	Jim Bunning	3.00
38	Jim Palmer	3.00
39	Jimmie Foxx	5.00
40	Joe Morgan	3.00
41	Johnny Bench	5.00
42	Johnny Mize	3.00
43	Juan Marichal	3.00
44	Kirby Puckett	4.00
45	Larry Doby	3.00
46	Lefty Grove	3.00
47	Lou Boudreau	3.00
48	Lou Brock	4.00
49	Luis Aparicio	3.00
50	Mel Ott	4.00
51	Mickey Cochrane	4.00
52	Monte Irvin	3.00
53	Orlando Cepeda	3.00
54	Ozzie Smith	5.00
55	Paul Molitor	4.00
56	Pee Wee Reese	3.00
57	Phil Niekro	3.00
58	Phil Rizzuto	3.00
59	Pie Traynor	3.00
60	Ralph Kiner	3.00
61	Red Schoendienst	3.00
62	Richie Ashburn	3.00
63	Rick Ferrell	3.00
64	Robin Roberts	3.00
65	Robin Yount	5.00
66	Rod Carew	3.00
67	Rogers Hornsby	4.00
68	Rollie Fingers	3.00
69	Roy Campanella	4.00
70	Steve Carlton	3.00
71	Tony Perez	3.00
72	Warren Spahn	5.00
73	Whitey Ford	4.00
74	Willie McCovey	4.00
75	Willie Stargell	4.00
76	Yogi Berra	5.00
77	Babe Ruth	8.00
78	Honus Wagner	4.00
79	Lou Gehrig	6.00
80	Mickey Mantle	15.00
81	Ty Cobb	6.00
82	Ryne Sandberg	5.00
83	Satchel Paige	5.00
84	Wade Boggs	4.00
85	Reggie Jackson	4.00
86	Babe Ruth	8.00
87	Christy Mathewson	4.00
88	Cy Young	4.00
89	Honus Wagner	5.00
90	Joe DiMaggio	6.00
91	Lou Gehrig	6.00
92	Mickey Mantle	15.00
93	Mike Schmidt	6.00
94	Nolan Ryan	8.00
95	Satchel Paige	5.00
96	Stan Musial	5.00
97	Ted Williams	6.00
98	Tom Seaver	4.00
99	Ty Cobb	6.00
100	Walter Johnson	4.00

Gold

Gold (1-100): 1.5-2X
Production 25 sets

Green

Green (1-100): 1X
Production 200 sets

Rainbow

No Pricing
Production one set

Silver

Silver (1-100): 1-1.5X
Production 99 sets

Class of Cooperstown

NM/M

Production 50 sets
Gold: No Pricing
Production 5 sets
Silver: No Pricing
Production 15 sets
Rainbow: No Pricing
Production one set

LA1	Luis Aparicio	4.00
LA2	Luis Aparicio	4.00
EB1	Ernie Banks	6.00
EB2	Ernie Banks	6.00
BE1	Johnny Bench	6.00
BE2	Johnny Bench	6.00
YB1	Yogi Berra	5.00
YB2	Yogi Berra	5.00
GB1	George Brett	10.00
GB2	George Brett	10.00
GB3	George Brett	10.00
LB1	Lou Brock	4.00
JB1	Jim Bunning	4.00
JB2	Jim Bunning	4.00
RC1	Rod Carew	4.00
RC2	Rod Carew	4.00
SC1	Steve Carlton	4.00
SC2	Steve Carlton	4.00
SC3	Steve Carlton	4.00
SC4	Steve Carlton	4.00
GC1	Gary Carter	4.00
GC2	Gary Carter	4.00
OC1	Orlando Cepeda	4.00
BD1	Bobby Doerr	4.00
BD2	Bobby Doerr	4.00
DE1	Dennis Eckersley	4.00
BF1	Bob Feller	4.00
BF2	Bob Feller	4.00
RF1	Rollie Fingers	4.00
CF1	Carlton Fisk	4.00
CF2	Carlton Fisk	4.00
WF1	Whitey Ford	5.00
WF2	Whitey Ford	5.00
BG1	Bob Gibson	5.00
BG2	Bob Gibson	5.00
MI1	Monte Irvin	4.00
MI2	Monte Irvin	4.00
RJ1	Reggie Jackson	5.00
RJ2	Reggie Jackson	5.00
RJ3	Reggie Jackson	5.00
FJ1	Fergie Jenkins	4.00
AK1	Al Kaline	6.00
AK2	Al Kaline	6.00
AK3	Al Kaline	6.00
GK1	George Kell	4.00
HK1	Harmon Killebrew	6.00
HK2	Harmon Killebrew	6.00
HK3	Harmon Killebrew	6.00
HK4	Harmon Killebrew	6.00
RK1	Ralph Kiner	4.00
RK2	Ralph Kiner	4.00
MA1	Juan Marichal	4.00
MA2	Juan Marichal	4.00
BM1	Bill Mazeroski	4.00
WM1	Willie McCovey	5.00
WM2	Willie McCovey	5.00
PM1	Paul Molitor	5.00

PM2 Paul Molitor 5.00
PM3 Paul Molitor 5.00
JM1 Joe Morgan 4.00
JM2 Joe Morgan 4.00
EM1 Eddie Murray 4.00
SM1 Stan Musial 6.00
SM2 Stan Musial 6.00
PN1 Phil Niekro 4.00
JP1 Jim Palmer 4.00
JP2 Jim Palmer 4.00
TP1 Tony Perez 4.00
GP1 Gaylord Perry 4.00
GP2 Gaylord Perry 4.00
KP1 Kirby Puckett 5.00
RR1 Robin Roberts 4.00
BR1 Brooks Robinson 5.00
BR2 Brooks Robinson 5.00
BR3 Brooks Robinson 5.00
FR1 Frank Robinson 5.00
FR2 Frank Robinson 5.00
NR1 Nolan Ryan 10.00
NR2 Nolan Ryan 10.00
NR3 Nolan Ryan 10.00
NR4 Nolan Ryan 10.00
MS1 Mike Schmidt 6.00
MS2 Mike Schmidt 6.00
MS3 Mike Schmidt 6.00
RS1 Red Schoendienst 4.00
TS1 Tom Seaver 5.00
TS2 Tom Seaver 5.00
OS1 Ozzie Smith 6.00
OS2 Ozzie Smith 6.00
SN1 Duke Snider 5.00
DS1 Don Sutton 4.00
BW1 Billy Williams 4.00
BW2 Billy Williams 4.00
BW3 Billy Williams 4.00
DW1 Dave Winfield 4.00
DW2 Dave Winfield 4.00
CY1 Carl Yastrzemski 6.00
CY2 Carl Yastrzemski 6.00
RY1 Robin Yount 6.00
RY2 Robin Yount 6.00

Class of Cooperstown Autograph

NM/M
Production 25 sets
Gold: No Pricing
Production 5 sets
Silver: No Pricing
Production 15 sets
Rainbow: No Pricing
Material Gold: No Pricing
Production 5 sets
Material Silver: No Pricing
Production 15 sets
Patch Gold: No Pricing
Production 5 sets
Patch Silver: No Pricing
Production 10 sets
LA1 Luis Aparicio 20.00
LA2 Luis Aparicio 20.00
EB1 Ernie Banks 50.00
EB2 Ernie Banks 50.00
BE1 Johnny Bench 40.00
BE2 Johnny Bench 40.00
YB1 Yogi Berra 60.00
YB2 Yogi Berra 60.00
GB1 George Brett 60.00
GB2 George Brett 60.00
GB3 George Brett 60.00
LB1 Lou Brock 35.00
JB1 Jim Bunning 25.00
JB2 Jim Bunning 25.00
RC1 Rod Carew 30.00
RC2 Rod Carew 30.00
SC1 Steve Carlton 20.00
SC2 Steve Carlton 20.00
SC3 Steve Carlton 20.00
SC4 Steve Carlton 20.00
GC1 Gary Carter 25.00
GC2 Gary Carter 25.00
OC1 Orlando Cepeda 25.00
BD1 Bobby Doerr 15.00
BD2 Bobby Doerr 15.00
DE1 Dennis Eckersley 20.00
BF1 Bob Feller 30.00
BF2 Bob Feller 30.00
RF1 Rollie Fingers 20.00
CF1 Carlton Fisk 30.00
CF2 Carlton Fisk 30.00
WF1 Whitey Ford 50.00
WF2 Whitey Ford 50.00
BG1 Bob Gibson 35.00
BG2 Bob Gibson 35.00
MI1 Monte Irvin 25.00
MI2 Monte Irvin 25.00
RJ1 Reggie Jackson 40.00
RJ2 Reggie Jackson 40.00
RJ3 Reggie Jackson 40.00
FJ1 Fergie Jenkins 20.00
AK1 Al Kaline 40.00
AK2 Al Kaline 40.00
AK3 Al Kaline 40.00
GK1 George Kell 20.00
HK1 Harmon Killebrew 40.00
HK2 Harmon Killebrew 40.00
HK3 Harmon Killebrew 40.00
HK4 Harmon Killebrew 40.00
RK1 Ralph Kiner 40.00
RK2 Ralph Kiner 40.00
MA1 Juan Marichal 25.00
MA2 Juan Marichal 25.00
BM1 Bill Mazeroski 40.00
WM1 Willie McCovey 40.00
WM2 Willie McCovey 40.00
PM1 Paul Molitor 30.00
PM2 Paul Molitor 30.00
PM3 Paul Molitor 30.00
JM1 Joe Morgan 25.00
JM2 Joe Morgan 25.00
EM1 Eddie Murray 50.00
SM1 Stan Musial 60.00
SM2 Stan Musial 60.00
PN1 Phil Niekro 20.00
JP1 Jim Palmer 20.00
JP2 Jim Palmer 20.00
TP1 Tony Perez 20.00
GP1 Gaylord Perry 20.00
GP2 Gaylord Perry 20.00
KP1 Kirby Puckett 40.00
RR1 Robin Roberts 25.00
BR1 Brooks Robinson 30.00
BR2 Brooks Robinson 30.00
BR3 Brooks Robinson 30.00
FR1 Frank Robinson 20.00
FR2 Frank Robinson 20.00
NR1 Nolan Ryan 90.00
NR2 Nolan Ryan 90.00
NR3 Nolan Ryan 90.00
NR4 Nolan Ryan 90.00
MS1 Mike Schmidt 50.00
MS2 Mike Schmidt 50.00
MS3 Mike Schmidt 50.00
RS1 Red Schoendienst 35.00
TS1 Tom Seaver 40.00
TS2 Tom Seaver 40.00
OS1 Ozzie Smith 40.00
OS2 Ozzie Smith 40.00
SN1 Duke Snider 40.00
DS1 Don Sutton 20.00
BW1 Billy Williams 20.00
BW2 Billy Williams 20.00
BW3 Billy Williams 20.00
DW1 Dave Winfield 30.00
DW2 Dave Winfield 30.00
CY1 Carl Yastrzemski 50.00
CY2 Carl Yastrzemski 50.00
RY1 Robin Yount 40.00
RY2 Robin Yount 40.00

Class of Cooperstown Calling

NM/M
Production 50 sets
Gold: No Pricing
Production 5 sets
Green: .75-1.5X
Production 25 sets
Silver: No Pricing
Production 15 sets
Rainbow: No Pricing
Production one set
LA1 Luis Aparicio 4.00
LA2 Luis Aparicio 4.00
EB1 Ernie Banks 6.00
BE1 Johnny Bench 6.00
YB1 Yogi Berra 5.00
WB1 Wade Boggs 5.00
WB2 Wade Boggs 5.00
WB3 Wade Boggs 5.00
GB1 George Brett 10.00
GB2 George Brett 10.00
LB1 Lou Brock 4.00
LB2 Lou Brock 4.00
JB1 Jim Bunning 4.00
RC1 Rod Carew 4.00
RC2 Rod Carew 4.00
SC1 Steve Carlton 4.00
SC2 Steve Carlton 4.00
GC1 Gary Carter 4.00
GC2 Gary Carter 4.00
GC3 Gary Carter 4.00
OC1 Orlando Cepeda 4.00
OC2 Orlando Cepeda 4.00
BD1 Bobby Doerr 4.00
BD2 Bobby Doerr 4.00
DE1 Dennis Eckersley 4.00
DE2 Dennis Eckersley 4.00
BF1 Bob Feller 4.00
BF2 Bob Feller 4.00
RF1 Rollie Fingers 4.00
RF2 Rollie Fingers 4.00
CF1 Carlton Fisk 4.00
CF2 Carlton Fisk 4.00
WF1 Whitey Ford 5.00
BG1 Bob Gibson 5.00
MI1 Monte Irvin 4.00
RJ1 Reggie Jackson 5.00
RJ2 Reggie Jackson 5.00
RJ3 Reggie Jackson 5.00
FJ1 Fergie Jenkins 4.00
FJ2 Fergie Jenkins 4.00
AK1 Al Kaline 6.00
AK2 Al Kaline 6.00
GK1 George Kell 4.00
HK1 Harmon Killebrew 6.00
HK2 Harmon Killebrew 6.00
RK1 Ralph Kiner 4.00
JM1 Juan Marichal 4.00
BM1 Bill Mazeroski 4.00
WM1 Willie McCovey 5.00
PM1 Paul Molitor 5.00
PM2 Paul Molitor 5.00
PM3 Paul Molitor 5.00
MO1 Joe Morgan 4.00
MO2 Joe Morgan 4.00
EM1 Eddie Murray 4.00
EM2 Eddie Murray 4.00
SM1 Stan Musial 6.00
SM2 Stan Musial 6.00
PN1 Phil Niekro 4.00
PN2 Phil Niekro 4.00
JP1 Jim Palmer 4.00
JP2 Jim Palmer 4.00
TP1 Tony Perez 4.00
TP2 Tony Perez 4.00
GP1 Gaylord Perry 4.00
GP2 Gaylord Perry 4.00
KP1 Kirby Puckett 5.00
KP2 Kirby Puckett 5.00
RR1 Robin Roberts 4.00
BR1 Brooks Robinson 5.00
BR2 Brooks Robinson 5.00
BR3 Brooks Robinson 5.00
FR1 Frank Robinson 5.00
NR1 Nolan Ryan 10.00
NR2 Nolan Ryan 10.00
NR3 Nolan Ryan 10.00
NR4 Nolan Ryan 10.00
SA1 Ryne Sandberg 6.00
SA2 Ryne Sandberg 6.00
SA3 Ryne Sandberg 6.00
MS1 Mike Schmidt 6.00
MS2 Mike Schmidt 6.00
MS3 Mike Schmidt 6.00
RS1 Red Schoendienst 4.00
TS1 Tom Seaver 5.00
OS1 Ozzie Smith 6.00
OS2 Ozzie Smith 6.00
OS3 Ozzie Smith 6.00
SN1 Duke Snider 5.00
DS1 Don Sutton 4.00
DS2 Don Sutton 4.00
DS3 Don Sutton 4.00
BW1 Billy Williams 4.00
BW2 Billy Williams 4.00
DW1 Dave Winfield 4.00
CY1 Carl Yastrzemski 6.00
CY2 Carl Yastrzemski 6.00
RY1 Robin Yount 6.00
RY2 Robin Yount 6.00
RY3 Robin Yount 6.00

Class of Cooperstown Calling Auto.

NM/M
Production 25 sets
Gold: No Pricing
Production 5 sets
Silver: No Pricing
Production 15 sets
Rainbow: No Pricing
Production one set
Material Gold: No Pricing
Production 5 sets
Material Silver: No Pricing
Production 15 sets
Patch Gold: No Pricing
Production 2 sets
Patch Silver: No Pricing
Production 10 sets
LA1 Luis Aparicio 20.00
LA2 Luis Aparicio 20.00
EB1 Ernie Banks 50.00
BE1 Johnny Bench 40.00
YB1 Yogi Berra 60.00
WB1 Wade Boggs 35.00
WB2 Wade Boggs 35.00
WB3 Wade Boggs 35.00
GB1 George Brett 60.00
GB2 George Brett 60.00
LB1 Lou Brock 35.00
LB2 Lou Brock 35.00
JB1 Jim Bunning 25.00
RC1 Rod Carew 30.00
RC2 Rod Carew 30.00
SC1 Steve Carlton 20.00
SC2 Steve Carlton 20.00
GC1 Gary Carter 25.00
GC2 Gary Carter 25.00
GC3 Gary Carter 25.00
OC1 Orlando Cepeda 25.00
OC2 Orlando Cepeda 25.00
BD1 Bobby Doerr 15.00
BD2 Bobby Doerr 15.00
DE1 Dennis Eckersley 20.00
DE2 Dennis Eckersley 20.00
BF1 Bob Feller 30.00
BF2 Bob Feller 30.00
RF1 Rollie Fingers 20.00
RF2 Rollie Fingers 20.00
CF1 Carlton Fisk 30.00
CF2 Carlton Fisk 30.00
WF1 Whitey Ford 50.00
BG1 Bob Gibson 35.00
MI1 Monte Irvin 25.00
RJ1 Reggie Jackson 40.00
RJ2 Reggie Jackson 40.00
RJ3 Reggie Jackson 40.00
FJ1 Fergie Jenkins 20.00
FJ2 Fergie Jenkins 20.00
AK1 Al Kaline 40.00
AK2 Al Kaline 40.00
GK1 George Kell 20.00
HK1 Harmon Killebrew 40.00
HK2 Harmon Killebrew 40.00
RK1 Ralph Kiner 40.00
JM1 Juan Marichal 25.00
BM1 Bill Mazeroski 40.00
WM1 Willie McCovey 40.00
PM1 Paul Molitor 30.00
PM2 Paul Molitor 30.00
PM3 Paul Molitor 30.00
MO1 Joe Morgan 25.00
MO2 Joe Morgan 25.00
EM1 Eddie Murray 50.00
EM2 Eddie Murray 50.00
SM1 Stan Musial 60.00
SM2 Stan Musial 60.00
PN1 Phil Niekro 20.00
PN2 Phil Niekro 20.00
JP1 Jim Palmer 20.00
JP2 Jim Palmer 20.00
TP1 Tony Perez 20.00
TP2 Tony Perez 20.00
GP1 Gaylord Perry 20.00
GP2 Gaylord Perry 20.00
KP1 Kirby Puckett 40.00
KP2 Kirby Puckett 40.00
RR1 Robin Roberts 40.00
BR1 Brooks Robinson 30.00
BR2 Brooks Robinson 30.00
BR3 Brooks Robinson 30.00
FR1 Frank Robinson 20.00
NR1 Nolan Ryan 90.00
NR2 Nolan Ryan 90.00
NR3 Nolan Ryan 90.00
NR4 Nolan Ryan 90.00
SA1 Ryne Sandberg 60.00
SA2 Ryne Sandberg 60.00
SA3 Ryne Sandberg 60.00
MS1 Mike Schmidt 50.00
MS2 Mike Schmidt 50.00
MS3 Mike Schmidt 50.00
RS1 Red Schoendienst 35.00
TS1 Tom Seaver 40.00
OS1 Ozzie Smith 40.00
OS2 Ozzie Smith 40.00
OS3 Ozzie Smith 40.00
SN1 Duke Snider 40.00
DS1 Don Sutton 20.00
DS2 Don Sutton 20.00
DS3 Don Sutton 20.00
BW1 Billy Williams 20.00

BW2 Billy Williams 20.00
DW1 Dave Winfield 30.00
CY1 Carl Yastrzemski 50.00
CY2 Carl Yastrzemski 50.00
RY1 Robin Yount 40.00
RY2 Robin Yount 40.00
RY3 Robin Yount 40.00

Cooperstown Cuts

NM/M
Production 1-20
JM Johnny Mize/20 180.00

Cooperstown Cuts Memorabilia

No Pricing
Production 1-20

Essential Enshrinement

NM/M
Production 50 sets
Gold: No Pricing
Production 5 sets
Silver: No Pricing
Production 15 sets
Rainbow: No Pricing
Production one set
LA1 Luis Aparicio 4.00
EB1 Ernie Banks 6.00
BE1 Johnny Bench 6.00
BE2 Johnny Bench 6.00
YB1 Yogi Berra 5.00
YB2 Yogi Berra 5.00
WB1 Wade Boggs 5.00
WB2 Wade Boggs 5.00
WB3 Wade Boggs 5.00
GB1 George Brett 10.00
GB2 George Brett 10.00
GB3 George Brett 10.00
LB1 Lou Brock 4.00
LB2 Lou Brock 4.00
JB1 Jim Bunning 4.00
RC1 Rod Carew 4.00
RC2 Rod Carew 4.00
SC1 Steve Carlton 4.00
SC2 Steve Carlton 4.00
GC1 Gary Carter 4.00
GC2 Gary Carter 4.00
OC1 Orlando Cepeda 4.00
BD1 Bobby Doerr 4.00
BD2 Bobby Doerr 4.00
DE1 Dennis Eckersley 4.00
BF1 Bob Feller 4.00
BF2 Bob Feller 4.00
RF1 Rollie Fingers 4.00
CF1 Carlton Fisk 4.00
CF2 Carlton Fisk 4.00
WF1 Whitey Ford 5.00
WF2 Whitey Ford 5.00
BG1 Bob Gibson 5.00
BG2 Bob Gibson 5.00
MI1 Monte Irvin 4.00
RJ1 Reggie Jackson 5.00
RJ2 Reggie Jackson 5.00
RJ3 Reggie Jackson 5.00
FJ1 Fergie Jenkins 4.00
FJ2 Fergie Jenkins 4.00
AK1 Al Kaline 6.00
AK2 Al Kaline 6.00
GK1 George Kell 4.00
HK1 Harmon Killebrew 6.00
HK2 Harmon Killebrew 6.00
RK1 Ralph Kiner 4.00
JM1 Juan Marichal 4.00
BM1 Bill Mazeroski 4.00
WM1 Willie McCovey 5.00
PM1 Paul Molitor 5.00
PM2 Paul Molitor 5.00
PM3 Paul Molitor 5.00
MO1 Joe Morgan 4.00
MO2 Joe Morgan 4.00
MO3 Joe Morgan 4.00
EM1 Eddie Murray 4.00
EM2 Eddie Murray 4.00
SM1 Stan Musial 6.00
SM2 Stan Musial 6.00
PN1 Phil Niekro 4.00
PN2 Phil Niekro 4.00
JP1 Jim Palmer 4.00
JP2 Jim Palmer 4.00
TP1 Tony Perez 4.00
GP1 Gaylord Perry 4.00
GP2 Gaylord Perry 4.00
KP1 Kirby Puckett 5.00
KP2 Kirby Puckett 5.00
RR1 Robin Roberts 4.00
BR1 Brooks Robinson 5.00
BR2 Brooks Robinson 5.00
BR3 Brooks Robinson 5.00
FR1 Frank Robinson 5.00
FR2 Frank Robinson 5.00
NR1 Nolan Ryan 10.00
NR2 Nolan Ryan 10.00
NR3 Nolan Ryan 10.00
NR4 Nolan Ryan 10.00
SA1 Ryne Sandberg 6.00
SA2 Ryne Sandberg 6.00
SA3 Ryne Sandberg 6.00
MS1 Mike Schmidt 6.00
MS2 Mike Schmidt 6.00
RS1 Red Schoendienst 4.00
TS1 Tom Seaver 5.00
OS1 Ozzie Smith 6.00
OS2 Ozzie Smith 6.00
SN1 Duke Snider 5.00
SN2 Duke Snider 5.00
DS1 Don Sutton 4.00
DS2 Don Sutton 4.00
BW1 Billy Williams 4.00
BW2 Billy Williams 4.00
DW1 Dave Winfield 4.00
CY1 Carl Yastrzemski 6.00
CY2 Carl Yastrzemski 6.00
CY3 Carl Yastrzemski 6.00
RY1 Robin Yount 6.00
RY2 Robin Yount 6.00
RY3 Robin Yount 6.00

Essential Enshrinement Autograph

NM/M
Production 25 sets
Gold: No Pricing
Production 5 sets
Silver: No Pricing
Production 15 sets
Rainbow: No Pricing
Production one set
Material Gold: No Pricing
Production 5 sets
Material Silver: No Pricing
Production 15 sets
Patch Gold: No Pricing
Production 5 sets
Patch Silver: No Pricing
Production 10 sets
LA1 Luis Aparicio 20.00
EB1 Ernie Banks 50.00
BE1 Johnny Bench 40.00
BE2 Johnny Bench 40.00
YB1 Yogi Berra 60.00
YB2 Yogi Berra 60.00
WB1 Wade Boggs 35.00
WB2 Wade Boggs 35.00
WB3 Wade Boggs 35.00
GB1 George Brett 60.00
GB2 George Brett 60.00
GB3 George Brett 60.00
LB1 Lou Brock 35.00
LB2 Lou Brock 35.00
JB1 Jim Bunning 25.00
RC1 Rod Carew 30.00
RC2 Rod Carew 30.00
SC1 Steve Carlton 20.00
SC2 Steve Carlton 20.00
GC1 Gary Carter 25.00
GC2 Gary Carter 25.00
OC1 Orlando Cepeda 25.00
BD1 Bobby Doerr 15.00
BD2 Bobby Doerr 15.00
DE1 Dennis Eckersley 20.00
BF1 Bob Feller 30.00
BF2 Bob Feller 30.00
RF1 Rollie Fingers 20.00
CF1 Carlton Fisk 30.00
CF2 Carlton Fisk 30.00
WF1 Whitey Ford 50.00
WF2 Whitey Ford 50.00
BG1 Bob Gibson 35.00
BG2 Bob Gibson 35.00
MI1 Monte Irvin 25.00
RJ1 Reggie Jackson 40.00
RJ2 Reggie Jackson 40.00
RJ3 Reggie Jackson 40.00
FJ1 Fergie Jenkins 20.00
FJ2 Fergie Jenkins 20.00
AK1 Al Kaline 40.00
AK2 Al Kaline 40.00
GK1 George Kell 20.00
HK1 Harmon Killebrew 40.00
HK2 Harmon Killebrew 40.00
RK1 Ralph Kiner 40.00
JM1 Juan Marichal 25.00
BM1 Bill Mazeroski 40.00
WM1 Willie McCovey 40.00
PM1 Paul Molitor 30.00
PM2 Paul Molitor 30.00
PM3 Paul Molitor 30.00
MO1 Joe Morgan 25.00
MO2 Joe Morgan 25.00
MO3 Joe Morgan 25.00
EM1 Eddie Murray 50.00
EM2 Eddie Murray 50.00
SM1 Stan Musial 60.00
SM2 Stan Musial 60.00
PN1 Phil Niekro 20.00
PN2 Phil Niekro 20.00
JP1 Jim Palmer 20.00
JP2 Jim Palmer 20.00
TP1 Tony Perez 20.00
GP1 Gaylord Perry 20.00
GP2 Gaylord Perry 20.00
KP1 Kirby Puckett 40.00
KP2 Kirby Puckett 40.00
RR1 Robin Roberts 25.00
BR1 Brooks Robinson 30.00
BR2 Brooks Robinson 30.00
BR3 Brooks Robinson 30.00
FR1 Frank Robinson 20.00
FR2 Frank Robinson 20.00
NR1 Nolan Ryan 90.00
NR2 Nolan Ryan 90.00
NR3 Nolan Ryan 90.00
NR4 Nolan Ryan 90.00
SA1 Ryne Sandberg 60.00
SA2 Ryne Sandberg 60.00
SA3 Ryne Sandberg 60.00
MS1 Mike Schmidt 50.00
MS2 Mike Schmidt 50.00
RS1 Red Schoendienst 35.00
TS1 Tom Seaver 40.00
OS1 Ozzie Smith 40.00
OS2 Ozzie Smith 40.00
SN1 Duke Snider 40.00
SN2 Duke Snider 40.00
DS1 Don Sutton 20.00
DS2 Don Sutton 20.00
BW1 Billy Williams 20.00
BW2 Billy Williams 20.00
DW1 Dave Winfield 30.00
CY1 Carl Yastrzemski 50.00
CY2 Carl Yastrzemski 50.00
CY3 Carl Yastrzemski 50.00
RY1 Robin Yount 40.00
RY2 Robin Yount 40.00
RY3 Robin Yount 40.00

Hall of Fame Materials

NM/M
Production 25 sets
Gold: No Pricing
Production 5 sets
Silver: No Pricing
Production 15 sets
Rainbow: No Pricing
Production one set
Green: No Pricing
Production 10 sets
RC1 Roberto Clemente 120.00
RC2 Roberto Clemente 120.00
RC3 Roberto Clemente 120.00
TC1 Ty Cobb 100.00
TC2 Ty Cobb 100.00
TC3 Ty Cobb 100.00
MC1 Mickey Cochrane 40.00
DD1 Dizzy Dean 80.00
DD2 Dizzy Dean 80.00
JD1 Joe DiMaggio 90.00
JD2 Joe DiMaggio 90.00
JD3 Joe DiMaggio 90.00
JF1 Jimmie Foxx 60.00
JF2 Jimmie Foxx 60.00
LG1 Lou Gehrig 180.00
LG2 Lou Gehrig 180.00
LG3 Lou Gehrig 180.00
RH1 Rogers Hornsby 80.00
MM1 Mickey Mantle 250.00
MM2 Mickey Mantle 250.00
MM3 Mickey Mantle 250.00
JM1 Johnny Mize 30.00
JM2 Johnny Mize 30.00
JM3 Johnny Mize 30.00
MO1 Mel Ott 40.00
MO2 Mel Ott 40.00
SP1 Satchel Paige 50.00
SP2 Satchel Paige 50.00
SP3 Satchel Paige 50.00
JR1 Jackie Robinson 60.00
JR2 Jackie Robinson 60.00
JR3 Jackie Robinson 60.00
BR1 Babe Ruth 250.00
BR2 Babe Ruth 250.00
BR3 Babe Ruth 250.00
GS1 George Sisler 40.00
GS2 George Sisler 40.00
TW1 Ted Williams 85.00
TW2 Ted Williams 85.00
TW3 Ted Williams 85.00

Hall of Fame Seasons

NM/M
Production 50 sets
Gold: No Pricing
Production 5 sets
Silver: No Pricing
Production 15 sets
Rainbow: No Pricing
Production one set
LA1 Luis Aparicio 4.00
EB1 Ernie Banks 6.00
BE1 Johnny Bench 6.00
BE2 Johnny Bench 6.00
YB1 Yogi Berra 5.00
YB2 Yogi Berra 5.00
WB1 Wade Boggs 5.00
WB2 Wade Boggs 5.00
WB3 Wade Boggs 5.00
GB1 George Brett 10.00
GB2 George Brett 10.00
LB1 Lou Brock 4.00
LB2 Lou Brock 4.00
JB1 Jim Bunning 4.00
RC1 Rod Carew 4.00
RC2 Rod Carew 4.00
GC1 Gary Carter 4.00
SC1 Steve Carlton 4.00
SC2 Steve Carlton 4.00
SC3 Steve Carlton 4.00
OC1 Orlando Cepeda 4.00
BD1 Bobby Doerr 4.00
DE1 Dennis Eckersley 4.00
DE2 Dennis Eckersley 4.00
DE3 Dennis Eckersley 4.00
BF1 Bob Feller 4.00
BF2 Bob Feller 4.00
RF1 Rollie Fingers 4.00
CF1 Carlton Fisk 4.00
CF2 Carlton Fisk 4.00
WF1 Whitey Ford 5.00
WF2 Whitey Ford 5.00
BG1 Bob Gibson 5.00
BG2 Bob Gibson 5.00
MI1 Monte Irvin 4.00
RJ1 Reggie Jackson 5.00
RJ2 Reggie Jackson 5.00
RJ3 Reggie Jackson 5.00
FJ1 Fergie Jenkins 4.00
FJ2 Fergie Jenkins 4.00
AK1 Al Kaline 6.00
AK2 Al Kaline 6.00
AK3 Al Kaline 6.00
GK1 George Kell 4.00
HK1 Harmon Killebrew 6.00
HK2 Harmon Killebrew 6.00
HK3 Harmon Killebrew 6.00
RK1 Ralph Kiner 4.00
JM1 Juan Marichal 4.00
BM1 Bill Mazeroski 4.00
WM1 Willie McCovey 5.00
PM1 Paul Molitor 5.00
PM2 Paul Molitor 5.00
PM3 Paul Molitor 5.00
MO1 Joe Morgan 4.00
MO2 Joe Morgan 4.00
EM1 Eddie Murray 4.00
EM2 Eddie Murray 4.00
SM1 Stan Musial 6.00
SM2 Stan Musial 6.00
PN1 Phil Niekro 4.00
PN2 Phil Niekro 4.00
JP1 Jim Palmer 4.00
JP2 Jim Palmer 4.00
JP3 Jim Palmer 4.00
TP1 Tony Perez 4.00
GP1 Gaylord Perry 4.00
GP2 Gaylord Perry 4.00
KP1 Kirby Puckett 5.00
KP2 Kirby Puckett 5.00
RR1 Robin Roberts 4.00
BR1 Brooks Robinson 5.00
BR2 Brooks Robinson 5.00
BR3 Brooks Robinson 5.00
FR1 Frank Robinson 5.00
FR2 Frank Robihson 5.00
NR1 Nolan Ryan 10.00
NR2 Nolan Ryan 10.00
NR3 Nolan Ryan 10.00

NR4 Nolan Ryan 10.00
SA1 Ryne Sandberg 6.00
SA2 Ryne Sandberg 6.00
MS1 Mike Schmidt 6.00
MS2 Mike Schmidt 6.00
MS3 Mike Schmidt 6.00
RS1 Red Schoendienst 4.00
TS1 Tom Seaver 5.00
TS2 Tom Seaver 5.00
OS1 Ozzie Smith 6.00
OS2 Ozzie Smith 6.00
SN1 Duke Snider 5.00
DS1 Don Sutton 4.00
DS2 Don Sutton 4.00
BW1 Billy Williams 4.00
BW2 Billy Williams 4.00
DW1 Dave Winfield 4.00
CY1 Carl Yastrzemski 6.00
CY2 Carl Yastrzemski 6.00
RY1 Robin Yount 6.00
RY2 Robin Yount 6.00

Hall of Fame Seasons Autograph

NM/M

Production 25 sets
Gold: No Pricing
Production 5 sets
Silver: No Pricing
Production 15 sets
Rainbow: No Pricing
Production one set
Material Gold: No Pricing
Production 5 sets
Material Silver: No Pricing
Production 15 sets
Patch Gold: No Pricing
Production 5 sets
Patch Silver: No Pricing
Production 10 sets
LA1 Luis Aparicio 20.00
EB1 Ernie Banks 50.00
BE1 Johnny Bench 40.00
BE2 Johnny Bench 40.00
YB1 Yogi Berra 60.00
YB2 Yogi Berra 60.00
WB1 Wade Boggs 35.00
WB2 Wade Boggs 35.00
WB3 Wade Boggs 35.00
GB1 George Brett 60.00
GB2 George Brett 60.00
LB1 Lou Brock 35.00
LB2 Lou Brock 35.00
JB1 Jim Bunning 25.00
RC1 Rod Carew 30.00
RC2 Rod Carew 30.00
GC1 Gary Carter 25.00
SC1 Steve Carlton 20.00
SC2 Steve Carlton 20.00
SC3 Steve Carlton 20.00
OC1 Orlando Cepeda 25.00
BD1 Bobby Doerr 15.00
DE1 Dennis Eckersley 20.00
DE2 Dennis Eckersley 20.00
DE3 Dennis Eckersley 20.00
BF1 Bob Feller 30.00
BF2 Bob Feller 30.00
RF1 Rollie Fingers 20.00
CF1 Carlton Fisk 30.00
CF2 Carlton Fisk 30.00
WF1 Whitey Ford 50.00
WF2 Whitey Ford 50.00
BG1 Bob Gibson 35.00
BG2 Bob Gibson 35.00
MI1 Monte Irvin 25.00
RJ1 Reggie Jackson 40.00
RJ2 Reggie Jackson 40.00
RJ3 Reggie Jackson 40.00
FJ1 Fergie Jenkins 20.00
FJ2 Fergie Jenkins 20.00
AK1 Al Kaline 40.00
AK2 Al Kaline 40.00
AK3 Al Kaline 40.00
GK1 George Kell 20.00
HK1 Harmon Killebrew 40.00
HK2 Harmon Killebrew 40.00
HK3 Harmon Killebrew 40.00
RK1 Ralph Kiner 40.00
JM1 Juan Marichal 25.00
BM1 Bill Mazeroski 40.00
WM1 Willie McCovey 40.00
PM1 Paul Molitor 30.00
PM2 Paul Molitor 30.00
PM3 Paul Molitor 30.00
MO1 Joe Morgan 25.00
MO2 Joe Morgan 25.00
EM1 Eddie Murray 50.00
EM2 Eddie Murray 50.00
SM1 Stan Musial 60.00
SM2 Stan Musial 60.00
PN1 Phil Niekro 20.00
PN2 Phil Niekro 20.00
JP1 Jim Palmer 20.00
JP2 Jim Palmer 20.00
JP3 Jim Palmer 20.00
TP1 Tony Perez 20.00
GP1 Gaylord Perry 20.00
GP2 Gaylord Perry 20.00
KP1 Kirby Puckett 40.00
KP2 Kirby Puckett 40.00
RR1 Robin Roberts 25.00
BR1 Brooks Robinson 30.00
BR2 Brooks Robinson 30.00
BR3 Brooks Robinson 30.00
FR1 Frank Robinson 20.00
FR2 Frank Robinson 20.00
NR1 Nolan Ryan 90.00
NR2 Nolan Ryan 90.00
NR3 Nolan Ryan 90.00
NR4 Nolan Ryan 90.00
SA1 Ryne Sandberg 60.00
SA2 Ryne Sandberg 60.00
MS1 Mike Schmidt 50.00
MS2 Mike Schmidt 50.00
MS3 Mike Schmidt 50.00
RS1 Red Schoendienst 35.00
TS1 Tom Seaver 40.00
TS2 Tom Seaver 40.00
OS1 Ozzie Smith 40.00
OS2 Ozzie Smith 40.00
SN1 Duke Snider 40.00
DS1 Don Sutton 20.00
DS2 Don Sutton 20.00
BW1 Billy Williams 20.00
BW2 Billy Williams 20.00
DW1 Dave Winfield 30.00
CY1 Carl Yastrzemski 50.00
CY2 Carl Yastrzemski 50.00
RY1 Robin Yount 40.00
RY2 Robin Yount 40.00

Hall Worthy

NM/M

Production 50 sets
Gold: No Pricing
Production 5 sets
Silver: No Pricing
Production 15 sets
Rainbow: No Pricing
Production one set
LA1 Luis Aparicio 4.00
EB1 Ernie Banks 6.00
BE1 Johnny Bench 6.00
BE2 Johnny Bench 6.00
YB1 Yogi Berra 5.00
WB1 Wade Boggs 5.00
WB2 Wade Boggs 5.00
WB3 Wade Boggs 5.00
GB1 George Brett 10.00
GB2 George Brett 10.00
GB3 George Brett 10.00
LB1 Lou Brock 4.00
LB2 Lou Brock 4.00
JB1 Jim Bunning 4.00
RC1 Rod Carew 4.00
RC2 Rod Carew 4.00
SC1 Steve Carlton 4.00
SC2 Steve Carlton 4.00
GC1 Gary Carter 4.00
GC2 Gary Carter 4.00
OC1 Orlando Cepeda 4.00
OC2 Orlando Cepeda 4.00
BD1 Bobby Doerr 4.00
DE1 Dennis Eckersley 4.00
DE2 Dennis Eckersley 4.00
DE3 Dennis Eckersley 4.00
DE4 Dennis Eckersley 4.00
BF1 Bob Feller 4.00
BF2 Bob Feller 4.00
RF1 Rollie Fingers 4.00
RF2 Rollie Fingers 4.00
CF1 Carlton Fisk 4.00
CF2 Carlton Fisk 4.00
WF1 Whitey Ford 5.00
BG1 Bob Gibson 5.00
MI1 Monte Irvin 4.00
RJ1 Reggie Jackson 5.00
RJ2 Reggie Jackson 5.00
RJ3 Reggie Jackson 5.00
RJ4 Reggie Jackson 5.00
FJ1 Fergie Jenkins 4.00
FJ2 Fergie Jenkins 4.00
FJ3 Fergie Jenkins 4.00
AK1 Al Kaline 4.00
AK2 Al Kaline 4.00
GK1 George Kell 4.00
HK1 Harmon Killebrew 6.00
HK2 Harmon Killebrew 6.00
RK1 Ralph Kiner 4.00
JM1 Juan Marichal 4.00
BM1 Bill Mazeroski 4.00
WM1 Willie McCovey 5.00
PM1 Paul Molitor 5.00
PM2 Paul Molitor 5.00
MO1 Joe Morgan 4.00
MO2 Joe Morgan 4.00
EM1 Eddie Murray 4.00
EM2 Eddie Murray 4.00
EM3 Eddie Murray 4.00
SM1 Stan Musial 6.00
PN1 Phil Niekro 4.00
PN2 Phil Niekro 4.00
JP1 Jim Palmer 4.00
JP2 Jim Palmer 4.00
TP1 Tony Perez 4.00
TP2 Tony Perez 4.00
GP1 Gaylord Perry 4.00
GP2 Gaylord Perry 4.00
KP1 Kirby Puckett 5.00
RR1 Robin Roberts 4.00
BR1 Brooks Robinson 5.00
BR2 Brooks Robinson 5.00
FR1 Frank Robinson 5.00
FR2 Frank Robinson 5.00
NR1 Nolan Ryan 10.00
NR2 Nolan Ryan 10.00
NR3 Nolan Ryan 10.00
NR4 Nolan Ryan 10.00
SA1 Ryne Sandberg 6.00
SA2 Ryne Sandberg 6.00
SA3 Ryne Sandberg 6.00
MS1 Mike Schmidt 6.00
MS2 Mike Schmidt 6.00
MS3 Mike Schmidt 6.00
RS1 Red Schoendienst 4.00
TS1 Tom Seaver 5.00
TS2 Tom Seaver 5.00
OS1 Ozzie Smith 6.00
OS2 Ozzie Smith 6.00
SN1 Duke Snider 5.00
SN2 Duke Snider 5.00
DS1 Don Sutton 4.00
DS2 Don Sutton 4.00
DS3 Don Sutton 4.00
BW1 Billy Williams 4.00
DW1 Dave Winfield 4.00
CY1 Carl Yastrzemski 6.00
CY2 Carl Yastrzemski 6.00
RY1 Robin Yount 6.00
RY2 Robin Yount 6.00

Hall Worthy Autograph

NM/M

Production 25 sets
Gold: No Pricing
Production 5 sets
Silver: No Pricing
Production 15 sets
Rainbow: No Pricing
Production one set
Material Gold: No Pricing
Production 5 sets
Material Silver: No Pricing
Production 15 sets
Patch Gold: No Pricing
Production 5 sets
Patch Silver: No Pricing
Production 10 sets
LA1 Luis Aparicio 20.00
EB1 Ernie Banks 50.00
BE1 Johnny Bench 40.00
BE2 Johnny Bench 40.00
YB1 Yogi Berra 60.00
WB1 Wade Boggs 35.00
WB2 Wade Boggs 35.00
WB3 Wade Boggs 35.00
GB1 George Brett 60.00
GB2 George Brett 60.00
GB3 George Brett 60.00
LB1 Lou Brock 35.00
LB2 Lou Brock 35.00
JB1 Jim Bunning 25.00
RC1 Rod Carew 30.00
RC2 Rod Carew 30.00
SC1 Steve Carlton 20.00
SC2 Steve Carlton 20.00
GC1 Gary Carter 25.00
GC2 Gary Carter 25.00
OC1 Orlando Cepeda 25.00
OC2 Orlando Cepeda 25.00
BD1 Bobby Doerr 15.00
DE1 Dennis Eckersley 20.00
DE2 Dennis Eckersley 20.00
DE3 Dennis Eckersley 20.00
DE4 Dennis Eckersley 20.00
BF1 Bob Feller 30.00
BF2 Bob Feller 30.00
RF1 Rollie Fingers 20.00
RF2 Rollie Fingers 20.00
CF1 Carlton Fisk 30.00
CF2 Carlton Fisk 30.00
WF1 Whitey Ford 50.00
BG1 Bob Gibson 35.00
MI1 Monte Irvin 25.00
RJ1 Reggie Jackson 40.00
RJ2 Reggie Jackson 40.00
RJ3 Reggie Jackson 40.00
RJ4 Reggie Jackson 40.00
FJ1 Fergie Jenkins 20.00
FJ2 Fergie Jenkins 20.00
FJ3 Fergie Jenkins 20.00
AK1 Al Kaline 40.00
AK2 Al Kaline 40.00
GK1 George Kell 20.00
HK1 Harmon Killebrew 40.00
HK2 Harmon Killebrew 40.00
RK1 Ralph Kiner 40.00
JM1 Juan Marichal 25.00
BM1 Bill Mazeroski 40.00
WM1 Willie McCovey 40.00
PM1 Paul Molitor 30.00
PM2 Paul Molitor 30.00
MO1 Joe Morgan 25.00
MO2 Joe Morgan 25.00
EM1 Eddie Murray 50.00
EM2 Eddie Murray 50.00
EM3 Eddie Murray 50.00
SM1 Stan Musial 60.00
PN1 Phil Niekro 20.00
PN2 Phil Niekro 20.00
JP1 Jim Palmer 20.00
JP2 Jim Palmer 20.00
TP1 Tony Perez 20.00
TP2 Tony Perez 20.00
GP1 Gaylord Perry 20.00
GP2 Gaylord Perry 20.00
KP1 Kirby Puckett 40.00
RR1 Robin Roberts 25.00
BR1 Brooks Robinson 30.00
BR2 Brooks Robinson 30.00
FR1 Frank Robinson 20.00
FR2 Frank Robinson 20.00
NR1 Nolan Ryan 90.00
NR2 Nolan Ryan 90.00
NR3 Nolan Ryan 90.00
NR4 Nolan Ryan 90.00
SA1 Ryne Sandberg 60.00
SA2 Ryne Sandberg 60.00
SA3 Ryne Sandberg 60.00
MS1 Mike Schmidt 50.00
MS2 Mike Schmidt 50.00
MS3 Mike Schmidt 50.00
RS1 Red Schoendienst 35.00
TS1 Tom Seaver 40.00
TS2 Tom Seaver 40.00
OS1 Ozzie Smith 40.00
OS2 Ozzie Smith 40.00
SN1 Duke Snider 40.00
SN2 Duke Snider 40.00
DS1 Don Sutton 20.00
DS2 Don Sutton 20.00
DS3 Don Sutton 20.00
BW1 Billy Williams 20.00
DW1 Dave Winfield 30.00
CY1 Carl Yastrzemski 50.00
CY2 Carl Yastrzemski 50.00
RY1 Robin Yount 40.00
RY2 Robin Yount 40.00

Signs of Cooperstown Duals

NM/M

Production 50 sets
Gold: No Pricing
Production 5 sets
Silver: No Pricing
Production 15 sets
Rainbow: No Pricing
Production one set
AB Ernie Banks, Luis Aparicio 6.00
AS Luis Aparicio, Ozzie Smith 8.00
BC Steve Carlton, Jim Bunning 4.00
BF Frank Robinson, Brooks Robinson 5.00
BG George Brett, Brooks Robinson 10.00
BM Lou Brock, Stan Musial 8.00
BR Jim Bunning, Robin Roberts 4.00
BS Ernie Banks, Ryne Sandberg 10.00
CM Orlando Cepeda, Willie McCovey 4.00
CS Tom Seaver, Gary Carter 4.00

DB Wade Boggs, Bobby Doerr 4.00
EF Dennis Eckersley, Rollie Fingers 4.00
FB Johnny Bench, Carlton Fisk 6.00
FC Bob Feller, Steve Carlton 4.00
FP Bob Feller, Gaylord Perry 4.00
GC Bob Gibson, Steve Carlton 5.00
GF Bob Gibson, Whitey Ford 5.00
IM Monte Irvin, Willie McCovey 5.00
JJ Joe Morgan, Johnny Bench 6.00
JM Reggie Jackson, Willie McCovey 5.00
JW Reggie Jackson, Dave Winfield 5.00
JY Yogi Berra, Johnny Bench 6.00
KK Al Kaline, George Kell 6.00
KP Kirby Puckett, Harmon Killebrew 6.00
LO Lou Brock, Ozzie Smith 8.00
MK Bill Mazeroski, Ralph Kiner 5.00
MP Joe Morgan, Tony Perez 4.00
MY Robin Yount, Paul Molitor 6.00
NS Steve Carlton, Nolan Ryan 10.00
PM Gaylord Perry, Juan Marichal 4.00
PN Gaylord Perry, Phil Niekro 4.00
PR Rod Carew, Paul Molitor 5.00
RC Rod Carew, Nolan Ryan 10.00
RP Jim Palmer, Brooks Robinson 5.00
RS Tom Seaver, Nolan Ryan 10.00
RW Ryne Sandberg, Wade Boggs 10.00
SB George Brett, Mike Schmidt 10.00
SC Mike Schmidt, Steve Carlton 10.00
SK Ralph Kiner, Duke Snider 5.00
SM Ozzie Smith, Stan Musial 8.00
SP Gaylord Perry, Don Sutton 4.00
SR Mike Schmidt, Brooks Robinson 10.00
SS Red Schoendienst, Ozzie Smith 8.00
SW Billy Williams, Ryne Sandberg 10.00
WB Billy Williams, Ernie Banks 6.00
WJ Billy Williams, Fergie Jenkins 4.00
WS Ozzie Smith, Dave Winfield 6.00
WY Yogi Berra, Whitey Ford 6.00
YF Carlton Fisk, Carl Yastrzemski 6.00
YJ Reggie Jackson, Carl Yastrzemski 6.00

Signs of Cooperstown Duals Auto.

NM/M

Production 20 sets
Gold: No Pricing
Production 5 sets
Silver: No Pricing
Production 10 sets
Rainbow: No Pricing
Production one set
AB Ernie Banks, Luis Aparicio 80.00
AS Luis Aparicio, Ozzie Smith 60.00
BC Steve Carlton, Jim Bunning 35.00
BF Frank Robinson, Brooks Robinson 60.00
BG George Brett, Brooks Robinson 90.00
BM Lou Brock, Stan Musial 100.00
BR Jim Bunning, Robin Roberts 60.00
BS Ernie Banks, Ryne Sandberg 120.00
CM Orlando Cepeda, Willie McCovey 50.00
CS Tom Seaver, Gary Carter 80.00
DB Wade Boggs, Bobby Doerr 50.00
EF Dennis Eckersley, Rollie Fingers 35.00
FB Johnny Bench, Carlton Fisk 75.00
FC Bob Feller, Steve Carlton 40.00
FP Bob Feller, Gaylord Perry 40.00
GC Bob Gibson, Steve Carlton 60.00
GF Bob Gibson, Whitey Ford 75.00
IM Monte Irvin, Willie McCovey 60.00
JJ Joe Morgan, Johnny Bench 80.00
JM Reggie Jackson, Willie McCovey 100.00
JW Reggie Jackson, Dave Winfield 80.00
JY Yogi Berra, Johnny Bench 150.00
KK Al Kaline, George Kell 85.00
KP Kirby Puckett, Harmon Killebrew 80.00
LO Lou Brock, Ozzie Smith 65.00
MK Bill Mazeroski, Ralph Kiner 75.00
MP Joe Morgan, Tony Perez 50.00
MY Robin Yount, Paul Molitor 85.00
NS Steve Carlton, Nolan Ryan 150.00
PM Gaylord Perry, Juan Marichal 40.00
PN Gaylord Perry, Phil Niekro 40.00
PR Rod Carew, Paul Molitor 50.00
RC Rod Carew, Nolan Ryan 150.00
RP Jim Palmer, Brooks Robinson 50.00
RS Tom Seaver, Nolan Ryan 180.00
RW Ryne Sandberg, Wade Boggs 100.00
SB George Brett, Mike Schmidt 140.00
SC Mike Schmidt, Steve Carlton 85.00
SK Ralph Kiner, Duke Snider 65.00
SM Ozzie Smith, Stan Musial 120.00
SP Gaylord Perry, Don Sutton 40.00
SR Mike Schmidt, Brooks Robinson 75.00
SS Red Schoendienst, Ozzie Smith 65.00
SW Billy Williams, Ryne Sandberg 90.00
WB Billy Williams, Ernie Banks 90.00
WJ Billy Williams, Fergie Jenkins 50.00
WS Ozzie Smith, Dave Winfield 75.00
WY Yogi Berra, Whitey Ford 100.00
YF Carlton Fisk, Carl Yastrzemski 100.00
YJ Reggie Jackson, Carl Yastrzemski 100.00

Signs of Cooperstown Quads

NM/M

Production 50 sets
Gold: No Pricing
Production 5 sets
Silver: No Pricing
Production 15 sets
Rainbow: No Pricing
Production one set
BMYC George Brett, Rod Carew, Robin Yount, Paul Molitor 10.00
BSAY Ernie Banks, Robin Yount, Luis Aparicio, Ozzie Smith 8.00
FCBB Yogi Berra, Johnny Bench, Carlton Fisk, Gary Carter 6.00
FGRC Bob Feller, Bob Gibson, Steve Carlton, Nolan Ryan 10.00
KCPM Tony Perez, Orlando Cepeda, Harmon Killebrew, Willie McCovey 6.00
KYBM Al Kaline, Lou Brock, Carl Yastrzemski, Stan Musial 8.00
MBKM Ernie Banks, Eddie Murray, Harmon Killebrew, Willie McCovey 8.00
MDMC Bill Mazeroski, Rod Carew, Joe Morgan, Bobby Doerr 5.00
MRKS Eddie Murray, Mike Schmidt, Frank Robinson, Harmon Killebrew 10.00
RBKS George Brett, Mike Schmidt, Brooks Robinson, George Kell 10.00
SPNS Tom Seaver, Phil Niekro, Don Sutton, Gaylord Perry 6.00
SPSF Tom Seaver, Jim Palmer, Whitey Ford, Don Sutton 6.00
SRCS Tom Seaver, Steve Carlton, Don Sutton, Nolan Ryan 10.00
WYKM Billy Williams, Ralph Kiner, Carl Yastrzemski, Stan Musial 8.00
YWMM Eddie Murray, Carl Yastrzemski, Stan Musial, Dave Winfield 8.00

Signs of Cooperstown Triple Auto.

NM/M

Production 20 sets 75.00
Gold: No Pricing
Production 5 sets
Silver: No Pricing
Production 10 sets
Rainbow: No Pricing
Production one set
ASY Robin Yount, Luis Aparicio, Ozzie Smith 140.00
BFJ Jim Palmer, Frank Robinson, Brooks Robinson 80.00
BSB George Brett, Mike Schmidt, Wade Boggs 185.00
BSY Ernie Banks, Robin Yount, Ozzie Smith 150.00
CMI Monte Irvin, Orlando Cepeda, Willie McCovey 75.00
DFY Carlton Fisk, Carl Yastrzemski, Bobby Doerr 125.00
DYB Carl Yastrzemski, Wade Boggs, Bobby Doerr 125.00
FRC Bob Feller, Steve Carlton, Nolan Ryan 200.00
GSM Bob Gibson, Ozzie Smith, Stan Musial 185.00
JFB Yogi Berra, Reggie Jackson, Whitey Ford 185.00
JPR Nolan Ryan, Gaylord Perry, Fergie Jenkins 150.00
KPC Rod Carew, Kirby Puckett, Harmon Killebrew 120.00
KSR Ralph Kiner, Duke Snider, Frank Robinson 120.00
MBP Joe Morgan, Tony Perez, Johnny Bench 160.00
MCM Orlando Cepeda, Willie McCovey, Juan Marichal 100.00
MSC Joe Morgan, Rod Carew, Ryne Sandberg 125.00
MYF Robin Yount, Paul Molitor, Rollie Fingers 125.00
PMC Rod Carew, Kirby Puckett, Paul Molitor 100.00
RAP Jim Palmer, Luis Aparicio, Brooks Robinson 80.00
RBC Steve Carlton, Jim Bunning, Robin Roberts 85.00
RBS George Brett, Mike Schmidt, Brooks Robinson 200.00
SRC Mike Schmidt, Steve Carlton, Robin Roberts 150.00
WJB Reggie Jackson, Wade Boggs, Dave Winfield 120.00
WSP Dave Winfield, Ozzie Smith, Gaylord Perry 120.00
YKM Ralph Kiner, Carl Yastrzemski, Stan Musial 140.00

Signs of Cooperstown Triples

NM/M

Production 50 sets
Gold: No Pricing
Production 5 sets
Silver: No Pricing
Production 15 sets
Rainbow: No Pricing
Production one set
ASY Robin Yount, Luis Aparicio, Ozzie Smith 8.00
BFJ Jim Palmer, Frank Robinson, Brooks Robinson 5.00
BSB George Brett, Mike Schmidt, Wade Boggs 10.00
BSY Ernie Banks, Robin Yount, Ozzie Smith 8.00
CMI Monte Irvin, Orlando Cepeda, Willie McCovey 5.00
DFY Carlton Fisk, Carl Yastrzemski, Bobby Doerr 8.00
DYB Carl Yastrzemski, Wade Boggs, Bobby Doerr 8.00
FPE Bob Feller, Dennis Eckersley, Gaylord Perry 4.00
FRC Bob Feller, Steve Carlton, Nolan Ryan 10.00
FSE Dennis Eckersley, Rollie Fingers, Don Sutton 4.00
GCE Bob Gibson, Dennis Eckersley, Steve Carlton 4.00
GSM Bob Gibson, Stan Musial, Ozzie Smith 8.00
JFB Yogi Berra, Reggie Jackson, Whitey Ford 8.00
JPR Nolan Ryan, Gaylord Perry, Fergie Jenkins 10.00
KKB Al Kaline, George Kell, Jim Bunning 6.00
KPC Rod Carew, Kirby Puckett, Harmon Killebrew 6.00
KSR Ralph Kiner, Duke Snider, Frank Robinson 5.00
KWR Al Kaline, Frank Robinson, Dave Winfield 6.00
MBP Johnny Bench, Tony Perez, Joe Morgan 6.00
MCM Orlando Cepeda, Willie McCovey, Juan Marichal 5.00
MMS Joe Morgan, Red Schoendienst, Bill Mazeroski 4.00
MRJ Eddie Murray, Reggie Jackson, Frank Robinson 5.00
MSC Rod Carew, Joe Morgan, Ryne Sandberg 6.00
MYF Robin Yount, Paul Molitor, Rollie Fingers 6.00
PMC Rod Carew, Kirby Puckett, Paul Molitor 6.00
RAP Jim Palmer, Luis Aparicio, Brooks Robinson 5.00
RBC Steve Carlton, Jim Bunning, Robin Roberts 4.00
RBS George Brett, Mike Schmidt, Brooks Robinson 10.00
RSR Robin Roberts, Don Sutton, Nolan Ryan 10.00
SRC Mike Schmidt, Steve Carlton, Robin Roberts 8.00
WBI Billy Williams, Monte Irvin, Lou Brock 4.00
WBJ Billy Williams, Ernie Banks, Fergie Jenkins 6.00
WJB Reggie Jackson, Wade Boggs, Dave Winfield 6.00

WSP Dave Winfield, Ozzie Smith, Gaylord Perry 6.00
YKM Ralph Kiner, Carl Yastrzemski, Stan Musial 8.00

2005 UD MINI JERSEY COLLECTION

NM/M
Complete Set (100): 15.00
Common Player: .15
Pack (3 + mini jersey): 6.00
Box (18): 90.00
1 Garret Anderson .25
2 Vladimir Guerrero .75
3 Luis Gonzalez .15
4 Shawn Green .25
5 Troy Glaus .25
6 Andruw Jones .50
7 Chipper Jones .75
8 John Smoltz .40
9 Tim Hudson .40
10 Miguel Tejada .50
11 Sammy Sosa 1.00
12 Curt Schilling .75
13 David Ortiz .75
14 Johnny Damon .75
15 Manny Ramirez .75
16 Greg Maddux 1.00
17 Kerry Wood .50
18 Mark Prior .75
19 Nomar Garciaparra 1.00
20 Frank Thomas .50
21 Adam Dunn .50
22 Ken Griffey Jr. 1.50
23 Travis Hafner .25
24 Victor Martinez .15
25 Todd Helton .50
26 Ivan Rodriguez .50
27 Magglio Ordonez .15
28 Carlos Delgado .40
29 Miguel Cabrera .75
30 Jeff Bagwell .50
31 Lance Berkman .25
32 Roger Clemens 2.00
33 Roy Oswalt .25
34 Mike Sweeney .15
35 Eric Gagne .15
36 J.D. Drew .15
37 Ben Sheets .40
38 Johan Santana .50
39 Torii Hunter .15
40 Carlos Beltran .50
41 Mike Piazza 1.00
42 Pedro Martinez .75
43 Alex Rodriguez 1.50
44 Derek Jeter 2.00
45 Hideki Matsui 1.50
46 Mike Mussina .40
47 Randy Johnson .75
48 Bobby Crosby .40
49 Eric Chavez .40
50 Bobby Abreu .40
51 Jim Thome .50
52 Jason Bay .15
53 Oliver Perez .15
54 Jake Peavy .40
55 Khalil Greene .40
56 Jason Schmidt .15
57 Moises Alou .40
58 Adrian Beltre .40
59 Ichiro Suzuki 1.50
60 Albert Pujols 2.00
61 Jim Edmonds .40
62 Mark Mulder .40
63 Scott Rolen .75
64 Aubrey Huff .15
65 Alfonso Soriano .50
66 Hank Blalock .40
67 Mark Teixeira .50
68 Roy Halladay .40
69 Jose Vidro .15
70 Livan Hernandez .15
71 Atlanta Braves .15
72 Chicago Cubs .15
73 Chicago White Sox .15
74 Cincinnati Reds .15
75 Cleveland Indians .15
76 Houston Astros .15
77 L.A. Angels of Anaheim .15
78 Los Angeles Dodgers .15
79 New York Yankees .15
80 Oakland Athletics .15
81 Philadelphia Phillies .15
82 Pittsburgh Pirates .15
83 San Diego Padres .15
84 San Francisco Giants .15
85 Texas Rangers .15
86 Cal Ripken Jr. 2.00
87 Derek Jeter 2.00
88 Hank Blalock .40
89 Hideo Nomo .40
90 Joe DiMaggio 1.00
91 Joe Morgan .50
92 Ken Griffey Jr. 1.50
93 Larry Doby .50
94 Pedro J. Martinez .75
95 Randy Johnson .75
96 Rick Ferrell .15
97 Roger Clemens 2.00
98 Stan Musial 1.00
99 Ted Williams 1.50
100 Torii Hunter .15

Replica Flannel Jerseys

NM/M
Inserted 1:18
1 Ted Williams 20.00
2 Jackie Robinson 15.00
3 Satchel Paige 15.00
4 Ty Cobb 15.00
5 Babe Ruth 30.00
6 Joe DiMaggio 20.00
7 Lou Gehrig 25.00
8 Mickey Mantle 30.00
9 Roberto Clemente 20.00

Mini Jerseys

NM/M
1 Vladimir Guerrero 5.00
2 Chipper Jones 5.00
3 Curt Schilling 5.00
4 Johnny Damon 5.00
5 Manny Ramirez 5.00
6 Kerry Wood 5.00
7 Nomar Garciaparra 5.00
8 Ken Griffey Jr. 5.00
9 Miguel Cabrera 5.00
10 Roger Clemens 10.00
11 Eric Gagne 5.00
12 Johan Santana 5.00
13 Carlos Beltran 5.00
14 Mike Piazza 5.00
15 Pedro Martinez 5.00
16 Alex Rodriguez 5.00
17 Derek Jeter 15.00
18 Hideki Matsui 8.00
19 Randy Johnson 5.00
20 Jim Thome 5.00
21 Ichiro Suzuki 8.00
22 Albert Pujols 10.00

Mini Jersey Autograph

NM/M
Inserted 1:480
1 Ken Griffey Jr. 150.00
2 David Wright 50.00
3 Miguel Cabrera
4 Johan Santana
5 Adrian Beltre 50.00
6 Derek Jeter

2005 UD ORIGINS

NM/M
Complete Set (200):
Common Player: .50
Tin (20): 50.00
1 Jim Edmonds .75
2 Jason Schmidt .75
3 J.D. Drew .75
4 Luis Gonzalez .50
5 Nomar Garciaparra 2.00
6 Jake Peavy .75
7 Rafael Furcal .50
8 Craig Biggio .75
9 Ken Griffey Jr. 3.00
10 Mike Piazza 2.00
11 Jose Vidro .50
12 Ivan Rodriguez 1.00

13 Carl Crawford .50
14 Roger Clemens 4.00
15 Kerry Wood 1.00
16 Vernon Wells .50
17 Carlos Guillen .50
18 Tim Hudson .75
19 Carl Pavano .50
20 Carlos Beltran 1.00
21 Pedro Martinez 1.50
22 Hideki Matsui 3.00
23 Frank Thomas 1.00
24 Curt Schilling 1.50
25 Manny Ramirez 1.50
26 Alex Rodriguez 4.00
27 Aubrey Huff .50
28 David Ortiz 1.50
29 Mark Prior 1.50
30 Albert Pujols 4.00
31 Miguel Cabrera 1.50
32 Brad Penny .50
33 Carlos Delgado .75
34 Aramis Ramirez 1.00
35 Josh Beckett .75
36 Rafael Palmeiro 1.00
37 Bret Boone .50
38 Lance Berkman .75
39 Carlos Zambrano .75
40 Adam Dunn 1.00
41 Livan Hernandez .50
42 Mike Mussina .75
43 Ben Sheets .75
44 Derek Jeter 4.00
45 Kazuo Matsui .50
46 Bobby Abreu .75
47 Jeff Bagwell 1.00
48 Travis Hafner .50
49 Torii Hunter .75
50 Kevin Brown .50
51 Alfonso Soriano 1.50
52 Jim Thome 1.00
53 John Smoltz .75
54 Mike Sweeney .50
55 Andy Pettitte .75
56 Chipper Jones 1.50
57 Randy Johnson 1.50
58 Steve Finley .50
59 Larry Walker .75
60 Troy Glaus .75
61 Greg Maddux 2.50
62 Shawn Green .50
63 Roy Halladay .75
64 Jeff Kent .50
65 Scott Podsednik .50
66 Miguel Tejada 1.00
67 Lyle Overbay .50
68 Bernie Williams .75
69 Todd Helton 1.00
70 Melvin Mora .50
71 Magglio Ordonez .50
72 Carlos Lee .75
73 Roy Oswalt .75
74 Victor Martinez .50
75 Scott Rolen 1.50
76 Eric Chavez .75
77 Paul Konerko .75
78 Jose Reyes .50
79 Barry Larkin .75
80 Johnny Damon 1.00
81 Eric Gagne .75
82 Andruw Jones 1.00
83 Gary Sheffield 1.00
84 Richie Sexson .75
85 Sammy Sosa 2.50
86 Mark Teixeira 1.00
87 Vladimir Guerrero 1.50
88 Michael Young .50
89 Johan Santana 1.00
90 Adrian Beltre .75
91 Tom Glavine .75
92 Hank Blalock .75
93 Preston Wilson .50
94 Jason Kendall .50
95 Mike Lowell .50
96 Craig Wilson .50
97 Ichiro Suzuki 3.00
98 Mark Mulder .75
99 Garret Anderson .75
100 Brian Giles .50
101 Robin Yount 3.00
102 Ernie Banks 3.00
103 Mike Schmidt 5.00
104 Enos Slaughter 1.00
105 Red Schoendienst 1.00
106 Hoyt Wilhelm 1.00
107 Lou Brock 2.00
108 Rollie Fingers 1.00
109 Gaylord Perry 1.00
110 Bobby Doerr 1.00
111 Larry Doby 1.00
112 Al Lopez 1.00
113 Joe Morgan 1.50
114 Luis Aparicio 1.00
115 Willie McCovey 2.00
116 Bob Lemon 1.00
117 Early Wynn 1.00
118 Bob Feller 2.00
119 Cal Ripken Jr. 8.00
120 George Kell 1.00
121 Juan Marichal 1.50
122 Monte Irvin 1.50
123 Harmon Killebrew 3.00
124 Lou Boudreau 1.00
125 Mickey Mantle 8.00
126 Richie Ashburn 1.00
127 Pee Wee Reese 1.50
128 Whitey Ford 2.00
129 Tom Seaver 2.00
130 Phil Rizzuto 2.00
131 Yogi Berra 3.00
132 Warren Spahn 2.00
133 Billy Williams 1.50
134 Jim Bunning 1.00
135 Ralph Kiner 1.00
136 Ted Williams 6.00
137 Rick Ferrell 1.00
138 Robin Roberts 1.00
139 Brooks Robinson 3.00
140 Hal Newhouser 1.00
141 Jim "Catfish" Hunter 1.00
142 Phil Niekro 1.00
143 Fergie Jenkins 1.00
144 Al Kaline 3.00
145 Stan Musial 4.00
146 Joe DiMaggio 6.00
147 Willie Stargell 2.00
148 Nolan Ryan 6.00
149 Babe Ruth 6.00
150 Bob Gibson 2.00
151 David DeJesus .50
152 Chris Burke .50
153 Chad Cordero .50
154 Kevin Youkilis .50
155 Bucky Jacobsen .50
156 B.J. Upton .50
157 Aaron Rowand .50
158 Jose Capellan .50
159 David Wright 2.00
160 Jason Bay .50
161 Edwin Jackson .50
162 Scott Kazmir .50
163 J.D. Closser .50
164 Chase Utley 1.00
165 Nick Swisher .50
166 Casey Kotchman .50
167 Bobby Crosby .50
168 Zack Greinke .50
169 Gavin Floyd .50
170 Jeff Francis .50
171 Dallas McPherson .50
172 Gabe Gross .50
173 Brandon Claussen .50
174 Wily Mo Pena .50
175 Robb Quinlan .50
176 Oliver Perez .50
177 Guillermo Quiroz .50
178 Ryan Howard 1.00
179 Gerald Laird .50
180 Jayson Werth .50
181 Bobby Madritsch .50
182 Laynce Nix .50
183 Eddy Rodriguez .50
184 Rickie Weeks 1.00
185 Scott Proctor .50
186 Adam LaRoche .50
187 Yhency Brazoban .50
188 Adrian Gonzalez .50
189 Jason Lane .50
190 Ryan Wagner .50

191 Roman Colon .50
192 Alexis Rios .50
193 Joe Mauer 1.00
194 Garrett Atkins .50
195 Daniel Cabrera .50
196 Khalil Greene 2.00
197 Joe Blanton .50
198 Jason Dubois .50
199 Angel Guzman .50
200 Jesse Crain .50

Black

No Pricing
Production One Set

Blue

Stars (1-200): 2X-4X
Production 50 Sets

Gold

No Pricing
Production 20 Sets

Red

Stars (1-200): 2X-3X
Production 99 Sets

Origins Materials Jersey

NM/M

Inserted 2:tin
Old Judge: 1X
JB Jeff Bagwell 8.00
CB Carlos Beltran 8.00
AB Adrian Beltre 5.00
LB Lance Berkman 5.00
HB Hank Blalock 5.00
MC Miguel Cabrera 8.00
EC Eric Chavez 5.00
JD J.D. Drew 5.00
GL Troy Glaus 5.00
KG Ken Griffey Jr. 10.00
VG Vladimir Guerrero 8.00
TG Tony Gwynn SP 10.00
HE Todd Helton 5.00
TH Tim Hudson 5.00
HU Torii Hunter 5.00
DJ Derek Jeter 15.00
RJ Randy Johnson 8.00
AJ Andruw Jones 5.00
CJ Chipper Jones 8.00
GM Greg Maddux 10.00
HM Hideki Matsui 15.00
KM Hideki Matsui 5.00
DO David Ortiz 8.00
PI Mike Piazza 8.00
MP Mark Prior 8.00
AP Albert Pujols 15.00
MR Manny Ramirez 8.00
CR Cal Ripken Jr. SP 25.00
IR Ivan Rodriguez 8.00
SR Scott Rolen 8.00
NR Nolan Ryan SP 30.00
CS Curt Schilling 8.00
BS Ben Sheets 5.00
GS Gary Sheffield 5.00
AS Alfonso Soriano 8.00
SS Sammy Sosa 8.00
IS Ichiro Suzuki 20.00
MT Mark Teixeira 5.00
TE Miguel Tejada 8.00
FT Frank Thomas 8.00
JT Jim Thome 8.00
KW Kerry Wood 8.00

Origins Nostalgic Signs

NM/M

One sign per tin
CB Carlos Beltran 8.00
AB Adrian Beltre 5.00
HB Hank Blalock 5.00
MC Miguel Cabrera 8.00
EC Eric Chavez 5.00
RC Roger Clemens 15.00
TC Ty Cobb 20.00
JD Joe DiMaggio 20.00
LG Lou Gehrig 15.00
KG Ken Griffey Jr. 12.00
VG Vladimir Guerrero 8.00
TH Todd Helton 8.00
DJ Derek Jeter 15.00
RJ Randy Johnson 8.00
WJ Walter Johnson 15.00
CJ Chipper Jones 8.00
PM Pedro Martinez 8.00
HM Hideki Matsui 20.00
DO David Ortiz 8.00
SP Satchel Paige 12.00
MP Mike Piazza 10.00
MPR Mark Prior 8.00
AP Albert Pujols 20.00
MR Manny Ramirez 8.00
CR Cal Ripken Jr. 25.00
JR Jackie Robinson 12.00
AR Alex Rodriguez 12.00
IR Ivan Rodriguez 8.00
SR Scott Rolen 8.00
BR Babe Ruth 20.00
NR Nolan Ryan 20.00
JS Johan Santana 8.00
CS Curt Schilling 10.00
AS Alfonso Soriano 8.00
SS Sammy Sosa 10.00
IS Ichiro Suzuki 12.00
MT Miguel Tejada 8.00
FT Frank Thomas 8.00
JT Jim Thome 8.00
HW Honus Wagner 10.00
TW Ted Williams 25.00

Origins Old Judge

NM/M

Common Player: .50
Blue: 2X-3X
Red: 1X-2X
Gold: No Pricing
1 Jake Peavy 1.00
2 Derek Jeter 5.00
3 Adrian Beltre 1.00
4 Hank Blalock 1.00
5 Preston Wilson .50
6 Randy Johnson 2.00
7 Pedro Martinez 2.00
8 Michael Young 1.00
9 Steve Finley .50
10 Shawn Green .75
11 Carlos Beltran 1.50
12 Bernie Williams 1.00
13 Brian Giles .50
14 Kevin Brown .50
15 Barry Larkin 1.00
16 Troy Glaus 1.00
17 Bret Boone .50
18 Jason Kendall .50
19 Johnny Damon 1.50
20 Josh Beckett 1.00
21 Carl Pavano .50
22 Chipper Jones 2.00
23 Ivan Rodriguez 1.50
24 Kerry Wood 1.50
25 Ken Griffey Jr. 3.00
26 Greg Maddux 3.00
27 Kazuo Matsui .50
28 Albert Pujols 5.00
29 Victor Martinez .50
30 Johan Santana 1.50
31 Bobby Abreu .75
32 Paul Konerko .75
33 Gary Sheffield 1.00
34 Jose Vidro .50
35 Alex Rodriguez 4.00
36 Alfonso Soriano 1.50
37 Mark Teixeira 1.50
38 Nomar Garciaparra 2.50
39 Sammy Sosa 3.00
40 Garret Anderson 1.00
41 Eric Chavez 1.00
42 Magglio Ordonez .50
43 Larry Walker 1.00
44 Brad Penny .50
45 Jeff Bagwell 1.50
46 Craig Biggio .75
47 Torii Hunter .75
48 Mike Lowell .50
49 Ben Sheets 1.00
50 Miguel Tejada 1.50
51 Jim Edmonds 1.00
52 Mark Mulder 1.00
53 Curt Schilling 1.50
54 Roger Clemens 5.00
55 Jason Schmidt .50
56 Rafael Furcal .50
57 Scott Rolen 2.00
58 Carlos Zambrano .75
59 Mike Sweeney .50
60 Vladimir Guerrero 2.00
61 Miguel Cabrera 2.00
62 Lance Berkman .50
63 Lyle Overbay .50
64 Livan Hernandez .50
65 Aramis Ramirez 1.00
66 Ichiro Suzuki 4.00
67 Roy Oswalt .50
68 Carl Crawford .50
69 Craig Wilson .50
70 Carlos Lee .75
71 J.D. Drew .50
72 Rafael Palmeiro 1.50
73 Jeff Kent .50
74 Adam Dunn 1.50
75 Andy Pettitte 1.00
76 Luis Gonzalez .50
77 Frank Thomas 1.50
78 John Smoltz 1.00
79 Hideki Matsui 3.00
80 Tom Glavine .50
81 Jose Reyes .50
82 Jim Thome 1.50
83 Mark Prior 2.00
84 Roy Halladay .75
85 Carlos Delgado 1.00
86 Melvin Mora .50
87 David Ortiz 2.00
88 Travis Hafner .50
89 Carlos Guillen .50
90 Tim Hudson .50
91 Vernon Wells .50
92 Andruw Jones 1.50
93 Mike Mussina 1.00
94 Mike Piazza 3.00
95 Richie Sexson 1.00
96 Aubrey Huff .50
97 Scott Podsednik .50
98 Eric Gagne .50
99 Manny Ramirez 2.00
100 Todd Helton 1.50
101 Joe Morgan 1.00
102 Billy Williams 1.00
103 Pee Wee Reese 1.00
104 Lou Boudreau 1.00
105 Richie Ashburn 1.00
106 Jim Bunning 1.00
107 Hal Newhouser 1.00
108 Rick Ferrell 1.00
109 Ted Williams 5.00
110 Ralph Kiner 1.00
111 Warren Spahn 2.50
112 George Kell .50
113 Willie Stargell 2.00
114 Jim "Catfish" Hunter .50
115 Tom Seaver 2.00
116 Cal Ripken Jr. 8.00
117 Al Lopez .50
118 Ernie Banks 3.00
119 Lou Brock 2.00
120 Robin Yount 3.00
121 Nolan Ryan 6.00
122 Larry Doby 1.00
123 Al Kaline 2.00
124 Willie McCovey 2.00
125 Stan Musial 3.00
126 Phil Niekro 1.00
127 Babe Ruth 6.00
128 Rollie Fingers 1.00
129 Juan Marichal 1.00
130 Early Wynn 1.00
131 Luis Aparicio 1.00
132 Brooks Robinson 3.00
133 Mike Schmidt 5.00
134 Gaylord Perry 1.00
135 Bob Lemon 1.00
136 Monte Irvin 1.50
137 Mickey Mantle 8.00
138 Phil Rizzuto 1.50
139 Robin Roberts 1.50
140 Bobby Doerr 1.00
141 Bob Gibson 2.00
142 Enos Slaughter 1.00
143 Yogi Berra 3.00
144 Whitey Ford 2.00
145 Red Schoendienst 1.00
146 Joe DiMaggio 5.00
147 Harmon Killebrew 2.00
148 Hoyt Wilhelm 1.00
149 Fergie Jenkins 1.00
150 Bob Feller 1.50
151 Scott Proctor .50
152 Adam LaRoche .50
153 Ryan Howard 1.00
154 Laynce Nix .50
155 Garrett Atkins .50
156 Chris Burke .50
157 Oliver Perez .50
158 Wily Mo Pena .50
159 B.J. Upton .50
160 Gavin Floyd .50
161 Jesse Crain .50
162 Khalil Greene 3.00
163 Eddy Rodriguez .50
164 Edwin Jackson .50
165 Scott Kazmir .50
166 Ryan Wagner .50
167 Nick Swisher .50
168 Joe Blanton .50
169 Alexis Rios .50
170 Chad Cordero .50
171 Jason Dubois .50
172 Chase Utley 1.00
173 David DeJesus .50
174 Zack Greinke .50
175 Bobby Crosby 1.00
176 Angel Guzman .50
177 Adrian Gonzalez .50
178 Guillermo Quiroz .50
179 Gerald Laird .50
180 Rickie Weeks 1.00
181 Jayson Werth .50
182 Buck Jacobsen .50
183 J.D. Closser .50
184 Jason Bay .50
185 Roman Colon .50
186 Casey Kotchman .50
187 Yhency Brazoban .50
188 Bobby Madritsch .50
189 Gabe Gross .50
190 Brandon Claussen .50
191 Aaron Rowand .50
192 Jeff Francis .50
193 David Wright 2.00
194 Jose Capellan .50
195 Jason Lane .50
196 Daniel Cabrera .50
197 Joe Mauer 1.00
198 Kevin Youkilis .50
199 Dallas McPherson .50
200 Robb Quinlan .50

Origins Old Judge Autographs

NM/M

Common Auto: 12.00
Bronze: No Pricing
JB Jason Bay 15.00
CB Carlos Beltran/15
AB Adrian Beltre 12.00
MC Miguel Cabrera 25.00
CC Carl Crawford Exch 12.00
BC Bobby Crosby Exch 15.00
BD Bobby Doerr 15.00
BF Bob Feller 25.00
MG Marcus Giles Exch 15.00
DG Dwight Gooden 15.00
GR Khalil Greene 20.00
KG Ken Griffey Jr. 75.00
RG Ron Guidry 15.00
TG Tony Gwynn 50.00
TH Travis Hafner 15.00
RH Rich Harden 15.00
KH Keith Hernandez 15.00
FH Frank Howard 20.00
HO Ryan Howard 20.00
AH Aubrey Huff 8.00
DJ Derek Jeter 150.00
SK Scott Kazmir 20.00
DK Dave Kingman 15.00
CK Casey Kotchman 15.00
SL Sparky Lyle 12.00
VM Victor Martinez 15.00
MA Don Mattingly 65.00
DM Dallas McPherson 12.00
PM Paul Molitor 40.00
OS Roy Oswalt 15.00
AO Akinori Otsuka 15.00
JP Jim Palmer 15.00
PE Jake Peavy 25.00
OP Oliver Perez 15.00
CR Cal Ripken Jr./25
BR Brooks Robinson 30.00
RO Al Rosen 15.00
JS Johan Santana Exch 35.00
RS Ron Santo 25.00
MS Mike Schmidt 75.00
BS Ben Sheets 12.00
ST Shingo Takatsu 15.00
MT Mark Teixeira 25.00
BU B.J. Upton 15.00
CU Chase Utley 25.00
RW Rickie Weeks 15.00
DW David Wright 50.00

RY Robin Yount 50.00
CZ Carlos Zambrano 20.00

Origins Old Judge Materials Jersey

NM/M
Common Jersey: 5.00
JB Jeff Bagwell 8.00
CB Carlos Beltran 8.00
AB Adrian Beltre 5.00
LB Lance Berkman 5.00
HB Hank Blalock 5.00
MC Miguel Cabrera 8.00
EC Eric Chavez 5.00
JD J.D. Drew 5.00
GL Troy Glaus 5.00
KG Ken Griffey Jr. 10.00
VG Vladimir Guerrero 8.00
TG Tony Gwynn SP 10.00
HE Todd Helton 5.00
TH Tim Hudson 5.00
HU Torii Hunter 5.00
DJ Derek Jeter 15.00
RJ Randy Johnson 8.00
AJ Andruw Jones 5.00
CJ Chipper Jones 8.00
GM Greg Maddux 10.00
HM Hideki Matsui 15.00
KM Kazuo Matsui 5.00
DO David Ortiz 8.00
PI Mike Piazza 8.00
MP Mark Prior 8.00
AP Albert Pujols 15.00
MR Manny Ramirez 8.00
CR Cal Ripken Jr. SP 25.00
SR Scott Rolen 8.00
NR Nolan Ryan SP 30.00
CS Curt Schilling 8.00
BS Ben Sheets 5.00
GS Gary Sheffield 5.00
AS Alfonso Soriano 8.00
SS Sammy Sosa 8.00
IS Ichiro Suzuki 20.00
MT Mark Teixeira 5.00
TE Miguel Tejada 8.00
FT Frank Thomas 8.00
JT Jim Thome 8.00
KW Kerry Wood 8.00

Origins Signatures

NM/M
Common Auto: 12.00
Bronze: No Pricing
Production 5 Sets
JB1 Jason Bay 15.00
CB1 Carlos Beltran/5
AB1 Adrian Beltre 12.00
MC1 Miguel Cabrera 25.00
CC1 Carl Crawford Exch 12.00
BC1 Bobby Crosby Exch 15.00
BD1 Bobby Doerr 15.00
BF1 Bob Feller 25.00
MG1 Marcus Giles 15.00
DG1 Dwight Gooden 15.00
GR1 Khalil Greene 20.00
KG1 Ken Griffey Jr. 75.00
RG1 Ron Guidry 15.00
TG1 Tony Gwynn 50.00
TH1 Travis Hafner 15.00
RH1 Rich Harden 15.00
KH1 Keith Hernandez 15.00
FH1 Frank Howard 20.00
HO1 Ryan Howard 20.00
AH1 Aubrey Huff 8.00
DJ1 Derek Jeter 150.00
SK1 Scott Kazmir 20.00
DK1 Dave Kingman 15.00
CK1 Casey Kotchman 15.00
SL1 Sparky Lyle 12.00
VM1 Victor Martinez 15.00
MA1 Don Mattingly 65.00
DM1 Dallas McPherson 12.00
PM1 Paul Molitor 40.00
OS1 Roy Oswalt 15.00
AO1 Akinori Otsuka 15.00
JP1 Jim Palmer 15.00
PE1 Jake Peavy 25.00
OP1 Oliver Perez 15.00
CR1 Cal Ripken Jr./25
BR1 Brooks Robinson 30.00
RO1 Al Rosen 15.00
JS1 Johan Santana Exch 35.00
RS1 Ron Santo 25.00
MS1 Mike Schmidt 75.00
BS1 Ben Sheets 12.00
ST1 Shingo Takatsu 15.00
MT1 Mark Teixeira 25.00
BU1 B.J. Upton 15.00
CU1 Chase Utley 25.00
RW1 Rickie Weeks 15.00
DW1 David Wright 50.00
RY1 Robin Yount 50.00
CZ1 Carlos Zambrano 20.00

Origins Tins

NM/M
Common Tin: 5.00
TC Ty Cobb 5.00
DJ Derek Jeter 10.00
WJ Walter Johnson 5.00
HW Honus Wagner 5.00

2005 UD PAST TIME PENNANTS

NM/M
Complete Set (90): 20.00
Common Player: .20
Pack (5): 4.00
Box (20): 70.00
1 Al Kaline .50
2 Al Rosen .20
3 Bert Blyleven .20
4 Bill Mazeroski .20
5 Billy Williams .20
6 Bob Feller .50
7 Bob Gibson .75
8 Bob Lemon .20
9 Bobby Doerr .40
10 Brooks Robinson .75
11 Bruce Sutter .30
12 Bucky Dent .20
13 Cal Ripken Jr. 2.00
14 Carl Yastrzemski .75
15 Carlton Fisk .40
16 Jim "Catfish" Hunter .20
17 Dale Murphy .40
18 Dave Parker .20
19 Don Larsen .50
20 Don Mattingly 1.00
21 Don Newcombe .20
22 Duke Snider .50
23 Early Wynn .20
24 Eddie Matthews .75
25 Eddie Murray .50
26 Enos Slaughter .20
27 Ernie Banks .75
28 Fergie Jenkins .20
29 Frank Howard .20
30 Frank Robinson .50
31 Fred Lynn .20
32 Gary Carter .20
33 Gaylord Perry .20
34 George Brett 1.50
35 George Kell .20
36 Rich "Goose" Gossage .20
37 Graig Nettles .20
38 Harmon Killebrew .75
39 Jack Morris .20
40 Jim Bunning .20
41 Felipe Alou .20
42 Jim Palmer .40
43 Jim Rice .20
44 Joe DiMaggio 1.50
45 Joe Morgan .20
46 Johnny Bench .75
47 Johnny Podres .20
48 Juan Marichal .20
49 Keith Hernandez .20
50 Kirby Puckett .75
51 Larry Doby .20
52 Lou Brock .40
53 Luis Aparicio .20
54 Luis Tiant .20
55 Maury 4illis .20
56 Mickey Mantle 2.00
57 Mike Schmidt 1.50
58 Monte Irvin .20
59 Nolan Ryan 1.50
60 Orlando Cepeda .20
61 Ozzie Smith .75
62 Paul Molitor .50
63 Pee Wee Reese .20
64 Phil Niekro .20
65 Phil Rizzuto .50
66 Ralph Kiner .20
67 Richie Ashburn .20
68 Rico Petrocelli .20
69 Robin Roberts .20
70 Robin Yount .75
71 Rocky Colavito .20
72 Rod Carew .40
73 Rollie Fingers .20
74 Ron Guidry .20
75 Ron Santo .20
76 Tony Gwynn .75
77 Sparky Lyle .20
78 Stan Musial 1.00
79 Steve Carlton .40
80 Rick Ferrell .20
81 Tom Seaver .75
82 Tommy John .20
83 Tony Perez .20
84 Wade Boggs .50
85 Warren Spahn .75
86 Whitey Ford .40
87 Will Clark .50
88 Willie McCovey .50
89 Willie Stargell .40
90 Yogi Berra .75

Gold

Gold: 4X-8X
Production 50 Sets

Silver

Gold: 3X-5X
Production 100 Sets

Mitchell & Ness Jersey Redem

No Pricing
Total Production
Per Player 36-37

Mitchell & Ness Pennants

NM/M
Common Pennant: 15.00
Inserted 1:hobby box
1903 1903 Boston Americans/100 20.00
1905 1095 New York Giants/100 20.00
1906 1906 Chicago White Sox/100 20.00
1907 1907 Detroit Tigers/100 20.00
1908 1908 Chicago Cubs/105 25.00
1909 1909 Pittsburgh Pirates/125 20.00
1910 1910 Philadelphia A's/125 20.00
1912 1912 Boston Red Sox/125 20.00
1914 1914 Boston Braves/125 20.00
1915 1915 Phildelphia Phillies/125 20.00
1916 1916 Brooklyn Robins/200 20.00
1917 1917 New York Giants/200 20.00
1918 1918 Boston Red Sox/200 20.00
1919 1919 Chicago White Sox/200 20.00
1920 1920 Cleveland Indians/200 15.00
1921 1921 New York Yankees/200 25.00
1922 1922 New York Giants/200 20.00
1924 1924 Washington Senators/200 20.00
1925 1925 Pittsburgh Pirates/200 15.00
1926 1926 Saint Louis Cardinals/200 20.00
1927 1927 New York Yankees/500 25.00
1928 1928 New York Yankees/500 25.00
1929 1929 Chicago Cubs/337 20.00
1930 1930 Philadelphia A's/337 15.00
1931 1931 Saint Louis Cardinals/337 20.00
1932 1932 Chicago Cubs/337 20.00
1934 1934 Detroit Tigers/337 15.00
1935 1935 Chicago Cubs/337 20.00
1936 1936 New York Yankees/337 25.00
1937 1937 New York Giants/337 20.00
1938 1938 New York Yankees/337 25.00
1939 1939 Cincinnati Reds/337 15.00
1940 1940 Cincinnati Reds/337 15.00
1941 1941 Brooklyn Dodgers/337 25.00
1942 1942 Saint Louis Cardinals/337 20.00
1943 1943 New York Yankees/500 25.00
1944 1944 Saint Louis Browns/337 15.00
1945 1945 Chicago Cubs/337 20.00
1946 1946 Boston Red Sox/337 20.00
1947 1947 Brooklyn Dodgers/337 25.00
1948 1948 Boston Braves/337 15.00
1949 1949 New York Yankees/337 25.00
1950 1950 Philadelphia Phillies/337 15.00
1951 1951 New York Giants/337 15.00
1952 1952 Brooklyn Dodgers/500 20.00
1953 1953 New York Yankees/337 25.00
1954 1954 Cleveland Indians/337 15.00
1955 1955 Brooklyn Dodgers/337 25.00
1956 1956 Brooklyn Dodgers/500 25.00
1957 1957 Milwaukee Braves/337 20.00
1958 1958 New York Yankees/500 25.00
1959 1959 Los Angeles Dodgers/337 20.00
1960 1960 Pittsburgh Pirates/337 15.00
1961 1961 Cincinnati Reds/337 15.00
1962 1962 San Francisco Giants/337 20.00
1963 1963 Los Angeles Dodgers/337 20.00
1964 1964 Saint Louis Cardinals/337 20.00
1965 1965 Minnesota Twins/337 15.00
1966 1966 Baltimore Orioles/337 20.00
1967 1967 Boston Red Sox/337 20.00
1968 1968 Detroit Tigers/337 15.00
1969 1969 New York Mets/337 20.00
1970 1970 Baltimore Orioles/337 20.00
1971 1971 Pittsburgh Pirates/337 15.00
1972 1972 Oakland A's/337 20.00
1973 1973 Oakland A's/337 20.00
1974 1974 Los Angeles Dodgers/337 20.00
1977 1977 New York Yankees/337 25.00
1978 1978 Los Angeles Dodgers/337 20.00
1979 1979 Pittsburgh Pirates/337 15.00
1980 1980 Philadelphia Phillies/337 20.00
1981 1981 Los Angeles Dodgers/337 20.00
1982 1982 Milwaukee Brewers/337 20.00
1983 1983 Baltimore Orioles/337 20.00
1984 1984 San Diego Padres/337 15.00
1985 1985 Kansas City Royals/337 15.00

1986 1986 Boston Red Sox/337 25.00
1988 1988 Los Angeles Dodgers/337 20.00
1975B 1975 Boston Red Sox/337 25.00
1975C 1975 Cincinnati Reds/337 20.00

Mitchell & Ness Penn Autograph

NM/M

Production 86-87
JB Johnny Bench/87 80.00
SC Steve Carlton/87 60.00
RF Rollie Fingers/87 40.00
CF Carlton Fisk/87 60.00
SG Steve Garvey/40 40.00
KG Kirk Gibson/87
AK Al Kaline/87 75.00
PM Paul Molitor/87 75.00
GN Graig Nettles/87 50.00
DN Don Newcombe/87 40.00
JP Jim Palmer/87
BR Brooks Robinson/87 75.00
TS Tom Seaver/87 80.00
CY Carl Yastrzemski/86 80.00

Signatures Bronze

NM/M

SP's Production 3-25
FA Felipe Alou 15.00
RB Rick Burleson 10.00
DC David Cone 15.00
LD Lenny Dykstra 12.00
SF Sid Fernandez 10.00
BF Bill Freehan 10.00
DG Dwight Gooden 15.00
KG Ken Griffey Sr. 10.00
GU Don Gullett 8.00
PG Pedro Guerrero 10.00
HO Ken Holtzman 10.00
BH Burt Hooton 10.00
WH Willie Horton EXCH 12.00
FH Frank Howard 15.00
HR Kent Hrbek 15.00
RH Randy Hundley 10.00
TJ Tommy John 15.00
WJ Wally Joyner 15.00
DK Dave Kingman 10.00
KN Ray Knight 10.00
SL Sparky Lyle 10.00
BM Bill Madlock 10.00
BO Bobby Murcer 15.00
RP Rico Petrocelli 12.00
BP Boog Powell 25.00
AR Al Rosen 15.00
SS Steve Sax 10.00
SC Mike Scioscia EXCH 15.00
WI Mookie Wilson 15.00

Signatures Dual

Production 15-24

Signatures Gold

NM/M

Many not priced due to scarcity
FA Felipe Alou 20.00
RB Rick Burleson 15.00
LD Lenny Dykstra 20.00
SF Sid Fernandez 15.00
BF Bill Freehan 15.00
KG Ken Griffey Sr. 15.00
PG Pedro Guerrero 15.00
GU Don Gullett 10.00
HO Ken Holtzman 15.00
BH Burt Hooton 15.00
WH Willie Horton EXCH 15.00
HR Kent Hrbek 20.00
RH Randy Hundley 10.00
DK Dave Kingman 15.00
KN Ray Knight 15.00
SL Sparky Lyle 15.00
BM Bill Madlock 15.00
BO Bobby Murcer 25.00
RP Rico Petrocelli 15.00

Signatures Silver

NM/M

FA Felipe Alou 10.00
LA Luis Aparicio 20.00
BB Bert Blyleven 15.00
BR Lou Brock 30.00
JB Jim Bunning EXCH 15.00
RB Rick Burleson 10.00
ST Steve Carlton 35.00
GC Gary Carter 20.00
OC Orlando Cepeda 20.00
CC Chris Chambliss 15.00
WC Will Clark 40.00
RC Rocky Colavito 65.00
DC David Cone 15.00
DE Bucky Dent 12.00
BD Bobby Doerr 15.00
LD Lenny Dykstra 10.00
CE Carl Erskine EXCH 12.00
EV Dwight Evans 30.00
FE Bob Feller 30.00
SF Sid Fernandez 10.00
RF Rollie Fingers 20.00
BF Bill Freehan 10.00
DG Dwight Gooden 15.00
GG Rich "Goose" Gossage 15.00
KG Ken Griffey Sr. 10.00
GU Don Gullett 8.00
PG Pedro Guerrero 10.00
KH Keith Hernandez 15.00
HO Ken Holtzman 10.00
BH Burt Hooton 10.00
WH Willie Horton EXCH 10.00
FH Frank Howard 15.00
HR Kent Hrbek 15.00
RH Randy Hundley 10.00
MI Monte Irvin 25.00
FJ Fergie Jenkins 20.00
TJ Tommy Jones 15.00
WJ Wally Joyner 15.00
AK Al Kaline 50.00
GK George Kell 15.00
HK Harmon Killebrew 50.00
RK Ralph Kiner 40.00
DK Dave Kingman 10.00
KN Ray Knight 10.00
DL Don Larsen EXCH 30.00
SL Sparky Lyle 10.00
FL Fred Lynn 15.00
BM Bill Madlock 10.00
JU Juan Marichal EXCH 20.00
MA Bill Mazeroski 30.00
PM Paul Molitor 40.00
MO Joe Morgan 20.00
JM Jack Morris 15.00
BO Bobby Murcer 20.00
MU Dale Murphy 25.00
GN Graig Nettles 20.00
DN Don Newcombe 15.00
JP Jim Palmer 30.00
DP Dave Parker 20.00
TP Tony Perez EXCH 40.00
GP Gaylord Perry 15.00
RP Rico Petrocelli 15.00
PO Johnny Podres 25.00
BP Boog Powell 20.00
JR Jim Rice 20.00
RO Brooks Robinson 60.00
AR Al Rosen 15.00
RS Ron Santo 25.00
SS Steve Sax 10.00
SC Mike Scioscia EXCH 20.00
BS Bill "Moose" Skowron 15.00
SU Bruce Sutter 15.00
LT Luis Tiant 15.00
BW Billy Williams EXCH 15.00
MW Maury Wills 20.00

2005 UD ULTIMATE SIGNATURE EDITION

NM/M

Complete Set (110):
Common (1-100): 2.00
Production 825
Common (101-110):
Production 225
Tin (3): 90.00
1 Al Kaline 4.00
2 Babe Ruth 10.00
3 Billy Williams 2.00
4 Bob Feller 2.00
5 Bob Gibson 3.00
6 Brooks Robinson 3.00
7 Carlton Fisk 2.00
8 Cy Young 3.00
9 Dizzy Dean 3.00
10 Don Drysdale 2.00
11 Eddie Mathews 4.00
12 Enos Slaughter 2.00
13 Ernie Banks 5.00
14 Fergie Jenkins 2.00
15 Eddie Murray 3.00
16 Harmon Killebrew 4.00
17 Honus Wagner 3.00
18 Jackie Robinson 5.00
19 Jimmie Foxx 4.00
20 Joe DiMaggio 6.00
21 Joe Morgan 2.00
22 Juan Marichal 2.00
23 Larry Doby 2.00
24 Jim Palmer 2.00
25 Johnny Bench 4.00
26 Lou Brock 2.00
27 Lou Gehrig 6.00
28 Mel Ott 3.00
29 Mickey Cochrane 2.00
30 Mickey Mantle 12.00
31 Mike Schmidt 5.00
32 Nolan Ryan 8.00
33 Pee Wee Reese 2.00
34 Phil Rizzuto 3.00
35 Ralph Kiner 2.00
36 Robin Yount 3.00
37 Ozzie Smith 4.00
38 Roy Campanella 3.00
39 Satchel Paige 4.00
40 Stan Musial 5.00
41 Ted Williams 8.00
42 Thurman Munson 4.00
43 Tom Seaver 3.00
44 Ty Cobb 4.00
45 Walter Johnson 3.00
46 Warren Spahn 4.00
47 Whitey Ford 3.00
48 Willie McCovey 3.00
49 Willie Stargell 3.00
50 Yogi Berra 4.00
51 Adrian Beltre 8.00
52 Albert Pujols 6.00
53 Alex Rodriguez 3.00
54 Alfonso Soriano 2.00
55 Andruw Jones 2.00
56 B.J. Upton 2.00
57 Ben Sheets 2.00
58 Bret Boone 2.00
59 Brian Giles 2.00
60 Carlos Beltran 3.00
61 Carlos Delgado 2.00
62 Chipper Jones 4.00
63 Curt Schilling 4.00
64 David Ortiz 4.00
65 Derek Jeter 8.00
66 Eric Chavez 2.00
67 Frank Thomas 3.00
68 Gary Sheffield 2.00
69 Greg Maddux 5.00
70 Hank Blalock 2.00
71 Hideki Matsui 6.00
72 Ichiro Suzuki 6.00
73 Ivan Rodriguez 3.00
74 Jason Schmidt 2.00
75 Jeff Bagwell 2.00
76 Jim Thome 3.00
77 Johnny Damon 4.00
78 Jose Vidro 2.00
79 Ken Griffey Jr. 5.00
80 Kerry Wood 3.00
81 Manny Ramirez 4.00
82 Mark Prior 3.00
83 Mark Teixeira 2.00
84 Miguel Cabrera 3.00
85 Miguel Tejada 3.00
86 Mike Mussina 2.00
87 Mike Piazza 4.00
88 Mike Sweeney 2.00
89 Oliver Perez 2.00
90 Pedro Martinez 4.00
91 Rafael Palmeiro 3.00
92 Randy Johnson 4.00
93 Roger Clemens 8.00
94 Sammy Sosa 5.00
95 Scott Rolen 3.00
96 Tim Hudson 2.00
97 Todd Helton 2.00
98 Torii Hunter 2.00
99 Victor Martinez 2.00
100 Vladimir Guerrero 4.00
101 Adrian Gonzalez 8.00
102 *Ambiorix Burgos* 25.00
103 *Ambiorix Concepcion* 20.00
104 Dan Meyer 15.00
105 Ervin Santana 25.00
106 Gavin Floyd 20.00
107 Joe Blanton 20.00
108 Eric Crozier 10.00
109 Mark Teahen 25.00
110 Ryan Howard 15.00

Platinum

Cards (101-110):
Production one set

Immortal Inscriptions

NM/M

Production 10-99
Platinum: No Pricing
Production One Set
WB Wade Boggs/75 100.00
JB Jim Bunning/99 60.00
SC Steve Carlton/99 40.00
GC Gary Carter/15
WC Will Clark/99 60.00
RC Roger Clemens/15
EG Eric Gagne/99 80.00
KG Ken Griffey Jr./99 200.00
TG Tony Gwynn/50 140.00
RJ Randy Johnson/10 10.00
GM Greg Maddux/10
DM Don Mattingly/75 150.00
WM Willie McCovey/15
SM Stan Musial/25
CR Cal Ripken Jr./10
BR Brooks Robinson/99 50.00
NR Nolan Ryan/10
TS Tom Seaver/25 90.00
OS Ozzie Smith/75 80.00
FT Frank Thomas/50 100.00

Signature Cuts

Production One Set

Signature Cy Young

NM/M

Production 1-250
CM David Cone, Greg Maddux/35 140.00
EG Eric Gagne, Dennis Eckersley/200 50.00
ES Dennis Eckersley, Bruce Sutter/250 30.00
GF Ron Guidry, Whitey Ford/250 65.00
GM Bob Gibson, Denny McLain/175 40.00
LC Sparky Lyle, Steve Carlton/250 30.00
MS Tom Seaver, Denny McLain 50.00
NF Don Newcombe, Whitey Ford 80.00
PC Gaylord Perry, Steve Carlton/250 40.00
PS Jim Palmer, Tom Seaver/100 75.00

Signature Decades

NM/M

Some not priced due to scarcity
Platinum: No Pricing
Production One Set
LA Luis Aparicio 20.00
LA1 Luis Aparicio 20.00
EB Ernie Banks/10
CB Carlos Beltran/99 35.00
BE Johnny Bench/15
YB Yogi Berra/25 80.00
WB Wade Boggs/25 65.00
WB1 Wade Boggs/25 65.00
GB George Brett/10
LB Lou Brock/50 35.00
JB Jim Bunning 20.00
MC Miguel Cabrera 30.00
JC Jose Canseco/99 40.00
CA Rod Carew/15
SC Steve Carlton 20.00
SC1 Steve Carlton 20.00
GC Gary Carter/50 25.00
OC Orlando Cepeda 15.00
WC Will Clark/99 40.00
CL Roger Clemens/10
RC Rocky Colavito 50.00
RC1 Rocky Colavito 50.00
AD Andre Dawson 15.00
BD Bobby Doerr 15.00
DE Dennis Eckersley 25.00
BF Bob Feller 25.00
RF Rollie Fingers 15.00
CF Carlton Fisk/15
WF Whitey Ford/15
NG Nomar Garciaparra/10
BG Bob Gibson/15
KG Ken Griffey Jr. 65.00
RG Ron Guidry 25.00
TG Tony Gwynn/15
KH Keith Hernandez 10.00
KH1 Keith Hernandez 10.00
MI Monte Irvin 20.00
BJ Bo Jackson/50 60.00
FJ Fergie Jenkins/50 20.00
DJ Derek Jeter/99 160.00
RJ Randy Johnson/10

CJ	Chipper Jones/10	
AK	Al Kaline/99	30.00
GK	George Kell	15.00
HK	Harmon Killebrew/99	40.00
RK	Ralph Kiner/99	30.00
DL	Don Larsen/99	25.00
FL	Fred Lynn	15.00
GM	Greg Maddux/10	
JM	Juan Marichal/99	25.00
DM	Don Mattingly/25	85.00
BM	Bill Mazeroski/99	40.00
WM	Willie McCovey/10	
PM	Paul Molitor/99	25.00
MO	Joe Morgan/50	25.00
MU	Dale Murphy	25.00
SM	Stan Musial/10	
DN	Don Newcombe/99	20.00
PN	Phil Niekro	20.00
DO	David Ortiz	40.00
RO	Roy Oswalt	15.00
JP	Jim Palmer	20.00
TP	Tony Perez	25.00
GP	Gaylord Perry	15.00
GP1	Gaylord Perry	15.00
MP	Mike Piazza/10	
JR	Jim Rice	20.00
CR	Cal Ripken Jr./10	
BR	Brooks Robinson	30.00
FR	Frank Robinson/25	40.00
AR	Al Rosen	15.00
NR	Nolan Ryan/10	
NR1	Nolan Ryan/10	
SA	Ryne Sandberg/15	
JS	Johan Santana	40.00
RS	Ron Santo	25.00
MS	Mike Schmidt/15	
TS	Tom Seaver/10	
BS	Ben Sheets	15.00
DS	Duke Snider/10	
SU	Don Sutton	15.00
MT	Mark Teixeira	25.00
LT	Luis Tiant	15.00
LT1	Luis Tiant	15.00
BU	B.J. Upton	15.00
RW	Rickie Weeks	20.00
BW	Billy Williams	20.00
MW	Maury Wills	15.00
CY	Carl Yastrzemski/10	
RY	Robin Yount/25	70.00

Signature Hits

NM/M

Production 1-125

BM	Stan Musial, Lou Brock/35	125.00
MY	Robin Yount, Paul Molitor/125	75.00
YB	Wade Boggs, Carl Yastrzemski/35	100.00

Signature HRs

NM/M

Production 1-250

BS	Mike Schmidt, Ernie Banks/25	180.00
GM	Ken Griffey Jr., Willie McCovey/250	100.00
KM	Willie McCovey, Harmon Killebrew/35	75.00
RG	Frank Robinson, Ken Griffey Jr./250	85.00

Signature MVPs

NM/M

Production 1-250

BM	Don Mattingly, Yogi Berra/175	100.00
BS	Ernie Banks, Ryne Sandberg/25	200.00
CM	Stan Musial, Orlando Cepeda/100	75.00
DS	Ryne Sandberg, Andre Dawson/175	80.00
EF	Dennis Eckersley, Rollie Fingers/250	30.00
FC	George Foster, Rod Carew/125	40.00
GM	Joe Morgan, Ken Griffey Jr./250	75.00
HY	Robin Yount, Keith Hernandez/200	50.00
KC	Harmon Killebrew, Rod Carew/100	80.00
KM	Harmon Killebrew, Willie McCovey/35	80.00
LM	Fred Lynn, Joe Morgan/200	30.00
LW	Maury Wills, Barry Larkin/250	35.00
MB	Joe Morgan, Johnny Bench/100	60.00
MG	Denny McLain, Bob Gibson/175	40.00
MY	Robin Yount, Dale Murphy/175	60.00
PR	Dave Parker, Jim Rice/250	40.00
SF	Mike Schmidt, Rollie Fingers/175	60.00
SS	Mike Schmidt, Ryne Sandberg/75	140.00
TB	Frank Thomas, Jeff Bagwell/50	90.00
YC	Orlando Cepeda, Carl Yastrzemski/100	65.00
YS	Carl Yastrzemski, Jim Rice/100	75.00

Signature No-Hitters

NM/M

Production 1-250

BG	Bob Gibson, Jim Bunning/125	60.00
CL	Don Larsen, David Cone/250	40.00
FR	Nolan Ryan, Bob Feller/25	150.00
GP	Bob Gibson, Jim Palmer/125	50.00

Signature Numbers

NM/M

Production 1-49

Platinum: No Pricing

Production One Set

WB	Wade Boggs/26	40.00
MC	Miguel Cabrera/24	50.00
JC	Jose Canseco/33	50.00
CA	Rod Carew/29	35.00
SC	Steve Carlton/32	25.00
OC	Orlando Cepeda/30	25.00
WC	Will Clark/22	60.00
CL	Roger Clemens/22	200.00
RF	Rollie Fingers/34	20.00
CF	Carlton Fisk/27	40.00
EG	Eric Gagne/38	40.00
BG	Bob Gibson/45	25.00
GL	Tom Glavine/47	40.00
RG	Ron Guidry/49	65.00
TG	Tony Gwynn/19	80.00
MI	Monte Irvin/20	30.00
FJ	Fergie Jenkins/31	20.00
RJ	Randy Johnson/41	75.00
MA	Juan Marichal/27	40.00
DM	Don Mattingly/23	125.00
WM	Willie McCovey/44	40.00
DO	David Ortiz/34	40.00
RO	Roy Oswalt/44	20.00
JP	Jim Palmer/22	30.00
PI	Mike Piazza/31	100.00
MP	Mark Prior/22	80.00
KP	Kirby Puckett/34	85.00
FR	Frank Robinson/20	50.00
SR	Scott Rolen/27	40.00
NR	Nolan Ryan/34	120.00
TS	Tom Seaver/41	75.00
JS	John Smoltz/29	60.00
FT	Frank Thomas/35	80.00
BW	Billy Williams/26	30.00
DW	Dave Winfield/31	35.00
KW	Kerry Wood/34	40.00
RY	Robin Yount/19	75.00

Signature ROYs

NM/M

Production 1-250

CM	Willie McCovey, Orlando Cepeda/75	65.00
CS	Rod Carew, Tom Seaver/25	100.00
DM	Andre Dawson, Eddie Murray/25	70.00
FB	Carlton Fisk, Johnny Bench/35	80.00
FL	Fred Lynn/125, Carlton Fisk/125	60.00
GR	Nomar Garciaparra, Scott Rolen/200	85.00
GS	Dwight Gooden, Tom Seaver/100	60.00
JG	Derek Jeter, Nomar Garciaparra/75	185.00
RA	Frank Robinson, Luis Aparicio/125	50.00
RJ	Derek Jeter, Cal Ripken Jr./75	300.00
SG	Dwight Gooden, Darryl Strawberry/250	40.00
WD	Andre Dawson, Billy Williams/250	30.00

Signature Supremacy

NM/M

Production 15-99

LA	Luis Aparicio/50	40.00
JB	Jeff Bagwell	75.00
EB	Ernie Banks/20	
CB	Carlos Beltran/50	
BE	Johnny Bench/25	60.00
YB	Yogi Berra/25	60.00
HB	Hank Blalock/50	25.00
WB	Wade Boggs/25	60.00
GB	George Brett/15	
LB	Lou Brock/25	40.00
BU	Jim Bunning/99	25.00
MC	Miguel Cabrera/99	40.00
JC	Jose Canseco/25	60.00
CA	Rod Carew/25	35.00
SC	Steve Carlton/99	25.00
GC	Gary Carter/25	
OC	Orlando Cepeda/99	20.00
EC	Eric Chavez/99	15.00
WC	Will Clark/50	40.00
CL	Roger Clemens/15	
RC	Rocky Colavito/25	
AD	Andre Dawson/99	20.00
BD	Bobby Doerr/99	20.00
BF	Bob Feller/99	25.00
RF	Rollie Fingers/99	15.00
CF	Carlton Fisk/25	40.00
WF	Whitey Ford/25	
EG	Eric Gagne/50	25.00
NG	Nomar Garciaparra/15	
BG	Bob Gibson/25	
KG	Ken Griffey Jr./99	80.00
VG	Vladimir Guerrero/20	
RG	Ron Guidry/99	20.00
TG	Tony Gwynn/25	
TH	Tim Hudson/50	25.00
MI	Monte Irvin/99	20.00
FJ	Fergie Jenkins/25	
DJ	Derek Jeter/50	200.00
RJ	Randy Johnson/15	
CJ	Chipper Jones/25	
AK	Al Kaline/50	60.00
GK	George Kell/99	25.00
HK	Harmon Killebrew/50	40.00
RK	Ralph Kiner/25	40.00
GM	Greg Maddux/15	
JU	Juan Marichal/25	50.00
MA	Don Mattingly/25	80.00
BM	Bill Mazeroski/50	40.00
WM	Willie McCovey/20	
PM	Paul Molitor/50	40.00
JM	Joe Morgan/25	30.00
MM	Mark Mulder/99	15.00
DM	Dale Murphy/99	25.00
EM	Eddie Murray/15	
MU	Stan Musial/25	125.00
DN	Don Newcombe/99	20.00
DO	David Ortiz/99	40.00
RO	Roy Oswalt/99	15.00
JP	Jim Palmer/99	25.00
TP	Tony Perez/99	25.00
PI	Mike Piazza/15	
MP	Mark Prior/25	75.00
KP	Kirby Puckett/20	
JR	Jim Rice/99	15.00
CR	Cal Ripken Jr./15	
RR	Robin Roberts/99	30.00
BR	Brooks Robinson/99	30.00
FR	Frank Robinson/25	40.00
IR	Ivan Rodriguez/25	
SR	Scott Rolen/25	50.00
AR	Al Rosen/99	25.00
NR	Nolan Ryan/15	
SA	Ryne Sandberg/25	85.00
JS	Johan Santana/99	40.00
RS	Ron Santo	25.00
MS	Mike Schmidt/25	100.00
TS	Tom Seaver/25	50.00
BS	Ben Sheets/99	20.00
OS	Ozzie Smith/25	50.00
SM	John Smoltz/25	50.00
DS	Duke Snider/20	
AS	Alfonso Soriano/25	40.00
MT	Mark Teixeira/99	25.00
TE	Miguel Tejada/25	
FT	Frank Thomas/25	80.00
BW	Billy Williams/99	25.00
DW	Dave Winfield/25	40.00
KW	Kerry Wood/25	
CY	Carl Yastrzemski/25	100.00
RY	Robin Yount/25	75.00

Signs of October

NM/M

Production 1-250

BW	Mookie Wilson, Bill Buckner/250	40.00
CS	John Smoltz, Joe Carter/250	50.00
EG	Kirk Gibson, Dennis Eckersley/200	40.00
FM	Carlton Fisk, Joe Morgan/100	50.00
GB	Bob Gibson, Lou Brock/100	70.00
GG	Ron Guidry, Steve Garvey/250	30.00
GL	Mickey Lolich, Bob Gibson/100	40.00
JG	Derek Jeter, Tony Gwynn/250	185.00
LB	Yogi Berra, Don Larsen/250	85.00
MP	Jack Morris, Kirby Puckett/100	85.00
PS	Ozzie Smith, Kirby Puckett/35	125.00
RR	Frank Robinson, Brooks Robinson/250	65.00
SB	George Brett, Ozzie Smith	150.00
SY	Ozzie Smith, Robin Yount/100	85.00
TG	Kirk Gibson, Alan Trammell/250	40.00

Z

1995 ZENITH

NM/M

Complete Set (150):		15.00
Common Player:		.10
Pack (6):		1.50
Wax Box (24):		17.50
1	Albert Belle	.20
2	Alex Fernandez	.10
3	Andy Benes	.10
4	Barry Larkin	.10
5	Barry Bonds	2.50
6	Ben McDonald	.10
7	Bernard Gilkey	.10
8	Billy Ashley	.10
9	Bobby Bonilla	.10
10	Bret Saberhagen	.10
11	Brian Jordan	.10
12	Cal Ripken Jr.	2.50
13	Carlos Baerga	.10
14	Carlos Delgado	.35
15	Cecil Fielder	.10
16	Chili Davis	.10
17	Chuck Knoblauch	.10
18	Craig Biggio	.10
19	Danny Tartabull	.10
20	Dante Bichette	.10
21	Darren Daulton	.10
22	Dave Justice	.10
23	Dave Winfield	.75
24	David Cone	.10
25	Dean Palmer	.10
26	Deion Sanders	.20
27	Dennis Eckersley	.75
28	Derek Bell	.10
29	Don Mattingly	1.50
30	Edgar Martinez	.10
31	Eric Karros	.10
32	Erik Hanson	.10

33	Frank Thomas	.75
34	Fred McGriff	.10
35	Gary Sheffield	.45
36	Gary Gaetti	.10
37	Greg Maddux	1.25
38	Gregg Jefferies	.10
39	Ivan Rodriguez	.75
40	Kenny Rogers	.10
41	J.T. Snow	.10
42	Hal Morris	.10
43	Eddie Murray (3,000 hit)	.50
44	Javier Lopez	.10
45	Jay Bell	.10
46	Jeff Conine	.10
47	Jeff Bagwell	.75
48	*Hideo Nomo*	2.00
49	Jeff Kent	.10
50	Jeff King	.10
51	Jim Thome	.75
52	Jimmy Key	.10
53	Joe Carter	.10
54	John Valentin	.10
55	John Olerud	.10
56	Jose Canseco	.50
57	Jose Rijo	.10
58	Jose Offerman	.10
59	Juan Gonzalez	.75
60	Ken Caminiti	.10
61	Ken Griffey Jr.	1.75
62	Kenny Lofton	.10
63	Kevin Appier	.10
64	Kevin Seitzer	.10
65	Kirby Puckett	1.25
66	Kirk Gibson	.10
67	Larry Walker	.10
68	Lenny Dykstra	.10
69	Manny Ramirez	.75
70	Mark Grace	.20
71	Mark McGwire	2.00
72	Marquis Grissom	.10
73	Jim Edmonds	.10
74	Matt Williams	.10
75	Mike Mussina	.60
76	Mike Piazza	1.75
77	Mo Vaughn	.10
78	Moises Alou	.10
79	Ozzie Smith	1.25
80	Paul O'Neill	.10
81	Paul Molitor	.75
82	Rafael Palmeiro	.75
83	Randy Johnson	.75
84	Raul Mondesi	.10
85	Ray Lankford	.10
86	Reggie Sanders	.10
87	Rickey Henderson	.75
88	Rico Brogna	.10
89	Roberto Alomar	.25
90	Robin Ventura	.10
91	Roger Clemens	1.50
92	Ron Gant	.10
93	Rondell White	.10
94	Royce Clayton	.10
95	Ruben Sierra	.10
96	Rusty Greer	.10
97	Ryan Klesko	.10
98	Sammy Sosa	1.50
99	Shawon Dunston	.10
100	Steve Ontiveros	.10
101	Tim Naehring	.10
102	Tim Salmon	.25
103	Tino Martinez	.10
104	Tony Gwynn	1.25
105	Travis Fryman	.10
106	Vinny Castilla	.10
107	Wade Boggs	1.25
108	Wally Joyner	.10
109	Wil Cordero	.10
110	Will Clark	.15
111	Chipper Jones	1.25
112	C.J. Nitkowski	.10
113	Curtis Goodwin	.10
114	Tim Unroe	.10
115	Vaughn Eshelman	.10
116	Marty Cordova	.10
117	Dustin Hermanson	.10
118	Rich Becker	.10
119	Ray Durham	.10
120	Shane Andrews	.10
121	Scott Ruffcorn	.10
122	*Mark Grudzielanek*	.25
123	James Baldwin	.10
124	*Carlos Perez*	.10
125	Julian Tavarez	.10
126	Joe Vitiello	.10
127	Jason Bates	.10
128	Edgardo Alfonzo	.10
129	Juan Acevedo	.10
130	Bill Pulsipher	.10
131	*Bob Higginson*	.50
132	Russ Davis	.10
133	Charles Johnson	.10
134	Derek Jeter	2.50
135	Phil Nevin	.10
136	LaTroy Hawkins	.10
137	Brian Hunter	.10
138	Roberto Petagine	.10
139	Jim Pittsley	.10
140	Garret Anderon	.10
141	Ugueth Urbina	.10
142	Antonio Osuna	.10
143	Michael Tucker	.10
144	Benji Gil	.10
145	Jon Nunnally	.10
146	Alex Rodriguez	2.00
147	Todd Hollandworth	.10
148	Alex Gonzalez	.10
149	*Hideo Nomo*	2.00
150	Shawn Green	.30
---	Numeric checklist	.10
---	Chase program checklist	.10

All-Star Salute

		NM/M
Complete Set (19):		16.00
Common Player:		.50
1	Cal Ripken Jr.	3.00
2	Frank Thomas	1.00
3	Mike Piazza	2.00
4	Kirby Puckett	1.50
5	Manny Ramirez	1.00
6	Tony Gwynn	1.50
7	Hideo Nomo	1.00
8	Matt Williams	.50
9	Randy Johnson	1.00
10	Raul Mondesi	.50
11	Albert Belle	.60
12	Ivan Rodriguez	1.00
13	Barry Bonds	3.00
14	Carlos Baerga	.50
15	Ken Griffey Jr.	2.00
16	Jeff Conine	.50
17	Frank Thomas	1.00
18	Cal Ripken Jr., Barry Bonds	2.00

Rookie Roll Call

		NM/M
Complete Set (18):		20.00
Common Player:		.60
1	Alex Rodriguez	4.00
2	Derek Jeter	4.50
3	Chipper Jones	3.00
4	Shawn Green	1.25
5	Todd Hollandsworth	.60
6	Bill Pulsipher	.60
7	Hideo Nomo	2.00
8	Ray Durham	.60
9	Curtis Goodwin	.60
10	Brian Hunter	.60
11	Julian Tavarez	.60
12	Marty Cordova	.60
13	Michael Tucker	.60
14	Edgardo Alfonzo	.60
15	LaTroy Hawkins	.60
16	Carlos Perez	.60
17	Charles Johnson	.60
18	Benji Gil	.60

Z-Team

		NM/M
Complete Set (18):		85.00
Common Player:		2.00
1	Cal Ripken Jr.	15.00
2	Ken Griffey Jr.	10.00
3	Frank Thomas	6.00
4	Matt Williams	2.00
5	Mike Piazza	10.00
6	Barry Bonds	15.00
7	Raul Mondesi	2.00
8	Greg Maddux	7.50
9	Jeff Bagwell	6.00
10	Manny Ramirez	6.00
11	Larry Walker	2.00
12	Tony Gwynn	7.50
13	Will Clark	2.50
14	Albert Belle	2.00
15	Kenny Lofton	2.00
16	Rafael Palmeiro	4.50
17	Don Mattingly	9.00
18	Carlos Baerga	2.00

1996 ZENITH

		NM/M
Complete Set (150):		15.00
Common Player:		.10
Common Artist's Proofs:		2.00
Star Artist's Proofs:		12X
Pack (6):		1.50
Wax Box (24):		25.00
1	Ken Griffey Jr.	2.00
2	Ozzie Smith	1.50
3	Greg Maddux	1.50
4	Rondell White	.10
5	Mark McGwire	2.50
6	Jim Thome	.75
7	Ivan Rodriguez	1.00
8	Marc Newfield	.10
9	Travis Fryman	.10
10	Fred McGriff	.10
11	Shawn Green	.25
12	Mike Piazza	2.00
13	Dante Bichette	.10
14	Tino Martinez	.10
15	Sterling Hitchcock	.10
16	Ryne Sandberg	1.50
17	Rico Brogna	.10
18	Roberto Alomar	.35
19	Barry Larkin	.10
20	Bernie Williams	.20
21	Gary Sheffield	.50
22	Frank Thomas	1.00
23	Gregg Jefferies	.10
24	Jeff Bagwell	1.00
25	Marty Cordova	.10
26	Jim Edmonds	.10
27	Jay Bell	.10
28	Ben McDonald	.10
29	Barry Bonds	3.00
30	Mo Vaughn	.10
31	Johnny Damon	.25
32	Dean Palmer	.10
33	Ismael Valdes	.10
34	Manny Ramirez	1.00
35	Edgar Martinez	.10
36	Cecil Fielder	.10
37	Ryan Klesko	.10
38	Ray Lankford	.10
39	Tim Salmon	.25
40	Joe Carter	.10
41	Jason Isringhausen	.10
42	Rickey Henderson	1.00
43	Lenny Dykstra	.10
44	Andre Dawson	.25
45	Paul O'Neill	.10
46	Ray Durham	.10
47	Raul Mondesi	.10
48	Jay Buhner	.10
49	Eddie Murray	1.00
50	Henry Rodriguez	.10
51	Hal Morris	.10
52	Mike Mussina	.75
53	Wally Joyner	.10
54	Will Clark	.10
55	Chipper Jones	1.50
56	Brian Jordan	.10
57	Larry Walker	.10
58	Wade Boggs	1.50
59	Melvin Nieves	.10
60	Charles Johnson	.10
61	Juan Gonzalez	1.00
62	Carlos Delgado	.35
63	Reggie Sanders	.10
64	Brian Hunter	.10
65	Edgardo Alfonzo	.10
66	Kenny Lofton	.10
67	Paul Molitor	1.00
68	Mike Bordick	.10
69	Garret Anderson	.10
70	Orlando Merced	.10
71	Craig Biggio	.10
72	Chuck Knoblauch	.10
73	Mark Grace	.20
74	Jack McDowell	.10
75	Randy Johnson	1.00
76	Cal Ripken Jr.	3.00
77	Matt Williams	.10
78	Benji Gil	.10
79	Moises Alou	.10
80	Robin Ventura	.10
81	Greg Vaughn	.10
82	Carlos Baerga	.10
83	Roger Clemens	1.75
84	Hideo Nomo	1.00
85	Pedro Martinez	1.00
86	John Valentin	.10
87	Andres Galarraga	.10
88	Andy Pettitte	.35
89	Derek Bell	.10
90	Kirby Puckett	1.50
91	Tony Gwynn	1.50
92	Brady Anderson	.10
93	Derek Jeter	3.00
94	Michael Tucker	.10
95	Albert Belle	.20
96	David Cone	.10
97	J.T. Snow	.10
98	Tom Glavine	.35
99	Alex Rodriguez	2.50
100	Sammy Sosa	2.00
101	Karim Garcia	.25
102	Alan Benes	.10
103	Chad Mottola	.10
104	*Robin Jennings*	.10
105	Bob Abreu	.10
106	Tony Clark	.10
107	George Arias	.10
108	Jermaine Dye	.10
109	Jeff Suppan	.10
110	*Ralph Milliard*	.10
111	Ruben Rivera	.10
112	Billy Wagner	.10
113	Jason Kendall	.10
114	*Mike Grace*	.10
115	Edgar Renteria	.10
116	Jason Schmidt	.10
117	Paul Wilson	.10
118	Rey Ordonez	.10
119	*Rocky Coppinger*	.10
120	*Wilton Guerrero*	.20
121	Brooks Kieschnick	.10
122	Raul Casanova	.10
123	Alex Ochoa	.10
124	Chan Ho Park	.10
125	John Wasdin	.10
126	Eric Owens	.10
127	Justin Thompson	.10
128	Chris Snopek	.10
129	Terrell Wade	.10
130	*Darin Erstad*	3.00
131	Albert Belle	.10
132	Cal Ripken Jr.	1.50
133	Frank Thomas	.60
134	Greg Maddux	.75
135	Ken Griffey Jr.	1.00
136	Mo Vaughn	.10
137	Chipper Jones	.75
138	Mike Piazza	1.00
139	Ryan Klesko	.10
140	Hideo Nomo	.60
141	Roberto Alomar	.20
142	Manny Ramirez	.60
143	Gary Sheffield	.10
144	Barry Bonds	1.50
145	Matt Williams	.10
146	Jim Edmonds	.10
147	Derek Jeter	1.50
148	Sammy Sosa	1.00
149	Kirby Puckett	.75
150	Tony Gwynn	.75

Artist's Proofs

	NM/M
Common Player:	2.00
Stars:	12X

(See 1996 Zenith for checklist and base card values.)

Diamond Club

		NM/M
Complete Set (20):		17.50
Common Player:		.45
Diamond Versions:		12X
1	Albert Belle	.60
2	Mo Vaughn	.45
3	Ken Griffey Jr.	1.50
4	Mike Piazza	1.50
5	Cal Ripken Jr.	2.50
6	Jermaine Dye	.45

7 Jeff Bagwell 1.00
8 Frank Thomas 1.00
9 Alex Rodriguez 2.00
10 Ryan Klesko .45
11 Roberto Alomar .75
12 Sammy Sosa 1.50
13 Matt Williams .45
14 Gary Sheffield .75
15 Ruben Rivera .45
16 Darin Erstad .75
17 Randy Johnson 1.00
18 Greg Maddux 1.25
19 Karim Garcia .60
20 Chipper Jones 1.25

Mozaics

NM/M

Complete Set (25): 30.00
Common Card: .45
1 Greg Maddux, Chipper Jones, Ryan Klesko 3.00
2 Juan Gonzalez, Will Clark, Ivan Rodriguez 1.00
3 Frank Thomas, Robin Ventura, Ray Durham 1.00
4 Matt Williams, Barry Bonds, Osvaldo Fernandez 5.00
5 Ken Griffey Jr., Randy Johnson, Alex Rodriguez 4.00
6 Sammy Sosa, Ryne Sandberg, Mark Grace 4.00
7 Jim Edmonds, Tim Salmon, Garret Anderson .45
8 Cal Ripken Jr., Roberto Alomar, Mike Mussina 5.00
9 Mo Vaughn, Roger Clemens, John Valentin 3.00
10 Barry Larkin, Reggie Sanders, Hal Morris .45
11 Ray Lankford, Brian Jordan, Ozzie Smith 1.50
12 Dante Bichette, Larry Walker, Andres Galarraga .45
13 Mike Piazza, Hideo Nomo, Raul Mondesi 4.00
14 Ben McDonald, Greg Vaughn, Kevin Seitzer .45
15 Joe Carter, Carlos Delgado, Alex Gonzalez .60
16 Gary Sheffield, Charles Johnson, Jeff Conine .45
17 Rondell White, Moises Alou, Henry Rodriguez .45
18 Albert Belle, Manny Ramirez, Carlos Baerga 1.00
19 Kirby Puckett, Paul Molitor, Chuck Knoblauch 1.50
20 Tony Gwynn, Rickey Henderson, Wally Joyner 2.00
21 Mark McGwire, Mike Bordick, Scott Brosius 4.00
22 Paul O'Neill, Bernie Williams, Wade Boggs 1.50
23 Jay Bell, Orlando Merced, Jason Kendall .45
24 Rico Brogna, Paul Wilson, Jason Isringhausen .45
25 Jeff Bagwell, Craig Biggio, Derek Bell 1.00

Z-Team

NM/M

Complete Set (18): 100.00
Common Player: 3.00
1 Ken Griffey Jr. 12.50
2 Albert Belle 3.25
3 Cal Ripken Jr. 20.00
4 Frank Thomas 7.50
5 Greg Maddux 10.00
6 Mo Vaughn 3.00
7 Chipper Jones 10.00
8 Mike Piazza 12.50
9 Ryan Klesko 3.00
10 Hideo Nomo 7.50
11 Roberto Alomar 4.00
12 Manny Ramirez 6.00
13 Gary Sheffield 3.50
14 Barry Bonds 20.00
15 Matt Williams 3.00
16 Jim Edmonds 3.00
17 Kirby Puckett 10.00
18 Sammy Sosa 12.50

1997 ZENITH

NM/M

Complete Set (50): 15.00
Common Player: .10
Pack (5 cards, 2 8x10): 2.00
Wax Box (12): 25.00
1 Frank Thomas .75
2 Tony Gwynn 1.00
3 Jeff Bagwell .75
4 Paul Molitor .75
5 Roberto Alomar .30
6 Mike Piazza 1.25
7 Albert Belle .20
8 Greg Maddux 1.00
9 Barry Larkin .10
10 Tony Clark .10
11 Larry Walker .10
12 Chipper Jones 1.00
13 Juan Gonzalez .75
14 Barry Bonds 2.00
15 Ivan Rodriguez .75
16 Sammy Sosa 1.25
17 Derek Jeter 2.00
18 Hideo Nomo .75
19 Roger Clemens 1.00
20 Ken Griffey Jr. 1.25
21 Andy Pettitte .25
22 Alex Rodriguez 1.50
23 Tino Martinez .10
24 Bernie Williams .25
25 Ken Caminiti .10
26 John Smoltz .10
27 Javier Lopez .10
28 Mark McGwire 1.50
29 Gary Sheffield .50
30 David Justice .10
31 Randy Johnson .75
32 Chuck Knoblauch .10
33 Mike Mussina .50
34 Deion Sanders .20
35 Cal Ripken Jr. 2.00
36 Darin Erstad .50
37 Kenny Lofton .10
38 Jay Buhner .10
39 Brady Anderson .10
40 Edgar Martinez .10
41 Mo Vaughn .10
42 Ryne Sandberg 1.00
43 Andruw Jones .75
44 Nomar Garciaparra 1.50
45 *Hideki Irabu* .25
46 Wilton Guerrero .10
47 *Jose Cruz Jr.* .45
48 Vladimir Guerrero .75
49 Scott Rolen .65
50 Jose Guillen .10

V-2

NM/M

Complete Set (8): 45.00
Common Player: 5.00
1 Ken Griffey Jr. 7.50
2 Andruw Jones 5.00
3 Frank Thomas 6.00
4 Mike Piazza 7.50
5 Alex Rodriguez 9.00
6 Cal Ripken Jr. 12.00
7 Derek Jeter 12.00
8 Vladimir Guerrero 5.00

Z-Team

NM/M

Complete Set (9): 60.00
Common Player: 3.00
1 Ken Griffey Jr. 9.00
2 Larry Walker 3.00
3 Frank Thomas 6.00
4 Alex Rodriguez 10.00
5 Mike Piazza 9.00
6 Cal Ripken Jr. 12.50
7 Derek Jeter 12.50
8 Andruw Jones 5.00
9 Roger Clemens 7.50

8x10 and 8x10 Dufex

NM/M

Complete Set (24): 20.00
Common Player: .50
Dufex versions: 1X
Samples: 1X
1 Frank Thomas 1.00
2 Tony Gwynn 1.50
3 Jeff Bagwell 1.00
4 Ken Griffey Jr. 2.00
5 Mike Piazza 2.00
6 Greg Maddux 1.50
7 Ken Caminiti .50
8 Albert Belle .50
9 Ivan Rodriguez .75
10 Sammy Sosa 2.00
11 Mark McGwire 2.50
12 Roger Clemens 1.75
13 Alex Rodriguez 2.50
14 Chipper Jones 1.50
15 Juan Gonzalez 1.00
16 Barry Bonds 3.00
17 Derek Jeter 3.00
18 Hideo Nomo 1.00
19 Cal Ripken Jr. 3.00
20 Hideki Irabu .50
21 Andruw Jones 1.00
22 Nomar Garciaparra 2.00
23 Vladimir Guerrero 1.00
24 Scott Rolen .75

1998 ZENITH

NM/M

Complete Set (100): 25.00
Common Player: .10
Pack (3): 2.50
Wax Box (18): 35.00
1 Larry Walker .10
2 Ken Griffey Jr. 1.75
3 Cal Ripken Jr. 2.50
4 Sammy Sosa 1.75
5 Andruw Jones 1.00
6 Frank Thomas 1.00
7 Tony Gwynn 1.50
8 Rafael Palmeiro 1.00
9 Tim Salmon .25
10 Randy Johnson 1.00
11 Juan Gonzalez 1.00
12 Greg Maddux 1.50
13 Vladimir Guerrero 1.00
14 Mike Piazza 1.75
15 Andres Galarraga .10
16 Alex Rodriguez 2.00
17 Derek Jeter 2.50
18 Nomar Garciaparra 1.75
19 Ivan Rodriguez 1.00
20 Chipper Jones 1.50
21 Barry Larkin .10
22 Mo Vaughn .10
23 Albert Belle .20
24 Scott Rolen .75
25 Sandy Alomar Jr. .10
26 Roberto Alomar .35
27 Andy Pettitte .35
28 Chuck Knoblauch .10
29 Jeff Bagwell 1.00
30 Mike Mussina .40
31 Fred McGriff .10
32 Roger Clemens 1.50
33 Rusty Greer .10
34 Edgar Martinez .10
35 Paul Molitor 1.00
36 Mark Grace .20
37 Darin Erstad .60
38 Kenny Lofton .10
39 Tom Glavine .35
40 Javier Lopez .10
41 Will Clark .10
42 Tino Martinez .10
43 Raul Mondesi .10
44 Brady Anderson .10
45 Chan Ho Park .10
46 Jason Giambi .75
47 Manny Ramirez 1.00
48 Jay Buhner .10
49 Dante Bichette .10
50 Jose Cruz Jr. .10
51 Charles Johnson .10
52 Bernard Gilkey .10
53 Johnny Damon .25
54 David Justice .10
55 Justin Thompson .10
56 Bobby Higginson .10
57 Todd Hundley .10
58 Gary Sheffield .50
59 Barry Bonds 2.50
60 Mark McGwire 2.00
61 John Smoltz .10
62 Tony Clark .10
63 Brian Jordan .10
64 Jason Kendall .10
65 Mariano Rivera .20
66 Pedro Martinez 1.00
67 Jim Thome .75
68 Neifi Perez .10
69 Kevin Brown .10
70 Hideo Nomo 1.00
71 Craig Biggio .10
72 Bernie Williams .20
73 Jose Guillen .10
74 Ken Caminiti .10
75 Livan Hernandez .10
76 Ray Lankford .10
77 Jim Edmonds .10
78 Matt Williams .10
79 Mark Kotsay .10
80 Moises Alou .10
81 Antone Williamson .10
82 Jaret Wright .10
83 Jacob Cruz .10
84 Abraham Nunez .10
85 Raul Ibanez .10
86 Miguel Tejada .10
87 Derek Lee .10
88 Juan Encarnacion .10
89 Todd Helton .75
90 Travis Lee .10
91 Ben Grieve .10
92 Ryan McGuire .10
93 Richard Hidalgo .10
94 Paul Konerko .15
95 Shannon Stewart .10
96 Homer Bush .10
97 Lou Collier .10
98 Jeff Abbott .10
99 Brett Tomko .10
100 Fernando Tatis .10

Z-Silver

NM/M

Common Player: 1.00
Stars/RCs: 2X

Inserted 1:7
(See 1998 Zenith for checklist and base card values.)

Z-Gold

	NM/M
Common Player:	3.00
Stars/Rookies 12X	

Production 100 sets
(See 1998 Zenith for checklist and base card values.)

5x7

		NM/M
Complete Set (80):		30.00
Common Player:		.25
Impulse Silvers:		1.5X
Inserted 1:7		
1	Nomar Garciaparra	2.50
2	Andres Galarraga	.25
3	Greg Maddux	2.00
4	Frank Thomas	1.00
5	Mark McGwire	3.00
6	Rafael Palmeiro	1.00
7	John Smoltz	.25
8	Jeff Bagwell	1.00
9	Andruw Jones	1.00
10	Rusty Greer	.25
11	Paul Molitor	1.00
12	Bernie Williams	.25
13	Kenny Lofton	.25
14	Alex Rodriguez	3.00
15	Derek Jeter	4.00
15s	Derek Jeter ("SAMPLE" overprint on back)	4.00
16	Scott Rolen	.75
17	Albert Belle	.25
18	Mo Vaughn	.25
19	Chipper Jones	2.00
20	Chuck Knoblauch	.25
21	Mike Piazza	3.00
22	Tony Gwynn	2.00
22s	Tony Gwynn ("SAMPLE" overprint on back)	2.00
23	Juan Gonzalez	1.00
24	Andy Pettitte	.35
25	Tim Salmon	.25
26	Brady Anderson	.25
27	Mike Mussina	.50
28	Edgar Martinez	.25
29	Jose Guillen	.25
30	Hideo Nomo	1.00
31	Jim Thome	1.00
32	Mark Grace	.35
33	Darin Erstad	.65
34	Bobby Higginson	.25
35	Ivan Rodriguez	1.00
36	Todd Hundley	.25
37	Sandy Alomar Jr.	.25
38	Gary Sheffield	.35
39	David Justice	.25
40	Ken Griffey Jr.	2.50
40s	Ken Griffey Jr. ("SAMPLE" overprint on back)	2.50
41	Vladimir Guerrero	1.00
42	Larry Walker	.25
43	Barry Bonds	4.00
44	Randy Johnson	1.00
45	Roger Clemens	2.25
46	Raul Mondesi	.25
47	Tino Martinez	.25
48	Jason Giambi	.75
49	Matt Williams	.25
50	Cal Ripken Jr.	4.00
51	Barry Larkin	.25
52	Jim Edmonds	.25
53	Ken Caminiti	.25
54	Sammy Sosa	2.50
55	Tony Clark	.25
56	Manny Ramirez	1.00
57	Bernard Gilkey	.25
58	Jose Cruz Jr.	.25
59	Brian Jordan	.25
60	Kevin Brown	.25
61	Craig Biggio	.25
62	Javier Lopez	.25
63	Jay Buhner	.25
64	Roberto Alomar	.50
65	Justin Thompson	.25
66	Todd Helton	1.00
67	Travis Lee	.25
68	Paul Konerko	.35
69	Jaret Wright	.25
70	Ben Grieve	.25
71	Juan Encarnacion	.25
72	Ryan McGuire	.25
73	Derrek Lee	.25
74	Abraham Nunez	.25
75	Richard Hidalgo	.25
76	Miguel Tejada	.25
77	Jacob Cruz	.25
78	Homer Bush	.25
79	Jeff Abbott	.25
80	Lou Collier	.25
	Checklist	.10

5x7 Impulse Silver

	NM/M
Common Player:	2.00
Stars/RCs:	1.5X

Inserted 1:7
(See 1998 Zenith 5x7 for checklist and base card values.)

Impulse Gold

	NM/M
Common Player:	5.00
Stars/RCs:	20X

Inserted 1:7
(See 1998 Zenith 5x7 for checklist and base card values.)

Raising the Bar

		NM/M
Complete Set (15):		25.00
Common Player:		1.25
Inserted 1:25		
1	Ken Griffey Jr.	3.00
2	Frank Thomas	1.25
3	Alex Rodriguez	3.50
4	Tony Gwynn	2.50
5	Mike Piazza	3.00
6	Ivan Rodriguez	1.25
7	Cal Ripken Jr.	4.50
8	Greg Maddux	2.50
9	Hideo Nomo	1.25
10	Mark McGwire	3.50
11	Juan Gonzalez	1.25
12	Andruw Jones	1.25
13	Jeff Bagwell	1.25
14	Chipper Jones	2.50
15	Nomar Garciaparra	3.00

Rookie Thrills

		NM/M
Complete Set (15):		20.00
Common Player:		1.50
Inserted 1:25		
1	Travis Lee	2.00
2	Juan Encarnacion	1.50
3	Derrek Lee	1.50
4	Raul Ibanez	1.50
5	Ryan McGuire	1.50
6	Todd Helton	3.00
7	Jacob Cruz	1.50
8	Abraham Nunez	1.50
9	Paul Konerko	2.00
10	Ben Grieve	1.50
11	Jeff Abbott	1.50
12	Richard Hidalgo	1.50
13	Jaret Wright	1.50
14	Lou Collier	1.50
15	Miguel Tejada	1.50

Z-Team

		NM/M
Complete Set (18):		35.00
Common Player:		1.25
Golds:		2X
Inserted 1:175		
1	Frank Thomas	2.50
2	Ken Griffey Jr.	3.50
3	Mike Piazza	3.50
4	Cal Ripken Jr.	6.00
5	Alex Rodriguez	5.00
6	Greg Maddux	3.00
7	Derek Jeter	6.00
8	Chipper Jones	3.00
9	Roger Clemens	3.25
10	Ben Grieve	1.25
11	Derrek Lee	1.25
12	Jose Cruz Jr.	1.25
13	Nomar Garciaparra	3.50
14	Travis Lee	1.50
15	Todd Helton	2.50
16	Paul Konerko	1.75
17	Miguel Tejada	1.25
18	Scott Rolen	2.00

Z-Team 5x7

		NM/M
Complete Set (9):		40.00
Common Player:		3.00
Inserted 1:35		
1	Frank Thomas	3.00
2	Ken Griffey Jr.	5.00
3	Mike Piazza	5.00
4	Cal Ripken Jr.	7.50
5	Alex Rodriguez	6.00
6	Greg Maddux	4.00
7	Derek Jeter	7.50
8	Chipper Jones	4.00
9	Roger Clemens	4.50

LATE ADDITIONS

-Bonus Pricing

2005 BOWMAN HERITAGE

NM/M

Complete Set (349):
Common Player (1-300): .15
Common SP (301-349): 3.00
Inserted 1:3
Draft Pick Variations (325-349) 1-1.5X
One DPV pack per hobby box
Pack (8): 4.00
Box (24): 75.00
Unlisted Stars (1-300): .25-2.00
230 *Stephen Drew* 4.00
301 Jason Bay 3.00
302 Tim Hudson 3.00
303 Miguel Tejada 4.00
304 Jeremy Bonderman 3.00
305 Alex Rodriguez 10.00
306 Rickie Weeks 3.00
307 Manny Ramirez 6.00
308 Nick Johnson 3.00
309 Andruw Jones 4.00
310 Hideki Matsui 6.00
311 Jeremy Reed 6.00
312 Dallas McPherson 3.00
313 Vladimir Guerrero 5.00
314 Eric Chavez 3.00
315 Chris Carpenter 3.00
316 Aaron Hill 3.00
317 Derrek Lee 5.00
318 Mark Loretta 3.00
319 Garrett Atkins 3.00
320 Hank Blalock 3.00
321 Chris Young 5.00
322 Roy Oswalt 3.00
323 Carlos Delgado 4.00
324 Pedro Martinez 5.00
325 *Jeff Clement* 6.00
326 *Jimmy Shull* 4.00
327 *Daniel Carte* 4.00
328 *Travis Buck* 3.00
329 *Chris Volstad* 3.00
330 *Andrew McCutchen* 8.00
331 *Cliff Pennington* 4.00
332 *John Mayberry* 4.00
333 *C.J. Henry* 5.00
334 *Ricky Romero* 6.00
335 *Aaron Thompson* 5.00
336 *Cesar Carrillo* 4.00
337 *Jacoby Ellsbury* 6.00
338 *Matt Garza* 6.00
339 *Colby Rasmus* 6.00
340 *Ryan Zimmerman* 10.00
341 *Ryan Braun* 6.00
342 *Brent Lillibridge* 3.00
343 *Jay Bruce* 6.00
344 *Matt Green* 4.00
345 *Brent Cox* 6.00
346 *Jed Lowrie* 4.00
347 *Beau Jones* 3.00
348 *Eli Iorg* 4.00
349 *Chaz Roe* 4.00

Mahogany

Stars (1-300): 1-2X
SP's (301-349): .5-1X
Inserted 1:1

Mini

Stars (1-300): 1-2X
SP's (301-349): .5-1X
Inserted 1:1

Future Greatness

NM/M

Common Player: 4.00
Unlisted Stars: 6-8.00
BT Brad Thompson 15.00

Pieces of Greatness

NM/M

Common Player: 4.00
Unlisted Stars: 6-10.00
BB Barry Bonds 20.00
RC Roger Clemens 10.00
JG Josh Gibson 15.00
AP Albert Pujols 20.00
AR Alex Rodriguez 15.00
IS Ichiro Suzuki 15.00
DWR David Wright 15.00

Signs of Greatness

NM/M

Common Player: 6.00
RB Ryan Braun 20.00
JB Jay Bruce 20.00
PB Patrick Bryant 10.00
MB Matt Bush 20.00
TC Travis Chick 6.00
TD Thomas Diamond 10.00
SE Scott Elbert 10.00
MG Matt Green 8.00
AG Angel Guzman 8.00
JH J.P. Howell 8.00
PH Philip Humber 15.00
ZJ Zach Jackson 8.00
JJ Jason Jaramillo 10.00
DJ Dan Johnson 15.00
BL Brent Lillibridge 10.00
DL Donald Lucey 8.00
EM Eddy Martinez-Esteve
JM John Mayberry 15.00
AM Andrew McCutchen 25.00
JP Jon Papelbon 40.00
DP David Purcey 8.00
RR Ricky Romero 15.00
HS Huston Street 20.00
CT Curtis Thigpen 10.00
JU Justin Upton
WW Wes Whisler 10.00
JZ Jon Zeringue 8.00
RZ Ryan Zimmerman 50.00

2005 BOWMAN STERLING

NM/M

Pack (5): 50.00
Box (6): 265.00
First Year Autographs
MA *Matt Albers* 10.00
RB *Ryan Braun* 30.00
TC *Travis Chick* 10.00
MG *Matt Green* 10.00
CH *C.J. Henry* 25.00
GK *George Kottaras* 15.00
EM *Eddy Martinez-Esteve* 20.00
JM *John Mayberry* 20.00
GO *Garrett Olson* 15.00
CP *Cliff Pennington* 15.00
HS *Humberto Sanchez* 10.00
BS *Brandon Sing* 15.00
AT *Aaron Thompson* 20.00
CV *Chris Volstad* 15.00
SW *Steven White* 10.00
Autographed First Year Relics
TB *Trevor Bell* 20.00
MB *Michael Bowden* 30.00
JB *Jay Bruce* 40.00
MC *Mike Conroy* 15.00
BC *J. Brent Cox* 15.00
JE *Jacoby Ellsbury* 25.00
JG *Josh Geer* 15.00
PH *Philip Humber* 20.00
EI *Eli Iorg* 20.00
BJ *Beau Jones* 25.00
BL *Bobby Livingston* 15.00
JL *Jed Lowrie* 25.00
SM *Steve Marek* 10.00
RM *Russell Martin* 20.00
BM *Brandon McCarthy* 35.00
AM *Andrew McCutchen* 50.00
TM *Tyler Minges* 15.00
JCN *John Nelson* 15.00
JN *Jeff Niemann* 20.00
JO *Justin Olson* 15.00
CPP *Carmen Pignatiello* 15.00
CR *Colby Rasmus* 30.00
CRO *Chaz Roe* 20.00
CS *C.J. Smith* 10.00
RT *Raul Tablado* 15.00
JV *Justin Verlander* 35.00
Autographed Prospect Base Relics
BB Billy Buckner 15.00
SE Scott Elbert 15.00
BE Brad Eldred 20.00
JF Josh Fields 15.00
AL Adam Lind 15.00
CN Chris Nelson 15.00
DP Dustin Pedroia 25.00
CT Curtis Thigpen 15.00
First Year Base Cards
BA *Brian Anderson* 10.00
BRB *Brian Bogusevic* 4.00
CBU *Clay Buchholz* 6.00
TBU *Travis Buck* 6.00
BBU *Billy Butler* 15.00
CC *Cesar Carrillo* 6.00
DC *Daniel Carte* 4.00
JC *Jeff Clement* 20.00
MCO *Mike Constanzo* 8.00
BCR *Brad Corley* 4.00
JDR *John Drennen* 8.00
SD *Stephen Drew* 20.00
JEG *Jon Egan* 6.00
YE *Yunel Escobar* 6.00
MGA *Matt Garza* 4.00
TG *Tyler Greene* 6.00
BH *Brett Hayes* 4.00
CHE *Chase Headley* 8.00
THE *Tyler Herron* 4.00
NH *Nick Hundley* 4.00
TI *Tadahito Iguchi* 8.00
HI *Hernan Iribarren* 4.00
CI *Craig Italiano* 6.00
CJ *Chuck James* 8.00
PK *Paul Kelly* 8.00
ACL *Andy LaRoche* 10.00
JLY *Jeff Lyman* 6.00
MAM *Matt Maloney* 6.00
JMA *Jacob Marceaux* 6.00
MMC *Mark McCormick* 4.00
RMO *Ryan Mount* 6.00
PP *P.J. Phillips* 4.00
CRA *Cesar Ramos* 4.00
NR *Nolan Reimold* 6.00
RR *Ricky Romero* 6.00
HAS *Henry Sanchez* 8.00
ZS *Zach Simons* 4.00
KS *Kevin Slowey* 6.00
BSN *Brandon Snyder* 8.00
DT *Drew Thompson* 4.00
CLT *Chuck Tiffany* 6.00
MTO *Matt Torra* 6.00
WT *Wade Townsend* 4.00
TT *Troy Tulowitzki* 10.00
JW *Josh Wall* 6.00
JWE *Jered Weaver* 8.00
NW *Nick Webber* 4.00
KW *Kevin Whelan* 4.00
TW *Travis Wood* 4.00
RZ *Ryan Zimmerman* 25.00

Refractors

Rookies: 1.5-2X
Rookie Auto.: 1-2X
Rookie Relic Auto.: 1-2X
Production 199 sets

Black Refractors

No pricing
Production 25 sets

Original Autographs

Production 1-160
AJ4 Andruw Jones 02 B/122 25.00
AJ6 Andruw Jones 03 B/112 25.00
AJ8 Andruw Jones 04 B/71 25.00
DL1 Derrek Lee 95 B/27 25.00
DL2 Derrek Lee 96 B/29 25.00
DL5 Derrek Lee 98 B/22 25.00
DL6 Derrek Lee 04 B/92 20.00
DL7 Derrek Lee 04 BC/26 25.00
DW1 David Wright 04 BD/98 60.00
DW3 David Wright 05 B/139 60.00
GA1 Garret Anderson 04 BC/36 20.00
GA2 Garret Anderson 05 B/48 20.00
JR1 Jeremy Reed 04 BD/82 15.00
JR2 Jeremy Reed 04 BCD/48 20.00
MC2 Miguel Cabrera 02 BD/26 50.00
MC4 Miguel Cabrera 03 BD/27 50.00
MC5 Miguel Cabrera 03 BCD/25 50.00
MC6 Miguel Cabrera 04 B/127 25.00
MC7 Miguel Cabrera 04 BC/25 50.00
MC8 Miguel Cabrera 05 B/154 25.00
MC9 Miguel Cabrera 05 BC/25 50.00
MK3 Mark Kotsay 98 B/56 15.00
MK5 Mark Kotsay 99 B/75 15.00
MK7 Mark Kotsay 05 B/160 10.00
MK8 Mark Kotsay 05 B C/46 15.00
MY1 Michael Young 04 B/148 15.00
MY2 Michael Young 04 BC/64 15.00
MY3 Michael Young 05 B/92 15.00

MLB Logo Patch

No pricing
Production one set

Relics

NM/M

Common Player: 4.00
Refractor: 1-1.5X
Production 199 sets
Black Refractor: 2-4X
Production 25 sets
Unlisted Stars: 6-10.00
BLB Barry Bonds 20.00
JGI Josh Gibson 15.00
GM Greg Maddux 10.00
HM Hideki Matsui 15.00
DO David Ortiz 10.00
AP Albert Pujols 20.00
AR Alex Rodriguez 20.00

2005 SP LEGENDARY CUTS

NM/M

Complete Set (90): 25.00
Common Player: .25
Pack (4): 14.00
Box (12): 150.00
1 Al Kaline 1.00
2 Babe Ruth 3.00
3 Bill Mazeroski .25
4 Billy Williams .25
5 Bob Feller .50
6 Bob Gibson 1.00
7 Bob Lemon .25
8 Bobby Doerr .25
9 Brooks Robinson 1.00
10 Carl Yastrzemski 1.50
11 Carlton Fisk .75
12 Casey Stengel .50
13 Jim "Catfish" Hunter .25
14 Christy Mathewson 1.00
15 Cy Young .50
16 Dennis Eckersley .25
17 Dizzy Dean .50
18 Don Drysdale .25
19 Don Sutton .25
20 Duke Snider .75
21 Early Wynn .25
22 Eddie Mathews 1.00
23 Eddie Murray .75
24 Enos Slaughter .25
25 Ernie Banks 1.00
26 Fergie Jenkins .25
27 Frank Robinson 1.00
28 Gary Carter .25
29 Gaylord Perry .25
30 Reggie Jackson 1.00
31 George Kell .25
32 George Sisler .25
33 Hal Newhouser .25
34 Harmon Killebrew 1.00
35 Honus Wagner 1.00
36 Jackie Robinson .50
37 Jim Bunning .25
38 Jim Palmer .50
39 Jimmie Foxx .75
40 Joe DiMaggio 2.00
41 Joe Morgan .50

42 Johnny Bench 1.00
43 Johnny Mize .25
44 Juan Marichal .50
45 Kirby Puckett .75
46 Larry Doby .25
47 Lefty Grove .25
48 Lou Boudreau .25
49 Lou Brock .50
50 Lou Gehrig 2.00
51 Luis Aparicio .25
52 Mel Ott .50
53 Mickey Cochrane .25
54 Mickey Mantle 4.00
55 Mike Schmidt 1.50
56 Monte Irvin .50
57 Nolan Ryan 2.00
58 Orlando Cepeda .25
59 Ozzie Smith 1.00
60 Paul Molitor .50
61 Pee Wee Reese .25
62 Phil Niekro .25
63 Phil Rizzuto .50
64 Ralph Kiner .25
65 Red Schoendienst .25
66 Richie Ashburn .25
67 Rick Ferrell .25
68 Robin Roberts .25
69 Robin Yount 1.00
70 Rod Carew .50
71 Rogers Hornsby .50
72 Rollie Fingers .25
73 Roy Campanella .50
74 Ryne Sandberg 1.00
75 Satchel Paige 1.00
76 Stan Musial 1.00
77 Steve Carlton .25
78 Ted Williams 2.00
79 Thurman Munson 1.00
80 Tom Seaver 1.00
81 Tony Gwynn 1.00
82 Tony Perez .25
83 Ty Cobb 1.50
84 Wade Boggs .50
85 Walter Johnson 1.00
86 Warren Spahn 1.00
87 Whitey Ford 1.00
88 Willie McCovey .50
89 Willie Stargell .75
90 Yogi Berra 1.00

Holofoil

Holofoil: 3-5X
Production 50 Sets

Classic Careers Autograph

NM/M
Common Player: 15.00
Production 25 Sets
LA Luis Aparicio 20.00
HB Harold Baines 25.00
JB Jay Buhner 30.00
CA Jose Canseco 40.00
GC Gary Carter 20.00
OC Orlando Cepeda 30.00
JC Jack Clark 20.00
WC Will Clark 25.00
DC David Cone 20.00
AD Andre Dawson 20.00
BD Bobby Doerr 20.00
LD Lenny Dykstra 20.00
CE Carl Erskine 20.00
SF Sid Fernandez 15.00
CF Carlton Fisk 35.00
GF George Foster 25.00
BF Bill Freehan 25.00
DG Dwight Gooden 15.00
GG Rich "Goose" Gossage 20.00
MG Mark Grace 30.00
RG Ron Guidry 35.00
GU Don Gullett 15.00
KH Keith Hernandez 20.00
BH Bob Horner 15.00
FJ Fergie Jenkins 25.00
BL Barry Larkin 40.00
SL Sparky Lyle 20.00
BM Bill Madlock 20.00
DE Dennis Martinez 15.00
GM Gary Mathews 15.00
MA Don Mattingly 60.00
JM Jack Morris 20.00
MU Bobby Murcer 30.00
DM Dale Murphy 35.00
PN Phil Niekro 20.00
GN Graig Nettles 20.00
TO Tony Oliva 20.00
GP Gaylord Perry 20.00
JP Johnny Podres 15.00
TR Tim Raines 20.00
JR Jim Rice 25.00
CR Cal Ripken Jr. 125.00
AR Al Rosen 20.00
ST Dave Stewart 15.00
DS Darryl Strawberry 20.00
SU Bruce Sutter 25.00
DO Don Sutton 20.00
LT Luis Tiant 20.00
AV Andy Van Slyke 30.00
CY Carl Yastrzemski 50.00

Classic Careers Jersey Autograph

NM/M
Production 25 Sets
LA Luis Aparicio 20.00
HB Harold Baines 25.00
JB Jay Buhner 30.00
GC Gary Carter 20.00
OC Orlando Cepeda 30.00
JC Jack Clark 20.00
WC Will Clark 25.00
DC David Cone 20.00
AD Andre Dawson 20.00
BD Bobby Doerr 20.00
LD Lenny Dykstra 20.00
CE Carl Erskine 20.00
SF Sid Fernandez 15.00
GF George Foster 25.00
BF Bill Freehan 25.00
DG Dwight Gooden 15.00
GG Rich "Goose" Gossage 20.00
MG Mark Grace 30.00
RG Ron Guidry 35.00
GU Don Gullett 15.00
KH Keith Hernandez 20.00
BH Bob Horner 15.00
FJ Fergie Jenkins 25.00
BL Barry Larkin 40.00
SL Sparky Lyle 20.00
BM Bill Madlock 20.00
DE Dennis Martinez 15.00
GM Gary Mathews 15.00
MA Don Mattingly 60.00
JM Jack Morris 20.00
MU Bobby Murcer 30.00
DM Dale Murphy 35.00
PN Phil Niekro 20.00
GN Graig Nettles 20.00
TO Tony Oliva 20.00
GP Gaylord Perry 20.00
JP Johnny Podres 15.00
TR Tim Raines 20.00
JR Jim Rice 25.00
CR Cal Ripken Jr. 125.00
AR Al Rosen 20.00
ST Dave Stewart 15.00
DS Darryl Strawberry 20.00
SU Bruce Sutter 25.00
LT Luis Tiant 20.00
AV Andy Van Slyke 30.00
CY Carl Yastrzemski 50.00

Classic Careers Patch Autograph

NM/M
Production 25 Sets
HB Harold Baines 40.00
JB Jay Buhner 50.00
JC Jack Clark 35.00
WC Will Clark 40.00
DC David Cone 35.00
AD Andre Dawson 35.00
BD Bobby Doerr 35.00
LD Lenny Dykstra 35.00
SF Sid Fernandez 25.00
GF George Foster 40.00
BF Bill Freehan 40.00
DG Dwight Gooden 25.00
GG Rich "Goose" Gossage 35.00
MG Mark Grace 50.00
GU Don Gullett 25.00
KH Keith Hernandez 35.00
BL Barry Larkin 60.00
DE Dennis Martinez 25.00
GM Gary Mathews 25.00
JM Jack Morris 35.00
GN Graig Nettles 35.00
TO Tony Oliva 35.00
GP Gaylord Perry 30.00
TR Tim Raines 30.00
JR Jim Rice 40.00
CR Cal Ripken Jr. 200.00
ST Dave Stewart 25.00
DS Darryl Strawberry 30.00
AV Andy Van Slyke 40.00

Classic Careers Jersey

NM/M
Common Player: 4.00
Gold: 1X
Production 75 Sets
Unlisted Stars: 6-10.00
MA Don Mattingly 12.00
CR Cal Ripken Jr. 20.00
CY Carl Yastrzemski 15.00

Classic Careers Patch

NM/M
Production 50 Sets
HB Harold Baines 10.00
JB Jay Buhner
CA Jose Canseco 15.00
JC Jack Clark 10.00
WC Will Clark 20.00
DC David Cone 15.00
AD Andre Dawson 15.00
BD Bobby Doerr 15.00
LD Lenny Dykstra 15.00
SF Sid Fernandez 10.00
GF George Foster 10.00
BF Bill Freehan 12.00
DG Dwight Gooden 15.00
GG Rich "Goose" Gossage 12.00
MG Mark Grace 20.00
KH Keith Hernandez 12.00
BL Barry Larkin 25.00
DE Dennis Martinez 10.00
GM Gary Mathews 10.00
JM Jack Morris 10.00
GN Graig Nettles 10.00
GP Gaylord Perry 12.00
TR Tim Raines 10.00
JR Jim Rice 15.00
CR Cal Ripken Jr. 40.00
AV Andy Van Slyke 15.00
ST Dave Stewart 10.00
DS Darryl Strawberry 12.00

Glory Days Autograph

NM/M
Common Player: 15.00
Production 25 Sets
HB Harold Baines 25.00
YB Yogi Berra 50.00
LB Lou Brock 30.00
JB Jay Buhner 30.00
CA Jose Canseco 40.00
JC Jack Clark 20.00
WC Will Clark 25.00
DC David Cone 20.00
AD Andre Dawson 20.00
BD Bobby Doerr 20.00
LD Lenny Dykstra 20.00
SF Sid Fernandez 15.00
WF Whitey Ford 40.00
GF George Foster 25.00
BF Bill Freehan 25.00
KG Kirk Gibson 20.00
DG Dwight Gooden 15.00
RG Ron Guidry 35.00
GU Don Gullett 15.00
TG Tony Gwynn 40.00
KH Keith Hernandez 20.00
BH Bob Horner 15.00
FJ Fergie Jenkins 25.00
BL Barry Larkin 40.00
SL Sparky Lyle 20.00
FL Fred Lynn 15.00
BM Bill Madlock 20.00
MA Juan Marichal 25.00
DE Dennis Martinez 15.00
GM Gary Mathews 15.00
PM Paul Molitor 40.00
JM Jack Morris 20.00
MU Bobby Murcer 25.00
DM Dale Murphy 35.00
GN Graig Nettles 20.00
TO Tony Oliva 20.00
JP Jim Palmer 25.00
TR Tim Raines 20.00
JR Jim Rice 25.00
CR Cal Ripken Jr. 125.00
AR Al Rosen 20.00
NR Nolan Ryan 100.00
RS Red Schoendienst 20.00
SN Duke Snider 40.00
ST Dave Stewart 15.00
DS Darryl Strawberry 20.00
BS Bruce Sutter 25.00
LT Luis Tiant 20.00
AV Andy Van Slyke 30.00
RY Robin Yount 50.00

Glory Days Patch Autograph

NM/M
Production 25 Sets
HB Harold Baines 40.00
JB Jay Buhner 50.00
JC Jack Clark 35.00
DC David Cone 35.00
AD Andre Dawson 35.00
BD Bobby Doerr 35.00
LD Lenny Dykstra 35.00
SF Sid Fernandez 25.00
GF George Foster 40.00
DG Dwight Gooden 25.00
KH Keith Hernandez 35.00
BH Bob Horner 25.00
FJ Fergie Jenkins 40.00
BL Barry Larkin 60.00
BM Bill Madlock 25.00
DE Dennis Martinez 25.00
GM Gary Mathews 25.00
JM Jack Morris 35.00
DM Dale Murphy 40.00
GN Graig Nettles 35.00
TO Tony Oliva 35.00
JP Jim Palmer 40.00
TR Tim Raines 30.00
JR Jim Rice 40.00
RS Red Schoendienst 30.00
DS Darryl Strawberry 30.00
BS Bruce Sutter 25.00
LT Luis Tiant 25.00
AV Andy Van Slyke 40.00

Glory Days Jersey

NM/M
Common Player: 4.00
Gold: 1X
Production 75 Sets
Unlisted Stars: 6-10.00
CR Cal Ripken Jr. 20.00
NR Nolan Ryan 15.00

Glory Days Memorabilia Autograph

NM/M
Production 25 Sets
HB Harold Baines 25.00
YB Yogi Berra 50.00
JB Jay Buhner 30.00
JC Jack Clark 20.00
WC Will Clark 25.00
DC David Cone 20.00
AD Andre Dawson 20.00
BD Bobby Doerr 20.00
LD Lenny Dykstra 20.00
SF Sid Fernandez 15.00
WF Whitey Ford 40.00
GF George Foster 25.00
BF Bill Freehan 25.00
KG Kirk Gibson 20.00
DG Dwight Gooden 15.00
BG Ron Guidry 35.00
GU Don Gullett 15.00
TG Tony Gwynn 40.00
KH Keith Hernandez 20.00
BH Bob Horner 15.00
FJ Fergie Jenkins 25.00
BL Barry Larkin 40.00
SL Sparky Lyle 20.00
FL Fred Lynn 15.00
BM Bill Madlock 20.00
MA Juan Marichal 25.00
DE Dennis Martinez 15.00
GM Gary Mathews 15.00
PM Paul Molitor 40.00
JM Jack Morris 20.00
MU Bobby Murcer 25.00
DM Dale Murphy 35.00
GN Graig Nettles 20.00
TO Tony Oliva 20.00
JP Jim Palmer 25.00
TR Tim Raines 20.00
JR Jim Rice 25.00
AR Al Rosen 20.00
NR Nolan Ryan 100.00
RS Red Schoendienst 20.00
SN Duke Snider 40.00
ST Dave Stewart 15.00
DS Darryl Strawberry 20.00
BS Bruce Sutter 25.00
LT Luis Tiant 20.00
AV Andy Van Slyke 30.00
RY Robin Yount 50.00

Glory Days Patch

NM/M
Production 50 Sets
HB Harold Baines 10.00
JC Jack Clark 10.00
DC David Cone 15.00
AD Andre Dawson 15.00
BD Bobby Doerr 15.00
LD Lenny Dykstra 15.00
SF Sid Fernandez 10.00
GF George Foster 10.00

DG Dwight Gooden 15.00
KH Keith Hernandez 12.00
BH Bob Horner 10.00
FJ Fergie Jenkins 15.00
BL Barry Larkin 25.00
GM Gary Mathews 10.00
JM Jack Morris 10.00
DM Dale Murphy 20.00
GN Graig Nettles 10.00
JP Jim Palmer 15.00
TR Tim Raines 10.00
RS Red Schoendienst 15.00
DS Darryl Strawberry 12.00
BS Bruce Sutter 15.00
LT Luis Tiant 15.00
AV Andy Van Slyke 15.00

Lasting Legends Autograph

NM/M

Common Player:
Production 25 Sets
LA Luis Aparicio 20.00
EB Ernie Banks 60.00
BE Johnny Bench 50.00
YB Yogi Berra 60.00
WB Wade Boggs 40.00
LB Lou Brock 25.00
RC Rod Carew 35.00
SC Steve Carlton 25.00
GC Gary Carter 25.00
OC Orlando Cepeda 25.00
BD Bobby Doerr 20.00
DE Dennis Eckersley 25.00
RF Rollie Fingers 20.00
CF Carlton Fisk 35.00
WF Whitey Ford 40.00
BG Bob Gibson 40.00
DG Dwight Gooden 15.00
TG Tony Gwynn 50.00
KH Keith Hernandez 20.00
FG Fergie Jenkins 25.00
AK Al Kaline 40.00
BL Barry Larkin 40.00
MA Juan Marichal 25.00
DM Don Mattingly 60.00
BM Bill Mazeroski 35.00
PM Paul Molitor 40.00
JM Joe Morgan 25.00
MU Dale Murphy 40.00
EM Eddie Murray 50.00
SM Stan Musial 60.00
GN Graig Nettles 20.00
PN Phil Niekro 25.00
JP Jim Palmer 25.00
TP Tony Perez 20.00
GP Gaylord Perry 20.00
KP Kirby Puckett 50.00
JR Jerry Rice 25.00
CR Cal Ripken Jr. 125.00
BR Brooks Robinson 40.00
FR Frank Robinson 25.00
NR Nolan Ryan 100.00
SA Ryne Sandberg 50.00
MS Mike Schmidt 50.00
RS Red Schoendienst 20.00
OS Ozzie Smith 60.00
SN Duke Snider 40.00
BS Bruce Sutter 25.00
DS Don Sutton 20.00
CY Carl Yastrzemski 50.00
RY Robin Yount 50.00

Lasting Legends Jersey Autograph

NM/M

Production 25 Sets
LA Luis Aparicio 20.00
EB Ernie Banks 60.00
BE Johnny Bench 50.00
YB Yogi Berra 60.00
WB Wade Boggs 40.00
LB Lou Brock 25.00
RC Rod Carew 40.00
SC Steve Carlton 25.00
GC Gary Carter 25.00
OC Orlando Cepeda 25.00
BD Bobby Doerr 20.00
DE Dennis Eckersley 25.00
RF Rollie Fingers 20.00
CF Carlton Fisk 40.00
WF Whitey Ford 40.00
BG Bob Gibson 40.00
DG Dwight Gooden 15.00
TG Tony Gwynn 50.00
KH Keith Hernandez 20.00
FG Fergie Jenkins 25.00
AK Al Kaline 50.00
BL Barry Larkin 40.00
MA Juan Marichal 25.00
DM Don Mattingly 60.00
BM Bill Mazeroski 40.00
PM Paul Molitor 40.00
JM Joe Morgan 25.00
MU Dale Murphy 40.00
SM Stan Musial 60.00
GN Graig Nettles 20.00
PN Phil Niekro 25.00
JP Jim Palmer 25.00
TP Tony Perez 20.00
GP Gaylord Perry 20.00
JR Jim Rice 25.00
CR Cal Ripken Jr. 140.00
BR Brooks Robinson 40.00
FR Frank Robinson 25.00
NR Nolan Ryan 100.00
SA Ryne Sandberg 50.00
MS Mike Schmidt 50.00
RS Red Schoendienst 20.00
OS Ozzie Smith 60.00
SN Duke Snider 40.00
BS Bruce Sutter 25.00
CY Carl Yastrzemski 50.00
RY Robin Yount 50.00

Lasting Legends Patch Autograph

NM/M

Production 25 Sets
WB Wade Boggs 50.00
LB Lou Brock
RC Rod Carew 50.00
SC Steve Carlton 35.00
GC Gary Carter 35.00
OC Orlando Cepeda 30.00
DE Dennis Eckersley 35.00
RF Rollie Fingers 25.00
DG Dwight Gooden 25.00
KH Keith Hernandez 25.00
FJ Fergie Jenkins 35.00
BL Barry Larkin 50.00
MA Juan Marichal 35.00
PM Paul Molitor 50.00
JM Joe Morgan 35.00
PN Phil Niekro 35.00
JP Jim Palmer 40.00
TP Tony Perez 30.00
GP Gaylord Perry 30.00
JR Jim Rice 35.00
BR Brooks Robinson 50.00
NR Nolan Ryan 140.00
SA Ryne Sandberg 80.00
OS Ozzie Smith 75.00
BS Bruce Sutter 30.00
RY Robin Yount 65.00

Lasting Legends Material

NM/M

Common Player: 4.00
Gold: 1X-1.5X
Production 75 Sets
Platinum: No Pricing
Production One Set
LA Luis Aparicio 4.00
EB Ernie Banks 10.00
BE Johnny Bench 8.00
YB Yogi Berra 8.00
WB Wade Boggs 6.00
LB Lou Brock 6.00
RC Rod Carew 6.00
SC Steve Carlton 4.00
GC Gary Carter 4.00
OC Orlando Cepeda 4.00
BD Bobby Doerr 6.00
DE Dennis Eckersley 6.00
RF Rollie Fingers 4.00
CF Carlton Fisk 6.00
WF Whitey Ford 6.00
BG Bob Gibson 8.00
DG Dwight Gooden 4.00
TG Tony Gwynn 8.00
KH Keith Hernandez 4.00
FJ Fergie Jenkins 4.00
AK Al Kaline 10.00
BL Barry Larkin 6.00
MA Juan Marichal 6.00
DM Don Mattingly 10.00
BM Bill Mazeroski 6.00
PM Paul Molitor 6.00
JM Joe Morgan 4.00
MU Dale Murphy 6.00
EM Eddie Murray 6.00
SM Stan Musial 10.00
GN Graig Nettles 4.00
PN Phil Niekro 4.00
JP Jim Palmer 6.00
TP Tony Perez 4.00
GP Gaylord Perry 4.00
KP Kirby Puckett 8.00
JR Jim Rice 4.00
CR Cal Ripken Jr. 20.00
BR Brooks Robinson 6.00
FR Frank Robinson 6.00
NR Nolan Ryan 15.00
SA Ryne Sandberg 8.00
MS Mike Schmidt 10.00
RS Red Schoendienst 4.00
OS Ozzie Smith 8.00
SN Duke Snider 6.00
BS Bruce Sutter 4.00
DS Don Sutton 4.00
CY Carl Yastrzemski 15.00
RY Robin Yount 8.00

Lasting Legends Patch

NM/M

Production 50 Sets
WB Wade Boggs 20.00
LB Lou Brock 15.00
RC Rod Carew 15.00
SC Steve Carlton 15.00
GC Gary Carter 12.00
OC Orlando Cepeda 15.00
DE Dennis Eckersley 15.00
RF Rollie Fingers 10.00
CF Carlton Fisk 15.00
DG Dwight Gooden 10.00
KH Keith Hernandez 10.00
FJ Fergie Jenkins 15.00
BL Barry Larkin 25.00
MA Juan Marichal 15.00
JM Joe Morgan 15.00
PN Phil Niekro 15.00
JP Jim Palmer 15.00
TP Tony Perez 15.00
GP Gaylord Perry 12.00
KP Kirby Puckett 25.00
JR Jim Rice 15.00
BR Brooks Robinson 20.00
FR Frank Robinson 15.00
SA Ryne Sandberg 25.00
OS Ozzie Smith 25.00
BS Bruce Sutter 15.00
DS Don Sutton 12.00
RY Robin Yount 25.00

Legendary Battery Cuts

NM/M

Production 6-99
SC Stan Coveleski/25 140.00
BD Bill Dickey/22 200.00
DD Don Drysdale/31 200.00
LG Lefty Gomez/77 160.00
JH Jesse Haines/28 200.00
WH Waite Hoyt/58 125.00
CH Carl Hubbell/99 140.00
HN Hal Newhouser/32 140.00
WS Warren Spahn/43 150.00
EW Early Wynn/32 125.00

Legendary Cornerstone Cuts

NM/M

Production 1-79
DC Dolph Camilli/79 120.00
RD Ray Dandridge/27 125.00
EM Eddie Mathews/50 150.00
JM Johnny Mize/44 150.00
WS Willie Stargell/36 150.00

Legendary Cuts

NM/M

Production 1-108
LA Luke Appling/55 125.00
RI Richie Ashburn/83 150.00
EA Earl Averill/91 90.00
JB Cool Papa Bell/78 300.00
LB Lou Boudreau/99 100.00
MC Max Carey/84 140.00
HC Happy Chandler/39 125.00
JC Jocko Conlan/40 140.00
ST Stan Coveleski/71 140.00
CR Joe Cronin/76 140.00
RD Ray Dandridge/76 100.00
BD Bill Dickey/95 150.00
JD Joe DiMaggio/56 500.00
LD Larry Doby/32 200.00
DD Don Drysdale/50 200.00
DU Leo Durocher/57 150.00
FE Rick Ferrell/80 125.00
NF Nellie Fox/12 12.00
CF Carl Furillo/25 200.00
CG Charlie Gehringer/97 120.00
GO Lefty Gomez/68 150.00
HG Hank Greenberg/44 280.00
BU Burleigh Grimes/99 125.00
GR Lefty Grove/41 250.00
HA Chick Hafey/52 150.00
JH Jesse Haines/90 150.00
GH Gabby Hartnett/50 180.00
BH Billy Herman/99 90.00
WH Waite Hoyt/99 140.00
CH Carl Hubbell/99 150.00
HU Jim "Catfish" Hunter/65 140.00
JJ Jackie Jensen/48 180.00
JO Judy Johnson/39 150.00
CK Charlie Keller/98 140.00
HK Harvey Kuenn/33 165.00
BL Bob Lemon/108 100.00
LE Buck Leonard/71 140.00
LI Freddie Lindstrom/19 250.00
LO Ernie Lombardi/29 200.00
HM Heinie Manush/25 175.00
RU Rube Marquard/80 150.00
EM Eddie Mathews/80 150.00
RO Roy McMillan/23 140.00
MI Johnny Mize/90 125.00
HN Hal Newhouser/96 125.00
PR Pee Wee Reese/69 180.00
SR Sam Rice/41 180.00
ER Edd Roush/99 100.00
JS Joe Sewell/76 140.00
ES Enos Slaughter/99 100.00
WA Warren Spahn/92 140.00
WS Willie Stargell/63 165.00
CS Casey Stengel/61 250.00
BW Bucky Walters/34 150.00
JW Hoyt Wilhelm/48 100.00
EW Early Wynn/89 120.00

Legendary Cuts Material

NM/M

Production 75 unless noted
Gold: No Pricing
Production 15 Sets
CA Roy Campanella 40.00
RC Roberto Clemente 80.00
TC Ty Cobb 140.00
CO Mickey Cochrane 50.00
CR Joe Cronin 15.00
DE Dizzy Dean 60.00
BD Bill Dickey 35.00
JD Joe DiMaggio 120.00
DD Don Drysdale 15.00
JF Jimmie Foxx 60.00
LG Lou Gehrig 175.00
HG Hank Greenberg 35.00
HO Gil Hodges 40.00
RH Rogers Hornsby 80.00
HU Jim "Catfish" Hunter 10.00
TK Ted Kluszewski 20.00
TL Tony Lazerri 40.00
BL Bob Lemon 25.00
MM Mickey Mantle 150.00
RM Roger Maris 60.00
EM Eddie Mathews 40.00
CM Christy Mathewson 125.00
MI Johnny Mize 25.00
TM Thurman Munson 35.00
MO Mel Ott 50.00
SP Satchel Paige 75.00
PR Pee Wee Reese 25.00
JR Jackie Robinson 65.00
BR Babe Ruth 180.00
SI George Sisler 35.00
ES Enos Slaughter 15.00
WA Warren Spahn 40.00
CS Casey Stengel 40.00
HW Honus Wagner/22 140.00
JW Hoyt Wilhelm 15.00
TW Ted Williams 75.00
EW Early Wynn 10.00

Legendary Duels Material

NM/M

Production 25 Sets
Patch: No Pricing
Production 10 Sets
BM Ernie Banks, Stan Musial 50.00
CC Jose Canseco, Will Clark 40.00
DM Paul Molitor, Lenny Dykstra 25.00
EG Dennis Eckersley, Kirk Gibson 25.00
FB Carlton Fisk, Johnny Bench 25.00
FR George Foster, Jim Rice 15.00
JY Reggie Jackson, Carl Yastrzemski 40.00

MC Rod Carew, Paul Molitor 25.00
MH Don Mattingly, Keith Hernandez 35.00
SF Duke Snider, Whitey Ford 35.00
SG Ron Guidry, Don Sutton 15.00
SS Ozzie Smith, Ryne Sandberg 60.00
YS Mike Schmidt, Robin Yount 35.00

Legendary Duos Material

NM/M

Production 25 Sets
Patch: No Pricing
Production 10 Sets
CO Tony Oliva, Rod Carew 20.00
ES Duke Snider, Carl Erskine 15.00
FB Yogi Berra, Whitey Ford 40.00
GS Ryne Sandberg, Mark Grace 50.00
JG Reggie Jackson, Ron Guidry 25.00
MB Joe Morgan, Johnny Bench 35.00
MY Robin Yount, Paul Molitor 40.00
RB Wade Boggs, Jim Rice 20.00
RC Will Clark, Cal Ripken Jr. 50.00
RM Cal Ripken Jr., Eddie Murray 50.00
RR Brooks Robinson, Frank Robinson 25.00
SC Mike Schmidt, Steve Carlton 30.00
SG Darryl Strawberry, Dwight Gooden 15.00

Legendary Glovemen Cuts

NM/M

EA Earl Averill/39 120.00
CP Cool Papa Bell/29 350.00
MC Max Carey/50 140.00
JD Joe DiMaggio/75 400.00
ES Enos Slaughter/65 120.00

Legendary Lineage Auto.

NM/M

Common Player: 15.00
Production 25 Sets
Gold: No Pricing
Production 10 Sets
Platinum: No Pricing
Production One Set
HB Harold Baines 25.00
JB Jay Buhner 30.00
CA Jose Canseco 40.00
SC Steve Carlton 25.00
JC Jack Clark 20.00
WC Will Clark 25.00
DC David Cone 20.00
AD Andre Dawson 20.00
BD Bobby Doerr 20.00
LD Lenny Dykstra 20.00
EC Dennis Eckersley 25.00
SF Sid Fernandez 15.00
BF Bill Freehan 25.00
DG Dwight Gooden 15.00
GG Rich "Goose" Gossage 20.00
MG Mark Grace 30.00
RG Ron Guidry 35.00
GU Don Gullett 15.00
TG Tony Gwynn 40.00
KH Keith Hernandez 20.00
BH Bob Horner 15.00
RJ Reggie Jackson 40.00
FJ Fergie Jenkins 25.00
BL Barry Larkin 40.00
SL Sparky Lyle 20.00
BM Bill Madlock 20.00
DE Dennis Martinez 15.00
GM Gary Matthews 15.00
MA Don Mattingly 60.00
PM Paul Molitor 40.00
JM Jack Morris 20.00
MU Bobby Murcer 25.00
DM Dale Murphy 35.00
GN Graig Nettles 20.00
TO Tony Oliva 20.00
JP Jim Palmer 25.00
KP Kirby Puckett 50.00
TR Tim Raines 20.00
JR Jim Rice 25.00
CR Cal Ripken Jr. 125.00
BR Brooks Robinson 40.00
AR Al Rosen 20.00
MS Mike Schmidt 60.00
OS Ozzie Smith 50.00
SN Duke Snider 40.00
DS Dave Stewart 15.00
ST Darryl Strawberry 20.00
SU Bruce Sutter 25.00
LT Luis Tiant 20.00
AV Andy Van Slyke 30.00

Legendary Lineage Jersey Auto.

NM/M

Production 25 Sets
Gold: No Pricing
Production 10 Sets
Platinum: No Pricing
Production One Set
HB Harold Baines 25.00
JB Jay Buhner 30.00
CA Jose Canseco 40.00
SC Steve Carlton 25.00
JC Jack Clark 20.00
WC Will Clark 25.00
DC David Cone 20.00
AD Andre Dawson 20.00
BD Bobby Doerr 25.00
LD Lenny Dykstra 20.00
EC Dennis Eckersley 25.00
SF Sid Fernandez 15.00
BF Bill Freehan 25.00
DG Dwight Gooden 15.00
GG Rich "Goose" Gossage 20.00
MG Mark Grace 30.00
RG Ron Guidry 35.00
GU Don Gullett 15.00
TG Tony Gwynn 40.00
KH Keith Hernandez 20.00
BH Bob Horner 15.00
RJ Reggie Jackson 40.00
FJ Fergie Jenkins 25.00
BL Barry Larkin 40.00
SL Sparky Lyle 20.00
BM Bill Madlock 20.00
DE Dennis Martinez 15.00
GM Gary Matthews 15.00
MA Don Mattingly 60.00
PM Paul Molitor 40.00
JM Jack Morris 20.00
MU Bobby Murcer 25.00
DM Dale Murphy 35.00
GN Graig Nettles 20.00
TO Tony Oliva 20.00
JP Jim Palmer 25.00
KP Kirby Puckett 50.00
TR Tim Raines 20.00
JR Jim Rice 25.00
CR Cal Ripken Jr. 150.00
BR Brooks Robinson 40.00
AR Al Rosen 20.00
MS Mike Schmidt 60.00
OS Ozzie Smith 50.00
SN Duke Snider 40.00
DS Dave Stewart 20.00
ST Darryl Strawberry 20.00
SU Bruce Sutter 25.00
LT Luis Tiant 20.00
AV Andy Van Slyke 30.00

Legendary Lineage Patch Auto.

NM/M

Production 25 Sets
Gold: No Pricing
Production 5 Sets
Platinum: No Pricing
Production One Set
HB Harold Baines 40.00
JB Jay Buhner 50.00
JC Jack Clark 35.00
WC Will Clark 40.00
DC David Cone 35.00
AD Andre Dawson 35.00
BD Bobby Doerr 35.00
BF Bill Freehan 40.00
DG Dwight Gooden 25.00
GG Rich "Goose" Gossage 35.00
MG Mark Grace 50.00
TG Tony Gwynn 70.00
KH Keith Hernandez 35.00
BH Bob Horner 25.00
BL Barry Larkin 60.00
BM Bill Madlock 25.00
DE Dennis Martinez 25.00
PM Paul Molitor 50.00
JM Jack Morris 35.00
DM Dale Murphy 40.00
GN Graig Nettles 35.00
TR Tim Raines 30.00
JR Jim Rice 40.00
CR Cal Ripken Jr. 200.00
MS Mike Schmidt 90.00
DS Dave Stewart 25.00
ST Darryl Strawberry 30.00
LT Luis Tiant 25.00
AV Andy Van Slyke 40.00

Legendary Lineage Jersey

NM/M

Common Player: 4.00
Gold: 1X-1.5X
Production 75 Sets
Platinum: No Pricing
Production One Set
HB Harold Baines 4.00
JB Jay Buhner 4.00
CA Jose Canseco 8.00
SC Steve Carlton 6.00
JC Jack Clark 4.00
WC Will Clark 6.00
DC David Cone 4.00
AD Andre Dawson 6.00
BD Bobby Doerr 6.00
LD Lenny Dykstra 4.00
EC Dennis Eckersley 6.00
SF Sid Fernandez 4.00
BF Bill Freehan 6.00
DG Dwight Gooden 4.00
GG Rich "Goose" Gossage 4.00
MG Mark Grace 8.00
RG Ron Guidry 4.00
GU Don Gullett 4.00
TG Tony Gwynn 8.00
KH Keith Hernandez 4.00
BH Bob Horner 4.00
RJ Reggie Jackson 8.00
FJ Fergie Jenkins 6.00
BL Barry Larkin 6.00
SL Sparky Lyle 4.00
BM Bill Madlock 4.00
DE Dennis Martinez 4.00
GM Gary Matthews 4.00
MA Don Mattingly 12.00
PM Paul Molitor 6.00
JM Jack Morris 4.00
MU Bobby Murcer 4.00
DM Dale Murphy 8.00
GN Graig Nettles 4.00
TO Tony Oliva 4.00
JP Jim Palmer 6.00
KP Kirby Puckett 8.00
TR Tim Raines 4.00
JR Jim Rice 6.00
CR Cal Ripken Jr. 20.00
BR Brooks Robinson 6.00
AR Al Rosen 6.00
MS Mike Schmidt 10.00
OS Ozzie Smith 8.00
SN Duke Snider 8.00
DS Dave Stewart 4.00
ST Darryl Strawberry 4.00
SU Bruce Sutter 4.00
LT Luis Tiant 4.00
AV Andy Van Slyke 4.00

Legendary Lineage Patch

NM/M

Production 50 Sets
Gold: No Pricing
Production 10 Sets
Platinum: No Pricing
Production One Set
HB Harold Baines 10.00
JB Jay Buhner 15.00
JC Jack Clark 10.00
WC Will Clark 20.00
DC David Cone 15.00
AD Andre Dawson 15.00
BD Bobby Doerr 15.00
BF Bill Freehan 12.00
DG Dwight Gooden 15.00
GG Rich "Goose" Gossage 12.00
MG Mark Grace 20.00
TG Tony Gwynn 20.00
KH Keith Hernandez 12.00
BH Bob Horner 10.00
BL Barry Larkin 25.00
BM Bill Madlock 10.00
DE Dennis Martinez 10.00
JM Jack Morris 10.00
DM Dale Murphy 20.00
GN Graig Nettles 10.00
TR Tim Raines 10.00
CR Cal Ripken Jr. 40.00
MS Mike Schmidt 25.00
DS Dave Stewart 10.00
ST Darryl Strawberry 12.00
LT Luis Tiant 10.00
AV Andy Van Slyke 15.00

Middlemen Cuts

NM/M

Production 2-99
LA Luke Appling/32 150.00
LB Lou Boudreau/99 100.00
JC Joe Cronin/30 140.00
CG Charlie Gehringer/95 140.00
BH Billy Herman/90 90.00
PW Pee Wee Reese/39 200.00
JS Joe Sewell/76 140.00

2005 TOPPS CHROME UPDATE

NM/M

Complete Set (237):
Common Player: .25
Common Rookie (106-215): .50
Common Rk Auto (221-237): 10.00
Pack (4): 4.00
Box (20): 70.00
UH1 Sammy Sosa 1.00
UH2 Jeff Francoeur .50
UH3 Tony Clark .25
UH4 Michael Tucker .25
UH5 Mike Matheny .25
UH6 Eric Young .25
UH7 Jose Valentin .25
UH8 Matt Lawton .25
UH9 Juan Rivera .25
UH10 Shawn Green .50
UH11 Aaron Boone .25
UH12 Woody Williams .25
UH13 Brad Wilkerson .25
UH14 Anthony Reyes .25
UH15 Gustavo Chacin .25
UH16 Mike Restovich .25
UH17 Humberto Quintero .25
UH18 Matt Ginter .25
UH19 Scott Podsednik .50
UH20 Byung-Hyun Kim .25
UH21 Orlando Hernandez .25
UH22 Mark Grudzielanek .25
UH23 Jody Gerut .25
UH24 Adrian Beltre .50
UH25 Scott Schoeneweis .25
UH26 Marlon Anderson .25
UH27 Jason Vargas .25
UH28 Claudio Vargas .25
UH29 Jason Kendall .25
UH30 Aaron Small .25
UH31 Juan Cruz .25
UH32 Placido Polanco .25
UH33 Jorge Sosa .25
UH34 John Olerud .25
UH35 Ryan Langerhans .25
UH36 Randy Winn .25
UH37 Zachary Duke .50
UH38 Garrett Atkins .25
UH39 Al Leiter .25
UH40 Shawn Chacon .25
UH41 Mark DeRosa .25
UH42 Miguel Ojeda .25
UH43 A.J. Pierzynski .25
UH44 Carlos Lee .25
UH45 LaTroy Hawkins .25
UH46 Nick Green .25
UH47 Shawn Estes .25
UH48 Eli Marrero .25
UH49 Jeff Kent .25
UH50 Joe Randa .25
UH51 Jose Hernandez .25
UH52 Joe Blanton .25
UH53 Huston Street .25
UH54 Marlon Byrd .25
UH55 Alex Sanchez .25
UH56 Livan Hernandez .25
UH57 Chris Young .25
UH58 Brad Eldred .25
UH59 Terrence Long .25
UH60 Phil Nevin .25
UH61 Kyle Farnsworth .25
UH62 Jon Lieber .25
UH63 Antonio Alfonseca .25
UH64 Tony Graffanino .25
UH65 Tadahito Iguchi 1.00
UH66 Brad Thompson .25
UH67 Jose Vidro .25
UH68 Jason Phillips .25
UH69 Carl Pavano .25
UH70 Pokey Reese .25
UH71 Jerome Williams .25
UH72 Kazuhisa Ishii .25
UH73 Felix Hernandez .50
UH74 Edgar Renteria .50
UH75 Mike Myers .25
UH76 Jeff Cirillo .25
UH77 Endy Chavez .25
UH78 Jose Guillen .25

UH79	Ugueth Urbina	.25
UH80	Zach Day	.25
UH81	Javier Vazquez	.25
UH82	Willy Taveras	.25
UH83	Mark Mulder	.50
UH84	Vinny Castilla	.25
UH85	Russ Adams	.25
UH86	Homer Bailey	.25
UH87	Ervin Santana	.25
UH88	Bill Bray	.25
UH89	Thomas Diamond	.25
UH90	Trevor Plouffe	.25
UH91	James Houser	.25
UH92	Jake Stevens	.25
UH93	Anthony Whittington	.25
UH94	Phillip Hughes	.25
UH95	Greg Golson	.25
UH96	Paul Maholm	.25
UH97	Carlos Quentin	.25
UH98	Dan Johnson	.25
UH99	Mark Rogers	.25
UH100	Neil Walker	.25
UH101	Omar Quintanilla	.25
UH102	Blake DeWitt	.25
UH103	Taylor Tankersley	.25
UH104	David Murphy	.25
UH105	Chris Lambert	.25
UH106	*Drew Anderson*	.50
UH107	*Luis Hernandez*	.50
UH108	*Jim Burt*	.50
UH109	*Mike Morse*	.50
UH110	*Elliot Johnson*	.50
UH111	*C.J. Smith*	.50
UH112	*Casey McGehee*	.50
UH113	*Brian Miller*	.50
UH114	*Chris Vines*	.50
UH115	*D.J. Houlton*	.50
UH116	*Chuck Tiffany*	2.00
UH117	*Humberto Sanchez*	.50
UH118	*Baltazar Lopez*	.50
UH119	*Russell Martin*	2.00
UH120	*Dana Eveland*	1.00
UH121	*Johan Silva*	.50
UH122	*Adam Harben*	1.00
UH123	*Brian Bannister*	1.00
UH124	*Adam Boeve*	.75
UH125	*Tom Oldham*	.75
UH126	*Cody Haerther*	1.50
UH127	*Dan Santin*	.75
UH128	*Daniel Haigwood*	1.00
UH129	*Craig Tatum*	.50
UH130	*Martin Prado*	.75
UH131	*Errol Simonitsch*	.50
UH132	*Lorenzo Scott*	.75
UH133	*Hayden Penn*	.50
UH134	*Heath Totten*	.50
UH135	*Nick Masset*	.50
UH136	*Pedro Lopez*	.75
UH137	*Benjamin Harrison*	.50
UH138	*Michael Spidale*	.50
UH139	*Jeremy Harts*	.50
UH140	*Danny Zell*	.50
UH141	*Kevin Collins*	.50
UH142	*Tony Arnerich*	.50
UH143	*Matt Albers*	.75
UH144	*Ricky Barrett*	.50
UH145	*Hernan Iribarren*	.75
UH146	*Sean Tracey*	.50
UH147	*Jerry Owens*	1.00
UH148	*Steve Nelson*	.50
UH149	*Brandon McCarthy*	2.00
UH150	*David Shepard*	.75
UH151	*Steve Bondurant*	.75
UH152	*Billy Sadler*	.75
UH153	*Ryan Feierabend*	.75
UH154	*Stuart Pomeranz*	.75
UH155	*Shawn Marcum*	.50
UH156	*Erik Schindewolf*	.50
UH157	*Stefan Bailie*	.50
UH158	*Mike Esposito*	.50
UH159	*Buck Coats*	.75
UH160	*Andy Sides*	.50
UH161	*Micah Schnurstein*	.75
UH162	*Jesse Gutierrez*	.50
UH163	*Jake Postlewait*	.50
UH164	*Willy Mota*	.50
UH165	*Ryan Speier*	.50
UH166	*Frank Mata*	.50
UH167	*Jair Jurrjens*	1.00
UH168	*Nick Touchstone*	.50
UH169	*Matthew Kemp*	3.00
UH170	*Vinny Rottino*	.50
UH171	*J.B. Thurmond*	.50
UH172	*Kelvin Pichardo*	.50
UH173	*Scott Mitchinson*	.50
UH174	*Darwinson Salazar*	.50
UH175	*George Kottaras*	1.00
UH176	*Ken Durost*	.75
UH177	*Jonathan Sanchez*	.75
UH178	*Brandon Moorhead*	.75
UH179	*Kennard Bibbs*	.75
UH180	*David Gassner*	.50
UH181	*Micah Furtado*	.50
UH182	*Ismael Ramirez*	.50
UH183	*Carlos Gonzalez*	3.00
UH184	*Brandon Sing*	.75
UH185	*Jason Motte*	.50
UH186	*Chuck James*	2.00
UH187	*Andy Santana*	.50
UH188	*Manny Parra*	1.00
UH189	*Chris Young*	2.00
UH190	*Juan Senreiso*	.50
UH191	*Franklin Morales*	.75
UH192	*Jared Gothreaux*	.50
UH193	*Jayce Tingler*	.50
UH194	*Matt Brown*	.50
UH195	*Frank Diaz*	1.50
UH196	*Stephen Drew*	10.00
UH197	*Jered Weaver*	4.00
UH198	*Ryan Braun*	4.00
UH199	*John Mayberry*	2.00
UH200	*Aaron Thompson*	2.00
UH201	*Ben Copeland*	4.00
UH202	*Jacoby Ellsbury*	2.00
UH203	*Garrett Olson*	1.50
UH204	*Cliff Pennington*	2.00
UH205	*Colby Rasmus*	3.00
UH206	*Chris Volstad*	1.50
UH207	*Ricky Romero*	2.00
UH208	*Ryan Zimmerman*	10.00
UH209	*C.J. Henry*	2.00
UH210	*Nelson Cruz*	1.00
UH211	*Josh Wall*	1.50
UH212	*Nick Webber*	.50
UH213	*Paul Kelly*	1.00
UH214	*Kyle Winters*	1.50
UH215	*Mitch Boggs*	.75
UH216	Craig Biggio	.50
UH217	Greg Maddux	1.00
UH218	Bobby Abreu	.25
UH219	Alex Rodriguez	2.00
UH220	Trevor Hoffman	.25
UH221	*Trevor Bell*	20.00
UH222	*Jay Bruce*	30.00
UH223	*Travis Buck*	20.00
UH224	*Cesar Carrillo*	20.00
UH225	*Mike Costanzo*	25.00
UH226	*Brent Cox*	15.00
UH227	*Matt Garza*	20.00
UH228	*Josh Geer*	10.00
UH229	*Tyler Greene*	20.00
UH230	*Eli Iorg*	20.00
UH231	*Craig Italiano*	15.00
UH232	*Beau Jones*	20.00
UH233	*Mark McCormick*	15.00
UH234	*Andrew McCutchen*	40.00
UH235	*Micah Owings*	15.00
UH236	*Cesar Ramos*	15.00
UH237	*Chaz Roe*	15.00

Black Refractor

Black (1-105): 2-4X
Black (106-215): 2-3X
Production 250
Black Auto (221-237): 1-2.5X
Production 200

Red X-Fractor

Red (1-105): 4-8X
Red (106-215): 6-12X
Production 65
Red Auto (221-237): No Pricing
Production 25

Refractor

NM/M

Stars (1-105): 2-3X
Rookies (106-215): 1-2X
Inserted 1:5
Refractor Auto (221-237): 1-1.5X
Production 500

Barry Bonds Home Run History

NM/M

Complete Set (15): 40.00
Common Bonds: 3.00
Inserted 1:12
Refractor: 1-2X
Inserted 1:71
Black Refractor: 2-3X
Production 200 sets
Red X-Fractor: 4-6X
Production 25 sets
Gold Super: No pricing
Production one set

2005 TOPPS ROOKIE CUP

NM/M

Complete Set (160): 35.00
Common Player (1-150): .15
Common Rookie Auto (151-160): 8.00
Inserted 1:62
Pack (7): 4.00
Box (24): 75.00

1	Pat Corrales	.15
2	Ron Santo	.25
3	Joe Torre	.40
4	Boog Powell	.15
5	Tom Tresh	.15
6	Jonny Gomes	.15
7	Rico Carty	.15
8	Bert Campaneris	.15
9	Tony Oliva	.25
10	Ron Swoboda	.15
11	Tony Perez	.40
12	Joe Morgan	.40
13	Davey Johnson	.15
14	Cleon Jones	.15
15	Tom Seaver	.75
16	Rod Carew	.50
17	Rick Monday	.15
18	Johnny Bench	.75
19	Bobby Cox	.15
20	Jerry Koosman	.15
21	Al Oliver	.25
22	Lou Piniella	.25
23	Larry Bowa	.25
24	Chris Chambliss	.15
25	Bill Buckner	.15
26	Don Baylor	.15
27	Buddy Bell	.15
28	Carlton Fisk	.50
29	Gary Mathews	.15
30	Davey Lopes	.15
31	Bob Boone	.15
32	Bill Madlock	.15
33	Claudell Washington	.15
34	Jim Rice	.25
35	Gary Carter	.15
36	Willie Randolph	.15
37	Chet Lemon	.15
38	Andre Dawson	.25
39	Eddie Murray	.50
40	Paul Molitor	.50
41	Ozzie Smith	1.00
42	Jeffrey Leonard	.15
43	Lonnie Smith	.15
44	Mookie Wilson	.15
45	Tim Wallach	.15
46	Tim Raines	.25
47	Fernando Valenzuela	.15
48	Cal Ripken Jr.	2.00
49	Ryne Sandberg	1.00
50	Willie McGee	.15
51	Darryl Strawberry	.15
52	Julio Franco	.15
53	Brook Jacoby	.15
54	Dwight Gooden	.15
55	Roger McDowell	.15
56	Ozzie Guillen	.15
57	Vince Coleman	.15
58	Pete Incaviglia	.15
59	Wally Joyner	.15
60	Jose Canseco	.50
61	Cory Snyder	.15
62	Devon White	.15
63	Walt Weiss	.15
64	Mark Grace	.40
65	Ron Gant	.15
66	Chris Sabo	.15
67	Jay Buhner	.15
68	Gary Sheffield	.40
69	Gregg Jefferies	.15
70	Ken Griffey Jr.	1.50
71	Tom Gordon	.15
72	Jim Abbott	.15
73	David Justice	.25
74	Larry Walker	.25
75	Sandy Alomar	.15
76	Chuck Knoblauch	.15
77	Jeff Bagwell	.50
78	Luis Gonzalez	.25
79	Ivan Rodriguez	.50
80	Eric Karros	.15
81	Jeff Kent	.15
82	Kenny Lofton	.15
83	Moises Alou	.25
84	Reggie Sanders	.15
85	Jeff Conine	.15
86	J.T. Snow	.15
87	Tim Salmon	.25
88	Mike Piazza	1.00
89	Manny Ramirez	.75
90	Ryan Klesko	.15
91	Javy Lopez	.15
92	Chipper Jones	.75
93	Ray Durham	.15
94	Garret Anderson	.25
95	Shawn Green	.15
96	Hideo Nomo	.25
97	Jermaine Dye	.15
98	Tony Clark	.15
99	Joe Randa	.15
100	Derek Jeter	2.00
101	Jason Kendall	.15
102	Billy Wagner	.15
103	Andruw Jones	.50
104	Dmitri Young	.15
105	Scott Rolen	.50
106	Nomar Garciaparra	.75
107	Jose Cruz Jr.	.15
108	Scott Hatteberg	.15
109	Mark Kotsay	.15
110	Todd Helton	.50
111	Miguel Cairo	.15
112	Magglio Ordonez	.25
113	Kerry Wood	.25
114	Preston Wilson	.15
115	Alex Gonzalez	.15
116	Carlos Beltran	.50
117	Rafael Furcal	.25
118	Pat Burrell	.15
119	Adam Kennedy	.15
120	Terrence Long	.15
121	Jay Payton	.15
122	Bengie Molina	.15
123	Albert Pujols	2.00
124	Craig Wilson	.15
125	Alfonso Soriano	.50
126	Jimmy Rollins	.15
127	Adam Dunn	.50
128	Ichiro Suzuki	1.50
129	Roy Oswalt	.25
130	C.C. Sabathia	.15
131	Brad Wilkerson	.15
132	Nick Johnson	.15
133	Eric Hinske	.15
134	Austin Kearns	.25
135	Dontrelle Willis	.40
136	Mark Teixeira	.50
137	Rocco Baldelli	.15
138	Scott Podsednik	.25
139	Brandon Webb	.15
140	Jason Bay	.25
141	Adam LaRoche	.15
142	Khalil Greene	.25
143	Joe Mauer	.25
144	Matt Holliday	.15
145	Chad Tracy	.15
146	Garrett Atkins	.15
147	Tadahito Iguchi	1.00
148	Russ Adams	.15
149	Huston Street	.15
150	Dan Johnson	.15
151	*J. Brent Cox*	15.00
152	*John Drennen*	20.00
153	*Ryan Tucker*	10.00
154	*Yunel Escobar*	25.00
155	*Jacob Marceaux*	10.00
156	*Mark Pawelek*	70.00
157	*Brandon Snyder*	25.00
158	*Wade Townsend*	15.00
159	*Troy Tulowitzki*	35.00
160	*Kevin Whelan*	12.00

Blue

Blue (1-150): 3-6X
Blue (151-160): 1-2X
Production 50 sets

Green

Green (1-150): 2-4X
Production 199
Green (151-160): 1-2X
Production 99

Orange

Orange (1-150): 1.5-3X
Production 399
Orange (151-160): 1X
Production 299

Red

Red (1-150): 1-2X
Production 499
Red (151-160): 1X
Production 399

Yellow

Yellow (1-150): 2-3X
Production 299
Yellow (151-160): 1X
Production 199

Autographs

NM/M

Common Autograph:
Silver: No Pricing
Production Five Sets
Gold: No Pricing

Production One Set
JBA Jason Bay 20.00
JB Johnny Bench 65.00
AD Andre Dawson 15.00
JD Jermaine Dye 8.00
RF Rafael Furcal 12.00
MG Mark Grace 25.00
DRJ Dan Johnson 15.00
DJ Davey Johnson 8.00
AJ Andruw Jones 40.00
CJ Chipper Jones 35.00
DJ David Justice 20.00
EK Eric Karros 8.00
MK Mark Kotsay 8.00
CK Chuck Knoblauch 20.00
RM Roger McDowell 10.00
PM Paul Molitor 50.00
BP Boog Powell 15.00
MR Manny Ramirez 50.00
JR Jim Rice 30.00
RSA Ron Santo 25.00
TS Tom Seaver 50.00
GS Gary Sheffield 25.00
DS Darryl Strawberry 15.00
RS Ron Swoboda 10.00
JT Joe Torre 25.00
BW Brad Wilkerson 8.00
DW Dontrelle Willis 20.00

Dual Autographs

NM/M
Inserted 1:118
GS Mark Grace, Ron Santo 80.00
BW Jason Bay, Dontrelle Willis 50.00
WD Brad Wilkerson, Andre Dawson 50.00
CS J. Brent Cox, Tom Seaver 40.00
RTW Ryan Tucker, Dontrelle Willis 20.00
EF Yunel Escobar, Rafael Furcal 20.00
MM Jacob Marceaux, Roger McDowell 20.00
SP Brandon Snyder, Boog Powell 25.00
TS Wade Townsend, Tom Seaver 50.00
TW Troy Tulowitzki, Walt Weiss 30.00
WM Kevin Whelan, Roger McDowell 15.00

Reprints

NM/M
Complete Set (150): 60.00
Common Player: .25
Reprints: 1X-2X base card
2 per hobby pack
1 per retail pack

2005 UPPER DECK TRILOGY

NM/M
Complete Set (100): 40.00
Common Player: .50
Pack (5): 20.00
Box (9): 170.00
1 A.J. Burnett .50
2 Adam Dunn 1.00
3 Adrian Beltre .50
4 Albert Pujols 4.00
5 Alex Rodriguez 3.00
6 Alfonso Soriano 1.00
7 Andruw Jones 1.00
8 Aramis Ramirez .50
9 Ben Sheets .75
10 Bobby Abreu .75
11 Bobby Crosby .50
12 *Ryan Zimmerman* 12.00
13 Brian Giles .50
14 Brian Roberts .50
15 Carl Crawford .50
16 Carlos Beltran 1.00
17 Carlos Delgado .75
18 Carlos Zambrano .75
19 Chipper Jones 1.00
20 Corey Patterson .50
21 Craig Biggio .50
22 Curt Schilling 1.50
23 Dallas McPherson .50
24 David Ortiz 1.50
25 David Wright 1.50
26 Delmon Young 1.00
27 Derek Jeter 4.00
28 Derrek Lee 1.00
29 Dontrelle Willis 1.00
30 Eric Chavez .50
31 Eric Gagne .50
32 Francisco Rodriguez .50
33 Gary Sheffield 1.00
34 Greg Maddux 2.00
35 Hank Blalock .50
36 Hideki Matsui 2.50
37 Ichiro Suzuki 3.00
38 Ivan Rodriguez 1.00
39 J.D. Drew .50
40 Jake Peavy .75
41 Jason Bay .50
42 Jason Schmidt .50
43 Jeff Bagwell 1.00
44 Jeff Kent .50
45 *Jeff Niemann* 2.00
46 Jeremy Bonderman .50
47 Jim Edmonds .75
48 Jim Thome 1.00
49 Joe Mauer .75
50 Johan Santana 1.00
51 John Smoltz .75
52 Johnny Damon 1.00
53 Jose Reyes .50
54 Jose Vidro .50
55 Josh Beckett .50
56 Justin Morneau .50
57 *Justin Verlander* 4.00
58 Ken Griffey Jr. 3.00
59 *Kendry Morales* 4.00
60 Kerry Wood .75
61 Khalil Greene .75
62 Lance Berkman .75
63 Luis Gonzalez .50
64 Manny Ramirez 1.50
65 Mark Buehrle .75
66 Mark Mulder .50
67 Mark Prior 1.00
68 Mark Teixeira 1.00
69 Michael Young .50
70 Miguel Cabrera 1.50
71 Miguel Tejada 1.00
72 Mike Mussina 1.00
73 Mike Piazza 1.50
74 Nomar Garciaparra 1.00
75 Pat Burrell .50
76 Paul Konerko .75
77 Pedro Martinez 1.50
78 *Philip Humber* 2.00
79 Prince Fielder 8.00
80 Randy Johnson 1.50
81 Richie Sexson .75
82 Rickie Weeks .75
83 Roger Clemens 4.00
84 Roy Halladay .75
85 Roy Oswalt .75
86 Sammy Sosa 1.50
87 Scott Kazmir .50
88 Scott Rolen 1.00
89 *Stephen Drew* 8.00
90 *Tadahito Iguchi* 4.00
91 Tim Hudson .75
92 Todd Helton 1.00
93 Tom Glavine .75
94 Torii Hunter .75
95 Travis Hafner .75
96 Troy Glaus .75
97 Vernon Wells .50
98 Victor Martinez .50
99 Vladimir Guerrero 1.50
100 Zack Greinke .50

Generation Future Lumber Silver

NM/M
Production 100 sets
Gold: 1X
Production 60 sets
RC Robinson Cano 20.00
CA Jorge Cantu 6.00
GF Gavin Floyd 4.00
BH Brad Halsey 4.00
JJ J.J. Hardy 4.00
RH Ryan Howard 20.00
LN Laynce Nix 4.00
JP Jhonny Peralta 6.00
JR Jeremy Reed 4.00
AR Alexis Rios 6.00
RI Juan Rivera 4.00
BJ B.J. Upton 6.00
JW Jayson Werth 4.00
YO Kevin Youkilis 6.00

Generations Future Sig. Silver

NM/M
Common Player: 8.00
Production 50-199
Bronze: 1-1.5X
Production 35 sets
Gold: No pricing
Production 15 sets
GA Garrett Atkins/199 10.00
JB Jason Bartlett/199 8.00
BE Colter Bean/199 8.00
BL Joe Blanton/99 10.00
YB Yhency Brazoban/199 10.00
AB Ambiorix Burgos/199 8.00
CB Chris Burke/199 15.00
DC Daniel Cabrera/199 12.00
JO Jose Capellan/199 10.00
JD J.D. Closser/99 10.00
AC Ambiorix Concepcion/199 8.00
DD David DeJesus/99 12.00
SD Stephen Drew/75 125.00
DU Jason Dubois/99 10.00
PF Prince Fielder/75 90.00
GF Gavin Floyd/99 10.00
JF Jeff Francis/99 12.00
AG Adrian Gonzalez/99 10.00
JG Jared Gothreaux/199 8.00
GG Gabe Gross/99 10.00
JJ J.J. Hardy/199 15.00
JH John Hattig Jr./199 10.00
FH Felix Hernandez/60 80.00
HO Dennis Houlton/199 10.00
RH Ryan Howard/99 40.00
PH Philip Humber/75 20.00
TI Tadahito Iguchi/75 175.00
EJ Edwin Jackson/99 8.00
KO Casey Kotchman/99 10.00
JL Jason Lane/99 10.00
ML Matt Lindstrom/199 8.00
PL Pedro Lopez/189 10.00
RM Russell Martin/199 15.00
KM Kendry Morales/199 100.00
JN Jeff Niemann/75 40.00
PO Peter Orr/199 15.00
TP Tony Pena/199 8.00
RQ Robb Quinlan/199 8.00
AR Alexis Rios/99 15.00
CR Casey Rogowski/199 10.00
RR Russel Rohlicek/199 8.00
SS Steve Schmoll/199 8.00
LS Luke Scott/199 10.00
TS Tim Stauffer/199 8.00
NS Nick Swisher/99 15.00
MT Mark Teahen/199 8.00
TH Charles Thomas/199 12.00
BJ B.J. Upton/50 20.00
CU Chase Utley/50 15.00
JV Justin Verlander/75 50.00
RW Rickie Weeks/50 25.00
JW Jayson Werth/99 15.00
KY Keiichi Yabu/199 25.00
YO Kevin Youkilis/99 20.00
DY Delmon Young/50 40.00
RZ Ryan Zimmerman/150 125.00

Generations of Materials Triple

NM/M
Common Trio: 10.00
Production 50 sets
Unlisted Stars: 15-25.00
LJU B.J. Upton, Barry Larkin, Derek Jeter 35.00
LYU Barry Larkin, Michael Young, B.J. Upton 35.00
MCG Don Mattingly, Sean Casey, Adrian Gonzalez 30.00
MMJ Don Mattingly, Derek Jeter, Bobby Murcer 60.00
RJC Derek Jeter, Cal Ripken Jr., Bobby Crosby 50.00
RRM Brooks Robinson, Cal Ripken Jr., Melvin Mora 50.00
RRT Miguel Tejada, Cal Ripken Jr., Brooks Robinson 50.00
SGU Ryne Sandberg, Chase Utley, Marcus Giles 35.00
SRU Chase Utley, Mike Schmidt, Jimmy Rollins 40.00

Generations of Signatures

NM/M
Production 35 sets
CTG Will Clark, Mark Teixeira, Adrian Gonzalez 80.00
FPH Rich Harden, Mark Prior, Bob Feller 75.00
JKM Casey Kotchman, Kendry Morales, Wally Joyner 80.00
LJU Barry Larkin, Derek Jeter, B.J. Upton 250.00
MBV Justin Verlander, Jack Morris, Jeremy Bonderman 90.00
MMJ Derek Jeter, Don Mattingly, Bobby Murcer 260.00
PPS Jake Peavy, Tim Stauffer, Gaylord Perry 40.00
RCD Tim Raines, David DeJesus, Carl Crawford 40.00
RJC Bobby Crosby, Cal Ripken Jr., Derek Jeter 450.00
RSH Nolan Ryan, John Smoltz, Philip Humber 165.00
SBT Mark Teahen, Adrian Beltre, Ron Santo 75.00
SBW Adrian Beltre, Mike Schmidt, David Wright 100.00

Generations Past Lumber

NM/M
Common Player: 4.00
Production 115 unless noted
Gold: 1-1.5X
Production 25-75
LA Luis Aparicio 8.00
HB Harold Baines 4.00
DB Dusty Baker 6.00
JB Johnny Bench 10.00
WB Wade Boggs 8.00
BB Bill Buckner 6.00
CA Rod Carew 8.00
SC Steve Carlton 6.00
GC Gary Carter 6.00
OC Orlando Cepeda 6.00
CY Ron Cey 4.00
JC Jack Clark 4.00
WC Will Clark 8.00
TC Ty Cobb/99 100.00
MC Mickey Cochrane/99 25.00
ED Eric Davis 8.00
AD Andre Dawson 6.00
JD Joe DiMaggio/99 65.00
BD Bobby Doerr 8.00
LD Lenny Dykstra 4.00
DE Dwight Evans 6.00
CF Carlton Fisk 6.00
GF George Foster 4.00
JF Jimmie Foxx/99 50.00
FR Bill Freehan 4.00
LG Lou Gehrig/99 140.00
DG Dwight Gooden 4.00
GR Lefty Grove/99 40.00
TG Tony Gwynn 10.00
KH Keith Hernandez 6.00
RH Rogers Hornsby/99 40.00
FH Frank Howard 6.00
BJ Bo Jackson 10.00
RJ Reggie Jackson 10.00
JO Wally Joyner 4.00
GK George Kell 8.00
JK John Kruk 4.00
BL Barry Larkin 6.00
DL Davey Lopes 4.00
BM Bill Madlock 4.00
MA Don Mattingly 25.00
FM Fred McGriff 6.00
JM Johnny Mize 4.00
TM Thurman Munson 20.00
MU Bobby Murcer 4.00
DM Dale Murphy 8.00
MY Eddie Murray 8.00
SM Stan Musial 20.00
GN Graig Nettles 6.00
TO Tony Oliva 6.00
MO Mel Ott 25.00
TP Tony Perez 6.00
GP Gaylord Perry 6.00
RP Rico Petrocelli 6.00
BP Boog Powell 4.00
TR Tim Raines 4.00
RI Jim Rice 6.00
CR Cal Ripken Jr. 25.00
RO Brooks Robinson 8.00
JR Jackie Robinson 4.00
AR Al Rosen 10.00
BR Babe Ruth/99 140.00
NR Nolan Ryan 25.00
SA Ryne Sandberg 15.00
RS Ron Santo 10.00
MS Mike Schmidt 15.00
SI George Sisler 20.00
SK Bill "Moose" Skowron 6.00
OS Ozzie Smith 20.00
SN Duke Snider 10.00
DS Darryl Strawberry 6.00
AT Alan Trammell 8.00
AV Andy Van Slyke 8.00
FW Frank White 4.00

WW	Willie Wilson	4.00
YA	Carl Yastrzemski	25.00

Generation Past Material Silver

NM/M

Common Player: 4.00
Production 99 unless noted
Gold: 1-1.5X
Production 25 sets

LA	Luis Aparicio	8.00
HB	Harold Baines	4.00
DB	Dusty Baker	6.00
JB	Johnny Bench	10.00
WB	Wade Boggs	8.00
BU	Jim Bunning	6.00
RC	Roy Campanella	20.00
CA	Rod Carew	8.00
SC	Steve Carlton	6.00
GC	Gary Carter	6.00
OC	Orlando Cepeda	6.00
CY	Ron Cey	4.00
JC	Jack Clark	4.00
WC	Will Clark	8.00
DC	David Cone	4.00
ED	Eric Davis	8.00
AD	Andre Dawson	6.00
DD	Dizzy Dean/75	40.00
JD	Joe DiMaggio/75	85.00
DR	Don Drysdale	10.00
LD	Lenny Dykstra	4.00
BF	Bob Feller	10.00
CF	Carlton Fisk	8.00
LG	Lou Gehrig/75	150.00
DG	Dwight Gooden	4.00
RG	Ron Guidry	8.00
TG	Tony Gwynn	10.00
KH	Keith Hernandez	6.00
RH	Rogers Hornsby/75	65.00
FH	Frank Howard	6.00
HR	Kent Hrbek	8.00
BJ	Bo Jackson	10.00
RJ	Reggie Jackson	10.00
JO	Wally Joyner	6.00
JK	John Kruk	8.00
BL	Barry Larkin	6.00
DL	Davey Lopes	4.00
BM	Bill Madlock	4.00
EM	Eddie Mathews/75	20.00
CM	Christy Mathewson/75	80.00
MA	Don Mattingly	25.00
JM	Johnny Mize	15.00
JA	Jack Morris	4.00
TM	Thurman Munson	20.00
MU	Bobby Murcer	8.00
DM	Dale Murphy	8.00
MY	Eddie Murray	8.00
SM	Stan Musial	20.00
GN	Graig Nettles	6.00
TO	Tony Oliva	6.00
MO	Mel Ott/75	30.00
SP	Satchel Paige/75	50.00
JP	Jim Palmer	6.00
TP	Tony Perez	6.00
GP	Gaylord Perry	6.00
RP	Rico Petrocelli	6.00
BP	Boog Powell	4.00
TR	Tim Raines	4.00
RI	Jim Rice	6.00
CR	Cal Ripken Jr.	25.00
RO	Brooks Robinson	10.00
AR	Al Rosen	10.00
NR	Nolan Ryan	25.00
SA	Ryne Sandberg	15.00
MS	Mike Schmidt	15.00
AV	Andy Van Slyke	8.00
OS	Ozzie Smith	15.00
SN	Duke Snider	10.00
DS	Darryl Strawberry	6.00
FW	Frank White	4.00
WW	Willie Wilson	4.00
YA	Carl Yastrzemski	15.00

Generations Past Auto. Silver

NM/M

Common Player: 10.00
Production 24-99
Bronze: 1-1.5X
Production 10 or 35
No pricing for prod. of 10
Gold: No pricing
Production 5-15

LA	Luis Aparicio/50	20.00
HB	Harold Baines/199	15.00
DB	Dusty Baker/25	20.00
WB	Wade Boggs/50	35.00
BB	Bill Buckner/50	15.00
BU	Jim Bunning/99	20.00
CA	Rod Carew/25	35.00
SC	Steve Carlton/25	20.00
CY	Ron Cey/199	15.00
JC	Jack Clark/199	10.00
WC	Will Clark/25	40.00
DC	David Cone/99	15.00
ED	Eric Davis/199	15.00
AD	Andre Dawson/99	20.00
BD	Bobby Doerr/199	15.00
LD	Lenny Dykstra/199	15.00
DE	Dwight Evans/50	20.00
BF	Bob Feller/99	25.00
GF	George Foster/199	10.00
FR	Bill Freehan/199	15.00
RG	Ron Guidry/199	15.00
TG	Tony Gwynn/25	
KH	Keith Hernandez/199	15.00
FH	Frank Howard/199	15.00
HR	Kent Hrbek/199	15.00
BJ	Bo Jackson/50	50.00
RJ	Reggie Jackson/25	50.00
JO	Wally Joyner/199	15.00
GK	George Kell/199	15.00
JK	John Kruk/199	20.00
BL	Barry Larkin/99	25.00
DL	Davey Lopes/199	10.00
BM	Bill Madlock/199	10.00
MA	Don Mattingly/25	75.00
FM	Fred McGriff/199	25.00
JA	Jack Morris/199	15.00
MU	Bobby Murcer/199	25.00
DM	Dale Murphy/99	25.00
SM	Stan Musial/25	80.00
GN	Graig Nettles/199	15.00
TO	Tony Oliva/99	15.00
JP	Jim Palmer/50	20.00
TP	Tony Perez/25	30.00
GP	Gaylord Perry/199	15.00
BP	Boog Powell/199	15.00
TR	Tim Raines/199	15.00
RI	Jim Rice/99	15.00
CR	Cal Ripken Jr./24	
RO	Brooks Robinson/50	30.00
AR	Al Rosen/199	15.00
NR	Nolan Ryan/25	100.00
SA	Ryne Sandberg/50	60.00
RS	Ron Santo/199	30.00
MS	Mike Schmidt/25	60.00
SK	Bill Skowron/199	15.00
OS	Ozzie Smith/25	50.00
DS	Darryl Strawberry/99	15.00
AT	Alan Trammell/50	20.00
AV	Andy Van Slyke/199	20.00
FW	Frank White/199	15.00
WW	Willie Wilson/199	15.00

Generation Present Lumber Silver

NM/M

Common Player: 4.00
Production 115 sets
Gold: 1X
Production 75 sets
Unlisted Stars: 6-10.00

RC	Roger Clemens	12.00
KG1	Ken Griffey Jr.	20.00
KG2	Ken Griffey Jr.	20.00
KG3	Ken Griffey Jr.	20.00
DJ	Derek Jeter	20.00
GM	Greg Maddux	15.00
AP	Albert Pujols	20.00
DW	David Wright	20.00

Generations Present Signatures

NM/M

Common Player: 10.00
Production 25-199
Bronze: 1-1.5X
Production 10 or 35
No pricing for prod. of 10
Gold: No pricing
Production 5-15

GA	Garret Anderson/25	20.00
JB	Jason Bay/199	15.00
BI	Craig Biggio/25	35.00
BO	Jeremy Bonderman/199	15.00
MC	Miguel Cabrera/25	40.00
SC	Sean Casey/50	15.00
CC	Carl Crawford/99	15.00
BC	Bobby Crosby/99	15.00
AD	Adam Dunn/95	25.00
RF	Rafael Furcal/99	15.00
BG	Brian Giles/99	12.00
MG	Marcus Giles/199	10.00
GR	Khalil Greene/135	25.00
ZG	Zack Greinke/199	15.00
KG1	Ken Griffey Jr./199	75.00
KG2	Ken Griffey Jr./199	75.00
KG3	Ken Griffey Jr./199	75.00
HA	Travis Hafner/99	15.00
RH	Rich Harden/199	15.00
AH	Aubrey Huff/199	15.00
HU	Torii Hunter/25	25.00
DJ	Derek Jeter/99	150.00
DL	Derrek Lee/25	40.00
BL	Brad Lidge/99	25.00
ML	Mark Loretta/99	15.00
VM	Victor Martinez/99	15.00
JM	Joe Mauer/25	25.00
ME	Melvin Mora/199	10.00
MO	Justin Morneau/99	15.00
MM	Mark Mulder/99	15.00
DO	David Ortiz/25	50.00
RO	Roy Oswalt/25	30.00
JP	Jake Peavy/99	15.00
WM	Wily Mo Pena/199	15.00
SP	Scott Podsednik/99	20.00
MP	Mark Prior/25	40.00
AR	Aramis Ramirez/99	15.00
BR	Brian Roberts/99	15.00
BS	Ben Sheets/99	15.00
GS	Gary Sheffield/25	35.00
SM	John Smoltz/25	50.00
MT	Mark Teixeira/25	50.00
TE	Miguel Tejada/25	40.00
FT	Frank Thomas/25	50.00
VI	Jose Vidro/99	10.00
WI	Dontrelle Willis/25	30.00
DW	David Wright/135	50.00
MY	Michael Young/199	15.00

Signature Dual Material

NM/M

Common Player: 20.00
Production 75 sets

HB	Harold Baines	25.00
AB	Adrian Beltre	25.00
BI	Craig Biggio	40.00
WB	Wade Boggs	50.00
MC	Miguel Cabrera	50.00
SC	Sean Casey	25.00
OC	Orlando Cepeda	40.00
CL	Jack Clark	20.00
WC	Will Clark	50.00
CC	Carl Crawford	20.00
BC	Bobby Crosby	30.00
ED	Eric Davis	35.00
AD	Andre Dawson	30.00
DU	Adam Dunn	40.00
LD	Lenny Dykstra	20.00
BG	Brian Giles	20.00
GI	Marcus Giles	20.00
KG	Ken Griffey Jr.	150.00
TG	Tony Gwynn	60.00
TH	Travis Hafner	30.00
FH	Frank Howard	30.00
RH	Ryan Howard	60.00
AH	Aubrey Huff	20.00
HU	Torii Hunter	30.00
DJ	Derek Jeter	300.00
WJ	Wally Joyner	40.00
BL	Barry Larkin	40.00
MA	Bill Madlock	25.00
VM	Victor Martinez	25.00
DM	Don Mattingly	90.00
BM	Bobby Murcer	35.00
GN	Graig Nettles	30.00
TO	Tony Oliva	25.00
DO	David Ortiz	75.00
CP	Corey Patterson	20.00
WP	Wily Mo Pena	25.00
TP	Tony Perez	40.00
SP	Scott Podsednik	50.00
AP	Albert Pujols	250.00
TR	Tim Raines	30.00
RA	Aramis Ramirez	35.00
RE	Jose Reyes	40.00
RI	Jim Rice	35.00
CR	Cal Ripken Jr.	150.00
BR	Brooks Robinson	50.00
RS	Ryne Sandberg	80.00
MS	Mike Schmidt	75.00
MT	Mark Teixeira	60.00
MI	Miguel Tejada	50.00
BU	B.J. Upton	25.00
AV	Andy Van Slyke	30.00
JV	Jose Vidro	20.00
JW	Jayson Werth	20.00
DW	David Wright	75.00
KY	Kevin Youkilis	20.00

2005 UPPER DECK UPDATE

NM/M

Complete Update Set (186):
Common Player (1-100): .15
Common Rookie (101-177): 3.00
Production 599
Common Rk Auto (178-186): 10.00
Production 75
Pack (5): 5.00
Box (24): 110.00

1	A.J. Burnett	.15
2	Adam Dunn	.50
3	Adrian Beltre	.25
4	Albert Pujols	2.00
5	Alex Rodriguez	2.00
6	Alfonso Soriano	.50
7	Andruw Jones	.50
8	Aramis Ramirez	.25
9	Barry Zito	.25
10	Bartolo Colon	.25
11	Ben Sheets	.25
12	Bobby Abreu	.25
13	Bobby Crosby	.25
14	Michael Cuddyer	.15
15	Brian Giles	.15
16	Brian Roberts	.15
17	Carl Crawford	.15
18	Carlos Beltran	.50
19	Carlos Delgado	.40
20	Carlos Lee	.15
21	Carlos Zambrano	.25
22	Chase Utley	.25
23	Chipper Jones	.75
24	Chris Carpenter	.25
25	Craig Biggio	.25
26	Curt Schilling	.75
27	David Ortiz	.75
28	David Wright	1.00
29	Derek Jeter	2.00
30	Derrek Lee	.50
31	Dontrelle Willis	.25
32	Eric Chavez	.25
33	Eric Gagne	.25
34	Francisco Rodriguez	.15
35	Gary Sheffield	.40
36	Greg Maddux	1.00
37	Hank Blalock	.25
38	Hideki Matsui	1.50
39	Ichiro Suzuki	1.50
40	Ivan Rodriguez	.50
41	J.D. Drew	.15
42	Jake Peavy	.25
43	Jason Bay	.25
44	Jason Schmidt	.15
45	Jeff Bagwell	.40
46	Jeff Kent	.25
47	Jeremy Bonderman	.15
48	Jim Edmonds	.40
49	Jim Thome	.50
50	Joe Mauer	.25
51	Johan Santana	.50
52	John Smoltz	.25
53	Johnny Damon	.75
54	Jose Reyes	.15
55	Jose Vidro	.15
56	Josh Beckett	.25
57	Justin Morneau	.15
58	Ken Griffey Jr.	1.50
59	Kenny Rogers	.15
60	Kerry Wood	.25
61	Khalil Greene	.25
62	Lance Berkman	.25
63	Livan Hernandez	.15
64	Luis Gonzalez	.15
65	Manny Ramirez	.75
66	Mark Buehrle	.25
67	Mark Mulder	.25
68	Mark Prior	.50
69	Mark Teixeira	.50
70	Michael Young	.25
71	Miguel Cabrera	.75
72	Miguel Tejada	.50
73	Mike Mussina	.40
74	Mike Piazza	.75
75	Moises Alou	.25
76	Morgan Ensberg	.25
77	Nomar Garciaparra	.50
78	Pat Burrell	.25
79	Paul Konerko	.75
80	Pedro Martinez	.75
81	Randy Johnson	.75
82	Rich Harden	.25
83	Richie Sexson	.25
84	Rickie Weeks	.25
85	Robinson Cano	.25
86	Roger Clemens	2.00
87	Roy Halladay	.25
88	Roy Oswalt	.25
89	Sammy Sosa	.75
90	Scott Kazmir	.15
91	Scott Rolen	.75
92	Shawn Green	.25
93	Tim Hudson	.25

94 Todd Helton .50
95 Tom Glavine .25
96 Torii Hunter .25
.25 Travis Hafner .15
.25 Troy Glaus .15
99 Vernon Wells .15
100 Vladimir Guerrero .75
101 *Adam Shabala* 3.00
102 *Ambiorix Burgos* 3.00
103 *Anibal Sanchez* 6.00
104 *Bill McCarthy* 3.00
105 *Brandon McCarthy* 6.00
106 *Brian Burres* 3.00
107 *Carlos Ruiz* 3.00
108 *Casey Rogowski* 3.00
109 *Chad Orvella* 3.00
110 *Chris Resop* 5.00
111 *Chris Roberson* 3.00
112 *Chris Seddon* 3.00
113 *Colter Bean* 3.00
114 *Dae-Sung Koo* 3.00
115 *David Gassner* 3.00
116 *Brian Anderson* 5.00
117 *D.J. Houlton* 3.00
118 *Derek Wathan* 3.00
119 *Devon Lowery* 3.00
120 *Enrique Gonzalez* 3.00
121 *Eude Brito* 3.00
122 *Francisco Butto* 3.00
123 *Franquelis Osoria* 5.00
124 *Garrett Jones* 3.00
125 *Geovany Soto* 3.00
126 *Hayden Penn* 5.00
127 *Ismael Ramirez* 3.00
128 *Jared Gothreaux* 3.00
129 *Jason Hammel* 3.00
130 *Jeff Miller* 3.00
131 *Joel Peralta* 3.00
132 *John Hattig Jr.* 5.00
133 *Jorge Campillo* 3.00
134 *Juan Morillo* 3.00
135 *Ryan Garko* 6.00
136 *Keiichi Yabu* 6.00
137 *Luis Hernandez* 5.00
138 *Luis Pena* 5.00
139 *Luis Rodriguez* 3.00
140 *Luke Scott* 3.00
141 *Marcos Carvajal* 5.00
142 *Mark Woodyard* 5.00
143 *Matt Smith* 5.00
144 *Matt Lindstrom* 5.00
145 *Miguel Negron* 3.00
146 *Mike Morse* 5.00
147 *Nate McLouth* 3.00
148 *Nelson Cruz* 3.00
149 *Nick Masset* 3.00
150 *Oscar Robles* 3.00
151 *Paulino Reynoso* 3.00
152 *Pedro Lopez* 3.00
153 *Peter Orr* 5.00
154 *Randy Messenger* 3.00
155 *Randy Williams* 3.00
156 *Raul Tablado* 3.00
157 *Ronny Paulino* 3.00
158 *Russel Rohlicek* 5.00
159 *Russell Martin* 3.00
160 *Scott Baker* 5.00
161 *Scott Munter* 5.00
162 *Sean Thompson* 5.00
163 *Sean Tracey* 3.00
164 *Shane Costa* 3.00
165 *Steve Schmoll* 5.00
166 *Tony Giarratano* 5.00
167 *Tony Pena* 3.00
168 *Travis Bowyer* 5.00
169 *Ubaldo Jimenez* 3.00
170 *Wladimir Balentien* 5.00
171 *Yorman Bazardo* 5.00
172 *Yuniesky Betancourt* 5.00
173 *Chris Denorfia* 5.00
174 *Dana Eveland* 5.00
175 *Jermaine Van Buren* 3.00
176 *Mark McLemore* 5.00
177 *Ryan Spilborghs* 5.00
178 *Ambiorix Concepcion* 10.00
179 *Jeff Niemann* 25.00
180 *Justin Verlander* 40.00
181 *Kendry Morales* 100.00
182 *Philip Humber* 25.00
183 *Prince Fielder* 150.00
184 *Stephen Drew* 150.00
185 *Tadahito Iguchi* 150.00
186 *Ryan Zimmerman* 100.00
Common Artifacts RC (201-285): 3.00
Production 799
201 *Adam Shabala* 3.00
202 *Ambiorix Burgos* 3.00
203 *Ambiorix Concepcion* 5.00
204 *Anibal Sanchez* 5.00
205 *Bill McCarthy* 3.00
206 *Brandon McCarthy* 6.00
207 *Brian Burres* 3.00
208 *Carlos Ruiz* 3.00
209 *Casey Rogowski* 3.00
210 *Chad Orvella* 3.00
211 *Chris Resop* 5.00
212 *Chris Roberson* 3.00
213 *Chris Seddon* 3.00
214 *Colter Bean* 3.00
215 *Dae-Sung Koo* 3.00
216 *David Gassner* 3.00
217 *Brian Anderson* 5.00
218 *D.J. Houlton* 3.00
219 *Derek Wathan* 3.00
220 *Devon Lowery* 3.00
221 *Enrique Gonzalez* 3.00
222 *Eude Brito* 3.00
223 *Francisco Butto* 3.00
224 *Franquelis Osoria* 5.00
225 *Garrett Jones* 3.00
226 *Geovany Soto* 3.00
227 *Hayden Penn* 5.00
228 *Ismael Ramirez* 3.00
229 *Jared Gothreaux* 3.00
230 *Jason Hammel* 3.00
231 *Jeff Miller* 3.00
232 *Jeff Niemann* 5.00
233 *Joel Peralta* 3.00
234 *John Hattig Jr.* 5.00
235 *Jorge Campillo* 3.00
236 *Juan Morillo* 3.00
237 *Justin Verlander* 8.00
238 *Ryan Garko* 5.00
239 *Keiichi Yabu* 5.00
240 *Kendry Morales* 8.00
241 *Luis Hernandez* 5.00
242 *Luis Pena* 5.00
243 *Luis Rodriguez* 3.00
244 *Luke Scott* 3.00
245 *Marcos Carvajal* 5.00
246 *Mark Woodyard* 5.00
247 *Matt Smith* 5.00
248 *Matt Lindstrom* 3.00
249 *Miguel Negron* 3.00
250 *Mike Morse* 5.00
251 *Nate McLouth* 3.00
252 *Nelson Cruz* 3.00
253 *Nick Masset* 3.00
254 *Oscar Robles* 3.00
255 *Paulino Reynoso* 3.00
256 *Pedro Lopez* 3.00
257 *Peter Orr* 5.00
258 *Philip Humber* 8.00
259 *Prince Fielder* 15.00
260 *Randy Messenger* 3.00
261 *Randy Williams* 3.00
262 *Raul Tablado* 3.00
263 *Ronny Paulino* 3.00
264 *Russel Rohlicek* 5.00
265 *Russell Martin* 3.00
266 *Scott Baker* 5.00
267 *Scott Munter* 5.00
268 *Sean Thompson* 5.00
269 *Sean Tracey* 3.00
270 *Shane Costa* 3.00
271 *Stephen Drew* 10.00
272 *Steve Schmoll* 5.00
273 *Tadahito Iguchi* 8.00
274 *Tony Giarratano* 5.00
275 *Tony Pena* 3.00
276 *Travis Bowyer* 5.00
277 *Ubaldo Jimenez* 3.00
278 *Wladimir Balentien* 5.00
279 *Yorman Bazardo* 5.00
280 Yuniesky Betancourt 5.00
281 *Ryan Zimmerman* 15.00
282 *Chris Denorfia* 5.00
283 *Dana Eveland* 5.00
284 *Jermaine Van Buren* 3.00
285 *Mark McLemore* 5.00
Common Reflections RC (201-286): 1.00
201 *Adam Shabala* 1.00
202 *Ambiorix Burgos* 1.00
203 *Ambiorix Concepcion* 3.00
204 *Anibal Sanchez* 1.00
205 *Bill McCarthy* 1.00
206 *Brandon McCarthy* 3.00
207 *Brian Burres* 1.00
208 *Carlos Ruiz* 1.00
209 *Casey Rogowski* 1.00
210 *Chad Orvella* 1.00
211 *Chris Resop* 3.00
212 *Chris Roberson* 1.00
213 *Chris Seddon* 1.00
214 *Colter Bean* 1.00
215 *Dae-Sung Koo* 1.00
216 *Yuniesky Betancourt* 3.00
217 *David Gassner* 1.00
218 *Brian Anderson* 3.00
219 *Dennis Houlton* 1.00
220 *Derek Wathan* 1.00
221 *Devon Lowery* 1.00
222 *Enrique Gonzalez* 1.00
223 *Ryan Zimmerman* 6.00
224 *Eude Brito* 1.00
225 *Francisco Butto* 1.00
226 *Franquelis Osoria* 1.00
227 *Garrett Jones* 1.00
228 *Geovany Soto* 1.00
229 *Hayden Penn* 2.00
230 *Ismael Ramirez* 2.00
231 *Jared Gothreaux* 1.00
232 *Jason Hammel* 1.00
233 *Chris Denorfia* 2.00
234 *Jeff Miller* 1.00
235 *Jeff Niemann* 2.00
236 *Dana Eveland* 2.00
237 *Joel Peralta* 1.00
238 *John Hattig Jr.* 1.00
239 *Jorge Campillo* 1.00
240 *Juan Morillo* 1.00
241 *Justin Verlander* 3.00
242 *Ryan Garko* 3.00
243 *Keiichi Yabu* 1.00
244 *Kendry Morales* 3.00
245 *Luis Hernandez* 1.00
246 *Jermaine Van Buren* 1.00
247 *Luis Pena* 1.00
248 *Luis Rodriguez* 1.00
249 *Luke Scott* 1.00
250 *Marcos Carvajal* 1.00
251 *Mark Woodyard* 1.00
252 *Matt Smith* 1.00
253 *Matt Lindstrom* 1.00
254 *Miguel Negron* 1.00
255 *Mike Morse* 1.00
256 *Nate McLouth* 1.00
257 *Nelson Cruz* 1.00
258 *Nick Masset* 1.00
259 *Mark McLemore* 1.00
260 *Oscar Robles* 1.00
261 *Paulino Reynoso* 1.00
262 *Pedro Lopez* 1.00
263 *Peter Orr* 1.00
264 *Philip Humber* 2.00
265 *Prince Fielder* 5.00
266 *Randy Messenger* 1.00
267 *Randy Williams* 1.00
268 *Raul Tablado* 1.00
269 *Ronny Paulino* 1.00
270 *Russel Rohlicek* 1.00
271 *Russell Martin* 1.00
272 *Scott Baker* 1.00
273 *Scott Munter* 1.00
274 *Sean Thompson* 1.00
275 *Sean Tracey* 1.00
276 *Shane Costa* 1.00
277 *Stephen Drew* 5.00
278 *Steve Schmoll* 1.00
279 *Ryan Spilborghs* 2.00
280 *Tadahito Iguchi* 2.00
281 *Tony Giarratano* 1.00
282 *Tony Pena* 1.00
283 *Travis Bowyer* 1.00
284 *Ubaldo Jimenez* 1.00
285 *Wladimir Balentien* 2.50
286 *Yorman Bazardo* 1.00
Common Origins RC (201-286): .75
201 *Adam Shabala* .75
202 *Ambiorix Burgos* .75
203 *Ambiorix Concepcion* 1.00
204 *Anibal Sanchez* 1.00
205 *Bill McCarthy* 1.00
206 *Brandon McCarthy* 2.00
207 *Brian Burres* .75
208 *Carlos Ruiz* 1.00
209 *Casey Rogowski* 1.00
210 *Chad Orvella* .75
211 *Chris Resop* 1.00
212 *Chris Roberson* 1.00
213 *Chris Seddon* .75
214 *Colter Bean* 1.00
215 *Dae-Sung Koo* .75
216 *Yuniesky Betancourt* 2.00
217 *David Gassner* .75
218 *Brian Anderson* 1.50
219 *Dennis Houlton* 1.00
220 *Derek Wathan* 1.00
221 *Devon Lowery* 1.00
222 *Enrique Gonzalez* 1.00
223 *Ryan Zimmerman* 5.00
224 *Eude Brito* 1.00
225 *Francisco Butto* 1.50
226 *Franquelis Osoria* 1.00
227 *Garrett Jones* 1.00
228 *Geovany Soto* .75
229 *Hayden Penn* 1.00
230 *Ismael Ramirez* 1.00
231 *Jared Gothreaux* .75
232 *Jason Hammel* .75
233 *Chris Denorfia* 2.00
234 *Jeff Miller* .75
235 *Jeff Niemann* 1.50
236 *Dana Eveland* 1.00
237 *Joel Peralta* .75
238 *John Hattig Jr.* 2.00
239 *Jorge Campillo* 1.00
240 *Juan Morillo* 1.50
241 *Justin Verlander* 2.00
242 *Ryan Garko* 3.00
243 *Keiichi Yabu* 1.00
244 *Kendry Morales* 3.00
245 *Luis Hernandez* 1.00
246 *Jermaine Van Buren* 1.00
247 *Luis Pena* 1.00
248 *Luis Rodriguez* 2.00
249 *Luke Scott* 1.00
250 *Marcos Carvajal* 1.00
251 *Mark Woodyard* 1.00
252 *Matt Smith* 1.00
253 *Matt Lindstrom* 1.00
254 *Miguel Negron* 1.50
255 *Mike Morse* 1.50
256 *Nate McLouth* 1.00
257 *Nelson Cruz* 1.00
258 *Nick Masset* .75
259 *Mark McLemore* 1.00
260 *Oscar Robles* .75
261 *Paulino Reynoso* .75
262 *Pedro Lopez* 1.50
263 *Peter Orr* 1.50
264 *Philip Humber* 1.50
265 *Prince Fielder* 5.00
266 *Randy Messenger* .75
267 *Randy Williams* 1.00
268 *Raul Tablado* .75
269 *Ronny Paulino* 1.00
270 *Russel Rohlicek* .75
271 *Russell Martin* 1.50
272 *Scott Baker* 1.50
273 *Ryan Spilborghs* 1.50
274 *Scott Munter* .75
275 *Sean Thompson* 1.00
276 *Sean Tracey* 1.00
277 *Shane Costa* 1.00
278 *Stephen Drew* 3.00
279 *Steve Schmoll* 1.00
280 *Tadahito Iguchi* 2.00
281 *Tony Giarratano* .75
282 *Tony Pena* .75
283 *Travis Bowyer* .75
284 *Ubaldo Jimenez* 1.50
285 *Wladimir Balentien* 2.00
286 *Yorman Bazardo* 1.50
Common SP Authentic Auto (101-186): 8.00
Production 185
101 *Adam Shabala* 10.00
102 *Ambiorix Burgos* 10.00
103 *Ambiorix Concepcion* 10.00
104 *Anibal Sanchez* 40.00
106 *Brandon McCarthy* 35.00
107 *Brian Burres* 10.00
108 *Carlos Ruiz* 8.00
109 *Casey Rogowski* 10.00
110 *Chad Orvella* 10.00
111 *Chris Resop* 12.00
112 *Chris Roberson* 12.00
113 *Chris Seddon* 10.00
114 *Colter Bean* 15.00
116 *David Gassner* 12.00
117 *Brian Anderson* 60.00
120 *Devon Lowery* 10.00
121 *Enrique Gonzalez* 10.00
122 *Eude Brito* 8.00
123 *Francisco Butto* 10.00
124 *Franquelis Osoria* 15.00
125 *Garrett Jones* 10.00
126 *Geovany Soto* 10.00
127 *Hayden Penn* 15.00
128 *Ismael Ramirez* 8.00
129 *Jared Gothreaux* 12.00
130 *Jason Hammel* 15.00
131 *Jeff Miller* 8.00
132 *Jeff Niemann* 25.00
133 *Joel Peralta* 10.00
134 *John Hattig Jr.* 15.00
135 *Jorge Campillo* 8.00
136 *Juan Morillo* 10.00
137 *Justin Verlander* 65.00
138 *Ryan Garko* 30.00
139 *Keiichi Yabu* 20.00
140 *Kendry Morales* 140.00
141 *Luis Hernandez* 12.00

143 Luis Rodriguez 12.00
144 Luke Scott 15.00
145 Marcos Carvajal 12.00
146 Mark Woodyard 10.00
147 Matt Smith 8.00
148 Matt Lindstrom 10.00
149 Miguel Negron 15.00
150 Mike Morse 25.00
151 Nate McLouth 15.00
152 Nelson Cruz 25.00
153 Nick Masset 8.00
155 Paulino Reynoso 12.00
156 Pedro Lopez 20.00
157 Peter Orr 15.00
158 Philip Humber 20.00
159 Prince Fielder 200.00
160 Randy Messenger 8.00
162 Raul Tablado 10.00
163 Ronny Paulino 15.00
164 Russel Rohlicek 10.00
165 Russell Martin 30.00
166 Scott Baker 30.00
167 Scott Munter 12.00
168 Sean Thompson 10.00
169 Sean Tracey 15.00
170 Shane Costa 15.00
171 Stephen Drew 140.00
172 Steve Schmoll 10.00
173 Tadahito Iguchi 100.00
174 Tony Giarratano 15.00
175 Tony Pena 8.00
176 Travis Bowyer 10.00
177 Ubaldo Jimenez 15.00
178 Wladimir Balentien 25.00
179 Yorman Bazardo 20.00
181 Ryan Zimmerman 200.00
182 Chris Denorfia 30.00
184 Jermaine Van Buren 15.00
185 Mark McLemore 10.00
Common SPx Auto (101-179): 8.00
Production 185
101 Adam Shabala 15.00
102 Ambiorix Burgos 10.00
103 Ambiorix Concepcion 15.00
104 Anibal Sanchez 35.00
106 Brandon McCarthy 35.00
107 Brian Burres 12.00
108 Carlos Ruiz 8.00
109 Casey Rogowski 10.00
110 Chad Orvella 12.00
111 Chris Resop 15.00
112 Chris Roberson 15.00
113 Chris Seddon 10.00
114 Colter Bean 15.00
115 David Gassner 10.00
116 Brian Anderson 50.00
118 Devon Lowery 8.00
119 Enrique Gonzalez 10.00
120 Eude Brito 15.00
121 Francisco Butto 15.00
122 Franquelis Osoria 15.00
123 Garrett Jones 10.00
124 Geovany Soto 10.00
125 Hayden Penn 15.00
126 Ismael Ramirez 8.00
127 Jared Gothreaux 10.00
128 Jason Hammel 15.00
129 Jeff Miller 8.00
130 Jeff Niemann 25.00
131 Joel Peralta 10.00
132 John Hattig Jr. 15.00
133 Jorge Campillo 8.00
134 Juan Morillo 8.00
135 Justin Verlander 50.00
136 Ryan Garko 30.00
137 Kendry Morales 120.00
138 Luis Hernandez 10.00
140 Luis Rodriguez 10.00
141 Mark Woodyard 10.00
142 Matt Smith 8.00
143 Matt Lindstrom 10.00
144 Miguel Negron 15.00
145 Mike Morse 20.00
146 Nate McLouth 15.00
147 Nelson Cruz 25.00
148 Nick Masset 8.00
150 Paulino Reynoso 12.00
151 Pedro Lopez 20.00
152 Philip Humber 20.00
153 Prince Fielder 150.00
154 Randy Messenger 8.00
156 Raul Tablado 10.00
157 Ronny Paulino 15.00
158 Russel Rohlicek 10.00
159 Russell Martin 25.00
160 Scott Baker 25.00
161 Scott Munter 12.00
162 Sean Thompson 10.00
163 Sean Tracey 15.00
164 Shane Costa 15.00
165 Stephen Drew 125.00
166 Tony Giarratano 15.00
167 Tony Pena 8.00
168 Travis Bowyer 8.00
169 Ubaldo Jimenez 15.00
170 Wladimir Balentien 25.00
171 Yorman Bazardo 15.00
173 Ryan Zimmerman 150.00
174 Chris Denorfia 25.00
176 Jermaine Van Buren 15.00
177 Mark McLemore 8.00
179 Ryan Speier 10.00
Common Sweet Spot RC (91-174): .75
91 Adam Shabala .75
92 Ambiorix Burgos .75
93 Ambiorix Concepcion 1.00
94 Anibal Sanchez 1.50
95 Bill McCarthy .75
96 Brandon McCarthy 2.00
97 Brian Burres .75
98 Carlos Ruiz .75
99 Casey Rogowski .75
100 Chad Orvella .75
101 Chris Resop 1.00
102 Chris Roberson 1.00
103 Chris Seddon .75
104 Colter Bean 1.00
105 Dae-Sung Koo .75
106 Ryan Zimmerman 6.00
107 David Gassner .75
108 Brian Anderson 1.50
109 D.J. Houlton 1.00
110 Derek Wathan .75
111 Devon Lowery .75
112 Enrique Gonzalez .75
113 Chris Denorfia 1.50
114 Eude Brito .75
115 Francisco Butto 1.00
116 Franquelis Osoria 1.00
117 Garrett Jones .75
118 Geovany Soto .75
119 Hayden Penn 1.00
120 Ismael Ramirez .75
121 Jared Gothreaux .75
122 Jason Hammel .75
123 Dana Eveland 1.50
124 Jeff Miller .75
125 Jermaine Van Buren 1.00
126 Joel Peralta .75
127 John Hattig Jr. 1.00
128 Jorge Campillo .75
129 Juan Morillo .75
130 Ryan Garko 3.00
131 Keiichi Yabu 1.50
132 Kendry Morales 3.00
133 Luis Hernandez .75
134 Mark McLemore 1.00
135 Luis Pena .75
136 Luis Rodriguez .75
137 Luke Scott 1.00
138 Marcos Carvajal 1.00
139 Mark Woodyard 1.00
140 Matt Smith .75
141 Matt Lindstrom 1.00
142 Miguel Negron 1.00
143 Mike Morse 2.00
144 Nate McLouth 1.00
145 Nelson Cruz 1.00
146 Nick Masset .75
147 Ryan Spilborghs 1.00
148 Oscar Robles .75
149 Paulino Reynoso .75
150 Pedro Lopez 1.50
151 Peter Orr 1.50
152 Prince Fielder 5.00
153 Randy Messenger .75
154 Randy Williams 1.00
155 Raul Tablado .75
156 Ronny Paulino 1.00
157 Russel Rohlicek .75
158 Russell Martin 1.50
159 Scott Baker 1.50
160 Scott Munter .75
161 Sean Thompson 1.00
162 Sean Tracey 1.00
163 Shane Costa 1.00
164 Stephen Drew 4.00
165 Steve Schmoll .75
166 Ryan Speier 1.00
167 Tadahito Iguchi 2.00
168 Tony Giarratano 1.00
169 Tony Pena .75
170 Travis Bowyer .75
171 Ubaldo Jimenez 1.00
172 Wladimir Balentien 2.00
173 Yorman Bazardo 1.50
174 Yuniesky Betancourt 2.00
Common Ultimate Signature Ed.(111-193): 8.00
Production 125
111 Adam Shabala 12.00
112 Anibal Sanchez 30.00
114 Brandon McCarthy 30.00
115 Brian Burres 10.00
116 Carlos Ruiz 8.00
117 Casey Rogowski 10.00
118 Chad Orvella 10.00
119 Chris Resop 12.00
120 Chris Roberson 12.00
121 Chris Seddon 12.00
122 Colter Bean 15.00
124 David Gassner 10.00
125 Brian Anderson 50.00
128 Devon Lowery 12.00
129 Enrique Gonzalez 10.00
130 Eude Brito 8.00
131 Francisco Butto 10.00
132 Franquelis Osoria 15.00
133 Garrett Jones 10.00
134 Geovany Soto 10.00
135 Hayden Penn 15.00
136 Ismael Ramirez 8.00
137 Jared Gothreaux 15.00
138 Jason Hammel 15.00
139 Jeff Miller 10.00
140 Jeff Niemann 25.00
141 Joel Peralta 10.00
142 John Hattig Jr. 15.00
143 Jorge Campillo 10.00
144 Juan Morillo 15.00
145 Justin Verlander 60.00
146 Ryan Garko 30.00
147 Keiichi Yabu 20.00
148 Kendry Morales 20.00
149 Luis Hernandez 10.00
151 Luis Rodriguez 15.00
152 Luke Scott 15.00
153 Marcos Carvajal 15.00
154 Mark Woodyard 12.00
155 Matt Smith 10.00
156 Matt Lindstrom 10.00
157 Miguel Negron 15.00
158 Mike Morse 20.00
159 Nate McLouth 15.00
160 Nelson Cruz 20.00
161 Nick Masset 8.00
162 Mark McLemore 10.00
164 Paulino Reynoso 10.00
165 Pedro Lopez 15.00
166 Peter Orr 15.00
167 Philip Humber 20.00
168 Prince Fielder 140.00
169 Randy Messenger 8.00
171 Raul Tablado 12.00
172 Ronny Paulino 15.00
173 Russel Rohlicek 8.00
174 Russell Martin 25.00
175 Scott Baker 30.00
176 Scott Munter 10.00
177 Sean Thompson 10.00
178 Sean Tracey 15.00
179 Shane Costa 15.00
180 Stephen Drew 120.00
181 Steve Schmoll 10.00
182 Tadahito Iguchi 100.00
183 Tony Giarratano 10.00
184 Tony Pena 8.00
185 Travis Bowyer 10.00
186 Ubaldo Jimenez 15.00
187 Wladimir Balentien 20.00
188 Yorman Bazardo 20.00
190 Ryan Zimmerman 140.00
191 Chris Denorfia 25.00
192 Ryan Speier 10.00
193 Jermaine Van Buren 12.00

Gold

Gold (101-177): 1-1.5X
Production 150
Gold (178-186): No Pricing
Production 10 sets

Link to Future Dual Autographs

NM/M
Common Duo: 15.00
Production 35 Sets
BR Wladimir Balentien, Jeremy Reed 20.00
BW Dontrelle Willis, Yorman Bazardo 40.00
CD David DeJesus, Shane Costa 15.00
DD J.D. Drew, Stephen Drew 125.00
DJ Stephen Drew, Derek Jeter 250.00
FO Prince Fielder, Lyle Overbay 85.00
FT Prince Fielder, Mark Teixeira 100.00
FW Prince Fielder, Rickie Weeks 150.00
GO Roy Oswalt, Jared Gothreaux 25.00
HF Luis Hernandez, Rafael Furcal 20.00
HG Tom Glavine, Philip Humber 50.00
MB Jason Bay, Nate McLouth 30.00
MK Casey Kotchman, Kendry Morales 50.00
NK Scott Kazmir, Jeff Niemann 40.00
NW Vernon Wells, Miguel Negron 20.00
OB Yhency Brazoban, Franquelis Osoria 20.00
OG Peter Orr, Marcus Giles 30.00
PV Javier Vazquez, Tony Pena 15.00
RH Roy Halladay, Ismael Ramirez 30.00
SK Chris Seddon, Scott Kazmir 25.00
SL Jason Lane, Luke Scott 30.00
VB Justin Verlander, Jeremy Bonderman 75.00
VC Roger Clemens, Justin Verlander 140.00
ZC Ryan Zimmerman, Chad Cordero 100.00

Link to the Past Dual Autographs

NM/M
Common Duo: 20.00
Production 25 Sets
BC Steve Carlton, Eude Brito 25.00
BM Juan Marichal, Brian Burres 25.00
CS Darryl Strawberry, Ambiorix Concepcion 20.00
GT Alan Trammell, Tony Giarratano 30.00
HG Dwight Gooden, Philip Humber 35.00
HS Philip Humber, Tom Seaver 50.00
IA Luis Aparicio, Tadahito Iguchi 125.00
IC Tadahito Iguchi, Rod Carew 125.00
JH Kent Hrbek, Garrett Jones 50.00
JJ Jack Morris, Justin Verlander 50.00
MC Rod Carew, Kendry Morales 40.00
MJ Kendry Morales, Wally Joyner 50.00
MV Andy Van Slyke, Nate McLouth 40.00
NB Miguel Negron, George Bell 40.00
NR Nolan Ryan, Jeff Niemann 150.00
PP Jim Palmer, Hayden Penn 50.00
RD Lenny Dykstra, Chris Roberson 25.00
TP Gaylord Perry, Sean Thompson 20.00
VM Justin Verlander, Denny McLain 60.00